The New GROVE® Dictionary of OPERA

Volume One

A-D

The New GROVE® Dictionary of OPERA

Edited by

STANLEY SADIE

Managing Editor

CHRISTINA BASHFORD

Volume One

A-D

MACMILLAN REFERENCE LIMITED, LONDON
GROVE'S DICTIONARIES OF MUSIC INC., NEW YORK, NY

The New Grove ® Dictionary of Opera

edited by STANLEY SADIE, in four volumes, 1992

First published in hardback 1992 by Macmillan Reference Limited, London.
In the United States of America and Canada, Macmillan Reference
has appointed Grove's Dictionaries of Music Inc.,
New York, NY, as sole distributor.

First published in paperback, 1998

Database creation and typesetting by Morton Word Processing Limited, Scarborough, Great Britain

Printed and bound in Hong Kong by China Translation and Printing Services Limited.

British Library Cataloguing in Publication Data

New Grove Dictionary of Opera
I.Sadie, Stanley
782.103

Library of Congress Cataloguing in Publication Data

The New Grove dictionary of opera/edited by Stanley Sadie
p. cm.
"First published in hardback 1992 by Macmillan Reference Limited, London" -
- T.p. verso
Includes bibliographical references.
ISBN 1-56159-228-5 Paperback
1. Opera - Dictionaries. I Sadie, Stanley
ML102.O6N5 1992 92-36276
782.1'03-dc20 CIP
MN

ISBN 0-333-73432-7

ISBN 1-56159-228-5

Contents

Preface

The New Grove Dictionary of Opera is the fourth, and the last, of the family of multi-volume specialist dictionaries to have developed from *The New Grove Dictionary of Music and Musicians* (1980). I write 'developed' rather than 'been developed', because the present dictionary, like most offspring, has taken on a life of its own in the course of its compilation. Like its parent, and its elder siblings, it has ended a good deal larger than was contemplated at the time of its conception. New lexicographical opportunities and challenges have presented themselves as work proceeded, and we have tried to respond to them.

Some of these have arisen from the breadth of the constituency, or the range of readership, that is peculiar to a dictionary of opera: from the opera-goer, the theatre-goer and the lover of singing to the serious student of any of the several arts of which opera is compounded. On the one hand, opera has increasingly been a favoured field of academic study in recent years, as witness the number of dissertations on operatic topics, the growth in the number of scholarly journals devoted to opera, and the extensive projects designed to provide a thorough documentation of its history (ventures that would hardly have been possible until the age of the computer); on the other, there has been an enormous rise in the interest in opera among a wider public, as is attested by the large repertory and large choice of CD opera recordings and video performances now available, the founding of new opera magazines, and the prevailing sense that opera is no longer merely a glamorous entertainment for the noble and the rich. The world plays football to operatic excerpts.

This, then, would seem to be a well-chosen moment to be publishing a dictionary of opera. It would be good to be able to claim that this represents an astute and far-sighted piece of planning, but that is not actually the case. The idea of an opera dictionary related to *The New Grove* was first mooted in the early 1980s, but set aside as too difficult, too complex and too unpredictable an endeavour. After the publication in 1986 of *The New Grove Dictionary of American Music* we contemplated a dictionary of singers, something that had never been attempted on a substantial scale in English, and to which we felt we could bring, through our access to scholars working on opera traditions over four centuries, a new historical depth. As that project developed, however, we began to feel it was too limited in scope to be rewarding, and in 1987 we scrapped it, having got as far as putting together a large database of singers' names. That, pruned of its non-operatic side, and of course topped up to keep pace with recent developments, served as the basis for the coverage of singers in the present dictionary.

I referred above to this dictionary as one of the series that has developed from *The New Grove*. The term 'spin-off' has from time to time been used of the various publications issued in the wake of the large dictionary (although these have not been direct reprints). There is none of our publications to which the term would be less applicable than the present work. Virtually no article has been reprinted as it stood; a considerable number on singers, some on lesser composers and a handful of others are based on those in *The New Grove* where the originals were appropriate to serve, after revision, the rather different purpose and the particular focus of the present dictionary. The commissioning policy has fundamentally been the same as that of *The New Grove*: to choose the best available author for each and every topic. Where a good choice existed we have sought to call on authors half a generation younger than those we used before, although in some subject areas the *New Grove* authors remain the leading (and sometimes the only) authorities. The present dictionary is certainly at least 80%, and probably closer to 90%, newly written. The editorial methods, described in the Introduction that follows, are close to those of *The New Grove*, with a number of modifications apt to the content of this dictionary.

*

'The time', wrote Oscar Sonneck in 1914, 'for an absolutely comprehensive and accurate opera dictionary has passed for ever. The task is altogether too formidable and too complicated'. A truly comprehensive opera dictionary is indeed far beyond reach; the Towers *Dictionary-Catalogue* of 1910 already listed more than 25 000 titles. Accuracy, of course, is another matter. But probably even Sonneck could not have contemplated the range of topics that, to an opera lexicographer of today, clamour for inclusion, if opera is to be treated as what it is (or can be), a *Gesamtkunstwerk*, or a compound of many arts.

Alongside the composers (and their operas) and the singers and conductors who have a fair claim to a high proportion of the dictionary's columnage – and we elected to have fairly brief entries on performers, by and large, to permit a generous number to be included – space needed to be found for the poets and other writers, stage designers, producers and directors, representatives of dance, managers, patrons and impresarios, and numerous others whose contributions make opera what it is. Then there are opera houses themselves, which (in pursuance of the policy in *The New Grove*) are treated within articles on the cities where they belong, so that their activities may be seen as part of a broader picture of local or national operatic life. National opera traditions, of composition as well as performance, are considered in entries on countries (these vary widely in approach: clearly an entry on France or Germany will need to deal with issues quite different from those applicable to smaller countries with shorter traditions, while that on Italy, as the *fons et origo* and much else, is perforce on a different scale from any other). There is also the terminology relating to opera, which is treated in the accepted *Grove* tradition with definitions and historical entries as appropriate. And there is a series of entries treating the terrain surrounding opera, its history, its practice and its reception, dealing with such topics as Allegory, Analysis, Benefit, Casting, Censorship, Copyright, Costume, Editing, Filming and Videotaping, Machinery, Orchestra, Periodicals, Publishing, Rock Opera, Sacred Opera, Season, Seating, Sociology, Stamps, Theatre Architecture, Tonality, Travelling Troupes and Versification. There is no article as such on Singing, but a series of individual articles considering each voice type (Soprano, Tenor etc.) and sub-type, its operatic history, its use and its exponents; and there is a comprehensive bibliography under Singing, listing works that bear on singing as it relates to opera. *The New Grove Dictionary of Music and Musicians* has no article under 'Music' (on the principle 'si monumentum requiris ...'), nor has *The New Grove Dictionary of Musical Instruments* one under 'Instrument'; but the present dictionary, following rather the precedent of *The New Grove Dictionary of Jazz*, does have an entry 'Opera', treating the origins and the nature of the phenomenon. The relationship between opera, literature and ideas is further explored in the entry Libretto, which is supported by an extended and wide-ranging bibliography.

One class of entry that lies outside the established *Grove* tradition is that devoted to individual operas; in the past, *Grove* dictionaries have not normally included entries on particular works. We have elected to place these not within or adjacent to the entries on their composers but under the titles of the operas themselves, for convenience and immediacy of reference, and to avoid unwieldy entries on the most important or most prolific opera composers. These entries normally give historical information and a plot outline, or a fuller account for operas of greater importance, with a discussion of any special features, musical or otherwise; they are designed to be complementary to the entries on composers (opera entries do not include bibliographies, which are subjoined to composer entries: composer entries are the main repository of hard information). The choice of operas for individual entry has been dictated by a variety of factors: their popularity (present-day or historic), their merit, their historical or aesthetic significance, their aptness and availability for study, or almost any other good reason. We have been receptive to suggestions from the many among our authors who have offered entries on operas that they felt merited inclusion.

Another group of entries discusses specific opera librettos and favoured opera topics. This, I believe, is a departure in opera lexicography. The history of opera is not only a history of composers but also of the words that composers set and the ideas behind them; the charting of significant, much-used librettos and their treatment, or of dramas that recur in the work of different librettists and composers, is a part of the story. As our understanding of historical attitudes develops – including the attitudes of audiences who listened contentedly to an opera in happy ignorance of its composer's identity (or even whether it was the work of a single composer or assembled from a variety of existing pieces) – new modes of interpretation need to be devised, and these entries represent a modest attempt to take a wider and differently angled view of operatic history.

In discussing the scope of this dictionary, and indeed in the planning of it, one question has constantly to be addressed: what is an opera? 'Opera' is here understood to mean, primarily, a work belonging to the genre that arose in Italy about 1600. Broadly, we have aimed to regard that genre as comprehending works designed for performance in a theatre, embodying an element of continuing drama articulated through music, with words that are sung with instrumental support or punctuation. But the more one works with opera the fuzzier its demarcation lines become; and decisions demand to be made about inclusion and exclusion. No one is likely to agree with all of them. Opera has many close relatives, among them *intermedio*, masque, *ballet de cour*, serenata and *festa teatrale* at one end of its history (not to mention such subsidiary genres as *componimento drammatico*, *favola boschareccia*, *divertissement* and the like), pantomime, zarzuela and melodrama at various periods, and at the other end operetta, Posse, musical, music theatre, happening and much else. Most opera-related genres are defined and discussed in the dictionary, as are many of their composers, but very few individual works in these categories are assigned entries of their own. Our lists appended to composers' entries include all their works that can securely be reckoned as operas but may not include works in the more distantly related genres; where however we have felt that a true and balanced picture of a composer's stage output needs particularly to take account of such works, we have felt free to cite them. The pursuit of a wholly consistent policy here would have been not only impossible but also constricting; in any case, consistency of this sort is a chimera. Decisions that seem arbitrary will usually have some kind of reasoning behind them, but if sometimes they are genuinely arbitrary I make no apology, as it could not have been otherwise.

This is not, then, a comprehensive dictionary of musical theatre. It deals, as I indicated above, with the genre that arose in Italy about 1600 and soon spread through the Western world. No attempt is made to treat the musical drama of earlier periods or other cultures. There is no discussion of medieval music drama or of 20th-century concert music with dramatic content, nor of Javanese dance-drama, Beijing Opera or Japanese noh. Non-Western musical drama is not related to opera, the topic of this dictionary, in its history or its traditions, and is not considered here; it is a substantial topic and any merely cursory treatment would be inappropriate.

*

It remains to outline here certain aspects of editorial policy and procedures.

An English-language opera dictionary has to face a number of problems analogous to those that confront opera houses in English-speaking countries in the matter of the claims of English versus original language. Details of our solutions to specific problems are to be found in the Introduction, especially in §§2 and 8; here it need be said only that we have tried to accommodate the needs both of scholarship, by providing titles, names and suchlike information in original-language form, and of the general reader, by also giving information in English. The goodly supply of cross-references should make it easy to find what one is seeking.

A particularly vexed question, in this context, is that of how to express role names. Do we talk of the characters of Gluck's *Orfeo ed Euridice* as Orpheus and Eurydice, or as Orfeo and Euridice? Is Henry VIII, in an Italian opera, to be Enrico Otto? In cast-lists and entries on operas, we have chosen to cite first the original-language name form, but thereafter to prefer standard English forms, where they exist, for roles that are (*a*) classical, (*b*) biblical, (*c*) English historical (or any historical, where there is a standard English form; e.g. Philip II rather than Filippo II, Joan of Arc rather than Jeanne d'Arc or Giovanna d'Arco), and (*d*) from an English literary source. We believe that such a policy has advantages for a primarily English-speaking readership in that it helps the reader relate the roles to myths or historical stories with which he or she may be familiar.

This policy – like any other – does however raise certain difficulties and demand certain exceptions. First, operas on classical stories often introduce fictional characters, whose names may be anglicized (or, in practice, latinized); we have generally preferred to retain such names in the form given in the language of the opera, though we have allowed occasional exceptions, particularly where there are only a few, for the sake of consistency within a plot (usually these are minor roles, but they can be characters as important as Mozart's Idamantes, an invention apparently of the early 18th century). Italian forms are not anglicized when applied to characters not from 'real' mythology; for example, 'Leandro' is retained in a late 18th-century *opera buffa* because the character has nothing to do with the man we know as Leander, the classical lover of Hero. Secondly, it is not always immediately obvious which operas do in fact have an English literary source; there are several, for example, treating Romeo and Juliet that make no use, or only marginal use, of Shakespeare. Thirdly, there are certain common usages in the world of opera that one defies only at the price of being suspected of rampant pedantry; so we retain Lucia, rather than Lucy, of Lammermoor, and Verdi's (and Rossini's) Otello. In the former opera, too, it would be obscurantist to call Donizetti's Raimondo by the name of Scott's Bide-the-Bent. Readers will, I hope, find that our usages temper consistency with common sense.

In this context, it may be useful to draw attention to Appendix A, an extensive list of roles, which lists 'cognate' forms (such as Orpheus/Orphée/Orfeo), and to which readers may in any case sometimes wish to refer when using articles on singers – where we have avoided the tiresome citation of opera titles to an extent that may occasionally test readers' knowledge.

The political events in Europe and parts of Central Asia during the years of this dictionary's preparation have given rise to a new series of problems for the lexicographer. We have tried to take full account of the Soviet Union's transformation into a series of independent republics in our statements of nationality, our arrangement of articles and our usages in work-lists and in such articles as that on libraries. The same applies to the fragmentation of the former Yugoslavia. At the time of closing for press the division of Czechoslovakia is pending and we have tried to take account of sensibilities over matters of nationality here too.

*

The New Grove Dictionary of Opera has been written by some 1300 people, and it no doubt embodies many contradictions. Differences on matters of interpretation or opinion are not unwelcome; the dictionary properly represents a variety of standpoints. Contradictions of fact are a different matter. We have endeavoured to draw these to our contributors' attention, and to reconcile them, but that has been a particularly arduous task in this dictionary because of the high factual (or would-be factual) content of the material, because of the diversity and the haphazard survival of primary sources, and because of the variability of much of the existing reference material. Users of the dictionary are invited to write to the editorial office (c/o Macmillan, Little Essex Street, London WC2R 3LF) to notify us of errors or omissions so that they may be recorded and considered in the future.

Introduction

1. Alphabetization. 2. Usages. 3. Signatures. 4. Cross-references. 5. Biographical entries. 6. Lists of works. 7. Bibliographies. 8. Opera entries. 9. Libretto entries. 10. Appendices. 11. Transliteration.

1. ALPHABETIZATION. The system of alphabetization in this dictionary follows that of *The New Grove Dictionary of Music and Musicians*. Words are alphabetized as if continuous, ignoring spaces, hyphens, apostrophes, accents, modifications and diacritical marks; German *ä*, *ö* and *ü* are read as *a*, *o* and *u*, not as *ae*, *oe* and *ue*. Parenthesized and bracketed material is ignored. If two words are identical up to the first punctuation mark, the principles are applied afresh after it if it is a comma. Where two full headings are still identical, precedence is given according to the following factors, in this order: (i) unaccented words over accented, counting letters from the beginning; (ii) roman type over italic (as used for opera titles: see §8 below); and (iii) capital letters over lower-case ones. If the headings remain identical, one will be labelled **(i)**, the next **(ii)**, etc. Roman numerals are alphabetized as if they were letters; arabic numerals are placed after 'z', in numerical sequence. Some of these points are illustrated by the following (partly hypothetical) sequences.

Lee, Dai-Keong
Lee, George Alexander
Lee, Ming Cho
Leeds
Lees, Benjamin
Leeuw, Ton de
LeFanu, Nicola (Frances)
Lefanu, Nicola
Lefèbvre, Charles Edouard
Lefebvre, Joseph
Lefèbvre, Joseph
Léfebvre, Joseph
Lefêbvre, Louise-Rosalie
Leffler-Burckhardt, Martha
Le Flem, Paul
Le Froid de Méreaux, Nicolas-Jean
Legard, Jóhn
Légende de Saint Christophe, La
Legend of Shota Rustaveli, The
Legend of the Invisible City of Kitezh
Leggate, Robin

Opera
Opera
Opéra (i)
Opéra (ii)
Opera America
Opéra-ballet
Opera ballo
Opéra Bastille
Opéra bouffe
Opera Colorado
Opera Comique
Opéra-Comique
Opéra comique
Opera Delaware
Opéra du Nord
Opéra du Rhin
Opera Factory
Opéra féerie
Opera for All
Opera glasses
Opera Iowa
Opera North
Opera of the Nobility
Opera Pacific
Opera Restor'd
Opera semiseria
Opera seria
Opera South
Opera-torneo
Opera 80
Opera 100
Operetta

All listed material in the body of the dictionary follows these principles. Normally, the article, definite or indefinite, is not included in alphabetization; it is however included in the alphabetization of the appendices.

As a general principle, we have tried to place every entry where the majority of readers would expect to find it. Common sense and established usage are important factors. Cross-references are supplied to lead the reader from alternative headings to the information they are seeking.

'St' is alphabetized as 'Saint' and 'Ste' as 'Sainte', 'S' as 'San', 'Santa' or 'São' as appropriate. 'Mac', 'Mc' and 'M'' are treated as 'Mac'. 'Mr' is treated as 'Mister', 'Mrs' as 'Mistress', 'M' as 'Monsieur'. Unless there are reasons that dictate otherwise, names incorporating prefixes in the Romance languages are alphabetized under the particle when it incorporates the definite article, though established usage requires many exceptions. Cross-references are supplied as necessary.

2. USAGES. Orthography normally follows accepted British practices. Original sources are, of course, followed in quoted matter, including generic titles (discrepancies between 'dramma' and 'drama', for example, are intentional). Obsolete and foreign letter forms (such as the Gothic 'β' and the Italian long 'i') are replaced by their modern equivalents. Usages in such matters as italicization and capitalization broadly follow those of *The New Grove*. In accordance with accepted practice for reference works drawing on many languages, we follow a general policy of using capital letters sparingly for titles of books, articles, operas etc. in languages other than English (and German). British practice is followed in technical musical vocabulary (minims, crotchets and quavers etc. are preferred to half-, quarter- or eighth-notes; bar to measure, conjunct to stepwise, part-writing to voice-leading).

In accordance with British usage in the spoken theatre, universal American usage and increasing practice in British opera houses, 'director' is preferred to 'producer'.

Abbreviations are confined to those listed on pp.xxvii–xl (pp.vii–xx in subsequent volumes). An oblique stroke (/) normally signifies an alternative; an asterisk (*), in a list of works, signifies an autograph.

Act numbers are given in arabic numerals, scene numbers in small roman; '3.iv' means Act 3 scene iv.

Dates. Dates are normally given according to the Gregorian calendar. Those for Greater Russia (most of which changed to New Style only on 14 February 1918) are given, generally, in dual form, Old Style/New Style (thus Borodin was born on 31 Oct/12 Nov 1833). British dates follow the Julian calendar up to the change in 1752; absolute consistency cannot be guaranteed for some early German and Italian dates as usages varied and sources are often unclear. It should be noted that opera house carnival seasons running from 26 December to the following Lent are identified by the later year number (that is, the season from 26 December 1672 to Lent 1673 is called 'Carnival 1673'; we have aimed to express early Venetian dates, where the old year's number was retained up to Lent, according to the modern calendar or with special explanation). Methods of citing dates that are approximate or conjectural are outlined in §5 below. When a period is expressed in the form '*c*1630–48' both dates are approximate, whereas the form '*c*1630–1648' means that only the first is.

A date given with an opera title in running text, unless there is an indication to the contrary, is the date of first performance, not of composition. Date and place are normally given in the form '(1800, London)', rather than the more conventional '(London, 1800)', to distinguish performance information from publication information.

Pitch notation. The system used is a modified version of Helmholtz's: middle C is c', with octaves above as c'', c''' etc. and octaves below as *c*, C, C′, C″ etc. Octaves are reckoned from C upwards. Italic type is used for specific pitches; pitch-classes are given in capital roman letters.

Place names. These represent a particularly intractable and sensitive issue. For cities and towns the usage of *The Times Atlas of the World* is followed except for those cities where there is a traditional and universally applied English name (for example Lyons, Milan, Munich, Naples, Rome, Venice and Vienna) or those recently changed in the former Soviet Union. Where a city name has changed in the course of history, we normally try to use the name relevant for the period under discussion, identifying it too by its modern name (e.g. 'Temesvár [now Timişoara]') – while of course recognizing that different groups in such cities as Bratislava/Pressburg/Poszony or L'viv/Lwów/Lemberg have always used different names. Common sense demands flexibility in the application of this rule, like most others. As noted in the Preface, we have tried to take account of recent political changes in and around Europe; references to (for example) East Germany (the German Democratic Republic), the USSR, Yugoslavia and Czechoslovakia (still however a single country at the time of writing) are thus historical.

3. SIGNATURES. The names of authors appear, in the form chosen by authors themselves, beneath the entries to which they apply. Where authorship is joint or multiple this is indicated, showing (by reference to the numbered sections of an entry) which author is responsible for which sections. Where two or more names appear, separated only by a comma, the entire authorship is joint or the contributions are fused to a degree where it would be impractical to assign responsibility more exactly. This applies particularly to entries of which part was originally written for *The New Grove* and new material has been provided specific to the subject's involvement in opera. An oblique stroke between the two names signifies that the second-named author has revised the work of the first. The symbol '/R' following an author's name indicates that the author's work has been revised and updated editorially, by scholars attached to the Grove office or external advisers. Unsigned entries are either the work of a group of editors working collectively or revisions of *New Grove* entries where too little of the original is retained for acknowledgment to the original author to be appropriate. A signature of the form

MARY BROWN (with JOHN SMITH)

indicates that Mary Brown is the principal author but that John Smith has contributed material substantial or significant enough for specific acknowledgment.

4. CROSS-REFERENCES. Cross-references are distinguished by the use of small capital letters, with a large capital for the initial letter of the entry referred to. Thus, for example, a reference in the form MICHEL-RICHARD DE LALANDE would show that the entry is under **Lalande, Michel-Richard de,** not **De Lalande, Michel-Richard.** Cross-references give the title of the entry in exactly the form in which it is printed in bold type at the head of the entry (excluding any parenthesized material). The word *see* is printed in italic when, and only when, the reference is to another entry in this dictionary.

Cross-references are of two kinds: (i) those that direct the reader to the form in which a particular entry appears, and (ii) those that indicate to the reader that an entry on a particular topic exists and that by turning to it he or she may discover material supplementary to that in the article he or she is reading. There are a number of automatic cross-references: at the beginnings of entries on operas (see §8 below) to the composer, librettist and (where applicable) author of the literary source of the opera in question; and at the end of the text of each entry on a composer, to the individual entries on his or her operas (similarly with a librettist and individual libretto entries, and also a country and individual city entries). In general, however, cross-references are not used simply to draw attention to the existence of an article; that would be inappropriate and confusing in a dictionary on this scale.

Cross-references directing the reader to the heading under which a particular entry is to be found may take the following forms:

Acoustics. *See* THEATRE ARCHITECTURE, §7.
City Opera. American company, founded in New York in 1943 as the City Center Opera Company; *see* NEW YORK, §3.
Coblenz. KOBLENZ.
Concertato. *See* PEZZO CONCERTATO.
Convitato di pietra, Il. Opera by Giuseppe Gazzaniga; *see* *DON GIOVANNI* (i).
Delalande, Michel-Richard. *See* LALANDE, MICHEL-RICHARD DE.
Pikovaya dama. Opera by P. I. Tchaikovsky; *see* *QUEEN OF SPADES, THE.*
Pique dame. Opera by P. I. Tchaikovsky; *see* *QUEEN OF SPADES, THE.*
Pressburg. BRATISLAVA.

5. BIOGRAPHICAL ENTRIES. Entries on persons begin with the subject's name and place and date of birth and death, followed by a statement of nationality and description, thus:

Smith, John (*b* London, 1 Jan 1800; *d* London, 31 Dec 1870). English composer.

Parentheses and brackets have specific meanings:

Smith, John (Robert) – full name 'John Robert Smith', 'Robert' not normally used
Smith, John R(obert) – same name, normally given as 'John R. Smith'
Smith [Smythe], **John** – the name 'Smith' sometimes appears in the form 'Smythe'
Smith, John [Schmidt, Johann] – the entire name sometimes appears as 'Johann Schmidt' (certain obvious alternatives, such as Carl and Karl, may not be noted)
Smith, John [Brown, Thomas] – either 'John Smith' was Thomas Brown's pseudonym or stage name, or vice versa (this should be made clear in the text)
Smith, Buster [John] – 'Buster Smith' is the name under which John Smith was generally known
Smith [née Brown], **Mary** – 'Smith', the married name of Mary Brown, is the name under which she is generally known
Smith [Brown], **Mary** – either Mary Smith has the married name, pseudonym or stage name Brown, or Mary Brown is generally known under the name Smith (this should be made clear in the text)
Smith, Mrs – no first name is known.

Names of titled persons are shown thus:

Smith, Sir **John**
Smith, John, 5th Earl of Sussex

but

Sussex, 5th Earl of [Smith, John]

would imply that John Smith, the 5th Earl of Sussex, was normally referred to by his title, as Earl of Sussex or Lord Sussex. In general, each person is entered under the form of name by which he is most commonly known.

Where dates of baptism (but not birth) and burial (but not death) are known, these are given and specified as such:

Smith, John (*b* London, bap. 1 Jan 1800; *d* London, bur. 31 Dec 1870).

If the year of birth is known but not the month or exact date, the parenthesis would appear:

(*b* London, 1800; *d* London, 31 Dec 1870).

According to the state of knowledge, the date of birth may be given with less precision, e.g. '1800–08', '*c*1800' (around that year) or '?1800' (to imply conjecture). A question mark is placed immediately before the statement it qualifies; where there is a space, it qualifies the series of statements that follows. Here are some examples:

(*b* ?London, 1 Jan 1800 ...) – born on 1 January 1800, conjecturally in London
(*b* London, ?Jan 1800 ...) – born in London in 1800, conjecturally in January
(*b* London, ?1800 ...) – born in London, conjecturally in 1800
(*b* ? London, 1800 ...) – born conjecturally in London, conjecturally in 1800
(*b* London, 1/2 Jan 1800 ...) – born in London, 1 January or 2 January 1800
(*b* London, 1–5 Jan 1800 ...) – born in London on a date between 1 January and 5 January inclusive.

Where a birthdate cannot be conjectured, dates when the subject flourished ('floruit') may be given: '*fl* 1815–35', '*fl* early 19th century'. Where nothing is known or can appropriately be conjectured, nothing is stated.

The opening statement gives the subject's nationality as it might be most generally and fairly understood. It may not take account of naturalization, or birth, or ancestry. 'American conductor of German birth and Hungarian descent' would be excessively elaborate; if the subject is normally regarded as American he or she will be so described, and the German birth will be clear from the initial parenthesis while the Hungarian descent may be referred to in the text. Where a double affiliation seems of especial importance, that may be noted: 'American conductor of German birth', 'German conductor, naturalized American'. Account may be taken of the sensibilities of living subjects on such points. The brief initial description essentially outlines the reason for the subject's inclusion in the dictionary. A composer who is entered in the dictionary as such should not expect to be described as 'composer, pianist, conductor, writer on music and teacher'. Exceptions have occasionally to be made; for example, Gustav Mahler earns a place in this particular dictionary as a conductor, but it would be absurd not to describe him first as a composer.

6. LISTS OF WORKS. Lists of works for composers in this dictionary are, of course, confined to operas. For some lists, as explained in the Preface, the term 'opera' has to be flexibly defined, to include certain closely related genres; that is particularly the case where a composer's operatic output would be misleadingly presented if such works were not listed, or where works defined as operas cannot readily be distinguished from those that are described otherwise. Readers seeking information about a composer's other works must look elsewhere, although non-operatic works, especially those of a dramatic character, are often referred to in entry texts.

The form of citation follows that in *The New Grove*. First is given the title, followed in brackets by any alternative title (and English translation if appropriate); then follows the date of composition (this is included only if the première is considerably later). Next, in parentheses, the sub-genre (if any) is named, with the number of acts, the librettist, and any literary source. Then comes the city of the première and the name of the theatre (the word 'theatre' is normally omitted), with the date. Genres and theatres may be identified by sigla, which will be explained at the head of the list (unless they are exclusively standard abbreviations used throughout the dictionary). Next follows source information (using RISM sigla, printed in italics, for libraries with manuscript material) and publication information (full score unless otherwise indicated). RISM sigla (listed on pp.xxxv–xl) are given in alphabetical order of countries, and in alphabetical order within countries. National sigla stand until contradicted: thus in '*I-Nc*, *Vnm*, *P-La*' the central sigillum means *I-Vnm*. This applies from item to item; a reader finding an isolated library sigillum should look back to discover what national sigillum qualifies it. Manuscript information is given, generally speaking, for works up to about 1800. An asterisk next to a sigillum indicates the composer's autograph. A revised version is noted 'rev.'. Where it is known whether particular sources correspond to the original version or a revised one, that is made clear by the placing of the relevant RISM sigla. Where a composer is known to have reset a text, successive settings will be listed as distinct works, indicated as '1st version', '2nd version', etc.; but where a later setting is simply a revision it will be noted within the listing of the original. Occasionally, locations are noted for printed librettos of early operas, though only, generally speaking, where they are the sole surviving evidence of an opera's existence (Italian librettos before 1800 are in any case listed in C. Sartori: *I libretti italiani a stampa dalle origini al 1800: catalogo analitico*, 1990–). Lists are chronological; where the order of composition differs considerably from that of performance, the former is followed. At the end of a list, works to which the composer contributed music, works in which his music appeared, and doubtful works may be separately listed (true collaborations are of course indicated as such). Pre-1800 works listed without source information should be taken as lost.

The following fictional example may help clarify the foregoing:

> Alessandro [Alessandro il grande; Il grande], 1738 (os, 3, A. Zariati, after J. Racine: *Phèdre*), Milan, Regio Ducal, 26/27 Jan 1747, *F-Pn*, *I-Mc** (*R*1980: IOB, cvii), *Vnm* (arias); rev. as Il vincitor, Lisbon, S Carlos, carn. 1756, *D-Mbs*, *Rtt*, *GB-Lbl*, *I-Nc*, *P-La*, ov. and 2 arias (London, 1762); ed. M. Grey (New York, 1990)

The opera is called, and was initially performed as, *Alessandro*; in some sources the title appears as *Alessandro il grande* or *Il grande*. It was composed in 1738. It is an *opera seria* ('os' is a standard abbreviation: see pp.xxvii-xxx) in three acts, to a libretto by A. Zariati based on Racine's *Phèdre*. It was first performed at the Regio Ducal Teatro, Milan, on either 26 January or 27 January 1747; there are manuscript scores at the libraries denoted by *F-Pn* and *I-Mc*, the latter an autograph (which has been reprinted in facsimile as vol. cvii in the series represented by IOB), and arias are at the library *I-Vnm*. The opera was revised as *Il vincitor* and given on an unknown date during the 1756 carnival season at the Teatro São Carlos, Lisbon, and scores of that version are found at the libraries listed at that point; the overture and two arias were published in London in 1762. (Details of revivals may not be given unless they are identifiable with revised source material; it is an assumption that any opera revival of this period is likely to entail some degree of revision.) Lastly, a modern edition, by M. Grey, was published in New York in 1990.

Lists of librettos, in entries on librettists, are presented in chronological order of known setting. Titles are printed in italics. Against each, the following information is given: genre (which may not be the same as the genre named in the corresponding entry in the composer's work-list); composer and year of first setting (the place and exact date can be found from the composer's work-list) – where no composer's name is known, that is stated along with the year; later settings, with the name of the composer and the year (and the opera's title if it differs from that of the original libretto). Within a year, librettos are listed chronologically where possible, otherwise alphabetically. Sources are not normally given for manuscript librettos. For librettists of particular importance, fuller information may be provided, including place of première when the composer's name is unknown. Lists for librettists are not claimed as comprehensive. In some cases, apparent discrepancies may be found between dates in composers' lists and librettists'; these are usually accounted for by carnival seasons, where, for example (as noted in §2 above), 'carn. 1757' may cover from 26 December 1756 (in some situations even earlier) until the following Lent.

Lists of works by playwrights, novelists and other literary men or women on which operas have been based are usually presented in chronological order, but for convenience certain longer ones (for example that for Shakespeare) are given in alphabetical order. In these lists, which are not claimed as comprehensive, titles of derived operas are given where they differ significantly from those of the originals.

7. BIBLIOGRAPHIES. As in *The New Grove*, bibliographies normally include studies on which authors have drawn as well as further reading. They are not intended to represent complete lists of the literature on the topic. Writings that are ephemeral, trivial or superseded, unless of historiographical interest, are excluded; general histories (or ones of specific periods or regions) may be cited where they contain material of particular importance on the topic in question. In entries on composers and singers, standard theatre histories, chronologies, listings and catalogues are not cited (except where there is some special reason for doing so); had these been included whenever authors had consulted them, the dictionary would have been hugely and unreasonably swollen. Readers should assume that such works have routinely been consulted, and will find citations under the appropriate city entry. Standard reference works too are not cited unless there is particular reason for doing so.

Bibliographies are chronologically arranged (within categories when a bibliography is categorized); items are listed in order of first (or cited) publication. Items published within the same year are listed alphabetically by author, and, for the same author, by title. Certain works of reference for which abbreviations are used are placed at the head of bibliographies, listed in alphabetical order of abbreviation (for larger works, authors' names are specified). In some cases, bibliographies may be situated at the ends of sections of text.

The procedures of citation are broadly self-evident, but it may be helpful to outline the main principles (the reader should also refer to the list of bibliographical abbreviations, pp.xxxi–xxxiv of this volume, pp.xi–xiv of subsequent volumes, and its prefatory note). For books that have appeared in several editions, the first and the most recent are cited unless there is particular reason to note intermediate ones (or to omit early ones, where the relevant material is not included). English translations are normally noted and their titles given if not obvious direct translations of the original ones. For items in less familiar languages, translations into other western European languages may be noted. Places of publication are given for the earliest edition cited. Multi-volume books are not cited as such but (unless they are through-paginated) page references will include the volume number (in lower-case roman numerals, which are used for volume numbers throughout the dictionary). Periodicals reckoned by issue rather than volume are expressed in arabic numerals. For periodicals that are not through-paginated, the fascicle number within the volume is indicated after an oblique stroke (e.g. xiv/3). Terminal page numbers are normally given for articles. Dissertations, doctoral or other, are noted as such and the institution and acceptance date are named; when a dissertation is published, the citation may refer only to the published version. A standard form is adopted for articles in congress reports, following J. Tyrrell and R. Wise: *A Guide to International Congress Reports in Music 1900–1975* (London, 1979), giving a short title for the congress, followed by the name of the city where it took place and the year (for example *Venezia e il melodramma nel seicento: Venice 1972*); items in congress reports are listed according to the date of the congress (i.e. when the material was first made public) rather than the date of publication of the report.

Lists of writings appended to entries on scholars or critics are organized according to the same principles. Such lists are selective, normally citing books and particularly substantial articles.

8. OPERA ENTRIES. Headwords for entries on operas are printed in italic bold type (thus: ***Götterdämmerung***) and cross-references to them are shown in italic small capitals (*GÖTTERDÄMMERUNG*).

Operas composed to librettos in Romance or Teutonic languages are entered under their original-language titles; familiar English titles are however also entered as headwords, with simply a cross-reference. For operas in Slavonic and other languages, English titles are used as the headword only where a familiar, recognized one exists. (At the end of each composer entry, the cross-references to his or her operas entered separately will show the form in which each is entered.) Thus while *Le nozze di Figaro* is entered as such, or rather as ***Nozze di Figaro, Le*** (the article is inverted), *Prodaná nevěsta* is considered under ***Bartered Bride, The,*** with the original title shown in brackets. (Cross-references, under ***Marriage of Figaro, The*** and ***Prodaná nevěsta,*** will guide the reader to the correct heading.) For non-English titles, an English translation is given. These examples will clarify the foregoing:

Bartered Bride, The [*Prodaná nevěsta*]. Comic opera in three acts by ...
Prodaná nevěsta. Opera by Bedřich Smetana; *see BARTERED BRIDE, THE.*

Marriage of Figaro, The. Opera by W. A. Mozart; *see NOZZE DI FIGARO, LE.*
Nozze di Figaro, Le ('The Marriage of Figaro'). *Opera buffa* in four acts by ...

Where an opera is widely known by a title that is not a translation, that title is given along with the translation: for example

Deux journées, Les ('The Two Days' [*The Water Carrier*]).

Where an opera is usually called by a title shorter than its actual one, the heading will show first the customary title with the full one bracketed (and the full one will be translated):

Flavio [*Flavio, re di longobardi* ('Flavius, King of the Lombards')].

Where an opera is often called by a title neither in its original language nor an English one, that title is also shown:

Golden Cockerel, The [*Zolotoy petushok* (*Le coq d'or*)].

In the light of the inconsistency of early practice regarding the use, in Italian titles, of the definite article before a personal name, the article is excluded from the headword, although if it appears widely in sources it may be shown as a fuller alternative, both in the entry on the opera –

Calisto [*La Calisto*] ('Callisto')

– and in the composer's list of works.

A different terminological issue is raised by the words used to identify the sub-genre to which an opera belongs. When as central a work as *Don Giovanni* is described by its librettist as a *dramma giocoso* and its composer as an *opera buffa*, clearly there is no simple right or wrong. It may be that such terms are interchangeable, or that one represents a sub-category of the other; it may also be that the descriptive terminologies for librettos and for musical scores, or those favoured by poets and by musicians, are somewhat different. We have tried, in lists of works and in entry headings, to follow contemporary descriptions wherever possible, although sometimes there has been reason to recognize that an understood modern usage could have advantages over a confusing historical one. Genre descriptions are normally given in the original language for Romance and Teutonic languages.

The initial paragraph of an opera entry normally states, after the title, the genre, the number of acts, the composer, the librettist and if relevant the author of any literary source (the existence of separate entries on these is signified by the use of cross-reference type), and the place and date of first performance (with additional information, if applicable, on the première of any revised version). A cast-box follows for those operas treated more extensively, showing the *dramatis personae*, with names in the original language and, where apposite, anglicized forms (as used throughout the entry, as explained in the Preface; such characters as 'A Nurse' or 'A Soldier' are given only in English). Voice-types are identified. The setting of the opera is also noted.

The entry normally proceeds with an account of the work's background, composition and performance history, with a synopsis (or for operas considered more briefly, a résumé) and some discussion of its music and its historical significance. Where two or more operas on the same plot appear in succession, the plot will not normally be discussed in each except to point out divergences. Opera entries do not carry bibliographies; any specific reference (such as 'Ashbrook 1982') found in an opera entry should be sought in the appropriate composer bibliography.

9. LIBRETTO ENTRIES. There are two kinds of entry on librettos, those on specific texts and those on topics; headwords are printed in normal bold type. The former kind gives the title of the libretto, in its original language, with the name of the librettist (incorporating a cross-reference) and details of the first setting; it continues with a synopsis, which if appropriate will relate the libretto to any historical background, and will give an account of the history of the libretto and its principal settings. The latter kind outlines the history of the topic in its operatic treatment; here the headword, unless there is reason otherwise, is given in anglicized form. Such topics as Julius Caesar, Orpheus and Faust are considered in these articles; in the case of subjects treated over a long period a list of operas may be subjoined.

10. APPENDICES. Attention should be drawn to the appendices. Appendix A is an index of opera roles; the reader may find from it to what opera a named character belongs, as well as the voice-type. Appendix B is an index of incipits of opera arias, duets etc.: the reader unable to place an aria title will be able to find it and discover to which opera, which act and which role it belongs. It should be emphasized that these indexes are not, of course, in any sense comprehensive; they are intended to cover the main operatic repertory and the first layers of the fringe repertory. Appendix C is a list of contributors and their last known place of work or residence; where no place is named, it should be taken that he or she is no longer living. Appendix D is a list of illustration sources.

11. TRANSLITERATION. The system used for transliteration from Cyrillic scripts (including Bulgarian [Bulg.], Serbian [Serb.] and Ukrainian [Ukr.]), a slightly modified version of the one used in *The New Grove*, is shown on p.xxii.

Common usage, and common sense, demand a number of exceptions. Place names such as Moscow and Kiev are given in their standard forms. The names of Prokofiev and Tchaikovsky are spelt in their accepted English ways, as are Tcherepnin (the spelling still used by the family), Koussevitzky (the spelling used by the Foundation) and Cui (a name of Western origins). Several popular transliterations that do not originate in English and are apt for pronunciation only in other languages (usually German or French) have been avoided: thus Dyagilev (not Diaghilev or Diaghileff), Glier (not Glière) and Rakhmaninov (not Rachmaninoff or Rachmaninov). Strict transliteration is used in bibliographical contexts; the orthography in a bibliography may thus differ from that in the text of the article to which it belongs.

We are indebted for advice on transliteration to several of our contributors and especially to Albina and Jeremy Howard. Dr V. Nersessian has advised us on Armenian.

Cyrillic	*Roman*	*Cyrillic*	*Roman*
а	a	п	p
б	b	р	r
в	v	с	s
г	g; Ukr. h/g	т	t
д	d	у	u
е	e/ye[1]	ф	f
ё	yo	х	kh; Serb. h
є	ye	ц	ts; Serb. c
ж	zh; Serb. ž	ч	ch; Serb. č
з	z	ш	sh; Serb. š
і	i	щ	shch; Bulg. sht
и	i; Ukr. y	ъ	' ; Bulg. a
й	y	ы	ï
к	k	ь	' ; Bulg. a
л	l	э	e
м	m	ю	yu
н	n	я	ya
о	o	ї	Ukr. ï

[1]ye, after ъ, ь and vowels and as initial letter
[2]terminations -iy or -ïy are given as -y in personal names
[3]кс may be given as x in personal names (e.g. Alexey)

Bulgarian: ж-a; ѣ-ee/ay; ай (final) -y.
Serbian: ђ-dj; љ-lj; њ-nj; ћ-ć; џ-dž; j-j.

Acknowledgments

The preparation of a reference work of this kind involves, in accordance with the traditions of *Grove* dictionaries, a large-scale and extended collaboration among many authors, most of them the leading authorities on the topics they are treating, as well as numerous advisers and a team of editors, along with administrative, clerical, publishing and printing staff. It is not possible to acknowledge here everyone who has contributed in some way to this dictionary, but I may here thank collectively all those who are not individually named.

*

Thanks are due, first of all, to the people who actually wrote the dictionary: the contributors, some 1300 in all. Their names are listed in full in Appendix C. Some of their articles were written in the first place for *The New Grove Dictionary of Music and Musicians* or *The New Grove Dictionary of American Music.* I am especially grateful to the large number of contributors who have taken much trouble over the thankless task of revising their material to bring it up to date or into line with recent research, or in particular to extend and elaborate the operatic part of material written previously for a general dictionary; this has often involved looking more deeply into source material and actual music, and going back over work done some years ago. I am grateful, too, for the understanding and generosity of those contributors who, when unable to pursue further inquiries themselves, or when their own interests have moved on, have permitted their material to be enlarged upon or in various ways adjusted by others currently working in their former research area. Many of our contributors have drawn our attention to matters that would otherwise have eluded us, or have warned us of sources of error, often in spheres outside those of their immediate work, and thus helped us to make the dictionary more comprehensive and more accurate. I am very conscious that, in the course of detailed work on the dictionary, we have had to trouble our contributors with numerous, and often intractable, queries, and we are grateful for the pains that many of them have taken in response to our importunities: all, we believe, to the advantage of the dictionary and thus in turn of future opera scholarship. I should also here thank those who are not contributors, but simply interested members of the public, who have drawn our attention to possible errors or omissions.

The names of our team of editorial consultants are listed in full on p.vi. Those who advised on the planning and editorial management of specific subject areas are as follows: Italian opera, Ellen Rosand, Lowell Lindgren (Baroque), Marita P. McClymonds (Classical), Roger Parker

(19th century) and John C. G. Waterhouse (20th century); German and north European opera, Thomas Bauman (up to 1800), Barry Millington (19th century), Andrew Clements and Elizabeth Forbes (20th century); French opera, Graham Sadler (Baroque), David Charlton (Classical and early Romantic), Elizabeth Forbes, Richard Langham Smith and Andrew Clements (later 19th and 20th centuries); English opera, Curtis Price (up to 1800), Leanne Langley (19th century) and Andrew Clements (20th century); Russian opera, Richard Taruskin (18th, 19th and early 20th centuries) and Laurel Fay (middle and late 20th century); east central European opera, John Tyrrell; Hispanic opera, Lionel Salter and Robert Stevenson, with Malena Kuss; north American opera, Steven Ledbetter, Harry Haskell, Andrew Stiller and Gaynor Jones; Australian opera, Thérèse Radic; operetta, Andrew Lamb, with Patrick O'Connor and Kurt Gänzl; singers, Elizabeth Forbes, John B. Steane and John Rosselli, with David Cummings and initially with Will Crutchfield; librettists and writers of the post-1800 period, Arthur Jacobs; and impresarios and patrons, John Rosselli. On the coverage of cities, we have had valuable help from Lorenzo Bianconi (Italy), Charles Pitt (France) and Imre Fabian (the German-speaking countries), as well as Richard Taruskin (Russia), John Tyrrell (east central Europe), Nancy Malitz (the USA) and Robert Stevenson (Latin America). On stage design, we have been grateful for the help of Marina Henderson and Mercedes Viale Ferrero; and on directors, Barry Millington. We have been specially grateful for the assistance of a group of scholars, notably Richard Macnutt, John Rosselli and Roger Parker, along with Patrick O'Connor, in the planning of the miscellaneous articles dealing principally with historical practices in and around opera houses.

This is the place to note our gratitude to some of the numerous contributors whose help went far beyond the line of duty, into the borderlines of editorial planning. These include Evan Baker (on matters to do with production), Xoán M. Carreira (recent Spanish opera), Andrew Clark (recent Swiss and German opera), Roger Covell (Australian opera and singers), Juan Pedro Franze (Argentine opera), David J. Hough (stage design), Masakata Kanazawa (Japanese opera), Alison Latham (conductors and critics), George Leotsakos (Greek opera), Raffaele Pozzi (recent Italian opera), Adrienne Simpson (New Zealand singers), and a group of scholars who have helped us ensure a proper coverage of operatic matters in newly independent countries, Virko Baley (Ukraine), Arnolds Klotiņš (Latvia), Adeodatas Tauragis (Lithuania) and Koraljka Kos (Croatia). Dale E. Monson has generously helped see through the contributions of the late Dennis Libby; Don Neville, Dorothea Link and John Black are among the others who have helped in a variety of ways to improve the accuracy of the dictionary. Marita McClymonds and Julie McClymonds-Smith have done much to amplify our work-lists and source citations for Italian composers of the 18th century. Nigel Simeone helped supplement our bibliographical citations. Julian Budden's ready and wide-ranging help should be warmly acknowledged, and so, again, should that of Elizabeth Forbes, who has so generously and willingly drawn on her capacious files and extensive knowledge to make the dictionary more comprehensive and accurate; she also did much towards the compilation of Appendix B.

I have been singularly fortunate to have, at the head of the editorial team, two scholars of exceptional enthusiasm and vitality, with whom it has been an outstanding pleasure to work. One is the Managing Editor,

Christina Bashford, whose command of organizational matters coupled with editorial and scholarly skills proved fundamental to the smooth execution of a highly complex, interlocking series of administrative and musicological tasks. In this she was much helped by the efficient and resourceful administration of Stephanie Farrow and Caroline Perkins (working with computer systems devised by Danny Doyle). The other is Leanne Langley, whose careful, far-sighted planning of the editorial procedures and alert supervision of their execution have done much to ensure the clear and sensible presentation of the dictionary's material. These two have made tremendous efforts on the dictionary's behalf; without their loyal support and their ready wit the production of the dictionary would have been far slower and would have seemed infinitely so.

Among the editorial team, I should like first to express my gratitude to a number of former *Grove* editors who have worked with us at various stages, including Paulène Fallows, Judith Nagley, Audrey Twine, Michael Wood and latterly Julie Woodward; other editors central to the preparation of the dictionary have been Lucy Temperley and Jennifer Doctor, along with Madeleine Ladell (who took charge of the music examples). Further former *Grove* editors recalled to the colours have been Laura Langley, Fiona Little, Elizabeth McKim, Malcolm Boyd and Nigel Fortune. New editors to have made a valued contribution include Elisabeth Cook, Paul Corneilson, Marija Đurić, Laura McGeary, Andrew Mikolajski and Steve Taviner. We were fortunate to have an editor of Elisabeth Ingles's experience to help us at various critical stages, the final ones especially; and Sarah Roberts deserves special mention for her careful management of a number of lengthy tasks, among them the compilation of the vast index that ensured the consistent reference to roles and led to the creation of Appendix A. Maureen Buja proved a dependable bibliographic bloodhound.

The enterprise and resourcefulness of the picture editors, Elisabeth Agate and Helen Ottaway, is plain for all to see. They and I would particularly like to thank the many contributors who have taken trouble to guide them towards interesting illustrative matter, foremost among them Elizabeth Forbes, Richard Macnutt, Roger Parker, Evan Baker and Sven Hansell, who have been especially generous in lending their own materials. We are indebted to the many collectors, librarians and archivists (listed in full in Appendix D) and in particular to Maria Teresa Muraro (Fondazione Giorgio Cini, Venice), Martine Kahane and Nicole Wild (Bibliothèque de l'Opéra, Paris), John Cavanagh (Mottisfont Abbey, Hampshire), Jiří Hilmera and Olga Hilmerová (Prague), Francesca Franchi (Royal Opera House, Covent Garden), Giancarlo Costa (Milan), the staff of the Theatre Museum (Victoria and Albert Museum), Philip Taylor (Collet's Bookshop), Vivian Liff and many more whom it would be impossible to thank here individually.

We have had assistance, in the gathering and checking of material, from many sources, far too many to name – including those (librarians, opera house and festival administrators and others) who have completed our questionnaire forms. Many artists, too, have completed questionnaire forms; we are particularly grateful to those singers who have broken with lexicographic tradition and supplied correct dates of birth. I would particularly like to acknowledge help from the editorial office and the archives at the Royal Opera House, Covent Garden; the offices of many other opera houses and festival organizations; several Music Information Centres, among which the one in London and those in the Low

Countries (Donemus and CeBeDeM) have been especially helpful; several embassies and cultural attachés; many artists' agents; and of course numerous libraries and their staff, of which I would mention in particular the British Library, the libraries of the Senate House and King's College of London University, the Music Faculty Library, Oxford (John Wagstaff), and New York Public Library (John Shepard).

Lastly, I should like to express my gratitude to my wife, for her tolerance of the heavy demands on me of such a mistress as this dictionary, and to my colleagues at Macmillan Press: Alyn Shipton, Simon Littlewood and Hugh Jones, for planning in the early stages, John Peacock, who ensured the smooth running of production matters, and especially, for his steadfast support, Christopher Paterson, who in the first place pressed us to go ahead with a modest-scaled opera dictionary and did his best to conceal his increasing alarm as it grew to its present size.

London, September 1992 STANLEY SADIE

General Abbreviations

A	alto, contralto [voice]
AB	Bachelor of Arts
ABC	American Broadcasting Company; Australian Broadcasting Commission
Abt.	Abteilung [section]
acc(s).	accompaniment(s); accompanied by
AD	anno Domini
add, addl	additional
add(s), addn(s)	addition(s)
ad lib	ad libitum
AK	Alaska (USA)
AL	Alabama (USA)
Alta.	Alberta (Canada)
AM	Master of Arts
a.m.	ante meridiem [before noon]
Amer.	American
AMS	American Musicological Society
Anh.	Anhang [appendix]
anon.	anonymous(ly)
appx	appendix
AR	Arkansas (USA)
arr(s).	arrangement(s); arranged (by/for)
ASCAP	American Society of Composers, Authors and Publishers
attrib.	attribution, attributed to
Aug	August
aut.	autumn
AZ	Arizona (USA)

B	bass [voice]
b	bass [instrument]
b	born
BA	Bachelor of Arts
bap.	baptized
Bar	baritone [voice]
bar	baritone [instrument]
BBC	British Broadcasting Corporation
BC	British Columbia (Canada)
BC	before Christ
bc	basso continuo
Bd.	Band [volume]
Berks.	Berkshire (GB)
Berwicks.	Berwickshire (GB)
BFA	Bachelor of Fine Arts
bk	book
BL	British Library
BLitt	Bachelor of Letters; Bachelor of Literature
BM	Bachelor of Music; British Museum
BME, BMEd	Bachelor of Music Education
BMI	Broadcast Music, Inc. (USA)
BMus	Bachelor of Music
bn	bassoon
Bros.	Brothers
BS, BSc	Bachelor of Science
Bucks.	Buckinghamshire (GB)
Bulg.	Bulgarian
bur.	buried

c	circa [about]
CA	California (USA)
Cambs.	Cambridgeshire (GB)
cap.	capacity
carn.	Carnival
cb	contrabass [instrument]
CBC	Canadian Broadcasting Corporation
CBE	Commander of the Order of the British Empire
CBS	Columbia Broadcasting System (USA)
CBSO	City of Birmingham Symphony Orchestra
CD	compact disc
cel	celesta
cf	confer [compare]
CG	Covent Garden, London
CH	Companion of Honour
chap.	chapter
Chin.	Chinese
Cie	Compagnie
cl	clarinet
cm	centimetre(s)
cmda	comédie mêlée d'ariettes
CNRS	Centre National de la Recherche Scientifique (F)
CO	Colorado (USA)
Co.	Company; County
col(s).	column(s)
coll.	collection, collected by
collab.	collaborator, in collaboration with
comp.	composer, composed
conc.	concerto
cond.	conductor, conducted by
cont	continuo
contrib(s).	contribution(s)
Corp.	Corporation
CRI	Composers Recordings, Inc. (USA)
CSc	Candidate of Historical Sciences
CT	Connecticut (USA)
Ct	countertenor
CUNY	City University of New York
CVO	Commander of the Royal Victorian Order
Cz.	Czech

D	Deutsch catalogue [Schubert]
d	died
d.	denarius, denarii [penny, pence]
Dan.	Danish
db	double bass
DBE	Dame Commander of the Order of the British Empire
dbn	double bassoon
DC	District of Columbia (USA)

DE	Delaware (USA)
Dec	December
ded.	dedication, dedicated (to)
Dept	Department
Derbys.	Derbyshire (GB)
DFA	Doctor of Fine Arts
dg	dramma giocoso
dir.	director, directed by
diss.	dissertation
DLitt	Doctor of Letters; Doctor of Literature
DMA	Doctor of Musical Arts
DMus	Doctor of Music
DPhil	Doctor of Philosophy
Dr	Doctor
DSc	Doctor of Science; Doctor of Historical Sciences

E.	east, eastern
EBU	European Broadcasting Union
ed(s).	editor(s); edited (by)
edn(s)	edition(s)
e.g.	exempli gratia [for example]
elec	electric, electronic
EMI	Electrical and Musical Industries
Eng.	English
eng hn	english horn
ENO	English National Opera
ens	ensemble
esp.	especially
etc.	et cetera [and so on]
ex., exx.	example, examples

f	forte
f., ff.	folio, folios
facs.	facsimile
fasc.	fascicle
Feb	February
ff	following pages
ff	fortissimo
fff	fortississimo
fig.	figure [illustration]
FL	Florida (USA)
fl	flute
fl	floruit [he/she flourished]
fp	fortepiano
Fr.	French
frag(s).	fragment(s)

GA	Georgia (USA)
Ger.	German
Gk.	Greek
Glam.	Glamorgan (GB)
glock	glockenspiel
Gloucs.	Gloucestershire (GB)
GmbH	Gesellschaft mit beschränkter Haftung [limited-liability company]
govt.	government
GSM	Guildhall School of Music and Drama, London
gui	guitar

H	Hoboken catalogue [Haydn]
Hants.	Hampshire (GB)
Heb.	Hebrew
Herts.	Hertfordshire (GB)
HI	Hawaii (USA)
HMS	His/Her Majesty's Ship
HMV	His Master's Voice
hn	horn
Hon.	Honorary; Honourable
hpd	harpsichord
HRH	His/Her Royal Highness
Hung.	Hungarian
Hunts.	Huntingdonshire (GB)
Hz	Hertz [cycle(s) per second]

IA	Iowa (USA)
IAML	International Association of Music Libraries
ibid	ibidem [in the same place]
ID	Idaho (USA)
i.e.	id est [that is]
IL	Illinois (USA)
IMS	International Musicological Society
IN	Indiana (USA)
Inc.	Incorporated
inc.	incomplete
incl.	includes, including
inst(s)	instrument(s); instrumental
int	intermezzo
IRCAM	Institut de Recherche et de Coordination Acoustique/Musique (F)
ISAM	Institute for Studies in American Music
ISCM	International Society for Contemporary Music
ISM	Incorporated Society of Musicians (GB)
It.	Italian

Jan	January
Jap.	Japanese
Jb	Jahrbuch [yearbook]
Jg.	Jahrgang [year of publication/volume]
jr	junior

K	Köchel catalogue [Mozart; no. after / is from 6th edn]
kbd	keyboard
KBE	Knight Commander of the Order of the British Empire
KCVO	Knight Commander of the Royal Victorian Order
Kgl	Königlich [royal]
kHz	kilohertz [1000 cycles per second]
km	kilometre(s)
KS	Kansas (USA)
KY	Kentucky (USA)

£	libra, librae [pounds, pounds sterling]
LA	Louisiana (USA)
Lancs.	Lancashire (GB)
Lat.	Latin
Leics.	Leicestershire (GB)
lib(s).	libretto(s)
Lincs.	Lincolnshire (GB)
LittD	Doctor of Letters; Doctor of Literature
LlB	Bachelor of Laws
LlD	Doctor of Laws
LP	long-playing record
LPO	London Philharmonic Orchestra
LSO	London Symphony Orchestra
Ltd	Limited

m	metre(s)
M.	Monsieur
MA	Master of Arts
MA	Massachusetts (USA)
mand	mandolin

mar	marimba
MBE	Member of the Order of the British Empire
MD	Maryland (USA)
ME	Maine (USA)
Met	Metropolitan Opera, New York
Mez	mezzo-soprano
mf	mezzo-forte
MFA	Master of Fine Arts
MI	Michigan (USA)
MLitt	Master of Letters; Master of Literature
Mlle(s)	Mademoiselle(s)
MM	Master of Music
M.M.	Metronome Maelzel
mm	millimetre(s)
Mme	Madame
MMus	Master of Music
MN	Minnesota (USA)
MO	Missouri (USA)
mod	modulator
Mon.	Monmouthshire (GB)
movt	movement
MP	Member of Parliament (GB)
mp	mezzo-piano
MPhil	Master of Philosophy
Mr	Mister
Mrs	Mistress
MS(S)	manuscript(s); Master of Science
MS	Mississippi (USA)
MSc	Master of Science
MT	Montana (USA)
Mt	Mount
MusB, MusBac	Bachelor of Music
MusD, MusDoc	Doctor of Music
MusM	Master of Music

N.	north, northern
nar	narrator
NBC	National Broadcasting Company (USA)
NC	North Carolina (USA)
ND	North Dakota (USA)
n.d.	no date (of publication)
NE	Nebraska (USA)
NEA	National Endowment for the Arts (USA)
NEH	National Endowment for the Humanities (USA)
NET	National Educational Television (USA)
NH	New Hampshire (USA)
NHK	Nippon Hōsō Kyōkai [Japanese national broadcasting system]
NJ	New Jersey (USA)
NM	New Mexico (USA)
no(s).	number(s)
Nor.	Norwegian
Northants.	Northamptonshire (GB)
Notts.	Nottinghamshire (GB)
Nov	November
n.p.	no place (of publication)
nr	near
NSW	New South Wales (Australia)
NV	Nevada (USA)
NY	New York State (USA)
NZ	New Zealand

ob	opera buffa; oboe
obbl	obbligato
OBE	Officer of the Order of the British Empire
OC	Opéra-Comique [company]
oc	opéra comique [genre]
Oct	October
OH	Ohio (USA)
OK	Oklahoma (USA)
OM	Order of Merit
Ont.	Ontario (Canada)
op	opera [genre]
op., opp.	opus, opera
opt.	optional
OR	Oregon (USA)
orch	orchestra, orchestral, orchestration
orchd	orchestrated (by)
org	organ
orig.	original(ly)
ORTF	Office de Radiodiffusion-Télévision Française
os	opera seria
OUP	Oxford University Press
ov(s).	overture(s)
Oxon.	Oxfordshire (GB)

P	Pincherle catalogue [Vivaldi]
p	piano
p., pp.	page, pages
PA	Pennsylvania (USA)
p.a.	per annum
PBS	Public Broadcasting Service (USA)
perc	percussion
perf(s).	performance(s); performed (by)
pf	piano(forte)
PhD	Doctor of Philosophy
pic	piccolo
pl(s).	plate(s); plural
p.m.	post meridiem [after noon]
PO	Philharmonic Orchestra
Pol.	Polish
pop.	population
Port.	Portuguese
posth.	posthumous(ly)
POW	prisoner of war
pp	pianissimo
ppp	pianississimo
pr.	printed
PRO	Public Record Office, London
prol.	prologue
PRS	Performing Right Society
Ps, ps	psalm
pseud.	pseudonym
pt(s)	part(s)
pubd	published
pubn	publication

qnt	quintet
qt	quartet

/R	(editorial) revision [in signature]
R	photographic reprint
r	recto
RAF	Royal Air Force
RAI	Radio Audizioni Italiane
RAM	Royal Academy of Music, London
RCA	Radio Corporation of America
RCM	Royal College of Music, London
rec	recorder
recit(s).	recitative(s)
red.	reduction, reduced for
repr.	reprinted
Rev.	Reverend
rev(s).	revision(s); revised (by/for)
RI	Rhode Island (USA)
RIdIM	Répertoire International d'Iconographie Musicale
RILM	Répertoire International de Littérature Musicale

RISM	Répertoire International des Sources Musicales
RMCM	Royal Manchester College of Music
RNCM	Royal Northern College of Music, Manchester
RO	Radio Orchestra
Rom.	Romanian
r.p.m.	revolution(s) per minute
RPO	Royal Philharmonic Orchestra (GB)
RSFSR	Russian Soviet Federated Socialist Republic
RSO	Radio Symphony Orchestra
RTE	Radio Telefís Éireann (Ireland)
RTF	Radiodiffusion-Télévision Française
Rt Hon.	Right Honourable
Russ.	Russian
RV	Ryom catalogue [Vivaldi]
S	San, Santa, Santo, São [Saint]; soprano [voice]
$	dollar(s)
S.	south, southern
s	soprano [instrument]
s.	solidus, solidi [shilling, shillings]
SACEM	Société d'Auteurs, Compositeurs et Editeurs de Musique (F)
Sask.	Saskatchewan (Canada)
sax	saxophone
SC	South Carolina (USA)
SD	South Dakota (USA)
Sept	September
ser.	series
Serb.	Serbian
sf, *sfz*	sforzando, sforzato
sing.	singular
SO	Symphony Orchestra
Sp.	Spanish
Spl	Singspiel
SPNM	Society for the Promotion of New Music (GB)
spr.	spring
sq	square
sr	senior
SS	Saints
Ss	Santissima, Santissimo
SSR	Soviet Socialist Republic
St	Saint, Sankt, Sint, Szent
Staffs.	Staffordshire (GB)
Ste	Sainte
str	string(s)
sum.	summer
SUNY	State University of New York (USA)
suppl(s).	supplement(s); supplementary
Swed.	Swedish
sym(s).	symphony (symphonies); symphonic
synth	synthesizer
T	tenor [voice]
t	tenor [instrument]
timp	timpani
TN	Tennessee (USA)
tpt	trumpet
Tr	treble [voice]
tr	treble [instrument]
trans.	translation, translated by
transcr.	transcription, transcribed by
trbn	trombone
TV	television
TX	Texas (USA)
U.	University
UCLA	University of California at Los Angeles (USA)
UHF	ultra-high frequency
UK	United Kingdom of Great Britain and Northern Ireland
Ukr.	Ukrainian
unacc.	unaccompanied
unattrib.	unattributed
UNESCO	United Nations Educational, Scientific and Cultural Organization
UNICEF	United Nations International Children's Emergency Fund
unperf.	unperformed
unpubd	unpublished
US	United States [adjective]
USA	United States of America
USSR	Union of Soviet Socialist Republics
UT	Utah (USA)
v, vv	voice, voices
v	verso
v., vv.	verse, verses
VA	Virginia (USA)
va	viola
vc	cello
VHF	very high frequency
vib	vibraphone
viz	videlicet [namely]
vle	violone
vn	violin
vol(s).	volume(s)
vs	vocal score, piano-vocal score
VT	Vermont (USA)
W.	west, western
WA	Washington (USA)
Warwicks.	Warwickshire (GB)
WI	Wisconsin (USA)
Wilts.	Wiltshire (GB)
wint.	winter
WNO	Welsh National Opera
WoO, WOO	Werk(e) ohne Opuszahl [work(s) without opus number]
Worcs.	Worcestershire (GB)
WV	West Virginia (USA)
ww	woodwind
WY	Wyoming (USA)
xyl	xylophone
Yorks.	Yorkshire (GB)
Z	Zimmerman catalogue [Purcell]
zar	zarzuela
*	autograph manuscript

Bibliographical Abbreviations

The bibliographical abbreviations used in this dictionary are listed below. Full bibliographical information is not normally supplied for national biographical dictionaries and general music reference works, or if details may be found elsewhere in this dictionary under the heading 'Dictionaries and guides' or 'Editions' (relevant items are indicated with D or E, respectively). General music periodicals are shown with dates only; for those in existence before 1980 full information may be found in the list forming part of the article 'Periodicals' in *The New Grove Dictionary of Music and Musicians*. Opera periodicals, listed in the present dictionary under the heading 'Periodicals', are shown here with an asterisk and serial number in brackets.

In this list, and throughout the dictionary, italic type is used for periodicals and reference works, and roman type for anthologies of music, series etc.

AcM — *Acta musicologica* (1928/9–)
ADB — *Allgemeine deutsche Biographie* (Leipzig, 1875–1912)
AllacciD — L. Allacci: *Drammaturgia* D
AMe (*AMeS*) — *Algemene muziekencyclopedie* (and suppl.) (Antwerp and Amsterdam, 1957–63; suppl., 1972)
AMf — *Archiv für Musikforschung* (1936–43)
AMI — L'arte musicale in Italia E
AMw — *Archiv für Musikwissenschaft* (1918/19–)
AMZ — *Allgemeine musikalische Zeitung* (1798/9–1882)
AMz — *Allgemeine Musik-Zeitung* (1874–1943)
AnM — *Anuario musical* (1946–)
AnMc — *Analecta musicologica* (some vols. in series Studien zur italienisch-deutschen Musikgeschichte), Veröffentlichungen der Musikabteilung des Deutschen historischen Instituts in Rom (Cologne, 1963–)

Baker6(–8) — *Baker's Biographical Dictionary of Musicians* (New York, 6/1978, 7/1984, 8/1992)
BAMS — *Bulletin of the American Musicological Society* (1936–48)
BDA — *A Biographical Dictionary of Actors, Actresses, Musicians, Dancers, Managers & Other Stage Personnel in London, 1660–1800* D
BeJb — *Beethoven-Jahrbuch* (1953/4–)
BMB — Bibliotheca musica bononiensis E
BMw — *Beiträge zur Musikwissenschaft* (1959–)
BNB — *Biographie nationale [belge]* (Brussels, 1866–86)
BordasD — *Dictionnaire de la musique* (Paris: Bordas, 1970–76)
Bouwsteenen: JVNM — *Bouwsteenen: jaarboek der Vereeniging voor Nederlandsche muziekgeschiedenis* (1869/72–1874/81)
BSIM — *Bulletin français de la S[ociété] I[nternationale de] M*[usique] [previously *Le Mercure musical*; also other titles] (1905–14)
BUCEM — *British Union-Catalogue of Early Music*, ed. E. Schnapper (London, 1957)
BurneyFI — C. Burney: *The Present State of Music in France and Italy* (London, 1771, 2/1773); ed. P. A. Scholes, *Dr. Burney's Musical Tours in Europe* (London, 1959)
BurneyGN — C. Burney: *The Present State of Music in Germany, the Netherlands, and United Provinces* (London, 1773, 2/1775); ed. P. A. Scholes, *Dr. Burney's Musical Tours in Europe* (London, 1959)
BurneyH — C. Burney: *A General History of Music from the Earliest Ages to the Present* (London, 1776–89) [p. nos. refer to edn of 1935]

CBY — *Current Biography Yearbook* (New York, 1940–)
CHM — *Collectanea historiae musicae* (in series Biblioteca historiae musicae cultores) (Florence, 1953–)
CMc — *Current Musicology* (1965–)
CMI — I classici musicali italiani E
ČMm — *Časopis Moravského musea* [Journal of the Moravian Museum] (*c*1915–)
CMz — *Cercetări di muzicologie* (1969–)
COJ — *Cambridge Opera Journal* [*Great Britain 27]
CroceN — B. Croce: *I teatri di Napoli* D
ČSHS — *Československý hudební slovník* (Prague, 1963–5)
CSPD — *Calendar of State Papers (Domestic)* (London, 1856–1972)

DAB — *Dictionary of American Biography* (New York, 1928–36; 8 suppls., 1944–88)
DAM — *Dansk aarbog for musikforskning* (1961–)
DBF — *Dictionnaire de biographie française* (Paris, 1933–)
DBI — *Dizionario biografico degli italiani* (Rome, 1960–)

DBL — *Dansk biografisk leksikon* (Copenhagen, 1887–1905, 2/1933–)
DBP — *Dicionário biográfico de músicos portuguezes* (Lisbon, 1900–04)
DDT — Denkmäler deutscher Tonkunst E
DEUMM — *Dizionario enciclopedico universale della musica e dei musicisti* (Turin, 1985–8)
DJbM — *Deutsches Jahrbuch der Musikwissenschaft* (1957–)
DMV — Drammaturgia musicale veneta E
DNB — *Dictionary of National Biography* (London, 1885–1901, suppls.)
DTB — Denkmäler der Tonkunst in Bayern E
DTÖ — Denkmäler der Tonkunst in Österreich E

EDM — Das Erbe deutscher Musik E
EIT — *Ezhegodnik imperatorskikh teatrov* (1892–1915)
EitnerQ — R. Eitner: *Biographisch-bibliographisches Quellen-Lexikon* (Leipzig, 1900–04, 2/1959–60)
EitnerS — R. Eitner: *Bibliographie der Musik-Sammelwerke des XVI. und XVII. Jahrhunderts* (Berlin, 1877)
EMC — *Encyclopedia of Music in Canada* (Toronto, 1981)
EMc — *Early Music* (1973–)
EMDC — *Encyclopédie de la musique et dictionnaire du Conservatoire* (Paris, 1920–31)
ERO — Early Romantic Opera E
ES — *Enciclopedia dello spettacolo* D
EwenD — D. Ewen: *American Composers: a Biographical Dictionary* (New York, 1982)

FAM — *Fontes artis musicae* (1954–)
FasquelleE — *Encyclopédie de la musique* (Paris: Fasquelle, 1958–61)
FétisB (*FétisBS*) — F.-J. Fétis: *Biographie universelle des musiciens* (and suppl.) (Brussels, 2/1860–65; suppl., 1878–80)
FlorimoN — F. Florimo: *La scuola musicale di Napoli e i suoi conservatorii* (Naples, 1880–83)
FO — French Opera in the 17th and 18th Centuries E

GänzlBMT — K. Gänzl: *The British Musical Theatre* D
GerberL — E. L. Gerber: *Historisch-biographisches Lexikon der Tonkünstler* (Leipzig, 1790–92)
GerberNL — E. L. Gerber: *Neues historisch-biographisches Lexikon der Tonkünstler* (Leipzig, 1812–14)
GfMKB — *Gesellschaft für Musikforschung Kongressbericht* (1950–)
GiacomoC — S. Di Giacomo: *I quattro antichi conservatorii musicali di Napoli* (Milan and Naples, 1924–8)
GMB — *Geschichte der Musik in Beispielen*, ed. A. Schering (Leipzig, 1931)
GOB — German Opera 1770–1800, ed. T. Bauman E
Grove1(–5) — G. Grove, ed.: *A Dictionary of Music and Musicians* (London, 1878–90; 2/1904–10 ed. J. A. Fuller Maitland, 3/1927–8 and 4/1940 ed. H. C. Colles, 5/1954 ed. E. Blom with suppl. 1961, all as *Grove's Dictionary of Music and Musicians*)
Grove6 — S. Sadie, ed.: *The New Grove Dictionary of Music and Musicians* (London, 1980)
GroveAM — H. W. Hitchcock and S. Sadie, eds.: *The New Grove Dictionary of American Music* (New York, 1986)
GroveI — S. Sadie, ed.: *The New Grove Dictionary of Musical Instruments* (London, 1984)
GSL — *Grosses Sängerlexikon* D
GV — *Le grandi voci: Dizionario critico-biografico dei cantanti con discografia operistica* D [where two authors are separated by a semi-colon, the second one compiled the discography]

HawkinsH — J. Hawkins: *A General History of the Science and Practice of Music* (London, 1776) [p. nos. refer to edn of 1853]
HayJb — *Haydn-Jahrbuch/Yearbook* (1962–71, 1975–8, 1980–)
HiFi — *High Fidelity* (1951/2–1965)
HiFi/MusAm — *High Fidelity/Musical America* (1965–87)
HJb — *Händel-Jahrbuch* (1928–33, 1955–)
HJbMw — *Hamburger Jahrbuch für Musikwissenschaft* (1975–)
HMT — *Handwörterbuch der musikalischen Terminologie* (Wiesbaden, 1972–)
HMw — Handbuch der Musikwissenschaft, ed. E. Bücken (Potsdam, 1927–) [monograph series]
HMYB — *Hinrichsen's Musical Year Book* (1944–61)
HPM — Harvard Publications in Music E
HR — *Hudební revue* (1908–20)
HRo — *Hudební rozhledy* (1948/9–)
HS — Handel Sources E
HV — *Hudební věda* (1961–)

IIM — *Izvestiya na Instituta za muzika* (1952–)
IMa — Instituta et monumenta E
IMSCR — *International Musicological Society Congress Report* (1930–)
IMusSCR — *International Musical Society Congress Report* (1906–11)
IOB — Italian Opera 1640–1770, ed. H. M. Brown E
IOG — Italian Opera 1810–1840, ed. P. Gossett E
IRASM — *International Review of the Aesthetics and Sociology of Music* (1971–)
IRMAS — *The International Review of Music Aesthetics and Sociology* (1970–71)
IRMO — S. L. Ginzburg: *Istoriya russkoy muzïki v notnïkh obraztsakh* (Moscow, 2/1968–70)
ISAMm — Institute for Studies in American Music, monograph series

JAMS — *Journal of the American Musicological Society* (1949–)
JbMP — *Jahrbuch der Musikbibliothek Peters* (1895–1941)
JbO — *Jahrbuch für Opernforschung* [*Germany 60]
JM — *Journal of Musicology* (1983–)
JMT — *Journal of Music Theory* (1957–)
JRBM — *Journal of Renaissance and Baroque Music* (1946–7)
JRMA — *Journal of the Royal Musical Association* (1987–)
JVNM — see *Bouwsteenen: JVNM*

KJb — *Kirchenmusikalisches Jahrbuch* (1886–1911, 1930–35, 1936/8, 1950–)
KM — *Kwartalnik muzyczny* (1911/13–1913/14, 1928/9–1933, 1948–50)
Kobbé10 — G. Kobbé: *Complete Opera Book* (New York and London, 10/1987) D

LaborD	*Diccionario de la música Labor* (Barcelona, 1954)
LaMusicaD	*La musica: dizionario* (Turin, 1968–71)
LaMusicaE	*La musica: enciclopedia storica* (Turin, 1966)
LM	*Lucrări di muzicologie* (1965–)
LoewenbergA	A. Loewenberg: *Annals of Opera 1597–1940* D
LS	*The London Stage, 1660–1800* D
MA	*The Musical Antiquary* (1909/10–1912/13)
MAS	Musical Antiquarian Society [Publications] E
MB	Musica britannica E
MD	*Musica disciplina* (1948–)
ME	*Muzïkal'naya entsiklopediya* (Moscow, 1973–82)
Mf	*Die Musikforschung* (1948–)
MGG	*Die Musik in Geschichte und Gegenwart* (Kassel and Basle, 1949–68; suppl., 1973–9, index 1986)
MJb	*Mozart-Jahrbuch des Zentralinstituts für Mozartforschung* (1950–)
ML	*Music and Letters* (1920–)
MLE	Music for London Entertainment, 1660–1800 E
MM	*Modern Music* (1925–46)
MMA	*Miscellanea musicologica* [Australia] (1966–70, 1972, 1975, 1977–)
MMC	*Miscellanea musicologica* [Czechoslovakia] (1956–62, 1965–1971/3, 1975–)
MMg	*Monatshefte für Musikgeschichte* (1869–1905)
MMR	*The Monthly Musical Record* (1871–1960)
MMS	Monumenta musicae svecicae E
MO	*Musical Opinion* (1877/8–)
MQ	*The Musical Quarterly* (1915–)
MR	*The Music Review* (1940–)
MS	*Muzïkal'nïy sovremennik* (1915/16–1916/17)
MSD	Musicological Studies and Documents, ed. A. Carapetyan (Rome, 1951–)
MT	*The Musical Times* (1844/5–)
MusAm	*Musical America* (1898–1964, 1987–92)
MZ	*Muzikološki zbornik* (1965–)
NA	*Note d'archivio per la storia musicale* (1924–7, 1930–43)
NAW	*Notable American Women* (Cambridge, MA, 1971; suppl., 1980)
NBJb	*Neues Beethoven-Jahrbuch* (1924–5, 1927, 1930, 1933, 1935, 1937–9, 1942)
NBL	*Norsk biografisk leksikon* (Oslo, 1921–)
NDB	*Neue deutsche Biographie* (Berlin, 1953–)
NicollH	A. Nicoll: *A History of English Drama, 1660–1900* (Cambridge, 1952–9)
NMA	W. A. Mozart: Neue Ausgabe sämtlicher Werke, ed. E. F. Schmid, W. Plath and W. Rehm (Kassel, 1955–91)
NNBW	*Nieuw Nederlandsch biografisch woordenboek* (Leiden, 1911–37)
NÖB	*Neue österreichische Biographie* (Vienna, 1923)
NOHM	*The New Oxford History of Music*, ed. E. Wellesz, J. A. Westrup and G. Abraham (London, 1954–)
NRMI	*Nuova rivista musicale italiana* (1967–)
NZM	*Neue Zeitschrift für Musik* (1834–1943, 1950–74, 1979–)
OC	*Opera in Canada* [*Canada 1]
OHM	*The Oxford History of Music*, ed. W. H. Hadow (Oxford, 1901–5, enlarged 2/1929–38)
OM	*Opus musicum* (1969–)
ÖMz	*Österreichische Musikzeitschrift* (1946–)
ON	*Opera News* [*USA 13]
OQ	*The Opera Quarterly* [*USA 28]
OW	*Opernwelt* [*Germany 42]
PAMS	*Papers of the American Musicological Society* (1936–8, 1940–41)
PÄMw	Publikationen älterer praktischer und theoretischer Musikwerke E
PBC	Publicaciones del departamento de música de la Biblioteca de Catalunya E
PEM	*Pipers Enzyklopädie des Musiktheaters* D
PMA	*Proceedings of the Musical Association* (1874/5–1943/4)
PNM	*Perspectives of New Music* (1962/3–)
PRM	*Polski rocznik muzykologiczny* (1935–6)
PRMA	*Proceedings of the Royal Musical Association* (1944/5–1984/5)
PSB	*Polskich słownik biograficzny* (Kraków, 1935)
QRaM	*Quaderni della Rassegna musicale* (1964–72)
Rad JAZU	*Rad Jugoslavenske akademije znanosti i umjetnosti* (Zagreb, 1867–)
RaM	*La rassegna musicale* (1928–43, 1947–62)
RBM	*Revue belge de musicologie* (1946–)
RdM	*Revue de musicologie* (1917/19–1943, 1945–)
RdMc	*Revista de musicología* (1978–)
ReM	*La revue musicale* (1920–40, 1946–)
RHCM	*Revue d'histoire et de critique musicales* (1901); *La revue musicale* (1902–11)
RicordiE	*Enciclopedia della musica* (Milan: Ricordi, 1963–4)
RiemannL 11,12	H. Riemann: *Musik-Lexikon* (Leipzig, 1882, 11/1929 rev. A. Einstein, 12/1959–75 rev. W. Gurlitt, H. H. Eggebrecht and C. Dahlhaus)
RIM	*Rivista italiana di musicologia* (1966–)
RISM	*Répertoire international des sources musicales* (Munich and Duisburg, 1960–; Kassel, 1971–)
RMARC	*R[oyal] M[usical] A[ssociation] Research Chronicle* (1961–)
RMFC	*Recherches sur la musique française classique* (1960–)
RMG	*Russkaya muzïkal'naya gazeta* (1894–1917)
RMI	*Rivista musicale italiana* (1894–1932, 1936–43, 1946–55)
RosaM	C. de Rosa, Marchese di Villarosa: *Memorie dei compositori di musica del Regno di Napoli* (Naples, 1840)
RRAM	Recent Researches in American Music E
RRMBE	Recent Researches in the Music of the Baroque Era E
RRMCE	Recent Researches in the Music of the Classical Era E
SBL	*Svenska biografiskt leksikon* (Stockholm, 1918–)
SchmidlD (SchmidlDS)	C. Schmidl: *Dizionario universale dei musicisti* (and suppl.) (Milan, 1887–90, 2/1928–9; suppl., 1938)
SCMA	Smith College Music Archives E
SeegerL	H. Seeger: *Musiklexikon* (Leipzig, 1966)
SH	*Slovenská hudba* (1957–71)
SIMG	*Sammelbände der Internationalen Musik-Gesellschaft* (1899/1900–1913/14)

SM — *Studia musicologica Academiae scientiarum hungaricae* (1961–)
SMA — *Studies in Music* (1967–) [Australia]
SML — *Schweizer Musiker Lexikon* (Zürich, 1964)
SMN — *Studia musicologica norvegica* (1968, 1976–)
SMP — *Słownik muzyków polskich* (Kraków, 1964–7)
SMw — *Studien zur Musikwissenschaft* (1913–16, 1918–34, 1955–6, 1960–66, 1977–)
SMz — *Schweizerische Musikzeitung/Revue musicale suisse* (1861–)
SOI — *Storia dell'opera italiana*, ed. L. Bianconi and G. Pestelli (Turin, 1987–)
SouthernB — E. Southern: *Biographical Dictionary of Afro-American and African Musicians* (Westport, CT, 1982)
SovM — *Sovetskaya muzika* (1933–41, 1946–)
StiegerO — F. Stieger: *Opernlexikon* D
STMf — *Svensk tidskrift för musikforskning* (1919–)

TVNM — *Tijdschrift van de Vereniging voor Nederlandse muziekgeschiedenis* (1885–)

VintonD — J. Vinton, ed.: *Dictionary of Contemporary Music* (New York, 1974)
VMw — *Vierteljahrsschrift für Musikwissenschaft* (1885–94)
VogelB — E. Vogel: *Bibliothek der gedruckten weltlichen Vocalmusik Italiens, aus den Jahren 1500 bis 1700* (Berlin, 1892); rev., enlarged, by A. Einstein (Hildesheim, 1962); further addns in *AnMc*, nos.4, 5, 9 and 12; further rev. by F. Lesure and C. Sartori as *Bibliografia della musica italiana vocale profana pubblicata dal 1500 al 1700* (Geneva, 1978)

WaltherML — J. G. Walther: *Musicalisches Lexicon oder Musicalische Bibliothek* (Leipzig, 1732)
WE — The Wellesley Edition E
WurzbachL — C. von Wurzbach: *Biographisches Lexikon des Kaiserthums Oesterreich* (Vienna, 1856–91)

ZfM — *Zeitschrift für Musik* (1920–55)
ZIMG — *Zeitschrift der Internationalen Musik-Gesellschaft* (1899/1900–1913/14)
ZL — *Zenei lexikon* (Budapest, 1930–31, 2/1965)
ZMw — *Zeitschrift für Musikwissenschaft* (1918/19–1935)

Library Sigla

The system of library sigla in this dictionary follows that used in its publications (Series A) by Répertoire International des Sources Musicales, Kassel, by permission. Below are listed the sigla to be found; a few of them are additional to those in the published RISM lists, but have been established in consultation with the RISM organization. Some original RISM sigla that have now been changed are retained here.

In the dictionary, sigla are always printed in *italic*. In any listing of sources a national sigillum applies without repetition until it is contradicted.

Within each national list below, entries are alphabetized by sigillum, first by capital letters (showing the city or town) and then by lower-case ones (showing the institution or collection).

A: AUSTRIA

Gk(h)	Graz, Hochschule für Musik und Darstellende Kunst und Landesmusikschule
Gmi	——, Musikwissenschaftliches Institut der Universität
HE	Heiligenkreuz, Zisterzienserstift
KR	Kremsmünster, Benediktinerstift
LA	Lambach, Benediktinerstift
LIm	Linz, Oberösterreichisches Landesmuseum
M	Melk an der Donau, Benediktinerstift
Sca	Salzburg, Museum Carolino Augusteum
Sm	——, Mozarteum (Internationale Stiftung Mozarteum)
Ssp	——, St Peter (Erzstift oder Benediktiner-Erzabtei)
Su	——, Universitätsbibliothek
SPL	St Paul, Stift
ST	Stams, Zisterzienserstift
Wdtö	Vienna, Gesellschaft zur Herausgabe von Denkmälern der Tonkunst in Österreich
Wgm	——, Gesellschaft der Musikfreunde
Wm	——, Minoritenkonvent
Wn	——, Österreichische Nationalbibliothek, Musiksammlung
Wst	——, Stadtbibliothek, Musiksammlung

ARG: ARGENTINA

BAc	Buenos Aires, Teatro Colón

AUS: AUSTRALIA

CAnl	Canberra, National Library of Australia
Msl	Melbourne, State Library of Victoria
NLwm	Nedlands, Wigmore Music Library, University of Western Australia
Scm	Sydney, New South Wales State Conservatorium of Music
Sfl	——, Fisher Library, University of Sydney

B: BELGIUM

Aa	Antwerp, Stadsarchief
Aac	——, Archief en Museum voor het Vlaamse Culturleven
Ac	——, Koninklijk Vlaams Muziekconservatorium
Ba	Brussels, Archives de la Ville
Bc	——, Conservatoire Royal de Musique
Bcdm	——, Centre Belge de Documentation Musicale [CeBeDeM]
Bmichotte	——, Michotte private collection
Br	——, Bibliothèque Royale Albert 1er/Koninklijke Bibliotheek Albert I
Gc	Ghent, Koninklijk Muziekconservatorium
Gu	——, Rijksuniversiteit, Centrale Bibliotheek
Lc	Liège, Conservatoire Royal de Musique
Lg	——, Musée Grétry

BR: BRAZIL

Rem	Rio de Janeiro, Escola Nacional de Música, Universidade do Brasil
Rn	——, Biblioteca Nacional

C: CANADA

HNu	Hamilton, McMaster University, Mills Memorial Library
Lu	London, University of Western Ontario, Lawson Memorial Library
On	Ottawa, National Library of Canada
Qsl	Quebec, Séminaire de Québec
Tp	Toronto, Metropolitan Toronto Library, Music Department
Tu	——, University of Toronto, Edward Johnson Music Library

CH: SWITZERLAND

Bu	Basle, Öffentliche Bibliothek der Universität, Musiksammlung
BEl	Berne, Schweizerische Landesbibliothek
E	Einsiedeln, Kloster
EN	Engelberg, Stift
Gc	Geneva, Conservatoire de Musique
Lmg	Lucerne, Allgemeine Musikalische Gesellschaft

Lz	——, Zentralbibliothek
LAcu	Lausanne, Bibliothèque Cantonale et Universitaire
MONbonynge	Montreux, Richard Bonynge, private collection
N	Neuchâtel, Bibliothèque Publique et Universitaire
Zschmitt	Zürich, Schmitt private collection
Zz	——, Zentralbibliothek

CS: CZECHOSLOVAKIA

Bm	Brno, Ústav Dějin Hudby Moravského Musea, Hudebněhistorické Oddělení
Bu	——, Universitní Knihovna
K	Český Krumlov, Pracoviště Státního Archívu Třeboň, Hudební Sbírka
KRa	Kroměříž, Státní Zámek a Zahrady, Historicko-Umělecké Fondy, Hudební Archív
KU	Kutná Hora, Oblastní Muzeum
Pk	Prague, Archív Státní Konservatoře v Praze
Pnd	——, Archiv Národního Divadla
Pnm	——, Národní Muzeum, Hudební Oddělení
Pr	——, Československý Rozhlas, Hudební Archív Různá Provenience
Pu	——, Národní Knihovna v Praze, Universitní Knihovna

CU: CUBA

Hin	Havana, Instituto Nacional de la Música
Hn	——, Biblioteca Nacional

D: GERMANY

As	Augsburg, Staats- und Stadtbibliothek
Au	——, Universitätsbibliothek
ALa	Altenburg, Historisches Staatsarchiv
AN	Ansbach, Regierungsbibliothek
B	Berlin, Staatsbibliothek Preussischer Kulturbesitz, Musikabteilung
Ba	——, Amerika-Gedenkbibliothek (Berliner Zentralbibliothek); Deutsche Akademie der Künste
Bbb	——, Bote & Bock Archiv
Bdhm	——, Deutsche Hochschule für Musik Hanns Eisler
Bds	——, Deutsche Staatsbibliothek (formerly Königliche Bibliothek; Preussische Staatsbibliothek; Öffentliche Wissenschaftliche Bibliothek), Musikabteilung
Bdso	——, Deutsche Staatsoper
Bhbk	——, Staatliche Hochschule für Bildende Kunst
Bhm	——, Staatliche Hochschule für Musik und Darstellende Kunst
Bko	——, Komische Oper
Bmm	——, Märkisches Museum
Bp	——, Pädagogisches Zentrum
Bsommer	——, Sommer private collection
Bsp	——, Sprachkonvikt
BAs	Bamberg, Staatsbibliothek
BAL	Ballenstedt, Stadtbibliothek
BAR	Bartenstein, Fürszt zu Hohenlohe-Bartensteinsches Archiv [in *NEhz*]
BB	Benediktbeuern, Pfarrkirche
BMs	Bremen, Staats- und Universitätsbibliothek
BNu	Bonn, Universitätsbibliothek
BS	Brunswick, Öffentliche Bücherei (Stadtarchiv und Stadtbibliothek)
Cl	Coburg, Landesbibliothek
Dl	Dresden, Bibliothek und Museum Löbau [in *Dlb*]
Dla	——, Staatsarchiv
Dlb	——, Sächsische Landesbibliothek
Ds	——, Staatstheater
DEl	Dessau, Stadtbibliothek (formerly Universitäts- und Landesbibliothek)
DI	Dillingen an der Donau, Kreis- und Studienbibliothek
DL	Delitzsch, Museum und Bibliothek
DO	Donaueschingen, Fürstlich Fürstenbergische Hofbibliothek
DS	Darmstadt, Hessische Landes- und Hochschulbibliothek
DT	Detmold, Lippische Landesbibliothek
DÜl	Düsseldorf, Landes- und Stadtbibliothek
Es	Eichstätt, Staats- und Seminarbibliothek [in *Eu*]
Eu	——, Universitätsbibliothek
Ew	——, Benediktinerinnen-Abtei St Walburg
EB	Ebrach, Katholisches Pfarramt
F	Frankfurt am Main, Stadt- und Universitätsbibliothek
FS	Freising, Dombibliothek
Ga	Göttingen, Staatliches Archivlager
Gs	——, Niedersächsische Staats- und Universitätsbibliothek
Hmb	Hamburg, Hamburger Öffentliche Bücherhallen, Musikbibliothek
Hs	——, Staats- und Universitätsbibliothek Carl von Ossietzky
HAmi	Halle an der Saale, Martin-Luther-Universität, Sektion Germanistik und Kulturwissenschaften, Fachbereich Musikwissenschaft (formerly Institut für Musikwissenschaft)
HAu	——, Universitäts- und Landesbibliothek
HG	Havelberg, Prignitz-Museum
HR	Harburg über Donauwörth, Fürstlich Oettingen-Wallerstein'sche Bibliothek [in *Au*]
HVl	Hanover, Niedersächsische Landesbibliothek
HVs	——, Stadtbibliothek
Ju	Jena, Universitätsbibliothek der Friedrich-Schiller-Universität
Kl	Kassel, Landesbibliothek und Murhardsche Bibliothek der Stadt
KA	Karlsruhe, Badische Landesbibliothek
KIl	Kiel, Schleswig-Holsteinische Landesbibliothek
KNha	Cologne, Historisches Archiv der Stadt Köln
KNu	——, Universitäts- und Stadtbibliothek
Lr	Lüneburg, Ratsbücherei und Stadtarchiv
LEm	Leipzig, Musikbibliothek der Stadt Leipzig
LEmi	——, Sektion Kulturwissenschaften und Germanistik der Karl-Marx-Universität, Wissenschaftsgebiet Musikwissenschaft (formerly Institut für Musikwissenschaft) [in *LEu*]
LEu	——, Universitätsbibliothek der Karl-Marx-Universität
LÜh	Lübeck, Bibliothek der Hansestadt
Mbm	Munich, Metropolitankapitel [in *FS*]
Mbn	——, Bayerisches Nationalmuseum
Mbs	——, Bayerische Staatsbibliothek
Mh	——, Staatliche Hochschule für Musik
Mo	——, Opernarchiv
Mth	——, Theatermuseum (Clara-Ziegler-Stiftung)
MEIr	Meiningen, Staatliche Museen mit Reger-Archiv
MGmi	Marburg an der Lahn, Musikwissenschaftliches Institut der Philipps-Universität
MGs	——, Staatsarchiv und Archivschule
MH	Mannheim, Wissenschaftliche Stadtbibliothek und Universitätsbibliothek
MHrm	——, Städtisches Reiss-Museum
MÜp	Münster, Diözesanbibliothek, Bischöfliches Priesterseminar und Santini-Sammlung
MÜs	——, Santini-Bibliothek [in *MÜp*]
MÜu	——, Universitätsbibliothek
Ngm	Nuremberg, Germanisches National-Museum
Nst	——, Stadtbibliothek
NEhz	Neuenstein, Hohenlohe-Zentralarchiv

OB	Ottobeuren, Benediktiner-Abtei
Rp	Regensburg, Bischöfliche Zentralbibliothek
Rtt	——, Fürst Thurn und Taxis Hofbibliothek
RH	Rheda, Fürst zu Bentheim-Tecklenburgische Bibliothek [in *MÜu*]
ROmi	Rostock, Institut für Musikwissenschaft der Universität
ROu	——, Wilhelm-Pieck-Universität, Universitätsbibliothek
RUl	Rudolstadt, Staatsarchiv
Sl	Stuttgart, Württembergische Landesbibliothek
SHs	Sondershausen, Stadt- und Kreisbibliothek
SHsk	——, Schlosskirche [in *SHs*]
SWl	Schwerin, Wissenschaftliche Allgemeinbibliothek (formerly Mecklenburgische Landesbibliothek)
SWth	——, Mecklenburgisches Staatstheater
Tu	Tübingen, Eberhard-Karls-Universität, Universitätsbibliothek
W	Wolfenbüttel, Herzog-August-Bibliothek
Wa	——, Niedersächsisches Staatsarchiv
WD	Wiesentheid, Musiksammlung des Grafen von Schönborn-Wiesentheid
WEY	Weyarn, Pfarrkirche [in *FS*]
WIbh	Wiesbaden, Breitkopf & Härtel, Verlagsarchiv
WRdn	Weimar, Deutsches Nationaltheater
WRl	——, Staatsarchiv (formerly Landeshauptarchiv)
WRtl	——, Thüringische Landesbibliothek, Musiksammlung [in *WRz*]
WRz	——, Zentralbibliothek der deutschen Klassik
WS	Wasserburg am Inn, Chorarchiv St Jakob, Pfarramt [in *FS*]
WÜsa	Würzburg, Stadtarchiv
ZI	Zittau, Stadt- und Kreisbibliothek

DK: DENMARK

Kk	Copenhagen, Det Kongelige Bibliotek
Kmk	——, Det Kongelige Danske Musikkonservatorium
Km(m)	——, Musikhistorisk Museum
Sa	Sorø, Sorø Akademis Bibliotek

E: SPAIN

Bc	Barcelona, Biblioteca de Cataluña
Bcd	——, Centro de Documentación Musical
Bim	——, Instituto Español de Musicología
Bit	——, Instituto del Teatro (formerly Museo del Arte Escénico)
Boc	——, Biblioteca Orfeó Catalá
Fbaudot	El Ferrol, G. Baudot-Puentes, private collection
La	León, Catedral
Mc	Madrid, Conservatorio Superior de Música
Mcns	——, Congregación de Neustra Señora
Mm	——, Biblioteca Municipal
Mn	——, Biblioteca Nacional
Mp	——, Palacio Real
Msa	——, Sociedad General de Autores de España
SC	Santiago de Compostela, Catedral
Zac	Saragossa, Archivo de Música del Cabildo

EIRE: IRELAND

Dam	Dublin, Royal Irish Academy of Music
Dtc	——, Trinity College

F: FRANCE

A	Avignon, Bibliothèque Municipale Livrée Ceccano (formerly Musée Calvet)
AG	Agen, Archives Départementales
AIXc	Aix-en-Provence, Conservatoire
AIXm	——, Bibliothèque Municipale, Bibliothèque Méjanes
AM	Amiens, Bibliothèque Municipale
BER	Bernay, Bibliothèque Municipale
BO	Bordeaux, Bibliothèque Municipale
BOLbrindejoint	Boulogne, Y. Brindejoint, private collection
CLO	Clermont-de-l'Oise, Bibliothèque
COGbuckley	Cognac, W. Buckley, private collection
COM	Compiègne, Bibliothèque Municipale
Dc	Dijon, Bibliothèque du Conservatoire
Dm	——, Bibliothèque Municipale
Lm	Lille, Bibliothèque Municipale
LYm	Lyons, Bibliothèque Municipale
Mc	Marseilles, Conservatoire de Musique et de Déclamation
MAC	Mâcon, Bibliothèque Municipale
ML	Moulins, Bibliothèque Municipale
MON	Montauban, Bibliothèque Municipale
NAc	Nancy, Conservatoire
NS	Nîmes, Bibliothèque Municipale
Pa	Paris, Bibliothèque de l'Arsenal
Pbourdon	——, M.-M. Bourdon, private collection
Pc	——, Fonds du Conservatoire National de Musique [in *Pn*]
Pcf	——, Comédie-Française, Bibliothèque
Pi	——, Bibliothèque de l'Institut de France
Pim	——, Institut de Musicologie de l'Université
Plambert	——, Lambert private collection
Pm	——, Bibliothèque Mazarine
Pmeyer	——, André Meyer, private collection
Pn	——, Bibliothèque Nationale
Po	——, Bibliothèque-Musée de l'Opéra
Poffenbach	——, P. Comte-Offenbach, private collection
Prt	——, Office de Radiodiffusion-Télévision Française
Psal	——, Editions Salabert
R(m)	Rouen, Bibliothèque Municipale
Sim	Strasbourg, Institut de Musicologie de l'Université
SA	Salins, Bibliothèque Municipale
SMcusset	St-Maud, F. Cusset, private collection
SRPalmeida	St-Rémy-de-Provence, A. de Almeida, private collection
TLm	Toulouse, Bibliothèque Municipale
V	Versailles, Bibliothèque Municipale

GB: GREAT BRITAIN

ABu	Aberystwyth, University College of Wales
ALb	Aldeburgh, Britten-Pears Library
Bu	Birmingham, University of Birmingham, Barber Institute of Fine Arts
BEL	Belton (Lincs.), Belton House
BRu	Bristol, University of Bristol Library
Ccl	Cambridge, Central Library
Cfm	——, Fitzwilliam Museum
Ckc	——, King's College, Rowe Music Library
Cpl	——, Pendlebury Library of Music
Cu	——, University Library
CDp	Cardiff, Public Libraries, Central Library [in *CDu*]
CDu	——, University of Wales College of Cardiff (formerly University College of South Wales and Monmouthshire)
DRc	Durham, Cathedral
En	Edinburgh, National Library of Scotland
Er	——, Reid Music Library, University of Edinburgh
Ge	Glasgow, Euing Music Library
Gm	——, Mitchell Library
Gu	——, University Library
Lam	London, Royal Academy of Music

Lbl	——, British Library (formerly *Lbm*, British Museum)
Lcm	——, Royal College of Music
Lfm	——, Faber Music
Lgc	——, Gresham College (Guildhall Library)
Lkc	——, University of London, King's College
Lmic	——, British Music Information Centre
Lpro	——, Public Record Office
Lu	——, University of London, Music Library
Lue	——, Universal Edition
Lva	——, Victoria and Albert Museum
Lwa	——, Westminster Abbey
LEbc	Leeds, University of Leeds, Brotherton Collection
LVp	Liverpool, Public Libraries, Central Library
Mp	Manchester, Central Public Library, Henry Watson Music Library
NWr	Norwich, Norfolk and Norwich Record Office
Ob	Oxford, Bodleian Library
Ouf	——, University, Faculty of Music
SOp	Southampton, Public Library
T	Tenbury, St Michael's College [dispersed: now principally in *F-Pn*, *V*, *GB-Ob*]
TWmacnutt	Tunbridge Wells, Richard Macnutt, private collection
WC	Winchester, Chapter Library

GR: GREECE

Aels	Athens, Ethniki Lyriki Skini
Akounadis	——, Panayis Kounadis, private collection
Aleotsakos	——, George Leotsakos, private collection
Am	——, Mousseio ke Kendro Meletis Ellinikou Theatrou
An	——, Ethniki Vivliothiki tis Ellados [National Library of Greece]

H: HUNGARY

Bn	Budapest, Országos Széchényi Könyvtára
Bo	——, Állami Operaház

HV: CROATIA

Zu	Zagreb, Nacionalna i Sveučilišna Biblioteka

I: ITALY

Ac	Assisi, Biblioteca Comunale
Af	——, S Francesco [in *Ac*]
AC	Acicatena, Biblioteca Comunale
Baf	Bologna, Accademia Filarmonica
Bas	——, Archivio di Stato
Bc	——, Civico Museo Bibliografico Musicale
Bsf	——, Convento di S Francesco
Bsp	——, Basilica di S Petronio
Bu	——, Biblioteca Universitaria
BAc(n)	Bari, Biblioteca Nazionale (Consorziale)
BAn	——, Biblioteca Nazionale Sagarriga Visconti-Volpi
BGc	Bergamo, Biblioteca Civica Angelo Mai
BGi	——, Civico Istituto Musicale Gaetano Donizetti
BRc	Brescia, Conservatorio di Musica
BRq	——, Biblioteca Queriniana
BZtoggenburg	Bolzano, Count Toggenburg, private collection
CAS	Cascia, Archivio di S Rita
CATc	Catania, Biblioteche Riunite Civica e Antonio Ursino Recupero
CATm	——, Museo Belliniano
CCc	Città di Castello, Biblioteca Comunale
CF	Cividale del Friuli, Archivio Capitolare
CHf	Chioggia, Archivio dei Padri Filippini
CMbc	Casale Monferrato, Biblioteca Civica
CNM	Civitanova-Marche, Biblioteca Comunale
CORc	Correggio, Biblioteca Comunale
CR	Cremona, Biblioteca Statale
Fa	Florence, Ss Annunziata
Fas	——, Archivio di Stato
Fbecherini	——, Becherini private collection
Fc	——, Conservatorio di Musica Luigi Cherubini
Fm	——, Biblioteca Marucelliana
Fn	——, Biblioteca Nazionale Centrale
Folschki	——, Olschki private collection
FAN	Fano, Biblioteca Comunale Federiciana
FEc	Ferrara, Biblioteca Comunale Ariostea
FEd	——, Duomo
FERc	Fermo, Biblioteca Comunale
FERd	——, Duomo
FOc	Forlì, Biblioteca Civica Aurelio Saffi
FZc	Faenza, Biblioteca Comunale
Gi(l)	Genoa, Istituto (Liceo) Musicale Paganini; see *Gl*
Gl	——, Conservatorio di Musica Nicolò Paganini
Gim	——, Istituto Mazziniano
Gu	——, Biblioteca Universitaria
IBborromeo	Isola Bella, Borromeo private archive
IE	Iesi, Biblioteca Comunale
La	Lucca, Archivio di Stato
Li	——, Istituto Musicale Luigi Boccherini (incl. Bottini Collection)
Ls	——, Seminario Arcivescovile
LI	Livorno, Biblioteca Comunale Labronica Francesco Domenico Guerrazzi
Mb	Milan, Biblioteca Nazionale Braidense
Mc	——, Conservatorio di Musica Giuseppe Verdi
Mcom	——, Biblioteca Comunale
Mr	——, Archivio Storico Ricordi
Ms	——, Biblioteca Teatrale Livia Simoni
Msartori	——, Claudio Sartori, private collection
Mt	——, Biblioteca Trivulziana e Archivio Storico Civico
MAav	Mantua, Accademia Virgiliana di Scienze, Lettere ed Arti
MAC	Macerata, Biblioteca Comunale Mozzi-Borgetti
MC	Monte Cassino, Biblioteca dell'Abbazia
MOa	Modena, Accademia Nazionale di Scienze, Lettere ed Arti
MOe	——, Biblioteca Estense
MOs	——, Archivio di Stato
Na	Naples, Archivio di Stato
Nc	——, Conservatorio di Musica S Pietro a Majella
Nf	——, Biblioteca Oratoriana dei Padri Filippini
Nlp	——, Biblioteca Lucchesi-Palli [in *Nn*]
Nn	——, Biblioteca Nazionale
OS	Ostiglia, Fondazione Greggiati
Pc	Padua, Biblioteca Capitolare
Pca	——, Biblioteca Antoniana, Basilica del Santo
Pci	——, Museo Civico, Biblioteca Civica e Archivio Comunale
Pi(l)	——, Istituto Musicale (Biblioteca del Liceo Musicale); see *Pl*
Pl	——, Istituto Musicale Cesare Pollini
PAc	Parma, Conservatorio di Musica Arrigo Boito
PAi	——, Istituto di Studi Verdiani
PAt	——, Teatro Regio
PAVu	Pavia, Biblioteca Universitaria
PCcon	Piacenza, Conservatorio di Musica Giuseppe Nicolini
PEc	Perugia, Biblioteca Comunale Augusta
PEl	——, Conservatorio di Musica Francesco Morlacchi
PEsp	——, S Pietro
PEA	Pescia, Biblioteca Comunale Carlo Magnani
PESc	Pesaro, Conservatorio di Musica Gioacchino Rossini

PESr	——, Fondazione Rossini
PIv	Pisa, Teatro Verdi
PLa	Palermo, Archivio di Stato
PLcom	——, Biblioteca Comunale
PLcon	——, Conservatorio Vincenzo Bellini
PS	Pistoia, Cattedrale
PSrospigliosi	——, Rospigliosi private collection
Rasc	Rome, Archivio Storico Capitolino
Rc	——, Biblioteca Casanatense
Rdp	——, Archivio Doria-Pamphili
Ria	——, Istituto di Archeologia e Storia dell'Arte
Rli	——, Accademia Nazionale dei Lincei e Corsiniana
Rmalvezzi	——, Malvezzi private collection
Rmassimo	——, Massimo princes, private collection
Rn	——, Biblioteca Nazionale Centrale Vittorio Emanuele III
Rp	——, Biblioteca Pasqualini [in *Rsc*]
Rps	——, Archivio dei Padri Scolopi (Chiesa di S Pantaleo)
Rrai	——, Radiotelevisione Italiana
Rrostirolla	——, Giancarlo Rostirolla, private collection
Rsc	——, Conservatorio di Musica S Cecilia
Rsp	——, Santo Spirito in Sassia
Rvat	——, Biblioteca Apostolica Vaticana
REm	Reggio Emilia, Biblioteca Municipale
RIM	Rimini, Biblioteca Civica Gambalunga
RVI	Rovigo, Accademia e Biblioteca dei Concordi
Sac	Siena, Accademia Musicale Chigiana
Sc	——, Biblioteca Comunale degli Intronati
SA	Savona, Biblioteca Civica Anton Giulio Barrili
SML	Santa Margherita Ligure, Biblioteca Comunale Francesco Domenico Costa
Tci	Turin, Biblioteca Civica Musicale Andrea della Corte
Tco	——, Conservatorio Statale di Musica Giuseppe Verdi
Tf	——, Accademia Filarmonica
Tmc	——, Museo Civico
Tn	——, Biblioteca Nazionale Universitaria
Tr	——, Biblioteca Reale
TAc	Taranto, Biblioteca Civica Pietro Acclavio
TLp	Torre del Lago, Museo Puccini
TOL	Tolentino, Biblioteca Comunale Filelfica
TRc	Trent, Biblioteca Comunale
TSmt	Trieste, Civico Museo Teatrale di Fondazione Carlo Schmidl
TVco	Treviso, Biblioteca Comunale
UDc	Udine, Biblioteca Comunale Vincenzo Soppi
Vas	Venice, Archivio di Stato
Vc	——, Conservatorio di Musica Benedetto Marcello
Vcg	——, Biblioteca Casa di Goldoni
Vgc	——, Biblioteca e Istituto della Fondazione Giorgio Cini
Vlevi	——, Fondazione Ugo Levi
Vmc	——, Museo Civico Correr
Vnm	——, Biblioteca Nazionale Marciana
Vqs	——, Fondazione Querini-Stampalia
Vs	——, Seminario Patriarcale
Vsm	——, Procuratoria di S Marco
Vt	——, Teatro La Fenice
VEc	Verona, Biblioteca Civica
VEs	——, Seminario Vescovile

J: JAPAN

Tn	Tokyo, Nanki Music Library, Ohki Collection [in Tokyo College of Music Library]

N: NORWAY

Ou	Oslo, Universitetsbiblioteket

NL: THE NETHERLANDS

At	Amsterdam, Toonkunst-Bibliotheek
DHgm	The Hague, Gemeentemuseum
DHk	——, Koninklijke Bibliotheek

NZ: NEW ZEALAND

Wt	Wellington, Alexander Turnbull Library

P: PORTUGAL

Em	Elvas, Biblioteca Municipal
EVc	Évora, Arquivo da Catedral
EVp	——, Biblioteca Pública
La	Lisbon, Palácio Nacional da Ajuda
Lan	——, Arquivo Nacional de Torre do Tombo
Lc	——, Conservatorio Nacional
Ln	——, Biblioteca Nacional
Lt	——, Teatro Nacional de S Carlos
VV	Vila Viçosa, Casa da Bragança, Museu-Biblioteca

PL: POLAND

CZp	Częstochowa, Klasztor OO. Paulinów na Jasnej Górze
Kc	Kraków, Muzeum Narodowe, Biblioteka Czartoryskich
Kj	——, Biblioteka Jagiellońska
Kp	——, Biblioteka Polskiej Akademii Nauk
KA	Katowice, Biblioteka Śląska
LA	Łańcut, Muzeum
Wn	Warsaw, Biblioteka Narodowa
Wtm	——, Biblioteka Warszawskiego Towarzystwa Muzycznego
Wu	——, Biblioteka Uniwersytecka
WRol	Wrocław, Biblioteka Ossolineum Leopoldiensis; see *WRzno*
WRzno	——, Polska Akademia Nauk Zakład Narodowy imienia Ossolińskich

R: ROMANIA

Bc	Bucharest, Biblioteca Centrală de Stat

RU: RUSSIA

KAu	Kaliningrad, Universitetskaya Biblioteka
Mcl	Moscow, Gosudarstvennïy Tsentral'nïy Literaturnïy Arkhiv
Mcm	——, Gosudarstvennïy Tsentral'nïy Muzey Muzïkal'noy Kul'turï imeni M. I. Glinki
Mk	——, Gosudarstvennaya Konservatoriya imeni P. I. Chaykovskogo, Nauchnaya Muzïkal'naya Biblioteka imeni S. I. Taneyeva
Mrg	——, Rossiyskaya Gosudarstvennaya Biblioteka (formerly *Ml*, Lenin Library)
SPan	St Petersburg, Biblioteka Rossiyskoy Akademii Nauk
SPia	——, Gosudarstvennïy Tsentral'nïy Istoricheskiy Arkhiv
SPil	——, Institut Russkoy Literaturï
SPit	——, Gosudarstvennïy Institut Teatra, Muzïki i Kinematografii
SPk	——, Biblioteka Gosudarstvennoy Konservatorii imeni N. A. Rimskogo-Korsakova
SPsc	——, Gosudarstvennaya Ordena Trudovogo Krasnogo Znameni Publichnaya Biblioteka imeni M. E. Saltïkova-Shchedrina
SPtob	——, Tsentral'naya Muzïkal'naya Biblioteka Gosudarstvennogo Akademicheskogo Mariinskogo Teatra Operï i Baleta

S: SWEDEN

L Lund, Universitetsbiblioteket
Sdt Stockholm, Drottningholms Teatermuseum
Sic ——, Informationscentral för Svensk Musik
Sk ——, Kungliga Biblioteket
Skma ——, Statens Musiksamlingar (formerly Kungliga Musikaliska Akademiens Bibliotek)
Sm ——, Musikhistoriska Museet [in *Skma*]
Smf ——, Stiftelsen Musikkulturens Främjande
Ssr ——, Sveriges Radio
St ——, Kungliga Teaterns Biblioteket [in *Skma*]
Uu Uppsala, Universitetsbiblioteket

SF: FINLAND

A Turku [Åbo], Sibelius Museum Musikvetenskapliga Institutionen vid Åbo Akademi, Bibliotek & Arkiv
Hy Helsinki, Helsingin Yliopiston Kirjasto

[*SLN*]: SLOVENIA

Lf Ljubljana, Knjižnica Frančiskanškega Samostana
Lu ——, Narodna in Univerzitetna Knjižnica

UA: UKRAINE

Kan Kiev, Tsentral'na Naukova Biblioteka, Akademii Nauk
LV L'viv, Biblioteka Derzhavnoï Konservatorii imeni N. V. Lysenka

US: UNITED STATES OF AMERICA

AA Ann Arbor, University of Michigan, Music Library
AUS Austin, University of Texas
Bm Boston, University, Mugar Memorial Library
Bp ——, Public Library, Music Department
BApi Baltimore, Peabody Conservatory of Music; Peabody Institute
BAT Baton Rouge, Louisiana State University Library
BE Berkeley, University of California, Music Library
BLl Bloomington, Indiana University, Lilly Library
BLu ——, Indiana University, School of Music Library
BUu Buffalo, State University of New York at Buffalo
Chs Chicago, Chicago Historical Society
Cn ——, Newberry Library
CA Cambridge, Harvard University Music Libraries
CDs Concord, New Hampshire State Library
CHH Chapel Hill, University of North Carolina, Music Library
DN Denton, North Texas State University, Music Library
Eu Evanston, Northwestern University Libraries
FAlewis Farmington (CT), Wilmarth S. Lewis, private collection
G Gainesville, University of Florida Library, Rare Book Collection
I Ithaca, Cornell University, Music Library
KBrobbin Key Biscayne (FL), Leon Robbin, private collection
KC Kansas City, University of Missouri, Kansas City Conservatory of Music
LAu Los Angeles, University of California, Walter H. Rubsamen Music Library
LAuc ——, University of California, William Andrews Clark Memorial Library
LOu Louisville, University, School of Music Library
MAhs Madison, Wisconsin Historical Society
MED Medford (MA), Tufts University Library
MSu Minneapolis, University of Minnesota, Music Library
NH New Haven (CT), Yale University, School of Music Library
NYcu New York, Columbia University, Music Library
NYgs ——, G. Schirmer, Inc.
NYj ——, Juilliard School of Music
NYlibin ——, Laurence Libin, private collection
NYp ——, Public Library at Lincoln Center, Library and Museum of the Performing Arts
NYpm ——, Pierpont Morgan Library
NYyellin ——, Victor Yellin, private collection
PHci Philadelphia, Curtis Institute of Music
PHf ——, Free Library of Philadelphia
PHhs ——, Historical Society of Pennsylvania
PHlc ——, Library Company of Philadelphia
PHu ——, University of Pennsylvania Libraries (Otto E. Albrecht Music Library; Van Pelt Library; Rare Book Collection)
PRu Princeton, University, Harvey S. Firestone Memorial Library
R Rochester (NY), University, Eastman School of Music, Sibley Music Library
Su Seattle, University of Washington, Music Library
SB Santa Barbara, University of California at Santa Barbara Library
SFp San Francisco, Public Library, Fine Arts Department, Music Division
SFsc ——, San Francisco State University (formerly State College) Library, Frank V. de Bellis Collection
SLug St Louis, Washington University, Gaylord Music Library
SM San Marino (CA), Henry E. Huntington Library and Art Gallery
SPmoldenhauer Spokane (WA), Hans Moldenhauer, private collection
STu Stanford, University, Division of Humanities and Social Sciences, Music Library
U Urbana, University of Illinois, Music Library
Wc Washington, DC, Library of Congress, Music Division
Ws ——, Folger Shakespeare Library
Wsi ——, Smithsonian Institution, Music Library
WM Waltham (MA), Brandeis University Library, Music Library, Goldfarb Library
WS Winston-Salem (NC), Moravian Music Foundation

YU: YUGOSLAVIA

(for libraries in the former republic of Yugoslavia, see also under *HV*, Croatia; and [*SLN*], Slovenia)

Bn Belgrade, Narodna Biblioteka N. R. Srbije

Aachen (Fr. Aix-la-Chapelle). City in western Germany. In the 1780s and early 90s Johann Böhm's company performed annually in the Komödienhaus (completed 1751), where their productions included *Die Entführung aus dem Serail* (1785) and *Die Zauberflöte* (1794). Dramatic performances in German were suspended during Napoleon's occupation of the western Rhineland but were resumed under the rule of Prussia, which acquired Aachen after the Congress of Vienna in 1815. In 1825 the Neues Schauspielhaus (designed by Johann Peter Cremer and decorated by Karl Friedrich Schinkel) opened with Spohr's *Jessonda*. Shortly afterwards Albert Lortzing and his wife were engaged there, he as 'second lover and tenor'. The theatre was renovated in 1900–01; only the portico, by Schinkel, remained unchanged, as a historical monument. In the 19th century and the early 20th the building continued to be rented out to private theatrical companies, with variable artistic results. It was taken over by the city in 1920 but after bombing in World War II only the foyer and portico remained intact; operatic activity resumed in 1947 in the assembly hall of the rebuilt Institute of Technology. The old civic theatre was renovated and it reopened in 1951 with *Die Meistersinger von Nürnberg*. With a capacity of about 900, the auditorium contains stalls, two circles, two side boxes and a central box. The season lasts at least ten and a half months, with opera performed on more than a hundred evenings. About six operas are performed, usually including a modern work and two or three lighter works. Notable conductors who have appeared at Aachen include Leo Blech, Fritz Busch, Karl Elmendorff, Herbert von Karajan (1934–42), Paul van Kempen, Wolfgang Sawallisch and Wilhelm Pitz; soloists have included Carl Burrian, Ludwig Suthaus, Maria Janowska, Tiana Lemnitz, Margarete Teschemacher, Marta Fuchs, Irmgard Seefried and Kurt Moll. GÁBOR HÁLASZ

Aarhus (Old Dan.). ÅRHUS.

Abaris. Opera by J.-P. Rameau; *see* BORÉADES, LES.

A basso porto ('In the Lower Port'). Lyric drama in three acts by NICOLA SPINELLI to a libretto by Eugenio Checchi ('Tom') after Goffredo Cognetti's play *Scene napoletane*; in German, translated by Ludwig Hartmann and Otto Hess as *Am untern Hafen*, Cologne, Stadttheater, 18 April 1894 (first Italian performance, Rome, Teatro Costanzi, 11 March 1895).

The action takes place in the via Acquaquilia, in the port area of Naples, among *camorristi* (a mafia-type secret society). Se' Maria (dramatic soprano) and Ciccillo o' Luciano, a *camorristo* (baritone), were betrothed, but almost at once he fell in love with Carmela, against whom the jealous Maria made false accusations which led to Carmela's early death and Ciccillo's imprisonment; Maria then married another man. Now she feels remorse ('Se è ver, Ciccillo, che un giorno solo'), but Ciccillo, full of hatred, swears to avenge himself by reducing Maria to poverty and ruining her children, Luigino (tenor) and Sesella (soprano). In Act 2, the *camorristi*, led by Si' Pascale o' cantiniere (bass), are worried that there is a traitor among them, and Ciccillo insinuates that Luigino is the spy. He entices Sesella to run away with him. In the opera's climactic scene Maria convinces Sesella of the truth ('S'era con me da un mese fidanzato') and that the spy is Ciccillo. The two women denounce him, and Luigino is detailed to kill him. In Act 3, Ciccillo learns of the plan from Maria, who is still prepared to save him if he forgets his hatred of her children. When he refuses she kills him.

A basso porto is Spinelli's most famous opera and was performed in many European and American cities, including London, New York, Amsterdam, Budapest, Berlin, Salzburg, St Petersburg, Prague and Riga. In its leaning towards *verismo* it is one of the many descendants of Mascagni's *Cavalleria rusticana*, but it lacks that work's considerable tragic tension. The harmonies are somewhat contrived, with frequent enharmonic modulation. In the continuous musical texture, which includes ensemble pieces, there are conspicuous recurrent motifs which are interwoven and modified, among them Carmela's pathetic theme, on which most of the prelude to the first act is based, and the tragic theme of Maria, which runs through the whole opera.

Local colour is provided by Luigino's barcarolle with chorus 'Mare d'argento', with its traditional accompaniment of mandolins and guitars, and the prelude to the third act, which includes a *stornello* motif on the mandolin. FRANCESCO BUSSI

Abbadia, Luigia (*b* Genoa, 1821; *d* Milan, 1896). Italian mezzo-soprano. She studied with her father, the composer and teacher Natale Abbadia, making her début in 1836 at Sassari. In Vienna she sang Corilla in Donizetti's *Le convenienze ed inconvenienze teatrali* (1840). At La Scala she created Giulietta in Verdi's *Un giorno di regno* (1840) and Ines in Donizetti's *Maria Padilla* (1841) and sang Marie (*La fille du régiment*). Her roles included Elvira (*Ernani*), Emilia (Mercadante's *La vestale*) and Pacini's Sappho. After retiring from the stage she taught in Milan. She had a fine voice, secure technique and a strong temperament.

ELIZABETH FORBES

Abbado, Claudio (*b* Milan, 26 June 1933). Italian conductor. Son of the violinist and teacher Michelangelo Abbado, he heard Debussy's *Nocturnes* as a small boy and was immediately fired with the ambition to become a conductor. He attended rehearsals by both Furtwängler and Toscanini in Milan soon after the war, and began to establish his own philosophy of conducting, eschewing Toscanini's dictatorial approach in favour of a gentler, less aggressive manner. During his training as a conductor, first at the Milan Conservatory and later with Hans Swarowsky at the Vienna Academy of Music, he developed a technique so sure that, even in Italy, he was able to command perfect discipline using the quietest manner and the minimum of verbal instructions.

His début as an operatic conductor took place in Trieste in 1958, with *The Love for Three Oranges*, and throughout his career he has sought to include 20th-century operas alongside the regular repertory. His 1960 début at La Scala was in a concert celebrating the 300th anniversary of the birth of Alessandro Scarlatti; the following year he began to conduct opera there, and in 1968 his performance of *I Capuleti e i Montecchi* opened the Scala season. The same year, conducting Verdi for the first time, he made his Covent Garden début with *Don Carlos*. Notable among his later successes at the Royal Opera House was *Boris Godunov* in 1983.

He became resident conductor of La Scala in 1969, music director two years later, artistic director in 1977, and finally chief conductor from 1980 to 1986. During his years there he was always adventurous in developing the repertory, reviving rare Italian operas and introducing new ones; he conducted the premières of both the original and revised versions of Nono's *Al gran sole carico d'amore* (1975 and 1978). He also gave special attention to composers close to his heart, among them Berg, Musorgsky, Debussy and Rossini. He took the Scala company on tour in Europe, the USA and Japan. He conducted the company in a landmark performance of *Simon Boccanegra* at Covent Garden in 1976.

Abbado made his début at the Vienna State Opera in 1984 in *Simon Boccanegra*, and two years later was appointed music director; however, he resigned in 1991 on grounds of ill-health. His successes there included new presentations of *Wozzeck*, *Khovanshchina*, *Un ballo in maschera*, *Don Carlos*, *L'italiana in Algeri* and *Il viaggio a Reims*. He had already rescued *Il viaggio* from oblivion in 1985 in performances at the Pesaro Festival with the Chamber Orchestra of Europe, of which he was also the artistic director; the recording he made then was among his most successful ever. With the same orchestra he revived Schubert's *Fierrabras*, both in the opera house and on record. Though in his highly active recording career he has concentrated mainly on orchestral repertory, he has recorded many operas too, not only at La Scala and in Vienna, but in London with the LSO, of which he was principal conductor, and later music director, from 1979 to 1986. His appointment as chief conductor of the Berlin PO in 1990 still allowed him time to conduct opera in Vienna and elsewhere, though more than ever concert work took priority.

Though as a personality he is quiet and not at all flamboyant, his direction of opera is generally electrifying in its clarity, freshness and concern for structure. Like the most successful of his younger Italian colleagues, he consistently avoids the vulgarities of the old Italian tradition in opera and adopts a scholarly approach to texts.

EDWARD GREENFIELD

Abbate, Carolyn (*b* New York, 20 Nov 1955). American musicologist. She studied at Yale, Munich and Princeton. Her dissertation, on Wagner's Parisian *Tannhäuser*, was completed in 1984 at Princeton, where she taught from 1982. Her early writings focus mainly on Wagner, and include important essays on the relationship of *Pelléas* and *Tristan* (*19th Century Music*, v, 1981–2, pp.117–41) and on *Tannhäuser* (*JAMS*, xxxvi, 1983, pp.73–123). Her more recent work, which includes a further, often-cited essay on *Tristan* (*COJ*, i, 1989, pp.33–58), had been much concerned with the problematic manner in which current concerns in literary theory may intersect with musical, and particularly operatic, criticism, an interest dealt with at length in her *Unsung Voices: Opera and Musical Narrative in the Nineteenth Century* (Princeton, 1991). The book, which also explores aspects of voice and performance, has consolidated her position as a leading opera scholar and critic of her generation.

Abbatini, Antonio Maria (*b* Città di Castello, 26 Jan 1595; *d* Città di Castello, ? after 15 March 1679). Italian composer. His birth date, hitherto unknown, is reported by Ciliberti (1986). After moving back and forth between positions in Rome and in his native Umbria, Abbatini was appointed *maestro di cappella* at S Maria Maggiore in Rome in 1640 and began to train boy sopranos including Domenico Dal Pane, who later sang in operas in Paris and Rome. During Abbatini's second tenure there (1649–57), Giulio Rospigliosi, the former librettist of the Barberini family, became prefect. They collaborated with Rospigliosi's nephew Giacomo and with the composer Marco Marazzoli on *Dal male il bene* (1654), based on a Spanish play. Beginning in 1657, Abbatini's activity and authority increased: he served as *maestro* at S Luigi dei Francesi (to 1667), as member of the Congregation of S Cecilia (to 1676), and as head of a monthly academy that discussed musical theory and composition. In 1667 he was appointed *bussolante extra muros* to the new pope Clement IX, who was none other than Rospigliosi. In this fertile period Abbatini composed two more operas. *Ione*, based on the Greek story of Io, may have been commissioned by Cardinal Carlo Carafa for the wedding of the Habsburg emperor (see Andrae 1986); no performance is recorded, although the score is dated 1666. In 1668 the Rospigliosi staged *La comica del cielo*, which tells the story of a Spanish actress who abandons the theatre for exile as a penitent. After working again at S Maria Maggiore (1672–7), Abbatini returned to the cathedral in Città di Castello where Dal Pane succeeded him in September 1679, an indication, but not proof, of Abbatini's death earlier that year.

Though he lived at the same time as Luigi Rossi, Abbatini's three operas were composed after 1650 and are more contemporary with the works of Antonio Cesti, whose *Orontea* Abbatini could have heard in Rome in 1661. The two Spanish dramas have small casts and require very little ensemble music, while *Ione* has 12 solo roles and closes each act with a choral finale. All three operas have a mixture of humorous and serious characters, offering opportunities for variety of musical expression. The languid lyricism of the 1640s is largely absent; the predominantly syllabic melodies of the arias integrate sequences and quick ornamental figures into clear phrases. In a variety of forms, the arias are also metrically diverse, with rhythmic motifs, active bass lines and imitative instrumental parts associated with later Baroque style. The six varied duets for the principal character in *Comica del cielo* often mark a dramatic resolution. Abbatini's recitative abandons earlier styles, with curtailed lyrical contours, increased speed of declamation and quick phrase endings, all over broadened harmonic rhythm. The resulting flexibility permits vivid characterization, whether for a vengeful Juno, an anti-military soldier or an overemotional actress.

See also DAL MALE IL BENE.

Dal male il bene (dramma musicale, 3, G. and G. Rospigliosi, after A. Sigler de Huerta: *No ay bien sin ageno daño*), Rome, Palazzo Barberini alle Quattro Fontane, 12 Feb 1654, *D-MÜs* (Act 1), *I-Bc*, *IBborromeo*, *Rsc* (Acts 2 and 3), *Rvat** (2 copies, 1 partly autograph); collab. M. Marazzoli

Ione (dramma [musicale], 3), unperf., *A-Wn* [Roman MS dated 1666]

La comica del cielo (dramma musicale, 3, Giulio Rospigliosi, after L. Vélez de Guevara, A. Coelho and F. de Roxas: *La Baltasara*), Rome, Palazzo Rospigliosi a S Lorenzo in Lucina, 1 Feb 1668, *I-Rvat* (partly autograph)

A. Ademollo: *I teatri di Roma nel secolo XVII* (Rome, 1888)
H. Goldschmidt: *Studien zur Geschichte der italienischen Oper im 17. Jahrhundert* (Leipzig, 1901) [incl. musical extracts, 325–48]
M. Fuchs: *Die Entwicklung des Finales in der italienischen Opera buffa vor Mozart* (diss., U. of Vienna, 1932), 6–11; repr. in Ciliberti (1986)
M. Vezzosi: *La commedia musicale romana nel Teatro di Palazzo Barberini nel secolo XVII* (diss., U. of Rome, 1940)
N. Pirrotta: 'Cesti e Abbatini: Opera', *Santa Cecilia*, ii/3 (1953), 31–4
C. Masson: 'Papal Gifts and Roman Entertainments in Honour of Queen Christiana's Arrival', *Analecta Réginensia*, i (1966), 244–61
I. Küffel: *Die Libretti Giulio Rospigliosis: ein Kapitel frühbarocken Operngeschichte in Rom* (diss., U. of Vienna, 1968)
M. Murata: 'Il carnevale a Roma nel secolo XVII', *RIM*, xii (1977), 83–99
——: *Operas for the Papal Court* (Ann Arbor, 1981) [incl. musical extracts, 352–68; 393–434]
K. Andrae: *Ein römischer Kapellmeister im 17. Jahrhundert, A. M. Abbatini (ca. 1600–1679): Studien zu Leben und Werk* (Herzberg, 1986) [incl. musical extracts, 318–58]
G. Ciliberti: *A. M. Abbatini e la musica del suo tempo (1595–1679): Documenti per una ricostruzione bio-bibliografica* (Selci-Umbro, 1986)
B. Brumana: 'Il Tasso e l'opera nel Seicento: una "Gerusalemme 'interrompue' " nella *Comica del cielo* di Rospigliosi-Abbatini', *Tasso, la musica, i musicisti* (Florence, 1988), 137–64

MARGARET MURATA

Abbiati, Franco (*b* Verdello, 14 Sept 1898; *d* Bergamo, 22 Jan 1981). Italian music critic. He studied composition and musicology in Turin before working in Milan as a critic, first on *Secolo sera* (1928–34) and then on *Corriere della sera* until his retirement (1972). In 1949 he founded the monthly journal *La Scala: Revista dell'opera*, which he edited until its closure in 1963. He wrote a multi-volume history of music but was particularly interested in opera, especially its authentic performance. His four-volume work on Verdi, *La vita e le opere di G. Verdi* (Milan, 1959), contains many letters not previously published; another book, *Alti e bassi del Simon Boccanegra*, was published in Verona in 1973.

CAROLYN GIANTURCO

Abbott, Emma (*b* Chicago, 9 Dec 1850; *d* Salt Lake City, 5 Jan 1891). American soprano. After studying in New York, she went in 1872 to Europe, studying further in Milan and with Mathilde Marchesi, Wartel and Delle Sedie in Paris. She made her début in London on 2 May 1876 and first appeared in New York on 8 February 1877, singing Marie (*La fille du régiment*) on both occasions in Italian. Her favourite role was said to be Gounod's Marguerite. She earned critical disapproval for interpolating hymns into Donizetti and Bellini operas. In 1878 she formed, under her husband's management, a small touring company which did much to popularize opera and operetta in the USA and Canada.

S. E. Martin: *The Life and Professional Career of Emma Abbott* (Minneapolis, 1891)
O. Thompson: *The American Singer* (New York, 1937), 127ff

H. WILEY HITCHCOCK

Abduction from the Harem, The. Opera by W. A. Mozart; *see* ENTFÜHRUNG AUS DEM SERAIL, DIE.

Abendroth, Irene (*b* Lemberg [now L'viv], 14 July 1872; *d* Weidling, nr Vienna, 1 Sept 1932). Polish soprano of Austrian parentage. She first appeared as a child prodigy, singing operatic arias in her native town. At 13 she entered the Vienna Conservatory; she later studied in Milan, becoming highly proficient in florid singing while developing a voice of considerable power. She made her début (1889) in *La sonnambula* at the Vienna Opera. In the Munich première of *Falstaff* she sang Mrs Ford, and at Dresden in 1902 sang Tosca in the opera's German première. She retired in 1908, having sung some 70 operatic roles, ranging from coloratura parts such as the Queen of Night and Lucia to dramatic roles including Sieglinde and Venus. A few rare gramophone records made in 1902 display some dubious stylistic qualities along with an extraordinary fluency in decorative work and a warm, limpid tone characteristic of the Lamperti school.

L. Riemens: 'Irene Abendroth', *Record Collector*, vi (1951), 77–85

J. B. STEANE

Abert, Anna Amalie (*b* Halle, 19 Sept 1906). German musicologist, daughter of Hermann Abert. She studied with Abert, Blume and Sachs at the University of Berlin where she took the doctorate in 1934. She held posts at the University of Kiel, where she completed the *Habilitation* in 1943 with a work on Monteverdi and music drama, and was on the editorial staff of *Die Musik in Geschichte und Gegenwart* (1949–58). Her main field of research is opera, on whose history she has written books and articles which deal especially with sources, librettos and aesthetics and with the relationship between speech and music.

Claudio Monteverdi und das musikalische Drama (Lippstadt, 1954)
Christoph Willibald Gluck (Zürich, 1960)
ed., with L. Finscher: C. W. Gluck: *Orfeo ed Euridice*, Sämtliche Werke, i/1 (Kassel and Basle, 1963)

Die Opern Mozarts (Wolfenbüttel, 1970; Eng. version in NOHM, vii, 1973)
Richard Strauss: die Opern (Velber, 1972)
with H. C. R. Landon: 'Opera in Italy and the Holy Roman Empire', NOHM, vii (1973), 1–199

*

K. Hortschansky, ed.: *Opernstudien: Anna Amalie Abert zum 65. Geburtstag* (Tutzing, 1975) [incl. F. Blume: 'Anna Amalie Abert', 9–12, and bibliography, 227–38]

HANS HEINRICH EGGEBRECHT

Abert, Hermann (*b* Stuttgart, 25 March 1871; *d* Stuttgart, 13 Aug 1927). German musicologist. He took the doctorate at Berlin in 1897 and in 1902 he completed the *Habilitation* at the University of Halle. He held university posts at Halle, Leipzig and Berlin and in 1925 was the first musicologist to be elected a member of the Prussian Academy of Sciences. Abert was one of the leading German musicologists of his generation. His interest in 19th-century and contemporary music led him to confront specific problems of opera. His articles on composers including Piccinni, Gluck, Meyerbeer and J. C. Bach, exemplary editions of important operatic works, his editorship of the *Gluck-Jahrbuch* (1913–18) and many monographs preceded his great Mozart biography, modestly called the fifth edition of Jahn's though in almost every respect an independent work and still one of the great standard works of music literature.

WRITINGS

Niccolò Jommelli als Opernkomponist (Halle, 1908)
W. A. Mozart (Leipzig, 1919–21, 3/1955–6) [enlarged 5th edn of O. Jahn: *W. A. Mozart*, Leipzig, 1856–9; essay on *Don Giovanni*, Eng. trans., 1976]
Goethe und die Musik (Engelhorn, 1922)

EDITIONS

N. Jommelli: *Fetonte*, DDT, xxxii, xxxiii (1907)
C. W. von Gluck: *Le nozze d'Ercole e d'Ebe*, DTB, xxvi, Jg.xiv/2 (1914); *Orfeo ed Euridice*, DTÖ, xliva, Jg.xxi/4 (1914)
B. Pallavicino: *La Gerusalemme liberata*, DDT, lv (1916)

*

F. Blume, ed.: *Gedenkschrift für Hermann Abert von seinen Schülern* (Halle, 1928) [incl. complete list of writings]

LOTHAR HOFFMANN-ERBRECHT

Abert, Johann Joseph (*b* Kochowitz, nr Leitmeritz, Bohemia, 20 Sept 1832; *d* Stuttgart, 1 April 1915). Bohemian composer. After studying at the Prague Conservatory, he was engaged in 1853 as a double-bass player at the Stuttgart Hofkapelle where he then served as Kapellmeister from 1867 to 1888. Between 1852 and 1894 he composed orchestral and chamber music in addition to sacred and secular vocal works. He was most important in the field of operatic composition, his six operas winning him acclaim as one of the masters between Meyerbeer and Wagner. His first opera, *Anna von Landscron* (1858), was firmly rooted in the German Romantic opera tradition. However *König Enzio*, produced four years later, clearly showed the influence of French grand opera, which the composer had studied first-hand during a long visit to Paris. He was especially successful in 1866 with his third opera, *Astorga*, whose less dramatic text allowed scope for his primarily lyrical style to develop. In 1875 he produced an entirely new version of *König Enzio*, entitled *Enzio von Hohenstaufen*, but despite the addition of vivid and lively folk scenes it was not as successful as the first version. In *Ekkehard* (1878), Abert's first opera to have its première outside Stuttgart, he adapted his musical language to the new demands of Wagnerian music drama. Abert failed in a similar attempt, however, in his last opera, *Die Almohaden* (1890); following its première this work disappeared from the stage entirely, like so many of the works of those of his contemporaries cogently described by Theodor Kroyer as 'circumpolar' composers.

Anna von Landscron (4, C. G. Nehrlich), Stuttgart, 19 Dec 1858, *D-Sl*
König Enzio (4, A. B. Dulk), Stuttgart, 4 May 1862, *Sl*; rev. as Enzio von Hohenstaufen, Stuttgart, 11 April 1875, *Sl**
Astorga (romantische Oper, 3, E. Pasqué), Stuttgart, 20 May 1866, vs (Leipzig, 1867), *Sl*
Ekkehard (5, after J. V. von Scheffel), Berlin, 11 Oct 1878, vs (Leipzig, 1879), *Sl*
Die Almohaden (4, A. Kröner, after D. J. Palon y Col: *Die Glocke von Almudaina*), Leipzig, 13 April 1890, *Sl*

*

H. Abert: *Johann Joseph Abert (1832–1915), sein Leben und seine Werke* (Leipzig, 1916, enlarged 2/1983)
T. Kroyer: 'Die circumpolare Oper', *JbMP 1919*, 16–33
A. A. Abert: 'Ein Circumpolarer zwischen Tradition und Fortschritt', *Festschrift Heinz Becker* (Laaber, 1982), 214–36

ANNA AMALIE ABERT

Abesalom da Eteri ('Absalom and Etery'). Opera in four acts by ZAKHARY PETROVICH PALIASHVILI to a libretto by P. Mirianashvili after the Georgian legend *Eteriani*; Tbilisi, Georgian National Opera House, 21 February 1919.

Paliashvili began work on *Absalom and Etery* in 1909, three years after co-founding the Fraternity for the Creation of Opera in the Georgian Language. His studies with Taneyev (1900–03) and his experience as collector and editor of Georgian folk music had given him the resources he needed for the creation of a style that was both technically secure and national in character. In addition, Taneyev had shown him how oriental folk styles could be synthesized with elements from traditional western European music, rather than simply grafted on – the besetting sin, Taneyev felt, of the Russian Five. Paliashvili was by no means the first Georgian composer to attempt such a synthesis in opera, but no work before *Absalom and Etery* aroused the same degree of enthusiasm. It is now accepted as a milestone in the development of Georgian music and continues to play an important part in the repertory.

The story of Absalom and Etery exists in varying forms. Mirianashvili based his libretto on a verse narrative of the early 19th century, although he altered parts of it for greater effect, such as removing Etery's parents and providing her with a wicked stepmother. In this version the beautiful shepherdess Etery (soprano) is wooed and eventually married by Absalom (tenor), son of Abio (bass), King of Cartalinia; but she is loved too by his vizier, Murman (baritone), who presents Etery with a poisoned necklace that destroys her beauty. On her insistence she and Absalom part and she accepts Murman's protection. Her beauty later returns but she refuses to go back to Absalom, although he is sick with longing for her, as he has rejected her and broken his vows of fidelity; eventually, however, after Queen Natela (mezzo-soprano) has pleaded in vain, she is persuaded by the singing of Absalom's sister Marich (soprano, accompanied on the *tohonguri*, a form of lute). Soon after the lovers are reunited, however, Absalom dies, and Etery kills herself with the golden dagger he had earlier given her as a token of his love.

Paliashvili's assimilation of native musical styles was highly successful and attention is often drawn to the modal writing, the oriental-sounding melismas, the use of Georgian-style vocal ornamentations and ensembles and orchestral passages in the unison style of oriental vocal music. The opera is organized so that a basic 'number' structure can be discerned, despite the frequent organic linking of recitative and aria sections. This not only makes for easier comprehension but also allows the incorporation of folk-style songs and dances and the repetition of sections without incongruity. Paliashvili was also able to draw on his experience of church music in the choral writing, and this, combined with the retention of recitative and aria as important structural elements and the unhurried flow of the action, has led several commentators to describe *Absalom and Etery* as oratorio-like or even ritualistic.

STEPHEN JOHNSON

Abingdon. English town on the Thames, near Oxford. It was an important centre for Handel revivals in the 1960s and 70s. Performances, modest in scale but noted for their spirit and enthusiasm, were given in the Unicorn Theatre (built in the granary of the 14th-century abbey) and twice in a civic hall, were directed and translated by Alan Kitching and were conducted and costumed (until her death in 1968) by Frances Kitching. Given by amateurs and advanced students until 1970, when they became professional, they began with *Orlando* in 1959; then followed, from 1961 to 1964, *Partenope*, *Floridante*, *Agrippina* and *Admeto*, and from 1966 to 1974 *Poro*, *Giustino*, *Flavio*, *Sosarme*, *Il pastor fido*, *Arminio*, *Tolomeo* and *Arianna in Creta* (*Lotario* was also given by the company, at Henley, in 1975). Most were modern premières. Several performances were repeated elsewhere, notably three at the City of London Festival.

*

A. Kitching: *Handel at the Unicorn: an Adventure* (Abingdon, 1981)

STANLEY SADIE

Abos [Abosso, Avos, Avosso], **Girolamo** (*b* La Valetta, 16 Nov 1715; *d* Naples, Oct 1760). Maltese composer of Spanish descent. Probably he studied at the Neapolitan conservatory Poveri di Gesù Cristo, where his principal teachers would have been Francesco Durante and Gerolimo Ferraro. Abos's first major work was an *opera buffa*, *Le due zingare simili*, staged in 1742. In that year he also took posts at two conservatories: Poveri di Gesù Cristo (under Francesco Feo), which however closed in 1743, and S Onofrio a Capuana (*maestro*, 1748–60), where his pupils included Giovanni Paisiello and the alto castrato Giuseppe Aprile. He also taught at the Conservatorio della Pietà dei Turchini (*secondo maestro*, 1754–9).

Abos was a respected composer of *opere buffe* and *serie*, which were performed in Italy and beyond with varying success. In 1756 his *Tito Manlio* was presented in London. Walsh printed its 'favourite airs', but Burney commented that 'none were favoured by the public'. However, even after Abos's death his arias appeared in pasticcios in London (*Love in a Village*, 1763; *The Maid of the Mill*, 1765). That he was the *maestro al cembalo* in London for *Tito Manlio* is often stated but not established. In older literature information about Abos was confused with that on the composer Giuseppe Avossa, and mistaken attributions of their works exist among manuscript copies.

Le due zingare simili (ob, A. Palomba), Naples, Nuovo, spr. 1742
Il gelosa (commedia, Palomba), Naples, Fiorentini, spr. 1743, lib. *I-Nn*
Le furberie di Spilletto (commedia), Florence, Cocomero, spr. 1744, *Bc*
La serva padrona (ob, A. Federico), Naples, 1744
La moglie gelosa (commedia, ?Palomba), Naples, Fiorentini, 1745
Artaserse (os, P. Metastasio), Venice, Grimani, carn. 1746
Pelopida (os, G. Roccaforte), Rome, Argentina, spr. 1747, *F-Pc**, arias *GB-Lbl*
Alessandro nelle Indie (os, Metastasio), Ancona, Fenice, sum. 1747, arias *F-Pc*, lib. *I-Bc*
Arianna e Teseo (os, P. Pariati), Rome, Dame, 26 Dec 1748, arias *F-Pc*, lib. *I-Bc*
Adriano in Siria (os, Metastasio), Rome, Argentina, 1750 [or, according to Pavan, ? Florence, Pergola, 1746]
Tito Manlio (os, ?Roccaforte), Naples, S Carlo, 30 May 1751, *A-Wn*, Act 2 *I-Mc*; airs (London, 1756)
Erifile (os), Rome, Dame, spr. 1752, arias *GB-Lbl*
Lucio Vero o sia Il vologeso (os, A. Zeno), Naples, S Carlo, 18 Dec 1752, *A-Wn*
Il Medo (os, C. I. Frugoni), Turin, Regio, carn. 1753, *I-Rsc*

Doubtful: Andromeda (os), *A-Wn*

Songs in: Armida placata, 1750; Nerone, 1753; Creso, 1758; Love in a Village, 1763; The Maid of the Mill, 1765

*

LoewenbergA
C. A. de Rosa, Marchese di Villarosa: *Memorie di compositori di musica del regno di Napoli* (Naples, 1840) [Abos and Avossa are confused]
G. Pavan: *Saggio di cronistoria dei teatro fiorentini* (Milan, 1901)
S. di Giacomo: *I quattro antichi conservatorii di musica a Napoli* (Palermo, 1924)
U. Rolandi: *Musica e musicisti in Malta* (Livorno, 1932)
R. Weaver: *A Chronology of Music in the Florentine Theatre 1590–1750* (Detroit, 1978), 309
G. Hardie: 'Neapolitan Comic Opera, 1707–1750: some Addenda and Corrigenda for The New Grove', *JAMS*, xxxvi (1983), 124–7, esp.125

HANNS-BERTOLD DIETZ

Abott [née Pickens], **Bessie** (*b* Riverside, NY, 1878; *d* New York, 9 Feb 1919). American soprano. She appeared first with her sister Jessie in vaudeville, then, in London, in operetta; she was heard there in 1898 by Jean de Reszke, who helped her to study in Paris with Victor Capoul and Mathilde Marchesi. Her début at the Opéra as Juliet in 1901 brought success in France, followed in 1906 by a moderately successful career at the Metropolitan; in that year her roles included Mimì, Marguerite and Micaëla, which she was singing at San Francisco on the night of the earthquake. She appeared in the première of Alban de Polhes' *Nariste* (1909, Monte Carlo). She retired shortly after marriage in 1911. A few recorded solos and the quartet from *Rigoletto* with Caruso as the Duke preserve something of the 'lovely timbre' and 'impeccable purity' admired by critics at her New York début.

J. B. STEANE

Abraham, Gerald (Ernest Heal) (*b* Newport, Isle of Wight, 9 March 1904; *d* Midhurst, 18 March 1988). English musicologist. He was largely self-taught in music. His first book, a study of Borodin (1927), established his authority in Russian music. He contributed to numerous journals in the ensuing years, among them *Music & Letters*, *The Musical Times* and *The Musical Standard*, which he also edited; many of his articles dealt with Russian music, especially opera, and opera (Wagner in particular) occupied an important place in his *A Hundred Years of Music* (1938). He was closely associated with the BBC, working for the *Radio Times*, *The Listener* and as head of the gramophone department; he later helped launch the Third Programme, and was Assistant Controller of Music, 1962–7. Other posts included the editorship of *Monthly Musical Record* (1945–60) and the first professorship of music at Liverpool University (1947–62); he was also secretary to the editorial board and editor of five volumes of the *New Oxford History of Music*. Abraham was a wide-ranging scholar, as his *Concise Oxford History of Music* (1979) shows; his particular sympathies embraced Handel, Schubert, Schumann and Bartók, but it was opera and Slavonic music that interested him above all. His command and distinction as both historian and critic, as well as his lucid and engaging style, are seen in his collections *Slavonic and Romantic Music* (1968) and *Essays on Russian and East European Music* (1985).

A list of Abraham's writings is to be found in *Slavonic and Romantic Music: Essays in Honour of Gerald Abraham* (ed. M. H. Brown and J. Wiley, Ann Arbor and Oxford, 1985).

Ábrányi, Emil (*b* Budapest, 22 Sept 1882; *d* Budapest, 11 Feb 1970). Hungarian composer and conductor. He studied composition, organ and piano at the Budapest Academy of Music, and spent a year with Nikisch in Leipzig. From 1904 he was a theatre conductor in Cologne, and from 1907 in Hanover. In 1911 he returned to Budapest to become conductor at the Royal Hungarian Opera House; he was director there (1919–20) and then at the Budapest Municipal Theatre (1921–6). He taught conducting at the Budapest Academy of Music.

Ábrányi was the most prolific Hungarian opera composer of his generation; between 1903 and 1923 five of his operas and a Singspiel were produced at the Budapest Opera House and the Municipal Theatre. Ábrányi did not shun international competition by seeking refuge in old-fashioned Hungarian romantic national opera style or folklore; on the contrary, he tried to challenge it, composing in a 'cosmopolitan' style. His choice of eclectic, colourful and erotic subjects corresponded, in some cases literally, to that of leading opera composers of the time. While the youthful ballad *A ködkirály* ('The King of Mist') still shows romantic traits, his next two works display a more modern approach and indulge in artificially sensuous melody typical of both Italian and German *Jugendstil*. In *Don Quijote* Ábrányi followed the more lyrical, declamatory style of French opera.

Though Ábrányi was frequently employed by the Budapest Opera House as a composer and conductor (partly, perhaps, out of reverence towards the merits of his father, an eminent poet, and his grandfather, a leading musical personality in Hungary), his operas never gained lasting popularity even in his outwardly most successful years. From the mid-1920s on, he gradually disappeared from the Budapest music scene, and his later operas were not performed. The première of his great historical opera *Bizánc* ('Byzantium') was planned but ultimately hindered by World War II.

first performed at the Royal Hungarian Opera House, Budapest, unless otherwise stated

A ködkirály [The King of Mist] (1, Á. Pásztor), 17 May 1903
Monna Vanna (3, E. Ábrányi sr, after M. Maeterlinck), 2 March 1907
Paolo és Francesca [Paolo and Francesca] (3, Ábrányi sr, after Dante: *Commedia*), 13 Jan 1912
Don Quijote (3, Ábrányi sr, after M. de Cervantes), 30 Nov 1917
Ave Maria: Májusi intermezzo [A May Intermezzo] (1), Budapest, Municipal, 25 Feb 1922
A vak katona [The Blind Soldier] (Spl, 1, E. Sas), Budapest, Municipal, 11 June 1923
Az éneklő dervis [The Singing Dervish], 1937 (2, N. W. Khayatt), unperf.
Liliomos herceg [The Prince of the Lilies], 1938 (3, Bohdaneczky), unperf.
Bizánc [Byzantium], 1942 (3, E. Innocent-Vincze, after F. Herczeg), unperf.
Éva boszorkány [Eva the Witch], 1944 (3, Herczeg), unperf.
Balatoni rege [A Balaton Legend], 1945 (3, Herczeg), unperf.
A Tamás-templom karnagya [The Cantor of the St Thomas Church], 1947 (3, G. Láng), unperf.

*

G. Staud, ed.: *A budapesti operház száz éve* [100 Years of the Budapest Opera House] (Budapest, 1984)
K. Szekeres: 'Emil Ábrányi', *Zenei lexikon*, i (Budapest, 1984)

TIBOR TALLIÁN

Abravanel, Maurice (de) (*b* Thessaloniki, 6 Jan 1903). American conductor of Spanish-Portuguese Sephardic descent. He studied composition with Weill in Berlin and made his début there in 1924, then worked in various German theatres until Hitler came to power. He moved to Paris, then to Australia, and on the recommendation of Walter and Furtwängler he was engaged at the Metropolitan Opera, 1936–8, making his début with *Samson et Dalila* and conducting mostly French repertory and some Wagner. A victim of internal politics, he moved to Broadway, where he conducted Weill's *Knickerbocker Holiday* (1938). He became known as a specialist in Weill's work for which, in 1990, he received the Kurt Weill Foundation's first distinguished achievement award. He conducted opera at Chicago, 1940–41, but his later career was mainly in concert work, including over 30 influential years with the Utah SO, 1947–79. From 1954 to 1980 he also directed the Music Academy of the West at Santa Barbara, and during the period 1970–76 was a member of the National Arts Council.

*

L. Durham: *Abravanel!* (Salt Lake City, 1989)

MICHAEL STEINBERG, NOËL GOODWIN

Abreise, Die ('The Departure'). *Musikalisches Lustspiel* in one act by EUGEN D'ALBERT to a libretto by Ferdinand von Sporck after a comedy by August von Steigentesch (1828); Frankfurt, 28 October 1898.

The action takes place in late 18th-century Germany. Gilfen (baritone), whose relationship with his wife Luise (soprano) has cooled, debates whether or not to go on a long-planned but much delayed journey: an absence might help his marriage, but he is suspicious of the motives of his friend Trott (tenor) in encouraging the journey and making the necessary arrangements. Finally Gilfen pretends to leave, but returns almost at once, to discover that Trott has wasted no time before pressing his attentions on Luise. Gilfen and his wife are reconciled, while it is Trott who takes the journey he has so carefully planned.

D'Albert's lighthearted score shows little or no trace of the *verismo* style that he cultivated in *Tiefland* and some of his later works. The influence of Cornelius and of the German romantics such as Lortzing is much stronger, though d'Albert, a musician of mixed cultural heritage, also owed, at least in this delightful piece, a certain allegiance to French style at the end of the 19th century as represented by Chabrier. ELIZABETH FORBES

Abstrakte Oper no.1 ('Abstract Opera no.1'). Opera in one act, op.43, by BORIS BLACHER to a libretto by WERNER EGK; Mannheim, Nationaltheater, 17 October 1953 (previously broadcast on Hessischer Rundfunk, 28 June 1953).

This 35-minute opera scored for soprano, tenor and baritone, mixed choir and instrumental ensemble is divided into seven self-contained scenes entitled Angst

(Fear), Liebe I (Love 1), Schmerz (Pain), Verhandlung (Negotiation), Panik (Panic), Liebe II (Love 2) and Angst (Fear). There is no conventional plot as such; rather the opera, constructed in arch-form, offers an exploration of various states of mind. The vocal writing dispenses with comprehensible speech and relies on syllables and stage gestures to make its effect. In the opening scene the dialogue between the three soloists consists entirely of primeval wails based on the sound patterns of 'ooh' and 'aah'. Following this is the first love scene which ends in hilarity when a dressmaker's dummy is shot by the soprano. At the centre of the work lies the fourth scene, 'Verhandlung', in which an infantile and barely comprehensible discussion between a Russian (baritone) and American diplomat (tenor) breaks down through lack of communication. With the return to the 'Angst' scene at the end of the opera comes an overriding feeling of the futility of modern life.

Although the musical idiom of *Abstrakte Oper no.1* owes little to the postwar avant garde, its experimental use of phonetics anticipates some of the more radical music-theatre works of the 1960s such as Mauricio Kagel's *Sur scène* (1960) and György Ligeti's *Aventures* (1962) and *Nouvelles aventures* (1965). ERIK LEVI

Abu Hassan. Singspiel in one act, J106, by CARL MARIA VON WEBER to a libretto by Franz Carl Hiemer after Antoine Galland's story *Le dormeur éveillé*; Munich, Residenztheater, 4 June 1811.

Hiemer based his libretto on the second part of Galland's version of the well-known tale of 'Abu Hassan, or The Sleeper Awakened' from the Arabian *Thousand and One Nights*. In the opera Abu Hassan (tenor), cupbearer to the Caliph, and his devoted wife Fatime (soprano) are being pressed for payment of debts by the moneylender Omar (bass), who is also unsuccessfully making advances to Fatime. Abu Hassan hits on the idea of pretending that his wife has died and claiming money from the Caliph (speaking role) for her funeral, while Fatime does the same with the Caliph's wife, Zobeide (speaking role). They succeed in their plot, but when the Caliph and Zobeide try to discover which of them is really dead they both feign death. Abu Hassan, however, leaps up and reveals the subterfuge when he hears the Caliph offer 10 000 gold dinars to anyone who can clear up the mystery. For about half the opera Omar is imprisoned in a cupboard, where he has been forced to hide because of the unexpected return of Abu Hassan while Omar was trying to make love to the reluctant Fatime. Fatime explains to her husband, in an undertone, what has happened, and they decide to punish Omar by leaving him there in fear of discovery. When the Caliph is informed of Omar's activities by Abu Hassan, at the end of the opera, he orders the cupboard to be taken to the city prison.

Weber received the text of *Abu Hassan* from Hiemer at the end of March 1810, but did not begin to work seriously on it for some time. It was not until late summer, shortly before the première of *Silvana* in Frankfurt, that he started to commit the new opera to paper. He began, in August, with the chorus of creditors, 'Geld! Geld! Geld!', an appropriate choice in view of his own recent experiences with moneylenders. The other seven numbers of the original version followed in haphazard succession during the remainder of the year, and on 12 January he completed the overture. In this form it was given in Munich some five months later. For a performance in Gotha in 1813 he added a new duet for Abu Hassan and Fatime, and for a revival in Dresden in 1823 he composed Fatime's lament over the supposed death of Abu Hassan.

Like Mozart's *Die Entführung aus dem Serail*, which seems to have acted as Weber's inspiration, *Abu Hassan* contains far greater richness and variety than the majority of Singspiels. Mozart's musical influence is particularly evident in such ensembles as the Terzetts 'Ich such' in allen Ecken' and 'Ängstlich klopft es mir im Herz' as well as in several of the solo numbers. But the opera also contains many instances of Weber's own individuality, and his gift for lively characterization is apparent throughout. The two added numbers, the full-blooded love duet 'Thränen, Thränen' and Fatime's sentimental lament 'Hier liegt', are splendid in their own right, though somewhat out of style with the rest of the opera. Weber's instrumentation is full of delightful touches: he augmented the standard orchestra with a pair of guitars that are tellingly employed in Abu Hassan's aria 'Ich gebe Gastereien', and made use of 'Turkish' percussion in several numbers. CLIVE BROWN

Académie Royale de Musique. The first permanent operatic institution in France, created by Louis XIV in 1669 and exercising a monopoly over all operatic productions in that country until the 19th century. In spite of several changes in name, the company has been known familiarly as the Paris Opéra throughout its long history. It has occupied several theatres, including the Palais Royal, the Salle Le Peletier, the Palais Garnier and, since 1990, the Opéra Bastille; *see* PARIS, §§2(i), 3(i), 4(ii), 5(ii) and 6(i, ii).

Academy of Music (i). Theatre in New York City, presenting regular operatic seasons from 1854 to 1886; *see* NEW YORK, §1.

Academy of Music (ii). Theatre in PHILADELPHIA, built in 1857.

Academy of Music Opera Company. Name for a group of American travelling companies drawn from resident troupes of the New York Academy of Music, 1854–86, variously under the management (1854–77) of Maurice Strakosch, Bernard Ullman, Max Maretzek and others. Under this umbrella were a variety of individual companies, including the Strakosch Opera Company, Ullman-Strakosch Opera Company and Academy of Music Company, all of which made extensive tours of the USA. From 1878 to 1886 James Mapleson was manager of the Academy companies. *See* TRAVELLING TROUPES, §5(iv, v).

Acante et Céphise [*Acante et Céphise, ou La sympathie* ('Acante and Céphise, or Empathy')]. *Pastorale-héroïque* in three acts by JEAN-PHILIPPE RAMEAU to a libretto by JEAN FRANÇOIS MARMONTEL; Paris, Opéra, 19 November 1751.

To protect Acante (*haute-contre*) and Céphise (soprano) from the menacing genie Oroès (bass), the fairy Zirphile (soprano) gives the lovers a talisman. This provides them with the telepathic power ('la sympathie' of the subtitle) to sense each other's feelings even when separated. The work, which celebrated the Duke of Burgundy's birth, includes more inventive music than such a puerile plot deserves, and incorporates the earliest surviving clarinet parts in French opera. The overture, a representation of the nation's joy at the royal birth, uses cannon fire in its portrayal of fireworks.

GRAHAM SADLER

Accademia dei Discordati (It.: 'Academy of the Discordant Ones'). Academy associated (in Lucca, 1645; Bologna, 1647; Ferrara, 1648) with the touring opera company or companies known as the FEBIARMONICI: either they were one and the same, or the Febiarmonici were in some way managed by the academy.

Acciaiuoli, Filippo (*b* Rome, 24 Feb 1637; *d* Rome, 7 Feb 1700). Italian impresario and deviser of spectacles. He was descended from a noble Florentine family and studied at the Seminario Romano, where he performed in Latin tragedies and *intermedi* produced during the carnivals of 1651–3. He was admitted to the Accademia degli Immobili, Florence, in January 1657 and then travelled extensively. He became a Knight of Malta in 1666. After his return to Rome he devised two operas for production at the Palazzo Colonna: *Girello*, with music by Jacopo Melani and Alessandro Stradella, and *L'empio punito*, with music by Alessandro Melani. Their librettos, often attributed to him, were apparently versified by G. F. Apolloni, who also collaborated with Acciaiuoli on Bernardo Pasquini's *La sincerità con la sincerità, overo Il Tirinto* and P. S. Agostini's *Gl'inganni innocenti, overo L'Adalinda*, produced at the Palazzo Chigi in Ariccia in 1672 and 1673 respectively. There is no evidence to support Morei's claim that Acciaiuoli wrote both music and text for the dramma burlesco, *Chi è cagion del suo mal pianga se stesso* (1682, Rome, Palazzo Colonna); the attribution in the libretto is 'text by Ovid and music by Orfeo'.

Acciaiuoli's reputation as a theatrical mastermind undoubtedly resulted from his behind-the-scenes control of many spectacles. In 1671–3 he was impresario and deviser of *intermedi* for the inaugural seasons of the Tordinona, the first public opera house in Rome, and for the theatre in Ariccia. From 1679 he may have managed the Teatro Capranica, Rome. He has been credited incorrectly with the design of the puppets used at S Moisè, Venice, 1680–82, but according to Morei he invented a puppet theatre for the young Ferdinando, Grand Prince of Tuscany, and wrote for it a work involving 124 marionettes, all manipulated by himself. The Trojan horse that he designed for the Florentine production of *Il Greco in Troia* (1689; libretto by M. Noris) was so complicated that he had to be called to Florence to operate it. He devised at least one intermezzo, *La noce di Benevento, o sia Il consiglio delle streghe*, for the extravagant production of Pasquini's *La caduta del regno degli Amazzoni* (libretto by G. D. DeTotis; 1690, Rome, Palazzo Colonna). His precise role in such productions is difficult to determine, as details of intermezzos and machines were rarely included in librettos. Raguenet's description of one of Acciaiuoli's feats led the editor of the English translation (probably Nicola Haym) to report that Acciaiuoli devised 'many more equally surprizing' spectacles during the 1690s, including the 'Intermede of Hell' in *Nerone fatto Cesare* (1695), which attracted 'great Numbers of Foreigners' who 'confess'd ... that it far exceeded the Expectations Fame had given 'em of it'.

*

DBI (C. Rotondi); *ES* (B. Brunelli)

G. M. Crescimbeni: *Comentarii all'istoria della volgar poesia*, i (Rome, 1702), 211

F. Raguenet: *Paralèle des italiens et des françois en ce qui regarde la musique et les opéra* (Paris, 1702); Eng. trans., *A Comparison between the French and Italian Musick and Opera's* (London, 1709), 57–60

M. G. Morei: 'Filippo Acciajuoli', *Notizie istoriche degli Arcadi morti*, ed. G. M. Crescimbeni, i (1720), 357–61

G. Mazzuchelli: *Gli scrittori d'Italia*, i/1 (Brescia, 1753), 46

F. Fuà: *L'opera di Filippo Acciaiuoli* (Fossombrone, 1921)

R. Lefevre: 'Pippo Acciajoli: Accademico Sfaccendato', *Strenna dei romanisti*, xvii (1956), 256–61

——: 'Gli Sfaccendati', *Studi romani*, vii (1960), 154–65, 288–301

G. Ugurgieri della Berardenga: *Gli Acciaioli di Firenze nella luce dei loro tempi (1160–1834)*, Biblioteca Storia Toscana, xii (Florence, 1962), 726–9

E. Tamburini: 'Filippo Acciajoli: un "avventuriere" e il teatro', *Teatro Oriente/Occidente*, ed. A. Ottai, Biblioteca teatrale, xlvii (Rome, 1986), 449–76

S. Franchi: *Drammaturgia romana: repertorio bibliografico cronologico dei testi drammatici pubblicati a Roma e nel Lazio, secolo XVII* (Rome, 1988)

LOWELL LINDGREN

Accompagnato (It.: 'accompanied'). Term used for *recitativo accompagnato* ('accompanied recitative'; Fr. *récitatif accompagné*) to signify recitative 01accompaniec by orchestra. The term, though strictly applicable to any recitative with orchestral accompaniment, is generally reserved for solemn scenes in which the voice declaims to sustained string harmonies (as opposed to *recitativo obbligato*, with a more active accompaniment). *See* RECITATIVE.

Accorimboni [Accoramboni, Accorimbeni], **Agostino** (*b* Rome, 28 Aug 1739; *d* Rome, 13 Aug 1818). Italian composer. Both Gerber and Eitner list him under the name Agosti. The abbot Lucantonio Benedetti noted that his opera *Il marchese di Castelverde* drew a large crowd of noblemen 'because the composer also belonged to the patrician class'. Between 1768 and 1785 he wrote several operas, all but one of them comic, and he is also known to have composed an oratorio and sacred music. His *Il regno delle Amazzoni* enjoyed particular success, with restagings in Bologna, Florence, Genoa and Prague.

Le scaltre contadine di Montegelato (farsetta, 2, A. Gatta), Rome, Tordinona, 2 Jan 1768

Le contadine astute (farsetta, 2, T. Mariani), Rome, Tordinona, 8 Jan 1770

L'amante nel sacco (farsetta, 2, G. Mancinelli), Rome, Tordinona, 2 Jan 1772

Le finte zingarelle (farsetta, 2, G. B. Lorenzi), Rome, Tordinona, 31 Jan 1774

Il finto cavaliere (farsetta, 2), Rome, Pace, carn. 1777; also known as Das Herbstabentheuer

Nitteti (os, 3, P. Metastasio), Florence, Pallacorda, carn. 1777

L'amore artigiano (int, 2, C. Goldoni), Rome, Tordinona, 7 Jan 1778

Le virtuose bizzarre (int, 2), Rome, Tordinona, 29 Dec 1778

Il marchese di Castelverde (ob, 3), Rome, Dame, carn. 1779

Lo schiavo fortunato, o sia La marchesina fedele (int, 2), Rome, Pace, carn. 1783

Il regno delle Amazzoni (ob, 2, G. Petrosellini), Parma, Ducale, 27 Dec 1783, *I-Fc* (? autograph)

Il governatore delle Isole Canarie (int, 2, C. Mazzolà), Rome, Valle, carn. 1785

Il podestà di Tufo antico, o sia Il tutore burlato (farsetta, 1, F. Ballani), Rome, Valle, sum. 1786

*

EitnerQ; *GerberL*; *GerberNL*

D. Silvagni: *La corte e la società romana nei secoli xviii e xix*, ii (Florence, 2/1883), 150

MICHAEL F. ROBINSON

Acevedo Guajardo, Remigio (*b* Santiago, 1863; *d* Santiago, 29 May 1911). Chilean composer. He studied theory and singing at the National Conservatory, and the organ and composition privately. He was organist at Santiago Cathedral, and occasionally conducted zarzuelas. In 1902 he composed the first act of his opera-ballet *Caupolicán*; based on the 16th-century poem *La araucana* by Alonso de Ercilla, the libretto is by Pedro Antonio Pérez and Adolfo Urzúa Rozas. The première of Act 1 took place at the Teatro Municipal, Santiago, in June 1902. Acevedo then received an award that enabled him to study in Milan, where he composed the last two acts of *Caupolicán*. The complete work, comprising three acts and 11 scenes, was given its first performance at the Teatro Municipal, Santiago, on 8 December 1942, more than 30 years after the composer's death. Acevedo also composed masses and other religious works, but the public, devoted to Italian opera at that time, never accepted his music.

*

M. Cánepa: *La opera en Chile (1839–1930)* (Santiago, 1976)

SAMUEL CLARO-VALDÉS

Aceves (y Lozano), Rafael (*b* La Granja de S Ildefonso, Segovia, 20 March 1837; *d* Madrid, 21 Feb 1876). Spanish composer. In 1853 he entered the Madrid Conservatory, where his composition teacher was Emilio Arrieta; he won a gold medal for composition in 1858. For an opera competition in 1869 he composed, in collaboration with Antonio Llanos (1841–1906), the prize-winning *El puñal de misericordia*; he also wrote some religious music. However, he was influenced mainly by Arrieta towards the composition of zarzuelas. His works in this genre were well received in his time, particularly *Sensitiva* (1870), but his fame has now been eclipsed by that of contemporaries such as Barbieri and Oudrid (in collaboration with whom he composed *El testamento azul*) and Caballero (with whom he composed *El trono de Escocia*).

El manco de Lepanto (1), Madrid, Circo, 23 April 1867
El puñal de misericordia, Madrid, 1869, collab. A. Llanos
Sensitiva (3, M. Pina), Madrid, Alhambra, 24 Dec 1870
Dos cómicos de provincia (2, R. M. Liern), Madrid, 1870
Mambrú, Madrid, 1870
El teatro en 1876 (revista, Liern), Madrid, ? 20 July 1871, collab. A. Rubio
La bola negra (1, Zapater), Madrid, Zarzuela, 1872
El testamento azul [Act 3] (3, Amalfi [Liern]), Madrid, Buen Retiro, 20 July 1874, collab. F. A. Barbieri and C. Oudrid
El trono de Escocia (3, R. Puente y Brañas), Madrid, Zarzuela, 28 March 1875, collab. M. F. Caballero
El teatro en 1876, collab. A. Rubio
El destierro del amor (1), Madrid, Buen Retiro, 24 July 1878, collab. Rubio
La canción de amor, Madrid, 1878
El carbonero de Subiza (1, S. M. Granés and M. Ramos Carrión), Madrid, 1878, collab. Rubio
Dates unknown: Los cuatro sacristanes; La sobrina del rector; Los titiriteros

*

A. Peña y Goñi: *La ópera española y la música dramatica en España en el siglo XIX* (Madrid, 1881, abridged 1967 as *España desde la ópera a la zarzuela*)
'Aceves y Lozano (Rafael)', *Enciclopedia universal ilustrada europeo-americana* (Barcelona, 1907–30)

JOSÉ LÓPEZ-CALO, ANDREW LAMB

Achille ('Achilles'). *Melo-dramma eroico* in two acts by FERDINANDO PAER to a libretto by GIOVANNI DE GAMERRA after HOMER's *Iliad*; Vienna, Kärntnertortheater, 6 June 1801.

One of Paer's best early operas, *Achille* was particularly admired by Napoleon. In De Gamerra's version of the story, the armies of Achilles (tenor), King of Thessaly, and Agamemnon (bass), leader of the Greek armies, are preparing to attack the city of Lyrnessus, which is allied with the Trojans. Achilles wishes to be reunited with Briseis (soprano), daughter of Briseus (bass), King of Lyrnessus. Upon defeating Briseus's army, both Achilles and Agamemnon demand Briseis in exchange for clemency. She chooses Achilles, but Agamemnon later has her kidnapped. Suspecting foul play by his purported ally, Achilles refuses to lead his army against the Trojans, although he does eventually send them into battle under the command of his companion Patroclus (bass), cloaked in Achilles' armour. After Patroclus is killed, Achilles relents and finally agrees to fight when Agamemnon surrenders Briseis. The opera ends with Achilles' defeat of Hector and the Trojans.

SCOTT L. BALTHAZAR

Achille in Sciro ('Achilles on Scyros'). Libretto by PIETRO METASTASIO, first set by Antonio Caldara (1736, Vienna). The title *Il trionfo della gloria* was used for later versions of this libretto.

In order to circumvent the destiny that awaits Achilles in the Trojan War, his mother, Thetis, has asked Chiron, his old tutor, to conceal him on the island of Scyros; Chiron has placed his charge among the women at the court of King Licomede [Lycomedes].

ACT 1 In female attire, and with the assumed name of Pirra [Pyrrha], Achilles is able to remain the constant companion of the king's daughter, Deidamia, whom he loves. The disguise, however, hangs ill upon the warrior, and the demands of Deidamia for his constant presence soon become a burden. His distress is intensified when Lycomedes promises his daughter to Teagene [Theagenes], Prince of Chalcis, and when Ulisse [Ulysses] arrives on the island on the pretext of mustering the armed strength of Scyros. In reality, Ulysses seeks Achilles who he knows is vital to Greek victory.

ACT 2 Ulysses employs various stratagems to force the disguised hero to reveal himself and succeeds when Achilles leaps into action to quell a pre-arranged fight.

ACT 3 Theagenes graciously relinquishes Deidamia who is now promised to Achilles upon his return from Troy. With his newly betrothed thus assured, Achilles can follow the call to arms and depart with Ulysses and the Scyros fleet, but not before Glory, Love and Time descend in a cloud, and with their retinue sing the praises of the happy pair.

* * *

Classical sources include Apollodorus, *Bibliotheca* (book 3); Comes, *Mythologiae* (book 9); Hyginus, *Fabulae* (no.96); and Statius, *Achilliad* (book 1). Close parallels, however, between Metastasio's plot and that of Ippolito Bentivoglio (text set by Giovanni Legrenzi, 1663), suggest that the Bentivoglio libretto may have provided a more immediate model for a work that Metastasio and Caldara had to prepare in haste. The occasion was the wedding of Maria Theresa and Francis, Duke of Lorraine, the couple honoured allegorically in the opera's last act. Aware of its lack of real dramatic conflict and its supernatural *licenza*, quite apart from the hero's appearance throughout in women's clothes, Metastasio designated *Achille in Sciro* a 'dramma immaginato' rather than simply a 'dramma'. These factors, coupled with the use of chorus and the impressive staging engineered by Antonio and Giuseppe Galli-Bibiena, launched this work as a *festa teatrale* as much as a *dramma per musica*. Although this text gained only moderate popularity, it was set with some regularity until the end of the 1770s. Sarro's version for

Naples (1737) inaugurated the Teatro S Carlo, where several subsequent settings also had premières, and Jommelli's for Vienna (1749) gained Metastasio's particular commendation. Pietro Coppola extended the life of this text into the 19th century with a setting for Catania in the 1820s; performed in Naples in 1832, it won the praise of Donizetti, Rossini and Pietro Raimondi.

For a list of settings *see* METASTASIO, PIETRO. DON NEVILLE

Achté [née Ströer], **Emmy (Charlotte)** (*b* Oulu, 14 Nov 1850; *d* Helsinki, 2 Dec 1924). Finnish soprano. After studying in Paris, Stockholm and Dresden, she was engaged at Helsinki in 1875, where for six years she sang roles such as Lucia, Norma, Pamina, Leonora (*Il trovatore*) and Marguerite. Her voice, bright, pure-toned and flexible, was managed with great expertise. She was married to the Finnish baritone and conductor Lorenz Achté (1838–1900); their daughter Aïno Ackté became the finest and best-known Finnish soprano of her generation. ELIZABETH FORBES

Acis and Galatea. Masque or serenata in one (later two) acts by GEORGE FRIDERIC HANDEL to words by JOHN GAY and others; Cannons, summer 1718 (revised version in three acts, incorporating Italian words by Nicola Giuvo, London, King's Theatre, 10 June 1732).

During the period 1717–20 Handel spent much of his time at Cannons, the seat of James Brydges, Earl of Carnarvon (later Duke of Chandos), at Edgware, a short distance north-west of London. As resident composer, he supplied his patron with church music, principally anthems, and two dramatic works, *Esther* (the first English oratorio) and *Acis and Galatea*, which has variously been described as a serenata, a masque, a pastoral or pastoral opera, a 'little opera' (in a letter while it was being written), an entertainment and even (incorrectly) an oratorio. Whether or not it was originally fully staged, given in some kind of stylized semi-dramatic form or simply performed as a concert work is uncertain; local tradition holds that it was given in the open air on the terraces overlooking the garden (the recent discovery of piping to supply an old fountain, suitable for the closing scene, might fancifully be invoked as support). It was performed on an unknown date, probably during the summer, in 1718.

Acis and Galatea, Handel's first dramatic work in English, had its models in the English pastoral operas by Pepusch (his colleague at Cannons), Galliard and others that had been given in 1715–18 at the Drury Lane theatre in rivalry to the Italian opera. The theme, drawn from Ovid's *Metamorphoses* (xiii. 750), had been the subject of a setting in 1701 by John Eccles, to a text by P. A. Motteux, but Pepusch's *Apollo and Daphne*, to a libretto by John Hughes, seems to have been a more specific inspiration for Handel's work. Gay's libretto – it is not certain how much he actually wrote himself – has features indicating that it was originally designed for only three characters, and subsequently expanded, perhaps by Hughes and Pope (it includes lines by both, and also Dryden), but there is no clear evidence that Handel considered setting it in that form. The Cannons version was almost certainly intended for just five singers – a soprano, three tenors and a bass – serving as 'chorus' as well as principals (Coridon, omitted from all modern editions, sings one air, added at a late stage to words by Hughes); the instrumental music could be supplied by seven players (strings, and oboes doubling recorders), though probably the violins were doubled, and some early copies indicate slightly fuller scoring including a bassoon.

Most of the music was published in 1722, and at least one early amateur performance is known of (in Wells, Somerset, in February 1719); but the work was not heard publicly until 1731, when it was given a single performance, without Handel's involvement, in London. The next year it was revived by an English opera company under Thomas Arne (father of the composer), performing at the Little Theatre in the Haymarket, immediately opposite the King's, where Handel gave Italian operas. It was claimed as 'with all the Grand Chorus's, Scenes, Machines, and other Decorations; being the first Time it ever was performed in a Theatrical Way'. Handel retaliated by converting it into a three-act serenata, performed by his Italian company, with substantial revisions and additions and 'a great Number of the best Voices and Instruments'. His revisions involved the incorporation of material from a cantata he had written in Italy on the same topic, *Aci, Galatea e Polifemo* (1708), and other music mainly from his Italian cantatas and operas; the result was an over-extended work, in three acts, oddly shaped, mixed in style and language. He used this version, or revisions of it, up to 1741, but also gave English performances from 1739; it was at this point that the English version reached its two-act form, with a chorus added to conclude the first act. Handel never gave *Acis and Galatea* in the form in which it is generally heard today. It became very popular, however, in his own time and was easily the most widely performed of his dramatic works. In 1788 it was arranged by Mozart. It has remained popular and has been many times revived, on the stage and otherwise, during the 19th and 20th centuries.

The work, even if not staged by Handel, may be imagined in the kind of setting described in his advertisement for his 1732 performances: 'There will be no Action on the Stage, but the Scene will represent, in a Picturesque Manner, a rural Prospect, with Rocks, Groves, Fountains and Grotto's; amongst which will be disposed a Chorus of Nymphs and Shepherds, Habits, and every other Decoration suited to the Subject'.

ACT 1 Nymphs and shepherds take delight in 'the pleasure of the plains'. Galatea (soprano), a part-divine sea-nymph, is in love with Acis, and attempts to silence the birds that inflame her desire ('Hush, ye pretty warbling quire!'). She and the shepherd Acis (tenor) continue to seek each other, with occasional counsel from another shepherd, Damon (tenor); when they meet he sings a delectable siciliana-style serenade, 'Love in her eyes sits playing'. Their duet ('Happy we') is echoed by a chorus (not in the Cannons original).

ACT 2 The amorous, pastoral mood now darkens at the threat to their love. The chorus, knowing of the approach of the 'monster Polypheme', warns the 'Wretched lovers', in sombre, fugal minor-key music, that 'no joy shall last'; the heavy steps of the hideous giant are heard in their music. The jealous Polyphemus (bass) enters in a part-comic *furioso* accompanied recitative, 'I rage, I melt, I burn', which is followed by his air 'O ruddier than the cherry', in which he is counterpointed by a small recorder ('a hundred reeds of decent growth', according to his recitative). He threatens force; another shepherd, Coridon (tenor), impartially counsels gentler wooing ('Would you gain the tender creature'). In militant tones, Acis determines to resist ('Love sounds th' alarm'), taking no heed of Damon's warning of the transience of amorous delight ('Consider, fond shepherd'). The lovers swear eternal devotion in what begins as a duet ('The flocks shall leave the mountains') but becomes a trio as the enraged Polyphemus intrudes and finally crushes Acis with a 'massy ruin'. The chorus mourn, joined by Galatea ('Must I my Acis still bemoan'); but they remind her of her deity – she can transform him into a fountain. In a sublime climax, a *larghetto* air with the string tone softened by a pair of recorders, she exerts her powers ('Heart, the seat of soft delight'). The chorus celebrate his watery immortality.

* * *

Acis and Galatea represents the high point of the pastoral opera in England, indeed perhaps anywhere. Intended, typically of the genre, as a courtly entertainment about the simple, rural life, with many witty hints of self-parody in its words, it rises above itself through the elegance and the sensual force of Handel's music to its first act and the elegiac power of that to its second: and that in spite of the humour maintained by the composer in his treatment of the secondary characters, Polyphemus and Damon, and their utterances, which in no way lessens the depth of the pathos with which the death of Acis and the grief of Galatea are depicted. The work is unique in Handel's output (though he tried to recapture elements of it in such works as *L'Allegro, il Penseroso ed il Moderato*, 1739, and *Semele*, 1744); the influence of Purcell has been claimed, and musical ideas indebted to Keiser and others have been noted, but in approach it owes more to the Drury Lane pastoral operas than to any other source and in inspiration, conception and execution it remains wholly individual.

STANLEY SADIE

Acis et Galatée ('Acis and Galatea'). *Pastorale-héroïque* in a prologue and three acts by Jean-Baptiste Lully (*see* LULLY family, (1)) to a libretto by JEAN GALBERT DE CAMPISTRON after OVID's *Metamorphoses*; Anet, château (without machines), 6 September 1686, and Paris, Opéra, 17 September 1686.

This work was privately commissioned by the Duke of Vendôme for a celebration to honour the dauphin; it subsequently enjoyed public success. Lully turned to Galbert de Campistron because Quinault, his usual collaborator, had withdrawn from theatrical work. In keeping with the conventions of the *pastorale-héroïque* genre, the plot involves a love triangle that mixes gods and mortals: the sea-nymph Galatea (soprano), the mortal Acis (*haute-contre*) and the monster Poliphème [Polyphemus] (baritone). Acis is violently murdered by Polyphemus (in full view of the audience) but restored to life and transformed into a river by Neptune (baritone). The musical conventions are those of Lully's mature *tragédies en musique*.

For illustration *see* PARIS, fig.11. LOIS ROSOW

Acis y Galatea ('Acis and Galatea'). Zarzuela in two acts with music by ANTONIO DE LITERES to a libretto by José de Cañizares; Madrid, Alcázar palace or Coliseo del Buen Retiro, 19 December 1708.

A partly sung zarzuela on the story of Acis, Galatea and Polifemo [Polyphemus], it was composed for King Philip V's birthday and performed by the combined companies of Joseph Garcés and Juan Bautista Chavarría. The characters also include Doris, Glauco [Glaucus], Tisbe [Thisbe], Telemo [Telemus], Momo [Momus] and Tíndaro [Tyndareus], as well as choruses. In the original cast only Polyphemus, Telemus and Tyndareus were played by men. After its first performance at court, the work entered the repertory of the public theatres in Madrid when the company of Garcés performed it in the Teatro del Príncipe for an extended run in January 1710. Subsequent revivals in 1713, 1714, 1721, 1725 and 1727 were largely successful, such that the work may represent Madrid's most popular zarzuela of the first half of the 18th century. In style it exemplifies the hybrid nature of the early 18th-century zarzuela in its absorption of foreign musical forms and procedures within Spanish musical-theatrical conventions. It is also typical of Literes's theatrical scores in its restricted use of recitative and juxtaposition of set pieces in traditional Spanish style with expressly italianate arias.

LOUISE K. STEIN

Ackermann, Otto (*b* Bucharest, 18 Oct 1909; *d* Wabern, nr Berne, 9 March 1960). Swiss conductor. After studying at the Royal Academy in Bucharest and the Berlin Hochschule für Musik, he became Kapellmeister at the Düsseldorf Opera House, and in 1932 chief Kapellmeister and opera director at the German Theatre in Brno. He was chief Kapellmeister at the Berne Municipal Theatre (1935–47) and from 1949 to 1955 he worked in the Zürich Opera House. In 1955 he became music director at the Cologne Opera House; during this period he gave guest performances with the Vienna Staatsoper, and in opera houses in Monaco and Italy. In 1958 he returned to the Zürich Opera but soon became seriously ill. Ackermann was internationally renowned as an opera conductor, and was a particularly sympathetic interpreter of Johann Strauss's operettas and Mozart's operas.

*

W. Reich: 'Otto Ackermann', *SMz*, c (1960), 194–5

JÜRG STENZL

Ackté [Achté], **Aïno** (*b* Helsinki, 23 April 1876; *d* Nummela, 8 Aug 1944). Finnish soprano. She studied with her mother, Emmy Achté (a soprano of the Helsinki Opera), and at the Paris Conservatoire. She appeared at the Opéra in 1897 as Gounod's Marguerite. Her success there and in other European cities led to her engagement for two seasons (1903–5) at the Metropolitan, where she sang Marguerite, Micaëla, Brünnhilde (*Siegfried*) and Eva; the last role she repeated, with Elsa, Elisabeth and Senta, in Van Dyck's 1907 German Opera Season at Covent Garden. Of her Salome (see overleaf), in the first English performances (1910, Covent Garden) of Strauss's opera under Beecham, Newman wrote that she 'acted and sang with unflagging spirit and striking characterisation', and she was commended for performing the Dance of the Seven Veils herself. Her later career was largely in Finland. She helped to found the Finnish Opera in 1911, and for one year (1938–9) was its director. She wrote the libretto for Merikanto's *Juha*. Her few, rare recordings show the flexibility of her strong, dramatic voice. She wrote two autobiographical books, *Muistojeni kirja* ('The Book of my Recollections', Helsinki, 1925) and *Taiteeni taipaleelta* ('My Life as an Artist', Helsinki, 1935).

*

C. L. Brunn: 'Aino Ackté', *Record News* [Toronto], v (1960–61), 83–9 [with discography]

J. B. STEANE

Aïno Ackté in the title role of Richard Strauss's 'Salome'

Acoustics. *See* THEATRE ARCHITECTURE, §7.

Act (Fr. *acte*; Ger. *Aufzug*; It. *atto*). A self-contained section of an opera or music drama marked off by an interval (normally with applause and curtain-calls for the artists). It may last anything between 15–20 minutes (Act 3 of *La bohème*, 1896) and more than two hours (Act 1 of *Götterdämmerung*, 1876). The number of acts in an opera may vary from one to five. Five is common in early operas, in the French *tragédie lyrique* and in grand opera. Three is the standard number in 18th-century Italian opera, both serious and comic. In the early part of the century the first two acts of a serious opera each normally ended with a bravura aria for a main character, sometimes a pathetic one or a duet; the last act generally ended with a 'coro' sung by all the principals. Comic operas rarely had more than three acts (an exception is *Le nozze di Figaro*, 1786, with four), and towards the end of the century their third acts became progressively shorter; eventually a two-act structure came to be preferred (this applies too, in a lesser degree, to serious opera). From soon after the middle of the century it was traditional in comic opera to end Act 1 (and sometimes Act 2 of a three-act work) with an ensemble of confusion. This practice continued into Rossini's time, and beyond; a bravura aria for the prima donna (with chorus) commonly ended the last act.

Until the mid-19th century, even in through-composed operas, acts were divided into finite scenes based on the entry and exit of one or more principal characters (*see* SCENE). From then on there was an increasing tendency, following Wagner's example, to construct each act as an organic unit, akin to a movement of a symphony. In Italian opera it was customary to place a huge ensemble of confrontation at the centre of the opera's action – at the end of the first act, if there were only two, the second if there were three, the second or third if there were four. In French grand opera each act normally ends with a spectacular tableau. Although this pattern can be traced as late as Wagner's *Die Meistersinger* (1868), German and Russian operas of the later 19th century normally follow the course of the dramatic idea without resorting to formula. By the 1890s French and Italian composers preferred to end their acts with the equivalent of the curtain line of a play, e.g. 'Elle est d'un autre!' (*Werther*, Massenet, 1892), 'E avanti a lui tremava tutta Roma!' (*Tosca*, Puccini, 1900). With the present century's abandonment of such structural devices as *leitmotif* and thematic reminiscence there has been some return to formal procedures of a more consciously artificial nature, as in Berg's *Wozzeck* (1925) and Stravinsky's *The Rake's Progress* (1951), though on occasion composers have preferred to avoid specific act structure in favour of casting a work in a number of distinct scenes which may be grouped at convenience. JULIAN BUDDEN

Acte de ballet (Fr.). A French 18th-century stage work in one act, akin to the *opéra-ballet* and performed at the Académie Royale de Musique (the Opéra). Like the *opéra-ballet*, an *acte de ballet* includes airs, duets, choruses (particularly *choeurs dansés*) and sometimes other vocal music as well as instrumental dances. Being in a single act, it had a continuous, though slight, dramatic action: the plot was often designed to provide maximum opportunities for colourful scenic displays. Under the title 'Fragments', an evening's performance at the Opéra might be made up of several *actes de ballet* by different authors or one with other short works; popular *entrées* from *opéra-ballets* were taken out of their original context and given as *actes de ballet*.

The earliest example is *Zélindor, roi des silphes* by Rebel and Francoeur (to a libretto by F.-A. P. de Moncrif, 1745), termed a *divertissement*. As a designation in scores and librettos, *acte de ballet* is most frequently found in the works of Rameau: *Pigmalion* (B. de Sovot, 1748) and *La guirlande, ou Les fleurs enchantées* (J.-F. Marmontel, 1751) are two examples. J. B. Cardonne's *Ovide et Julie* (L. Fuzelier, 1773) was one of the last specifically so called.

The heyday of the *acte de ballet* was the third quarter of the 18th century. The practice of giving several different works on the same programme continued at the Opéra, but in the late 18th century and the early 19th the short *ballet d'action* or opera was combined with a longer work. Later in the 19th century (particularly in the 1830s) extracts from favourite repertory items (like the second act of Rossini's *Guillaume Tell*) were another option.

See DANCE and OPÉRA-BALLET. M. ELIZABETH C. BARTLET

Actéon ('Actaeon'). *Pastorale* in six scenes by MARC-ANTOINE CHARPENTIER; Paris, Hotel de Guise, 1683–5.

Actaeon (*haute-contre*) and a chorus of hunters are tracking game while Diane [Diana] (soprano) and her companions are bathing in a nearby spring. Actaeon takes leave of his party to find a quiet glade to sleep. Encountering the bathers, he attempts to hide but is immediately discovered. To prevent him from boasting of what he has seen, Diana transforms him into a stag. The hunters come looking for Actaeon to invite him to join their hunt, but Junon [Juno] (mezzo-soprano) appears and announces the death of Actaeon, who has been torn to pieces by his own hounds. A miniature *tragédie lyrique*, *Actéon* approaches other works by Charpentier, such as *David et Jonathas* and *Médée*, in its psychological dimensions. Charpentier's music, through affective choices of key, orchestral colour and vocal style, faithfully reflects the rapid succession of moods within the drama's short span. Especially moving is the poignant instrumental plaint that accompanies Actaeon's transformation into a stag. JOHN S. POWELL

Action musicale (Fr.). A translation of Wagner's 'Handlung für Musik', his designation of the *Lohengrin* libretto, used by French Wagnerians (e.g. d'Indy, on the title-pages of his *Fervaal* and *L'étranger*) to suggest something more elevated than a mere opera.

Act music. Instrumental (rarely vocal) music performed before and during the intervals of late 17th- and early 18th-century English plays and semi-operas (*see* SEMI-OPERA). A full suite of act music comprises nine pieces: two pieces each of 'first music' and 'second music', played to entertain the audience waiting for the play to begin; an overture, usually in the French style, sounded after the prologue was spoken and just before the curtain was raised; and four 'act tunes' played immediately at the end of each act of a five-act play or semi-opera (except the last).

The earliest known suites of act music were composed by MATTHEW LOCKE in the 1660s for various unidentified productions of the Duke's Company, London; the first set to be published was Locke's for the 1674 'operatic' production of Dryden and Davenant's *The Tempest*, which includes the remarkable overture or 'curtain tune' in imitation of a storm. The full score includes indications of expression and dynamics ('lowder by degrees', 'violent', 'soft and slow by degrees'). After *The Tempest*, act music was designed increasingly to reflect the dramatic content of the play for which it was commissioned, and act tunes in particular, besides signalling the ends of acts (as the curtain was not lowered until the end of the play), attempted to capture the mood of the scene they immediately followed. An act tune might therefore repeat the melody of a song in the preceding act or comment on the action in some obvious way, such as Godfrey Finger's punning 'Cuckoo' tune in *The Husband his own Cuckold* (1696) by John Dryden the younger.

The most important collection of act music is that by Henry Purcell published posthumously in *Ayres for the Theatre* (1697), which includes orchestral music for 13 plays and semi-operas. Apart from a few rondeaux and pieces on ground basses, most act tunes are in simple binary form, with two repeated strains of eight to 16 bars each. The overtures are all of the French type, with stately or grave introductions and brisk, quasi-contrapuntal canzonas; a few have conclusions recalling the style of the opening section. Purcell's act music is distinguished from that of his contemporaries by its depth and range of expression and attention to the inner parts.

In 1701 John Walsh began a huge periodical collection of act music under the general title *Harmonia Anglicana, or the Musick of the English Stage*, which includes more than 60 sets composed up to 1710. Among the last suites of act music to be published is that for a 1710 production of Jonson's *The Alchemist* composed by 'an Italian master'. This is in fact the overture and instrumental music from Handel's *Rodrigo* (1707); the composer himself did not arrive in England until late 1710. After this, no new act music is known to have been commissioned; instead, theatre managers used popular pieces, including Corelli sonatas and concertos, as the preliminary music and act tunes, and this kind of music ceased to have an explicitly dramatic function.

*

C. A. Price: *Music in the Restoration Theatre* (Ann Arbor, 1979)
——: Introduction to *Instrumental Music for London Theatres, 1690–1699*, MLE, A3 (1987)
P. Holman: Introduction to M. Locke: *The Rare Theatrical*, MLE, A4 (1989)
CURTIS PRICE

Actor's Revenge, An. Opera by Minoru Miki; *see* ADA.

Act tune. A piece of music played, in English semi-operas and plays of the late 17th century and the early 18th, at the end of each act (except the last). *See* ACT MUSIC.

Ada ('Revenge') [*An Actor's Revenge*]. Opera in two acts by MINORU MIKI to a libretto by James Kirkup after Otokichi Mikami; London, Old Vic, 5 October 1979.

In a Zen monastery, Yukinojō (tenor), once a popular kabuki actor specializing in female roles, reminisces over his past with remorse, seeing a vision of his beloved Namiji (soprano). He was destined to avenge his parents' death by killing Lord Dobe (bass), a corrupt magistrate, and his henchman Kawaguchiya (tenor). He accomplished the deed successfully and also caused the downfall of Hiromiya (bass), a dishonest rice dealer, but it was done at the price of the life of Namiji, Lord Dobe's daughter, promised to the Shogun (tenor). The music consists principally of declamatory solo singing with few ensembles, and exploits the tone colours of individual instruments. The orchestra is small and includes three Japanese instruments: koto, shamisen and percussion. The writing is spare but dramatically effective. At the première the role of Yukinojō was performed by two artists: a singer and a dancer.

MASAKATA KANAZAWA

Adam, Adolphe (Charles) (*b* Paris, 24 July 1803; *d* Paris, 3 May 1856). French composer. The son of Louis Adam (*b* Muttersholtz, Bas-Rhin, 3 Dec 1758; *d* Paris, 8 April 1848), a pianist, composer and teacher, Adolphe was not encouraged to become a musician but, influenced by his friendship with Ferdinand Hérold (12 years his senior), he decided at an early age that he wished to compose and particularly to compose theatre music. At 17 he entered the Paris Conservatoire, where he studied composition with Boieldieu, the chief architect of his musical development. By the age of 20 he was already contributing songs to the Paris vaudeville theatres; he played in the orchestra at the Gymnase-Dramatique, later becoming chorus master there. He helped Boieldieu with the preparation of *La dame blanche*, produced by the Opéra-Comique on 10 December 1825. While touring the Netherlands, Germany and Switzerland in summer 1826 with a friend, he met Eugène Scribe in Geneva. Adam had already written music for a one-act vaudeville by Scribe (and Mazères), *L'oncle d'Amérique*, given at the Gymnase on 14 March 1826; now he obtained from the librettist the text of a one-act comic opera, *Le mal du pays, ou La batelière de Brientz*, which was produced at the Gymnase on 28 December 1827. Just over a year later, on 9 February 1829, *Pierre et Catherine*, his first work to be accepted by the Opéra-Comique, was given in a double bill with Auber's *La fiancée* and achieved over 80 performances.

Adam's next piece for the Opéra-Comique, the three-act *Danilowa*, was successfully produced in April 1830, but its run was interrupted by the July Revolution. After the Revolution theatrical conditions became difficult in Paris, and Adam went to London, where his brother-in-law, Pierre François Laporte, was manager of the King's Theatre. In 1832 Laporte leased the Theatre Royal, Covent Garden, and on 1 October, as an afterpiece to *The Merchant of Venice*, he presented *His First Campaign*, a 'military spectacle' with music by Adam, which featured the 12-year-old Elizabeth Poole as a drummer boy. *The Dark Diamond*, a historical melodrama in three acts, which followed on 5 November, failed to repeat the success of *His First Campaign*. Adam returned to Paris for the première of Hérold's *Le pré aux clercs* (15 December) and then achieved one of his greatest popular successes with *Le chalet*. A one-act *opéra comique* with text by Scribe and Mélesville (based on Goethe's *Jery und Bätely*), it was first produced on 25 September 1834 and received its 1000th performance by the Opéra-Comique in 1873. Boieldieu, who died 13 days after the première, was present at his pupil's triumph. Adam then accepted a libretto from de Leuven and Brunswick provisionally entitled *Une voix*. This opera, now called *Le postillon de Lonjumeau*, was given its successful première by the Opéra-Comique on 13 October 1836 with the tenor Jean Baptiste Chollet (who also created the title roles of Auber's *Fra diavolo* and Hérold's *Zampa*) as the postilion Chapelou.

Four more works for the Opéra-Comique followed in quick succession, then in September 1839 Adam left Paris for St Petersburg, where his ballet *La fille du Danube* was given immediately after his arrival. *Le brasseur de Preston*, first heard in Paris in 1838 and dedicated to Tsar Nicholas I, was performed in February 1840 by the German opera company in St Petersburg, with Adam conducting. Back in Paris, Adam composed the work by which he is now best known, the ballet *Giselle*, and reorchestrated Grétry's *Richard Coeur-de-lion*, revived for King Louis Philippe at Fontainebleau with its original sets. He also completed *Lambert Simnel*, an opera left unfinished by Hippolyte Monpou. Adam's first 'grand opera', *Richard en Palestine*, was produced at the Opéra in 1844, arousing little interest.

That same year, having quarrelled with Alexandre Basset, the new director of the Opéra-Comique, who vowed never to perform a work by Adam at his theatre, the composer found his main source of income removed. He made plans to open a third opera house in Paris, to be called the Opéra-National. A large amount of money was required, and after some difficulty was borrowed. The Opéra-National opened on 15 November 1847 and for a few months flourished, then in February 1848 revolution again broke out in Paris, and on 26 March the Opéra-National closed down. Adam was completely ruined. Assigning all his royalties to pay off the debt, he turned to journalism as a means of earning some money and contributed reviews and articles to *Le constitutionnel* and the *Assemblée nationale*. He also became a professor of composition at the Conservatoire, a post he held until his death. Meanwhile Basset had left the Opéra-Comique and Adam was able to return to his spiritual home. In July 1850 one of his best works, the opera *Giralda, ou La nouvelle Psyché* (with a text by Scribe, originally intended for Auber), was produced there. He also wrote the very successful *Si j'étais roi* for the Théâtre Lyrique (the successor to the ill-fated Opéra-National), where it was performed with different casts on 4 and 5 September 1852. That year no fewer than six new works of his were produced, and by the end of it his debts were finally cleared. During the remaining three years of his life Adam composed as prolifically as ever, including arranging Donizetti's *Betly*, on the same subject as his own opera *Le chalet*, for the Opéra (27 December 1853). His final dramatic work, the charming one-act operetta *Les pantins de Violette*, was produced at the Bouffes-Parisiens, where it shared the bill with Poise's *Le thé de Polichinelle*, on 29 April 1856. Four nights later Adam died in his sleep.

Adam wrote with extreme facility, but a large proportion of his huge output – which includes piano arrangements, potpourris of operatic arias and songs – is of purely ephemeral interest. He composed about 70 operatic works, some of which, especially those for the Opéra-Comique, achieved considerable and lasting success. Several operas and ballets (above all *Giselle*) are not merely delightful examples of their kind, but are also scores full of genuine inspiration. *Le chalet*, his first significant success, was Adam's most popular opera in France throughout the 19th century, but *Le postillon de Lonjumeau* outdistanced it in other European countries, particularly in Germany, where every tenor who could boast the necessary top notes indefatigably performed the title role. The score is imbued with a sense of theatre, the inborn gift that Adam brought so abundantly to all his stage works, even the weakest. The most stylish, tuneful and accomplished of his later operas are *Giralda* and *Si j'étais roi*, the overtures to both pieces being particularly graceful and charming.

See also CHALET, LE; POSTILLON DE LONJUMEAU, LE; and SI J'ÉTAIS ROI.

first performed in Paris unless otherwise stated; works performed at the Gymnase-Dramatique, Vaudeville and Nouveautés are mainly vaudevilles, the remaining works are opéras comiques unless otherwise stated; printed works published in Paris

PG – *Théâtre Gymnase-Dramatique* PL – *Théâtre Lyrique*
PN – *Théâtre des Nouveautés* POC – *Opéra-Comique*
PVD – *Théâtre du Vaudeville*

Pierre et Marie, ou Le soldat ménétrier (1), PG, 22 Jan 1824
Le baiser au porteur (1), PG, 9 June 1824
Le bal champêtre (1), PG, 21 Oct 1824
La haine d'une femme (1), PG, 14 Dec 1824
L'exilé (2), PV, 9 July 1825
La dame jaune (1, P. F. A. Carmouche and E. J. E. Mazères), PVD, 7 March 1826
L'oncle d'Amérique (1, E. Scribe and Mazères), PG, 14 March 1826
L'anonyme (2, Jouslin de la Salle, C. Dupeuty and F. de Villeneuve), PVD, 29 May 1826
Le hussard de Felsheim (3, Dupeuty, Villeneuve and A. Villain de Saint-Hilaire), PVD, 9 March 1827
L'héritière et l'orpheline (2, T. Anne and Henry), PVD, 12 May 1827
Perkin Warbeck (2, M. Théaulon, Brazier and Carmouche), PG, 15 May 1827
Mon ami Pierre (1, Dartois), PN, 8 Sept 1827
Monsieur Botte (3, Dupeuty and Villeneuve), PN, 15 Nov 1827
Le Caleb de Walter Scott (1, Dartois and Planard), PN, 12 Dec 1827
Le mal du pays, ou La batelière de Brientz (1, Scribe and Mélesville [A.-H.-J. Duveyrier]), PG, 28 Dec 1827, vs (?1828)
Lidda, ou La jeune servante (1, Anne), PN, 16 Jan 1828
La reine de seize ans (2, Bayard), PG, 30 Jan 1828

Le barbier châtelain, ou La loterie de Francfort (3, Anne and Théaulon), PN, 7 Feb 1828
Les comédiens par testament (1, Picard and Laffite), PN, 14 April 1828
Les trois cantons, ou La Confédération suisse (3, Villeneuve and Dupeuty), PVD, 16 June 1828
Valentine, ou La chute des feuilles (2, Saint-Hilaire and Villeneuve), PN, 2 Oct 1828
Le clé (3, Leroi and Hyppolyte), PVD, 5 Nov 1828
Le jeune propriétaire et le vieux fermier (3, Dartois), PN, 6 Feb 1829
Pierre et Catherine (2, J.-H. Vernoy de Saint-Georges), POC (Feydeau), 9 Feb 1829 (?1829)
Isaure (3), PN, 1 Oct 1829
Henri V et ses compagnons [pasticcio] (3), PN, 27 Feb 1830
Danilowa (3, J. B. Vial and P. Duport), POC (Ventadour), 23 April 1830 (?1830)
Rafaël [pasticcio] (3), PN, 26 April 1830
Les trois Catherine (3), PN, 26 July 1830, collab. C. Gide
Trois jours en une heure (1, Gabriel [J. J. G. de Lurieu] and A. M. B. G. Masson), POC (Ventadour), 21 Aug 1830, collab. H. Romagnesi
Joséphine, ou Le retour de Wagram (1, Gabriel and Delaboullaye), POC (Ventadour), 2 Dec 1830 (?1830)
Le morceau d'ensemble (1, Carmouche and F. de Courcy), POC (Ventadour), 7 March 1831 (?1831)
Le grand prix, ou Le voyage à frais communs (3, Gabriel and Masson), POC (Ventadour), 9 July 1831 (?1831)
Casimir, ou Le premier tête-à-tête (2), PN, 1 Dec 1831
His First Campaign (military spectacle, 2), London, CG, 1 Oct 1832
The Dark Diamond (historical melodrama, 3), London, CG, 5 Nov 1832
Le proscrit, ou Le tribunal invisible (3, Carmouche and J. X. V. Saintine), POC (Bourse), 18 Sept 1833 (?1833)
Une bonne fortune (1, Féréol [L. Second] and Edouard), POC (Bourse), 28 Jan 1834 (1834)
Le chalet (1, Scribe and Mélesville, after J. W. von Goethe: *Jery und Bätely*), POC (Bourse), 25 Sept 1834 (1834)
La marquise (1, Saint-Georges and A. de Leuven), POC (Bourse), 28 Feb 1835 (1835)
Micheline, ou L'heure d'esprit (1, Saint-Hilaire, Masson and Villeneuve), POC (Bourse), 29 June 1835 (1835)
Le postillon de Lonjumeau (3, de Leuven and Brunswick [L. Lhérie]), POC (Bourse), 13 Oct 1836 (?1836)
Le fidèle berger (3, Scribe and Saint-Georges), POC (Bourse), 6 Jan 1838 (1838)
Le brasseur de Preston (3, de Leuven and Brunswick), POC (Bourse), 31 Oct 1838 (1838)
Régine, ou Les deux nuits (2, Scribe), POC (Bourse), 17 Jan 1839 (?1839)
La reine d'un jour (3, Scribe and Saint-Georges), POC (Bourse), 19 Sept 1839 (?1839)
Die Hamadryaden (opéra-ballet, 2, Colombey), Berlin, Court Opera, 28 April 1840
La rose de Péronne (3, de Leuven and A. P. d'Ennery), POC (Favart), 12 Dec 1840
La main de fer, ou Le mariage secret (3, Scribe and de Leuven), POC (Favart), 26 Oct 1841, vs (?1841)
Le roi d'Yvetot (3, de Leuven and Brunswick), POC (Favart), 13 Oct 1842 (1842)
Lambert Simnel (3, Scribe and Mélesville), POC (Favart), 14 Sept 1843, vs (1843) [completion of work begun by H. Monpou]
Cagliostro (3, Scribe and Saint-Georges), POC (Favart), 10 Feb 1844 (?1844)
Richard en Palestine (opéra, 3, P. Foucher), Opéra, 7 Oct 1844, vs (?1844)
La bouquetière (opéra, 1, H. Lucas), Opéra, 31 May 1847, vs (?1847)
Les premiers pas (scène-prologue, G. Vaëz and A. Royer), Opéra-National, 15 Nov 1847, collab. Auber, Carrafa and Halévy
Le torédor, ou L'accord parfait (2, T. Sauvage), POC (Favart), 18 May 1849 (?1849)
Le Fanal (opéra, 2, Saint-Georges), Opéra, 24 Dec 1849, vs (?1849)
Giralda, ou La nouvelle Psyché (3, Scribe), POC (Favart), 20 July 1850 (?1850)
La poupée de Nuremberg (1, de Leuven and A. de Beauplan, after E. T. A. Hoffmann: *Der Sandmann*), Opéra-National, 21 Feb 1852 (1852)
Le farfadet (1, F. A. E. de Planard), POC (Favart), 19 March 1852, vs (1852)
Si j'étais roi (3, d'Ennery and J. Brésil), PL, 4 Sept 1852 (?1852)
La faridondaine (drama with songs, 5, Dupeuty and E. Bourget), Porte-St-Martin, 30 Dec 1852, collab. L. A. de Groot
Le sourd, ou L'auberge pleine (3, F. Langlé and de Leuven, after P. J. B. Choudard Desforges), POC (Favart), 2 Feb 1853, vs (?1853)
Le roi des halles (3, de Leuven and Brunswick), PL, 11 April 1853, vs (?1853)
Le bijou perdu (3, de Leuven and P. A. A. Pittaud de Forges), PL, 6 Oct 1853, vs (?1854)
Le muletier de Tolède (3, d'Ennery and L. F. Clairville), PL, 16 Dec 1854, vs (1854)
A Clichy (1, d'Ennery and E. Grangé), PL, 24 Dec 1854, vs (*c*1855)
Le houzard de Berchini (2, E. Rosier), POC (Favart), 17 Oct 1855, vs (1855)
Falstaff (1, Saint-Georges and de Leuven, after W. Shakespeare: *The Merry Wives of Windsor*), PL, 18 Jan 1856, vs (1856)
Mam'zelle Geneviève (2, Brunswick and Beauplan), PL, 24 March 1856
Les pantins de Violette (operetta, 1, L. Battu), Bouffes-Parisiens, 29 April 1856, vs (?1856)

*

J. Lardin: *Zémire et Azor par Grétry: quelques questions à propos de la nouvelle falsification de cet opéra* (Paris, 1846)
——: *Adrien François Boieldieu: Adolph Adam: Biographien* (Kassel, 1855)
A. Adam: *Souvenirs d'un musicien ... précédés de notes biographiques* (Paris, 1857, many later edns)
——: *Derniers souvenirs d'un musicien* (Paris, 1859, many later edns)
F. Halévy: *Notice sur la vie et les ouvrages de M. Adolphe Adam* (Paris, 1859); repr. as 'Adolphe Adam' in Halévy: *Souvenirs et portraits* (Paris, 1861)
P. Scudo: *Critique et littérature musicales*, ii (Paris, 1859)
F. Clément and P. Larousse: *Dictionnaire lyrique* (Paris, 1867–81); ed. A. Pougin, *Dictionnaire des opéras* (2/1897, 3/1905)
F. Clément: *Les musiciens célèbres depuis le seizième siècle jusqu'à nos jours* (Paris, 1868, enlarged 4/1887)
E. de Mirecourt: *Adolphe Adam* (Paris, 1868)
A. Pougin: *Adolphe Adam: sa vie, sa carrière, ses mémoires artistiques* (Paris, 1877)
ELIZABETH FORBES

Adam, Frédéric (*b* Hinsbourg, 4 Jan 1904; *d* Illkirch-Graffenstaden, 7 Sept 1984). French conductor, composer and opera administrator. He studied in Strasbourg with Erb and in Paris with Koechlin and Gédalge. He joined the Strasbourg Opera in 1933 as a répétiteur and stayed until he retired in 1972, being successively chorus master (1933–6), conductor from 1936, co-director (with Ernest Bour) from 1955 to 1960 and director (1960–72).

Adam sought to create a balanced repertory of French, German and Italian classics, together with contemporary works (such as Jean Martinon's *Hécube*, 1956, which was specially commissioned) and revivals of rarely given masterpieces such as *Les Troyens* (1960) and Roussel's *Padmâvatî* (1967). He gave the first French performances of Bizet's *Don Procopio* (1958), Françaix's *L'apostrophe* (1958), Dallapiccola's *Il prigioniero* (1961), Strauss's *Die Frau ohne Schatten* (1965), Britten's *A Midsummer Night's Dream* (1965), Henze's *Der junge Lord* (1967) and Smetana's *Dalibor* (1968). In 1959 the Strasbourg Opera became the first French company to mount *Wozzeck*, which had already been performed in Paris but by a visiting German company. He brought performances of Wagner operas to a high standard with *Tannhäuser* in 1966, in which Birgit Nilsson made her French début; the *Ring* was given in 1956 and 1963 with Bayreuth casts, and his *Parsifal* of 1961 featured Régine Crespin in her first appearance as Kundry. Although widely recognized as one of the foremost French Wagnerian conductors, he never sought international fame, being content to remain in Strasbourg building up the musical and visual levels of productions; he later collaborated with the producers Bronislav Horowicz, Rudolf Hartmann and Hans Hotter. In addition to two ballets and symphonies, he composed two operas: *Judith* (1948, Strasbourg) and *Le voyage vers l'étoile* (1954, Strasbourg).

CHARLES PITT

Adam, Theo(dor) (*b* Dresden, 1 Aug 1926). German bass-baritone. He studied in Dresden and Weimar, making his début in 1949 as the Hermit (*Freischütz*) at the Dresden Staatsoper and singing the same role at the re-opening of the Semper-Oper in 1985. At Bayreuth he graduated from Ortel (*Meistersinger*) in 1952 to King Henry, Titurel, Wotan, the Dutchman, Amfortas and Hans Sachs, then Pogner and Gurnemanz (1980). A member of the Berlin Staatsoper since 1957, he had a repertory ranging from Handel's Julius Caesar, Don Giovanni and Philip II to La Roche (*Capriccio*) and Dessau's Einstein, which he created in 1974. At Salzburg he has sung Ochs (1969), Wozzeck (1972) and Cerha's Baal (1981), which he created, as well as Prospero in Berio's *Un re in ascolto* (1984). He made his débuts at Covent Garden in 1967 as Wotan and at the Metropolitan in 1969 as Hans Sachs. He appeared at the Vienna Staatsoper and the Theater an der Wien, where in 1970 he sang Pizarro (*Fidelio*) for the Beethoven bicentenary. He directed many operas for the Berlin Staatsoper and other theatres, including *Capriccio* at the Munich Festival in 1989, when he also sang La Roche. He recorded Wotan for Böhm, then Alberich (*Rheingold*) for Haitink (1989). His voice was an expressive though not always ingratiating instrument. As an actor, he was commanding in presence and intelligent.

ALAN BLYTH

Adamberger, (Josef) Valentin (*b* Munich, 6 July 1743; *d* Vienna, 24 Aug 1804). German tenor. In 1755 he studied singing with J. E. Walleshauser (Giovanni Valesi) while at the Domus Gregoriana, a Jesuit institution in Munich. In 1760 he joined the Kapelle of Duke Clemens and on Clemens's death in 1770 was taken into the elector's Hofkapelle. He sang leading tenor roles in *opere serie* at Modena, Venice, Florence, Pisa and Rome from 1775 to 1777, then at the King's Theatre in London until 1779, and again in Italy until he joined the National Singspiel at Vienna, where he made his début on 21 August 1780. In 1781 he married the Viennese actress Marie Anne Jacquet (1753–1804). On the demise of the National Singspiel in 1783 Adamberger joined the Italian company that replaced it at the Burgtheater, then in 1785 the new German troupe under imperial subvention at the Kärntnertortheater, and on its dissolution in 1789 the Italian company at the Burgtheater once again. He retired from the stage in 1793 but continued as a member of the imperial Hofkapelle and as an eminent singing teacher.

Adamberger's voice was universally admired for its pliancy, agility and precision, although Schubart and Mount Edgcumbe also remarked on its nasal quality. Mozart wrote the part of Belmonte in *Die Entführung* (1782) and Vogelsang in *Der Schauspieldirektor* (1786) for him, as well as several arias (K420 and K431) and the cantata *Die Maurerfreude* (K471).

Before coming to Vienna, Adamberger created leading tenor parts in serious operas by J. C. Bach, Sarti, Pietro Guglielmi, Sacchini, Bertoni and others. The arias they wrote for his voice reveal a fondness for moderate tempos, B♭ major, obbligato clarinets and expressive chromatic inflections. At Vienna Mozart (*Die Entführung*), Umlauf (*Das Irrlicht*) and Dittersdorf (*Doktor und Apotheker*) perpetuated these features, which made Adamberger 'the favourite singer of softer hearts', according to a local journalist (Michtner, p.360).

*

C. F. D. Schubart: *Deutsche Chronik*, i (1774) [journal]
J. F. von Schönfeld: *Jahrbuch der Tonkunst von Wien und Prag* (Vienna, 1796)
R. Mount Edgcumbe: *Musical Reminiscences* (London, 1824, 4/1834)
H. Killer: *Die Tenorpartien in Mozarts Opern* (Kassel, 1929)
O. Michtner: *Das alte Burgtheater als Opernbühne* (Vienna, 1970)
H. Barak: *Belmontes Familie* (Vienna, 1991)
T. Bauman: 'Mozart's Belmonte', *EMc*, xix (1991), 557–63

THOMAS BAUMAN

Adami, Carl. *See* ADAMS, CHARLES R.

Adami, Giuseppe (*b* Verona, 4 Nov 1878; *d* Milan, 12 Oct 1946). Italian playwright, librettist and journalist. After graduating in law at the University of Padua he devoted himself to literature, first as theatre critic of the *Arena* (Verona), then as playwright. His first stage work was the one-act comedy *I fioi di Goldoni* in Venetian dialect; thereafter he proved remarkably successful in a comic-sentimental vein with such plays as *Una capanna e il tuo cuore* (1913), *Capelli bianchi* (1915), *Felicità Colombo* (1935) and its sequel *Nonna Felicità* (1936). In 1911 he made the acquaintance of Giulio Ricordi, head of the publishing firm, of whom he left a valuable memoir in his *Giulio Ricordi e i suoi musicisti* (Milan, 1933, 2/1945 as *Giulio Ricordi, amico dei musicisti*). It was Ricordi who first put him in touch with Puccini, who briefly considered setting his Spanish-derived libretto *Anima allegra* written with Luigi Motta; it was eventually set by Franco Vittadini, for whom Adami wrote a number of ballet scenarios. His first collaboration with Puccini was on *La rondine* (1917), which he adapted as a full-length verse libretto from a German operetta text by Willner and Reichert. There followed *Il tabarro* (1918) and *Turandot* (1926), the last being written in partnership with Renato Simoni. To Adami we owe the first collection of Puccini's letters to be published, *Giacomo Puccini: epistolario* (Milan, 1928; Eng. trans., 1931, 2/1974), as well as one of the earliest biographies of the composer (Milan, 1935), based on personal recollections. From 1931 to 1934 he was music critic for *La sera* (Milan) and of the review *La comoedia*. To the end of his life he maintained a connection with the house of Ricordi, for whom he acted as publicist.

La rondine, Puccini, 1917; *Il tabarro*, Puccini, 1918; *La via della finestra*, Zandonai, 1919; *Anima allegra* (with L. Motta), Vittadini, 1921; *La monacella della fontana*, Mulè, 1923; *Nazareth*, Vittadini, 1925; *Turandot* (with R. Simoni), Puccini, 1926; *La Sagredo*, Vittadini, 1930; *Taormina*, Mulè, 1938; *La zolfara*, Mulè, 1939; *Fiammetta e l'avaro* (with G. Forzano), Vittadini, 1951

*

R. Simoni: *Trent'anni di cronaca drammatica* (Turin, 1955)

JULIAN BUDDEN

Adams, Charles R. [Adami, Carl] (*b* Charlestown, MA, 9 Feb 1834; *d* West Harwich, MA, 4 July 1900). American tenor. He studied in Boston and, after concert and opera appearances in the West Indies and the Netherlands, in Vienna with Carlo Barbieri. He was then engaged by the Berlin Königliche Oper. From 1867 to 1876, except for one year, he was principal tenor of the Vienna Hofoper;

his roles there included Gennaro, Raoul, Edgardo, Faust, Lohengrin and Tannhäuser. He also appeared at La Scala and Covent Garden. Returning to the USA, he sang the title role in the first American production of *Rienzi*, in New York on 4 March 1878. As a teacher, after his retirement from the stage, he numbered Melba and Eames among his pupils.

*

O. Thompson: *The American Singer* (New York, 1937), 85–9

H. WILEY HITCHCOCK

Adams, Donald (*b* Bristol, 20 Dec 1928). English bass. He was a chorister at Worcester Cathedral and later became an actor. After singing in the D'Oyly Carte Opera chorus, from 1953 to 1969 he was principal bass of the company. In 1963 he co-founded 'G&S for All', with whom he toured extensively in Australia and the USA. In 1983 he sang the Mikado in Chicago, returning for Baron Mirko Zeta and the Theatre Director/Banker (*Lulu*). He made his Covent Garden début in 1983 as a Frontier Guard (*Boris Godunov*), and later sang Quince and Frank. For the ENO (1985–92) he has sung Dikoj (*Kát'a Kabanová*), Mozart's Bartolo, and Pooh-Bah; for the WNO (1985–7) his roles included Monterone and Rossini's Bartolo. He also appeared at Glyndebourne (Dikoj, Quince and Swallow), Amsterdam, Los Angeles, San Francisco and Geneva. In 1991 he sang Schigolch in *Lulu* for the Canadian Opera. A superb comic actor with an imposing presence, meticulous diction and a resonant voice, he made a magnificent Ochs in *Der Rosenkavalier* for the WNO in 1990.

ELIZABETH FORBES

Adams, John (**Coolidge**) (*b* Worcester, MA, 15 Feb 1947). American composer and conductor. One of the foremost minimalist composers, Adams established his reputation in the late 1970s with a series of electronic, chamber and orchestral works, and completed his first opera, *Nixon in China*, in 1987.

He studied the clarinet as a child, and began his studies in conducting at Dartmouth College in 1965. At Harvard University he studied composition with Leon Kirchner and worked as a freelance musician. He took up a teaching post at the San Francisco Conservatory of Music in 1972, leaving it a decade later. In 1978 he was appointed New Music Adviser to the San Francisco Symphony Orchestra, for which he was composer-in-residence until 1985.

In his earliest works Adams composed in a conservative, tightly structured academic style, but by the early 1970s was experimenting not only with electronics but also with combinations of Classical, folk and popular forms (e.g. *American Standard*, 1973). In the late 1970s he took a decisive step towards the minimalist style, while maintaining an element of individuality with an outgoing use of chromaticism. He also made use of rapid changes of chord sequence, dynamics, scoring and direction more typical of the neo-romantics than of the minimalists, as exemplified in works such as *Harmonium* and *Grand Pianola Music* (both 1980). *Nixon in China* was conceived in 1982 by the controversial theatre and opera director Peter Sellars, who wanted to work on an opera based on an episode in contemporary history rather than a distant or fictional one. In Richard Nixon's 1972 visit to China he found a subject that was not only recent enough for virtually everyone in the work's first audiences to remember but which also contained the kind of noble intentions, grand situations and flawed, complex characters to which mythological attributes might be applied.

The team Sellars assembled included Adams, the poet Alice Goodman as librettist and the choreographer Mark Morris. All those involved have insisted that the work was an equal, four-way collaboration, which implies that the production and choreography will survive into future performances. They relied on newspaper, magazine and television coverage of the event for their sources and kept close to the public record, with the exception of the final scene.

Adams's music for *Nixon* is in many ways the culmination of the style he had been developing since *American Standard*. The eclecticism of that work and *Grand Pianola Music* is heard in amalgams of Gershwin and Wagner with a brand of minimalist figuration closer to that of Philip Glass's works (most notably *Satyagraha*) than to the more novel style of Adams's string septet *Shaker Loops* (1978) and other works. His characterizations, if sometimes exaggerated, serve as recognizable caricatures of the people concerned.

The première of *Nixon in China* (Houston, Grand Opera, 22 October 1987) received generally enthusiastic notices, the dissenters being mainly opponents of minimalism. The Houston production was videotaped for television broadcast early in 1988, at around the time the work was being performed in Washington, DC. It had its New York première on 4 December 1987 (Brooklyn Academy of Music) and was recorded during its New York run.

Adams's second opera, *The Death of Klinghoffer*, also to a libretto by Alice Goodman, had its première on 19 March 1991 (Brussels, Monnaie). Like *Nixon in China* it was directed by Sellars and choreographed by Morris and is based on recent occurrences, this time the hijacking of the cruise ship *Achille Lauro* in 1985. The story unfolds in meditations and narratives, punctuated by choruses, rather than in action.

See also NIXON IN CHINA.

*

R. H. Kornick: *Recent American Opera: a Production Guide* (New York, 1991), 3–5

ALLAN KOZINN

Adams, Suzanne (*b* Cambridge, MA, 28 Nov 1872; *d* London, 5 Feb 1953). American soprano. She studied with Mathilde Marchesi and Bouhy in Paris and made her début at the Opéra in 1895 as Juliet, a role which, together with Marguerite in *Faust*, she seems to have studied with Gounod, who greatly admired her brilliant yet flexible tone and fine technique. She sang at Covent Garden (1898–1904), where she created Hero in Stanford's *Much Ado about Nothing*; she was also a member of the Metropolitan Opera (1899–1903). Her repertory included Eurydice, Donna Elvira, Micaëla and Marguerite de Valois. She retired in 1904 and then taught singing in London.

*

O. Thompson: *The American Singer* (New York, 1937), 199–201

J. Freestone: 'Suzanne Adams, 1873–1953', *Gramophone*, xxxi (1953–4), 37 [with discography]

Addison, John (*b* London, *c*1766; *d* London, 30 Jan 1844). English composer. He displayed a taste for music at an early age and learnt to play several instruments. About 1793 he married the singer Miss Willems, a niece of F. C. Reinhold, and decided to become a professional musician. As Mrs Addison she appeared at Vauxhall Gardens, where her husband was a cellist. They went to

Liverpool and then to Dublin, where Addison became director of an amateur theatre orchestra. In 1796 they returned to London, Mrs Addison appearing at Covent Garden as Rosetta in a revival of *Love in a Village*. After a three-year engagement at Dublin and a spell in the provinces they returned to London, where Addison shared with Michael Kelly the management of his music business and produced his own theatrical music, chiefly comic works given at the Lyceum. He was also engaged at the King's Theatre as a double bass player. He published a singing treatise in London in 1836.

all first performed in London

The Sleeping Beauty (play, L. St G. Skeffington), Drury Lane, 6 Dec 1805, vs (London, 1805)
Maids and Bachelors, or My Heart for Yours (comedy, Skeffington), CG, 6 June 1806
False Alarms, or My Cousin (comic op, J. Kenney), Drury Lane, 12 Jan 1807, collab. J. Braham and M. P. King
The Russian Impostor, or The Siege of Smolensko (H. Siddons and S. J. Arnold), Lyceum, 22 July 1809, vs (London, 1809)
My Aunt (operatic farce, Arnold), Lyceum, 1 Aug 1815, vs (London, 1813)
Bobinet the Bandit, or The Forest of Monte-Scarpini (musical entertainment), CG, 4 Dec 1815, vs (*c*1815)
Two Words, or The Silent not Dumb! (play, Arnold), Lyceum, 2 Sept 1816, vs (1816)
Free and Easy (comic op, Arnold), Lyceum, 16 Sept 1816, vs (1816)
My Uncle (operetta, S. Beazley), Lyceum, 23 June 1817, vs (1817)

Music in: W. Shield: Robin Hood, 1813; H. R. Bishop and T. Welsh: England Ho!, 1813; and other works

Addison, Joseph (*b* Milston, Wilts., 1 May 1672; *d* Kensington, 17 June 1719). English librettist and writer on opera. He studied at Oxford, then held minor political offices and toured on the continent (1699–1704), hearing performances in the most important operatic centres: Lully's *Proserpine* in Paris (1699), Italian opera in Venice and Florence, and perhaps a work of Keiser's in Hamburg. While in Venice he seems to have written his play *Cato* after seeing what he considered an absurd opera on the subject (C. F. Pollarolo's *Catone Uticense*, 1701). He documented his impressions of opera in his *Remarks upon Several Parts of Italy* (1705), commenting perceptively on the differences between the Italian, French and English poetic styles and criticizing the dramatic vacuity of Italian opera librettos. He wrote a libretto on the story of Rosamond, mistress of Henry II (1133–89), and an epilogue to George Granville's dramatic opera *The British Enchanters* (1706). With other poets, Addison may have decided to capitalize on the recent success of opera in London, particularly that of *Arsinoe* by Thomas Clayton. Clayton's setting of Addison's *Rosamond* (1707) was not successful, however, partially because of the composer's ineptitude. The libretto, while not Addison's best work, is an elegant attempt to create an opera on a British theme and shows that Addison had studied the dramatic and technical sides of opera. Not only does the plot allow for musical presentations of all the basic affections, it even calls for the use of standard operatic scenery and stage machinery (to lower two angels into a grotto). Addison explored a variety of poetic metres and experimented with word repetition to create unusual rhythmic effects. The libretto contains an extraordinarily heavy use of imagery related to the sense of hearing, mixes serious and comic elements in a skilful manner, and embodies a highly moralistic, if artificial, conclusion. It was set successfully by T. A. Arne (1733) and, in a revised form and with less success, by Samuel Arnold (1767).

In his contributions to *The Tatler* (1709–11) and *The Spectator* (1711–12) Addison made his most extensive comments on the London opera scene and put forward suggestions for the improvement of British opera. He opposed multilingual performances where singers of different nationalities performed in their native tongues and insisted that, if translations from the Italian be used, they remain true to the original meaning. He ridiculed Handel's *Rinaldo* (1711) and the mixing of realistic stage props (such as live sparrows) with unrealistic ones (pasteboard seas, painted dragons etc.). He had serious reservations about the quality of Italian librettos, particularly when (as in *Rinaldo*) they were the product of 'poets of different nations'. Addison rejected the florid literary style of Italian librettists and complained that the British public seemed to enjoy any opera – no matter how foolish the plot – as long as it was in a language they could not understand. But he expressed admiration for the Italian performers in London, particularly the castrato Nicolini, whom he praised for his acting ability. He pointed out that Italian recitative style needed to be adapted to the rhythms of the English language, and exhorted British composers to follow Lully's model and to create native opera traditions.

Addison's essays had a considerable impact on the development of musical aesthetics and criticism. Mattheson translated and adapted many of them in *Die Vernünftler* (1713–14) and used Addison's arguments to support his advocacy for the creation of a German operatic tradition. Gottsched knew Addison's works (and in 1732 wrote his own *Der sterbende Cato*), although his attacks on opera were far less moderate than Addison's. Gottsched's wife translated Addison's contributions to *The Spectator* as well as his *Cato* and *The Drummer*. J. A. Scheibe mentions Addison frequently in *Der critische Musicus* (1745), particularly to bolster his arguments for a recitative style matching the German tongue. *The Spectator* had many imitators, including Pierre Marivaux's *Le spectateur française* (1721–4) and the *Discourse der Mahlern* (1721–3) by the Swiss writers Bodmer and Breitinger. Addison's ideas are cited by mid-century operatic reformers, particularly Algarotti, whose pupil Calzabigi also knew Addison's works. Addison's emphasis on naturalness in opera, the need for librettos of high literary quality and for national opera independent of Italian models helped to prepare the way for the operatic revolution of Gluck.

*

'Critical Discourse on Opera's and Musick in England', in F. Raguenet: *A Comparison between French and Italian Musick and Opera's* (London, 1709) [Eng. trans. of *Paralèle des italiens et des françois, en ce qui regarde la musique et les opéra* (1702)]
W. Graham, ed.: *The Letters of Joseph Addison* (London, 1941)
S. Betz: 'The Operatic Criticism of the Tatler and Spectator', *MQ*, xxxi (1945), 318–30
P. Smithers: *The Life of Joseph Addison* (Oxford, 1954, 2/1968)
D. Arundell: *The Critic at the Opera* (London, 1957)
M. Tilmouth: 'Music and British Travellers Abroad, 1600–1730', *Source Materials and the Interpretation of Music: a Memorial Volume to Thurston Dart* (London, 1981), 357–82
D. Boomgaarden: *Musical Thought in Britain and Germany During the Early Eighteenth Century* (Berne, 1987)
L. Lindgren: 'The Accomplishments of the Learned and Ingenious Nicola Haym (1678–1729)', *Studi musicali*, xvi (1987), 247–380

DONALD R. BOOMGAARDEN

Adelaide. Australian city, capital of South Australia. It was originally settled in 1836 and had its first opera production, Auber's *La muette de Portici*, in 1840. Like other Australian capitals, it depended on visits from touring companies, such as those of W. S. Lyster in the 1860s and 70s, Martin Simonsen (1887), George Musgrove (1901, 1907), Melba-Williamson (1924, 1928) and J. C. Williamson (1949), culminating in the Sutherland-Williamson season of 1965; all these companies performed standard repertory works in the Theatre Royal (opened 1868).

In 1957 a small amateur group, Intimate Opera, began the staging of short modern works; it developed into New Opera in 1973 and into the State Opera of South Australia in 1976. In 1977 the company acquired Her Majesty's Theatre (formerly the Tivoli) as its permanent home; refurbished and with seating reduced to 1000, it was renamed the Opera Theatre. In 1988 the theatre was sold to alleviate the company's financial crisis. The newly formed Australian Opera, based in Sydney, visited Adelaide in 1956 with its inaugural all-Mozart season, but has not appeared annually.

From the founding of the Adelaide Festival of the Arts in 1960, the city began to achieve a prominence in Australian operatic history, setting it apart even from the more important opera centres of Sydney and Melbourne: the biennial festival has staged many important Australian premières, including works not repeated elsewhere. Here Australian Opera gave the Australian premières of *Salome* (1960), *Ariadne auf Naxos* (1962), *Troilus and Cressida* (1964), *Porgy and Bess* (with the New Zealand Opera Company, 1966), *The Rape of Lucretia* (1972), *Wozzeck* (1976) and, after a gap, the world première of Richard Meale's *Voss* in 1986. The local company has also had an innovatory presence at the festival, with one-act works from Intimate Opera, *The Excursions of Mr Brouček* from New Opera in 1974, and larger-scale works from State Opera: *The Midsummer Marriage* (1978), *Death in Venice* (1980), *The Makropulos Affair* (1982), *Lady Macbeth of the Mtsensk District* (1984) and *The Fiery Angel* (1988). Early festival performances were given in a variety of venues until the opening of the Festival Theatre in 1973. Since the selling of the Opera Theatre in 1988, State Opera, giving seasons of three or four operas a year, has also performed there.

*

R. Holmes, ed.: *Through the Opera Glass: a Chronological Register of Opera Performed in South Australia, 1836 to 1988* (Adelaide, 1991)

A. I. GYGER

Adelaide [*L'Adelaide*]. *Dramma per musica* in three acts by ANTONIO SARTORIO to a libretto by Pietro Dolfin; Venice, Teatro S Salvatore, 1672 (libretto dedicated 19 February 1672).

The libretto is based on historical events of AD 951 (for a fuller account of these events, *see LOTARIO*, by Handel). Adelaide (soprano), the widow of Lotario, King of Italy, is commanded by Berengario (bass), the second King of Italy, to marry his son Adalberto (soprano). She steadfastly resists all Adalberto's attempts to force her into marriage and is repeatedly imprisoned. She receives aid from Ottone [Emperor Otto] (soprano), who has come disguised as a fisherman to ask for her hand in marriage himself. He rescues her three times and eventually frees her from Berengario's clutches. The subplot centres on the imaginary character of Gissilla (soprano), daughter of Adelaide's uncle Annone (alto), Duke of Canossa; Gissilla is in love with Adalberto. The secondary characters include the courtier, Lindo (tenor), and the old woman Delma (tenor), as well as the shepherd Armondo (bass) and General Amedeo (tenor). Although the main action adheres closely to historical fact, the opera is embellished with a number of stock scenic and dramatic features from Venetian opera, including spectacular scenes such as a leap into a lake, disguises, cases of mistaken identity, attempted poisonings and unexpected rescues. A scene in a marble quarry indicates a realistic tendency.

The two versions of the opera differ to some extent in the instrumental accompaniment: the sinfonia, famous as the first evidence for the use of trumpets in opera, occurs only in the Venetian score. Outstanding among the arias (about 75 in all, some 20 with written-out accompaniment) are Adalberto's lament (2.vii) and the wide-ranging opening aria of Act 1 which sets out the theme of the drama, the virtue of steadfastness personified in the heroine. NORBERT DUBOWY

Adelaide di Borgogna ('Adelaide of Burgundy'). *Dramma* in two acts by GIOACHINO ROSSINI to a libretto by GIOVANNI SCHMIDT; Rome, Teatro Argentina, 27 December 1817.

The setting is 10th-century Italy (as in Sartorio's *ADELAIDE*). Lotario, the King of Italy, has been murdered by Berengario (bass). Lotario's wife, Adelaide (soprano), has survived but is under siege in a fortress waiting for a promised intervention by Ottone (contralto), the German King Otto I, who has a longstanding treaty with the peoples of Italy. In the opera's first concerted number, Adelaide rejects Berengario's sly suggestion that his son Adelberto (tenor) should marry Adelaide in return for her restoration to Lotario's throne. Ottone arrives and is also offered false peace terms, this time by the wily Adelberto. In the Act 1 finale Ottone finds himself immured in the fortress. At the start of Act 2, the fortress is still under siege, though Ottone has fled to rally forces that will eventually rout Berengario. Apart from the closing victory arias by Adelaide and Ottone, Act 2 is notable for the development of Adelberto's character, caught between his military duties, his growing love for the widowed Adelaide, and his love for his mother, Eurice (mezzo-soprano). Fearful for her husband's life, Eurice has thrown confusion into his plans and Adelberto's by proposing a truce and the peaceful exchange of Adelaide and Berengario under Ottone's auspices. But the plan only causes further confusion and the opera ends with the defeat of Berengario and the crowning of Ottone as the new king. Despite the somewhat grey atmosphere of feudal militarism and the relative anachronism of the *travesti* Ottone, the opera has a certain cogency and energy and offers challenges and some rewards to the interpreters of the roles of Adelaide, Adelberto and Ottone. RICHARD OSBORNE

Adelheit von Veltheim. *Schauspiel mit Gesang* in four acts by CHRISTIAN GOTTLOB NEEFE to a libretto by GUSTAV FRIEDRICH WILHELM GROSSMANN; Frankfurt, Theater in der Junghof, 23 September 1780.

Achmet, Pasha of Tunis, so loves the captive German Adelheit von Veltheim that he has raised her to the status of his sole wife. Her fiancé Karl von Bingen, also a captive, works in the Pasha's garden. He is the object of the attentions of Donna Olivia, a hot-headed Italian in the Pasha's harem who is furious over the preferment shown to Adelheit. Karl, intent on abducting Adelheit, plays along with Olivia's scheme to escape with him. With a ladder she has provided, he and Adelheit flee to a waiting frigate, but the Pasha's forces overtake them and the Maltese knights on board. Asked to judge Karl's behaviour, the knights condemn him to death, but the Pasha forgives the couple and frees them and the rest of his harem.

Grossmann's libretto shares many traits with C. F. Bretzner's contemporaneous *Belmont und Constanze* (Mozart's source for *Die Entführung aus dem Serail*), but also shows some decisive differences: it is far more exaggerated in tone and characterization, throws significant musical and dramatic weight on the various European ladies in the Pasha's harem, and treats the Pasha as a principal singing part. Neefe's music is much closer to Benda's style than to Mozart's. It includes a melodrama, marches, a battle entr'acte and arias in bravura as well as lied style, but has static ensembles and only a brief finale at the end of Act 2.

THOMAS BAUMAN

Adelson e Salvini ('Adelson and Salvini'). *Opera semiseria* in three acts by VINCENZO BELLINI to a libretto by ANDREA LEONE TOTTOLA after François-Thomas de Baculard d'Arnaud's novella *Adelson et Salvini: Anecdote anglaise* and Prospère Delamarre's play *Adelson et Salvini*; Naples, Conservatorio di S Sebastiano, some time between 11 and 15 February 1825.

The action takes place in 17th-century Ireland at the castle of Lord Adelson (bass). While Adelson is abroad an Italian painter, Salvini (tenor), has fallen in love with his fiancée, Nelly (mezzo-soprano). Nelly rejects the infatuated Salvini, who tries to commit suicide. In Act 2 Adelson's enemy, Struley (bass), enlists the help of Salvini in his plot to abduct Nelly. During the ensuing struggle a shot is heard and Salvini mistakenly believes that Nelly has been killed. In Act 3 (mostly cut in Bellini's second version) Adelson stages a trial of Salvini, who confesses his guilt. When Nelly revives, Salvini recovers from his infatuation and she prepares to marry Adelson.

Bellini's first opera, composed to bring his student career in Naples to an end, is an *opera semiseria* with numbers separated by spoken dialogue. The Tottola libretto was the one earlier set by Valentino Fioravanti for Naples in 1816; it makes provision for a comic character (the only such example in a Bellini opera) in the person of Salvini's friend, Bonifacio (bass), who sings in Neapolitan dialect, but it was nevertheless the elegiac and sentimental elements of the story that Bellini chose to emphasize. The melodic lines are characterized by varied rhythmic shapes and the tendency to oppose relative major and minor tonalities. It is significant that Bellini's melodic individuality should already appear in Nelly's *romanza* 'Dopo l'oscuro nembo' (re-used in *I Capuleti e i Montecchi*) and Salvini's 'Sì cadro ... ma estinto ancora'. A two-act revision (1826 or 1828–9), using recitative and in Italian throughout, was not performed but was later published in vocal scores by Schonenberger and Ricordi. SIMON MAGUIRE

Ademira. *Opera seria* in three acts by ANGELO TARCHI to a libretto by FERDINANDO MORETTI; Milan, Teatro alla Scala, 27 December 1783.

Ademira (soprano) has fallen in love with her captor, the Roman emperor Flavio Valente (soprano castrato). Her father Alarico [Alaric] (tenor), King of the Goths, has sworn vengeance on the emperor because he killed his son in battle. In an attempt on the emperor's life, Alaric mistakenly stabs his own ambassador Eutarco (contralto castrato), who reveals that the man whom he thought to be his son had actually been switched at birth with Auge (soprano), Ademira's sister, now posing as her friend. Alaric then embraces his newly found daughter and blesses the union of the lovers. The opera is innovatory for incorporating large choruses and dance: an antiphonal chorus serves as an introduction, a chorus with central solo section is used in Act 1, and a divertimento with dance and chorus opens Act 2. A conventional duet and a trio conclude each of the first two acts, but a dramatic cavatina *a terzo* grows out of the highly charged emotional situation at the end of Act 3.

MARITA P. McCLYMONDS

Adenis, Jules [Colombeau, Jules-Adenis] (*b* Paris, 28 June 1823; *d* Paris, Jan 1900). French playwright and librettist. He studied at the Collège Bourbon (Lycée Condorcet) and began his career as a dramatist with *Le fils du bonnetier* (1841), a vaudeville written with Ludger Berton. For the next decade, however, he was employed in business and on the editorial staff of the daily newspaper *Le corsaire* (1847–9). He began writing more vaudevilles and comedies in the 1850s, usually in collaboration with others. He was a member of the Société des Gens de Lettres and secretary of the Société des Auteurs et Compositeurs Dramatiques.

From 1856 onwards Adenis, in collaboration or alone, produced the librettos for more than two dozen *opéras comiques*, *opérettes* and *opéras*. He worked with Bizet, also a good friend, and with Guiraud and Massenet early in their careers. Contemporary critics occasionally judged his work harshly but he seems to have been generally regarded as competent and dependable, if unoriginal. His sons Eugène and Edouard also wrote plays and librettos; their work is sometimes confused with that of their father.

Le postillon en gage (opérette, with E. Plouvier), Offenbach, 1856; *Le docteur Tam-Tam* (opérette, with F. Tourte), F. Barbier, 1859; *Le ménétrier de Meudon* (oc, with Guillard), J.-B. Weckerlin, 1861; *Madame Pygmalion* (opérette bouffe, with Tourte), Barbier, 1863; *Sylvie* (oc, with J. Rostaing), Guiraud, 1864; *La bouquetière de Trianon* (oc, with Laurencin [P. D. A. Chapelle]), Barbier, 1864; *Valse et menuet* (oc, with J. Méry), P.-L. Deffès, 1865; *Les deux chasseurs et la laitière* (oc [rev. of L. Anseaume]), Gevaert, 1865 [rev. of E. Duni, 1763]

La fiancée d'Abydos, Paladilhe, comp. 1864 (A. Barthe, 1865); *Le fantôme du Rhin* (oc, with Méry), Deffès, 1866; *Le sorcier* (oc [rev. of A. A. H. Poinsinet]), Poise, 1867 [rev. of Philidor, 1764]; *La grand'tante* (oc, with C. Grandvallet), Massenet, 1867; *La jolie fille de Perth* (with J.-H. Vernoy de Saint-Georges), Bizet, 1867; *La contessina, ou Stella d'Amalfi* (opera semiseria, with Saint-Georges, rev. A. de Lauzières), J. Poniatowski, 1868; *Mlle Marguerite, s.v.p.* (opérette, with Tourte), A. Dumey and T. de Lajarte, 1868; *Les trois souhaits* (oc), Poise, 1873

Le trompette de Chamboran (oc, with A. de Leuven), Deffès, 1877; *La fée des bruyères* (oc, with E. Scribe), S. David, 1878; *Le portrait* (oc, with Laurencin), Lajarte, 1883; *Les templiers* (with A. Silvestre and L. Bonnemère), Litolff, 1886; *Juge et partie* (oc, after Montfleury), E. Missa, 1886; *La devineresse* (opérette), Lajarte, 1886; *Le roi Lear* (with E. Adenis), Litolff, 1890; *Jessica* (with H. Boisseaux), Deffès, 1898; *Le légataire universel* (ob, with Bonnemère), G. Pfeiffer, 1901; *Marcella* (with H. Cain, trans. L. Stecchetti), Giordano, 1907

DBF (M. Bécet)

G. Vapereau: *Dictionnaire universel des contemporains* (Paris, 6/1893)

M. Curtiss: *Bizet and his World* (New York, 1958)

T. J. Walsh: *Second Empire Opera* (London, 1981)

LESLEY A. WRIGHT

Adina [*Adina, o Il califfo di Bagdad* ('Adina, or the Caliph of Baghdad')]. *Farsa* in one act by GIOACHINO ROSSINI to a libretto by Marchese Gherardo

Bevilacqua-Aldobrandini; Lisbon, Teatro de S Carlos, 22 June 1826.

The opera was written in 1818, to a libretto adapted from FELICE ROMANI's *Il califfo e la schiava*, as a private commission for a Portuguese patron. The Caliph of Baghdad (bass) plans to marry the beautiful young slave-girl Adina (soprano). She, for reasons which are not immediately evident, is not unsympathetic to the Caliph but the reappearance of her one-time lover Selimo (tenor) puts her in a dilemma. Aided by his servant Mustafà (*buffo* bass), a gardener in the royal palace, Selimo persuades Adina to elope with him; which is just as well for it turns out that Adina is the Caliph's longlost daughter. The abduction goes awry, however, leading to a vivid little scene among the fishermen of the Tigris as the lovers are arrested. Selimo is sentenced to death and Adina faints, but a medallion round her neck happily reveals her true identity to the Caliph. This eminently stageable work is a pen-and-ink sketch rather than a full-scale drawing, notable for the tender, elaborate music provided for Adina (the only woman in the cast), for the crystal-clear orchestration, and for a mood which is prevailingly sad. There is no overture, nor is there any evidence that Rossini ever heard the piece in performance. RICHARD OSBORNE

Adini, Ada [Chapman, Adele] (*b* Boston, 1855; *d* Dieppe, Feb 1924). American soprano. She studied with Pauline Viardot and Giovanni Sbriglia in Paris. Her début role was Meyerbeer's Dinorah, at Varese in 1876. She appeared with the Mapleson Company in New York and after returning to Europe sang at the Opéra from 1887, notably in the 1890 première of *Ascanio* by Saint-Saëns. At Covent Garden she was heard as Donna Anna (1894, 1897). She was successful in the Wagnerian repertory and sang Brünnhilde in the Italian première of *Die Walküre* (1893, La Scala). Her second husband was Paul Milliet, the librettist of Massenet's *Hérodiade*. DAVID CUMMINGS

Adler, Guido (*b* Eibenschütz [now Ivančice, Moravia], 1 Nov 1855; *d* Vienna, 15 Feb 1941). Austrian musicologist. He was a pupil of Bruckner and Dessoff at the Vienna conservatory, also studying law at the university, where he lectured on Wagner's *Ring* (1875–6; the lectures were published as a book, 1904). He took the doctorate in music history in 1880 and became professor in Prague in 1885, succeeding Hanslick at the University of Vienna in 1898; there he founded the Musikwissenschaftliche Institut. He was founder and general editor of the Denkmäler der Tonkunst in Österreich series, in which he edited the then known portions of Cesti's *Il pomo d'oro* (vi, Jg.iii/2, 1896; ix, Jg.iv/2, 1897). He taught many composers (among them Wellesz and Webern) and musicologists, and was a close friend of Mahler's. He was noted for his analytical work, his studies in Austrian (and especially Viennese Classical) music, and above all for the wide-ranging and systematic foundations he laid for the discipline of musicology.

Adler, Kurt Herbert (*b* Vienna, 2 April 1905; *d* Ross, CA, 9 Feb 1988). American conductor and director of Austrian birth. He was educated at the Musikakademie and the University in Vienna, and made his début in 1925 as a conductor for the Max Reinhardt theatre, then conducted at the Volksoper and opera houses in Germany, Italy and Czechoslovakia. He assisted Toscanini in Salzburg (1936) and went to the USA in 1938 for an engagement with the Chicago Opera. He worked for the San Francisco Opera from 1943 to 1981, initially as chorus master, than as artistic director from 1953 and general director from 1956. Although he occasionally conducted, most of his time was devoted to administrative duties. During his regime the San Francisco Opera became increasingly adventurous in repertory and became noted for the engagement of unproven talent and the implementation of modern staging techniques. By 1972 Adler had lengthened the season from five weeks to ten and he also organized subsidiary organizations in San Francisco to stage experimental works, to perform in schools and other unconventional locales, and to train young singers. His work received citations from the governments of Italy, Germany, Austria and Russia.

K. Lockhart, ed.: *The Adler Years* (San Francisco, 1981)

MARTIN BERNHEIMER

Adler, Peter Herman (*b* Jablonec, 2 Dec 1899; *d* Ridgefield, CT, 2 Oct 1990). American conductor of Czech birth. After studying composition and conducting with Alexander Zemlinsky at the Prague Conservatory, he became music director of the Bremen Staatsoper (1929–32) and the Ukrainian State Philharmonia, Kiev (1932–7). He left for the USA in 1939 and made his début with the New York PO in 1940. From 1949 to 1959 he was music and artistic director of the NBC-TV Opera Company. After a period as music director of the Baltimore SO (1959–68), he became music and artistic director of WNET (National Educational Television). His Metropolitan Opera début was in 1972 with *Un ballo in maschera*, and he directed the American Opera Center at the Juilliard School, New York, 1973–81. Adler was a pioneer director of television opera in the USA and commissioned many operas for television, among them Menotti's *Amahl and the Night Visitors* and *Maria Golovin* (of which he conducted the première at the 1958 Brussels World Fair), Dello Joio's *The Trial at Rouen* and Martinů's *The Marriage* (all for NBC), Pasatieri's *The Trial of Mary Lincoln* and Henze's *La cubana*. ELLIOTT W. GALKIN

Adler, Samuel (Hans) (*b* Mannheim, 4 March 1928). American composer. His family moved to the USA in 1939 and he attended Boston and Harvard universities; he studied composition with Copland, Fromm, Hindemith and others, and conducting with Koussevitzky. After joining the US Army in 1950 he organized the Seventh Army SO, and also conducted concerts and operas throughout Europe and the USA. He was appointed professor of composition at North Texas State University (1957) and then joined the faculty of the Eastman School of Music (1966), where he has been chairman of the composition department since 1974.

Adler is a prolific composer whose music embraces a wide variety of contemporary styles. His works exhibit great rhythmic vitality, with a predilection for asymmetrical rhythms and metres, a colourful orchestral palette and a keen sensitivity to counterpoint. The diatonicism of his pre-1969 works shows in his first opera, *The Outcasts of Poker Flat* (composed 1959). Set in the Sierras, it is the tragic tale of Uncle Billy, a drunk, Mr Oakhurst, a gambler, and his lover, Dutchess, a 'madam', who are cast out of Poker Flat by a group of

Townsmen. A snowstorm threatens their lives and eventually Dutchess dies of starvation and Mr Oakhurst commits suicide. When the Townsmen finally appear as rescuers, it is to take back their 'brother and sister' and lay them to rest. In *The Wrestler* (1971), a dramatic depiction of the biblical story of Jacob, and *The Lodge of Shadows* (1973), a variation of the Orpheus story as told by American Indians, Adler includes occasional improvisatory and aleatory elements. These works also feature quarter-tones, clusters and vocal effects such as falsetto, flutter-tonguing, whispering and *Sprechstimme*. However, Adler's overture and accompaniments for the reconstructed first American ballad opera, Andrew Barton's *The Disappointment* (1767), are executed in an 18th-century style; the opera, a social and political satire set in Philadelphia, is believed to contain the earliest use of *Yankee Doodle*. A number of Adler's works have been recorded and more than 300 have been published.

The Outcasts of Poker Flat (1, J. Stampfer), Dallas, April 1961 (New York, 1961)
The Wrestler (1, Stampfer), Dallas, June 1972 (New York, 1972)
The Lodge of Shadows, 1973 (musical drama, J. Ramsey), Fort Worth, Texas Christian U., May 1988 (New York, 1975)
Ov. and accompaniments for A. Barton: The Disappointment; or, The Force of Credulity (2, Barton), Washington DC, Library of Congress, Nov 1976, ed. J. C. Graue and J. Layng in RRAM, iii–iv (1976)

*

EwenD
J. D. Lucas: *The Operas of Samuel Adler: an Analytical Study* (diss., Louisiana State U., 1978)

MARIE ROLF

Adlgasser, Anton Cajetan (*b* Inzell, Upper Bavaria, 1 Oct 1729; *d* Salzburg, 22 Dec 1777). German composer. A chorister at the choir school of the Salzburg court chapel in 1744, he may have learnt composition with J. E. Eberlin; while a student he sang and acted in many school plays. He became court and cathedral organist in 1750, and was sent by the archbishop, who was fond of Italian opera and was apparently pleased with his services, to study in Italy, 1764–5. After 1760 he was also organist at the Trinity church, Salzburg. In 1769 he married the court singer Maria Anna Fesemayr.

As a composer Adlgasser represents the transitional period from south German and Austrian late Baroque style to the Classicism found in the young Mozart's works. He wrote an Italian opera to a text by Metastasio, *La Nitteti* (1766, lost), several Singspiels and other German dramatic works (*Schuldramen*, *Finalkomödien*) performed at the Salzburg Benedictine University. He also composed many oratorios (one in collaboration with Michael Haydn and Mozart, 1767), liturgical music and instrumental pieces. Of his stage works, several consist of musical dramas within spoken plays, sometimes with insertions of comic scenes.

*

S. Keller: 'Biographische Mitteilungen über Anton Cajetan Adlgasser', *MMg*, v (1873), 41–5
C. Schneider: 'Zur Lebensgeschichte des Salzburger Komponisten A. C. Adlgasser', *Salzburger Museumsblätter*, iv/2 (1925), 1–3
——: *Geschichte der Musik in Salzburg* (Salzburg, 1935)
W. Rainer: 'Verzeichnis der Werke A. C. Adlgassers', *MJb 1962–3*, 280–91
M. H. Schmid: *Mozart und die Salzburger Tradition* (Tutzing, 1976)

REINHARD G. PAULY

Admeto [*Admeto, rè di Tessaglia* ('Admetus, King of Thessaly')]. Opera in three acts by GEORGE FRIDERIC HANDEL to a libretto anonymously adapted from ORTENSIO MAURO's *L'Alceste* (1679, Hanover) after Antonio Aureli's *L'Antigona delusa da Alceste* (1660, Venice); London, King's Theatre, 31 January 1727.

Admeto [Admetus] *King of Thessaly*	alto castrato
Alceste [Alcestis] *his wife*	soprano
Ercole [Hercules]	bass
Orindo *gentleman of the court*	contralto
Trasimede [Thrasymedes] *prince, Admetus's brother*	alto castrato
Antigona *Trojan princess, disguised as a shepherdess*	soprano
Meraspe [Meraspes] *her governor*	bass
Oracle of Apollo	bass

Setting Larissa, capital of Thessaly, in ancient times

Admeto was Handel's tenth full-length opera for the Royal Academy of Music, and the second of the group of five operas in which the leading roles were designed for the rival sopranos Francesca Cuzzoni and Faustina Bordoni; they sang Antigona and Alcestis. The other singers were the alto castratos Senesino and Antonio Baldi (Admetus and Thrasymede), the contralto Anna Vincenza Dotti (Orindo), and the basses Giuseppe Boschi and Giovanni Palmerini (Hercules and Meraspes). The opera achieved an excellent opening run of 19 performances to 18 April (during which period the act giving Handel British nationality was passed); two new arias seem to have been provided for Faustina during the run.

The opera was revived for six performances at the King's Theatre from 30 September 1727, the opening of the next season, and for three more from 25 May 1728; in the latter group, if not the former, the soprano Mrs Wright sang a new aria in the role of Orinda, a 'Lady of the Court' substituted for Orindo. In Handel's last revival, on 7 December 1731, this role was completely removed, and there were many other cuts and alterations, with only Senesino surviving from the original cast. Alcestis was sung by the contralto Anna Bagnolesi and Hercules by the tenor Giovanni Pinacci. There was one further revival at the King's Theatre, the last production of any Handel opera in the composer's lifetime, on 12 March 1754, when the theatre was under the management of Vanneschi. It is unlikely Handel himself was concerned with this production, but the fact that both the autograph and conducting score of *Admeto* are lost suggests that he may have lent them out for the occasion. There were productions at Brunswick in 1729, 1732 and 1739, and at Hamburg, in a German version by C. G. Wendt, on 23 January 1730 and subsequently to 1736. The first modern production, in a version by Hans Dütschke, was at Brunswick on 14 October 1925; the first in Britain was at the Unicorn Theatre, Abingdon, on 7 May 1964. Chrysander's edition gives the original 1727 version as its main text; his appendix contains only the two early additional arias for Faustina and one of Alcestis' new arias of the 1731 version ('Mostratevi serene'), erroneously assigned to Orindo.

The libretto is a highly elaborated version of the classical myth best known from the play by Euripides and Quinault's libretto for Lully's *Alceste* (*see* ALCESTIS). Handel treated the subject again in his incidental music for Smollett's lost play *Alceste* (1749–50).

AN

EPISTLE

FROM

S——r S——O

TO

S——a F——A.

Percurris agili corpus arte tractatrix
Manumq; doctam spargis omnibus membris.
Martial. Epig.

Infelix operis summâ, quia ponere totum
Nescio: —— Hor. Ar. Poet.

LONDON:
Printed for J. Roberts at the *Oxford-Arms* in *Warwick-Lane*.
M DCC XXVII. [Price *6 d.*

Vignette (with the text 'Si caro, caro si') from Handel's 'Admeto' showing by implication the last scene from the opera where the lovers Admetus and Alcestis (played by Senesino and Faustina Bordoni) are united; from the title-page of a satirical pamphlet 'An Epistle from S[igno]r S[enesin]o to S[ignor]a F[austin]a', published on 8 March 1727 (a few weeks after the première of 'Admeto') at the height of the rivalry between Faustina and Francesca Cuzzoni

Act 1 Admetus lies ill and near to death in his palace. The courtier Orindo mentions that Admetus's brother Thrasymedes has fallen madly in love with a woman whom he knows only through a portrait. Hercules, who has been staying with Admetus, takes his leave. The queen, Alcestis, prays to Apollo for the recovery of her husband. In answer, a voice emerges from the statue of the god declaring that Admetus can live only if a friend will die in his place; Alcestis resolves to be that friend.

In a nearby wood the Trojan princess Antigona, accompanied by her governor Meraspes, laments her fate: she was once betrothed to Admetus (though he had not seen her) and believes his illness is punishment for betraying her. They decide to go to the palace in disguise, she as a shepherdess, he as her father.

In the palace garden Alcestis, with a dagger in her hand, bids farewell to her companions. Admetus appears fully recovered, but his joy swiftly vanishes as news is brought of the death of Alcestis: the back of the stage opens to show her body with the dagger through her heart. Admetus asks Hercules to release Alcestis from Hades. Meraspes brings the news to Antigona, who sees a chance to regain Admetus's love. They meet the distracted Thrasymedes, who recognizes Antigona as the woman in his portrait; but she claims to be only a shepherdess, called Rosilda. Thrasymedes conveniently invites her and Meraspes (under the name of Fidalbo) to become gardeners at the palace, a situation of which they intend to take full advantage.

Act 2 In the underworld, Alcestis, chained to a rock, is tormented by furies. Hercules releases her and leads her back to earth. In the palace, Antigona is saved from the unwelcome attentions of Orindo by the arrival of Thrasymedes; he throws away her portrait which Orindo secretly picks up. Orindo shows it to Admetus, saying that it shows Antigona, believed dead. Admetus is struck by its beauty, but says it is not Antigona, whose portrait Thrasymedes once gave him. Antigona and Meraspes present themselves, still in disguise. Admetus shows Antigona the picture: she says it is that of Antigona, the woman who resembles her and on whom Thrasymedes dotes. Admetus realizes he has been deceived: when Thrasymedes was commissioned to bring Antigona from Troy, he fell in love with her himself and gave Admetus a false portrait. Antigona understands that Admetus did not deliberately betray her. She asks if he would marry Antigona if she were alive, but his uncertain answer dashes her rising hopes.

In a nearby wood, Alcestis explains to Hercules that she wishes to return to the palace disguised as a warrior so that she can see if Admetus is keeping faithful to her; Hercules is to report that he was unable to find her in Hades. Admetus broods despairingly on the supposed deaths of both his first love and his wife. Thrasymedes and his soldiers take Antigona prisoner. A page brings him a portrait of Admetus in mistake for that of Antigona; he is ordered to take it back, but inadvertently drops it. Antigona eagerly picks it up and addresses it with a declaration of her love. The disguised Alcestis overhears, and questions Antigona. Antigona again confesses her love, but refuses to say if she expects to become Admetus's wife. Alcestis is tormented with jealousy, but wonders if Antigona is lying.

Act 3 Meraspes reports the abduction of Antigona and explains to Admetus who she really is. Orindo is despatched to rescue her. Hercules tells Admetus that he was unable to find Alcestis in Hades; Admetus, thinking that his old love for Antigona may now be renewed, seems unconcerned. Alcestis, still disguised as a warrior, finds Antigona kissing the portrait of Admetus. As she angrily snatches the picture from Antigona's hands, Orindo arrives and, assuming that Alcestis is the abductor of Antigona, takes her prisoner. Hercules appears and orders Orindo to release Alcestis into his custody; he tells Alcestis that Admetus is in love with another woman. Back at court Antigona forgives Thrasymedes for his treatment of her and is received by Admetus as his new bride. The jealous Thrasymedes attempts to kill Admetus, but Alcestis takes the sword from his hand. She is arrested by mistake, but is recognized by Admetus. Hercules explains. Admetus forgives Thrasymedes for the attempt on his life. Antigona relinquishes her claim to Admetus's love, giving Thrasymedes new hope. Admetus declares that the images of both Antigona and Alcestis will always be imprinted on his heart.

* * *

Admeto is the finest of the Cuzzoni-Faustina operas, with a wealth of distinctive music. The obvious contrast between a noble couple (Admetus and Alcestis) and a lighter and more unstable one (Thrasymedes and Antigona) is more subtle than first appears, since the arias for the latter pair by no means exclude deep feelings; both the crazed Thrasymedes and the cheated Antigona are partly tragic figures despite the brilliance of their music. Each act has a major soliloquy for Admetus, none more compelling than that which opens the opera; first a dance for spectres holding bloody daggers (a vision of Admetus's fevered brain), then a long accompanied recitative in which the king rails against his afflictions, and finally, emerging almost imperceptibly, a cavatina expressing a longing for death. Horns add colour to the orchestral score, and are a particular feature of Thrasymedes' aria 'Se l'arco avessi e i strali'.

ANTHONY HICKS

Admission. The circumstances governing admission to opera houses before the 19th century are ill documented; full understanding awaits more research. Conditions varied; no theatre, however, met those looked for today – common access for all operagoers by means of tickets entitling them to specific seats, priced according to seating area.

Theatres were rarely full, save on special occasions; some court theatres were extensions of the ruler's palace; in France, before the Revolution, nobles came attended by retinues of servants: hence a vast, sometimes amorphous list of persons entitled to free admission, and much giving out of free tickets to singers and staff, in part as a means of eking out wages. Even those who paid to get in did not all pay the same price for the same seats: nobles might pay more than ordinary citizens, army officers and civil servants less.

In opera houses of the Italian type the audience was physically divided into the owners or renters of boxes, the stalls audience, and the gallery (if there was one): each area had separate access (an arrangement that survives for the gallery of older theatres), but only the boxes had numbered seats; this meant a rush to get into the stalls on special occasions, and into the gallery on most nights. In Italy, each section of the audience might buy its tickets from a different source: boxholders were often entitled to re-let their boxes in competition with the management, and the gallery was generally sub-let to a separate impresario. A separate charge was made for admission to the building (*ingresso*) and, in the stalls, for a few locked seats with arm rests; the bulk of the stalls audience sat on benches or stood. There and elsewhere, many bought season tickets.

French theatres were never as dominated by boxholders as Italian ones; by the late 18th century they had a more complex plan, with 'amphitheatres' (raked tiers of seats) around the stalls or in front of some of the boxes. Under the impact of revolution (in 1789 and again in 1830) they came to apply tests of commercial rationality rather than of status. The Paris Opéra in 1831 brought in numbered seats in the stalls area; it cut down the free list, as La Scala, Milan, had already done in 1789. Their example was gradually followed by other opera houses, which also turned some boxes into open seating areas. By the 1880s the all-seated stalls area, filled with chairs with arm rests, was the rule, and the Italian *ingresso* entitled one to no more than (restricted) standing room. The unnumbered gallery survived in many places till after World War II.

See also SEATING and TICKET.

*

ES ('Palchi, palchetti': E. Povoledo)

M. L. Quicherat: *Adolphe Nourrit: sa vie*, i (Paris, 1867), 90, 101

J. Rosselli: *The Opera Industry in Italy from Cimarosa to Verdi* (Cambridge, 1984), 40–45, 47–8

J. F. Fulcher: *The Nation's Image: French Grand Opera as Politics and as Politicised Art* (Cambridge, 1987), 14–15

JOHN ROSSELLI

Adolfati, Andrea (*b* Venice, 1721–2; *d* Padua, 28 Oct 1760). Italian composer. After studying with Galuppi, he became *maestro di cappella* of S Maria della Salute, Venice. In 1745 he left to serve the Modenese court. He provided recitatives, choruses and six arias for Hasse's *Lo starnuto d'Ercole* (P. G. Martelli) which was performed with puppets at a Venetian palace in 1745 (according to the 1755 edition of the Allacci *Drammaturgia*); it was staged conventionally at the Teatro S Girolamo, Venice, during Carnival 1746. From 1748 until early 1760 Adolfati held a church post in Genoa, then moved to Padua.

Adolfati was not highly regarded by Metastasio, who heard his *La clemenza di Tito* in 1753 and wrote to him in 1755 and 1757. Although Adolfati's style is in general conventional, he composed an aria in 5/4 time and, as a youth, even attempted to use 7/4. As well as operas he wrote cantatas, sacred music and instrumental pieces.

La pace fra la virtù e la bellezza (divertimento da camera, Liborati, after P. Metastasio), Modena, Ducale, 1 Jan 1746, *I-MOe*

Didone abbandonata (Metastasio), Venice, S Girolamo, carn. 1747 [perf. with puppets]

Arianna (P. Pariati), Genoa, Falcone, wint. 1750

La gloria ed il piacere (introduzione per musica alla festa da ballo), Genoa, Falcone, carn. 1751

Adriano in Siria (Metastasio), Genoa, Falcone, aut. 1751

Il giuoco dei matti (commedia per musica, 3), Genoa, Falcone, aut. 1751 [according to Stieger]

Ifigenia (dramma per musica, 3), Genoa, Falcone, 26 Dec 1751

Ipermestra (Metastasio), Modena, Rangoni, carn. 1752, aria *Fc*

Vologeso (after A. Zeno: *Lucio Vero*), Genoa, Falcone, carn. 1752, 4 arias *Gl*

La clemenza di Tito (Metastasio), Vienna, Burg, 15 Oct 1753, *A-Wn*

Sesostri re d'Egitto (Zeno), Genoa, Falcone, carn. 1755, *I-Gl*

Music in: J. A. Hasse: Lo starnuto d'Ercole, 1745

Doubtful: Il corsaro punito (dg, 3), Pavia, Omodeo, spr. 1750 [attrib. Adolfati by Stieger, but lib. mentions 'diversi autori']

*

AllacciD; *StiegerO*

R. Giazotto: *La musica a Genova* (Genoa, 1951)

B. Brunelli, ed.: *Tutte le opere di Pietro Metastasio*, iii (Milan, 1951)

SVEN HANSELL

Adolphe, Bruce (*b* New York, 31 May 1955). American composer. A graduate of the Juilliard School (1976), he has taught at the New York University Tisch School of the Arts since 1983 and at Yale University (1984–5). He was composer-in-residence at the Santa Fe Chamber Music Festival (1989), Music from Angel Fire (1988) and the 92nd Street Y School Concert Series (1988–90). His first opera, *The Tell-Tale Heart*, based on the short story by Edgar Allan Poe, assigns roles to characters other than Poe's narrator and creates a female character, Helen. Several of Poe's poems are interpolated in the basic plot: 'To Helen', 'The City in the Sea' and 'The Happiest Day'. The musical effects, especially the pounding of the heart, are skilfully handled.

Adolphe's later operas investigate aspects of his Jewish heritage. *Mikhoels the Wise* (1982) examines Jewish life in the Soviet Union at the beginning of the 20th century, focussing on the life of Solomon Mikhoels, a Yiddish actor who wedded Jewish thought to communist ideals and whose achievements in elevating Jewish theatre to new heights were cut short by his murder, indicative of the demise of Jewish culture under Stalin's rule. The story is treated episodically in seven scenes covering the period 1918–48. The music is eclectic, incorporating Yiddish comic theatre, folk, liturgical, pop and jazz elements. Dance rhythms in some pieces show the influence of Kurt Weill. *The False Messiah* (1983) portrays the life of the Turkish Jew Shabtai Zvi, a self-proclaimed Messiah. Set in 17th-century Gaza, the opera takes much of its material from the historical studies of Gershom Scholem. The composer's stated intention was to try 'to capture the exoticism and passion of the movement'. His music draws heavily on dervish rhythms and improvisation, giving the work a mystical feel.

The Tell-Tale Heart, 1978 (1, Adolphe, after E. A. Poe), Boston, Boston and New England Conservatories, 22 Jan 1982
Mikhoels the Wise (2, M. Gordon), New York, Kaufmann Auditorium (92nd Street Young Men's-Young Women's Hebrew Association), 8 May 1982
The False Messiah (2, Gordon, after G. Scholem: *Life of Shabtai Zvi*), New York, Kaufmann Auditorium, 9 April 1983

*

R. H. Kornick: *Recent American Opera: a Production Guide* (New York, 1991), 5–11 JAMES P. CASSARO

Adorno, Theodor W(iesengrund) (*b* Frankfurt, 11 Sept 1903; *d* Canton Valais, Switzerland, 6 Aug 1969). German philosopher, sociologist and music theorist. He was a prominent member of the Frankfurt School of Critical Theory. Of partly Jewish extraction, he went into exile during the Nazi period, first to Oxford (1934–8), then to the USA (1938–49). Adorno taught philosophy at Frankfurt University, and was co-director of the Frankfurt Institut für Sozialforschung from 1950 to 1969. In the 1950s and 1960s Adorno was a frequent contributor to the Darmstadt Summer School, and played an important role in the debate on the 'new music'. His small compositional output includes sketches for an opera, *Der Schatz des Indianer Joe*, based on Mark Twain's *Tom Sawyer*. He wrote numerous reviews of performances at the Frankfurt Opera (1921–34), over 40 essays and articles on various aspects of opera, and a major book, *Versuch über Wagner*. There is also discussion of operatic questions in *Philosophie der neuen Musik*, *Berg: Der Meister des kleinsten Übergangs* and, in particular, *Einleitung in die Musiksoziologie*.

In his philosophy of music history (concerned exclusively with the 'bourgeois period' from the Enlightenment to the mid-20th century) Adorno drew on the Hegelian Marxism of his contemporaries Lukács, Bloch and Benjamin, and incorporated elements of Freudian psychoanalytic theory and of Max Weber's concept of the progressive rationalization of life in the industrialized and bureaucratized world of advanced capitalism. He set out to decipher the contradictory relationship between the apparently autonomous and 'irrational' sphere of music and the social and historical context of its production and consumption. The Wagnerian music dramas exemplified this relationship because of their claims to synthesis and universality. He saw the mythological subject-matter of the *Ring* as a retreat from the political frustrations of post-1848 Germany and the realities of the age of industry. He also perceived a contradiction between the dynamism of Wagner's radical harmonic procedures and the essentially static character of the leitmotif technique.

He identified Wagner's legacy in the extremes of both the early 20th-century avant garde (particularly Schoenberg's *Erwartung* and Berg's *Wozzeck* and *Lulu*) and the commodity forms of the 'culture industry' (for instance the Hollywood movie score, into which the idea of the *Gesamtkunstwerk* had migrated). While he regarded sympathetically attempts by Weill, Eisler, and even Stravinsky (in *L'histoire du soldat*) to encompass these extremes, he nevertheless argued that it is no longer possible for music to reconcile the conflicting demands of authenticity and accessibility within a seamless aesthetic unity – a synthesis in his view last achieved by Mozart in *Die Zauberflöte*. The fractured character of music in the modernist period becomes a metaphor for a fractured society.

Often condemned for its cultural pessimism, Adorno's modernist aesthetic has attracted renewed interest in debates over postmodernism.

with M. Horkheimer: *Dialektik der Aufklärung* (Amsterdam, 1947; Eng. trans., 1972)
Philosophie der neuen Musik (Tübingen, 1949; Eng. trans., 1973) [incl. discussion of stage works by Schoenberg, Berg and Stravinsky]
Minima Moralia (Frankfurt, 1951; Eng. trans., 1974)
Versuch über Wagner (Berlin, 1952, 2/1964; Eng. trans., 1981)
Mahler: eine musikalische Physiognomik (Frankfurt, 1960)
Einleitung in die Musiksoziologie (Frankfurt, 1962; Eng. trans., 1976) [incl. chapter on opera]
Negative Dialektik (Frankfurt, 1966; Eng. trans., 1973)
Berg: der Meister des kleinsten Übergangs (Vienna, 1968, Eng. trans., 1991)
with H. Eisler: *Komposition für den Film* (Munich, 1969) [orig. in Eng. as H. Eisler: *Composing for the Films* (1947)]
Ästhetische Theorie (Frankfurt, 1970; Eng. trans., 1984)
Gesammelte Schriften, ed. R. Tiedemann and others (Frankfurt, 1970–86) [incl. list of reviews of works perf. at Frankfurt Opera, 1922–34 (vol.xix); other articles and essays on opera written 1921–69]

*

R. Leibowitz: 'Der Komponist Theodor W. Adorno', in M. Horkheimer: *Zeugnisse* (Frankfurt, 1963), 355–9
C. Dahlhaus: 'Soziologische Dechiffrierung von Musik: zu Theodor W. Adornos Wagnerkritik', *International Review of Music, Aesthetics and Sociology*, i/2 (1970), 137–47
S. Buck-Morss: *The Origin of Negative Dialectics* (Brighton, 1977)
O. Kolleritsch, ed.: *Adorno und die Musik* (Graz, 1979)
L. Sziborsky: *Adornos Musikphilosophie* (Munich, 1979)
J. Deathridge: 'Theodor Adorno, *In Search of Wagner*', *19th Century Music*, vii (1983–4), 81–5 [review]
M. Jay: *Adorno* (London, 1984)
M. Paddison: 'Adorno's *Aesthetic Theory*', *Music Analysis*, vi/3 (1987), 355–77 [review article] MAX PADDISON

***Adriana Lecouvreur*.** Opera in four acts by FRANCESCO CILEA to a libretto by ARTURO COLAUTTI after EUGÈNE SCRIBE and Ernest Legouvé's play *Adrienne Lecouvreur*; Milan, Teatro Lirico, 6 November 1902.

Adriana Lecouvreur was commissioned by the publisher Edoardo Sonzogno following the success of Cilea's *L'arlesiana*. Cilea chose the subject for its mixture of comedy and tragedy, its 18th-century ambience, the loving intensity of its protagonist and the moving final act; three other operas use the story of Adrienne Lecouvreur (by Edoardo Vera, Tommaso Benvenuti and Ettore Perosio). Colautti reduced the intricate mechanism of Scribe's plot to a serviceable operatic framework, occasionally at the expense of clarity. The première,

Poster for Cilea's 'Adriana Lecouvreur' printed for the publisher Edoardo Sonzogno at the time of the first production at the Teatro Lirico, Milan, in 1902

Adriana Lecouvreur of the Comédie Française		soprano
Maurizio *Count of Saxony*		tenor
Prince of Bouillon		bass
Princess of Bouillon		mezzo-soprano
Michonnet *stage director of the Comédie Française*		baritone
Quinault	*members of the Comédie*	bass
Poisson		tenor
Mlle Jouvenot		soprano
Mlle Dangeville		mezzo-soprano
Abbé of Chazeuil		tenor

Ladies, gentlemen, mute extras, stage hands, valets and dancers

Setting Paris, March 1730

however, was outstandingly successful, with a cast that included Enrico Caruso (Maurizio), Angelica Pandolfini (Adriana) and Giuseppe De Luca (Michonnet). The conductor was Cleofonte Campanini. The first London performance took place at Covent Garden in 1904 in the presence of the composer with Rina Giachetti (Adriana), Giuseppe Anselmi (Maurizio) and Mario Sammarco (Michonnet), again under Campanini. Three years later the opera arrived at the Metropolitan Opera, New York, with Caruso (Maurizio), Lina Cavalieri (Adriana) and Antonio Scotti (Michonnet). Since then *Adriana Lecouvreur* has proved the only one of Cilea's three surviving operas to stay in the international repertory, mainly due to the opportunities it affords to an experienced prima donna who has already passed her prime. Famous among postwar exponents of the title role are Maria Caniglia, Renata Tebaldi, Magda Olivero, Renata Scotto and Joan Sutherland.

ACT 1 *The foyer of the Comédie Française* The curtain is about to rise. Actors and actresses are snapping at one another and at Michonnet, who protests that he has only one pair of hands. The evening's tragedy is Corneille's *Bajazet*, featuring both Adriana and her rival Mlle Duclos. The Prince of Bouillon, La Duclos' lover, arrives with the Abbé of Chazeuil and pays affected compliments to the players. Adriana enters reading her lines; she tells her admiring hearers that she is merely the poet's handmaid ('Io son l'umile ancella'), to a melody which will serve as her theme throughout the opera. Alone with Adriana, Michonnet, who has recently come into an inheritance, is about to propose marriage to the actress, with whom he has been in love for years, when she gives him to understand that she herself loves an officer in the service of the Count of Saxony who will be in the theatre that night. But the man who now enters is the Count himself, who is wooing Adriana under a false identity. In a brief solo, 'La dolcissima effigie sorridente', he pours out his feelings for her. A love duet develops, after which Adriana leaves to go on stage, having given Maurizio a nosegay of violets and agreed to meet him after the performance. Meanwhile the Abbé has managed to intercept a letter addressed to Maurizio from, as he thinks, La Duclos arranging a tryst for that evening at the love-nest by the Seine in which the Prince has installed her. The Prince decides to surprise the guilty pair by organizing a party in the same house at the appointed hour. Receiving the letter, Maurizio is well aware that the writer is not La Duclos but the Princess of Bouillon, whose lover he has been in the past; and he decides for political reasons to keep the assignation. He therefore has a note conveyed to Adriana breaking their appointment. Adriana is duly upset; but on being invited to join the Prince's party, at which, she is told, the Count of Saxony himself will be one of the guests, she consents to come in order to have the opportunity of furthering her lover's career.

ACT 2 *Mlle Duclos' villa by the Seine* The Princess is waiting anxiously for Maurizio ('Acerba voluttà, dolce tortura'). When he arrives she notices the nosegay and at once suspects another woman. With great presence of mind he offers it to her. She tells him that she has spoken on his behalf to the Queen of France, but finds his gratitude inadequate. Reluctantly he admits to another liaison. At the sound of a second carriage arriving she darts into the adjoining room. The Prince and the Abbé enter laughing and congratulate Maurizio on his latest conquest, whom they take to be La Duclos. Maurizio, grasping the situation, decides to keep up the deception. Adriana arrives, to be made aware for the first time of her lover's true identity. Their duet of happiness is interrupted by Michonnet, who has come with a message for La Duclos. He is told by the Abbé that she is somewhere in the villa, whereupon Adriana assumes that Maurizio has come for a secret rendezvous with her; but this he solemnly denies. There is indeed a woman in the next room, he says, with whom his relations are purely political. Adriana must see to it that no one enters that room and, once the guests have gone in to supper, must extinguish the lights and help the unknown visitor to escape in the dark. Adriana follows his instructions. However, the few words exchanged between the women in darkness make it apparent that both are in love with Maurizio. As lights are seen approaching Adriana determines to expose her rival. But the Princess has escaped, dropping a bracelet, which Michonnet picks up and hands to Adriana.

ACT 3 *The Palais Bouillon* Preparations for a party are in train, under the supervision of the Abbé, who flirts discreetly with the Princess until her husband joins them. An amateur chemist, he has discovered a poisonous powder which, when inhaled, will induce delirium followed by death. (All this he describes to the Abbé and the Princess in a passage cut from certain editions of the opera.) Adriana arrives without her jewellery, which she has pawned in order to effect the release of Maurizio, imprisoned by order of the jealous Princess. Seeming to recognize her voice as that of her rival, the Princess lays a trap for Adriana. She tells her that Maurizio has been fatally wounded in a duel. The actress duly comes over faint; but she revives spectacularly when Maurizio himself enters and entertains the guests with tales of his military exploits ('Il russo Mencikoff'). A company of dancers perform *The Judgment of Paris*. In the general conversation that follows the Princess and Adriana fence with each other verbally. The Princess mentions a nosegay of violets. Adriana produces the compromising bracelet which the Prince identifies as his wife's. To distract attention the Princess proposes that the great actress should recite from one of her famous roles. At the Prince's suggestion she chooses a passage from Racine's *Phèdre*, where the heroine denounces lustful women; and as she declaims the lines she looks straight at her rival. All applaud her performance except the Princess who, white with fury, determines on revenge.

ACT 4 *Adriana's house* It is her birthday, but convinced that Maurizio no longer loves her Adriana has retired into solitude. Michonnet visits her in a vain attempt to bring her comfort. They are joined by four of her fellow artists, each with a present for her. Michonnet too offers a gift – Adriana's jewellery which he has redeemed with the inheritance from his uncle. Deeply touched, Adriana declares that she will return to the stage. Her colleagues entertain her with a gossipy madrigal. The maid comes in with a package labelled 'from Maurizio'. While the actors retire Adriana opens it and finds inside the nosegay of violets she had given him, now withered – a sign, she thinks, that their love is at an end. She pours out her grief in the aria 'Poveri fiori'; then she presses the flowers to her lips and throws them into the fire. But Michonnet has already summoned Maurizio, who now arrives, protests his undying devotion and offers her his hand in marriage. Adriana joyfully accepts, then suddenly turns pale. Her mind starts to wander. Clearly the nosegay was sprinkled with the poisonous powder, sent not by Maurizio but by the Princess. Adriana tries desperately to cling to life, but she is beyond help and dies in Maurizio's arms.

* * *

The texture of *Adriana Lecouvreur* is more richly woven and the style somewhat less emphatic than in most *verismo* operas of the time. The ensemble scenes, especially in Act 1, owe something to Verdi's *Falstaff*, though the orchestral figuration is often curiously pianistic. Abundant use is made of recurring motifs, several of which anticipate the solos from which they derive. Some (e.g. that of the violets) are insufficiently theatrical for their associations to register. There are touches of period stylization in the dances of Act 3, but in the main Cilea is content to evoke a generalized elegance, varied by characteristic moments of lyrical effusion. Particularly effective is his recourse to unsung speech to point up Adriana's recitation at the end of the third act. JULIAN BUDDEN

Adriano in Siria ('Hadrian in Syria'). Libretto by PIETRO METASTASIO, first set by Antonio Caldara (1732, Vienna). The title *Farnaspe* was used for a later version of this libretto.

In Antioch, the Emperor Hadrian has conquered the Parthian king Osroa [Osroes] and, in spite of being betrothed to Sabina, a Roman noblewoman, has fallen in love with Emirena, Osroes' daughter. He has invited several Asian princes to Antioch, but his invitation to Osroes is refused. Osroes, however, has come in disguise, as a follower of Farnaspe [Pharnaspes], the Parthian prince to whom Emirena is betrothed.

ACT 1 Hadrian consents to Emirena's departure with Pharnaspes if she so chooses. But Aquilio [Aquilius], Hadrian's confidant, because he himself loves Sabina, desires a marriage between Emirena and Hadrian; he warns Emirena of Hadrian's supposed anger, cautioning her to conceal her true feelings for Pharnaspes, who is astounded by Emirena's subsequent coldness. Hadrian's hopes for Emirena are thus revived, and he is confused when Sabina arrives unexpectedly. Meanwhile, Osroes sets fire to the palace, and Pharnaspes is blamed. He and Emirena reaffirm their love.

ACT 2 On Aquilius's advice, Emirena feigns love for Hadrian, but convinces Sabina that her real love is for Pharnaspes, thus gaining Sabina's help for an escape attempt. Sabina confronts Hadrian, who admits his love for Emirena. An outbreak of fighting traps the escaping lovers who meet Osroes holding a bloodied sword. He claims to have killed Hadrian, and hides. Hadrian, unharmed, accuses Pharnaspes of attempted regicide. Emirena, however, points out the culprit, unaware that it is Osroes, her father; he is unrepentant, and Hadrian, furious, imprisons all three.

ACT 3 Aquilius urges Hadrian to ask Osroes for Emirena's hand in exchange for the return of his throne. Instead of giving his consent, Osroes instructs his daughter to let Hadrian languish. Pharnaspes, however, distraught, persuades Emirena to offer herself to the Emperor as the only means of saving both Osroes and Asia. Aquilius's treachery is exposed and Sabina

'Adriano in Siria', Act 3 scene xi (HADRIAN: *'And to you, now deemed worthy of you, I yield myself'): engraving from the 'Opere' of Pietro Metastasio (Paris: Hérissant, 1780–82)*

volunteers to stand aside if Hadrian still desires Emirena. Impressed by the willing sacrifices of those around him, Hadrian frees Osroes and Aquilius, accepts Sabina, and unites Pharnaspes and Emirena.

* * *

Metastasio created this text as a fiction built around Osroes and Hadrian, who are mentioned in Dio Cassius's *Historiarum* (Xiphilinus, *Epitome*, books 68–9) and Spartianus, *Vita Hadriani* (no.12). *Adriano in Siria* became one of the popular Metastasian dramas, with regular new settings dating from the first by Caldara (to celebrate the name day of Emperor Charles VI) to Cherubini's for Livorno in 1782, after which date new settings were more sporadic. Mercadante's version for Lisbon (1828) was the last of the 19th-century operas to be based on this text. For Genoa, in 1734, Sandoni wrote the part of Emirena for his wife, Francesca Cuzzoni, who sang the same role the following year, in London, in a setting by Veracini. This, Veracini's first opera, was staged by the Opera of the Nobility, Handel's rival company; the cast included Senesino as Hadrian and Farinelli as Pharnaspes. Beginning late in 1752, Metastasio created a shorter version of this text at the request of Farinelli, then employed in Madrid. In a revision of Conforto's setting, it was performed to celebrate Ferdinand VI's birthday in 1757. A French version, *Adrien*, set by Méhul, was performed in Paris in 1799.

For a list of settings *see* METASTASIO, PIETRO. DON NEVILLE

Adriano in Siria (i) ('Hadrian in Syria'). *Dramma per musica* in three acts by ANTONIO CALDARA to a libretto by PIETRO METASTASIO (*see* ADRIANO IN SIRIA above), with ballet music by Nicola Matteis; Vienna, Hoftheater (Teatro Grande), 9 November 1732.

Caldara's 13th opera for the name-day celebrations of the Habsburg emperor Charles VI has the Roman emperor Adriano [Hadrian] (tenor) as its nominal hero. The plot deals with his amorous dalliance with Emirena (soprano), a captive Parthian princess, his arrogant dismissal of Farnaspe [Pharnaspes] (alto), Emirena's lover, and his deception of his wife Sabina (soprano). In the *lieto fine* Metastasio's allusion to the incorruptible position of the Holy Roman Emperor is obvious, as Hadrian rises above temptation to impart further dignity to his imperial role.

Caldara's setting, however, emphasizes the three characters most affected by Hadrian's illicit desires. Hadrian himself is drawn rather shallowly in arias that (apart from the tender 'Dal labbro che t'accende', 1.i) are mostly stereotyped but superficially impressive gestures of rage and revenge, such as 'Tutti nemici' (2.ix). The two minor characters, Osroa [Osroes] (tenor), Emirena's father, and Aquilio [Aquilius] (bass), Hadrian's treacherous confidant, likewise react conventionally to their situations, although the former's 'Sprezzo il furor del vento' (1.iii) and the latter's 'Saggio guerriero antico' (2.v) include clever pictorialisms. In contrast, Caldara accords Emirena, Sabina and Pharnaspes a series of intimate arias that capture moods of estrangement, abandonment and desolation, as well as reconciliation and optimism, and maintain a level of lyricism rarely surpassed in his other operas. Sensitive scorings, with relatively few contrapuntal devices in the accompaniments, enhance the emotional tension, especially in Pharnaspes' 'Doppo un tuo sguardo' (1.v) and Sabina's 'Numi sì giuste siete' (1.xi).

The *introduzione*, with its double trumpet scoring typical of the name-day operas, is notable for the virtuoso solo cello passages that relieve the customary antiphonal block structures of such pieces.

BRIAN W. PRITCHARD

Adriano in Siria (ii) ('Hadrian in Syria'). *Opera seria* in three acts by GIOVANNI BATTISTA PERGOLESI to a libretto by PIETRO METASTASIO (*see* ADRIANO IN SIRIA above); Naples, Teatro S Bartolomeo, 25 October 1734.

In May 1734 the Kingdom of Naples was recaptured from the Austrian Habsburgs by Charles Bourbon (later Charles III) of Spain. To celebrate the birthday of the queen mother, Elisabeth Farnese, the Teatro S Bartolomeo staged a new work by Pergolesi, *Adriano in Siria*. This was the third of the four *opere serie* written by Pergolesi, and his first to a libretto by Metastasio. For Pergolesi the libretto was much altered. Of Metastasio's 27 original aria texts, only ten were retained: ten substitute arias and a new duet were inserted, and several alterations to the recitatives were made to accommodate those changes. Most of these alterations can be attributed to the magnificent cast hired by the new king, with his typically Spanish emphasis on theatrical splendour. Caffarelli was the primo uomo; he received all new texts, and the position of some of them was shifted to give him a more prominent role: his character sings at the end of the first two acts. Caffarelli's music is the most careful, extensive and lyrical in the opera, and includes the particularly exquisite 'Lieto così tal volta', with obbligato oboe, and 'Torbido in volto e nero', for double orchestra (this aria must have been particularly effective since it was later borrowed, without change, for *L'olimpiade*). These arias are full of the type of brilliant virtuosity and lyric expression in which Caffarelli excelled. Likewise, the role of the seconda donna, Sabina (sung by Catarina Fumagalli), is extraordinary in its virtuoso expression: 'Splenda per voi sereno' has a wide range, rapid leaps of over an octave and a half and extensive passage-work. The reception of Pergolesi's *Adriano*, despite its evident genius, was apparently mediocre, as attested by contemporary *avvisi* and the few manuscript copies. Unlike *L'olimpiade* and his comic intermezzos, there were apparently no revivals or pasticcios based on the work in the 18th century. The first of several modern revivals was given in June 1985 at the Maggio Musicale Festival in Florence.

DALE E. MONSON

Adriano in Siria (iii) ('Hadrian in Syria'). *Dramma per musica* in three acts by PASQUALE ANFOSSI to a libretto by PIETRO METASTASIO (*see* ADRIANO IN SIRIA above); Padua, Teatro Nuovo, June 1777.

The libretto is much altered from the 1752 version, incorporating some elements from the 1732 original but giving the three Parthian characters – Osroa [Osroes], Emirena and Farnaspe [Pharnaspes] – greater prominence. Anfossi used a substantial amount of accompanied recitative and he wrote a trio for Emirena, Pharnaspes and Osroes to conclude Act 2. Act 3, greatly shortened in accordance with the conventions of the period, ends with simple recitative. Osroes and Aquilio [Aquilius] (whose role is cut substantially) are written for tenors, while the four lovers are soprano roles. Apart from a few cavatinas, the arias retain the textual structure of da capo arias but are through-composed. Many are in a sonata-form design in which the *A* sections constitute the exposition and recapitulation and the *B* section functions as a retransition or development; the remainder have similar *ABA* structures, with the *A* section closing in the tonic. The opera has a reprise overture.

STEPHEN C. FISHER

Aeneas i Cartago [*Aeneas i Cartago, eller Dido och Aeneas* ('Aeneas in Carthage, or Dido and Aeneas')]. Lyric tragedy in a prologue and five acts by JOSEPH MARTIN KRAUS to a libretto by JOHAN HENRIK KELLGREN after an outline by GUSTAVUS III based on Jean-Jacques Le Franc de Pompignan's play *Didon*; Stockholm, Royal Opera, 18 November 1799.

The opera begins with a prologue depicting winds chained to a rock in the sea. Eol [Aeolus] (bass) refuses to release them until asked by Juno (soprano) to allow them to sink the escaping Trojan fleet. After a storm, Neptun [Neptune] (bass) calms the waves and Aeneas (tenor) is cast ashore on the coast of Carthage. His mother Venus (soprano) directs him to seek aid from Queen Dido (soprano). In Act 1, she welcomes the strangers and asks that they help dedicate a new temple in homage to Juno, who refuses to accept it. In Act 2 a hunt is interrupted by a storm that drives Dido and Aeneas to a cave for shelter; they pledge their love, only to be interrupted by the ghost of Dido's first husband, Siché [Sychaeus] (bass), who warns of their impending doom. In Act 3, the Numidian King Jarbas (tenor or baritone) arrives disguised as his own ambassador to ask for Dido's hand; he is rejected and vows revenge. Aeneas and Dido then appear before the temple of Juno to be married, but an earthquake occurs, followed by the appearance of Ära (soprano), who orders Aeneas to leave Carthage. As the Trojans prepare to set sail, Dido unsuccessfully asks Aeneas to stay. Her servant Clelié [Cloelia] (soprano) then arrives with news of the approaching Numidian army. In Act 5 a battle takes place in which Aeneas slays Jarbas and defeats the Numidians before leaving Carthage. Dido, at first encouraged by his victory, sees his ships departing and immolates herself. The goddess Iris (soprano) arrives and tells the Carthaginians that Dido has been apotheosized. Finally Jupiter (baritone) receives Dido in Olympus.

The work was originally intended to open the new Royal Opera in 1782, but the performance was cancelled (and Naumann's *Cora och Alonzo* substituted) when the prima donna, Caroline Müller, left Stockholm abruptly. Both Kellgren and Kraus waited in vain for ten years to see the première, making extensive revisions in both text and music. Court intrigue prevented the work from being performed until 1799, and then only in a heavily truncated version lasting three hours, half the original length. A revival of part of Act 3 took place in 1966 at the Drottningholm Theatre, and a shortened concert version was performed in Stockholm and New York in 1980 under the direction of Newell Jenkins.

Aeneas is regarded as the epitome of Swedish Gustavian opera. In its treatment of the text, the opera focusses on the psychological characteristics and situations rather than on Virgil's story. Kraus's music is bold and striking, using progressive leitmotivic ideas that anticipate Beethoven and Wagner in addition to showing the strong influences of Gluck and the German *Sturm und Drang*. The work contains a wide variety of special effects designed to show off the new theatre's machinery.

BERTIL H. VAN BOER

Aeneas in Latium. Libretto subject used chiefly in the 17th and 18th centuries. Its principal source is VIRGIL's *Aeneid*. Operas on the subject appear under various titles including *Enea nel Lazio*, *Enea in Italia* and *Enea e Lavinia*, and in French as *Enée et Lavinie*.

In opera Aeneas is most widely known for his desertion of Dido (particularly in Nahum Tate's poetry for Purcell in 1689, in Metastasio's *Didone abbandonata*, found in numerous 18th-century settings, and in Berlioz's *Les Troyens*) in order to appease the gods and fulfil his destiny, the founding of the Roman empire. Homer, and later Cato and Virgil, recounted the many trials and disasters to which Aeneas was subjected after the fall of his native Troy. In Virgil's version of the episode in Latium, which follows Cato's account, Aeneas arrives in Italy (having left Carthage and Dido) and is offered, by oracular decree, both the kingdom and the hand of King Latinus's only daughter, Lavinia. Turnus, a foreign prince to whom these favours have previously been promised, wages a jealous war with his Rutolian forces against the king. Aeneas leads the king's army to victory, however, and Turnus is slain. This account was the basis for numerous librettos of the 17th and 18th centuries. In the 17th century Bussani's libretto, *Enea in Italia* (1670, with various musical settings as late as 1686), was particularly popular, adding intrigue by combining the Dido and Lavinia legends; Enea [Aeneas] is forced to choose between the two women. Rolli fashioned his *Enea nel Lazio* for Porpora (1734, London). Cigna-Santi's libretto for Turin (again as *Enea nel Lazio*, 1760), with music by Traetta, altered the legend somewhat. Aeneas's captain, Segesto, is revealed in the end to be Aeneas's mother, Venus, in disguise; she intervenes, granting Turno [Turnus] his life and a marriage to the princess Ersinda. Unusual are the numerous battle and crowd scenes, as well as the *deus ex machina* ending. Fontenelle's French text, *Enée et Lavinie*, was first set by Collasse (1690, Paris), but later found new life in the mid-18th century: it was revived by Dauvergne (1758, Paris) and then by Traetta (1761, Parma, in a translation by Sanvitale), and was widely imitated. It was presumably the model for Jommelli's *Enea nel Lazio* for the French Stuttgart court (1755, lost), later revised for Lisbon in 1767. This was followed by a rendition for Sacchini (*Enea e Lavinia*) in London (1779; perhaps by Bottarelli). New dramatic elements in the mid-18th century include the decree of the oracle of Faun (Latinus's father) that Lavinia herself must choose between Aeneas and Turnus by following her heart; Juno's stirring up of enmity against Aeneas in Amata, Latinus's wife, and in Turnus; Lavinia's struggle with the new-found knowledge of Aeneas's desertion of Dido and what that may mean for her own fate; and in the end hand-to-hand combat between Aeneas and Turnus on the battlefield to resolve the feud. The best-known late 18th-century libretto to this legend was that set by Guglielmi in 1785 (also as *Enea e Lavinia*), jointly attributed to Sertor and de Stefano, again with much of Fontenelle's intrigue; this was repeated at least nine times over the ensuing ten years. De Filistri wrote an *Enea nel Lazio* for Berlin in 1793, with music by Righini, that closely adhered to Virgil's account and detailed Aeneas's final battle with Turnus. Other versions appeared in librettos by the Duca di San Angelo Morbilli of Naples (1769) and Belmont (1778, Naples).

DALE E. MONSON

Aeschylus [Aischylos] (*b* Eleusis [now Elevsina], 525 BC; *d* Gela [now Terranuova], Sicily, 456 BC). Greek dramatist, author of some 80 tragedies and satyr plays. Seven tragedies have survived, though doubt has been cast on the authenticity of the *Prometheus*. Aeschylus fought at Marathon (490 BC) and describes in detail the battle of Salamis (480 BC) in what is probably his earliest play, *The Persae* (472 BC). Excepting *The Persae*, Aeschylus usually produced for the Great Dionysia at Athens three tragedies and a satyr play thematically linked. The only trilogy to survive is *The Oresteia* (458 BC), consisting of the *Agamemnon*, *Choephori* and *Eumenides*. *The Suppliants* (*c*463 BC) is the first play in an otherwise lost cycle dealing with the 50 daughters of Danaus (the Danaides) and the murder of their husbands except Lynceus, saved by Hypermnestra. *The Seven against Thebes* is the last play in an Oedipus cycle and describes the death of his sons Eteocles and Polynices. Early opera generally avoided the craggy splendour of Aeschylus, perhaps agreeing with Quintilian that he was uncouth, though Metastasio's libretto *Ipermestra* (1744) was set by some 30 composers and Salieri set a French translation of one by Calzabigi (*Les Danaides*, 1784). More recently the *Prometheus* (Fauré, Maurice Emmanuel, Orff, Wagner-Régeny), *The Suppliants* (Emmanuel's *Salamine*) and *Oresteia* (Taneyev, Weingartner, Milhaud, Eaton's *The Cry of Clytaemnestra*) have provided operatic inspiration.

*

M. Ewans: *Wagner and Aeschylus: the 'Ring' and the 'Oresteia'* (London, 1982)

ROBERT ANDERSON

Afanas'yev, Nikolay Yakovlevich (*b* Tobol'sk, 31 Dec 1820/12 Jan 1821; *d* St Petersburg, 22 May/3 June 1898). Russian composer. He studied with his father, a violinist, and made his début as a violinist in Moscow in 1836, becoming leader of the Bol'shoy Theatre Orchestra in 1838. He resigned in 1841 to become conductor of the serf orchestra maintained by a landowner near St Petersburg. In 1846 he decided to pursue a career as a solo violinist and toured widely, settling in St Petersburg in 1851. There he led the orchestra of the Italian opera, sometimes deputizing for the regular conductor. In 1853 he became a piano teacher at the Smolny Institute and relinquished his orchestral post. He visited western Europe in 1857.

On his return to Russia, Afanas'yev decided to devote himself to composition. He was a prolific composer, at his best in small-scale works, where there is less evidence of the uneven technique resulting from his very informal musical education. His nine operas met with little success: *Ammalet-bek* was performed at the Mariinsky Theatre in 1870, but has not been revived. *Sten'ka Razin* was rejected by the censor, and *Vakula-kuznets* ('Vakula the Smith'), entered for the competition which was won by Tchaikovsky, was never performed. Other operas, as well as several orchestral works, remain in manuscript. Many of Afanas'yev's more attractive pieces reflect his interest in Russian folk music.

all unpublished; some MSS in RU-SPk

Taras Bulba, 1860s (after N. V. Gogol)

Vakula-kuznets, 1860s [Vakula the Smith] (op, after Gogol: *Noch' pered rozhdestvom* [Christmas Eve])

Ammalet-bek (4, A. F. Weltmann, after A. A. Bestuzhev-Marlinsky), St Petersburg, Mariinsky, 11/23 Nov 1870

Sten'ka Razin

*

ME

A. Ulïbïshev: 'Russkiy skripach N. Ya. Afanas'yev', *Severnaya pchela* (9 Nov 1850)

N. Ya. Afanas'yev: 'Vospominaniya' [Reminiscences], *Istoricheskiy vestnik*, xli (1890), 23, 255

Obituary, *RMG* (1898), 659

N. Shelkov: 'Nikolay Afanas'yev', *Muzïkal'naya zhizn'* (1962), no.10, p.17

JENNIFER SPENCER

Affair, The. Opera in one act, op.99, by FELIX WERDER to a libretto by Leonard Radic; Sydney, Opera House, 14 March 1974.

Lady Celia (soprano) sets a trap for her apparently unfaithful husband, Sir Reginald (tenor), the Australian High Commissioner, who spends too much time with Olivia Tomas (mezzo-soprano), the wife of the South American Ambassador. Lady Celia plans an opera performance to celebrate the Queen's birthday and offers Sir Reginald and Olivia roles. When the opera begins, it becomes clear that the plot is a slice of Sir Reginald's own life. He tries to break out of the scene but cannot. When Olivia shoots him as rehearsed, the 'dummy' gun turns out to be real and Sir Reginald collapses. Neither woman is responsible: Gregory Jones (baritone), the Second Secretary, loaded the gun knowing that it would be fired at his superior, a man who had long denied him promotion and had incessantly ridiculed him.

The Affair is an expressionistic anti-tonal work using parlando throughout, as well as jagged orchestral note-clusters and the extremes of vocal and instrumental ranges. Arias and other traditional forms are used ironically. *The Affair* was first performed by Australian Opera on a double bill with Larry Sitsky's *Lenz*, the company's first presentation of opera by Australian composers.

THÉRÈSE RADIC

Affre, Agustarello (*b* St Chinian, 23 Oct 1858; *d* Cagnes-sur-Mer, 27 Dec 1931). French tenor. For 20 years he was a principal lyric-heroic tenor at the Opéra in Paris. Its director, Pierre Gailhard, had heard him in the provinces and arranged for lessons with Victor Duvernoy. Affre's house début in 1890 coincided with Melba's, in *Lucia di Lammermoor*. He developed a large repertory, appearing in Gluck's *Armide* and also in the first performances at the Opéra of *Entführung* and *Pagliacci*. In 1891 he sang in the première of *Le mage* by Massenet, who found his voice 'vibrant as pure crystal'. At Covent Garden in 1909 his roles were Faust and Saint-Saëns' Samson. He went to the USA in 1911, appearing at San Francisco and New Orleans where in 1913 he became director of the Opera. He was a prolific recording artist and sang Romeo in one of the earliest complete operatic recordings (1912), the firmness and power of his tone showing why he was often described as the French Tamagno.

*

Mrs Vellacott and J. Dennis: 'Gustarello Affre', *Record Collector*, iii (1948), 84–8, 131–3
M. Scott: *The Record of Singing* (London, 1977) J. B. STEANE

Africaine, L' ('The African Maid'). Grand opera in five acts by GIACOMO MEYERBEER to a libretto by EUGÈNE SCRIBE; Paris, Opéra, 28 April 1865.

Sélika *a slave*	soprano
Vasco da Gama *a naval officer*	tenor
Inès *daughter of Don Diégo*	soprano
Nélusko *a slave*	baritone
Don Pédro *president of the Royal Council*	bass
Don Diégo *an admiral*	bass
Anna *Inès's confidante*	mezzo-soprano
Don Alvar *council member*	tenor
Grand Inquisitor of Lisbon	bass
High Priest of Brahma	bass/baritone

Councillors, naval officers, bishops, Brahmins, Indians, soldiers, sailors

Setting Lisbon and an island in the Indian Ocean, *c*1500

The genesis of *L'Africaine* is more complex than that of any other Meyerbeer opera. A first contract between Meyerbeer and Scribe for the production of the libretto was signed in May 1837; the point of departure for the plot seems to have been 'Le mancenillier', a poem by Millevoye about a young girl who sits under a tree that emits poisonous fragrances and is rescued by her lover. Doubts about the viability of the libretto, and the illness of Cornélie Falcon, for whom the title role was intended, caused Meyerbeer to abandon the project in favour of *Le prophète* in summer 1838. He returned to *L'Africaine* at the end of 1841, when the draft of *Le prophète* was almost complete. *L'Africaine* was set aside when Meyerbeer completed a draft in 1843, only to be taken up again eight years later when he decided to revise the work substantially. The original libretto was set in Spain during the reign of Philip III and features in the tenor role an obscure naval officer named Fernand, who purchases Sélika in a slave market; he sails for Mexico in Act 3, but a storm drives his ships to the coast of Africa and Sélika's realm on the Niger river. In the revision Portugal and India became the backdrop and the explorer Vasco da Gama was made the protagonist of the work; the working title was changed from *L'Africaine* to *Vasco da Gama*.

Meyerbeer dropped the project once more in 1853, briefly did some work on it in 1857, and settled upon *Vasco da Gama* in 1860. Since Scribe died in 1861, a number of other librettists had a hand in the final stages of preparation, including Charlotte Birch-Pfeiffer and Camille Du Locle. The work was fully orchestrated by November 1863 and the way cleared for a production at the Opéra, with Marie Sasse in the role of Sélika, when Meyerbeer died in May 1864. His widow placed the eminent Belgian musicologist and critic, F.-J. Fétis, in charge of the rehearsals; Naudin was engaged for the role of Vasco and Faure for Nélusko. As Meyerbeer himself would have been compelled to do, Fétis made a large number of cuts to the long score. He also made changes to the libretto. The most striking of these concerns the title and setting of the last two acts. Thinking *Vasco da Gama* too long and Sélika the most important character, Fétis reinstated *L'Africaine* as the title. The last two acts must therefore take place in Africa; though not explicit, the suggestion in the libretto, particularly in the Act 2 duet, is that Sélika's homeland is Madagascar. Nonetheless, confusion about the setting must inevitably arise in modern productions, since references to the Indian gods Brahma, Vishnu and Shiva were not expunged from the text.

ACT 1 *The council room in the Admiralty of Lisbon* Inès has been called to attend a meeting of the council and tells her confidante, Anna, that she suspects news may be revealed about Vasco, who has been away at sea for two years. Inès is to marry Vasco upon his return; in a *romance* ('Adieu mon beau rivage') she recalls his final farewell beneath her balcony; thus, in a telescopic manner endemic to eventful grand opera librettos, Vasco's position as Inès's lover is not established in a long duet, but rather through her recollection of his words in a more compact solo number. The piece exhibits the progression from minor to major characteristic of the genre, but an unusual effect evocative of Vasco's desolation before his departure is created in the minor section by alternating the voice with melodic fragments in the wind instruments. Don Diégo and Don Pédro appear to a pompous melody. The former insists that his daughter marry Don Pédro. The music projects complete nonchalance as they report to her that Vasco is among those who have perished on the ill-fated journey of the Portuguese fleet. In a brief trio the two men express irritation at Inès's lyrical effusion about her lover's death. Inès is led off just before the Grand Inquisitor, bishops and members of the council enter with a march-like strain and an imposing unison prayer. Don Diégo asks whether a rescue party should be launched and the end of the first part of the finale is articulated by a reprise of the prayer. Much to everyone's surprise, Vasco da Gama suddenly appears in the room, all impetuosity and hubris. He asks for support to explore uncharted regions beyond Africa. As evidence of his previous explorations he produces two slaves, Sélika and Nélusko, to a mildly exotic figure in the piccolo. Sélika, a queen in her native land, remains taciturn in the face of questions. Vasco attempts to coax her into responding and gives evidence of some attachment to her, since his words are accompanied by a melody for *divisi* cellos strongly reminiscent of a similarly scored passage before the *romance*, Inès's earlier recollection of his love for her. Nélusko seethes with anger and through manifold reiteration of the same musical figure staunchly refuses to reveal anything about himself. Vasco leaves and members of council deliberate, with the Inquisitor intoning the previously heard prayer and arguing that to speak of a land unmentioned in the Bible is heresy. The council does not support the request for a new fleet. When Vasco learns of the decision, he baldly accuses the tribunal of envy and jealousy. A prompt condemnation to life imprisonment by the Inquisitor brings the fulminations of a concluding *strette*, with Vasco's supporters outnumbered by his detractors.

ACT 2 *An Inquisition prison in Lisbon* Sélika watches Vasco while he sleeps, racked by nightmares; much to her chagrin he expresses love for Inès. With the 'Air du sommeil', 'Sur mes genoux, fils du soleil', from her native land, Sélika attempts to calm him; the use of the triangle and short ornamental runs in muted strings and winds lend an exotic flavour to the piece, though the dialogue between voice and flute in one of the episodes of this rondo design was a common operatic device. In another episode (with a verbal commonplace of the kind that is liberally distributed in Scribe's work) she beseeches the High Priest of Brahma to extinguish 'the flames of her heart'. Nélusko appears and moves to stab the sleeping man. Sélika restrains him and asks why his intentions are murderous. He responds in an *air* ('Fille des rois'), first by paying homage to Sélika's royal blood in stately double-dotted rhythms, and then, in the *cabalette*, by alluding with bravado to his love for her. Vasco awakens, sends Nélusko away and ignores Sélika while he rages about his fate. On a map she shows him a way to reach her island in the Indian Ocean. Convinced that this is the route to his own glory, the explorer warms towards her and the two combine in cantabile parallel singing. Suddenly Inès, Anna, Don Pédro and Don Alvar burst in. In a vocal line punctuated by rests to suggest her sobbing, Inès informs Vasco that she has bought his freedom. He seeks to convince her that he feels no affection for Sélika by offering the African queen to Inès as a slave, and Inès leads an ensemble with a lyrical line expressing her realization that Vasco loves her after all. To a figure in the orchestra that brims with overconfidence, Don Pédro informs Vasco that he himself has been equipped with a fleet; the injury is magnified when Vasco learns that Inès has actually married Don Pédro. Following a conventional unison 'frozen moment' in which all give voice to conflicting emotions, musical interest is bestowed upon Inès (and not upon Vasco, as one might expect): to one of the most famous melodies of the opera ('Eh bien, sois libre par l'amour') she leads a concluding ensemble by advising him to place his own glory above his love for her.

ACT 3 *Aboard Don Pédro's ship* It is dawn and, in a scene-setting chorus accompanied by gentle rocking motion in the low strings, Inès's attendants sing of the quick progress of the ship across the waves. The sailors are roused from sleep and anticipate the day's work ahead; Inès joins them in a prayer for safe passage. Nélusko has been made pilot of the boat by Don Pédro, who ignores Don Alvar's warnings that the slave is steering them towards danger. The suspicions are well founded, however: in a fiery strophic *ballade*, 'Adamastor, roi des vagues profondes', Nélusko tells the sailors of the deadly sea monster, Adamastor. His macabre laughter and mock jovial music suggest that he expects the wrath of the monster will soon avenge him. Another Portuguese vessel is sighted and a small boat from it pulls beside Don Pédro's ship. Vasco disembarks and boldly informs Don Pédro that, out of concern for the safety of Inès, he has come to warn him that the course his ship has taken will lead to disaster. Don Pédro bristles at the impudence of Vasco and both hurl threats at each other; the *cabalette* of their duet is a static moment as, with swords drawn, both stand ready to duel. Suddenly a storm wells up. In the major scenic coup of the opera, the ship is driven against a reef; compatriots of Sélika and Nélusko stream on board the vessel and capture the Europeans (for illustration *see* MACHINERY, fig.19).

ACT 4 *Outside a Brahmin temple* Priestesses, priests, Amazons, jugglers and warriors enter in succession during a balletic *divertissement*. To a hymn-like strain the entire assembly expresses allegiance to its queen, Sélika. Nélusko gleefully informs her that all the Portuguese men who landed save one have been executed and that the women are being led to the manchineel tree, the poisonous fragrances of which will kill them. Vasco is the sole Portuguese male survivor; he appears, accompanied by a rapturous clarinet melody beneath flute tremolo, a musical translation of his bedazzlement by the lush surroundings. He takes up the clarinet tune in the slow section of a *grand air* ('O paradis sorti de l'onde'); his ecstatic music about the discovery of a new land is interrupted by shouts for his blood, and in the *cabalette* he begs the warriors for mercy. Just as he is to be beheaded, Sélika appears and orders her subjects to stop. She claims that Vasco must be spared since she is married to him and forces Nélusko reluctantly to confirm this. In a solemn ceremony Sélika and Vasco are united according to local custom and drink a philtre from the same cup. As the populace processes into the temple, Sélika tells Vasco that he may escape. Suddenly overcome with affection for the queen, Vasco refuses her offer. They both give voice to mutual love in a duet and, with a magical modulation from F♯ major to E♭ major, Vasco openly accepts Sélika as his wife. The *cortège* returns from the temple and celebrates the union while the voices of the expiring Portuguese women are heard in the distance.

ACT 5.i *The queen's gardens* Inès has escaped from the deadly perfume of the manchineel tree and has sought refuge in Sélika's gardens. Vasco sees her and declares that he must resist his rekindled love since he is married to another. Sélika's fury is aroused when she sees the two together. The ensuing duet for Sélika and Inès is too extended in its position at the dénouement of the opera, especially since there are no developments in the drama across its various parts: both slow section and *cabalette* develop musically the distress of the women, Inès because she believes she can never have Vasco, and Sélika because Vasco's true love does not appear directed towards her. After the number Sélika instructs Nélusko to lead Inès and Vasco to safety. She resolves to go to the manchineel tree.

5.ii *A promontory overlooking the sea, with the manchineel tree* Sélika arrives at her final place of rest ('D'ici je vois la mer'). She forgives Vasco and bids him farewell. She gathers the blossoms and presses them to her face. As a lyrical cello strain is heard in tonalities successively a major 3rd apart, she begins to hallucinate. To the accompaniment of harps and with light staccato singing, she envisages Vasco returning to her in a swan-drawn chariot. Nélusko, displaying musically a depth of

'L'Africaine' (Meyerbeer), Act 4 (outside a Brahmin temple), designed by Charles-Antoine Cambon and Joseph Thierry for the original production at the Paris Opéra (Salle Le Peletier), 28 April 1865: engraving from 'L'illustration' (6 May 1865)

emotion not associated with him before in the opera, joins her in death.

* * *

In *L'Africaine*, Meyerbeer and Scribe placed love relationships into greater relief than in their previous grand opera collaborations. Vasco is the common denominator in no fewer than three triangles: he challenges Don Pédro for Inès, causes Sélika's anguish in continuing to love her rival and, in turn, arouses Nélusko's jealousy. Combined with the political backdrop and obligatory enactments of ritual, love is stretched rather thinly across the five-act frame of *L'Africaine*; as usual with Meyerbeer, intensity of emotion takes second place to manoeuvring of the characters into sensationalistic dramatic situations, especially in *finales*. The Vasco–Don Pédro–Inès and Vasco–Sélika–Inès triangles are played off against each other in the Act 2 *finale*, leaving Vasco (temporarily) with little more than his massive ego, and the Vasco–Nélusko–Sélika triangle generates suspense in the Act 4 *finale* as Nélusko ponders whether to reveal Sélika's ruse. Nélusko is arguably the most interesting character in the opera, an echo of Marcel in *Les Huguenots* in combining musical grotesqueries with a more heartfelt core. Sélika, for her part, is an operatic forerunner to self-annhilating non-Europeans such as Lakmé and Madama Butterfly. The connection of female sexuality to the exotic, however, is less explicit in *L'Africaine* than in many later works, in part because of restrained use of musical *couleur locale* in Sélika's role (and in the opera as a whole) and also because Vasco's attraction to her occurs, in the first instance, as a result of his exploratory zeal and, later on, because of a philtre administered by the high priest. STEVEN HUEBNER

Afterpiece. Term used for the smaller dramatic work in a double bill, the theatrical programme which was the staple diet of London theatre audiences from the 1714–15 season to the 19th century. The term probably first appears in 1779, when Richard Holcroft, writing on 30 October to Richard Hughes, refers to Sheridan's *The Critic* as 'a new afterpiece'. It was included in the 1822 revision of Johnson's *Dictionary*, described as 'A Farce or any smaller entertainment after the play'. However, the *Oxford English Dictionary* is wrong to interpret 'smaller entertainment' as including 'any extra item' and the epilogue. An afterpiece must have dramatic coherence; songs and dances or miscellaneous entertainments between the acts are therefore excluded. Most afterpieces are in two acts and had to be reasonably short; when *The Critic* ran for two and a half hours in November 1779, the *Morning Chronicle* remarked that 'it must of necessity be considerably shortened', while the libretto for Hook's comic opera *Wilmore Castle* (1800) notes that 'The Opera being found, on the first Night of its Performance, to exceed the time usually allotted to After-pieces, the Passages marked with inverted Commas, were afterwards omitted in the Representation'. An afterpiece often contained most of the music in an evening's entertainment.

Among the genres used as afterpieces are pantomimes, farces, burlettas and occasional pieces such as serenatas and masques. Some popular works began life as unsuccessful mainpieces, Kane O'Hara's burletta *Midas* (1760) and John Burgoyne's entertainment *The Maid of the Oaks* (1774) among them. Afterpieces were interchangeable; even when a work was written or adapted for a particular mainpiece on a certain occasion, it was nearly always staged later with a different work. Dibdin's burletta *Poor Vulcan*, first given on 4 February 1778, received 22 performances that season. The mainpieces it accompanied were plays as widely differing as *King Lear*, *Henry V*, *She Stoops to Conquer*, *Iphigenia*, *Jane Shore* and *The Countess of Salisbury*. Afterpieces were rarely if ever included on bills on which the main work was a full-length opera (an exception was the pasticcio *Il soldano generoso* given after Sacchini's *La contadina in corte* at the King's Theatre on 14 December 1779). The genres used as afterpieces did not usually require actors and singers of the first talent, and the much vaunted transformations in works such as masques generally required only stock scenery.

The inclusion of an afterpiece as a matter of course

seems to have been the result of competition between the Theatre Royal, Drury Lane and the theatre in Lincoln's Inn Fields in the 1714–15 season. Performance figures show a small but regular use of the double bill from the beginning of the century until that season, when the increase was in the order of 700%. The introduction of the pantomime during the 1720s again increased the number of multiple bills; the 1723–4 season included 165 afterpieces in a total of 370 theatrical programmes. Thereafter it became part of the regular diet for London theatre audiences. Interludes of the late 17th and earlier 18th centuries, such as Motteux's *Acis and Galatea* (?1700) or William Taverner's *Ixion* (?1697), sometimes referred to as 'afterpieces', in fact tend to be much shorter works, and grew out of the interpolated masque tradition.

The early development of the afterpiece in part parallels the continental tradition of the comic intermezzo, a response to the creation of *opera seria.* Unlike the afterpiece, however, the subjects and characteristics of the intermezzo form a distinct genre. The ground they and the afterpiece have in common is that initially both were repositories for ideas and music considered inappropriate for inclusion in the mainpiece of the evening. Both could also be crucial to a larger work's reception; as Burney remarked of the later intermezzo, 'few operas would go down without this coarse sauce', while Cumberland wrote of his play *The West Indian* (1771) that it had run for 'eight and twenty successive nights without the buttress of an afterpiece, which was not then the practice of attaching to a new play' (*Memoirs of Richard Cumberland*, London, 1807, i, 296). The popularity of both forms was due in no small measure to their brevity, their subjects and the welcome relief they provided the audience from the not infrequently tedious mainpieces.

*

L. Hughes: 'Afterpieces, or That's Entertainment', *Restoration and Eighteenth-Century Theatre Research*, iv (1965), 55–70

R. Fiske: *English Theatre Music of the Eighteenth Century* (London, 1973, 2/1986)

D. F. Cook: 'Venus and Adonis: an English Masque "After the Italian manner"', *MT*, cxxi (1980), 553–7

K. Pry: 'Theatrical Competition and the Rise of the Afterpiece, 1700–24', *Theatre Notebook*, xxxvi (1982), 21–7

M. Burden: 'The Wedding Masques for Anne, the Princess Royal', *MMA*, xvii (1990), 87–113

MICHAEL BURDEN

Agache, Alexandru (*b* Cluj, 16 Aug 1955). Romanian baritone. After studying at Cluj, he made his début there in 1979 as Silvano (*Ballo*), followed in 1980 by Sharpless. During the next decade he sang Don Giovanni, Malatesta, Germont, Luna, Posa (*Don Carlos*), the title role of *Nabucco*, and Schaunard at Cluj. He also appeared at Budapest, Dresden, Ankara and the Deutsche Staatsoper, Berlin, with whose company he toured Japan in 1987 as Almaviva. He made his Covent Garden début in 1988 as Renato in *Ballo*, later singing Enrico Ashton and Boccanegra (1991). He made his début at La Scala in 1989 as Belcore in *L'elisir d'amore.* Other roles include Gounod's Méphistophélès, and Escamillo. His powerful, flexible voice and imposing stage presence make him an ideal interpreter of Verdi's baritone roles.

ELIZABETH FORBES

Agamemnon. Opera in one act by FELIX WERDER to his own libretto after AESCHYLUS' play, translated by Gilbert Murray; Melbourne, Grant Street Theatre, 1 June 1977 (broadcast of earlier version, *The Agamemnon of Aeschylus*, ABC, 1967).

The plot follows precisely the words of Gilbert Murray's translation of Aeschylus' *Agamemnon.* On his return from the Trojan wars, King Agamemnon of Mycenae (bass) is greeted by his wife Clytemnestra (soprano) and her lover, Aegisthus (countertenor), who together plot the king's murder. Warned of the plot against him by the prophetess Cassandra (soprano), a princess of Troy and concubine of Agamemnon, the king ignores all advice. The lovers kill him, fulfilling the destiny predicted not only for themselves but for their doomed House of Atreus.

Composed in 1967, the opera, then titled *The Agamemnon of Aeschylus*, was performed for a radio broadcast in the same year; the composer reworked and retitled the piece shortly thereafter. Through-composed in 25 sections and serially constructed, with the first 12-note row having strong tonal implications, *Agamemnon*'s structural approach was further developed in Werder's later opera, *Medea* (1988). In both works the soloists and chorus sing from fixed positions while their alter egos, actor-dancers, mime the external and internal drama. The musical and dramatic climax of *Agamemnon* occurs during the confrontation between Clytemnestra and Cassandra, a scene of extreme musical tension in which rage and madness are graphically apparent in the score's dissonance and final dissolution. Music from the opera was incorporated into *Banker*, a percussion play Werder composed in 1971.

THÉRÈSE RADIC

Agazzari, Agostino (*b* ?1579–81; *d* Siena, Dec 1641–Jan 1642). Italian composer. Having lived in Siena from before 1596, he and his father were made nobles by the Grand Duke of Tuscany in 1601. Some time after 1603 Agazzari became *maestro di cappella* at the Seminario Romano where during Carnival 1606 his young students performed his *dramma pastorale Eumelio* (prol., 3, T. de Cuppis and F. Tirletti). In 1607 the composer returned to Siena, apparently having been blacklisted by the Sistine Chapel singers; he served as organist and *maestro di cappella* at the cathedral there, remaining in Siena until his death.

The staging of school plays had long been part of Jesuit academic tradition; *Eumelio* was different because it was sung throughout and its score published (Venice, 1606). Two Jesuits collaborated on the libretto (in *F-Pn*), a simple morality play set in a schoolboy's Arcadia. The shepherd boy Eumelio (soprano) is tempted by the Vices to follow the path of pleasure. When he is dragged down to hell, the other shepherds beg Apollino [Apollo] (tenor) and Mercurio [Mercury] (alto) to rescue him. The two gods are ferried by Caronte [Charon] (tenor) to Plutone [Pluto] (bass), who, after appeasing the demons protesting his release, allows the boy to return to Arcadia. The composer stated that from lack of time and for ease of learning, he did not vary 'all the melodies for all the words'. Agazzari's straightforward monodic style relies heavily on repetition, in the many strophic texts and in several restatements of whole musical passages. *Eumelio* was restaged in Amelia in 1614 with additional *intermedi*, though the libretto does not specify that Agazzari's music was sung. A modern revival took place at the Holland Festival in 1974.

*

ES (N. Pirrotta)

A. Bonaventura: 'I primi melodrammi a Roma e l'*Eumelio* di A. Agazzari', *Bulletino senese di storia patria*, xxxvii (1930), 301–4
——: 'A. Agazzari', ibid, new ser., ii (1931), 285–8
G. Barblan: 'Contributo a una biografia critica di A. Agazzari', *CHM*, ii (1956–7), 33–63
T. Culley: *Jesuits and Music*, i: *A Study of the Musicians connected with the German College in Rome during the 17th Century and of their Activities in Northern Europe* (St Louis, 1970), 113–18
M. F. Johnson: 'Agazzari's *Eumelio*, a "dramma pastorale"', *MQ*, lvii (1971), 491–505
S. Leopold: 'Das geistliche Libretto im 17. Jahrhundert: zur Gattungsgeschichte der frühen Oper', *Mf*, xxxi (1978), 245–57
C. Gianturco: 'Nuove considerazioni su *Il tedio del recitativo* delle prime opere romane', *RIM*, xviii (1982), 212–39
A. Mazzeo: *Arie e madrigali a voce sola di compositori senesi del 1600* (Florence, 1984), 5–8 [incl. music from *Eumelio*]
C. A. Reardon: *A. Agazzari and the Performance of Sacred Music in the Sienese Cathedral during the Early Baroque* (diss., U. of California, Los Angeles, 1987) MARGARET MURATA

Agesilao, re di Sparta ('Agesilaus, King of Sparta'). *Opera seria* in three acts by GAETANO ANDREOZZI to a libretto by Francesco Ballani; Venice, Teatro S Benedetto, Carnival 1788.

Leucade [Leotychidas] (soprano castrato) is taken prisoner in an uprising against Agesilaus (soprano castrato), initiated by the Congiutati under the leadership of Leotychidas' father, Lisandro [Lysander] (tenor), a military hero and supposed friend of the king. Outraged by his perfidy, Erissa (soprano), Queen of Paphlagonia and Leotychidas' betrothed, condemns him to death and offers her hand to the king, much to the dismay of Lysander's daughter, Aglatide (soprano), who loves the king. When Lysander attempts to take power Leotychidas interposes himself between his father's sword and the king, thereby earning clemency for both of them.

Based on a new libretto by the young Roman author Ballani, the opera enjoyed half a dozen revivals in the years before the Republic. Though still an 'aria' opera, with ensembles to end Acts 1 and 2 and a chorus in each act, it contains a few novelties: an aria interrupted by a second character, and a short quartet ('cavatina a quattro') when the captured Leotychidas is brought in. When it was revised for Florence in the autumn of 1788 the choruses were cut and it was reduced to two acts. The second act concludes with an action ensemble finale.

Andreozzi's music is outstanding for its skilful musical characterizations, the dramatic intensity of the obbligato recitatives and ensembles, and the lavish use of wind instrument colour, chromaticism and dynamic contrasts, particularly the crescendo.

MARITA P. McCLYMONDS

Aggházy, Károly (*b* Pest, 30 Oct 1855; *d* Budapest, 8 Oct 1918). Hungarian composer. He studied at the National Conservatory in Pest (1867–70), the Vienna Conservatory (1870–73), and the Academy of Music in Budapest (1875–8) with Liszt and Volkmann, twice winning the Liszt scholarship. He was made a professor of piano at the National Conservatory in 1882. On Liszt's recommendation he taught at the Stern and Kullak conservatories in Berlin (1883–9), then returned to teach at the National Conservatory in Budapest until the end of his life.

Aggházy composed about 170 works, mainly short pieces for piano, but including two two-act operas. *Maritta, a korsós Madonna* ('Maritta, the Madonna with Jug'; I. Fuhrmann; Budapest, Opera House, 14 Oct 1897) is set in and around the monastery of S Yuste in Spain in the 16th century; the plot contains no real dramatic conflict, and the music is consequently predominantly lyrical, albeit high-flown. Although traces of Gounod, Massenet, even Mascagni can be discovered, it is principally Wagner whose music had the most influence. While there are some numbers, arias among them, the style is typically declamatory, with arioso passages. Despite a successful première it remained in the repertory only eight weeks. The manuscript is in the National Széchényi Library. *A ravennai nász* ('The Wedding in Ravenna', 1908; D. Orbán) was not performed. Aggházy also wrote incidental music for the theatre, and a pantomime, *A müvészet diadala* ('Triumph of the Arts', 1894).

DEZSŐ LEGÁNY

Agnelli [Angello], **Salvatore** (*b* Palermo, 1817; *d* Marseilles, 1874). Italian composer. He studied first at Palermo Conservatory, then at Naples Conservatory (1830–34), where his teachers included Zingarelli and Donizetti. Donizetti supported his theatrical début, the *opera buffa I due pedanti* (1838, Naples). Nine other comic operas by Agnelli were performed in Naples and Palermo between 1838 and 1842. In 1846 he moved to Marseilles. His other works include five unperformed operas, three ballets and sacred music. Agnelli was an imitator of Donizetti and Mercadante without great distinction.

I due pedanti (A. Passaro), Naples, Nuovo, 25 Feb 1838
Il lazzarone napolitano (R. D'Ambra), Naples, Nuovo, 1838
Una notte di carnevale, Palermo, Carolino, 1838
I due forzati ovvero Giovanni Vallese (P. Giaramicca), Palermo, Carolino, 1839
I due gemelli (G. B. Lorenzi), Palermo, Carolino, 1839
La locandiera di spirito (G. Sapio, after C. Goldoni), Naples, Nuovo, 1839
La sentinella notturna (Passaro), Naples, Partenope, 1840
I due pulcinelli simili, Naples, La Fenice, 1841
L'omicida immaginario, Naples, La Fenice, 1841
Il fantasma (F. Romani), Naples, La Fenice, 1842
La jacquerie, Marseilles, Grand, 22 April 1849
Léonore des Médicis, Marseilles, Grand, 21 March 1855
Les deux avares (F. de Falbaire), Marseilles, Grand, 22 March 1860

Unperf.: Cromwell (4); Stefania (3); Gli Sforza (4); Il debitore; Le nozze di un principe

*

DBI (R. Bonvicini); *DEUMM*; *ES*
F. Florimo: 'Salvatore Agnelli', *Cenno storico sulla scuola musicale di Napoli*, ii (Naples, 1871), 2152–6 [incl. list of works held in *I-Nc*] GIOVANNI CARLI BALLOLA

Agnese. *Dramma semiserio per musica* in two acts by FERDINANDO PAER to a libretto by Luigi Buonavoglia after Filippo Casari's play *Agnese di Fizendry*; Parma, Villa Scotti, Teatro Ponte d'Attaro, October 1809.

Seven years before the opera takes place, Agnese (soprano) has driven her father Uberto (bass) to madness by marrying Ernesto (tenor), whom Uberto despises. Confined to an asylum and believing Agnese to be dead, Uberto has been ignored by his daughter until Ernesto's infidelity causes her to seek him out again. With the help of Don Pasquale (bass), superintendent of the asylum, and Don Girolamo (tenor), her father's caretaker, she gradually convinces him that she is still alive. Uberto finally recognizes her, and he recovers his sanity completely when she performs a song that she often sang to him before their estrangement; Agnese forgives Ernesto after he repents of his indiscretions. The kindly Don Pasquale, himself a contented father, and his loyal daughter Carlotta (soprano) serve as dramatic foils to Uberto and Agnese and provide comic relief.

Agnese is Paer's last *opera semiseria* and the one in which comic and serious elements are most skilfully integrated. Its situations have been perceived as anticipating those of such intense psychological *melodrammi* as Donizetti's *Lucia di Lammermoor* and Verdi's *I masnadieri* which became common after 1830; other authorities have noted a similarity in Donizetti's *Il furioso all'isola di San Domingo*, as both there and in *Agnese* the mad scene involves the participation of a 'buffo' – clearly a throwback to the 18th century when male dementia was regarded as entertaining rather than tragic. SCOTT L. BALTHAZAR

Agnesi, Luigi [Agniez, Louis-Ferdinand-Léopold] (*b* Erpent, Namur, 17 July 1833; *d* London, 2 Feb 1875). Belgian bass and composer. He studied in Brussels where his opera *Hermold le Normand* was performed at the Théâtre de la Monnaie on 16 March 1858. After a period of study in Paris he toured Germany and the Netherlands with Merelli's Italian company, then in 1864, after further studying in Paris with Gilbert Duprez, he sang Assur (*Semiramide*) at the Théâtre Italien. He made his London début at Her Majesty's Theatre (1865) and sang at Drury Lane (1871–4). His repertory included Henry VIII (*Anna Bolena*) and Alfonso (*Lucrezia Borgia*). A stylish singer with a secure technique, he was an excellent interpreter of Rossini.

ELIZABETH FORBES

Agnesi-Pinottini, Maria Teresa (*b* Milan, 17 Oct 1720; *d* Milan, 19 Jan 1795). Italian composer. Her first theatrical work, the *cantata pastorale Il ristoro d'Arcadia*, was successfully presented in Milan at the Regio Ducal Teatro in 1747. At about this time she dedicated collections of her own arias and instrumental pieces to the rulers of Saxony and Austria; according to Simonetti the Empress Maria Theresa sang from a collection of arias that Agnesi-Pinottini had given her. She used her own libretto for the opera *Ciro in Armenia* (1753) and possibly for a *componimento drammatico* (1766) and a serenata. She was also known as a harpsichordist and singer. Her portrait hangs in the theatre museum of La Scala; other portraits are reproduced in the encyclopedia *Storia di Milano* (vols. xii, xiv).

Ciro in Armenia (dramma serio, 3, Agnesi-Pinottini), Milan, Regio Ducal, 26 Dec 1753, *I-Mc* (Acts 2 and 3 only), *IBborromeo* (Act 2 only)
Il rè pastore (dramma serio, 3, P. Metastasio), ?1756, *A-Wn*
Sofonisba (dramma eroico, 3, G. F. Zanetti), Naples, 1765, *Wgm*, *Wn*
Nitocri (dramma serio, 3, A. Zeno), Venice, 1771

*

MGG (S. Simonetti)
G. M. Mazzuchelli: *Gli scrittori d'Italia*, i (Brescia, 1753), 198–9
C. de Brosses: *Lettres historiques et critiques sur l'Italie* (Paris, 1798–9; It. trans., 1957)
L. Anzoletti: *Maria Gaetana Agnesi* (Milan, 1900)
G. Seregni: 'La cultura Milanese nel settecento', *Storia di Milano*, xii (1959), 567–640
G. Barblan: 'Il teatro musicale in Milano: il settecento', *Storia di Milano*, xii (1959), 965–96 SVEN HANSELL

Agnes von Hohenstaufen. *Grosse historisch-romantische Oper* in three acts by GASPARE SPONTINI to a libretto by Ernst Raupach; Berlin, Königliches Opernhaus, 12 June 1829.

Although banished by Emperor Henry VI (baritone), Heinrich (tenor), son of the Emperor's Guelph opponent Henry the Lion, is in Mainz incognito in the year 1194 to win his beloved Agnes (soprano), a cousin of the Emperor. He is arrested; however, he not only escapes from prison but also secretly marries Agnes and triumphs over his rival, King Philip of France (baritone). The angry Emperor is finally persuaded by the imperial knights and the intercession of his brother Philip (tenor) and Agnes's mother Irmengard (soprano) to bow to the triumph of love.

Spontini worked for many years on this, his last opera, which he considered his major work. Only the first act was ready for performance at the scheduled première on 28 May 1827. After extensive revisions of the completed work, which was first performed on 12 June 1829, a second version was performed on 6 December 1837. *Agnes von Hohenstaufen* breaks with all the conventions of its time: the large number of royal characters in the cast – in the 1837 version Henry the Lion (bass) also appears – is matched by a huge orchestra and a concept in which the few arias are subordinate to complex ensembles of vast extent. Long-winded monologues and countless *coups de théâtre* prevent the suspense from building up effectively, a failing due not only to the inexperience of the librettist but also to Spontini's determined search for grandiose through-composed *tableaux* and his intention to introduce neo-classical grandeur into German Romantic opera. However, the unique significance of this monumental work was not generally recognized until it had its first performance outside Berlin, in Florence in 1954, in an abridged Italian version, prepared and conducted by Gui. The cast included Corelli, and Lucille Udovick in the title role. Muti conducted an RAI broadcast in 1970, with Caballé in the title role. ANSELM GERHARD

Agostinelli(-Quiroli), Adelina (*b* Verdello, Bergamo, 23 Nov 1882; *d* Buenos Aires, 6 July 1954). Italian soprano. She studied in Milan and made her début in 1903 at Pavia as Fedora. She sang throughout Europe, in South America and in Russia. After an engagement at the Manhattan Opera House, New York (1909–10), she appeared at La Scala, as Amelia in *Simon Boccanegra* (1910), the Marschallin in *Der Rosenkavalier* (1911) and in Mascagni's *Isabeau* (1912). She made her Covent Garden début in 1912 as Puccini's Manon Lescaut and later sang Mimì there. Her repertory also included Elisabeth de Valois (*Don Carlos*) and Nedda (*Pagliacci*). A stylish singer, she had a fine, even-toned voice.

ELIZABETH FORBES

Agostini, Giuseppe (*b* Verona, 21 July 1874; *d* Abington, PA, 26 July 1951). Italian tenor. He made his début in 1895 at Nuovi Ligure. In 1897, after singing Rodolfo for the first time at Cagliari, he took the role in the American première of *La bohème* at Los Angeles and in the New York première (1898) with the Italian opera company at Wallack's Theater. He also sang Rodolfo in Lisbon, Barcelona, Mexico City and elsewhere. He sang Giorgio in Mascagni's *Amica* at Palermo (1910) and toured extensively in the USA with the San Carlo opera company. He retired in 1921, but sang one performance of *Faust* in an emergency in 1929. He had a strong, serviceable voice with ringing top notes. ELIZABETH FORBES

Agostini [Augustini], **Pietro** [Pier] **Simone** (*b* Forlì, *c*1635; *d* Parma, 1 Oct 1680). Italian composer. His profligate manner of living resulted in his banishment from several Italian cities, including his native Forlì.

During his short military career, he participated in the war against the Turks in Crete, for which he was made a Knight of the Golden Spur. His first datable dramatic music was a prologue and interludes for *Tolomeo*, a play presented in 1658 by the Accademici Imperturbabili at the Teatro S Apollinare, Venice. Although the last of his six operas was also written for Venice, most were for Milan or Genoa. The primary centre of his activity during the 1670s was Rome, where he cultivated a style of greater contrapuntal density than that of his Venetian contemporaries, such as Giovanni Legrenzi, Carlo Pallavicino and Antonio Sartorio.

Agostini's first two operas, *La regina Floridea* and *Ippolita reina delle amazzoni* of 1670, like many operas for Milan, were collaborative efforts. *La regina Floridea* was restaged four more times in the 17th century, but it is unclear whether any of the later productions used the Milanese music. Agostini may not have been on hand for the production of *Ippolita* in 1670, since Lodovico Busca supplied additional arias to Act 2 and Agostini was responsible for the production of his own *Eliogabalo* in Genoa the same season. In Rome he enjoyed the patronage of Cardinal Flavio Chigi, which is reflected in his setting *Gl'inganni innocenti, ovvero L'Adalinda* for performance by the Accademici Sfaccendati at the Villa Chigi outside Rome in 1673; four years later Cardinal Chigi sponsored another production of it in Siena. In 1679 Agostini accepted the position of *maestro di cappella* to Ranuccio II Farnese, Duke of Parma. The next year he wrote his last opera, *Il ratto delle Sabine*, for the Teatro S Giovanni Grisostomo, Venice, the luxurious theatre opened by the Grimani family two years earlier. The librettist, G. F. Bussani, dedicated the work to Agostini's employer, but *Il ratto delle Sabine* was not well received and, perhaps for this reason, was replaced by a restaging of the theatre's inaugural work, Pallavicino's *Vespasiano*.

Like those of his contemporaries Agostini's arias are short and numerous; for *Il ratto delle Sabine*, for example, he wrote 48. Da capo format predominates, and arias are usually accompanied by continuo alone. He cultivated a rich interplay between voice and instruments, in which the vocal declamation unfolds freely above a conspicuously independent continuo part, often marked by a modulating ostinato or walking bass. The tensions arising between the vocal and instrumental lines, rather than the tunes themselves, are the source of appeal here.

dates are of first performance unless specified as dedication dates

La regina Floridea [Act 3] (dramma musicale, 3, P. Manni), Milan, Ducale, ?1669 [Act 1 by F. Rossi, Act 2 by L. Busca]; as Floridea regina di Cipro, Reggio Emilia, carn. 1677; as Floridea (lib. rev. G. Pancieri), Venice, SS Apostoli, aut. 1687, lib. (Venice, 1687)

Ippolita reina delle amazzoni [Act 2] (3, C. M. Maggi), Milan, Ducale, 1670, *I-Nc* [Act 1 and arias added to Act 2 by Busca, Act 3 by P. A. Ziani]

La costanza di Rosmonda (melodramma, A. Aureli), Genoa, Falcone, 1670

Eliogabalo (dramma musicale, Aureli), Genoa, Falcone, ded. 28 Jan 1670

Gl'inganni innocenti, ovvero L'Adalinda (favola drammatica musicale, 3, G. F. Apolloni), Ariccia, nr Rome, aut. 1673; rev. Bologna, 1675; as Adalinda, Florence, Casino di S Marco, 1679; rev. with orig. title and new arias, Milan, Ducale, ded. 12 Jan 1679, *MOe*

Il ratto delle Sabine (dramma, 3, G. F. Bussani), Venice, S Giovanni Grisostomo, carn. 1680, *Bc*, *Vnm*

*

H. C. Wolff: *Die venezianische Oper in der zweiten Hälfte des 17. Jahrhunderts: ein Beitrag zur Geschichte der Musik und des Theaters im Zeitalter des Barocks* (Berlin, 1937)

H. S. Saunders: *The Repertoire of a Venetian Opera House (1678–1714): the Teatro Grimani di San Giovanni Grisostomo* (diss., Harvard U., 1985)

HARRIS S. SAUNDERS

Agram (Ger.). ZAGREB.

Agreeable Surprise, The [*The Agreeable Surprise, or The Secret Enlarged*]. Comic afterpiece, op.16, in two acts by SAMUEL ARNOLD to a libretto by JOHN O'KEEFFE; London, Little Theatre in the Haymarket, 4 September 1781.

This opera, which played for 200 performances over the rest of the century, chiefly owed its popularity to the novelty of the acting, especially that of John Edwin as Lingo (baritone), the schoolmaster-turned-butler who is continually misquoting Latin tags. The plot is a parable of rustic virtue and innocence set against the deceptions of the town; tuneful strophic airs are appropriate in the representation of comic country characters and Arnold's score has some good examples. Lingo's 'Amo, amas, I love a lass' became famous as a student song.

ROBERT HOSKINS

Agricola [née Molteni], **Benedetta Emilia** (*b* Modena, 1722; *d* Berlin, 1780). Italian soprano, wife of JOHANN FRIEDRICH AGRICOLA. A pupil of Porpora, Hasse and Salimbeni, she made her début in Berlin as prima donna in C. H. Graun's *Cesare e Cleopatra* (1743). The arrival of Giovanna Astrua in 1748 forced her to take second place, and she sang more in oratorio, until her dismissal on her husband's death in 1774. Burney (*Present State of Music in Germany*, 1773) wrote of her, 'she is now near fifty years of age, and yet sings songs of *bravura*, with amazing rapidity ... her compass extends from A in the base, to D in *alt*, and she has a most perfect shake and intonation'.

E. EUGENE HELM

Agricola, Johann Friedrich (*b* Dobitschen, Saxe-Altenburg, 4 Jan 1720; *d* Berlin, 2 Dec 1774). German composer and writer on music. His mother may have been related to Handel. From 1738 to 1741 he studied at the University of Leipzig, and was also a pupil of J. S. Bach. He heard Hasse's operas in Dresden. In 1741 he moved to Berlin, became a pupil of Quantz, made the acquaintance of C. P. E. Bach, C. H. Graun and their contemporaries, and embarked on a musical career of remarkable versatility, notably as a writer. He published pseudonymous pamphlets (1749) on French and Italian taste (taking the part of Italian music), collaborated with C. P. E. Bach on an obituary of J. S. Bach (1754), translated and edited Tosi's singing treatise and corresponded with Padre Martini and the dramatist Lessing. In his contribution to the 1769 and 1771 volumes of Friedrich Nicolai's *Allgemeine deutsche Bibliothek* he displayed his inability to appreciate the significance of Gluck's 'reform' operas.

Agricola's career as a thoroughly italianized composer of opera was fostered and then blighted by the patronage of Frederick the Great. His first intermezzo, *Il filosofo convinto in amore*, was performed with much success at Potsdam in 1750, and Frederick appointed him a court composer in 1751. But in the same year he married Benedetta Emilia Molteni, one of the singers of the Opera, against the king's rule that the singers must remain single. Frederick punished the pair by reducing their joint salary to 1000 thalers, whereas Molteni's single salary had been 1500 thalers. When Graun, Frederick's chief opera composer, died in 1759,

Agricola was appointed musical director of the Opera without the title of Kapellmeister, and his output as a composer in that genre began to decline. Within a few years his operas were little more than pallid imitations of Graun's. His extant dramatic works show him to have been a thoroughly professional craftsman, able to enrich the Italian lyrical-homophonic ideal with contrapuntal touches, but essentially uninspired. In October 1767, after hearing the rehearsals of Agricola's *Amor e Psiche*, Frederick wrote to his attendant Pöllnitz: 'You will tell Agricola that he must change all of Coli's arias – they are worthless – as well as those of Romani, along with the recitatives, which are deplorable from one end to the other'. An effort of 1772 entitled *Oreste e Pilade*, ordered by Frederick as entertainment for a visit by the Queen of Sweden and the Duchess of Brunswick, proved to be so far from what Frederick wanted that the entire opera had to be rewritten and retitled *I greci in Tauride*.

Besides operas, Agricola composed oratorios, sacred cantatas, numerous songs and odes and some keyboard pieces. He was also a distinguished organist and singing master.

Il filosofo convinto in amore (int), Potsdam, 1750, *D-Dlb*
La ricamatrice divenuta dama (int), Berlin, 1 Nov 1751, lost
Cleofide (3, P. Metastasio), Berlin, carn. 1754, *B*
La nobiltà delusa (dg), 1754, ?*ROmi*
Achille in Sciro (os), 16 Sept 1765, *B*
Amor e Psiche (A. Landi), Oct 1767, lost
Il re pastore (?L. Villati), Sept–Oct ?1770, lost
Oreste e Pilade (Landi), early 1772; rev. as I greci in Tauride, Potsdam, March 1772; both lost

*

C. C. Rolle: *Neue Wahrnehmungen zur Aufnahme und weitern Ausbreitung der Musik* (Berlin, 1784)
L. Schneider: *Geschichte der Oper und des königlichen Opernhauses in Berlin* (Berlin, 1852)
H. Wucherpfennig: *J. Fr. Agricola* (diss., U. of Berlin, 1922) [incl. some letters]
E. E. Helm: *Music at the Court of Frederick the Great* (Norman, OK, 1960)

E. EUGENE HELM

Agricola, Johann Paul (*b* Hilpoltstein, nr Nuremberg, 1638–9; *d* Neuburg an der Donau, bur. 3 July 1697). German composer. He was educated at the Jesuit Gymnasium of St Salvator, Augsburg, and in 1660 wrote the music for a play performed there. After studying at the University of Ingolstadt, in 1663 he became a chamber musician and court organist at Neuburg an der Donau to Count Palatine Philipp Wilhelm. When the count's eldest son, Johann Wilhelm, married the Archduchess Maria Anna, sister of the Emperor Leopold I, in 1679, two operas – *Streit der Schönheit und der Tugend* and *Die gesuchte, verlorene, und endlich wiedergefundene Freiheit in der Begebnis zweier sicilianischer Princessinnen Salibene und Rosimene* – and a pastoral by him, and another work, *Freudens-Triumph des Parnassus* (with an equestrian ballet), that was probably by him, were performed (librettos in *D-Mbs*); the music is all lost. On the occasion of the wedding of Princess Maria Sophia Elisabeth and King Pedro II of Portugal, celebrated lavishly in 1687 at Heidelberg with a performance of Sebastiano Moratelli's opera *La gemma Ceraunia*, Agricola received two ornamental goblets and a present of money 'for his many and varied labours over the comedy and other matters'. No music that he may have written on this occasion can be identified. His only surviving works are motets.

F. Walter: *Geschichte des Theaters und der Musik am kurpfälzischen Hof* (Leipzig, 1898)
A. Einstein: 'Italienische Musiker am Hofe der Neuburger Wittelsbacher, 1614–1716', *SIMG*, ix (1907–8), 336–424
C. Sachs: 'Die Ansbacher Hofkapelle unter Markgraf Johann Friedrich (1672–1686)', *SIMG*, xi (1909–10), 105–37
P. Winter: 'Musikpflege am Pfalz-Neuburger Hof (1505–1718)', *Neuburg, die junge Pfalz und ihre Fürsten*, ed. J. Heider (Neuburg, 1955)

LINI HÜBSCH-PFLEGER

Agrippina. *Drama per musica* in three acts by GEORGE FRIDERIC HANDEL to a libretto by VINCENZO GRIMANI; Venice, Teatro S Giovanni Gristostomo, 26 December 1709.

Handel's second and last opera written in Italy, *Agrippina* effectively established his international reputation. According to Mainwaring's *Memoirs of the Life of … Handel* (1760) it was performed 27 times (not an unusual run for the main opera of the Venetian carnival) and was enthusiastically received with cries of 'Viva il caro Sassone!'. The original cast included Margherita Durastanti (a former colleague from Rome) in the title role, Diamante Maria Scarabelli as Poppaea, Antonio Francesco Carli as Claudius, Francesca Vanini as Otho and her husband Giuseppe Maria Boschi as Pallas. Nero and Narcissus were sung by the castratos Valeriano Pellegrini and Giuliano Albertini. Elena Croce (listed as the Agrippina in one MS source) may have replaced Durastanti in some performances. The opera was subjected to revision before performance and possibly during its initial run: there are significant differences between Handel's autograph and the printed wordbook of 1709 and between the autograph and most other MS sources, the latter generally conforming to the wordbook. Arnold's edition of *c*1795, based on an MS in his possession (and now lost), is probably a reasonable reflection of the early performances, though inaccurate over detail. Chrysander's edition is an unfortunate attempt to reconcile the autograph text with Arnold and the wordbook, the result being a composite version of no authority. A new scholarly edition is needed.

Handel did not himself revive *Agrippina* after leaving Italy, but he included two arias in *Rinaldo* (1711, London), and the overture and four vocal numbers (including 'Pensieri' and the popular 'Ho un non so che nel cor', originally written for *La Resurrezione*) appeared in four other operas produced in London during the period 1710–14. There were independent revivals in Naples (1713, with additional music by Mancini), Hamburg (1718 and later, retaining the Italian text) and Vienna (1719 – a pasticcio with music also by Fux and Caldara). The first modern revival was at Halle in 1943; it was given in Leipzig in 1959, at Abingdon in 1963 (its British première) and, among other revivals, in London in 1965, by Kent Opera in 1982, at Venice in 1983 and at Drottningholm in 1985.

The story, set in Rome, is fictional, though it involves historical characters and touches on real events around AD50. The Emperor Claudio [Claudius] (bass) is away in Britain and his death is reported. His wife Agrippina (soprano) uses the opportunity to secure the succession for Nerone [Nero] (soprano), her son by a previous marriage. She obtains help from her henchmen and putative lovers Pallante [Pallas] (bass) and Narciso [Narcissus] (alto), but her plans are upset by the unexpected return of Claudius, announced by his servant Lesbo (bass); his life has been saved by Ottone [Otho] (alto) who has been granted the succession as reward.

Agrippina then takes advantage of Claudius's passion for Poppea [Poppaea] (soprano), also wooed by Otho and Nero, and by various deceits uses her to turn Claudius against Otho. Otho is denounced as a traitor, but he manages to convince Poppaea that he is faithful to her. Agrippina tries to trick Pallas and Narcissus into murdering Otho and each other. To help Otho, Poppaea arranges for her three lovers to come to her house in quick succession, each hiding as the next arrives, and contrives to get Nero exposed to Claudius as an importunate rival. Pallas and Narcissus, joining forces, tell Claudius about Agrippina's double-dealing. Nevertheless Agrippina cunningly convinces her husband that she was acting throughout for his own good. Claudius finally attempts to satisfy everyone by awarding the succession to Otho, and Poppaea to Nero; but Nero protests that it would be double punishment to gain a wife and lose an empire, and so Claudius names Nero as his successor after all and Poppaea is given to Otho. The goddess Giunone [Juno] (alto) descends to bless their marriage.

* * *

Handel to some extent ensured the opera's success by drawing on the best music from works written earlier in Rome and Florence (the opera *Rodrigo*, the oratorio *La resurrezione* and cantatas), as well as making use of some memorable thematic fragments from Reinhard Keiser's *Der verführte Claudius* (1703, Hamburg). The effectiveness of the opera as a whole also owes much to Cardinal Grimani's witty and skilfully worked-out libretto – a typically Venetian anti-heroic comedy, in which all the main characters, apart from Otho, cheerfully and cynically intrigue for their own ends. They are nevertheless redeemed by certain underlying virtues – Agrippina's single-minded ambition is for her son rather than herself – and by the music, which always expresses genuine emotion. Otho is an entirely serious character – his F minor lament in Act 2 ('Voi che udite il mio lamento') is the most tragic moment in the opera – but the dominant role is, rightly, that of Agrippina herself, always confident and occasionally menacing. A sense of triumph is present in her very first aria ('L'alma mia fra le tempeste', based on one of Handel's favourite tunes) and she is at her most formidable in the great scena 'Pensieri, voi mi tormentate' of Act 2, when in desperation she plans a triple murder. ANTHONY HICKS

Agthe, Rosa. *See* MILDE-AGTHE, ROSA VON.

Aguiari [Agujari], **Lucrezia** ['La Bastardina', 'La Bastardella'] (*b* Ferrara, 1743; *d* Parma, 18 May 1783). Italian soprano. Traditions explaining her nickname describe her variously as a foundling raised by Leopoldo Aguiari, his natural daughter or that of Marchese Bentivoglio, while her pronounced limp was supposedly the result of having been partly eaten in infancy by a dog or hog. She studied in Ferrara with Brizio Petrucci and Abbé Lambertini. After her opera début (1764, Florence) and initial successes (Padua and Verona, 1765; Genoa, Lucca and Parma, 1766), she settled in Parma, where she met the composers Mysliveček, with whom she had an affair, and Giuseppe Colla, the new *maestro*; in 1768 the court at Parma appointed her *virtuosa di camera*. She became one of Europe's most sought-after sopranos.

After singing in Paisiello's *Le nozze di Peleo e Tetide* for a royal wedding in Naples (1768) and in Gluck's *Le feste d'Apollo* in Parma (1769), she began her nearly exclusive devotion to the works of Colla, whose pastorale *Licida e Mopsa* she also sang then. Their association took them to Venice for his *Vologeso* (1770) and Genoa for his *L'eroe cinese* (1771). Between 1772 and 1775 she sang in works by Colla in Turin, Parma and Milan. After visits to Paris and London (1775–7) she appeared in Florence and Venice (1778–80) before leaving the stage. By 1780 she and Colla were married. She died of tuberculosis – not, as rumoured, of slow poisoning by jealous rivals.

Aguiari's voice was an object of wonder to her contemporaries, especially her range of three and a half octaves and her facility in executing the most difficult passage-work. 'I could not believe that she was able to reach C sopra acuto' wrote Leopold Mozart on 24 March 1770, 'but my ears convinced me'. In a postscript Wolfgang notated bravura passages she had sung. Burney called her 'a truly wonderful performer. The lower part of her voice was full, round, of an excellent quality and its compass ... beyond any one who had then [been] heard ... Her shake was open and perfect, ... her execution marked and rapid; and her style of singing ... grand and majestic'. According to Fanny Burney, Aguiari's voice had 'a mellowness, a sweetness, that are quite vanquishing ... She has the highest taste, with an expression the most pathetic'. As an actress, Sara Goudar wrote that she 'depicts on the stage any character whatsoever with the greatest realism'.

*

BurneyH; *DBI* (R. Nielsen)
S. Goudar: *Remarques sur la musique et la danse* (Venice, 1773; It. trans., n.d.), 30
F. D'Arblay: *Memoirs of Doctor Burney*, ii (London, 1832), 21ff, 42
Castil-Blaze: *L'opéra italien de 1548 à 1856* (Paris, 1856), 159ff, 209ff, 213
E. Greppi and A. Giulini, eds.: *Carteggio di Pietro e di Alessandro Verri*, vi (Milan, 1923), 83, 183, 185
N. Pelicelli: 'Musicisti in Parma nel sec. XVIII', *NA*, xi (1934), 239–81, esp. 280
E. Anderson, ed.: *The Letters of Mozart and his Family* (London, 1938, 3/1985) KATHLEEN KUZMICK HANSELL

Aguirre Lizaola, Avelino de (*b* Bilbao, 10 Aug 1838; *d* Mendoza, Argentina, 19 July 1901). Spanish composer. He studied in Madrid, Paris, and then Milan, where he was a pupil of Lauro Rossi. He held conducting posts in Bilbao and Madrid before settling in Buenos Aires in 1876, where he conducted at the Teatro de la Opera. He sometimes acted as impresario, and his final appointment was as director of the National Conservatory of Music.

Most of Aguirre's music is lost, including the opera *Gli amanti di Teruel* (first performed at the Teatro Principal in Valencia on 16 December 1865). With an Italian text (by Rosario Zapater) and cast with Italian singers, the opera reflected the domination of Italian opera in Spain at the time. It was favourably received in the press, but comparisons made with Rossini, Bellini and Donizetti suggest it was of no great originality. Aguirre wrote two other operas, *Guzmán el Bueno* and *Covadonga* (1875), and two zarzuelas, *Lo que puede el mate* (1877) and *Nicolasita* (1885).

EMILIO CASARES

Ägyptische Helena, Die ('The Egyptian Helen'). *Oper* in two acts by RICHARD STRAUSS to a libretto by HUGO VON HOFMANNSTHAL; Dresden, Staatsoper, 6 June 1928 (revised version, Salzburg, Festspielhaus, 14 August 1933).

Helena [Helen] of Troy	soprano
Menelas [Menelaus] *her husband*	tenor
Hermione *their daughter* [role omitted in 1933 version]	soprano
Aithra *a sorceress*	soprano
Altair *a nomad chieftain*	baritone
Da-ud *his son*	tenor
The Omniscient Seashell	contralto
Two Servants of Aithra	soprano, mezzo-soprano
Three Elves	two sopranos, contralto

Elfin chorus, warriors, serving-maidens, boys and eunuchs

Setting Aithra's palace on a Mediterranean island, after the Trojan War; then a palm grove below Mount Atlas

After Strauss completed *Die Frau ohne Schatten* in 1917 there was a long hiatus in his operatic partnership with Hofmannsthal. In the early 1920s Hofmannsthal made abortive sketches for a Semiramis libretto (which Strauss had yearned for since *Elektra*) and on the Danae myth (left for Joseph Gregor to realize 17 years later); but among several classical candidates they agreed at last upon Helen. Strauss saw her as a role for Maria Jeritza, their original Ariadne and Empress, who had first entranced him in the title role of Offenbach's *La belle Hélène*. He and Hofmannsthal assured each other that this opera would be buoyant and sparkling in three acts with ballet-interludes, much spoken dialogue and light arioso. But the Helen who fascinated the writer came from a more sophisticated legend, a poetical conjecture by Stesichorus (6th century BC). Seeking to reconcile her unforgivable part in the Trojan War with Homer's report of her serene reunion with her husband, the poet explained that the 'Helen' who absconded with Paris to Troy was a phantom double; the real, faithful Helen had been spirited away by the gods to await post-war collection by Menelaus.

Though Euripides took up that unlikely idea, it would not now bear a literal retelling. Hofmannsthal's twist was to make the story a wilful fraud, with a new angle: there is only the one (guilty) Helen – but by Aithra's sorcery the vengeful Menelaus is made first to believe in the blameless 'original' and then, by reliving his past struggles, to recognize and accept his real wife as she is. For this psychical scenario Hofmannsthal failed to hit upon a plausible operatic form. Strauss soon saw that the lofty effusions of Helen and Menelaus would need full-blooded treatment beyond the original plan, and yet the visible action was mere exotic pantomime; the notion of spoken dialogue was dropped. He alarmed Hofmannsthal by proposing to make young Da-ud a mezzo (like Octavian), where the writer had imagined a romantic baritone like Alfred Jerger; they compromised with a tenor. The score was completed only in October 1927. In 1932, at the producer Lothar Wallenstein's behest, Strauss tried to improve Act 2 by some dramatic reordering and a little recomposing.

Since the Dresden Staatsoper could not afford the glamorous Jeritza, the first Helen – over Hofmannsthal's protests – was Elisabeth Rethberg, a fine soprano but homely. Curt Taucher (and then Max Lorenz) sang Menelaus, Maria Rajdl Aithra and Friedrich Plaschke Altair. The conductor was the ailing Fritz Busch, absent from many rehearsals, and the première went badly. Strauss himself conducted the opera in Vienna five days later, on his 64th birthday, and with Jeritza as Helen it was better received. But the opera has never entered the repertory, not even in the 1933 version; perhaps it awaits bold re-imagining by another producer, in some theatrical form that would make the most of Strauss's expertly fluent score.

ACT 1 *A hall in Aithra's palace, opening upon a terrace and the sea* An introductory scene begins with eight bars of faery skittering, hinting at some main themes, and settling into D minor by curtain-rise (the opera will end in D major). While a maidservant strums a harp, Aithra pines after her absent lover Poseidon ('Das Mahl ist gerichtet'). The mystical Seashell – originally imagined as a large rococo *objet*, with a speaking-horn for the contralto – explains that he is unavoidably detained in Ethiopia. The maid recommends lotus juice, the consoling draught of Forgetfulness. Suddenly the Seashell reports a distant sighting: on a ship at sea a man is about to slay his wife, and they are Menelaus and Helen of Troy. Aithra conjures up a storm which sweeps the foundering ship towards shore, and soon the embattled couple wade to safety. The music falls silent as Menelaus, still with a dagger between his teeth, drags in his recaptured Helen. Espying a mirror, she calmly rearranges her hair (Hofmannsthal conceived her as serene but 'demonic').

Blinking in the palatial lamplight, Menelaus is bent implacably upon murder; Helen is all sweet dignity, confident that he will forgive and forget. She woos him in rich flat keys – a pervasive motif recalls Delilah's 'Mon coeur s'ouvre à ta voix' – and hymns their old, glorious nights together ('Bei jener Nacht'). Menelaus resists bitterly, over disapproving comments from the hidden Aithra, and resolves that their daughter Hermione must never see her disgraced mother again. As the duologue becomes a strenuous C minor duet, both call upon 'Earth and Night, Moon and Sea' for help (with top Cs at the end, but Strauss provided a variant with mere Gs). The lamps fade; with dagger again upraised, Menelaus freezes before Helen's beauty in the moonlight.

The sorceress calls up her Elves to distract him. They draw him away into a spectral battle which mimics the Trojan scene, *scherzando* – there is a mocking 'Paris', and a ghostly 'Helen'; meanwhile, Aithra declares herself Helen's friend.

The maids restore Helen's youthful radiance, and ply her with the Forgetfulness potion. The ladies join hands: 'Women who trust each other are stronger than warriors, richer than kings'. Helen sinks into a happy daze, and while she is put to bed the mock-battle shifts nearer again.

Menelaus staggers in, convinced that he has not only slain Paris for a second time but Helen too. Aithra offers him a sly welcome, a dram of the potion, and then a fantastic alibi. The 'Helen' whom Paris took to Troy – and whom Menelaus has now killed – was a deceptive wraith; ever since her supposed seduction, his own, chaste wife has dwelt with Aithra and her sisters on the slopes of Mount Atlas, and will now be restored to him. He is bewildered.

The finale begins in a suave E major glow (with organ, and ironic laughter from unseen Elves); Helen is revealed asleep. Menelaus's resistance melts away. She wakes, and the intended reunion succeeds (elaborate trio, with Elvish obbligato). Mindful for their future, Aithra prescribes regular doses of the potion, and since

'Die ägyptische Helena' (Richard Strauss), Act 1 (a hall in Aithra's palace): the original production at the Staatsoper, Dresden, 6 June 1928, with Elisabeth Rethberg (Helen, centre), Maria Rajdl (Aithra, left) and Curt Taucher (Menelaus)

Helen fears a premature return to their familiar home she promises them an enchanted interlude where nobody knows their distressful history and it can be forgotten. The Elves jeer softly.

ACT 2 *A pavilion in a palm-grove at the foot of Atlas; dawn* Helen rhapsodizes at length (in B major) over her second wedding night ('Zweite Brautnacht'). As her husband wakes, she seeks a goblet for his next dose of the potion – and lets slip the dagger of Paris, the one with which Menelaus slew him and later threatened Helen. Menelaus refuses to drink, for his doubts are revived: is this newly irresistible 'Helen' only the ultimate illusion?

Desert warriors gallop in (a striking orchestral sketch) led by their chieftain Altair, who holds this land in fief to Aithra and her sisters. All are entranced by Helen, Altair no less than his susceptible son Da-ud, and they bring lavish gifts. Menelaus bridles angrily: in Da-ud he recognizes another Paris. Altair treats this servantless foreign king with civil disdain, and invites him to a hunt. Though Da-ud demands to ride beside Helen (Strauss recycled the music of his rapt protestations for the central *Arabella* duet), eventually only the men go off.

Aithra and her maids come to warn Helen that two similar vials were packed by mistake: one of Forgetfulness, the other of Recollection – which would be fatal. To Aithra's horror, Helen commands the maids to lace the wine with the latter. Whatever the consequences, she cannot bear that Menelaus should take her for anyone other than herself. Altair returns alone to press his suit, virile and overbearing. While Helen gives him a teasing rebuff, the maids watch the distant hunt: pursuing the same gazelle as Da-ud, Menelaus strikes him dead. But Altair, who has sons aplenty, is not deflected from his purpose; a skirling offstage band announces the great feast he has decreed.

To a sombre, poignant march, Da-ud's corpse is borne in by black slaves. Menelaus follows like a sleepwalker. Gently, Helen makes him understand that this wanton murder was another echo of his vengeance upon Paris. He admits that he was reaching out to his lost wife, not to the comforting 'Helen'-twin of the moment. As Altair's feast begins, Menelaus takes gratefully – like Tristan – the brew she offers him, expecting it to be lethal; instead, he finds himself recollecting and embracing his whole, unique Helen. (For his climactic profession the music attains Strauss's beloved D♭ major, and stays there for a grand trio with Aithra.) Altair and his men rise in menace, but Aithra calls up Poseidon's forces to forestall them. Like a young goddess Hermione steps forth: 'Father, where is my beautiful mother?' Pausing only for a unison duet in full cry, her parents gallop off with her on horseback towards home.

* * *

Though the visible story of *Helena* is arbitrary and silly, Strauss's score is loyally inventive. The 'thematic transformations' are endless, the orchestral pictures fresh, the pace well varied. If the musical tagging of every dramatic element sounds like period routine, the opera has a saving lyrical grace: more relaxed and fluid than either his preceding Hofmannsthal opera, *Die Frau ohne Schatten*, or the more recent *Intermezzo* to his own text. The original operetta-style intention survives in the undisguised 'numbers', the frank reprises towards the end, and the unusually limpid musical texture (despite the assiduous working of themes). The trouble is with the principal roles. Since Helen, unlike the Empress or Arabella, actually *does* next to nothing, she needs all the wiles of a seductive diva to make her a real character, and so does the all-too-mysterious Aithra. Poor Menelaus, a constant dupe, can only bawl aloud, alternating baffled rage with baffled rapture – a thankless task. When the old Strauss regretted never having learnt to write for tenor, it must have been Menelaus he regretted most, not Bacchus or the Emperor. It is still debatable whether the fault lay in Hofmannsthal's dramaturgy or in Strauss's failure to capture its suave ironies.

DAVID MURRAY

Ahlefeldt, Countess **Maria Theresia** (*b* Regensburg, 28 Feb 1755; *d* Prague, 4 Nov 1823). German composer. The daughter of Prince Alexander Ferdinand of Thurn und Taxis, she married the Danish diplomat Count Ferdinand Ahlefeldt in 1780 and until 1791 lived at the court of the last Margrave of Ansbach, Karl Alexander, where she was active in musical and literary spheres; she was highly thought of as a pianist. After the dissolution of the court, she moved to Denmark with her husband, who was superintendent of the royal theatre in Copenhagen, 1792–4. There, as in Ansbach, she came to public notice as a composer, having particular success with the four-act opera-ballet *Telemak på Calypsos Øe* (Copenhagen, Royal, 28 Dec 1792; vs, Copenhagen, 1794; score, 1805, *DK-Kk*), for which she composed orchestral numbers throughout and vocal numbers in Act 2. Based on a libretto by Vincenzo Galeotti, the renowned Italian ballet-master, it ran for 37 performances until 1813 in Copenhagen alone. The work is rooted in the period of *galanterie* and sensibility, but owes something to operetta and in places shows expressive qualities and a Classical shape reminiscent of Gluck; her natural wealth of feeling, however, exceeded her technical abilities. She also wrote the libretto and possibly the music for the two-act comic opera *La folie, ou Quel conte!* (music lost, lib. in E. Craven: *Nouveau théâtre*, ed. E. Asimont, i, Ansbach, 1789).

*

G. Schilling: *Encyclopädie der gesammten musikalischen Wissenschaften oder Universal-Lexikon der Tonkunst* (Stuttgart, 1835–42)

DIETER HÄRTWIG

Ahlersmeyer, Matthieu (*b* Cologne, 29 June 1896; *d* Garmisch-Partenkirchen, 23 July 1979). German baritone. He studied with Karl Niemann in Cologne and made his début at Mönchengladbach in 1929 as Wolfram. He sang at the Kroll Opera, Berlin (1930–31), at the Hamburg Staatsoper (1931–3 and 1946–61), and at the Dresden Staatsoper (1934–44), where he created the Barber in *Die schweigsame Frau*. In 1938 he created the title role in Egk's *Peer Gynt* at the Berlin Staatsoper. He appeared at Covent Garden in 1936 with the Dresden Staatsoper as Don Giovanni and Count Almaviva, and at the Edinburgh Festival with the Hamburg Opera in 1952 as Hindemith's Mathis. In 1947 he shared the title role in *Dantons Tod* with Paul Schöffler at the Salzburg Festival, and in 1963 he created Count Almaviva in Klebe's *Figaro lässt sich scheiden* at Hamburg. He retired in 1973. HAROLD ROSENTHAL/R

Ahlstrom, David (*b* Lancaster, NY, 22 Feb 1927). American composer. He studied at the Cincinnati Conservatory of Music, the Eastman School and the California Institute of Asian Studies. His principal teachers were Alan Hovhaness, Henry Cowell and Bernard Rogers. He taught at Northwestern University (1961–2), Southern Methodist University (1962–7) and Eastern Illinois University (1967–76) before moving to San Francisco as a freelance composer and writer. In 1982 he founded VOICES/SF, Bay Area Youth Opera, an ensemble specializing in new American musical theatre. Ahlstrom's one-act chamber opera *Three Sisters who are not Sisters*, to a libretto by Gertrude Stein, was first performed on 1 March 1953 at the Cincinnati Conservatory. Two years later he set another Stein text, *Doctor Faustus Lights the Lights*; it was first performed by VOICES/SF on 29 October 1982. Both works recall the Thomson–Stein operas in their mixture of straightforward tonality and sophisticated prosody. Ahlstrom's small-scale orchestrations call for a wide variety of percussion and keyboard instruments; *Doctor Faustus* contains an optional electronic dance sequence. His musical comedy *America, I love, You*, to poems by E. E. Cummings, was first heard in New Orleans on 6 January 1981. Ahlstrom has also written numerous children's operas and 'mini-operas' intended for both children and adults, in which the influence of Carl Orff is apparent. HARRY HASKELL

Åhlström, Olof (*b* Åletorp, Värdinge, 14 Aug 1756; *d* Stockholm, 11 Aug 1835). Swedish composer. After early musical education with a local organist, he moved in 1772 to Stockholm, where he was instructed in composition by Ferdinand Zellbell the younger. In 1777 he was appointed organist at the Marian church and in 1786 at the Jakobskyrka. Though he made his livelihood mainly in government posts, he was active as a music publisher from 1787 to 1823, under royal privilege; in the journals he founded, *Musikaliskt tidsfördrif* ('Musical Pastimes') and *Skaldestycken satte i musik* ('Poetry Set to Music') he often published his own piano reductions of portions of the most popular operas in Stockholm during the period. His own operatic works, beginning with the nationalist comedy *Frigga* (1787; for illustration *see* DESPREZ, LOUIS-JEAN), demonstrate a good sense of lyrical line coupled with influences from the *opéras comiques* of Grétry and Dalayrac. His orchestration is often fairly dense, and sometimes rich in texture.

all first performed and published in Stockholm

Frigga (Spl, 1, C. G. Leopold), Royal Opera, 31 May 1787, *SF-A*

Den bedragne Bachan [The Deceived Bacchus] (Spl, 1, Gustavus III), Bollhuset, 29 April 1789, *S-Skma*

Tanddoctoren [The Dentist] (comedy with song, 3, C. G. Nordfoss), Royal Opera, 16 May 1800, *Skma, St*

De begge Crisperne, eller Tvillingsbröderne [The Two Crispins, or The Twin Brothers] (oc, 1, Lemière), Royal Opera, 17 Aug 1801, *Skma*

Arias in Eremiten, 1798, *Skma*

*

F. Dahlgren: *Anteckningar om Stockholms teatrar* (Stockholm, 1866)

A. Afzelius: *Tonsättaren Olof Åhlströms minne* (Stockholm, 1867)

BERTIL H. VAN BOER

Ahna, Pauline de. *See* DE AHNA, PAULINE.

Ahnsjö, Claes Håkan (*b* Stockholm, 1 Aug 1942). Swedish tenor. He studied at the Stockholm Opera School with Erik Saedén, Aksel Schiøtz and Max Lorenz. From 1969 he has appeared at the Royal Opera, Stockholm, notably in works by Mozart and Rossini (début as Tamino). At Drottningholm he has sung in many revivals of Baroque operas. He left Stockholm in 1973 and has since been engaged at the Staatsoper in Munich, where he sang in *Lulu*, *Mathis der Maler* and the premières of Sutermeister's *Le roi Bérenger* (1985) and Penderecki's *Ubu Rex* (1991). Haydn's *Orlando Paladino*, *La vera costanza* and *L'infedeltà delusa* are among his recordings. DAVID CUMMINGS

Aiblinger, Johann Kaspar (*b* Wasserburg, Bavaria, 23 Feb 1779; *d* Munich, 6 May 1867). German composer. He studied at the Benedictine Abbey at Tegernsee and the Gymnasium in Munich, also having lessons in composition from Joseph Schlett. He went to Italy as a pupil of Simon Mayr, studying in Vicenza (1804–11), Venice and Milan. In 1819 he returned to Munich, where he became Kapellmeister of the Italian Opera. In 1823 he was appointed assistant conductor at the Hof- und Nationaltheater, and became court Kapellmeister there in 1826.

Aiblinger's talents were best displayed in his numerous sacred works. He was less well equipped for dramatic music, and his two-act opera *Rodrigo und Chimene* (1821, Munich), on a text by J. Sendtner after Pierre Corneille's *Le Cid*, is flawed by its libretto and lack of stylistic unity (a medley of Italian and French operatic conventions). Aiblinger also wrote an earlier opera, *La burla fortunata, ossia I due prigionieri* (1811, Venice), and several arias for operas by other composers.

*

P. Hötzl: *Zum Gedächtnis Aiblingers* (Munich, 1867)

SIEGFRIED GMEINWIESER

Aida. Opera in four acts by GIUSEPPE VERDI to a libretto by ANTONIO GHISLANZONI after a scenario by Auguste Mariette; Cairo, Opera House, 24 December 1871.

The King of Egypt	bass
Amneris *his daughter*	mezzo-soprano
Aida *an Ethiopian slave*	soprano
Radames *Captain of the Guards*	tenor
Ramfis *Chief Priest*	bass
Amonasro *King of Ethiopia, Aida's father*	baritone
The High Priestess	soprano
A Messenger	tenor

Priests, priestesses, ministers, captains, soldiers, functionaries, Ethiopian slaves and prisoners, Egyptian populace, etc.

Setting Memphis and Thebes, during the reign of the Pharaohs

During the late 1860s the search for suitable librettos began to cause Verdi increasing problems. One of his most active helpers was the French librettist and impresario CAMILLE DU LOCLE, with whom Verdi had collaborated in the making of *Don Carlos.* Du Locle sent Verdi a stream of possible subjects covering a wide variety of genres: from comic plots that might have continued the manner of *Un ballo in maschera* to large-scale topics suitable for conversion into grand opera. But Verdi became more and more difficult to please, finding the comic subjects structurally or temperamentally unsuitable, while often complaining of the 'patchwork' quality of grand opera, its inherent lack of coherence. The breakthrough came in the early months of 1870, when Du Locle sent Verdi a scenario by the archaeologist and Egyptologist Auguste Mariette, based on an invented story set in Egyptian antiquity. Verdi had the previous year refused to supply an inaugural hymn as part of the celebrations to open the Suez Canal; but he accepted this new Egyptian idea – which was to open the new Cairo Opera House – almost immediately, appointing as librettist Antonio Ghislanzoni, his collaborator in the revised *La forza del destino.* Work on the opera, whose scenario was adapted and enlarged by both Du Locle and Verdi, proceeded through 1870, Verdi as usual taking a considerable hand in the libretto's formation, even in minor details of line length and wording.

As the composer decided not to attend the Cairo première, he proceeded to complete the orchestration of his score in Italy; but by that stage it was clear that production of the opera would be delayed by the Franco-Prussian war, the siege of Paris having trapped the sets and costumes in the French capital. There were in addition a series of intense struggles over the première cast, in which as usual Verdi took a close interest. Eventually *Aida* was first performed in Cairo – with predictable success – in late 1871, directed by the famous double bass player Giovanni Bottesini, with a cast including Eleonora Grossi (Amneris), Antonietta Anastasi-Pozzoni (Aida), Pietro Mongini (Radames) and Francesco Steller (Amonasro). Verdi also devoted great attention to the Italian première at La Scala, making various slight changes to the score and minutely rehearsing a carefully chosen group of principals. This second performance, conducted by Franco Faccio, took place on 8 February 1872, and included Maria Waldmann (Amneris), Teresa Stolz (Aida), Giuseppe Fancelli (Radames) and Francesco Pandolfini (Amonasro). It was again hugely successful with the public, although some critics voiced reservations about passages they found conventional or old-fashioned. Verdi was reluctant to allow further performances in Italy without assurances of a sensitive staging, but by the mid-1870s the opera had entered the general repertory, where it has remained to the present day. Some time before the Milanese première, Verdi wrote a full-scale overture; but after hearing it rehearsed he decided to withdraw it and reinstate the prelude.

The prelude juxtaposes and combines two themes: the first, chromatic and presented on high strings, will be associated with Aida throughout the opera; the second, scalar idea, contrapuntally developed, will be associated with the priests.

ACT 1.i *A hall in the King's palace in Memphis* To the accompaniment of a restrained development of motifs from the prelude, Ramfis and Radames are in conversation: Ramfis advises that the Ethiopian enemy is again on the attack, and that Isis has named the commander of the Egyptian troops. As Ramfis departs, Radames eagerly anticipates becoming that leader, and then muses on his beloved Aida in the *romanza* 'Celeste Aida', a ternary-form piece shot through with atmospheric instrumental effects. Radames is then joined by Amneris, who loves the young warrior, but whose sinuous string melody underlines her suspicions about the direction of his affections. Their agitated duet, 'Quale inchiesta!', is interrupted by the appearance of Aida (and her characteristic theme), and Radames's longing glances confirm Amneris's jealousy. The duet turns into a trio as Amneris relentlessly questions the confused lovers.

A series of fanfares heralds the King of Egypt, Ramfis and a large group of followers. A messenger announces that Amonasro, King of the Ethiopians, is leading an army against them; the King of Egypt reveals that Isis has named Radames as their commander. All join in the martial hymn, 'Su! del Nilo', Aida's syncopated line underlining her distress at the forthcoming battle. After a final unison cry of 'Ritorna vincitor!' ('Return victor!'), the crowd disperses, leaving Aida alone. Her long, multi-sectioned arioso, which begins with an anguished verbal echo of the chorus's 'Ritorna vincitor!', explores in depth her predicament: Amonasro is her father, but the victory of her family would see the defeat of her beloved Radames. The soliloquy ends with a delicate but intense prayer, 'Numi, pietà', in which she begs the gods to have pity on her suffering.

1.ii *Inside the temple of Vulcan in Memphis* The scene is an old-fashioned tableau, so beloved of French grand opera. An opening chorus, 'Possente Fthà', has many gestures to local colour, notably in its use of the melodic diminished 3rd. There follows a priestesses' dance during which Radames is conducted to the altar. In solemn tones, Ramfis bids Radames protect the homeland, and then leads off the concertato 'Nume, custode e vindice', which gradually gains in power, mingles with the opening strains of the scene, and culminates in a triumphant cry of 'Immenso Fthà!' (For Verdi's annotated libretto, *see* VERDI, GIUSEPPE, fig.4.)

ACT 2.i *A room in Amneris's apartments* A chorus of female slaves, singing of Radames's recent victories, is followed by a dance of Moorish slaves, Amneris punctuating the choral song with a languorous appeal for her warrior to return. Aida is seen approaching and Amneris dismisses her slaves, to begin one of the great confrontational duets of Verdi's later operas, a number that has echoes of the traditional four-movement form though with equally significant divergences. First comes a succession of contrasting episodes, 'Fu la sorte dell'armi', in which Amneris, with her characteristic sinuous chromaticism, attempts to trap Aida into admitting her love for Radames. Aida's confusion crystallizes into an anguished statement of her identifying theme, but Amneris continues the interrogation by announcing Radames's death, and then by contradicting the news. The intensity of Aida's reactions leaves no doubt of her feelings and, in an *adagio* second movement, 'Pietà ti prenda del mio dolore', she begs in vain for Amneris to show mercy. They are interrupted by fanfares, and an offstage chorus singing the Act 1 'Su! del Nilo' (Verdi revised this final section after the first performance in Cairo). Over the choral musical background, Amneris and Aida sing a cabaletta substitute, 'Alla pompa che s'appresta', Amneris's line matching the martial atmosphere of the chorus, Aida's minor-mode answer – with syncopated accompaniment – in sharp contrast. Amneris storms out, to leave Aida alone for a last, desperate reprise of 'Numi, pietà'.

2.ii *One of the city gates of Thebes* The grand concertato finale – one of Verdi's most spacious – begins with a chorus, 'Gloria all' Egitto', which features interludes for a female group and for the priests, who have a version of their characteristic contrapuntal theme. The stage gradually fills to strains of the famous march for 'Egyptian' trumpets; then comes a ballet sequence, full of harmonic and instrumental local colour; then a reprise of 'Gloria all'Egitto' during which the victorious Radames finally appears. Amneris places a laurel wreath on Radames's head, and the King grants him any wish he may desire. Radames asks that the prisoners be brought forth and Aida sees among them Amonasro. She inadvertently reveals to all that he is her father, but Amonasro quickly stops her from disclosing his identity. The Ethiopian king now takes centre stage to lead off the central Andante, which begins with his account of the battle and then shades into the main lyrical passage, a prayer for clemency, 'Ma tu, Re, tu signore possente'. The prayer is taken up by Aida and the prisoners, is sharply rejected by the priests (who demand death for the defeated), and develops into a broad and lengthy tutti. The set piece over, Radames asks the Egyptian king for clemency to be shown to the prisoners; Ramfis objects, but Radames carries the day. In a final gesture the king gives him a last reward: Amneris's hand in marriage. The scene concludes with a reprise of 'Gloria all'Egitto', varied and expanded to allow the principals to express their reactions to the new situation.

ACT 3 *The banks of the Nile* A single note, G, is sustained by a complex blend of orchestral sonorities to invoke moonlight on the banks of the Nile. An offstage chorus adds to the effect by chanting a hymn to Isis, 'O tu che sei d'Osiride'. Amneris and Ramfis disembark from a boat and enter the temple to pray on the eve of Amneris's marriage. Aida's theme emerges as she cautiously enters for a clandestine meeting with Radames. In a *romanza* that Verdi added to the opera only at the last minute, 'Oh, patria mia', she invokes her long-lost homeland, the restless accompaniment and harmonies combining with a formal layout of remarkable freedom, even for the later Verdi.

The ensuing duet with Amonasro is best seen as the first half of a conventional four-movement structure. After a brief scena in which Amonasro shows that he knows of her love for Radames, the first movement, 'Rivedrai le foreste imbalsamate', is the usual juxtaposition of contrasting lyrical sections: Amonasro invokes their beautiful homeland and reminds Aida of the cruelty of their enemies, but when she refuses to ask Radames about the route his troops will take, and so help the Ethiopians ambush the Egyptians, he angrily reproaches her in 'Su, dunque, sorgete'. Aida is by now broken down, and in the *andante* second movement, 'Padre! ... a costoro', painfully accepts her duty to the homeland: her fragmented line is 'healed' by Amonasro, and finally flowers into a lyrical acceptance of her fate. As Amonasro hides, Radames appears and a second, more conventional four-movement duet ensues. In a hectic first movement, Radames assures Aida of his love but warns that he must again lead his troops in battle. The *andantino* second movement, 'Fuggiam gli ardori inospiti', sees Aida recall the musical idiom of 'Oh, patria mia' in an effort to persuade Radames to run away with her. A brief transition movement, in which Aida accuses the still-reluctant Radames of not loving her, leads to the duet cabaletta, 'Sì: fuggiam da queste mura', in which Radames emphatically agrees to join her in flight. The cabaletta ceases abruptly before its final cadences as Aida asks Radames of the route his army will take. As soon as Radames discloses the information, Amonasro emerges from the shadows, triumphantly announcing that his troops will be there to meet the Egyptians. In a closing terzetto, 'Tu! ... Amonasro!', Radames rails at his lost honour. Aida and Amonasro try to comfort him, but they delay too long: Amneris and Ramfis discover them; Amonasro tries to kill Amneris but is prevented by Radames; and, as father and daughter rush off, Radames gives himself up to justice at the hands of the priests.

ACT 4.i *A hall in the King's palace* After an orchestral prelude based on the main theme of the terzetto in Act 1 scene i, Amneris sings an extended arioso in which she determines to save Radames. He is led on by the guards, and yet another multi-section duet ensues. In the first movement, 'Già i sacerdoti adunansi', there is a patterned alternation of declamatory periods

'Aida' (Verdi), Act 4 scene ii (the temple of Vulcan, with a vault below): engraving after Philippe Chaperon's design for the production at the Paris Opéra (Salle Garnier), 22 March 1880

as Amneris begs Radames to defend himself and Radames refuses, having lost all interest in life. The central lyrical movement, 'Ah! tu dei vivere', allows Amneris to declare her love, but Radames still wishes only for death. The main melody of the opening movement returns in the third as Amneris reveals that Aida, whom Radames believed dead along with Amonasro, is still alive. This revelation eventually precipitates a brief cabaletta, 'Chi ti salva', in which Amneris explodes with renewed jealousy and Radames rejoices that he can now die to protect his beloved.

Radames is led back to the dungeon, and a restrained version of the priests' theme, punctuated by anguished cries from Amneris, sounds as the priests and Ramfis follow him in. They chant a solemn prayer, 'Spirto del Nume', before beginning Radames's trial. Radames is accused by Ramfis three times: each time he refuses to answer, the priests brand him traitor ('Traditor!') and Amneris begs the gods for mercy. The priests then pronounce the horrible sentence: he will be entombed alive below the altar of the god he has outraged. In an unrestrained arioso, Amneris begs for mercy; but the priests are inflexible. As they depart, she is left to hurl after them a bitter curse, 'Empia razza! Anatema su voi!'

4.ii *The scene is on two levels: the upper represents the interior of the temple of Vulcan, gleaming with gold and light; the lower is a vault* Priests close the stone over Radames's head as he sings his opening recitative, full of thoughts of Aida. But he hears a groan and quickly finds his beloved: she has stolen into the vault to die in his arms. Their duet has none of the usual contrasting movements, but is rather a sustained piece of delicate lyricism with three main ideas. First comes Radames's 'Morir! sì pura e bella!', in which he laments her death; Aida counters with 'Vedi? ... di morte l'angelo', whose scoring and vocal style suggest that the heroine is already speeding to a celestial haven. And finally, with the background addition of chanting from above, comes the most substantial lyrical idea, 'O terra addio', whose extreme simplicity of formal outline is matched, perhaps permitted, by the unusually angular melodic arch. In the final moments, with the lovers singing 'O terra addio' in unison, Amneris kneels above the vault and implores peace for the soul that lies beneath.

* * *

Although *Aida* is still one of Verdi's most popular operas, its reputation has perhaps declined slightly of late, overtaken for the first time by works such as *Don Carlos* and *Simon Boccanegra*. The reasons for this reverse are doubtless complex, but the comparative conservatism of *Aida* must surely have played a part. If any rough division of Verdi's mature output were made according to 'experimental' versus 'conservative' works (with, say, *Rigoletto*, *La traviata* and *La forza del destino* in the first category, and *Il trovatore* and *Un ballo in maschera* in the second), then *Aida* would undoubtedly figure with the latter group. In formal terms it concentrates on the conventional set pieces of grand opera: the grand ceremonial scene and – most of all – the large-scale multi-sectional duet, of which there are several. True, there is a considerable array of variants within the recurring duet scheme, but both contemporary critics and more recent commentators have nevertheless seen certain elements of these formal structures as uncomfortable throwbacks to an earlier aesthetic. The level of musical characterization is also indicative of this conservative stance. In common with the characters of *Trovatore* and *Ballo*, the principal roles in *Aida* – with the partial exception of Amneris – hardly develop during the opera, tending to remain within their conventional vocal personalities as the plot moves their emotions hither and thither.

But to regard the restricted focus of *Aida* purely in these terms is to take a one-sided view of Verdi's capacities as a musical dramatist, and to lend an unfair aesthetic privilege to the radical aspect of his personality. Indeed, *Aida*'s greatest artistic successes are born of this 'conservatism': in magnificently controlled ceremonial scenes such as Act 2 scene ii – in which a kind of flexible variation technique allows episodes such as the opening chorus to reappear as the culmination of the scene; or in the telling effects gained when various multi-movement duets dovetail into each other, as in the sequence that closes Act 3.

There is, moreover, one important aspect in which *Aida* remains the most radical and 'modern' of Verdi's scores: its use of local colour. *Aida*, constantly alluding to its ambience in harmony and instrumentation, is the one Verdi opera that could not conceivably be transported to another geographical location. In this respect it was an important indication of the influence local colour would come to have over *fin-de-siècle* opera, and an object lesson on the delicacy and control with which this colour could be applied to the standard forms and expressive conventions of Italian opera.

For an illustration of Act 2 scene ii, *see* GRAND OPÉRA, fig.5.

ROGER PARKER

Aiglon, L' ('The Young Eagle'). *Drame musical* in five acts by ARTHUR HONEGGER and JACQUES IBERT to a libretto by HENRI CAIN after Edmond Rostand's play; Monte Carlo, Opéra, 10 March 1937.

It was the first of two stage works by Honegger and Ibert (the other being an operetta, *Les petites Cardinal*). Apparently after each composer had separately refused involvement in *L'aiglon*, they were brought together through the breakdown of a car and agreed to collaborate, Honegger contributing the central three acts. Its potentially serious subject – a war where the Duc de Reichstadt, Napoleon's son (nicknamed 'L'aiglon'; soprano), is torn between his Austrian roots and his French allegiances – is treated lightly. Military strategies are planned with toy soldiers, and Act 3 is a ball which introduces characters from the *commedia dell'arte*. Ibert's pastiches of waltzes and of 18th-century music are here given full rein and both composers seem to have fulfilled the commission (from the impresario Raoul Gunsbourg) for 'music easily accessible to the public'. RICHARD LANGHAM SMITH

Aimon, Pamphile-Léopold-François (*b* L'Isle-sur-Sorgue, 4 Oct 1779; *d* Paris, 2 Feb 1866). French composer, son of the composer and cellist Esprit Aimon (1754–1828). A pupil of his father, he was initially director of the orchestra at the theatre in Marseilles and from 1817 worked in Paris, where he was director at the Théâtre Français from 1822. His works include instrumental music and eight operas, three of which remained unperformed.

Les jeux floraux (opéra, 3, J. N. Bouilly), Paris, Opéra, 16 Nov 1818 (Paris, 1818)
La fée Urgèle (oc, 1, C. S. Favart), Paris, Gymnase, 6 Jan 1821
Les sybarites, ou Les franc-maçons de Florence (drame lyrique, 3, J. Lafitte), Paris, Nouveautés, Nov 1831 (Paris, 1831), collab. Castil-Blaze and others
Abufar, 1820 (opéra, 3, Laverpillière and S. de Montferrier), Marseilles, 1852
Velleda (opéra, 5, M. de Jouy), Paris, 1824

Unperf.: Alcide et Omphale; Les cherusques; Les deux Figaros

*

DEUMM; *StiegerO*

Air (Fr.: 'song'). A term used in French vocal music from the late 16th century, an approximate counterpart to the Italian ARIA, for a solo or ensemble song, often qualified to indicate the style (e.g. *air tendre* for a sentimental text and *air à boire* for a lighthearted drinking song); by extension, an *air* in opera is a self-contained piece, either vocal or instrumental.

In the late 17th century and the early 18th, tables of contents of published opera scores by Lully and his successors sometimes used *air* in the most general sense: under *airs à chanter* are listed not only solos (including important *récitatifs*) but also duets, terzets, other ensembles and choruses, whereas the category *airs à jouer* embraces overtures, dances, entr'actes and other instrumental music. By the mid-18th century Rousseau excluded *récitatif* from the vocal *air* category and noted that shorter solo *airs* were most often in binary form and longer ones in ternary. Here he was thinking of the distinction in operas by Rameau and his contemporaries between the more declamatory *airs* in the French tradition and the virtuoso italianate pieces often called *ariettes*. (Other solo vocal pieces in opera were called *couplets*, strophic songs; *romances*, songs in a tender and melancholic vein, also strophic; and *cavatines*, short, through-composed songs.)

Although Rousseau continued to include within the category of *air* music for more than one voice, in practice the term came increasingly to be restricted to solo pieces during the second half of the 18th century. For dances the general term preferred was *air de ballet* or *air de danse*, or, like the overtures, marches and so on, they received more specific designations as to type. Later in the century composers experimented with forms for major vocal *airs*; the da capo *air*, for example, was virtually replaced by sonata-ternary procedures (as in the operas of Gluck and Piccinni). Outside opera, in solo instrumental pieces, the term *air* was replaced by sonata, fantasia, etc., except for variation sets (known as 'air et variations'). By the Romantic period *pas* became as frequent as *air de danse*. For vocal *airs*, as well as forms continuing French traditions (such as *romances*), composers of *grands opéras* and *opéras comiques* also borrowed the cavatina-cabaletta form from the Italian and, particularly in *grand opéra*, *airs* were often a part of larger ensembles of scene complexes. *Air* continues to be the preferred designation for lyric pieces in the late 19th century and the 20th century, although the musical fluidity of some scores makes the lines of demarcation not always clear.

*

J.-J. Rousseau: 'Air', 'Cavatine', 'Couplet', 'Romance', 'Rondeau', *Dictionnaire de musique* (Paris, 1768)
J.-B. A. Suard: 'Air', *Encyclopédie méthodique: Musique*, ed. N. Framery, P. L. Ginguené, and [vol. 2] J.-J. de Momigny (Paris, 1791–1818)
Castil-Blaze [F. H. J. Blaze]: 'Air', *Dictionnaire de musique moderne* (Paris, 1821, 2/1825)

M. ELIZABETH C. BARTLET

Aitken, Hugh (*b* New York, 7 Sept 1924). American composer. He studied at the Juilliard School (where he later taught) with Persichetti, Bernard Wagenaar and Robert Ward. In 1970 he was appointed chairman of the music department at William Paterson College in Wayne, New Jersey, where he became professor of music in 1973.

Aitken has written two operas, *Fables* (chamber op, 2, after La Fontaine; Wayne, NJ, William Paterson College, 23 Oct 1975) and *Felipe* (1980; 3, L. Tapia, after M. de Cervantes: *El viejo celoso*; unperf.). The first is based on ten of Aesop's fables as retold by the 17th-century French poet La Fontaine. Translated and expanded by the composer, these tales explore issues of manners and morals and questions such as selfishness versus altruism and the nature of morality. The 30 roles are shared between four singers, and the episodic nature of the work is held together by a framing device in which the singers portray a band of travelling players. The composer characterizes the mainly tonal music as 'eclectic', employing various musical styles resulting in 'affectionate parody'. Musical quotations, largely from Rameau, appear with ironic effect at certain moments in the plot. Rhythmic intricacy is evident throughout a score that is governed by subtlety of metre changes and nuance.

Felipe, set in 16th-century Seville, focusses on the unforeseen and serious consequences of a lighthearted attempt at seduction. The music is freely tonal, melodic, and rhythmically and metrically sophisticated. The use of Spanish Renaissance tunes, along with some Spanish text and guitar-like accompaniments, gives the opera its regional and cultural flavour.

M. Redmond: 'Music in New Jersey: Fabulous *Fables*', *The Star-Ledger* (25 Oct 1975)

D. Rollman: 'The Illusive Simplicity of *Fables*', *MUSE* (Aug 1976)

R. H. Kornick: *Recent American Opera: a Production Guide* (New York, 1991), 12–14

JAMES P. CASSARO

Aix-en-Provence. Town in southern France, ancient capital of Provence. From the 13th century to the 18th, music flourished chiefly at St Sauveur and in court circles. The town was too small to support an opera company and was dependent on Marseilles, Avignon and even Nice. It had visits from travelling troupes, and in particular from Gautier's Marseilles troupe in 1695 and 1696. In the 18th century the town built an opera house, the Théâtre Municipal, where Mme de Saint-Huberty performed regularly. The annual festival, now the most famous in France, was founded in 1948 by André Bigonnet and Gabriel Dussurget and takes place in July and early August. With Dussurget as artistic director for over 20 years and Hans Rosbaud as chief conductor for the first ten years, it rapidly became the French equivalent of Glyndebourne or Salzburg. Most performances take place in the theatre specially constructed each year in the courtyard of the archbishop's palace. This theatre, designed by Casandre in 1949, was modified in 1974–5 and in 1984–5, and enlarged to a capacity of 1640. Because plans for the building of a new theatre have never been implemented, some performances have been given at other locations: in the town, at Place des Quatre Dauphins, the courtyard of the Gendarmerie, and even at the little, rarely used Théâtre Municipal; outside the town, in the natural décor of Les Baux-de-Provence (where *Mireille* was given in 1954), in the park of the Château de Tholonet (*Carmen*, 1957), and at the Roman arena of Arles (*Elisabetta, regina d'Inghilterra* with Caballé, 1975, and *Medée* with Rysanek, 1976). None of these secondary theatres has proved really satisfactory or lasting for the purposes of the festival.

From the beginning, when the festival was inaugurated with *Così*, that opera, *Figaro* and *Don Giovanni* have been the pillars of the repertory, with *Zauberflöte* added in 1958. Gradually the repertory was extended to include the works of Haydn (the first performance in France of *Il mondo della luna* in 1959), Monteverdi, Gluck, Cimarosa, Grétry, Rossini (both comic and serious operas), Handel, Campra (born in Aix), Rameau (with the first ever stage performance of *Les Boréades*, 1982) and even Strauss (*Ariadne auf Naxos* with Jessye Norman, 1963) and Verdi (*Falstaff*, 1964; *Luisa Miller*, 1974; *Traviata*, 1976). Works by Menotti, Britten, Sauguet, Poulenc, Milhaud (also born in Aix) and Stravinsky have been performed, and there have also been commissions – Henri Barraud's *Lavinia* (1961), Jacques Charpentier's *Beatris* (1971) and Claude Prey's *Le rouge et le noir* (1989). Dussurget's talent-spotting was exceptional. Berganza and Massard made their first appearances at Aix as unknown singers, with Stich-Randall, Sciutti, Berbié, Eda-Pierre, Capecchi, Simoneau, Arie, Alva, Wunderlich and others singing at the earliest stages of their careers. Such success could not be sustained and gradually the lack of renewal made itself felt. Bernard Lefort succeeded to the artistic direction (1973–80), and by calling on established stars – Caballé, Horne, Bumbry, Rysanek, Carreras – and imaginative new directors – Lavelli, Auvray, Lehnhoff – as well as adding a massive stiffening of British artists, singers, conductors and orchestras, again raised the level of the festival. Since 1981 it has been under the direction of Louis Erlo, also director of the Lyons Opéra. Of the five annual productions, one is usually a co-production with Lyons (in 1989, *The Love for Three Oranges*). He has introduced sponsorship, important to a festival that is more reliant on self-financing than most. Adrian Noble's production of Purcell's *The Fairy-Queen*, conducted by William Christie, was the outstanding success of the 1989 season; it affirmed a movement towards performance on period instruments. In autumn 1991 the Théâtre Municipal was reopened for an annual lyric season.

Les opéras du festival d'Aix-en-Provence (Aix-en-Provence, 1982)

CHARLES PITT

Aix-la-Chapelle (Fr.). AACHEN.

Ajo nell'imbarazzo, L' ('The Tutor in a Jam'). *Melodramma giocoso* in two acts by GAETANO DONIZETTI to a libretto by JACOPO FERRETTI after Giovanni Giraud's *L'ajo nell'imbarazzo* (1807, Rome); Rome, Teatro Valle, 4 February 1824 (revised as *Don Gregorio*, Naples, Teatro Nuovo, 11 June 1826).

This was the first sustained success of Donizetti's career. A father, Marchese Giulio (baritone), having been maltreated by a woman, insists that his two sons grow up without knowing any females. Their tutor, Don Gregorio (*buffo* bass), vainly tries to persuade the boys to follow this edict. The elder, Enrico (tenor), however, secretly married to Gilda (soprano) for a year, has fathered a son; the younger, Pipetto (tenor), is smitten by an aged serving-woman, Leonarda (mezzo-soprano). Anxious to acknowledge his bride, Enrico tries to enlist Don Gregorio's help, producing Gilda and the baby to strengthen his arguments. Returning home inopportunely, the Marchese learns the truth about his sons, and sings a scena and aria expressing his fury and his sorrow. Hearing his decision to disinherit Enrico in favour of Pipetto, Gilda threatens to kill herself and the baby. The Marchese relents, acknowledges Enrico's marriage and, dismissing Leonarda, sends Pipetto off on a tour of Europe.

Donizetti's score shows his aptitude for musical characterization and mimicry; and the duet for Gilda and Don Gregorio carries more than a hint of his way of humanizing comedy with an underlining of pathos.

WILLIAM ASHBROOK

Akhnaten. Opera in three acts by PHILIP GLASS to a libretto by the composer, Shalom Goldman, Robert Israel and Richard Riddell; Stuttgart, Staatsoper, 24 March 1984.

Glass has called *Einstein on the Beach*, *Satyagraha* and *Akhnaten* a trilogy of 'portrait' operas. From a purely dramatic standpoint such a grouping makes sense, although all of the composer's later operas bear closer musical resemblance to *Satyagraha* (1980) than they do to the *sui generis Einstein on the Beach* (1976). In *Satyagraha* Glass developed his own distinctive mutation of 'traditional' opera and the works which have followed are cast in a related musical mould.

Akhnaten opens in 1875 BC in Egypt. On the death of his father, Akhnaten (counter-tenor) is crowned as the new King Amenhotep IV. Immediately he abolishes the Amon traditions of his father, deposing Amon priests, and proposes instead the monotheistic worship of Aten. He builds a temple, Akhetaten, in honour of Aten, and refuses to practise polygamy, preferring to remain true to his wife, Nefertiti. As he becomes increasingly isolated from his people by his preoccupations, the Amon priests incite the people to overthrow him. Akhnaten and his family are left roaming the ruined Akhetaten, mourning the passing of their epoch.

Though *Akhnaten* is written for 12 solo voices, chorus and narrator, in general it is less determinedly 'operatic' than *Satyagraha*, with long orchestral interludes and much spoken text; moreover, the scoring is clarified, pared down (the large orchestra includes a range of percussion instruments but there are no violins), and almost neo-classical in its economy of means. One also finds a use of dissonance unprecedented in the composer's mature work; Akhnaten's 13-minute 'Hymn' in the second act is probably the most chromatic music Glass has written since his student days and has something of the spirit of the spare, chant-like late compositions of Stravinsky. (The exciting 'Funeral Music' in Act 1 was excerpted for use in the Jerome Robbins ballet *Glass Pieces*.)

Akhnaten was inspired by the writings of Immanuel Velikovsky (*Worlds in Collision*, *Earth in Upheaval* and especially *Oedipus and Akhnaten*), in which he contends that events in the fictional life of Oedipus occurred hundreds of years earlier in the life of Akhnaten. Glass acknowledges that Velikovsky's cataclysmic theories are generally regarded as spurious and unscientific but considers him a 'lively, interesting and provocative writer'. Glass had hoped to work with Velikovsky himself on the opera but the writer died in November 1979. Looking to other collaborators, Glass began work on the libretto in 1982: Shalom Goldman excerpted the vocal text, in English, Hebrew and Egyptian, from sources ranging from the Egyptian Book of the Dead to the King James version of the Bible to James H. Breasted's *A History of Egypt*. 'Decrees, titles, letters, fragments of poems, etc., were all left to be sung in their original languages, thereby emphasizing the artifactual slant of our approach', Glass wrote. Only the 'Hymn' is always sung in the language of the audience.

Akhnaten met with mixed reviews in Europe and America; an unsympathetic American première, presented in both New York and Houston, was blamed for the opera's unfavourable reception in the USA. However, David Freeman's revised version of the same production was immediately successful in London and the opera has become part of the repertory of the ENO. For many, it was only with the release of the composer-supervised recording in 1987 that *Akhnaten* was recognized as one of Glass's major works.

For an illustration *see* STAGE DESIGN, fig.27. TIM PAGE

Akutagawa, Yasushi (*b* Tokyo, 12 July 1925; *d* Tokyo, 31 Jan 1989). Japanese composer. He studied composition with Kunihiko Hashimoto, Akira Ifukube and others at the Tokyo Music School. In 1949, the year of his graduation, he won first prize in the Japanese radio competition, and the next year his Music for Symphonic Orchestra attracted attention. With Dan and Mayuzumi he formed the Sannin no Kai (Group of Three) in 1953 and visited Moscow for the first time in 1954, returning frequently to the USSR. In 1956 he organized the New Symphony Orchestra of Japan; he remained its director and conductor until his death. In 1960 a successful performance of his opera *Kurai Kagami* ('Dark Mirror'), to a libretto by Kenzaburō Ōe, was given at Yomiuri Hall, Tokyo (27 March); the work was also broadcast on radio that month. Seven years later he revised it for television with the new title *Hiroshima no Orufe* ('Orpheus in Hiroshima'; NHK TV, 27 August 1967) and it won an Anerkennungspreis at the 1968 Salzburg Festival; its stage version has enjoyed a number of revivals, and it was included among the repertory of the Stanislavsky–Nemirovich-Danchenko Music Theatre, Moscow, in 1985. Akutagawa held a number of administrative posts, including those of president of the Japan Federation of Composers (1980–89) and president of the Japanese Performing Rights Society (1981–9).

See also HIROSHIMA NO ORUFE. MASAKATA KANAZAWA

Alaimo, Simone (*b* Villabate, *c*1952). Italian bass. He studied in Palermo and Milan, making his début in 1978 as Don Pasquale and taking part in Soliva's *La testa di bronzo* at La Piccola Scala (1980). He has appeared throughout Italy, singing in Rome, Naples, Bologna, Turin and many other cities. A Rossini specialist, he has sung Dandini, Alidoro, Selim, Don Basilio, Assur, Asdrubale, Pharaoh (*Mosè*) and Polidoro (*Zelmira*). Other roles include Count Robinson, Dulcamara, Belcore, Murena (*L'esule di Roma*), Henry VIII (*Anna Bolena*), Nottingham (*Roberto Devereux*), Torquato Tasso, Rodolfo (*La sonnambula*) and Issachar (Apolloni's *L'ebreo*). He made his American and British débuts at Chicago (1987) and Covent Garden (1988) as Mustafà and sang Mahomet at San Francisco (1988). A superb comic actor, he is equally convincing in tragic opera, while the exceptional range of his keenly focussed and flexible voice enables him to sing Verdi baritone roles such as Miller, as well as the *basso buffo* characters at which he excels. ELIZABETH FORBES

Alaleona, Domenico (Ottavio Felice Gaspare Maria) (*b* Montegiorgio, Ascoli Piceno, 16 Nov 1881; *d* Montegiorgio, 28 Dec 1928). Italian musicologist, conductor and composer. He studied at the Liceo di S Cecilia, Rome, where from 1912 he was professor of aesthetics and music history, and also at Rome University, graduating with a thesis, subsequently expanded into a book, on the Italian oratorio. His writings helped lay the foundations of Italian musicology, he was a bold and innovatory theorist, and he worked for the improvement of Italian music education. His only completed opera, *Mirra*, written in 1908–12 to a libretto based on part of Vittorio Alfieri's tragedy of the same name, is unconvincingly eclectic but shows enterprise in its brief use of a specially constructed 'pentaphonic harmonium', tuned to a scale in which the octave is divided into five equal parts (cf Indonesian *slendro*). The opera had only one stage production (Rome, Costanzi, 31 March 1920), although the orchestral intermezzo was more widely performed.

DBI
A. De Angelis: *L'Italia musicale d'oggi: dizionario dei musicisti* (Rome, 1918, 3/1928)
E. G. Rovira: 'In attesa della Mirra di Domenico Alaleona', *Musica* [Rome], xiv/2 (1920), 1–2
J. C. G. Waterhouse: *The Emergence of Modern Italian Music (up to 1940)* (diss., U. of Oxford, 1968), 181–3, 584–5
D. Tampieri, ed.: *Aspetti e presenze del novecento musicale: scritti e ricerche dedicate a Domenico Alaleona (1881–1928)* (Montegiorgio, 1980), esp. 95–123

JOHN C. G. WATERHOUSE

Alan, Hervey (*b* Whitstable, 22 Feb 1910; *d* Croydon, 12 Jan 1982). English bass. After studying with Roy Henderson, he was engaged at Sadler's Wells Opera (1947–52), singing Colline, Don Basilio, Zuniga, Simone (*Gianni Schicchi*), Alfio, the Grand Inquisitor, the Commendatore, and Cancian (*I quatro rusteghi*). At Glyndebourne (1949–59) he sang Tom (*Un ballo in maschera*), Alidoro (*La Cenerentola*), Trulove and Padre Guardiano. He created Mr Redburn in *Billy Budd* at Covent Garden (1951). For the WNO (1952–61) he sang Sparafucile, Procida, Barbarossa (Verdi's *La battaglia di Legnano*), Melcthal (*Guillaume Tell*) and Mephistopheles (Gounod and Boito). He had a dark-toned, resonant voice, especially effective as Zaccaria in *Nabucco*. ELIZABETH FORBES

Alarie, Pierrette (**Marguerite**) (*b* Montreal, 9 Nov 1921). Canadian soprano. She studied in Montreal and with Elisabeth Schumann in Philadelphia. She made her début in 1938 in Montreal with the Variétés Lyriques, later singing in *La fille du régiment*, *Barbiere*, *Traviata* and *Mireille*. In 1943 she sang Mozart's Barbarina under Beecham. She made her Metropolitan début in 1945 in *Un ballo in maschera* under Bruno Walter after winning the Auditions of the Air. In 1949 she made her début at the Opéra as Olympia, remaining in Paris for several seasons and appearing frequently with the tenor Léopold Simoneau, whom she had married in 1946. She sang at the 1959 Salzburg Festival in *Die schweigsame Frau*. She retired from the stage in 1966. For some years she taught in Montreal before moving to San Francisco in 1972, and to Victoria, British Columbia, in 1986. She directed some productions of Canada Opera Piccola, a company of young singers headed by her husband, and taught at Banff from 1972 to 1978.

*

R. Maheu: *Pierrette Alarie, Léopold Simoneau, deux voix, un art* (Montreal, 1988) GILLES POTVIN

Alayrac, Nicolas-Marie d'. *See* DALAYRAC, NICOLAS-MARIE.

Albanese [Albanèse, Albaneze], (**Egide-Joseph-Ignace-**) **Antoine** (*b* Albano Laziale, nr Rome, 1729; *d* Paris, 1800). French composer of Italian origin. Educated in Naples, he went to Paris in 1747 and found employment in the royal chapel of Louis XV. From 1752 to 1762 he was a prominent soloist in the Concert Spirituel, appearing frequently in performances of Pergolesi's *Stabat mater* as a castrato. He apparently retired from public performance about 1764–5 and thereafter taught singing and composed vocal music. In 1774 he received a life pension of 2000 livres. He wrote the music for two lyric scenes performed by the Petits Comédiens du Bois de Boulogne, *Les adieux d'un soldat* (24 October 1778) and *Le soldat français* (1 June 1779; a collaboration with Stanislas Champein). KENNETH LANGEVIN

Albanese, Francesco (*b* Torre del Greco, Naples, 13 Aug 1912). Italian tenor. He studied in Rome and made his début in 1942 at La Fenice as Ramiro in *La Cenerentola*. After touring in Hungary and Germany, he was engaged by the S Carlo and sang with that company at Covent Garden in 1946 as Almaviva (*Il barbiere di Siviglia*) and the Duke (*Rigoletto*). He sang Rinaldo in Rossini's *Armida* (Florence, 1952); Alfredo in *La traviata* (Venice and Rome, 1953); Jason in *Médée* (Rome, 1955); and Pylades in *Iphigénie en Tauride* (Florence, 1957), all with Maria Callas. He had a fine voice but his singing lacked style. ELIZABETH FORBES

Albanese, Licia (*b* Bari, 22 July 1913). American soprano of Italian birth. After study with Giuseppina Baldassare-Tedeschi, her career began at the Teatro Lirico, Milan, where in 1934 she was an emergency replacement for an indisposed Butterfly in the second half of the opera. The same opera, always closely identified with her, occasioned her formal début at Parma (1935) and her début at the Metropolitan (1940). During her career she made more than 1000 appearances in 48 roles, in the lyric or *lirico spinto* repertory, including Mozart (Donna Anna, Zerlina, Susanna) and French opera (Micaëla, Manon, Gounod's Marguerite) as well as the obvious Italian challenges; her speciality was the Puccini heroines. A singer of extraordinary technical skill and emotional intensity, she was the Violetta and Mimì in Toscanini's recorded NBC broadcasts. Active in the movement to save the old Metropolitan Opera House, she never rejoined the company at Lincoln Center. In later years she taught, and sang sporadically in concert and in roles the Metropolitan had, perhaps wisely, denied her, such as Aida and Santuzza.

*

GV (E. Gara, R. Celletti; R. Vegeto)
J. Hines: *Great Singers on Great Singing* (Garden City, NY, 1982), 19–24 MARTIN BERNHEIMER

Albani [Lajeunesse], Dame **Emma** (**Marie Louise Cécile**) (*b* Chambly, nr Montreal, 1 Nov 1847; *d* London, 3 April 1930). Canadian soprano. She studied in Paris from 1868 with Duprez and later in Milan with Lamperti. In 1870 she made her début at Messina as Amina, repeating the role for her London début on 2 April 1872 at Covent Garden. She sang there nearly every season until 1896, notably as Elsa (1875) and Elisabeth (1876) in the first London performances of *Lohengrin* and *Tannhäuser* (see overleaf). She made her American début at the New York Academy of Music as Amina (21 October 1874), and first appeared at La Scala in January 1882 as Lucia and at the Metropolitan Opera on 23 December 1891 as Gilda. Later she was successful as Eva, and as Desdemona in the first Covent Garden and Metropolitan productions of *Otello*. The last and greatest triumph of her career was on 26 June 1896, as Isolde with Jean and Edouard de Reszke.

Albani's voice was a rich soprano, of exceptional beauty in its higher register, and she perfected the art of singing *mezza voce*.

*

E. Albani: *Forty Years of Song* (London and Toronto, 1911)
H. Charbonneau: *L'Albani* (Montreal, 1938)
N. A. Ridley: 'Emma Albani', *Record Collector*, xii (1958–60), 77–101 [with discography by W. R. Moran]

Albania. The cradles of music and, ultimately, opera in Albania were Shkodër in the north and Korçë in the

Emma Albani as Elisabeth in Wagner's 'Tannhäuser'

south, where the first theatres opened towards the end of the 19th century. Among the theatrical works of that period was Andrea Zadeja's *Rozafa*, which, in its musical version by Michele Koliqi, may (according to the *Enciclopedia dello Spettacolo*) be considered an opera. However, the earliest attempts in the genre were two works by Martin Gjoka (1890–1940), a Franciscan monk and a pioneer of Albanian music, active as a composer and teacher in Shkodër: his *Juda Makabe* ('Judas Maccabaeus'), composed 1917–19 (but uncompleted because of material difficulties in performance), and *Shqiptarja e qytetnueme* ('The Civilized Albanian Woman'), both to texts by the poet Gjergj Fishta (1871–1940). The first Albanian singers were the bass Petraq Marko and, more importantly, the lyric tenor Dhimitër Mihali (1888–1962), who as 'Toskani' had an international career. It is not yet known whether Toskani ever sang in Albania, but the sopranos Georgjia Filçe-Truja (*b* 1909), TEFTA TASHKO-KOÇO, Maria Paluca-Kraja (*b* 1911) and Gjysepina Kosturi (1912–85), and the tenors Mihal Ciko (1900–86) and Kristaq Antoniou (1907–79) were active there in the 1930s or earlier. In 1933 Kristo Kono presented excerpts from Verdi's *I Lombardi* and *Ernani* in Korçë, but the Italian invasion of the country in 1939 and the difficulty Albanian composers experienced in receiving any advanced training before the late 1940s virtually halted further development of the genre, and a visit by an Italian company in 1942–3 was largely ignored by the indigenous population. The first step towards a national opera company was taken with the foundation in Tirana in 1947 of the Albanian Philharmonia, an organization comprising the radio orchestra, a chorus, ballet and singers. This was succeeded in November 1953 by the Theatre of Opera and Ballet, which has its own chorus and orchestra. The first performance of an opera with an all-Albanian cast was of Dargomïzhsky's *Rusalka* in Tirana on 27 November 1953. A feature of the company's activity is the regular performance of new Albanian operas (which are sometimes also televised), though the standard repertory, mainly Italian and Russian works, was included until at least 1961 (when Albania's breach with the USSR led to a shift of cultural policy). From that time foreign works were almost totally ignored; until the production of *Il trovatore* on 9 November 1991 the last new staging of any non-Albanian opera was in 1966 (Mozart's *Le nozze di Figaro*). Operas and operettas are occasionally performed in the cultural centres of Shkodër and Korçë, and there are theatres in Durrës, Vlora, Elbasan, Fier, Berat and Gjirokastër.

Albanian composers approached opera cautiously, starting with operetta: the earliest included Kono's *Agimi* ('The Dawn', 1954) and Daija's *Lejla* (1957). The first operas were Prenkë Jakova's *Mrika* (1958), which remains popular; Daija's *Pranvera* ('Spring', 1960); and Kono's *Lulja e kujtimit* ('The Flower of Remembrance', 1961). National history, tradition and literature as well as socialist life (e.g. *Mrika*) form the basis of Albanian opera subjects. Many of the librettos, especially those from the mid-1960s onwards, are by major authors such as Llazar Siliqi and Dritëro Agolli.

The current available repertory comprises 20 operas (including three by Mula and two each by Jakova, Kono, Daija, Zoraqi, Harapi, Nova and Gaci), of which 16 have been performed, and 26 operettas (including three each by Kono and Daija, two by Harapi, and one each by Jakova, Mula and Zoraqi), of which 21 have been performed.

For further information on operatic life in the country's principal centre *see* TIRANA.

*

ES

S. Vani: *Kur dëgjomë operën* [Listening to Opera] (Tirana, 1979)

S. Gjoni: 'L'opéra et le ballet en Albanie', *Les lettres albanaises* (1980), no.3, pp.218–22

S. Kalemi: *Arritjet e artit tonë muzikor: vepra dhe krijues të muzikës Shqiptare* [Achievements of our Musical Art: Creations and Creators of Albanian Music] (Tirana, 1982)

'Muzike skenike' [Music for the Stage], *Historia e muzikës Shqiptare* [History of Albanian Music] (Tirana, 1983), ii, 273–327 [pubn of Superior Institute of Arts, Tirana]

T. Zadeja: 'Martin Gjoka, 1890–1940', *Nëntori* (1983), no.3, pp.191–8

P. Bello: 'Le mouvement musical à Korça depuis la fin du XIXe siècle jusqu'à la libération du pays', *Les lettres albanaises* (1987), no.3, pp.172–80

GEORGE LEOTSAKOS

Albano, Ippolito d'. Pseudonym of GIROLAMO ALESSANDRO BIAGGI.

Albarelli, Luigi ['Il Luigino'] (*fl* 1692–1706). Italian contralto castrato. His name first appears in a libretto in 1692 as Silandro in *Pausania* (composer unknown) at Crema, and he sang frequently thereafter in the principal Italian centres in lead and second-lead male parts. In Venice he appeared at S Giovanni Grisostomo in operas by C. F. Pollarolo (*Tito Manlio*, *Marzio Coriolano*, *La fortuna per dote* and *Il Dafni*). Galliard (1743), in the notes to his translation of Tosi's treatise, indicated that he was a pupil of Pistocchi in the service of Emperor Josef I, but there is no record of such service. He served the Duke of Modena from 1694. Tosi cites him as Pistocchi's successor only in terms of style. He was one of the best representatives of the generation of castratos after Pistocchi.

*

P. F. Tosi: *Opinioni de' cantori antichi e moderni* (Bologna, 1723; Eng. trans. by J. E. Galliard, 1742, 2/1743, as *Observations on the Florid Song*), 65

L. Riccoboni: *Réflexions historiques et critiques sur les différents théâtres de l'Europe* (Amsterdam, 1740), 38

O. Termini: 'Singers at San Marco in Venice: the Competition between Church and Theatre (ca. 1675-ca. 1725)', *RMARC*, no.17 (1981), 65–96

F. Marri: 'Muratori, la musica e il melodramma negli anni milanesi (1695–1700)', *Muratoriana*, xvi (1988), 19–124

SERGIO DURANTE

Albéniz, Isaac (Manuel Francisco) (*b* Camprodón, Gerona, 29 May 1860; *d* Cambo-les-Bains, 18 May 1909). Spanish composer and pianist. When he was a year old he moved with his family to Barcelona. His musical propensities soon became apparent, and his sister Clementina gave him piano lessons when he was about three and a half. A child prodigy, he made his first public appearance at about five, at the Teatro Romea in Barcelona. Soon afterwards he began lessons with Narciso Oliveras. In 1867 he was taken to Paris where, it is said, he studied privately with Antoine Marmontel, eventually taking the entrance exam for the Paris Conservatoire; though impressed with his talent, the jury is said to have refused him admission because he was too immature. In 1868 Albéniz's father lost his government post, and, to earn money, took Isaac and Clementina on recital tours of the Spanish provinces. In 1869 the family moved to Madrid, where Albéniz was enrolled in the Escuela Nacional de Música y Declamación (now the Real Conservatorio Superior de Música). His studies were constantly interrupted; having experienced the life of a travelling virtuoso, he repeatedly ran away from home, giving impromptu recitals in the provinces or wherever fate took him. He returned intermittently to Madrid and studied for a time with Eduardo Compta and José Tragó. His last escapade took him to Puerto Rico and Cuba in 1875 before he finally settled down to serious studies.

Albéniz returned to Europe and enrolled at the Leipzig Conservatory in May 1876 but remained there for only two months; by summer he was back in Madrid seeking financial aid. Through the intercession of Guillermo Morphy, secretary to King Alfonso XII, he obtained a pension to attend the Brussels Conservatory. There he studied the piano to 1879, first with Franz Rummel and then with Louis Brassin, obtaining a first prize. He did not, as many biographers claim, go on to study with Liszt, though he seems to have travelled to Budapest in August 1880 with the goal of meeting the Abbé. By mid-September 1880 Albéniz was again in Madrid pursuing his performing career. He made tours of Spain and appearances in the Spanish-speaking Americas. He also began to conduct, and by 1882 he had become administrator and conductor of a touring zarzuela company in Spain. It is probably from this time that his earliest attempts at zarzuela originate – *El canto de salvación*, *¡Cuanto más viejo …!* and *Catalanes de Gracia* (nothing more than the titles of these works survives). In 1883 he moved to Barcelona where he studied composition with Felipe Pedrell. While still continuing to perform he gave piano lessons, and on 23 June 1883 married his pupil Rosina Jordana. By the end of 1885 they moved to Madrid, where, through the protection of his old friend Morphy, Albéniz firmly established himself in Madrid's musical life, performing in the homes of nobility, organizing and participating in concerts and teaching. By 1886 he had written over 50 works, principally for piano. By 1889 he was well known as a pianist-composer, and in March gave concerts in Paris and London. The London appearances proved so successful that he made repeated visits. In June 1890 he placed himself under exclusive contract as a composer and performing musician to the manager Henry Lowenfeld and moved with his wife and family to London by the end of the year.

Through Lowenfeld, who was associated with musical theatre, Albéniz agreed to compose music for a comic opera, *The Magic Opal*, written by Arthur Law. He also came into contact with Horace Sedger, manager of the Lyric Theatre, and became involved with its production of *Incognita* (an adaptation of Charles Lecocq's *Le coeur et la main*, opening 6 October 1892), for which he arranged the Act 2 finale, 'Oh! Horror! Horror!'. On 19 January 1893 *The Magic Opal* had its première at the Lyric. After a successful run, it was revised slightly and staged at the Prince of Wales Theatre as *The Magic Ring* (11 April 1893) with Albéniz conducting. The next offering at the Prince of Wales, *Poor Jonathan* (15 June 1893), was an adaptation of Carl Millöcker's *Der arme Jonathan* to which Albéniz contributed some numbers and acted as musical director.

About this time he acquired exclusive rights to the celebrated tragedy *Mar i cel* by the Catalan poet and playwright Angel Guimerá. The play was to form the basis of Albéniz's next operatic undertaking, but was set aside when the composer was asked by Francis Burdett Money-Coutts, an amateur poet and playwright, to write an opera based on his own tale of the Wars of the Roses, *Henry Clifford*. Money-Coutts, heir to the banking fortune of Coutts & Co. and financial investor in both the Prince of Wales and Lyric theatres, had become a partner with Lowenfeld in the contract concerning Albéniz's musical talents; by 31 June 1894 Money-Coutts would become Albéniz's sole patron.

After *The Magic Ring* closed, Albéniz moved back to the continent because of illness, settling in Paris. He soon resumed his performing activities in Spain, at the same time working on *Henry Clifford*. He spent the summer of 1894 in Paris completing the score as well as composing yet another stage work, *San Antonio de la Florida*, a one-act zarzuela to a libretto by Eusebio Sierra; this was first given in Madrid, at the Teatro de Apolo on 26 October 1894, the composer conducting. Because it was more ambitious musically than the typical zarzuela in the accepted *género chico* style, *San Antonio* was not entirely successful. A month later Albéniz conducted his *Magic Opal* (presented in Sierra's Spanish translation under the title of *La sortija*) at the Teatro de la Zarzuela and was again criticized for writing a work that did not conform to the established mould. Disgusted, he returned to Paris. Albéniz was not the only Spanish composer to encounter resistance from the establishment. Efforts to elevate the artistic content of the zarzuela as well as to create a Spanish national opera (vigorously supported by Tomás Bretón and Felipe Pedrell) repeatedly faced deep-rooted prejudices.

On 8 May 1895 Albéniz conducted the première of *Henry Clifford* at the Gran Teatro del Liceo in Barcelona. As was the custom there, the work was performed in Italian. Though not appreciated by the general public it proved a success with the critics, who felt that the music showed promise. Money-Coutts's and Albéniz's next endeavour was an opera based on the novel *Pepita Jiménez* by Juan Valera. It had its première on 5 January 1896 at the Gran Teatro del Liceo (in Italian) to the decidedly enthusiastic applause of the general public; the press however were disappointed, having hoped for something more substantial from the composer of *Henry Clifford*. By September Albéniz had expanded *Pepita* to two acts and, though he continued to give concerts, much of 1896–7 was devoted to promoting the opera's performance. On 22 June 1897 *Pepita*, conducted by Frank Schalk, was produced in German at the German Theatre in Prague to great praise. Angelo Neumann, manager of the theatre, contracted Albéniz to compose two stage works, which did not however materialize. Instead, the composer embarked on a trilogy, *King Arthur*, to a libretto by Money-Coutts. Albéniz's talent for inventing attractive vocal lines woven around a vibrant orchestral fabric had formed the compositional basis for *Clifford* and *Pepita*, operas that succeed from moment to moment. The immense undertaking of a trilogy, however, daunted rather than excited Albéniz's imagination. Contrary to his usual speed, Albéniz took four years to finish *Merlin* (1898–1902), *Lancelot* was left incomplete after the beginning of the second act and *Guenevere* remained untouched.

Meanwhile, from 1896, Albéniz wrote songs, many on texts by Money-Coutts, music for solo piano and for orchestra and the opening pages of a one-act lyric drama, *La sérénade* (1899), by an unidentified author. From 1898 to 1900 he taught advanced piano at the Schola Cantorum; he had to resign because of poor health and in 1900 left Paris for the warmer climate of Spain. In Barcelona he became associated with Enrique Morera and the movement to promote the performance of Catalan lyrical works. He made repeated attempts to have *Merlin* and *Pepita Jiménez* produced in both Madrid and Barcelona but met constant opposition from the establishment. Despite his arrangement with Money-Coutts, in 1902 Albéniz agreed to compose a three-act zarzuela to a libretto by Cristóbal de Castro, *La real hembra*. He set little more than the prelude and first two scenes however, and Castro never completed the libretto. Though Albéniz had support from the press, his international reputation was a liability. He was viewed as a Spaniard 'in foreign attire' and thus not only lacked commitment from the public and the impresarios but also suffered from their intrigues and jealousies. Since all efforts to have his lyric works performed failed, Albéniz returned to France where, esteemed by colleagues there, he felt he could more effectively advance the cause of Spanish music.

Suffering from Bright's disease, he spent much of the rest of his life at Nice. He resumed work on *Lancelot*, eventually putting it aside to revise the orchestration of *Pepita* for a performance in French at the Théâtre de la Monnaie of Brussels. *Pepita*, along with *San Antonio de la Florida* (translated into French as *L'ermitage fleuri*), was given on 3 January 1905 to enthusiastic reviews. Albert Carré, director of the Paris Opéra-Comique, expressed interest in *Pepita*, but it was not given there until 1923. Although the Monnaie announced plans to perform *Merlin* the next winter in a French translation by Maurice Kufferath, the production did not materialize. In April 1905 Albéniz began a lyric drama in four acts entitled *La morena*, but this too was left incomplete. Heeding the advice of his friends and the dictates of his conscience, he returned to the composition of piano music. From 1905 to 1907 he wrote his masterpiece, *Iberia*, wherein he captured and immortalized the sounds and rhythms of his native country. *Navarra*, originally conceived as part of *Iberia*, and *Azulejos* remained unfinished at his death.

See also MAGIC OPAL, THE and PEPITA JIMÉNEZ.

El canto de salvación, ?end of 1881 (zar, 2), lost
¡Cuanto más viejo ...! (zar, 1, Zapino), Bilbao, Feb 1882, lost
Catalanes de Gracia (zar, 1, R. L. Palomino de Guzmán), Madrid, Salón Eslava, 25 March 1882, lost
The Magic Opal (comic op, 2, A. Law), London, Lyric, 19 Jan 1893, *E-Bc**, vs (London, 1893); rev. as The Magic Ring, London, Prince of Wales, 11 April 1893; as La sortija, Madrid, Zarzuela, 23 Nov 1894
Mar i cel, *c*1893–5 (after A. Guimerá), *Bc**, inc.
San Antonio de la Florida (zar, 1, E. Sierra), Madrid, Apolo, 26 Oct 1894, *Bc**, *Boc*, vs (Barcelona, ?1894); as L'ermitage fleuri, Brussels, Monnaie, 3 Jan 1905
Henry Clifford (3, Mountjoy [F. B. Money-Coutts]), in It. as Enrico Clifford, Barcelona, Liceo, 8 May 1895, *Bc**, *Boc*, vs (Barcelona, ?1895); also known as Le deux Roses
Pepita Jiménez (lyric comedy, 1, Money-Coutts, after J. Valera), in It. trans., Barcelona, Liceo, 5 Jan 1896, *Bc**; rev. in 2 acts, Ger. trans., Prague, Neues Deutsches, 22 June 1897, full score and vs (Leipzig, 1896); rev., Fr. trans., Brussels, Monnaie, 3 Jan 1905, *Bc**, full score and vs (Leipzig, 1904); new Fr. trans., Paris, OC (Favart), 18 June 1923, vs (Paris, 1923); rev. P. Sorozábal in 3 acts, Sp. trans., Madrid, Zarzuela, 6 June 1964, vs (Madrid, 1963)
King Arthur [La table ronde] (trilogy, Money-Coutts, after T. Malory: *Morte d'Arthur*)
  Merlin, 1898–1902 (3), Barcelona, Tívoli, 18 Dec 1950, *Bc**, vs (Paris, 1906)
  Lancelot, 1902–3 (3), *Bc**, inc.
  Guenevere (4), not comp.
La sérénade, 1899 (lyrical drama, 1), *Bc**, inc.
La real hembra, 1902 (zar, 3, C. de Castro), *Bc**, inc.
La morena, 1905 (lyrical drama, 4, A. Mortier), *Bc**, inc.

1 number ('Oh! Horror! Horror!') in Incognita (F. C. Burnand, after C. Lecocq: *Le coeur et la main*), London, Lyric, 6 Oct 1892, vs (London, 1892); numbers for Poor Jonathan (after C. Millöcker: *Der arme Jonathan*), London, Prince of Wales, 15 June 1893, *Bc**

*

G. Morphy: 'Porvenir de los compositores españoles', *La correspondencia de España* (30 Dec 1894)
J. Roca y Roca: 'La semana en Barcelona', *La vanguardia* (12 May 1895)
H. Klein: 'Music and Musicians: *Pepita Jiménez*', *The Sunday Times* (5 Jan 1896)
J. Pena: 'Musichs que fugen', *Joventut*, iii (1902), 383–5
R. Mitjana: 'Música del porvenir: *La celestine* – La trilogía del *Rey Artus, Emporium*', *¡Para música vamos!: estudios sobre el arte musical contemporáneo en España* (Valencia, 1909), 189–212
E. Newman: 'Music and Musicians: Albéniz and his *Merlin*', *New Witness*, x (1917), 495–6
H. Klein: 'Albéniz's opera *Pepita Jiménez*', *MT*, lix (1918), 116–17
H. Klein: *Musicians and Mummers* (London, 1925)
M. Casamada: '*Merlin* de Isaac Albéniz', *La vie musicale*, ii (1951–2), 8–10
G. Laplane: *Albéniz: sa vie, son oeuvre* (Geneva, 1956; Sp. trans., 1972)
A. Laborda: 'Unas cartas de Albéniz sobre el estreno de *Pepita Jiménez* en Praga', *ABC* [Madrid] (5 July 1964)
M. Falces Sierra: *Contribución a la recuperación de la obra vocal de Isaac Albéniz: estudio linguistico-musical del tratamiento dado a textos literarios ingleses* (diss., U. of Granada, 1991)
F. Barulich: *Isaac Albéniz: a Biography and Thematic Catalogue of his Work* (diss., New York U., 1992)
W. A. Clark: 'Isaac Albéniz's Faustian Pact: A Study in Patronage', *MQ*, lxxvi (1992)
——: *'Spanish Music with a Universal Accent': Isaac Albéniz's Opera 'Pepita Jimenez'* (diss., UCLA, 1992)

FRANCES BARULICH

Albers, Henri (*b* Amsterdam, 1 Feb 1866; *d* Paris, 12 Sept 1925). Flemish baritone. He began as an actor in comedy, and in 1889 made his operatic début as Méphistophélès in *Faust* at Amsterdam. Massenet heard him in Antwerp and arranged for him to study in Paris with Jean-Baptiste Faure. He then travelled widely in France and the USA, making his début at the Metropolitan in 1898. He appeared at Covent Garden between 1894 and 1899, mostly in the French repertory but also as a French-singing Wotan in *Die Walküre*. In Paris he sang in the first performances there of *Götterdämmerung* and *Tristan*. His finest role was generally considered to be Hamlet in Thomas' opera. Recordings show an exemplary voice-production and an assured style. J. B. STEANE

Albert, Eugen (Francis Charles) d' (*b* Glasgow, 10 April 1864; *d* Riga, 3 March 1932). German composer. His parents, who were living in Newcastle upon Tyne at the time of his birth, were German, but his paternal grandmother was French, while the family came originally from Italy. D'Albert later took Swiss nationality. Having shown great musical aptitude at an early age, he studied the piano, and also composition with Sir Arthur Sullivan in London. In 1882 he won the Mendelssohn Prize for travel abroad and went first to Vienna, where he studied with Hans Richter, then to Weimar, where he worked with Liszt, before embarking on a highly successful career as a concert pianist. In 1907 he became director of the Berlin Hochschule für Musik.

His first opera, *Der Rubin*, was produced at Karlsruhe in 1893 and, during the remaining 40 years of his life, despite a demanding career as piano virtuoso and teacher, he found time to compose 19 more, most of which were first performed in Germany. Among the exceptions were *Tiefland* (1903), his best-known, most successful opera and the only one to retain a place in the general repertory, and *Flauto solo* (1905), a comic piece that obtained an initial popularity; the premières of both were at the Neues Deutsches Theater in Prague.

D'Albert's very varied cultural and artistic background is reflected in the subject and style of his operas, which range from the charming one-act comedy of manners *Die Abreise* (1898) to the music drama *Der Golem* (1926), both first produced in Frankfurt; from *Der Improvisator* (1902, Berlin), based on the Victor Hugo tragedy *Angelo, tyran de Padoue* (the play that provided Boito with a libretto for Ponchielli's *La Gioconda*), to *Die schwarze Orchidee* (1928, Leipzig), an opera burlesque that was favourably compared with *Jonny spielt auf*, the jazz opera by Krenek first heard in Leipzig the previous year.

The stylistic influences on d'Albert's music are equally varied. The shadow of Wagner is inescapable, but his earlier operas also show the influence of the German Romantic composers, particularly Cornelius in *Die Abreise*. In *Tiefland*, based on *Terra baixa* ('The Lowlands'), a drama by the Catalan playwright Angel Guimerá, the strongest influence is Italian *verismo*. Though an attempt to repeat the success of *Tiefland* with *Liebesketten* (1912, Vienna), also adapted from a play by Guimerá, was a failure, his next opera, *Die toten Augen* (1916), achieved quite a triumph on its first production in Dresden. In this score the major influences are Wagner's *Parsifal*, Richard Strauss's *Salome* and, in the orchestration, Debussy.

D'Albert's later operas (with the exception of *Der Golem* and *Die schwarze Orchidee*) were even less successful than the earlier ones had been. The last of all, *Mister Wu*, adapted from the well-known play by H. M. Vernon and H. Owen, was unfinished at the composer's death in 1932. Completed by Leo Blech, it was posthumously produced at the Dresden Staatsoper later the same year, but only received a few performances. *Tiefland* remains d'Albert's greatest legacy and his operatic masterpiece.

See also ABREISE, DIE; TIEFLAND; and TOTEN AUGEN, DIE.

Der Rubin (musikalisches Märchen, 2, d'Albert, after C. F. Hebbel), Karlsruhe, 12 Oct 1893
Ghismonda (3, d'Albert, after K. L. Immermann), Dresden, 28 Nov 1895
Gernot (G. Kastropp), Mannheim, 11 April 1897
Die Abreise (musikalisches Lustspiel, 1, F. von Sporck, after A. von Steigentesch), Frankfurt, 28 Oct 1898
Kain (musikalische Tragödie, 1, H. Bulthaupt), Berlin, Hofoper, 17 Feb 1900
Der Improvisator (3, G. Kastropp, after V. Hugo: *Angelo, tyran de Padoue*), Berlin, Hofoper, 26 Feb 1902
Tiefland (Musikdrama, prol., 2, R. Lothar [Rudolph Spitzer], after A. Guimerá: *Terra baixa*), Prague, Neues Deutsches, 15 Nov 1903
Flauto solo (musikalisches Lustspiel, 1, H. von Wolzogen), Prague, Neues Deutsches, 12 Nov 1905
Tragaldabas, oder Der geborgte Ehemann (komische Oper, 4, Lothar, after A. Vacquerie), Hamburg, 3 Dec 1907
Izeÿl (Musikdrama, 3, Lothar, after A. Silvestre and E. Morand), Hamburg, 6 Nov 1909
Die verschenkte Frau (komische Oper, 3, Lothar and R. Batka, after E. Antony), Troppau, 3 Feb 1912
Liebesketten (3, Lothar, after Guimerá), Vienna, 12 Nov 1912
Die toten Augen (Bühnendichtung, prol., 1, H. H. Ewers and M. Henry [A. G. d'Ailly-Vaucheret], after Henry: *Les yeux morts*), Dresden, Hofoper, 5 March 1916
Der Stier von Olivera (3, Batka), Leipzig, 10 March 1918
Revolutions Hochzeit (2, F. Lion, after S. Michaelis), Leipzig, 26 Oct 1919
Scirocco (3, L. Feld and K. M. von Levetzow), Darmstadt, 18 May 1921
Mareike von Nymwegen (Legendenspiel, 3, H. Alberti), Hamburg, 31 Oct 1923
Der Golem (Musikdrama, 3, Lion, after A. Holitschev), Frankfurt, 14 Nov 1926
Die schwarze Orchidee (opera grottesca, 3, Levetzow), Leipzig, Neues, 2 Dec 1928
Mister Wu (3, Levetzow, after H. M. Vernon and H. Owen), inc.; completed by L. Blech, Dresden, Staatsoper, 29 Sept 1932

*

J. Korngold: *Deutsches Opernschaffen der Gegenwart* (Leipzig, 1921)
W. Raupp: *Eugen d'Albert: ein Kunstler- und Menschenschicksal* (Leipzig and Vienna, 1930)
H. Heisig: *D'Alberts Opernschaffen* (diss., U. of Leipzig, 1942)
ELIZABETH FORBES

Albertarelli, Francesco (*fl* late 18th century). Italian bass. From 1788 until 1790 he was a member of the *opera buffa* company in Vienna. He made his début as Biscroma in Salieri's *Axur, rè d'Ormus*, appeared in Paisiello's *La modista raggiratrice*, sang the title role in the first Vienna performance of Mozart's *Don Giovanni*, and created the role of the Marchese in Weigl's *Il pazzo per forza*. Mozart contributed an aria for him in his role of Don Pompeo for the 1788 version of Anfossi's *Le gelosie fortunate*. Albertarelli sang Brunetto in Da Ponte's 1789 pasticcio *L'ape musicale*. In 1790 he sang Rusticone in Salieri's *La cifra* in Milan, and in 1791 he appeared at the King's Theatre in London. DOROTHEA LINK

Albertazzi [née Howson], **Emma** (*b* London, 1 May ?1814; *d* London, 25 Sept 1847). English contralto. She made her début in 1830 in London at the King's Theatre as Pippo in *La gazza ladra*. In 1831 she went to Italy and married a lawyer; she continued to sing, appearing at the Teatro della Cannobiana (1832), Madrid (1833) and the Théâtre Italien in Paris (1835–7). In 1837 she returned to the King's Theatre, later Her Majesty's, and in 1838 again appeared at the Théâtre Italien, as Sarah, Duchess of Nottingham, in the French première of *Roberto Devereux*. In the 1840s she sang in English opera at Sadler's Wells Theatre. She was reported to have a weighty but flexible voice that she used with style; the progressive weakening of her voice forced her early retirement. ELIZABETH FORBES

Albert Herring. Comic opera in three acts, op.39, by BENJAMIN BRITTEN to a libretto by ERIC CROZIER, after Guy de Maupassant's short story *Le rosier de Madame Husson*; Glyndebourne, 20 June 1947.

Lady Billows *an elderly autocrat*	soprano
Florence Pike *her housekeeper*	contralto
Miss Wordsworth *head teacher at the church school*	soprano
Mr Gedge *the vicar*	baritone
Mr Upfold *the mayor*	tenor
Superintendent Budd	bass
Sid *a butcher's shophand*	baritone
Albert Herring *from the greengrocer's*	tenor
Nancy *from the bakery*	mezzo-soprano
Mrs Herring *Albert's mother*	mezzo-soprano
Emmie } *village children*	soprano
Cis } *village children*	soprano
Harry } *village children*	treble

Setting Loxford, a small market town in East Suffolk, during April and May of 1900

After the stormy inception of *Peter Grimes* at Sadler's Wells, Britten and Eric Crozier were among those who decided to launch a new, independent and progressive opera company. The English Opera Group was first associated with Glyndebourne, but this relationship gave rise to problems (connected with touring *The Rape of Lucretia*), and in the early days of 1947 the fully independent English Opera Group was finally established. Even so, Britten's second chamber opera was first performed, under his direction, at Glyndebourne, alongside a revival of *Lucretia*, with Peter Pears in the title role, Joan Cross as Lady Billows and a supporting cast including Nancy Evans and Margaret Ritchie. But Britten and his friends were now determined to establish their own centre for performance. The Aldeburgh Festival was set up, and *Albert Herring* was the first opera performed there, in the Jubilee Hall in June 1948. Since then there have been many productions worldwide, the opera's strong local flavour proving no hindrance to its appeal. *Herring* returned to Glyndebourne in 1985 in an acclaimed production by Peter Hall, which was televised, and in 1989 the same production was presented at Covent Garden. A complete recording with Peter Pears as Herring and Britten conducting was made in 1964.

ACT 1.i *The breakfast room of Lady Billows's house* The fast-moving, often parodic style of this scene, with a mixture of piano-accompanied recitatives and through-composed solos and ensembles, sets the tone for the whole opera. The various dignitaries of Loxford assemble for their annual task of choosing a Queen of the May, but it soon becomes clear that none of the young women proposed meet the exacting moral standards of Lady Billows. It is the police superintendent who eventually proposes a radical solution: that they elect instead a King of the May. He has in mind one Albert Herring, and although Lady Billows is initially opposed to the idea, the only alternative seems to be to cancel the festival altogether. After further discussion she decisively announces her approval, and leads the committee in an exuberant contrapuntal ensemble. Scene ii follows after an orchestral interlude.

1.ii *Mrs Herring's shop* Sid is teasing Albert about his strait-laced subservience to his mother, and sings of the joys of poaching and courting; when Sid's sweetheart Nancy arrives, and they start flirting, Albert grows increasingly agitated and embarrassed. Left alone, he reflects on his lot, and shows the first signs of a desire to kick over the traces. Then Miss Pike, Lady Billows's housekeeper, arrives, followed by her ladyship and the rest of the festival committee. They give Albert and his mother their news. To Albert 'the whole thing's daft!', but his mother, excited at the prospect of a gift of £25, shouts down his dissent.

ACT 2.i *Inside a marquee set up in the Vicarage garden* It is the day of the ceremony, and tables are set out in the marquee for a festive tea. Sid tells Nancy about the special church service which has been taking place, with Albert 'on tenterhooks' throughout. After Miss Wordsworth has rehearsed the schoolchildren in a song of welcome for the new May King, Sid adds a tot of rum to the glass of lemonade which has already been placed by Albert's plate, to 'loosen him up and make him feel bright'. Now Albert arrives, with the local worthies in attendance. The children present Albert and his mother with flowers; Lady Billows embarks on a rambling homily; then the mayor, the schoolmistress and the police superintendent all offer the May King gifts or advice. Albert, called on to respond, is overcome by shyness and can only stammer out, after a painful silence, 'Thank you very much'. Then the entire company sing the anthem 'Albert the Good', at the end of which, to a short instrumental fantasia on the *Tristan* chord, the May King drains his rum-laced glass. As he is smitten with hiccups, the feast begins.

2.ii *Mrs Herring's shop, the same evening* Again an instrumental interlude links the new scene to its predecessor. Albert enters, thoroughly tipsy and rebellious, but still reluctant to take advantage of what he imagines to be Nancy's interest in him. Sid and Nancy pass by the shop and sing a lighthearted love duet after Sid has told Nancy that he thinks it's time for Albert to sow a few wild oats. As they leave, Albert, in increasing agitation, tosses one of the sovereigns that were his prize as May King. 'Heads for Yes and tails for No!' It comes down heads, and by the time Mrs Herring arrives home, worn out by the day's events, her son has set off in search of excitement and experience.

ACT 3 *Mrs Herring's shop, the afternoon of the following day* Albert has not yet returned, and Nancy is miserable, Sid unrepentant at their part in encouraging his defection. Mrs Herring is convinced that he is dead, and the other characters assemble to offer condolences. When the orange-blossom crown presented to Albert as May King is brought in, 'found on the road to Campsey Ash, crushed by a cart', the evidence seems conclusive, and the nine principals join in an extended threnody, each in turn floating a solo line against the repeated refrain: 'In the midst of life is death, Death awaits us one and all, Death attends our smallest step, Swift and silent, merciful'. At the threnody's climax,

'Albert Herring' (Britten): Act 1 scene ii (Mrs Herring's shop) of the original production at Glyndebourne, 1947, with Frederick Sharp as Sid, Peter Pears as Albert (centre) and Nancy Evans as Nancy

Albert pokes his head round the shop door. With an instant change of atmosphere everyone turns on him and berates him for his lack of consideration in vanishing without warning. At first Albert responds reticently to their interrogation, but once he decides to offer an explanation he does so with increasing confidence. His revelations of drinking and fighting shock everyone except Nancy and Sid. Then Albert blames his mother for keeping him wrapped in cotton wool, so that the 'only way out was a wild explosion'. He then assures everyone that, grateful as he was for the prize-money that funded his adventure, he did not greatly enjoy the experience, and now wants to be left alone to get back to work. The worthies leave in disgust, Mrs Herring is put firmly in her place, and Sid and Nancy rejoice with Albert in his new-found self-possession.

* * *

Apart from Albert's extended scena in Act 2 scene ii, this is very much an ensemble opera. Other solos are relatively brief, and there is an emphasis on rapid dialogue, often with piano accompaniment played by the conductor. Even so, the 12-piece orchestra is used with the greatest skill, notably in the evocative night-music that frames Act 2 scene ii. Though *Albert Herring* may now seem rather dated in the treatment of its subject-matter, the energy and unaffected lyricism of Britten's music have not faded, reflecting his evident delight in the special possibilities of chamber opera. It also confirms that he was perfectly capable of writing comic opera: in this respect *Albert Herring* fulfils the promise of *Paul Bunyan*, and many may regret that he made only one other contribution to the genre, *A Midsummer Night's Dream*. ARNOLD WHITTALL

Alberti, Domenico (*b* Venice, *c*1710; *d* Rome, 14 Oct 1746). Italian composer. Few reliable facts about his life are known. He reportedly studied counterpoint with Lotti and singing with Biffi. In the mid-1730s he went to Spain as secretary to a Venetian ambassador. Farinelli, who arrived there in 1737, paid tribute to his singing. By September 1737 Alberti must have returned to Venice, for his serenata *Endimione* (in *I-Mb*) was performed there on 24 September under the auspices of a society of merchants; another serenata on a text by Metastasio, *La Galatea* (in *F-Pn*, *I-Brc* and *MOe*), was performed before the same society later in the year. Alberti subsequently went to Rome in the company of the Marquis Giovanni Carlo Molinari, earning plaudits for his singing and harpsichord playing. His tomb lies in the Palazzo S Marco.

Alberti's posthumous fame has rested mainly on his harpsichord sonatas, although he composed at least as much sacred and secular vocal music. Besides the two serenatas there are several surviving operatic arias (in *A-Wn*, *D-Mbs*, *Bds*, *Dlb*, *Gb-Lbl* and *I-Bc*), which include settings of texts from Metastasio's *L'Olimpiade* and *Temistocle*. Since there are no reliable reports of productions of operas by Alberti, these may have been merely *arie di baule* for individual singers or contributions to pasticcios.

*

J.-B. de La Borde: *Essai sur la musique ancienne et moderne* (Paris, 1780), iii, 161–2 MICHAEL TALBOT

Albertini, Giuliano (*fl* 1701–38). Italian alto castrato. Probably from Florence, he had a long career there, singing in 24 operas, including works by Orlandini, Gasparini and Albinoni, 1701–38. He was employed by the Cardinal and later the Grand Duchess of Tuscany. He sang in Venice in 1705, 1709 (two operas by Lotti and Handel's *Agrippina*) and 1718–19, in Naples in 1707–9 (four operas, including A. Scarlatti's *Teodosio*), Bologna in 1711, Modena in 1716 and Rome in 1729. In *Agrippina* he played the freedman Narcissus, a part that makes slight demands on range and skill; its compass is *a* to *d″*. WINTON DEAN

Albertini, Joachim [Gioacchino] (*b* Pesaro, 30 Nov 1748; *d* Warsaw, 27 March 1812). Polish composer of Italian birth. He was known as an aria composer and 'young virtuoso' in 1777. Later he was conductor at Prince Karol Radziwiłł's residence at Nieśwież, and from 1782 *maître de chapelle* at King Stanisław August Poniatowski's court in Warsaw. In 1796 he went to Rome, and in autumn 1803 was back in Poland, where he spent the rest of his life. He is principally known for his opera *Don Juan albo Ukarany libertyn* ('Don Juan, or The Rake Punished'), believed to have been performed in Warsaw with an Italian text by G. Bertati in 1780–81; in 1783 it was performed in Polish, and it was later twice revised by Albertini for performances in 1790 and 1803.

La cacciatrice brillante (int, G. Mancinelli), Rome, Tordinona, Feb 1772
Don Juan albo Ukarany libertyn [Don Juan, or The Rake Punished] (3, G. Bertati, trans. W. Bogusławski), Warsaw, 23 Feb 1783; score (It. text), *I-Fc*, 2 fragments (It. text), *PL-ŁA*; Pol. lib. (Warsaw, 1783)
Circe und Ulisses (os), Hamburg, spr. 1785
Virginia (os, L. Romanelli), Rome, Dame, 7 Jan 1786; 1 song (London, *c*1788), arias *I-Mc*, *Rsc*, selections *Tn*
Scipione africano (os, N. Minato), Rome, 1789
La virgine vestale (os, M. Prunetti), Rome, Dame, carn. 1803
Kapelmajster polski [Polish Conductor] (int, L. A. Dmuszewski), Warsaw, 28 Oct 1808

*

SMP
U. Monferrari: *Dizionario universale delle opere melodrammatiche* (Florence, 1954)
A. Nowak-Romanowicz: *Z dziejów polskiej kultury muzycznej* [A Historical Survey of Musical Culture in Poland], ii (Kraków, 1966)
Z. Raszewski: 'Rondo alla Polacca', *Pamiętnik literacki* [Literary Review], ii (1970) ALINA NOWAK-ROMANOVICZ

Albery, Tim [Bronson Reginald] (*b* Harpenden, 4 June 1952). English director. Born into a distinguished theatrical family (his father was the impresario Donald Albery), he first gained a reputation in the British regional and avant-garde theatre with distinctive modern reappraisals of the classics marked by a cool, highly refined sense of visual style. His first opera production was of *The Turn of the Screw*, at the 1983 Musica Nel Chiostro festival at Batignano, Italy; this led to work with Opera North – Tippett's *Midsummer Marriage* (1985), *La finta giardiniera* (1989), and most notably the production of *Les Troyens* (begun in 1986) that was later shared between Opera North, Welsh National Opera and Scottish Opera. In each of these, but most particularly in his triumphant production of the Berlioz epic, Albery's invention of a modern visual and dramatic language that combined stillness, taut economy, intense feeling for states of psychological and poetic complexity, and deep musical responsiveness created a powerful impression of musico-dramatic revelation. For the ENO he produced Berlioz's *Béatrice et Bénédict* (1990) and Britten's *Billy Budd* (1988) and *Peter Grimes* (1991); European engagements include Catalani's *La Wally* at the 1990 Bregenz Festival and Berlioz's *Benvenuto Cellini* in Amsterdam (1991).

MAX LOPPERT

Albini, Srećko (*b* Županja, 10 Dec 1869; *d* Zagreb, 18 April 1933). Croatian composer and conductor. After leaving school he studied music in Graz, where he was Kapellmeister of the Stadttheater from 1893 to 1895. He was then conductor of the Zagreb Opera until 1902, when the company's activities were interrupted, and resumed this position in 1909 having spent the interim years composing in Vienna. As director and conductor at Zagreb (until 1919) he contributed a great deal to the expansion of the repertory, presenting many contemporary Croatian operas by, among others, Bersa, Hatze, Širola and Lhotka.

Albini's best and best-known compositions are his operettas. He is Croatia's most important composer of operetta in the period between Ivan Zajc and Ivo Tijardović. His works are in the tradition of the classical Viennese operetta, a genre he enriched with the local colour of stylized folk dances (*kolo*) and traditional tunes, particularly those from Slavonia, as in *Baron Trenck*. His genuine sense of drama and musical effect made his best operettas successful outside Croatia, notably in Austria and Germany.

operettas unless otherwise stated
Maričon (op, 3, M. Smrekar), Zagreb, 23 Nov 1901, vs (Zagreb, 1901)
Nabob (3, L. Krenn), Vienna, Carl, 23 Sept 1905; rev. as Die Barfusstänzerin (2, B. Jenbach), Leipzig, Altes, 28 Aug 909, vs (Leipzig, 1909); rev. as Bosonoga plesačica (D. Dubajić and Đ. Vaić), Zagreb, 23 April 1939
Madame Troubadur (3, Jenbach and R. Pohl), Zagreb, 3 April 1907, vs (Vienna, 1909)
Baron Trenck [Barun Trenk] (3, M. A. Willner and R. Bodanzky), Leipzig, Stadt, 1908, vs (Vienna, 1908)
Die kleine Baronesse (1, Bodanzky), Vienna, Apollo, 1 April 1909, vs (Vienna, 1908)
Pepeljuga [Cinderella] (Spl)

*

K. Kovačević: *Hrvatski kompozitori i njihova djela* [Croatian Composers and their Works] (Zagreb, 1960), 9–12
J. Andreis: *Music in Croatia* (Zagreb, 1974) KORALJKA KOS

Albinoni, Tomaso Giovanni [Zuane] (*b* Venice, 8 June 1671; *d* Venice, 17 Jan 1751). Italian composer. His father Antonio was a stationer and manufacturer of playing cards. Tomaso, the eldest son, served his apprenticeship as a stationer and for a while worked in this trade as a fully qualified 'master'; for this reason he liked to be described in his early published works and in the librettos of his first operas as a 'dilettante'. Before his father's death in 1709, however, he had abandoned the family business, leaving a brother to take charge.

There is little information about Albinoni's training as a musician, although Legrenzi has been mooted rather implausibly as a possible teacher. He certainly studied singing in his youth, although it was as a violinist that he first came to prominence. His aspirations as a composer developed rapidly after about 1690. From this time until he ceased composing, about ten years before his death, he divided his attention fairly equally between instrumental music (sonatas, ballettos and concertos) and vocal music (operas, comic intermezzos, oratorios, serenatas and solo cantatas), though with slight variations of emphasis at different stages of his career. Both his first published collection of instrumental music (*Suonate a tre*, op. 1) and his first opera (*Zenobia, regina de' Palmireni*) date from 1694.

In 1705 Albinoni married the soprano Margherita Raimondi, who had made her operatic début in Venice in 1699, aged about 15. Margherita continued her stage career intermittently until her death in 1721 but, strangely, never appeared in any work by her husband. Quietly industrious but remaining on the margin of Venetian musical life, Albinoni pursued a freelance career as a composer, seeking no official positions, though he was proposed unsuccessfully as the new *maestro di coro* at the Ospedale dei Derelitti in 1743. Caffi stated that he ran a successful school of singing. His few absences from Venice were mainly to officiate as a violinist at the premières of his new operas. In 1703 he travelled to Florence for the opening of *Griselda* and *Aminta*; in 1722 he was in Munich for *I veri amici* and *Il trionfo d'amore*.

Albinoni is known to have composed a total of 48 operas, although the libretto of his penultimate opera *Candalide* (1734) identifies it as his 80th; in addition, there are three sets of comic intermezzos and four shorter dramatic works (serenatas). Even if we accept the true total as nearer 50 than 80, Albinoni ranks among the most successful and productive operatic composers of his time, comparable with Vivaldi and Francesco Gasparini. Moreover, his operas held the stage in Venice over a longer period of time (1694–1741) than those of any contemporary. This was partly due to his longevity and permanent residence in Venice but it also reflects the success with which he was able to modify his style to suit changes in fashion, especially those brought about by the sudden rise to prominence of Neapolitan composers in the mid-1720s. He was not associated exclusively with any single Venetian opera house for any length of time; nor was he ever a dominating presence in a theatre after the fashion of Gasparini or C. F. Pollarolo, though he occasionally supplied all the operas heard during one season (as in 1700–01, 1717–18 and 1729–30 at S Angelo). On the whole, smaller theatres under the control of independent impresarios favoured him more than larger ones managed by noble proprietors; significantly, he received only one *scrittura*, in 1717, from the S Giovanni Grisostomo house, the most fashionable in Venice. 11 operas were written to commissions from outside Venice, mostly for centres in north and central Italy.

Albinoni's vocal and instrumental styles cross-fertilized each other throughout his life. He was a pioneer composer of violin and oboe concertos, and the idiomatic figurations of their solo and orchestral parts also inform the accompaniments of his dramatic music. Dance-rhythms encountered in his ballettos are found in the operas, though this fondness for mechanically repetitive rhythmic patterns based on dance-types is fairly general in Venetian operas of his period. He inclined towards a rather abstract style of vocal writing in which the demands of word-setting and word-painting are subordinated to a desire to write perfectly shaped, sensitively balanced melodies almost irrespective of context. Unexpectedly, the intricate counterpoint that characterizes Albinoni's instrumental works – a counterpoint derived more from the combination of dissimilar lines than from regular imitative patterns – rarely appears in his operas outside duets and other ensembles, though it has a notable presence in one of the serenatas (*Il nascimento de l'Aurora*). The most recognizably 'Albinonian' type of aria is homophonic, regularly phrased, cheerful in mood and marked by a beguiling naivety. Albinoni was in fact better at expressing mild emotions, which were in tune with the temperate climate of his natural musical language, than forceful ones. His surviving intermezzos, *Pimpinone* (1708), though primitive and musically unadventurous compared with Telemann's later setting of a version of the same libretto, evidence a distinct gift for comic writing, particularly in the duets, where the singers have effectively contrasted lines. In his early operas he handled recitative clumsily, but he became more expert as his career progressed; the opening recitative of *Statira* (1726), for instance, achieves great immediacy through careful shaping.

Albinoni rarely advanced beyond the conception of music, normal for the time and place, as 'clothing' for a dramatically self-sufficient literary composition. The prescriptions of his librettists (e.g. the choice of through-composed, strophic or da capo form for an aria) are for the most part faithfully observed. Just occasionally, however, a streak of inventiveness reveals itself. For instance, one short aria in *Zenobia*, Aurelian's 'Sì, spero di goder', is apparently conceived by the poet as through-composed, but Albinoni emphasized the interruption that follows by setting the words as a da capo aria broken off shortly after the start of the B section.

On the whole more conventional in his operatic than his instrumental music, Albinoni is a good representative of Venetian opera in the first half of the 18th century. To modern audiences his operas may seem to lack stageworthiness because the music takes a passive role in the unfolding of the drama. Although much of this criticism must be levelled at the conventions of his time, it cannot be denied that he was better as a musician *tout court* than as a musical dramatist; nevertheless his dramatic music deserves an occasional hearing on account of its distinctive musical voice.

See also PIMPINONE (i); STATIRA (ii); and ZENOBIA, REGINA DE' PALMIRENI.

first performed in Venice unless otherwise stated

VA – *Teatro S Angelo* VC – *Teatro S Cassiano*
VM – *Teatro S Moisè*

dm – *dramma per musica*

Zenobia, regina de' Palmireni (dm, 3, A. Marchi), SS Giovanni e Paolo, carn. 1694, *US-Wc* (*R*1979: IOB, xv), arias *A-Wn*
Il prodigio dell'innocenza (dramma, 3, F. M. Gualazzi), SS Giovanni e Paolo, carn. 1695
Zenone, imperator d'oriente (dm, 3, Marchi), VC, aut. 1696
Il Tigrane, re d'Armenia (dm, 3, Marchi), VC, carn. 1697
Primislao, primo re di Boemia (dm, 3, G. C. Corradi), VC, aut. 1697
L'ingratitudine gastigata (dm, 3, F. Silvani), VC, carn. 1698; as Alarico, Piacenza, Ducale, 1712
Radamisto (dm, 3, Marchi), VA, aut. 1698, arias *GB-Lgc*
Diomede punito da Alcide (dramma, 3, A. Aureli), VA, aut. 1700
L'inganno innocente (dm, 3, Silvani), VA, carn. 1701, arias *B-Br*; as Rodrigo in Algeri, addns by J. B. Stuck, Naples, S Bartolomeo, Dec 1702
L'arte in gara con l'arte (dm, 3, Silvani), VC, carn. 1702
Griselda (dm, 3, A. Zeno), Florence, Cocomero, carn. 1703, arias *I-Mc*; as L'umiltà esaltata, Naples, S Bartolomeo, 1734
Aminta (dramma regio pastorale, 3, Zeno), Florence, Cocomero, aut. 1703
Il più fedel tra i vassalli (dm, 3, Silvani), Genoa, Falcone, aut. 1705
La prosperità di Elio Sejano (dm, 3, N. Minato), Genoa, Falcone, carn. 1707
La fede tra gl'inganni (dm, 3, Silvani), VA, carn. 1707
La fortezza al cimento (melodramma, 2, Silvani), Piacenza, Ducale, 1707
Astarto (dm, 3, Zeno and P. Pariati), VC, aut. 1708, arias *D-MÜs, SWl, GB-Ob*
Pimpinone (3 comic intermezzos, Pariati), VC, aut. 1708, *A-Wn, D-MÜs* (Intermezzo 1 only), aria *SWl*; as La serva astuta, Bologna, Formagliari, spr. 1717; ed. in RRMBE, xliii (1983)
Engelberta [Acts 1–3] (dm, 5, Zeno and Pariati), VC, carn. 1709, *A-Wn, D-B*, arias *GB-Ob* [Acts 4 and 5 by Gasparini]
Il tradimento tradito (dm, 3, Silvani), VA, carn. 1709
Ciro (dm, 3, Pariati), VC, carn. 1710
Il tiranno eroe (dm, 3, V. Cassani), VC, carn. 1711, arias *B-Bc*
Il Giustino (dm, 5, Pariati, after N. Beregan), Bologna, Formagliari, spr. 1711
La pace generosa (dm, 3, Silvani), Genoa, Falcone, aut. 1711, lib. *I-SA*
Le gare generose (dm, 3, A. Zaniboni), VC, aut. 1712, arias *D-SWl*
Lucio Vero (dm, 3, Zeno), Ferrara, S Stefano, spr. 1713
L'amor di figlio non conosciuto (dm, 3, D. Lalli), VA, carn. 1716

Eumene (dm, 3, A. Salvi), S Giovanni Grisostomo, aut. 1717, arias *F-Pc*, *I-Bc*
Meleagro (dm, 3, P. A. Bernardoni), VA, carn. 1718
Cleomene (dm, 3, Cassani), VA, carn. 1718
Gli eccessi della gelosia (dm, 3, Lalli), VA, carn. 1722, arias *D-Hs*, *GB-Lbl*, *US-Wc*; as La Mariane, addl music by G. Porta, VA, carn. 1724 and 1725, aria *D-SWl*
I veri amici (dm, 3, Silvani, rev. Lalli, after P. Corneille), Munich, Hof, Oct 1722, arias *GB-Ob*
Eumene (dm, 3, Zeno), VM, carn. 1723, aria *Lbl*
Ermengarda (dm, 3, A. M. Lucchini), VM, aut. 1723, aria *I-CF*
Antigono, tutore di Filippo, re di Macedonia (tragedia, 5, G. Piazzon), VM, carn. 1724, collab. G. Porta, aria *D-ROu*
Scipione nelle Spagne (dm, 3, Zeno), S Samuele, Ascension 1724
Laodice (dm, 3, A. Schietti), VM, aut. 1724, arias *I-CF*
Didone abbandonata (tragedia, 3, P. Metastasio), VC, carn. 1725
Alcina delusa da Ruggero (dm, 3, Marchi), VC, aut. 1725; rev. as Gli evenimenti di Ruggero, VM, carn. 1732
I rivali generosi (dm, 3, Zeno), Brescia, Nuovo, 1725
Statira (dm, 3, Zeno and Pariati), Rome, Capranica, carn. 1726, *A-Wn* (microfilm), arias *GB-Cfm*, *Lbl*
Malsazio e Fiammetta (comic intermezzos), Rome, Capranica, carn. 1726
Il trionfo di Armida (dm, 3, G. Colatelli, after T. Tasso: *Gerusalemme liberata*), VM, aut. 1726
L'incostanza schernita (dramma comico-pastorale, 3, Cassani), S Samuele, Ascension 1727, arias *F-Pc*, *GB-Lbl*, *Ob*; as Filandro, VM, carn. 1729; as L'infedeltà delusa, Vicenza, Grazie, May 1729
Le due rivali in amore (dm, 3, Aureli), VM, aut. 1728
Il Satrapone (comic intermezzos, Salvi), Parma, Omodeo, 1729
Li stratagemmi amorosi (dm, 3, F. Passerini), VM, carn. 1730
Elenia (dm, 3, L. Bergalli), VA, carn. 1730
Merope (dramma, 3, Zeno), Prague, Sporck, aut. 1731 [music largely by Albinoni]
Il più infedele tra gli amanti (dm, 3, Schietti), Treviso, Dolfin, aut. 1731
Ardelinda (dramma, 3, B. Vitturi), VA, aut. 1732, arias *I-Bas*
Candalide (dm, 3, Vitturi), VA, carn. 1734
Artamene (dm, 3, Vitturi), VA, carn. 1741

Arias, presumably from operas, in *D-SWl*, *E-Mn*, *GB-Lgc*, *I-CF*, *Nc*, *S-L*

Shorter dramatic works: Il nascimento de l'Aurora (festa pastorale), ?Venice, Austrian ambassador's residence, *c*1710, *A-Wn*; Il trionfo d'amore (componimento poetico per servire ad un carosello, Pariati), Munich, Nov 1722; Il nome glorioso in terra, santificato in cielo (serenata, Cassani), Austrian ambassador's residence, 4 Nov 1724, *Wn*; Il concilio de' pianeti (serenata, G. Baruffaldi), French ambassador's residence, 16 Oct 1729

*

F. Caffi: *Storia della musica teatrale in Venezia* (MS, *I-Vnm*)
R. Giazotto: *Tomaso Albinoni: 'musico di violino dilettante veneto' (1671–1750)* (Milan, 1945)
J. E. Solie: 'Aria Structure and Ritornello Form in the Music of Albinoni', *MQ*, lxiii (1977), 31–47
H. C. Wolff: 'Neue Quellen zu den Opern des Tommaso Albinoni', *Studi musicali*, viii (1979), 273–89
M. Talbot: *Albinoni: Leben und Werk* (Adliswil, 1980)
H. C. Wolff: ' "Pimpinone" von Albinoni und Telemann – ein Vergleich', *HJbMw*, v (1981), 29–36
——: 'Zur Neuausgabe von Tommaso Albinonis Oper "Zenobia" (1694)', *Mf*, xxxvi (1983), 79–82
M. Talbot: *Tomaso Albinoni: the Venetian Composer and his World* (Oxford, 1990)
MICHAEL TALBOT

Albion and Albanius. Opera in three acts by LUIS GRABU to a libretto by JOHN DRYDEN; London, Dorset Garden Theatre, early June 1685.

In 1680–81 the reign of Charles II was gravely threatened by the Exclusion Crisis, an attempt by certain members of Parliament to block the succession of his brother, James, Duke of York, a Roman Catholic. With the defeat of the Exclusionists and the foiling of plots to assassinate him, Charles II requested 'something at least like an Opera' to celebrate his deliverance and the continuation of the Stuart line. The actor-manager Thomas Betterton was despatched to Paris in 1683 with instructions 'to carry over the Opera', that is, Jean-Baptiste Lully and members of the Académie Royale de Musique. When this proved impracticable, Betterton returned with Luis Grabu, former Master of the King's Music, who had been living in exile in Paris since 1679.

Apparently misunderstanding the king's request, John Dryden, the poet laureate, wrote a play in blank verse, 'adorn'd with Scenes, Machines, Songs and Dances', that is, *King Arthur*. But it was soon augmented with an allegorical prologue, which Grabu was invited to set to music. By August 1684 the two projects had become separated and for some unknown reason Dryden shelved *King Arthur* and expanded the prologue into a three-act opera, which was finished by Christmas 1684; this was called *Albion and Albanius*. King Charles attended at least three rehearsals at Whitehall Palace in January 1685, particularly enjoying Acts 1 and 3, but his unexpected death on 6 February made any public performance impossible. A few months later Dryden and Grabu altered the ending to allude to the king's death and the opera was finally performed at the Dorset Garden Theatre in early June. Unfortunately, the first run was cut short and the opera abandoned when news of the Duke of Monmouth's Rebellion reached London on 13 June.

Albion and Albanius is an allegory of the Restoration in which Albion (baritone) clearly represents Charles II, Albanius (tenor) the Duke of York (later James II), Archon (bass) General Monck (who secured Charles's actual return to London) and Acacia [Innocence] (soprano) possibly Catherine of Braganza. Act 1 represents the defeat of the opponents of monarchy, Democracy (alto) and Zelota [Zeal, i.e. Puritanism] (soprano), and the triumphal entry of the royal brothers into London. Acts 2 and 3 offer a remarkably frank account of the many crises of Charles's reign, including the Popish Plot, various assassination plots and the painful decision to send his brother into exile to appease the anti-Catholic faction. The final defeat of Democracy and Asebia [Atheism] (soprano) is followed by the apotheosis of Albion.

Dryden was forced to defend his choice of composer, Grabu, against whom a party 'of his own Profession', that is, 'some *English* Musicians, and their Scholars' had formed. The Spaniard's rapid promotion to Master of the King's Music in 1666 was still resented, and he had long been accused (unfairly) of professional incompetence. After praising Grabu's skill 'in diversifying the Recitative, the Lyrical part, and the Chorus', Dryden proclaimed: 'When any of our Country-men excel him, I shall be glad, for the sake of old *England*, to be shown my error', words he graciously ate after hearing Purcell's music for the second, revised version of *King Arthur* in 1691.

In 1687 Grabu published the full score of *Albion and Albanius*, the first full-length opera in English to survive. It resembles a Lullian *tragédie lyrique* in everything but language: the drama unfolds in units of intermingled recitative, arioso, airs, choruses and dances, and all the instrumental music (including the overture) is scored for five-part strings (violin, three violas and bass) in the French manner; but most curious is Grabu's adoption of Lully's style of *récit*, with its frequent change from duple to triple metre, which no other contemporaneous composer felt necessary for setting English. Grabu's occasional misaccentuation has been ridiculed by many writers, perhaps most devastatingly by Edward Dent, but some more recent scholars have defended Grabu's prosody and pointed to the high quality of his part-writing. The scene in Act 2 in which Albion agonizes over the decision to send his brother into exile contains some particularly expressive accompagnato, and the great C major chaconne at the end of the second act, 'Ye nymphs, the charge is royal' (some 57 pages of full score), is a remarkable achievement and clearly influenced Purcell's similar (though much shorter) ground-bass multi-pieces in *Dioclesian* and *King Arthur*.

The failure of *Albion and Albanius* was circumstantial rather than solely artistic, though the Duke's Theatre company lost a huge amount of money on the production. Booksellers continued to stock the score for several years, and parts of the libretto were revised by Daniel Purcell and incorporated into the semi-opera *Brutus of Alba, or, Augusta's Triumph* in October 1696. *Albion and Albanius* itself is last heard of in June 1697, four years after Grabu had left England, when M. de Beaulieu advertised a private performance.

CURTIS PRICE

Alboni, Marietta [Maria Anna Marzia] (*b* Città di Castello, 6 March 1823; *d* Ville d'Avray, 23 June 1894). Italian contralto. She studied at Cesena with Bagioli and in Bologna with Domenico Mombelli and with Rossini, who gave her free lessons for three years. She made her début in 1842 at the Teatro Comunale as Clymene in Pacini's *Saffo*, and also sang Maffio Orsini in *Lucrezia Borgia*. Under contract to the impresario Merelli, she achieved success at La Scala in Rossini's *Le siège de Corinthe* (30 December 1842) and Marliani's *Ildegonda*, Donizetti's *La favorite*, Salvi's *Lara*, *Norma* and Pacini's *L'ebrea*.

Her success took her to St Petersburg (1844–5) where she sang Gondi in Donizetti's *Maria di Rohan* and Arsace in Rossini's *Semiramide*. After playing Anziletto in the première of Gordigiani's *Consuelo* at Prague (1846), she sang Arsace again at the opening of the Royal Italian Opera at Covent Garden (1847). That season she appeared in leading roles by Rossini and Donizetti (where she outshone Giulia Grisi and Jenny Lind) and also sang Cherubino (performing with Henriette Sontag), the baritone role of Don Carlo in *Ernani* and Urbain in *Les Huguenots*, to which the composer added an aria for her. She first appeared in Paris at the Théâtre Italien (2 December 1847) as Arsace and then as Rossini's Cenerentola, returning, at the Opéra, in 1851 as Zerline at the première of Auber's *La corbeille d'oranges*. In 1849 she appeared in Brussels and at Her Majesty's Theatre, London; the next year she undertook a tour of France. She then toured Spain and the USA, arriving in New York in 1852, but abandoned her career in 1863. In 1868, however, she sang at Rossini's funeral and in April 1872 played Fidalma in Cimarosa's *Il matrimonio segreto* at the Théâtre Italien. Her voice, dramatic, flexible, rich and wide-ranging, was admired for its beauty, perfection and assured technique; she was one of the finest representatives of classical Italian bel canto.

Marietta Alboni (right) as Urbain and Pauline Viardot as Valentine in Meyerbeer's 'Les Huguenots', Act 1 scene ix (Covent Garden, 1848): lithograph from a contemporary sheet music cover

ES (F. d'Amico)
Obituary, *Le ménestrel*, xxvi (1894), 205–6
A. Pougin: *Marietta Alboni* (Paris, 1912)
G. Adami: *Tre romanzi dell '800* (Milan, 1943)
V. Rigoni: 'Centenario a Parigi', *Bollettino del Centro Rossiniano di Studi* (1956), 17
——: 'Una festa a Parigi', ibid (1956), 75–6
G. Gualerzi: 'I cantanti', *La Scala* (Milan, 1966)
H. Pleasants: *The Great Singers* (London, 1967), 223–4

GALLIANO CILIBERTI

Albrecht, Gerd (*b* Essen, 19 July 1935). German conductor. He studied conducting at Hamburg with Wilhelm Brückner-Rüggeberg, won various competitions and was répétiteur and conductor at the Stuttgart Opera (1958–61). He held conducting posts in Mainz, Lübeck and Kassel, was chief conductor at the Berlin Deutsche Oper, 1972–9, and became general music director at the Hamburg Staatsoper in 1988. His appearances abroad include operatic engagements in San Francisco and Buenos Aires; he made his British début at the 1983 Edinburgh Festival with the Hamburg company in a Zemlinsky double bill and first appeared at Covent Garden in 1986 conducting *Der fliegende Holländer*.

Albrecht's repertory embraces opera from three centuries, and he has conducted the premières of Fortner's *Elisabeth Tudor* (1972) at Berlin, and Reimann's *Lear* (1978) and *Troades* (1986), both at Munich. He made the first recordings of *Lear* and Schreker's *Der Schatzgräber*; his other operas on disc include *Cardillac* and early one-act operas by Hindemith. Albrecht is regularly admired for performances of pulsating spirit and expressive shading. He has shown special concern for children, participating in over 25 television films, books and recordings designed for them.

NOËL GOODWIN

Albuzzi [Albuzzio], **Ottavio** (*b* Milan, *c*1720; *d* after 1766). Italian tenor. He made his début in *opera seria* in Venice in autumn 1737, then sang with the Mingotti company in central Europe, resuming his Italian career in autumn 1740 when he was quickly recognized as a leading artist with engagements in the most important theatres. In Venice he sang in Gluck's *Ipermestra* (1744), Wagenseil's *Ariodante* (1745), Jommelli's

Sofonisba and Abos's *Artaserse* (both 1746). He retired after Carnival 1756 but in 1762 and 1766 sang in opera in Milan, where he was a singer at the cathedral and one of the teachers of the castrato Luigi Marchesi. Music written for him suggests a highly skilled singer with a mastery of bravura technique and a range about *c* to *b'*.

DENNIS LIBBY

Alcaide, Tomáz (de Aquino Carmelo) (*b* Estremoz, 16 Feb 1901; *d* Lisbon, 9 Nov 1967). Portuguese tenor. He studied in Portugal and in Milan (under Franco Ferrara). His beautiful lyric voice was flexible, with easy high notes and excellent breath control. He made his début in 1923 as Wilhelm Meister (*Mignon*) at the Teatro Carcano, Milan. A distinguished actor, he sang leading roles in about 30 operas (most frequently *Rigoletto*, *Faust*, *Les pêcheurs de perles*, *Manon*, *La bohème* and *Tosca*), at La Scala (début 1930), the Paris Opéra, La Monnaie, Brussels, the Vienna Staatsoper, and at the Salzburg Festival. He retired from the stage in 1948 and from 1963 produced for the Portuguese National Opera Company in Lisbon. He wrote his memoirs, *Um cantor no palco e na vida* (Lisbon, 1961).

JOÃO DE FREITAS BRANCO

Alceste (i) [*Alceste, ou Le triomphe d'Alcide* ('Alcestis, or The Triumph of Alcides')]. *Tragédie en musique* in a prologue and five acts by Jean-Baptiste Lully (*see* LULLY family, (1)) to a libretto by PHILIPPE QUINAULT after EURIPIDES' *Alcestis*; Paris, Opéra, 19 January 1674.

PROLOGUE

Nymph of the Seine	soprano
La Gloire [Glory]	soprano
Nymph of the Tuileries	soprano
Nymph of the Marne	soprano

TRAGEDY

Alceste [Alcestis] *Princess of Iolcos*	soprano
Admète [Admetus] *King of Thessaly*	haute-contre
Alcide [Alcides, or Hercules]	baritone
Licomède [Lycomedes] *brother of Thetis, King of Scyros*	bass
Lychas *confidant of Hercules*	haute-contre
Straton *confidant of Lycomedes*	bass
Céphise *confidante of Alcestis*	soprano
Cléante *knight of Admetus*	tenor
Pherès [Pheres] *father of Admetus*	tenor
Charon	baritone
Pluton [Pluto]	bass
Thétis [Thetis] *a sea-nymph*	soprano
Apollon [Apollo]	haute-contre
Proserpine [Proserpina]	soprano
The Ghost of Alcestis	silent role
Alecton [Alecto] *a Fury*	haute-contre
A Rebuffed Ghost	soprano
Eole [Aeolus] *King of the winds*	baritone
Diane [Diana]	soprano
Mercure [Mercury]	silent role

Followers of Glory, naiads, rustic divinities, river divinities, the Pleasures; Thessalians, pages and followers, sea divinities, sailors, four aquilons, four zephyrs; Lycomedes' soldiers, Thessalian soldiers, the Arts; afflicted women, sorrowful men; the shades, followers of Pluto; people of Greece, the nine Muses, the Games, shepherds and shepherdesses, herdsmen

Setting The city of Iolcos in Thessaly

This was Lully's second tragedy. The king and courtiers saw a rehearsal at Versailles in November 1673 and were enthusiastic. However, poets and musicians jealous of Lully's growing power and of the success of *Cadmus et Hermione* organized a cabal to discredit *Alceste* after its première. Only Perrault defended the work at length, pointing out that everybody 'knows by heart' and sings everywhere the little songs that are said to be worthless, that the many scenes judged 'useless' by the critics (mainly scenes dominated by secondary characters) all have their dramatic purposes, and that the conventions of opera are different from those of spoken tragedy and comedy (*Critique de l'opéra*, 1674, attrib. Charles or Pierre Perrault).

Despite the cabal, *Alceste* succeeded. It had its court première at Versailles on 4 July 1674, as part of an extended celebration of the victory over Franche-Comté (see fig.2 below). There were additional court productions at Fontainebleau in 1677 and Saint-Germain-en-Laye in 1678. The casts at the Paris and court premières are uncertain. At Fontainebleau in 1677 the principal singers included Saint-Christophle (Alcestis and the Nymph of the Seine), La Garde (Céphise and Glory), Gaye (Hercules), Cledière (Admetus), Langeais (Lychas), Morel (Straton) and Godonesche (Charon, Lycomedes and Pluto); the principal dancers (all male) included Faure, Favier, Lestang and Magny. There were Paris Opéra revivals regularly up to 1757. Between 1695 and 1730 *Alceste* was produced in Marseilles, Lyons, Brussels and other cities.

PROLOGUE *Paris, on the banks of the Seine in the Tuileries garden* The Nymph of the Seine longs for Louis XIV to return from battle (extended rondeau, 'Le héros que j'attens ne reviendra-t'il pas?'). She is assured that he follows Glory (whose descent is announced by trumpets and timpani) but will return. The pastoral divinities celebrate. The *air* 'L'art accord avec la nature', sung by the Nymph of the Tuileries, was a favourite of early audiences.

ACT 1 *A seaport* The tragedy begins at the wedding of Admetus and Alcestis. An undeclared suitor, Hercules, prepares to leave Iolcos. A jilted suitor, Lycomedes, abducts Alcestis under the guise of giving a

1. 'Alceste' (Lully): Jean Berain's design for the marine chariot of the sea-nymph Thetis for the original production at the Paris Opéra (Académie Royale de Musique) on 19 January 1674 (or possibly for the revivals of 1677–8)

2. *'Alceste' (Lully): performance in the Cour de Marbre, Versailles (4 July 1674) as part of the celebrations marking the victory over Franche-Comté: engraving by Jean Le Pautre showing the final scene in Act 4 (Hercules (right, wearing a lion-skin), heralded by the fury Alecto, invades the court of Pluto and Proserpina who are guarding Alcestis)*

party for the betrothed couple; his escape is aided by a storm at sea. The tempest scene, apparently inspired by an episode in Virgil's *Aeneid* (book 1), demonstrates well the flexible relationship between ballet and drama in the Lullian tragedy: after a series of dances and dance-songs, Lycomedes' invitation to Alcestis to join him on his ship (marked by a change of key) seems to signal the end of the *divertissement* and the return to high drama; yet the presentation of that drama relies on the conventions of court ballet. Lycomedes' sister, the sea-nymph Thetis (fig.1), rises from the sea on a marine chariot, and at her command four dancers representing storm winds stir up the water. The 'Entrée des Aquilons' is a dance in running semiquavers. In a soothing *air*, the wind god Aeolus calls on the gentle west winds to calm the sea. Four flying 'zephyrs' chase the four scurrying 'aquilons' into the sea, allowing Admetus's army (including Hercules) to pursue Lycomedes' ship.

A comic subplot, involving a love triangle among the confidants of the main characters, begins in Act 1; it continues in Acts 2 and 5. Céphise, a girl of 15 who makes a virtue of fickleness, is responsible for much of this opera's lyricism: she is frequently present and sings numerous charming little *airs*.

ACT 2 *City on the island of Scyros* The *divertissement* is a spectacular battle: half the chorus and dancers represent the 'besieging soldiers' and the other half the 'besieged soldiers'. Hercules triumphs and delivers Alcestis, but Admetus is mortally wounded. Alcestis and the dying Admetus say a moving farewell: intertwined solo fragments grow progressively shorter and gradually give way to a duet. Apollo offers immortal glory to anyone who volunteers to die in Admetus's stead.

ACT 3 *A monument raised by the Arts* A central altar will bear the image of the person who dies for Admetus. Only Alcestis will sacrifice herself. The *divertissement* is a monumental funeral scene including pantomime ballet; the introduction is organized around the choral refrain 'Alceste est morte!', and the conclusion is a choral chaconne during which the chorus and orchestra gradually fade. Hercules, who loves Alcestis, intends to try to bring her back from Hades and asks Admetus to relinquish her to him. In the hope of seeing Alcestis alive, Admetus agrees.

ACT 4 *The River Acheron, then Pluto's palace* The act opens with one of Lully's best-known passages. In the *air* 'Il faut passer tôt ou tard', over a bass line representing the flowing River Acheron, a frankly comic Charon sings cheerfully of the inevitability of death. In the doubled continuo *air* 'Donne, passe', he collects a fare from the shades with bourgeois efficiency. Hercules simply jumps into the ferryboat and demands passage. Despite a majestic entrance *prélude* for Pluto and his retinue, this is not a solemn underworld: in a light and stylish *fête*, the shades welcome Alcestis to eternal peace. The *divertissement* is interrupted by Hercules' arrival (fig.2), announced by the barking of Cerberus, cleverly represented by a male chorus. After hearing Hercules' entreaties, Proserpina persuades Pluto to allow Hercules to take Alcestis.

ACT 5 *A triumphal arch* In a *choeur en rondeau*, 'Alcide est vainqueur du trépas', different peoples of Greece, led by Admetus, cheer Hercules' triumph over death. Admetus and Alcestis sadly prepare to part. Hercules announces that, having conquered an army and conquered death, he will now conquer his own desires and allow Alcestis and Admetus to remain together. The final *divertissement* is a celebration of love and of Hercules' generosity.

* * *

Like most *tragédies en musique*, *Alceste* contains plenty of heroic action but no exploration of a tragic dilemma: the characters make their sacrifices without apparent second thoughts or discussion. In place of human dilemma and discussion, the genre offers human and supernatural spectacle, and these features were already fully developed in this early work. The ballet *divertissements* present a catalogue of stock topics, to which French librettists and composers would return many times: maritime celebration, tempest, battle scene, funeral, underworld scene and pastoral celebration. Compared with Lully's mature operas of the 1680s, *Alceste* makes sparing use of the full orchestra, and the recitative virtually never exploits subtle conflict between poetic and musical metre; still the composer's general manner of structuring dialogues was well developed and successful by this time. Finally, from a modern point of view, the presence of comic scenes – criticized at the time – is a virtue rather than a vice since Lully was a gifted musical comedian.

See also ALCESTIS below. LOIS ROSOW

Alceste (ii) ('Alcestis').

Italian version: *Tragedia* in three acts by CHRISTOPH WILLIBALD GLUCK to a libretto by RANIERI DE' CALZABIGI after EURIPIDES; Vienna, Burgtheater, 26 December 1767.

French version: *Tragédie opéra* in three acts by Gluck to a libretto by MARIE FRANÇOIS LOUIS GAND LEBLANC ROULLET after Calzabigi; Paris, Académie Royale de Musique, 23 April 1776.

The Italian *Alceste* was the second of Gluck's three so-called reform operas written with Ranieri de' Calzabigi (the others were *Orfeo ed Euridice* and *Paride ed Elena*) in which a noble simplicity in the action and the music was intended to replace the complicated plots and florid musical style of *opera seria*. Although *Orfeo* was the first, it is *Alceste* that contains, in the first edition of the score, the famous preface in which Gluck and Calzabigi outlined their principles and ideals (*see* GLUCK, CHRISTOPH WILLIBALD, §6). The opera was a great success; according to Calzabigi 60 performances were given in Vienna. It was choreographed not by Angiolini, the choreographer of *Orfeo* in 1762, but his rival JEAN-GEORGES NOVERRE, also an influential figure in the early *ballet d'action*. The principals in the first performance included Antonia Bernasconi (Alcestis), Giuseppe Tibaldi (Admetus), Filippo Laschi (Apollo and the High Priest), Antonio Pilloni (Evander) and Teresa Eberardi (Ismene).

In 1770, for further performances in Vienna, Gluck rewrote the tenor role of Admetus for the soprano castrato Giuseppe Millico (just as he had the role of Orpheus for performances in Parma the previous year). *Alceste* was revived in Vienna in 1781 and 1786; local premières elsewhere in Europe included Copenhagen in 1775, Padua 1777, Bologna 1778, Lille 1783, Hanover 1783, Naples 1785, Florence 1786, London 1795, Berlin 1796, St Petersburg 1798, Moscow 1803 and Trieste 1804.

Gluck's revision of *Alceste* for performance in Paris in 1776 amounts almost to a recomposition. His alterations were far more extensive than those he had made in his Paris adaptation of *Orfeo* (the table below shows the structure of the two versions side by side). The French *Alceste* had a new text by Roullet, Gluck's librettist for *Iphigénie en Aulide*, based on Calzabigi's libretto; but alterations to the plot and the order of events led to major differences between the two. The principals at the première of the French version included Rosalie Levasseur (Alcestis), Joseph Legros (Admetus), Henri Larrivée (Hercules), Moreau (Apollo) and Nicolas Gélin (High Priest).

At the first Paris performances of *Alceste* the Act 3 denouement was substantially different from the version familiar today, and closer to the Italian original. Gluck and Roullet, after much criticism, altered the act to incorporate a part for Hercules, who has no place in the Italian original. Just as Gluck was arranging more music to enlarge the final *divertissement*, again to please Parisian taste, he heard of the death of his adopted daughter Marianne in Vienna; he left Paris and assigned the completion of the *divertissement* to Gossec. This revised version, published in Paris in 1776, is the one that has nearly always been performed subsequently; the Italian version has rarely been revived since the 18th century, although it was recorded in 1956, with Kirsten Flagstad in the title role. The French version has rarely been long out of the repertory, though as with so many

ITALIAN VERSION

Alceste [Alcestis] *Queen of Pherae in Thessaly*	soprano
Admeto [Admetus] *her husband*	tenor
Eumelo [Eumelus] } *their children*	soprano
Aspasia }	soprano
Evandro [Evander] *a confidant of Admetus*	tenor
Ismene *a confidante of Alcestis*	soprano
A Herald	bass
High Priest of Apollo	baritone
Apollo	baritone
Oracle	bass
Infernal Deity	bass

Courtiers, citizens, Alcestis's maids of honour, priests of Apollo, gods of the underworld

Setting Classical Pherae, Thessaly

FRENCH VERSION

Alceste [Alcestis] *Queen of Thessaly*	soprano
Admète [Admetus] *her husband*	tenor
Their two children	silent
Evandre [Evander] *leader of the Pherae people*	tenor
A Herald of Arms	bass
High Priest of Apollo	bass
Apollo *protector of the house of Admetus*	baritone
Hercule [Hercules]	bass
Oracle	bass
Thanatos *an infernal deity*	bass
Chorus Leaders	soprano, contralto, tenor, bass

Officers of the palace, Alcestis's attendants, citizens of Pherae, infernal deities, priests and priestesses in the temple of Apollo

Setting Classical Pherae, Thessaly

of Gluck's operas (*Orfeo ed Euridice* apart) it has been performed far less often than the lip-service it receives might lead one to imagine. Important productions have included one at the Paris Opéra in 1825 with Alexandrine Caroline Branchu as Alcestis; Berlioz saw it, and it may have influenced the edition he prepared for Pauline Viardot at the Opéra in 1861. Germaine Lubin was a notable Alcestis in Paris in the 1920s, 30s and 40s, and sang the role at Covent Garden in 1937. *Alceste* has received only sporadic performances in Britain in recent times, notably at Glyndebourne in the 1950s and at the Edinburgh Festival in 1974; Janet Baker chose it for her farewell performances at Covent Garden in 1981. Notable performances elsewhere include those by Wilhelmine Schröder-Devrient in Dresden in 1846; a production conducted by Liszt in Weimar in 1857; one at the Metropolitan Opera in New York in 1952 with Kirsten Flagstad as Alcestis; and one at La Scala in 1954 with Maria Callas in the title role and Carlo Maria Giulini conducting (one of Callas's performances was recorded). Of the two recordings of the French *Alceste* to date (one with Jessye Norman, the other with Ethel Semser), neither is absolutely complete.

In the synopsis that follows, '*I*' stands for the Italian version, '*F*' for the French version (numerals in *italics* denote the French version); see Table 1 (pages 64–6) for a comparison of the two versions.

Act 1 *The great square in the city of Pherae, with the façade of Admetus' palace on one side, filled by a crowd of distressed courtiers and citizens; also, in F, an entrance to the temple of Apollo at the back of the stage* The sombre overture is one of the earliest to set the mood for a tragic drama, according to Gluck's principles as outlined in the preface to the printed score of the opera. The Italian overture ends with an imperfect cadence before the herald's D major fanfare; the French has the first of many marvellous additions to the original as the chorus interrupts the overture with a short, anguished plea to the gods to return Admetus to them, beginning with an arresting diminished seventh chord.

1.i (*I*, *F*) The herald informs the crowd that Admetus is about to die and that nothing can save him. The people sing the first of the opera's choral laments ('Ah di questo afflitto regno'/'O dieux! qu'allons-nous devenir?'). This scene is more extended in the Italian version (no.4): the choral refrain returns twice, enclosing duet and solo sections for Evander and Ismene, and it includes too a sombre ballet movement, a recitative in which Evander suggests that they consult the Oracle in Apollo's temple, and a repeat of 'Ah di questo' with a solo for Evander before his announcement of Alcestis's approach (no.8). The French revision includes one statement of the choral lament (no.5), ending with a contrapuntal Allegro, immediately followed by Evander's briefer announcement of Alcestis's approach and a choral recitative (no.6).

1.ii (*I*, *F*) Another chorus of mourning ensues, 'Misero Admeto!'/'O malheureux Admète!', with chromatic harmony and antiphonal effects. Alcestis enters with a recitative and aria. In the Italian original she has one of the opera's few examples of conventional *recitativo secco* accompanied only by continuo. Her words, also conventional, would not be out of place in an *opera seria*: 'Popoli di Tessaglia' ('People of Thessaly, never were your tears more justified; to you no less than to these innocent children is Admetus a father': no.10). Her very different entry in the French revision (no.*8*) illustrates, in words and music, how far Gluck's dramatic powers had advanced. Not only is the French recitative orchestrally accompanied; in the middle of it seven bars from the chorus 'O malheureux Admète' heighten the pathos. Alcestis's aria, in which she beseeches the gods to delay their cruel decree ('Io non chiedo'/'Grands dieux!'), is in several sections of contrasting tempos, beginning with a long phrase for solo oboe (recalling 'Che puro ciel' in *Orfeo ed Euridice* and anticipating 'O malheureuse Iphigénie' in *Iphigénie en Tauride*). An agitated Allegro follows in which Alcestis sings of her suffering; in the Italian version this incorporates a short duet for Alcestis's children. In the French version the children were reduced to non-singing roles and the aria was substantially shortened. In both, its impassioned ending leads into a repeat of the chorus 'Misero Admeto!'/'O malheureux Admète!' (with the words changed to 'Miseri figli' in the Italian version).

Alcestis now urges the people, in a recitative (no.13/*11*), to join her in the temple of Apollo to beg the gods for mercy. In the French version this leads to a repeat of 'O dieux! qu'allons-nous devenir?'; the Italian has the chorus's cries in recitative of 'Al tempio', followed by a poignant two-and-a-half bars for two oboes linking the recitative to a repeat of the chorus 'Ah di questo afflitto regno', which this time ends with the contrapuntal section used in the French version.

1.iii (*I*, *F*) *The temple of Apollo with a huge statue of the god in the middle* A slow pantomime covers the change of scene; low divided flutes and first violins play one of Gluck's most sublime melodies as priests, priestesses and people process into the temple. The three trombones, whose solemn colours were prominent in the overture and in the choruses of the Italian version, are heard again as the High Priest begins his prayer (no.16/*14*). A chorus led by the High Priest restores the anguished mood of scene i, accompanied by trombones and with agitated rhythms in wind and strings. As in scene i, the repetition of choruses is an important part of the structure.

1.iv (*I*, *F*) Alcestis asks the god to accept her offerings and prayers. A repeat of the preceding chorus in the Italian version is replaced in the French by a chromatic pantomime to accompany the sacrifice (the dance from scene i of the Italian version, no.5). The High Priest, in a recitative (no.24/*22*) largely built from an arpeggio figure hammered out in octaves at the start, tells Alcestis that Apollo hears her prayers and receives her gifts favourably, and exhorts everyone to listen to the Oracle. The Oracle pronounces that Admetus will die that day unless another dies for him; the soft accompaniment of slow-moving trombones, woodwind and muted strings is, in the French version, a variation on the choral outburst at the end of the overture. The astonished people give vent to their terror; in the Italian version this chorus is animated by an offstage group of basses singing 'fuggiamo' ('let us flee') on a monotone, an effect Gluck removed when he adapted the opera for Paris. In the main Allegro Gluck gives a vivid impression of the frightened people fleeing in all directions, with disjointed musical fragments repeated again and again, gradually dying away to *pianissimo*.

1.v (*I*), v–vii (*F*) Alcestis, left alone (in the French version; with her two children in the Italian), resolves to die for Admetus so that the people can retain their king. Then comes the first of the major differences between the two versions. So far, the Italian has been the longer; but here the French version is expanded. Alcestis's

TABLE 1: Italian and French versions of *Alceste* (ii)

N – new to 1776 version; R – revision of number in 1767 version; items in 1776 version neither N nor R are in effect direct transcriptions; italic numerals represent 1776 version

	Italian version, 1767		*French version, 1776*
	ACT 1		ACT 1
1	Intrada, d	*1*	Ouverture, d
Scene i		*Scene i*	
		2	Choeur: Dieux, rendez-nous, d (*N*)
2	Improvviso di tromba, D	*3*	Prélude de trompette, D
3	Recit. (Un banditore): Popoli, che dolenti	*4*	Récit (Le herault): Peuples écoutez!
4	Coro, Ismene, Evandro: Ah di questo afflitto, E♭	*5*	Choeur, Coryphée, Evandre: O dieux! qu'allons-nous, E♭ (*R*4)
5	Aria di Pantomimo, c		
6	Recit. (Evandro): Amorosi vassalli		
7	Coro, Ismene, Evandro: Ah di questo afflitto, E♭		
8	Recit. (Evandro): Tacete! Ah della reggia	*6*	Récit (Evandre, Choeur): Suspendez vos gémissements (*R*8)
Scene ii		*Scene ii*	
9	Coro: Misero Admeto!, g	*7*	Choeur: O malheureux Admète!, g
10	Recit. (Alceste): Popoli di Tessaglia	*8*	Récit (Alceste): Sujets du roi le plus aimé (*R*10), incl. choral repeat of last 7 sung bars of *7*
11	Aria (Alceste, Eumelo, Aspasia): Io non chiedo, E♭	*9*	Air (Alceste): Grands dieux! du destin, E♭ (*R*11)
12	Coro: Miseri figli!, g	*10*	Choeur: O malheureux Admète!, g
13	Recit. (Alceste, Coro): Non si perda	*11*	Récit (Alceste): Suivez-moi dans le temple (*R*13)
14	Coro, Ismene, Evandro: Ah di questo afflitto, E♭	*12*	Choeur, Coryphée, Evandre: O dieux! qu'allons-nous, E♭
Scene iii		*Scene iii*	
15	Ballo, G	*13*	Pantomime, G
16	Recit. (Gran Sacerdote): Dilegua il nero turbine, C	*14*	Récit (Le Grand-Prêtre): Dieu puissant, C
17	Coro, Gran Sacerdote: Dilegua il nero turbine, c	*15*	Choeur, Le Grand-Prêtre: Dieu puissant, c (*R*17)
18	Recit. (Gran Sacerdote): A te Nume del giorno	*16*	Récit (Le Grand-Prêtre): Dispensateur de la lumière (*R*18)
19	Coro: Dilegua il nero turbine, c	*17*	Choeur, Le Grand-Prêtre: Dieu puissant, c (*R*19)
20	Recit. (Gran Sacerdote): Sospendete, O ministri	*18*	Récit (Le Grand-Prêtre): Suspendez vos sacrés mystères (*R*20)
21	Ballo, G	*19*	Pantomime, G
Scene iv		*Scene iv*	
22	Recit. (Alceste): Nume eterno	*20*	Récit (Alceste): Immortel Apollon!
23	Coro: Dilegua il nero turbine, c		
		21	Pantomime pour la sacrifice, c (=5)
24	Recit. (Gran Sacerdote): I tuoi prieghi	*22*	Récit (Le Grand-Prêtre): Apollon est sensible (*R*24)
25	Recit. (Oraculo): Il Re morrà, b	*23*	Récit (L'Oracle): Le roi doit mourir, b
26	Coro, coro de'Bassi dentro la scena: Che annunzio funesto, b–G	*24*	Le Grand-Prêtre, Choeur: Quel oracle funeste, b–G (*R*26)
Scene v		*Scene v*	
27	Recit. (Alceste): Ove son?	*25*	Récit (Alceste): Où suis-je? (*R*27)
		26	Air (Alceste): Non, ce n'est point un sacrifice, D (*N*)
		27	Récit (Alceste): Arbitres du sort des humains (*R*34, bars 52–67)
		Scene vi	
		28	Récit (Le Grand-Prêtre): Tes destins sont remplis (*N*)
		29	Air (Le Grand-Prêtre): Déjà la mort s'apprête (*R*33)
		Scene vii	
28	Aria (Alceste): Ombre, larve, B♭	*30*	Air (Alceste): Divinités du Styx, B♭ (*R*28)
Scene vi			
29	Recit. (Evandro, Ismene, Alceste): Ah t'affetta		
30	Ismene, Evandro, Coro: E non s'offerse, g		
31	Coro: Chi serve, C		
	ACT 2		ACT 2
Scene i			
32	Recit. (Ismene, Alceste): Fermà. Perchè abbandoni		
33	Aria (Ismene): Parto ... ma senti, E♭		
Scene ii			
34	Recit. (Alceste, Numi infernale): Partì. Sola restai		
35	Aria (Alceste): Chi mi parlà?, F		
36	Coro: E vuoi morire, o misera, d–g		
37	Recit. (Alceste): Stelle! Chi mi risveglia		
38	Coro: Altro non puoi raccogliere, d–g		
39	Recit. (Alceste): Lo so, Numi		
40	Aria (Nume infernale): Dunque vieni, D		
41	Recit. (Alceste, Nume infernale): Uditemi, fermate!		
42	Aria (Alceste): Non vi turbate, no, E♭		
43	Pantomime de' Numi infernali, c		

Scene iii	*Scene i*
44 Coro: Dal lieto soggiorno, B♭	*31* Choeur: Que les plus doux transports, G (*N*)
45 Ballo, F	*32* Ballet:
	a) Légèrement, e (*N*)
	b) Légèrement, G (*N*)
46 Aria (Evandro): Or che Morte, F	
	c) Andante, g (*N*)
	d) Allegro, G (*N*)
47 Ballo, B♭	
	e) Lent, G (*N*)
48 Coro: Dal lieto soggiorno, B♭	
	33 Choeur: Que les plus doux transports, G (*N*)
Scene iv	*Scene ii*
49 Recit. (Evandro, Admeto): Signor, mai più sincero	*34* Récit (Choeur, Evandre, Admète): O mon roi! (incl. material from 50, 51)
	35 Coryphées, choeur: Vivez, aimez des jours A (*N*)
	36 Récit (Admète, Evandre): Alceste, chère Alceste! (*N*)
Scene v	*Scene iii*
50 Recit. (Admeto, Alceste): Adorata consorte	
	37 Récit (Admète, Alceste): Alceste! (*N*)
	38 Choeur, Alceste: Livrons-nous à l'allégresse, B♭ (*R*44)
	39 Récit (Admète): Transports flatteurs (*N*)
	40 Choeur et Coryphée: Parez vos fronts, G (*N*)
	41 Air (Alceste): O dieux! Soutenez mon courage, g (*N*)
	42 Choeur: Parez vos fronts, G (*N*)
	43 Récit (Admète, Alceste): O moment délicieux! (*N*)
	44 Air (Admète): Bannis la crainte, A (*N*)
51 Duetto (Admeto, Alceste): Ah perchè, d	
52 Recit. (Admeto, Alceste, Ismene, Evandro): Consorte!	*45* Récit (Alceste, Admète): Ciel! tu pleures? (partial *R*52)
	46 Air (Alceste): Je n'ai jamais, D (*N*)
	47 Récit (Admète, Alceste): Tu m'aimes (*N*)
	48 Choeur: O malheureux Admète, g (*N*)
	49 Récit (Admète, Alceste): O coup affreux! (partial *R*52)
53 Aria (Admeto): No, crudel, a	*50* Air (Admète): Barbare!, a (*R*53)
Scene vi	*Scene iv*
54 Recit. (Alceste): O tennerezza	
	51 Récit (Alceste): Grands dieux! (*N*)
55 Ismene, Coro: Oh come rapida, f	
56 Recit. (Ismene, Alceste): E il cor non mi spezza!	
57 Ismene, Coro: Così bella!, f	*52* Coryphées et choeur: Tant de graces, f (*R*57)
58 Aria (Alceste): Vesta, tu che fosti, F	
59 Coro: Oh come rapida, f	
60 Aria (Alceste): Oh casto, oh caro nuzial, F	
61 Ismene, Coro: Così bella, f	
62 Recit. (Ismene, Alceste): Regina, ecco i tuoi figli	
63 Duetto (Eumelo, Aspasia): Ah mia diletta madre!, g	
64 Recit. (Alceste): Figli, diletti figli!	
	53 Récit (Alceste): Dérobez-moi vos pleurs (*N*)
65 Aria (Alceste): Ah per questo, F	*54* Air (Alceste): Ah, malgré moi, F (*R*65)
66 Coro: O come rapida, f	*55* Choeur: Oh, que le songe de la vie, f (*R*66)
	56 Air (Alceste): Ciel! Quel supplice, F (part repeat of *54*)
	57 Choeur: Oh, que le songe de la vie, f
ACT 3	ACT 3
	Scene i
	58 Evandre, Coryphées: Nous ne pouvons trop, f (*N*)
	59 Choeur: Pleure, ô patrie!, c (*R*79)
	Scene ii
	60 Récit (Hercule, Évandre, Coryphée, Choeur): Après de longs travaux (*N*)
	61 Choeur: Pleure, ô patrie!, c (1st half of *59*)
	62 Récit (Hercule): Au pouvoir de la mort (*N*)
	63 Air (Hercule): C'est en vain, A (*N*)
	Scene iii
	64 Récit (Alceste): Grands dieux! (after 31, 33)
	65 Choeur: Malheureuse, où vas-tu?, f (*R*35)
	66 Air (Alceste): Ah, Divinités, F (*R*42)
	Scene iv
	67 Récit (Alceste, Admète): Ciel! Admète! (*N*)
	68 Air (Alceste): Vis pour garder, G (*N*)
Scene i	
67 Recit. (Admeto, Evandro): Ah mio fido!	

		69	Récit (Admète): Vivre sans toi! (*N*)
68	Aria (Admeto): Misero! E che farò!, c	*70*	Air (Admète): Alceste, au nom des dieux!, c (*R*68)
69	Recit. (Admeto): No, sì atroce costanza		
Scene ii			
70	Recit. (Alceste, Evandro, Ismene, Admeto): Sposo, Admeto		
		71	Récit (Alceste, Admète): Je les sens (*N*)
71	Duetto (Alceste, Admeto): Cari figli, E♭	*72*	Duo (Alceste, Admète): Aux cris de la douleur, F (*R*71)
		73	Air (Un Dieu infernal): Caron t'appelle, D (*R*40)
		74	Récit (Alceste): Qu'il vive! (*N*)
72	Ensemble (Ismene, Aspasia, Eumelo, Evandro, Admeto): Ma! qual suono	*75*	Choeur, Alceste, Admète: Alceste! (*R*72)
73	Coro: Vieni Alceste, g–f		
74	Recit. (Alceste, Numi infernali): Ahimè! Chi mi riscuote!		
75	Admeto, Alceste, Coro: Fermatevi! Udite!, E♭	*76*	Ensemble (Admète, Alceste, Choeur): Arrêtez! Barbares déités!, E♭
76	Recit. (Nume infernale, Admeto, Alceste): Vieni		
Scene iii			
77	Introduzione, c		
78	Recit. (Due voci, Evandro, Ismene): Mori? Non vive più?		
79	Coro: Piangi o patria, c		
80	Aria (Ismene): Alceste è morta!, c		
81	Coro: Piangi o patria, c		
82	Aria (Evandro): Morte trionfa, E♭–c		
83	Coro: Piangi o patria, c		
84	Duetto (Ismene, Evandro): Ogni virtù più bella, A♭–c		
85	Coro: Piangi o patria, c		
Scene iv			
86	Recit. (Admeto, Ismene, Evandro): Lasciatemi, crudeli		
		Scene v	
		77	Duo (Hercule, Admète): Ami, leur rage, f–C (*N*)
		78	Coro: Notre fureur est vaine, C (*N*)
		79	Récit (Hercule, Admète): Des mains de l'amitié (*N*)
		Scene vi	
		80	Récit (Apollon): Poursuis, ô digne fils (*N*)
Scene v		*Scene vii*	
87	Introduzione, G–g		
88	Recit. (Apollo, Admeto, Alceste): Admeto, in Ciel		
		81	Récit (Apollon): Et vous, qui vous montrez (*N*)
		Scene viii	
		82	Trio (Alceste, Admète, Hercule): Reçois, dieu bienfaisant, F (*N*)
		Scene ix	
		83	Récit (Admète, Alceste, Choeur): O mes amis! (*N*)
89	Coro: Regna a noi, G		
		84	Choeur: Qu'ils vivent à jamais, C (*R37*)
		Divertissement	
		85	Andante, G (*N*)
		86	Marche, D (*N*)
		87	Andante, A (*N*)
		88	Menuet, gracieux, D (*N*)
		89	Gavotte, A Add (*N*)
		90	Chaconne, D (*N*)

resolution takes place in a lengthy recitative in the original; in the French, a much shorter recitative is followed by an air, 'Non, ce n'est point un sacrifice', where Alcestis declares that she could not live without Admetus: to die that he may live is no sacrifice. The refrain alternates with expressions of her sorrow at leaving her husband and children. After a short arioso ('Arbitres du sort des humains'), the High Priest reappears to tell Alcestis that her destiny is decided and that the spirits of the underworld are awaiting her (air, 'Déjà la mort s'apprête'). Alone, Alcestis sings an air of defiance ('Ombre, larve'/'Divinités du Styx'). The trombones, the deliberate arpeggios in the bass and the syncopated rhythms in the upper strings urge on this mighty rondo, which provides a powerful conclusion to Act 1 of the French revision.

1.vi (*I*) In the original, when the aria is over, Alcestis is joined by Evander and Ismene, who tell her to hurry to the palace if she wants to see her husband alive – he is close to death, and calling for her. The priests and people gather round Evander and Ismene and the ensemble and chorus reveal that all are afraid to die to save Admetus (Alcestis has not informed anyone of her resolve to take his place, as she has in the French version). The act ends with a lively, almost frivolous chorus in which the people sing that the gods ask too much but that rulers and subjects alike must endure suffering.

ACT 2.i (*I*) *A dense forest sacred to the gods of the underworld; night* Ismene asks Alcestis why she is leaving her dying husband to go to the forest and abandon herself to grief (this recitative begins with the restless chromatic figure for low violins which Gluck was to use in the underworld scene of the French version; compare no.32 with no.64). Alcestis tells Ismene to leave her, but first Ismene begs Alcestis to tell her what she is hiding (Gluck also used this music in the French version, for no.29, the High Priest's air).

2.ii (*I*) Alone, Alcestis is terrified by the darkness and silence and the hoarse cries of a night-bird (semiquaver triplets on the first violins, minor 3rd cries on chalumeaux and bassoons); calling to the Lord of the Underworld, she is answered by the slow, bass voice of the Infernal Deity. She gives vent to her agitation (aria, 'Chi mi parla?'), with her music echoed by the woodwind and obsessive triplets in the strings.

This leads into another choral tableau, of invisible infernal deities: 'E vuoi morire' (the basses sing on a monotone while the orchestra weaves chromatic lines above them). Rushing string scales and calls on horns and trombones (no.40) introduce a short aria for an infernal deity, calling her to the underworld. But Alcestis begs to return to the palace to bid her husband and children farewell. The tenderness of her aria, 'Non vi turbate, no', with its sighing phrases, muted strings and prominent english horns, surely reflects her words, 'I will die of love and happiness'. A solemn pantomime of gods of the underworld ends the scene.

2.iii (*I*), i (*F*) *A room in the palace of Admetus* In the Italian version, to the first truly joyful music of the opera, the people celebrate the miraculous recovery of their king (chorus, 'Dal lieto soggiorno', followed by a dance, an aria for Evander, another dance and a reprise of the chorus). The French version opens with a different chorus, 'Que les plus doux transports', telling how joy follows unhappiness and how the gods have changed the Thessalians' misfortunes, in a lively 6/8 with solos; then follows a celebratory *divertissement* on an expanded scale, with five dances and a reprise of the chorus.

2.iv (*I*), ii (*F*) Admetus expresses his astonishment at his recovery and elicits from Evander the news of the Oracle's pronouncement, supposing that some unknown subject has given up his life to save him. In the French version this is followed by another celebratory chorus, richly-scored, rather like a minuet ('Vivez, aimez les jours dignes d'envie').

2.v (*I*), iii (*F*) Admetus and Alcestis are now reunited. In the Italian version, Admetus inquires why she is so sad. Most of their dialogue is in recitative, but there is a short, anguished duet ('Ah perchè con quelle lagrime'); eventually Alcestis reveals that it is she who is to die for him. The recitative moves to a frenzied *presto* as the distraught Admetus tells Alcestis he will not accept her gift and will go to the temple to question the Oracle. Admetus proclaims his hatred of the heavens, the world and himself before plunging into an aria of despair, full of chromatic harmony and anguished leaps ('No, crudel, non posso vivere').

The equivalent scene in the French revision makes characteristic use of tragic irony as the dialogue for Admetus and Alcestis is punctuated by choruses and dances as the people celebrate Admetus's return to health. These include the chorus which began the celebratory scene in the Italian original, 'Dal lieto soggiorno', as 'Livrons-nous à l'allégresse', and, with Alcestis's grief-stricken aside, the delightful chorus and dance 'Parez vos fronts de fleurs nouvelles' with its vocal solos and pizzicato accompaniment. Within this chorus Alcestis sings a moving lament ('O dieux! soutenez mon courage!'); it is akin to an instrumental piece with a subsidiary vocal part as flute and violas weave their desolate melody. Admetus, puzzled at her distress, tries to console her: 'Bannis la crainte et les alarmes' (the only da capo aria in the opera). This is more dramatic than the frenzied questioning in the corresponding scene in the Italian original, but when Admetus presses Alcestis for an answer (no.45) she sings a deceptively simple air in the manner of *Iphigénie en Aulide*: 'Je n'ai jamais chéri la vie', at once deceiving her husband by reassuring him that she lives only to love him, but also telling him the truth ('Je t'aimerai jusqu' au trépas, jusque dans la nuit éternelle': 'I will love you even to death, right up to eternal night' – an augmented sixth and a slower speed emphasize these words). Eventually Alcestis reveals that it is she who will die; the chorus breaks in with a cry of anguish on a repeated diminished seventh chord (as at the end of the overture of the French version); Admetus rages against the gods' cruelty, culminating in his air, 'Barbare! non, sans toi je ne puis vivre' (a revision of his aria at the corresponding point in the original). Before Admetus leaves, Alcestis interrupts briefly with a falling four-note scale figure, like a leitmotif for her in the French version.

2.vi (*I*), iv (*F*) Alcestis, growing weaker, asks Ismene to prepare her for making her final offerings to the gods. 'Oh come rapida nel suo bel fiore', Ismene sings, her lament taken up by the chorus (no.55), to begin another of Gluck's characteristic tableaux: this sombre F minor music with homophonic choral writing and falling orchestral figures alternates with another F minor chorus, led by Ismene ('Così bella! così giovane!'). In between come a recitative and two short arias, both for Alcestis, richly scored with pairs of chalumeaux, english horns, trombones and strings: in the first she prays to the goddess Vesta to look after her children, and in the second says that no new wife to Admetus could be more loving or faithful than her. After she has bidden her children farewell (they have a short duet), Alcestis sings an aria, 'Ah per questo', which again has an eloquent introduction for oboe before she gives expression to her emotions, especially (as the poignant final 6/8 section makes clear) her anguish at being parted from her children.

In the French revision, this scene is contracted to a single statement of the 'Così bella!' chorus (now 'Tant de graces') and two of the 'Oh come rapida' one ('Oh, que le songe de la vie'). The intervening material is cut too, except Alcestis's air 'Ah per questo' (now 'Ah, malgré moi', with solo flute rather than oboe). The fast part of this air is repeated after 'Oh, que le songe' and heard again to end the act with the same music that concluded Act 2 of the Italian original. The cuts reduce this final scene to seven musical numbers in the French version as opposed to the 13 of the original.

In Act 3 the differences are so extensive, with the order of events changed, that the two versions require separate discussion.

ACT 3.i (*I*) *A large, open-air entrance hall of Admetus's palace, decorated with statues and trophies* Admetus has returned from the temple; in a recitative (first *secco*, later orchestral) he tells Evander of the Oracle's edict: Alcestis must die if Admetus is to live. He gives vent to his sorrow in an aria, 'Misero! E che farò!', his agitation expressed both in the semiquaver arpeggios in the

Design by François-Joseph Bélanger for Act 3 of the revised version of Gluck's 'Alceste', first performed at the Paris Opéra (Académie Royale de Musique), 23 April 1776

second violins, the plangent oboes doubling the voice and the doleful bassoons imitating it. Finally it moves into passionate accompanied recitative: 'O Alceste, o figli, o divisione! O morte!'.

3.ii (*I*) The music changes from anguished minor to radiant major as Alcestis enters with her children and Ismene to bid him a final farewell; her noble resignation and calmness contrast with Admetus's impatient dotted rhythms (duet, 'Cari figli, ah! non piangete'). The gods of the underworld come to claim Alcestis. An ensemble, for Ismene, Evander, Admetus, Aspasia and Eumelus, begins with a sinister octave G♭, like the sounding of a death-knell; tremolandos, falling chromatic figures and diminished seventh chords abound as they cry out in horror. The infernal deities remind Alcestis of her promise in a chorus in octaves reminiscent of those for the Furies in Act 2 of *Orfeo*; Admetus begs them to take him too, but in vain. An infernal deity orders Alcestis to follow them; she dies and is taken away by the gods of the underworld.

3.iii (*I*) A brief Lento, 'a sinfonia expressing terror and dismay', introduces a great scene of mourning. Ismene, Evander and the courtiers lament Alcestis's death in a massive tableau in which short duets and arias alternate with four statements of the chorus of lamentation, 'Piangi o patria, o Tessaglia'.

3.iv (*I*) Admetus bursts in, angry that the courtiers have disarmed him and prevented him from killing himself. He is reminded of his duty to his kingdom and his children, but can think of nothing but his dead wife.

3.v (*I*) String scales and flashes of lightning announce the arrival of Apollo. He and Alcestis appear on clouds, and in a simple, succinct scene Apollo restores Alcestis to life and to her husband: the gods have taken pity on them. The opera ends with a lively chorus of rejoicing in praise of Alcestis ('Regna a noi con lieta sorte').

ACT 3.i (*F*) *A courtyard surrounded by colonnades in Admetus's palace* Evander and a female chorus leader sing a short lament for Alcestis ('Nous ne pouvons trop répandre des larmes'): this begins in F minor, with sighing phrases on oboes and violins, and a chromatically descending bass, continuing the mood and key of the end of the preceding act, as does the following chorus 'Pleure, ô patrie!' (a revision of no.79, 'Piangi o patria', in Act 3 of the original; much of this scene is based on the corresponding one in the Italian version). The translation of this chorus, 'Alcestis is going to die', points up an important difference between the two operas: in the original this scene of mourning takes place after she has actually died, but in the revision it precedes her confrontation with the spirits of the underworld – as far as the chorus is concerned at this point in the revision, she has gone to her death.

3.ii (*F*) After this sombre C minor chorus, bustling wind and strings in E♭ major introduce a character new to the revision, Hercules. As in the Euripides original, Hercules happens to visit his friend Admetus, to find the court in mourning for Alcestis. Hercules' recitative is interrupted by the astonished and delighted shout of the people at his arrival. Evander and the chorus-leader tell him what has happened; Hercules assures them he will bring back Alcestis from the underworld, expressing his strength and determination in a march-like air in A major with dotted rhythms, high horns and short, repeated melodic lines ('C'est en vain que l'enfer compte sur sa victime'). As in Euripides, Hercules is a grotesquely comic character, a foil lacking for the tragedy of the Italian original.

3.iii (*F*) *The entrance to the underworld; a ravaged scene with rocks, fallen trees and a gaping cavern, out of which smoke billows, with the altar of death visible on one side, adorned with a scythe; the light gradually dies* The first part of this scene is based on Act 2 scenes i and ii and Act 3 scene ii of the Italian original, beginning with the music that began Act 2 as Alcestis enters and is terrified by the place and what she has to do. The sinister night-bird of the original (Act 2 scene ii) is heard, Alcestis's fear and breathlessness here enhanced by a trembling rhythmic figure (three quavers and a quaver rest).

The voices of the gods of the underworld now call her, with their implacable repeated monotone 'Malheureuse, où vas-tu?' (no.*65*, based on no.35 of the original with the addition of parts for tenors and altos, and the more sombre clarinets replacing oboes; it is only heard once here, though twice in the original). It is followed by Alcestis's air 'Ah, divinités implacables!', an adaptation of 'Non vi turbate, no' of the original (Act 2 scene ii); Gluck changed it into a French air in two parts, each repeated, adding a G minor modulation in the second, making an even more poignant contrast, its F major following the bleak F minor of the chorus.

3.iv (*F*) Admetus appears (as in Act 2 scene v of the original, albeit in less congenial surroundings); he has followed Alcestis, determined to persuade her to live or else to die with her. Her response is one of the loveliest additions to the original, a short (13-bar) air, 'Vis pour garder le souvenir d'une épouse qui te fut chère', where pizzicato outer strings accompany the divided violas, the upper part doubling Alcestis's line. Admetus responds with the tormented air, 'Alceste, au nom des dieux!' (an adaptation of his aria no.68, in Act 3 scene i of the original), making more dramatic effect as he addresses Alcestis rather than Evander. There Admetus interrupted the air; here it is Alcestis (as earlier, in 'Barbare! non sans toi'); again we hear her four-note descending scale at the beginning of the recitative, and tension increases in their duet, 'Aux cris de la douleur', emphasizing their mutual love and its betrayal rather than their children as in the original. This leads to the air for the infernal deity (no.*73*, reworked from no.40 in the original). A chorus of infernal deities follows (the ensemble for Ismene, Evander and Admetus in Act 3 scene ii of the original, no.72, with the vocal parts adjusted); it leads, via Alcestis's four-note falling figure ('Adieu, cher époux'), to Admetus's raging against the obdurate gods of the underworld who are taking away his wife ('Arrêtez! barbares deités!'), swearing he will follow them to Hades.

3.v (*F*) But that is not necessary, because Hercules appears, to universal astonishment, and charges off after the gods of the underworld. The music rushes on into the next number, where he fights the infernal deities (this is new material written for the French revision); rushing scales and repeated notes depict him setting about his victims with his club while Admetus provides an excited commentary including frequent exclamations of encouragement. Hercules' victory is announced as the infernal deities, reduced to a shocked *pianissimo*, in a sudden move to C major accompanied by pulsating strings, sing 'Notre fureur est vaine, cédons à sa valeur'; Hercules brings back Alcestis and presents her to Admetus.

3.vi (*F*) Apollo now appears; this is not essential to the drama in its revised form, but since Hercules' restoration of Alcestis would appear to go against the gods' decree, his appearance restores all to order.

3.vii–ix (*F*) *A courtyard in Admetus's palace, thronging with people* The denouement is quite succinct, but it is expanded by Apollo's address to the Thessalian people, praising their devotion to their monarch, and a trio in praise of him for Alcestis, Admetus and Hercules, 'Reçois, dieu bienfaisant', which musically harks back to the mood of the celebratory numbers in Act 2. In a brief recitative Admetus, Alcestis and the chorus express their joy, Admetus singing similar words and identical music to that with which he made his first entry in this version of the opera (Act 2 scene ii). The final chorus comes from the end of Act 1 in the original; here it seems better placed.

The final *divertissement* is one of the largest in a Gluck opera. Of its six movements, three are known to be by Gluck: the Marche (no.*86*), the Andante with its flute solo reminiscent of the Dance of the Blessed Spirits from *Orphée et Eurydice* (no.*87*), and the lengthy concluding Chaconne (no.*90*). The others may be in whole or part by Gossec, bearing in mind Gluck's comment in a letter of 30 June 1776 concerning the work's publication: 'You can leave the opera as it stands; the little that Mr Gossec may have done for it can be of no consequence. This will make the opera no better and no worse, because it is the end of it'.

* * *

The two versions of *Alceste*, it will be clear, are in effect distinct operas, with distinct merits; unlike Gluck's Orpheus operas they are so different as to preclude a 'best of both worlds' solution by incorporating music from one into the other. That is in any case unnecessary, because the French revision retains virtually all the best music of the Italian original and adds much more. The only music whose omission might give cause for regret is the marvellously expressive ensemble with chorus near the end of Act 1, 'E non s'offerse', Alcestis's richly scored arias in Act 2 (nos.58 and 60) and the almost Berliozian *Introduzione* in Act 3 (no.77).

When he came to revise *Alceste* for Paris, Gluck took a different, more sophisticated and French-influenced view of the theatre. The original is to some extent hampered by its sheer size. The huge choral tableaux go a stage further than those in *Orfeo*; there the chorus comments on events rather in the manner of a Greek chorus, whereas in *Alceste* it assumes a character of its own – as the people of Thessaly, whose well-being depends on their king. Gluck's huge, monumental choral tableaux in the Italian version, although strikingly original as well as powerfully constructed, can with their sheer massiveness and their use of repeated sections seem static and unwieldy. As the table shows, there are far fewer repetitions of choruses in the French revision, and this greater concision leads to a more taut drama.

While due allowance has to be made for the different traditions – *opera seria* and *tragédie lyrique* – from which the works spring, the two principal characters emerge with greater humanity in the revised version. Arguably, Calzabigi went too far in his libretto in his quest for the 'beautiful simplicity' and 'strong passions' cited in his preface. The result is that the plot is basically reduced to a single incident – Alcestis's self-sacrifice – which is expressed in a language colder and more rhetorical than the passionate language of Calzabigi's two other reform operas. Further, the tension may flag after the dramatic climax of the opera in Act 2 scene ii; in his revision Roullet maintains it with his rearrangement of the order of events in Acts 2 and 3 and his postponement of the climax to Hercules' defeat of the infernal deities in Act 3 scene v. In tune with the changing times, and with French attitudes as opposed to Italian, Roullet's characters are today the more credible and sympathetic, and the relationship between Alcestis and Admetus (and their desire to die for each other rather than for their people) is expressed in more human terms. Admetus is more central, and Alcestis is transformed from a rather stiff and formal queen to a real wife, one of Gluck's greatest creations.

The revision focusses more strongly on the central drama by decreasing the role of the confidants; but it also introduces a new character, Hercules. The way in which he is introduced (not until Act 3, as a *homo ex machina*) and his music have been the subject of adverse criticism; but by restoring Hercules, so central and crucial in the Euripides original, Roullet and Gluck found an ideal foil for the predominant gloom of the rest of the tragedy.

The recitative in the French *Alceste* is orchestral throughout, like that in all French opera of the time and in *Orfeo ed Euridice*; why *secco* recitative occasionally appears in the Italian version – bearing in mind Gluck and Calzabigi's explicit renunciation of it in the preface – is a mystery. In spite of, or perhaps partially as a result of, the cuts, particularly in the choral scenes, the revised *Alceste* has a more continuous and fluid texture than the original; successive numbers often merge in structures more flexible than those of the more formal Italian original.

That is not to denigrate the boldness and power of what was in many ways Gluck's grandest conception. Had Gluck never revised his Italian *Alceste*, it would still be viewed as a great, if flawed, opera; but any comparisons with the French revision reflect favourably on the latter, which is a distillation of all that was best in the original, balanced by Gluck's increased musical and dramatic powers.

See also ALCESTIS below. JEREMY HAYES

Alceste **(iii)** ('Alcestis'). *Opera seria* in three acts by Pietro Alessandro Guglielmi (*see* GUGLIELMI family, (1)) to a libretto by RANIERI DE' CALZABIGI revised by Giuseppe Parini; Milan, Regio Ducal Teatro, 26 December 1768.

Shortly after the Viennese première of Gluck's *Alceste* (1767) the directors of the theatre in Milan negotiated with Calzabigi for a revised libretto. In indignant letters Calzabigi defended his refusal to 'add interesting characters' or make any other changes. The correspondence also offers important evidence about the subsequent Milanese production. It reveals the reviser of the text, unnamed in the libretto, as the poet Giuseppe Parini and documents the theatre management's unsuccessful attempts to secure a pre-publication copy of Gluck's score. In the event, Guglielmi provided an entirely new setting without reference to Gluck.

Parini substantially altered the libretto's structure and tone to suit Italian tastes and his own concept of opera, reducing the role of the chorus and cutting out the dances. While retaining all the characters, he shifted the emphasis away from the part of Alcestis by increasing the weight of the other roles. The greatest change was in the part of Apollo who, under the name of Evandro [Evander], is present throughout, swaying the course of the action. Parini added five new arias – three for Apollo/Evander and one each for Admeto [Admetus] and Ismene. In addition he replaced one of Calzabigi's arias for Alcestis and the final chorus with his own.

Parini's aria texts, with their double quatrains maintaining a single common metre throughout, are far more along Metastasian lines than Calzabigi's shorter verses in mixed metres of less traditional lengths. In at least three Parini pays explicit tribute to well-known Metastasian models. By shifting or eliminating the choral interjections and lines of recitative, originally freely woven together with the aria texts, Parini modified Calzabigi's structural innovations, preferring longer monologues crowned by clearly delimited solo arias, ensemble pieces or choral movements. Finally, in deference to Italian sensibilities, he omitted certain lines in order to achieve a more even tone and, perhaps, to avoid too strong expressions of passion (see Candiani 1988).

Guglielmi's setting, reflecting Parini's alterations, differs considerably from Gluck's. The principal roles of Alcestis and Admetus, as in Gluck's opera, are for soprano (Antonia Maria Girelli) and tenor (Guglielmo Ettore); but Apollo/Evander is for a soprano castrato (Giuseppe Nicolini) rather than a tenor. No longer merely ancillary, his part and that of Ismene (sung by the soprano Felicità Suardi) had the proper status of secondo uomo and seconda donna. In the arias to Parini's texts Guglielmi emphasizes the singers' virtuoso technique, and the settings are not only more self-contained but also far lengthier than Gluck's. His accompaniments feature the traditional mid-century Italian complement of strings, paired oboes and horns, only occasionally supplemented with separate parts for flutes, bassoons and trumpets. Although Gluck's unusual use of woodwind instruments (english horns, chalumeaux) and trombones has no counterpart in *opera seria*, Guglielmi's orchestration is conservative even by Italian standards. A Milanese copy of the score (at *F-Pn*) contains five alternative arias, at least four taken from other works, probably substituted by the singers during performance.

Guglielmi's *Alceste* also contains features that look forward to his later serious operas. These generally correspond to the unaltered parts of Calzabigi's libretto and include the ample use of orchestrally accompanied recitative, cavatinas, solo ensembles and choruses to build complex scenes. Contrapuntal writing enlivens the ten choral movements, some in fugal design. Here as in the more formally adventurous solo pieces the harmonic language too is bolder. Thematic returns and an effort at seamless transitions between sections indicate a concern to create larger musical units from the less traditionally organized scenes. The dualistic nature of the work's text and music, with both conservative and experimental features, probably explains its limited success. After the Milanese production Guglielmi's setting was not taken up again.

See also ALCESTIS below. KATHLEEN KUZMICK HANSELL

Alceste **(iv)** ('Alcestis'). Singspiel in five acts by ANTON SCHWEITZER to a libretto by CHRISTOPH MARTIN WIELAND, based on EURIPIDES' *Alcestis*; Weimar, Hoftheater, 28 May 1773.

Alcestis (soprano) learns of the Delphic oracle's pronouncement that the king is fatally ill from her sister and confidante, Parthenia (soprano), who cannot dissuade her from dying in her husband's place. Neither can Admet [Admetus] (tenor), who senses immediately what she has done and is carried off in a stupor after she takes a tearful leave of him and their children. Her sacrifice so moves Admetus's friend Herkules [Hercules] (bass) that he heads off resolutely to Orcus to fetch her back. After despairing monologues from Parthenia and

'Alceste' (Schweitzer), a scene from the opera composed for the Weimar court in 1773: engraving by J. G. Geyser after Steinhauer

Admetus, Hercules reappears with a beautiful woman to comfort Admetus. When Admetus registers indignation at the very suggestion, Hercules produces Alcestis, but refuses to explain how he rescued her.

Wieland's much-simplified version of the Alcestis myth includes only four singing parts, owing to the limited number of skilled singers at Weimar. Literary and dramatic values are similarly constricted. The mellifluous aria texts vie consciously with those of Metastasio, and the drama's emotional range is restricted to what Wieland thought music capable of expressing – 'warm feeling and glowing *Affekt*'. The absence of spectacle and of the seemingly obligatory scene in the Underworld underscores the opera's spiritual allegiance to the family-centred sentimentality of the *drame*. The young Goethe gave vent to his outrage over its *galant*, counter-Euripidean literary demeanour in a merciless persiflage, *Götter, Helden und Wieland*.

Although Schweitzer's music has virtually nothing in common with Gluck's *Alceste* (which he knew and did not admire), with its blend of mid-century *seria* style and German harmonic-contrapuntal complexity it marked a startling departure from the simple musical fare then in vogue on German stages. The dark French overture in G minor sets the tone from the outset; there follow at once two minor-mode arias, both for Alcestis. 'Unlucky the singer who falls into Schweitzer's hands,' wrote Mozart to his father on 11 September 1778, 'for all his life long he will never learn how to write singably.' The favourite aria from the opera was the least relevant dramatically: Parthenia's brilliant virtuoso effusion with obbligato violin in Act 4, written for the accomplished soprano Josepha Hellmuth. In the expressive obbligato recitatives Schweitzer is at his best. The opera's rather monochromatic melancholy turns incandescent in Admetus's lengthy and deeply felt 'O Jugendzeit' in Act 4, in which he recalls past golden days of joy and imagines his wife about to drink from the river Lethe. Alcestis's disorientated ruminations on returning from the Underworld, replete with the ethereal harmonic legerdemain at which Schweitzer excelled, form a final high point.

Despite its difficulties the opera achieved widespread popularity on German stages, both court and civic, in stage and concert productions. Further, it served as a model for other serious operas in German, most notably Holzbauer's *Günther von Schwarzburg* (1777, Mannheim). Wieland's libretto was later set by F. W. H. Benda (1786, Berlin) and E. W. Wolf (1786, Weimar).

See also ALCESTIS below. THOMAS BAUMAN

Alcestis. Libretto subject used chiefly in the 17th and 18th centuries, based on EURIPIDES' *Alcestis*. When Admetus, King of Pherae in Thessaly, is ill and about to die an oracle announces that he will be saved if someone else is willing to die in his stead. His wife Alcestis displays her conjugal devotion by offering herself; she dies and Admetus recovers. According to some versions, Hercules then brings Alcestis back from the Underworld and reunites her with Admetus.

In Aureli's *L'Antigona delusa da Alceste*, first performed in 1660 with music by P. A. Ziani and reset by several other composers (including Handel, *Admeto*, 1727), the story is embroidered with typically Venetian intrigue. Princess Antigona [Antigone] loves Admetus; dressed as a man, she goes in search of him. On hearing of Alcestis's death she reveals her identity to try to win Admetus. In the meantime, Hercules brings Alcestis back from the Underworld; now it is her turn to be disguised in male clothes. Hercules tells Admetus that he was unable to rescue Alcestis. Admetus decides to marry Antigone but changes his mind when Alcestis reveals her true identity and angrily accuses him of infidelity. In Philippe Quinault's *Alceste, ou Le triomphe d'Alcide*, set by Lully (1674), the focus is on a different amorous conflict: Hercules (the Alcide of the title) loves Alcestis and offers to retrieve her on condition that she be granted to him in marriage (she is not yet married to Admetus), but when he completes his mission he is moved by the love of Alcestis and Admetus and gives up his claim.

18th-century librettists found the story of Alcestis particularly attractive as a glorification of conjugal love, one of the virtues most valued by neo-classical artists and writers. These librettists tended to concentrate on Alcestis and Admetus and to avoid the amorous intrigues of 17th-century versions. In Calzabigi's *Alceste*, set by Gluck in 1767, Alcestis dies only in the third and final act, so she has ample opportunity to express her love for husband and children (children had no place in the Alcestis librettos of Aureli and Quinault) and to bid them farewell. Hercules does not appear, but Apollo makes a sudden appearance near the end of the opera to announce that he will restore Alcestis to life.

Under the influence of *tragédie lyrique*, Calzabigi enriched his libretto with choruses, ballets and opportunities for impressive scenery. The German poet and playwright C. M. Wieland, by contrast, avoided these as unnecessary; his five-act *Alceste* (set by Anton Schweitzer, 1773) is rather more lugubrious than Calzabigi's. By having Alcestis die in the middle of the opera he gave himself opportunity to explore the feelings of Admetus as deeply as those of Alcestis.

See also ADMETO [Handel]; *ALCESTE* (i) [Lully]; *ALCESTE* (ii) [Gluck]; *ALCESTE* (iii) [Guglielmi]; and *ALCESTE* (iv) [Schweitzer].

JOHN A. RICE

Alchevs'ky, Ivan [Jean] **Olexiyovych** (*b* Kharkiv, 15/27 Dec 1876; *d* Baku, 27 April/10 May 1917). Ukrainian tenor. He studied in St Petersburg and from 1901 to 1905 was a soloist at the Mariinsky Theatre there. In 1906 he sang in London, as Lensky in the first performance there of *Yevgeny Onegin*; he later appeared in the Beecham season of Russian opera, 1913–14. At the Paris Opéra (1908–10) he sang Shuysky in the local première of *Boris Godunov* as well as French roles (Gounod's Romeo, Faust, Raoul). He returned to Russia to sing at the Bol'shoy, Moscow (1910–14). Among his other roles were Lohengrin, Siegfried and Radames; he was also active in the promotion of Ukrainian music and he directed Gulak-Artemovsky's *Zaporozhets za Dunayem* ('Cossack beyond the Danube') at the Bol'shoy in 1915 and in Odessa the next year.

*

I. Lysenko and K. Myloslas'ky, eds.: *Ivan Alchevs'ky: spohady, materialy, lystuvannya* [Reminiscences, Documents, Letters] (Kiev, 1980)

VIRKO BALEY

Alchymist, Der [*Der Alchymist, oder Der Liebesteufel* ('The Alchemist, or The Love Demon')]. *Comische Oper* in one act by JOSEPH SCHUSTER to a libretto by AUGUST GOTTLIEB MEISSNER after Marc Antoine Le Grand's comedy *L'Amour diable*; Dresden, Kleines Kurfürstliches Theater, March 1778.

The old alchemist Tarnow (baritone) refuses to let his daughter Louise (soprano) wed until he has discovered the philosopher's stone. Her lover Bellnitz (tenor) has contrived a trap-door into her chamber in order to effect their escape. Bellnitz's servant Heinrich (bass) impersonates a devil that Tarnow believes he has conjured up in one of his experiments and demands either Tarnow or a young female in his place. Tarnow agrees to give him Louise. He tries to renege when the deception is revealed, but threats from Frau Tarnow (soprano) and the charge of having given his daughter to a devil convince him that he should give up alchemy, and allow his daughter to marry Bellnitz.

A mixture of stylish vocal and comic writing absorbed in Italy and popular traits enforced by the indifferent skills of many of Pasquale Bondini's singers, Schuster's opera was one of the most successful to come out of northern Germany. It was revived as recently as 1933.

THOMAS BAUMAN

Alcide al bivio ('Alcides at the Crossroads'). *Festa teatrale* in one act by JOHANN ADOLF HASSE to a libretto by PIETRO METASTASIO; Vienna, Grosse Redoutensaal, 8 October 1760.

Written to celebrate the wedding of Archduke Joseph to Princess Isabella of Parma, this *festa teatrale* antedates Gluck's *Orfeo ed Euridice* by only two years and may in fact have served as a model for some aspects of Gluck's 'reform'. The work is also the first in a series of three *feste teatrali* and three *opere serie* for the imperial court in the 1760s. The Alcides of the title is the youthful Hercules (soprano), who is led by his tutor, Fronimo (tenor), to a crossroads; there he is confronted by a choice between pleasure and virtue, represented by the goddesses Edonide (soprano) and Aretea (soprano). By choosing the latter Alcides earns the praise of the gods, expressed in an aria for their messenger Iride [Iris] (soprano). *Alcide* contains the features traditionally associated with the *festa teatrale*: extensive accompanied recitatives (sometimes within arias) and impressive choruses (usually with aria-like sections for soloists). In addition, the orchestration is infinitely richer than elsewhere in the composer's late *opere serie*. Edonide's entrance is accompanied by an onstage orchestra of flutes, oboes, english horn, bassoons and horns, and by flutes, oboes and muted strings offstage. Alcides' accompanied recitative (scene x), with full orchestra, contains contrasts of tempo and metre. The unidentified three-movement dance in scene vii (probably the 'Ballo' specified in the libretto) is a remarkable orchestral piece, comparable in length to the overture, which presents each pair of wind instruments in succession in an elaborate duet.

ERIC D. WEIMER

Alcide negli orti esperidi ('Alcides in the Gardens of the Hesperides'). *Opera seria* in two acts by GIAN FRANCESCO DE MAJO to a libretto by MARCO COLTELLINI; Vienna, Laxenburg, Privilegiato, 9 June 1764.

Alcides (alto castrato; the same mythological figure as Hercules) has fallen deeply in love with Elettra [Electra] (soprano), who is promised to Dardano [Dardanus] (soprano castrato). Taigete [Taygete] (soprano), Electra's sister, reports to King Atlante [Atlas] (tenor), their father, that pirates have taken Electra and Dardanus captive. Desperate for the safety of his daughter, Atlas promises her to his friend Alcides, if he will save her. Alcides returns victorious, and Atlas tells the rescued couple that Electra has been promised to him. Electra denounces Alcides for his unreasonable demands, and all leave in distress. Taygete explains the situation to the bewildered Alcides, who then kills the monster guarding the golden apple tree, which disappears. He releases the old king from his promise, thus reuniting Electra and Dardanus. Alcides is hailed as Atlas's successor. Esperide [Hesperis], Atlas's immortal wife, then emerges from the sea to join the company in a celebratory ballet.

Coltellini infuses an italianate libretto with French spectacular elements. A festive scene in Act 1 combines chorus with soloists, and the encounter with the pirates uses machine spectacle in the form of a raging sea and ballet pantomime. The chorus (either as pirates or Hesperides) becomes a character in the drama, frequently interacting with the principals. In Act 1 is an early example in an *opera seria* of an action ensemble, as Taygete bursts in to report the arrival of the pirates. Majo's music displays a mastery of musical characterization; melodic lines are strong, elegant or passionate as the situation demands. Two bassoons impart a sombre tone to Atlas's grief-stricken 'Giusti dei' in Act 1. The action trio is a triumph of musical dramatization, and some unusual orchestral music is provided for the appearance of Hesperis.

MARITA P. McCLYMONDS

Alcina. Opera in three acts by GEORGE FRIDERIC HANDEL to an anonymous libretto after Cantos vi and vii of LUDOVICO ARIOSTO's *Orlando furioso*, adapted from the libretto for Riccardo Broschi's *L'isola di Alcina* (1728, Rome); London, Covent Garden Theatre, 16 April 1735.

Alcina *a sorceress*	soprano
Morgana *her sister*	soprano
Ruggiero *a knight, betrothed to …*	alto castrato
Bradamante	contralto
Melisso *her governor*	bass
Oronte *Alcina's general*	tenor
Oberto	treble

Setting Alcina's magic island

Handel composed *Alcina* in the early months of 1735 while presenting his first season at John Rich's newly built theatre at Covent Garden (the last page of the autograph score is dated 8 April 1735, eight days before the first performance). The title role was sung by Anna Maria Strada del Pò, Ruggiero by the celebrated castrato Giovanni Carestini. John Beard, at the start of a long career, sang Oronte, and the talented William Savage (then a boy treble, later a bass) Oberto. (That role, which does not appear in the source libretto, seems to have been created specifically for Savage: the scenes involving him are all late additions to the score.) In common with Handel's other operatic productions in the same season (notably *Ariodante*) the opera contains dance sequences (originally performed by Marie Sallé and her company) and choruses. Though these features show the influence of the French opera of the period, the customary predominance of da capo arias and the general structure of the opera place *Alcina* firmly in the Italian *opera seria* tradition.

In 1735 *Alcina* achieved a good run of 18 performances up to 2 July, the end of the season. Handel revived it in shortened form (without the dances) for three performances at the start of his 1736–7 season at Covent Garden (opening on 6 November 1736) and gave two further performances (when arias from *Arianna* and *Admeto* were added) on 10 and 21 June 1737. (The wordbook for the 1736 revival was published as the 'Third Edition'; no second edition has been traced.) The Händel-Gesellschaft edition of 1868, prepared by Chrysander, mainly follows the version of first performance, except that Ruggiero's aria 'Di te mi rido' is printed in its transposed 1736 version (the original is in F, preceded by a recitative cadence in D minor) and the original close of Act 1 is shown in a footnote. The F major ('A') version of the chorus 'Questo è il cielo' was discarded before first performance.

There were two revivals of *Alcina* in Brunswick in 1738. The first modern revival was in Leipzig on 14 June 1928. In Britain the opera was revived by the Handel Opera Society at St Pancras Town Hall on 19 March 1957; Joan Sutherland's singing of the title role in that and in Zeffirelli's production of 1960 for Venice (also given in Dallas and London) did much to establish the opera in the modern operatic repertory.

ACT 1 The sorceress Alcina lures heroes to her enchanted island and transforms them into rocks, streams, trees or wild beasts. Her latest captive is the paladin Ruggiero, as yet untransformed. The opera begins with the arrival on the island of Ruggiero's betrothed, Bradamante, and her governor Melisso; Bradamante is disguised as her brother Ricciardo. The newcomers are met by Alcina's sister Morgana, who immediately begins to flirt with 'Ricciardo'. She brings them to Alcina's palace, where they find Ruggiero wholly captivated by Alcina and living a life of voluptuous luxury. He has no memory of his vows to Bradamante. Also on the island is the boy Oberto, searching for his father Astolfo. Bradamante and Melisso, realizing that Astolfo has been transformed by Alcina, evade the boy's questions. Alcina's general Oronte, who loves Morgana, is annoyed at Morgana's interest in 'Ricciardo'; Ruggiero is equally concerned that he may lose Alcina to 'Ricciardo'. Oronte warns him of the fate of Alcina's former lovers. Ruggiero, seeing no danger to himself, decides to persuade Alcina to transform 'Ricciardo'. Morgana warns 'Ricciardo' of this plan and openly declares her love for 'him'.

ACT 2 Melisso appears to Ruggiero as his old tutor Atlante and by use of a magic ring displays Alcina's island as a barren desert. On Melisso's instructions Ruggiero gets leave from Alcina to go hunting. Oberto appears again, and is assured by Alcina that he will soon see his father. Oronte brings news that Ruggiero has fled, leaving Alcina distraught and vengeful. Ruggiero, restored to his senses, finally recognizes Bradamante and they resolve to defeat Alcina together. Morgana, overhearing, flies to warn her sister as Ruggiero bids a resigned farewell to the illusory beauty of the island. Alcina, alone in a subterranean cavern, calls on her spirits to prevent Ruggiero's flight, but they refuse to obey her. She laments the loss of her powers. As she leaves spectres appear and dance.

ACT 3 Oronte pretends to be indifferent to Morgana, thus prompting her to confess her love for him. Alcina confronts Ruggiero and finds him resolute in his love for Bradamante: she vows vengeance, but will forgive him if he returns to her. Oronte reports to Alcina that her warriors have been rendered powerless. Oberto's cheerful expectation of finding his father annoys the sorceress: she gives him a spear and orders him to kill a lion with it, but Oberto recognizes the features of his father in the friendly beast and threatens Alcina instead. Ruggiero rejects Alcina's renewed pleas and obtains Oronte's support by offering him a sword and his freedom. Alcina and Morgana make a final appeal for mercy but Ruggiero shatters the urn that holds the source of Alcina's magic powers and she vanishes with Morgana. The transformed heroes return to their true forms: among them is Astolfo, reunited with Oberto. All rejoice at their release.

* * *

Alcina is one of the greatest and most popular of Handel's operas, thanks to the rich and expansive invention of the music, the emotional range and power demanded from the singers of the two leading roles (especially Alcina herself) and the fantasy of the story (inviting a variety of allegorical interpretations). The title role includes three deeply felt minor-key arias 'Ah! mio cor', 'Ombre pallide' and 'Mi restano le lagrime' – the second forming the climax of an extraordinary scena ('Ah! Ruggiero crudel') at the end of Act 2, in which Alcina's despair at the loss of her powers is conveyed by music of disturbing instability. Ruggiero's farewell to Alcina's island, 'Verdi prati', expresses yearning nostalgia with a melody of deceptive simplicity – according to Burney, Carestini at first refused to sing it and earned Handel's wrath – and his final resumption of true heroic status is aptly marked with the aria 'Sta nell'Ircana', a virtuoso piece in the fashionable 'Neapolitan' style with ringing high horns in the accompaniment. Bradamante's arias are also brilliant, portraying the doughty warrior maiden – except for her last, when she has abandoned her disguise and can sing with womanly warmth. Morgana's role includes the delectably seductive aria 'Tornami a vagghegiar', elaborated from an aria in Handel's early cantata *O come chiare e belle*; in 1736 Handel transferred it to Alcina – an unhappy translation, which some modern-day Alcinas have been too ready to adopt. All the minor roles are generously endowed with arias of high quality, and the dance music is delightful.

ANTHONY HICKS

Alcyone [*Alcione*]. *Tragédie en musique* in a prologue and five acts by MARIN MARAIS to a libretto by ANTOINE HOUDAR DE LAMOTTE after OVID; Paris, Opéra, 18 February 1706.

On the evidence of box-office takings and contemporary descriptions, this opera was 'much applauded' at the time of its first performance; it was revived on several occasions to 1771. Lamotte was criticized for remaining 'too close to the manner' in which Ovid had treated the subject in the *Metamorphoses* (a modernist, he had never before shown such respect for the writers of antiquity), but the libretto was generally considered 'well written, full of spirit and of sentiments which almost make one forget its failings' (François and Claude Parfaict, *Histoire de l'Académie royale de musique*). Most of the praise, however, went to the composer, whose score shows great merits. There is some excellent vocal writing in the moving *airs*, accompanied sometimes by continuo, sometimes by flutes or an oboe, sometimes by the string ensemble. Accompanied recitatives may derive their structure from the repetition of a melodic element and are generally reserved for the most dramatic scenes. Also remarkable are the duets, trios and expressive choruses, which sometimes incorporate a solo voice.

The love of Alcyone (soprano) and the king of Trachines, Ceix [Ceyx] (*haute-contre*), is opposed by Ceyx's friend Pelée [Peleus] (baritone) and by the magician Phorbas (baritone), who succeeds in separating the couple and causing the death of the young king in a terrible shipwreck. Alcyone, desperate, commits suicide, but Neptune (baritone) intervenes and brings the lovers back to life.

Alcyone owes its fame principally to its instrumental pieces, including the impressive overture and grand *chaconne* finale, picturesque sailors' dances with tambourine accompaniment, descriptive interludes such as the *symphonie* of sleep and the famous storm scene, which contains one of the earliest uses of a double bass in a French operatic score. According to Titon du Tillet (*Le Parnasse françois*, Paris, 1732), the effect created by this passage was 'prodigious': the bass line was further reinforced by 'drums not very tightly stretched, rolling all the time' and producing 'a hollow and lugubrious sound', which, in conjunction with the 'shrill tones' of the violins and oboes, was able to 'make one feel all the fury and horror of a rough sea, of a raging wind howling and whistling, in short of a real and effective tempest'.

JÉRÔME DE LA GORCE

Alda [Davis], **Frances (Jeanne)** [Fanny Jane] (*b* Christchurch, 31 May 1879 [not 1883]; *d* Venice, 18 Sept 1952). New Zealand soprano. She was born into a noted Australasian operatic family; her career began in light opera in Australia at the age of 18. She went to Europe in 1902, studying in Paris with Marchesi, who changed her stage name to Alda and arranged her European début (as Manon at the Opéra-Comique in 1904). She sang three highly acclaimed seasons at the Monnaie in Brussels (1904–7), also appearing at Covent Garden (1906) and La Scala (1908). She was engaged by the Metropolitan in 1908 (début as Gilda, opposite Caruso, 7 December) and remained a leading member of the company until her retirement on 28 December 1929.

Possessed of a secure technique and a pure, lyrical voice, Alda excelled as Desdemona, Manon Lescaut and Mimì. She created the leading soprano roles in three American operas: Damrosch's *Cyrano de Bergerac* (1913), Herbert's *Madeleine* (1914) and Hadley's *Cleopatra's Night* (1920). A successful recording artist, she was also a pioneer of opera on radio and toured widely as a recitalist. In 1910 she married Giulio Gatti-Casazza, General Manager of the Metropolitan, but divorced him in 1928, later (1941) marrying Ray Vir Den. She became an American citizen in 1939. Her memoirs reflect her flamboyant personality and her commonsense approach to the craft of singing.

*

F. Alda: *Men, Women and Tenors* (Boston, 1937) [autobiography]

A. Favia-Artsay: 'Frances Alda', *Record Collector*, vi (1951), 221–33 [with discography]

A. Simpson: '"This country may well be proud of her" – Frances Alda's 1927 Tour of New Zealand', *Music in New Zealand* (spring 1989), 36–61

——: 'New Zealand's most Famous Daughter', *Women's Studies Journal*, v/1 (1989), 61–73

A. Simpson and P. Downes: *Southern Voices: International Opera Singers of New Zealand* (Auckland, 1992), 11–23

ADRIENNE SIMPSON

Aldeburgh. Small coastal town in Suffolk, England. It is the location for the Aldeburgh Festival, an annual series of musical performances and related non-musical events begun in 1948 in and around the town where Benjamin Britten lived from 1947 until his death in 1976 (and which was the historical setting for his opera *Peter Grimes*). The festival was born from a suggestion by Peter Pears that a focus of cultural events should be established in East Anglia. Britten's taste, imagination and personality helped to give the festival an outstanding and distinctive musical character. The English Opera Group was responsible for the early productions but an international outlook was cultivated from strong local roots, with Britten's own music forming an important though not preponderant element in the programmes. The festival takes place in June and lasts for about 17 days, recently with an average of six staged or semi-staged opera performances.

Britten's operatic works first performed at successive festivals are *Let's Make an Opera*, incorporating *The Little Sweep* (1949); *Noye's Fludde* (1958); *A Midsummer Night's Dream* (1960); *Curlew River* (1964); *The Burning Fiery Furnace* (1966); *The Prodigal Son*(1968); *Death in Venice* (1973); and the first British production of *Paul Bunyan* (1976). Premières of works by Walton, Berkeley and Birtwistle, among others, have also been given. Until the opening of the Maltings concert hall in Snape in 1967 most works were staged in the tiny Jubilee Hall, with *Noye's Fludde* and the three church parables in nearby Orford Church. The Maltings (cap. almost 800, and with very fine acoustics) burnt down in 1969 but was rebuilt in time for the 1970 festival.

Following Britten's death the festival management was vested in a new Snape Maltings Foundation and events have been planned by a panel of executive artistic directors, among whom Steuart Bedford, Oliver Knussen and (until 1989) Murray Perahia have been notable. Sponsorship campaigns for additional funds have been initiated, but the rising costs of staging opera have meant that, from 1982, performances were presented with students from the operatic and instrumental summer courses at the Britten-Pears School of Advanced Musical Studies, Snape, giving operas mostly by Britten but also by other composers (Handel, Tchaikovsky, Bizet, Ravel and Copland); there have also been performances by visiting companies such as Kent Opera. Since the early 1980s a programme of musical events during the rest of the year has been mounted including occasional semi-staged opera performances (such as *Don Giovanni* in October 1989).

*

H. Rosenthal: 'Britten on Aldeburgh and the Future', *Opera* (1967), festival issue, 7–9 [interview; issue also incl. contributions by P. Pears, J. Cross, M. Harewood, I. Holst]

E. W. White: *Benjamin Britten: his Life and Operas* (London, 1970)

R. Blythe, ed.: *Aldeburgh Anthology* (Aldeburgh and London, 1972)

NOËL GOODWIN

Alden, Christopher (*b* New York, 16 Sept 1949). American director. After a brief period in the Broadway musical theatre, he was an assistant to Jean-Pierre Ponnelle from 1978 to 1982. Since then he has staged operas in many American cities, and has been director of production at the Long Beach Opera (California) and associate director of Opera at the Academy in New York City. For these two smaller companies, which encourage innovation, Alden has pursued an enlivening approach that has proved controversial but seldom dull; his version of Purcell's *Dido and Aeneas* was presented as a cautionary tale of the flesh for British schoolgirls, while Offenbach's *La vie parisienne* was updated to reflect the drug culture of present-day New York. The results may be sometimes debatable, but they invariably show a questing spirit, a lively theatrical imagination and genuine love for the work at hand. PETER G. DAVIS

Alden, David (*b* New York, 16 Sept 1949). American director, the twin brother of Christopher Alden. His early productions in America in the late 1970s were well-received but gave no hint of the Brechtian, often violent bent that later characterized his stagings in Europe. A new production, using Caspar Neher's existing sets, of *Wozzeck* at the Metropolitan in 1980 led to a new staging of the same work for Scottish Opera later that year that was hailed as 'far more exciting' (*Opera*, 1980, festival issue, 40) than anything seen in Europe that summer. This was a reversal of the disdain which had greeted his *Rigoletto* for the same company in 1979. A punk *Rake's Progress* (1982, Amsterdam) led to a notorious *Mazepa* (1984), his first work for the ENO, which with its chain-saws and strip lighting entered local operatic folklore as an extreme of director's folly. This, however, made his name, and his ENO *Simon Boccanegra* (1987) and *Un ballo in maschera* (1989), both designed by David Fielding, were seen as creating a new house style that, though controversial and alienating, was both musical and dramatically stimulating. He has also worked with the Long Beach company and the New Israeli Opera. He staged the American première of Matthus's *Judith* (1990, Santa Fe) and the world première of Bolcom's *Casino Paradise* (1990, Philadelphia).

*

R. Milnes: 'Genoa, Watergate and Trauma: the Theatrical World of Alden and Fielding', *Opera*, xxxix (1988), 1290–1301

PATRICK O'CONNOR

Aldenhoff, Bernd (*b* Duisburg, 14 June 1908; *d* Munich, 8 Oct 1959). German tenor. His first major success was at Frankfurt (Manrico and Riccardo, 1939). During World War II he appeared at opera houses in Erfurt, Darmstadt and Düsseldorf. At the Dresden Staatsoper (1944–52) he developed as a Heldentenor and he sang Siegfried at Bayreuth between 1951 and 1957. At the Staatsoper in Munich (1950–56) he sang in operas by Weber, Verdi and Strauss (*Die ägyptische Helena*). His sole London appearance was as Siegfried in *Götterdämmerung* in 1957. He appeared in the *Ring* performances at La Scala conducted by Furtwängler.

DAVID CUMMINGS

Aldighieri, Gottardo (*b* Lazise, Lake Garda, 6 Jan 1824; *d* Verona, 11 May 1906). Italian baritone. He studied in Verona and Milan, making his début in 1858 at Novara as Germont. For the next 20 years he sang at all the leading Italian theatres, including S Carlo, where he created Raoul in Donizetti's posthumously performed *Gabriella di Vergy* (1869), and La Scala, where he sang Barnaba in the first performance of Ponchielli's *La Gioconda* (1876). His other roles included Don Giovanni and William Tell. He had a powerful but flexible voice of attractive timbre. ELIZABETH FORBES

Aldighieri, Maria Spezia- (*b* Villafranca Veronese, 1828; *d* Colognola ai Colli, 1907). Italian soprano. She made her début in 1849 at Verona as Bellini's Beatrice di Tenda, also singing Donizetti's Maria Padilla. In 1854 at the Teatro S Benedetto, Venice, she scored a triumph as Violetta not long after the disastrous première of Verdi's *La traviata* at La Fenice. She also sang Violetta at the Teatro della Cannobiana, Milan, and at the S Carlo, Naples. She made her début at La Scala in 1857 as Valentine (*Les Huguenots*), returning in 1861 to sing Abigaille to her husband's Nabucco (she was married to the baritone Gottardo Aldighieri). Her repertory also included Norma, Rossini's Desdemona, Pacini's Sappho, Leonora (*Il trovatore*) and Léonor (*La favorite*), which she sang in Florence in 1875. ELIZABETH FORBES

Aldrovandini [Aldovrandini, Aldrovandin, Aldrovandon, Altrobrandino], **Giuseppe** [Gioseffo] **Antonio Vincenzo** [Giuseppe Maria] (*b* Bologna, 8 June 1671; *d* Bologna, 9 Feb 1707). Italian composer. He was a pupil of G. A. Perti and joined the Accademia Filarmonica in Bologna in 1695; he was chosen *principe* by lot in 1701. His name appears in librettos from 1702 as honorary composer to the Duke of Mantua and *maestro di cappella* at the Accademia dello Spirito Santo in Ferrara, titles which he used himself in the preface to his trio sonatas op.5 (Bologna, 1706). He drowned in the canal port in Bologna as he was preparing to leave for Venice.

Aldrovandini was highly valued as a teacher of singing in Florence, and Prince Ferdinand sent his *virtuosi* to him for further training. As a composer of oratorios he was active only in Bologna, but he was more widely known and appreciated for his operas. Those partly or entirely in Bolognese dialect enjoyed lasting fame locally. *Gl'inganni amorosi scoperti in villa*, after a problematic opening because of *doubles entendres* that were promptly eliminated, was performed several times up to 1759 (it is not certain whether this success should be credited to the music or to Landi's text). *Amor torna in 's al 'so* was performed until 1733 and, together with *Gl'inganni amorosi*, represents an early *buffa* tradition independent of Naples but in many ways close to models in the Italian language. In Bologna Aldrovandini wrote other kinds of opera as well, such as the elegant pastoral comedy *Dafni* by the Arcadian poet Eustachio Manfredi. The high point of his short career is probably represented by works to Venetian librettos by Francesco Silvani (*La fortezza al cimento*, 1699) and Apostolo Zeno (*Pirro*, 1704).

Surviving librettos, which represent various genres and styles, show Aldrovandini as a versatile and professional musician. His music does not stray beyond the working conventions of the day but exploits them fully by the varied application of available stylistic resources: da capo structure predominates, sometimes relieved by simple canzonas; duets and trios are found within rather than at the ends of acts, and their brevity reflects contemporary practice. Aldrovandini stands out for his relatively varied instrumentation and for his arias with instrumental obbligato, particularly for solo violin (which were, however, fairly common in Bologna); his harmony serves to express the text, as also does his melismatic writing, which is never employed merely for display.

drammi per musica in three acts unless otherwise stated

NB – *Naples, Teatro di S Bartolomeo*

Gl'inganni amorosi scoperti in villa (scherzo giocoso, 3, L. M. Landi), Bologna, Formagliari, 28 Jan 1696

Dafni (favola boschereccia, prol., 3, E. Manfredi), Bologna, Malvezzi, 18 Aug 1696

Ottaviano (N. Beregan), Turin, Regio, carn. 1697

Amor torna in 's al 'so, over L'nozz dla Checha e d' Bdett (scherzo drammatico rusticale, A. M. Monti), Bologna, Formagliari, carn. 1698; as Amor Torna in 's al 'so, over L'nozz dla Flippa e d' Bdett, Bologna, Marsigli-Rossi, carn. 1733 [the erroneous title Amor torna in 5 al 50 first appeared in *AllacciD*]

La fortezza al cimento (F. Silvani), Venice, S Salvatore, Feb 1699

Cesare in Alessandria (F. M. Paglia), NB, sum. 1699, *D-Dlb* (scena buffa and int Mirena e Floro), *F-Pn*, *I-Nc* (1700, with int Mirena e Lesbina and Mirena e Floro)

Le due Auguste (P. P. Seta), Bologna, Formagliari, 16 Aug 1700

Semiramide (? G. A. Moniglia), Genoa, Falcone, carn. 1701, *D-Dlb* (scena buffa), *F-Pn*, *I-Nc*

Mitridate in Sebastia (G. Maggi), Genoa, Falcone, aut. 1701; with adds by G. Vignola, NB, 1706, *I-Mc*

Turno Aricino (? S. Stampiglia), Genoa, Falcone, carn. 1702

Pirro (dramma per musica, 5, A. Zeno), Venice, S Angelo, wint. 1704

L'odio e l'amore (melodramma, 3, M. Noris), NB, ?Dec 1704, 8 arias *Nc*

L'incoronazione di Dario (S. Stampiglia, after A. Morselli), NB, carn. 1705; rev. as Li tre rivali al soglio, Bologna, Marsigli-Rossi, 2 Jan 1711, *Mc*, *Nc*

Il più fedel tra vassalli (melodramma, 3, Silvani, with adds by G. Convò and Stampiglia), NB, ?spr. 1705

Doubtful: L'orfano, Naples, 1699; Il Trace in catena, Venice, 1704; Berenice, ?pasticcio, Venice, 1705; Muzio Scevola, 1705; Amore non vuol rispetti, Cento, 1719; Zelida; Perseo

*

O. Penna: *Catalogo degli aggregati della Accademia Filarmonica di Bologna* (MS, *I-Baf*, 1736/*R*1971) [sometimes attrib. G. B. Martini]

C. Goldoni: *Mémoires*, ii (Paris, 1787), chap. 24; in *Tutte le opere di Carlo Goldoni*, ed. G. Ortolani (Milan, 1935–56), i, 346ff

C. Ricci: *I teatri di Bologna nei secoli xvii e xviii: storia aneddotica* (Bologna, 1888), esp. 92, 95ff, 376ff, 386, 388–9, 398, 428

L. Busi: *Il Padre G. B. Martini, musicista-letterato del Secolo xviii* (Bologna, 1891), 130ff

R. L. Weaver and N. W. Weaver: *A Chronology of Music in the Florentine Theatre, 1590–1750* (Detroit, 1978)

L. Bianconi and G. Morelli, eds.: *Antonio Vivaldi: teatro musicale, cultura e società: Venice 1981*

SERGIO DURANTE

Aleko. Opera in one act by SERGEY VASIL'YEVICH RAKHMANINOV to a libretto by VLADIMIR IVANOVICH NEMIROVICH-DANCHENKO after ALEXANDER SERGEYEVICH PUSHKIN'S dramatic narrative poem *Tsïganï* ('The Gypsies', 1824); Moscow, Bol'shoy Theatre, 27 April/9 May 1893.

Aleko was an official graduation piece, assigned not only to the 19-year-old Rakhmaninov but to all three members of Arensky's class in free composition at the Moscow Conservatory in 1892 (the settings by Lev Conus [Konyus] and Nikita Morozov were not published or performed; another opera on the same libretto, by Paul Juon, was performed in Tbilisi in 1897). Starting with the two gypsy dances, which were done by 23 March/4 April, Rakhmaninov completed the full score something over three weeks later, on 16/28 April. The work effectively launched the young composer's professional career, earning him not only the highest possible grade and a gold medal but also his first publication (vocal score, 1892; the full score was issued posthumously, in 1953) and a most prestigious première, under Ippolit Al'tani, at which it received the approbation of Tchaikovsky, who proposed that *Aleko* share a double bill with his own *Iolanta*.

The title character (baritone or bass) is a jaded sophisticate who joins a gypsy caravan in search of a more meaningful existence. There he falls in love with a gypsy girl, Zemfira (soprano), with whom he lives happily for a time. When she tires of him and takes a young gypsy lover (tenor), Aleko reacts according to the false 'civilized' values in which he had been reared, kills the couple in a fit of jealous rage and is expelled from the tribe. The libretto underscores the parallel with *Cavalleria rusticana*, then the latest sensation, by providing a lyrical orchestral intermezzo immediately before the murder.

Otherwise, perhaps befitting the utilitarian circumstances in which it was commissioned, the libretto, while fashioned almost entirely out of Pushkin's original verses, is a primitive, disjointed affair providing a string of numbers covering a variety of operatic forms but little in the way of dramatic continuity or motivation. (A Soviet recording under Golovanov, about 1950, effectively addressed this problem by interspersing readings from Pushkin's poems between the musical numbers.) Rakhmaninov made some attempt to give shape to the opera through thematic consistency (especially obvious is a three-note leitmotif ascending and descending by a semitone that corresponds in rhythm and contour to the pronunciation of the title character's name), and by the use of reprises, some dramatically significant, others purely formal. There is much that is understandably studentish and derivative about the work: the gypsies are characterized musically by a stereotyped 'oriental' idiom handed down from Glinka by way of Borodin; reference in the finale to their noble-savage mores is accompanied by a conventionally 'wild' whole-tone bass progression; a chorus at the denouement, meant to register horror, is cast in the form of a fugal exposition, academically faultless. Perhaps needless to add, the musical style is educed from Tchaikovsky (see especially the duettino for Zemfira and the 'Young Gypsy'). But the writing is admirably fluent, the scoring is both economical and sumptuous, and in the best number – Aleko's cavatina 'Ves' tabor spit' ('The whole camp sleeps'), also the best known thanks to recordings by Shalyapin, who established its performance tradition – a hint of Rakhmaninov's mature lyrical manner may be detected in the dejected falling sequences that pick up flats as they descend.

Aleko makes modest demands on performers; it is a good vehicle for opera workshops and amateur troupes, and these have kept the work marginally alive in Russia.

RICHARD TARUSKIN

Aler, John (*b* Baltimore, 4 Oct 1949). American tenor. He trained at Catholic University, Washington, DC (1969–72), and at the American Opera Center at the Juilliard School (1972–6). While at the latter he made his début as Ernesto and in 1977 he won two first prizes at the Concours International de Chant de Paris; his European début, two years later, was as Belmonte at the Théâtre Royal de la Monnaie, Brussels. He first sang at the Santa Fe Opera in 1978, and has subsequently appeared at Glyndebourne, the New York City Opera and the San Diego Opera. He made his Covent Garden début in 1986 as Ferrando, returning in 1988 as Percy (*Anna Bolena*). Aler's light, clear and appealing voice is best suited to the operas of Mozart, Rossini, Donizetti and Bellini, in which he can demonstrate his tone and vocal agility. He has sung less familiar music, including Rameau's Hippolytus at Aix-en-Provence.

MICHAEL WALSH

Alessandri, Felice (*b* ?Rome, 24 Nov 1747; *d* Casinalbo, nr Modena, 15 Aug 1798). Italian composer. Possibly born at S Damaso, near Modena, he studied in Naples and gained recognition as a harpsichordist and conductor in Turin and Paris before visiting Verona and Venice to prepare his first operas for Carnival 1767. At about this time he married the *buffa* singer Maria Lavinia Guadagni (*b* Lodi, 21 Nov 1735; *d* Padua, *c*1790), sister of the celebrated castrato Gaetano Guadagni; both were employed by the King's Theatre, London, for which Alessandri composed the comic operas *La moglie fedele* and *Il re alla caccia*. Although he must have visited Vienna for the première of his opera *L'argentino* (1768), he was again in London as a harpsichordist in 1770.

Alessandri's career has not been thoroughly investigated. Simonetti stated that he was summoned from Genoa to Dresden in 1773 to direct a performance of his *L'amor soldato*, but this opera was written by a composer with whom he is sometimes confused: Alessandro Felici. From 1773 until April 1775 he was mainly in Turin, where he had three operas performed. A *Medonte* (carn. 1774, Milan) is attributed to Luigi Alessandri in a printed libretto in the Brera library, Milan, but to Felice in the *Gazzetta di Milano* of 28 December 1774. Two comic operas composed for Venetian theatres (not for London as stated by Fétis) received first performances later in 1775, *La sposa persiana* and *La novità*, and another for Lucca, *Sandrina* (not composed with Sacchini as claimed by Gerber).

Alessandri then worked for two years with Joseph Legros in Paris. In December 1778 his *Calliroe* was staged at Milan's new Teatro alla Scala, and during the next few years he had other operas staged in various Italian cities, including Padua, where he was highly regarded by the direction of the Teatro Nuovo. In 1783 the nobility of Padua commissioned him to set the cantata *Le virtù rivali* honouring Alvise Mocenigo, the retiring governor. After a period in St Petersburg as a singing teacher, he moved in autumn 1789 to Berlin where he was named assistant director of the court opera, reportedly at the instigation of the prima donna Luisa Todi. The works he composed were not well received, however. Gerber reported that his first opera, *Il ritorno di Ulysse a Penelope*, was generally admired, and yet the composer encountered difficulties with J. F. Reichardt and other colleagues and displeased his patron Friedrich Wilhelm II with his second opera, *L'ouverture du grand opéra italien à Nankin*. His next opera, *Dario*, proved a disaster, as did his last effort, a pasticcio entitled *Vasco di Gama*. Finally, the king withdrew the *scrittura* for another opera, *Alboino*, and dismissed him (4 July 1792).

Alessandri remarried and returned in autumn 1792 to Italy, where his *Virginia* was performed (1793, Venice). He rejected an offer to compose a *Medea* for the Paris Opéra, but travelled to Vienna and Berlin in 1794 in search of commissions. Later that year *Zemira* and *Armida* received great applause in Padua, and he was named honorary member of the Modenese Accademia dei Filarmonici. His last opera, of unknown title, was given at the Teatro Rangoni, Modena, shortly before his death.

See also CALLIROE (ii).

Ezio (os, 3, P. Metastasio), Verona, Filarmonica, carn. 1767, *I-Mc*
Il matrimonio per concorso (ob, 3, G. Martinelli, after C. Goldoni), Venice, S Moisè, carn. 1767, *A-Wn*
La moglie fedele (ob, 2), London, King's, 27 Feb 1768
L'argentino (ob, 2), Vienna, Burg, spr. 1768
Arianna e Teseo (pasticcio), London, King's, 11 Oct 1768
Il re alla caccia (ob, 3, Goldoni), London, King's, 1 March 1769
Argea (os, 3, G. Boggio), Turin, Regio, carn. 1773
Creso (os, 3, G. Pizzi), Pavia, Quattro Signori, spr. 1774
La cameriera per amore (ob, 2, F. Livigni), Turin, Carignano, aut. 1774
Medonte re d'Epiro (os, 3, G. De Gamerra), Milan, Ducale, 26 Dec 1774
Alcina e Ruggero (os, 3, V. A. Cigna-Santi, after L. Ariosto), Turin, Regio, carn. 1775
La novità (ob, 2, G. Bertati), Venice, S Moisè, aut. 1775, *I-Mc*
La sposa persiana (ob, 3, Goldoni), Venice, S Samuele, aut. 1775, *MOe*, *D-Dlb*
Sandrina, ossia La contadina di corte (ob, 2, Goldoni), Lucca, Pubblico, 1775
Calliroe (os, 3, M. Verazi), Milan, Scala, 26 Dec 1778
Adriano in Siria (os, 3, Metastasio), Venice, S Benedetto, 26 Dec 1779

Erifile (os, 3, G. B. Neri or De Gamerra), Padua, Nuovo, 12 June 1780
Attalo re di Bitinia (os, 3, F. Casorri or A. Salvi), Florence, Pergola, Sept 1780, *F-Pn*
Il vecchio geloso (ob, 2, Bertati), Milan, 1 Oct 1781, *I-Bc, Fc* (inc.); ? rev. as Il marito geloso, Livorno, Nuovo, carn. 1784
Arbace (os, 3, G. Sertor), Rome, Argentina, 29 Dec 1781
La finta principessa, ossia Li due fratelli Pappamosca (ob, 2, Livigni), Venice, S Moisè, aut. 1782, *D-DS, I-CR*, ov., aria *Gl*
I puntigli gelosi (ob, 2, Livigni), Venice, S Samuele, carn. 1783
Demofoonte (os, 3, Metastasio), Padua, Nuovo, 12 June 1783
Artaserse (os, 3, Metastasio), Naples, S Carlo, 4 Nov 1783
L'imbroglio delle tre spose (ob, 2, Bertati), Florence, Pergola, spr. 1784
La villanella rapita (ob, 2, Bertati), Bologna, Formagliari, aut. 1784
Il ritorno di Ulysse a Penelope (os, 3, A. Filistri), Potsdam, court theatre, 25 Jan 1790, *D-B*
L'ouverture du grand opéra italien à Nankin [La compagnia d'opera a Nanchino] (2, Filistri), Berlin, Kleines, 16 Oct 1790
Dario (os, 3, Filistri), Berlin, Königliches, Jan 1791, *B*
Vasco di Gama (pasticcio, 3, Filistri), Berlin, Königliches, 20 Jan 1792
Virginia (os, 3, A. Pepoli), Venice, Fenice, 26 Dec 1793
Zemira (os, 2, Sertor), Padua, Nuovo, 12 June 1794
Armida (os, 2, G. M. Foppa), Padua, Nuovo, 1 July 1794, *I-Bc**, duets *PAc, Vnm*
I sposi burlati (ob, 2), Mantua, Nuovo Nazionale, 26 Dec 1798

*

DBI (S. Simonetti); *ES* (E. Zanetti); *FétisB*; *GerberNL*; *LS*; *MGG* (S. Simonetti)
L. Schneider: *Geschichte der Oper und des königlichen Opernhauses in Berlin* (Berlin, 1852)
L. F. Valdrighi: *Felice Alessandri maestro di cappella di Federico Guglielmo II re di Prussia (1790–92)* (Modena, 1896)
R.-A. Mooser: *Annales de la musique et des musiciens en Russie au XVIIIme siècle*, ii (Geneva, 1951)
U. Manferrari: *Dizionario universale delle opere melodrammatiche*, i (Florence, 1954)
SVEN HANSELL

Alessandria. Italian city in Piedmont. It acquired its first theatre in 1729 when the hall of the palace of Marchese Filippo Guasco Gallarati di Solerio was inaugurated. The Teatro Civico opened in 1775 and in 1779 Cherubini's first opera, *Il Quinto Fabio*, was performed there during the Alessandria fair. Restored in 1853–4, the theatre was particularly active in the second half of the 19th century, and became an essential platform for singers and dancers who aspired to perform in the major theatres. The auditorium was restructured several times before its destruction by bombing in 1944. The Teatro Comunale, built in 1978, houses opera, concerts, plays and entertainments staged by the 'Laboratorio Lirico' (formed in 1980 by the Azienda Teatrale Alessandrina). This arrangement continues the venture organized by the 'Teatro Lirico di avviamento artistico' which took place in Alessandria from 1937 to 1943. Every summer, young singers, instrumentalists, assistant conductors and directors are selected by competition, and after a month working together they present a lyric opera as final test. The Teatro Lirico has staged two world premières: Lorenzo Ferrero's *Mare Nostro* (1985) and Marco Tutino's *Cirano* (1987).

*

A. Civalieri: 'Il Teatro Civico di Alessandria', *Rivista di storia, arte e archeologia per le provincie di Alessandria e di Asti* (1924)
A. Scansetti: 'Il Teatro Municipale di Alessandria', *Bollettino storico-bibliografico subalpino* (1929)
A. Tafuri: *La vita musicale di Alessandria (1729–1868)* (Alessandria, 1968)
C. Beltrami: *Musica e melodramma. Testimonianze di vita teatrale nell'ottocento alessandrino* (Turin, 1988)
PAOLO GALLARATI

Alessandro ('Alexander'). Opera in three acts by GEORGE FRIDERIC HANDEL to a libretto by PAOLO ANTONIO ROLLI based on ORTENSIO MAURO's *La superbia d'Alessandro* (1690, Hanover); London, King's Theatre, 5 May 1726.

Alessandro Magno [Alexander the Great]		alto castrato
Tassile [Taxiles] *king of India*		alto castrato
Clito [Clitus]	*Macedonian captains*	bass
Cleone [Cleon]	*Macedonian captains*	contralto
Leonato [Leonnatus]	*Macedonian captains*	tenor
Rossane [Roxana]		soprano
Lisaura		soprano

Setting Oxidraca, 4th century BC

Alessandro was Handel's ninth full-length opera for the Royal Academy of Music and the first of the group of five in which the leading female roles were designed for the rival sopranos Francesca Cuzzoni and Faustina Bordoni; they sang Lisaura and Roxana. The other singers included the castratos Senesino (Alexander) and Antonio Baldi (Taxiles), the tenor Luigi Antinori (Leonnatus), the contralto Anna Vincenza Dotti (Cleon) and the bass Giuseppe Boschi (Clitus). The opera was completed on 11 April 1726, less than a month before its production as the last of the 1725–6 season, but had been begun some months earlier in anticipation of Faustina's arrival in London (Handel broke off composition to write *Scipione*). Owen Swiney, writing from Venice on 4/15 March 1726, was no doubt correct in assuming that the subject of the opera, in which 'there is to be a Struggle between the Rival Queen's, for a Superiority', had been deliberately intended to reflect the real-life contention of the two sopranos (or at any rate of their supporting factions).

During the initial run of 13 performances Handel replaced two of Roxana's arias. He revived *Alessandro* on 26 December 1727, and in a much abridged version on 25 November 1732, when Roxana and Lisaura were sung by Anna Strada del Pò and Celeste Gismondi. There were revivals at Hamburg on 18 November 1726 (in a version by C. G. Wendt) and at Brunswick on 17 August 1728 (as *Der hochmütighe Alexander*). On 8 November 1743 the opera was produced at the King's Theatre under the title *Rossane*. Handel may have given permission for this revival as a concession to Lord Middlesex, who earlier in the year had pressed him to resume composing for the opera house, but had been refused. The score was probably arranged by Lampugnani, who added a version of the *Samson* aria 'Return, oh God of Hosts' with Italian text as well as a number of arias not by Handel; some are preserved in a manuscript in the Hall collection (*US-PRu*). This version was revived on 24 February 1747 and 20 February 1748. The first modern revival was at the Staatsoper, Dresden, in 1959, and the first in Britain (apart from a concert performance at Oxford in 1966) was by Opera 70 at the Assembly Rooms, Chichester, on 7 July 1981.

The story is largely fictional, but involves the historical character of Alexander the Great (356–23 BC) and persons associated with him, and is set in the period of his Indian campaign (*c*327 BC).

ACT 1 Alexander, claiming to be the son of Jupiter, is leading an assault on the walls of 'Oxidraca', described as 'a city in India'. (The Oxydracae were actually a tribe; presumably the reference is to the incident described in Arrian's *Anabasis*, vi.9, in which Alexander leads the charge on an unnamed town belonging to the Mallians, neighbours of the Oxydracae.) With encouragement from his captain Leonnatus, he enters the city. Two women, the captive princess Roxana and Lisaura, are in love with him. The Indian king Taxiles, who owes allegiance to Alexander, brings the news to Roxana, but finds Lisaura (whom he loves) equally interested. Alexander is received in triumph by Taxiles, Leonnatus and his other captains, Cleon and Clitus. Cleon, in love with Roxana, turns Alexander's attention to Lisaura. The jealous Roxana reflects on her unhappiness. Cleon leads a sacrifice to Alexander in the temple of Jupiter Ammon, but Clitus refuses to acknowledge Alexander as a god and Alexander knocks him to the ground. The two women try to pacify Alexander, prompting him to interrupt his military campaign for the claims of love.

ACT 2 In a garden, Alexander first declares love for Roxana (feigning sleep) and then for Lisaura; each overhears, and each sarcastically quotes back to Alexander the song with which he wooed the other. Taxiles presses his suit to Lisaura, but she is not yet prepared to abandon her hopes for Alexander. Roxana tests Alexander's further protestations of love by demanding her freedom; he agrees, but she indicates that she prefers to be his prisoner. Alexander sees that he must abandon Lisaura and hints as much to her. He assumes the throne and distributes the lands of his conquests to his captains: Clitus, offered the Indies, refuses to accept them from one who claims to be the son of Jupiter rather than of his true father Philip. Alexander threatens to kill him, but is prevented by Taxiles. At this moment the canopy above the throne falls 'by conspiracy', just missing Alexander. He accuses Clitus of treachery and has him imprisoned. Roxana faints at the news, convincing Alexander of the sincerity of her love. Leonnatus reports an uprising among the local people, inspired by false news of Alexander's death. Alexander leads his men to battle, promising Roxana the fulfilment of her love when he returns victorious.

ACT 3 The imprisoned Clitus receives an unwelcome visit from Cleon; Leonnatus arrives with armed men, releases Clitus and imprisons Cleon in his place. Leonnatus says the Macedonians are ready to join Clitus in deposing Alexander and leaves with Clitus. Cleon, released by his own men, goes to warn Alexander. Lisaura and Roxana amicably resolve to glory in their joint love for Alexander. Alexander persuades Lisaura to reward Taxiles' fidelity. Roxana tells Alexander of the Macedonian plot to depose him. He goes to meet the conspirators and challenges them to oppose him. They are overawed; Clitus begs a general pardon and receives it. In the final scene, again in the temple of Jupiter, Alexander proclaims a festival, pledging friendship to Lisaura and love to Roxana.

* * *

The precise equalization of the roles of Roxana and Lisaura is a significant feature of the opera: they are first heard in a duet recitative in which neither has prominence over the other, and for the finale Handel links in one continuous sequence a duet for each soprano with Alexander, a trio for the three of them, and the customary *coro*. To achieve this equality Rolli sacrificed much of the coherence of Mauro's original libretto with more than his usual disregard for dramatic values, and Handel did not give the rival roles the contrast of character that he achieved in his later Cuzzoni-Faustina operas. In broad effect *Alessandro* is a series of stunning numbers for the three main characters, mostly in fast tempos and in major keys, but sufficiently varied with enjoyable arias for the minor characters and reflective accompanied recitatives to make the musical feast pleasantly digestible. ANTHONY HICKS

Alessandro nelle Indie ('Alexander in India'). *Opera seria* in two acts by GIOVANNI PACINI to a libretto by ANDREA LEONE TOTTOLA after PIETRO METASTASIO (*see* ALESSANDRO NELL' INDIE below); Naples, Teatro S Carlo, 29 September 1824.

Pacini's *Alessandro* resembles other 19th-century adaptations of 18th-century librettos in a number of respects. It centres on a love triangle involving the invading Greek general Alexander (tenor), Cleofide [Cleophis] (soprano), queen of one part of India, and her lover Poro [Porus] (soprano), king of another part of India, who suspects unjustly that Cleophis has betrayed him. It also presents a horrifying climax in which the heroine threatens to immolate herself rather than marry Alexander, and it gives a primary role to ensembles of conflict. Yet it retains elements of Metastasian intrigue in the use of assumed identities by Porus and his general Gandarte [Gandartes] and in Alexander's twofold attempt to coerce Cleophis's affection. Moreover, it ends happily, when Alexander relents and reunites the couple.

Alessandro was Pacini's first new work for Naples, and the composer recalled that the creative process had been 'arduous' because of his concerns regarding the sophisticated and critical Neapolitan public. Yet its première was a tremendous success, and it received 70 consecutive performances at the Teatro S Carlo.

SCOTT L. BALTHAZAR

Alessandro nell'Indie ('Alexander in India'). Libretto by PIETRO METASTASIO, first set by Leonardo Vinci (1730, Rome). Versions of the libretto also appear with such titles as *Alessandro e Poro*, *Cleofide*, *La generosità di Alessandro* and *Poro, rè dell'Indie*.

ACT 1 Poro [Porus], an Indian king, defeated by Alessandro Magno [Alexander the Great], resolves to save Cleofide [Cleophis], queen of another part of India. Disguised as his general, Gandarte [Gandartes], and taking the name Asbite [Asbites], he is dispatched by Alexander to offer peace to Porus. Timagene [Timagenes], Alexander's confidant, loves Erissena [Eryxene], Porus's sister. When he leads her in as captive, Eryxene's obvious admiration of Alexander, who releases her, arouses Timagenes' jealousy of his king. Cleophis visits Alexander, but 'Asbites' (Porus) interrupts to relay Porus's refusal of Alexander's peace offer. Recognizing him, and angered by his jealousy, Cleophis invites Alexander to return her visit.

ACT 2 Fighting breaks out upon Alexander's arrival in Cleophis's realm. Alexander is victorious, and the vanquished Porus flees with Cleophis, who reaffirms her love for him. Porus is captured, but Timagenes, turned traitor, frees him and offers, in a letter, to help him assassinate Alexander. Gandartes (disguised as Porus) surrenders to Alexander, who magnanimously frees him. He orders 'Asbites' (Porus) released, but Eryxene reports that he has killed himself. Gandartes urges Eryxene to leave with him, but she reminds him of their duty to India.

ACT 3 Porus lives, however, and gives Timagenes' letter to Eryxene, who passes it to Alexander. Timagenes is forgiven by Alexander and can no longer help Porus kill him. Porus, believing that Cleophis is to

'Alessandro nell'Indie', Act 3 scene xii (CLEOPHIS: *'Say no more. It is the hour of death, not of Love'): engraving from the 'Opere' of Pietro Metastasio (Paris: Hérissant, 1780–82)*

marry Alexander, vows to kill them both. When Cleophis announces, however, that she will immolate herself on his funeral pyre, Porus reveals himself. Alexander forgives all and unites the lovers.

* * *

Details of the confrontation between Alexander and Porus are recorded in Arrian, *Anabasis* (book 5) and Curtius Rufus, *Historiarum* (book 8). The subject is also treated briefly in Diodorus Siculus, *Bibliotheca* (book 17); Justin's epitome of the Trogus, *Historiae* (book 12); and Plutarch's *Vitae* (Alexander). Claude Boyer's drama *Porus ou La générosité d'Alexandre* (1648) shares not only an alternative title for Metastasio's libretto but also the common practice of creating a plot through the imposition of love intrigues on a classical narrative; Racine's *Alexandre le grand* (1665) provides another example. Incidents in these dramas have parallels in Metastasio's version, the libretto lying closer to Boyer than to Racine. Even stronger are the similarities between *Alessandro nell'Indie* and *L'amante eroe* (1693), a libretto by Domenico David, whose *La forza del virtù* had been a model for Metastasio's first opera libretto, *Siface*, in 1723. Late in 1753, Metastasio reluctantly began work on a shortened version for Carlo Broschi (Farinelli), in Madrid, but he eventually expressed satisfaction at the resultant increase in movement, interest and intensity. In popularity, *Alessandro nell'Indie* was to hold second place only to *Artaserse*, with which it initially shared the same carnival season in Rome, both operas in settings by Vinci. For Hasse, this was his first opera for Dresden (as *Cleofide*, 1731), for Luigi Gatti, his first for Mantua (1768), and for Giovanni Pacini, his first for Naples (1824). Handel's setting (1731, as *Poro*), with Senesino in the title role, was admired for its dramatic impact. The Lisbon presentation of the second version of Perez (1755) was impressively staged by Giovanni Galli-Bibiena, and J. C. Bach's settings of *Catone in Utica* and *Alessandro nell'Indie* for Naples (1761–2) would have ensured further commissions for the S Carlo but for his departure for London.

For a list of settings *see* METASTASIO, PIETRO. *See also* CLEOFIDE [Hasse] and PORO [Handel].

DON NEVILLE

Alessandro Severo (i) ('Alexander Severus'). *Dramma per musica* in three acts by ANTONIO LOTTI to a libretto by APOSTOLO ZENO; Venice, Teatro S Giovanni Grisostomo, Carnival 1717.

The plot is based loosely on Roman history. Giulia Mammea [Julia Mamaea] (soprano), mother of the emperor Alexander Severus (soprano castrato), desires to retain power as she did throughout her son's reign (222–35). According to historical record, she succeeded in banishing her son's wife Sallustia (soprano) and father-in-law after the latter's foiled conspiracy against the emperor. But in the opera Sallustia selflessly offers her own life in order to save Julia Mamaea from the conspirators; overcome by the magnanimity of her gesture, Julia Mamaea is reconciled to Sallustia. A completely ahistorical subplot involves Albina (contralto), dressed as a man, testing the fidelity of her lover Claudio [Claudius] (soprano castrato).

This was the last opera Lotti set for Venice before leaving to take up his new post in Dresden and the last libretto Zeno wrote for Venice before becoming imperial poet in Vienna. It was the only production for the 1717 carnival at the Teatro S Giovanni Grisostomo, the pre-eminent Venetian opera house of the day, and may have been performed as early as 26 December 1716. Between 1717 and 1763 it was produced at least 19 times, in 14 different Italian cities and in London, but Lotti's setting was never performed again in its entirety.

The opera begins and ends with choruses and contains 30 arias and two duets. With minimal orchestral forces Lotti nonetheless provided effective characterizations through his choice of melodic material and judicious use of coloratura; the leading roles of the imperious Julia Mamaea and the more tender Sallustia were well suited to their first interpreters, Maria Anna Benti Bulgarelli and Faustina Bordoni respectively. The energetic Albina was played by Diana Vico.

HARRIS S. SAUNDERS

Alessandro Severo (ii) ('Alexander Severus'). Opera in three acts by GEORGE FRIDERIC HANDEL to a libretto anonymously adapted from APOSTOLO ZENO as revised for Milan, 1723; London, King's Theatre, 25 February 1738.

Like *Oreste* (1734), *Alessandro Severo* is a pasticcio opera created by Handel from his own works: the arias, duets, entr'actes and final *coro* are taken (with verbal changes) from earlier operas (mainly those of the previous London season – *Arminio, Giustino* and *Berenice*); the overture and recitatives are new. The story is based on an incident in the reign of the Roman emperor Alexander Severus (222–35) as related by Herodian (vi, 1.9). Alexander (mezzo-soprano castrato) is dominated by his mother Giulia [Julia] (contralto), whose jealous rage at being outranked by Alexander's wife Sallustia (soprano) generates the main action; Alexander is tricked into repudiating Sallustia, who bears her humiliation patiently and eventually saves Julia from being murdered in a conspiracy organized by Sallustia's father Marziano [Marcianus] (bass). Alexander's minister Claudio [Claudius] (soprano castrato) is also involved in the conspiracy, but his role is discovered by his discarded lover Albina (soprano) and she wins back his love by protecting him.

Some of the arias seem a little light in style for the usually strong dramatic contexts, but the final act is very effective and is memorable for a powerful scene set in Julia's bedroom in which Sallustia confronts her father and his fellow conspirators and foils their murderous plans. The opera was given six performances in Handel's last full opera season at the King's Theatre, with a cast consisting of the castrato Gaetano Majorano (Caffarelli) as Alexander, Elisabeth Duparc (La Francesina) as Sallustia, Antonia Margherita Merighi as Julia, Margherita Chimenti (La Droghierina) as Claudius, Maria Antonia Marchesini (La Lucchesina) as Albina, and Antonio Montagnana as Marcianus. It has yet to be revived. ANTHONY HICKS

Alessandro Stradella. Romantic opera in three acts by FRIEDRICH FLOTOW to a libretto by W. FRIEDRICH; Hamburg, Stadttheater, 30 December 1844.

The plot is a mild and comic extract from the turbulent life of the 17th-century Italian composer. In Act 1, set in and around St Mark's Square, Venice, Stradella (tenor) is discovered in a gondola with some of his music students as they sing first a hymn to Venice and then a serenade to his beloved Leonore (soprano). She appears on the balcony and warns him against her guardian, Bassi (bass), a rich Venetian who has incarcerated her and plans to marry her the next day against her will. Stradella arranges to flee with Leonore, and the pair take advantage of a conniving, tumultuous carnival procession to elope. While Bassi gets caught up among the masked revellers, Stradella and Leonore slip away in the gondola.

Act 2 takes place in front of Stradella's country house near Rome. Leonore, in bridal array, rejoices in her good fortune. To the sound of the bells Stradella leads her amid a procession of guests to the wedding ceremony. Malvolino (bass), a bandit who has been engaged by Bassi to assassinate Stradella, now arrives and is surprised to find that his associate, the bandit Barbarino (tenor), is there with the same mandate. When the marriage procession returns, the bandits introduce themselves to Stradella as pilgrims. He invites them to join in the celebrations, then sings a romance which describes the compassion and kindness that lie deep in the hearts of all robbers and bandits who help the poor and grant asylum to the wandering minstrel. This song so moves Malvolino and Barbarino that they abandon their murderous plan.

Act 3 begins in an antechamber in Stradella's country house. Stradella, Leonore and the bandits sing in praise of the beauty of Italy. The young couple move on to join a group of pilgrims, and Bassi appears to see whether his instructions have been carried out. Overhearing the two assassins declare that they no longer have the heart to kill Stradella, he substantially increases his fee, upon which they agree to perform the task. The three conspirators creep up on Stradella just as he starts rehearsing the hymn 'Jungfrau Maria! Himmlisch Verklärte!' for the festival of the Virgin Mary the following day. This hymn, describing how the Virgin will lead all evildoers back to the paths of righteousness and forgiveness, is the culmination of the opera, and still survives as a tour de force for tenors. The assassins are once again so overwhelmed by the pious strains that they all kneel down and join in song. Leonore enters just as Stradella notices them kneeling with daggers drawn. Bassi makes an emotional confession and he and the bandits are forgiven by Stradella. The scene changes to a hill near Rome. Stradella is borne on a litter of branches to the picture of the Madonna, where the pilgrims await the divine grace which his music will elicit.

Flotow had in 1837 written some of the music used in this work for a one-act *comédie mêlée de chant* on the same subject for performance in Paris. Although the work is through-composed and has no spoken dialogue, it fits the description of *opéra comique* better than that of romantic opera. Its 'romantic' aspect lies not in its style or subject but rather in Flotow's musical interpretation of the text. Notwithstanding the comic relief offered by Bassi and the two bandits, the opera, set against the background of a lyrically idealized Italy, is an apotheosis of the pious musician using his art to improve society. As in many of his works Flotow pays close attention to cyclic overall form, using several reminiscence themes: the hymn 'Jungfrau Maria!', for example, occurs in the overture and is repeated in varied forms in each act. This, combined with an inexorable drive towards large climaxes in each scene, conveys a feeling of compelling dramatic truth. The work's wide range of expression comprises atmospheric Venetian water music ('In des Mondes Silberhelle'), a nocturne ('Durch die Täler'), Leonore's exacting recitative and aria ('So wär' es denn erreicht'), buffo humour ('An dem linken Strand der Tiber'), a hearty drinking ensemble ('Bei Schmaus und Sang und Becherklang') and the hymnal climax ('Wie freundlich strahlt der Tag'). Two instrumental ballets, the second in Act 2 having five movements, add an important dimension.

PETER COHEN

Alewijn, Abraham (*b* Amsterdam, 16 Nov 1664; *d* Batavia, Dutch East Indies, 4 Oct 1721). Netherlands poet and playwright. Born into a wealthy family, he studied law in Leiden and Utrecht. He was one of the most important and prolific Netherlands poets and playwrights of the decades around 1700, although his works are now little esteemed. He wrote numerous song texts, as well as librettos for *zangspelen* (Singspiels) such as *Amarillis* (1693, possibly by D. Petersen); *Hardersspel ter Bruiloft van Frederik Willem Mandt en Maria van Blyswyk* (1699, S. de Konink); and *Orpheus*, for which no score exists. In 1707 Alewijn left for the Dutch East Indies, where he became an administrator in Batavia (now Jakarta).

J. A. Worp: 'Mr. Abraham Alewijn', *Tijdschrift voor Nederlandse Taal- en Letterkunde*, v (1885), 246–75 RUDOLF A. RASCH

Alexander, Carlos (*b* Utica, NY, 15 Oct 1915). American bass-baritone. He studied in New York, making his début in 1941 in St Louis as Masetto. In 1955 he went to Germany and sang in Cologne, Düsseldorf, Munich, Berlin and Stuttgart, where he was engaged for a decade, and where he created the title role in Orff's *Prometheus* (1968). He also appeared in Vienna, Florence and at Glyndebourne, where he sang Mittenhofer in the first

British performance of *Elegy for Young Lovers* (1961). At Bayreuth he sang Beckmesser (1963–4). His repertory included the Dutchman, Wotan, Iago, Baron Prus (*The Makropulos Affair*), John the Baptist, Mandryka and Cardinal Borromeo (*Palestrina*). A powerful singing actor, he excelled in roles such as Dr Schön (*Lulu*), Schoenberg's Moses and Father Grandier (*The Devils of Loudun*), in which his musical and dramatic gifts were effectively displayed.

ELIZABETH FORBES

Alexander, John (*b* Meridian, MS, 21 Oct 1923; *d* Meridian, 8 Dec 1990). American tenor. He trained at the Cincinnati Conservatory and made his début as Faust with the Cincinnati Opera in 1952. He joined the New York City Opera as Alfredo five years later and made his Metropolitan début as Ferrando in 1961. Important European engagements found him singing in Korngold's *Die tote Stadt* at the Vienna Volksoper (1967), *La bohème* at the Vienna Staatsoper (1968), and Pollione at Covent Garden (1970). The Bellini opera became one of his specialities, and he has sung it in a single season opposite the three most celebrated Normas of the time, Sutherland, Caballé and Sills; he recorded the opera, and Rossini's *Semiramide* (singing Idreno) with Sutherland. In May 1973 he sang the title role in the American première of the original French version of *Don Carlos*, staged by the Boston Opera. Alexander's value to leading American opera companies rested partly with his remarkable versatility and reliability in an enormous repertory, spanning bel canto at one extreme and such Germanic roles as Bacchus and Walther von Stolzing at the other. Although his acting sometimes lacked ardour and his singing was not invariably notable for dynamic finesse, he made the most of taste, fervour, stamina and a voice that commanded an exceptionally brilliant ring at the top.

*

J. Hines: *Great Singers on Great Singing* (Garden City, NY, 1982), 25–9

MARTIN BERNHEIMER

Alexander, Roberta (*b* Lynchburg, VA, 3 March 1949). American soprano. She graduated in voice studies at the University of Michigan, and continued her training at the Royal Conservatory, The Hague (with Herman Woltman), and the Netherlands Opera Studio, with which she made her début in *La cambiale di matrimonio* (Rossini). Making her home in Amsterdam, she sang a variety of roles with the Netherlands Opera, one of them in the première of Ullmann's *Der Kaiser von Atlantis* (1975). Her European engagements also included both West and East Berlin, the latter in 1982 as Mimì in Harry Kupfer's Komische Oper production of *La bohème*. She returned to the USA for her operatic début there as Pamina at Houston, in 1980; she sang Strauss's Daphne at Santa Fe (1981) and Zerlina at the Metropolitan Opera (1983), where she later sang Bess (Gershwin), Jenůfa and Mimì. Her British operatic début was at Covent Garden as Mimì (1984), and her Viennese (1985) as Cleopatra (*Giulio Cesare*) at the Theater an der Wien; she later sang Donna Elvira at the Staatsoper (1986). She sang Jenůfa at Glyndebourne in 1989. Her roles include Mozart's Vitellia and Electra. An accomplished singing actress with a smoothly produced soprano of wide expressive range, she also has a flourishing concert career.

NOËL GOODWIN

Alexandre [Alessandro], **Charles-Guillaume** (*b c*1735; *d* Paris, late 1787 or early 1788). French composer. He was active as a violinist throughout his career, playing with the orchestra of the Opéra-Comique from 1753 to 1755 and arranging numerous *airs* (mainly for string quartet) from popular operas by Grétry and Dalayrac among others. In addition to two *spectacles à machines* performed at the Théâtre des Tuileries in the mid-1750s (La Borde, in his *Essai sur la musique*, claims a third), he wrote three *opéras comiques* and collaborated with various composers on a fourth, *Le tonnelier*, one of the most popular works given by the Comédie-Italienne during the 1770s and 80s. His own operas met with a more modest success. *Georget et Georgette*, which contains two scenes loosely based on Shakespeare's *The Tempest*, was criticized for its weak libretto. *Le petit-maître en province*, which exposed the morals of 18th-century society, was performed 12 times in the first month (although the critic Friedrich Grimm called Alexandre 'un faiseur de notes'). Both works include *ariettes*, a small number of ensembles and vaudeville finales. *L'esprit du jour* was apparently performed only once.

first performances in Paris; printed works published in Paris

Georget et Georgette (oc, 1, Harny de Guerville), Foire St Laurent, 28 July 1761 (1761)

Le tonnelier (oc, 1, N.-M. Audinot and A.-F. Quétant), Comédie-Italienne (Hôtel de Bourgogne), 16 March 1765 (*c*1767), collab. Ciapalanti, Gossec, Kohaut, F.-A. D. Philidor, Schobert and J.-C. Trial

Le petit-maître en province (comédie avec des ariettes, 1, Harny de Guerville), Comédie-Italienne (Hôtel de Bourgogne), 7 Oct 1765 (*c*1765)

L'esprit du jour (oc, 1, Harny de Guerville), Comédie-Italienne (Hôtel de Bourgogne), 22 Jan 1767, airs pubd in contemporary anthologies

ELISABETH COOK (text), MICHEL NOIRAY (work-list)

Alexandrov, Anatoly Nikolayevich (*b* Moscow, 13/25 May 1888; *d* Moscow, 16 April 1982). Russian composer. He studied with Taneyev, Vasilenko and Konstantin Igumnov at the Moscow conservatory (1910–16), where from 1923 until 1964 he was a composition professor. In general his music is characterized by emotional depth and colourfulness, and by its close links with 19th-century Russian traditions. His six operas, which span his creative career, are lyrical, melodic and expressively direct with flexible and varied vocal parts. These works incorporate folk melodies and employ leitmotif technique. *Bela*, commissioned by the Bol'shoy Theatre for the centenary of Lermontov's death, ran for a year after its first performance on 10 December 1946. The music includes melodies collected in the Caucasus by Taneyev in 1885. Although the opera has not been revived and its final version, completed in 1949, was never staged, Alexandrov derived four later works (op.51a–d) from its music. *Dikaya Bara* ('Wild Bara'), composed between 1954 and 1957, is based on Božena Němcová's collection of Czech folktales. Alexandrov's final opera, *Levsha* ('Lefty'), received over 100 performances after its première at the Detskiy Muzïkal'nïy Teatr (Children's Music Theatre) in Moscow on 8 February 1976. This children's opera, which comprises 24 scenes in two acts, has the subtitle 'A Tragicomic Performance with Song, Dance, Dialogue, Symphonic Music and a Shoed Flea'. A mixture of Russian fairground farce and 18th-century comic opera, the music features three Russian folksongs: 'Vdol' po rechke' ('Along the River'), 'Vo kuznitse' ('In the Smithy') and 'Posledniy chas razluki' ('The Last Hour of Parting').

Ten' Fellidï [The Shadow of Fellida], 1915 (V. Morits, after M. Kuz'min), inc.; 1 song, Moscow, 31 January 1919, pubd as op.8a (Moscow, 1926)
Dva mira [Two Worlds], 1916 (after A. Maykov); rev. of Act 1, 1974
Sorok perviy [The Forty-First] op.41, 1933–5 (B. Gusman and Morits, after B. Lavrenyov), broadcast perf., Moscow, All-Union Radio, 1935; inc.
Bela op.51, 1940–45 (prol., 4, Yu. Stremin, after M. Yu. Lermontov: *A Hero of our Time*), Moscow, Bol'shoy, 10 Dec 1946; rev. 1949, unperf.; vs (Moscow, 1988)
Dikaya Bara [Wild Bara] op.82, 1954–7 (3, S. Severtsev, after B. Němcová), excerpts, concert perf., Moscow, 2 March 1957, vs (Moscow, 1962); incl. music from Sorok perviy, 1933–5
Levsha [Lefty] op.103 (children's op, 2, N. Sats, after N. Leskov, lyrics V. Viktorov), Moscow, Detskiy Muzïkal'nïy, 8 Feb 1976, vs (Moscow, 1979)

*

V. Kokushkin and A. Khokhlovkina: '"Bela" – opera An. Aleksandrova', *SovM* (1946), no.11, pp.19–34
O. Stepanov: 'Tragikomicheskoye predstavleniye: opera *Levsha*' [A Tragicomic Performance: the Opera 'Lefty'], *SovM* (1976), no.8, pp.76–9
V. M. Blok, ed.: *A. N. Aleksandrov: vospominaniya, stat'i, pis'ma* [Reminiscences, Articles, Letters] (Moscow, 1979) [incl. article by Alexandrov on *The Forty-First*]
V. Kokushkin: *Anatoly Aleksandrov* (Moscow, 1987)

GALINA GRIGOR'YEVA

Alfano, Franco (*b* Posillipo, nr Naples, 8 March 1875; *d* Sanremo, 27 Oct 1954). Italian composer. After studying at the Conservatorio S Pietro a Majella in Naples, he moved in 1895 to Leipzig in order to continue his studies with Jadassohn. From 1899 until 1905 he lived in Paris, writing ballet music and travelling in northern Europe as far as Russia. After the success of *Risurrezione* (1904) Alfano moved back to Italy, first to Milan, then in 1914 to Sanremo where he continued to live until his death. From 1916 he taught composition at the Liceo Musicale of Bologna, becoming its director in 1918; in 1921 his opera *La leggenda di Sakùntala* was successfully given in Bologna. From 1923 until 1939 he acted as director of the Turin Conservatory. Alfano's close association with Italian fascism from 1925, when he collaborated on the 'Manifesto degli intellettuali del fascismo', led to personal contact with Mussolini. However, Alfano refused to sign the manifesto of 1932, which included a condemnation of all modernist tendencies in Italian music. Having retired from his position in Turin he was director of the Teatro Massimo in Palermo (1940–42) and then directed the Liceo Musicale in Pesaro from 1947 to 1950. As the full score of *La leggenda di Sakùntala* had been destroyed during the war, Alfano devoted the following years to its reconstruction; the new version received its première as *Sakùntala* (1952, Rome).

Alfano's early operas reflect the transition of musical style at the turn of the century. Influences from Naples, Leipzig and Paris all left their mark on his output. The première of *Risurrezione*, a traditional Italian opera in a somewhat crude *verismo* style devoid of Puccini's subtleties of orchestration, profoundly changed the composer's career and established his fame. The gradual refinement of Alfano's style during the following years is most obvious in his settings of poems by Tagore in 1918; these prepared the ground for *La leggenda di Sakùntala* (1921) for which the composer himself wrote the libretto. This work, one of the first Italian operas written on a prose libretto, is without doubt his major artistic achievement; it may best be characterized as a very personal adaptation of Debussy's and Ravel's innovations in orchestration and musical declamation, sometimes combined with a curious lack of sense of harmonic coherence. Alfano's choice of Kalidasa's drama for the opera betrays the influence of *fin de siècle* exoticism, and his transformation of dramatic conflicts into lyrical, almost pastoral dialogues yields an astonishing example of a thoroughly French influence on Italian music well after the *fin de siècle* period.

After Puccini's death in 1924, Alfano was asked by the Ricordi company on Toscanini's recommendation to decipher Puccini's sketches for the second part of Act 3 of *Turandot*, to orchestrate those passages for which Puccini had provided music in piano-vocal score and to compose new music for those passages of the libretto for which no sketches by Puccini existed. Alfano resolved this difficult task with considerable musical craftsmanship, using some material from his own *Sakùntala*, but failed to familiarize himself thoroughly with Puccini's full score of the first two and a half acts of the opera. The resulting music, already far from being an adequate finale for Puccini's work, was heavily cut on Toscanini's demand and was not performed in its original version until 1982.

Between 1921 and 1927 Alfano's style changed radically again, showing a general decline in harmonic complexity as well as in richness of orchestral texture. The composer had obviously adopted the official simple neo-classical style of Italian fascist music in his later scores, and his habitual lack of harmonic coherence appears now undisguised by full-bodied orchestral textures. With the exception of the reconstruction of *Sakùntala* his operas after *Madonna Imperia* (1927) have been largely forgotten.

See also CYRANO DE BERGERAC; SAKÙNTALA; and *RISURREZIONE*.

Miranda, 1896 (Alfano, after A. Fogazzaro), unperf.
La fonte di Enschir (L. Illica), Breslau, 8 Nov 1898
Risurrezione (dramma, 4, C. Hanau, after L. N. Tolstoy), Turin, Vittorio Emanuele, 30 Nov 1904
Il principe Zilah (dramma lirico, 2, Illica, after J. Claretie), Genoa, Carlo Felice, 3 Feb 1909
I cavalieri e la bella, 1910 (G. Adami and T. Monicelli), inc.
L'ombra di Don Giovanni (dramma lirico, 3, E. Moschino), Milan, Scala, 2 April 1914; rev. as Don Juan de Manara, Florence, 28 May 1941
La leggenda di Sakùntala (3, Alfano, after Kalidasa), Bologna, Comunale, 10 Dec 1921; reconstructed as Sakùntala, Rome, Reale, 9 Jan 1952
Madonna Imperia (commedia lirica, 1, A. Rossato, after H. de Balzac), Turin, Torino, 5 May 1927
L'ultimo lord (os, 3, M. Falena and Rossato, after U. Falena), Naples, S Carlo, 19 April 1930
Cyrano de Bergerac (commedia eroica, 4, H. Cain, after E. Rostand), Rome, Reale, 22 Jan 1936
Il dottor Antonio (op lirica, 3, M. Ghisalberti, after G. Ruffini), Rome, 30 April 1949

Completion of Puccini: Turandot, Milan, Scala, 26 April 1926

*

ES; *LoewenbergA*
G. M. Gatti: 'Franco Alfano', *Musicisti moderni d'Italia e di fuori* (Bologna, 1920, 2/1925), 9; Eng. trans., as 'Some Italian Composers of Today, ii: Franco Alfano', *MT*, lxii (1921), 158–61
G. Cesari: '*La leggenda di Sakùntala* di Franco Alfano', *RMI*, xxviii (1921), 666–76
A. Veretti: 'La leggenda di Sakùntala di Franco Alfano', *Pensiero musicale*, i (Bologna, 1921), 30
M. Castelnuovo-Tedesco: 'Sakùntala di Franco Alfano', *Lo spettatore*, i/1 (Rome, 1922), 78
G. M. Gatti: 'Franco Alfano', *MQ*, ix (1923), 556–77
G. Pannain: *La leggenda di Sakùntala di F. Alfano* (Milan, 1923)

G. Rossi-Doria: 'Franco Alfano', *Musikblätter des Anbruch*, vii (1925), 402–5
F. Brusa: '*Madonna Imperia* di Franco Alfano', *RMI*, xxxiv (1927), 248–56
L. Perrachio: 'Madonna Imperia di Franco Alfano', *Musica d'oggi*, 1st ser., ix (Milan, 1927), 149–51
G. M. Gatti: 'Madonna Imperia von Franco Alfano', *Melos*, vii (1928), 534–7
A. Della Corte: *Ritratto di Franco Alfano* (Turin, 1935)
F. Mompellio: 'Franco Alfano: biografia minima', *Ricordiana* [Milan], new ser., i (1955), 2
J. C. G. Waterhouse: 'Franco Alfano', *Ricordiana* [London], xi/4 (1966), 1–3
——: *The Emergence of Modern Italian Music (up to 1940)* (diss., U. of Oxford, 1968)
G. Vigolo: 'Sakùntala: tramonto in uno specchio', *Mille e una sera all'opera e al concerto* (Florence, 1971), 139
M. Bruni: 'Franco Alfano e la cerchia della "generazione dell'80" ', *Musica Italiana del primo Novecento: "La generazione dell'80"*, ed. F. Nicolodi (Florence, 1981), 97–109
J. Maehder: 'Puccini's "Turandot": A Fragment – Studies in Franco Alfano's Completion of the Score', *Turandot*, ed. N. John, ENO Opera Guide, xxvii (London, 1984), 35–53
——: 'Studien zum Fragmentcharakter von Giacomo Puccinis "Turandot" ', *AnM*, xxii (1984), 297–379
F. Nicolodi: *Musica e musicisti nel ventennio fascista* (Fiesole, 1984)
J. Maehder, ed.: *Esotismo e colore locale nell'opera di Puccini* (Pisa, 1985)
K.-M. Lo: *Turandot auf der Opernbühne* (diss., U. of Heidelberg, 1988)
W. Ashbrook and H. Powers: *Puccini's 'Turandot': the End of the Great Tradition* (Princeton, 1991) JÜRGEN MAEHDER

Alfiero [Alfieri], **Giuseppe** (*b* Naples, 1630; *d* Naples, 21 Jan 1665). Italian composer. He studied at the Conservatorio dei Poveri di Gesù Cristo and about 1658 was named *maestro di cappella* of the city of Naples. In 1655 he composed for the Teatro S Bartolomeo *La fedeltà trionfante* (G. C. Sorrentino), one of the first operas originally written for Naples. Prota-Giurleo ascribed to him two other dramatic works: *Le magie amorose* (1653, Naples) and *Il trionfo della pace* (G. Gastaldo; 1658, Naples). The former certainly is not by him: it is a renamed version of Cavalli's *La Rosinda*. Alfiero's only surviving work is a hymn.

*

CroceN; *DBI* (U. Prota-Giurleo)
U. Prota-Giurleo: *Francesco Cirillo e l'introduzione del melodramma a Napoli* (Gruma Nevano, 1952)
L. Bianconi: 'Funktionen des Operntheaters in Neapel vor 1700 and die Rolle Alessandro Scarlattis', *Colloquium Alessandro Scarlatti: Würzburg 1975*, 13–116 THOMAS WALKER

Alfonso und Estrella ('Alfonso and Estrella'). *Oper* in three acts by FRANZ SCHUBERT to a libretto by Franz von Schober; Weimar, Hoftheater, 24 June 1854.

Mauregato *usurping king of León*	baritone
Estrella *daughter of Mauregato*	soprano
Adolfo *Mauregato's army commander*	bass
Froila *exiled former king of León*	baritone
Alfonso *Froila's son*	tenor
Young Girl	soprano
Young Boy	tenor
Peasants, courtiers, servants, soldiers, hunters and huntresses	

Setting The kingdom of Asturia (here called León): a mountainous valley and the royal residence of King Mauregato, in the Middle Ages

In September 1821, enjoying the recent minor successes of three of his compositions in Vienna theatres, Schubert left Vienna with his friend Schober to spend several weeks in the country working on their new opera. Schober, a year older than Schubert and a dilettante of letters, music and the theatre, was full of enthusiasm for this collaboration. Both authors were influenced by the theories on opera of Ignaz von Mosel, a highly respected government official and man of the theatre and one of Schubert's patrons, who supported Gluck's operatic ideals. The young men may have followed his advice in omitting all spoken dialogue, thus breaking away from the German Singspiel tradition. The story, in which the son of a usurped monarch falls in love with the daughter of the usurper, and brings about a conciliation, might owe something to Shakespeare's *As you Like it* and *The Tempest*, but it is more likely that Schober adapted the plot from a Spanish source, as yet unidentified. Before the work was completed Schubert was asked to submit a German opera for the court opera theatre in Vienna (the Kärntnertortheater) by the director. As soon as *Alfonso und Estrella* was completed Schubert offered it, in high hopes, and was bitterly disappointed when it was rejected. The part of Froila was designed for Johann Michael Vogl, a fine operatic high baritone, friend and patron of Schubert, and that of Estrella for the popular soprano Anna Milder-Hauptmann. The critical reaction of both singers to the finished opera did nothing to enhance its chances of performance. Despite Schubert's considered opinion that this was his finest opera, it remained unperformed for more than 30 years. Then Liszt, probably persuaded by Schober, who was for a while his secretary, conducted the première; Schubert's overture was replaced by one by Anton Rubinstein. The opera was revived in Kassel in 1881 in a new version – in fact a travesty – by J. N. Fuchs, and it was repeated in this form in Vienna and several German cities. Since then, it has received a few performances and broadcasts and has been recorded. In spite of some marvellous music, however, it has not been successful because of its serious dramatic weaknesses. On 28 September 1991 Schubert's original version was given for the first time at the Graz Opera, conducted by Mario Venzago, to considerable acclaim.

ACT 1.i *An idyllic valley* Froila, former king of León, lives incognito with his son Alfonso, much loved and respected by the local community. In a long and static opening scene, a series of pastoral choruses in Singspiel vein, arias and duets serve to establish identities and relationships. A fine aria for Froila, 'Sei mir gegrüsst, O Sonne', in a style approaching that of grand opera, is in four sections and is marked by typical Schubertian woodwind interpolations above a mainly harmonic string accompaniment.

1.ii *Inside Mauregato's castle* The remainder of Act 1 is conceived on a grander operatic scale and with some dramatic flair. While the ladies of the court prepare for a hunt, Estrella has more romantic thoughts. In the second part of a lively hunting chorus, 'Zur Jagd!', Estrella voices her desire for peace and calm in a melody with syncopated rising 3rds and 4ths and some major–minor ambiguity; the huntresses respond with interjections containing wider intervals (5ths and 6ths) in a firmly major key.

Adolfo, newly returned victorious from the wars, seeks to win Estrella's affection and hand in a concise, vigorous and characterful aria in E♭ minor, 'Doch im

Getümmel der Schlacht', featuring a persistent and ominous dotted rhythmic pattern heard in much of Adolfo's music. As he describes how the sweet memory of Estrella has inspired him on the battlefield, a melody featuring a rising augmented 4th presages a brief shift to the major. The following duet, in which Estrella rejects Adolfo's advances, is in three sections: the first (C major) tender and lyrical, the second angry and tense (C minor) with a return of the dotted rhythm and some elegant interweaving of the vocal lines, and the third (C major) threatening, in very fast tempo and with a climactic ending. This is followed by an equally impressive grand finale during which Mauregato sides with his daughter against Adolfo's demand for her hand; her chosen husband must wear the Chain of Eurich (a motif associated with the Chain is first heard here). Adolfo swears vengeance. This is a finale of striking dramatic intensity and it includes some outstanding passages of accompanied recitative, and a canon in three parts (in which the chorus eventually joins), probably modelled on the four-part canon ('Mir ist so wunderbar') in *Fidelio*.

ACT 2.i *Froila's valley* At Alfonso's request, his father sings the ballad of the 'Cloud Maiden', 'Der Jäger ruhte', a graceful 12/8 andante con moto with prominent harp (Schubert's melody, as the young huntsman of the ballad follows the mysterious damsel up the mountain, foreshadows that of 'Täuschung' in *Winterreise*). In a telling ending, the music moves from G to A♭ and A minor before the hunter, after hovering on a seventh chord on C♯, plunges to his death on the tonic G. Alfonso, left alone in a romantic daze, is surprised by the appearance of Estrella, whom he at first imagines to be the fictitious Cloud Maiden; he falls under her spell. In a lengthy series of duets and arias, mostly of Singspiel character though often of considerable charm and sweet lyricism, the young pair declare their love, Alfonso sealing his vow by presenting her with the Chain of Eurich which his father has given him.

2.ii *The rebel conspirators' den* A short, sinister pianissimo introduction sets a scene of treachery. Two groups of Adolfo's followers meet in a male-voice chorus in D minor, for Schubert a key often associated with passion and alienation. There is an unremitting string bass line in steady crotchets. When Adolfo arrives, with a characteristic dotted rhythm, the already fast tempo increases. The basic key is now F major, but the music passes rapidly through almost every tonality, major or minor, before settling in B – a noteworthy example of Schubert's excursions into unrelated keys to stress the intensity or (as here) turbulence of a dramatic situation. By the end of this long and, for Adolfo, demanding ensemble, again on the grand operatic scale, the conspirators have unanimously proclaimed Adolfo their leader and future king.

2.iii *Inside Mauregato's castle* Estrella has not returned from the hunt. Mauregato, distraught, can find no joy in living. At last she appears. Amid general rejoicing, Mauregato recognizes the chain that she is wearing, but her explanation as to how she came by it is interrupted by an alarm: rebels, led by Adolfo, are approaching. The effect of this scene is marred by its flawed handling of dramatic pace.

ACT 3 *Froila's valley; a hut in the background* An orchestral introduction, painting a scene of battle between the armies of Mauregato and Adolfo, rises to a climax in which darting arrows are depicted by rapid flute scales. The duet of an anxious young girl and boy, observing the battle from afar, is interrupted by the cries of fleeing refugees accompanied by orchestral music taken from the introduction. The music dies away as the stage empties, but rises as the victorious Adolfo runs in, dragging Estrella. His triumphant cry 'Du wirst mir nicht entrinnen!', beginning their duet, flows straight on from the previous ensemble. On a falling F minor arpeggio in triple time, it is accompanied by full unison orchestra, including trombones. This long duet ends with another cry – this time Estrella's, for help. Again, the music flows directly into the following ensemble, without recitative, as Alfonso arrives to overpower Adolfo – rather too quickly to make a convincing dramatic effect – who is led off captive. In another series of duets thoughts of war give way to those of love as Alfonso and Estrella are reunited. The music, by turns tender and noble as the text requires, reaches a climax in a splendid descriptive recitative as Alfonso – unaware of his royal status and learning that Estrella is a princess – determines to prove himself worthy of her by rescuing her father. He blows his horn to summon his followers, a call answered in by now conventional operatic manner. The followers are heard approaching to another lively hunting chorus, for male voices, which ends with an italianate stretta.

Froila appears and, in recitative dialogue with the young pair, overcomes his initial horror at his son's wish to marry the daughter of his old enemy. He will protect Estrella while Alfonso searches for Mauregato. The scene ends with a short, rousing ensemble in D minor and major. The stage empties. Mauregato enters, alone and despairing. His aria 'Wo find' ich nur den Ort', its melody doubled by the cellos, rises to a climax as Froila, who has been sheltering in the hut with Estrella, appears before him and Mauregato imagines he is seeing a ghost (in a short, powerful passage with persistent trombones, syncopated and chromatic). Froila steps forward: his opening words in the ensuing duet ('Kein Geist, ich bin am Leben') are accompanied only by lower strings. The music turns to the minor for Mauregato's answer, nervous and supported by agitated string figures. Reconciliation is achieved and in the finale all loose ends are happily tied: Froila abdicates the throne returned to him by Mauregato in favour of Alfonso, whose betrothal to Estrella is blessed by both parents; and Adolfo repents and is forgiven. All this takes place in a series of concise recitatives and lyrical ensembles leading to a conventional and spirited final chorus, with full orchestral colour enriched (as in the Act 2 finale) by bass drum and cymbals.

* * *

Although Schubert was attempting with *Alfonso* to compose a grand romantic opera, using a large chorus and orchestra, he retained in several places the simpler style of his earlier Singspiels, using song-like melodies, light orchestration coloured by lyrical woodwind comment, and simpler harmonic patterns. At other times, in keeping with the manner of grand opera, the vocal lines are more declamatory, the orchestration richer and the harmonic progressions more violent and disturbing. In such sections Schubert shows not only his genius for setting words to music and his sensitivity to orchestral colours but also his ability to manage the large resources of big operatic ensembles.

ELIZABETH NORMAN McKAY

Alfred. Heroic opera in three acts by ANTONÍN DVOŘÁK to a German libretto by THEODOR KÖRNER; Olomouc, Czech Theatre, 10 December 1938 (in Czech).

The plot concerns the English King Alfred (bass), and his bride Alwina (soprano), who is a prisoner of the Danes. In the first act, the general of the triumphant Danes, Harald (tenor), attempts to persuade Alwina to marry him. Another Danish leader, Gothron (baritone), has premonitions of an English victory. Act 2 introduces Alfred and his companion, Sieward (baritone), and concludes with Alfred's freeing of Alwina. In Act 3 Alfred, with the assistance of the noble Dorset (tenor), wins a victory, and Harald commits suicide.

Dvořák completed *Alfred* in 1870, but throughout his life, with the possible exception of an occasion in 1874 when he may have shown the score to Smetana, he neglected to draw attention to its existence. This may have been because, alone among his operas, and most of those of his contemporaries, *Alfred* is a setting of a German text. The libretto was written in 1811, as *Alfred der Grosse*; its clear divisions suited the conventions of Singspiel, but not the musical language of the late 1860s. Dvořák's alterations to the text, including changing it from two acts to three, show a burgeoning theatrical instinct. Many of the broader aspects of musical structure, motif and recitative anticipate Dvořák's mature operas. JAN SMACZNY

Algarotti, Francesco (*b* Venice, 11 Dec 1712; *d* Pisa, 3 May 1764). Italian writer on opera. He was well educated at Rome and Bologna, from where he was welcomed into the learned circles of London and Paris. He lived for a time with Voltaire. In 1740 Frederick the Great took him into his personal service and gave him the title of count. From 1742 to 1747 he was also adviser to Augustus III, Elector of Saxony and King of Poland. At both Berlin and Dresden he was actively engaged in operatic productions, arranging and versifying Italian librettos to the taste of his patrons. He returned to Italy in 1753 because of ill-health. His *Saggio sopra l'opera in musica* was written the following year and first published in 1755. It attacks the unruliness prevalent in Italian public theatres, which compared unfavourably with the well-regulated and varied spectacles beginning to emerge at the court theatres of northern Europe. Other contemporary essayists such as Charles de Blainville, John Brown, Ranieri de' Calzabigi, C. G. Krause, Giammaria Ortes and Giacomo Durazzo said much the same in condemning the dominance of the singers over every other aspect of serious opera in Italy.

The *Saggio* was the best-grounded and most wide-ranging of these critiques, also the one that received the widest diffusion through reprinting and translations. It proposed that all parts of music, including singing, be subordinated to a unifying poetic idea, preferably a remote or exotic tale because the fabulous lent itself most readily to the extreme stylization endemic to the operatic genre. Graun's *Montezuma* for Berlin was held up as a model. Metastasio's librettos were dismissed with faint praise; only two of them, *Didone abbandonata* and *Achille in Sciro*, were mentioned as providing sufficient opportunity for spectacle. An ideal collaboration between poet and musician was achieved by Philippe Quinault and Lully. Algarotti concluded the *Saggio* with two examples of the path to be followed: a sketch for an *Enea in Troia*, after Virgil, and a fully-fledged French libretto for an *Iphigénie en Aulide*, after Euripides and Racine. The latter represented a bold departure from the Metastasian canon in the direction of a Greek-like severity and simplicity. It lacked amorous intrigue and confidants; choruses, ballets and spectacle were integrated into its action. Two years later Denis Diderot proclaimed the same subject to be the salvation of serious opera, but without mention of Algarotti. A spate of operas more or less indebted to Algarotti's *Iphigénie* followed in the last third of the century, the best-known being Gluck's for Paris, which Algarotti did not live to see. He did witness and to a small extent supervise the reform operas of Traetta and C. I. Frugoni for Parma, beginning in 1759, an attempt to wed Rameau's style of *tragédie lyrique* and *opera seria* that was timid by comparison with the thoroughgoing integration achieved by Gluck in Vienna and Paris. The revolution in taste during the 1750s that saw the Rococo style dethroned found an eloquent voice in the *Saggio*, described by Voltaire as 'the foundation for the reform of the castrato's realm'. The ensuing wave of archaeological neoclassicism is already apparent in Algarotti's work, particularly in his call for large, sparely adorned opera houses, with semicircular halls modelled after ancient arenas. Practical man of the theatre that he was, Algarotti tempered this antique-inspired vision of the future with advice about the materials and dimensions likely to produce the best acoustic, and about the compromises necessary between proscenium stage and arena for maximum sight lines.

*

E. Newman: *Gluck and the Opera* (London, 1895)

C. Malherbe: 'Un précurseur de Gluck: le comte Algarotti', *RHCM*, ii (1902), 369, 414

H. Goldschmidt: 'Die Reform der italienischen Oper des 18. Jahrhunderts und ihre Beziehnugen zur musikalischen Aesthetik', *IMusSCR*, iii (Vienna 1909), 196–206

I. Treat: *Un cosmopolite italien du XVIIIème siècle: Francesco Algarotti* (Trévoux, 1913)

E. Wellesz: 'Francesco Algarotti und seine Stellung zur Musik', *SIMG*, xv (1913–14), 427–39

G. Roncaglia: 'Il Conte Francesco Algarotti e il rinnovamento del melodramma', *Chigiana*, xxi (1964), 63–75

P. Petrobelli: 'Tartini, Algarotti e la corte di Dresda', *AnMc*, no.2 (1965), 72–84

D. Heartz: 'From Garrick to Gluck: the Reform of Theatre and Opera in the mid-Eighteenth Century', *PRMA*, xciv (1967–8), 111–27

——: 'Operatic Reform at Parma: *Ippolito ed Aricia*', *Atti del convegno sul settecento Parmense nel 2o centenario della morte di C. I. Frugoni* (Parma, 1969), 271–300

DANIEL HEARTZ

Algeria. Country in North Africa. Opera was swiftly introduced after the French conquest in 1830. The hall of the Djenina Palace in Algiers was converted into a theatre and in 1836 the 700-seat Théâtre de la rue de l'Etat Majeur was built; *opéras comiques* and vaudevilles were performed by French troupes, and operas by visiting Italian companies in summer – *Semiramide* in 1837, *Belisario* in 1838 and *Lucia* in 1839. With the success of these seasons, scores began to be printed locally. A larger theatre (1120 places in stalls and three galleries) was designed by the French architect Frédéric Chassériau and inaugurated in 1853 as the Théâtre Impérial d'Algers; in 1856 a further 300 seats were added. When Napoleon III visited in 1865 he attended a gala performance of *Rigoletto* given by an Italian company. The opera house was known after 1870 as the Théâtre Municipal; its interior was destroyed by fire in 1882 and rebuilt in eight months with a larger stage, the new machinery being modelled on that of the Paris Châtelet and able to produce magnificent feric effects. The theatre was run as a typical French provincial opera house, and stars of the Paris Opéra and Opéra-Comique visited as guest artists. Ernest Reyer was closely associated with the house from the 1840s, first as accompanist, then conductor and musical director. His opera *Sigurd* was given in 1891. Saint-Saëns supervised productions of *Samson et Dalila* and *Henry VIII* in 1910. The 1927–8 season was typical in its attraction of the Paris stars; Alice Raveau sang in *Orphée*, Rose Heilbronner in *Faust* and *Fidelio* and Miguel Villabella in *La dame blanche*, *Manon* and *Lakmé*. The *Ring* was given in 1931. But opera put down no roots in the local Arab population and when the French left in 1962 and Algeria became independent, the theatre became the Théâtre National Algérien and operas were no longer performed. Théâtres Municipaux were built by the French during the late 19th century at Oran and Bône (now Annaba).

*

F. Arnaudès: *L'Opéra d'Algers* (Algiers, 1941)
L. Lepagnot: 'Le théâtre en Algérie, 1830–1860', *Revue d'histoire des colonies*, xxxix (1952), 76–102

CHARLES PITT

Alghisi [Algisi], **Paris Francesco** (*b* Brescia, 19 June 1666; *d* Brescia, 30 or 29 March 1733). Italian composer. Except for two years in the service of the King of Poland (1681–3), he resided in Brescia, where he became a minorite and entered the Congregazione dell'Oratorio. He studied law and philosophy, in addition to music, which was taught to him from an early age by Orazio Pollarolo, organist of the cathedral. Alghisi wrote at least nine oratorios between 1689 and 1705, but his operatic output is restricted to two three-act works to librettos by G. C. Corradi, written for the Teatro SS Giovanni e Paolo in 1690; *L'amor di Curzio per la patria* was for carnival (arias in *I-Rvat*) and *Il trionfo della continenza* for the autumn season (arias in *MOe* and *Rvat*). There is no evidence that either was restaged. Although neither survives in full score, the existing arias, mainly in da capo form, reveal him as a fluent writer of vocal melodies; their declamatory style is reflected also in the supporting continuo parts.

*

DBI (L. F. Tagliavini)
G. M. Mazzuchelli: *Gli scrittori d'Italia*, i, pt 1 (Brescia, 1753)

HARRIS S. SAUNDERS

Al gran sole carico d'amore ('In the bright sunshine heavy with love'). *Azione scenica* in two acts by LUIGI NONO to a libretto by the composer and YURI LYUBIMOV after texts by BERTOLT BRECHT, Tania Bunke, Fidel Castro, Ernesto Che Guevara, Georgy Dimitrov, Maxim Gorky, Antonio Gramsci, Vladimir Lenin, Karl Marx, Louise Michel, Cesare Pavese, Arthur Rimbaud, Celia Sanchez, Haydée Santamaria and popular sources; Milan, Teatro Lirico, 4 April 1975 (revised, definitive version, Milan, Teatro Lirico, 11 February 1978).

Each half of this work brings together texts and images that gravitate around a central theme: in the first half, the Paris Commune, in the second, the Russian revolt of 1905. The two themes echo and complement each other. Both revolts were crushed, yet both have served to inspire subsequent struggles for social justice. Central to both halves is the role played by women within those struggles.

Act 1 charts the progress of the Commune with images taken from Brecht's *Tage der Commune*. Interleaved with these are commentaries from Marx and Lenin on the significance of the Commune, fragments from the self-defence of Louise Michel, one of the heroines of the Commune, which are complemented by excerpts from poems by Tania Bunke, written before going to join the *guerrilla* war in Bolivia, and a setting of lines from Rimbaud's *Les mains de Jeanne-Marie*, from which the title of the work is also drawn. Many of the most vivid moments of action are wordless, accompanied only by orchestra and/or tape. The orchestra also contributes four actionless 'Reflections'. The politicians – Thiers (tenor), Favre (bass) and Bismarck (bass) – who appear only briefly, are impersonated by male soloists in normal operatic fashion. The works of Michel and Bunke are sung by a quartet of sopranos and are thus distanced from the pathos of individual impersonation. But as Nono himself emphasized, the main protagonist is the chorus, whose aural and physical presence (vividly deployed by the producer, Lyubimov) dominates the action.

A frame for Act 2 is once again provided by words from Brecht, this time his adaptation of Gorky's novel *The Mother* (in turn based on real events). Again, Nono found more recent parallels to this story of industrial protest and its repression in the Turin of the 1950s, evoked through the words of Cesare Pavese. Similarly, two women's commentaries on the battle for the Moncada barracks at the start of the Cuban revolution emphasize the continuity between more recent events and those that provide the focus for this work. In this act the main symbol of resistance to a hostile industrial environment, the Mother, is sung by a contralto soloist, while the quartet of sopranos sings fragments associated by Nono with Pavese's character, Deola, the resilient prostitute from industrial Turin.

'Al gran sole carico d'amore' (Nono), Act 1: scene from the definitive version performed at the Teatro Lirico, Milan, 1978, showing the use of layers of movable staging

Through sheer multiplicity of musical resources (orchestra, tape, large chorus, small chorus, soloists) Nono is able to differentiate the elements of this interacting network of images, complementing Lyubimov's resourceful articulation of an empty stage through the deployment of a mass of singers, movable banks of lights, and elementary movable structures (scaffolding and platforms). In its confrontation between instrumental and taped sound, its generation of substantial structures from fixed harmonic fields, its derivation of musical building-blocks from a range of revolutionary songs (though without any direct or obvious quotation), and its diffraction of texts through complex choral textures, *Al gran sole* summarizes many of the most individual technical features of Nono's work over the previous two decades. DAVID OSMOND-SMITH

Alibert. Theatre in Rome, built in 1716–17 by Antonio Alibert; also known as the Teatro delle Dame from Carnival 1726. *See* ROME, §§2, 3(i, ii).

Alibert, Giacomo d' (*b* ?*c*1625–6; *d* Rome, 1713). Franco-Italian theatre builder and impresario. A French nobleman from Orléans, he became secretary in 1662 to Queen Christina of Sweden (resident in Rome after her abdication), in whose service he remained till her death in 1689; he managed her musical and theatrical entertainments, opera included. Under her patronage he built in 1669 the Teatro di Tordinona, the first notable opera house in Rome; he also built tennis courts and once ran a lottery combined with an exhibition of mirrors. When a new pope in 1676 forbade the reopening of the Tordinona, and Christina's income from Sweden was held up by war, d'Alibert went to Turin; there he built and, in 1678, managed another opera house, the Teatro Ducale (later Regio). After the opening season he judged it to be doubtfully profitable and returned to Rome, where he kept gambling tables in his own house and entertained his customers with plays, music and puppet shows. After the demolition of the Tordinona in 1697 on the orders of the pope, he served another queen, who was resident in Rome, Maria Casimira of Poland, and from 1708 managed the operas she put on in a small theatre in her palace.

Antonio (1670–1731), Giacomo's son by a Corsican noblewoman, in 1716–17 built the Teatro delle Dame, also known as the Alibert, as a speculation. He failed and died in poverty. But the Tordinona (rebuilt in 1733) and the Alibert remained for the rest of the century two of the three leading Rome opera houses.

See also ROME, §§1(iii) and 2.

*

A. Cametti: *Il Teatro di Tordinona poi di Apollo*, i (Tivoli, 1938), 16–22

A. De Angelis: *Il Teatro Alibert o delle Dame nella Roma papale (1717–1863)* (Tivoli, 1951)

A. Basso, ed: *Storia del Teatro Regio di Torino* (Turin, 1976–86), i

JOHN ROSSELLI

Alina, regina di Golconda ('Alina, Queen of Golconda'). *Melodramma* in two acts by GAETANO DONIZETTI to a libretto by FELICE ROMANI after MICHEL-JEAN SEDAINE's text for Pierre-Alexandre Monsigny's *Aline, reine de Golconde* (1766, Paris), itself based on Stanislas-Jean de Boufflers' novel of the same title; Genoa, Teatro Carlo Felice, 12 May 1828 (revised version, Rome, Teatro Valle, 10 October 1829).

Alina, Queen of Golconda (soprano), delays accepting the proposal that she marry Seide (tenor), when the newly arrived French ambassador Volmar (baritone) and his servant Belfiore (*buffo* bass) turn out to be the long-lost husbands of Alina and her maid Fiorina (soprano). Ultimately, the machinations of Seide are foiled and the happy couples are reunited to the joy of the populace.

Alina, one of the more serious of Donizetti's comedies, includes some incipiently romantic touches, as in the episode in which Alina recalls the Provençal landscape where she and Volmar had first fallen in love. Notable, too, is the casting of the antagonist Seide, Alina's Indian suitor, as a tenor.

The musical gem of Donizetti's score is the Act 1 quartet, 'Ho inteso ... ho sentito', where Donizetti's skill at gradually building up the intensity of an ensemble is revealed to fine effect. Grateful, too, are the extensive midpoint concertato and the soprano's aria-finale. It is difficult to account for the neglect of this rich work that contains so many intimations of Donizetti's future achievement, except that the demands of the vocal writing, in terms of both range and agility, are daunting. The 1987 revival at Ravenna and the resulting recording prove that the work repays closer acquaintance.

WILLIAM ASHBROOK

Aline, reine de Golconde ('Aline, Queen of Golconda'). *Ballet-héroïque* in three acts by PIERRE-ALEXANDRE MONSIGNY to a libretto by MICHEL-JEAN SEDAINE after Stanislas-Jean de Boufflers' story *La reine de Golconde*; Paris, Opéra, 15 April 1766.

The opera opens with a ceremony during which Saint Phar (baritone), ambassador to the Indies (where France had trading stations at the time), comes to pay his respects to Aline, Queen of Golconda (soprano). Aline, who is of French origin herself, recognizes Saint Phar as the man she once loved when she was a simple peasant girl and hides her true identity behind a veil. In Act 2 she dresses as a shepherdess and is recognized by Saint Phar in a valley resembling the one where they first loved one another. She then leaves him, in order to test his love. In the final act Saint Phar refuses the hand of the Queen of Golconda out of faithfulness to the shepherdess he has found again, but Aline reveals that shepherdess and queen are the same woman and the lovers are reunited.

The libretto is an apologia for true love transcending social class and surviving years of separation, but it is possible to understand the opera in a very different way through comparison with the original source. Boufflers' characters are far from being examples of the moral purity proper to those in a *ballet-héroïque*. Saint Phar arrives in the kingdom of Golconda after a life of adventures and debauchery, while Aline (who has borne a son by him) has an even less elevating past: after living as a courtesan, she deceived an old gentleman she had married in Paris, became the slave of an Indian merchant and was then married for a second time to the King of Golconda, whom she deceives to be reunited with her former lover. A study of the two texts suggests that the sweeping idealization in which Sedaine's libretto indulged is not to be taken entirely at face value, but contains implicit criticism of the conventions of the Opéra: it is up to the spectators to reconstruct the 'real' story of Aline and Saint Phar in their minds.

On a formal plane, Sedaine and Monsigny observe the structural rules of an *opéra-ballet*; indeed, the style of the libretto is so flat that it is difficult not to detect a tendency towards caricature. The chief innovations introduced are in the musical treatment of the principal parts: simple recitative is reduced to the minimum, while *récitatif obligé* and arias expressing emotion (like Aline's romance 'Ma bouche n'a qu'un langage') predominate in those parts of the opera that are not just ornamental. The composer and librettist were thus entering, if tentatively, upon the reform of French serious opera for which more and more critics were calling.

Several other composers wrote operas on this plot, among them Berton (1803), Boieldieu (1804), Donizetti (1828) and Berwald (1864–5, as *Drottningen av Golconda*). MICHEL NOIRAY

Aliprandi, Bernardo (*b* ?Milan, *c*1710; *d* Frankfurt, *c*1792). Italian composer. One of the numerous Italian musicians who found careers north of the Alps, he worked as a cellist for the Bavarian court at Munich from 1731. In 1737 he became composer of chamber music, and in 1744 Konzertmeister; he retired in 1778.

Aliprandi's works for the Bavarian court opera include *Mitridate* (B. Pasqualigo; 1738, vs *D-Dlb*) and *Semiramide riconosciuta* (P. Metastasio; 1740, vs *F-Pn*); he also wrote a *festa teatrale* for Nymphenburg, *Apollo trà le muse in Parnasso* (Perozzo do Perozzi, 1737), two works for the Munich College of Jesuits (1737–8), a *Stabat mater* (1749) and some instrumental music. The *Iphigenia in Aulide* (1739, Munich, vs *F-Pn*) sometimes attributed to Aliprandi was probably by Giovanni Porta. In Münster's judgment Aliprandi's style was conservative, isolated from the newer Italian operatic developments.

*

MGG (R. Münster)

F. J. Lipowsky: *Baierisches Musik-Lexicon* (Munich, 1811)

F. M. Rudhart: *Geschichte der Oper am Hofe zu München* (Freising, 1865), 125–6, 131, 166 JAMES L. JACKMAN

Alizard, Adolphe-Joseph-Louis (*b* Paris, 29 Dec 1814; *d* Marseilles, 23 Jan 1850). French bass-baritone. He began his career as a violinist, studying under Chrétien Urhan, but switched to singing in 1834, enrolling at the Paris Conservatoire. After earning first prize there in 1836, he made his début the following year as Saint-Bris (*Les Huguenots*). Alizard was associated with the Opéra, primarily in minor roles, until 1842 when he accepted a two-year appointment in Brussels. A throat problem, possibly induced by higher baritone roles, forced him to take leave from 1844 to 1846. Following a short recuperative sojourn in Italy, he enjoyed a brief second success in Paris from 1846 to 1848. A recurrence of his ailment necessitated his permanent retirement to the balmier climate of Marseilles, where he died. Contemporary critics described his voice as powerful and of a flattering timbre. His short and overly muscular stature, however, compromised his popularity with the public. LAURIE C. SHULMAN

Allacci [Allacius, Allatius], **Leone** [Lione] (*b* Chios, 1588; *d* Rome, 19 Jan 1669). Italian theologian and scholar of Greek origin. He came to Italy as a child and studied in Rome from 1599 to 1610. He was later employed in the Vatican Library and in 1661 became chief curator. He wrote on a wide range of subjects, and is significant for the history of music by virtue of his *Drammaturgia … divisa in sette indici* (Rome, 1666), a compendious and surprisingly accurate list of dramatic works of all kinds, including opera librettos, published in Italy; it also lists many unpublished works. A second, vastly enlarged and updated edition by Giovanni Cendoni, Apostolo Zeno, Giovanni degli Apostoli and others unnamed (Venice, 1755) adds the names of composers to *drammi per musica* and remains a major work of reference for Italian drama studies, although it must be used with caution. Many of Allacci's manuscripts and his large collection of printed dramas are now in the Vatican Library.

*

DBI (D. Musti)

C. Jacono: *Bibliografia di Leone Allacci (1588–1669)* (Palermo, 1962)

N. Savarese: 'Per una nuova *Drammaturgia* (vicende, problemi, bibliografia)', *Biblioteca teatrale*, iv (1972), 73

THOMAS WALKER

Allan, Richard Van. *See* VAN ALLAN, RICHARD.

Allegory. The treatment of a subject in the guise of another which it resembles; in opera, investing plots, characters and scenography with symbolical or metaphorical meaning.

1. The 17th century. 2. The 18th century. 3. The Romantic era. 4. The 20th century. 5. Allegory and interpretation.

1. THE 17TH CENTURY. From the beginning opera was to some extent allegorical, borrowing what was essentially a literary device already well established in spoken drama, the *intermedi*, *ballet de cour* and masque and especially in the visual arts. Three basic levels of allegorical content may be identified in opera, often coexisting in the same work: *(i)* Parable: the singers personify abstractions such as The Soul, Love, Innocence, Greed, Folly and so forth. The obvious example is Cavalieri's *Rappresentatione di Anima, et di Corpo* (1600); but the many allegorical prologues of early Venetian opera, often involving classical deities, include elements of parable as well as mythological symbolism. *(ii)* Mythological symbolism: characters drawn from classical mythology or later fables (especially those of Ariosto and Tasso) carry conventional or specific symbolism. Jupiter sometimes represents the Power of the State, Orpheus the Power of Music, Rinaldo Youthful Impetuosity, and so forth; or, by extension, a character in the drama is designed as, or may be construed as, an idealized representation of the prince or nobleman under whose auspices the opera was produced. *(iii)* Topical or political allusion: mythological, Arcadian or historically based plots are chosen or adapted to reflect or comment on current events, often as a deliberate instrument of court or state propaganda. Without a clear statement of authorial intention or a contemporaneous key to the 'real' identities of the characters represented, political allegory is difficult to prove (in either opera or plays), and there is always the danger that a harmless or conventional plot might be 'explained into a satire'. Distinction should therefore be made between *politicized* operas, in which plot and characters are liable to application to current affairs, and *partisan* operas, for which there is evidence of a deliberate political design.

The themes and subjects of some early operas appear to reflect or comment obliquely on the special occasions for which they were composed. For example, Peri and Caccini's settings of *Euridice* (1600, Florence), which were wedding gifts to Maria de' Medici and Henri IV, dramatize marriage, bereavement and reunion (both spiritual and corporal). There is no evidence that the operas were intended as political allegories or that

Orpheus and Eurydice were meant to reflect the real bride and bridegroom. But the festive occasion may have dictated Rinuccini's happy ending, a radical departure from the Orpheus myth.

Plots based on parables and familiar myths are common in opera throughout the 17th century; librettists wishing to politicize the more recent classics such as *La Gerusalemme liberata* could turn to Tasso's own 'Allegoria del Poema' for a key to the symbolism attached to certain episodes and characters. Partisan operas usually operate simultaneously on two or more allegorical levels. Marco Marazzoli's setting of Francesco Buti's *Il giuditio della Ragione* (1643, Rome) is both a simple moral parable (the characters include Beauty, Reason, Jealousy and Caprice) and an extended metaphor of the international manoeuvring to elect a new pope (True Love could be taken to represent France, Beauty the Vatican and Caprice the Austrian Empire). Since the production may have been sponsored by Cardinal Mazarin, an interested party in papal affairs, the allegory was not made explicit and therefore such interpretation, however plausible, must remain speculative.

As Italian opera developed and spread across Italy and over the Alps, certain themes and allegories came to be associated with particular areas or cities. Venice was fond of operas based on historical or heroic subjects, from which audiences could perhaps draw parallels between the ancient Roman and the modern Venetian states. Naples, the largest kingdom in 17th-century Italy, preferred heroic operas with prologues in praise of the monarchy. Vienna copied Venetian operatic practice, making even plainer the connections between historical-heroic plots and the politics of the Austrian Empire. French opera, which was completely state-controlled, avoided such themes, preferring instead mythological-pastoral plots with allegorical prologues in praise of Louis XIV. Besides these regional peculiarities, one also notices a correlation between plots and the circumstances of the prince or sovereign of the time. For example, many serious dramas (including Italian operas) produced in London during the reign of Queen Anne (1702–14) were so-called 'she-dramas' in which a woman (usually a queen or princess) thwarts treachery or overcomes disaster to preserve her line: *Arsinoe*, *Camilla*, *Thomyris*, *Semele*, *Rosamond* and *Clotilda* are but a few operatic examples. While none explicitly allegorizes the end of the Stuart dynasty, collectively they reflect Queen Anne's problems over the succession.

In Vienna during the second half of the 17th century, little attempt was made to hide or deny political allegory. For example, a manuscript key to the identity of the *dramatis personae* was inserted into some copies of the libretto of Antonio Draghi's *La lanterna di Diogene* (1674), which reveals that Alexander the Great represented Emperor Leopold. This linkage became traditional in later *opera seria*. In dedicating *Muzio Scevola* (1721, London) to George I, the librettist Paolo Rolli explains that Alexander Severus is a portrait of the king himself; later, the eponymous hero of various settings of Metastasio's *Alessandro nell'Indie* was taken to represent the reigning monarch.

The *tragédies en musique* of Lully and Quinault are allegorically the richest of all Baroque opera. Designed to reflect *la gloire* of France and to flatter Louis XIV, Quinault's *livrets* blend the myth- and fable-based drama of the French classical theatre with the traditional symbolism of *ballet de cour*, in which royal triumphs and tribulations were represented with surprising frankness, sometimes with the future king himself dancing his allegorical counterpart. The prologues to most of Lully's operas ostentatiously praise the king's recent achievements; for example, that for *Persée* (1682) alludes to France's victories in the Dutch wars. The allegorical content of the operas themselves is less apparent, though some plots were liable to application, sometimes misapplication. Quinault was banned from court for two years after the production of *Isis* (1677), which tells the story of Jupiter's affair with the river nymph Io. Jupiter would naturally have been seen as Louis XIV, but the depiction of Juno as Mme de Montespan and Io as Mme de Ludres, the king's new mistress, was thought to be too close to the mark. Of course, Quinault protested his innocence, but there are other examples of tasteless or mishandled royal allegories in French opera, whether or not deliberate. Perhaps the most notorious was Rameau's *Platée* (1745), a *comédie lyrique* performed in honour of the marriage of the dauphin and the rather plain Princess Maria Theresa of Spain. In Le Valois d'Orville's *livret*, Platée is mercilessly ridiculed for her ugliness.

2. The 18th century. Political allegory becomes increasingly less obvious in 18th-century opera. The French repertory ossified and Quinault's original political intent was forgotten. *Opera seria* relied for many decades on the morally fastidious and unflinchingly monarchist librettos of Metastasio, while Italian comic opera, though rife with topical allusions and local colour, was not a good vehicle for covert designs. Standing outside European practice is England, with its long tradition of political satire in drama and literature. John Gay's *The Beggar's Opera* (1728) was, on one level at least, a biting attack on the prime minister, Sir Robert Walpole. But with the passage of the Licensing Act in 1737, strict censorship was imposed on all stage works, including Italian opera, and England came into line with most other opera-producing countries.

Where it exists at all in late 18th-century opera, allegory either takes the form of panegyric or, if political, is well hidden. Being musically and textually the most sophisticated of Classical operas, Mozart's have been scoured for sub-texts. Metastasio's *La clemenza di Tito*, the story of a ruler who suppresses personal feelings for the greater good, was an obvious choice to mark the coronation of Leopold II in Prague in September 1791, but there seem to be no close parallels between the Roman Titus (even as redrawn by Caterino Mazzolà, who adapted Metastasio's libretto for Mozart) and the new emperor: any allegory is a generalized one of imperial benevolence and generosity. *Die Zauberflöte*, which is undeniably a parable of Enlightenment and rich in masonic symbolism, was instead interpreted in the early 1790s as an allegory of the French Revolution, with the Queen of Night as the *ancien régime*, Pamina as Freedom, and so forth; the search for darker masonic secrets did not begin until the 19th century, when lodges had been banned and members of the craft were being persecuted.

3. The Romantic era. The inconsistencies in the allegorical fabric of *Die Zauberflöte* (1791) and the persistent difficulty in decoding it prefigure the imperfect, protean and usually fugitive forms in which allegory intermittently asserts itself in operas of the 19th and 20th centuries. One could say that fugato rather

than strict fugue points the way forward. Allegory had previously served extra-artistic goals of instruction, reinforcing religious, moral, political and even social precepts. This didactic function tended to disappear after 1800 as beliefs in absolute values continued to crumble. The ascendant Romantic impulse shied away from creating works with allusions to authoritarian principles, beliefs and moral precepts. When allegory resurfaces its imagery reflects the dramas enacted in the artist's soul and in man's search for new gods.

Romanticism conversed in symbols because they were absolute and resisted explication. Goethe's fragmentary textual sequel to *Die Zauberflöte* (1795–) is a typical response to this impulse. E. T. A. Hoffmann's opera *Undine* (1816) appealed to Weber 'as a dramatized fairytale in which many an inner connection might well have been more definitely and distinctly clarified'. Weber saw that its characters 'are all encircled by – or better, creatures of – that ghostly, fabulous world whose awesome stimulations are the peculiar property of the fairytale'. *Undine* belongs (as do Weber's *Der Freischütz*, 1821, and the operas of Marschner) to that genre of *Schauerromantik* works which are not so much allegories of the supernatural as direct conjurations of it in the style of folktale and legend. The dramaturgy uses symbols to present meanings in themselves rather than in the allegorical manner of saying one thing and implying another, or in using characters who are less important in themselves than for their representation of abstract qualities.

Allegory did not re-emerge with any coherent force until Wagner linked it to his use of Nordic and Germanic myth. The gods, giants, men and Nibelungs are also embodiments of ideas, a principle that extends to the music, most famously in the leitmotifs. Wagner keeps faith with Romantic tradition in that his works are allegories not only of a world-view but also of the battles raging in his heart and mind. He worked on the *Ring* in confident expectation that a plurality of allegorical and other interpretations, compliant with the work's central concern with power and love, were of its essence.

Wagner regarded the *Ring* as the key to man's history and nature, a crucial departure from earlier allegory being that this one is not troubled by a measure of inconsistency. A positive, Feuerbachian view grounded in political optimism coexists with a later negative gospel deriving from Schopenhauer. In *sentimentalisch* vein, allegory no longer advocates certainties but puts possibilities on trial. It is a means for investigating, even validating, the co-existence of contraries. The allegorical programme is not concealed but itself participates in the action. The theory and practice of artistic creation are principal actors in *Die Meistersinger*, which may be seen as an allegory of art's supremacy over social and political ordinance. In *Parsifal* allegory mediates between good and evil, between art and religion.

The 19th century saw many instances of opera as a means of circumventing censorship by allegorizing political protest. Austrian rule in Italy made it impossible for the voice of nationalist indignation to speak openly. Opera channelled political and social protest by transporting the immediate concerns to a distant place and time. (A much later instance is Brecht and Weill's *Aufstieg und Fall der Stadt Mahagonny*, 1930, which uses the never-never-land of America as a stalking horse for European malaise.) The famous 'Va pensiero' chorus of the Israelites in Egypt in *Nabucco* (1842) has been widely taken as alluding to Italian misery under Austrian rule, as has the opera as a whole. Sometimes it was the censor who compelled the composer to adjust the story, thus inventing a genre of 'enforced allegory'. Although Verdi had not planned *Un ballo in maschera* (1859) as about anything but the assassination of the Swedish king, Gustavus III, in 1792, the censor, responding to an attempt in 1858 on the life of Napoleon III, insisted on the story being recast as the death of an English governor in the safely obscure city of Boston. Verdi had no option but grudgingly to comply. No allegory had been intended, but the opera-goer wishing to experience the drama as Verdi imagined it has the task of translating Boston and its conspirators back to the court of Gustavus III.

4. THE 20TH CENTURY. Thomas Mann, culpably forgetting Mozart, celebrated Wagner as the first depth-psychologist among composers, and this is a role consciously embraced by composers of the generation after him. For towards the end of the 19th century the explanatory power of psychology began to overwhelm that of myth and religion. Allegory is now called on to bridge a new credibility gap – that between a mythological narrative and the feeling that the myth masks unresolved turbulence which it is the musical dramatist's task to lay bare. Although Freud and Jung both extolled the explanatory power of myth, in its artistic form the psychologizing impulse turns against myth, which it distrusts and seeks to explicate. In *Die Frau ohne Schatten* (1919) Hofmannsthal takes Strauss to the further shores of allegorical abstraction, whither the composer complained he was not always able to follow. The spiritual and temporal pairs are figures representing those concepts in a mystery play about marriage and fertility which consciously echoes Goethe's allegorical postscript to *Die Zauberflöte*. Debussy's *Pelléas et Mélisande* (1902) engages in a *faux-naïf* flirtation with allegory, but its symbolist aesthetic is antithetical to the defining requirement of a palpable relationship between surface and deeper meanings. In Strauss and Hofmannsthal's *Elektra* (1909) the story is retold so that words and music allegorize it as a drama of the neuroses. As in Wagner, the characters behave both as themselves and as abstract components of an archetypal psyche whose conflicts they are constrained to enact.

Schoenberg's *Erwartung* (1909, first staged 1924) and *Die glückliche Hand* (1913, also 1924) are psychodramas where the characters are named no more explicitly than 'the man', 'the woman' etc., and the scenarios are rudimentary shorthand for the Id and Superego's struggles for mastery of the Ego unfolded in the music. The narrative is subsumed into the exploratory demands of expressionistic music drama. Other composers using psycho-allegory include Franz Schreker, although works like *Der ferne Klang* (1912) and *Die Gezeichneten* (1918) do not sacrifice the comprehensibility of the scenario to the demands of the musical drama as uncompromisingly as Schoenberg did. Bartók's *Bluebeard's Castle* (1918) allegorizes the innermost secrets of the psyche and the catastrophic consequences of forcibly unveiling them. The mythic characters are also agents of their own analysis. Bluebeard is constrained by Judith to tear away the seven veils of the psychopathology of their relationship.

Psycho-music drama does not concern itself with the great problems of religion and morality, save those of the artist's duty to be true to himself. Composers for whom music represented a moral as well as an aesthetic calling emerged from the ultimately frustrating expressionist quest to seek whatever timeless subject matter might offer proof against the critical devastations of psychodrama. Yet in *Moses und Aron* (1930–31, unfinished, first staged 1957), Schoenberg's dramatization of the Judaic dialectic between the unknowable god and the need to make assertions about him in order to compel others to abjure false gods, Moses and Aaron are also to be read as personifying the two sides of every artist's debate with himself. The effect of the opera is less an affirmation of Judaic belief than a *de profundis* cry of the absolute isolation of the absolute artist. The debate between the speaking Moses and the singing Aaron is not only about the incommunicability of religious revelation but also signals the risk of the means of expression betraying, because inadequately representing, the artist's vision.

Other works allegorizing the composer's search for historical and legendary models to validate his identity and mission include Pfitzner's *Palestrina* (1917), Busoni's *Doktor Faust* (1925) and Hindemith's *Cardillac* (1926, rev. 1952) and *Mathis der Maler* (1938). Vaughan Williams's point of departure for *The Pilgrim's Progress* (1951) is Bunyan's classic, but the composer, in tune more with scepticism than belief, transmutes religious allegory into 'A Morality', significantly changing the hero's name from 'Christian' to 'Pilgrim'.

The didactic moralizing streak in the poet W. H. Auden has kept the allegorical mode alive in the postwar operatic renaissance evident in Britten and Henze. *Paul Bunyan* (1941) draws on a legendary account of the birth of America and was also intended by Auden as an allegory of the emergence of individual responsibility within a society governed by Christian principles. But Britten found realism a more congenial vehicle for the moral concerns of his subsequent operas. Although the literary source for *Billy Budd* (1951) is almost as famous an example of Melville's allegorizing as *Moby Dick*, E. M. Forster and Eric Crozier's libretto does not overstress symbolical allusion. The referential frames of Britten's church parables (1964–8) are a skilful amalgam of East-Western religious mythology and spiritual symbolism, but stop short of allegory. Auden's libretto for *The Rake's Progress* transmutes Hogarth's story-board morality into a transparent allegory with Anne Trulove and Nick Shadow as the good and evil angels competing for the soul of the prodigal Tom. Working with Henze on *The Bassarids* (1966), Auden interrupts Euripides' story of *The Bacchae* for an allegorical intermezzo, 'The Judgement of Calliope'. This supplies a commentary on the fantasies of the sexually repressed Pentheus, enacted in the style of an 18th-century French court charade. This playful interlude demonstrates that allegory can function no less instructively as a comical divertissement in serious context than as the other way about. In Strauss's valedictory *Capriccio* (with Clemens Krauss, 1942), opera allegorizes itself in a setting borrowed from the aesthetic battleground of Paris in the 1770s. The perennial debate about the relative priorities of words, music, dance, stage direction etc., is ingeniously embodied in characters (Olivier the poet, Flamand the composer etc.) representative of their respective claims.

Although Tippett's operas are profuse in their range of reference and appeal to symbolic and metaphoric structures, their allegorical gestures are fragmentary, acknowledging the discontinuities of modern experience which the composer presents as trials that must be endured in the hope of personal and cosmic renewal. Tippett's theory and practice of opera presuppose an external action which refers to an unseen, internal world of Jungian archetypes, images of component parts of the psyche (especially the *anima* and *animus*) which undergo painful processes in order to effect a higher synthesis of new possibility. The events of *The Midsummer Marriage* (1955) are an allegory whose purpose is to dispel the characters' illusions about themselves. In Tippett's words, 'only in the course of the plot do the characters become aware of their real selves'. The composer intends that we should sense, 'especially at certain designed moments, another world within or behind the stage set' (he was much influenced by T. S. Eliot's verse plays). The allegory declares a quest for spiritual growth and integration on terms to be discovered. The objective is cross-reference between the raw energies of modern life and the timeless patterns of myth and symbol which alone give it meaning and value. '*The Midsummer Marriage*', Tippett wrote, 'is what I have called a collective imaginative experience, dealing with the interaction of two worlds, the natural and the supernatural'. The characters are allegorical intermediaries between modernity and mythological precedent. Tippett's royal pair, Mark and Jenifer, deliberately hark back to Tamino and Pamina; his down-to-earth mechanic (Jack) and secretary (Bella) to Papageno and Papagena. 'The eventual marriage of the first pair becomes a spiritual, even supernatural symbol, transcending the purely social and biological significance of the eventual marriage of the second pair.' Tippett acknowledged that *The Midsummer Marriage* is in the same Quest tradition as *Die Zauberflöte*, where the incidents 'are traditionally extraordinary and supernatural, depicting as they do some continuous illumination of the hero'. *King Priam* (1962) contains its own allegorical instruction scene in Hecuba, Andromache and Helen's impersonation of the three Graces between whom Paris has to choose. In a highly significant interlude in the third act, Hermes enters as 'a messenger of death' but his song reveals him as agent of the 'timeless music played in time' which speaks from beyond Priam's and every other grave.

Tippett's characters tend to begin as predominantly allegorical figures (e.g. Mangus's first words in *The Knot Garden* (1970): 'So, if I dream,/It's clear I'm Prospero:/Man of power./He put them all to rights.') from which their flesh-and-blood individuality only slowly and painfully emerges. In the third act of *The Knot Garden* the characters specifically re-enact episodes from *The Tempest* which is allegorized in and through them. The surface events of *The Ice Break* (1977) are drawn from modern America (as are those of *New Year*, 1989), but far more important than the contemporaneity is the conversation between the foreground and the fathomless background represented by the ever-present chorus which, in Tippett's words, 'serves to remind us of the world of stereotypes, peaceful and aggressive, from which the individual seeks rebirth'. Tippett believed it significant that whereas Romantics like E. T. A. Hoffmann prized allegory and symbol as revelations of the numinous, the 20th-century mind is never untouched by critical or analytical judgment. Music has both to embody and transcend the surface structure. Its task for this composer is to help 'suspend the critical and analytical judgment, without which happening, no experience of the numinous can be immediate at all'. Here Tippett is fortunate in that the musical images and metaphors are always dominant, often preceding the text – whose oddities are often attributable to this process – 'I sensed the musical metaphors before I searched for the verbal'.

5. ALLEGORY AND INTERPRETATION. Because allegory deals in meanings that are veiled or coded, it poses the need for interpretation. Many operas after 1800 permit and even invite several legitimate interpretations of their allegorical content. Interpretation can therefore make an important contribution of its own. Critical exposition becomes absorbed into how operas speak to us.

Early commentators on the *Ring* were concerned with the pagan mythologies and their challenge to the precepts of a nominally Christian society. For Shaw, the work allegorized the class struggle and the social effects of industrialization. For Nietzsche, Wagner had restaged the ancient antagonism between Dionysus and Apollo, while Thomas Mann saw Wagner as a precursor of Freud, whose ideas have coloured such readings as that of Robert Jacobs (*Wagner*, 1935, 2/1965), for whom the *Ring* pushes 'the antithesis between power and love ... into the realm of sexuality as seen through the distorting mirror of the Oedipus Complex'. Robert Donington's Jungian analysis (*Wagner's 'Ring' and its Symbols*, 1963) has been influential, while other persuasive readings have been advanced by social anthropologists and lawyers.

The most important contributions to interpretation are made in the theatre, for every operatic performance is also an interpretation. In recent years stage directors have sought to expose obscurities and inconsistencies, bridging credibility gaps by constructing 'more relevant' dramatic foregrounds. The original text is treated as a problem which it is the production's task to solve. Thus Bill Bryden's charismatic Christians replacing the Knights of the Grail in *Parsifal* at Covent Garden (1988), or Peter Sellars's substitution of a West Coast Bhagwan-style commune for Sarastro's masonic fraternity in *Die Zauberflöte* at Glyndebourne (1990), are both responses to a palpable embarrassment with works which deal with communities of belief. Where the Baroque invented opera so that men could be seen to act as gods, and the 19th century was eager to demonstrate that man had become his own god, the modern mind tips all divinities from their thrones, with allegory a secondary casualty.

For Wieland Wagner at Bayreuth from 1951, Wagner's characters were filtered through a psychological lens (very much in line with Donington's later interpretation). Joachim Herz (1973–6, Leipzig), and Patrice Chéreau (1976, Bayreuth) rejected psychologizing and, albeit in very different ways, staged the Shavian view of the *Ring*. Such coherent interpretations have been followed by post-modern deconstructions which are impatient of allegory. Aggressive fragmentations challenge the audience to find their own sense, acknowledging that the only indisputable content is the drama manifest in the composer's score.

*

W. Benjamin: *Ursprung des deutschen Trauerspiels* (Frankfurt, 1928, 2/1963; Eng. trans., as *The Origin of German Tragic Drama*, 1977 [esp. 'Allegory and Trauerspiel', 159–235])

M. Bukofzer: 'Allegory in Baroque Music', *Journal of the Warburg Institute*, iii (1939–40), 1–21

C. Sasse: 'Die Texte der Londoner Opern Händels in ihren gesellschaftlichen Beziehungen', *Wissenschaftliche Zeitschrift der Martin-Luther-Universität-Halle-Wittenberg*, iv (1954–5), 627–46

N. Frye: *Anatomy of Criticism* (Princeton, 1957)

M. Tippett: *Moving into Aquarius* (London, 1959)

A. Fletcher: *Allegory: the Theory of a Symbolic Mode* (Ithaca, 1964)

R. M. Isherwood: *Music in the Service of the King: France in the Seventeenth Century* (Ithaca, 1973)

P. Conrad: *Romantic Opera and Literary Form* (London, 1977)

R. Strohm: *Essays on Handel and Italian Opera* (Cambridge, 1985)

T. Walker and L. Bianconi: 'Production, Consumption and Political Function of Seventeenth-Century Italian Opera', *Early Music History*, iv (1985), 209–96

D. Chisholm: 'Handel's *Lucio Cornelio Silla*: its Problems and Context', *EM*, xiv (1986), 64–70

C. Price: 'Political Allegory in Late Seventeenth-century English Opera', *Music and Theatre: Essays in Honour of Winton Dean* (Cambridge, 1987), 1-29

R. D. Hume: *Henry Fielding and the London Theatre 1728–1737* (Oxford, 1988)

N. Zaslaw: 'The First Opera in Paris: a Study in the Politics of Art', *Jean-Baptiste Lully and the Music of the French Baroque: Essays in Honor of James R. Anthony* (Cambridge, 1989), 7–23

CURTIS PRICE (1,2), PATRICK CARNEGY (3,4,5)

Allegra, Salvatore (*b* Palermo, 17 July 1898). Italian composer. He studied at the Conservatorio Vincenzo Bellini, Palermo, with Cilea and Antonio Favara, graduating in 1917. He held office as President of the Cassa Nazionale Assistenza Musicisti and as Honorary President of the Italian Musicians' Union. He is known mainly as a composer of operettas and operas in which he followed closely the typical melodic style of the popular Italian lyric tradition. His operettas, of which *Mademoiselle Ultra* (1926) and *Mitizi* (1928) are representative, exploit the vein of *petit bourgeois* sentimentality which was highly successful between 1910 and 1930. In the 1930s, when operetta lost its appeal with Italian audiences, he turned to opera, with works such as *Ave Maria* (1934) and *Romulus* (1946), whose style is that of late *verismo*.

operettas unless otherwise stated

La maschera nuda (3, F. Paolieri and L. Bonelli), Naples, Politeama Giacosa, 26 June 1925 [based on sketches by Leoncavallo]

Mademoiselle Ultra (3, Paolieri and Bonelli), Turin, Balbo, 1926

Mitizi (3, N. Vitali), Brindisi, 1928

La fiera dell'Impruneta (3, G. Bucciolini), Genoa, 1929

Il gatto in cantina (Vitali), Florence, 1930

Maremma (Yambo [G. E. Novelli]), Florence, 1931

Cappuccetto rosso (3, Yambo), Florence, 1932

Le avventure di Pippo Fallatutti (4 scenes, Bucciolini), Florence, 1934

Ave Maria (op, A. Donini, after G. Zorzi), Perugia, Morlacchi, 1934

I viandanti (poema lirico-sinfonico, 1, after V. Andreaus), Kassel, 1938, as Rast vor dem Jenseits

Il medico suo malgrado (op, Donini, after Molière), Kassel, 1938

Romulus (op, 3, E. Mucci), Naples, Floridiana, 1946

Il ritratto (op, after R. Nathan), Cluj, 1958

RAFFAELE POZZI

Allegranti, (Teresa) Maddalena (*b* Venice, 1754; *d* Ireland, after 1801). Italian soprano. She made her début in 1770 in Venice and in 1771 went from Florence to Mannheim, where her teacher, Holzbauer, employed her as second soubrette in the court opera. In 1772 she made her début in Gassman's *L'amore artigiano* (Angiolina) and Sacchini's *La contadina in corte* (Tancia); Burney gave a glowing report of her. The libretto of Salieri's *La fiera di Venezia* (1772) calls her 'virtuosa da camera'. She sang in Venice and Florence in 1778; Horace Walpole ranked her success highly when she made her London début in 1781 in Anfossi's *I viaggiatori felici*, but Parke was later critical of her. In 1783 she was engaged by Bertholdi as *prima donna* *buffa* at the Dresden court opera, where Mozart heard her and placed her above Ferrarese (letter of 16 April 1789). She returned by way of Venice (1798) to London where she sang in *Il matrimonio segreto* (1799) and taught singing for a few years from 1801. She is said to have retired with her husband to Ireland.

*

BurneyGN
W. T. Parke: *Musical Memoirs* (London, 1830)
F. Walter: *Geschichte des Theaters und der Musik am kurpfälzischen Hofe* (Leipzig, 1898) ROLAND WÜRTZ

Allen [Lee], **Betty** [Elizabeth] (**Louise**) (*b* Campbell, OH, 17 March 1930). American mezzo-soprano. She studied at Wilberforce University and the Hartford School of Music, later with Sarah Peck More, Zinka Milanov and Paul Ulanowsky. Chosen by Leonard Bernstein to sing in a performance of his *Jeremiah* Symphony in 1951, she made her opera début the following year in Thomson's *Four Saints in Three Acts*, and later took part in the first complete recording. She made her début with the New York City Opera as Queenie in Kern's *Show Boat*; her other roles included Azucena, Mistress Quickly, Jocasta, Eurycleia in *Il ritorno d'Ulisse in patria*, Teresa in *La sonnambula* and the title role in Joplin's *Treemonisha*. She first appeared at the Colón, Buenos Aires, in 1964 as Jocasta in *Oedipus Rex*, and has also sung with Boston, Houston, San Francisco and Santa Fe opera companies. In the 1970s her tone acquired a contralto-like deepening, which can be heard on her recording of Prokofiev's *Alexander Nevsky* under Ormandy. From 1971 she taught at the Manhattan School of Music, and in 1979 she became the executive director of the Harlem School of the Arts. Beginning in 1987 she taught at the Curtis Institute of Music in Philadelphia.

*

J. Gruen: 'Betty is busy figuring out Betty', *New York Times* (19 Aug 1973)
J. Gray: *Blacks in Classical Music* (Westport, CT, 1988)

Allen, Henry Robinson (*b* Cork, 1809; *d* London, 27 Nov 1876). Irish baritone. He studied at the RAM and appeared as Damon in a stage production of Handel's *Acis and Galatea* at Drury Lane in 1842. In 1846 he was engaged at Drury Lane, where he created Basilius in Macfarren's *An Adventure of Don Quixote*; Chorley considered him the most complete artist on the English operatic stage. After retiring as a performer about 1856, Allen devoted himself to teaching and the composition of ballads.

*

H. F. Chorley: Review of Macfarren: *Don Quixote*, *The Athenaeum*, no.954 (1 Feb 1846), 156
J. E. Cox: *Musical Recollections of the Last Half-Century* (London, 1872), ii, 138–9

Allen, Thomas (**Boaz**) (*b* Seaham Harbour, Co. Durham, 10 Sept 1944). English baritone. He studied at the RCM (1964–8) and made his début in 1969 as Marchese d'Obigny (*La traviata*) with the WNO in Haverfordwest. After a summer in the Glyndebourne chorus he rejoined the WNO, where his roles included Rossini's Figaro, Mozart's Count Almaviva, Guglielmo and Papageno, Falke, Billy Budd, Posa, Yevgeny Onegin and Germont. In 1971 he made his Covent Garden début as Donald in *Billy Budd*, and he joined the company the following year. There he has sung Belcore, Paolo (*Simon Boccanegra*), Patroclus (*King Priam*), Pelléas, Marcello, Sharpless, Ford, Ned Keene, Wolfram (*Tannhäuser*, 1984) and Janáček's Forester (1990). His solo Glyndebourne début was as Papageno in 1973, and he returned as Mozart's Figaro (1974), Guglielmo (1975) and Don Giovanni (1977); he made his Metropolitan début in 1981 (Papageno). At Salzburg he sang Monteverdi's Ulysses in 1985 and Count Almaviva in 1991. He sang Faust in the British stage première of Busoni's opera for the ENO in 1986. His Chicago début was as Rossini's Figaro in 1991; the following year he sang Gluck's Orestes at La Scala. His vocal range is wide, encompassing Orff's *Carmina burana* and Mozart's Figaro with equal ease; his voice is evenly produced and clearly projected, agile in florid passages and firm in tone. As Musgrave's Count (*The Voice of Ariadne*), a role he created at the 1974 Aldeburgh Festival, he shows his ability to generate dramatic tension. He is also a deft comedian.

*

M. Loppert: 'People, 117: Thomas Allen', *Opera*, xxix (1978), 671–7 HELEN SIMPSON, ELIZABETH FORBES

Allin, Norman (*b* Ashton-under-Lyne, 19 Nov 1884; *d* Hereford, 27 Oct 1973). English bass. He studied in Manchester and made his début in 1916 with the Beecham Opera Company in London, as the Old Hebrew (*Samson et Dalila*); he later sang Dosifey when *Khovanshchina* was first given in English at Drury Lane. At Covent Garden in 1919 he appeared as Khan Konchak, Boris and Gurnemanz. In 1922 he became a director and principal bass with the British National Opera Company, adding Méphistophélès, King Mark, Hagen, Hunding, Ochs, Nicolai's Falstaff, Osmin and Sarastro to his roles and taking part in the international seasons (1926–33). He sang Mozart's Bartolo at the first Glyndebourne season in 1934 and then appeared with the Carl Rosa Company (1942–9). He had a voice of comparative rarity, a true, voluminous bass of considerable agility and vitality.

*

J. B. Richards and J. Fryer: 'Norman Allin', *Record Collector*, x (1955–6), 101–42 [with discography by Richards] ALAN BLYTH

Alliteration. *See* STABREIM.

Allman, Robert (*b* Melbourne, 8 June 1927). Australian baritone. He began his career with Gertrude Johnson's National Theatre Movement. He left Australia in 1954 for further study in Paris and worked at Covent Garden from 1956; in 1959 he moved to Germany, where he was based for the next decade, appearing in Frankfurt, Hamburg, Berlin and Munich, and becoming a principal baritone at Cologne until 1967. After appearances in Australia in 1959 (Rigoletto, Michele in *Il tabarro*, John the Baptist), 1964 (Macbeth, Escamillo) and 1965 (Germont, Valentine, Belcore, Enrico), he settled in Australia and appeared there as Don Carlo, Iago, Rigoletto, Amonasro, Tonio, Wolfram, Alfonso, Telramund and Nabucco. One of the most familiar and dependable of Australian Opera principals, he has a powerful, resolute voice, albeit limited in expression and dramatic range, and an air of implacable force which have made him almost ideal in Verdi, Donizetti and Bellini. ROGER COVELL

Alma-Ata. Capital of Kazakhstan, to 1921 known as Vernïy. A provincial outpost of the Russian empire, it occasionally received touring groups and produced some original works of lyric theatre, but regular operatic activity did not begin until 1933, when the musical troupe of the Kazakh National Dramatic Theatre became independent. Yevgeny Brusilovsky's *Kïz-Zhibek*, the first Kazakh national opera, was given its première at the theatre on 7 November 1934, beginning a long association with the composer. The Gosudarstvennïy Ob'yedinyonnïy Teatr Kazakhskoy i Russkoy Operï (State United Theatre of Kazakh and Russian Opera), formed by a merger of this troupe with a Russian troupe from Kuybyshev, in 1937 became the Kazakhskiy Gosudarstvennïy Teatr Operï i Baleta, moving to a new 1243-seat theatre in Kalinin Street in 1941 (designed by N. Prostakov, incorporating elements of native art). The theatre was closely associated with the local composer Mukhtan Tulebayev, whose *Birzhan i Sara* ('Birzhan and Sara') was first performed in 1946 and won a USSR State Prize in 1949. The season traditionally opens with *Abay* (1944), an opera by A. Zhubanov and L. Khamidi based on the life of the national poet Abay Kunanbayev, after whom the theatre was named the Kazakhskiy Gosudarstvennïy Akademicheskiy Teatr Operï i Baleta imeni Abaya (Abay Kazakh State Academic Theatre of Opera and Ballet) in 1945.

*

ME (V. F. Erzakovich)
B. Mekishe and G. Bisenova: *Kazakhskiy gosudarstvennïy akademicheskiy teatr operï i baleta imeni Abaya* (Alma-Ata, 1954)
B. Messman: *Vozrozhdeniye pesni* [The Revival of the Song] (Alma-Ata, 1958)
V. Forsky and N. Rovensky, eds.: *Desyat' nezabïvayemïkh dney: dekada kazakhskovo iskusstva i literaturï v Moskve* [Ten Unforgettable Days: a Decade of Kazakh Art and Literature in Moscow] (Alma-Ata, 1961)
Muzïkal'nïy teatr kazakhskovo naroda [The Musical Theatre of the Kazakh People] (Alma-Ata, 1961) [in Kazakh]
N. I. L'vov: *Kazakhskiy teatr: ocherk istorii* [Kazakh Theatre: a Historical Study] (Moscow, 1961)
G. Bernandt: *Slovar' oper vperviye postavlennïkh ili izdannïkh v dorevolyutsionnoy Rossii i v SSSR 1736–1959* [Dictionary of Operas First Performed or Published in Pre-revolutionary Russia and in the USSR 1736–1959] (Moscow, 1962), 535
B. G. Erzakovich: *Muzïkal'noye iskusstvo Kazakhstana* [The Art of Music in Kazakhstan] (Alma-Ata, 1962)
'Opernoye iskusstvo' [The Art of Opera], *Ocherki po istorii kazakhskoy sovetskoy muzïki* [Essays on the History of Kazakh Soviet Music] (Alma-Ata, 1962)
P. Mominov: *Kazakhskoye opernoye iskusstvo* [The Art of Kazakh Opera] (Alma-Ata, 1963)
Yu. V. Keldish, ed.: *Istoriya muzïki narodov SSSR* [History of the Music of the Soviet Peoples], i–v (Moscow, 1970–74)
A. Mukhambetova: 'Dan' pamyati geroyev' [A Tribute in Memory of Heroes], *SovM* (1983), no.8, pp.33–9 GREGORY SALMON

Almahide. Pasticcio opera in three acts arranged by JOHN JACOB HEIDEGGER, including music by GIOVANNI BONONCINI and ATTILIO ARIOSTI; London, Queen's Theatre in the Haymarket, 10 January 1710.

Almahide (soprano) has been brought up as a man in order to kill her father's enemy, Almiro (alto castrato), but has fallen in love with him. He loves Celinda (soprano), who is loved by the king, Almanzor (alto castrato). Celinda loves the disguised Almahide. After much jealousy and several threats of death, all ends happily in two marriages.

According to Burney (*A General History of Music*), 'This was the first opera performed in England, *wholly in Italian*, and by *Italian singers*; who were Nicolini, Valentini, Cassani, Margarita, and Isabella Girardeau'. The work was based on Ariosti's *Amor tra nemici* (1708), but most of the arias were replaced by the music of other composers, including six arias from Bononcini's *Turno Aricino* (1707) and 11 from his *Mario fuggitivo* (1708).

In the libretto Heidegger acknowledged the absurdity of recent mixed-language operas, with their questions posed in Italian and answered in English. He concluded that since the main performers could not sing in English the whole work had to be in Italian. Audiences were assisted by a parallel English translation in the libretto, and entertained by English comic intermezzos between the acts, sung by Thomas Doggett, Mary Lindsey and Letitia Cross. John Walsh published *Songs in the New Opera, Call'd Almahide* soon after the première and the opera was successful for three seasons, but Burney later dismissed the music as 'neither dramatic, passionate, pathetic, nor graceful'. OLIVE BALDWIN, THELMA WILSON

Almast. Opera in two acts by ALEXANDER SPENDIARYAN to a libretto by the composer and S. Parnok after Hovhannes Tumanyan's poem *Tmkabert aṙumē* ('The Capture of Tmkabert'); Moscow, Bol'shoy Theatre, 1930.

The opera is set in the Crimea in the 18th century. Almast (soprano), a frail and beautiful girl of noble descent, is betrothed to Tatul, the ruler of the Armenian fortress of Tmkabert, which is under threat from the armies of Nadir, Shah of Persia. At first Almast is faithful to Tatul and to his people, but a Persian musician (tenor), sent as a spy by Nadir, persuades her by the power of his art that marriage to the Shah would mean greatness for herself and her country. Almast betrays Tatul to Nadir, but the Armenian people rise up, liberate the fortress and collectively sentence Almast to exile. Her fate in the opera is therefore very different from that related by Tumanyan, where she is killed by the bored Nadir.

Spendiaryan worked on *Almast* from around 1918, having first met Tumanyan in Petrograd (now St Petersburg) in 1916, until his death in 1928. The orchestration and the short score of the last two scenes, left only in sketch by Spendiaryan, were completed by T. Akhumyan. *Almast* is widely recognized as Spendiaryan's *magnum opus*, the work in which his lifelong preoccupation with the folk music of the Near East and of his native Armenia in particular came to fruition. It was well received at its Moscow première, and the first Erevan performance, in the newly completed Alexander Spendiaryan Theatre (1933), was hailed as a major landmark in the development of Armenian national opera. Although *Almast* is well grounded in the Russian grand operatic tradition and employs an intricate system of leitmotifs, it also makes extensive use of Armenian and Persian folksongs and dances and imitates the sound of their folk instruments, with parts for oriental percussion in some of the dance episodes. It has been objected that *Almast* is not a real 'singer's opera', since with the exception of the celebrated 'Ashug song', sung by the Persian musician-spy as he attempts to win Almast to Nadir's cause, the orchestra has most of the melodic writing. For a long time after the première, however, *Almast* was held up as a model for opera composers in Armenia and other eastern Soviet republics. It was given as the opening production at the Erevan State Opera Theatre in 1933.

STEPHEN JOHNSON

Almeida, Antonio (Jacques) de (*b* Neuilly-sur-Seine, 20 Jan 1928). French conductor. He studied with Ginastera in Argentina and with Hindemith, Koussevitzky and

Szell in the USA, joining the opera department at the University of Southern California and setting up and directing the opera school of Occidental College, Los Angeles. He became conductor of the Portuguese Radio SO in Lisbon, 1957–60, which involved him in opera there, and worked at the Paris Opéra, 1965–7. After returning to concert work in the USA and elsewhere, and serving as music director for the Friends of French Opera, New York, in 1976 he was appointed music director of the Nice PO, serving a busy opera, as well as concert, schedule. He appeared at Covent Garden in 1990 in a special production of *Idomeneo* for the English Bach Festival. His recordings include Haydn's *L'infedeltà delusa* (in collaboration with H. C. Robbins Landon, 1969), the first recording of Bizet's *Le Docteur Miracle* (1974), and Halévy's *La Juive* (1989). A conductor of elegance and fastidious detail, his work as an editor includes a thematic catalogue of Offenbach's works. He has received the French Ordre des Arts et Lettres and the Légion d'honneur.

CHRISTIANE SPIETH-WEISSENBACHER, NOËL GOODWIN

Almeida, Francisco António de (*b* *c*1702; *fl* 1722–52). Portuguese composer. He studied in Rome between 1722 and 1728, where he presented the sacred works *Il pentimento di Davidde* (1722) and *La Giuditta* (1726). A 1724 caricature of him describes him as 'bravissimo compositore di Concerti e di musica da Chiesa'. He returned to Lisbon probably in 1726, and in 1733 his opera *La pazienza di Socrate*, the first Italian opera to be performed in Portugal, was presented at the court of João V. According to José Mazzo, Almeida was organist of the Royal and Patriarchal chapel at Lisbon in 1738.

Praised by Andrea Trabucco (in the preface to his libretto for Almeida's *Il pentimento*) for his immediate mastery of the Italian language, Almeida not only completely assimilated the characteristic idioms of current Italian church music but also those of the reigning Neapolitan *opera buffa* style. His orchestra was that of Alessandro Scarlatti: paired oboes and horns with strings. In *La Spinalba, ovvero Il vecchio matto*, his only opera to have survived complete, the male roles are assigned not to castratos but to standard male voices. He may have died in the Lisbon earthquake of 1755.

See also SPINALBA.

all performed in Lisbon

Il trionfo della virtù (componimento poetico [serenata], 1, L. Giovine), da Mota Palace, 22 April 1728

Il trionfo d'amore (scherzo pastorale [serenata]), Ribeira Palace, 27 Dec 1729, *P-VV*

Gl'incanti d'Alcina (dramma per musica da cantarsi [serenata], 2), Ribeira Palace, 27 Dec 1730

La pazienza di Socrate (dramma comico da cantarsi, 3, ? A. de Gusmão), Ribeira Palace, carn. 1733, Act 3 *La*

La finta pazza (dramma per musica, 3), Ribeira Palace, carn. 1735

La virtù trionfante (serenata, 1, A. Tedeschi), Palace of the Patriarch, 1738

La Spinalba, ovvero Il vecchio matto (dramma comico, 3), Ribeira Palace, carn. 1739, *La*, ed. in PM, ser. B, xii (1969)

L'Ippolito (serenata, 1, Tedeschi), Ribeira Palace, 4 Dec 1752

*

DBP (E. Vieira)

J. Mazza: *Dicionário biográfico de músicos portugueses* (Lisbon, 1944–5), 23, 68–9

J. A. Alegria: *Biblioteca do Palacio Real de Vila Viçosa: catálogo das fundos musicais* (Lisbon, 1989), 21, 88, 164

M. C. de Brito: *Opera in Portugal in the Eighteenth Century* (Cambridge, 1989)

——: 'Um retrato inédito do compositor Francisco António de Almeida', *Estudos de historia da música em Portugal* (Lisbon, 1989), 123–6

LUISA CYMBRON, ROBERT STEVENSON

Almeida Mota [Almeyda Motta, de Almeida, Almeida y Mota], **João Pedro** [Juan Pedro, Giovanni Pietro, Carlos Francisco] (*b* Lisbon, 24 June 1744; *d* Madrid, *c*1817). Portuguese tenor and composer active in Spain. He sang in Lisbon, Braga, Santiago de Compostela and Mondeñedo (after October 1772) and as maestro de capilla in Lugo (after July 1775) and Astorga (after March 1783). He then went to Madrid as *maestro de música* at the Real Capilla.

Most of his compositions are liturgical, but some secular works have survived, including two arias for soprano and orchestra, 'Mi sento il cor trafiggere' and 'Quegl' occhietti si fur', which may be fragments of an opera.

On 15 August 1774 his *opera buffa Il matrimonio per concorso* was first performed at Mondoñedo. The libretto was by Gaetano Martinelli, a poet at the Portuguese court and the author of several other librettos. The score is lost but programmes have survived, with text in Italian and Spanish.

*

X. M. Carreira: 'Almeida Mota, João Pedro', *Diccionario de la música española e hispanoamericana* (Madrid, 1992)

XOÁN M. CARREIRA

Almena. Opera in three acts by MICHAEL ARNE and JONATHAN BATTISHILL to a libretto by Richard Rolt; London, Theatre Royal, Drury Lane, 2 November 1764.

The sultan of Persia has been desposed and killed by the villain Mohammed (bass) who then makes advances to the sultan's widow Aspatia (soprano), who is also loved by the sultan's Vizier (bass). Aspatia's daughter Almena (soprano) is wooed by the hero Mirza (soprano castrato), the late sultan's nephew. He has also aroused the affection of Zara (soprano), Mohammed's sister. When Mirza is thrown into prison, Zara assumes a disguise and rescues him, without overturning his love for Almena. Eventually all ends happily with the lovers reunited. Michael Arne provided the arias for the hero and heroine, whereas Battishill was responsible for Mohammed and Zara's arias and the choruses. Strangely, their contributions were published separately. Arne's florid music includes Almena's aria 'No fears alarm' which features a remarkable mandolin obbligato.

JOHN A. PARKINSON

Almira [*Der in Krohnen erlangte Glücks-Wechsel, oder Almira, Königin von Castilien* ('The Change of Fortune gained with a Crown, or Almira, Queen of Castile')]. Singspiel in three acts by GEORGE FRIDERIC HANDEL to a libretto by FRIEDRICH CHRISTIAN FEUSTKING after Giulio Pancieri's *L'Almira* (1691, Venice); Hamburg, Theater am Gänsemarkt, 8 January 1705 (according to Mattheson; relevant wordbooks are dated 1704).

Handel's first opera, produced when he was 19, is strongly influenced by the example of the leading Hamburg composer Reinhard Keiser in its brilliant fusion of French, German and Italian styles. The libretto was in fact intended for Keiser, and was set by him for production in Hamburg in 1704; but it was not performed and (according to the account in Mainwaring's *Memoirs of the Life of … Handel*, which there is no reason to doubt) Keiser had to leave Hamburg hastily, having 'involved himself in debts', and the opera house manager 'therefore applied to Handel, and furnished him with a drama [i.e. *Almira*] to set'. (Keiser's setting reached performance only in revised versions, one at Weissenfels in 1704 and another at Hamburg in 1706, the latter having the title *Der durchlauchtige Secretarius, oder: Almira, Königin in Castilien.*) All three acts of Handel's version contain dance music, apparently fully extant (with the possible exception of some middle parts) in the sole surviving score (*D-B*, reproduced with minor inaccuracies in Chrysander's edition); the final aria of Act 1 and most of a chorus in Act 3 are lost, however. 15 arias have Italian texts taken from Pancieri; the rest of the libretto is in German. The original cast is not known, though it is likely that Fernando was sung by Johann Mattheson.

The story, set in Valladolid in an unspecified era, is fictional. Almira (soprano) has reached her 20th birthday and in accordance with her father's will she is crowned Queen of Castile by her guardian Consalvo, Prince of Segovia (bass). There is further provision that she should marry a member of Consalvo's family, which seems to mean that she must be betrothed to his son, Osman (tenor). She, however, is in love with her secretary Fernando (tenor), an orphan found and brought up by Consalvo; he also loves her, though dares not admit it. Osman, ambitious for the throne, abandons his former love, the Princess Edilia (soprano). A series of intrigues and misunderstandings follows, in which Bellante, Princess of Arando (soprano), Fernando's comic servant Tabarco (tenor), and Raymondo, King of Mauritania (bass), are also involved (the last as an unsuccessful suitor of Almira). Eventually Fernando is discovered to be Consalvo's youngest son Floralbo, thought to have been drowned in a shipwreck: he therefore satisfies the terms of the will and becomes Almira's consort. Osman marries Bellante; Raymondo marries Edilia.

Despite signs of the young composer's inexperience (notably the structural awkwardness of certain arias and some ungrateful passages of quasi-instrumental vocal writing), the music is full of lively invention and often prophetic of Handel's mature style, especially at moments of quiet reflection (such as Fernando's aria 'Liebliche Wälder' in Act 1) and of deep feeling (Almira's aria 'Geloso tormento' in Act 1, for example, or Fernando's prison scene in Act 3). Dances, low comedy and the opportunities for spectacle in the coronation scene of Act 1 and in the masque of the continents at the start of Act 3 provide the variety typical of Hamburg operas of this period, though dramatic coherence is occasionally sacrificed to make way for them. The only revival in Handel's lifetime was at Hamburg in 1732, in a version revised by Telemann. In 1878 the Hamburg Stadttheater staged a severely truncated version (prepared by J. N. Fuchs) as part of a triple bill celebrating the bicentenary of the Hamburg Opera. *Almira* was revived at Leipzig in 1985.

ANTHONY HICKS

Alonso (López), Francisco (*b* Granada, 9 May 1887; *d* Madrid, 18 May 1948). Spanish composer. He displayed musical ability from an early age but studied medicine before turning to music. At 18 he became director of a military band, conducted the Granada Philharmonic Society, and composed his first zarzuela, *La niña de los cantares*. He moved to Madrid to further a theatrical career, and in the 1920s produced a succession of works that proved hugely popular for their colourfully orchestrated scores and rousing melodies. A particular feature of his output was the dedication of works to various provinces of Spain. He composed about 150 works for the stage; besides zarzuelas, he wrote many individual songs and complete scores for revues.

selective list

La niña de los cantares (zar, 1, R. Dominguez and V. Herreros), Granada, Cervantes, 20 June 1905; Armas al hombro (zar, 1, C. Dotesio), Madrid, Martín, 3 Nov 1911; El bueno de Guzmán (zar, 1, R. Asensio Más), Madrid, Cómico, 1913; Música, luz y alegría (revista, F. de Torres and A. Varela), Madrid, Novedades, 20 May 1916; Las corsarias (humorada cómico-lírica, E. Paradas and J. Jiménez), Madrid, Martín, 1919; La linda tapada (zar, 2, J. Tellaeche), Madrid, Cómico, 19 April 1924; La bejarana (zar, L. Fernández Ardavín), Madrid, Apolo, June 1924, collab. E. Serrano

Curro el de Lora (zar, Tellaeche and M. de Góngora), Madrid, Apolo, 1925; La calesera (zar, 3, E. González del Castillo and L. Martínez Román), Madrid, Zarzuela, 12 Dec 1925; Las castigadores (revista, F. Lozano and J. Mariño), Madrid, Eslava, 13 May 1927; La parranda (zar, 3, Fernández Ardavín), Madrid, Calderón, 24 April 1928; La mejor del puerto (zar, 2, L. Fernández de Sevilla and A. C. Carreño), Madrid, Novedades, 11 Sept 1928; Las cariñosas (sainete), Madrid, Maravillas, 1928; Coplas de Ronda (zar, C. Arniches and J. de Lucio), Madrid, 1929

La picarona (zar, 3, González del Castillo and Martínez Román), Madrid, Eslava, 6 Feb 1930; Las leandras (sainete lírico, 1, González del Castillo and J. Muñoz Román), Madrid, Pavón, 12 Nov 1931; Me llaman la Presumida (sainete lírico, 3, F. Ramos de Castro and Carreño), Madrid, Ideal, 4 Dec 1935; Rosa la pantalonera (sainete, P. Llabrés and J. Lerena), San Sebastián, Príncipe, 1938; Doña Mariquita de mi corazón (revista), Madrid, Martín, 1942; Tres días para quererte (revista, F. Lozano), 1945

*

A. Fernández-Cid: *Cien años de teatro musical en España (1875–1975)* (Madrid, 1975)

J. Arnau and C. Gomez: *Historia de la zarzuela* (Madrid, 1979)

R. Alier and others: *El libro de la zarzuela* (Barcelona, 1982, 2/1986 as *Diccionario de la zarzuela*)

J. Montero Alonso: *Francisco Alonso* (Madrid, 1987)

ANDREW LAMB

Alonso e Cora ('Alonso and Cora'). *Opera seria* in three acts by FRANCESCO BIANCHI to a libretto by GIUSEPPE MARIA FOPPA, after FERDINANDO MORETTI's libretto *Idalide*; Venice, Teatro S Benedetto, 7 February 1786.

The plot, a romance between the conquistador Alonso (soprano castrato) and the Inca sun-maiden Cora (soprano), closely follows Moretti's libretto as set by Giuseppe Sarti (*see* VERGINE DEL SOLE, LA). Bianchi's setting is unusual for the large number of concertato choruses (including *introduzioni* to both Acts 1 and 3), its three ensembles (two duets and a quintet), and the ballet that is incorporated into the final scene complex in Act 1. Act 3 is one enormous scene complex, large parts of which are set in obbligato recitative with orchestral accompaniment; there are several choruses, and a vocal rondò for Alonso, 'Nella sede degli amanti'. Foppa enhanced the spectacle with a stormy sea, a disembarkation and a volcanic eruption, complete with ballet and chorus. In pairing *Alonso e Cora* with Tarchi's new setting of Coltellini's French-inspired *Ifigenia in Tauride* (to which a spectacular new *introduzione* was added) the Teatro S Benedetto offered its patrons carnival entertainment of unprecedented richness that was unrivalled until 1792.

MARITA P. McCLYMONDS

Alpar, Gitta (*b* Budapest, 5 March 1903). Hungarian soprano. After study with Laura Hilgermann she sang in Budapest from 1923. In Munich, Berlin and Vienna her agile coloratura was admired in the roles of Gilda, Rosina and the Queen of Night. She had her greatest success in operetta, appearing in Millöcker's *Der Bettelstudent* at the Metropoltheater, Berlin, and singing in the première of Lehár's *Schön ist die Welt* (1930). She sang the title role of Millöcker's *Gräfin Dubarry* in 1931 but was obliged to leave Germany with the rise of the Nazis. After arriving in America in 1936 she resumed her career in operetta and appeared in films (her second husband was the director Gustav Fröhlich).

DAVID CUMMINGS

Alpenkönig und der Menschenfeind, Der ('The King of the Alps and the Misanthrope'). *Romantisch-komisches Zauberspiel* by WENZEL MÜLLER to a libretto by FERDINAND RAIMUND; Vienna, Theater in der Leopoldstadt, 17 October 1828.

Probably the masterpiece of both dramatist and composer, *Der Alpenkönig und der Menschenfeind* can stand comparison with Molière in its depiction of the two sides of the character of a misanthrope. Herr von Rappelkopf (tenor) is cured of his misanthropy through the intervention of Astragalus (spoken), the King of the Alps, with whom under duress he exchanges appearances. Rappelkopf's eviction of the charcoal burner's family, a scene considered by some to be chillingly proto-naturalistic, is accompanied by the ensemble 'So leb denn wohl, du stilles Haus'. The scenes of domestic life, with well-drawn comic servants, are more effective than those depicting young love; best of all is the role of Rappelkopf (which Raimund wrote for himself), with its lively and attractive songs. If the five choruses lack any great individuality the ensembles, and especially the solo numbers for Rappelkopf (for example the explosive entry song 'Ha! Ja, das kann nicht mehr so bleiben'), are simple but highly effective. Raimund played the part to great acclaim both in Vienna and during his guest seasons in Germany. The play was successfully performed in London (Adelphi Theatre) in 1831, translated by Lord Stanhope, and it has continued to be one of the most popular of all Viennese Singspiels. Leo Blech's new setting, *Alpenkönig und Menschenfeind*, was performed in Dresden in 1903.

PETER BRANSCOMBE

Alsen, Elsa (*b* Obra, Poland, 7 April 1880; *d* New York, 31 Jan 1975). Polish-American soprano. Born of a French mother and Norwegian father, she trained in Breslau as a contralto and sang first in public at short notice and from memory in the *St Matthew Passion*. Her operatic début followed in 1902 at Heidelberg as Azucena in *Il trovatore*, a role she sang later in Germany with Caruso. In 1912 she reappeared as a dramatic soprano specializing in the roles of Isolde and Brünnhilde. She joined the Chicago Civic Opera in 1925 and made her final appearance as Isolde at Detroit in 1937. She also had a considerable concert career and appeared with Lawrence Tibbett in the film *The Rogue Song*. Recordings made in the 1920s show a well-placed heroic voice and a convincing dramatic style.

*

E. Vesper: 'Elsa Alsen', *Record Collector*, xv (1963–4), 5–12, 142, 180

J. B. STEANE

Alsen, Herbert (*b* Hildesheim, 12 Oct 1906; *d* Vienna, 25 Oct 1978). German bass. He studied at the Berlin Musikhochschule and made his début at Hagen in 1929 as Rocco. After engagements in Dessau and Wiesbaden he sang Gurnemanz at the Vienna Staatsoper in 1935, remaining with the company until 1949. He was heard at the Salzburg Festival from 1936 as Pogner, Caspar and Rocco, and in the 1947 première of *Dantons Tod.* He sang Osmin and Sarastro during the 1937 season at Glyndebourne and appeared at Covent Garden ten years later. Banquo and Philip II in *Don Carlos* were among his most successful roles.

DAVID CUMMINGS

Al'tani, Ippolit (Karlovich) (*b* S. Ukraine, 15/27 May 1846; *d* Moscow, 17 Feb 1919). Ukrainian conductor. He studied at the St Petersburg Conservatory with Anton Rubinstein and Nikolay Zaremba. He was chorus master at the Kiev Opera from 1868 and conducted Tchaikovsky's *Oprichnik* there shortly after its St Petersburg première in 1874. His association with the music of Tchaikovsky continued at the Bol'shoy (1882–1906), where he conducted the première of *Mazepa* (1884) and the first Moscow performance of *The Queen of Spades* (1891). He also conducted *Boris Godunov* (1888), Rimsky-Korsakov's *Snow Maiden* and Rakhmaninov's *Aleko* (both 1893).

DAVID CUMMINGS

Alternative title [secondary title]. The tradition of giving dramatic works alternative titles is an old one, belonging initially to spoken theatrical works. Most Shakespeare plays have alternative titles. Normally, the 'alternative title' is not a genuine alternative but is intended to be read alongside the principal title and to elucidate it or elaborate upon it. Examples are Campra's *Aréthuse, ou La vengeance de l'Amour* (1701); Arne's *Thomas and Sally, or The Sailor's Return* (1760); Mozart's *Il dissoluto punito, ossia Il Don Giovanni* (1787) and his *Così fan tutte, ossia La scuola degli amanti* (1790); Rossini's *Almaviva, ossia L'inutile precauzione* (better known as *Il barbiere di Siviglia*, 1816) and *Otello, ossia Il moro di Venezia* (1816); Wagner's *Das Liebesverbot, oder Die Novize von Palermo* (1836); and Sullivan's *HMS Pinafore, or The Lass that Loved a Sailor* (1878).

True alternative titles may also be found, particularly in the 18th century, when an opera was revised for a later performance. Cimarosa's *I due baroni di Rocca Azzura* (1783) was later given as *La sposa in contrasto* (1802) and as *Il barone deluso* (1805). Sometimes operas were re-titled to preclude confusion with an existing work, for example Rossini's *Il barbiere*; Verdi's *Otello*, similarly, was initially to have been called *Iago*.

Althouse, Paul (Shearer) (*b* Reading, PA, 2 Dec 1899; *d* New York, 6 Feb 1954). American tenor. Educated at Bucknell University, he studied with P. D. Aldrich in Philadelphia and Oscar Saenger and P. R. Stevens in New York. The first American tenor without European experience to sing at the Metropolitan Opera, he made his début there as Grigory in the American première of *Boris Godunov* under Toscanini (1913); between then and 1920 he participated in its first productions of Giordano's *Madame Sans-Gêne*, Herbert's *Madeleine*, De Koven's *Canterbury Pilgrims*, Cadman's *Shanewis* and Breil's *The Legend*. His voice was described as a 'lyric tenor of the more robust Italian type'. During part of the 1920s he devoted himself exclusively to concerts, but after a visit to Bayreuth, he decided to retrain as a Heldentenor. In 1933 he sang Tristan in San Francisco, and returned to the Metropolitan as Siegmund, which he repeated in 1935 at Flagstad's début. Until the 1939–40 season he shared the principal Wagner roles at the Metropolitan with Melchior. After a final appearance as Loge in 1941, he devoted himself to teaching; among his pupils were Tucker, Steber, Simoneau and Dalis. PHILIP LIESON MILLER

Altmeyer, Jeannine (**Theresa**) (*b* La Habra, CA, 2 May 1948). American soprano. She studied with Lotte Lehmann in Santa Barbara and later at Salzburg. After winning the Illinois Opera Guild Auditions in 1971, she made her début at the Metropolitan as the Heavenly Voice in Verdi's *Don Carlos*. She sang Freia at the Chicago Lyric Opera (1972), Salzburg (1973) and Covent Garden (1975). After several seasons at Stuttgart (1975–9) she sang Sieglinde in Patrice Chéreau's production of the *Ring* (1979) at Bayreuth, where she also sang Isolde (1986). Apart from her Wagnerian roles (which include Elsa, Eva, Elisabeth, Gutrune and Brünnhilde), Altmeyer sings Agathe (*Der Freischütz*), Strauss's Salome and Chrysothemis, Lisa (*The Queen of Spades*) and Leonore, which she sang at La Scala in 1990. The radiant tone of her voice and the intensity of her expression make her a particularly fine interpreter of Wagner and Strauss. ELIZABETH FORBES

Alto (It.: 'high'; Fr. *alto*; Ger. *Alt*). Term used in English to denote a singer whose voice lies in the region *f-d″*. A female singer is more frequently described as CONTRALTO; a male may be a COUNTERTENOR (or in early French music an HAUTE-CONTRE), or a FALSETTO singer; a CASTRATO may also sing at this pitch.

Altrobrandino, Giuseppe Antonio Vincenzo. *See* ALDROVANDINI, GIUSEPPE ANTONIO VINCENZO.

Alva, Luigi [Alva Talledo, Luis Ernesto] (*b* Lima, 10 April 1927). Peruvian tenor. He studied in Lima with Rosa Morales and in Milan with Emilio Ghirardini and Ettore Campogalliani. He made his début in 1949 in *Luisa Fernanda* at Lima, where he sang Beppe (*Pagliacci*) the following year. His European début was at the Teatro Nuovo, Milan, in 1954 as Alfredo. He sang Paolino in *Il matrimonio segreto* to open the Piccola Scala in 1955, repeating the role in Edinburgh in 1957. At La Scala in 1956 he sang Almaviva, a role in which his highly developed sense of comedy and lack of exaggeration were to win him widespread admiration. He sang regularly in Milan (where he appeared in the premières of Luciano Chailly's *Una domanda di matrimonio* and Riccardo Malipiero's *La donna è mobile*), at Covent Garden (1960–77), at Chicago (1961–77) and at the Metropolitan (1964–76), where he made his début as Fenton and later sang Ernesto, Lindoro and Tamino. He appeared at the festivals of Aix-en-Provence and Salzburg and sang Nemorino at Glyndebourne in 1961. His elegant and refined style was specially suited to Mozart and Rossini, and he continued to sing Paolino, at Naples (1978), the Piccola Scala (1979) and Bordeaux (1980). He taught in Lima from 1982 and retired as a singer in 1989.

*

GV (G. Gualerzi; R. Vegeto) HAROLD ROSENTHAL/R

Alvares, Eduardo (*b* Rio de Janeiro, 10 June 1947). Brazilian tenor. He studied in Rio, Rome and Vienna, making his début in 1970 at Linz as Don José. He has appeared in Vienna, Munich, Oslo and Rio, as the Duke, Alfredo, Gabriele Adorno, Don Carlos, Don Alvaro, Faust, Werther and Lensky. At Wexford he sang Konrad in *Hans Heiling* (1983) and Lukas in Smetana's *The Kiss* (1984). He has sung with Opera North as Manrico; with Scottish Opera as Calaf, Herod and Alwa (*Lulu*); and with the ENO as Radames and Cavaradossi. His originally lyric voice has acquired a heroic timbre, and in 1988 he sang Bacchus in Rio. ELIZABETH FORBES

Alvarez, Albert [Gourron, Raymond] (*b* nr Bordeaux, 16 Jan 1861; *d* Nice, 26 Feb 1933). French tenor. He studied in Paris and made his début in 1886 at Ghent as Gounod's Faust. From 1892 until 1906 he was engaged at the Opéra, where he created Nicias in Massenet's *Thaïs* (1894) and roles in Holmès' *La montagne noire* (1895), Duvernoy's *Hellé* (1896), Bruneau's *Messidor* (1897), Vidal's *La burgonde* (1898), Leroux's *Astarte* (1901), Erlanger's *Le fils de l'étoile* (1904) and Guiraud's *Frédégonde* (1905). At Covent Garden he sang Leicester in the first performance of De Lara's *Amy Robsart* (1903) and created Araquil in Massenet's *La navarraise* (1904). In Monte Carlo he sang Paris in the first performance of Saint-Saëns's *Hélène* (1904). His large repertory included Romeo, Samson, Don José, Fernand (*La favorite*), Raoul (*Les Huguenots*), John of Leyden (*Le prophète*), Rodrigue (*Le Cid*), Mathô (*Salammbô*), Hoffmann, Berlioz's Faust, Reyer's Sigurd, Radames, Canio and Otello, as well as Lohengrin, Tannhäuser, Walther, Siegmund and Tristan. A stylish singer, he excelled in heroic French roles. ELIZABETH FORBES

Alvarez [Alvarez de Rocafuerte], **Marguerite d'.** *See* D'ALVAREZ, MARGUERITE.

Alvary [Achenbach], **Max**(**imilian**) (*b* Düsseldorf, 3 May 1856; *d* Grosstabarz, Thuringia, 7 Nov 1898). German tenor. He studied in Frankfurt with Julius Stockhausen and in Milan with Francesco Lamperti. He made his début in 1879 at Weimar, under the name of Max Anders, in the title role of *Alessandro Stradella* and remained there until 1885. He made his Metropolitan début in 1885 as Don José. He was the USA's first Siegfried (in *Siegfried*), his most celebrated role, in 1887; his roles at the Metropolitan included Adolar (1887), Alvar in *Fernand Cortez* (1888) and Loge (1889). In 1890 he was engaged by the Munich Hofoper and in 1891 by the Hamburg Stadttheater. He sang Tristan and Tannhäuser at Bayreuth in 1891, and the following year he made his Covent Garden début as Siegfried. He returned to London in 1893 and 1894 to sing Max, Florestan, Lohengrin, Siegmund and his earlier Wagner roles. As the result of an accident, he retired from the stage in 1897. Notable for dramatic force and refined interpretation, he broke tradition by performing Tristan and other heroic parts without a beard.

*

A. von Mensi-Klarbach: 'Max Alvary', *Alt-Münchner Theater-Erinnerungen* (Munich, 1924), 154–9 HAROLD ROSENTHAL/R

Alyab'yev, Alexander Alexandrovich (*b* Tobol'sk, Siberia, 4/15 Aug 1787; *d* Moscow, 22 Feb/6 March 1851). Russian composer. Best remembered for his chamber music and for his songs, including the ubiquitous *Solovey* ('The Nightingale'), he was nevertheless a leading composer for the stage during the brief heyday of Romanticism in Russia. He had the turbulent biography of a Romantic. After serving in the army (1812–23), he was imprisoned and then exiled for his dubious political associations on trumped-up murder charges; he spent his middle years on the fringes of the Russian empire, where he was drawn to the local folk music and laid the foundations for the stereotyped Russian 'oriental' idiom. In 1836 he moved to Moscow, where he remained, with only brief absences, until his death.

Besides operas and other sung dramatic works, Alyab'yev wrote ballets, melodramas, scenic cantatas, incidental music to prose stage works and a number of 'triumphal prologues' to civic ceremonies. His main theatrical genre was the 'opera-vaudeville', a situation comedy in verse (usually adapted from a French original), furnished with an overture, entr'actes and simple musical numbers in strophic or couplet form, often patter songs which the actors could sing, if sufficiently skilled, or simply recite to music. Between 1822 and 1836 Alyab'yev wrote music for 23 such works (mostly in collaboration with other composers, chiefly Alexey Verstovsky), including eight by Alexander Pisarev (1803–28), the great specialist in the genre. *Lunnaya noch'* ('Moonlit Night'), his first opera, so called, was only slightly more elaborate than his vaudevilles: the difference between the genres has been aptly characterized as one of theatrical stance – the degree to which the 'fourth wall' separating the actors from the spectators is respected. Alyab'yev's music is heavily indebted to Dalayrac, Isouard and Méhul, the early protagonists of *opéra comique*, whose works were frequently performed on the Russian stage; in the opinion of the great Moscow connoisseur V. F. Odoyevsky, Alyab'yev's operas and vaudevilles were 'in no way inferior' to their models.

The more ambitious theatrical works of Alyab'yev's maturity, notably his five romantic operas, never achieved performance in their entirety because of his exile and the jealousy of Verstovsky, who was not only a rival composer but also, as the intendant of the imperial theatres in Moscow, a powerful bureaucrat. Nonetheless, individual numbers from them became popular in concert performance, and the scores were well known to Alyab'yev's younger contemporaries, including Dargomïzhsky, who acknowledged their influence. Two of the three 'magic' operas, *Burya* ('The Tempest') and *Volshebnaya noch'* ('The Enchanted Night', after *A Midsummer Night's Dream*) were based on Shakespeare, while the third, *Rïbak i rusalka* ('The Fisherman and the Mermaid'), now partly lost, was based on Alexander Veltman's completion of Pushkin's dramatic poem *Rusalka* (later adapted by Dargomïzhsky for his most successful opera). *Edvin i Oskar* ('Edwin and Oscar'), a heroic opera of military valour and self-sacrifice after E. de Parny, is incomplete.

Alyab'yev's last opera, *Ammalat-Bek*, after a popular novella of the Caucasian wars by his fellow exile Alexander Bestuzhev (pen-name 'Bestuzhev-Marlinsky'), reflects the romantic vogue for 'bilingualism', in which a work of art is shaped by contrasting national idioms (both of Glinka's completed operas are examples, and there are famous literary prototypes by Pushkin and Lermontov). To capture the confrontation of Russian and Caucasian forces Alyab'yev resorted to multifarious citations: Russian soldiers' songs, mountaineers' dances and sinuous 'oriental' melodies, which he had transcribed while living in the northern Caucasus in 1831–2. At the dramatic turning-point, where Ammalat-Bek is forced to kill a Russian officer who had befriended him, a Russian march and a Circassian melody are juxtaposed contrapuntally. Another typical number is a chorus of mountaineers preparing for battle with the Russians, set to a 'Kabardinian Song' that Alyab'yev had previously published as a solo with piano accompaniment. Excerpts from *Ammalat-Bek* were performed in 1847 at a concert in Moscow, where they were heard by Nikolay Afanas'yev, whose opera on the same libretto was performed at the Mariinsky Theatre in St Petersburg in 1870. Alyab'yev's score is lost; our knowledge of the opera is based only on surviving sketches.

Undoubtedly Alyab'yev's most enduring contribution to the operatic repertory was *The Nightingale*, which, suitably embellished, was frequently interpolated into the singing-lesson scene in Rossini's *Il barbiere di Siviglia* by many 19th-century divas – and not only in Russia – including Viardot, Patti and Sembrich.

all unpublished; MSS in RU-Mcm

Lunnaya noch', ili Domovïye [Moonlit Night, or The Domestic Sprites] (comic op, 2, P. A. Mukhanov and P. N. Arapov), St Petersburg, Bol'shoy, 7/19 June 1823, ov. (Moscow, 1976)

Edvin i Oskar [Edwin and Oscar] (4, ? D. Davïdov, after E. de Parny: *Isnel et Aslėga*), early 1830s, sketches, excerpts and MS lib. survive

Burya [The Tempest] (3, ? A. A. Shakhovskoy, ? N. M. Satin, ? M. A. Gamazov, after W. Shakespeare), unperf.

Volshebnaya noch' [The Enchanted Night] (3, A. F. Veltman, after Shakespeare: *A Midsummer Night's Dream*), rehearsed Moscow, sum. 1838, unperf., lib. (1844)

Rïbak i rusalka, ili Zloye zel'ye [The Fisherman and the Mermaid, or The Evil Potion], 1841–3 (3, Veltman, after A. S. Pushkin: *Rusalka*), unperf., inc., orch. excerpt ed. G. Kirkor (Moscow, 1865)

Ammalat-Bek (5, Veltman, after Bestuzhev-Marlinsky [A. Bestuzhev]), concert perf. of excerpts, 1847; lost, sketches survive, lib. (1871, in connection with Afanas'yev's setting)

Opera-vaudevilles: Novaya shalost', ili Teatral'noye srazheniye [A Novel Prank, or A Theatrical Battle] (1, N. I. Khmel'nitsky), St Petersburg, Bol'shoy, 12/24 Feb 1822, collab. A. N. Verstovsky and L. Maurer; Derevenskiy filosof [The Village Philosopher] (1, M. N. Zagoskin), Moscow, Mokhovaya, 11/23 Jan 1823; Medved' i pasha [The Bear and the Pasha] (1, Arapov, from Fr.), St Petersburg, 4/16 March 1823 [arr. of popular tunes]; Puteshestvuyushchaya tantsovshchitsa, ili Tri sestrï-nevestï [The Wandering Dancing Girl, or The Three Sister-Brides] (Arapov, from Fr.), St Petersburg, 8/20 Jan 1824 [music as for Derevenskiy filosof, 1823]

Uchitel' i uchenik, ili V chuzhom piru pokhmel'ye [Teacher and Pupil, or Your Carousing, my Hangover] (1, A. I. Pisarev, from Fr.), Moscow, Mokhovaya, 24 April/6 May 1824, collab. Verstovsky and F. E. Shol'ts; Prositel' [The Petitioner] (1, Pisarev), Moscow, Mokhovaya, 29 May/10 June 1824, collab. Verstovsky, M. I. Vil'khorsky and Shol'ts; Khlopotun, ili Delo mastera boitsya [Mr Bustle, or Work Fears the Master] (1, Pisarev, from Fr.), Moscow, Malïy, 4/16 Nov 1824, collab. Verstovsky; Vstrecha dilizhansov [The Stage-coaches Meet] (1, Pisarev, Arapov and M. A. Dimitriyev), Moscow, Bol'shoy, 23 Jan/4 Feb 1825, collab. Verstovsky

Zabavï Kalifa, ili Shutki na odni sutki [The Caliph's Amusements, or Jokes Around the Clock] [Act 2] (3, Pisarev), Moscow, Bol'shoy, 9/21 April 1825 [Act 1 by Shol'ts, Act 3 by Verstovsky]; Tri desyatki, ili Novoye dvukhdnevnoye priklyucheniye [The Three Tens, or A New Two-day Adventure] (3, Pisarev, from Fr.), Moscow, Bol'shoy, 19 Nov/1 Dec 1825, collab. Verstovsky; Utro i vecher, ili Veter peremenilsya [Morning and Evening, or The Wind has Changed] (2, R. Zotov), St Petersburg, 1/13 Nov 1826; Dve zapiski, ili Bez vinï vinovat [The Two Chits, or Guilty though Innocent] (1, Pisarev, from Fr.), Moscow, Bol'shoy, 27 Jan/8 Feb 1827, collab. Verstovsky

Pastushka, starushka, volshebnitsa, ili Chto nravitsya zhenshchinam [Shepherdess, Crone and Sorceress, or What Women Like] (3, Pisarev, after C. S. Favart), Moscow, Bol'shoy, 20 May/1 June 1827, collab. Verstovsky; Moya zhena vïkhodit zamuzh [My Wife is Getting Married] (2, N. I. Malïshev, from Fr.), Moscow, Bol'shoy, 6/18 Oct 1827; Molodaya mat' i zhenikh v 48 let, ili Domashniy spektakl' [The Young Mother and her 48-year-old Bridegroom, or A Domestic Spectacle] (2, Shakhovskoy, from Fr.), Moscow, Bol'shoy, 25 Nov/7 Dec 1827; Nerazdel'nïye, ili

Novoe sredstvo platit' dolgi [The Inseparables, or A New Way to Pay one's Debts] (1, N. Shatilov, from Fr.), Moscow, Bol'shoy, 25 Nov/7 Dec 1827, collab. Shol'ts

Luchshiy den' v zhizni, ili Urok bogatïm zhenikham [The Best Day of Your Life, or A Lesson to Rich Bridegrooms] (2, Malïshev, from Fr.), Moscow, Bol'shoy, 21 Dec 1827/2 Jan 1828, collab. Verstovsky and Shol'ts; Redkaya nasmeshnitsa, ili Muzh po zaveshchaniyu [A Rare Scoffer, or A Husband from A Will], 1827; Muzh i zhena [Man and Wife] (1, D. T. Lensky, from Fr.), Moscow, Bol'shoy, 23 May/4 June 1830, collab. Verstovsky, Maurer and Shol'ts; Starïy gusar, ili Pazhi Fridrikha II [The Old Hussar, or The Pages of Frederick II] (3, Lensky, from Fr.), Moscow, Bol'shoy, 5/17 June 1831, collab. I. I. Genishta, Maurer and Shol'ts, addns by Isouard; Ivan Savel'yich [ov.] (1, F. Koni), Moscow, 18/30 Oct 1835; Nakazannïy za obman [Punished for Deception], 1835; Novïy Paris [The New Paris], 1836

*

A. Gozenpud: *Muzïkal'nïy teatr v Rossii* (Leningrad, 1959)

B. V. Dobrokhotov: *Aleksandr Aleksandrovich Alyab'yev: tvorcheskii put'* [Creative Path] (Moscow, 1966)

S. Karlinsky: *Russian Drama from its Beginnings to the Age of Pushkin* (Berkeley and Los Angeles, 1985)

Ye. Levashov: 'A. A. Alyab'yev', *Istoriya russkoy muziki*, ed. Yu. Keldïsh and others, v (Moscow, 1988), 29–96

RICHARD TARUSKIN

Alyff, Mrs. *See* AYLIFF.

Alzira. *Tragedia lirica* in a prologue and two acts by GIUSEPPE VERDI to a libretto by SALVADORE CAMMARANO after VOLTAIRE's play *Alzire, ou Les Américains*; Naples, Teatro S Carlo, 12 August 1845.

Alvaro	*father of Gusmano, initially Governor of Peru*	bass
Gusmano	*Governor of Peru*	baritone
Ovando	*a Spanish Duke*	tenor
Zamoro	*leader of a Peruvian tribe*	tenor
Ataliba	*leader of a Peruvian tribe*	bass
Alzira	*Ataliba's daughter*	soprano
Zuma	*her maid*	mezzo-soprano
Otumbo	*an American warrior*	tenor

Spanish officers and soldiers, Americans of both sexes

Setting Lima and other regions of Peru, about the middle of the 16th century

There were two reasons why *Alzira*, Verdi's eighth opera, was something of a special event. It was the first he had written specially for the famous Teatro S Carlo of Naples, and so offered him an opportunity to confront a significant public and theatre with whom he had so far had little success. And it presented a chance to collaborate with Salvadore Cammarano, resident poet at the S Carlo, certainly the most famous librettist still working in Italy, renowned for his string of successes in the previous decade with Gaetano Donizetti. Because of Cammarano's fame, Verdi seems to have taken little active part in the formation of the libretto (this in contrast to the works he prepared with his principal librettist of the period, Piave), being for the most part happy to accept the dictates of Cammarano's highly professional instincts. Work on *Alzira*, begun in the spring of 1845, was delayed by illness and by the fact that Verdi had to add an overture when the work proved too short for a full evening's entertainment. The cast for the première was unusually strong, including Filippo Coletti (Gusmano), Gaetano Fraschini (Zamoro) and Eugenia Tadolini (Alzira), but the first performance was at best only a partial success. Subsequent revivals fared little better, and the opera soon disappeared entirely from the repertory. It has occasionally been revived in modern times, but remains one of the composer's two or three least-performed operas.

The overture is in three movements. The first is an Andante mosso in which woodwind and percussion attempt to impose a generic local colour on the exotic ambience; the second juxtaposes warlike calls to arms with a lachrymose clarinet solo; the third is a march-like Allegro brillante.

PROLOGUE ('The Prisoner') *A vast open plain, irrigated by the river Rima* A bloodthirsty tribe of 'Americans' led by Otumbo drag on Alvaro in chains, tie him to a tree and mock him with the driving 6/8 chorus 'Muoia, muoia coverto d'insulti'. They are about to dispatch him horribly when a boat is sighted carrying Zamoro, their leader whom they believed dead. Zamoro, strangely moved by the sight of Alvaro, has him released and orders him returned to his people. With Alvaro gone, Zamoro's unusually extended Andante, 'Un Inca ... eccesso orribile!', tells the tribe of his brutal treatment at the hands of the wicked Spaniard Gusmano. The Andante over, Zamoro hears that his beloved Alzira is imprisoned with her father in Lima. Zamoro swears to rescue them, and joins his warriors in a bellicose cabaletta, 'Dio della guerra'.

ACT 1 ('A Life for a Life').i *The main piazza of Lima* A robust choral movement, reinforced by the *banda*, introduces Alvaro, who announces that he is ceding power to his son Gusmano. The latter immediately declares a general peace with the Inca chief Ataliba, reminding him that Ataliba's daughter Alzira has been agreed as Gusmano's reward. But in the Andante of his double aria, 'Eterna la memoria', Gusmano admits that Alzira's feelings for her former lover remain too powerful for him to overcome. Ataliba urges Gusmano to be patient; but the new Governor can brook no delay and, in the forceful cabaletta 'Quanto un mortal può chiedere', declares that he must possess Alzira immediately.

1.ii *Ataliba's apartments in the Governor's palace* Tremolando strings introduce a sleeping Alzira, who awakes to utter Zamoro's name and tell her attendants of a strange dream. 'Da Gusman, su fragil barca' narrates how she dreamt of fleeing Gusmano in a boat, being caught in a storm and rescued by her beloved; the aria boldly follows the pattern of the tale rather than duplicating the form of a conventional Italian Andante. Despite the warnings of her entourage, she proudly declares her love for Zamoro in the ornamental cabaletta 'Nell'astro che più fulgido'.

Ataliba comes on, dismisses Zuma and the chorus, and in simple recitative begs Alzira to marry Gusmano. She will have none of it, and asks instead for death. As Ataliba leaves, Zuma announces a 'member of the tribe', and Alzira is ecstatic to see none other than Zamoro. The first movement of their duet, 'Anima mia!', is a rapid exchange of loving words, held together in the traditional manner by a driving orchestral melody. With little else needing to be said, Cammarano and Verdi moved immediately to the sprightly cabaletta, 'Risorge ne' tuoi lumi'.

The lovers are discovered by Gusmano, Ataliba and a host of attendants. Gusmano orders Zamoro to instant execution and, in a fiery Allegro, Zamoro taunts Gusmano with cowardice. The stage is now set for an unusually grand slow concertato, 'Nella polve, genuflesso', one which begins with a freer dialogue structure than usual and, perhaps for this reason, builds to an uncommonly impressive final climax. The concertato over, wild, exotic music is heard in the distance: a messenger reports that a hostile army is without, demanding the return of Zamoro. Gusmano decides to release him, thus offering a life for the life of his father; but in leading off the concluding stretta, 'Trema, trema ... a ritorti fra l'armi', he warns Zamoro that they will meet again on the battlefield.

ACT 2 ('The Revenge of a Savage').i *Inside the fortifications of Lima* The Incas have again lost the battle; victorious Spanish soldiers indulge in a riotous brindisi, 'Mesci, mesci', interrupted only briefly by the mournful sight of Zamoro and his followers trudging across the stage. Gusmano promises his soldiers rich spoils, and loudly pronounces a death sentence on Zamoro. At this Alzira rushes on to beg for clemency, and Gusmano offers her a polite version of Count di Luna's bargain in *Il trovatore*: Zamoro's life for Alzira's hand in marriage. The impasse is explored in an Andante, 'Il pianto ... l'angoscia', Alzira's breathless sobs contrasting with Gusmano's smooth (perhaps *too* smooth) cantabile. Eventually she agrees, and the pact is sealed by a lively duet cabaletta, 'Colma di gioia ho l'anima'.

2.ii *A dreary cave* A sombre orchestral introduction, appropriate to the desolate scene, introduces Otumbo, who tells his friends that he has secured the release of Zamoro by bribing his Spanish guards. Zamoro appears, and in the Andante 'Irne lungi ancor dovrei' declares himself desolate without his beloved Alzira. Otumbo makes matters worse by telling him that Alzira is about to marry Gusmano. Nothing can restrain Zamoro's fury, and in the cabaletta 'Non di codarde lagrime' he resolves to take stern revenge.

2.iii *A great hall in the Governor's residence* A bridal chorus, 'Tergi del pianto America', looks forward to the peace that this marriage will bring, and Gusmano welcomes all to the ceremony. He is about to take Alzira's hand when Zamoro (disguised as a Spanish soldier) bursts upon the scene, plunges a dagger into Gusmano's heart, and awaits bloody retribution. But Gusmano has a surprise in store: he has learnt from Alzira the joys of peace and mercy, and in a final aria accompanied by the chorus ('I numi tuoi'), gives the two lovers his blessing. It is an impressive close, with the chorus gradually taking the lyrical thread as Gusmano loses strength and the mode shifts from minor to major.

* * *

Verdi pronounced *Alzira* 'proprio brutta' ('downright ugly') in later life, and the opera is without doubt one of the least likely of his works to be performed, even in today's revival-conscious atmosphere. Perhaps, as happened on other occasions, the esteem in which Verdi held his librettist was a disadvantage, inhibiting him from following freely his dramatic instincts. However, like all Verdi's minor operas, *Alzira* has many fine passages, the large ensembles in particular. Even its moments of comparative failure are interesting, coming as they often do in numbers such as Alzira's Act 1 narration, in which the composer attempted something startlingly new in formal terms. In today's critical atmosphere, when it is commonplace to single out for particular praise those passages that break decisively with tradition, it is at least salutary to observe an opera in which the conventional moments succeed far better than those that challenge accepted norms.

ROGER PARKER

Amadei, Filippo (*fl* 1690–1730). Italian composer. He has been variously called 'Sigr Pippo' or 'Pipo' (in English documents of the years 1719–21), 'Filippo Mattei' (in Mattheson's *Critica musica*, 1722–3), and 'Pippo Amadio' (in Gerber's *Lexikon*, 1812). He played the cello in Rome under the patronage of Cardinal Pietro Ottoboni between 1690 and 1696, and was also known as a composer of oratorios and cantatas. *Teodosio il giovane*, his first known opera, was given in the cardinal's palace in 1711 with sets designed by Filippo Juvarra (for illustration *see* JUVARRA, FILIPPO). By early 1719 he was in London where, as Sigr Pippo, he gave several concerts. In 1720 he was a member of the orchestra of the newly founded Royal Academy of Music of which Handel was a musical director. He also served the academy as composer, adding 14 arias to Orlandini's opera *Amore e maestà*, given under the title of *Arsace* (1 February 1721). The next Academy production (15 April 1721) was *Muzio Scevola*, Act 1 of which was composed by Amadei, Act 2 by G. Bononcini and Act 3 by Handel. Amadei was still in London in 1723; later he returned to Rome, serving Cardinal Ottoboni until 1729. The date and place of his death are unknown. His Act 1 to *Muzio Scevola* (in *GB-Lbl*) is his only surviving operatic music.

See also MUZIO SCEVOLA.

*

DBI (C. Petrucci)

H. J. Marx: 'Die Musik am Hofe Pietro Kardinal Ottobonis unter Arcangelo Corelli', *AnMc*, no.5 (1968), 104–77

MICHAEL F. ROBINSON

Amadigi di Gaula ('Amadigi of Gaul'). Opera in three acts by GEORGE FRIDERIC HANDEL to an anonymous libretto adapted from ANTOINE HOUDAR DE LAMOTTE's libretto *Amadis de Grèce* (1699, Paris); London, King's Theatre, 25 May 1715.

The original cast of *Amadigi* consisted of the castrato Nicolini (Amadigi), the contralto Diana Vico (Dardano), Anastasia Robinson (Oriana) and Elisabetta Pilotti-Schiavonetti (Melissa). (The singer of Orgando's role, which consists only of brief recitatives, is unknown.) Robinson fell ill after the first night and was probably replaced by Caterina Galerati. (It may have been at this point that Oriana's last aria in Act 2, 'Affannami, tormentami', was replaced by 'Ch'io lasci mai d'amare'.) Further changes were made for revivals of the opera in the following seasons (1716 and 1717). A total of five new arias seems to have been added to the opera at various times, but the absence of wordbooks for the later performances makes the textual history difficult to trace. There were two productions in Hamburg in 1717, both with additional characters and music. The first modern revival was in Osnabrück in 1929, conducted by Horst-Tanu Margraf; the first in Britain was by Unicorn Opera at the Abbey Hall, Abingdon, conducted and directed by Frances and Alan Kitching. In the absence of Handel's autograph score the task of editing *Amadigi* requires particularly careful evaluation of the many MS copies. J. Merrill Knapp's edition for the Hallische Händel-Ausgabe (1971) is an improvement on Chrysander's of 1874, especially for its inclusion of all additional arias (one in the critical report); but neither takes full account of textual details (mainly affecting orchestration) found in the earliest MSS.

The place and period of the action are unspecified. The hero Amadigi (mezzo-soprano castrato) and Dardano, Prince of Thrace (alto), are each in love with the princess Oriana (soprano). The sorceress Melissa (soprano), infatuated with Amadigi, has imprisoned Oriana in a tower and Amadigi in her garden, in company with Dardano. The plot involves deceptions, visions and anguish for the true lovers, Amadigi and Oriana, who in the end are united when Melissa, finding herself impotent against the gods, stabs herself; Oriana's uncle Orgando (soprano) descends in a chariot and announces an end to the lovers' torments. He unites the couple and all celebrate their happiness.

* * *

The impresario J. J. Heidegger dedicated the libretto to the Earl of Burlington, noting that the opera was 'compos'd in Your own Family' – presumably while Handel was staying at Burlington House. Haym may have been the author, as the text, like that of Haym's *Teseo*, is adapted from a French original; but (perhaps because of haste) it is clumsily assembled and the author may have been reluctant to acknowledge his work. It was, however, sufficient to draw music of surprising variety and power from Handel, perhaps because the characters are in tense emotional states almost throughout. The sorceress Melissa is more than a worthy successor to her predecessors in *Rinaldo* and *Teseo*, since she seems more human; her first aria 'Ah! spietato', mourning Amadigi's rejection of her, is mostly a poignant lament, the anguish of the vocal line intensified by imitative phrases on a solo oboe and further emphasized by a brief outburst of rage before the da capo. The rest of her music is more conventionally vigorous (a solo trumpet makes 'Desterò dall'empia Dite' especially brilliant) until the sad sequence of accompanied recitative and cavatina as she dies. Oriana also has several striking arias, including the profound F minor lament 'S'estinto è l'idol mio', as does Dardano, especially in Act 2. Amadigi himself is not sharply characterized, but most of his music is effective in its own right, from his opening contemplation of the night to his final aria of jubilation with solo trumpet.

ANTHONY HICKS

Amadis [*Amadis de Gaule* ('Amadis of Gaul')]. *Tragédie en musique* in a prologue and five acts by Jean-Baptiste Lully (*see* LULLY family, (1)) to a libretto by PHILIPPE QUINAULT after Nicolas Herberay des Essarts' adaptation of Garcí Rodríguez de Montalvo's *Amadís de Gaula*; Paris, Opéra, 18 January 1684.

Lully's last three *tragédies* were based on tales of chivalry rather than ancient mythology; *Amadis* was the earliest, and the subject chosen by Louis XIV. The title is sometimes given as *Amadis de Gaule* to avoid confusion with Destouches' *Amadis de Grèce*. The première was in Paris instead of at court because the queen had died in July 1683; a court production without scenery or machines took place at Versailles in March 1685. The principal singers at the première included Moreau (Oriane), Le Rochois (Arcabonne), Dumesnil (Amadis) and Dun (Florestan); the principal male dancers were Beauchamp, Pécour and Lestang, and the principal female dancers La Fontaine, Carré and Pesan. There were eight Paris revivals between 1687 and 1771; for the 1759 production François Rebel composed new dances and made other revisions. Between 1687 and

PROLOGUE

Alquif *celebrated sorcerer, husband of Urgande*	baritone
Urgande *celebrated sorceress, wife of Alquif*	soprano

TRAGEDY

Amadis *son of King Perion of Gaule*	haute-contre
Oriane *daughter of King Lisuart of Great Britain*	soprano
Florestan *natural son of King Perion*	baritone
Corisande *ruler of Gravesande*	soprano
Arcabonne *sorceress, sister of Arcalaus and Ardan Canile*	soprano
Arcalaus *sorcerer knight, brother of Arcabonne and Ardan Canile*	baritone
Ghost of Ardan Canile	baritone

Male followers of Alquif, female followers of Urgande; knights; followers and soldiers of Arcalaus, demons disguised as monsters, nymphs, shepherds and shepherdesses; captives and gaolers, flying demons; followers of Urgande, infernal demons, demons of the air; enchanted heroes and heroines

Setting Medieval Britain

1729 *Amadis* was produced in Amsterdam, Marseilles, Rouen, Brussels, The Hague, Lunéville, Lyons and Dijon. In the 1930s Henry Prunières, realizing that he would not live to finish the complete edition of Lully's works, abandoned his chronological approach to the operas and edited *Amadis*. The score is celebrated mainly for its wealth of melody and includes Lully's best known *air*, 'Bois épais'. The libretto was criticized by early commentators for its profusion of events that lack unity and direction.

PROLOGUE Ever since the medieval hero Amadis died, the sorceress Urgande and her husband Alquif have chosen to lie in an enchanted sleep. Now that an even more glorious hero (Louis XIV) controls the world's destiny, they and their followers awaken and celebrate.

ACT 1 *The palace of King Lisuart* The opening scene, a dialogue between Amadis and Florestan made up of seven little *airs* and only a small amount of recitative, establishes the tone of lyricism in this opera. Amadis's first words, 'J'aime, hélas!' over a chromatic bass, set the mood. He and Oriane love each other, though her father has betrothed her to another. Oriane, however, thinks Amadis unfaithful and spurns him in the *air* 'Juste dépit, brisez ma chaîne'. Meanwhile, their confidants, Corisande and Florestan, enjoy each other's love. While knights engage in war games for Oriane's entertainment (*divertissement* with trumpets and timpani), she hides her pain.

ACT 2 *A forest* The sorceress Arcabonne is lovesick over a nameless knight who once saved her life (monologue *air*, 'Amour que veux-tu de moi?'). Her brother Arcalaus eventually distracts her with talk of their enemy Amadis, who killed their brother Ardan Canile; at the moment of distraction a chain of six adjacent *airs* in the same key is broken by modulatory recitative that leads to a climactic imitative duet, 'Irritons notre barbarie'. Meanwhile, Amadis, while trying to hide his sadness in the shadows of the forest (monologue *air*, 'Bois épais'), meets Corisande, who weeps because Florestan has been lured away by an unknown enchantress. They find Arcalaus, who holds Florestan

'Amadis' (Lully), Act 5: design by Jean Berain probably for the original production at the Paris Opéra (Académie Royale de Musique) on 18 January 1684 (the heroes and heroines receive Amadis and Oriane)

prisoner and now takes Corisande as well. Arcalaus calls on the demons to help him fight Amadis: in the *divertissement* demons disguised as monsters fail to defeat him, but those disguised as nymphs and shepherds succeed in enchanting him with love. Thinking one of the nymphs to be Oriane, Amadis puts down his weapons and follows her.

ACT 3 *An old ruined palace* To avenge her dead brother Arcabonne plans to kill not only Amadis but all the prisoners, including Corisande and Florestan. The opening of the act is *divertissement*-like in structure: a static mosaic of fragments for double chorus (prisoners and gaolers), soloists and ensembles, emphasizing minor characters. The dramatic entrance *préludes*, moreover, make use of the machinery and dance troupe: during one of them Arcabonne is carried in by flying demons, and during another the prisoners crawl from their dungeons.

The ghost of Ardan Canile rises briefly from his tomb to predict that Arcabonne will fail to carry out her planned vengeance; their encounter is set as orchestrally accompanied *récitatif mesuré* throughout, the orchestra providing ghostly moans and mysterious thumps in the bass. Then, seeing Amadis for the first time, Arcabonne realizes (in simple recitative) that he is the stranger who once saved her. She cannot kill him, and frees all the others at his request. The former captives rejoice (*divertissement*).

ACT 4 *A pleasant island* As part of Amadis's punishment, Arcalaus has taken Oriane prisoner. Arcabonne agrees to participate in their torture, not out of hatred but out of jealous love. Oriane, lamenting her fate and Amadis's supposed unfaithfulness, suddenly sees Amadis, stretched out on his bloody weapons and apparently dead. In a monologue scene, 'Que vois-je?', she blames herself and faints. As the evil siblings plot their next move, a flaming rock approaches; the flames subside, revealing a ship in the form of a great dragon, which carries the good sorceress Urgande and her followers. In the *divertissement* Urgande's followers undo the evil enchantment and take Amadis and Oriane into the dragon ship with them. In a pantomime ballet during the reprise of a *prélude*, infernal demons come to help Arcalaus and Arcabonne but are vanquished by good demons of the air. Brother and sister together renounce life.

ACT 5 *The enchanted palace of Apollidon* Encouraged by Urgande, Amadis approaches Oriane. She rejoices to find him alive, and he succeeds in convincing her that he loves only her. Urgande offers to obtain the consent of Oriane's father, then directs their attention to an 'arch of loyal lovers'. Florestan, despite his love for Corisande, is prevented by invisible people from passing through the arch; only Amadis succeeds, and as he does, the chorus of invisible people praises his faithful love. A forbidden chamber opens, revealing heroes and heroines who have been held there under an enchantment while awaiting the most faithful of lovers. Their enchantment ended, they receive Amadis and Oriane; this *divertissement* is dominated by a lengthy chaconne.

* * *

Amadis was the first *tragédie en musique* to be based on medieval romance rather than ancient mythology. The score contains a profusion of melody with brief *airs* dominating much of the dialogue. Some, such as the monologue *airs* 'Bois épais' and 'Amour que veux-tu de moi?' – the latter sung by 'every cook in France', according to Le Cerf de la Viéville (*Comparaison*, 1704–6) – became well known. In general, the music represents Lully's most mature style. LOIS ROSOW

Amadis de Gaule ('Amadis of Gaul') [*Amadis des Gaules* ('Amadis of the Gauls')]. *Tragédie lyrique* in three acts by JOHANN CHRISTIAN BACH to a libretto by PHILIPPE QUINAULT revised by Alphonse-Denis-Marie de Vismes du Valgay; Paris, Opéra, 14 December 1779.

Johann Christian Bach's only French opera entered the repertory of the Académie Royale de Musique (with the *haute-contre* Joseph Legros in the title role) between Gluck's *Echo et Narcisse* (24 September 1779) and Piccinni's *Atys* (22 February 1780) and, predictably, satisfied neither the supporters of these two composers nor the traditionalists. The revision of Quinault's 1684 libretto for Lully's *Amadis* was undertaken according to the principles of Marmontel by the cavalry-officer brother of the director of the Opéra. The original prologue and five acts were reduced to three and the subplot involving Florestan and Corisande was eliminated. This drew fierce criticism, which led to the withdrawal of the work from the repertory after the third performance for revision; by the time it returned, following illness among the cast, public interest had cooled and its run ended after only seven performances.

Amadis is Bach's most ambitious opera, with large choral scenes and extensive ballet sequences. It shows a significant enlargement of his harmonic language, with a much greater use of the minor mode and chromaticism.

Dramatically too, Bach seems to have extended his range, as the Gluckian opening of Act 2 in particular shows. The orchestra, used throughout, includes for the first time in Bach's output piccolos ('petites flûtes') and trombones. ERNEST WARBURTON

Amadis de Grèce ('Amadis of Greece'). *Tragédie en musique* in a prologue and five acts by ANDRÉ CARDINAL DESTOUCHES to a libretto by ANTOINE HOUDAR DE LAMOTTE; Paris, Opéra, ?26 March 1699.

After about 1700 chivalric subjects became a popular alternative to mythology for French opera librettos; alongside this went a growing taste for horror and the supernatural, supplied here by the intervention of the sorceress Mélisse (soprano). The plot concerns Amadis (bass) and the Prince of Thrace (*haute-contre*), rival suitors for Niquée (soprano), daughter of the King of Thebes. An *ombre*, the spirit of the Prince, is summoned by Mélisse to help her thwart Amadis's intentions, but pronounces instead the gods' support of Niquée and Amadis. The casting of the *haute-contre* as the unsuccessful lover is unusual. The music contains many illustrations of natural and supernatural phenomena. The scene of the *ombre* in Act 5 (i and ii) gives the orchestra a prominent role: first in the evocation, with irregular flurries of activity in the *prélude* and Mélisse's air and recitative, and then in an obsessive rhythmic motif which accompanies the *ombre*'s appearance and pronouncement. Lamotte's libretto was later adapted for Handel's *Amadigi di Gaula* (1715).

CAROLINE WOOD

Amadori, Giovanni. *See* TEDESCHI, GIOVANNI.

Amahl and the Night Visitors. Opera for television in one act by GIAN CARLO MENOTTI to his own libretto; NBC, New York, 24 December 1951.

The stage is in two parts. One is the stark interior of a shepherd's hut; surrounding it is the exterior showing distant hills, a road winding offstage to the left and reappearing among the hills, and a starry sky with the star of Bethlehem shining brightly. After a very short prelude of soft, tender music Amahl (boy soprano, about 12 years old), who is crippled, is seen and heard (oboe) playing his shepherd's pipe. It is a cheerful C major tune, totally diatonic, over a drone C–G bass 5th. He is seated outside the hut wearing an oversized cloak. His mother (soprano) calls him to go to bed. He delays as long as possible but finally takes his crutch and hobbles into the hut. He tells her of the large bright star and she replies that he is a chronic liar and complains of their poverty. Amahl begins a short duet – comforting his mother – which closes with 'Good night'. While they sleep, he on a bed of straw and she on a bench, the voices of the Three Kings are heard in the distance: Kaspar (tenor), Melchior (baritone) and Balthazar (bass). Amahl wakes up and hobbles to the window. He tells his mother that he sees three kings and, of course, she does not believe him. The kings and a page (baritone) are allowed in by the bewildered mother. They settle in, the kings seated on the bench and the page on a stool, to a stately but sprightly march from the orchestra. During the following conversation there is a humorous song by Kaspar – 'This is my box'. He shows off the precious gems in his box, but most important is the liquorice. He gives some to Amahl. In staged performances this song is often sung with Kaspar walking among the audience tossing out sweets.

The kings speak of the Child they seek, led by the star, and Melchior begins a very moving quartet. Immediately following the quiet close of the quartet the shepherds arrive to a joyful four-part chorus. This is followed by a lively ballet for the shepherds. They then depart on a quiet chorus of good night and farewell which fades into a return of the tender opening music of the opera. All sleep except the mother, who is envying the king's riches. She thinks that they won't miss a little of it, but as she is about to take some she is caught by the page. The kings are stunned and angry at first and Amahl reacts to seeing his mother in the clutches of the page by beating him with his crutch. But Melchior forgives her in a beautiful aria accompanied by the tender opening music. As the kings are about to leave Amahl offers them his crutch, that he made himself, to take to

Set design by Eugene Berman for Menotti's 'Amahl and the Night Visitors': ink and watercolour drawing dated 1952 and dedicated to Thomas Schippers who conducted the original production

the Child: a miracle occurs – he can walk! There is amazement and joy and Amahl begins a lively quintet. They grant Amahl's request to go with the kings and take the crutch to the Child himself. The shepherds are heard in the distance singing of the dawn of peace. Amahl plays his shepherd's pipe as they leave, recapitulating his C major tune from the beginning which gradually fades to silence.

Amahl was the first opera written expressly for American television. The head of the NBC Opera Company, Samuel Chotzinoff, suggested that NBC commission Menotti to write an opera. Menotti at first seemed not very interested in the idea and it lay dormant for several years. A visit to the Metropolitan Museum of Art brought the inspiration, when Menotti was deeply impressed by *The Adoration of the Magi* by the Flemish Renaissance artist Hieronymus Bosch. He began the opera only weeks before the scheduled broadcast on Christmas eve 1951, and rehearsals were begun before the score was completed. The première was a great success and for years the opera was transmitted on Christmas eve. *Amahl* is scored for a small orchestra: two oboes and one each of flute, clarinet, bassoon, horn, trumpet, harp and piano, plus percussion and strings. This factor and the non-virtuoso vocal writing has allowed *Amahl* to be performed by church, college and community opera groups. The music has tonal charm, is diatonic and non-dissonant, and has many memorable melodies. BRUCE ARCHIBALD

Amante di tutte, L' ('The Lover of All Women'). *Dramma giocoso* in three acts by BALDASSARE GALUPPI to a libretto by ANTONIO GALUPPI; Venice, Teatro S Moisè, 15 November 1760.

Don Orazio (bass) suspects his wife Lucinda (soprano) of indiscretion and offers the peasant Mingone (tenor) a reward to spy for him. His suspicions are confirmed when Lucinda invites Marchese Canoppio (alto castrato) and Clarice (soprano), a woman of the most delicate affectation, and receives a third guest, Conte Eugenio (soprano castrato), who by his own admission is hopelessly in love with whichever woman is nearby; he alternately courts Clarice, Lucinda and even the servant Dorina (soprano). Surprised at dinner by Orazio, who has been warned by Mingone, the guests discover they cannot leave, since their coach has departed. Later, Orazio and Mingone thwart a rendezvous between Eugenio and Lucinda. Lucinda, Dorina and Canoppio threaten Mingone for his treachery, and Orazio is outraged; Dorina is given her salary and dismissed, and Canoppio is insulted. In the end Clarice and Eugenio become engaged, Orazio forgives Lucinda, and she reciprocates with an apology. Everyone sings, 'What has happened has happened, and we shouldn't dwell on the past'.

The libretto, by Galuppi's son Antonio, is closely modelled in design on those of Goldoni, but it contains more slapstick than they do (Orazio and Mingone bump heads in the dark, for example). The music for the finale of Act 2, in which Orazio and Mingone wait to catch Clarice and Eugenio, is wonderfully comic and varied; it is one of Galuppi's most accomplished finales. DALE E. MONSON

Amanti generosi, Gl' ('The Generous Lovers'). *Dramma per musica* in three acts by FRANCESCO MANCINI to a libretto by GIOVANNI PIETRO CANDI revised by Giulio Convò and SILVIO STAMPIGLIA; Naples, Teatro S Bartolomeo, ?Carnival 1705.

The opera was the fourth by Mancini to be performed at the S Bartolomeo; the revised libretto included new or additional material by the Neapolitan Abate Convò and comic scenes by Stampiglia. The tale concerns the Persian king Artaserse [Artaxerxes] (contralto) and his problems with two pairs of lovers: his nephew Idaspe [Hydaspes] (soprano) and Berenice (soprano), whom Artaxerxes wants for himself, and his brother Dario [Darius] (contralto) and Mandane (soprano), daughter of the King of Media and a captive of Artaxerxes. Another pair of 'generous lovers' written in by Stampiglia – Ircano (bass), one of Darius's soldiers, and Mandane's maid Drosilla (soprano) – offers comic relief. Artaxerxes plans, with the aid of his captain Arbace [Arbaces] (soprano), to put his rival Hydaspes to death. Arbaces becomes disillusioned with the actions of his king and joins Darius, who attacks Artaxerxes' capital city, Susa. But when Artaxerxes' life is threatened by Darius's soldiers, Darius and Hydaspes protect him, whereupon he admits his past mistakes and gives Berenice to Hydaspes and Mandane to Darius.

In musical style, the opera is typical of the Italian mid to late Baroque, with contrapuntal textures, active bass lines, and short arias mostly in da capo form; continuo arias are usually followed by short ritornellos. The comic scenes depart from this pattern, and are more fluid in structure and progressive in style, with the siciliano metre predominating.

The singers in the original production were Elena Garofalina (Artaxerxes), Angiola Magliani (Darius), Maria Angelica Bracci (Mandane), Caterina Galerati (Berenice), Nicolini (Hydaspes), Maria Maddalena Fratini (Arbaces), Livia Dorotea Nannini (Drosilla) and Giuseppe Ferrari da Ferrara (Ircano). A revision of the work was performed in London at the Queen's Theatre in the Haymarket on 23 March 1710, and again in 1712, under the title *L'Idaspe fedele* or *Hydaspes*. A great success, it was the first opera given in London to be sung entirely in Italian. The same libretto with English translation was published for both runs; in addition to other changes to the Neapolitan version, the comic scenes were deleted. The link between Naples and London was probably Nicolini, who signed the dedication and sang Hydaspes. The scenery for the 1710 production was painted by Marco Rizzi of Venice.

Gl'amanti generosi was also performed in the Teatro del Falcone, Genoa, in 1711 with additional arias (librettist unknown) by Francesco Duni, *maestro di cappella* of Matera and the father of Antonio and Egidio Duni. STEPHEN SHEARON

Amara [Armaganian], **Lucine** (*b* Hartford, CT, 1 March 1927). American soprano of Armenian descent. She studied at San Francisco, where she sang in the opera chorus (1945–6). At the Metropolitan she made her début (1950) as the Heavenly Voice (*Don Carlos*). By her 25th anniversary performance there, as Micaela, she had sung 41 roles in 35 operas, with regular appearances as Leonora (*Il trovatore*), Aida, Butterfly, Mimì, Donna Anna, Pamina, Antonia, Tatyana, Gluck's Eurydice, Nedda and Ellen Orford; she later sang Mother Marie there (1987). At Glyndebourne (1954–8), she sang Ariadne and Donna Elvira. Her voice was clear, cool and refined in timbre and used with sure musicianship though she sometimes lacked dramatic projection. ALAN BLYTH

Amarillo. American city in northwest Texas. It is an important cultural centre of the Texas and Oklahoma panhandles and eastern New Mexico. It has one professional opera company, the Amarillo Opera (founded in 1988 by Mila Gibson), which gives four to five operas annually at the Amarillo Civic Center (2400 seats) and the Amarillo Little Theater (450 seats) during two two-week seasons in September and March. As well as professional musicians from the area the company includes personnel from opera workshops and choral organizations at Amarillo College and nearby West Texas State University (Canyon), and sponsors guest artists from major operatic centres for leading roles; Giorgio Tozzi and Richard Cassilly are among recent guests. Although it performs works from all segments of the repertory, its speciality is opera on American folk topics. The company gave Leonardo Balada's *Hangman, Hangman* in 1989 and Carlisle Floyd's *Susannah* in 1991, and has staged premières of two one-act comic operas by Gene Erwin Murray: *Whirligig*, after O. Henry's *Whirligig of Life* (22 August 1990), and *Dear Doctor* (16 October 1991). It tours extensively and regularly collaborates with other professional musical organizations, notably the Amarillo Symphony and Lone Star Ballet. A. DEAN PALMER

Amato, Pasquale (*b* Naples, 21 March 1878; *d* Jackson Heights, NY, 12 Aug 1942). Italian baritone. He studied in Naples and made his début there in 1900 as Germont. Soon in much demand, he sang at Covent Garden (1904) and at La Scala with Toscanini (1907–8) before making his début at the Metropolitan Opera as Germont in *La traviata* on 20 November 1908. He quickly established himself there, and remained a member of the company until 1921, singing all the principal roles of the Italian repertory, as well as Valentin, Escamillo and many other French parts, and Kurwenal and Amfortas in German. He often sang with Caruso; they appeared together in the 1910 première of Puccini's *La fanciulla del West*, in which Amato sang Jack Rance. He also created the title role in Damrosch's *Cyrano de Bergerac* (1913) and Napoleon in Giordano's *Madame Sans-Gêne* (1915). His voice was of fine quality and extensive range, with brilliant resonance in the upper register; and he made himself into a reliable and complete artist in every respect. His qualities are well shown in a long series of recordings, at first for the Italian firm of Fonotipia (1907–10) and subsequently for Victor (1911–15) and Homocord (1924); the Victor series included some notable Verdi duets with Caruso, Gadski and Hempel.

For illustration *see* FANCIULLA DEL WEST, LA.

*

GV (R. Celletti; R. Vegeto)

P. Kenyon and C. Williams: 'Pasquale Amato', *Record Collector*, xxi (1973–4), 3–47 [with discography]

DESMOND SHAWE-TAYLOR

Amato [D'Amato, De Amato, Di Amato], **(Epifanio) Vincenzo** (*b* Ciminna, nr Palermo, 5 Jan 1629; *d* Palermo, 29 July 1670). Italian composer. His younger brother Paolo was one of Sicily's greatest architects and scenographers; their sister or cousin Eleonora was the mother of Alessandro Scarlatti. Vincenzo spent his life at Palermo, where he obtained a degree in theology and took holy orders. In 1665 he was appointed *maestro di cappella* at the cathedral. Allacci mentions a prose work, *Isauro* (printed at L'Aquila in 1666), by a homonymous author; some lexicographers – probably on this basis – ascribe two operas, *Isaura* (1664, Palermo) and *Aquila* (1666), to Amato. Both are lost, but some of Amato's sacred music survives.

*

AllacciD

G. Bertini: *Dizionario storico-critico degli scrittori di musica e dei più celebri artisti*, i (Palermo, 1814), 28; suppl. (Palermo, 1815), 2

R. Pagano: 'La vita musicale a Palermo e nella Sicilia del Seicento', *NRMI*, iii (1969), 439–66 PAOLO EMILIO CARAPEZZA

Amazone corsara, L' [*L'amazone corsara, ovvero L'Alvilda regina de' Goti* ('The Amazon Pirate, or Alvilda Queen of the Goths')]. *Dramma per musica* in three acts by CARLO PALLAVICINO to a libretto by GIULIO CESARE CORRADI; Venice, Teatro SS Giovanni e Paolo, shortly after 1 February 1686.

L'amazone corsara was produced twice at the Teatro SS Giovanni e Paolo, in 1686 and 1688. Six unattributed productions for other Italian cities between 1688 and 1697 may have used some of Pallavicino's music, although the libretto was reset by Alessandro Scarlatti in 1689. Corradi provides no historical sources for his plot, which is presumably completely fanciful. By the standards of the day, the staging requirements are modest; there are only seven human characters. The allegorical character Fame (soprano) appears in a flying chariot to deliver the prologue. Alvilda, Queen of the Goths (soprano), has become a pirate rather than marry, but Alfo, King of Denmark (tenor), who loves her, has at length defeated and captured her. Alfo's brother Olmiro (soprano) is in love with Gilde (soprano), but her father Ernando (bass) intends her to become a nun. Delio, a courtier (alto), and Alvilda's companion Irene (soprano) also fall in love. Repeatedly rejected by Alvilda, Alfo pretends to marry Gilde and to give the pirate to her as a servant. Finally Alvilda agrees to marry Alfo and the other two couples also unite.

The 62 arias of *L'amazone corsara* include fine examples of Pallavicino's smoothly flowing vocal lines, supported by a continuo that shares the declamatory style of the voice part. Most of these arias follow the refrain form of da capo design. Only ten call for upper melodic instruments in addition to continuo. The instrumental scoring is for five parts (presumably two violins, two violas and cello) along with continuo. Although the libretto refers to trumpets, there is no reference to trumpets in the score (*D-Mbs*). The single walking bass, in Delio's aria 'Sono in traccia del mio bene', is a clear instance of word painting. Two other arias have exceptional continuo parts: steady quavers are maintained throughout Olmiro's 'A dispetto delle stelle' while Alfo's 'Amor, assistimi' has the same rhythmic ostinato in a descending scalar pattern. Gilde's 'Non ha tante stelle il ciel' has an obbligato bass part, presumably for cello. STEPHEN C. FISHER, HARRIS S. SAUNDERS

Ambigu-Comique. Theatre in Paris, founded in the late 18th century. In 1807 it became one of the four official secondary theatres. It was little used for opera after 1815 and burnt down in 1827. *See* PARIS, §4 (i, vii).

Ambleto ('Hamlet'). *Dramma per musica* in three acts by FRANCESCO GASPARINI to a libretto by APOSTOLO ZENO and PIETRO PARIATI after Saxo Grammaticus: *Historiae Danicae*; Venice, Teatro S Cassiano, Carnival 1706.

Ambleto was first performed during the week before 16 January 1706, with the alto castrato Nicolini in the title role. The libretto is based on Saxo Grammaticus, one of Shakespeare's indirect sources. The characters in *Ambleto* parallel those in Shakespeare's play: Ambleto (alto castrato) corresponds to Hamlet, Veremonda (soprano) to Ophelia, Gerilda (soprano) to Gertrude, Fengone (bass) to Claudius and Valdemaro (soprano castrato) to Fortinbras. There is neither incest theme nor ghost, but love complications abound. Fengone and Valdemaro are both in love with Veremonda, a princess in her own right, who is true to Hamlet. Another Danish princess, Ildegarde (contralto), who was Fengone's mistress before he usurped the throne, is also in love with Hamlet. Twice Hamlet foils Fengone's attempts to unmask his madness as pretence. The usurper's resolve to repudiate Gerilda and marry Veremonda precipitates the crisis. Fengone forces Gerilda and Veremonda to bow to his wishes by threatening to kill Hamlet; but during a bacchanalian revel, Hamlet arranges to administer a sleeping draught to him and he awakens in chains. As the newly acknowledged king, Hamlet sentences Fengone to a slow death, but the officer in charge takes it upon himself to dispatch him swiftly. Hamlet will marry Veremonda and reign along with his mother; Valdemaro will marry Ildegarde.

Ambleto was among the first Italian operas produced on the London stage; Nicolini was probably behind the production, which opened at the Haymarket on 27 February 1712. He again assumed the title role and was probably responsible for introducing arias from other Venetian productions in which he had participated. Hamlet's feigned madness provided brilliant display pieces for his acting talents. The publication in London (1712) of songs from *Ambleto* is the most important musical source for the opera. The arias that survive from the London production illustrate Gasparini's taut musical language, in particular his graceful vocal melodies and his contrapuntal instrumental parts. By varying key, metre, instrumentation and declamatory style, Gasparini skilfully highlights affective contrasts from one aria to the next. HARRIS S. SAUNDERS

Ambrogietti [Ambrogetti], **Giuseppe** (*b* 1780; *d* after 1833). Italian bass. He sang in Italy from about 1807, then appeared at the Théâtre Italien, Paris (1815). Engaged at the King's Theatre, London, he made his début as Count Almaviva, then sang Don Giovanni (1817), Dr Bartolo in *Il barbiere di Siviglia* (1818), Taddeo in *L'italiana in Algeri* (1819) and Don Magnifico in *La Cenerentola* (1820), all first British performances. He also sang Uberto in Paer's *Agnese*, Count Robinson in *Il matrimonio segreto*, Don Rospolone in Paisiello's *La molinara* and Papageno. Superbly comic in *buffo* roles, he was an elegant Don Giovanni, while his tragic acting was compared to that of Kemble and Kean. He became a Trappist monk in 1833. ELIZABETH FORBES

Ambros, Vladimír (*b* Prostějov, 18 Sept 1890; *d* Prostějov, 12 May 1956). Czech composer. He studied at Brno and Frankfurt, where he was taught composition by Knorr. He was répétiteur at the Frankfurt Opera (1911–13), conductor of the Carl Rosa company and répétiteur at Covent Garden (1915–18). After returning to Czechoslovakia in 1921 he worked in Prostějov as a teacher, choirmaster and conductor, and was head of the Břeclav School of Music, 1926–8. At first influenced by Janáček, as in the opera *Ukradené štěstí* ('Stolen Happiness'), Ambros later successfully assimilated Novákian impressionism. In a final period (1945–56) he turned to a socialist realist technique, basing his works on contemporary subjects, though his only opera from this period, *Maryla* (1949–51), is an idyll set in the 15th century. Ambros was most successful, however, with miniatures and works for children.

Ukradené štěstí [Stolen Happiness] (3, Zahradníkova-Krapková, after I. Frank), Brno, 19 Feb 1925, vs (Prostějov, 1926)
El Christo de la Luz [Christ of the Light] (radio op, 3, based on J. Zeyer), Czechoslovak radio, 30 March 1929; stage, Bratislava, 18 Sept 1930
To mě těší [The Pleasure is Mine], 1931 (comic op), unperf.
Ozvěna [The Echo], 1936 (radio op), inc.
Maryla (3, after A. Jirásek), Olomouc, 10 Oct 1953

*

J. Hutter and Z. Chalabala, eds.: *České umění dramatické*, ii: *Zpěvohra* [Czech Dramatic Art: Opera] (Prague, 1941)
V. Gregor: *Vladimír Ambros* (Prostějov, 1969)

VLADIMÍR HUDEC

Ambrosch, Joseph Karl [Ambrož, Josef Karel] (*b* Český Krumlov, 6 May 1759; *d* Berlin, 8 Sept 1822). German tenor and composer of Czech descent. He studied with J. A. Kozeluch in Prague and made his début in Bayreuth in 1784. From 1791 to 1811 he was first tenor of the Königliches Opernhaus in Berlin, where he remained a prominent and respected musical figure until his death. His published lieder include two complete volumes (1796) and contributions to contemporary anthologies. His daughter Wilhelmine Ambrosch Becker (*b* Berlin, 1791) was a pianist and singer in Berlin and later first soprano of the Hamburg city theatre.

Ambrosio, Giacomo [Jacovo] **d'.** Italian 18th-century composer and singer; *see* VENTURA, GIUSEPPE.

Amelia al ballo ('Amelia Goes to the Ball'). *Opera buffa* in one act by GIAN CARLO MENOTTI to his own libretto; Philadelphia, Academy of Music, 1 April 1937 (in English).

Written when Menotti was 23, *Amelia al ballo* became his first major success. It was given its première, in an English translation by George Mead, by members of the Curtis Institute of Music (where Menotti had studied). It was performed at the Metropolitan Opera in New York on 3 March 1938; the first performance in Italian was at San Remo on 4 April 1938. Amelia (soprano) is dressing for a ball when her husband (baritone) storms in, having found a love letter to her. He leaves angrily and her lover (tenor) enters through a window; they sing a duet. The husband returns and during the ensuing argument Amelia, becoming ever more impatient at not going to the ball, breaks a vase on her husband's head. She blames her lover when the police arrive: her husband goes to the hospital, her lover to gaol. But Amelia has her wish, as the chief of police (bass) takes her to the ball. A joyful C major chorus from the gathered crowd closes the opera.

Amelia was begun in Vienna while Menotti and Samuel Barber were on holiday together. The work is in traditional *buffa* format with set numbers (*duettino*, *romanza*, etc.) connected by accompanied recitatives, so that the music is continuous as in late Verdi and Puccini. The music is rhythmically energetic or pleasantly lyrical in a conservative, tonal language with only slight touches of dissonance. BRUCE ARCHIBALD

Amendola, Giuseppe (*b* ?Palermo, *c*1750; *d* ? Palermo, 1808). Italian composer. Between 1772 and 1792 he was active in Palermo where an *Orfeo* of his was given at the Teatro S Cecilia. His only known opera, the *dramma giocoso Il Begliar-Bey di Caramania* (probably to a libretto by G. Tonioli; scores *F-Pn*, *D-Dlb*, *Rtt*), was apparently first performed in Madrid in 1776; it was probably given in Bologna in 1778 (as *La schiava fedele*), and subsequently achieved notable success in other European capitals. About 1790 he is believed to have given the young Isouard lessons in harmony involving study of the operas of Leo and Durante.

U. Rolandi: *Musica e musicisti in Malta* (Livorno, 1932), 67–8

JAMES L. JACKMAN

American Opera Company. Company, also known as the National Opera Company, founded by Jeannette Thurber in 1885 to encourage the cultivation of American singers and the performance of foreign-language works in English; under the direction of Theodore Thomas, it toured the north-east in 1886 and again in 1887, collapsing in Buffalo and disbanding after a few performances in its 1887–8 season. *See* TRAVELLING TROUPES, §5(ii).

Amicis, Anna Lucia de. *See* DE AMICIS, ANNA LUCIA.

Amico, Fedele d'. *See* D'AMICO, FEDELE.

Amico Fritz, L' ('Friend Fritz'). *Commedia lirica* in three acts by PIETRO MASCAGNI to a libretto by P. Suardon (Nicola Daspuro) from ERCKMANN-CHATRIAN's story *L'ami Fritz*; Rome, Teatro Costanzi, 31 October 1891.

The sensational success of *Cavalleria rusticana* in 1890 aroused hopes that the precarious state in which Italian opera had existed for some decades was reaching a turning-point. In the next year Mascagni fulfilled those high hopes with *L'amico Fritz*, consolidating his already international reputation as the most promising composer of the younger generation. The première, hailed as the most important operatic event since that of *Otello*, was a triumph, and the work immediately had many further performances; it seemed at first that it would be just as successful as Mascagni's first opera. With Fritz Kobus's house and estate in Alsace, Mascagni had again chosen a rural setting, but the choice of a sentimental subject in the *comédie larmoyante* tradition shows that he was deliberately aiming for a contrast with the stark realism of *Cavalleria*.

The action of the piece (described, like *Falstaff* later, as a 'commedia lirica') is extremely innocuous, offering no scope for moments of intense drama and outbursts of passion. The prosperous landowner Fritz Kobus (tenor), a confirmed bachelor, leads a contented life, sufficient to himself, until his friend, the rabbi and enthusiastic matchmaker David (baritone), tricks him out of his epicurean attitude and marries him to the attractive Suzel (soprano), daughter of the steward of his estate. In this opera the absence of external drama led Mascagni inevitably to a psychologically subtler depiction of the characters and their emotions: Fritz and Suzel, in the torments of unavowed love and in their happiness after they have declared themselves, are drawn in more detail than the characters of *Cavalleria*.

Much of the orchestral writing has the limpid quality of chamber music, mellow and impressionistic; the woodwind instruments are given prominence to emphasize the pastoral setting or, as in the Preludietto, the humorous undertones and lighter character of the piece. It is noteworthy that almost as much attention is paid to atmosphere as to the action. The introduction of two genuine Alsatian folksongs provides direct local colour, but in addition the greatest care is lavished on the depiction of the idyllic ambience in general. For instance, Mascagni keeps the chorus out of sight behind the set, using it purely to establish mood, a novelty which also preserves the intimate character of the action.

Stylistic variety distinguishes the treatment of the voices: the spectrum ranges from voluptuous cantilena, as in the second part of the famous Cherry Duet, to the surprisingly novel, flexible and elegant conversational tone Mascagni employs for the dialogue at the beginning of the opera. Parlando, often overlying a sustained orchestral melody, is used to singular effect, as are also (far more than in *Cavalleria*) vocal themes recurring in the orchestra, so that there is a high degree of musical unity, particularly within each act. As to genre, the fundamental tone of sensibility in the opera, which finds expression in the prevalence of elegiac colours, suggests in combination with the idyllic setting that it belongs in the category of *opera semiseria*. In this respect *L'amico Fritz* shows close points of contact with Bellini's *Sonnambula* and may be regarded as a late example of that independent genre standing between *opera seria* and *opera buffa*.

PETER ROSS

Amiconi [Amigoni], **Jacopo** (*b* Venice or Naples, 1682; *d* Madrid, 1752). Italian designer. He studied in Naples and with Belluchi in Düsseldorf, and was employed at the court of Bavaria (1717–27). He went to England with Farinelli and Bononcini in 1729, and probably through their influence was engaged as principal painter at the King's Theatre in London. According to Henry Angelo (*Reminiscences*, i, London, 1828, pp.12–13), 'nothing had been seen equally splendid and imposing with this department of stage effect, in England, before this epoch'. Rich engaged him for the opening of the Covent Garden Theatre in 1732, for which he designed the ceiling and where he worked as scene painter with Lambert and Harvey. He returned to Venice in 1739 and was also in Paris and at the court of St Petersburg. He returned to the King's Theatre in 1741, remaining there for only one season, after which he became court painter at Madrid.

SYBIL ROSENFELD

Amirov, Fikret (Meshadi Jamil') (*b* Gyandzha, 22 Nov 1922; *d* Baku, 20 Feb 1984). Azerbaijani composer. The son of a famous *tar* player and singer, he studied at the Kirovabad Music College and Baku College, and from 1939 at the Azerbaijan State Conservatory where his teachers included Zeydman and Hajibeyov. His studies were interrupted by the war, in which he served and was wounded. Returning to the conservatory, he submitted his first opera, *Ulduz*, for his diploma in 1948; written to a text by I. Idayat-zade, it has never been staged. Amirov's passionate interest in his native music bore its finest fruit in his two symphonic *mugam* (1948), based on the indigenous song-dance form of that name, and in his second opera, *Sevil'* (1953, Baku), in four acts, to a libretto by Talet Eyubov. *Sevil'* was published in 1953 and revised twice, in 1955 and 1959. In 1956, after holding important musical posts in Azerbaijan, Amirov was appointed secretary to the Azerbaijani Composers'

Union; he was director of the Azerbaijani Theatre of Opera and Ballet, 1956–9. He became National Artist of the USSR in 1965.

See also SEVIL'.

L. Karagicheva and G. Ismaylova: '*Sevil'* (Opera Fikreta Amirova)', *SovM* (1954), no.4, 39–46

D. Danilov: *Opera 'Sevil' ' Fikreta Amirova* (Baku, 1959)

S. Kasimova: 'Narodnïye istoki muzïkal'nogo yazïka operï *Sevil'* Amirova' [The Folk Origins of the Musical Language of Amirov's Opera *Sevil'*], *Uchyonïye zapiski Azerbaydzhanskoy gosudarstvennoy konservatorii* [Transactions of the Azerbaijan State Conservatory] (1964), no.1, p.37

YURIY GABAY/STEPHEN JOHNSON

Amleto (i) ('Hamlet'). *Opera seria* in two acts by GAETANO ANDREOZZI to a libretto by GIUSEPPE MARIA FOPPA after a tragedy by Jean-François Ducis; Padua, Teatro Nuovo, 12 June 1792.

Amleto (soprano castrato) is tormented by his father's ghost demanding revenge for his murder. In an attempt to learn who committed the deed, all gather at his funeral urn. As Amleto's mother Geltrude (soprano) and her lover Claudio (tenor) approach, the urn bursts into flames. Amleto holds Claudio responsible. Amelia (mezzo-soprano), Claudio's daughter and Amleto's betrothed, reports to Geltrude and Noresto (mezzo-soprano castrato) that conspirators are seeking Amleto's death. In the final scene Claudio fatally wounds Geltrude. Amleto captures him and bids a heartbroken farewell to his dying mother.

Typical of the 1790s, the opera opens with an *introduzione* – a dialogue for Claudio and a chorus of conspirators in obbligato recitative, arioso and ensemble. The body of the work is principally a succession of recitatives and arias. New to *opera seria* are Geltrude's dialogue with chorus (1.x) and Amleto's cavatina (1.vi) and aria (2.vii), with *pertichini* (interjections) by others and sometimes by the chorus. The middle section of Amleto's aria encompasses action as the guilty couple step forward and the urn bursts into flames; the aria concludes with the reaction of Amleto and a chorus of witnesses. Andreozzi uses obbligato recitative sparingly, and only in the final scene does it depart from its traditionally static function. The opera is unusual for its lavish use of winds, in solos and as a section. Both rounded and unrounded ternary arias appear, often with two or three tempos and ranging from a terse declamatory style to broad melodies that gather embellishments and move into melismatic display. The full orchestra gives way to minimal accompaniments when the voice enters, but returns in vocal caesuras to contribute motivic commentary or *forte-piano* contrasts and to support the voice in long crescendos. MARITA P. McCLYMONDS

Amleto (ii) ('Hamlet'). *Tragedia lirica* in four acts by FRANCO FACCIO to a libretto by ARRIGO BOITO after WILLIAM SHAKESPEARE's play *Hamlet*; Genoa, Teatro Carlo Felice, 30 May 1865 (revised, Milan, Teatro alla Scala, 9 February 1871).

The second and last of Faccio's operas, *Amleto* commands attention for two reasons. First, it marks an effort of two prominent members of the Scapigliatura (a late Romantic reform movement in northern Italy in the 1860s and 70s) to renew the tradition of Italian opera. Second, as the first of Boito's librettos derived from Shakespeare, it reveals the future poet of *Otello* and *Falstaff* collaborating with a far less experienced and gifted composer than Verdi. The libretto gives an Italian equivalent for many of the famous passages and images of Shakespeare's text, but it possesses a decidedly un-Shakespearean flavour due to its metrical variety and self-consciously wide range of vocabulary. Undeniably it is a literary tour de force: learned, but callow.

Act 1 contrasts the celebration of the coronation of Claudio [Claudius] (baritone) with Orazio [Horatio] and Marcello's account of the ghost. Amleto [Hamlet] (tenor) then sees the ghost (bass), who, as one from Purgatory, addresses him in *terza rima*. The second act begins with the interview between Hamlet and Ofelia [Ophelia] (soprano); this is followed by the announcement of the players' arrival, and then the play within the play. In Act 3 the king prays, and Hamlet confronts his mother (soprano); Laerte [Laertes] (tenor) leads a revolt, and Claudius reveals that Hamlet is responsible for the death of Polonio [Polonius] (bass); then follows Ophelia's mad scene. The final act takes place at Ophelia's grave; Laertes duels with Hamlet, who disarms him and then stabs the king. The opera ends with Hamlet begging Ophelia's forgiveness.

WILLIAM ASHBROOK

Amor coniugale, L' ('Conjugal Love'). *Farsa sentimentale* in one act by SIMON MAYR to a libretto by GAETANO ROSSI after JEAN-NICOLAS BOUILLY's libretto *Léonore, ou L'amour conjugal*; Padua, Teatro Nuovo, 26 July 1805.

Mayr's opera is the third of four works based on Bouilly's story; the others are by Gaveaux (*Léonore, ou L'amour conjugal*, 1798), Paer (*Leonora, ossia L'amore conjugale*, 1804) and, of course, Beethoven (*Leonore*, later *Fidelio*). In contrast to the other Italian opera on the story by Paer and his librettist Giovanni Schmidt, which adheres closely to the original source, Mayr's incorporates numerous revisions. With the action moved from Spain to 17th-century Poland, it joined the vogue for Polish rescue operas at the turn of the century which included Cherubini's *Lodoïska* (1791, reset by Mayr in 1796) and *Faniska* (1806). Rossi reduced the number of acts from two to one, rearranged several scenes, eliminated the chorus, renamed most of the characters and changed their personalities. He transformed the politically motivated, vindictive Pizarre into the love-crazed, cowardly Moroski (bass), made Léonore into the ardently passionate, yet somewhat naive Zeliska/Malvino (soprano), gave the saucy wench Marcelline an idealistic, serious side as the character Floreska (soprano), and treated her father, now Peters (bass) instead of Roc, as an object of ridicule. The hero, Amorveno (tenor), is rescued by his brother Ardelao (tenor).

Mayr's *Amor coniugale* was one of his most successful operas, receiving performances during the years following its première in Bologna, Naples, Milan and many other European cities. It is notable for its high proportion of action ensembles and for Mayr's skilful blending of comic and serious elements.

SCOTT L. BALTHAZAR

Amor contrastato, L'. Opera by Giovanni Paisiello; *see* MOLINARA, LA.

Amor d'un ombra e gelosia d'un aura. Opera by Domenico Scarlatti; *see* NARCISO.

Amore artigiano, L' ('Love among the Artisans'). *Opera buffa* in three acts by FLORIAN LEOPOLD GASSMANN to a libretto by CARLO GOLDONI; Vienna, Burgtheater, 26 April 1767.

One of Gassmann's most enduring successes, this opera was performed throughout Austria, Italy and Germany, sometimes in translation as *Die Liebe unter den Handwerksleuten*; Haydn oversaw three productions at Eszterháza. The libretto, first set in 1760 by Gaetano Latilla, is the second instalment in a trilogy depicting love among the various classes of society. The artisans of the title include the blacksmith Titta (tenor), the carpenter Giannino (tenor) and the elderly cobbler Bernardo (bass), who run adjacent shops in the village square; romantic entanglements involve Rosina, a dressmaker and Bernardo's daughter (soprano), and the milliner Angiolina (contralto). The cast is completed by Madame Costanza, a wealthy widow of a certain age (soprano), in love with her French valet Girò (tenor). In fact, the libretto is an extensive revision of Goldoni's original, expanding the ensemble finales of all three acts from three sections to four or even five; sudden shifts in the action are matched by changes, sometimes abrupt, of key, tempo and metre. The role of the valet is also expanded, and his French nationality (Gassmann's invention) gives rise to many gently satirical invocations of French music (generally the minuet). JOSHUA KOSMAN

Amore dei tre re, L' ('The Love of Three Kings'). *Poema tragico* in three acts by ITALO MONTEMEZZI to a libretto by SEM BENELLI after his play; Milan, Teatro alla Scala, 10 April 1913.

The action is set in the Middle Ages in a remote castle in Italy 40 years after a barbarian invasion. In the first act Baron Archibaldo (bass), old and blind, is wandering restlessly around his castle at night, reflecting on his heroic youth when he, a barbarian, had conquered Italy. His son Manfredo (baritone) is away fighting, and Manfredo's young Italian wife Fiora (soprano) has been left in the castle, where she meets her lover Avito (tenor), also an Italian, at night. Archibaldo guesses that they have an adulterous relationship and interrogates Fiora, but his blindness prevents him from discovering the truth and he has to repress his hatred of her. When Manfredo returns, innocently happy at seeing Fiora again, she receives him with cold courtesy.

In the second act Manfredo departs again, embittered and full of foreboding; he asks Fiora to climb to the top of the castle tower and send him on his way, waving a white scarf. Fiora, moved by her husband's goodness, promises to do so, but after he has left she is joined on the tower by Avito; she at first tries to repel his advances, but falls once more into his arms. Archibaldo arrives; Avito manages to avoid him, but the baron has heard his footsteps and insists that Fiora reveal the name of her lover. When she proudly refuses he strangles her just before Manfredo returns in haste.

In the third act the people pay their respects to the dead Fiora in the castle crypt; when they leave, Avito enters and as he kisses his dead beloved he sways and falls. Manfredo appears and tells him that Archibaldo has sprinkled Fiora's lips with poison in order to discover the identity of her lover. But Manfredo does not wish for revenge; alone and in despair, he in turn kisses Fiora's lips. His old father gropes his way into the crypt and, hearing a groan, thinks he has caught the adulterer, but finds in his arms his dying son.

The story has clear echoes of *Tristan* in the lovers' rapturous desire for annihilation and in a structure centring on the great love duet of the second act, and of *Pelléas* in the presence of symbolist elements and the impersonality of three young people whose unwitting actions seem to be governed by a fatal destiny. Against them the powerful figure of the old blind baron stands out, struggling against his own physical impotence and providing the mainspring of the action (he is on stage at the end of each act). But there are also contrasting ethnic and moral elements, as the ferocity of the old barbarian is set against the nobility of the young Italians and the Italian-born Manfredo. The music is also affected by the two poles of Wagner and Debussy. The extraordinary density of the orchestral writing and the harmonic language suggest Wagner, notably when personalities and the relationships of the characters are depicted (for example the furious anger of Archibaldo and the inevitable chromatic writing of the love scenes), while Debussy is recalled in the enigmatic evocation of atmosphere and in the trance-like suspended sonorities (the text repeatedly refers to a dream state in which the characters move). The subtle orchestration is indebted to both composers. The plot is advanced through dialogue: the 'hidden arias' typical of early 20th-century Italian opera occur only rarely (for Archibaldo at the beginning of the first act, for Manfredo at the beginning of the second), but the only relationships that are developed are those between the two lovers and between Fiora and Archibaldo. The character of Manfredo is hardly comprehensible, especially given the extreme brevity of the third act in which he might have been made the leading figure. There are leitmotifs of various kinds throughout the opera, some with a clear thematic outline such as those for the love between Fiora and Avito and for Archibaldo's ferocity, and others more allusive, such as the sequence of rhythmically irregular chords signalling the approach of the blind baron. The ostinato figures have an essential function. In some cases they have a precise meaning, such as the swift dactylic rhythm associated with barbarity, war and invasion; elsewhere they combine to form groups of suspended sonorities. The orchestration itself has a strong semantic value: a good example is provided by the sustained chords of pairs of woodwind linked to the cold courtesy with which Fiora addresses her husband.

After the success of the first performance at La Scala, *L'amore dei tre re* was heard by Toscanini and Gatti-Casazza, who decided to stage it in New York, and thus began the extraordinary worldwide rise of the opera, hailed on its appearance as one of the great masterpieces of the 20th century, equal to those of Debussy and Strauss. Grout described it as 'without doubt the greatest Italian tragic opera since Verdi's *Otello*' (*A Short History of Opera*, 1947, p.444). It was always more popular in the USA than in Europe, but like Montemezzi's other operas, it has in recent decades practically disappeared from the repertory, despite occasional revivals. LUCA ZOPPELLI

Amore medico, L' [*Der Liebhaber als Arzt*] ('Love the Doctor'). Comic opera in two acts by ERMANNO WOLF-FERRARI to a libretto by ENRICO GOLISCIANI after MOLIÈRE's play *L'amour médecin*; Dresden, Hoftheater, 4 December 1913.

After his uncharacteristic excursion into post-Mascagnian *verismo* in *I gioielli della Madonna* (1911), Wolf-Ferrari returned, in this sixth of his published operas, to that special vein of lighthearted satirical comedy in which he most often gave of his best. *L'amore medico* may not be quite as unfailingly polished and spontaneous as *I quatro rusteghi* (1906), but there is no question of mere self-repetition: the music contains some notable new departures, as well as having more than enough typically Wolf-Ferrarian sparkle to make it surprising that the work has remained so little known.

Whereas the composer's two most remarkable previous comic operas had been quite closely based on plays by Goldoni, Golisciani's adaptation of one of Molière's shorter comedies is somewhat freer: in addition to converting the text (for much of the time) into Italian rhyming verse, he added many picturesque and theatrically effective details. Nevertheless the basic drift of the plot remains unchanged. Arnolfo (baritone) – equivalent to Molière's Sganarelle – has a daughter Lucinda (soprano) whom he jealously wants to keep as his companion for the rest of his life. But the girl develops a mysterious debilitating illness. Ignoring the down-to-earth advice of his quick-witted servant Lisetta (soprano) – who insistently identifies the malady as the need for a husband – Arnolfo sends simultaneously for four doctors (tenor, two baritones and a bass), who pompously give contradictory diagnoses and are clearly interested only in their fees. Meanwhile, however, Lisetta has found a physician of a very different sort: he is in fact Clitandro (tenor), whom Lucinda already loves from afar. With Lisetta's help this new young 'doctor' persuades Arnolfo to let him demonstrate his special technique: he declares that by 'pretending' to be a suitor, and by continuing the 'charade' right up to and including a 'false' marriage ceremony, he will surely and irreversibly cure the girl's sickness, which is a sickness of the soul. Only when it is too late does it dawn on Arnolfo that not only was Clitandro's wooing genuine, but so was the wedding itself.

In *L'amore medico* the musico-dramatic approach relates to the *opera buffa* tradition in much the same free yet unmistakable way as in the composer's preceding Goldoni operas. Moreover the satire is again from time to time reinforced by overt musical parody: for example the ensemble in which the four doctors solemnly state their various diagnoses is introduced by a wilfully tortuous yet ruthlessly academic fugue. However, Wolf-Ferrari's harmonic language was now reaching out, at least intermittently, well beyond that used in his previous operas, towards a more pervasive and versatile chromaticism: the resultant unassuming but fresh and unpredictable sound-world in some ways parallels that of certain lighter pieces by Busoni.

JOHN C. G. WATERHOUSE

Amorevoli, Angelo (Maria) (*b* Venice, 16 Sept 1716; *d* Dresden, 15 Nov 1798). Italian tenor. After establishing his reputation in Porpora's *Mitridate* and *Siface* (1730, Rome) and Hasse's *Dalisa* (1730, Venice), he sang in Milan (1731–5) and Naples (1736–40), where he appeared in ten productions, including Sarro's *Achille in Sciro*, which inaugurated the Teatro S Carlo (1737). Horace Mann heard him in Giuseppe Scarlatti's *Arminio* (1741, Florence) and recommended him to Horace Walpole, who reported that the pasticcio *Alexander in Persia* (1741, London) owed its success entirely to Amorevoli. After singing in ten other operas at the King's Theatre (1742–3) and in Milan (1744–5), he made Dresden his home from 1745 in order to sing Hasse's music, except for visits to Vienna (where Metastasio praised his singing in 1748) and Milan (1748–9 and 1760–61). He retired from the stage in 1764. Burney wrote that he had heard better tenor voices 'but never, on the stage, more taste and expression'.

*

BurneyH; *ES* (E. Zanetti)

B. Brunelli, ed.: *Tutte le opere di Pietro Metastasio*, iii (Milan, 1951), 352, 605f, 1223, 1240

W. S. Lewis, ed.: *The Yale Edition of Horace Walpole's Correspondence: Horace Walpole's Correspondence with Sir Horace Mann*, i–ii (New Haven, 1955)

SVEN HANSELL

Amori di Ergasto, Gli ('The Loves of Ergasto'). Pastoral in a prologue and three acts by JAKOB GREBER to a libretto after A. Amalteo; London, Queen's Theatre, Haymarket, 9 April 1705.

Gli amori di Ergasto, the music of which does not survive, was the first Italian opera produced in London in Italian and inaugurated John Vanbrugh's Haymarket Theatre, the principal opera house in London until 1789. Vanbrugh and his partner William Congreve were planning to open with either a play or perhaps Eccles's English opera *Semele*, but the unexpected success of Thomas Clayton's *Arsinoe* at the rival Drury Lane Theatre prompted them to opt for an Italian opera. Greber, a German who had studied in Italy before his arrival in England about 1703, evidently composed the score at short notice. In *Roscius anglicanus* (1708), the prompter John Downes said that *Gli amori* was performed 'by a new set of Singers, Arriv'd from *Italy*; (the worst that e're came from thence) for it lasted but 5 Days, and they being lik'd but indifferently by the Gentry; they in a little time marcht back to their own Country'. It is, however, unlikely that any singers were specially imported for this opera, which requires only four: Licori (probably doubling as Cupid in the prologue), Phillis, Ergasto and Filandro. Greber was closely associated with Margherita de l'Epine, one of the sopranos in *Arsinoe*; but the only singer known to have taken part in *Gli amori di Ergasto* is Joanna Maria Lindelheim ('The Baroness'). In a diary kept while he was in London, Kusser recorded that Greber was paid 1000 guineas for the opera, which was supposedly scheduled for only six performances. This sum is hardly credible: the Baroness received just 50 guineas for her services, half what Vanbrugh and Congreve originally promised her.

There is some doubt whether *Gli amori* was sung in Italian. Its main competitors *Arsinoe* and *Camilla* were sung in English, and no London opera is certain to have been performed entirely in Italian until 1709. Yet its libretto is printed in Italian with a parallel English translation on facing pages, an arrangement which strongly suggests a foreign-language performance. Based on a libretto by A. Amalteo (Vienna, 1661), the plot is a slight tale of pastoral love, in which one of the couples, Phillis and Filandro, are revealed in Act 3 as long-lost brother and sister. The hunting scene in Act 1, during which Ergasto comes upon Licori singing 'in her sleep', is reminiscent of scenes in the English operas *Venus and Adonis* and *Dido and Aeneas*; and it may be no coincidence that the dog that assists Ergasto in killing a wild boar shares its name with one of Adonis's pack, Melampus. The opera included mainly da capo arias, perhaps as many as 20, plus two duets and a final chorus. In 1711 Greber composed another opera called *Gli amori di Ergasto* for Vienna, but this appears to bear no relation to the London libretto, except in its title. CURTIS PRICE

Amor non vuole inganni, L'. Opera by Alessandro Scarlatti; *see* EQUIVOCI NEL SEMBIANTE, GLI.

Amor vuol sofferenza ('Love Demands Pain') [*La frascatana* ('The Woman from Frascati'); *Il cioè* ('Mr That-is-to-Say')]. *Commedia per musica* in three acts by LEONARDO LEO to a libretto by GENNARO ANTONIO FEDERICO; Naples, Teatro Nuovo, autumn 1739.

Amor vuol sofferenza is one of the finest surviving examples of the Neapolitan dialect comedy tradition, with the librettist at pains to ensure cohesion between the *seria* and *buffa* characters by a complex web of relationships. The three *buffa* characters recall masks from the *commedia dell'arte*: Mosca (bass), the scheming coachman, as Brighella, out to fleece a rich foreigner; Fazio Tonti (bass), the rich, gullible Lucchese, as Pantaloon the dupe; and Vastarella (soprano), the baker, as the flirtatious and streetwise soubrette. Typical of this genre, the comicality depends on intrigue and misunderstanding, on characterization in the *buffa* parts, and on spoofs of the *opera seria*, including incongruous use of Metastasian clichés. The music is in the *galant* style; the *buffa* arias draw, for their characterization, on techniques explored typically in the contemporary intermezzos. The *seria* story follows the stock *commedia* procedure in which, at the outset, all the male characters have strayed to the 'wrong' partners, and the couples are happily reunited only after much 'sofferenza'. The first production of this opera drew from Charles de Brosses the much-quoted remark: 'Quelle invention! quelle harmonie! quelle excellente plaisanterie musicale!' After Federico's death, an anonymous librettist was employed to recast the comedy as *La finta frascatana* (1744), leaving Vastarella as the only Neapolitan role. Leo died shortly after starting work on the new version, and the music was completed by Matteo Capranica. A completely Tuscan version reached London in 1749, and a setting by Gioacchino Cocchi, as *Li matti per amore*, now lacking the *seria* soprano roles of Alessandro and Camilla, was performed in Venice in 1754 and in Berlin in 1764.

GRAHAM HARDIE

Amour, fléchy par la constance, L' ('Love Moved by Constancy'). *Pastorale* in nine scenes by MICHEL-RICHARD DE LALANDE; Fontainebleau, autumn 1697.

An occasional piece for the French court, *L'amour, fléchy par la constance* represents the reduced scope of Lalande's middle-period stage compositions following the War of the League of Augsburg. The work played twice at Fontainebleau in autumn 1697 as a *concert*, and may have been repeated with dancing at Versailles in December for the wedding of the Duc and Duchesse de Bourgogne. The theme is one of disrupted and then reconciled love among shepherds and the setting is a forest near a temple to Amour; the librettist is unknown. Tircis (*haute-contre*) with Philis (soprano) and Climene (soprano) with Daphnis (baritone) lament love's travails, while the chorus affirms its pleasures. The nine scenes display organic unity: for example, solo and ensemble singing is well balanced by choral music and the extended chorus and instrumental *passacaille* in Scene 5 form the centrepiece of the composition. Climene's *air* in Scene 3 contains the only written-out *double* in Lalande's stage works. The 1697 production included four soloists, four-part chorus and an orchestra of five-part strings, three winds and continuo.

BARBARA COEYMAN

Amour des trois oranges, L'. Opera by Sergey Prokofiev; *see* LOVE FOR THREE ORANGES, THE.

Amours déguisés, Les ('The Disguised Loves'). *Opéra-ballet* in a prologue and three entrées by THOMAS-LOUIS BOURGEOIS to a libretto by LOUIS FUZELIER; Paris, Opéra, 22 August 1713.

This work, which takes its title from a ballet of 1664 by Lully, was so successful that it was revived in 1714 with a new act, *La reconnaissance*, and again in 1726. The three entrées treat different disguised emotions. In *La Haine*, love triumphs over evil; in *L'Amitié*, passion is revealed; and in *L'Estime*, modesty is allowed to declare its flame. With its prologue anticipating Watteau in the description of an embarkation for Cythera, its 'consort of small flutes' imitating birdsong, its *airs* for musettes and its mimes, it is one of the best surviving reflections of the aesthetic of early 18th-century France.

JÉRÔME DE LA GORCE

Amours de Ragonde, Les [*Les amours de Ragonde, ou La soirée de village* ('The Loves of Ragonde, or The Village Evening')]. *Comédie lyrique* in three acts by JEAN-JOSEPH MOURET to a libretto by Philippe Néricault-Destouches; Sceaux, December 1714, as *Le mariage de Ragonde et de Colin, ou La veillée de village* (revised version, Paris, Opéra, 30 January 1742, as *Les amours de Ragonde, ou La soirée de village*).

Ragonde (tenor), an aged widow with only 'four teeth', proposes marriage to the young shepherd Colin (*haute-contre*), who loves Ragonde's daughter Colette (soprano). Colette, however, loves Lucas (bass). Ragonde will agree to their union only when she herself is betrothed to Colin. Demons and sprites released by Ragonde surround Colin in the *divertissement* of Act 2, threatening him unless he agrees to marry Ragonde. In Act 3 all the villagers celebrate the double wedding of Lucas to Colette and of the hapless Colin to Ragonde.

Only the libretto is extant from the performance at Sceaux in 1714. The reduced score, printed by Mouret's widow in 1742, bears a privilege date of 1738, the year of the composer's death. Although a genuine lyric comedy, *Les amours de Ragonde* is called a 'comédie-ballet' in the printed score, a 'comédie en musique' in the 1742 libretto and a 'divertissement comique' in the *Approbation* at the end of the libretto. Musically it is a charming, though slight, work. By omitting a prologue, the authors anticipated Rameau's *Zoroastre* by 35 years, while by using a concluding vaudeville and popular melodies they followed contemporary practice at the Parisian fair theatres. JAMES R. ANTHONY

Amphion. *Opéra-ballet* in a prologue and one act by JOHANN GOTTLIEB NAUMANN to a libretto by Gudmund Göran Adlerbeth after Antoine Léonard Thomas's play; Stockholm, Bollhus Theatre, 24 January 1778.

Antiope (soprano) loves Mercury's son, Amphion (tenor), who is able to calm the passions of beasts through his song. She is threatened by the Chieftain of the barbarians (bass), who demands her love. Rejected, he captures and threatens both her and Amphion with death, but Amphion disarms the barbarians by singing. They promise to reform themselves, and Amphion weds Antiope.

Newly arrived in Stockholm from Dresden, Naumann wrote *Amphion* as a test piece to gauge both his ability with Swedish and public reaction to his style. It was an unqualified success in Stockholm, with more than 20 performances: arias from the opera are still in the Swedish repertory. The music, which shows both French and Italian influences, displays Naumann's gift for word painting and a singable melody, coupled with often brilliant orchestration. BERTIL H. VAN BOER

Amram, David (Werner) (*b* Philadelphia, 17 Nov 1930). American composer and conductor. He studied at Oberlin College, George Washington University and the Manhattan School of Music, but is largely self-taught in composition. His first involvement with dramatic music began in 1951–2, when he wrote music for plays at Ford's Theater in Washington. He was music director at Joseph Papp's New York Shakespeare Festival (1956–67), creating incidental music for 28 productions. Later theatrical positions included work with two New York theatres, the Phoenix (1958–60) and Lincoln Center Repertory (1963–5); he has worked on Broadway and for films as well. Amram has written more than a hundred orchestral and chamber works. His two operas date from the 1960s: *The Final Ingredient* (television op, 1, A. Weinstein, after R. Rose) and *Twelfth Night* (2, J. Papp, after W. Shakespeare).

The Final Ingredient was first performed on 11 April 1965 on 'Directions '65', an ABC television production, with the composer conducting. Its story is of concentration camp prisoners who break out to find an egg, the final ingredient for their forbidden Passover supper.

Twelfth Night, composed between 1965 and 1968, was first produced at the Lake George Opera Festival, Glens Falls, New York, on 1 August 1968. One of Amram's most successful works, it is a comic drama in 14 fast-moving scenes; its rich, fluid, colourful music includes conventional arias, duets and expansive ensemble finales.

*

VintonD

D. Amram: *Vibrations: the Adventures and Musical Times of David Amram* (New York, 1968)

David Amram (New York, 1980) [brochure, incl. biography, list of works, discography; pubn of BMI] BARBARA A. PETERSEN

Amsterdam. Capital of the Netherlands. It is the largest city in the kingdom. In 1634 Jan Hermanszoon Krul founded the Musyck Kamer, a society formed to discuss the relationship of music to drama. However, the first opera house, built on the Leidsegracht by Theodoro Strijker, did not open until 1680, when P. A. Ziani's *Le fatiche d'Ercole per Deianira* was staged. Despite considerable public success the house was declared bankrupt after only three years; Amsterdam, unlike The Hague, saw no other opera companies survive for more than a few decades. From 1638 until 1772 operas (including works by the Dutch composers Hacquart, De Konink and Johannes Schenck) were occasionally staged in the Schouwburg on the Keizersgracht, though plays were given priority. At this time, the regents of the civic orphanage and home for the elderly had jurisdiction over Amsterdam's theatres, but they were unfavourably disposed towards operatic ventures. Thus some theatres just outside the city boundaries, like the Blankenburg, achieved more success than companies performing in the centre. Dutch, Italian and German operas predominated in Amsterdam, whereas in The Hague French opera was most popular. J. F. D. Neyts's Flemish troupe played in the Schouwburg with great success; the theatre burnt down in 1772, and thereafter Neyts's company staged opera first in nearby Haarlem, then in the Overtoomse Weg in Amsterdam and finally in the Leidseplein. There the Stadsschouwburg (Municipal Theatre) opened in 1774, under the musical direction of the composer and translator Bartholomeus Ruloffs, whose *Zemire en Azor* enjoyed much success in 1784 and has been occasionally revived since. Works by Mozart, Pergolesi, Kreutzer, Dittersdorf and Grétry were given there, all in translations by Ruloffs. The Théâtre Français, on the Amstel River, opened in 1788; it was originally for members only but opened to the general public after the French Revolution; now called the Kleine Komedie, it is still used for musicals and cabarets. The Hoogduitse Schouwburg (High German Theatre) on the Amstelstraat was built in 1791 and staged opera regularly until 1853. Its six-week season in 1794 comprised four operas by Mozart, four by Dittersdorf and one by Salieri, and from 1798 to 1801 it boasted as its leading soloist Aloysia Lange, Mozart's sister-in-law. The theatre (cap. 519) had an orchestra of 30 and a chorus of 24 and was also used by the Joods Hoogduitse opera society.

Whereas companies presenting German and French opera thrived, Italian companies did not survive for long, apart from a brief period under the patronage of Louis Napoleon; foreign troupes presenting Italian opera, however, made frequent appearances in the Stadsschouwburg and the Hoogduitse Schouwburg. The post-Napoleonic period marked the start of a declining interest in French opera in Amsterdam, though the demand for German opera increased throughout the 19th century. From 1845 to 1859 J. E. de Vries's Hoogduitse Opera in the Stadsschouwburg presented so many noteworthy productions, especially of German repertory, that the Hoogduitse Schouwburg had to close. 1858 saw the Netherlands première of *Tannhäuser*, before the work reached London or Paris. After the departure of De Vries in 1859, the Stadsschouwburg was used by visiting companies, principally the Royal French Theatre from The Hague and the Hoogduitse Opera from Rotterdam. In 1883 two *Ring* cycles were staged in the Paleis voor Volksvlijt, a venue not well suited to opera production and which burnt down in 1929. The 1880s saw a brief surge of nationalism in the city's operatic activity: the Hollandse Opera, under J. G. de Groot, gave only works sung in Dutch, in the Parkschouwburg (later destroyed), and artists from his company later formed the Nederlandse Opera, directed by C. van der Linden, which performed five times every fortnight in the new Stadsschouwburg on the Leidseplein. (This, the present-day Stadsschouwburg, seating 989 and with three balconies, opened in 1894.)

In 1883 Henri Viotta founded the Wagner Society, and from 1884 until 1919 he conducted 93 Wagner performances, including *Parsifal* in 1905 (much to the distress of Cosima Wagner, who maintained that the work could be staged only in Bayreuth). Not restricting its activities to Wagner, the society staged *Boris Godunov* in 1932 (with Shalyapin in the title role) and Dukas' *Ariane et Barbe-bleue* (with Germaine Lubin), and Richard Strauss conducted his *Ariadne auf Naxos* in 1924 and *Arabella* in 1934 for it. The society, which was instrumental in the formation of the opera class at the Amsterdam Conservatory in 1933, gave its last

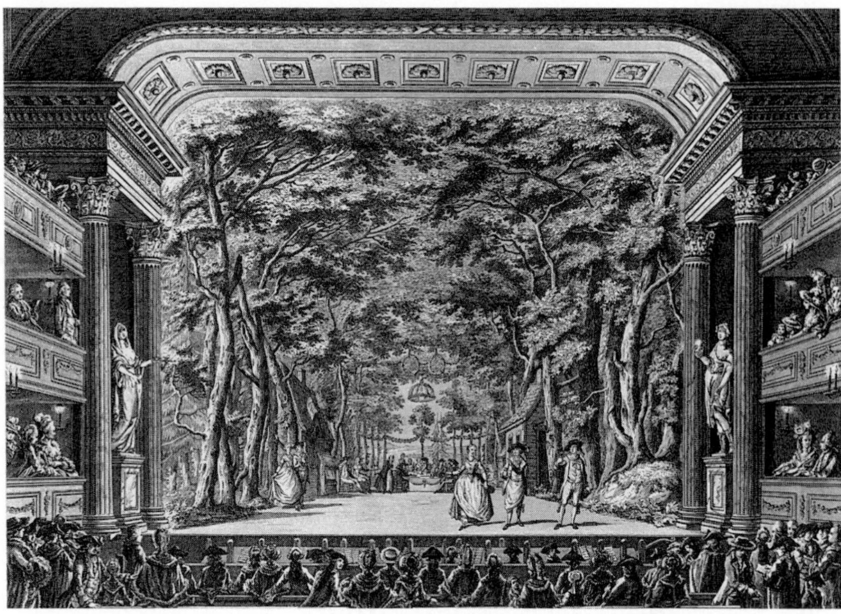

Interior of the Stadsschouwburg, Amsterdam, during a performance of Bartholomeus Ruloffs's 'De bruiloft van Kloris en Roosje': engraving by De Wit and Jonxis after Henning and J. Balthuis (1787)

performance in 1959, at the annual Holland Festival (founded 1948).

In 1929 the city council, with a slim majority, rejected plans for an opera house on the Museumplein, opposite the Concertgebouw; the Opera thus continued to share the Stadsschouwburg with 'straight' theatre. The German occupation saw an increase in operatic activity there, and backstage facilities were considerably expanded. After World War II, however, there were protests against artists who had performed for the Gemeentelijk Theaterbedrijf (Municipal Theatre Company); the tenor singing Florestan was kidnapped after a performance of *Fidelio*, and mice were released on stage during *Madama Butterfly*.

In 1946 the first opera company to be financed by the government, the Stichting de Nederlandsche Opera, was formed. Circumstances were difficult: the company shared the Stadsschouwburg with theatre and ballet companies, and rehearsals had to be held in more than ten locations in Amsterdam, The Hague, Rotterdam and Utrecht. In 1964 the Nederlandse Operastichting was formed, with a permanent chorus but without its own orchestra. Under the intendancy of Maurice Huisman, director of the Brussels opera, premières were given of works by the Dutch composers Ton de Leeuw, Guillaume Landré, Peter Schat and Ton de Kruyf. A training programme, the Opera Studio, was founded in 1966.

With Hans de Roo as Intendant, 1971–86, productions of Baroque and early Classical operas attracted international attention. There were numerous premières in The Hague, and Amsterdam saw world premières of Schat's *Houdini* (1977) and *Aap verslaat de knekelgeest* (1980), and Theo Loevendie's *Naima* (1985). *Der Kaiser von Atlantis*, written by Viktor Ullmann in Theresienstadt concentration camp, received its première at the Bellevue Theater in December 1975.

In 1986 the first purpose-built opera house in the Netherlands opened in Amsterdam with the première of Otto Ketting's *Ithaka*. The Muziektheater has some 1600 seats, two balconies and one of the best-equipped stages in Europe. A new company, the Nederlandse Opera, was formed, with Jan van Vlijmen as Intendant. In 1988 Pierre Audi took over as artistic director and Truze Lodder as business administrator. The company gives about a hundred performances of some ten works annually, usually only in Amsterdam. The world première of Alfred Shnitke's first opera, *Life with an Idiot*, was given by Nederlandse Opera on 13 April 1992. The Muziektheater Foundation occasionally stages operas in the new theatre, among them the premières of Kees Olthuis's *De naam van de maan*, and Philip Glass's *The Making of the Representative for Planet 8*, jointly commissioned with London, Houston and Kiel and first performed at Houston in 1988. The touring company Opera Forum brings most of its productions from Enschede to the Amsterdam Stadsschouwburg.

D. J. Balfoort: *Het muziekleven in Nederland in de 17de en 18de eeuw* (Amsterdam, 1938)

S. A. M. Bottenheim: *De opera in Nederland* (Amsterdam, 1946, 2/1983)

E. Reeser: *Een eeuw Nederlandse muziek, 1815–1915* (Amsterdam, 1950, 2/1986)

T. Coleman, ed.: *Een noodzakelijke luxe* (Zutphen, 1986)

MICHAEL DAVIDSON

Amy Robsart. Opera in three acts by ISIDORE DE LARA to a libretto by Augustus Henry Glossop Harris and Frederick Edward Weatherly, after WALTER SCOTT's novel *Kenilworth*; London, Covent Garden, in a French translation by Paul Milliet, 20 July 1893.

The Earl of Leicester (tenor) fears that he will lose the favour of Queen Elizabeth (mezzo-soprano) if she learns of his secret marriage to Amy Robsart (soprano). Amy is therefore kept secluded at Cumnor Hall in the care of Leicester's wicked retainer Varney (baritone). Her childhood sweetheart Tressilian (tenor), ignorant of her marriage, petitions the Queen for her release. Varney, fearful for his own ambitions, plots Amy's murder; Leicester arrives at Cumnor to rescue her but, to his horror, she plunges to her death through a hidden trapdoor previously set by Varney.

Amy Robsart is written in De Lara's early style in which the influence of Massenet predominates. The opera was given at Paris, Boulogne, Monte Carlo and St Petersburg in 1894, and at Florence in 1896. The first performance with the original English text took place at Croydon, 14 May 1920. NIGEL BURTON

Anacréon ('Anacreon'). *Acte de ballet* by JEAN-PHILIPPE RAMEAU to a libretto by LOUIS DE CAHUSAC; Fontainebleau, 23 October 1754.

Intended for a projected *opéra-ballet, Les beaux jours de l'Amour*, this is one of two independent works by Rameau with the same title (the other, to a libretto by Pierre-Joseph Bernard, eventually became part of *Les surprises de l'Amour*). The ageing poet Anacreon (bass) prepares a betrothal celebration for his two protégés Chloë (soprano) and Bathylle (*haute-contre*) but teasingly pretends that it is for his own betrothal to Chloë. The insubstantial score, possibly incomplete (it contains fewer dances than usual), begins with a one-movement overture. GRAHAM SADLER

Anagilda [*L'Anagilda, o vero La fede ne tradimenti* ('Anagilda, or Faith Despite Betrayal')]. *Dramma per musica* in three acts by ANTONIO CALDARA to a libretto by GIROLAMO GIGLI; Rome, Palazzo Bonelli, 4 January 1711.

This opera, commissioned by Francesco Maria Ruspoli for Carnival 1711, was staged 13 times by 5 February and was perhaps the most frequently performed of all Caldara's operas. Its plot is based on an incident in Bartolommeo de Rogatis's *Storia della perdita e riacquisto della Spagna* (1648) in which Fernando (soprano), Count of Castile, defeats Sancio, King of Navarra, and is betrothed to his enemy's daughter Sancia (Anagilda, soprano, in the opera) but incarcerated by her brother Garzia (alto castrato). Eventually Anagilda rescues Fernando and they escape to Castile. Elvira (contralto), Fernando's warrior sister, who confronts Garzia only to fall in love with him, is apparently Gigli's invention. He further adapted the libretto for its Roman première, providing additional arias and, at Ruspoli's request, comic scenes within the acts as well as independent intermezzos for Dorina (alto) and Grullo (bass).

The music marks a departure from the rather static, heavy-textured writing of Caldara's extant Venetian operas. Light accompaniments for two- and three-part strings predominate, foreshadowing the three-part scoring of most of his succeeding Roman oratorios; numerous short continuo-accompanied arias, usually based on rhythmic ostinato figures, provide further variety and enhance the dramatic flow. The diverse aria forms possibly reflect Caldara's concentration at the time on the composition of cantatas; strophic and curtailed ritornello structures are particularly notable, as is the powerful intrusion of the Neapolitan minuet. The recitatives, especially as they move into and out of arioso passages in Acts 2 and 3, display a plasticity seldom recaptured in Caldara's Metastasian operas.

BRIAN W. PRITCHARD

Analysis. The analysis of opera seeks to interpret one or more of opera's three basic systems: its visual, verbal and musical substance. Thus in the broadest sense opera analysis encompasses diverse literary endeavours that our institutions tend to separate, and embraces criticism as it does focussed and technical description. Such analysis can be considered in terms of its history, its stances towards its object, its choice of emphasis (visual element and stage action; words; music), its use of historical arguments to buttress interpretation and how in turn it is conditioned by history.

1. History. 2. Ideologies.

1. HISTORY. Detailed analyses of operatic music can be distinguished from the rich tradition of aesthetic or literary writings on operatic music and librettos (such as Marcello's *Teatro alla moda*, Stendhal's *Rossini* or E. T. A. Hoffmann's operatic fantasies) in that analysis claims to deal objectively with operatic composition. Opera analysis in this sense arose in the mid-19th century, as one component in a newly invented machine, the science of musicology. Beyond this, it also arose as a subjective response to adverse criticism, either of specific composers and their works or of opera itself.

19th-century opera analysis inherited certain precepts from its precursors, 17th- and 18th-century aesthetic writing on opera, which articulated a disapproval of operatic music that would become a recurring motif in the reception of the genre. The question of the relation of music to the other systems of opera was from the outset a central problem of opera analysis, as it had been in aesthetic criticism of opera. Classic aesthetic wrangles of the 18th century (the salvos exchanged by Raguenet and Le Cerf de la Viéville, the Querelle des Bouffons, the Gluckist–Piccinnist debate), though couched in nationalist terms and overtly concerned with the relative merits of French and Italian opera, are fundamentally judgments about the sterility of any music lacking a relationship to poetry, spectacle and the drama. Thus, in Le Cerf's pro-French *Comparaison de la musique italienne et de la musique française* (1704–6), Italian opera is accused of an obsession with the process of melodic ornamentation; in isolating and exalting this purely musical element, such opera becomes incapable of expression. Indeed, much pre-Romantic aesthetic writing on opera deemed the music unsatisfactory when music becomes the pretext for overt singing performance: that is, when music maximizes something that is purely musical and so refers only to itself (a position perhaps most clearly articulated in Francesco Algarotti's *Saggio sopra l'opera in musica*, 1755). But the fault is neither exclusively Italian nor French, for the accusation could simply be inverted; in his *Lettre sur la musique française* (1753), Rousseau discovered in the extreme formality of French opera a solipsistic music that paradoxically lacks the expressive precision of music that traces passions or images, that is grounded in the human world. He later reinforced this position, coming to suggest (in the *Essai sur l'origine des langues*, 1760) that music, tracing emotion, made fruitful alliances with other (verbal or dramatic) realms. Music would thus strive to transcend itself. Operatic music above all had the potential to be an ideal music, expressive in translating and exalting what was represented in the visual and textual systems.

The notion that such music might fruitfully transpose a non-musical element into its own body was taken, especially by the German Romantics, as a prescriptive norm. Idealization of the signifying power of operatic music continued as an aesthetic force through the 19th century, reaching its culmination in the writings of Liszt and Wagner. Yet at the same time the structure of prestige was inverted; operatic absolutists such as Otto Jahn (as well as Nietzsche, in *The Birth of Tragedy*) proposed an alternative orthodoxy, in which operatic music was of value only as far as it could attain instrumental music's capacity for autonomy.

This opposition fuelled analysis of operatic music, which may indeed be said to have begun in a serious way in the mid-19th century. Analytical essays on contemporary operatic music appeared in French, Italian and German musical periodicals, and after 1830 with some frequency. About the same time, writers on opera turned their attention to non-contemporary composers, foremost among them Mozart and Gluck. Thus operatic analysis arose as well as a consequence of the (largely German) historicist and revivalist impulses of the early 19th century, as an attempt not only to criticize modern operas but to understand earlier achievements. Many opera analysts (including both Hanslick and Wagner) adopted a historical approach, comparing modern works to 18th-century predecessors.

All 19th-century analyses, no matter what their object (contemporary or older music), articulate a fundamental schism that defined the two main thrusts of opera analysis: formalist (exclusively musical) versus symbolic interpretation of operatic music. One can observe the schism, gaining momentum up to the middle of the century, reflected in the first two comprehensive studies of Mozart's operas. Oulibicheff's *Mozarts Opern: kritische Erläuterungen* (1849) was one of the earliest (and, in several senses, fabulous) analytic studies of opera of any kind; Oulibicheff hears symbolic meanings shouted at every musical moment, pauses (for instance) to speculate on the transcendent significance of the sustained G that saturates the first number in the Act 1 finale of *Die Zauberflöte*. The analytical discussions in Otto Jahn's *W. A. Mozart* (1856), on the other hand, laud the absolutely musical. Jahn, who had read Oulibicheff, strives to undermine the symbolist stance, and repeats obsessively that Mozart's operas commit no 'Effektmalerei', 'Tonmalerlei' or 'Wortmalerei', insisting upon reading opera's musical themes as elements that simply work to build musical *Struktur*.

Jahn's *Gesammelte Aufsätze über Musik* (1866), as well as Eduard Hanslick's writings of the 1840s and 50s, are coloured by the larger trend towards generic formal analysis, a trend which took its greatest impetus from the writings of A. B. Marx, whose *Gluck und die Oper* (1863) reflects his own inclination towards analysis as typology and definitions of form. Hanslick's 1845 analysis of Wagner's *Tannhäuser* can stand as a classic instance. Hanslick sets the form of the numbers in *Tannhäuser* against pedigreed contemporary operatic forms (for instance, the finale concertato) and criticizes departures from traditional models. Joachim Raff's *Die Wagnerfrage: kritisch beleuchtet* (1854), the first book devoted to Wagner's music, is equally concerned with formal genres but allows Wagner rather more success in conforming to them. Abramo Basevi's *Studio sulle opere di Giuseppe Verdi* (1859), another locus classicus of the generic formal tradition, similarly treats opera analysis in part as the description and typography of formal types (e.g. typical aria or ensemble structures) and identification of their pedigree in earlier operas.

Hanslick's *Die moderne Oper* (1875), which deals with opera from Gluck to Johann Strauss, can stand as the early ideological summary of the formalist method. In it Hanslick articulates eloquently several classic positions: the familiar prejudice that Mozart's finales and ensembles are the *summa* of his operatic work, as well as the notion that Wagner's (as well as Weber's) operas became 'formless' because they gave themselves over to a too-intense, too-thoroughgoing symbolization of poetic meaning. But it is important to note that the 19th-century formalist analysts had inherited Rousseauian aesthetic prejudices, and generally (if somewhat paradoxically) claim that structural beauties turn sterile when lacking dramatic expressive force. Thus Hanslick (1875) criticizes *Così fan tutte*, for all its musical suasions, as merely filling out conventional formal types for numbers, and *Fidelio* for a typically Beethovenian concentration on the absolute, instrumental musicality of themes.

What might be called the symbolist tradition essentially sought to identify moments at which operatic music could be understood as exemplifying not musical perfection *per se* but music's capacity to reflect emotion, dramatic events or poetic images. Documentation of leitmotifs (the term was coined by F. W. Jähns in *Carl Maria von Weber in seinen Werken*, 1871) became one central preoccupation, even obsession, in the tradition of symbolic analysis. Liszt's 1851 essay on Wagner's *Tannhäuser* and *Lohengrin*, while hardly the first analysis to identify recurring motifs in operatic music, stands out for its careful dissection of the phenomenon, but more for the centrality accorded to the musical consequences of such symbolism.

Wagner's own writings on opera, which essentially adopt a symbolist stance, influenced operatic analysis in ways that should not be underestimated. Wagner never espoused the vision of operatic music as perfect or absolute music. Indeed, his counterclaim (most forcefully asserted in *Oper und Drama*, and never fully retracted) was that operatic music makes expressive gestures that both stem from and enhance dramatic reality. Integration of musical analysis with perception of opera's dramatic, poetic and visual suasions is thus a fundamentally Wagnerian move. Wolzogen's *Thematischer Leitfaden durch die Musik zu Richard Wagners Festspiel 'Der Ring des Nibelungen'* (1876), the first and classic leitmotivic analysis of Wagner's music, degraded Wagner's complex vision to a dictionary of themes and images, yet became in effect a model for all subsequent leitmotivic opera analysis to the present day.

The mid-19th-century split between formalist analysis (encompassing typologies of arias and ensemble types, descriptions of traditional forms such as sonata form in operatic incarnations and harmonic and tonal analysis) and symbolist analysis (consideration of how music traces and enhances non-musical forces in opera, the signifying force of recurring motifs) set the terms for subsequent opera analysis well into the 20th century. Operatic analysis – piggybacked on musical analysis and musicological writing in general – has been produced in immense quantities in the 20th century, yet has tended to repeat 19th-century positions, with one significant difference. In many 20th-century analyses, the last vestiges of Rousseauian guilt have disappeared, giving rise to an analytical tone in which purely musical structures, in themselves and independent of expressive capability, are asserted as the basis for aesthetic pleasure in opera. Alfred Lorenz's studies of Wagner's operas in the 1920s and 30s are a case in point, and have exercised a central influence on opera analysis in the 20th century, not only ideologically (in their insistence on formalism) but methodologically, as comprehensive discussions of single works collected in the form of a scholarly book (the appendix to Lorenz's *Ring* study is still the best bibliography of earlier music-analytical literature on Wagner). In particular, Lorenz popularized the analysis of tonal structures in opera (in works by Wagner as well as those of Mozart and Scarlatti); later tonal analyses, judiciously applying Lorenz's thought, have extended his general notion of large-scale tonal relations, and his ideas about the associative force of key, to composers from Monteverdi to Britten. Later Wagnerian analysts, such as Carl Dahlhaus, have reacted against the details of Lorenz's formalism, modifying yet not fundamentally changing the terms of his formalist methods.

In English, opera analysis of both symbolist and formalist bent is familiar to a broad audience from books on the works of important composers (Newman's *Wagner Nights*, Dent's *Mozart's Operas*, Budden's *The Operas of Verdi*). By the 1980s composers far less important, as well as composers outside Germany, Italy or France, had been honoured with their own monographs; at the same time the analytical methodologies formed in the 19th century for interpretation of the central repertory were extended back to opera before Mozart. More specialized analytical writing emerged from the European and American musicological industry of the 1960s, 70s and 80s, which produced music-analytical essays in great numbers; opera analysis constituted a significant part of this whole. Though pre-Romantic opera has tended to be analysed more in terms of formal types for numbers, 19th-century and later opera in terms of its tonal and harmonic structures and its musical symbolism, there has been no absolute association of a given historical era with a given methodology (the exception is atonal and 12-note opera in the 20th century, which has, of course, generated a special analytical medium). Composing a Catalogue Aria to this mass of later 20th-century analysis, however, is far less fruitful than examining the strategies and ideological assumptions underpinning the whole enterprise.

2. Ideologies. Telling the history of opera analysis, naming its most famous practitioners, constitutes a background to a more complicated issue: understanding the ideological and aesthetic problems that underpin analytical writing on opera. The central problem remains the necessity to cope with an art that mixes various languages (visual, verbal, musical); this problem has affected every writer on opera, and can be said to twist his or her own interpretative language. While opera combines three basic systems, an analytical methodology has yet to be developed that is capable of discussing these as they exist in an ideal experiential reality, as aspects of a single and simultaneously perceived entity. Virtually all operatic interpretation has been forced to dissect the operatic experience, focus separately upon the music, the text and the visual form of any operatic passage (i.e. 'while the text spoken is this, we see that on stage, and the music does this'). Opera analysis deals monophonically with what in performance is a visual-textual-musical polyphony. To be sure, analysis often seeks for a relationship between these systems, yet such a search is itself born of interpretation's inability directly to reflect or translate the complex simultaneities of opera. Analysing opera thus inevitably creates a fundamental schism, and its quest for relationships is perhaps driven by longing for a whole object that the act of analysis has itself unfused.

If opera analysis inevitably splits itself into separate interpretation of the different systems, each branch does not adopt the same strategies. Analysis of the text, 'librettology', has been shaped by two related precepts. One is practical and historical and reflects a concern with the genesis and individual alchemy of operatic works: the assumption that the creation of a libretto generally precedes that of the music that sets it. The second is aesthetic, and is (paradoxical as it might seem) one impetus for close readings of a libretto: an idea that the libretto text is a fundamentally incomplete utterance, a lesser line within a polyphony whose chief splendour is music.

The status accorded to a libretto is often determined by our knowledge of its genesis: did libretto or music come first in the making of a work? In all phases of opera history, but particularly those regarded as mannerist phases (the Baroque, the bel canto era), we know of cases where pre-existing music was simply fitted out with text. Abstract, *a priori* ideas of musical form may shape libretto content and structure. Versions of Cavalli's *Erismena* reveal how the nascent da capo aria stamped its identity upon a mutating text; Mozart's correspondence concerning his operas, as well as that of (among others) Verdi and Puccini, demonstrate that structure and scansion, as well as emotional trajectory, may be shaped by compositional demands for poetry to reflect set musico-rhetorical arcs. Historically literate critics, possessing knowledge that a text was invented merely to fill out music, may be inclined to belittle study of librettos *per se*, seeing operatic texts as mere verbal roughage, interesting only insofar as they reflect musical pressures applied by a specific individual composer or an historical era. Such knowledge may also serve, if not to block libretto analysis entirely, to direct its focus. Analyses influenced by historical certainty of a text's *a posteriori* status, for instance, tend to deal with the text's mechanical features (scansion, rhyme, verse structure) since prosody alone will determine whether it will actually fit under an *a priori* music. We know that the text of the Act 2 quartet of Verdi's *Otello* could be altered after the music was sketched because all that was needed for a substitution were alternative *quinario* verses, whose actual meaning could be as different (or not) as wished. We know, beyond this, of instances where there seems to be no causal relationship between poem and music. Those cognizant of cases in which existing music was simply assigned an entirely new text (as happened frequently in Baroque *opera seria*) may take this as justification for denying the force of textual-musical connections in general. Thus historical knowledge may serve to relegate the verbal system to an ancillary position, and repress serious interpretations of libretto text, or of expressive links between music and text. The fact that Wagner originally conceived part of the *Tristan* music (Brangäne's Consolation in Act 1) as music for an entirely different text in Act 3 of *Siegfried* might be used to police interpretative desires to understand the music of *Tristan* as a symbolic transposition of the *Tristan* text.

A second, covert precept of librettology concerns the incompleteness of the libretto. Unless a more-or-less direct adaptation of a stage play, the libretto attends its own fulfilment in an overriding musical setting (Peter Conrad's *Romantic Opera and Literary Form* is in effect an extended meditation on this idea). This assumption might be imagined to discourage serious analysis of libretto texts, and institutional pleas for the establishment of librettology conventionally begin by refuting it and arguing that libretto analysis need not necessarily take account of the musical setting, even that such attention to music will distort an independent text-centred view. In reality, however, the covert assumption of the partial and fragmentary being of the libretto has served as an aesthetic dispensation, excusing librettistic epigones, literary infelicities and the flaws that might otherwise have excluded librettos from attaining a pedigree as worthy of critical attention. It is precisely that which is absent from librettos – primarily the music, but opera's visual and spectacular element as well – that lends the aura needed to attract our interpretative scrutiny. (This disconcerting irony is, of course, obvious in any analysis that focusses largely on the libretto yet refers to 'Mozart's' – not 'Da Ponte's' – *Don Giovanni*, for example Ivan Nagel's controversial book *Autonomie und Gnade*.) Throughout operatic history, librettos have been considered as objects of criticism in isolation from music; more recently they have been analysed by means of strategies familiar in modern literary criticism. These have included decontextualizing approaches such as deconstruction (e.g. examining paradoxical rhetorical structures in the *Parsifal* poem), generic interpretations of texts as exemplifying theatrical or poetic types (the libretto of Monteverdi's *Orfeo* and pastoralism) and sociological interpretations seeking for literary traces of contemporary culture (*Carmen* as building a plot around a 19th-century xenophobic exclusion of the Other). Whatever the method adopted, interpretation of these texts has been driven by the fact of their association with a music that may well go (significantly) unremarked. Thus the plea of librettology that librettos merit discussion in their own right paradoxically wishes to create a full art-form from one whose claim on our intellectual energies is powerful only because that art-form – as one part of an opera – is inevitably incomplete.

Analysis of the music of opera tends to display similar methodological ironies. The 19th-century formalists' view of operatic music as musical structure allowed our casual understanding of opera analysis as music analysis. While librettos have been seen as partial or incomplete texts, music has more often been regarded as a full text in its own right, needing no prosthetic aura (lent by the verbal or visual) to command our attention. The autonomy of operatic music is less secure than it might seem, and analysis of operatic music, like that of librettos, is often characterized by nervous sensitivity to the absent discursive systems, verbal and visual.

Adopting the two strategies established in the 19th century, the analysis of operatic music assumes either that music has the capacity to retrace meanings that originate in the visual or verbal systems and that analysis should seek these transpositions, or prefers to neutralize the question of representation, regarding operatic music as self-sufficient or exemplifying procedures found in instrumental music and, in thus establishing its autonomy, lend it prestige.

Reading operatic music as representation means invoking various forms of symbolic translation. There are musical gestures whose trajectory repeats a spatial image; in Monteverdi's *L'incoronazione di Poppea*, Otho's first line, concerning his 'return...to the centre', returns musically (and often) to the tonic pitch. Contextually odd sonorities act as indexes, drawing attention to the words they set, as in *Così fan tutte*, with that sudden diminished seventh chord above a dominant pedal in the terzetto at 'ai nostri desir', sensitizing us so clearly to the dangerous word, 'desire'. Music can establish a system of arbitrary signs, as with the leitmotifs and symbolic tonalities in the *Ring* (and in all the post-Wagnerian operas that followed Wagnerian habits); it can devise elaborate harmonic equivalents for semantic patterns. On a broader level, musical forms may constitute a ground against which the figure is some formal disruption that plays out the stage action, as in the vaudeville finale to *Die Entführung aus dem Serail*, where Osmin's anger breaks a happy pattern of similar verses. Such examples could be multiplied. Analysis of operatic music as representation may espouse a larger hermeneutic agenda, a totalizing project in which all mysteries of operatic music are neatly explained; in popularized forms (e.g. leitmotif analyses in record sleeve notes), it may attempt to suggest that operatic music can be understood as a series of decodable symbols. While such analyses may investigate many different representational possibilities, what they share is a view of such gestures as driving music to extremes it would not otherwise attain. Thus the metaphorical field within which such analysis occurs presupposes an image of operatic music, or an operatic number or passage, as noumenally 'whole', 'unified' or 'coherent' but goaded to a higher, richer being in phenomenal reality by the sonorous inflections of musical allegory.

The antithetic analytic strategy, descended from 19th-century formalism, prefers to neutralize the question of representation. This can be done in various ways. Verbal and visual systems, even when seen as corresponding to music in a closed tautology of interrelatedness, may be assumed innocent of disrupting music. A causal argument may be adduced to assert that verbal or visual elements were themselves invented to reflect a self-contained and autonomous music. The musical consequences of representation can simply be denied. Representational gestures may be trivialized as 'incidental' or 'small'. They can be interpretatively erased by readings that seek larger-scale phenomena and hence set up a conceptual opposition between foreground and background, or surface and depths, lending particular authority to the second term. This is a critical swerve – favouring background or deep structure – that traditional music analysis holds in common with familiar humanistic methodologies such as Marxism or structuralism. Thus Alfred Lorenz identified musical patterns such as *Barform*, exemplified both locally and globally; a Schenkerian analysis of any opera can describe contrapuntal relationships between musical infra- and superstructure, and a tonal reading can unveil successions of keys as a hierarchical system, a purely musical background control of foreground modulations. Such analyses may well reveal significant musical facts (as do 'representational' analyses). Yet they, too, are hardly free of ideology. By invoking methodologies familiar in analysis of instrumental music, such readings plead (in the case of Lorenz, overtly) that operatic music fundamentally operates in ways identical with those of music uninflected by verbal or visual systems. This move strives to reinforce the notion that, in opera, music alone attains the status of a full text.

This repression of the non-musical is itself as complex a phenomenon as arguments about the musical consequences of symbolization. Operatic music has, over the course of its history, attracted to itself a rich fund of negative judgments: as formally uncontrolled, illogical, excessive, subjective, vulgar, immoral, feminine. Associating operatic music with instrumental music may seem straightforwardly to reflect an historical-stylistic reality (e.g. that da capo aria rhetoric resembles Baroque concerto forms). Yet whether accomplished through analytical demonstration or an act of naming (for example, by referring to Wagner's operas as 'symphonies'), it inevitably bespeaks a desire to purify operatic music through a purgative association with genres uncorrupted by non-musical systems; significantly, it reflects as well a recuperation of operatic music to a masculine objectivity.

This purifying gesture seems doomed to fail. Opera analysis will inevitably face the necessity of acknowledging the polyphony between visual, verbal and musical, in an object it seems compelled to unlayer. This polyphony is nonetheless not merely a matter of parallel 3rds and 6ths. While opera analysis has often sought the 'relationships' between the visual, verbal and musical systems in terms of parallelisms or correspondence, these three frequently come together in adversarial meetings. The *music* for the Act 2 finale of *Le nozze di Figaro* generates full closure through modulations of tempo and through harmonic design, yet on stage (in the verbal and visual systems) 'open' chaos reigns. Thus though we might well see the music of the finale *per se* as autonomous, this autonomy is in phenomenal reality set against a contradictory system, a juxtaposition that alters the music without changing a single note. John Cage's *Europeras* celebrates possibilities for non-coincidence of staging, text and music: in it the three systems, existing together in time, are combined at random, and whatever animated connections may ricochet between the three are *constructed* by the spectator-listener. Analytical accounts of opera might strive to become what might be called dramaturgical interpretations, seeking, in such non-congruent nodes, the drama of opera, a polyphony beyond mere coincidence of monophonic lines that constitute the virtual essence of opera. The dialogue-like nature of opera seems in the end to suggest a general rejection of totalizing approaches, and an adoption of plural strategies with the capacity to acknowledge its diversity and richness.

*

Bibliographies to the entries on individual composers should be consulted for fuller lists of interpretative essays; the present list is intended as a selective point of departure.

A. Oulibicheff: *Mozarts Leben, nebst einer Übersicht der allgemeinen Geschichte der Musik und einer Analyse der Hauptwerke Mozarts* (Stuttgarg, 1847)
——: *Mozarts Opern: kritische Erläuterungen* (Leipzig, 1848)
A. Morel: *Le prophète: analyse critique de la nouvelle partition de Giacomo Meyerbeer* (Paris, 1849)
F. Liszt: *Lohengrin et Tannhäuser de Richard Wagner* (Leipzig, 1851; Ger. trans., 1852)
J. Raff: *Die Wagnerfrage: kritisch beleuchtet, 1: Wagners letzte künstlerische Kundgebung im 'Lohengrin'* (Brunswick, 1854)
O. Jahn: *W. A. Mozart* (Leipzig, 1856, 2/1867)
A. Basevi: *Studio sulle opere di Giuseppe Verdi* (Florence, 1859)
A. B. Marx: *Gluck und die Oper* (Berlin, 1863, 2/1866)
O. Jahn: *Gesammelte Aufsätze über Musik* (Leipzig, 1866)
F. W. Jähns: *Carl Maria von Weber in seinen Werken* (Berlin, 1871)
E. Hanslick: *Die moderne Oper: Kritiken und Studien* (Berlin, 1875)
H. von Wolzogen: *Thematischer Leitfaden durch die Musik zu Richard Wagners Festspiel 'Der Ring des Nibelungen'* (Leipzig, 1876)
G. Adler: *Richard Wagner: Vorlesungen gehalten an der Universität zu Wien* (Munich, 1904, 2/1923)
K. Grunsky: 'Wagner als Symphoniker', *Richard Wagner Jb*, i (1906), 227–44
E. J. Dent: *Mozart's Operas: a Critical Study* (London, 1913, 2/1947)
A. Lorenz: *Das Geheimnis der Form bei Richard Wagner* (Berlin, 1924)
——: *Alessandro Scarlattis Jugendoper* (Augsburg, 1927)
——: 'Das Finale in Mozarts Meisteropern', *Die Musik*, xix (1926–7), 621–32
H. Abert: *Grundprobleme der Operngeschichte* (Leipzig, 1926)
P. Bekker: *Wandlungen der Oper* (Leipzig, 1934)
W. Schuh: *Über Opern von Richard Strauss* (Zürich, 1947)
S. Levarie: *Mozart's 'Le nozze di Figaro': A Critical Analysis* (Chicago, 1952)
J. Kerman: *Opera as Drama* (New York, 1956, 2/1988)
U. Weisstein: *The Essence of Opera* (New York, 1964)
J. Chailley: *'La flûte enchantée', opéra maçonnique: essai d'explication du livret et de la musique* (Paris, 1968; Eng. trans., 1972)
V. Klotz: *Geschlossene und offene Form im Drama* (Munich, 4/1969)
C. Dahlhaus: 'Formprinzipien in Wagners "Ring des Nibelungen"', *Beiträge zur Geschichte der Oper*, ed. H. Becker (Regensburg, 1969), 95–129
——: 'Zur Geschichte der Leitmotivtechnik bei Wagner', *Das Drama Richard Wagners als musikalisches Kunstwerk* (Regensburg, 1970), 17–36
J. Budden: *The Operas of Verdi*, i: *From Oberto to Rigoletto* (London, 1973); ii: *From Il trovatore to La forza del destino* (London, 1978); iii: *From Don Carlos to Falstaff* (London, 1981)
E. T. Cone: *The Composer's Voice* (Berkeley, 1974)
P. Gossett: 'Verdi, Ghislanzoni, and *Aida*: the Uses of Convention', *Critical Inquiry*, i (1974), 291–334
P. Conrad: *Romantic Opera and Literary Form* (Berkeley, 1977)
F. Noske: *The Signifier and the Signified* (The Hague, 1977)
C. Clément: *L'opéra ou la défaite des femmes* (Paris, 1979; Eng. trans., *Opera, or the Undoing of Women*, 1988)
R. Strohm: *Die italienische Oper im 18. Jahrhundert* (Wilhelmshaven, 1979)
A. Newcomb: 'The Birth of Music out of the Spirit of Drama: an Essay in Wagnerian Formal Analysis', *19th Century Music*, v (1981–2), 38–66
P. Petrobelli: 'Music in the Theatre (a propos of *Aida*, Act III)', *Themes in Drama 3: Drama, Dance, and Music*, ed. J. Redmond (Cambridge, 1981), 129–42
A. Whittall: 'The Music', in L. Beckett: *Richard Wagner: Parsifal* (Cambridge, 1981), 61–86
U. Weisstein: 'Librettology: the Fine Art of Coping with a Chinese Twin', *Komparistische Hefte*, v–vi (1982), 23–42
H. Lindenberger: *Opera: the Extravagant Art* (Ithaca, 1984)
I. Nagel: *Autonomie und Gnade: über Mozarts Opern* (Munich, 1985)
S. Kunze: *Mozarts Opern* (Munich, 1986)
M. Poizat: *L'Opéra ou le cri de l'ange* (Paris, 1986)
G. Tomlinson: *Monteverdi and the End of the Renaissance* (Berkeley, 1987)
I. Bent: *Analysis* (New York and London, 1988)
L. Bianconi: 'Introduzione', *La drammaturgia musicale*, ed. L. Bianconi (Bologna, 1988), 7–51
E. T. Cone: 'The World of Opera and its Inhabitants', *Music: a View from Delft* (Chicago, 1988), 125–38
C. Dahlhaus: 'Drammaturgia dell'opera italiana', *Storia dell'opera italiana*, ed. L. Bianconi and G. Pestelli, vi (Turin, 1988), 79–162
A. Groos and R. Parker, eds.: *Reading Opera* (Princeton, 1988)
P. Kivy: *Osmin's Rage* (Princeton, 1988)
P. Robinson: 'A Deconstructive Postscript: Reading Libretti and Misreading Opera', *Reading Opera*, ed. A. Groos and R. Parker (Princeton, 1988), 328–46
C. Abbate and R. Parker: 'Introduction: On Analyzing Opera', *Analyzing Opera: Verdi and Wagner*, ed. C. Abbate and R. Parker (Berkeley, 1989), 1–24
E. Rosand: 'Monteverdi's Mimetic Art', *COJ*, i (1989), 113–37
C. Dahlhaus: 'What is a Musical Drama?', *COJ*, ii (1990), 95–111
C. Abbate and R. Parker: 'Dismembering Mozart', *COJ*, ii (1990), 187–95
J. Webster: 'Mozart's Operas and the Myth of Musical Unity', *COJ*, ii (1990), 197–218
A. Whittall: '"Forceful Muting" or "Phatic Dithering"? Some Recent Writing on Opera', *ML*, lxxi (1990), 65–71
P. Petrobelli: *Music in the Theater: Essays on Verdi and Other Composers* (Princeton, 1991)
J. Webster: 'The Analysis of Mozart's Arias', *Mozart Studies*, ed. C. Eisen (Oxford, 1991), 101–99

CAROLYN ABBATE

Anchorage. City in Alaska, USA. Anchorage Opera, a nationally recognized regional non-profit-making company founded by Elvera Voth, its artistic director, presented *Pagliacci* as its first production in 1975, followed by *The Ballad of Baby Doe* to celebrate America's 1976 bicentenary, then *La bohème* in 1977. In 1979 *Lucia di Lammermoor* became the first fully produced non-English opera to be presented in its original language in Alaska. Since 1978 the company has presented two or three full productions annually. Anchorage Opera became a full member of Opera America in 1981. Recent productions include *Carmen*, *Rigoletto*, *Roméo et Juliette*, *Die Fledermaus* and *Figaro*. The casts include guest artists who perform with Alaskan singers and instrumentalists. SUSAN WINGROVE

Ancona. Italian city in the Marche region. The constitution of the Accademia dei Caliginosi (founded 1624) provided for the performance of *drammi per musica*, but it is not known whether this was ever put into practice. In 1658 the municipal authorities granted a group of noblemen permission to create a permanent theatre in part of the Arsenal (which had already been used for theatrical purposes). They installed 54 boxes in three tiers and ran the theatre for their own profit, although technically the theatre was 'public' since it occupied municipal premises. It opened in 1664 with Cavalli's *Giasone* and was used every season until destroyed by fire on 20 November 1709. In 1711 it was replaced by La Fenice, a municipal theatre that staged operas until it was declared unsafe in 1818 (demolished 1822). Tartini performed in the orchestra there in 1714, and Anna Guidarini, Rossini's mother, made her début in 1798.

In 1821 Marco Organari transformed his arena, built in 1806 outside Porta Farina, into a theatre with three rows of boxes, and organized operatic seasons there. It fell into decline after the opening of the Teatro delle Muse and was closed in about 1848. The Muse, a municipal theatre designed by Pietro Ghinelli, was begun in 1822 in the block containing the Palazzo del Podestà and the Carcere (now the Piazza della Repubblica). Built on a truncated oval groundplan, it had 99 boxes in four tiers plus a gallery, and opened on 28 April 1827 with Rossini's *Aureliano in Palmira*. Its principal season of *opera seria* and *buffa* was in April and May; and there was a minor season of *opera semiseria* and *opera buffa* at Carnival. Until about 1870 two to four works, each having 25 to 40 performances, were produced in a season; after that, activity was halved, and in the early 1900s the carnival season was often abandoned. Activity revived in 1919–25, but the theatre suffered war damage in 1943 and was later demolished. Smaller theatres occasionally staging opera or, more usually, operetta included the Teatro Vittorio Emanuele, which opened with Achille Peri's *Vittore Pisani* and was in use from 1860 to 1927, and the Politeama Goldoni, inaugurated in 1880 with *Lucia di Lammermoor* and since 1900 used for variety and as a cinema.

*

ES (A. M. Bonisconti)
O. Morici: *Il Teatro delle Muse di Ancona nelle vicende e nella tradizione* (Rome, 1907)
——: *I cento anni del Teatro delle Muse di Ancona* (Ancona, 1927)
F. Sternini: *Piccola storia del teatro delle Muse di Ancona dalla celebrazione del suo primo centenario (1872) alla distruzione per cause belliche (1943)* (Ancona, 1972)
A. Fazi: *I teatri di Ancona* (Falconara, 1980)
M. Salvarini: 'Tornei ed intermedi all' "Arsenale" di Ancona (1603–1623)', *RIM*, xxiv (1989), 306–29 PAOLO FABBRI

Ancona, Mario (*b* Livorno, 28 Feb 1860; *d* Florence, 23 Feb 1931). Italian baritone. Having made his début in 1889 at Trieste as Scindia in *Le roi de Lahore*, in 1890 he sang the King (*Le Cid*) at La Scala. He created Silvio in *Pagliacci* at the Teatro dal Verme, Milan (1892) and made his Covent Garden début as Tonio in the British première of Leoncavallo's opera (1893). His Metropolitan début was also as Tonio, and he appeared as Riccardo (*I puritani*) at the Manhattan Opera House on its opening night (3 December 1906). His repertory embraced Mozart (Don Giovanni and Figaro), Verdi (Germont, Rigoletto, Amonasro, Iago and Don Carlo in *Ernani*), Wagner (Wolfram, Telramund and Hans Sachs), Puccini (Lescaut and Marcello), Mascagni (Alfio and David in *L'amico Fritz*) and many French roles, including Nevers, Escamillo and Valentin (*Faust*). He retired in 1916. An elegant and stylish singer, he possessed a voluminous voice and an impeccable technique.

*

ES (F. Gara)
A. Bonaventura: *Musicisti livornesi* (Livorno, 1930)
ELIZABETH FORBES

Anday, Rosette (*b* Budapest, 22 Dec 1903; *d* Vienna, 28 Sept 1977). Hungarian mezzo-soprano. She studied with Mme Charles Cahier and Georges Anthes. After her début at the National Theatre, Budapest, she sang at the Vienna Staatsoper from 1921 (début as Carmen), appearing there regularly until 1961. At Salzburg she was heard from 1922 as Dorabella, Cherubino, Orlofsky, Orpheus, Brangäne and Clytemnestra. Her Covent Garden appearances were in 1928 and 1929, as Erda, Fricka, Waltraute and Hatred in Gluck's *Armide*. She retired in 1961, after singing Clytemnestra at the Vienna Staatsoper. DAVID CUMMINGS

Ander [Anderle], **Aloys** (*b* Libiče nad Doubravkou, 13 Oct 1817; *d* Sedmihorsky, 11 Dec 1864). Bohemian tenor. After studying in Vienna, he made his début there in 1845 as Flotow's Alessandro Stradella at the Hofoper, where he was engaged until his death. The first Viennese John of Leyden (*Le prophète*) in 1850, he also sang Raoul (*Les Huguenots*), Lyonel (*Martha*) and Faust. In 1861 he sang Lohengrin in the first performance of the opera heard by Wagner, who for a time considered him a possible creator of Tristan. Ander's voice, however, was lyrical rather than heroic in timbre. He sang Arnold (*Guillaume Tell*) shortly before his final collapse and premature death.

ELIZABETH FORBES

Anders, Hendrik (*b* Oberweissbach, Thuringia *c*1657; *d* Amsterdam, bur. 14 March 1714). Netherlands composer of German birth. After having attended the gymnasium of Rudolstadt, he settled in Amsterdam around 1680. From 1683 to 1694 he was organist of the Lutheran church, and from about this time until his death his name occurs in the records of the Amsterdam Stadsschouwburg, where he certainly served as a musician. He composed instrumental ensemble music (possibly intended as introductory and entr'acte music for the city theatre), continuo songs, and music for five Dutch *zangspelen* (theatre plays with a mixture of spoken and sung parts), on texts by A. du Moulin (*Harderszang*, libretto published 1687), Dirk Buysero (*Min- en Wynstrydt*, libretto 1697; *Venus en Adonis*, libretto 1698), and Cornelis Sweerts (*De verliefde Rykaard*, libretto ?1694; *Apollo en Dafne*, libretto 1698). Unfortunately only a few songs from these plays are extant in such songbooks as Sweerts's *Mengelzangen en zinnebeelden* (Amsterdam, 1694; nine songs from *De* *verliefde Rykaard*) and his *Verscheide nieuwe zangen* (Amsterdam, 1697; four songs from *Apollo en Dafne*).

*

H. Philips: 'Uit het leven van Hendrik Anders', *Mens en Melodie*, i (1946), 372–83

A. Jansen: *Het leven van Hendrik Anders* (thesis, U. of Amsterdam, 1965) RUDOLF A. RASCH

Anders, Max. *See* ALVARY, MAX.

Anders, Peter (*b* Essen, 1 July 1908; *d* Hamburg, 10 Sept 1954). German tenor. He studied first at the Berlin Academy and then with Lula Mysz-Gmeiner, who became his mother-in-law. In 1931 he appeared in *La belle Hélène* in Berlin; he made his operatic début the following year at Heidelberg. Engagements at Darmstadt, Cologne and Hanover followed, and from 1938 to 1940 he was at the Munich State Opera where he sang in the première of Strauss's *Friedenstag*. He then returned to Berlin where he remained at the State Opera till 1948, singing also at Salzburg in 1941 and 1942. His roles at this time included Tamino, Belmonte, Cavaradossi and Leukippos in *Daphne*, but from 1948, when he joined the Hamburg Opera, he undertook dramatic roles such as Florestan, Lohengrin and even Otello. In 1950 he sang Bacchus in *Ariadne auf Naxos* at the Edinburgh Festival, and in 1951 appeared at Covent Garden in *Fidelio* and *Die Meistersinger*. He died after a car accident. His many recordings, including several complete operas, are impressive for fine tone and technique as well as for the intelligence of his lieder singing.

*

A. G. Ross: 'Peter Anders', *Record News* [Toronto], iii/1 (1958–9), 3–16 [with discography]

F. W. Pauli: *Peter Anders* (Berlin, 1963) J. B. STEANE

Andersen, Hans Christian (*b* Odense, 2 April 1805; *d* Copenhagen, 4 Aug 1875). Danish writer and librettist. Best known for his collection of fairy-tales (158 published 1835–72), he originally aspired to be an actor or singer and worked in the Royal Theatre, Copenhagen. From 1832 he also wrote librettos, including adaptations of Walter Scott's novel *The Bride of Lammermoor*, as Bredal's *Bruden fra Lammermoor* (1832), and Alessandro Manzoni's novel *I promessi sposi*, as Gläser's *Brylluppet ved Como-Söen* ('The Wedding by Lake Como', 1849). His tales, with their timeless characters, universal subject matter and richness of imagination, have been a popular source for opera and ballet librettos, inspiring dozens of works in the past hundred years.

FAIRY-TALES ON WHICH OPERAS HAVE BEEN BASED

Fyrtøjet [The Tinderbox]: Chevreuille, 1950, as D'un diable de briquet; N. E. Fougstedt, 1950, as Tulukset

Grantraet [The Christmas Tree]: Rebikov, 1903, as Yolka

Historien om en moder [The Story of a Mother]: Petyrek, 1923, as Die arme Mutter und der Tod; Sternefeld, 1935, as Mater dolorosa; E. Reesen, 1941; Vlad, 1951; Hollingsworth, 1954, as The Mother; T. H. Koppel, 1965

Hyrdinden og skorstensfejeren [The Shepherdess and the Chimney-sweep]: Schultz, 1953; J. Smith, 1966

Ib og lille Christine [Ib and Little Christina]: F. Leoni, 1901

Kejserens nye klæder [The Emperor's New Clothes]: C. Kjerulf, 1888; Kósa, 1926, as A király palástja; Høffding, 1928; Wagner-Régeny, 1928, as Der nackte König; G. Confalonieri, 1930; E. Werdin, 1948; D. S. Moore, 1949; Kalmanoff, 1950, as Fit for a King; H. Lofer, 1953; Ránki, 1953, as Pomádé király új ruhája; O. Kaufmann, 1954; H. Hayashi, 1955, as Hadaka no osama; B. Hummel, 1957; Beneš, 1969, as Cisárove Nové Šaty; W. W. Glaser, 1973, as En naken kung; Avidom, 1976, as Bigdei haMelech

Klodshans [Clumsy Hans]: S. Brandholt, 1913

Klokken [The Clock]: K. S. Clausen, 1934

Den lille havfrue [The Little Mermaid]: J. L. Weissberg, 1923, as Rusalotsjka; Maliszewski, 1928, as Syrena; L. Samuel, 1946, as La sirène au pays des hommes; A. Moeschinger, 1948; M. More, 1951; Tailleferre, 1960

Den lille pige med svovlstikkerne [The Little Match Girl]: Enna, 1897; Veretti, 1934, as Una favola di Andersen

Nattergalen [The Nightingale]: Enna, 1912; I. Stravinsky, 1914, as Solovej; F. Frischenschlager, 1937, as Der Kaiser und die Nachtigall; A. Irmler, 1939; H. Schanazara, 1947; B. Rogers, 1955; Strouse, 1982; Bjelinski, 1984, as Slavuj

Paradisets have [The Garden of Eden]: Bruneau, 1923; E. Němeček, 1933, as Rajská zahrada

Prinsessen på ærten [The Princess on the Pea]: Enna, 1900; Toch, 1927

Rejsekammeraten [The Travelling Companion]: Stanford, 1925; E. Hamerik, 1946

Snedronningen [The Snow Queen]: A. Guzewski, 1907, as Dziewica lodowców; Asaf'yev, 1908, as Snezhnaya koroleva; Silver, 1909, as Neigilde

Sneglen og rosenhækken [The Snail and the Rose Tree]: Nørholm, 1949

Stoppenålen [The Darning Needle]: S.-E. Johanson, 1973

Store Claus og lille Claus [The Clever Knapsack]: W. Wendland, 1909, as Das kluge Felleisen

Svinedrengen [The Swineherd]: J. Bartholdy, 1886; Hallström, 1887, as Per Svinaherde; Poldini, 1903, as Vagabund und Prinzessin; Chemin-Petit, 1905; Frischenschlager, 1913, as Der Schweinehirt; O. Ring, 1923; Sekles, 1926, as Die zehn Küsse; Rota, 1926, as Il principe porcaro; H. Reutter, 1938, as Die Prinzessin und der Schweinehirt; S. S. Schultz, 1970; Spasov, comp. 1980, as Printessata i svinaryat

Librettos: *Bruden fra Lammermoor* [The Bride of Lammermoor], I. F. Bredal, 1832; *Ravnen eller Broderprøven* [The Raven, or The Brother's Test], J. P. E. Hartmann, 1832; *Festen på Kenilworth* [The Feast at Kenilworth], Weyse, 1836; *Liden Kirsten* [Little Christina], Hartmann, 1846; *Brylluppet ved Como-Söen* [The Wedding by Lake Como], Gläser, 1849; *Nøkken* [The Water-Sprite], Gläser, 1853; *Kong Saul* [King Saul], Hartmann, comp. *c*1865, inc. (J. A. Krygell, comp. *c*1874–95, inc.)

*

G. Hetsch: *H. C. Andersen og Musiken* (Copenhagen, 1930) CLAUS RØLLUM-LARSEN

Andersen [Strecker], **Ludwig** (*b* Mainz, 13 Jan 1883; *d* Wiesbaden, 15 Sept 1978). German librettist and publisher. In 1909 he joined his father Ludwig Strecker (1853–1943) as a partner in the music publishing house of Schott in Mainz, becoming a director with his brother Willy Strecker (1884–1958) in 1920. From an early age he had shown a deep interest in literature and poetry, and during the 1930s began to develop his skills as a librettist, adopting the professional pseudonym of Ludwig Andersen. His first efforts were in oratorio, but he soon moved on to opera, adapting Franz Graf von Pocci's tale *Die Zaubergeige* (1935) for Werner Egk, Karl Simrock's version of the medieval puppet play *Doktor Johannes Faust* (1936) for Hermann Reutter, and Hermann Heinz Ortner's drama *Tobias Wunderlich* (1937) for Joseph Haas. The first two of these works ranked among the most frequently performed contemporary operas in Nazi Germany and were largely responsible for securing Schott's reputation as the pre-eminent German publisher of music-theatre works of the period. During World War II Andersen completed librettos for two comic operas, Wolf-Ferrari's *Gli dei a Tebe* (as *Der Kuckuck von Theben*, 1943) and Haas's *Die Hochzeit des Jobs* (1944), neither of which achieved any lasting success. Subsequently he resumed his collaboration with Reutter, providing the texts for *Don Juan und Faust* (1950) and *Die Witwe von Ephesus* (1954); but his most successful postwar partnership was with Cesar Bresgen, for whom he devised the scenarios of the popular school operas *Der Igel als Bräutigam*

(1948, rev. 1951), *Brüderlein Hund* (1953) and *Der Mann im Mond* (1960). Andersen also translated a number of operas into German, most notably Manuel de Falla's *La vida breve*.

*

C. Dahlhaus, ed.: *Festschrift für einen Verleger: Ludwig Strecker zum 90. Geburtstag* (Mainz, 1973) ERIK LEVI

Anderson, Beth [Barbara Elizabeth] (*b* Lexington, KY, 3 Jan 1950). American composer. She studied composition at the University of California, Davis, where she was a pupil of Larry Austin, John Cage and Richard Swift; she also studied at Mills College, Oakland, with Robert Ashley and Terry Riley. In 1973 she presented a one-act opera, *Queen Christina*, using pageantry, popular music, tape collage and live performance, with three principals, three smaller roles and chamber orchestra. Following her move to New York in 1975, she turned to performance art, dance accompaniment, teaching and criticism. Her *Zen Piece* and *Soap Tuning* (both 1976) are conceptualist avant-garde theatre pieces. The former, to her own libretto and first performed at The Kitchen, is in a question and answer format; the latter, using borrowed textual material, discards the answers, retaining only questions quoted from daytime television dramas. Anderson has also composed two musicals exploring social issues, *Nirvana Manor* (1981) and *Elizabeth Rex* (1984); *Riot Rot* (1984, book and lyrics by Anderson), a text-sound chamber work for two speakers and one singer (unspecified range), juxtaposing New York street riots with internal turmoil of an unloved and rejected character; and instrumental music as well as work for tape, live electronics and film.

CHARLES SHERE

Anderson, June (*b* Boston, 30 Dec 1952). American soprano. She studied at Yale University and made her début in 1978 as the Queen of Night at the New York City Opera, where she also sang Rosina, Gilda, Olympia and Lora (*Die Feen*). In 1982 she made her European début at the Rome Opera in *Semiramide*. She has sung at La Scala and in many other European cities, as well as in Chicago and San Francisco. She made her British début in 1984 with the WNO as Violetta and first sang at Covent Garden in 1986 in a concert performance of *Semiramide*, returning as Lucia, Gilda and Elvira in *I puritani* (1992). Concentrating on the bel canto repertory, she has sung Rossini's Desdemona, Anna (*Maometto II*), Zoraida and Armida; Bellini's Amina, Juliet, Elvira and Beatrice; Donizetti's Marie (*La fille du régiment*), Verdi's Lida (*La battaglia di Legnano*) and Gulnara (*Il corsaro*). Her voice, both strong and very flexible, is perfectly suited to Isabelle in *Robert le diable*, which she sang at the Paris Opéra (1985). She made her Metropolitan début as Gilda in 1989.

ELIZABETH FORBES

Anderson, Marian (*b* Philadelphia, 17 Feb 1899). American contralto. She studied with Giuseppe Boghetti and Frank La Forge. She made concert appearances in the USA and London, and toured Germany and Scandinavia, winning from Toscanini the reported tribute: 'A voice like yours is heard only once in a hundred years'. At the invitation of Rudolf Bing, she made a belated operatic début at the Metropolitan as Ulrica (1955). Although her voice was past its best, as the first black singer there she paved the way for others. After leaving the Metropolitan in 1956, she continued her concert career. Anderson's voice was large and striking, if not even throughout the range; she was above all admired for her artistic integrity.

DENNIS K. McINTIRE, MAX DE SCHAUENSEE

Anderson, Sylvia (*b* Denver, 1938). American mezzo-soprano. She studied at the Eastman School, Rochester, and in Cologne. After her stage début (Cologne, 1962, as Fyodor in *Boris Godunov*) she appeared widely in Germany, notably at Hamburg, Frankfurt, Mannheim and Düsseldorf. In 1968 she sang Ophelia in the Hamburg première of Searle's *Hamlet*, and in 1973 she took part in the première of Orff's *De temporum fine comoedia* at Salzburg. Returning to the USA, she appeared with the City Opera and at the Metropolitan Opera in New York as well as in Washington, DC, Santa Fe and San Francisco. Her repertory ranged from Gluck and Purcell through Rossini, Verdi and Wagner to contemporary music.

DAVID CUMMINGS

Andersson, Einar (*b* Västerås, 13 July 1909; *d* 11 Jan 1989). Swedish tenor. He studied in Stockholm, making his début there in 1938 as Fenton (*Die lustigen Weiber von Windsor*) at the Royal Opera where he was engaged until his retirement in 1963. At first he sang lyrical parts such as Tamino, Ferrando, Nicias (*Thaïs*), Lensky, the Duke, Alfredo and the title role in Atterberg's *Aladdin*, which he created in 1941. By the 1950s he was singing heavier roles: Faust, Vladimir (*Prince Igor*), Grigory, Pinkerton and Cavaradossi. An excellent actor with a serviceable voice, he was a thoroughly reliable artist.

ELIZABETH FORBES

Andersson, Laila (*b* Lösen, Blekinge, 30 March 1941). Swedish soprano. She studied in Stockholm, joining the Royal Opera in 1964. She created roles in Blomdahl's *Herr von Hancken* (1965), Gunnar Bucht's *Tronkrärna* (1966) and Maurice Karkoff's *Gränskibbutzen* (1975) and sang Lulu in the Swedish première of Berg's opera (1977). Her early repertory included Alcina, Susanna, the Queen of Night, Konstanze, Donna Elvira, Mathilde (*Guillaume Tell*) and Ebba Brahe (Georg Josef Vogler's *Gustav Adolf och Ebba Brahe*), which she sang at Drottningholm (1973). Her vibrant voice remained flexible as it grew more powerful, and she took on roles such as Leonora (*Il trovatore*), Alice Ford, Abigaille, Amelia (*Ballo*), Butterfly, Musetta, Salome, Jenůfa, Marie (*Wozzeck*) and the three Brünnhildes, which she sang at Århus (1987).

ELIZABETH FORBES

An der Wien. Theatre in Vienna built in 1801 and used for opera and operetta throughout the 19th century and in the first half of the 20th; from October 1945 until the reopening of the rebuilt Staatsoper am Ring in 1955 the Theater an der Wien was the home of the Staatsoper company. *See* VIENNA, §§3; 4 (ii); and 5.

Andolfati, Pietro (*b c*1755; *d c*1829). Italian impresario and librettist. His family was from Vicenza. Though trained as a lawyer, he chose instead to become an actor like his parents, and joined first Pietro Rossi's company in Venice and then, around 1777, the Compagnia Nazionale Toscana in Florence, directed by Giovanni Roffi. His first tragedy, *Le glorie della religione di Malta*, had success in many Italian theatres. He succeeded Roffi as impresario of the Teatro del Cocomero in 1785 and served until 1795, visiting Milan for a season in 1792.

Andolfati's greatest importance lies in his cultivation of Florentine poets and composers for the Cocomero's musical repertory. His contract there required him to translate French farces into Italian; in addition to the librettos listed below that are almost certainly his work, he probably wrote the otherwise anonymous librettos for most of the *farse* and some of the intermezzos given at the theatre during his tenure.

all farse

La pianella persa [L'inverno], ? Neri Bondi, 1789; *I vendemmiatori*, 1789; *Gli amori d'estate*, ? Neri Bondi, 1789; *Il diavolo a quattro*, 1790; *La Tarantola* [in *Il teatro moderno applaudito*, xl (1799), 38]

*

DBI (G. de Caro)
F. Bartoli: *Notizie istoriche de' comici italiani* (Padua, 1782), 4–7
F. Regli: *Dizionario biografico dei più celebri poeti ed artisti melodrammatici, tragici, e comici* (Turin, 1860)
L. Rasi: *I comici italiani* (Florence, 1897)
R. L. and N. Weaver: *A Chronology of Music in the Florentine Theater 1751–1800* (Warren, MI, 1992)

ROBERT LAMAR WEAVER

Andrade, Francisco d'. *See* D'ANDRADE, FRANCISCO.

André, Johann (*b* Offenbach, 28 March 1741; *d* Offenbach, 18 June 1799). German composer and publisher of Huguenot extraction. As a child of ten he inherited the family silk business, run by his mother and uncle until he reached his majority. While preparing to assume direction of the firm he also acquired some informal training as a dilettante composer. In 1761 he saw at Frankfurt the French operatic troupe of Renaud, described by Goethe in his autobiography. The naive charm and artless grace of the melodies in the *opéras comiques* performed by the company made a deep impression on André. His own melodic style, on which his subsequent success as a composer largely rested, remained under the sway of these and similar French models throughout his career.

André's theatrical skills became more fully formed during his association in 1771–2 with the troupe of Theobald Marchand, one of the finest itinerant companies in Germany, for which he translated French comic operas into German (for use with the original music). A year later André provided the text to his own first opera, *Der Töpfer* (1773, Hanau), a one-act farce dedicated to Marchand. More serious projects ensued – collaboration with Goethe on his Rousseau-influenced pastoral opera *Erwin und Elmire* (composed 1774–5), and a setting of G. A. Bürger's dramatic ballad *Lenore* (1775) which gained André widespread attention. At this time André also both translated and wrote incidental music for Beaumarchais' *Le barbier de Séville*.

The theatrical entrepreneur Theophil Döbbelin, prompted by the immense popularity of *Erwin und Elmire* on his stage at Berlin, offered André the position of music director in his company (one of the largest in Germany). He held the post from 1777 to 1784, composing 13 new operas for the company. He also wrote music for most of the celebratory occasional pieces and ballets they performed, and contributed a substantial amount of incidental music for spoken dramas (including *Macbeth* and *King Lear*). André's new operas for Berlin fared well at first, but by 1782 his manner had begun to lose its appeal for his audiences who were increasingly interested in Italian and Austrian operas rather than the German and French works that dominated Döbbelin's repertory. In 1784 business difficulties and the death of his mother in Offenbach persuaded André to resign his post and return to the Rhineland. At this time the Margrave Friedrich Heinrich of Schwedt, in the province of Brandenburg, named André honorary Kapellmeister of his private theatre. In return André supplied copies of his earlier operas but composed no new works and indeed wrote only one further opera after leaving Berlin, in 1796. He devoted the last 15 years of his life to the music publishing firm he had founded at Offenbach in 1774 and which was to gain even greater renown under his son Johann Anton André.

'He played a subordinate role, but still a role', Goethe once wrote of a lesser light in the German theatrical scene of his day. The same might be said of André during the formative years of German opera after the Seven Years War. Less original and experimental than Georg Benda, less genial and craftsmanlike than Hiller, André nonetheless contributed a series of stageworthy works spanning a decade in which a largely French-inspired genre sought fresh dramatic and musical modes of expression within the confines of the German troupe system. He combined a fondness for bluff and at times earthy humour with a popular, relentlessly foursquare melodic style that made all his operas easily apprehensible. Only for Döbbelin's brilliant, virtuoso leading lady Marie Niklas did he essay italianate bravura arias. He adopted virtually every novelty of his day – melodrama, Romanze, male chorus, thematic recall – but without devising any of his own. He was among the first to seek out fashionable new opera texts dealing with the exotic (*Das tartarische Gesetz*, *Belmont und Constanze*, *Der Barbier von Bagdad*), the supernatural (*Das wütende Heer*) and the unbridled (*Claudine von Villa Bella*, *Laura Rosetti*) but did not contribute substantially to their musical delineation.

His son, Johann Anton André (1775–1842), wrote two operas: *Rinaldo und Alcina* (L. von Baczko; ? 1799, Dresden) and *Die Weiber von Weinsberg* (of which the vocal score was published: Offenbach, 1800).

See also BELMONT UND CONSTANZE (i); *ERWIN UND ELMIRE* (i); and TÖPFER, DER.

all Berlin premières at Döbbelin's Theater in der Behrenstrasse

Der Töpfer (komische Oper, 1, André), Hanau, Fürstliches, 22 Jan 1773 (Offenbach, 1773/*R*1986: GOB, ix)

Erwin und Elmire (Schauspiel mit Gesang, 2, J. W. von Goethe, after the ballad 'Angelica and Edwin' in O. Goldsmith: *The Vicar of Wakefield*), private perf., Frankfurt, May 1775; Berlin, 17 July 1775, *A-Wn*, *D-B*, *US-Wc*; orch pts, vs (Offenbach, 1776)

Der alte Freyer (komische Oper, 1, André), Berlin, 2 Oct 1775

Die Bezauberten (komische Oper, 1, André, after Mme Favart: *Les ensorcelés*), Berlin, 18 Oct 1777, *D-B* (inc.)

Der Alchymist (Operette, 1, A. G. Meissner, after M. A. Le Grand: *L'amour diable*), Berlin, 11 April 1778

Laura Rosetti (Schauspiel mit Gesang, 3, B. C. d'Arien), Berlin, 23 May 1778, *B*

Azakia (Spl, 3, C. F. Schwan), Berlin, 26 Nov 1778

Claudine von Villa Bella, 1778 (Schauspiel mit Gesang, 3, Goethe), unperf.

Die Schadenfreude, 1778 (Operette, 1, C. F. Weisse), ?unperf., *B*

Das tartarische Gesetz (Schauspiel mit Gesang, 3, F. W. Gotter, after C. Gozzi: *I pitocchi fortunati*), Berlin, 31 May 1779, *B-Bc*, *D-B*, *Rtt*

Alter schützt für Thorheit nicht (Operette, 1, F. L. W. Meyer), Mannheim, 20 June 1779, *Rtt*; rev. as Kurze Thorheit ist die beste, Berlin, 18 July 1780, *B*

Das wütende Heer, oder Das Mädchen im Thurme (Operette, 3, C. F. Bretzner), Berlin, 22 Nov 1780, *B*

Belmont und Constanze, oder Die Entführung aus dem Serail (Operette, 3, Bretzner), Berlin, 25 May 1781, *B*, *US-Wc*

Elmine (Schauspiel mit Gesang, 3, C. W. von Drais), Berlin, 14 Feb 1782, *Wc*, vs (Berlin, 1782)

Eins wird doch helfen, oder Die Werbung aus Liebe (komische Oper, 2, J. D. Sander), Berlin, 24 Aug 1782, *D-DS*

Der Liebhaber als Automat oder Die redende Maschine (Operette, 1, André, after C. Dorbeil: *L'amant statue*), Berlin, 11 Sept 1782, *B, Bhbk, DS*

Der Barbier von Bagdad (Oper, 2, André), Berlin, 19 Feb 1783, *B, US-Wc*

Der Bräutigam in der Klemme (Spl, 1, Meyer, after Molière: *Le mariage forcé*), Frankfurt, 1796

*

C. F. von Bonin: *Berliner Theater-Journal für das Jahr 1782* (Berlin, 1783)

E. Schramm: 'Musikalisches Rokoko in Offenbach', *Alt-Offenbach*, v (1929), 31–5

W. Stauder: *Johann André: ein Beitrag zur Geschichte des deutschen Singspiels* (diss., U. of Frankfurt, 1936); extracts in *AMf*, i (1936), 318–60

T. Bauman: *North German Opera in the Age of Goethe* (Cambridge, 1985)

THOMAS BAUMAN

Andrea Chénier. *Dramma istorico* in four acts ('tableaux') by UMBERTO GIORDANO to a libretto by LUIGI ILLICA; Milan, Teatro alla Scala, 28 March 1896.

Andrea Chénier *a poet*	tenor
Carlo Gérard *a servant, later a sans-culotte*	baritone
Maddalena de Coigny	soprano
Bersi *her maid, a mulatto*	mezzo-soprano
Madelon *an old woman*	mezzo-soprano
La Contessa de Coigny	mezzo-soprano
Roucher *a friend of Chénier*	bass/baritone
Pietro Fléville *a novelist*	bass/baritone
Fouquier Tinville *the Public Prosecutor*	bass/baritone
Mathieu *a sans-culotte*	baritone
An Incroyable	tenor
The Abbé *a poet*	tenor
Schmidt *a gaoler at St Lazare*	bass
Master of the Household	bass

Ladies, gentlemen, abbés, footmen, musicians, servants, pages, valets, shepherdesses, beggars, sans-culottes, the National Guard, soldiers of the Republic, gendarmes, shopkeepers

Setting In and around Paris, 1789–93

Illica's libretto, inspired by the life of the French poet André Chénier (1762–94), was ceded to Giordano in 1894 by Alberto Franchetti, for whom it was written. The opera was completed in mid-November the following year. After some hesitation it was accepted for performance at La Scala on the strong recommendation of Mascagni, and it proved the only success of a disastrous season given at that theatre under the management of the publisher Sonzogno, who excluded from the cartello all works belonging to his rival, Ricordi. The principals were Giuseppe Borgatti (Chénier), then at the start of his career, Evelina Carrera (Maddalena) and Mario Sammarco (Gérard); the conductor was Rodolfo Ferrari. *Andrea Chénier* at once raised the composer to the front rank of the 'giovane scuola', along with Mascagni, Puccini and Leoncavallo. Today it remains the most widely performed of Giordano's operas, mainly as an effective vehicle for a star tenor. Borgatti owed to it the start of a notable Italian career. Outstanding exponents in recent times have included Franco Corelli and Placido Domingo.

ACT 1 *A salon in the Château Coigny* Preparations are in hand for a party, viewed with disgust by Gérard. He inveighs against the idleness and cruelty of the aristocracy in whose service his aged father has slaved all his life as a gardener. The Countess enters and gives orders to the servants. With her are Maddalena and her maid, Bersi, who discuss clothes. The guests begin to arrive; Fléville, the novelist, presents two friends, the Italian pianist Florinelli and the poet Andrea Chénier. They are joined by the Abbé, who brings the latest news from Paris. The King has taken the advice of Necker and summoned the Third Estate; the statue of Henri IV has been defaced by an unruly mob. To cheer the dejected company Fléville calls on the musicians to perform a madrigal to his own words, 'O pastorelle, addio'. Maddalena and her friends determine to tease Chénier out of his silence. Will he not recite a poem for them? He replies that poetry, like love, cannot be compelled; nonetheless he obliges with the Improvviso, 'Un dì all'azzurro spazio'. His love, he says, is the fair land of France, whose peasants are suffering while its clergy grows fat. The guests are offended; but the Countess begs their indulgence for a poet's wayward fancy. She commands a gavotte. But hardly has it begun when a lugubrious chant is heard from outside. Gérard comes in leading a crowd of beggars. Furious, the Countess orders them out of the house. Gérard's father goes on his knees to her; but his son raises him up, strips off his own livery and leads him and the beggars away. Recovering from a faint, the Countess declares herself totally bewildered – had she not always been generous to the poor? She bids the dance resume.

ACT 2 *The Café Hottot, by the Pont de Peronnet* Three years have passed. Mathieu is present with a number of *sans-culottes*; Chénier sits at a table apart. Paper-boys announce the arrest of the King. Bersi arrives, followed by an Incroyable whom she suspects of spying on her as an enemy of the Revolution. Accordingly she bursts out in its praise and joins in the cheers as a cartload of condemned prisoners passes by, to the strains of 'Ah, ça ira'. However, the Incroyable has seen her looking at Chénier and decides not to let her out of his sight. Roucher comes with a passport for Chénier, whom he advises to leave France with all speed. But Chénier has been intrigued by the receipt of letters written in a female hand and signed 'Hope'. A crowd gathers to watch the People's Representatives crossing the bridge. Among them the Incroyable notices Gérard, and draws him aside. From their conversation it appears that Gérard is in pursuit of Maddalena. The Incroyable promises to bring her to him that evening. Bersi now approaches Roucher; she has a message for Chénier: he must wait for 'Hope' at the nearby altar of Marat. She is overheard by the Incroyable. As Mathieu sings the *Carmagnole* a patrol passes by. Maddalena arrives, reveals her identity to Chénier and throws herself on his protection. The Incroyable goes off to summon Gérard. There follows a love duet between Maddalena and Chénier, 'Ecco l'altare', at the end of which Gérard appears. The two men fight. Gérard, severely wounded, tells Chénier to save himself and protect Maddalena. When the *sans-culottes* return and ask him who his assailant was, Gérard professes ignorance.

ACT 3 *The Hall of the Revolutionary Tribunal* To an assembled audience Mathieu declares that the country is in danger, threatened by rebellion from within and invasion from foreign powers. Gérard enters, to receive congratulations on his recovery. He calls on the women to give their sons and their jewelry to the nation. Old Madelon comes forward. Her son, she says, died

'Andrea Chénier' (Giordano), Act 3 (the Hall of the Revolutionary Tribunal): engraving showing the original production at La Scala, Milan, 28 March 1896, from 'L'illustrazione italiana' (12 April 1896)

fighting for his country; but she gladly offers her 15-year-old grandson to take his father's place. Much moved, the crowd disperse to the strains of the *Carmagnole*. Newspaper vendors proclaim the arrest of Andrea Chénier. The Incroyable assures Gérard that this will draw Maddalena into the trap. As he makes out the papers of accusation Gérard reflects in a famous monologue, 'Nemico della patria', that, once the slave of the aristocracy, he has now become a slave to his own passions. Maddalena is brought before him. To his ardent declaration of love she replies with an account of her miserable existence since her mother died and their castle was burnt, 'La mamma morta', until the voice of love bade her take heart and hope. Nonetheless she is prepared to yield to Gérard if she can thereby save Chénier's life. The court assembles and the accused are led in, among them Chénier. Fouquier Tinville reads aloud the charges against him. Chénier stoutly defends himself as a patriot and a man of honour ('Si, fui soldato'). Tinville calls for witnesses, whereupon Gérard springs up and insists that all the accusations against his rival are false. The court is astonished, but resolved nonetheless on Chénier's execution.

ACT 4 *The courtyard of the St Lazare prison* Chénier sits at a table, writing. Schmidt, the gaoler, admits Roucher, to whom Chénier reads his final poem, 'Come un bel dì di maggio', in which he compares the sunset of his life to that of a fine spring day. Roucher leaves; the distant voice of Mathieu can be heard singing the *Marseillaise*. Then Gérard is introduced together with Maddalena. She bribes the gaoler to allow her to take the place of one of the condemned. When Gérard has left she and Chénier join in a heroic duet, 'Vicino a te s'acqueta', before being taken to the guillotine.

* * *

Like most *verismo* operas of the period *Andrea Chénier* is built, act by act, as a loosely organized continuity bound together by variegated orchestral figuration in which motifs, repeated at short range and in different keys, play a prominent part. Thematic recollection, however, is rare, being confined here to the final strain of Maddalena's 'La mamma morta'. The vocal delivery is naturalistic, freely mixing conversational, lyrical and declamatory elements. Solos and duets arise directly and without preparation from the dialogue and are rarely marked off by a full close. The aristocratic ambience of Act 1 is conveyed by touches of period stylization such as the gavotte, while snatches of the *Carmagnole*, 'Ah, ça ira', and the *Marseillaise* evoke the atmosphere of the Revolution. JULIAN BUDDEN

Andreae, Volkmar (*b* Berne, 5 July 1879; *d* Zürich, 18 June 1962). Swiss conductor and composer. He was a pupil of Wüllner in Cologne (1897–1900). Following a one-year engagement as répétiteur at the Munich Hofoper, in 1902 he settled in Zürich where he dominated musical life for the next half-century, as a conductor, musical director and teacher; he also worked extensively abroad. He was president of the Schweizerische Tonkünstlerverein from 1920 to 1925.

Like most of his output, his operas date from the early part of his career: *Ratcliff* op.25, after Heine's tragedy, was first staged in Duisburg (25 May 1914), and *Abenteuer des Casanova* op.34, a group of four one-act works to a libretto by Ferdinand Lion, in Dresden (17 June 1924). They are rooted in the Romantic tradition, with Straussian orchestration.

*

E. Tobler: 'Volkmar Andreae', *Wissen und Leben*, xvi (1923), 1007–17

Volkmar Andreae: Festgabe (Zürich, 1949)

Volkmar Andreae zum 70. Geburtstag (Zürich, 1949)

F. Giegling: *Volkmar Andreae*, Neujahrsblatt der Allgemeinen Musikgesellschaft Zürich, no.143 (Zürich, 1959)

PETER ROSS

Andreini, Giovanni [Giovan] **Battista** (*b* Florence, 9 Feb ?1579; *d* Reggio Emilia, 7 or 8 June 1654). Italian dramatist and poet. His parents were among the foremost actors of their time; they were both good musicians, and his mother Isabella was also a poet. He appears to have studied at the University of Bologna. In 1594, taking the stage name 'Lelio', he joined the Gelosi, the comic troupe to which his parents belonged, and in 1601 he married the actress and singer Virginia Ramponi ('La Florinda'). By the time the Gelosi had disbanded in 1604 he had already formed his own company, the Comici Fedeli, which served the dukes of Mantua, with brief interruptions, until about 1647–50, playing throughout northern and central Italy. In 1613 Maria de' Medici invited the Fedeli to France; their visit, which lasted from September 1613 to July 1614, was so successful that they performed there again from January 1621 to March 1622, December 1622 to March 1623 and December 1623 to June 1625. In 1627 they visited Prague, and in 1628 Vienna: Andreini's wife died during this tour, or during the plague of 1630. Soon after, he married Virginia Rotari, an actress in his company for whom he had harboured an ill-concealed passion since about 1620. In 1643 the Fedeli returned to France, and in 1647, the year in which Luigi Rossi's *Orfeo* was performed in Paris, Andreini dedicated a presentation copy of his comedy *La Ferinda* to Cardinal Mazarin, evidently in the hope of having it set to music. He was the subject of eulogies and sonnets and belonged to the Accademia degli Spensierati of Florence.

Andreini was a prolific writer. About ten of his stage works straddle the borderline between spoken drama and opera. For example, in writing *La Ferinda* (Paris, 1622) he tried to take account of the operas he had seen at Florence and Mantua: though typical of the *commedia dell'arte* in its mixing of dialects and languages, it is entirely in verse; Andreini described it as a 'commedietta musicale', and much of it was sung. *La Centaura* (also Paris, 1622) married comedy and pastoral with tragedy. It too included sections that were sung, as well as choruses at the end of each act, and most of the other comedies allowed for isolated pieces of music such as songs and dances. Andreini wrote two sacred dramas, both in verse and in five acts, which are well on the way to being operas. *L'Adamo* (Milan, 1613; ed. E. Allodoli, Lanciano, 1913), which may have inspired Milton's *Paradise Lost*, includes scenes with directions for music. *La Maddalena* (1617, Mantua), performed by the Fedeli at the festivities for the wedding of Duke Ferdinando Gonzaga and Caterina de' Medici, had portions set to music by Monteverdi, Muzio Effrem, Salamone Rossi and Alessandro Ghivizzani: Andreini published the settings as *Musiche de alcuni eccellentissimi musici ... per La Maddalena* (Venice, 1617). Andreini based this 'sacra rappresentazione' on his poem of the same name (Venice, 1610), and it was later revised in three acts as *La Maddalena lasciva e penitente* (1652, Milan). The interest of all these works is heightened by the fact that he combined personal experience of both the traditional *commedia dell'arte* and the practical and musical aspects of contemporary 'literary' drama. He helped to pave the way for Italian opera in France and for the *comédie-ballet* of Molière and Lully.

DBI (F. A. Frajese); *ES* (A. Fiocco and C. E. Tanfani)

G. M. Mazzuchelli: *Gli scrittori d'Italia*, i (Brescia, 1753), 708–11

F. Bartoli: *Notizie istoriche de' comici italiani* (Padua, 1782), i, 13–30

C. Magnin: 'Teatro celeste (Les comédiens en paradis): les commencements de la comédie italienne en France', *Revue des deux mondes*, xx (1847), 1090–1109

A. Baschet: *Les comédiens italiens à la cour de France* (Paris, 1882)

A. Valeri (Carletta): 'Un palcoscenico del seicento: Lelio e Fritellino', *Nuova rassegna*, i/48 (1893), 797–800

E. Bevilacqua: 'Giambattista Andreini e la Compagnia dei "Fedeli"', *Giornale storico della letteratura italiana*, xxiii (1894), 76–155; xxiv (1894), 82–165

L. Rasi: *I comici italiani*, i (Florence, 1894 [dated 1897]), 117–39

A. E. Picot: 'Gli ultimi anni di Giovan Battista Andreini in Francia', *Rassegna bibliografica delle lettere italiane*, ix (1901), 61–7

M. Ortiz: 'Filodrammatici e comici di professione in una commedia di Giovanni Battista Andreini', *Rivista teatrale italiana*, viii/13 (1908–9), 257–73

V. Mazzetti: *Un famoso comico e autore drammatico del seicento* (Reggio Emilia, 1915)

COLIN TIMMS with TIM CARTER

Andreini [née Ramponi], **Virginia** ['La Florinda'] (*b* Milan, 1 Jan 1583; *d* ?Bologna, ?1630). Italian singer, wife of Giovanni Battista Andreini. She joined her husband in the Comici Fedeli; her stage name derived from her performance in his tragedy *Florinda* (1603, Florence), and she played the eponymous role of the inamorata in a number of his comedies. In spring 1608 she was required at short notice to take the place of Caterina Martinelli as the protagonist of Monteverdi's *Arianna* in the celebrations for the wedding of Prince Francesco Gonzaga and Margherita of Savoy; according to Antonio Costantini, she learnt the part in six days. She also sang in Monteverdi's *Ballo delle ingrate* in the same festivities. Contemporary accounts suggest that her performance in *Arianna* was exceptionally powerful; indeed, her talents as a singer were recalled with praise by Severo Bonini in his *Discorsi e regole* (1649–50). Her later career was marred by her rivalry with Orsola Cecchini ('La Flaminia' in the Comici Accesi) and then her husband's affair with Virginia Rotari. She may have died during a tour by the Fedeli in Austria in 1628, but more likely in Bologna during the plague two years later.

ES (E. Zanetti)

P. Fabbri: *Monteverdi* (Turin, 1985)

TIM CARTER

Andreoni, Giovanni Battista (*b* Lucca; *d* Lucca, 23 April 1797). Italian mezzo-soprano castrato. In 1736 he was appointed first soprano to the Palatine Chapel in Lucca. In 1738–9 he sang in Venice in operas by Pergolesi, Lampugnani, Hasse and Porpora, then for three seasons in London: in Lord Middlesex's experimental opera season at the New Haymarket Theatre (1739–40), Handel's final, unsuccessful opera season at Lincoln's Inn Fields (1740–41), and in Lord Middlesex's King's Theatre company as second man to Monticelli, mostly in pasticcios (1741–2). Under Handel he created the parts of Tirinthus in *Imeneo* and Ulysses in *Deidamia* and sang in several non-operatic works. Burney called him 'a good singer of the second class'; his Handel parts indicate a capable technique and a voice and compass (*b* to *a''*) similar to Carestini's. He was immensely fat, and according to Horace Mann had no trill. Andreoni sang at Florence in 1742–3 and 1747–8 (in Lampugnani's *L'Olimpiade* and *Tamerlano*), then in Spain, where he was robbed by a servant, which so disgusted him that he went to Rome and was ordained priest. WINTON DEAN

Andreozzi, Gaetano (*b* Aversa, 22 May 1755; *d* Paris, 21 or 24 Dec 1826). Italian composer. He studied singing, harmony and counterpoint with Fenaroli and P. A. Gallo at the Conservatorio di S Maria di Loreto, Naples. He was called 'Jommellini' after his maternal uncle, Niccolò Jommelli, with whom he also studied. Following his début work, the oratorio *Giefte* (1779, Rome), he established himself as a regular contributor of comic operas for Florence and Venice, but he did not write an *opera seria* for Venice until 1788. After Carnival 1784 he travelled to St Petersburg, where his *Didone abbandonata* was performed (Mooser). During his visit he may also have written *Giasone e Medea* (Florimo), though he must soon have been back in Naples, for he wrote an opera for Carnival 1785. The following spring he was again in Florence, where he married his student, the soprano Anna de Santi (*b* Florence, *c*1772; *d* nr Dresden, 2 June 1802). She had made her début as prima donna at the Teatro S Benedetto in Venice during the carnival season of 1786 and thereafter pursued a successful career, occasionally as the principal in her husband's operas. As well as singing in many Italian operatic centres including Naples and Palermo, she appeared for a season in Madrid (May–December 1791).

In 1786 Andreozzi wrote his first version of *Catone in Utica*, which enjoyed a number of revivals. Equally successful was his *Agesilao* (1788, Venice), which established his reputation as a composer of *opera seria*; thereafter his serious operas outnumber his comic works by more than three to one. For the next seven years he wrote operas on new texts by all the most important librettists of the period and for all the major operatic centres. He was also invited to revise successful operas by others. For most of his career he worked in northern Italy, returning frequently to Naples to compose operas. Beginning in 1790, he was called upon to write an occasional carnival opera for Rome. He also probably accompanied his wife on her Madrid trip, during which his *Angelica e Medoro* and *Didone abbandonata* were given at the Caños del Peral, although there is no evidence to support Fétis's claim that Andreozzi wrote a new opera for the city, *Gustavo, re di Svezia*. His Lenten opera, *Saulle* (1794, Naples), enjoyed numerous revivals through the first decade of the 19th century.

During the Napoleonic wars Andreozzi experienced a sharp decline in demand for his services. He and his wife separated by 1801; he returned to Naples, and she accepted a contract in Dresden, where she died in a carriage accident in 1802. From January 1802 to September 1803 Andreozzi produced five new operas. When political complications attending the French occupation of Naples cut short his service as impresario at the S Carlo in 1806, he began to teach singing. In 1825, ten years after his last opera was performed in Rome, he moved to Paris, where with the patronage of his former pupil Maria Carolina, the Duchess of Berry and daughter of King Francesco I of Naples, he was able to earn enough to assist his family, which had remained in Naples.

Andreozzi's serious operas of the late 1780s show that the move towards more ensembles and choruses and fewer arias had already begun. Some of the ensembles are conceived as arias with interjections by other characters which serve either as transitions or as commentary during the soloist's caesuras. Most of his arias are in through-composed, ternary form, in one or two tempos. There are a few minuets and an occasional shortened rondò or *dal segno* aria. Two-tempo rondòs are reserved for the principals, and shorter binary and simple ternary arias are more prevalent in the second and third acts. Extensive obbligato recitative is still reserved for the principals and does not accompany action. Andreozzi's ensembles tend to move from *largo* to *presto* in successively faster tempos. He skilfully imbued them with a sense of dramatic motion, though not in the same way as an action-filled comic finale. In his ensembles and in his choruses, which can be extensive, antiphonal pieces with solo and ensemble components, he used imitative writing and counterpoint. His sinfonias are in a single movement with two themes, a short development and a partial recapitulation; an extended crescendo and stretto articulate each section.

By the late 1790s *ABA′* aria forms almost disappeared from Andreozzi's operas. The number of arias decreased, while the number of cavatinas, choruses and ensembles increased. *Introduzioni*, scene complexes and multi-sectional, action-ensemble finales are all used. Freely constructed ensembles often contain some action and may fluctuate in the numbers of personnel. The varying components in scene complexes are tonally unified and interconnected with obbligato recitative. Choruses interact with the principals in recitative and ensemble. As a result of the fashion for tragic endings and for operas in two acts, when *Angelica e Medoro* was revived in Florence in 1792 the third act was cut so that the unhappy conclusion of Act 2 prevailed. Andreozzi's comic operas have the usual *introduzioni* and multi-sectional action-ensemble finales, as well as an additional ensemble in the middle of each act. By the mid-1790s these internal ensembles also incorporate action and become more like the finale.

Andreozzi was a skilled and original composer. He often contrasted wind and string sonorities and used solo instruments in dialogue or to provide obbligato embellishment or a simple countermelody to the voice. The English horn, clarinet and bassoon, as well as horns and oboes, heighten the effect of obbligato recitatives. His lean accompaniments often take the form of motivic, rhythmic or syncopated beat-keeping, using arpeggiated, oscillating or repeated note figures. Simple string accompaniment for the vocal phrases are in strong contrast with motivic tutti commentaries in orchestral passages and ritornellos. Andreozzi often establishes a dialogue between voice and orchestra, and occasional examples of motivic, textural or harmonic word-painting can be found. Andreozzi's prominent use of wind instruments, crescendo passages, chromaticism, modality and disguised recapitulations, as well as his tonally unified scene complexes, all point to Jommelli's influence.

See also AGESILAO, RE DI SPARTA and AMLETO (i).

L'equivoco (dg, 3), Florence, Pergola, spr. 1781, *I-Fc*

Arbace (os, G. Sertor), Livorno, S Sebastiano, aut. 1781, *P-La*; in 2 acts, Florence, Palla a Corda, spr. 1785, *I-Fc*

I pazzi per disimpegno (dg, 2, P. A. Bagliacca), Venice, S Moisè, carn. 1782

Olimpiade (os, 3, P. Metastasio), Pisa, Prini, spr. 1782

Bajazet (os, 3, A. Piovene), Florence, Pergola, carn. 1783, *Fc*

Medonte, re d'Epiro (os, G. De Gamerra), Alessandria, Città, Oct 1783

L'amore industrioso (int, 2, G. Casorri), Florence, Palla a Corda, aut. 1783

Quello che può accadere (dg, 2), Venice, S Samuele, carn. 1784

Didone abbandonata (os, 3, Metastasio), St Petersburg, Hermitage, 1784

Giasone e Medea (os, 2), ? St Petersburg, 1785 [according to Florimo]; Naples, S Carlo, 4 Nov 1793, *Nc*

Le tre fanatiche (ob, 2, G. Palomba), Naples, Fondo, carn. 1785

Catone in Utica (os, 3, Metastasio), Cremona, Società, carn. 1786; in 2 acts, Livorno, Armeni, aut. 1789

Virginia (os, after S. Stampiglia: La caduta dei Decemviri), Genoa, S Agostino, carn. 1787; as La caduta dei Decemviri, Florence, Palla a Corda, spr. 1788

Agesilao, re di Sparta (os, 3, F. Ballani), Venice, S Benedetto, carn. 1788, *F-Pn*; in 2 acts, Florence, Pergola, aut. 1788, *I-Fc**, *P-La*
Arminio (os, 3, F. Moretti), Venice, S Benedetto, 7 May 1788, *F-Pn*, *P-La*
Teodelinda (os, 3, G. D. Boggio), Turin, Regio, carn. 1789, *La*
Giovanna d'Arco, ossia La pulcella d'Orléans (os, 4, A. S. Sografi), Vicenza, Nuovo, 27 June 1789
Artaserse (os, Metastasio), Livorno, Armeni, aut. 1789
La morte di Giulio Cesare (os, 3, Sertor), Rome, Argentina, carn. 1790, *I-Gl*
Il finto cieco (ob, ?Trinchera), Naples, Nuovo, 1791
Angelica e Medoro (os, 2, Sertor, after Metastasio), Florence, Intrepidi, spr. 1792 [? or 1783]
Amleto (os, 2, G. M. Foppa, after J.-F. Ducis), Padua, Nuovo, 12 June 1792, *Pl*
Gli amanti in Tempe (pastorale, 2, De Gamerra), Florence, Palla a Corda, 4 Aug 1792
Sofronia ed Olindo (azione tragica, 2, C. Sernicola), Naples, S Carlo, 17 Feb 1793, *Bc*, *Fc*, *Nc*; as Amelia ed Ottiero, Trieste, Regio, 7 Nov 1797
Ines de Castro (os, 2, C. Giotti), Florence, Pergola, 8 Sept 1793
Le nozze inaspettate (ob, 2), Naples, Fiorentini, 1793
Saulle [L'ombra di Samuele, ossia La morte di Saulle] (os, 2, F. Salfi), Naples, Fondo, Lent 1794, *Fc*
La principessa filosofa, ossia Il contravveleno (ob, 2, Sografi, after A. Moreto: *Donna Diana*), Venice, 6 Oct 1794, *Bc*; rev. as Il disprezzo vinto dal disprezzo, Naples, Fondo, 2 Aug 1795
Arsinoe (os, 2, M. Rispoli), Naples, S Carlo, 13 Aug 1795, *Nc*
Il trionfo di Arsace (os, F. Ballani), Rome, Argentina, carn. 1796, *GB-Lbl* (Act 2)
La vergine del sole (os, C. L. Rossi, after J. F. Marmontel), Palermo, S Cecilia, aut. 1797, *?F-Pn*; in 2 acts (F. Casòli), Livorno, Avvalorati, aut. 1799, *I-Fc*
Argea (os, 3, G. Boggio), Turin, Nazionale, carn. 1799
Pamela nubile (comic-serious, 2), Parma, Corte, carn. 1800, *PAc*
Sesostri (os, 2, ?A. Zeno), Naples, S Carlo, 12 Jan 1802, *GB-Lbl*, *I-Nc*
Armida e Rinaldo (os, 2, after T. Tasso: *Gerusalemme liberata*), Naples, S Carlo, 2 Sept 1802, *Nc*
Il trionfo di Alessandro (os, 2, A. Passaro), Naples, S Carlo, 1803, *Nc*
Piramo e Tisbe (os, 2, G. Schmidt), Naples, S Carlo, 30 May 1803, *Nc*
Il trionfo di Claudia (os, 2), Florence, Pergola, 8 Sept 1803, *Fc*
Sedesclavo (os, M. Prunetti), Rome, Alibert, carn. 1805
Il trionfo di Tomiri (os, F. Cammarano), Naples, S Carlo, Lent, 1807
Tutti i torti son dei mariti (burletta, 1), Florence, Cocomero, 7 June 1814
Il trionfo di Alessandro Magno il Macedone (os, Passaro), Rome, Argentina, carn. 1815

Doubtful: Gustavo, re di Svezia (os), Madrid, 1791; La morte di Cleopatra (os, 3, G. Rossi and Sografi), Palermo, S Cecilia, 1797

*

ES (E. Zanetti); *FétisB*; *FlorimoN*; *StiegerO*
F. Piovano: 'Notizie storico-bibliografiche sulle opere di Pietro Carlo Guglielmi (Guglielmini) con appendice su Pietro Guglielmi', *RMI*, xvi (1909), 243–70, esp. 263–5; xvii (1910), 822–77, esp. 866
A. Della Corte: *L'opera comica italiana nel '700: studi ed appunti* (Bari, 1923)
R.-A. Mooser: *Annales de la musique et des musiciens en Russie au XVIIIme siècle* (Geneva, 1948–51)
U. Prota-Giurleo: '"Jommellino" e Signora', *Nostro tempo*, iv (Naples, 1955)
U. Zelaski: *L'opéra italien jusqu'en 1900* (Brussels, 1982)
M. Conati: Introduction to G. Andreozzi: *Amleto* (Milan, 1984)
M. McClymonds: '*La morte di Semiramide ossia La vendetta di Nino* and the Restoration of Death and Tragedy to the Italian Operatic Stage in the 1780s and 90s', *Atti del XIV Congresso della Società Internazionale di Musicologia: Bologna 1987*, iii: *Free Papers*, 285–92
——: 'The Venetian Role in the Transformation of Italian Opera Seria during the 1790s', *I vicini di Mozart*, ed. M. T. Muraro (Florence, 1989), 221–40

MARITA P. McCLYMONDS

Andrésen, Ivar (Frithiof) (*b* Christiania [now Oslo], 27 July 1896; *d* Stockholm, 24 Nov 1940). Norwegian bass. He studied in Stockholm, making his début there in 1919 as the King in *Aida*. In 1925 he sang in the première of Atterberg's *Bäckahästen*, then joined the Dresden Staatsoper. At Bayreuth (1927–36) he sang King Mark, Gurnemanz, the Landgrave, Hunding and Titurel. He also sang at Covent Garden (1928–31), the Metropolitan (1930–2) and the Berlin Staatsoper (1934–6). As well as Wagner, his repertory included Sarastro and Osmin, which he sang at Glyndebourne in 1935, and Abul Hassan in Cornelius's *Barbier von Bagdad*. He had a beautiful voice and was an artist of the first rank.

HAROLD ROSENTHAL/R

Andriessen, Hendrik (*b* Haarlem, 17 Sept 1892; *d* Haarlem, 12 April 1981). Dutch composer. He studied the organ and composition at the Amsterdam Conservatory, and in 1926 was appointed to teach composition and analysis there; he also taught the organ in Utrecht, where he became organist of the cathedral (1934) and later director of the conservatory. In 1949 he was appointed director of the conservatory in The Hague, and from 1952 to 1962 was professor at Nijmegen University.

Andriessen's large output includes much sacred choral music and works in most other genres. The opera *Philomela* (3, J. Engelman), completed in 1948 and first performed at the Holland Festival (Amsterdam, Stadsschouwburg, 16 June 1950), is based on an episode from Ovid's *Metamorphoses*, and is notable for the profound symphonic working of its leitmotifs. The prelude has the character of a symphonic exposition, orchestral interludes constitute developments of the ideas, and the ballet forms a scherzo. The finale, where the musical developments reach their climax, is also the culmination of the drama: the gods, in compassion for the people who destroy all in their unfettered passion, change them into birds, and so the conflicts are resolved in the triumph of eternal song. Broad, flowing melody, individual modal harmony and colourful orchestration make this one of Andriessen's most striking works. His chamber opera *De spiegel van Venetië* ('The Venetian Mirror'; 1, H. Nolthenius) concerns a fictitious moment in the life of Dirck Janszoon Sweelinck, the son of the Dutch composer. Andriessen complemented a drama full of passion and humour with a mixture of Romantic and neo-Baroque music, taking late Baroque style as a model but using genres such as madrigals, ricercares and dances. The work was performed only once, on Dutch television (KRO, 5 October 1967).

JOS WOUTERS/LEO SAMAMA

Andriessen, Louis (*b* Utrecht, 6 June 1939). Dutch composer. He studied composition with his father, Hendrik Andriessen, and later with Kees van Baaren and Berio. Since 1978 he has taught at the Royal Conservatory in The Hague.

At first Andriessen experimented with serial and aleatory procedures, but after discovering American minimalist music he created his own musical language. He shares with Stravinsky a strong anti-romantic attitude in his music, and has employed medieval and renaissance techniques. In 1969 he collaborated with four Dutch composers and two Dutch writers on the 'morality' *Reconstructie*.

His most elaborate music-theatre piece is *De materie* ('Matter'; composed 1984–8), first performed at the Holland Festival in 1989. The libretto is a compilation of existing texts based on the ideas and lives of four historical figures: Piet Mondrian, Madame Curie, the

17th-century philosopher David Gorleus and the 13th-century mystic and poet Hadewijch. Each of the four parts explores the relationship between mind and matter in a different perspective: science, mysticism, art and poetry. As well as incorporating musical forms such as the toccata, ballad, passacaglia and pavane, the third part in particular contains elements of boogie-woogie and funk music.

See also RECONSTRUCTIE.

all first performed in Amsterdam

Reconstructie [Reconstruction] (morality, 2 pts, H. Mulisch and H. Claus), Carré, 29 June 1969, collab. R. de Leeuw, M. Mengelberg, Schat, van Vlijmen

Mattheus Passie (music theatre, 2 pts, L. Ferron), Shaffy, 3 Nov 1976

Orpheus (music theatre, 3, L. de Boer), Shaffy, 19 Oct 1977

George Sand (music theatre, 3, M. Meijer), 29 May 1980

Dr. Nero (music theatre, 2, de Boer), Appel, 13 April 1984

De materie [Matter] (music theatre, 4 pts, Andriessen and R. Wilson), Muziek, 1 June 1989

*

A. Coenen: 'Louis Andriessen's "De materie"', *Key Notes*, xxv (1988–9), 3–12

P. Peters: 'De enige kunstvorm is de labyrintische: Louis Andriessen over "De materie"', *Mens en melodie*, vi (1989), 336–44

MICHAEL VAN EEKEREN

Andriessen, Pelagie. *See* GREEFF-ANDRIESSEN, PELAGIE.

Andromaca (i) ('Andromache'). *Opera seria* in three acts by FRANCESCO FEO to a libretto by APOSTOLO ZENO after Euripides, Seneca, Corneille and Racine; Rome, Teatro della Valle, 5 February 1730.

At the end of the Trojan war Andromache (soprano), Hector's faithful widow, her son Astianatte [Astyanax] (alto) and his 'brother' Telemaco [Telemachus] (soprano), Ulysses' child, whom she had abducted and raised as her own, are held captive by Pirro [Pyrrhus] (soprano), King of Epirus, who desires Andromache although she rejects his love. She fears for the life of Astyanax, whom the Greeks regard as heir to Hector's strength. The Spartan princess Ermione [Hermione] (soprano), betrothed to Pyrrhus, is overcome with jealousy at her lover's betrayal, and wants to eliminate her rival. Ulisse [Ulysses] (tenor) comes to press Pyrrhus into honouring his commitment to Hermione, to punish Andromache for the abduction and murder (he thinks) of his son, and to kill Astyanax. Protected by Pyrrhus, Andromache hides the boys in Hector's tomb. When Ulysses discovers them, she reveals that one of them is his son. After Hermione identifies Telemachus, and Astyanax is taken to be executed, Pyrrhus commands that Telemachus too must die. Ulysses then relents and their lives are spared. Pyrrhus, hearing that Andromache would kill herself if forced to be his wife, accepts Hermione.

Andromaca is typical of Feo's mature style, and abounds with effective and affective da capo arias. The last act, which includes a duettino, a quartet and two orchestral recitatives, is musically the most varied and dramatically the strongest of the three acts. Of special interest is the quartet 'Cederai superbo ingrato', in which the protagonists interact and address each other with statements and interjections projected through contrasting, profiled phrase gestures (ex.1), a procedure that may have influenced Pergolesi and anticipates an aspect of the action ensembles of later *opera buffa*. The quartet also offers an example of Feo's approach to a more fluid kind of orchestration, using wind instruments to set momentary dynamic or tutti accents. The last aria of the opera, Pyrrhus's 'Alma bella ombra diletta', with its bold unison passages, brings to mind Burney's praise of Feo for his 'fire, invention, and force in the melody'.

Ex.1

[Andromache: 'Yes, return to your first love' Astyanax: 'Ah, he appeases you, unjust destiny' Andromache: 'Pay attention' Ulysses: 'Go' Andromache: 'Listen' Pyrrhus: 'Be silent']

See also ANDROMACHE below.

HANNS-BERTOLD DIETZ

Andromaca (ii) ('Andromache'). *Dramma per musica* in three acts by LEONARDO LEO to a libretto by ANTONIO SALVI after JEAN RACINE's play *Andromaque*; Naples, Teatro di S Carlo, 4 November 1742.

Andromaca was the alternative title of Salvi's libretto *Astianatte*. Leo's setting – his penultimate *opera seria* – was performed for the name-day of King Charles III. The opera represents a decisive advance in the composer's powers of dramatic expression. The stylistic language is leaner and simpler, but more profound, than that found in his earlier works. In addition to powerfully emotive accompanied recitatives one finds choruses and marches; modified da capo arias are the norm, but where the drama requires greater flexibility it is given; and the use of orchestration and dynamics is more sophisticated than in *L'olimpiade* of only five years before. As in *L'olimpiade*, Leo employed his students from the conservatory of S Maria della Pietà dei Turchini to sing the simple choruses, unusual in any form in Neapolitan opera.

The scenery for the production was painted by Vincenzo Re and the dances created by Francesco Savuter. The singers were the soprano Giovanna Astrua (Andromaca [Andromache]), the soprano castrato Caffarelli (Oreste [Orestes]), the soprano Giovanna Jozzi (Ermione [Hermione]), the soprano castrato Lorenzo Ghirardi (Pirro [Pyrrhus]), the tenor Ottavio Albuzzi (Pilade [Pylades]) and the contralto Giuseppa

Barbieri (Clearte [Cleartes]). The work seems never to have been revived, although the autograph score has survived (*I-Nc*).

See also ANDROMACHE below. STEPHEN SHEARON

Andromache. Libretto subject popular in the 18th century. HOMER's *Iliad* recounts the unfortunate early life of Andromache, daughter of Eëtion, the king of Thebes in Cilicia. Andromache's husband Hector, as well as her father and brothers, are killed in the Trojan war, and her son Astyanax (also known as Scamandrius) is thrown from the walls. (In some versions of the legend he survives; librettos using this story are sometimes entitled *Astianatte* rather than *Andromaca*.) Virgil, in the *Aeneid*, tells of her subsequent enslavement by Pyrrhus (Neoptolemus), the son of Achilles, of her journey with him to Epirus where he is king, and of her bearing his son, Molossus. Pyrrhus later deserts her for Helen's daughter, Hermione, but Orestes, consumed with jealousy for Hermione, kills him. Andromache marries Helenus, Hector's brother.

Two famous dramas on this epic preceded the several opera librettos of the 18th century: the *Andromache* of EURIPIDES and JEAN RACINE's *Andromaque* (1667), both of which addressed the stormy and wanton actions of Pyrrhus, although to different ends. Racine's play set the tone for operatic productions, establishing variations that he later felt compelled to defend. Since 'one cannot imagine Andromache loving another husband or another son', Pyrrhus is made only to press a marriage suit on Andromache, threatening the life of Astyanax (still living) if she refuses. Orestes, son of Agamemnon, is messenger to this king of Epirus: Pyrrhus must not marry the wife of their defeated enemy, Hector, but rather Menelaus's daughter by Helen, Hermione (whom Orestes has long loved). Greece also demands that Astyanax be killed lest he inspire the rise of fallen Troy. Angered by Andromache's refusal to marry him, Pyrrhus threatens to hand the boy over to Greece and marry Hermione; faced with the certain death of her son, Andromache consents, but plots suicide. In a jealous rage, Hermione persuades Orestes to murder Pyrrhus at the altar, but he is pre-empted in his assassination by attending Greek soldiers. Yet Hermione still scorns Orestes; she rushes off to view the carnage and, on seeing the fallen Pyrrhus, plunges a dagger in her own breast. Orestes goes mad, loses consciousness, and is carried off by his soldiers.

Antonio Salvi's libretto *Astianatte* ('Astyanax'), first set by G. A. Perti at the Villa di Pratolino in 1701, acknowledges its debt to Racine in the *argomento* though it diverges sharply in his last act. At the end of Act 2, Pirro [Pyrrhus] himself is about to slay Astyanax when Andromaca [Andromache] relents and agrees to marriage. At the urging of Ermione [Hermione], Oreste [Orestes] wounds the king and flees. In Act 3, Andromache fears for Astyanax's life; Pyrrhus captures and condemns Orestes; yet now Hermione pleads for Orestes' life, which leads to a confession of love between her and Orestes. Pilade [Pylades], Orestes's compatriot, snatches Astyanax from Andromache, but is confronted by Pyrrhus. Pylades threatens to strike down the boy should Pyrrhus advance; Pyrrhus agrees to free Orestes in exchange for the boy's life. This noble act liberates Pyrrhus from all Grecian wrath. Pyrrhus and Andromache, and Orestes and Hermione, pledge their futures. This libretto was revived or reset more than 40 times, at first as *Astianatte* but by 1740 more widely known as *Andromaca* (presumably since Salvi's title character did not speak; in most productions the role of Astyanax was omitted altogether). Among the more important later settings of Salvi were those by Gasparini (1719), Vinci (1725), G. B. Bononcini (1727), Jommelli (1741), Leo (1742), Lampugnani (1748), Sacchini (1761), Bertoni (1771) and Nasolini (1790).

Other early *Andromaca* librettos are those by Pietro d'Averara (1701, Milan; composer unknown) and Zeno (1724, Vienna, music by Caldara; reset by Feo for Rome, 1730), both of which address the same portion of the story. The anonymous libretto for Paisiello's *Andromaca* (1797) is loosely based on Salvi's but the acts are reduced to two by the removal of the love between Orestes and Hermione. Ulysses, King of Ithaca, tries to steal away Astyanax by force (in some versions of the legend he kills him in Troy); Andromache is so taken with Pyrrhus's honour in defending the boy that she offers him her heart. Tottola's libretto for Rossini's *Ermione* (1819) returns to Racine's *Andromaque*, which it follows closely.

See also *ANDROMACA* (i) [Feo]; *ANDROMACA* (ii) [Leo]; *ASTIANATTE* [G. Bononcini]; and *ERMIONE* [Rossini]. For a list of operas based on Racine's *Andromaque*, *see* RACINE, JEAN. DALE E. MONSON

Andromeda. Libretto subject used chiefly in the 17th and 18th centuries. Its source is Greek mythology.

The story of Perseus' rescue of Andromeda from a sea monster was one of the most popular subjects of early opera, with over 25 independent librettos before 1800 (operas on the subject were also entitled *Andromeda e Perseo*, *Andromeda liberata*, *Persée* and *Perseo*). Perseus, the son of Danaë and Zeus, cast into the sea with his mother by the King of Argos (Danaë's father, Acrisius), grew up on the island of Seriphus. Later in life he saved his mother from the advances of Polydectes with the aid of the head of Medusa, which he cut off with a magic sword while shielded by godly armaments. An apparently middle-eastern addition to this legend concerns Perseus' rescue of Andromeda. Andromeda's mother, Cassiopeia, dared compare her beauty to the Nereids, so Poseidon sent a sea monster to plague the town. King Cepheus, Andromeda's father, was told through Zeus' oracle that the town could be saved only by sacrificing Andromeda to the monster. On his return from slaying Medusa, Perseus fell in love with the chained Andromeda, turned the monster to stone by exposing it to Medusa's head and took Andromeda for his wife.

Opera librettos generally ignored the broader legend and concentrated on Andromeda's rescue. Early versions, such as Ferrari's (set by Manelli) for the opening of the Venetian public theatres in 1637 and Bassi's (set by Tortona) for Piacenza in 1662, often included much of the mythological account, and particularly emphasized the role of the gods in both punishing and saving Andromeda. Ferrari suggests that Andromeda was saved, through Perseus, both out of pity (particularly represented by Venus) and justice (Astraea). The staged battle scenes between Perseus and the monster were often embellished by magnificent stage machinery; later they became platforms for inserted ballet. A particularly popular variant introduced another suitor for Andromeda's hand, usually a foreign prince who will marry her out of duty or by decree; Quinault's libretto for Lully's *Persée* (1682, Paris) used this scenario. Cigna-Santi's version, one of his most popular works, was the most influential libretto on this variant; it was set by at least four composers: Cocchi (1755, Turin), Fiorillo (1770, Kassel), Colla (1772, Turin) and Paisiello (1774, Milan). Here Andromeda is to marry the successor to King Acrisius of Argos, thought to be Euristeo. Andromeda and Perseus (known only as a valorous prince) must see their developing love thus dissolved. The wedding is cancelled, however, when Andromeda's name is drawn by lottery as the sacrifice victim to the oppressing sea monster. Perseus slays the beast (with sword alone) and in the end is discovered to be the rightful heir of Argos and the son of Zeus; Euristeo is united with his own former promised bride, Erminia. In Filistri's libretto set by Reichardt (1788, Berlin), the third suitor, Fineo, tries to steal away Andromeda. Bertati's serenata set by Zingarelli (1796, Venice) allows Perseus to intervene in Andromeda's fate by saving her, but not to alter her affections for Fineo. A Viennese spoken drama with background music (in the manner of a *duodramma*) from 1780 centres the entire episode around the rock where Andromeda has been chained; Perseus again slays the monster unaided by magical weapons.

See also ANDROMEDA [Manelli] and *PERSÉE* [Lully].

DALE E. MONSON

Andromeda. Opera in a prologue and three acts by FRANCESCO MANELLI to a libretto by BENEDETTO FERRARI; Venice, Teatro S Cassiano, Carnival 1637, before 25 February.

The opera, based on the myth of Perseus and Andromeda, is set in Ethiopia and required two stage sets. The account that follows is a conflation of the 1637 libretto and scenario. The curtain opens on to scenery depicting a rocky seashore at sunrise against which Aurora [Dawn], borne across the stage on a cloud, sings the prologue. Giunone [Juno] enters in a golden chariot drawn by peacocks, and Mercurio [Mercury] flies on to the stage. Cassiope [Cassiopeia], Queen of Ethiopia, has angered Juno by boasting that she is more beautiful than the goddess. Juno has resolved that her punishment will be to see her daughter Andromeda devoured by a sea monster. The scene changes to woodland, and Andromeda enters with a chorus of nymphs. They praise the beauty of the woods and depart to hunt a boar which has been terrorizing the countryside. The scene changes back to the seashore. Mercury brings Juno's orders to Nettuno [Neptune], who summons Protheo [Proteus] from the depths and orders him to release the most ferocious of his sea monsters. The act ends with a madrigal sung behind the scenes, followed by an intermezzo – a dance performed by three boys dressed as Cupids.

As Act 2 opens, Astrea [Astraea] appears in the sky and Venere [Venus] on the sea in a shell drawn by swans. Astraea declares that justice cannot be served by Andromeda's death. She returns to the sky to plead with Giove [Jupiter], while Venus exits to implore Neptune not to release the monster. Against the woodland scene, Andromeda and her nymphs enter and celebrate her slaying of the boar with a ballet (choreographed by G. B. Balbi) danced by six of the nymphs. Suddenly, the magician Astarco rises through the stage and warns Andromeda to flee if she would avoid death. She resolves to accept Heaven's will, and departs to give thanks to Jupiter for the boar's death. The heavens open to reveal Jupiter and Juno enthroned. Jupiter pleads for Andromeda, but Juno remains unmoved. The act ends with a madrigal sung behind the scenes, and an intermezzo follows in the form of a ballet, choreographed by Balbi, danced by 12 nymphs.

Act 3 is dominated by the spectacular use of stage machinery. Astraea reveals that it was she who sent Astarco to warn Andromeda; Venus has failed to prevent the departure of the sea monster. As they sing a duet, Mercury enters. The sky opens and Jupiter orders Mercury to tell Perseo [Perseus] to hasten to Andromeda's rescue. The royal palace of Andromeda suddenly appears, and from it comes the courtier Ascalà. In a lengthy monologue he laments Andromeda's decision to die and pictures her chained to a rock. The palace disappears and we see Andromeda awaiting death. In a long lament she reflects on the vanity of earthly greatness and bids death come. The monster appears and threatens her; Perseus arrives on the winged horse Pegasus and kills the monster. Releasing Andromeda, he asks for her hand in marriage. The sky opens to reveal the gods: Juno's heart has softened, and Jupiter bids Perseus and Andromeda rise to heaven. They do so to the accompaniment of a chorus of voices and instruments.

Andromeda was the first opera to be presented before a paying public and thus inaugurated the modern tradition of commercial opera performances. It was given in the newly refurbished Teatro S Cassiano by a company of singers and instrumentalists headed by Ferrari and Manelli, who staged it at their own expense. Manelli, a bass, sang two roles (Neptune and Astarco), and Ferrari, who acted as impresario, played the theorbo and also presumably directed the instrumental ensemble. The score is lost, but the text was published after 6 May 1637 to commemorate the performances; the publication also includes descriptions of the sets, costumes and stage action. The text of the prologue is not given in the 1637 libretto, but appears in Ferrari's *Poesie drammatiche* (Milan, 3/1659). The 12 solo roles of the opera were distributed between seven singers. The only woman, Maddalena Manelli, wife of the composer, took the roles of Andromeda and Dawn. The remaining female roles were sung by men, all of them soprano castratos and members of the choir of St Mark's, Venice: Juno by Francesco Angeletti, Astraea by Girolamo Medici and Venus by Anselmo Marconi. The other solo roles were also taken by members of the choir of St Mark's: Mercury, Perseus and the courtier Ascalà by the tenor Annibale Graselli; Proteus and Jupiter by the bass G. B. Bisucci. The libretto mentions a chorus of 12 nymphs – six archers and six dancers – and a chorus of gods. The latter appears only in the finale of the last act and probably did not require a separate group of singers.

See also ANDROMEDA above.

JOHN WHENHAM

Andzhelo ['*Angelo*']. Opera in four acts by CÉSAR ANTONOVICH CUI to a libretto by Viktor Burenin after VICTOR HUGO's *Angelo, tyran de Padoue*; St Petersburg, Mariinsky Theatre, 1/13 February 1876.

Despite its subtext of political liberation, Hugo's play was pre-eminently an erotic one: a love rectangle, one has to call it, among Angelo Malipieri (bass in the opera), the ruler of Padua, his wife Caterina (soprano) and his mistress Thisbe (mezzo-soprano), both of whom love not him but Ezzelino da Romano, alias Rodolfo (tenor), scion of the former ruling clan of Padua. Caterina is saved from a life-threatening plot by the self-sacrificing Thisbe, who accidentally learns that Caterina had saved her mother's life long ago in Venice. It is interesting to compare the libretto of Cui's opera with the one 'Tobia Gorrio' (Arrigo Boito) fashioned from the same play for Ponchielli's exactly contemporary *La Gioconda*. The whole first act of *La Gioconda* depicts actively the Venetian episode that is (very characteristically) cast as a static narrative in Cui's piece. On the other hand, Cui and Burenin, emulating the final scene of Musorgsky's *Boris Godunov*, fabricate a subplot of insurrection against Angelo's tyranny, headed by Rodolfo, to which an elaborat but dramatically inconsequential choral scene in Act 3 is devoted.

The best music in *Angelo* is in the two love duets. The one for Rodolfo and Thisbe in Act 1 is interesting for the musically delineated contrast of a sincere lover with an evasive, insincere one. That for Rodolfo and Caterina in Act 3, where both characters love genuinely, lends some credence to Vladimir Stasov's hyperbolic praise of Cui's powers of musical love portraiture. Within the peculiarly unlibidinous 'mighty kuchka', at any rate, he was love-poet supreme. RICHARD TARUSKIN

Anelli, Angelo (*b* Desenzano, 1 Nov 1761; *d* Pavia, 9 April 1820). Italian librettist. He was trained as a classical scholar, and between 1808 and 1816 he was Professor of Forensic Oratory in Milan; later he was Professor of Judicial Procedure in Pavia. He wrote more than 40 librettos, some of which became the most famous of the day. They include *La Griselda*, set by Piccinni and Paer, and *Ser Marcantonio*, which was set by Pavesi and later used by Ruffini as the basis for the libretto of Donizetti's *Don Pasquale*. The Pappataci rituals in *L'italiana in Algeri* (set by L. Mosca and Rossini) may reflect Anelli's interest in freemasonry. The same opera also reveals his propensity to use real-life situations in his librettos: in 1805 a Milanese girl, Antonietta Frapollo, was kidnapped and taken to the court of Mustapha-ibn-Ibrahim in Algiers. A number of his librettos were published under the pseudonyms of Lauro Fifferi, Marco Landi, P. Latanzio, Nicolo Liprandi, Tomasso Menucci, Giovanni Scannamusa and Gasparo Scopabirba.

Il castello d'Atlante (dg), Martín y Soler and others, 1791; *Cinna* (dramma), B. Asioli, 1792 (M. A. Portugal, 1793; Paer, 1795); *Egilina* (dramma), Borghi, 1793; *L'oro fa tutto* (dg), Paer, 1793; *La Griselda* (dramma eroicomico), N. Piccinni, 1793 (Paer, 1798, as La virtù al cimento); *La lanterna di Diogene* (dramma), P. A. Guglielmi, 1793 (M. Arici, 1810; F. Paini, 1820); *La secchia rapita* (dg), Zingarelli, 1793 (Bianchi, 1794; F. Celli, 1823); *Oro non compra amore* (dg), Caruso, 1794 (Portugal, 1804; P. C. Guglielmi, 1811; Zamboni, 1825); *L'amor sincero* (dg), G. Farinelli, 1799; *I fuorusciti* (dramma), V. Pucitta, 1801 (Paer, 1802)

Il podestà di Chioggia (dg), F. Orlandi, 1801; *Il marito migliore* (dg), Gazzaniga, 1801 (1807, as I due gemelli, ? with addl music by P. Generali); *Le lettere* (commedia), Orlandi, 1804; *L'impostore* (dg), F. B. Dussek, 1797 (Generali, 1815; Paini, 1815); *Nè l'un nè l'altro* (dg), Mayr, 1807; *Belle ciarle e tristi fatti* (dg), Mayr, 1807; *L'italiana in Algeri* (dg), L. Mosca, 1808 (Rossini, 1813); *Arminia* (dramma), S. Pavesi, 1810; *Chi s'è visto s'è visto* (dramma), V. Lavigna, 1810 (Generali, 1812, as L'orbo che ci vede); *I filosofi al cimento* (melodramma giocoso), E. Paganini, 1810; *Ser Marcantonio* (dg), Pavesi, 1810; *Il cicisbeo burlato* (dg), Orlandi, 1812

Le bestie in uomini (dg), G. Mosca, 1812 (G. Tadolini, 1815); *Arrighetto* (dramma), C. Coccia, 1813; *La nemica degli uomini* (ob), C. Mellara, 1814; *I begl'usi di città* (dg), Coccia, 1815 (Azzali, 1825, as La moglie avveduta; G. Speranza, 1840; C. Dominiceti, 1841); *Bettina vedova*, Pacini, 1815; *La cameriera astuta* (dg), Paini, 1815; *Il matrimonio per procura*, Pacini, 1815; *La chiarina*, Pacini, 1816 (Farinelli, 1816); *Il carnevale de Milano*, Pacini, 1817; *Dalla beffa il disinganno, ossia La poetessa* (dramma buffo), Pacini, 1817; *Piglia il mondo come viene* (dg), Pacini, 1817 (G. Persiani, 1825); *Amore ed equivoco* (drama), Q. Pecile, 1827

G. Bustico: 'Un librettista antiromantico (Angelo Anelli)', *RMI*, xxviii (1921), 53–81

RICHARD OSBORNE (text), JOHN BLACK (work-list)

Anfossi, Pasquale (*b* Taggia, 5 April 1727; *d* Rome, ? Feb 1797). Italian composer. According to the *Dizionario biografico degli italiani*, in 1744 he entered the Loreto conservatory, Naples, where he specialized in the violin. Having left the conservatory about 1752, he played in the orchestra of one of the small Neapolitan theatres; after about ten years in that profession (Ginguené) he decided to become a composer and took composition lessons from Sacchini and Piccinni. His first opera, *La serva spiritosa*, was produced at the Teatro Capranica, Rome, in Carnival 1763, but he only gradually established himself as a leading opera composer. According to Burney, he wrote some music for Sacchini's operas at the composer's request, while Ginguené and Grossi stated that Piccinni obtained opera commissions for him between 1771 and 1773 at the Teatro delle Dame, Rome, and that he achieved success with only the third of these, *L'incognita perseguitata* (1773). There is no doubt of the success of *L'incognita*, which gained for Anfossi a degree of celebrity he had not previously enjoyed.

During the 1770s Rome and Venice were the main centres of Anfossi's activities. For part of this period he was *maestro di coro* at the Venetian girls' conservatory called the Derelitti or Ospedaletto, for which he wrote music between 1773 and 1777. It has not been possible, however, to determine from the surviving conservatory records (now in *I-Vas*) the exact dates of his appointment or resignation. It is said that he went to Paris in 1780, but if so, he composed no new operas there. The statement in the *Dizionario biografico degli italiani* that he moved directly from Paris to London is dubious. His first opera for London, *Il trionfo della costanza*, was produced at the King's Theatre on 19 December 1782, and there is no evidence that he was in London much before then; the new operas that he had performed in Venice and Rome between 1780 and 1782 prove that he must have been working in Italy during this period. Off and on during the years 1782–6 he served as music director for the King's Theatre, where five new operas as well as several of his earlier works were produced. He also supervised the production of operas by other composers, including a version (first staged at the King's in May 1785) of Gluck's *Orfeo* with additional music by Handel and J. C. Bach. His last London opera, *L'inglese in Italia*, was unsuccessful, being performed only twice (20 and 27 May 1786); an extract from the *General Advertiser* for 22 May reads, 'The music evidently labours under a tedious monotony'.

By the following autumn Anfossi was back in Venice. At the start of 1787 he was in Rome for the production of his *Le pazzie de' gelosi*, a work which, according to Gerber, caused a fresh wave of enthusiasm for his music among the Romans. In 1790, however, his production of new operas, uninterrupted since the 1770s, came to an abrupt stop and he spent his last years in the service of the church. In August 1791 he was promised the post of *maestro di cappella* at St John Lateran, Rome, on G. B. Casali's resignation or death; he was appointed in July 1792 and held this position until his death.

The total number of Anfossi's operas, both heroic and comic, has not been established, but is certainly over 60 and possibly 70 or more. He also composed a considerable amount of church music, including about 20 sacred oratorios in Latin (composed for female voices and orchestra and first performed in Venice) or Italian (composed for mixed voices and orchestra and first performed in Rome). Anfossi's early style is close to Piccinni's, a reflection of their close professional relationship. His harmonies are diatonic and bland and his textures within any single number discreetly varied, though perhaps a little heavy at times because of constant note repetitions in the bass. His melodies, although not all equally inspired, contain moments of elegance and warmth. Several stylistic changes are noticeable in his later works: textures are lighter, and there is more effective use, both in accompaniments and melody, of pauses and rests; there are fewer embellishments and ornamental notes in the melodic parts; the orchestration is more colourful, partly because of a more imaginative use of wind instruments.

Anfossi employed the old-fashioned da capo form in arias of his early heroic operas and oratorios, though not in those of his comic operas, where freer forms prevail; by the mid-1770s, however, he abandoned the form altogether in favour of freer structures. Gerber noted the originality of his finales, although part of the credit is due to the high quality of the librettos by Bertati and others. Anfossi was particularly successful at depicting sentimental characters and situations: Giannetta in *L'incognita perseguitata* is one of his loveliest creations. But his operas betray evidence of haste in composition, and his operatic music has sometimes been criticized for not sufficiently enhancing characterization or creating dramatic impact. His *buffo* characters lack both Paisiello's witty terseness and Cimarosa's extravagant prolixity, while the music for most of his *seria* characters is overwhelmingly formulistic. In these respects he was far inferior to Mozart, whose superiority as a music dramatist can be seen from a comparison of Anfossi's *La finta giardiniera* (1774) with Mozart's setting of the same libretto a year later.

See also ADRIANO IN SIRIA (iii); AVARO, L'; CLEOPATRA (ii); CURIOSO INDISCRETO, IL; FINTA GIARDINIERA, LA (i); GELOSO IN CIMENTO, IL; NITTETI (ii); VERA COSTANZA, LA (i); VIAGGIATORI FELICI, I; and ZENOBIA DI PALMIRA.

LKH – *London, King's Theatre in the Haymarket*
RA – *Rome, Teatro Argentina*
RD – *Rome, Teatro delle Dame* RV – *Rome, Teatro Valle*
VB – Venice, *Teatro S Benedetto* VM – *Venice, Teatro S Moisè*
VS – *Venice, Teatro S Samuele*

cm – *commedia per musica* dg – *dramma giocoso*
dm – *dramma per musica* int – *intermezzo*

La serva spiritosa, o siano I ripieghi della medesima (farsetta, 2 pts), Rome, Capranica, carn. 1763, *?I-Gl* (as La serva spiritata)
Lo sposo di tre e marito di nessuna (cm, 3, A. Palomba), Naples, Nuovo, aut. 1763, collab. P. A. Guglielmi, *A-Wn*, *I-Bc*, *Nc*
Il finto medico (cm, 3), Naples, Nuovo, wint. 1764
Fiammetta generosa [Acts 2 and 3] (cm, 3), Naples, Fiorentini, carn. 1766 [Act 1 by Piccinni]
I matrimoni per dispetto (cm, 3), Naples, Nuovo, carn. 1767
La clemenza di Tito (dm, 3, P. Metastasio), RA, carn. 1769; Naples, S Carlo, 30 May 1772; *I-Nc*, *Rvat*, *Rc*, *F-Pn*, *P-La* (2 copies)
Armida (dm, 3, J. Durandi, after T. Tasso: *Gerusalemme liberata*), Turin, Regio, carn. 1770, *F-Pn*, *P-La*
Cajo Mario (dramma serio, 3, G. Roccaforte), VB, aut. 1770, *I-Rc**, *P-La* (2 copies)
Quinto Fabio (dm, 3, A. Zeno), RD, carn. 1771, *La*
Nitteti (dm, 3, Metastasio), Naples, S Carlo, 13 Aug 1771; rev. VB, 1780; *D-Mbs*, *F-Pn* (2 copies), *I-Nc*, *P-La* (2 copies)
Alessandro nell'Indie (dm, 3, Metastasio), RA, carn. 1772, *D-MÜs*, *F-Pn*, *I-Fc*, *P-La*
L'amante confuso (cm, 3, F. S. Zini), Naples, Fiorentini, aut. 1772, *GB-Lcm*
Il barone di Rocca Antica [Act 2] (int, 2, G. Petrosellini), Dresden, 1772 [Act 1 by Franchi; ? rev. of Franchi op of 1771]; rev. as La finta cingara [zingara] per amore (farsa, 2), Rome, Tordinona, carn. 1774; Venice, S Giovanni Grisostomo, carn. 1780; *D-Dlb*, *Rtt*, *F-Pn*, *I-Fc*
L'incognita perseguitata (dg, 3, Petrosellini, after C. Goldoni), RD, carn. 1773; as Metilda ritrovata, Vienna, 1773; as La Giannetta, Bologna, 1773; as Il capitano Asdrubale, Rovigo, 1773; as La Giannetta perseguitata, Dresden, 1774; in Fr. trans., Fontainebleau, 1776, Versailles, 1781 (Paris, 1781); *A-Wgm*, *Wn* (both as La Metilda ritrovata), *B-Bc*, *D-B*, *?Dlb* (La Giannetta perseguitata), *HR*, *F-Pn**, *Po*, *GB-Cpl* (Act 1), *Lbl*, *H-Bn*, *I-Bc*, *Fc*, *Mc* (La Giannetta), *Rdp*, *Rmas*, *Rn*, *Vnm*, *P-La*, *US-Bp*, *Wc*
Demofoonte (dm, 3, Metastasio), RA, carn. 1773, *D-MÜs*
Antigono (dm, 3, Metastasio), VB, Ascension 1773, excerpts (Venice, 1773)
Achille in Sciro (dm, 3, Metastasio), RA, carn. 1774, *I-Rc* (? autograph), *Rsc*
La finta giardiniera (dg, 3), RD, carn. 1774; as La marchesa giardiniera, London, 1775; as Die edle Gärtnerin, Frankfurt, 1782; *B-Bc*, *D-B*, *F-Pn*, *Po*, *GB-Lbl* (Acts 1 and 2), *Lcm*, *H-Bn*, *I-Fc*, *Mc*, *Rc*, *P-La*, *US-Wc* (as La contadina in corte)
Lucio Silla (dm, 3, G. De Gamerra), VS, Ascension 1774, *D-Mbs*, selections *F-Pn*
Il geloso in cimento (dg, 3, G. Bertati, after Goldoni: *La vedova scaltra*), Vienna, Burg, 25 May 1774; as La vedova galante, Graz, 1779; as La vedova scaltra, Castelnuovo, 1785; as La vedova bizzarra, Naples, 1788; *A-K*, *Wn*, *D-B* (as Die Eifersucht auf der Probe), *DS*, *Wa*, *F-BO*, *Pn*, *Po*, *GB-Lbl*, *H-Bn*, *I-Fc*, *Gl*, *Pl*, *P-La* (2 copies), *S-Ssr* (in Ger.), *US-Wc*
Olimpiade (dm, 3, Metastasio), VB, 26 Dec 1774, *D-Hs*, *Mbs*, *F-Pn*, *I-Rc*, *P-La*
La contadina incivilita (dg, 3, N. Tassi), VS, carn. 1775; as La contadina in corte, RD, 1775; as Il principe di Lago Nero, o sia L'innocenza premiata, Florence, Cocomero, spr. 1777, *US-Wc*
Didone abbandonata (dm, 3, Metastasio), VM, Ascension 1775, *F-Pn*, *I-Nc*, *P-La*
L'avaro (dg, 3, Bertati), VM, aut. 1775; as La fedeltà nelle angustie, Florence, 1777; as Li contrasti amorosi, Venice, S Giacomo di Corfù, aut. 1778; as Il sordo e l'avaro, Brunswick, 1782; *D-B*, *DS*, *Rtt*, *F-Pn*, *GB-Lbl*, *I-Bc*, *Fc*, *P-La*, *US-Wc*; as Le tuteur avare, Paris, 1787 (Paris, *c*1787)
La vera costanza (dg, 3, F. Puttini), RD, 2 Jan 1776; as La pescatrice fedele, VM, 1776; *A-Wgm*, *GB-Lbl*, *I-Fc*, *US-Wc*
Motezuma (dm, 3, V. A. Cigna-Santi), Reggio Emilia, Pubblico, Fair 1776
Isabella e Rodrigo, o sia La costanza in amore (dg, 2, Bertati), VS, aut. 1776, *D-DS*, *Dlb*, *Rtt*, *H-Bn*, *I-Fc*, *Mc* (as L'avventure di Donna Isabella e Don Rodrigo), *US-LOu*
Il curioso indiscreto (dg, 3, ? Bertati or Petrosellini, after M. de Cervantes: *Don Quixote*), RD, carn. 1777; in Fr., Paris, 1790; *F-Pn*, *Po*, *H-Bn*, *I-Nc* (Act 1), *Tf* (Act 3), *US-Bp*
Gengis-Kan (dm, 3), Turin, Regio, carn. 1777, *D-B*, *I-Tf*, *P-La* (2 copies)
La vaga frascatana contrastata dagli amorosi (dg), Ravenna, Nobil, May 1777
Adriano in Siria (dm, Metastasio), Padua, Nuovo, June 1777, *F-Po*, *I-Pl*, *P-La*; ed. in DMV, xxiv (1983)
Lo sposo disperato (dg, 2, Bertati), VM, aut. 1777; as Il zotico incivilito, Bologna, 1777; as Gli sposi in contrasto, Faenza, Accademica, carn. 1780; *B-Bc*, *D-B*, *F-Pn*, *H-Bn*, *I-Fc*, *US-Bp*
Il controgenio, ovvero Le speranze deluse (int, 2, ?Petrosellini), RV, carn. 1778, *I-Tf*
Ezio (dramma serio, 3, Metastasio), VM, Ascension 1778, *F-Pn*, *P-La*
La forza delle donne (dg, 2, Bertati), VM, aut. 1778; as Il valore delle donne, Turin, aut. 1780; as Il trionfo delle donne, Vienna, Hof, 1786; *D-Wa*, *F-Pn*, *I-Fc*, *Vnm*, *S-Skma*, *US-Bp*, *Wc*
L'americana in Olanda (dg, 2, N. Porta), VS, aut. 1778
Cleopatra (dramma serio, 3, M. Verazi), Milan, Scala, carn. 1779, *F-Pn*, *P-La*

Il matrimonio per inganno (dg, 2, ?Bertati, after Cervantes: *El casamiento engañoso*), Florence, Cocomero, spr. 1779, *D-Wa*, *F-Pn*, *Po*, *H-Bn*, *US-Wc*
Azor, re di Kibinga (dg, 2, Bertati), VM, aut. 1779
Amor costante (int, 2), Rome, Capranica, carn. 1780
Tito nelle Gallie (dm, 3, P. Giovannini), RD, carn. 1780
I viaggiatori felici (dg, 2, F. Livigni), VS, aut. 1780, *A-Wn*, *D-B*, *DS*, *Rtt*, *F-Pn*, *H-Bn*, *I-Fc*, *US-Bn*, *Wc*, Favourite Songs (London, *c*1782)
La donna volubile, Piacenza, carn. 1781
Lo sposo per equivoco (int, 2), Rome, Capranica, carn. 1781
Il trionfo d'Arianna (dm, 2, G. Lanfranchi Rossi), VM, Ascension 1781, *I-Vc*, *P-La*
L'imbroglio delle tre spose (dg, 2, Bertati), VM, aut. 1781, *I-Fc*, *Tf* (Act 2), *P-La*
Gli amanti canuti (dg, 2, Lanfranchi Rossi), VS, aut. 1781, ?*D-Dlb*, *US-Wc*
Zemira (dm, 2, G. Sertor), VB, carn. 1782, *Wc*
Il disprezzo (azione drammatica giocosa, 1), VS, carn. 1782, perf. with Act 2 of Gli amanti canuti
Il trionfo della costanza (dg, 2, C. F. Badini), LKH, 19 Dec 1782, Favourite Songs (London, *c*1783)
I vecchi burlati (dg, 2), LKH, 27 March 1783
Issipile (dm, 2, after Metastasio), LKH, 8 May 1784, Favourite Songs (London, *c*1784)
Le due gemelle (dg, 2, G. Tonioli), LKH, 12 June 1784
La pazza per amore (dg), Correggio, Pubblico, carn. 1785
L'inglese in Italia (dg, 2, Badini), LKH, 20 May 1786
Le gelosie fortunate (dg, 2, Livigni), VS, aut. 1786, *F-Pn*, *H-Bn*
Le pazzie de' gelosi (farsetta, 2), RV, carn. 1787, *F-Pn*
Creso (dm, 3, G. Pizzi), RA, carn. 1787
L'orfanella americana (cm, 4, Bertati), VM, aut. 1787
La maga Circe (farsetta, 1), RV, carn. 1788, *F-Pn*, *I-Gl*, *Rsc*, *US-Wc*
Artaserse (dm, 2, Metastasio), RD, carn. 1788, *F-Pn*
I matrimoni per fanatismo (dg, 2, ? C. Sernicola), Naples, Fondo, 1788
La gazzetta, o sia Il bagiano deluso (farsa, 2), RV, carn. 1789
Zenobia di Palmira (dm, 3, Sertor), VB, 26 Dec 1789, *I-Bc*, *Fc*
Gli artigiani (dg, 2, G. Foppa, after Goldoni: *L'amore artigiano*), VM, spr. 1793; as L'amor artigiano, Pavia, 1797; *D-MÜs*, *F-Pn*, *GB-Lbl*, *I-Gl*, *Rmassimo*, *S-St*, *US-Wc*

Music in: La finta principessa, o sia Li due fratelli Papamosca, 1785

Doubtful: Lucio Papirio, Rome, 1771; I visionari, Rome, 1771; Orlando paladino, Vienna, 1778; Le gelosie villane, Casale Monferrato, 1779; La finta ammalata, Parma, carn. 1782–3; Chi cerca trova, Florence, 1783 or 1789; Gli sposi in commedie, Piacenza, 1784; Il cavaliere per amore, Berlin, 1784; La villanella di spirito, Rome, 1787; L'antiquario, Paris, 1789

*

BurneyH; *DBI*; *GerberL*; *PEM* (S. Leopold and others); *RosaM*
P. L. Ginguené: *Notice sur la vie et les ouvrages de Nicola Piccinni* (Paris, an IX [1800–01])
G. B. G. Grossi: 'Pasquale Anfossi', *Biografia degli uomini illustri del regno di Napoli*, ed. D. Martuscelli, vi (Naples, 1819)
H. Kretzschmar: 'Mozart in der Geschichte der Oper', *Gesammelte Aufsätze über Musik*, ii (Leipzig, 1911), 257, esp.268
L. de Angelis: 'Musiche manoscritte inedite dei secoli xvi–xvii dell' Archivio del Pio Sodalizio dei Piceni in Roma', *NA*, xvi (1939), 29–31
M. Pedemonte: 'Musicisti liguri: Pasquale Anfossi', *Genova*, xxii (1942), 32
G. Tintori: *L'opera napoletana* (Milan, 1958)
R. Angermüller: 'Wer war der Librettist von *La finta giardiniera*', *MJb 1976/7*, 1–20
J. Joly: 'Metastasio e le sintesi della contraddizione', preface to P. Anfossi: *Adriano in Siria*, DMV, xxiv (1983)
R. Angermüller: 'Die Wiener Fassung von Pasquale Anfossis "Il curioso indiscreto"', *I vicini di Mozart: Venice 1987*, 35–98

MICHAEL F. ROBINSON, MARY HUNTER

Ange de feu, L'. Opera by Sergey Prokofiev; *see* FIERY ANGEL, THE.

Angel, Marie (*b* Pinnaroo, South Australia, 30 July 1953). Australian soprano. After appearing in Australia she joined Opera Factory Zürich, with whom she made her London début in 1980 as Galatea. With Opera Factory London (1982–92) she has sung Pretty Polly (*Punch and Judy*), Lucy (*The Beggar's Opera*), Denise (*The Knot Garden*), Juno and Callisto, Gluck's Iphigenia, Fiordiligi, Donna Anna, Countess Almaviva and Poppaea, and took part in the première of Osborne's *Hell's Angels* (1986). For ENO she sang Monteverdi's Eurydice and Hope (1983) and Queen Tye (*Akhnaten*), which she had already sung at Houston and for New York City Opera (1984), and created Oracle of the Dead/Hecate in *The Mask of Orpheus* (1986). She sang the Queen of Night for WNO (1986), Musetta for Opera North (1988) and Jo Ann in Tippett's *New Year* for Glyndebourne Touring Opera (1990), as well as creating Morgan le Fay in Birtwistle's *Gawain* at Covent Garden in 1991. The tonal purity, accuracy and flexibility of her voice are as admirable in 18th-century music as they are in that of the 20th century.

ELIZABETH FORBES

Angelica e Medoro ('Angelica and Medoro'). Libretto subject used chiefly in the 17th, 18th and 19th centuries. Its source is LUDOVICO ARIOSTO's epic poem *Orlando furioso* (1516); operas based on the story were also entitled *Orlando*, *Roland*, *Orlando paladino* and *Le pazzie di Orlando*.

Orlando (in French, Roland), nephew of Charlemagne, is one of several warriors infatuated with the pagan Angelica, daughter of the Great Khan of Cathay. The issue comes to a head with the appearance (in Canto xviii:165ff) of Medoro, an African prince. Medoro is seriously injured attempting to rescue the body of Prince Dardinello from the Christian camp. Angelica (xix:17) heals his wounds and, as they rest in a shepherd's house, falls in love with him: the account of Angelica and Medoro's union as they dally in forest groves carving their names on trees and rocks (xix:26–36) produces some of Ariosto's most sensual verse. The couple leave for Spain; Angelica rewards the shepherd with a bracelet given to her by Orlando. Orlando, arriving in the forest (xxiii:101), is incensed to see the carvings and even more distraught on hearing the shepherd's tale and seeing the bracelet. Mad with rage, he runs naked through the land, wreaking havoc and destruction (xxiii:129–xxiv:14). He catches up with Angelica and Medoro in Spain (xxix:58–67), kills Medoro's horse and pursues Angelica, who escapes only by virtue of a magic ring. Orlando continues on the rampage (xxx:4–15), swimming the straits of Gibraltar to Africa. Orlando's allies hear of his madness (xxxi:42–8, 61–4), and St John the Evangelist explains (xxxiv:62–6) to Astolfo, Prince of England, that it is divine punishment for his loving a pagan. They fly to the moon to recover Orlando's wits, stored there in a phial. Orlando arrives at Astolfo's camp (xxxix:35), is forcibly restrained by the Christians, and (xxxix:57) has his wits restored. Sane, he is no longer in love, and he continues the campaign against the infidels. Angelica and Medoro's fate is less clear, although we are told (xlii:38) that they sail to India where (xxx:16) he will become king.

Angelica's love for Medoro inspired over 50 operas. It provided the basis for an early musico-dramatic entertainment by Marco da Gagliano and Jacopo Peri (*Lo sposalizio di Medoro et Angelica*, 1619; libretto by Andrea Salvadori): here another Ariosto character, Sacripante, is the scorned lover. But later operas, understandably, prefer to focus on Orlando. Metastasio's *Angelica*, a serenata first set by Porpora in 1720, treats the early stages of the story straightforwardly (with a secondary love interest between Tirsi and Licori): Orlando concludes the work with a rather genteel lament. In contrast, Vivaldi's *Orlando* (1727), to a libretto by Grazio Braccioli, takes considerable liberties, conflating the tale with that (Cantos vi-viii) of the wicked sorceress Alcina, who is infatuated with Ruggiero (in turn loved by Bradamante). Alcina, who rescues Medoro from shipwreck and near-death, becomes Angelica's accomplice in imprisoning Orlando within a mountain, which he destroys (along with Alcina's power) before blessing Angelica and Medoro's union. Alcina also appears in Haydn's *Orlando paladino* (1782, to a libretto by C. F. Badini revised by Nunziato Porta): this time her magic is more white than black – Orlando is turned into a rock only as a temporary punishment for his excesses, and is cured of his madness by Charon and the waters of the River Lethe. Haydn introduces another Ariosto character, the pagan Rodomonte, as well as near-comic figures.

Lully's *Roland* (1685, libretto by Quinault) and Handel's *Orlando* (1733, libretto adapted from Capece) stay closer to the poem. The focus in Lully's opera is on Orlando's unworthy love for a pagan: he recovers his manhood by the example of the shades of past heroes and by the intervention of La Gloire [Glory], La Renommée [Fame] and La Terreur [Terror]. In Handel, Zoroaster is introduced as the magician who will bring Orlando to his senses, while a secondary love interest is provided by Dorinda (taking the place of Ariosto's shepherd), in love with Medoro. In both, the spectacular elements are in keeping with the epic poem, as too is the moral, which demonstrates (according to the Argument of Handel's libretto) 'the imperious Manner in which Love insinuates its Impressions into the Hearts of Persons of all Ranks; and likewise how a wise Man should be ever ready with his best Endeavours to re-conduct into the right Way, those who have been misguided from it by the Illusion of their Passions'.

See also *MEDORO* [Lucio]; *ORLANDO* (i) [Vivaldi]; *ORLANDO* (ii) [Handel]; *ORLANDO PALADINO* [Haydn]; *ROLAND* (i) [Lully]; and *ROLAND* (ii) [Piccinni]. For a list of operas based on Ariosto's *Orlando furioso see* ARIOSTO, LUDOVICO. TIM CARTER

Angelini, Giovanni Andrea. *See* BONTEMPI, GIOVANNI ANDREA.

Angélique. Farce in one act by JACQUES IBERT to a libretto by Nino (pseudonym of Michel Veber); Paris, Théâtre Bériza, 28 January 1927.

Set in a port, the opera concerns a woman, Angélique (soprano), who has been put up for sale by her husband Boniface (baritone) with the aid of Charlot (baritone), who takes money from three would-be buyers: an Italian (tenor), an Englishman (tenor) and a negro (bass), all characterized by clever musical pastiches. None of them can cope with her ebullience, and despairingly Boniface cries 'the devil take her!'. Obediently the devil appears and takes her, but even he cannot keep her and he too gives her back to the despairing Boniface: she is destined to be always for sale. A drinking-chorus finishes off this concise and fast-moving work, where each set piece is clearly defined.

The ridiculous situation, somewhat reminiscent of *commedia dell'arte*, is captured with 'wrong-note' harmonies, bitonality and a constantly nervous rhythmic drive, which includes African cross-rhythms to portray the negro's inspection, and what Ibert called 'de choeurs rythmés-parlés' – a chorus in speaking rhythm. His eclectic style and technique were well suited to the pastiche set pieces of this, his most successful opera. He was always pleased with it, considering it innovatory for a stage work: 'Using the voices to the limits of their possibilities, I did not spare the orchestra, using the minimum of instruments for the maximum result'.

RICHARD LANGHAM SMITH

Angelis, Nazzareno de. *See* DE ANGELIS, NAZZARENO.

Angelo. Opera by C. A. Cui; *see* *ANDZHELO*.

Angerer [von Rupp], **Margit** (*b* Budapest, 6 Nov 1903; *d* London, 31 Jan 1978). Hungarian soprano. She studied at the Budapest Academy and made her début in Vienna in 1926 as Leonora (*La forza del destino*). She remained in Vienna until 1938, achieving success in roles as diverse as Pamina, Tosca, Elsa, Eva, Octavian, Marguerite and Aithra in *Die ägyptische Helena*. At the Salzburg Festival she appeared in operas by Strauss, and she sang Octavian at Covent Garden in 1931. She moved to London in 1938 and continued her career as a concert singer. DAVID CUMMINGS

Angeri, Anna D'. *See* D'ANGERI, ANNA.

Angermüller, Rudolph (*b* Gadderbaum, Bielefeld, 2 Sept 1940). German musicologist. He studied musicology in Mainz (1961–5), Münster (1965–7) and Salzburg (1967–70) with Arnold Schmitz, Günther Massenkeil, Hellmut Federhofer and Croll. He received the doctorate at Salzburg University with a dissertation on Antonio Salieri in 1970, published as *Antonio Salieri: sein Leben und seine weltlichen Werke* (Munich, 1971–), and taught at Salzburg University (1968–72). While continuing to teach there, in 1972 he became academic librarian of the Internationale Stiftung Mozarteum, a post in which he worked with Otto Schneider on the preparation of a valuable series of Mozart bibliographies. In his Salieri studies, which brought him international recognition, he edited the opera *Tarare* (1978). He edited for the Neue Mozart-Ausgabe (of which he was editor-in-chief from 1973) *Bastien und Bastienne* (1974), and (with D. Berke) *La finta giardiniera* (1978). He has published studies of aspects of these works, on opera reform and on 19th-century operatic topics as well as an illustrated study of the production history of Mozart's operas (*Mozart: die Opern von der Uraufführung bis heute*, Fribourg, 1988; Eng. trans., 1989).

Angers. Town in western France. The first theatre in which opera was performed was built in 1738. It was replaced by the first Grand Théâtre in 1773. After a series of bankruptcies the theatre was acquired by the municipality in 1820 and reinaugurated in 1825 with *Il barbiere di Siviglia*. At this time Angers and Nantes shared a lyric troupe. In 1846 the public demanded their own troupe to play for eight months of the year, but this was not accorded until 1855, when the stars of Paris appeared as guest artists. Persiani sang in *Lucia* in 1849 and in 1858 the 15-year-old Massenet accompanied the tenor G.-H. Roger in a recital. After the theatre burnt down in 1865, opera and concerts were transferred to the hastily built Théâtre du Cirque by the river, now only recently demolished. The present Grand Théâtre, on the rue Duboys, was built in 1871 by the architect

Magne; seating nearly 1800, it was one of the largest French provincial theatres of its time (the capacity has been reduced to 1000 comfortable places). It was decorated by the local artists Roux, Maindron and Daubon and the ceiling was painted by the Angevin artist Lenepveu, who had painted the ceiling of the Paris Opéra in the rue Le Peletier. Known as the Théâtre Musical d'Angers, it has a season running from October to May with productions of some five operas and several operettas (often co-productions with other opera houses, particularly Nantes). Two to four performances of each work are put on, generally on Friday evenings and as Sunday matinées. CHARLES PITT

Anghelopoulos, Yannis (*b* Athens, 21 Jan 1881; *d* Piraeus, 5 Dec 1943). Greek baritone. He studied at the Lottner Conservatory in Athens and later with the soprano Nina Phoka. He made his début with the Elliniko Melodrama, probably in 1906, and it was on tour with this company (reportedly in 1910) that he first sang Rigoletto, which was to become his greatest role. After further study in Milan on a scholarship in 1920, he repeated the role in 1922 at the Teatro Massimo, Palermo, opposite Toti dal Monte's Gilda. He was engaged at the Teatro Carcano, Milan, for the 1923–4 season and then appeared with an Italian opera group in Egypt before returning to Greece in 1924, where he continued to sing with the Elliniko Melodrama for the next 15 years. His roles included Enrico Ashton, Gounod's Valentin, Ernani, Scarpia, Rossini's Figaro, Amonasro, Escamillo, Marcello, Luna and King Alfonso. He also created roles in some of the most important new works of the Greek repertory, among them Sakellaridis's *Perouze* (1911) and Kalomiris's *The Master Builder* (1916) and *The Mother's Ring* (1917). His many recordings (arias by Verdi, Donizetti and Leoncavallo and songs by Samaras and Hadjiapostolou) reveal a rich, sonorous voice, homogeneous and highly expressive; this, combined with a fine acting ability – he constantly sought to renew his interpretations, exploring the emotional overtones of both text and music – make him one of the greatest exponents of Greek lyric art.

*

G. Leotsakos: *Elliniko Lyriko Theatro, 100 chronia, 1888–1988* (YP 4–6, A/A 14564–6, 1988), 100–13 [record notes]

GEORGE LEOTSAKOS

Angiola, Maria Angiosa. *See* PAGANINI, MARIA ANGIOLA.

Angiolini, (Domenico Maria) Gasparo [Gaspare, Gaspero] [Gasparini, Domenico Maria Angiolo] (*b* Florence, 9 Feb 1731; *d* Milan, 6 Feb 1803). Italian choreographer and dancer. He began his dance career in Lucca (1747) and then danced in Venice (1747–8, 1750), Turin and Spoleto (1751), Lucca again, this time also working as a choreographer, and Rome (1752–3) before moving to Vienna. There, in 1754, he married his partner Maria Teresa Fogliazzi (1733–92) notwithstanding the rivalry of Casanova. During Carnival 1756–7 Angiolini produced ballets for the operas given at the Teatro Regio, Turin, also performing as *primo ballerino*. He returned to Vienna as *premier danseur* at the French theatre, and when Hilverding departed for Russia in November 1758, the director Giacomo Durazzo named Angiolini as his successor. Gluck succeeded Joseph Starzer as composer of ballet music.

Angiolini had misgivings over this appointment, and indeed early reports on his dancing and his ballets hardly hint at the power of his later creations. In a 1762 essay he implied that the chore of producing repertory ballets had inhibited his artistic development; with the hiring of assistant choreographers and the arrival in Vienna in 1761 of Ranieri de' Calzabigi, Angiolini gave up some of his duties and embarked on a series of major dance-dramas informed by the ideals of ancient pantomime. Calzabigi wrote or co-wrote at least some of Angiolini's printed essays for these works, providing literary polish and theoretical rigour. Angiolini himself insisted on concision, clarity and respect for classical poetics. In the interest of audience comprehension, the three main ballets in this series – *Le festin de pierre* (*Don Juan*), *Citera assediata* and *Sémiramis* – were based on well-known plays or operas. (Angiolini later staged a five-act version of his *Sémiramis* ballet, to his own music.) During this same period Angiolini contributed ballets to *opéras comiques*, and to *opere serie* including reform operas by Traetta and Gluck in which dance formed an integral part of the action. He called particular attention to the classical sources of his ballets for Gluck's *Orfeo ed Euridice*. Still, Angiolini was proudest of his independent ballets, which he saw as requiring far greater force of imagination.

The death of Emperor Francis in 1765 closed all theatres in Vienna, and prevented performances in Innsbruck of Angiolini's last ballet to music by Gluck, *Achille in Sciro*, based on Metastasio's libretto. Shortly thereafter Angiolini succeeded Hilverding at St Petersburg, making his début (September 1766) with another ballet derived from Metastasio, *Le départ d'Enée, ou Didon abandonnée*, to his own music. During this stay in Russia Angiolini presented several new ballets, restaged others from Vienna, and composed dances for a number of Italian operas. He worked next (1772–3) in Venice and Padua, and then in Milan, where he published an impassioned defence of his teacher Hilverding as the inventor of the *ballet en action*, and of his own ideals, against the claims of priority of the choreographer Jean-Georges Noverre, who had succeeded him in Vienna. (Their polemic over the next few years involved several figures in the Milanese enlightenment.) In his *Lettere … a Monsieur Noverre* (prompted also by a critical pamphlet on ballet by Ange Goudar) Angiolini clarified his attitudes on matters such as the contradictory languages of gestures and words, and the proper conduct of a tragic action. He also chided Noverre for neglecting technique, for relying on long explanatory programmes, and for his insufficient knowledge of music; Angiolini was by this time accustomed to writing his own music for his ballets.

The rivals traded posts in 1774, Noverre being hired at the Teatro Regio Ducale in Milan, and Angiolini returning to Vienna; this stay proved unsuccessful. In 1776 Angiolini was called again to St Petersburg, where he composed ballets for several operas by Paisiello. Between 1779 and 1782 Angiolini worked in opera houses in Milan, Venice, Turin and Verona, composing ballets, most of which (typically for Italian practice at the time) were independent in plot from the operas they accompanied. During his final sojourn in St Petersburg (1782–6) he became involved in the newly founded ballet school, and also in disputes with the impresario Yelagin. Between Carnival 1789 and 1791 Angiolini worked at La Scala, Milan, at Turin, and at S Benedetto in Venice. Thereafter his theatrical activities became increasingly politicized, and his republican sympathies cost him two years' imprisonment and exile; he was released in 1801 following the Peace of Lunéville.

It is not only Angiolini's revival of ancient pantomime drama that marks him as a major figure in 18th-century ballet, but also his sophisticated thinking on the relationship between dance, words and music. Remarkably many of his independent ballets were derived from operas, including *La caccia di Enrico IV* (1773, after Sedaine and Collé), *Il disertore* (1773, after the 1769 *opéra comique* by Sedaine and Monsigny), *Il sagrificio di Dircea* (1773, after Metastasio's *Demofoonte*), *Solimano II* (1781, after Favart and Marmontel) and *Il diavolo a quattro* (1782, after Sedaine). In the programmes for several of these works Angiolini discusses with rare perspicacity the changes made necessary by different means of expression. He was a sensitive and intelligent collaborator with opera composers, but his own music for his independent ballets was less than distinguished; his most important creations are those to music by Gluck.

Angiolini's nephew Pietro Angiolini (*b* ?Florence, *c*1760; *d* after 1836), also a dancer and choreographer, worked in opera houses throughout Italy as well as in London and Lisbon. He should not be confused with a son of Gasparo, also named Pietro, who was born in 1764.

Ballets in: Bertoni: Lucio Vero, Turin, 1757; Numa al trono (?pasticcio), Vienna, 1760; Rousseau: Le devin du village, Vienna, 1760; Hasse: Alcide al bivio, Vienna, 1760; G. Scarlatti: Issipile, Vienna, 1760; Traetta: Armida, Vienna, 1761; Rousseau: Le devin du village, Vienna, 1761; Gluck and others: Le diable à quatre, Vienna, 1761; Gluck: L'arbre enchanté, Vienna, 1761; Hasse: Il trionfo di Clelia, Vienna, 1762; Gluck and others: Le diable à quatre, Vienna, 1762; Gluck, arr.: Arianna, Vienna, 1762; Gluck: Orfeo ed Euridice, Vienna, 1762; Scarlatti: L'isola disabitata, Vienna, 1763; Traetta: Ifigenia in Tauride, Vienna, 1763; Gluck: La rencontre imprévue, Vienna, 1764; Galuppi: Ifigenia in Tauride, St Petersburg, 1768; Traetta: L'Olimpiade, St Petersburg, 1769; Paisiello: Nitteti, St Petersburg, 1777; Paisiello: Achille in Sciro, St Petersburg, 1778; ? F. Todi: Polinnia, St Petersburg, 1784; F. Bianchi: Nitteti, Milan, 1789; Federici: L'Olimpiade, Turin, 1789; Tarchi: L'apoteosi d'Ercole, Venice, 1791

*

ES (G. Tani)
Reports from Vienna in *Journal encyclopédique* (Dec 1759) and *Journal étranger* (May 1760–Aug [appeared after Oct] 1762)
G. Angiolini [with R. de' Calzabigi]: Preface to *Le festin de pierre* [*Don Juan*] (Vienna, 1761)
——: Preface to *Citera assediata* (Vienna, 1762)
[G. Angiolini and R. de' Calzabigi]: *Dissertation sur les ballets pantomimes des anciens, pour servir de programme au ballet pantomime tragique de Sémiramis* (Vienna, 1765)
J. von Stählin: 'Nachrichten von der Musik in Russland', *Beylagen zum neuveränderten Russland*, ed. J. J. Haigold [A. L. von Schlözer] (Riga and Leipzig, 1769–70)
G. Angiolini: *Lettere ... a Monsieur Noverre sopra i balli pantomimi* (Milan, 1773)
A. Goudar: *De Venise: remarques sur la musique et la danse ou Lettres de Mr. G ... à Milord Pembroke* (Venice, 1773)
G. Angiolini: *Riflessioni sopra l'uso dei programmi nei balli pantomimi* (Milan, 1775)
R. Haas: 'Die Wiener Ballet-Pantomime im 18. Jahrhundert und Glucks Don Juan', *SMw*, x (1923), 6–36
——: *Gluck und Durazzo im Burgtheater* (Vienna, 1925)
——: 'Der Wiener Bühnentanz von 1740 bis 1767', *JbMP 1937*, 77–93
R.-A. Mooser: *Opéras, intermezzos, ballets, cantates, oratorios joués en Russie durant le XVIIIe siècle* (Basle, 1945, 3/1964)
——: *Annales de la musique et des musiciens en Russie au XVIIIe siècle* (Geneva, 1948–51)
R. Engländer: Preface to C. W. Gluck: *Don Juan, Sémiramis*, Sämtliche Werke, ii/1 (Kassel, 1966)
L. Tozzi: *Il balletto pantomimo del settecento: Gaspare Angiolini* (L'Aquila, 1972)
M. H. Winter: *The Pre-Romantic Ballet* (London, 1974)
M. Viale Ferrero: 'Appunti di scenografia settecentesca, in margine a rappresentazioni di opere in musica di Gluck e balli di Angiolini', *Chigiana*, xxix–xxx (1975), 513–34
K. K. Hansell: *Opera and Ballet at the Regio Ducal Teatro of Milan, 1771–1776* (diss., U. of California, Berkeley, 1980)
——: 'Il ballo teatrale e l'opera italiana', *SOI*, v (1988), 175–306
B. A. Brown: *Gluck and the French Theatre in Vienna* (Oxford, 1991)
BRUCE ALAN BROWN

Anglés, Amalia (*b* Badajoz, 3 Nov 1827; *d* Stuttgart, 1 May 1859). Spanish soprano. A pupil at the Royal Conservatory in Madrid, she was appointed répétiteuse there in 1847 and held that position until April 1851. She was also singing teacher to the royal princesses. She performed in the last two operatic seasons of the Teatro del Real Palacio (which was suppressed in June 1851), singing in *La straniera* (1850) and *Luisa Miller* (1851), and perhaps other roles, before going to Italy. She made her début at La Scala as Gilda in the first Milan performance of *Rigoletto* (18 January 1853), and thereafter had a successful career which took her to the Opéra in Paris for ten months, to Italy and then to Germany, where she died suddenly.

*

B. Saldoni: *Diccionario biográfico-bibliográfico de efemérides de músicos españoles*, iii (Madrid, 1880)
A. Penã y Goñi: *La ópera española y la música dramática en España en el siglo XIX: a puntes históricos* (Madrid, 1881; abridged E. Rincón, as *España desde la ópera a la zarzuela*, 1967)
Almanaque musical Salón Romero (Madrid, 1895)
E. Cotarelo y Mori: *Historia de la zarzuela, o sea el drama lírico en España* (Madrid, 1934)
XOÁN M. CARREIRA

Anglesi, Domenico (*b* ? between *c*1610 and 1615; *d* after 28 Aug 1669). Italian composer. He became an instrumentalist and composer to the Grand Duke of Tuscany at Florence in 1638, and for several years was also in the household of Cardinal Giovan Carlo de' Medici. Mentioned by Atto Melani for his contrary opinion of Cavalli's *Ipermestra* (letter of 1654 to Prince Mattias de' Medici; cited in Ademollo, 1884, p.70), he wrote the comic opera *La serva nobile* (G. A. Moniglia; Florence, Pergola, 1660), staged by the Accademia degli Immobili, whose patron was Cardinal Giovan Carlo. The music is lost, but Anglesi's surviving Italian songs show him to have been a sensitive and progressive composer.

*

A. Ademollo: *I primi fasti della musica italiana a Parigi* (Milan, 1884), 70
——: *I primi fasti del Teatro di Via della Pergola in Firenze (1657–1661)* (Milan, 1885), 14
R. L. Weaver: *Florentine Comic Operas of the Seventeenth Century* (diss., U. of North Carolina, 1958), 62ff
——: 'Opera in Florence: 1646–1731', *Studies in Musicology: Essays in Memory of Glen Haydon* (Chapel Hill, 1969), 60–71
N. W. Weaver: *A Chronology of Music in the Florentine Theater 1590–1750* (Detroit, 1978), 130, 239
NIGEL FORTUNE

Angora. ANKARA.

Angri [Angry, D'Angri], **Elena** (*b* Corfu, 14 May 1824; *d* Barcelona, after 1860). Greek contralto and mezzo-soprano. The earliest known Greek singer to pursue an international career, she appeared at La Scala (1844–7) in 131 performances of 12 operas, including Mercadante's *Il giuramento*, Pacini's *Saffo*, Rossini's *Semiramide*, Donizetti's *Linda di Chamounix* and Gnecco's *La prova d'un opera seria*. Donizetti mentions her in two of his letters from Vienna (15 April 1845 and 6 May 1848). In spring 1846, her success in Vienna earned her the title of *cantante di camera* from the Emperor. She subsequently sang in St Petersburg (1847–9, according to Kutsch and Riemens), Paris and London, and toured in Spain and North America. Contemporary reviews praise her agility and precision in passages of vocal virtuosity, her charm on stage and her vivid characterization of Corilla in Gnecco's opera. In 1860 she retired from the theatre and settled in Barcelona. Nothing is known about her thereafter.

*

GSL
G. Zavadini: *Donizetti: vita, musiche, epistolario* (Bergamo, 1948), 807–8, 809–10 GEORGE LEOTSAKOS

Angrisani, Carlo (*b* Reggio Emilia, *c*1765; *fl* 1786–1826). Italian bass. Between 1786 and 1794 he sang in some of the leading theatres in Italy, including those at Bologna, Florence, Venice, Turin and Milan. In 1794 he went to Vienna, singing in operas by Cimarosa and Paisiello at the Hoftheater until 1800. In the first decade of the 19th century he returned to La Scala, also singing in Verona and Vicenza. He made his début at the King's Theatre in London in 1816–17 and during the following seasons appeared with Pasta, Fodor-Mainvielle, Naldi and Ambrogietti. His diverse repertory included Mozart's Figaro and Sarastro and Rossini's Bartolo. In 1825–6 Angrisani made a tour of North America and appeared in the first New York performances of *Don Giovanni*, *Tancredi*, *La Cenerentola* and *Il turco in Italia*. Nothing is known of his last years.

*

GSL
T. Fenner: *Leigh Hunt and Opera Criticism: the 'Examiner' Years, 1808–1821* (Lawrence, KS, 1972) THEODORE FENNER

Anhalt, István (*b* Budapest, 12 April 1919). Canadian composer of Hungarian birth. He studied composition with Kodály at the Budapest Academy (1937–41) and in 1945 became assistant conductor at the Hungarian State Opera. From 1946 to 1948 he studied in Paris with Nadia Boulanger (composition), Fourestier (conducting) and Soulima Stravinsky (piano). He moved to Canada in 1949 and taught at McGill University where, in 1964, he installed an electronic music studio which he directed until 1971. From 1971 until his retirement in 1984 he was head of the music department at Queen's University in Kingston, Ontario.

Anhalt's works display no influence of Kodály and Boulanger (except through the meticulous care with which they are crafted) and they are an uncompromising document of his own voyage of discovery. Autobiographical references are a subtle undercurrent in his substantial scores. Having initially composed much serial and electronic music, he combines, in his two operas, tonal and atonal idioms. The music is rich and expressive, even given the complex harmonies and intricate rhythmic sonorities, and this personal and powerful intensity is most compelling in *La tourangelle*, a musical tableau for five singer-narrators, a 16-piece orchestra and pre-recorded tapes requiring five operators, first given in Toronto in 1975. *La tourangelle*, in seven sections or scenes, is based on the life of Sister Marie de l'Incarnation, who founded the Ursuline Order in Quebec in 1639. Anhalt took seven years to compose his second opera, *Winthrop*, a musical pageant about the 17th-century Englishman John Winthrop (1588–1649), who founded the city of Boston. Completed in March 1983, it is in two acts with ten scenes and is scored for six solo singers, a mixed choir, a boys' choir and an instrumental ensemble of at least 30 players. It was first given at the Centre in the Square in Kitchener on 6 September 1986, on the 50th anniversary of the CBC and as part of the celebrations for the International Year of Canadian Music.

The operas are similar in using a historical person with a mission as their basis, but neither unfolds as a conventional narrative; rather they delve into the spiritual and personal existence of the protagonists. Both Marie and Winthrop have three different singers to represent different phases in their lives. Anhalt drew from various sources in writing both librettos: *La tourangelle* is bilingual, with Marie singing and speaking in French contrasted with English for commentary and elsewhere. In each opera he explores the possibilities of the sound quality of the voice as well as the implications of the text, and the long gestation period for both works stimulated his book on writing for the voice, *Alternative Voices* (1984).

*

J. Beckwith: 'Vocal Frontier Pushed Back in New Anhalt Works', *The Music Scene*, no.281/Jan–Feb (1975), 4–5
I. Anhalt: 'Winthrop: The Work, The Theme, The Story', *Canadian University Music Review*, iv (1983), 184–95
——: '"What Tack to Take?": an Autobiographical Sketch (Life in Progress…)', *Queen's Quarterly*, xcii (1985), 96–107
——: 'Text, Context, Music', *Canadian University Music Review*, ix/2 (1988–9), 1–21
——: 'Music: Context, Text, Counter-Text', *Contemporary Music Review*, v/1 (1989), 101–35
G. E. Smith: '"Deep Themes, not so Hidden" in the Music of Istvan Anhalt', *Queen's Quarterly*, xcviii (1991), 99–119
GAYNOR G. JONES

Aniara. 'Revue about man in time and space' in two acts by KARL-BIRGER BLOMDAHL to a libretto by Erik Lindegren after Harry Martinson's poem; Stockholm, Royal Opera, 31 May 1959.

The space-ship Aniara has left the desolated and poisoned Earth and is travelling to Mars. Through Mimaroben (bass-baritone), operator of the Mima (tape), a computer which is the master of Aniara, the emigrants learn about the cruelty of man. During the midsummer celebration Aniara is thrown off its course and panic breaks out. The commander, Chefone (baritone), says that the passengers are now doomed to travel towards the constellation Lyra until the ends of their lives. The Chief Technician I (tenor) compares the journey to the movement of an air-bubble through glass. A beam from the Mima blows up the Earth. The comedian Sandon (high *buffo* tenor) jokes that everyone is safe, but he falls silent when the Deaf Mute (mute role), in sign language, describes the end of the world. After this the Mima cannot survive. Chefone blames Mimaroben and takes him and the pilot Isagel (dancer) away. Despair and moral decline spread. A scene in the Hall of Mirrors shows Daisy Dodd (soprano) and her lesbian partner Libidel (dancer), passengers dancing lasciviously, and the Blind Poetess (high soprano), whose Light cult has replaced the Mima. Next the 20th anniversary of the departure from the Earth is celebrated, and the dead body of the Chief Technician I is shot into space. The Blind Poetess falls into ecstasy because she has seen the city of heaven, but she is taken away by men in white coats. In the final scene, on the last night in the ship, Isagel dances her swan-song. The Blind Poetess sings about the bliss of death, and a beam of light sweeps over the dead passengers; Mimaroben prepares for the end of the journey.

Aniara is one of the most successful Swedish operatic works, employing a text of the highest literary quality and a powerful musical language which mixes such different elements as jazz, hymns, cabaret, serial technique and electronic tape. It is a collective drama; there is almost no dialogue, and the story is told by Mimaroben and the chorus, which plays an important part. Blomdahl's virtuoso treatment of the tonal forces is striking, and his idiom constituted a landmark in the development of modern music. ANDERS WIKLUND

Anima allegra ('A Lively Spirit'). Opera in three acts by FRANCO VITTADINI to a libretto by GIUSEPPE ADAMI and Luigi Motta partly after Serafín and Joaquín Álvarez Quintero's comedy *El genio alegre*; Rome, Teatro Costanzi, 15 April 1921.

Vittadini's biggest operatic success, which was performed in several foreign countries (including the USA) as well as in Italy, is blessed with a libretto of great charm, originally intended for Puccini. The plot centres on the beneficial effect that youthful exuberance can have on older people if only they can be persuaded to open their minds. Donna Sacramento (mezzo-soprano), Marchioness of Arrayanes, has become set in her ways, and her house has become so gloomy and forbidding that her son Pedro (tenor) spends as little time there as possible, preferring to live in Granada. But during one of his brief visits to his mother, his young cousin Consuelo (soprano), whom he has not seen for ten years, turns up unannounced, and her effervescent personality completely transforms the atmosphere of the place: she and Pedro fall in love; Donna Sacramento (after initial resistance) eventually warms to her charms, encouraged by the fact that Pedro no longer wants to keep his distance from the family home; and even the Marchioness's crusty old administrator Don Eligio (bass) reveals an unsuspected humanity when Consuelo insists on regarding him, too, as a friend.

Firmly traditional in style, the opera (composed in 1918–19) is notable for its refined harmony and orchestration, for the simple but telling definition of the principal characters and for vivid picturesque and atmospheric effects, ranging from the Spanish local colour in Act 2 (analogous to that in Zandonai's *Conchita*) to the Puccinian tenderness of the final pages of Acts 1 and (especially) 3. JOHN C. G. WATERHOUSE

Anima del filosofo, L' [*L'anima del filosofo, ossia Orfeo ed Euridice* ('The Spirit of the Philosopher, or Orpheus and Eurydice')]. *Dramma per musica* in four or five acts by JOSEPH HAYDN to a libretto by CARLO FRANCESCO BADINI; Florence, 9 May 1951.

This opera, commissioned by Johann Peter Salomon in 1791 for the reopening of the King's Theatre in the Haymarket, London, was never performed in Haydn's lifetime. The project fell through when George III denied a licence to Sir John Gallini, the impresario of the theatre, and no other arrangements were made to stage the work. It is not certain whether the opera is complete. The sources indicate only four acts, but Haydn's letter of 14 March 1791 indicates that five were intended. In the modern edition in Hadyn's complete works the last scene of the fourth act is designated as Act 5. The meaning of the work's title is obscure; neither the identity of 'the philosopher' nor his relevance to the story of Orpheus and Eurydice has been explained. The most likely candidate for the role of philosopher is Creonte [Creon], whose first-act aria is among the more philosophical texts in the piece, but that leaves open the relevance of his spirit to the rest of the opera.

The splendid overture moves from a slow introduction in C minor to a faster C major sonata form with an impressive symphonic development section. The drama begins as Eurydice (soprano) laments her forthcoming marriage to Arideo [Arideus] ('Sventurata, che fo?'); a chorus of Furies warns her of the dangers of the location ('Ferma il piede, o principessa'). This chorus owes a lot to Gluck's famous *coro di furie* in its key (C minor), in the unison writing for chorus and orchestra and in the interaction between Eurydice and the chorus. Eurydice tells the Furies in accompanied recitative that she is not afraid to die in the pyre they have prepared for her ('Che chiedete da me'). A two-tempo aria with extensive coloratura follows, in which Eurydice compares herself to the abandoned Philomena ('Filomena abbandonata'). Orpheus (tenor) arrives and calms the Furies, first with the music of his harp (accompanied recitative), and then by singing an aria, 'Cara speme'. The rippling triplets in the accompanied recitative are also used by Gluck; like the C minor chorus, however, this was also a well-known convention in late 18th-century opera. The aria has the desired effect, dispersing the Furies and leading to a male-voice chorus in praise of harmony ('O poter dell'armonia'). In the third scene Eurydice's father, Creon (baritone), agrees to let Eurydice marry Orpheus rather than Arideus. Creon sings a moralizing hymn ('Il pensier sta negli oggetti') about the tyranny of the emotions; the music is among the loveliest in the opera. The melody seems to aim at grace and naturalness rather than intensity or virtuosity (anticipating the Haydn of *The Creation* and *The Seasons*). Orpheus and Eurydice end the first act in typical *opera seria* fashion with a duet, 'Come il foco allo splendore'.

Act 2 begins with a chorus of Cupids extolling the pleasures of love ('Finché circola il vigore'). The music to this chorus is taken from the Act 2 finale to *Orlando paladino* (1782). Eurydice is left alone while Orpheus investigates a disturbance; she is almost captured by one of Arideus's men. But a snake bites her, and after an accompanied recitative and a short aria ('Dov'è l'amato bene?' and 'Del mio core il voto estremo') she dies. This brings about a stormy accompanied recitative and a minor-mode rage aria for Orpheus ('Dov'è quell'alma audace' and 'In un mar d'acerbe pene'). The act ends with a heroic aria for Creon after he has learnt of his daughter's death.

Mourning choruses open Act 3 as Orpheus grieves ('Ah, sposo infelice'). Creon sings another moralizing aria about the pointlessness of life without love ('Chi spira e non spera'). Orpheus consults the Genio [Sibyl] (soprano), who promises to lead him to the Underworld to retrieve Eurydice. The Sibyl prefaces the journey with the virtuoso aria 'Al tuo seno fortunato', the opera's most brilliant number. The act ends with a chorus.

Act 4 begins on the shores of the river Lethe with a chorus of unhappy shades ('Infelici ombre dolenti') – one of the many jewels of this opera. Orpheus receives Pluto's permission to enter the Elysian fields in search of Eurydice; the orchestra plays a cheerful intermezzo. Orpheus finds Eurydice, and the chorus (using the tune of the intermezzo) warns him not to look at his wife. The fateful glance occurs in the course of a short recitative, and the scene changes back to a representation of Hades. In the recitative and aria 'Mi sento languire'

Set design by Anisfeld for the Royal Palace in the original production of Prokofiev's 'The Love for Three Oranges' at the Civic Auditorium, Chicago, 30 December 1921: gouache

Orpheus elaborates on his grief. As the final scene opens, he is still grieving. He is interrupted by a chorus of Bacchantes praising pleasure and love ('Vieni, vieni, amato Orfeo'). They offer him a cup of poison as they repeat the same music to the words 'Bevi, bevi in questa tazza'. Orpheus dies, and the Bacchantes set off for the island of delight but drown.

The libretto is an unsuccessful attempt to reshape a strong myth to accommodate the conventions of late 18th-century *opera seria.* Haydn's music, despite its many beauties, tends to respond to individual moments rather than to the continuity of the drama; it seems better suited to concert performance than to the stage. The work was first recorded in a performance conducted by Hans Swarowsky and issued by the Haydn Society of Boston in 1951.

See also ORPHEUS. MARY HUNTER

Anisfeld, Boris Izrayelevich (*b* Bel'tsï, Bessarabiya, 2/14 Oct 1879; *d* Waterford, CT, 4 Dec 1973). American painter and stage designer of Russian birth. He studied at the Odessa Drawing School (1895–1901) and at the Academy of Arts in St Petersburg (1901–9), and exhibited with the Russian avant garde, including Dyagilev's St Petersburg exhibition of young painters in 1905 and his Paris Salon d'Automne exhibition (1906). Anisfeld went to America in 1918, and was appointed professor of Advanced Drawing and Painting at the Chicago Art Institute in 1928, a post he held until he retired in 1968.

In 1910 he began scene painting and designing for Dyagilev's Ballets Russes and in 1911 designed and painted the costumes and the set for Fokine's opera-ballet *Le royaume sous-marin* (1911), which was based on Rimsky-Korsakov's *Sadko*; it was described as 'full of a fantastic beauty'. Anisfeld brought a 'blazing brush' to designs for the Metropolitan Opera, although none were kept in the repertory for more than one season. They included the first American production of Xavier Leroux's *La reine Fiammette* (1919), Albert Wolff's *L'oiseau bleu* (1919) and Boito's *Mefistofele*, which was Gigli's Metropolitan début in 1920. He designed Prokofiev's *Love for Three Oranges* for the world première (1921, Chicago; see illustration). His works are exhibited in the Hermitage, Chicago Art Institute and the Brooklyn and Philadelphia Museums.

DAVID J. HOUGH

Anitua, Fanny (*b* Durango, 22 Jan 1887; *d* Mexico City, 4 April 1968). Mexican contralto. She studied in Mexico City and in Italy, making her début in 1909 at Rome as Gluck's Orpheus. The following year she sang at La Scala, in 1911 at the Colón, Buenos Aires, and in 1913 she toured the USA with the Western Metropolitan Opera Company. She took part in the first performance of Pizzetti's *Fedra* at La Scala (1915) and sang Rosina (in the original key) at Pesaro, Rome and Parma during 1916, the centenary year of Rossini's *Barbiere*. She had a rich, flexible voice and also sang Cenerentola and other coloratura contralto roles, as well as Mistress Quickly (*Falstaff*). ELIZABETH FORBES

Ankara [Angora]. Capital of the Republic of Turkey. The foundation of the Turkish Republic in 1923 was followed by the concentration of cultural activities in the new capital, which had been an important commercial city since ancient times. In 1934 the first operas by Turkish composers were produced at the Ankara Halkevi Theatre (opened 1930, cap. 638): *Özsoy* and *Taş bebek* by Ahmed Adnan Saygun, and *Bayönder* by Necil Kâzím Akses. The opening of the Ankara Conservatory in 1936 was followed by the foundation in 1939 of an opera workshop led by the German opera director Carl Ebert, who remained at the Conservatory for nine years and appointed eminent teachers including Elvira de Hidalgo, Giannina Arangi-Lombardi and Apollo Granforte. Trial productions by the Opera Workshop began in 1940 with *Bastien und Bastienne*, *Fidelio*, Act 2 of *Tosca* and Act 1 of *Madama Butterfly*. In 1948 the Palais des Expositions (built 1934) was converted into a theatre, the Büyük Tiyatro (Grand Theatre), with 650 seats. There the Ankara Devlet Opera ve Balesi (Ankara State Opera and Ballet

Company) stages six new productions each year, between September and July, of operas and operettas from the standard international repertory, usually two productions in Italian and four in Turkish. Local soloists perform with invited foreign singers; notable among the latter have beem Gianni Raimondi, Luciano Pavarotti and Nicola Martinucci.

*

A. C. Konuralp: *Devlet opera v balesi: Ankara, Istanbul, Izmir* [The State Opera and Ballet: Ankara, Istanbul, Izmir] (Ankara, 1991)

FARUK YENER

Anna Amalia [Amalie], Duchess of Saxe-Weimar (*b* Wolfenbüttel, 24 Oct 1739; *d* Weimar, 10 April 1807). German amateur musician and patron, daughter of Duke Karl I of Brunswick and niece of Frederick the Great. After the early death of her husband in 1756 she conducted the regency until 1775. Despite heavy official responsibilities she cultivated intellectual interests, especially music. She took lessons from the leading musician in Weimar, Ernst Wilhelm Wolf (later the court Kapellmeister), and gathered round her a group of scholars, poets and musicians, including Wieland, Herder and eventually Goethe. Anna Amalia herself played a significant part in bringing together the poetry of 'Weimar Classicism' and the music of the time. J. A. Hiller's most successful Singspiel, *Die Jagd* (dedicated to the duchess), was first performed in Weimar in 1770, and Weimar was also the scene of the première in 1773 of Anton Schweitzer's setting of Wieland's *Alceste*. After the destruction of the castle theatre by fire in 1774 Anna Amalia continued the tradition of the Singspiel with performances in the amateur court theatre of her own compositions to texts by Goethe: *Erwin und Elmire* (1776) and *Das Jahrmarktsfest zu Plundersweilern* (1778). The former, without being eclectic in effect, reveals an intimate familiarity – remarkable for an amateur – with both the German Singspiel of Hiller and contemporary Italian opera, on which she had been raised at Brunswick, and shows thorough technical competence and spontaneous invention. The majority of pieces are beholden to the manner of Hiller and Wolf. But Anna Amalia's significance lies mainly in the decisive influence exerted by her artistic convictions on German intellectual life at the period of its flowering in Weimar.

*

W. Bode: *Amalie, Herzogin von Weimar* (Berlin, 1908)
H. Abert: *Goethe und die Musik* (Stuttgart, 1922)
A. Krille: *Beiträge zur Geschichte der Musikerziehung und Musikübung der deutschen Frau* (Berlin, 1938)
R. Münnich: 'Aus der Musiksammlung der Weimarer Landesbibliothek, besonders dem Nachlass der Anna Amalia', *Aus der Geschichte der Landesbibliothek zu Weimar und ihrer Sammlungen: Festschrift zur Feier ihres 250jährigen Bestehens* (Jena, 1941)
O. Heuschele: *Herzogin Anna Amalia* (Munich, 1947)

ANNA AMALIE ABERT

Anna Bolena ('Anne Boleyn'). *Tragedia lirica* in two acts by GAETANO DONIZETTI to a libretto by FELICE ROMANI after Ippolito Pindemonte's *Enrico VIII ossia Anna Bolena* and Alessandro Pepoli's *Anna Bolena*; Milan, Teatro Carcano, 26 December 1830.

This was Donizetti's first great international success, giving him his initial exposure to Paris and London audiences. Pasta (Anne) and Rubini (Percy) sang in the première. Immensely popular for almost half a century, it re-entered the modern repertory following a triumphant revival at La Scala with Callas in 1957. Since then the work has proved a favourite vehicle for such bel canto specialists as Sutherland, Sills and Caballé.

It was long a commonplace of criticism that with *Anna Bolena* Donizetti at a single stroke emerged from the shadow of Rossini into a more personal style, yet one influenced by Bellini. Now, however, thanks to our greater familiarity with the operas that precede *Anna* in the Donizetti canon, this fallacious notion has been superseded by our understanding that it is, rather, a logical extension of directions that Donizetti had already explored. The part of the score that has been regarded as most 'Bellinian', Anne's Larghetto in the final scene, has on closer acquaintance turned out to be a reworking of an aria from Donizetti's first performed opera, *Enrico di Borgogna* of 1818 – seven years before the première of Bellini's first opera. The presence of other self-borrowings of material adapted from five of Donizetti's Neapolitan operas of the 1820s further strengthens the case that *Anna Bolena* is more a product of a self-motivated maturation than had been recognized.

Anne Boleyn (soprano) is unhappy at the coolness of Enrico [Henry VIII] (bass) towards her (cavatina, 'Come, innocente giovane'); indeed his neglect of her also troubles Giovanna Seymour [Jane Seymour] (mezzo-soprano), who has yielded to the king's advances. In an interview with Henry, Jane is dismayed at his dark threats about Anne's future and upset at his talk of marriage to her while he is still Anne's husband. In their duet, 'Oh qual parlar', one of those powerful scenes of confrontation that are a Donizettian speciality, the composer modified the conventional structure inherited from Rossini in ways that underscore the conflict.

Rochefort (bass), Anne's brother, is amazed to see Percy (tenor), her first love, returned from exile. Percy confides to Rochefort that he has heard rumours of Anne's distress, further admitting that his own life has been a misery since he was separated from her. Percy's *sortita* takes the expected form of a double aria, but the jagged melody of the cabaletta with its daunting tessitura reveals at once his rash, passionate nature. Henry appears with a hunting party, having arranged Percy's return as a trap for Anne, and is grimly amused at their emotion when they meet again. The Larghetto of the quintet, 'Io sentii sulla mia mano', with its canonic entrances, is adapted from the *benedizione* in the opening scene of *Otto mesi in due ore* of 1827.

Smeton (mezzo-soprano), Anne's household musician and in love with her, tries to return her miniature portrait, but he is forced to hide when Rochefort persuades Anne against her better judgment to admit Percy, who pleads his love. Anne, distressed, begs him to find another love. Their duet effectively mirrors the shifting course of their feelings: hers, gradual loss of composure; his, increasingly persuasive and desperate. Percy draws his sword to kill himself; whereupon Smeton rushes forward, just as Henry bursts in and orders their arrest. Smeton, pleading Anne's innocence, inadvertently drops the miniature at the king's feet; Henry is enraged and Anne faints. The sextet 'In quegli sguardi impresso', which develops into a groundswell of emotion, shows Donizetti's consummate skill at creating vocal ensembles that expand in an apparently inevitable way the dramatic tension of the moment. Protesting, Anne, Percy and Smeton are led off.

In Act 2 Jane comes to Anne and tells her that the king will spare her if she will confess to loving Percy. When

Giuditta Pasta in the title role of Donizetti's 'Anna Bolena' (the mad scene in Act 2), which she created at the Teatro Carcano, Milan, 26 December 1830: painting by Alexandre Brülloff (1798–1877)

Jane allows that Henry loves another woman, Anne demands to know her identity; unable to restrain herself, Jane confesses. This powerful duet moves ahead in a series of cogent solo passages, the *a due* being confined to the coda. At Anne's trial Smeton lies and admits to being Anne's lover, hoping to save her, but in fact he seals her fate. Anne and Percy are summoned before the council. Jane pleads with the king to spare Anne's life (aria, 'Per questa fiamma'). In the Tower, Percy urges Rochefort to live (aria, 'Vivi tu'), but both refuse clemency when they learn it does not extend to Anne. In her cell, Anne's mind wanders as she recalls her girlhood love for Percy (aria, 'Al dolce guidami castel natio'). When cannons announce the king's new marriage, Anne calls on heaven not to curse the royal couple but to have mercy on them.

This final 20 minutes of *Anna Bolena* reveals for the first time Donizetti's mature ability to flesh out an aria-finale so that it provides the substance of a gripping scene. After a fine F minor chorus ('Chi può vederla'), Anne enters to a regal string prelude, with which her appearance – clothes in disarray, her mind unhinged – makes an ironic contrast. Her recitative reflects her abruptly shifting moods, underpinning them with short motivic ideas. Gradually she lapses into nostalgia, thinking of Percy and the time they first fell in love. An english horn introduces the melody, later functioning as an obbligato to its wistfully expansive measures. Unlike the slow movements of Bellini's aria finales, characteristically ternary, Donizetti uses a binary form, each section repeated and varied. After her fellow prisoners come in, the *tempo di mezzo* is expanded to include what amounts to an extra little aria with *pertichini*, scored for chamber orchestra, an exquisite variant of the tune best known as 'Home, sweet home'. An irruption of cannon and bells heralds the premature marriage of Henry and Seymour, producing a shock that restores Anne's reason. Aware of her desperate situation, she launches into her hard-driving, wide-ranging cabaletta with its formidable series of trills, granting her at the last a hysterical apotheosis. Nothing Donizetti had done before approaches the scope and multiform intensity of this magnificent scene. WILLIAM ASHBROOK

Anna Karenina. Opera in three acts by IAIN HAMILTON to his own libretto, after LEV NIKOLAYEVICH TOLSTOY; London, Coliseum, 7 May 1981.

Hamilton's opera centres on the relationship between Anna (soprano), her husband Karenin (baritone) and her lover Vronsky (tenor). Act 1 depicts the growth of Anna's passion for Vronsky and its effects on family and friends. Act 2 explores further the relationship between Karenin and Anna, and ends, after Anna has borne Vronsky's child, with the reconciliation of husband and lover brought about by Anna. Act 3 begins after Anna and Vronsky have returned from Italy and ends with Anna's suicide.

Hamilton makes use of a lyrical, romantic, tonally based idiom and adopts many of opera's traditional forms and devices. Conflicts among the emotions of the characters are expressed in ensembles such as the trio in Act 2, in which Anna's husband, her brother Stiva (baritone), and her lover give vent to their feelings. Tonalities are used to define character: throughout the opera, Anna and Vronsky's underlying incompatibility is stressed by the tonal clash between Anna's D and Vronsky's E♭. As in many operas of the last century, a chain of ballroom dances provides the background for dramatic action. Big ensemble and chorus scenes at the station, in the ballroom and at the racecourse presuppose a large-scale and spectacular production, such as the opera received at the Coliseum in 1981, when Colin Graham was the producer. HUGO COLE

Annibali, Domenico [Dominichino; 'Balino'] (*b* Macerata, *c*1705; *d* ?Rome, 1779 or later). Italian alto castrato. After appearances in Rome (Porpora's *Germanico*, 1725) and Venice (1727 and 1729), he was engaged in 1729 for Dresden, where he sang in Hasse's *Cleofide* (1731) and *Caio Fabricio* (1734). He also sang in Rome (1730, 1732 and 1739) and Vienna (1731), where his performance in Caldara's *Demetrio* won the approval of Metastasio, and in Handel's company in London (1736–7). He made his London stage début in a revival of *Poro*, when he introduced two arias by Ristori and one by Vinci (one of only two occasions on which Handel is known to have allowed this in his own operas). Annibali was in the first performances of Handel's *Arminio*, *Giustino* and *Berenice*, a revival of *Partenope* and the pasticcio *Didone*.

He returned to Dresden where he was particularly associated with Hasse's operas, appearing in *Tito Vespasiano*, *Demetrio*, *Lucio Papirio*, *Arminio*, *Semiramide*, *Demofoonte*, *Attilio Regolo* and *Adriano in Siria*(1738–52). The court pensioned him in 1764.

According to Burney 'his abilities during his stay in England seem to have made no deep impression', but Mrs Pendarves wrote that Annibali had 'the best part of Senesino's voice and Caristini's, with a prodigious fine taste and good action'. This is confirmed by the compass of the parts Handel wrote for him, Giustino, Arminius and Demetrio (*Berenice*), which is *a* to *g''* (Hasse took him down to *g* in *Demofoonte*, 1748). Other accounts emphasized his brilliant and flexible coloratura, though some found his acting wooden.

For illustration *see* ATTILIO REGOLO. WINTON DEAN

Annunzio, Gabriele D'. *See* D'ANNUNZIO, GABRIELE.

Ansani, Giovanni (*b* Rome, ?20 ?Feb 1744; *d* Florence, 5 July 1826). Italian tenor. He began in *opera seria* in 1768 at Bologna and Venice, then appeared at Udine in 1770. He sang in Copenhagen (Sarti's *Demofoonte*, 1771) and Germany, resuming his Italian career in August 1773, when he was engaged at leading houses to Carnival 1795. He appeared in Mysliveček's *Calliroe* at Pisa in 1779, and in Anfossi's *Tito nelle Gallie* and Cimarosa's *Cajo Mario* in Rome in 1780; in that year he was also at the King's Theatre, London. In 1778 he married the prima donna Giuseppina Maccherini (or Maccarini; *fl* 1765–91). Burney described his voice as 'sweet, powerful, even, and of great compass and volubility'; others speak of a *timbro stupendo*, especially in the middle and lower registers, which, joined to his forceful acting, frequently created a furore, making him a prime agent in the shifting of focus in *opera seria* from castrato to tenor. He was 'tall, thin, and had the look of a person of high rank' (Burney), with an irascible personality that brought him into conflict with colleagues. DENNIS LIBBY/R

Anseaume, Louis (*b* Paris, ?1721; *d* Paris, ?7 July 1784). French librettist. From the 1750s he held various posts at the Opéra-Comique, and was probably *sous-directeur* under Monnet. He wrote more than 30 *opéra comique* librettos during a period of important stylistic transition, in addition to numerous *compliments* for the opening and closing of seasons. His earliest works, in particular *Bertholde à la ville* and *Le chinois poli en France* (both 1754), were greatly reliant on vaudevilles and material parodied from the Bouffons' repertory; during this period he collaborated frequently with the playwright Pierre-Augustin Lefèvre de Marcouville (1722–after 1760). These were followed by collaborations with Laruette and Egidio Duni, the two composers most influential in the transition to the *comédie mêlée d'ariettes*.

Anseaume is best remembered for his extremely successful partnership with Duni, beginning with *Le peintre amoureux de son modèle* (1757), although he also wrote important librettos for Philidor (*Le soldat magicien*, 1760) and Grétry (*Le tableau parlant*, 1769). His naturalism and lyric qualities were praised by Grimm, and he met Diderot's pleas for a more realistic style of acting, particularly through use of gesture, by including detailed stage directions (see, for example, duets in *Mazet*, Act 1 scene vi, and *La clochette*, scene xvi). The emphasis on movement and action is exemplified further in Anseaume's treatment of the ensemble. In constructing complex and irregular texts in which up to seven characters could voice conflicting sentiments, he pioneered a dramatic, progressive type of ensemble in contrast to the traditional tableau effect of earlier operatic concerted writing. He developed, in particular, the ensemble of perplexity, an outstanding example of which is the septet finale to Act 2 of *L'école de la jeunesse* (1765). Previously, and in conjunction with Marcouville, he had introduced the first known sextet in an *opéra comique* (*L'isle des foux*, 1760).

Anseaume's works enjoyed great public acclaim; *Les deux chasseurs et la laitière* (1763) and *La clochette* (1766) numbered among the most popular *opéras comiques* of the period, and *Le tableau parlant* remained in the repertory of the Opéra-Comique for almost one hundred years. Many librettos were published in the three-volume *Théâtre de M. Anseaume* (Paris, 1766).

Le monde renversé (oc, after A.-R. Lesage and D'Orneval), 1753 (Gluck, 1758, as L'ile de Merlin, ou Le monde renversé); *Le boulevard* (oc, with F. de Hautemer), Laruette, 1753; *Bertholde à la ville* (oc, with G. C. de Lattaignant and P.-A. Lefèvre de Marcouville), after Ciampi, 1754; *Le chinois poli en France* (intermède), after Sellitto, 1754; *La nouvelle Bastienne* (oc, with J.-J. Vadé), ?Vadé, 1754; *Les amants trompés* (oc, with Marcouville), Laruette, 1756; *La fausse aventurière* (oc, with Marcouville), Laruette, 1757 (Gluck, 1758, as La fausse esclave); *Le peintre amoureux de son modèle* (oc), E. Duni, 1757 (rev. 1758); *Le docteur Sangrado* (oc, with J.-B. Lourdet de Santerre), Duni and Laruette, 1758

Le médecin de l'amour (oc, with Marcouville), Laruette, 1758 (Maldere, 1766); *Cendrillon* (oc), Laruette, 1759; *L'ivrogne corrigé, ou Le mariage du diable* (oc, with Lourdet de Santerre), Laruette, 1759 (Gluck, 1760); *Les épreuves de l'amour* (oc), J.-B. de La Borde, 1759; *Le maître d'école* (oc, with Marcouville), 1760; *Le procès des ariettes et des vaudevilles* (pièce, with C.-S. Favart), 1760; *Les précautions inutiles* (oc, with Achard), Chrétien, 1760; *La nouvelle troupe* (comédie, with Favart and C. H. Fusée de Voisenon), 1760; *Le soldat magicien* (oc), Philidor, 1760; *L'écosseuse* (oc, with Pannard), 1760; *L'isle des foux* (cmda, with Marcouville, after C. Goldoni), Duni, 1760; *Le dépit généreux* (oc, with A.-F. Quétant), Laruette, 1761

Mazet (cmda), Duni, 1761 (L. Kozeluch, 1780/86); *L'amant corsaire* (oc, with Salvert), Lasalle d'Offemont, 1762; *Le milicien* (cmda), Duni, 1762; *Les deux chasseurs et la laitière* (cmda), Duni, 1763; *L'école de la jeunesse, ou Le Barnevelt françois* (cmda), Duni, 1765 (A. Prati, 1779); *La clochette* (cmda), Duni, 1766; *Le tableau parlant* (comédie-parade), A.-E.-M. Grétry, 1769; *La coquette du village, ou Le baiser pris et rendu* (oc), L. J. Saint-Amans, 1771; *Le poirier* (oc, after Vadé), Saint-Amans, 1772; *La ressource comique, ou La pièce à deux acteurs* (cmda), N.-J. Le Froid de Méreaux, 1772; *Le rendez-vouz bien employé* (parade), J.-P.-E. Martini, 1773; *Le retour de tendresse* (cmda), Méreaux, 1774; *Achmet et Almanzine* (oc, after Lesage and D'Orneval), 1776

Doubtful: *La vengeance de Melpomène*, 1753 [attrib. J. Fleury]; *Le dormeur éveillé* (oc), La Borde, 1764 [according to Brenner]; *Sémire et Mélinde, ou Le navigateur* (comédie), Philidor, 1773 [attrib. Fenouillot de Falbaire]

M. Tourneux, ed.: *Correspondance littéraire, philosophique et critique par Grimm, Diderot, Raynal, Meister, etc.* (Paris, 1877–82)

P. Wechsler: *Louis Anseaume und das französische Singspiel* (Leipzig, 1909)

C. D. Brenner: *A Bibliographical List of Plays in the French Language 1700–1789* (Berkeley, 1947, 2/1979)

E. A. Cook: *The Operatic Ensemble in France, 1673–1775* (diss., U. of East Anglia, 1989), 218–77 ELISABETH COOK

Anselmi, Giuseppe (*b* Nicolosi, nr Catania, 6 Oct 1876; *d* Zoagli, nr Rapallo, 27 May 1929). Italian tenor. He first appeared at the age of 13 as a violinist in his native city. After some experience in operetta he made his operatic début, by his own account, at Patras, Greece, *c*1896–8, singing various leading Italian roles. Serious studies with the conductor Mancinelli led to appearances in Genoa (1900) and soon afterwards at the S Carlo, Naples. In 1901 (and again in 1904 and 1909) he sang at Covent Garden; his success was still greater in Buenos Aires, Warsaw, Moscow and St Petersburg, and greatest of all in Spain. His warm, beautiful timbre and impassioned delivery (clearly evident in his many Fonotipia records made between 1907 and 1910) were helped by vivid enunciation as well as by a romantic appearance. He retired in 1918 and made his final public appearance, once more as a violinist, at Rapallo in 1926. Also a composer, he wrote songs, chamber music and a *Poema sinfonico* for orchestra.

*

GV (R. Celletti; R. Vegeto)
D. Shawe-Taylor: 'Giuseppe Anselmi', *Opera*, vii (1956), 146–151
L. Lustig, C. Williams and T. Kaufman: 'Giuseppe Anselmi', *Record Collector*, xxxii (1987), 51–109 [with discography]

DESMOND SHAWE-TAYLOR

Ansermet, Ernest (*b* Vevey, 11 Nov 1883; *d* Geneva, 20 Feb 1969). Swiss conductor. He studied composition with Ernest Bloch and conducting with Nikisch before making his début as an orchestral conductor in 1910. His close friendship with Stravinsky (then living in Switzerland) led to an appointment in 1915 as principal conductor for Dyagilev's Ballets Russes, and in 1922 Ansermet conducted the première of Stravinsky's *Reynard* at the Paris Opéra. Three more premières followed: *The Rape of Lucretia* (1946, Glyndebourne), *Der Sturm* (1956, Vienna Staatsoper) and *Monsieur de Pourceaugnac* (1963, Geneva), the latter two by his compatriot Frank Martin. At Geneva his productions of *Boris Godunov*, *Die Zauberflöte* and *Pelléas et Mélisande* were well received; he also conducted five performances of *Pelléas* at the Metropolitan in 1962.

Ansseau, Fernand (*b* Boussu-Bois, nr Mons, 6 March 1890; *d* Brussels, 1 May 1972). Belgian tenor. A pupil of Demest in Brussels, he made his début at Dijon in 1913 as John the Baptist in *Hérodiade*. The war delayed his international recognition, but in 1918 he sang at La Monnaie, and from 1919 to 1928 he appeared at Covent Garden, singing Massenet's Des Grieux, Faust, Romeo, Don José, Canio and Cavaradossi. At the Opéra-Comique (1920–21) he was the first tenor Orpheus in Paris since Nourrit and Duprez; at the Opéra (1922–34) his roles included John the Baptist, Alain (*Grisélidis*), Samson, Lohengrin and Tannhäuser. Mary Garden engaged him for Chicago (1923–8). The Paris Opéra selected him for Admetus in *Alceste* (with Lubin) and Lohengrin. From 1930 he sang mostly at La Monnaie, taking the role of Masaniello in *La muette de Portici*, performed to celebrate the centenary of the 1830 Revolution. His extremely beautiful voice suited him for lyrical roles, but with its inner animal drive and dramatic verve he gave vivid stage performances of heavier roles such as Tannhäuser and Don Alvaro later in his career.

*

GV (R. Celletti; R. Vegeto)
A. De Cock: 'Fernand Ansseau', *Record Collector*, ix (1954), 5–20 [with discography]

ANDRÉ TUBEUF, ELIZABETH FORBES

Antefatto. *See* ARGOMENTO.

Antheil, George [Georg] (**Carl Johann**) (*b* Trenton, NJ, 8 July 1900; *d* New York, 12 Feb 1959). American composer of German descent. In 1926, Antheil was hailed by Aaron Copland as the most promising of a trio of radical composers (the others were Roger Sessions and Henry Cowell). In less than a year, however, his Parisian supporters were denouncing his turn from iconoclasm to neo-classicism and American critics were rejecting him following the disastrous American première of his *Ballet mécanique*. Faced with artistic dethronement, Antheil accepted the critic H. H. Stuckenschmidt's invitation to participate in the operatic renaissance in Germany, and in 1928 he moved to Vienna to begin work on his 'political' opera *Transatlantic*, a work he later viewed as the beginning of his search to shape a 'fundamentally American style'. A wild caricature of an American presidential election and a burlesque of the American temperament in the 1920s, the opera was first performed in Frankfurt on 25 May 1930 to modest critical acclaim (its American première was given more than 50 years later, as was its German revival). Antheil electrifies the drama with fast cinematographic staging: the final act is played on an arrangement of four stages and a screen that allow quick cuts between scenes. Musically, the modular structure, jazz-inspired rhythms and parody of popular American tunes reinforce the pace of the plot and underline the satirical tone of the opera.

While Antheil prepared for the production of his first opera, he also worked on several other dramatic compositions including his unsuccessful second opera, *Helen Retires* (1930–31). He returned permanently to the USA in 1933 and spent more than a decade trying to recover the compositional momentum of his early European years. The decade witnessed his continued search for an 'American style' in several short works for orchestra; his brief involvement with what he identified as 'a new theater movement – musical ballet-opera theater'; his move to Hollywood in 1936 and his composition of film scores to make a living; and numerous fantastic money-making ventures.

By 1942 Antheil had regained his equilibrium both compositionally and financially, and in 1949, he returned to music drama: opera, ballet, musical theatre and music for films and television. *Volpone* is the most successful of a set of four operas completed in the early 1950s. The libretto is farcical and fast-moving and the music not only supports but, in the manner of Antheil's film music, expertly enhances the comedy. The heterogeneous harmonic language, the thematic versatility, the rhythmic continuum, the mosaic construction and the colourful timbres used programmatically all combine to reinforce the drama. Antheil's ubiquitous sense of parody in *Volpone* is perhaps the most attractive element in his music for the stage and cinema and probably one of the most effective aspects of his non-dramatic works. His talent for satire and caricature, when matched by rhythmic energy, colourful harmonic juxtapositions and melodic invention, infuses much of his music with wit and poignancy.

Transatlantic: the People's Choice [orig. Glare], 1927–8 (3, Antheil); lib. rev. Antheil and W. Lowenfels, trans. R. S. Hoffmann as Transatlantik, Frankfurt, Opera, 25 May 1930, vs (Vienna and Leipzig, 1929); rev. version (D. Jewett), reorchd F. Johnson, Trenton, NJ, 23 Oct 1981
Flight [Ivan the Terrible], 1927–30 (op-ballet, 1, Antheil and B. Antheil), unperf., *US-Wc**
Helen Retires, 1930–31 (3, J. Erskine), New York, Juilliard School of Music, 28 Feb 1934, *Wc**, lib. (New York, 1934)
Volpone, 1949–52 (satire in music, 3, A. Perry, after B. Jonson), Los Angeles, U. of S. California, Bovard Auditorium, 9 Jan 1953, vs *LAusc*
The Brothers (1, Antheil), U. of Denver, ?Little, 28 July 1954, *Wc*
Venus in Africa, 1954 (1, M. Dyne), U. of Denver, Little, 24 May 1957, vs *Wc*
The Wish, 1954 (4 scenes, Antheil), Louisville, 2 April 1955

Correspondence in *US-NYp*, *PRu*, *Wc* and Yale University, Beinecke Rare Book and Manuscript Library
G. Antheil: 'Mr. Antheil's Opera', *New York Times* (13 April 1930)
——: 'Opernregie von morgen', *Das Kunstblatt*, xiv (1930), 234–5
——: 'Voraussetzungen für meine Oper "Transatlantic"', *Anbruch*, xii (1930), 8–10
——: 'Wanted – Opera by and for Americans', *MM*, vii/4 (1930), 11–13; repr., abridged, in *Composers on Music*, ed. S. Morgenstern (New York, *c*1956), 528–31
——: 'Zurück zur romantischen Oper', *Der Querschnitt*, x (1930), 235–6
T. Wiesengrund-Adorno: 'George Antheil: Transatlantik', *Die Musik*, xxii (1930), 754–6
——: 'Transatlantic', *MM*, vii/4 (1930), 38–41
G. Antheil: 'Musical Theatre', *New Review*, i/1 (1931), 59–60
——: 'Opera – a Way Out', *MM*, xi/2 (1934), 89–94
P. Rosenfeld: 'The Latest Helen', *New Republic* (14 March 1934)
G. Antheil: *Bad Boy of Music* (Garden City, NY, 1945) [autobiography]
——: 'So you want to compose an opera', *The Score*, v (1953), no.2, pp.4–5; no.3, p.14
——: 'Volpone as an American Opera', *Arts Magazine* [Los Angeles], ii/1 (1953), 14–16
L. Whitesitt: *The Life and Music of George Antheil, 1900–1959* (Ann Arbor, 1983)
R. Ermen: 'Das letzte Glanzstück der Amerikaoper: Antheils *Transatlantik* in Bielefeld und Ulm', *Musica*, xli (1987), 249–51
S. Cook: 'George Antheil's *Transatlantic*: an American in the Weimar Republic', *JM*, ix (1991), 498–519 LINDA WHITESITT

Anthony, Charles [Caruso, Calogero Antonio] (*b* New Orleans, 15 July 1929). American tenor. He studied at New Orleans and in Rome, making his début in 1954 as the Holy Fool (*Boris Godunov*) at the Metropolitan, where he sang for 30 years in a wide variety of lyric and character roles. They included Almaviva, Ernesto, Nemorino, Beppe (*Pagliacci*), David (*Die Meistersinger*) and the four comic tenor roles in *Les contes d'Hoffmann*. He also sang at Boston, Dallas and Santa Fe. A reliable singer and a good actor, he had a sweet-toned though not very large voice. ELIZABETH FORBES

Anthony, James R(aymond) (*b* Providence, RI, 18 Feb 1922). American musicologist. He attended Columbia University, the Sorbonne and the University of Southern California, where he took the doctorate with a dissertation on André Campra's *opéra-ballets* (1964). He taught at the University of Montana (1948–50), then became a professor at the University of Arizona (from 1952). His particular area of study is French opera of the 17th and early 18th centuries, on which he has published articles and reviews in American, French and British journals. His *French Baroque Music from Beaujoyeulx to Rameau* (London, 1973, rev. 2/1978, rev. Fr. trans., 1981) is a valuable introduction to that era and its music.

*

J. Hajdu Heyer, ed.: *Jean-Baptiste Lully and the Music of the French Baroque: Essays in Honor of James R. Anthony* (Cambridge, 1989) [incl. list of Anthony's writings]

Antier, Marie (*b* Lyons, 1687; *d* Paris, 3 Dec 1747). French soprano. Trained as a singer and actress by Marthe le Rochois, she made her début at the Opéra in the 1711 revival of Michel de La Barre's *ballet La vénitienne* (1705). For 30 years she sang major roles in up to five productions each season, and she retired with a generous pension at Easter 1741. After her début she was immediately given important roles in new productions, beginning with Campra's *Idomenée* (1712) and Salomon's *Médée et Jason* (1713); 23 years later she sang the same role, Cléone, in a revival of the Salomon opera and was warmly praised by the *Mercure* (December 1736). Antier appeared in almost two dozen Lully revivals. In 1720 she became *première actrice* of the Académie Royale de Musique and in 1721 was appointed *musicienne de la chambre du roi*.

In the early 1720s Antier sang at the Château des Tuileries in private performances of *opéras-ballets*, in which Louis XV danced. She became *maîtresse en titre* to the Prince of Carignan and on her marriage in 1726 to Jean Duval, *inspecteur du grenier à sel de Paris*, she received lavish gifts from the royal family. After an imprudent affair in 1727 with Le Riche de La Pouplinière she was installed for a time in the Convent of Chaillot while apparently continuing to appear at the Opéra. But her career had passed its zenith: major roles were increasingly given to her younger colleagues – Le Maure, Pélissier, Eremans and Petitpas. Destouches commented on her in a letter of 8 February 1728 (translated from Tunley):

> Mlle Antier has a most beautiful voice, of noble quality and fantastic flexibility; it is a pity that she does not possess an extra semitone at both ends of her range. She sings all styles – gracious, tender, expressive .... As nothing is perfect in this world these fine qualities are balanced by faults. Sometimes she lacks intonation; her tendency to sing light music has somewhat diminished the beauty of her trills and takes away that intensity of tone so necessary when expressing terror.

Nevertheless, she sang in such new productions as Montéclair's *Jephté* (1732), Rameau's *Hippolyte et Aricie* (1733) in the demanding role of Phaedra, *Les Indes galantes* (1735) and *Castor et Pollux* (1737). She spent her last years living rent-free in the Magasin de l'Opéra. Her younger sister sang in the Opéra chorus, 1719–43. She was the mother of the soprano Mlle de Maiz.

*

Mémoire pour servir à l'histoire de l'Académie royale de musique (*F-Po*, Amelot), 284
J.-B. Durey de Noinville: *Histoire du théâtre de l'Académie royale de musique en France* (Paris, 2/1757), ii, 67–8
J.-B. de La Borde: *Essai sur la musique ancienne et moderne* (Paris, 1780), iii, 491–2
A. Pougin: *Pierre Jélyotte et les chanteurs de son temps* (Paris, 1905), 45ff
D. Tunley: *The Eighteenth-Century French Cantata* (London, 1974), 9, 17, appx B JULIE ANNE SADIE

Antigona ('Antigone'). *Opera seria* in three acts by TOMMASO TRAETTA to a libretto by MARCO COLTELLINI; St Petersburg, Imperial Theatre, 11 November 1772.

A terrifying introduction, combining pantomime, dance, recitative and chorus, opens each act: in Act 1 Antigone's brothers engage in mortal combat; in Act 2 Antigone (soprano) prepares a secret, nocturnal funeral; and in Act 3, condemned by Creon (tenor), Antigone prepares for her death. Unusual for an *opera seria* are the trios (in Acts 1 and 2), the arias that merge into ensembles, and the duet for the hero, Emone (alto castrato), and Antigone's sister Ismene (soprano), replacing the usual love duet at the close of Act 1. The opera has French-inspired elements, including many choruses and dances within the action, arias with chorus and a joyous final chorus and ballet. The music, especially rich in the expressive use of wind instruments (including clarinet and bassoon), reveals Traetta in full command of his mature powers. Passages of orchestrally accompanied recitative reach levels of profound dramatic expression. For both Traetta and Coltellini, this masterpiece represented the culmination of a decade of effort to breathe new life into Italian opera through a Franco-Italian synthesis as envisioned in Algarotti's

Saggio sopra l'opera in musica (1755) – an effort that had begun with their collaboration on *Ifigenia in Tauride* for Vienna in 1763.

See also ANTIGONE below. MARITA P. MCCLYMONDS

Antigonae ('Antigone'). Tragedy in five acts by CARL ORFF to SOPHOCLES' drama translated into German by Friedrich Hölderlin; Salzburg, Felsenreitsschule, 9 August 1949.

After the death of Oedipus, King of Thebes, his sons Eteocles and Polyneices were supposed to share the throne. But the brothers quarrelled and Polyneices fled to Argos to organize an army in order to occupy Thebes. The revolt was suppressed when the brothers killed each other. The opera begins as Creon (baritone) succeeds to the throne. He decrees that anyone who contemplates burying Polyneices will be put to death. But Oedipus's daughter Antigone (dramatic soprano) is determined to accord her brother the true rites of burial. She attempts to enlist the support of her sister Ismene (soprano), but Ismene, fearful of the consequences, tries to discourage Antigone. Antigone ignores her and visits her brother's corpse alone. As she scatters earth on the body she is seized by soldiers and taken prisoner by Creon. Ismene, ashamed of her former cowardice, admits complicity in the deed and is also imprisoned. Creon's son Haemon (tenor), to whom Antigone is betrothed, goes to the king to plead for mercy, threatening to kill himself if either of the sisters is put to death. But while Creon releases Ismene he condemns Antigone to solitary confinement. The blind soothsayer Tiresias (tenor) appears and prophesies disaster for the king if he does not release Antigone and give Polyneices an honourable burial. Creon bows to this pressure but is unable to forestall a dreadful sequence of events. Antigone has already hanged herself with her sash and Haemon, clinging to her body, kills himself with his sword. When Creon's wife Euridice [Eurydice] (contralto) hears this news, she also takes her own life. Creon is now in despair and longs for death, but is unable to effect complete absolution. The final words in the opera are reserved for the Chorus: only in wisdom can there be peace of mind and man should not profane the teachings of the gods.

Antigonae marks a point of departure in Carl Orff's output, away from the scenic cantata *Carmina burana* and the fairy-tale operas *Der Mond* and *Die Kluge* towards the exploration of tragedy, a vein further pursued in later stage works such as *Oedipus der Tyrann* and *Prometheus*. The idiom is much more austere than in previous works with darker orchestral accompaniment (double basses, woodwind, brass and a vast array of percussion instruments), a penchant for extended ostinato patterns and an intoned, sometimes deliberately monotonous vocal line which follows the natural rise and fall of speech.

See also ANTIGONE below. ERIK LEVI

Antigone. Libretto subject used chiefly in the 18th century, derived from plays by SOPHOCLES and EURIPIDES. Italian librettos on the subject were entitled *Antigona* or occasionally *Creonte*.

The plot concerns Antigone, daughter of Oedipus and Jocasta. Her brothers Polynices and Eteocles have died, each at the other's hand; their maternal uncle Creon, who is acting as regent in Oedipus's absence, has forbidden the proper burial of Polynices, but Antigone defiantly attempts to bury him. In Sophocles' version of the story Creon inters her alive in a vault and her betrothed Haemon kills himself; in Euripides' version Creon hands Antigone over to Haemon to be executed, but instead he hides her among shepherds and she bears his child.

Early operas on the subject take up the story when Antigone's daughter is a young woman. The earliest libretto may be Benedetto Pasqualigo's *Antigona* in five acts, for G. M. Orlandini (1718), much performed early in the century. At the beginning of the opera, Antigone's daughter Jocasta has appeared after a long absence and is not recognized. Creonte [Creon] has ordered Antigone's husband, here called Osmene, to marry Jocasta, not knowing she is his daughter. Antigone returns to Thebes, identifies herself and attempts to stab Creon. Osmene is again ordered to kill his wife, but Creon dies in a popular insurrection and the couple are reunited with their daughter.

Roccaforte provided a new version for Galuppi (1751), whose opera enjoyed numerous revivals; the libretto was reset by many others including Casali (1752), Latilla (1753), Giuseppe Scarlatti and Bertoni (1756), Vincenzo Ciampi (1762), De Majo (1768), Mysliveček (1774), Mortellari (1776) and Giuseppe Gazzaniga (1781). Here Antigone is Antiope, a high priestess and interpreter of the oracle of Apollo. She prevents the marriage of Ermione (not yet recognized as her daughter) to Euristeo, her husband and Creon's son. She tries to save Ermione from the sacrificial dagger by stabbing Creon, but Euristeo intercepts the blow; now she reveals her identity publicly and is taken prisoner. Creon demands that Euristeo kill her, but he refuses. Alceste tells them that Ermione is their daughter; they join in a trio. The people revolt: Creon is taken prisoner and Antigone made queen. Marco Coltellini wrote a less complex version for Traetta (1772), returning to the earlier events of Antigone's life, in which Antigone and her betrothed, Creon's son Emone, are condemned to death because they disobeyed Creon's orders to leave Polynices unburied. Creon finally relents. Operas by Bortnyansky (*Creonte*, 1776), Campobasso d'Alessandro (1788), Winter (1791) and Basili (1799) are based on this text. Marmontel wrote a French *Antigone* libretto which Zingarelli set for Paris in 1790.

Apart from incidental music by Mendelssohn (1841) and Saint-Saëns (1894) *Antigone* was largely left alone by opera composers in the 19th century. The 20th saw a revival of interest with Honegger's opera to Cocteau's version of the story (1927) and Orff's setting of a direct translation of Sophocles' play by Friedrich Hölderlin (1949). Recent settings have taken varied forms: Krejčí's was staged in Prague in 1934 and revised for television in 1964; Joubert composed a radio opera (1954); and Lyubomir Pipkov's *Antigona '43* (1963) put the story in a contemporary political context.

See also *ANTIGONA* [Traetta] and *ANTIGONAE* [Orff].
MARITA P. MCCLYMONDS

Antigono ('Antigonus'). Libretto by PIETRO METASTASIO, first set by Johann Adolf Hasse (1743, Hubertusburg). The title *Alessandro, rè d'Epiro* was used for a later version of the libretto.

ACT 1 Princess Berenice of Egypt is engaged to Antigonus, King of Macedonia, but loves his son Demetrio [Demetrius]. Antigonus banishes Demetrius who returns to warn his father that King Alessandro [Alexander] of Epirus, previously spurned by Berenice, seeks revenge in a campaign against the Macedonians. Ismene, Antigonus's daughter, confesses to Berenice her love for Alexander. During the battle, Demetrius disobeys his father in order to ensure the safety of Berenice, and the Macedonians are defeated. Antigonus, after banishing his son, is captured by Alexander along with Ismene and Berenice who steadfastly resists her captor's protestations of love.

ACT 2 Demetrius begs Alexander to release Antigonus, offering himself in his father's place. Alexander accepts, provided Berenice becomes his consort, a condition that Demetrius must persuade her to accept. This Demetrius does, but not before he and Berenice have renewed their vow of mutual love. Antigonus, however, is still held hostage, a situation that remains unchanged even after a victory won by the reorganized Macedonian army.

ACT 3 Antigonus refuses to give up Berenice and is imprisoned in a cell from which he can be released only by someone wearing Alexander's ring. Demetrius compels Alexander to give him the ring and, having freed Antigonus, plans suicide to escape his position as rival to his father. Clearco [Clearchus], Alexander's captain and Demetrius's friend, prevents this act. Meanwhile, Antigonus consents to Ismene's marriage to Alexander and, moved by his son's constancy, he grants Demetrius Berenice's hand.

* * *

The story of the invasion of Macedonia by Alexander of Epirus, his initial victory over Antigonus II (Gonatas) and his defeat at the hands of the young Demetrius (the future Demetrius II), son of Antigonus, is recorded in Justin's epitome of the Trogus *Historiae* (book 26). Claude Boyer's drama *La mort de Démétrius* (1660) contains the type of complex love relationships that Metastasio was to impose upon this basic plot, including the love of Ismene for Alexander, and may also have been a source. With well over 40 settings between 1743 and 1798 (at least six each for Naples and Rome), *Antigono* was the most popular of the Metastasian dramas for which Hasse provided the first setting. Conforto made his début at the Teatro di S Carlo in Naples with a successful setting of *Antigono* in 1750. This, Conforto's first serious opera, was destined for further success in London seven years later. Durán was instrumental in bringing the Italian style to Barcelona with his *Antigono* of 1760 as well as being among the first Spanish composers to write opera for that city. Johann Poissl and Antonio Gandini extended the life of the libretto into the 19th century with settings in 1808 and 1824.

Because of the closeness of Metastasio's title to the *Antigona* librettos of Roccaforte and Coltellini, there has been some confusion over attributions.

For a list of settings *see* METASTASIO, PIETRO. DON NEVILLE

Antill, John (Henry) (*b* Sydney, 8 April 1904; *d* Sydney, 29 Dec 1986). Australian composer. After training as a chorister, he studied composition with Alfred Hill. His interest in music for theatre began at 11, when he commenced work on the libretto and music of an opera, *Ouida* (1915). He began work on several more in the following decade, including *Heroida* and *Dorothea* (*c*1920), *Sleeping Princess* (*c*1921), *Endymion* and *The Glittering Mask* (*c*1922) and *The Gates of Paradise* (*c*1924), but only *Endymion*, after the poem by Keats, was staged. In a prologue, two parts and an epilogue, it was first performed in 1953 at the Tivoli Theatre in Sydney by the New South Wales National Opera Company, with the composer conducting. Besides ballets, oratorios and film music, Antill also wrote two one-act operas, *The Music Critic* (*c*1952), based on an event in Tasmania, and *The First Christmas* (to a libretto by Pat Flower), first broadcast by ABC Radio on 25 December 1969. On his retirement in 1969 as Federal Music Editor for the ABC, he was made an OBE for services to Australian music; in 1981 he was made a Companion of the Order of St Michael and St George.

*

L. McCallum: 'John Antill', *Canon*, viii (1955), 353–6

B. Dean and V. Carell: *Gentle Genius: a Life of John Antill* (Sydney, 1987)

GEORGINA BINNS

Antimasque. *See* MASQUE.

Antinori, Luigi (*fl* 1719–34). Italian tenor. A native of Bologna, he sang in Rome (G. Bononcini's *Etearco*, 1719), Ferrara (1724) and other Italian cities, and was engaged on Owen Swiney's recommendation by the Royal Academy in London, replacing Francesco Borosini in revivals of *Elpidia* (by Vinci and Orlandini) and *Rodelinda* (Handel) in 1725, and appearing in the unsuccessful pasticcio *Elisa* in 1726. Handel composed the parts of Laelius in *Scipione* and Leonnatus in *Alessandro* (only one aria) for him and evidently had little confidence in his powers; but Fétis described him as a fine singer with an excellent method. The compass is *d* to *a'*, the tessitura fairly high. Antinori sang in Venice (1726 in Porpora's *Imeneo in Atene*, 1731), Genoa (1728, 1732), Livorno (1731), Reggio Emilia (1732) and Florence (1733–4). WINTON DEAN

Anton (Clemens Theodor) of Saxony (*b* Dresden, 27 Dec 1755; *d* Dresden, 6 June 1836). German prince and amateur composer. The third son of Friedrich Christian of Saxony and Maria Antonia Walpurgis, a noted patroness and composer, he married Maria Antonia of Sardinia in 1781, and after her death Maria Theresa of Austria (1787). Throughout most of his life he remained outside government, and instead pursued his favourite pastimes, musical composition and genealogy. On the death of his brother King Friedrich August I in 1827 he succeeded to the throne of Saxony. Religious controversies and his advancing age led to a co-regency with his nephew Friedrich August in 1830, and a constitutional monarchy in 1831.

Anton of Saxony was a skilful musical dilettante and one of the most prolific composers of the House of Wettin. His works (which fill more than 50 manuscript volumes in *D-Dlb*) include several operas and some 30 cantatas, and were performed by other amateurs at Dresden and Pillnitz to celebrate court occasions. Anton also composed sacred music, instrumental works and secular vocal pieces. Though Weber described the cantata *Il trionfo d'Imene* as being 'full of talent', Anton's compositions are rather monotonous with regard to harmony and motif. They belong to the *galant*, early Classical style, and hardly reflect the move towards early Romanticism which was occurring in Dresden.

MSS in D-Dlb unless otherwise stated

L'isola disabitata (int), 1775

Der Triumph der Treue (operette, 2), 1779

Vathek (2), 1781

Le cinesi (componimento drammatico, 1), 1784

Tamas (opera drammatica, 3), 1785

Il poeta ridicolo (dg, 2), 1786

La nascità del sole (componimento drammatico, L. Orlandi), 1797

Prometeo vendicato (componimento drammatico), 1798
Die Liebesgaben (operette, 1, F. J. Kind), Dresden, Sächsischer Hof, 22 Oct 1819, lost
Il fosso incantato (3)

*

M. M. von Weber: *Carl Maria von Weber*, ii (Leipzig, 1864), 192ff
M. Fürstenau: *Die musikalischen Beschäftigungen der Prinzessin Amalie, Herzogin zu Sachsen* (Dresden, 1874)
O. Schmid: *Das sächsische Königshaus in selbstschöpferischer musikalischer Bethätigung* (Leipzig, 1900)
——, ed.: *Musik am sächsischen Hofe*, iii, v (Leipzig, 1900–03)
O Schmid: *Fürstliche Komponisten aus dem sächsischen Königshause* (Langensalza, 1910) DIETER HÄRTWIG

Antonacci, Anna Caterina (*b* Ferrara, 5 April 1961). Italian soprano. She studied in Bologna and made her début in 1986 at Arezzo as Rosina, then sang Flora (*La traviata*) at Bologna. In 1988, after winning the Pavarotti Competition, she sang Elizabeth (*Maria Stuarda*) in Bari. Others of her roles are Horatia (*Gli Orazi ed i Curiazi*, Cimarosa) at Rome in 1989 and Lisbon, and the next year Fiordiligi at Venice and Macerata, Adalgisa at Catania, Polyxena in Manfroce's *Ecuba* and the title role of Paisiello's *Elfrida* at Savona. She also sang Mayr's *La rosa bianca e la rosa rossa* at Bergamo. Her beautiful, dark-toned, flexible voice and dramatic temperament have been finely displayed in Rossini, as Dorliska at Savona, Ninetta (*La gazza ladra*) at Philadelphia, Anaï (*Moïse*) at Bologna, Semiramide at Catania and in the title role of *Ermione* at Rome (1991) and London (1992). ELIZABETH FORBES

Antoni, Antonio d' (*b* Palermo, 25 June 1801; *d* Trieste, 18 Aug 1859). Italian composer and conductor. He was taught first by his grandfather and father, both composers and conductors. At the age of 12 he conducted his own mass for St Cecilia's Day. In 1817 he made his début in Palermo, as both conductor and composer, with the opera *Un duello per equivoco, ossia Gli amanti in disturbo*. He travelled in Europe as a conductor and as an impresario; in Trieste he met Meyerbeer, who encouraged him to write *Amina, ovvero L'innocenza perseguitata* (based on the same libretto as *La sonnambula*). *Amina* was a great success (1825, Trieste), and was believed to be by Meyerbeer. Another opera soon followed: *Amazilda e Zamoro* was performed in Florence in March 1826. In about 1828 d'Antoni settled in Trieste, as musical director of the newly-formed Società Filarmonico-Drammatica. He wrote a cantata for the official inauguration (1829) and composed the vaudeville *La festa dell'Archibugio* for the Società in the same year. He contributed greatly to raising the musical standards of Trieste.

Un duello per equivoco, ossia Gli amanti in disturbo (dg, 2), Palermo, Carolino, 1817
Amina, ovvero L'innocenza perseguitata (op semiseria, 2, F. Romani), Trieste, Grande, carn. 1825
Amazilda e Zamoro (dramma, 2), Florence, Pergola, 31 March 1826

According to *StiegerO*: Gli amanti burlati (2), Siracusa, carn. 1821; Il pellegrino (2), Malta, carn. 1823; Giovanna Gray, ?1847
FRANCESCO BUSSI

Antonicek, Theophil (*b* Vienna, 22 Nov 1937). Austrian musicologist. He studied with Erich Schenk and Othmar Wessely at the University of Vienna, taking the doctorate there in 1962 with a dissertation on Ignaz von Mosel; in 1967 he spent a year of study with Remo Giazotto in Italy. In 1963 he was appointed research musicologist for the Music Research Commission of the Austrian Academy of Sciences; concurrently he has served as secretary of the Gesellschaft zur Herausgabe der Denkmäler der Tonkunst in Österreich (1963–75) and of the Österreichische Gesellschaft für Musikwissenschaft (appointed 1973), becoming editor of its *Mitteilungen* in November 1973. He is also editor (since 1976; with C. Harten) of the series Musicologia Austriaca. His chief areas of research have been Austrian (particularly Viennese) music history from the 17th century to the 19th, and relations between Italian and Austrian music of the same period; his publications include articles on Cavalieri, Cesti, Monteverdi and Beethoven.

Zur Pflege Händelscher Musik in der 2. Hälfte des 18. Jahrhunderts (Vienna, 1966)
Musik im Festsaal der Österreichischen Akademie der Wissenschaften (Vienna, 1972)
'Die Damira-Opern der beiden Ziani', *AnMc*, no.14 (1974), 176–207
with C. Harten: *Franz Schmidt, 1874–1939, Ausstellung zum 100. Geburtstag* (Vienna, 1974) [catalogue]
ed., with R. Flotzinger and O. Wessely: *De ratione in musica: Festschrift Erich Schenk* (Kassel, 1975)

Antoniou, Theodore (*b* Athens, 10 Feb 1935). Greek composer. He studied composition with Iōhannēs Papaioannou and Günter Bialas and then taught composition at Stanford University (1969–70), the University of Utah (1970), the Philadelphia Music Academy (1970–75) and the University of Pennsylvania (1978) before joining the faculty at Boston University in 1979. A prolific composer of music-theatre works, incidental and film music, he has composed only one opera, *Periander* (1977–9). This mixed media work in two acts portrays several episodes in the life of the second tyrant of Corinth. Musically it has its roots in the Second Viennese School, especially in the works of Berg. An unmistakable lyricist, Antoniou is capable of sensitive combinations of sounds and delicate orchestral shadings, and he shows considerable creativity in his treatment of the chorus. While musically appealing, *Periander* has been criticized as dramatically weak. The English libretto, by George Christodoulakis, is loosely constructed; various sequences depicting Periander's misuse of power, senseless murder and ultimate self-destruction are arbitrarily linked together with no driving dramatic force. Nowhere is it mentioned that this despot was also a patron of literature and was considered one of the Seven Wise Men of Greece.

For Antoniou, music is not a decorative art but must reflect what is happening around him, and *Periander* is obviously a commentary on the political events occurring in his homeland at the time. It was performed in a German translation (by P. Kertz) at the Gärtnerplatztheater in Munich on 6 February 1983. Some of his music-theatre works are also based on Greek history, for example *Clytemnestra* (1967) and *Cassandra* (1969). These are generally scored for singers/narrators, actors, dancers, chorus and orchestra, and often use projections and electronic tape.

*

Anderson2; *Baker7*; *VintonD*
D. Rosenberg and B. Rosenberg: *The Music Makers* (New York, 1979), 71–8
I. Fabian: 'Szenen aus dem Leben eines Tyrannen', *Opernwelt*, xxiv/4 (1983), 26–7
R. H. Kornick: *Recent American Opera: a Production Guide* (New York, 1991), 16–18 JAMES P. CASSARO

Antony and Cleopatra. Opera in three acts, op.40, by SAMUEL BARBER to a libretto by FRANCO ZEFFIRELLI after

'Antony and Cleopatra' (Barber), Act 2 scene vii (aboard a Roman galley): design by Franco Zeffirelli for the original production which opened the Metropolitan Opera House, New York, 16 September 1966

WILLIAM SHAKESPEARE's play; New York, Metropolitan Opera, 16 September 1966.

Commissioned for the opening of the new opera house at Lincoln Center, the original version of *Antony and Cleopatra* consisted entirely of Shakespeare's words (*see also* CLEOPATRA), which Franco Zeffirelli condensed to 16 scenes set in Rome and Egypt, plus one scene aboard a Roman galley omitted in the revised version. Antony (bass-baritone) leaves Egypt and his mistress, the Egyptian Queen Cleopatra (soprano). Returning to Rome, he is pressed to marry Octavia, sister of Octavius Caesar (tenor). When he goes to Cleopatra instead, Caesar declares war and defeats him. Antony kills himself and Cleopatra commits suicide soon after.

The alternating geographical settings are mirrored in the character of the music: sinuous melodies, luminescent harmonies and exotic orchestral timbres in the Egyptian scenes and for Cleopatra contrast with the angular declamations and driving, irregular rhythms of the brash 'Roman' music. Conventional forms support the dramatic action: a fugato and ominous passacaglia, for example, dominate the tense meeting of Antony and Caesar in the Roman Senate (Act 1 scene ii). Recurring motives reinforce dramatic associations through transformation or expansion, giving audible unity to the opera: the Prologue's brass fanfare opens the Roman scenes in Acts 1 and 2; Cleopatra's serpentine phrase 'If this be love indeed' returns in the orchestral accompaniment to her suicide; her spinechilling 'my man of men' (Act 1 scene iii) returns as the climax of her death scene in Act 3; the haunting choral evocation 'Cleopatra' accompanies the vision of her barge on the Nile and pervades the orchestral texture as well. Unusual instrumental combinations are strikingly effective: an electronic instrument and double bass provide an eerie background to the 'Music i' the air' episode, and a solo flute and timpani are chilling accompaniment to the suicides of Antony and Enobarbus. Some of the most sensuous and soaring lyrical passages were composed especially for Leontyne Price, who created the role of Cleopatra. Two arias – 'Give me some music' (from Act 1) and the suicide monologue 'Give me my robe, put on my crown, I have immortal longings in me' (from Act 3) – were expanded in 1968 into independent concert scenes.

Initial appreciation of the opera, which contained some of Barber's most dramatic vocal music and a skilfully crafted score, was handicapped by an inflated production with problematic technical apparatus, gaudy costumes, overcrowded stage forces and a press overly attentive to the social glitter of the occasion. Six years after the première, Barber began revising the score and libretto in collaboration with Gian Carlo Menotti, who condensed the work further, diminishing elements of grand opera spectacle in favour of a more intimate production in which the chorus, as in Greek tragedy, sings from each side of the stage. Musical revisions place the lovers in sharper focus and diminish the importance of the world at large: the opening chorus was reduced by half and the ensuing duet between Cleopatra and Antony lengthened; the elimination of interruptive scenes in Rome and discourses by supporting characters permit Cleopatra expanded episodes of lyric meditation that were lacking in the original version. A voluptuously tender love duet was added: 'Oh take, oh take those lips away' (the text is from Beaumont and Fletcher's *The Bloody Brother*). Menotti staged four performances in the American Opera Center at the Juilliard School (6–10 February 1975); subsequent performances were mounted at the Spoleto Festival of Two Worlds in Charleston and Italy in 1983 and by the Lyric Opera of Chicago in 1991, the latter being the opera's first production in a major house since its première.

BARBARA B. HEYMAN

Antoš, Jan (*fl* 1772–92). Czech composer. He was a teacher in Nemyčeves near Jičín (1772–92), then in Kopidlno. Most of his work output consists of church music, but he also wrote the *Opera de rebellione boëmica rusticorum quae contigit anno 1777*, which deals with the great peasant rebellion in East Bohemia of 1775. The work seems to have gained popularity in its time: it appears in several musical collections, and also as a spoken drama. The opera is composed in a late Baroque idiom, with Rococo features; to highlight the contrast between the lives of peasants and the nobility, it uses elements of folk and art music.

*

J. Němeček: *Lidové zpěvohry a písně z doby roboty* [Folk Operas and Songs from the Time of Serfdom] (Prague, 1954)

T. Volek: 'První české zpěvohry' [The First Czech Singspiels], *Dějiny českého divadla*, ed. F. Černy, i: *Od počátku do sklonku osmnáctého století* [History of Czech Theatre, i: From the Beginning to the End of the 18th Century] (Prague, 1968), 331–2

J. Trojan: *České zpěvohry 18. století* [Czech Singspiels of the 18th Century] (Brno, 1981) MICHAELA FREEMANOVÁ

Antwerp (Fr. Anvers; Flem. Antwerpen). Belgian city and port on the River Scheldt. Although Lully's *Proserpine* was performed there in 1682, two years after its première in Paris, harpsichord making and church music dominated in the city's musical life until the late 18th century. Taste was then dictated by the Italian and (chiefly) French opera performed at the Théâtre Royal (1802–1933). In 1890 Peter Benoit, who had founded the Vlaamsche Muziekschool in 1867, helped form the Nederlandsch Lyrisch Toneel (Netherlands Lyric Theatre) at Kipdorpbrug. Despite having been Offenbach's assistant conductor at the Bouffes-Parisiens, he did not like opera and gave instead plays with incidental music – *Egmont*, *L'arlésienne* and his own *Charlotte Corday*, written for the opening – but with little success. The Flemish bass Hendrik Fontaine became director and transformed the company, which in 1893 became the Vlaamse Opera. Its first production was *Der Freischütz*, sung in Flemish. In 1907 the company moved to its newly built house, the Vlaamsch Lyrisch Toneel (Flemish Lyric Theatre), on Frankrijkiel (1050 seats), which is still in use; in 1920 it became the Koninklijke Vlaamse (Royal Flemish) Opera.

Originally the repertory consisted mostly of Flemish versions of the works of Weber, Lortzing, Marschner, Mozart, d'Albert and above all Wagner (the *Ring* has been given regularly from 1910, and *Parsifal* every Good Friday), but with the closing in 1933 of the Théâtre Royal, French and Italian works were added, although everything except gala performances was sung in Flemish. Nearly a hundred original Flemish works have been produced, the most successful being *De Herbergprinses* ('The Princess of the Inn', 1896) and *De Bruid der Zee* ('The Bride of the Sea', 1901) by Jan Blockx. The company has also given the Belgian premières of *Kát'a Kabanová* (1960), *The Nose* (1965), *A Midsummer Night's Dream* (1962), Pizzetti's *L'assassinio in cattedrale* (1963), Suchoň's *The Whirlpool* (1968) and Martinů's *The Greek Passion* (1969). In 1982 the company joined with the Koninklijke Opera of Ghent to form the Opera voor Flaanderen (Flanders Opera), since when the association has more than once dissolved and reformed (under a variety of names); since 1988 it has been known as the Vlaamsoper (Flemish Opera). The group now produces stagione rather than repertory performances in both cities from the end of September to the end of July, sung in the original language. Since 1959 the Vlaamse Kameropera has given one-act operas and works using smaller forces.

*

A. Monet: *Een halve eeuw Nederlandsch lyrisch tooneel en Vlaamsche opera te Antwerpen* (Antwerp, 1939)

A. M. Pols: *Vijftig jaar Vlaamsche opera* (Antwerp, 1943)

CHARLES PITT

Anush. Opera in four acts by ARMEN TIGRAN TIGRANYAN, orchestrated by G. Ya. Burkovich, to his own libretto after Hovhannes T'umanyan's poem; Alexandrapol (now Kumayrï), People's City Hall, 4/17 August 1912.

Anush was the first opera to receive its première in Armenia, in amateur productions which helped to disseminate its popular melodies. It also helped establish the foundations for a national operatic style. In 1935 it was revived for Erevan in a revised version (in five acts and reorchestrated) given by the Spendiaryan Armenian Theatre of Opera and Ballet; the same company later performed *Anush* in Moscow at the Bol'shoy (22 October 1939). T'umanyan's lyric poem – a timeless tragedy of lovers sacrificed on the altar of social prejudice – to which Tigranyan turned in 1908 was rich in local colour and atmosphere, features enhanced by the music. Although only one folksong is quoted, Tigranyan's score is permeated with traces of Armenian folklore: modal melodic inflections and ornate embellishments, song forms, improvisatory flexibility, evocative instrumental colour and native drumming styles, and the traditional forms of wedding and ritual music.

The action takes place among the nomadic peoples of the Lori mountains in Armenia at the end of the 19th century. Although the first version of the opera began, like its literary original, with spirits lamenting the fates of Anush and Saro in song and dance, in the revised version this scene was replaced with a symphonic prologue and an interpolated choral episode. In scene i Anush (soprano), working with her mother (mezzo-soprano), hears in the distance the shepherd Saro (tenor) singing of his love for her and runs to the spring, jug in hand. In scene ii she breaks away from the chorus of maidens to reflect on her love for Saro; the two are blissfully reunited.

Act 2 takes place during the Ascensiontide festival of song and dance. The crowd tries to coax Saro to wrestle with the shepherd Mosi (baritone), Anush's brother, but Mosi reminds them of the ancient mountain injunction never to knock a friend to the ground in front of others. The young women begin telling fortunes, singing excitedly. One, however, makes a terrible prediction that death by point-blank bullet awaits another's lover. This is the lot drawn by Anush. Inconsolable, she falls senseless to the ground.

In Act 3 Anush and Saro attend a wedding. Saro and Mosi are persuaded to wrestle in fun, but in the heat of conflict Saro forgets the sacrosanct custom and knocks down Mosi, who, infuriated, challenges Saro to a genuine fight. When, in a reconciliatory gesture, Saro extends a goblet from which he has sipped, Mosi dashes it to the ground and grasps his dagger. Anush interposes herself between her brother and lover; Mosi exits quickly.

Act 4 finds Anush and Saro in the mountains, fugitives from their angry relatives. Mosi has set fire to a haystack, blaming Saro, to incite the peasants against him. Mosi vows to kill Saro.

In Act 5 scene i, Saro is alone in the mountains while Anush entreats her mother's permission to marry. Mosi finds and shoots him. Saro's mother (mezzo-soprano) prostrates herself on her son's body. In the concluding scene, Anush, demented with grief, wanders near the scene of the murder, oblivious to all but the voice of Saro calling her to him. Responding with devotion, she throws herself into the river. LAUREL E. FAY

Anvers (Fr.). ANTWERP.

Apell [Capelli], **David August von** (*b* Kassel, 23 Feb 1754; *d* Kassel, 30 Jan 1832). German composer. He worked in the treasury at Kassel, receiving musical instruction from local court musicians, then concentrated on composition (public performances date from 1780) and conducting. In 1792 Count Wilhelm IX (later Elector Wilhelm I) made him Intendant of the court theatre, and he remained at Kassel throughout the wars with France. In 1822, however, possibly as the result of intrigues, he was relieved of all theatrical duties. Despite receiving many honours in the course of his career, he died alone and in poverty.

Apell's operatic works are all lost except *Anacreon*. One aria from *Griselda* also survives (*D-Bds*), but it is possible that this is a cantata, not an operatic fragment. These, along with his vocal music and instrumental pieces, were admired by his contemporaries, including Gerber, but he outlived their fame. His published account of the musicians of Kassel from the 16th century (1806) remains his principal achievement.

La clemenza di Tito (3, P. Metastasio), Kassel, 1787
Tancrède (after Voltaire), Kassel, 1790
L'amour peintre ou Le jaloux dupé (oc, 1), Kassel, 1794
Anacreon (Spl, 1, C. H. Bindseil), Kassel, 1803, *D-Ds*

*

GerberNL
W. Lyncker: *Geschichte der Musik und des Theaters in Kassel* (Kassel, 1865, 2/1886)
R. Lebe: *Ein deutsches Hoftheater* (Kassel, 1964)
JEFFRY MARK, DAVID CHARLTON

ApIvor, Denis (*b* Collinstown, 14 April 1916). Irish composer of Welsh origin. His early musical education was as a chorister, at Christ Church, Oxford, and at Hereford Cathedral. Since his parents were not in favour of a musical career he studied medicine at London University, remaining essentially self-taught as a composer until, from the age of 21, he had private lessons with Patrick Hadley and Alan Rawsthorne. ApIvor regarded World War II as 'a severe set-back' in his development as a composer; he had reached a decisive stage only to find that almost all musical activity was impossible for six years. Nevertheless, in 1942 he began work on the libretto of his first opera, *She Stoops to Conquer*. The basically light style of this and other early pieces is, in part, a reflection of Constant Lambert's influence. Lambert helped to obtain a commission from Covent Garden for a ballet (*A Mirror for Witches* op.19) and he conducted the première of ApIvor's setting of T. S. Eliot's *The Hollow Men* in 1951.

She Stoops to Conquer can be regarded as completing the first phase of ApIvor's development. He next explored a serial method which did not necessarily eliminate all tonal references. When the Sadler's Wells Trust commissioned an opera in 1955 he chose to base it on García Lorca's tragedy *Yerma*. The work remained unstaged though a radio version was broadcast in 1961. After *Yerma*, ApIvor's style became more radical, the serialism atonal and athematic; his music of this period includes two larger compositions, the opera *Ubu Roi* and a ballet, *Corporal Jan*. Most of the works of this period exploit short forms, smaller groups and more polyphonic textures; from 1968 he favoured a freer serialism. Between 1971 and 1974 he wrote a three-act opera with prologue, *Bouvard et Pécuchet*. The extent of his development – from post-Warlock to post-Webern – is obvious enough, and the fact that his music has been little played or published may be due in part to the stylistic distance he has travelled.

She Stoops to Conquer op.12, 1942–7 (4, ApIvor, after O. Goldsmith)
Yerma op.28, 1955–9 (3, M. Slater, after F. García Lorca), BBC, 17 Dec 1961
Ubu Roi op.40, 1966–7 (op pataphysica, 3, ApIvor, after A. Jarry)
Bouvard et Pécuchet op.49, 1971–4 (ob, prol., 3, ApIvor, after G. Flaubert)

*

D. C. F. Wright: 'Denis ApIvor', *MR*, l (1989), 53–63
ARNOLD WHITTALL

Apollo. Theatre in Rome, completed in 1795 on the site of the former Teatro Tordinona; *see* ROME, §3(i, ii).

Apollo et Hyacinthus ('Apollo and Hyacinthus'). Intermezzo in three acts, K38, by WOLFGANG AMADEUS MOZART to a Latin libretto by Rufinus Widl; Salzburg, Benedictine University, 13 May 1767.

Mozart's first stage work, *Apollo et Hyacinthus* is an intermezzo, written for performance by students with the five-act Latin tragedy *Clementia Croesi* by the Benedictine Gymnasium teacher, Widl.

Hyacinthus (boy soprano), son of Oebalus (tenor), King of Lacedonia, is murdered by Zephyrus (boy alto) to incriminate Apollo (boy alto), his rival for the hand of Oebalus's daughter Melia (boy soprano). She denounces Apollo; but the dying Hyacinthus, in a moving recitative, reveals the truth. Zephyrus is banished, Apollo and Melia marry, and the god turns Hyacinthus into the flower that bears his name.

The musical idiom is not yet characteristic, but is never less than expressive. Although the singers were aged between 12 and 23, the solo numbers (an aria for each character, two duets and a trio) are neither short nor particularly easy. There is a single-movement overture and an opening chorus. JULIAN RUSHTON

Apolloni [Apollonio, Appolloni], **Giovanni Filippo** (*b* Arezzo, *c*1635; *d* Arezzo, ?15 May 1688). Italian librettist. The name Apollonio Apolloni is spurious and refers to Giovanni Filippo (see Pirrotta 1953). In 1653 he entered the service of Archduke Ferdinand Karl of Austria at Innsbruck, perhaps at the instigation of Cesti, where he wrote the librettos for *Mars und Adonis*, *L'Argia* and *La Dori*. He returned to Italy by 1659 and entered the service of Cardinal Flavio Chigi at Rome in May 1660, remaining in that post until his death; at some point he was given an abbotship. Like Cesti he belonged to the circle of Salvator Rosa and G. B. Ricciardi. He set to verse *L'empio punito* of Filippo Acciaiuoli for the Teatro Tordinona, Rome, in 1669; he apparently did the same for Acciaiuoli's *Girello* (Rome, 1668), for which he certainly wrote the prologue. In addition to the dramatic works he wrote three oratorio texts.

Crescimbeni recognized Apolloni as 'one of the best followers' of G. A. Cicognini. The work that most clearly shows him in that tradition is *La Dori*, which rivalled *Giasone* and *Orontea* as one of the most widely performed Italian operas of the 17th century. *La Dori* relies heavily on mistaken identity and misunderstanding in its concentrated love plot, which makes little use of historical or pseudo-historical superstructure; it has in common with Cicognini's dramas much rapid dialogue, direct and lively language, strong but traditional comic elements and a 'surprise' resolution of the plot.

L'Argia, Cesti, 1655; *Mars und Adonis*, ?Cesti, 1655; *La Dori*, Cesti, 1657; *La Circe* (operetta), Stradella, 1668; *La forza d'amore* (cantata scenica), P. P. Cappellini, n.d. (B. Pasquini, 1672, rev. as Con la forza d'amor si vince amor, 1679); *La sincerità con la sincerità, overo Il Tirinto* (favola drammatica per musica, with F. Acciainoli), B. Pasquini, 1672; *Gl'inganni innocenti, ovvero L'Adalinda* (with Acciaiuoli), P. S. Agostini, 1673; *L'Amor per vendetta, ovvero L'Alcasta*, Pasquini, 1673

*

Apolloni poesie (MS, *I-Rn* Ebor.26) [incl. texts set by Cesti and Stradella; others in *I-Fn* Palat.285.ix and *Rvat* Ferrajoli 1]
G. M. Crescimbeni: *L'istoria della volgar poesia* (Rome, 2/1714)
L. Allacci and others: *Drammaturgia* (Venice, 1755)
N. Pirrotta: 'Tre capitoli su Cesti', *La scuola romana: G. Carissimi – A. Cesti – M. Marazzoli*, Chigiana, x (1953), 27–79, esp. 59
N. Burt: 'Opera in Arcadia', *MQ*, xli (1955), 145–70
F. Schlitzer: *Intorno alla 'Dori' di Antonio Cesti* (Florence, 1957)
C. Schmidt: *The Operas of Antonio Cesti* (diss., Harvard U., 1973)
——: 'Antonio Cesti's "La Dori": a Study of Sources, Performance Traditions and Musical Style', *RIM*, x (1975), 455–98
—— '"La Dori" di Antonio Cesti: sussidi bibliografici', *RIM*, xi (1976), 197–229
M. Murata: 'Il carnevale a Roma sotto Clemente IX Rospigliosi', *RIM*, xii (1977), 83–99 THOMAS WALKER

Apolloni, Giuseppe (*b* Vicenza, 8 April 1822; *d* Vicenza, ?30 Dec 1889). Italian composer. He studied the piano and composition in Vicenza, where he lived until 1848, when his political involvement forced him to leave the city for Florence. Upon his return to Vicenza in 1852 his first opera, *Adelchi*, was staged there. His most widely produced work was *L'ebreo*, first performed at Venice in 1855, and then in Barcelona and Malta; it was given a different title in Rome and Bologna, *Lida* [*Leila*] *di Granata*, at the insistence of the censors. On the strength of its very successful production at the Fenice, the management there invited Apolloni to revise *Adelchi* for a revival. Besides his operas, which follow Verdi's middle-period style at a distance, he composed an orchestral rhapsody, *I canti dell'Appennino*, using folk melodies, and a number of religious works.

Adelchi (melodramma tragico, 5, G. B. Nicolini, after A. Manzoni), Vicenza, Eretenio, 14 Aug 1852; rev. version, Venice, Fenice, 26 Dec 1856
L'ebreo [Leila di Granata, Lida di Granata] (melodramma tragico, prol., 3, A. Boni, after E. Bulwer-Lytton: *Leila*), Venice, Fenice, 27 Jan 1855
Pietro d'Abano (melodramma serio, 3, Boni), Venice, Fenice, 8 March 1856
Il conte di Königsmark (melodramma, 3), Florence, Pergola, 17 March 1866
Gustavo Wasa (os, 4, U. Poggi), Trieste, Comunale, 16 Nov 1872

*

T. G. Kaufman: *Verdi and his Major Contemporaries* (New York and London, 1990), 1–10 WILLIAM ASHBROOK

Apolloni [Appoloni, Appolini], **Salvatore** [Salvadore] (*b* Venice, *c*1704). Italian composer. According to Caffi, he was closely associated with Baldassare Galuppi. Like Galuppi's father, he was a barber by trade and a part-time violinist. He was a friend of Galuppi's from childhood and it is likely that they both received early musical training from the elder Galuppi. A libretto of 1727 names him as first violinist of the Teatro di S Samuele, Venice. Caffi said that Apolloni was one of Baldassare Galuppi's few students, and eventually Galuppi made a place for him in the orchestra of the ducal chapel of St Mark's.

Apolloni is reputed to have had a lively, cheerful disposition, a trait according well with the lighthearted subjects of his music (of which none is known to survive). He gained an early local reputation as a composer of songs in the style of the Venetian gondoliers (barcarolles), serenatas and other occasional works. As a theatrical composer, he worked almost exclusively for Giuseppe Imer's troupe of comedians (non-professional singers), suggesting that his musical style must have been relatively simple. His intermezzos and parodies of *opera seria* catered to a taste for musical satire which according to Dent ('Giuseppe Maria Buini', *SIMG*, xiii, 1911–12, p.331) was peculiarly Venetian. Such parodies are a curious mixture of the *opera seria* and *buffa* conventions then current in Venice: the characters are people of high social degree (but one of the kings speaks in Venetian dialect); da capo exit arias are regularly used, but so are ensemble finales and short arias to open scenes. The works are much shorter than normal operas, whether serious or comic, and they contain about half as many musical numbers. Although early historians spoke slightingly of Apolloni's talents as a composer, performance records attest to his popularity at home and even beyond the Alps.

His works, all for the Teatro di S Samuele, are: *La fama dell'onore* (M. Miani; May 1727; revived in Vienna, 1730); *Le metamorfosi odiamorose* (A. Gorì, carn. 1732; revived in Dresden, 1747, as *La Contesa di Mestre e Malghera*); and possibly *La pelarina* (Goldoni ?and Gorì, carn. 1734), and *Il pastor fido* (carn. 1739). Both Apolloni and Giacomo Maccari have been suggested as possible composers of settings of Goldoni intermezzos; although Maccari is the more likely, either composer's authorship is doubtful.

*

J.-B. de La Borde: *Essai sur la musique ancienne et moderne* (Paris, 1780), iii, 165
F. Caffi: *Storia della musica nella già cappella ducale di San Marco in Venezia dal 1318 al 1797* (Venice, 1854–5), i, 402–3; ii, 67–8
T. Wiel: *I teatri musicali veneziani del settecento* (Venice, 1897), 132
G. Ortolani, ed.: *Tutte le opere di Carlo Goldoni:* (Milan, 1935–56), i, 716 and passim on Imer's troupe; x, 1217, 1226, 1232, 1234 JAMES L. JACKMAN

Apostolou, Yannis [Ioannis, Yangos] (*b* Athens or Menidi, Attica, ?1860; *d* Naples, 28 Aug 1905). Greek tenor. From boyhood he sang in the Royal Chapel and other Athens church choirs, and later studied, probably at the Athens Conservatory, with Alexandros Katakouzenos and Napoleon Lambelet. He made his operatic début in the first production staged by the newly-formed Elliniko Melodrama company, Spyridon Xyndas's *The Parliamentary Candidate* (1888). As the company's leading tenor he sang principal roles in its tours of Egypt and Turkey (1889), Marseilles, Romania, Odessa and Constantinople (1889–90), including Fernand, Edgardo and Elvino. In 1890 he left Greece for Milan, and after six months of further training began to appear in Italian opera houses. From 1895 he sang leading roles from the French and Italian repertories at the S Carlo, La Fenice and La Scala; he also made successful guest appearances in Russia. At Monte Carlo in 1897 he sang Alfredo to Adelina Patti's Violetta and Edgardo to her Lucia; and in 1904 in Naples he sang Riccardo to Battistini's Duke de Chevreuse in Donizetti's *Maria di Rohan*. Apostolou became extremely popular in his own country, and after the invention of the gramophone he was the first Greek soloist to gain international acclaim. Critics praised the restrained, silvery sweetness of his voice and his exceptionally clear diction; his voice may be heard on two rare recordings of 1903.

*

T. N. Synadinos: *Istoria tis neoellinikis moussikis, 1824–1919* [History of Modern Greek Music, 1824–1919] (Athens, 1919), 166, 278, 302–6

G. Leotsakos: *Elliniko Lyriko Theatro, 100 chronia, 1888–1988* (YP 4–6, A/A 14564–6, 1988), 18–25 [record notes]

GEORGE LEOTSAKOS

Apotheker, Der. Opera by Joseph Haydn; *see* SPEZIALE, LO (ii).

Apotheker und der Doktor, Der. Opera by C. D. von Dittersdorf; *see* DOKTOR UND APOTHEKER.

Appia, Adolphe (François) (*b* Geneva, 1 Sept 1862; *d* Nyon, 29 Feb 1928). Swiss theatrical theorist and stage designer. He studied at Geneva (1879–89), and at the conservatories of Leipzig and Dresden, at the same time acquainting himself with contemporary theatrical practice by attendance at the Bayreuth Festival (from 1882), and the court opera houses of Dresden (1889) and Vienna (1890). After 1890 he pursued his interests as a writer and artist and led a secluded existence in the vicinity of Lake Geneva.

Like many contemporary artists Appia reacted against the economic and social conditions of his day, registering a Romantic protest by aspiring to a theatrical art independent of reality and determined solely by the creative imagination of the artist. Wagner's music dramas were the focal point of his ideas. Whereas Wagner's music and text as a product of the 'first and primordial idea of creation' was to his mind free from the conventions of the real world, its stage representation had been taken over by the 'conventional influence of the milieu'. For Appia, the solution followed on from the insight that in Wagner the music constituted not only the time element but also that of space, taking on 'bodily form' in the staging itself. However, this could come about only if there were a hierarchical order of the factors of presentation to guarantee that the music, as the prime revelation of the artist's soul, would determine all the relationships on the stage. Appia's hierarchical synthesis – a departure from the equal participation of the arts in Wagner's *Gesamtkunstwerk* – gives the central role to the actor trained in dance and rhythm. His actions, pre-formed by the score, transfer the music on to the stage, whose 'arrangement' must match its physical properties: a 'scenic construction set up in an ad hoc manner, with its surfaces and their various angles extending unconcealed in space'; electrical lighting takes on the function of articulating the stage area, while painting and costumes are reduced to a colouring agent with the task of 'simplification'. His aesthetics, which appear to turn away from the conventions of the industrial era, are however subservient to them, because his stage art was not only dominated by the new technology of electricity, but (as a result of his negation of the producer's creativity) ultimately aimed at an automatic process, at an art of machines set in motion by the music. Appia had his first opportunity of trying out his theories at the theatre of the Comtesse de Béarn in Paris in 1903 with scenes from Schumann's *Manfred* and Bizet's *Carmen*, using a new lighting system developed by Mariano Fortuny. A decisive influence on his later work was his encounter (1906) with Emile Jaques-Dalcroze, in whose rhythmical gymnastics he saw the realization of the synthesis of music with the living body that was essential to his theatrical ideas – reflected in his 'espaces rythmiques' from 1909 onwards. They demonstrated the principles of 'living space', not formulated until *L'oeuvre d'art vivant* (1921). In order to correspond to the form and movements of the living actors, this space consists of freely adaptable, purpose-built stage structures formed of a limited number of linear elements, on which each transformation or each fresh combination happens in full view of the audience. The concept was demonstrated in Jaques-Dalcroze's *Echo und Narzissus* (1912) and Gluck's *Orfeo ed Euridice* in the Jaques-Dalcroze educational institute in Dresden.

Appia is the father of non-illusionist musical theatre. All anti-realistic tendencies of the moderns can more or less be traced back to him. Like EDWARD GORDON CRAIG, who was comparable to him in many respects, his influence found a more effective medium in his theoretical writings than in his practical activities. Only after his ideas were already widespread and to some extent even superseded was he recalled to the public stage: in 1923 he designed *Tristan und Isolde* for La Scala and in 1924 and 1925 *Das Rheingold* and *Die Walküre* for the Stadttheater at Basle. In Bayreuth, Cosima Wagner, to whom his reforming projects were primarily addressed, rejected them; it was only with the 'new' Bayreuth of Wieland and Wolfgang Wagner that his ideas made a deep mark on stage design at the Festspielhaus.

For illustrations of Appia's designs *see* PRODUCTION, fig.18 and STAGE DESIGN, fig.16.

La mise en scène du drame wagnérien (Paris, 1895; Eng. trans., 1982)

Die Musik und die Inszenierung (Munich, 1899; Eng. trans., 1962)

L'oeuvre d'art vivant (Geneva, 1921; Eng. trans., 1960)

Art vivant ou nature morte? (Milan, 1923)

Album de reproductions, ed. O. L. Forel, E. Junod and J. Mercier (Zürich, 1929)

Oeuvres complètes, ed. M. L. Bablet-Hahn (Lausanne, 1983–)

*

J. Mercier: 'Adolphe Appia: The Re-birth of Dramatic Art', *Theatre Arts Monthly*, xvi (1932), 615–30

L. Simonson: 'Appia's Contribution to the Modern Stage', ibid, 631–48

E. Stadler: 'Adolphe Appia', *Maske und Kothurn*, v (1959), 144–56

F. Marotti: *La scena di Adolphe Appia* (Milan, 1963)

E. Stadler: *Mostra dell'opera di Adolphe Appia* (Venice, 1963) [exhibition catalogue]

W. R. Volbach: *Adolphe Appia: Prophet of the Modern Theatre* (Middletown, CT, 1968)

G. Giertz: *Kultus ohne Götter: Emile Jaques-Dalcroze und Adolphe Appia: der Versuch einer Theaterreform auf der Grundlage der rhythmischen Gymnastik* (Munich, 1975)

Adolphe Appia, 1862–1928: acteur, espace, lumière (Zürich, 1979; Eng. trans., 1982) [exhibition catalogue]

R. Beecham: 'Adolphe Appia and the Staging of Wagnerian Opera', *OQ*, i/3 (1983–4), 114–39

——: *Adolphe Appia, Theatre Artist* (Cambridge, 1987)

MANFRED BOETZKES

Applausus musicus (Lat.). A genre of 18th-century Austrian cloister theatre: a compact, Latin operetta or semi-dramatic cantata in one act or part, of a congratulatory character. It consisted of a row of solo ariosos or arias alternating with recitative and at least one ensemble number (duet, trio or quartet), as well as a final chorus that usually functioned as a LICENZA. The arias, ensembles and choruses were cast predominantly in da capo form, and the whole was introduced by an orchestral overture ('intrada', 'introduzione', 'sinfonia') that typically followed the Italian three-movement pattern. The weight of the concluding chorus and the elaborate scoring (a feature possibly derived from the Italian serenata) were characteristic. Joseph Haydn's *Applausus* HXXIVa:6, composed in 1768 for the Cistercian cloister at Zwettl, is in some respects representative. The title *Singgedicht* ('sung poem') was employed for works following the identical format as the *applausus*, but composed on German texts.

The *applausus* was often performed scenically on a stage with costumes. It may have evolved out of the musical prologue and epilogue encasing the acts of the old Baroque cloister drama (LUDI CAESAREI), the plots of which had increasingly become more independent. It had in common with the old prologue-epilogue the mythological and allegorical characters and the *licenza*-like function of the final chorus.

R. N. Freeman: *The Practice of Music at Melk Abbey, based upon the Documents, 1681–1826*, Österreichische Akademie der Wissenschaften, philosophisch-historische Klasse, Sitzungsberichte, dxlviii (Vienna, 1989) ROBERT N. FREEMAN

Appoggiatura (It.; Fr. *appoggiature, port de voix, chute, accent, appuy, coulé*; Ger. *Vorschlag, Accent*). A 'leaning-note'; a dissonant note sounded on a strong beat, 'leaning' and resolving on to the following note, which is normally one step below (occasionally above). It may be notated as an ordinary note, or as an ornament in smaller notation, or, in certain understood contexts, it may not be notated at all. In opera the unnotated appoggiatura is of particular importance, primarily in recitative but also elsewhere, during the Baroque and Classical periods and to some extent in the Romantic period too; if the convention regarding its insertion is not correctly applied the natural accentuation of the words is not reflected, as it ought to be and as composers intended it to be, in the music.

Theorists during the late Baroque period and the Classical period agree that, when 'feminine endings' to a phrase – in recitative and, generally, in lyrical music – are notated with a pair of notes at the same pitch, the first of them accented, the first note must be executed as an appoggiatura (the 'prosodic appoggiatura') in accordance with the verbal accentuation. The most common contexts are where the voice falls by a 3rd to the tonic, when the appoggiatura will be sung to the supertonic, or a 4th to the dominant, when the tonic will be reiterated (ex.1*a* and *b*); more rarely, and chiefly when the words embody a question, it may be a step below (ex.1*c*), usually a semitonal step. The 'blunt ending', with a note repeated from a strong accent to a weak one at the end of a phrase, was always avoided. The rule applied not only to final cadences but also to intermediate breaks at line endings, and even to repeated notes in the middle of a line when the first falls on a strong beat. Examples from later in the 18th

Ex.1

(a)

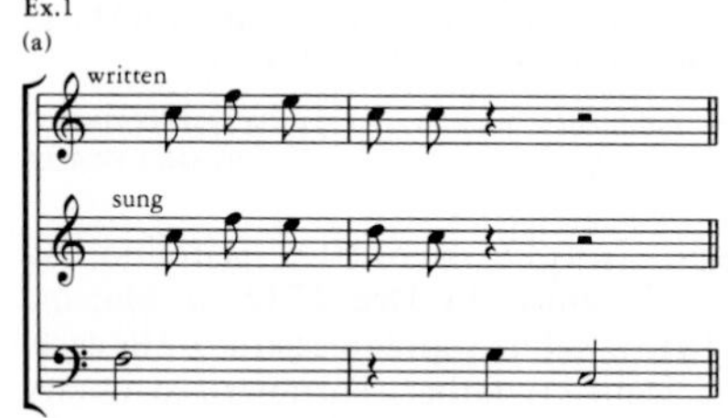

(b)

(c)

(d) Hiller: *Anweisung* (1780)

(e) Sacchini: *Perseo* (1774), taken from Corri (*c*1779)

Nor te - mer i - dol mi - o! no! che a tal se - gno non
so - no in - giu - sti i nu - mi all' ara in -
- nan - zi, cor - ro vo - lo a pros - trar - mi, ah si! s'è
ve - ro che di quei nu - mi i - stes - si nel - le
ve - ne mi scor - ra, il di - vin
san - gue, av - ran di me, di te pie - tà

•realized appoggiatura

(f)

century show a wide variety of practices (ex.1*d* and *e*), including leaping from below the accented note and approaching it from above. The creation of a harmonic clash does not require the omission of the appoggiatura, as Telemann makes clear (ex.1*f*, from *Der harmonische Gottesdienst*, 1725).

The convention of the prosodic appoggiatura is mentioned and illustrated by many contemporary theorists, among them Tosi (1723, who objected to the implied reflection on singers when composers notated it as it was to be performed), Telemann (1725), Agricola (1757), Marpurg (1763), Hiller (1774, 1780), Mancini (1777), Corri (1779), Rellstab (1786–7), Lasser (1798), Schubert (1804), Lanza (1809), Garaudé (1810) and Ferrari (1818). Corri refers to 'either an air or a recitative'; Lanza states that 'This Rule applies to Songs, as well as Recitative'; and Lasser prints several phrases from arias with appoggiaturas on feminine endings. Ferrari prints a table showing how a number of standard phrases are modified, indicating different treatment according to the nature of the metre (ex.2). It is applicable equally to Italian and German music; while Italian writers tend to emphasize the avoidance of successive syllables at the same pitch when the first is accented, Germans stress the filling-in of the melodic interval. Many writers refer to the possibility of adding appoggiaturas on masculine endings (to fill the gap of a 3rd or simply to reflect the fall of the voice, as at the end of ex. 1*e*), in the middles of phrases and to notes that are already appoggiaturas, generally advising caution and regarding them as a matter of taste and judgment. Although no exceptions are contemplated by theorists to the rule as applied to 'blunt endings', it is uncertain whether phrases that acquire their character from a note repetition (such as the passages in the trio 'Cosa sento?' from Act 1 of *Le nozze di Figaro*, 'In mal punto' etc.) should in fact be modified. That performers exercised certain options about the insertion of appoggiaturas is clear; among modern writers Neumann (1982, 1986) takes the view that these options were extensive.

Practical examples from contemporary sources bear out the theorists' rules. Written-out, elaborated versions of arias invariably show the modification of blunt endings, and transcriptions of arias for instruments include additional appoggiaturas (for examples, see Crutchfield 1989).

The convention continued to apply well into the 19th century. Composers, however, came increasingly to write appoggiaturas into their scores; Rossini and Donizetti, conservatively, often left them to the singers, but Bellini and Verdi did not. The traditional application of appoggiaturas can still be heard in many early recordings. In the early and middle 20th century, the false supposition that the alteration of the printed note represented a violation of the composer's intentions led to a more literal interpretation of notation and the virtual abandonment of appoggiaturas, an interpretative misapprehension which the 'early music' movement has endeavoured, with limited success, to correct since the 1970s.

S. H. Hansell: 'The Cadence in 18th-Century Recitative', *MQ*, liv (1968), 228–48

W. Dean: 'The Performance of the Recitative in Late Baroque Opera', *ML*, lviii (1977), 389–402

F. Neumann: 'The Appoggiatura in Mozart's Recitative', *JAMS*, xxxv (1982), 115–37; rev. repr. in *Ornamentation and Improvisation in Mozart* (Princeton, 1986), 184–215

W. Crutchfield: 'Vocal Ornamentation in Verdi: the Phonographic Evidence', *EMc*, vii (1983–4), 3–54

H. M. Brown and S. Sadie, eds.: *Performance Practice: Music after 1600* (London, 1989), chaps. 5, 15, 21

W. Crutchfield: 'The Prosodic Appoggiatura in the Music of Mozart and his Contemporaries', *JAMS*, xlii (1989), 229–71

For primary sources and further bibliography *see* Ornamentation.

STANLEY SADIE

Aprile, Giuseppe [Scirolo, Sciroletto, Scirolino] (*b* Martina Franca, Taranto, 28 Dec 1732; *d* Martina Franca, 11 Jan 1813). Italian soprano castrato. His early musical training from his father, Fortunato (a notary and church singer), was followed when he was 19 by study with Gregorio Sciroli in Naples (thus his nickname). He made his début in Sciroli's *Lo barone deluso* (1752, Rome). Until 1757 he sang in Naples (in the royal chapel, 1752–6), Turin and Rome; during the next few years he travelled, visiting Venice, Madrid and Stuttgart. After a brief engagement in Italy, he returned to Stuttgart for the period 1762–9 (with one Italian interlude), appearing in Jommelli's *Didone abbandonata* (1763), *Demofoonte* (1764) and *Fetonte* (1768), among other works, and enjoying a salary comparable to Jommelli's own. The depletion of the duke's *cappella* provoked his departure; he left behind him large debts. In 1770 Burney heard him in Naples; Mozart heard him there, in Bologna and Milan, remarking that 'Aprile, first man, sings well and has a beautiful, even voice', which was 'unsurpassed'. Aprile collaborated with Jommelli in Naples on several further occasions. He was first soprano in the royal chapel (replacing Caffarelli) by 1783. His last known performance was in 1785, and he was pensioned in 1798. Aprile was well known as a teacher (his students included Michael Kelly and Cimarosa, and his 1791 vocal method – published in English, as *The Modern Italian Method of Singing* – was widely reprinted); he also composed vocal chamber music. He possessed an agile voice, with a wide range and diversity of expression, and was a good actor. Schubart, writing in Stuttgart, praised his manner of varying arias and noted his great importance to Jommelli. DALE E. MONSON

Aquilanti [Aquilante], **Francesco** (*fl* 1719–42). Italian choreographer and dancer. He was probably a native of Florence, since he is often cited in librettos as 'Francesco Aquilanti, Fiorentino' or 'da Firenze'. His early choreographic work was concentrated in Venice, where he provided ballets for 17 operas at the Teatro S Giovanni Grisostomo (1721–34; including Leo's *Catone in Utica*, Porpora's *Semiramide riconosciuta* and works by Gasparini, Orlandini, Vinci and others), and for five operas during Ascension seasons at the Teatro S Samuele (1722–35; including Vivaldi's *Griselda*). During this time he is also listed as a choreographer in Reggio Emilia (1725, Porpora's *Didone abbandonata*) and as a dancer for opera productions in Turin (1727–8, 1729–30), along with Chiara Aquilanti who may have been his wife, sister or daughter. He spent two seasons in Naples as a choreographer, first for operas at the Teatro S Bartolomeo (1736–7; Leo's *Farnace* and Hasse's or Sarro's *Alessandro nell'Indie*) and then for the opening season of the Teatro S Carlo (1737–8; Sarro's *Achille in Sciro* and works by Leo and Federico). Francesco and Chiara Aquilanti are also listed as dancers for his productions at S Carlo. Throughout his career Aquilanti returned to Florence, where he provided ballets for operas at the Pergola. The last notice of his activity is as a choreographer for two operas at the Regio Ducal Teatro in Milan during the 1741–2 season – Gluck's *Artaserse* and Brivio's *Alessandro nell'Indie*. A Chiaretta Aquilanti appeared in London, dancing at Drury Lane in 1742, and many years later a long letter printed in the *Theatrical Review* (London, 18 March 1763) was addressed 'to the Signora Chiara Aquilante (the famous opera Broker) at Naples'.

BDA

L. C. degli Albizzi: Letters, 1732–7: Florence, Palazzo Guicciardini library, A770 and A771

R. L. Weaver and N. W. Weaver: *A Chronology of Music in the Florentine Theater, 1590–1750* (Detroit, 1978) IRENE ALM

Arabella. *Lyrische Komödie* in three acts by RICHARD STRAUSS to a libretto by HUGO VON HOFMANNSTHAL; Dresden, Staatsoper, 1 July 1933.

Arabella	soprano
Zdenka *her sister*	soprano
Count Waldner *their father, a retired cavalry officer*	bass
Adelaide *their mother*	mezzo-soprano
Mandryka *a Croatian landowner*	baritone
Matteo *a young officer*	tenor
Count Elemer *one of Arabella's suitors*	tenor
Count Dominik *another*	baritone
Count Lamoral *a third*	bass
The Fiakermilli *belle of the Coachmen's Ball*	coloratura soprano
A Fortune-Teller	soprano
Welko, Djura, Jankel *Mandryka's servants*	spoken
Hotel Porter	spoken
A Chaperone, Three Card Players, a Doctor, a Waiter	silent

Coachmen, waiters, ball guests, hotel residents

Setting Vienna in the 1860s, on Carnival Day (Shrove Tuesday)

This opera was the last of the Hofmannsthal–Strauss collaborations: which fact is poignantly registered in the opera itself, not to its advantage. A few days after the writer had sent Strauss his final version of Act 1, his only son committed suicide, and within 36 hours Hofmannsthal himself suffered a fatal stroke. Out of respect, the grieving composer resolved to set both the provisional draft of Act 2 and the still more tentative draft of Act 3 just as they stood, though Act 1 – one of the best-made first acts in the repertory – had been the result of long and strenuous reworking by the partners. A certain diffuseness in the later acts is disguised by their best scenes (the betrothal duet and the final making-up) and sometimes also by performers who can make the most of their sympathetic characters even when the action limps. Despite a triumphal première, *Arabella* did not repeat the unassailable success of *Der Rosenkavalier*.

After their metaphysical excursions with *Die Frau ohne Schatten* and *Die ägyptische Helena*, they had agreed to try Viennese period-comedy again. Hofmannsthal proposed not one idea but two or three, to be woven together. The first was a 'psychological' sketch he had published in 1910 (subtitled 'Characters for an Unwritten Comedy') as *Lucidor* – the alias of Lucile, a 17-year-old tomboy in a youth's clothes, who befriends a rejected Slav suitor to her coquettish sister and falls in love with him, keeps him on hand by forging love-notes from 'Arabella', and at last impersonates her in bed with him. She would become our Zdenka/'Zdenko' in *Arabella*, bringing much of her doubtful family situation with her. The other, newer idea was to exploit a 19th-century Viennese institution, the annual *Fiakerball*, for picturesque effect. The *Fiaker* – coachmen, a robust Viennese clan – had been the colourful subjects of many an old play, including two by Mozart's librettist Emanuel Schikaneder. Though shy, anxious little Zdenka could not make a Strauss soprano lead, charming Arabella could, if sufficiently enhanced by a romantic-idealist dimension. Her transformation from seeming coquette to devout bride-to-be would become the heart of the drama; the original Slavonic swain would be split into two, the green-stick object of Zdenka's affection and a Croatian rough diamond who takes Arabella by surprise (though mysteriously foreseen). All the intrigues and misunderstandings could be arranged around the Coachmen's Ball, in a seedy, *déclassé* Vienna quite different from the imperial capital of *Rosenkavalier*.

As the opera grew, two flaws in the plan appeared. With the story newly adjusted – Arabella's betrothal above Zdenka's romantic deception – and elevated beyond mere operetta, the *Fiakerball* could add nothing but trivial colour, like the showy role of the 'Fiakermilli' herself. (Originally, Act 1 was to have introduced each of Arabella's vain suitors in his ludicrous ball-costume; in its final version only Elemer appears, and only to propose a sleigh-ride. Rather wildly, Strauss suggested inflating the ball itself with an expansive ballet on Balkan folk tunes, but Hofmannsthal was horrified.) Then the 'Lucidor' plot, *risqué* but touching, was not so easily relegated to the background. Strauss feared from the outset that the new Arabella-Mandryka 'drama' would make tame theatre, and though Zdenka's role dwindles after Act 1 to dramatic semaphoring the action still pivots upon her. The composer nurtured her so tenderly at the outset that he must surely have demanded more for her later had not fate abruptly withdrawn Hofmannsthal from further debate.

The fact that Strauss broke off composing *Arabella* to re-write Mozart's *Idomeneo*, in 1930–31, may have betokened misgivings. Eventually he set the principals' heartfelt confessions searchingly and with grace, the provisional comic scenes in no better than routine style – Mandryka's drunken, stagy recoil, the Fiakermilli's yodelling, the farcical duel-of-honour – and did what he could with the meagre parts Hofmannsthal had sketched for Zdenka and her baffled Matteo. The story can seem over-stretched; many producers and conductors prefer some adaptation of the 'two-act version' which Strauss soon agreed to permit. The lusty closing chorus of Act 2 is cut to make an immediate transition to the Act 3 prelude. To save time some of the Fiakermilli's warblings may be stifled too, and usually the plot revelations of Act 3 are trimmed – often, sadly, at the cost of Zdenka's last intimate exchange with her sister. There is no 'right' solution. In abbreviated versions, however, the risk of romantic blandness that Strauss foresaw is real; and any principal pair engaging and subtle enough to scotch it could carry the fuller version just as well.

Scored for a normal Romantic-size orchestra (plus a fourth clarinet and Elemer's sleighbells), *Arabella* was dedicated to the conductor Fritz Busch and the première contracted to Dresden. When the time came, the Nazis had already had Busch sacked. The composer first insisted upon having him back, then threatened to withdraw the score; at last he agreed to fulfil the contract only with performers of his own choice, and so Clemens Krauss conducted his first Strauss première. Later Krauss would marry the first Arabella, Viorica Ursuleac; her Mandryka had been Alfred Jerger, with Margit Bokor as Zdenka and Friedrich Plaschke as Waldner (and Kurt Böhme, a future Waldner, as young Count Dominik). In Vienna Lotte Lehmann had a greater success as the heroine. From the 1950s the fortunes of the opera waxed with a peerless central pair, Lisa della Casa and Dietrich Fischer-Dieskau.

ACT 1 *The drawing-room of the Waldners' smart hotel lodgings* While Zdenka, in her customary 'Zdenko' guise, fends off creditors at the door, her mother listens eagerly to the fortune-teller's obscure reading of Arabella's prospects from the cards. (As such prophecies go, this one proves remarkably accurate, and at suitable points Strauss insinuates some of the main themes to come.) We learn that only a rich marriage for Arabella can rescue the Waldner family from its straits, and that Zdenka's preferred boyish garb has been a lucky economy – dressing both of their daughters to a high social standard would have been ruinous. The ladies withdraw for further divination, and in a *prestissimo* monologue Zdenka worries that Arabella's rejected swain Matteo, her only friend, may become suicidal. Her fears are confirmed when he calls by (to a doleful little waltz): in the face of Arabella's rebuffs, he has begun to doubt 'her' precious letters and to despair. As he slips off, she swears to press his suit with her sister once more.

Arabella returns from a walk (the music, until now chromatic and volatile, settles into a warm, limpid F major) and is disappointed to learn that the fresh roses come merely from Matteo, not from the fur-coated stranger who watched her in the street with wide, serious eyes. Pleading vainly for her friend, Zdenka protests that she would rather be a 'boy' forever than an icy coquette like Arabella. Calmly and sweetly, Arabella explains ('Aber der Richtige') that she will recognize the Right One for her – if there is one; but certainly not Matteo, nor perhaps any of the three counts who are besieging her – when he comes along. Aside, Zdenka admits incomprehension, but is ready to do anything for her sister's happiness; their voices entwine in Strauss's most rapturous soprano duet (he adapted here one of the tunes he had found in a Balkan folksong collection).

Sleighbells herald Count Elemer, passionately overweening, who has won the toss to take Arabella for a ride today. She plays the tease, insists that 'Zdenko' must come along and sends Elemer downstairs to wait. As she goes to get ready, she espies the stranger again in the street below. The senior Waldners come in fantasizing about possible financial rescues; Waldner reveals that he has even sent Arabella's photograph to an old fellow-officer, rich, romantic Mandryka. No sooner has Adelaide drifted out than Count Mandryka himself is announced: not, however, the old Croatian friend, who has died, but his rustic-elegant nephew and heir (the stranger, of course – specified as 'no more than 35'). Bewitched by the photograph, he has sold a forest to make this trip and plead for Arabella's hand. He explains himself at length, with intense candour, and wins her father's heart by pressing a large loan upon him ('Teschek, bedien' dich!'). With an introduction promised for later, Mandryka leaves him alone and bedazzled.

Collecting himself, Waldner strolls grandly out to rejoin affluent society at the gambling tables. The worried 'Zdenko', still not dressed for the outing, promises Matteo that he will get another note from Arabella at the ball tonight. Her sister reappears to say that the horses are impatient; 'The horses – and your Elemer!' snaps Zdenka as she goes off. Arabella repeats 'Mein Elemer!' over a peculiar, deflating cadence: she resists the very idea, without knowing what she wants instead. Perhaps the stranger? – though surely he is a married man, and may never be seen again. In any case, she is about to be the carefree Queen of the *Fiakerball*;

'Arabella' (Richard Strauss): set for Act 3 (the main hall of the Waldners' hotel) designed by Adolf Mahnke for the original production at the Staatsoper, Dresden, in 1933; it is not known to what extent this design was actually used in the production

but then ... ? (Strauss demanded this rich closing soliloquy from Hofmannsthal; with a prominent solo viola the music draws earlier themes together, fluently and suggestively.) Zdenka returns, and they hurry off towards the sleighbells.

ACT 2 *A public ballroom* Though the Coachmen's Ball is gaily under way, the curtain music is an elevated sigh of relief in B♭: with her mother, Arabella is descending the great staircase towards Mandryka and Waldner. For a moment she hesitates; then the introduction is briefly effected, and she and her exotic suitor feel their way towards their destined rapport. (Meanwhile counts Dominik and Lamoral, and later Elemer, in turn invite her to waltz, but are put off.) Cautiously coquettish, Arabella asks why he has come; Mandryka declares honestly what she already knows, and further that he is a widower with great possessions in his remote Austro-Hungarian province, where he hopes she will join him forever. They recognize each other as their longed-for partners, and unite in a rapt E major duet of mutual surrender (on another Balkan tune – but a folksong may be developed in many ways: in Strauss's treatment this one becomes a refined version of Da-ud's devotion-theme in *Die ägyptische Helena*). Then Arabella begs liberty for the rest of the evening to say her maiden farewells – which she does, gracefully and irrevocably, to each of the disconcerted counts.

First the Fiakermilli, cued by Dominik, acclaims her as Queen of the Ball. During the subsequent chain of sub-*Rosenkavalier* waltzes not only does Arabella play out her tender goodbyes, but desperate 'Zdenko' proffers secret hope to the amazed Matteo with the key to Arabella's bedroom. Their exchange is overheard by Mandryka, who is appalled by this unconventional 'farewell' and then frantic. Arabella has gone; he flirts drunkenly with the Fiakermilli, invites the whole company to be his guests, horrifies the Waldners with sarcastic gibes about their daughter's Viennese morals, and reels off home with them to ascertain the facts. The company toasts him cheerfully.

ACT 3 *The main hall of the Waldners' hotel, late at night* In Strauss's musical iconography, the long, unbridled orchestral prelude in E signifies Erotic Tumult, and the participants are identified by Zdenka's themes and an electrified version of Matteo's hesitation-waltz. (It carries no operatic conviction: nothing we have seen of those nervy adolescents fits the luxuriant passion represented in the music.) At curtain-rise Matteo, jacketless, is musing at the top of the hotel staircase, but retreats when the entry-bell rings. It is Arabella, reflecting (in G, folksong-style) upon her new life to come. Matteo reappears: he cannot understand why his bedded love of half an hour ago is 'returning' in cloak and ball-gown, and she is offended by his fond familiarity. As they dispute on the stairs Mandryka and the Waldners burst in, demanding explanations and heightening the confusion. Mandryka, bitterly disappointed, will not be taken for a fool; Arabella protests her innocence and requests corroboration from Matteo, who does the gentlemanly thing and lies – but after a tell-tale hesitation. Now everyone becomes furious, except some other hotel guests who arrive in their night-clothes to enjoy the show. Waldner challenges Mandryka to a duel.

Suddenly Zdenka rushes down in her negligée, ashamed and utterly distraught, on her way to drown herself in the Danube. While Arabella comforts her, all is revealed; Waldner is more relieved than shocked (unlike Adelaide), Matteo astounded but also excited, Mandryka overcome with guilt. The younger couple discover themselves in love. Though Mandryka generously persuades Waldner to accept Matteo as a prospective son-in-law, Arabella retreats upstairs with tight-lipped dignity, merely asking for a glass of water to be brought to her. The onlookers go back to bed. Alone and abject, Mandryka curses his loutishness. Then Arabella reappears above, and descends – to the staircase music that began Act 2, but brighter now in B major – bearing the glass of water which symbolizes, in a village custom Mandryka described earlier, a maiden's betrothal. Pausing on the last step, she confesses her joy at finding him waiting ('Das war sehr gut, Mandryka'), for she knows still better now that he is the Right One. She ends her fervent testimony in E; Mandryka's full-hearted response comes in sturdy C major, and once he has drunk the water, smashed the glass and made a last plea ('Will you always remain what you are?' – 'I can't be anything else; you must take me as I am!') the opera flashes to a buoyant close in F.

* * *

When *Arabella* makes its best overall impression, it is affectingly limpid. That is only in part because of the homely folktunes Strauss adapted for its central confessional scenes, reserving any chromatic turmoil for transient farce and melodrama (but for the overheated

Act 3 prelude, the one place where the orchestra is given its head); and it would be tendentious to judge that he fell back on folk material because his own lyrical invention was drying up. Rather, he and Hofmannsthal had developed the structure of their opera – doubtless without intending it so – in the sentimental vein of late-Viennese operetta, quite distinct from Rossini or the younger Johann Strauss. Any repartee, suspense or strife in *Arabella* is relegated to mere by-play: it could have been shaped into musical numbers which advanced the action decisively, like almost every 'number' in their earlier operas, but there are none such here. Instead the musically expansive passages crystallize, make explicit, feelings which the action has already predicted, in line with the whimsically 'predestined' course of the story. They are serene apotheoses in which dramatic time is stretched or suspended, and they borrow their folksong-tinges to colour deeper instinctual motives than Viennese urbanity could capture. Arabella, too, like plucky little Zdenka, is a heroine to baffle and infuriate modern feminists: a spirited, confident mistress of her own fate, she chooses nevertheless to become an all-forgiving wife, in radiantly melting music. When faithfully sung in its dramatic context, the central submission-duet 'Und du wirst mein Gebieter sein' ('And you will be my master') commands sympathetic responses – tears of wishful recognition, for example – that transcend gender, political fashion and even common sense. DAVID MURRAY

Aragall (y Garriga), Giacomo [Jaume] (*b* Barcelona, 6 June 1939). Spanish tenor. He studied in Barcelona and Milan. In 1963 he won the Verdi Busseto competition, made his début at La Fenice as Gaston in *Jérusalem* and was offered a three-year contract at La Scala, making his first appearance in the title role of *L'amico Fritz*. He then sang in Barcelona, Munich, Vienna, Verona and Covent Garden, where he made his début (1966) as the Duke, returning for Edgardo, Rodolfo, Cavaradossi, Werther and Riccardo (*Ballo*) in 1988. The Duke was also his début role at the Metropolitan (1968) and at San Francisco (1972). His repertory includes Romeo (*I Capuleti e i Montecchi*, in the adaptation of the role prepared by Claudio Abbado in 1966), Gerardo (*Caterina Cornaro*), Fernand (*La favorite*), Gounod's Faust, Alfredo, Don Carlos which he sang in 1990 at Orange and Maurizio (*Adriana Lecouvreur*). A stylish singer, he has an open, keen-edged voice which he uses with sensitivity, though some of the roles he has undertaken strain its lyric tone. His many recordings include Gennaro (*Lucrezia Borgia*), Roland (*Esclarmonde*), and Gabriele Adorno (*Simon Boccanegra*). ALAN BLYTH

Araia [Araja], **Francesco** (*b* Naples, 25 June 1709; *d* Bologna, 1770). Italian composer. No information is available on his musical education. In 1729 he wrote a comic opera for Naples, *Lo matremmonejo pe' mennetta*; this is the only comic opera that has been attributed to him. His first heroic opera was *Berenice* (1730, Pratolino). In 1731 he composed two operas for Rome. Another opera, *La forza dell'amore e dell'odio*, was presented in Milan in 1734, and yet another, *Lucio Vero*, in Venice early in 1735. It is in the libretto of this last that Araia is called for the first time '*maestro di cappella* of Her Majesty, ruler of all the Russias'. The invitation to go to Russia was probably extended to him in Venice by the violinist Pietro Mira, who had been ordered to assemble an Italian opera troupe for the Empress Anne. Araia arrived in St Petersburg late in 1735. He presented a new production of his *La forza dell'amore e dell'odio* in 1736, and wrote two further operas, *Il finto Nino* (1737) and *Artaserse* (1738). When the Empress Anne died in 1740 he returned to Italy to recruit personnel for the opera troupe, returning in 1742 with performers and a production team that included the librettist Giuseppe Bonecchi. He continued to write operas for the court until 1755. The most famous of these is undoubtedly *Tsefal i Prokris* ('Cephalus and Procris'), the first opera known to have been sung in the vernacular rather than in Italian.

In 1757 a comic-opera troupe led by the impresario Giovanni Battista Locatelli arrived in St Petersburg, and the court's taste then seems to have swung away from heroic opera, Araia's preferred genre, in favour of comic opera. From this time he wrote only occasional pieces for the various royal residences in St Petersburg, and in 1759 he obtained leave to retire to Italy. He was recalled to write music for the coronation of the new tsar, Peter III, in 1762, but finally withdrew to Bologna later that year after the deposition of Peter by his wife, the Empress Catherine.

Apart from operas, Araia's works include an oratorio, cantatas and keyboard capriccios. Only one aria of his is known to have been published in his lifetime, 'Felice ai dì sereni', in Walsh's Favourite Airs from the pasticcio *Orfeo* (London, 1736). Information on his music in MSS in Russia is given by Mooser.

Lo matremmonejo pe' mennetta (ob, T. Mariani), Naples, Fiorentini, aut. 1729
Berenice (os, A. Salvi), Florence, Pratolino, 1730
Ciro riconosciuto (os), Rome, Dame, carn. 1731
Il Cleomene (os, V. Cassani), Rome, Dame, spr. 1731
La forza dell'amore e dell'odio (os), Milan, Ducale, Jan 1734, *A-Wn*
Lucio Vero (os, A. Zeno), Venice, S Angelo, carn. 1735
Il finto Nino, overo La Semiramide riconosciuta (os, F. Silvani), St Petersburg, 28 Jan/9 Feb 1737, *D-B*, *GB-Lbl*
Artaserse (os, P. Metastasio), St Petersburg, 28 Jan/9 Feb 1738
Seleuco (os, G. Bonecchi), Moscow, 26 April/7 May 1744
Scipione (os, Bonecchi), St Petersburg, 23 or 24 Aug/4 or 5 Sept 1745
Mitridate (os, Bonecchi), St Petersburg, 26 April/7 May 1747
L'asilo della pace (festa teatrale, Bonecchi), St Petersburg, 26 April/7 May 1748
Bellerofonte (os, Bonecchi), St Petersburg, 28 Nov/9 Dec 1750
Eudossa incoronata, o sia Teodosio II (os, Bonecchi), St Petersburg, 28 April/9 May 1751
Tsefal i Prokris (os, A. P. Sumarokov), St Petersburg, 27 Feb/10 March 1755
Amor prigioniero (dialogo per musica, Metastasio), Oranienbaum, 16/27 June 1755
Alessandro nell'Indie (os, Metastasio), St Petersburg, 18 Dec/29 Dec 1755

*

DBI (U. Prota-Giurleo)
R. A. Mooser: *Annales de la musique et des musiciens en Russie au XVIIIme siècle*, i (Geneva, 1948), 121–31
G. Hardie: 'Neapolitan Comic Opera, 1707–1750: Some Addenda and Corrigenda for The New Grove', *JAMS*, xxxvi (1983), 126
MICHAEL F. ROBINSON

Araiza, Francisco (*b* Mexico City, 4 Oct 1950). Mexican tenor. He began singing with a university choir, and became a pupil of the Mexican soprano Irma Gonzalez at the Conservatorio Nacional de Música. His début as the First Prisoner in *Fidelio* (1970) was followed in 1973 by appearances as Des Grieux (Massenet) and Rodolfo. He went to Europe in 1974 and studied in Munich with Richard Holm and Erik Werba; he then took a two-year contract at Karlsruhe, where he made his European début as Ferrando in 1975 and sang other lyric roles in Mozart and Italian operas. He sang the Steersman in *Der fliegende Holländer* at Bayreuth (1978), and appeared at the Vienna Staatsoper as Tamino, a role he recorded with Karajan. His British début was as Ernesto (*Don Pasquale*) at Covent Garden in 1983; his American début the next year was at San Francisco in *La Cenerentola*, and he appeared as Belmonte at the Metropolitan Opera later the same year. He sang Gounod's Romeo at Zürich, Lohengrin in Venice (1990) and Titus at Salzburg (1991). A lyric tenor whose voice has developed with experience, he now takes leading Verdi and Puccini roles and also sings Werther and Faust.

*

S. von Buchau: 'Conquistador', *ON*, xlviii/14 (1983–4), 30–32

NOËL GOODWIN

Arakishvili, Dimitri Ignat'yevich (*b* Vladikavkaz, 11/23 Feb 1873; *d* Tbilisi, 13 Aug 1953). Georgian composer and ethnomusicologist. He was one of the founding fathers of Georgian classical music. He studied at the Music and Drama College of the Moscow Philharmonic Society until 1901, after which he took part in four expeditions to Georgia to collect songs; their publication aroused a great interest in Georgian music. His first opera, *Tkmuleba Shota Rustavelze* ('The Legend of Shota Rustaveli', 1919, Tbilisi), in three acts, to a libretto by A. Khakhanashvili after a Georgian folk legend, uses elements of both urban and rural Georgian folksong; on its appearance in 1919 it was regarded as a national triumph. His second, *Sitsotskhle sikharulia* ('Life is a Joy'), on a text by Dinara, was completed in 1926. Arakishvili continued to exert considerable influence in Georgia through composing and teaching, and he received many decorations, among them People's Artists of the Georgian SSR (1929), the USSR State Prize (1950) and the Badge of Honour.

See also TKMULEBA SHOTA RUSTAVELZE.

*

P. Khuchua: 'Sovetskaya opera i balet', *Gruzinskaya musikal'naya Kul'tura*, ed. A. Balanchivadze and others (Moscow, 1957), 177–227

YEVGENY MACHAVARIANI, STEPHEN JOHNSON

Arana, Lucrecia (*b* Haro, Logroño, 23 Nov 1871; *d* Madrid, 1 May 1927). Spanish soprano. After completing her musical studies, she began her stage career in Madrid in June 1889 in Audran's *La mascotte*. She then appeared at various Madrid theatres before being engaged as principal soprano at the Teatro de la Zarzuela for 12 years from 1895. She became a popular favourite there, creating leading roles in Giménez's *El baile de Luis Alonso* (1896), Nieto's *El gaitero* (1896), Caballero's *La viejecita* (1897) and *Gigantes y cabezudos* (1898), Pérez Soriano's *El guitarrico* (1900), Vives's *La balada de la luz* (1900), and Giménez and Vives's *El húsar de la guardia* (1904). She later made guest appearances in Barcelona, Murcia and elsewhere. She was noted for a beautiful soprano voice of considerable range, combined with natural acting ability and a dominating stage presence.

ANDREW LAMB

Arangi-Lombardi, Giannina (*b* Marigliano, Naples, 20 June 1891; *d* Milan, 9 July 1951). Italian soprano. She studied in Naples, making her début as a mezzo-soprano in 1920 at the Teatro Costanzi, Rome, as Lola (*Cavalleria rusticana*). After further study, she made a second début as a soprano in 1924 at La Scala as Helen (*Mefistofele*). Her other roles at La Scala included Santuzza, Aida, La Gioconda, Leonora (*Il trovatore*) and Donna Anna, which she also sang at Salzburg (1935). She appeared in Buenos Aires, notably as Asteria (*Nerone*), in 1926 and throughout Europe, including Turin, as Ariadne (1925) and Florence, as Lucrezia Borgia (1933). She had a large, beautiful voice but lacked dramatic ability.

HAROLD ROSENTHAL/R

Arapov, Boris Alexandrovich (*b* St Petersburg, 30 Aug/12 Sept 1905; *d* St Petersburg, 27 Jan 1992). Russian composer. He studied music from earliest childhood in Poltava, at first with his mother, and by the age of ten had begun to compose. He lived from 1921 in Petrograd, where he continued piano studies, but a disease of the hand forced him to abandon his career as a pianist and in 1923 he entered the Petrograd Conservatory to study composition and theory. After graduating (1930) he was invited to join the teaching staff and in 1940 was appointed professor; his pupils included Sergey Slonimsky. He took an active part in the Composers' Union from its foundation (1932) and he received several honours and awards. His compositions, which include three operas, are mainly of large scale and are programmatic in the broadest sense, abounding in picturesque images, to which highly coloured and resourceful orchestration makes an important contribution. In *Khodzha Nasreddin* (1944) the composer incorporates folk melodies, with untraditional harmonizations, and employs ostinato rhythmic formulas, or *usul*. The historic drama *Fregat 'Pobeda'* ('The Frigate "Victory"', 1957); was composed in commemoration of the 250th anniversary of the founding of St Petersburg. The chamber opera *Dozhd'* ('Rain'; 1967) is notable for its psychological acuteness and its vivid musical expression, effected through colourful orchestration.

Khodzha Nasreddin (oc, 7 scenes, V. Vitkovich and G. Radomissky, after Solov'yov: *Vozmutitel' spokoystviya* [Disturber of the Peace], Yangiyul', Uzbekistan, National, 1944, unpubd

Fregat 'Pobeda' [The Frigate 'Victory'], 1957 (historic drama, 4, V. Rozhdestvensky and A. Ivanovsky, after A. S. Pushkin: *The Negro of Peter the Great*), Leningrad radio, 12 Oct 1959, unpubd

Dozhd' [Rain] (chamber op, 5 scenes, T. Todorova and Arapov, after W. S. Maugham); concert perf., Leningrad, Academic Chapel, 25 April 1967, vs (Leningrad, 1984)

*

A. Kenigsberg: *Boris Aleksandrovich Arapov* (Moscow and Leningrad, 1965)

L. Dan'ko: 'Na puti obnovleniya muzïkal'nogo teatra' [On the Way to a Renewal of the Musical Theatre], *Muzïka i zhizn'* [Music and Life], iii (Leningrad and Moscow, 1975), 3–20 [on *Dozhd'* and the ballet *Portret Doriana Greya*]

——: *Boris Arapov* (Leningrad, 1980)

ABRAHAM I. KLIMOVITSKY

Araújo, João Gomes de. *See* GOMES DE ARAÚJO, JOÃO.

Arbace. *Opera seria* in three acts by FRANCESCO BIANCHI to a libretto by GAETANO SERTOR; Naples, Teatro S Carlo, 20 January 1781.

Arbace (soprano castrato) poses as his own murderer, Belesi, in order to rescue his wife Semiri (soprano) from his enemy Scitalce (tenor), ruler of Assyria. Arbace's true identity is exposed when he declines to marry Scitalce's sister Alsinda (soprano), and Semiri cannot bring herself to take revenge on her husband's supposed murderer. Condemned to death, the pair are confined in a terrible subterranean prison. The soldiers of their friend Idaspe (soprano) take the city and release the prisoners. They learn that Scitalce has set fire to himself and his treasures in the seraglio. All celebrate the release from tyranny and hail Arbace as their new ruler.

Contrary to Italian dramaturgical tradition in which Acts 1 and 2 reach a central peak and then decline in action towards the end, each act of this opera mounts steadily towards a strong conclusion. The final scenes are through-composed, moving through various styles of obbligato recitative and cavatinas before the final ensembles. Wind instruments (including clarinet and bassoon) and the unearthly sounds of the *voce umana* intensify the eerie gloom of the prison scene – a foreshadowing of romanticism. The use of tonality, modality, chromaticism and strong dynamic contrasts for expressive purposes, as well as the liberal use of wind instruments, suggests Jommelli's influence.

MARITA P. McCLYMONDS

Arbell, Lucy [Wallace, Georgette] (*b* Paris, Sept 1882; *d* Paris, 1947). French mezzo-soprano. She made her début in 1903 at the Paris Opéra as Delilah, then sang Amneris, Maddalena (*Rigoletto*), Uta (*Sigurd*) and Fricka (*Die Walküre*). In 1906 she sang Persephone in *Ariane*, the first of six roles that she created in operas by JULES MASSENET. The others were the title role of *Thérèse* (1907, Monte Carlo), Queen Amahelli in *Bacchus* (1909, Opéra), Dulcinée in *Don Quichotte* (1910, Monte Carlo; for illustration *see* DON QUICHOTTE), Postumia in *Roma* (1912, Monte Carlo) and Colombe in *Panurge* (1913, Théâtre Lyrique de la Gaîté, Paris). She also sang Charlotte (*Werther*) at the Opéra-Comique, where in 1924 she appeared as Dulcinée for the last time. Her warm, clear voice and sparkling personality inspired Massenet to continue composing operas in the last years of his life.

ELIZABETH FORBES

Arbore di Diana, L' ('The Tree of Diana'). *Dramma giocoso* in two acts by VICENTE MARTÍN Y SOLER to a libretto by LORENZO DA PONTE; Vienna, Burgtheater, 1 October 1787.

For his third collaboration with Martín, commissioned for the marriage of Joseph II's niece, Maria Theresa, Da Ponte 'wanted a gentle subject, suited to the sweetness of his melodies which are felt in the soul but which few can imitate'. Da Ponte drew his 'gentle subject' from the repository of pastoral scenarios cultivated by the *commedia dell'arte*, derived from the late 16th-century pastoral; the libretto is peopled with conventional nymphs and swains and the mythological figures of Diana, Endymion and Cupid. Diana (soprano) and her three nymphs devote themselves to lives of chastity on a beautiful island. Their chastity is regularly tested by a magic apple tree, which gives off exquisite sound and light for the virtuous but pelts the guilty with deadly black apples. Amore [Cupid] (soprano), offended by the tree, undertakes to make Diana fall in love. He spirits three youths onto the island to woo the maidens. The shepherd Endymion (tenor) grazes Diana with one of Cupid's arrows. After a desperate struggle, Diana succumbs to love and Cupid converts her realm into a garden of love.

The libretto has all the standard plot elements of a comic pastoral: the amorous pursuits of the pastoral characters, the antics of the comic characters and the powers of the magician (Cupid). Like many pastorals, the libretto has an allegorical dimension. According to Da Ponte, the story endorses Joseph II's policy of liquidating contemplative monasteries and redirecting the funds into public service. Following the traditional features of the genre, the libretto is laced with eroticism; Da Ponte claimed *L'arbore di Diana* was 'the best of all the operas I have ever composed both as regards the conception and the verse: it was voluptuous without overstepping into the lascivious'.

The music is unusually lyrical. 'Sweet melodies' are to be found in almost all the numbers, which are predominantly short, periodic, lyrical and vocally insubstantial. This applies especially to those for Cupid, a trouser role, whose five short arias demand greater acting than singing skills, but also to the other roles, except for Diana's, which alone includes two large-scale virtuoso arias in the *seria* style. Endymion has no corresponding aria, nor does the comic Doristo have a fully-fledged *buffa* aria; instead, varying degrees of lyricism are blended with appropriate *seria* and *buffa* characteristics. The ensembles are for the most part in a single section and homophonically conceived. The opera, consequently, is almost entirely singable by the amateur, and this contributed in no small measure to its popularity. The original cast included Anna Morichelli (Diana), Vincenzo Calvesi (Endymion), Luisa Laschi (Cupid), Stefano Mandini (Doristo), Nicolò del Sole (Silvio) and Maria Mandini (Britomarte).

DOROTHEA LINK

Arbre enchanté, L' [*L'arbre enchanté, ou Le tuteur dupé* ('The Enchanted Tree, or The Duped Tutor')]. *Opéra comique* in one act by CHRISTOPH WILLIBALD GLUCK to a libretto after JEAN-JOSEPH VADÉ's *opéra comique Le poirier* (1752); Vienna, Schönbrunn Schlosstheater, 3 October 1759 (revised version, Versailles, 27 February 1775).

Based on a tale from Boccaccio's *Decameron*, as retold by La Fontaine, *L'arbre enchanté* concerns the attempt of Claudine (soprano) and her lover Lubin (under the name of Pierrot, tenor) to outwit her lecherous tutor Monsieur Thomas (baritone). Lubin climbs a supposedly enchanted pear tree and pretends to see Thomas embracing his pupil below; the tutor climbs to see for himself, whereupon the lovers actually do embrace, then remove the ladder, and run to seek protection from the village Seigneur. Throughout the opera they receive forthright encouragement from Claudine's younger sister Lucette (soprano), and from the fisherman Blaise (tenor), who speaks mainly in dialect.

L'arbre enchanté is on an intimate scale, with unpretentious *ariettes* interspersed among vaudevilles and prose, and no chorus, apart from the final ensemble of principals. Much of the lovers' music is in a lyrically French style, and that for Thomas comically grotesque. The Paris version, revised by Pierre Louis Moline, retains the same small scale, but (rather incongruously) substitutes verse for the vaudevilles and prose. At the beginning of the 1775 version of the opera Gluck added (for Lubin) an *ariette* parodied from his *Le cadi dupé* of 1761.

BRUCE ALAN BROWN

Arcà, Paolo (*b* Rome, 12 May 1953). Italian composer. He studied composition with Irma Ravinale at the Rome Conservatory, then attended Donatoni's courses in Rome and Siena. In 1982 he won a composition prize at Avignon, and three years later composed his first opera, *Angelica e la luna*, a free reworking of a popular fairy-tale to a libretto in one act by Giovanni Carli Ballola (Ferrara, 3 June 1985). Arcà and Ballola again avoided realism in the one-act *Il carillon del gesuita* (Fermo, 28 July 1989). Intended to celebrate the bicentenary of the

French Revolution, it has nothing to do with the Revolution itself but concerns the mysterious fate of the dauphin, Louis XVI's son. At the start, it appears to have a realistic setting (the prison where the dauphin is confined), but this gives way to a lyrical, oneiric mood when the musical box of a beheaded Jesuit is given to the dauphin and proves to have mysterious powers. The shades of the *ancien régime* (chorus) are summoned, and they carry off the dauphin to save him from the guillotine. In 1989–90 Arcà wrote an opera for puppets, *Lucius, Asinus Aureus* (after Apuleius), in which the voices of the characters are provided by instruments; it was commissioned by Henze for the Munich festival (29 April 1990). Arcà avoids both radicalism and direct borrowing from the past; he is motivated by a desire to communicate and to maintain a relationship with traditional vocal forms. PAOLO PETAZZI

Arcadia in Brenta, L'. *Dramma giocoso* in three acts by BALDASSARE GALUPPI to a libretto by CARLO GOLDONI; Venice, Teatro S Angelo, 14 May 1749.

Fabrizio Fabroni da Fabriano (bass), who owns a villa overlooking the river Brenta, entertains a variety of guests and foreigners in his idyllic Arcadia, now a year old. But, as Foresto (bass) insistently tries to tell him (though he cannot rouse Fabrizio from his slumber), there is no more money – and more visitors are expected! Rosanna, Laura and Giacinto (sopranos), three of his guests, sing praises to their peaceful life and natural surroundings, and the women lead Fabrizio to believe that they are enamoured of him and seek his attentions. Madama Lindora (soprano) soon joins their ranks; she is of the most extreme affectation and complains of too much walking (a few steps), noises that are too loud and too many bad smells out of doors, etc. After bitter complaints about Fabrizio and his household, she wanders off. Count Bellezza (tenor) is another caricature. He simply cannot cease praising Fabrizio and his Arcadia, and this in the most outrageous hyperbole in rhymed couplets. Fabrizio is at first flattered, then impatient and annoyed as he cannot make him stop this patter. He finally threatens, 'Either you go, Signore, or I will'. Left alone, he laments that, with two more fools in the company, his 'Arcadia in Brenta' is now at an end. He sings an aria explaining how he hopes at least to sell off his possessions to maintain the ladies' favour ('Per Lauretta vezzosetta la carrozza vada pure'). The first act finale describes a meeting with Lindora and the Count. Fabrizio offers the two tobacco, which makes everyone sneeze, particularly the sensitive Lindora.

Fabrizio is offended in Act 2 as his wooing of his three lady guests is politely rebuffed and the presents he offers them are given to their male friends. Foresto placates Fabrizio by returning the presents, and in the end announces the intention of the Count that everyone improvise a comedy that very evening. The Count will play the young lover Cintio, with Lindora as his love Diana. Other roles fall to Laura as Columbina Menarella, Diana's servant, and Fabrizio as the comic servant, Pulcinella; the most blatant and comic role is reserved for Foresto: Pantalon, the father of Diana. As this drama within a drama unfolds, Columbina falls in love with Pulcinella and sings a poignant aria commenting on the limitations of romance and social class ('Se i padroni fra lor fanno l'amore'). Soon afterwards Galuppi's first extended finale, masterfully crafted, begins; its shifting rhythms, metres, keys and expressive nuances carefully outline the lovers' pleas for the father's consent to their marriage, his refusal and eventual blessing ('Vezzosetta mia diletta'). The next day (Act 3) the house is truly desolate; not even a cup of chocolate remains. Eventually everyone, including the reluctant Fabrizio, agrees to go off to the villa of Rosanna, where they can continue their Arcadian dreams. A final *coro* frames this happy decision.

L'Arcadia in Brenta was a landmark in the history of comic opera, and the first of a long series of collaborations between Galuppi and Goldoni that was to continue in the 1750s. It already exhibits most of the significant features of their efforts. Goldoni's witty, polite social satire, elevated by high poetry and comedy alike, coupled with Galuppi's extraordinary sense of musical drama are everywhere evident. The finale to Act 2, while considerably shorter than comparable finales of five years later, is extraordinary in its skilful blending of affective melody, sharp disjunction (harmonic, rhythmic and textural) and comic relief in local events to establish the fast pace and diversity of the poetic dialogue. Goldoni's Arcadia, in this instance, is a thin satire on the summer retreats of the Venetian nobility of the day rather than a direct parody of the elevated and intellectual Roman Arcadia. With Francesco Baglioni as Fabrizio and Francesco Carrattoli as Foresto, the opera was exceptionally well received and established the Goldoni-Galuppi venture as the most important operatic development in comic opera of the mid 18th century.

For illustration *see* GALUPPI, BALDASSARE. DALE E. MONSON

Arcadian Academy. Association formed in Rome in 1690 for the reform or 'purification' of opera, following ideas earlier put forward in Venice (for example in the works of Apostolo Zeno). The intention was to eliminate comedy and feature pastoral Arcadians or heroic, historical figures. The chief patron was Cardinal Pietro Ottoboni; composers associated with the movement include Alessandro Scarlatti and Giovanni Bononcini. *See* ROME, §3(ii); for bibliography *see* LIBRETTO (ii), §III, B(i).

Arcais, Francesco d'. *See* D'ARCAIS, FRANCESCO.

Archer, Neill (*b* Northampton, 31 Aug 1961). English tenor. He studied at the Brevard Music Center in North Carolina, and sang the part of Sandy in Maxwell Davies's *The Lighthouse* for Thameside Opera at Bracknell in 1986. He made his official début in 1987 with Kent Opera as Tamino. At Buxton (1987 and 1988) he sang the title role of Conti's *Don Chisciotte in Sierra Morena* and Ubaldo in Haydn's *Armida*. For the WNO he has sung Don Ottavio, Almaviva and Cassio; for Opera North, Almaviva and Achilles (*King Priam*). He has sung Ferrando for Scottish Opera, Opera Factory and Glyndebourne Touring Opera. In 1990 he made his Covent Garden début as Jaquino (*Fidelio*) and his ENO début as Tamino. He has sung Edward IV in Cesti's *Riccardo III* at Turin, Andres (*Wozzeck*) at Parma, and Pylades (*Iphigénie en Tauride*) at Basle (1991). A very stylish singer with a lyrical voice well suited to Mozart and Rossini, he also has a special facility for 20th-century music. ELIZABETH FORBES

Archilei [née Concarini], **Vittoria** ['La Romanina'] (*b* Rome, 1550; *d* 1620s or later). Italian soprano. She was a protégée of Cavalieri in Rome, where she began her apparently lifelong service with the Medici. In 1588, she went with her husband, Antonio Archilei, to Florence, where she became one of the day's most famous singers.

She had a major part in the spectacular 'intermedii et concerti' for the comedy *La pellegrina* during the celebration in 1589 of the marriage of Ferdinando de' Medici and Christine of Lorraine. The opening piece, as published in a highly elaborated form, suggests her extraordinary virtuosity in improvisatory passage-work and ornamentation. Her performance in Cavalieri's *Disperazione di Fileno* (1590–91) was said to have moved the audience to tears. She was in touch with modern tendencies in Florentine music; both Giulio Caccini and Jacopo Peri cited her as having performed their music in the new monodic style. Caccini (preface to *L'Euridice*, 1600) wrote that she had 'long ago' adopted the new manner of passage-work 'invented' by him. Peri (preface to *L'Euridice*, 1600/01) said that she adorned his music not only with brilliant *passaggi* but with graces too subtle to write out. The perhaps more impartial composer Sigismondo d'India lauded her (preface to *Le musiche ... da cantar solo ...* , 1609) as 'above any other' as an excellent singer, 'most intelligent' and having a sweet and tender voice. From about 1610 she is mentioned in Medici court chronicles mainly as a singer of sacred music.

ES (E. Zanetti)

A. Solerti: *Musica, ballo e drammatica alla corte medicea dal 1600 al 1637* (Florence, 1905)

F. Hammond: 'Musicians at the Medici Court in the Mid-seventeenth Century', *AnMc*, no.14 (1974), 151–69

H. WILEY HITCHCOCK

Arcis [Arcy], **François-Joseph d'**. *See* DARCIS, FRANÇOIS-JOSEPH.

Arcoleo, Antonio (*b* Venice; *fl* 1685–90). Italian librettist. He lived at Candia (now Iraklion), Crete. He wrote the librettos for Domenico Gabrielli's *Il Clearco in Negroponte* (1685) and G. A. Perti's *La Rosaura* (1689) and *Brenno in Efeso* (1690). They treat historical subjects in a heroic-comic manner; each, by concealing the true identity of a principal character, has a happy ending.

K. Leich: *Girolamo Frigimelica Robertis Libretti (1694–1708): ein Beitrag insbesondere zur Geschichte des Opernlibrettos in Venedig* (Munich, 1972)

R. S. Freeman: *Opera without Drama: Currents of Change in Italian Opera, 1675–1725* (Ann Arbor, 1981)

KARL LEICH

Arcy, Paul d'. Joint pseudonym of LUDOVIC HALÉVY and HECTOR-JONATHAN CRÉMIEUX.

Arden must Die [*Arden muss sterben*]. Opera in two acts, op.21, by ALEXANDER GOEHR to a libretto by Erich Fried (English version by Geoffrey Skelton); Hamburg, Staatsoper, 5 March 1967.

The murder of Arden (bass), a prosperous businessman, is planned by his wife, Alice (mezzo-soprano), and her lover, Mosbie (tenor). Two landowners ruined by Arden, Greene (baritone) and Reede (bass), and two disaffected servants, Susan (soprano) and Michael (tenor), are also involved in the conspiracy. After three bungled attempts, the hired assassins Shakebag (tenor) and Black Will (bass) murder Arden at a reconciliation banquet arranged by him for his so-called friends. In the concluding court scene, Alice and Mosbie admit their guilt, while the others attempt to deny their complicity.

The libretto draws both on Holinshed's account of the 1551 murder and on the anonymous 16th-century *Arden of Faversham*, translating its theme of guilt from the middle-class, Christian context of the original into the contemporary world of Brechtian epic theatre. The cuckolding of Arden, which is the source of discord and retribution, becomes no more than another incident in the game of power and possession played by all the characters. And in the courtroom scene, justice is shown to be unrelated not only to moral precept, but to any precepts whatsoever apart from those of self-interested gain – in which, by virtue of the intervention of Arden's neighbour, Mrs Bradshaw (contralto), the audience also shares.

In its genuinely musico-dramatic distinction between the libretto's strophic forms and narrative recitative, passages of elaborate tone-painting – the ferry-boat scene for example – and characteristic use of variation and parody to symbolize levels of hypocrisy among the characters, Goehr's score is the culmination of 16 years of intense compositional activity. A concert work drawn from the opera, *Three Pieces from Arden must Die*, was first performed in January 1969 by the LPO under Sir Charles Mackerras. The British première of the opera was given at Sadler's Wells, London, on 17 April 1974, conducted by Meredith Davies and directed by Jonathan Miller.

NICHOLAS WILLIAMS

Arderíus (y Bardán), Francisco (de) (*b* Portugal, 1836; *d* Madrid, 21 May 1886). Spanish impresario, actor and singer. He first became popular in comic roles at the Teatro de la Zarzuela in Madrid. In 1866 he formed his own company, the Bufos Madrileños, modelled on Offenbach's Bouffes-Parisiens. It was an instant success. By 1870 he had begun a second company in Barcelona. In addition to operettas by Offenbach and Lecocq, Arderíus staged new works by Spanish composers, including F. A. Barbieri and P. J. E. Arrieta. The dance routines and brief costumes of the female chorus were indispensable to the appeal of the Bufos, and were among the features that incited critics to condemn the genre as frivolous and a hindrance to the development of serious opera in Spanish. By the beginning of 1873 the company's popularity had ended, and Arderíus had become director at the Teatro de la Zarzuela. Thereafter he championed the cause of national opera, attempting, without success, to launch a Spanish opera series in 1881. From 1871 he edited the weekly periodical *La correspondencia de los Bufos*.

F. Arderíus: *Confidencias de Arderíus: Historia de un bufo* (Madrid, 1870)

——: *La ópera española y la zarzuela* (Madrid, 1882)

A. Barrera: *Crónicas del género chico y de un Madrid divertido* (Madrid, 1983)

'Arderius, Francisco', *Enciclopedia universal ilustrada europeo-americana* (Madrid and Barcelona, n.d.), vi, 6–7

ROLAND J. VÁZQUEZ

Arditi, Luigi (*b* Crescentino, Piedmont, 22 July 1822; *d* Hove, Sussex, 1 May 1903). Italian conductor and composer. He studied the violin and composition at Milan Conservatory, where his teachers included Nicola Vaccai. His first opera, *I briganti*, was given there in 1841. After working in Vercelli and Milan, 1842–6, he went with Bottesini to Havana, where he worked at the Teatro Imperial and directed a one-act opera, *Il corsaro*, at the Teatro Tacón in 1847. He later conducted in Canada (1853) and the USA (1854–6), and his opera *La spia* was produced in New York in 1856. His later compositions were mostly occasional orchestral pieces and songs, notably the famous vocal waltz, *Il bacio*.

After European tours Arditi settled in London as conductor at Her Majesty's Theatre in 1858. He remained there for 11 years, conducting Italian operas and taking the company on tours, especially to Dublin. He made many tours to Europe, chiefly with Italian opera companies. In 1869 he succeeded Costa at Covent Garden for one year, and followed this with seasons at the St Petersburg Italian Opera (1871 and 1873). From 1870 he conducted annually in Vienna, and from 1874 to 1877 directed the promenade concerts at Covent Garden. Between 1878 and 1894 Arditi was largely concerned with Mapleson's annual opera tours of the USA, but he also worked at London theatres and toured with the Carl Rosa company (1894). His *Reminiscences* were published in London in 1896. Shaw wrote of him: 'He can conduct anything, and come off without defeat'. Arditi's considerable contribution to London musical life included the introduction of 23 important operas; these included new works, among them Verdi's *Un ballo in maschera* (1861) and *La forza del destino* (1867), Gounod's *Faust* (1863), Thomas' *Hamlet* and *Mignon* and Wagner's *Der fliegende Holländer* (1870), Boito's *Mefistofele* (1880) and Mascagni's *Cavalleria rusticana* (1891); and also works of historical significance such as Cherubini's *Médée* (1865) and Gluck's *Iphigénie en Tauride* (1866).

I briganti (1), Milan, Conservatorio, 1841
Il corsaro (Spanish op, 1, after Byron), Havana, Tacón, carn. 1847
Gulnara (2, R. María Mendine), Havana, Tacón, 4 Feb 1848
La spia (os, 3, F. Manetta, after J. F. Cooper: *The Spy*), New York, Academy of Music, 24 March 1856

*

L. Arditi: *My Reminiscences* (London, 1896)
P. Bertini: 'L. Arditi', *La nuova musica*, viii (Florence, 1903)
T. G. Kaufman: *Verdi and his Major Contemporaries: A Selected Chronology of Performances with Casts* (New York, 1990), 11–13

NIGEL BURTON, KEITH HORNER

Arefece, Antonio. *See* OREFICE, ANTONIO.

Arena, Giuseppe (*b* Malta, 1713; *d* Naples, 6 Nov 1784). Italian composer. In 1725 he entered the Conservatorio di Gesù Cristo in Naples where he remained for ten years; among his teachers were Gaetano Greco and Francesco Durante, and Pergolesi was a fellow pupil. Arena composed operas for Rome, Turin, Venice and Naples, and some of his music was included in *Alessandro in Persia*, a pasticcio performed on 31 October 1741 in London. According to the libretto of *Il vecchio deluso* (1746), Arena served the Prince of Bisignano; he was also an organist. None of his operas survives complete, although individual numbers are in libraries in Naples, Bologna, Milan, Florence, Brussels and London.

Achille in Sciro (os, 3, P. Metastasio), Rome, Dame, 7 Jan 1738
La clemenza di Tito (os, 3, Metastasio), Turin, Regio, 26 Dec 1738
Artaserse (os, 3, Metastasio), Turin, Regio, carn. 1741
Tigrane (os, 3, F. Silvani, rev. G. Goldoni), Venice, S Giovanni Grisostomo, 18 Nov 1741
Farnace (os, 3, A. M. Lucchini), Rome, Capranica, 23 Jan 1742; completed by G. Sellitto
Il vecchio deluso (op comica, 3, G. Palomba), Naples, Nuovo, carn. 1746

Music in: Alessandro in Persia, 1741

GORDANA LAZAREVICH

Arensky, Anton [Antony] **Stepanovich** (*b* Novgorod, 30 June/12 July 1861; *d* nr Terioki, Finland [now Zelenogorsk, Russia], 12/25 Feb 1906). Russian composer. He is best remembered for his chamber and piano music. He studied composition with Rimsky-Korsakov at the St Petersburg Conservatory, graduating in 1882. From then until 1895 he lived in Moscow, where he taught theory and composition at the Conservatory alongside Taneyev, his pupils including Rakhmaninov and Glier. Since this was the period in which he made his reputation, since virtually his entire oeuvre was brought out by the Moscow publishing house of Jurgenson, since many of his important premières (including those of all his operas) took place in the second capital and since he modelled himself in many ways on Tchaikovsky, an admired friend, Arensky is often thought of as a 'Moscow composer'. He spent his last and most productive decade, however, back in St Petersburg, succeeding Balakirev as director of the imperial court chapel choir, a post he held until 1901, when he retired on a pension. From then until his death (from tuberculosis exacerbated by alcoholism) Arensky held a professorship at the St Petersburg Conservatory, and toured widely as pianist and conductor both in Russia and abroad.

Arensky's career as an operatic composer began in 1882 in Rimsky-Korsakov's composition class, for which he set on assignment several passages from Alexander Ostrovsky's verse play *Voyevoda, ili Son na Volge* ('The Provincial Governor, or A Dream on the Volga'). After moving to Moscow, Arensky enlisted Taneyev's help in procuring from Tchaikovsky the libretto he and Ostrovsky had fashioned from the play some 15 years earlier for Tchaikovsky's long-since-withdrawn first opera, *Voyevoda*. Arensky completed his opera, *Son na Volge*, op.16, in 1888, and it was staged at the Bol'shoy Theatre, Moscow, on 21 December 1890/2 January 1891. Although sharing a great deal of text matter (especially in Act 1, where the libretto was actually by Ostrovsky), the two operas on the same play turned out quite differently. Where Tchaikovsky, characteristically, had stripped the drama down to its love intrigue, Arensky, true to his Korsakovian upbringing, sought a panoply of period and local colour: songs and dances in the first of the four acts, a traditional bridal-party (*devichnik*) scene in Act 3, variations à la Glinka on the folksong 'Down by the Mother Volga' (Act 4), and a concluding folklike chorus in 5/4 time. These, plus the modesty of its formal structures compared with Tchaikovsky's, its reliance on 'recitative-arioso' (or what Cui called 'melodic recitative'), and its Balakirevesque harmonizations in the natural minor, made *Son na Volge* a retrospective monument to the naive 'high Kuchkism' of the 1860s and 70s. It was a nostalgic favourite among composers in the latterday Rimsky-Korsakov circle.

Arensky's second opera, the one-act *Rafael'* ('Raphael'), op.37, is subtitled 'Musical Scenes from the Renaissance'; the libretto is by A. A. Kryukov. Its plot consists of a sentimental fiction ostensibly drawn from the life of the great Florentine painter. Condemned by the jealous Cardinal Bibiena for a presumed illicit love affair with his model Fornarina, Raphael shames his accuser by unveiling a new Madonna for which Fornarina had posed. The matchless purity of his inspiration puts an end to speculation as to the painter's morals. Commissioned by and dedicated to the Moscow Society of Art Lovers, *Rafael'* was first performed on 24 April/6 May 1894 in the Hall of Nobles by a cast of Moscow Conservatory students for the delegates to the First All-Russian Congress of Painters. The music is strikingly reminiscent of Tchaikovsky's last opera, the one-act *Iolanta*, first performed a year and a half previously. One number, the ballad 'Strast'yu i negoyu serdtse trepeshchet' ('My heart is aquiver with passion and bliss'), sung by an offstage singer to the tune of an Italian folk melody, enjoyed some popularity on the recital stage as a vehicle for the great tenor Leonid Sobinov.

The libretto of Arensky's third and last opera, *Nal' i Damayanti* ('Nal and Damayanti'), op.47, was the work of Modest Tchaikovsky, the late composer's brother. Drawn from the Mahābharata, the epic of ancient India, in Vasily Zhukovsky's translation, the plot concerns the steadfast love of Damayanti, daughter of King Bhima of Vidarba, for Nal Punyaloka, the saintly King of Nishada, and their triumph, with the help of benevolent deities, over the evil designs of the goddess Kali.

The work, staged at the Bol'shoy Theatre on 9/22 January 1904, disappointed contemporary audiences by its straightforward number format, its dramatic blatancy (here the librettist was characteristically to blame) and its pallidly conventional style. Despite the exotic setting, Arensky seems to have made an in-principle renunciation of decorative local colour in favour of an all-purpose religiosity reminiscent of *Lohengrin*. The elegantly coloured orchestration was a saving grace. Reviewers singled out Arensky's use of the bass clarinet as the characteristic timbre for the demonic realm of Kali. Rimsky-Korsakov, on the other hand, was unimpressed. In *Memories and Commentaries* (1959), Stravinsky – evidently confusing *Nal' i Damayanti* with *Son na Volge* – recalled his teacher's comment that 'the noble bass clarinet should not be put to such ignominious use'. To Vasily Yastrebtsev, Rimsky-Korsakov complained that the opera consisted of 'commonplaces out of Tchaikovsky, Cui, Verdi and the rest'. After a short-lived St Petersburg production (Mariinsky Theatre, opening on 15/28 January 1908), the opera – and with it Arensky's dramatic oeuvre – disappeared from the stage.

See also SON NA VOLGE.

*

V. Cheshikhin: *Istoriya russkoy operï* (Moscow, 2/1905)
G. Tsïpin: *A. S. Arensky* (Moscow, 1966) RICHARD TARUSKIN

Argenta, Nancy (Maureen Herbison) (*b* Nelson, BC, 17 Jan 1957). Canadian soprano. She studied at the University of Western Ontario (1978–80), then privately in Düsseldorf and London. Her teachers included Peter Pears, Gérard Souzay and Vera Rozsa. As a concert singer she rapidly gained recognition throughout Europe and America, her light, clear voice making her much sought after in the Baroque and Classical repertory. She made her operatic début in Rameau's *Hippolyte et Aricie* (doubling as the High Priestess and Huntress) at the 1983 Aix-en-Provence Festival, and returned to the festival in 1990 in Purcell's *The Fairy-Queen*. At Lyons in 1985 she sang Asteria in Handel's *Tamerlano* and Susanna in *Figaro*. She has also appeared as Monteverdi's Poppaea (1988, QEH), Vespina in Haydn's *L'infideltà delusa* (1990, Antwerp; she also recorded the role) and Purcell's Dido (1991, Hämeenlinna Festival).

Argenti [Argentio], **Bonaventura** [Bonaventura Perugino] (*b* Cascia Spolentina, Perugia, 1620/21; *d* Rome, 7 Feb 1697). Italian castrato soprano. One of the most celebrated singers of his day, he was active in Rome and sang oratorios by Carissimi at the Collegio Germanico Ungarico between 27 March 1638 and 13 December 1646. On 15 August 1645 he entered the Sistine Chapel choir without competition, and was successively *puntatore* (1665), chamberlain (1660), *maestro di cappella* (1661), pensioner (1670) and dean (1694). He also performed cantatas, serenades and music dramas at the courts of the Roman aristocracy, and from June 1645 to December 1647 he was in the service of Prince Camillo Pamphili and his wife Olimpia Aldobrandini. On 31 January 1656 he took the title role of Vita in Marazzoli's *La vita humana*, performed in the Palazzo Barberini, Rome in honour of Queen Christina of Sweden; he may also have sung in Marazzoli and Abbatini's *Dal male il bene*. Athanasius Kircher praised his voice as one that could move his hearers to tears. Pier Leone Ghezzi made a caricature portrait of him (*I-Rvat*, Ott.Lat. 3113, c.127).

*

A. Kircher: *Musurgia Universalis*, i (Rome, 1650), 674
M. Murata: *Operas for the Papal Court 1631–1668* (Ann Arbor, 1981), 386
C. Annibaldi: 'L'archivio musicale Doria Pamphili: saggio sulla cultura aristocratica a Roma fra XVI e XVIII secolo', *Studi musicali*, xi (1982), 295
G. Rostirolla: 'La musica nelle istituzioni religiose romane al tempo di Stradella', *Chigiana*, xxxix (1982), 704–7
G. Ciliberti: *Antonio Maria Abbatini e la musica del suo tempo (1595–1679): Documenti per una ricostruzione bio-bibliografica* (Perugia, 1986), 267 GALLIANO CILIBERTI

Argentina (i). Of all the Latin American countries, Argentina can claim the most intense operatic activity, running in an unbroken line from about 1850. This activity is primarily concentrated on the capital, Buenos Aires, and its civic opera house, the Teatro Colón, opened in 1908. Since 1926 the Colón has had its own permanent orchestra, chorus, ballet ensemble and children's chorus. Inland, the Teatro Argentino (founded 1890) of La Plata, capital of the province of Buenos Aires, has its own permanent company and administration, as does the theatre (built 1891) of Córdoba. Rosario, Bahia Blanca, Tucumán and Mendoza also have an operatic tradition.

During the Spanish colonial period the area now covered by Argentina belonged to Peru and was governed by its viceroy. Cultural influences from Lima, Potosí and Chuquisaca (now Sucre) enriched the north-western regions of what is now Argentina. The centrally situated town of Córdoba had performances of school dramas and rhetorical allegories. Eastern towns, on the other hand, were influenced by the Jesuit missions to the Guaraní Indians, and guest performances (of allegorical 'operas' as well as other works) took place in Buenos Aires and Santa Fe. The first theatre in Buenos Aires, a 'Casa de Operas y Comedias' (1757), where Bartolomé Mazza's *Las variedades de Proteo* had its première in 1760, did not last long. The Viceroy's theatre opened in 1783; known as the Teatro de la Ranchería, it gave many performances of *tonadillas* with musicians, dancers and singers. The theatre burnt down in 1792 and was replaced in 1804 by the Coliseo Provisional, while building began on a large-scale Coliseo (never completed). In 1810, after the independence movement, the provisional theatre was renamed the Teatro Argentino, and it continued in use until 1870. The first contact with the Portuguese court opera of Rio de Janeiro also took place in 1810, with a visit by the singer

Pietro Angelelli. Rio de Janeiro and Buenos Aires exchanged artists and repertories until 1860 and from 1830 also with Montevideo; the Buenos Aires orchestra was considered among the finest in the continent during the early part of this period. Attempts to produce Italian opera were begun in 1816. The founding of the Sociedad del Buen Gusto en el Teatro the following year was a landmark, and so was that of the Sociedad Filarmónica directly afterwards. These institutions aimed to set up a permanent opera company; performances began at the end of September 1825 with *Il barbiere di Siviglia*. The tenor Mariano Rosquellas and the baritone Miguel Vaccani were prominently involved in successful productions (chiefly of Rossini but also Mozart) up to 1832. The Italian violinist Giacomo Massoni (1798–1878) was the musical director in the early years, and the first prima donna, Angelita Tani, was much admired.

From 1832 to October 1848 there were only partial, concert performances of opera. In 1838 a second theatre, the Teatro de la Victoria, opened and a new era of activity began with the first performance in the country of *Lucia di Lammermoor*. By 1849 the repertory included works by Bellini and Verdi, and within a few years the leading works of the French repertory were being produced. In 1854, 53 different works could be heard in Buenos Aires, 30 of them new to the city. The first Teatro Colón, built on the site of the unfinished Coliseo, opened in 1857. Until 1888 it was Argentina's major theatre, giving French operas (by Meyerbeer, Halévy and Auber) as well as Italian ones; German operas sung in Italian were added in the 1860s, notably *Martha* and *Der Freischütz*. More opera houses were soon founded, including the Teatro de la Opera (1872–1935, its heyday being 1889–1908), the Politeama (1872–1950), the San Martín and the Coliseo. Local impresarios often brought over entire operatic productions from Milan (La Scala) or Rome (Costanzi) from about 1870 to 1915, so great was the enthusiasm for international star singers.

The Teatro de la Opera inherited the mantle of the old Teatro Colón. *Lohengrin* was mounted in 1883 and *Der fliegende Holländer* in 1887 (both in Italian). The latter work had its first Argentine performance in La Plata even before it was produced at the Teatro Colón the same year. Other Wagnerian productions were of *Tannhäuser* (1894), *Die Meistersinger* (1898) and *Die Walküre* (1899). New Italian and French works almost always came straight to Buenos Aires after their premières in Europe, so that the city can boast of many first performances for the entire American continent. Rosario too was receptive: the first performance of *Tosca* in the New World took place there within months of the Rome première. After the opening of the new Teatro Colón in May 1908, parallel operatic seasons were still given in Buenos Aires at the Coliseo (also a new building) and the Teatro de la Opera. Gradually, however, after the 1920s the new Colón became the most important opera house in the cultural life of the capital. Of more than 100 premières of Argentine operas that have taken place since 1908, the Colón has staged 58.

The first Argentine composers to turn to lyric drama were Francisco Hargreaves and Miguel Rojas (1845–1904); other pioneers included Juan Gutiérrez (1840–1906) and Zenón Rolón (1856–1902). The first important and successful operas with South American settings were *Pampa* (1897) and *Yupanki* (1899) by Arturo Berutti, whose successors included Héctor Panizza, and Constantino Gaito. Gaito studied the themes, rhythms and tonal language of both pre-Columbian and Creole folk music and headed a generation of idealistic composers of nationalist opera which included Pascual de Rogatis and Felipe Boero; Boero's *El Matrero* (1929) has been aptly described as the most Argentinian opera ever composed.

The major figure of the 1940s and 50s was Juan José Castro, who, besides his success with opera after works by García Lorca, won the Verdi Prize in Milan in 1951 for his *Proserpina y el extranjero*. The most celebrated Argentine composer of the 20th century, however, was Alberto Ginastera, whose *Don Rodrigo* (1964), *Bomarzo* (1967) and *Beatrix Cenci* (1972) all postdate his periods of 'objective' and 'subjective' nationalism. Later generations of Argentine composers, from Pompeyo Camps (*b* 1924), Valdo Sciammarella and Rodolfo Arizaga (1926–85) to Juan Carlos Zorzi and Mario Perusso (both *b* 1936), have worked imaginatively in lyric drama while distancing themselves to some extent from traditional opera and drawing on a wide range of compositional styles.

For further information on operatic life in the country's principal centre *see* BUENOS AIRES.

*

V. Gesualdo: *Historia de la música en la Argentina* (Buenos Aires, 1961)

R. Caamaño, ed.: *La historia del Teatro Colón (1908–1968)* (Buenos Aires, 1969)

M. E. Kuss: *Natavistic Strains in Argentine Operas premièred at the Teatro Colón (1908–1972)* (diss., UCLA, 1976)

R. García Morillo: *Estudios sobre música argentina* (Buenos Aires, 1984)

J. Rosselli: 'The Opera Business and the Italian Immigrant Community in Latin America, 1820–1930: the Example of Buenos Aires', *Past and Present*, no 127 (1990), 155–82

JUAN PEDRO FRANZE

Argentina (ii). Theatre in Rome, built in 1731 and inaugurated on 13 January 1732; *see* ROME, §3(i, ii).

Argento, Dominick (*b* York, PA, 27 Oct 1927). American composer. Although born to Sicilian immigrants, he was attracted to music through the works of Gershwin. Piano lessons and a self-taught course in theory and analysis ended when he was drafted into the army. On his discharge in 1947 he entered the Peabody Conservatory in Baltimore, where he turned from the piano to composition, studying with Nicolas Nabokov; he also began working with the Baltimore composer Hugo Weisgall, who stimulated his interest in opera. After graduating (BM 1951), he spent a year in Florence on a Fulbright fellowship, studying with Dallapiccola at the Conservatorio Cherubini; here he experienced a weakening in his aversion to 12-note composition. He later returned to Florence on two Guggenheim fellowships (1957–8, 1964–5) and has resided there each summer since the mid-1960s. Back at Peabody (MM 1954), Argento studied composition with Cowell and became musical director of the Hilltop Musical Company, of which Weisgall was artistic director. John Scrymgeour (professionally John Olon-Scrymgeour, or John Olon), the group's stage director, became Argento's librettist. Their *Sicilian Limes* (1954), the first of seven collaborations, was followed three years later by the engaging one-act work, *The Boor*, after Chekhov. It was completed and produced while Argento was at the Eastman School (PhD 1957), where his teachers were Rogers, Hovhaness and Hanson. In 1958 he began teaching theory and composition at the University of Minnesota, Minneapolis, where he has remained since his promotion to Regents' Professor in 1979.

Argento was recognized early as an important regional composer and received commissions from nearly every type of performing organization in Minneapolis and St Paul. A small commission came from the local chapter of Phi Mu Alpha music fraternity for the one-act opera *Christopher Sly* (1963) to a student's libretto; this boisterous piece, drawn from Shakespeare's *The Taming of the Shrew*, was the first opera in which Argento explored 12-note writing within a tonal context. The opening of the Guthrie Theatre in 1963 brought requests for incidental scores (including *St Joan*, 1964 and *Volpone*, 1964), as well as fruitful discussions about opera with the director Tyrone Guthrie. The following year Argento and Olon-Scrymgeour formed the Center Opera Company (later the Minnesota Opera), whose inaugural performance included their collaboration *The Masque of Angels*. Eschewing 17th-century models, they created a one-act opera in which a band of angels promotes mortal romance in the face of contemporary defeatism. The score is memorable for its arias, polychoral writing and mixture of medieval and modern sonorities. Argento's decision to remain in the upper Mid-west in the mid-1960s was prompted largely by the desire to develop his compositional approach (revisionist, lyrical and selective), unhindered by trends. His rich harmonic palette often disguises discreet 12-note usage. In his operas of the 1960s and 70s, he sought to create a different vocal idiom for each work – a form of expression unique to the dramatic requirements – which may be viewed as an outgrowth of his overriding concern for the voice. During the 1970s, he moved towards more adventurous librettos, non-linear narratives and use of the play-within-a-play device.

National recognition came with the success of *Postcard from Morocco* (1971). This surreal and most eclectic of his operas remains a favourite with directors. It was followed by a more emotional and straightforward work, the monodrama for male voice, *A Water Bird Talk* (1977). The success of Argento's libretto after Chekhov and Audubon inspired him later to write the texts for his own full-length operas, and prompted Olon-Scrymgeour to write the text for a companion monodrama for soprano, *Miss Havisham's Wedding Night* (1981). This piece is also the Epilogue of the 1979 opera, *Miss Havisham's Fire*, a commission from the New York City Opera that proved musically strong but dramatically disappointing. In 1975 Argento won the Pulitzer Prize for the song cycle *From the Diary of Virginia Woolf*, written for Janet Baker. In 1975–6 he composed his critically acclaimed full-length opera, *The Voyage of Edgar Allan Poe*, on a bicentenary commission from the University of Minnesota with a libretto by Charles Nolte, a university colleague. Poe (tenor), depicted at the end of his life, often rises to the stature of a Wozzeck – outcast, persecuted and half mad with poverty and desperation – through a series of scenes following only nightmarish logic. The score contains a seamless flow and free application of 12-note music, with a prevailing compact, syllabic and intense vocal idiom.

In the 1980s Argento enjoyed success with two operas on his own librettos. *Casanova's Homecoming* (1983), a full-bodied *opera buffa* based on Casanova's memoirs, is unabashedly theatrical. Quotations from Jommelli's 1770 version of *Demofoonte* are overlaid with Argento's own music in a dramatic scene in an opera house, demonstrating the composer's tendency to borrow or paraphrase pre-existing works or styles to well-conceived dramatic purpose. *The Aspern Papers* (1988), after Henry James, explores an extensive flashback plot through a score having both 12-note and bel canto implications. Argento's new operas now attract singers of international stature, and the diversity of his operatic accomplishments is beginning to be recognized.

See also ASPERN PAPERS, THE; BOOR, THE; CASANOVA'S HOMECOMING; POSTCARD FROM MOROCCO; and WATER BIRD TALK, A.

Sicilian Limes (1, J. Olon-Scrymgeour [pseud. of J. Scrymgeour], after L. Pirandello), Baltimore, Peabody Conservatory, spr. 1954

The Boor (ob, 1, J. Olon [Scrymgeour], after A. P. Chekhov: *The Bear*), Rochester, NY, Eastman School of Music, 6 May 1957, vs (New York, 1960)

Colonel Jonathan the Saint, 1958–61 (comic op, 4, Olon-Scrymgeour), Denver, Loretto Heights College, 31 Dec 1971

Christopher Sly (comic op, 2, J. Manlove, after W. Shakespeare: *The Taming of the Shrew*), Minneapolis, U. of Minnesota, 31 May 1963, vs (New York, 1968)

The Masque of Angels (1, Olon-Scrymgeour), Minneapolis, Tyrone Guthrie, 9 Jan 1964, vs (New York, 1964)

The Shoemaker's Holiday (ballad op, 2, Olon-Scrymgeour, after T. Dekker), Minneapolis, Tyrone Guthrie, 1 June 1967, vs (New York, 1971)

Postcard from Morocco (1, J. Donahue), Minneapolis, Cedar Village Theater, 14 Oct 1971, vs (New York, 1972)

A Water Bird Talk, 1974–6 (monodrama, 1, Argento, after Chekhov and J. J. Audubon), Brooklyn, Brooklyn Academy of Music, 19 May 1977, vs (New York, 1980)

The Voyage of Edgar Allan Poe (2, C. Nolte), St Paul, O'Shaughnessy Auditorium, 24 April 1976, vs (New York, 1979)

Miss Havisham's Wedding Night, 1978 (monodrama, 1, Olon-Scrymgeour, after C. Dickens: *Great Expectations*), Minneapolis, Tyrone Guthrie, 1 May 1981, vs (New York, 1981)

Miss Havisham's Fire (2, Olon-Scrymgeour, after Dickens), New York, New York State, 22 March 1979

Casanova's Homecoming (ob, 3, Argento, after J. Casanova: *L'histoire de ma vie*), St Paul, Ordway, 12 April 1985, vs (New York, 1985)

The Aspern Papers (2, Argento, after H. James), Dallas, Music Hall at Fair Park, 19 Nov 1988, vs (1991)

H. Cole: 'Recordings: Dominick Argento: *Postcard from Morocco*', *Tempo*, new ser., no.103 (1972), 55–7

M. Steele: 'Dominick Argento', *HiFi/MusAm*, xxv/9 (1975), MA8–9

P. Altman: 'The Voyage of Dominick Argento', *ON*, xl/21 (1975–6), 12–15

D. J. Speer, ed.: *Commemorating the World Premiere of 'The Voyage of Edgar Allan Poe'* (St Paul, 1976)

A. Porter: 'By a Route Obscure', *New Yorker* (17 May 1976) [*The Voyage of Edgar Allan Poe*]

H. Heinsheimer: 'Great Expectations', *ON*, xliii/18 (1978–9), 34–5 [*Miss Havisham's Fire*]

A. Kozinn: 'Argento at Ease', *World of Opera*, i (1979), 1–13

A. Porter: 'Fire in April', *New Yorker* (9 April 1979) [*Miss Havisham's Fire*]

M. Swales: *Characterization in Dominick Argento's Opera 'Postcard from Morocco': a Director's Guide* (diss., U. of Iowa, 1983)

A. Porter: 'Musical Events', *New Yorker* (2 Dec 1985) [*Casanova's Homecoming*]

H. Sigal: *The Concert Vocal Works of Dominick Argento: A Performance Analysis* (diss., New York U., 1985)

J. Sutcliffe: 'The Argento Papers', *ON*, liii/5 (1988–9), 14–18 [*The Aspern Papers*]

V. Saya: *The Current Climate for American Musical Eclecticism as Reflected in the Operas of Dominick Argento* (diss., U. of Cincinnati, 1989)

R. H. Kornick: *Recent American Opera: A Production Guide* (New York, 1991), 18–32

VIRGINIA SAYA

Argomento (It.: 'argument') [*antefatto*, *premessa*]. Heading normally given to the prefatory material of a printed libretto (*see* LIBRETTO (i)) in which the background to the plot ('the story so far') is outlined. Its purpose is to inform the audience of relevant events supposed to have taken place before the rise of the curtain and thus to help elucidate what follows.

Argonauti in Colco, Gli [*Gli Argonauti in Colco, o sia La conquista del vello d'oro* ('The Argonauts in Colchis, or the Conquest of the Golden Fleece')]. *Opera seria* in three acts by GIUSEPPE GAZZANIGA to a libretto by SIMEONE ANTONIO SOGRAFI; Venice, Teatro S Samuele, Carnival 1790.

Eeta [Aeetes] (tenor), King of Colchis, welcomes Giasone [Jason] (tenor) and the Argonauts. The high priestess Medea (soprano), daughter of Aeetes, warns Jason of danger: another stranger, Frisso [Phrixus], husband of her sister Calciope [Chalciope] (soprano), has already been killed by monsters leaving four children, among them Argo (soprano castrato). Jason resolves to earn the golden fleece by battling with the monsters and succeeds with Medea's help; Phrixus's ghost (bass) appears in the midst of the rejoicing to demand revenge. Aeetes condemns Medea to be sacrificed, but Jason returns to save her, and she and Chalciope set sail with Jason, Argo and the Argonauts, leaving Aeetes alone on shore.

This is the first of Sografi's innovative librettos in which departures from the strict delineations between recitative and formal set pieces allow a free interplay of textural options – solo, ensemble, and chorus. Sografi goes a step beyond such constructions as the multi-sectional action ensemble or the scene complex, which were often unified with obbligato recitative. The procedures pioneered here led after 1795 to a new style in opera librettos in which the chorus, as a freely participating character in the drama, is central to the new flexibility. The chorus of Argonauts sing in the *introduzione*, combine in duo with Jason in 'Tremar! ... non sa chi in petto' (1.vi), link his cavatina with Aeetes' aria in 'Contro i feroci Tauri' (1.viii), and join in an action duet with Medea and Jason at the end of Act 1. In Act 2 the opening of the celebration scene combines two choruses with dance and solo commentary. The appearance of Phrixus's ghost occasions an ensemble leading into chorus and then into tutti dialogue with the ghost. The Argonauts interrupt in pantomime during Jason's farewell aria; in Act 3 they sing with him while preparing for departure and perform a chorus as Aeetes rages on shore.

With so much chorus, there are only 11 solo exit arias, five of which are Medea's. Many of Jason's are with chorus and only one is a solo. The second-ranking singers have two each, the High Priest one, and Chalciope none. Both principals have one aria incorporating action. A few arias are in rounded ternary form, but most go through the entire text once or twice without rounding. Gazzaniga's accompaniments are relatively active, providing countermelodies, embellishing or elaborating the vocal line, or adding a duo part in thirds. Winds, including bassoon, assume solo roles and perform as a section. Obbligato recitative, often with full orchestra, combines with sustained, tremolo, and occasional measured accompaniments for the voice; moving beyond its traditional role in monologues, it heightens the most dramatic episodes, such as the dialogue between Jason and Medea at the end of Act 1 and the ghost scene in Act 2.

MARITA P. McCLYMONDS

Århus (Old Dan. Aarhus). Second largest city in Denmark. The Jyske Opera (Jutland Opera) is a permanent institution, founded in 1947. Until 1970 the conductor Gerhard Schepelern and Holger Boland made their mark with productions of the classical and modern repertories in the Århus Teater. From 1962 there were also summer productions in the Helsingør Teater in the Old Town museum. Guest performances outside the city were initiated in 1975; two years later they became established under the law on regional theatre which places the Jutland Opera among the national opera companies having support from regional orchestras and local choirs. Annual operational expenditure is underwritten by the Danish government and the 14 Danish counties. The Jutland Opera still has its base in Århus, where in 1982 the Musikhuset Århus (Århus House of Music) was opened. Apart from its continuing seasonal programmes, this is where, since 1983, the Opera has presented outstanding productions of the *Ring*, *Tristan und Isolde* and other Wagner operas under the direction of the general manager, Francesco Christofoli. The company has also earned distinction for its many productions of new Scandinavian music drama.

NILS SCHIØRRING

Aria (It.: 'air'). A closed lyrical piece for solo voice (exceptionally, for more than one), either independent or forming part of an opera or other large work; in the 17th and 18th centuries it was also sometimes applied to instrumental music. Strictly, its Italian sense may be rendered as 'style, manner or course', as of a melody. In Italian vocal music of the 16th and 17th centuries it was a closed form, normally strophic, with or without instrumental accompaniment. The term derives from the Latin *aer*, meaning 'air, atmosphere', and in the writings of theorists of the 14th and 15th centuries implies 'manner', 'way' or 'mode'; a 16th-century reference is to 'per intendere l'aere veneziano', 'to hear the Venetian way' or 'the Venetian type of melody'. During the 16th century it came to mean specifically a song or a way of singing.

The aria, from the 17th century to the 19th, was the chief expressive vehicle for the solo singer in Italian opera.

1. 17th century. 2. 18th century: (i) The da capo aria. (ii) The dal segno aria. (iii) Later aria types. 3. 19th century: (i) Italy. (ii) Other countries. 4. 20th century.

1. 17TH CENTURY. Although around 1600 the term did not have a strong connotation of music for solo voice, 'aria' played a leading role in the early development of monody. Settings of such poetic forms as strophic quatrains (particularly in prologues), ottavas and *capitoli* abound in opera from Jacopo Peri and Jacopo Corsi's setting of *Dafne* (Ottavio Rinuccini; 1597–8) onwards (see Porter 1965). 'Possente spirto' from Monteverdi's *Orfeo* (Alessandro Striggio (ii); 1607) is a particularly elaborate example of an 'aria per cantar terza rima'.

In general, the only distinction between monodic madrigal and solo aria in the early 17th century is in the matter of repetitive – usually strophic – poetic form. A similar distinction existed between 'cantata' and 'aria'. Strophic variations are common throughout the first half of the 17th century; most are in recitative style but some use more regular rhythms. These include pieces, often laments (*see* LAMENT), built on ostinatos, particularly in the 1630s and 40s; the practice may have been borrowed from instrumental music. Occasionally a series of strophes is distributed over two or more musical units. There is a curious instance, marked 'aria', sung by Cupid towards the end of Act 2 of Monteverdi's *L'incoronazione di Poppea* (Busenello; 1642–3). Four verses are separated by the same ritornello; the first and fourth have the same music, although in different notation, while the second and third, though not identical, are closely allied. The form (noting the ritornello, *R*) is *ARBRB'RA*. Variation forms, including those built on ostinatos, except for modulating ones, are rare after 1650.

'Recitative' and 'aria' are not musically exclusive terms in the early 17th century. The former refers to style whereas the most reliable implication of the latter is formal: thus 'aria recitativa di sei parti' (six-strophed aria in recitative style) in Domenico Mazzocchi's *La catena d'Adone* (1626), which also continues to indicate strophic ensemble pieces as arias. In this work Mazzocchi introduced the term 'mezz' aria' for passages having the lyrical character expected of an aria but lacking its strophic form (for a slightly different view, see Reiner 1968); in that category are probably the several non-strophic pieces, without ritornellos, for solo voice ('aria' in the score), mostly using a walking bass. Recitative intrusions into more regular movement occur in Cavalli's earlier operas but went out of fashion in the early 1650s, as did recitative arias generally. The opposite phenomenon, a lyrical moment ('arioso') in the setting of poetry meant for recitative, remained an essential ingredient of Italian opera throughout the 17th century.

In Venetian operas before 1660 (most surviving works are by Cavalli), most arias are in triple time or a mixture of triple and duple; the same applies to Michelangelo Rossi's opera *Erminia sul Giordano* (1633). Before 1630, however, duple time often held its own. Many early arias have four or five strophes, or even more; after 1650, in opera at least, two rapidly became the standard number. Most 17th-century opera arias have continuo accompaniment to the vocal line and ritornellos for three to five parts between the strophes.

Arie concertate, in which an instrumental ensemble intervenes between vocal phrases within a strophe or accompanies the voice, first penetrated opera to any extent in the 1640s; early Cavalli works offer several examples. Although their number grows during the second half of the century, they remain a minority until the age of *opera seria*. Their accompaniment nearly always consists of string orchestra and continuo, just as for ritornellos. The only wind instrument to gain currency before 1690 (except in such isolated court extravaganzas as Cesti's *Il pomo d'oro*, 1668, Vienna) was the trumpet, used in dialogue with the voice from about 1670, apparently first in Venice and Bologna. The texts of trumpet arias express bellicose sentiments and the voice imitates the instrument's characteristic figures.

Aria strophes exhibit great variety of form, but the same procedure of composition underlies most of them: the text is set line by line, by and large syllabically despite isolated flourishes, and often with modest repetition of single words or phrases; the end of each line – or sometimes couplet – is marked by a cadence, with or without a rhythmic hiatus. Two formal schemes, each corresponding to a distinct poetic type, account for the bulk of arias in the later 17th century. In the so-called *ABB* (better *ABB'*) aria, the last line or group of lines is rendered twice to similar music, having a cadence on the tonic only the second time; the repeat may involve anything from simple transposition to complete reworking of material. The form at its most complete consists of two strophes and ritornellos, for example, *ABB'RABB'R* as in 'Adorisi sempre' (*Orontea*, Cesti, 1656); some arias, however, have only a single strophe. The two poetic strophes often have parallel or identical final lines, with an epigrammatic or emphatic quality that justifies their musical repetition: an example is 'Frena il cordoglio' from Cavalli's *Ormindo* (1644). In the other type of aria the first line or couplet is repeated as a refrain at the end of the same strophe; the music for the repeated text is often varied in pieces of the 1650s and 1660s (*ABA'*, as in 'Chi mi toglie' from *Ormindo*) but comes increasingly to be a literal restatement of the opening (*ABA*; or, giving the complete form, *ABARABAR*). This is the source of the da capo aria.

An extension of the possibilities of prosody continued throughout the period 1640–80, yielding line lengths of nine, ten and 12 syllables and a range of internal rhythms, of which the anapest was particularly favoured. The object of this extension was to inspire variety of musical rhythm, just as Caccini had sought inspiration in the poetic licence of Chiabrera. The generation of P. A. Ziani, Antonio Sartorio, Legrenzi and Carlo Pallavicino had to hand poetry of this sort, which moreover often changed pattern in mid-strophe – a procedure not unknown to the early 17th century, but less assiduously applied. These changes usually produced a corresponding change of musical metre. In general the range of figure and type of movement greatly expanded during these years.

Most arias even of the later 17th century are short and simple, commensurate with their number (30 to 50 per opera is a fair average; see, for example, Alessandro Scarlatti's *Gli equivoci nel sembiante*, 1679, and *Eraclea*, 1700). Many have rhythmic patterns in which some writers have seen a relationship to contemporary dance music, but it remains uncertain to what extent the resemblance is a by-product of regular text accent in a syllabic setting.

Passage-work, often associated with a conventionally placed text image, waxed during the 1670s. The aria with motto opening, or 'Devisenarie', came into vogue; in it a brief vocal proclamation is repeated by the accompaniment, then taken up again by the voice and given its continuation, as in 'Gigli alteri' (*Gli equivoci nel sembiante*). A parallel development is the 'tag' ending, or repeated final short phrase, for example in 'Pastorella tutta bella' (*Gli equivoci*). The works of Legrenzi and his contemporaries afford numerous further examples of these, and of bass lines built on a single melodic or rhythmic idea, or on a modulating ostinato as in 'Onde, fero, fiamme e morte' (*Gli equivoci*). The sections of many arias are marked off as if for repetition.

By 1680 the da capo aria occupied a dominant position, though its dimensions remained small into the early 18th century. The trend seems first to have taken hold in Venice, still the principal market-place of opera. It does not have the connection with Alessandro Scarlatti that many writers, mainly out of a limited knowledge of the repertory, have suggested. With the establishment of the hegemony of the da capo, and in any case by 1690, the second strophe disappeared.

2. 18TH CENTURY.

(i) The da capo aria. The da capo form dominated the Italian aria by the beginning of the 18th century, but there was then still some fluidity in its relationship to the words. There is usually a binary construction of the setting of the first part of the text, although arias from this date tend to be so short that this binary structure often consists only of two periods with a half cadence, rather than a modulation, at the end of the first (and the second often repeated); see 'Penso far ciò che brami' in Scarlatti's *Eraclea*. The text of this, the *A* part of the *ABA* (or five-part *AA'BAA'*) da capo structure, usually consists of two to four lines of verse. If a couplet, it was nearly always repeated completely in the second part of the binary form, but this was not yet always the case with quatrains, in which sometimes only the second couplet was repeated. The middle or *B* section of the aria was often treated exactly like the *A* section, even occasionally using the so-called 'motto' beginning, which remained popular in the early years of the century – an example is 'Saper tu vuoi' in *Eraclea*. In many arias of this period the *A* and *B* sections of the aria are equal in length and musical weight, but in others (for example 'Chi lascia la sua bella', *Eraclea*) the *A* is as much as twice as long as *B*, and when the text of *B* consists of a quatrain it is seldom repeated in full. The accompaniment of arias in this period also tended towards diversity. The continuo aria continued into the 1720s but became increasingly rare. In the works of conservative composers at the beginning of the century, independent ritornellos in several parts following a continuo aria are still occasionally found; and arias in which the voice is accompanied only by continuo, but with instruments playing between the phrases, are quite common (see *Gli equivoci nel sembiante*). More individual textures, such as the accompaniment of the voice in unison and octaves or with several instruments weaving contrapuntal parts above the voice as lowest sounding part, also had periods of vogue. A considerable variety of instruments in combination or solo were used.

By the 1720s, longer arias were favoured, but not to such an extent as to destroy the intimacy of the relationship between music and text. This might be called the 'classic' moment in the development of the da capo aria, especially as it was accompanied by the rise to prominence of a generation of composers – Vinci, Hasse, Pergolesi etc. – who were to be regarded as the originators of the modern style of 18th-century music, as well as the appearance of a poet, Metastasio, who provided a body of aria poetry that was to be the main source for composers and the model for other poets until near the end of the century.

The standard da capo aria pattern, although traditionally expressed *ABA'*, can more usefully be seen as a five-part one, *AA'BAA'*, with each part delineated by ritornellos, *RARA'RBRARA'R*. It begins with an instrumental introduction, or ritornello, varying in length but self-contained, with a full close in the tonic. The aria is normally based on two quatrains of poetry, the second couplet of the first quatrain embodying a change of sentiment that offers a textual motive for a change of key to the dominant (or, in a minor key, to the relative major). A further ritornello in the secondary key, usually shorter, leads to the second setting (*A'*) of the first quatrain, which might begin in either the new key or the tonic. A third ritornello brings the section to a close (it will also close the aria, after the da capo). The setting of the second quatrain (the *B* section) might be in a contrasting style and a different metre and tempo; it was often more lightly accompanied and it commonly moved through several related keys – often ending in the minor, or on a Phrygian cadence – before preparing for a return to the tonic key and the introductory ritornello. Cadenzas could be inserted at the ends of the statements of both stanzas, and the da capo provided an opportunity for the singer to add ornamentation; fioriture often appeared in the final line of the first quatrain.

A specific example, Vinci's setting of 'L'onda dal mar' from *Artaserse* (Metastasio; 1730), may illustrate the relationship between text and music:

L'onda dal mar divisa
Bagna le valle e'l monte,
Va passeggiera in fiume,
Va prigioniera in fonte,
Mormora sempre e geme
Fin che non torna al mar;

Al mar dov'ella naque,
Dove acquistò gli umori,
Dove da' lunghi errori
Spera di riposar.

(The wave parted from the sea bathes the valley and the mountain, it travels in the stream and is captured in the fountain; it always murmurs and laments until it returns to the sea – at the sea that gave it birth, where it acquired its moods, where after its long wanderings it hopes to find repose.)

These lines embody a simple natural metaphor concerning the motion of water. That they were made expressly for music is evident from their sounds (predominance of liquid consonants, the ideal sound of 'mar' at the end of the first stanza, where tradition dictated melismas) as well as from their sense: several opportunities for painting individual words, a motion of travelling and returning that allows parallels with the binary tonal scheme of the *AA'* section and then 'wandering' with hopes of repose to suggest the tonal function of the *B* section. The first line, set syllabically, receives three bars; the second is extended to five so that the depth of 'valle' can be contrasted with the height of 'monte'. The modulation to the dominant sets in with the third line (at a verb of motion), a three-bar phrase which is then repeated, and is confirmed by the setting of the fourth line, again three bars, to the accompaniment of gently agitated semiquavers in the strings in order to suggest perpetual murmuring and shuddering. The final line is extended to seven bars by repeating the two-bar melisma on 'mar', the whole then deftly extended by an interrupted cadence, allowing a final melodic peak and a graceful descent into the cadence.

Metastasio and many critics – particularly those who held that the opera belonged to the tragic genre – compared the function of the aria with that of the chorus in Greek tragedy. This accounts for the large number of aria texts in his works and those of his imitators that might, like 'L'onda dal mar', be said to trope the action sententiously or imagistically (as in the so-called 'simile' aria) rather than forming a direct part of it. Such a function for the aria helped justify it for critics of a primarily literary orientation, but it was seen as a grave defect by reformers later in the century, who began to form a concept of the opera in which music was to take a more central role in the drama. Dramatic arias, however, are by no means lacking in Metastasio's work as a whole.

As the da capo form was nearly universal, a dramatic effect could be won by playing on its very predictability. Thus the opening ritornello could be jettisoned if the situation suggested that the singer should begin impetuously without one; this happened a few times in most operas. Handel's operas provide many examples of this technique and of others that vary the form for dramatic ends. Eduige's 'Lo farò' from Act 1 of *Rodelinda* (1725), a 'motto aria', shows a character responding immediately in a situation where a ritornello would be out of place, as does Polissena's 'Barbaro! partirò', from Act 3 of *Radamisto* (1720), where the ritornello is simply omitted. In some, much rarer, cases the dramatic situation might cause the aria to be interrupted before its completion; an example is Rodrigo's 'Sommi Dei' from *Rodrigo* (or *Vincer se stesso*, 1707), where what seems to be the middle section of a short aria has just begun when a call to arms intervenes and the singer breaks off. There are examples of an aria's breaking off with the vocal part unfinished because the character dies or seems to die, or (as in *Orlando*, 1733) goes to sleep. Another variation of the scheme involved the introduction of a recitative as a substitute for the middle section (Elvira's 'Notte cara', in Act 2 of *Floridante*, 1722) or between the middle section and the return of the first (Cleopatra's 'V'adoro, pupille', *Giulio Cesare*, Act 2, 1724).

Within the da capo form itself a considerable variety of musical treatment was possible, for example in thematic and tonal relationships. The voice usually entered with the material heard at the beginning of the ritornello. As in instrumental binary forms, the second solo might begin with the same phrase transposed to the dominant, or a developmental transformation of it; if however the preceding ritornello itself states this idea, it was likely to begin with different material, and examples can be found where the opening idea reappears only at the beginning of the middle section. Similarly, again as in instrumental binary forms, the tonal treatment of the second solo had many possibilities. It could begin in the tonic; it could return to the tonic almost immediately; or it could put off that return for some time. The variety in the treatment of the middle section was even greater. The accompaniment was often reduced, for a chiaroscuro effect, and there could be a complete musical contrast, with different tempo and metre.

During the 1730s and 40s the music of the main section of the da capo continued to expand in length. The text, however, did not; and that led to a weakening of the closeness of their previous union. The text had now to be much more repeated, in whole or in part, and this tended to dissolve it into the music. Perhaps partly for this reason, a chronological survey of Metastasio's arias reveals that while in his earlier work he had used a considerable variety of metres and stanza lengths, in his later ones arias in quatrains of *settenario* (seven-syllable) verse increasingly predominate. By the 1720s the first two solos each occasionally have a second statement of all or most of the text as a coda-like appendage to the main statement, with music that is an extension or reinforcement of the new key in the first or the return to the original one in the second. This became the standard format for the da capo, as a result of which the first stanza was heard eight times in a complete performance of an aria, the second usually only once; composers in this period often set the middle section in a contrasting tempo and metre (usually a moderate 3/8 if the main section was an Allegro in common time, as it usually was) as if to emphasize it and relieve the sameness. The aria and the *opera seria* in general underwent increasing criticism after the middle of the century, both from those who felt that musical expansion was now out of hand in the arias and that the old balance should be restored, and those, including Gluck and Calzabigi, who wanted an altogether new relationship.

(ii) The dal segno aria. By the middle of the century, however, a tendency to retrenchment had set in with regard to aria form. At first this was entirely mechanical, replacing the da capo with the dal segno, that is, the indication of a return not to the beginning of the piece but to a point marked with a sign within it. The dal segno (or 'da capo al segno') had been used earlier, with the sign placed at the first vocal entry, to eliminate the repeat of the opening ritornello or part of it. But from about 1760 composers used the sign to shorten the *A'* section substantially. Often it was placed at the beginning of the second solo, as in 'Al destin che la minaccia' (*Mitridate*, Mozart, 1770), though where the second solo began in the dominant they sometimes preferred to write out the beginning of the return in the tonic, placing the sign at the point where the music had originally returned to the tonic in preparation for closure as in 'Dopo un tuo sguardo' (*Adriano in Siria*, J. C. Bach, 1765). If the second solo had begun with new material, the same procedure might be used to create a rounded form by providing a recapitulation of the first solo adjusted to remain in the tonic as in 'Disperato mar turbato' from *Adriano* (*AA'BA*); but just as often only the second solo was retained (*AA'BA'*) as in 'Cara la dolce fiamma' (*Adriano*). Occasionally the setting of the opening words after the middle section would be different from either the first or the second solo though closely related rhythmically and melodically (*AA'BA"*); an example is 'Son quel fiume' from Jommelli's *Fetonte* (1768). There were also dal segno arias in which the first couplet of text never returned. When the final section was severely shortened, the formal proportions of the aria were so radically changed that the middle section had the effect of an episode within the second part of a binary structure.

Most arias had only a three-part string accompaniment. Some added oboes and horns to enhance the affections expressed in the aria, to swell the crescendos, to add force to ritornellos and to sustain harmonies. Jommelli appears almost unique in detaching the cello and viola from the continuo. The bassoon, which played when horns and oboes were scored, was seldom specified or detached from the continuo until late in the century. During the vocal sections, composers commonly varied the accompaniment style from one phrase to another and assigned contrasting tasks to the two violin parts. One might double or elaborate on the vocal part while the other maintained a beat-keeping motive or played repeated notes or arpeggiation. Brief *B* sections were usually distinguished by the omission of wind instruments. The compound *A* sections of arias gradually grew to more than one hundred bars, overpowering the *B* sections.

(iii) Later aria types. Early in the 1770s, the dal segno aria gave way to a through-composed, compound ternary aria: *AA'BA"A'"* (see Table 1, section 2.a), as in 'Se dal suo braccio oppreso' (*Armida*, Haydn, 1784) and 'Se il tuo duol' (*Idomeneo*, Mozart, 1781); and *AA'BA"* (see Table 1, section 2.b), as in 'L'odio nel cor frenate'

TABLE 1: Aria Forms in the 18th Century

1.a Five-part da capo

sections		*A*		*A′*		‖ *B*	*da capo (A, A′)*
	tutti	solo	tutti	solo	tutti	solo	
thematic		a		b (a′)		x	
poetic lines		1–2, 3–4		1–2, 3–4		5–8	
tonal plan { I		I—V		—I[1]		related keys	
tonal plan { i		i—III		—i[1]		related keys	

1.b Da capo al segno

sections		*A*		*A′*		‖ *B*		*da capo al segno (A, A′)*
	tutti	·𝄋· solo	tutti	solo	tutti	solo	tutti	·𝄋·
thematic		a		b (a′)		x		
poetic lines		1–2, 3–4		1–2, 3–4		5–8		
tonal plan { I		I—V		—I[1]		related keys		
tonal plan { i		i—III		—i[1]		related keys		

1.c Dal segno

sections		*A*		*A′*		‖ *B*		*either* { *dal segno (A′)*	*(A″) dal segno*[2]
	tutti	solo	tutti	·𝄋· solo ·𝄋·	tutti	solo	tutti	·𝄋·	(solo)
thematic		a		b (a′)		x		*or*	(a, b, c)
poetic lines		1–2, 3–4		1–2, 3–4		5–8			(1–2)
tonal plan { I		I—V		—I[1]		related keys			(—I[1])
tonal plan { i		i—III		—i[1]		related keys			(—i[1])

2.a Through-composed, compound ternary, compound return

sections		*A*		*A′*		*B*		A″		A‴	
		exposition				development		recapitulation			
	tutti	solo	tutti	solo	tutti	solo	tutti	solo	tutti	solo	tutti
thematic		a		b (a′)		x		a (c)		b (c, d)	
poetic lines		1–4		1–4		5–8		1–4		1–4	
tonal plan { I		I–V		V		related or V		—I[1]		I	
tonal plan { i		i—III		III		related or III		—i[1]		i	

2.b Through-composed, compound ternary, compressed return

sections		*A*		*A′*		*B*		*A″*	
	tutti	solo	tutti	solo	tutti	solo	tutti	solo	tutti
thematic		a		b (a′)		x		a (c)	
poetic lines		1–4		1–4		5–8		1–4	
tonal plan { I		I—V		V		related or V		—I[1]	
tonal plan { i		i—III		III		related or III		—i[1]	

2.c Simple ternary

sections		*A*		*B*		*A′*	
	tutti	solo	tutti	solo	tutti	solo	tutti
thematic		a		x		a (b)	
poetic lines		1–4		5–8		1–4	
tonal plan { I		I—V		related or V		—I[1]	
tonal plan { i		i—III		related or III		—i[1]	

3 Compound binary (with stretta)

sections		*A*		*B*		*A′*		*B′*		*(C*		*C′)*[3]	
	tutti	solo	tutti	solo	tutti	solo	tutti	solo	tutti	(solo	tutti	solo	tutti)
thematic		a		b		a (c)		b (c, d)		(c, d, e)		(c, d, e)	
poetic lines		1–4		5–8		1–4		5–8		5–8 (9–12)		5–8 (9–12)[4]	
tonal plan { I		I—V		V		—I[1]		I		(I)			
tonal plan { i		i–III		III		—i[1]		i		(i or I)			

1 The return to tonic is variable but usually near the beginning of the section.
2 The placement of the ·𝄋· varies; it may be at the beginning of *A′* or within it (the beginning of *A′* is often rewritten following the *B* section, becoming *A″*).
3 An additional section in a faster tempo may be added, as in the rondò.
4 Texts of variable length, either new or extracts from lines 1 to 8.
NB: tutti sections may not always be present.

(*Mitridate*, Mozart). The form with the compound return is close in tonal and thematic plan to both the contemporary instrumental sonata-form pattern and the classical concerto form in which the double exposition and ritornellos parallel those in the aria. Here the first solo moves to the dominant or major mediant, the second presents new material in the newly established key, in which it closes, and the middle section provides thematic, textural and tonal or modal contrast before a return to the tonic for a recapitulation of the first or second solos, or both, adjusted to close in the tonic. An example is 'Se colà ne' fati' from *Idomeneo*. Unlike the instrumental sonata, the middle section of an aria is seldom developmental in the instrumental sense; arias only rarely have large, tonally and motivically unstable transitional or development sections. Developmental figuration and coloratura usually function as closing material following a simple and direct modulation. Similarly, the middle section usually consists of melodically stable phrases even when there is a modulation (or more than one). By the 1780s, arias frequently remained in the dominant throughout the middle section. After the initial statement of the opening lines of the first stanza, fragmentation of the text and the lack of articulating ritornellos sometimes make it difficult to talk of the number of complete statements of the first stanza. Depending on the style, there may be as many as three or four or as few as one preceding the middle section and the same or fewer following it. Unlike its instrumental counterpart, in an aria the recapitulation may not begin in the tonic, and the thematic material for one or both solos may be disguised, varied or totally new as in 'Se il tuo duol' with a new second solo and 'Nò, la morte' with a new first solo (*Idomeneo*; see Table 1, section 2.a). The return usually presents a clear recapitulation of earlier material within a few phrases but it may be so heavily reworked as to qualify as another version of the material, as in 'L'odio nel cor frenate' (*Mitridate*, Mozart).

By the 1780s, operas contained only a few long arias, usually concentrated in the first act. The rest were relatively short; the shortest dispensed with the second stanza of poetry and simply set the first stanza twice – the first moving to the dominant and the second returning to the tonic. The composer also might shorten the aria by reducing the number of statements of the first stanza (*ABA'*) as in 'Se tu sequir mi vuo (*Armida*, Haydn; see Table 1, section 2.c). For longer arias the composer had a number of options besides the compound ternary. The single-tempo rondo (*ABAB'(C)A*), introduced into Italian opera in the 1760s, appeared occasionally, as in 'Torna pure al cara bene' (*Armida*), and in the 1780s the da capo form returned to *opera seria* in the shape of the newly-fashionable minuet ('minue' or 'minuetto'). Arias might also take compound binary form in which the composer simply sets two stanzas of text twice through in more equal proportions (*ABA'B'*; see Table 1, section 3) with a tonal plan similar to the first and second solos in a da capo aria (moving to the dominant for *B* and back during *A'*), as in 'Padre, germani, addio' (*Idomeneo*). The Neapolitan poet Saverio Mattei – who called this form (*Elogio del Jommelli*, 1785) 'shortened rondo', though this does not accord with modern terminological usage – advocated such a form because it maintained the original order of the poetry; he took credit for having persuaded Piccinni to use it in his *opere serie* by the early 1770s. The form may also be viewed as a borrowing from comic opera, where it had been in use since the 1750s. Arias in this form may carry little or no contrast between the settings of the first and second stanzas, as in 'Colla bocca, e non core' (*La finta semplice*, Mozart, 1769). The stanzas may be set apart with changes of tempo, metre or style to produce strong contrasts, as in 'Senti l'eco, ove t'aggiri' (*La finta semplice*). In comic opera during the 1770s such arias acquired either a coda or a faster closing section in the tonic (stretta). The addition of the stretta produces the form *ABA'B':CC'*, for example 'Non sparate ... mi disdico' (*La vera costanza*, Haydn, 1779), or 'Non mi dir' (*Don Giovanni*, Mozart, 1787). This form is similar to that of the two-tempo RONDÒ (slow–fast) which was developing in *opera seria* during the same decade. The serious version usually had a short reprise of the opening material before moving to the faster tempo for a third stanza of text. Its simplest and earliest serious form appears to be a two-tempo Mattei-type 'shortened rondo' (slow–fast–slow–fast) that avoids the return to the *primo tempo* for the reprise of the first solo (*A:BA'B'*); an example is 'Non ho colpa' in *Idomeneo*. Rondòs based on only two strophes of poetry persist into the 1790s, but those using three strophes are more numerous and offer an almost endless variety of textual repetition patterns. A reprise of at least the first couplet normally precedes the change of tempo. In the fast section, a resetting of the second stanza appears between the initial setting of the third stanza and its reprise (*ABA':CB'C'*), as in 'Dei pietosi' (*Armida*). As the fast section became longer and more complex, composers alternated texts from all three stanzas. By the end of the decade the two-tempo rondòs had become showpieces for the leading singers; and not more than one or two were to be found in any opera. With their increasing vogue, about which the more serious critics complained, they became more frequent, the prototype of the cantabile–cabaletta of the early 19th century. The insertion of recitative into arias again begins to be found after 1770 with increasing frequency, as in 'Non temer' (K490, a 1786 addition by Mozart to *Idomeneo*); after 1785, so too do *pertichini* (the name for other characters or chorus when they intrude into a solo number; see 'Ah chi mi dice mai' from *Don Giovanni*) and from about that period in centres where a chorus was available the use of the chorus in solo numbers increased (see 'Deh ti placa' in Andreozzi's *Amleto*, 1792).

In the 1790s composers continued to prefer the compound binary with or without the stretta for comic opera and ternary forms (for example 'Torna di Tito a lato', *La clemenza di Tito*, Mozart, 1791) plus the two-tempo rondò ('Non più di fiori', *La clemenza di Tito*) for *opera seria*. Occasionally each stanza has the same closing text to be set as a refrain, as in 'È vero che in casa' (*Il matrimonio segreto*, Cimarosa, 1792). In the middle section, by the late 1780s, the dominant began to be replaced by third-related keys of the flat major mediant and submediant as in 'Tempra il duol' (*Amleto*) as well as keys of the subdominant and supertonic minor and major as in 'S'altro che lagrime' (*La clemenza di Tito*), thus placing this section in much starker contrast with the rest of the aria than had been the practice earlier in the 1780s. A few of the arias for the principals acquire yet a fourth stanza, presenting an even greater contrast in length with the rest of the arias in the opera. These were usually set in three or four tempos, either gradually growing quicker in tempo or in an alternating fast–slow–fast pattern (see 'A vendicar un padre', *Amleto*). Arias acquire sections in recitative style, and the combination of a slow cantabile, a 'tempo di mezzo' in recitative style and a fast final section akin to the cabaletta in 19th-century opera makes an appearance ('Caro è vero', *Armida*, Haydn). During the decade there are steadily fewer independent solo arias in each opera until they almost disappear. Many incorporate *pertichini*, as individuals, in groups and in chorus as in

'Deh ti placa' (*Amleto*). Many solo pieces function as cavatinas in scene complexes that move freely from declamatory to lyrical sections without clear articulations; an example is 'Ah non ferir' from *Armida*.

Arias in comic operas were generally freer and more varied in form than in the *opera seria*. Few comic operas are extant from the first half of the 18th century, but the da capo aria appears to have been widely used in them as well; see, for example, 'A Serpina penserete' (*La serva padrona*, Pergolesi, 1733). The *parti serie* sang much in the style as well as the form of the *opera seria* (for example 'Furie di donna irata', *La buona figliuola*, Piccinni, 1760). It is in the arias of the most farcical characters that texts tend to become longer, and the development of a rapid patter style for such characters, as in 'Gia sento i cani' from *La serva padrona*, may have contributed to this. In the second half of the century the form in which the whole text is stated completely and then run through a second time, as in 'Che superbia maledetta' (*La buona figliuola*), became very common, as did multi-tempo arias, particularly those with a slow beginning and a conclusion in a 6/8 Allegro movement (for example 'È pur bella la cecchina', *La buona figliuola*).

By contrast, the *parti serie* continued to be given arias in da capo forms, such as 'So che fedel m'adora' in *La buona figliuola*, until they disappeared from the *opera seria* repertory; after that the two-tempo rondò was used, as in 'Non mi dir' (*Don Giovanni*). In the 1770s, texts are no longer divided into two clear stanzas; musically, each stanza tends to fall into three sections, the first in the tonic, the second moving to the dominant and the third either remaining in the dominant or returning to the tonic in preparation for the second setting of the text (it may not have a clear reprise of the opening material; see 'Voi vedrete in una sala', *L'italiana in Londra*, Cimarosa, 1779, or 'Veramente ho torto', *Il barbiere di Siviglia*, Paisiello, 1782). Paisiello returned from Russia in 1783 with a setting of Goldoni's *Il mondo della luna* in which nearly all the aria texts are new; many have three settings of the complete text, the central one functioning as a development. In Cimarosa's *Il matrimonio segreto* (1792), many arias have either a short *stretta* or a sizeable concluding fast section. The section preceding the tempo change may assume the characteristics of the old middle section by moving into a contrasting tonality or carrying developmental characteristics.

3. 19TH CENTURY.

(i) Italy. In an age of vocal virtuosity the solo set piece continued to occupy pride of place in opera. The aria in two contrasting tempos, the first slow and expressive, the second fast and brilliant, prepared by a half close in the dominant key, survived as late as Rossini's *Semiramide* (1823; 'Ah, qual giorno'). By this time, the general practice was to separate the movements into two self-contained units, the 'cantabile' and 'cabaletta', the latter repeated at first in part (as in 'Io sono docile', *Il barbiere di Siviglia*, 1816), later complete, with an intervening orchestral ritornello which is resumed in the coda. The singer was expected to embellish the repetition with decorations of his or her own. Three-movement arias are occasionally to be found, such as 'Ah sì, per voi già sento' (*Otello*, Rossini, 1816). As the formal units of Italian opera expanded so it became usual to widen the gap between cantabile and cabaletta so as to allow the action to evolve in the meantime. Each aria would be preceded by a recitative, part declamatory, part arioso, described as 'scena'. The cantabile would end with a cadenza tailored to the means of the original singer. A 'tempo di mezzo' would follow, consisting of short phrases in strict time punctuated by instrumental figuration and leading to the cabaletta, the opening strain of which would be anticipated by the orchestra. Rossini frequently bridged the gap between scena and cantabile by starting the latter with a succession of declamatory flourishes that give way to a more periodic motion (for example 'Pensa alla patria', *L'italiana in Algeri*, 1813). His successors, especially Bellini, favoured a lyrical character from the start (again with orchestral anticipation). Choral intervention is common, particularly in the cabaletta. A classic instance of the grand aria is 'Casta diva' (*Norma*, Bellini, 1831), where the 'tempo di mezzo' includes a snatch of music from the stage band. The cantabile itself provides an instance of extended, non-repeating melody of which Bellini was a master (see also 'Ah! non credea mirarti', *La sonnambula*, 1831). A more common design may be summarized as *AA′BA″* followed by a coda, as in 'Ah! per sempre' (*I puritani*, Bellini, 1835), 'Io sentii tremar la mano' (*Parisina*, Donizetti, 1833) or 'Come rugiada al cespite' (*Ernani*, Verdi, 1844). Several arias feature an obbligato wind instrument – horn in 'Languir per una bella' (*L'italiana in Algeri*, Rossini, 1813), clarinet in 'Fatal Goffredo' (*Torquato Tasso*, Donizetti, 1833), trumpet in 'Cercherò lontana terra' (*Don Pasquale*, Donizetti, 1843). A variant is the *aria con pertichini* to which the occasional intervention by a minor character, as in 'Ah rimiro il bel sembiante' (*Maria Stuarda*, Donizetti, 1835) or even a principal, as in 'Cedi, cedi, o più sciagure' (*Lucia di Lammermoor*, Donizetti, 1835) gives the sense, if not the form, of a duet. When an aria marks the singer's first appearance it is termed a 'cavatina'; if it concludes the opera it is called a 'rondò finale', for example 'Era desso il mio figlio' (*Lucrezia Borgia*, Donizetti, 1833) or 'Sciagurata, in questi lidi' (*Oberto*, Verdi, 1839).

After 1850, aria patterns became more various. 'Ah fors'è lui' (*La traviata*, Verdi, 1853) has a cantabile in two strophes, each of which finishes with a major-key refrain in the manner of a French couplet. The same melody recurs in the ritornello and coda of the cabaletta as a *pertichino* allocated to a different voice. The cantabile of 'Come in quest'ora bruna' (*Simon Boccanegra*, Verdi, 1857) follows a ternary design with a modulating episode and a reprise of the opening section. With the gradual disappearance of the cabaletta, single-movement arias start to prevail. An early instance is 'Cortigiani, vil razza dannata!' (*Rigoletto*, Verdi, 1851), articulated in three sections, each expressing a different sentiment. In 'Eri tu che macchiavi quell'anima' (*Un ballo in maschera*, Verdi, 1859) and 'Madre, pietosa vergine' (*La forza del destino*, Verdi, 1862), the minor–major design associated mostly with the *romanza* but also certain cantabile arias – such as 'Regnava nel silenzio' (*Lucia di Lammermoor*) or 'Ah sì, ben mio' (*Il trovatore*, Verdi, 1853) – is expanded into a unit of larger proportions. 'Ma dall'arido stelo divulsa' (*Un ballo in maschera*) offers an elementary species of bar-form with refrain, which Verdi defined more sharply in 'Piangea cantando nell'erma landa' (*Otello*, 1887). Until 1860 the rule was for all movements in the minor key to end with at least a cadence in the major; even in 'Addio, del passato' (*La traviata*) it is left to the oboe to bring back the key of A minor after the singer's last note. But in 'Morrò, ma prima in grazia' (*Un ballo in maschera*) the music, for the first time, remains in the minor key throughout.

Tradition allowed greater freedom of form to narrative arias, for example 'Nella fatal di Rimini' (*Lucrezia Borgia*), 'Un ignoto, tre lune or saranno' (*I masnadieri*, Verdi, 1847), and 'Condotta ell'era in ceppi' (*Il trovatore*). With the invasion of Italian theatres by foreign works, especially French, during the 1860s, the same freedom came to be extended to those that depict a complex emotional state. In 'Ritorna vincitor!' (*Aida*, Verdi, 1871) and 'Dio! mi potevi scagliar' (*Otello*) the form is dictated purely by the ebb and flow of the singer's feelings. A varied strophic form is also common, as in 'Cielo e mar' (*La Gioconda*, Ponchielli, 1876), where the second strophe, initially abbreviated, is expanded into near-symmetry with the first by means of a codetta. Instances of couplet form abound: extended in Meyerbeer's manner in 'Son lo spirito che nega' (*Mefistofele*, Boito, 1868), subtly varied in 'Sul fil d'un soffio etesio' (*Falstaff*, Verdi, 1893). But in the age of Italian grand opera (1870–90) it is the French ternary form with modulating episode that prevails, as in 'Suicidio!' (*La Gioconda*), 'Mio bianco amor' (*Dejanice*, Catalani, 1883) and 'Ebben, ne andrò lontano' (*La Wally*, Catalani, 1892). With Puccini and his generation the last traces of conventional formalism disappear from the aria, whose construction varies according to the sense of the text, as for example in 'Voi lo sapete, o mamma' (*Cavalleria rusticana*, Mascagni, 1890), 'La mamma morta' (*Andrea Chénier*, Giordano, 1896), 'È la solita storia del pastore' (*L'arlesiana*, Cilea, 1897) and 'Sola, perduta, abbandonata' (*Manon Lescaut*, Puccini, 1893). Only Leoncavallo, who wrote his own librettos, would often allow his verse-forms to impose a similar regularity on his settings, as in 'Vesti la giubba' (*Pagliacci*, 1892) and 'Testa adorata' (*La bohème*, 1897). Puccini, who tended to organize his acts motivically, showed considerable skill in incorporating cardinal motifs into his arias, as in 'Che gelida manina' (*La bohème*, 1896) and 'Vissi d'arte' (*Tosca*, 1900). During the 19th century and the early 20th, with few exceptions – and those mainly by Puccini, such as 'Un bel dì vedremo' (*Madama Butterfly*, 1904), 'Ch'ella mi creda libero e lontano' (*La fanciulla del West*, 1910), 'O mio babbino caro' (*Gianni Schicchi*, 1918) and 'Nessun dorma' (*Turandot*, 1926) – arias become increasingly difficult to divorce from their context, and thus effectively cease to exist as such.

(ii) Other countries. In France the two most characteristic aria designs are the ternary with modulating central episode and the couplet. The first, inherited from Gluck and his contemporaries, remained the model for large-scale pieces for most of the century. Among earlier examples are 'Toi que j'implore avec effroi' (*La vestale*, Spontini, 1807), 'Ah quel plaisir d'être soldat' (*La dame blanche*, Boieldieu, 1825) and 'Quand je quittai la Normandie' (*Robert le diable*, Meyerbeer, 1831). Later, the central section might be set in a different tempo, as in 'Avant de quitter ces lieux' (*Faust*, Gounod, 1859, rev. 1862), or even time signature, as in 'Je dis que rien ne m'épouvante' (*Carmen*, Bizet, 1875). The same pattern, modified and loosened up, can be found as late as 'Reste au foyer, petit grillon' (*Cendrillon*, Massenet, 1899). The couplet, which originates in *opéra comique*, found its way into grand opera after 1830. It consists of two strophes, each ending with the same strain set to the same words, sometimes echoed by the chorus. It may form the basis of a narrative ballade, as in 'Jadis régnait en Normandie' (*Robert le diable*), a character piece, as in 'Piff, paff, piff, paff' (*Les Huguenots*, Meyerbeer, 1836), or even a love song, as in 'Plus blanche que la blanche ermine' (*Les Huguenots*). A classic instance of couplets with chorus is 'Votre toast' (*Carmen*). Offenbach's operettas depend on this form almost exclusively for all their solo numbers; not surprisingly its last appearance in serious opera is with the same composer's 'Les oiseaux dans la charmille' (*Les contes d'Hoffmann*, 1881). Meyerbeer, in his later operas, enlarged both couplet and ternary designs with a multiplicity of ideas.

During the Rossinian ascendancy of the 1820s the cantabile–cabaletta pattern is sometimes found, as in 'A celui que j'aimais' (*La muette de Portici*, Auber, 1828). 'O beau pays de la Touraine' (*Les Huguenots*) has a slow movement followed by a fast one, both in ternary design. However, the two contrasted movements of 'Je vais le voir' (*Béatrice et Bénédict*, Berlioz, 1862) have no connection with an Italian form which had become obsolete even in its country of origin. As in Italy, the aria structured according to the text was soon making headway: an example is 'La fleur que tu m'avais jetée' (*Carmen*).

In Germany during the first two decades of the century opera was dominated by a mixture of Italian and French forms. In Beethoven's *Fidelio* (1805), 'O wär' ich schon mit dir vereint' is in couplet form, while 'Komm, Hoffnung' follows the current Italian bipartite pattern, as does 'In des Lebens Frühlingstagen', though the concluding movement in the revision, where the melody is shared between voice and oboe, blazes a new trail of formal freedom. Weber and his successors conceived the aria more dramatically from the start. The three small movements (ending in a new key) of 'Durch die Wälder' (*Der Freischütz*, Weber, 1821) are determined purely by the conflict of the singer's feelings; while 'Leise, leise' (*Der Freischütz*), though set out in two substantial contrasting movements, entirely avoids the formalism of the cantabile–cabaletta design. The tradition of ending an aria with a section in faster time persists as late as 'Die Frist ist um' (*Der fliegende Holländer*, Wagner, 1843). Both couplet and ternary forms are found in the early Wagnerian canon, together with the strophic aria, such as 'O du mein holder Abendstern' (*Tannhäuser*, 1845). In the music dramas of Wagner's maturity the aria has no place (neither the Prize Song from *Die Meistersinger* (1868) nor even 'Winterstürme' (*Die Walküre*, composed 1855) can qualify as such). His contemporaries, operating within the more restricted area of Singspiel, mostly followed the path of Weber, while drawing sometimes on the aria forms of *opéra comique*. Only Nicolai, who had served his operatic apprenticeship in Italy, availed himself here and there of Italian techniques in *Die lustige Weiber von Windsor* (1849). During the last quarter of the 19th century the term 'Arie' virtually disappears from German opera.

In English opera, which up to the mid-19th century mostly followed the pattern of *opéra comique* with spoken dialogue, the aria is usually cast in the form of the Victorian strophic ballad with *couplet* refrain, for example 'I dreamt that I dwelt in marble halls' (*The Bohemian Girl*, Balfe, 1843). In later, through-composed scores the detachable solo piece is still sometimes found, such as the recitative and aria 'Woo thou thy snowflake' (*Ivanhoe*, Sullivan, 1892). A late instance is Hugh's 'Song of the Road' (*Hugh the Drover*, Vaughan Williams, 1924). In the Slavonic countries, in spite of obvious folk elements, the aria was accepted as a natural form of expression, for example Lyudmila's aria (which even includes a cadenza) in Act 4 of Glinka's *Ruslan and Lyudmila* (1842), Tatyana's Letter Song in Act 1 and Lensky's aria in Act 2 of Tchaikovsky's *Yevgeny Onegin* (1879) and Premsyl's 'Již plane slunce' ('The sun now burns') in Smetana's *Libuše* (composed 1872), even if Smetana's operas owe more to Wagner than to Italian models. The operas of The Five, however, except in the lyrical music apt to love scenes, tend rather to follow the continuous arioso-like pattern of heightened declamation found in Dargomïzhsky's *The Stone Guest* (written in the 1860s). This is particularly well suited to the great contemplative monologues such as that of Musorgsky's Boris Godunov (composed in the late 1860s), which, like several arias by Borodin and Rimsky-Korsakov, keeps to a free, ternary design.

4. 20TH CENTURY. If Debussy's *Pelléas et Mélisande* brought the Wagnerian operatic model (and *Parsifal* in particular) to the brink of modernism, abandoning almost all distinctions between an organization based upon vocal set pieces and through-composed music drama, subsequent 20th-century composers did not forsake 'number opera' altogether. While a heterogeneous collection of composers from Schoenberg (in *Von heute auf morgen*, 1930) and Stravinsky (*The Rake's Progress*, 1951) to Hindemith (*Cardillac*, 1926) and Henze (from *Boulevard Solitude*, 1952, to *Elegy for Young Lovers*, 1961) evoked the aria and other close vocal forms in a selfconsciously historical, neo-classical sense, Berg, in *Lulu* (1935), utilized the aria so as to develop its function musically and dramatically in a way that was not compromised by a Wagnerian *durchkomponiert* symphonism. Both the large-scale aria for Dr Schön in the second act, and the 'Lied der Lulu' that interrupts it are embedded in a hierarchy of musical forms that ramified through the operatic structure. Such examples bear directly upon Britten's operas, whose set pieces in works such as *Peter Grimes* (1945), *Billy Budd* (1951) and *Death in Venice* (1973) merge such ideas with Puccinian melodic rapture, and even Zimmermann's *Die Soldaten* (1965) contains passages that may be related back to the Bergian archetype.

Even in those examples, however, the dramatic function of the aria was blurred, and its purpose combined with those of monologue and narration: in the operas of Janáček too the distinctions between such constructions seem more concerned with terminology than musical effectiveness. In opera since 1945 especially the term 'aria' has come to signify any large-scale solo vocal item that could be distinguished musically and dramatically from the surrounding structure: in Birtwistle's *The Mask of Orpheus* (1986), for instance, the narration for Orpheus that provides the substance of the second act may not be an aria in any strict historical sense, but the term seems to describe its character and its dramatic effect more truthfully than any other.

*

J.-J. Rousseau: *Dictionnaire de musique* (Paris, 1768; Eng. trans., 1771)
J. G. Sulzer: *Allgemeine Theorie der schönen Künste* (Leipzig, 1771–4, 4/1792–9)
H. C. Koch: *Versuch einer Anleitung zur Composition* (Rudolstadt and Leipzig, 1782–93)
——: *Musikalisches Lexicon* (Frankfurt, 1802, 2/1817)
Castil-Blaze [F.-H.-J. Blaze]: *Dictionnaire de musique moderne* (Paris, 1821, 3/1828)
P. Lichtenthal: *Dizionario e bibliografica della musica* (Milan, 1826)
G. Cesare: 'Aria come termine musicale', *Enciclopedia italiana*, iv (Milan, 1929)
H. C. Wolff: *Die venezianische Oper in der zweiter Hälfte des 17. Jahrhunderts* (Berlin, 1937)
N. Fortune: 'Italian Secular Monody from 1600 to 1635: an Introductory Survey', *MQ*, xxxix (1953), 171–95
E. Downes: *The Operas of Johann Christian Bach as a Reflection of the Dominant Trends in Opera Seria 1750–1780* (diss., Harvard U., 1958)
H. S. Powers: 'Il *Serse* trasformato', *MQ*, xlvii (1961), 481–92; xlviii (1962), 73–92
M. Robinson: 'The Aria in Opera Seria, 1725–1780', *PRMA*, lxxxviii (1961–2), 31–43
B. Hjelmborg: 'Aspects of the Aria in the Early Operas of Francesco Cavalli', *Natalicia musicologica Knud Jeppesen* (Copenhagen, 1962), 173–98
——: 'Om den venezianske arie indtil 1650', *DAM*, iv (1964–5), 91–112
M. Chusid: 'The Organization of Scenes with Arias: Verdi's Cavatinas and Romanzas', *I° congresso internazionale di studi verdiani: Venice 1966*, 59–66
R. Celletti: 'Il vocalismo italiano da Rossini a Donizetti', *AnMc*, no.5 (1968), 267; no.7 (1969), 214–47
N. Pirrotta: 'Early Opera and Aria', *New Looks at Italian Opera: Essays in Honor of Donald J. Grout* (Ithaca, 1968), 39–107
S. Reiner: 'Vi sono molt'altre mezz'arie', *Studies in Music History: Essays for Oliver Strunk* (Princeton, 1968), 241–58
S. Döhring: 'Die Arienformen in Mozarts Opern', *MJb 1968–70*, 66–76
——: *Formgeschichte der Opernarie vom Ausgang des achtzehnten bis zur Mitte des neunzehnten Jahrhunderts* (Marburg, 1969)
F. Lippmann: 'Vincenzo Bellini und die italienische Opera seria seiner Zeit', *AnMc*, no.6 (1969), 1–104
E. Rosand: 'Aria as Drama in the Early Operas of Francesco Cavalli', *Venezia e il melodramma nel seicento: Venice 1972*, 75–96
F. Lippmann: 'Der italienische Vers und der musikalische Rhythmus: zum Verhältnis von Vers und Musik in der italienischen Oper des 19. Jahrhunderts, mit einem Rückblick auf die 2. Hälfte des 18. Jahrhunderts', *AnMc*, no.12 (1973), 253–369; no.14 (1974), 324–410; no.15 (1975), 298–33
S. Döhring: 'La forma dell'aria in Gaetano Donizetti', *CSD 1975*, 149–78
R. A. Moreen: *Integration of Text Forms and Musical Forms in Verdi's Early Operas* (diss., Princeton U., 1975)
R. Dalmonte: 'La canzone nel melodramma italiana del primo ottocento: ricerche di metodo strutturale', *RIM*, xi (1976), 230–312
E. Rosand: 'Comic Contrast and Dramatic Continuity: Observations on the Form and Function of Aria in the Operas of Francesco Cavalli', *MR*, xxvii (1976), 92–105
R. Strohm: *Italienische Opernarien des frühen Settecento (1720–1730), AnMc*, no.16 (1976)
F. L. Millner: *The Operas of Johann Adolf Hasse* (Ann Arbor, 1979)
M. McClymonds: *Niccolò Jommelli: the Last Years, 1769–1774* (Ann Arbor, 1980)
C. Rosen: *Sonata Forms* (New York, 1980)
R. S. Freeman: *Opera without Drama: Currents of Change in Italian Opera, 1675 to 1725* (Ann Arbor, 1981)
M. K. Hunter: *Haydn's Aria Forms: a Study of the Arias in the Operas Written at Eszterháza, 1766–1783* (Ann Arbor, 1982)
E. Weimer: *Opera Seria and the Evolution of Classical Style* (Ann Arbor, 1984)
S. L. Balthazar: 'Ritorni's *Ammaestramenti* and the Conventions of Rossinian Melodramma', *Journal of Musicological Research*, vii (1989–90), 281–311
A. B. Caswell, ed.: *Embellished Opera Arias* (Madison, 1989)
J. Platoff: 'The Buffa Aria in Mozart's Vienna', *COJ*, ii (1990), 99–120
M. F. Robinson: 'The Da Capo Aria Seria as Symbol of Rationality', *La musica come linguaggio universale*, ed. R. Pozzi (Florence, 1990), 51–63
G. Buschmeier: *Die Entwicklung von Arie und Szene in der französischen Oper von Gluck bis Spontini* (Tutzing, 1991)
J. Webster: 'The Analysis of Mozart's Arias', *Mozart Studies*, ed. C. Eisen (Oxford, 1991), 101–99

JACK WESTRUP (1), MARITA P. McCLYMONDS (2),
JULIAN BUDDEN (3), ANDREW CLEMENTS (4)
(with THOMAS WALKER, DANIEL HEARTZ, DENNIS LIBBY)

Ariadna. Opera by Martinů; *see* ARIANE (ii).

Ariadne. Libretto subject used chiefly during the 17th, 18th and 20th centuries (also as *Ariane* or *Arianna*). Its source is Greek mythology. Ariadne, daughter of Minos, king of Crete, fell in love with the Athenian hero Theseus, who came to Crete to slay the Minotaur, the monstrous offspring, half-bull, half-man, of Minos's wife Pasiphae; she helped him to escape the Labyrinth by providing him (in one version) with a ball of string that he unwound as he penetrated it, thus enabling him to find his way out. Ariadne accompanied Theseus to the island of Naxos, where he abandoned her. In some versions she dies of grief; in others she is rescued by the god Dionysus (Bacchus), whom she weds.

Most librettos about Ariadne deal with either the events on Crete or those on Naxos but not both. *Ariane*, by Catulle Mendès, set by Massenet (1906), is one of the few that follow Ariadne and Theseus from one island to the other and show both Theseus's victory over the Minotaur and his abandonment of Ariadne. Act 2 of this libretto, reminiscent of Act 1 of *Tristan*, takes place on a boat carrying Theseus and Ariadne from Crete to Naxos.

Of librettos about Ariadne on Crete the most important is that of Pietro Pariati, *Arianna e Teseo*, first performed with music by Porpora (1714) and reset by many composers, including Leo, Broschi, Sarti and Galuppi, throughout most of the 18th century. Handel's *Arianna in Creta* (1734) is the best-known setting of the text, which begins with the arrival in Crete, accompanied by Theseus, of Athenian youths to be sacrificed to the Minotaur. The story is enriched with new characters, the lovers Alceste [Alcestes] (a young man) and Carilda (an intended victim), and new subplots (Ariadne thinks that Theseus loves Carilda). The drama ends with Theseus's victory over the Minotaur and his reconciliation with Ariadne.

An interesting reinterpretation of the Cretan story transforms it into a penetrating psychological study: Martinů's one-act *Ariane* (1958), to a libretto by the composer after a play by Georges Neveux, *Le voyage de Thésée*. Here the Minotaur looks exactly like Theseus, who recognizes him as a part of his own personality. In killing the Minotaur, he kills his love for Ariadne; thus in his Cretan triumph the seeds are sown for his betrayal of her on Naxos.

This latter episode has proved even more attractive to librettists and composers than the Cretan story. It served for Ottavio Rinuccini's libretto *Arianna*, Monteverdi's setting of which (1608) is lost. This is a close study of emotional turmoil. As Ariadne sleeps Theseus painfully reaches his decision to leave her. She awakens; at first reassured by her confidante, she finally learns that Theseus has gone and expresses her grief in the great lament, the only part of the score to survive. Bacchus arrives in the fifth and final act and the opera ends with his wedding to Ariadne.

20th-century librettists and composers have tended to treat the episode on Naxos with a good deal of irony. In Hugo von Hofmannsthal's *Ariadne auf Naxos*, set by Richard Strauss (1912), the story is presented as an opera within a play, with comic and serious singers forced to perform together; the abandoned Ariadne is unmoved by the actors' attempts to cheer her. When Bacchus arrives Ariadne thinks that he is Death and welcomes him; in the final scene she rises with him into heaven, where the pleasures of love await her. Another lighthearted treatment is Milhaud's *L'abandon d'Ariane*, to a libretto by Henri Hoppenot (1927). This 'opéra-minute' in five scenes, which takes about 12 minutes to perform, is a comic mixture of myth and fantasy. Theseus, having abandoned Ariadne, now has second thoughts; but Dionysus, disguised as a blind beggar, gets him so drunk that he goes off with Ariadne's sister Phaedra instead, and Dionysus transforms Ariadne into a star.

See also ARIADNE AUF NAXOS (i) [Benda]; ARIADNE AUF NAXOS (ii) [Strauss]; ARIANE (i) [Cambert and Grabu]; ARIANE (ii) [Martinů]; ARIANNA [Monteverdi]; ARIANNA IN CRETA [Handel]; and ARIANNA IN NASSO [Porpora].

JOHN A. RICE

Ariadne auf Naxos (i) ('Ariadne on Naxos'). Duodrama (melodrama for two principal characters) in one act by Georg Benda (*see* BENDA family, (1)) to a text by JOHANN CHRISTIAN BRANDES after Heinrich Wilhelm von Gerstenberg's cantata of the same name; Gotha, Schloss Friedenstein, 27 January 1775.

Ariadne (spoken role), having fled from Crete with Theseus (spoken role), awakens on the desolate island of Naxos to learn that he has abandoned her. Feelings of disbelief, anger, grief and love swirl in her mind along with tender memories. A storm mounts and at its height she throws herself from a cliff into the sea.

In 1773 Brandes had given his text, written for his wife Charlotte, to Anton Schweitzer, whose setting remained incomplete; he gave the text to Benda in late 1774. The première marked the first use of historical costuming on the German stage (Duke Ernst II chose Charlotte's flowing robe). Benda's score, which at a stroke defined the German melodrama, swept triumphantly through Germany, and to France and Italy; its musical language, derived from obbligato recitative, includes much text painting, but there is also a firm consciousness of overall design. After Theseus's weak opening scene the music builds impressively to the catastrophe, where Ariadne speaks over, rather than between, the orchestra's utterances.

See also ARIADNE above. For illustration *see* MELODRAMA.

THOMAS BAUMAN

Ariadne auf Naxos (ii) ('Ariadne on Naxos'). *Oper* by RICHARD STRAUSS to a libretto by HUGO VON HOFMANNSTHAL, existing in two versions: '*Ariadne* I', in one act, to be played after a German version of MOLIÈRE's *Le bourgeois gentilhomme*, and '*Ariadne* II', in a prologue and one act; I, Stuttgart, Hoftheater (Kleines Haus), 25 October 1912, and II, Vienna, Hofoper, 4 October 1916.

In early 1911, while *Der Rosenkavalier* – the first wholly purpose-built collaboration between Hofmannsthal and Strauss – enjoyed its triumphant first performances, ideas for three new projects came to them. One was to thank Max Reinhardt for his productions of Wilde's *Salomé* and Hofmannsthal's *Elektra* (which had inspired Strauss's third and fourth operas), and unofficially of *Der Rosenkavalier* itself, by turning a Molière comedy into a German words-and-music piece for his Berlin company. Another was for a half-hour chamber-opera on the Ariadne myth, in which *commedia dell'arte* characters would collide with 18th-century operatic stereotypes, and the third was for a 'sombre' but 'fantastic' opera *Das steinerne Herz*, after a fairy-tale by Hauff. This last would grow into *Die*

PROLOGUE (II) AND OPERA (I, II)

The Prima Donna (later Ariadne)		soprano
The Tenor (later Bacchus)		tenor
Zerbinetta		coloratura soprano
Harlequin	*commedia dell'arte players*	baritone
Scaramuccio		tenor
Truffaldino		bass
Brighella		tenor

PROLOGUE (II)

The Composer	mezzo-soprano
His Music-Master	baritone
The Dancing-Master	tenor
A Wigmaker	baritone
A Footman	bass
An Officer	tenor
The Major-Domo	spoken

Servants

OPERA (I, II)

Naiad	*nymphs*	high soprano
Dryad		contralto
Echo		soprano

Setting A large, under-furnished room in the house of a rich man (originally Molière's 'bourgeois gentilhomme' Monsieur Jourdain, but in the revised version an unseen, nameless Viennese *parvenu*), in which later the opera-within-the-opera will be performed

Frau ohne Schatten; before that, however, the first two ideas coalesced into one project. The ironical-comical Ariadne miniature could serve as a closing *divertissement* for Molière's *Le bourgeois gentilhomme*, newly translated by Hofmannsthal, with room earlier in the play for scene music by Strauss. With Reinhardt's actors and with distinguished singers, it would make a gala performance.

As often during their partnership, the writer was more excited by his literary-dramatic idea than was Strauss by the prospect of composing it; but as usual, once the composer had warmed to his task the playing time stretched out far beyond their first intentions. For *Feuersnot* Strauss had already raided his 1900 sketches for *Die Insel Kythere*, a grand mock-Rococo ballet inspired by Watteau's *L'embarquement pour Cythère* – like Debussy's 1904 piano piece *L'isle joyeuse*, and later Poulenc; now he drew upon it again, with better historical excuse, for two of the dances in the play and a main tune of Ariadne's aria (at 'Bald aber naht ein Bote'). Meanwhile Hofmannsthal became fascinated with his heroine, and rather against the grain of the original plan – *opera seria* pretensions subverted by down-to-earth comics – he elaborated her metaphysical plight to the point where Strauss begged to have her lines explained. Her climactic duologue with Bacchus swelled to Wagnerian scale, taxing Strauss's 36-strong band proportionately. In turn, the composer was adamant about giving their wryly pragmatic, promiscuous Zerbinetta a huge coloratura scena to vie with the *Lucia di Lammermoor* Mad Scene. Eventually Molière was compressed into two acts, each with a prelude and other musical numbers, and *Ariadne auf Naxos* became a long Act 3.

With the composer conducting, Reinhardt duly produced this Molière-Hofmannsthal-Strauss confabulation as *Der Bürger als Edelmann*, with his own Berlin troupe and with Maria Jeritza as Ariadne, Margarethe Siems (Strauss's first Chrysothemis and Marschallin) as Zerbinetta and Hermann Jadlowker as Bacchus. It had a mixed reception: respectful reviews, but discomfited factions in the audience wanting either less of the spoken acts or less of the expansive operatic one. Though the work was soon staged in several other

1. 'Ariadne auf Naxos' (Richard Strauss): Maria Jeritza as Ariadne (left) and Margarethe Siems as Zerbinetta in the original production (with sets and costumes by Ernst Stern) which opened the Kleines Haus of the Hoftheater, Stuttgart, 25 October 1912; see also COSTUME, *fig.13*

cities, the cost of employing two different troupes was likely to discourage revivals. The authors soon agreed upon a salvage operation.

A shortened *Ariadne* – with alterations notably to Zerbinetta's brilliant rondo and to the final scene (described below) – would now follow a new, operatic prologue-act. This would re-create the circumstances of the opera-within-the-opera as in *Der Bürger*, omitting Molière's 'bourgeois gentilhomme', while of course retaining Hofmannsthal's new twist: the Master's absurd command that the *commedia dell'arte* and the lofty *opera seria* be played simultaneously, so as to end in time for his firework display. Freshly developed characters would lend human interest to this Prologue – the young Composer of the opera-within-the-opera, falling victim to Zerbinetta's wily coquetry, and his protective Music-Master. Though Hofmannsthal, who imagined the Composer as a mature youth, was appalled at his becoming a mezzo breeches-role like the *Rosenkavalier* Octavian, Strauss retorted that any opera company could field an intelligent mezzo – and besides, there were already three tenors in the piece. The sympathy he felt for the beleaguered young artist may explain the intricate score he wrote for the prologue, where Hofmannsthal had expected (and doubtless wanted) little more than *recitativo secco*.

The 1916 première of the operatic two-act revision, '*Ariadne* II', which had Jeritza once again, Selma Kurz as Zerbinetta, Béla Környei's Bacchus, Lotte Lehmann's Composer and Hans Duhan as both Harlequin and the Music-Master, has been the established version ever since. In it Maria Ivogün, Adele Kern, Rita Streich, Erika Köth and Edita Gruberová have been famous Zerbinettas; after Lehmann, Elisabeth Schumann and Sena Jurinac were much admired as the Composer, and Ariadne has been memorably sung by Lehmann and by Elisabeth Schwarzkopf. It may still be argued that the original, longer *Ariadne* deserves reinstatement, with the new prologue or the old play-with-music. But Strauss wasted nothing: he licensed a revised *Bürger als Edelmann* theatre score without *Ariadne* (besides the Act 1 overture and the Act 2 prelude it includes pictorial dinner-music, songs and dances, some adapted from Lully), and also an orchestral suite extracted from it. All these alternatives count as belonging to his 'op.60'.

PROLOGUE [*Ariadne* II only] The orchestral prelude in C, eager and volatile, shares only its key with the *Bürger als Edelmann* overture. The latter had begun with sturdy mock-Baroque music for strings and continuo (i.e. pianoforte, prominent in all versions of op.60) – which returned with the smug *gentilhomme* himself to put an end to *Ariadne* I, thus setting wry quotation marks around the entire affair. But with Monsieur Jourdain expunged from the new libretto, *Ariadne* II needed a fresh start and a different conclusion: the new prelude is a candidly romantic potpourri of the best tunes, the Composer's new ones along with Bacchus-and-Ariadne's old ones and the Comedians' ditties – and the 'new' close would simply extend the D♭ raptures of the blessed pair, instead of putting them ironically in their place.

The stage and backstage area in the house of a rich Viennese The curtain rises to show the reverse side of a stage backcloth: anxious preparations for the rich man's post-prandial entertainment are under way. An overweening Major-Domo is telling the outraged Music-Master that immediately after *Ariadne*, his beloved pupil's *opera seria*, a vulgar *opera buffa* will be performed before the nine o'clock fireworks. As an officer thrusts his way into the dressing-room of Zerbinetta, star of the *commedia*, the young Composer arrives in hope of a last-moment rehearsal and hears the bad news. The Dancing-Master comments cynically, and the self-absorbed principals of both troupes preen and fret. The Major-Domo reappears with worse news still: to safeguard the timetable – and also to enliven the desert-isle *Ariadne* scene, which the Master thinks too mean for his status as grandee-host – he wants their shows played 'gleichzeitig', at the same time. That will involve severe cuts.

General horror soon gives way to canny professional reactions. Only the naive Composer tries to make a defiant stand. His guardian knows too well what the career cost of an angry withdrawal might be, and the Dancing-Master backs him up. The Ariadne-soprano and the Bacchus-tenor treacherously urge cuts in each other's roles. Zerbinetta sets out to extract the details of the *opera seria* from its author, charming him into compliance while calculating where her comedians can best intervene. She is at least intrigued, though not remotely persuaded, by the impassioned metaphysical gloss he puts on the story. Ariadne, who gave Theseus the clue to the Labyrinth, is the archetype of a one-man woman. After Theseus abandons her on Naxos (never in fact a 'desert' island: it is the most fertile of the Cyclades) she abandons herself to Death, for whom later she happily mistakes the young god Bacchus, and is thereby 'transformed' and eternally fulfilled.

Until here, the music has been nervy, suggestive, bitty – unless in the hands of an *echt*-Straussian conductor who can make it seem a continuous web. As Zerbinetta teases the Composer tenderly, their duologue expands into a rapt E major idyll, if not quite a love duet. It is stopped abruptly by the order for curtain-rise. Still captivated and exalted, the Composer improvises a paean to the holy art of music ('Musik ist eine heilige Kunst'); then the clowns prance in, and he realizes too late the compromise he has been distracted into accepting. While he rushes away in despair, the prologue ends with his motif arrested by a stern C minor cadence – but the show goes on.

THE OPERA ('Ariadne auf Naxos') There is a winding, melancholy overture in G minor, with an Allegro of dismay and alarm just before the curtain of the stage-within-the-stage rises. Ariadne is prostrate before her rocky cave. Three Nymphs lament her inconsolable state, but their trio slips into light, flowing G major – Mozart's Three Ladies are not far off – as they admit that her ceaseless moaning has become as familiar to them as the lapping waves on the shore. Now she cries aloud, soullessly echoed by Echo, and tries to recapture a lost dream. (Until now Strauss's harmonium has been only a discreet sustaining instrument, but from here he entrusts specially plangent harmonies to its dusky tones.) From the wings the Comedians watch her with concern, doubting whether they can possibly cheer her up. Dimly she recalls something beautiful that used to be called Theseus-Ariadne ('Ein Schönes war'); then, transported from E♭ to softly radiant G♭ and back, she imagines herself a chaste maiden, calmly awaiting a pure death. The Comedians find her dementia deeply affecting. Zerbinetta urges Harlequin, the romantic baritone of the company, to try a philosophical little song, which

2. *'Ariadne auf Naxos' (Richard Strauss); scene from the original production of the second version (Hofoper, Vienna, 4 October 1916), with (left to right) Julius Betetto (Truffaldino), Hermann Gallos (Scaramuccio), Maria Jeritza (Ariadne, in the background), Selma Kurz (Zerbinetta), Hans Duhan (Harlequin) and Georg Moisel (Brighella)*

he does ('Lieben, hassen') to salon-style piano. Like Pedrillo's serenade in Mozart's *Entführung* it has odd sideslips of harmony, and a touching gravity disproportionate to its span.

Ariadne ignores him, and returns to her visionary G♭ for 'Es gibt ein Reich': only in the realm of the Dead is everything pure, and soon Hermes will summon her there to self-forgetting freedom (lyric ecstasy in B♭). This is altogether too morbid for the Comedians, who burst in with a buoyant, rackety song-and-dance number, a *Biergarten* quartet with descant by Zerbinetta. When it fails to have any therapeutic effect she sends them off, and addresses Ariadne ('Grossmächtige Prinzessin!') confidentially, woman-to-woman: do we not *all* want each lover to be once-and-forever? and surely we get over it in time for the irresistible next one to come along? She cites her own erotic adventures as confirmation. This is her monster coloratura showpiece – glittering recitatives, a pair of delectable ariettas and a spectacular rondo with variations and competing flute. In *Ariadne* I the central sections are in E, with top F♯; for *Ariadne* II not only did Strauss prudently lower their pitch by a whole tone, but he abbreviated the first arietta, erased the central cadenza and wrote an entirely new coda. In either version the showpiece is much more than a virtuoso exercise: besides the disarmingly winsome tunes, all the roulades and trills – as the best Zerbinettas know – can have the force of witty, self-mocking gestures.

During this performance Ariadne has withdrawn into her cave, refusing to hear. (Understandable, but damaging to the original plan: since the confronting sopranos simply deliver their lengthy main effusions one after the other, the intended comic friction between genres – and human types – dwindles to mere alternation.) Zerbinetta's monologue is followed and completed by the Comedians' principal scene, in which each privately seeks her favours but only Harlequin wins them. This stylized vaudeville builds to a lusty quick-waltz climax in D, whereupon they all disperse.

Suddenly, with C♯ fanfares, the excited Nymphs announce the arrival of 'Bacchus' – more correctly the 'Dionysus' of ancient Greek cults, not the merely bibulous Roman god – on a ship, and while awaiting him they recount the supernatural events of his young life. From afar his heroic tenor is heard, exulting over his escape from the witch-seductress Circe (it was his first affair). Ariadne, who expects a messenger of Death, is strangely stirred, and the Nymphs answer his defiant song with a melting lullaby. (In *Ariadne* I naughty Zerbinetta reappears here, bringing the music down to earth in C major as she rhapsodizes over the handsome intruder – 'What a man!' – for Ariadne's benefit; but Strauss chose to excise that passage, and also the following orchestral one which illustrated the hero's striding advent.)

In *Ariadne* II, just eight bars of ascending white-note chords bring him on. Startled, Ariadne takes him momentarily for Theseus, but then welcomes him more calmly (in B♭) as the ordained messenger. They are both bemused. Bacchus explains that he is a god; during a long duet of high-flown intensity, with intermittent support from the invisible trio of nymphs, she gives herself up to the heaven-sent stranger. The rocky island disappears, a baldachin descends from a starry sky to enfold them, and (in this version) Zerbinetta appears briefly during an orchestral interlude to whisper again: 'When the new god comes, we surrender dumbly'. The lovers' entwined voices rise to an epiphany in D♭ with a fervent peroration by Bacchus, and the orchestra reiterates it in pompous *fortissimo* before shimmering away into silence. (*Ariadne* I was better ordered:

Zerbinetta returned immediately *after* the duet, pulling the music cheerily back into D major, and the Comedians danced on to join her in a reprise of their chorus, 'That a heart should so fail to understand itself!' Upon their jocular exit, amid light scatter-shot chords, Monsieur Jourdain reappeared blinking in C major, puzzled to find that all his guests had slipped away. A quick coda recalled the *Bürger als Edelmann* overture, and concluded the whole piece in its original mischievous terms.)

* * *

First conceived as a little number opera, *Ariadne* offered Strauss no scope for the lyric interplay he had perfected in *Der Rosenkavalier*. Instead he relished composing the contrasted numbers, unlike almost everything in his previous operatic successes, and drawing brave effects from his unaccustomedly modest band (some of their calculated, off-colour appeal is lost when a large opera house deploys extra strings). If, as Stravinsky complained, the 'serious' music trades continually on the pathos of 6–4 chordal harmony, the Bavarian music-hall numbers set it in ironic focus – at least in *Ariadne* I. The inflated close of *Ariadne* II flatters neither the romantic element nor the original point of the piece. Though the *opera seria*, despite its meagre action and Hofmannsthal's overwrought poesy, now seems meant to win, it does not persuade: not because of any intrinsic weakness, but because the very terms of the entertainment undermine it. Probably Strauss should bear the blame for the first fatal step. His insistence on an extravagant, period-pastiche tour de force for Zerbinetta incurred a matching solo scena for Ariadne, leaving too little room for comic dissonance between their troupes. Yet the divided spirit of the piece is beautifully captured in the score; the task of bringing it to theatrical life remains a challenge for a producer. It would be an easier task if the *Ariadne* I conclusion could be adapted to the purpose, putting inverted commas around the *opera seria* apotheosis instead of succumbing to it.

See also ARIADNE above.

DAVID MURRAY

Ariane (i) [*Ariane, ou Le mariage de Bacchus* ('Ariadne, or The Marriage of Bacchus')]. *Opéra* in a prologue and five acts by ROBERT CAMBERT and LUIS GRABU to a libretto by PIERRE PERRIN; London, Theatre Royal, Drury Lane, 30 March 1674.

In Perrin's libretto the story of Bacchus's wooing of Ariadne on Naxos is complicated by the unsuccessful attempts by Mars, god of war, and Silene [Silenus], Bacchus's foster-parent, to dissuade him from subordinating war and wine to love.

The work originated as a simple *comédie en musique*, written by Perrin and Cambert in 1659 at the time of the wedding of Louis XIV but never formally performed. In about 1671–2 Perrin revised and enlarged the libretto, using a bigger cast, more complex plot, *corps de ballet* and spectacular machine effects; but the opera remained unperformed until 1674, when a troupe of French players visited London and, under Grabu's direction, inaugurated Charles II's Royal Academy of Musick with *Ariane* (in French). The text for a new, allegorical prologue was added in London, possibly by Sébastien Brémond; it celebrated the recent marriage (1673) of James, Duke of York, and Mary of Modena and rendered topical the opera's story. Librettos in French and English were produced by Thomas Newcomb, the royal printer; they carried a long dedication to the king, extolling England's political and strategic prowess. The whole venture was thus seen to be highly royalist and, as a result of anti-Catholic and anti-royalist feelings, not well received and consequently short-lived. No music survives; although it is unclear whether Cambert had revised the score by the time he left Paris in 1673, the

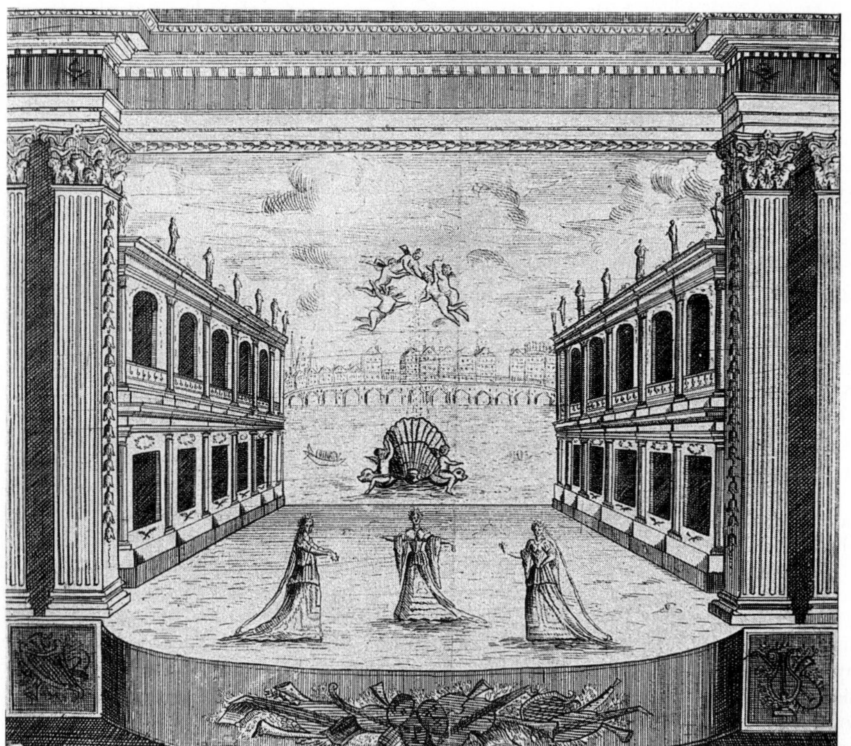

Design for the prologue of Cambert and Grabu's 'Ariane, ou Le mariage de Bacchus' showing London and the River Thames with three nymphs representing the Thames, Tiber and Seine: engraving from the libretto (London, 1674)

librettos indicate that Grabu wrote at least some of the extra music.

See also ARIADNE above. CHRISTINA BASHFORD

Ariane (ii) [*Ariadna*] ('Ariadne'). Opera in one act (three tableaux) by BOHUSLAV MARTINŮ to his own libretto after Georges Neveux's play *Le voyage de hésée*; Gelsenkirchen, 2 March 1961.

A significant factor determining the style and nature of this opera was Martinů's admiration for the singing of Maria Callas, accounting for the bravura writing in the part of Ariadne (soprano). For his text Martinů returned to the author of the play on which he had based *Julietta*; and he had already used some lines from *Le voyage de Thésée* to preface the third of his orchestral *Paraboly* (1958). With the author's permission, Martinů took passages from the second, third and fourth acts of the play.

After a sinfonia – the first of three in the opera – and a prologue in which a Watchman (bass) records the safe return of Theseus (baritone), the first Tableau deals with the arrival of the Athenians at Knossos. Theseus and Ariadne meet and fall in love. Ariadne fears that the Minotaur (bass) will kill him and, as evening falls, she senses the monster's presence. The climax of the Tableau comes not with the appearance of the Minotaur, but the announcement that the king's daughter, Ariadne, will marry the stranger, Theseus. The second Tableau presents Theseus's encounter with the Minotaur. Knowing that no man would willingly kill his double, the Minotaur takes on Theseus's shape. Theseus recognizes the Minotaur as the image of himself which enjoyed the bliss of a wedding night with Ariadne, and it is this which he kills. The third Tableau sees the departure of Theseus followed by a long aria of farewell ('Thésée, je respire une dernière fois') from Ariadne.

Completed in summer 1958, *Ariane* shares the warm, mainly tonal lyricism cultivated so successfully by Martinů in the last decade of his life. Characteristically flexible vocal writing is on occasion enlivened by neo-Baroque rhythmic patterns and in the cabaletta-like fast sections of Ariadne's farewell coloratura.

See also ARIADNE above. JAN SMACZNY

Ariane et Barbe-bleue ('Ariane and Bluebeard'). Tale in three acts by PAUL DUKAS to a libretto by MAURICE MAETERLINCK after Charles Perrault; Paris, Opéra-Comique (Salle Favart), 10 May 1907.

Barbe-bleue [Bluebeard]		bass
Ariane		mezzo-soprano
The Nurse		contralto
Sélysette	*Bluebeard's former wives*	mezzo-soprano
Ygraine	*Bluebeard's former wives*	soprano
Mélisande	*Bluebeard's former wives*	soprano
Bellangère	*Bluebeard's former wives*	soprano
Alladine	*Bluebeard's former wives*	mime
An Old Peasant		bass
Second Peasant		tenor
Third Peasant		bass

Peasants

Setting Bluebeard's castle

Maeterlinck's many-sided, symbolic libretto (originally considered and rejected by Grieg) was written for his companion Georgette Leblanc, actress and singer. He claimed that it was based on actual experiences of hers. With typical Maeterlinckian ambiguity, questions are posed but not answered. We know by the end that the former wives are still attracted to their torturer and that they have refused Ariane's offer of liberty. Bluebeard's power is broken but uncertainty remains. In spite of her composure Ariane has achieved little except, as Dukas suggested (in a note published in 1936 in the special Dukas number – no.166 – of the *Revue musicale* also containing a valuable study of *Ariane* by Olivier Messiaen), the possibility of liberating herself. *Ariane*, completed in 1906 after seven years' work, won and has retained the high regard of musicians and particularly composers, including Schoenberg, Berg and Messiaen. Yet though it is one of the foremost examples of the abundantly productive post-Wagnerian phase in French opera it has never gained popular success. Even in Paris productions have been infrequent (one of them was brought to London for two performances at Covent Garden during the 1937 season). The complex principal role requires a singer of strong personality, vocal stamina and impeccable declamation (notable interpreters have included Suzanne Balguerie and Germaine Lubin; for an illustration of Lubin in the role, *see* LUBIN, GERMAINE).

ACT 1 Through the windows of the great hall can be heard the cries of peasants attempting to rescue Ariane, whom Bluebeard is bringing home as his sixth wife. Accompanied by her nurse, Ariane appears. She does not believe the rumours that her five predecessors are dead. Bluebeard has given her seven keys, six silver ones for the silver-locked doors beneath the six windows, and a golden one for the seventh, forbidden, and so far invisible door on which Ariane's curiosity is concentrated. She knows that the six doors conceal Bluebeard's hoard of jewels, and since these do not interest her she allows the nurse to open them one by one. Out of the alcoves tumble successive cascades of amethysts, sapphires, pearls, emeralds and rubies and finally a cataract of diamonds so overpoweringly brilliant that Ariane is momentarily distracted until, at the back of the alcove, she notices the golden lock of the forbidden seventh door. To the nurse's alarm she turns the key. Out of the darkness come the voices, faint at first but gradually filling the hall, of the former wives, singing of the five daughters of Orlamonde searching for daylight and finding only a closed door which they fear to open. As the song reaches its climax, Bluebeard enters. 'You too?', he asks Ariane. 'I, above all', she answers. He tries to seize her. She cries out, and as they struggle, shouts are heard outside. The nurse opens the central door to reveal the peasants massed on the threshold. Ariane calmly tells them: 'He has done me no harm'. They go. Bluebeard ruefully contemplates his drawn sword.

ACT 2 Ariane and the unwilling nurse have made their way past the seventh door, down to a vaulted subterranean chamber where there is no light except for Ariane's lamp. She discovers a group of motionless figures huddled together. The lamp reveals the five former wives, haggard, blinking, their clothes in rags. Shyly they begin to talk about their imprisonment. As she moves her hands over the wall at the back, Ariane feels huge shutters, bolted and barred. When she prises them open there is a faint glimmer, but when she breaks a pane of glass with a stone, a ray of bright light shines through. As she shatters more panes, the light becomes blinding. Urged on by Ariane, the women climb up to the broken window and gaze enraptured at countryside and sea. Midday strikes. Dancing with joy, they follow Ariane into the sunlight.

ACT 3 In the great hall the alcove doors are still open. In Bluebeard's absence Ariane encourages her 'sisters' to prepare for their approaching freedom by adorning themselves with the jewels. The nurse appears in distress to announce the return of Bluebeard. From the gallery beneath the open windows the wives describe how Bluebeard's coach is attacked by the peasants, armed with scythes and pitchforks. They haul him out, bind him and drag him towards the castle. Ariane opens the central door. Awed by her presence, the insurgents carry in their bound master. Ariane thanks them and closes the door. Bluebeard's wounds are bleeding. The wives gather round to tend him; one of them furtively kisses him. Ariane calls for a dagger to cut the cords. Bluebeard rises slowly, looks at each wife in turn and then fixes his gaze on Ariane, who holds out her hand in a gesture of farewell. Informing the wives that she is going far away where there is work for her to do, she asks if they will follow her. Not one accepts. Ariane and the nurse leave the castle. The women look at one another, then at Bluebeard.

* * *

Formally *Ariane* is carefully considered. Act 1 has a sequence of appropriately brilliant variations for the discovery of the jewels and an unusual *coup de théâtre* in the swelling offstage song of the daughters of Orlamonde (a folktune also used by d'Indy in his Second Symphony), a theme much heard subsequently. The second act contains another, longer, more elaborate crescendo in the gradual progression, as Ariane discovers and then breaks the barred window, from darkness to light (C major against the prevailing tonalities of F♯ minor and major). Act 3, after a mournful prelude implying that the offer of liberation is a failure before it has been made, is a free recapitulation of the first, reflecting the jewel variations (which Dukas had left short enough – with the exception of the extended diamond section – to allow further development), the offstage revolt of the peasants and the return of Bluebeard, this time as a silent captive. The strong framework is matched with musical craftsmanship of outstanding excellence. The orchestration, polished to a luminosity surpassing Rimsky-Korsakov, has a sombre glow beneath the enamelled surface. Nothing illustrates Dukas' independent position better than the contrast between *Ariane* and *Pelléas*. There is enough in common in the two musical styles, for instance in the use of the whole-tone scale, for brief quotations identifying Mélisande to sound perfectly natural, but the more deliberate dramatic pace, the less soloistic writing and generally richer, more solid sonorities are essentially different.

RONALD CRICHTON

Arianna ('Ariadne'). *Tragedia* in one act by CLAUDIO MONTEVERDI to a libretto by OTTAVIO RINUCCINI; Mantua, ducal palace, 28 May 1608.

Arianna was written for the celebrations following the marriage of Francesco Gonzaga, elder son of the Duke of Mantua, to Margherita, daughter of the Duke of Savoy. Monteverdi probably received the libretto in October 1607, and it was originally intended that the opera should be performed towards the end of Carnival (that is, before 18 February) 1608. The title role was to have been taken by Caterina Martinelli, a young singer trained under Monteverdi's supervision. In the event the Gonzagas' original intentions proved impossible to realize. Arrangements for the marriage were beset by political problems, causing the celebrations to be delayed until after Lent, and on 7 March 1608 Caterina Martinelli died of smallpox. Her place was taken by Virginia Andreini, one of a company of actors called to Mantua for the celebrations, and the opera was finally given on 28 May in a temporary theatre constructed for the purpose within the ducal palace. The role of Theseus was taken by Francesco Rasi. According to Federico Follino, chronicler of the occasion, the performance lasted two and a half hours and was played before an audience of several thousand people.

The single set for the opera represented a rocky island washed by the movement of the sea; the instrumentalists were placed behind the scenes. Apollo descended in a cloud and sang the prologue in which he paid compliments to the bride and introduced the action to follow. He was succeeded on stage by Venere [Venus] and Amore [Cupid] who provide what is essentially a second introduction to the opera. Venus reveals that Ariadne will that day be abandoned on the island by Teseo [Theseus] but that soon afterwards the god Bacco [Bacchus] will arrive. Cupid is to inflame Bacchus and Ariadne with mutual desire. As they see Theseus's ship approaching, Venus exits, but Cupid remains, invisible, to watch the new arrivals. Theseus and Ariadne, journeying to Athens after Theseus's triumph over the Minotaur, disembark on the island to rest. They are greeted by a chorus of fishermen, who first celebrate Theseus's triumph and then, at the end of the scene, celebrate the advent of night. While Ariadne sleeps, Theseus's counsellor advises him to abandon her and return alone to Athens; a messenger announces that the ships are prepared, and the three leave.

The chorus announces the dawn. Ariadne enters with her confidante Dorilla. She cannot find Theseus. Dorilla tries to reassure her, and the chorus join in, though half in pity. Ariadne and Dorilla leave for the seashore, and the chorus are left to reflect on what they have seen. A messenger describes to the chorus the departure of Theseus's ships and Ariadne's anguished cries as she discovers that she has been deserted. Ariadne enters and sings the lament which formed the main focus of the opera. Its first four sections are each followed by short choral responses. In the five sections of the lament which follow, Ariadne continues to lament her loss, while Dorilla at first sympathizes and then, as she sees ships approaching, tries to rouse Ariadne. They leave, and the scene ends with a chorus. (According to the Modenese ambassador to Mantua, writing the day after the performance, the lament was accompanied by viols and violins. This may, however, mean no more than that they played between the sections of the lament.) Tirsi [Thyrsis] announces that it is not Theseus who is returning but a new husband for Ariadne. He tells of Bacchus's arrival and his wooing of Ariadne. Bacchus, Ariadne and Cupid enter, accompanied by Bacchus's soldiers, some of whom perform a dance while the others join in the exchanges of the choral finale. Cupid and Ariadne sing of her love for Bacchus. They are joined by Venus, who rises from the sea, and Jove, who is revealed in the heavens. Jove invites the couple to take their seat above the stars, and the opera ends as Bacchus foresees the happy years that Ariadne will enjoy among the gods.

In the first instance Rinuccini probably constructed his text as a continuous action shaped into a prologue and five scenes, each ending with a formal chorus, corresponding to the structure of a classical tragedy. At a meeting on 26 February 1608, however, the Duchess of Mantua pronounced the opera as it stood 'very dry' and required Rinuccini to provide additional material (probably the initial dialogue between Venus and Cupid, and elements of the spectacular finale).

Several copies of the score of *Arianna* were made during Monteverdi's lifetime, the last probably for a performance of the opera at the Teatro S Moisè, Venice, during Carnival 1640; none of these has yet come to light. Ariadne's lament has, however, survived in several printed and manuscript versions. Monteverdi himself made a five-part arrangement of the first four sections in 1610 and published it in his sixth book of madrigals (1614); he issued the first five sections of the lament for solo voice at Venice in 1623, and in the same year these were also published at Orvieto in Giovanni Battista Rocchigiani's anthology *Il maggio fiorito*. Manuscript copies of the version for solo voice survive; some include all nine sections of Ariadne's speech in the lament scene, but none supplies the responses of the chorus and of Ariadne's confidante Dorilla which appear in Rinuccini's libretto. Monteverdi published a sacred contrafactum of the first four sections of the lament for solo voice – the *Pianto della Madonna* – in his *Selva morale e spirituale* (Venice, 1640). The lament in *Arianna* is different in kind from the laments in Monteverdi's *Orfeo*, both in its length and in the fact that the repetition structures that Monteverdi uses are fully supported by Rinuccini's text. It seems to have provided a model during the first third of the 17th century for other operatic laments and for independent lament settings found in manuscript and published song collections.

See also ARIADNE above. JOHN WHENHAM

Arianna in Creta ('Ariadne in Crete'). Opera in three acts by GEORGE FRIDERIC HANDEL to a libretto anonymously adapted from PIETRO PARIATI's *Teseo in Creta* (1715) as revised for Naples (1721) and Rome (1729); London, King's Theatre, 26 January 1734.

Handel completed the score of *Arianna in Creta* on 5 October 1733. It was his only new opera of his 1733–4 season at the King's Theatre, and the subject may have been deliberately chosen to complement Porpora's *Arianna in Nasso* at Lincoln's Inn Fields, the first production of the newly-formed 'Opera of the Nobility'. The libretto elaborates the mythical tale of Theseus's visit to Crete and his slaying of the Minotaur with the help of Ariadne, daughter (though she is unaware of it) of King Minos; there is a subplot involving Ariadne's jealousy when Theseus champions Carilda, the intended first victim of the Minotaur, who herself secretly loves Theseus but is loved by Alcestes, Theseus's friend, and more violently courted by Tauris, captain of Minos's guards. The mezzo-soprano castratos Giovanni Carestini and Carlo Scalzi sang the roles of Teseo [Theseus] and Theseus's friend Alceste [Alcestes]; the other singers were Anna Maria Strada del Pò as Ariadne (soprano), Margherita Durastanti (Handel's old colleague from his time in Italy) as the Cretan general Tauride [Tauris] (mezzo-soprano), Maria Caterina Negri as the Athenian maiden Carilda (contralto) and Gustavus Waltz as King Minos (bass). Waltz probably also sang the small part of Sonno [Somnus], God of Sleep. *Arianna* had a continuous run of 14 performances up to 12 March, and two more on 16 and 20 April. Handel revived the opera on 27 November 1734, in his first season at Covent Garden, when dances were added for Marie Sallé and her company, the roles of Alcestes and Carilda were adapted for tenor (John Beard) and soprano (Maria Rosa Negri), and the role of Tauris was transferred to Maria Caterina Negri (for whom a new aria was inserted). There were revivals at Brunswick in August 1737 and February 1738, after which the opera remained unheard until the first modern revival, at Göttingen on 30 June 1946, in an arrangement by Fritz Lehmann. The first British revival was at the Unicorn Theatre, Abingdon, on 6 September 1974.

In *Arianna*, Handel took care to respond to the talents of Carestini, his new leading castrato, and much of the best music is found in the part of Theseus; it includes the beautiful E major aria in Act 1 ('Sdegnata sei con me') in which Theseus assures Ariadne of his love, two fine accompanied recitatives (the sleep scene in Act 2 and the entrance into the labyrinth in Act 3) and several examples of virtuoso writing of which the aria of Theseus' challenge to the Minotaur ('Qui ti sfido') is the most exciting (the final ritornello is extended to cover the combat). His final aria 'Bella sorge', which continues into the final *coro*, has great melodic grace. Alcestes has a reflective aria with cello obbligato ('Son qual stanco pellegrino') and Tauris a brilliant one with horns ('Qual leon'). The female roles, unusually, are less compelling, perhaps because the women are not in sufficiently strong dramatic situations. The minuet of the overture achieved early popularity as the 'Minuet in Ariadne' and remains the opera's most famous number.

See also ARIADNE above. ANTHONY HICKS

Arianna in Nasso ('Ariadne in Naxos'). *Dramma per musica* in three acts by NICOLA PORPORA to a libretto by PAOLO ANTONIO ROLLI; London, Lincoln's Inn Fields, 29 December 1733.

The action takes place on the island of Naxos where the lovers Teseo [Theseus] (alto castrato) and Ariadne (soprano), forced ashore by a storm, come into contact with Theseus's wife Antiope (soprano), with the god Libero [Dionysus] (contralto), in the guise of his high priest Onoro, who loves Ariadne, and with Piritoo (bass), who becomes friendly with Theseus and acts as his accomplice. By the use of various threats, Dionysus persuades Theseus to leave Naxos with his wife rather than with Ariadne. He then discloses his true identity to Ariadne and successfully woos her.

Arianna in Nasso was the first of five operas composed by Porpora during his stay in London (1733–6) as musical director of the Opera of the Nobility company, set up in 1733 in competition with Handel and the Royal Academy of Music. The cast of the first production included several singers who had forsaken Handel's company to join Porpora's: the alto castrato Senesino (in the role of Theseus), the soprano Celeste Hempson (Antiope), the contralto Francesca Bertolli (Dionysus), and the bass Antonio Montagnana (Piritoo) [Piritous]. The soprano Maria Segatti sang the title role but was later replaced by Francesca Cuzzoni. Intended for English audiences, *Arianna in Nasso* has a simpler plot and greater musical diversity than is common in Porpora's earlier operas written for Italy or Austria (*see* SEMIRAMIDE RICONOSCIUTA). The proportion of accompanied to simple recitatives and of short arietta to da capo arias is higher than usual and contributes greatly to the variety of musical characterization.

See also ARIADNE above. MICHAEL F. ROBINSON

Ariarate. *Opera seria* in three acts by ANGELO TARCHI to a libretto by FERDINANDO MORETTI; Milan, Teatro alla Scala, January 1786.

Ariarate (soprano castrato), true heir to the throne of Cappadocia, has been reared as Eumene by Attalo [Attalus] (tenor), King of Pergamum and father of Stratonica (soprano), Ariarate's betrothed. Orossene (contralto castrato), usurper of the Cappadocian throne, is betrothed to Laodice (soprano), but wishes to put her aside in favour of Stratonica. By trickery, Orossene learns of Eumene's true identity. He takes Ariarate and Attalus prisoner and forces Stratonica to choose who will be put to death. When Laodice's supporters take the city, they are saved, and Orossene's powers are broken.

Tarchi's most successful opera in terms of the number of revivals, *Ariarate* is outstanding for the beauty and drama of its music and the suspense of its plot. It is a traditional 'aria' opera with a duet and a quartet at the close of Acts 1 and 2. The formally innovatory quartet dispenses with the usual initial quatrains for each participant, replacing them with short-breathed statements that spring dramatically from the dynamics of the action. MARITA P. McCLYMONDS

Ariè [Arie], **Raffaele** [Rafael, Raphael] (*b* Sofia, 22 Aug 1922; *d* Switzerland, 17 March 1988). Bulgarian bass. He studied the violin in Sofia, then turned to singing, making a concert début in 1939. He joined the National Opera in Sofia in 1945, and the next year won first prize in the Geneva International Competition. This led to further studies in Italy with Riccardo Stracciari, Apollo Granforte and Carlo Tagliabue, and to his début at La Scala as the King in *The Love for Three Oranges*. At Venice in 1951 he created Trulove in *The Rake's Progress*, and after appearing as the Commendatore at the Salzburg Festival in 1953 he developed a career in Europe and America. He recorded Raimondo (*Lucia*) with Callas. His deep, easily produced and fine-textured voice came to be widely admired in the role of Boris and other bass parts of the Russian and Italian repertories.

NOËL GOODWIN

Arienzo, Marco d'. *See* D'ARIENZO, MARCO.

Arienzo, Nicola d'. *See* D'ARIENZO, NICOLA.

Arietta (It., diminutive of *aria*). A term usually applied to vocal chamber music, but occasionally to be found in opera for a small-scale aria. Examples are Mozart's 'Voi, che sapete' (*Le nozze di Figaro*, 1786) and Rossini's 'Quando mi sei vicina' (*Il barbiere di Siviglia*, 1816), both of which could more precisely have been described as *canzoni* or *canzonette*, and Verdi's 'A buon mercato' (*La forza del destino*, 1862). JULIAN BUDDEN

Ariette (Fr., from It. *arietta*, diminutive of aria). In French 18th-century opera, *opéra-ballet* and *opéra comique*, *ariette* denotes two different types of vocal solo. In the works of Campra, Rameau and their contemporaries, it is a substantial da capo piece, much longer than an *air*, in italianate style and at a lively tempo. The melodic writing is florid, challenging the virtuosity of the singer; the orchestra frequently has a prominent role. Conventionally, *ariettes* were placed in *divertissements* for, as expressions of joy or triumph, they did not advance the dramatic action. 'Règne, Amour, fais briller tes flammes' from Rameau's *Pygmalion*, with its lengthy melismas on 'règne' (reign), 'briller' (shine), 'lance' (hurl), is an excellent example. By the late 18th' century *grand air*, or simply *air*, came to be the preferred designation for its successor (in *A-B-A'* form), but occasionally *ariette* was used, as in Méhul's 'Quand le guerrier vole aux combats' (*Euphrosine*, 1790).

In *opéras comiques* from the mid-century, *ariettes* are short pieces in strophic or other simple forms where a tuneful melody dominates and the orchestra generally provides a basic accompaniment. Tempo, mood and subject matter vary greatly. They appear as 'set' songs (i.e. where the dialogue includes reference to the actual fact of performance, such as singing for the entertainment of those on stage) and as expressions of emotion or illustrations of character. They are frequent in the scores of Egidio Duni, Philidor, Grétry and others, as the contemporary term for the genre, *comédie mêlée d'ariettes*, suggests. During the Revolution *ariettes* are still occasionally found. By the 19th century short pieces in French opera came to be called *romances*, *chansons* or *airs*.

*

J.-J. Rousseau: *Lettre sur la musique française* (Paris, 1753, 2/1753); Eng. trans., abridged, in O. Strunk, ed.: *Source Readings in Music History* (New York, 1950)

P. J. B. Nougaret: *De l'art du théâtre*, ii (Paris, 1769)

J. J. O. de Meude-Monpas: *Dictionnaire de musique* (Paris, 1787)

N. E. Framery, P. L. Ginguené and [for vol.ii] J.-J. de Momigny: *Encyclopédie méthodique: musique* (Paris, 1791–1818)

Castil-Blaze [F. H. J. Blaze]: *Dictionnaire de musique moderne* (Paris, 1821, 2/1825) M. ELIZABETH C. BARTLET

Arigoni, Giovanni Giacomo. *See* ARRIGONI, GIOVANNI GIACOMO.

Arimondi, Vittorio (*b* Saluzzo, 3 June 1861; *d* Chicago, 15 April 1928). Italian bass. Gifted with a commanding stage presence and a sonorous voice, he studied singing while training for business. After his début at Varese in Gomes's *Il Guarany* in 1883 he sang in the provinces, going to La Scala in 1893, first as Sparafucile in *Rigoletto* and then as Pistol in the première of *Falstaff*. His international career dates from 1894, when he sang Don Basilio to Patti's Rosina at Covent Garden, with a New York début at the Metropolitan in 1896. From 1905 he spent most of his time in the USA, having sung in Russia, Poland and Austria. He joined Hammerstein's Manhattan Opera Company, singing Arkel in the American première of *Pelléas et Mélisande*, and at the Metropolitan appeared as Nero, originally a tenor role, in Nouguès's *Quo vadis?*. His greatest personal success remained Méphistophélès in *Faust*. He joined the Chicago Opera Company in 1910 and later taught at the Chicago Music College. His few recordings suggest a voice more remarkable for bulk than beauty, though he was described in his prime as a graceful singer.

J. B. STEANE

Ariodant [*Ina*]. *Drame mêlé de musique* in three acts by ETIENNE-NICOLAS MÉHUL to a libretto by FRANÇOIS-BENOÎT HOFFMAN after LUDOVICO ARIOSTO's poem *Orlando furioso* (cantos v–vi); Paris, Opéra-Comique (Salle Favart), 11 October 1799.

Ina (soprano), a princess at the Scottish court, becomes betrothed to Ariodant (*haute-contre*). Othon (*haute-contre*/tenor), spurned earlier by the heroine, challenges Ariodant to a duel over her, and they arrange to meet that night. Meanwhile, at the *fête* given by her father, King Edgard (tenor), to celebrate the engagement, a bard (*haute-contre*) accompanied by a harp entertains the guests with a touching *romance* ('Femme sensible, entends-tu le ramage'). Ina worries that Othon will prove treacherous and seeks to dissuade her lover from keeping the rendez-vous. A model of chivalry, Ariodant insists on defending her honour. Left alone, she expresses her conflicting emotions (her love for and confidence in Ariodant and her fear of Othon) in a magnificent *récitatif et air* ('Mais que dis-je? femme timide ... O des amans le plus fidèle'). The villain tricks the hero into believing that his fiancée is unfaithful; in reality, it is her lady-in-waiting, Dalinde (soprano), who, also deceived by Othon, admits him into her mistress's private chambers at night. Ariodant flees in despair. While in the forest he rescues Dalinde, whom the villain has ordered to be killed. Back at the court Ina is put on trial for her (seeming) promiscuity against the laws of the country; Othon offers to save her by claiming that she has been secretly married to him, but Ina rejects the offer. Ariodant arrives and with Dalinde's help reveals Othon's perfidy. Ina is acquitted, and the lovers are reunited.

To match the 'chevaleresque' tone and the dramatic requirements of the libretto, Méhul wrote his best score of the 1790s. The characterization of the villain is particularly vivid, and, to underline his jealousy bordering on madness, the composer created a striking musical symbol in the orchestra in which unprepared dissonances show the vehemence of Othon's fury. It is introduced on his first appearance, in the air 'O démon de la jalousie', and recurs in nine other numbers. Highly theatrical conflict is expressed effectively in the Act 1 finale (Othon's challenge) and in that of Act 2 (Ariodant's deception) as rewritten for the second season. The time and setting of the plot also needed a musical response: Méhul adopted an intentionally 'antique' style (however historically inaccurate), which is apparent in the modal ambiguity in Ariodant's *romance*, 'Amour, amour, si je succombe', and the contrapuntal, trio-sonata-like texture in a section of the overture. Finally, for all the variety in the score, Méhul experimented extensively in linking pieces by tonal and motivic interconnections. The result was a much more integrated work than was typical for the Opéra-Comique and one that set an important precedent for later composers in France and Germany (particularly Weber's *Euryanthe*). M. ELIZABETH C. BARTLET

Ariodante. Opera in three acts by GEORGE FRIDERIC HANDEL to a libretto anonymously adapted from ANTONIO SALVI's *Ginevra, principessa di Scozia* (1708, Pratolino) after LUDOVICO ARIOSTO's poem, *Orlando furioso*, cantos iv–vi; London, Covent Garden Theatre, 8 January 1735.

Ariodante was the first new opera produced by Handel in his first season at Covent Garden Theatre. It was mostly written between 12 August and 24 October 1734, though some pre-performance revisions (such as the alteration of Dalinda's part from contralto to soprano) may have been made later. The original cast consisted of the castrato Giovanni Carestini (Ariodante), Anna Maria Strada del Pò (Ginevra), the contralto Maria Negri (Polinesso), John Beard (Lurcanio), Cecilia Young (Dalinda), Gustavus Waltz (King of Scotland) and Michael Stoppelaer (Odoardo). In common with the other operas of Handel's 1734–5 season *Ariodante* contains dance sequences in each act, written for Marie Sallé and her company. (These originally included a ballet of Good and Bad Dreams at the end of Act 2, representing Ginevra's troubled thoughts and concluding with an accompanied recitative in which she wakes up; but the sequence seems to have been replaced before performance by a short 'Entrée de Mori' and transferred – without the recitative – to *Alcina*.) *Ariodante* received 11 performances before giving way to a series of oratorio concerts, all in competition with the opera season organized by the 'Opera of the Nobility' at the King's Theatre. It was revived (without the dances) for just two performances on 5 May 1736, apparently as a stopgap before the première of *Atalanta*. The soprano castrato Gioacchino Conti, who took over the title role, presumably did not have sufficient time to learn his part and was allowed to include several non-Handelian arias from his earlier continental repertory (their bass lines, not all identified, survive in the original keyboard score at Hamburg). There were no further performances until the revival at Stuttgart on 28 September 1928 in an arrangement by A. Rudolph. The first British revival was at the Barber Institute, Birmingham, on 7 May 1964.

The King of Scotland	bass
Ariodante *a vassal prince*	mezzo-soprano
Ginevra *daughter of the King of Scotland, betrothed to Ariodante*	soprano
Lurcanio *Ariodante's brother*	tenor
Polinesso *Duke of Albany*	alto
Dalinda *attendant on Ginevra, secretly in love with Polinesso*	soprano
Odoardo *favourite of the king*	tenor

Setting Edinburgh and its vicinity

ACT 1 The action is set in Edinburgh (though there is no local colour in the music). The opening scene is Ginevra's dressing room, where she confesses to Dalinda that she is in love, with her father's approval. Polinesso presumptuously enters and declares love for Ginevra, but she says he is odious to her and leaves. Dalinda tells Polinesso that Ariodante is his rival for Ginevra and coyly hints at her own love for Polinesso. He decides to use her to destroy Ariodante.

In the royal gardens, Ariodante and Ginevra pledge faith. The King gives them his blessing and tells Odoardo to prepare for their wedding the following day. Polinesso deceitfully convinces Dalinda that he loves her, and asks her to help him take revenge on Ginevra: she is to dress that night in Ginevra's clothes and lead him into the royal apartments. Ariodante's brother Lurcanio tells Dalinda that he loves her, but she says she is not for him. In a beautiful valley, Ariodante and Ginevra are entertained by the singing and dancing of the local shepherds and shepherdesses.

ACT 2 In a ruined place, from which a private door leads into the royal apartments, Polinesso meets Ariodante by moonlight and pretends to be amazed when Ariodante says that he will soon be married to Ginevra. Polinesso claims (overhead by Lurcanio, in hiding) that he already enjoys Ginevra's favours, as

Ariodante will see for himself. The door to the apartments is opened by the disguised Dalinda, and Polinesso is admitted. Ariodante, horrified, and overwhelmed with grief is about to kill himself but is prevented by Lurcanio, who urges him to avenge his betrayed love. Unaware of what she has done, Dalinda leaves Polinesso to exult in his deceit.

In a gallery of the palace, Odoardo brings terrible news to the King: Ariodante has been seen to plunge from a high cliff into the sea and is presumed drowned. Ginevra is told and faints with grief. Lurcanio claims the cause of Ariodante's death is the wantonness of Ginevra: he presents the King with a signed account of what he believes was her assignation with Polinesso and is prepared to defend its truth with his sword. The King denounces Ginevra as a whore, leaving her in profound despair.

ACT 3 Ariodante is in a wood; he is revealed to have survived and curses the gods for letting him live. He meets and rescues Dalinda, fleeing from assassins employed by Polinesso; she is now aware of Polinesso's treachery and explains to Ariodante how he was deceived.

Back at the palace Polinesso hypocritically presents himself to the King as Ginevra's champion against Lurcanio. Ginevra, under sentence of death for her alleged unchastity, is brought to the King. She begs to kiss his hand for the last time; moved, the King allows her to do so, and insists that Polinesso be her champion despite her protests.

On the tournament field, Lurcanio challenges Polinesso to a duel and mortally wounds him; he offers a further challenge, which the King himself is about to take up, when a new champion appears with the visor of his helmet down. The newcomer reveals himself to be Ariodante and promises to explain everything if Dalinda is granted a pardon. Odoardo announces that Polinesso has died after confessing his crimes. The King orders rejoicing. The chastened Dalinda yields to Lurcanio's assurance of his love.

Ginevra, in prison, resigns herself to death, but her despair is swiftly turned to joy with the appearance of Ariodante and the King, who renews his blessing on the lovers. In a royal hall the two couples are entertained with the dances of knights and ladies.

* * *

Ariodante is one of Handel's most appealing operas: the story is romantic and unusually straightforward, and the characters are portrayed with warm humanity. It is also one of the greatest: the music is of consistently high quality, making considerable technical demands on the singers, and covers a remarkable range of emotional expression. Despite the expansiveness there is always a sense of intimacy, partly suggested by the general modesty of the scoring (trumpets appear only in the public scenes of Act 3, horns being used for the King's aria 'Voli colla sua tromba la fama' and for pastoral scenes) and by minor deviations from the strict pattern of recitatives and da capo arias. Three scenes begin with short arioso songs – that for Ariodante in the garden scene of Act 1, with its oboe solo, is especially lovely – and the King's genial interruption of the Act 1 duet for Ariodante and Ginevra is a delightful moment. The formal arias for the main characters are among Handel's finest, with superb examples of optimism and joy expressed through vocal virtuosity (Ginevra's 'Volate amori' and Ariodante's 'Con l'ali di costanza' in Act 1, the latter's 'Dopo notte' in Act 3) contrasted with the bleak despair of Ariodante's 'Scherza infida' in Act 2 (coloured by a mournful obbligato for bassoons with muted upper strings and pizzicato bass) and Ginevra's moving farewell to her father in Act 3 ('Io ti bacio', significantly echoed by Iphis in Act 3 of *Jephtha*). Dramatic tension is compellingly maintained through the whole of Act 2, which begins with an evocative sinfonia suggesting the rising of the moon. The dances and choruses in the final scenes of Acts 1 and 3, though peripheral to the story, are essential to the structure and include a pair of musettes touched by the melancholy yearning for a golden age often found in Handel's pastoral music. If *Ariodante* has not achieved the place in the modern repertory which its attractiveness would seem to justify, the reasons are largely practical: the length of the work, the presence of the dance episodes and the need for singers of special quality. If these demands are met, the opera reveals itself as an outstanding example of Baroque musical drama. ANTHONY HICKS

On the tournament field: woodcut illustrating Canto V of Ludovico Ariosto's 'Orlando furioso' (Venice: Valvassori, 1553)

Arioso (It.). The term, an Italian adjective, is usually encountered in English as a noun; it means 'in the manner of an aria'.

1. Baroque. 2. Classical and Romantic.

1. Baroque. The term has two usages in reference to 17th-century music: a passage in the style of an aria, or a passage that is aria-like for some other reason.

A recitative in the standard Italian poetic metres of seven- or eleven-syllable lines may have one or two of its lines, rarely three, set in a contrasting song style, most often at the final line or closing couplet of a speech (or a section of one). First lines of recitatives (or of sections in long ones) may also be in aria style, as in scores by Virgilio Mazzocchi or Francesco Cavalli. The change of style is rarely noted in the sources. Domenico Mazzocchi, in his index to the arias and choruses of *La catena d'Adone* (1626, Rome), wrote: 'Vi sono molt'altre mezz'Arie sparse per l'Opera, che rompono il tedio del recitativo' ('there are many other semi-arias scattered throughout the work, which interrupt the tedium of the recitative'). There is an example in Monteverdi's *Il ritorno d'Ulisse* (1640, Venice) of an arioso developing into an aria: when Minerva assures Ulysses in recitative that he will return in disguise to find the suitors impudent and Penelope faithful, he twice exclaims in arioso 'O fortunato Ulisse', which at the end of the ensuing scene becomes the opening phrase of an aria. In later scores, arioso phrases may be marked 'in aria' or 'alla battuta', the latter direction distinguishing them from the normally metrically free delivery of recitative. The term 'arioso' appears as early as 1638 in the libretto to a chamber dialogue, but the word itself never became exclusively attached to the appearance of phrases or groups of phrases in aria style within recitatives. (Using arioso as a normal Italian word, Scarlatti wrote in the dedication of *Lucio Manlio*, 1705: 'Dove è segnato grave, non intendo malenconico; dove andante, non presto, ma arioso': 'where the music is marked "grave" I do not mean "melancholy"; where it is marked "andante", not fast but "arioso"' – meaning 'in a flowing melodic style'.)

Recitatives that temporarily break into lyric melodies in triple metre or into strongly profiled phrases over walking basses are common in Italian operas from the 1640s to the 1660s, for example in works by Cavalli, Cesti and Legrenzi; they continue to appear in Alessandro Scarlatti's operas. From the 1670s the adjective Cavata also became associated with aria-like passages in recitatives.

Handel used 'arioso' to mean a short aria, for example Melissa's 'Io già sento l'alma in sen' (*Amadigi*, 1715), where it is preceded by an accompanied recitative, Dorinda's 'Quando spieghi i tormenti' (*Orlando*, 1733) or Rosmene's 'Al voler di tua fortuna' (*Imeneo*, 1740); other similar solos in his operas are not always described as ariosos.

Long recitatives or even whole scenes in recitative have been called 'arioso' by some modern writers to emphasize their heightened melodic plasticity or interest, which usually results from the expression of intense emotion. Though often described as having a vocal line midway between the recitative and aria styles of a period, they do not depend on those aria styles. A frequently cited example is Octavia's farewell, 'Addio, Roma', in Monteverdi's *L'incoronazione di Poppea* (1643, Venice).

2. Classical and Romantic. In the Classical era the term 'arioso' may still be applied to segments of recitative where the composer temporarily abandons the normally declamatory recitative style for a brief lyrical expression of one or more phrases. In Italian scores, short arias occurring within recitative are usually labelled Cavatina and set apart with a key signature, a time signature and a tempo marking, and often with additional instruments. Short lyrical moments within recitative are not set apart though they may occasion a contrasting tempo indication. They appear more often in obbligato recitative, where they may be accompanied with sustaining upper strings in *accompagnato* style (see Mozart's *Idomeneo*, Act 3, Idamantes' 'Padre, mio caro padre!'). A lyrical expression may also have a rhythmically regular instrumental accompaniment (*Idomeneo*, Act 3, Electra's 'Ah, no, il germano Oreste'). Arioso is sometimes equated with measured recitative, but lyrical expressions are not necessarily rhythmically regular, nor does a rhythmic instrumental accompaniment ensure the presence of a lyrical vocal style (*Idomeneo*, Act 3, Idamantes' 'Odo? o sol quel, che brama'). Since an arioso style remains a frequent option in 18th-century French opera, arioso passages appear particularly in Italian operas on French models, such as Gluck's *Orfeo* (a notable example is 'Che puro ciel') and *Alceste*, and indeed *Idomeneo*. They grow more common in Italian opera during the 1780s and 90s as orchestrally accompanied recitative gradually becomes more extensive.

In the 19th century the term is applied to a lyrical recitative, usually to be sung in strict time. Arioso passages that have the importance of an aria are especially common in Bellini's operas, for example 'Teneri, teneri figli' (*Norma*, 1831). Cardinal recitatives such as 'Pari siamo' from Verdi's *Rigoletto* (1851) and 'O monumento' from Ponchielli's *La Gioconda* (1876) combine arioso with declamatory elements. As the aria becomes ever more closely integrated into the operatic texture, the arioso tends to disappear as a separate category.

*

A. A. Abert: *Claudio Monteverdi und das musikalische Drama* (Lippstadt, 1954), 174

N. Pirrotta: 'Falsirena e la più antica delle cavatine', *CHM*, ii (1956), 355–66; rev. in his *Scelte poetiche di musicisti* (Venice, 1987), 255–63

S. Reiner: '"Vi sono molt'altre mezz'arie ..."', *Studies in Music History: Essays for Oliver Strunk* (Princeton, NJ, 1968), 241–58

C. Gianturco: 'Caratteri stilistici delle opere teatrali di Stradella', *RIM*, vi (1971), 211–45

M. Murata: *Operas for the Papal Court* (Ann Arbor, 1981)

C. Gianturco: 'Nuove considerazioni su *Il tedio del recitativo* delle prime opere romane', *RIM*, xviii (1982), 212–39

P. Fabbri: 'Recitativo e cavata', *Storia dell' opera italiana*, vi (Turin, 1988), 180–85

MARGARET MURATA, MARITA McCLYMONDS, JULIAN BUDDEN

Ariosti, Attilio (Malachia [Clemente]) (*b* Bologna, 5 Nov 1666; *d* London, sum. 1729). Italian composer. Between about 1672 and 1684 he was a *chierico* (an altar-boy) at S Petronio, where he presumably received his musical training. As Frate Ottavio he entered the monastic Order of the Servites at the age of 21 and served as organist at their basilica, S Maria de' Servi, in Bologna. He was referred to as 'Padre Attilio' in Catholic lands, but no record of his ordination has been found, and he signed dedications and letters with 'frate' rather than 'padre', so he apparently never attained the rank of priest. He often substituted Clemente for his baptismal name Malachia. His first two oratorios (Modena, 1693, and Bologna, 1694) or his *Divertimenti da camera* for violin and cello (Bologna, 1695) must have attracted the attention of the music-loving duke of Mantua, who took Ariosti into his service in 1696. After composing his first opera, *Erifile* (1697), he was sent by the duke to work for the electress Sophie Charlotte in Berlin; as the electoral court was Protestant, the Servite Order was highly displeased by his move to Berlin and repeatedly commanded him to return to Bologna. However, he had managed quickly to become Sophie's favourite musician, and she successfully manoeuvred to extend his visit, enlisting Italian dukes and cardinals as well as the German philosopher Leibnitz to support the cause. As Leibnitz said, Ariosti was not easy to replace, because he could sing, perform on several instruments and write dramatic texts (he wrote the libretto for *Polifemo*, set by G. Bononcini in 1702) as well as music. Sophie did not capitulate until mid-1703, whereupon Ariosti prudently declared his readiness to return to his Order by way of Vienna, though as Sophie commented to Leibnitz: 'Don't tell anyone, but he is dying for fear of returning to his monastery'.

Having contrived to extend his Berlin visit to six years, Ariosti stretched his time in Vienna from a break in his journey to a period of seven and a half years in the imperial service. He was greatly esteemed by Joseph I, who in 1707 gave him the portfolio of imperial minister and agent for all the princes and states of Italy. As such he was received by his monastic order in Bologna in May 1708, and during the last four years of Joseph's reign he may well have spent more time as a diplomat in Italy than as a composer in Vienna. A Bolognese memoir of 1711 (*I-Bu*, MS 770) records indignantly that the monk Ariosti, upon returning to Italy, wore a secular costume with gold brocade and a grandiose hat, and received visitors with great pomp; for such worldly behaviour he was banned from the Austrian realm by the widow of Joseph I and from Catholic lands by the pope. According to Leibnitz, his post as imperial agent in Italy ended with the death of Joseph, after which he 'entered the service of the Duke of Anjou, with a huge salary'. The duke was none other than the future Louis XV; if Ariosti was employed in his service, he presumably held a ministerial rather than a musical post. So far, all that is known of his activities during the period from 1711 to 1716 is contained in a letter he wrote from Paris on 15 February 1716 to his brother Giovanni Battista (Frate Odoardo, *b* 1668): 'I have been received with great honour by all rulers wherever I went, that is, Bavaria, Württemberg, Durlach, Baden, Lorraine and, at present, by the Duke of Orléans, regent of this realm'.

Ariosti's career before he went to England in 1716 is thus full of diplomatic intrigue, by means of which he sidled with surprising ease from one lofty court position to another. Perhaps because he served the courts mainly as a teacher and statesman, his output as a composer is rather small when compared with that of other Italians writing at the time. During his first 50 years he is known to have produced only five three-act operas, eight or nine serenatas, five oratorios, some 75 cantatas, two sets of instrumental pieces and a few sacred works. In general, Ariosti's extant works written before 1716 contain little that seems extraordinary for their time and place of composition. He did, however, provide dramatically effective settings, and one writer (von Besser, 1720) relates that the chromaticism and dissonance in the 'infernal symphony' of *L'Inganno vinto dalla Costanza* (1700) depicted the rage and despair of Atys so successfully that listeners were alternatively overcome with horror and pity.

The only one of Ariosti's Viennese works that certainly reached London before he did was *Amor tra nemici* (1708), which had been brought by the Viennese ambassador. Ariosti's score was treated there in the customary manner by editors and singers: they replaced all but 11 of its 43 arias, mainly by pieces drawn from recent Viennese works of Giovanni Bononcini. The resulting pasticcio was given as *Almahide* in 1710. While in London Ariosti composed a highly successful series of some 20 suites for the viola d'amore; he published six of them by subscription, together with six cantatas, in 1724, and may thereby have realized as much as £1600.

His first dramatic work written for London was *Tito Manlio*, which was the culminating work of the 1716–17 season. In addition to the typical da capo arias alternating with *recitativo semplice*, *Tito Manlio* has nine long accompanied recitatives and five duets. 31 of the 35 arias and all of the accompanied recitatives employ unusually colourful treble instrumentation to underline the affect in each scene (e.g. pizzicatos and tremolos depict madness). The work must have prompted the Directors of the newly founded Royal Academy of Music to commission him to write an opera for their first season, 1719–20; but Ariosti did not agree to write an opera for the Royal Academy until its fourth season, apparently because he remained active as a diplomat from 1717 to 1723. (Such activities were still remembered after his death; an anti-popish pamphleteer wished in 1733 that 'his mischievous Negociations could sleep with him'.) He was with diplomats in Paris at the beginning of 1720 and seems to have stayed there until shortly before the production of his *Caio Marzio Coriolano* (1723), the first and by far the most successful of his seven operas for the Royal Academy of Music. Its success owed a great deal to the prima donna, Francesca Cuzzoni, who had made her sensational London début one month earlier (in Handel's *Ottone*), but it likewise owed much to Ariosti's expressive setting of Pariati's excellent libretto. The dramatic high point is the prison scene for the title character (portrayed by Senesino) in the middle of Act 3. The chromatic accompagnato with which it begins was cited by Rameau in his *Génération Harmonique* (1737) as an admirable example of the 'enharmonic genre'. The ensuing aria, in F minor, begins with a *largo* section, but continues with a furious, modulatory presto. Hawkins found this scene to be 'wrought up to the highest degree of perfection that music is capable of' and noted that it was 'said to have drawn tears from the audience at every representation'. The success of the work led Ariosti to publish an almost complete collection of its numbers; in 1724 he did the same for *Vespasiano*, his next opera.

Vespasiano is filled with languishing rather than lively airs, and the satirical poem *The Session of Musicians* expressed Londoners' disappointment: 'Of *Ti[tu]s Ma[nli]us* you may justly boast, but dull *Ves[pasi]an* all that Honour lost'. Indeed, he never again had a notable success: of his five later operas, only *Artaserse* had more than six performances. Ariosti did not undertake to publish any pieces from these works, but John Walsh published four collections of 'Favourite Songs', which preserve arias from four of them. Nearly all are either relatively simple tunes that can easily be performed by amateurs or virtuoso airs that illustrate the agility of the stars; they cannot represent entire operas, but they do show the tendency noted in *Vespasiano*, away from the vigour of the Baroque and towards the languor of the pre-classical idiom.

Ariosti was among the 'renowned triumvirate' (Burney) of composers employed by the Royal Academy of Music. Handel was engaged during all eight seasons, Bononcini during five (1720–24 and 1726–7), and Ariosti also during five (1722–5 and 1726–8). In the spring of 1727, the Directors of the Academy resolved to commission operas in turn from Handel, Ariosti and Bononcini, so that their theatre, which could 'boast of the three best Voices in Europe, and the best Instruments', would likewise have 'three different Stiles of composing'; but the closing of the Academy's doors in 1728 precluded these plans. At least during its final season, the Academy may have paid Ariosti poorly, because he was reportedly living in poverty at the beginning of 1728. He may, however, have been a spendthrift; the librettist and poet P. A. Rolli wrote a mordant epitaph for him: 'Here lies Attilio Ariosti, he'd borrow still, could he accost ye. Monk to the last, whate'er betide, at other's cost he lived – and died'.

See also ALMAHIDE and VESPASIANO, IL.

Tirsi (dramma pastorale, 5, A. Zeno), Venice, S Salvatore, aut. 1696, arias *B-Bc*, collab. A. Caldara and A. Lotti [according to Allacci (1755)]

Erifile (dramma per musica, 3, G. B. Neri), Venice, S Salvatore, carn. 1697

L'Inganno vinto dalla Costanza [Atys, Atide] (pastorale, 3, O. Mauro), Berlin, Lützenburg, 6 June 1700

La fede ne' tradimenti (dramma per musica, 3, after G. Gigli), Berlin, Lützenburg, 12 July 1701, *GB-Lbl*

Il bene dal male (trattenimento carnavalesco), Vienna, Hof, ?1704, Act 1 *Wgm*

Amor tra nemici (dramma per musica, 3, P. A. Bernardoni), Vienna, Hof, 4 Sept 1708, *Wn*, Act 3 *Wgm*; rev. as Almahide, London, Queen's, 10 Jan 1710, incl. arias by G. Bononcini, Songs (London, 1710)

Tito Manlio (op, ? N. F. Haym), London, King's, 4 April 1717, *Lbl*

Caio Marzio Coriolano (drama, Haym, after P. Pariati), London, King's, 19 Feb 1723, excerpts (London, 1723/*R*1984: BMB, iv/75)

Il Vespasiano (drama, Haym, after G. C. Corradi), London, King's, 14 Jan 1724, excerpts and lib. (London, 1724/*R*1977: IOB, xxvi and lx)

Aquilio consolo (drama, ?Haym, after F. Silvani: *Arrenione*), 21 May 1724, Favourite Songs (London, 1724)

Artaserse (drama, 3, Haym, after Pariati ?and Zeno), London, King's, 1 Dec 1724, Favourite Songs (London, 1724)

Dario (drama per musica, ?Haym, after Silvani: *L'inganno scoperto per vendetta*), London, King's, 10 April 1725, Favourite Songs (London, 1725)

Lucio Vero, imperator di Roma (drama, 3, ?Haym, after Zeno), London, King's, 7 Jan 1727, Favourite Songs (London, 1727)

Teuzzone (melo-drama, 3, ?Haym, after Zeno), London, King's, 21 Oct 1727 [possibly arr., rather than composed by, Ariosti]

Music in: Almahide, 1710

*

BurneyH; *HawkinsH*; *LS*
J. von Besser: *Schriften* (Leipzig, 2/1720), 348–62
The Session of Musicians (London, 1724, repr. in Deutsch 1955)
P. Rolli: *Marziale in Albion*, ed. G. Tondini (Florence, 1776)
A. Ebert: *Attilio Ariosti in Berlin (1697–1703)* (Leipzig, 1905)
R. Doebner, ed.: *Briefe der Königin Sophie Charlotte von Preussen und der Kurfürstin Sophie von Hannover an hannoversche Diplomaten* (Leipzig, 1905)
A. Einstein: 'Italienische Musiker am Hofe der Neuberger Wittelsbacher (1614–1716)', *SIMG*, ix (1907–8), 412–17
C. Sachs: *Musik und Oper am kurbrandenburgischen Hof* (Berlin, 1910)
E. Wellesz: 'Die Opern und Oratorien in Wien von 1660–1708', *SMw*, vi (1919), 85–8
L. Frati: 'Attilio Ottavio Ariosti', *RMI*, xxxiii (1926), 551–7
R. Casimiri and A. Vicentini: 'Attilio Ottavio Ariosti: nuovi documenti', *NA*, ix (1932), 1–20
O. E. Deutsch: *Handel: a Documentary Biography* (London, 1955)
W. C. Smith: '"Do you know what you are about?": a Rare Handelian Pamphlet [of 1733]', *MR*, xxv (1964), 114–19
L. Lindgren: 'Parisian Patronage of Performers from the Royal Academy of Musick (1719–28)', *ML*, lviii (1977), 4–28
——: 'Six Newly Discovered Letters of Attilio Ariosti, O.S.M. (1666–1729)', *Studi storici dell'Ordine dei Servi di Maria*, xxx (1980), 125–37
——: 'Ariosti's London Years, 1716–29', *ML*, lxii (1981), 331–51
——: 'The Accomplishments of the Learned and Ingenious Nicola Francesco Haym (1678–1729)', *Studi musicali*, xvi (1987), 247–380
——: 'Musicians and Librettists in the Correspondence of Gio. Giacomo Zamboni', *RMARC*, no.24, xxiv (1991) [whole issue]

LOWELL LINDGREN

Ariosto, Ludovico (*b* Reggio Emilia, 8 Sept 1474; *d* Ferrara, 6 July 1533). Italian poet and playwright. His career was spent as a courtier and diplomat in the service of Cardinal Ippolito d'Este (1502–17), then of Ippolito's brother, Alfonso I d'Este, duke of Ferrara. Ariosto's five plays, which include *La cassaria* (1508) and *I suppositi* (1509), are important early Italian comedies, but his major work was the epic poem *Orlando furioso* (the first redaction was substantially completed by 1509: the poem was published in 1516, with revised editions in 1521 and 1532). Begun as a completion of the *Orlando innamorato* by Matteo Maria Boiardo (*d* 1494; two parts published in 1483), it soon surpassed its model, developing into a 46-canto romance of chivalry and magic in the time of Charlemagne. The epic focusses on Orlando, nephew of Charlemagne, who is rendered mad ('furioso') by his love for Angelica (who eventually marries the Saracen Medoro), daughter of the Great Khan of Cathay. But Ariosto paints a broad canvas, filling his poem with a rich variety of spectacular episodes that seem almost designed for the theatre.

In the 16th century *Orlando furioso* was often performed to music by means of improvised recitational schemes (offering one precedent for the *stile recitativo*), and its *ottava rima* stanzas were also frequently set by madrigalists, whether singly or in cycles (e.g. Jacquet de Berchem's *Capriccio … sopra le stanze del Furioso*, 1561). Such settings of *Orlando furioso* or its rival, Tasso's *Gerusalemme liberata*, encouraged a dramatic focus in the madrigal, establishing a context for early opera. In the early 17th century the mythological subjects of the first operas gave way to plots drawn from epic poetry: the first Ariosto operas were Marco da Gagliano and Jacopo Peri's *Lo sposalizio di Medoro et Angelica* (1619) and Francesca Caccini's *La liberazione di Ruggiero dall'isola d'Alcina* (1625), both performed in Florence. Thereafter, Orlando's passion for Angelica (*see* ANGELICA E MEDORO) was the favoured subject for Ariosto-based operas; however, the tales of the sorcerer Atlante (ii:37–57; iv passim; xxii passim), Ariodante and Ginevra (iv:57ff; v–vi:15), Ruggiero and the sorceress Alcina (vi:16–viii:13) and Olimpia (ix:9–x:34; xi:33ff) also provided rich material for the 'magic' operas of the Baroque period: the failure of the all-powerful Alcina to secure her love for Ruggiero (in turn loved by Bradamante) proved a particularly poignant subject. Ariosto (like Tasso) was particularly popular in Italy up to the 1650s, in France in the second half of the century, then in Italy and England (perhaps under French influence, and also that of the Arcadians) in the early 18th century, reaching a peak in Handel's three *Orlando furioso* operas of the 1730s. A few *Orlando* operas, however, such as Vivaldi's *Orlando finto pazzo* (1714), were based instead on Boiardo. A full list of operas and other dramatic works drawing on Ariosto's epic has yet to be compiled: the one that follows is inevitably incomplete.

ORLANDO, ANGELICA, MEDORO

Gagliano and J. Peri, *Lo sposalizio di Medoro et Angelica* (A. Salvadori), Florence, 1619; O. Vernizzi, *Angelica legata* (intermedi, S. Branchi), Bologna, 1623; Cignani, *Il ritorno d'Angelica nell'Indie* (O. Tronsarelli), Rome, 1628; comp. unknown, *La pazzia d'Orlando* (intermedi, P. Bonarelli), lib. pubd (Venice, 1635); comp. unknown, *Angelica in India* (P. P. Bissari), Venice, 1656; F. Lucio, *Il Medoro* (A. Aureli), Venice, 1658; Lully, *Roland* (P. Quinault), Versailles, 1685; Steffani, *Orlando generoso* (O. Mauro), Hanover, 1691; G. Griffini, *La fortunata sventura di Medoro, o La pazzia d'Orlando* (G. Giovanalli), Lodi, 1697; D. Scarlatti, *Orlando, ovvero La gelosa pazzia* (C. S. Capece), Rome, 1711; Ristori, *Orlando furioso* (G. Braccioli), Venice, 1713 (rev. Vivaldi, Venice, 1714); Fux, *Angelica vincitrice di Alcina* (P. Pariati), Vienna, 1716; Porpora, *Angelica* (P. Metastasio), Naples, 1720; Schürmann, *Orlando furioso* (Braccioli), Brunswick, 1722; comp. unknown, *Angelica y Medoro* (Canizares), Madrid, 1722; Bioni, *Orlando furioso* (Braccioli), Guckuksbade, 1724; O. Polaroli, *Orlando furioso* (Braccioli), Mantua, 1725; Vivaldi, *Orlando* (Braccioli), Venice, 1727; various comps., *Orlando furioso* (Braccioli), Brussels, 1727; Handel, *Orlando* (Capece), London, 1733; Latilla, *Angelica ed Orlando* (F. A. Tullio), Naples, 1735; Lampugnani, *Angelica* (C. Vedova), Venice, 1738; Pescetti, *Angelica e Medoro* (Vedova), London, 1739; I. Fiorillo, *L'Angelica*, Padua, 1744; comp. unknown, *Roland* (parody, C. F. Panard and Sticotti), Paris, 1744; comp. unknown, *Orlando furioso*, Venice, 1746; G. B. Mele, *Angelica e Medoro* (Metastasio), Madrid, 1747; Graun, *Angelica e Medoro* (L. de Villati), Berlin, 1749; comp. unknown, *Angelica* (Metastasio), Wolfenbüttel, 1751; F. Brusa, *L'Angelica* (Metastasio), Venice, 1756; N. Piccinni, *Il nuovo Orlando*, Modena, 1764; I. von Beecke, *Roland*, Paris, after 1770; P. A. Guglielmi, *Le pazzie di Orlando* (C. F. Badini), London, 1771 (rev. with addns by various comps. as *Orlando paladino*, lib. rev. N. Porta, Prague, 1775; Vienna, 1777); J. Touchemoulin, *I furori di Orlando* (D. Friggieri), Regensburg, 1777; J. de S. Carvalho, *L'Angelica* (Metastasio), Lisbon, 1778; N. Piccinni, *Roland* (J. F. Marmontel), Paris, 1778; Haydn, *Orlando paladino* (N. Porta), Eszterháza, 1782; Andreozzi, *Angelica e Medoro* (G. Sertor), Venice, 1791 (rev. Florence, 1792); Mortellari, *Angelica*, Padua, 1796; P. Vannacci, *Angelica e Medoro*, Livorno, 1802; A. Tozzi, *Angelica e Medoro* (Sertor), Barcelona, 1805; G. Nicolini, *Angelica e Medoro, ossia Orlando* (Sertor), Turin, 1810; A. Loffredo, *Orlando furioso*, Naples, 1831; A. Thomas, *Angélique et Médor* (T. M. F. Sauvage), Paris, 1843; J. J. Schneider, *Orlando* (F. Adami), Schwerin, 1848; L. C. Desormes, *Roland furieux* (Péricaud and Delormel), Paris, 187?

ALCINA, RUGGIERO, BRADAMANTE

F. Caccini, *La liberazione di Ruggiero dall'isola d'Alcina* (opera-ballet, F. Saracinelli), Florence, 1625; Luigi Rossi, *Il palazzo incantato, overo La guerriera amante* (G. Rospigliosi), Rome, 1642; Sacrati, *L'isola di Alcina* (F. Testi), Bologna, 1648; S. Martinelli, *Alcina*, Trent, 1649; ?Cavalli, *Bradamante* (P. P. Bissari), Venice, 1650; comp. unknown, *Libertà di Ruggiero*, Modena, 1651; Sabadini, *Il Ruggiero* (G. Tamagni), Parma, 1699; Campra, *Alcine* (A. Danchet), Paris, 1705; L. de Lacoste, *Bradamante* (P.-C. Roy), Paris, 1707; Albinoni, *Alcina delusa da Ruggero* (A. Marchi), Venice, 1725 (rev. as *Gli evenimenti di Ruggero*, 1732); various comps., *Alcina maga*, Bologna, 1725; Broschi, *L'isola di Alcina* (A. Fanzaglia), Rome, 1728; Handel, *Alcina*, London, 1735; P. A. Guglielmi, *Ruggiero* (C. Mazzolà), Venice, 1769; Hasse, *Il Ruggiero, ovvero L'eroica gratitudine* (P. Metastasio), Milan, 1771; G. Gazzaniga, *L'isola d'Alcina* (G. Bertati), Venice, 1772 (rev. G. Rust, Bologna, 1772); F. Alessandri, *Alcina e Ruggiero* (V. A. Cigna-Santi), Turin, 1775; J. Schuster, *Bradamante* (Mazzolà), Padua, 1779; various comps., *L'isola d'Alcina*, Naples, 1785; M. T. von Paradis, *Rinaldo und Alcina* (L. von Baczko), Prague, 1797; P. C. Guglielmi, *La fata Alcina* (G. M. Foppa), Venice, 1800; Reichardt, *Bradamante* (H. J. von Collin), Vienna, 1809; comp. unknown, *Il ritorno del Ruggiero* (S. Serofano), Naples, 1810; A. Gandini, *Il Ruggiero, ovvero L'eroica gratitudine* (Metastasio), Modena, 1822; J. B. Giraud, *Ruggiero e Bradamante*, 183?; S. Holmes, *Ruggiero*, Naples, 1838

GINEVRA, ARIODANTE

G. M. Costa, *Ariodante* (G. A. Pisani and G. A. Spinola), Genoa, 1655; Bassani, *La Ginevra, infanta di Scozia* (G. C. Grazzini), Ferrara, 1690; Perti, *Ginevra principessa di Scozia* (A. Salvi), Florence, 1708; C. F. Pollarolo, *Ariodante* (Salvi: *Ginevra*), Venice, 1716; Sarro, *Ginevra principessa di Scozia* (Salvi), Naples, 1720; A. S. Fiorè, *Ariodante* (Salvi), Milan, 1722; F. Faleoni, *Ginevra principessa di Scozia* (Salvi), Rome, 1724; G. Sellitto, *Ginevra* (Salvi), Venice, 1733; Handel, *Ariodante* (Salvi), London, 1735; Vivaldi, *Ginevra principessa di Scozia* (Salvi), Florence, 1736; Wagenseil, *Ariodante* (Salvi), Venice, 1745; F. Bertoni, *Ginevra* (Salvi), Venice, 1753; Isouard, *Ginevra di Scozia*, Malta, *c*1798; Méhul, *Ariodant* (F.-B. Hoffman), Paris, 1799; Mayr, *Ginevra di Scozia* [*Ariodante*] (Gaetano Rossi), Trieste, 1801; G. Tritto, *Ginevre e Ariodante* (D. Piccinni), Naples, 1801; G. Mosca, *Ginevra di Scozia, ossia Ariodante* (Rossi), Turin, 1802; M. A. Portugal, *Ginevra di Scozia* (Rossi, rev. G. Caravita), Lisbon, 1805; V. Noberasco, *Ginevra di Scozia* (Bonelli), Milan, 1852; L. Petrali, *Ginevra di Scozia* (M. Marcello), Mantua, 1854; G. Rota, *Ginevra di Scozia* (Marcello), Parma, 1862; F. Lombardi, *Ginevra di Scozia*, Florence, 1877

OLIMPIA

D. Freschi, *Olimpia vendicata* (A. Aureli), Venice, 1681 (rev. as *Olimpia placata*, Parma, 1687); A. Scarlatti, *Olimpia vendicata* (Aureli), Naples, 1685 (rev. as *Amor vince lo sdegno, o vero L'Olimpia placata*, Rome, 1692); Heinichen, *Olimpia vendicata* (Aureli), Naumburg, 1709; comp. unknown, *Olimpia in Ebuda* (P. A. Rolli), London, 1740; Latilla, *Olimpia nell'isola di Ebuda* (A. Trabucco), Naples, 1741; G. de Majo, *Il sogno d'Olimpia* (R. de Calzabigi), Naples, 1747; A. Sacchini, *Olimpia tradita*, Naples, 1758; G. Paisiello, *Olimpia* (Trabucco), Naples, 1768

OTHERS

D. Gabrielli, *Carlo il grande* (A. Morselli), Venice, 1688; M. A. Gasparini, *Rodomonte sdegnato* (G. Braccioli), Venice, 1714; comp. unknown, *Il castello d'Atlante*, Brescia, 1791; H. M. Berton, *Montano et Stéphanie* (J. E. B. Dejaure), Paris, 1799; C. Jachino, *Giocondo e il suo re* (G. Forzano), Milan, 1924

*

A. Einstein: '*Orlando furioso* and *La Gerusalemme liberata* as Set to Music during the Sixteenth and Seventeenth Centuries', *Notes*, viii (1950–51), 623–30

C. Girdlestone: *La tragédie en musique (1673–1750) considérée comme genre littéraire* (Geneva, 1972)

R. Döring: *Ariostos 'Orlando furioso' im italienischen Theater des Seicento und Settecento* (Hamburg, 1973)

G. Schmidgall: *Literature as Opera* (New York, 1977)

M. A. Balsano, ed.: *L'Ariosto, la musica, i musicisti* (Florence, 1981)

A. L. Bellina, B. Brizi and M. G. Pensa: *I libretti vivaldiani* (Florence, 1982), 85–96

L. Bianconi and T. Walker: 'Production, Consumption and Political Function of Seventeenth-Century Italian Opera', *Early Music History*, iv (1984), 209–96

M. Collins and E. K. Kirk, eds.: *Opera & Vivaldi* (Austin, 1984)

B. A. Brown: '*Le Pazzie d'Orlando*, *Orlando Paladino* and the Uses of Parody', *Italica*, lxiv (1987), 583–605

TIM CARTER

Aristo e Temira ('Aristo and Temira'). Dramma per musica in one act by FERDINANDO BERTONI to a libretto by Conte de' Salvioli; Venice, Teatro S Benedetto, 3 January 1776.

Performed alongside Bertoni's *Orfeo ed Euridice* and described variously as a pastorale (*D-Mbs*) and cantata (*F-Pn*), *Aristo e Temira* is in nine short scenes and outlines the separation and reunion of a pair of lovers. It gives each of the four singers an opportunity for virtuosic display of their voices, in contrast to the companion work. Aristo (soprano) was sung by Lorenzo Piatti and Temira (soprano) by Camilla Passi Sarti, who also sang Euridice in *Orfeo*. Egina (soprano) was sung by Lucia Alberoni and Alceo (tenor) by Giacomo Davide, who sang Imene in *Orfeo*. Scene iv comprises a complex of recitative (marked *accompagnato* in *D-Mbs*), cavatina ('Senza te, mio caro bene') sung alternately by Temira and Aristo, a bravura aria for Aristo, and a rhapsodic duet for the reunited pair. Scene vi contains a bravura aria ('Il fato à voi concede') with lengthy *passaggi* for Alceo (copy in *A-Wgm*) and is similar to the aria 'Sò che dal ciel discende' from *Tancredi* (1767). Scene viii contains an even longer coloratura aria ('In questo amico amplesso') for Tamira, who is required to sing up to *g‴*.

Subsequent revivals were staged in Munich (1781), Florence (1784) and Venice (1783) where it was revised by Bertoni's student Simon Mayr as *Temira e Aristo* (1795). GEORGE TRUETT HOLLIS

Aristophanes [Aristophanēs] (*b* Athens, *c*450 BC; *d* Athens, *c*385 BC). Greek comic dramatist, author of some 40 plays, of which 11 have survived. Most belong to the Old Comedy in style, though the *Plutus* (388 BC) more properly belongs to Middle Comedy in the reduced role of the chorus. The lasting appeal of Aristophanes depends on the exuberance of his dialogue and riotous delight in the improbable. Such scenes as Socrates suspended aloft in a basket (his 'thinking-shop'), a hero's flight to heaven on a dung beetle, the god of the sea trying to hide from Zeus beneath an umbrella, and the highly formal trial of a dog, delighted ancient Athens and still have comic vitality. The attacks Aristophanes made on contemporary morals and political abuses have inevitably lost topicality. The *Lysistrata* (411 BC), which declares a female sex strike until men see sense and make peace, attracted Schubert (*Die Verschworenen*) and Paul Kont (1961), and Walter Braunfels made a libretto and opera from the deliciously fanciful *The Birds* ('Die Vögel'). ROBERT ANDERSON

Arizona Opera. American company, based in PHOENIX and TUCSON, Arizona.

Arkansas Opera Theatre. American company, founded in 1973 and based in LITTLE ROCK, Arkansas; in 1989 it was renamed Opera Theatre at Wildwood.

Arkas, Mykola Mykolayovych (*b* Mykolaïv, 26 Dec 1852/7 Jan 1853; *d* Mykolaïv, 13/26 March 1909). Ukrainian composer. He was the author of a comprehensive history of Ukraine, *Istoriya Ukrainï-Rusi* (St Petersburg, 1908) and collected over 80 Ukrainian folksongs. After graduating from Odessa University, he worked at the Mykolaïv Naval Office until 1899, then established a Ukrainian-language school, which was closed by authorities after only two years. He began composing the opera *Kateryna*, to his own libretto based on the poem by Taras Shevchenko, in the late 1880s, completing it in 1891; it was later edited and orchestrated by Hlib Taranov. The piano score was published in 1897 and two years later, on 12 February 1899, Marko Kropyvnytsky staged it in Moscow. The style of *Kateryna* is essentially lyrical, making much use of folksongs and dance rhythms. Although its structure and harmonic language is at times quite primitive, it nevertheless derives considerable emotional power from its melodic and psychological interest.

*

L. Kaufman: *M. Arkas* (Kiev, 1958) VIRKO BALEY

Arkhipova, Irina (Konstantinovna) (*b* Moscow, 2 Dec 1925). Russian mezzo-soprano. She graduated in 1948 from the Moscow Institute of Architecture, where she learnt singing in N. Malïsheva's group, and in 1953 from L. Savransky's class at the Moscow Conservatory. She sang with the Sverdlovsk Opera (1954–6) and made her Bol'shoy début as Carmen in 1956. Her voice, of wide range, is remarkable for its emotional warmth and variety of tone-colour. Her roles include Lyubasha (*Tsar's Bride*), Pauline and Lyubov' (*Queen of Spades* and *Mazepa*), Amneris and Eboli, and Massenet's Charlotte. She has participated in many Bol'shoy first performances, including Khrennikov's *Mat'* ('Mother'; Nilovna, 1957), *War and Peace* (Hélène, 1959) and *Story of a Real Man* (Klavdiya, 1960), Shchedrin's *Ne tol'ko lyubov'* ('Not Love Alone'; Varvara, 1961) and Kholminov's *Optimisticheskaya tragediya* ('An Optimistic Tragedy'; Commissar, 1965). She has sung throughout eastern Europe and in the USA, Japan, Austria and Scandinavia. After appearances in Naples in 1960, as Carmen, she sang Hélène with the Bol'shoy at La Scala in 1964, returning as Marfa (1967 and 1971) and Marina (1968). She scored a great success as Azucena at Orange in 1972, and this led to her Covent Garden début in the same role in 1975; she has been praised for her intensely dramatic performance. She sang Ulrica at Covent Garden in 1988.

I. M. YAMPOL'SKY

Arkor, André d'. *See* D'ARKOR, ANDRÉ.

Arlberg, (Georg Efraim) Fritz (*b* Leksand, 21 March 1830; *d* Oslo, 21 Jan 1896). Swedish baritone. He studied at Uppsala, making his début in 1854 at the Mindre Theatre, Stockholm. Engaged at the Royal Opera, Stockholm (1858–74, 1877–83), he also sang in Oslo and in Germany. His repertory, ranging from Mozart to Wagner, included Don Giovanni, Count Almaviva, Figaro (Mozart and Rossini), Hans Heiling, Belcore, Don Carlo (*Ernani*), the Dutchman and Telramund. He had a strong, flexible voice and was also employed as director and translator.

ELIZABETH FORBES

Arlecchino [*Arlecchino, oder Die Fenster* ('Arlecchino, or The Windows')]. *Theatralisches Capriccio* in one act, op.50, by FERRUCCIO BUSONI to his own libretto; Zürich, Stadttheater, 11 May 1917.

The action is divided into four movements (Busoni uses the word *Satz*, which can also signify a leap or skip); the scene is a street in Bergamo. In 'Arlecchino as Rogue' the hero (speaking role) dallies with the lovely Annunziata (silent role) while her aging husband, the tailor-master Ser Matteo del Sarto (bass-baritone), reads Dante. Arlecchino persuades him that the town is surrounded by barbarians, hurries him into the house, locks the door and pockets the key. The Abbate Cospicuo (baritone) and Dr Bombasto (bass) pass by, taking their evening stroll. They are alarmed at Matteo's news and set off in haste to inform the mayor, but vanish instead into a nearby tavern.

'Arlecchino as Warrior' shows Ser Matteo being called up for military service. Arlecchino grants him permission to take his Dante into battle: 'Nobody shall say that culture was allowed to perish in the war'.

'Arlecchino as Husband' depicts the hero's confrontation with his wife Colombina (mezzo-soprano). She scolds him for his infidelity, but he, feigning reconciliation, sneaks away. Enter Leandro (tenor), cavalier and wandering minstrel, who regales Colombina with extravagant, operatic advances. His wooing is interrupted by Arlecchino who, in the role of betrayed husband, challenges him to a duel. Colombina is escorted to safety; Leandro falls.

'Arlecchino as Victor' begins with the Abbate and Dr Bombasto emerging from the inn with Colombina. They stumble over Leandro's inert body and hoist the wounded cavalier into a cart drawn by a donkey. Singing the praises of the 'asinus providentialis' in a quartet, they set off for the infirmary. The coast is clear, and Arlecchino enters triumphantly to elope with Annunziata. Ser Matteo returns, bemused, to his sewing table. The curtain falls. Arlecchino reappears, outlines his mocking philosophy of marriage and dances off.

In the first-draft libretto for his opera *Doktor Faust* (1910), Busoni intended the serious action to be interspersed with comic Casperle episodes, as in the 16th-century puppet plays. He decided to write these in advance – a few loosely connected scenes, in the spirit of a baroque operatic intermezzo – as a musical study for *Doktor Faust*. Inspired by a visit to Bergamo, the traditional home-town of Arlecchino, and by Schoenberg's *Pierrot lunaire*, he drafted a libretto during the summer of 1913. He revised it early the following year and, due to the outbreak of war, modified it again in October 1914. The title role was conceived for (and later first performed by) Alexander Moissi, a celebrated actor in Max Reinhardt's Berlin company. Work on the score was begun in December of the same year but abandoned three weeks later.

In 1915 the extant musical material of *Arlecchino* was transformed into an orchestral work, the *Rondò arlecchinesco* op.46. The biting sarcasm of an 'opera which itself turns against opera' virtually obscured the surface humour, and Busoni saw little future for the work, least of all in New York where he was then living. In October he took refuge in Switzerland from the war. The first performance of the *Rondò* (Rome, 5 March 1916) and a visit to a Rossini opera performed by marionettes encouraged him to resume work on *Arlecchino*, which he completed in August 1916.

Stylistically the score bridges the gap between Busoni's experimental pre-war compositions and the later works written in the spirit of 'Junge Klassizität'. An important source of inspiration was the *Sonatina ad usum infantis* (1915), a deceptively simple piano piece which seems to turn its back on the war and seek the naivety of childhood; Colombina's music in *Arlecchino* includes several passages from it. The element of operatic parody in the score gives rise to all manner of quotations and allusions, from Gluck to Wagner, and bel canto to ragtime. These are unified through harmonic cunning and brilliant use of a modestly sized orchestra. Arlecchino's rhythmic speech (precisely notated but unpitched) etches his role against the musical background and stylizes him to an 'über-marionette' (to use Edward Gordon Craig's term), a comic mask whose counterpart is Faust, the tragic mask and *Übermensch*.

'I have been reproached for *Arlecchino* because it is considered scornful and inhuman,' wrote Busoni. But he insisted that he wrote the work 'out of sympathy for mankind', describing it (in the MS) as a Marionettentragödie and (in a dedication) as 'mia confessione giocosa'. The opera, which lasts an hour, has enjoyed a certain enduring popularity, although the extreme rapidity of the action and the hard, brilliant effect of the music serve even today to alienate rather than to entertain. ANTONY BEAUMONT

Arlen, Stephen (Walter) (*b* Birmingham, 19 Oct 1913; *d* London, 19 Jan 1972). English administrator. He began his theatrical life in 1929 as an actor, but soon turned to stage management. After World War II he became general manager of the Old Vic and in 1951 was appointed general manager of Sadler's Wells, and then administrative director. In 1959 he advised Maurice Huisman on the reorganization of La Monnaie in Brussels. In 1966 he was appointed managing director of Sadler's Wells and in 1968 was responsible for the company's move from Rosebery Avenue, Islington, to the London Coliseum. He was made CBE in 1968.

E. Tracey: 'Stephen Arlen, 1913–72', *Opera*, xxiii (1972), 219–21

HAROLD ROSENTHAL

Arlesiana, L' ('The Girl from Arles'). Opera in four acts by FRANCESCO CILEA to a libretto by Leopoldo Marenco after Alphonse Daudet's play *L'arlésienne*; Milan, Teatro Lirico, 27 November 1897 (revised in three acts, 1898).

The action takes place at the farm of Rosa Mamai (soprano) in Provence. Of her two sons, the younger, known as L'Innocente (mezzo-soprano), is a simpleton. The elder, Federico (tenor), is madly in love with a girl from Arles, whom he intends to marry, much to his mother's concern, since nothing is known about her. The old shepherd, Baldassare (baritone), is entertaining L'Innocente with a nursery tale. Rosa Mamai tells her foster-daughter, Vivetta (soprano), how Federico first set eyes on the girl ('Era un giorno di festa'). Vivetta is distressed, since she is in love with Federico herself. The young man arrives with his uncle Marco (bass), who gives a satisfactory account of the bride's family. While the others are celebrating the forthcoming wedding, Rosa Mamai and Baldassare receive a visit from the drover, Metifio (baritone), with letters proving that the girl from Arles has been his mistress. Baldassare borrows them to show to Federico, who is overcome with despair.

Baldassare tries vainly to persuade Federico to go with him to the mountains; L'Innocente attempts to distract him with one of Baldassare's stories, but falls asleep. Federico pours out his feelings in a famous aria ('È la solita storia del pastore'). At length he pulls himself together and decides to marry Vivetta. During the preparations for their wedding, Metifio reappears asking for the return of his letters. He tells Baldassare that he intends to carry away the girl from Arles on his horse. Overheard by Federico, his words reawaken the young man's passion and he has to be restrained from attacking the drover. That night while Rosa Mamai is reflecting sadly on the trials of motherhood ('Esser madre è un inferno'), she is joined by L'Innocente, who is at last showing signs of intelligence. His mother has misgivings, since an old Provençal tradition has it that a fool in the family brings good luck. Next morning her fears prove justified. All night long Federico has wrestled with his grief, like the goat with the wolf in Baldassare's story, but to no avail. In desperation he plunges from a high window to his death.

It was at the première of *L'arlesiana* that the young Enrico Caruso first established his reputation. For a revival at the Teatro Lirico on 22 October 1898, Cilea reduced the original four acts to three. When the opera was performed in Rome in 1937, with a cast that included Tito Schipa and Margherita Carosio, he added a prelude based on themes from the opera. From the outset Cilea established the idyllic, pastoral background against which the tragedy would take place. Among the few recurring motifs is a descending figure of interlocking broken octaves associated with L'Innocente, which is skilfully woven into Federico's aria in the second act. In general the opera shows Cilea's melodic invention at its freshest and most spontaneous. JULIAN BUDDEN

Armand, Mlle (*fl* 1704–7). French soprano. After making her début at the Paris Opéra in 1704, as Venus and La Jeunesse in Destouches' *Le carnaval et la folie*, she sang Iris in the revival of Lully's *Isis* later that year. She created the role of Electra in Desmarets and Campra's *Iphigénie en Tauride*, also in 1704, and alternated with Journet in the role of Clorinde at the first revival of Campra's *Tancrède* in 1707. This revival presented a revised denouement; the Parfaict brothers record laconically that 'the heroic character of Clorinde was not greatly appreciated at the Opéra, where weakness enjoys greater favour than virtue.' Shortly after this Armand retired.

*

F. Parfaict and C. Parfaict: *Histoire de l'Académie royale de musique depuis son établissement jusqu'à présent* (MS, 1741, *F-Pn*), ff.105, 107–8, 117 PHILIP WELLER

Arme Heinrich, Der ('Poor Heinrich'). *Musikdrama* in three acts by HANS PFITZNER to a libretto by James Grun (with Pfitzner) after the medieval poem by Hartmann von Aue; Mainz, Stadttheater, 2 April 1895.

Heinrich *a German knight*	tenor
Dietrich *one of his vassals*	baritone
Hilde *Dietrich's wife*	soprano
Agnes *their daughter, aged 14*	soprano
The Physician *a monk in the monastery of Salerno*	bass
Monks	

Setting Heinrich's castle in Swabia (Acts 1 and 2) and the monastery of Salerno (Act 3), *c*1100

Pfitzner completed this, his first opera, in 1893, when he was 24 and still without a permanent post. Its first performance was secured with the assistance of the librettist's influential sister, Frances Grun. The title role was sung by Bruno Heydrich, and the work's favourable reception (sealed by an appreciative review by Humperdinck) marked the beginning of Pfitzner's reputation as a significant post-Wagnerian composer (productions at Frankfurt and Darmstadt followed in 1897). In Hartmann's original, more closely adhered to by Gerhart Hauptmann in his similarly titled play of 1902, Heinrich had suffered from leprosy, which could only be cured by the blood of a young girl who would voluntarily sacrifice herself. The daughter of the farmer with whom Heinrich had taken refuge agreed to do so. Struck by her beauty, Heinrich had nevertheless prevented the girl's sacrifice and been rewarded with a miraculous recovery; he later married her. Pfitzner himself started a libretto on Hartmann's subject and wrote the initial feverish 'dream' narration of his own more mysteriously ailing knight. The rest was the work of his friend James Grun, who adhered throughout to a somewhat slavishly Wagnerian manner of poetic diction.

ACT 1 *A room in a tower of Heinrich's castle* After an overture presenting the main leitmotif associated with the sick knight (ex.1), the curtain rises on the sleeping Heinrich. Beside him stands Agnes, who with her

mother, Hilde, has been tending the knight while her father is travelling to seek the advice of a famous physician-monk in Salerno. Dietrich's return is signalled by a horn, and Agnes goes to greet him. With Hilde in attendance, Heinrich slowly wakens from a fevered dream of former friends and deeds, now lost in the past. Dietrich enters and explains what the Physician has said, but only after giving a long account of his journey to Italy, begun in autumn and now ended in spring. This elaborate, orchestrally illustrated narrative was performed separately as *Dietrichs Erzählung* before the opera's première (1893, Berlin, and 1894, Frankfurt) and has continued to be regarded as the finest single episode in the opera (it was recorded by Fischer-Dieskau in 1979). Dietrich comes to the Physician's grim pronouncement: only the willing sacrifice of a pure young virgin can effect the knight's recovery from his debilitating malady of the soul and nerves – a malady which is to be regarded as a divine punishment for 'youthful wantonness'. During the course of Dietrich's narration the sky has clouded over and the stage grown dark. Heinrich resignedly takes leave of the weapons he had formerly wielded, and collapses after fruitlessly attempting to pull his sword from its scabbard. Agnes is deeply affected. The act ends in C minor with a sad tableau, during which Dietrich and Hilde anxiously meet each other's gaze.

ACT 2 *The bedchamber of Dietrich and Hilde at night* After a slow orchestral introduction, beginning, like the overture to Act 1, with a statement of the primary motif, the curtain rises on a scene of anxious tension between Dietrich, standing, and his disconsolately reclining wife. Hilde cannot, however, bring herself to speak of her fearful premonition. Agnes then comes into their room and the rest of the act is devoted to her increasingly eloquent entreaty to her horrified parents: they must let *her* be the sacrificial victim. The life of the hero-knight is more valuable than hers. An ecstasy of divinely inspired commitment transforms her and convinces her parents. The act concludes with a trio of prayerful reconciliation whose intensity causes Hilde to faint; the music closes in a portentous E♭ minor.

ACT 3 *An open courtyard in the monastery of Salerno at daybreak* After a slow and ceremonial overture in D minor, Dietrich is found trying to comfort Hilde as monks sing from the church. They exit, and Agnes and Heinrich enter, to be greeted by the Physician from the double doors that lead into the sacrificial chamber. Heinrich now wishes to prevent the sacrifice but is too weak to be forceful. To the accompaniment of an offstage 'Dies irae' sung by the monks, the Physician makes sure that Agnes is willing to sacrifice herself. Having prepared himself with flagellation, he is impressed by her resolve. In her eagerness to comfort Heinrich, she envisages her own 'seligster Liebestod' before entering the chamber with the Physician, who closes the doors. Heinrich lies as if dead but is suddenly galvanized by the mental picture of the sacrifice. He is refused entry to the chamber. Lightning and a roll of thunder symbolically release his anger, and he pulls an iron torch-holder from the wall, batters his way into the chamber and releases the still-living Agnes. Organ music (in C major) is heard as the monks process from the church and form an astonished audience to the 'miracle' of Heinrich's recovery; Dietrich and Hilde also now return. Heinrich greets the risen sun and is embraced by Dietrich, who then kneels before him. The monks stretch out their hands towards Agnes, and the Physician kisses the hem of her garment as the music moves from D minor into a 'transfigured' A major.

* * *

As the synopsis indicates, the opera inhabits the world of the Pre-Raphaelites, and at times the singers are directed to hold positions that create appropriate tableaux. Dealing with passivity, *Weltschmerz* and none but spiritual ecstasies, the libretto lacks the psychological depth of its models (*Parsifal* and the third act of *Tristan*) but signals its high aims in the epigraph from Goethe's *Faust* which appears in the libretto (but not the score): the Mater Gloriosa's 'Hebe dich zu höheren Sphären!/ Wenn er dich ahnet, folgt er nach'. For the most part it comprises lengthy formal exchanges which avoid obvious theatrical effect. Julius Korngold commented on the Wagnerism of the libretto in 1915: 'without rich Richard there could have been no poor Heinrich'.

From a purely musical viewpoint, however, the opera, and particularly its first act, must be seen as a landmark of 1890s intellectual Wagnerism. The harmonic language, accomplished and surprisingly adventurous, aspires always to a sinewy contrapuntal logic that Pfitzner seems anxious not to overload or overcolour in any 'decadent' fashion. Significantly the opera opens with a form of unprepared French sixth (F♯–D–A♭–C) whose whole-tone implications are nevertheless restricted by the chamber-music texture (four muted violas) and strict four-part writing (see ex.1). The tempo and dynamic range are predominantly restrained and solemn, the use of leitmotifs orthodox, although the latter rarely generate orchestral episodes divorced from literal association with the characters on stage. Imaginative word-painting in *Dietrichs Erzählung* represents a rare stretch of colouristic indulgence in a score that less devoted Wagnerians were to find controlled to the point of monotony. After 1900 few were able to welcome without question the revitalization of Pfitzner's not wholly attractive German knight by the Senta-like decision of a child to embrace a violent death, most explicitly described to Dietrich by the oddly characterized Physician of Salerno. PETER FRANKLIN

Armenia. For discussion of opera in Armenia *see* EREVAN.

Armida. Libretto subject used from the 17th century to the early 20th. Its source is TORQUATO TASSO's epic poem *Gerusalemme liberata* (1581). Almost 100 operas and ballets draw upon the love of the Saracen sorceress Armida for the Christian warrior Rinaldo (in French called Armide and Renaud), with such titles as *Armida*, *Rinaldo*, *Armida e Rinaldo*, *Armida abbandonata* and *Armida al campo d'Egitto*.

In Canto iv of *Gerusalemme liberata*, Armida, niece of Idraoto, King of Damascus, lures Christian warriors (commanded by Goffredo) who are laying siege to Jerusalem in the First Crusade (1099). Their imprisonment, then rescue by the noble Rinaldo (in temporary disgrace for his murder of Gernando), is narrated in Canto x, and Armida's vengeful pursuit of Rinaldo is recounted (Canto xiv) by a wizard to Carlo, a Danish knight, and Ubaldo, who are to bring him back to the Christian camp. Armida encounters Rinaldo, is attracted to him and, torn by love and hate, takes him to an enchanted island. Rinaldo, bewitched, spends languorous days with Armida in her palace (this recalls the episode of Alcina and Ruggiero in Ariosto's *Orlando furioso*). Carlo and Ubaldo reach the palace – the scene (Canto xvi) produces some of Tasso's most eloquent evocations of nature – successfully resisting monsters and other spells. Rinaldo is shown his reflection in a shield, recognizes his dishonourable state and resolves to abandon Armida, even though he still loves her. She vows revenge, summons demons to destroy the palace, and returns to Syria on her chariot drawn by two dragons.

In Canto xvii, Armida arrives in Egypt to recruit an army to attack the Christians, offering herself to whomever will kill Rinaldo: Adrasto, Tisaferno and Altomoro become her champions. Meanwhile Rinaldo has rejoined his colleagues (Canto xviii). He is required to conquer a forest enchanted by the pagan sorcerer Ismeno – the Christians need the wood for their war machines – and succeeds in destroying the magic myrtle, despite the enticements offered by a vision of Armida. Jerusalem is taken, and the Egyptians arrive for the final battle (Canto xx). Armida meets Rinaldo but, still in love, is unable to kill him (her champions also perish). In desperation, she attempts suicide but is prevented by the warrior, who promises to restore her kingdom. They are reconciled, with the implication, at least, that Armida will convert to Christianity and that the two may marry.

Tasso's splendid evocation of Armida's fury on being abandoned by Rinaldo was popular among madrigalists in the late 16th and early 17th centuries, and Monteverdi wrote a (now lost) dramatic cantata on the scene (1626). Armida soon reached the operatic stage with works by Marco Scacchi (1638, to a libretto by Virgilio Puccitelli), Benedetto Ferrari (1639, libretto by the composer) and Marco Marazzoli (1641, libretto by Ascanio Pio di Savoia). Quinault's *Armide*, set by Lully in 1686, focusses on the first stage of the story (up to Rinaldo's departure from the enchanted palace), and exploits the dramatic potential of a sorceress both hating and loving her enemy and a hero torn between pleasure and duty. Handel's *Rinaldo* (1711, libretto by Giacomo Rossi to a scheme by Aaron Hill) is more complex: Hill acknowledged that he had 'vary'd from the Scheme of Tasso, as was necessary for the better forming a Theatrical Representation'. Rinaldo is betrothed to Goffredo's daughter Almirena, and Armida is loved by Argante, King of Palestine. Armida kidnaps Almirena to lure Rinaldo to her island; Argante falls in love with Almirena; and Armida, now seeking a double revenge, seduces Rinaldo in the guise of Almirena. Goffredo and Eustazio rescue Rinaldo and Almirena from Armida's palace, which they destroy, returning the scene to Jerusalem. Armida and Argante, reconciled, fight the Christians and are captured; Rinaldo and Almirena are reunited; and Armida and Argante turn to Christianity and are freed by Goffredo.

Quinault's libretto is reworked in French or Italian settings by C. H. Graun (1751), Traetta (1761), Astarita

(1773) and Gluck (1777). A number of other Armida operas also appeared in the 1770s and 1780s: in some circles the subject may have gained renewed popularity in the light of Carlo Gozzi's recommendations for the supernatural on the operatic stage. Coltellini (set by Salieri in 1771 and Vincenzo Righini in 1782, among others) locates the action exclusively on the magic island, ending with the destruction of Armida's palace. However, in other operas (and as with Handel) the future of Rinaldo and Armida again becomes an issue: Tasso's reconciliation (doubtless a product of Counter-Reformation sensibilities) is somewhat contrived, but theatrical exigency requires at least some more rounded conclusion. Giacomo Duranti's libretto for Anfossi (1770) introduces a secondary love-interest: the Dane (here Clotarco) falls for Zelmira, betrothed to the King of Damascus (here Idreno), and Armida resolves to replace Clotarco in Idreno's intended sacrifice, only to be rescued (and again abandoned) by Rinaldo. Sacchini's setting of this libretto (1772, often wrongly attributed to G. De Gamerra) later gained some popularity in London and Paris in revisions and pasticcios. Francesco de Rogatis (set by Jommelli in 1770) extends the tale to the magic forest, with Armida defeated a second time (Giuseppe Gazzaniga's *Armida* of 1773 conflates this libretto with Duranti's). Giovanni Bertati (J. G. Naumann, 1773) adds Armida's attempted suicide which is prevented by Rinaldo – she ends swearing revenge – while reconciliation is suggested in Antonio Tozzi's *Rinaldo* (1775, librettist unknown). These various treatments become further conflated in operas by Bertoni (1781), Cherubini (1782), Mortellari (1785) and Zingarelli (1786). Haydn's *Armida* (1784) follows Tozzi's libretto, although the opera ends as Naumann's with the sorceress crying revenge.

Rossini's setting (1817, libretto by G. F. Schmidt) reverts to earlier formats: the action covers Armida in the Christian camp, Rinaldo and Armida on the magic island, and Gernando and Uberto's rescue of Rinaldo – the opera ends with the destruction of Armida's palace. Dvořák's *Armida* (1904, libretto by Jaroslav Vrchlický) follows similar lines but once more takes things further. The Danish prince (now Sven) and Ubald rescue Rinaldo at the prompting of Ismen, who is in love with Armida; and Armida and Rinaldo later meet on the battlefield. Rinaldo kills the sorceress unbeknown to him (the scene derives from the story of Tancredi and Clorinda); on her deathbed, Armida is baptized.

See also *ARMIDA* (i) [Traetta]; *ARMIDA* (ii) [Salieri]; *ARMIDA* (iii) [Sacchini]; *ARMIDA* (iv) [Naumann]; *ARMIDA* (v) [Haydn]; *ARMIDA* (vi) [Rossini]; *ARMIDA* (vii) [Dvořák]; *ARMIDA ABBANDONATA* [Jommelli]; *ARMIDE* (i) [Lully]; *ARMIDE* (ii) [Gluck]; and *RINALDO* [Handel]. For a list of operas based on Tasso's *Gerusalemme liberata*, *see* TASSO, TORQUATO. TIM CARTER

***Armida* (i).** *Azione teatrale* in one act by TOMMASO TRAETTA to a libretto by GIOVANNI AMBROGIO MIGLIAVACCA and Giacomo Durazzo after PHILIPPE QUINAULT's *Armide*, itself based on TORQUATO TASSO's epic poem *Gerusalemme liberata*; Vienna, Burgtheater, 3 January 1761.

The five acts of Quinault's *Armide* have here been reduced to a single act of 20 scenes. Armida (soprano), her uncle Idraoto (tenor) and a band of Saracens, including Fenicia (soprano) and Argene (soprano), plot to capture a group of crusaders, among them Rinaldo (soprano castrato). During a confrontation Armida and Rinaldo fall in love. When Artemidoro (soprano castrato) and Ubaldo (tenor) restore Rinaldo's reason, he leaves Armida, who falls into a rage, summons her dragon-drawn chariot and reduces the scene to flames and smoke.

This work appeared in Vienna a year before Gluck's *Orfeo*, also a French-inspired piece. Following its French model, Lully's *Armide*, Traetta's work is rich in divertimentos incorporating chorus, dance and pantomime. It has several duets, and choruses occur in combination with one of the duets and a few of the arias. Nearly all the arias are in full da capo form. Traetta unified extensive scene complexes of recitative and cavatina through obbligato recitative, introducing programmatic material when appropriate. In the first, and most charming, such scene Rinaldo becomes enchanted with the limpid brooks and singing birds in Armida's garden and falls asleep. Flutes, harp and muted strings depict his seduction. Armida enters, intent on killing him, but is dismayed to find herself falling in love with him instead. In the end she is abandoned, and like Metastasio's Dido she expresses her emotions in a concluding scena with cavatinas. The work was divided into three acts and performed in Naples (1763), and Traetta composed a new version for Venice (1767).

See also ARMIDA above. MARITA P. MCCLYMONDS

***Armida* (ii).** *Dramma per musica* in three acts by ANTONIO SALIERI to a libretto by MARCO COLTELLINI after TORQUATO TASSO's epic poem *Gerusalemme liberata*; Vienna, Burgtheater, 2 June 1771.

Salieri's opera takes as its subject the story of Armida and Rinaldo, already the subject of operas by Lully and Traetta among others. Like Traetta a decade earlier, Salieri used the story as an opportunity to combine the dramatic and musical devices of French and Italian opera. Following in Traetta's footsteps, Salieri successfully exploited the melodic richness of Italian opera within the dramatic framework of French *tragédie lyrique*, anticipating many aspects of Gluck's *Armide* (1977). Like Traetta, Salieri kept the number of soloists to a minimum; there are only four characters: Armida (soprano), her confidante Ismene (soprano), Rinaldo (tenor) and Ubaldo (tenor). Salieri's *Armida* was much praised by critics; it was one of the few Italian operas to be published in Germany in the 18th century (Leipzig, 1783).

In accordance with Gluck's preface to *Alceste* (1769), Salieri's overture is closely connected with the opera: with the aid of his annotations in the autograph score, we can follow the overture as a action-filled programmatic work setting the stage for the drama to come. Salieri used italianate coloratura with dramatic effect in several arias, including Armida's 'Tremo, bell'idol mio' and Rinaldo's 'Vieni a me' (both in Act 2). He skilfully used accompanied recitative, often effectively bridging numbers, as when the chorus of demons, 'Qual sibilo orrendo', leads straight into Ubaldo's accompanied recitative, 'Eterno proveder'. Choruses play a crucial role in *Armida*, and in several numbers a soloist alternates with chorus.

See also ARMIDA above. JOHN A. RICE

***Armida* (iii).** *Opera seria* in three acts by ANTONIO SACCHINI to a libretto by JACOPO DURANDI after TORQUATO TASSO's epic poem *Gerusalemme liberata*; Milan, Regio Ducal Teatro, Carnival 1772.

Armida incorporates elements previously associated with French opera: choruses, ballets, spectacle, machines and monsters. The characters are Armida (soprano), Rinaldo (soprano castrato), Ubaldo (tenor, but sung in Milan by G. B. Zonca), Zelmira (soprano), Idreno (alto castrato), and Clotarco (alto castrato). Sacchini's music reflects the special character of the libretto by being carefully composed, including numbers in minor keys. 'Idol mio, se più non vivi' is one of the earliest instances of a vocal rondò being employed as a showpiece for the primo uomo, and its success probably contributed to what became a vogue for this genre.

Sacchini used this subject twice more: as *Rinaldo* (1780, London), and as his first French opera, *Renaud* (1783, Paris), to a libretto by Pellegrin and Leboeuf. Although *Renaud* was not successful, Sacchini dedicated the score to Marie Antoinette, whose support made this failure less disastrous for his career in France than it would have been otherwise. Details of the relationships between the three scores have yet to be fully investigated.

See also ARMIDA above. DENNIS LIBBY

Armida **(iv).** *Dramma per musica* in three acts by JOHANN GOTTLIEB NAUMANN to a libretto by GIOVANNI BERTATI after TORQUATO TASSO's epic poem *Gerusalemme liberata*; Padua, Nuovo Teatro, 13 June 1773.

Composed in only three weeks, *Armida* was one of the last works of Naumann's student years in Italy. The opera depicts the bitter struggle between Armida (soprano), who magically controls her lover Rinaldo (soprano castrato), and Ubaldo (tenor), the leader of the French army, who wants Rinaldo to come away and fight with them for Jerusalem. Their intrigues involve Armida's father Idreno (bass) and her confidante Zelmira (alto). After much scheming and struggling, Armida relents; Rinaldo promises that he will return to her after the battle, and goes off with the army. The music is heavily influenced by the reformist styles of Traetta and Jommelli. Naumann favours ensembles and short, through-composed cavatinas. Selections from *Armida* were first published in Venice, and a German translation of the opera gained recognition throughout central Europe.

See also ARMIDA above. BERTIL H. VAN BOER

Armida **(v).** *Dramma eroico* in three acts by JOSEPH HAYDN to a libretto by NUNZIATO PORTA, after TORQUATO TASSO's epic poem *Gerusalemme liberata*; Eszterháza, 26 February 1784.

Armida	soprano
Rinaldo	tenor
Ubaldo *a Frankish knight*	tenor
Idreno *King of Damascus*	bass
Zelmira *destined bride of Idreno*	soprano
Clotarco *a Danish knight*	tenor

Setting Damascus

The original cast featured Matilde Bologna (Armida), Prospero Braghetti (Rinaldo), Antonio Specioli (Ubaldo), Paolo Mandini (Idreno), Costanza Valdesturla (Zelmira) and Leopold Dichtler (Clotarco). *Armida*, the most performed opera at Eszterháza, received 54 performances between its première and 1788. It enjoyed modest success outside Eszterháza; most later performances were in German. Artaria published a collection of 'favourite songs' from the opera in 1787. Haydn's work derives originally from an episode in Tasso's *Gerusalemme liberata* (published in 1581), but relies more immediately on librettos on the same subject by Durandi, De Rogatis, Bertati and an unknown adapter (set by Tozzi, 1775). Today *Armida* is among the most admired of Haydn's operas. There is at least one recording (with Jessye Norman in the title role), and there were several staged performances in the 1980s, including one given at the 1981 Monadnock Festival in Keene, New Hampshire, directed by Peter Sellars and set in Vietnam.

The overture is in three parts. The *allegretto* middle section anticipates the music of the magic grove in Rinaldo's Act 3 *scena*; the outer *vivace* sections anticipate no themes exactly, but musical topics relevant to the characters and situations of the opera are explored.

ACT 1.i–iii *A council chamber in the royal palace of Damascus* Idreno announces the arrival of the Frankish crusaders in Damascus. Rinaldo offers to help defend Damascus, singing 'Vado a pugnar contento', a heroic C major aria with military motifs and virtuoso coloratura. Armida fears for his safety, but Idreno promises that if Rinaldo defeats the enemy, he will have the right to rule Damascus ('Se dal suo braccio oppresso'). Idreno's aria is another heroic piece, but with less vocal virtuosity and more orchestral bluster than Rinaldo's. Armida, left alone, worries that she might have encouraged Rinaldo to go to his death (accompanied recitative, 'Parti Rinaldo'). Her succeeding aria, 'Se pietade avete o Numi', is a hybrid two-tempo form in A major whose principal motif echoes the opening of the recitative. The piece ends with extensive coloratura and several opportunities for cadenzas. The intensity, variety and sustained virtuosity of this aria establish Armida as the emotional centre of the opera.

1.iv–v *A steep mountain, on whose peak Armida's palace can be seen* Scene iv begins with a short march for wind band, recalling the march theme in the overture. Ubaldo's accompanied recitative ('Valorosi compagni') reveals that he is becoming bewitched. His *largo* aria, 'Dove son' (published separately in 1802), includes particularly beautiful wind writing. The aria moves directly into a burst of accompanied recitative in which Ubaldo recovers his courage and decides to ascend Armida's mountain. Clotarco warns him that the mountain is swarming with monsters and soldiers, but Ubaldo fights his way to the top. In scene v Zelmira explains to the audience that she has been co-opted by Armida and Idreno to entice the crusaders to their deaths. Seeing Clotarco, she is struck by his beauty, and sings a charming G major aria persuading him to follow her ('Se tu seguir mi vuoi').

1.vi–ix *Armida's rooms* Armida begs Rinaldo to hide from the crusaders, then Ubaldo tries to shame him into remembering his original obligations. Rinaldo starts to follow Ubaldo, but Armida restrains him in a passionate accompanied recitative, preceding their duet, 'Cara, sarò fedele'. This piece follows the usual progression: a tender opening gives way to a disturbed middle section, leading to a cheerful conclusion in parallel 3rds and 6ths.

ACT 2.i–vi *A garden in Armida's palace* Idreno reveals his plan to ambush the crusaders on their way back down the mountain and Zelmira tries unsuccessfully to dissuade him. In the following scenes Clotarco and Ubaldo plead for peace and persuade Rinaldo to return to his people; but (scene v) Rinaldo is torn between love and duty. His accompanied recitative and aria ('Armida ... oh affanno' and 'Cara, è vero', published separately in 1827), in which he bids Armida an agonized farewell, form the centrepiece of the opera. Armida moves from grief to rage in her accompanied recitative, 'Barbaro! e ardisci ancor', then sings the most celebrated aria in the opera, 'Odio, furor, dispetto, dolor'. This piece is justly famous for its concentration and its intensity; eschewing coloratura, the voice spits out brief syllabic motifs and howls long high notes over a turbulent accompaniment. It is the only minor-mode piece in the opera.

2.viii–x *The crusaders' encampment* Ubaldo welcomes Rinaldo, singing 'Prence amato'. Armida arrives, and the act ends with a trio in which Rinaldo is torn between Armida and Ubaldo ('Partirò, ma pensa, ingrato').

The second act is notable for the through-composition of scenes v–vii. These scenes are also the first exploration of Rinaldo's divided loyalties, and the continuous music focusses attention on the emotions of the characters.

ACT 3.i *Part of the forest, near the enchanted grove* Ubaldo reminds Rinaldo of his task.

3.ii–iii *A fearsome grove, with a bushy myrtle tree in the middle* Rinaldo is almost overcome by the enchantments of the grove. The orchestral accompaniment to his recitative 'Questa dunque è la selva?' conjures up streams, birds, monsters and sweet odours as he imagines and then describes them. Zelmira tries to persuade him to return to Armida ('Torna pure al caro bene'; published separately in 1802). Rinaldo resists bewitchment ('Qual tumulto d'idee'), and is about to strike the sacred myrtle when Armida appears out of the tree and stays his hand, singing a deeply felt *largo* aria, 'Ah, non ferir'. She departs, 'making gestures with her magic branch' and darkening the stage in the process, while the orchestral music depicts the infernal scene. Rinaldo's final aria, 'Dei pietosi', is a two-tempo piece which juxtaposes a tender and reflective first section with a valiant then panic-stricken second section. He strikes the myrtle, the furies and the grove disappear, and the crusaders' encampment reappears to a series of increasingly soft scales in the orchestra. The entire scene is through-composed. In the final scene, Armida curses Rinaldo and calls for her infernal carriage. The finale consists of two march-like choral sections in which all participants lament their cruel fates; these frame a brief central section in which Armida berates Rinaldo, who almost weakens again, after which Ubaldo reminds him of his duty once more.

* * *

Armida may be Haydn's best opera. The long through-composed scenes with accompanied recitatives at the ends of the second and third acts allowed Haydn opportunities to exercise his formidable powers of orchestral illustration; they also project a remarkably natural dramatic rhythm; Armida's 'Ah, non ferir' in Act 3 scene ii is effective partly because she can begin it as an interruption of Rinaldo's recitative. The rather slow pace of dramatic action also suits Haydn's interest in extended explorations of character and situation. Armida is by far the most fully characterized role; like Amaranta in *La fedeltà premiata*, she portrays a wide and convincing range of emotional positions. Rinaldo has a comparable variety of music; his aria 'Dei pietosi' is a powerful expression of incompatible sentiments; nevertheless, vacillation is a less operatically compelling condition than naked desire. In contrast to the central characters, the secondary figures seem flat and undifferentiated. They fade into the landscape, whose physical features and transformations are more vividly illustrated than the human qualities of its inhabitants.

See also ARMIDA above; for an illustration of a costume design for *Armida*, *see* HAYDN, JOSEPH. MARY HUNTER

***Armida* (vi).** *Dramma* in three acts by GIOACHINO ROSSINI to a libretto by GIOVANNI SCHMIDT after TORQUATO TASSO's epic poem *Gerusalemme liberata*; Naples, Teatro S Carlo, 11 November 1817.

The Paladin Knights, led by Goffredo (tenor), are preparing to elect a successor to the deceased Dudone, but the election is interrupted by a weeping noblewoman demanding protection from Idraote who has usurped the throne of Damascus. The woman is the sorceress Armida (soprano) and the plea is a ruse. With the disguised Idraote (bass) as one of her followers, she has come to Jerusalem to enslave the knights in general and Rinaldo (tenor) in particular. The knights elect Rinaldo, to the fury of his closest rival, Gernando (tenor). Armida begins to seduce Rinaldo but is interrupted by Gernando's insults. The two men fight a duel and Gernando is slain. Horrified by what he has done, Rinaldo flees the camp with Armida. Act 2 begins in a Fury-infested forest where Armida's follower Astarotte (bass) rules over his demon empire. Rinaldo appears with Armida who transforms the forest into a vast Baroque palace. Love music and an extended ballet dominate the act. In Act 3 Carlo (tenor) and Ubaldo (tenor) arrive to recover Rinaldo. After a further duet with Armida, Rinaldo is shown his besotted image in the knights' adamantine shield; this is the cue for the celebrated trio for three tenors 'In quale aspetto imbelle'. The opera's final scene, the lovers' parting and Armida's demented flight, is part realistic, part allegorical as Armida is confronted by the spirits of Vengeance and Love.

This traditionally spectacular subject was chosen by Rossini and the impresario Domenico Barbaia for the opening of the rebuilt Teatro S Carlo. It is a work of a kind rare among the composer's operas, that shows the darker, more sensual side of his nature; the first and third acts in particular contrast the brilliant daylit world of chivalric endeavour with the gloomier, more sensuously alluring world of Armida herself. The libretto draws freely on Tasso's original poem.

Armida's final scene, and much of her preceding music provides a brilliant showcase for soprano; Rossini uses the bel canto style to suggest the enchantress caught in the toils of her own fantasy. Similarly, the bright texturing of the tenor voice is used by Rossini to create the special atmosphere of the world of the Paladin knights. The fact that seven tenor roles are listed has helped create the legend of the opera's unperformability. In practice, six are comprimario roles that can effectively be shared between three singers, as happened at the première in 1817.

See also ARMIDA above. RICHARD OSBORNE

***Armida* (vii).** Opera in four acts by ANTONÍN DVOŘÁK to a libretto by JAROSLAV VRCHLICKÝ, after TORQUATO

TASSO's epic poem *Gerusalemme liberata*; Prague, National Theatre, 25 March 1904.

With a common root in Tasso's *Gerusalemme liberata*, Vrchlický's libretto bears clear resemblances to Quinault's for Lully. The first act is set in Damascus as the Crusaders are advancing. The magician Ismen (baritone) persuades King Hydraot of Damascus (bass) to send his daughter Armida (soprano) to distract the Christian knights. Armida only agrees when Ismen conjures a picture of the camp and she recognizes the knight Rinald (tenor), whom she had seen and fallen in love with in a dream. In Act 2 there is already discontent at the slowness of the campaign in the Crusaders' camp. A hermit Petr (bass), who senses that Armida will indeed cause a distraction, attempts to have her removed, but Rinald intervenes and takes her under his protection. In a frenzy of passion Armida and Rinald attempt to flee the camp but are discovered by Petr. As he calls the guards, Ismen appears in a chariot drawn by dragons and sweeps them away.

Set in Armida's magic gardens, Act 3 sees the development of her and Rinald's love. She rebuffs the suit of Ismen who, in revenge, gives Sven (tenor) and Ubald (bass), knights who have come in search of Rinald, the diamond shield of the archangel Michael with which they attract Rinald away allowing Ismen to destroy Armida's magic palace. Rinald awakes in an oasis in the desert at the beginning of Act 4. Inspired by the singing of pilgrims he joins battle against the Moor and slays Ismen. At this point Vrchlický interpolated the episode in *Gerusalemme liberata* in which Tancred unwittingly kills Clorinda, substituting Rinald and Armida. At the end of the opera, to the song of the pilgrims, Rinald christens Armida as she dies.

Armida marks the peak of Dvořák's interest in Wagner although much of it, not least the Act 1 aria 'Za štíhlou gazelou' ('After a slender gazelle') for Armida, Ismen's Act 3 aria 'Div nezšílel jsem bezmála' ('A wonder nearly drove me mad') and Rinald's Act 4 monologue 'Sám, v poušti sám' ('Alone in the desert, alone'), is wholly typical of Dvořák and completely successful. The old-fashioned structure of the libretto, quite outside the *verismo* trends in Czech opera at the time, found little favour, and *Armida* has only held a marginal place in the modern Czech repertory.

See also ARMIDA above. JAN SMACZNY

Armida abbandonata ('Armida Abandoned'). *Opera seria* in three acts by NICCOLÒ JOMMELLI to a libretto by FRANCESCO SAVERIO DE ROGATIS after TORQUATO TASSO's *Gerusalemme liberata*; Naples, Teatro di S Carlo, 30 May 1770.

Armida abbandonata was the first opera Jommelli wrote for Naples after having spent 17 years in the service of the Duke of Württemberg. It is unusually rich in spectacular elements, especially the depiction of rage at the end of Act 2, when Armida (soprano) calls down thunder and lightning to destroy her palace and then leaves in a chariot drawn by winged dragons. Such theatrical effects were rare in Naples but more common in Jommelli's operas for the new theatre at Ludwigsburg, which had been designed to accommodate spectacle in the French style. Ballet and choruses were also introduced, and in Act 1 Tancredi (tenor) converses with silent dancers. The programmatic recitative in Act 3, describing the progress of Rinaldo (soprano castrato) through Armida's enchanted forest, originated in this opera; it was set by half a dozen other composers before it was later incorporated into Haydn's *Armida* (1783). The ending was also different from earlier versions which ended with Armida's destructive rage. Rogatis went on with the story: after Rinaldo locates the magic myrtle and destroys it, Armida and her spectres disappear, and all returns to normal.

Jommelli's opera had a superb cast of singers equal to the expressive and the virtuoso challenges of his music. Giuseppe Aprile (Rinaldo) and Arcangelo Cortoni (Tancredi) had followed Jommelli to Naples from Stuttgart; Anna Lucia De Amicis (Armida) later sang Giunia in Mozart's *Lucio Silla* (1772). But Neapolitan audiences did not respond well to Jommelli's dense orchestration, chromaticism and rhythmic complexities. The attention to dramatic detail that he lavished on obbligato recitative was lost in the noise of the theatre. Mozart's reaction was mixed. On 29 May after having seen a rehearsal, he wrote that the opera was 'well composed' and that he liked it. Later, in a letter dated 5 June, he wrote that it was 'beautiful but too serious and old-fashioned for the theatre'. Despite its supposed lack of success, copies of the full score and of individual arias enjoyed a wider distribution throughout Europe than any of Jommelli's other works. The opera received the unusual honour of three other Neapolitan revivals (1771, 1780 and 1786), and it was performed in Lisbon (1773) and Florence (1775).

See also ARMIDA above. MARITA P. McCLYMONDS

***Armide* (i).** *Tragédie en musique* in a prologue and five acts by Jean-Baptiste Lully (*see* LULLY family, (1)) to a libretto by PHILIPPE QUINAULT after TORQUATO TASSO's epic poem *Gerusalemme liberata*; Paris, Opéra, 15 February 1686.

PROLOGUE

La Gloire [Glory]	soprano
La Sagesse [Wisdom]	soprano

TRAGEDY

Armide *magician, niece of Hidraot*	soprano
Renaud *a knight*	haute-contre
Phénice } *confidantes of Armide*	soprano
Sidonie }	soprano
Hidraot *magician, King of Damascus*	baritone
Aronte *guard of Armide's captive knights*	tenor
Artémidore *a knight*	tenor
La Haine [Hatred]	tenor
Ubalde *a knight*	baritone
The Danish Knight *companion of Ubalde*	haute-contre
A Demon in the form of a Water Nymph	soprano
A Demon in the form of Lucinde, the Danish Knight's beloved	soprano
A Demon in the form of Mélisse, Ubalde's beloved	soprano

Heroes who follow Glory, nymphs who follow Wisdom; people of Damascus; demons disguised as nymphs and as shepherds and shepherdesses, flying demons disguised as zephyrs; followers of Hatred, the Furies, Cruelty, Vengeance, Rage etc.; demons disguised as rustics; Pleasures, demons disguised as happy lovers

Setting Damascus, during the First Crusade

The last tragedy by Lully and Quinault was regarded during the 18th century as their masterpiece. It is their only opera to concentrate on the sustained psychological development of an individual character. According to Le Cerf de la Viéville, it was known as 'the ladies' opera', presumably a reference to Armide's internal conflict.

Louis XIV chose the subject, but because of illnesses and scheduling clashes, the initial production had no court première (although unstaged chamber performances were sponsored by the dauphine). Apart from Le Rochois (Armide) and Dumesnil (Renaud), the principal singers at the Paris première are uncertain; they probably included either Dun or Beaumavielle (Hidraot), Moreau (Sidonie), Desmatins (Phénice) and Frere (Hatred). *Armide* was revived regularly at the Paris Opéra between 1692 and 1766, the 1745–7 revival being a joint production with the court at Versailles. By the end of the 17th century the last scene of Act 4 (the Ubalde–Mélisse encounter) had been permanently cut; for the production of 1761 François Francoeur comprehensively reworked *Armide* to conform with contemporary taste; and in 1766 Pierre-Montan Berton rewrote the Act 5 *divertissement*. Between 1686 and 1751 *Armide* was produced repeatedly in Marseilles, Brussels and Lyons; it had single productions in The Hague, Lunéville, Berlin (with revisions by Carl Heinrich Graun) and perhaps Metz; and there were apparently concert performances in Rome on two occasions. There have been a few modern productions.

PROLOGUE *A palace* Glory and Wisdom, assisted by their followers, celebrate their relative power over an unnamed hero (Louis XIV): in time of war Glory holds the upper hand, while Wisdom dominates in peacetime. Their hero has invited them to watch Renaud follow Glory away from the palace where he loved Armide. A comment on a 'monster' that the hero has vanquished is thought to refer to the Edict of Nantes (revoked in 1685).

ACT 1 *A great square, decorated by an arch of triumph* In an extended passage set as recitative and brief *airs* Phénice and Sidonie congratulate Armide on using her womanly charms and her power over the underworld to capture almost all the Crusaders in Godefroy's camp. Armide's eventual entrance into the conversation, set as simple modulatory recitative, begins with an affective progression to the relative minor. Titon du Tillet wrote that 'in the moment when Mademoiselle Rochois spread her arms and raised her head with a majestic air, singing

> Je ne triomphe pas du plus vaillant de tous
> L'indomptable Renaud échappe à mon courroux.

her two confidantes seemed, so to speak, eclipsed; one no longer saw anybody but her on the stage, and she seemed to fill it alone'. Renaud, the most famous knight from Godefroy's camp, has eluded Armide; in powerful accompanied recitative she tells Phénice and Sidonie of a terrible dream, in which she fell in love with Renaud as he was about to kill her. When Hidraot says he wishes to see his niece marry, Armide expresses interest only in 'the conqueror of Renaud (if someone can be that)'. Rameau later wrote that by setting the parenthetical phrase in the subdominant key – the flat side, representing weakness – Lully showed Armide's ambivalence. Neither the suggestion that Renaud is unconquerable nor the bad dream is in Tasso. Still trying to reassure Armide, the people of Damascus praise her beauty and glorious victories; the *divertissement* begins with a large-scale bass *air* and chorus, 'Armide est encore plus aimable', and continues with an intricately organized set of *sarabandes en rondeau*. When Aronte brings word that Renaud has singlehandedly freed the captive knights, all vow revenge.

ACT 2 *The countryside, where a river forms an agreeable island* Renaud assures Artémidore, whom he has freed from captivity, that he is indifferent to Armide's charms, and then sends him away. Demons, following the instructions given by Armide and Hidraot in the extended duet 'Esprits de haine et de rage', disguise themselves under pleasant exteriors and lull Renaud to sleep. Renaud's well-known monologue *air de sommeil*, 'Plus j'observe ces lieux', in which recorders and muted strings paint the flowing river, is followed by a pastoral *divertissement* for demons transformed into nymphs, shepherds and shepherdesses. In Lully's most famous recitative monologue, 'Enfin il est en ma puissance' – criticized at length by Rousseau (1753) and defended in a detailed analysis by Rameau (1754) – Armide stands over the sleeping Renaud, dagger in hand, but is overcome with love for him and cannot kill him. During the entr'acte, demons disguised as zephyrs transport them both to a faraway desert where Armide might hide her shame; a drawing survives of the machine used in an early production.

ACT 3 *A desert* In an orchestrally accompanied monologue *air*, 'Ah! si la liberté', Armide declares herself unable to hate Renaud. She then confesses to Phénice and Sidonie that she is nonetheless too ashamed to enjoy his love since she needed the help of magic to win it; a recurring cadential phrase insists, 'Hélas! que son/mon amour est différent du mien/sien!'. In the monologue *air* 'Venez, venez, Haine implacable', over a savage repeated-note bass line, Armide calls to Hatred to save her from her love; the invocation and ensuing dialogue between Armide and Hatred are accompanied entirely by the orchestra. Hatred and her followers – an all-male chorus and dance troupe – attempt to obey in a *divertissement* that includes the breaking of Cupid's bows and arrows in a pantomime ballet, but Armide stops them. Hatred tells Armide never to seek her help again and disappears.

ACT 4 *The desert* Ubalde and the Danish Knight search for Renaud. Armide has filled the desert with traps, and the knights must cope first with monsters and open chasms, then (after the desert appears to change into pleasant countryside) with seduction. In a pastoral *divertissement* Lucinde and demons disguised as rustic folk attempt to seduce the Danish Knight, but Ubalde uses a magic sceptre to make the demons disappear. Mélisse then attempts to seduce Ubalde; the Danish Knight rescues him, using some of the same musical phrases uttered earlier by Ubalde under parallel circumstances.

ACT 5 *Armide's enchanted palace* In the only love scene in the opera Renaud, unarmed and wearing garlands of flowers, responds to Armide's premonitions of trouble mainly with loving rhetorical questions. The mutual declarations of love in the ensuing duets do little to reassure her. She departs to consult the underworld, leaving Pleasures and happy lovers to entertain Renaud in her absence; this well-known *divertissement* is an extended *passacaille* with vocal interludes as well as danced portions. Ubalde and the Danish Knight find

'Armide' (Lully), Act 5 (the destruction of Armide's enchanted palace, with the departure of Renaud in the foreground): engraving by J. Dolivar after Jean Berain's design for the original production at the Paris Opéra (Académie Royale de Musique) on 15 February 1686, from the first edition of the libretto (1686)

Renaud and break the spell Armide has cast over him. When Armide returns, Renaud expresses pity for her, states that Glory requires love to yield to duty, then leaves. (The often-reproduced frontispiece from the libretto of 1686, see illustration, conflates Renaud's departure with the destruction of the palace at the end of the opera; Renaud is shown in a boat, accompanied by Glory.) The celebrated final monologue, accompanied entirely by the orchestra, begins with the *air* 'Le perfide Renaud me fuit' and continues in recitative; this is the only Lullian tragedy that ends intimately rather than with a *divertissement* or other crowd scene. In the monologue Armide flies into a rage, then descends into despair; she orders the demons to destroy the magical palace and, with it, her fatal love. As the demons obey, Armide departs in a flying chariot. The famous stage-machine palace, by Jean Berain, was probably made up of a series of small panels with different images painted on each side; they could turn individually, giving the effect of a gradually crumbling building.

* * *

Armide represents Lully and Quinault's style at its most mature. As in *Roland*, Quinault's exploration of a character's inward conflict is subtly complemented by the details of Lully's music. The recitatives contain a greater degree of rhythmic and tonal subtlety than those in any previous opera, and 18th-century observers recognized this feature, praising *Armide* as a model of expressive text declamation. As in the other operas of the mid-1680s, Lully makes particularly effective use of the orchestra in certain vocal passages: the nightmare in Act 1, Renaud's *air de sommeil*, Armide's encounter with Hatred and all of the final monologue.

See also ARMIDA above. LOIS ROSOW

Armide (ii). *Drame héroïque* in five acts by CHRISTOPH WILLIBALD GLUCK to a libretto by PHILIPPE QUINAULT after TORQUATO TASSO's epic poem *Gerusalemme liberata*; Paris, Opéra, 23 September 1777.

Armide *a sorceress, Princess of Damascus*	soprano
Renaud *one of the most famous crusaders*	tenor
Phénice } *a confidante of Armide*	soprano
Sidonie } *a confidante of Armide*	soprano
Hidraot *magician, King of Damascus and Armide's uncle*	baritone
La Haine [Hatred]	contralto
The Danish Knight } *crusaders sent to look for Renaud*	tenor
Ubalde } *crusaders sent to look for Renaud*	baritone
A demon in the form of Lucinde, The Danish Knight's beloved	soprano
A demon in the form of Mélisse, Ubalde's beloved	soprano
Artémidore *one of Armide's prisoners freed by Renaud*	tenor
Aronte *guard in charge of Armide's prisoners*	bass
A Naiad	soprano
A Shepherd	soprano
A Pleasure	soprano

People of Damascus, nymphs, shepherds and shepherdesses, attendants of Hatred, demons, pleasures

Setting Damascus at the time of the First Crusade

Armide was the fifth of the seven operas that Gluck wrote for the Académie Royale de Musique in Paris. In it, after the successes of *Iphigénie en Aulide*, *Orphée et Eurydice* and *Alceste*, Gluck paid homage to, and also confronted, the operatic traditions of Lully and Rameau by setting complete (except for the prologue) the libretto Quinault had written nearly 90 years earlier for Lully's last *tragédie lyrique*. The principals in the first performance were Rosalie Levasseur (Armide), Joseph Legros (Renaud), Mlle Lebourgeois (Phénice), Mlle Châteauneuf (Sidonie), Nicolas Gélin (Hidraot), Mlle Durancy (Hatred), Etienne Lainé (The Danish Knight) and Henri Larrivée (Ubalde).

Performances of *Armide* since the 18th century have not been frequent. Among important revivals was one in Paris in 1825 when Alexandrine Caroline Branchu sang the title role and was much admired by Berlioz. Meyerbeer conducted it in Berlin in 1843, the year Wagner conducted it in Dresden with Wilhelmine Schröder-Devrient in the title role; and Berlioz conducted Act 3 the following year at the Paris Exhibition with 900 performers. Another extraordinary performance took place in Karlsruhe in 1853 when *Armide* was performed in German translation with new recitatives by Joseph Strauss. Toscanini conducted the opera at La Scala and at the Metropolitan Opera in New York. In 1905 Lucienne Bréval sang Armide in a Paris revival, and between 1906 and 1928 there were ten performances at Covent Garden with Bréval, Emmy Destinn and Frida Leider as Armide.

In recent times *Armide* has had only occasional performances at festivals, in student productions and in concert performances. A controversial production by Wolf-Siegfried Wagner at the 1982 Spitalfields Festival in London was followed by a recording, the opera's only complete commercial recording to date.

ACT 1 *A public square decorated by a triumphal arch in the city of Damascus* Armide's two confidantes Phénice and Sidonie are celebrating her recent victory over the crusaders and trying to distract her from her preoccupation with the idea of defeating Renaud, the most valiant crusader of them all. Armide describes how she has recently seen him in a dream in which she fell in love with him at the very moment he struck her a fatal blow. Gluck claimed that in *Armide* he managed to differentiate the expression of the characters to a degree that one can instantly tell whether Armide or another is singing. This is true from the opening scene of the opera where the lyrical, dance-like music for Phénice and Sidonie is sharply distinguished from the martial dotted rhythms and minor-key harmony of Armide's.

Hidraot and his retinue enter. He congratulates Armide on her victory over the crusaders but urges her to marry. His blustering music, almost from the world of *opera buffa*, contrasts vividly with Armide's: her *ariette* 'La chaîne de l'hymen m'étonne' is like an instrumental movement into which the vocal part has been fitted, its radiant major key and caressing phrases belying her words ironically. She confesses that, if she marries, it will only be to the man who defeats Renaud.

The people of Damascus celebrate Armide's victory with singing and dancing. Their rejoicing is interrupted by Aronte who staggers in, wounded, and tells them that all their prisoners have been rescued by one soldier, single-handed – Renaud. The act ends with the soloists and chorus swearing vengeance on him.

ACT 2 *The countryside outside Damascus* Renaud tells Artémidore, one of the knights he has rescued, to return to the camp of the crusaders; he himself cannot do so because he has been banished by their leader, Godefroi. Artémidore warns him to beware of Armide, but in a short, martial air ('J'aime la liberté') Renaud declares his indifference to the danger she poses.

As they leave, Armide and Hidraot come in and invoke the spirits of the underworld to put a spell on Renaud (duet, 'Esprits de haine et de rage'). When Renaud appears, he is entranced by the beauty of the countryside, and sings an air ('Plus j'observe ces lieux') in which the solo flute represents birdsong and the constant quaver motion in the muted violins a gently flowing stream. Evil spirits transformed into naiads, nymphs, shepherds and shepherdesses lull him to sleep with songs and dances.

Armide suddenly appears, ready to stab the sleeping Renaud. But she cannot bring herself to do so, her indecision being expressed in a fine example of Gluck's suggestive orchestration as her avowals of hatred for Renaud are belied by warmer, more sensual music in the orchestra. She determines to make him love her, thereby avenging herself by seducing him from the field of battle. In shame and desperation she calls on her spirits to take them both far away to the end of the universe ('Venez, venez, secondez mes désirs'). Their enchanted flight is vividly depicted by fleeting semiquaver triplets on the flute and violins, a syncopated accompaniment on divided violas and above them all a high, angular line for solo oboe which leads Armide's vocal part on ever higher.

ACT 3 *A desert* Alone, Armide reflects that although, by means of her magic, she has made Renaud love her, she has failed to control her own amorous feelings for him (air, 'Ah! si la liberté me doit être ravie'). Phénice and Sidonie assure her that she has him completely in her power, but she knows she must choose between her love for Renaud and hatred and revenge on him (this scene includes Armide's air 'De mes plus doux regards Renaud sut se défendre'). Left alone, Armide summons Hatred to rescue her and exorcise love from her heart (air, 'Venez, venez, Haine implacable!').

Hatred and her demonic entourage appear from the underworld and, in a series of three airs with chorus, separated by two dances, they begin their incantations. But this is too much for Armide and, her mind made up, she joins in, rejecting Hatred's help. Armide's anguish is strikingly portrayed as her voice is suddenly left isolated, rising higher in a crescendo as she declares it impossible to take away her love for Renaud without breaking her heart.

Hatred scornfully predicts Armide's abandonment, saying that she could not punish her more harshly than by leaving her to the powers of Love. She then leads a mocking chorus ('Suis l'Amour, puisque tu le veux') before leaving Armide trembling with fear for her fate and putting her trust in Love. For this Gluck added four lines to Quinault's libretto; in them the persistent ostinato rhythms which have characterized Hatred continue to torment Armide in spite of the consoling phrases from the strings.

ACT 4.i *A desert* The Danish Knight and Ubalde, sent to Armide's palace to find Renaud and bring him back to the war, find their way barred by Armide's monsters. They overcome these with the help of a talismanic diamond shield and a golden sceptre given them by a magician to counter Armide's magic powers.

4.ii The desert changes into beautiful countryside and the two knights are in turn tempted by demons who have been transformed by Armide to resemble their beloveds. They dispel these visions with the golden sceptre and go on their way towards Armide's palace, singing a duet of heroic resolution ('Fuyons les douceurs dangereuses').

ACT 5 *Armide's enchanted palace* Armide is now committed to loving Renaud but fears she will lose him (as Hatred predicted). His langorous sighing phrases at the opening are followed by an extended love duet containing some of the most passionate music Gluck ever wrote (as he must have realized when, in later years, he said that if he suffered damnation it would be for having written this duet).

Armide goes to consult her evil powers and leaves Renaud to be entertained by her retinue until she returns. They take the form of Pleasures who sing and dance for him in a lengthy *divertissement*. This begins and ends with a chaconne; in between there are airs with chorus and other dances. But Renaud cannot enjoy anything without Armide, and banishes the Pleasures with his lovesick air, 'Allez, éloignez-vous de moi'.

Ubalde and the Danish Knight enter and show Renaud the diamond shield; this breaks Armide's spell and awakens him to his desertion. As he is leaving with his companions, Armide returns: in an anguished recitative ('Renaud! Ciel! O mortelle peine!') with solo oboe she expresses her horror at seeing her fears of his betrayal confirmed. The chromatic, languishing phrases of Renaud's love music now give way to conventional, straightforward recitative as he bids Armide farewell; but there is a hint of his looking back at her longingly in the chromatic descending phrase 'Trop malheureuse Armide, Que ton destin est déplorable'.

After the knights have left Armide alternates between despair and desire for vengeance. This final scene of the opera, an extended arioso whose opening grows from Renaud's parting words 'Que ton destin est déplorable', is one of Gluck's finest. At first Armide laments the departure of the perfidious Renaud; then the music becomes more violent and distraught as she regrets not having killed him when he was in her power (the orchestra vividly depicts her stabbing him in her imagination). Finally she orders the demons to destroy her enchanted palace, and she leaves on a flying chariot to seek revenge on Renaud.

* * *

Armide is the only one of Gluck's late operas to end tragically, with no *deus ex machina* appearing to put all to rights; instead its conclusion is the logical outcome of the events of the drama. It is also unique as a setting of a libretto which was so much a part of an earlier French operatic tradition, with its five acts and abundance of spectacular effects and *divertissements*. That Gluck brought these to life with such success is a measure of his versatility, for the music is constantly on an inspired level. Gluck himself said that whereas *Alceste* 'must call forth tears', *Armide* must 'produce a voluptuous sensation', and the opera contains some of the most sheerly beautiful and sensuous music that he ever wrote, notably Renaud's slumber scene in Act 2 and much of the fourth and fifth acts. But Gluck's evocation of evil and the supernatural in Act 3 is also as vivid as anything in *Orfeo ed Euridice* or *Alceste*.

There is more action *per se* in *Armide* than in any other of Gluck's major operas, and its structure is very fluid and continuous with comparatively few self-contained airs or set numbers of any length. Instead there are short airs, arioso and recitative; arguably *Armide* contains the most successful continuous arioso and recitative of any Gluck opera, for example in the last two scenes of Act 5. And it is in the recitative and arioso that Armide herself is most fully characterized. She dominates the opera, a Kundry-like combination of sorceress and seductress, one of Gluck's great heroines and possibly his most rounded and fascinating female character. Posterity has undervalued this opera which Gluck regarded as 'perhaps the best of all my works'.

See also ARMIDA above. JEREMY HAYES

Arminio ('Arminius'; 'Hermann'). Opera in three acts by GEORGE FRIDERIC HANDEL to a libretto anonymously adapted from ANTONIO SALVI's *Arminio* (1703, Pratolino); London, Covent Garden Theatre, 12 January 1737.

Handel composed *Arminio* immediately after drafting *Giustino*, completing the 'filling-out' of the score on 14 October 1736. It was the first new opera in Handel's season of 1736–7 at Covent Garden Theatre, when for the last time his productions competed with those of the 'Opera of the Nobility' at the King's Theatre. Salvi's libretto is founded on the account by Tacitus (*Annals of Imperial Rome*, i.54–ii.21) of events in the Roman war against the Germans in 15 and 16 AD, and involves the historical characters of the rebel chieftain Hermann or Arminius (Prince of the Cauchi and Cherusci), the collaborating chieftain Segestes (Prince of the Catti), Segestes' son Sigismond and the Roman general Publius Quinctilius Varus. Arminius (alto castrato), betrayed by Segeste [Segestes] (bass) and imprisoned by Varo [Varus] (tenor), is freed through the courage of his wife Tusnelda [Thusnelda] (soprano) and his sister Ramise [Ramisa] (contralto), who loves Sigismondo [Sigismond] (soprano castrato), and ultimately of Sigismond himself; he and his allies defeat the Romans and peace is restored.

Arminius was sung by Domenico Annibali, Thusnelda by Anna Maria Strada del Pò, Ramisa by Francesca Bertolli, Thusnelda's father Segestes by Henry Reinhold, her brother Sigismond by the soprano castrato Gioacchino Conti ('Gizziello'), Varus by John Beard and the tribune Tullio [Tullius] by the contralto Maria Caterina Negri. (Tullius, originally written for bass, was reassigned before performance.) The opera received only six performances and was not heard again until its revival at Leipzig on 23 February 1935, arranged by H. J. Moser and Max Seiffert. The first British revival was by Unicorn Opera at Abingdon on 12 September 1972.

Handel's return to an older-style heroic libretto for *Arminio* after the romance and fantasy of *Ariodante*, *Alcina* and *Atalanta* is surprising and not altogether successful. The string of melodramatic confrontations, falling in quick succession because of the ruthless condensation of the recitative, obscures the individuality of the characters and the music does not fully restore it. The arias vary between short single-section songs and elaborate set pieces not particularly expressive of their dramatic contexts, but Arminius has some very fine numbers, notably his noble declaration of faith to his country ('Al par della mia sorte'), with its suggestion of a chaconne bass, and his prison aria 'Vado a morir'. Thusnelda's 'Rendimi il dolce sposo', ending Act 2, is an attractive *siciliana* and Varus' expansive Act 3 aria 'Mira il ciel' makes evocative use of oboes and horns.

ANTHONY HICKS

Armstrong, Karan (*b* Horne, MT, 14 Dec 1941). American soprano. She studied singing privately and with Lotte Lehmann in Santa Barbara. She made her début as Elvira (*L'italiana in Algeri*) at San Francisco in 1966, and a year later sang for the first time at the Metropolitan as the Dew Fairy (*Hänsel und Gretel*). She appeared at Santa Fe (1968) as Adina, and was a member of the New York City Opera from 1975 to 1978. She made her European début in 1974 as Micaëla at Strasbourg, where she later sang Salome, a role she repeated in Munich, Vienna, Berlin, Hamburg, Cologne and elsewhere. She made her Bayreuth début in 1979 as Elsa, took the role of Death in the première of Einem's *Jesu Hochzeit* in Vienna (1980) and made her Covent Garden début as Lulu in 1981, the year she created the title role of Sinopoli's *Lou Salomé* at Munich. In 1984 she took part in the première of Berio's *Un re in ascolto* at Salzburg. Her repertory includes Fiordiligi, Violetta, the Marschallin, Mélisande, Tosca, Butterfly and Minnie; her strong voice, striking appearance and acting ability are particularly effective in roles such as Marie (*Wozzeck*), Lulu, Katerina Izmaylova, Regina (*Mathis der Maler*) and Marietta (Korngold's *Die tote Stadt*), which she sang at the Deutsche Oper, Berlin (1983) and in Los Angeles (1985) where she also sang Mrs Alice Ford and Leonore (*Fidelio*). In 1991 she returned to Covent Garden as Sieglinde and Gutrune. She is married to the director Götz Friedrich in many of whose productions she has appeared. ELIZABETH FORBES

Armstrong, Richard (*b* Leicester, 7 Jan 1943). English conductor. An organ scholar at Corpus Christi College, Cambridge, he joined the musical staff of Covent Garden in 1966, moving to the WNO in December 1968 as assistant musical director to James Lockhart. He made his conducting début with *The Marriage of Figaro* in 1969, and he was musical director from 1973 until 1986 (when he became principal guest conductor at Frankfurt). This covered the company's biggest expansion, including several foreign visits. His conducting repertory included a cycle of five Janáček operas, the first Welsh *Ring* cycles, André Engel's production of *Salome*, and numerous Verdi productions, including the Peter Stein *Otello*.

He conducted two *Ring* cycles when the WNO became the first regional company to visit Covent Garden in 1986, and took their *Falstaff* to New York and Milan in 1989. In May 1990 he conducted the première of John Metcalf's *Tornrak*, also for the WNO. Overseas operatic engagements have included Berlin, Geneva, Brussels and Amsterdam.

*

K. Loveland: 'Richard Armstrong', *Opera*, xxxvii (1986), 1354–8

KENNETH LOVELAND

Armstrong Gibbs, Cecil. *See* GIBBS, CECIL ARMSTRONG.

Arnaboldi, Cristoforo ['Il Comaschino'] (*b* Como, *c*1750–55; *d* after 1798). Italian castrato singer. Most of his career was spent in Russia. He sang the female leads in three successive seasons at the Teatro Argentina, Rome (1772–4), starting with Anfossi's *Alessandro nell'Indie*, then appeared in Venice and Vienna, and reached St Petersburg in 1778. From 1780 to 1789 he was a leading singer at the court theatre, where he sang Orpheus in the Russian première of Gluck's *Orfeo ed Euridice* (1782); he created Peter in Paisiello's oratorio *La passione di Gesù Cristo* (1783). He retired in 1789 but stayed on until 1794 in Moscow; in 1795 he was at the court of the king of Poland. While based in Russia he made several trips abroad to recruit singers and buy materials for the imperial theatres. Mooser deduces (perhaps wrongly) that he pimped for the foreign minister, Alexander Bezborodko. On his return to Italy he bought lands formerly belonging to the noble Visconti family. No description of his singing appears to be known.

*

C. A. Vianello: *Teatri, spettacoli, musiche a Milano nei secoli scorsi* (Milan, 1941), 283–4

R. A. Mooser: *Annales de la musique et des musiciens en Russie au XVIIIe siècle* (Geneva, 1951), ii, 247–8, 331, 347–8

M. Rinaldi: *Due secoli di musica al Teatro Argentina* (Florence, 1978)

JOHN ROSSELLI

Arnaud, François (*b* Aubignan, Carpentras, 27 July 1721; *d* Paris, 2 Dec 1784). French man of letters. He came to Paris from Provence in 1752 as attaché to Prince Louis of Württemberg. A classical scholar and accomplished linguist and translator, he collaborated with his close friend J. B. A. Suard (whose wife was said to be his mistress) on the *Journal étranger*, *Gazette littéraire de l'Europe*, *Variétés littéraires* and other writings. His humour, historical knowledge and vigorous polemical style make him stand out among the many literary writers on music of the second half of the 18th century.

Arnaud was a member of the Encyclopedist generation and deeply influenced by its ideas, but he did not share Marmontel's or Rousseau's exclusive admiration for Italian music. The *Lettre sur la musique* of 1754 sketches an unrealized plan for a major historical work; La Borde included it in his *Essai sur la musique*. Arnaud was particularly interested in prosody, arguing that every language should have its own melody or 'déclamation lyrique'; his ideas had considerable influence on Grétry. Arnaud had long advocated operatic reform, and his fervent admiration for Gluck, who seemed to revive antique tragedy, led to his being nicknamed the Gluckists' High Priest. He engaged in a duel of wits with Marmontel, in whose *Polymnie* he figures as Trigaut. He saw Gluck's synthesis of French and Italian elements as the logical outcome of Encyclopedist ideas, especially those of d'Alembert, and attacked the superficiality of Italian opera in his 'Profession de foi en musique' (*Journal de Paris*, 1777). The pamphlet *La soirée perdue à l'Opéra* is attributed to him in his posthumous *Oeuvres*, in the *Mémoires pour servir à l'histoire de la révolution opérée dans la musique par M. le Chevalier Gluck*, and by Bricqueville, but it may be the work of Pascal Boyer.

Oeuvres complètes, ed. L. Boudon (Paris, 1808) [incl. 'Lettre sur un ouvrage italien intitulé Il Teatro alla Moda'; 'Essai sur le mélodrame ou drame lyrique'; 'Lettre à Mme D'[Augny] et à la comtesse de B ... sur l'Iphigénie de Gluck', 1774; 'La soiree perdue à l'opéra', 1776; 'Le souper des enthousiastes', 1776; 'Lettre au P. Martini', 1776; 'Lettre à l'ermite de la forêt de Sénart', 1777; 'Profession de foi en musique, d'un amateur des beaux-arts, à M. de la Harpe', 1777; 'Lettre sur l'Iphigénie en Tauride de M. le Chevalier Gluck', 1779]

*

L. G. Michaud: *Biographie universelle* (Paris, 1842–65)

E. de Bricqueville: *L'Abbé Arnaud et la réforme de l'opéra au XVIII siècle* (Avignon, 1881)

——: *Un critique musical au siècle dernier* (Paris, 1883)

——: *Deux abbés d'opéra au siècle dernier: J. Pellegrin, F. Arnaud* (Avignon, 1889)

JULIAN RUSHTON

Arndt-Ober, Margarethe (*b* Berlin, 15 April 1885; *d* Bad Sachsa, 17 March 1971). German contralto. She studied in Berlin and married her second teacher, Arthur Arndt. Her début was in *Trovatore* at Frankfurt in 1906, and she sang with Berlin State Opera from 1907 until her retirement in 1944. Her roles there included Amneris, which she sang with Caruso in 1908, and Kostelnička in the Berlin première of *Jenůfa*. In 1913 she made a highly praised début at the Metropolitan as Ortrud and then sang Octavian in the house première of *Rosenkavalier*. Later her Waltraute was praised as 'one of the grand figures of the drama'. In 1914 she sang in Toscanini's revival of *Euryanthe*, but on America's entry into the war was dismissed from the company and interned. Back in Germany she resumed her career at the Berlin Opera, singing in the première of Egk's *Peer Gynt* (1938), and appeared regularly at the Zoppot Festival. Her voice recorded well, being sumptuous in tone and unfailingly steady in production.

J. B. STEANE

Arne, Mrs. English soprano; *see* YOUNG family, (1).

Arne, Michael (*b* *c*1740; *d* Lambeth, 14 Jan 1786). English composer, illegitimate son of Thomas Augustine Arne (Burney). His aunt, Mrs Cibber, was responsible for his upbringing. Under her guidance he is said to have made his stage début as the Page in Thomas Otway's play, *The Orphan*. He first appeared as a singer in 1750, but his career as a performer was brief. Burney comments that 'his father tried to make him a singer, but he was naturally idle and not very quick. However he acquired a powerful hand on the harpsichord'. He showed an early gift as a composer. *The Floweret*, the first of his seven collections of songs (1750), contains 'The Highland Laddie', a song in the Scottish style, which became popular and as late as 1775 was adapted for *The Duenna*, the comic opera by Thomas Linley and his son.

On 5 February 1751 he first performed one of his father's organ concertos, of which he remained the principal exponent for 30 years. Thereafter he found his true vocation as keyboard player and composer to the theatres and pleasure gardens. From 1756 onwards he wrote some 15 complete operas and contributed songs to various dramatic productions; in 1764 he collaborated with Jonathan Battishill in setting Rolt's *Almena*, which enjoyed a limited success. His most famous song, 'The Lass with the delicate air', first appeared in 1762. On 5 November 1766 he married Elizabeth Wright, a young singer whom he had heard at Ranelagh in 1763. His wife sang the leading roles in many Drury Lane productions, including his setting of Garrick's *Cymon* in 1767, which proved to be Arne's biggest success. In the same year he is reputed to have built a laboratory at Chelsea in order to study alchemy, which led him to a debtor's prison. When Mrs Arne died on 1 May 1769, Burney placed the blame for her early death on the overwork to which her husband had subjected her.

In 1771–2 he toured Germany with a pupil, Ann Venables, and conducted the first public performance in Germany of Handel's *Messiah* on 21 May 1772. On his return to England he married Miss Venables. In December 1776 he was engaged by Thomas Ryder to produce *Cymon* in Dublin, where his second wife proved a popular attraction. But the lure of alchemy again drove him into debt. While in detention in Dublin he was assisted by Michael Kelly's father, who provided him with a piano in return for young Kelly's daily lesson. Returning to London, he was engaged as composer to Covent Garden for several seasons. After his father's death he retained many of Dr Arne's unpublished manuscripts, and announced his intention of publishing them. But he died, leaving his second wife destitute, without having done so. His daughter Jemima, who had nursed him in his last illness, was a leading singer at Drury Lane from 1795 to 1800.

His operas show a wide variety of melodic invention, with occasional coloratura passages and a nice sense of verbal accentuation. *Cymon* remained in the repertory until 1827, but his other works were less successful.

See also ALMENA and CYMON.

LCG – *London, Covent Garden* LDL – *London, Drury Lane*

The Humorous Lieutenant (F. Beaumont and J. Fletcher), LCG, 10 Dec 1756
Harlequin's Invasion, or A Christmas Gambol (pantomime, D. Garrick), LDL, 31 Dec 1759, songs (London, n.d.); collab. T. Ayleward and W. Boyce
The Heiress, or The Antigallican (Mozeen), LDL, 21 May 1759
Edgar and Emmeline (entertainment, 2, J. Hawkesworth), LDL, 31 Jan 1761
Hymen (interlude, Allen), LDL, 23 Jan 1764, excerpts (London, 1764)
Almena (op, 3, R. Rolt), LDL, 2 Nov 1764, excerpts (London, 1764); collab. J. Battishill
Cymon (dramatic romance, 5, Garrick, after J. Dryden: *Cymon and Iphigenia*), LDL, 2 Jan 1767 (London, 1767); rev. version, LDL, 17 Jan 1778
Linco's Travels (interlude, Garrick), LDL, 6 April 1767 (London, 1767); collab. J. Vernon
The Maid of the Vale (T. Holcroft, after C. Goldoni: *La buona figliuola*), Dublin, Smock Alley, 15 Feb 1775
Emperor of the Moon (farce, after A. Behn), London, Patagonian, 22 March 1777
The Fathers, or The Good-natured Man (comedy, H. Fielding), LCG, 30 Nov 1778, 1 song (London, 1778)
The Belle's Stratagem (comedy, H. Cowley), LCG, 22 Feb 1780, excerpts (London, 1780)
The Artifice (comic op, 2, W. A. Miles), LDL, 14 April 1780
The Choice of Harlequin, or The Indian Chief (pantomime, Messink), LCG, 26 Dec 1781, excerpts (London, 1782)
Vertumnus and Pomona (M. Feilde), LCG, 21 Feb 1782
The Positive Man (comedy, J. O'Keeffe), LCG, 16 March 1782, songs (London, 1782), collab. S. Arnold
The Capricious Lady (Beaumont, Fletcher and W. Cooke), LCG, 17 Jan 1783, 1 glee (London, 1783)
Tristram Shandy (farce, L. McNally, after L. Sterne), LCG, 26 April 1783, songs (London, 1783)

Music in: Florizel and Perdita, or The Winter's Tale, 1756; Harlequin Sorcerer, 1757; A Midsummer Night's Dream, 1763 [as The Fairy Tale, 1777]; Tom Jones, 1769; All Alive at Jersey, 1779; The Conscious Lovers, 1779; Love in a Village, 1779; The Maid of the Mill, 1782

C. Burney: 'M. Arne', *Rees's Cyclopaedia* (London, 1802–19)
M. Kelly: *Reminiscences of the King's Theatre* (London, 1826, 2/1826); ed. R. Fiske (London, 1975)
W. H. Cummings: *Dr. Arne and Rule Britannia* (London, 1912)
M. Sands: *Invitation to Ranelagh* (London, 1946)
J. A. Parkinson: *Index to the Vocal Works of Thomas and Michael Arne* (Detroit, 1972)
T. J. Walsh: *Opera in Dublin 1705–1797* (Dublin, 1973)
R. Fiske: *English Theatre Music in the Eighteenth Century* (London, 1973, 2/1986)

JOHN A. PARKINSON

Arne, Susanna Maria. *See* CIBBER, SUSANNA MARIA.

Arne, Thomas Augustine (*b* London, 12 March 1710; *d* London, 5 March 1778). English composer and violinist, the leading figure in English theatrical music in the mid-18th century. He was born and spent most of his life in Covent Garden. His father was a successful upholsterer and undertaker who sent his son to Eton intending him for the legal profession, though he allowed him to study the violin with the composer Michael Festing. A chance encounter in a friend's house when he found his son leading the orchestra caused Thomas Arne senior to consent to the choice of a musical career.

In 1732 Arne joined Henry Carey and J. F. Lampe to form a company with the aim of performing English operas 'after the Italian manner'. First they gave Lampe's *Amelia*, in which Arne's sister Susanna, a naturally gifted singer, made her first appearance. Their success encouraged them to mount Handel's *Acis and Galatea*, announced as the first dramatic performance of the work, which drove Handel to put on his own production as a riposte. In the autumn of 1732 the partners split up. Lampe opened a season at the Haymarket, but Arne headed a rival company at Lincoln's Inn Fields, which produced *Teraminta*, J. C. Smith's first opera. Arne's father provided the financial backing and acted as ticket agent. *Teraminta* was staged four times, followed by Arne's first attempt at opera, a setting of Addison's *Rosamond* (7 March 1733). Susanna took the title role and her younger brother Richard made his début; later he was loaned to Lampe's company for a performance of Lampe's *Tom Thumb*. A severe financial crisis threatened Arne's group, but it soon abated when they merged with Theophilus Cibber's company at the New Theatre, Haymarket. Their first joint production, in the autumn of 1733, was Arne's version of *Tom Thumb*, in which Richard Arne again took the title role.

It enjoyed great success, completely out-staging Lampe's version.

By the spring of 1734 Arne's father had given up his once prosperous business and the family faced financial ruin. They were saved by Cibber, who had formed an attachment to Susanna and was now able to return to Drury Lane. He did so, taking the entire Arne family with him – Thomas as composer and musical director, Susanna and Richard as singers and their father as 'numberer', responsible for counting the numbers of the audience. The price of this transaction was the unwilling hand of Susanna, who was persuaded to marry Cibber in April 1734. She promptly became pregnant and retired temporarily from the stage, making a successful return in 1736 in Aaron Hill's *Zara* with incidental music by her brother. Thereafter, as Mrs Cibber, she was renowned more as a tragic actress than a singer.

In 1737 Arne married Cecilia Young, a noted singer and member of a well-known musical family. He continued to provide incidental music for Drury Lane until in 1738 he was invited to compose the music for Milton's masque of *Comus*. Produced in March 1738, it was an immediate and lasting success, establishing Arne as a composer of the first rank. Early in 1740 he was commissioned to write the music for James Thomson's patriotic masque *Alfred*. Frederick, Prince of Wales, Thomson's patron, negotiated a performance before the stage production as part of the celebrations for his daughter's third birthday. The principal performers of both London theatres were engaged and the work was given in an open-air theatre at the Prince's residence at Cliveden on 1 August 1740. London audiences did not hear *Alfred* until 1745, when the final chorus, 'Rule, Britannia', immediately became popular. The threat of the 1745 rebellion provoked a patriotic fervour that responded not only to 'Rule, Britannia' but also to 'God save the King', sung for the first time at Drury Lane in an arrangement by Arne.

The 1740–41 seasons saw a succession of Shakespeare revivals, including *The Tempest*, *As You Like It*, *Twelfth Night* and *The Merchant of Venice*, for which Arne provided some of his finest, most enduring songs. In 1742, following Handel's example, Arne and his wife visited Dublin; they gave performances of his works including his first oratorio, *The Death of Abel*. Returning to London in 1744, Arne resumed his duties at Drury Lane, then managed by Charles Fleetwood, who engaged David Garrick as principal actor. Fleetwood later decamped to avoid his creditors and in 1747 Garrick took over as actor-manager. He had little ear for music and Arne had a lean time until he finally transferred his services to John Rich at Covent Garden.

In 1754 Arne composed a new opera *Eliza* to a libretto by Richard Rolt. After a single performance it ran into difficulties and was not heard again until the autumn of 1755, during Arne's second visit to Dublin. This time he was accompanied not only by his wife but by a brilliant young pupil, Charlotte Brent. They performed *Eliza* and other works with much success, but at the end of the 1756 season Arne returned to London with Miss Brent, leaving his wife in Ireland. Their stormy marriage, bedevilled by Mrs Arne's frequent indispositions and fits of temper as well as by Arne's infidelity (his illegitimate son Michael had been born in about 1740), had come to an acrimonious end.

Back in London Arne prepared his gifted but inexperienced pupil for her stage début. After offering her services to Garrick, who remained unimpressed, he found a sympathizer in the singer John Beard, who had taken over as manager at Covent Garden. In 1759 Arne was admitted to the degree of Doctor in Music at Oxford. Later that year Miss Brent appeared with Beard in *The Beggar's Opera* and scored a spectacular success, much to Garrick's chagrin. In 1760 they repeated their success in Arne's comic opera *Thomas and Sally*, with a libretto by Isaac Bickerstaff. The same author was responsible for the text of Arne's oratorio *Judith*, produced at Drury Lane in 1761. The following year Arne achieved the pinnacle of success with his English opera *Artaxerxes*, staged at Covent Garden in February 1762.

In lighter vein the pasticcio *Love in a Village* (8 December 1762), for which Arne provided most of the music, was extremely popular. But this was the last time he was to enjoy the services of Bickerstaff, who fled the country to avoid charges of homosexuality. Thrown back on his own resources Arne sustained a setback in December 1764, when his comic opera *The Guardian Outwitted* lasted only six nights at Covent Garden. His attempt at an Italian opera, *L'Olimpiade* (27 April 1765), of which not a note survives, proved another disaster. This catalogue of misfortunes continued in 1766 with the death of his sister Mrs Cibber and the loss of Miss Brent, who married the violinist Thomas Pinto.

For some years Arne was dogged by ill-health and ostracized by the theatre managers. In 1769 his fortunes revived when he was invited to compose an ode for Garrick's Shakespeare Jubilee at Stratford. Garrick later invited him to provide additional music for a revival of Purcell and Dryden's *King Arthur* in 1770, followed by the masque *The Fairy Prince* in 1771. The next year another comic opera, *The Cooper*, achieved some success and *Elfrida*, an opera in Greek style, enjoyed a lengthy run. Seeking a replacement for Miss Brent, Arne discovered fresh talent in Anne Catley, who excelled in *Achilles in Petticoats* (1773), a burlesque opera on Gay's play. Another of his discoveries was Margaret Farrell (later Mrs Kennedy); a contralto of exceptional quality, she was particularly successful in masculine roles such as Macheath in *The Beggar's Opera*. Another young singer, Harriet Abrams, took the leading role in Arne's last opera, *May-Day, or The Little Gipsy* (1775), which shows little falling-off in the 65-year-old composer's ability. Shortly before his death Arne and his wife were reconciled and in his will he left all his possessions, including his MSS, to 'my beloved wife Cecilia and my only son Michael'.

In a career spanning 45 years Arne composed music for some 90 stage works, including plays, pantomimes, masques and operas. Few of his MSS have survived; probably most of them were lost in the Covent Garden fire of 1808. Those works that were printed in score usually omit the recitatives and choruses, making reconstruction difficult. *Comus* is a happy exception, surviving in full score, but *Alfred*, which underwent several revisions as masque, oratorio and opera, remains a problem for the editor. *Comus* was successful from the start, showing Arne's lyrical genius at its best in a succession of melodies combining italianate fluency with a typically English pastoral quality. *The Judgment of Paris* (1740) also stands out as a fine early example, although the choruses are lost. But Arne was not content to adhere to Handelian baroque patterns. He responded to changes in public taste and his later works mark a progress towards a lighter *opera buffa* style, notably in *Thomas and Sally*. *Artaxerxes* was a tour de force designed to exploit Charlotte Brent's brilliant coloratura; it remained in the repertory longer than any of his other works.

See also ARTAXERXES; COMUS; COOPER, THE; ELIZA; FAIRY PRINCE, THE; LOVE IN A VILLAGE; and THOMAS AND SALLY.

all printed works published in London

Cliveden – *Cliveden House, Berks.*
DSA – *Smock Alley Theatre, Dublin*
LCG – *Covent Garden*
LDL – *Drury Lane*
LKH – *Kings Theatre, Haymarket*
LLH – *Little or New Theatre, Haymarket*
LLIF – *Lincoln's Inn Fields*
LMG – *Marylebone Gardens*
LSW – *Sadler's Wells*

title	*genre, acts*	*librettist*	*first performance*	*sources and revivals*
Rosamond	3	J. Addison	LLIF, 7 March 1733	2 songs (1734, 1762), 9 songs, *GB-Lbl*
The Opera of Operas, or Tom Thumb the Great	op, 3	E. Haywood and W. Hatchett, after H. Fielding	LLH, 29 Oct 1733	1 song (1734), lib. lists 17 others
Dido and Aeneas		B. Booth	LLH, 12 Jan 1734	2 songs in The British Musical Miscellany (1734)
Love and Glory	masque, 2	T. Phillips	LDL, 21 March 1734	lib. lists 14 numbers, lost; revived as Britannia, 29 April 1734
Harlequin Orpheus, or The Magical Pipe	pantomime		LDL, 3 March 1735	lost
Harlequin Restor'd, or The Country Revels	pantomime		LDL, 18 Oct 1735	medley ov., comic tunes (1736)
Zara		A. Hill, after Voltaire	LDL, 12 Jan 1736	march (*c*1746)
The Fall of Phaeton		Pritchard	LDL, 28 Feb 1736	1 song in The Songs in As You Like It (1741), lib. lists 5 others
Comus	masque, 3	J. Dalton, after J. Milton	LDL, 4 March 1738	score (1740); *Lbl*; ed. in MB, iii (1951)
An Hospital for Fools	ballad op, 1	J. Miller	LDL, 15 Nov 1739	4 songs pubd in lib.
Don John, or The Libertine Destroy'd		T. Shadwell	LDL, 13 Feb 1740	songs, Dance of Shepherds, Dance of Furies, lost
Alfred	masque, 3	J. Thomson and D. Mallett	Cliveden, 1 Aug 1740	expanded LDL, 20 March 1745; revived as Alfred the Great, LCG, 12 May 1753; score (1756)
The Judgment of Paris	masque, 1	W. Congreve	Cliveden, 1 Aug 1740	London, LDL, 12 March 1742 (but see Fiske 1966); revived with adds, LCG, 3 April 1759; score (*c*1745); final chorus, *Lbl*
Oedipus, King of Thebes		J. Dryden and N. Lee	LDL, 19 Nov 1740	song, sacrificial scene, lost
The Blind Beggar of Bethnal Green	ballad op, 2	R. Dodsley	LDL, 3 April 1741	6 songs, 1 duet (*c*1742)
Miss Lucy in Town	ballad farce	Fielding	LDL, 6 May 1742	lib. lists 10 songs, lost; revived as The Country Madcap in London, LDL, 10 June 1770
The Temple of Dullness		after interludes in L. Theobald: *The Happy Captives*	LDL, 17 Jan 1745	lib. lists 16 songs, incl. 3 from Miss Lucy in Town, lost; revived as Capochio and Dorinna, LMG, 28 July 1768, music lost
The Picture, or The Cuckold in Conceit		Miller, after Molière	LDL, 11 Feb 1745	lib. lists 5 numbers, lost
King Pepin's Campaign	comic op, 3	J. Shirley	LDL, 15 April 1745	lib. lists 19 numbers, lost
Harlequin Incendiary, or Columbine Cameron	pantomime		LDL, 3 March 1746	lib. lists 14 numbers, lost
Lethe, or Aesop in the Shades		D. Garrick	LDL, 18 Jan 1749	1 song in The Agreeable Musical Choice, vi (*c*1752), other music by Boyce
The Triumph of Peace	masque	Dodsley	LDL, 21 Feb 1749	1 song in A Favourite Collection of English Songs (1757), lib. lists 6 other numbers
The Muses' Looking Glass		T. Randolph	LCG, 9 March 1749	Masque: War, Peace and Plenty, lost
Henry and Emma, or The Nut-brown Maid [1st setting]	pastoral	M. Prior	LCG, 31 March 1749	lib. lists 14 numbers; ov. as no. 3 of Eight Overtures (1751)
Don Saverio	comic op	Arne	LDL, 15 Feb 1750	lib. lists 18 numbers; 1 song in London Magazine (1752)
Harlequin Sorcerer	pantomime	after Theobald	LCG, 11 Feb 1752	comic tunes, 4 songs in Vocal Melody, iv (1752)
The Drummer, or The Haunted House		Addison	LCG, 8 Dec 1752	dialogue Damon and Florella in Vocal Melody, iv (1752), later added to Harlequin Sorcerer; other music lost
The Sheep-shearing, or Florizel and Perdita		after W. Shakespeare: *The Winter's Tale*	LCG, 25 March 1754	revived LCG, 22 Dec 1760 with added song, Come let us all be blithe and gay, in The Winter's Amusement, xiii (1761); other music lost
Eliza	3	R. Rolt	LLH, 29 May 1754	score (1758)
Britannia	masque, 2	Mallett	LDL, 9 May 1755	score (1755)

title	genre, acts	librettist	first performance	sources and revivals
Injured Honour, or The Earl of Westmoreland		H. Brooke	DSA, 8 March 1756	anthem, dirge, triumphal hymn, lost
The Pincushion		J. Gay	DSA, 20 March 1756	songs, duet, lost
Mercury Harlequin	pantomime	H. Woodward	LDL, 27 Dec 1756	1 song (1757)
The Sultan, or Solyman and Zayde			LCG, 23 Nov 1758	masque for The Prophetess: duet in A Choice Collection of Songs, xii (1761)
The Beggar's Opera	ballad op, 2	Gay	LCG, 10 Oct 1759	hornpipe, country dance; (1769); revived 17 Oct 1777, with new finale by Arne
The Jovial Crew	ballad op, 2	E. Roome, after R. Brome	LCG, 14 Feb 1760	7 songs in A Collection of Songs, ix (*c*1760) revived as The Ladies' Frolic, 1770
Thomas and Sally, or The Sailor's Return	comic op, 2	I. Bickerstaff	LCG, 28 Nov 1760	score (1761)
Artaxerxes	3	Arne, after P. Metastasio	LCG, 2 Feb 1762	score (1762/*R*1986), vs (?1785/*R*1977) add recit. air (1777)
Love in a Village	3	Bickerstaff	LCG, 8 Dec 1762	pasticcio, incl. 19 songs by Arne; compiled by E. Toms
The Arcadian Nuptials			LCG, 19 Jan 1764	pastoral dialogue (1764)
The Guardian Outwitted	comic op, 3	Arne	LCG, 12 Dec 1764	score (1764)
L'Olimpiade	os, 3	G. G. Bottarelli, after Metastasio	LKH, 27 April 1765	only lib. survives
King Arthur, or The British Worthy	3	Garrick, after Dryden	LDL, 13 Dec 1770	ov., numbers for Purcell's semi-opera, score (*c*1770)
The Fairy Prince	masque, 3	G. Colman, after B. Jonson: *Oberon*	LCG, 12 Nov 1771	score (1771)
Squire Badger	comic op, 2	Arne, after Fielding: *Don Quixote in England*	LLH, 16 March 1772	lib. lists 15 songs, only The Dusky Night survives; revived as The Sot, LKH, 16 Feb 1775
The Cooper	comic op, 2	Arne, after Audinot and Quétant: *Le tonnelier*	LLH, 10 June 1772	score (1772)
Elfrida	3	G. Colman, after W. Mason	LCG, 21 Nov 1772	score (1772)
The Rose	comic op, 3	?Arne	LDL, 2 Dec 1772	lib. lists 19 songs, lost; ov. later used with A Trip to Portsmouth
Alzuma		Murphy	LCG, 23 Feb 1773	Procession of virgins, Ode to the Sun, lost
Achilles in Petticoats	burlesque op, 3	Colman, after Gay	LCG, 16 Dec 1773	score (1774)
Henry and Emma [2nd setting]		H. Bate, after Prior	LCG, 13 April 1774	lib. lists 4 songs, lost
May-day, or The Little Gipsy	musical play, 2	Garrick	LDL, 28 Oct 1775	score (1776)
Phoebe at Court		Arne, after R. Lloyd: *Capricious Lovers*	LKH, 22 Feb 1776	lost
Caractacus		Mason	LCG, 6 Dec 1776	lib. lists 21 numbers, lost
The Birth of Hercules	masque	Shirley		rehearsed 1763, not perf.; lib. (1765) lists 19 numbers, lost

Contribs. to: The Temple of Peace, 1749; The Summer's Tale, 1765; Lionel and Clarissa, 1768; Tom Jones, 1769; The Pigmy Revels, 1772; The Golden Pippin, 1773; A Trip to Portsmouth, 1773; The Seraglio, 1776; Love Finds the Way, 1777; Poor Vulcan, 1778; All Alive at Jersey, 1779; Summer Amusement, 1779; Tom Thumb, 1780; The Castle of Andalusia, 1782; Fontainbleau, 1784; The Battle of Hexham, 1789; The Crusade, 1790.

BurneyH; *HawkinsH*; *LS*

B. Victor: *History of the Theatres of London and Dublin* (London, 1761–7)

C. Burney: 'Arne', *Rees's Cyclopaedia* (London, 1802–20)

J. Genest: *Some Account of the English Stage* (London, 1832)

G. Hogarth: *Memoirs of the Musical Drama* (London, 1838)

B. H. Horner: *Life and Works of Dr. Arne* (London, 1893)

H. Saxe Wyndham: *Annals of Covent Garden Theatre* (London, 1906)

W. H. G. Flood: 'Dr Arne's Visits to Dublin', *MA*, i (1909–10), 215–33

F. Kidson: 'T. A. Arne: a Bicentenary Appreciation', *MT*, li (1910), 153–4

W. H. Cummings: *Dr Arne and Rule Britannia* (London, 1912)

H. Langley: *Dr Arne* (Cambridge, 1938)

P. C. Roscoe: 'Arne and "The Guardian Outwitted"', *ML*, xxiv (1943), 237–45

E. W. White: *The Rise of English Opera* (London, 1951)

J. Herbage: 'The Vocal Style of T. A. Arne', *PRMA*, lxxviii (1951–2), 83–96

——: 'The Opera of Operas', *MMR*, lxxxix (1959), 83–9

C. L. Cudworth: 'Boyce and Arne', *ML*, xli (1960), 136–45

J. Herbage: 'T. A. Arne', *MT*, ci (1960), 623–5

——: 'Young Master Arne', *MMR*, xc (1960), 14–16

——: 'Arne, his Character and Environment', *PRMA*, lxxxvii (1960–61), 15–29

C. Farncombe: 'Arne and Artàxerxes', *Opera*, xiii (1962), 159–61

J. Herbage: 'Artaxerxes', *Opera*, xiii (1962), 333–5

C. L. Cudworth: 'Two Georgian Classics, Arne and Stevens', *ML*, xlv (1964), 146–53

P. Lord: 'The English-Italian Opera Companies 1732–3', *ML*, xlv (1964), 239–51

R. Lonsdale: *Dr. Charles Burney: a Literary Biography* (Oxford, 1965)

R. Fiske: 'A Cliveden Setting', *ML*, xlvii (1966), 126–9

J. A. Parkinson: *An Index to the Vocal Works of Thomas Augustine Arne and Michael Arne* (Detroit, 1972)

R. Fiske: *English Theatre Music in the Eighteenth Century* (London, 1973, 2/1986)

T. J. Walsh: *Opera in Dublin 1705–1797* (Dublin, 1973)
A. Scott: 'Arne's "Alfred"', *ML*, lv (1974), 385–97

JOHN A. PARKINSON

Arniches (y Barrera), Carlos (*b* Alicante, 11 Oct 1866; *d* Madrid, 15 or 16 April 1943). Spanish zarzuela librettist. He came from a poor family and was forced as a child to contribute to the family income. Having moved from Alicante to Barcelona, he worked in a bank and then in the local branch of the Singer sewing-machine company. His literary interests led to his becoming a reporter for *La vanguardia* before moving to Madrid. There he became a prolific and successful author of some 300 plays and zarzuela librettos, usually in collaboration, most notably with Celso Lucio (1865–1915), Enrique García Álvarez (1873–1931) and José López Silva (1860–1925). He was perhaps the most prolific librettist of the one-act *género chico*, his greatest successes including *El cabo primero* (Caballero, 1895), *El puñao de rosas* (Chapí, 1902), *El pobre Valbuena* (Torregrosa and Valverde, 1904) and *La alegría del batallón* (Serrano, 1909). His works were noted for their theatricality and ingenuity, allied to an essentially popular touch.

selective list; all zarzuelas

Ortografía (with G. Cantó), Chapí, 1888; *Panorama nacional* (with C. Lucio), A. Brull, 1889; *Calderón* (with Lucio), M. Nieto, 1890; *La leyenda del monje* (with Cantó), Chapí, 1890; *Los aparecidos* (with Lucio), M. F. Caballero, 1892; *Los secuestradores* (with Lucio), Nieto, 1892; *Las campanadas* (with Lucio and Cantó), Chapí, 1892; *Via libre* (with Lucio), Chapí, 1893; *Los descamisados* (with J. López Silva), Chueca, 1893; *El reclamo* (with Lucio), Chapí, 1893; *Las amapolas* (with Lucio), Torregrosa, 1894; *Los mostenses* (with Cantó and Lucio), Chapí, 1894

Los puritanos (with Lucio), Q. Valverde *hijo* and Torregrosa, 1894; *El cabo primero* (with Lucio), Caballero, 1895; *Tabardillo* (with Lucio), Torregrosa, 1895; *La banda de trompetas*, Torregrosa, 1896; *El coche correo* (with López Silva), Chueca, 1896; *La expulsion de los judios* (with Lucio), Caballero, 1896; *La fantasia de Carmen* (with Lucio), Valverde, 1896; *Los camarones* (with Lucio and M. Labra), Valverde, 1897; *La guardia amarilla* (with Lucio), J. Jiménez, 1897; *El santo de la Isidra*, Torregrosa, 1898; *La fiesta de San Antón*, Torregrosa, 1898

Instantáneas (with López Silva), Valverde and Torregrosa, 1899; *El último chulo* (with Lucio), Valverde and Torregrosa, 1899; *La cara de Díos*, Chapí, 1899; *El escalo* (with Lucio), Vives, 1900; *María de los Angeles* (with Lucio), Chapí, 1900; *Sandías y melones*, E. Montero, 1900; *El siglo XIX* (revista, S. Delgado and López Silva), E. Montesinos, 1901; *El tio de Alcalá*, Montesinos, 1901; *Doloretes*, Vives and M. Quislant, 1901; *Los niños llorones* (with A. Paso and E. García Álvarez), T. Barrera, Torregrosa and Valverde, 1901; *El puñao de rosas* (with R. Asensio Más), Chapí, 1902

La canción del náufrago, Morera, 1903; *El terrible Pérez* (with García Álvarez), Torregrosa and Valverde, 1903; *Los pícaros celos* (with C. Fernández Shaw), J. Jiménez, 1904; *El pobre Valbuena* (with García Álvarez), Torregrosa and Valverde, 1904; *Las estrellas*, J. Serrano and Valverde, 1904; *El iluso Cañizares* (with García Álvarez), Valverde and Calleja, 1905; *El perro chico* (with García Álvarez), Serrano and Valverde, 1905; *El maldito dinero* (with Fernández Shaw), Chapí, 1906; *La pena negra*, Valverde, 1906; *La noche de reyes*, Serrano, 1906

Alma de Dios (with García Álvarez), Serrano, 1907; *La alegría del batallón* (with F. Quintana), Serrano, 1909; *El metodo Górritz* (with García Álvarez), V. Lleó, 1909; *El fresco de Goya* (with García Álvarez and A. Dominguez), Valverde, 1912; *El principe casto* (with García Álvarez), Valverde, 1912; *El amigo Melquíades*, Serrano and Valverde, 1914; *La estrella del Olympia*, Calleja, 1915; *La flor del barrio*, Calleja and L. Foglietti, 1919; *Don Quintín el amargao, o el que siembra vientos*, Guerrero, 1924; *Coplas de ronda* (with J. de Lucio), Alonso, 1929; *Marí Eli* (with E. Garay), Guridi, 1936

ANDREW LAMB

Arnold, Elizabeth. *See* CLENDINING, ELIZABETH.

Arnold, György (*b* Paks, 1781; *d* Szabadka, 1848). Hungarian composer. He studied with his father, József Arnold, cantor at Hajós and Pál Pőhm, and conductor at the cathedral in Kalocsa. Between 1800 and 1848 he was a member of the Szabadka choir. His political activities included membership of the town council and of the Temporary Peace Commission (1848). In 1815 he composed a great offertorium to celebrate the return of Pope Pius VII from French captivity, a work acknowledged in a letter from the pope. Arnold composed mainly church music. His stage works include the opera *Kemény Simon* based on K. Kisfaludy's drama and first performed in Baja in 1827; a melodrama, *A gotthardhegyi boszorkány* ('The Witches of the Gotthard Mountains'), to a text by Antal Schuster, 1837; incidental music to Ignác Nagy's play *Tisztújitás* ('Re-election'); and four songs based on Hungarian melodies for Jószef Heinish's musical *Mátyás király válazstása* ('The Election of King Matthias'). Kálmán Isoz published a biography of Arnold in 1908.

Arnold, Malcolm (Henry) (*b* Northampton, 21 Oct 1921). English composer. He won a scholarship in 1938 to the RCM, where he studied composition with Gordon Jacob and the trumpet with Ernest Hall. In 1941 he joined the LPO, becoming first trumpet in 1942. After winning the Mendelssohn scholarship in 1948 he abandoned professional playing and quickly established a reputation as a versatile and practical composer with an inexhaustible capacity for inventing memorable tunes. His instrumental works include nine symphonies, more than 20 concertos, four ballets and chamber works. He has also composed more than 80 film scores and much occasional music. He was made a CBE in 1970.

The list of his vocal works is short, but includes two one-act operas. *The Dancing Master*, a comedy of intrigue and misunderstanding, is a number opera with several full-scale ensembles which has something in common with 18th-century ballad opera; it also resembles the lighter operas of Wolf-Ferrari in flirting with pastiche, in transparent orchestration and in the ingenious manipulation of tuneful material. *The Open Window* (1956), composed for television and based on a story by Saki, is a comedy involving two main characters: Mr Nuttel (tenor), a hypochondriac in search of a peaceful retreat, and Vera (soprano), a young girl who invents lurid stories to terrify him. The music moves at brisk conversational pace with little concerted singing, and establishes character and mood economically and vividly. The *Song of Simeon*, a Nativity masque, was written for a charity matinee in 1960.

The Dancing Master op.34, 1952 (1, J. Mendoza, after W. Wycherley: *The Gentleman Dancing Master*), London, Barnes Music Club, 1 March 1962

The Open Window op.56 (1, S. Gilliat, after Saki), BBC TV, 14 Dec 1956; stage, Horton-cum-Becking, Lincoln Opera Group, April 1958

Song of Simeon op.69 (Nativity masque, 3 scenes, C. Hassall), London, Drury Lane, 5 Jan 1960

*

H. Cole: *Malcolm Arnold: an Introduction to his Music* (London, 1989)

HUGO COLE

Arnold, Samuel (*b* London, 10 Aug 1740; *d* London, 22 Oct 1802). English composer. He was the son of Thomas Arnold, a commoner, and, according to some sources, the Princess Amelia. Arnold received his education as a Child of the Chapel Royal (*c*1750 to August 1758) and on leaving became known as an organist, conductor and teacher, and composed prolifically. In autumn 1764 he was engaged by John Beard as harpsichordist and composer to Covent Garden, and he compiled several pastiche operas, including the popular *The Maid of the Mill* (1765), which is among the supreme examples of the form. In 1769 Arnold bought Marylebone Gardens, and during the next six summers produced several short all-sung burlettas, composing or at least contributing to four new examples (now lost). These productions were simply written (from the literary point of view at least) and would have appealed to an audience with no previous experience of operatic music.

In 1771 Arnold married Mary Ann Napier, sometimes described as wealthy; but whatever the family fortune, the criminal activities of an employee at Marylebone lost Arnold most of his money and the Gardens were sold. The eldest of Arnold's four children, Samuel James, his only son, was the author of some weak opera librettos which his father set; he became the first manager of the Lyceum Theatre. Unsurprisingly, Arnold pursued his early composing career with a sequence of oratorios on biblical subjects; *The Prodigal Son* (1773) was performed at Oxford at the installation of Lord North as Chancellor at the Encaenia of 1773. The university also offered Arnold the honorary degree of Doctor of Music, but he declined, preferring to take it in the ordinary manner.

Arnold resumed his professional association with the patent theatres when, in 1777, he was engaged by George Colman the elder as composer and music director for the Little Theatre in the Haymarket. As a result of an inheritance, Colman had just bought the theatre; he and Arnold had collaborated when they were on the Covent Garden staff in the 1760s, and were always close friends. Arnold composed for the Little Theatre for 25 years; from 1789 George Colman the younger was manager. There is little documentary material related to Arnold's residency at the theatre, except through evidence of the production and reception of his works performed there. With his afterpiece opera *Lilliput* (1777) and an arrangement of the full-length ballad opera *Polly* (text by Gay and original music attributed to Pepusch) – Arnold's only operatic material to survive orchestrally – was begun a successful series of his stage works, which achieved maturity in the full-length pasticcio 'comic opera' *The Castle of Andalusia* (1782). By that time Arnold was in a position to combine his summer directorship at the Little Theatre with several other posts in London, as organist and conductor. He was organist and composer to the Chapel Royal (from 1783) and organist to Westminster Abbey (from 1793). Of importance to English musicology was the appearance in 1786 of Arnold's proposals for a complete Handel edition, 180 parts of which were published between 1787 and 1797. In autumn 1798 Arnold fell off his library steps, suffering injuries which eventually led to his death; he was buried on 29 October 1802 in Westminster Abbey. During his last three years he wrote three novel pantomimes and a short oratorio, *The Hymn of Adam and Eve*.

Arnold's achievement was greatest as a dramatic composer who, besides pantomimes and incidental music, wrote, or contributed to, over 70 operas. Although some of his writing is lacking in compositional finesse, having been produced at great speed and with little thought, the number of editions and stage productions of his operas testifies to Arnold's popularity in the last quarter of the 18th century. Statistics show that Arnold's more successful operas, such as *The Agreeable Surprise* (1781) and *Inkle and Yarico* (1787), were among the most frequently performed of all operas of the time. No doubt Arnold's prominence as a musical figure and his position at the Little Theatre had something to do with the frequency of performances, but we can be sure that the operas found appreciative audiences. Arnold well knew the resources of his stage, the capabilities of his actor-singers and the taste of his audience, and in his best comic operas he managed to attain some individuality and to write dramatically vivid music. In his early works, Arnold closely adhered to the tradition of the Italian burletta, and in his first surviving all-sung opera, *The Portrait* (1770), he not only revealed an ability to write effective italianate ensembles full of bustling and amusing stage action, but also demonstrated how flexible the burletta form was and how easily it could be adapted to commentary on contemporary life.

For the Little Theatre Arnold wrote 'dialogue' operas, but whereas the operas of his middle creative period – for instance, *The Castle of Andalusia*, *The Spanish Barber* (1777), *Two to One* (1784) and *Turk and No Turk* (1785) – are bound to the conventions of English comic opera, with its mixture of serious and comic elements, Arnold attempted in his later works, such as *The Battle of Hexham* (1789), *The Surrender of Calais* (1791), *The Mountaineers* (1793) and *Zorinski* (1795), to develop a historical-hybrid form – a play for the chief characters but an opera for the subsidiary ones, set in the distant past – which released the romantic strain in his imagination. If the middle-period operas are principally successful in the portrayal of individual characters in music, for freely constructed ensembles as finales, for the frequent use of folktunes and for music composed in the folk idiom, the operas of Arnold's last period make greater dramatic use of the overture and chorus, and intermittently include instrumental music of an illustrative or 'programmatic' character and also ballet. Whereas the serious characters are generally allotted full-scale arias with florid vocal divisions, the comic characters sing mostly simple melodies in ballad style. Of special importance are the ensembles, which often show that Arnold clearly understood the nature of music drama and was moved to match dramatic event with musical gesture. The tempo, the rhythm, the key, and the number of singers are constantly varied; duetting is mainly confined to 3rds and 6ths, and block chordal harmony predominates in the choruses. There is an excellent trio at the end of Act 1 of *The Siege of Curzola* (1786), and striking choral writing in *The Surrender of Calais* and in *The Shipwreck* (1796); the last was composed for Drury Lane and reveals how effectively Arnold could write for large instrumental and vocal resources. Judging by the orchestral cues given in many of the published vocal scores, Arnold's instrumentation was remarkable for its variety and originality; wind cues abound, and there is occasional use of such instruments as the flageolet (in *The Children in the Wood*, 1793), harp (*Cambro-Britons*, 1798) and tubalcain, a glockenspiel in its original form of a miniature carillon (*The Veteran Tar*, 1801). Arnold showed his professionalism chiefly in his regard for singers – almost every aria is adapted to the special character and qualities of the person assigned to the role. Among his best are the coloratura arias with flute obbligato written for Elizabeth Bannister, such as 'The tuneful lark' in *The Agreeable Surprise* and 'Ah solitude' in *The Castle of Andalusia*. The use of English folksongs is one of the most important features of Arnold's operas, for example 'Peggy of Derby O' in *Two to One* and 'We go up Holborn Hill' in *Peeping Tom* (1784). Arnold set a number of previously unrecorded songs; for instance, *The Children in the Wood* includes a version of 'The Truth sent from above' that in the 20th century has been associated with Vaughan Williams. Colourful Irish songs in Arnold's scores are the result of his successful collaboration with an Irish librettist, John O'Keeffe, who sometimes wrote lyrics to fit the tunes he remembered from his youth. Arnold's long theatrical experience gave him sufficient knowledge to borrow sensibly.

See also Agreeable surprise, the; Castle of andalusia, the; and Inkle and yarico. For an illustration of a design for the pastiche opera *The Maid of the Mill see* Richards, john inigo.

LCG – *Covent Garden* LDL – *Drury Lane*
LLH – *Little Theatre in the Haymarket*
LMG – *Marylebone Gardens*

aft – *afterpiece* a-s – *all-sung*

dialogue operas unless otherwise stated; vocal scores and librettos published in London soon after first performance, unless otherwise stated

The Maid of the Mill (pasticcio, 3, I. Bickerstaff, after S. Richardson: *Pamela*, and J. Fletcher and W. Rowley), LCG, 31 Jan 1765, 4 nos. by Arnold

Daphne and Amintor (aft, pasticcio, 1, Bickerstaff, after G. de Saint-Foix and S. M. Cibber), LDL, 8 Oct 1765, music selected by author, collab. Arnold

The Summer's Tale (pasticcio, 3, R. Cumberland), LCG, 6 Dec 1765, 6 nos. by Arnold; rev. as Amelia (2), LDL, 14 Dec 1771, music unpubd

Harlequin Dr Faustus (pantomime, aft, 1, H. Woodward and others), LCG, 18 Nov 1766, music pubd

Rosomond (aft, a-s, 1, rev. of J. Addison), LCG, 21 April 1767, music unpubd

The Royal Garland (aft, a-s, 1, Bickerstaff), LCG, 10 Oct 1768, music unpubd

Tom Jones (pasticcio, 3, J. Reed and A. L. H. Poinsinet, after H. Fielding), LCG, 14 Jan 1769, 7 nos. by Arnold

Amintas (aft, pasticcio, 2, G. Tenducci, after R. Rolt and P. Metastasio), LCG, 15 Dec 1769, 2 nos. by Arnold

The Servant Mistress (aft, a-s, 2, S. Storace trans. of *La serva padrona*), LMG, 16 June 1770, Pergolesi's music arr. and airs added by Arnold, unpubd

The Madman (aft, pasticcio, a-s, 1), LMG, 28 Aug 1770, music unpubd

The Portrait (aft, a-s, 3, G. Colman (i), after L. Anseaume: *Le tableau parlant*), LCG, 22 Nov 1770, vs lacks recits

Mother Shipton (pantomime, aft, 1, Colman (i)), 26 Dec 1770, music pubd, no lib. extant

The Magnet (aft, a-s, 1, D. Dubois), LMG, 27 June 1771, music unpubd

The Cure for Dotage (aft, a-s, 1), LMG, 3 Aug 1771

Don Quixote (aft, a-s, 1, D. J. Piguenit, after M. de Cervantes), LMG, 30 June 1774, music unpubd

The Weathercock (aft, pasticcio, 2, T. Forrest), LCG, 17 Oct 1775; ov. by Arnold, music unpubd

The Seraglio (aft, 2, C. Dibdin and E. Thompson), LCG, 14 Nov 1776, music by Dibdin with 3 nos. by Arnold

Lilliput (aft, 1, D. Garrick, after J. Swift: *Gulliver's Travels*), LLH, 15 May 1777, revival, new music by Arnold

Polly (ballad op, 3, J. Gay, rev. Colman (i)), LLH, 19 June 1777, full score *US-CA* (with Arnold's addns: ov. and 7 airs)

A Fairy Tale (aft, pasticcio, 2, D. Garrick, after W. Shakespeare, rev. Colman (i)), LLH, 18 July 1777, music by J. C. Smith and M. Arne with epilogue song by Arnold, unpubd

The Sheep Shearing (3, pasticcio, Colman (i), after Shakespeare), LLH, 18 July 1777, music by T. Arne with 2 airs by Arnold, music unpubd

April Day (a-s, 3, K. O'Hara, after G. Carey: *The Magic Girdle*), LLH, 22 Aug 1777, music unpubd

The Spanish Barber op.17 (3, Colman (i), after P.-A. Beaumarchais), LLH, 30 Aug 1777, music and song words pubd

Poor Vulcan (aft, a-s, 2, Dibdin, after P. A. Motteux), LCG, 4 Feb 1778, music by Dibdin with 2 nos. by Arnold

The Gipsies (aft, 2, Dibdin, after C.-S. Favart: *La Bohémienne*), LLH, 3 Aug 1778, music unpubd

Summer Amusement, or An Adventure at Margate (part pasticcio, 3, M. P. Andrews and W. A. Miles), LLH, 1 July 1779, 6 nos. by Arnold, facs. of vs (Miami, 1977)

The Son in Law op.14 (aft, 2, J. O'Keeffe), LLH, 14 Aug 1779, only pirated lib. extant

Fire and Water (aft, 2, Andrews), LLH, 8 July 1780, 2 songs and lib. pubd

The Wedding Night (aft, part pasticcio, 1, J. Cobb), LLH, 12 Aug 1780, music and lib. unpubd

The Genius of Nonsense op.27 (pantomime, aft, part pasticcio, 1, Colman (i)), LLH, 2 Sept 1780, music and song words pubd

The Dead Alive op.18 (aft, 2, O'Keeffe, after *The Thousand and One Nights*), LLH, 16 June 1781, only pirated lib. extant

Baron Kinkvervankotsdorsprakingatchdern (part pasticcio, 3, Andrews, after Lady Craven), LLH, 9 July 1781, music unpubd

The Silver Tankard (aft, part pasticcio, 2, Lady Craven), LLH, 18 July 1781, music and lib. unpubd, incl. music by Giordani, Arne and others

Hodge-podge (aft, Colman (i)), LLH, 28 Aug 1781, unpubd

The Agreeable Surprise, or The Secret Enlarged op.16 (aft, 2, O'Keeffe), LLH, 4 Sept 1781, only pirated lib. extant

The Banditti (part pasticcio, 3, O'Keeffe), LCG, 28 Nov 1781, song words pubd; rev. as The Castle of Andalusia op.20 (part pasticcio), LCG, 2 Nov 1782, MLE (in preparation)

None so blind as those who won't see (aft, 2, Dibdin, after L. Dorvigny), LLH, 2 July 1782, music and lib. unpubd

The Female Dramatist (aft, 2, Colman (i)), LLH, 16 Aug 1782, unpubd

Harlequin Teague op.19 (pantomime, aft, part pasticcio, 1, Colman (i) and O'Keeffe), LLH, 17 Aug 1782, music and song words pubd

The Birth Day, or The Prince of Arragon op.21 (aft, 2, O'Keeffe, after Saint-Foix), LLH, 12 Aug 1783

Gretna Green op.22 (aft, pasticcio, 2, C. Stuart and O'Keeffe), LLH, 28 Aug 1783

Two to One op.24 (3, G. Colman (ii)), LLH, 19 June 1784

Hunt the Slipper op.26 (aft, 2, H. Knapp), LLH, 21 Aug 1784, only pirated lib. extant (1792)

Peeping Tom op.25 (aft, part pasticcio, 2, O'Keeffe), LLH, 6 Sept 1784, only pirated lib. extant

Turk and No Turk op.28 (3, Colman (ii)), LLH, 9 July 1785, music and song words pubd

Here and There and Everywhere (pantomime, aft, 1, C. Delpini), LLH, 31 Aug 1785, song pubd, music and lib. unpubd

The Siege of Curzola op.29 (3, O'Keeffe), LLH, 12 Aug 1786, music and song words pubd

Inkle and Yarico op.30 (comic dialogue op, 3, Colman (ii), after R. Steele), LLH, 4 Aug 1787, facs. of vs (Miami, 1977)

The Gnome (pantomime, aft, 1, R. Wewitzer and K. Invill), LLH, 5 Aug 1788, 1 song pubd, song words pubd

Ut Pictora Poesis!, or The Enraged Musician op.31 (aft, a-s, 1, Colman (i), based on W. Hogarth), LLH, 18 May 1789

The Battle of Hexham op.32 (3, Colman (ii)), LLH, 11 Aug 1789

New Spain, or Love in Mexico op.33 (3, J. Scawen), LLH, 16 July 1790

The Basket Maker (aft, 2, O'Keeffe), LLH, 4 Sept 1790, music unpubd

The Surrender of Calais op.33 (3, Colman (ii)), LLH, 30 July 1791

The Enchanted Wood op.35 (3, W. Francis, after Shakespeare and T. Parnell), LLH, 25 July 1792

The Mountaineers op.34 (3, Colman (ii), after Cervantes: *Don Quixote*), LLH, 3 Aug 1793

The Children in the Wood op.35 (aft, 2, T. Morton), LLH, 1 Oct 1793

Harlequin Peasant (pantomime, aft, 1), LLH, 26 Dec 1793, music unpubd, song words pubd

Thomas and Sally (aft, a-s, 2, Bickerstaff), LLH, 24 Feb 1794, music by T. Arne with new finale by Arnold, music unpubd

Auld Robin Gray op.36 (aft, 2, part pasticcio, S. J. Arnold), LLH, 26 July 1794

How to be Happy (comedy, 5, G. Brewer), LLH, 9 Aug 1794, 1 song pubd, lib. unpubd

Rule Britannia (aft, pasticcio, 2, J. Roberts), LLH, 18 Aug 1794, music unpubd

Britain's Glory (aft, part pasticcio, 1, R. Benson), LLH, 20 Aug 1794, 3 songs pubd

The Death of Captain Faulkner (aft, part pasticcio, 1, W. Pearce), LCG, 6 May 1795, ov. by Arnold, music unpubd
Zorinski op.37 (3, Morton, after H. Brooke: *Gustavus Vasa*), LLH, 20 June 1795
Who Pays the Reckoning? (aft, 2, S. J. Arnold), LLH, 16 July 1795, 2 songs pubd, lib. unpubd
Love and Money op.38 (aft, part pasticcio, 1, Benson), LLH, 29 Aug 1795
Love and Madness! (tragicomedy, 5, F. Waldron, after Shakespeare and J. Fletcher: *Two Noble Kinsmen*), LLH, 21 Sept 1795, music unpubd, song words pubd
Bannian Day op.39 (aft, 2, Brewer, after J. Cross: *The Apparition*), LLH, 11 June 1796
The Shipwreck op.40 (aft, 2, S. J. Arnold), LDL, 10 Dec 1796
The Hovel (aft, 2), LDL, 23 May 1797, music and lib. unpubd
The Irish Legacy (aft, 2, S. J. Arnold), LLH, 26 June 1797, music and lib. unpubd
The Italian Monk op.43 (3, J. Boaden, after A. Radcliffe), LLH, 15 Aug 1797, incl. only ov. and 4 songs
Throw Physic to the Dogs! (aft, 2, H. Lee), LLH, 8 July 1798, 1 song and song words pubd
Cambro-Britons op.45 (3, Boaden), LLH, 21 July 1798
False and True op.46 (3, G. Moultrie), LLH, 11 Aug 1798
Obi, or Three-Fingered Jack op.48 (pantomine, aft, 2, J. Fawcett, after B. Moseley), LLH, 2 July 1800
The Review op.52 (aft, 2, Colman (ii), after Lee and T. Dibdin), LLH, 1 Sept 1800
Virginia (3, D. Plowden), LDL, 30 Oct 1800, ov. and song accs. by Arnold, tunes by Plowden
The Veteran Tar op.50 (aft, 2, S. J. Arnold, after G. Pigault-Lebrun: *Le petit matelot*), LDL, 29 Jan 1801
The Corsair op.51 (pantomime, aft, 2, C. Farley), LLH, 29 July 1801
The Sixty-third Letter (aft, 2, W. C. Oulton), LLH, 18 July 1802
Fairies' Revels, or Love in the Highlands (ballet-pantomime, aft, 1, Fawcett, after T. Moore: *The Ring*), LLH, 14 Aug 1802

Doubtful: The Revenge (aft, a-s, 1, T. Chatterton), unperf., music unpubd

*

LS
W. C. Oulton: *A History of the Theatre in London, 1771–95* (London, 1796)
'Biographical Sketch of the Late Dr. Arnold', *The Monthly Mirror*, x (1803), 147–52, 225–6
T. Busby: *Concert Room and Orchestra Anecdotes*, iii (London, 1825), 148ff
J. O'Keeffe: *Recollections in the Life of John O'Keeffe, written by himself*, ii (London, 1826)
G. Colman the younger: *Random Records*, i (London, 1830)
'Memoir of Samuel Arnold, Mus. Doc.', *Harmonicon*, viii (1830), 137–41 [probably by William Ayrton, Arnold's son-in-law]
W. S. Ayrton: *Memoir* [1876] *and Correspondence of Marianne Ayrton, c1793–1834* (MS, *US-Wc*)
R. Fiske: *English Theatre Music in the Eighteenth Century* (London, 1973, 2/1986)
R. Hoskins: *Dr. Samuel Arnold (1740–1802): an Historical Assessment*, ii (diss., U. of Auckland, 1984)
——: 'Samuel Arnold's *The Spanish Barber*', *Early Music New Zealand*, iv (1985), 11–14
——: 'The Pantomimes and Ballets of Samuel Arnold', *Studies in Music*, xix (1985), 80–93
——: 'Theatre Music, 1760–1800', *The Blackwell History of Music in Britain*, iv: *The Eighteenth Century*, ed. H. D. Johnstone and R. Fiske (Oxford, 1990)
ROBERT HOSKINS

Arnold, Samuel James (*b* ?London, 1774; *d* Walton upon Thames, 16 Aug 1852). English librettist and impresario, son of Samuel Arnold. Though trained as an artist, from the mid-1790s he worked with his father at the Little Theatre in the Haymarket, writing words for afterpieces set by the elder Arnold. He himself wrote the words and music for one such work there, *Foul Deeds Will Rise* (18 July 1804). In 1809, when Drury Lane burnt down and its company moved to the Lyceum Theatre in Wellington Street off the Strand, Arnold then became associated with that theatre (benefiting from the guest company's licence for putting on musical works), and began to stage his own plays with music. The Drury Lane company left in 1812 and Arnold retained the Lyceum, naming it the English Opera House during summer seasons. In 1815 he obtained the lease and had the theatre almost completely rebuilt; it was formally opened as the English Opera House on 15 June 1816, presenting original works, many to Arnold's own texts, as well as adaptations of foreign pieces. Until his productions of *Der Freischütz* in 1824 and *Tarare* in 1825 (the earliest of those works in England), such adaptations had mostly been revivals of popular English plays with borrowed music, notably Mozart or Rossini, rather than versions of genuine continental operas. The Lyceum (uninsured) burnt down in February 1830, but after a successful public subscription it reopened in July 1834 as the English Opera House, Royal Lyceum, for 'the presentation of English operas and the encouragement of indigenous musical talent'. From this period dates the first real flowering of authentic English Romantic operas, by Loder (notably *Nourjahad*, to an S. J. Arnold libretto), Barnett, Thomson, and later Balfe and Macfarren. Arnold retired in the mid-1840s.

Auld Robin Gray (pastoral entertainment), S. Arnold, 1794; *Who Pays the Reckoning?* (musical entertainment), Arnold, 1795; *The Shipwreck* (comic op), Arnold, 1796; *The Irish Legacy* (operatic farce), Arnold, 1797; *The Veteran Tar, or A Chip of the Old Block* (comic op), Arnold, 1801; *Foul Deeds Will Rise* (musical drama), S. J. Arnold, 1804; *Up All Night, or The Smuggler's Cave* (comic op), M. P. King, 1809; *Britain's Jubilee* (musical entertainment), 1809; *The Maniac, or The Swiss Banditti* (comic op), Bishop, 1810; *Plots!, or The North Tower*, King, 1810; *The Americans* (comic op), King and Braham, 1811
The Devil's Bridge, or The Piedmontese Alps (operatic romance), Horn and Braham, 1812; *The Woodman's Hut* (musical drama), Horn, 1814; *Frederick the Great, or The Heart of a Soldier* (operetta), T. S. Cooke, 1814; *Jean de Paris* (farce, after Saint-Just play), 1814; *The Unknown Guest* (musical drama), 1815; *Charles the Bold, or The Siege of Nantz* (musical drama), 1815; *My Aunt* (operatic farce), J. Addison, 1815; *The Waltz* (comic op, after W. Wycherley: *The Gentleman Dancing Master*), 1815; *The King's Proxy, or Judge for Yourself* (comic op), Cooke, 1815
The Maid and the Magpye, or Which is the Thief? (musical entertainment, after Caigniez and D'Aubigny: *La Pie Voleuse*), H. Smart, 1815; *Two Words, or The Silent not Dumb!* (musical drama), Addison, 1816; *Free and Easy* (comic op), Addison, 1816; *The Election*, Horn, 1817; *The Wizard, or The Brown Man of the Moor* (musical drama), Horn, 1817; *Broken Promises, or The Colonel, the Captain, and the Corporal* (ballad op), 1825; *Tarare, the Tarter Chief* (after P.-A. Beaumarchais: *Tarare*), 1825; *Tit for Tat, or The Tables Turned* (operetta, after L. da Ponte: *Così fan tutte*), 1828; *Nourjahad*, Loder, 1834

*

DNB (E. D. Cook); *NicollH*
'Rebuilding of the English Opera House', *The Times* (23 March 1830)
F. Boase: 'Arnold, Samuel James', *Modern English Biography* (London, 2/1965)
BRUCE CARR, LEANNE LANGLEY

Arnoldson, Sigrid (*b* Stockholm, 20 March 1861; *d* Stockholm, 7 Feb 1943). Swedish soprano. She studied in Paris and made her début in 1885 at Prague as Rosina. In 1887 she made her London début at Drury Lane and the following year was engaged at Covent Garden, where she sang Zerlina, Rosina, Cherubino, Papagena and Oscar (*Ballo*). She returned to Covent Garden in 1892 to sing Baucis in Gounod's *Philémon et Baucis*, the role of her Metropolitan début in 1893. She sang Sophie in the first New York and London performances of *Werther* (1894). Her repertory included Marguerite de Valois (*Les Huguenots*), Nedda (*Pagliacci*), Micaëla and Carmen, which she took over from an indisposed Calvé at Covent Garden (1903). A charming personality allied to fine technique made her a great favourite with audiences. ELIZABETH FORBES

Arnould [Arnoult], (**Magdeleine** [Madeleine]) **Sophie** (*b* Paris, 13 Feb 1740; *d* Paris, 22 Oct 1802). French soprano. Her performance in sacred music impressed the royal family and Mme de Pompadour, and she was appointed to the Opéra, studying declamation with Clairon and singing with Fel. Her voice was sweet and expressive, not powerful, supported by fine diction and acting. She was the leading Opéra soprano from 1757 (début in Mouret's *Les amours des dieux*) to 1778. She sang over 30 roles, by Lully, Rameau, Rousseau (*Le devin du village*) and others; several she created, but her greatest was Telaira in Rameau's *Castor et Pollux*. She adapted to Italian-influenced music such as Monsigny's *Aline*, and the climax of her career was in *Iphigénie en Aulide* (1774; at Fontainebleau as late as 1777). Less successful as Eurydice, she was mortified by Gluck's choice of Levasseur for *Alceste*. The Dorothy Parker of her day, she entertained the *philosophes* while alienating colleagues; she bore three illegitimate children to the Count of Lauraguais. Her colourful career inspired several biographies, two comedies, and an opera by Pierné.

For illustration *see* IPHIGÉNIE EN AULIDE.

*

ES (E. Zanetti)
C. Y. Cousin d'Avalon: *Grimmiana* (Paris, 1813)
[A. Deville]: *Arnoldiana, ou Sophie Arnould et ses contemporaines* (Paris, 1813)
F. Fayolle: *L'esprit de Sophie Arnould* (Paris, 1813)
E.-L. Lamothe-Langon, ed.: *Mémoires de mademoiselle Sophie Arnoult* (Paris, 1837)
E. and J. de Goncourt: *Sophie Arnould d'après sa correspondance et ses mémoires inédits* (Paris, 1857, 2/1859)
H. Sutherland Edwards: *Idols of the French Stage* (London, 1889)
R. Douglas: *Sophie Arnould: Actress and Wit* (Paris, 1898)
F. Rogers: 'Sophie Arnould', *MQ*, vi (1920), 57–61
B. Dussanc: *Sophie Arnould: la plus spirituelle des bacchantes* (Paris, 1938)
JULIAN RUSHTON

Aroldo. Opera in four acts by GIUSEPPE VERDI to a libretto by FRANCESCO MARIA PIAVE after their earlier opera *STIFFELIO*; Rimini, Teatro Nuovo, 16 August 1857.

Aroldo *a Saxon knight*	tenor
Mina *his wife*	soprano
Egberto *her father, an old knight, vassal of Kent*	baritone
Briano *a pious hermit*	bass
Godvino *an adventurer knight, guest of Egberto*	tenor
Enrico *Mina's cousin*	tenor
Elena *also her cousin*	soprano
Jorg *Aroldo's servant*	spoken

Crusader knights, ladies and gentlemen of Kent, squires, pages, heralds, huntsmen, Saxons, Scottish peasants

Setting In Egberto's castle in Kent, and on the shores of Loch Lomond in Scotland, in about 1200

The first performance of *Stiffelio*, at Trieste in November 1850, had encountered severe problems with local religious censorship, particular objection being made to the final scene, which had to be changed radically and – Verdi thought – damagingly. The few subsequent revivals also tended to run into trouble, and in 1854 Verdi decided to collaborate with Piave on rescuing the opera by setting it to a different, less sensitive plot. In 1856 they started work, changing the tale of a 19th-century Protestant pastor into that of a 13th-century Saxon knight returned from the Crusades, Verdi taking the opportunity to make a number of further modifications. The brilliant young conductor Angelo Mariani directed the première at Rimini, whose cast included Emilio Pancani (Aroldo), Marcellina Lotti (Mina) and Gaetano Ferri (Egberto). The revised opera was a huge success, but revivals fared less well and *Aroldo* soon disappeared from the general repertory, receiving only the occasional performance. In the discussion below, musical detail will be mentioned only if a passage differs substantially from *Stiffelio* or is new to *Aroldo*.

ACT 1.i *A drawing room in Egberto's home* The overture is substantially that of *Stiffelio*, but the opening of the act is new to *Aroldo*. A festive unaccompanied chorus, 'Tocchiamo! a gaudio insolito', welcomes Aroldo home from the Crusades. After an intense orchestral introduction, Mina enters to give voice to her remorse and offer a brief prayer, 'Salvami tu, gran Dio', an opening that immediately makes her a more forceful presence than was Lina in *Stiffelio*. Aroldo now arrives and introduces the hermit Briano, who saved his life in battle. His ensuing double aria carries frequent anguished interpolations from Mina. The Andante, 'Sotto il sol di Siria', which describes how his thoughts on the battlefield were always for his wife, takes its theme from the overture; but (as in *Stiffelio*) the absence of Mina's ring arouses suspicions which he voices in the cabaletta 'Non sai che la sua perdita'.

Mina, left alone, decides to write to her husband. She is interrupted by Egberto; the words and music of the ensuing duet are, apart from a few details, identical with those in *Stiffelio*.

1.ii *A suite of rooms illuminated for a grand celebration* To a further theme borrowed from the overture, ladies and knights appear downstage as Godvino slips a letter to Mina into a book, observed – though only from behind – by Briano. In the interval between bursts of choral celebration, Enrico comes on, dressed like Godvino, and takes up the book. Briano is now convinced that Enrico placed the letter there, and warns Aroldo. Egberto enters, and asks for a returning warrior to narrate the adventures of King Richard in Palestine. Aroldo obliges with 'Vi fu in Palestina', a largely declamatory episode that tells of a dishonourable man who betrayed his guests by writing a secret love letter to the lady of the house. He takes up the book to further illustrate the point, finds it locked and tells a terrified Mina to open it. The ensuing concertato, 'Oh qual m'invade ed agita', is taken directly from *Stiffelio*, though with various expansions and musical changes, in particular to the main melodic line of the stretta.

ACT 2 *An old graveyard in the castle in Kent* The opening part of the scene, together with Mina's prayer 'Ah! dagli scanni eterei', is taken from *Stiffelio*, but at the appearance of Godvino new music takes over in preparation for a new cabaletta, 'Ah dal sen di quella tomba', which – in line with the changes made to Mina's role in Act 1 – requires an impressive musical and emotional range from the soprano. The remainder of the act follows *Stiffelio*: Egberto's duel with Godvino is interrupted by Aroldo; Egberto reveals to Aroldo that

Godvino is Mina's seducer; and Briano narrowly prevents Aroldo from fighting a duel with Godvino.

ACT 3 *An antechamber in Egberto's home* The act is identical with Act 3 scene i of *Stiffelio*, although with occasional alterations to and expansions of Mina's role. Egberto contemplates suicide in his double aria; Aroldo and Godvino have a brief scene; and finally there is the long duet of confrontation between Aroldo and Mina, during which Egberto murders Godvino.

ACT 4 *A deep valley in Scotland* An opening chorus, 'Cade il giorno', offers generic local colour to mark the new geographical location. Aroldo and Briano, dressed as hermits, join the chorus in a prayer, 'Angiol di Dio', that makes prominent use of contrapuntal effects. A storm has been brewing and now breaks out to an orchestral accompaniment as elaborate in its instrumental virtuosity as anything Verdi had written to date. To the relief of the chorus, a boat seen approaching on the lake survives the storm, and as the bad weather subsides the boat moors and from it disembark Mina and Egberto. They go to the hermit's cottage to seek shelter. The ensuing Quartetto finale breaks into two large sections. First comes an Allegro, 'Ah da me fuggi', in which sharply differing emotional reactions are juxtaposed: Aroldo's violent rejection of his wife, then Egberto's narration of his and Mina's painful exile after Godvino's death, and finally Mina's disjointed pleas for forgiveness. But Mina takes control and leads off the final Largo, 'Allora che gl'anni', in which she begs Aroldo at least to forgive her when she is old and near death. At last the conflicting voices join, and a sententious phrase about forgiveness from Briano eventually persuades Aroldo to pronounce the words 'Sei perdonata!' ('You are forgiven!').

* * *

As will be clear from the above, *Aroldo* differs from *Stiffelio* primarily in its first and last acts. However, there is surprisingly little stylistic disparity in the later opera, a fact that in part demonstrates the forward-looking nature of so much of *Stiffelio*. The relative merits of the operas are not such as to recommend one firmly over the other. *Aroldo* has a more forceful soprano presence, and its final act makes a weightier close than the brief though effective choral finale of *Stiffelio*. On the other hand, Lina's reticence in the earlier opera is one of its most effective dramatic ploys, and *Stiffelio's* compelling sense of religious claustrophobia is somewhat diffused by the *Aroldo* story, which wavers uncertainly between the warlike and the religious. It is tempting to conclude that both operas deserve more performances than they at present receive.

ROGER PARKER

Arquier [D'Arquier], **Joseph** (*b* Toulon, 1763; *d* Bordeaux, Oct 1816). French composer. He went to Paris in 1790 or 1791, attracted by the proliferation of theatres following the abolition of the privilege system. The impresario and founder of the Théâtre Molière, Boursault-Malherbe, engaged him first as a cellist and then, after Scio left for the Théâtre Feydeau in 1792, as orchestral conductor. Arquier was subsequently appointed conductor at the Théâtre de la Gaîté (1793) and, with some periods of absence, at the Théâtre des Jeunes-Elèves between 1800 and 1807. When Napoleon closed that theatre he moved back to the south of France, where he had begun his career as a composer. His most notable work is probably *Marie-Christine* (1793), a trenchant satire on the aristocratic society of the Austrian Netherlands at the time of the French army's invasion; its music was judged to be 'pleasant'.

L'Indienne, Carcassonne, 1788
Le pot au noir et le pot aux roses, ou Daphnis et Hortense (pastorale mêlée d'ariettes, 1, Saint-Priest), Marseilles, Elèves Privilégiés de Mgr le duc d'Orléans, 16 Feb 1789
Le pirate (3), Toulon, 1789, or Marseilles, 1790
Le mari corrigé (2), Paris, Français Comique et Lyrique, 21 Feb 1791
La peau de l'ours (oc, 1), Paris, Molière, 1791
Le congé des volontaires (oc, 1), Paris, Montansier, 1792 or 1793
Le bon hermite (opéra-vaudeville, 1, Provost-Montfort), Paris, Palais-Variétés, 2 May 1793
L'hôtellerie de Fontainebleau, Paris, Montansier, 18 May 1793
Marie-Christine, ou La tigresse du Nord (oc, 2, P. Desriaux), Paris, Lycée des Arts, 12 Nov 1793
Les Péruviens, Tours, 1798
Les deux petits troubadours (oc, 1), Paris, Jeunes-Elèves, 1800
L'hôtellerie de Sarzanno (1, Desriaux, after C. Goldoni), Paris, Jeunes-Elèves, 22 April 1802
Le désert, ou L'oasis, New Orleans, ?1802
La fée Urgèle (4, C.-S. Favart), Brest, 1804
L'hermitage des Pyrennées (comédie mêlée de chant, 1, Périn), Paris, Jeunes-Elèves, 5 March 1805
Montrose et Zisac (3), Marseilles, Pavillon, 1810
La suite du médecin turc, Marseilles, 1811
Zipéa et Adèle, ou La fuite précipitée (3), Perpignan, Dec 1812

*

H. Duval: *Dictionnaire des ouvrages dramatiques* (MS, *c*1850, *F-Pn*)

MICHEL NOIRAY

Arresti [Aresti], **Floriano** (*b* Bologna, *c*1660; *d* Bologna, 1719). Italian composer. He studied keyboard and composition in Rome with Bernardo Pasquini. By 1684 he had returned to Bologna, where he became a member of the Accademia Filarmonica, serving as its *principe* in 1714. In 1692 he became second organist at S Petronio; by 1717 he was named in librettos as 'Organista della Metropolitana'. He composed a quantity of music for both the stage and the church, but all his major works are lost.

L'enigma disciolta (trattenimento pastorale, G. Neri), Bologna, Formagliari, carn. 1710
Crisippo (os, G. Braccioli), Ferrara, Bonacosi, May 1710; perf. with puppets, Bologna, (?)Barbellini, 1710
L'inganno vince l'inganno; perf. with puppets, Bologna, Dec 1710
La costanza in cimento con la crudeltà (os, Braccioli), Venice, Sant'Angelo, carn. 1712; as La costanza in cimento, ossia Il Radamisto, Bologna, Marsigli-Rossi, 1715
Il trionfo di Pallade in Arcadia, Bologna, Marsigli-Rossi, 1716

*

J.-B. de La Borde: *Essai sur la musique ancienne et moderne* (Paris, 1780), iii, 165
N. Morini: *La Reale accademia filarmonica di Bologna* (Bologna, 1930), 92, 95

JAMES L. JACKMAN

Arriaga (y Balzola), Juan Crisóstomo (Jacobo Antonio) [de] (*b* Bilbao, 27 Jan 1806; *d* Paris, 17 Jan 1826). Basque composer. The precocious Arriaga had written an octet before he was 11 and an opera at about 15. From 1821 he attended the Paris Conservatoire; his teacher Fétis praised him lavishly, as did Cherubini, but he made little mark outside his native Bilbao in the Spanish musical circles of his day. In 1824, when only 18, he was appointed répétiteur in harmony and counterpoint there; his three string quartets, which have since had considerable success, were published in Paris the same year.

Arriaga's only opera, *Los esclavos felices*, an *opera seria* in one act to a libretto by L. F. Comella (written some 25 years earlier for an opera by Laserna), was composed by 1820 and performed in Bilbao in that year; its teasingly attractive overture is well known in Spain, yet the opera has attracted surprisingly little attention. Written in the literary tradition of the confrontation between Christian and Moor going back to Cervantes and beyond, it tells how a Spanish nobleman and his loyal wife, faced with humiliation, death and the harem by their Moorish captors, are saved by their valour and constancy matched finally by the noble clemency of the King of Algiers and his son. His operatic potential is also seen in the 'biblical scene' *Agar* and in the 'lyric-dramatic scene' *Erminia*, both for soprano and orchestra and probably written after *Los esclavos felices*. The unforced way Arriaga neatly combined his own individual touch with fashionable italianate operatic styles in his earlier works, and the elegant correctness later demanded by the Conservatoire, goes some way towards justifying his sobriquet as 'the Spanish Mozart'.

*

FétisB

J. de Eresalde: *'Los esclavos felices', ópera de J. C. de Arriaga: antecedentes, comentarios, argumentos y algunas noticias bio-bibliográficas* (Bilbao, 1935)

C. A. Figuerido: *El arte y la mente del músico J. C. de Arriaga* (Bilbao, 1948)

S. Juan Jalón: *Juan Crisóstomo de Arriaga* (Bilbao, 1979)

C. Gómez Amat: *Historia de la música española*, v: *Siglo XIX* (Madrid, 1987)

JACK SAGE

Arrieta (y Corera), Pascual (Juan) Emilio (*b* Puente de la Reina, Navarra, 21 Oct 1823; *d* Madrid, 11 Feb 1894). Spanish composer. Orphaned very early and brought up by a sister in Madrid, at 15 he took himself, by way of a smuggler's coaster, to Milan, where he managed to enter the Conservatory to study composition under Vaccai (with Ponchielli as a fellow-student and friend). He was in such abject poverty that he used to faint from hunger in classes. A grant from Count Litta (to whom in gratitude he later dedicated several works) enabled him to continue and to win acclaim in 1845 for his student opera *Ildegonda* (libretto by Solera), which, after his return to Madrid, was repeated in the little theatre in Isabel II's palace on 19 October 1849. She appointed him her singing teacher and encouraged him to write a further Italian opera with Solera, *La conquista di Granata* (1850). Arrieta then spent a year in Italy supervising performances of his works, but on his return found Madrid agog over the efforts of a group of composers to re-establish the zarzuela (Barbieri's three-act *Jugar con fuego* had created a sensation). He decided to take up this form, which he had hitherto despised, and won immediate successes in 1853 with the three-act *El dominó azul* (every number of which was encored) and the one-act *El grumete*. He followed these up in 1855 with his greatest triumph, *Marina* (converted into an opera 16 years later), which still remains in the repertory. The several dozen zarzuelas he composed in the following quarter-century are, however, no longer heard. In 1857 Arrieta was appointed professor of composition at the Madrid Conservatory, where Chapí and Bretón were among his pupils. In 1868 he became its director, holding the post until his death. He brought a much-needed technical polish to the popular nationalist zarzuela, though in some quarters he was regarded as 'the least romantic, the most academic and circumspect Spanish musician of his time'.

See also MARINA.

Ildegonda (2, T. Solera), Milan, Conservatory, 1845

La conquista di Granata [La conquista de Granada; Isabel la Católica] (3, Solera), Madrid, Palacio, 10 Feb 1850

Marina (3, M. Ramos Carrión), Madrid, Real, 6 March 1871 [rev. of zarzuela of 1855]

Zarzuelas (all first performed in Madrid): Al amanecer (1, M Pina), Circo, 8 May 1851; El dominó azul (3, F. Camprodón), Circo, 12 Feb 1853; El grumete (1, A. García Gutiérrez), Circo, 6 June 1853; La estrella de Madrid (3, A. Lopez de Ayala), Circo, 13 Oct 1853; La cacería real (3, García Gutiérrez), Circo, 11 March 1854; La dama del rey (1, N. Villoslada), Circo, 7 Feb 1855; Guerra a muerte (3, Ayala), Circo, 22 June 1855; Marina (2, Camprodón), Circo, 21 Sept 1855; La zarzuela (1), Zarzuela, 1 Oct 1856, collab. F. A. Barbieri and J. R. Gaztambide; La hija de la Providencia (T. Rodriguez), Circo, 12 May 1856

El sonámbulo (1, A. Hurtado), Zarzuela, 11 Oct 1856; El planeta Venus (3, V. de la Vega), Zarzuela, 27 Feb 1858; Azón Visconti (3, García Gutiérrez), Zarzuela, 12 Nov 1858; Quien manda, manda (2, Camprodón), Zarzuela, 6 May 1859; Los Circasianos [El caudillo de Baza] (3, L. Olona), Zarzuela, 8 April 1860; Llamada y tropa (2, García Gutiérrez), Circo, 8 March 1861; El hombre feliz (1, C. Frontaura), Circo, 6 April 1861; Un ayo para el niño (1, García Gutiérrez), Circo, 6 April 1861; Dos coronas (3, García Gutiérrez), Circo, Dec 1861; El agente de matrimonios (3, Ayala), Zarzuela, 1 March 1862

La tabernera de Londres (3, García Gutiérrez), Circo, 14 Nov 1862; Un trono y un desengaño (3, Pina), Circo, 14 Dec 1862; La vuelta del corsario (3, García Gutiérrez), Circo, 18 Nov 1863; Cadenas de oro (3, R. de Navarrete and L. M. de Larra), Circo, 1 Sept 1864; De tal palo tal astilla (1, J. Selgas), Circo, 1 Sept 1864; El toque de ánimas (3, D. Cespedes), Circo, 26 Nov 1864; La ínsula Barataria (3, de Larra after M. de Cervantes: *Don Quixote*), Circo, 24 Dec 1864; El capitán negrero (3, García Gutiérrez), Zarzuela, 19 Dec 1865; El conjuro (1, Ayala, after P. Calderón de la Barca), Variedades, 24 Nov 1866

Un sarao y una soirée (2, Ramos Carrión and Lustonó), Variedades, 12 Dec 1866; La suegra del diablo (3, E. Blasco), Variedades, 23 March 1867; Los enemigos domésticos (2, J. Picón), Variedades, 16 Nov 1867; El figle enamorado (1, Ramos Carrión), Circo, 24 Dec 1867; Los novios de Teruel (2, Blasco), Circo, 24 Dec 1867; A la humanidad doliente (1, Blasco), 30 Jan 1868; Los misterios del Parnaso (1, de Larra), Circo, 5 Sept 1868; Los progresos del amor (3, Blasco), Circo, 19 Dec 1868; Las fuentes del Prado (1, M. Godino), Circo, 6 May 1870; El potosí submarino (3, G. Santisteban), Circo, 19 Dec 1870

De Madrid a Biarritz (1, Carrión and Coello), Zarzuela, Dec 1870; El motin contra Esquilache (3, Retez and Echevarria), Zarzuela, 12 Sept 1871; La sota de espadas (3, Pina), Zarzuela, 16 Dec 1871; Las manzanas de oro (3, Blasco), Español, Dec 1873; Un viaje a Cochinchina (1, Picón), Zarzuela, Nov 1875; Entre el alcalde y el rey (3, N. de Arco), Zarzuela, 23 Dec 1875, collab. M. F. Caballero; La guerra santa (1, de Larra and D. Escrich), Zarzuela, 4 March 1879; El amor enamorado [Heliodora] (3, J. E. Hartzenbusch), Apolo, 28 Sept 1880; San Franco de Sena (3, J. de Estremera), Apolo, 27 Oct 1883; El guerrillero (3, F. Muñoz), Apolo, Jan 1885, collab. Caballero and Chapí

*

A. Peña y Goñi: *La ópera española y la música dramática en España en el siglo XIX* (Madrid, 1881, 2/1967, as *España desde la ópera a la zarzuela*)

F. de Arteaga: *Celebridades musicales* (Barcelona, 1887)

J. Subirá: *El teatro del real palacio* (Madrid, 1950)

A. Sagardía: *Gatzambide y Arrieta* (Pamplona, 1986)

LIONEL SALTER

Arrieu, Claude (*b* Paris, 30 Nov 1903; *d* ?Paris, 7 March 1990). French composer. She studied at the Paris Conservatoire, where her teachers included Roger-Ducasse and Dukas, taking a *premier prix* for composition in 1932. In 1935 she began working for French Radio, where she remained until 1947 when she devoted herself to composition. A prolific composer, she retained in her music the ease of flow and elegance of structure that typified Parisian neo-classicism, while avoiding the often concomitant frivolity. *Noé* is remarkable for its extensive use of *Sprechgesang*, while *Cadet Roussel* returns to the alternating speech and song of the *opéra comique*. *Balthazar* is a *commedia dell'arte* story, and *Un clavier pour un autre* concerns a party of classical musicians forced to spend the night in the customs hall of a railway station. A doctor arrives and ruins the voice of one of the singers, but teaches a secretary to sing; she swaps her typewriter keyboard for that of a piano. Her several radio productions must place Arrieu as one of the most important contributors to the concept of radio opera, although *La cabine téléphonique* was later transferred to the stage (Tours, 5 March 1977).

Noé, 1931–4 (imagerie musicale, 3, A. Obey), Strasbourg, Opéra, 29 Jan 1950
Cadet Roussel, 1938–9 (ob, 5, A. de La Tourrasse after J. Limozin), Marseilles, Opéra, 2 Oct 1953
La Coquille à planètes (opéra radiophonique, P. Schaeffer), RTF, 1944
Les deux rendez-vous, 1948 (oc, 1, P. Bertin, after G. de Nerval), RTF, 22 June 1951
Le chapeau à musique (opéra enfantine, 2, Tourrasse and P. Dumaine), RTF, 1953
La princesse de Babylone, 1953–5 (ob, 3, P. Dominique, after Voltaire), Reims, Opéra, 3 March 1960
La cabine téléphonique (ob, 1, M. Vaucaire), RTF, 15 March 1959
Cymbeline, 1958–63 (2, J. Tournier and M. Jacquemont, after W. Shakespeare), ORFT, 31 March 1974
Balthazar ou Le mort-vivant, 1966 (ob, 1, Dominique), unperf.
Un clavier pour un autre (ob, 1, J. Tardieu), Avignon, Opéra, 3 April 1971
Barbarine, 1972 (3, after A. de Musset), inc.
Les amours de Don Perlimpin et Belise en son jardin (imagerie lyrique, 4 tableaux, after F. García Lorca), Tours, Grand, 1 March 1980

*

P. Landormy: *La musique française après Debussy* (Paris, 1943)
F. Masset: 'Le théâtre lyrique de Claude Arrieu', *Le théâtre lyrique français 1945–1988*, ed. D. Pistone (Paris, 1987), 193–202

RICHARD LANGHAM SMITH

Arrigo, Girolamo (*b* Palermo, 2 April 1930). Italian composer. He studied at the Palermo conservatory and with Max Deutsch in Paris, where he settled in 1954. In the 1960s he won various scholarships and composition prizes. Initially influenced by the contemporary Parisian school (particularly Boulez), in his works of the 1960s and 70s he arrived at a personal synthesis that cannot be classified as belonging to any specific trend. His first opera was *Orden*, a fiercely political work critical of Franco and the civil war in Spain. It was first performed at the Avignon Festival in 1969. Arrigo addressed social problems again in *Addio Garibaldi*, composed to his own libretto, which had its première in Paris and was also given in Strasbourg by the newly-formed Opéra du Rhin. *Il ritorno di Casanova* (based on Schnitzler's 1918 novella) was commissioned by Radio France and first given at the Grand Théâtre, Geneva, in 1985.

Orden (1, P. Bourgeade, R. Alberti and P. Levi), Avignon, July 1969
Addio Garibaldi (epopea musicale, 1, Arrigo), Paris, OC, aut. 1972
Il ritorno di Casanova (2, G. di Leva, after A. Schnitzler: *Die Heimkehr des Casanova*), Geneva, Grand, 18 April 1985

RAFFAELE POZZI

Arrigoni, Carlo (*b* Florence, 5 Dec 1697; *d* Florence, 19 Aug 1744). Italian composer. He was principally associated with Florence, where he was a theorbo player, violinist and singer. By 1722 Arrigoni was a member of the Accademia Filarmonica of Bologna; his opera *La vedova* was staged at Foligno in that year. His presence in London in 1732–6 coincided with the lifespan of the Opera of the Nobility, rival to Handel's company, which presented four performances of his *Fernando* (P. A. Rolli, after G. Gigli: *La fede ne'tradimenti*) at Lincoln's Inn Fields Theatre beginning on 5 February 1734. He also took part in concerts. In 1736 Arrigoni was back in Florence, and some of his music was given in Vienna in 1737 and 1738. His last two known operas, *Scipione nelle Spagne* and *Sirbace*, were performed in Florence during Carnival 1739; both are now lost.

His only operatic music known to survive is from *Fernando* (eight arias, *GB-Lbl*), though several oratorios and cantatas are extant. He was a composer of modest ability. His arias often seem to be constructed of brief, unrelated phrases which awkwardly return to a few pitches and thus lack directional flow, but he does show a command of fashionable stylistic conventions.

*

LS

W. Dean: 'An Unknown Handel Singer: Carlo Arrigoni', *MT*, cxviii (1977), 556–8

JOHN WALTER HILL

Arrigoni [Arigoni], **Giovanni Giacomo** (*b* S Vito al Tagliamento, 10 March 1597; *d* S Vito al Tagliamento, 8 June 1675). Italian composer. He was organist of the Imperial Hofkapelle in Vienna from 1632 to 1638. After 1638 there is evidence that he was in S Vito and Venice, and from 1652 to 1655 he managed an opera company in Udine. However, he did not break off his connections with Vienna, as witness the dedication to Emperor Leopold I of his three-act *festa teatrale* (probably of 1657–8) *Gli amori d'Alessandro Magno e di Rosane*, to a libretto by G. A. Cicognini. There is no record of the opera's having been performed in Vienna or anywhere else (the prologue, first act, and a German translation of the libretto are preserved in *A-Wn*). Characteristic of the work are its short, song-like arias, its large number of recitatives, the setting for small orchestra, and several comic scenes.

*

L. von Köchel: *Die kaiserliche Hof-Musikkapelle in Wien von 1543–1867* (Vienna, 1869)
R. Haas: *Die Musik des Barocks* (Potsdam, 1928)
T. Morsanuto: *Giovanni Giacomo Arrigoni (1597–1675): un compositore seicentesco fra Venezia, Vienna ed Udine* (Cremona, 1991)

JOSEF-HORST LEDERER

Arroio, João Marcelino (*b* Oporto, 4 Oct 1861; *d* Colares, 18 May 1930). Portuguese composer of Spanish descent. A politician and member of the Coimbra University law faculty, he practised music as an amateur. His most significant work, the three-act *drama lirico Amore e Perdizione*, to a libretto by Francisco Braga, is based on Camilo Castelo Branco's Portuguese classic *Amor de Perdição*. First performed at the S Carlos, Lisbon, on 2 March 1907, *Amore* was later translated into German as *Liebe und Verderben* for a Hamburg performance of 1910, one of the first Portuguese operas to be staged in Germany. Arroio's second *drama lirico*, the four-act *Leonora Telles*, was published in 1910 to his own libretto, but so far only the second act has been staged (1941, Sociedade de Musica da Câmara, Lisbon). Dramatically, Arroio's operas are similar to the nationalist operas of his compatriots Noronha, Keil and Ferreira Veiga. At a stylistic level, however, they attempt to escape from the Italian style prevalent in Portugal through an intensive use of chromaticism (particularly in *Leonora Telles*) more akin to that of Wagner. LUISA CYMBRON

Arroyo, José Francisco (*b* Oyarzun, nr San Sebastián, 14 Jan 1818; *d* Oporto, 20 Sept 1886). Spanish composer. He spent most of his life in Portugal, where his operas were performed with varying success. The first, *Bianca de Mauleon*, was criticized in the press after its première, but a more favourable review appeared later in the *Revista Universal Lisboense* (signed 'Y', but probably by Arroyo himself), comparing the work to Verdi's *I Lombardi* and *Ernani*. According to Pedrell, all of Arroyo's music is influenced by Italian models. In 1858–9 Arroyo was impresario at the Teatro das Variedades in Oporto, a post he held with Braz Martins (the librettist of *Recordações da guerra Peninsula*), but competition from the Teatro Baquet soon caused the theatre to close. None of Arroyo's operas was published.

first performed in Oporto unless otherwise stated

Bianca de Mauleon, S João, 11 March 1846
Francesca Ventivoglio, unperf.
O segredo do tio Vicente (1, A. C. Lousada), Variedades, 27 Oct 1858
Recordações da guerra Peninsula (5, B. Martins), Variedades, 13 Nov 1859
Santo Gonçalo d'Amarante (3), Variedades, 13 March 1859
Os Monges de Toledo (1), S João, 3 May 1862

*

DBP
F. Pedrell: *Diccionario biográfico y bibliográfico de músicos y escritores de musica* (Barcelona, 1897) JAVIER SUAREZ PAJARES

Arroyo, Martina (*b* New York, 2 Feb 1936). American soprano. She studied at Hunter College, New York, and won the 1958 Metropolitan Opera auditions. That year she sang in the American première of Pizzetti's *Assassinio nella cattedrale* at Carnegie Hall. After taking minor roles at the Metropolitan, she sang at Vienna, Düsseldorf, Berlin, Frankfurt, and Zürich (1963–8). In 1965 she was a substitute Aida for Nilsson at the Metropolitan where she has played all the major Verdi parts that form the basis of her repertory, as well as Donna Anna, Norma, Butterfly, Liù, Santuzza, La Gioconda, Turandot and Elsa. She made her London début as Valentine (*Les Huguenots*) in concert in 1968, the year she first sang at Covent Garden. She retired in 1989. Her rich, powerful voice, heard to greatest advantage in Verdi, was flexible enough for Mozart; she had a dignified though undramatic stage presence. Her recordings include Hélène (*Les vêpres siciliennes*), Amelia (*Ballo*) and Leonora (*La forza*).

*

J. B. Steane: *The Grand Tradition* (London, 1974), 413ff
ALAN BLYTH

Arsace. *Dramma per musica* in three acts by DOMENICO NATALE SARRO to a libretto by ANTONIO SALVI after THOMAS CORNEILLE's tragedy *Le comte d'Essex*; Naples, Teatro S Bartolomeo, 10 December 1718.

Salvi's text (originally set by Giuseppe Orlandini as *Amore e Maestà* in 1715) is one of the few early 18th-century Italian librettos which end with the death of the hero or heroine. During the course of the opera the hero Arsace (soprano castrato) is arrested for having led an uprising against his queen, Statira (soprano). He contributes to his downfall by refusing to answer Statira, who loves him and would save him if she could, about the reason for his rebellion. The real reason, as he explains to his friend Megabise (soprano), is that he is secretly in love with the princess Rosmiri (soprano) and wants to prevent her enforced marriage to Mitrane (alto castrato). A false report linking Arsace with Dario, pretender to the throne, is spread by his enemy Artabano (tenor) and contributes to Statira's decision to sign the death warrant. She hears the truth too late to stay execution, and is stricken with grief at the news of his death.

In Sarro's setting some light relief is provided by a 'lady of the court', Merilla (contralto), and a court servant, Morante (bass), who enact a 'Prologue' for the queen at the start of the opera and who later reappear in comic scenes at the end of Acts 1 and 2, and in the middle of Act 3.

Arsace is a transitional work. Many of the arias exhibit the semi-contrapuntal techniques of older operas; others however are written in the homophonic style typical of operatic music of the late 1720s and the 1730s. Uncharacteristic of opera of the period but in keeping with the tragic denouement, the work ends with an accompanied recitative for Statira and Megabise, and without a chorus. MICHAEL F. ROBINSON

Arsinoe [*Arsinoe, Queen of Cyprus*]. Opera in three acts by THOMAS CLAYTON to a libretto by TOMMASO STANZANI, translated by PETER ANTHONY MOTTEUX; London, Drury Lane, 16 January 1705.

The opera opens with the hero Ormondo (countertenor) foiling an assassination attempt on Queen Arsinoe (soprano) instigated by Dorisbe (soprano), a princess who holds the Queen responsible for her father's death. Arsinoe and Ormondo fall in love, but

Drawing by James Thornhill for Act 1 scene i of Clayton's 'Arsinoe' performed at Drury Lane, London, 16 January 1705: pen, ink and watercolour

Dorisbe is in love with Ormondo and is herself loved by Feraspe (bass), the captain of the Queen's Guard. After much misunderstanding and jealousy, a duel between Ormondo and Feraspe, a second murderous attack on Arsinoe, a prison scene with Ormondo in chains in which Arsinoe realizes that he is of royal birth and a suicide attempt by Dorisbe the opera ends with Arsinoe about to marry Ormondo and the forgiven Dorisbe united with Feraspe. Light relief is provided by Ormondo's servant Delbo (bass) and Dorisbe's old nurse (contralto).

Arsinoe was the first all-sung opera in the Italian style to be performed on the English stage. The first three performances were by subscription and the opera was performed at court on Queen Anne's birthday (6 February). It then received regular performances until the failure of Clayton's second opera, *Rosamond*, in March 1707. In his preface to the libretto Clayton claimed that the singers were 'the Best that were to be found in England' and indeed the cast, and James Thornhill's handsome sets, must have played a large part in the opera's success (see illustration). Arsinoe was the first dramatic role for the new English singing star Catherine Tofts, and she was supported by the lively Letitia Cross as Dorisbe, Francis Hughes as Ormondo and Richard Leveridge as Feraspe. At the first performance Tofts's rival, Margherita de l'Epine, was advertised as performing 'several Entertainments of Singing in Italian and English' before and after the opera. *Arsinoe* provided a shorter evening's entertainment than audiences were accustomed to and after the first three months was generally accompanied by part of a play.

16 songs from *Arsinoe* appeared in issues of the *Monthly Mask of Vocal Music* between April 1705 and February 1706; later two selections from the opera were published and were combined to form a complete set. The recitatives, the feature which distinguished *Arsinoe* from all earlier English operas, survive in the manuscript of the complete opera (*GB-Lbl*).

Clayton had studied in Italy and returned eager to promote opera in the Italian style in England. He brought with him the *Arsinoe* libretto, first set by Franceschini in 1676. Since Clayton's name is absent from the illustrated title-page to the complete set of songs and from some, but not all, of the individual songs it has been suggested that the opera was not all his own music but a pasticcio using Italian airs. However, some copies of the complete *Songs* have a title page including Clayton's name; and the absence or presence of the composer's name on the heading of an individual song depended on whether or not the song was intended to be sold singly. Charles Burney was later to claim of the music that it was 'too mean in melody and incorrect in counterpoint' to be the work of an Italian. It is clear that *Arsinoe* succeeded because of its novelty, its action-filled libretto and the skill of its performers.

OLIVE BALDWIN, THELMA WILSON

Artaserse ('Artaxerxes'). Libretto by PIETRO METASTASIO, first set by Leonardo Vinci (1730, Rome).

ACT 1 King Serse [Xerxes] of Persia has banished Arbace [Arbaces], a friend of his son, Prince Artaxerxes, because he is the beloved of his daughter, Princess Mandane. Arbaces' father, Artabano [Artabanus], assassinates Xerxes and, finding Arbaces secretly returned to visit Mandane, exchanges swords with him

*'Artaserse', Act 2 scene xi (*ARTABANUS*: 'I condemn my son: Arbaces shall die'): engraving from the 'Opere' of Pietro Metastasio (Paris: Hérissant, 1780–82)*

so that Arbaces may hide the murder weapon. Artabanus then convinces Artaxerxes that his brother Prince Darius is the assassin and, acting quickly upon Artaxerxes' first reactions, immediately has Darius executed. Arbaces is subsequently accused and arrested, and although Artabanus urges punishment, Artaxerxes is reluctant to condemn his friend and the brother of Semira, the woman he loves.

ACT 2 Artabanus makes possible his son's escape, but Arbaces refuses. Semira begs Artaxerxes to pardon Arbaces while Mandane, despite her love, demands vengeance. Perplexed, Artaxerxes passes the responsibility of judgment to Artabanus who, to everyone's consternation, condemns his son to death. Secretly, however, he plans to oust Artaxerxes and place Arbaces on the throne.

ACT 3 Artaxerxes visits Arbaces in prison and contrives his escape. Artabanus comes to rescue him, finds the cell empty, and assumes that his son is dead. Mandane is disconsolate, and Arbaces, overhearing her cries, claims her love. Meanwhile Artabanus has poisoned the wine in the cup from which Artaxerxes will drink at his coronation. As he is about to drink, news comes of an insurrection. Arbaces is suspected as its instigator, but is soon absolved when his suppression of the rebellious forces is discovered. Reconciled with Arbaces, Artaxerxes bids him affirm his innocence by drinking from the coronation cup. Horrified, Artabanus confesses. He is banished and the couples are united.

* * *

Accounts of the assassination of Xerxes by Artabanus, the execution of Darius, the identification of the true assassin and the revenge of Artaxerxes are to be found in Ctesias, *Persica* (book 16); Diodorus Siculus, *Bibliotheca* (book 11); and Justin's epitome of the Trogus, *Historiae Philippicae* (book 3). Mandane's conflict between duty to a slain father and love for his supposed murderer parallels that of Chimène in Pierre Corneille's *Le Cid* (1637), and the death of Darius and the execution of the conspirator who threatens the throne concludes Boyer's *Artaxerce* (1683). The closest parallels to Metastasio are found in the *Xercès* (1714) by Crébillon, although, as with other French works, the focus of the action differs from that of Metastasio's drama. *Artaserse* abounds in conflicts of considerable moment from which no character is immune, while a theme of injustice, unresolved until the final scene, pervades the whole. Thus the composer is afforded ample opportunity for characterization and musical drama. That *Artaserse*, in 1730, should then have been Vinci's last opera (with Carestini as Arbaces) and Hasse's first Metastasian opera, with Cuzzoni and Farinelli (Carlo Broschi) heading the cast, provided the work with a propitious launching. With over 90 settings, 50 between 1730 and 1760, *Artaserse* was to become Metastasio's most popular text. Vinci's opera, admired by Metastasio, was staged for a gala at the new Teatro di S Carlo in Naples in 1738 and served to inaugurate the new Dresden opera house in 1746. Similarly, Graun's 1743 setting inaugurated the Stuttgart opera house in 1750 and a revision of Galuppi's 1749 setting opened the Teatro Nuovo in Padua in 1751. Hasse's setting reached London in 1734 with additional music by Riccardo Broschi, brother of Farinelli, who made his London début in it with a cast including Cuzzoni and Senesino. *Artaserse* was a first opera for both Gluck (1741, Milan) and J. C. Bach (1760, Turin), and was the only Metastasian opera to be set by Isouard (1794, Livorno). Thomas Arne achieved great success with his setting of an English translation for London in 1762.

For a list of settings *see* METASTASIO, PIETRO. DON NEVILLE

Artaserse (i) ('Artaxerxes'). *Dramma per musica* in three acts by LEONARDO VINCI to a libretto by PIETRO METASTASIO (*see* ARTASERSE above); Rome, Teatro delle Dame, 4 February 1730.

Artaserse and its companion piece *Alessandro nell'Indie* were the last of a series of successful collaborations between Vinci and Metastasio before the poet departed for Vienna. They were first performed during the same season in which Porpora presented two operas at the neighbouring Teatro Capranica. According to Burney, Vinci set both operas 'for half price, to gratify his enmity to Porpora'. Marpurg describes how each composer had his own theatre, group of singers and partisan followers, and even his own coffee-house where these followers gathered to discuss the merits of the two masters. The rivalry came to a climax when the Vinci party tried to sabotage the première of Porpora's second opera, *Siface* – an unnecessary effort since both Vinci operas were successful. *Artaserse* went on to become one of the few classics of the *dramma per musica* genre and was primarily responsible for Vinci's posthumous reputation. Even in France *Artaserse* had admirers, such as the *bouffonnist* De Rochemont who declared it to be 'the most beautiful opera from Italy, somewhat as *Armide* is the masterpiece of French composition'.

The role of Arbace [Arbaces], written for Carestini, is perhaps the finest in the opera; from the agitated 'Fra cento affanni' after his father Artabano [Artabanus] commits regicide in Act 1, to the dignified cantilena of 'Per quel paterno amplesso' after he has been unjustly condemned for this crime by his father in Act 2, to the prison scene, with its suggestion of cavatina-cabaletta form and the sentimental reconciliation duet with Mandane in Act 3, Arbaces' music exemplifies Vinci's talents. The heroic coloratura simile aria 'Vò solcando un mar' became one of the most popular arias of the 18th century, the reason, according to Grétry, being that 'the melody and above all the accompaniment absolutely match the words'. This aria is a perfect example of the early Classical style that Vinci and his Neapolitan colleagues cultivated during the 1720s, and its stylistic links with the late century are probably the reason Grétry considered it to be 'the first ray of light towards the truth'. Nonetheless vestiges of the old style can be found, such as Mandane's 'Dimmi, che un' empio sei' which is also one of the few full-length arias by Vinci not in da capo form.

The run of the opera was cut short by the death of Pope Benedict XIII on February 21. It was revived with even greater success the following year (after Vinci's unexpected death in May), the first of many revivals during the 18th century. KURT MARKSTROM

Artaserse (ii) ('Artaxerxes'). *Opera seria* in three acts by JOHANN ADOLF HASSE to a libretto by PIETRO METASTASIO (*see* ARTASERSE above); Venice, Teatro S Giovanni Grisostomo, February 1730, with text much changed by DOMENICO LALLI or Giovanni Boldini (revised version, Dresden, Court Theatre, 9 September 1740; recomposed version, Naples, Teatro S Carlo, 20 January 1760 and summer 1762 with, for the most part, Metastasio's original text).

Hasse's first and third settings of this libretto illustrate his style when he was about to take up his duties as Kapellmeister in Dresden (1731) and again when he was about to give them up (1763). His style underwent significant change during his association with Dresden, so that little in the work of 1760 and 1762 resembles the scores of 1730 and 1740. The rhythmic variety and exciting exploitation of vocal range, typical of his later arias, guaranteed the spontaneity that pleased audiences and gratified singers more and more with each decade. On the basis of musical style, it would seem that Hasse viewed Arbaces, his father and his sister as commoners (if this were an accepted interpretation of the libretto, that would help explain its exceptional popularity in the later 18th century).

Hasse's consistent use of specific keys to underline the psychological states of characters and, at times, the expectations of persons addressed, is nicely illustrated in all three versions of *Artaserse*. For example, D major is not only the key of the sinfonia but of arias presenting issues central to the plot. With D as a foil, E♭ expresses noble sentiments like virtuous duty; B♭ denotes royalty, G major qualities of the common man; E major communicates extreme emotion or intense anguish, A major sensuous love, and so on.

Unfortunately, no version of the opera has been revived in the 20th century. Its modern history may be said to begin with Sonneck's article of 1912–13, which describes differences among the three versions but, regrettably, praises the first (1730) while condemning the last (1760/62). Since it is faithful to Metastasio's original text, the last version deletes the accompanied recitative and aria for Mandane (concluding Act 1), in which she calls upon the ghost of her father, King Xerxes, a scene illustrating the romantic inclination of Hasse's early period and of Venetian taste of the time. But the classical elegance of Hasse's style of the 1760s not only justified but required the deletion.

At the 1730 première, Arbace [Arbaces] was sung by the celebrated castrato Farinelli, and Mandane by Francesca Cuzzoni; Faustina Bordoni, the composer's wife, took the latter role in 1740. As primo uomo and prima donna, Arbaces and Mandane each had five arias, or two more than Artaxerxes, the secondo uomo (and between one and three more than other characters depending on the version of the opera).

Most manuscript copies of arias for Arbaces are of the 1730 version. The many copies of 'Per questo dolce amplesso' in E major (Act 2 scene xi), following his father's condemnation, and 'Se al labbro mio non credi' in A major (1. xiv), a love song to Mandane, may be attributed to Farinelli's popularity. The 18th-century interest in Hasse's setting of 1730 is otherwise implied by widespread knowledge of the libretto: other composers and arrangers in the 1730s and 40s combined the Venetian text Hasse used with Metastasio's original text for Rome. The 1730 version, at least in part, was produced at Lucca in 1730, Ferrara (1731), Verona (1733), Bergamo (1738), Ljubljana (1740) and Ferrara (1745) and possibly supplied the basis for pasticcios in Venice (1734), Modena (1739) and elsewhere. The only complete score in Hasse's own hand (in *I-Mc*) is marked 'Naples 1762' (for illustration *see* HASSE, JOHANN ADOLF). SVEN HANSELL

Artaserse (iii) ('Artaxerxes'). *Opera seria* in three acts by BALDASSARE GALUPPI to a libretto by PIETRO METASTASIO (*see* ARTASERSE above); Vienna, Burgtheater, 27 January 1749.

This was Galuppi's first setting of Metastasio's most popular text; it was revised for Padua in 1751. The text is heavily cut throughout, with many lines of new recitative added to bridge awkward transitions. The most extensive variation is the insertion of a quartet for the principals, Arbace [Arbaces] (soprano), Artaxerxes (soprano), Artabano [Artabanus] (tenor) and Mandane (alto, sung by Vittoria Tesi), in Act 1 scene xi and the deletion of the rest of the act following (five arias and four scenes, including Arbaces's pleas for clemency and claims of innocence). The work's popularity rode on the tails of *Demetrio*, performed at the Burgtheater on 16 October 1748, which broke all box office records. Metastasio complained bitterly about his mangled text.

DALE E. MONSON

Artaxerxes. Opera in three acts by THOMAS AUGUSTINE ARNE probably to his own libretto after PIETRO METASTASIO's *Artaserse*; London, Covent Garden, 2 February 1762.

Artaxerxes was Arne's first and only attempt at a full-length English opera on the Italian model. For his libretto he seems to have made an English version of Metastasio's well-known text himself, already set numerous times by such composers as Hasse and J. C. Bach. The opera was chiefly intended as a display piece for his pupil Charlotte Brent, whose part of Mandane contains coloratura writing of awesome difficulty. Semira, the other female role, also demands an accomplished singer. John Beard first sang the part of

Artaxerxes *son of Xerxes, King of Persia*	contralto
Artabanes *generalissimo to the king*	tenor
Arbaces *his son*	soprano
Rimenes *general in the king's army*	tenor
Mandane *sister to Artaxerxes, in love with Arbaces*	soprano
Semira *sister to Arbaces, in love with Artaxerxes*	soprano

Nobles, guards and attendants

Setting In and near the royal palace in ancient times

the villain Artabanes, whose complex character and mixture of motives is reflected in his music. Artaxerxes and Arbaces, two castrato roles, were sung by the Italians Peretti and Tenducci respectively, which brought some criticism from those opposed to 'the vile race of eunuchs'. Tenducci's music requires expressiveness as well as a measure of virtuosity, and is more demanding than that given to Peretti. The part of the treacherous Rimenes, sung by George Mattocks, was of a suitably unsubtle nature.

The first performance was an outstanding success, but a later one, on 24 February 1763, was the occasion of a riot (see illustration). A gang of ruffians, headed by one Fitzpatrick, demanded the return of their privilege of entry for the third act at half price. When refused, they caused damage to the theatre estimated at £2000. Despite this setback, seven more performances were given before the end of the season and the opera remained in the repertory until well into the 19th century, presenting a challenge to all the outstanding sopranos of the time. The part of Mandane was sung in successive revivals by Anne Catley, Anna Maria Crouch, Mrs Billington, Mara and many others. The work was first given in Dublin on 18 February 1765, and in Edinburgh in 1769, when Tenducci (whose wife also took part) sought local approval by inserting three Scots airs with words by Robert Ferguson. It was revived at Covent Garden on 23 September 1813 for the début of Catherine Stephens, with additional music by Bishop and Braham, and was given in New York on 31 January 1828, reorchestrated by C. E. Horn. On 14 March 1962 *Artaxerxes* was revived in London at the Camden Festival by the Handel Opera Society. The aria 'The soldier tir'd' has been recorded by Joan Sutherland.

The full score of the opera, printed by John Johnson and originally sold by the composer, was advertised on 16 December 1762. A vocal score was published later by James Harrison. As usual, the recitatives and final chorus were omitted; the MS was apparently lost in the Covent Garden fire of 1808. But an edition of about 1820 by John Addison includes the recitatives used in Bishop's production of 1813, some of which may be by Arne. Haydn witnessed a performance in London in 1791 and professed amazement at such a work by an English composer. Charles Lamb recorded his youthful memories of it in his essay 'My First Play'.

ACT 1.i *An inner garden belonging to the palace of the King of Persia* The lovers Mandane and Arbaces must part, since Arbaces, on account of his love, has been banished by her father Xerxes. In the moonlight they sing a tender aubade 'Fair Aurora, prithee stay', in which the strings are silent for 24 bars while the ritornello, an evocation of dawn, is entrusted to oboes,

Riot at a performance of Thomas Arne's 'Artaxerxes' at Covent Garden on 24 February 1763, caused by the decision to suspend half-price entry for latecomers: engraving

bassoons, horns and double basses. Mandane leaves. Artabanes enters, holding the blood-stained sword with which he has just killed Xerxes. He exchanges swords with Arbaces and bids him escape. Arbaces expresses his anguish in the aria 'Amid a thousand racking woes', in which Arne introduces a chilling change of harmony at the words 'I feel cold blood thro' every vein distil'. Arbaces departs and Artaxerxes enters, asking Artabanes to discover the identity of his father's assassin. Artabanes voices the murdered king's call for revenge in the aria 'Behold on Lethe's dismal strand', which opens slowly with imaginative scoring, leading to a raging presto and a calmer final section. Semira enters and reproaches Artaxerxes, her lover, for his coldness. He responds with the aria 'Fair Semira, lovely maid', but is impelled by duty to depart, leaving Rimenes to explain. Rimenes takes the opportunity to express his own affection for Semira ('When real joys we miss'). Left alone, Semira deplores her fate.

1.ii *The palace* Artabanes tells Mandane and Artaxerxes that he has avenged Xerxes' death by killing the crown prince Darius, whom he accuses of the king's murder. Semira denies Darius's guilt, since Arbaces has been caught red-handed with the murder weapon. Arbaces is brought in a captive and asserts his innocence, but is rejected by his father in the aria 'Thy father! away'. Semira bids him defend himself ('Acquit thee of this foul offence'). Mandane believes him guilty and struggles with her conscience, torn between love and duty, in the brilliant aria 'Fly, soft ideas, fly', in which the bravura passages span two octaves.

ACT 2.i *The royal apartments* Artaxerxes recalls his childhood friendship with Arbaces in the tender, deliberately simple 'In infancy our hopes and fears'. He orders the prisoner to be brought before the generalissimo and leaves them alone. Artabanes then confides his intention of putting Arbaces on the throne and tells him to make good his escape. Arbaces refuses, knowing that this will appear to confirm his guilt. When his father angrily rejects him, Arbaces sings 'Disdainful you fly me' before he is taken back to prison. Rimenes enters and Artabanes offers him the hand of Semira if he will assist in the plot to kill Artaxerxes. He agrees, and when Semira enters Rimenes woos her, in a fashion reminiscent of Polyphemus wooing Galatea, in the aria 'To sigh and complain'. Mandane enters, still believing Arbaces guilty, and attempts to subdue her love for him in the aria 'If o'er the cruel tyrant love'.

2.ii *The throne room* Artaxerxes summons Artabanes to be the judge in his own son's case and Artabanes, maintaining the pretence, condemns him to death. Mandane vents her rage at such an inhuman act in the furious aria 'Monster, away!'. Left alone, Artabanes soliloquizes on his secret design for his son's enthronement, singing 'Thou like the glorious sun'.

ACT 3.i *A prison cell* Arbaces in melancholy mood asks, 'Why is death for ever late?'. Artaxerxes enters and, convinced of Arbaces' innocence, allows him to escape, after he has sung the famous aria 'Water parted from the sea'. Artabanes, who later finds his son gone, conspires with Rimenes to present Artaxerxes with a poisoned cup at the coronation ceremony.

3.ii In Mandane's apartment Semira reproaches her for her lack of pity, but Mandane defends herself in 'Let not rage thy bosom firing'. Arbaces takes the risk of meeting Mandane and they sing a love duet 'For thee I live, my dearest'.

3.iii *The temple prepared for the coronation ceremony* Just as Artaxerxes takes the poisoned chalice Semira enters with the news that the palace is surrounded by mutinous troops led by Rimenes. Artaxerxes prepares to defend his life, but Mandane promptly arrives announcing that Arbaces has slain Rimenes and single-handedly put down the rebellion. In triumph Mandane sings the florid aria 'The soldier tir'd of war's alarms'. Arbaces is received joyfully and to him Artaxerxes proffers the poisoned cup. But Artabanes strikes it from his son's lips and admits his own guilt. Artaxerxes spares his life but sentences him to banishment. All join in a final chorus of acclamation, 'Live to us, to empire live'.

* * *

Artaxerxes shows a remarkable advance on Arne's previous work. In it he avoids the old-fashioned da capo aria and writes music that vividly reflects the mood of the characters and their response to each new situation. The overture too breaks new ground with its three interconnected movements; the larghetto middle section enjoyed particular popularity and reappeared in a number of guises, including that of a hymn. Burney's criticism of the work, that Arne 'crouded the airs, particularly in the part of Mandane for Miss Brent, with most of the Italian divisions and difficulties which had ever been heard at the opera', was repeated unthinkingly by many later commentators. But even Burney, Arne's strongest critic, was unable to deny the success which the opera deservedly gained. JOHN A. PARKINSON

Arteaga, Esteban de [Arteaga, Stefano] (*b* Moraleja de Coca, nr Segovia, 26 Dec 1747; *d* Paris, 30 Oct 1799). Spanish aesthetician and opera historian. After entering the Society of Jesus (1763) he studied in Madrid, Corsica and Italy, after which he abandoned the Society (1769) and attended Bologna University (1773–8). There at Padre Martini's behest he wrote the first critical history of opera, *Le rivoluzioni del teatro musicale italiano dalla sua origine fino al presente* (Bologna, 1783–8, 2/1785), which met with immediate success and was translated into German (1789) and French (1802). He moved to Venice and to Rome, where he prepared works on ideal beauty (1789) and ancient and modern rhythm. His last years were spent in travel.

The original edition of *Le rivoluzioni* began with chapters on opera aesthetics and on the suitability of Italian as a language for music. In the first edition of 1782, his somewhat muddled history did not get beyond the advent of Metastasio. He viewed the early 18th century as the Golden Age of Music, singling out the composers Vinci and Jommelli as exemplary and crediting Metastasio with having raised opera to the greatest perfection possible. The second, 'enlarged, varied and corrected' edition of 1785 acquired a detailed critique of the decadence into which opera had fallen since that time. Much of his criticism centres on the failure of composers to set the words in a natural way that conveyed the meaning and moved the listener. He deplored accompaniments that obscured the words, distorted the meaning, and were too noisy and heavily orchestrated, especially with winds. On the other hand, he praised Gluck for his sensitive text settings and the unity he achieved by means of continuous string accompaniments for recitative, credited Piccinni with having substituted the rondò for the distortions of da capo form, and cited other composers (Traetta, Paisiello, Sacchini and Sarti) and performers (Ferrari, Jarnovich, Lolli, Somis and Chiabrano, among others) whose work he believed had merit. Calzabigi countered with a sarcastic *Risposta* (Venice, 1790).

*

M. Batllori: 'Estudio preliminar', *E. de Arteaga: I. Lettere . . . II. Del ritmo sonoro* (Madrid, 1944)

R. Allorto: 'Stefano Arteaga e "Le rivoluzioni del teatro musicale italiano"', *RMI*, lii (1950), 124–47

V. Borghini: *Problemi d'estetica e di cultura nel Settecento spagnolo: Feijóo – Luzán – Arteaga* (Genoa, 1958)

E. M. K. Rudat: *The Aesthetic Ideas of Esteban de Arteaga: Origin, Meaning and Current Value* (diss., U. of California, Los Angeles, 1969; pubd as *Las ideas estéticas de Esteban de Arteaga: origenes, significado y actualidad*, Madrid, 1971)

R. Freeman: *Opera Without Drama* (Ann Arbor, 1981), 93–6

MARITA P. McCLYMONDS

Artémis ('Artemis'). Opera ('lyric episode') in one act by ALBERTO NEPOMUCENO to a libretto by Coelho Neto; Rio de Janeiro, Teatro São Pedro de Alcântara, 14 October 1898.

Helio (tenor), a sculptor from Athens, falls in love with a statue of the goddess Artemis which he has just completed. He kills his own daughter, Delia, tearing her heart out with the aim of giving life to the statue. Surprised by his wife, Hestia (soprano), he becomes confused and throws the statue to the ground, destroying it. He realizes then that his blind passion has caused the useless sacrifice of his daughter. While the subject appeared rather insignificant and artificial at the time, the opera was considered by Luiz Heitor Corrêa de Azevedo a 'musical jewel'. GERARD BÉHAGUE

Artemovsky, Semyon [Simeon] **Stepanovich.** *See* GULAK-ARTEMOVSKY, SEMYON STEPANOVICH.

Artôt, (Marguerite-Joséphine) Désirée (Montagney) (*b* Paris, 21 July 1835; *d* Berlin, 3 April 1907). Belgian mezzo-soprano, later soprano. She studied with Pauline Viardot in London and Paris. On Meyerbeer's recommendation she was engaged for the Opéra in 1858, making her début as Fidès. Deciding to concentrate on the Italian repertory, she toured in France and Belgium as Rosina and Leonora (*Il trovatore*). In 1859 she sang in Italy, and at the Victoria-Theater, Berlin, won acclaim as Rosina, Angelina, Leonora (*Il trovatore*) and even as Maddalena (*Rigoletto*). Thereafter the greater part of her career was spent in Germany, singing soprano and mezzo roles.

In 1863 Artôt sang at Her Majesty's Theatre, London, as Marie (*La fille du régiment*), Adalgisa and Violetta. Her appearances at Covent Garden in 1864 and 1866 were her last in England. She married the Spanish baritone Mariano Padilla y Ramos in 1869 and sang with him in Italian opera in Germany, Austria and Russia until her retirement.

Their daughter, the soprano Lola Artôt de Padilla (*b* Sèvres, 5 Oct 1876; *d* Berlin, 12 April 1933), made her début in Paris in 1904, then sang in Berlin at the Komische Oper (1905–8) and the Hofoper (1909–27), where in 1911 she was the first Octavian heard in Berlin. Her other successful roles included Zerlina, Countess Almaviva, Oscar and Micaëla.

*

ES (B. Horowicz)

La Mara [pseud. of M. Lipsius]: *Musikalische Studienköpfe*, v (Leipzig, 1882) HAROLD ROSENTHAL/R

Artpark. Park and site of an annual festival in LEWISTON.

Arts florissants, Les ('The Flourishing Arts'). *Opéra* in five scenes by MARC-ANTOINE CHARPENTIER; Paris, Hôtel de Guise, 1685–6.

La Musique [Music] (soprano), La Peinture [Painting] (*haute-contre*), La Poésie [Poetry] (soprano) and L'Architecture [Architecture] (mezzo-soprano) flourish together under the reign of La Paix [Peace] (soprano) and the benign influence of Louis XIV. Each allegorical character begins with a statement of his attributes and concludes by paying homage to the king, patron of the arts and founder of the royal academies. Confronting the evils personified by La Discorde [Discord] (bass) and the furies, Peace finally triumphs and the arts unite to restore universal harmony through choral song and dance. The dramatic framework and symmetrical design of *Les arts florissants* (with the confrontation between Peace and Discord serving as its axis) recall those of Charpentier's pastoral prologue to *Le malade imaginaire.* JOHN S. POWELL

Aruhn, Britt-Marie (*b* Motala, 11 Nov 1943). Swedish soprano. She studied in Stockholm, making her début there at the Royal Opera in 1974 as Olympia. Later roles included Violetta, Gilda, Sophie, Norina and Adina. In 1978 she made her Covent Garden début as Zerbinetta and in Stockholm she created the Chief of Secret Police in Ligeti's *Le Grand Macabre*, repeating the role at the Paris Opéra (1981), where she also sang Zdenka (*Arabella*). At the Théâtre de la Monnaie she has sung the Fairy Godmother (*Cendrillon*), Musetta, Mélisande, Susanna, Cinna (*Lucio Silla*), Adele (*Die Fledermaus*) and Sandrina (*La finta giardiniera*). In 1987 she sang Helen in Gluck's *Paride e Elena* at Drottningholm. Her voice is light and very flexible.

ELIZABETH FORBES

Arundell [Arundel], **Dennis (Drew)** (*b* London, 22 July 1898; *d* London, 10 Dec 1988). English director and writer. At St John's College, Cambridge (1919–29), he read classics and music (his teachers included Stanford) and became a Fellow. He made appearances as an actor, singer and director from 1926. An influential figure in English musical-theatrical life for many years, his opera and masque productions cover a remarkably wide historical range: from Locke (*Cupid and Death*, 1929, London), Purcell (*The Fairy-Queen*, 1927, in Hyde Park, London, which he conducted; also 1930, Cambridge), John Eccles (*The Judgment of Paris*, 1923, Cambridge) and Handel (*Semele*, stage première, 1925, Cambridge) to Janáček (*Kát'a Kabanová*, British première, 1951, London), Britten (*Peter Grimes*, 1949, Helsinki), Honegger (*Le roi David*, British stage première, 1929, Cambridge) and Stravinsky (*The Soldier's Tale*, British première, 1928, Cambridge).

As a director, he also collaborated with Beecham in reviving Balfe's *The Bohemian Girl* (1951, Covent Garden) and in the first production of Delius's *Irmelin* (1953, Oxford). To the standard repertory he brought dramatic vigour and stage mastery: his productions of *I quattro rusteghi* (as *School for Fathers*, 1946), *Der fliegende Holländer* (1958) and *Tosca* (1960) for Sadler's Wells Opera were considered exemplary. Purcell and Mozart were among his chief enthusiasms: he edited *King Arthur* (1928), and wrote an introduction to *Le nozze di Figaro* and *Così fan tutte* (1971). His breadth of historical inquiry and sometimes deliberately provocative approach were manifest in his book *The Critic at the Opera*, which extends well beyond the implications of its title. Other publications include an authoritative history of Sadler's Wells Theatre. His many opera translations were stylish and readily singable: they include *Háry János*, *Švanda the Bagpiper*, *Jeanne d'Arc au bûcher*, *From the House of the Dead*, *Il matrimonio segreto* and *Les contes d'Hoffmann* (the last for the Beecham-Powell-Pressburger film).

selective list

Henry Purcell (London, 1927)
Dryden and Howard (London, 1929)
The Critic at the Opera (London, 1957)
The Story of Sadler's Wells (London, 1965, 2/1978)
Introduction to Le nozze di Figaro and Così fan tutte (London, 1971)

ARTHUR JACOBS

Arutyunyan, Alexander Grigori. *See* HARUT'YUNYAN, ALEXANDER GRIGOR.

Asaf'yev, Boris Vladimirovich [Glebov, Igor] (*b* St Petersburg, 17/29 July 1884; *d* Moscow, 27 Jan 1949). Russian musicologist and composer. He graduated in history and philology from St Petersburg University (1908) and studied with Rimsky-Korsakov and Lyadov at the St Petersburg conservatory (1904–10). From 1910 he was répétiteur at the Mariinsky Theatre. After the 1917 revolution, he helped organize the music department of the Petrograd Institute for the History of the Arts (now the St Petersburg Institute of Theatre, Music and Cinematography), and from 1920 was director of music history there. From 1925 to 1943 he was professor at the Leningrad conservatory, where he founded the musicology department and also in the 1920s, arranged concerts of contemporary Western music and contributed articles to journals. In 1943 he became professor and director of research at the Moscow conservatory, a senior research fellow at the Institute for the History of the Arts, and a consultant to the Bol'shoy Theatre; he was also chairman of the Union of Soviet Composers (1948–9).

Asaf'yev began to be known as a musicologist in the 1920s with writings on 19th-century Russian music, and produced the first Russian book on Stravinsky (1929); he also wrote about Stravinsky's (and Tchaikovsky's) ballets in *Simfonicheskiye etyudï* (Leningrad, 1922), a seminal collection of analytical essays on 19th- and early 20th-century Russian stage music, including operas by Glinka, Dargomïzhsky, Rimsky-Korsakov and Serov. During the 1930s, when he was occupied primarily with composition, he wrote several operas and ballets, as well as incidental music to a number of plays; his ballets achieved some success, but none of his 11 operas was staged in a major theatre, and eight of them were not performed at all. He returned to academic work in the 1940s with further writings and the second volume of *Muzïkal'naya forma kak protsess* ('Musical Form as a Process', Moscow, 1947), in which he expounded his influential theories of 'intonation', a term which, in Russian, embraces the diverse expressive aspects of musical form. On the basis of this theory, he produced several analyses of the Russian classics, including Tchaikovsky's *Yevgeny Onegin* and *The Sorceress*. He was also responsible, with Pavel Lamm, for important studies of Musorgsky's manuscripts.

Zolushka [Cinderella] (children's op, 2, L. A. Levandovskaya, after C. Perrault), St Petersburg, winter 1906–7 (private perf.)
Snezhnaya koroleva [The Snow Queen] (children's op, 4, S. M. and V. M. Mart'yanov, after H. C. Andersen), St Petersburg, 20 Jan/2 Feb 1908 (private perf.)
Kaznacheysha [The Treasurer's Wife] (6 scenes, prologue and epilogue, A. A. Matveyev, after M. Yu. Lermontov: *Tambovskaya kaznacheysha*), Leningrad, Pakhomov Sailors' Club, 1 April 1937 (amateur perf.); pf score (Moscow and Leningrad, 1946)
Faust i Mefistofel' [Faust and Mephistopheles] (dramatic scene, after A. S. Pushkin), 1936
Minin i Pozharsky (4, M. A. Bulgakov), 1936–8
Altïnchech [The Girl with the Golden Hair] (6 scenes, M. Dzhalil'), 1938
Mednïy vsadnik [The Bronze Horseman] (symphony-monodrama, 8 episodes, prologue and epilogue, after Pushkin), 1939–40
Groza [The Storm] (5, after A. N. Ostrovsky), 1939–40
Pir vo vremya chumï [A Feast in Time of Plague] (dramatic scene, after Pushkin), 1940
Slavyanskaya krasavitsa (Volshebnïy zamok) [The Slavonic Beauty (The Magic Castle)] (4, G. Ismailov, after G. Nizami: *The Seven Beauties*), 1940
Alyonushka i bratets Ivanushka [Little Elena and her brother Ivan] (children's op, 4, Yu. Dantsiger), 1945

WRITINGS

Selective list. Items marked with an asterisk written under the name Asaf'yev; all others written under the pseudonym Igor Glebov

Pyotr Il'ich Chaykovsky: ego zhizn' i tvorchestvo [Life and Works] (Petrograd, 1922)

Simfonicheskiye etyudï [Symphonic studies] (Petrograd, 1922, 2/1968)
Musorgsky: opït kharakteristiki [An attempt at Characterisation] (Moscow, 1923)
Kniga o Stravinskom [A Book about Stravinsky] (Leningrad, 1929)
**M. I. Glinka: k 100-letiyu so dnya pervogo predstavleniya operï Ruslan i Lyudmila* [Glinka: On the Centenary of the First Performance of *Ruslan and Lyudmila*] (Leningrad, 1942)
**Yevgeny Onegin, liricheskiye stsenï P. I. Chaykovskogo: opït intonatsionnogo analiza stilya i muzïkal'noy dramaturgii* [*Yevgeny Onegin*, Tchaikovsky's Lyric Scenes: an Attempt at Intonation, Analysis of Style and Musical Dramaturgy] (Moscow and Leningrad, 1944; Ger. trans., 1949)
**Nikolay Andreyevich Rimsky-Korsakov (1844–1944): k 100-letiyu so dnya rozhdeniya* [Rimsky-Korsakov: On the Centenary of his Birth] (Moscow and Leningrad, 1944)
**Charodeyka, opera P. I. Chaykovskogo: opït raskrïtiya intonatsionnogo soderzhaniya* [Tchaikovsky's Opera *The Sorceress*: an Attempt to Reveal its Intonation Content] (Moscow and Leningrad, 1947)
**Glinka* (Moscow, 1947, 2/1950)
Ob opere: izbrannïye stat'i (Leningrad, 1976) [collected opera criticism]

*

B. V. Asaf'yev: 'Moy put' [Autobiography], *SovM* (1934), no.8, 47–50
V. Bogdanov-Berezovsky: *B. V. Asaf'yev* (Moscow and Leningrad, 1937)
D. B. Kabalevsky: *B. V. Asaf'yev – Igor Glebov* (Moscow, 1954)
E. M. Orlova: 'Rabotï B. V. Asaf'yev o A. G. Rubinshteyne, A. K. Glazunove, A. K. Lyadove, S. I. Taneyeve, S. V. Rakhmaninove i drugikh russkikh kompositorakh-klassikakh' [Asaf'yev's Works on Rubinstein, Glazunov, Lyadov, Taneyev, Rakhmaninov and other Classical Russian Composers], *B. V. Asaf'yev: izbrannïye trudï* [selected works], ii, ed. E. M. Orlova and V. V. Protopopov (Moscow, 1954)
——: 'Rabotï B. V. Asaf'yeva o Musorgskom, Rimskom-Korsakove, Borodine, Balakireve i Stasove', *B.V. Asaf'yev: izbrannïye trudï*, iii, ed. E. M. Orlova (Moscow, 1954)
V. A. Vasina-Grossman: 'Russkaya muzïkal'naya kul'tura v rabotakh B.V. Asaf'yeva' [Russian Musical Culture in the Works of Asaf'yev], *B.V. Asaf'yev: izbrannïye trudï*, iv, ed. T. N. Livanova and V. A. Vasina-Grossman (Moscow, 1955)
D. B. Kabalevsky: 'Sovetskaya muzïka v rabotakh B.V. Asaf'yeva' [Soviet Music in Asaf'yev's Works], *B. V. Asaf'yev: izbrannïye trudï*, v, ed. D. B. Kabalevsky and others (Moscow, 1957)

GEOFFREY NORRIS

Ascanio. *Opéra* in five acts and seven tableaux by CAMILLE SAINT-SAËNS to a libretto by LOUIS GALLET after Paul Meurice's play *Benvenuto Cellini*; Paris, Opéra, 21 March 1890.

Composed in 1887–8, *Ascanio* makes a grand opera of a play of intrigue set in Paris in 1539. Meurice, whom Saint-Saëns knew well, had collaborated with Alexandre Dumas *père* on his novel *Benvenuto Cellini*, published in 1843, and had fashioned a successful play from the story in 1852. To avoid confusion with Berlioz's opera the title was changed (even though Cellini is still the principal character in the drama) and a scene in the play where Cellini runs out of metal when casting a statue was not included. The choice of an episode from Cellini's life that took place in France at the court of François I satisfied Saint-Saëns' longstanding desire to base his operas on French history, and by casting the third act as a *fête* at Fontainebleau (a departure from Meurice's play) he found an opportunity for an extensive *divertissement* of 12 dances very much in the spirit, and to some extent in the style, of French Baroque opera. The opera was not well received and was not revived until 1921, at the very end of Saint-Saëns' life.

HUGH MACDONALD

Ascanio in Alba. *Festa teatrale* in two acts, K111, by WOLFGANG AMADEUS MOZART, to a libretto by Giuseppe Parini (1729–99); Milan, Regio Ducal Teatro, 17 October 1771.

Mozart's second Milan opera, following *Mitridate* (1770), is in the courtly genre beloved of the Habsburgs. It was included in the celebrations for the wedding of Archduke Ferdinand to Maria Ricciarda Berenice d'Este, with Hasse's *Il Ruggiero* which (according to Leopold Mozart) it put in the shade, and it was repeated three or four times.

Ascanio (soprano castrato; originally sung by Mozart's former singing instructor, Giovanni Manzuoli) is the son of Aeneas and grandson of Venere [Venus] (soprano, representing Maria Theresa). He is destined to marry Silvia (soprano), a descendant of Hercules (alluding to Duke Ercole d'Este). In an allegory of arranged marriage, Venus contrives to have Silvia fall in love with a dream-image of Ascanio, while he is allowed to see her but may not identify himself. This slender plot develops amid pastoral scenes with shepherds, votaries of Venus led by Fauno (soprano castrato) and the priest Aceste (tenor). During an entr'acte (a ballet, for which only the bass parts have survived), the city of Alba Longa miraculously springs up; in Act 2 a little dramatic tension is generated by Silvia's uncertainty about whether her beloved really is Ascanio. Several scenes are structured by repeated choruses; there is one trio. The arias, particularly Fauno's second and those for Ascanio and Silvia, are exceptionally brilliant. Mozart's growing maturity is revealed in the solo scene for Silvia (aria, 'Infelici affetti miei') and in the skilful blend of counterpoint and homophony in what is perhaps the work's most distinctive feature, its choral writing.

JULIAN RUSHTON

Aschieri, Catterina (*b* ?Rome, *c*1720; *d* after 1755). Italian soprano. She is first found in comic opera in Naples in 1735–6, and was expelled from the kingdom for unknown reasons, probably her sexual conduct. She was seconda donna in *opera seria* in Parma in Carnival 1737 and rose to prima donna in Carnival 1738 in Milan, where she appeared in the premières of Gluck's *Sofonisba* (1744) and *Ippolito* (1745). She became a favourite there, returning for seven carnivals until 1755, when she left the stage. In 1746–7 she was in Vienna and in 1748–9 at the S Carlo, Naples. She had a good stage presence and was an accomplished musician with a rather small voice, low in tessitura (range about *e'*-*b''*).

DENNIS LIBBY

Ashbrook, William (Sinclair) (*b* Philadelphia, 28 Jan 1922). American scholar and musicologist. He studied at Harvard University (MA 1947) and from 1955 taught English in the humanities department at Indiana State University, Terre Haute, eventually becoming Distinguished Professor Emeritus. Ashbrook is an enthusiastic writer on Italian opera and has contributed numerous articles to *Opera News* and other journals. His studies of Donizetti and Puccini are particularly valuable for the careful presentation of biographical material, the discussion of the literary and dramatic aspects of the operas and the description of the various revisions.

Donizetti (London, 1965)
The Operas of Puccini (New York, 1968, 2/1985)
Donizetti and his Operas (Cambridge, 1982)
with H. S. Powers: *Puccini's Turandot: the End of the Great Tradition* (Princeton, 1991)

PAULA MORGAN

Ashkhabad. Capital of Turkmenistan. Although the Turkmen Dramatic Theatre, founded in 1929, presented some opera, regular productions came only with the establishment of an opera studio in 1937. The opera-ballet studio of the Turkmenskiy Muzïkal'nïy Teatr (founded 1940) formed the basis of the Turkmenskiy Teatr Operï i Baleta, which opened on 10 February 1941 with the first Turkmen national opera, *Sud'ba bakhshi* ('The Fate of Bakhshi') by G. Kakhiani, director of the opera theatre in Baku. Early premières included a number of national operas: A. G. Shaposhnikov's *Gyul' i bil'bil'* ('Rose and Nightingale', 1943), Yu. S. Meytus and D. Ovezov's *Leyli i Medzhun* ('Leyli and Medzhun', 1946) and Shaposhnikov and V. Mukhatov's *Kemine i kazï* ('Poet and Judge', 1947). The repertory mixes Russian and European classics with new national operas, performed in Turkmen and in Russian. In 1948 Ashkhabad was struck by an earthquake which destroyed the theatre. In 1950 a new theatre was built, which was renamed the Turkmenskiy Teatr Operï i Baleta imeni Makhtumkuli (Makhtumkuli Theatre of Opera and Ballet) in 1956.

*

ME ('Turkmenskiy teatr operï i baleta'; K. A. Mamilev)
G. Bernandt: *Slovar' oper vpervïye postavlennïkh ili izdannïkh v dorevolyutsionnoy Rossii i v SSSR 1736–1959* [Dictionary of Operas First Performed or Published in Pre-revolutionary Russia and in the USSR 1736–1959] (Moscow, 1962), 535–6
K. Kerimi: *Turkmenskiy teatr* (Moscow, 1964)
Yu. V. Keldïsh, ed.: *Istoriya muzïki narodov SSSR* [History of the Music of the Soviet Peoples], i–v (Moscow, 1970–74)
Arkhitektura sovetskogo teatra (Moscow, 1986), 170, 366
F. A. Abukova: *Turkmenskaya opera: puti formirovaniya, zhanrovaya tipologiya* [Turkmen Opera: Paths of Development, Genre Typology] (Ashkhabad, 1987)
GREGORY SALMON

Ashley, Robert (Reynolds) (*b* Ann Arbor, 28 March 1930). American composer. He studied music theory at the University of Michigan (1948–52) and piano and composition at the Manhattan School of Music, then returned to Ann Arbor to study acoustics and composition (1957–60). His teachers in composition included Riegger, Finney, Bassett and Gerhard. As a composer and founder-member Ashley was active with Milton Cohen's space theatre (1957–64), the ONCE Festivals and ONCE Group (*c*1958–69) and the Sonic Arts Union (1966–76). From 1969 to 1981 he directed the Center for Contemporary Music at Mills College, Oakland, California.

Even in his instrumental pieces, Ashley's subject matter is frequently theatrical in conception. During the 1960s he became a pioneer in mixed-media performance art with a series of carefully 'scored' and rehearsed works. He became preoccupied with language and its levels of meaning, and also with creating musical simultaneities: in *The Trial of Anne Opie Wehrer and Unknown Accomplices for Crimes Against Humanity* (1968), for example, a taped voice interrogates the protagonist while her two surrogates on stage reply, and all three are questioned by two additional interrogators; the resulting multi-level composition frequently dislocates the listener's sense of time.

Since the mid-1970s Ashley's interests have been concentrated on televised opera. *Music with Roots in the Aether* (1976) and *Perfect Lives (Private Parts)* (1977–83) are operatic portraits in television-episode format, highly unconventional in their use of the medium. Striking spoken texts and visual imagery contribute to lyrical and aurally varied compositions and help to reveal the deeper musical structures. Subsequent operas of the *Atalanta* (1982–9) and *Now Eleanor's Idea* (1986–9) groups have continued along that path, always with an eye towards both stage and television performance and towards open-ended or multiple interpretations.

for television unless otherwise stated; librettos by Ashley

in memoriam ... Kit Carson (stage op), Ann Arbor, 1964
That Morning Thing (stage op), Ann Arbor, 8 Feb 1968
Music with Roots in the Aether, Paris, 1976
Title Withdrawn, Paris, 1976
Perfect Lives (Private Parts), 1980, Great Britain, 1984
The Lessons, New York, 1981 [may be perf. as part of Perfect Lives (Private Parts)]
Atalanta (Acts of God), Paris, 1982; subsequently rev. as trilogy: Requirements of Desire M, 1989; Wuh ... Mountain Country Courtship, 1991; Odalisque B with Leopards, 1988
Atalanta Strategy, Montreal, 1985
Now Eleanor's Idea, 1986–9, cycle of 4 ops: Improvement (Don leaves Linda), 1986; Foreign Experiences, 1987; Now Eleanor's Idea, 1988; When Opportunity Knocks, 1989
Gentlemen of the Future, 1986–90
eL/Aficionado, Marseille, stage perf., 1988
Yellow Man with Heart with Wings, 1989–90

*

N. Osterreich: 'Music with Roots in the Aether', *PNM*, xvi/1 (1977), 214–28
J. Howell: 'Robert Ashley's Perfect Lives (Private Parts)', *Live: Performance Art*, iii (1980), 3–7
T. De Lio: 'Sound, Gesture and Symbol: the Relationship between Notation and Structure in American Experimental Music', *Interface*, x (1981), 199–219
——: 'Structural Pluralism: Open Structures in the Musical and Visual Arts of the Twentieth Century', *MQ*, lxvii (1981), 527–43
M. Sumner, K. Burch and M. Sumner: 'Robert Ashley', *The Guests Go In To Supper* (Oakland, CA, 1986), 96–168
K. Potter: 'Robert Ashley and Post-Modernist Opera', *Opera*, xxxviii (1987), 388–94
R. James: 'The ONCE Phenomenon: Microcosm of the 1960s Musical and Multi-Media Avant-Garde', *American Music*, v/4 (1987), 359–90
RICHARD S. JAMES

Ashman, Mike [Michael] (**Vincent Crocker**) (*b* Hertford, 16 April 1950). English director. After a period as staff director for the WNO (1979–84) and Covent Garden (1984–6), and an impressive début with *Parsifal* for the WNO in 1983, he was responsible for a series of strongly characterized productions both at home and abroad. His *Fliegender Holländer* (1986) and *Médée* (1989), with their references to social and political conditions obtaining at the time of composition, both alienated large sections of their Covent Garden audiences. The cogency of his *Paul Bunyan* for the RCM (1988) was praised, as was his imaginative use of minimal resources in John Metcalf's *Tornrak* (WNO, 1990). BARRY MILLINGTON

Ashmedai. Opera in two acts (16 scenes) by JOSEF TAL to a libretto (in Hebrew) by Israel Eliraz; Hamburg, Städtische Oper, 9 November 1971 (in German).

Inspired by an ancient Talmudic legend, and an allegory about totalitarianism, the opera is set in an idyllic, peaceful country. The King (lyric baritone) hates the Queen (mezzo-soprano), whom he married only to prevent war with her father, and is in love with the Landlady (soprano). In Act 1, the devil Ashmedai (tenor) appears one night to the King and suggests that if he, Ashmedai, could rule as king for a year, he could turn the peace-loving citizens into bloodthirsty savages while the King could live happily with the Landlady. The King has such faith in his people that he agrees to the bet, but as soon as Ashmedai assumes the physical traits of the King and ascends the throne the citizens turn into intolerant, aggressive killers. A terrible war breaks out, causing total destruction. In Act 2, Ashmedai has won his bet, but the real King refuses to reclaim the throne because his faith in his people has been shattered. Ashmedai changes into a rooster and is devoured, unknowingly, by the Queen and her entourage. The King returns to his throne but refuses to continue the war, despite the advice of his Son (tenor), the commander of the army, and is lynched by the furious masses. Ashmedai appears to the people but they refuse to believe the truth. In an apocalyptic scene the physical world disintegrates, leaving only the King's naked body with his anguished, faithful Daughter (soprano) leaning over him.

Ashmedai's libretto provides an optimal link between theatre and music. Words, music, action, sets and lighting undergo continually changing internal relationships through a permutation technique, in keeping with the title character, Ashmedai, 'the Switcher'. The music is composed in 12-note technique with some parlando and speech-song intervals. The work is scored for a large symphony orchestra with a substantial percussion section. For the most part Tal blends electronic and orchestral music, though the five-minute overture contains electronic music only. WILLIAM Y. ELIAS

Ashrafi, Mukhtar (*b* Bukhara, Uzbekistan, 29 May/11 June 1912; *d* Tashkent, 15 Dec 1975). Uzbek composer. He studied composition at Samarkand, Moscow Conservatory (1934–7) and Leningrad Conservatory (1941–3); in 1944 he settled in Tashkent and taught at the conservatory there.

His music is dedicated mainly to the heroic subjects of Central Asia, and his first opera, *Buran*, which was orchestrated by Vasilenko, was considered the first authentic grand opera of Soviet Uzbekistan. It recounts the revolutionary activities of Uzbek patriots in 1916. Vasilenko's orchestration uses exquisite colouring but the success of the opera at its première was due to Ashrafi's melodious talent and his excellent knowledge of Uzbek harmony, polyphony and rhythm.

Two years later, Ashrafi again collaborated with Vasilenko in the compositon of *Velikiy Kanal* ('The Great Canal'), based on the heroic efforts of the Uzbek Kolhoz masses in the construction of the Fergana Canal. He wrote two other operas, *Dilorom* in 1958 and *Dusha Poeta* ('A Poet's Soul') in 1960, the latter based on the life of the Ukrainian poet, Taras Shevchenko.

Ashrafi's works include two ballets, two symphonies, five symphonic suites and numerous film scores.

Buran (5, Y. Nughmanov), Tashkent, 12 June 1939, collab. S. Vasilenko
Velikiy Kanal [The Great Canal] (5, M. Burkhanov), Tashkent, 19 Jan 1941, collab. S. Vasilenko
Dilorom (4, K. Yashen and M. Mukhamedov, after A. Navoi: *The Seventh Planet*), Tashkent, 5 Feb 1958
Dusha Poeta [A Poet's Soul] (3, I. Sultan), Tashkent, 13 July 1960

*

R. Moisenko: *Realist Music: 25 Soviet Composers* (London, 1949)
G. B. Bernandt: *Slovar Oper* [Dictionary of Opera] (Moscow, 1962)
J. R. Bennett: *Melodiya: a Soviet Russian LP Discography* (Westport, CT, 1981) MARTIN S. LIPPMAN

Ashton, Sir **Frederick (William Malandaine)** (*b* Guayaquil, 17 Sept 1904; *d* Eye, Suffolk, 19 Aug 1988). British choreographer. A central figure in the growth of the Royal Ballet from its earliest days, and its director from 1963 to 1970, he was the most celebrated British choreographer of his time and created many classics of the repertory. In the field of opera his collaboration with Britten is specially important. His production of *Albert Herring* (1947) delighted the composer, and his choreography for *Death in Venice* (1973) was integral to the work. Ashton also directed the historic revival at Covent Garden (1953) of Gluck's *Orfeo ed Euridice*.

*

D. Vaughan: *Frederick Ashton and his Ballets* (London, 1977)
Obituary, *Opera*, xxxix (1988), 1194 IVOR GUEST

Asioli, Bonifazio (*b* Correggio, nr Reggio Emilia, 30 Aug 1769; *d* Correggio, 18 May 1832). Italian composer. Born into a family of musicians, he was essentially self-taught; while still a boy he was a successful harpsichordist and improviser. At the age of 14 he taught at the Collegio Civico in Correggio, and in 1786 was appointed *maestro di cappella*. *La volubile*, performed in Correggio in 1785 with the intermezzo *Il ratto di Proserpina*, marked the beginning of his career as an opera composer. In the retinue of the Marchese Gherardini, he moved to Turin, Venice and then Milan, where his opera *Cinna* had already been staged at La Scala (1792). In 1805 he was appointed *maestro di cappella* and music director at the court of the viceroy Eugène Beauharnais. In 1808 he became the first director of the newly founded Milan Conservatory, and he devoted the rest of his life to teaching by the production of a series of theoretical works; from 1814 he was back in Correggio, where he established a music school in his house.

Asioli's music, which also includes many cantatas, is now forgotten, though the brilliance of his talent was widely acknowledged by his contemporaries.

La volubile (ob), Corregio, 1785; perf. with Il ratto di Proserpina (int)
La contadina vivace (ob), Parma, 1785
La gabbia de' pazzi (ob), Venice, 1785
La discordia teatrale (ob), Milan, 1786
Le nozze in ville (ob), Correggio, 1786
Cinna (dramma serio, 2, A. Anelli), Milan, Scala, 26 Dec 1792, *I-CORc**, *Mr**, *Fc*, *PAc*
Pigmalione (azione teatrale), 1796, *F-Pn*, *I-Bc*, *BGc*, *CORc**, *Fc*, *Gl*, *Mc*, *PAc*, vs (London, ?1800)
Gustava al Malabar (dramma serio), Turin, 1802, *CORc**, *Tn*

*

'Verzeichniss sämmtlicher Compositionen nebst einer kurzen Biographie des Herrn Bonifacio Asioli', *AMZ*, xxii (1820), 667–70
A. Coli: *Vita di Bonifazio Asioli da Correggio* (Milan, 1834)
I. Saccozzi: 'Di Bonifazio Asioli', *Notizie biografiche e letterarie in continuazione della Biblioteca Modenese del Cavalier Abate G° Tiraboschi*, ii (Reggio Emilia, 1834) [incl. letters and Asioli's *Riflessioni sopra l'opera del Signor di Momigni intitolata 'La sola e vera teorica della musica'*]
G. Roncaglia: 'Bonifazio Asioli', *Deputazione di storia patria per le antiche provincie modenesi: atti e memorie*, 8th ser., ix (1957), 202–13
R. Finzi: *Celebrazione del musicista Bonifazio Asioli (1769–1832) nel secondo centenario della nascita* (Reggio Emilia, 1969)
A. Zecca Laterza: 'Bonifacio Asioli maestro e direttore della real musica', *Chigiana*, xxvi-xxvii (1969–70), 61–76
SERGIO LATTES

Askold's Grave [*Askol'dova mogila*]. Romantic opera in four acts by ALEXEY NIKOLAYEVICH VERSTOVSKY to a libretto by Mikhail Nikolayevich Zagoskin after his novel (1833); Moscow, Bol'shoy Theatre, 16/28 September 1835.

Though largely forgotten today, *Askold's Grave* was the most popular Russian opera of the 19th century. It was first published in vocal score in 1836 and there have been many subsequent editions. The action takes place in 10th-century Kiev, during the reign of Svyatoslav Igorevich. Nadezhda (soprano), the daughter of Alexey (bass), a Christian fisherman, is betrothed to Vseslav (tenor), the pagan ruler's orphan ward. A mysterious figure called Neizvestnïy ('The Unknown'; bass) appears to Vseslav, informs him of his descent from the glorious line of Prince Askold, and tries unsuccessfully to enlist Vseslav's aid in overthrowing the dissolute Svyatoslav. In Act 2 the Unknown has Nadezhda abducted by one of Svyatoslav's minions; Vseslav kills the latter and is forced to become an outlaw. In Act 3 Nadezhda, immured in Svyatoslav's palace, is assisted by Toropka Golovan (tenor), a kindly minstrel, who distracts Svyatoslav's retinue with a ballad while Vseslav steals in and rescues his bride. In the final act Svyatoslav's steward Vïshata (bass) learns the lovers' whereabouts with the aid of the witch Vakhrameyevna (contralto). Surrounded, Vseslav and Nadezhda are about to leap into the Dnepr to their deaths when Svyatoslav's groom, Stemid (tenor), announces their pardon. The Unknown, foiled in his attempt to topple the Kievan Prince, is swallowed up by the river and perishes. The assembled populace praise God.

Though Verstovsky set great store by the dramatic qualities of his opera – particularly the Unknown's three stormy arias and the Act 3 finale (confusion following the rescue of Nadezhda) – and felt that he was entitled to claim precedence over Glinka as the founder of the Russian national operatic school, in fact *Askold's Grave* remains a Singspiel not far removed from the style and spirit of the 'opera-vaudevilles' on which the composer had made his early reputation. What made the work so popular with audiences was its wealth of tuneful decorative numbers: the realistically folksy fishermen's choruses in Act 1 (replete with intoner and group response), Toropka's songs in Acts 2 and 3 (one of them transposing a familiar drinking-song of 18th-century urban origin to the opera's archaic setting), and especially the immured maidens' choruses and dances *à la polonaise* in the third act. Alexander Serov praised the last effusively in his capacity as critic, and as composer copied them in *Rogneda*, his own Kievan farrago (meanwhile fashioning his Jester on Toropka). Not at all coincidentally, the same episodes in *Askold's Grave* became a favourite target of parodists, as in Borodin's early pastiche operetta *Bogatïri*. The melodrama in Vakhrameyevna's cave (Act 4), so obviously indebted to Weber's Wolf's Glen (*Der Freischütz*), also found echoes in *Rogneda*.

Except in Kiev, its setting, where a favourite scenic spot overlooking the Dnepr still bears its name, and where it was revived in 1959, *Askold's Grave* did not survive the Revolution. That single Soviet production employed a new libretto by N. G. Biryukov that attempted to do for Verstovsky's opera what Sergey Gorodetsky had done for Glinka's *A Life for the Tsar*, while the score, freely expanded by the musicologist Boris Vasil'yevich Dobrokhotov, incorporated not only some extra numbers Verstovsky had added for a revival in the late 1850s but also a considerable number of items from Verstovsky's other operas. Thus, while unreliable as a source for *Askold's Grave*, the vocal score of this version (Moscow, 1963) is valuable as the only modern edition of several numbers adapted from *Pan Tvardovsky* (1828) and *Gromoboy* (1857), as well as the sole publication of music from *Vadim* (1832), *Toska po rodine* ('Homesickness'; 1839) and *Son nayavu* ('A Waking Dream'; 1844). RICHARD TARUSKIN

Aspa, Mario (*b* Messina, 17 Oct 1797; *d* Messina, 14 Dec 1868). Italian composer. He studied at the Palermo conservatory and with Zingarelli in Naples. He taught singing privately, and counterpoint at the Buon Pastore Institute in Palermo. He composed 42 operas, none of which has survived in the repertory, although his subjects include several that were later set by other more successful hands, including *Carlotta e Werther*, 1849 and *Paolo e Virginia*, 1843.

selective list; first performed in Naples unless otherwise stated

Bannier [Giovanni Bannier; L'assedio di Arolte] (2, D. Gilardoni), Fondo, 6 June 1829
Il carcere d'Ildegonda (2, Gilardoni), Nuovo, Oct 1830
I litiganti senza lite (2, A. L. Tottola), Nuovo, 1831
Federico II re di Prussia [La calunnia] (G. Checcherini), Nuovo, Nov 1833
Il quadro parlante e la muta orfanella (Checcherini), Nuovo, Nov 1834
Bartolomeo del Piambo (3, G. di Giurdignano), Nuovo, Dec 1836
I due Savoiardi (2, L. Tarantini), Fondo, 4 March 1838
Allan Mac-Auley (Giurdignano), Nuovo, 29 July 1838
Il Marinajo (2, Giurdignano), Nuovo, 1839
Maria d'Arles (2, Tarantini), Nuovo, 26 Sept 1840
Il proscritto (2, M. d'Arienzo), Nuovo, 2 Sept 1841
Guglielmo Colmann (2, d'Arienzo), Nuovo, 1842
Paolo e Virginia (3, J. Ferretti), Rome, Metastasio, 29 April 1843
Un travestimento (Giurdignano), Fondo, Dec 1845
Carlotta e Werther (A. Spadetta), Nuovo, 1849
Il muratore di Napoli (D. Bolognese), Nuovo, 16 Oct 1850; as Gli Aragonesi in Napoli, Rome, June 1880
Il coscritto (Spadetta), Fondo, Aug 1851
Pietro di Calais, Messina, Teatro Vittorio Emanuele, 6 March 1872

ES (E. Zanetti); *StiegerO* PATRICK O'CONNOR

Aspen. American town in Colorado. It is the home of the Aspen Music Festival. The town grew quickly from 1878, when silver was discovered, and in 1889 the financier Jerome B. Wheeler built the Wheeler Opera House. But the death of the silver standard ruined Aspen overnight and by 1900 it was a ghost town. In 1947 the area was redeveloped as a winter ski resort.

The Goethe Bicentennial Convocation and Music Festival, held in 1949 as an experiment to attract summer visitors, grew into the Aspen Music Institute. Its founders included Milhaud and Mack Harrell, and from the beginning there was an opera programme taught by Madeleine Milhaud and Martial Singher. Other early tutors included Hans Hotter (1949–54) and Mack Harrell (1949–58), followed by Dorothy Maynor, Adele Addison, Jennie Tourel and Jan DeGaetani, who gave her last professional performances at the festival in 1989. The institute's reputation quickly grew, and in 1954 it began a nine-week summer festival which would eventually attract more than 80 000 people each year.

James Levine made his opera début at Aspen in 1964, conducting Stravinsky's *Mavra*; Leonard Slatkin's début followed four years later, in the American première of Walton's *The Bear*. The many American premières, frequently performed under the composers' supervision, included Henri Sauguet's *La contrebasse* (1962), Humphrey Searle's *Diary of a Madman* (1967), Alexander Goehr's *Naboth's Vineyard* (1970), Peter Maxwell Davies's *The Martyrdom of St Magnus* (1978) and Laszlo Vidovsky's *Narcissus and Echo* (1988). In 1979 Richard Duffallo conducted Peter Schat's circus opera *Houdini*, which featured three performers (a dancer, a singer and a magician) in the title role and involved a sealed barrel escape trick on stage. The programme was renamed the Aspen Opera Theater Center in 1985.

Most performances take place at the restored Wheeler Opera House (488 seats; with expanded wing and fly space), but the Music Tent (1700 seats) is also used, as it was for *The Martyrdom of St Magnus*, which featured scenery specially designed by the sculptor Ann Sperry for the performance area's unusual, three-sided configuration. Many successful artists have made their débuts at Aspen, including Barbara Hendricks and Gwendolyn Killebrew. NANCY MALITZ

Aspern Papers, The. Opera in two acts by DOMINICK ARGENTO to his own libretto based on HENRY JAMES's novella of the same title; Dallas, Music Hall at Fair Park, 19 November 1988.

Argento moved the setting of Henry James's story of conflict between artistic and personal values from Venice to the shores of Lake Como. The fictional 19th-century poet, Jeffrey Aspern, became a composer modelled loosely after Vincenzo Bellini, and the papers sought by a scholar after Aspern's death were changed from love letters into an opera manuscript suppressed by Aspern's mistress.

The opera, set in 1895, includes a series of flashbacks to 1835 which come to a climax when Aspern (tenor) drowns while attempting to swim across Lake Como to the home of the woman he loves (Sonia, mezzo-soprano), instead of remaining with his mistress, the diva Juliana Bordereau (soprano). These events illuminate the action of 60 years later when the elderly Juliana finds her reclusive life invaded by a Lodger (baritone) who is secretly in search of Aspern's supposedly destroyed opera *Medea*. Juliana has hoarded the pages of *Medea* which Aspern completed for her just before his death, and the Lodger, suspecting this, ingratiates himself with Tina (mezzo-soprano), Juliana's plain, middle-aged niece, as a way of gaining access to the manuscript. To his dismay, his attentions raise powerful feelings in Tina and his scholarly obsession contributes to Juliana's death. Tina, as her aunt's heir, makes an awkward proposal of marriage as the condition for obtaining the papers, and when the Lodger falters, her pride leads her to resolve to destroy the manuscript. Although the Lodger decides that he is ultimately willing to pay Tina's price, she deceives him and burns the papers in the final scene.

The work is rich in layers of reference, among them similarities drawn between the couples Aspern/Juliana and the legendary Jason/Medea. In the music, bel canto references occur, such as in the Act 1 scene iv duet 'O seaborn goddess', and fade in and out of focus to depict the congealing and dissolving perspective of memory. The opera's general musical style is expansively phrased, loosely dodecaphonic and infused with strong tonal underpinnings. The psychologically powerful scenes between Tina and the Lodger are highlights of the score and point to Argento's admiration for Britten. Of particular note are the desolate, unaccompanied exchange in Act 1 scene v, and the duet expanded to sextet and chorus in their final encounter.

For illustration *see* VON STADE, FREDERICA. VIRGINIA SAYA

Aspirate. When a syllable is sung to more than one note, some singers are in the habit of inserting a light aspirate, as in 'Cele-heste Aida'. In Italy, Spain and Latin America this appears not to be considered a major stylistic fault (if one at all), but in Britain and, on the whole, the USA and Germany the practice is generally condemned. Gramophone records suggest that in standard operatic work the habit grew during the first half of the century, and that criticism has subsequently had some effect: Domingo and Pavarotti, for instance, are not habitual aspiraters, unlike their predecessors such as Gigli and Pertile. More insidious are the means used to 'separate' notes in the florid music of Baroque composers, where on the one hand they are defended as ensuring greater clarity, and on the other attacked as the makeshift devices of a defective technique. J. B. STEANE

Asplmayr [Aspelmayr, Aspelmeier, Asplmeyr, Aschpellmayr, Appelmeyer etc.], **Franz** (*b* Linz, bap. 2 April 1728; *d* Vienna, 29 July 1786). Austrian composer and violinist. The only known musical training he received was from his father. He was a member of the imperial Hofkapelle in Vienna and served as secretary to Count Morzin, 1759–61. Named a court composer in 1761, he wrote a good deal of instrumental (mostly chamber) music. In the early 1770s he composed several ballet scores for the choreographer Noverre, who brought his French troupe to Vienna and achieved much success there. With Starzer and Gluck, Asplmayr counted among the leading composers of ballet pantomimes in Vienna. Throughout the 1770s he composed melodramas and operas, including the first German-language melodrama (a translation of Rousseau's *Pygmalion*), performed in the Kärntnertortheater in 1772. He was a founding member of the Tonkünstler-Sozietät and was acquainted with the Mozarts (according to Leopold Mozart's letter to his daughter of 21 February 1785). He wrote two works based on Shakespeare, a pantomime on *Macbeth* (1771) and incidental music to *The Tempest* (1779–80); both are lost.

Among Asplmayr's best-known operas was *Die Kinder der Natur* (1778), commissioned for the Viennese National Singspiel's first full season. Though most Austrian and south German composers borrowed heavily from Italian and French techniques during this period, Asplmayr in *Kinder der Natur* favoured a more popular, native style. The arias are dominated by syllabic declamation, regular two- or four-bar phrases, gentle dotted rhythms, 2/4 metre (mostly Andantino or Allegretto) and modest orchestral accompaniments. Therese's aria 'So gut wie er mir schiene' stands alone in its use of coloratura, extremes of vocal range and a lengthy orchestral introduction; the only recitative is a solo 'Recitativo' for Theodor. Asplmayr draws mostly on binary, ternary and rondo forms in the arias. In the quartet, the closing number and the duets, Asplmayr usually assigns successive solo stanzas to the characters; in the rarer instances when the voices come together, they sing in simple 3rds or 6ths, and in only one short passage in the quartet is there four-part homophony (no polyphony between the voices is used). *Die Kinder der Natur* was withdrawn after only three performances and not given thereafter. Possibly audiences preferred more Italian- or French-influenced pieces or found the text unconvincing (its distribution of musical numbers is certainly unusual: two characters perform all ten numbers in the first act). Though Asplmayr experimented eagerly with new genres, in his melodramas and Singspiels as well as in his ballet scores, his works found little long-term recognition.

Pygmalion (melodrama, 1, J.-J. Rousseau, trans. J. G. von Laudes), Vienna, Kärntnertor, 19 Feb 1772, pubd. lib. *A-Wn*

Die Kinder der Natur (Singspiel, 2, J. F. von Kurz, after J. F. Schmidt: *Wer ist in der Liebe unbeständig*, after P. C. de Chamblain de Marivaux: *La dispute*), Vienna, Burg, 15 July 1778, *Wn*

Orpheus und Euridice (melodrama, Bursay, trans. von Laudes), 1779–80

Undated: Montgolfier, oder die Luftkugel

*

E. Istel: *Die Entstehung des deutschen Melodramas* (Berlin, 1906)

R. Haas: 'Einleitung' to Umlauf: *Die Bergknappen*, DTÖ, xxxvi, Jg. xviii/1 (1911), ix–xxxiv

——: 'Die Musik in der Wiener deutschen Stegreifkomödie', *SMw*, xii (1925), 3–64

H. Riessberger: *Franz Aspelmayer* (diss., U. of Innsbruck, 1954)

O. Michtner: *Das alte Burgtheater als Opernbühne: von der Einführung des deutschen Singspiels (1778) bis zum Tod Kaiser Leopolds II. (1792)* (Vienna, 1970)

G. Zechmeister: *Die Wiener Theater nächst der Burg und nächst dem Kärntnerthor von 1747 bis 1776* (Vienna, 1971)

LINDA TYLER

Asrael. *Leggenda* in four acts by ALBERTO FRANCHETTI to a libretto by FERDINANDO FONTANA; Reggio Emilia, Teatro Municipale, 11 February 1888.

In his libretto, which combines features from *Mefistofele* and *Lohengrin*, Fontana tried to depict the combat between the spirit of evil (Asrael) and the incarnation of Christian love (Nefta, in the guise of Suor Clotilde). Act 1, divided between Hell and Heaven, seems like a real rehash of the prologue of *Mefistofele*; even Bioto's experiments with poetic metres are imitated, on a lower level. Nefta (soprano), in love with the sinful spirit Asrael (tenor), prays to be sent to Earth to rescue his soul. In Acts 2 and 3, set in Brabant by the river Escaut, the confrontation is seen in a vaguely medieval ambience. Act 4 is set in a convent where Nefta eventually conquers a demons' chorus to redeem Asrael's soul; the convent is transformed into Heaven and angels' choruses are heard.

The opera, Franchetti's first, typifies the peculiarities of Italian Wagnerism. Fontana's librettos from the 1880s show the predilection for plots from German fairy-tales (notable in Catalani's operas); he had already written *Le villi* for Puccini and was later to write for him *Edgar*, also set in medieval Brabant. Although written long after *Lohengrin*, the Wagnerian opera *par excellence* for Italian audiences, *Asrael* shows a concept of musico-dramatic structure closer to Meyerbeer or to *Rienzi* than to true 'music drama'. Franchetti's knowledge of *Tristan*, however, is often obvious, notably in the love duet for Loretta (mezzo-soprano) and Asrael in Act 3. Fontana's libretto was limiting to Franchetti's imagination and precluded the establishment of a consistent musico-dramatic unity. JÜRGEN MAEHDER

Assassinio nella cattedrale ('Murder in the Cathedral'). Opera in two acts and an intermezzo by ILDEBRANDO PIZZETTI to his own libretto, shortened and adapted from Alberto Castelli's translation of T. S. Eliot's play *Murder in the Cathedral*; Milan, Teatro alla Scala, 1 March 1958.

The partial recovery of Pizzetti's operatic inspiration in the 1950s, after its long sag during the previous two decades and more, was undoubtedly helped by happy choices of subjects and texts. Nowhere is this more the case than in *Assassinio nella cattedrale* (composed in 1956–7), for Eliot's great play contained several elements that were likely to bring out the best in him: plentiful choruses; a central character tormented by moral dilemmas; ethical discourses controlled by a literary talent greater than the composer's own; a pervading elevated atmosphere in a religious context.

Thomas Becket (bass-baritone), Archbishop of Canterbury, has just returned from a long exile in France that resulted from deep disagreements with King Henry II. He is welcomed by Canterbury women and by priests, who nevertheless fear for his future and for their own. Four tempters (tenor and three baritones) try to tempt him in ways relating both to his past life and to his present situation: Thomas's struggle to resist them culminates in a turbulently impressive monologue at the end of Act 1. Before Act 2 there is an 'intermezzo', in which Thomas's Christmas sermon is represented (controversially) by two sung fragments separated by a purely orchestral interlude. Likewise questionable is the depiction of the four knights (tenor, two baritones and bass), who in due course murder Thomas for his refusal to submit to the king's will. Their musical characterization seems tame and over-simple, and their final self-justifying address to the audience is reduced, in Pizzetti's version, to a few token phrases. The orchestration, too, may seem disappointing, even at times ineffective, compared with that of the composer's masterpiece *Dèbora e Jaéle*. But the intensity and variety of the choral writing, together with the compelling depiction of the protagonist, show the composer back on something approaching his very best form.

One may regret that this is still the only Pizzetti opera to have been staged in Britain and performed several times in North America. The choice, however, is understandable, in view of the subject. The work's tepid reception at its British première (Coventry, 12 June 1962), after big successes elsewhere, was aggravated by the unsympathetic critical climate of the 1960s, which also tended to cut the composer's English contemporaries severely down to size. A revival might well be much better received; however, Pizzetti's declamatory lines undoubtedly lose much when divorced from the Italian language, by which they are so closely and sensitively moulded.

JOHN C. G. WATERHOUSE

Assedio di Calais, L' ('The Siege of Calais'). *Melodramma lirico* in three acts by GAETANO DONIZETTI to a libretto by SALVADORE CAMMARANO after Luigi Marchionni's *L'assedio di Calais*, with details from Luigi Henry's 1827 ballet *L'assedio di Calais*, both ultimately derived from Pierre Du Belloy's *Le siège de Calais*; Naples, Teatro S Carlo, 19 November 1836.

The action, set in 1347, involves the latter stages of Edward III's siege of Calais. On the king's offer to raise the siege if seven leading citizens will sacrifice their lives, six burghers come forward. When they appear in the English camp, led by the mayor (baritone) and his son (mezzo-soprano), the resolute bravery of the Frenchmen moves the English queen (soprano) to plead for their lives; Edward (bass) accedes.

In the 19th century *L'assedio di Calais* had no more than a single run of performances at the S Carlo between 1836 and 1840. An enterprising recording by Opera Rara in 1989 opened the public's eyes to the work's many merits. Originally designed by Donizetti as a passport to the Paris Opéra, it contains an integral *divertissement* (in which however only two of the four dances are Donizetti's). This was then an unusual feature as almost all Italian operas of the period were performed as double bills along with full-length ballets. The first two acts of *L'assedio* contain some excellent ensembles, particularly the prayer at the close of Act 2 ('O sacro polve'), sung as the hostages leave the city hall. The last act, which includes the dances, is on a lower level than the rest of the opera. WILLIAM ASHBROOK

Assisi. Italian city in Umbria. In 1656 the Accademia degli Eccitati rose from the ashes of the earlier Accademia dei Disiosi, and the following year it presented a *dramma per musica*, *La Dafne* (libretto by U. Fiumi). The academy was then renamed the Accademia dei Rinati in 1750, the Colonia Arcadica Properziana in 1774 and in 1810 the Accademia Properziana del Subasio; Giuseppe Verdi became a member in 1874.

In 1755 a wooden theatre was built within the great hall of the Palazzo Comunale which came to be known as the Teatro del Leone (from the arms of the city); here many musical works were staged including, in Carnival 1760, Gian Francesco de Majo's *Ricimero re dei Goti* and David Perez's *Il Farnace*. In 1780 there was a performance of Giovanni Ricci's *La caduta di Erebo*, to a libretto by Agesilao Leucadio, custodian of the Accademia Properziana. Cimarosa's *I due baroni di Rocca Azzurra* was performed for Carnival 1785. In 1836 the Accademia Properziana commissioned the architect Lorenzo Carpinelli to build the Teatro Metastasio, which was inaugurated in autumn 1840 with Mercadante's *Emma d'Antiochia*.

Since 1946 some of the productions of the Sagra Musicale Umbra have taken place at Assisi.

*

Brevi cenni sulla costruzione e attivazione del Teatro Metastasio in Assisi e i suoi rispettivi regolamenti impressi per cura del municipio (Assisi, 1864)

Notizie relative al Teatro Metastasio di Assisi (Assisi, 1881)

C. Sartori: *Assisi: la cappella della Basilica di S. Francesco*, i: *Catalogo del fondo musicale della Biblioteca comunale di Assisi* (Milan, 1962)

G. Zaccaria: 'Ricordi di Saverio Mercadante in Assisi', *Altamura: Bollettino dell' Archivio, Biblioteca museo civico*, xiii (1971), 133

GALLIANO CILIBERTI

Assoluto, assoluta (It.: 'absolute'). As applied to a singer, the term crept into opera bills and contracts with the general inflation of titles that set in towards the end of the 18th century. In theory it meant 'unique': a particular singer was the only member of the company engaged for a season entitled to be called prima donna (or *primo tenore*, *primo basso* etc.), and she or he could refuse parts that did not fit the description. In practice, nearly every leading singer now wished to be called 'absolute', however illogically; in Naples the impresario Domenico Barbaia, backed up by Rossini, was still resisting the trend in the 1820s, but in vain. By 1877 the tenor-impresario Italo Campanini could write of *parti assolute*, meaning simply leading parts; these included Marguerite de Valois in *Les Huguenots*, one of two leading women's parts in that work (letter of 29 July 1877, *I-Ms* Coll. Casati 233). Thus devalued into meaninglessness, the term seems to have vanished from opera by the early 20th century. It is still occasionally used – in its original sense – of an outstanding ballerina.

*

G. Valle: *Cenni teorico-pratici sulle aziende teatrali* (Milan, 1823), 35–45 JOHN ROSSELLI

Astarita [Astaritta], **Gennaro** (*b* ?Naples, *c*1745–9; *d* after 1803). Italian composer. In the summer of 1765 he contributed to Piccinni's comic opera *L'orfana insidiata* at the Teatro dei Fiorentini, Naples; this has led tô the suggestion that he may have been Piccinni's pupil. He left Naples after producing two operas at the Fiorentini (1765–6); in 1768 an *azione drammatica* by him was performed in Palermo, and in 1770–71 he had two comic operas performed in Turin. From Carnival 1772 to autumn 1779 he produced a series of operas in Venice and other northern and central Italian cities, including Florence (1773) and Bologna (1778). In 1779 he completed his friend Traetta's last opera and in 1780 was at Pressburg (now Bratislava) where he produced three operas. After a long gap in his output he went to Moscow as music director of the Petrovsky Theatre (1784); he then moved to St Petersburg (1786), where he may have had an opera performed in 1787 (according to a score with that date in St Petersburg). He evidently spent the rest of his life working in Italy and Russia: several new operas were performed in Venice and Florence between 1789 and 1793, and in 1794 he was sent by the director of the imperial theatres to engage an Italian opera company. He returned to St Petersburg in 1795 as its *maestro compositore*, and in 1796 he composed for it a comic opera, *Rinaldo d'Asti*; in 1799 the company was taken into the imperial service. In July 1803 he announced his departure from Russia.

Astarita wrote over 40 operas, almost all of which are comic. La Borde called him a 'very pleasant modern composer' who appealed more to the public than to connoisseurs; he singled out the rondò 'Come lasciar poss'io l'anima mia che adoro' as one of the best known.

selective list

Il corsaro algerino (ob, G. Palomba), Naples, Fiorentini, aut. 1765

L'astuta cameriera (dg), Turin, aut. 1770

Gli amanti perseguitati (semi-seria, P. Donzel), Turin, 1770

Il re caccia, Turin, 1770, ov. *D-Bds**

La critica teatrale, Turin, aut. 1771

La contessa di Bimbimpoli [Il divertimento in campagna] (dg, G. Bertati), Venice, S Moisè, carn. 1772, *Dlb*

I visionari (dg, Bertati), Venice, aut. 1772, *I-Mr*, *Tf*, *P-La* (as I filosofi immaginari), *RU-SPit*, *US-Wc*

La contessina (dg, M. Coltellini, after C. Goldoni), Livorno, S Sebastiano, aut. 1772

L'avaro in campagna (dg, Donzel), Turin, 1772

L'isola disabitata (dramma per musica, 1, P. Metastasio), Florence, Accademia degl'Ingegnosi, 1773, *A-Wn* (as perf. Pressburg, 1780)

Le finezze d'amore, o sia La farsa non si fa, ma si prova (farsa, ?Bertati), Venice, S Cassiano, 1773; rev. Milan, 1791, *I-Mr* (as Non si fa ma si prova)

Le cinesi (Metastasio), 1773

Il principe ipocondriaco (dg, Bertati), Venice, S Moisè, carn. 1774, *P-La* (Act 3 missing)

La villanella incostante (dg), Cortona, Nuovo, spr. 1774

Il marito che non ha moglie (dg, Bertati), Venice, S Moisè, aut. 1774

Li astrologi immaginari (dg), Lugo, 1774

Il mondo della luna (dg, Goldoni), Venice, S Moisè, carn. 1775

Li sapienti ridicoli, ovvero Un pazzo ne fa cento (Bertati), Prague, Regio, 1775

L'avaro (Bertati), 1776

L'isola del Bengodi (dg, Goldoni), Venice, S Moisè, aut. 1777, *I-Fc**

Armida (Migliavacca), Venice, S Moisè, 1777, *I-Fc*, *Gl*, *P-La* (as Rinaldo)

La dama immaginaria (dg, P. A. Bagliacca), Brescia, 1777

Il marito indolente (dg), Bologna, Zagnoni, aut. 1778

Il francese bizzarro (dg), Milan, Nuovo Regio Ducale, spr. 1779, *D-Dlb*, *F-Pn*, *H-Bn* (with addns by Haydn)

Le discordie teatrali (dg), Florence, Borgo Ognissanti, aut. 1779

Nicoletto bellavita, ?Naples, ?1779, *I-Mr*

La Didone abbandonata (dramma per musica), Pressburg, 1780, *A-Wn**

Il diavolo a quattro (farsa), Naples, S Carlino, carn. 1785

I capricci in amore (dg), ?St Petersburg, ?1787, *RU-SPit**

Il curioso accidente (dg, Bertati), Venice, S Moisè, aut. 1789, *I-Fc*

Ipermestra (dramma per musica), Venice, Vernier, 1789

La nobilità immaginaria (int), Florence, Intrepidi, carn. 1791

L'inganno del ritratto (dg), Florence, Risoluti, 1791
Il medico parigino (Palomba), Venice, 1792, *RU-SPit*
Le fallaci apparenze (dg, G. B. Lorenzi), Venice, S Samuele, aut. 1793
Rinaldo d'Asti, St Petersburg, 1796, *P-La, RU-SPit*
Gl'intrighi per amore, *SPit*

Music in: L'orfana insidiata, 1765; Gli eroi dei campi elisi, 1779

*

J.-B. de La Borde: *Essai sur la musique ancienne et moderne* (Paris, 1780)
S. di Giacomo: 'Paisiello e i suoi contemporanei', *Musica e musicisti*, lx (1905), 762–8; repr. in *Napoli: figure e paesi* (Naples, 1909), 211–26, and *Opere*, ii (Milan, 1946), 532–9
R.-A. Mooser: *Annales de la musique et musiciens en Russie au XVIIIme siècle* (Geneva, 1949–51)

DENNIS LIBBY (text), MARITA McCLYMONDS (work-list)

Astarto. *Dramma per musica* in three acts by GIOVANNI BONONCINI to a libretto by PAOLO ANTONIO ROLLI after APOSTOLO ZENO and PIETRO PARIATI's libretto of the same title (1708); Rome, Teatro Capranica, January 1715 (revised, London, King's Theatre, 19 November 1720).

Elisa (soprano castrato), Queen of Tyre, loves her admiral Clearco (alto castrato) and is ready to marry him. Their union is opposed by Fenicio (alto castrato), supposed father of Clearco, Agenore (tenor), who loves Elisa, and Sidonia (soprano castrato), who loves Clearco rather than Nino (soprano castrato). Only Fenicio knows that Clearco is really Astarto, the son of the king who was slain when Elisa's father usurped the throne. Clearco learns his true identity near the end of Act 2, and in the end reveals his identity to all and is united with Elisa.

The Roman libretto includes intermezzos at the end of the first two acts, but they are not in the only extant score (in *D-MÜs* MS 4137). Richard Boyle, the Earl of Burlington, saw the Roman production, and he was largely responsible for inviting Rolli, then Bononcini, to London. Bononcini's first work for the King's Theatre, *Astarto* opened the second season of the Royal Academy of Music, where it succeeded partly because Senesino made his London début in the title role. He must have enjoyed the role since he instigated the revival of the opera at Lincoln's Inn Fields in 1734. The first London production included 33 arias for six characters; all except Fenicio (bass) were sopranos. The most popular pieces in London were the two tender arias sung by Nino (Matteo Berselli), 'No più non bramo no' and 'L'esperto nocchiero', and the duet sung by Nino and Sidonia, 'Mio caro ben non sospirar'. Although Burney (*A General History of Music*, ii, pp.707–12) examined each song in the collection, he could not 'discover that tenderness and pathos, for which Bononcini has been so celebrated, even by those who denied his invention and science'. LOWELL LINDGREN

Astianatte ('Astyanax'). *Drama* in three acts by GIOVANNI BONONCINI to a libretto by NICOLA FRANCESCO HAYM after JEAN RACINE's play *Andromaque* (1667) by way of ANTONIO SALVI's libretto (1701, Pratolino); London, King's Theatre, 6 May 1727.

The child Astyanax (silent role) and his mother Andromaca [Andromache] (soprano), widow of Hector, are at the court of Pirro [Pyrrhus] (mezzo-soprano), son of Achilles. Pyrrhus loves Andromache, thus slighting and arousing the vengeful ire of Ermione [Hermione] (soprano), whom he is contracted to marry. Hermione is loved by Oreste [Orestes] (contralto), son of Agamemnon, who asks for the sacrifice of Astyanax so that he will not grow up to wreak vengeance upon Greece. Pyrrhus accedes to the request, halts the slaughter when Andromache appeals to him, then is himself wounded by Orestes, who had been spurred on by Hermione. Orestes is captured, but his friend Pilade [Pylades] (contralto) abducts Astyanax with the intention of killing him. This is prevented when Pyrrhus's captain, Creonte (bass), exchanges Orestes for Astyanax.

The production marked the culmination of the noisy war between partisans of Francesca Cuzzoni (Andromache) and Faustina Bordoni (Hermione), who had been the 'rival' prima donnas in London since 5 May 1726. The raucousness of the audience had affronted Princess Amelia at a performance of Handel's *Admeto* on 4 April 1727. Faustina and Cuzzoni, who were presumably horrified rather than flattered by such a racket, thereafter suffered from successive 'indispositions', which delayed the première of *Astianatte* for two weeks. The audience presumably resumed battle at its première, but we hear nothing about the noise until the performance on 6 June, when the same princess unwisely attended, and the din forced the omission of everything between the end of Act 2 and the closing chorus. The bemused reporter for *The Country Journal* wondered at first if the harsh pipe called the 'cat-call' was 'an awkward Design to improve and fill up *Bononcini's* Musick, which is condemn'd by some of our very fine Gentlemen for its too great *Simplicity*', but then he noticed that the performers were gentry in the pit and upper gallery, who were 'as much out of time as they were out of tune'. There is no evidence that Cuzzoni and Faustina themselves fought on stage, which is implied in parodies of the event (e.g. *The Beggar's Opera*).

No score survives, but 13 of the 32 arias and a minuet are extant. The favourites were the minuet (played when Astyanax is led to the sacrificial altar in Act 2) and 'Ascolta o figlio quell'augellino', a moving tune sung by Andromache to her son after his rescue in Act 3. Hawkins printed Andromache's sorrowful 'Deh! lascia o core di sospirar' at the end of Act 2, which was 'greatly admired for the sweetness of the air and the originality of the accompaniment'. Quantz, who attended both *Admeto* and *Astianatte* in 1727, clearly preferred Handel's counterpoint to Bononcini's tunes, for in his autobiography of 1754 he judged that 'Händels Grundstimme überwog Bononcinis Oberstimme'.

See also ANDROMACHE. LOWELL LINDGREN

Astorga, Baron **Emanuele (Gioacchino Cesare Rincón) d'** [Giuseppe del Chiaro] (*b* Augusta, Sicily, 20 March 1680; *d* ?Madrid, ?1757). Italian composer. He came of a Spanish family that acquired a Sicilian barony in the early 17th century. He had shown signs of musical talent at an early age, and in 1698 an opera of his, *La moglie nemica*, had been performed privately in Palermo by aristocratic amateurs, with him and his brother in the leading female parts. In later years he gave salon performances of his own solo cantatas, which make up the bulk of his compositions. Going to Rome, Astorga became part of the circle of the Duke of Osseda, Spain's papal ambassador; there he made friends with the Neapolitan poet Sebastiano Biancardi, who provided the texts for some of his cantatas. They went to Genoa, where they were robbed by their servant, and to raise money Astorga wrote an opera, *Dafni*, performed there on 21 April 1709. Under the assumed names Giuseppe del Chiaro and Domenico Lalli, they then visited Tortona, Mantua and Venice. Probably late in 1709 or early in 1710 Astorga was summoned to Barcelona by Charles III, the Habsburg claimant to the Spanish throne, who had been impressed by *Dafni* when it was performed at Barcelona in summer 1709. In 1711 Charles III became emperor as Charles VI and returned to Vienna; Astorga went there at about the same time and may have composed the anonymous one-act opera, *Zenobia*, produced in Vienna in 1712.

Astorga left Vienna (and a number of debts) in spring 1714, returning to Palermo the following year. In 1721 he left Sicily and seems to have visited Lisbon, Livorno, London and Bohemia during the next years. The date and place given for his death are known only from a manuscript in the Santini collection (*D-MÜs*).

Dafni was revived at Parma in 1715 and Breslau in 1726. Only the first act is extant (in *A-Wn* and *D-Dlb*); the overture and some arias were published in 1902.

S. Biancardi: *Rime* (Venice, 1732)
H. Volkmann: *Emanuel d'Astorga* (Leipzig, 1911–19) [incl. list of works]
L. Genvardi: 'Emmanuele Rincon d'Astorga, musicista siciliano del secolo XVIII', *Archivio storico siciliano*, new ser., xxxvi (1912), 488–92
G. Sorge: *I teatri di Palermo* (Palermo, 1926)
F. Walker: 'Emanuele d'Astorga and a Neapolitan Librettist', *MMR*, lxxxi (1951), 90–96
O. Tiby: 'Emanuele d'Astorga: aggiunte e correzioni da apportare alle richerche del Prof. Hans Volkmann', *IMSCR*, v *Utrecht 1952*, 398–403

Astor Place Opera Company. American travelling company, nominally based at the Astor Place Opera House in New York from November 1847 until March 1853. The 1847–8 company was managed by Antonio Sanquirico and Salvatore Patti and the 1848–9 troupe by Edward Fry; Max Maretzek took over in March 1849 and retained control until 1853. It performed Italian opera extensively along the eastern seaboard from Boston to Charleston, with Maretzek frequently dividing the ensemble into smaller groups to perform simultaneously in different cities. In 1852 the troupe appeared in New Orleans and Mexico, then disbanded. *See* TRAVELLING TROUPES, §5(iv).

Astrologi immaginari, Gli. Opera by Giovanni Paisiello; *see FILOSOFI IMMAGINARI, I*.

Astrua, Giovanna (*b* Graglia, nr Vercelli, 1720; *d* Turin, 28 Oct 1757). Italian soprano. After study with Bravio in Milan she made her début at the Teatro Regio, Turin, in *Il Ciro riconosciuto* by Leonardo Leo (1739). She sang at the Teatro S Samuele, Venice, from 1739 and appeared with Caffarelli at the S Carlo, Naples (1745–6), where she was the butt of his outrageous on-stage behaviour. She was engaged at the Hofoper, Berlin (1746–56), earning 6000 thaler a season and appearing in the premières of Graun's *Britannico* and *La Merope* (1751, 1756) and in operas by Benda. She achieved particular success in the bravura aria 'Mi paventi' in *Britannico*. She lost her voice the year before her early death. DAVID CUMMINGS

Astuzie femminili, Le ('Female Shrewdness'). *Commedia per musica* in two acts by DOMENICO CIMAROSA to a libretto by GIUSEPPE PALOMBA; Naples, Teatro dei Fiorentini, 26 August 1794.

The orphan Bellina (soprano) is the ward of Don Romualdo (bass), an ignorant elderly man who aspires to marry her. He is upset to discover that, according to her father's will, she will receive a large dowry if she marries Don Gianpaolo Lasagna (bass), an old family friend. When the crude and cowardly Lasagna, who sings exclusively in Neapolitan dialect, comes to claim his bride he is rejected and ridiculed by Bellina. The object of her affections is Filandro (tenor), and for his sake she also rejects Romualdo's amorous advances. Two other women live in Romualdo's household: the governess Leonora (soprano), who is anxious to marry Romualdo and is jealous of his attentions toward Bellina; and Bellina's friend Ersilia (soprano), who is happy with her unmarried status.

Through Leonora's intrigues, Romualdo, Lasagna and Filandro realize that they are all rivals for Bellina's hand. Bellina and Filandro attempt to pawn Leonora and Ersilia off on to Lasagna in order to extricate Bellina from her marital obligation to him, and later the couple disguise themselves as Hussars, speaking broken German. They finally succeed in tricking Lasagna and Romualdo into blessing their marriage. After the men's initial anger at having been duped, the story concludes with a happy ending as Romualdo unites with Leonora and Lasagna with Ersilia.

With the colourful character of Lasagna and his lively and naturalistic expressions this libretto was tailored expressly to Neapolitan taste. One of Palomba's most successful librettos, it abounds with elements of slapstick and disguise (the use of broken German was a favourite comic device in Neapolitan intermezzos and comic operas). Cimarosa scored for a large orchestra including brass, oboes, clarinets, strings and bassoons. Although the strings usually either carry the melodic material or function as accompaniment to the vocal line, there are also sections of independent instrumental writing, as in the Act 1 finale where Lasagna and Romualdo's opening lilting duet in 6/8, 'Signor Gianpaolo padron mio caro', has passages of alternating strings and wind. This sectional chain finale includes masterly comic characterization, as well as some expressive writing, such as Filandro's 'Qui dolcemente spira soave zeffiretto', accompanied by a solo clarinet.

The opera enjoyed considerable success in Italy and abroad: in the first two decades after its première it was performed in Barcelona, Lisbon, Paris, London, Milan, Bologna, Florence and elsewhere. It was revived in Naples, London, Bologna and Florence in 1871, as well as in other cities in the last quarter of the 19th century. In 1920 it was given in Paris as an opera-ballet, choreographed by Massine, directed by Dyagilev and re-orchestrated by Respighi. GORDANA LAZAREVICH

Asunción. Capital of Paraguay. The advent of operatic activity in Paraguay was delayed by the disastrous war against Argentina, Uruguay and Brazil during the period 1865–70. A touring French operetta company gave works by Offenbach at the Teatro Nacional in 1875. It was not until 1887 that the first Italian operas (Pedrotti's *Tutti in maschera*, *Lucia* and *La traviata*) were given, by another touring company. Further repertory followed fairly quickly thereafter, with other touring companies performing at the Teatro Nacional in the late 1890s and several times more in the early 20th century. These companies rarely featured well-known artists, being generally composed of merely adequate singers, many of whom had extensive careers in lesser houses.

*

J. Pla: *Cuatro Siglos de Teatro en el Paraguay* (Asuncion, 1990–91)

TOM KAUFMAN

Atalanta. Opera in three acts by GEORGE FRIDERIC HANDEL to a libretto anonymously adapted from Belisario Valeriano's *La caccia in Etolia* (1715, Ferrara); London, Covent Garden Theatre, 12 May 1736.

Handel completed the score of *Atalanta* on 22 April and performed it as part of a short spring opera season at Covent Garden to celebrate the marriage of Frederick, Prince of Wales, to Augusta, Princess of Saxe-Gotha. (Handel had declined to offer a full season in deference to the dominance of the productions of the 'Opera of the Nobility' at the King's Theatre.) The eight performances were preceded by two of *Ariodante*. Frederick, the leading supporter of the Nobility Opera, ostentatiously refused to attend the first night, but Handel was as usual supported by the king and the royal princesses. The young soprano castrato Gioachino Conti (known as Egizziello) and Handel's regular soprano Anna Strada del Po sang the roles of Meleagro [Meleager], King of Etolia, and Atalanta, Princess of Arcadia. Maria Negri (contralto) sang the shepherdess Irene, John Beard (tenor) the shepherd Aminta [Amyntas], and the two basses Gustavus Waltz and Henry Reinhold sang the old shepherd Nicandro [Nicander] and the god Mercurio [Mercury] respectively. A significant last-minute revision (perhaps made during the first run) was the inclusion of a duet in Act 3 in place of Meleager's brilliant aria 'Tu scolcasti' in scene vi; the second of the two issues of the wordbook shows that the aria was not cut (as suggested in Chrysander's edition) but was given a revised text and moved to close scene iii. Handel revived the opera for two performances on 20 November 1736, probably with the same cast (Waltz may have been replaced). It was not heard again until the revival by Kent Opera at Hintlesham Hall, Suffolk, on 17 July 1970.

The action, which takes place in a single set depicting the countryside with cottages, with woods on either side, treats of Meleager's love for Atalanta. She has refused his offer of marriage, preferring the pleasures of the hunt, and lives in the woods under the name of Amarilli [Amaryllis]. Meleager, disguised as the shepherd Tirsi [Thyrsis], has followed her. After a series of misunderstandings, involving the shepherd Amyntas and his beloved, Irene, misdelivered gifts, supposed betrayals and jealousy, as well as Atalanta's proud resistance, both pairs of lovers are reconciled and the royal lineage of the principal couple is revealed. Mercury descends on a cloud to declare that Jupiter has decreed the royal union in response to the 'fervent prayers of the British people'; he calls for general rejoicing, which takes the form of bonfires and fireworks accompanied by trumpets and drums.

Though *Atalanta* begins and ends in celebratory style (the overture is a miniature concerto for solo trumpet, owing much to movements in Telemann's *Musique de table*), it displays a range of feeling well beyond that to be expected in a purely occasional work. The first vocal number, Meleager's 'Care selve' (still often sung as a recital piece), is surprisingly reflective in mood, suggesting the seriousness of the character, while Atalanta's first solos, with their imitations of trumpet or horn motifs, gently caricature the determined huntress. Act 2 opens with a expansively jubilant chorus (in which Handel employs horns in B♭, apparently *in alt*) but soon touches profounder emotions with Atalanta's C minor aria 'Lassa! ch'io t'ho perduta' and her duet with Meleager, where the suspensions and the use of stabbing repeated-note figures on the violins hauntingly suggest strong feelings held in check. The minor characters are also given ample opportunity to make a mark. Throughout the opera the vocal writing is demanding (Meleager's part has the highest tessitura required by Handel in a castrato role, touching *c'''*); with singers who are equal to it *Atalanta* makes a most satisfying entertainment.

ANTHONY HICKS

Atanasov [Athanassov], **Georgi** (*b* Plovdiv, 6 May 1882; *d* Fasana, Lake Garda, Italy, 17 Nov 1931). Bulgarian composer and conductor. At the age of 14 he began formal music studies in Bucharest. He studied composition with Mascagni at the Pesaro Conservatory (1901–3), then returned to Bulgaria, where he became well known as a military bandmaster. In 1922–3 he conducted the Sofia National Opera. Atanasov was the first Bulgarian professional opera composer. His lyrical, Romantic style shows the influence of late 19th-century Italian opera, but is primarily melodic and also bears traces of folk idioms. He achieved dramatic effects by the alternation of contrasting numbers. His most frequently performed opera is *Gergana*, the first Bulgarian opera to make an individual character the centre of the plot. The opera *Tsveta* is similar in its clearly expressed dramatic conflict. In *Kosara* (1924) Atanasov used a mystical-romantic style and a leitmotif technique; in *Altzec* he developed these stylistic features using ancient Slav motifs. His works also include a comic operetta, *Moralisti*, as well as children's operettas and songs.

all first performed in Sofia

Borislav (N. Popov, after I. Vasov), Balgarska Operna Druzhba, 4 March 1911

Gergana (P. Bobevski, after P. R. Slaveykov: *Izvorat na Belonogata*), Balgarska Operna Druzhba, 6 June 1917

Zapustyalata vodenitsa [The Abandoned Mill] (A. Morfov), National Opera, 31 March 1923

Tsveta (V. Chernodrinski), Cooperative Operetta, 31 Oct 1925

Kosara (B. Danovsky), National Opera, 20 Nov 1929

Altzec (P. Karapetrov), National Opera, 15 Sept 1930

Moralisti (comic operetta, A. Milenkov), Jan 1916

Children's operettas

*

V. Krastev: *Ocherki varkhu razvitiyeto na balgarskata muzika* [Essays on the Development of Bulgarian Music] (Sofia, 1954)

L. Sagaev: *Maestro Georgi Atanasov* (Sofia, 1960)

MAGDALENA MANOLOVA

Atelier de Recherche et de Création pour l'Art Lyrique [ARCAL]. A touring chamber-opera group founded in 1982 by the countertenor Henri Ledroit and the producer Christian Gangneron to take productions to French provincial towns and Paris suburbs that usually see no opera, and to employ young singers taking their first steps in the profession. It is subsidized by the French Cultural Ministry. Each production is given between 10 and 30 performances; the repertory ranges from the Baroque – Handel's *Orlando* (1983), Cavalli's *L'Ormindo* (1986), Blow's *Venus and Adonis* coupled with Locke and Gibbons's *Cupid and Death* (1986) – to modern works – Britten's *The Turn of the Screw* (1987), Milhaud's *Les malheurs d'Orphée* and *Le pauvre matelot* (1988) and Frederic Rzewski's *Les perses* (1985), the last specially commissioned. In towns where there are no theatres, the group has performed on specially constructed platforms in churches; its production of Milhaud's *Le pauvre matelot* in the version with piano accompaniment was performed in cafés. The company has also presented productions in Stockholm and in London. CHARLES PITT

Athalie ('Athaliah'). Opera in five acts by JOHANN ABRAHAM PETER SCHULZ to his own libretto (with C. F. Cramer) after JEAN RACINE; Rheinsberg, French Theatre of Prince Heinrich, 1785.

Athaliah has usurped the throne after the death of her son Ahaziah and has massacred all the members of the royal house except her grandson Joash, who was rescued by an aunt. The opera opens after Athaliah has been ruling for seven years and as supporters of Joash are conspiring to elevate him to his rightful place on the throne. Athaliah is assassinated during the final struggle and Joash is crowned King of Judah. Schulz wrote his opera, in French, in 1785 for performance at the court, and revised it the following year for the French Theatre in Berlin. The work was musically successful but Schulz's dedication of it to Princess Amalie (with its unfortunate subject of regicide) misfired, leading to his resignation.

The instrumental writing shows the influence of C. P. E. Bach, while Schulz's blending of solo voices and choir foreshadows Beethoven. The popularity of the opera is probably due to the songlike quality of the vocal writing, which reflects Schulz's work in the art song genre with his *Lieder im Volkston*.

RAYMOND A. BARR

Athanassov, Georgi. *See* ATANASOV, GEORGI.

Athens (Gk. Athinai). Capital of Greece. From the beginning of its existence the state subsidized the importing of Italian opera companies for the entertainment of diplomats and financial potentates, a policy still pursued. The earliest opera performances, of *Il barbiere di Siviglia*, were given in 1837 at the Melis Theatre. Early in 1840 the Boukouras Theatre, named after an impresario who undertook to provide performances by an Italian company for eight months each year, was inaugurated with *Lucia di Lammermoor*; for 40 years it was the only theatre in Athens. It had three tiers of boxes and 113 stalls seats; it ceased to be used in 1897. From the beginning opera drew hostile press comment for alleged immorality and because governments spent heavily on it.

In 1871 operetta was introduced by a French company, gaining a foothold that was reinforced by state subsidy and increasing popularity. Meanwhile outdoor theatres had been opened, one in the resort of Phaleron, where in 1875 Pavlos Carrer's *Marcos Botsaris* and *Kyra Frossyni* were given their Athens premières by an Italian company; there, in 1883, operettas by Tigran Tchukhatjian were added to the French repertory by a touring Armenian company.

The Dhimotikon Theatron Athinon (Athens Municipal Theatre), an imposing neo-classical building seating 1500, was inaugurated on 15 October 1888 with *Mignon*, given by a French company; it was demolished in the late 1930s. The dawn of Greek lyric theatre had been marked earlier in 1888 by a performance at the Boukouras Theatre of Spyridon Xyndas's comic opera *O ypopsifios vouleftis* ('The Parliamentary Candidate') – by a Greek composer, to a Greek text on a Greek subject, with a mostly Greek cast, presented by the Elliniko Melodrama (Greek Opera Company). The company was revived in 1888 at the Municipal Theatre with a predominantly Italian and Greek repertory; it was disbanded in 1890, Italian and French companies having once more gained ascendancy. Two operas by Spyridon Samaras were however given by visiting companies in 1889 and 1906, as well as *Lohengrin* in 1903.

A new Elliniko Melodrama, established by the composer-conductors Dionyssios Lavrangas and Ludovicos Spinellis (*c*1871–1904), first appeared at the Municipal Theatre in 1900 with *La bohème*, sung in Greek by an all-Greek cast. This began one of the most illustrious periods in the operatic life of Athens; the company was a training-ground for many leading singers. It sometimes joined with short-lived companies such as the Ellinikos Moussikos Thiassos (Greek Music-Theatre Company) and the Neos Moussikos Thiassos (New Musical Company), both of which gave premières of works by Manolis Kalomiris: *O protomastoras* ('The Master Builder', 1916) and *To dakhtylidi tis manas* ('The Mother's Ring', 1917) respectively. One of its principal activities was touring. From 1916 it often performed at the new Olympia Theatre (inaugurated with *Ernani*).

The building of new theatres in the early years of the 20th century was perhaps not unconnected with the formation of the first Greek operetta companies in 1908: the opera school of the Conservatory gave Offenbach's *Le mariage aux lanternes* at the Vassilikon Theatron (Royal Theatre, 750 seats) and the actor-director Thomas Ikonomou presented *Die Fledermaus* and *La belle Hélène* at the Panellinion Theatre. Paramount among the new companies was Elliniki Operetta, founded by the comic actor and director Ioannis Papaioannou, a disciple of Ikonomou. It was established as a permanent company in 1909. On 11 May 1916 it inaugurated its own theatre, the Papaioannou. The company left a deep imprint on Greek musical life lasting well beyond the 20 years of its existence, during which time it presented some 65 operettas; the Greek repertory included 13 works by Sakellaridis.

The last full-scale attempt to form a private opera company was Kalomiris's Ethnikos Melodramatikos Omilos (National Opera Company), inaugurated in Salonica in August 1933. Its appearances in Athens that autumn at the Kyvelis Theatre (the former Syndagma, converted into an indoor theatre seating 701) started with Samaras's *La martire*; apart from two of Kalomiris's operas the repertory was drawn from the popular Italian and French classics.

It is difficult not to consider the foundation of the Ethniki Lyriki Skini (National Opera) as a branch of the National Theatre during Metaxas's dictatorship (1936–41) as one aspect of an attempt to control the artistic and mass media. It was inaugurated in 1940 at the Olympia Theatre with *Die Fledermaus*; four years later it became independent, under Kalomiris's directorship. It now has a virtual monopoly of opera production in Greece and operates as part of the Ministry of Culture. Promising young singers have often preferred to make their careers abroad, mainly in Germany; many return as guests. The Olympia Theatre, rebuilt several times, has traditionally been the company's home; its main season runs from November to May. The repertory is restricted by the dimensions of the building, with its narrow stage and small pit; there are 433 stalls seats, with a further 519 in two tiers of boxes and galleries. By the early 1990s the company had staged a total of 162 works. The average season consists of six operas and two operettas (usually including a popular Greek one). The repertory is conservative; 18th- and 20th-century operas have been given mainly by visiting artists and are rarely revived. In the late 1960s the company's repertory broadened to include several 19th-century Russian operas; among 20th-century operas Dallapiccola's *Il prigioniero* was given in 1977.

Operettas have been presented in summer at the Kyvelis and other open-air theatres; each summer the company stages a spectacular production, from 1955 as part of the Athens Festival, at the open-air theatre of Herodes Atticus (built in AD 161), with a capacity of over 5000. The festival has staged only one production of its own, Peggy Glanville-Hicks's *Nausicaa* (1961). For Callas's appearances in 1960–61 in *Norma* and *Medea* the ancient theatre at Epidaurus was used for the summer production.

A strong impulse was imparted to Greek musical life by the opening in 1991 of the new, multi-purpose Megaro Moussikis Athinon (Athens Concert Hall). Its functional areas include two auditoriums suited to opera (2000 and 500 seats), containing advanced stage, acoustic and technical equipment.

T. N. Synadinos: *Istoria tis neoellinikis moussikis, 1824–1919* [History of Modern Greek Music, 1824–1919] (Athens, 1919)

N. I. Laskaris: *Istoria tou neoellinikou theatrou* [History of Modern Greek Theatre] (Athens, 1938–9)

A. Hadjiapostolou: *Istoria tou ellinikou melodramatos* [History of the Hellenic Opera Company] (Athens, 1949)

Y. Sideris: *Istoria tou neou ellinikou theatrou, 1794–1944* [History of Modern Greek Theatre, 1794–1944] (Athens, *c*1949)

I. Prineas: 'To melodrama'; 'I operetta', *Neoteron engyklopedikon lexikon 'Iliou'*, vii: *Hellas* [Greece] (Athens, ?1950), 1125–6; 1126–8

Y. Sideris: 'I. Papaioannou', *Imera tou ithopoiou 1958* [Actor's Day 1958], 5–17 [programme book]

T. Hadjipandazis and L. Maraka: *I athinaiki epitheorissi* [The Athenian Revue] (Athens, 1977)

T. Hadjipandazis: '"Flora mirabilis": i opera tou Samara ke i proti paroussiasi tis stin Athina' [*Flora mirabilis*: Samaras's Opera and its Athens Première], *Proini* (Athens, 26 April and 3 May 1979)

——: *To komidhyllio* [The Greek Vaudeville] (Athens, 1981)

T. Karalivanos: *Elliniko melodrama: istoriko 1886–1943, ke Ethniki lyriki skini, 1940–1982* [The Hellenic Opera Company: a History, 1886–1943, and the National Opera, 1940–82] (MS, 1982, *GR-Aleotsakos*)

T. Bourlos: *Me to Manoli Kalomiri* [With Manolis Kalomiris] (Athens, 1983)

Y. Pilichos: 'Bastias, Kostis', *Pangosmio viografiko lexiko* [*Ekpedeftiki elliniki engyklopedia*, i–ix b], vi (Athens, 1987), 341–3

G. Leotsakos: *Elliniko lyriko theatro: 100 chronia, 1888–1988* (YP 4–6, A/A 14564–6, 1988) [record notes]

E. Fessa-Emmanuil: *I architektoniki tou neoellinikou theatrou, 1720–1940* [The Architecture of Modern Greek Theatres, 1720–1940] (diss., Greek National Polytechnic School, Athens, 1989)

M. A. Raptis: *Epitomi istoria tou Ellinikou melodramatos ke tis Ethnikis lyrikis skinis, 1888–1988* [One-Volume History of the Hellenic Opera Company and the National Opera] (Athens, 1989)

GEORGE LEOTSAKOS

Atherton, David (*b* Blackpool, 3 Jan 1944). English conductor. He played clarinet with the National Youth Orchestra and studied at Cambridge University. While training as a répétiteur at the London Opera Centre he returned to conduct University performances of *Ariadne auf Naxos*, *Béatrice et Bénédict* and *Oberon*, which brought him to the attention of Georg Solti, who engaged him at Covent Garden. At 24 Atherton became the youngest conductor there on his début in *Il trovatore*; he remained a staff conductor for 12 years. His repertory ranged from Mozart and Verdi to Britten and Tippett, and he conducted the première of Henze's *We Come to the River* in 1976. With the English Opera Group at the Aldeburgh Festival he conducted the premières of Birtwistle's *Punch and Judy* (1968) and Crosse's *The Grace of Todd* (1969). He has conducted *Peter Grimes* and *Billy Budd* at the Metropolitan and for English National Opera. Meticulous preparation in contemporary works is complemented by stylistic concern in the Classical and Romantic repertory. He co-founded the London Sinfonietta and was music director from 1968 to 1973, including a notable Schoenberg-Gerhard series; he later returned to work on a Ravel-Varèse cycle and another of Kurt Weill. In 1991 he conducted the first London performance since World War II of Meyerbeer's *Les Huguenots*, at Covent Garden.

NOËL GOODWIN

Atherton, James (**Peyton, jr**) (*b* Montgomery, AL, 27 April 1943; *d* St Louis, 20 Nov 1987). American tenor and director. He studied at the Peabody Conservatory, chiefly with Singher but also with Ponselle, and made his début with the San Francisco Opera in 1971 as Goro. With the Santa Fe Opera from 1973 he sang Sir Philip Wingrave in the American stage première of Britten's opera, as well as Janáček's Schoolmaster, Fenton, Jo (*The Mother of Us All*), Monsieur Triquet, Antonio (Oliver's *Duchess of Malfi*), Leukippos (*Daphne*) and Pluto (*Orphée aux enfers*). He sang with the Canadian Opera Company in 1976 as Fritz in Offenbach's *La Grande-duchesse de Gérolstein* and with the Metropolitan in 1977 as the Holy Fool in *Boris Godunov*, returning as Valzacchi and Jaquino; he made his English début at Glyndebourne in 1979 in Haydn's *La fedeltà premiata*. He appeared at Dallas, Miami, Toronto, Houston, Philadelphia and other cities; his repertory included Shuysky, the Four Servants (*Les contes d'Hoffmann*), David (*Die Meistersinger*) and Don Ottavio. From 1977 he also worked as a director of opera. His flexible vocal technique and dramatic abilities made him highly respected as a character performer and he was equally successful in lyrical roles.

JAMES WIERZBICKI, ELIZABETH FORBES

Atlanta. American city, capital of Georgia. References to opera in Atlanta date from 1866, when Max Strakosch's Italian opera company performed *Il trovatore*, *Norma* and *Il barbiere di Siviglia* in the newly constructed Bell-Johnson Opera House (seating 600). Other companies soon followed, including Isabella McCulloch's opera troupe in 1868. The growing demand for opera led to the opening of the Belgian consul Laurent DeGive's Opera House (seating 2000) in 1870. Increasingly frequent visits by major companies followed, including the New York-based Metropolitan Opera in 1901 and 1905. However, the critical event in the city's operatic history occurred in spring 1910, when the Metropolitan returned to perform in the new Municipal Auditorium, a visit which set new attendance records for the company's tours. Among the attractions were the singers Enrico Caruso (in *Aida* and *Pagliacci*), Geraldine Farrar, Louise Homer and Pasquale Amato. From 1911 to 1923 Atlanta was the only city outside the North-east to which the Metropolitan toured, and annual visits continued with few interruptions until the company's national tours ceased after the 1986 season.

Other venues for its performances were the Fox Theatre (seating 4518) and the Civic Center (seating 4580).

Because of the Metropolitan's presence, Atlanta was slow in forming its own companies, and those that were created were short-lived. Between 1964 and 1967 a local director, Christopher Manos, presented Puccini and Verdi as part of his outdoor summer series 'Theater under the Stars', featuring leading American singers, among them Robert Merrill, Beverly Wolff, Phyllis Curtin and Richard Tucker. Buoyed up by the success of the series, Manos created the Atlanta Municipal Theater, which combined a professional dance and theatre company with the Atlanta Opera Company (with Blanche Thebom as artistic director).

When the Atlanta Memorial Arts Center (later Robert W. Woodruff Memorial Arts Center) opened in 1968, one of the first performances there was the American première on 30 October of Purcell's *King Arthur* (Alliance Theatre, seating 784), in an elaborate production by the combined Atlanta Municipal Theater companies (48 performances were given over six weeks). In December 1968 the opera company presented its first independent endeavour, a controversial production of *La bohème* set in the 1920s and featuring a nude woman. Although both productions were artistically successful, the company became bankrupt on 14 January 1969.

During the early 1970s, when there was no permanent major local company, the Atlanta Symphony Orchestra, directed by Robert Shaw, gave concert performances of operas and the stage première on 28 January 1972 of Scott Joplin's *Treemonisha*, with an all-black cast (Woodruff Arts Center, Symphony Hall; seating 1762).

Two ambitious professional companies emerged in the mid-1970s. The Atlanta Lyric Opera (1976) was founded by William Noll, who also served as artistic director. Its first production, *Madama Butterfly* with Lorna Haywood in the title role, attracted capacity audiences for two performances at the Fox Theatre. The company presented two seasons of four operas there. Meanwhile, in 1974, Patricia Heuerman, who had been active in semi-professional productions of opera at Emory University, established the Music Theater Guild of Atlanta. This gave performances by local professionals with piano accompaniment, most at the Center Stage Theater (seating 750). In 1977 Heuerman moved to the Woodruff Arts Center, renamed the company the Georgia Opera, and added an orchestra under the direction of John Naskiewicz. Over the next two years Georgia Opera presented Robert Ward's *The Crucible* at the Alliance Theatre and *Il barbiere di Siviglia*, *Tosca*, *Lucia di Lammermoor* and *Rigoletto* at Symphony Hall, with nationally prominent singers, including Jan Peerce.

In 1979 the two companies combined forces for *La traviata* and Thomas Pasatieri's *The Seagull* (Fox Theatre) and soon afterwards merged to form the Atlanta Civic Opera. Pasatieri became the artistic director, with Noll as principal conductor. Despite artistic achievements, financial problems mounted and both Noll and Pasatieri had left the company by 1984. The company was reorganized in 1985 as the Atlanta Opera, with William Fred Scott as conductor and artistic director, and in 1991 continued to be the city's principal source of staged opera, performing in the Woodruff Arts Center; it presents three productions a year in Symphony Hall.

Several smaller companies employ local and regional talent. The Shoestring Opera Company, founded in 1978, used minimal sets, simple costumes and piano accompaniment. It evolved into the Atlanta Repertory Opera Company and, under the artistic direction of Naskiewicz, presented memorable productions of *Così fan tutte* (1987) and *Le nozze di Figaro* (1988) with chamber orchestra, but financial difficulties prevented further productions. The longest-surviving company is the Southeastern Savoyards (founded 1980), a Gilbert and Sullivan troupe which has given an uninterrupted series of performances of consistently high quality. It presents three productions a year, with six performances of each, in the Center Stage Theater. In 1988 Onyx Opera, a company designed to feature black American performers from Georgia in both traditional operas and works by black American composers, was founded by local singers, with Uzee Brown jr as artistic director. Their first presentation of a complete opera, William Grant Still's *A Bayou Legend*, was planned for 1992.

DERRICK HENRY

Atlantov, Vladimir (Andreyevich) (*b* Leningrad [now St Petersburg], 19 Feb 1939). Russian tenor. The son of an opera singer, he graduated from Bolotina's class at the Leningrad Conservatory in 1963, and had further training as a student-artist (1963–5) at La Scala opera school. He won the 1966 Tchaikovsky and the 1967 Sofia international competitions. In 1963 he made his début at the Kirov Theatre, and in 1967 he joined the Bol'shoy. His voice is full and ample, but capable of great beauty and delicacy; he has a strong temperament and a gift for character portrayal. His roles include Hermann, Vladimir (*Prince Igor*), Alfredo and Don José. He has toured in Europe, Canada and Japan, and was made People's Artist of the RSFSR in 1972. He made his Covent Garden début in *Otello* in 1987, and sang Canio there in 1989. I. M. YAMPOL'SKY

Atomtod ('Atomic Death'). Opera in two acts by GIACOMO MANZONI to a libretto by Emilio Jona; Milan, Piccola Scala, 27 March 1965.

Incorporating video and electronic music with a graphic dodecaphonic score, *Atomtod* is set inside and outside a group of private nuclear shelters. The Proprietor (baritone) chooses those who are to join him inside the spherical shelters: the Constructor who made them (tenor), a General (tenor), a Priest (bass), and to minister to their needs a Servant (bass) and Slam (soprano), the provider of carnal pleasures. As preparations for war multiply on all sides, the Speaker, on video, assures the populace that 'there is no cause for alarm'. Individual voices from the crowd (soprano, mezzo-soprano, baritone and bass) sing of general foreboding: normal life has been abandoned. The Proprietor's shelter emerges from the ground; those outside desperately try to gain entrance. Inside the spheres, bourgeois social ritual is pursued in a mounting frenzy of emptiness; outside, crowds are driven hither and thither by loudspeakers around the theatre. Both reach their peak as the bomb explodes. In its wake, as a 'new crust' forms on the earth, the mutated chorus lament their fate. A multitude of shelters emerge from the ground. Their occupants, glassy-eyed and half smiling, advance on the audience, while from the auditorium loudspeakers a chant, lacerated by electronic incursions, proclaims their newly acquired immortality.

DAVID OSMOND-SMITH

Atresio Geonuntino. *See* STANZANI, TOMMASO.

Attaque du moulin, L' ('The Attack on the Mill'). *Drame lyrique* in four acts by ALFRED BRUNEAU to a libretto by LOUIS GALLET after EMILE ZOLA; Paris, Opéra-Comique (Salle Favart), 23 November 1893.

The opera concerns the plight of a miller's family when war breaks out. The daughter, Françoise (soprano), has fallen in love with a stranger, Dominique (tenor). After scenes stressing the family's love of their work and announcing the marriage of the pair, the Town Crier (bass) warns of war. Marcelline (mezzo-soprano), wife of the miller Merlier (baritone), fears that it can bring only destruction.

As hostilities begin, Bruneau responds with realistic clarion calls and military marches. Françoise is appalled by the carnage; emphasis on realist detail to elicit a moral reaction is characteristic of the opera. The enemy captain appears, accusing Merlier and Dominique of complicity. Merlier will be shot at dawn.

In Act 3 as Marcelline engages a look-out in conversation Françoise enters stealthily and kills him. When the body is discovered Dominique is blamed. Françoise confesses but her father tries to persuade the captain to punish him instead.

Dominique reappears and escapes to summon help. Bruneau gives two possible endings: in the first, Merlier is shot the moment before the French soldiers arrive and it is left to Marcelline to underline the moral of the tale –'Oh! la guerre! Héroïque leçon et fléau de la terre' ('Oh! war! A lesson in heroism and the scourge of the earth'). In the second, a happier but weaker conclusion, the soldiers arrive in the nick of time.

Bruneau's compositional approach to this opera is less imaginative than in his earlier works, if more unified. The mill itself is predictably underlined with a Schubertian figure, while the main conflict is depicted in a contrast between pastoral and military music. The opera was widely performed throughout Europe and in the USA until the outbreak of World War I, and revived in 1922. RICHARD LANGHAM SMITH

Atterberg, Kurt (Magnus) (*b* Göteborg, 12 Dec 1887; *d* Stockholm, 15 Feb 1974). Swedish composer. Trained as a civil engineer, he spent his working life (1912–68) in the patent office. As a composer he was largely self-taught although he studied briefly with Hallén at the Stockholm Conservatory (1910–11), and in Germany (1911 and 1913). He made his début as a conductor at Göteborg in 1912, and from 1916 to 1922 was *kapellmästare* at the Royal Dramatic Theater, Stockholm. He was co-founder and president (1924–47) of the Swedish Composers' Society and held other posts in musical administration; he was music critic of the *Stockholms-tidningen* (1919–57).

With Rangström, Atterberg was one of the leading Swedish composers in the generation after Peterson-Berger, Stenhammar and Alfvén. His compositions include nine symphonies and incidental music; some of his operas and ballets had many performances in Europe during the 1920s and 30s, particularly in Germany. The opera *Bäckahästen* ('The White Horse'), with its naive folkloristic tone and Singspiel character, met with success, and *Fanal* is an effective, ballad-style drama of freedom in 16th-century Germany. All Atterberg's stage works rely on decorative effect rather than psychological profundity.

all first performed in Stockholm, Royal Opera; autographs in S-Sic

Härvard harpolekare [Härvard the Harpist] op.12 (4, Atterberg), 29 Sept 1919; rev. as Härvards återkomst [Härvard's Homecoming] (3, Atterberg), 3 April 1954

Bäckahästen [The White Horse] op.24 (Scanian fairy play, 4 pranks, A. Österling), 23 Jan 1925

Fanal op.35 (3, O. Ritter and I. M. Welleminsky, after H. Heine, trans. Atterberg), 27 Jan 1934

Alladin [Aladdin] op.43 (fairy op, 3, B. Hard-Warden and Welleminsky, trans. K. Atterberg and M. Atterberg), 18 March 1941

Stormen [The Tempest] op.49 (7 tableaux, Atterberg, after W. Shakespeare), 19 Sept 1948

HANS ÅSTRAND, ANDERS WIKLUND

At the Boar's Head. Musical interlude in one act by GUSTAV HOLST to a libretto based on the tavern scenes from WILLIAM SHAKESPEARE's *King Henry IV* Parts I and II (with two of Shakespeare's sonnets and some traditional songs); Manchester, Opera House, 3 April 1925.

Holst composed *At the Boar's Head* in 1924 at Thaxted, Essex, while convalescing from the effects of a fall from the rostrum while conducting. He noticed, after reading Shakespeare's *Henry IV*, that the words fitted some of the tunes in Playford's *English Dancing Master* (1651). 'Immediately', Imogen Holst relates in her biography, 'he succumbed to the fascinating task of seeing how many other tunes he could find that would "fit" the rest of the words. And then he settled down to enjoy himself'.

Something like 40 traditional tunes, taken mainly from collections by Chappell and Cecil Sharp, were pressed into service. Holst himself supplied only three original tunes. The results might have been thought to sound artificial and contrived, but Holst's astonishing feat was to compose a score that flows easily and smoothly, one tune succeeding another without any suggestion of being forced into a mould. Yet when the work was new, it was strongly criticized for being a mere exercise in ingenuity and for slowing down the action of Shakespeare's comedy. It took almost 50 years for the score to be recognized as an exhilarating and brilliant creation. Its many felicities were fully revealed in its first recording (1982). Its awkward length, about an hour, has undoubtedly militated against its more frequent stage revival.

The opera is set in a room in the Boar's Head, Eastcheap, London. Falstaff (bass) accuses Prince Hal (tenor) and Poins (bass) of cowardice for failing to support him in a highway robbery that he and his followers had attempted. After listening to Falstaff's tall tale of the episode, Hal reveals that he and Poins had set on Falstaff and robbed him of the money that he had taken earlier from unarmed travellers. A messenger from the court brings news of civil war. Falstaff suggests Hal should practise what he will say on returning to his father, the king. Falstaff impersonates the king and later they exchange roles.

Hal and Poins disguise themselves as servants to watch Falstaff wooing Doll Tearsheet (soprano). The disguised Hal sings a song of which Falstaff disapproves – it is about the onset of old age. Bardolph (baritone) brings news of the king, and Hal and Poins doff their disguises and leave for Westminster. Pistol (baritone) arrives seeking his crony Falstaff. Doll and the Hostess (soprano) regard Pistol with extreme disfavour and throw him out. Bardolph tells Falstaff that he is needed in the war. The women are in tears as he leaves – but Bardolph returns to whisper to the Hostess: 'Bid Mistress Tearsheet come to my master'. MICHAEL KENNEDY

Attila. *Dramma lirico* in a prologue and three acts by GIUSEPPE VERDI to a libretto by TEMISTOCLE SOLERA (with additional material by FRANCESCO MARIA PIAVE) after Zacharias Werner's play *Attila, König der Hunnen*; Venice, Teatro La Fenice, 17 March 1846.

Attila *King of the Huns*	bass
Ezio *a Roman general*	baritone
Odabella *the Lord of Aquileia's daughter*	soprano
Foresto *a knight of Aquileia*	tenor
Uldino *a young Breton, Attila's slave*	tenor
Leone *an old Roman*	bass

Leaders, kings and soldiers, Huns, Gepids, Ostrogoths, Heruls, Thuringians, Quadi, Druids, priestesses, men and women of Aquileia, Aquileian maidens in warlike dress, Roman officers and soldiers, Roman virgins and children, hermits, slaves

Setting Aquileia, the Adriatic lagoons and near Rome, in the middle of the 5th century

Verdi had read Werner's ultra-Romantic play as early as 1844, and initially discussed the subject with Piave. However, for his second opera at La Fenice, the composer eventually fixed on Solera, the librettist with whom – at least until then – he seems to have preferred working. Solera set about preparing the text according to his usual format, with plenty of opportunity for grand choral tableaux such as are found in *Nabucco* and *I Lombardi*; but the progress of the opera was beset with difficulties. First Verdi fell seriously ill, and then Solera went off to live permanently in Madrid, leaving the last act as only a sketch and necessitating the calling in of the faithful Piave after all. Verdi instructed Piave to ignore Solera's plans for a large-scale choral finale and to concentrate on the individuals, a change of direction that Solera strongly disapproved of. The première, whose cast included Ignazio Marini (Attila), Natale Costantini (Ezio), Sophie Loewe (Odabella) and Carlo Guasco (Foresto), was coolly received, but *Attila* went on to become one of Verdi's most popular operas of the 1850s. After that it lost ground; however, it has recently been more than occasionally revived. In 1846 Verdi twice rewrote the *romanza* for Foresto in Act 3: the first time for Nicola Ivanoff, the second for Napoleone Moriani.

The prelude follows a pattern that later became common in Verdi's work: a restrained opening leads to a grand climax, then to the beginnings of melodic continuity that are quickly fragmented. It is the drama *in nuce*.

PROLOGUE.i *The piazza of Aquileia* 'Huns, Heruls and Ostrogoths' celebrate bloody victories and greet their leader Attila who, in an impressive recitative, bids them sing a victory hymn. A group of female warriors is brought on, and their leader Odabella proclaims the valour and patriotic zeal of Italian women. Odabella's double aria is a forceful display of soprano power, its first movement, 'Allor che i forti corrono' showing an unusually extended form which allows Attila to insert admiring comments. Such is the force of this movement that the cabaletta, 'Da te questo', merely continues the musical tone, though with more elaborate ornamentation.

As Odabella leaves, the Roman general Ezio appears for a formal duet with Attila. In the Andante 'Tardo per gli anni, e tremulo', Ezio offers Attila the entire Roman empire if Italy can be left unmolested. Attila angrily rejects the proposal, and the warriors end with a cabaletta of mutual defiance, 'Vanitosi! che abbietti e dormenti'.

PROLOGUE.ii *The Rio-Alto in the Adriatic lagoons* The scene opens with a sustained passage of local colour (strongly suggesting that Verdi now had his eye on the fashions of the French stage). First comes a violent orchestral storm, then the gradual rising of dawn is portrayed with a passage of ever increasing orchestral colours and sounds. Foresto leads on a group of survivors from Attila's attack on Aquileia. In an Andantino which again shows unusual formal extension, 'Ella in poter del barbaro', his thoughts turn to his beloved Odabella, captured by Attila. In the subsequent cabaletta, 'Cara patria, già madre', the soloist is joined by the chorus for a rousing conclusion to the scene.

ACT 1.i *A wood near Attila's camp* A melancholy string solo introduces Odabella, who has remained in Attila's camp in order to find an opportunity to murder him. In a delicately scored Andantino, 'Oh! nel fuggente nuvolo', Odabella sees in the clouds the images of her dead father and Foresto. Foresto himself appears: he has seen her with Attila and accuses her of betrayal. Their duet takes on the usual multi-movement pattern: Foresto's accusations remain through the minor-major Andante, 'Sì, quello io son, ravvisami', but Odabella convinces him of her desire to kill Attila, and they lovingly join in a unison cabaletta, 'Oh t'innebria nell'amplesso'.

1.ii *Attila's tent, later his camp* Attila tells his slave Uldino of a terrible dream in which an old man denied him access to Rome in the name of God ('Mentre gonfiarsi l'anima'). But he dismisses the vision with a warlike cabaletta, 'Oltre quel limite'.

A bellicose vocal blast from Attila's followers is interrupted by a procession of women and children led by the old man of Attila's dream. His injunction precipitates the Largo of the concertato finale, 'No! non è sogno', which is led off by a terrified Attila, whose stuttering declamation is answered by a passage of sustained lyricism from Foresto and Odabella. The concertato takes on such impressive proportions that Verdi saw fit to end the act there, without the traditional stretta.

ACT 2.i *Ezio's camp* The scene is no more than a conventional double aria for Ezio. In the Andante, 'Dagl'immortali vertici', he muses on Rome's fallen state. Foresto appears and suggests a plan to destroy Attila by surprising him at his camp. In a brash cabaletta, 'È gettata la mia sorte', Ezio eagerly looks forward to his moment of glory.

2.ii *Attila's camp* Yet another warlike chorus begins the scene. Attila greets Ezio, the Druids mutter darkly of fatal portents, the priestesses dance and sing. A sudden gust of wind blows out all the candles, an event that precipitates yet another concertato finale, 'Lo spirto de' monti', a complex movement during which Foresto manages to tell Odabella that Attila's cup is poisoned. The formal slow movement concluded, Attila raises the cup to his lips, but is warned of the poison by Odabella (who wishes a more personal vengeance); Foresto admits to the crime, and Odabella claims the right to punish him herself. Attila approves, announces that he will marry Odabella the next day, and launches the concluding stretta, 'Oh miei prodi! un solo giorno'; its dynamism and rhythmic bite prefigure similar moments in *Il trovatore*.

ACT 3 *A wood* Foresto is awaiting news of Odabella's marriage to Attila, and in a minor–major *romanza*, 'Che non avrebbe il misero', bemoans her apparent treachery. Ezio arrives, urging Foresto to speedy battle. A distant chorus heralds the wedding procession, but suddenly Odabella herself appears, unable to go through with the ceremony. Soon all is explained between her and Foresto, and they join Ezio in a lyrical Adagio.

Attila now enters, in search of his bride, and the stage is set for a Quartetto finale. In the Allegro, 'Tu, rea donna', Attila accuses the three conspirators in turn, but in turn they answer, each with a different melodic line. At the climax of the number, offstage cries inform us that the attack has begun. Odabella stabs Attila, embraces Foresto, and the curtain falls.

* * *

The final act is, as several have pointed out, more than faintly ridiculous in its stage action, and parts of Verdi's setting seem rather perfunctory; perhaps Solera's original plan for a grand choral finale would have been more apt. Perhaps, indeed, the central problem with *Attila* is that it falls uncomfortably between being a drama of individuals (like *Ernani* or *I due Foscari*) and one that is essentially public (like *Nabucco* or *I Lombardi*). It is surely for this reason that two of the principals, Ezio and Foresto, are vague and undefined, never managing to emerge from the surrounding tableaux. On the other hand, Odabella and Attila, both of whom assume vocal prominence early in the opera, are more powerful dramatic presences. As with all of Verdi's early operas, there are impressive individual moments, particularly in those grand ensemble movements that constantly inspired the composer to redefine and hone his dramatic language. ROGER PARKER

Attilio Regolo ('Attilius Regulus'). Libretto by PIETRO METASTASIO, first set by Johann Adolf Hasse (1750, Dresden).

ACT 1 Regulus, the former Roman consul, who has been a prisoner in Carthage for five years, returns to Rome with the Carthaginian ambassador, Amilcare [Hamilcar], to discuss a possible exchange of prisoners, the first gesture in a move for peace. If Hamilcar's offer is rejected, Regulus must return to Carthage to be executed. To save the honour of Rome, Regulus nevertheless counsels the Senate to reject the proposal.

ACT 2 Regulus persuades his son, Publio [Publius], to argue his case in the Senate. Publius is torn between filial love and patriotic duty. Regulus' daughter Attilia and her beloved, Licinio [Licinius], along with Barce, a Carthaginian slave, plot to save Regulus. Publius returns to announce the Senate's rejection of the Carthaginian offer.

ACT 3 A crowd gathers, angered by the Senate's verdict. Regulus addresses them and convinces them and his family not to let emotion mar a victory for Rome. All bid him farewell as he returns to Carthage to face death and glory.

* * *

Among the sources that refer to the self-sacrifice of Regulus are: Appian, *Historia* (books 5 and 8); Cicero, *De officiis* (book 3); Florus, *Epitome* (book 1); Horace, *Carmina* (book 3, no.5); Silius, *Punica* (book 6); and Zonaras, *Annals* (book 8). Although sentiments from the second act of Zeno's *Eumene* are reflected in *Attilio Regolo*, Jacques Pradon's *Régulus* (1688), which has an almost identical plot, would have been a more influential contemporary model. Metastasio could have read this drama in the original French or in the Italian translation by Girolamo Gigli for a performance in Rome in 1711. The libretto by Matteo Noris, best known in the adaptation set by Alessandro Scarlatti (1719, Rome), begins where Metastasio was to conclude. It was initially intended that Metastasio's libretto be set for performance in Vienna on 4 November 1740 to celebrate the name day of Emperor Charles VI. Charles's death on 20 October, however, put paid to a Vienna performance, but over the next nine years Metastasio made several revisions and on occasion the work was read at court. The text eventually came to the notice of Frederick Augustus II of Saxony whose interest in it led to Hasse's successful setting for Dresden. Indeed, Hasse closely followed some instructions that Metastasio sent him in a letter dated 20 October 1749, directives that have since provided important insights into Metastasio's views on the interaction of text and music in general. Jommelli's version (1753, Rome), was staged in London the following year. Here, the final words of Regulus, set in obbligato recitative, were encored at every performance. This unusual tribute to a recitative was appropriate to a work which Metastasio, a writer of literary dramas, regarded as the most solidly structured of his texts. He seemed to realize, however, that literary excellence would impose limitations upon composers, for soon after the Dresden première, he predicted that the work would not be popular. That the libretto was set only three more times proved the validity of this prognosis.

For a list of settings *see* METASTASIO, PIETRO. DON NEVILLE

Attilio Regolo ('Attilius Regulus'). *Opera seria* in three acts by JOHANN ADOLF HASSE to a libretto by PIETRO METASTASIO (*see* ATTILIO REGOLO above) after the historical writings of Silicus Italicus, *Punica* vi and passages of Horace and Cicero; Dresden, Hoftheater, 12 January 1750.

The libretto almost wholly lacks dramatic development or significant incidents, though two events are worthy of notice. Barce (soprano), the slave in the house of Pubblio [Publius] (soprano), is given her freedom to return to Africa with her former lover, Amilcare [Hamilcar] (soprano); and the mayor of Rome, Manlius (tenor), accepts the arguments of Regolo [Regulus] (contralto) in Act 2 scene ii, the scene Metastasio said he liked most (letter of 20 October 1749 to Hasse). A sinfonia (1.vii) and the very long orchestrally accompanied recitatives for Regulus (in 1.ii, vii, 2.vii and the last scene of the work) conform closely to the instructions Metastasio sent Hasse. The entire score is a tour de force involving richly varied melodic invention and the use of different keys, major and minor, to depict fluctuating states of mind. Since Hasse was the first to set the libretto, not a single word was left out; this was the first of a series of librettos by Metastasio that Hasse was the first to set. At the opera's première Hasse's wife Faustina Bordoni sang Attilia and the alto castrato Domenico Annibali sang the title role. SVEN HANSELL

Atto (It.). ACT.

Designs by Francesco Ponte for the costumes of Publius (sung by Regina Mingotti, left) and Regulus (sung by Domenico Annibali) in the original production of Hasse's 'Attilio Regolo' at the Hoftheater, Dresden, 12 January 1750 (see also BORDONI, FAUSTINA*)*

Attwood, Thomas (*b* London, bap. 23 Nov 1765; *d* London, 24 March 1838). English composer. The son of a coal merchant and musician in the King's Band, he was a chorister in the Chapel Royal and then a Page of the Presence to the Prince of Wales; he was later sent by his patron to study in Europe, with Felipe Cinque and Gaetano Latilla in Naples, 1783–5, and then with Mozart in Vienna from August 1785 until February 1787. Kelly's account of Mozart's view of Attwood is well known: 'Attwood is a young man for whom I have a sincere affection and esteem; he conducts himself with great propriety and I feel much pleasure in telling you, that he partakes more of my style than any scholar I ever had; and I predict, that he will prove a sound musician'. Attwood's studies with Mozart in harmony, counterpoint and freer styles of composition survive; they say a great deal about the young Attwood's ability as well as betraying the secrets of Mozart's teaching methods and sources (C. P. E. Bach, Rameau and Fux).

Attwood returned to England in the company of Kelly and the Storaces, and he soon received royal appointments, becoming music teacher to the Duchess of York (1791) and the Princess of Wales (1795), organist of St Paul's Cathedral and composer to the Chapel Royal (both 1796), Musician in Ordinary to the king (1825) and organist of the Chapel Royal (1836). In addition, he was one of the directors of the Chapel Royal, 1816–20 and 1824–32, and became one of the first professors at the Royal Academy of Music in 1823.

Although Attwood's career resulted in a large output of sacred music, particularly after 1800, he was one of London's most successful composers for the stage in the 1790s. He composed for all three London opera houses and worked with the leading librettists of his day. Most of his works are afterpieces consisting of songs and simpler types of ensemble which supplement the spoken dialogue of the play; such dramas did not allow for the more elaborate types of scena that he must have seen Mozart composing in the previous decade. But Mozart was close to the centre of Attwood's operatic activity: in two of his earlier collaborations with the librettist John Rose, *The Prisoner* (1792) and *Caernarvon Castle* (1793), Attwood included pieces from *Le nozze di Figaro*, 'Non più andrai' and 'Sull'aria' respectively. *The Adopted Child* (1795) contains a song, 'In seclusion's sacred bower', that had formed part of Attwood's study with Mozart ten years before.

Attwood's contribution to these works ranges from responsibility for the complete music (e.g. *The Fairy Festival*, 1797) to the composition of one or two songs only (e.g. *Guy Mannering*, 1816). His most ambitious ensemble writing is found in the last scene of *The Castle of Sorrento*; in collaborative ventures, he seems to have been responsible for ensembles and finales rather than songs or simple choruses.

all first produced in London; published in vocal score in same year unless otherwise indicated; MSS of most librettos in US-SM, Larpent Collection

LCG – *Covent Garden* LDL – *Drury Lane*
LHM – *Theatre Royal, Haymarket*

The Prisoner (musical romance, 3, J. Rose, after J. M. Boutet de Monvel), LHM, 18 Oct 1792, finale by G. M. Giornovichi, incl. music by Mozart

Ozmyn and Daraxa (musical romance, 2, J. Boaden), LHM, 7 March 1793, incl. music by Mozart and Giornovichi, only songs and choruses pubd
The Mariners (musical entertainment, 2, S. Birch), LHM, 10 May 1793, incl. music by T. Shaw, J. P. A. Martini, B. Ferrari, Mozart, 'Miss Bannister' and Dittersdorf
Caernarvon Castle, or The Birth of the Prince of Wales (entertainment, 2, Rose), LHM, 12 Aug 1793, incl. music by Mozart
The Packet Boat, or A Peep behind the Veil (musical farce, 2, Birch), LCG, 13 May 1794, unpubd
The Adopted Child (musical farce, 2, Birch), LDL, 1 May 1795
The Poor Sailor, or Little Ben and Little Bob (musical drama, 2, J. Bernard), LCG, 29 May 1795
The Smugglers (musical drama, 2, Birch), LDL, 13 April 1796, incl. music by R. Suett and J. G. Distler
The Fairy Festival (masque, 1, Rose), LDL, 13 May 1797, only 4 songs pubd
The Irish Tar, or Which is the Girl? (musical piece, 1, W. C. Oulton), LHM, 24 Aug 1797, unpubd
Fast Asleep (farce, 2, Birch, after J. Powell), LDL, 28 Oct 1797, only 2 songs pubd
Britain's Brave Tars!! or All for St Paul's (musical farce, 1, J. O'Keeffe), LCG, 19 Dec 1797, only 1 song pubd
The Devil of a Lover (musical farce, 2, G. Moultrie), LCG, 17 March 1798, unpubd
Reform'd in Time (comic op, 2, H. Heartwell), LCG, 23 May 1798, unpubd
A Day at Rome (musical farce, 2, C. Smith), LCG, 17 Oct 1798, unpubd
The Mouth of the Nile, or The Glorious First of August (musical entertainment, 1, T. J. Dibdin), LCG, 25 Oct 1798, incl. music by Dibdin and J. Mazzinghi
Albert and Adelaide, or The Victim of Constancy (grand heroic romance, 3, Birch, after B. J. Marsollier and Boutet de Monvel), LCG, 11 Dec 1798, pf score of ov. (Paris, n.d.), collab. D. Steibelt, incl. music by Cherubini
The Magic Oak, or Harlequin Woodcutter (pantomime, 2, Dibdin), LCG, 29 Jan 1799, collab. F. Attwood
The Old Clothesman (comic op, 3, T. Holcroft), LCG, 2 April 1799, ov. by ?W. Parke
The Castle of Sorrento (comic op, 2, Heartwell and G. Colman (ii), after A. V. P. Duval), LHM, 13 July 1799, incl. music by Paisiello
The Red Cross Knights (play, 5, J. G. Holman, after F. von Schiller), LHM, 21 Aug 1799, incl. music by S. Arnold, J. W. Calcott and Mozart
True Friends (musical farce, 2, Dibdin), LCG, 19 Feb 1800
St David's Day (musical piece, 2, Dibdin), LCG, 25 March 1800
The Hermione, or Valour's Triumph (musical piece, 1, Dibdin), LCG, 5 April 1800, unpubd
Il Bondocani, or The Caliph Robber (serio-comic musical drama, 3, Dibdin), LCG, 15 Nov 1800, collab. J. Moorehead, incl. music by Mozart
Harlequin's Tour, or The Dominion of Fancy (pantomime, 1, Dibdin), LCG, 22 Dec 1800, collab. Moorehead
The Sea-Side Story (operatic drama, 2, W. Dimond), LCG, 12 May 1801, unpubd
The Escapes, or The Water Carrier (musical entertainment, 2, Holcroft, after J. N. Bouilly), LCG, 14 Oct 1801, incl. music by Cherubini
Adrian and Orilla, or A Mother's Vengeance (play, 5, Dimond), LCG, 15 Nov 1801, only 2 songs by Attwood pubd, collab. M. Kelly
The Curfew (farce, 5, J. Tobin), LDL, 19 Feb 1807, only 1 song pubd
Guy Mannering, or the Gipsey's Prophesy (musical play, 3, D. Terry, after W. Scott), LCG, 12 March 1816, collab. H. R. Bishop
Elphi Bey, or the Arab's Faith (musical drama, 3, R. Hamilton), LDL, 17 April 1817, only 3 songs by Attwood pubd, collab. C. E. Horn and H. Smart, incl. music by Mozart
David Rizzio (serious op, 3, Hamilton), LDL, 17 June 1820, only 1 song by Attwood pubd, collab. J. Braham, T. S. Cooke and W. Reeve
The Hebrew Family, or A Traveller's Adventures (play, 3), LCG, 8 April 1825, collab. P. Cianchettini, J. Whitaker and J. Watson

*

LS; *NicollH*
M. Kelly: *Reminiscences of the King's Theatre* (London, 1826, 2/1826); ed. R. Fiske (London, 1975), 116
Obituaries: *Musical World*, viii (1838), 220–21, 227–8
D. Baptie: *Sketches of the English Glee Composers* (London, 1895)
C. B. Oldman: 'Thomas Attwood, 1765–1838', *MT*, cvi (1965), 844–5
——: 'Attwood's Dramatic Works', *MT*, cvii (1966), 23–7

MARK EVERIST

Atys (i) ('Attis'). *Tragédie en musique* in a prologue and five acts by Jean-Baptiste (*see* LULLY family, (1)) to a libretto by PHILIPPE QUINAULT after OVID's *Fasti*; St Germain-en-Laye, court, 10 January 1676.

PROLOGUE

Le Temps [Time] *God of Time*	baritone
Flore [Flora] *a goddess*	soprano
Melpomène [Melpomene] *the tragic Muse*	soprano
Iris *a goddess*	soprano
A Zephyr	haute-contre
Hercule [Hercules], Antée [Antaeus], Etheocle [Eteocles], Polinice [Polynices], Castor, Pollux	dancers

TRAGEDY

Atys [Attis] *relative of Sangaride and favourite of Celaenus*	haute-contre
Sangaride *nymph, daughter of the River Sangarius*	soprano
Cybèle [Cybele] *a goddess*	soprano
Celenus [Celaenus] *King of Phrygia and son of Neptune, in love with Sangaride*	baritone
Idas *friend of Attis and brother of Doris*	bass
Doris *nymph, friend of Sangaride, sister of Idas*	soprano
Mélisse *confidante and priestess of Cybele*	soprano
Le Sommeil [Sleep] *God of Sleep*	haute-contre
Morphée [Morpheus] } *sons of sleep*	haute-contre
Phobétor } *sons of sleep*	bass
Phantase } *sons of sleep*	tenor
The God of the River Sangar [Sangarius] *father of Sangaride*	bass
Alecton [Alecto] *a Fury*	silent role

The Hours of the Day and Night, nymphs who follow Flora, four little zephyrs, heroes who follow Melpomene; Phrygians; followers of Celaenus, zephyrs, people attending the celebration of Cybele; Pleasant Dreams, Baleful Dreams; gods of the rivers and brooks, nymphs of the springs; gods of the woods and waters, Corybantes

Setting Ancient Phrygia

Lully's fourth tragedy was known as 'the king's opera', according to Le Cerf de la Viéville (who gave no explanation). Voltaire (*Le siècle de Louis XIV*, 1751) singled out *Atys*, along with *Armide*, to exemplify Quinault's mastery of the genre. 20th-century scholars have often cited *Atys* as marking the start of a style period, primarily for its avoidance of subplots and comic interludes in the Venetian manner, along with its 'Racinian serenity' (Lionel de La Laurencie's phrase).

Principal singers at the première included Baumavielle (Time), Verdier (Flora), Beaucreux (Melpomene), Cledière (Attis), Morel (Idas), Aubry (Sangaride), Brigogne (Doris), Saint Christophle (Cybele) and Gaye (Celaenus); principal dancers (all male) were Beauchamp, Dolivet, Faure, Favier, Lestang, Magny and Pécour. Additional productions at St Germain took place in 1677, 1678 and 1682; Lully wrote

'Atys' (Lully), Act 5 (Attis is transformed into a pine tree by Cybele): engraving by Lalouette after F. Chauveau's drawing of Berain and Vigarani's designs (probably for the original production at St Germain-en-Laye, 10 January 1676), from the first edition of the libretto (1676)

supplementary dances for the 1682 production, and courtiers danced alongside the professional dancers. The public première was at the Paris Opéra in April (not August) 1676; there were seven Opéra revivals between 1689 and 1747 and a production (without the prologue) at Louis XV's court at Fontainebleau in 1753. In the Paris production of 1738 the final *divertissement* was suppressed; it 'had always seemed superfluous, after such a sad catastrophe' (C. and F. Parfaict, 1741). Between 1687 and 1749 *Atys* was produced in Amsterdam, Marseilles, Lyons, Rouen, Brussels, Metz, Lille and The Hague. A highly successful modern production was directed by William Christie in Paris and elsewhere from 1987 and recorded.

PROLOGUE *Time's palace* Time and the chorus of Hours of the Day and Night praise a glorious 'hero' (Louis XIV). During a *menuet en rondeau* danced by flower-bearing nymphs, the goddess Flora enters, led by a dancing zephyr. Flora has come in winter to avoid missing her hero, for Glory will surely call him to war in the spring. Flora's celebrations are interrupted by the arrival of the tragic muse Melpomene, whose followers – Hercules, Antaeus and other heroes – enact their battles in a pantomime ballet. The goddess Iris, acting on Cybele's command, arrives to unite nature (Flora) and art (Melpomene) for the drama to follow. All celebrate.

ACT 1 *A mountain consecrated to Cybele* The tragedy appears to begin with a brief monologue *air* for Attis, prefigured by its *ritournelle*, but as more characters gradually join him the *air* turns out to have been the first statement of a varied refrain: 'Allons, allons, accourez tous / Cybèle va descendre'. While they await the arrival of the goddess Cybele, Attis admits privately to Idas that he has been wounded by love, but tells Sangaride, whom he congratulates on her impending marriage, that he is indifferent to love. The modulatory phrase that announces the next segment of the act begins in the continuo alone but ends with a strong vocal cadence: 'Atys est trop heureux!'. Alone with Doris, Sangaride confides that she loves Attis rather than her fiancé Celaenus and that she envies Attis his indifference. 'Atys est trop heureux!', the introductory remark, is later expanded into a brief lament over a descending tetrachord ostinato. The next change of key marks Attis's return. In a much praised recitative scene he and Sangaride gradually reveal their love to each other. They hide their feelings as the Phrygians gather to honour Cybele's arrival (*divertissement*). The goddess's spectacular descent in her chariot, the climax of the act, is followed by the *air* and chorus 'Vous devez vous animer d'une ardeur nouvelle', over an intermittent ground bass. (This chorus became the basis for an English dance form of the period 1690 to 1710, called the 'Cibell'.)

ACT 2 *Cybele's temple* Celaenus begs Attis for reassurances of Sangaride's love; Attis responds that, as Celaenus's wife, Sangaride will follow duty and glory. Their dialogue culminates in a pair of adjacent *airs*, contrasting the joy of indifference with the torment of love.

Cybele, alone with Celaenus, tells him that she has chosen Attis to be her great Sacrificer. Alone with Melisse, Cybele admits that she loves Attis. Flying zephyrs appear in dazzling glory; zephyrs and people from different nations pay homage to the new Sacrificer (*divertissement*).

ACT 3 *The palace of the great Sacrificer of Cybele* Attis, alone and troubled, is approached by Idas and Doris, who warn him that Sangaride intends to declare the truth to Cybele. Attis is torn between loyalty to Celaenus and his own desires. Left alone, he grows drowsy; Cybele has asked the god of Sleep to announce her love in a dream. This famous *divertissement*, the 'sommeil' scene, is an elaborate structure composed of a hypnotic passage for recorders and strings; solos and ensembles for Sleep and his sons ('Dormons tous'); dances for the Pleasant Dreams, who demonstrate Cybele's love to the sleeping Attis; and dances for the Baleful Dreams, who demonstrate, in jagged rhythms, the danger of resisting the goddess's love. An all-male chorus of Baleful Dreams hammers home a warning in insistent repeated chords. After a final dance, Attis awakes in fright; Cybele is there, asking for his love. When Sangaride enters and begs to be released from her engagement to Celaenus, Attis prevents her from announcing their love for each other. Cybele, however, senses a problem (monologue *air*, 'Espoir si cher et si doux').

ACT 4 *The palace of the River Sangarius* Having misunderstood Attis's motives, Sangaride confides to Doris and Idas that Attis no longer loves her – the scene culminates in a painfully sweet trio – then promises herself to Celaenus. Sangaride and Attis then accuse each other of infidelity but eventually reaffirm their love. The god of the River Sangarius presents Celaenus to the water divinities, who approve his choice of husband for his daughter and celebrate with him; the *divertissement* is a series of exuberant dance-songs. However, the Sacrificer Attis – acting in Cybele's name – refuses to approve the marriage. The zephyrs carry Attis and Sangaride away as the chorus protests.

ACT 5 *A pleasant garden* Cybele and Celaenus angrily confront Attis and Sangaride, their conversation consisting entirely of alternating duet fragments. Cybele calls on the Fury Alecto. During a brief *prélude* characterized by running semiquavers and dotted rhythms, Alecto arrives from the underworld and waves a torch over Attis's head, rendering him insane. As Phrygians and Cybele's priestesses watch in horror, Attis mistakes Sangaride for a monster; he chases and kills her (the murder occurs offstage and is reported by Celaenus). Cybele ends Attis's insanity so that he might know what he has done. A choral refrain, 'Atys lui-même fait périr ce qu'il aime!', unifies the mad scene and its aftermath. As Cybele, alone with Mélisse, regrets the severity of the punishment, Attis enters: he has stabbed himself and is dying. Cybele transforms him into a pine tree that she will love for ever. The final *divertissement* is a scene of mourning; the gentle weeping of the nymphs is juxtaposed with the frenzy of the Corybantes.

* * *

Atys combines the brilliant use of spectacle and intricately structured *divertissements* in Lully's earlier operas with more subtly structured recitative dialogues and a new seriousness of dramatic content. Burlesque scenes and subplots are absent for the first time and do not return in subsequent operas. Inward conflict, a prominent feature of the late tragedies *Roland* and *Armide* but virtually absent from most of Quinault's other librettos, is present here. Although *Atys* is not Lully's only opera to end sorrowfully, it is the only one to conclude with unmitigated tragedy.

For an illustration of Act 3, *see* PRODUCTION, fig.5; *see also* COSTUME, fig.4*a*.

LOIS ROSOW

***Atys* (ii)** ('Attis'). *Tragédie lyrique* in three acts by Niccolò Piccinni (*see* PICCINNI family, (1)) to a libretto by JEAN FRANÇOIS MARMONTEL after PHILIPPE QUINAULT; Paris, Opéra, 22 February 1780.

Marmontel's libretto follows Quinault's (set by Lully, 1676) except for the tragic end. In this later version, Cybele (soprano) does not transform Attis (alto) into a pine tree; rather, the opera ends with the suicide of Attis and choral mourning. Marmontel also omitted the Prologue and the divertissements, limited the accessory singing roles to two companions, Idas (alto) and Doris (soprano), added aria texts and regularized some recitative verses. At the 1783 revival in Paris, which was more successful than the première, a happy ending was substituted.

Piccinni's music is remarkable for its startling effects, unexpected dynamic shifts and striking textures. This is evident at the beginning of the overture: a quiet semibreve chord in the strings is joined halfway through the bar by the winds, *forte*; the entire orchestra makes a crescendo, followed by a *piano* and a bar of sighing figures marked *smorzando*. This figure is repeated several times in the course of the overture, and crescendos followed by *piano* are a regular feature of the opera. Piccinni modulates with unusual frequency to remote keys such as F♯ major and E♭ minor; in the middle of Sangaride's aria 'Est-il un destin plus cruel' there is a remarkable progression around the circle of fifths from B♭ minor to G minor. B♭ minor is also the key of the middle section of Sangaride's 'Malheureuse, hélas'. The arias range from simple, song-like utterances as in Attis's 'L'amour fait verser trop de pleurs' (1.iii) to elaborate, italianate virtuoso numbers as in Cybele's 'Tremblez, ingrats, de me trahir' (2.v). The chorus plays a relatively small but impressive role.

Atys was the third of Piccinni's nine serious operas for Paris, and the second based on a drama by Quinault. It was performed over 60 times in Paris until 1792, and productions were also given in Copenhagen, Stockholm and St Petersburg.

For an illustration of the Stockholm production, *see* TRAGÉDIE EN MUSIQUE, fig.4.

MARY HUNTER

Auber, Daniel-François-Esprit (*b* Caen, 29 Jan 1782; *d* Paris, 12 May 1871). French composer, principally of *opéras comiques*, and the foremost representative of this genre in 19th-century France.

1. Early life and works. 2. Collaboration with Scribe. 3. Style and influence.

1. EARLY LIFE AND WORKS. Auber studied the piano with Ignace Antoine Ladurner, and he also learned to play the violin. Among his earliest compositions were several *romances*, at least one string quartet, a piano trio and a concerto for violin, viola, cello and piano. At first he intended to go into his father's business (dealing in art materials), and after the Peace of Amiens in 1802 he went to London to study commerce and learn English. He seems to have had some success in London as a performer and as a composer of *romances* and quartets,

but the outbreak of war between France and England in 1803 brought him back to Paris.

His first stage work, *Julie*, was composed in 1805 for an amateur society that met in the Salle Doyen. Here Auber met the artist Ingres (they remained friends until the latter's death in 1867). At the same time Auber began taking private lessons from Cherubini, with whom he studied composition for three years; he subsequently composed a fugue on a theme from Cherubini's *Faniska*. During this period Auber spent several months every year at the Belgian chateau of the Count of Caraman and Prince of Chimay, who was an active member of a theatrical group. Auber composed a mass for the chapel of this chateau; the theme of the Prière in *La muette de Portici* is taken from its Agnus Dei. In 1812 he wrote his second opera, *Jean de Couvain*, for the theatrical group. That year, encouraged by his parents and by Cherubini, Auber decided to compose a one-act opera, *Le séjour militaire*, for the Salle Feydeau, but the work was not very successful. For the next seven years, until his father's death, he led a carefree life. His decision to devote himself seriously to opera composition arose from the bankruptcy of his father, which forced Auber to provide for his family.

His next opera, *Le testament et les billets doux*, to a libretto by François-Antoine-Eugène de Planard, was staged on 18 September 1819. It was dropped from the repertory after only a few performances, but Auber achieved success with *La bergère châtelaine* (1820) and *Emma* (1821), both to librettos by Planard; they were also successful in their first performances in Germany.

2. Collaboration with Scribe. At this time he entered upon what soon became a very close collaboration with Eugène Scribe. With five *opéras comiques* and the *drame lyrique Léocadie*, Scribe and Auber became the leading exponents of *opéra comique* in France, enjoying success too in the German-speaking states, Denmark and (though only with *Le maçon*) England – reflected in the numbers of translations of the librettos and piano arrangements of the scores.

As early as 1825 Delavigne wrote a libretto for a three-act opera on a revolutionary theme entitled *Masaniello, ou La muette de Portici*. The idea of an entirely new type of libretto, conceived by Scribe only after the completion of this three-act version, and the censor's insistence on alterations, meant that much of the original revolutionary content was subsequently removed, and with it the logical motivation for the dramatic action of the main characters and the chorus. But the result was a new operatic genre, Grand opéra. The work was first performed on 29 February 1828. Despite its inconsistencies of plot, the opera was regarded as politically revolutionary, and the collaboration of the director Solomé and the designer Ciceri provided it with magnificent scenery and sensational stage effects. Its connection with the Belgian revolution of 22 August 1830 made it a general symbol of revolutionary ideas, and Auber's music played an important part. Wagner regarded it as 'something quite new' because of its 'unusual concision and drastic concentration of form'. Besides being the first grand opera, *La muette de Portici* was one of the great operatic successes of the 19th century. By 1882 it had had 505 performances in Paris, and it was performed in translated versions throughout Europe. Auber consolidated his international reputation with *La fiancée* and *Fra Diavolo*; the latter is still frequently revived, especially in Germany.

From the 1820s until 1840 he wrote at least one new opera a year, mostly *opéras comiques*, but he also composed more serious works for the Paris Opéra: *Le dieu et la bayadère*, *Le philtre*, *Le serment*, *Le cheval de bronze*, the 'grand historical opera' *Gustave III* and *Le lac des fées*. According to Véron, *Gustave III* originally failed in Paris because of the unfortunate design of costumes and sets in the Louis XV style, which were a hindrance to the singers in their attempts to express passionate feeling.

As the extant correspondence between Auber and Scribe shows, their conception of characters and musical numbers in their comic operas depended a good deal on the performers available to them, and was not determined solely by aesthetic criteria. Scribe's letter of 25 August 1843 describes the casting of *La sirène*:

> I have managed to arrange for Roger to play the lead. This will mean a good deal of work for me, but none for you, because – and this is what made the problem difficult to solve – I have not changed anything affecting the music, except in the finale of the first act which you have not written.
>
> When I wrote the part for Chollet, having no alternative, I was very uneasy about it. Though he can still be good in big parts which are not naturalistic, Chollet is terrible when verisimilitude, animation and above all interest are required. It is impossible for him to be interesting, but now, with Roger, I shall have animation, interest and comedy. Moreover, I have placed the little aria of which you gave me the rough sketch for Mlle Lavoye, and I may add a little smuggler's song for Roger, which will not detract from his second-act aria.
>
> We still have to cast our lover, who in any case would always have been a secondary role. See if young Giraud, whom you introduced to me and of whom you had great hopes, could sing and act the part. That would be a fine thing, since with Giraud, Roger and Mlle Lavoye we should instantly have a new, young cast for our piece, something unusual at the Opéra-Comique, and almost a guarantee of success. What's more – and keep him up to this – Crosnier [director of the Opéra-Comique] has promised me that Mlle Lavoye will not appear in any other new piece before ours.

Scribe's reference to a rough sketch (*monstre*) denotes a procedure known to have been employed in French opera since its early days, and Scribe and Auber frequently adopted it. Auber often composed solo arias before he received Scribe's verses; next the composer gave his librettist a 'rough sketch' with the metre and sometimes certain key words, and Scribe would use this sketch to write the text to be sung.

Rossini had taken the opera-going public by storm with the Paris première of *Il barbiere di Siviglia* on 26 October 1819. In his early comic operas Auber was accused of falling under Rossini's influence, not only in the coloratura passages of his arias, but also in the number of ensembles, many more than in the works of his predecessors and having considerable dramatic and musical weight. But he soon developed his own style, which was regarded throughout Europe as typically French and typically Parisian.

3. Style and influence. In Auber's *opéras comiques*, the introductions to the first acts are generally comparable in importance to the finales. As a rule, the climax is reached at the latest with the finale of the second act, in a manner similar to Verdi's. Only in *Fra Diavolo* is the climax delayed until the finale of the third act, as in Auber's grand operas. In the important and more serious works of his middle creative period (*L'ambassadrice*, 1836; *Le domino noir*, 1837; *Les diamants de la couronne*, 1841; *La part du diable*, 1843; and *Haydée*, 1847) the solo arias gain in individuality,

musical expressiveness and harmonic depth, influenced by the *drame lyrique*. On the whole, however, the ensemble is also pre-eminent in these works. The first-act, or more rarely the second-act, finale is the richest in action and musical content. In these mature works and in his last creative period Auber usually opens the first act with an aria (only *Le premier jour de bonheur*, 1868, and *Rêve d'amour*, 1869, begin with introductions).

The belief that Auber's last comic operas are sterile and unimaginative is refuted by the great variety of arias they contain and their individuality of form. In *L'enfant prodigue* (1850) he broke new ground yet again by his exoticism and the biblical plot, a model in some respects for Gounod and Félicien David, in a manner which, naturally enough, was in contrast to the ideas of Berlioz. At the age of 86, only three years before his death and at a time when the repertory in Paris was dominated by Offenbach's *opéras bouffes* and the operas of Verdi, Auber had another great success in France and Germany with *Le premier jour de bonheur*.

Unlike many of his Romantic contemporaries, Auber did not seem to have any lofty sense of mission. He was inclined to express himself ironically. Throughout his career he introduced into his operas easily accessible melodies that lodged in the memory after a single hearing and became popular in all classes of society. In this he was following a typically French tradition, dating back to the *airs de vaudeville* Lully used in his *tragédies*. Besides the various types of aria, Auber made use of such vocal genres as the *couplet*, barcarolle, ballade, nocturne, rondeau, chanson, *valse chantée*, bolero, galop and *mélodie*, both as solo numbers and within the ensembles. They made him one of the most popular, successful and influential composers of his time, particularly during the 1830s and 40s. The music for Fenella's pantomime in *La muette de Portici* is as masterly as that for most of his ballets and ball scenes. The galop in his *Gustave III* stimulated a fashion all over Europe.

Although Auber lived in Paris almost uninterruptedly, the popularity of his operas led to a flood of publication of his works throughout Europe and in America. Editions of the individual opera librettos and piano arrangements were printed in immense quantities, and particularly successful numbers gave rise to more than 400 transcriptions and free instrumental arrangements – sonatinas, fantasias, potpourris and *mélanges* – ranging from the piano to military bands and salon orchestras. The overtures of most of his operas were among the most popular items played at concerts, as well as in salons and private homes. Auber's historical significance is comparable to that of Rossini, although his operas have not endured in the repertory. Berlioz was among his sternest critics in France, while the hostile attitudes of Schumann and Mendelssohn in Germany were in marked contrast to the enthusiastic views of Wagner.

See also DOMINO NOIR, LE; FRA DIAVOLO; GUSTAVE III; LAC DES FÉES, LE; MANON LESCAUT (i); and MUETTE DE PORTICI, LA.

unless otherwise stated, works were first performed in Paris and published in Paris in the year of first performance

Julie [L'erreur d'un moment] (comédie, 1, J.-M. Boutet de Monvel), Salle Doyen, 1805, unpubd

Jean de Couvain [Le château de Couvain] (oc, 3, N. Lemercier), Belgium, Château de Chimay, Sept 1812, unpubd

Le séjour militaire (oc, 1, J.-N. Bouilly and E. Mercier-Dupaty), OC (Feydeau), 27 Feb 1813

Le testament et les billets doux (comédie mêlée de chant, 1, F.-A.-E. de Planard), OC (Feydeau), 18 Sept 1819

La bergère châtelaine (oc, 3, Planard), OC (Feydeau), 27 Jan 1820

Emma, ou La promesse imprudente (oc, 3, Planard), OC (Feydeau), 7 July 1821

Leicester, ou Le château de Kenilworth (oc, 3, E. Scribe and Mélesville [A.-H.-J. Duveyrier], after W. Scott: *Kenilworth*), OC (Feydeau), 25 Jan 1823

La neige, ou Le nouvel Eginard (oc, 4, Scribe and G. Delavigne), OC (Feydeau), 9 Oct 1823

Vendôme en Espagne (drame lyrique, 1, A.-J.-S. d'Empis and E. Mennechet), Opéra, 5 Dec 1823, collab. Hérold

Les trois genres (scène lyrique, Scribe, Dupaty and M. Pichat), Odéon, 27 April 1824, collab. A. Boieldieu

Le concert à la cour, ou La débutante (oc, 1, Scribe and Mélesville), OC (Feydeau), 5 May 1824

Léocadie (drame lyrique, 3, Scribe and Mélesville, after M. de Cervantes: *La fuerza de la sangre*), OC (Feydeau), 4 Nov 1824

Le maçon (oc, 3, Scribe and Delavigne), OC (Feydeau), 3 May 1825

Le timide, ou Le nouveau séducteur (oc, 3, Scribe and Saintine [X. Boniface]), OC (Feydeau), 2 June 1826

Fiorella (oc, 3, Scribe), OC (Feydeau), 28 Nov 1826

La muette de Portici [Masaniello] (opéra, 5, Scribe and Delavigne), Opéra, 29 Feb 1828

La fiancée (oc, 3, Scribe), OC (Feydeau), 10 Jan 1829

Fra Diavolo, ou L'hôtellerie de Terracine (oc, 3, Scribe), OC (Ventadour), 28 Jan 1830

Le dieu et la bayadère, ou La courtisane amoureuse (opéra, 2, Scribe), Opéra, 13 Oct 1830

Le philtre (opéra, 2, Scribe), Opéra, 15 June 1831

La marquise de Brinvilliers (drame lyrique, 3, Scribe and Castil-Blaze [F.-H.-J. Blaze]), OC (Ventadour), 31 Oct 1831, collab. Batton, H.-M. Berton, Blangini, A. Boieldieu, Carafa, Cherubini, Hérold and Paer

Le serment, ou Les faux-monnoyeurs (opéra, 3, Scribe and E.-J.-E. Mazères), Opéra, 1 Oct 1832

Gustave III, ou Le bal masqué (opéra historique, 5, Scribe), Opéra, 27 Feb 1833

Lestocq, ou L'intrigue et l'amour (oc, 4, Scribe), OC (Bourse), 24 May 1834

Le cheval de bronze (opéra-féerie, 3, Scribe), Opéra, 28 March 1835; rev. as opéra-ballet, Opéra, 21 Sept 1857

Actéon (oc, 1, Scribe), OC (Bourse), 23 Jan 1836

Les chaperons blancs (oc, 3, Scribe), OC (Bourse), 26 March 1836

L'ambassadrice (oc, 3, Scribe), OC (Bourse), 21 Dec 1836

La fête de Versailles (intermède, Scribe), Versailles, 10 June 1837

Le domino noir (oc, 3, Scribe), OC (Bourse), 2 Dec 1837

Le lac des fées (opéra, 5, Scribe and Mélesville), Opéra, 1 April 1839

Zanetta, ou Jouer avec le feu (oc, 3, Scribe and J.-H. Vernoy de Saint-Georges), OC (Favart), 18 May 1840

Les diamants de la couronne (oc, 3, Scribe and Saint-Georges), OC (Favart), 6 March 1841

Le duc d'Olonne (oc, 3, Scribe and Saintine), OC (Favart), 4 Feb 1842

La part du diable (oc, 3, Scribe), OC (Favart), 16 Jan 1843

La sirène (oc, 3, Scribe), OC (Favart), 26 March 1844

La barcarolle, ou L'amour de la musique (oc, 3, Scribe), OC (Favart), 22 April 1845

Les premiers pas (scène-prologue, A. Royer and G. Vaez), Opéra-National, 15 Nov 1847, collab. A. Adam, Carafa, Halévy

Haydée, ou Le secret (oc, 3, Scribe, after P. Mérimée: *Six et quatre*), OC (Favart), 28 Dec 1847

L'enfant prodigue (opéra, 5, Scribe), Opéra, 6 Dec 1850

Zerline, ou La corbeille d'oranges (opéra, 3, Scribe), Opéra, 16 May 1851

Marco Spada (oc, 3, Scribe and Delavigne), OC (Favart), 21 Dec 1852; rev. as Marco Spada, ou La fille du bandit (ballet, J. Mazilier), Opéra, 1 April 1857

Jenny Bell (oc, 3, Scribe), OC (Favart), 2 June 1855

Manon Lescaut (oc, 3, Scribe, after A.-F. Prévost), OC (Favart), 23 Feb 1856

La circassienne (oc, 3, Scribe), OC (Favart), 2 Feb 1861

La fiancée du Roi de Garbe (oc, 3, Scribe and Saint-Georges), OC (Favart), 11 Jan 1864

Le premier jour de bonheur (oc, 3, A.-P. Dennery and E. Cormon), OC (Favart), 15 Feb 1868

Rêve d'amour (oc, 3, Dennery and Cormon), OC (Favart), 20 Dec 1869

*

X. Eyma and A. de Lucy: *Auber* (Paris, 1841)

L. de Loménie: *Auber* (Paris, 1842)

L. Véron: *Mémoires d'un bourgeois de Paris*, iii (Paris, 1854)

E. de Mirécourt: *Auber* (Paris, 1857)

B. Jouvin: *Auber: sa vie et ses oeuvres* (Paris, 1864)
E. Hanslick: *Geschichte des Concertwesens in Wien* (Vienna, 1869) [incl. 'Ein Besuch bei Auber', ii, 479–82, and 'Auber', ii, 530–34]
R. Wagner: 'Erinnerungen an Auber', *Gesammelte Schriften und Dichtungen* (Leipzig, 1871–3), ix (1873), 51–73; Eng. trans. (London, 1893–1900), v, 35–55
V. Massé: *Notice sur la vie et les travaux de D. F. E. Auber* (Paris, 1873)
A. Pougin: *Auber: ses commencements, les origines de sa carrière* (Paris, 1873)
J. Carlez: *L'oeuvre d'Auber* (Caen, 1874)
E. Hanslick: 'Auber', *Die moderne Oper* (Berlin, 1875), 123–37
H. Blaze de Bury: 'Scribe et Auber', *Revue des deux mondes*, xxxv (1879), 43–75
A. Kohut: *Auber* (Leipzig, 1895)
L. Douriac: *La psychologie dans l'opéra français* (Paris, 1897)
E. Prout: 'Auber's Le philtre and Donizetti's L'elisire d'amore: a comparison', *MMR*, xxx (1900), 25–7, 49–53, 73–6
J. Chantavoine: 'Quelques lettres inédites d'Auber', *RHCM*, iii (1903), 161ff
C. Malherbe: *Auber* (Paris, 1911)
H. Grierson: 'My Visit to Auber', *English Review*, xviii (1914), 173–86
J. Tiersot: 'Auber', *ReM*, no. 140 (1933), 265–78
A. B. Benson: 'Gustavus III in the Librettos of Foreign Operas', *Scandinavian Studies Presented to George T. Flom* (Urbana, IL, 1942), 92–105
A. Ringer: 'Fra Diavolo', *MQ*, xxxviii (1952), 642–4
R. Longyear: *D. F. E. Auber: a Chapter in French Opéra Comique, 1800–1870* (diss., Cornell U., 1957)
——: 'La muette de Portici', *MR*, xix (1958), 37–46
F. D'Amico: 'Il Ballo in maschera prima di Verdi', *Bollettino quadrimestrale dell'Istituto di Studi Verdiani*, i (1960), 1251–328
W. Börner: *Die Opern von Daniel-François-Esprit Auber* (diss., Leipzig U., 1962)
R. Longyear: 'Le livret bien fait: the Opéra Comique Librettos of Eugène Scribe', *Southern Quarterly*, i (1962–3), 169–92
C. Casini: 'Tre Manon', *Chigiana*, xxviii (1973), 171–217
K. Pendle: 'Scribe, Auber and the Count of Monte Cristo', *MR*, xxxiv (1973), 210–20
——: *Eugène Scribe and the French Opera of the Nineteenth Century* (Ann Arbor, 1979)
S. Slatin: 'Opera and Revolution: *La muette de Portici* and the Belgian Revolution of 1830 Revisited', *Journal of Musicological Research*, iii (1979), 45–62
Auber et l'opéra romantique (Paris, 1982) [exhibition catalogue]
L. Finscher: 'Aubers La muette de Portici und die Anfänge der Grand opéra', *Festschrift Heinz Becker* (Laaber, 1982), 87–105
A. Gier: '*Manon Lescaut* als Fabel von der Grille und der Ameise: D. F. E. Auber (1856)', *JbO*, i (1985), 73–89
J. Mongrédien: 'Variations sur un thème, Masaniello: du héros de l'histoire à celui de "La Muette de Portici"', *JbO*, i (1985), 90–121
D. Kämper and P.-E. Knabe: 'Un requiem pour Manon', *Les écrivains français et l'Opéra*, ed. J.-P. Capdevielle and P.-E. Knabe (Cologne, 1986), 185–95
D. Rieger: '*La Muette de Portici* von Auber/Scribe: eine Revolutionsoper mit antirevolutionärem Libretto', *Romanistische Zeitschrift für Literaturgeschichte*, x (1986), 349–59
J. Fulcher: *The Nation's Image: French Grand Opera as Politics and Politicized Art* (Cambridge, 1987)
H. Schneider: 'Die Barkarole und Venedig', *L'opera tra Venezia e Parigi*, ed. M. T. Muraro (Florence, 1988), 11–56
H. R. Cohen, ed.: *The Original Staging Manuals for Twelve Parisian Operatic Premières* (Stuyvesant, NY, 1991) [incl. production books for *Fra Diavolo* and *La muette de Portici*]
A. Gerhard: *Die Verstäderung der Oper* (Stuttgart, 1992)
P. Vendrix, ed.: *Grétry et l'Europe de l'opéra-comique* (Liège, 1992)
H. Schneider and N. Wild: *La Muette de Portici. Kritische Ausgabe des Librettos und Dokumentation ihrer ersten Inszenierung* (Tübingen, in preparation)
H. Schneider: *Thematischer Katalog sämtlicher Werke von D. F. E. Auber* (in preparation)
——: 'Verdis Parlante und seine französischen Vorbilder', *Festschrift für A. A. Abert* (in preparation)

HERBERT SCHNEIDER

Aubert, Jacques [*le vieux, le père*] (*b* Paris, 30 Sept 1689; *d* Belleville, nr Paris, 17/18 May 1753). French composer. He had a varied early career as a dancing-master, violinist and composer, working at the Théâtres de la Foire before entering the service of the Prince of Condé, for whom he composed a *divertissement* and a ballet to entertain the infant Louis XV at Chantilly in 1722. He then joined the 24 Violons du Roi (1727–46), later becoming *premier violon* of the Opéra orchestra (1747). Parallel to these activities, he composed and performed works for the Concert Spirituel.

His early stage works are *opéras comiques* to texts by Lesage and d'Orneval, composed for the Théâtres de la Foire in the burlesque manner of the Regency. The music is simple and direct, without pretension. From 1716 Lesage and d'Orneval worked with the librettist Fuzelier, who invented the *ballet-héroïque* in 1723. In 1725 Fuzelier provided Aubert with the libretto for perhaps his most interesting stage work, *La reine des Péris*, which, in keeping with its more serious tone, was staged at the Opéra. Called a *comédie persane*, the work has a continuous plot and is fully sung. It is thus one of the earliest examples of French comic opera with sung dialogue. Fuzelier was fond of exotic plots (he also wrote the text for Rameau's *Les Indes galantes*), and was said to have researched his subjects thoroughly. Aubert's music has an italianate simplicity, but retains French poise and grace. It does not attempt exotic effects, but presents the dialogue with clarity and discrimination of sentiment. Its distinction is wholly European, as is the vein of feeling and of moralism which counterbalances the remote and fantastic world of the Persian imagery. The use of oriental mythology plausibly allowed sumptuous costumes, picturesque sets, spectacular scene changes and supernatural magic. The work was parodied by Lesage and d'Orneval (music in *F-Pn*), but was not itself revived; the brothers Parfaict recorded its lack of success with regret.

opéras comiques unless otherwise stated; printed works published in Paris

PSG – *Paris, Foire St Germain* PSL – *Paris, Foire St Laurent*

Arlequin gentilhomme malgré lui, ou L'amant supposé (3, A.-R. Lesage and d'Orneval), PSG, 3 Feb/27 March 1716; Act 3 perf. as Les arrêts de l'amour (1), PSG, 17 July 1716, airs in Le Théâtre de la foire, ii (1721)
Arlequin Hulla, ou La femme répudiée (1, Lesage and d'Orneval), PSL, 24 July 1716, airs in Le Théâtre de la foire, ii (1721)
Les animaux raisonnables (1, L. Fuzelier and M.-A. Legrand), PSG, 25/27 Feb 1718, collab. Gillier, airs in Le Théâtre de la foire, iii (1721)
Le regiment de la calotte (1, Fuzelier, Lesage and d'Orneval), PSL, 1 Sept 1721, airs in Le Théâtre de la foire, v (1724)
Fête royale (divertissement), Chantilly, Nov 1722; pubd (1722), see La Laurencie
Le ballet de 24 heures (comédie, prol., 4, Legrand), Chantilly, 5 Nov 1722; as op.6 (1723); music possibly known as Le ballet de Chantilly (1723)
La reine des Péris (comédie persane, prol., 5, Fuzelier), Paris, Opéra, 10 April 1725; as op.5 (1725)
Symphonie for T.-L. Bourgeois' Diane, 1721

*

Mercure de France (March 1725), 567–70; (April 1725), 787–800
F. Parfaict and C. Parfaict: *Histoire de l'Académie royale de musique* (MS, 1741, *F-Pn*), f.33
—— *Dictionnaire des théâtres de Paris* (Paris, 1756), iv, 408ff
L. de La Laurencie: *L'école française de violon de Lully à Viotti*, i (Paris, 1922), 203

PHILIP WELLER

Aubert, Louis(-François-Marie) (*b* Paramé, Ille-et-Vilaine, France, 19 Feb 1877; *d* Paris, 9 Jan 1968). French composer. Something of a child prodigy, Aubert sang under Fauré at the Madeleine, and as a boy treble took the solo part in the first performance of his Requiem. He entered the Paris Conservatoire in 1887 and became a pupil of Marmontel, Lavignac and Diémer and subsequently of Fauré whose style was the most decisive influence on his music. Aubert wrote songs and church music as well as several ballets and sets of incidental music but left only one opera, *La forêt bleue* (3, J. Chenevière, after C. Perrault). Aubert began the work in 1904; the second act was given in Paris in 1911 by the Société Musicale Indépendante and the whole opera was first performed in Geneva, 7 January 1913. It was not staged in Paris until 1924 when it was mounted at the Opéra-Comique (Salle Favart). Several times successfully revived, it is a fairy-tale opera with a happy ending and engagingly characterizes the Sleeping Beauty and her Prince Charming, as well as the Ogre, Little Red Riding-Hood, Tom Thumb and the other magical characters of Perrault's original.

*

J.-G. Prod'homme: 'Gustave Doret, Paul Ladmirault, Louis Aubert, Jacques Ibert', *Le théâtre lyrique en France* (Paris, 1937–9) [pubn of Poste National/Radio-Paris], iii, 172–81

L. Aubert: 'Propos impromptu', *Courrier musical de France*, xiv (1966)

M. Landowsky and G. Morançon: *Louis Aubert* (Paris, 1967)

RICHARD LANGHAM SMITH

Aubin, Tony (Louis Alexandre) (*b* Paris, 8 Dec 1907; *d* Paris, 21 Sept 1981). French composer. He studied at the Paris Conservatoire (1925–30) with Samuel-Rousseau, Noël Gallon and Dukas, winning the Prix de Rome in 1930. Having studied conducting with Gaubert (1934–5) he worked for French radio (1937–60), for whom he recorded *Ariane et Barbe-Bleue*. In 1945 he was appointed professor of composition at the Conservatoire and in 1969 he was elected to the Institut. His single opera *Goya*, to a libretto by R. Escholier and the composer, was written in two parts. The first part, dealing with the painter's more optimistic early work, was first performed in an ORTF concert under the title *La jeunesse de Goya*. The second part, in three tableaux, deals with the tragic events of Goya's later life. *Goya* was first staged by the Opéra de Lille on 28 November 1974. With its passionate, expressive vocal writing the work springs from the mainstream tradition of Grand Opera.

*

'Propos impromptu: Tony Aubin', *Courrier musical* (1968), no.23

PAUL GRIFFITHS, RICHARD LANGHAM SMITH

Aubry, Marie (*b c*1656; *d* Paris, 1704). French singer. She sang at a young age in the musical establishment of Philip, Duke of Orleans, and first appeared on stage in 1671 before the court at Versailles, as Diana in Sablières' *Les amours de Diane et d'Endymion*. Her performance impressed Robert Cambert, who cast her in the role of Phyllis in his pastoral *Les peines et les plaisirs de l'amour* (1671). In 1672 Lully recruited her for the Académie Royale de Musique. She created the leading roles of Aegle in *Thésée* (1675), Sangaride in *Atys* (1676), Io in *Isis* (1677), Philonoé in *Bellérophon* (1679) and Andromeda in *Persée* (1682), and sang the title role in *Proserpine* at the first Paris performance in November 1680. Mlle Fanchon Moreau, not Mlle Aubry as the Parfaict brothers claim (*Histoire de l'Académie Royale de Musique*, *F-Pn*), sang Oriane in Lully's *Amadis* (1684). Aubry retired from the Opéra in 1684, according to the Parfaicts 'not because of her age but because she had assumed such a prodigious size that she could not walk and that she appeared to be *toute ronde*'.

Aubry, as a former lover of Guichard, and her brother Sébastien were key witnesses in the sensational trial brought against Guichard by Lully. It was Aubry who first informed Lully that Guichard had asked her brother to murder him by mixing arsenic with his tobacco.

JAMES R. ANTHONY

Aucassin et Nicolette [*Aucassin et Nicolette, ou Les moeurs du bon vieux temps* ('Aucassin and Nicolette, or The Customs of the Good Old Days')]. *Comédie mise en musique* in four acts by ANDRÉ-ERNEST-MODESTE GRÉTRY to a libretto by MICHEL-JEAN SEDAINE after Jean-Baptiste de la Curne de Sainte-Palaye's fable *Les amours du bon vieux tems*; Versailles, 30 December 1779.

The troops of Bongars, Comte de Valence (bass), are besieging the chateau of the elderly Garins, Comte de Beaucaire (baritone/bass). Aucassin (tenor), Garins' son, is unwilling to defend his family since his father has forbidden him to marry the orphan Nicolette (soprano), but he finally goes off to fight the intruders on condition that he will be allowed to bid farewell to her after a victorious battle. When the Vicomte de Beaucaire (tenor) and Garins learn from Nicolette that she cannot reject Aucassin, she is imprisoned in the castle's tower. Aucassin returns victorious from the battle, but Garins refuses to fulfil the promise he made to him. In revenge, Aucassin sets his prisoners free and an enraged Garins orders his son to be thrown into the dungeon. Nicolette escapes from the prison tower while two sympathetic, humorous officers, Marcou (tenor) and Bredau (bass), look on. In vain she implores Aucassin to submit to his father's will before she flees. Aucassin, too, is freed by his father, who assumes that Nicolette will die in the surrounding woods. A shepherd (bass) helps Aucassin to find her. Meanwhile Bongars returns to the chateau declaring that Nicolette is his daughter: she had been abducted by the Beaucaire family, who were unaware of her identity. Aucassin and Nicolette meet in the final act, but she again fails to persuade him to give her up. The couple are ready to commit suicide as Garins, Bongars and their troops approach. After Nicolette's identity is revealed her marriage to Aucassin is announced.

Performed publicly at the Comédie-Italienne (Hôtel de Bourgogne) on 3 January 1780, Grétry's opera was reduced to three acts in 1782. Using new scenic effects, Sedaine adapted the conventional plot of the mysterious orphan rejected by her prospective father-in-law, and in a sensational scene Nicolette escapes from her prison tower by tying her sheets into a rope. Audiences would also have been excited by Aucassin's disobedience and his determination to commit suicide with Nicolette. Yet despite these dramatic climaxes, emotional relationships remain almost unchanged, reflecting the ideal of male moral steadfastness promoted in the original fable from the 13th century. Only Nicolette's emotions continually vary between resignation and love. Altogether ten arias are shared between six characters, weakening the impact of the main characters. The serious treatment of a medieval topic was ambitious, particularly since Grétry chose in places to employ a historical musical style to further the illusion: Charlton (*Grétry and the Growth of Opéra-Comique*, 1986) notes 'sequential 6–3 chords and non-directional harmony' as well as 'old-fashioned melody for gothic words'. These features are juxtaposed with modern traits such as an overture interspersed with cries by Garins, a quartet in which two people remain invisible and heroic war scenes richly scored for brass instruments.

MICHAEL FEND

Auden, W(ystan) H(ugh) (*b* York, 21 Feb 1907; *d* Vienna, 29 Sept 1973). English poet and librettist, later naturalized American. Of all the mid-century poets, Auden was the most actively concerned with music; the third part of his *Collected Poetry* (New York, 1945) consists of 38 'songs and other musical pieces', including arias from Britten's 'choral operetta' *Paul Bunyan* (1941). With Britten he collaborated on films, broadcasts, plays, the 'symphonic cycle' *Our Hunting Fathers* (1936) and cabaret songs. Then, in 1948, Auden declared himself an 'opera addict'; his friend CHESTER KALLMAN 'was the person who was responsible for arousing my interest in opera, about which previously, as you can see from *Paul Bunyan*, I knew little or nothing'. In that year Kallman and Auden collaborated on the libretto for Stravinsky's *The Rake's Progress*. In 1953 they published *Delia*, a delicate masque, written for Stravinsky, but unset. Thereafter for Henze they produced two librettos, *Elegy for Young Lovers* and *The Bassarids*, and for Nabokov adapted *Love's Labour's Lost*. Auden's (and Kallman's) last libretto, *The Entertainment of the Senses*, was an antimasque for insertion into the Gibbons-Locke *Cupid and Death* (1653, 1659). It was posted to its composer, John Gardner, a few days before Auden's death.

About half of *The Rake's Progress* and, by Auden, 'about 75%' of *Elegy* has been credited to Kallman – though, in a joint essay, the collaborators described themselves as a 'corporate personality'. Their theories about opera (among them, 'a good libretto plot is a melodrama in both the strict and the conventional sense of the word; it offers as many opportunities as possible for the characters to be swept off their feet by placing them in situations which are too tragic or too fantastic for "words" ') were set out in several essays; their practice produced the most elegantly wrought librettos of the day. *Elegy*, for example, opens with full-voiced pentameters, linked by patterns of alliteration and internal rhyme:

At dawn by the window in the wan light of today
My bridegroom of the night, nude as the sun, with a brave
Open sweep of his wonderful Samson-like hand

and, among its variety of carefully planned forms, includes simple songs:

On yonder lofty mountain
a lofty castle stands
where dwell three lovely maidens,
the fairest in the land

and scherzo patter:

Blood-pressure drops,
Invention stops;
Upset tum,
No images come

as well as conversational exchanges for recitative, conventional declarations of love, and a chorale.

Despite his preference for opera in the original, Auden was also drawn to fit words to existing scores, and with Kallman he made several opera translations. These are mellifluous, elegant, and better poetry than anything else of their kind; but on occasion they stray far from the original – quite deliberately so, since 'a too-literal translation of the original text may sometimes prove to be a falsification'.

Ideas and some verses from *The Sea and the Mirror*, Auden's *Tempest* 'commentary', were used in Berio's *Un re in ascolto* (1984). Mendelson's collected edition (1992) contains critical texts of all the librettos and of the *Magic Flute* translation, together with ample commentary.

Librettos: *Paul Bunyan*, Britten, 1941
with C. Kallman: *The Rake's Progress*, Stravinsky, 1951; *Elegy for Young Lovers*, Henze, 1961; *The Bassarids*, Henze, 1966; *Love's Labour's Lost*, Nabokov, 1973; *The Entertainment of the Senses*, John Gardner, 1974

Translations, with C. Kallman: Die Zauberflöte, Mozart, 1956; Die sieben Todsünden, Weill, 1958; Don Giovanni, Mozart, 1960; Aufstieg und Fall der Stadt Mahagonny, Weill [1960, unperf. (Boston, 1976)]; Arcifanfano, Dittersdorf, 1965

Essays: 'Opera on an American Legend: Problems of Putting the Story of Paul Bunyan on the Stage', *New York Times* (4 May 1941); 'A Public Art', *Opera*, xii (1961), 12–15; [with C. Kallman] 'Genesis of a Libretto', *Elegy for Young Lovers* (Mainz, 1961); *The Dyer's Hand* (New York, 1962), 463–527 ['Notes on Music and Opera', 'Cav & Pag', 'Translating Opera Libretti' (with Kallman), 'Music in Shakespeare']; 'The World of Opera', *Secondary Worlds* (London, 1969); *Forewords and Afterwords* (New York, 1973), 244–55, 256–61, 345–50, 432–5 ['The Greatest of Monsters' (Gutman's *Wagner*), 'A Genius and a Gentleman' (Verdi's letters), 'A Marriage of True Minds' (the Strauss-Hofmannsthal correspondence) and 'A Tribute' (to Stravinsky)]

*

J. Kerman: 'Opera à la mode', *Hudson Review*, vi (1954), 560–77; rev. in *Opera as Drama* (New York, 1956, 2/1988), 190–202
——: 'Auden's Magic Flute', *Hudson Review*, x (1957), 309–16
I. Stravinsky and R. Craft: *Memories and Commentaries* (New York, 1960), 144ff
M. K. Spears: *The Poetry of W. H. Auden: the Disenchanted Island* (New York, 1963), 105ff, 262ff
I. Stravinsky and R. Craft: *Dialogues and a Diary* (New York, 1963)
H. W. Henze: *Essays* (Mainz, 1964), 95ff
J. C. Blair: *The Poetic Art of W. H. Auden* (Princeton, 1965), 163ff
I. Stravinsky and R. Craft: *Themes and Episodes* (New York, 1966), 56ff
——: *Retrospectives and Conclusions* (New York, 1969), 145ff, 160ff, 173ff
U. Weisstein: 'Reflections on a Golden Style: W. H. Auden's Theory of Opera', *Comparative Literature*, xxii (1970), 108–24
B. C. Bloomfield and E. Mendelson: *W. H. Auden: a Bibliography* (Charlottesville, VA, 2/1972)
E. Mendelson, ed.: *W. H. Auden and Chester Kallman: Libretti and Other Dramatic Writings* (Princeton, 1992)

ANDREW PORTER

Audinot [Odinot, Oudinot], **Nicolas-Médard** (*b* Bourmont-en-Bassigny, Haute-Marne, 7 June 1732; *d* Paris, 21 May 1801). French impresario, singer and dramatist. He first made his name as a singer with the Opéra-Comique (after about 1758), chiefly in artisan roles; no doubt it was to exploit this special talent that he was allowed to put on an *opéra comique* of his own, *Le tonnelier*, after La Fontaine's *Le cuvier* (Foire St Laurent, 28 September 1761). The work failed but Audinot nevertheless joined the Comédie-Italienne when that company merged with the Opéra-Comique in 1762. Audinot revised the libretto of *Le tonnelier* with A.-F. Quétant, and the work was revived on 16 March 1765 at the Comédie-Italienne with new *ariettes* and ensembles by various composers. In this new version it had considerable success in France, Holland and Germany alike. Audinot left the Comédie-Italienne in 1767 and soon became one of the principal impresarios of the Paris stage. After attracting crowds to his puppet show at the Foire St Germain, he opened the Théâtre de l'Ambigu-Comique on 9 July 1769, remaining its owner-manager until 1796 (for his many disputes with the political authorities see Isherwood, 187–91). The Ambigu-Comique used child actors at first; Audinot then employed adolescents, whom he exploited in morally dubious circumstances. On the other hand, the repertory of his theatre, initially dominated by skits and coarse farces, was enriched during the 1780s by moral plays and heroic and romantic pantomimes. It is difficult to evaluate the place of music at the Ambigu-Comique, but such composers as Botson, Andre-Jean Rigade and Papavoine were regularly employed there in the 1770s.

*

DBF (M. Prévost); *ES* (R. Averini and E. Zanetti)

Les spectacles des foires et des boulevards de Paris, vi (1778)

[Mayeur de Saint Paul]: *Le désoeuvré ou L'espion du boulevard du Temple* (London, 1781)

Almanach général de tous les spectacles de Paris, i (1791), 172–81, 244; ii (1792), 291–3

N. Brazier: *Histoire des petits théâtres de Paris depuis leur origine* (Paris, 1838), 28–37

E. Campardon: *Les spectacles des Foires depuis 1595 jusqu'à 1791* (Paris, 1877), i, 29–74

C. D. Brenner: *A Bibliographical List of Plays in the French Language, 1700–1789* (Ann Arbor, 1947, 2/1979)

R. M. Isherwood: *Farce and Fantasy: Popular Entertainment in Eighteenth-Century Paris* (New York and Oxford, 1986)

N. Wild: *Dictionnaire des théâtres parisiens au XIXe siècle* (Paris, 1989)

MICHEL NOIRAY

Audran, Edmond (*b* Lyon, 11 April 1840; *d* Tierceville, nr Gisors, Oise, 17 Aug 1901). French composer. Son of Marius-Pierre Audran (1816–87), at one time a tenor at the Opéra-Comique, he studied under Jules-Laurent Duprato at the Ecole Niedermeyer and won the composition prize in 1859. In 1861 he moved with his family to Marseilles, where his father became a singing teacher and later director of the conservatory. He himself became organist at the church of St Joseph, for which he wrote religious music including a mass (1873) which was also performed at St Eustache in Paris. His other compositions include a funeral march on the death of Meyerbeer and some songs in Provençal dialect. His attempts at *opéra bouffe* finally brought an invitation to Paris from Louis Cantin, director of the Bouffes-Parisiens, also a native of Marseilles. With *Les noces d'Olivette* (1879) and *La mascotte* (1880) Audran established himself in Paris as a rival to Lecocq and gained international fame. *La cigale et la fourmi* (1886) also became well known, particularly in its 1890 English version; his later works, apart from *Miss Helyett* (1890) and *La poupée* (1896), were less popular. Audran sustained through all his large output great melodic appeal and rhythmic variety in his music. During his last years he suffered a mental and physical breakdown which caused his withdrawal from Paris society and eventually led to his death.

La mascotte, an involved story of matchmaking in 17th-century Italy, is Audran's most lastingly successful operetta. The best-known number of its lively and tuneful score is the Act 1 duet for Bettina (the 'mascot' of the title) and Pippo, in which she tells him, with appropriate farmyard noises, that she loves him just as much as her beloved turkeys. In *La cigale et la fourmi* the grasshopper and the ant of La Fontaine's fable are personified by two sopranos, of which the grasshopper, Thérèse, has the star role, with the lively 'Chanson de la cigale' and the celebrated gavotte 'Ma mère, j'entends le violon'.

first performed in Paris unless otherwise stated; publications are vocal scores published in Paris

L'ours et le pacha (oc, 1, after E. Scribe and J. X. B. Saintine), Marseilles, Grand, 1862

La chercheuse d'esprit (oc, 1, after C. Favart), Marseilles, Grand, ? April 1866 (1882)

La nivernaise (oc, 1), Marseilles, Gymnase, December 1866

Le petit poucet (opérette, 3), Marseilles, Gymnase, April 1868

Le grand mogol (ob, 3, H. Chivot and A. Duru), Marseilles, Gymnase, 24 Feb 1877; rev. in 4 acts, Paris, Gaîté, 19 Sept 1884 (1884)

La Saint-Valentin (opérette, 1, St Armand-Cercle), Paris, 1878

Les noces d'Olivette (opérette, 3, Chivot and Duru), Bouffes-Parisiens, 13 Nov 1879 (1880)

La mascotte (oc, 3, Chivot and Duru), Bouffes-Parisiens, 29 Dec 1880 (1881)

Gillette de Narbonne (oc, 3, Chivot and Duru), Bouffes-Parisiens, 11 Nov 1882 (1883)

Les pommes d'or (opérette, 4, Chivot, Duru and Blondeau-Monréal), Menus-Plaisirs, 12 Feb 1883 (1883)

La dormeuse éveillée (oc, 3, Chivot and Duru), Bouffes-Parisiens, 29 Dec 1883 (1884)

Pervenche (opérette, 3, Chivot and Duru), Bouffes-Parisiens, 31 March 1885

Serment d'amour (oc, 3, M. Ordonneau), Nouveautés, 19 Feb 1886 (1886)

Indiana (oc, 3, H. B. Farnie), Manchester, Comedy, 4 Oct 1886; London, Avenue, 11 Oct 1886 (London, 1886)

La cigale et la fourmi (oc, 3, Chivot and Duru), Gaîté, 30 Oct 1886 (1887)

Le paradis de Mahomet (opérette, 3), Brussels, Alhambra, 1887

La fiancée des Verts-Poteaux (oc, 3, Ordonneau), Menus-Plaisirs, 8 Nov 1887 (1887)

Le puits qui parle (oc, 3, Beaumont, Nuitter and Burani), Nouveautés, 15 March 1888 (1888)

Miette (opérette, 3, Ordonneau), Renaissance, 24 Sept 1888

La petite fronde (oc, 3, Chivot and Duru), Folies-Dramatiques, 16 Nov 1888 (1888)

La fille de Cacolet (vaudeville-opérette, Chivot and Duru), Variétés, 10 July 1889

L'œuf rouge (oc, 3, A. Vanloo and W. Busnach), Folies-Dramatiques, 14 March 1890 (1890)

Miss Helyett (opérette, 3, M. Boucheron), Bouffes-Parisiens, 12 Nov 1890 (1890)

L'oncle Célestin (opérette, Ordonneau and H. Kéroul), Menus-Plaisirs, 24 March 1891 (1891)

Article de Paris (opérette, 3, Boucheron), Menus-Plaisirs, 17 March 1892 (1892)

Sainte Freya (oc, 3, Boucheron), Bouffes-Parisiens, 4 Nov 1892 (1892)

Madame Suzette (opérette, 3, A. Sylvane and Ordonneau), Bouffes-Parisiens, 29 March 1893 (1893)

Mon prince! (oc, 3, Sylvane and C. Clairville), Nouveautés, 18 Nov 1893 (1893)

L'enlèvement de la Toledad (opérette, 3, F. Carré), Bouffes-Parisiens, 17 Oct 1894 (1894)

La duchesse de Ferrare (opérette, 3, Boucheron), Bouffes-Parisiens, 25 Jan 1895 (1895)

Photis (oc, 3, L. Gallet), Geneva, Grand, Feb 1896

La reine des reines (opérette, 3, P. L. Flers), Eldorado, 14 Oct 1896

La poupée (oc, 4, Ordonneau, after E. T. A. Hoffmann: *Der Sandmann*), Gaîté, 21 Oct 1896 (1896)

Monsieur Lohengrin (opérette, 3, Carré), Bouffes-Parisiens, 30 Nov 1896 (1896)

Les petites femmes (opérette, 4, Sylvane), Bouffes-Parisiens, 11 Oct 1897 (1897)

Les sœurs Gaudichard (oc, 3, Ordonneau), Gaîté, 21 April 1899 (1899)

Le curé Vincent (opérette, 3, Ordonneau), Gaîté, 25 Oct 1901

*

GänzlBMT; StiegerO

R. Traubner: *Operetta: a Theatrical History* (New York, 1983)

ANDREW LAMB

Auenbrugger, Joseph Leopold (*b* Graz, 19 Nov 1722; *d* Vienna, 18 May 1809). Austrian librettist. Educated in medicine at the University of Vienna, he made a name for himself as the inventor of the percussion method of diagnosing diseases of the chest cavity (1761). In 1775 he stood witness at the wedding of the court composer Antonio Salieri, for whom he wrote his only stage work, the libretto for *Der Rauchfangkehrer*, first performed by the National-Singspiel on 30 April 1781. The opera enjoyed considerable success, although in a letter of 10 December 1783 Mozart called the text 'a miserable original piece'. THOMAS BAUMAN

Aufstieg und Fall der Stadt Mahagonny ('Rise and Fall of the City of Mahagonny'). Opera in three acts by KURT WEILL to a libretto by BERTOLT BRECHT; Leipzig, Neues Theater, 9 March 1930.

Leokadja Begbick	contralto/mezzo-soprano
Fatty [Willy] *the 'attorney'*	tenor
Trinity Moses [Dreieinigkeitsmoses]	baritone
Jenny Hill	soprano
Jim Mahoney [Johann Ackerman or Hans]	tenor
Jack O'Brien	tenor
Bill, alias Sparbüchsenbill [Heinz, alias Sparbüchsenheinrich]	baritone
Joe [Josef Lettner], alias Alaskawolfjoe	bass
Tobby Higgins (can be doubled with the role of Jack)	tenor

Six girls from Mahagonny, the men of Mahagonny

Weill's correspondence with his publishers (Universal Edition) records how his collaboration with Brecht began in April 1927 with the idea of using the poet's 'Mahagonny-Gesänge' (from the collection *Hauspostille*) as the basis for the Songspiel *Mahagonny* (see MAHAGONNY (i). Later, however, in his article 'Zur Aufführung der Mahagonny-Oper' (*Leipziger Neueste Nachrichten*, 8 March 1930), he describes the Songspiel as 'a stylistic study by way of preparation for the operatic work, which was already begun and, the style having been tried out, was then continued'.

That the composer wished retrospectively to relegate the Songspiel to the status of a mere 'Stilstudie' is understandable. But why he should also claim, by backdating the genesis of the full-scale opera, that this was his intention all along remains unclear. He obviously wished to stress the importance of the latter work to his theatrical output, partly no doubt because of Brecht's rather negative assessment, made public in his 'Notes', 'Anmerkungen zur Oper *Aufstieg und Fall der Stadt Mahagonny*' (*Versuche*, ii, Berlin, 1930). Another factor may have been the charge of plagiarism levelled at Weill and Brecht by the playwright Walter Gilbricht: the earlier the inception of their work, the less likely they could have known Gilbricht's *Die Grossstadt mit einem Einwohner*, completed in 1928. What is certain, however, is that the actual composition of the Songspiel preceded the full-length opera *Aufstieg und Fall der Stadt Mahagonny*. Moreover, although the Songspiel is related both thematically and stylistically to the later work, Weill's musical language evinces a change of attitude during the two-year genesis (1927–9) of the opera. Comparison of the music adapted from the Songspiel – especially the 'Alabama Song' – readily reveals those differences: the earlier harmonizations have been divested of their harsher dissonances.

As the composition of the opera progressed, Weill gradually distanced himself from the earlier acerbic 'song style' (though not from the song style as such, as *Happy End*, 1929, shows), cultivating 'a perfectly pure, thoroughly responsible style', as he himself described it in a letter to his publishers. The development culminates in the exquisite 'Cranes' Duet', added in October 1929 in response to strong criticism from the publishers, who urged that some of the work's more risqué material should be removed. It is indicative of the difficulties surrounding the opera that the question of where to place the love duet has never been satisfactorily solved, either dramatically or musically. It is also characteristic of the work's fate that Otto Klemperer, having been enthusiastic about the Songspiel, should reject the opera after the Kroll Oper, Berlin, had committed itself to giving the first performance under his direction. Like the publishers, Klemperer was perturbed by the depravity of the libretto. The work was therefore entrusted to the Neues Theater in Leipzig, where the first night provoked one of the greatest scandals in the history of 20th-century music (the producer was Walther Brügmann, the conductor Gustav Brecher, the stage designer Caspar Neher). Further productions followed in Brunswick and Kassel, with both houses insisting on cuts for moral, religious and political reasons. Fuelled by Nazi sympathizers, protests nonetheless continued both in and out of the opera house. The work did not reach Berlin until December 1931, when, at the instigation of the impresario Ernst Josef Aufricht, it was given at the Theater am Kurfürstendamm in a radically reduced and shortened version by a team of singer-actors associated with *Die Dreigroschenoper*, with Zemlinsky as conductor. Members of the same ensemble, starring Lotte Lenya and conducted by Hans Sommer, contributed to the recording of highlights released in 1932. Lenya also starred (with her part rewritten) in the first complete recording (1956), conducted by Wilhelm Brückner-Rüggeberg.

The various cuts demanded by German opera houses in the early 1930s are indicated in the published vocal score, though their precise origin is not specified. The text published in Brecht's *Versuche* in 1930 and in the new complete edition of his works (*Grosse kommentierte Berliner und Frankfurter Ausgabe, Stücke* 2, 1988) represents a later version, in which – among other things – the ideological nature of divine authority is made less explicit. There are three authorized English translations: by Michael Feingold, by David Drew and Michael Geliot, and by Arnold Weinstein and Lys Symonette. The original published vocal score contains a note suggesting that because 'the pleasure city Mahagonny is in every sense international' the names of the characters may be replaced by names appropriate to the country of performance. Several alternatives for German performance are given, for example 'Willy' instead of 'Fatty', as used in the opera's première.

ACT 1.i Scene captions are projected on to a small white curtain which can be pulled aside. Inscriptions are also used for epic narration. As the music begins a 'wanted' poster appears, with photographs of Leokadja Begbick, Trinity Moses and Fatty; they are charged with procuring and fraudulent bankruptcy, and described as 'Fugitives from Justice'. Above the projection is an inscription: 'The Founding of the City of Mahagonny'. The backdrop depicts a desolate place. A large dilapidated truck arrives on stage. The engine stalls, and Trinity Moses climbs down from the driver's seat and crawls under the bonnet. Fatty gets out of the back of the vehicle and the dialogue begins. They are unable to continue on their way, so they found Mahagonny, 'the city of nets [Netzestadt]' – 'you get gold more easily from men than from rivers'. Begbick, Fatty and Moses sing together: 'Mahagonny only exists because

'Aufstieg und Fall der Stadt Mahagonny' (Weill): Act 1 scene i (the founding of the city of Mahagonny) from the original production at the Neues Theater, Leipzig, 9 March 1930, with (left to right) Marga Dannenberg as Begbick, Hanns Fleischer as Willy (the role later known as Fatty) and Walther Zimmer as Moses

everything is so bad, because there's no peace and no contentment and because there's nothing to hold on to'.

1.ii A city has quickly emerged. Jenny and the six girls sing the 'Alabama Song', in which they state their need for whisky and dollars.

1.iii The backdrop projection shows a huge city and photographs of large numbers of men. Fatty and Moses recruit the dissatisfied men to move to Mahagonny.

1.iv The caption reads: 'In the following years the malcontents from all continents descended on Mahagonny, city of gold'. Jim, Jack, Bill and Joe sing the praises of Mahagonny's whisky, women, horses and poker – and of the beautiful green moon of Alabama.

1.v The caption reads: 'Among those who came to the city of Mahagonny at that time was Jim Mahoney, and it is his story that we want to relate to you'. Jim, Jack, Bill and Joe stand next to a sign pointing to Mahagonny. Begbick introduces herself and tries to interest the men in 'fresh girls'. Jim gets to know Jenny.

1.vi The projection shows a map of Mahagonny. Jim and Jenny emerge, singing as they pass. Jenny asks Jim whether he likes her to wear underwear or not. He answers in the negative and inquires about her wishes. 'It's perhaps a little early to talk about that', she replies.

1.vii The caption reads: 'All great enterprises have their crises'; the backdrop displays statistics relating to crime and finance in Mahagonny. Inside the Hotel Rich Man, Fatty and Moses are sitting at a bar table. Begbick rushes in wearing white make-up. Business is bad. Fatty and Moses confront Begbick with the bitter truth: 'Cash breeds passion'.

1.viii The caption reads: 'Those who truly seek shall be disappointed'; the projection is of the wharf at Mahagonny. Jim arrives, coming away from the town; he is fed up, but his friends persuade him to stay and they all return to the city.

1.ix In front of the Hotel Rich Man the men of Mahagonny are smoking and drinking, listening to music and dreamily observing a white cloud moving across the sky. They are surrounded by placards: 'Treat my chairs with respect', 'Do not make any noise', 'Avoid offensive songs'. The onstage pianist plays Tekla Bądarzewska-Baranowska's *The Maiden's Prayer*. Jack declares, 'That's timeless art', but Jim is still dissatisfied: 'No one will ever be happy with this Mahagonny, because there's too much peace and too much harmony, and because there's too much to hold on to'. The lights go out.

1.x On the backdrop, in gigantic letters, 'A typhoon' is followed by the inscription 'A hurricane moving towards Mahagonny'. The orchestra plays a fugue and the company bemoans the 'frightful phenomenon'. People flee and a wind blows leaves and scraps of paper across the stage. An inscription reads 'On this night of horror a simple lumberjack by the name of Jim Mahoney discovered the laws of human happiness'.

1.xi On the night of the hurricane, Jenny, Begbick, Jim, Jack, Bill and Joe sit on the ground, propped up against a wall. All are feeling desperate except for Jim, who is smiling. On the wall are placards inscribed 'It is forbidden'. The male chorus sings a chorale pleading for fearless acceptance of the hurricane's force, but Jim claims that people are just as destructive as hurricanes and challenges everyone to ignore what is forbidden and do whatever they please. The lights go out. In the background is a diagram with an arrow indicating the path of the hurricane.

Act 2.i In a pale light the girls and men are waiting on the road outside Mahagonny. The projection again shows the arrow moving towards Mahagonny. A loudspeaker makes intermittent announcements during the orchestral ritornello, plotting the hurricane's progress, until the danger is past. The chorus praises the 'miraculous resolution'.

2.ii The inscription reads: 'Business flourishes in Mahagonny after the great hurricane'. In silence, projections depict the transition from a simple goldmining town to a modern city. The male chorus intones the agenda: 'First, don't forget, comes grub; second the act of love; third don't forget boxing; fourth boozing, according to contract.' The men go on stage and take part in the proceedings. On the backdrop is the word 'Eating'. Men sit at individual tables, piled high with meat. Jack, now known as The Glutton, eats incessantly. After boasting that he has eaten two calves and would like to eat himself, he dies. The chorus laments him as 'a man without fear'.

2.iii On the backdrop is 'Love'. The men queue in front of the Mandalay brothel; erotic pictures appear on a screen. A small band is on stage, but no girls. Begbick admonishes the men to spit out their chewing gum, wash their hands, give her time and exchange a few words with her. Moses asks the men, who are being admitted in groups of three, to be patient. The male chorus expresses lyrical urgency.

2.iv In front of the backdrop, on which 'Boxing' is projected, a boxing ring is being set up under Fatty's supervision. On a platform at the side a wind band is playing. Joe arrives with Jim and Bill. He bets all his money on himself but is slain by Moses.

2.v 'Boozing': the men sit down, put their feet on the table and drink. Jim, Bill and Jenny play pool. Jim orders a round but when Begbick asks for payment he realizes he has no money left. They have made a 'ship' using the pool table, a curtain rod and the like. Jim, Bill and Jenny get on it, and South Sea landscapes appear on the backdrop. The men indicate a storm by whistling and howling. Expecting to land elsewhere, they are disappointed to find themselves still at Mahagonny. Jim's friends leave him and, unable to pay, he is arrested. Jenny reaffirms the moral: 'You lie in the bed that you yourself make, no one else pulls up the covers, and if someone's going to do the kicking, it's me, if someone's going to be kicked, it's you'. Jim is removed. The chorus intones a new chorale: 'Don't be led on, there is no return. The end is nigh; you can already feel the nocturnal wind. There will be no more tomorrow'.

ACT 3.i At night Jim lies with one foot chained to a lamp-post and sings a defiant aria against the coming day.

3.ii The inscription reads: 'The courts in Mahagonny were no worse than anywhere else'. A tent serves as a court room. Seated on the judge's chair is Begbick, on the defence's chair Fatty, on the prosecution bench, Tobby Higgins. Moses is selling tickets for the proceedings. Higgins is charged with premeditated murder but eventually offers a sufficiently large sum to be acquitted. Jim is charged with the indirect murder of a friend, disturbing the peace, the seduction of a girl named Jenny and failing to pay for Begbick's whisky and curtain rod, above all for lack of money. The 'Benares Song' is sung as the men read in their newspapers of an earthquake in Benares. There is nowhere left to go.

3.iii The inscription reads 'Execution and death of Jimmy Mahoney. Many people may prefer not to see the following execution of Jimmy Mahoney. But we believe that even you, ladies and gentlemen, would not wish to pay for him. Such is the respect for money in our time'. The projection is of Mahagonny, peacefully illuminated. Small groups of people stand around. Jim enters, accompanied by Moses, Jenny and Bill. Jim and Jenny are ordered to the front of the stage, where a duet is sung and leave is taken of Bill. All but Jim sing of God coming to Mahagonny.

3.iv On the backdrop, Mahagonny burns. Begbick, Fatty and Moses are standing and singing 'Aber dieses ganze Mahagonny ...' A group of men arrive carrying placards: 'For money', 'For the battle against all'. A second group arrives with placards reading: 'For property', 'For love', 'For the saleability of love', 'For life without limits', 'For unlimited murder'. In another procession the placards read: 'For the unjust distribution of worldly goods', 'For the just distribution of unworldly goods'. A group of girls arrive with Jenny, carrying Jim's shirt and, on a cloth cushion, his ring, watch and revolver. They sing a reprise of the 'Alabama Song'. Bill, at the head of a procession of men bearing Jim's coffin, carries a placard: 'For justice'. The male chorus intones 'Can't help a dead man'. Moses, Begbick and Fatty enter with three more processions, each bearing different placards. They all move forward as if to march into the audience. The entire cast sings 'Can't help us and you and nobody!'.

* * *

Aufstieg und Fall der Stadt Mahagonny is on various levels an awkward work. Up to a point, that was the authors' purpose. But by the time Brecht came to write his *Anmerkungen* in 1930, he was all too willing to emphasize the more overtly destructive aspects, especially the generic ones. Weill's essays, written shortly before, convey more constructive ambitions and no doubt prompted Brecht's notes. The difficulty that any prospective producer faces, notwithstanding the work's intentionally 'uncomfortable' aspects, stem in part from tensions in the Brecht-Weill partnership itself: 'The very nature of the work compels us to continue searching for ideal solutions long after we have recognized there are none to be found'. Thus David Drew, summarizing his fascination with a work which he sees in terms of 'the collision of two congenial yet incompatible minds' (*Kurt Weill: a Handbook*, p.185). For all its reliance on the 'song' idiom, musically the work aspires to be much more than the mere sum of its parts. Weill described it as a 'structure based on purely musical laws'. Just how incompatible his views were with Brecht's can be measured from the collaborators' divergent attitudes towards the use of the projected inscriptions. Weill was concerned with 'giving the links between the musical numbers a form that obstructs as little as possible the musical design of the whole'. For Brecht, on the other hand, the inscriptions constituted an important means of 'defamiliarization' (*Verfremdung*), something central to his theory of epic theatre. Just as the emergence of the opera out of the Songspiel reflects conflicts in the Weill-Brecht partnership, with Brecht's theorizing about the opera anticipating his later experiments in the genre of didactic theatre (the *Lehrstück*), so the opera itself invites producers and conductors to take sides in those conflicts.

For further illustration *see* STAGE DESIGN, fig.22.

STEPHEN HINTON

Aufzug (Ger.). ACT.

Augenarzt, Der ('The Oculist'). Singspiel in two acts by ADALBERT GYROWETZ to a libretto by Johann Emanuel Veith; Vienna, Kärntnertortheater, 1 October 1811.

The story is based on the libretto (by Armand Croizette and Armand François Chateauvieux) for Louis-Sébastien Lebrun's opera *Les petits aveugles de Franconville* (1802, Paris). A shy ex-regimental doctor, Berg (tenor), falls in love with Marie (soprano), the daughter of Pastor Reinfeld (bass). Berg is supported by his friend and patron, the Duke of Steinau (bass), but his wooing is complicated by a crafty rival, Igel (tenor), major-domo of the ducal palace. Pastor Reinfeld has two blind wards, Philipp and Wilhelmine (both sopranos), who have grown to love each other. Berg carries out a successful operation to restore their sight and discovers Wilhelmine to be his long-lost sister. Marie finally admits her love for Berg and the two couples are united, amid general rejoicing.

Contemporary commentators noted the stylistic similarity of *Der Augenarzt* to *Die Schweizerfamilie* (1809) by Gyrowetz's colleague in Vienna, Joseph Weigl. Despite this, the score was generally praised for its attractively melodic nature and economy of means. The convoluted libretto was criticized by E. T. A. Hoffmann, writing in the *Allgemeine musikalische Zeitung* (30 December 1812), who considered it sentimental and not very suitable for the operatic stage. It nevertheless became Gyrowetz's most popular stage work, being widely performed throughout German-speaking lands until well into the 1820s, and even translated for a Paris production in 1826. Like many works of the same genre, it was ultimately eclipsed by changing musical fashions. ADRIENNE SIMPSON

Augér, Arleen (*b* Long Beach, CA, 13 Sept 1939). American soprano. She graduated in voice studies at the University of California. After giving concerts with the Los Angeles PO she worked as a schoolteacher in Chicago and studied with Ralph Errolle. She won an audition at the Vienna Staatsoper, where she was engaged as the Queen of Night for her stage début under Josef Krips in 1967; she sang the same role with the New York City Opera in 1969. She sang regularly in the Vienna ensemble until 1974, then moved to Frankfurt, after which she developed a major international career, singing at La Scala (1975) and the Metropolitan Opera (1978, as Marzelline) and in German centres. Her British opera début was in *Alcina* (Handel) at the City of London Festival in 1985; she returned in 1988 as Monteverdi's Poppaea. By 1990 she had made more than 140 recordings, including Poppaea and operas by Handel, Mozart and Strauss. She is admired for her coloratura technique and style in Baroque music, as for her sensibility to word and phrase and her clarity of articulation. NOËL GOODWIN

Augsburg. Cathedral city and industrial centre in Bavaria, southern Germany. In the 13th century it became an imperial free city; in the 16th it was the seat of the diet that evaluated the new Lutheran faith. The first operas (by Kusser) were given in the late 17th century, and by the early 1800s operatic life was flourishing, though chiefly dependent on visiting Italian troupes. Weber's *Peter Schmoll* had its first performance there in 1803. The Stadttheater in Kasernstrasse was built in 1877 by the architects Ferdinand Fellner and Hermann Helmer in neo-Renaissance style, with a tiered auditorium. It opened on 26 November with a production of Beethoven's *Fidelio*. Its repertory was extensive, and famous artists gave guest performances. *Die Meistersinger* was first staged on 1 March 1878, *Carmen* and *Der Bettelstudent* in 1883, and the *Ring* in 1888–93. Plays were also performed. In the 1890s the theatre's financial situation was precarious, and there were even ideas of merging the company with that of the Munich Hoftheater. But Carl Häusler, the administrator from 1903 to 1928, rescued it from its longstanding difficulties, permitting all the major works of Wagner, Mozart and Verdi to be performed. *Parsifal* was given in 1914, immediately after the work's release for general performance, and there was also a large operetta repertory. Small-scale productions were staged during World War I.

In 1919 the theatre was handed over to the civic authorities, and the inflationary period saw the company dissolved; from 1924 to 1929 small companies from Munich made guest appearances. In January 1929 *Die Dreigroschenoper* was performed in Augsburg, Brecht's birthplace. The stage was renovated in 1938–9, and the auditorium extended, but the theatre was destroyed in an air raid in February 1944. In 1954–6 the Stadttheater was rebuilt (with 994 seats), opening on 10 November 1956 with *Figaro*. It now concentrates, as indeed it did before 1944, on 20th-century works, notably by Honegger, Poulenc, Berg, Werner Egk (who grew up in Augsburg) and Von Einem. During a special season for the 1972 Olympics, Rafael Kubelik's *Cornelia Faroli* received its first performance. Conductors and singers who began their careers in Augsburg include Heinz Wallberg, István Kertész, Wolfgang Sawallisch, Hans Hopf and Benno Kusche. Pfitzner, Strauss and Egk have appeared as guest directors. The season runs from the end of September to the beginning of June; the musical director since 1989 has been Michael Luig. In June and July, the company plays for a four-week festival (founded 1929) in the open-air theatre at the Rote Tor (2117 seats), staging one opera and one operetta. The Deutsche Mozart Festival (founded 1951) stages operas at various venues in either spring or autumn. KLAUS J. SEIDEL

Augusta. American city in eastern Georgia. Augusta is the only city in Georgia outside the Atlanta area to have a fully professional opera company. The city's serious commitment to opera began in 1967, when the Augusta Opera Association was founded to present opera and musical theatre sung in English by young American artists. It is now the oldest continuously active opera company in Georgia, and the only one to tour regularly throughout the south-eastern USA. Edward Bradberry has been general director since 1973. In 1983 the Augusta Opera's production of *Madama Butterfly* was broadcast on a 28-state public television network.

The company presents four productions annually, usually two operas and two operettas or Broadway musicals. The 1990–91 season consisted of *La bohème*, *Die lustigen Weiber von Windsor*, *South Pacific* and *Annie Get Your Gun*. All performances are at the Imperial Community Theater (seating 800–850).

DERRICK HENRY

Augustini, Pietro [Pier] **Simone.** *See* AGOSTINI, PIETRO SIMONE.

Auletta, Pietro (*b* S Angelo, Avellino, *c*1698; *d* Naples, Sept 1771). Italian composer. He completed his musical training at the Neapolitan conservatory of S Onofrio. Some time before 1724 (according to Prota-Giurleo) he was appointed *maestro di cappella* of the important Neapolitan church S Maria la Nova. In 1725 he composed his first comic opera, *Il trionfo dell'amore, ovvero Le nozze tra amici*, for production at the Teatro Nuovo in Naples. His second comic opera, *Carlotta*, appeared in Naples in 1726, and his first heroic opera, *Ezio*, in Rome in 1728. After eight years, at Carnival 1737, he re-emerged as a dramatic composer with the first production in Naples of his comic opera *Orazio*. This work, which was extremely popular, had a long subsequent history, being continually modified as it was performed in city after city and quickly turned into a pasticcio. In that form it was sometimes ascribed to Auletta and sometimes to other composers. One famous production, a much-shortened version of the original *Orazio*, took place in Paris in 1752 under the title *Il maestro di musica*. The score printed in Paris in 1753 attributed the music to Pergolesi, but in fact it was by several composers including Auletta, who was represented by four items from his original opera. As a pasticcio it was also known as *Le maître de musique*, *La scolara alla moda*, and perhaps *El maestro de capilla*. An anonymous *Impresario abbandonato* (*D-Dlb*) is identified in the library catalogue as a revised version of *Orazio* and was probably performed in Munich in 1749 and 1758.

For a few years after the first production of *Orazio* Auletta was much in favour among the Neapolitans. Between 1738 and 1740 he wrote no fewer than four comic operas for Naples, as well as an intermezzo for the marriage of the Infante Felipe in Madrid. After 1740, for a reason as yet unknown, his operatic output fell sharply. It is noteworthy that, in the librettos of certain of his operas, including *Il trionfo dell'amore* (1725), *Carlotta* (1726), *Ezio* (1728), *Il Marchese Sgrana* (1738) and *L'impostore* (1740), Auletta is called *maestro di cappella* to the Prince of Belvedere.

The small amount of Auletta's surviving music contains much that is of high quality. The two arias of his earliest surviving composition, the cantata *Sulla nascente herbetta* (1718), may be criticized for some awkward harmonies; their melodies, however, are most attractive. The melodic styles are surprisingly modern for a Neapolitan composition of 1718, exhibiting the lilting, buoyant qualities commonly associated with Neapolitan music of the late 1720s and 1730s; ex.1,

['(Love, I understand you,) if you wish to jest. You can hear even though you are asleep.']

from the vocal line of the second aria, typifies the style. Of Auletta's extant operas the short, two-act *La locandiera* is probably the most appealing. Written in 1738 to celebrate the marriage of Queen Maria Amalia to King Charles III of Naples that year, it rivals Pergolesi's comic operas of the same period in its subtle musical characterization, its grotesque humour (especially in the parts for the elderly characters) and its portrayal of the playful yet tender feelings of youth – all achieved with the utmost economy of technical means. Once again, Auletta's attractive melodies are a crucial factor in the success of the work. His accompaniments are discreet and his orchestration never overbearing.

Il trionfo dell'amore, ovvero Le nozze tra amici (opera comica, 3, C. de Palma), Naples, Nuovo, aut. 1725, *D-MÜs*

La Carlotta (opera comica, 3, B. Saddumene), Naples, Fiorentini, spr. 1726

Ezio (opera eroica, 3, P. Metastasio), Rome, Dame, 26 Dec 1728

L'amor costante (opera comica, 3, A. Palomba), Naples, Fiorentini, Spr. 1734, *I-Nn*

Orazio (opera comica, 3, Palomba), Naples, Nuovo, carn. 1737; as pasticcio Il maestro di musica, Paris, 1752 (Paris, 1753); as Impresario abbandonato, ? Munich, 1749, *D-Dlb*; as Orazio, Turin, 1748, *Dlb*, *Wa*, *I-Fc*

Il Marchese Sgrana (opera comica, 3, Palomba), Naples, Nuovo, spr. 1738

La locandiera (scherzo comico per musica, 2, G. A. Federico), Naples, S Carlo, 10 July 1738, *Nc*

Don Chichibio (opera comica, 3), Naples, Nuovo, carn. 1739

Intermezzo for the marriage of the Infante Felipe, Madrid, 1739

L'impostore (opera comica, 3, C. Fabozzi), Naples, Fiorentini, aut. 1740

Caio Fabricio (opera eroica, 3, A. Zeno), Turin, Regio, carn. 1743

Il Marchese di Spartivento, ovvero Il cabalista ne sa'men del caso (farsetta), Rome, Valle, carn. 1747, addns B. Micheli

Il conte immaginario (int), Venice, S Cassiano, aut. 1748

Didone (opera eroica, 3, Metastasio), Florence, Pergola, aut. 1759, *Fc*

*

DBI (U. Prota-Giurleo)

F. Walker: 'Two Centuries of Pergolesi Forgeries and Misattributions', *ML*, xxx (1949), 297–320

——: 'Orazio: The History of a Pasticcio', *MQ*, xxxviii (1952), 369–83

M. F. Robinson: *Naples and Neapolitan Opera* (Oxford, 1972)

G. Hardie: 'Neapolitan Comic Opera, 1707–1750: Some Addenda and Corrigenda for *The New Grove*', *JAMS*, xxxvi (1983), 124–7

MICHAEL F. ROBINSON

Aureli, Aurelio (*b* Murano, Venice; *fl* 1652–1708). Italian librettist. He wrote some 50 librettos, including a few adaptations. Until 1687 he seems to have lived mainly in Venice (except for a brief sojourn in 1659 at the Viennese court), where he was a member of the Accademia degli Imperfetti. From 1688 to 1694 he was employed by the Duke of Parma; during this period he produced about a dozen dramatic works, all set by the court composer Bernardo Sabadini. Most of his subsequent librettos were written for Venice and other cities of the Venetian republic. He occasionally revised texts of other librettists, including Moniglia and Morselli. His works are whimsical and at times bizarre transformations of the most disparate historical and mythological source material. They reflect the evolution of Venetian taste (to which he admittedly pandered) from the libretto's first point of stability to the era of Arcadian reform.

selective list

dm – *dramma per musica*

L'Erginda (favola per musica), G. Sartorio, 1652; *Erismena* (dm), Cavalli, 1655; *Le fortune di Rodope e di Damira* (dm), P. A. Ziani, 1657 (M. A. Ziani, 1680, as Damira placata); *Medoro* (dm), F. Lucio, 1658; *La virtù guerriera* (invenzione drammatica), G. Tricarico, 1659; *Antigona delusa da Alceste* (dm), P. A. Ziani, 1660; *Gl'amori infruttuosi di Pirro* (dm), A. Sartorio, 1661; *Gli scherzi di Fortuna subordinato al Pirro* (dm), P. A. Ziani, 1662; *Le fatiche d'Ercole per Deianira* (dm), P. A. Ziani, 1662; *Eliogabalo* (dm), G. A. Boretti, 1669; *Artaserse, ovvero L'Ormonda costante* (dm), C. Grossi, 1669

Claudio Cesare (dm), Boretti, 1672; *Orfeo* (dm), A. Sartorio, 1672; *Medea in Atene* (dm), A. Giannettini, 1675; *Helena rapita da Paride* (dm), D. Freschi, 1677; *Alessandro Magno in Sidone* (dm), M. A. Ziani, 1679; *Alcibiade* (dm), M. A. Ziani, 1680; *Pompeo Magno in Cilicia* (dm), Freschi, 1681; *Olimpia vendicata* (dm), Freschi, 1681 (A. Scarlatti, 1685); *Massimo Puppieno* (dm), C. Pallavicino, 1685 (B. Sabadini, 1692, as Il Massimino; A. Scarlatti, 1695); *Ermione raquistata* (dm), A. Giannettini, 1686; *Hierone tiranno di Siracusa* (dramma), Sabadini, 1688

(A. Scarlatti, 1692); *Il favore degli dei* (dramma fantastico musicale), Sabadini, 1690
La gloria d'amore (spettacolo festivo), Sabadini, 1690; *Diomede punito da Alcide* (dramma), Sabadini, 1691 (T. G. Albinoni, 1700); *Circe abbandonata da Ulisse* (dramma), Sabadini, 1692 (C. F. Pollarolo, 1697); *Talestri innamorata d'Alessandro Magno* (dramma), Sabadini, 1693; *Il riso nato fra il pianto* (dm), Sabadini, 1694; *La ninfa bizzarra* (dramma pastorale per musica), M. A. Ziani, 1697; *Rosane imperatrice degli Assiri* (dm), 1699; *Prassitele in Gnido* (dramma pastorale per musica), A. B. Coletti, 1700; *Creso tolto a le fiamme* (dm), G. Polani, 1705; *La pace fra Pompeiani e Cesariani* (dm), 1708; *Igene regina di Sparta* (dm), C. F. Pollarolo, 1708

*

E. Rosand: ' "Ormindo travestito" in Erismena', *JAMS*, xxviii (1975), 268–91
L. Bianconi: 'L'Ercole in Rialto', *Venezia e il melodramma nel Seicento*, ed. M. T. Muraro (Florence, 1976), 259–72
E. Rosand: Introduction to A. Aureli and A. Sartorio: *L'Orfeo*, DMV, vi (Milan, 1983)
G. Morelli: Introduction to A. Aureli and F. Lucio: *Il Medoro*, DMV, iv (Milan, 1984) [also incl. T. Walker: ' "Ubi Lucius": Thoughts on Reading *Medoro*', pp.cxxxi–clxiv]
P. Fabbri: *Il secolo cantante: per una storia del libretto d'opera nel Seicento* (Bologna, 1990)

THOMAS WALKER (text), NORBERT DUBOWY (work-list)

Aureli [Oreli, Orelia, Averara], **Diana Margherita** (*fl* 1691–6). Italian singer. She is described in contemporary documents as 'torinese', although that may refer to her service in the court of Turin; she is also described as '*musica di camera* to His Royal Highness of Savoy' in the libretto of *La pace fra Tolomeo e Seleuco* by C. F. Pollarolo (1691, Piacenza). A singer of no particular distinction, she usually took second female parts. Among the most important productions in which she appeared were those at the Teatro S Giovanni Grisostomo in Venice, where she sang with the best singers of the time: G. F. Tosi's *L'incoronazione di Serse* (1691) and C. F. Pollarollo's *Ibraim sultano*, *Onorio in Roma* (both 1692), *Rosimonda* and *Ercole in Cielo* (both 1696) and *L'Ulisse sconosciuto* (1698). By 1695 Aureli had married the librettist Pietro d'Averara. She seems not to have been related to the Bolognese family of singers of the same name.

*

S. Cordero di Pamparato: 'Un duca di Savoia impresario teatrale e i casi della musica Diana', *RMI*, xlv (1940), 240–60

SERGIO DURANTE

Aureliano in Palmira ('Aurelianus in Palmira'). *Dramma serio* in two acts by GIOACHINO ROSSINI to a libretto by FELICE ROMANI, after GAETANO SERTOR's libretto for Anfossi's *Zenobia di Palmira* (1789); Milan, Teatro alla Scala, 26 December 1813.

Despite its outwardly heroic subject matter and its being a commission from La Scala, *Aureliano in Palmiro* is in effect a Rossinian chamber opera. The heroic and militaristic elements are strongly stylized and the opera's finest and most characteristic music is written in an idyllic, pastoral vein. There are three central characters: the Roman emperor, Aurelianus (tenor), who has seized Antioch and freed a number of hostages, including Publia (mezzo-soprano); the brilliant Queen Zenobia (soprano) whose expansionist sallies into Syria, Egypt and Asia Minor have angered the Roman leadership; and the Persian prince Arsace, Zenobia's lover and fearless ally, a part originally written for the celebrated castrato, Giovanni Battista Velluti. The score's distinctive colour derives in large measure from the character of Arsace, a comely and affecting young man who seems most at home amid the hills and woods of the Euphrates. Under his influence, Zenobia is transformed from a warrior queen to a woman of sensibility, conforming to the mood of an opera where the woods are apostrophized as the source of true, inner freedom, and where a prisoners' plea for clemency, salvaged from the finale of the revised *Tancredi*, is a characteristic moment. Aurelianus, by contrast, is portrayed as a divided man, by turns assertive and humane. After numerous battles and confrontations between the warring parties it is Aurelianus, the confident Roman victor, who puts aside ideas of revenge and his own feelings for Zenobia, to allow her union with Arsace in return for an oath of allegiance to the Roman Empire.

RICHARD OSBORNE

Auric, Georges (*b* Lodève, 15 Feb 1899; *d* Paris, 23 July 1983). French composer. He studied at the conservatory in Montpellier and at the Paris Conservatoire, as well as at the Schola Cantorum under d'Indy during the first years of World War I. It was at this time that he became acquainted with Satie, Milhaud and Honegger, and with Jean Cocteau, whose ideals of a renewal of art were seminal in bringing Auric together with these composers to form Les Six. He wrote several ballets and contributed to stage works that defy the conventional boundaries of opera and ballet. Most celebrated among them are the jointly composed *Les mariés de la tour Eiffel* (1920) and the *ballet chorégraphique Phèdre* (1949).

Auric's short one-act opera, *Sous le masque*, dates from 1927, by which time Les Six had lost its cohesion as a group. It displays several of the ideals adhered to by Les Six – clarity and simplicity of expression, and a rejection of the profound content of expressionism or symbolism and of the textures of impressionism. It is characterized by the four-square phrase lengths of Parisian popular music, simple ostinatos and uncluttered textures. The text, by Louis Laloy, is treated with a sense of humour tinged with light irony. The opera is a modern day *Fête galante* in the form of a masked ball with the characters delighting in the 'pleasure of pretence'. At the end of the piece the characters give thanks to the 'indiscretions of night', having enjoyed their disguises but now discarding them. If there is a moral behind the tale it is that dreams must not be confused with reality: art is there simply to entertain.

Until the early 1940s Auric was also active as a music critic. Among other things, he wrote an interesting article on Debussy's *Pelléas* for *La nouvelle revue française* (January 1941), on the occasion of the opera's revival. His memoirs, *Quand j'étais là* (Paris, 1979), vividly recall many musicians and their works from the 1920s onwards and include some material on the operas of the period. He was director of the Paris Opéra and the Opéra-Comique, 1962–8.

*

A. Schaeffner: *Georges Auric* (Paris, 1928)
P. Landormy: *La musique française après Debussy* (Paris, 1943)
A. Goléa: *Georges Auric* (Paris, 1958)
C. Samuel: *Panorama de l'art musical contemporain* (Paris, 1962)
P. Collaer: *La musique moderne* (Brussels, 1963)

RICHARD LANGHAM SMITH

Aurisicchio [Euresicchio, Eurisechio, Orisicchio], **Antonio** (*b* Naples, *c*1710; *d* Rome, 3 or 4 Sept 1781). Italian composer. He studied in Rome and, like so many southern Italian composers of his generation, made his professional début in Naples with a comic opera in the

Teatro dei Fiorentini (1734). He was assistant *maestro* (1751), then *maestro di cappella* (1756–66) of the church of S Giacomo degli Spagnuoli, Rome, and a director of the *maestri* at the Accademia di S Cecilia (1776–9).

Though his reputation lay chiefly in his church music, he obviously did not disdain the quick income brought by an occasional opera commission. However, many of these commissions were for a species of operatic hack work: for intermezzos (or 'farsette', as they had come to be called in Rome, where the genre stayed in fashion much longer than elsewhere in Italy, transformed in style and shape into miniature *opere buffe*) or for the revision of works by other composers. An aria by Aurisicchio was sufficiently admired to be included in the pasticcio *Attalo* for London in 1758 (and subsequently printed by Walsh in his *Favourite Songs*), but Burney said it was his 'only air that was ever sung on our stage'. His style is characteristic of the period, with simply constructed but appealing melodic surfaces over essentially tonic–dominant harmonic foundations.

Chi dell'altrui si veste presto si spoglia (commedia, 2, T. Mariani), Naples, Fiorentini, wint. 1734
L'inganno deluso (int), Rome, Argentina, carn. 1743
Il cicisbeo consolato (farsetta, C. Mazzarelli), Rome, Pace, carn. 1748
Chi la fà l'aspetta (int), Rome, Pace, carn. 1752
Andromaca (os, A. Salvi), Rome, Argentina, carn. 1753, collab. A. G. Pampani, 6 arias *GB-Lbl*
Eumene (os, G. Pizzi), Rome, Argentina, carn. 1754, *P-La*
Lo sposalizio all'usanza (farsetta), Rome, Valle, carn. 1757

Arias in: Didone abbandonata, 1745; Alessandro nell'Indie, *I-FZc*

*

BurneyFI; *BurneyH*
Diario ordinario, no.689 (Rome, 8 Sept 1781), 9
C. Goldoni: *Mémoires* (Paris, 1787); ed. G. Ortolani in *Tutte le opere di Carlo Goldoni* (Verona, 1935–56), i, 404–5
M. Grétry: *Mémoires, ou Essais sur la musique* (Paris, 1789), 85–6
D. Corri: Foreword to 'Life of Domenico Corri', *The Singers Preceptor* (London, after 1794)

JAMES L. JACKMAN

Aurora. Opera in three acts and an intermezzo by HÉCTOR PANIZZA to a libretto by Héctor Quesada and LUIGI ILLICA; Buenos Aires, Teatro Colón, 5 September 1908.

The story takes place in Córdoba, Argentina, during the Revolution of May 1810 and concerns the love of Aurora (soprano), the daughter of the royalist leader in the city, and Mariano (tenor), a young patriot on the Revolutionary side. He is arrested and condemned to death, but a friend of Aurora's, Chiquita (soprano), enables them to meet and tries to help them flee. They escape but are surprised by the guard, and Aurora, fatally wounded, dies in the arms of her beloved, singing, 'Mirad! Es la aurora, Dios la escribe en el cielo con el sol y en la tierra con mi sangre' ('Behold the dawn [aurora], God draws it on the sky with the sun and on the earth with my blood'). The sun symbolizes liberty on the flag and arms of Argentina, and dawn, a new age.

The work was composed and given its first performance in Italian, but was reworked by its author and translated into Spanish in 1945; it is this version which is normally performed. The intermezzo 'Canción a la bandera' ('Song to the Flag') has become a patriotic song in Argentina. Stylistically the work belongs to the Italian lyric tradition rather than to Argentinian nationalism, in spite of its heroic national theme.

CARLOS SUFFERN

Ausensi, Manuel (*b* Barcelona, 8 Oct 1919). Spanish baritone. He studied in Barcelona and made his début there in 1948. In the following years he established himself as the most popular Spanish baritone of his time, singing with great success in Madrid and throughout South America, where he made his début in 1954 at the Teatro Colón, Buenos Aires. His North American début followed in 1960, when he sang a 'suavely elegant' Sharpless in *Madama Butterfly* at Dallas, returning there and to Philadelphia regularly during the decade. Heavier roles, such as Nabucco, Amonasro and Scarpia, which he increasingly undertook at this time, also brought acclaim, but by 1969 he was reported to be sounding tired, his high notes no longer steady. His robust but polished style and resonant tone distinguish many opera and zarzuela recordings widely circulated in Spain; elsewhere he is remembered chiefly for his Figaro in *Il barbiere di Siviglia* (with Teresa Berganza), notable less for personality than for the quality of his singing.

J. B. STEANE

Aussig (Ger.). ÚSTÍ NAD LABEM.

Austin. American city, capital of Texas. It was first settled in 1834. It is the centre of state government and seat of the University of Texas at Austin. The earliest evidence of operatic activity dates from the late 1860s when operatic selections were given in concerts. On 21 September 1871 the new Austin Opera House presented *La fille du régiment* in English. During the 1880s and 90s numerous operas involving small casts of local artists were performed under William Besserer, born in Austin, who had received his musical education in Germany.

With the extension of the railways Austin, like other Texas cities, received several professional touring opera companies, including the Carleton Opera Company (1887), the Whitney Mockridge Grand Opera Company (1900), the Henry W. Savage English Opera Company (1908), the Boston Opera Company (1917), the Creatore Grand Opera Company (1919) and the San Carlo Opera Company (1914, 1920, 1923–5, 1935–6). Local productions were also presented. The Austin Civic Opera Company, organized in 1927, presented two performances of *Martha* (1928), two of *The Bohemian Girl* (1929), one of *Die lustige Witwe* (1930) and one of *The Mikado* (1931) before disbanding.

More recent activity has centred on four different organizations. The university music department presents at least two productions a year, in the large, modern Performing Arts Center or the more intimate Opera Laboratory Theater. Jess Walters, a member of the university's voice faculty, has independently directed an opera annually since 1981, sung in English by local artists. The Austin Lyric Opera, which presented its inaugural performance (*Die Zauberflöte*) in 1987 under the directorship of Joe McClain, presents three productions each season in the university Performing Arts Center or in an old opera house now known as the Paramount Theater; the company employs professional set and costume designers and singers for the leading roles. A Gilbert and Sullivan Society also exists but its productions are more sporadic.

*

L. Spell: *Music in Texas* (Austin, 1936)
M. James-Reed: *Music in Austin 1900–1956* (Austin, 1957)
M. Barkley: *History of Travis County and Austin 1839–1899* (Waco, 1963)

GARY GIBBS

Austin, Elizabeth (*b* Leicester, *c*1800; *d* after 1835). English singer. Performances in Dublin in 1821 led to engagements at the Theatre Royal, Drury Lane (début on 23 November 1822) and the English Opera House. On 10 December 1827 she made her American début at the Chestnut Street Theatre, Philadelphia, in Arne's *Love in a Village*; her New York début was at the Park Theatre on 2 January 1828. For the next six years she was America's reigning prima donna, performing principally in New York, Boston, Providence, Philadelphia, Baltimore and Washington. Her repertory ranged from *The Beggar's Opera* to *Der Freischütz*; she was most closely identified, however, with Rossini's *Cenerentola* (adapted by M. R. Lacy), which she introduced to the United States. She had a high, sweet and flexible voice, but was only a mediocre actress. Her prestige began to decline after the arrival in the USA of Mary Anne Paton Wood in late 1833; in May 1835 she returned to England and retired from the stage.

*

'Mrs. Austin', *The Euterpiad: an Album of Music, Poetry, and Prose*, i (1830), 147

'Mrs. Austin', *American Musical Journal* (1835), April, 114–15

F. C. Wemyss: *Twenty-Six Years of the Life of an Actor and Manager* (New York, 1847)

K. K. Preston: *Travelling Opera Troupes in the United States, 1825–1860* (diss., City U., New York, 1989)

WILLIAM BROOKS, KATHERINE K. PRESTON

Austin, Frederic (*b* London, 30 March 1872; *d* London, 10 April 1952). English baritone. His operatic career began when he sang Gunther in the Covent Garden 1908 *Ring* under Richter, and he sang a variety of roles (in *Les contes d'Hoffmann*, *Tiefland* and *Così fan tutte*) in the ensuing seasons. He was a leading bass-baritone in the Beecham Opera Company and took an active part in Boughton's Glastonbury festivals. In 1920 he sang Peachum in *The Beggar's Opera*, which he had arranged for what proved to be a highly successful and long surviving revival (his arrangement of *Polly* was staged two years later), and in 1924 he was appointed artistic director of the British National Opera Company. He was also a composer, mostly of orchestral music.

Austin, Sumner (Francis) (*b* London, 24 Sept 1888; *d* London, 9 July 1981). English baritone and director. He studied at Oxford, making his début in 1919 with the Carl Rosa Opera Company, then sang with the O'Mara Opera Company and at the Old Vic. For Oxford University Opera Club (1925–31) he sang Monteverdi's Orpheus and Nero, Max (a tenor role) and Kecal (*The Bartered Bride*). Engaged at Sadler's Wells Theatre (1931–40), he directed *La bohème*, Collingwood's *Macbeth*, Stanford's *The Travelling Companion*, *Faust*, *Falstaff*, *Die Walküre*, *Don Carlos* and Smyth's *The Wreckers*. His wide repertory included Amonasro, Escamillo, Beckmesser and Gianni Schicchi, but he was principally admired as a Mozart singer. He staged *Wozzeck* (1952) and *Tannhäuser* (1955) at Covent Garden.

ELIZABETH FORBES

Austral [Fawaz, Wilson], **Florence** (*b* Melbourne, 26 April 1894; *d* Newcastle, NSW, 15 or 16 May 1968). Australian soprano. Her real name was Wilson, but she was also known by that of her stepfather, Fawaz, before she adopted her familiar professional name. Having studied at Melbourne Conservatory and with Sibella in New York, she is said to have been offered a contract with the Metropolitan Opera, but preferred to make her career in England. In 1922 she appeared at Covent Garden with the British National Opera Company as Brünnhilde in the complete *Ring* cycle, and this role was to remain her most famous; she was also successful as Isolde and Aida. Less forceful and more lyrical than many Wagnerian dramatic sopranos, she maintained a consistent beauty and evenness of tone through these arduous parts, which she also sang in the international Covent Garden seasons of 1924 and later. She married the flautist John Amadio, and toured widely with him in Australia and America. Her many admirable recordings for HMV include the pioneer late-acoustic English-language series of excerpts from the *Ring*; in the early-electric German-language series, as at Covent Garden, she shared the role with Frida Leider.

*

D. White: 'Florence Austral', *Record Collector*, xiv (1961–2), 5–29 [with discography by W. Hogarth and D. White]

DESMOND SHAWE-TAYLOR

Australia. Touring and adept mimicry are factors that made extensive activity in operatic performance possible in Australia for about a hundred years, from the middle of the 19th century to the middle of the 20th; along with this there emerged a surprisingly large number of proficient solo singers of opera, some of high international renown (Melba, Sutherland, Austral, Marjorie Lawrence). Touring as a way of life for Australian operatic performance finally destroyed itself because of the costs implicit in the large distances between the country's major population centres. But in its heyday touring fed and satisfied a remarkable appetite for opera. That this was not simply a by-product of a special kind of colonial society in a particular period is evidenced by the size of its continuing audience. The Australian Opera (formerly Elizabethan Trust Opera) performs in Sydney on most nights for about seven months of the year and for about four months in Melbourne; it visits Brisbane and Adelaide irregularly for short seasons and occasionally Perth and Hobart. Melbourne, Brisbane, Adelaide and Perth each support a resident company of high professional competence, using a nucleus of artistic and administrative staff to prepare limited series of city performances and country or suburban tours. The Australian Opera repertory may reach 20 or more operas in a year, that of the regional companies from three or four in the smaller capitals to six or eight in Melbourne.

The earliest kind of opera known to have been performed in Australia belonged to the vernacular English genre of the later 18th century (such as Shield's *The Poor Soldier*, 1796, Sydney – eight years after white settlement began), and works of this or related kinds were prominent in those years, up to 1840, when Sydney and Hobart were the principal centres. At least seven operas, including Bishop's travesty of *Le nozze di Figaro*, were given at Barnett Levey's Theatre Royal in Sydney, for example, as part of the 1833 season. The dominance of touring coincided with the onset of the gold rushes, from 1851, and the tendency of touring companies to favour what is already recognizable as the basis of a modern repertory based on Italian opera, with strong infusions from French grand opera and *opéra comique* and a few German works. The remarkable scope of touring later in the century and the speed with which some Verdi works, for example, found their way to Australia reflected the enterprise of the Irish impresario W. S. Lyster, whose companies toured

Australia almost continuously for 20 years from 1861 and whose greatest success, among a vast repertory, seems to have been *Les Huguenots*.

Lyster's companies played months at a time in Melbourne and Sydney, and some singers in touring companies chose to settle in Australia. Accordingly, Australians with ambitions in opera singing had models of professionalism and experienced practitioners under whom to study. Melba's first teacher was a retired Italian veteran of the Lyster era before she had her few months with Marchesi in Paris. At the level of singing accurately, rapidly, very loudly or very softly and unusually high or low, opera offered the same kind of opportunities for a gifted colonial to excel in a measurable way as sport. Eisteddfods, imported from Wales and vigorously cultivated, and, later, handsomely sponsored aria competitions provided recognizable and clearly defined ladders of individual progress. These help explain why Australia has produced an unusually large number of singers who have made careers in challenging environments: they have had a thorough grounding, through frequent competitions, in responding to the opportunities for instant demonstration provided by auditions and have developed their competitive instinct and technique.

Operatic conducting was a profession less quick to breed local imitation, partly because it depended on wider cultural and repertorial bases. For most of the middle-to-later history of opera in Australia, the notable conductors were foreigners who arrived with touring companies and stayed (such as Alberto Zelman senior, Gustav Slapoffski and, later, Georg Tintner, a member of the Vienna Boys' Choir stranded by war). Joseph Post was the first Australian-born musician to conduct opera with distinction; Sir Charles Mackerras became an important international professional, Richard Bonynge a specialist in 19th-century repertories and Stuart Challender, German-trained, a noted interpreter of Richard Strauss, Wagner and 20th-century works.

The composition of theatre works, a clearly defined and by no means intimidating occupation in the period of earlier white settlement, began much earlier. After the introduction of English ballad operas, an Irish convict and former medical student, Edward Geoghegan, put together (to existing tunes) a creditable and workable comic opera in one act, *The Currency Lass* (1844, Royal Victoria Theatre, Sydney). Isaac Nathan, the musician for whom Byron had written his *Hebrew Melodies*, has not been dislodged from the claims made for his *Don John of Austria* as the first opera written and performed (1847) in Australia, again on an English vernacular model. August Juncker and other practical theatre musicians contributed pieces in the 1890s that were remembered for a song or two, but their more ambitious scores remained unperformed. The stormy Australian career of George W. L. Marshall-Hall introduced bemused and sometimes alarmed Melburnians to a composer of Nietzschean ideals whose fierce championship of Wagner and mostly frustrated efforts on behalf of his own operas appear to have had no local progeny; however, his example might well have sustained such musicians as the Englishman, Fritz Hart, composer of 18 operas during his 20 years in Melbourne (most of them not performed) and the Melbourne-born Alfred Hill, whose belief in the importance of opera led him to compose a series of works and to become co-founder of the Australian Opera League with the idea of establishing a national repertory. It is no accident that the two most professionally equipped Australian opera composers of the post-World War II period, Arthur Benjamin and Malcolm Williamson, undertook their operatic writing in and for London; and the late Peggy Glanville-Hicks, an expatriate in the USA and Greece during her opera-writing years, composed the two most distinctive of her four operas with an avowed debt to Greek and Indian traditions of highly rhythmic monophony and heterophony. Australia was still in the process of establishing a national resident company and its first years were too under-funded for it to risk mounting the substantial works of expatriate or resident Australian composers (among them George Dreyfus and Felix Werder). When Dreyfus's *Garni Sands* was given in 1972 (University of New South Wales Opera) it was the first performance by a professional cast of a full-length opera since Hill's *Tapu* in 1904. In this decade and earlier, most performances of Australian works (by James Penberthy, Werder, Barry Conyngham, Donald Hollier, Alison Bauld and, later, Gillian Whitehead, Brian Howard, Nigel Butterley, Andrew Ford and others) were by specialized local groups, regional companies or ABC TV. Apart from a number of short operas, and Peter Sculthorpe's *Rites of Passage* (swiftly abandoned by Australian Opera when its character as a piece of symbolic musical theatre puzzled audiences), the first Australian work to receive vigorous launching and sustained support by the Australian Opera was Richard Meale's *Voss*, which disconcerted some listeners by demonstrating that Australia had forgotten its own musical past: Meale, instead of referring glancingly to Sydney dance music of the 1840s, quoted it extensively and literally, reviving the musical past as he commented on it.

Touring companies in Australia did sufficiently well up to the 1960s for the late J. Nevin Tait of the J. C. Williamson management to be confident of making a profit from the Sutherland-Williamson company of 1965. He was disappointed not to succeed in that, though the margin of loss was very small by operatic standards. But it was now obvious that in Australia, as elsewhere, opera must be subsidized, especially when it toured. The late Robert Quentin, founding general manager of what is now the Australian Opera, estimated that touring on the scale practised in 1957 accounted for one-third of the company's costs. Now that operatic performances are centred in the customary way on particular buildings in the capital cities, it is tempting to criticize the 'edifice complex' that overtook Australian state governments and municipalities in the 1970s and 1980s in building expensive performing arts centres: the idea is sometimes expressed in the notion that it is more important to support companies than the boards they tread on. But it can be argued, in the light of recent Australian experience, that nothing seems to work better in persuading governments of the value of opera and kindred arts than the presence of costly public theatres and the need to avoid the embarrassment of not using them.

It may be instructive to compare the centres that now house opera. The politically motivated changes made in Utzon's plan for Sydney Opera House meant that opera on a day-to-day basis was relegated to the smaller of the main halls with limited seating and a pit meant for light or intimate opera. With this example, it seems even more extraordinary that the ample and handsome State Theatre of the Victorian Arts Centre in Melbourne was equipped with a pit no more adequate for large opera orchestras. As Perth opted for the refurbishment of a traditional all-purpose theatre, the only opera auditoriums with adequate pits are those in Brisbane and Adelaide. Given the rapid growth of Brisbane and the wealth of the state on which it draws it would not be a complete surprise if that city were to become a principal centre for large-scale opera.

For further information on operatic life in the country's principal centres *see* ADELAIDE; BRISBANE; CANBERRA; MELBOURNE; PERTH; SYDNEY; and TRAVELLING TROUPES, §7.

*

R. Covell: *Australia's Music: Themes of a New Society* (Melbourne, 1967), esp. chap. 8, 'Australians and Opera'
B. and F. McKenzie: *Singers of Australia: from Melba to Sutherland* (Adelaide, 1967)
E. R. Irvin: *Theatre Comes to Australia* (St Lucia, Queensland, 1971)
E. Wood: '1840–1965: Precedents and problems for Australian opera composers', *Quadrant*, xvii/3 (1973), 27–37
R. Covell: 'Opera', *The Australian Encyclopaedia* (Sydney, 1977–83)
C. D. Throsby and G. A. Withers: *The Economics of the Performing Arts* (Melbourne, 1979)
H. Love: *The Golden Age of Australian Opera* (Sydney, 1981)
H. H. Guldberg: *The Australian Music Industry* (Sydney, 1987)
A. Gyger: *Opera for the Antipodes* (Sydney, 1990)

ROGER COVELL

Australian Opera. Company based in SYDNEY, founded in 1956 as the Australian Opera Company, and renamed as the Elizabethan Trust Opera Company in 1957 and as the Australian Opera in 1970.

Austria. *See* GERMANY, AUSTRIA; *see also* BADEN BEI WIEN, BAD ISCHL, BREGENZ, GRAZ, INNSBRUCK, KLAGENFURT, KREMSMÜNSTER, LINZ, MELK, SALZBURG and VIENNA.

Auto (Sp.: 'act'). A Spanish dramatic composition originally of religious or allegorical character. Developed from medieval liturgical drama, it attained its typically Spanish form in the 16th-century *autos sacramentales* performed in the streets during the feast of Corpus Christi. A 15th-century antecedent, Gómez Manrique's *Representación del nacimiento de Nuestro Señor*, includes a cradle song, various pastoral choruses and a closing villancico; this combination of music and drama was amplified in the *autos* of Juan del Encina and his contemporary Gil Vicente. The *auto* engaged the talents of many leading Spanish poets, including Lope de Vega and Calderón, and of composers such as Cristóbal Galán, Manuel de León Marchante, Gregorio de la Rosa and Juan Romero.

Autos sacramentales generally consisted of one act with a *loa* (prologue) or other introduction and a finale in praise of the Sacrament. Although spoken verse predominated, the main characters often expressed their emotions in song, and an offstage chorus commented on the action. There were frequent interruptions for *intermedios*, which often included *bailes* or *danzas*. In the 18th century these interpolations grew, incorporating popular songs, *seguidillas*, *entremeses* and *tonadillas* (e.g. Luis Misón's *Los jardineros*, a *tonadilla*, was composed for *De lo que va, ó El hombre de Dios*, 1761, Madrid). The performances moved from the streets to the theatre and employed professional actors and musicians. This secularization led to prohibition by royal decree in 1765, but *autos* continued to be performed in small cities and villages for a considerable time.

Music drama derived from the Spanish *auto* survives in the south-western USA. There are two types, one based on the Old Testament (e.g. *Comedia de Adán y Eva*, based on an *auto* first presented in Mexico City in 1532) and the more popular cycle based on the New Testament, of which the best known is *Los pastores*, a re-enactment of the Nativity story.

*

M. Latorre y Badillo: 'Representación de los autos sacramentales en el periodo de su mayor florecimiento (1620 à 1681)', *Revista de archivos, bibliotécas y museos*, xxv (1911), 189–211; xxvi (1912), 236–62
M. N. Hamilton: *Music in Eighteenth Century Spain* (Urbana, 1937)

Auvray, Jean-Claude (*b* Saint Lô, 14 May 1942). French director. At Toulouse in 1974 he directed *Manon*, which won the Cultural Ministry's prize for best production of the year. He staged *Elisabetta, regina d'Inghilterra* at Aix and *Le roi d'Ys* at Wexford (1975), *Carmen* at Toulouse and *La bohème* for ENO (1977). A production of *Rigoletto* (1981) set in New York during Prohibition began a long association with Basle, where he directed *Il trittico*, *Roméo et Juliette*, *Lucia di Lammermoor*, *La clemenza di Tito*, *Die Zauberflöte*, *Idomeneo*, *Les contes d'Hoffmann* and *Falstaff*. Spectacular stagings of *Don Carlos* and *Boris Godunov* at Orange, *La Gioconda* at Verona and *Il ritorno d'Ulisse* at Mézières, above Lausanne, were all praised. Though Auvray sometimes overloads his productions with detail, they are never uninteresting. ELIZABETH FORBES

Avaro, L' ('The Miser'). *Dramma giocoso* in three acts by PASQUALE ANFOSSI to a libretto by GIOVANNI BERTATI; Venice, Teatro S Moisè, autumn 1775.

L'avaro is in many ways a conservative work, relying on a traditional *commedia dell'arte* plot. The miser, Signor Orgasmo (bass), chooses an old, deaf, but rich suitor, Macobrio (bass), for his daughter, Rosalinda (soprano), but she wants to marry the young and attractive Felicino (tenor). Signor Orgasmo's son Steffanello (bass) wants to marry Laurina (soprano), a young woman whom the miser himself desires. A servant, Tortora (soprano), plays a minor role. In order to remove his son from amorous competition, Signor Orgasmo plans to send him to America; by pretending to prefer the old man to his son, Laurina persuades him to keep Steffanello at home. Felicino manages to enter the miser's home in the guise of a Moluccan astrologer and predicts that he is to become extremely rich. The two plots eventually converge in the Act 2 finale, where the miser is duped into signing marriage contracts in the belief that this will expedite the promised fortune.

One of Anfossi's most popular operas, *L'avaro* had over 30 productions throughout Europe and remained in the repertory until at least 1791, and possibly 1793. It was also known as *La fedeltà nelle angustie*, *Il sordo e l'avaro* and in French as *Le tuteure avare*. For this rather old-fashioned subject Anfossi wrote mostly short arias with relatively undemanding vocal parts and few tempo changes. Comic highlights include two duets for Signor Orgasmo and Macobrio, in which both librettist and composer explored the possibilities of discontinuity.

MARY HUNTER

Avdeyeva, Larisa (Ivanovna) (*b* Moscow, 21 June 1925). Russian mezzo-soprano. She studied singing and dramatic art at the Stanislavsky Opera Studio (1945–6). From 1947 she was a soloist at the Stanislavsky Music

Theatre, Moscow, where she sang Suzuki, La Périchole, Kosova and Varvara (Khrennikov's *V buryu* and *Frol Skobeyev*) and Mistress of the Copper Mountain (Molchanov's *Kamenniy tsvetok* ['The Stone Flower']). In 1952 she moved to the Bol'shoy Theatre, where she sang the leading Rimsky-Korsakov and Musorgsky mezzo roles, Tchaikovsky's Enchantress, Borodin's Konchakovna, Akhrosimova in *War and Peace* and the Commissar (Kholminov's *Optimisticheskaya tragediya*). She married Yevgeny Svetlanov. She has toured widely, in the USA, Canada, Japan and Europe and was made People's Artist of the RSFSR in 1964.

I. M. YAMPOL'SKY

Aventures, Nouvelles aventures. Pair of music-theatre pieces by GYÖRGY LIGETI to his own text; Stuttgart, Württemberg Staatstheater, 19 October 1966.

Ligeti's achievement in *Aventures* is a theatre without words, owing less to Blacher than to Beckett, silent films, comic strips and the interest in vocal acoustics he discovered when he arrived in Cologne in 1956. There are three singers (soprano, contralto, baritone) and seven instrumentalists (flute, horn, cello, double bass, harpsichord, piano doubling celesta, percussion), joining in a stream of episodes that includes a nonsense 'conversation' without accompaniment, a male solo of drunken exhibitionism, a chattering hubbub interrupted by isolated cries, and finally, a contralto 'aria' of solitariness and expectation. The result, as Ligeti has said, is 'an imaginary stage action that is undefined as to content but precisely defined as to the emotions displayed ... one experiences a sort of "opera", imagining the fantastic vicissitudes of imaginary persons on an imaginary stage'. The new vocal techniques explored by Stockhausen, Berio, Kagel and others provide the means for this precise definition of emotions, while the speed and suddenness of the cutting guarantee that pathos is subverted by wit, mystery by earthiness, lyricism by bathos.

Composed in 1962 (performed in Hamburg, 4 April 1963), this original work was cut short for lack of time, and in 1965 Ligeti completed a companion piece, *Nouvelles aventures*, which effectively provides the last two movements of a three-movement composition. To quote Ligeti again: 'There are still more human feelings than in *Aventures*, but the most intense emotions and expressions are in a way dissected and laid out, so that they become completely cool'. *Nouvelles aventures* is more intricately composed, faster in pace and odder, the episodes more compact and elusive. It also makes the whole into a substantial concert item, playing for 23 minutes. Both pieces were performed in Hamburg on 26 May 1966.

In 1966 Ligeti further expanded the work in his stage version *Aventures & Nouvelles aventures*, introducing mimes, dancers and extras in a rush of invented dramatic situations, though it is the concert form that has joined the repertory of avant-garde classics.

PAUL GRIFFITHS

Averara, Diana Margherita. *See* AURELI, DIANA MARGHERITA.

Averara, Pietro d' (*b* Bergamo; *d* ?Turin, by aut. 1720). Italian librettist. In Bergamo, he was a member of the Accademia degli Arioni. By 1686 he had moved to Venice and in 1687 he moved to Turin, by which time he was an *abbate*. In 1692 or 1693 he resigned his order to marry the singer Diana Margherita Aureli; they settled in Turin in 1697.

In the preface to *Angelica nel Cataj*, Averara claims to have written over 40 librettos, a number yet to be confirmed by bibliographic sources. His documented librettos were produced for Venice, Turin and Milan. In Turin, he also acted as impresario for two seasons, 1688–9 and 1689–90. From the preface to *Filindo*, it is clear that he had died by autumn 1720.

The fact that Averara drew many of his subjects from mythology reflects the preferences of the court of Savoy and the Spanish dependency of Milan. *Andromaca* is exceptional in his output because it combines elements from Euripides and Racine. *Filindo* (under various titles) and *Aretusa*, both pastorals, proved to be his most popular works.

Publio Elio Pertinace, Legrenzi, 1684; *L'amante fortunato per forza*, Varischino, 1684; *Silvio, re degli albani*, D. Gabrielli, 1689; *I gemelli rivali*, Turin, Regio, 1690; *Aiace*, Lonati, Magni and Ballarotti, 1694; *Rosilde*, Turin, Regio, 1696; *Demofoonte*, Milan, Regio, 1698; *Aristomene*, Turin, Regio, 1698; *Esione*, Ballarotti, 1699; *Ariovisto*, Perti, Magni and Ballarotti, 1699 (Palermo, S Cecilia, 1705, as L'amore fra l'armi, ovvero L'Ariovisto); *Arsiade*, Martinenghi, 1700; *L'inganno di Chirone*, C. F. Pollarolo, 1700; *Andromaca*, Milan, Regio, 1701; *Admeto re di Tessaglia*, Magni, 1702; *Ascanio*, C. F. Pollarolo, 1702; *Angelica nel Cataj*, Milan, Regio, 1702; *Aretusa*, Monari, 1703; *Alba Cornelia*, Milan, Regio, 1704; *Filindo* (pastorale eroica), G. M. Buini, 1720 (A. Pollarolo, 1728, as Nerina; Venice, S Margherita, 1729, as Dori); *Il trionfo della virtù*, Brusa, 1724

*

AllacciD; *DBI* (M. Quattrucci); *ES* (E. Zanetti)
C. Ivanovich: *Minerva al tavolino* (Venice, 1681, 2/1688)
G. Bonlini: *Le glorie della poesia e della musica* (Venice, 1730)
A. Groppo: *Catalogo di tutti i drammi per musica recitati ne' teatri di Venezia* (Venice, 1745)
B. Belotti: *Storia di Bergamo e di bergamaschi*, ii (Milan, 1940), 705, 712
S. Cordero di Pamparato: 'Un duca di Savoia impresario teatrale e i casi della musica Diana', *RMI*, xlv (1941), 108–32, 237–63
M. Viale Ferrero: *Storia del Teatro regio di Torino*, iii: *La scenografia dalle origini al 1936* (Turin, 1980)
E. Selfridge-Field: *Pallade veneta: Writings on Music in Venetian Society, 1650–1750* (Venice, 1985)
C. Sartori: *I libretti italiani a stampa dalle origini al 1800* (Cuneo, 1990–)

HARRIS S. SAUNDERS

Aviatore Dro, L' ('Dro the Aviator'). Opera in three acts by FRANCESCO BALILLA PRATELLA to his own libretto; Lugo di Romagna, Teatro Comunale Rossini, 4 September 1920.

Although Pratella was the one trained musician to sign the first few futurist manifestos, this most famous of his operas (composed 1911–14) only incidentally celebrates the machine age: basically it is a naive symbolic drama about escape from the flesh into pure spirit. Dro (tenor) becomes disgusted with the decadent sensuality that surrounds him: he therefore seeks refuge by the sea, and then flies upwards, in a primitive monoplane, towards 'that other, inverted sea, even deeper and more limitless'. The plane crashes almost at once; but Dro expires only gradually, beside its shattered remains, serenely identifying himself with the sky above him.

Pratella's music is most convincing when it is least futuristic – especially in passages where contemplation of Nature is expressed in radiant arabesques reflecting the composer's interest in Romagnan folksong. His crude use of 'modern' dissonance relies much too heavily on parallel motion and the whole-tone scale. However, the opera has the historical interest of using Luigi Russolo's futurist 'noise machines' (*intonarumori*) to represent the sounds of motor cars and the monoplane. JOHN C. G. WATERHOUSE

Avidom [Mahler-Kalkstein], **Menahem** (*b* Stanislav, 6 Jan 1908). Israeli composer of Polish origin. He studied at the Paris Conservatoire with Henri Rabaud, but considered himself self-taught. In 1925 he emigrated to Palestine (now Israel) where he was greatly influenced by Jewish and local (mainly oriental) folk music, although since the late 1950s his compositions have been mostly serial. A prolific composer, Avidom has produced nine operas, ten symphonies, songs for voice and piano, choral works and many chamber works, some written for educational purposes. His works have been awarded many prizes, the most important being the 1961 Israel State Prize for his opera *Alexandra haHashmonait* in which he used special themes for various characters (not unlike leitmotifs). Each scene in *Alexandra* is a complete entity within the structure of the opera. The plot revolves around Alexandra (soprano), the last descendant of the Hasmonean dynasty which ruled Judea for several generations during the period of the second Temple. Herod the Edomite (baritone), with the help of the Romans, overthrows the Hasmonean and usurps the Judean throne. Alexandra attempts to liberate her country from the yoke of Herod. Two arias from *Alexandra* are often performed as lieder; and the Bacchanalia (finale of Act 2) and ballet music are both attractive pieces which are also performed as short orchestral works.

Four of Avidom's operas were written for special commissions: *Bechol dor vador* ('In Every Generation') for the Ein-Gev Festival in 1955; *Bigdei haMelech* ('The Emperor's New Clothes') for the Israel Festival in 1976; and his dramatic scene *Me'arat Yodfat* ('The Cave of Jotapata') for the Festival of 1978. *HaRamay* ('The Crook'), to a libretto by Efraim Kishon, is a humorous chamber opera of one hour's duration about the burden of taxation in a country where the government has run out of ideas and decides to impose a tax on the air that its citizens breathe. It was commissioned by the Israel Chamber Ensemble and given its first performance under the baton of Gary Bertini in 1967. Except for his first three operas, all are written using 12-note technique. The first three – *Alexandra*, *In Every Generation* and *David the Boy and Goliath the Giant* – are written more traditionally in the so-called Mediterranean style, incorporating elements of the indigenous music of the area. In all cases, his operas display skilful orchestration. His 1971 radio opera *HaPreida* ('The Farewell') is a work depicting complex psychological situations. However, apart from a radio broadcast of *Alexandra* in the late 1960s in the USA by radio station KFIZ, Avidom's operas have not been performed outside Israel.

Bechol dor vador [In Every Generation] (ballad op, 3, L. Goldberg), Kibbutz Ein Gev, April 1955
David the Boy and Goliath the Giant, 1958 (children's op, L. Kipnis)
Alexandra haHashmonait, 1953 (3, A. Ashman), Tel-Aviv, 15 Aug 1959
HaRamay [The Crook] (comic op, 2, E. Kishon), Tel-Aviv, 22 April 1967
HaPreida [The Farewell; Louise] (chamber op, 1, D. Hertz), Radio Jerusalem, Nov 1971
Bigdei haMelech [The Emperor's New Clothes] (M. Ohad, after H. C. Andersen), Tel-Aviv, July 1976
Me'arat Yodfat [The Cave of Jotapata] (dramatic scene, S. Shalom), Tel-Aviv, 16 Aug 1978
The End of King Og (children's op, S. Tani), 1980
Hahet Harishon [The First Sin] (satirical op, A. Maged), 1981

D. Rabinovich: 'Ha'ôperah Alexandrah me'et Menahem 'Avidom', *Tatzlil*, x/18 (1978), 9–20 WILLIAM Y. ELIAS

Avignon. Ancient town in southern France. It was the seat of the papacy in the 14th century. The Jeu de Paume de Pompée Catilina was one of several theatres in use by the end of the 17th century, and its façade is still visible in the Place Crillon. Duhamel gives 1622 as the date of the first opera performed there, *Le duel de la juste rigueur et de la clémence* by Chanoine Internet; Loewenberg gives Lully's *Phaëton*, in 1687. Pierre Gautier's opera company from Marseilles had great success at Avignon during the last years of the 17th century, and Nicolas Ranc directed a permanent local company from 1705. The Jeu de Paume was restored in 1734. A new and much larger opera house was constructed in the Place de l'Hôtel de Ville in 1825, which burnt down in 1846. The new Théâtre Municipal (1000 seats) was built by the architects Charpentier and Feuchères. Today the season runs from October to June, with six productions of operas usually given three performances each, and six productions of operettas each given five or six performances. The audience typically prefers star singers rather than intricate productions. The Avignon Festival (July and August each year) was inaugurated in 1946. Though principally devoted to drama, since 1972 it has introduced contemporary music-theatre works in its programmes, performed in the cloisters in which Avignon abounds. Performances have included premières of works by composers such as Maurice Ohana, Claude Prey, Antoine Duhamel, André Boucourechliev and Philip Glass (the première of *Einstein on the Beach*, 25 July 1976).

LoewenbergA
L. Duhamel: 'Le théâtre d'Avignon aux XVIIe et XVIIIe siècles', *Annuaire du Vaucluse*, xxii (1909)
J. Robert: 'Les Ranc d'Avignon, propagateurs de l'opéra à la fin du XVIIe siècle', *RMFC*, vi (1966), 95–115
P. Puaux: *Avignon en festivals* (Paris, 1983)
L. J. Brote: 'A propos du répertoire lyrique des théâtres français', *Le Théâtre lyrique français 1945–1985*, ed. D. Pistone (Paris, 1987), 51–73 CHARLES PITT

Avoglio [Avolio; née Croumann or Graumann], **Christina Maria** (*b* ? Mainz or Frankfurt; *fl* 1727–46). German soprano. She sang in the Peruzzi company at Brussels, 1727–8, and was at Hamburg in 1729, where she sang Cleopatra in Handel's *Giulio Cesare* and Rodelinda in Telemann's *Flavius Bertaridus*. She sang two roles at the Sporck theatre in Prague in the 1730–31 season, where she is noted as 'in attuale servizio di S. M. il Re di Svezia, e Landgravio di Hassia-Kassel'; her husband, Giuseppe Avoglio, was a musician at the Hesse-Kassel court. She went to Russia with her husband, singing in Moscow in 1731 and St Petersburg, 1731–8. She was briefly in Italy in 1738 and then went to England. She may be 'La Muscovita' mentioned in the *London Daily Post* on 26 February 1739. She is next heard of in Handel's letter of 29 December 1741 to Jennens from Dublin: 'Sig[ra] Avolio, which I brought with me from London pleases extraordinary'. His leading soprano throughout the Dublin season, she sang the principal soprano part at the first performance of *Messiah* on 13 April 1742; other roles included Rosmene in *Imeneo*. She was a member of Handel's company in the Covent Garden oratorio seasons of 1743 and 1744, singing Iris in *Semele*; in 1744 she created Hecate in Samuel Howard's pantomime *The Amorous Goddess* at Drury Lane. Her Handel parts in 1742–3 require a moderate compass (*d'* to *a''*) but considerable flexibility.

WINTON DEAN, DANIEL FREEMAN

Avondano, Pedro António (bap. Lisbon, 16 April 1714; *d* Lisbon, 1782). Portuguese composer of Italian ancestry. He studied with his father, a Genoese violinist of the Portuguese royal chapel and a composer, and himself became a violinist in the same chapel; others of his family were also members. His duties as a court musician included composing the music for the ballets which accompanied the operas. He also promoted concerts in his own house in the Rua da Cruz, and was a Knight of the Order of Christ. He wrote a *dramma giocoso*, *Il mondo della luna* (3, C. Goldoni; Salvaterra de Magos, Court, carn. 1765; *P-La*) and several oratorios and instrumental works. Three further individual arias which survive (in *P-Ln*, *D-B* and *B-Bc* respectively) were probably intended for the Lisbon productions of Perez's *La Didone* (1765), Majo's *Antigono* (1772) and Galuppi's *Il filosofo di campagna*.

*

DBP; *MGG* (C. Schröder-Auerbach)

J. Mazza: 'Dicionário biográfico de músicos portugueses', *Ocidente*, xxv (1945); also pubd separately, ed. J. A. Alegria (Lisbon, 1944–5)

M. C. de Brito: *Opera in Portugal in the Eighteenth Century* (Cambridge, 1989)

MANUEL CARLOS DE BRITO

Avos [Avosso], **Girolamo.** *See* ABOS, GIROLAMO.

Avossa [d'Avossa, Avosa, Avos, d'Anossa], **Giuseppe** (*b* Paola, Cosenza, 1708; *d* Naples, 9 Jan 1796). Italian composer, often confused with his contemporary Girolamo Abos, several of whose *opere serie* are sometimes attributed to him. The family is reputed to have been of Spanish origin. After studying in Naples he became a *maestro di cappella* there and possibly taught singing. By 1749 he was a *maestro di cappella* in Pesaro and conductor of the municipal theatre orchestra there. His principal fame derives from his highly popular comic opera *La pupilla*, but he probably wrote mainly church music. Surviving works have concertato textures, contrapuntal facility, a certain adventurousness in tonal thinking and, in some cases, an essentially symphonic conception of a whole movement. Avossa also wrote sacred operas: *La nuvoletta d'Ella*, which was given in Ancona in 1746, and *La felicità de' tempi* and *Il giudizio di Salomone* for Pesaro (1749 and 1751).

Don Saverio (commedia per musica, A. Palomba), Venice, S Moisè, aut. 1744

Lo scolaro alla moda (dramma comico), Reggio Emilia, Cittadella, carn. 1748

Il baron gonfianuvoli (dramma comico-giocoso), Salzburg, carn. 1750

I tutori (commedia per musica), Naples, Nuovo, wint. 1757

La pupilla (commedia per musica, Palomba), Naples, Fiorentini, carn. 1763, *H-Bn*; in *A-Wn* and *US-Wc* as Il ciarlone

*

DBI (U. Prota-Giurleo); *LoewenbergA*; *RosaM*; *SchmidlDS*

M. Scherillo: *L'opera buffa napoletana durante il settecento: storia letteraria* (Naples, 1883, 2/1917), 280, 282

C. Cinelli: 'Memorie cronistoriche del Teatro di Pesaro (1637–1897)', *La cronaca musicale* (Pesaro, 1897), ii, 431–2

U. Prota-Giurleo: *Ricordi digiacomiani* (Naples, 1956), 10

JAMES L. JACKMAN, DALE MONSON

Avshalomov, Aaron (*b* Nikolayevsk, Siberia, 31 Oct/12 Nov 1894; *d* New York, 26 April 1965). American composer of Siberian origin. After studying at the Zürich Conservatory in 1913–14, he spent more than 30 years in China, where he composed symphonic and dramatic works, collected Chinese folk music, and became head librarian of the Municipal Library of Shanghai (1928–43) and conductor of the Shanghai City Government Symphony (1943–6). He arrived in the USA in 1947, joining his American wife and his son, the composer and conductor Jacob Avshalomov (*b* Tsingtao, China, 28 March 1919). He continued to compose, but his work never achieved much recognition in the USA.

Avshalomov was much interested in the integration of Western music with elements of traditional Chinese music. He made use of authentic Chinese themes in many of his symphonic and dramatic works, including tone poems and four pantomime ballets. His three operas were composed in China. *The Great Wall*, written between 1933 and 1941, was first performed in Shanghai in 1945 and repeated in Nanjing under the sponsorship of Madame Chiang Kai-shek. It requires a minimum of 40 singers, dancers and actors, a chorus and orchestra.

Kuan Yin (C. Lunt), Beijing, 24 April 1925

The Twilight Hour of Yang Kwei Fei, 1933 (1, A. E. Grantham)

The Great Wall [Meng Jianghu], 1933–41 (Avshalomov), Shanghai, 26 Nov 1945

*

VintonD

American Composers Alliance Bulletin, x/2 (1962), 18–19

BARBARA A. PETERSEN

Axur, re d'Ormus ('Axur, King of Ormus'). *Dramma tragicomico* in five acts by ANTONIO SALIERI to a libretto by LORENZO DA PONTE after PIERRE-AUGUSTIN BEAUMARCHAIS' libretto *Tarare*; Vienna, Burgtheater, 8 January 1788.

The opera was first conceived as a translation into Italian of Salieri's last opera for Paris, *TARARE* (1787), but Da Ponte and Salieri abandoned the translation in favour of a new opera based freely on Beaumarchais' libretto. Da Ponte's text follows *Tarare* in general, but the two operas differ in many details and in some aspects of characterization. Beaumarchais' King Atar is now called Axur (bass; sung by Francesco Benucci); Beaumarchais' hero Tarare is now called Atar (tenor; Vincenzo Calvesi). In giving the hero the name of the original villain, Da Ponte may have been developing a point made by Beaumarchais himself when he gave his two principal characters names whose relation to one another are so clear (Atar – Axur; Tarare – Atar). Originally in five acts, *Axur* was later performed in a four-act version in which Salieri combined Acts 1 and 2.

In creating an opera for Joseph II's *opera buffa* troupe, Da Ponte and Salieri gave *buffo* elements a prominent place; one can see this, for example, in the character of King Axur. Unlike Beaumarchais' Atar, Axur became, probably with the influence of Benucci, something of a caricature – a *buffo* tyrant, much less threatening than Atar. The role of the eunuch Biscroma (tenor, Beaumarchais' Calpigi), a former castrato singer, was already a source of some humour in *Tarare*; Da Ponte took this humour much further. Atar and his beloved Aspasia (soprano, Beaumarchais' Astasie) represent the *parti serie* that one would expect in most late 18th-century *opere buffe*. Yet this is no *opera buffa.* Da Ponte preserved much of the spectacle of Beaumarchais' drama and many of its most powerful scenes, including Axur's onstage suicide, so that *Axur* fully deserves the generic categorization of 'dramma tragicomico' that Da Ponte and Salieri gave it.

The extensive use of chorus and the preference for accompanied over simple recitative (though simple recitative is not excluded entirely) both point to the work's origins as a French opera and differentiate it from the other operas written for Joseph's *opera buffa* troupe. Salieri's early biographer Mosel alluded to the more serious qualities of *Axur* when he praised it as 'the most excellent of all serious Italian operas – even including Mozart's *La clemenza di Tito*'.

First performed in celebration of the marriage of Archduke Franz, Joseph's nephew, *Axur* was an immediate and lasting success. It was said to have been Joseph's favourite opera, and it found favour with the Viennese public as well. With 100 performances between 1788 and 1805, *Axur* was one of the most often performed operas in the Viennese court theatres during this period. Many performances in Germany, mostly in German translation, attest to its popularity during the last decade of the 18th century and the first decade of the 19th. JOHN A. RICE

Ayliff [Aylif, Alyff, Ayloff, Ayloffe], Mrs (*fl* 1692–6). English soprano and actress. She sang in *The Fairy-Queen* at Dorset Garden Theatre in May 1692 and soon became Purcell's leading soprano. In the *Gentleman's Journal* for August 1692 Peter Motteux referred to her performance of Purcell's italianate 'Ah me to many deaths decreed' in Crowne's play *Regulus* as 'divinely sung'. Well over a dozen of Purcell's songs and dialogues were published as sung by her, including 'When first I saw the bright Aurelia's eyes', written for a revival of *Dioclesian.* In 1695 she sang in *Bonduca* at Drury Lane and worked with Betterton's company at Lincoln's Inn Fields. Her last recorded appearance was in November 1696 when she sang in *The Loves of Mars and Venus*, a masque with music by Eccles and Finger.

*

BDA; *LS*

O. Baldwin and T. Wilson: 'Purcell's Sopranos', *MT*, cxxiii (1982), 602–9

C. A. Price: *Henry Purcell and the London Stage* (Cambridge, 1984)

OLIVE BALDWIN, THELMA WILSON

Ayrton, William (*b* London, 22 Feb 1777; *d* London, 8 May 1858). English impresario. He was director of the Italian opera at the King's Theatre, London, for three memorable seasons, 1817, 1821 and 1825. A founding member (1813) and concert director (1814) of the Philharmonic Society, he was known for his musical taste and administrative skill when, in summer 1816, the theatre's proprietor, Edmund Waters, hired him as managing director. He went to Paris to secure the best available singers, notably Pasta, Ambrogetti and Angrisani, and filled out the company with Camporese and Crivelli; all made their London débuts in 1816–17. With Fodor-Mainvielle and Naldi from the previous season, this made the strongest team at the theatre in years. The repertory too was of a high order: Cimarosa's *Penelope*, Paer's *Agnese* and Paisiello's *La molinara* were joined by *Figaro*, *Così*, *La clemenza di Tito* and, for the first time complete on an English stage, *Don Giovanni* (12 April 1817). The last, given 23 times in the season, was a huge success and consolidated Ayrton's high standing in the musical world; to the end of his career – mainly as a writer on music – it was his proudest professional achievement.

As director, Ayrton believed himself responsible not only for personnel, repertory and the mundane aspects of theatre administration (instrument dealers, copyists, moneytakers, doorkeepers), but also the artistic policy of the house. He insisted on his own casting, on artists' attendance at rehearsals and, as far as possible, faithfulness to the score: a singer's whimsical interpolations (or a patron's preference in sopranos) were not to be tolerated. When Waters overruled him on one of these points in 1817, he stepped down in frustration and had to go to court for his remuneration; he was awarded damages of £700 against his claim of £1200.

In 1821 John Ebers took over the lease of the faltering theatre on the express condition that Ayrton be director. It was a profitable season. *La gazza ladra* was a successful novelty, Ronzi de Begnis and Alberico Curioni attractive acquisitions. Ayrton's salary came to £1500. But again his authority over singers was interfered with, and he withdrew before the season's end. Back in 1825, he presided over a much talked-about season: Pasta and Curioni were great favourites, Malibran and the castrato Velluti made their London débuts and Meyerbeer's *Il crociato in Egitto* was highly acclaimed. But when through royal influence the notorious N. C. Bochsa was appointed conductor for the following season, Ayrton retired in disgust, Velluti taking his place. Finally, in July 1827 Ayrton concocted a plan to lease the King's Theatre himself. His proposal – for a three-year period – was turned down by the assignors and he thenceforward gave up all official connection with the theatre, concentrating instead on his work for *The Harmonicon*, *The Examiner* and other literary projects.

*

Ayrton Collection, *GB-Lbl* (esp. Add. MSS 52335 and 52336)

[R. M. Bacon]: Review of 'La gazza ladra', *Quarterly Musical Magazine and Review*, iii (1821), 252–63 [with a prospectus of the season]

J. Ebers: *Seven Years of the King's Theatre* (London, 1828)

S. D.: 'Chronicles of the Italian Opera in England: Season 1817', *The Harmonicon*, viii (1830), 246–7

L. Langley: *The English Musical Journal in the Early Nineteenth Century* (diss., U. of North Carolina, Chapel Hill, 1983), 284–317

LEANNE LANGLEY

Ayton, Fanny [?Frances] (? bap. Macclesfield, 1804; *d* 1832 or later). English soprano. She studied in Florence and first appeared in Italy. In 1827–8 she was engaged at the King's Theatre, London, where she sang Ninetta in *La gazza ladra* as well as the principal roles in *Il turco in Italia* and Pacini's *La schiava in Bagdad.* In 1828 she also sang at Drury Lane, in an English version of *Il turco* and as Rosetta in *Love in a Village.* The next year she appeared with Malibran under Michael Costa. In 1831–2 she sang Creusa in Mayr's *Medea* at the King's Theatre and Isabel in a mutilated version of *Robert le diable* at Drury Lane.

*

J. Ebers: *Seven Years of the King's Theatre* (London, 1828), 333

H. F. Chorley: *Thirty Years' Musical Recollections* (London, 1862), i, 240

Azerbaijan. For discussion of opera in Azerbaijan *see* BAKU.

Azevedo, Luiz Heitor Corrêa de (*b* Rio de Janeiro, 13 Dec 1905). Brazilian musicologist. He studied at the Instituto Nacional de Música, Rio de Janeiro, in the mid-1920s and was active as a pianist and composer from 1929 to 1937, specializing in musicology and music criticism. He became librarian at the institute in 1932 and founded and directed the *Revista brasileira de Música* (1934–42). In 1939 he received his doctorate from the University of Brazil. His monograph *Relação das óperas de autores brasileiros* (Rio de Janeiro, 1938) was the first historical work on Brazilian opera. Besides general studies on Latin American music history, he has published definitive works on Brazilian 19th- and 20th-century music and musicians, with special attention to the Brazilian operatic repertory. GERARD BÉHAGUE

Azione sacra (It.: 'sacred action', 'sacred plot'). One of several terms commonly applied to the SEPOLCRO, composed to texts in Italian for the Habsburg court in Vienna in the second half of the 17th century. The term was also one of many used for the Italian ORATORIO of the 18th century and for the 'staged oratorio', or *opera sacra*, of the late 18th and early 19th centuries (*see* SACRED OPERA). Although oratorio was essentially an unstaged genre, the *sepolcro* was presented with a minimum of staging and action and the *opera sacra* was fully staged and acted in the manner of an opera.

From the 1780s to about 1820, the theatres of Naples often presented staged oratorios during Lent and usually designated them *azione sacra*. Such works differed little from the *opera seria* of the time except for their subject matter, which was that of the traditional oratorio. P. A. Guglielmi's *Debora e Sisara: azione sacra* (1788, Naples) was favoured by numerous performances, both staged and unstaged, throughout Europe, as was Rossini's *Mosè in Egitto*, called *azione tragico-sacra* in the libretto printed at Naples in 1818.

*

R. Schnitzler: *The Sacred Music of Antonio Draghi* (diss., U. of North Carolina, 1971)
H. E. Smither: *A History of the Oratorio*, i (Chapel Hill, 1977)
——: 'Oratorio and Sacred Opera, 1700–1825: Terminology and Genre Distinction', *PRMA*, cvi (1979–80), 88–104

HOWARD E. SMITHER

Azione teatrale (It.: 'theatrical action', 'theatrical plot'). The term was coined by Metastasio to denote a species of SERENATA that, unlike many works in this genre, contained a definite plot and envisaged some form of simple staging. The 12 works by Metastasio so described begin with *Endimione* (1721, Naples, set by Sarro) and end with *La corona* (1765, Vienna, set by Gluck). One of the most celebrated was *L'isola disabitata* (1752), first performed in Madrid with music by Bonno. Gluck's *Orfeo ed Euridice*, to a libretto by Ranieri de' Calzabigi (1762), was originally described as an *azione teatrale*.

MICHAEL TALBOT

Azuma, Atsuko (*b* Osaka, 11 Dec 1939). Japanese soprano. She studied in Tokyo, then in Milan and Parma, making her début in 1963 at Reggio Emilia as Suzel (*L'amico Fritz*). She sang at La Scala and elsewhere in Italy; in France, Belgium, Germany and Austria; in North and South America and with Fujiwara Opera in Tokyo. She took part in the première of Joachim Ludwig's *Rashomon* at Augsburg (1972). Her repertory, which extended from Mozart to Strauss, included Violetta, Micaëla, Mimì and Iris, but her most admired interpretation was undoubtedly Butterfly, which suited her extremely well vocally as well as dramatically. She used her round, full-toned voice with taste and artistry. ELIZABETH FORBES

Azzali, Augusto (*b* Ravenna, 1863; *d* Atlantic City, NJ, July 1907). Italian conductor, composer and impresario. His career was largely spent in touring Latin America and the Caribbean, sometimes as the conductor for other impresarios, sometimes as both conductor and impresario of his own company.

His four-act opera *Ermengarda*, to a libretto by P. Martini, had its première at the Teatro Andreini in Mantua on 27 November 1886. Azzali embarked for Colombia in 1891. A six-month season in Bogotà was followed by an extended tour of the country and another season in the capital in 1893. During that season his *Lhidiak* (2, V. Fontana), based on an Indian legend, the first opera to be written for Colombia, had its première at the Colón theatre (12 August). In 1895–6 he started another tour that included Guatemala City, Quezaltenango, Bogotà and Medellin. Later he also visited San Salvador, San José, Mexico and Puerto Rico. He died in Atlantic City while trying to save a young chorus member from drowning.

*

J. I. Perdomo Escobar: *La Opera en Colombia* (Bogota, 1979)

TOM KAUFMAN

Azzolini, Caterina (*fl* 1700–08). Italian soprano. Sometimes known as 'La Valentina', and probably of Ferrarese birth, she was employed at the Mantuan court until she entered the service of Ferdinando de' Medici at Pratolino in 1700. A specialist in male roles, she appeared in ten operas there and in Florence, including Handel's *Rodrigo* (1707), in which she played Evanco. She sang in C. F. Pollarolo's *Venceslao* in Venice in 1703. Handel wrote for her within the narrow compass of *f′* to *a″*. WINTON DEAN

B

Babbi, Gregorio (Lorenzo) (*b* Cesena, 16 Nov 1708; *d* Cesena, 2 Jan 1768). Italian tenor. Active from 1730 to 1760, he was renowned for his powerful voice and wide range (*c* to *c″*, full voice; *c″* to *g″*, falsetto), his dramatic and expressive manner and his mastery of the improvised bel canto style. Babbi sang in the major theatres of Italy (notably in Florence, Venice, Rome, Turin, Padua and Naples) and Portugal (Lisbon), in heroic *opere serie* by Hasse, Vivaldi, Albinoni, Galuppi, Porpora and Jommelli, among others. After a brief period as 'virtuoso' to the Grand Duke of Tuscany (*c*1730), Babbi obtained the patronage of Charles III, King of Naples and the Two Sicilies and Palermo. From 1747 until his retirement in 1759, he performed almost exclusively for Charles's court in Naples. Burney called him a 'dignified, splendid and powerful performer', with the 'sweetest, most flexible, and most powerful voice of its kind, that his country could boast at the time', and P. L. Ghezzi considered him worthy of a caricature (MS, *I-Rvat* Cod. Lat. Ottoboniensis 3117, f.161). Babbi's first wife Giovanna Guaetti [Guaetta, Guaitti], a soprano, sang in many operas with him. His son Cristoforo Bartolomeo Babbi (1745–1814) was a violinist and composer, and his grandson Gregorio Babbi was also a singer (bass) and composer; both were active at the electoral court in Dresden.

*

DBI (A. Zapperi); *ES* (E. Zanetti); *FétisB*; *GerberNL*; *SchmidlD*
C. Burney: 'Gregorio Babbi', *Rees's Cyclopaedia*, iii (London, 1819)
N. Trovanelli: 'Due celebri cantanti cesenati del secolo scorso', *Il cittadino: giornale della domenica*, v/30 (Cesena, 25 July 1897)

GLORIA EIVE

Babbini [Babini], **Matteo** (*b* Bologna, 19 Feb 1754; *d* Bologna, 22 Sept 1816). Italian tenor. He studied with Arcangelo Cortoni and made his début in 1773 in Modena. After singing in various Italian cities, he was engaged at the court operas of Berlin and then St Petersburg (1777–81), where he was much admired in works by Paisiello. He appeared in Lisbon, Madrid, Vienna, at the King's Theatre, London (1786–7), and in Paris. Returning to Italy in 1789, he sang in Naples, Rome, Turin and Bologna, where in 1802 he made his farewell. Reputed to be a stylish singer with a flexible voice, he took part in Cimarosa's *Gli Orazi ed i Curiazi*, Nicolini's *Manlio* and Mayr's *Misteri eleusini*.

ELIZABETH FORBES

Babylons Pyramiden ('The Pyramids of Babylon'). *Heroisch-komische Oper* in two acts by JOHANN MEDERITSCH (Act 1) and PETER WINTER (Act 2) to a libretto by EMANUEL SCHIKANEDER; Vienna, Freihaus-Theater auf der Wieden, 25 October 1797.

This work received over 60 performances at the Theater auf der Wieden and played successfully in other cities as well. Like Mozart's *Die Zauberflöte* and other heroic-comic works, it is rich in temple scenes, sacred rites, priests, processions, magic and folk humour. The circuitous plot culminates in a ceremony at the pyramid, where Queen Ragunka (soprano) is instructed by the high priest Senides (bass) to choose the future king. She selects the young Timoneus (tenor) to the joy of his lover Cremona (soprano). The villains Artandos (bass) and Pitagoleus (bass) are defeated, while the servants Forte (bass) and Piana (soprano) provide comic relief. Each act features an introduction and a finale. The arias range from simple folklike numbers to elaborate, pathos-laden solos (Cremona's 'Ohne Mutter, ohne Gatten' in Act 2 is an excellent example of the latter). The second half of the opera, composed by Winter, is distinguished by a fuller orchestral texture and more expansive polyphonic passages.

LINDA TYLER

Bacarisse, Salvador (*b* Madrid, 12 Sept 1898; *d* Paris, 5 Aug 1963). Spanish composer. He studied in Madrid, where Conrado del Campo was his composition teacher. A leader of the Grupo de los Ocho formed in Madrid in emulation of Les Six to combat conservatism, as director of Unión Radio until 1936 he was able to pursue with particular success the difficult task of promoting new music. During the Civil War he held an administrative post in the Consejo Central de la Música, which enabled him to initiate a series of music publications, the journal *Música* and the National Orchestra. From 1939 until his death he worked in Paris as a Spanish-language broadcaster.

The first performances of Bacarisse's works brought violent reaction from a very conservative public unable to accept their harsh dissonance and polytonality. Bacarisse also inclined towards impressionism and Falla-like, though quite individual, nationalism. He used texts from classical and contemporary Spanish writers in vocal and stage works of a direct impact, though in some cases, perhaps swayed by the aesthetic of Les Six, he preferred a humorous, amiable, witty manner, as in the opera *Charlot*.

A certain neo-Romantic tendency, noticeable in some youthful works, developed in much of his Parisian output; yet on other occasions he introduced a more fluent, personal, Spanish vein. In 1958 he won a French radio competition with the opera *El tesoro de Boabdil*, and he repeated that success with *Font aux cabres*, a radio version of *Fuenteovejuna* broadcast in 1962. His music is brilliantly orchestrated, and the dramatic temperament with which he was endowed is often perceptible.

Charlot (3, R. Gómez de la Serna), 1933
El tesoro de Boabdil (A. Camp and F. Puig), 1958
Fuenteovejuna (J. Camp, after F. Lope de Vega), 1962; as Font aux cabres, RTF, 1962

Undated: L'étudiant de Salamanque; Le sang d'Antigone (mistero tragico, J. Bergamin, after Sophocles) ENRIQUE FRANCO

Baccaloni, Salvatore (*b* Rome, 14 April 1900; *d* New York, 31 Dec 1969). Italian bass. He studied with Kaschmann and made his début at the Teatro Adriano, Rome, in 1922 as Dr Bartolo. In 1926 he was engaged at La Scala, where he sang regularly until 1940, first in serious roles and then, on Toscanini's advice, specializing in roles like Dulcamara, the two Bartolos and the *buffo* roles in Wolf-Ferrari's operas. He appeared at Covent Garden (1928–9) and at Glyndebourne (1936–9), where his Leporello, Dr Bartolo and Don Pasquale set a standard of excellence. He made his North American début in Chicago in 1930 as Melitone and sang at the Teatro Colón (1931–41, 1947). In 1940 he joined the Metropolitan, and sang there regularly until 1962, giving 297 performances, mostly in the Italian *buffo* repertory. He sang Falstaff at San Francisco (1944) and made numerous tours of the USA. Portly in build and good-humoured, Baccaloni had a communicative dramatic gift for comedy and was noted for his musicianship.

GV (R. Celletti; R. Vegeto)

Salvatore Baccaloni in the title role of Donizetti's 'Don Pasquale'

Baccanti, Le ('The Bacchanals'). Opera in a prologue and three acts by GIORGIO FEDERICO GHEDINI to a libretto by Tullio Pinelli after EURIPIDES' tragedy *The Bacchae*; Milan, Teatro alla Scala, 22 February 1948.

Composed in 1941–4 during his most richly creative period, *Le baccanti* is much the most impressive of Ghedini's operas. Pinelli's libretto remains true to the outline of Euripides' tragedy, with a prominent part assigned to the chorus and a simple, boldly sculpted action. The total effect is stylized and oratorio-like: the musical influence of *Oedipus rex*, though by no means all-dominating, is appropriate enough as far as it goes.

Thebes is in the grip of the orgiastic new religion of Dionysus, much to the chagrin of the young king Pènteo [Pentheus] (tenor), whose own mother Agave (soprano) has become a devotee of the cult. When brought face to face with the god (Dioniso, baritone), Pentheus at first does not recognize him and rashly tries to imprison him. But he eventually agrees to go with Dionysus to Mount Cithaeron, the gathering-place of the maenads, whom he hopes to challenge but who promptly tear him to pieces. His head is then brought back to Thebes impaled on a thyrsus staff, carried by Agave: in her crazed state of mind, she is unable to recognize it as that of her son, not (as she had imagined) of a lion; and only on reaching the city is she forced to see the truth by her father the old king Cadmo [Cadmus] (bass). Agave is condemned by Dionysus to spend the rest of her life as a wanderer, mourning Pentheus.

As well as owing a fair amount to Stravinsky, Ghedini's music also shows some kinship with Frank Martin. Yet in total effect it is powerfully individual, with a distinctive interval-structure striking a fine balance between tonal and quasi-serial forces. The orchestration is highly original: often stark and lapidary in effect, but with quieter interludes that give scope for a cold, hypnotic lyricism, unlike anything by any other composer. Though certainly one of the two or three finest Italian operas of a decade which also saw the birth of Dallapiccola's *Il prigioniero*, *Le baccanti* had to wait a long time for adequate recognition, even in Italy. Only when it was revived in Milan in 1972 was the work's stature properly appreciated; and even today it still awaits the international currency it deserves.

JOHN C. G. WATERHOUSE

Bacewicz, Grażyna (*b* Łódź, 5 Feb 1909; *d* Warsaw, 17 Jan 1969). Polish composer and violinist. She studied at the Warsaw Conservatory with Kazimierz Sikorski and others, then (1932–4) in Paris with Nadia Boulanger and Carl Flesch. Bacewicz's music from 1945 to 1960 demonstrates her particular gift for vigorous and idiomatic writing for strings and for piano. Her comic radio opera, *Przygoda króla Artura* ('The Adventure of King Arthur'; 1, E. Fischer, after S. Undset; Polish Radio, 10 Nov 1959) deftly blends a choral idiom derived from Stravinsky's *The Wedding* with orchestral effects associated with comedy films of the period. The story of

Arthur's battle of wits with a marauding Giant (in which the former is rescued by the guile of a Witch and the apparent self-sacrifice of Gawain) concerns a familiar fairy-tale moral based on the riddle 'What do all women want?'

*

L. Erhardt: 'Telewizyjna "Przygoda króla Artura" ', *Ruch muzyczny* (1960), no.15, p.6

E. Derewecka: 'Opery radiowe', ibid, no.21, p.12 [on *Przygoda króla Artura*] ADRIAN THOMAS

Bach, Jan (Morris) (*b* Forrest, IL, 11 Dec 1937). American composer. He studied with Kenneth Gaburo, Donald Martino, Aaron Copland and others. The recipient of many awards and grants, including the Koussevitzky Award (1961) and an NEA grant (1975), he has taught at Northern Illinois University since 1966.

Bach has contributed two works to the operatic repertory: *The System* (1974) and *The Student from Salamanca* (1980). Winner of the Mannes College of Music Opera Competition in 1973, *The System* was given its première by the Mannes Opera Workshop on 5 March 1974. The libretto, by the composer, is based on *The System of Doctor Tarr and Professor Fether* by Edgar Allan Poe. Bach employs sounds reminiscent of 19th-century music halls to enrich his score. His use of ensembles is ingenious, but has been criticized as too complex to allow full comprehension of the text.

The Student from Salamanca was awarded the one-act opera competition prize given by the American Music Center on behalf of the New York City Opera. This led to the work's première by the City Opera on 9 October 1980. The libretto, freely adapted by the composer from two interludes of Cervantes (*La cueva de Salamanca* and *El viejo celoso*), deals with an *opera buffa* cliché involving the cuckolded aging husband and his adventurous wife and servants. The score is highly chromatic; the vocal lines use themes heard earlier in the orchestra; and contrapuntal handling of the voices is a cornerstone of the ensembles. Major flaws of the opera are its excessive length and an iterative rhyme scheme that prevents the work from exploring other means of portraying the comic aspects of the story.

*

Anderson2

R. H. Kornick: *Recent American Opera: a Production Guide* (New York, 1991), 36–9 JAMES P. CASSARO

Bach, Johann [John] **Christian** (*b* Leipzig, 5 Sept 1735; *d* London, 1 Jan 1782). German composer, youngest son of Johann Sebastian Bach and the only member of the Bach family to compose operas. He probably began lessons in keyboard playing and theory with his father in 1743 or 1744. After his father died, in 1750, he went to live in Berlin with his brother Carl Philipp Emanuel with whom he continued his keyboard studies and took composition lessons. There he first had the opportunity to attend opera performances on a regular basis.

In 1754 he went to Italy, where he found a congenial teacher in Padre Martini of Bologna and a generous patron in Count Agostino Litta of Milan. Both teacher and patron directed Bach, who had embraced Roman Catholicism, towards a safe career as a church musician. However, as early as 1756 he may have written some substitute arias for an opera (Gioacchino Cocchi's *Emira*), at the Regio Ducal Teatro, Milan, and in December 1758 his aria 'Misero pargoletto' was sung in place of Antonio Ferradini's original setting, which had failed to please during the early performances of his *Demofoonte*.

Bach's own first full-length opera, *Artaserse*, came two years later in response to a commission from the Teatro Regio, Turin, where it opened the 1761 carnival season. The opera's reception was affected first by the illness of the Prince of Piedmont and then by the indisposition of Gaetano Guadagni, the primo uomo, and it received only seven performances. The next invitation came from Naples: the opera was *Catone in Utica*, first performed at the Teatro S Carlo in November 1761. This was the first of Bach's four operas in which the German tenor Anton Raaff created the title role, and it was easily his most successful work for the stage, with nine productions in all. Its success resulted in Bach's being commissioned to compose a second opera, and a cantata to precede it, for S Carlo the same season. *Alessandro nell'Indie* was less well received, but it yielded Bach's most famous aria, 'Non so d'onde viene'.

In the spring of 1762 Bach received an invitation to compose two operas for the King's Theatre in London. His first contracted opera, *Orione*, given 13 times, was (according to Burney) admired chiefly for the richness of its harmony and particularly its orchestral writing. The reception of *Orione* was helped by Bach's having persuaded the popular *buffo* singer Anna Lucia de Amicis to undertake the principal female role, a début which launched her on a second career as a prima donna in serious opera. Bach's second contracted opera, *Zanaida*, entered the repertory in May 1763, so late in the season that, although it was well received, there was time for only six performances.

At the end of the season Bach decided to make London his home. In due course he became music master to the queen, founded the Bach-Abel concerts with his compatriot Carl Friedrich Abel, appeared frequently as a keyboard soloist and orchestra director and was one of a group of three involved in the building of a new concert hall, the Hanover Square Rooms. Some of his Italian arias, together with a few newly composed pieces, were used in translation on the English stage and he composed one original theatre work in English, *The Fairy Favour* (1767). From time to time he also contributed to the seasons of Italian opera at the King's Theatre, with either complete operas or arias inserted into pasticcios. *Adriano in Siria* (1765) featured G. F. Tenducci in the title role and Giovanni Manzuoli as Pharnaspes. Wolfgang and Leopold Mozart were in London during the run of seven performances; one of them, probably Leopold, wrote a set of embellishments K293*e* for Pharnaspes' aria 'Cara, la dolce fiamma'. *Carattaco* followed in 1767; in the title role was Tommaso Guarducci, who had created major roles in both of Bach's Neapolitan operas. It had only six performances, but (as with *Adriano in Siria*) individual arias were much admired and frequently performed. Bach's insertion arias in London pasticcios were mostly taken from his first three operas, but his arrangement of Gluck's *Orfeo ed Euridice* (7 April 1770), with the original Orpheus, Gaetano Guadagni, in the cast, contained much new material. The role of Eurydice was taken by Cecilia Grassi, whom Bach married later in the decade.

In November 1772 Bach was in Mannheim for the first performance of his *Temistocle* at the court theatre, with Anton Raaff, Dorothea and Elisabeth Wendling and the castrato Francesco Roncaglia in the leading

'Artaserse' (J. C. Bach), Act 3 scene v (private chamber in the apartments of Mandane): design by Fabrizio Galliari for the original production at the Teatro Regio, Turin, 26 December 1761

roles. Two of his serenatas, *Endimione* and *Amor vincitore*, composed for concert performance in London, were revived there. A second Mannheim opera, *Lucio Silla*, had its première on 5 November 1775 (not, as has long been supposed, 1774: the planned performance, for which a libretto was prepared, was postponed). This was a setting of the libretto written by De Gamerra for Mozart in 1772, revised, with substantial changes to improve the dramaturgy of Act 2, by the Mannheim court poet Mattia Verazi. The invention is not generally on as high a level as that of *Temistocle*, though the Act 1 finale, set around the urn of the dead emperor, is one of Bach's most effective scenes, including an accompanied recitative thematically linked to the solemn choral invocation that follows it, and a duet for the reunited lovers; he received no further commissions from Mannheim.

Orione was revived at the King's Theatre in London in the summer of 1777 in a revised version, which ran for four performances; Bach's final London opera, *La clemenza di Scipione* (1778), fared better with eight. The cast included Valentin Adamberger, future creator of the role of Belmonte in Mozart's *Die Entführung aus dem Serail*, and two Mannheim artists, Roncaglia and the coloratura soprano Franziska Danzi. Her aria with four obbligato instruments, 'Infelice, in van m'affanno', may have been the model for 'Martern aller Arten' in *Die Entführung*.

In 1778 Bach was commissioned to compose an opera for the Académie Royale de Musique in Paris, where the rivalry between Gluck and Piccinni was just beginning. *Amadis de Gaule* (1779) was his most ambitious score and once again individual numbers were much admired. Yet the work as a totality failed to please and, after a much interrupted run of only seven performances, it was dropped from the repertory. Nevertheless, according to Michel Brenet, Bach was under contract for a second French opera, *Omphale*, at the time of his death.

Johann Christian Bach was one of the most versatile composers of the late 18th century, but his stage works were comparatively few and intermittent. He was, however, unusually responsive to local conditions and taste and his ten *opere serie* and single *tragédie lyrique*, composed for five distinct operatic centres, offer a glimpse of his perception of the locally prevailing fashions. Bach's Italian operas came at a time when the da capo aria was giving way to the through-composed, the impersonal texts of Metastasio were yielding to the dramatically more apt verses of his successors, and plots were becoming simpler, with a consequent decline in the extent of the *secco* recitative. Perhaps Bach's greatest contribution lies in the ever-increasing emphasis he placed on the role of the orchestra, both in its participation in the musical argument and in the palette of colour offered by the larger number of wind instruments involved.

See also Amadis de Gaule; Catone in Utica (ii); Clemenza di Scipione, La; Lucio Silla (ii); Orione; and Temistocle.

Edition: *The Collected Works of Johann Christian Bach*, ed. E. Warburton (New York, 1984–) [W]

LCG – *London, Covent Garden*
LKH – *London, King's Theatre in the Haymarket*

Artaserse (os, 3, P. Metastasio), Turin, Regio, 26 Dec 1760, *GB-Lbl** (inc.), *I-Tf*, *P-La* (2 copies), W i

Catone in Utica (os, 3, Metastasio), Naples, S Carlo, 4 Nov 1761, *La*, W ii

Alessandro nell'Indie (os, 3, Metastasio), Naples, S Carlo, 20 Jan 1762, private collection* (Act 3 only, inc.), *F-Pn* (inc.), *I-Mc*, *Nc* (inc.), *P-La*, W iii; staged with his Cantata a tre voci

Orione, ossia Diana vendicata (os, 3, G. G. Bottarelli), LKH, 19 Feb 1763, *GB-Lbl* (inc.), *Ob* (inc.), Favourite Songs (London, 1763), W iv and xii; rev. LKH, 24 May 1777

Zanaida (os, 3, Bottarelli), LKH, 7 May 1763, Favourite Songs (London, 1763), W iv and xii
Adriano in Siria (os, 3, Metastasio), LKH, 26 Jan 1765, *P-La*, Favourite Songs (London, 1765), W v
The Fairy Favour (masque, 1, T. Hull), LCG, 29 Jan 1767, lib. W xlv, music lost [perf. by children as afterpiece]
Carattaco (os, 3, Bottarelli), LKH, 14 Feb 1767, *B-Bc** (inc.), orch pts *GB- Lbl* (inc.), Favourite Songs (London, 1768), W vi
Endimione (serenata/azione drammatica, 2, Metastasio, rev. Bottarelli), LKH, 6 April 1772, *Cfm** (pt 1); rev. (M. Verazi), with addns by Jommelli, Mannheim, ? Feb 1774, *D-DS*; W xiv
Temistocle (os, 3, Metastasio, rev. Verazi), Mannheim, Hof, 5 Nov 1772, *B* (2 copies), *Dlb*, *DS*, *F-Pn* (Act 1 only), *GB-Cfm** (Acts 1 and 3), *US-NH*, W vii
Amor vincitore (cantata/azione teatrale, 1), LKH, 15 April 1774, *D-DS*, *F-Pc*, W xv
Lucio Silla (os, 3, G. De Gamerra, rev. Verazi), Mannheim, Hof, 5 Nov 1775, *D-DS*, W viii
La clemenza di Scipione (os, 3), LKH, 4 April 1778 (London, 1778), W ix
Amadis de Gaule (tragédie lyrique, 3, P. Quinault, rev. A.-D.-M. de Vismes du Valgay), Paris, Opéra, 14 Dec 1779, *F-Pc* (Acts 1 and 2, ballet music); (Paris, *c*1782), W x

Music in: A. Cocchi: Emira, 1756, 3 arias in *F-Pn* and *I-OS*, W xii; A. Ferradini: Demofoonte, 1758, aria in *A-Wgm*, *D-SWl* and *F-Pc*, W xii; Astarto, re di Tiro, LKH, 4 Dec 1762, aria, W ix, duet lost; Berenice, LKH, 1 Jan 1765, aria lost; The Maid of the Mill, LCG, 31 Jan 1765, duet, W xxv; The Summer's Tale, LCG, 6 Dec 1765, aria, W xxv; L'olimpiade, LKH, 11 Nov 1769, aria, W ix; Gluck: Orfeo ed Euridice, LKH, 7 April 1770, 4 arias, W ix, other music lost; Gluck: Orfeo ed Euridice, Naples, S Carlo, 4 Nov 1774, 3 arias in *I-Nc* and *P-La*, W xi

Arias in *D-Mbs*, *GB-Lbl* and *I-Nc*, W xii

*

BurneyH
M. Brenet: 'Un fils du grand Bach à Paris', *Guide musical*, xlviii (1902), 551–3, 571–3
H. Abert: 'Joh. Christian Bachs italienische Opern und ihr Einfluss auf Mozart', *ZMw*, i (1918–19), 313–28
C. S. Terry: *John Christian Bach* (London, 1929, 2/1967)
A. Wenk: *Beiträge zur Kenntnis des Opernschaffens von J. Christian Bach* (diss., U. of Frankfurt, 1932)
R. Seebandt: *Arientypen Johann Christian Bachs* (diss., Humboldt U., Berlin, 1956)
E. O. D. Downes: *The Operas of Johann Christian Bach as a Reflection of the Dominant Trends in Opera Seria 1750–1780* (diss., Harvard U., 1958)
S. Kunze: 'Die Vertonungen der Arie "Non so d'onde viene" von J. Chr. Bach und W. A. Mozart', *AnMc*, no.2 (1965), 85–111
E. Warburton: 'J. C. Bach's Operas', *PRMA*, xcii (1965–6), 95–106
——: *A Study of Johann Christian Bach's Operas* (diss., U. of Oxford, 1969)
J. Rushton: *Music and Drama at the Académie Royale de Musique, Paris, 1774–1789* (diss., U. of Oxford, 1970)
E. Warburton: 'J. C. Bach's La clemenza di Scipione', *MT*, cxiii (1972), 356–7
R. Fiske: *English Theatre Music in the Eighteenth Century* (London, 1973, 2/1986)
F. C. Petty: *Italian Opera in London 1760–1800* (Ann Arbor, 1980)
E. Weimer: *Opera Seria and the Evolution of Classical Style 1755–1772* (Ann Arbor, 1984)
E. Warburton: 'Lucio Silla, by Mozart and J. C. Bach', *MT*, cxxvi (1985), 726–30
H. Gärtner: *Johann Christian Bach: Mozarts Freund und Lehrmeister* (Munich, 1989)
C. Esch: *'Lucio Silla': vier Opera-seria-Vertonungen aus der Zeit zwischen 1770 und 1780* (diss., U. of Göttingen, 1991)
L. Finscher, ed.: *Die Mannheimer Hofkapelle im Zeitalter Carl Theodors* (Mannheim, 1991) ERNEST WARBURTON

Bach, P. D. Q. Persona invented by PETER SCHICKELE.

Bachelet, Alfred (*b* Paris, 26 Feb 1864; *d* Nancy, 10 Feb 1944). French composer. After studying with Guiraud at the Paris Conservatoire he won the Prix de Rome in 1890. He became chorus master and subsequently conductor at the Paris Opéra and succeeded Ropartz as head of the Conservatoire in Nancy in 1919. In 1929 he replaced Messager on the Académie des Beaux-Arts.

His first opera, *Scemo*, derives its title from the nickname of its hero Lazaro (tenor), who is supposed to have the evil eye and is distrusted by the inhabitants of his Corsican village. Lazaro's childhood companion Francesca (soprano), now married, is strangely drawn to him. Her husband and father collaborate to exile Lazaro, and Francesca falls into a seemingly incurable and interminable sleep. Easter bells awaken her and she visits Lazaro in exile, only to find he has been blinded. This hot-blooded opera ends as the blind Scemo touches his beloved for the last time. The combination of passionate chromaticism, bucolic interludes and interpolated plainchant was common to many operas of its period. It was revived at the Opéra-Comique in 1926.

Receiving over 50 performances immediately following its première, *Quand le cloche sonnera*, a *verismo* opera in one act lasting over an hour and a half, has only three roles and is set in Russia during World War I. Manoutchka (soprano) is called upon by her father Akimitch (*basse chantante*) to ring the belfry bell, thus giving the signal to soldiers to blow up a bridge under which she knows her lover, Yascha (tenor), is waiting.

Un jardin sur l'Oronte, a grand 'oriental' opera, tells of Oriante (soprano), who is at first the lover of the Christian invader Guillaume (tenor); finally, driven by thirst from her desert abode, she becomes that of his enemy the Prince of Antioch. The opera, which had a large cast, was drastically cut for its creation at the Paris Opéra. Bachelet's score is opulent and richly orchestrated, with sweeping melodies used for the most dramatic moments. In both *Scemo* and *Un jardin sur l'Oronte* local colour is introduced by the use of modal gestures.

Scemo (drame lyrique, 3, C. Méré), Paris, Opéra, 6 May 1914, vs (Paris, 1914)
Quand la cloche sonnera (drame musical, 1, Y. de Hansewick and P. de Wattyne), Paris, OC (Favart), 6 Nov 1922 (Paris, 1922)
Un jardin sur l'Oronte (drame lyrique, 4, Franc-Nohain, after M. Barrès), Paris, Opéra, 3 Nov 1932, vs (Paris, 1932)

*

G. Samazeuilh: 'Alfred Bachelet', *Le théâtre lyrique en France* (Paris, 1937–9) [pubn of Poste National/Radio-Paris], iii, 219–28
M. Kelkel: *Naturalisme, vérisme et réalisme dans l'opéra de 1890 à 1930* (Paris, 1984) RICHARD LANGHAM SMITH

Bachmann, Hermann (*b* Kottbus, 7 Oct 1869; *d* Berlin, 5 July 1937). German baritone. He made his début at Halle in 1890 and from 1894 sang for three seasons at Nuremberg. He then joined the Berlin Staatsoper, where he remained until 1917, serving also as stage manager from 1910 onwards. At Bayreuth he sang first in 1894 as the Herald in *Lohengrin*, then in 1896 as Donner and Wotan. He later taught in Berlin. Other notable roles include the Dutchman and Verdi's Falstaff. His recordings, mostly Wagnerian, include the role of Escamillo in the first 'complete' *Carmen* (1908); they show a fine, resonant voice and stylish usage. J. B. STEANE

Bachmann, Ingeborg (*b* Klagenfurt, 25 June 1926; *d* Rome, 17 Oct 1973). Austrian librettist. She studied in Vienna, completing a doctoral thesis on the philosophies of Wittgenstein and Heidegger, before establishing her reputation as a poet with *Die gestundete Zeit* (1953) and *Anrufung des grossen Bären* (1956). She first collaborated with Henze in 1952 on the ballet-pantomime *Der Idiot* after Dostoyevsky, and her poetry supplied the texts for his orchestral song-cycle

Nachtstücke und Arien (1957) and the Choral Fantasy (1964). She acted as librettist for *Der Prinz von Homburg* (1960), an adaptation of Kleist's *Prinz Friedrich von Homburg*, and for *Der junge Lord* (1965), which is based on a short story by Hauff. The two operas are sharply contrasted: *Der Prinz von Homburg* is less overtly nationalistic than Kleist's drama, and Bachmann and Henze emphasize the poetic aspirations of the central character at the expense of his military ambitions; *Der junge Lord* is a dark-hued comedy, eventually turning to sharp tragedy. ANDREW CLEMENTS

Bachschmidt [Bachschmid], **(Johann) Anton (Adam)** (*b* Melk, Lower Austria, 11 Feb 1728; *d* Eichstätt, 29 Dec 1797). German composer of Austrian birth. From 1751 to 1753 he was *Thurnermeister* (director of instrumental music) in Melk. He then travelled as a violin virtuoso and may have been employed briefly at Würzburg (or Wurzbach) before settling in Eichstätt. There he established himself as a versatile musician in the court orchestra of Prince-Bishop Johann Anton II, rising steadily in rank to Kapellmeister (1773). Although known as a church composer, Bachschmidt wrote a number of dramatic works for Eichstätt's theatres. His turn from Latin-school drama (he wrote five, the music of which is now lost) to Italian opera reflects the closing of the Jesuit theatre in Eichstätt in 1773.

first performed in Eichstätt, autographs in D-Es

Il re pastore (P. Metastasio), 1774
La clemenza di Tito (Metastasio), 1776
Antigono (Metastasio), 1778

Lost: Erstickter Neid und Eifersucht, 1762; Die Liebe zum Vaterland, 1766; L'eroe cinese (Metastasio), 1775; Demetrio (Metastasio), 1777; Ezio (A. Raimund), 1780

*

F. J. Lipowsky: *Baierisches Musiklexikon* (Munich, 1811)
R. Schlecht: *Musikgeschichte der Stadt Eichstätt* (MS, 1883, *D-Es*) [with thematic catalogue]
J. Sax: 'Musik und Theater in der fürstbischöflichen Residenzstadt Eichstätt bis zum Jahre 1802', *Jahresbericht des Historischen Vereins für Mittelfranken* [Ansbach], xlvi (1898), 6–28
J. Gmelch: *Die Musikgeschichte Eichstätts* (Eichstätt, 1914)
K.W. Littger: *Musik in Eichstätt* (Tutzing, 1988)

ROBERT N. FREEMAN

Bäck, Sven-Erik (*b* Stockholm, 16 Sept 1919). Swedish composer. He studied the violin, then played the viola in the Barkel Quartet (1944–53). From 1940 to 1945 he also received tuition in composition from Rosenberg, who was a decisive influence on him. Bäck subsequently took a leading position in Swedish musical life, in administrative posts (he was on the board of the Theatre and Music Council), as a performer, and as a teacher of interpretation and performance in Renaissance, Baroque and contemporary music. He has worked often with artists in other media, notably in his most successful opera *Tranfjädrarna* ('The Crane Feathers', 1956). Bäck's works are often concise in form, and show a variety of influences: the 'pointillist' style of Webern, the lyricism of Berg, Renaissance musical and harmonic structures and Asian music; the latter is particularly evident in *Tranfjädrarna*. He has also written semi-dramatic works combining music, singing, dance, lighting and sculpture.

Tranfjädrarna [The Crane Feathers] (chamber op, 5 scenes, B. Malmberg, after J. Kinoshita), Swedish Radio, 28 Feb 1957; stage, Stockholm, Blanche, 19 Feb 1958
Gästabudet [The Banquet] (2, Ö. Sjöstrand), Stockholm, Blanche, 12 Nov 1958
Fågeln [The Bird] (chamber op, 1, P. Verner-Carlson, after A. Obrenovic), Swedish Radio, 14 Feb 1961; stage, Södra, Södra Theatre, 14 Oct 1970

ANDERS WIKLUND

Bacocco e Serpilla. Intermezzo by G. M. Orlandini; *see* *MARITO GIOCATORE E LA MOGLIE BACCHETTONA, IL.*

Bacquier, Gabriel (-Augustin-Raymond-Théodore-Louis) (*b* Béziers, 17 May 1924). French baritone. Having gained a *premier prix* and two opera prizes at the Paris Conservatoire he began his career in Beckman's Compagnie Lyrique (1950–52). After three years at La Monnaie, Brussels (début as Rossini's Figaro), he joined the Opéra-Comique (1956) singing Sharpless, Alfio, Albert (*Werther*), Zurga, Ourrias, Yevgeny Onegin and Gianni Schicchi. At the Opéra (1958–81) his roles included Germont, Rigoletto, Valentin, Escamillo, Boris, Boccanegra and Leporello; at Aix-en-Provence (1960–89) he sang Don Giovanni, Don Alfonso, Golaud, Falstaff, Don Pasquale and the King of Clubs. In 1962 he made his British début at Glyndebourne as Mozart's Count Almaviva and in 1964 sang Riccardo in *I puritani* at Covent Garden and the High Priest in *Samson et Dalila* at the Metropolitan, where his later roles (until 1981) included Melitone, the Hoffmann villains, Massenet's Lescaut, and Iago. His voice became richer and firmer during the early 1970s, his command of vocal and dramatic nuance increasingly skilful. His Scarpia was the more formidable for being sophisticated, his Dr Bartolo the more humorous for being stripped of buffoonery; his Don Alfonso, if suave, was also dominating. Bacquier's repertory ranges from a witty Dulcamara to (on record) a strong William Tell. He was made a Chevalier of the Légion d'honneur in 1975. During the 1980s he sang Sancho Panza, the Father (*Louise*) and the Viceroy (*La Périchole*) with great success. In 1990 he returned to Covent Garden as Rossini's Dr Bartolo.

*

S. Segalini: 'Gabriel Bacquier', *Opera*, xxxiii (1982), 577–81

ANDRÉ TUBEUF, ELIZABETH FORBES

Baczko, Ludwig von (*b* Lyck, East Prussia, 8 June 1756; *d* Königsberg, 27 March 1823). German librettist. At 21, after studying law at Königsberg, he went blind. Thereafter he taught history at an artillery academy and wrote novels, several works on Prussian history and musical texts for local use. Three of his librettos were published in 1794. He had sent one of them, his magic opera *Rinaldo und Alcina*, to the blind composer-pianist Maria Theresia von Paradis several years earlier, but her setting (1797, Prague) is lost.

Die Kantons-Revision (komische Oper), W. F. Halter, 1792; *Die Singschule* (komische Oper), N. Mühle, 1794; *Rinaldo und Alcina* (komische Oper), F. A. L. Löwe, 1797 (M. T. von Paradis, 1797); *Das ländliche Fest* (Prolog), J. P. S. Schmidt, 1798

THOMAS BAUMAN

Bada, Angelo (*b* Novara, 27 May 1876; *d* Novara, 23 March 1941). Italian tenor. He made his début in 1898 in Italy and sang there for a decade. In 1908 he went to New York, where he made his Metropolitan début as the Messenger in *Aida*. He remained as chief comprimario at the Metropolitan for 30 years, creating roles in Puccini's *Fanciulla del West* (1910), *Il tabarro* (Tinca) and *Gianni Schicchi* (1918, Gherardo) and taking part in many New York first performances. In 1928–9 he sang at Covent Garden as Shuysky (*Boris Godunov*) and in 1935 appeared at the Salzburg Festival as Dr Caius (*Falstaff*). He made his last appearance at the Metropolitan in 1938 at Martinelli's silver jubilee concert. ELIZABETH FORBES

Baddeley [née Snow], **Sophia** (*b* London, ?1745; *d* Edinburgh, 1 July 1786). English actress and soprano. Daughter of the trumpeter Valentine Snow, she eloped with the actor Robert Baddeley and in 1764 made her début as Ophelia at Drury Lane. Although the prompter Hopkins found her Ophelia 'very bad, all but the singing', she made a charming heroine in genteel and Shakespearean comedy. In English operas she was particularly successful as Patty (*The Maid of the Mill*) and Rosetta (*Love in a Village*). She created roles in Dibdin's *Ephesian Matron* and *Recruiting Sergeant* and her performance of his song in praise of Shakespeare, 'Sweet Willy O', was the hit of the Garrick *Jubilee*. Her beauty gained her many admirers, but her scandalous private life, extravagance and indulgence in laudanum eventually destroyed her. After 1780 she appeared only in Dublin, the provinces and finally Edinburgh, where she died in poverty.

*

H. Kelly: *Thespis*, i (London, 1766)
E. Steele: *The Memoirs of Mrs Sophia Baddeley* (London, 1787)
C. H. Wilson: *The Myrtle and Vine* (London, 1802)
J. Boaden: *The Life of Mrs Jordan*, i (London, 1831)
R. Fiske: *English Theatre Music in the Eighteenth Century* (London, 1973, 2/1986) OLIVE BALDWIN, THELMA WILSON

Badea, Christian (*b* Bucharest, 10 Dec 1947). Romanian conductor. He was a boy chorister at the Budapest Opera, studied the violin at the conservatory and joined the Opera as a répétiteur. After leaving Romania in 1970 he studied further in Brussels and Salzburg and at the Juilliard School. He was music director at the Spoleto Festival of Two Worlds in Italy from 1978 and directed the festivals in both Italy and Charleston, South Carolina, from 1980 to 1986, conducting a variety of operas ranging from Mozart and Verdi to Menotti and Shostakovich. During this time he conducted the first European production of Menotti's *The Hero* (1980) and made his British début in 1983 with Prokofiev's *The Gambler* for the ENO. He has worked with Canadian Opera, Netherlands Opera and at Verona, and made the first recording (with the Spoleto Festival Orchestra) of Barber's *Antony and Cleopatra* in 1985. His performances have been praised for theatrical vitality, secure phrasing and balance and an awareness of the wider potential of music theatre. NOËL GOODWIN

Baden-Baden. Spa town in Baden-Württemberg, Germany, on the Rhine. A musical theatre ensemble existed there as early as 1657, and comedies with music were given at the Jesuit College up to 1771. True operatic activity is recorded only from the mid-19th century, when Baden-Baden became important as a spa. L. A. Piccinni, grandson of the composer, directed operas and operettas there in the 1840s; and in 1860 Gounod's *La colombe* had its première there. The new Theater der Stadt (cap. 512) was inaugurated in 1862, with a season including Conradin Kreutzer's *Der Nachtlager in Granada*, the première under Berlioz of his *Béatrice et Bénédict*, composed for the occasion, and two weeks later that of Reyer's *Erostrate*. The following year Berlioz conducted a revival of Pergolesi's *La serva padrona*. Baden-Baden was popular with musicians, among whom Pauline Viardot, who performed there in the 1860s, settled in the town. A festival was inaugurated in 1906, and from 1918 many opera seasons were given at the Kurhaustheater by visiting companies, among them the Mannheim Nationaltheater (the *Ring* under Furtwängler), the Berlin Staatsoper under Walter, Knappertsbusch and Stransky, and the Metropolitan of New York under Kleiber and Bodanzky; Stephan's *Die ersten Menschen* was given under Fritz Busch. Premières there include Weill's *Kleine Mahagonny*, Hindemith's *Hin und zurück*, Toch's *Die Prinzessin auf der Erbse* and Milhaud's *L'enlèvement d'Europe* (all in 1927) and the Brecht-Weill-Hindemith *Der Lindberghflug* (1929).

*

Hundert Jahre Theater Baden-Baden (Baden-Baden, 1962)

Baden bei Wien. Spa town in Austria, 28 km south of Vienna. It is Austria's most famous sulphur spa, with a climate and landscape that have always drawn the citizens of the capital. In the early 19th century it was the summer residence of Franz II. Beethoven loved the surrounding woodlands and Constanze Mozart often stayed there to enjoy the healing waters. The Sommerarena (657 seats) was built in 1906 by the architect Krausz, and the attractive Stadttheater (702 seats), designed by the architects Hellmer and Fellner, was opened in 1909 (as the Jubiläums-Stadttheater). Performances usually take place twice daily, except Mondays, from March until June, with additional local touring. In July and August (during the festival) they are given in the summer amphitheatre, equipped with a movable glass roof for bad weather. Three or four operettas are performed in the season, each for a run of three weeks. Besides the operettas and plays mounted in the main season (June–March), there is one comic opera on the programme each year. The company of about 75 members is largely supported by the Federal and Lower Austrian government. HARALD GOERTZ

Badescu, Dinu (*b* Craiova, 17 Oct 1904). Romanian tenor. Originally a baritone, he studied at the Bucharest Conservatory and made his début at Cluj in 1931, as Germont; later the same year he sang the tenor roles of Flotow's Lyonel (*Martha*) and Stradella. At the Bucharest Opera (1934–61) he was successful in the lyric Italian repertory and appeared as guest in Warsaw as Calaf and Faust (1937). He appeared at the Vienna Volksoper during World War II and from 1948 sang more than 50 roles at the Staatsoper. Further guest appearances took him to Italy, the Netherlands, Germany, Czechoslovakia and Russia. He taught in Bucharest after his retirement. DAVID CUMMINGS

Badia, Carlo Agostino (*b* ?Venice, 1672; *d* Vienna, 23 Sept 1738). Italian composer. His earliest known work is the oratorio *La sete di Cristo in croce*, a *sepolcro* written for Innsbruck in 1691. At the beginning of 1692 he may have lived in Rome, where his earliest secular dramatic works were produced. By spring 1692 he was a court composer at Innsbruck. He gained the enthusiastic patronage of Eleonora Maria (1653–97), widow of both King Michael Wisniowiecki of Poland and Duke Charles of Lorraine, and stepsister of the Emperor Leopold I. Besides the 1691 oratorio, Badia composed for Innsbruck two operas in 1692, as well as two *sepolcri* for Holy Week 1693. With the support of Eleonora Maria, who moved to Vienna late in 1693, and with a recommendation from the King of Poland, he was appointed *Musik-Compositeur* at the imperial court on 1 July 1694, receiving an initial monthly salary of 60 florins backdated to 1 July 1693. Badia thus became the first in a succession of distinguished late Baroque musicians (including Fux, Giovanni Bononcini, P. F. Tosi and Francesco Conti) to hold the title of court composer at Vienna.

After initial successes, Badia was sent by the emperor to Rome, probably in 1695, to complete his musical education, but because of a lack of funds he returned to Vienna before the end of that year. Until 1697 he seems to have composed only oratorios for Vienna. His first opera for the Habsburg court, *Bacco, vincitore dell'India*, was produced during Carnival 1697 and dedicated to Eleonora Maria. During 18 years at the courts of Leopold I (*d* 1705) and Joseph I (*d* 1711), Badia enjoyed a period of remarkable creative activity, producing at least 34 oratorios and 20 secular dramatic works. He also composed more than 50 chamber cantatas and duets. His salary was increased by 30 florins in 1699 and by an additional 30 in 1702, making him one of the highest-paid musicians at the court. He seems to have become a favourite of Leopold I, and was praised by Draghi as a 'guter Virtuoso' and by Draghi's successor Pancotti as 'gar guten Talento und ungeheimer prontezza'.

The date of Badia's marriage to the prima donna Anna Maria Elisabetta (Lisi) Nonetti, who arrived in Vienna in 1700, is unknown. In 1706 he probably accompanied her to Venice, where she appeared at the Teatro S Giovanni Grisostomo. Badia's operas and oratorios continued to be performed in northern Italy, but there is no evidence that he had a direct hand in any of the productions. In 1709 he was commissioned to write the opera *Gli amori di Circe con Ulisse* for Dresden; the performance took place during a visit by the King of Denmark. It seems unlikely that Badia travelled to Dresden for the performance, which was directed by Baron Francesco Ballerini, one of the most famous singers at the imperial court. Badia composed less prolifically during the reign of Joseph I, who favoured the Bononcini brothers, Giovanni and Antonio Maria, but the emperor frequently supplemented Badia's income with secret sums of money that apparently rescued him from persistent debts. After the death of Joseph I, the imperial chapel was reorganized and many musicians were released. But on 1 October 1711 the contracts of both Badias were renewed, and Carlo remained in the employ of the Habsburgs until his death, serving 44 years as court composer.

Under Charles VI (*d* 1740), who preferred the more progressive composers Fux and Caldara, Badia's activity declined sharply. Between 1712 and 1738 he is known to have composed only six oratorios and secular dramatic works. Anna Maria Lisi died on 7 January 1726, and by 1729 he had married Anna Maria Sophia Novelli, his first wife's niece; a son, Antonius Nicolaus, was born in 1729. In his last years Badia was closely associated with G. J. Dornberger, a pupil of Caldara.

Badia was the first of a group of Italian composers (including the Bononcinis, M. A. Ziani and Conti) who introduced the stylistic innovations of the late Baroque era to the Viennese court, long dominated by the conservative Draghi. Badia's style underwent a gradual maturing process (as Wellesz, 1919, showed). The numerous early works are characterized by smooth melodic writing, lyric grace and a lack of contrapuntal complexity. He can be credited with increasing the importance of idiomatic string writing at Vienna. The ritornellos and sinfonias of his operas and oratorios are longer than those of his predecessors, and he also called for more frequent solo obbligatos. He appears to have been the first composer at Vienna to use concerto grosso contrasts: in the trio 'Quanti e di grande' from *Le gari dei beni* (1700) he called for two large opposing groups (he may have been influenced by Torelli, who visited Vienna in 1699–1700). The overture to one of his best works, *Ercole, vincitore di Gerione*, is unusual in consisting of four movements, the third a minuet. In his oratorios and his secular dramatic works Badia made extensive use of vocal ensemble numbers, especially trios. *La concordia della Virtù e della Fortuna* (1702) ends with a trio, a technique that foreshadows the use of ensemble finales in the operas of Fux and Caldara.

It seems likely that Badia was related to the two other musicians of the name at the Habsburg court. Giuseppe (*b c*1642; *d* Vienna, 31 March 1706) served at the court of the Dowager Empress Eleonora Gonzaga for many years. After her death in 1686, he went with his large family to Italy and received a recommendation from Eleonora Maria of Innsbruck for an appointment to the chapel of Duke Ferdinando Carlo Gonzaga of Mantua. However, he returned to Vienna and was engaged as a bass at the imperial court on 1 January 1690; from 1694 to 1702 his name appears in the list of tenors. Giovanni Giuseppe was active in Vienna as a singer about the same time. A letter from Parma from a Carlo Francesco Badia to Giacomo Antonio Perti is preserved (*I-Bc*) and was reproduced by Nemeth, who indicated that the author was definitely not C. A. Badia.

performed in Vienna unless otherwise stated

Amor che vince lo sdegno, ovvero Olimpia placata (A. Aureli), Rome, Capranica, carn. 1692

La Rosaura, ovvero Amore figlio della gratitudine (O. Malvezzi), Innsbruck, April 1692

L'amazone corsara, ovvero L'Alvilda, regina de' goti (dramma per musica, G. C. Corradi), Innsbruck, aut. 1692, *A-Wn*

La ninfa Apollo (favola pastorale o scherzo scenica, F. de Lemene), Rome and Milan, 1692

Bacco, vincitore dell'India (festa teatrale, D. Cupeda), 14 Feb 1697

La pace tra i numi discordi nella rovina di Troia (serenata, N. Minato), 21 May 1697, *Wn*

L'idea del felice governo (serenata, Cupeda), Laxenburg, 9 June 1698

Lo squittinio dell'eroe (componimento per musica da camera), Neue Favorita, 26 July 1698

Imeneo trionfante (serenata), 28 Feb 1699, *Wn*

Il Narciso (favola boschereccia, Lemene), Laxenburg, 9 June 1699, *Wn*

Il commun giubilo del mondo (musica da camera, Cupeda), Neue Favorita, 26 July 1699, *Wn*

Cupido fuggitivo da Venere e ritrovato a' piedi della Sacra Reale Maestà d'Amalia (trattenimento carnevalesco, G. Spedazzi), carn. 1700

Diana rappacificata con Venere e con Amore (trattenimento musicale), Schönbrunn, 28 April 1700, *Wn*

La costanza d'Ulisse (dramma per musica, Cupeda), Neue Favorita, 29 June 1700

Le gare dei beni (applauso poetico per musica), 25 July 1700, *Wn*

L'amore vuol somiglianza (dramma per musica, P. A. Bernardoni), 18 Jan 1702

La concordia della Virtù e della Fortuna (poemetto drammatico, Bernardoni), Neue Favorita, 21 April 1702, *Wn*

Enea negli Elisi (poemetto drammatico, Bernardoni), 9 June 1702, *Wn*

L'Arianna (poemetto drammatico, Bernardoni), Favorita garden, 22 July 1702

La Psiche (poemetto drammatico, Bernardoni), 22 July 1703, *Wn*

Napoli ritornata ai romani (componimento per musica, S. Stampiglia), Neue Favorita, 1 Oct 1707, *Wn*

Ercole, vincitore di Gerione (poemetto drammatico, Bernardoni), 4 Nov 1708, *Wn*

Gli amori di Circe con Ulisse (dramma per musica, G. B. Ancioni), Dresden, 20 June 1709
Il bel genio dell'Austria ed il Fato (dialogo), Nov 1723, *Wn*

*

AllacciD
S. von Molitor: *Biographische und kunstgeschichtliche Stoffsammlung* (MS, *A-Wn*)
L. von Köchel: *Die kaiserliche Hof-Musikkapelle in Wien von 1543–1867* (Vienna, 1869)
A. von Weilen: *Zur Wiener Theatergeschichte* (Vienna, 1901)
A. Koczirz: 'Exzerpte aus den Hofmusikakten des Wiener Hofkammerarchivs', *SMw*, i (1913), 278–303
E. Wellesz: 'Die Opern und Oratorien in Wien von 1660–1708', *SMw*, vi (1919), 5–138
R. Haas: *Die Musik des Barocks* (Wildpark-Potsdam, 1928)
L. Ferrari: 'Per la bibliografia del teatro italiano in Vienna', *Studi di bibliografia e di argomento romano in memoria di Luigi de Gregori* (Rome, 1949)
E. Wellesz: *Essays on Opera* (London, 1950)
W. Senn: *Musik und Theater am Hof zu Innsbruck* (Innsbruck, 1954)
F. Hadamowsky: 'Barocktheater am Wiener Kaiserhof', *Jb der Gesellschaft für Wiener Theaterforschung 1951–52* (1955), 7–117
C. Nemeth: 'Zur Lebensgeschichte von Carlo Agostino Badia (1672–1738)', *Anzeiger der phil.-hist. Klasse der Österreichischen Akademie der Wissenschaften*, xcii (1955), 224–36
R. Brockpähler: *Handbuch zur Geschichte der Barockoper in Deutschland* (Emsdetten, 1964)
H. Knaus: *Die Musiker im Archivbestand des Kaiserlichen Obersthofmeisteramtes (1637–1705): Sitzungsberichte der Österreichischen Akademie der Wissenschaften, philosophisch-historische Klasse*, no.254 (1967); no.259 (1968); no.264 (1969)
O. Deutsch: 'Das Repertoire der höfischen Oper, der Hof- und der Staatsoper', *ÖMz*, xxiv (1969), 369–421
H. Knaus: 'Die Musiker in den geheimen kaiserlichen Kammerzahlamtsrechnungsbüchern (1669, 1705–1711)', *Anzeiger der phil.-hist. Klasse der Österreichischen Akademie der Wissenschaften*, cvi (1969), 14–38
H. Seifert: 'Die Musik der beiden Kaiserinnen Eleonora Gonzaga', *Festschrift Othmar Wessely zum 60. Geburtstag* (Tutzing, 1982), 527–54
——: *Die Oper am Wiener Kaiserhof im 17. Jahrhundert* (Tutzing, 1985) LAWRENCE E. BENNETT

Badiali, Cesare (*b* Imola, *c*1803; *d* Imola, 17 Nov 1865). Italian bass. He studied in Milan, making his début in 1827 at Trieste. He appeared at La Scala (1830–32), in Lisbon, Madrid, Bergamo, Rome, Vienna, Venice, London, where he sang Don Giovanni at Drury Lane (1858), and Paris, where he took part in a Rossini pastiche *Un curioso accidente* (1859) at the Théâtre Italien. A singer with superb coloratura technique, he excelled in roles such as Assur (*Semiramide*), Count Robinson (*Il matrimonio segreto*), Donizetti's Belisarius, Alfonso (*Lucrezia Borgia*) and King Pedro (*Maria Padilla*). ELIZABETH FORBES

Badings, Henk (*b* Bandung, Java, 17 Jan 1907; *d* Maarheeze, 26 June 1987). Dutch composer. Born of Dutch parents, he went to the Netherlands in 1915 as an orphan. His wish to follow a musical career met with opposition from his guardian, who forced him to train at the Technical University in Delft; after his graduation (1931) he was a demonstrator in palaeontology and historical geology there. During his student years he taught himself composition and music theory, and in 1930 briefly studied with Pijper. From 1934 he taught at the conservatories in Rotterdam and Amsterdam, and was director of The Hague Conservatory from 1941 to 1945; for the next decade and a half he worked as a freelance composer. In 1961 he was appointed to teach acoustics at Utrecht University and between 1962 and 1972 was professor of composition at the Staatliche Hochschule für Musik, Stuttgart; he also lectured in Australia and the USA.

Badings's compositions include 15 symphonies, a large number of choral works, and operas; many show a preoccupation with non-diatonic tonalities and micro-intervals yet the composer's gift for striking instrumentation and his care for formal integration are always evident. The wartime opera, *De nachtwacht* (composed 1942), one of his finest scores, takes Rembrandt as its subject: the painter's *Nightwatch*, his love for his wife, and his commitment to producing more elevated works of art than the usual mere depictions of the Amsterdam merchant class. Lighter in style – more Gallic than Germanic – and with more transparent orchestration is *Liefde's listen en lagen* of 1945. In about 1952 Badings began to experiment with electronic music. The radio opera *Orestes* attracted great international acclaim (it was awarded the Italia Prize in 1954); this was his first composition to combine purely electronic music with an instrumental score, and in it he realized previously unavailable pitches, timbres and rhythms. For example, in one section a fearsome effect for the Eumenides is achieved by using a recording of a male chorus played at accelerated speed, and in another choral section a slower speed is used to attain extreme bass notes. Variable speed techniques are also employed with instrumental sounds, as well as reversed recordings of cymbals and tam-tams.

A second radio opera, *Asterion*, commissioned by South African radio, followed in 1957, and the television opera *Salto mortale*, commissioned by, and first performed on, Nederlandse Televisie Stichting received a prize in the 1959 International Competition of Television Societies in Salzburg. The latter work is the first opera with a fully electronic accompaniment. With his last opera, *Martin Korda, DP* (a DP being a Displaced Person), Badings returned to the traditional forces of voices and orchestra that he had used in *De nachtwacht*, and proved once again his strength as a composer of highly expressive and moving dramatic music.

De nachtwacht, 1942 (dramatic op, 3, T. Bouws), Antwerp, Flemish, 13 May 1950
Liefde's listen en lagen [Love's Ruses and Snares], 1945 (chamber op, 3, Badings and Bouws), Radio Hilversum, 6 Jan 1948
Orestes (radio op, Badings and Starink), Florence, 24 Sept 1954
Asterion (radio op, P. N. van Wijk Louw), Johannesburg, 1957
Salto mortale (television chamber op, 12 scenes, Badings and Belcampo), Nederlandse Televisie Stichting, 19 June 1959
Martin Korda, DP (dramatic choral op, 3, Badings and A. van Eijk), Amsterdam, Stadsschouwburg, 1960

*

J. Wouters: 'Henk Badings', *Dutch Composers' Gallery*, i: *Nine Portraits of Dutch Composers* (Amsterdam, 1971), 50–70
L. Samama: *Zeventig jaar nederlandse muziek (1915–1985)* (Amsterdam, 1986), 138–48 JOS WOUTERS/LEO SAMAMA

Badini, Carlo Francesco (*fl* 1770–93). Italian librettist and journalist. His origins are obscure, though he claimed to hold degrees from 'the Royal University of Turin'. Badini was in London by 1769, when he wrote the libretto for Pugnani's comic opera *Nanetta e Lubino*. Probably supplementing his income by translating and teaching Italian, he wrote a few librettos for the King's Theatre during the 1770s, including *Le pazzie di Orlando* (set by Pietro Alessandro Guglielmi in 1771), a witty, ambitious work which Nunziato Porta adapted for Haydn as *Orlando paladino* (1782, Eszterháza). Badini's other works from this period include *Il disertore* (1770), set by Guglielmi and revived in Lisbon in

1772, and *L'ali d'amore* (1776), which was set by Venanzio Rauzzini.

An early sign of the individuality which marks Badini's later works is found in the libretto for Bertoni's *La governante*. This is a free translation of the popular English dialogue opera *The Duenna* by R. B. Sheridan, who just happened to be the new co-owner of the King's Theatre where *La governante* was performed. While Badini retained many of Sheridan's lyrics (translated into Italian, of course), he reworked the original drama into a typical three-act burletta whose arias, unlike Sheridan's, advance the plot. Another example of Badini's interest in English drama is *Il duca d'Atene* (set by Bertoni in 1780), the plot of which is partly drawn from *The Taming of the Shrew*.

Badini kept abreast of the latest continental developments in opera, as evidenced in *Il trionfo della costanza* (set by Anfossi in 1782). Indebted to Sedaine's *Le roi et le fermier*, this highly melodramatic libretto includes an exceptionally long first-act finale comparable to those of Casti and Da Ponte in its depiction of domestic chaos. Badini later expressed contempt for his fellow Italian librettists. In the preface to his libretto *L'amore protetto dal cielo, o sia La vestale* (1787), an *opera seria* with music composed and assembled by Rauzzini, he wrote: 'the present Opera has a better claim to the indulgence of an English audience than the operatical rhapsodies commonly imported from Italy'.

Badini's fortunes fluctuated widely during his later career. In 1779 he was sued by the King's Theatre manager, Antoine Le Texier, and bound over to keep the peace. Two years later he was sued again, this time by the harpsichord maker Jacob Kirckman, and sentenced to Debtors' Prison, being discharged on 17 November 1781. Beginning with the 1783–4 season, he was employed by the King's Theatre as one of two house poets, receiving an annual salary of £100 which rose to £150 (some reports say £250) in the following seasons. In 1785 he was appointed principal librettist at the Haymarket and became a close associate of the manager, Giovanni Andrea Gallini. Badini received special concessions for supplying librettos to the royal family and was allowed to raise the price per copy from 1s. to 1s. 6d., of which he kept 9d. as profit. In 1788 it was reported that he had been editor of the *Morning Post* for a short time a few years earlier. With his compatriot Andrea Carnavale, he was accused of writing a libellous pamphlet, the *Case of the Opera-House Disputes* (1784), a vicious attack on the former owner-manager of the King's Theatre William Taylor, Gallini's arch-enemy. Da Ponte later wrote that Badini 'kept a noose around Taylor's neck by virtue of his pen' and claimed that he also exercised his excellent command of English and biting satire as critic for several newspapers. This claim cannot be verified, however, because such journalism was at the time almost entirely anonymous and available to anyone willing to pay to see his words in print.

Deeply mistrusted by Robert Bray O'Reilly, the manager of the Pantheon Opera House, Badini naturally sided with Gallini in the struggle during 1789–92 for control of Italian opera in London. In his capacity as house poet at the new King's Theatre in the Haymarket, which opened in early 1791, he was commissioned to write a libretto for Haydn during his first visit to London: this was *L'anima del filosofo* (*Orfeo ed Euridice*), which Haydn worked on between January and April 1791 but never quite finished. The Lord Chamberlain, a secret financial backer of the rival Pantheon, refused to grant the King's Theatre the necessary licence, and the opera could not be performed. Badini's brilliant though flawed libretto is one of the most peculiar of all *opere serie*. Taking a completely different approach from Calzabigi and Gluck, though Haydn slyly recalls the tune of 'Che farò senz'Euridice', Badini reverts to Virgil's violent ending, with Orpheus killed by the Bacchantes. The libretto is rich in learned and arcane allusion, including an exact quotation of two lines from Rinuccini's *Euridice* of 1600; thus did Badini attempt to span the whole history of opera. That this extraordinary work, Haydn's last opera, was not finished and performed during the composer's lifetime is much to be regretted.

On 11 February 1792 Badini wrote a letter containing this claim: 'having, from a cruel persecution, been deprived of my bread at the Opera-House, I am so reduced, as to be literally starving'. He was subsequently reappointed house poet at the King's Theatre, its monopoly on Italian opera now restored. But he faded from the picture and was soon eclipsed by another Haymarket librettist, Lorenzo da Ponte, who arrived in London in 1792.

Nanetta e Lubino (ob), Pugnani, 1769; *Il disertore* (dg), P. A. Guglielmi, 1770; *Le pazzie di Orlando* (dg), Guglielmi, 1771; *Il bacio* (comic op), Vento, 1776 (Giordani, 1782); *La vestale* (comic op), Vento, 1776; *L'ali d'amore* (op comica, after P. Metastasio), V. Rauzzini, 1776; *La governante* (burletta, after R. B. Sheridan: *The Duenna*), Bertoni, 1779; *Rinaldo* (after G. De Gamerra: *Armida*), Sacchini, 1780; *Il duca d'Atene* (comic op, after W. Shakespeare: *The Taming of the Shrew*, and *Arlecchino finto principe*), Bertoni, 1780; *Mitridate*, Sacchini, 1781 (replacement scene); *Il trionfo della costanza* (dg), Anfossi, 1782; *L'inglese in Italia* (dg), Anfossi, 1786; *Alceste* (after Metastasio: *Demetrio*), Gresnick, 1786; *L'amore protetto dal cielo, o sia La vestale* (os), Rauzzini, 1787; *La generosità di Alessandro* (dramma per musica, after Metastasio: *Alessandro nelle Indie*), Tarchi, 1789; *Andromache* (after A. Salvi), Nasolini, 1790; *L'anima del filosofo, ossia Orfeo ed Euridice* (dramma per musica), Haydn, comp. 1791

BDA

Documents in *GB-Lpro*: PRIS 10/51; C31/239/203 (Chancery Affidavits); C38/754 (Masters' Reports); C107/201 (Masters' Exhibits); LC 7/3

L. da Ponte: *Memorie* (New York, 1823; Eng. trans., London and Philadelphia, 1929)

H. C. Robbins Landon: *Haydn in England 1791–1795* (London, 1976)

F. C. Petty: *Italian Opera in London 1760–1800* (Ann Arbor, 1980)

C. Price, J. Milhous and R. D. Hume: 'The Rebuilding of the King's Theatre, Haymarket, 1789–1791', *Theatre Journal*, xliii (1991), 421–44

CURTIS PRICE

Badini, Ernesto (*b* S Colombano al Lambro, 14 Sept 1876; *d* Milan, 6 July 1937). Italian baritone. He was trained at the Milan Conservatory, first appearing as Figaro (*Barbiere*) in his native town. He sang regularly at La Scala, where his greatest success was as Gianni Schicchi. He sang this role at the first performances of the opera in Milan and at Covent Garden in 1920. Other premières in which he took part included Mascagni's *Il piccolo Marat*, Giordano's *La cena delle beffe* and Wolf-Ferrari's *Sly*. He was also a favourite in South America and at Salzburg, and made many recordings including the first complete one of *Don Pasquale*. His voice was serviceable rather than rich, but he acted with an assured style and economy of gesture.

J. B. STEANE

Bad Ischl. Spa town in Upper Austria. A theatre was established as early as 1827, when the first spa treatments were devised. Franz Josef I chose the town for his summer residence, where he spent every summer from 1849 to 1914, and his presence attracted royalty, artists and moneyed aristocracy. Johann Strauss (the younger) and Brahms were frequent guests there. Bad Ischl developed into such a centre for operetta that it became known as 'the operetta stock exchange' because of the immense number of contracts signed. Franz Lehár, who wrote many of his works in the town ('I always have the best ideas in Bad Ischl'), became an honorary citizen. His villa, filled with art treasures, is now a museum. Emmerich Kálmán, Robert Stolz, Richard Tauber (Lehár's favourite tenor) and many others stayed and took part in Bad Ischl's activities.

After a period of stagnation in the interwar years, in 1961 the International Operetta Society was founded. Since then, there has been a regular summer operetta season, the Operettenwochen, consisting of two operettas (one always a Lehár work) in 24 performances altogether. The spa hotel in the Herrengasse, where the performances now take place, has a capacity of 800. In 1962 Nico Dostal's *Die ungarische Hochzeit* received its première, as, in 1963, did Rudi Gfaller's *Der feurige Elias* (which refers jokingly to the local railway, closed down in 1957). Once a season there is a town festival with a firework display, to which some 40 000 spectators come. The company has about 120 members, and the orchestra is named after Lehár. In 1985 a special postage stamp was issued to commemorate the 25th anniversary of the Operettenwochen. HARALD GOERTZ

Badoaro [Badoer, Badoero, Badovero], **Giacomo** [Iacopo] (*b* Venice, 1602; *d* Venice, 1654). Italian librettist. He was a member of the Venetian nobility. His reputation as a librettist rests on Monteverdi's supposed predilection for his work in his *Il ritorno d'Ulisse in patria* (1640) and *Le nozze d'Enea in Lavinia* (1641). The latter text, however, is by another (unidentified) poet, as its printed scenario makes clear. Badoaro's next libretto, *L'Ulisse errante* (1644, music by Sacrati), also drew on the Odyssey; each of its five acts presents an independent episode of Ulysses' adventure. The deliberate, even selfconscious rejection of Aristotelian unity of action may have been inspired by Giacomo Torelli, who created sets and machinery for the production. Chronicles of Venetian opera also attribute to Badoaro *Helena rapita da Theseo* (1653, music possibly by Cavalli), which is not, *pace* Ivanovich, based on a plot by Giovanni Faustini. His works were given only single productions in Venice, except for the Bolognese performance of *Il ritorno d'Ulisse* (also 1640), one of several works exported there during the first decade of public opera in Venice. The presence at Vienna of the sole surviving score of *Il ritorno d'Ulisse* has led some scholars to suppose that it was used for a performance there. Like many of the other early Venetian librettists, Badoaro was a member of the cynical and libertine Accademia degli Incogniti.

C. Ivanovich: *Minerva al tavolino* (Venice, 1681, 2/1688)

R. Haas: 'Zur Neuausgabe von Claudio Monteverdis "Il ritorno d'Ulisse in patria"', *SMw*, ix (1922), 3–42

A. A. Abert: *Claudio Monteverdi und das musikalische Drama* (Lippstadt, 1954)

W. Osthoff: 'Zu den Quellen von Monteverdis "Ritorno d'Ulisse in patria"', *SMw*, xxiii (1956), 67–78

——: 'Zur Bologneser Aufführung von Monteverdis Ritorno d'Ulisse im Jahr 1640', *Anzeiger der phil.-hist. Klasse der Österreichischen Akademie der Wissenschaften*, xcv (1958), 155–60

——: *Das dramatische Spätwerk Claudio Monteverdis* (Tutzing, 1960)

T. Walker: 'Gli errori di "Minerva al tavolino": osservazioni sulla cronologia delle prime opere veneziane', *Venezia e il melodramma del Seicento: Venice 1972*, 7–20

L. Bianconi and T. Walker: 'Dalla "Finta pazza" alla "Veremonda": storie di Febiarmonici', *RIM*, x (1975), 379–454

E. Rosand: *Opera in Seventeenth-Century Venice: the Creation of a Genre* (Berkeley and Los Angeles, 1991) THOMAS WALKER

Badura-Skoda [née Halfar], **Eva** (*b* Munich, 15 Jan 1929). Austrian musicologist. She studied at the Vienna Academy and at universities in Heidelberg, Regensburg, Vienna and Innsbruck, where she received the doctorate in 1953. She taught at the International Summer Academy of the Salzburg Mozarteum, 1962–3, and at the University of Wisconsin, 1964–74. Her research has centred on 18th-century topics (particularly the music of the Scarlattis), on Viennese composers including Mozart and Haydn, and also on Schubert. She has written on the development of various genres of comic opera such as Singspiel, *opera buffa* and *opéra comique* and has been particularly concerned with the operas of Haydn and their sources in Viennese popular theatre. She is married to the pianist Paul Badura-Skoda.

Baeyens, August (*b* Antwerp, 5 June 1895; *d* Antwerp, 17 July 1966). Belgian composer. He studied at the Royal Flemish Conservatory in Antwerp. Shortly after World War I he became the leader of the expressionist school in Flemish music, his principal fellow members being Karel Albert and Jef van Durme. He was secretary of the Koninklijke Vlaamse Opera in Antwerp from 1931 to 1944, when he was made director, and was also a leading viola player. His stage works include the burlesque *De liefde en de kakatoe* ('Love and the Cockatoo', comp. 1928; 1, R. Avermaete), the radio opera *Coriolanus* (comp. 1940; 1, L. A. J. Burgersdijk, after W. Shakespeare), which was staged by the Vlaamse Opera on 27 November 1941, and *Ring van Gyges*, composed in 1943 (A. Monet; Vlaamse Opera, 15 Dec 1945). CORNEEL MERTENS

Baglioni. Italian family of singers.

(1) **Francesco** [Carnace] **Baglioni** (*fl* 1729–62). Bass. He was a comic opera singer who began singing intermezzos in the late 1720s in Foligno and Pesaro. He launched his comic opera career in Rome in 1738 with Gaetano Latilla's *La finta cameriera* and *Madama Ciana* and Rinaldo di Capua's *La commedia in commedia.* Productions throughout northern Italy of these operas along with another first performed in Rome, Rinaldo's *La libertà nociva* (1740), dominated Baglioni's career for the next decade. In 1749 he appeared in the *dramma giocoso L'Arcadia in Brenta* in Venice, the first collaboration between Galuppi and Goldoni, and for the remainder of his career he primarily sang texts written by Goldoni, in cities along the axis from Venice to Turin. According to the libretto of *Lo speziale* (1755, Venice; music by Vincenzo Pallavicini and Domenico Fischietti), Baglioni was a member of Girolamo Medebach's opera troupe. Three of his daughters appeared in productions with him: Giovanna from 1752, Clementina from 1753 and Vincenza from 1757. His other children include the singers Costanza, Rosina

and perhaps Antonio, Camilla and Giuseppe. Francesco's range encompassed *B♭* to *f'*, and music written for him is predominantly syllabic.

(2) **Giovanna Baglioni** (*fl* 1752–1770s). Soprano, daughter of (1) Francesco Baglioni. She began her career singing with her father in productions of comic opera. Her first role was Eugenia, a serious part in Galuppi's comic *Arcifanfano, re dei matti* (1752, Parma). She continued to sing serious roles in productions of comic opera in northern Italy with her father and her sisters in the early 1760s; by 1765 she was singing comic roles as well. Her range encompassed *c♯'* to *a''*, and she was able to execute lengthy melismatic lines.

(3) **Clementina Baglioni** [Poggi] (*fl* 1753–88). Soprano, daughter of (1) Francesco Baglioni. In 1753–9 she toured northern Italy with her father and one or two sisters, appearing in five comic operas at Venice in 1754–5. She also performed there in 1760–65 and 1775–8. Although best known for comic roles, she also sang in *opera seria*, appearing at Turin in 1759–60 (Galuppi's *La clemenza di Tito*, Traetta's *Enea nel Lazio*) and at Parma in 1761 and 1763 (J. C. Bach's *Catone in Utica*). In 1762 she was in Milan and Vienna (Hasse's *Il trionfo di Clelia*) and in 1767 in Naples, by which time she had married Domenico Poggi. She returned to Vienna where, in 1768, Mozart wrote for her the elaborate part of Rosina in *La finta semplice*, which however she never performed. She sang in Vienna in 1772–4 with her sisters Costanza and Rosina, and may have done so in Paris in 1778–9. Her range was *c'–b''*. J. von Sonnenfels praised her 'silvery' and 'agile' voice, but Burney thought it rather small. She also sang in Pisa in 1775 and Parma in 1780–81, was at Graz in 1783 and went with her husband to Brunswick in 1788.

BurneyFI; *BurneyGN*; *DBI* (R. Meloncelli); *ES* (E. Zanetti); *GSL*
J. von Sonnenfels: *Gesammelte Schriften*, v (Vienna, 1784), 300
V. Alfieri: *Memoirs* (Eng. trans., London, 1810), 39

BARBARA DOBBS MACKENZIE (1–2), COLIN TIMMS (3)

Baglioni, Antonio (*fl* 1780s–90s). Italian tenor and singing teacher. He may have been related to Francesco Baglioni. He sang in productions of comic opera, particularly in Venice during the late 1780s and early 1790s, and of serious opera. Two of his most important roles were Don Ottavio in the first production of Mozart's *Don Giovanni* (1787, Prague) and Titus in *La clemenza di Tito* (1791, Prague). His range encompassed *e* to *b♭'*. He was said to have had a well-trained, pure and expressive voice. As a singing teacher, he taught, among others, Giulietta da Ponte, the niece of Mozart's librettist, Lorenzo da Ponte, who claimed that Baglioni was 'a man of perfect taste and great musical knowledge who had trained the most celebrated singers in Italy'. Baglioni also wrote music, including a set of vocal exercises.

DBI (R. Meloncelli); *ES* (E. Zanetti)
A. Capacio: *Poesia e lodi della cattedrale di Cracovia* (Warsaw, 1790)

BARBARA DOBBS MACKENZIE

Baglioni, Bruna (*b* Frascati, 8 April 1947). Italian mezzo-soprano. She studied in Rome, making her début in 1970 at Spoleto as Maddalena (*Rigoletto*), and then sang at all the leading Italian theatres, including La Scala, the Rome Opera, La Fenice and S Carlo. Her repertory includes Amneris, Eboli, Ulrica, Azucena, Preziosilla, Laura (*La Gioconda*), Léonor (*La favorite*), Jane Seymour (*Anna Bolena*), Charlotte (*Werther*) and Marina (*Boris Godunov*). She uses her rich voice with great effect.

ELIZABETH FORBES

Bagnolesi, Anna Maria Antonia (*fl* 1726–43). Italian contralto. A Florentine employed by the Grand Duchess of Tuscany, she was married to the tenor G. B. Pinacci (1732). She sang in Florence (1725–6), Bologna (1726–8), Naples (1727, in operas by Vinci and Hasse) and Milan (1728). She may have been the Anna Bolognesi who appeared in Venice in 1729. She sang in Turin in 1731. Engaged by Handel for the London season of 1731–2, she made her début at the King's Theatre as Alcestis in *Admeto* and sang in *Ezio*, *Sosarme*, *Giulio Cesare*, *Flavio*, the bilingual *Acis and Galatea*, Ariosti's *Coriolano*, and the pasticcio *Lucio Papirio dittatore*. The two parts Handel composed for her, Valentinian in *Ezio* and Erenice in *Sosarme*, are restricted in compass (*b♭* to *e♭''* in the arias) and not technically difficult, but the scope and quality of the music suggest confidence in her powers of expression; her affected delivery, however, reminded Horace Mann of 'a person talking upon a close stool'. She sang in Naples in operas by Hasse, Pergolesi and N. Conti (1733–4), Venice (1739–40) and Florence (1732–3, 1739, 1741–3). She often took male roles.

WINTON DEAN

Baguer, Carlos [Carlets] (*b* Barcelona, ? March 1768; *d* Barcelona, 1 March 1808). Catalan composer. He served as organist of Barcelona Cathedral from 1786 until his death. Though known throughout Spain in his day as a composer of organ music and oratorios (of which he wrote at least four), he scored a notable success with his only opera, *La princesa filósofa, o sea El desdén con el desdén*, to a libretto by Carlo Gozzi after the 17th-century Spanish comedy by Agustín Moreto. First given at the Teatro de Santa Cruz in Barcelona (4 November 1797), it was performed several times in 1797 and again at the rebuilt Teatro de Santa Cruz in 1798, alongside highly regarded works by Haydn and Sor. MS scores of the opera are extant, not only in Catalonia (*E-Bc*) but also elsewhere in Spain (*E-E*). The surviving parts of the score suggest that the composer succeeded in capturing Moreto's comic-serious tone.

M. A. Ester Sala: 'Algunos datos biográficos de Carlos Baguer (1768–1808), organista de Barcelona', *Revista de musicología*, vi (1983), 223–52
A. Martín Moreno: *Historia de la música española*, iv: *Siglo XVIII* (Madrid, 1985), 156–7, 373

JACK SAGE

Bahia. Familiar name for Salvador da Bahia de todos os Santos, capital of the state of Bahia, Brazil; *see* SALVADOR.

Bahn, Monsieur (*b c*1700; *d* after 1726). German bass. He was mentioned in the Hamburg *Relations-Courier* (4 Dec 1724) as 'the new bass Mons. Bahn', who was billed to sing Argante in Handel's *Rinaldo* at the Gänsemarkt theatre. He had previously made his début as Mars on 2 November in Giovanni Porta's *Die heldenmütigen Schäfer Romulus und Remus*, a German version of *Numitore*, under Telemann's direction. In 1725 he sang in more than ten operas, prologues and serenatas, among them works by J. P. Kunzen and Gasparini, as well as Telemann and Keiser, and two

Handel roles: Leo in *Tamerlano* and Achillas in *Giulio Cesare*, both in German. The following year he sang in several works by Keiser; it is not known where he went after that.

*

K. Zelm: 'Die Sänger der Hamburger Gänsemarkt-Oper', *HJbMw*, iii (1978), 35–73, esp. 45–6, 48 HANS JOACHIM MARX

Bahr-Mildenburg, Anna (*b* Vienna, 29 Nov 1872; *d* Vienna, 27 Jan 1947). Austrian soprano. Having studied with Rosa Papier and presented herself in 1895 to the Hamburg impresario Pollini, she was immediately engaged there, and made her first appearance as Brünnhilde in *Die Walküre* on 12 September 1895 in a performance conducted by Mahler. This event led to a relationship between singer and conductor-composer which was emotional and somewhat tempestuous, but artistically fruitful. In 1898 Mildenburg followed Mahler to Vienna, where she remained a much valued member of the company until 1916, returning as a guest in 1920 and 1921. She excelled in all the great Wagner roles (including Kundry, which she often sang at Bayreuth between 1897 and 1914), as the heroines of *Fidelio*, *Oberon* and *Don Giovanni* (Donna Anna), and as Norma and in other Italian roles. She was seen at Covent Garden in 1906, and in 1910 under Beecham's direction made a great impression there as Clytemnestra in Strauss's *Elektra*. Such heavy use produced signs of vocal deterioration, which led her to undertake directional work at Bayreuth (with Cosima Wagner) and later at Munich, and to make appearances as a stage actress. Her solitary recording (1904) is of the recitative only of Weber's 'Ozean' aria, and gives a good, though tantalizing, impression of her brilliant voice and commanding style. The familiar hyphenated form of her name dates from her marriage, in 1909, to the Viennese author Hermann Bahr (1863–1934).

Anna Bahr-Mildenburg as Kundry in Wagner's 'Parsifal'

WRITINGS

with H. Bahr: *Bayreuth und das Wagner-Theater* (Leipzig, 1910; Eng. trans., 1912)
Erinnerungen (Vienna and Berlin, 1921)

*

P. Stefan: *Anna Bahr-Mildenburg* (Vienna, 1922)

DESMOND SHAWE-TAYLOR

Bailey, Norman (Stanley) (*b* Birmingham, 23 March 1933). English baritone. He studied at Rhodes University, South Africa, and at the Vienna Music Academy, making his début with the Vienna Chamber Opera as Tobias Mill in Rossini's *La cambiale di matrimonio* in 1959. He sang at Linz (1960–63) and in Germany (1963–7), where his roles included Rigoletto, Boccanegra, Nabucco and Renato. He joined the Sadler's Wells Opera (later the ENO) in 1967, making his British début in Manchester as Mozart's Count Almaviva; he celebrated his 25th anniversary with the company in 1992 as Sharpless. His London début, as Hans Sachs under Goodall (1968), established him as a Wagnerian of more than local importance, and he later undertook the role at Covent Garden, in Hamburg, Brussels and Munich, and at Bayreuth. He was an equally impressive Wotan (in a new production of the *Ring* at the London Coliseum, 1970–73), while at Bayreuth (Gunther, Amfortas) and elsewhere he expanded his Heldenbariton repertory. In 1972, starting with Count di Luna at the Coliseum, he resumed the big Italian roles of his early days in Germany. At the Coliseum he has sung Pizarro, Kutuzov (*War and Peace*), the Forester and Prince Gremin. His La Scala début was in 1967 as Dallapiccola's Job. In 1975 he sang Hans Sachs with the New York City Opera and in 1976 made his début with the Metropolitan in the same role. In 1985 at Duisburg he created Johann Matthys in Goehr's *Behold the Sun*. He was made a CBE in 1977. His timbre is definite, individual, firm, not rich or romantic in an italianate manner. Clarity, incisiveness and high musical intelligence distinguish his interpretations. His command of musical gesture, his vivid projection and his 'three-dimensional' presentation of a character have given his performances at once romance and uncommon dramatic power.

*

E. Forbes: 'Norman Bailey', *Opera*, xxiv (1973), 774–80

ANDREW PORTER

Baillou [Baylou, Baillon, Ballion, Ballioni, Baglioni], **Luigi** [Louis] **de** (*b* Milan, *c*1735; *d* Milan, *c*1809). Italian composer. He was a violinist at the Stuttgart court from 1762 to 1774 and thereafter worked in Milan. In 1779 he became opera orchestra director of the new Teatro alla Scala, a prestigious position which he held for 23 years. He was not, as Burney suggests, related to the 18th-century Baglioni family of opera singers; his error has led scholars mistakenly to distinguish Luigi Baglioni the Stuttgart court violinist from the Milanese Luigi (Louis) de Baillou.

Baillou wrote scores for many ballets (music lost), some of which were choreographed by J.-G. Noverre, but he also composed instrumental works and possibly two operas: *Tancredi* (Stuttgart, Hof, 1770 or 1777), probably identical to his ballet of the same title (1777), and the comic opera *Il casino di campagna* (Stuttgart, Hof, 1777). There is an aria by Baillou in an otherwise unattributed opera *Gli avventurieri* (*I-Tf*).

BurneyGN; *FétisB*; *MGG* (G. Grigolato)
J. Sittard: *Zur Geschichte der Musik und des Theaters am württembergischen Hofe*, ii (Stuttgart, 1891)
R. Krauss: 'Das Theater', *Herzog Karl Eugen von Württemberg und seine Zeit*, i/7 (Esslingen, 1907), 507, 530
W. Pfeilsticker: *Neues Württembergisches Dienerbuch* (Stuttgart, 1957), i, §885
C. Gatti: *Il teatro alla Scala nella storia e nell'arte (1778–1963)* (Milan, 1964), ii KATHLEEN KUZMICK HANSELL

Bain, Wilfred Conwell (*b* Shawville, Quebec, 20 Jan 1908). American administrator. He was educated at Houghton College (BA 1929), Westminster Choir College (BMus 1931) and New York University (MA 1936, EdD 1938). Between 1929 and 1947 he held posts at Wesleyan Methodist College, Central, South Carolina, Houghton College and North Texas State University, and from 1947 to 1973 was dean of the School of Music at Indiana University. After retiring from that post he became artistic director of the Opera Theater at Indiana University. The eminence of the Indiana School of Music, especially its excellent facilities for operatic production, is largely due to his efforts, and he was instrumental in engaging professional artists, including the mezzo-soprano Margaret Harshaw, to teach at the music school. PATRICK J. SMITH

Bainbridge, Elizabeth (*b* Rawtenstall, Lancs., 28 March 1930). English contralto. She studied in London, making her début in 1963 at Glyndebourne as Pallas Athene (*L'incoronazione di Poppea*) and Third Lady (*Die Zauberflöte*). In 1964 she sang Azucena for the WNO and a Valkyrie at Covent Garden the following year, joining the Royal Opera, of which she was still a member in 1991. Her large repertory includes Amneris, Ulrica, Mistress Quickly, Mamma Lucia, Suzuki, Erda, Filippyevna (*Yevgeny Onegin*), the Innkeeper (*Boris Godunov*), Grandmother Buryjovka (*Jenůfa*), Evadne (*Troilus and Cressida*), She-Ancient (*Midsummer Marriage*) and, her best-known role, Auntie (*Peter Grimes*), which she sang on the 25th anniversary of her début at Covent Garden, and also in Florence (1988). At Wexford in 1990 she sang Widow Sweeney in Maw's *The Rising of the Moon*. She has a rich voice, strong in the lower register. ELIZABETH FORBES

Bainton, Edgar (Leslie) (*b* London, 14 Feb 1880; *d* Sydney, 8 Dec 1956). English composer and teacher. He studied at the RCM under Stanford and Franklin Taylor. At the outbreak of World War I he was interned at Ruhleben. He was principal of the Newcastle upon Tyne conservatory before his appointment as director of the New South Wales State Conservatorium of Music in Sydney in 1934. Just before leaving England he was elected Fellow of the RCM and awarded the degree of Hon. DMus by the University of Durham. One of his early achievements at the Conservatorium was the establishment of the Opera School, with Florent Hoogstoel as musical director and Hilda Mulligan as stage director. The first work chosen was Gluck's *Orfeo ed Euridice*; the performance received encouraging critical acclaim. Other early productions included Stanford's *Shamus O'Brien*, *The Bartered Bride* and *Die Zauberflöte*. Following a broadcast performance of his one-act opera *The Crier by Night* (1919) in 1942, Bainton was encouraged to mount a production of his opera *The Pearl Tree* which, although composed in 1927, remained unperformed until the Sydney production in 1944. In their continuous flow of melody, their use of dramatic motifs, colourful harmony and rich orchestration, his operas reveal a debt to the music drama of Wagner and Strauss. Yet even the exotic nature of *The Pearl Tree* does not hide Bainton's distinctively English style, not least through the sensitive, yet unaffected melodic line.

See also PEARL TREE, THE.

Oithona, 1915, lost
The Crier by Night, 1919 (1, G. Bottomley), ABC, 8 Aug 1942, *AUS-NLwm*
The Pearl Tree, 1927 (opera phantasy, 2, R. Trevelyan), Sydney, Conservatorium Opera School, 20 May 1944, *Scm*

*

H. Bainton: *Remembered on Waking* (Sydney, 1960)
D. Tunley: 'Thoughts on the Music of Edgar Bainton', *Westerly* (1963), no.2, pp.55–7
M. Jones: 'Edgar Bainton: Musical and Spiritual Traveller', *Journal of the British Music Society*, xii (1990), 19–40 DAVID TUNLEY

Baird, Julianne (*b* Statesville, NC, 10 Dec 1952). American soprano. She took the BM and MM degrees at the Eastman School, where she studied singing with Masako Ono Toribara, and the PhD at Stanford University with a dissertation on P. F. Tosi. She also studied with Berry and Harnoncourt and at the Salzburg Mozarteum. She began her singing career in New York as a member of the Waverly Consort and Concert Royal, with which she made her stage début in 1980 in *Il pastor fido*. She has since sung in many operas by Charpentier, Gagliano, Gluck, Mozart, Purcell and others, in Los Angeles, Philadelphia, Santa Fe, Washington, DC and elsewhere, and has recorded *Amadis de Gaule*, *Imeneo*, *Orfeo* (Monteverdi) and *La serva padrona*. A respected specialist in Baroque vocal music, she teaches at Rutgers University and has written articles published in *Continuo* (1984) and *Early Music* (1987); her performances are distinguished by pristine vocalism, fluent coloratura and expressive, imaginative ornamentation founded in serious scholarship.
CORI ELLISON

Baird, Tadeusz (*b* Grodzisk Mazowiecki, 26 July 1928; *d* Warsaw, 2 Sept 1981). Polish composer. During World War II he studied composition with Kazimierz Sikorski and Bolesław Woytowicz, and subsequently (1947–51) with Piotr Perkowski and Piotr Rytel at the Warsaw Conservatory. His most significant works date from 1958 onwards, when he developed a lyrical-dramatic language drawing on the vocal and orchestral examples of Mahler, Berg and, to a lesser extent, Webern. His one-act opera *Jutro* ('Tomorrow'), with a libretto by J. S. Sito based on Joseph Conrad's short story of the same name, was first performed at the Wielki Theatre, Warsaw, on 18 September 1966, and its stature as a major new Polish chamber opera was quickly established. The starkly simple libretto concerns three alienated characters – the blind Joshua (baritone), his daughter Jessica (mezzo-soprano) and the old, deluded Ozias (bass) – whose fantasies about the return of Ozias's prodigal son Harry (a speaking role) are cruelly and violently shattered. Set on the edge of civilization – an isolated fishing post – *Jutro*'s dramatic world of human self-deception has in fact more in common with *Peter Grimes* than with *Riders to the Sea*. Its musical language, however, with its terse concentration on sinuous chromatic lines, belongs to post-Bergian central European traditions and marks the liberation of mid-20th-century Polish opera from its overtly national ties.

J. Kański: 'Dramat muzyczny Tadeusza Bairda', *Ruch muzyczny* (1966), no.23, pp.4–5

E. Nehrdich: 'Utwory z tekstem w drugim okresie twórczości Tadeusza Bairda (1958–1970)' [Works with Text from Tadeusz Baird's Second Period (1958–1970)], *Muzyka*, xxix/1–2 (1984), 71–82

ADRIAN THOMAS

Bajazet. *Dramma per musica* [*tragedia*] in three acts by FRANCESCO GASPARINI to a libretto, *Tamerlano*, by AGOSTIN PIOVENE (revised by Ippolito Zanelli) after Jacques Pradon's tragedy *Tamerlan, ou La mort de Bajazet*; Reggio Emilia, Teatro Pubblico, Spring Fair 1719 (revised as *Bajazette*, Venice, Teatro S Samuele, Ascension Fair 1723; original version as *Tamerlano*, Venice, Teatro S Cassiano, 24 January 1711).

Of Gasparini's three settings of this libretto, *Tamerlano*, the 1711 original, may have formed the basis for productions in Verona (1715), Udine (1716), Florence (Carnival 1717), Livorno (Carnival 1719) and Ancona (1719). For this second version he added new music, and Ippolito Zanelli, the Modena court poet, extensively rewrote Piovene's libretto, notably in the final scene. The third setting, *Bajazette*, restores that scene to its original form; here the original Bajazet, Giovanni Paita, assumed the same role.

Bajazet (tenor), the Ottoman emperor, has been defeated and captured by Tamerlano [Tamerlane] (alto castrato), the Turko-Mongol conqueror. Tamerlane, though betrothed to Irene (soprano), Princess of Trebizond, whom he has never seen, determines to wed Bajazet's daughter Asteria (soprano), ignorant of her love for Andronico [Andronicus] (contralto), a Greek prince and Tamerlane's dependant. Bajazet rejects the proposed marriage, but Asteria pretends to agree to it as part of a plot to kill Tamerlane; the plot is however foiled when Irene, disguised as a handmaiden, intervenes. A grateful Tamerlane consents to marry Irene, and, moved by Bajazet's suicide, pardons Asteria and allows her to marry Andronicus.

In the Reggio Emilia version of 1719 the role of Bajazet was taken by Francesco Borosini, Tamerlane by Antonio Bernacchi, Asteria by Maria Anna Bulgarelli and Irene by Faustina Bordoni; all but Borosini had sung in *Tamerlano* in 1711. The 1719 revisions present Bajazet's suicide in an extensive final scena in which Bajazet virtually dies before the audience's eyes; his leading tenor role is exceptional for its time. The trio in Act 2, in which Tamerlane rages against Bajazet and Asteria, who both offer to die rather than placate Tamerlane, is another high point. The score calls for one flute, two oboes, two horns, four-part strings and basso continuo (possibly with bassoon). The libretto for Handel's *Tamerlano* (1724), by Nicola Haym, is based on the 1719 *Bajazet* (*see* TAMERLANO).

HARRIS S. SAUNDERS

Bajić, Isidor (*b* Kula, 10 Aug 1878; *d* Novi Sad, 15 Sept 1915). Serbian composer. He was a pupil of Hans Koessler in Budapest and later became an organizer of musical life in Novi Sad, where from 1901 until his death he taught at the high school. He was editor of the magazine *Srpski muzički list* in 1903 as well as a series of music by Serbian composers (1903–4); he also founded a music school in 1909. His Romantic national opera *Knez Ivo od Semberije* ('Prince Ivo of Semberia'; 1, B. Nušić; Belgrade, 6 Jan 1911) deals with the trading of Serbian slaves during the Serbian uprising against the Turks in the 19th century. Although rather naive and deficient in technique, it is interesting for its musical differentiation between Serbian and Turkish characters. Its main characteristics are its sentimental idiom, emphasized by the use of augmented 2nds, the Balkan minor scale and leitmotifs, and the arioso melodies and *čoček* dances. Bajić also composed music for stage plays by Serbian writers.

S. Đurić-Klajn: 'Razvoj muzičke umetnosti u Srbiji' [The Development of the Art of Music in Serbia], in J. Andreis, D. Cvetko and S. Đurić-Klajn: *Historijski razvoj muzičke kulture u Jugoslaviji* [The Historical Development of Musical Culture in Yugoslavia] (Zagreb, 1962), 529–709

V. Peričić: *Muzički stvaraoci u Srbiji* [Musical Creators in Serbia] (Belgrade, 1969)

ROKSANDA PEJOVIĆ

Bakala, Břetislav (*b* Fryšták, nr Holešov, 12 Feb 1897; *d* Brno, 1 April 1958). Czech conductor. At Brno he studied composition with Janáček, conducting with Neumann and the piano with Vilém Kurz. He became a répétiteur and conductor at the Brno Opera, making his début with Gluck's *Orfeo* and in 1930 he gave the première of Janáček's posthumous *From the House of the Dead*, completing the score with Osvald Chlubna. He was an intellectual conductor, of sparse gesture, who conveyed precisely the internal structure of a work through firm rhythmic control and careful balance.

J. Trojan: 'Břetislav Bakala: Janáčkovský interpret', *Sborník Janáčkový akademie muzickych umění*, v (1965), 91ff

ALENA NĚMCOVÁ

Baker, Dame **Janet (Abbott)** (*b* Hatfield, Yorks., 21 Aug 1933). English mezzo-soprano. She studied in London with Helene Isepp and Meriel St Clair, making her début in 1956 as Miss Róza in *The Secret* (Oxford University Opera Club). In 1959 she sang Eduige in the Handel Opera Society's *Rodelinda*; other Handel roles included Ariodante (1964) and Orlando (1966), which she sang at the Barber Institute, Birmingham. With the English Opera Group at Aldeburgh she sang Purcell's Dido (1962), Polly (Britten's version of *The Beggar's Opera*) and Lucretia. At Glyndebourne she appeared again as Dido (1966) and as Diana/Jupiter (*Calisto*) and Penelope (*Il ritorno d'Ulisse*). For Scottish Opera she sang Dorabella, Dido (*Troyens*), Octavian, the Composer and Gluck's Orpheus. At Covent Garden, having made her debut in 1966 as Hermia, she sang Berlioz's Dido, Kate in *Owen Wingrave* (the role she created in its original television version in 1971), Mozart's Vitellia and Idamantes, Walton's Cressida and Gluck's Alcestis (1981). For the ENO she sang Poppaea, Donizetti's Mary Stuart, Charlotte (*Werther*) and Handel's Julius Caesar. In 1982 she retired from opera, after singing Mary Stuart at the ENO and Gluck's Orpheus at Glyndebourne. She described her final opera season and her career in *Full Circle* (London, 1982). Complete emotional identification with her roles, many of which she recorded, and a rich, expressive and flexible voice enabled her to excel in florid as well as dramatic music. She was created a DBE in 1976.

A. Blyth: *Janet Baker* (London, 1973) [with discography by M. Walker]

J. B. Steane: *The Grand Tradition* (London 1974), 500ff

ALAN BLYTH

Baklanov [Bakkis], **Georgy** (**Andreyevich**) (*b* Riga, 23 Dec 1880/4 Jan 1881; *d* Basle, 6 Dec 1938). Russian baritone of Latvian birth. He studied with Pets in Kiev, Pryanishnikov in St Petersburg and Vanza in Milan. He made his début (1903, Kiev) as Rubinstein's Demon, sang with the Zimin Private Opera in Moscow and was engaged in 1905 by the Bol'shoy, creating the Baron in Rakhmaninov's *The Miserly Knight* (1906) and remaining until 1909. That year he sang Barnaba (*La Gioconda*) at the inaugural performance of the Boston Opera House. At Covent Garden he appeared as Rigoletto (début, 1910), Scarpia and Amonasro; in 1911 he repeated the first two roles at the Komische Oper, Berlin. He sang in Boston (1915–18), then with Chicago Opera (1917–26), and also in New York, where he later became a mainstay of the Russian Opera Company. His repertory included Yevgeny Onegin, Hamlet, Boris, Méphistophélès, the Father (*Louise*), Golaud, Telramund and Wotan. He was greatly admired for his dramatic talents, and his voice was rich and vibrant, particularly in the middle and upper registers. Between 1910 and 1930 he made a number of recordings. HAROLD BARNES, KATHERINE K. PRESTON

Baku. Capital of Azerbaijan. After the annexation of Azerbaijan by Russia in 1806 a theatrical tradition developed only gradually, under the influence of Russian residents. The first local theatre, the Teatr G. Z. A. Tagiyeva (built in 1880), featured some music in its productions, including musical-dramatic performances by singers and instrumentalists during intervals. Concert life developed only at the end of the 19th century, although touring Russian and Italian opera troupes appeared earlier. Efforts by the Nijat society, which directed the Tagiyev Theatre, led to the production of the first Azerbaijani opera, *Leyli i Mejnun* by Uzeir Hajibeyov, on 12/25 January 1908 and later to other operas by Hajibeyov, including *Sheykh Sanan* in 1909 and *Rustam i Zokhrab* in 1910. A 1281-seat opera theatre, built in 1910–11 and reconstructed in 1938, opened in 1911 with a performance of *Boris Godunov* and has since devoted itself to the performance of Russian and Azerbaijani classics. In 1920 the theatre was nationalized after the incorporation of Azerbaijan into the USSR; it became known as the Azerbaijanskiy Gosudarstvennïy Teatr (Azerbaijan State Theatre), and separate Russian and Azerbaijani troupes formed within it. The two troupes merged in 1924 to form the Azerbaijanskiy Teatr Gosudarstvennïy Operï i Baleta; renamed after the Dramaturg M. F. Akhundov in 1930, the theatre became known as the Azerbaijanskiy Akademicheskiy Teatr Operï i Baleta imeni F. Akhundova (Akhundov State Academic Theatre of Opera and Ballet). Early premières at the theatre included Hajibeyov's *Kyor-oglï* ('A Blind Man's Son', winner of the USSR State Prize, 1941), A. B. Beadalbeyli's *Gnev narodniy* ('The People's Wrath', 1941), Mahomayev's *Nergiz* (1935) and Karayev and Hajiyev's *Veten* ('Homeland', 1945; State Prize, 1946). A separate Teatr Muzïkal'nïy Komedii, opened in 1938, presents operettas and other lighter works of musical theatre; in 1967 it was renamed after Sh. Kurbanov.

*

ME (K. Kasimov)

U. Gadzhibekov: *Ot 'Leyli i Medzhnuna' do 'Kyor-oglï': iskusstvo azerbaydzhanskogo muzïkal'nogo naroda* [From *Leyli i Mejnun* to *Kyor-oglï*: the Musical Art of the Azerbaijani Peoples] (Moscow and Leningrad, 1938)

K. Kasimov: 'Zarozhdeniye i razvitiye azerbaydzhanskogo muzïkal'nogo teatra' [The Origins and Development of Azebaijan Music Theatre], *Iskusstvo Azerbaydzhana* [The Art of Azerbaijan], iii (Baku, 1950)

S. Korev: *Uzer Gadzhibekov i ego operï* [Uzeir Hajibeyov and his Operas] (Moscow, 1952)

S. Dadashev: *50-letiye Azerbaydzhanskogo ordena Lenina teatra operï i baleta im. M. F. Akhundova* [50 years of the Azerbaijan Akhundov Opera and Ballet Theatre] (Baku, 1958) [in Azeri]

A. Badalbeyli and K. Kasimov: *Azerbaydzhanskiy gosudarstvennïy ordena Lenina teatr operï i baleta imeni M. F. Akhundova* [The Azerbaijan State Akhundov Opera and Ballet Theatre] (Moscow, 1959)

G. Bernandt: *Slovar' oper vpervïye postavlennïkh ili izdannïkh v dorevolyutsionnoy Rossii i v SSSR 1736–1959* [Dictionary of Operas First Performed or Published in Pre-revolutionary Russia and in the USSR 1736–1959] (Moscow, 1962), 536

A. I. Isazade: *Letopis' muzïkal'noy zhizni Sovetskogo Azerbaydzhana, 1920–1925*, ed. K. A. Kisimov [A Chronicle of Musical Life in Soviet Azerbaijan (1920–25)] (Baku, 1965)

A. G. Sarabsky: *Vozniknoveniye i razvitiye Azerbaydzhanskogo muzïkal'nogo teatra (do 1917.g.)* [The Origins and Development of Azerbaijan Music Theatre (Pre-1917)] (Baku, 1968)

E. Abasova and K. Kasimov: *Ocherki muzïkal'nogo iskusstva Sovetskogo Azerbaydzhana 1920–56* [Studies on Music in Soviet Azerbaijan, 1920–56] (Baku, 1970)

Yu. V. Keldïsh, ed.: *Istoriya muzïki narodov SSSR* [History of the Music of the Soviet Peoples], i-v (Moscow, 1970–74)

A. I. Isazde and T. G. Akhundov: *Letopis' muzïkal'noy zhizni Sovetskogo Azerbaydzhana (1926–1932gg)* [A Chronicle of Musical Life in Soviet Azerbaijan (1926–32)] (Baku, 1982)

GREGORY SALMON

Balada, Leonardo (*b* Barcelona, 22 Sept 1933). American composer of Spanish birth. He was trained as a tailor and as a pianist, and attended the Barcelona Conservatory. In 1956 he won a scholarship to study at the New York College of Music; he graduated from the Juilliard School in 1960. His composition teachers included Copland, Tansman and Persichetti. He taught at the United Nations International School (1963–70), then joined the music faculty at Carnegie-Mellon University, Pittsburgh, where he became professor in 1975.

Before 1975, Balada composed mainly instrumental works that used note clusters, dense textures and aleatory methods. He favoured bright colours, aggressive rhythms and percussive sounds, and has shown what he called 'a dislike for obvious melodic lines'.

Melody, an expression of 'ethnic values', reasserted itself after 1975 as a counterbalance to the 'cultural uniformity' towards which he felt international music was moving. This reaction not only opened the way for him to compose operas, but suggested the subject matter for them. While Balada's operas abound in local colour (sometimes using folk melodies), each also deals with the moral issues of a society in transition, and represents conflict and change by surrealistic distortions of the themes (inspired, Balada says, by the paintings of Salvador Dali). The orchestra carries much of the expressive burden, using the vivid dissonant effects of his earlier style; his vocal melodies are usually diatonic, of a traditional *verismo* cast, and well matched to the text.

His first opera, *Hangman, Hangman!* (1982) is a tragi-comic satire of greed and corruption with a romantic thief as its central character, and is based on popular songs and dances of the Old West. Its première was given in Barcelona by the Chamber Opera of Catalonia. With *Zapata* a more operatic vocal style emerges, although the orchestra still dominates, with quotations of Mexican folksongs and an aggressive dissonance.

Cristóbal Colón marks an advance in style and stagecraft. Telling the story of Columbus's voyage, through scenes on the ship and through flashbacks, Balada favours polyphonic (sometimes polytonal) writing for voice and orchestra, suggestive of Richard Strauss in its denser moments and of Leoncavallo at other times. He uses his familiar colouristic dissonances selectively, to evoke such things as the sailors' anger and the sounds of wind, waves and birds. Melodic characterizations are also subtly woven through the score; Catalan, Andalusian, Jewish, American Indian and ecclesiastical elements of the story add colour to the music at appropriate times.

Hangman, Hangman! (chamber op, 1, Balada, after a traditional cowboy ballad), Barcelona, 10 Oct 1982
Zapata, 1982–4 (2, T. Capobianco and G. Roepke), unperf.
Cristóbal Colón (2, A. Gala), Barcelona, Liceu, 24 Sept 1989

*

P. E. Stone: 'He writes for the audience, but on his own terms', *New York Times* (21 Nov 1982)
Leonardo Balada (Pittsburgh, 1982) [brochure; pubn of Carnegie-Mellon University]
P. E. Stone: 'Leonardo Balada's First Half Century', *Symphony*, xxiv/3 (1983), 85
B. Holland: 'Columbus comes home from the New World', *New York Times* (30 Sept 1989)
O. Roca: 'Opera tribute to Columbus is glorious musical theater', *Washington Times* (3 Oct 1989) DAVID WRIGHT

Balanchivadze. Georgian family.

(1) **Meliton Antonovich Balanchivadze** (*b* Banodzha, 12/24 Dec 1862; *d* Kutaisi, 21 Nov 1937). Composer and singer. He studied music from an early age, sang in church choirs and from 1880 was a member of the chorus of the Tbilisi opera theatre, where he subsequently appeared as soloist. He later lived in St Petersburg (1889–1915), where he was a pupil of Rimsky-Korsakov at the conservatory. Much of his life was devoted to the promotion of Georgian music, either researching, recording or performing his country's folk music, or taking an active part in the organization of musical life, especially in Tbilisi (after 1921), Batimi (1929–31) and latterly in Kutaisi, where he founded a music college. His music, which enjoyed great popularity in Georgia, is distinguished by its melodic quality, striking lyricism and use of folk music intonations. Excerpts from *Tamara kovornaya* (after A. Tsereteli), one of the first Georgian national operas, were performed in St Petersburg in 1897. The work was revised twice: the second version was performed in Tbilisi on 6 April 1926 as *Daredzhan kovornoya* (also known as *Daredzhan tsbieri*, 'Perfidious Daregani'; V. Velichko and K. Potskhverashvili), and the third was given there in 1937.

(2) **George Balanchine** [Balanchin; Balanchivadze, Georgy Melitonovich] (*b* St Petersburg, 9/22 Jan 1904; *d* New York, 30 April 1983). Choreographer, later naturalized American, son of (1) Meliton Balanchivadze. He was trained at the Imperial Ballet School, St Petersburg, making his stage début at the Mariinsky Theatre in *La jota aragonesa* (music by Glinka) in 1916. He created his first opera-ballet, *Le coq d'or*, for the Maliy Theatre in 1923, and gained further experience under Dyagilev, choreographing *divertissements* for ten operas (including *Carmen*, *Thaïs*, *Manon*, *Faust* and *Hérodiade*) at the Monte Carlo Opera in 1925. In the same year, he choreographed the première of Ravel's *L'enfant et les sortilèges*, giving it a fantastic quality through the grotesque metamorphoses of everyday objects into dancers who threaten to stampede the cruel child with their intricate footwork. After the collapse of the Ballets Russes in 1929 Balanchine continued at Monte Carlo, in 1932 creating dances for as many as 18 operas, including *Tannhäuser*, *Les contes d'Hoffmann*, *Le prophète* and *Samson et Dalila*. From 1935–1938 he was ballet-master for the Metropolitan Opera, but the 1936 season was marked by critics' jibes at his avant-garde works and angry public confrontations between the choreographer and administration officials. He claimed to tire of their space limitations and trite conventions, preferring to focus on pure or 'plotless' ballets. However, he did not lose contact with opera, working with other companies in New York (1942–3, 1944), as well as in Los Angeles and San Francisco (1944), Mexico City (1945), Paris (1947, 1975), Milan and Florence (1953), Hamburg (1963, 1969) and Berlin (1973). Balanchine choreographed dances for 76 different operas, a significant proportion of his ballet output. His collaboration with Stravinsky began with *Le chant du rossignol*, revised by the composer as a ballet for Dyagilev (1920), and continued throughout his life for a total of 28 ballets to Stravinsky's music. He also directed the staging of *The Rake's Progress* at its first American performance (New York, Metropolitan, 14 February 1953).

*

B. Taper: *Balanchine* (New York, 1963, enlarged 2/1984)
N. Reynolds, ed.: *Choreography by George Balanchine: a Catalogue of Works* (New York, 1983)

(3) **Andrey Melitonovich Balanchivadze** (*b* St Petersburg, 19 May/1 June 1906). Composer, son of (1) Meliton Balanchivadze. He spent his childhood in St Petersburg and first studied the cello, then the piano. In 1917 the family moved to Georgia and in 1921 he entered the Tbilisi conservatory, where he studied composition with Ippolitov-Ivanov. After graduating he was active in the work of the Georgian Proletkul't and composed for the Theatre of the Working Association of Youth. He then studied at the Leningrad Conservatory (1927–31). After returning to Georgia in 1931 he composed for the first Georgian sound films and took up forms new to Georgian music, including symphonies and concertos. From 1935 he taught at the Tbilisi conservatory, as professor from 1942 and head of composition from 1963; he also held musical and government administrative posts, and appeared as pianist and conductor in his own works. He was made People's Artist of the USSR (1968) and received many other honours and awards. The development of Georgian music from the 1920s is inseparably linked with Balanchivadze's work. With a group of contemporaries he furthered the establishment of musical forms and modes of thought new to Georgia, seeking an organic link between distinctive national traditions and those of European music generally.

Arsen, 1935 (Sh. Dadiani, after S. Shanshiashvili)
Schast'ye [Happiness], 1939 (M. Lakerbay)
Mziya (lyric comedy, V. Pataraya and Lakerbay), concert perf., Tbilisi, 1949; stage, Tbilisi, 28 Oct 1950
Zolotaya svad'ba [Golden Wedding], Tbilisi, 1969

*

P. Khuchua: 'Sovetskaya opera i balet', *Gruzinskaya muzïkal'naya kul'tura* [Georgian Musical Culture] (Moscow, 1957)
G. Ordzhonikidze: *Andrey Balanchivadze* (Tbilisi, 1967)

YEVGENY MACHAVARIANI (1, 3),
MAUREEN NEEDHAM COSTONIS (2)

Balasanian, Sergey Artem'yevich (*b* Ashkhabad, 13/26 Aug 1902; *d* Moscow, 3 June 1982). Tajik composer. He received his musical education in Tbilisi and at the Moscow Conservatory. From 1936 to 1943 he lived in Tajikistan and was instrumental there in organizing the national musical theatre. In 1939 he composed the first Tajik opera, *Vosstaniye Vose* ('Vose's Uprising'), first performed that year in Stalinabad (now Dushanbe). In this operatic treatment of a peasant revolt at the end of the 19th century Balasanian used many Tajik melodies. His attraction to the folk traditions of Tajikistan as well as Armenian, Afghan and other eastern cultures is reflected in many other works, including two more Tajik operas: *Kuznets Kova* ('Kova the Smith', 1941), to a libretto based on episodes from a poem by Firdousi, and *Bakhtiyor i Nisso* ('Bakhtiyor and Niso', 1954), to a libretto based on a novel by Luknitsky. Balasanian returned to Moscow in 1943 and from 1948 taught at the Moscow Conservatory, heading the composition department there for many years.

See also VOSSTANIYE VOSE.

Vosstaniye Vose [Vose's Uprising] (4, A. Dekhoti and M. Tursunzade), Stalinabad, Tajik Musical Theatre, 16 Oct 1939; rev., Stalinabad, Ayni Tajik Theatre of Opera and Ballet, 13 Jan 1959

Kuznets Kova [Kova the Smith] (4, A. Lakhuti, after A. K. Firdousi: *Shakh-name*), Moscow, Tajik Theatre of Opera and Ballet, 15 April 1941, collab. Sh. N. Bobokalonov

Bakhtiyor i Nisso [Bakhtiyor and Niso] (4, S. A. Tsenin, after P. N. Luknitsky: *Nisso*), Stalinabad, Ayni Theatre of Opera and Ballet, 25 Oct 1954

*

N. Shakhnazarova and G. Golovinsky: *S. Balasanian* (Moscow, 1972)

LAUREL E. FAY

Balassa, Sándor (*b* Budapest, 20 Jan 1935). Hungarian composer. He worked first as a factory mechanic, but after hearing Verdi's *Il trovatore* he decided to study choral conducting at the Budapest Conservatory (1952–6). From 1960 to 1965 he attended the Budapest Music Academy as a composition pupil of Endre Szervánszky and was a music producer for Hungarian Radio from 1964 to 1980. In 1981 he was appointed to teach orchestration at the Budapest Academy of Music, at the same time pursuing a career as a freelance composer. He has won many prizes.

Balassa developed his style in a freely dodecaphonic idiom with strong leanings towards diatonicism resulting from his use of traditional Hungarian material. His music shows great sympathy for the voice and sensitivity to poetry. In spite of that and his early fascination with opera, it took him five years with several interruptions to complete his one-act opera, commissioned by Hungarian Radio, *Az ajtón kivül* ('The Man Outside'; G. Fodor, after W. Borchert; Budapest, Hungarian State Opera House, 20 October 1978). The division into five movements rather than acts or scenes underlines the essentially lyrical character of his writing. *The Man Outside* is a series of *danse macabre* variations for the stage, with allegorical characters. The Berg-inspired chromatic declamatory style is set against powerful choruses, which mark the point of departure for Balassa's next large-scale vocal work, *A harmadik bolygó* ('The Third Planet'), an apocalyptic vision of man's pollution of nature, written in 1987 to his own libretto and first performed in a concert version (1989, Budapest). In this work choral commentaries predominate over unnamed solo parts, so that the general impression, despite the subtitle 'opera', is of a cantata.

A. Boros: *Harminc év magyar operái 1948–1978* [30 Years of Hungarian Opera, 1948–78] (Budapest, 1979)

G. Staud, ed.: *A budapesti operaház száz éve* [100 Years of the Budapest Opera House] (Budapest, 1984)

TIBOR TALLIÁN

Balázs, Béla (*b* Szeged, 4 Aug 1884; *d* Budapest, 17 May 1949). Hungarian librettist. His libretto *Bluebeard's Castle*, a response to the Maeterlinck play set by Dukas, was written for either of the two composers to whom he was tied by links of friendship and nationalist artistic ideals: Bartók and Kodály. The former took it on, and also used a Balázs scenario for his second stage work, the ballet *The Wooden Prince* (1914–16), while the latter collaborated with Balázs much later on the Singspiel *Czinka Panna* (1946–8). Between 1919 and 1945 Balázs, as a communist, had been in exile. His reputation in Hungary is largely that of a pioneering writer about the cinema.

PAUL GRIFFITHS

Balbi, Giovan Battista [Giambattista, Giovanni Battista; 'Il Tasquino'] (*fl* 1636–57). Italian choreographer, dancer, stage designer and impresario. Probably born in Venice, he apparently was well known in 1637 when, in the libretto for Francesco Manelli's *Andromeda*, he was cited as 'Veneziano Ballarino celebre'. Over the next seven years he continued to provide choreography for Venetian operas, including Manelli's *La maga fulminata* (1638), Cavalli's *Le nozze di Teti e di Peleo* (1639) and Francesco Sacrati's *L'Ulisse errante* (1644). In 1645 Balbi and the Febiarmonici, a travelling company, obtained permission to stage their production of Sacrati's *La finta pazza* in Florence, exactly as they had presented it in Venice in 1641. While Balbi was in Florence, Anne of Austria sent a request through her cousin Duke Odoardo Farnese of Parma, asking him to collaborate with the Comédie-Italienne in Paris. The stage designer Giacomo Torelli also went, and together they mounted a celebrated production of *La finta pazza* at the Salle du Petit Bourbon on 14 December 1645. Balbi's fanciful ballets incorporated monkeys, bears, ostriches, Indians and parrots. He published a description of the three ballets, each illustrated with six engravings by Valerio Spada (see illustration), under the title *Balletti d'invenzione nella Finta Pazza di Giovanbatta Balbi* (n.p., *c*1658).

In 1647 Balbi created ballets for the French production of *Orfeo* by Francesco Buti and Luigi Rossi. The following year Archduke Leopold Wilhelm of Austria, governor of the Low Countries, called a number of artists, including Balbi, to his court at Brussels. Balbi created a grand 'balet a entrées' in honour of the wedding of Philip IV and Maria Anna of Austria. Entitled *Le balet du monde*, it was presented in Brussels during Carnival 1650, between the acts of Gioseffo Zamponi's opera *Ulisse all'isola di Circe*.

Balbi returned to Florence in 1650 and with the Febiarmonici staged Cavalli's *La Deidamia*, first performed in Venice at the Teatro Novissimo in 1644. During the carnival of 1651 Balbi was once again in Venice, where he created the choreography and stage design for Cesti's *Alessandro vincitor di se stesso* at the Teatro SS Giovanni e Paolo. In December 1652 Balbi and the Febiarmonici produced *Veremonda l'amazzone di Aragona* (possibly by Cavalli) in Naples for celebrations of the recapture of Barcelona. This production and *La finta pazza*, presented earlier that year, served to introduce Neapolitan audiences to the innovations of Venetian stage design, machinery and ballet. For the

Balbi's final ballet for 'La finta pazza' in which Indians release five parrots, performed at the Salle du Petit Bourbon, Paris, 14 December 1645: engraving by V. Spada

1653 carnival season Balbi created the set designs and choreography for *Le magie amorose* (composer unknown) and for Provenzale's *Il Ciro* in Naples, and restaged *Veremonda* at SS Giovanni e Paolo in Venice. The following year *Ciro* was restaged at SS Giovanni e Paolo with new music by Cavalli, and in the preface to the libretto Balbi noted that the opera had been adapted for Venetian taste. The final notice of his activities comes in 1657 from Palermo, where he is credited with the sets, machinery and ballets for a production of *Ciro*. Balbi's importance in the field of choreography may be likened to that of Torelli in stage design. He not only established a place for ballet in the Venetian theatres, but also played a significant role in taking Venetian opera to France, and with the Febiarmonici promoted its export to other Italian cities.

DBI (F. Marotti); *ES* (E. Povoledo)

H. Prunières: *L'opéra italien en France avant Lulli* (Paris, 1913)

G. Morelli and T. Walker: 'Tre controversie intorno al San Cassiano', *Venezia e il melodramma nel seicento: Venice 1972*, 97–120

L. Bianconi and T. Walker: 'Dalla *Finta pazza* alla *Veremonda*: storie di Febiarmonici', *RIM*, x (1975), 379–454

R. L. Weaver and N. W. Weaver: *A Chronology of Music in the Florentine Theater, 1590–1750* (Detroit, 1978)

G. Donato: 'Su alcuni aspetti della vita musicale in Sicilia nel seicento', *La musica a Napoli durante il seicento*, ed. D. A. d'Alessandro and A. Ziino (Rome, 1987), 567–623 IRENE ALM

Baldassari, Benedetto [Benedetti] (*fl* 1708–25). Italian soprano castrato. He was in the service of the Elector Palatine at Düsseldorf, *c*1708–14, where he sang a female part in Steffani's *Tassilone* (1709). In 1712 he went to London and sang in revivals of Mancini's *Idaspe fedele* and Gasparini's *Antioco* at the Queen's Theatre, playing a female part in the latter, and in the pasticcio *Ercole*. He was much applauded, again in a female role, in Gasparini's *Lucio Papirio* in Rome in 1714, and sang in operas by C. F. Pollarolo and Orlandini in Venice in 1718. Returning to London in 1719, he sang, as an original member of the Royal Academy company, in Porta's *Numitore*, Handel's *Radamisto* (where he demanded to be elevated from a captain of the guard to a princely lover) and Roseingrave's adaptation of Domenico Scarlatti's *Narciso* in 1720, and in original productions of Handel's *Floridante* (1721) and Giovanni Bononcini's *Crispo* and *Griselda* (1722).

Handel's two parts for him, Fraarte in *Radamisto* and Timante in *Floridante*, show a high soprano (compass *e'* to *a''*), but the two leading male roles in *Radamisto* were allotted to women, implying that Handel did not rate him as a front-rank castrato. WINTON DEAN

Baldi, Antonio (*fl* 1722–35). Italian alto castrato. He came from Cortona and sang in 13 operas in Venice (1722–4, 1729 and 1733–5), including works by Gasparini, Orlandini, Giacomelli, Hasse and Leo, in Milan (1725), Florence (1730–31) and Rome (1731). He was engaged for three seasons (1725–8) by the Royal Academy in London, making his début in a revival of the Vinci-Orlandini *Elpidia*. He sang in ten operas by Handel (four of them revivals), the pasticcio *Elisa*, Ariosti's *Lucio Vero* and *Teuzzone* and Giovanni Bononcini's *Astianatte*. The six parts Handel composed for him, Scipio, Taxiles in *Alessandro*, Trasimede in *Admeto*, Oronte in *Riccardo Primo*, Mendarse in *Siroe* and Alessandro in *Tolomeo*, indicate a narrow compass (*a* to *d''*) and a tessitura similar to Senesino's but with far less brilliance. Owen Swiney described him in 1725 as a tolerable actor and neither a good nor a bad singer. Burney called him 'a singer of no great abilities' and suggested, of one of his arias in *Siroe*, that Handel assigned 'the chief part of the business to the instruments, which, so employed, were better worth hearing than the voice'; but Burney can never have heard Baldi sing. WINTON DEAN

Baldini, Lucrezia (*b* ?Venice, 1700 or 1701; *d* Venice, 1 Feb 1733). Italian singer. Having sung contralto roles in operas performed in the provinces from as early as 1720, she made her Venetian début in Vignati's *I rivali generosi* at S Samuele in 1726. Her career was short; the last opera in which she is known to have appeared was Orlandini's *Adelaide* (S Cassiano, Carnival 1729). A contract that she made with Vivaldi on 13 October

1726 shows her to have been a worthy seconda donna; for singing in only one opera (Vivaldi's *Farnace*, given at S Angelo, Carnival 1726–7) she was to receive 200 ducats, payable in instalments before, during and after the performances. Her retirement may have been caused by her marriage to a Venetian spicer, Angelo Venzoli. She died from an injury sustained when a carnival booth in St Mark's Square collapsed.

*

R. Giazotto: *Antonio Vivaldi* (Turin, 1973) MICHAEL TALBOT

Balducci, Marina (*b* ?Genoa, ?1758; *d* after 1784). Italian soprano. She was said to have come from an impoverished noble Genoese family, her real name being Maria Bertaldi. Although she sang in *opera seria* alone from 1778 to 1784, retiring after her marriage, she made a great impression and was long remembered. She appeared at Pavia, Venice, Milan (as seconda donna in the distinguished company that opened La Scala in 1778), Mantua, Florence, Turin and Palermo, and sang for three seasons at the S Carlo, Naples, where she was greatly admired for her beauty, her acting and especially her high-register singing (to *g‴*). DENNIS LIBBY

Bâle (Fr.). BASLE.

Balerini, Francesco. *See* BALLERINI, FRANCESCO.

Balfe, Michael William (*b* Dublin, 15 May 1808; *d* Rowney Abbey, Herts., 20 Oct 1870). Irish composer and singer. The most successful composer of English operas in the 19th century, and the only one whose fame spread throughout Europe, he gained wide international recognition with *The Bohemian Girl*.

1. LIFE. Balfe received his earliest musical instruction from his father, a dancing-master and violinist, and the composer William Rooke. When his father died in January 1823, Balfe went to London and became the articled pupil of C. F. Horn, earning a living as a violinist in the Drury Lane orchestra. He developed a fine baritone voice and made his stage début at Norwich as Caspar in a bowdlerized version of *Der Freischütz*. In 1825 he went to Rome, where he studied composition with Paer, and then to Milan to study counterpoint with Federici and singing with Filippo Galli. That autumn his first stage work, *Il naufragio di La Pérouse*, a *ballo pantomimo serio*, was given there at the Teatro alla Cannobiana.

During the next four years Balfe pursued his career as an opera singer. He returned to Paris where Cherubini, whose good opinion he had already won en route to Rome, introduced him to Rossini. On hearing Balfe sing 'Largo al factotum', Rossini promised to recommend him to the Théâtre des Italiens, if he would first study for a year with Bordogni. Balfe agreed, and made his Paris début as Figaro in *Il barbiere* at the Théâtre des Italiens in 1827. After two seasons there he returned to Italy, appearing as Valdeburgo in Bellini's *La straniera* at the Teatro Carolino, Palermo, on 1 January 1830. Towards the end of the carnival season, a dispute between the chorus and the management resulted in his being commissioned to compose a short opera without chorus, *I rivali di se stessi*, which was written and produced in about 20 days. His singing engagements took him next to Piacenza and to Bergamo, where he met and shortly afterwards married the Hungarian singer Lina Roser.

In spring 1831 he was invited to write an opera for the Teatro Fraschini, Pavia, the *farsa giocosa Un avvertimento ai gelosi*. His third opera, the more ambitious *Enrico Quarto al passo della Marna*, was given at the Teatro Carcano, Milan (not La Scala, as is often stated) on 19 February 1833, with himself and his wife in leading roles. Later that year Balfe renewed his friendship with Maria Malibran, whom he had known in Paris. She persuaded the management at La Scala to engage him to sing there with her, and recommended that he return to England, which he did in 1834.

Balfe's position as the most popular native composer in Britain was established overnight in London by the triumph of *The Siege of Rochelle* (1835, Drury Lane) which ran for 73 performances during its first season. Almost equal success attended *The Maid of Artois* (1836, Drury Lane), written for Malibran. In 1838 Balfe was honoured by a commission for the Italian Opera at Her Majesty's Theatre, which resulted in *Falstaff*, one of his best scores; it was sung there by a star cast which included Giulia Grisi, Albertazzi, Rubini, Antonio Tamburini and Lablache. After this he successfully toured Ireland and the west of England.

Balfe was now determined to become his own manager with a view to establishing English opera on a permanent footing. Even though his backers included Queen Victoria and the Prince Consort, his venture was doomed to failure. He leased the Lyceum Theatre (English Opera House) and brought out his latest work, *Këolanthé* (1841), with his wife making her London début in the title role. This was successful, but receipts dwindled when subsequent works were performed, and eventually he was forced to abandon the project. He informed the audience that he would never again appear before them in the capacity of a manager, and he kept his word.

Disheartened by this reverse, Balfe decided to try his luck in Paris. He had nearly completed *Elfrida* for the Théâtre des Italiens when Grisi, who was to have taken a leading role, announced that she was pregnant and unable to take part. Balfe's plans appear to have been frustrated, therefore, for the opera was never finished; but fortunately the librettist Scribe, who attended a concert of his works, offered to collaborate with him on a comic opera, *Le puits d'amour* (1843, Opéra-Comique), which was an instantaneous success. In the meantime Alfred Bunn, who had managed Balfe's earlier successes at Drury Lane, had extricated himself from bankruptcy, and *The Bohemian Girl*, on which Balfe had been working for some years, was produced at Drury Lane on 27 November 1843; it was the greatest triumph of his career, and the only 19th-century British opera to enjoy a genuine international reputation.

In 1845 *L'étoile de Séville* was given at the Paris Opéra, where it ran for 15 performances. In 1846 Balfe took over from Michael Costa as conductor of the Italian Opera at Her Majesty's Theatre, remaining until the theatre closed in 1852. During the 1850s he toured extensively abroad, visiting Berlin, Vienna (where Johann Strauss hailed him as the 'King of Melody'), St Petersburg and Trieste (where his opera *Pittore e duca* was unsuccessfully produced in 1854). In 1857 the inception of the Pyne-Harrison Opera Company at the Lyceum provided the impetus for a final period of remarkable creativity. *The Rose of Castille* was the first of a series of operas produced for the company between 1857 and 1863, and probably the most popular, after which the company moved to Covent Garden.

'The Rose of Castille' (Balfe), finale of Act 1, from the original production by the Pyne-Harrison Opera Company (Lyceum Theatre, London, 29 October 1857) with Louisa Pyne as Elvira and William Harrison (left) as Manuel the Muleteer: engraving from 'The Illustrated London News' (21 November 1857)

In 1864 Balfe decided to retire to the country, and bought a small estate in Hertfordshire, Rowney Abbey, which his wife succeeded in running profitably. His congenital acute spasmodic asthma troubled him increasingly. He was unable to complete his last opera, *The Knight of the Leopard* (based on Scott's novel *The Talisman*), on which he bestowed extraordinary care; it was produced posthumously by Costa as *Il talismano* at Drury Lane in 1874. Towards the end of the summer of 1870 he caught cold and his condition gradually deteriorated until he died on 20 October.

2. WORKS. When attempting to evaluate Balfe's works, it should be remembered that two distinct traditions of British opera existed during his lifetime, of which he was only too well aware. The English ballad opera was viewed by the public simply as entertainment, a genre set apart from the more elevated style of 'highbrow' opera. Of Balfe's operas, only *Falstaff* and *Il talismano* belong to the latter category, though it is also notable that he took more trouble over the works for Paris and Italy than for those written for production in London. Throughout his life, Rossini was his mentor to an extent that has hitherto been underestimated: both men possessed the same shrewdness of artistic judgment, the same inexhaustible musical facility, and the same chameleon-like ability to adapt themselves to the situation in hand. In musical terms, the Rossinian influence is most pronounced in the early Italian works, in *Falstaff*, and in the English operas written up to 1852. The second most prevalent idiom is French; derived principally from Auber, it finds its most natural expression in *Le puits d'amour*, *Les quatre fils Aymon* and *L'étoile de Séville*, though in this last work, as in some of the later Pyne-Harrison scores, a Meyerbeerian influence is present. Yet the music that made Balfe famous – the ballads which no one surpassed – remains indisputably his own. His operas, and his livelihood, relied on these 'hit' numbers in a manner similar to the 20th-century musical.

Balfe, however, was never less than thoroughly musically literate: the unusual key relationship between the appearances of the second subject in *The Bohemian Girl* overture demonstrates that. His feeling for local colour is especially remarkable in *The Siege of Rochelle*, *The Sicilian Bride* and *The Rose of Castille*. His knowledge of the voice was exceptional: the pyrotechnics of Elvira's Scherzo in *The Rose of Castille* are the work of a composer who understood every aspect of vocal art. His music is never dull, if only because of its rhythmic vitality; when this quality is wedded to striking musical ideas the effect is intoxicating, as, for example, in the quintet 'C'est dit, c'est entendu' from *Les quatre fils Aymon*. The critic Henry Chorley considered this opera to be Balfe's masterpiece, and he was right: of all Balfe's unknown works, it most merits revival. The later operas, such as *Bianca* (1860) and *The Puritan's Daughter* (1861), are more homogeneous in style, but although they are better through-composed, they lack the freshness of inspiration that characterizes their predecessors. In *Il talismano*, Balfe updated his vocabulary to reach a par with middle-period Verdi, but the price paid for stylistic consistency is melodic weakness.

Balfe's music bespeaks his personality: he was the most honest, genial and charming of men. William Harrison recalled that when asked if he ever borrowed from other men's works, he admitted, astonishingly, to stealing snatches of Beethoven: '"Ye can't do better", he said with a beaming face, "than to go to the fountain-head, and come away with a cupful! There are two composers I've never scrupled to borrow from – one's Beethoven, the other's meself!"'.

See also BOHEMIAN GIRL, THE and SIEGE OF ROCHELLE, THE.

For an illustration of a scene from *Satanella*, *see* PYNE, LOUISA.

unless otherwise stated: first performed in London, autograph MSS in GB-Lbl, scores (all vocal) published in London
LDL – *Drury Lane Theatre* LCG – *Covent Garden Theatre*

Atala (after F. R. de Chateaubriand), Paris, between 1826 and 1828, inc., lost

I rivali di se stessi (2, A. Alcazar, after C. A. G. Pigault-Lebrun: *Les rivaux d'eux-mêmes*), Palermo, Carolino, ?Feb 1830, lost

Un avvertimento ai gelosi (farsa giocosa, 1, G. Foppa), Pavia, Fraschini, spr. 1831, lost

Enrico Quarto al passo della Marna (1), Milan, Carcano, 19 Feb 1833, lost

The Siege of Rochelle (grand op, 2, E. Fitzball, after Comtesse de Genlis: *Le siège de La Rochelle*), LDL, 29 Oct 1835 (1836)
The Maid of Artois (grand serious op, 3, A. Bunn, after A.-F. Prévost: *L'histoire du Chevalier des Grieux et de Manon Lescaut*), LDL, 27 May 1836 (1837)
Adelwina, between 1836 and 1843, inc.
Catherine Grey (grand op, 3, G. Linley), LDL, 27 May 1837 (1837)
Caractacus (historical play, J. R. Planché), LDL, 6 Nov 1837, lost
Joan of Arc (grand op, 3, Fitzball, after R. Southey), LDL, 30 Nov 1837 (1839)
Diadesté, or The Veiled Lady (opéra bouffe, 2, Fitzball, after L. Pillet and Marquis de St Hilaire), LDL, 17 May 1838, 1 song (1838)
Falstaff (ob, 2, S. M. Maggioni), Her Majesty's, 19 July 1838 (?1845)
Elfrida, begun 1840 (Maggioni), inc.
Këolanthé, or The Unearthly Bride, 1840 (romantic op, 2, Fitzball), English Opera House, 9 March 1841, selections (1840), MS lost
Le puits d'amour (oc, 3, E. Scribe and A. de Leuven), Paris, OC (Favart), 20 April 1843 (Paris, 1843); as Geraldine, or The Lover's Well (G. Soane), Princess's, 14 Aug 1843, selections (1843)
The Bohemian Girl, 1840–43 (grand op, 3, Bunn, after J.-H. Vernoy de Saint-Georges: *La gypsy*, from M. de Cervantes: *La gitanilla*), LDL, 27 Nov 1843 (1844)
Les quatre fils Aymon (oc, 3, de Leuven and Brunswick [L. Lhérie]), Paris, OC (Favart), 15 July 1844 (Paris, 1844); as The Castle of Aymon, or The Four Brothers (Fitzball), Princess's, 20 Nov 1844
The Daughter of St Mark (grand serious op, 3, Bunn, after Saint-Georges: *La reine de Chypre*), LDL, 27 Nov 1844 (1845)
The Enchantress (grand op, 3, Bunn, after Saint-Georges), LDL, 14 May 1845 (1845)
L'étoile de Séville (grand op, 4, H. Lucas, after F. Lope de Vega: *La estrella de Sevilla*), Paris, Opéra, 17 Dec 1845 (Paris, 1846), MS lost
Le jour de Noël (Scribe), Paris, ?1845, lost
The Bondman (grand op, 3, Bunn, after Mélesville [A.-H.-J. Duveyrier]: *Le Chevalier de Saint-George*), LDL, 11 Dec 1846 (1847)
The Maid of Honour (grand op, 3, Fitzball), LDL, 20 Dec 1847 (1848)
The Sicilian Bride (4, Bunn, after Saint-Georges), LDL, 6 March 1852, selections (1852)
The Devil's in it (comic op, prol., 3, Bunn, after C. Coffey: *The Devil to Pay*), Surrey, 26 July 1852; as Letty, the Basket-Maker (prol., 3, J. P. Simpson), Gaiety, 14 June 1871 (1873)
Pittore e duca (prol., 3, F. M. Piave), Trieste, Comunale, 21 Nov 1854, lost; as Moro, or The Painter of Antwerp (grand op, prol., 3, W. A. Barrett), Her Majesty's, 28 Jan 1882 (1882), MS lost
Lo scudiero, 1854 (Piave), unperf., lost
The Rose of Castille (3, A. G. Harris and E. Falconer, after A. P. d'Ennery and Clairville: *Le muletier de Tolède*), Lyceum, 29 Oct 1857 (1858)
Satanella, or The Power of Love (romantic op, 4, Harris and Falconer, after A. R. Lesage: *Le diable boiteux*), LCG, 20 Dec 1858 (1876)
Bianca, or The Bravo's Bride (4, Simpson, after M. G. Lewis: *Rugantino*), LCG, 6 Dec 1860
The Puritan's Daughter (3, J. V. Bridgeman), LCG, 30 Nov 1861 (1861)
Blanche de Nevers (4, J. Brougham, from his *The Duke's Motto*, after M. Feval: *Le bossu*), LCG, 21 Nov 1862 (1864)
The Armourer of Nantes (grand romantic op, 3, Bridgeman, after V. Hugo: *Marie Tudor*) LCG, 12 Feb 1863 (1863)
The Sleeping Queen (operetta, 1, H. B. Farnie), Gallery of Illustration, 31 Aug 1864 (1874); 2-act version (1868)
The Knight of the Leopard (3, A. Matthison, after W. Scott: *The Talisman*), inc.; arr. M. Costa as Il talismano (G. Zaffira), LDL, 11 June 1874 (1874); as The Talisman, New York, 10 Feb 1875; MS as The Talisman

Addl nos. for Zingarelli: Giulietta e Romeo, between 1826 and 1828, lost
It. recits for Beethoven: Fidelio, 1851, lost

*

Musical World, xviii (1843), 395 [on *The Bohemian Girl*]; xxiii (1848), 209–11
E. Fitzball: *Thirty-five Years of a Dramatic Author's Life* (London, 1859)
H. Phillips: *Musical and Personal Recollections during Half a Century* (London, 1864)
H. St Leger: *Reminiscences of Balfe* (London, 1871)
J. E. Cox: *Musical Recollections of the Last Half-Century* (London, 1872)
C. L. Kenney: *Memoir of Michael William Balfe* (London, 1875)
W. A. Barrett: *Balfe: his Life and Work* (London, 1882)
C. Harrison: *Stray Records* (London, 1892), i, 95–108
M. W. Disher: *Victorian Song* (London, 1955), 95–8, 100, 117
D. Arundell: *The Critic at the Opera* (London, 1957), 324, 326–8
N. Temperley, ed.: *Music in Britain: the Romantic Age, 1800–1914* (London, 1981)
E. W. White: *A History of English Opera* (London, 1983)

NIGEL BURTON

Balino. *See* FABRI, ANNIBALE PIO.

Balkwill, Bryan (Havell) (*b* London, 2 July 1922). English conductor. After studies at the RAM, in 1947 he joined the New London Opera Company at the Cambridge Theatre as a répétiteur; he made his début there that year conducting Carl Ebert's production of *Rigoletto*. He went to Glyndebourne as a répétiteur in 1950, returning (1953–8) as chorus master and associate conductor, working closely with Vittorio Gui on the Italian repertory. During that period he was also principal conductor at the Wexford Festival. In 1959 he became a resident conductor at Covent Garden, where he remained until 1965, giving over 200 performances of 16 operas. He toured with the English Opera Group to the USSR and Portugal, conducting *Albert Herring* and *A Midsummer Night's Dream*. From 1963 to 1967 he was music director of the WNO. He first conducted the Sadler's Wells Opera in 1957, and returned to it as joint music director (1966–9), giving the first performance of Richard Rodney Bennett's *A Penny for a Song* (1967). After a period working as a freelance conductor (from 1969), he became a member of the music department of Indiana University, USA, where he taught from 1979 to 1992 and conducted opera, specializing in Rossini and Britten.

NOËL GOODWIN

Ballabile (It.: 'suitable for dancing'). A movement intended for dancing; the term is mostly applied to choruses during which there is dancing, e.g. 'Chi dona luce al cor?' (*Attila*, Verdi, 1846) and 'Ondine e silfidi' (*Macbeth*, 1847). Verdi himself often used the term loosely to indicate the movements of a self-contained ballet such as those of *Jérusalem*, *Les vêpres siciliennes* and *Don Carlos*, whose omission in Italian performances he regularly sanctioned. Dance *divertissements* in Meyerbeer's operas are titled *1°, 2° ballabile* etc.

JULIAN BUDDEN

Ballad of Baby Doe, The. Opera in two acts by DOUGLAS S. MOORE to a libretto by John Latouche; Central City, Colorado, Opera House, 7 July 1956.

Moore had been attracted to the story of Elizabeth 'Baby Doe' Tabor as early as 1935, when he read accounts of her being found frozen to death near the abandoned mine where she had maintained a vigil since the death of her husband 36 years earlier. Nonetheless, no opera resulted until the Central City Opera Association suggested that subject in 1953. Following the première, projected revisions were halted by the death of Latouche (August 1956), after one new scene (Act 2 scene ii) and an additional aria for Baby Doe had been added. The revised version was first performed by the New York City Opera on 3 April 1958, with Beverly Sills as Baby Doe.

The complicated story is a true one, though some

events have been compressed in time or space. The opera opens outside the Tabor Opera House, Leadville, Colorado, in 1880. A drunken miner (tenor) is thrown out of a neighbouring saloon. He has been rowdily celebrating the sale of his silver mine, the Matchless, to Horace Tabor (baritone) for a large sum. Tabor, who built the new opera house and 'owns the whole dam[n] town', now appears with his rough cronies to take the air during the interval. He relishes the lively street life he finds there and dances with the saloon girls before being interrupted and upbraided by his dour wife, Augusta (mezzo-soprano), who is obsessed with propriety and respectability. As he is going back into the opera house, Tabor is accosted by Baby Doe (soprano), newly arrived in town, who asks for directions to the Clarendon Hotel.

Outside the hotel later that evening (Act 1 scene ii) Tabor overhears the saloon girls gossiping about Baby Doe. Apparently she has a husband in Central City and was given her nickname by the miners. Through her hotel-room window, she can be seen and heard singing her famous 'Willow Song' ('Willow, where we met together'); Tabor applauds and she responds with flirtatious flattery. Tabor is hopelessly smitten ('Warm as the autumn light').

In the Tabors' apartment several months later (Act 1 scene iii) Augusta, while sorting through her husband's desk, finds a gift intended for Baby. She confronts him with it; he is unrepentant and Augusta threatens to create a scandal by publicizing their affair. In the lobby of the hotel (Act 1 scene iv) Baby is preparing to leave. As she explains in a letter home ('Dearest Mama, I am writing'), the situation is impossible, and the affair with Tabor must end. She confirms this to Augusta, who has come to confront her, but when Augusta contemptuously ridicules Tabor, Baby tears up the letter and rushes into Tabor's arms when he arrives. Augusta's friends (Act 1 scene v) are determined to create a scandal, but Augusta now resolves to maintain a dignified silence.

Augusta's reticence is in vain for by 1883 (Act 1 scene vi) the two lovers have divorced their spouses and married each other, a marriage Tabor wishes to make respectable with a formal Catholic wedding in Washington, DC, where he has been appointed to a seat in the Senate. As the couple and the priest arrive for the reception at the Willard Hotel (boycotted by the other senators' wives), Mama McCourt (contralto), Baby's mother, vociferously supportive of her daughter, calumniates both Augusta and Baby's former husband Harvey Doe. The priest, unaware of the divorces, is scandalized, and a scene is avoided only by the arrival of President Arthur (tenor).

Back in Denver (Act 2 scene i), the couple are universally snubbed, but are so much in love that they are unconcerned. Augusta, who has mellowed, has heard from Washington that the USA is about to take its currency off the silver standard – which will ruin Tabor – and she warns Baby that the Matchless Mine must be sold before it is too late. Tabor angrily rejects this advice and makes Baby promise that she will always keep the mine. Two years later (Act 2 scene ii) Tabor, in serious financial trouble, throws in his lot with William Jennings Bryan (bass-baritone) and his 'free silver' platform. Bryan makes a rousing speech at the gate of the Matchless Mine (Act 2 scene iii) but his campaign is doomed. Mama McCourt goes to Augusta (Act 2 scene iv) to seek help for the now impoverished Tabors, but is gently rebuffed by Augusta, who knows that Tabor would never accept her money.

The final scene (Act 2 scene v) abandons realism. In 1899 Tabor, dying and delirious, stumbles onto the darkened stage of his opera house in Leadville. There he relives his past and foresees the future: one of his daughters will disown him, the other will turn to prostitution. Baby arrives to comfort his dying moments and then is seen as an old woman. Slowly she crosses to the Matchless Mine (now visible on the stage) to take up her lonely vigil.

The mixture of romance and frontier rowdiness in the tale of Baby Doe ideally suited Moore's musical and dramatic strengths, allowing both for Broadway-like production numbers (the opening scene, Bryan's speech) and for set-piece songs in the early Tin Pan Alley style of the composer's youth (Baby Doe's 'Willow Song' and letter aria). Outside such high points the music relaxes into a bland arioso reminiscent of Moore's teacher D'Indy, and of Puccini.

For an illustration of a set design for the original production, *see* OENSLAGER, DONALD.

ANDREW STILLER

Ballad opera.

1. Definition, terminology. 2. Origins, *The Beggar's Opera*. 3. Successors.

1. DEFINITION, TERMINOLOGY. A distinctively English form in which spoken dialogue alternates with songs set to traditional or popular melodies and sung by the actors themselves. A vogue for the form was sparked by the enormous popularity of John Gay's *THE BEGGAR'S OPERA* (January 1728) but faded out by the mid-1730s. Some 80 such works were written in these years, but only a handful remained in the repertory. The genre was invented by Gay as a complex vehicle for both harsh and subtle satire; for most of his successors it quickly became little more than a way of padding out farces with popular music.

The term 'ballad opera' is a misnomer. The works so described are plays (almost always comic, usually farcical) into which a variety of songs have been worked. Fewer than half the songs are actually popular ballads: the sources of the music vary widely, ranging from D'Urfey's *Wit and Mirth, or, Pills to Purge Melancholy* to arias from Handel's operas and movements of Italian concertos. Sources have been found in *The English Dancing Master* (1651 and its derivatives), traditional favourites such as *Lilliburlero* and *Tweedside*, and most of the popular composers of the time. Among the acknowledged sources are Thomas Arne, Giovanni Bononcini, Henry Carey, Corelli, Francesco Gasparini, Francesco Geminiani, John Baptist Grano, Leveridge and Pepusch; among those identified by later scholars are Blow, Jeremiah Clarke, Giovanni Battista Draghi, John Eccles, Galliard, John Frederick Lampe, Locke, Henry Purcell and Weldon. In every instance, however, the music is fitted with new words, and the songs are integrated into the dramatic structure of the play, not simply interpolated as variety or entr'acte entertainment.

2. ORIGINS, *THE BEGGAR'S OPERA*. The sudden appearance of ballad opera in 1728 remains one of the mysteries of 18th-century theatre history. Late 17th-century English plays were heavily laden with music, and many works included integral songs sung by the

actors themselves. But these roles were confined to a few specialists, such as Thomas Doggett and Anne Bracegirdle, and the music was freshly written by mainstream composers. Gay's innovation was twofold: to have all the characters sing as much as they speak, and to use tunes well known to everyone. Such generic precursors as can be found are surprisingly remote in both date and kind. Thomas Duffett's *The Mock-Tempest* (1674) and *Psyche Debauch'd* (1675) are vulgar musical travesties of the semi-operas from which they take their names; Newcastle's *The Triumphant Widow* (1674) has also been pointed out as a proto-ballad opera. Perhaps the closest antecedent is Richard Estcourt's musical farce *Prunella* (1708), a crude satire on Giovanni Bononcini's Italian opera *Camilla* (London première, 1706). Here one finds striking parallels with the later ballad opera: low-life characters singing their own songs, which were evidently parodies of arias from the opera itself; there is also a certain amount of poking of fun at the conventions of Italian opera. Unfortunately, the music is lost. Whether Gay was familiar with any of these works is uncertain. He may have known contemporaneous plays of the Théâtre Italien and the Théâtres de la Foire in Paris, which included popular tunes fitted with new verses. The immediate inspiration for *The Beggar's Opera* seems to have been provided by Jonathan Swift, who suggested that Gay write 'a Newgate [prison] Pastoral, among the Whores and Thieves there'. None of this detracts from Gay's originality, for *The Beggar's Opera* was radically new: 'instead of cardboard heroes of antiquity, Gay offered very real modern Londoners; instead of noble sentiments, every crime in the calendar' (Fiske). Today *The Beggar's Opera* is usually performed as a charming period piece, but in 1728 it provoked denunciations for incitement to immorality. More to the point, it confronted the audience with an ironic exaltation of criminals and whores that was in radical contrast to the usual decorum of the 18th-century theatre. This was an innovation in which Gay was not followed by his successors.

As Gay conceived it, ballad opera is a fast-moving satirical drama of low-life characters in which the actors frequently break into song. *The Beggar's Opera* contains 69 songs; they are rarely separated by more than a page of spoken dialogue. The familiarity of the music renders it rich in extra-textual references which could either enhance the emotional impact of the dramatic situation or (more often) render it delightfully preposterous. Gay's snide incongruities between his new words and the old ones are a particular pleasure of the piece. For example, in Act 1 scene ix, Peachum's rather lame attack on the legal profession, 'A fox may steal your hens, sir', was set to Eccles's 'A soldier and a sailor' (from Congreve's *Love for Love*) whose notoriously rude original verses would have added an unspoken barb to Gay's message. By no means all the songs in ballad operas were satirical; for sentimental scenes, Gay often chose similarly sentimental music. Many of his less gifted imitators were insensitive to musical reference and simply searched through the popular collections, especially the volumes of Scotch airs, for any tune that would suit a particular verse, regardless of the character of the music itself.

The Beggar's Opera has often been said to be a savage satire on Italian opera as Handel was producing it at the King's Theatre, Haymarket, in the 1720s; it has even been credited with the demise of the Royal Academy of Music in 1728. Neither claim is true. Gay certainly satirized some of the conventions of *opera seria* and its squabbling performers, but he was by no means hostile to Handel, and the troubles of the Italian opera were not caused by competition from popular English fare. Nonetheless, Gay's allusions probably tickled opera fanciers. In the introduction to *The Beggar's Opera*, the Beggar says that, in setting the roles, he has 'observed such a nice Impartiality to our two Ladies [Lucy Lockit and Polly Peachum] that it is impossible for either of them to take Offence'. This is a clear allusion to the rivalry between the sopranos Faustina and Cuzzoni, for whom Handel in *Alessandro* (1726) had written parts of almost exactly equal weight. Gay's improbable happy ending is also a parody of the perfunctory *lieto fine* of Italian opera. But not all reference was satirical. Macheath's brilliantly dramatic soliloquy in 'the Condemn'd Hold' (Act 3 scene xiii), an unbroken chain of ten airs or snatches of tunes, while ultimately modelled on the mad-song concatenations of Purcell or Eccles, is remarkably similar in style to some of Handel's big accompanied recitatives and uncannily anticipates the mad scene in *Orlando* (1733).

The Beggar's Opera was originally produced at Lincoln's Inn Fields by John Rich after it was refused at Drury Lane. In its first partial season it ran for 62 performances, a total far surpassing any play in the recorded history of the London theatre. As early as summer 1728 it was pirated at the Little Haymarket, and the rival Drury Lane company naturally hastened to commission and produce ballad operas. At first these were, like Gay's original, ambitious three-act 'mainpieces' (*see* AFTERPIECE): Charles Johnson's *The Village Opera* (Drury Lane, 1729 – ultimately the basis for Isaac Bickerstaff's pasticcio comic opera, *Love in a Village*, 1762), Ebenezer Forrest's *Momus turn'd Fabulist* (Lincoln's Inn Fields, 1729), James Ralph's *The Fashionable Lady, or Harlequin's Opera* (Goodman's Fields, 1730), Joseph Mitchell's *Highland Fair* and *The Jovial Crew* (both Drury Lane, 1731). None of these expensive experiments entered the repertory. *Polly*, Gay's sequel to *The Beggar's Opera*, was suppressed by the Lord Chamberlain in December 1728: Sir Robert Walpole did not fancy having himself impersonated as a pirate who meets a richly deserved end on the gallows and kept it off the boards, though Gay made a small fortune by publishing this rather heavy-handed satire. Rich's failure to mount more ballad opera has occasioned surprise among modern commentators, given the fortune he made out of the first one, but in fact Lincoln's Inn Fields was heavily committed to Rich's pantomimes, which were themselves both musical and wildly popular. Rich did not need to invest in another musical genre, and aside from a handful of farce-with-music ballad-opera afterpieces he left the form to his competitors.

3. SUCCESSORS. An enormous variety of ballad operas were produced between 1728 and about 1735. Historical subjects were tried, as in the anonymous *Robin Hood* (1730) and Walter Aston's *The Restauration of King Charles II* (suppressed in 1732 on suspicion of Jacobite implications). John Mottley and Thomas Cooke's *Penelope* (Little Haymarket, 1728) is a delightful little classical spoof: Sergeant Ulysses, who went off to Marlborough's wars, is now living with Circe in Rotterdam, drinking gin; his faithful wife Penelope keeps a London pub and finds herself courted by the local tinker, tailor and butcher. Another such satire is John Breval's *The Rape of Helen* (1733). The

best known of this 'classical' group is Gay's posthumous *Achilles* (1733), a rather sodden reprise of the hero-in-petticoats story. Gay's last attempt at the form (unperformed) was *The Rehearsal at Goatham*, which presents a puppet show whose innocent allusions outrage the bumpkins in the small town where it is performed. The idea was better than the execution: Gay never came close to recapturing the charm and bite of his first effort.

With the exception of *The Beggar's Opera*, ballad operas which entered the repertory were all afterpieces, including some which started out as full-length mainpieces. Colley Cibber's *Love in a Riddle* (Drury Lane, 1729) was probably the victim of audience hostility to the author; cut down as *Damon and Phillida*, and produced anonymously at the Little Haymarket the same year, it was long popular. It is a good example of the form's penchant for sentimentalized country low-life and improbable romance plots. Charles Coffey's *The Devil to Pay* (1731) had a disastrous first night in the off season; the songs were cut from 48 to 16 by Theophilus Cibber and the piece became one of the century's most enduring entertainments. It was based on Thomas Jevon's *The Devil of a Wife* (1686), a magical identity-swap farce without much substance but with proven audience appeal. Ballad operas of the early 1730s could be as chastely pastoral and moral as George Lillo's *Sylvia* (Lincoln's Inn Fields, 1730) or as essentially lower-class sentimental as Carey's *The Honest Yorkshireman* (Little Haymarket, 1735), but most tend towards the farcical.

The most important practitioner of ballad opera after Gay was Henry Fielding, now remembered largely as a novelist (*Tom Jones*). Yet Fielding was the foremost English dramatist of his time, and among his 30 plays are about ten that can be plausibly classified as ballad opera, though they vary considerably in the amount of music employed. Fielding's first attempt at the form was *The Author's Farce* (Little Haymarket, 1730, radically revised in 1734), a boisterous spoof on Grub Street life and a brazen attack on theatre managers at Drury Lane and Lincoln's Inn Fields. *The Welsh Opera* (Little Haymarket, 1731) is an impudent political allegory that helped get the theatre suppressed: Fielding exhibits King George II, Queen Caroline, the Prince of Wales, Walpole and Pulteney as master, mistress, not-so-hopeful heir and principal servants in the disorganized household of Squire Ap-Shinken, an amiable Welshman whose only wish is peace and quiet in which to smoke and drink. Fielding expanded the work as *The Grub-Street Opera* (a much more dangerous satire), but the authorities closed the Little Haymarket and appear to have bribed Fielding to withdraw the play, though it received a pirate printing. *Don Quixote in England* (written 1728; staged at Drury Lane, 1734) was a failure, a scrappy farce with incidental music. *Deborah, or A Wife for you All* (Drury Lane, March 1733) survived just one night and was not printed. It appears to have been a satire on Handel's oratorio *Deborah*, for which the composer had tried to double prices. Deutsch suggests that Fielding parodied Humphreys's word-book, but ridicule of a biblical story would have been risky and Fielding may well just have attacked Handel's prices and foreign singers' difficulty with English. The title role was taken by Kitty Clive (then still Miss Raftor), a splendid and popular singer-actress.

Several of Fielding's most lastingly successful plays were part of the series of ballad-opera farces concocted for Kitty Clive at Drury Lane: *The Lottery* (1732), *The Mock Doctor* (1732), *The Intriguing Chambermaid* (1734), *An Old Man Taught Wisdom* (1735, usually performed as *The Virgin Unmask'd*), *Eurydice* (1737) and *Miss Lucy in Town* (1742). Except for the last two, all remained theatrical staples throughout the 18th century. *The Lottery* and *The Intriguing Chambermaid* are lightweight musical farce – the latter adapted from Jean François Regnard's *Le retour imprévu* (1700), turning the clever valet into the maid Lettice as a vehicle for Clive. *The Mock Doctor* is a free translation of Molière with just nine songs worked in. *The Virgin Unmask'd* exemplifies Fielding's comic skills: Old Goodwill decides to marry off his silly 15-year-old daughter; she listens to proposals from five boobies (an apothecary, a dancing-master, an Oxford student, a singing-master and a lawyer), accepts three of them – and then elopes with a footman whose fine clothes and elegant *coiffure* have gone to her head. The work offers more ridicule than satire, and Fielding quickly reduced his original 20 songs to 12. It was designed solely to display the talents of Kitty Clive, and both she and her successors found that it worked to perfection.

Fielding's most interesting and ambitious ballad operas are his last two, both of which burlesque Italian opera. Unfortunately the music is lost, so one can only guess at the impact of the originals. *Eurydice* died in one night, ruined by a footmen's riot at Drury Lane. As an opera spoof the piece requires two outstanding singers, and Fielding had them in Stoppelaer (Orpheus) and Clive (Eurydice). The piece is a flippant travesty-satire. Orpheus and Eurydice are society wastrels from London, and hell is populated by fops and courtiers. No one believes that a man could want to recover his wife. Eurydice, appalled at the idea of returning to her husband, tricks him into looking back so that she can return to the social whirl in hell. Pluto is amusingly henpecked; Orpheus becomes a swipe at Farinelli, the reigning castrato star of the Opera of the Nobility. Fielding makes plain his ferocious contempt for Italian opera and castratos. Nine airs and a 'Grand Dance' and 'Chorus' are included, the airs preceded by 'Recitativo' in English. *Orfeo* (a pasticcio with a text by Rolli) had been a hit the previous season, and Fielding goes after it in a decidedly sour spirit. It is not known who arranged or composed the music.

Miss Lucy in Town is a sequel to *The Virgin Unmask'd.* The ex-footman brings his wife to town; they mistakenly lodge in a bordello, where the visitors competing for her services include Lord Bawble (one of the directors of the opera – evidently a hit at Lord Middlesex), Mr Ballad (an English singer) and Signor Cantileno (an Italian opera singer, played by Beard). Horace Walpole wrote to a friend that 'Mrs Clive mimics the Muscovita [Lord Middlesex's mistress] admirably, and Beard Amorevoli intolerably'. The piece, published anonymously, may be a collaboration between Fielding and the young David Garrick. With the music lost and the composer unknown one can hardly guess at its effect, but it proved quite popular for a season.

Ballad opera was short-lived. *The Beggar's Opera* proved that there was a large, untapped audience in London, and contributed to the establishment of Goodman's Fields theatre, the increasing use of the Little Haymarket, and the construction of Covent Garden in 1732. Among Gay's successors only Fielding really understood how to use the form to good advantage in several sorts of plays, and in the operatic travesties we find him moving into what must have been newly composed pieces that take us into the realm of burletta. A handful of influential ballad operas continued to be performed throughout the rest of the 18th century, but the later burlettas and English operas of Arne, Dibdin, Storace, the Linleys and others, though often including ballad tunes, bear little resemblance to true ballad opera.

One reason for the relatively brief popularity of the original form is that the quality of the musical performances cannot have been very high. Most of the actors were not trained singers, though the demands of the genre helped to produce a new generation of actors who possessed the necessary musical skills. The extent to which the singers were accompanied is unknown. The arrangements provided by Pepusch, Carey and Seedo are often crude in the extreme, even eschewing the original (and easily obtainable) basses of the pieces they were arranging. Nor was much care taken to preserve the integrity of 'composed' melodies of Purcell, Handel and others. Nevertheless, the theatres which produced ballad operas maintained fairly large orchestras (a dozen or so, mostly strings), and paylists show that the instrumentalists attended every night. Given the presence of the orchestra, we must presume that it was used.

Only *The Beggar's Opera* is now performed, and just a handful of other ballad operas retain even much historical interest. The form is important, however, for its contribution to the musicalization of the British theatre which is one of its most conspicuous features in the second half of the 18th century.

*

W. B. Squire: 'An Index of Tunes in the Ballad Operas', *MA*, ii (1910–11), 1–17

F. Kidson: *The Beggar's Opera: its Predecessors and Successors* (Cambridge, 1922)

W. Schultz: *Gay's Beggar's Opera: its Content, History, and Influence* (New Haven, 1923)

A. Nicoll: *A History of Early 18th Century Drama, 1700–1750* (Cambridge, 1925, 3/1952)

E. Gagey: *Ballad Opera* (New York, 1937)

B. Bronson: 'The Beggar's Opera', *Studies in the Comic*, U. of California Publications in English, viii/2 (1941), 197–231

W. Rubsamen: 'The Ballad Burlesques and Extravaganzas', *MQ*, xxxvi (1950), 551–61

——: 'The Jovial Crew: History of a Ballad Opera', *IMSCR*, vii *Cologne 1958*, 240–43

E. Roberts: 'Eighteenth-Century Ballad Opera: the Contribution of Henry Fielding', *Drama Survey*, i (1961–2), 77–85

——: 'Fielding's Ballad Opera *The Lottery* (1732) and the English State Lottery of 1731', *Huntington Library Quarterly*, xxvii (1963–4), 39–52

——: 'Mr Seedo's London Career and his Work with Henry Fielding', *Philological Quarterly*, xlv (1966), 179–90

H. Moss: *Ballad-Opera Songs: a Record of the Ideas Set to Music, 1728–1733* (diss., U. of Michigan, 1970)

L. Morrissey: 'Henry Fielding and the Ballad Opera', *Eighteenth-Century Studies*, iv (1971), 386–402

R. Fiske: *English Theatre Music in the Eighteenth Century* (London, 1973, 2/1986)

W. Rubsamen, ed.: *The Ballad Opera: a Collection of 171 Original Texts of Musical Plays Printed in Photo-Facsimile* (New York, 1974)

C. Kephart: 'An Unnoticed Forerunner of "The Beggar's Opera" ', *ML*, lxi (1980), 266–71

L. Lindgren: '*Camilla* and *The Beggar's Opera*', *Philological Quarterly*, lix (1980), 44–61

A. Hume: 'The 1734 *Penelope*: a Ghost', *Notes and Queries*, ccxxviii (1983), 39–40

R. Hume: *Henry Fielding and the London Theatre, 1728–1737* (Oxford, 1988) CURTIS PRICE, ROBERT D. HUME

Ballarotti, Francesco (*b c*1660; *d* Bergamo, April 1712). Italian composer. The approximate date of his birth derives from the dedication of his *Balletti, arie, gighe, corrente, alemande, sarabande, capricci da camera*, op.1 (Milan, 1681), in which he describes himself as 'a youth of tender years'. From 12 April 1692 until his death he worked in Bergamo as *maestro di cappella* of S Maria Maggiore and as a teacher in the Congregazione di Carità. He composed, either on his own or in collaboration, many theatrical works, all but two of which are lost; most of the others are known only from librettos. He also shared in the composition of pasticcios by a number of different composers.

Ballarotti's operatic writing does not differ in any significant way from that of other contemporary composers; the sinfonia to *Ottaviano in Sicilia* is in five parts (not an uncommon feature at the time) and the arias are for the most part accompanied by strings in three or four parts or by basso continuo only. The ritornellos and the brief instrumental interjections separating the vocal phrases are typical of the period, as also is the inclusion of the servant Gildo (bass), who is given a parody of a battle aria, 'A battaglia, a battaglia'. The war element is also expressed in the *aria di tromba*, 'Su, fieri guerrieri', of Pompeo [Sextus Pompeius] (alto) and in 'Fra gli applausi', sung by Ottaviano [Octavianus] (alto) when he disembarks. Ballarotti's choice of vocal figuration and affect is not always impeccably related to the meaning of the text.

Enea in Italia (dramma per musica, 3, G. F. Bussani), Milan, Ducale, 1686, 3 arias *I-MOe*, collab. C. A. Lonati and P. Magni

Dialogo musicale fra Nettuno e Bergamo, Bergamo, 1688

Il merito fortunato (F. Roncalli), Bergamo, 1691

Ottaviano in Sicilia (dramma per musica, 3), Reggio Emilia, 1692, *MOe**

L'Aiace (dramma per musica, 3, P. d'Averara), Milan, Ducale, 1694, *US-Cn*, collab. Lonati and Magni

Ariovisto [part of Act 3] (dramma per musica, 3, d'Averara), Milan, 1699 [Act 1 by Perti, Act 2 and part of Act 3 by Magni]

La caduta dei Decemviri (dramma per musica, 3, S. Stampiglia), Reggio Emilia, 1699

Esione (dramma per musica, 3, d'Averara), Turin, Regio, 1699

Alciade, ovvero L'eroico amore [La violenza d'amore; Act 3] (opera tragicomica, 3, M. A. Gasparini), Bergamo, 1709 [Act 1 by F. Gasparini, Act 2 by C. F. Pollarolo]

*

ES (E. Zanetti)

G. Donati-Petteni: *L'arte della musica in Bergamo* (Bergamo, 1930)

A. Geddo: *Bergamo e la musica* (Bergamo, 1958)

M. Donà: *La stampa musicale a Milano fino all'anno 1700* (Florence, 1961) SERGIO DURANTE, SERGIO LATTES

Ballata (It.: 'danced'; 'ballad'). (1) A light-hearted song in dance-like rhythm, e.g. 'Questa o quella per me pari sono' (*Rigoletto*, Verdi, 1851), 'Stridono lassù liberamente' (*Pagliacci*, Leoncavallo, 1892). 'Ben venga maggio' (*I Medici*, Leoncavallo, 1893) is an isolated instance of the term used in its original, 15th-century sense as a dance-song – and indeed the words are taken from a 'ballata' by Poliziano.

(2) A narrative song, more formal than a *racconto*, being the Italian equivalent of a French *ballade*, e.g. 'Per sua madre andò una figlia' (*Linda di Chamounix*, Donizetti, 1842), 'Son Pereda, son ricco d'onore' (*La forza del destino*, Verdi, 1862). A variant of this usage denotes a strophic song describing a mysterious figure, e.g. 'Voltea la terra' (*Ballo*, Verdi, 1859). See in this connection 'Voyez sur cette roche' (*Fra Diavolo*, Auber, 1830) and 'Trefft ihr das Schiff in Meere an' (*Der fliegende Holländer*, Wagner, 1843). JULIAN BUDDEN

Ballerina amante, La ('The Ballerina in Love'). *Commedia per musica* in three acts by DOMENICO CIMAROSA to a libretto by GIUSEPPE PALOMBA; Naples, Teatro dei Fiorentini, 6 October 1782.

Madama Rubiconda Zampetti (soprano), a ballet dancer of some reputation, and the prima donna Ortensia (soprano) both believe that they will never suffer from a lack of masculine attention and mistakenly see themselves as rivals in love. Rubiconda however is in love with Don Totomaglio (bass), a foolish and ignorant doctoral student, and Ortensia with a rich Englishman, Cavaliere Bireno (tenor). Complications arise through the machinations of the innkeeper Bettina (soprano), Mazzacogna (bass; also known as Sgranerino), Don Petronio (bass), who pretends to be Ortensia's father, and the young Frenchman Monsù Franchiglione (tenor), who earlier had jilted Ortensia. In the end, Bireno, disgusted by the infidelity of women, refuses to marry; Franchiglione marries Ortensia and Rubiconda marries Totomaglio.

At the première the role of Totomaglio was sung in Neapolitan dialect; for performances outside Naples, however, Totomaglio's text was changed to Tuscan Italian, peppered with garbled Latin to caricature his pseudo-scholarly aura. Of particular musical interest is Totomaglio's effective *buffo* patter line that weaves its way through the Act 1 trio 'Il mio babbo'. In most European cities the opera was given in a reduced two-act version. For a later performance in Eszterháza, Haydn added a bassoon obbligato to Totomaglia's aria 'State adagio, aspetta un poco'.

GORDANA LAZAREVICH

Ballerini [Ballarini, Balerini, Ballarino, Baron Ballerini], **Francesco** (*b* Florence; *fl* 1680–1717). Italian contralto castrato. The earliest reference to him is in 1680, when he sang in *Le pompose feste di Vicenza* (composer unknown) in Vicenza and the role of Tazio in P. S. Agostini's *Il ratto delle Sabine* in Venice. In 1682 he took the leading role in Legrenzi's *Ottaviano Cesare Augusto* at Mantua, and from that year until at least 1693 he styled himself 'musician to Ferdinando Carlo Gonzaga, Duke of Mantua'. From 1684 he sang in many Italian cities. In 1700 he appeared in Ariosti's *Lucio Vero* in Florence (Pratolino) and in his *La festa d'Imeneo* in Berlin. From 1708 he was in Vienna in the service of the Emperor Joseph I, and he took part in the production of C. A. Badia's *Gli amori di Circe con Ulisse* (1709) and the intermezzo *Vespetta e Milo* (1717; by A. Scarlatti and F. Conti) in Dresden. Tosi mentioned him (as Baron Ballerini) for his qualities as an actor, and in particular for his masterly execution of dramatic recitative.

PAOLA BESUTTI

Ballet. In its broadest sense, any theatrical exhibition of dance and pantomimic action (or the music accompanying it). Ballet has traditionally had an important place in opera, serving in earlier periods as an adjunct to the action or a relief from it. Ballet was traditionally presented in the intervals or at some other break in Italian serious opera, linked symbolically if at all with the main action and usually composed by a house ballet composer. Later, after the era of Gluckist reform and the rise of the *ballet d'action*, it came to be more closely integrated with the opera, as it generally had been in France, where it remained central throughout the 19th century. For a fuller discussion, *see* DANCE.

Ballet d'action [ballet en action, ballet pantomime; pantomime ballet] (Fr.). A stage work in which a dramatic story is conveyed through gesture, dance and instrumental music. It developed in part as a reaction against the *divertissement* in opera, in which dance is designed to delight the eye and depict a general mood, and the *opéra-ballet*, where vocal music has an important role and plots are loosely constructed. Some consider it as analogous to the 'reform opera' of Gluck. Key exponents in France in the second half of the 18th century and the first part of the 19th were the choreographers Jean-Georges Noverre, Gaetano Vestris and the Gardel brothers. Their successors, among them Pierre Aumer and Filippo Taglioni, followed this tradition, and with changes in technique and costuming are credited with the creation of the Romantic ballet.

See also DANCE.

M. ELIZABETH C. BARTLET

Ballet de cour (Fr.). French court entertainment of the late 16th and 17th centuries in which dances, elaborate machines and costumes and vocal pieces are combined in impressive and expensive displays, often mixing the noble and the grotesque. It was a vehicle for exalting royal power and authority; the patronage of Louis XIII and Louis XIV (for the first half of his reign), as well as their predecessors, was decisive. Its components were *récits*, *vers* (printed texts distributed to the spectators), entrées and usually a concluding *grand ballet* (in which nobles and sometimes the king himself participated). Overtures became a common addition in the second half of the 17th century.

In its early stage (to 1621) it differs from its predecessor, the court *divertissement* or *fête* (which continued to be popular), principally in presenting a more unified and continuous dramatic action. Among the first was Baltasar de Beaujoyeulx's *Circé, ou Le balet comique de la Royne* (1581; music by Jacques Salmon and Lambert de Beaulieu), which, according to Anthony (1973), shows the strong aesthetic and musical influence of Baïf's Académie. Later, however, it became a series of entrées, loosely related at best, but each illustrative of the subject announced in the title. Isaac de Benserade's *Ballet de la nuit* (1653) with music by Jean de Cambefort and machines devised by Giacomo Torelli is an excellent example (see illustration overleaf); in four entrées it traces the progress from dusk to dawn in three-hour segments (the last presenting the young Louis XIV symbolically as the rising sun). The same year Lully was appointed a court composer, and writing *ballets de cour* soon became his principal occupation. He is credited with introducing new dances, particularly several at brisker tempos, and giving more emphasis to the vocal component both in dramatically expressive *récitatif* and in choruses (see, for example, the *Ballet des muses* of 1666). His works in the genre served as his dramatic apprenticeship. With Louis XIV's retirement from dancing in 1670, the *ballet de cour* declined in importance, but there were occasional examples at court until the 1720s (one of the last was Lalande's *L'inconnu* of 1720, in which Louis XV danced) and annual ones at the Collège Louis-le-Grand until the expulsion of the Jesuits in 1761 (*see* JESUIT DRAMA). Nevertheless, the *opéra-ballet* owes much to its 17th-century predecessor.

*

Saint-Hubert: *La manière de composer et faire réussir les ballets* (Paris, 1641)

'Ballet de la nuit' (Salle du Petit Bourbon, Paris, 23 February 1653), third of the four entrées (Sabbath): at the approach of two spectators (one played by Louis XIV) the cave, in front of which is a flaming fire where dragons and witches sport, opens suddenly to reveal a banqueting hall; wash and gouache drawing, workshop of Henry de Gissey

M. de Pure: *Idée des spectacles anciens et nouveaux* (Paris, 1668)
P. Lacroix: *Ballets et mascarades de cour de Henri III à Louis XIV* (Paris, 1868–70)
H. Prunières: *Le ballet de cour en France avant Benserade et Lully* (Paris, 1914)
M. M. McGowan: *L'art du ballet de cour en France, 1581–1643* (Paris, 1963)
M.-F. Christout: *Le ballet de cour de Louis XIV, 1643–1672* (Paris, 1967)
J. R. Anthony: *French Baroque Music from Beaujoyeulx to Rameau* (London, 1973, 2/1978; Fr. trans., 1981)
M. M. McGowan: 'Les jésuites à Avignon: les fêtes au service de la propagande politique et religieuse', *Les fêtes de la Renaissance*, iii, ed. J. Jacquot and E. Konigson (Paris, 1975), 153–71
A. Verchaly: 'Ballet de cour', *Dictionnaire de la musique: science de la musique*, ed. M. Honegger (Paris, 1976)
M.-F. Christout: *Le ballet de cour au XVIIe siècle* (Geneva, 1987)
J. L. Schwartz and C. J. Schlundt: *French Court Dance and Dance Music: a Guide to Primary Source Writings* (New York, 1987)
L. E. Auld: 'The Non-Dramatic Art of *Ballet de cour*: Early Theorists', *Beyond the Moon: Festschrift Luther Dittmer* (Ottawa, 1990), 360–93 M. ELIZABETH C. BARTLET

Ballet des saisons ('Ballet of the Seasons'). *Opéra-ballet* in a prologue and four entrées by PASCAL COLLASSE to a libretto by Abbé Jean Pic; Paris, Opéra, 14, 15 or 18 October 1695.

The *Ballet des saisons* is an important precursor of the full-blown *opéra-ballet*. Like Campra's *L'Europe galante* (1697), the *Ballet des saisons* is a series of self-contained entrées linked by a common thread, but unlike its successor, it still features the gods and mythological characters of the *tragédie en musique* and its *divertissements*. After a conventional prologue extolling Louis XIV, each scene features a different couple to illustrate love's 'seasons': Zephyrus (*haute-contre*) and Flora (soprano) for spring ('L'amour coquet'); Vertumnus (bass) and Pomona (soprano) for summer ('L'amour constant et fidèle'); Bacchus (bass) and Ariadne (soprano) for autumn ('L'amour paisible'); and Boreas (bass) and Orithyia (soprano) for winter ('L'amour brutal'). In the score of 1700, Collasse reinstates some instrumental numbers by Lully which in his preface he says he had been unable to print in the first edition. CAROLINE WOOD

Ballet en action. *See* BALLET D'ACTION.

Ballet-héroïque (Fr.). A type of French *opéra-ballet* during the reign of Louis XV which is distinguished by having as its principal characters heroic, noble figures, often from antiquity, classical gods and goddesses, or exotic personages, rather than the comic bourgeois and tender heroines of other *opéras-ballets*. While its treatment of subject is in a loftier tone than the latter, the *ballet-héroïque* also differs from the contemporary *tragédie lyrique* in that the events portrayed are generally festive and gay, not dramatic and terrifying. While dance, of course, remains prominent, in some works there is greater use of vocal music than in other *opéras-ballets*.

The earliest use of the term appears in the libretto of Fuzelier's *Les fêtes grecques et romaines* set by Collin de Blamont (1723). Among the most famous examples are those by Rameau: *Les Indes galantes* (1735), *Les fêtes de Polymnie* (1745), *Les fêtes de l'Hymen et de l'Amour* (1747) and *Zaïs* (1748) are all specifically called *ballets-héroïques*, and others could justly be considered to belong to the same genre. All but the latter follow the standard *opéra-ballet* model of prologue and entrées whose separate stories illustrate a single theme; *Zaïs* is exceptional in that it has a unified plot (and there are a few more examples in the oeuvre of Rameau's contemporaries). The last successful *ballet-héroïque* performed at the Opéra was E. J. Floquet's *L'union de l'Amour et des arts* (1773). The term was also occasionally applied to a single entrée in an *opéra-ballet* (for example, to *Euthyme et Lyris* by L.-B. Desormery in 1776).

See also PASTORALE-HÉROÏQUE.

R. de Saint-Mard: *Réflexions sur l'opéra* (Paris, 1741)
L. de Cahusac: 'Ballet', *Encyclopédie, ou Dictionnaire raisonné des sciences, des arts et des métiers*, ed. D. Diderot, J. d'Alembert and others (Paris, 1751–65; suppls. Amsterdam and Paris, 1776–7, 1780)
P. M. Masson: 'Le ballet héroïque', *ReM*, ix/8 (1927–8), 132–54
J. R. Anthony: *French Baroque Music from Beaujoyeulx to Rameau* (London, 1973, 2/1978; Fr. trans., 1981)
M. ELIZABETH C. BARTLET

Ballet pantomime. *See* BALLET D'ACTION.

Balling, Michael (*b* Heidingsfeld, nr Würzburg, 28 Aug 1866; *d* Darmstadt, 1 Sept 1925). German conductor. He trained as a violist and played in the opera orchestras of Mainz and Schwerin. After touring Australia and New Zealand (1892–5) he went to England in 1895 as musical director of Frank Benson's Shakespearean company. The following year he returned to Germany and played in the orchestra at the Bayreuth Festival. Here his conducting talents were discovered by Felix Mottl and Cosima Wagner and he acted as an assistant for the festivals of 1896, 1899, 1901 and 1902. After posts in Hamburg, Lübeck and Breslau he succeeded Mottl in 1903 as musical director in Karlsruhe. He became a regular conductor at Bayreuth (1904–14, 1924–5) conducting the *Ring*, *Parsifal* and *Tristan*. In 1910 he conducted the first *Ring* performances in Scotland, and in 1911 succeeded Hans Richter as conductor of the Hallé Orchestra. He was in Bayreuth at the outbreak of war in August 1914 and never resumed his Manchester post. From 1912 he was editor for Breitkopf & Härtel of a projected critical Wagner edition. His final post was as musical director in Darmstadt (1919–25). In 1908 he married the widow of Hermann Levi. CHRISTOPHER FIFIELD

Ballo (It.: 'dance'). A term sometimes used as an alternative to *balletto* ('ballet') but otherwise rarely found in Italian opera (Monteverdi's *Il ballo delle ingrate*, 1608, is not an opera). Many of the grand operas of the 1870s and 80s, however, were described as 'opera ballo' if they contained a central ballet (*see* DANCE). Puccini's *Le villi* (1884) is subtitled 'opera ballo' since the *corps de ballet* takes a prominent part in the action. JULIAN BUDDEN

Ballo in maschera, Un ('A Masked Ball'). *Melodramma* in three acts by GIUSEPPE VERDI to a libretto by ANTONIO SOMMA after EUGÈNE SCRIBE's libretto *Gustave III, ou Le bal masqué*; Rome, Teatro Apollo, 17 February 1859.

Riccardo *Count of Warwick, Governor of Boston*	tenor
Renato *a Creole, his secretary, and husband of Amelia*	baritone
Amelia	soprano
Ulrica *a negro fortune-teller*	contralto
Oscar *a page*	soprano
Silvano *a sailor*	bass
Samuel } *enemies of the Count*	bass
Tom }	bass
A Judge	tenor
Amelia's Servant	tenor

Deputies, officers, sailors, guards, men, women, children, gentlemen, associates of Samuel and Tom, servants, masks, dancing couples

Setting In and around Boston, at the end of the 17th century

By February 1857 Verdi had agreed to write a new opera for the Teatro S Carlo in Naples, to be performed in the carnival season 1857–8. His first idea was to use *King Lear*, a setting of which he had planned with the playwright Antonio Somma, but (not for the first time) the S Carlo singers were not to his liking and the project was postponed. By September 1857 the composer was becoming anxious about his approaching deadline, and eventually proposed to Somma and the S Carlo – albeit with some reservations about the libretto's conventionality – that he set a remodelled and translated version of an old Scribe libretto entitled *Gustave III, ou Le bal masqué*, written for Auber in 1833. Somma and the theatre agreed, and Verdi set to work advising his librettist, who had no experience of writing for the musical theatre, on the necessary poetic proportions of the subject.

As soon as a synopsis reached the Neapolitan censors, it became clear that the opera, which dealt with the assassination of the Swedish king Gustavus III, would have to be changed considerably if it was to be performed in Naples. Verdi agreed to change the king into a duke and to set the action back in time, and a new version of the story was patched together. However, soon after the composer arrived in Naples the censor rejected this version, making a series of new, more stringent demands, notably that Amelia become a sister rather than a wife, that there be no drawing of lots by the conspirators, and that the murder take place offstage. The authorities of the S Carlo attempted to answer these objections by cobbling together a new version entitled *Adelia degli Adimari*, but this Verdi angrily rejected. Eventually, negotiations broke down, the planned performances fell through, and Verdi undertook to satisfy his contract at a later date.

When it became clear that Naples would not stage the opera, Verdi decided to have it given at the Teatro Apollo, in Rome, even though it soon became clear that Roman censorship, though far less exigent than that at Naples, would require at least a change of locale and the demoting of the king to some lesser noble. Eventually, however, Somma and Verdi established Riccardo, Conte di Warwick and a setting in North America, although as a protest Somma did not allow his name to appear on the printed libretto. The première, given with a cast including Gaetano Fraschini (Riccardo), Leone Giraldoni (Renato), Eugenia Julienne-Dejean (Amelia) and Zelina Sbriscia (Ulrica), was a great success, and *Un ballo in maschera* became one of Verdi's most popular operas. Though not attaining the dissemination of *Rigoletto*, *Il trovatore* or *La traviata*, it has never lost its place in the international repertory. Many modern performances restore the opera to its original, 18th-century Swedish setting, even though such restoration seems not to have had Verdi's explicit approval. In the Swedish setting the names are as follows:

Riccardo	Gustavus III *King of Sweden*
Renato	Captain Anckarstroem *Gustavus's secretary*
Amelia	Amelia
Ulrica	Mam'zelle Arvidson
Oscar	Oscar
Silvano	Christian
Samuel	Count Ribbing
Tom	Count Horn
A Judge	Armfelt *Minister of Justice*

The brief prelude presents three of the main musical ideas of the opening scene, first a chorale-like opening chorus, then a fugato associated with the conspirators and finally Riccardo's first aria; the whole argument is punctuated by a tiny rhythmic figure first heard in the second bar.

ACT 1.i *A ball in the Governor's house* The opening chorus, 'Posa in pace, a' bei sogni ristora', continues the prelude's musical juxtaposition of Riccardo's loyal followers with the conspirators, led by Samuel and Tom. Riccardo appears and, in a style reminiscent of *opera buffa*, reviews with Oscar the guest list for the coming masked ball. At seeing the name of Amelia, however, Riccardo is visibly moved, and advances to the footlights to sing a brief aria privately expressing his guilty love for her, 'La rivedrà nell'estasi'. Its opening phrase, with an expressive chromaticism and rising 5th, will return later as a musical symbol of the love around which the story of the opera revolves. As the chorus disperses, Renato enters to warn Riccardo of plots against his life. His aria, 'Alla vita che t'arride', though formally more extended than Riccardo's, displays the same tendency towards condensation of traditional elements. Next to appear is a judge, requesting that Riccardo exile Ulrica, a fortune-teller suspected of supernatural practices. Oscar chooses to defend Ulrica in the ballata 'Volta la terrea', a French two-stanza form studded with that light coloratura typical of the page. Riccardo decides that he and his followers will disguise themselves and pay a personal call on Ulrica. He leads off the final stretta, 'Ogni cura si doni al diletto', a number that continues the Gallic atmosphere in its celebration of the pleasures of life, despite the continued mutterings of the conspirators in the musical background.

1.ii *The fortune-teller's dwelling* After an atmospheric orchestral introduction, full of low woodwind sonorities and sinister tritones, Ulrica sings the invocation 'Re dell'abisso', an aria that begins in the minor, is interrupted by Riccardo's entrance in disguise, and continues with a cabaletta substitute in the major. The atmosphere of foreboding is rudely interrupted by Silvano, a sailor who has seen no preferment and who – in the brief, sprightly solo 'Su, fatemi largo' – asks Ulrica to divine his future. Ulrica predicts wealth and a commission, something that Riccardo promptly brings to pass by secreting gold and the appropriate papers into Silvano's pocket. Silvano discovers his new-found wealth and all join in praise of Ulrica. They are interrupted by Amelia's servant, who requests for her mistress an interview with Ulrica. Ulrica dismisses the crowd; but Riccardo, who has recognized the servant, remains in his hiding place.

In an impassioned arioso, Amelia asks Ulrica to rid her of the love that torments her. Ulrica's reply is the sinuous, chromatic 'Della città all'occaso', which tells of a healing plant that grows in the gallows-field nearby. In the brief terzetto that ensues, 'Consentimi, o Signore', Amelia prays that she may be healed, while Ulrica tries to comfort her and Riccardo, still hidden, vows to follow her on her quest. As Amelia departs, the stage is filled with Riccardo's entourage. Riccardo poses as a fisherman and sings the characteristic two-stanza canzone 'Di' tu se fedele', replete with the conventions of maritime musical language. He presents his hand to Ulrica who, in an imposing arioso, predicts that he will soon die by the hand of a friend. Riccardo attempts to disperse the tension by leading off the famous quintet 'È scherzo od è follia', in which his breathless, 'laughing' line is accompanied by sinister chattering from Samuel and Tom, and by a sustained, high-lying melody for Oscar. Riccardo asks the identity of his murderer: Ulrica says it will be the first person who shakes his hand, a prophecy seemingly made absurd by Renato, who hurries on soon after and immediately clasps his master's hand. The act closes with a martial hymn, 'O figlio d'Inghilterra', in which the principals emerge from the vocal mass to restate their differing positions.

ACT 2 *A lonely field on the outskirts of Boston* Amelia's grand scene is preceded by a lengthy, impassioned orchestral prelude which features her melody from the Act 1 terzetto. She is terrified by her surroundings and in the aria 'Ma dall'arido stelo divulsa' prays for assistance in her ordeal. The aria, with the mournful english horn obbligato that is a traditional pointer of the isolated heroine, is interrupted by a terrifying vision as midnight sounds, but her final prayer re-establishes a kind of resigned calm. Riccardo appears, and so begins one of Verdi's greatest soprano-tenor duets, a number that, as was becoming common in middle-period Verdi, has a succession of contrasting 'dialogue' movements before its more conventional close with a cabaletta *a due*. In the opening Allegro agitato the pace of exchange is rapid as Riccardo declares his love and Amelia begs him to leave; the musical continuity comes for the most part from a driving string melody. In a second movement, 'Non sai tu che se l'anima mia', their individual attitudes are explored at greater length, with a particularly impressive modulation as the discourse turns from Riccardo to Amelia; but eventually Riccardo's pleas win the day and, to a passionate, soaring melody sustained by a pedal A major chord, Amelia admits her love for him. A brief linking section leads to the cabaletta, 'Oh qual soave brivido', whose two stanzas and lively arpeggiated melody are separated by yet another impassioned declaration of mutual love.

The couple separate at the sound of footsteps: Riccardo recognizes Renato; Amelia, terrified, lowers her veil. In the first movement of the ensuing trio, 'Per salvarti da lor', Renato warns of the approaching conspirators, and lends his cloak to Riccardo in order to effect the latter's escape. Riccardo will leave only after muffled pleas from Amelia, and he solemnly charges Renato to escort her, still veiled, to the gates of the city. Before Riccardo rushes off, the three principals pause for a furiously paced second trio movement, 'Odi tu come fremono cupi', in which the driving rhythm encloses a strictly patterned alternation of solo statements. Riccardo is safely away when the conspirators appear, singing the contrapuntal music first heard in the prelude to the opera. They are challenged by Renato and, finding their prey has disappeared, decide to amuse themselves by seeing the face of the mysterious woman. When it becomes clear that Renato will fight rather than permit this, Amelia herself raises her veil. Renato is astounded: the conspirators cannot contain their mirth at the notion of Renato's nocturnal assignation with his own wife, and break into the nonchalant 'laughing' chorus, 'Ve' se di notte qui colla sposa'. In between statements of the main idea, Renato accuses Amelia while she begs for mercy. As a parting gesture, Renato arranges a meeting with Samuel and Tom later that morning; the conspirators stroll off together, still vastly amused, their laughter echoing as the curtain comes down.

ACT 3.i *A study in Renato's house* A stormy orchestral introduction ushers in Renato and Amelia. In an impassioned arioso, Renato insists that his wife must die. Although she admits her love for Riccardo, she insists that she has not betrayed her husband. Renato,

Title page of the first edition of the vocal score of Verdi's 'Un ballo in maschera' (Milan: Ricordi, c1859) showing the final scene in Act 3

however, is inflexible, and in the sorrowful aria 'Morrò, ma prima in grazia', Amelia begs to see her child before dying, a cello obbligato adding to the pathos of the scene. Renato agrees to her request and once she has departed hurls furious insults at the portrait of Riccardo, which has a prominent place in his study. His anger coalesces into the famous aria 'Eri tu', a minor–major *romanza* which in the second part turns from angry accusations to the pain of his lost love.

Yet again the contrapuntal theme introduces Samuel and Tom. Renato shows them that he knows of their conspiracy, but now offers to join in its execution, offering his son's life as proof of his good word. Samuel and Tom accept his word, and all three swear blood brotherhood in the martial hymn 'Dunque l'onta di tutti sol una'. They elect to draw lots to decide who will strike the fatal blow, and Renato takes advantage of Amelia's return to force her to draw the name from an urn. To dotted rhythms and tremolando strings, Amelia draws Renato's name, and the conspirators again join in the martial hymn, this time with a terrified descant from Amelia.

In one of those abrupt changes of mood so characteristic of the opera, Oscar now appears, bringing with him the musical atmosphere of French comic opera. He has an invitation to tonight's masked ball, which Renato, Samuel and Tom all accept. To close the scene, they join in a stretta led off by Oscar, 'Di che fulgor', in which the terror and exultation of the principals are subsumed under Oscar's delicate musical idiom.

3.ii *The Count's sumptuous study* In an opening recitative, Riccardo decides to sign a paper sending Renato and Amelia back to England. He then muses on the loss of his love in the *romanza* 'Ma se m'è forza perderti', which moves from minor to major, but via an unusual intermediate section in which he feels a strange presentiment of death. Dance music is heard offstage, and Oscar brings an anonymous message warning Riccardo that he risks assassination at the ball. But Riccardo, as ever heedless of the danger, concludes the scene with a passionate recollection of his Act 1 aria of love for Amelia.

3.iii *A vast, richly decorated ballroom* The opening chorus, 'Fervono amori e danze', repeats the music heard offstage in scene ii. As Renato, Samuel, Tom and their followers appear, a new, minor-mode theme emerges over which the conspirators exchange passwords and search for the Count. A third theme is heard as Oscar recognizes Renato. However, in spite of Renato's anxious questions, Oscar refuses to reveal the Count's costume, singing instead a lively French couplet form, 'Saper vorreste'. The opening chorus is heard again, and Renato renews his questions, pleading important business. Oscar finally reveals that the Count is wearing a black cloak with red ribbon, after which he mingles with the crowd to yet more of the opening chorus. A new dance melody, this time a delicate mazurka, underpins a stifled conversation between Amelia and Riccardo: Amelia begs the Count to escape; he reiterates his love but tells her that she is to return to England with her husband. They are bidding a last, tender farewell when Renato flings himself between them and stabs Riccardo. In the subsequent confusion, Oscar rips off Renato's mask and the chorus expresses its fury in a wild Prestissimo. But then the gentle mazurka briefly returns (the offstage dance orchestra as yet unaware of the events) as Riccardo bids his people release Renato. Leading off the final concertato, 'Ella è pura', Riccardo assures Renato that Amelia's honour is intact. He bids his subjects farewell, and a brief stretta of universal horror brings down the curtain.

* * *

Un ballo in maschera, as many have remarked, is a masterpiece of variety, of the blending of stylistic elements. Verdi's experiment with a 'pure' version of French grand opera in the mid-1850s, *Les vêpres siciliennes*, was not entirely happy; here we see him instead gesturing to the lighter side of French opera, primarily with the character of Oscar, but also in aspects of Riccardo's musical personality. The juxtaposition of this style with the intense, interior version of Italian serious opera that Verdi had preferred in the early 1850s is extremely bold, particularly in sections such as Act 1 scene ii (where Riccardo confronts Ulrica) or in the finale to Act 2 (the so-called laughing chorus), in both of which the two styles meet head on with little mediation. One of the reasons why the blend is so successful is that Verdi's treatment of the traditional forms at the backbone of his 'Italian' manner were themselves changing, adapting towards the more elliptical manner of French models. *Ballo* is notable for the shortness and intensity of its principal arias, for the absence of grand design.

Another reason for the opera's success undoubtedly lies in its delicate balance of musical personalities. At the outer limits of the style, as it were, lie two musical extremes; Oscar, whose role is throughout cast in an unambiguously Gallic mould of light comedy; and Ulrica, whose musical personality is unrelievedly dark and austere. Within these two extremes lie Renato and Amelia, characters cast in the Italian style, fixed in their emotional range, but from time to time infected by the influence of their 'French' surroundings. And at the centre comes Riccardo, who freely partakes of both worlds, and who mediates between them so movingly and persuasively. ROGER PARKER

Balochino [Balocchi, Balocco], **Carlo** (*b* Vercelli, 1770; *d* Milan, 1850). Italian impresario. He began as a *croupier*, and in later life deceived Berlioz and others by saying that he had been a *tailleur* ('tailor', but less obviously 'card-cutter'). Gambling threw him together with Domenico Barbaia, whose assistant he became in his manifold enterprises as a gambling promoter and opera impresario, first in Venice from 1807, where he managed La Fenice, then in Naples, Palermo and Milan. When Barbaia withdrew from Milan in 1828, Balochino stayed on at La Scala, working again as assistant to leading impresarios, in particular Bartolomeo Merelli. From 1835 to 1848 he was Merelli's partner and representative in charge of the Kärntnertortheater, Vienna, besides sharing in Merelli's operatic agency business. Balochino therefore dealt, through the heyday of early 19th-century Italian opera, with some of the most notable artists of the time. He seems, however, to have been a canny, stubborn businessman without much artistic flair; late in his career he rejected a work by his own musical director, Otto Nicolai – *Die lustigen Weiber von Windsor*, one of the best and most successful of German comic operas. He was apparently well educated for an impresario. His papers are in the Stadtbibliothek, Vienna.

Luigi Balocchi (Louis Balochy; 1766–1832), Carlo's brother, wrote the librettos of several of Rossini's Paris operas – *Il viaggio a Reims* and, in collaboration with others, *Le siège de Corinthe* and *Moïse et Pharaon*.

*

F. Regli: *Dizionario biografico dei più illustri poeti e artisti melodrammatici* (Turin, 1860)

J. Rosselli: *The Opera Industry in Italy from Cimarosa to Verdi* (Cambridge, 1984)

JOHN ROSSELLI

Balslev, Lisbeth (*b* Åbenrå, 21 Feb 1945). Danish soprano. She studied at the Esbjerg Conservatory and at the opera school of the Royal Theatre, Copenhagen, where she made her début as Yaroslavna (*Prince Igor*) and joined the Danish Royal Opera in 1975. Her roles included Fiordiligi, Leonora (*Il trovatore*) and Senta, the last of which she sang at Bayreuth in 1978 and in the six following years. She was a member of the Hamburg Staatsoper, 1979–83, making her début as Elsa, and later sang in other leading German centres and in Amsterdam, Brussels and Moscow, notably in Wagner roles and as Strauss's Salome, Chrysothemis and Empress. In 1988 she sang Isolde in Turin and Florence. Her singing is admired for its emotional vibrancy and strong dramatic commitment. NOËL GOODWIN

Balsys, Eduardas (*b* Nikolayev, Ukraine, 20 Dec 1919; *d* Druskininkai, 3 Nov 1984). Lithuanian composer. He studied at the Lithuanian conservatory in Vilnius, where he later taught composition, graduating in 1950, and at the Leningrad conservatory. Established as one of the leading Lithuanian composers of his generation, from 1962 to 1971 he was the chairman of the Lithuanian Composers' Union. His only opera, *Kelionė į Tilžę* ('A Journey to Tilsit'), was given its first performance in Vilnius on 29 June 1980. In a prologue and two acts, it is based on Hermann Sudermann's short story *Die Reise nach Tilsit*, and tells of love, self-sacrifice and betrayal. The music reveals the composer's enthusiasm for Berg, especially *Lulu*, but the use of strict dodecaphonic procedures does not preclude deep emotionality and expressiveness. The opera presents some production difficulties because of its lack of stage action; however, it has a stylistic unity and psychological realism that were relatively new for Lithuanian opera of this period. Balsys also wrote incidental music for films and plays, as well as three violin concertos.

*

O. Narbutienė: *Eduardas Balsys* (Vilnius, 1971)

ADEODATAS TAURAGIS

Balthrop, Carmen Arlen (*b* Washington DC, 14 May 1948). American soprano. She studied at the University of Maryland, College Park, and at the Catholic University of America. She made her début in 1973 as Virtue (*L'incoronazione di Poppea*) at Washington, DC, where in 1974 she sang Minerva in the American première of *Il ritorno d'Ulisse*. In 1975 she sang the title role of Scott Joplin's *Treemonisha* at Houston and later on Broadway, also recording the opera. Having won the 1975 Metropolitan Auditions, she made her début with the company as Pamina in 1977, then sang Climene in Cavalli's *Egisto* at Wolf Trap. In 1978 she sang the first Mermaid (*Oberon*) and Ruggiero (*Tancredi*) with Opera Orchestra of New York at Carnegie Hall. She sang Monteverdi's Poppaea at Spoleto (1979), Innsbruck (1980) and Santa Fe (1986), and Gluck's Eurydice (1982) and Poppaea in Handel's *Agrippina* (1983) in Venice. She appeared with Michigan Opera Theater (1982–4) as Treemonisha and Pamina. Of diminutive stature, she was noted for a fresh, pleasing voice, a refined style and an alluring stage presence.

ELIZABETH FORBES

Baltimore. American city, the largest in Maryland. Beginning in the late 19th century it was visited by touring opera companies including the Metropolitan Opera. The Baltimore Civic Opera, formed in the early 1930s by Eugene Martinet, was Maryland's first opera company. It performed in the Maryland Casualty Auditorium until 1952, when it moved to the Lyric Opera House (built in 1894 as the Lyric Theatre), opening there with *Aida*. The American soprano Rosa

Ponselle, who had been closely involved with the company's administration since her retirement from singing in 1937, was made artistic director at that time and remained in the position until the late 1970s. Limited backstage space and facilities at the Lyric preclude elaborate staging, but the company's productions have covered a broad repertory including *Don Giovanni* with Beverly Sills and Norman Treigle (1966), *Rigoletto* with Sherrill Milnes (1970), the première of Thomas Pasatieri's *Ines de Castro* (1976), and *Die Walküre* (1984) in which James Morris sang his first Wotan. The group, which became known as the Baltimore Opera Company in 1970, stages four operas a season, giving three or four performances of each work. Their educational project, Eastern Opera Theatre, brought fully staged opera productions with a recorded orchestra into Maryland state schools for a decade beginning in 1972, including Donizetti's *Rita* and Menotti's *The Old Maid and the Thief*.

The Peabody Art Theatre (from 1976 the Peabody Opera Theatre) was formed in the 1960s to feature singers from the Peabody Conservatory. Past productions have included a double bill of *The Beggar's Opera* and *Die Dreigroschenoper*, Bononcini's *Il trionfo di Camilla* and Argento's *Postcard from Morocco*. Besides at least two main productions each year, the theatre presents workshops on operas by young composers.

ROBERT E. BENSON

Baltsa, Agnes (*b* Lefkas, 19 Nov 1944). Greek mezzo-soprano. She studied in Athens, Munich and Frankfurt, where she made her début in 1968 as Cherubino. In 1969 she sang Octavian at the Vienna Staatsoper and in 1970 appeared at the Deutsche Oper, Berlin, and the Salzburg Festival. She made her American début in 1971 at Houston as Carmen and first sang at La Scala in 1974 as Dorabella. She made her Covent Garden début in 1976 as Cherubino and first appeared at the Metropolitan in 1979 as Octavian. Her repertory includes Orpheus, Sextus, Rosina, Cenerentola, Isabella (*L'italiana in Algeri*), Romeo (*I Capuleti e i Montecchi*), Eboli, Adalgisa, Dido (*Les Troyens*), the Composer (*Ariadne auf Naxos*), Herodias (*Salome*), Delilah, Charlotte and Giulietta (*Les contes d'Hoffmann*). A powerful singer, she often sacrifices beauty of tone to dramatic effect, but in roles such as Carmen she is unrivalled.

*

N. Goodwin: 'Agnes Baltsa', *Opera*, xxxvi (1985), 483–8

ELIZABETH FORBES

Balyozov, Rumen (*b* Sofia, 6 Sept 1949). Bulgarian composer. He studied at the Bulgarian State Conservatory (1971–6), then worked as a cellist in the Symphony Orchestra of Bulgarian Radio and Television. Balyozov came to prominence as a composer in the 1970s and 80s. Drawing on the aesthetics of Cage and Kagel, he sought to embody the idea of music as the illumination of the intellect in his works, which include elements of self-irony, games, paradoxes and a sense of the absurd. Moral and ethical issues determine the themes of the stage works. In *Kogato kuklite ne spyat* ('When Dolls are not Asleep') Balyozov imaginatively evokes the world of fairy-tales. In *Zelenata igra* ('The Green Game') contemporary social issues are dealt with alongside more universal human questions; music is the medium by which the text and visual aspects of the work are linked.

Malkiyat Prints [The Little Prince], 1975 (television op, R. Balyozov, after A. de Saint-Exupéry)

Kogato kuklite ne spyat [When Dolls are not Asleep] (children's op, L. Mileva), Blagoevgrad, Nov 1980

Zelenata igra [The Green Game] (music-theatre work, I. Radoev), Sofia, National Palace of Culture, 13 Oct 1987

*

M. Manolova: *Opus musicum* (Brno, 1985)

V. Dicheva: 'Rumen Balyozov', *Bulgarska muzika* (1989), no.8, p.10

MAGDALENA MANOLOVA

Bambini, Eustachio (*b* Pesaro, 1697; *d* Pesaro, 1770). Italian impresario. After serving as *maestro di cappella* at Cortona and Pesaro, he spent some time in Moravia, where his operas *Partenope* (1733) and *La pravità castigata* (1734) were performed. He became impresario of the Regio Ducal Teatro Nuovo in Milan in 1745 and director of Italian opera at the city theatre in Strasbourg five years later. On 24 May 1752 he agreed to provide seven singers and an orchestra for performances in Rouen later that year, but this contract was revoked by the Opéra and the singers were summoned to Paris. Their part in the QUERELLE DES BOUFFONS has been overemphasized: generally considered an integrated and talented troupe that took Paris by storm, the Bouffons were in reality a group of minor actors on the periphery of the Italian operatic world. Few of them had performed together before meeting in Strasbourg and, except for Bambini's wife, the soprano Anna Tonelli, none had enjoyed widespread success in Italy. The eventual popularity of early performances such as Pergolesi's *La serva padrona* and *Il maestro di musica*, which required a cast of only three, encouraged Bambini to stage more ambitious works, and his troupe eventually comprised nine singers. Contemporary reviews indicate that he knew how to satisfy his critics and accommodate productions to prevalent taste. Presumably he returned to Italy after his troupe's final performances in March 1754.

ELISABETH COOK

Bambini, Felice (*b* Bologna, *c*1743; *d* ?after 1787). French composer of Italian origin, son of Eustachio Bambini. He went to Paris in July 1752 at the same time as the company of Bouffons directed by his father. Jean-Jacques Rousseau mentioned him in the *Lettre sur la musique française*, drawing a favourable comparison between his light manner of playing the continuo (usually in two parts) and the stiff style of the Opéra's harpsichordist. La Borde added that Bambini composed 'several *ariettes* for addition to the *intermèdes* performed at the time'. He stayed in Paris after the departure of the Italian company and studied with André-Jean Rigade. The music of his principal opera, *Nicaise*, is relatively rudimentary, and more reminiscent of the Italian intermezzos of the 1740s and 50s than the more elaborate *opéras comiques* of Duni, Monsigny and Philidor. After the failure of *Nicaise* no more of Bambini's works were performed at the Comédie-Italienne, and during the 1780s he had to be content with the modest Théâtre des Beaujolais.

all first performed in Paris; all printed works published in Paris

Les amans de village (comédie mêlée de musique, 2, A. F. Riccoboni), Comédie-Italienne (Bourgogne), 26 July 1764, 2 airs (1771)

Nicaise (oc, 1, J.-J. Vadé, rev. N. E. Framery, after La Fontaine), Comédie-Italienne (Bourgogne), 15 July 1767, collab. Fridzeri (1767)

Les fourberies de Mathurin (opéra bouffon, 1, Davesne), Beaujolais, 5 Aug 1786

L'amour l'emporte (opéra bouffon, 1, Mayeur de Saint-Paul), Beaujolais, 20 Oct 1787

*

J.-B. de La Borde: *Essai sur la musique ancienne et moderne* (Paris, 1780), iii, 384
M. Tourneux, ed.: *Correspondance littéraire, philosophique et critique par Grimm, Diderot, Raynal, Meister etc.* (Paris, 1877–82), vii, 372
C. D. Brenner: *A Bibliographical List of Plays in the French Language, 1700–1789* (Ann Arbor, 1947) MICHEL NOIRAY

Bampton, Rose (Elizabeth) (*b* Lakewood, nr Cleveland, OH, 28 Nov 1908). American mezzo-soprano, later soprano. She studied at the Curtis Institute, made her début in 1929 at Chatauqua as Siébel, and then sang secondary roles with the Philadelphia Grand Opera. She made her Metropolitan début in 1932 as Laura (*La Gioconda*), and sang as a mezzo until 1937, when she made her soprano début as Leonora (*Il trovatore*); other roles included Aida and Amneris (in the same season), Donna Anna, Alcestis, Elisabeth, Elsa, Sieglinde and Kundry. She appeared at Covent Garden (1937) as Amneris; in Chicago (1937–46), where her roles included Maddalena de Coigny; at the Teatro Colón, Buenos Aires (1942–8), where she sang the Marschallin as well as Daphne in the South American première of Strauss's opera; and San Francisco (1949). She retired in 1950. She had a fine, if not a great, voice, and her sovereign musicianship was admired by Toscanini, for whom she recorded the title role of *Fidelio*.

DENNIS K. McINTIRE, ELIZABETH FORBES

Banda (It.: 'band'). *See* STAGE BAND.

Banderali, Davidde (*b* Lodi, 12 Jan 1789; *d* Paris, 13 June 1849). Italian tenor and singing teacher. He made his début at the Teatro Carcano, Milan, in 1806, but after a few years as a singer, specializing in *buffo* roles, he turned to teaching. In 1814 he became director of the Teatro dei Filodrammatici, Milan, where in the following year the 18-year-old Giuditta Negri, later to be known as Pasta, made her début in Scappa's *Le tre Eleanore*. He taught in Milan from 1821 to 1828, and then for 20 years in Paris. His pupils included Pasta, the sopranos Adelaide Comelli-Rubini and Henriette Méric-Lalande, and the baritone Paolo Barroilhet.

ELIZABETH FORBES

Banditti, The. Opera by Samuel Arnold; *see* CASTLE OF ANDALUSIA, THE.

Bandrowski-Sas [Brandt]**, Aleksander** (*b* Lubaczów, 22 April 1860; *d* Kraków, 28 May 1913). Polish singer. He sang in Lwów from 1881 as a baritone in operetta under the name Aleksander Barski. After studying in Milan and Vienna, he became one of the finest tenors of his time, excelling in Wagner (under the stage name Brandt). From 1887 to 1899 he sang in many of the principal west European houses; he had a permanent contract in Frankfurt (1889–1901). At Dresden in 1901 he created the title role in Paderewski's *Manru*, which he later sang in Lwów, Philadelphia, Boston, Chicago and at the Metropolitan. Bandrowski-Sas wrote three opera librettos: *Stara baśń*, after J. I. Kraszewski (music by W. Żeleński, 1907), *Bolesław Śmiaty*, after S. Wyspiański (L. Różycki, 1909) and *Twardowski* (Wallek-Walewski, 1911); he also translated into Polish various excerpts from Wagner's librettos and the whole of *Die Meistersinger*.

K. Michałowski: *Opery polskie* (Kraków, 1954)
Słownik biograficzny teatru polskiego 1765–1965 (Warsaw, 1973)

IRENA PONIATOWSKA

Banevich, Sergey (*b* Okhansk, 2 Dec 1941). Russian composer. He studied at the Rimsky-Korsakov College of Music and the Leningrad Conservatory. He has shown a clear preference for writing music for the theatre, and his works include operas, musical comedies and musicals; he has also collaborated on radio and television works, and has composed prolifically for children.

The opera *Beleyet parus odinokiy* ('Lone White Sail'; 3, V. Roshchin, after V. Katayev), written and staged in 1969 at Odessa, tells of the adventures of a boy, Gavrik, and his grandfather during the revolutionary period in Odessa. The themes for the main characters are close to the styles of Dargomïzhsky, Musorgsky and Prokofiev, and Banevich also used phrases from specific revolutionary songs. In his subsequent works, there was a sharp change to a more everyday style, with popular song, dance tunes and energetic march rhythms.

The roots of the vivid tunefulness of *Ferdinand Velikolepnïy* ('Ferdinand the Magnificent'; 3, V. Dreyer, after J. Kern), an opera first performed at the Malïy Theatre in Leningrad in 1974, lie in Soviet opera of the 1930s and the music of Cole Porter, Frederick Loewe and Michel Legrand; the style is also reminiscent of Puccini and Saint-Saëns. In the plot the dog Ferdinand first mistakes thieves for friends, swears an oath to find the criminals and finally keeps his promise; the swiftly moving action and unusual musical humour have made the opera popular with both children and adults.

One of Banevich's most mature works is the musico-philosophical parable *Istoriya Kaya i Gerdï* ('The Story of Kai and Gerda'; 2, T. Kalinina, after H. C. Andersen: *The Snow Queen*), performed in 1981 at the Kirov Theatre in Leningrad. It is based on the moral conflict between Kai's coldheartedness and Gerda's warmth and selflessness, and lyricism permeates the subject matter and inner meaning throughout. The symbolic themes are marked by a breadth of melodic style; the harshness of the musical language – the predominant intervals are seconds, sevenths and ninths – is concealed by a tendency to sequential development.

In the two-act opera *Gorodok v tabakerke* ('The Town in the Snuff-box'; G. Khmel'nitsky, after V. Odoyevsky; Leningrad, Children's Theatre, 1988), Banevich resurrects the traditions of the Romantic theatre with its world of great deeds and exalted dreams. The subject of the opera – the Princess of Melody chased out of town in a snuff-box by an important general, thus silencing the musical mechanism of the toys – recreates a style epitomized by Tchaikovsky's *Nutcracker* and Stravinsky's *Petrushka*.

In 1991, Banevich completed an opera entitled *Rusalochka* ('The Little Mermaid'), intended for performance by children. MARINA NEST'YEVA

Banff. Town in south-western Alberta, Canada, in Banff National Park. The Banff Festival of the Arts was established in 1971 with productions of operas and musicals such as Carlisle Floyd's *Susannah* (1971), Healey Willan's *Deirdre* (1972), Cole Porter's *Kiss Me, Kate* (1976), and *Così fan tutte* (1978, 1990 and 1992). Performers are faculty members and students from the Banff Centre School for the Arts out of which the festival evolved. The school maintains an opera programme and since

1956 has toured with full-length operas through the western provinces. GAYNOR G. JONES

Bánffy, Count **Miklós** (*b* Kolozsvár [now Cluj-Napoca], 30 Dec 1874; *d* Budapest, 6 June 1950). Hungarian opera director, designer and writer. After studying law at the universities of Kolozsvár and Budapest he entered the service of the state. From 1912 to 1917 he was director of the Hungarian State Theatres (the Royal Opera House and the National Theatre), and in 1917–18 was general director of the Budapest opera house, where he undertook the renewal of the outmoded repertory and 19th-century traditions of staging. Although World War I thwarted some of his plans, he succeeded in bringing new life to the repertory by introducing works such as *Salome* (1912), *Boris Godunov*, *Die Entführung* and *L'enfant prodigue* (all 1913), Handel's *Judas Maccabaeus* (1914), Franz Schmidt's *Notre Dame* (1916), Bartók's *Bluebeard's Castle* (1918) and many ballets. Bánffy smoothed Bartók's path to the stage, and not just as director: his set, reminiscent of naive folk art, for the ballet *The Wooden Prince*, and the symbolist-constructivist scenery that he designed for *Bluebeard's Castle*, contributed greatly to the success of these works' premières. His period as director saw the first guest performance of Dyagilev's Ballets Russes in Budapest (Dec 1912 to Jan 1913), including the first performance in Hungary of Stravinsky's *The Firebird*, which had a lasting influence on the development of Hungarian ballet.

Bánffy was his country's Foreign Minister, 1921–2, and from 1913 to 1927 he was chairman of the Hungarian Council for the Fine Arts. In 1926 he moved to Transylvania, where he played a leading part in Hungarian literary life. Under the pseudonym Miklós Kisbán he wrote several plays and a trilogy of novels. Kodály wanted to set his play *A nagyúr* ('The Great Lord') as an opera, but Bánffy withheld the rights. Bánffy figures as an eccentric amateur according to Bartók's librettist, Béla Balázs, but in fact he was a versatile, cultured and gifted innovator in the world of Hungarian literature and the Hungarian stage.

*

B. Balázs: 'Hz oszthatatlan ember' [The Indivisible Man], *Forum* [Budapest], iii (1948), 956–64 FERENC BÓNIS

Bánk bán. Historical dramatic opera in three acts by FERENC ERKEL to a libretto by BÉNI EGRESSY after József Katona's play *Bánk bán*; Pest, National Theatre, 9 March 1861.

Bánk bán *Palatine of Hungary*	tenor
Melinda *his wife*	soprano
Endre II *King of Hungary*	baritone
Gertrud *his wife*	contralto
Otto *Duke of Meran, Gertrud's brother*	tenor
Petur bán *Lord Lieutenant of Bihar*	bass-baritone
Biberach *a knight-errant*	baritone
Tiborc *a peasant*	baritone

Courtiers, guests, insurgents, soldiers

Setting The Hungarian royal palace and by the River Danube in the 13th century

While King Endre II was at war over the Carpathian Mountains, which formed the frontier of Hungary, his power-drunk wife, Gertrud, from Meran in the Tyrol, filled the royal household with her foreign courtiers and lived with them in the greatest luxury. Eventually she and her courtiers were killed in a revolt in 1213. Katona's fine drama (1815) based on this story of tragic conflict between strong historical characters is a mirror of Hungary's centuries-old struggle against foreign despotism. For that reason its performance was forbidden by the censor. The play was published in book form but was forgotten for two decades before being staged successfully. After the failure of the war of independence in 1848–9, it was again banned for many years.

It is impossible to tell when Erkel began to compose the opera; the only reliable information is that the librettist died in 1851. A newspaper mentioned in 1844 that Erkel intended to write an opera entitled *Bánk bán*, but the libretto could not have been ready at that time. During 1850 and 1851 it was repeatedly stated in the newspapers that Erkel was writing the opera, though he could not at that time have hoped for permission to perform it. When the oppression began to decline in 1860, Erkel must have been close to finishing the work: according to the dates on the score it was completed between August and October 1860.

The première in the National Theatre was conducted by Erkel and was enormously successful. It was performed by the theatre's best singers at the time, including József Ellinger as Bánk bán, Kornélia Hollósy as Melinda, Lajos Bignio as Endre II and Zsófia Hofbauer as Gertrud. Within Hungary it was not staged as widely as *Hunyadi László* because it was more difficult to perform. Important premières were given in 1866 at Kolozsvár (now Cluj-Napoca, Romania), Nagyvárad (now Oradea, Romania) and Arad (now in Romania); in 1872 at Debrecen; in 1877 at Székesfehérvár, Pozsony (now Bratislava, Czechoslovakia) and Veszprém; in 1881 at Pécs; and in 1882 at Sopron. By 1990 it had been performed 900 times in Budapest. The finest foreign performer to sing Melinda in the 19th century was Marie Wilt. In 1939 Nándor Rékai revised the music of the opera and Kálmán Nádasdy and Gusztáv Oláh wrote a new libretto, closer to Katona's play and in faultless verse. It is now performed in this revised version, with some small modifications to the music of Act 3 scene i made by Jenő Kenessey in 1953. Rékai made many deletions in the score, and thoroughly rearranged the music to fit the rewritten libretto. Outside Hungary only the 1939 version was performed; it had premières in Novosibirsk (in Russian), Opava (in Czech) and Dessau (in German) in 1955; in Moscow in 1958 (in a Hungarian performance by the Budapest opera) in the Nemirovich-Danchenko Music Theatre and in 1959 (in Russian) at the Bol'shoy Theatre; in Helsinki (in Finnish) in 1959, in Ghent (in Flemish) in 1960 and in London (in English) at University College in 1968. In 1990 only the 1939 version was available on record and in an edition. The musical discussion below therefore follows this version.

ACT 1.i *The ceremonial hall of the royal palace at Visegrád* There is an overture and a short introduction including Melinda's principal melody; this is in a slow *verbunkos* (a Hungarian dance) style, similar in mood to the famous 'Death Song' in *Hunyadi László*. The curtain rises. Otto tells the intriguer Biberach of his intention to seduce Melinda. Both of them, in common with all the 'negative' characters, are depicted in non-nationalistic idioms, and Otto always by richly sentimental music.

Petur, the chief of the rebels, enters accompanied by the rebels' chorus and sings a 'Keserű bordal' ('Drinking Song of Bitterness') to words by M. Vörösmarty, first composed separately from the opera; he protests against the carousing of Gertrud and her courtiers and voices the misery of the people. The rebels have sent a messenger to ask Bánk to come and help them and the country. A delegate from the King arrives, reporting that his army has gained a great victory, and a rejoicing chorus containing folklike tunes follows. In his portrayal of Petur and the other 'positive' characters, Erkel succeeded in combining *verbunkos* dance rhythms with vocal melodies often reminiscent of actual folk music, and in developing them on an operatic level. There is a short ensemble for Otto, Gertrud and Melinda, whom Gertrud has summoned to her court in order to give Melinda as prey to Otto. After a repetition of the rejoicing chorus Bánk arrives. In a duet with Petur, he is made aware of the rebels' plans and of Melinda's danger (confirmed by Biberach). Bánk promises to be with the rebels that night and hurries away. The court returns, followed by the rebels' chorus and that of the courtiers and then by a dance in the form of a *csárdás* (a derivative of the *verbunkos*). The curtain falls, but the orchestra continues to play, linking the first scene to the next. Throughout the opera the orchestra has an important role, not only delineating the principal characters with their motifs but also participating actively in the dramatic development and providing local colour where necessary, sometimes as a folklike chamber ensemble.

1.ii *The stairway of the royal palace* Otto lays siege to Melinda's heart, but she resists. Melinda's musical character, like that of the other main figures in the opera, undergoes constant development: first presented in the introduction as strongly nationalistic, later – in the royal court full of foreign courtiers – it begins to assume international stylistic traits, but by the end of scene i Melinda is once again represented by the nationalistic theme of the introduction with its variants and by another group of closely related themes. Bánk witnesses the encounter between Otto and Melinda, having been set up by Biberach, who wants to take revenge on Gertrud, Otto, Melinda and everybody for not respecting his importance in the court. Though Bánk is convinced of Melinda's devotion, he is tormented by jealousy. As with Melinda earlier, his character is not yet fully established, shown by a love aria that is typical of many in French and Italian opera. Biberach gives Otto a powder that will make Melinda lose consciousness, so that Otto can have his way with her. At the same time he is turning Bánk against Gertrud, who is the original instigator of Otto's plan. In a powerful finale Gertrud dismisses her guests, except for Melinda.

ACT 2.i *The porch of the royal palace, facing the Danube* Bánk, in an impassioned aria 'Hazám, hazám, te mindenem!' ('Homeland, Homeland, my Everything'), worries about the fate of his country. Tiborc, an old peasant, enters and tells him of his family's misery. Biberach arrives with the news that Otto can now accomplish his evil plan. Melinda enters, staggering as though insane. In her despair she begs Bánk to kill her, only asking that he will be compassionate to their child. In this duet the tragedy of their situation is increasingly suggested by sharper rhythms and wider-ranging melodic patterns. Bánk places Melinda and the child in the care of Tiborc, who is to take them to Bánk's remote castle. The folklike chamber ensemble that accompanies them, including a cimbalom and a viola d'amore, brilliantly evokes their tragic situation.

2.ii *The Queen's room* Bánk enters. He and Gertrud confront one another in an increasingly violent exchange of accusations. Otto appears briefly, then vanishes. Both Bánk and Gertrud maintain their musical characters; Gertrud sings in a wilful, aristocratic manner, but gradually adopts Bánk's *verbunkos*-inspired style as she becomes more fearful for her own safety. This is in vain, however: it is she who has handed Melinda over, reduced the country to destitution and seized power for her courtiers, and her change of tone does not help her. She draws a dagger against Bánk, who stabs her with it.

ACT 3.i *The banks of the River Tisza by moonlight, before a storm* In a short introduction inspired by folk music, two piccolos wonderfully evoke the landscape and the prevailing mood. Tiborc urges Melinda to cross the river without delay. The storm, the rough water and the lightning are only hinted at in the music, all attention being concentrated on Melinda, who has collapsed. She is mad and uncomprehending, and sings a rapid succession of arias, in which her characteristic motifs and intonation are merged with the *verbunkos* form, quickening towards a climax at which, clasping her infant, she throws herself into the river and dies. A solemn entr'acte follows.

3.ii *The state room of the royal palace* Endre II sits in one of the two thrones; the other is empty. A chamber beyond is hidden by curtains. The scene takes place in semi-darkness, lit only by torches. The King and court are in deep mourning. Endre II accuses the lords of murder. The curtains are drawn back, revealing Gertrud's body on a catafalque; round it kneel their children and pages. The King persists in his violent accusations. The chorus of rebels denies the murder and reveals the misery that Gertrud has caused. Bánk then enters and throws down the emblem of his rank in front of the catafalque, claiming that he killed the queen, that her crimes are widely known and that anyone else would have done the same. The King commands him to be arrested. Bánk exclaims that only the nation may judge between the King and him. The King draws his sword to fight a duel with Bánk. A shepherd's pipe sounds in the distance, and Tiborc enters, followed by other peasants bearing the bodies of Melinda and the infant. Bánk, stricken with grief, asks to be buried with them. Everybody kneels. After a short funeral chorus the orchestra brings the opera to a close.

* * *

With its strongly national theme, its critical timing in relation to political events, and its readiness to draw on the world of folk melody and the formal principles of the Hungarian *verbunkos*, *Bánk bán* represents an important stage in the development of Hungarian opera. It is widely regarded as the most significant Hungarian opera of its time, for although not as widely popular in Hungary as *Hunyadi László*, it shows a broader command of dramatic characterization and greater skill in accommodating a national idiom. As the fruit of many years of idiomatic development, *Bánk bán* represents a high point in Erkel's output; his development thereafter took different directions and he never again succeeded in writing with such naturalness and vitality.

DEZSŐ LEGÁNY

Bannister. English family of singers.

(1) **Charles Bannister** (*b* Newland, Gloucs., 1741; *d* London, 19 Oct 1804). Bass and actor. He had a fine, untaught voice and sang roles including Macheath and Hawthorne in Norwich before his Drury Lane début as Merlin in Michael Arne's *Cymon* (1767). In 1768 he created Don Diego in *The Padlock* and for over 20 years was given leading roles in musical pieces by Dibdin, Shield and Arnold. Tom Tug in *The Waterman* and Steady in *The Quaker* were two of his successes; he was also admired for his Grimbald (*King Arthur*), Hecate and Caliban. According to the *Thespian Dictionary* his voice 'was a strong, clear bass, with one of the most extensive falsettos ever heard'. In the early 1780s he was an incomparable Polly in travesty performances of *The Beggar's Opera*. There, as in his famous imitations of the castratos, the humour lay in brilliantly accurate mimicry and not in exaggerated burlesque. Convivial, improvident, witty and good-natured, he was said to attribute his vocal stamina to gargling with port wine.

*

BDA; *LS*
D. Pinn: *Roscius* (Norwich, 1767, 2/1767)
T. Bellamy: *The London Theatres* (London, 1795)
C. Dibdin: *A Complete History of the English Stage*, v (London, 1800)
The Thespian Dictionary (London, 1802, 2/1805)
C. H. Wilson: *The Myrtle and Vine* (London, 1802)
J. Adolphus: *Memoirs of John Bannister, Comedian* (London, 1839)
R. Fiske: *English Theatre Music in the Eighteenth Century* (London, 1973, 2/1986)

(2) **Elizabeth Bannister** [née Harper] (*b* *c*1757; *d* London, 15 Jan 1849). Soprano. She was admired as a charming woman with a pure voice and unadorned singing style. Most of her stage career was spent in summer seasons at the Haymarket, where she sang from 1778 and created many roles in operas by Shield and Arnold, including Eliza in *The Flitch of Bacon* and Laura in *The Agreeable Surprise*. She also sang in concerts and was at Covent Garden from 1781 to 1786, creating the title role in Shield's *Rosina*. She married the actor (3) John Bannister in 1783, reputedly teaching him to sing and turning him into a model husband and father. She retired in 1792 to 'trim Friendship's lamp round her family fire'.

*

BDA; *LS*
A. Pasquin [pseud. of J. Williams]: *The Children of Thespis*, ii (London, 1787, 13/1792)
'Mrs Bannister', *Thespian Magazine*, i (1792), 117–18
J. O'Keeffe: *Recollections*, ii (London, 1826)

(3) **John Bannister** (*b* Deptford, London, 12 May 1760; *d* London, 7 Nov 1836). Actor and baritone, son of (1) Charles Bannister. During his career he played, according to his *Memoirs*, well over 400 different parts. He became a favourite comic actor and after his marriage to the soprano Elizabeth Harper in 1783 he began to take singing roles. Robson praised his voice as 'full, round, clear, manly, and intelligible' and declared: '*everybody* loved Jack Bannister'. In Storace's operas, from *The Haunted Tower* (1789) onwards, he and Nancy Storace were frequently paired as the secondary lovers and Kelly later wrote roles for him. In Storace's exuberant afterpiece *The Three and the Deuce* (1795) he played identical triplets, while as Walter, the saviour of the babes in Arnold's *The Children in the Wood*, he delighted audiences from 1793 until his farewell performance in 1815.

BDA; *LS*
W. Oxberry: 'Memoir of John Bannister', *Dramatic Biography*, iv (1826), 128–38
J. Adolphus: *Memoirs of John Bannister, Comedian* (London, 1839)
W. Robson: *The Old Play-Goer* (London, 1846)

OLIVE BALDWIN, THELMA WILSON

Banshchikov, Gennady Ivanovich (*b* Kazan', 9 Nov 1943). Russian composer. He studied composition at the Moscow Conservatory with Sergey Balasanian, and then at the Leningrad Conservatory with Boris Arapov, completing his studies in 1969; since 1973, he has been on the faculty there. In his choice of operatic subjects, Banshchikov has been attracted by the classics of Russian satirical literature, exploring the distance between ironic and human dimensions. His musical setting for *Opera o tom, kak possorilsya Ivan Ivanovich s Ivanom Nikiforovichem* ('Opera about how Ivan Ivanovich Quarrelled with Ivan Nikiforovich') features a natural declamatory style against a finely-etched orchestral backdrop balancing a lushly romantic, lyrical impulse with grotesque elements.

Ostalas' legenda [The Legend Remained], 1967 (radio op for children, F. Naftul'yev)
Lyubov' i Silin [Love and Silin] (chamber op, 3, S. Volkov, after K. Prutkov), Leningrad, Conservatory, 1968
Kradenoye solntse [The Stolen Sun], 1969 (television op for children)
Opera o tom, kak possorilsya Ivan Ivanovich s Ivanom Nikiforovichem [Opera about how Ivan Ivanovich Quarrelled with Ivan Nikiforovich] (1, M. Lobodin, after N. V. Gogol: *Povest' o tom, kak possorilsya Ivan Ivanovich s Ivanom Nikiforovichem*), Leningrad, Kirov, 1973
Smert' korneta Klyauzova [The Death of Cornet Klyauzov], 1976 (1, A. Kleyman, after A. P. Chekhov: *The Phosphorus Match*)
Gore ot uma [Woe from Wit], 1982 (2, Banshchikov, after A. S. Griboyedov), Krasnoyarsk, State Opera and Ballet Theatre, 1985

*

E. Finkel'shteyn: *Gennady Banshchikov: monograficheskiy ocherk* (Leningrad, 1983)

LAUREL E. FAY

Banská Bystrica. Town in central Slovakia. Its first theatre, built in 1826, and which burnt down in 1906, was occasionally visited by travelling Hungarian troupes. Since 1959 it has had what is still the youngest and smallest Slovak opera company, housed in the Národný Dom (National House, built 1927). Calling itself the Opera of the Jozef Gregor-Tajovský Theatre, it gives almost half its performances on tour, and has developed remarkable dramaturgical strength. In 1963, after more than a decade during which two distorted Stalinist versions were perpetrated, it presented Suchoň's *Krútňava* ('The Whirlpool') with its original ending. In 1967 the company gave the Czechoslovak première of Menotti's *The Old Maid and the Thief*; in 1969 it mounted a reconstruction of J. S. Kusser's *Erindo*; in 1977 it gave the Slovak première of Kholminov's *Optimisticheskaya tragediya*; and in 1978 it put on Ibert's *Angélique*. Conductors have included Ján Kende, Anton Buranovský and Miroslav Šmíd. Among the artists who began their careers with the company are Drahomíra Drobková (now a principal with the Prague National Theatre), Jozef Konder (a principal with the Košice Opera), Milan Kopačka (a principal with the Bratislava Opera), and Edita Gruberová. IGOR VAJDA

Banti, Brigida Giorgi (*b* Monticelli d'Ongina, nr Cremona, *c*1756; *d* Bologna, 18 Feb 1806). Italian soprano. Daughter of a street singer and mandoline player, she made her début at the Paris Opéra in 1776, singing between the acts of Gluck's *Iphigénie en Aulide*. After lessons from Sacchini, she went to London in 1779, met (and later married) the dancer Zaccaria Banti, but seems at first to have been a bad and lazy singer despite a very beautiful voice. She sang in Vienna (1780), Venice (1782–3) and other Italian cities, Warsaw (1789) and Madrid (1793–4) with increasing fame. She returned to London in 1794, singing in Bianchi's *Semiramide*, and became principal soprano at the King's Theatre from then until her retirement in 1802.

Banti's fame was truly international, and she was particularly admired by Mount Edgcumbe, who composed *Zenobia* for her in 1800, called her 'far the most delightful singer I ever heard', and wrote in his *Musical Reminiscences* (London, 1824, 4/1834): 'Her voice was of most extensive compass, rich and even, and without a fault in its whole range – a true *voce di petto* throughout'. He also praised her acting. Her son, Giuseppe Banti SJ, published a short biography of her in 1869 (copy in *I-Bc*).

W. T. Parke: *Musical Memoirs* (London, 1830), i, 183–4, 254, 297–8

C. Lozzi: 'Brigida Banti, regina del teatro lirico nel secolo xviii', *RMI*, xi (1904), 64–76

BRUCE CARR

Bantock, Sir **Granville** (*b* London, 7 Aug 1868; *d* London, 16 Oct 1946). English composer. He studied with Frederick Corder at the RAM (1889–93), where he was the first winner of the Macfarren Scholarship. From 1893 to 1896 he edited the *New Quarterly Musical Review* and gained much experience as a conductor of light music, taking the musical comedy *The Gaiety Girl* on a world tour in 1894–5 and then directing music at The Tower, New Brighton (1897–1900). His serious aspirations bore fruit when he was appointed principal of the Birmingham and Midland School of Music in 1900 and Peyton Professor of Music at Birmingham University in 1908. During this period his mature, large-scale compositions were written, including his choral masterpiece *Omar Khayyám*, and until World War I his reputation was second only to Elgar's, though it is doubtful whether he was ever considered great. He retired in 1934 and moved to London, where he taught and examined for Trinity College of Music.

Romantically eclectic and enthusiastic by temperament to the point of ill-discipline, Bantock was forever drawn towards the exotic, particularly the oriental and the Celtic, as evidenced by his operas *Caedmar* and *The Seal-Woman*. *Caedmar* (1892) is Wagnerian and dramatically effective. *The Seal-Woman* (1917–24) owes much to the example of his friend and colleague Rutland Boughton, who hoped to produce it at one of his festivals. In *The Immortal Hour* Boughton had shown a way forward in the use of indigenous myth and modest local resources, though Bantock goes further in the retreat from Wagnerian rhetoric by basing his opera on folksongs. Yet he explored no operatic centre between these two poles, his early venture into musical comedy lying even further beyond; his witty numbers for *ABC* (1898) were written, under the pseudonym 'Graban', for Marie Lloyd, who toured with the show.

See also SEAL-WOMAN, THE.

Eugene Aram (4, after E. Bulwer Lytton and T. Hood), inc., *GB-Bu**, pubd as a recitation (1892)

Caedmar (romantic op, 1, Bantock), London, Olympic, 25 Oct 1892, *Bu**, vs (London, 1893)

The Pearl of Iran (romantic op, 1, Bantock), *Bu**, vs (Leipzig, 1894)

The ABC, or Flossie the Frivolous (musical comedy, 2, R. Henry [R. W. Butler and H. Chance Newton]), Wolverhampton, Grand, 21 March 1898, collab. G. Chandoir and others

Sweet Brier (musical comedy-drama, 3, H. Shelley and H. Hertford), vs (London, 1898)

Harlequinade, or Only a Clown, 1899 (musical play, 1, Bantock), unpubd

The Seal-Woman, 1917–24 (Celtic folk op, 2, M. Kennedy-Fraser, after her collection, *Songs of the Hebrides*), Birmingham, Repertory, 27 Sept 1924, *Bu**, vs (London, 1924)

GänzlBMT

H. O. Anderton: *Granville Bantock* (London, 1915)

M. Bantock: *Granville Bantock: a Personal Portrait* (London, 1972)

T. Bray: *Granville Bantock* (diss., U. of Cambridge, 1972)

——: 'Bantock's "Seal-Woman" ', *MT*, cxvi (1975), 431–3

D. Laurence, ed.: *Shaw's Music*, ii (London, 1981), 723–4

L. Foreman: 'British Opera Comes of Age: 1916–61', *British Opera in Retrospect* (n.p., 1986) [pubn of the British Music Society], 109–10

STEPHEN BANFIELD

Bär, Olaf (*b* Dresden, 19 Dec 1957). German baritone. He studied in Dresden, singing Nardo (*La finta giardiniera*) and creating the title role of *Meister Mateh* by his fellow student, Jan Trieder. In 1985 he joined the Dresden Staatsoper, singing Kilian (*Der Freischütz*) at the reopening of the Semper Oper and creating the Marquis in Matthus's *Die Weise von Liebe und Tod des Cornets Christoph Rilke*. In 1985 he also made his Covent Garden début as Harlequin (*Ariadne auf Naxos*), a role he repeated at Aix- en-Provence in 1986, the year of his début at La Scala as Papageno. He sang the Count in *Capriccio* at Glyndebourne (1987), returning as Don Giovanni in 1991, and has appeared at Frankfurt, Vienna and Berlin in a repertory that includes Count Almaviva, Guglielmo, Silvio (*Pagliacci*) and Wolfram. In 1989 he created Hoffmann in Eckehard Mayer's *Der goldene Topf* at Dresden. An excellent actor with a fine stage presence, he has a flexible, warm-toned voice and excels in Mozart.

ELIZABETH FORBES

Barab, Seymour (*b* Chicago, 9 Jan 1921). American composer. Between 1940 and 1960 he played the cello in several American orchestras; he also played the viola da gamba in the New York Pro Musica. During the 1960s he taught at Rutgers and at the New England Conservatory. A sojourn in Paris in 1952 fostered Barab's interest in composition. He is best known for his more than 30 operas, most of which are in one act and ideally suited for student or amateur productions. The most frequently performed are *Chanticleer*, *A Game of Chance*, *Little Red Riding Hood* and *The Toy Shop*.

selective list

Chanticleer (comic op, 1, M. C. Richards, after G. Chaucer: *The Nun's Priest's Tale*), Aspen, CO, Wheeler Opera House, 4 Aug 1956, vs (New York, 1964)

A Game of Chance (comic op, E. Manacher, after F. and C. Ryerson: *All on a Summer's Day*), Rock Island, IL, 11 Jan 1957, vs (New York, 1960)

Little Red Riding Hood (children's op, 1, Barab, after J. L. and W. C. Grimm), New York, Carl Fischer Hall, 13 Oct 1962, vs (New York, 1965)

A Piece of String, 1965 (3, Barab, after G. de Maupassant), Greeley, CO, U. of North Colorado Opera Theatre, 23 May 1985

Phillip Marshall, 1967 (2, Barab, after F. Dostoyevsky: *The Idiot*), Chautauqua, NY, Chautauqua Institution, 12 July 1974

The Toy Shop (children's op, 1, Barab), New York, City Opera Theatre, 3 June 1978, vs (New York, 1980)

Not a Spanish Kiss (ob, 1, Barab), New York, Singing Teachers Association 77, 2 May 1981

Fortune's Favourites (comedy, 1, Barab, after H. H. Munro: *Baker's*

Dozen), New York, Theater in the Park, 19 June 1982, vs (New York, 1986)

*

H. J. Parr: *Descriptive Analysis of Three One-Act Operas by Seymour Barab* (diss., Ohio State U., 1982)

R. H. Kornick: *Recent American Opera: a Production Guide* (New York, 1991), 39–43

Barabas, Sari (*b* Budapest, 14 March 1918). Hungarian soprano. She planned to be a dancer, but following an injury she turned to singing and made her début at the National Opera in Budapest in 1939 as Gilda. Resuming her career after the war, she joined the Staatsoper in Munich in 1949 and made a reputation there and in Vienna as a coloratura soprano of agile technique and glamorous personality, especially beguiling in operetta. She made her American début at San Francisco in 1950 as the Queen of Night, and sang that role and Gilda at Covent Garden in 1951–2. At Glyndebourne she sang Konstanze in 1953, but was most admired there in 1954 as Adèle in Rossini's *Le comte Ory*, which she recorded with the Glyndebourne cast in 1956. NOËL GOODWIN

Baranović, Krešimir (*b* Šibenik, 25 July 1894; *d* Belgrade, 17 Sept 1975). Croatian composer. He studied the piano and the horn, and composition at the Vienna Akademie (1912–14). From 1915 to 1943 he was a conductor at the Zagreb Opera (which he directed between 1929 and 1940), and in 1927–8 he made a European tour with a ballet troupe led by Pavlova. He was later a professor at the Belgrade Academy of Music (1946–61) and director of the Belgrade PO (1952–61). As a conductor he contributed much to improving the artistic standards and professionalism of Yugoslav music making; he was particularly interested in the performance of Slavonic works.

Until the late 1930s Baranović was one of the representatives of the so-called national style, building his works on the characteristics of the folk music of Croatian Zagorje. His music is rich in fantasy and invention, its dramatic character underlined by means of colourful orchestration. He composed two comic operas, *Striženo-košeno* ('Shorn-mown'; G. Krklec; Zagreb, 4 May 1932) and *Nevjesta od Cetingrada* ('The Bride from Cetingrad'), composed in 1942 (M. Fotez, after A. Šenoa; Belgrade, 12 May 1951); the overture and symphonic scherzo from the former entered the Yugoslav orchestral repertory. The best of his stage works, however, is the ballet *Licitarsko srce* ('Gingerbread Heart'), a work influenced by Stravinsky's *Petrushka*; it became a model of the genre.

*

K. Kovačević: *Hrvatski kompozitori i njihova djela* [Croatian Composers and their Works] (Zagreb, 1960), 17–31

I. Supičić: 'Estetski pogledi u novijoj hrvatskoj muzici: pregled temeljnih gledanja četrnaestorice kompozitora' [Aesthetic Approaches in Contemporary Croatian Music: a Survey of the Basic Views of 14 Composers], *Arti musices*, i (1969), 23–61

J. Andreis: *Music in Croatia* (Zagreb, 1974), 283–8

K. Kovačević: 'Krešimir Baranović (1894–1975)', *Arti musices*, vii (1976), 5–17

M. Veselinović: *Krešimir Baranović: stvaralački uspon* [Krešimir Baranović: Creative Rise] (Zagreb, 1979)

KREŠIMIR KOVAČEVIĆ/KORALJKA KOS

Baratta [Baratti], **Pietro** (*b* ?Massa; *fl* 1723–41). Italian singer. He was in the service of the Duke of Massa and Carrara in 1724–5, the Landgrave of Hesse-Darmstadt in 1729 and the Hereditary Prince of Modena from 1730 to 1736. He appeared in eight operas at Florence between 1723 and 1737 and 11 at Venice, 1724–37, including new works by Albinoni, Antonio Pollarolo, Orlandini, Vivaldi and Porpora. He also sang at Livorno in 1727 and at Naples in 1740–41. He may have been married to Teresa Baratta, who appeared at Florence and Venice in 1735–7, Naples in 1739–41 and Turin in 1742–3. She may possibly be identified (according to Weaver) with the soprano (Maria) Teresa Pieri, who performed at Florence (1727–32), Naples (1728–30 and 1740–41) and Venice (1734–5); if so, she appeared as both Baratta and Pieri in 1740–41.

*

R. L. Weaver and N. W. Weaver: *A Chronology of Music in the Florentine Theater, 1590–1750* (Detroit, 1978) COLIN TIMMS

Barbaia, Domenico (*b* Milan, ?1778; *d* Posillipo, 19 Oct 1841). Italian impresario. He first earned his living as a scullion in local cafés and bars. In 1806 he obtained the lease of the gambling tables in the foyer of La Scala and on 7 October 1809 was appointed manager of the royal opera houses in Naples (originally the S Carlo and Nuovo theatres, to which were later added the Fondo and Fiorentini). After the S Carlo burnt down in 1816, he obtained the contract for rebuilding it. Through the Austrian ambassador he also secured the management of the Viennese Kärntnertortheater and the Theater an der Wien from 1821 to 1828. For several years from 1826 he ran La Scala and the Cannobiana in Milan.

The most famous impresario of his day, Barbaia played an important role in early 19th-century opera. His Neapolitan seasons were of an unparalleled brilliance, with stars like the tenors Giovanni David, Nozzari, García and, later, Rubini, the contralto Benedetta Rosmunda Pisaroni and the soprano Isabella Colbran. His operatic tastes ranged widely. He introduced Spontini's *La vestale* (1811) and Gluck's *Iphigénie en Aulide* (1812), so inaugurating the new tradition of Italian *opera seria* in which all recitative was orchestrally accompanied (early examples include Mayr's *Medea in Corinto*, 1813, and the Rossinian canon beginning with *Elisabetta, regina d'Inghilterra*, 1815). He was among the first to recognize Rossini's genius and in 1815 engaged him at Naples with a six-year contract with the obligation to compose two operas a year and to direct revivals of older works, all for the yearly sum of 12 000 francs and part of the proceeds of the gambling tables. It was to Rossini that Barbaia lost his mistress, Isabella Colbran (later Colbran-Rossini), though relations between the two men remained cordial. In 1822 he produced Rossini in Vienna with great success and the following year mounted Weber's *Euryanthe* at the Kärntnertor. Throughout his life he showed a flair for discovering young talent. Mercadante, Pacini, Carafa and Generali all owed to him many of their earliest opportunities. Through him Bellini first gained a footing at the S Carlo and La Scala. In 1827 Barbaia signed Donizetti to a three-year contract that obliged him to write four operas a year for Naples.

Rough in his manners and poorly educated, Barbaia was held in high esteem by both singers and composers (his word, said Pacini, was as good as a written contract), and his death was mourned throughout Italy. His personality inspired Emil Luka's novel *Der Impresario* (Vienna, 1937), and he figures as a character in Auber's opera *La sirène* (1844).

*

G. Radiciotti: 'Il Barbaia nella leggenda e quello della storia', *L'arte pianistica*, vii/3 (1920), 5–6

A. Canti: 'Impresari d'altri tempi', *Città di Milano*, xl (1943), 17

J. Rosselli: *The Opera Industry in Italy from Cimarosa to Verdi* (Cambridge, 1984) JULIAN BUDDEN

Barbe-bleue ('Bluebeard'). *Opéra bouffe* in three acts by JACQUES OFFENBACH to a libretto by HENRI MEILHAC and LUDOVIC HALÉVY; Paris, Théâtre des Variétés, 5 February 1866.

Widowed for the fifth time, squire Bluebeard (tenor) sends his alchemist Popolani (baritone) to find a virtuous peasant girl to become wife number six. Popolani holds a raffle for the honour, but the winner is the promiscuous Boulotte (soprano). Meanwhile Count Oscar (baritone), court chamberlain to King Bobèche (baritone), has recovered the King's 18-year-old daughter, Princess Hermia (soprano), abandoned as a baby and now living as the shepherdess Fleurette. In Act 2, in King Bobèche's palace, the King attempts to persuade Princess Hermia to marry Prince Saphir (tenor), but she refuses until she discovers that the Prince is none other than her own shepherd lover. Boulotte soon proves too much for Bluebeard, but Popolani rebels at being required to dispose of yet another wife. It transpires that the previous five have merely been given sleeping draughts, and Popolani sets off with them from his laboratory to the palace, bent on revenge. In Act 3 the wedding procession of the Prince and Princess is under way in the palace when Bluebeard arrives, announces Boulotte's demise, and claims the Princess for his next wife. Then Popolani arrives with the six wives, accompanied by five courtiers supposedly put to death for flirting with the Queen. The situation is resolved by marrying off the five ex-wives and five supposed lovers, leaving Princess Hermia to Prince Saphir, and Bluebeard to Boulotte.

Offenbach's *Barbe-bleue* is a satirical version of the medieval story; highlights include the sprightly Fleurette-Saphir duet 'Tous les deux, amoureux', Boulotte's song as she enters the lottery, 'V'là z'encor' de drôl's de jeunesses', Bluebeard's entrance song 'Je suis Barbe-bleue ogué', his triumphant battle-cry 'Amours nouvelles, changer de belles', and Count Oscar's description of court subservience 'Q'un bon courtesan s'incline'. The original cast included José Dupuis as Bluebeard, Hortense Schneider as Boulotte, Kopp as Bobèche and Grenier as Count Oscar. In modern times the work has been best known through the long-lived production by Walter Felsenstein at the Komische Oper, Berlin. ANDREW LAMB

Barber, Samuel (*b* West Chester, PA, 9 March 1910; *d* New York, 23 Jan 1981). American composer. One of the most honoured and most frequently performed American composers in the Americas and Europe during the middle of the 20th century, Barber followed, throughout his career, a path marked by vocally inspired lyricism and a commitment to the tonal language and many of the forms of late 19th-century music. Modernist elements – increased dissonance, chromaticism, tonal ambiguity and limited serialism – appear in his music after 1939 only in so far as he could pursue, without compromise, principles of tonality and lyrical expression. Almost all his published works (48 opus numbers including at least one composition in nearly every genre) entered the repertory soon after he wrote them, and many continue to be performed, gaining new significance within the current trend of 'New Romanticism'.

From the age of seven, Barber displayed a prodigious talent for composing both vocal and instrumental music. At 14, with the encouragement of his aunt and uncle – the celebrated opera singer Louise Homer and the composer Sidney Homer, who was Barber's mentor for more than 25 years – he entered the newly founded Curtis Institute of Music and distinguished himself in three areas of study: piano, with Isabelle Vengerova; voice, with Emilio Edoardo de Gogorza; and composition with Rosario Scalero. For a brief period during the mid-1930s he pursued a career as a singer. Barber gained early recognition as a composer, winning a Rome Prize, which enabled him to spend two years at the American Academy (1935–7). His international stature was firmly established in 1938, when Toscanini and the NBC Symphony Orchestra gave a nationwide broadcast of the first *Essay* and the Adagio for Strings.

After 1939, almost all Barber's instrumental works were composed on commission and for specific virtuoso performers or groups; he was also a prolific composer of songs. His works for the stage include two major operas and one chamber opera. *The Rose Tree*, an early 'operetta' written when he was ten to a libretto by Annie Brosius Noble Sullivan, exists in manuscript at the Chester County Historical Society. *Vanessa* (1957), a four-act opera with a libretto by Barber's long-time companion Gian Carlo Menotti, was first performed by the Metropolitan Opera on 15 January 1958 and won Barber the Pulitzer Prize in 1958. It was the first American opera performed at the Salzburg Festival (1958). *Antony and Cleopatra*, commissioned for the opening of the new Metropolitan Opera House at Lincoln Center (16 September 1966), suffered from an overladen production and overwhelmingly negative reviews until revised by Barber and restaged by Menotti in 1975, when it received its rightful critical accolades. *A Hand of Bridge* (libretto by Menotti), a bitingly witty nine-minute opera for four soloists and chamber orchestra, was composed for the 1959 Festival of Two Worlds in Spoleto.

Barber's operas are marked by continuous lyricism (even in recitative passages), sensitivity to textual rhythms and a rich harmonic language. The orchestra is an important partner to the voice in achieving dramatic expression. Whereas the music of *Vanessa* is predominantly diatonic, that of *Antony and Cleopatra* is infused with chromaticism and disjunct melodic lines and shows less distinction between arias and recitatives. These differences seem to derive less from a change in Barber's style over the nine-year interim than from the different requirements of the operas' subjects.

See also ANTONY AND CLEOPATRA and VANESSA.

The Rose Tree, 1920 (A. B. N. Sullivan), inc., unpubd

Vanessa op.32 (4, G. C. Menotti), New York, Met, 15 Jan 1958, cond. D. Mitropoulos; rev. (3), New York, Met, 13 March 1965, cond. W. Steinberg

A Hand of Bridge op.35 (1, Menotti), Spoleto, 17 June 1959

Antony and Cleopatra op.40 (3, F. Zeffirelli, after W. Shakespeare), New York, Met, 16 Sept 1966, cond. T. Schippers; rev., New York, 6 Feb 1975, cond. J. Conlon

*

S. Barber: 'On Waiting for a Libretto', *ON*, xxii/13 (1957–8), 4–6

——: 'Birth Pangs of a First Opera', *New York Times* (12 Jan 1958)

J. Harrison: 'Samuel Barber Discusses "Vanessa"', *New York Herald Tribune* (12 Jan 1958)

P. H. Lang: '"Vanessa" Opens at Met', *New York Herald Tribune* (16 Jan 1958)

I. Kolodin: 'Barber, Menotti and *Vanessa*', *Saturday Review* (25 Jan 1958)

W. Sargeant: 'Musical Events', *New Yorker Magazine* (25 Jan 1958)
E. Helm: '"Vanessa" in Salzburg', ibid (13 Sept 1958)
E. Coleman: 'Samuel Barber and Vanessa', *Theatre Arts*, xlii/1 (1958), 69–87
H. Klein: 'The Birth of an Opera', *New York Times Magazine* (28 Aug 1966)
H. W. Heinsheimer: 'Birth of an Opera', ibid (17 Sept 1966)
I. Kolodin: 'Music to my Ears: Barber's Antony, after Zeffirelli', *Saturday Review* (1 Oct 1966)
H. W. Heinsheimer: 'Vanessa Revisited', *ON*, xlii/21 (1977–8), 22–5
A. Porter: *Music of Three Seasons: 1974–1977* (New York, 1978)
R. Dyer: record notes, *Antony and Cleopatra* (New World Records, NW 322–24, 1984)
B. Heyman: *Samuel Barber: a Documentary Study of his Works* (diss., City U., New York, 1989)
R. H. Kornick: *Recent American Opera: a Production Guide* (New York, 1991), 43–6
B. Heyman: *Samuel Barber: the Composer and his Music* (New York, 1992) BARBARA B. HEYMAN

Barberillo de Lavapiés, El ('The Little Barber of Lavapiés'). Zarzuela in three acts by FRANCISCO ASENJO BARBIERI to a libretto by Luis Mariano de Larra; Madrid, Teatro de la Zarzuela, 18 December 1874.

The plot (loosely based on historical fact) is set in 1766 during the reign of Carlos III. Lamparilla (tenor), a latter-day Figaro, is barber and general factotum in a working-class district of Madrid. He and his sweetheart Paloma (mezzo-soprano), a seamstress, inadvertently become caught up in a plot hatched by the Infanta to replace the hated Italian prime minister Grimaldi by Floridablanca. The Infanta's lady-in-waiting, the Marquesita Estrella (soprano), has come to the park of El Pardo for a clandestine meeting with Don Juan (bass), one of the chief conspirators, but they are seen in furtive conversation by her fiancé, Don Luis (tenor), Grimaldi's nephew, who not unnaturally draws the wrong conclusions and reproaches her for infidelity, though she endeavours to reassure him. Their discovery by Luis makes it essential to send a warning to Floridablanca. The Marquesita needs someone to escort her discreetly across the city, and Paloma (whom she knows) persuades Lamparilla to do so; but the chief of police has been tipped off, and Lamparilla, to his bewilderment, finds himself under arrest. At the beginning of Act 2 he is released, and is again induced to divert attention – by organizing a crowd to smash street lamps – from the conspirators' spiriting Floridablanca into the royal palace through a secret passage. In Act 3 the Marquesita, who is being hunted by the police, is kept hidden by Paloma, who disguises her as a working girl and, with the help of Lamparilla and Luis (who has decided that his love is more important than his political loyalties), plans her escape. The police raid Paloma's workshop, but Lamparilla suddenly brings the news that the king has dismissed Grimaldi and they are now safe – all but Luis, who has to go into exile, but with Estrella happy to go with him.

This is one of the most famous of all zarzuelas; several of its numbers – including Paloma's entry song 'Cómo nací en la calle de la Paloma', two of Lamparilla's patter songs, a *jota* and a seguidilla – have become familiar parts of Spanish popular culture. LIONEL SALTER

Barberini. Italian family of patrons. Of Tuscan origin, the family gained its fortune in Rome beginning with the ecclesiastical career of Maffeo (1568–1644), who became a cardinal and then Pope Urban VIII (1623–44). He raised two of his nephews to the purple, Francesco (1597–1679) and Antonio (1607–71), and a third, Taddeo (1603–47), headed the line of the princes of Palestrina, followed by his son Maffeo (1631–85) and grandson Urbano (1664–1722). All were active patrons of music in various arenas, with singers, instrumentalists and often librettists such as Francesco Buti and Arcangelo Spagna in their private households. Under the three brothers, particularly Francesco, annual private presentations of opera became established in Rome by 1632, possibly as early as 1628.

Cardinals Francesco and Antonio acquired several young protégés, castratos, who sang in the Barberini productions. Access to the Sistine Chapel provided other fine singers as well as convenient posts for their favourites. Nine operas and a ballet were mounted in 11 carnival seasons between 1631 and 1643, with some restaged out of season. Three further works were presented in 1654 and 1656. Giulio Rospigliosi contributed 11 librettos, set by six different composers (Landi, Virgilio Mazzocchi, Michelangelo and Luigi Rossi, Marazzoli and Abbatini), and three were published as folio scores with engravings representing staging, scenery and special effects. Among the stage designers were the well-known artists Francesco Guitti, G. L. Bernini, G. F. Grimaldi, Cortona and Sacchi. The operas were staged in four different palaces. The so-called Teatro Barberini, in an annexe to the palace in via Quattro Fontane, was internally a partly temporary construction and used for the 1639 *Chi soffre speri*, plays and perhaps again for opera in 1656. It was said to seat 3000 or more. The family had a similar ground-floor hall reserved for plays and opera at their palace in Palestrina. The earlier operas were often given in honour of foreign dignitaries and influenced the dissemination of the taste for opera and Italian music in France, Poland, Vienna and Germany.

Diplomatic visits and sojourns by Taddeo within the papal states occasioned further operatic performances outside Rome, principally in Ferrara and Bologna. Antonio's enthusiasm for opera was shared by Cardinal Mazarin, prime minister of France, and this resulted in their joint production of Luigi Rossi's *Orfeo* in Paris in 1647.

Prince Maffeo's activities, less well-documented, included presenting *Il finto amante* to a libretto by his brother (Palestrina, 1669) and at least four operatic productions between 1678 and 1684 of the domestic, pastoral type of comedy with small casts that were common to Roman private productions after 1675, by contrast with the heroic, Venetian-style spectacles associated with the commercial theatres.

Prince Urbano avidly supported opera. An agent regularly collected music from Venetian operas for him, and 11 volumes of Venetian and Roman opera arias in the Barberini Library bear his arms. He supported the Teatro Capranica, and the librettos of four operas staged there in 1695–6 bear dedications to his second wife, suggesting that he was then a substantial sponsor. His two known private productions were Spagna's *La gelosa di se stessa* (1689) for his sister's wedding and *Dagl'inganni alle nozze* (1714), performed in celebration of his third marriage.

*

A. Ademollo: *I teatri di Roma nel secolo XVII* (Rome, 1888)
R. Rolland: 'La première représentation du *San Alessio*', *RHCM*, ii (1902), 29–36, 74–5
H. Prunières: *L'opéra italien en France avant Lulli* (Paris, 1913)
U. Rolandi: 'La prima comedia musicale rappresentata a Roma nel 1639', *Nuova antologia*, lxii (1927), 523–8
H. Prunières: 'Les musiciens du Cardinal Antonio Barberini',

Mélanges de musicologie offerts à M. L. de Laurencie (Paris, 1933), 117–22
M. Vezzosi: *La commedia musicale romana nel Teatro di Palazzo Barberini* (diss., U. of Rome, 1940)
G. Masson: 'Papal Gifts and Roman Entertainments in Honour of Queen Christina's Arrival', *Analecta reginensia*, i (1966), 244–61
M. Aronberg Lavin: *Seventeenth-Century Barberini Documents and Inventories of Art* (New York, 1975)
F. Hammond: 'Girolamo Frescobaldi and a Decade of Music at Casa Barberini: 1634–1643', *AnMc*, no.19 (1979), 94–124
M. Murata: *Operas for the Papal Court* (Ann Arbor, 1981)
L. Bianconi and T. Walker: 'Production, Consumption and Political Function of Seventeenth-century Opera', *Early Music History*, iv (1984), 209–96
F. Hammond: 'More on Music in Casa Barberini', *Studi musicali*, xiv (1985), 235–61
V. Kapp: 'Das Barberini-Theater und die Bedeutung der römischen Kultur unter Urban VIII', *Literaturwissenschaftliches Jb*, new ser., xxvi (1985), 75–100
P. Waddy: *Seventeenth-Century Roman Palaces: Use and the Art of the Plan* (New York, 1990)

MARGARET MURATA

Barberis, Mansi (*b* Iaşi, 12 March 1899; *d* Bucharest, 10 Oct 1986). Romanian composer. She studied music at the Iaşi Conservatory (1918–22), completing her education in Berlin and in Paris (1926–7) with d'Indy (conducting) and Gallon (composition), then taught singing and the violin in Iaşi and Bucharest. In addition to incidental music for the theatre, she wrote several operas based on Moldavian folklore, which are post-romantic in style, gentle rather than strongly dramatic, and orchestrated in delicate, pastel colours. Barberis also wrote orchestral music (including a piano concerto), chamber and choral works and more than 120 songs; her autobiography, *Din zori pînă în amurg* ('From Daylight until Twilight'), was published in Bucharest in 1989.

Prinţesa îndepărtată [The Distant Princess], 1946 (3, M. Codreanu, after E. Rostand), inc.; rev. 1971 as Domniţa din depărtări [The Princess Far Away] (3, M. Barberis), Iaşi, Romanian Opera, 9 May 1976

Apus de soare [Sunset], 1958 (3, G. Teodorescu, after B. Ştefănescu-Delavrancea), Bucharest, Romanian Opera, 30 Dec 1967; rev. 1968

Kera Duduca, 1963 (television op, 3, A. Ionescu-Arbore, after N. Filimon: *Ciocoii vechi şi noi* [The Old and New Boyars]); rev., Romanian TV, 26 July 1970

Căruţa cu paiaţe [The Cart with Clowns], 1981 (3 acts and 2 tableaux, A. Ionescu-Arbore, after M. Ştefanescu), Iaşi, Romanian Opera, 10 May 1982

VIOREL COSMA

Barbier, (Henri-)Auguste (*b* Paris, 29 April 1805; *d* Nice, 13 Feb 1882). French poet. He was renowned as an acerbic satirist from the time of the July Revolution of 1830, and his election to the Académie Française in 1869 was interpreted as an anti-Imperial gesture. When Berlioz met him in Rome in 1832 he asked for a libretto after *Romeo and Juliet*; Barbier was unwilling to oblige, but later he had a large share in the preparation of the libretto for *Benvenuto Cellini*. In his *Etudes dramatiques* (Paris, 1874) Barbier recorded that Berlioz first asked the distinguished poet Alfred de Vigny (1797–1863) to compose the text; Vigny refused (though he was prevailed on to help at a much later stage) and recommended Léon de Wailly (1804–63), a minor dramatist and a translator of English and Scottish literature. The latter turned for aid, probably with versification, to Barbier. When after many delays and alterations *Cellini* was performed, critics tended to blame the librettists for its failure; in his *Mémoires* Berlioz ostensibly defended them but did not forbear to mention problems over plot and wording. Lachner also composed a setting of *Cellini*, first performed in 1849.

A. Barbier: *Souvenirs personnels et silhouettes contemporaines* (Paris, 1883)
E. Dupuy: 'Alfred de Vigny et Hector Berlioz d'après des lettres inédites', *Revue des deux mondes*, 6th ser., ii (1911), 837–65
P. Citron, ed.: *Mémoires de Hector Berlioz* (Paris, 1969), ii, chap. xlviii
——: *H. Berlioz: correspondance générale*, ii (Paris, 1975), 299–300 [no.473]; iii (Paris, 1978), 184–5 [no.905]

CHRISTOPHER SMITH

Barbier, Jane (*b* *c*1692; *d* London, will proved 9 Dec 1757). English contralto. She first appeared in *Almahide* (November 1711) and the *Spectator* commented on her becoming shyness and her 'agreeable Voice, and just Performance'. She had three seasons with the Italian opera, generally taking male roles, singing in Handel's *Rinaldo*, *Il pastor fido* and *Teseo*. She was Telemachus in Galliard's *Calypso and Telemachus* which had an English libretto by John Hughes, whose poem *The Hue and Cry* described her dark good looks and headstrong nature. From 1714 to 1716 she appeared in masques by Pepusch and then, after a short-lived elopement, sang with John Rich's company in musical afterpieces, pantomimes and English operas. In 1732–3 she was in two new operas by J. C. Smith and played King Henry in Arne's *Rosamond*. Her career petered out after this; in 1737 her death was erroneously reported in the *Gentleman's Magazine*.

BDA; *LS*
R. Fiske: *English Theatre Music in the Eighteenth Century* (London, 1973, 2/1986)
W. Dean and J. Knapp: *Handel's Operas 1704–1726* (Oxford, 1987)

OLIVE BALDWIN, THELMA WILSON

Barbier, Jules (*b* Paris, 8 March 1825; *d* Paris, 16 Jan 1901). French librettist and playwright. His career illustrates the evolution of theatrical taste in Paris through the 19th century. He started by writing little comedies while in his teens, and his early works belong to the tradition of ephemeral entertainments spiced with topicality and enlivened by songs adapted to popular tunes of the day. Gradually he became more ambitious, and his *Jeanne d'Arc* (1873), for instance, in five acts and with incidental music by Gounod, was rated highly by contemporary critics; this play was one of the sources Tchaikovsky used in compiling his own libretto for *The Maid of Orléans* (1881). As a librettist he generally followed the Parisian practice of writing both plays and librettos in collaboration, mostly with the prolific Michel Carré until the latter's death in 1872 and then with his own son, Pierre Barbier (*b* 1854; *d* 1903 or later). With them he responded to the challenge of adapting the significant literary works that some French composers of his period wished to set as operas. He was never again to have a share in so great a success as Gounod's setting of Goethe's *Faust* in 1859. Few operas have been so popular for so long, but the work now appears dated, not least because the libretto trivializes the masterpiece on which it is based, quarrying conventional operatic scenes out of great drama. Passion becomes sentimentality, and great characters are reduced to merely effective roles. The language of the libretto, though clear, lacks the depth, vigour and rhythm of the original. The gulf between Goethe's *Faust* and Barbier's is an indication of the librettist's limitations, and the consequence is a work that is too much of its time to transcend the age in which it was written. Nonetheless he worked with all the major French composers of the day (and with Anton Rubinstein) and was responsible for a succession of adaptations of classics ranging from Corneille's Christian tragedy *Polyeucte* (Gounod, 1878) to Shakespeare's *Romeo and Juliet* (Gounod, 1867) and *Hamlet* (Thomas, 1868), as well as the libretto for Offenbach's *Les contes d'Hoffmann* (1881).

Galathée (oc, with M. Carré), Massé, 1852; *Les noces de Jeannette* (oc, with Carré), Massé, 1853; *Les papillotes de M. Benoist* (oc, with Carré), H. Heber, 1853; *Les sabots de la marquise* (oc, with Carré), E. H. A. Boulanger, 1854; *Le roman de la rose* (oc, with J. Delahaye), P. Pascal, 1854; *Miss Fauvette* (oc, with Carré), Massé, 1855; *L'anneau d'argent* (oc, with Carré), L. P. Deffès, 1855; *Deucalion et Pyrrhe* (oc, with Carré), A. Montfort, 1855; *Les saisons* (oc, with Carré), Massé, 1855

Le chercheur d'esprit (oc, with Carré and E. Foussier), F. Besanzoni, 1856; *Valentine d'Aubigny* (oc, with Carré), Halévy, 1856; *La parade* (opérette, with Brésil), Jonas, 1856; *Psyché* (oc, with Carré), Thomas, 1857; *Le médecin malgré lui* (oc, with Carré, after Molière), Gounod, 1858; *Faust* (opéra dialogué, with Carré, after J. W. von Goethe), Gounod, 1859; *Le pardon de Ploërmel* (oc, with Carré), Meyerbeer, 1859; *Philémon et Baucis* (oc, with Carré), Gounod, 1860

Gil Blas (oc, with Carré), T. A. E. Semet, 1860; *La colombe* (oc, with Carré, after La Fontaine), Gounod, 1860; *L'éventail* (oc, with Carré), Boulanger, 1860; *La statue* (oc, with Carré), Reyer, 1861; *La nuit aux gondoles* (oc, with Carré), Pascal, 1861; *La reine de l'onde* (oc, with Carré), E. F. Péan de la Roche-Jagu, 1862; *La reine de Saba* (with Carré, after G. Nerval), Gounod, 1862; *La fille d'Egypte* (oc, with P.-E.-F. Gille), J. Beer, 1862; *Le cabaret des amours* (oc, with Carré), Pascal, 1862

La guzla de l'émir (with Carré), Bizet, comp. 1862 (T. Dubois, 1873); *Peines d'amour perdues* (with Carré) [music from Mozart: Così fan tutte], 1863; *Fleur de lotus* (oc), Pascal, 1864; *Le mariage de Don Lope* (oc), E. de Hartog, 1865; *Les dragées de Suzette* (oc, with Delahaye), H. Salomon, 1866; *Mignon* (oc, with Carré, after Goethe), Thomas, 1866; *Roméo et Juliette* (with Carré, after W. Shakespeare), Gounod, 1867

Hamlet (with Carré, after Shakespeare), Thomas, 1868; *L'amour mouillé* (with A. de Beauplan), Hartog, 1868; *Don Quichotte* (oc, with Carré, after M. de Cervantes), Boulanger, 1869; *L'amour et son hôte* (oc, with Carré and C. de Beauplan), Hartog, 1872; *L'esclave* (oc, with Foussier and F. J. E. Got), E. Membrée, 1874; *Don Muscarad* (oc, with Carré), Boulanger, 1875; *Les amoureux de Cathérine* (oc, after Erckmann-Chatrian), Maréchal, 1876

Le magnifique (oc), J. Philipot, 1876; *Paul et Virginie* (with Carré, after B. de Saint-Pierre), Massé, 1876; *Le timbre d'argent* (with Carré), Saint-Saëns, 1877; *Graziella* (with Carré), A. Choudens, 1877; *Polyeucte* (with Carré, after P. Corneille), Gounod, 1878; *La reine Berthe*, Joncières, 1878; *Néron*, A. Rubinstein, 1879; *Les contes d'Hoffmann* (with Carré, after E. T. A. Hoffmann), Offenbach, 1881; *La taverne des Trabans* (oc, with Erckmann-Chatrian), Maréchal, 1881

Françoise de Rimini (with Carré, after Dante), Thomas, 1882; *Une nuit de Cléopâtre* (oc, after T. Gautier), Massé, 1885; *Bianca Capello* (with Mestépès), Salomon, 1886; *Les fiançailles de Pasquin* (oc, with L. de Maupertuis), E. dell'Acqua, 1888; *Jehan de Saintré* (oc, with P. Barbier), F. d'Erlanger, 1893; *Lovelace* (with Choudens), H. Hirschmann, 1898; *Daphnis et Chloë* (with P. Barbier), Maréchal, 1899; *Le Tasse* (with P. Barbier), E. D'Harcourt, 1903; *4e dragons* (oc), C. L. Hess, 1904

CHRISTOPHER SMITH

Barbier, Marie-Anne (*b* Orléans, *c*1670; *d* Paris, 1745). French dramatist. After writing four tragedies for the Théâtre Français, she is thought to have collaborated with the Abbé Pellegrin, who gave her advice, on several librettos: *Les fêtes de l'été* (1716), set by Montéclair, and *Le jugement de Pâris* (1718) and *Les plaisirs de la campagne* (1719), both with music by Bertin de la Doué. *Les caractères de l'amour* (1738), for Collin de Blamont, is also attributed to her, but was actually written by Pellegrin. She is credited with 'wit', 'good sense' and 'natural, easy, elegant versification'.

See also PELLEGRIN, SIMON-JOSEPH.

E. Titon du Tillet: *Le Parnasse françois*, suppl. ii (Paris, 1755)
J.-M.-B. Clément and J. de la Porte: *Anecdotes dramatiques* (Paris, 1775)
L.-F. Beffara: *Dictionnaire alphabétique des auteurs* (MS, *F-Po*)

JÉRÔME DE LA GORCE

Barbier, René (**Auguste Ernest**) (*b* Namur, 12 July 1890; *d* Ixelles, Brussels, 24 Dec 1981). Belgian composer. He studied at the conservatories of Brussels and Liège and won the Belgian Prix de Rome in 1920. Professor of harmony at Liège (1920–49) and then Brussels, he also directed the Namur Conservatory and worked as a conductor. In 1968 he was elected to the Belgian Royal Academy. Barbier's music is notable for the richness of its orchestration, recalling Dukas and Wagner. His theatre works, apparently intended to please provincial audiences, include the *comédie lyrique Yvette* (2 tableaux, E. Grésini; Namur, Royal, 4 Jan 1912), the *conte lyrique La fête du vieux tilleul* (2; Namur, July 1913) and the operetta *Une sultane à Paris* (3, M. Henrion; Namur, 4 March 1934).

D. von Volborth-Danys: *CeBeDeM and its Affiliated Composers* (Brussels, 1977–80)

HENRI VANHULST

Barbiere di Siviglia, Il (i) [*Il barbiere di Siviglia, ovvero La precauzione inutile* ('The Barber of Seville, or The Useless Precaution')]. *Dramma giocoso* in four acts by GIOVANNI PAISIELLO to a libretto probably by GIUSEPPE PETROSELLINI after PIERRE-AUGUSTIN BEAUMARCHAIS' play *Le barbier de Séville*; St Petersburg, Hermitage, 15/26 September 1782.

Count Almaviva *nobleman under the assumed name of Lindoro*	tenor
Figaro *a barber*	baritone
Rosina *orphan and pupil of Bartolo*	soprano
Bartolo *doctor, tutor to Rosina*	bass
Don Basilio *music teacher to Rosina*	bass
Lo svegliato *young simpleton, servant to Bartolo*	bass
Giovinetto *servant to Bartolo*	tenor
Alcade	tenor
Notary	tenor

Soldiers in disguise, servants

Setting Don Bartolo's house in Seville in the 18th century

The text is a free adaptation of *Le barbier de Séville*, the first play of Beaumarchais' Figaro trilogy. The second play, *Le mariage de Figaro, ou La folle journée*, was reworked by Da Ponte and set to music by Mozart as *Le nozze di Figaro* (1786). The success of Beaumarchais' *Le barbier de Séville*, performed in St Petersburg in 1780, prompted Paisiello to write an opera based on the play. His dedication to Catherine II refers to the earlier work: 'Since Your Imperial Majesty had a taste of *Le barbier de Séville*, I thought that the same piece set as an opera would not displease you; consequently I have made an extract from it which I have attempted to render as short as possible, conserving ... the expressions of the original piece without adding anything'.

The singers who appeared in the première of the opera included the best of the Italian troupe at the imperial court: Anna Davia de Bernucci (Rosina); Guglielmo Jermolli (Almaviva), who came to St

Petersburg from Eszterháza; G. B. Brocchi (Figaro); Baldassare Marchetti (Bartolo), who had sung in Paisiello's *La discordia fortunata* (1775, Venice); and Luigi Pagnanelli (Don Basilio). After its première Paisiello's opera was snapped up by theatres across Europe, including Naples, Venice, Vienna, Amsterdam, London, Lisbon and Madrid. The work was translated into French, parodied by Framery and performed at Versailles in 1784; two years later it was translated into German by G. F. W. Grossmann as *Der Barbier von Seville, oder Die unnütze Vorsicht* and performed at Cologne. For the Teatro dei Fiorentini, Naples, in 1787, it was reduced to three acts by Giambattista Lorenzi and Paisiello himself reworked some of the original numbers. The new material included Rosina's 'La carta che bramate' (1. xviii), the Act 1 finale and Almaviva's 'Serena il bel sembiante' (3.vi).

The opera met with such acclaim during its initial production in Vienna in August 1783 that it remained in the repertory with performances, alternately in Italian and German, at the Burgtheater, Schönbrunn, Laxenburg, the Theater an der Wien and the Kärntnertortheater. Between 1783 and 1804 it received close to 100 performances in Vienna. Mozart composed 'Schon lacht der holder Frühling' (K580) for inclusion in a German version of the opera in 1789, but the aria, written for his sister-in-law Josepha Hofer, was not used and the orchestration is incomplete.

ACT 1 *A street in front of Bartolo's house* The short, one-movement overture for flutes, oboes, bassoons, horns, trumpets and strings is in binary form and displays a bubbly exuberance through a compilation of short motifs. Count Almaviva, under the assumed name of Lindoro, eagerly awaits a nocturnal assignation with Rosina. He unexpectedly encounters his former servant Figaro, who is in Seville in search of employment. In the opening scene, in which recitative is intermingled with an aria and a duet, Figaro is composing a song, 'Diamo alla noja il bando'. In his 'Scorsi già molti paesi', permeated with syllabic patter phrases, he offers his services to Almaviva. Rosina appears at the window with a letter in hand and is apprehended by her jealous guardian, Bartolo, who is secretly planning to marry her the following day. Rosina lets the letter drop and, while Bartolo runs down to retrieve it, beckons to Lindoro to pick it up. Bartolo looks foolish in his attempt to find it. Figaro, in his capacity as Bartolo's barber, offers to help the lovesick Lindoro get into the house by disguising him as a drunken officer. Once inside, Lindoro will be able to talk to his beloved Rosina.

ACT 2 *Rosina's room* Figaro enters to announce Lindoro's love for Rosina, who is in the process of writing Lindoro a letter. Figaro is interrupted however by the sounds of Bartolo approaching, and he hides in the room. On his way to Rosina's room, Figaro had administered a sleeping potion to one of Bartolo's servants and a sneezing potion to another. In a wonderful trio between Bartolo and the two servants, dominated by slapstick elements, a furious Bartolo is unable to find out who visited the house in his absence because of the constant yawning and sneezing of the two servants. Bartolo receives a visit from Rosina's music teacher, Don Basilio, who brings news of Count Almaviva's presence in Seville, incognito. Basilio advises Bartolo to destroy his rival by maligning him. His aria, 'La calunnia, mio signore', is a clever depiction of the way a rumour grows, spreads and gathers momentum; the strings, which for the most part double and embellish the vocal line, and the rest of the orchestra are involved in the crescendo.

Figaro, who has been a witness to all the events, warns Rosina of Bartolo's nuptial intentions. Disguised as a drunken soldier, Almaviva arrives at Bartolo's house. Inside he informs Rosina of his identity and secretly gives her a letter, while he gives Bartolo an order that his soldiers are to be given a night's lodging. The ensuing trio, involving Rosina, Almaviva and Bartolo, is filled with quick musical exchanges and *double entendres* as Almaviva, playing the drunken soldier, furtively receives a handkerchief and letter from Rosina. The trick quickly begins to wear off as Bartolo grows increasingly suspicious. The act ends with Rosina's E♭ major cavatina 'Giusto ciel', praying for some peace of mind from her jealous guardian.

ACT 3 *Rosina's room* In his continuing attempt to rescue Rosina from Bartolo's household and to steal a few moments alone with her, Almaviva, at Figaro's suggestion, has assumed the disguise of Alonso, a music teacher. In a duet with Bartolo, 'O che umor', Almaviva gains access to Rosina's room by saying that he is a pupil of Basilio and has been sent in his place because Basilio is ill and cannot attend Rosina's music lesson. Through the persistent one-note intonations of his greeting, 'Joy and peace', he is a cause of considerable annoyance to Bartolo. Rosina's ensuing aria, 'Già riede primavera', a piece she is supposedly learning under Alonso's tutorship, is a parody of a rigid da capo aria. Preceded by an extensive orchestral introduction and peppered with ritornellos, it has a lovely *largo* as its middle section, a siciliana with melodic inflections on the flattened second and sixth degrees of the scale.

Figaro steals the key to Rosina's window, and Almaviva promises to come for her that evening. Figaro's intrigues are foiled, however, when Basilio unexpectedly appears. The quintet, 'Don Basilio', is a masterpiece of cross-communication. For various reasons, everyone tries to convince Basilio that he is sick and should go home to rest; totally confused, Basilio agrees and leaves, and his 'buona sera' ('good night'), answered in unison by the other four, is a humorous musical touch. In order to distract Bartolo, Figaro gives him a shave and obstructs his view of Rosina while Almaviva discusses with her the details of their nocturnal escape. The finale ends in general disarray as everyone comments on Bartolo's anger.

ACT 4 *Rosina's room* The final act opens with orchestral music depicting a storm. Bartolo apprehends Rosina, who is waiting to elope with her lover; producing a letter as evidence, he tells her that Alonso is an impostor and agent of Count Almaviva. Still unaware of her lover's identity, and thus believing 'Lindoro' to be unfaithful to her, the gullible and naive Rosina reveals the plans for the secret rendezvous and decides to marry Bartolo. But shortly thereafter Almaviva, who reaches her room by ascending the ladder, reveals his true identity, and a stunned Rosina falls into his arms. The last number, 'Cara sei tu il mio bene', is an extended chain finale. Beginning as a love duet for Rosina and Almaviva, it becomes *allegro moderato* with Figaro's excited entry announcing that the ladder – their only means of escape – has been removed. In the following *andante* with Rosina, Almaviva, Figaro, the Notary and Don Basilio, Almaviva bribes the Notary to perform a hurried marriage ceremony, so that the deed is done by the time Bartolo returns. Two more sections follow, and in the happy ending all the characters convene on stage.

* * *

As an expression of the aesthetic values and tastes of the late 18th century, Paisiello's *Il barbiere di Siviglia* is a masterpiece. It pales, however, in comparison with Rossini's opera of the same title (1816). Paisiello's orchestration is thin and functions for the most part as an accompaniment to the vocal lines; Rossini's is fuller and features writing independent of the vocal lines. Paisiello's opera is not vocally demanding, except in parts of Rosina's role; Rossini's vocal writing is much more brilliant. Rossini's harmonic vocabulary, in the early 19th-century Romantic style, is richer and more imaginative. While Paisiello does not provide layers of complexity in the depiction of his characters, the techniques of musical slapstick, the humorous complications with dialogues at cross-purposes and his facility at depicting comic situations show him to be a superb composer of comic opera in the context of *opera buffa* of his time. GORDANA LAZAREVICH

Barbiere di Siviglia, Il (ii) ('The Barber of Seville') [*Almaviva, ossia L'inutile precauzione* ('Almaviva, or The Useless Precaution')]. *Commedia* in two acts by GIOACHINO ROSSINI to a libretto by CESARE STERBINI after PIERRE-AUGUSTIN BEAUMARCHAIS' *Le barbier de Séville* and the libretto often attributed to GIUSEPPE PETROSELLINI for Giovanni Paisiello's *Il barbiere di Siviglia* (1782, St Petersburg); Rome, Teatro Argentina, 20 February 1816.

Count Almaviva	tenor
Bartolo *a doctor in Seville*	baritone
Rosina *well-to-do ward of Dr Bartolo*	contralto
Figaro *a barber*	baritone
Don Basilio *music teacher, hypocrite*	bass
Fiorello *Count Almaviva's servant*	bass
Ambrogio *Bartolo's servant*	bass
Berta *Bartolo's old housekeeper*	mezzo-soprano
Officer	baritone
Notary	silent

Musicians, soldiers, police officers

Setting Seville, in the 18th century

Beaumarchais' play *Le barbier de Séville* had been used as a subject for opera by a number of composers before Rossini. Of these, by far the most successful was Paisiello; indeed, the continuing popularity of his *Il barbiere di Siviglia* (1782) obliged Rossini to issue a number of public and private disclaimers in which he extolled the virtues of Paisiello's art and affirmed the newness of his own treatment of the Beaumarchais play. This was further underlined by Rossini's choice of an alternative title for his opera, *Almaviva*. The present title was not used until the Bologna revival of August 1816, two months after Paisiello's death. Rossini had signed the contract for the opera on 15 December 1815, just over two months before the first night. Legend has it that he wrote the work in 13 days (nine days, in some versions). However, conceiving a work and writing it are two very different matters and there can be little doubt that Beaumarchais' play (and Paisiello's decorative and conservative treatment of it) had long been in Rossini's sights. The initial launch of the opera was a fiasco. The commissioning impresario Duke Sforza-Cesarini died on 6 February, and the opening night a fortnight later was marred by stage accidents and persistent disruption by followers of Paisiello. Rossini, who directed the first performance, was considerably affected by the furore. Despite contractual obligations, he declined to direct any subsequent performances. He did, however, sanction the introduction into the opera of the now famous overture, originally written for his *Aureliano in Palmira* (1813). One must also assume that he was agreeable to having the first Rosina, Geltrude Righetti-Giorgi, take over Almaviva's lengthy Act 2 bravura aria 'Cessa di più resistere' for the Bologna revival in August 1816. This proved to be a temporary expedient; the following year, Rossini adapted the music for Righetti-Giorgi as part of the finale of *La Cenerentola*.

The singers at the first performance of the opera, in addition to Righetti-Giorgi, included Manuel García as Almaviva (his singer's fee higher than Rossini's commissioning fee), Luigi Zamboni as Figaro, Zenobio Vitarelli as Don Basilio and Bartolomeo Botticelli as Dr Bartolo. Though the opera was by no means the most popular of Rossini's works with contemporary audiences, its fame rapidly spread. In London in March and April 1818 it played 22 times at the King's Theatre, Haymarket; it quickly reached Paris, Berlin and St Petersburg (where Paisiello's version had first been heard in 1782); and it became the first opera to be sung in Italian in New York when the García family troupe visited the Park Theatre in November 1825. To name a selection of interpreters of the main roles in the course of the opera's subsequent stage history would be invidious, given the vast number of singers the leading roles have attracted. However, it is important to record the degree to which singers have sometimes distorted Rossini's intentions. The most serious distortion has been the upward transposition of the role of Rosina, turning her from a lustrous alto into a pert soprano. Parallel to this was a longstanding tradition, now happily largely redundant, of turning the Act 2 'music lesson' into a show-stopping cabaret. Adelina Patti's repertory in this scene included Arditi's 'Il bacio', followed by the Bolero from *I vespri siciliani*, the Shadow Song from *Dinorah* and 'Home Sweet Home'. Melba provided a similar programme, accompanying herself on the piano in the final number. Patti should have known better; as a young girl she gave an unusually florid rendering of 'Una voce poco fa' during one of Rossini's Saturday soirées, only to be met by the composer's polite inquiry, 'Very nice, my dear, and who wrote the piece you have just performed?'. The difficulty of Bartolo's 'A un dottor della mia sorte' led *buffo* basses of the period to opt for a substitute aria by Pietro Romani, 'Manca un foglio', an aria that replaced Rossini's own in many printed editions. Rossini's carefully written recitatives were also replaced by simple *parlato*.

The result of all these changes was to simplify and schematize the opera, turning Rossini's shrewdly drawn realizations of Beaumarchais' characters into stage marionettes. Vittorio Gui's detailed work on original source materials for his 1942 revival of the opera at the Teatro Comunale, Florence, did much to root out the worst mistreatments and adaptations that tradition had imposed on the opera; and since the publication of Alberto Zedda's critical edition (Ricordi) Rossini's original text has been restored to general circulation, and soprano Rosinas are few and far between. But the

Costumes for early productions of Rossini's 'Il barbiere di Siviglia' at the Théâtre Italien, Paris: Rosina (sung by Henriette Sontag for the first time in 1826), Don Basilio (sung by Giuseppe de Begnis at the Paris première in 1819; centre) and Figaro (sung by Vincenzo-Felice Santini); engravings from A. Martinet, 'La petite galerie dramatique'

tradition of treating *Il barbiere* as a vulgar romp or an impersonal farce rather than a comedy of character has not entirely vanished.

ACT 1.i *A square in Seville* Dr Bartolo lives in a secluded piazza in a household that consists of two servants and his wealthy young ward, Rosina. Determined to marry her himself, Bartolo keeps her very much under lock and key. Unfortunately for him, she has already attracted the attention of a young Spanish nobleman, Count Almaviva. He has followed her from Madrid, disguised as the student Lindoro, for if Rosina is ever to be the Countess Almaviva, it must be for himself and not for his land and money. As the curtain rises, it is shortly before dawn and the Count is preparing to serenade Rosina, aided by Fiorello and a band of musicians. The serenade 'Ecco, ridente in cielo' is musically eloquent but strategically ineffective. Frustrated by Rosina's lack of response, Almaviva pays off the musicians – even their noisy gratitude fails to rouse the household – and determines to keep vigil alone.

Suddenly, the voice of a rumbustious, roistering sort of fellow is heard in the distance. It is Figaro, barber and general factotum to the city of Seville. As he explains in his famous cavatina 'Largo al factotum della città', he is in demand everywhere. And we can believe it. The explosive energy of the music establishes Figaro as a typically Rossinian creation full of impulse and concentrated energy. Figaro and Almaviva, it now turns out, have met before. Almaviva explains why he is in Seville incognito and is overjoyed to discover that Figaro is barber, wigmaker, surgeon, gardener, apothecary, vet – in short, Jack-of-all-trades – to the Bartolo household. Figaro is also able to tell him that Rosina is Bartolo's ward, not his daughter. While they are talking, Rosina appears on the balcony with a note she has written to the handsome young stranger who has been visiting the square. Unfortunately, her guardian is just behind her; but amid much kerfuffle and a good deal of excited coming and going by Dr Bartolo, the note floats safely down to the waiting Almaviva. Alarmed by his ward's furtive behaviour, Bartolo determines to expedite his marriage plans, leaving instructions that while he is away no one, not even the music teacher Don Basilio, should be admitted to the house.

With Rosina still hovering behind the shutters, Figaro persuades Almaviva to answer her note in another serenade. In Beaumarchais' play, Almaviva makes clear how nervous he is about his guitar-playing. This is omitted in Sterbini's libretto but the number he and Rossini concocted brilliantly captures Almaviva's unease. Though the minor-key 'Se il mio nome' can be sung as a piece of fine bel canto (De Lucia made some famous recordings of it), it is also a telling portrait of a man sick with nerves. Sterbini's verse lines are irregular and deliberately awkward, and Rossini's music is also awkward in key and in the lie of the phrasing and the vocal line. The number is almost a parody of the conventional aubade, and as such is precisely the kind of effect we look for in vain in Paisiello's much blander setting. Rosina is about to respond to the serenade when she is interrupted, making it obvious to Figaro and Almaviva that some kind of entry to the house must be effected. Stimulated by the promise of gold from Almaviva (duet, 'All'idea di quel metallo'), Figaro helps formulate a plot. A regiment is due in town that day and, posing as a soldier, the Count will ask at the house for a billet. To help the ploy further, the Count will also act drunk. As they are about to part, Almaviva calls Figaro back: 'Where can I find you? Where's your shop?'. In Paisiello's setting this is the only section of the scene to be given extended musical treatment. With Rossini it comes as a dazzling and increasingly exciting cabaletta-like Allegro that rounds off a multisection movement which began, *allegro maestoso*, with Figaro's contemplation of his reward and develops with a particularly fine interweaving of rapid patter and accompanied recitatives.

1.ii *A room in Dr Bartolo's house* Thrilled by the sound of her admirer's voice, Rosina launches into her cavatina 'Una voce poco fa'. Verdi once referred to Rossini's 'accuracy of declamation', a point that is well illustrated in this cavatina, which Rossini adapted from a smooth-running aria for Queen Elizabeth in his *Elisabetta, regina d'Inghilterra* (1815). In its new context, it is a keenly pointed, sharply observed portrait in words and music of a beguiling, vixenish creature. Rosina's minatory pointing of the word 'ma' – 'but' – is enough to send a shiver down any man's spine.

Figaro has meanwhile inveigled his way into the house and had a brief meeting with Rosina. Bartolo, angry with Figaro's busybodying and disrespect, quizzes Rosina about the meeting; he also quizzes his servants – Berta who is always sneezing and Ambrogio who is forever yawning, a delightful scene in Paisiello that Rossini does not even attempt to challenge. When the musician-cum-marriage-broker Don Basilio arrives, Bartolo informs him of the new urgency in the situation. Basilio agrees; the Count Almaviva is said to be in Seville and it may be prudent to run him out of the town on a tide of slander. Dr Bartolo is not so sure about this, but Basilio insists in his aria 'La calunnia è un venticello': 'calumny is a little breeze, a gentle zephyr which insensibly, subtly, lightly and sweetly begins to whisper ... to gather force ... and finally explodes like a cannon'. Here Rossini gratefully deploys Beaumarchais' original list of dynamic extremes – *piano*, *pianissimo*, *rinforzando*, the famous *crescendo* itself – and also revels in musical onomatopoeia as the buzzing sound of scandal makes its poisonous progress through the community. Figaro having overheard the conversation, now seeks out Rosina to tease her a little and prepare the ground for the entrance of her mystery lover, the penniless Lindoro. But Figaro soon discovers, in their duet 'Dunque io son', that Rosina is already several moves into the game. 'Donne, donne, eterni Dei' he exclaims – 'Women, women, eternal gods, who can attempt to make you out?'.

Dr Bartolo is equally maddened and intoxicated by Rosina's wiles, but his dignity is offended when her protestations of innocence fail to square with inky fingers, sharpened quills and missing sheets of paper. In his aria 'A un dottor della mia sorte', he advises Rosina to dream up better excuses when dealing with a man of his intellect. The aria is in two parts: a grandiloquent Andante maestoso and a lightning Allegro vivace which, as befits the doctor's academic status, is in full sonata form. Stage directors underestimate Rossini's Dr Bartolo at their peril. The first act ends with Almaviva's appearance in Bartolo's house disguised as the drunken officer. This is one of the most powerful and amusing of all Rossini's first-act finales, Beethovenian in the sheer disruptiveness of its comic energies. This is particularly evident in Almaviva's initial appearance and in the violence of his response when Bartolo unearths his exemption from the military billet. Equally, there are some surprising interludes amid the mayhem, such as the sly pathos of Rosina's 'sempre un' istoria' as she bewails her sad fate. The arrival of Basilio and Figaro adds to the confusion and with the appearance of the local militia there is a crazed Vivace: a dazzling canonic passage in which the characters, locked by the music into febrile acts of imitation, vehemently protest to the officers about each other's behaviour. An attempt to arrest Almaviva is aborted when he passes a document to the officer in charge, leaving everyone, and not least Dr Bartolo, totally confused about the day's events.

ACT 2 *A music room in Dr Bartolo's house with a window and balcony nearby* Almaviva presents himself to Dr Bartolo in a new disguise: as 'Don Alonso', music-teacher, and pupil of the 'indisposed' Don Basilio. Like Paisiello, Rossini gives Don Alonso a solemn nasal whine for his aria of greeting 'Pace e gioia sia con voi!', but Rossini's setting is funnier, with excruciating violin colours and lightning-quick parlando outbursts from the double-dealing Count. Further to gain Bartolo's confidence, Don Alonso reveals that he has intercepted a note from Count Almaviva to Rosina. With this note as evidence, he hopes to use his 'music lesson' to convince Rosina of the Count's duplicity. Bartolo falls for the story and hurries off to fetch Rosina to her lesson. She performs a rondo from *L'inutile precauzione* ('The Useless Precaution') and while Bartolo dozes she and 'Lindoro' express their mutual affection. Bartolo awakes and, bored by contemporary music, performs an example of the music of his youth, 'Quando mi sei vicina'.

Figaro now arrives to shave Bartolo. When Bartolo sends him out to fetch shaving materials, Figaro takes the opportunity to steal the key to the balcony. He then smashes a pile of glass and crockery to lure the fretful Bartolo away from the music-room. All is going to plan when Don Basilio appears. But he is offered money and in a wittily crafted quintet, 'Buona sera, mio signore', he accepts the conspirators' story that he is suffering from scarlet fever, and makes a lugubrious withdrawal. The shaving of Bartolo now resumes to the accompaniment of one of Rossini's frothiest allegros while Rosina is alerted to Figaro's plot to spirit the lovers away at midnight. But Bartolo is not entirely off his guard. Creeping over to the piano, he overhears Almaviva talk of disguise. 'Il suo travestimento!' exclaims Bartolo, and once more the game is temporarily up for the lovers.

Berta is left to comment on the foolishness of old men wanting to marry young wives, 'Il vecchiotto cerca moglie'. When Dr Bartolo discovers that Don Basilio has never heard of Don Alonso he determines to marry Rosina straight away. To help advance his case, he presents Rosina with her letter to Lindoro, claiming that he obtained it from a certain Count Almaviva on whose behalf Lindoro is clearly acting. A storm rages. As it settles, Figaro and Almaviva make their entrance over the balcony only to be confronted by Rosina, furious at being 'used' by Lindoro to further the Count's wicked plans. Almaviva is forced to reveal his true identity which Rosina accepts without demur. Time now being of the essence, Figaro becomes increasingly frustrated (trio, 'Ah! qual colpo') as the lovers bill and coo together. Figaro's mockery is conveyed by a simple echo effect at the end of the lover's simpering phrases. Here Rossini redeploys ideas originally used in his early cantata *Egle ed Irene* to ingenious comic effect. There is also another of Rossini's sophisticated musical jokes as the lovers' delay is prolonged by the duet's need to end with a fully worked-out cabaletta. When they finally try to leave, the ladder has been removed from the balcony. But the situation is saved by Basilio arriving with the notary Dr Bartolo has hastily engaged. Bribed with a valuable ring and threatened with a couple of bullets through the head, Basilio agrees to stand witness to the marriage of Rosina and Almaviva. Bartolo arrives with soldiers, but it is too late. It is vain to resist, Almaviva tells him, in the lengthy and expendable aria 'Cessa di più resistere'. Bartolo accepts that he has been beaten and the opera ends with a jaunty vaudeville in which Figaro, Rosina and the Count celebrate their good fortune with the company at large.

* * *

In earlier years, the comic radicalism of Rossini's setting daunted some contemporary audiences who had been brought up, not on works like *Falstaff*, *Gianni Schicchi* and *Albert Herring*, but on the more genteel offerings of Cimarosa, Paisiello and others. Rossini's *Il barbiere* came, in Lord Derwent's phrase, as 'a nervous outburst of vitality', a quality that clearly commended the work to Beethoven (who allegedly said to Rossini 'Be sure to write more *Barbers*!') and to Verdi. Beyond the physical impact of a piece like Figaro's 'Largo al factotum' there is Rossini's ear for vocal and instrumental timbres of a peculiar astringency and brilliance, his quick-witted word-setting, and his mastery of large musical forms with their often brilliant and explosive internal variations. Add to that what Verdi called the opera's 'abundance of true musical ideas', and the reasons for the work's longer-term emergence as Rossini's most popular *opera buffa* are not hard to find.

RICHARD OSBORNE

Barbieri, Antonio (*b* Reggio Emilia; *fl* 1720–43). Italian tenor. From 1720 to 1731 (at least) he was in the service of the Landgrave of Hesse-Darmstadt, governor of Mantua, where he made his earliest known appearance, in the première of Vivaldi's *Candace* (1720). The composer seems then to have engaged him for Venice, where he sang in 23 operas from 1720 to 1738. He became well known throughout Italy, appearing in Reggio (1720), Rome (from 1724), Parma and Florence (both 1725 and 1734–5), Naples (1727–9) and Turin (1739–40). In 1731 he sang at Pavia in Vivaldi's *Farnace* alongside his wife, Livia Bassi Barbieri, who also performed at Venice and Florence in 1734–5; it is not known whether he was related to the contralto Santi Barbieri who appeared in eight operas at Florence from 1730 to 1743. Later he was *maestro di maniera* at the Ospedale dei Mendicanti, Venice, from 1736 until (apparently) 1767 and at the Derelitti, 1741–3.

COLIN TIMMS

Barbieri [de Barbieri], **Carlo Emanuele** (*b* Genoa, 22 Oct 1822; *d* Pest, 28 Sept 1867). Italian conductor and composer. He received his musical training at the Naples Conservatory, studying singing with Crescentini and composition with Mercadante. Although he wrote operas and vaudevilles and some sacred music, he was known principally as a theatre conductor in central and northern Europe. From 1844 he conducted at the Carltheater in Vienna for two years, also serving as vocal coach at the Kärntnertortheater and composing music for several vaudevilles and pantomimes. He travelled extensively as an opera conductor: to Berlin, for the Königstädter Theater, in 1847–8, Dresden in 1849, Hamburg in 1850, Bremen in 1853, and Rio de Janeiro in 1854. From 1856 to 1862 he lived in Vienna, conducting in various Austrian cities, and from 1862 to 1867 he was conductor at the National Theatre in Buda. Barbieri's one important opera, *Perdita* (1865), is a free adaptation of Shakespeare's *The Winter's Tale*. Its musical structure is continuous (without separable numbers) in the Wagnerian manner, but the music itself is old-fashioned: for example, the large orchestra usually accompanies or doubles the voices. The overture is a potpourri of tunes from the opera and the mostly diatonic melodies are frequently in lilting 6/8. The choruses are simple and squarely homophonic.

La casa dei matti (ob, 2), Vienna, Kärntnertor, 16 Sept 1843
Doktor und Friseur (posse, prol., 2, F. Kaiser), Vienna, An der Wien, 25 Jan 1845
Finette, das Gärtnermädchen, oder Mit dem Feuer spielen ist gefährlich (vaudeville, 3, I. F. Castelli, after E. Scribe), Vienna, An der Wien, 15 Feb 1845
Die Pariserin (operetta, 2), Vienna, An der Wien, 28 March 1845 [music arranged from Carl Maria von Weber]
Braut, Gattin und Witwe in einer Stunde (melodrama, 4), Vienna, An der Wien, 30 Nov 1845
Der Ritter von der Stande, oder Die beiden Josefinen (vaudeville, 2, K. Braun, after a French text), Vienna, Leopoldstrasse, 23 March 1846
Der Lumpensamler von Paris (melodrama, 5, F. Pyat and W. H. Claepius), Berlin, Königstädter, 14 Oct 1847
Cristoforo Colombo (4, F. Romani), Berlin, Königstädter, 20 Dec 1848
Nisida, die Perle von Procida (3, J. Krüger), Hamburg, 20 Sept 1852
Arabella (3, A. de Lauzières), Turin, Angennes, 20 May 1857
Carlo und Carline (operetta, 3, E. Nessl), Vienna, An der Wien, 21 March 1859; as Harlekin, Vienna, An der Wien, 11 April 1859
Perdita, oder Ein Wintermärchen (4, K. Gross, after W. Shakespeare: *The Winter's Tale*), Leipzig, Opernhaus, 11 Jan 1865
Der Herr Hauptmann (operetta, 1, Nessl), Vienna, Carl, 21 Nov 1865
Die Abenteuer auf Vorposten, oder Zuanen in Algier (operetta, 1, Nessl), Vienna, Harmonie, 20 Jan 1866
Bursche vom Leder (operetta, 1, K. Wolff), Vienna, Harmonie, 7 April 1866
Die Federschlange (operetta, 1, F. Zell), Pest, Deutsches, 16 Feb 1867

MARVIN TARTAK

Barbieri, Fedora (*b* Trieste, 4 June 1920). Italian mezzo-soprano. She studied at Trieste with Luigi Toffolo and in Florence, where she made her début in 1940 as Fidalma (*Il matrimonio segreto*). At the Maggio Musicale in 1941 she sang Dariola in Alfano's *Don Juan de Mañara*, and also appeared in Monteverdi revivals. She sang regularly at La Scala from 1942, and at the Metropolitan (début in 1950 as Eboli in *Don Carlos*), where she gave 95 performances of 11 roles from 1950 into the 1970s. She first visited England with the Scala company in 1950, as Mistress Quickly and in Verdi's *Requiem*; she returned to Covent Garden in 1957–8 and in 1964. Her voice, of fine quality and considerable power, was well suited to the dramatic mezzo-soprano parts of Verdi and also capable of majestic calm in the music of Monteverdi, Pergolesi and Gluck.

*

GV (E. Gara; R. Vegeto)
A. Natan: 'Barbieri, Fedora', *Primadonna: Lob der Stimmen* (Basle, 1962) [with discography]

HAROLD ROSENTHAL, DESMOND SHAWE-TAYLOR

Barbieri, Francisco Asenjo (*b* Madrid, 3 Aug 1823; *d* Madrid, 17 Feb 1894). Spanish composer and musicologist. Initially intended for medicine and then for engineering, he frequented the performances of Italian opera at the Teatro de la Cruz, of which his uncle was manager, and entered the Madrid Conservatory in 1837, studying the piano and clarinet, singing and composition. After his father died and his mother moved from Madrid, he led a varied existence for some years as a clarinettist in a military band and in theatre orchestras, a music copyist, chorus master and prompter to a travelling company, a singer and singing teacher and a composer of songs and dance music. In 1846 he settled in Madrid, where he became music critic of *La ilustración*, founded the periodical *La España musical* and campaigned for opera (his own *Il buontempone*, to an Italian libretto, composed in 1847, was not staged). His first zarzuela, *Gloria y peluca*, was sufficiently well received for him to pursue this genre with enthusiasm, and in 1851 he created a sensation with the three-act *Jugar con fuego* (previous zarzuelas had had two acts at the most), which saved the future of the Teatro del Circo, newly acquired by a group of composers whom it stimulated to follow his example. Together with Arrieta, Gaztambide and others, he organized a society to build a theatre to be devoted to zarzuelas: this opened in 1856 and witnessed a long series of his successes.

In all, Barbieri wrote over 70 zarzuelas, some of which – notably *Jugar con fuego*, *Pan y toros* and *El barberillo de Lavapiés* – quickly became classics of the repertory and are still played today. Inevitably much influenced at first by Italian models, both melodically and in construction (e.g. the large-scale second-act finale of *Jugar con fuego*), his works became increasingly Hispanic in character, not merely by the inclusion of national dances but also in their whole idiom and ethos. His other compositions have been forgotten, but he was also active in other spheres. In 1859 he founded an orchestra (later to develop into the Sociedad de conciertos de Madrid) which presented, besides works of Mozart, Beethoven, Weber and others, the first Wagner extract to be heard in Madrid (the overture to *Tannhäuser*); for the year 1869 he was conductor at the Teatro Real. He helped to found the Sociedad de bibliofilos españoles and carried out extensive research into Spanish musical history, assembling a large library of scores and documents (later bequeathed to the Biblioteca Nacional) and in 1890 transcribed and published the *Cancionero musical de los siglos XV y XVI*. He was professor of music history at the Madrid Conservatory and wrote articles and books, of which the most important is *El Teatro Real y el Teatro de la Zarzuela* (Madrid, 1877). He received many honours, and in 1892 was made a member of the Royal Spanish Academy, the first musician to be elected to it.

See also BARBERILLO DE LAVAPIÉS, EL; *JUGAR CON FUEGO*; and *PAN Y TOROS*.

all zarzuelas; first performed in Madrid

MDC – *Teatro del Circo* MDV – *Teatro des Variedades*
MDZ – *Teatro de la Zarzuela*

Gloria y peluca (1, V. del Valle), MDV, 9 March 1850; Tramoya (1, L. Olona), Basilios, 27 June 1850; Escenas en Chamberi (1, J. Olona), MDV, 19 Nov 1850, collab. Oudrid, Hernando and Gaztambide; La picaresca (2, Doncel y Asquerina), MDC, 29 March 1851, collab. Gaztambide; Jugar con fuego (3, V. de la Vega), MDC, 6 Oct 1851; Por seguir a una mujer (4, L. Olona), MDC, 24 Dec 1851, collab. Gaztambide, Inzenga, Hernando and Oudrid; La hechicera (3, R. Rubi), MDC, 24 April 1852

El Manzanares (1, M. Pina), MDC, 19 June 1852; Gracias a Dios que está puesta la mesa (1, L. Olona), MDC, 24 Dec 1852; La espada de Bernardo (3, A. García Gutiérrez), MDC, 14 Jan 1853; El Marqués de Caravaca (2, Vega), MDC, 12 April 1853; Don Simplicio Bobadilla (3, M. and V. Tamayo y Baus), MDC, 7 May 1853, collab. Gaztambide, Inzenga and Hernando; Galanteos en Venecia (3, L. Olona), MDC, 24 Dec 1853

Un día de reinado (3, García Gutiérrez and L. Olona), MDC, 11 Feb 1854, collab. Gaztambide, Inzenga and Oudrid; Aventura de un cantante (1, G. de Alba), MDC, 16 April 1854; Los diamantes de la corona (3, F. Camprodón, after E. Scribe), MDC, 15 Sept 1854; La cola del diablo (L. Olona), MDC, 1854, collab. M. S. Allu and Oudrid; Mis dos mujeres (3, L. Olona), 26 March 1855; Los dos ciegos (1, L. Olona), MDC, 25 Oct 1855; El Vizconde (1, Camprodón), MDC, 1 Dec 1855

El sargento Federico (4, L. Olona), MDC, 22 Dec 1855, collab. Gaztambide; Entre dos aguas (3, A. Hurtado), MDC, 4 April 1856, collab. Gaztambide; Gato por liebre (1, Hurtado and L. Olona), MDC, 21 June 1856; La zarzuela (1), MDZ, 10 Oct 1856, collab. P. E. Arrieta and Gaztambide; El diablo en el poder (3, Camprodón), MDZ, 11 Dec 1856; El relámpago (3, Camprodón), MDZ, 15 Oct 1857; Por derecha de conquista (1, Camprodón), MDZ, 5 Feb 1858

Amar sin conocer (3, L. Olona), MDZ, 24 April 1858, collab. Gaztambide; Un caballero particular (1, C. Frontaura), MDZ, 28 June 1858; El robo de las Sabinas (2, García Gutiérrez), MDZ, 17 Feb 1859; El niño (1, Pina), MDZ, 15 June 1859; Compromisos del no ver (1, Pina), MDZ, 14 Oct 1859; Entre mi mujer y el negro (2, L. Olona), MDZ, 14 Oct 1859; Un tesoro escondido (3, Vega), MDZ, 19 Nov 1861; Los herederos (1, F. del Rio), MDZ, 5 June 1862

El secreto de una dama (3, L. Ribera), MDZ, 20 Dec 1862; Dos pichones del Turia (1, R. M. Lieru), MDZ, 28 Nov 1863; Pan y toros (3, J. Picón), MDZ, 22 Dec 1864; Gibraltar en 1890 (1, Picón), MDZ, 22 Jan 1866; El rábano por las hojas (1, R. Puente y Branas), MDZ, 22 Jan 1866; Revista de un muerto (1), MDC, 3 Feb 1866, collab. J. Rogel; De tejas arriba (1, M. Gil), MDV, 22 Dec 1866; El pavo de Navidad (1, Puente y Branas), MDV, 24 Dec 1866

El pan de la boda (2, Camprodón), MDC, 24 Oct 1868; El soprano (1, M. Pastorfido), MDZ, 23 Feb 1869; Robinson (3, R. Santisteban), MDC, 18 March 1870; Los holgazanes (3, Picón), MDZ, 25 March 1871; Don Pacifico (3, A. M. Segovia), MDZ, 14 Oct 1871; El hombre es débil (1, Pina), MDZ, 14 Oct 1871; El tributo de las cien doncellas (3, Santisteban), MDZ, 7 Nov 1872; Sueños de oro (3, L. M. de Larra), MDZ, 21 Dec 1872; El proceso del cancán (2, Lieru), Buen Retiro, 10 July 1873

Los comediantes de antaño (2, Pina), MDZ, 13 Feb 1874; La despedida (1, Santisteban), Real, March 1874; El domador de fieras (1, Ramos Carrión and C. Arana), MDZ, 14 April 1874; El testamento azul (3, L. Amalfi), Buen Retiro, 20 or 28 July 1874, collab. R. Aceves and Oudrid; El barberillo de Lavapiés (3, Larra), MDZ, 18 Dec 1874; Chorizos y polacos (3, Larra), Príncipe Alfonso, 18 Aug 1875; La vuelta al mundo (3, Larra), MDC, 18 Aug 1875, collab. Rogel

Juan de Urbina (3, Larra), MDZ, 6 Oct 1876; La Confitera (1, Pina), Comedia, 22 Dec 1876; Artistas para la Habana (1, Lieru), Comedia, 10 April 1877; El loro y la lechuza (1, M. Fernandez), Español, 23 Dec 1877; Los carboneros (1, Pina), Comedia, Dec 1877; El triste Chactas (1, Barrera), Eslava, 9 March 1878; El diablo conjuelo (3, Ramos Carrión and P. Dominguez), Príncipe Alfonso, 18 June 1878; Los chichones (1, Pina), Comedia, 23 Dec 1879

¡Ojo a la niñera! (1, Santisteban), Comedia, 24 Dec 1879; Anda, valiente (1, Pina), Comedia, 13 Dec 1880; A Sevilla por todo (2, J. de Burgos), Comedia, 22 Dec 1880; La filoxera (1, Pina), Lara, 23 Dec 1882; De Getafe al Paraíso [La familia del tío Maroma] (2, R. de la Vega), MDV, 5 Jan 1883; Hoy sale, hoy (1, Burgos and Dominguez), Eslava, 13 Sept 1884, collab. F. Chueca, Hernandez and Nieto [some sources suggest first perf. Variedades, 16 Jan 1884]; Los fusileros (2, Dominguez), Jovellanos, Dec 1884; Novillos en Polvoranca (3, Vega), MDV, 1885; El señor Luis el tumbón (1), 1891

*

A. Peña y Goñi: *Nuestros músicos: Barbieri* (Madrid, 1875)
——: *La ópera española y la música dramática en el siglo XIX* (Madrid, 1881; abridged by E. Rincón as *España desde la ópera a la zarzuela*, 1967)
E. Cotarelo y Mori: 'Ensayo histórico sobre la zarzuela, ó sea el drama lirico español desde su origen a fines del siglo XIX', *Boletín de la Real Academia Española*, xix–xxiii (1932–6); pubd separately as *Historia de la zarzuela, ó sea el drama lírico* (Madrid, 1934)
G. Chase: 'Barbieri and the Spanish zarzuela', *ML*, xx (1939), 32–9
A. Martinez Olmedilla: *El maestro Barbieri y su tiempo* (Madrid, 1941)
A. Salcedo: *Francisco Asenjo Barbieri: su vida y su obra* (Madrid, n.d.)

LIONEL SALTER

Barbieri, Giovan Domenico (*b* ?Parma, *c*1674; *d* *c*1740). Italian stage designer. A pupil of Ferdinando Galli-Bibiena, he was active as a painter of perspective scenery in many theatres of northern Italy: the Teatro Malvezzi, Bologna, Teatro Regio, Turin, Teatro di S Agostino, Genoa and the Teatro Omodeo, Pavia. In Milan he worked sporadically from 1709 (Gasparini's *Amor generoso* at the Teatro delle Commedie) and then

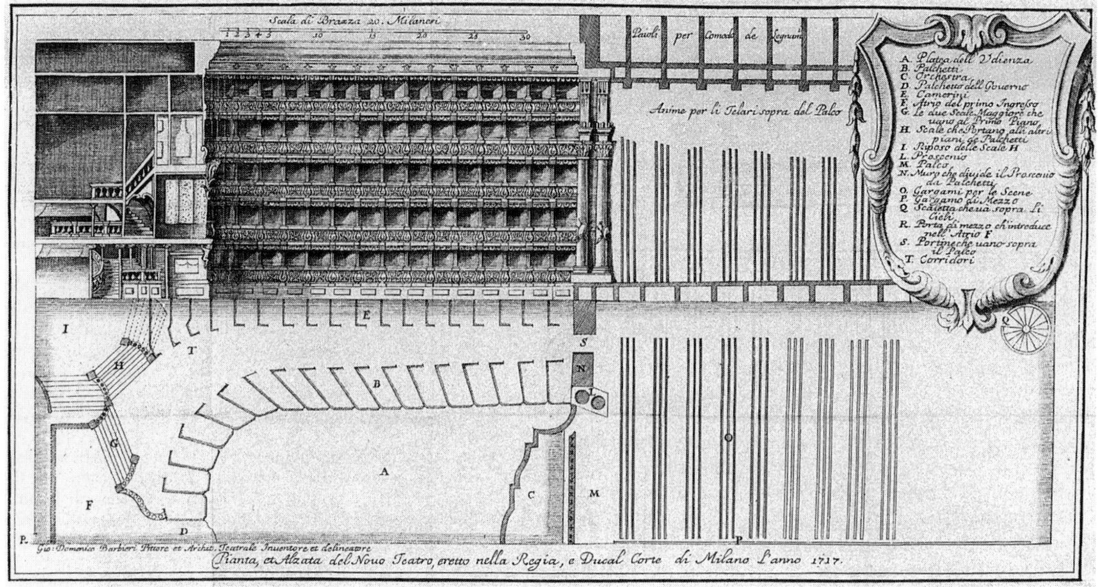

Plan and cross-section of the interior of the Regio Ducal Teatro, Milan designed by Giovan Domenico Barbieri: engraving, 1717, from S. Latuada, 'Descrizione di Milano', ii (Milan, 1738)

continuously from 1722 to 1736, mostly at the Regio Ducal Teatro where his productions included Gasparini's *Flavio Anicio Olibrio* (1722) and Broschi's *Adriano in Siria* (1736). His usual collaborator as decorator and figure painter was another of Galli-Bibiena's pupils, Giovan Battista Medici (who in librettos of 1737–42 is named alone or with Fabrizio Galliari). Barbieri was also a theatre architect and designed the interior of the Regio Ducal, inaugurated on 26 December 1717 and destroyed by fire in 1776. Its appearance is known from an autograph drawing (Milan, Civica Raccolta delle stampe A. Bertarelli) and two engravings (reproduced by Latuada; see illustration): the auditorium was U-shaped, with five tiers each of 36 boxes. There is no reliable pictorial evidence for Barbieri's long career as a stage designer.

S. Latuada: *Descrizione di Milano*, ii (Milan, 1738)
F. S. Quadrio: *Della storia e della ragione d'ogni poesia*, iii/2 (Milan, 1744)
R. Gironi: 'Sulle decorazioni sceniche ed in ispezie su quelle dell'Imp. R. Teatro alla Scala in Milano', in G. Ferrario: *Storia e descrizione de' principali teatri* (Milan, 1830), 292–314
A. Paglicci-Brozzi: *Il Regio Ducal Teatro di Milano nel secolo XVIII* (Milan, 1893–4)
C. A. Vianello: *Teatri, spettacoli, musiche a Milano nei secoli scorsi* (Milan, 1941)
D. Manzella and E. Pozzi: *I teatri di Milano* (Milan, 1971)
D. Lenzi: 'Giovan Domenico Barbieri', *L'arte del Settecento emiliano. Architettura, scenografia, pittura di paesaggio* (Bologna, 1979), 246–7 [exhibition catalogue]
G. Ricci: 'Nuovo Regio Ducal Teatro a Milano', ibid, 174–6

MERCEDES VIALE FERRERO

Barbieri-Nini, Marianna (*b* Florence, 18 Feb 1818; *d* Florence, 27 Nov 1887). Italian soprano. After study with Luigi Barbieri, Pasta and Vaccai, in 1840 she made a disastrous first appearance at La Scala in Donizetti's *Belisario*. Shortly afterwards she broke her contract with the impresario Merelli and joined Lanari's troupe in Florence. Here she made a second, this time triumphant, début in Donizetti's *Lucrezia Borgia*. For the next 15 years she sang with great success throughout Italy and in Barcelona, Madrid and Paris. She was a highly dramatic singer with a powerful voice, particularly effective in the title roles of Donizetti's *Anna Bolena* and Rossini's *Semiramide*. She appeared in the first performances of three Verdi operas, singing Lucrezia in *I due Foscari* (1844, Rome), Lady Macbeth (1847, Florence) and Gulnara in *Il corsaro* (1848, Trieste). She retired in 1856. ELIZABETH FORBES

Barbier von Bagdad, Der ('The Barber of Baghdad'). *Komische Oper* in two acts by PETER CORNELIUS (i) to his own libretto after a story from *The Thousand and One Nights*; Weimar, Hoftheater, 15 December 1858.

The Caliph	baritone
Baba Mustapha *a Cadi*	tenor
Margiana *his daughter*	soprano
Bostana *a relative of the Cadi*	mezzo-soprano
Nureddin	tenor
Abul Hassan Ali Ebn Bekar *a barber*	bass
First Muezzin	bass
Second Muezzin	tenor
Third Muezzin	tenor

Servants of Nureddin, friends of the Cadi, wailing women, followers of the Caliph, people of Baghdad

Setting Baghdad in ancient times

Cornelius began writing the text of *Der Barbier von Bagdad* in September 1855. His friend and patron Liszt initially disapproved of the subject matter, but later became intimately involved with the work's evolution. The text was finished in November 1856 and the music in February 1858. The première in Weimar succeeded musically, with Liszt conducting, Roth appearing as the Barber, Caspari as Nureddin and Rosa von Milde-Agthe as Margiana, but the occasion was marred by a demonstration against the conductor; Liszt left his position at Weimar and the opera was never performed again in Cornelius's lifetime.

Der Barbier remained closely associated with Liszt. It was he who orchestrated the new overture that Cornelius wrote shortly before his death, and who subsequently interested Felix Mottl in the work. Mottl first conducted his shortened and revised form of the opera in Karlsruhe on 1 February 1881. Hermann Levi restored some of the cut material for the Munich première, on 15 October 1885, and it was this version that Kahnt published in Leipzig in 1886. Despite these efforts to ensure the opera's popularity, it never really gained an audience until Max Hasse successfully reintroduced the original version at the Weimar Hoftheater on 10 June 1904. Since then it has retained a place, if only a minor one, in German opera houses. It opened the Munich opera festival in 1984, with Kurt Moll as the Barber, Lucia Popp as Margiana and Peter Seiffert as Nureddin. The first recording was made by Erich Leinsdorf in 1956, with Czerwenka, Schwarzkopf and Gedda; the BBC broadcast the opera in 1965 with Forbes Robinson, April Cantelo and Gerald English.

ACT 1 *Nureddin's house* Cornelius's second overture introduces many of the opera's themes, whereas the original one restricts itself to setting the mood, mingling lyrical and burlesque elements. As the curtain rises, Nureddin reclines in bed while his servants serenade him ('Sanfter Schlummer'); lingering chromaticism underlines their fear that his death from unrequited love is near. He responds with an incongruously healthy outpouring to his Margiana ('Komm deine Blumen'). As the servants imagine him in paradise ('In Strahlen ew'gen Lichts'), their song's tripping rhythms also suggest earthly rather than heavenly joys, joining Nureddin's love song in reassuring harmony.

Left alone, Nureddin indulges his feelings in one of the opera's few uninterrupted aria sections ('Vor deinem Fenster'). The mood changes abruptly at the entrance of Bostana, her speech punctuated by garrulous wind figures as she reveals that Margiana has agreed to a meeting. In his excitement Nureddin joins in with her comically exaggerated expressions, calling Bostana a dove and his heart a writhing snake, all with appropriate illustrations from the orchestra. Their unanimity of mood is perfectly expressed in a swiftly moving canonic duet ('Wenn zum Gebet') as they rehearse the details of the lovers' rendezvous. There is only one moment of solemnity, when Bostana recommends a barber to restore Nureddin's looks. As Nureddin awaits the barber, scurrying strings show his impatience. His flow of feelings is checked somewhat by the imposing figure of Abul Hassan, and the scene is set for a humorous conflict between Nureddin's youthful ardour and the barber's ponderousness. The latter repeats his formal greeting so often that the sequence appears to be never-ending ('Mein Sohn, sei Allah's Frieden hier'). Nureddin interrupts while the barber discusses whether the stars are auspicious for such a shaving. The wind join Nureddin in urging the music forward, while the strings mimic the old man's exaggerated gestures.

Yet the barber has more resources at his command than at first appear. When Nureddin tries to dismiss him, he recites all his attributes in a virtuoso patter song rich in textual as well as musical invention ('Bin Akademiker'). Nureddin is left speechless, unable to prevent Abul Hassan from embarking on the story of his six brothers, with comic asides from the wind and percussion as he invents oriental-style epithets. Nureddin tries to throw the old man out. The servants bustle in, but faced with the mock heroic resistance of the barber, razor in hand, they bustle out again.

Nureddin appeases the barber and the shaving finally begins. Abul Hassan accompanies himself with a love song to a past loved one also named Margiana; interesting rhythmic and harmonic twists give his melody an irresistibly haunting quality ('Lass dir zu Füssen wonnesam mich liegen'). Nureddin joins in, forgetting his impatience, until Abul Hassan embarks on italianate cadenzas. Breaking in, Nureddin seeks to hurry the barber by telling him of his assignation. This provokes more witty exchanges, for Margiana's father, the Cadi, is an enemy of Abul Hassan's (because he shaves himself). The barber thus proposes to escort Nureddin to his meeting, despite the young man's objections.

While Nureddin leaves to adorn himself, Abul muses on the dangers of love ('So schwärmet Jugend'), the bassoon echoing his solemn refrain, 'Liebe'. Nureddin's final recourse on finding the barber still there is to convince his servants that Abul is ill, with a comic recitation of symptoms worthy of the barber himself. The servants respond with an equally fast list of remedies. For once the musical pace wrests the initiative from Abul Hassan; he is smothered with blankets, leaving Nureddin free to meet Margiana alone.

ACT 2 *The Cadi's house* A prelude establishes a mood of exotic languor; this music, the most oriental of the opera, later serves to call the faithful to prayer. The focus changes to more immediate emotions as Margiana awaits Nureddin, joined sympathetically by Bostana ('Er kommt! Er kommt!'). The entry of the Cadi unexpectedly changes the duet into a trio, adding tension because he is awaiting not Nureddin, but his old friend Selim as Margiana's suitor. Margiana echoes her father's praises of Selim's trunk of gifts. Yet while she and Bostana answer the Cadi's flowing phrases and join him in three-part harmony, they whisper to each other that a young lover is the only true treasure.

As the Muezzin's distant call draws the Cadi to the mosque, its dream-like quality sets the scene for Nureddin's appearance, and with an accompaniment of solo cellos his love song ('O, holdes Bild in Engelschöne') sustains the delicate mood. The lovers' passion emerges only gradually as their voices rise in unison ('So mag kein anders Wort erklingen'). Their restraint is offset by an expansive phrase from Abul Hassan, escaped to come to Nureddin's aid after all and now encouraging the lovemaking from beneath the window. Although this causes some comic disruption, Abul's singing adds much to the musical momentum of the scene once the lovers decide to ignore him.

A slave's warning cry represents a far more serious disruption, the arrival of the Cadi. A light and continuous rhythmic patter conveys the confusion as Abul thinks Nureddin is being attacked, while Margiana and Bostana hide the young man in Selim's trunk. The action reaches a crisis when Abul begins to remove the trunk (to funereal brass chords), thinking it contains Nureddin's dead body. His way is barred by the Cadi, who calls him a thief for removing his treasures. In the manner of a large-scale passacaglia, the same phrase is repeated many times over, with one side calling out theft and the other murder, the ensemble swollen by a growing crowd of servants, wailing women and townspeople.

This musical continuity is broken by the entry of the Caliph, cutting through the barber's wordy explanations and offering the simple solution of opening the trunk. As Nureddin's apparently lifeless body is revealed, the Cadi, Caliph and barber seem themselves to fall into a trance, repeating the same unaccompanied phrases. Margiana and Bostana try to recall Nureddin to life, but it is the barber's love song, aided by the scent of Margiana's flowers, which achieves the miracle, dissolving all barriers to the lovers' union, including her father's opposition. Although the Caliph then arrests the barber, this is only so that he can take him to the palace to hear the old man's stories. Abul sings the Caliph's praises in a final display of invention, and the chorus repeats his ceremonial greeting, 'Salamaleikum'.

* * *

The virtuosity with which Cornelius spins out musical details to follow the twists and turns of this plot has gained *Der Barbier von Bagdad* a high reputation despite its chequered performance history. With the libretto, he created a sophisticated comedy out of mimicking the exaggerated inflections of oriental speech and gesture, a sophistication matched throughout by the opera's orchestral, harmonic and melodic features. Some of this subtle characterization is lost in theatrical performance, for Cornelius lacked the ability to project details as large-scale dramatic gestures. However, the refined nature of the humour of *Der Barbier* and the integrity of the relationship between libretto and music succeeded in creating a new ideal for German comic opera. Cornelius may not have fully realized this ideal himself, but his influence upon operas such as Hugo Wolf's *Der Corregidor* and Wagner's *Die Meistersinger* is unmistakable. AMANDA GLAUERT

Barbier von Seville, Der ('The Barber of Seville'). *Komische Oper* in four acts by Friedrich Ludwig Benda (*see* BENDA family, (3)) to a libretto by GUSTAV FRIEDRICH WILHELM GROSSMANN, adapted from PIERRE-AUGUSTIN BEAUMARCHAIS' play *Le barbier de Séville*; Leipzig, Theater am Rannstädter Tor, 7 May 1776.

Grossmann originally translated Beaumarchais' play more or less faithfully for the Seyler company. Seyler persuaded him to adapt it as a comic opera and it was in this form, with Benda's music, that the play was generally performed in Germany during the 18th century. Unlike the simple tunes Beaumarchais had gathered and published with the original text, Benda's vocal numbers – 13 in all – have nothing Spanish about them. Italianate showpieces for the company's best voices predominate; the part of Rosina (soprano) is particularly ornate and virtuoso, a vehicle for the prima donna Josepha Hellmuth. THOMAS BAUMAN

Barbirolli, Sir **John** [Giovanni Battista] (*b* London, 2 Dec 1899; *d* London, 29 July 1970). English conductor of Italian-French descent. After winning scholarships to Trinity College of Music and the RAM, in 1916 he became the youngest member of the Queen's Hall Orchestra. He gained his first experience of conducting in the army, with a voluntary orchestra, and was invited to conduct the British National Opera Company on tour and later (1928) in London. From 1929 to 1933 he was guest conductor for the Covent Garden international and English seasons. He conducted at Sadler's Wells in 1934 and returned to Covent Garden for the coronation season of 1937.

Up to 1937 Barbirolli seemed set to become the leading British opera conductor after Beecham, but the two men were incompatible, and Barbirolli subsequently accepted a post with the New York PO. His later devotion to the Hallé Orchestra may have discouraged a more durable connection with the postwar regime at Covent Garden, at which he appeared as guest conductor for three seasons between 1951 and 1954 (the 1953 season including Gluck's *Orfeo* with Kathleen Ferrier making her final appearance). In his last years, when he recorded *Madama Butterfly* and *Otello*, and conducted *Aida* in 1969 at the Rome Opera, he appeared to be picking up the threads of his frustrated operatic career. As a technician he understood the orchestra from the inside, and as an interpreter could persuade audiences to share his enthusiasms. His musical tastes were conventional, showing a marked fondness for the late Romantics, British composers included. His recording career extended from the pre-electric days of 1911 to the month of his death. Barbirolli was made a Companion of Honour in 1969 and was knighted in 1949. He was first married to Marjorie Parry, the singer, and then to Evelyn Rothwell, the oboist.

*

M. Kennedy: *Barbirolli* (London, 1971) [with discography by M. Walker] RONALD CRICHTON

Barbot, Joseph-Théodore-Désiré (*b* Toulouse, 12 April 1824; *d* Paris, 1 Jan 1879). French tenor. He studied with the younger Manuel García in Paris, where he made his début at the Opéra in 1848. For a decade he toured Italy, singing at Bologna, Turin, Rome, Milan and Naples. In 1859 he returned to Paris and created the title role of Gounod's *Faust* at the Théâtre Lyrique. Then he continued touring in Italy and Russia with his wife, the soprano Caroline Barbot-Douvry (*b* 27 April 1830; *d* after 1875), who sang Leonora at the first performance of *La forza del destino* in St Petersburg (1862). After retiring from the stage, Barbot taught in Paris. ELIZABETH FORBES

Barcarola (It.; Fr. *barcarolle*). A boating song, often to be found in operas set in a marine ambience; usually an Andantino in 6/8 time. Examples include 'Amis, la matinée est belle' (*La muette de Portici*, Auber, 1828), 'Or che in ciel alta è la notte' (*Marino Faliero*, Donizetti, 1835), 'Tutta è calma la laguna' (*I due Foscari*, Verdi, 1844) and, best known of all, 'Belle nuit, ô nuit d'amour' (*Les contes d'Hoffmann*, Offenbach, 1881). 'O matutini albori' (*La donna del lago*, Rossini, 1819) has the character of a *barcarola*, though not labelled as such. 'Io son ricco e tu sei bella' (*L'elisir d'amore*, Donizetti, 1832), an Allegro in 2/4, is entitled 'barcarola' for no better reason than that the scene it portrays is laid in Venice. 'Pescator, affonda l'esca' (*La Gioconda*, Ponchielli, 1876) is an unusually vigorous example, in keeping with the character who sings it. The so-called barcarola from Mascagni's *Silvano* (1895) forms no part of the opera as such, being merely a free arrangement of some of the music. JULIAN BUDDEN

Barcelona. Spanish city, the capital of Catalonia. During the War of the Spanish Succession (1702–13) Barcelona regained its status as a court. In 1705, with military help from England, the Catalans proclaimed Archduke Charles of Austria King of Catalonia and all Spain, but Barcelona fell to Castile again in 1714. Celebrations on the occasion of Charles's marriage to Elisabet Kristina in 1708 included opera, now seen in Barcelona for the first time; Italian composers, singers and the stage designer F. Galli-Bibiena gave a lavish opera season (1708–09) with Caldara's *Il più bel nome* and works by Porsile, Emanuele d'Astorga and others.

The Barcelona theatre, the Teatre de la Santa Creu (Teatro de la Santa Cruz), which belonged to the local hospital, was never used for such performances: it was an undistinguished playhouse and lacked sufficient prestige to be attended by royalty. Performances there always included some music, but the usual fare was straight theatre and most of those who attended were from the middle classes of the city whose interest was in popular plays and magic pieces.

After the war, however, performances of italianate zarzuela (*c*1729) and the establishment of an Italian opera company in Barcelona from 1750 changed this trend. Opera was brought to the S Creu by Captain-General Jaime-Miguel de Guzmán-Spínola, Marquis of La Mina, who had fought in the Spanish wars in Italy for many years. He used opera as a way of amusing his large garrison and took a general delight in showing off his taste for the genre and grandly presiding over premières at the theatre as some kind of royal delegate. The Barcelona bourgeoisie soon developed a genuine interest in opera, and when the Barcelona hospital tried to suppress it to cut expenses, it proved impossible to do so. Other captain-generals, such as the Count of Ricla (1767–73), also dabbled in theatrical affairs: he tried to impose Italian opera in Spanish translations, but the singers were of low quality and the impresario, Carlos Vallés, lost his credit, so opera in Italian had to be resumed. The count was further discredited by his relationship with a ballerina, Nina Bergonzi.

The Barcelona opera house's main fare was Neapolitan opera (both *buffa* and *seria*), Venetian opera (mainly works by Galuppi or Scolari) and a small number of Viennese operas by composers such as Gassmann, Bonno and, later on, Gluck (*Orfeo*, 1780) and Mozart (*Così fan tutte*, 1798). After 1780 Neapolitan *opera buffa* took precedence over *opera seria*, and the main works of Guglielmi, Anfossi, Paisiello and Cimarosa were performed. Cimarosa was probably the most popular composer at the time; his *Il matrimonio segreto* reached Barcelona soon after its première and was particularly successful. At this time Barcelona was often the first city outside Italy where successful operas were performed. No French work was given until 1802, when *opéras comiques* by Boieldieu, Gaveaux and Grétry were staged, but without success.

Among those Catalan composers to have their works performed were Terradellas (*Sesostri*, 1754), Josep Durán (*Antígona*, 1760, *Temístocles*, 1762), Fernando Sor (*Telemaco*, 1796) and Carlos Baguer, organist of Barcelona Cathedral (*La principesa filósofa*, 1797). The Valencian Martín y Soler's operas, such as *Una cosa rara* (1790) or *L'arbore di Diana* (1791), were also well received. By then, Barcelona audiences were becoming more discriminating about singers, and some divas acquired a large following: particularly famous were the *prima buffa* Orsola Fabrizi-Bertini, who was in Barcelona from 1788 to 1795 and was responsible for having composer Vincenzo Fabrizi's operas performed, and Benedetta Marchetti, who sang in Barcelona from 1796 to 1799. Tenors such as Luigi Pacini (father of the composer Giovanni), who was in the city from 1798 to 1801 and also sang at many private concerts, were also well received. During the 18th century the S Creu was additionally used for masked balls and as a concert hall. The standard fare was instrumental music, by Haydn and Pleyel for example, but audiences began to show a preference for arias by such composers as Cimarosa, Paisiello, Guglielmi, Anfossi, Jommelli, Traetta and Antonio Tozzi (then the musical director of the opera house). Tozzi also wrote several operas for the S Creu, some of which were successful, such as *El amor a la patria* (1793), written in honour of the war with France.

The war against Napoleon (1808–14) interrupted the opera seasons at the S Creu as the Italian singers fled to Madrid. The theatre was reopened in 1810, with French plays and occasional *opéras comiques* (by Boieldieu, Grétry, Pleyel and others), which were largely ignored by the civilian population. On the other hand, the French occupation severed the former Viennese connection, and after the war musical life in Barcelona became even more italianate. In 1815 the Catalan composer Carnicer was sent to Italy to hire the best available singers as well as the composer Pietro Generali. With the new company came the first Rossini operas to be heard in Barcelona, beginning with *L'italiana in Algeri* (1815), which was a great success and was followed by *L'inganno felice* and *La cambiale di matrimonio* (1816), *Tancredi* and *Elisabetta* (1817), *La Cenerentola* and *Il barbiere di Siviglia* (1818), the last two enhanced by the excellent *buffo* bass Filippo Galli. Rossini influenced the new generation of Catalan composers, such as Carnicer himself (who wrote an overture for *Barbiere*, the score of which had reached Barcelona with no sinfonia), Mateu Ferrer (1788–1864), Mariano Obiols and Ramón Vilanova (1801–70). During the following years Italian opera continued to be the staple fare in Barcelona; first Paer and Mayr, then Bellini, Donizetti, Mercadante and Pacini were very popular, along with Meyerbeer, Vaccai, Persiani, Nicolai and Coccia. Other Catalan composers tried their luck in the genre: Vicenc Cuyás y Borés, whose Bellinian *La fattuchiera* (1838) was a great success; Eduardo Domínguez (1814–80), Baltasar Saldoni, Nicolau Guanyabéns (1826–83), whose *Arnaldo di Erill* (1857) started the trend of incorporating in an Italian language libretto elements drawn from local medieval history; and Nicolau Manent, who also wrote Catalan zarzuelas.

When the S Creu lost its privilege in 1833 opera began to be performed in a small theatre at the Liceu de Mont Sion, the first Barcelona conservatory (1838); this eventually gave birth to the Gran Teatre del Liceu (Gran Teatro del Liceo) (1847), which opened with a cantata by Obiols (*Il regio Imene*) and, a few days later, Donizetti's *Anna Bolena.* Meanwhile the S Creu was renamed the Teatre Principal; it also had a regular opera season until after 1890. A few other theatres offered opera, such as the Nou (Nuevo) and the Circo Barcelonés. The Liceu burnt down in 1861 but was immediately reconstructed and opened again on 20 April 1862 with Bellini's *I puritani.* At that time summer theatres were thriving on the outskirts of the rapidly growing city. The main houses were to be found along what is now the Passeig de Gràcia, among them the Teatre dels Camps Elisis, where French romantic opera and *opéra comique* were well received. The most important operas given at the Camps Elisis were also put on at the Liceu with mounting success, especially those by Gounod, Thomas, Halévy and Meyerbeer, and Auber's *Fra Diavolo*.

After a belated start (*Lohengrin* in 1882 at the S Creu and in 1883 at the Liceu) Wagnerian influence became very strong in Barcelona. The Associació Wagneriana (founded in 1901) translated all Wagner's operas into Catalan and even printed full scores with Catalan translations. Some composers, such as Albéniz and Granados, were under the influence of Spanish nationalism, but their operas had little success. Enric Morera was a Catalan musical nationalist who sometimes imitated Wagner in his operas (e.g. *La fada*, 1897), while Jaime Pahissa developed a personal, expressionist style (*Gala Placidia*, 1913). Amadeo Vives was famous for his zarzuelas; his few operas, such as *Artús* (1897), are now forgotten. Once the Wagnerian influence had diminished, Russian opera became the rage in the 1920s with performances of many works by Musorgsky, Borodin, Rimsky-Korsakov and Tchaikovsky, among others. Fewer operas were given, and the Liceu remained as the sole opera house, except for occasional performances elsewhere. Some popular works were constantly repeated, while others (such as the operas of Meyerbeer) gradually disappeared from the repertory.

The Liceu's constitution was based on a private ownership scheme which gave every shareholder a seat or a box in the house, the theatre being managed by an impresario chosen by the board of shareholders. From 1915 to 1947 the impresario was Joan Mestres i Calvet who, from the beginning of his tenure, encouraged audiences to accept Mozart's operas. His successor was Joan Antoni Pàmias, during whose 33 years in office Wagner's music once more became important (in 1955 the Bayreuth Festival company performed at the Liceu with great success). When Pàmias died in 1980, the private ownership system was superseded: a Consorci del Gran Teatre del Liceu was founded to reduce the former owners' status and to provide state and local government subsidies.

Many internationally famous singers, including Viñas, Capsir, Barrientos, Supervía, Pareto, Los Angeles, Caballé, Aragall, Giménez, Carreras and Gonzales were born or were trained in Barcelona. A singing competition, created in 1963 and named after Viñas, has won international renown.

*

F. Virella Cassañes: *La ópera en Barcelona* (Barcelona, 1888)
M.-J. Bertrán: *El Gran Teatre del Liceu* (Barcelona, 1930)
J. Subirà: *La ópera en Barcelona* (Barcelona, 1946)
R. Alier: *L'òpera* (Barcelona, 1979)
——: *Historia del Gran Teatro del Liceo* (Barcelona, 1983) [collected articles pubd in *La vanguardia*, 28 Dec 1982–11 April 1983]

ROGER ALIER

Bardari, Giuseppe (*b* Pizzo, Calabria, May 1817; *d* Naples, 22 Sept 1861). Italian librettist. He was 17 when he wrote the *tragedia lirica Maria Stuarda*, based on Maffei's verse translation of Schiller's play, for Donizetti, but he pursued a legal career, becoming a Crown Judge, only to be dismissed in 1848 following his supposed participation in the uprisings. Despite his liberal sympathies, he was eventually able to resume his career and became, briefly, Prefect of Police in Naples. *Maria Stuarda* is a first-rate libretto, full of striking situations, despite a slow start, and almost certainly betrays the hand of the experienced composer. Either as a result of the prohibition of this opera in Naples or because of the demands of his legal duties, Bardari wrote no other librettos.

*

J. Commons: 'Giuseppe Bardari', *Journal of the Donizetti Society*, iii (1977), 85–96

JOHN BLACK

Bardi, Giovanni de', Count of Vernio (*b* Florence, 5 Feb 1534; *d* Sept 1612). Italian literary critic, poet, playwright and composer. As host to the CAMERATA and patron of Vincenzo Galilei and Giulio Caccini (*see* CACCINI family, (1)) he gave the main impetus to the movement that led to the first experiments in lyrical and dramatic MONODY, and hence to opera.

Bardon, Henry (*b* Český Těšín, 19 June 1923; *d* Melbourne, 19 July 1991). British painter and set designer of Czech birth. He fled his homeland after the German invasion of 1938–9 and was trained at Dundee College of Art. In his early career Bardon designed for repertory theatre and in London for several West End plays, but from the 1960s he concentrated on opera and ballet. He quickly established a reputation as a master of the decorative Baroque-Rococo style as interpreted through the pictorial technique of the 19th-century stage, providing ideally Romantic frameworks for satisfyingly conventional stagings (*Werther*, 1966, Glyndebourne).

The frequent partnership of Bardon (sets) and David Walker (costumes) has resulted in some memorable productions, most notably the ravishingly pretty *Così fan tutte* (1968, Covent Garden) and *Semele* (1982, Covent Garden), which revived the scenic conventions of the Baroque stage with delicacy, wit and flowing inventiveness. Bardon, whose work was influenced by that of Lila De Nobili, worked extensively in North America before settling in Australia. At his death he was working on a new production of *Alcina* for Covent Garden.

*

Obituary, *The Times* (27 July 1991)

MARINA HENDERSON

Barenboim, Daniel (*b* Buenos Aires, 15 Nov 1942). Israeli conductor. He began his career as a pianist, but turned to orchestral conducting in 1962. His experience as a conductor of opera began with *Don Giovanni* at the Edinburgh Festival in 1973, at the instigation of the director Peter Diamand (always an enthusiast for Barenboim's work); this was followed in 1975 by *Le nozze di Figaro*.

In 1978 he undertook *Samson et Dalila* at the Orange Festival. He also recorded all three works. In 1981 he made his début at Bayreuth with *Tristan und Isolde* and conducted the *Ring* in Harry Kupfer's new production in 1988. In the late 1980s he was appointed to the directorship of the new Bastille opera house in Paris, where for years he had conducted the Orchestre de Paris, but political circumstances forced him to renounce the engagement before he had conducted a single performance. In 1990 he embarked on a new set of recordings of Mozart's Da Ponte operas with the Berlin PO and in 1991 his acclaimed recording of *Parsifal* appeared. The same year he was appointed music director of the Deutsche Staatsoper, Berlin, to take effect from 1993.

Whether on stage or in the studio, Barenboim's opera interpretations are distinguished by the long period of preparation that he considers a *sine qua non*, hence the comparative rarity of his appearances. As in the orchestral repertory, his performances lay emphasis on freedom of expression and allow for many changes in tempos and a careful disclosure of detail. At the other extreme, as in the climaxes of the second act of *Tristan* or the third act of *Die Walküre*, he attempts a kind of incandescence that recalls Furtwängler. He approaches Mozart unfashionably, very much through 19th-century eyes and ears, using a comparatively large orchestra and eschewing period instruments. The most positive aspect of his readings is the flexibility and quick sensitivity that also mark his performances on the piano. His autobiography *A Life in Music* was published in London in 1991.

ALAN BLYTH

Bärenhäuter, Der ('The Bear-Skinner'). Opera in three acts by Siegfried Wagner (*see* WAGNER family, (3)) to his own libretto; Munich, Königliches Hof- und Nationaltheater, 22 January 1899.

Based on two fairy-tales by the brothers Grimm, the opera is set in medieval Franconia. Hans Kraft (tenor), a young soldier, returns home to find his mother dead. Refused hospitality by the villagers, he accepts an offer from the Devil (*buffo* bass) to work in hell, guarding the souls of sinners. There he is visited by a Stranger (baritone), who is really St Peter in disguise. They play a game of dice, which results in Hans's losing all the souls to heaven. Hans is subsequently punished by the Devil, who sentences him to wander the earth dressed only in a bearskin, covered with soot and unable to wash. He can be redeemed only by a faithful woman. On his travels he stops at an inn (Act 2) and helps the mayor, Melchior Fröhlich (bass), by paying his debts to the landlord, Nikolaus Spitz (*buffo* tenor), from his bag of never-ending gold, a gift from the Devil. The mayor promises to reward him with the hand of one of his three daughters. In the night the landlord tries to steal Hans's bag but is attacked by the Devil's imps. He is rescued by Hans. The mayor's daughters, Lene, Gunda and Luise (all sopranos), arrive the next morning, but Lene and Gunda reject him. Luise promises to wait for him, taking half his ring as a keepsake. The landlord incites the villagers to turn against Hans, but Luise helps him to escape. Three years later (Act 3) Hans returns to claim his bride, but he again encounters the Stranger, who tells him to go to Plassenburg to wake the guards and save the fortress from the Wallenstein forces. Corporal Kaspar Wild (baritone) tells the villagers how an unknown man has saved Plassenburg. When Hans arrives in the village he asks for a bandage and some water. Luise brings them and when Hans drops his ring into the cup she recognizes him. All the people praise her faithfulness and offer their thanks to the angels.

The overture gives a symphonic summary of the plot: Hans's challenging horn theme is answered by a 'cloven-hoof' motif (the Devil), but Luise's 'eternal feminine nature' protects Hans, and love wins the struggle. Despite unbroken continuity, the music contains closed forms such as ballad, song, prayer, duet, waltz and set chorus. Among the many significant melodious inventions is the musically grotesque characterization of the Devil, the most exciting figure in the opera, which shows the influence of Mephisto in Liszt's *Faust* symphony. The final ensemble prayer 'Lasset uns die Engel loben' ('Only be the angels praised') indicates Marschner's *Der Vampyr* as a musical model. In *Der Bärenhäuter* Siegfried Wagner in some ways emulated his father's work, particularly in its orchestration, which strongly resembles that of *Der fliegende Holländer*, and in its scenic development and dramatic situations. However, the musical language itself is unlike that of Richard Wagner in its post-Romantic style and use of themes derived from folksong. PETER P. PACHL

Barga. Town in central Italy, in the province of Lucca. In July and August each year the festival Opera Barga takes place there. It was founded in 1967 by Peter and Gillian Hunt with the collaboration of Peter Gellhorn. The aim is educational, and the performances are staged by pupils following specialized courses; the pupils, coming from all over the world, are selected by audition. The repertory consists of rarely performed works of the 18th and 19th centuries, such as Donizetti's *I pazzi per progetto* (1977), Raimondi's *Il ventaglio* (1978) and Rossini's *Demetrio e Polibio* (1979), each given its first modern performance at Barga, as well as of contemporary operas and operettas; there are also jazz concerts. Up to 1983 the venue was the Teatro dei Differenti, built in 1793 (400 seats). Since then, performances have been given at open-air locations.

ARRIGO QUATTROCCHI

Bargielski, Zbigniew (*b* Łomża, 21 Jan 1937). Polish composer. He studied at the Warsaw Conservatory with Tadeusz Szeligowski and at Katowice with Bolesław Szabelski before becoming a pupil of Boulanger in Paris and pursuing further studies at Graz. By the late 1960s his dramatic use of violent orchestral sonorities showed an affinity with Lutosławski and the early works of Górecki. Bargielski's operas, which include a discarded first attempt at a French revolutionary theme, on the death of Marat (1968, libretto after P. Weiss), include a number of ironic and even aggressive approaches to the genre and usually incorporate a large measure of spoken dialogue. In *Mały książę* ('The Little Prince') the text takes precedence over musical considerations, while *Alicja w krainie czarów* ('Alice in Wonderland'), cast for ten actors, uses electronic means to distort the vocal lines of all the characters except Alice, who uses speech alone. *Danton* is conceived as theatre within theatre: the drama is articulated by a 'performance leader', and every attempt is made to divest the musical drama of what the composer called 'singing corpses'. Bargielski's most unusual opera is *Widma nie kłamią* ('Phantoms do not Lie', 1972), the first version of *W małym dworku* ('In a Little Manor'). The original story by Poland's leading writer of the early 20th century, Stanisław Ignacy Witkiewicz (or 'Witkacy'), parodies the foibles and grotesque perversions of human life through the medium of the ghostly Anastasia (sung by a bass in this earlier version), whose peccadilloes come to torture her surviving husband, lovers and family. The orchestral palette is carefully controlled so as to reach full brilliance in the final act, when Bargielski further emphasizes the cumulative parody by exchanging male with female voices for several of the characters.

all librettos by the composer

Mały książę [The Little Prince], 1966 (musical tale, 1, after A. de Saint-Exupéry), Warsaw, Wielki, 19 Nov 1970

Danton, czyli Kilka obrazów z dziejów wielki rewolucji francuskiej [Danton, or some pictures from the History of the Great French Revolution], 1968–9 (pseudo-historical op, 3, after G. Büchner: *Dantons Tod* and A. L. de Saint-Just), unperf.

Alicja w krainie czarów [Alice in Wonderland] (youth op, after L. Carroll), Lublin, Puppet and Actors' Theatre, 21 Oct 1972

Widma nie kłamią [Phantoms do not Lie], 1971–2 (comic op, 3, after S. I. Witkiewicz); rev. 1979 as W małym dworku [In a Little Manor], Wrocław, State, 10 June 1981

*

T. Marek: '*The Little Prince* by Zbigniew Bargielski', *Polish Music* (1969), no.4, pp.7–9

——:'Composer's Workshop: Zbigniew Bargielski' [*Danton*], *Polish Music* (1970), no.1, pp.24–7

Z. Bargielski: 'Of my Opera "Phantoms Do Not Lie" ', *Polish Music* (1973), no.1, pp.10–15

O. Pisarenko: 'Witkacy z muzyką' [*W małym dworku*], *Ruch muzyczny* (1983), no.16, pp.4–5 ADRIAN THOMAS

Bari. City in Apulia, southern Italy. Despite the many musical associations of the region, Bari had no real theatre until the mid-19th century. From 1815 to 1835 the Teatro del Sedile, the only building capable of holding even 250 people, presented recitals, concerts, drama and opera. Between 1840 and the opening of the multi-purpose Teatro Comunale Piccinni (on corso Ferdinando, later corso Vittorio Emanuele) the temporary site of the Circo Olimpico was used.

The series of theatres opened over a 60-year period – the Piccinni in 1854, the Petruzzelli in 1903 and the Margherita in 1914 – reflected the social and economic development of the city. (Apulia, and Bari as its chief town, were always important components of the kingdom of the Two Sicilies.) The architect chosen was Antonio Niccolini from Naples, considered with Alessandro Sanquirico to be the father of Italian scene-painting and renowned internationally for his restoration of the S Carlo opera house and his studies on theatre acoustics. The Piccinni (named after the composer, a native of Bari) was the only 'teatro di pianta' he designed; its horseshoe plan had 312 stalls seats and 64 boxes (the capacity eventually reached 1200 seats). The building was both sumptuous and elegant; built entirely with public money, it was inaugurated on 4 October 1854 with Donizetti's *Poliuto*.

After the unification of Italy the principal towns and cities of the kingdom of Naples enjoyed little operatic activity of their own, centred as that was on Naples and its theatres, and the difficulty of forging a link with a national circuit after decades of isolation was decisive for the development of opera in Bari and for the fortunes of the Piccinni. Under a succession of inexperienced and short-sighted municipal managements the theatre gradually lost revenue and became less accessible to the populace during the 1860s. The operas performed in the years 1854–1965 were drawn mainly from the standard Italian repertory, with a few unadventurous forays into contemporary works including Mercadante's *Leonora* in 1855 and De Giosa's *Napoli di carnevale* and *Don Checco* in 1880. The seasons lasted between one and two months each with the Italian repertory predominating, performed by a locally recruited orchestra and chorus with conductors and soloists engaged for the occasion. The theatre was closed between 1902 and 1914, and thereafter was a secondary house. Its operatic offerings became increasingly inferior in both quantity and quality to those of the Petruzzelli theatre, and it is not surprising that after the 1964 season (26 November to 13 December, with 14 performances) the operatic life of the municipal theatre of Bari finally ended.

In March 1891 protests over the poor quality of the singers at the Piccinni during a performance of *Cavalleria rusticana* had led to popular demand for a new and larger theatre as an alternative to the municipal theatre. The Politeama Petruzzelli was therefore planned, whose size was conceived from the first to be commensurate with the city's growth (the population reached 100 000 in 1911). The new theatre had to be flexible enough for both popular entertainment and more lofty occasions; to the latter end its programme of productions was linked to the national circuit. The design, by Angelo Cicciomessere (later Messeni), was a mixture of French-style parterre boxes, two and a half tiers of 91 closed boxes, and capacious stepped galleries, amounting to 3000 places; together with the large stage and 30 dressing rooms, the Petruzzelli was the fourth largest theatre in Italy after the S Carlo, the Massimo in Palermo, and La Scala. The theatre opened on 14 February 1903 with *Les Huguenots* and the season, which continued until 30 April, included (besides the Meyerbeer) *Andrea Chénier*, *Trovatore*, *Aida* and *Dea*, by the local composer Pasquale La Rotella, a total of 47 performances. The proprietors and the impresario, Antonio Quaranta, were encouraged by attendances, and the theatre entered the orbit of Italian musical life, the traditional centres providing it with soloists and conductors. Two tendencies were soon evident: a propensity for grand opera and its derivatives – *Il Guarany* (1914) and Massenet's *La Navarraise* (1904), *Le Roi de Lahore* (1905) and *Hérodiade* (1913) for example; and a marked preference for the works of Mascagni (116 performances between 1903 and 1926). Wagner, on the other hand, was heard only infrequently: *Lohengrin* in 1906 and 1922, *Tannhäuser* in 1913 and *Tristan und Isolde* in 1915.

The death of Quaranta in 1928 marked a downturn in musical life in Bari. Theatres such as the Margherita and the Politeama Barese (1929) were smaller and more provincial, and did not contribute to the opera season. The old cultural and social order was faced with a new style of politically approved management which continued to determine the Petruzzelli's opera seasons until 1970. The number of occasions on which opera was given declined steadily in favour of films and variety shows to a total of 20 days a year, though up and coming singers such as Bergonzi, Cappuccilli and Chiara continued to be presented. The reform of the organization of Italian musical life approved by the government in 1968 portrayed the Petruzzelli as a secondary theatre in a provincial city, built by private citizens and under private management with some public subsidy.

Up to the end of the 1980s the Italian repertory was well represented, but there were also unjustifiable omissions: only a handful of performances had been given of *Boris Godunov*, *Don Giovanni*, *Così fan tutte*, *Die Walküre*, *Macbeth*, *Figaro*, *Tristan und Isolde* and *The Rake's Progress*, and none at all of *Pelléas*, *Lulu*, *Wozzeck*, *Fidelio*, *Die Zauberflöte* or *Rosenkavalier*, nor any first performances of contemporary operas. Singers of international stature have appeared over the years, although there has never been a true year-round system, but instead limited seasons usually amounting to three or four months a year; the theatre still has no permanent orchestra, chorus or ballet. The year 1979, however, marked the beginning of a change of organization which resulted in greater awareness being shown of the civic and cultural requirements of Bari and Apulia. The Ente Artistico Teatro Petruzzelli, a private company that has returned the building to its original purpose as a *politeama* for various forms of entertainment, has also ensured its re-establishment at national and international level. In addition to ballet the Petruzzelli presented, in April 1986, the world première of the 1835 Naples version of Bellini's *I puritani*, written for Malibran but never staged; in December 1986 Niccolò Piccinni's *Iphigénie en Tauride* (the opera that occasioned the Gluckistes–Piccinnistes dispute); and in September 1987 a memorable performance of *Aida*, in Egypt at the foot of the Pyramids. On 27 October 1991, however, the Petruzzelli theatre was completely destroyed by fire.

*

G. Gargiulo: *Cenno intorno al gran teatro di Bari* (Bari, 1854)
G. Petroni: *Del gran teatro di Bari* (Bari, 1854)
A. Vinaccia: 'Il nuovo Politeama Petruzzelli', *Rassegna tecnica pugliese*, ii (1903), 65, 81
S. La Sorsa: *Teatro Piccinni di Bari: stagione lirica del centenario 1854–1954* (Bari, 1954)
P. Marino: *Bari: Teatro comunale Piccinni* (Bari, 1964)

A. Giovine: *L'opera in musica in teatri di Bari* (Bari, 1969)
——: *Il Teatro del Sedile, primo teatro di Bari* (Bari, 1969)
——: *Il Teatro Petruzzelli di Bari* (Bari, 1970)
——: *Il Teatro Piccinni di Bari* (Bari, 1970)
C. Ricci: *Teatri d'Italia dalla Magna Grecia all'ottocento* (Milan, 1971)
F. Mancini: *Scenografia napoletana dell'ottocento: Antonio Niccolini e il neoclassicismo* (Naples, 1980)
V. A. Melchiorre, ed.: *Il Teatro Petruzzelli di Bari* (Bari, 1981)
A. Giovine: *Il Teatro Petruzzelli di Bari: stagioni liriche dal 1903 al 1983* (Bari, 1983)
V. Melchiorre and L. Zingarelli: *Il Teatro Piccinni di Bari* (Bari, 1983)
P. Moliterni, V. Attolini and E. Persichella: *Vissi d'arte: gli 80 anni del Petruzzelli: il mito e le vicende* (Bari, 1983)
P. Moliterni, ed.: *Puglia: l'organizzazione musicale* (Rome, 1986)
F. Picca: *Bari 'capitale' a teatro: il Politeama Petruzzelli 1877–1914* (Bari, 1987)

PIERFRANCO MOLITERNI

Barilli-Patti, Caterina Chiesa. *See* PATTI, SALVATORE.

Baritone (from Gk. *barytonos*, 'deep-sounding'; Fr. *baryton*; Ger. *Bariton*; It. *baritono*). A male voice in compass and depth between the tenor and the bass, with a normal compass of about *A* to *f′* which may be extended at either end.

1. Terminology and early history. 2. Voice types. 3. Singers and roles: the 19th century: (i) French, Italian and Russian opera (ii) German opera. 4. Singers and roles: the 20th century.

1. TERMINOLOGY AND EARLY HISTORY. The term 'baritonans' was first used in Western music in the late 15th century, principally in French polyphonic sacred music, where it may signify a voice lower than the *bassus*. Gaffurius (*Practica musicae*, 1496) uses it for the lowest of the four normal voices; 'baritonus' is used in John Dowland's translation (1609) of Ornithoparcus (*Musicae activae micrologus*, 1517: 'a deep voice, which is called *Baritonus*'). In 17th-century Italy the term appears to refer to a rather ordinary type of choral singer who sang low parts. Monteverdi used it of a singer ('he is a baritone, not a bass') in a letter of 1627. J. G. Walther (*Musicalisches Lexicon*, 1732) writes that a baritone 'must have the high range of the tenor as well as some depth in the bass'. The term was not, however, used in normal operatic parlance until the 19th century, although many roles of the 18th call for what is now considered a baritone voice. These include, for example, the parts written by Handel for the 'bass' G. M. Boschi, and such Mozart roles as Count Almaviva, perhaps Don Giovanni, and Papageno, all normally sung by baritones today; the *basso buffo* roles in Mozart's late comic operas (Figaro, Leporello, Guglielmo), written for or sung by Francesco Benucci, are also often considered baritone roles, as are similar ones in other *opere buffe* of the middle and late 18th century. The connotation of 'deep' or 'heavy' sound has largely disappeared today; a description of a singer as 'a heavy baritone' would not seem tautologous. The French counterpart to the Italian 'baritono' is *basse-taille*; Sébastien de Brossard (*Dictionaire de musique*, 1703) defined it as a voice 'going high and low. Those who sing Mozart's part can serve as *tailles* or *basses* if needs be'. Although Lully wrote several important roles such as Cadmus, Alcides (*Alceste*) and Aegeus (*Thésée*) in the baritone clef (the F clef on the middle line), their ranges do not exceed *G* to *e′*, even if several lie in a high tessitura (pitch was approximately a whole tone lower than today's). The solo *basse-taille*, making frequent use of the top of the range, did not emerge as one of the three favourite solo voices (with *dessus* and *haute-contre*) until the 18th century. Rameau's operas include several such roles, extending from *F* or *G* to *f′* or *f♯′*, such as Teucer and Ismenor in *Dardanus* and Pollux and Jupiter in *Castor et Pollux* (and these at a time when the pitch had apparently risen by a semitone from that used in Lully's day). The most notable *basse-taille* of Rameau's day was Claude Louis Dominique Chassé (*fl*1720–56), noted for his acting more than his singing, but sufficiently versatile to take the *haute-taille* role of Medusa in a revival of Lully's *Persée* in 1738. D'Hannetaire (1764) attributed Chassé's 'haughtiness of attitude, [and] nobility of gesture' to the masterpieces of sculpture and painting 'which he has observed for the purpose'. The *basse-taille*, although a separate constituent of the five-part chorus in sacred music, had no specific line in the four-part opera chorus, where singers in this range joined either with the *tailles* or, more generally, judging from extant lists of performers, with the *basses*.

2. VOICE TYPES. Like the mezzo-soprano among women, the baritone is generally considered the 'normal' voice among men. If an average male speaking voice is made to sing, some sort of baritone is probably what will be heard. To some extent this normality is reflected in the operatic repertory. For example, the roles in Mozart commonly sung by a baritone have a range and tessitura that suit the 'normal' voice quite comfortably. They will require a *B♭* and an *f′*, with the occasional extension of a note or two on either side. Similarly, Wagnerian roles generally accepted as being appropriate to the baritone rather than the bass-baritone – Wolfram in *Tannhäuser*, Kurwenal in *Tristan und Isolde*, Gunther in *Götterdämmerung*, for example – require characteristics of compass and tone that are very 'central'. In a wider field, the operatic baritone has to extend himself well beyond this comfortable norm, and in particular the roles which are to be undertaken by what is now thought of as 'the Verdi baritone' probably lie as far outside the capabilities of an average vocalist as do the tenor and bass roles themselves.

Italian opera usually has a well-defined hero and heroine, sung, respectively, by tenor and soprano; but in Verdi's operas the baritone regularly plays an important part and in four of them is the protagonist. *Nabucco*, *Rigoletto*, *Simon Boccanegra* and *Falstaff* are the operas that, in the Italian repertory, most conspicuously raise the status of the baritone and place him in the centre of the stage. Correspondingly, they make great demands. They are, for one thing, roles in which an exceptionally large portion of the singer's attention has to be directed towards his acting: an unofficial item of operatic lore has been that while both the tenor and the bass, in their different ways, can rely on a number of postures to see them through their obligations, the baritone is expected to do some real acting. The vocal demands are more strenuous still. Rigoletto, in particular, is a role which lies high in the voice: though the score (as opposed to tradition) asks for nothing beyond the high *g′♭*, there are many passages which, as it were, assume comfort in the upper regions of the voice, the area around *e′* and *f′*. In other words, the top of a bass's voice is assumed to be an easily habitable region for the baritone, and this in turn assumes a considerable extension of range above, available in emergency, perhaps never to be called upon but still reliably there. Baritones are sometimes cautioned not to undertake the role of Rigoletto unless they feel that under dire compulsion they could sing it a semitone higher: often (allowing for temperament) it is shrewd advice and, if heeded, would avert many a mishap.

The development of the high dramatic baritone coincided broadly with that of the dramatic tenor. Before the 1840s the baritone certainly may have been required to cope with a high tessitura, as with Rossini's Figaro, but the orchestration was less heavy and the dramatic expression less forceful. The history of opera in the 19th century does not resound with the names of great baritones who achieved a 'breakthrough' comparable to that of tenors such as Duprez and Tamberlik; first to gain wide fame in fact was Victor Maurel, creator of Verdi's Iago and Falstaff and of Tonio in *Pagliacci*, whose distinction lay in the style and intelligence of his performances rather than in his possession of the range and resonance we now expect of 'the Verdi baritone'. It was rather later, in the early years of the 20th century, that the type of robust, powerful baritone who glories in the high notes came to rival the tenor in popular acclaim, as did Titta Ruffo, said to be the one singer against whose voice Caruso had qualms about matching his own.

Ruffo is one of three Italian baritones active in this period who may stand as representatives of the principal types. Giuseppe De Luca exemplifies the lyric baritone who cultivates a well rounded beauty of tone and evenness of production. Mattia Battistini, some 20 years senior to these, may serve as a double archetype, for he commanded a high degree of technical virtuosity and was also closer in timbre to the tenor than to the bass. Of this latter type the French school made a speciality. As early as Gluck and Spontini, composers writing for the French opera provided for high baritones, and in the early decades of the 19th century a notable exponent was Jean-Blaise Martin whose name has long been evoked to designate such singers (the 'baryton Martin'). The German school also developed high baritones, and the Russians have encouraged a line of singers with sufficient ease in the high register and often a tenor-like quality on upper notes, to sing roles such as Onegin and Yelitsky.

In 20th-century opera the baritone voice has appealed to such composers as Strauss, who wrote sympathetically for the lyrical, medium-dramatic voice in *Arabella*; Berg, whose Wozzeck provides perhaps the most important extension of the repertory; and Puccini, who with his Gianni Schicchi added delightfully to the relatively small store of effective comic roles. More recently Harrison Birtwistle has cast the baritone as Punch, and in John Adams's *Nixon in China* the principal baritone plays Chou En-Lai.

3. SINGERS AND ROLES: THE 19TH CENTURY.

(i) French, Italian and Russian opera. Jean-Blaise Martin, the French high baritone, enjoyed a career of more than 35 years, creating during the first two decades of the century roles in several operas by Boieldieu, Isouard, Méhul and Dalayrac. In 1833 Halévy composed a one-act opera, *Les souvenirs de Lafleur*, for Martin, then 67 but still singing 'with a voice of marvellous freshness and charm for one of his age'. With a high, light voice similar to Martin's, Henry also had a long career, at the Opéra-Comique, where he created even more roles, by Hérold, Auber and Adam, as well as Gaveston in Boieldieu's *La dame blanche* (1825; he was still singing it at the 700th performance), Mathéo in Auber's *Fra Diavolo* (1830) and Sulpice in *La fille du régiment* (1840). At the Opéra Henri-Bernard Dabadie had a shorter career. His flexible, warm-toned and high-lying voice is reflected in the Rossini roles that he was the first to sing, the Pharaoh in *Moïse et Pharaon* (1827), Raimbaud in *Le comte Ory* (1828) and the title role of *Guillaume Tell* (1829); he also created roles in Auber's *La muette de Portici* (1828), *Le philtre* (1831) and *Gustave III* (1833), as well as Ruggiero in Halévy's *La Juive* (1835). A year after singing Jolicoeur in *Le philtre*, he created Belcore (the same character as Jolicoeur) in Donizetti's *L'elisir d'amore* at Milan (1832).

Antonio Tamburini, a superb Belcore and the finest Italian baritone of the first half of the 19th century, took part in ten Donizetti premières between 1822 and 1843, among them *Marin Faliero* and *Don Pasquale* (as Dr Malatesta); his other Donizetti roles included Enrico Ashton, and Alfonso d'Este in *Lucrezia Borgia*. It was as a specialist in Bellini's baritone roles that Tamburini made his greatest individual contribution; he created Ernesto (*Il pirata*, 1827), Filippo (*Bianca e Fernando*, 1828), Valdeburgo (*La straniera*, 1829) and Riccardo (*I puritani*, 1835), displaying the perfectly even emission of his voice as well as its extreme agility. He also sang Rossini's Dandini, Figaro and Assur (*Semiramide*) as well as Iago, written for tenor but often adapted for baritone. However, he found the baritone role of Don Carlo in Verdi's *Ernani* too high and begged to be excused from singing it.

Giorgio Ronconi, another baritone for whom Donizetti wrote some splendid roles, including Cardenio (*Il furioso all'isola di San Domingo*), Torquato Tasso (both 1833) and Chevreuse (*Maria di Rohan*, 1843), was a very different kind of singer from Tamburini, although they sang many of the same roles. Ronconi's voice lacked smoothness and flexibility but his style was more dramatic; Chorley wrote: 'There are few instances of a voice so limited in compass (barely exceeding an octave), so inferior in quality, so weak, so habitually out of tune as his ... [yet] with his wondrously limited means so shaped and turned to account by Genius, as to make every limit, every defect, forgotten and forgiven'.

Although Ronconi was highly effective as Chevreuse, Alfonso d'Este and Dr Dulcamara (with Tamburini as Belcore), he scored his greatest triumphs in Verdi; having created the title role of *Nabucco* (1842) at La Scala, he sang Don Carlo in *Ernani*, the Doge in *I due Foscari* (both 1844) and, most successfully, Rigoletto to great acclaim at Covent Garden. Other baritones who sang in Verdi premières included Filippo Coletti, who created Gusmano (*Alzira*, 1845) and Francesco (*I masnadieri*, 1847) and later sang Rigoletto and Boccanegra with success; Filippo Colini, the first Giacomo (*Giovanna d'Arco*, 1845), Rolando (*La battaglia di Legnano*, 1849) and Stankar (*Stiffelio*, 1850), also made a powerful Nabucco and Macbeth.

Felice Varesi, the creator of Macbeth (1847) and Rigoletto (1851) and Germont at the première of *La traviata* (1853), was perhaps the most gifted of the early Verdi baritones, Ronconi apart. Achille De Bassini created Seid (*Il corsaro*, 1848), Miller (*Luisa Miller*, 1849) and Fra Melitone (*La forza del destino*, 1862). Leone Giraldoni, the first Boccanegra (1857) and Renato (*Un ballo in maschera*, 1859), created the title role of *Il duca d'Alba*, left unfinished by Donizetti and not performed until 1882. Giraldoni's son Eugenio, also a baritone, sang Scarpia in the première of *Tosca* (1900).

In Paris, a new generation of baritones was to prove

that Donizetti, and later Verdi, could be sung in bel canto style. Paolo Barroilhet, although of French birth, began his career in Italy, where he created Eustachio (*L'assedio di Calais*, 1836) and Nottingham (*Roberto Devereux*, 1837) and sang Torquato Tasso and Belisarius with great success; in Paris, he created two more Donizetti roles, Alphonse XI (*La favorite*, 1840) and Camoëns (*Dom Sébastien*, 1843), as well as Jacques de Lusignan (Halévy's *La reine de Chypre*, 1841) and the title role of Adam's *Richard en Palestine* (1844); his voice was less flexible, but he had a beauty of timbre to rival Tamburini. So too did Jean-Baptiste Faure, one of the greatest singers of the century. At the Opéra-Comique he created Hoël in Meyerbeer's *Le pardon de Ploërmel* (1859); at the Opéra, he sang Nélusko in the première of *L'Africaine* (1865), then sang Posa in the première of Verdi's *Don Carlos* (1867) and created the title role of *Hamlet* (1868), written by Thomas with his voice and personality in mind. His most popular role was Méphistophélès, which he sang at the first Opéra performance of *Faust* and repeated at Covent Garden and elsewhere. Paul Lhérie, the Posa at La Scala when *Don Carlos* was first given in the four-act version (1884), had earlier, as a tenor, created Don José in *Carmen* (1875). Later he sang Rabbi David in the première of Mascagni's *L'amico Fritz* (1891). Jacques Bouhy, the first Escamillo, also created the title role of Massenet's *Don César de Bazan* (1872).

Faure's successor at the Opéra, Jean Lassalle, was another baritone of exceptionally beautiful timbre: he created Scindia in Massenet's *Le roi de Lahore* (1877); Sévère in Gounod's *Polyeucte* (1878), Malatesta in Thomas' *Françoise de Rimini* (1882) and the title role of Saint-Saëns' *Henry VIII* (1883); he was also a notable William Tell and Hamlet. The French baritone Victor Maurel, after an inconspicuous début at the Opéra, went to Italy, where he created roles in two operas by Gomes, *Il Guarany* (1870) and *Fosca* (1873); as a gifted Verdi interpreter he sang Posa in the Italian première of *Don Carlos* at Naples (1872), Amonasro in the American première of *Aida* in New York, Renato, Don Carlo (*Ernani*) and Luna at Covent Garden, Germont and Rigoletto at Monte Carlo and, most significantly, the title role in the revised *Simon Boccanegra* at La Scala (1881). Verdi promised him Iago in *Otello* (1887), which he also sang at Covent Garden, the Metropolitan and the Opéra. When Verdi wrote *Falstaff*, it was to Maurel that the title role was entrusted (1893). He sang Herod (in Italian) at the Paris première of *Hérodiade* and created Tonio in *Pagliacci* (1892); as the character had no aria, Leoncavallo gave him the prologue, originally intended for the tenor. Maurel also sang Wagner, notably Wolfram and Telramund in the London premières of *Tannhäuser* and *Lohengrin* (in Italian).

These roles were also sung by Mattia Battistini, whose voice had an exceptional range, up to *a'*. Massenet adapted the tenor title role of *Werther* for him, and he sang other French parts, including Alphonse XI (*La favorite*), Nélusko (*L'Africaine*) and Thomas' Hamlet, as well as Don Carlo (*Ernani*), Rigoletto, Boccanegra and Scarpia. A meticulous stylist with a superb florid technique, Battistini was the most admired baritone in Europe; he was a frequent visitor to Russia, where he was an admired Yevgeny Onegin. Battistini and Maurel had a number of roles in common, but in *Faust* the former sang Valentin and the latter Méphistophélès. Jean-François Delmas was another excellent Méphistophélès, which he sang at the 1000th performance in Paris of Gounod's opera; the same year (1894) he created one of Massenet's finest roles for baritone, Athanaël (*Thaïs*). He had earlier created another Massenet role, Amron in *Le mage* (1891). His voice had a very wide compass; he was the first Wotan and Hans Sachs at the Opéra and also the first Hagen and Gurnemanz. At the Opéra-Comique Lucien Fugère, in a rather lighter repertory, was equally many-sided: he created Fritelli in Chabrier's *Le roi malgré lui* (1887) and sang in three Massenet premières: as Chevalier des Grieux (*Le portrait de Manon*, 1894), Pandolfe (*Cendrillon*, 1899) and the Devil (*Grisélidis*, 1901). His best-known role was the Father in *Louise* (1900), which he created. A role he sang in Paris, Boniface (*Le jongleur de Notre Dame*), was created by Maurice Renaud, an exceptionally rich-toned baritone, at Monte Carlo, where he sang the Philosopher in the première of *Chérubin* (1902).

The title role of *Boris Godunov* has always been disputed between baritones and basses. When Musorgsky's opera reached Paris in 1908, Boris was sung by Shalyapin, a bass; but the Tsar was first sung by Ivan Mel'nikov, a baritone who took part in the premières of many Russian operas: he created Tokmakov in Rimsky-Korsakov's *The Maid of Pskov* (1873) and the title roles of Rubinstein's *The Demon* (1875) and Borodin's *Prince Igor* (1890). As Tchaikovsky's favourite baritone, he sang Prince Vyazminsky in *The Oprichnik* (1874), the Devil in *Vakula the Smith* (1876), Prince Kurlyatev in *The Enchantress* (1887) and Tomsky in *The Queen of Spades* (1890), all first performances. Yevgeny Onegin was one of his less successful roles. The first professional Onegin was Pavel Khokhlov, who was also a fine Igor.

(ii) German opera. In the final version of *Fidelio*, Pizarro was sung by Anton Forti, an Austrian baritone of extraordinary range who sang several tenor roles (including Rossini's Otello and Max in *Der Freischütz*) and created Lysiart in Weber's *Euryanthe* (1823). Johann Wächter, the Austrian baritone who sang Orsini at the première of Wagner's *Rienzi* (1842), was a notable Sherasmin in Weber's *Oberon* and Brian de Bois-Guilbert in Marschner's *Der Templer und die Jüdin*; he also created the rather heavier title role of *Der fliegende Holländer* (1843). Other baritones to have sung important Marschner roles include Edward Genast, an actor as well as a singer with a powerful bass-baritone voice, who created Lord Ruthven, the title role of Marschner's *Der Vampyr* (1828), and Eduard Devrient, who first sang the title role of *Hans Heiling* (1833) and also wrote the libretto.

Anton Mitterwurzer, another Austrian baritone, sang Wolfram in the première of *Tannhäuser* (1845) and created Kurwenal in *Tristan und Isolde* (1865). Telramund in *Lohengrin* (1850) was first sung by Hans von Milde, a baritone who passed his entire career at Weimar, where he created the title role of Cornelius's *Der Barbier von Bagdad* (1858) and the High Priest in the stage première of *Samson et Dalila* (1877); he also sang the Dutchman, Kurwenal and Hans Sachs.

August Kindermann began his immensely successful 50-year career at Leipzig, where he was befriended by Lortzing, who dedicated to him the score of *Hans Sachs*, in which he sang the title role (1840); Kindermann also created Count Eberbach in *Der Wildschütz* (1842). Moving to Munich, he sang Wotan in the premières of *Das Rheingold* (1869) and *Die Walküre* (1870); later he created Titurel in *Parsifal* at Bayreuth (1882). He celebrated his 40-year jubilee at Munich as Stadinger in Lortzing's *Der Waffenschmied* and retired at 72.

Franz Betz, having created Hans Sachs in *Die Meistersinger* at Munich (1868), sang Wotan in the first complete *Ring* cycle (during which he created the Wanderer in *Siegfried*) at Bayreuth (1876). He was engaged for nearly 40 years at the Berlin Hofoper where he sang a wide repertory including Don Giovanni, Hans Heiling and Pizarro as well as Falstaff in the Berlin première of Verdi's opera. Theodor Reichmann, Amfortas at all performances of *Parsifal* at Bayreuth in 1882 when the other main roles were shared between two or three singers, was a baritone of extensive range, vocally and stylistically; he returned to Bayreuth for Sachs and Wolfram, while at the Metropolitan he sang Luna, Escamillo and William Tell as well as his Wagner roles.

4. SINGERS AND ROLES: THE 20TH CENTURY. The two baritones who took part in the première of *Pelléas et Mélisande*, at the Opéra-Comique in 1902, were of dissimilar types: Jean Périer (Pelléas) was a typical 'baryton Martin' with a comparatively light, high-lying voice (he also created Don Ramiro in *L'heure espagnole* and the title role of Rabaud's *Mârouf*), while Hector Dufranne (Golaud), a Belgian, had a heavier though still lyrical voice (the previous year he had created the Marquis de Saluces in Massenet's *Grisélidis*, and he sang the Father in *Louise*). Both sang in the American première of *Pelléas* by the Manhattan Opera.

Another fine baritone to sing with the Manhattan Opera was Mario Sammarco; having created Gérard (*Andrea Chénier*, 1896) and Cascart (*Zazà*, 1900) in Italy, he sang Enrico Ashton, Rigoletto and Scarpia in New York. Pasquale Amato, the first Italian Golaud at La Scala, sang for more than a dozen seasons at the Metropolitan, where he created Jack Rance in *La fanciulla del West* (1910), the title role of Damrosch's *Cyrano de Bergerac* (1913) and Napoleon in Giordano's *Madame Sans-Gêne* (1915). Giuseppe De Luca, who had created Michonnet (*Adriana Lecouvreur*, 1902), Gleby (Giordano's *Siberia*, 1903) and Sharpless (*Madama Butterfly*, 1904) in Italy early in his career, later sang at the Metropolitan for 20 years, creating Paquiro (*Goyescas*, 1916) and Gianni Schicchi (1918), while his huge repertory ranged from Figaro (Mozart and Rossini) to Rigoletto, his favourite role; that he could still perform this role at the age of 70 is a commentary on the masterly technique of this most accomplished and stylish of baritones.

Richard Strauss wrote several effective baritone roles, beginning with Kunrad (*Feuersnot*), sung at the Dresden première in 1901 by Karl Scheidemantel, who also created Faninal in *Der Rosenkavalier* (1911) and sang Wolfram, Amfortas and Hans Sachs at Bayreuth. Karl Perron, the bass-baritone who created John the Baptist (*Salome*, 1905), Orestes (*Elektra*, 1909) and Baron Ochs (*Der Rosenkavalier*), sang Amfortas and Wotan at Bayreuth as well as King Mark and Daland, more usually bass roles. Anton van Rooy, the Dutch bass-baritone who sang John the Baptist in the American première of *Salome* at the Metropolitan and in the American première of *Parsifal* (1903), had sung Wotan, Sachs and the Dutchman at Bayreuth.

The most famous interpreter of Ochs, Richard Mayr, who created Barak in *Die Frau ohne Schatten*, was really a bass. Friedrich Plaschke, the bass-baritone, took part in five Strauss premières at Dresden, where he was engaged for nearly 40 years; he sang minor roles in *Feuersnot* and *Salome*, Altair in *Die ägyptische Helena* (1928), Waldner in *Arabella* (1933) and Morosus in *Die schweigsame Frau* (1935), the last two properly bass roles. He also sang Barak and the title role of *Boris Godunov*, both Dresden premières. The baritone hero of *Arabella*, Mandryka, was created by Alfred Jerger, who also sang in the Vienna and London premières of the opera. The Barber in *Die schweigsame Frau* was first sung by Mathieu Ahlersmeyer, who also created Egk's Peer Gynt (1938) and Almaviva in Klebe's *Figaro lässt sich scheiden* (1963); a specialist in contemporary opera, he sang the title role in the British stage première of Hindemith's *Mathis der Maler* at Edinburgh. Other noted baritones of this era were Herbert Janssen, outstanding in the lighter Wagner roles, and Gerhard Hüsch, a warm, lyric singer specially admired as Papageno.

Two bass-baritones with generous voices, Friedrich Schorr and Rudolf Bockelmann, were renowned for their performances of Wagner between the wars; both were especially admired as Wotan and Hans Sachs. Schorr also sang Barak, Cardinal Borromeo (*Palestrina*), Busoni's Doctor Faust and Daniello in the American première of Krenek's *Jonny spielt auf*, while Bockelmann created the title role of Krenek's *Leben des Orest* (1930) at Leipzig.

Hans Hotter, in a career lasting over 60 years, began as a high baritone and progressed through bass-baritone to bass. He created the Commandant in Strauss's *Friedenstag* (1938) and Olivier in *Capriccio* (1942) and sang Jupiter at the unofficial première (the dress rehearsal) of *Die Liebe der Danae* (1944). During the 1950s he became the leading Wagnerian bass-baritone, unrivalled as Wotan, Kurwenal, Amfortas, Sachs and the Dutchman; he also sang Almaviva, Don Giovanni, Pizarro, the Grand Inquisitor and Cardinal Borromeo. Later he took on Wagner's bass roles, singing with equal success as Pogner, King Mark and Gurnemanz. He sang Schigolch in *Lulu* at San Francisco in 1989, repeating the role at Vienna, Madrid, Barcelona and Paris (1991), when his vitality and authority were undiminished. Paul Schöffler, who sang Jupiter at the official première of *Die Liebe der Danae* at Salzburg in 1952, began his career, like Hotter, as a lyric baritone before progressing to heavier roles in the bass-baritone range. At Salzburg he created Danton in Einem's *Dantons Tod* (1947) and sang La Roche, the theatre director, in *Capriccio*. His favourite and most popular role was Hans Sachs.

Three distinguished American baritones, Lawrence Tibbett, Leonard Warren and Robert Merrill, all noted interpreters of Verdi, spanned 52 years of Italian opera at the Metropolitan. Tibbett, a powerful actor as well as a superb singer, created roles in several American operas, including Colonel Ibbetson in Taylor's *Peter Ibbetson* (1931) and the title role of Gruenberg's *The Emperor Jones* (1933), one of his greatest triumphs. Warren, with an even larger, more lustrous voice that easily encompassed *a′*, concentrated on Verdi, singing Rigoletto, Iago, Amonasro, Luna, Macbeth and Boccanegra with particular success. Merrill, a lyric baritone, was outstanding as Germont (*La traviata*); his secure technique enabled him also to sing Rossini, Donizetti and Bellini.

John Brownlee, the Australian baritone and protégé of Melba, sang frequently in Paris, where his roles included Athanaël in *Thaïs* and Golaud; a fine Mozart stylist, he sang Don Giovanni, Count Almaviva and Don Alfonso at Glyndebourne in the 1930s. Another outstanding stylist was the Italian baritone Mariano Stabile, chosen by Toscanini to sing Falstaff at La Scala (1921–2); he also sang the role at Covent Garden, as well as Iago, Rigoletto and Scarpia, and appeared at Glyndebourne, making an excellent Figaro and a fine Dr Malatesta. In 1961, at the age of 73, he sang Falstaff in Siena. The mantle of Stabile descended in certain respects on Tito Gobbi, a magnificent comic actor as well as a powerful tragedian. The first Italian Wozzeck, Gobbi had over 100 roles in his repertory, but excelled in Verdi and Puccini; his Posa, Iago, Macbeth, Boccanegra and Falstaff were notable for their dramatic effectiveness, while as Scarpia, opposite the Tosca of Maria Callas, he has remained unrivalled.

Geraint Evans, the Welsh baritone who often sang Mozart's Figaro to Gobbi's Count and Leporello to Gobbi's Don Giovanni, became an excellent Falstaff, a role he first sang at Glyndebourne; Evans created Mr Flint (*Billy Budd*, 1951) and Mountjoy (*Gloriana*, 1953), and also sang Britten's Balstrode, Nick Bottom and Claggart, though his finest 20th-century role was Wozzeck. The Croatian baritone Marko Rothmüller, also a moving Wozzeck, created Truchsess in *Mathis der Maler* at Zürich (1938) and sang Macbeth and Nick Shadow (*The Rake's Progress*) at Glyndebourne; Nick Shadow had been created at Venice (1951) by Otakar Kraus, the dark-toned Czech bass-baritone whose most effective role was Alberich, which he sang at Bayreuth and Covent Garden.

Dietrich Fischer-Dieskau, whose large repertory embraces Mozart, Verdi, Wagner and Strauss (notably Barak and Mandryka), sings many roles in contemporary opera: he created Mittenhofer in Henze's *Elegy for Young Lovers* (1961) and the title role of Reimann's *Lear* (1978), both composed for him. An extremely effective actor, he has also sung Busoni's Faust, Mathis, Wozzeck and Dr Schön. Sherrill Milnes, the American baritone who succeeded to the roles once sung by Tibbett, Warren and Merrill, has also been successful in the French repertory, in particular as Thomas' Hamlet, Alphonse XI (*La favorite*) and Saint-Saëns' Henry VIII. Early in his career he sang Ruprecht in the American première of Prokofiev's *The Fiery Angel* and created Adam Brant in Levy's *Mourning Becomes Electra* (1967). A noted American bass-baritone, prominent as Wotan in the 1980s, is James Morris.

During the 1970s Piero Cappuccilli came to be regarded as the leading Verdi baritone in Italy, a position he held for nearly two decades. With some 16 Verdi roles in his repertory, he excelled in the more generous characters, such as Posa and Boccanegra, but was also vocally magnificent as Macbeth even if the evil side of the character escaped him. Another singer pre-eminent in the Verdi and Donizetti repertories was the Italian baritone, Renato Bruson. In Britain, Thomas Allen has become one of the most versatile baritones of his generation; he is especially noted for his Mozart roles (Figaro, Don Giovanni, Papageno), for his accomplishment in Verdi, his sombre Onegin and stirring Billy Budd.

The opening up of eastern Europe and the former USSR has revealed a formidable number of talented singers; they include the baritones Alexandru Agache from Romania, a Verdi specialist who is a magnificent Boccanegra and Renato, and the Russian-born Sergey Leiferkus, who sings Don Giovanni, Escamillo and Zurga (*Les pêcheurs de perles*) as well as Tomsky, Onegin, Prince Igor and Ruprecht in authentic style.

For bibliography *see* SINGING: A BIBLIOGRAPHY.

OWEN JANDER, LIONEL SAWKINS, J. B. STEANE, ELIZABETH FORBES

Barkworth, John (Edmond) (*b* Beverley, 20 May 1858; *d* Geneva, 18 Nov 1929). English composer. He studied music with Parry, Stanford, Humperdinck and others, took the Oxford BMus in 1890, and taught the organ at the Peabody Conservatory, Baltimore. He later settled in Cambridge. He wrote three operas: *Romeo and Juliet* (vs, London, 1926), performed at Middlesbrough in 1916 and in London in 1920 and 1926; *The Well of Wishes*; and *Fireflies*, given at the RCM in 1925. *Romeo and Juliet*, his principal work, is remarkable for setting Shakespeare's text almost unaltered.

*

W. Dean: 'Shakespeare and Opera', *Shakespeare in Music*, ed. P. Hartnoll (London, 1964), 89–175, esp. 151–2

Barlow, Samuel L(atham) M(itchell) (*b* New York, 1 June 1892; *d* Wyndmoor, PA, 19 Sept 1982). American composer. He was a pupil of Percy Goetschius and Franklin Robinson in New York, and of Philipp in Paris and Respighi in Rome (1923). His one-act opera *Mon ami Pierrot*, to a libretto by Sacha Guitry on the life of Lully and purporting to show the origin of the French children's song 'Au clair de la lune', was the first by an American to be performed at the Opéra-Comique in Paris (11 January 1935). He also wrote the operas *Amanda* (1936) and *Eugénie*, besides some novel orchestral pieces. His style was relatively conservative: he admitted that 'tunes which wouldn't shock Papa Brahms keep sticking their necks out'.

H. WILEY HITCHCOCK

Barmen. One of six towns that merged in 1929 to form the city of WUPPERTAL.

Barnett, John (*b* Bedford, 1 or 15 July 1802; *d* Leckhampton, 16 April 1890). English composer of German and Hungarian parentage. At the age of 11 he was articled to S. J. Arnold, proprietor of the Lyceum Theatre, London, making his first stage appearance in *The Shipwreck* on 22 July 1813, and he continued to sing on the stage until 1818. At the same time he studied the piano, and composition with William Horsley and C. E. Horn. Between 1826 and 1833, he wrote incidental music for farces, melodramas and burlesques. Though some of these were highly successful, particularly *The Pet of the Petticoats* (1832), and others contained songs that soon became popular favourites, the music in general was not of a high standard. In 1832 Lucia Vestris appointed him musical director at the Olympic Theatre.

On 14 July 1834 Arnold reopened the Lyceum and soon began to produce full-length English operas of a kind that had become almost obsolete, the only recent representatives being Bishop's *Aladdin* (1826), Weber's *Oberon* (1826) and Ries's *The Sorceress* (1831). Loder's *Nourjahad* was the first (21 July 1834). Barnett's *The Mountain Sylph* which followed (25 August) went even further than Loder's work by replacing most of the customary spoken dialogue with recitative; it was thus one of the first English operas to contain through-composed scenes since Arne's *Artaxerxes* (1762), a work for which Barnett had unbounded admiration. Barnett had written some of the music for a play at the Victoria Theatre, but he now 'heightened' it into a 'romantic grand opera'. He dedicated the published vocal score to Arnold 'for the spirit, zeal, and enthusiasm which he has shewn in the production of Native Operas, and in cherishing native talent'. However, Arnold's primary effort was towards the establishment of serious opera in the English language; he did not feel that either plot or music need be drawn from English traditions. The story of *The Mountain Sylph* was accordingly taken from French sources, and the music was a good deal less 'English' than most of Bishop's. But its success proved that audiences were now prepared to listen to dramatic music with an English text. It had an initial run of about 100 nights, and held its own on the stage for the rest of the century.

Barnett unfortunately quarrelled with Arnold, and publicly accused him of breaking a financial agreement. He had already been at odds with Alfred Bunn, another leading figure in the world of the theatre; later he was to add Mapleson to his mounting list of theatrical adversaries. His next two serious operas, *Fair Rosamond* and *Farinelli*, were produced at Drury Lane. Neither was through-composed, and both show a tendency to return to the older conception of English opera as a string of independent songs and ballads – some of which, however, are of good quality. In 1838 he joined with the dramatist Morris Barnett (unrelated to him) in an effort to set up a permanent English Opera House at St James's Theatre. But it closed after a week. After one more attempt to establish English opera, this time at the Prince's Theatre (1840), he abandoned the London stage. In 1841 he went to live in Cheltenham, where he became a highly successful singing teacher; soon afterwards he published two books about learning to sing. He lived nearly 50 years longer but never again attempted to produce an opera. An advanced 'freethinker', he became an inveterate controversialist, constantly writing trenchant letters of protest to the press: he engaged in a great battle with Leigh Hunt over the merits of English opera in the *Tatler*, claiming among other things that some of Bishop's music was worthy of Mozart.

Barnett's position was an eminent one, largely based on *The Mountain Sylph*. Macfarren wrote that 'its production opened a new period for music in this country, from which is to be dated the establishment of an English dramatic school, which, if not yet accomplished, has made many notable advances'. Barnett's failure to follow up his success must be attributed in great part to an irascible disposition verging on paranoia. His other works include sacred and secular vocal music as well as orchestral and chamber works.

See also MOUNTAIN SYLPH, THE.

all first performed in London; all printed works published in London; MS librettos in GB-Lbl

Robert the Devil (musical drama), Covent Garden, 2 Feb 1830, 1 song *Bp* [adapted from Meyerbeer]
The Deuce is in Her (operetta, 1, R. J. Raymond), Adelphi, 28 Aug 1830, 1 song (1830)
The Picturesque (operetta, T. H. Bayly), Adelphi, 25 Aug 1831, *Bp*, 1 song (?1840)
The Convent, or The Pet of the Petticoats (operetta, J. B. Buckstone), Sadler's Wells, 9 July 1832, *Bp**
Win Her and Wear Her (comic op, 3, S. Beazley, after S. Centlivre: *A Bold Stroke for a Wife*), Drury Lane, 18 Dec 1832, *Bp**
The Soldier's Widow, or The Ruins of the Mill (musical drama, E. Fitzball), Adelphi, 4 May 1833, *Bp**
The Mountain Sylph (grand op, 2, T. J. Thackeray), Lyceum, 25 Aug 1834, *Bp**, vs (1834)
Fair Rosamond (4, C. Z. Barnett and F. Shannon), Drury Lane, 28 Feb 1837, *Bp**, vs (1837)
Farinelli (serio-comic op, 2, Barnett), Drury Lane, 8 Feb 1839, *Bp*, selections (1839)
Kathleen, 1840 (J. S. Knowles), unperf., *Bp*
Queen Mab, 1841, unperf., *Bp*
Marie, 1845, unfinished

*

DNB; *Grove1* (E. F. Rimbault); *LoewenbergA*; *StiegerO*
'Theatrical Journal', *European Magazine*, lxiv/July (1813), 44–7, esp. 46
J. Sainsbury, ed.: *A Dictionary of Musicians* (London, 2/1825)
Monthly Supplement to the Musical Library, i (1834), 70, 84
Musical World, ii (1836), 139; iv (1837), 172, 188; xii (1839), 117; xiv (1840), 349, 365, 393
A. Bunn: *The Stage*, i (London, 1840), 138–40
G. A. Macfarren: 'Barnett, John', *The Imperial Dictionary of Universal Biography*, ed. J. F. Waller (London, 1859–63)
J. D. Brown and S. S. Stratton: *British Musical Biography* (Birmingham, 1897)
J. F. Barnett: *Musical Reminiscences and Impressions* (London, 1906)
H. M. Rogers: 'John Barnett, Musician', *Harvard Graduates' Magazine*, xxxiii (1924–5), 595; pubd separately (Cambridge, MA, 1925)
C. K. Rogers: *Memories of a Musical Career* (Norwood, MA, 1932)
P. A. Scholes: *The Mirror of Music 1844–1944* (London, 1947), 7–8
C. Rice: *The London Theatre in the Eighteen-Thirties* (MS, 1837); ed. A. C. Sprague and B. Shuttleworth (London, 1950), 16–17
E. W. White: *The Rise of English Opera* (London, 1951)
E. D. Mackerness: 'Leigh Hunt's Musical Journalism', *MMR*, lxxxvi (1956), 212–22, esp. 217
B. Carr: 'The First All-sung English 19th-century Opera', *MT*, cxv (1974), 125–6
E. W. White: *A History of English Opera* (London, 1983)
——: *A Register of First Performances of English Operas and Semi-Operas* (London, 1983)
N. Temperley: 'John Barnett: The Mountain Sylph', *PEM*, i (1986), 196–7 NICHOLAS TEMPERLEY, NIGEL BURTON

Barometermacher auf der Zauberinsel, Der ('The Barometer-Maker on the Enchanted Island'). *Zauberposse* in two acts by WENZEL MÜLLER to a libretto by FERDINAND RAIMUND; Vienna, Theater in der Leopoldstadt, 18 December 1823.

Subtitled 'parody of the fairy-tale: Prince Tutu', this play was based on the story 'Die Prinzessin mit der langen Nase' in Wieland's collection *Dschinnistan*. The shipwrecked Viennese barometer-maker Quecksilber (tenor) has come into possession of a magic staff but is tricked out of it by Princess Zoraide (spoken), who later also gains his magic horn and sash. He gets his own back by giving her magic figs that make her nose grow unattractively long and recovers his possessions by tricking her with an ineffective antidote, then marries her charming servant Linda (soprano) before setting off for home. Several of the 22 songs and dances are more extensive and adventurous than usual at this late stage of Müller's career, though it is the tuneful songs that have worn best. *Der Barometermacher* was widely performed in Raimund's lifetime (it was given nearly a hundred times in the Leopoldstadt) and is still frequently revived. PETER BRANSCOMBE

Baroness, The. *See* LINDELHEIM, JOANNA MARIA.

Baroni, Leonora. *See* BASILE, ADRIANA.

Barraud, Henry (*b* Bordeaux, 23 April 1900). French composer. He entered the Paris Conservatoire in 1926, studying composition with Dukas, fugue with Caussade and, on the advice of Florent Schmitt, orchestration and composition with Louis Aubert. He was soon expelled for writing a string quartet (now lost) that was considered outrageously innovatory. Together with Rivier, he helped to organize the Triton concerts in 1933. During the war he assisted with Resistance broadcasting in occupied France, afterwards becoming head of music for Radiodiffusion Française.

His main operatic success has been *Lavinia*, a full-length *opéra bouffe* first performed in 1961. The action takes place in Naples and centres on Gennaro, a vegetable seller (bass), his wife Nunziatina (contralto) and his 18-year-old daughter Maria-Stella (soprano). A young journalist, Carluccio (tenor), is in love with Maria-Stella and although she returns his love, her father disapproves. When Nunziatina gives birth to a second child, Carluccio announces the birth in his newspaper as a christening present, pointing out that the newborn has been given 'the name of Enée's [Aeneas's] wife, Lavinia'. This leads to a series of misunderstandings on the part of Peppino (tenor), a scrap-metal merchant, and various neighbours, who assume that the said Enée must be the father of the child, and that Nunziatina (despite her enormous size) has been unfaithful. When the mistake is finally pointed out, Gennaro gives his consent for Carluccio and Maria-Stella to marry, on condition that there will be no publicity.

The musical style of the opera reflects the influences of the composer's teachers: Barraud uses a tonal language rich in added-note harmony, and the orchestration is skilful and luxuriant. Barraud has written perceptively in his book *Les cinq grands opéras* (Paris, 1972) on *Don Giovanni*, *Tristan*, *Boris Godunov*, *Pelléas* and *Wozzeck*.

La farce de maître Pathelin, 1938 (1, G. Cohen, after medieval fable), Paris, OC (Favart), 24 June 1948
Numance, 1950–52 (2, S. de Madariaga, after M. de Cervantes), Paris, Opéra, 15 April 1955
Lavinia, 1959 (opéra bouffe, 3, F. Marceau), Aix-en-Provence, 20 July 1961
Le roi Gordogane, 1974 (chamber op, 3, R. Ivsic), Bordeaux, Grand, 6 Jan 1978
Tête d'or, 1980 (tragédie lyrique, 2, after P. Claudel), concert perf., Paris, Champs-Elysées, 1985

*

P. Pistone and P. de Prat: 'Henri Barraud et le Théâtre lyrique', *Le théâtre lyrique français, 1945–1985*, ed. D. Pistone (Paris, 1987), 203–8

RICHARD LANGHAM SMITH

Barrera [De Curtis], **Giulia** (*b* New York, 28 April 1942). American soprano. She studied in New York and made her début at the City Opera in 1963, as Aida. Other Verdi repertory includes Amelia (*Ballo*) and Leonora in *Il trovatore*. Her career is based in New York, but guest appearances have taken her to San Francisco, Pittsburgh, Washington, Seattle and New Orleans. She has also appeared with the WNO in Cardiff, and in Rome and Copenhagen. Further repertory includes Tosca, Turandot, Sieglinde, Donna Anna and Santuzza. DAVID CUMMINGS

Barrera (Saavedra), Tomás (*b* La Solana, Ciudad Real, 13 Feb 1870; *d* Madrid, 16 July 1938). Spanish composer. The son of a carpenter, he developed musical interests while working in a piano store. He moved to Madrid with an introduction to Ruperto Chapí, who found him a place in the orchestra of the Teatro de la Zarzuela and assisted the completion of his musical studies under Valentin Arín. Barrera later became conductor at the Teatro de la Zarzuela and was a prolific exponent of the zarzuela, composing in a fluent and direct style well suited to pleasing the undemanding audiences. He is best remembered for the tenor solo 'Granadinas' (from *Emigrantes*, 1905), popularized by Tito Schipa, Miguel Fleta and others.

selective list; mostly one-act zarzuelas

El petit buffete, 1899; A cuarto y a dos (parodía, G. Merino and C. Lucio), Madrid, 26 Jan 1900, collab. R. Calleja; La señora capitána (J. Jackson Veyán), Madrid, Romea, 21 March 1900, collab. Q. Valverde *hijo*; El fondo del baúl (Jackson Veyán), Madrid, 18 Sept 1900, collab. Valverde *hijo*; La cara de dios (parodía, Merino and Lucio), Madrid, Oct 1900, collab. Calleja; Floridor (G. Cantó), Madrid, Romea, Nov 1900; La maestra (E. Navarro Gonzalvo and J. López Silva), Madrid, Eslava, 19 Jan 1901, collab. Calleja and V. Lleó; Los monigotes del chico (Navarro Gonzalvo), Madrid, Moderne, June 1901, collab. Calleja
La tremenda (López Silva and Jackson Veyán), Madrid, Moderne, June 1901, collab. Valverde *hijo*; Los niños llorones (C. Arniches, A. Paso and E. García Alvarez), Madrid, 4 July 1901, collab. T. L. Torregrosa and Valverde *hijo*; El género infimo (pasillo, S. Alvarez Quintero and J. Alvarez Quintero), Madrid, Apolo, 17 July 1901, collab. Valverde *hijo*; El código penal (E. Sierra and J. Abati), Madrid, Cómico, 24 Dec 1901, collab. Valverde *hijo*; El olivar (A. Melantuche and G. Arista), Madrid, Jan 1902, collab. J. Serrano; Píquito de oro (Saenz), Madrid, Zarzuela, Oct 1902, collab. J. M. Guervós
Ideícas (Melantuche), Madrid, Zarzuela, Sept 1905; La vara del alcalde (Melantuche), Madrid, Zarzuela, 23 Dec 1905; Emigrantes, 1905, collab. Calleja; La silla de manos, 1905, collab. Caballero; Calínez, 1906; La cantinera, 1906; El maño, 1906; Manolo el afilador, 1906; La manzana de oro, 1906, collab. Calleja; La mujer de cartón, 1906; Villa alegre, 1906; El carro de las cortes de la muerte, 1907; El delfín, 1907; El celoso extremeño, Barcelona, April 1908; Cantos baturros, 1908; Cuentan de un sabio que un día, Madrid, 1908, collab. P. Marquina; El guarda jurao, 1908
La canción á la vida, 1908/9, collab. Calleja; ¡A. C. T! ... ¡Qué se va el tío! (epitafio cómico-lírico, 1, M. Fernández Palomero and E. Córdoba), Madrid, Zarzuela, 27 Feb 1909, collab. P. Luna; El Aretino (M. Castro and Boada), Madrid, Gran, Dec 1909, collab. Guervós; La tajadera, 1909; La luna del amor, Madrid, Martín, April 1910, collab. Calleja; El baile de la flor (sainete), Madrid, Gran, July 1912, collab. L. Foglietti; La hija del mar, 1912; Tenorio musical (humorada, Parcela), Madrid, Feb 1913; La suerta de la fea, Madrid, Novedades, April 1913
La socorito (A. Caamaño), Madrid, Novedades, Jan 1914, collab. Calleja; Las chulas de Madrid, Madrid, Gran, Feb 1914; El sueño de Pierrot, Madrid, Apolo, June 1914; El alma del Garibay (revista, 1, García Alvarez and A. López Monis), Madrid, Magic Park, July 1914; El caballero de Narunkestunkesberg, Madrid, Apolo, Dec 1914; El alma del querer, 1914, collab. A. Vives; Las dos reinas, 1914, collab. Calleja; La alegre Diana, 1916; El marido de la engracia (sainete, P. Muñoz Seca and P. Pérez Fernández), 1917, collab. J. Taboada
El agua del Manzanares, o Cuando el río suena, 1918; La última revista (revista, J. Romea), Madrid, Oct 1920, collab. M. Quislant; La del dos de mayo (sainete, 1, S. and J. Alvarez Quintero), Madrid, Apolo, 1920; Las tres cosas de Juanita (E. Polo and Romea), Madrid, Novedades, 8 June 1921, collab. Quislant; El niño de la suerte (J. Ramos Martín), 1922; La virgen capitana (Ramos Martín), Saragossa, 1923; ¡Que viene el lobo!, 1929; La payesa de Sarria (M. Fernández de la Puente, after L. Eguílaz), 1930

*

A. Peña y Goni: *La ópera española y la música dramática en el siglo XIX* (Madrid, 1881; abridged E. Rincón, as *España desde la ópera a la zarzuela*, 1967)
S. Delgado: *Mi teatro* (Madrid, 1905)
'Barrera Saavedra (Tomás)', *Enciclopedia universal ilustrada europeo-americana*, appx i (Madrid, 1930), 1348
A. Fernández-Cid: *Cien años de teatro musical en España (1875–1975)* (Madrid, 1975)

ANDREW LAMB

Barrientos, Maria (*b* Barcelona, 10 March 1884; *d* Ciboure, Basses-Pyrénées, 8 Aug 1946). Spanish soprano. After a short course of singing lessons at the Barcelona Conservatory, she made her début at the age of 14 at the Teatro Lirico in *La sonnambula*, followed by several other leading roles there and at the Teatro de Novidades. After further studies, she sang at Covent Garden (in *Il barbiere di Siviglia*, 1903), at La Scala (in Meyerbeer's *Dinorah* and in *Barbiere*, 1904–5), and at many leading theatres throughout the world. On 31 Jan 1916 she made her Metropolitan début in *Lucia di Lammermoor*, and appeared there regularly in the standard coloratura roles during the next four seasons. In later years she became an admired interpreter of French and Spanish songs, and made a valuable set of records, including de Falla's *Siete canciones populares españoles* and *Soneto a Córdoba* with the composer at the piano.

*

GV (R. Celletti; R. Vegeto)
C. Williams: 'Maria Barrientos', *Record Collector*, xxviii (1983), 71–95 [with discography] DESMOND SHAWE-TAYLOR

Barrington, Rutland [Fleet, George Rutland] (*b* Penge, 15 Jan 1853; *d* London, 31 May 1922). English baritone. From 1875 he appeared with the entertainer Mrs Howard Paul, joining her (as Dr Daly) in the original cast of *The Sorcerer* in 1877 and creating the further Gilbert and Sullivan roles of Captain Corcoran (*HMS Pinafore*), Sergeant of Police (*The Pirates of Penzance*), Grosvenor (*Patience*), Earl of Mountararat (*Iolanthe*), King Hildebrand (*Princess Ida*), Pooh-Bah (*The Mikado*), Sir Despard Murgatroyd (*Ruddigore*), Giuseppe (*The Gondoliers*), King Paramount (*Utopia Limited*) and Ludwig (*The Grand Duke*). Other works in which he created leading roles were Edward Solomon's *The Nautch Girl* (1891), Sidney Jones's *The Geisha* (1896) and Lionel Monckton's *A Country Girl* (1902). He reappeared in Gilbert and Sullivan roles under W. S. Gilbert at the Savoy in 1908–9.

ANDREW LAMB

Barroilhet, Paul(-Bernard) (*b* Bayonne, 22 Sept 1810; *d* Paris, April 1871). French baritone. After studying at the Paris Conservatoire, he went in 1830 to Italy, where he sang in Milan, Genoa, Verona, Trieste, Turin, Palermo and Rome. Engaged at S Carlo, he created roles in Donizetti's *L'assedio di Calais* (1836) and *Roberto Devereux* (1837) and in Mercadante's *Elena da Feltre* (1838) and *La vestale* (1840). On returning to Paris he was engaged at the Opéra, where he sang in the first performances of Donizetti's *La favorite* (1840) and *Dom Sébastien* (1843); Halévy's *La reine de Chypre* (1841) and *Charles VI* (1843); and Adam's *Richard en Palestine* (1843). His other roles included Don Giovanni, William Tell, Donizetti's Torquato Tasso, Enrico Ashton and Belisarius, and many others in the Italian and French repertories. In 1847 he left the Opéra and, apart from appearances in Madrid (1851–2), where he sang Don Carlo in *Ernani*, retired from the stage. His voice was beautiful in timbre, flexible and expressive.

*

J.-L. Tamvaco: 'Paul-Bernard Barroilhet', *Donizetti Society Journal*, ii (1975), 130–42 ELIZABETH FORBES

Barry, Gerald (*b* Clarecastle, 28 April 1952). Irish composer. He studied in Cork, and afterwards on a series of scholarships with Peter Schat in Holland, Kagel and Stockhausen in Cologne, and Cerha in Vienna. On leaving Cologne in 1981 he returned to Dublin; the following year he became a lecturer in music at Cork University, where he remained until 1986.

Barry's earliest acknowledged work, the 1977 setting of the Pillow Book of Sei Shonagon, *Things that Gain by Being Painted*, first performed at the Institute of Contemporary Arts, London, on 24 February 1980, counterpoints a miming soprano soloist with an unseen narrator and reveals most palpably the influence of Kagel's concepts of music-theatre, while the ballet *Unkrautgarten* (1980) served in 1981 as the source of two short theatre pieces, *Cinderella* and *Snow White*. Musically, however, his work of the 1980s showed more and more interest in Baroque figuration, ornament and sonority, harking back to his early training as an organist.

Baroque and Classical models were especially important in the conception of the three-act opera that Barry began to prepare with the librettist Vincent Deane on his return to Ireland. *The Intelligence Park* (1981–7) was commissioned by the Institute of Contemporary Arts, but was eventually performed at the Almeida Festival on 6 July 1990; meanwhile sections of the score had appeared as independent concert works. Set in Dublin in 1753 and proceeding through a mixture of discrete numbers and constantly developing sections, it is both an opera about writing an opera and an exploration of the boundaries of the creative process. With evocations of *opera seria* and the use of puppets, it tells of a composer who has lost his creative spark, and his love for a famous castrato. The musical material is derived principally from a collection of Bach chorales; the text switches between ornate English and stylized Italian, and the exceptionally demanding vocal lines range from elaborate coloratura to *Sprechgesang*. A second opera, *The Triumph of Beauty and Deceit*, was commissioned by Channel 4 Television, London; to a text by Meredith Oakes, it also has 18th-century antecedents, in Benedetto Pamphili's libretto for the masque *The Triumph of Time and Truth*.

*

A. Jack: 'Introducing Gerald Barry', *MT*, cxxix (1988), 389–93
A. Clements: 'A Short Journey around *The Intelligence Park*', *Opera*, xxxxi (1990), 804–7 ANDREW CLEMENTS

Barski, Aleksander. *See* BANDROWSKI-SAS, ALEKSANDER.

Barsova [née Vladimirova], **Valeriya Vladimirovna** (*b* Astrakhan', 1/13 June 1892; *d* Sochi, 13 Dec 1967). Russian soprano. She studied with her sister, Mariya Vladimirova, then in Umberto Mazetti's class at the Moscow Conservatory. She made her début with the Zimin Private Opera, Moscow, in 1919, later becoming a soloist at the Bol'shoy (1920–48). She also sang at Stanislavsky's and Nemirovich-Danchenko's opera studios. To a light, silvery tone and an agile technique she added warmth and depth of feeling. She sang Glinka and Rimsky-Korsakov roles; Gilda, Violetta and Leonora (*Il trovatore*); Butterfly and Musetta, Lakmé and Manon. After 1929 she toured in Germany, Britain, Turkey, Poland, Yugoslavia and Bulgaria.

*

G. Polyanovsky: *V. V. Barsova* (Moscow and Leningrad, 1941)

I. M. YAMPOL'SKY

Barstow, Josephine (**Clare**) (*b* Sheffield, 27 Sept 1940). English soprano. She studied in Birmingham and London, then sang with Opera for All. In 1967 she joined Sadler's Wells, singing the Second Lady, Cherubino, Eurydice and Violetta, her début role with the WNO, for whom she sang Countess Almaviva, Fiordiligi, Mimì, Amelia (*Boccanegra*), Elisabeth de

Valois, Lisa, Jenůfa, Ellen Orford and Tatyana. Having made her Covent Garden début in 1969 as a Niece (*Peter Grimes*), she created Denise in *The Knot Garden* (1970), Young Woman in *We Come to the River* (1976) and Gayle in *The Ice Break* (1977), also singing Mrs Ford, Santuzza, Odabella and Lady Macbeth, which she recorded on video for Glyndebourne. She has appeared in Paris, Berlin, Munich, San Francisco, Chicago, Boston and at the Metropolitan, where she made her début in 1977 as Musetta. For Sadler's Wells, later the ENO, she created Marguerite in *The Story of Vasco* (1974); she sang Jeanne with them in *The Devils of Loudun* (1973) and Autonoe with the New Opera Company in *The Bassarids* (1974), both British stage premières. Her repertory at the ENO includes Natasha, Leonore, Salome, Octavian, the Marschallin, Arabella, Leonora (*La forza*), Aida, Sieglinde, Emilia Marty, Katerina Izmaylova and Ellen Orford. In 1986 at Salzburg she created Benigna in Penderecki's *Schwarze Maske*, then sang Tosca and Amelia (*Ballo*), which she recorded with Karajan. A powerful actress with a vibrant, flexible voice of highly individual timbre, capable of expressing the strongest emotions, she excels in portraying distraught characters.

*

E. Forbes: 'Josephine Barstow', *Opera*, xxv (1974), 859–64

ALAN BLYTH

Bárta [Barrta, Bartha, Bartta], **Josef** (*b* Prague, *c*1746; *d* Vienna, 13 June 1787). Czech composer. He was active as an organist in two Prague monastic churches until 1772. Then he evidently moved to Vienna, where all his dramatic works were first performed. His comic operas were given alongside those of such composers as Umlauf, Benda, Asplmayr, and later Mozart and Dittersdorf, as part of the German National-Singspiel project founded by Emperor Joseph II. Some of Bárta's arias were sufficiently popular to be arranged for instrumental chamber ensembles.

all first performed in Vienna

La diavolessa (Spl, 3, C. Goldoni), Burgtheater, 18 July 1772

Da ist nicht gut zu rathen (comische Oper, 2, G. Stephanie the younger), Burgtheater, 8 Aug 1778, inst arrs. *CS-Pnm*

Der adeliche Taglöhner (komisches Originalsingspiel, 3, J. Weidmann), Burgtheater, 28 March 1780, 1 scene and duet *A-Wn*, 3 inst arrs. *CS-Pnm*

Il mercato di Malmantile (dg, 3, F. Bussani, after Goldoni), Burgtheater, 26 Jan 1784, *A-Wn*, *I-Fc*

*

C. Schoenbaum: 'Die böhmischen Musiker in der Musikgeschichte Wiens vom Barock bis zur Romantik', *SMw*, xxv (1962), 475–95

O. E. Deutsch: 'Das Repertoire der Höfischen Oper, der Hof- und der Staatsoper', *ÖMz*, xxiv (1969), 369–70, 379–421

MILAN POŠTOLKA

Bartali [Barthali, Bartaldi], **Antonio.** *See* BERTALI, ANTONIO.

Bartay, András (*b* Széplak, 7 April 1799; *d* Mainz, 4 Oct 1854). Hungarian composer. He came of an aristocratic family and first worked as a civil servant. In 1829 he was a co-founder of the earliest singing school in Pest, and he was one of the first to publish Hungarian folksongs (1833–4). On 16 December 1837 his two-act comic opera *Aurelia, oder Das Weib am Konradstein* (K. Haffner) had its première at the Pest Municipal Theatre, and on 29 April 1839 his comic opera *Csel* ('Ruse'; 2, I. Jakab) had its première at the Pest Hungarian Theatre. Bartay was director of the Hungarian National Theatre in 1843–4 and it was during this short period that the most popular Hungarian theatrical genre of the 19th century, the so-called folk play, including both folksongs and folkdances, began to flourish. Bartay composed one other opera, *A magyatok Nápolyban* ('The Hungarians in Naples'), the overture of which was performed in Pest on 3 March 1847, and a melodrama, *Árpád népe* ('The People of Árpád'; 1847); both of these works are lost. After the collapse of the Hungarian struggle for independence, in 1849 Bartay emigrated, first to France and then to Germany. His other works include oratorios, songs and piano pieces. Although his music shows him to be a cultivated creator, it has little originality.

*

MGG (F. Bónis)

B. Szabolcsi: *A XIX. század magyar romantikus zenéje* [Romantic Hungarian Music in the 19th Century] (Budapest, 1951)

FERENC BÓNIS

Bartered Bride, The [*Prodaná nevěsta*]. Comic opera in three acts by BEDŘICH SMETANA to a libretto by KAREL SABINA; Prague, Provisional Theatre, 30 May 1866 (definitive version, Prague, Provisional Theatre, 25 September 1870).

Krušina *a farmer*	baritone
Ludmila *his wife*	soprano
Mařenka *their daughter*	soprano
Mícha *a smallholder*	bass
Háta *his wife*	mezzo-soprano
Vašek *their son*	tenor
Jeník *Mícha's son from his first marriage*	tenor
Kecal *a village marriage-broker*	bass
Circus Master	tenor
Esmeralda } *circus artists*	soprano
Indian } *circus artists*	bass

Villagers, circus artists, boys

Setting A village at festival time in the afternoon and early evening

Smetana commissioned a libretto for a comic opera from Sabina, librettist for his first opera (*The Brandenburgers in Bohemia*) and, according to his diary entry on 5 July 1863, received it apparently in the form of a one-act piece. On 1 September 1864 the periodical *Slavoj* announced that Smetana had completed the overture to a two-act opera of which he had now received the first act. As yet the opera had no name: it may well be, as František Bartoš (1955) speculates, that the 'comic overture by Smetana' played at the Umělecká Beseda on 18 November 1863 (in a four-hand arrangement) was the already completed overture to *The Bartered Bride*. Smetana seems to have finished the piano sketch during the first months of 1865 (only then did he give a name to the opera); orchestration was completed on 15 March 1866, simultaneously with sketching his next opera, *Dalibor*. Two duets for the Circus Master and Esmeralda, not in the libretto, were added after this date. Smetana himself rehearsed and conducted the first performances; the producer was Josef Jiří Kolár, the designer Josef Macourek. The original cast included the chief prima donna of the company, the coloratura soprano Eleanora z Ehrenbergů, as Mařenka and the celebrated actor Jindřich Mošna as the Circus Master (this casting perhaps explains why the latter part places so few vocal demands on its interpreter).

At first the opera was far less successful than its predecessor, *The Brandenburgers in Bohemia*, and its popularity with the Czech public only gradual. Its worldwide popularity – for many years it was the only Czech opera in general repertory – dates from the performances given by the Prague National Theatre at the Vienna Music and Theatre Exhibition in 1892.

Its original version was much shorter, in two acts (the first act ended where the present second act ends), without dances and other numbers, and with spoken dialogue. Over the next four years many changes were made:

27 October 1866 (third performance): one duet for the Circus Master and Esmeralda (the couplet 'Ten staví

Terezie Rückaufová as Mařenka at a performance of Smetana's 'The Bartered Bride' at the Provisional Theatre, Prague, in 1867

se svatouškem': 'This man becomes a saint') excluded and the Act 1 ballet from *The Brandenburgers in Bohemia* (now labelled 'Gypsy ballet') inserted instead.

29 January 1869 (17th performance; 'second version'): Act 1 divided into two scenes (the second set in the inn, beginning with a newly composed drinking chorus). A newly composed polka opened Act 2 (before Vašek's aria) and Mařenka's final solo was extended.

1 June 1869 (21st performance; 'third version'): the opera divided into three acts corresponding to the final division except that the newly written *furiant* is at the end of Act 1 after the polka (now transferred to this position). Act 3 included a newly written *skočná* (to replace the *Brandenburgers* ballet) and introductory march for the circus troupe.

25 September 1870 (30th performance; 'fourth' and definitive version): newly composed recitatives replaced spoken dialogue, the *furiant* transferred to Act 2, after the drinking chorus.

ACT 1 *The village green beside a tavern* The long, separate overture is a tour de force of the genre: wonderfully spirited (it is marked 'Vivacissimo') and equally wonderfully crafted. Its most striking features are the extended string fugato (heard immediately after the opening unison tutti) and the climactic tutti with prominent syncopations and third-beat stresses. It is followed by a leisurely prelude, providing a genre description of the village at church festival time. The prelude (based on an earlier piano piece) includes one of the first bagpipe imitations in Czech opera: open 5th drones, and perky, decorated wind parts. The chorus that it prepares for, 'Proč bychom se netěšili?' ('Why shouldn't we be glad?', ex.1), was noted down untexted

as a 'Chorus for a comedy' in Smetana's 'Notebook of Motifs' in October 1862; Sabina was presumably instructed to fit his words to it. The solo middle section introduces the lovers Jeník and Mařenka, with ex.1 now inflected into the minor to suggest Mařenka's low spirits.

In the following recitative, originally of course prose dialogue, Mařenka explains her unhappiness. Mícha is due to arrive in the village to negotiate a marriage between her and his son Vašek. She fears that her parents will try to force her into it. Of course she will remain faithful to Jeník, but she knows so little of his past, as she explains in her aria; why had he left his native village? Jeník responds (in recitative) that he was the son of a wealthy father, but his mother died young, his father married again and his stepmother drove him from home. Their charming duet 'Jako matka' ('Like a mother') is followed by a brief recitative link that leads into the well-loved section about constancy ('Věrné milování'), with its lilting clarinet accompaniment in 6ths. They go off singly.

Another celebrated number follows: Kecal the marriage-broker, accompanied by Mařenka's parents Ludmila and Krušina, announces that everything is ready, 'Jak vám pravím pane kmotře' ('As I said to you'). Kecal's verbose and self-important character (his name means 'babbler') is immediately established by his music – at first limited to two pitches and then to rapid patter. Ludmila thinks they are moving too fast – there might be some obstacles. In his most portentous vein, Kecal declares that their wills and his cleverness will overcome all obstacles.

In the following recitative Krušina says that he knows Mícha, the father of the proposed bridegroom, but has never met his two sons – which one is being proposed? Kecal replies that it is the second, for the first is a good-for-nothing vagabond, and in a terzetto he provides a flattering character reference for Vašek. Mařenka enters. In the conversational quartet that follows, Kecal tells Mařenka that he has a husband for her, and Mařenka declares that there may be a problem: with the return of the lilting clarinet theme she explains that she already has a lover. In his typical staccato patter Kecal orders that the lover be sent packing; Mařenka responds in long notes, *con espressione*, that she has already given her heart. Little is resolved in the following recitative, especially when Kecal reveals that the prospective bridegroom is shy and not used to talking to women; Kecal resolves to talk to Jeník himself. The discussions are cut short by the polka that now breaks out as young people surge on to the stage and dance. The act concludes with choral voices added to the polka.

ACT 2 *A room in the tavern* The act opens with a strophic drinking song for the male chorus celebrating beer ('To pivečko'). Between the second and third verses Jeník and Kecal are heard, championing (respectively) love and money above alcohol. This chorus scene ends with a *furiant*, and paves the way for the chief business of the act: the separate attempts by Mařenka and Jeník to overcome the obstacles placed in their marital path. The fact that these are uncoordinated and unknown to each other leads to the near-tragedy of Act 3. First Mařenka seeks out Vašek, charms him and, painting her in the blackest colours, attempts to put him off his promised bride. Vašek does not of course realize that this gruesome creature is Mařenka herself and readily swears devotion to the engaging young woman he has just met. Vašek is introduced with a short solo, 'Má ma-ma-ma-tič-ka po-po-povídala' ('My m-m-mother s-s-said' – his stutter is a notable feature). Mařenka conducts her campaign first in recitative and then in a duet (Andante amoroso, 3/4), 'Známt' já jednu dívčinu' ('I know a girl who burns for you'), in which her lyrical lines and Vašek's stuttering responses are brilliantly contrasted. The music flows into a brisker 2/4 as Mařenka extracts her promise: its stretto ending leads to a triumphant *fortissimo* version of the opening 3/4 Andante.

Kecal and Jeník follow them on to the stage. Their duet 'Nuže, milý chasníku' ('Now, dear young fellow') is one of the longer musical structures of the opera. In the first section (2/4, Allegro comodo) Kecal learns that Jeník is from 'far away'; he recommends that he return home since the local girls aren't up to much. Maybe, Jeník responds, but Mařenka is a 'real diamond'. The next section (3/4, Moderato) is mostly a solo for Kecal in which he argues that all the beauties of the world will fade. In the final section (2/4, Allegro comodo), Kecal offers Jeník a rich bride and money, 'Znám jednu dívku' ('I know a girl who has ducats'), with Jeník happily repeating after Kecal all the wonders offered him. The real bargaining, however, happens in the final recitative, as Jeník pushes up Kecal's original offer for renouncing his bride to 300 florins. Jeník makes a decent show of unwillingness, but eventually agrees to 'sell' his bride (as the Czech title has it – 'bartered' is less accurate if more euphonious). But he makes his own conditions: Mařenka must marry no one but Mícha's son, and as soon as Mařenka and Mícha's son are married Mícha's debt to Mařenka's father must be cancelled. Kecal agrees and runs off triumphantly for witnesses to the contract.

'How can he believe that I would sell my Mařenka?' ('Jak možná věřit') Jeník asks in a short aria when left alone. The finale begins with a return to the opening of the overture as Kecal's witnesses (the entire chorus) flood on to the stage. Kecal dictates the terms and Jeník confirms them. Krušina is impressed by Jeník's 'good heart' in giving up Mařenka voluntarily, until he hears about the money that Jeník will receive. The chorus is similarly shocked at such callous behaviour and the growing groundswell of disapproval brings Act 2 to an end.

ACT 3 *The village green beside a tavern* Vašek is confused by the turn of events. As before he is seen alone; an orchestral prelude recalls the opening of his Act 2 aria and the duet music with which he was seduced. The music is dark (a rare minor key) and in its intensity he virtually loses his stutter. Once again he is the victim of others' machinations. The arrival of a small circus is announced with a brief, colourfully orchestrated march (trumpet, piccolo, percussion). In his opening patter the Circus Master describes his troupe: the dancer Esmeralda, an 'Indian' and, their greatest attraction, an American bear who will perform a can-can with Esmeralda. Their wares are further displayed in the brilliant *skočná* (a fast 2/4 folkdance). But there is a crisis: the Indian announces to the Circus Master that the 'bear' has got too drunk to appear. They need a substitute and come upon Vašek, seen admiring Esmeralda's legs. Esmeralda begins chatting him up, describing the life of 'artists' in glowing terms. The recitative leads into a sparkling strophic duettino between the Circus Master and Esmeralda, 'Milostné zvířátko uděláme z vás' ('We'll make a nice little animal of you').

The circus people go off, and Vašek is joined by his parents and Kecal. All are amazed (in the following quartet) when he is unwilling to sign the agreement, and ask what he has against his prospective bride. She will poison him, he declares: he has been told so by an unknown girl. Vašek withdraws, his place taken by Mařenka and her parents. Mařenka has just heard about Jeník's renunciation of her but refuses to believe it. A further complication occurs when Kecal calls back Vašek, who announces that the girl with his parents is the one who spoke to him, and who he is perfectly willing to marry. He goes off. One obstacle is thus removed, but Mařenka says she needs time and in a sextet Kecal and the parents encourage her to think it over ('Rozmysli si, Mařenko!') and then leave her.

Her aria 'Och, jaký žal' ('Oh, what pain'), was extended in the 1869 revision with a much more substantial section, 'Ten lásky sen' ('That dream of love'). Here, as Mařenka sings of her disappointment, Sabina abandoned his usual trochees in favour of a more formal iambic verse and Smetana responded with more passionate and darker music than anywhere else in the opera. By the time Jeník appears she is able to dismiss him as heroically as a prima donna, refusing even to listen to his explanations. She will marry Vašek, she declares. She is further provoked when Jeník cannot hide his amusement: both vent their frustration in a spirited polka-like duet. Kecal joins them and in the following trio Jeník attempts to pacify Mařenka, who simply wants to get the whole affair over. Then Jeník steps aside.

The finale begins with the entry of the chorus and two sets of parents wishing to know Mařenka's decision. She says she will go ahead with her marriage to Vašek, calling Jeník's bluff, as she thinks. But when Jeník steps out, addressing Mícha as 'father', Vašek's parents are astonished to see the long-lost elder son. Although seemingly unwelcome, as he observes, he can at least claim the right to marry Mařenka, being the son of Mícha – as the contract specifies. At last Mařenka understands Jeník's behaviour, and falls into his arms. Kecal acknowledges himself beaten and fears for his reputation. All this business has been conducted in solo dialogue; now, however, the ensemble grows, with the chorus providing a continuous background, the parents expressing their frustration, Kecal his shame and indignation, and the young couple their triumph. The ensemble builds up to a climax, interrupted by cries of terror offstage: boys from the village run on to say that the 'bear' has broken loose and is heading that way. And indeed it appears, only to take off its headdress and reveal itself to be Vašek. His mother is mortified and marches him off but Krušina takes the opportunity of suggesting to Mícha that Vašek is not ready for marriage, and, as recitative gives way to sustained orchestral background, Krušina and his wife Ludmila persuade Mícha to consent to the marriage of Mařenka and Jeník. He does so and blesses the young couple. The music of the opening chorus (ex.1) returns slowly in the orchestra and as it quickens in tempo and grows in volume chorus and soloists join to acknowledge that all has turned out well.

* * *

Czechs consider *The Bartered Bride* as quintessentially Czech. The characteristic dances (polka, *skočná* and *furiant*) support this claim, as do individual details such as the bagpipe imitation in the opening prelude, but there is little else that is concretely 'Czech'. Czech productions usually lavish attention on the authenticity of the setting and costumes, but this is a matter of staging which anyway dates back only to the production made for Vienna in 1892. A better claim for the opera's intrinsic 'Czechness' derives from the fact that the somewhat casually concocted libretto was one of the few Czech librettos of its time to be written mostly in trochees or even prose (rather than high-style iambs), thus matching the natural first-syllable stress of Czech. Another claim may be made from the closeness to Czech dance metres of many individual numbers. Smetana's settings fall mostly into two main types: fast duple and slow triple, thus corresponding to the polka (and related dances) and the slow, triple-time *sousedská*. The simplicity of the music must also have encouraged audiences to see a stronger folk base in it than contemporary, more declamatory and complicated works and indeed than in Smetana's next opera, *Dalibor*.

JOHN TYRRELL

Barthe, Adrien (**Grat-Norbert** [?Gratien-Norbert]) (*b* Bayonne, 7 June 1828; *d* Asnières, 13 Aug 1898). French composer and teacher. After studying with Leborne, he won the Prix de Rome in 1854. The music section of the Académie praised his *envoi*, the French opera *Don Carlos* (1857), for its craftsmanship, fine orchestration and strong sense of the stage, and in 1858 they awarded him the Prix Edouard Rodrigues for his oratorio *Judith*, over the only other competitor, Bizet.

The Théâtre Lyrique opened a competition in 1864 on Jules Adenis' libretto, *La fiancée d'Abydos*, for Prix de Rome winners whose work had not yet reached the stage. Barthe was the unanimous choice of the jury, above Emile Paladilhe and three others. Extensive changes were made during rehearsal and the première took place on 30 December 1865. Critics were largely positive, though they noted resemblances to Meyerbeer, Félicien David, Gounod and others, and found the libretto somewhat tedious. After 19 performances the work disappeared from the repertory.

In 1869 Barthe's score to the libretto *La coupe du roi de Thulé* was placed fourth (after Diaz de la Peña, Massenet and Guiraud) among 42 entered in the Opéra's competition in connection with the 1867 Exposition Universelle. Barthe then turned to teaching and in 1881 replaced Henri Duvernoy as professor of harmony (for women) at the Conservatoire.

Teresa e Claudio, 1855 (op semiseria, 1), unperf., *F-Pc**
Don Carlos, 1857–9 (3), unperf., *Pc**
La fiancée d'Abydos (4, J. Adenis [J.-A. Colombeau], after Byron), Paris, Lyrique, 30 Dec 1865, vs (Paris, 1866)
Le roi de Thulé, 1868–9 (3, L. Gallet and E. Blau), unperf., *Pc**
Le novice [Gioventù], 1876–7 (3), inc., *Pc**
Le retour (oc, 1), unperf., *Pc**

*

FétisBS
C. Le Senne: 'Période contemporaine: Adrien Barthe', *EMDC*, I/iii (Paris, 1921), 1791
W. Dean: *Georges Bizet: his Life and Works* (London, 1948, 3/1976)
T. J. Walsh: *Second Empire Opera: the Théâtre Lyrique Paris 1851–1870* (London, 1981)

LESLEY A. WRIGHT

Barthélemon, Mrs. English soprano; *see* YOUNG family, (6).

Barthelemon [Barthélemon], **François Hippolyte** (*b* Bordeaux, 27 July 1741; *d* Christ Church, Surrey, 20 July 1808). French composer active in England. Having studied the violin in Paris and played in the orchestra of the Comédie-Italienne, he went to England in 1764 to lead the band at the King's Theatre and, later, at Marylebone Gardens. He impressed David Garrick of Drury Lane with the quality of his Italian opera *Pelopida* (1766) and his speed of composition (he set a verse as quickly as Garrick could write the text). Essentially a composer in the *galant* style best suited to background music, he could compose in a variety of modes: the burletta *Orpheus* in Garrick's afterpiece *A Peep behind the Curtain* (1767), for instance, parodies the revenge aria and the sentimental English ballad. He enjoyed another success with *The Maid of the Oaks* (1774). This play concluded with a masque that he and John Burgoyne had originally written for a private *fête champêtre*. Barthelemon also composed ballet music for the King's Theatre. Parke approved his 'scientific' violin playing, but Zaslaw (*Grove6*) noted that his compositions lack a 'clearly developed personal style'.

first performed in London unless otherwise stated

LDL – *Drury Lane* LMG – *Marylebone Gardens*

Pelopida (3, ? G. Roccaforte), King's, 24 May 1766, selections, vs (London, 1766)
Orpheus (burletta, 2, D. Garrick), LDL, 23 Oct 1767, in A Peep behind the Curtain, or The New Rehearsal (farcical afterpiece), vs (London, 1768)
Oithona (dramatic poem, 3, after J. Macpherson's Ossianic epic), Theatre Royal, Haymarket, 3 March 1768 [only 2 acts perf., no further perfs.]
The Judgment of Paris (burletta, 2, R. Schomberg), Theatre Royal, Haymarket, 24 Aug 1768
La fleuve Scamandre (comic op, J. Renout, after J. de La Fontaine), Paris, Comédie-Italienne, 22 Dec 1768
The Magic Girdle (burletta, 2 pts, G. S. Carey, after J.-B. Rousseau), LMG, 17 July 1770
The Noble Pedlar, or The Fortune Hunter (burletta, 2 pts, Carey), LMG, 21 Aug 1770
The Portrait (burletta, 2 pts), Dublin, Rotunda, *c*1771 (Dublin, 1772)

The Wedding Day (burletta, 2 pts), LMG, 15 July 1773
La zingara, or The Gipsey (burletta, 2 pts), LMG, 25 Aug 1773
The Election (musical interlude, 1, M. P. Andrews), LDL, 19 Oct 1774, selections, vs (London, 1774)
The Maid of the Oaks (masque within a comedy, 5, J. Burgoyne, after J. F. Marmontel: *Sylvain*), LDL, 5 Nov 1774, vs (London, *c*1775); masque in Act 5 incl. music orig. for fête champêtre, Epsom, The Oaks, 9 June 1774
Belphegor, or The Wishes (comic op afterpiece, 2, Andrews, after J. F. Guichard and N. Castet: *Le bûcheron, ou Les trois souhaits*), LDL, 16 March 1778, vs (London, 1778)

Music in: C. Dibdin: Love in the City, 1767; Le vicende della sorte, or The Turns of Fortune, 1770

*

BDA; *DNB* (J. Maitland); *ES* (E. Zanetti); *Grove6* (N. Zaslaw); *LS*
W. T. Parke: *Musical Memoirs* (London, 1830)
C. F. Pohl: *Mozart und Haydn in London* (Vienna, 1867)
M. Pincherle: 'Sur François Barthélémon', *Mélanges de musicologie offerts à M. Lionel de la Laurencie* (Paris, 1933), 235–45
N. Slonimsky: 'Musical Oddities', *Etude: the Music Magazine*, lxxiv/4 (1956), 6
R. Dircks: '*Les fêtes champêtres 1774*: Literary and Theatrical Perspectives', *Philological Quarterly*, i (1971), 647–56
R. Fiske: *English Theatre Music in the Eighteenth Century* (London, 1973, 2/1986)
H. C. R. Landon: *Haydn: Chronicle and Works*, iii: *Haydn in England: 1791–1795* (London, 1976)
S. Lincoln: 'Barthelemon's Setting of Garrick's *Orpheus*', *The Stage and the Page: London's 'Whole Show' in the Eighteenth-Century Theatre*, ed. G. Stone (Berkeley and Los Angeles, 1981), 148–59
P. T. Dircks: *David Garrick* (Boston, 1985)
M. Sands: *The Eighteenth-Century Pleasure Gardens of Marylebone: 1737–1777* (London, 1987) LINDA V. TROOST

Bartók, Béla (Viktor János) (*b* Nagyszentmiklós, Hungary [now Sînnicolau Mare, Romania], 25 March 1881; *d* New York, 26 Sept 1945). Hungarian composer. He began lessons with his mother, who brought up the family after his father's death in 1888. In 1894 they settled in Bratislava, where he attended the Gymnasium (Dohnányi was an elder schoolfellow), studied the piano, and composed sonatas and quartets. In 1898 he was accepted by the Vienna Conservatory, but following Dohnányi he went to the Budapest Academy (1899–1903), where he studied the piano with Liszt's pupil István Thomán and composition with János Koessler. In 1904 he made his first Hungarian folksong transcription, beginning his collaboration with Kodály in 1905. He was appointed Thomán's successor at the Budapest Academy (1907), which enabled him to settle in Hungary and continue his folksong collecting, notably in Transylvania.

His single-act *A Kékszakállú herceg vára* ('Bluebeard's Castle'), composed in 1911, is crucial both to his own output and to the modern operatic repertory, but otherwise he left little evidence of interest in the genre. The only operas mentioned in his published letters, for example, are *Il barbiere di Siviglia*, which he saw on a tour of the Soviet Union in 1929, and several of Wagner's music dramas, which made a great impression on him while he was a student at the Budapest Academy. In 1904 he had been to Bayreuth and seen *Parsifal*, but during the next few years his interests turned to Strauss, Debussy, Schoenberg and, most decisively, Magyar folk music. This gave him the means to create a distinctively Hungarian music, and *Bluebeard's Castle*, for all its personal resonances, can be seen as part of that project: an opera in Hungarian, rooted in the modes and rhythms of Hungarian folksong, but also showing a knowledge of the languages of Strauss and Debussy, staking a claim for Hungarian art at the highest, most up-to-date, international level. The Budapest Opera failed to produce the work until 1918, however, and frustration may have been one reason for Bartók's subsequent operatic silence.

Other explanations, though, suggest themselves. His reticence, for instance, seems to have disinclined him from works speaking their meanings in words: apart from *Bluebeard's Castle* and various folksong arrangements, his only vocal pieces were 15 songs and the *Cantata profana*. In that respect *Bluebeard's Castle* had its successors in two dramatic works which dispense with words: the ballet *A fából faragott királyfi* ('The Wooden Prince', 1914–17) and the pantomime *A csodálatos mandarin* ('The Miraculous Mandarin', 1918–23). All three works have a central male-female couple and are concerned with the power, but also the hopelessness, of love. They also, as a trilogy, display a characteristic Bartókian movement from the ideal (the first two are based on fairy-tales by Béla Balázs) to the grotesque (Menyhert Lengyel's scenario for *The Miraculous Mandarin* being sordid and contemporary in its setting). They thus form a natural triple bill. Bartók wrote nothing for the stage after *The Miraculous Mandarin*, apart from a short-lived ballet idea whose sketches were rescued in the Concerto for Orchestra.

The eclipse of Bartók the dramatist can also be ascribed to his development during the 1920s and 30s of an almost geometrical musical language, which enabled him to draw whole works out from small cells, entailing a strictness, symmetry and singleness of purpose to which the theatre could add nothing. The favoured media were rather the string quartet, the orchestra, in *concertante* formations, and the piano, much of the piano music coming after 1926 when Bartók began an international career as a soloist. But his home remained in Hungary, where he taught at the Budapest Academy and pursued his folk-music studies until moving regretfully to the United States in 1940.

See also BLUEBEARD'S CASTLE.

*

H. Stevens: *The Life and Music of Béla Bartók* (New York, 1953, 2/1964)
G. Króo: 'Duke Bluebeard's Castle', *SM*, i (1961), 251–340
——: 'Adatok "A Kékszakállú herceg vára" keletkezéstörténetéhez' [Some Data on the Genesis of 'Bluebeard's Castle'], *Magyar zenetörténeti tanulmányok: Szabolcsi Bence 70 szuletés napjára* [Studies in Hungarian Musical History Dedicated to Benice Szabolcsi on his 70th Birthday] (Budapest, 1969), 333–58
J. Demény, ed.: *Béla Bartók Letters* (London, 1971)
J. Ujfalussy: *Béla Bartók* (Budapest, 1971)
F. Bónis: *Béla Bartók: his Life in Pictures and Documents* (Budapest, 1972, 2/1981)
T. Crow, ed.: *Bartók Studies* (Detroit, 1976)
B. Suchoff, ed.: *Béla Bartók Essays* (London, 1976)
E. Lendvai: *The Workshop of Bartók and Kodály* (Budapest, 1983)
P. Griffiths: *Bartók* (London, 1984) PAUL GRIFFITHS

Bartoletti, Bruno (*b* Sesto Fiorentino, Florence, 10 June 1926). Italian conductor. He studied at the Florence Conservatory, and became pianist at the centre for opera training attached to the Florence Teatro Comunale. He worked as assistant to many leading conductors including Rodziński, Mitropoulos, Gui and Serafin, and made his conducting début at the Teatro Comunale in 1953 with *Rigoletto*. He soon demonstrated the interpretative insight and versatility that enabled him to conduct contemporary works in addition to the Italian opera repertory from Rossini to Dallapiccola to which his career has mainly been devoted. He conducted the premières of Malipiero's *Il figliuol prodigo* and *Venere prigioniera* (1957) at Florence, Mortari's *La scuola delle mogli* (1959) at La

Scala and Ginastera's *Don Rodrigo* (1964) at the Teatro Colón, Buenos Aires. During this time he also introduced Egk's *Der Revisor*, Krenek's *Jonny spielt auf* and Shostakovich's *The Nose* to the Italian stage, and conducted the Italian repertory at the Kongelige Teater, Copenhagen, 1957–60. He made his American début at the Chicago Lyric Opera in 1956, and was appointed principal conductor and artistic director there in 1964. He was conductor at the Rome Opera from 1965 to 1973, and artistic director at the Maggio Musicale Fiorentino, 1986–91. His recordings include several Verdi and Puccini operas, and a video of *Tosca* (1976) filmed on location in Rome. LEONARDO PINZAUTI

Bartoli, Cecilia (*b* Rome, 4 June 1966). Italian mezzo-soprano. She studied in Rome at the Accademia di S Cecilia. Having sung the Shepherd-boy in *Tosca* as a child, she made her début in 1987 at the Teatro Filarmonico, Verona, then appeared in Berlin and Warsaw. In 1988 she sang Rosina at Cologne, Schwetzingen and Zürich, where she also sang Cherubino. She has sung Lucilla (*La scala di seta*) at Pesaro (1989); Giannetta (*Le cantatrice villane*) at the S Carlo (1990); and Isolier at La Scala, Despina in Rome, Dorabella in Florence and Rosina at Barcelona (1991). Her recordings of Cherubino, Dorabella, Cecilius (*Lucio Silla*) and Rosina won great praise. The beauty and flexibility of her voice are heard to particular advantage in Rossini; she has a delightful stage presence that will strengthen with maturity. ELIZABETH FORBES

Bartolozzi, Bruno (*b* Florence, 8 June 1911; *d* Florence, 12 Dec 1980). Italian composer and violinist. He studied at the Florence Conservatory, with Luigi Dallapiccola for composition, and went on to study conducting, which he later taught at the conservatory. His first compositions, dating from the early 1950s, were influenced by the 12-note system to which he had been introduced by Dallapiccola. In 1965 he began work on the *rappresentazione drammatica* in one act with prologue *Tutto ciò che accade ti riguarda*, completed in 1970, to his own libretto based on Günter Eich's radio play *Träume*; the opera received its première at the Teatro della Pergola, Florence, on 30 May 1972 (vocal score, Milan, 1970). The story concerns five people who have been shut up for a long time in a railway carriage on a train which is continuously increasing speed; none of the occupants knows where it is going. Through a crack in the carriage they become aware of the outside world, the existence of which each of them denies in an egotistical and self-absorbed manner; their personal anguish is finally expressed by the chorus in a question that is destined to remain unanswered: who will save us?

Bartolozzi's investigation of timbre and instrumentation, characteristic of his mature work, reaches a synthesis in *Tutto ciò che accade ti riguarda*. Libretto and musical substance are explicitly linked: for example the radical opposition between the outside world and the interior of the carriage is conveyed by the contrast between electronic and traditional instrumental sonorities, and by the treatment of the chorus, which follows and comments on the action with a wide range of vocal techniques, from song to whispering, from screams to speech. The opera's abrasive presentation of contemporary man's alienation and failure to communicate links it to the avant-garde theatrical works of the 1950s and 60s treating social themes – for example Nono's *Intolleranza 1960* and Manzoni's *Atomtod* (1965) – or investigating the problematic and violent relationships between the individual and society in the modern industrialized world.

*

Grove6 (C. Annibaldi)

R. Smith Brindle: 'Current Chronicle: Italy', *MQ*, xlix (1963), 98–101; lii (1966), 106–9

M. Pinzauti: 'I sogni di Bartolozzi', *La nazione* (31 May 1972)

F. D'Amico: 'Spogliatevi compagni', *L'espresso* (11 June 1972)

RAFFAELE POZZI

Baruffe chiozzotte, Le. Opera by G. F. Malipiero; *see* *TRE COMMEDIE GOLDONIANE*.

Bary, Alfred von (*b* La Valetta, Malta, 18 Jan 1873; *d* Munich, 13 Sept 1926). German tenor. He trained first for the medical profession, specializing in neurology at Leipzig University, and it was not until he was nearly 30 that his ability as a singer was discovered by Arthur Nikisch and he began to study singing with Richard Müller. He made his stage début in 1903 as Lohengrin in Dresden, remaining with the company until 1912 when he moved to Munich. From 1904 to 1914 he sang with great success at Bayreuth, as Siegmund, Siegfried, Lohengrin, Tristan and Parsifal. He retired in 1918 because of an eye disease that led to blindness. Only two recordings remain to testify to the power and steadiness of his voice, together with the fluid lyricism that distinguished him among the Wagnerian tenors of his time.

J. B. STEANE

Baryton Martin. A term used to characterize a particular type of BARITONE voice. It owes its origin to JEAN-BLAISE MARTIN (1768–1837), a baritone with a remarkably extensive upper range, sufficiently famous and distinctive for his name to continue in use long after his death to denote a high, lyric baritone, almost a tenor, usually bright of timbre and light of weight, but with a free, unthroaty production characteristic of the French school. Jean Périer, the first Pelléas, was probably typical, with Gabriel Soulacroix a distinguished predecessor and Camille Mauranne (*b* 1911) a notable representative in more recent times. It is always doubtful whether the term should be applied to 'foreign' baritones who might seem to qualify, such as Mattia Battistini or Yury Mazurok. The continued use of the term, so long after its originator has passed out of memory, might also be questioned. J. B. STEANE

Bascarán, Ermogene Imleghi. *See* PAOLI, ANTONIO.

Bas-dessus [second dessus] (Fr.: 'low soprano', 'second soprano'). Term used in French sources from the 17th century to the early 19th for a female voice with a range *b* to *g''* (pitch was as much as a whole tone lower than that now used). It is the equivalent of the MEZZO-SOPRANO. Solo roles were rarely assigned to a *bas-dessus*, although Rousseau (*Dictionnaire de musique*, 1768) praised a Paris Opéra singer, Mlle Gondré, as 'un fort beau Bas-Dessus' (her name appears on a 'Second Dessus' part for an 18th-century performance of Lully's *Armide*). Choral writing in French operas from Lully onwards frequently contrasted the normal four-part texture with a three-part high-voice *petit choeur*, where the middle part was for *bas-dessus* (and the lowest for the male *haute-contre*).

Rousseau also observed that 'a good *bas-dessus*, full and sonorous, is no less valued in Italy than clear and high voices, but in France no importance is attached to them'. In Rossini's *Guillaume Tell* (1829), both the upper voices in four-part choruses were labelled 'dessus', the lower voice corresponding to the range of the *bas-dessus*. (Both are written in the soprano clef, even though the upper part reaches *b*″.) Berlioz in his *Grande traité d'instrumentation* (Paris, 1844) drew attention to Gluck's choruses of priestesses in *Iphigénie en Tauride*, which are for *dessus* and *bas-dessus* only, and observed that 'it cannot be denied that in France, [Nature] is very sparing of [contraltos]'. The *bas-dessus* was thus the only lower female voice recognized in 17th-, 18th- and early 19th-century France.

*

L. Rosow: 'Performing a Choral Dialogue by Lully', *EMc*, xv (1987), 325–35
LIONEL SAWKINS

Baseggio [Basseggio], **Lorenzo** (*b* *c*1660; *d* in or after 1715). Italian composer. He wrote the operas *L'Adamiro* (B. Pisani) for Treviso in 1687 and *Laomedonte* (G. B. Guizzardi or G. B. Ruperti) for Venice, Teatro S Moisè, in 1715. There are two settings of texts by Francesco Passarini: *Amor e fortuna*, performed at the Teatro Campagnella in Rovigo in autumn 1712, and a *favola boschereccia Gli equivoci del caso*, given at Dolo (near Venice) in June of the same year. He was a member of the Venetian instrumentalists' guild.

*

AllacciD; *EitnerQ*; *FétisB*; *SchmidlD*
V. Coronelli: *Guida de' forastieri per la città di Venezia* (Venice, 1706), 19
G. C. Bonlini: *Le glorie della poesia e della musica* (Venice, 1730)
THOMAS WALKER

Basel (Ger.). Basle.

Basevi, Abramo (*b* Livorno, 29 Nov 1818; *d* Florence, 25 Nov 1885). Italian music critic. He studied composition with Pietro Romani and had two *opere serie* performed in Florence, *Romilda ed Ezzelino* (2, Basevi; Alfieri, 11 Aug 1840) and *Enrico Howard* (2, F. Guidi; Pergola, 28 May 1847); they were admired more by connoisseurs than the public. He gave up composition and became prominent in Florentine cultural life as a critic and organizer; among his enterprises was a concert cycle of dramatic music by such earlier Italian composers as Sacchini and Spontini. He was chiefly important, however, as a critic, and especially in the movement to reform the Italian musical scene by bringing in new influences while at the same time fostering Italian traditions.

Basevi was an early supporter of Wagner but did not advocate the adoption of his methods by Italians. Verdi he recognized as a skilful, sometimes inspired musician; his articles on Verdi's operas up to *Aroldo*, collected into a book (*Studio sulle opere di Giuseppe Verdi*, 1859), remain one of the most valuable and perceptive works of Verdi criticism. However, Basevi saw Verdi as one who followed the taste of the time rather than moulding and improving it. For him the most significant contemporary was Meyerbeer, whose work, seen as a synthesis of German learning and Italian melody, provided the most appropriate model for Italians. He published numerous articles, many of which were collected in books; in his later years he devoted himself chiefly to philosophy. LEONARDO PINZAUTI

Bashkortostan. *See* Ufa.

Basile [Baroni], **Adriana** [Adreana] (*b* Posillipo, nr Naples, *c*1590; *d* Rome, *c*1640). Italian singer. She worked from 1610 at the Mantuan court, with other members of her family: her brothers Giovanni Battista, a poet, and Lelio, a composer; her sisters Margherita and Vittoria, both singers; and her husband the nobleman Mutio Baroni and their children Camillo, Leonora and Caterina. Within a few months of her arrival, Monteverdi declared her more gifted than the Medici singer Francesca Caccini; she was awarded a barony by Duke Vincenzo Gonzaga and enjoyed further privileges under his son Ferdinando. She visited Florence, Naples, Rome and Modena between 1618 and 1620, and Venice in 1623. In Mantua in 1621 she performed in Alessandro Guarini's *Licori, ovvero L'incanto d'amore*. She was released from Mantuan service in 1626 and spent her remaining years, still performing, in Naples and (from 1633) Rome. She may also have composed: in 1616 Monteverdi recommended that she and her sisters write solos for a dramatic entertainment.

Her sister Margherita (*d* ? after 1636) was at Mantua from 1615 and in 1617 sang in Santi Orlandi's *Gli amori di Aci e Galatea*, staged on Ferdinando's marriage; she became the principal singer at the court in the 1620s and 30s and probably spent a period at Vienna in 1631.

Her daughter Leonora Baroni (*b* Mantua, Dec 1611; *d* Rome, 6 April 1670), sometimes known as L'Adrianella or L'Adrianetta, also became a famous singer. As a child she took part in concerts at the Mantuan court, and later enjoyed a successful career in Naples, Rome (in particular) and as a guest at the French court. She is not, however, known to have sung in opera.

*

DBI (L. Pannella); *ES* (E. Zanetti)
A. Ademollo: *La bell'Adriana ed altre virtuose del suo tempo alla corte di Mantova* (Città di Castello, 1888)
S. Parisi: *Ducal Patronage of Music in Mantua, 1587–1627: an Archival Study* (diss., U. of Illinois, 1989)
SUSAN PARISI

Basili [Basily], **Basilio** (*b* Macerata, 1803; *d* ?New York, ?*c*1895). Italian composer active in Spain. The son of the composer Francesco Basili, he started his career as an operatic tenor but turned to composition soon after arriving in Spain in 1827. In a musical climate monopolized by Italian opera, he tried to revitalize the tradition of Spanish musical theatre, composing several stage works in Spanish, with spoken dialogue. The dichotomy between Spanish and Italian music is presented allegorically in *El novio y el concierto*, in which the young hero's choice of bride symbolizes a choice between Italian opera and Spanish folksong. Basili conducted several seasons of Italian opera in Madrid during the late 1840s. In 1847 Basili, Hilarión Eslava and others formed España Musical, a group that promoted the cause of national music. Though none of Basili's dramatic works gained lasting fame, they paved the way for the successful revival of the zarzuela around 1849.

first performed in Madrid, Teatro de la Cruz, unless otherwise stated
L'assedio di Tarifa, 1 aria perf. Jan 1839
El novio y el concierto (comedia-zar, 1, M. Bretón de los Herreros), Madrid, Príncipe, 12 March 1839
Il carozzino da vendere (1), 5 Oct 1839
El sacristán de Toledo, before 1840 (ópera de magia, 3, A. G. Gutiérrez), collab. Carnicer and M. Ducassi
Los contrabandistas [El contrabandista] (ópera andaluz, 3, T. Rodríguez Rubí), Madrid, Liceo, 10 April 1841; as I contrabbandieri al Porto di S Maria, Paris, Ventadour, 1844
El ventorillo de Crespo (1, Rodríguez Rubí), 15 July 1841

Los solitarios (comedia-zar, 1, Bretón de los Herreros, after E. Scribe: *Les inconsolables*), Madrid, Príncipe, 9 Jan 1843
La pendencia (escena andaluz, 1, Sandoval), 7 Nov 1843
El diablo predicador (drama lírico, imitación de la comedia antigua española, 3, V. de la Vega, after L. de Belmonte y Bermudez), 5 March 1846

*

E. Cotarelo y Mori: *Ensayo histórico sobre la zarzuela* (Madrid, 1937)
R. J. Vázquez: *The Quest for National Opera and the Re-invention of the Zarzuela in Nineteenth-Century Spain* (diss., Cornell U., 1992)

ROLAND J. VÁZQUEZ

Basili [Basilii, Basilj, Basily], **Francesco** (*b* Loreto, 31 Jan 1767; *d* Rome, 25 March 1850). Italian composer. He studied first with his father, then with G. B. Borghi and finally with Giuseppe Jannaconi at the Accademia di S Cecilia in Rome. After passing his examinations in conducting in 1783 he was accepted as a member of the academy. For about 40 years he worked as a conductor, at Foligno (1786–9), Macerata (1789–1803) and Loreto (1809–27); during this time his 13 operas, of which *Gl'illinesi* (1819, Milan) was the most successful, were composed and produced. In 1827 he became director of the Milan Conservatory, where he was responsible for Verdi's failure to be admitted in 1832.

Basili was *maestro di cappella* of St Peter's in Rome from 1837 until his death. His style is similar to Spontini's, and is characterized by march-like rhythms and by melodies reminiscent of the Viennese Classical composers and of Schubert. In his earliest works he anticipated Rossini, and in that respect his style contrasts markedly with that of his contemporaries.

La bella incognita (farce, 2), Rome, Valle, carn. 1788
La locandiera (farce, 2) Rome, Capranica, carn. 1789
Il ritorno di Ulisse (dramma, 3, G. B. Moniglia), Florence, Pergola, 1 Sept 1798
Achille all'assedio di Troia (dramma, 2), Florence, Pergola, 26 Dec 1798
Antigona (dramma serio, 2, G. Rossi), Venice, Fenice, 5 Dec 1799
Conviene adattarsi (farce, 1), Venice, S Moisè, aut. 1801
L'unione mal pensata (dramma, 1), Venice, S Benedetto, 27 Dec 1801
Lo stravagante e il dissipatore (dg, 2, G. M. Foppa), Venice, Fenice, spr. 1805
L'ira di Achille (dramma serio, 3, P. Pola), Venice, Fenice, 30 Jan 1817
L'orfana egiziana (dramma, 3, B. Merelli), Venice, Fenice, Jan 1818
Gl'illinesi (melodramma, 2, F. Romani), Milan, Scala, 26 Jan 1819
Il califfo e la schiava (melodramma, 2, Romani), Milan, Scala, 21 Aug 1819
Isaura e Ricciardo (os, 2, C. Sterbini), Rome, Valle, 29 Jan 1820

*

Opere manoscritte autografe di musica di chiesa, di teatro, e di camera del celebre Francesco Basili Romano (Rome, n.d.) [list of works]

LEOPOLD M. KANTNER

Basilides, Mária (*b* Jolsva, 11 Nov 1886; *d* Budapest, 26 Sept 1946). Hungarian contralto. She studied at the Budapest Academy of Music under József Sík. In 1911, at the opening of the Budapest Municipal Theatre, she made her début in Jean Nouguès's *Quo vadis?*, and until 1915 played there in such roles as Azucena, Mignon, Carmen and Ulrica. She then joined the Budapest Opera, appearing there until her death. Her repertory was wide: noted in Verdi and Wagner, she also sang Gluck's Orpheus and Clytemnestra, Sylvia in Monteverdi's *Orfeo*, and created the Housewife in Kodály's *The Spinning Room*. She made frequent guest appearances abroad. An innate musicality, a voice of velvety beauty (at its peak), and avoidance of vocal artifice endeared her to Budapest audiences. In addition she was one of Hungary's most eminent concert singers and an enthusiastic supporter of Bartók and Kodály, whose folksong arrangements she recorded (with Bartók at the piano). The second and eighth books of Kodály's *Magyar népzene* were dedicated to her.

*

J. A. Molnár: *Basilides Mária* (Budapest, 1967)

PÉTER P. VÁRNAI

Basiola, Mario (*b* Annico, nr Cremona, 12 July 1892; *d* Annico, 3 Jan 1965). Italian baritone. He studied with Antonio Cotogni in Rome, where he made his début in 1918. Appearances in Florence and Barcelona led to an engagement with the San Carlo company which toured America in 1923, and this in turn brought him to the Metropolitan in 1925. His roles there included Amonasro, Escamillo and Count di Luna. In 1930 he appeared in the American première of Felice Lattuada's *Le preziose ridicole* and in that of Montemezzi's *La notte di Zoraima* the following year. He was also the Venetian guest in the first Metropolitan production of *Sadko* (1930). In 1933 he returned to Italy where for many years he was a leading baritone in Milan and Rome. The enthusiastic reports of his work there were not entirely borne out when, after a serious illness, he came to Covent Garden (as Iago, Amonasro and Germont) in 1939; nor are they well supported by the recordings he made of *Pagliacci* and *Madama Butterfly* with Gigli. In 1946 he joined a company touring Australia, and in 1951 he returned there as a teacher. His earlier recordings show the full-bodied tone and flowing style which earned him a high reputation among the singers of his time. His son, Mario Basiola jr (*b* Highland Park, IL, 1 Sept 1935), was also a successful baritone, singing in many leading houses including La Scala and the Vienna Staatsoper; his repertory includes the title role in *Wozzeck*. J. B. STEANE

Basle (Ger. Basel; Fr. Bâle). City in northern Switzerland. Opera was initially performed at the Theater auf dem Blömlein, built in 1834, then from 1875 at the Theater am Steineberg, which opened with *Don Giovanni*. A permanent ensemble was formed in 1892. The theatre was destroyed by fire in 1904, and a Stadttheater (cap. 1150), built on the same site at Elisabethenstrasse, opened on 20 September 1909 with *Tannhäuser*. Heinrich Sutermeister's *Titus Feuerfuchs* received its première there in 1958. Long considered inadequate, the theatre was demolished in 1975 to make way for a new Stadttheater (cap. 980), incorporating a studio theatre. The building is used for opera, ballet and drama, with five or six new opera productions in repertory from September to June, together with one or two revivals. The director from 1978 to 1988 was Horst Statkus, who established the company's reputation as the most progressive in Switzerland. A series of highly original productions was staged by the French director Jean-Claude Auvray, and musical standards were high under Armin Jordan, who was music director until 1989, when he was succeeded by Michael Boder. During the 1980s the Basle chorus gained an outstanding reputation in its own right under its director Werner Nitzer. The theatre hires the Basle SO or the orchestra of Radio Basel for opera performances. Singers who began their careers in the ensemble include Montserrat Caballé and Anne Sofie von Otter.

*

Stadttheater einst und jetzt, 1807–1975 (Berne, 1975)

ANDREW CLARK

Bass (Fr. *basse*; Ger. *Bass*; It. *basso*). The lowest male voice, normally written for within the range *F* to *e′*, which may be extended at either end.

1. The Baroque period. 2. The Classical period. 3. After 1800: (i) Introduction (ii) Voice types. 4. Singers and roles: the 19th century: (i) Italian and French opera (ii) German opera (iii) Russian opera. 5. Singers and roles: the 20th century.

1. The Baroque period. Italian composers in the late 16th century often wrote highly ornate parts for the bass voice, and this continued into the first three decades of the 17th. In opera, however, where bass roles were few and generally unimportant, ornate writing was relatively rare; the emphasis lay rather on dramatic portrayal. In the surviving operas of Monteverdi the bass already appears in some of what were to be its most important historical role types: as a god (particularly a god of the underworld: Pluto in *Orfeo*, 1607, Neptune in *Il ritorno d'Ulisse*, 1640), or as a sepulchral figure (Charon in *Orfeo*). In *Orfeo* Monteverdi called for special instrumentation (the regal, a trombone choir) which was itself to become a tradition in much operatic scoring associated with the bass voice. A further impressive use of the voice is for the role of Seneca in *L'incoronazione di Poppea* (1643), an early example of another archetype, the sage. The Seneca figure, however, is rare in 17th-century opera; the old tutor becomes, rather, a secondary comic role, typically an elderly lecher, as for example the pompous pseudo-philosopher Alfeo in Alessandro Scarlatti's *Eraclea* (1700), who is always seeking to meddle in the plot. The bass also appears as a drunken servant, again with a tendency to interfere with the plot; this stock figure is personified by Gelone in Cesti's *Orontea* (1656), who appears in no fewer than seven scenes. Other Scarlatti basses include Flacco (*La caduta de' decemviri*, 1697), the absurd wooer of an old crone, and Mustafà, the topical figure of the 'terrible Turk' in *La principessa fedele* (1710), who sings a bombastic, fulminating 'rage aria'. The arias Scarlatti composed for his comic basses already show exaggerated vocal leaps, plummetings or flights into extreme registers, preposterous roulades, rapid patter and implied staccato delivery – all to become the stock vocabulary of the *basso buffo* of the 18th century.

Most Handel operas include a role for bass who, though usually a secondary character, is of sufficient importance to be assigned three arias, one in each act. These roles are most often for kings or generals, whose noble arias declare pride in rank. Sometimes a villain (Achillas in *Giulio Cesare*, 1724, or Garibaldo in *Rodelinda*, 1725, for example) may be cast as a bass. A favourite type of aria is that of rage or defiance, often with huge leaps; James Miller wrote of Handel's Royal Academy bass G. M. Boschi, 'And Boschi-like, be always in a rage'. Boschi's parts are high-lying, in what would now be called a baritone range; but some of Handel's finest bass parts were for Montagnana, who sang down to *F* in the remarkable role of the magician Zoroastro in *Orlando* (1733). There are a number of love arias for basses, revealing an impressive potential for tenderness; but slow arias, calling for poignancy or tragedy, are on the whole few, the most notable being for Chosroes in *Siroe* (1728).

In French opera, the bass more often took serious roles. In his *Paralèle* of 1702 (Eng. trans., 1709) Raguenet wrote: 'When the Person of Gods or Kings, a Jupiter, Neptune, Priam or Agamemnon are brought on Stage, our Actors, with their deep Voices, give 'em an Air of Majesty, quite different from the feign'd voices [i.e. castratos] among the Italians'. In Cavalli's *Ercole amante* (1662), written for Paris, the title role is for bass. Lully followed the tradition of employing the bass voice in role types such as gods (Jupiter in *Cadmus et Hermione*, 1673, and *Isis*, 1677) and especially those of the underworld (Pluto in *Alceste*, 1674, and *Proserpine*, 1680; Neptune in *Isis* and *Acis et Galatée*) as well as for roles with comic elements (Charon in *Alceste*, Polyphemus in *Acis*). Only in *Roland* (1685) did he use the bass voice in a title role. His solos lie within the range *F* to *d′*, which, given the low pitch used at the time (about a tone below present-day pitch), indicates that they were true bass roles. A leading exponent of French bass and *basse-taille* (baritone) roles in the early years of the 18th century was Gabriel-Vincent Thévenard, who sang in many works by Destouches, Marais and Campra as well as in Lully revivals. The distinction between *basse* and *basse-taille* had become less marked by the time of Rameau's works, where impressive and extensive roles such as that of Theseus in *Hippolyte et Aricie* (1733), with a compass of *F* to *f′*, or Pollux in *Castor et Pollux* (1737), *G* to *f♯′* – both were created by the same singer, C. L. D. Chassé – require the use of a higher register. From Lully's *Bellérophon* (1679) onwards, *récits de basse* were usually accompanied by the full orchestra and the vocal line became increasingly independent of the continuo.

2. The Classical period. The true bass has only a modest role to play in Italian opera of the Metastasian period; he still usually appears only as a confidant, a general or occasionally a king (though by this date tenors are increasingly assigned king's roles). He retained his more important position in French opera, however, as Gluck's bass roles – such as Calchas (*Iphigénie en Aulide*, 1774), Hercules (*Alceste*, 1776) and Thoas (*Iphigénie en Tauride*, 1779) – illustrate. It is interesting to note that Mozart had hoped to recast his *Idomeneo* 'more in the French style', in which he envisaged the title role taken by a bass; he had originally, in 1781, expressed a wish that it could have been written not for a tenor but for the Mannheim-Munich bass G. B. Zonca (who had created central roles in Majo's *Ifigenia in Tauride*, 1764, and *Alessandro nell'Indie*, 1766). Mozart's most characteristic bass roles are Osmin, a comically savage overseer, in *Die Entführung aus dem Serail* (1782, written for Ludwig Fischer) and Sarastro, a high priest, in *Die Zauberflöte* (1791). Most of his roles nominally for bass in his *opere buffe* are now regarded as equally baritone roles, such as Count Almaviva (*Figaro*, 1786), Don Giovanni (1787) and Guglielmo (*Così fan tutte*, 1790), and in their lyric moments they look forward to 19th-century role types; but the characters of lower station, Figaro and Leporello, tend to be more often sung by basses and are essentially *basso buffo* roles, the former designed for (and both sung by) the outstanding Viennese exponent, Francesco Benucci. Such roles as the Commendatore and Masetto in *Don Giovanni* retain the traditional use of the bass for the elderly nobleman or the rough peasant, and Bartolo (*Figaro*) for the bumbling, ineffectual old man. The *basso buffo* tradition to which these and many other roles belong is in fact the hallmark of *opera buffa*. It goes back to the 17th century, with the Villifranchi libretto *Il Trespolo tutore balordo* (set by Pasquini in 1677 and Stradella in 1679); appears in

numerous intermezzo-type works, such as Pergolesi's *La serva padrona* (1733); is central to the entire repertory of operas to Goldoni's librettos and the principal works of Paisiello and Cimarosa; and continues well into the 19th century in the operas of Rossini and Donizetti.

3. After 1800.

(i) Introduction. Up to 1800, virtually every operatic role was composed with a particular singer and a particular occasion in mind. There was no expectation of creating an opera that would enter the repertory, as no consolidated repertory existed; most operas were never revived, and when they were they were subject to revision or recomposition to suit a new team of singers. Accordingly roles were designed less for voice types than for individual voices. This procedure continued, especially in Italy, into the late 19th century. But the growth of an established repertory – international, but with local variations – led to singers being required to perform music not written for them. This in time gave rise, because of the need for appropriate casting, to some degree of classification of roles and singers, and to the identification of different voice types (the *basse chantante*, the *basse noble* and the *basse profonde*, for example). Further, as the 19th century progressed, instead of a composer being required to suit his music to a particular voice, the composer wrote what he pleased and the voice had to be found to cope with his requirements.

(ii) Voice types. The most important development in the later history of the bass voice is the emergence around the turn of the century of the baritone and subsequently the bass-baritone as voice categories in their own right. Though they continued to share the bass clef, and retained some overlap in repertory, these three types with their various subdivisions became more distinct in general recognition, and the true operatic bass found himself increasingly a specialist in certain types of role.

The depth of his voice was commonly taken to suggest advanced age (though Puccini probably had the right idea when he made his aged Emperor in *Turandot* an enfeebled tenor). In Verdi's *Ernani* the bass is allotted the part of Silva, habitually addressed as 'vecchio', 'vecchio misero' and so forth. In his *I masnadieri* the bass's role is that of Count Massimiliano, old enough to have begotten the tenor and the baritone who play his sons. The voice-casting of *Simon Boccanegra* provides an example of the way in which operatic convention established an unwritten law to the effect that depth of voice was directly proportionate to advance in years: thus the tenor is the young hero in love with the daughter of the baritone who in turn loves the daughter of the bass.

With age comes – by a similar convention – authority. The bass may accordingly play King or High Priest, and in *Aida* both. In *Don Carlos* basses are both King and Grand Inquisitor, and the latter's superior authority is implied by his greater depth. Puccini, not greatly interested in basses as a rule, cast the Japanese priest, Madame Butterfly's interfering uncle, as a bass, and in *Turandot* the bass is the aged and deposed King Timur. The French oriental operas *Lakmé* and *Les pêcheurs de perles* each have a bass High Priest. Debussy cast *Pelléas et Mélisande* in accordance with the convention: the romantic Pelléas is a tenor or high baritone, the middle-aged Golaud a baritone or bass-baritone, and the blind old King Arkel a bass. Examples abound in most national schools of opera: the monk Pimen in *Boris Godunov*, Dosifey, leader of the Old Believers, in *Khovanshchina*; the Hermit in *Der Freischütz*, old Gurnemanz in *Parsifal*; in Walton's *Troilus and Cressida* the High Priest Calkas is predictably a bass, as is the He-Ancient in Tippett's *The Midsummer Marriage*.

The bass may also be seen in comedy, where he tends to be cast as the bibulous fat man, such as Falstaff in Nicolai's *Die lustige Weiber von Windsor*, or as the dotard whose fate it is to be outwitted by the bright young people, as Donizetti's Don Pasquale or Rossini's Dr Bartolo. The obverse of this is his frequent association with downright villainy. In *Il barbiere* the other bass role is Don Basilio, whose slander aria, however amusing, enunciates a poisonous ethical philosophy; of the various roles for bass in Wagner's *Ring* none is particularly amiable and the most effective of them, Hagen in *Götterdämmerung*, is known among his associates as 'Hagen der Grimme', the treacherous hero-slayer. Most famously the bass frequently plays the Devil himself; Méphistophélès in Gounod's *Faust* and the title role in Boito's *Mefistofele* are two of the bass's most coveted roles.

Though this repertory is thoroughly international, there have been some major national differences in characteristics among singers. The typical Italian bass has been endowed with a vibrant richness of tone, and in the early 19th century elegance and agility, as in several serious Rossini roles or Bellini's Oroveso. The French at best have valued freedom and grace (the 'basse chantante' or 'basse noble') rather than tremendous power or exceptional depth. The Russians are celebrated for their cavernous basses, though their opera singers rarely display the deep notes heard in Russian choirs. The German speciality has been the 'black' bass, a type in which the weight of the sound, a combination of power and depth, is often more evident than the beauty. All countries have made some distinction between what are most generally known as the 'basso cantante' (or 'basse chantante') and the 'basso profondo' (or 'basse profonde'), though there is no reason why the terms should be mutually exclusive. Perhaps the best example in practice of the difference between the two types is to be found in *Don Carlos*, in the scene between the King and the Inquisitor. Though the writing for the two parts shows little difference in range or tessitura, the Inquisitor is associated from the start with the deep sonority of the accompanying orchestration, and it is clearly more effective if contrasted voices are employed, the Inquisitor here being the deeper in timbre, closer in type to the Germanic 'black' bass.

4. Singers and roles: the 19th century.

(i) Italian and French opera. Rossini expected the bass singers in his operas to have voices as flexible as the tenors, or indeed the sopranos and mezzos. Nicola de Grecis, after singing in the premières of Generali's *Don Chisciotto* (1805) and P. C. Guglielmi's *La guerra aperta* (1807), was the first to inspire Rossini's *basso buffo* roles. He sang Mr Slook in *La cambiale di matrimonio* (1810) in Venice and created roles in *La scala di seta* (1812) and *Signor Bruschino* (1813). He later took part in the premières of Mercadante's *Elisa e Claudio* (1821) and Donizetti's *Chiara e Serafina* (1822). Rossini wrote eight roles, serious and comic, for

Filippo Galli, among them Tarabotto in *L'inganno felice* (1812) and Mustafà in *L'italiana in Algeri* (1813), the title role of *Maometto II* (1820) and Assur in *Semiramide* (1823); Galli's noble, flexible voice later inspired Donizetti to write the part of Henry VIII in *Anna Bolena* (1830). Michele Benedetti, reportedly a more dramatic singer than Galli, created bass roles in seven of Rossini's serious operas for Naples, including Elmiro in *Otello* (1816), the title role of *Mosè in Egitto* (1818) and Douglas in *La donna del lago* (1819). His later roles included Atkins in Donizetti's *Alfredo il grande* (1823) and Clemente in Bellini's *Bianca e Gernando* (1826). The title role of Rossini's *Mosè* (given as *Pietro l'Eremita*) was first sung in London by Giuseppe de Begnis, the versatile *buffo* bass who had created Dandini in *La Cenerentola* (1817) at Rome.

The illustrious Neapolitan bass Luigi Lablache, who made his début as Dandini, also sang in the première of *Elisa e Claudio*. Engaged at Naples (1826–32), he created roles in seven Donizetti operas, including *L'esule di Roma* and *Il giovedì grasso* (both 1828) and *Sancia di Castiglia* (1832); by then the most famous bass in Europe, he sang the title roles in two Donizetti premières in Paris, *Marino Faliero* (1835) and *Don Pasquale* (1843). In Paris he also created Giorgio in Bellini's *I puritani*; in London, his performance of the title role written for him in Balfe's *Falstaff* (1838) drew from Chorley the remark that he was 'such a protagonist as would have made Shakespeare's heart leap for joy', while the role of King Philip in Costa's *Don Carlos* (1844) gave scope to his great dramatic gifts. He also created Massimiliano in Verdi's *I masnadieri* (1847). Lablache was equally effective in comic and serious roles; he excelled as Dulcamara and as Don Pasquale, and was particularly admired as Elmiro (Desdemona's father) in Rossini's *Otello*, Henry VIII in *Anna Bolena* and Oroveso in *Norma*.

Carlo Porto, whose repertory also included Henry VIII, Oroveso and Giorgio, created roles in four Donizetti operas, among them Ernesto in *Parisina* (1833), Clifford in *Rosmonda d'Inghilterra* (1834), Talbot in *Maria Stuarda* and Raimondo in *Lucia di Lammermoor* (both 1835). Talbot was later sung by Ignazio Marini, another high bass with a strong, well-schooled voice who specialized in Donizetti; he created Guido in *Gemma di Vergy* (1834), Gran Siniscalco in *Gianni di Parigi* (1839) and Arnoldo in *Adelia* (1841). He sang Oberto in the première of Verdi's first opera (1839) and later created the title role of *Attila* (1846).

At the Paris Opéra, dominated early in the century by composers of Italian birth, Henri-Etienne Dérivis, a singer in the classical French tradition with an excellent coloratura technique, created roles in three Spontini operas: the Pontifex Maximus in *La vestale* (1807), Montezuma in *Fernand Cortez* (1809) and Antigone in *Olympie* (1819); he also sang in premières of works by Méhul, Cherubini and Isouard before creating Mahomet II in Rossini's *Le siège de Corinthe* (1826). His successor at the Opéra, Nicolas Levasseur, began his career in Italy, where he sang in the première of Meyerbeer's *Margherita d'Anjou* (1820), then in Paris he sang Don Alvaro in Rossini's *Il viaggio a Reims* at the Théâtre Italien (1825) and created many roles at the Opéra, among them Moses in *Moïse et Pharaon* (1827), the Tutor in *Le comte Ory* (1828), Walter Furst in *Guillaume Tell* (1829), Bertram in *Robert le diable* (1831), Count Ankastrom in Auber's *Gustave III* (1833), Cardinal Brogni in *La Juive* (1835), Marcel in *Les Huguenots* (1836), Balthazar in *La favorite* (1840) and Zacharie in *Le prophète* (1849). These are roles of the *basse noble* type: Levasseur had a magnificent voice of enormous range, better suited to Meyerbeer than to Rossini. His contemporary Prosper Dérivis (Henri-Etienne's son), who sang a Herald in the première of *La Juive* and later became a fine Cardinal Brogni, also had a large compass: he sang Melcthal in the 100th performance of *Guillaume Tell* at the Opéra (1834) and created Nevers in *Les Huguenots*, Balducci in *Benvenuto Cellini* (1838) and Félix in *Les martyrs* (1840). In Vienna he sang the Prefect in the première of *Linda di Chamounix* (1842) and he created roles in two Verdi operas at La Scala, Zaccaria in *Nabucco* (1842) and Pagano in *I Lombardi* (1843).

Louis-Henri Obin, another *basse noble* at the Opéra, sang Procida in the première of *Les vêpres siciliennes* (1855) and later created the Grand Brahmin in *L'Africaine* (1865) and Philip II in *Don Carlos* (1867); his repertory included Elmiro, Moses, Brogni and Balthazar. Jules-Bernard Belval, Don Pédro in the première of *L'Africaine*, also created King Solomon in Gounod's *La reine de Saba* (1862) and Claudius in Thomas' *Hamlet* (1868). Though by then virtually retired, he sang Brogni at the opening performance of the Palais Garnier in 1875.

Massenet took enormous pains to fit the roles in his operas to the singer. Léon Gresse, though French-born, created Phanuel in *Hérodiade* (1881) at the Théâtre de la Monnaie, Brussels, where he also sang Hagen in the première of Reyer's *Sigurd* (1884). In Paris he became the first Hunding in *Die Walküre* and Pogner in *Die Meistersinger* at the Opéra. His son André Gresse sang in the première of two Massenet operas, as Césaire in *Sapho* (1897) and as Sancho Panza in *Don Quichotte* (1910), whose title role was composed for the Russian bass Fyodor Shalyapin. Pol Plançon, an effective actor as well as a most stylish singer, created two Massenet roles, Count of Gormas in *Le Cid* at the Opéra (1885) and Garrido in *La Navarraise* (1894) at Covent Garden. Don Diègue in *Le Cid* was created by the Polish-born bass Edouard de Reszke. An equally fine interpreter of Italian, French and German opera, he created Ruben in Ponchielli's *Il figliuol prodigo* (1880) and sang Fiesco in the revised *Simon Boccanegra* at La Scala (1881); with his brother Jean in the tenor roles, he sang Phanuel in the Paris première of *Hérodiade*, Méphistophélès (his favourite role) in the 500th performance of *Faust* and Friar Laurence in the first performance of *Roméo et Juliette* (1867) at the Opéra. His prowess as a Wagner singer was legendary: at Covent Garden and the Metropolitan, usually with Jean, he excelled as King Henry, King Mark, Pogner, the Wanderer and Hunding.

(ii) German opera. In the early 1820s German basses were still mainly all-purpose singers; a good example was Heinrich Blume, who created Caspar in *Der Freischütz* (1821); although Don Giovanni was considered his best role he sang Masetto and the Commendatore with equal facility. As a youth of 19 in Leipzig, Carl Risse took part in the première of Marschner's *Der Templer und die Jüdin* (1829); later he created Cecco del Vecchio in *Rienzi* (1842) and the following year Daland in *Der fliegende Holländer*. His colleague Wilhelm Dettmer sang Steffano Colonna in *Rienzi* and the Landgrave in *Tannhäuser* (1845). August Zschiesche, engaged for 50 years at the Berlin Hofoper, created Falstaff in Nicolai's *Die lustigen Weiber von*

Windsor (1849); a genuine bass, he also sang Rocco, Osmin and Bertram with distinction.

Karl Formes, who sang Plumkett in the première in Vienna of Flotow's *Martha* (1847), sang for many years at Covent Garden, notably as Tsar Peter in the British première of Meyerbeer's *L'étoile du Nord*, and ended his career in New York, where he sang in the American premières of *Lohengrin* and *Der Templer und die Jüdin*. Gustav Hölzel, an Austrian bass of wide range, created Di Fiesco in Donizetti's *Maria di Rohan* (1843); later in Munich he sang Beckmesser in the première of *Die Meistersinger* (1868).

Ludwig Zottmayr, the first King Mark in *Tristan und Isolde* (1865), was probably a bass-baritone: his roles in Munich included Count di Luna and Hans Heiling. Caspar Bausewein, on the other hand, who created Pogner in *Die Meistersinger*, Fafner in *Das Rheingold* (1869) and Hunding in *Die Walküre* (1870), was a true bass who also sang Leporello, Caspar and Don Basilio. Karl Fischer, the first Munich Daland, created Kothner in *Die Meistersinger* and Alberich in *Das Rheingold*. His brother Emil, though technically a bass-baritone, sang many bass roles; he was the first American Hans Sachs, King Mark, Wotan (*Das Rheingold*), the Wanderer and Hagen as well as Lysiart in *Euryanthe*. Hagen had been created at Bayreuth by Gustav Siehr (1876), who later alternated as Gurnemanz in *Parsifal* with Emil Scaria, the bass who created the role (1882); Scaria, who had sung Escamillo at Vienna in the first performance of *Carmen* outside France, sang Wotan in the first complete Vienna, Berlin and London *Ring* cycles.

(iii) Russian opera. When Glinka's first opera, *A Life for the Tsar*, was given in 1836, the title role was entrusted to Osip Petrov; engaged at St Petersburg from 1830 until his death in 1878, Petrov also created Ruslan in *Ruslan and Lyudmila* (1842); the Miller in Dargomïzhsky's *Rusalka* (1856) and Leporello in *The Stone Guest* (1872); Ivan the Terrible in Rimsky-Korsakov's *The Maid of Pskov* (1873), Varlaam in *Boris Godunov* (1874) and the Mayor in Tchaikovsky's *Vakula the Smith* (1876). Vladimir Vasilyev, Pimen in the première of *Boris Godunov*, created roles in two Tchaikovsky operas, Prince Zhemchuznïy in *The Oprichnik* (1874) and the king in *The Maid of Orléans* (1881).

Fyodor Stravinsky, father of the composer, was equally gifted in comic and dramatic roles; he sang His Royal Highness and Dunois in the respective premières of *Vakula the Smith* and *The Maid of Orléans* and created Grandfather Frost in Rimsky's *The Snow Maiden* (1882), Mamirov in *The Enchantress* (1887), in which he was greatly praised by Tchaikovsky, and Skula the gudok player in *Prince Igor* (1890), and he also sang Varlaam and Falstaff. His contemporary Mikhail Koryakin was the first Thibaut in *The Maid of Orléans*, Kichiga in *The Sorceress* and Khan Konchak in *Prince Igor*; though a less subtle singer, he had a magnificent voice. So too did Vasily Petrov, who sang Susanin, Ruslan, Prince Gremin and Konchak at the Bol'shoy in Moscow, and King Dodon in the British première of *The Golden Cockerel* in 1914.

The outstanding singer in the London Russian seasons (1913–14) was Fyodor Shalyapin, the first exponent in Britain of Boris Godunov, Dosifey, Ivan the Terrible and both Prince Galitsky and Khan Konchak in *Prince Igor*. Shalyapin, an outsize personality and possessor of a highly individual voice, was found rather eccentric in his characterizations of non-Russian roles, which included Mephistopheles (both Gounod and Boito) and Don Basilio.

5. Singers and roles: the 20th century. When *Don Quichotte* was first performed in Paris the title role was sung by Vanni-Marcoux, a bass-baritone rather than a bass, who created Guido in Février's *Monna Vanna* (1909) and, at Monte Carlo, Séraphim Flambeau in *L'aiglon* (1937) by Honegger and Ibert. Félix Vieuille, engaged for many years at the Opéra-Comique, created, among other roles, the Junk-seller in *Louise* (1900), Arkel in *Pelléas et Mélisande* (1902), Bluebeard in Dukas' *Ariane et Barbe-Bleue* (1907) and the Sultan in Rabaud's *Mârouf* (1914).

The roles for bass in Puccini's later operas are mainly character parts: Adam Didur, the Polish-born bass who sang for 25 seasons at the Metropolitan, created Ashby, the Wells-Fargo agent in *La fanciulla del West* (1910), and Talpa in *Il tabarro* (1918), as well as the Woodcutter in *Königskinder* (1910). The first Boris Godunov, Prince Galitsky and Khan Konchak at the Metropolitan, Didur sang Baron Archibaldo in the London and New York premières of Montemezzi's *L'amore dei tre re*.

Baron Ochs in *Der Rosenkavalier* (1911) was created by the baritone Karl Perron, but the most famous exponent of the role was Richard Mayr, the Austrian bass who sang Ochs in the Viennese première. Mayr also sang Figaro, Leporello and Sarastro at Salzburg and Hagen, Gurnemanz and Pogner at Bayreuth. In Strauss he was unrivalled: he created Barak in *Die Frau ohne Schatten* (1919) and sang Count Waldner in the Viennese première of *Arabella*. Mayr became a much-loved Baron Ochs at Covent Garden, but the first London Ochs, as well as the first London Gurnemanz, was Paul Knüpfer, more notable as a Wagnerian.

Early in his career Ezio Pinza sang Wagner roles (Pogner, King Mark and Gurnemanz), in Italian, as well as bel canto parts such as Oroveso (*Norma*) and Rodolfo (*La sonnambula*); at La Scala he created the Blind Man in Pizzetti's *Dèbora e Jaéle* (1922) and Tigellinus in Boito's *Nerone* (1924). At the Metropolitan, where he sang for 22 seasons, he gave up Wagner; his enormous repertory was chiefly in Italian and French opera. As Don Giovanni and Figaro, Gounod's and Boito's Mephistopheles, Don Basilio and Dulcamara, Fiesco and Padre Guardiano, this velvet-toned bass dominated the stage dramatically and vocally.

During the 1920s and 30s there was no lack of strong-voiced basses to sing at Bayreuth: the Norwegian Ivar Andrésen sang Gurnemanz, King Mark and Pogner there and appeared at Salzburg and Glyndebourne (in 1935) as Sarastro and Osmin. Alexander Kipnis sang the same roles at Bayreuth and appeared at Salzburg and Glyndebourne as Sarastro. After World War II the supply continued: Ludwig Weber, the finest Gurnemanz of his generation, was admired as Rocco, Ochs and Barak. Gottlob Frick, a superb, black-voiced Hagen, was another notable Gurnemanz; he created Caliban in Sutermeister's *Zauberinsel*. Kurt Böhme sang Pogner, Fafner and Titurel at Bayreuth, but was best known as Ochs. Martti Talvela brought his large, resonant voice to such Wagner roles as Fasolt, King Mark and Daland, and was an impressive Sarastro.

The tremendous success of Verdi's *Don Carlos* in Europe and the USA produced four very different readings of Philip II: Boris Christoff, the Bulgarian bass who was also a magnificent Boris Godunov, Khan Konchak and Dosifey, offered a tyrannical, suspicious Spanish monarch; Nicolai Ghiaurov, also Bulgarian, but more practical and decisive, sang Padre Guardiano and Fiesco with similar authority; Cesare Siepi, whose favourite role was Don Giovanni, offered a more introspective interpretation; while Ruggero Raimondi, also an admired Don Giovanni, included Philip among a gallery of powerful Verdi characterizations (Fiesco, Procida, Attila, Silva and Padre Guardiano).

Britten's operas contain many rewarding roles for the bass: Owen Brannigan, who created Swallow in *Peter Grimes* (1945), Collatinus in *The Rape of Lucretia* (1946), Noye in *Noye's Fludde* (1958) and Bottom the Weaver in *A Midsummer Night's Dream* (1960), was a comic actor of great charm if not much subtlety. Frederick Dalberg, creator of John Claggart, the villainous Master-at-Arms in *Billy Budd* (1951) and Sir Walter Raleigh in *Gloriana* (1953), had a darker voice and a more forbidding personality. Michael Langdon, the first Ratcliffe in *Billy Budd* and Recorder of Norwich in *Gloriana*, also created the He-Ancient in Tippett's *The Midsummer Marriage* (1955) and the title role of Orr's *Hermiston* (1975); he was also a stylish Ochs and a sound Wagnerian. Forbes Robinson, who created the title role of Tippett's *King Priam* (1962), was a powerfully evil Claggart; he also took the role of Moses in the British stage première of Schoenberg's *Moses und Aron*.

The revival of interest in Rossini's operas, serious and comic, requires basses with agile voices and a good coloratura technique; Justino Díaz, who created Antony in Barber's *Antony and Cleopatra*, the opera which inaugurated the new Metropolitan at Lincoln Center in 1966, sang Mahomet in *Le siège de Corinthe* with some success. Samuel Ramey has also sung Mahomet, as well as Moses, Assur, Pasha Selim, Mustafà, the Podestà (*La gazza ladra*) and Douglas (*La donna del lago*); his flexible but powerful voice can encompass a repertory that runs from the Rossini roles written for Galli or Benedetti to Gounod's and Boito's Mephistopheles, Attila and the four villains in *Les contes d'Hoffmann*.

For bibliography *see* SINGING: A BIBLIOGRAPHY.

OWEN JANDER, LIONEL SAWKINS, J. B. STEANE, ELIZABETH FORBES

Bassani, Giovanni Battista (*b* Padua, *c*1657; *d* Bergamo, 1 Oct 1716). Italian composer. He is said to have studied in Venice with Legrenzi and Daniele da Castrovillari. From 1667 he was an organist in Ferrara. In 1677 he became a member of the Accademia Filarmonica at Bologna (which he later served briefly as *principe*) and *maestro di cappella* and organist of the Confraternità del Finale, Modena. Subsequently he was *maestro di cappella* at the court of Duke Alessandro II della Mirandola (from 1680), of the Accademia della Morte (from 1683 or 1684) and of Ferrara Cathedral (from 1686); because of his contribution to the musical life of that city he became known as 'Bassani of Ferrara'. He was also a celebrated violinist. From 1712 he was music director at S Maria Maggiore, Bergamo.

Bassani's music was prominent in the middle Baroque period in Italy, when the concertato style predominated. Although his fame has rested chiefly on his trio sonatas for strings, he was also a prolific composer of vocal music. His nine operas seem to be entirely lost except for ten arias from *Gli amori alla moda*, found in a small manuscript volume preserved in Modena. Some are for soprano, others for tenor, with basso continuo. They are extremely short, though in the da capo form, rhythmically lively and varied, and charming in effect. Among his other works are oratorios, solo cantatas (sacred and secular) and many other sacred pieces.

dm – *drama per musica*

L'amorosa preda di Paride (dm, 3), Bologna, Publico, 1683
Falaride, tiranno d'Agrigento (dm, 3, A. Morselli), Venice, S Angelo, 1683
L'Alarico, rè de' Goti (dm, 3), Ferrara, Conte Pinamonte Bonacossi, Feb 1685
Vitige [Vitige, rè de' Vandali] (dm, 3), Ferrara, Feb 1686
Gli amori alla moda (scherzo melodrammatico, 3), Ferrara, Bonacossi, 1688, 10 arias in *I-MOe*
Il trionfo di Venere in Ida (melodramma), Ferrara, 1688
La Ginevra, infanta di Scozia (dm, 3, G. C. Grazzini, after L. Ariosto), Ferrara, Bonacossi, 1690
Il coceio Nerva (dm, 3), Ferrara, Bonacossi, 1691
Gl'amori tra gl'odii, o sia Il Ramiro in Norvegia (dm, 3, M. A. Rimena), Verona, 1693

F. Pasini: 'Notes sur la vie de Giovanni Battista Bassani', *SIMG*, vii (1905–6), 581–607
U. Rolandi: 'Opere ed oratorii di G. B. Bassani', *La scuola veneziana (secoli XVI–XVIII): note e documenti*, Chigiana, iii (1941), 32–4
R. Haselbach: *Giovanni Battista Bassani* (Kassel and Basle, 1955)
A. Cavicchi: 'L'attività ferrarese di Giovan Battista Bassani', *Chigiana*, xxiii (1966), 43–58

PETER SMITH

Bassarids, The. *Opera seria* with intermezzo in one act (four movements) by HANS WERNER HENZE to a libretto by W. H. AUDEN and CHESTER KALLMAN after EURIPIDES' *The Bacchae*; Salzburg, Grosses Festspielhaus, 6 August 1966.

Dionysus *who also sings:* A Voice, A Stranger	tenor
Pentheus *King of Thebes*	baritone
Cadmus *his grandfather, founder of Thebes*	bass
Tiresias *an old blind prophet*	tenor
Captain of the Royal Guard	baritone
Agave *Cadmus's daughter and mother of Pentheus*	mezzo-soprano
Autonoe *her sister*	soprano
Beroe *an old slave, once nurse to the deceased Semele*	mezzo-soprano
Young woman *slave in Agave's household*	silent
Child *her daughter*	silent

Bassarids, Theban citizens, guards and servants

Setting The Royal Palace, Thebes, and Mount Cytheron, in antiquity

Henze's second collaboration with Auden and Kallman, after the successful première of *Elegy for Young Lovers*, was commissioned by the Salzburg Festival. The libretto was prepared in 1963, but Henze did not begin work on the score until more than a year later, after he had completed *Der junge Lord*. The first performance (in German) was conducted by Christoph von Dohnányi with a cast led by Ingeborg Hallstein, Kerstin Meyer, Vera Little, Loren Driscoll, Helmut Melchert, Kostas Paskalis, William Dooley and Peter Lagger; the première of the original English-language version took place at Santa Fe in 1967, conducted by the composer. In 1974 it was staged by the ENO at the London Coliseum, with a cast that included Josephine Barstow, Katherine Pring, Anne Collins, Gregory Dempsey, Kenneth Woollam, Norman Welsby and Tom McDonnell; Henze conducted and directed the performances. A concert

'The Bassarids' (Henze): scene from the original production at the Grosses Festspielhaus, Salzburg, 6 August 1966, designed by Filippo Sanjust

performance at the Deutsche Oper in Berlin in 1986, conducted by Gerd Albrecht, formed the basis of a subsequent commercial recording (1991), in which the intermezzo in the third movement was omitted (a cut approved by the composer).

FIRST MOVEMENT *The courtyard of the Royal Palace* Cadmus, founder of Thebes, has abdicated in favour of his grandson Pentheus. The citizens of Thebes gather to sing a hymn in praise of their new king, but Pentheus is in retreat, praying and fasting; he plans to convert his people gradually to a rational monotheism. Next to the palace is the grave of Semele, a daughter of Cadmus, who, according to legend, had borne a son by Zeus: Dionysus. An offstage Voice interrupts the hymn, proclaiming 'Ayayalya, the God Dionysus has entered Boeotia!', and the brass fanfares that underpinned the choral celebration give way to lyrical lines of flute and strings, while the chorus takes up the melismatic chant as, transformed into Bassarids, they follow the Voice to Mount Cytheron. Cadmus, Beroe, Agave and Tiresias discuss the Dionysian cult. Cadmus is fearful, Tiresias suspicious, Beroe clings to the old religion; only Agave welcomes the new faith.

The Bassarids' hymn continues in the background. Autonoe arrives as Agave praises the handsome Captain of the Guard, who reads a proclamation from Pentheus forbidding his people to believe that Dionysus is the son of Semele and Zeus. Pentheus himself reinforces his command by extinguishing the flame on Semele's grave, threatening death to anyone who relights it. Cadmus is horrified. Agave and Autonoe pledge their loyalty to Pentheus, but the offstage voice of Dionysus interrupts them with a seductive serenade, urging them to Mount Cytheron, to the land of eternal happiness. The sisters follow, as if hypnotized.

SECOND MOVEMENT Despite Cadmus's warnings, Pentheus sends his guards to imprison all those who celebrated the festival of the Bassarids. As the Bassarids' chorus is heard again, Pentheus confesses in a long aria to Beroe his fear of the Dionysian cult, and swears to abstain 'from wine, from meats, and from woman's bed'; she prays that the new king will be protected. Entranced detainees from Mount Cytheron are brought before Pentheus; they include his mother Agave, her sister Autonoe, Tiresias and a stranger suspected of being a Dionysian priest. Pentheus attempts to wake his mother, but she can only sing an aria describing the delights of Cytheron. He places her and Autonoe under house arrest, and orders the destruction of Tiresias's house. Beroe has recognized the stranger as Dionysus; when Pentheus threatens him with torture, he responds with an aria that describes Dionysus's voyage to Naxos.

THIRD MOVEMENT The Bassarids' hymn continues. As the stranger is tortured Thebes is struck by an earthquake; the prisoners escape and rush off to Mount Cytheron. The stranger offers Pentheus a vision in a mirror of the feast of the Bassarids.

In an intermezzo Pentheus is shown a rococo enactment of the Judgement of Calliope, in effect his own repressed sexual fantasies: Agave and Autonoe appear as Aphrodite and Persephone in erotic play with the Captain of the Guard as Adonis. The scene is accompanied by onstage mandolins and guitar, and the music itself is neo-classical, with recitative, arias, duets and a final quartet.

Pentheus is appalled by what has been brought from his own subconscious; the stranger suggests he disguise himself as a woman and follow him to Mount Cytheron. Beroe and Cadmus await Pentheus's return. On the mountain Pentheus hides to watch his people, transformed into Bassarids and Maenads. The voice of Dionysus tells them there is a spy among them; led by Agave, who fails to recognize her son's pleas, the Bassarids kill Pentheus.

FOURTH MOVEMENT While Cadmus and Beroe keep watch at dawn, a triumphant procession returns to Thebes. Agave displays the head of her son; still entranced, she believes she has killed a lion. Questioned by Cadmus, she comes gradually to her senses, and identifies the stranger as perpetrator of the murder. He admits he is Dionysus; he exiles the remainder of the Theban royal family and orders the burning of their palace. Among the flames he summons his mother

Semele from her grave and commits her to Mount Olympus as the goddess Thyone. When the flames subside Semele's grave is bedecked in vines, and adorned with statues of Dionysus and Thyone. In the morning sunshine, the people kneel to worship their new gods.

* * *

When Auden and Kallman took on the commission they specified that Henze listen to *Götterdämmerung* before composing the music. Henze in turn requested a libretto shaped into the four-movement plan of a symphony, and the music of *The Bassarids* represents a conscious attempt to come to terms with the post-Wagnerian tradition, continued through Mahler and Schoenberg. Though traditional operatic forms, arias and ensembles are embedded in the structure, each of the four movements has a symphonic archetype: the first is a sonata form in which the hard-edged Pentheus material and the more sensuous music for the Bassarids provide the two subject groups; the second is a scherzo made from a sequence of dances; the third a slow movement interrupted by the intermezzo and culminating in the music of the hunt for Pentheus; the fourth is founded on a 43-note theme that flows into a final passacaglia.

ANDREW CLEMENTS

Bass-baritone (Ger. *Bassbariton*, *Hoher Bass*). A male voice intermediate in pitch between BARITONE and BASS. This is a late 19th-century addition in the terminology of commonly recognized categories of the singing voice. It arose largely in response to the requirements of the great Wagner roles of the Dutchman, Wotan and Hans Sachs. Wagner used the term 'Hoher Bass' to designate the roles of Wotan, Alberich, Donner and Fasolt in *Das Rheingold* and *Die Walküre*. These have too high a tessitura to be comfortably sung by a bass, and yet they presuppose a deeper voice than the baritone as understood by writers of opera in Italy and France, especially by Verdi, the most influential among them. There is no corresponding term in general use relating to the female voice.

Though it may seem to be a somewhat specialized and perhaps unnecessary subdivision, it has proved useful. Other roles, in addition to the three in Wagner, have been found appropriate to the voice. In Mozart, Don Giovanni, Count Almaviva and Figaro are normally taken by baritones, but occasionally by basses, and they probably call for something in between. Pizarro in *Fidelio*, Caspar in *Der Freischütz* and John the Baptist in *Salome* are further examples in German opera. The cast-lists in Russian scores may specify five or six roles for bass, but when the voice-parts are examined few will be found to call on the deep reserves of the Russian *basso profondo*, and if they are sung by basses rather than baritones it may often be because the character (an old monk perhaps) is more effectively represented by the deep timbre. The part of Boris Godunov, though usually taken by a bass, is really for bass-baritone, and it may be argued that this is what its most famous exponent, Fyodor Shalyapin, more truly was, certainly in his later years.

Shalyapin was always known as a bass, but since his time the use of 'bass-baritone' as a descriptive term has become much more widespread. The dictionary of singers by Kutsch and Riemens (1982 edition) places just over 100 singers in this category as compared with roughly 170 basses and 520 baritones. Many of their ascriptions show how little of a science the business of categorizing voices can claim to be: there are anomalies in respect of both bass and baritone voices, for among those named as baritones are Friedrich Schorr and Rudolf Bockelmann, commonly known as bass-baritones and two of the most admired singers of the Wagnerian roles named above as constituting a prime *raison d'être* for the existence of the bass-baritone as a special category.

For a discussion of bass-baritone singers and roles, *see* BARITONE, §§3–4.

J. B. STEANE

Basse chantante. French term for a 'singing bass' voice, akin to the Italian BASSO CANTANTE. It is distinguished from other types of bass voice partly by having a timbre nearer to the bass-baritone than to the deep bass, partly by a style that favours smooth, melodic music rather than the more declamatory and dramatic, and partly by volume, which may not be sufficient for the heavier roles such as those in Wagner. Pre-eminent among French basses of the type was Pol Plançon who lacked neither volume nor depth, and who was also an expressive singer and a polished actor, yet whose prime excellence lay in the sheer beauty of his tone, its production and usage.

See also BASS.

J. B. STEANE

Basse noble. French term for a 'noble bass' voice. It is close kin to the BASSE CHANTANTE; both terms have often been applied to the same singer. A difference of connotation lies in the quality of voice and its dramatic purposes. In Gounod's *Roméo et Juliette*, for example, a *basse chantante* may sing the part of Capulet while Friar Laurence is for the *basse noble*. Sarastro in *Die Zauberflöte* requires a *basse noble* who must also have the smoothness and tonal beauty of the *chantante*. King Henry in *Lohengrin* may also be a *basse noble* in quality, the voice lying in terms of power somewhere between the *chantante* and the darker, weightier type cast as Hunding or Hagen. French basses of the type in this century would be well represented by Marcel Journet.

See also BASS.

J. B. STEANE

Basse-taille (Fr.). The lowest of the three male voices intermediate between the *dessus* (soprano) and the *basse* in Baroque and Classical French opera, with a range *c* to *g′* (pitch was as much as a whole tone lower than that now used). These three voices – the others were *haute-contre*, and [*haute-*]*taille*, later *ténor* – corresponded to the three *parties intermédiaires* of the string orchestra, all played by violas: *haute-contre de violon*, *taille de violon* and *quinte de violon*. Brossard (1703) equated the Italian 'baritono' and the French 'concordant' with *basse-taille*. In 1768 Rousseau, concurring, added that true *basses* were sometimes also called *basses-tailles*.

See also BARITONE.

Bassi, Amedeo (*b* Montespertoli, nr Florence, 29 July 1874; *d* Florence, 15 Jan 1949). Italian tenor. He trained in Florence, making his début at Castelfiorentino in Marchetti's *Ruy Blas* in 1897. After travelling widely in Italy he sang with great success in South America, where he performed regularly until 1912. He joined the Manhattan Opera Company in 1906 and made his Covent Garden début the following year; he returned in 1911 for the British première of *La fanciulla del West*, in which he also sang at the first performances in Rome and Chicago. At Monte Carlo in 1905 he participated in the première of Mascagni's *Amica* and in Naples the following year that of Frédéric d'Erlanger's *Tess*; he was also in the first American performances of *I gioielli della Madonna* (1912). In the 1920s at La Scala he began a second career, as an admired Wagnerian tenor. He taught in Florence where Ferruccio Tagliavini was among his pupils. Early recordings show a powerful voice produced in the typical *verismo* style.

GV (R. Celletti; R. Vegeto)
M. Scott: *The Record of Singing* (London, 1977) J. B. STEANE

Luigi Bassi in the title role of Mozart's 'Don Giovanni': engraving by Médard Thoenert (1787)

Bassi, Luigi (*b* Pesaro, 4 Sept 1766; *d* ?Dresden, 1825). Italian baritone. He studied in Senigallia with Pietro Morandi and appeared on the stage at the age of 13. He completed his studies with Laschi in Florence, where he appeared at the Pergola Theatre. In 1784 he joined Bondini's company in Prague and in 1786 sang Count Almaviva in the first Prague performance of *Le nozze di Figaro*; the next year he created the name part in *Don Giovanni* (1787). He is said to have asked Mozart to write him another air in place of 'Fin ch'han dal vino' and to have induced Mozart to rewrite 'Là ci darem' five times. In later years he stressed that no two performances were the same and that Mozart had specifically wished that he should improvise as long as he paid attention to the orchestra.

Bassi was praised in the *Gothaer Taschenkalendar* (1793):

> This rewarding singer was from the start the ornament of the company and he still is. His voice is as melodious as his acting is masterly. Immediately he comes on, joy and cheerfulness pervade the whole audience and he never leaves the theatre without unequivocal and loud applause.

In 1793 Bassi sang Papageno in Italian at Leipzig. But by 1800 his voice had deteriorated, although his histrionic ability remained unimpaired. According to the *Allgemeine musikalische Zeitung* (1800):

> Bassi was an excellent singer before he lost his voice, and he still knows very well how to use what remains. It lies between tenor and bass, and though it sounds somewhat hollow, it is still very flexible, full and pleasant. Herr Bassi is furthermore a very skilled actor in tragedy with no trace of burlesque, and with no vulgarity or tastelessness in comedy. In his truly artful and droll way he can parody the faults of the other singers so subtly that only the audience notices and they themselves are unaware of it. His best roles are Axur, Don Giovanni, Teodoro, the Notary in *La molinara*, the Count in *Figaro* and others.

In 1806 Bassi left Prague because of the war and relied on the patronage of Prince Lobkowitz, making occasional appearances in Vienna. In 1814 he returned to Prague, where Weber consulted him about *Don Giovanni*. In the autumn he was engaged for the Italian company in Dresden; and in 1815 he was made director. He still appeared in Mozart's operas; in 1816 he sang Count Almaviva, although he could no longer encompass the role vocally, but in 1817 he was well received as Guglielmo. He no longer performed Don Giovanni but sang Masetto, for which he was criticized because his figure was unsuited to the part. His contract with the Dresden company continued until his death.

CHRISTOPHER RAEBURN

Bassini, Achille de. *See* DE BASSINI, ACHILLE.

Basso, Alberto (*b* Turin, 21 Aug 1931). Italian musicologist. He took a degree in law at Turin University (1956) before being appointed in 1961 to teach music history at the Turin Conservatory; he became librarian in 1974. He was editor of *Opera*, a series of music guides (1973–5), and with Guglielmo Barblan edited the three-volume *Storia dell'opera* (1977). Active in various musical organizations, and a council member of the Teatro Regio, Turin (1968–78), he was coordinator of the five-volume *Storia del Teatro Regio di Torino* (1976–88) as well as chief editor of the 13-volume *Dizionario enciclopedico universale della musica e dei musicisti* (Turin, 1983–90). In 1991 he organized the exhibition and edited the catalogue for the 250th anniversary of the Turin Teatro Regio.

L'Amfiparnaso di O. Vecchi (Turin, 1960)
G. Verdi: autografi dell'Archivio Ricordi esposti per l'esecuzione del Simon Boccanegra (Turin, 1963)
Il Conservatorio G. Verdi di Torino: storia e documenti dalle origini al 1970 (Turin, 1971)
Il teatro della città, 1788–1936, Storia del Teatro Regio di Torino, ii (Turin, 1976)
ed., with G. Barblan: *Storia dell'opera* (Turin, 1977)
ed.: *Il Teatro Regio di Torino 1740–1990: L'Arcano incanto* (Milan, 1991) CAROLYN GIANTURCO

Basso buffo. Italian term for a 'comic bass' (or baritone) voice, the type principally used for comic roles in 18th-century opera (an exception is the tenor cast as Don Quixote in Paisiello's opera of that name). Dr Bartolo in the Figaro operas of Mozart and Rossini is typical of the continuing tradition, both as a character, ridiculous in pretensions and sense of outrage when not satisfied, and in the writing for voice which, while requiring no great skill in bel canto, asks for effective volume and proficiency in patter song. Mozart's Figaro (baritone or bass-baritone) and Leporello are further classic examples. The type of 'tricked' character ('basso buffo caricato') is exemplified by Donizetti's Don Pasquale, one of whose main assignments is his part in the patter duet. Latter-day examples include Gianni Schicchi (baritone) and, outside Italy, Henry Morosus in *Die schweigsame Frau*.

See also BARITONE; BASS; and BUFFO. J. B. STEANE

Basso cantante. Italian term, meaning the 'singing bass' voice of Italian tradition. A bass of this type, like his French counterpart (*see* BASSE CHANTANTE), sets out to offer beauty of tone, evenness of line and stylistic grace. Characteristic of the school, as represented by Francesco Navarrini and later by Ezio Pinza, is a well-rounded sonority, more vibrant than those of the French or German traditions, less deep in tone and range than the Russian. Typical roles are Count Rodolfo in *La sonnambula* and Silva in *Ernani*, both of whom have arias in which a prime requirement is a true legato. The term 'basso cantante' should not be taken to imply that lyrical and dramatic qualities are mutually exclusive; its use could be misleading if taken to denote a clear distinction between repertories. In practice, for example, a *basso cantante* may often take essentially dramatic roles such as Boris Godunov and Boito's Mefistofele.

The term has also been used for the lyrical bass-baritone or baritone roles of the period of Bellini and Donizetti, before the term 'baritone' came into general use.

See also BASS. J. B. STEANE

Basso continuo. *See* CONTINUO.

Basso profondo. Italian term for a 'deep bass' voice, distinguished from the *basso cantante* (or singing bass) not simply by depth of voice but also in the power and weighty tone expected of the singer. The type, which is comparatively rare, is nearer to the German 'black' voice, less vibrant in tone than the typical *basso cantante*; it is the kind of voice needed for the Grand Inquisitor in Verdi's *Don Carlos*. Vittorio Arimondi, the first Pistol in *Falstaff*, was an example, and Nazzareno de Angelis, the leading bass of his generation in Italy, was nearer to the specification than his internationally more famous near-contemporary Ezio Pinza. In England, Norman Allin was an outstanding representative in a line that is now almost extinct, not because singers have lost the ability to produce low notes but because there is little encouragement to cultivate that kind of tone.

Of the various national schools of singing, the Russian has been most noted for its supply of deep basses, yet the best-known of Russian exponents (Shalyapin, Reyzen) have not been remarkable for their depth, and the bass parts in Russian operas do not habitually make any great demands upon the lowest regions of the voice. Where the *basso profondo* is most essential in the normal operatic repertory today is in the Mozart operas, especially *Die Entführung aus dem Serail*, where Osmin's vocal line regularly dips to *G* and in his principal solo requires a sustained *D*.

See also BASS. J. B. STEANE

Bastianini, Ettore (*b* Siena, 24 Sept 1922; *d* Sirmione, 25 Jan 1967). Italian baritone. He studied with Flamio Contini in Florence and made his début in 1945, as a bass, singing Colline at Ravenna. He also sang Tiresias (*Oedipus rex*) at La Scala in 1948. After further study he made a second début in 1951, as a baritone, at Bologna as Germont. In 1953 he sang Andrey in the Western première of *War and Peace* at Florence and made his Metropolitan début as Germont, later singing Gérard, Marcello, Posa, Enrico Ashton, Scarpia and Amonasro. He returned to La Scala in 1954 as Yevgeny Onegin and continued to sing there until 1964. His only Covent Garden appearance was in 1962 as Renato. He was specially distinguished in Verdi roles such as Posa and Luna, which he sang in Vienna and Salzburg. At the peak of his short career his voice was rich and warm, his phrasing both musical and aristocratic.

GV (F. Serpa; R. Vegeto) HAROLD ROSENTHAL/R

Bastien und Bastienne ('Bastien and Bastienne'). Singspiel in one act, K50/46*b*, by WOLFGANG AMADEUS MOZART to a libretto by Friedrich Wilhelm Weiskern and Johann Müller and revised by Johann Andreas Schachtner after MARIE-JUSTINE-BENOÎTE FAVART and Harny de Guerville's *opéra comique Les amours de Bastien et Bastienne*; Vienna, F. A. Mesmer's house, September–October 1768.

Favart and Guerville's realistic parody of Rousseau's *Le devin du village* appeared in Vienna in 1755 and was translated in 1764. It was used in children's theatre and was possibly performed in Salzburg in 1766. For Mozart, Schachtner made alterations and improvements, including versification of the dialogue. The performance in Vienna at Mesmer's house in 1768 used spoken dialogue; Mozart later set some of it as recitative. The opera may have been revived in Salzburg in 1774.

Bastien (tenor) has shown signs of fickleness but Bastienne (soprano), advised by the 'magician' Colas (bass), wins him back by feigning indifference, even encouraging him to drown himself. Pastoral innocence is reflected in the short melodious arias (*La finta semplice* shows that their unsophisticated style derives from the subject, not Mozart's youthfulness). Variety is given by Colas's pseudo-magical invocation; by dividing a two-section aria between the angry lovers; and by a short recitative-arioso at the crux (the threat of suicide). A longer duet includes quarrel and reconciliation, and leads without a break into the final trio.

JULIAN RUSHTON

Bastin, Jules (*b* Brussels, 18 March 1933). Belgian bass. He studied in Brussels, making his début there at the Théâtre de la Monnaie in 1960 as Charon in Monteverdi's *Orfeo*. He has sung at Covent Garden, La Scala and the Paris Opéra; at the Salzburg, Florence, Aix-en-Provence and Edinburgh festivals; and in Toronto, Philadelphia, Buenos Aires and many European cities. His repertory includes Osmin, Mozart's and Rossini's Dr Bartolo, Sulpice, the Grand Inquisitor, Ramfis, Titurel, Balducci (*Benvenuto Cellini*), Graumann (*Der ferne Klang*), Varlaam, King Dodon (*The Golden Cockerel*), Würfl (*The Excursions of Mr Brouček*), Arkel, Le Bailli (*Werther*), the King of Clubs and Creonte (*The Love for Three Oranges*), and the Theatre Director and the Banker (*Lulu*). His fine, full-toned voice, presence and gift for comedy make him a superb Ochs. ELIZABETH FORBES

Baszny [Baschny], **Józef** (*d* Lwów, after 1862). Polish composer, probably of Czech descent. He was choirmaster at the cathedral in Lwów, and vice-director of the music society there (1838–44); later he taught singing and the flute in Kiev. He composed a three-act vaudeville, *Skalmierzanki*, to a libretto by J. N. Kamiński (1828; MS in *PL-Wn*), and three operas: *Syn i córka* ('Son and Daughter'), *Więzienie Jana Kazimierza we Francji* ('The Imprisonment of Jan Kazimierz in France') and *Twardowski na Krzemionkach*, a five-act comic opera to another libretto by Kamiński. He also wrote sacred music and some piano works.

*

SMP
K. Michałowski: *Opery polskie* (Kraków, 1954)
ELŻBIETA DZIĘBOWSKA

Ba-ta-clan. *Chinoiserie musicale* in one act by JACQUES OFFENBACH to a libretto by LUDOVIC HALÉVY; Paris, Théâtre des Bouffes-Parisiens (Salle Choiseul), 29 December 1855.

A lighthearted piece of nonsense, the work opened the winter (later permanent) home of the Bouffes-Parisiens in the Passage Choiseul. It parodies Bellini in a mock-Italian quartet, 'Morto! Morto! Infamio! Infamio! Morto!', and also Meyerbeer's *Les Huguenots*. The 'Ba-ta-clan' is the national anthem of the Chinese state of Ché-i-no-or, where a conspiracy is afoot, led by the chief of the imperial guard Ko-ko-ri-ko (baritone), to dethrone the Emperor Fé-ni-han (tenor). However, it turns out that both they and the mandarins Ké-ki-ka-ko (tenor) and Fé-an-nich-ton (soprano) are really Parisians, and all finally decide to return home together.

A café-concert named Ba-ta-clan opened in 1863 on the Boulevard Prince-Eugène (now Voltaire) and still exists. ANDREW LAMB

Bathori, Jane [Berthier, Jeanne Marie] (*b* Paris, 14 June 1877; *d* Paris, 25 Jan 1970). French mezzo-soprano and director. She studied singing at the Paris Conservatoire with the Belgian tenor Emile Engel, whom she married in 1908, and made her début at Nantes in 1900. Toscanini engaged her for the first La Scala performance of Humperdinck's *Hänsel und Gretel* (1902), and in Brussels she appeared in opera with her husband. Soon, however, she decided to devote herself to concert work. In Paris during World War I she managed the Théâtre du Vieux Colombier, producing such works as Chabrier's *Une éducation manquée*, as well as Debussy's *La demoiselle élue* and Honegger's *Le dit des jeux du monde*. In 1926 Bathori visited Argentina, to which she returned each year, taking part in many Latin American premières in Buenos Aires, including Honegger's *Judith*; she also appeared at the Teatro Colón, where in 1933 she sang Concepcion in Ravel's *L'heure espagnole*. Her book on singing, *Conseils sur le chant*, was published in Paris in 1928.

*

G. Jean-Aubry: 'Jane Bathori', *Recorded Sound* (1961), no.4, pp.102–10 [with biographical note, and discography by H. M. Barnes]
DAVID COX

Báthy, Anna (*b* Beregszàsz, 13 June 1901; *d* Budapest, 20 May 1962). Hungarian soprano. She studied at the Budapest Academy of Music with Bianca Maleczky, making her début in 1928 at the Budapest Municipal Theatre as Elisabeth in *Tannhäuser*. For her Budapest Opera début in 1929 she sang Amelia (*Ballo*) and went on to become the company's leading dramatic soprano. Her repertory there included Mozart, Verdi and the less heavy Wagner roles, Beethoven's Leonore, Tosca, Arabella (the first Hungarian to sing the role) and a fine Marschallin. She was also a notable oratorio singer and recitalist. With her accomplished musicality and sense of style, and her serious, even solemn artistic personality, she was particularly well suited to expressing the nobility of Leonore, Elisabeth, Agathe, Elisabeth de Valois and Desdemona.

*

V. Somogyi and I. Molnár: *Báthy Anna* (Budapest, 1969)
PÉTER P. VÁRNAI

Batignano. Village in Italy near Grosseto, Tuscany, the site of an opera festival since 1974. The festival, which takes place during July and August, was founded by the designer Adam Pollock on the site of a ruined monastery, Santa Croce; the theatre is an open-air cloister in which performances are given in the late evening by the company Musica nel Chiostro ('Music in the Cloister'). It was inaugurated by a performance of Purcell's *Dido and Aeneas*, sung by a mixture of Italian and British artists, in which scene changes were accomplished by moving the audience from one part of the building to another. The operas are always given in Italian. Works from the Baroque period (by Handel, Cavalli and Cesti, among others) have predominated; the company has also given J. C. Bach's *Temistocle* (1988), Mozart's *La finta semplice*, and *Zaide* with additional text by Italo Calvino (both 1981), Beethoven's *Leonore* (1987) and Offenbach's *Ba-ta-clan* (1988), as well as *The Turn of the Screw* in 1983 and *King Priam* in 1990, its first Italian performance. Two operas by Stephen Oliver were given their premières at the festival: *The Garden* in 1977 (as *Il giardino*) and *Beauty and the Beast* in 1984 (as *La bella e la bestia*); Oliver's completion of Mozart's *L'oca del Cairo* was first performed there in 1991. The orchestra is a professional body of players (initially recruited in Siena) and casts consist mainly of young professionals. Since 1978 the company has performed guest seasons in London, Venice and Paris.

Batistin. *See* STUCK, JEAN-BAPTISTE.

Batka, Richard (*b* Prague, 14 Dec 1868; *d* Vienna, 24 April 1922). Austrian critic and writer of Czech descent. After graduating in German and musicology at the German University in Prague he worked as an editor (*Neue Revue*, *Kunstwart*) and as a music critic (*Bohemia*, *Prager Tagblatt*). In 1908 he moved to Vienna, where he continued his activities, editing *Der Merker* with Richard Specht and writing reviews for the *Wiener Fremdenblatt*. He also taught history of opera at the academy (1909–14). His publications include *Aus der Opernwelt: Prager Kritiken und Skizzen* (Munich, 1907) and *Allgemeine Geschichte der Musik* (Stuttgart, 1909–15). In addition to his writings on music, where he was one of the first German-speaking writers to deal with Czech music, he translated Czech, Italian and French operas into German, and wrote several opera librettos himself.

Der polnische Jude (with V. Léon), K. Weis, 1901; *Das war ich*, L. Blech, 1902; *Alpenkönig und Menschenfeind*, Blech, 1903; *Aschenbrödel*, Blech, 1905; *Zierpuppen*, A. Goetzl, 1905;

Versiegelt (with A. S. Pordes-Milo), Blech, 1908; *Der Abmarsch*, K. Bastl, comp. 1911; *Der Kuhreigen*, W. Kienzl, 1911; *Der Sturm auf die Mühle*, Weis, 1912, as Útok na mlýn; *Die verschenkte Frau* (with R. Lothar), E. d'Albert, 1912; *Ländlische Liebesorakel*, T. Veidl, 1913; *Mila* (with M. Wassermann), G. Major, 1913; *Die himmelblaue Zeit* (with P. Wertheimer), C. Strauss, 1914; *Der Stier von Olivera*, d'Albert, 1918; *Eroica*, M. Frank, 1919; *Meister Schwalbe*, H. Marteau, 1921; *Ilse*, R. Stöhr, n.d.

*

E. Rychnovsky: *Leo Blech* (Prague, 1905)
——: 'Richard Batka', *Der Auftakt*, ii (1922), 181–4

JOHN TYRRELL

Baton Rouge. American city, capital of the state of Louisiana. Despite the proximity of Baton Rouge to New Orleans, whose operatic history dates back to 1796, professional opera was established much later in the smaller city. The first civic company was formed in the early 1950s, but lasted only two seasons. In 1981 Baton Rouge Opera was founded, with Henry Holt as artistic director and principal conductor (Marioara Trifan succeeded Holt in 1990). The first production was a performance of *Aida* in 1982. The company produces three operas or operettas each season, usually performed in the Louisiana State University Union Theatre (seating 1261).

Until the formation of Baton Rouge Opera the principal source of opera was the Louisiana State University opera department, established in 1929. LSU was one of the first academic institutions in the USA to present opera at a high level of excellence. In the mid-1930s two musicians from the Metropolitan Opera were brought in to head the opera programme: the baritone Pasquale Amato in 1935 and the conductor Louis Hasselmans in 1936; Amato remained only a few years, but Hasselmans stayed until 1948. Under the conductor Peter Paul Fuchs (1950–76) the university's opera programme grew to national prominence. Several premières were given, including Elie Siegmeister's *The Plough and the Stars* (1969), Fuchs's *Serenade at Noon* (1965) and Eugene Zádor's *The Magic Chair* (1966). The company also gave the American premières of Hermann Reutter's *Die Witwe von Ephesus* (1968–9 season, in a translation by Fuchs) and (in a double bill) Reutter's *Der Weg nach Freudenstadt* and Mario Peragallo's *La gita in campagna* (1955).

From 1987 the LSU Opera Theatre and Baton Rouge Opera collaborated in productions, with instrumental support from the LSU and Baton Rouge symphony orchestras.

DERRICK HENRY

Battaglia di Legnano, La ('The Battle of Legnano'). *Tragedia lirica* in four acts by GIUSEPPE VERDI to a libretto by SALVADORE CAMMARANO after Joseph Méry's play *La bataille de Toulouse*; Rome, Teatro Argentina, 27 January 1849.

The revolutions that swept through Italy and much of the rest of Europe in 1848 – and in particular Milan's 'cinque giornate', when the Milanese forced the Austrian soldiers from their city – inspired Verdi to attempt an opera in which the theme of patriotism would be overt. Together with his librettist Cammarano, he eventually decided to compose an opera set in 12th-century Italy, the epoch of the Lombard league, adapting for the purpose a recent French drama. Work on *La battaglia di Legnano* took up most of 1848, and by the time it was finished Milan and many other cities were long back in Austrian hands. But Rome was still a beleaguered republic, and the première of the opera took place there in what must have been highly charged circumstances. It was a clamorous success, with the entire final act encored. The cast included Filippo Colini (Rolando), Teresa De Giuli Borsi (Lida) and Gaetano Fraschini (Arrigo). However, the opera was extremely difficult to get past the censors in the repressive, counter-revolutionary atmosphere of the 1850s, and never firmly established itself in the repertory. In the mid-1850s Verdi voiced the intention of rehabilitating *La battaglia* by making a thorough revision of the libretto, but his ideas came to nothing, and the work virtually disappeared from the theatre until its occasional modern revivals.

Federico Barbarossa	bass
First Consul of Milan	bass
Second Consul of Milan	bass
Mayor of Como	bass
Rolando *a Milanese leader*	baritone
Lida *his wife*	soprano
Arrigo *a soldier from Verona*	tenor
Marcovaldo *a German prisoner*	baritone
Imelda *Lida's maid*	mezzo-soprano
Arrigo's Squire	tenor
A Herald	tenor

Knights of Death, magistrates and leaders of Como, Lida's maids, Milanese people, Milanese senators, soldiers from Verona, Novara, Piacenza and Milan, German army

Setting Milan and Como in 1176

The overture has the usual three-part structure, with the middle section slower and (in the manner of the *Guillaume Tell* overture) dominated by solo woodwind. But its inner workings and its sheer scale far outstrip any of Verdi's previous efforts, and the piece surely deserves revival in today's concert halls.

ACT 1: 'He Lives!'

1.i *A part of rebuilt Milan, near the city walls* Soldiers from various parts of northern Italy congregate to an Allegro marziale and sing an unaccompanied patriotic hymn, 'Viva Italia! Sacro un patto' (already heard as the opening subject of the overture). Arrigo emerges from the crowd of soldiers to greet his beloved Milan in 'La pia materna mano', an aria whose subtlety of orchestral detail and distant modulations immediately alert us to the developments taking place in Verdi's musical language. After a brief reprise of the hymn, Rolando joyously greets Arrigo, having thought him killed in battle. His *romanza*, 'Ah! m'abbraccia d'esultanza', functions dramaturgically as a cabaletta but is actually a French-influenced ternary form. The scene is rounded off by a solemn 'giuramento' in which all swear to defend Milan to the last drop of their blood.

1.ii *A shady place* A female chorus celebrating the arrival of the soldiers introduces Lida, who explains in an Andante, 'Quante volte come un dono', that she cannot be happy now that her father and brothers have been slain in battle. Again, unusually detailed orchestration and harmonic excursions underline a new manner in Verdi's style. Marcovaldo pays unwelcome court to Lida, but is interrupted by Imelda, who announces that Rolando has returned, bringing with him Arrigo. Lida's attempts to restrain her joy at the news that Arrigo is alive coalesce into her cabaletta 'A frenarti, o cor nel petto'.

Rolando ushers in Arrigo, saying that his friend must remain in the house as a guest. Left alone, Arrigo and Lida engage in a long, single-movement duet finale, 'È ver? ... Sei d'altri?', a piece quite unlike the usual multi-movement sequence and gaining its cohesion more from juxtapositions of key than from contrasting formal units.

ACT 2: 'Barbarossa!'

A magnificent room in the town hall of Como In the chorus 'Sì, tardi ed invano' the people of Como, ancient enemies of the Milanese, rejoice to hear of their rivals' difficulties with the German Emperor Barbarossa. Arrigo and Rolando enter to request military assistance, urging their cause with a passionate duet, 'Ben vi scorgo'. Hardly has the duet finished than Barbarossa himself appears, his impressive entrance immediately precipitating the concertato finale. The Adagio of the finale, 'A che smarriti e pallidi', is made up of patterned exchanges between Barbarossa and the two Milanese warriors, first in hesitant minor, then in more lyrically extended major, with the chorus firmly on Barbarossa's side. Barbarossa then has the windows thrown open to display the mass of German troops; but Arrigo still trusts the power of the people. In the closing stretta, 'Il destino d'Italia son io!', the fixed opposition between the two sides continues, Verdi lavishing much orchestral and harmonic detail on a section which had traditionally been of the most straightforward.

ACT 3: 'Disgrace!'

3i *A subterranean vault in the basilica of S Ambrogio, Milan* In a sombre opening chorus, 'Fra queste dense tenebre', the Knights of Death celebrate a pact to avenge the deaths of their forefathers. Arrigo is admitted to their ranks before all join in the solemn oath of allegiance, 'Giuriam d'Italia por fine ai danni'. The scene is reminiscent of *Ernani*, Act 3, though shot through with French-influenced atmospheric effects.

3.ii *Apartments in Rolando's castle* Lida has heard of Arrigo's enlistment with the Knights of Death, and has written him a letter which she now gives to Imelda. Her scene is without a formal aria but is full of those lyrical outpourings that will become one of Verdi's greatest strengths. Rolando enters to bid farewell to his wife and child and joins Lida in the tender duet 'Digli ch'è sangue italico'. As Lida and the child leave, Arrigo appears and Rolando confesses his fears for the coming battle. In the gentle, Bellinian Andante, 'Se al nuovo dì pugnando', he entrusts his family to the care of Arrigo should he die in battle. The friends embrace and Arrigo leaves. Marcovaldo now enters: he has intercepted Lida's letter, and shows it to Rolando. In a furious cabaletta, 'Ahi scellerate alme d'inferno', Rolando swears vengeance on his wife and friend.

3.iii *A room high in the tower* Arrigo, alone on the balcony as the curtain rises, decides to write a letter of farewell to his mother. Lida enters and the couple confess their love in a simple recitative. They are interrupted by Rolando, whose offstage voice causes Lida to hide on the balcony. Rolando appears and immediately discovers Lida, thus precipitating the Terzetto finale. The first movement, 'Ah! d'un consorte, o perfidi', is all flux and change, while in the central Andante, 'Vendetta d'un momento', the two lovers desperately call for death. But Rolando has other plans. The set piece finished, Arrigo hears trumpets calling him to the Knights of Death and prepares to leave; but Rolando has decided that his punishment will be 'disgrace' and rushes out, locking the door behind him. Arrigo cannot stand the shame that will result if he fails to join the Knights, and with a final cry of 'Viva Italia!' throws himself from the balcony into the moat below.

Title page of the first edition of the vocal score of Verdi's 'La battaglia di Legnano' (Florence: Ricordi & Jouhaud, 1850), showing the final scene in Act 4

ACT 4: 'To Die for the Homeland!'

The vestibule of a church, giving on to a piazza in Milan As a choir sings inside the church, Imelda tells Lida that Arrigo survived his fall and reached the Knights of Death. They join the chorus in a prayer. Distant sounds of rejoicing announce victory over the German army. All unite in a celebratory hymn, but at its close a funeral march is heard in the distance. Arrigo is brought in, mortally wounded. He again protests Lida's innocence and begins the final trio of reconciliation, 'Per la salvata Italia'. The last, soaring phrase, sung by Arrigo, Lida and then by the entire company, sums up the opera's message: 'Chi muore per la patria alma sì rea non ha!' ('He who dies for the homeland cannot have such an evil soul!').

* * *

La battaglia di Legnano was from the start dogged by the special circumstances of its creation: in the early years by problems with the censor, and later perhaps by its too intense association with a particular historical period. But Verdi's plans to revise the work in the 1850s are surely significant, suggesting that he thought the opera comparable to *Macbeth*, *Stiffelio* and *Luisa Miller*. *La battaglia* is impressive above all in its inner workings, which show the concern for orchestral and harmonic detail that never left Verdi after his decisive encounter with French operatic style. In today's climate, in which almost all Verdi's early operas are occasionally revived, *La battaglia* stands as one of Verdi's most unjustly neglected works. ROGER PARKER

Battaille, Charles (Amable) (*b* Nantes, 30 Sept 1822; *d* Paris, 2 May 1872). French bass. After studying in Paris with the younger Manuel García (1845–7), he made his début at the Opéra-Comique as Sulpice in *La fille du régiment* (22 June 1848). A versatile actor, capable of florid singing and possessing an extensive range, he was soon entrusted with principal roles in new operas by Halévy, Adam, Thomas and others, one of his best being that of Peter the Great in Meyerbeer's *L'étoile du nord* (1854). His career was interrupted by a throat ailment in 1857, but in 1860 he appeared at the Théâtre Lyrique as Jacques Sincère in Halévy's *Val d'Andorre* (a role he had created 12 years earlier) and in the première of Gounod's *Philémon et Baucis*. In the following year he sang at both the Théâtre Lyrique and the Opéra-Comique (in a revival of *L'étoile du nord*), but early in 1863 he retired from the stage. He taught at the Conservatoire and in 1861 published *Nouvelles recherches sur la phonation*. PHILIP ROBINSON

Battishill, Jonathan (*b* London, May 1738; *d* Islington, London, 10 Dec 1801). English composer. In 1747 he became a chorister of St Paul's Cathedral; later he developed a fine tenor voice and frequently appeared as a soloist in London concerts. He was William Boyce's deputy organist at the Chapel Royal and conductor at Covent Garden, directing from the harpsichord.

Most of Battishill's compositions date from 1760 to 1775, and reflect his many-sided activities; they include anthems, songs and glees. His only opera *Almena* (3, R. Rolt), a collaboration with Michael Arne, performed at Drury Lane, London, on 2 November 1764 (excerpts published in London, 1764), was not a great success, but that was attributed to dramatic faults on the part of the librettist rather than to deficiencies in the music.

Mattia Battistini as Renato in Verdi's 'Un ballo in maschera'

See also ALMENA.

*

LS
J. B. Trend: 'Jonathan Battishill: from the Unpublished Recollections of R. J. S. Stevens', *ML*, xiii (1932), 264–71
R. Fiske: *English Theatre Music in the Eighteenth Century* (London, 1973, 2/1986) PETER WARD JONES

Battistini, Mattia (*b* Rome, 27 Feb 1856; *d* Colle Baccaro, nr Rieti, 7 Nov 1928). Italian baritone. After a brief period of study with Venceslao Persichini and Eugenio Terziana, Battistini seized a sudden chance to sing the leading role of Alphonse XI in Donizetti's *La favorite* at the Teatro Argentina, Rome, on 11 December 1878, when his immediate success inaugurated a career of nearly 50 years. His early London appearances, in 1883 and 1887, attracted no special attention; his major English triumphs came at Covent Garden in 1905 and 1906, when he was heard in several of his leading roles, including Rigoletto, Germont, Amonasro and Yevgeny Onegin. By that time he was established throughout Europe, and especially in Russia, as a baritone without rival in the older repertory and scarcely less famous in later and widely varied roles. He was probably the most important singer of his day to have resisted the pull of the Metropolitan – owing, it was said, to his dread of the Atlantic crossing. When he reappeared in London at the Queen's Hall in 1922 and the two following years, his unimpaired tone and technique astonished audiences. His voice was an unusually high baritone, verging on the range of a tenor. The quality was noble: clear, strong, vibrant, capable also of a deliberately 'villainous' harshness when required; then suddenly melting into the extremes of tenderness and delicacy. Between 1903 and 1924, he made some 100 records, most of them excellent for their date.

*

GV (R. Celletti; R. Vegeto)
F. Palmegiani: *Mattia Battistini: il re dei baritoni* (Milan, 1949, 2/1977) [with discography by W. R. Moran]
J. Dennis: 'Mattia Battistini', *Record Collector*, viii (1953), 245–65
D. Shawe-Taylor: 'Mattia Battistini', *Opera*, viii (1957), 283–9
A. Kelly, J. F. Perkins and J. Ward: 'Mattia Battistini (1856–1928): a Discography', *Recorded Sound*, no.65 (1977), 652–6

DESMOND SHAWE-TAYLOR

Battle, Kathleen (*b* Portsmouth, OH, 13 Aug 1948). American soprano. She studied with Franklin Bens at the Cincinnati College-Conservatory, and in the early seventies she was engaged by James Levine for both the Ravinia Festival and the Metropolitan. She made her début in 1976 as Susanna with the New York City Opera. In 1977 she sang Oscar at San Francisco, then made her Metropolitan début as the Shepherd in *Tannhäuser*, subsequently singing Blonde, Pamina, Strauss's Zdenka and Sophie, and Handel's Cleopatra (1988). She made her British début in 1979 at Glyndebourne as Nerina (*La fedeltà premiata*) and sang Adina at Zürich in 1980. At Salzburg she has sung Despina, Susanna and Zerlina. She made her Covent Garden début in 1985 as Zerbinetta, returning as Norina in 1990. Battle is gifted with a high, sweet soprano of considerable charm, which she governs with technical finesse; she also has an attractive and vivacious stage presence, and her work is skilful and stylish, if not always highly individual.

RICHARD DYER, ELIZABETH FORBES

Batton, Désiré-Alexandre (*b* Paris, 2 Jan 1798; *d* Versailles, 15 Oct 1855). French composer. He was a pupil at the Paris Conservatoire from 1806 to 1817, winning the Prix de Rome in his final year. Before he left for Italy he produced a successful *opéra comique*, *La fenêtre secrète*. Dedicated to Luigi Cherubini, his former teacher, the work relies considerably on forms such as the *couplet*, *romance* and *cavatine*, but contains moments of graceful orchestration. It enjoyed some success outside France, notably in Brussels and Copenhagen. In Rome Batton wrote an opera, *Vellèda*. After his return to Paris his theatrical compositions met with little success, except for his part in the nine-man collaboration opera, *La marquise de Brinvilliers* (1831). *Le remplaçant*, his last attempt, was criticized for lack of melody and an uncharacteristically poor libretto by Eugène Scribe.

opéra comiques, first performed in Paris unless otherwise stated

La fenêtre secrète, ou Une soirée à Madrid (3, Des Essarts d'Ambreville), OC (Feydeau), 17 Nov 1818, selections, vs (Paris, *c*1819)
Vellèda, 1820 (1, after F. R. de Chateaubriand: *Les martyrs*), unperf., *F-Pc*
Ethelwina, ou L'exilé (3, P. de Kock and Mme Lemaignan), OC (Feydeau), 31 March 1827
Le prisonnier d'état (1, Mélesville [A.-H.-J. Duveyrier]), OC (Feydeau), 6 Feb 1828, *Pc*
Le camp du drap d'or (3, de Kock), OC (Feydeau), 23 Feb 1828, collab. L. V. E. Rifaut and Leborne
La marquise de Brinvilliers (drame lyrique, 3, E. Scribe and Castil-Blaze [F.-H.-J. Blaze]), OC (Ventadour), 31 Oct 1831 (Paris, 1831), collab. Auber, H.-M. Berton, Blangini, A. Boieldieu, Carafa, Cherubini, Hérold and Paer
Le remplaçant (3, Scribe and J. Bayard), OC (Nouveautés), 11 Aug 1837

Battu, Marie (*b* Paris, 1838; *d* Paris, 1888). French soprano. After appearing as a child in Offenbach's *Pépito* at the Théâtre des Variétés, Paris, she made her début in 1860 at the Théâtre Italien as Amina (*La sonnambula*). She sang Oscar in the first Paris performance of *Un ballo in maschera*. Transferring to the Opéra, in 1865 she created Inès in Meyerbeer's *L'Africaine* (1865) and sang Mathilde in the 500th performance of *Guillaume Tell* (1868). She made her Covent Garden début in 1862 as Gilda (*Rigoletto*) and also sang Elvire (*La muette de Portici*), Marguerite de Valois and Alice (*Robert le diable*). She retired in 1873. Her singing combined superb technique with faultless intonation.

ELIZABETH FORBES

Baudo, Serge (*b* Marseilles, 16 July 1927). French conductor. He studied at the Paris Conservatoire, winning *premiers prix* in conducting and other subjects, and making his début in 1950 at the Concerts Lamoureux. He was resident conductor at the Paris Opéra, 1962–5, and was invited by Karajan to conduct *Pelléas et Mélisande* at La Scala in 1962. He made his début at the Metropolitan in *Les contes d'Hoffmann* in 1971, returning in the following three seasons. Baudo conducted the premières of Menotti's *L'ultimo selvaggio* (as *Le dernier sauvage*) at Paris in 1963 and Milhaud's *La mère coupable* at Geneva in 1966. After becoming music director of the Orchestre de Lyon in 1971 he founded and directed an annual Berlioz Festival to include the composer's operas, but resigned in 1989 when a curtailment of funds required the operatic performances to stop. He has specialized in French and Russian music, giving performances imbued with subtlety and passion, and has composed a number of works including film scores.

CHRISTIANE SPIETH-WEISSENBACHER, NOËL GOODWIN

Baudot-Puente, Gregorio (*b* Colmenar Viejo, Madrid, 12 March 1884; *d* El Ferrol, Coruña, 4 Nov 1938). Spanish composer and conductor. He studied the flute and composition at the Madrid Conservatory, where he was a pupil of Tomás Bretón. After playing in chamber groups and touring abroad (1906–9), he was appointed director of music of a regiment in El Ferrol, where he spent the rest of his life except for a period in Africa, 1915–17. As well as a large amount of military music, three dramatic scenas and five symphonic poems, he composed many zarzuelas (alone and in collaboration), of which few survive. In 1928 he conducted the première of his opera *Cantuxa*, whose success led to further performances in Spain and at the Teatro Colón. A story of jealousy (including a death quarrel at a local folk festival) in rural Galicia, the opera exemplifies *verismo* in its continuous melodic tension, vocal characterization, immediacy of emotion and the anguish of its brutal ending. Of Baudot-Puente's other opera, *La figlia di Jorio*, only fragments survive.

zarzuelas unless otherwise stated

Aires de la Sierra (1, A. Osete), Madrid, Noviciado, 4 Feb 1909, *E-Msa*, collab. C. del Campo
La cruz de mayo (poema, 1, Osete), Barcelona, Cómico, 1909
La cola de Mariquita (1, Osete), before 1910, lost
El gallo Chantecler (1, Osete), before 1910, lost
Lo bello y lo útil (1), ? before 1910
La eterna paz, ? before 1910, *Msa*
Zoraya (leyenda, 2), *c*1916, *Fbaudot*
La figlia di Jorio (ópera, 3, after G. d'Annunzio), *c*1917, frags. *Fbaudot*

Cantuxa (opéra, 3, A. Torrado), Madrid, Zarzuela, 5 June 1928, *Msa*
La heredera (1, J. A. Torres y Lasso), ?1930, *Fbaudot*
Mari-Lorenza (2, J. Rosales and V. Escohotado), Madrid, Aug 1930, *Msa*
Luces de Verbena [completion of zar by R. Soutullo] (2, J. Tellaeche and F. Serrano-Anguita), Madrid, Calderón, 2 May 1935, *Msa*, collab. F. Moreno Torroba

*

A. Fernández-Cid: *Cien años de teatro musical en España (1875–1975)* (Madrid, 1975)
M. Soto-Viso and X. M. Carreira: 'Vida y obra del compositor Gregorio Baudot-Puente', *RdMc*, v (1982), 51–81
X. M. Carreira: 'El nacionalismo operístico en Galicia', *RdMc*, x (1987), 667–83 XOÁN M. CARREIRA

Baudron, Antoine Laurent (*b* Amiens, bap. 16 May 1742; *d* Paris, 1834). French composer. He studied the violin in Paris and in 1763 joined the orchestra of the Comédie-Française, succeeding François Grenier in 1766 as its first violinist and leader. Baudron composed incidental music for revivals as well as new plays. These included, according to Choron, Racine's *Athalie*, Rousseau's *Pygmalion* and Beaumarchais' *Le mariage de Figaro*. The *Mercure de France* also credits him with writing the music for *Le barbier de Séville*, which included the famous air 'Je suis Lindor' that Mozart later used as the theme of his 12 Variations K354/299*a*. Choron states that Baudron's final output numbered some 120 theatre pieces.

*

A.-E. Choron and F. Fayolle: *Dictionnaire historique des musiciens* (Paris, 1810–11) JOHN S. POWELL

Bauer als Millionär, Der. Opera by Joseph Drechsler; *see* MÄDCHEN AUS DER FEENWELT, DAS.

Bauermeister, Mathilde (*b* Hamburg, 1849; *d* Herne Bay, Kent, 15 Oct 1926). German, later British, mezzo-soprano. She studied in London at the RAM and made her début in Dublin in 1866. She first sang at Covent Garden in 1868, as Siébel in *Faust*, and returned there every year until 1905. From 1891 to 1906 she was engaged at the Metropolitan, making her début as Gertrude (*Roméo et Juliette*). Her repertory of more than a hundred roles included Aennchen (*Der Freischütz*), Magdalene (*Die Meistersinger*) and Mamma Lucia (*Cavalleria rusticana*). She also sang many soprano roles and was capable of taking over major parts such as Zerlina, Donna Elvira, Inès (*L'Africaine*) and Marguerite de Valois (*Les Huguenots*) at short notice. ELIZABETH FORBES

Baugé, André (*b* Toulouse, 4 Jan 1892; *d* Paris, 22 May 1966). French baritone. His mother was the soprano Anna Tariol-Baugé and his father, Alphonse, was a teacher of singing. His studies with them led to his début with the Opéra-Comique in 1917 as Frédéric in *Lakmé*. Other roles with the company included Don Giovanni and Pelléas, with the Rossini Figaro as his tour de force. At the Opéra in 1925 he sang Germont in *La traviata* and the title role in Rabaud's *Mârouf*. He appeared at Monte Carlo as Escamillo in 1924. His career took a new turn when at the Marigny Theatre in Paris he sang the title role in the French première of Messager's *Monsieur Beaucaire* in 1925, and from then onwards he became increasingly associated with operetta, enjoying a special success in Lehár's *Paganini*. He also appeared in some early French musical films and after World War II taught at the Ecole Normale. His recordings show a light, high baritone, firmly placed if somewhat dry-toned, better suited to Messager than to Rossini. J. B. STEANE

Baum, Kurt (*b* Cologne, 15 March 1900; *d* New York, 27 Dec 1989). German tenor, naturalized American. He won the international singing award at Vienna in 1932 and made his début in Zemlinsky's *Der Kreidekreis* at Zürich (1933). He sang in Prague and at various houses in Europe before moving to the USA in 1939. He made his début at the Metropolitan in 1941 as the Italian Singer in *Der Rosenkavalier* and was a leading heroic tenor there for over 20 years. He partnered Callas in some famous performances of *Aida*, *Il trovatore* and *Norma* at Mexico City in 1950, and again in *Aida* at Covent Garden in 1953. His only appearances at La Scala were in *Il trovatore* (1948–9). His strong voice and ability to bridge the German and Italian repertories were valued; less so the charmless style and increasingly tight voice production, which also limit the appeal of his recordings. J. B. STEANE

Bauman, Thomas (Allen) (*b* Marinette, WI, 10 March 1948). American musicologist. He studied at the University of California at Berkeley, under Daniel Heartz and others, writing a dissertation *Music and Drama in Germany: a Traveling Company and its Repertory, 1767–1781* (1977). He has taught at the University of Pennsylvania (1977–84), Stanford University (1984–9) and the University of Washington, Seattle. His interests centre on German opera in the late 18th and early 19th centuries, and he has written a valuable and carefully researched book, *North German Opera in the Age of Goethe* (Cambridge, 1985), and a perceptive study of Mozart's *Die Entführung aus dem Serail* (Cambridge, 1987) as well as editing and contributing to Heartz's *Mozart's Operas* (Berkeley and Los Angeles, 1990).

Baumgarten, Karl [Carl] **Friedrich** (*b* Lübeck, *c*1740; *d* London, 1824). German composer active in England. He had organ lessons at Lübeck before he settled in London, at about the age of 18, as organist of the Lutheran Chapel in the Savoy, also working as a teacher, composer and violinist. The imputation made by Haydn, who heard him in London in 1792, that his violin playing lacked energy seems to be contradicted by the fact that he was a well-known orchestral leader (at the Haymarket, at Covent Garden and in Dublin). In 1789 Burney wrote that Baumgarten had then 'been so long in England that his merit [was] unknown to his countrymen on the Continent'. He wrote a comic opera, *William and Nanny, or The Cottagers*, which was first performed at Covent Garden in 1779 (Shield later attached its overture to his *Robin Hood*), and contributed to the pasticcio *Netley Abbey*, but his music for the stage was only moderately successful. Baumgarten also had an interest in music theory and wrote an unpublished treatise (*GB-Lbl**).

*

Burney H
W. T. Parke: *Musical Memoirs* (London, 1830)
OWAIN EDWARDS

Bausewein, Kaspar (*b* Aub, nr Ochsenfurt, 15 Nov 1838; *d* Munich, 18 Nov 1903). German bass. He studied in Munich, making his début there in 1854 at the Hofoper, where he was engaged for 46 years. A fine actor, equally gifted for comic and serious opera, he had a wide repertory ranging from Mozart's Figaro and

Leporello and Rossini's Don Basilio to Caspar (*Der Freischütz*) and the three Wagner roles that he created: Pogner in *Die Meistersinger* (1868), Fafner in *Das Rheingold* (1869) and Hunding in *Die Walküre* (1870). He retired in 1900 after a farewell performance as Lord Cockburn in *Fra Diavolo*. ELIZABETH FORBES

Baussnern [Bauszneren], **Waldemar von** (*b* Berlin, 29 Nov 1866; *d* Potsdam, 20 Aug 1931). German composer. A gifted improviser, he studied in Berlin and later returned there as a teacher after holding positions in Cologne, Weimar and Frankfurt. He was a remarkably prolific composer who wrote in a style drawing largely on Brahms in its tendency towards motivic economy and thick scoring. Generally his music is heavily chromatic. Besides composing several operas, Baussnern also devoted himself to the task of editing Peter Cornelius's *Der Barbier von Bagdad*, *Der Cid* and *Gunlöd*, the latter completed from the composer's sketches.

Dichter und Welt (J. Petri), Weimar, 4 June 1897
Dürer in Venedig (3, A. Bartels), Weimar, 3 March 1901
Herbort und Hilde (2, heitere Heldenoper, E. König), Mannheim, Hof- und National, 15 Feb 1902
Der Bundschuh (3, O. Erler), Frankfurt, Stadt, 27 May 1904
Satyros (musikalische Komödie, 2, after J. W. von Goethe), Basle, 1922

*

MGG (G. Wehle); *StiegerO*
H. Keller: 'Waldemar von Baussnern', *Neue Musikzeitung*, xlviii (1926), 80
G. Wehle: 'Zum 100. Geburtstag Waldemar von Bausznern', *Musica*, xx (1966), 296 CHARLOTTE ERWIN

Bavarian State Opera. Bayerische Staatsoper, the principal opera company in Munich; the name was adopted in 1922 for the former Hofoper (court opera). *See* MUNICH, §3(i).

Baviera, Il. *See* SANTURINI, FRANCESCO (i).

Baxevanos, Peter (*b* Salonika, 29 Sept 1908; *d* Vienna, 24 June 1982). Greek tenor. He studied in Vienna and made his début in 1934 at the Vienna Volksoper in Wolf-Ferrari's *Sly*. At the Zürich Opera, where he sang until the outbreak of war, he sang Alwa in the first (incomplete) performance of Berg's *Lulu* (1937) and was the Cardinal in the delayed première of Hindemith's *Mathis der Maler* (1938). He returned to Vienna in 1940 and until his retirement was successful there and in Italy as Florestan, Manrico, Don Carlos, Don José and Cavaradossi. DAVID CUMMINGS

Bayard, Jean-François-Alfred (*b* Cherolles, 17 March 1796; *d* Paris, 19 Feb 1853). French librettist and dramatist. An obscure but representative figure among the large number of librettists in Paris in the first half of the 19th century, he belonged to the group of writers around Scribe (sneeringly described by Wagner as 'die Scribefabrik'). He began by writing one-act *opéras comiques* and in his last years wrote for the Opéra. Only one of the texts he participated in has survived, that for Donizetti's *La fille du régiment*; the other eight opera and *opéra comique* texts that he may be securely identified with – all joint efforts – have receded into obscurity. His works for the spoken stage seem to have been equally ephemeral.

La médecine sans médecin (oc, with E. Scribe), F. Hérold, 1832; *Alda* (oc, with P. Duport), A. Thys, 1835; *Le remplaçant* (oc, with Scribe), D.-A. Batton, 1837; *La fille du régiment* (oc, with J.-H. Vernoy de Saint-Georges), G. Donizetti, 1840; *Le diable à l'école* (oc, with Scribe), E.-H.-A. Boulanger, 1842; *Une voix* (oc, with C. Potron), Boulanger, 1845; *Le démon de la nuit* (with E. Arago), J. Rosenhain, 1851; *Le miroir* (with Davrecourt), L. Gastinel, 1853; *L'ombre d'Argentine* (with Biéville), A. Montfort, 1853 WILLIAM ASHBROOK

Bayerische Staatsoper. Bavarian State Opera, the principal opera company in Munich; the name was adopted in 1922 for the former Hofoper (court opera). *See* MUNICH, §3(i).

Bayka pro Lisu, Petukha, Kota da Barana. Opera by Igor Stravinsky; *see* RENARD.

Baylis, Lilian (**Mary**) (*b* London, 9 May 1874; *d* London, 25 Nov 1937). English theatre manager, originator of the Vic-Wells (later Sadler's Wells) Opera and Ballet companies. She received early musical instruction from her parents, who were touring concert-party artists; she joined them as a teenager, and formed the St James' Ladies Orchestra when she was 14. Accompanying her parents to South Africa, she began giving music lessons in Johannesburg, but returned to London in 1898 to help her aunt, Emma Cons, manage the Old Vic Theatre, where she included some opera in English. Baylis took sole charge from 1912, and by the 1920s opera productions were given there twice a week. She then campaigned for and raised £80 000 to rebuild the then derelict Sadler's Wells Theatre; the house reopened in 1931, and her first opera presentation there was *Carmen*, on 20 January. An indefatigable social worker in the Victorian temperance tradition, she gradually ensured regular seasons of opera and ballet at 'popular' prices without benefit of public subsidy: the basis of what later became the English National Opera and the Royal Ballet. She was appointed CH in 1929.

*

S. Thorndike and R. Thorndike: *Lilian Baylis* (London, 1938)
E. J. Dent: *A Theatre for Everybody: the Story of the Old Vic and Sadler's Wells* (London, 1945, 2/1946)
P. Roberts, ed.: *Lilian Baylis Centenary Festival Programme* (London, 1974) NOËL GOODWIN

Bayreuth. Town in Bavaria, southern Germany. It is internationally famous as the site of Richard Wagner's Festspielhaus (opened 1876). The town, dating back to 1231 and in the 17th and 18th centuries the seat of an independent margravate, is now the capital of the district of Upper Franconia and since 1975 has had a university. As well as the Festspielhaus it possesses two theatres in which opera is performed, the Markgräfliches Opernhaus and the modern Stadthalle.

1. Markgräfliches Opernhaus. 2. Stadthalle. 3. Wagner's Festspielhaus. 4. Wagner's successors: (i) Cosima Wagner (1886–1906) (ii) Siegfried Wagner (1908–30) (iii) Winifred Wagner (1931–44) (iv) Wieland and Wolfgang Wagner (1952–66) (v) Wolfgang Wagner (1967–). 5. Richard Wagner Foundation.

1. MARKGRÄFLICHES OPERNHAUS. In virtually all the kingdoms, principalities, dukedoms and margravates constituting Germany up to 1918, the cultivation of opera was an important part of court life. Bayreuth was no exception: the first opera to be performed there (in 1661) was *Sophia*, by an unknown composer, and in the next 55 years about four to six works by German and Italian composers (among them G. H. Stölzel, G. P. Telemann, C. F. Hurlebusch, Attilio Ariosti and Antonio Lotti) were staged each year, either in the Schlosssaal or in a theatre built within the palace

1. *The stage of the Markgräfliches Opernhaus, Bayreuth (built by Joseph Saint-Pierre, 1745–8; interior decoration by Carlo and Giuseppe Galli-Bibiena), seen from the margrave's box at the back of the auditorium (shown in* THEATRE ARCHITECTURE, *fig.5)*

grounds. However, it was not until the accession as margravine of Frederick the Great's sister Wilhelmine in 1735 that opera in Bayreuth became something beyond the ordinary. Wilhelmine (1709–58), the consort of Margrave Friedrich, was a skilled composer herself (her opera *Argenore*, performed in 1740, is lost, but some chamber works remain), and her excellent relations with her brother and the Prussian court ensured that eminent composers and musicians were willing to place themselves at her disposal.

Among the works known to have been performed in Bayreuth under the Kapellmeister Johann Pfeiffer (served 1734–61) were Hasse's operas *Ezio* and *Artaserse* and Bernasconi's *festa teatrale L'huomo*. These were staged in the new Markgräfliches Opernhaus, built in the street now known as Opernstrasse, close to the margrave's palace. One of the finest late Baroque theatres still in existence, this three-storey building was erected by the French architect Joseph Saint-Pierre in 1745–8, and the interior decoration was entrusted to the Italian theatre designer Giuseppe Galli-Bibiena and his son Carlo. The richly decorated auditorium is dominated by the large margrave's box at the back, with three tiers of boxes on either side, the stalls area being separated from the stage by an ornamental balustrade (see fig.1). The elaborate proscenium stage (14 metres wide, 15 metres high), which is slightly raised, is unusually deep (30 metres); it was this feature that first attracted Wagner to Bayreuth in the hope that it might prove suitable for the production of his *Ring* cycle. He at once saw, after inspecting it, that it would not do for his work as it was, and he wrote on 20 April 1871 to Lorenz Düfflipp, secretary to King Ludwig II of Bavaria: 'This theatre is probably the most fantastic example of rococo to be found anywhere, and not the least thing in it may be changed'.

Following Wilhelmine's death in 1758 and Friedrich's in 1763, the court moved to Ansbach, and Bayreuth reverted to the status of a provincial town. The Markgräfliches Opernhaus continued, however, to be used by travelling companies from neighbouring towns, mainly Bamberg and Coburg. No complete list is available of the operas presented there, but it is recorded that, to celebrate the 50th anniversary of Bayreuth's incorporation into Bavaria, a performance of Wagner's *Tannhäuser* was given on 30 June 1860 in a production from Coburg – an event of which Wagner himself appears to have been unaware. The Opernhaus was in continuous use until 1935, when, after a restoration that carefully preserved its original character, it became little more than a museum. It was brought into use again in 1948 (its bicentenary) as a venue for the Fränkische Festwochen, which take place annually in May/June and are devoted to performances of early operas and ballets in productions by the Bavarian Staatsoper, Munich. It is also used for occasional recitals and other events.

2. STADTHALLE. The Markgräfliches Opernhaus's former function as the regular venue of entertainment for the people of Bayreuth was taken over by the Stadthalle in Jean-Paul-Platz. It stands on the site of the former margraves' Reithalle (built 1747–8), which was converted into a theatre in 1935–6. The first Stadthalle was destroyed in an air attack in 1945, but the front wall remained intact and was incorporated in the new Stadthalle, opened in 1965. An all-purpose building also used for plays, concerts, congresses and balls, it contains two theatres with seating capacity of 930 (Grosses Haus) and 300 (Kleines Haus). Opera performances are given throughout the year by companies from Nuremberg, Hof, Coburg and other nearby towns.

3. WAGNER'S FESTSPIELHAUS. The Markgräfliches Opernhaus may have been the factor that first drew Wagner to Bayreuth, but it was by no means the begin-

2. The Bayreuth Festspielhaus in its original form before the addition (in 1882) of the entrance to the royal box, designed to give Ludwig II total privacy

ning of his vision of a theatre of his own. That was closely connected with the composition of *Der Ring des Nibelungen*, which he early recognized as unsuitable for presentation within the traditional operatic framework. In the preface to the full text of the *Ring* in 1863 he outlined the ideal theatre he had in mind:

> I would have to aim at one of the less large towns in Germany, favourably sited and capable of accommodating an unusual number of guests, and in particular a town in which there would be no danger of clashing with a large existing theatre and thus having to compete with large-city audiences and their established customs. Here a temporary theatre would be erected, as simple as possible, perhaps merely of wood, its sole criterion being the artistic suitability of its inner parts. I had already worked out in discussions with an intelligent and experienced architect a plan with an auditorium in the shape of an amphitheatre and with the great advantage of an orchestra invisible to the audience. To this theatre singers from German opera houses, chosen for their outstanding acting skills, would be summoned, probably in early spring, to rehearse the several parts of my work, uninterrupted by any other artistic activity.

Three performances of the complete cycle, Wagner went on to say, would be given at the height of summer on four successive evenings for 'art-lovers from near and far'.

Bayreuth met in all respects the conditions he had laid down in his *Ring* preface for the site of his festival performances. It had the additional advantages of being within the territories of his patron, King Ludwig, and of having civic authorities (in particular the mayor, Theodor Muncker, and the banker, Friedrich Feustel) eager to serve Wagner in the realization of his ambition. They offered him, free of charge, a site on a hill on the northern outskirts of the town (the Grünes Hügel) for the theatre, and he bought at his own expense a plot of land backing on to the grounds of the Neues Schloss (the margraves' former residence, by now the property of King Ludwig) for a family home. (Called Wahnfried, in Richard Wagner Strasse, it was the home of the Wagner family up to the death of Wieland Wagner in 1966, and is now the Richard Wagner Museum.)

After laying the foundation stone of the theatre on 22 May 1872 (a ceremony that included a performance of Beethoven's Ninth Symphony in the Markgräfliches Opernhaus, conducted by Wagner himself), he set out to raise funds for it by conducting concerts and selling certificates of patronage. The response was disappointing, and he was obliged to construct the building with the simplest and cheapest materials. This, as his *Ring* preface shows, is what he had always intended his Festspielhaus to be: a 'sketch of an ideal', a temporary structure that the German nation, if it chose, could eventually turn into a monumental building. It incorporated all his theatrical ideas, which (as mentioned in the *Ring* preface) had been translated into practical terms by the architect Gottfried Semper. Now, working with the architect Otto Brückwald and the stage machinist Karl Brandt, Wagner realized them.

The auditorium (originally 1460 seats with boxes, including a royal box, behind) is on a single raked level, converging fan-shaped on a stage 32 metres wide and 23 metres deep (40 metres including the backstage area). A particular feature is the duplication of the stage proscenium arch (13 metres wide, 11.8 metres high) by a wider one just beyond the orchestra and the continuation of this line by 'false' wooden pillars projecting from the side walls to the back of the auditorium (see fig.3). The orchestra is positioned in a deep well obscured from the audience's sight (*see* ORCHESTRA, figs.13 and 14). Wagner wrote: 'We called this the "mystic chasm", because its task was to separate the real from the ideal', and the result of this arrangement, together with the extended proscenium, was that 'the spectator has the feeling of being at a far distance from the events on stage, yet perceives them with the clarity of near proximity; in consequence, the stage figures give the illusion of being enlarged and superhuman'. The hood over the orchestra serves the additional function of throwing the orchestral sound on to the stage to blend with the vocal sound before being projected back to the auditorium. All these features, combined with the theatre's wooden ceiling covered with painted canvas, give the performances in the Festspielhaus a visual and acoustical flavour that is unique. (*See also* FILMING, VIDEOTAPING.)

With the aid of a loan from King Ludwig, Wagner was at last able, in August 1876, to produce the *Ring* for the first time in its entirety, having previously travelled through Germany and Austria with his wife Cosima to assemble singers and orchestral players prepared to work more for love than financial gain (a principle to which Bayreuth still adheres). Three complete cycles were given, the first attended by Emperor Wilhelm I of Germany and the last by King Ludwig. But Wagner's triumph was clouded by dissatisfaction with the production itself and dismay at the huge financial deficit remaining. Six years passed before he could afford to stage another festival, this time (1882) devoted exclusively to *Parsifal*, his only work written expressly for the completed Festspielhaus (a fact reflected in its orchestration) and intended by Wagner to be performed nowhere else. In all, 16 performances were given. At the last, Wagner took the baton for the final scene – his only conducting appearance in his own theatre. He died in the following year.

4. WAGNER'S SUCCESSORS.

(i) Cosima Wagner (1886–1906). The task of running the festival devolved on Wagner's widow Cosima, who dedicated herself to carrying out the composer's wishes exactly as she understood them. Wagner had intended that all his works from *Der fliegende Holländer* onwards should eventually be staged in his theatre, and Cosima's first production (1886) was *Tristan und Isolde*, followed by *Die Meistersinger* in 1888, *Tannhäuser* in 1891, *Lohengrin* in 1894, a new production of the *Ring* in 1896, and *Der fliegende Holländer* in 1901. Her achievement was laudable, but her priestess-like devotion to the voice of the master and her refusal to consider new ideas (such as those of the Swiss designer Adolphe Appia) threatened to turn the Festspielhaus into a museum. She did, however, move with the times to the extent of installing electric lighting in 1888 in place of the original gas. Cosima's choice of artists, though widened to include foreign singers, was based not on their star quality (the Bayreuth Festival prides itself on making reputations rather than profiting from them), but on the artists' willingness to submit to her rigid production style, in which prescribed movements were tied closely to musical phrases and clear diction was of paramount importance.

Cosima was assisted by her daughters Daniela and

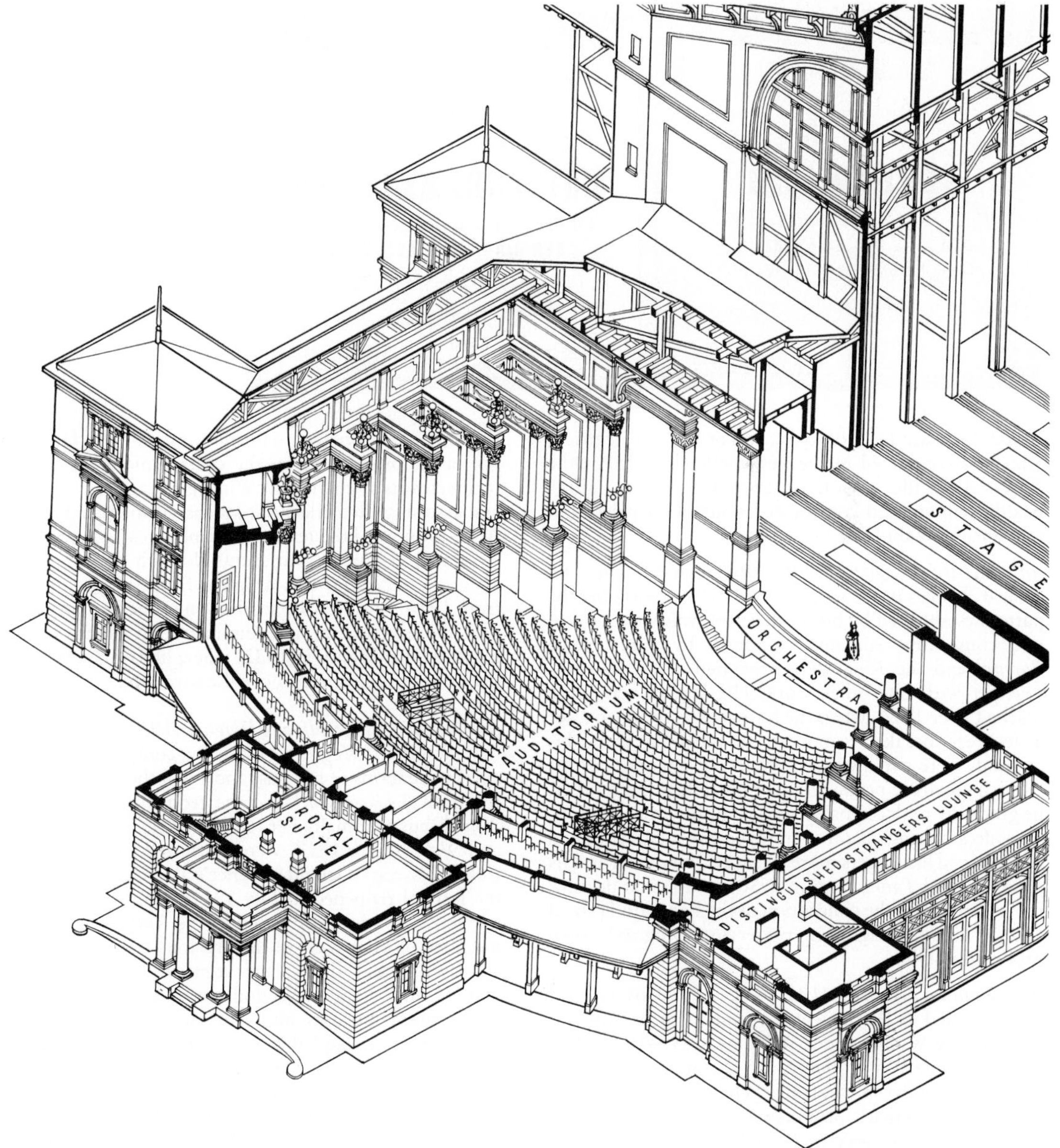

3. Diagram of the Bayreuth Festspielhaus after 1882 when the royal entrance was added: drawing by Richard Leacroft (see also THEATRE ARCHITECTURE, *fig.7)*

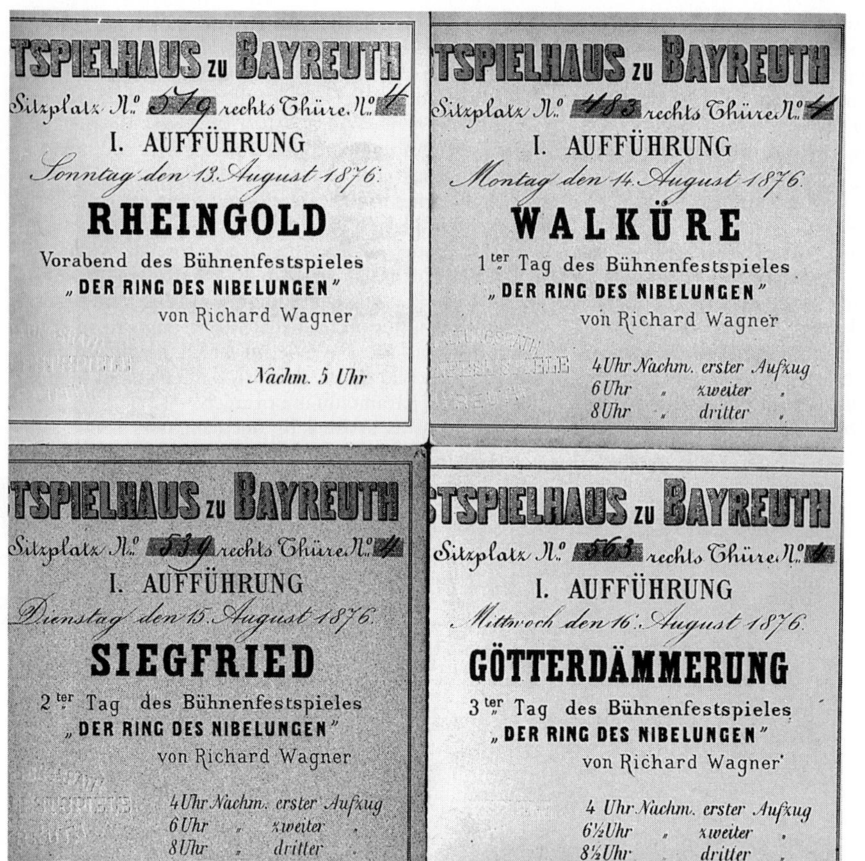

4. Four tickets for the first complete 'Ring' cycle at Bayreuth, 13–16 August 1876; the performances of 'Siegfried' and 'Götterdämmerung' were postponed for one day because of the indisposition of Franz Betz, who sang Wotan

Isolde (for costumes and so on) and by her son Siegfried, who first conducted in the Festspielhaus in 1896 (the *Ring*). After the festival of 1906 Cosima, in failing health, relinquished control in favour of Siegfried, but remained in Wahnfried.

(ii) Siegfried Wagner (1908–30). Siegfried made no radical changes in the years before 1914, continuing the pattern established by his mother: festivals were held in two consecutive summers, followed by a rest year; *Parsifal* and the *Ring* were presented at all festivals, together with one other work. His impact was more marked after 1924, when the festival was resumed after a ten-year break. A modest, unassuming man, his methods were evolutionary: while not abandoning the basically realistic productions of his father and mother, he gradually replaced painted backcloths with solid sets, extended the stage depth, improved the lighting system and allowed his singers more freedom of movement. His production of *Tannhäuser* in 1930 was the first decisive move away from the conception of the Bayreuth Festival as a museum religiously preserving Wagner's own production style.

(iii) Winifred Wagner (1931–44). Both Cosima and Siegfried died in 1930. Siegfried's successor, his British-born widow Winifred (née Williams, 1897–1980), had no pretensions as a producer, and she appointed the Intendant of the Berlin Staatsoper, Heinz Tietjen, as artistic director. Tietjen's productions, with scenic designs by Emil Preetorius (except *Parsifal*, redesigned in 1934 by Alfred Roller and in 1937 by Wieland Wagner), were lavish. If this period of the Bayreuth Festival's history is to some extent viewed with disapproval, the fault lies not in the productions or the stylized modified realism of Preetorius's sets, but in Winifred Wagner's personal association with Hitler, a frequent visitor to Bayreuth. At his command the festival became a yearly event from 1936 to 1944 (when war events closed it down), and at his request *Parsifal* was dropped from the programme from 1940. Winifred's contribution to the building itself was the erection of an administrative block on the north-west side and (in 1932) a new line of boxes at the back of the auditorium above the royal box.

(iv) Wieland and Wolfgang Wagner (1951–66). The fact that Winifred Wagner, politically compromised, was still by the terms of her husband's will the sole owner of the festival's assets delayed the reopening after World War II, but eventually her two sons Wieland (1917–66) and Wolfgang (*b* 1919) were permitted to assume control as lessees. Wieland Wagner's *Parsifal*, with which the festival reopened in July 1951, made a sensational impact, as did his production of the *Ring*. The realism, modified or otherwise, of the previous festivals had disappeared; what little stage scenery there was came mainly from light projections; costumes were simple and stylized; choruses, uniformly dressed, moved in precise formations; and the soloists matched their movements to the words rather than the music. It was a complete rejection of the tradition established by Cosima Wagner, but not, so Wieland Wagner claimed, a rejection of the ideas of his grandfather, whose works he defined as 'mystery plays', concerned more with inner conflicts than outward events.

The 'new Bayreuth style', as it came to be called, may have owed something of its origin to the need to change the festival's image after its Nazi associations, but it soon established an artistic validity, and before long directors everywhere were copying Wieland Wagner's methods. Wieland, whose production experience had been gained outside Bayreuth (in Nuremberg and Altenburg), acknowledged no masters, but his conception of the stage as an 'illuminated space' owes something to Appia as well as to Gordon Craig. In the years 1951–66, during which the festival was again an annual event, he used the Festspielhaus as an 'experimental workshop', bringing out new productions or modifying older ones in a constant search for new aspects. Like Cosima, he chose singers who were willing to follow his ideas: casts, which had been predominantly German under Winifred Wagner, again became international.

Wolfgang Wagner, who served his apprenticeship under Tietjen in Berlin, concentrated mainly on administrative duties until 1966. These included the restoration of the theatre itself. Although Richard Wagner, regarding it as a temporary structure, had set little store on its outward appearance, Wolfgang Wagner decided, in the interests of its unique visual and acoustic qualities, to retain the original form of the building both inwardly and outwardly, and simply to replace weak parts with more solid materials (steel, concrete, brick). He extended the stage still further, modernized technical equipment, increased the seating capacity (now 1925) and built new offices, dressing rooms and rehearsal stages.

(v) Wolfgang Wagner (1967–). During the period of joint control with his brother, Wolfgang Wagner staged his own productions of some of the works. These, though less radical than Wieland Wagner's, adhered in the main to the principles of the new Bayreuth style. Following Wieland Wagner's death in 1966, Wolfgang Wagner, while continuing to stage operas occasionally himself, adopted from 1969 a policy of inviting directors from outside the family to stage one of the works in turn, each production remaining in the repertory for a number of years (usually five). Guest directors up to 1989 were August Everding, Götz Friedrich, Harry Kupfer, Patrice Chéreau, Jean-Pierre Ponnelle, Peter Hall and Werner Herzog. The result of this policy was the disappearance of a recognizable Bayreuth style. Guest directors have been allowed the freedom to interpret the works each in his own way, untrammelled by any pious regard to the composer's expressed intentions. The tendency of most (though not all) of them has been to place a direct stress (through the use of modern clothing or alienation techniques, for instance) on the moral, sociological and political implications of the works rather than on the mythological guise in which Wagner chose more indirectly to present them. Whatever the directors' individual merits, they have served to maintain that spirit of controversy that has been a constant feature of Wagner's Festspielhaus from its very beginning.

The annual festivals run from the last week of July to the end of August; *Parsifal* and the *Ring* are usually given, together with two of the other works, and each festival normally contains one new production.

5. Richard Wagner Foundation. The festival was financially self-supporting until World War II, but after its postwar reopening it relied to some extent on public subsidies. In May 1973 exclusive family ownership of the festival ended with the creation of the Richard Wagner Foundation Bayreuth which assumed responsibility in perpetuity for the festival and took over its assets, including the Wagner archives in Wahnfried. The trustees of the foundation include members of the Wagner family and representatives of the Federal Republic of Germany, the Bavarian Land, the town of Bayreuth and the voluntary organization Die Freunde von Bayreuth. The foundation does not finance the festival, which continues to receive public subsidies, and sole artistic control remains in the hands of the appointed festival director (Wolfgang Wagner was appointed in 1973). In the choice of future directors the trustees undertake to give preference to members of the Wagner family.

*

R. Wagner: *Gesammelte Schriften*, vi: *Epilogischer Bericht* (Leipzig, 1872); ix: *Bayreuth* (Leipzig, 1873); x: *Das Bühnenweihfestspiel in Bayreuth 1882* (Leipzig, 1888)

L. Schiedermair: *Bayreuther Festspiele im Zeitalter des Absolutismus* (Leipzig, 1908)

A. von Puttkamer: *50 Jahre Bayreuth* (Berlin, 1927)

G. Skelton: *Wagner at Bayreuth: Experiment and Tradition* (London, 1965, 2/1976)

Z. von Kraft: *Der Sohn: Siegfried Wagners Leben und Umwelt* (Graz, 1969)

W. E. Schäfer: *Wieland Wagner: Persönlichkeit und Leistung* (Tübingen, 1970)

G. Skelton: *Wieland Wagner: the Positive Sceptic* (London, 1971)

Arbeitsgemeinschaft '100 Jahre Bayreuther Festspiele' (Regensburg and Munich, 1972–6)

H. Barth: *Der Festspielhügel* (Munich, 1973)

H. Barth, D. Mack and E. Voss, eds.: *Wagner: sein Leben und sein Welt in zeitgenössischen Bildern und Texten* (Vienna, 1975; Eng. trans., 1975)

C. Wagner: *Die Tagebücher 1869–1883* (Munich, 1976–7; Eng. trans., 1978–80)

S. Grossmann-Vendrey: *Bayreuth in der deutschen Presse: Beiträge zur Rezeptionsgeschichte Richard Wagner und seiner Festspiele* (Regensburg, 1977–83)

P. Burbidge and R. Sutton, eds.: *The Wagner Companion* (London, 1979)

H.-J. Bauer: *Barockoper in Bayreuth* (Laaber, 1982)

G. Skelton: *Richard and Cosima Wagner: Biography of a Marriage* (London, 1982)

S. Spencer and B. Millington, eds.: *Selected Letters of Richard Wagner* (London, 1987)

GEOFFREY SKELTON

Bayseitova, Kulyash (Gul'bakhram) Zhasïmovna (*b* Vernïy [now Alma-Ata], 20 April/2 May 1912; *d* Moscow, 6 June 1957). Kazakh soprano. She studied at the Vernïy Institute of Education (1924–8), sang with the Kazakh National Dramatic Theatre from 1934 and joined the Kazakh opera in 1937. Her voice was soft and of a distinctive timbre, and she was a good actress. She created many roles in operas in the Kazakh repertory by Brusilovsky, Tulebayev, Zhubanov and Kharmidi, combining in her interpretations a vocal style that was both strongly national and also European. She was the first Kazakh singer to perform Tatyana, Tamara (*The Demon*) and Butterfly. I. M. YAMPOL'SKY

Bazin, François (Emmanuel-Joseph) (*b* Marseilles, 4 Sept 1816; *d* Paris, 2 July 1878). French composer. He entered the Paris Conservatoire in 1834 and in 1840 won the Prix de Rome. On his return to Paris he quickly established a dual career as theatre composer and teacher. In 1846 his one-act *Le trompette de Monsieur le Prince* was successful, proving to be the first of a line that ceased only in 1870; his best-known work was *Le voyage en Chine* (1865) which survived well into the 20th century. He was a conservative within the Conservatoire, where he taught from 1844, succeeding Ambroise Thomas in 1871 as professor of composition.

Bazin's theatrical career was gradually eclipsed by that of Massenet, whom he had refused to have as a student in his Conservatoire class but who took over his class on his retirement in 1878. The style of Bazin's stage works is light and conventional in rhythm and harmony. The Bolero in *Le voyage en Chine*, however, is a strong contribution to the 'Spanish' repertory before *Carmen.*

all opéras comiques, first performed at the Salle Favart; printed works published in Paris

Le trompette de Monsieur le Prince (1, Mélesville [A.-H.-J. Duveyrier]), 15 May 1846 (1851)
Le malheur d'être jolie (1, C. Desnoyers), 18 May 1847, vs (1847)
La nuit de la Saint-Sylvestre (3, Mélesville and M. Masson, after J. H. Zschokke), 7 July 1849, vs (1849) [pubd as La St Sylvestre]
Madelon (2, T. Sauvage), 26 March 1852 (*c*1854)
Maître Pathelin (1, A. de Leuven and J. A. F. Langlé), 12 Dec 1856 (1857)
Les désespérés (1, de Leuven and J. Moinaux), 26 Jan 1858, vs (1858)
Marianne, 1861–2 (1, A. Challamel), unperf.
Le voyage en Chine (3, E. M. Labiche and A. Delacour), 9 Dec 1865 (1866)
L'ours et le pacha (1, E. Scribe and Saintine [J. X. Boniface]), 21 Feb 1870, vs (1870)

Unperf.: La belle au bois dormant; Mascarille

*

LoewenbergA; *StiegerO*
C. Le Senne: 'François Bazin', *EMDC*, I/iii (1923), 1759–61
J. Harding: *Massenet* (London, 1970) DAVID CHARLTON

Bazzani, Francesco Maria (*b* ?Parma, *c*1650; *d* Piacenza, *c*1700). Italian composer. He was elected *maestro di cappella* of Piacenza Cathedral in 1679 and held the post until at least 1693. A respected teacher, he taught his nephew Fortunato Chelleri among others. His operas, of which only some librettos survive, include *L'inganno trionfante* (1673, Parma), *Ottone in Italia* (1679, Parma) and *Il pedante di Tarsia* (1680, Bologna). The music of one oratorio, *La caduta del Gerico* (1693), survives (in *I-Moe*). JULIA ANN GRIFFIN

Bazzini, Antonio (*b* Brescia, 11 March 1818; *d* Milan, 10 Feb 1897). Italian composer. He began his concert career at an early age and became one of the most highly regarded violinists of his time. From 1841 to 1845 he lived in Germany, then briefly in Denmark before returning to Brescia to teach and compose. He toured Spain, then lived in Paris, and ended his concert career with a tour of the Netherlands (1864). Returning to Brescia, he devoted himself to composition. His works from this period include an opera, *Turanda* (A. Gozzoletti, after C. Gozzi; Milan, La Scala, 13 Jan 1867), and orchestral music, but he was most successful in chamber music. From 1873 he taught at the Milan Conservatory (director from 1882). Among his pupils there were Catalani, Mascagni and Puccini.

*

DBI (A. Pironti)
C. Sartori: 'Antonio Bazzini e il teatro lirico', *Il melodramma italiano dell'ottocento: studi e ricerche per Massimo Mila* (Turin, 1977) GIOVANNI CARLI BALLOLA

Beach [née Cheney], **Amy Marcy** [Mrs H. H. A. Beach] (*b* Henniker, NH, 5 Sept 1867; *d* New York, 27 Dec 1944). American composer and pianist. She was celebrated during her lifetime as the foremost woman composer of the USA. A member of the Second New England School of composers, she wrote and published more than 300 works in a wide variety of genres. The one-act chamber opera *Cabildo* op.149, Beach's only opera (1932), is a nationalist work by virtue of its subject and her use of Creole folk melodies. It was first performed at the Pound Auditorium in the University of Georgia, Athens, USA, on 27 February 1945 (MS, *US-KC*). The libretto by Nan Bagby Stephens is based on Stephens's play *Cabildo* and her novel *Bella Donna.* It concerns the pirate Pierre Lafitte who in about 1812 was imprisoned in the Cabildo, whence he mysteriously escaped. In this fictional treatment of the historical event, a visitor to the Cabildo dreams of Lafitte and his aristocratic beloved, Lady Valerie, who returns from the dead to free him.

Musically *Cabildo* is eclectic, combining late Romantic and folklike themes and treatments. Beach included a number of borrowings from Creole folksongs and from her own work in her melodic material; some of this – both original and borrowed – takes the form of motifs referring to characters and situations. The opening phrase of Beach's song *When Soul is Joined to Soul* op.62 (a setting of Elizabeth Barrett Browning, composed in 1905) appears briefly as a theme whenever Lady Valerie is mentioned, and the entire song, recomposed as a rhapsodic duet for Valerie and Pierre, is the musical climax of the opera.

*

A. F. Block: 'Why Amy Beach Succeeded as a Composer: the Early Years', *CMc*, no.36 (1983), 41–59
L. Petteys: '"Cabildo" by Amy Marcy Beach', *Opera Journal*, xxii/1 (1989), 10–20
A. F. Block: 'Dvořák, Beach and American Music', *A Celebration of American Music: Words and Music in Honor of H. Wiley Hitchcock* (Ann Arbor, 1990), 256–80 ADRIENNE FRIED BLOCK

Beach, John Parsons (*b* Gloversville, NY, 11 Oct 1877; *d* Pasadena, CA, 6 Nov 1953). American composer. A pupil of George Chadwick, he studied the piano in Boston and between 1900 and 1910 taught in Minneapolis, New Orleans and Boston. He then went to Europe, where his teachers included André Gédalge in Paris and Malipiero in Venice. On returning to Boston he took further composition lessons with Loeffler. He finally settled in Pasadena. Beach composed two operas: *Pippa's Holiday*, a one-scene monologue (after Browning: *Pippa Passes*), for mezzo-soprano and orchestra, staged at the Théâtre Réjane in Paris in 1915; and *Jorinda and Jorindel*, begun in 1909, a fairy-tale in 2 scenes for four characters (after J. L. and W. C. Grimm; MS, *US-NYp*, inc.). His output also includes ballets, in a style favouring the rich sonorities of late Romanticism.

ELIZABETH A. WRIGHT

Beach of Falesá, The. Opera in three acts, op.83, by ALUN HODDINOTT to a libretto by Glyn Jones after Robert Louis Stevenson's short story; Cardiff, New Theatre, 26 March 1974.

Wiltshire (baritone) and Case (baritone) are traders on a South Sea island. Case finds a half-caste bride for Wiltshire in Uma (mezzo-soprano) and then puts it about that she had been promised to one of the native chiefs. The islanders refuse to trade with Wiltshire, but with the help of the priest, Father Galuchet (tenor), he finds and destroys the voodoo shrine which is the source of Case's power over the natives. Case confronts him, reveals his own complicity in the deaths of previous traders, and is killed by Wiltshire. The music combines an evenly paced arioso style with vivid orchestral writing. MALCOLM BOYD

Bear, The. Extravaganza in one act by WILLIAM WALTON to a libretto by PAUL DEHN and Walton after a vaudeville by ANTON PAVLOVICH CHEKHOV; Aldeburgh, Jubilee Hall, 3 June 1967.

Madam Popova (mezzo-soprano), an attractive widow, is reproved by her manservant Luka (bass) for prolonging her period of mourning: she should start to go out again. Life is over, she says; she will mourn for the rest of her life. Luka points out that her husband had not been faithful and scarcely deserved this devotion. She should have the horse Toby put into harness and call on the neighbours. No, Popova replies, give Toby an extra bag of oats. Her reveries about the past are interrupted by Smirnov (baritone), who has forced his way in. He is a landowner and wants immediate payment of 1300 roubles owed by Popova's late husband for oats for the horse. She walks out in a huff and in her absence he laments that 'creditors appear and debtors vanish'. On her return, he parodies the Russian aristocrat's use of French ('Madame, je vous prie'). Put off these widow's weeds, he urges, and unveil like Salome (quotation from Strauss in the orchestra). They argue again. Are men more faithful in love than women, she asks rhetorically, and sings an aria ('I was a constant, faithful wife') in which she details her husband's frequent infidelities. Smirnov remarks that in spite of her mourning, she still powders her face. She calls him a boor and a bear and asks Luka to show him the door. This interchange leads to Smirnov's challenge to a duel – sex equality. By now he is genuinely attracted by her spirited behaviour and flashing eyes. Popova fetches her husband's pistol but Smirnov has to show her how to fire it and tells her he will fire into the air. 'Get out', she orders, but he pauses at the door and their eyes meet to a Puccinian motif in the orchestra. They continue their quarrel, but she has now fallen for him. No oats for Toby today, she decrees.

In his use of parody and his light and effective orchestration, Walton recaptured in *The Bear* something of the wit of *Façade* and the ebullience of *Scapino* and the Partita. The text is always clearly audible. Both librettist and composer sought to emulate Chekhov's caricatures of the three characters, and they succeeded.

MICHAEL KENNEDY

Beard, John (*b c*1717; *d* Hampton, 5 Feb 1791). English tenor. Trained by Bernard Gates at the Chapel Royal, he sang while still a boy in Handel's *Esther* (staged) in 1732. He won immediate success on his début as Silvio in *Il pastor fido* with Handel's Covent Garden company (1734) and began a long association with the composer from the late 1730s up to the 1750s. He sang more Handel parts under the composer than any other singer, appearing in ten operas, and created roles in *Ariodante* (Lurcanio, 1735), *Alcina* (Oronte, 1735), *Atalanta* (Amintas, 1736), *Arminio* (Varus, 1737), *Giustino* (Vitalian, 1737), *Berenice* (Fabio, 1737), and many oratorios including the title roles in *Samson* (1743) and *Jephtha* (1752) as well as Jupiter in *Semele* (1744). He also sang in many revivals.

Beard was not exclusively a Handel singer; from 1736, when he sang in Galliard's *The Royal Chace* at Covent Garden, he appeared in numerous ballad operas, pantomimes, burlesques and more serious pieces, and was a member of the Drury Lane company (1737–43, 1748–59) and at Covent Garden (1743–8, 1759–67). From 1737 he was a popular Macheath in *The Beggar's Opera* and appeared in J. C. Smith's *Rosalinda* (1740), *The Fairies* (1755) and *The Tempest* (1756). He also sang in many works by Lampe, Boyce and especially Arne, including *Comus*, *Rosamond*, *The Judgment of Paris*, *Alfred*, *Artaxerxes* and *Love in a Village*, in which he made his last appearance in 1767. (For illustration *see* LOVE IN A VILLAGE.)

In 1739 Beard married Lady Henrietta Herbert; she died in 1753 and in 1759 he married Charlotte Rich, daughter of the proprietor of Covent Garden, whom Beard succeeded in the management from 1761 until his retirement with the onset of deafness in 1767, when he sold the Covent Garden patent for £60 000. Burney said he 'constantly possessed the favour of the public by his superior conduct, knowledge of Music, and intelligence as an actor'. Dibdin considered him the finest English singer of the age. The heroic parts Handel composed for him established the importance of the tenor voice at a time when leading male roles were still often taken by castratos and women. The extreme compass of his Handel parts is *B* to *a'*, but they seldom go below *d*.

WINTON DEAN

Beatrice di Tenda. *Tragedia lirica* in two acts by VINCENZO BELLINI to a libretto by FELICE ROMANI after Carlo Tedaldi-Fores's play *Beatrice di Tenda*; Venice, Teatro La Fenice, 16 March 1833.

Filippo Maria Visconti *Duke of Milan, in love with Agnese*	baritone
Agnese del Maino *secretly in love with Orombello*	mezzo-soprano
Orombello *Signore of Ventimiglia*	tenor
Beatrice di Tenda *Filippo's wife, widow of Facino Cane*	soprano
Rizzardo del Maino *Agnese's brother, confidant to Filippo*	tenor
Anichino *former minister of Facino, friend to Orombello*	tenor

Courtiers, judges, guards, ladies-in-waiting

Setting The castle of Binasco, Milan, in 1418

By 24 May 1832 Bellini had agreed to write another opera for La Fenice, for which he had composed *I Capuleti e i Montecchi* in 1830. The new work would be expressly written for Giuditta Pasta; Romani had chosen the subject of *Cristina di Svezia* (after Dumas), but in October Bellini, for the first time in their collaboration, forced a new subject on Romani, *Beatrice di Tenda*, prompted by Pasta's enthusiasm for Monticini's ballet which she had recently seen in Milan. He hoped that Romani would play down the similarities to his libretto for Donizetti's *Anna Bolena* and would draw instead on Schiller's *Maria Stuart* for the ending.

Bellini reached Venice on 8 December 1832 in order to stage *Norma* with Pasta, but Romani was simultaneously at work on five other librettos and did not arrive until 1 January 1833. By mid-February Bellini still had the 'entire second act to do', and predicted a fiasco. At a late stage the role of Filippo was reassigned to the young Orazio Cartagenova, causing alterations to at least three pieces. Besides Pasta in the title role, the other singers

'Beatrice di Tenda' (Bellini), Act 1 scene iii (a grove in the gardens of the ducal palace): design by Francesco Bagnara for the original production at La Fenice, Venice, 16 March 1833

(disliked by Bellini) included Alberico Curioni as Orombello and Anna del Serre as Agnese. At the end of his preface to the original libretto Romani included an apology for his 'fragment' of melodrama, 'because inevitable circumstances have affected the plot, the colours, the characters. It requires the full indulgence of readers'. The unfortunate outcome was mutual recrimination and the eventual breach of their partnership.

The six performances were largely unsuccessful. In the years following Bellini's death, however, the opera achieved a respectable circulation. In 1837 it was performed in Trieste as *Il castello d'Ursino*; the same year Romani's libretto was set by Rinaldo Ticci for Siena. Bellini's Beatrice was a particular favourite of Erminia Frezzolini; other sopranos who sang the role included Giuseppina Ronzi de Begnis, Karoline Unger, Giuseppina Strepponi and Fanny Tacchinardi-Persiani. *Beatrice di Tenda* was the first opera by Bellini to be published in full score, in an edition by Pittarelli (Rome, *c*1840) that contains material not in the Ricordi scores, particularly some relevant to the problematical Act 2 finale.

Beatrice, the widow of Facino Cane, is now married to the avaricious and dissolute Duke Filippo. Having acquired Beatrice's lands, Filippo is more interested in her young lady-in-waiting, Agnese. The short prelude uses themes from the opera, notably that from Beatrice's arioso in the Act 1 finale.

ACT 1.i *The entrance hall of the castle of Binasco* A grand celebration is taking place. Meeting Filippo, a group of courtiers ask why he is leaving. Filippo, continuing their choral melody, replies that he can no longer bear his wife, and the courtiers sympathize. Agnese is heard off stage singing a romanza, 'Ah! non pensar che pieno sia nel poter diletto'. Filippo vows that he will find a way to free himself and expresses his feelings in 'Divina Agnese ... Come t'adoro, e quanto'.

1.ii *Agnese's quarters* Agnese, who loves Orombello, has sent him a letter, inviting him to a rendezvous. Orombello arrives, expecting to find Beatrice, and in his confusion, inadvertently discloses that he loves the Duchess. (Furious, Agnese, it is to be inferred, decides to give Filippo proof of his wife's infidelity by providing him with letters incriminating Beatrice.)

1.iii *A grove in the gardens of the ducal palace* In the cavatina 'Ma la sola, ohimè! son io', Beatrice laments to her ladies-in-waiting the suffering she has brought on everyone by marrying Filippo, who mistreats her subjects (the autograph of the cabaletta contains a less decorated vocal line than do the Ricordi scores). Filippo enters with Rizzardo, Agnese's brother, whom he instructs to watch Orombello. After wondering why his wife's unfaithfulness should annoy him, Filippo accuses Beatrice of infidelity and of treason. In the duet 'Odio e livore! – ingrato!' (part of whose accompaniment derives from *Zaira*), Beatrice rejects both accusations, but Filippo produces incriminating documents provided by Agnese. Beatrice demands justice and a fair trial.

1.iv *A remote part of the castle* In a chorus, 'Lo vedeste? Sì; fremente', the men-at-arms predict Orombello's downfall. Beatrice, kneeling before a statue of her late husband, Facino Cane, prays to his spirit for assistance in 'Deh! se mi amasti un giorno'. Orombello enters, swearing to protect her, and confessing that he loves her. Beatrice orders him to leave but he refuses. Filippo and the entire court crowd in to find the apparently guilty couple together. Both Beatrice and Orombello proclaim their innocence, but Filippo orders their arrest and they are surrounded by guards.

ACT 2.i *A hall in the castle* The courtiers and Beatrice's ladies discuss her forthcoming trial and the sufferings of Orombello under torture, which have led to an admission of his own and Beatrice's guilt. Filippo enters and, in spite of Anichino's warnings that popular sympathy for Beatrice may lead to an uprising, orders the trial to begin. Beatrice denies the judges' accusations and has an angry altercation with Filippo. Orombello is brought in and Agnese is mortified by the suffering that her jealousy has caused him. Upbraided by Beatrice for his disloyalty, Orombello recounts his tortures and retracts his confession. Their duet leads into the quintet with chorus 'Al tuo fallo ammenda festi' for Beatrice, Agnese, Orombello, Anichino, Filippo and the judges, the finest number in the score. Filippo suggests that the passing of sentence be postponed, but the judges demand further interrogation of both prisoners. Beatrice pleads with Filippo, until he orders that she and Orombello be taken away. The remorseful Agnese comes to beg forgiveness for Beatrice. Filippo refuses, then relents, acknowledging in 'Qui m'accolse oppresso, errante' the honour and power that Beatrice has brought him; but when news is brought of a popular uprising in support of Beatrice, Filippo signs her death warrant.

2.ii *A vestibule above the castle prison* Beatrice's maids lament her fate. She is brought in, proudly proclaiming that she said nothing under torture. Agnese confesses that she is the cause of Beatrice's downfall and asks for pardon. At first Beatrice is outraged, but the voice of Orombello, heard from his cell, urges her to forgive Agnese in 'Angiol di pace' (the melody of which comes from Orosmane's aria in *Zaira*, Act 2), and in the ensuing trio Beatrice's anger is transformed into forgiveness. A funeral bell announces the arrival of the death procession. Beatrice bids a moving farewell in the aria 'Ah! se un'urna è a me concessa', asking that flowers be laid on her grave. In the cabaletta (from *Bianca e Fernando*) she asserts that her death brings victory, not sorrow or pain.

* * *

Beatrice di Tenda marks a stage in the progress of Bellini's art both in the elaboration of its forms and in the variety of its harmonies. The design of the introduzione is something new: a dialogue between chorus and soloist followed by an offstage canzone for the comprimaria (a device copied by Mercadante in *Il bravo* of 1839) and a cantabile for the principal baritone in two strophes punctuated by a rapid choral ritornello which also functions as a concluding stretta. The first movement of the duet for Agnese and Orombello is extended into distantly related keys, while in their cabaletta the regularity of the phrase-structure is masked harmonically, giving a remarkably propulsive effect. The central cantabile of Beatrice's duet with Filippo spans a wide tonal orbit, ending, most unusually, in the tonic minor. The 'coro d'armigeri' ('Lo vedeste') arrests the attention with its often unpredictable progressions; while its allegro movement presages the courtiers' 'Scorrendo uniti' from *Rigoletto* in its rhythmic cut. The Act 1 finale impressed the young Verdi sufficiently for him to recommend it to Piave as a model of effective theatre. The judgment scene contains darker colours than have appeared in Bellini so far. Unfortunately the recourse to earlier material in the opera's final scenes betrays Bellini's haste. Beatrice deserves a less generic final cabaletta than the one borrowed from *Bianca e Fernando*. It is a pity, too, that Bellini had no time to set the duet for Beatrice and Agnese leading to their terzetto with Orombello, for which Romani had provided the text. Sketches for the music exist; and it is clear from a letter to Ricordi that Bellini intended to complete them. Another weakness lies in the portrayal of Filippo Visconti, an exceptionally odious villain (as Bellini himself recognized) who emerges as just another baritone antagonist, far more convincing in his movements of remorse than in his anger. All this doubtless explains why *Beatrice di Tenda*, despite many excellent qualities, has failed to establish itself in the repertory.

SIMON MAGUIRE, ELIZABETH FORBES, JULIAN BUDDEN

Béatrice et Bénédict ('Beatrice and Benedick'). *Opéra* in two acts by HECTOR BERLIOZ to his own libretto after WILLIAM SHAKESPEARE's *Much Ado about Nothing*; Baden-Baden, Theater der Stadt, 9 August 1862.

The celebrated overture, though not a pot-pourri in the usual sense, characterizes the substance of the opera by alluding to quite a number of passages to follow. The first act takes place in the garden of Léonato [Leonato] (spoken), governor of Messina in Sicily. The townspeople rejoice that the invading Moors have fled from Don Pedro (bass) and his force. Soon the victors will be home, and Héro [Hero] (soprano) will be reunited with her intended, Claudio (baritone). Less pleased is Béatrice [Beatrice] (soprano), her cousin, to contemplate the return of Bénédict [Benedick] (tenor), with whom she has long enjoyed 'a kind of merry war'. Those so far assembled dance a *sicilienne* based on Berlioz's first published song, *Le dépit de la bergère* (*c*1819) – an acknowledgment, perhaps, that he expected *Béatrice et Bénédict* to be his last work. Hero's aria is one of ecstasy at the thought of seeing Claudio again.

Don Pedro and his retinue arrive; at once Beatrice and Benedick, in their duet, begin to taunt each other. The wedding of Hero and Claudio will take place that evening – an example, it is noted, that should tempt Benedick. In his trio with Claudio and Don Pedro, Benedick insists he would much prefer the cloistered life to marriage: if ever he consents to that yoke, they can put a sign on his roof, 'Here you see Benedick, the married man'. Following his exit, his companions determine to trick Beatrice and Benedick into acknowledging their love.

Somarone (bass), *maestro di capella* of questionable gifts in composition, arrives with his choristers and oboists to rehearse the nuptial epithalamium, an absurd double fugue; a reprise with comic oboe ornamentation is offered before Don Pedro. Benedick, hidden behind a hedge, overhears an arranged conversation to the effect that Beatrice is indeed in love with him; suddenly he begins to consider some of the advantages of marriage. Hero and her attendant Ursula (mezzo-soprano), having arranged a similar ruse as regards Beatrice, come to the garden to escape the festive commotion within. During their famous Duo-Nocturne, 'Nuit paisible et sereine!', Hero's access of melancholy is calmed by the play of moonlight and shadows, the breeze's caress, the murmur of nightingale and crickets, the aroma of spring blossoms. The effect is much the same as in 'Nuit d'ivresse' from *Les Troyens*.

The entr'acte is a reprise of the *sicilienne*. Act 2 takes place in a great hall in the governor's palace, with the wedding banquet in an adjoining room offstage. The guests, drinking heavily, prevail on Somarone to improvise a song on the merits of the local wines, accompanied by a rustic band and the pounding of wine-glasses on the tables; with effort, on stage, he finishes a second verse. Beatrice, in her aria, acknowledges that she, too, has fallen victim to love. Hero and Ursula, recognizing the change, join her in a trio of promised joys and happiness; Beatrice is lost in thought as an offstage chorus summons the bride. In a chance encounter Beatrice and Benedick, each safe in the knowledge that the other has been uncontrollably smitten, continue mercilessly to bait each other. The bridal procession enters. After the bride and groom have signed their contract, the scribe produces a second, asking who else wishes to be married. Beatrice and Benedick take each other out of pity, and banners bearing the words 'Ici on voit Bénédict, l'homme marié' are duly proffered. A truce has been signed; the warring will recur on the morrow.

Béatrice et Bénédict represented for Berlioz a light-hearted turn away from the rigours of *Les Troyens*. Whereas the Virgilian tragedy summarizes the epic tendencies of his imagination, *Béatrice et Bénédict* affirms both his mordant wit and his overall good humour. He was pleased to return to Italian subject matter and to music of triple metres, street dances, tambourines and guitars. The concision of means, likewise, is the stuff of rebound from Troy. Somarone is Berlioz's invention; his line 'The piece which you are about to have the honour to perform is a masterpiece! Let us begin!' is said to have been uttered by Spontini at a rehearsal of *Olimpie* in Berlin. Elsewhere the text often follows Shakespeare closely. Contemporary vocal scores did not, however, include the spoken lines. These were reassembled from the materials used in Baden-Baden and first published in the New Berlioz Edition (1980). D. KERN HOLOMAN

Beatrix Cenci. Opera in two acts, op.38, by ALBERTO GINASTERA to a libretto by William Shand and Alberto Girri; Washington, DC, Kennedy Center for the Performing Arts, 10 September 1971.

The opera is set in Rome and Petrella at the end of the 16th century (the librettists claim that Shelley's verse-play *The Cenci* was not one of their basic sources). The insanely cruel, depraved and sadistic Count Francesco Cenci (baritone) has ordered a great banquet and ball which his daughter Beatrix (soprano) and her stepmother Lucrecia (mezzo-soprano) are commanded to attend. Beatrix, filled with forebodings of evil, asks her former suitor Orsino (tenor), now a priest, to take a letter to the Pope pleading for him to save her from her father's tyranny; but when she has gone he destroys the letter, wishing to be her sole protector. At the masked ball Cenci gloatingly announces that two of his sons have been killed in Spain; the guests leave in horror. Alone, the drunken Cenci voices his incestuous desire for Beatrix. Meanwhile Orsino tells her that the Pope has rejected her appeal; but on hearing Cenci approach he cravenly flees. Lucrecia hears Beatrix's terrified scream as Cenci rapes her. In Act 2 Beatrix, anguished by her violation, is hiding herself away. Her brother Giacomo (bass) hires two assassins to avenge his sister. Beatrix slips a sleeping-draught into the Count's wine, and he enters a delirium, believing he hears the voices of his enemies in the baying of his mastiffs (the representation of which is one of the dramatic high points of the work). Urged on by Beatrix, the assassins stab him. But later his body is found, and the family is arrested. Orsino, fearful for his own safety, abandons the family, who are all tortured, Beatrix on a wheel in a prison of the Castel Sant'Angelo. Bidding farewell to her young brother Bernardo (tenor), she goes forth calmly to execution.

The opera resembles Ginastera's previous opera *Bomarzo* in its theme – madness and evil – and its period setting, and both his other operas in its formal organization into separate scenes, 14 in this case. It employs a wide variety of musical techniques, from advanced serialism to aleatory writing, along with microtones and note-clusters. In keeping with this, the initial staging also employed such novel techniques as a simulation of cinematic slow motion in the danced delirium scene in Act 2; and its use of films and projections to convey the work's lurid and nightmarish aspects matched the composer's concept of an amalgam of opera and cinema. The dramatic pace is deliberate until the Act 1 ball scene (which contains dances in ancient style, with distortions) but then forges ahead in ever-increasing tension until the final scene. LIONEL SALTER

Beatty-Kingston, William (*b* 1837; *d* at sea, 4 Oct 1900). English librettist and translator. He wrote the librettos for Isidore de Lara's *The Light of Asia* ('a sacred legend') and Leonhard Emil Bach's *Irmengarda*, both produced without success at Covent Garden in 1892, and was the author of the English version of *Tosca*, published in the vocal score (1900). Its notoriously clumsy diction (opening with the rhymed couplet 'Ha! I have baulked them! Dread imagination/Made me quake with uncalled-for perturbation') clogged British performances for more than half a century.

ARTHUR JACOBS

Beauchamps [Beauchamp], **Pierre** (*b* Paris, 30 Oct 1631; *d* ?1705). French dancer and choreographer. He has been wrongly identified with Charles-Louis Beauchamps. Called the father of all ballet-masters, he codified the five ballet positions of feet and arms, and developed a rational system of dance notation which is now called after Raoul-Auger Feuillet, who published it (in his *Chorégraphie, ou L'art de décrire la dance*) in 1700.

Beauchamps was Louis XIV's personal dancing-master and favourite partner in *ballets de cour* in the 1650s. Throughout his career he collaborated with Lully, whom he first met as comic dancer in, and later as composer of, *ballets de cour*. Beauchamps choreographed *intermèdes* and dances for Molière's *comédies-ballets*, beginning with *Les fâcheux* (1661), as well as for Lully's *Le mariage forcé*, *La princesse d'Elide* (both 1664), *Monsieur de Pourceaugnac* (1669), *Les amants magnifiques* and *Le bourgeois gentilhomme* (both 1670). He was the first ballet-master of Pierre Perrin's Académies d'Opéra, creating dances for Cambert's *Pomone* (1671). He choreographed dances for the premières of Lully's *L'impatience* (1661), *Les amours déguisés* (1664), *La naissance de Vénus* (1665), *Les fêtes de l'Amour et de Bacchus* (1672), *Cadmus et Hermione* (1673), *Thésée* (1675), *Atys* (1676), *Isis* (1677) and *Le triomphe de l'Amour* (1681), in which he also danced the role of Mars. After Lully's death (1687), Beauchamps left the Opéra to choreograph and compose music for ballets at the Jesuit colleges (1669–97). Louis XIV bestowed many honours upon him: he was appointed *Intendant des ballets du roi* in 1661 and director of the Académie Royale de Danse in 1680 (although he was not, as many have assumed, a founder-member).

*

F. Derra de Moroda: 'The Dance Notation of the 18th Century: Lorin-Beauchamps-Feuillet' (typescript, 1971, London, Theatre Museum)

R. Kunzle: 'Pierre Beauchamp: the Illustrious Unknown Choreographer', *Dance Scope*, viii/2 (1974), 32–45

R. Astier: 'Pierre Beauchamps and the Ballets de Collège', *Dance Chronicle*, vi/2 (1983), 138–63

MAUREEN NEEDHAM COSTONIS

Beaumarchais, Pierre-Augustin (Caron de) (*b* Paris, 24 Jan 1732; *d* Paris, 18 May 1799). French writer. He is remembered today as the author of two genial stage comedies, *Le barbier de Séville, ou La précaution inutile* and *La folle journée, ou Le mariage de Figaro*, both destined for immortality also as opera librettos. To his contemporaries his notoriety had many other sources besides: he began his career in 1753 as a watchmaker, the king, Mme de Pompadour and other nobility at Versailles soon becoming his clients; then he served as harp teacher to Louis XV's four daughters (1757). He bought his way into the nobility (1761), became a judge (1763), later an occasional diplomat and even a spy. He was an eternal litigant, and the popularity of his witty – if unscrupulous – pamphlets pillorying his legal opponents rivalled that of the *Provincial Letters* of Pascal. He was also a supplier, or would-be supplier, of arms to both the American and the French Revolutions. In 1794, while he was abroad, mishaps caused his name to be inscribed on the list of criminal émigrés and his family placed under arrest. Returning to Paris in 1796, his finances and his health in disarray, he spent the remaining three years of his life recuperating his losses.

Beaumarchais also emerged as an important literary personality, indeed the last great writer of comedy of the *ancien régime.* His earliest surviving theatrical efforts were written (starting in about 1757 or 1758) for private performance at Etiolles, the estate of Mme de Pompadour's husband, and were never published during his lifetime. These pieces included vaudevilles and *comédies mêlées d'ariettes.* His first publicly staged plays were both 'drames', inspired mainly by Diderot: *Eugénie* (first performed 1767) and *Les deux amis* (1770). Beaumarchais' own *Essai sur le genre dramatique sérieux* (published with *Eugénie* in 1767), also owing much to Diderot, remains one of the clearest expositions of the 'drame' written during the century. Neither of these plays is performed today.

Le barbier de Séville, ou La précaution inutile, though belonging to the classical Molière tradition, was designed to be the first episode in a cycle that would finally include two more plays: *Le mariage de Figaro* and *La mère coupable* (the author had hoped to add still others). Apparently modelled after the Oedipus cycle of antiquity, this was a daringly original conception; it was unheard of before Beaumarchais to invent stage characters who, play by play, would grow older and change, and who were to be imagined as leading lives outside the texts the author wrote for them.

Both Figaro comedies, *Le barbier* and *Le mariage de Figaro*, lent themselves exceptionally well to musical setting. *Le barbier* was turned into opera at least four times, by F. L. Benda, Paisiello, Isouard and Rossini. The play in its original version (1772) had been intended as an *opéra comique* for the Comédie-Italienne. Even when it was revised as a stage play for the Comédie-Française, the plot featured various twists that were perfectly designed for the incidental music which Antoine-Laurent Baudron, principal violinist of the threatre orchestra, composed and orchestrated for it. Some of this music made its mark: Baudron's musical 'storm' between Acts 3 and 4 made a hit with the audience, a unique example of incidental music being remarked on at that theatre. 'Je suis Lindor' from Act 1 scene vi was used by Mozart for a theme and variations for piano (K354/299*a*).

Le mariage, the longest stage comedy of the century, overflowed with incidental songs, dances and musical ceremonies composed mainly by Baudron. It came closer to an *opéra comique* than any previous French play, a feature upon which Mozart and Da Ponte capitalized in *Le nozze di Figaro.* The structure of Beaumarchais' comedy largely survived the transformation into an opera libretto, and one of the enduring elements was Beaumarchais' innovatory strategy (part of his long-standing feminism) in giving the lead to women – the Countess and Suzanne – to devise the deceptions of the plot, rather than to males as was the more usual theatrical practice. Conservative Vienna demanded certain *adoucissements*, mainly political but also sexual. Figaro's enormous monologue, with its daring thrusts against the nobility, disappeared almost entirely. The sexual overtones of the relationship between the Countess and the young page, Chérubin, considered almost shocking in the original comedy, were played down, as were Marceline's feminist outbursts; the trial scene, unsuitable for opera, was excised completely. Though in Beaumarchais' play the Countess's final gesture of forgiveness was touching enough, it could never have had the sublimity it achieved in the Mozart-Da Ponte opera: his Countess was not so innocent as theirs.

In 1793 a heavily revised version of the Mozart-Da Ponte opera was produced at the Paris Opéra, in French translation. As in an *opéra comique*, extensive parts of Beaumarchais' original spoken dialogue were reinserted in place of the recitatives. The production had no success.

The last instalment of the Figaro trilogy, a 'drame' whose full title is *L'autre Tartuffe, ou La mère coupable*, was staged during the Revolution (1792), and in its painful emotions and dark-coloured settings intensely reflected the new spirit of the times. The 'guilty mother' is the Countess, who has had an illegitimate son by Chérubin, following a moment of *égarement* in which he forced his will upon her. Later Chérubin was killed in a far-off land, and his death seems to have drained the life and gaiety from the remaining characters. Just as in Molière's *Tartuffe*, the entire family in the last act faces financial disaster, but this time there is a hair's breadth escape thanks to Figaro's wits, while the Count is called upon to make a dramatic gesture of forgiveness towards the guilty mother, even as the Countess had earlier done for him. Although praised by connoisseurs such as Victor Hugo and Charles Péguy, the play is all but forgotten today. Grétry apparently offered to provide music for parts of the text, but the work became an opera only with Milhaud's setting (1966, Geneva). John Corigliano borrowed characters from the play for the plot of his opera *The Ghosts of Versailles* (1992).

In 1782 Beaumarchais submitted a revision of Voltaire's libretto *Samson* (music by Rameau, unperformed) to the Opéra. Although Voltaire's text was shortened from five acts to three, the action tightened, more emphasis placed on the love interest, and a new composer chosen for the music, the revised version was never put into rehearsal. Five years later Beaumarchais produced an opera libretto of his own making, *Tarare*, with music by Salieri; generally considered this composer's masterpiece, it was performed at the Opéra in 1787 and frequently revived there until 1826. Much influenced by Gluck, Beaumarchais' preface, 'Aux abonnés de l'Opéra qui voudraient aimer l'opéra', set forth a challenging conception of the relationships between plot, words and music – a theory that seems to prefigure the reforms of Wagner. In the opera proper, the semi-allegorical plot, based on a *conte arabe*, featured perilous escapes and grandiose scenic effects. Tarare's effort to liberate his imprisoned wife recalls, in a more sombre mode, the plot of *Le barbier*, while the moral lesson of the piece, that success depends on character rather than rank, looks back to Figaro and probably also to the materialism of Diderot.

L. de Loménie: *Beaumarchais et son temps* (Paris, 1856)
E. Lintilhac: *Beaumarchais et ses oeuvres* (Paris, 1887)
M. Rouff: 'Un opéra politique de Beaumarchais', *La Révolution française*, lix (1910), 212–29, 333–58
E. Giudici: *Beaumarchais nel suo e nel nostro tempo: 'Le Barbier de Séville'* (Rome, 1964)
F. Lesure: 'A propos de Beaumarchais', *RdM*, liii (1967), 175–8
S. Popper: *Beaumarchais and Music* (diss., Columbia U., 1969)
P. Rétat: 'La mort de Chérubin', *Revue d'histoire littéraire de la France*, lxxiv (1974), 1000–09
N. Pirrotta: 'Causerie su Beaumarchais e la musica teatrale', *Letterature comparate, problemi e metodo: studi in onore di Ettore Paratore* (Bologna, 1981), 1471–80
M. E. C. Bartlet: 'Beaumarchais and Voltaire's *Samson*', *Studies in Eighteenth-Century Culture*, xi (1982), 33–49
S. Dudley: 'Les premières versions françaises du *Mariage de Figaro* de Mozart', *RdM*, lxix (1983), 55–83
B. A. Brown: 'Beaumarchais, Mozart and the Vaudeville: Two Examples from "The Marriage of Figaro"', *MT*, cxxvii (1986), 261–5
W. E. Rex: '*Figaro*'s Games', *The Attraction of the Contrary: Essays on the Literature of the French Enlightenment* (Cambridge, 1987), 184–90
P. Larthomas and L. Larthomas, eds: *Pierre-Augustin Caron de Beaumarchais: Oeuvres* (Paris, 1988)
B. N. Morton and D. C. Spinelli: *Beaumarchais: a Bibliography* (Ann Arbor, 1988)
D. Heartz: 'From Beaumarchais to Da Ponte: Metamorphosis of *Figaro*', *Mozart's Operas*, ed. T. Bauman (Berkeley and Los Angeles, 1990), 107–21
P. Robinson: 'La musique des comédies de Figaro: éléments de dramaturgie', *Studies on Voltaire and the Eighteenth Century*, no.275 (1990), 359–499
J. Starobinski: 'Les âges de l'amour', *L'avant-scène opéra*, no.135 (1990) [*Le nozze di Figaro* issue], 140–44
WALTER E. REX

Beaumavielle, François (*d* 1688). French baritone (*basse-taille*). Recruited in Languedoc, he first sang in Paris in 1671, in Cambert's *Pomone* (as Vertumne) and *Les peines et les plaisirs de l'amour*. He joined the Opéra in 1672. The Parfaict brothers (MS, *F-Pn*) attributed the creation of the title role in *Cadmus* (1673) to Beaumavielle; Durey de Noinville (writing in 1753) to Gaye. The casts may have been different for the court and public performances, as in *Bellérophon* (1679), when Jobate was apparently sung by Gaye at St Germain but by Beaumavielle in Paris. Pluto (in Lully's *Proserpine*, 1680) was similarly divided between them.

The principal *basse-taille* roles between 1676 and 1686 were taken mostly by Gaye, and later by Dun. Those sung by Beaumavielle included four in further works by Lully: Time (*Atys*, 1676), Jupiter (*Isis*, 1677), Phineus (*Persée*, 1682, both in Paris and at Versailles; also the revival, 1687) and Priam (*Achille et Polyxène*, 1687). The Parfaicts described Beaumavielle as 'Languedocien, grand, laid, mais ayant l'air noble au théâtre'; Titon du Tillet allowed him a 'visage gracieux'. He sang Aegeus in the 1688 revival of Lully's *Thésée*, but died during rehearsals for Collasse's *Thétis et Pélée*. Beaumavielle is said to have bequeathed his furniture to Dumesnil, who apparently had it covered with cloth woven from ribbons he had prised from the 'actrices de l'Opéra'. PHILIP WELLER

Beaumesnil, Henriette Adélaïde Villard de (*b* Paris, 30 or 31 Aug 1748; *d* Paris, 1813). French singer and composer. Having specialized in soubrette roles in comedies from the age of seven, she made a successful début at the Paris Opéra on 27 November 1766, replacing Sophie Arnould in the title role of *Silvie* (P.-M. Berton and J.-C. Trial). Although she sang in many premières and revivals until her retirement in 1781, creating with Rosalie Levasseur the role of Iphigenia in Gluck's *Iphigénie en Tauride* (1779), her talents were overshadowed by those of Arnould and Levasseur. Grimm praised her acting ability and graceful figure, but considered her voice too small and dry for the demanding roles she was often required to sing.

Anacréon, a one-act opera and her first composition, received a private performance at the Brunoy residence of the Comte de Provence on 5 December 1781. Beaumesnil then achieved public success with her *acte de ballet Tibulle et Délie, ou Les Saturnales* (after L. Fuzelier: *Les fêtes grecques et romaines*; Paris, Opéra, 15 March 1784; MS *F-Po*) and, later, with the *opéra comique Plaire, c'est commander* (2, Marquis de La Salle; Paris, Théâtre de Montansier, 12 May 1792). She is further remembered for her part in a 'duel au pistolet' with the dancer Mlle Théodore.

H. Audiffret: 'Beaumesnil, Henrietta-Adélaïde Villard', *Biographie universelle*, ed. L. Michaud (Paris, 1843–65), iii, 407–8
V. Fournel: *Curiosités théâtrales anciennes et modernes* (Paris, 1859), 259
F. M. Grimm: *Correspondance littéraire, philosophique et critique* (Paris, 1813); complete edn., ed. M. Tourneux (Paris, 1877–82), vii, 200–01
E. Campardon: *L'Académie royale de musique au XVIIIe siècle* (Paris, 1884), i, 49–57
J. Gourret: *Dictionnaire des cantatrices de l'Opéra de Paris* (Paris, 1987), 23–4
ELISABETH COOK

Beccarina, La. *See* TORRI, ANNA MARIA.

Bechi, Gino (*b* Florence, 16 Oct 1913). Italian baritone. He studied in Florence with Raul Frazzi and Di Giorgi and made his début at Empoli in 1936 as Germont. He sang regularly in Rome (1938–52), and at La Scala (1939–53), where he sang the title role of *Nabucco* at the reopening of the theatre in 1946. He established himself as the leading Italian dramatic baritone of the day, especially in the Verdi repertory; his roles also included Gérard and Thomas' Hamlet. His performances with the Scala company at Covent Garden in 1950 as Iago and Falstaff found him in poor vocal form; those at Drury Lane as William Tell in 1958 were equally disappointing. His recordings reveal a powerful, dramatic voice and a 'growl' reminiscent of Titta Ruffo. He sang in the premières of Rocca's *Monte Ivnor* (1939, Rome) and Alfano's *Don Juan de Manara* (1941, Florence). Bechi continued to sing until 1961, when he appeared as Salieri's Falstaff at Siena and in *Il barbiere di Siviglia* at Adria. HAROLD ROSENTHAL/R

Becht, Hermann (*b* Karlsruhe, 19 March 1939). German baritone. He studied in Karlsruhe, making his début in Brunswick. In 1974 he became a member of the Deutsche Oper am Rhein. He sang Donner at Covent Garden in 1978, and at Bayreuth he has sung Alberich (from 1979) and Kurwenal (1981). He made his American début at San Francisco in 1982 as Telramund and has sung at Houston and Chicago. His repertory includes Amfortas, Klingsor, Pizarro, Faninal, Mandryka,

Falstaff, Borromeo (*Palestrina*), Dr Schön (*Lulu*) and the title roles of *Mathis der Maler* and Egk's *Peer Gynt*. He created the title role in Volker David Kirchner's *Belshazar* at the Staatsoper in Munich (1986). A powerful actor, he has a strong, dark-coloured voice.

ELIZABETH FORBES

Beck, Franz [François] **Ignaz** (*b* Mannheim, 20 Feb 1734; *d* Bordeaux, 31 Dec 1809). German composer and conductor active mainly in France. After learning the violin and other instruments, he gravitated towards the circle of Johann Stamitz, who had settled in Mannheim in 1741. For unknown reasons, but perhaps because of a duel resulting from jealousy over the favours he received from the Elector Palatine, he left Mannheim for Venice, where he studied with Galuppi and gave concerts as a violinist before travelling to Naples. He arrived in France in about 1760, and became leader of the Marseilles theatre orchestra. At the same period about 20 of his symphonies were published in Paris; his name appears as early as 1757 on a programme of the Concert Spirituel. Around 1761 he went to Bordeaux as conductor of the opera orchestra, an influential post that he held until 1798 when he fell out of favour with the city's theatrical director, though he resumed his duties in 1801. He was also active as a teacher, his pupils including Gaveaux and Henri Blanchard. In 1783 in Paris Marie Antoinette gave him the honorary title of *maître de chapelle*; his career culminated with his nomination in 1803 as a corresponding member of the Institut de France.

A prolific composer, Beck is thought to have begun work on more than 3000 pieces, including orchestral, keyboard and sacred vocal works. He also wrote for the stage – *opéras comiques*, ballets, *mélodrames*, incidental music, choruses for Racine's *Athalie* and *Esther* – though most of these works remain only in manuscript or have been lost. They were of considerable importance in Bordeaux, as Beck consistently set texts by authors of high repute, as well as local writers. His style is influenced by the German, Italian and French schools of the time, and his melodic forms are related to the writing of the Mannheim School in their frequent expressive use of appoggiaturas and augmented 2nds. He is at his most brilliant in his orchestral writing; his overtures, illustrating the various elements of the drama they precede, remained in fashion until late in the 19th century. That for *L'isle déserte*, for example, has four sections of contrasting tonality and dynamics, corresponding to the four stages of the plot. For his fine sense of dramatic action and skilful illustration of tragic texts, notably in the play *Le comte de Comminges* (1790), Beck is often regarded as having introduced the aesthetics of *Sturm und Drang* to France, thus anticipating the development of French opera in the direction of Romantic drama.

first performed in Bordeaux unless otherwise stated

Le combat des Muses (prol., L.-C. Leclerc), 1762, ?lost

Le nouvel an, ou Les étrennes de Colette (oc, S. Mamin), 1765, ?lost

La belle jardinière (bouquet, Caprez), 24 Aug 1767, pubd lib. *F-BO*

L'isle déserte (oc, C.-P.-H. Comte d'Ossun, after P. Metastasio), 14 Jan 1779, *Pn*

Le jugement d'Apollon (épisode, Blincourt), Grand, 7 April 1780

Les trois sultanes, ou Soliman second (comédie, 3, C.-S. Favart, after J.-F. Marmontel), Grand, 1784, 5 ariettes *Pn*

Belphégor, ou La descente d'Arlequin aux enfers (comédie, 3, ?J. Le Grand), Grand, 9 Feb 1789, parts *BO*

La loterie d'amour (oc, Vallier), Grand, 4 June 1789

Pandore (mélodrame, d'Aumale de Corsenville), Paris, Monsieur, 2 July 1789, pubd parts *BO*

Sargines, ou L'élève de l'amour (opéra buffon, 4, Mlle Renaud, after F.-T.-M. de Baculard d'Arnaud), Grand, 5 Dec 1789

Les peuples et les rois (oc), Grand, 1793, parts *BO*

*

H. Blanchard: 'Essais biographiques: I. Francesco Beck', *Revue et gazette musicale de Paris*, xii (1845), 212, 219, 225, 241

P. Courteault: *La Révolution et les théâtres de Bordeaux d'après les documents inédits* (Paris, 1926)

B. S. Carrow: *The Relationship between the Mannheim School and the Music of Franz Beck, Henri Blanchard and Pierre Gaveaux* (diss., New York U., 1956)

D. H. Foster: 'Franz Beck's Compositions for the Theater in Bordeaux', *CMc*, no.33 (1982), 7–35

PHILIPPE VENDRIX

Beck, Johann Nepomuk (*b* Budapest, 5 May 1827; *d* Bratislava, 9 April 1904). Hungarian baritone. He studied in Vienna and made his début in 1851 as the Speaker (*Die Zauberflöte*) at the Hofoper, where he was engaged from 1853 for over 30 years. He sang Don Giovanni at the opening of the new Opera (1869), Hans Sachs at the first Viennese performance of *Die Meistersinger* (1870) and Solomon in the première of Goldmark's *Die Königin von Saba* (1875). His repertory included William Tell, Pizarro, Tsar Peter (*L'étoile du nord*), Nélusko (*L'Africaine*), Rigoletto, Don Carlo (*Ernani*) and Mikéli (Cherubini's *Les deux journées*), with which he made his farewell to Vienna in 1885. He had a strong, flexible voice especially suited to French and Italian music.

ELIZABETH FORBES

Becker, Heinz (*b* Berlin, 26 June 1922). German musicologist. He studied with Vetter at the Humboldt University in Berlin, where he took the doctorate in 1951. After posts in Berlin (1951–5), he taught from 1956 to 1966 at Hamburg University, where he completed the *Habilitation* (1961), and was then professor of musicology at the Ruhr University in Bochum, retiring in 1987. Although Becker's research centres on the history of instruments, he has published many articles on the history of opera (especially on Meyerbeer and other French grand opera) and has also been general editor of the series Die Oper (Munich, 1975–).

ed.: G. Meyerbeer: *Briefwechsel und Tagebücher* (Berlin, 1960–)

ed.: *Beiträge zur Geschichte der Oper* (Regensburg, 1969)

ed.: *Die Couleur locale in der Oper des 19. Jahrhunderts* (Regensburg, 1976)

Giacomo Meyerbeer in Selbstzeugnissen und Bilddokumenten (Reinbek, 1980)

Quellentexte zur Konzeption der europäischen Oper im 17. Jahrhunderts (Kassel, 1981)

with G. Becker: *Giacomo Meyerbeer: ein Leben in Briefen* (Wilhelmshaven, 1983; Eng. trans., 1989)

HANS HEINRICH EGGEBRECHT

Becker, John J(**oseph**) (*b* Henderson, KY, 22 Jan 1886; *d* Wilmette, IL, 21 Jan 1961). American composer. He studied at the conservatories of Cincinnati (graduation, 1905) and Wisconsin (doctorate of composition, 1923). He was the only 'ultramodernist' composer associated with the American Midwest, where he held several academic and administrative appointments, including that of professor of music at Barat College in Lake Forest, Illinois (1943–57).

He wrote several pioneering multi-media stage works, but since none of them has been performed, he has had little impact on the modernization of opera. Around 1930 he came under the influence of the ultramodernists and decided that opera was outmoded, that it would be replaced by 'an entirely new form, which definitely co-ordinates all the arts – music, speaking, dancing, pantomime, and lighting'. Accordingly, he abandoned his unfinished operas *The City of Shagpat* (1926–7) and *Salome* (1931). From 1932 to 1943 he worked on *The Life of Man*, a 'polytechnic drama' using light, colour, sound, solo and group dance, dramatization and large orchestra. Though incomplete, it is notable for its abstract dramatic character and opening musical gesture of forearm clusters played on pianos placed around the audience.

Becker's most important completed stage work is *A Marriage with Space* (1933–5). In this hour-long 'drama in color, light, and sound', Emanuel Savoir, an architect, struggles against his regressive social environment in his effort to build a perfect 'city of the future'. The music is dissonant and transcendental in style with a prominent trumpet solo; the poem is spoken over the music, and indications are given for abstract choreography. The score includes material from Becker's Third Symphony, his most widely played composition.

In 1945 Becker wrote the one-act opera *Deirdre of the Sorrows* and in 1951 *Faust*, a 'television opera in the form of a monodrama' for tenor and piano; neither work was orchestrated. The one-act satire *Privilege and Privation* sets pompous Privilege against a group of tramps; the piece is a sharp-tongued critique of Depression-era economics.

The City of Shagpat [Almerle], 1926–7 (tragic oriental op, 3, Becker, after G. Meredith), inc.
Salome, *c*1931 (cinema op, 1, Becker), inc.
A Marriage with Space [Stagework no.3], 1933–5 (drama, M. Turbyfill), unperf.
Privilege and Privation, 1939 (1, A. Kreymborg), Amsterdam, 22 June 1982
The Life of Man [Stagework no.4], 1932–43 (polytechnic drama, after L. Andreiev), inc.
Deirdre of the Sorrows [Stagework no.6], 1945 (1, Becker, after J. M. Synge), unperf., unorchd
Faust, 1951 (television op, J. W. von Goethe, trans. B. Taylor), Los Angeles, 8 April 1965, unorchd
The Queen of Cornwall, 1956 (after T. Hardy), inc.

*

D. Gillespie: *John Becker: Midwestern Musical Crusader* (Ann Arbor, 1977)

KYLE GANN

Beckmann, Judith (*b* Jamestown, ND, 10 May 1935). American soprano. She studied in Los Angeles and with Lotte Lehmann in Santa Barbara. A Fulbright scholarship took her to study in Hamburg with Henny Wolff and in Düsseldorf with Franziska Martienssen-Lohmann; she made her stage début at Brunswick in 1962 as Fiordiligi. She became a member of the Deutsche Oper am Rhein, Düsseldorf, in 1964 and the Hamburg Staatsoper in 1967, also appearing at other leading German theatres, with débuts as Marguerite (*Faust*) at San Francisco, Violetta and other roles at the Vienna Staatsoper in 1973–4, and Tatyana at Covent Garden in 1974. Her well-produced lyric soprano is allied to a fine stage presence. Perhaps her finest role is the Marschallin, which she sang at Munich in 1990. She has taught at the Hamburg Musikhochschule.

NOËL GOODWIN

Beckwith, John (*b* Victoria, BC, 9 March 1927). Canadian composer. He studied with Alberto Guerrero in Toronto (1945–50) and Nadia Boulanger in Paris (1950–52), then joined the music faculty of Toronto University (1952), where he served as Dean from 1970 to 1977. From 1984 to his retirement in 1990 he was professor of Canadian music and director of the faculty's Institute for Canadian Music. A founder-member in 1951 of the Canadian League of Composers, he was also a regular broadcaster on CBC radio (1956–65) and music critic for the *Toronto Star* (1959–62, 1963–5). His compositional output is extensive and varied, and includes three operas. *Night Blooming Cereus*, commissioned by the CBC and begun in 1953 to a libretto by the Ontario writer James Reaney, was completed in 1958. It was given its radio première in 1959 and staged in Toronto the following year in a production by Beckwith's wife, the actress Pamela Terry. Like many of Beckwith's chamber pieces from the 1950s, it has a clarity reminiscent of Stravinsky. After receiving a Canada Council fellowship in 1965 Beckwith began work on *The Shivaree*, and in 1988 he completed *Crazy to Kill*, which was commissioned by the Guelph Spring Festival.

Beckwith's interest in Canadian music history resulted in his reconstruction (1989–90) of Quesnel's comic opera *Lucus et Cécile*. He was appointed a member of the Order of Canada in 1987.

Night Blooming Cereus (chamber op, 1, J. Reaney), CBC radio, 4 March 1959; stage, Toronto, Hart House, 5 April 1960
The Shivaree, 1978 (chamber op, 2, Reaney), Toronto, St Lawrence Centre, 3 April 1982
Crazy to Kill (detective op, 1, Reaney, after A. Cardwell), Guelph, Ont., 11 May 1989

*

EMC (I. Anhalt, K. Winters)

KEITH MACMILLAN/R

Bedford, Steuart (John Rudolf) (*b* London, 31 July 1939). English conductor. He studied at the RAM and while an organ scholar at Worcester College, Oxford, conducted university productions of *Albert Herring* and *The Consul*. In 1965–6 he joined the Glyndebourne music staff, and in 1967 the English Opera Group, with which he made his conducting début that year in *The Beggar's Opera* at Sadler's Wells Theatre. In 1965 he became a professor at the RAM and conductor of the opera class; there he conducted his own version of *L'incoronazione di Poppea* in 1969 (which he discussed in *Opera*, xx, 1969, pp. 94–100) and gave the first modern British performances of Donizetti's *Belisario* as an RAM centenary production (1972). Bedford conducted the première of Gardner's *The Visitors* (Aldeburgh Festival, 1972) and the first stage performances of *Owen Wingrave* (Covent Garden, 1973); he was widely praised for his preparation, conducting and recording of *Death in Venice* (Aldeburgh, 1973), of which he conducted many later performances at Covent Garden and on tour abroad as well as the first USA production, at the Metropolitan Opera in 1974 (his American début). In December 1973 he was appointed an artistic director of the Aldeburgh Festival, and in 1975 joint artistic director of the English Music Theatre Company, for which he conducted the première of Stephen Oliver's *Tom Jones* in 1976, and the first British production of *Paul Bunyan*. His later freelance work has included numerous performances of Britten's operas across the world.

NOËL GOODWIN

Bedini, Domenico (*b* ?Fossombrone, *c*1745; *d* after 1795). Italian soprano castrato. His career began intermittently in comic opera at Pesaro (1762) and Rome (1764), and as secondo uomo in *opera seria* at Venice (1768). In 1770–71 he was secondo uomo in five Italian houses and then entered the service of the Munich court, resuming his career in Italy in 1776 and soon becoming primo uomo in leading houses. He is mostly remembered as the first Sextus in Mozart's *La clemenza di Tito* (1791, Prague). He retired after singing at Florence in Carnival 1792 and by 1795 was in the *cappella* of the S Casa of Loreto in his native region.

DENNIS LIBBY

Beecham, Sir **Thomas** (*b* St Helens, Lancs., 29 April 1879; *d* London, 8 March 1961). English conductor. He studied composition privately in London and Paris, but as a conductor was self-taught, making the most of easy circumstances (his father, Sir Joseph Beecham, was a successful manufacturing chemist with a fondness for music) to attend opera and concerts. A career of prodigious enterprise began with the founding in 1909 of the Beecham SO, which gave adventurous concerts, toured, and played for opera and ballet. Beecham then embarked upon a period of intensive operatic activity at Covent Garden, His Majesty's and Drury Lane; in 1910 alone there were three London seasons, with Strauss and Bruno Walter among the guest conductors. He presented a number of operas new to Britain, including works by Russian composers, and by Strauss, Delius, Smyth, Stanford and Holbrooke, and he was also responsible for the first appearances in London of Dyagilev's Ballets Russes. In 1915 he formed with mainly British singers the Beecham Opera Company (*see* LONDON, §II, 1), which performed in London and the provinces; the latter (Manchester especially) owed to Beecham a significant widening of operatic experience. Joint Covent Garden seasons with the Grand Opera Syndicate followed in 1919 and 1920, but by now Beecham's financial affairs were such that he had to withdraw temporarily from musical life to put them in order. During the decade after his return in 1923, he attempted, unsuccessfully, to establish an Imperial League of Opera to be financed from private subscriptions, mounted a Russian opera season at the Lyceum Theatre, London (1931), and made various visits abroad.

In 1932, dissatisfied as usual with orchestral conditions in Britain and goaded by the inception of the BBC SO, Beecham formed the LPO, bringing it swiftly to the front rank. The Beecham Opera Company had in 1922 become the BRITISH NATIONAL OPERA COMPANY (not under Beecham's direction). This was absorbed in 1929 by Covent Garden, where Beecham returned in 1932 as artistic director. From 1935 until the theatre was closed at the outbreak of war in 1939 he was in sole control, inviting a number of distinguished guest conductors to the house, and himself conducting several *Ring* cycles among many other works. In 1940 he went to New York and, until his return to Britain in 1944, spent the war years mainly in the USA (he conducted at the Metropolitan in 1942 and 1943). At home in 1946 he created yet another orchestra, the RPO, and in 1951 returned to Covent Garden as guest conductor for *Die Meistersinger*. He conducted the première of Delius's *Irmelin* at Oxford in 1953. His last operatic performances were given at the Teatro Colón in Buenos Aires in 1958.

This dynamic, restless founder of orchestras and planner of opera seasons was described by Richard Capell as 'the most gifted executive musician England has ever produced'. During the first part of his career Beecham did more than anyone to foster the appreciation of Mozart's operas in England: three were included in his 1910 season at His Majesty's, among them the almost unknown *Così fan tutte*. He conducted the first British performances of *Salome*, *Elektra*, *Der Rosenkavalier* and *Ariadne auf Naxos*. A particular fondness for the music of his friend Delius made him a unique interpreter of the composer's work. Unfortunately, he had too little opportunity to show his affection for French opera, from Méhul to Massenet.

Beecham was knighted in 1916, succeeded to the baronetcy on his father's death in the same year, and was made a Companion of Honour in 1957. He wrote an autobiography, *A Mingled Chime* (London, 1944/*R*1976 as *The Lyric Stage*) and a book on Delius (London, 1958, 2/1975). His few complete opera recordings have always been much admired: they include the 1937 *Die Zauberflöte* made in Berlin with a German cast; the 1956 *La bohème* with Victoria de Los Angeles and Jussi Björling; and the *Carmen* of 1958–9 with de Los Angeles and Nicolai Gedda.

See also LONDON, §I, 10.

B. Shore: *The Orchestra Speaks* (London, 1938)
'List of Operas Conducted and/or Produced by Sir Thomas Beecham in England, 1910–1953', *Opera*, x (1959), 285–7
R. Capell: Obituary, *MT*, cii (1961), 283
N. Cardus: *Sir Thomas Beecham: a Memoir* (London, 1961)
Sir Thomas Beecham Discography (El Cerrito, CA, 1975)
A. Jefferson: *Sir Thomas Beecham: a Centenary Tribute* (London, 1979)
W. Legge: 'Sir Thomas', *Opera*, xxx (1979), 428–34, 536–44, 650–58

RONALD CRICHTON

Beecham Opera Company. Company organized in London by Thomas Beecham during World War I; *see* LONDON, §II, 1. In 1922 it became the BRITISH NATIONAL OPERA COMPANY.

Beecke, (Notger) Ignaz (Franz) von (*b* Wimpfen am Neckar, 28 Oct 1733; *d* Wallerstein, 2 Jan 1803). German composer. He served as a military officer early in the Seven Years War, possibly coming into contact with Dittersdorf; eventually Gluck became his teacher and model. In 1759 he arrived in Wallerstein, near Nördlingen, and was taken up as a courtier by Count Philipp Karl of Oettingen-Wallerstein, who maintained a small musical band. Beecke acquired increasing esteem as pianist and music director in Wallerstein, and was continually promoted; his journeys to Vienna, Paris and elsewhere brought far-reaching contacts and valuable stimuli to the small Swabian court.

Beecke first attracted attention as a composer in Paris in 1767; several years later a Parisian première of the opera *Roland*, which he had been encouraged to complete in Vienna in 1770 by Gluck and Hasse, was thwarted by intrigues between Mme Dubarry and Marie-Antoinette. For the German company at the Vienna Burgtheater Beecke wrote *Claudine von Villa Bella* (1780), which, despite a strong cast, was withdrawn after only two performances. In Mannheim in 1782 the Intendant Wolfgang Heribert von Dalberg had Beecke's *Die Jubelhochzeit* and *Die Weinlese* performed, although a planned performance of his setting of Klopstock's *Hermannschlacht* was not realized. In all he composed several stage works, as well as sacred, orchestral, chamber and keyboard music.

See also CLAUDINE VON VILLA BELLA (i).

Roland (after L. Ariosto), Paris, after 1770
Claudine von Villa Bella (Schauspiel mit Gesang, 1, J. W. von Goethe), Vienna, Burg, 13 June 1780, *A-Wn*

Die Jubelhochzeit (komische Oper, 3, C. F. Weisse), Mannheim, National, 9 June 1782
Die Weinlese (Spl, 2, W. C. D. Meyer, after Weisse), Mannheim, National, 10 Dec 1782
Don Quixotte (Spl, 3, H. Soden), 1784
List gegen List [Die Glocke] (Spl, Soden), ?*c*1785
Das Herz behält seine Rechte (Spl), Mainz, 1790
Nina (Spl, H. Spaur), Aschaffenburg, Hof, 1790
Die zerstörte Hirtenfeier (Pastorale, Spaur), Aschaffenburg, Hof, 1790

*

GerberL; *GerberNL*; *StiegerO*
F. J. Lipowsky: *Baierisches Musik-Lexikon* (Munich, 1811)
L. Schiedermair: 'Die Blütezeit der Öttingen-Wallersteins'chen Hofkapelle', *SIMG*, ix (1907–8), 83–130, esp. 107ff
E. F. Schmid: 'Ignaz von Beecke', *Lebensbilder aus dem bayerischen Schwaben*, i, ed. G. F. von Pölnitz (Munich, 1952), 343–64
ADOLF LAYER/THOMAS BAUMAN

Beer-Walbrunn, Anton (*b* Kohlberg, Bavaria, 29 June 1864; *d* Munich, 22 March 1929). German composer and teacher. He came from a family of schoolteachers and received his first musical instruction from his father, who however refused to let him make his career as a musician. He taught in Amberg and Eichstätt, where he was also cathedral organist. He later studied music in Munich, where he was a composition pupil of Rheinberger and where, for a decade, he was active as a freelance composer and teacher. From 1901 he taught at the Akademie der Tonkunst, and among his pupils there were Furtwängler and Einstein.

Beer-Walbrunn's compositions show a mixture of conservatism and new elements, and often have a folk-like quality, but they never achieved widespread acclaim. He was at his best in his chamber music and settings of Shakespeare's sonnets. Among his operas, the tragicomedy *Don Quijote* was the most successful. He also wrote incidental music to Shakespeare's *Hamlet* and *The Tempest*.

Die Sühne (tragische Oper, 2, Beer-Walbrunn, after T. Körner: *Liebe*), Lübeck, 16 Feb 1894, vs (Berlin, 1896); rev. *c*1910
Don Quijote (musikalische Tragikomödie, 3, G. Fuchs, after M. de Cervantes), Munich, 1 Jan 1908, vs (Munich, 1911)
Das Ungeheuer (musikalisches Lustspiel, 1, after A. P. Chekhov), Karlsruhe, 25 April 1914

*

NDB (A. Ott)
O. G. Sonneck: 'Anton Beer-Walbrunn', *Suum cuique* (New York, 1916), 155 [with complete list of works]
A. Beer-Walbrunn: Autobiography in *Neue Musikzeitung*, xxxviii (1917), 20–22, 38–9
W. Zentner: 'Anton Beer-Walbrunn', *NZM*, cviii (1941), 154–8
L. Schiedermair: *Musikalische Begegnungen* (Cologne and Krefeld, 1948)
GAYNOR G. JONES

Beeson, Jack (Hamilton) (*b* Muncie, IN, 15 July 1921). American composer and teacher. He attended the Eastman School as a pupil of Burrill Phillips, Bernard Rogers and Howard Hanson, and had private lessons with Bartók in New York (1944–5). In 1945 he began to teach at Columbia University, where he was also an accompanist and conductor for the opera workshop; he became MacDowell Professor of Music in 1967, lectured at the Juilliard School (1961–3) and other universities and has received the Marc Blitzstein Award for the Musical Theater (1968).

Beeson's operas may be considered to have some of the qualities of those of Douglas Moore, one of his predecessors at Columbia. Though his style is of a later generation, it shares with Moore's a feeling for lyrical line, occasionally suggesting an American folk idiom; and Beeson too has shaped successful opera subjects from American life and literature. The principal features of Beeson's operatic style have been maintained consistently throughout his career. In *Hello out There* (1953) his characters 'take on a real musical identity', as one critic has put it, and his orchestral writing supports them with atmospheric music; twelve years later, in *Lizzie Borden*, the aptitude for vocal characterization and orchestral atmosphere again shows itself. In *Captain Jinks* (1975) he exploits the 'period' charm of traditional opera forms just as he did earlier with that of evangelical hymns and flapper dances in *The Sweet Bye and Bye* (1957). Beeson borrows from a variety of sources – popular songs, folksong and dance, jazz, Italian opera – to enrich the musical and dramatic background; any theatrical work that lasts for two hours, Beeson has said, ought to have some range of style. He has expressed satisfaction with Nicolas Slonimsky's characterization of his style as 'marked by enlightened utilitarianism'.

See also LIZZIE BORDEN.

Jonah, 1950 (2 or 3, Beeson, after P. Goodman)
Hello out There (chamber op, 1, Beeson, after W. Saroyan), New York, Brander Matthews, 27 May 1954, vs (New York, 1960)
The Sweet Bye and Bye (2, K. Elmslie), New York, Juilliard Concert Hall, 21 Nov 1957, vs (New York, 1966)
Lizzie Borden (family portrait, 3, Elmslie, after R. Plant), New York, City Center of Music and Drama, 25 March 1965, vs (New York, 1967)
My Heart's in the Highlands (chamber op, 2 or 3, Beeson, after Saroyan), NET, 17 March 1970; stage, New York, Columbia U., Miller, 25 Oct 1988, vs (New York, 1973)
Captain Jinks of the Horse Marines (romantic comedy in music, 3, S. Harnick, after C. Fitch), Kansas City, Lyric, 20 Sept 1975, vs (New York, 1983)
Dr Heidegger's Fountain of Youth (chamber op, 1, Harnick, after N. Hawthorne), New York, National Arts Club, 17 Nov 1978, vs (New York, 1978)
Cyrano, 1990 (heroic comedy in music, 3, Harnick, after E. Rostand)

*

Q. Eaton: *Opera Production: a Handbook* (St Paul, 1961–74) [entries on *Hello out There*, *The Sweet Bye and Bye*, *Lizzie Borden* and *My Heart's in the Highlands*]
D. Johns: 'Connections: an Interview with Jack Beeson', *Music Educators Journal*, lxvi/2 (1979), 44–9
J. Beeson: 'The Autobiography of *Lizzie Borden*', *OQ*, iv/1 (1986–7), 15–42
R. H. Kornick: *Recent American Opera: a Production Guide* (New York, 1991), 53–7
HOWARD SHANET

Beethoven, Ludwig van (*b* Bonn, bap. 17 Dec 1770; *d* Vienna, 26 March 1827). German composer. He lived for 21 years in Bonn, where his father and grandfather served as musicians at the court of the Electorate of Cologne. He was already composing by the age of 11. By 1784 he held an official appointment as organist, assisting his teacher Christian Gottlob Neefe. His first-hand experience with opera probably began when he joined the court orchestra as a viola player in 1789. In his last Bonn years he wrote his first music related to the theatre: two arias for bass, an aria for soprano and the *Ritterballett*, a set of seven short dances in old German costume that was performed at a court entertainment in March 1791. It is not known whether the three vocal pieces were performed.

At the end of 1792 Beethoven went to Vienna to study with Joseph Haydn. He remained there for the rest of his life. During his first five years in Vienna he made his reputation as a pianist, and it was primarily music for the piano – sonatas, variations, a variety of chamber works and two concertos – that occupied him as a composer. This began to change in the late 1790s. He wrote three string trios, six quartets and finally his First Symphony, which was performed in his first important concert, in 1800. As his fame grew, so did his ambition. In the winter of 1800–01 he completed a large and successful ballet, *Die Geschöpfe des Prometheus*; two years later, in 1802–3, he wrote an oratorio, *Christus am Oelberge*. And during 1803 he began work on his first opera. The libretto was *Vestas Feuer* by Emanuel Schikaneder, who a dozen years earlier had written *Die Zauberflöte* for Mozart and was now director of the Theater an der Wien (where Beethoven took up residence).

Beethoven had been preparing for this commission. Already in 1795 or 1796 he had written a few individual operatic numbers: two arias for the Singspiel *Die schöne Schusterin* (by Ignaz Umlauf) and a scena and aria, 'Ah! perfido', on a text by Metastasio. Apparently he felt he needed more study, however, for he then went to Antonio Salieri, probably in 1801–3, for lessons in the setting of Italian texts. The result was a collection of brief studies, culminating in three large movements that were composed (with much sketching) in 1802–3: a scena and aria (to words by Metastasio) for soprano and strings, 'No, non turbarti', and two ensembles with orchestra, the duet 'Ne' giorni tuoi felici' (Metastasio) and the trio 'Tremate, empi, tremate' (Bettoni). At about the same time he worked through the article on recitative from J. G. Sulzer's *Allgemeine Theorie der schönen Künste*. And finally he copied out extended ensemble passages from operas by Mozart, Salieri and Cherubini.

It was time for an opera of his own, but Beethoven seems to have applied himself only half-heartedly to *Vestas Feuer*. Most of his energy in 1803 went into two large instrumental works, the Symphony no. 3 (*Sinfonia eroica*) and the Piano Sonata op.53 ('Waldstein'). By the end of the year he had completed only the first scene of the opera, consisting of two short duets, a transition and a trio (the music of the trio was later used in *Fidelio*). The libretto could not have inspired him. *Vestas Feuer* is set in ancient Rome, but Schikaneder's drama preserves little of the elevated style of classical tragedy that had sustained the operas of Gluck and the many settings of Metastasio. Nor does it combine its classical setting effectively with a newer kind of dramatic action; a few years later *La vestale* would rekindle the vestal flame more convincingly.

In 1803 an attractive alternative existed in the so-called rescue operas of Cherubini and his French contemporaries, which were much in vogue in Paris and had just achieved enormous success in Vienna. These operas had melodramatic plots of bravery in the face of political oppression – an obviously contemporary theme even when the locale and time were shifted to avoid problems with the censors – and they celebrated the virtue of common people. When the opportunity to set a libretto of this sort presented itself in the winter of 1803–4, Beethoven seized it. He set aside *Vestas Feuer* and took up *Léonore, ou L'amour conjugal*. The author was J. N. Bouilly, who had also written the libretto of Cherubini's *Les deux journées*.

The long and complex history of *Leonore*, which became *Fidelio* in Beethoven's setting, is described in detail in the separate entry for the opera. Beethoven worked at it throughout 1804 and the first half of 1805. The première was on 20 November 1805. It was not successful, and the opera was withdrawn after the third performance. Small changes were made in both the libretto and the music, and two performances of the revised version occurred on 29 March and 10 April 1806. *Fidelio* then left the stage for eight years, until 1814, when a more extensively revised third version was performed with greater success; it is in this third version that the opera has survived, though in our century the *Fidelio* (*Leonore*) of 1805 has occasionally been revived.

The story of Beethoven's involvement with opera after 1805 is one of reluctance and frustration. He searched more or less continuously for an acceptable libretto, but nothing offered to him fired his imagination more than briefly. Of his many attempts to establish a working relationship with a librettist, he came closest to success with Heinrich von Collin in 1808–11 and Franz Grillparzer in 1823–6.

The possibility of a collaboration with Collin was raised by three events of 1807: Beethoven's composition of an overture to Collin's play *Coriolan*, a much-discussed revival of *Iphigénie en Tauride* and other operas by Gluck, and some performances of Shakespeare's *Macbeth* in a translation by Schiller. Collin offered Beethoven the first act of a *Macbeth* libretto, and in sketchbooks of 1808 and 1811 Beethoven made a couple of entries concerning the opening chorus (including the comment 'Overture Macbeth leads directly into the chorus of witches'). But the project went no further. Collin died in 1811 with *Macbeth* still a fragment. Through procrastination, Beethoven also lost Collin's completed *Bradamante* (to J. F. Reichardt, whose setting was finished in 1809).

In 1823 Beethoven discussed several subjects with Franz Grillparzer. One was *Drahomira*, drawn from Bohemian legendary history. Grillparzer had already drafted parts of a libretto, but Beethoven evidently was not interested. His preference was for *Melusine*, which Grillparzer proceeded to write for him at great speed. A contract with the Kärntnertortheater may have been signed that same year. Beethoven kept the libretto until 1826, when he finally returned it with the excuse that it was too similar to the *Undine* (1816) of E. T. A. Hoffmann and Fouqué. Although he had assured Grillparzer at various times that the opera was well underway, even finished, in fact no sketches for it have survived. (*Melusine* was later set by Konradin Kreutzer in 1833.)

An extensive list of other aborted operatic projects can be compiled from Beethoven's correspondence and 'conversation books' and from the reminiscences of people who knew him. Some references, such as those to *Faust* and *Claudine von Villa Bella* (also by Goethe, and the source for one of Beethoven's Bonn arias), have a particular fascination. For reasons never fully understood, he found it easy to contemplate these projects and hard to commit himself to them. His own critical remarks about various librettos are often at odds with what we know of his activities. It is hard, for example, to reconcile his expressed aversion to the use of magic or the supernatural with the list of librettos that he considered seriously; *Vestas Feuer* was thus tainted, as were *Macbeth*, *Bradamante* and *Melusine* (not to mention *Faust*). Beethoven was grimly high-minded about opera. He found no merit in Rossini, and he was unnerved by the moral ambiguities in the operas Mozart wrote with Da Ponte. But his high-mindedness with respect to operatic subjects evidently did not extend to theatrical productions of other kinds, where he was content to associate himself with material that was decidedly second-rate.

On six occasions between 1807 and 1822 Beethoven provided music for a stage work in which he had no controlling hand. On the first two such occasions the results were impressive. These were the overture he supplied for Collin's *Coriolan* in 1807 and the more extended incidental music for Goethe's *Egmont* in 1810. But he must have found *König Stephan* and *Die Ruinen von Athen*(1811), *Tarpeja* (1813), *Leonore Prohaska* (1815) and *Die Weihe des Hauses* (1822) rewarding for financial rather than dramatic reasons. The overtures he wrote for *King Stephan*, *The Ruins of Athens* and *The Consecration of the House* (as they are known in English) are still often played as concert pieces. But the other movements (except perhaps the 'Marcia alla Turca' from *The Ruins of Athens*) remain largely unknown. The same is true of single movements he composed in 1814 and 1815 for two pasticcio Singspiels by G. F. Treitschke (both are finales, 'Germania' for *Die gute Nachricht* and 'Es ist vollbracht' for *Die Ehrenpforten*). Because this music was not written for accomplished singers, most of it is only incidentally operatic, comprising choruses and marches rather than arias and ensembles.

Throughout the 18th century opera held a central position in European musical life, offering to the successful composer greater fame and fortune than he might achieve in any other genre. This was still true in Beethoven's time, despite the growing importance of instrumental music. It is not surprising, therefore, that Beethoven should have been attracted to opera, and that in 1807, after the failure of *Fidelio*, he should have offered to compose an opera every year in exchange for a fixed income. But neither is it surprising, in view of his general irascibility and, from the time of *Fidelio* onwards, his progressive loss of hearing, that he should have found it difficult to accept the compromises and manage the personal relationships that are required in the production of opera. Indeed it is strange to contemplate what course an opera by Beethoven might have taken after 1814, when his deafness effectively ended his own performing career. Grillparzer, his most promising collaborator in the 1820s, evidently had doubts:

> Once I had the idea of writing a libretto ... I began to doubt if Beethoven, who meanwhile had become completely deaf and whose latest compositions without detracting from their high worth possessed a quality of harshness, who seemed to be in conflict with the treatment of the singing voice, – I doubted, I say, if Beethoven was still capable of composing an opera.

On the harshness of Beethoven's late style, Grillparzer continued:

> I also did not want to give Beethoven the opportunity to step still closer to the extreme limits of music which lay nearby, threatening like precipices, in partnership with material that was semi-diabolical.

The extreme limits of music have been redrawn many times since 1827, of course, but Grillparzer's caution still sounds sensible. And his explanation that he agreed to the collaboration in order to 'give a great man the opportunity for a work which would be at any rate of the first interest' still sounds generous, even inspired. That the great man himself sensed limits of a different sort leaves us free to imagine what a late opera might have sounded like. As for a *Macbeth* or a *Faust* from the time of the Fifth Symphony or the F minor Quartet, these live in a world whose sounds will lie for ever just outside earshot.

The best introduction to the subject of Beethoven and opera remains Winton Dean's essay in *The Beethoven Companion*. A more detailed study is provided in Willy Hess's *Das Fidelio-Buch*, which includes the complete libretto of Bouilly's *Léonore*, Paer's *Leonora* (Italian and German) and the 1805 *Fidelio*. The fragment of *Vestas Feuer* and the 1805 and 1806 versions of *Fidelio* have been published by Hess in his supplementary volumes to the old complete edition of Beethoven's works.

See also FIDELIO.

Editions: *L. van Beethovens Werke: Vollständige kritisch durchgesehene überall berechtigte Ausgabe*, i–xxiv (Leipzig, 1862–5), xxv [suppl.] (Leipzig, 1888) [GA]
L. van Beethoven: Sämtliche Werke: Supplemente zur Gesamtausgabe, ed. W. Hess (Wiesbaden, 1959–71) [HS]

no.	*title*	*libretto*	*composition; first performance*	*publication; remarks*	*GA; HS*
Hess 15	Vestas Feuer	E. Schikaneder	1803	(Wiesbaden, 1953); frag.	–; xiii
op.72	Fidelio [Leonore, oder Der Triumph der ehelichen Liebe]	J. Sonnleithner, after J. N. Bouilly: *Léonore, ou L'amour conjugal*	1st version (with Leonore ov. no.2), 1804–5; Vienna, Theater an der Wien, 20 Nov 1805	vs (Leipzig, 1905), (Leipzig, 1908–10) [private edn]; see also FIDELIO, Table 1	–; ii, xi–xiii
			2nd version (with Leonore ov. no.3), 1805–6; Vienna, Theater an der Wien, 29 March 1806	vs (Leipzig), 1810; 3 nos. pubd separately (Vienna, 1807)	–; xi–xiii
			final version (with 'Fidelio' ov.), 1814; Vienna, Kärntnertor, 23 May 1814	vs (Vienna, 1814); in Fr. (Paris, 1826); in Ger. (Bonn, 1847)	xx/206; –

Music in: I. Umlauff: Die schöne Schusterin, Vienna, ? 1795–6; Die gute Nachricht [finale] (Spl, G. F. Treitschke), Vienna, Kärntnertor, 11 April 1814; Die Ehrenpforten [finale] (Spl, Treitschke), Vienna, Kärntnertor, 15 July 1815

FIDELIO (LEONORE)

H. Berlioz: *A travers chants* (Paris, 1862), 65–82 [article written in 1860]

O. Jahn: 'Leonore oder Fidelio?', *Gesammelte Aufsätze über Musik* (Leipzig, 1866), 236–59 [repr. from *AMZ*, new ser., i (1863)]

G. Nottebohm: *Beethoveniana* (Leipzig and Winterthur, 1872, 2/1925), 60–78, 82–99

——: *Zweite Beethoveniana*, ed. E. Mandyczewski (Leipzig, 1887, 2/1925) [7 articles]

A. Levinssohn: 'Die Entstehungszeit der Ouvertüre zu Leonore Nr. 1 Op.138, mit anschliessenden kritischen Bemerkungen zu Nottebohm's Beethoveniana', *VMw*, ix (1893), 128–65

M. Hehemann: 'Leonore: die erste Fassung des "Fidelio"', *Die Musik*, v/1 (1905–6), 227–37

J.-G. Prod'homme: 'Léonore ou l'amour conjugal, de Bouilly et Gaveaux (à propos du centénaire de Fidelio)', *SIMG*, vii (1905–6), 636–9

L. Schiedermair: 'Über Beethovens "Leonore"', *ZIMG*, viii (1907), 115–26

A. Seidl: '"Leonoren"-Fragen', *Die Musik*, xi/2 (1911–12), 21–35

E. Istel: 'Beethoven's "Leonore" and "Fidelio"', *MQ*, vii (1921), 226–51

A. Heuss: 'Die Humanitätsmelodien im Fidelio', *ZfM*, xci (1924), 545–52

A. Sandberger: 'Léonore von Bouilly und ihre Bearbeitung für Beethoven durch Joseph Sonnleithner', *Ausgewählte Aufsätze zur Musikgeschichte*, ii (Munich, 1924), 141–53, 283–365

W. von Waltershausen: 'Zur Dramaturgie des Fidelio', *NBJb*, i (1924), 142–58

A. Schmitz: 'Cherubinis Einfluss auf Beethovens Ouvertüren', *NBJb*, ii (1925), 104–18

J. Braunstein: 'Gibt es zwei Fassungen von der Ouvertüre Leonore Nr.2?', *ZMw*, ix (1926–7), 349–60

H. Abert: 'Fidelio', *Beethoven-Almanach der deutschen Musikbücherei auf das Jahr 1927*, ed. G. Bosse (Regensburg, 1927), 304–19

J. Braunstein: *Beethovens Leonore-Ouvertüren* (Leipzig, 1927)

F. Cortolezis: 'Gedanken über eine stilgerechte Aufführung des "Fidelio"', *NBJb*, iii (1927), 91–102

R. Rolland: *Beethoven: les grandes époques créatrices I* (Paris, 1928 [many later edns], Eng. trans., 1929)

R. Engländer: 'Paërs "Leonora" und Beethovens "Fidelio"', *NBJb*, iv (1930), 118–32

M. Unger: 'Zur Entstehungs- und Aufführungsgeschichte von Beethovens Oper "Leonore"', *ZfM*, cv (1938), 130–39

J. Boyer: 'La Rivoluzione francese nel "Fidelio"', *RMI*, xliv (1940), 243–6

B. A. Wallner: 'Fidelio in Gotik und Barock', *NBJb*, x (1942), 78–103

A. Capri: '"Don Giovanni" e "Fidelio"', *RMI*, xlvii (1943), 188–211

M. Brunswick: 'Beethoven's Tribute to Mozart in Fidelio', *MQ*, xxxi (1945), 29–32

R. Steglich: 'Das melodische Hauptmotiv in Beethovens "Fidelio"', *AMw*, ix (1952), 51–67

W. Hess: *Beethovens Oper Fidelio und ihre drei Fassungen* (Zürich, 1953); enlarged as *Das Fidelio-Buch* (Winterthur, 1986)

K. Kobald: 'Eine Sternstunde der Menschheit: die Entstehung von Beethovens "Fidelio"', *ÖMz*, viii (1953), 131–8

W. Fürtwangler: 'Die Ouvertüren des "Fidelio"', *Ton und Wort* (Wiesbaden, 1954), 171–4 [written 1942]

R. M. Longyear: 'Notes on the Rescue Opera', *MQ*, xlv (1959), 49–66

E. Schenk: 'Salieris "Landsturm"-Kantate von 1799 in ihren Beziehungen zu Beethovens "Fidelio"', *Colloquium amicorum: Joseph Schmidt-Görg zum 70. Geburtstag* (Bonn, 1967), 338–54

W. Dean: 'Opera under the French Revolution', *PRMA*, xciv (1967–8), 77–96

W. Osthoff: 'Zum dramatischen Charakter der zweiten und dritten Leonoren-Ouvertüre und Beethovenscher Theatermusik allgemein', *Beiträge zur Geschichte der Oper*, ed. H. Becker (Regensburg, 1969), 11–24

A. Tyson: 'Beethoven's Heroic Phase', *MT*, cx (1969), 139–41

Internationaler Beethoven-Kongress: Berlin 1970, 249–99 [incl. J. Rudolph: 'Realismus und Antizipation in Werken Ludwig van Beethoven: zur Weckselwirkung der Künste am Beispiel der "Egmont"-Musik und des "Fidelio"-Problems in Shakespeares "Cymbeline"', 249–68; B. Jarustowski: 'Zum Problem der Entstehung des "Fidelio"', 269–74; H. Pischner: 'Zur Interpretation des "Fidelio"', 275–82; G. Kraft: 'Quellenstudien zur thematischen Konzeption des "Fidelio"', 283–90; K.-H. Viertel: 'Beethovens Oper "Leonore"', 291–300]

Internationaler musikwissenschaftlicher Kongress: Bonn 1970 [incl. W. Osthoff: 'Beethovens "Leonoren"-Arie', 191–9; H. Schmidt: 'Ein wiederaufgefundenes "Fidelio"-Libretto', 555–7]

E. Schenk: 'Über Tonsymbolik in Beethovens "Fidelio"', *Beethoven-Studien* (Vienna, 1970), 223–52

W. Dean: 'Beethoven and Opera', *The Beethoven Companion*, ed. D. Arnold and N. Fortune (London, 1971, and as *The Beethoven Reader*, New York, 1971), 331–86; repr. in Dean: *Essays on Opera* (Oxford, 1990), 123–63

R. Kramer: 'Beethoven and Carl Heinrich Graun', *Beethoven Studies 1*, ed. A. Tyson (New York, 1973), 18–44

M. Ruhnke: 'Die Librettisten des Fidelio', *Opernstudien: Anna Amalie Abert zum 65. Geburtstag* (Tutzing, 1975), 121–40

A. Tyson: 'The Problem of Beethoven's "First" *Leonore* Overture', *JAMS*, xxviii (1975), 292–334

E. Wellesz: 'Beethoven's "Fidelio" and the "Leonore" Overture no.3', *Essays on Opera and English Music in Honour of Sir Jack Westrup* (Oxford, 1975), 166–7

L'avant-scène opéra, no.10 (1977) [*Fidelio* issue]

O. Pulkert: 'Die Partitur der zweiten Fassung von Beethovens Oper "Leonore" in Musikarchiv des Nationaltheaters in Prag', *Internationaler Beethoven-Kongress: Berlin 1977*, 247–56

I. Singer: *Mozart & Beethoven: the Concept of Love in their Operas* (Baltimore, 1977)

A. Tyson: 'Yet Another "Leonore" Overture?', *ML*, lviii (1977), 192–203

——: 'Das Leonoreskizzenbuch (Mendelssohn 15): Probleme der Rekonstruktion und der Chronologie', *BeJb*, ix (1977), 469–99

R. W. Wade: 'Beethoven's Eroica Sketchbook', *FAM*, xxiv (1977), 254–89

M. Carner: *Major and Minor* (London, 1980), 186–252

N. John, ed.: *Fidelio*, ENO Opera Guide, iv (London, 1980)

A. Csampi and D. Holland, eds.: *Fidelio: Texte, Materialen, Kommentare* (Hamburg, 1981)

W. Hess: *Beethoven: Studien zu seinem Werk* (Winterthur, 1981)

M. Schuler: 'Unveröffentlichte Briefe von Ludwig van Beethoven und Georg Friedrich Treitschke: zur dritten Fassung des "Fidelio"', *Mf*, xxxv (1982), 53–62

M. Wagner: 'Rocco: Beethovens Zeichnung eines Funktionärs', *ÖMz*, xxxvii (1982), 369–79

P. Gossett: 'The Arias of Marzelline: Beethoven as a Composer of Opera', *BeJb*, x (1983), 141–83

M. Broyles: 'Stylistic Dualism in Early Beethoven and the *Leonore* Challenge', *JM*, v (1987), 419–47

T. Albrecht: 'Beethoven's *Leonore*: a New Compositional Chronology', *JM*, vii (1989), 165–90

BEETHOVEN'S OTHER STAGE WORKS AND OPERA PLANS

F. Grandaur: 'Die Handlung des Ballets: "Die Geschöpfe des Prometheus"', *AMZ*, new ser., ii (1867), 178–9

W. Altmann: 'Zu Beethovens "Fidelio" und "Melusine"', *Die Musik*, iii/3 (1903–4), 433–7

F. Grillparzer: 'Erinnerungen an Beethoven', in *Sämtliche Werke* (Vienna, 1909–48), i, 29–37 [written *c*1844–5]

H. Riemann: 'Beethovens Prometheus-Musik: ein Variationenwerk', *Die Musik*, ix/4 (1909–10), 19–34, 107–25

R. Lach: 'Zur Geschichte der Beethovenschen "Prometheus"-Balletmusik', *ZMw*, iii (1920–21), 223–37

R. Haas: 'Zur Wiener Ballettpantomime um den Prometheus', *NBJb*, ii (1925), 84–103

R. Biberhofer: '"Vestas Feuer", Beethovens erster Opernplan', *Die Musik*, xxii (1929–30), 409–14

D. W. MacArdle: 'Beethoven and Grillparzer', *ML*, xl (1959), 44–55

W. Hess: '"Vestas Feuer" von Emanuel Schikaneder', *BeJb*, iii (1959), 63–106 [first pubn of the complete lib.]

——: *Beethovens Bühnenwerke* (Göttingen, 1962)

——: 'Das Singspiel "Die schöne Schusterin"', *BeJb*, iv (1962), 143–86

——: 'Tarpeja', *BeJb*, v (1966), 92–147

——: 'Zwei patriotische Singspiele von Friedrich Treitschke', *BeJb*, vi (1969), 269–320

P. Mies: 'Beethoven–Collin–Shakespeare: zur Coriolan-Ouvertüre op.62', *BeJb*, vi (1969), 260–68 [written 1938]

G. Rienäcker: 'Zur Dialektik in der dramaturgischen Gestaltung der Beethovenschen Bühnenmusik zu Goethes "Egmont"', *Internationaler Beethoven-Kongress: Berlin 1970*, 301–13

E. Rebling: 'Probleme der Aufführung von Beethovens Ballett "Die Geschöpfe des Prometheus"', *Internationaler Beethoven-Kongress: Berlin 1977*, 329–34
A. Fecker: *Die Entstehung von Beethovens Musik zu Goethes Trauerspiel Egmont* (Hamburg, 1978)
C. Floros: *Beethovens Eroica und Prometheus-Musik* (Wilhelmshaven, 1978)
R. Pečman: *Beethovens Opernpläne* (Brno, 1981)
K. K. Polheim, ed.: *Zwischen Goethe und Beethoven: verbindende Texte zu Beethovens Egmont-Musik* (Bonn, 1982)

DOUGLAS JOHNSON

Beffroy de Reigny, Louis-Abel [Cousin Jacques] (*b* Laon, 6 Nov 1757; *d* Paris, 17 Dec 1811). French composer and librettist. He founded the satirical journal *Les lunes* in 1785 and was also known for his literary accounts of the Revolution. Under the pseudonym 'Cousin Jacques' he became the acknowledged playwright of the Revolution, writing the texts and occasionally the music to numerous farces and *pièces de circonstance* which enjoyed a popular vogue. Among these works is *Nicodème dans la lune* (1790), which had a run of 363 nights at the Théâtre-Français Comique et Lyrique, and was revived at the Théâtre-Français de la Cité in 1796 for another 200 performances. It was one of the first boulevard plays to succeed both as entertainment and as propaganda. A number of plays based on *Nicodème* followed, but none matched the success of the original. *Le retour du Champs-de-Mars* (1790), an instantaneous success, saved the Théâtre Beaujolais from bankruptcy.

first performed in Paris and texts by the composer unless otherwise stated; all printed works published in Paris

Les ailes de l'amour (divertissement, 1), Comédie-Italienne (Favart), 23 May 1786, airs (*c*1786)
Coriolinet, ou Rome sauvée, 1786 (folie héroï-comique, 3), ?unperf.
Les clefs du jardin, ou Les pots de fleurs (divertissement, 1), Comédie-Italienne (Favart), 24 March 1787 (1787)
La fin du bail, ou Le repas des fermiers (divertissement), Comédie-Italienne (Favart), 8 March 1788 (1788)
Jean-Bête (comédie, 3), Nicolet, 12 July 1790
La fédération du Parnasse (divertissement, 1), Beaujolais, July 1790
Le retour du Champs-de-Mars (divertissement, 1), Beaujolais, July 1790
Nicodème dans la lune, ou La révolution pacifique (folie, 3), Français Comique et Lyrique, 7 Nov 1790, orchd and ov. arr. Leblanc; 25 ariettas (1791)
L'histoire universelle (comédie mêlée de vaudevilles et d'airs nouveaux, 2), Monsieur, 16 Dec 1790, collab. Chardiny; 1 air by Gaveaux, 1 air by J.-P.-E. Martini
Apollon directeur (1), Beaujolais, 1790
Les folies dansantes (oc, 2), Délassement-Comique, 1790
Louis XII (comédie, 3, Valcour), Délassement-Comique, 1790
Le club des bonnes-gens, ou Le curé français [La réconciliation] (folie, 2), Feydeau, 24 Sept 1791 (1791), ov., several airs by Gaveaux
Les deux Nicodèmes, ou Les français sur la planète de Jupiter (opéra-folie, 2), Feydeau, 21 Nov 1791, air (n.d.)
Nicodème aux enfers (5), Feydeau, 1791 [see Pougin]
Les trois Nicodèmes, 1791, ?unperf.
Le vrai Nicodème, 1791, ?unperf.
Le retour de Nicodème, 1792 (4), ?unperf.
Allons ça va, ou Le Quaker en France (tableau patriotique, 1), OC (Feydeau), 28 Oct 1793
Démosthènes (tableau patriotique, 1), OC (Favart), 22 March 1794
Le petite Nannette (oc, 2), OC (Feydeau), 9 Dec 1796 (1796)
Turlututu, Empereur de l'isle vert (farce, 3), Cité-Variétés, 3 July 1797 (1797)
Jean-Baptiste (oc, 1), OC (Feydeau), 1 June 1798 (1798)
Un rien, ou L'habit de noces (folie, 1), Ambigu-Comique, 7 June 1798 (1797) [music rev. Gaveaux according to Pougin]
Le grand genre (oc, 1), Ambigu-Comique, 13 Jan 1799
Magdelon [Madelon] (oc, 1), Montansier, 4 June 1799 (1799)
Emilie, ou Les caprices (comédie, 3), Jeunes-Artistes, 9 July 1799 (1799)
Les deux charbonniers, ou Les contrastes (comédie, 2), Montansier, 24 Aug 1799 (1799)
Le bonhomme, ou Poulot et Fanchon (oc, 1), Montansier, 11 Dec 1799

Unperf. (dates are of announced performances, unless otherwise stated): L'amant poltron, 1784; Le poète amoureux (1), 1785; Prosper, ou Le malheur de plaire (2), 1786; Francisca, comp. 1790; Le diable, ou L'amour charbonnier, 1791, *F-Pn*; Armand, 1792

Attrib. Beffroy: Bordier aux enfers, 1789 (comédie, 1), ?unperf. (1789); Arlequin, général d'armée, 1790 (opéra bouffon, 2), ?unperf. (1790); Les capucins, ou Faisons la paix (comédie, 2), Feydeau, 26 Feb 1791

Librettos for other composers: *Honoré, ou L'homme célèbre*, Chardiny, comp. 1786; *L'ivrogne vertueux* (oc), Lemoyne, comp. *c*1791; *Sylvius Nerva, ou L'école des familles* [*La malédiction paternelle*] (drame lyrique), Lemoyne, comp. 1792; *Toute la Grèce, ou Ce que peut la liberté* (tableau patriotique), Lemoyne, 1794; *Le compère Luc, ou les dangers de l'ivrognerie* (oc), Lemoyne, 1794

*

ES ('Cousin-Jacques'; F. Lesure, Louis Allard)
A. Pougin: 'Le Cousin-Jacques', *Chronique musicale* (1875), Oct–Dec
M. Dietz: *Geschichte des musikalischen Dramas in Frankreich während der Revolution* (Vienna, 1886, 2/1893)
C. Westercamp: *Beffroy de Reigny, dit le cousin Jacques, 1757–1811: sa vie et ses oeuvres* (Laon, 1930)
M. Sajous: Introduction to L.-A. Beffroy de Reigny: *Nicodème dans la lune* (Paris, 1983), 7–51

LELAND FOX

Begg, Heather (*b* Nelson, 1 Dec 1932). New Zealand mezzo-soprano. She studied with Dame Sister Mary Leo in Auckland, at the New South Wales Conservatorium and at the London Opera Centre. Her Australian début (1954, Sydney) was as Azucena with the Sydney-based National Opera of Australia. She sang in England with the Carl Rosa company and from 1961 to 1964 at Sadler's Wells. After a return to Auckland for a period with New Zealand Opera (1964–6) she made guest appearances at Covent Garden, Bordeaux, Chicago and elsewhere. She was a principal at Covent Garden from 1972, then joined Australian Opera in 1976, where she had marked success in such diverse roles as Jane in *Patience* and Carmen. In 1990 she sang Mother Marie (*Dialogues des Carmélites*) at San Diego. She sang Marcellina in Ponnelle's film of *Le nozze di Figaro*. A versatile artist, Begg has a noted gift for comedy.

*

A. Simpson and P. Downes: *Southern Voices: International Opera Singers of New Zealand* (Auckland, 1992)

ROGER COVELL

Beggar's Opera, The. Ballad opera in three acts arranged by JOHANN CHRISTOPH PEPUSCH to a libretto by JOHN GAY; London, Lincoln's Inn Fields, 29 January 1728.

The Beggar's Opera took London by storm, and it remains one of the most frequently performed operatic works in English. There was no precedent or model for the work. Gay was a disappointed seeker of court patronage at the time of the première. A friend of Pope and Swift, he had written seven mostly undistinguished plays and a fair quantity of verse.

The ballad opera form that he created virtually out of nothing consists of spoken dialogue interspersed with thematically relevant songs, taken from a variety of mostly popular sources. Of the 69 songs, 28 have been traced to English ballads and 23 to popular Irish, Scottish and French tunes. The remaining 18 are drawn from Purcell (3), John Barrett (2), Jeremiah Clarke (2), Handel (2), Henry Carey (2), Bononcini, John Eccles, possibly Geminiani, John Wilford, Pepusch, Frescobaldi

Macheath *celebrated highwayman and womanizer*	tenor/baritone
Peachum *a seller of stolen goods*	bass
Mrs Peachum *his wife*	soprano
Polly Peachum *his daughter and Macheath's wife*	soprano
Lockit *a corrupt gaoler*	baritone/bass
Lucy Lockit *his daughter and Macheath's mistress*	soprano
Filch *a thief in Peachum's employment*	tenor
Diana Trapes	soprano
Beggar	speaking role
Player	speaking role

Macheath's Gang (Matt of the Mint, Jemmy Twitcher, Crook-Finger'd Jack, Wat Dreary, Robin of Bagshot, Nimming Ned, Harry Padington, Ben Budge), Women of the Town (Jenny Diver, Mrs Coaxer, Dolly Trull, Mrs Vixen, Betty Doxy, Mrs Slammekin, Suky Tawdry, Molly Brazen), constables, Drawer, Turnkey

Setting London in 1727

and Lewis Ramondon. The overture is based on 'One evening, having lost my way', an air in Act 3. The musical arrangement is usually credited to Pepusch, but there is no definite evidence to support this statement. Most of the tunes were extremely familiar to the original audience, and Gay was clever at creating ironic overtones and interplay between the music and his new lyrics. For example, the heroic overtones of the original words for Purcell's melody clang oddly against the very ugly sexual realities of Polly's 'Virgins are like the fair Flower'.

Gay offered the work to Drury Lane, where it was refused by Colley Cibber, perhaps because of its genuine oddity or because of its unflattering allusions to the Whig Prime Minister, Sir Robert Walpole, in the characters of Macheath and Peachum. John Rich agreed to mount it at Lincoln's Inn Fields, where its success was unprecedented in the history of the London theatre. It received 62 performances during its first, partial season and was immediately pirated. The first production created a popular craze for *Beggar's Opera* fans, playing cards, porcelain figures and illustrations (Hogarth's are the best known). The piece was performed in London every season for the rest of the century and productions were mounted in the 18th century throughout the English-speaking world, including Dublin, Dover, Norwich, Bath, Newcastle, Canterbury, Bristol, Glasgow, Edinburgh, Jamaica, New York, Boston, Philadelphia, Providence, Newport, Baltimore, Richmond, Williamsburg, Norfolk and Charleston. It was less often performed during the 19th century but returned to hit status in the famous Frederic Austin arrangement given at the Lyric Theatre, Hammersmith, on 5 June 1920 – a production that ran a startling 1463 nights and was frequently revived.

In 1928 Bertolt Brecht created a German adaptation with music by Kurt Weill, *Die Dreigroschenoper* ('The Threepenny Opera'). Despite that work's enormous international popularity, *The Beggar's Opera* continues to hold the stage. Loewenberg reported numerous productions before 1940, and since then they have, if anything, multiplied. The work has been revived regularly in the commercial theatre in London and New York, as well as in the National Theatre, London. It has also been made into a film by Sir Laurence Olivier (1953). Most late 20th-century productions have been executed with little comprehension of the musical and dramatic style of the original, which was designed for performance by actors rather than singers.

The first edition of *The Beggar's Opera* (1728) gave the tunes of the songs, the second (also 1728; *see* PUBLISHING, fig.8) added the overture on four staves, and the third (1729) included the basses of the songs, and also the text and songs from Gay's sequel, *Polly*. No MS orchestral parts of *The Beggar's Opera* survive, but parts for other ballad operas suggest that the songs were performed with short orchestral preludes and postludes derived from the tunes themselves; perhaps because of economy these were never published. Thus the third edition of *The Beggar's Opera* is almost a full score, for such songs were normally accompanied by strings alone with only the harpsichord to fill in between tune and bass. More elaborate accompaniments have been provided by Linley, Addison, Hatton, Austin, Dent, Bliss and Britten, among others.

Introduction (followed by the overture). The Beggar explains his 'Opera' to the Player: 'I have introduc'd the Similes that are in all your celebrated *Operas* ... Besides, I have a Prison Scene which the Ladies always reckon charmingly pathetick. As to the Parts, I have observ'd such a nice Impartiality to our two Ladies [i.e. Polly and Lucy – a jibe at the Faustina–Cuzzoni rivalry], that it is impossible for either of them to take Offence. I hope I may be forgiven, that I have not made my Opera throughout unnatural, like those in vogue; for I have no Recitative'.

ACT 1 *Peachum's house* Peachum is going over his accounts and gives us his view of the world: 'Through all the Employments of Life / Each Neighbour abuses his Brother ... All Professions be-rogue one another ... And the Statesman, because he's so great, / Thinks his Trade as honest as mine'; doctors, priests, lawyers and statesmen live by 'Cheats', just as he does. Filch enters with questions about various thieves in Peachum's employment who have been arrested. Peachum says Black Moll may plead her belly (i.e. pregnancy); that he will collect the £40 reward when Tom Gagg is hanged, etc. Peachum returns to his review of his affairs, going over a list of thieves with whom he deals, including '*Robin* of *Bagshot*, alias *Gorgon*, alias *Bluff Bob*, alias *Carbuncle*, alias *Bob Booty* ... he spends his Life among Women' – and hence should be impeached for the reward (this is a manifest allusion to Walpole). Mrs Peachum enters, and the two of them discuss the dashing Captain Macheath. She regrets that 'the Captain hath not more Discretion. What business hath he to keep Company with Lords and Gentlemen? He should leave them to prey upon one another'.

Peachum expresses horror at the idea of his daughter's marrying and putting her husband in possession of the family secrets, and goes off to berate Polly and warn her against matrimony. Filch enters and gives Mrs Peachum the seven handkerchiefs he has just stolen at the opera. He admits that he has promised Polly he will not tattle on her, and Mrs Peachum takes him off for a drink while she worms the truth out of him. Polly and her father enter, with Polly insisting that 'A Woman knows how to be mercenary, though she hath never been in a Court or at an Assembly. ... If I allow Captain *Macheath* some trifling Liberties, I have this Watch and other visible Marks of his Favour to show for it'. In an

'The Beggar's Opera': fan, possibly by a French artist after the satirical etching (1728) attributed to Hogarth. The main characters on the central platform are represented with animal heads (Lockit a bull, Lucy a pig, Macheath an ass, Mr and Mrs Peachum a dog and a weasel, Polly a cat); winged 'Harmony' turns its back to face the performance of an Italian opera (right). (The following words appear under the original etching: 'Britons attend – view this harmonious stage and listen to those notes which charm the age. Thus shall your tastes in sound and sense be shown, and Beggar's Op'ras ever be your own'.)

air she tells us that 'Virgins are like the fair Flower in its Lustre ... when once pluck'd, 'tis no longer alluring, / To Covent-Garden 'tis sent, (as yet sweet,) / There fades, and shrinks, and grows past all enduring, / Rots, stinks, and dies, and is trod under feet'. As Polly comments, 'A Girl who cannot grant some Things, and refuse what is most material, will make but a poor hand of her Beauty, and soon be thrown upon the Common'. Mrs Peachum, however, enters 'in a very great Passion' singing 'Our Polly is a sad Slut!', having discovered the horrible truth: Polly has secretly married Macheath. Her parents abuse her ('Do you think your Mother and I should have liv'd comfortably so long together, if ever we had been married? Baggage! ... thou foolish Jade, thou wilt be as ill-us'd, and as much neglected, as if thou hadst married a Lord!'). Polly defends herself: 'I did not marry him (as 'tis the Fashion) coolly and deliberately for Honour and Money. But, I love him'. Mrs Peachum is horrified: 'Love him! worse and worse! I thought the Girl had been better bred', and has to be revived with two stiff drinks. Peachum realizes that they 'must all endeavour to make the best of it', and proposes that Polly 'Secure what he hath got, have him peach'd the next Sessions, and then at once you are made a rich Widow'. Polly protests that her duty to her husband forbids this; her mother says her duty to her parents requires obedience: 'Away, Hussy. Hang your Husband, and be dutiful'. Alone for an exaggeratedly 'pathetic' scene, Polly imagines the execution at Tyburn ('I see him at the Tree! ... even Butchers weep!'). She has hidden Macheath in her room, and they take romantic leave of each other in a series of five songs, including 'Pretty Polly, say' and 'O what Pain it is to part!'. Macheath swears fidelity, and Polly assures him 'I have no Reason to doubt you, for I find in the Romance you lent me, none of the great Heroes were ever false in Love'.

ACT 2 *A Tavern near Newgate* Macheath's gang are discovered congratulating themselves upon their 'try'd Courage, and indefatigable Industry' and saying that all of them would die for the sake of a friend ('Show me a Gang of Courtiers that can say as much'). Macheath enters and explains that he will have to go into hiding. To the strains of the 'March in [Handel's] *Rinaldo*' they sing 'Let us take the Road' and disperse. Macheath remains chatting with the Drawer, singing 'If the Heart of a Man is depress with Cares, / The Mist is dispell'd when a Woman appears', while women are fetched. Macheath frolics, sings and dances with the whores. Jenny sings 'Before the Barn-door crowing, / The Cock by Hens attended'. The women signal Peachum, who enters with constables and arrests Macheath.

Macheath arrives at the prison in Newgate, where Lockit demands 'Garnish' in return for lighter fetters. Macheath laments his condition, especially when Lucy Lockit enters and berates him. He promises to marry her at the first opportunity and denies his marriage to Polly. In another part of the prison Peachum and Lockit try to settle their joint accounts, proclaiming that 'Business is at an end – if once we act dishonourably', – piety quickly degenerating into a quarrel in which they 'collar' one another and threaten impeachment and hanging. Just as Macheath is trying to persuade Lucy to help him raise money to escape ('Money well tim'd, and properly apply'd, will do any thing'), Polly enters and proclaims herself his wife – to Lucy's fury. Macheath sings 'How happy could I be with either, / Were t'other dear Charmer away!'; Polly and Lucy sing 'I'm bubbled', and Peachum enters and hauls Polly off. Macheath tries to explain himself to Lucy, who agrees to help him escape and concludes the act with 'I like the Fox shall grieve, / Whose Mate hath left her side'.

ACT 3 *Newgate* Lockit abuses Lucy – not for letting Macheath escape, but for failing to get paid for it. While Macheath is in a gaming house, Peachum and Lockit plot his recapture in Peachum's Lock. Diana Trapes enters and tells them how to find him. Back in Newgate, Lucy has 'the Rats-bane ready' for Polly. They exchange insincere commiserations; Polly drops the poisoned glass when Macheath is hauled in again; Lucy concludes grumpily that 'she was not happy enough to deserve to be poison'd'. The two women squabble furiously over the unhappy Macheath (though Peachum says 'Away Hussies! This is not a time for a Man to be hamper'd with his Wives'). 'A Dance of Prisoners in Chains' covers the trial, offstage. Macheath, in the 'Condemn'd Hold', seeks consolation in drink and sings ten rousing songs in quick succession to bolster his spirits, concluding with 'Since Laws were made for ev'ry Degree ... I wonder we han't better Company, / Upon Tyburn Tree!' (to the tune of 'Green Sleeves'). Macheath expresses distress that Jemmy Twitcher should testify against him, saying glumly 'Tis a plain Proof that the World is all alike, and that even our Gang can no more trust one another than other People'. Polly and Lucy enter to take leave of their husband, but when 'Four Women more ... with a Child a-piece' are announced Macheath says 'This is too much'; he is ready to be hanged.

At this point we return to the frame with the entry of the Player and the Beggar. The Beggar says he intends to have Macheath hanged for the sake of 'doing strict poetical Justice'. The Player objects that this would make 'a down-right deep Tragedy. The Catastrophe is manifestly wrong, for an Opera must end happily'. The Beggar accepts the objection and orders a reprieve, saying that 'in this kind of Drama, 'tis no matter how absurdly things are brought about ... All this we must do, to comply with the Taste of the Town'. The work concludes with a dance and an air, 'Thus I stand like the Turk, with his Doxies around' (to the tune 'Lumps of Pudding').

* * *

The Beggar's Opera has been called everything from 'a sentimental lollipop' to 'a terse social fable'. Most critics have been anxious to find as much significance and serious satire as possible in the work. It is witty at the expense of a number of obvious targets, notably Sir Robert Walpole, the conventions of Italian opera at the Royal Academy of Music in the 1720s, the generic customs of both tragedy and comedy of sentiment, and society's structure and conventional assumptions. The radical inversions of high and low life are startling and amusing, and the many comparisons of humans with animals ('Of all Animals of Prey, Man is the only sociable one', 3.ii) must have disconcerted the original audience. In elementary ways, however, the work fails to function effectively as a satire on its obvious targets. Gay offers no genuine alternatives: he demeans high life, but without suggesting that low life is better. Macheath's revelation that 'the World is all alike' seems to reflect Gay's own view of things – and if all the world is irremediably corrupt, then there is little point to satire, which attacks evil in support of the good. The tone is lighthearted, but the ultimate ideological implications are exceedingly bleak – far more so than in *Die Dreigroschenoper*, where evils are angrily attacked on the assumption that the world can be changed.

The Beggar's Opera may fairly be called 'frivolously nihilistic'. Ironically, it is almost always now staged as a period romp, and appears to have been given in an equally superficial way during the 18th century. Other kinds of production are possible, as David Freeman demonstrated in his Opera Factory production of 1982, replete with punk rock additions but giving the text the ugliness and despair that are almost always masked in performance by surface jollity.

See also BALLAD OPERA and *DREIGROSCHENOPER, DIE*.

ROBERT D. HUME

Begley, Kim (*b* Birkenhead, 23 June 1952). English tenor. He studied at the Guildhall School of Music, London, making his début in 1983 as the Archangel Gabriel (*Taverner*) at Covent Garden, where during the next five years he sang many character roles: Andres (*Wozzeck*), Borsa (*Rigoletto*), Snout and Lysander (*A Midsummer Night's Dream*), Bardolph (*Falstaff*), Heinrich der Schreiber and Walter von der Vogelweide (*Tannhäuser*), Pang (*Turandot*), Scaramuccio (*Ariadne auf Naxos*), Guido Bardi (*A Florentine Tragedy*), Basilio (*Le nozze di Figaro*), Cassio and Froh. He has also sung Alfredo (Sadler's Wells), Don Ottavio (Glyndebourne Touring Opera), Nadir (Scottish Opera) and Boris Grigorjevič (*Kát'a Kabanová*). In 1990 he sang Pelegrin in the Glyndebourne première of Tippett's *New Year* and, with Opera North in 1992 (Leeds), Fritz in *Der ferne Klang*. A capable and versatile singer, he is also a convincing actor.

ELIZABETH FORBES

Begnis, Giuseppe de (*b* Lugo, 1793; *d* New York, Aug 1849). Italian bass. He made his début at Modena in 1813 in Pavesi's *Ser Marcantonio*, and soon became a leading exponent of *buffo* roles in Italy. In 1816 he married the soprano Giuseppina Ronzi and the same year sang at La Scala, in Mayr's *Ginevra di Scozia*. He created the role of Dandini in Rossini's *La Cenerentola* at the Teatro Valle, Rome, in 1817. Two years later he and his wife appeared in Paris as Don Basilio and Rosina in *Il barbiere di Siviglia*, and as Geronio and Fiorilla in *Il turco in Italia*. They repeated the latter roles at their début in London at the King's Theatre in 1821. De Begnis took part in a concert performance of *Mosè in Egitto* at Covent Garden in 1822, three months before Rossini's opera was staged, as *Pietro l'eremita*, at the King's Theatre. In the following year he sang in the first London performance of Rossini's *Matilde di Shabran*, and in 1824 he took the part of Don Febeo in Mayr's *Che originali* (*Il fanatico per la musica*), staged for Catalani's return to London after a long absence. During his last season at the King's Theatre (1827), he appeared in Pacini's *La schiava in Bagdad*. Equally proficient as an actor and as a singer, he was an ideal interpreter of Rossini's comic operas.

ELIZABETH FORBES

Begrez, Pierre (Ignace) (*b* Namur, 23 Dec 1787; *d* London, 19 Dec 1863). French tenor. He made his début at the Paris Opéra in 1815, but much of his career was spent in England. He first sang in London at the King's Theatre in 1816 (billed as Signor Begri) in Paer's *Griselda*; that season he also sang Guglielmo (*Così fan tutte*), and the following year appeared in Paisiello's *La molinara* and Mozart's *La clemenza di Tito* (as Annius). In 1819 he sang Don Ottavio and Monostatos; and in 1824 he appeared in two Rossini operas, as Roderigo (*Otello*) and as Narciso (*Il turco in Italia*). He had neither a remarkable voice nor a virtuoso technique, but his musicality and his dependability made him a valuable member of the Italian opera company in London.

*

W. C. Smith: *The Italian Opera and Contemporary Ballet in London 1789–1820* (London, 1955)

ELIZABETH FORBES

Behold the Sun [*Die Wiedertäufer* ('The Anabaptists')]. Opera in three acts by ALEXANDER GOEHR to a libretto by John McGrath and the composer; Duisburg, Deutsche Oper am Rhein, 19 April 1985.

In 1534 two Dutch Anabaptist prophets, the idealistic Matthys (baritone) and the insidious Bokelson (tenor), preach news of the Second Coming and turn the prosperous city of Münster into the 'City of God'. Inflamed by desire for a better world, the people cast aside material and sexual conventions. Their hope is expressed through the chorus (*turba*), while the historical forces are projected on to a small group of individuals, the Berninck family. As in Goehr's *Sonata about Jerusalem* (1970), treating a similar subject, the outcome is a double betrayal of the collective dream: from within, by the people's misplaced trust in the delusions of the megalomaniacal Bokelson; and from without, by the power of the establishment represented by the local Prince Bishop (baritone), for whom the Anabaptists' disruption of traditional values is a dangerous source of social anarchy. Münster is finally recaptured, and the Anabaptists massacred. But in the work's closing bars, the figure of Divara (soprano), emblematic of the pure messianic spirit, confirms the permanence of the flawed Utopian ideal.

Dramatically, the besieged city becomes an exemplary scenario for the conflicts aroused by fundamentalism in action. The historically accurate libretto, with its scriptural references, quotations from Milton and Shelley and the recorded utterances of the Anabaptists themselves, is rich in millenarian vigour, the result of a discarded attempt to present the story in terms of biblical parallels. For his musical language, the composer deliberately avoided expressionism in order to re-create a Baroque dramaturgy more suited to his social theme. The music evolves through statuesque fugal choruses and refrains, which draw on traditional material, as well as through arias and recitatives; the brilliant showpiece aria 'Behold the sun', sung by the Bernincks' son, Christian (coloratura soprano), has also been performed separately.

Though a BBC studio recording subsequently revealed the music's strengths, at the première its theatrical power was vitiated by severe cuts and transpositions made with the deliberate aim of subverting the opera's message from that of timeless Utopian parable to anti-revolutionary tract, conceived against the background of contemporary German politics as an expressionistic costume drama. These alterations were made expressly against the composer's wishes, and the opera awaits a satisfactory stage production.

NICHOLAS WILLIAMS

Behrend, Fritz (*b* Berlin, 3 March 1889; *d* Berlin, 29 Dec 1972). German composer. He studied composition with Humperdinck and others. After an engagement as coach at the Brunswick Hoftheater (1911–12), he served in the German army, and was then active as a pianist and teacher. Since his music was considered 'undesirable' by the Nazi regime, he established a reputation as a composer only after World War II. In his most important works he emulated Strauss.

König Renés Tochter op.22, 1919 (1, H. Hertz), unperf.
Der schwanger Bauer, 1927 (1), Berlin, Städtische Oper, 22 May 1949 [pt of 3 Hans Sachs-Spiele op.53]
Die lächerliche Preziösen op.57, 1928 (1, after Molière), Berlin, Städtische Oper, 22 May 1949
Die Tänzerin des Himmels op.54 (Märchenpantomime), Augsburg, Stadt, 12 Nov 1929
Almansor op.61, 1929–31 (3, after H. Heine)
Dornröschen op.76, 1933–4 (Märchenoper, 3)
Der Wunderdoktor op.98, 1947 (komische Oper, 3, Behrend, after Molière)
Der Spiegel op.100, 1949–50 (komische Oper, 1, Behrend, after Chin. fairy-tale)
Romantische Komödie op.111, 1953 (komische Oper, 3, Behrend, after G. Büchner)

*

R. Bauer: 'Berliner Komponisten', *Musikstadt Berlin zwischen Krieg und Frieden* (Berlin, 1956)

JOHN MORGAN

Behrens, Hildegard (*b* Varel, nr Oldenburg, 9 Feb 1937). German soprano. She studied in Freiburg, making her début there in 1971 as Mozart's Countess Almaviva. She then sang at Düsseldorf and Frankfurt in roles including Fiordiligi, Agathe, Elsa, Eva, Kát'a, and Marie (*Wozzeck*). In 1976 she made her début at Covent Garden as Leonore (*Fidelio*) and at the Metropolitan as Giorgetta (*Il tabarro*). She sang Salome at Salzburg (1977) and Brünnhilde at Bayreuth (1983-6). Her later repertory also includes Electra (*Idomeneo*), Tosca, Senta, Isolde, Donna Anna, Strauss's Electra, which she first sang at the Paris Opéra (1986), and Emilia Marty (*The Makropulos Affair*), which she sang at the Bayerische Staatsoper, Munich (1988). She sang both Marie and Brünnhilde at the Metropolitan in 1990. A highly intelligent singer with a rich-toned voice, she excels in Wagner and Strauss.

*

A. Blyth: 'Hildegard Behrens', *Opera*, xlii (1991), 502–8

ELIZABETH FORBES

Behrens, Jack (*b* Lancaster, PA, 25 March 1935). Canadian composer. He studied at the Juilliard School of Music with William Bergsma, Vincent Persichetti and Peter Mennin and at Harvard University with Leon Kirchner and Roger Sessions. In the 1960s he also studied with Milhaud, Wolpe and Cage. From 1976 to 1980 he taught theory and composition at the University of Western Ontario, then served as Dean of the Faculty of Music (1980–86). He has also had an active performing career as pianist and conductor. His comic opera *The Lay of Thrym* was written for the Canadian Centennial Commission for Festival Canada and celebrates the Scandinavian origins of a sizeable section of the Canadian population. The libretto, by C. Keith Cockburn, is based on a poem from the Icelandic Elder Edda; Behrens carried out research into Viking literature, art and music in Iceland and Scandinavia in 1965 before composing the opera, which received its première on 13 April 1968 at Regina, Saskatchewan. It is an atonal work, divided into four scenes. The work does not focus on dazzling displays of vocal technique but rather offers a sensitive and humorous treatment of the subject in which chance music and improvisation play an important part.

GAYNOR G. JONES

Beiden Pädagogen, Die ('The Two Pedagogues'). Singspiel in one act by FELIX MENDELSSOHN to a libretto by Johann Ludwig Casper after EUGÈNE SCRIBE's comedy *Les deux précepteurs, ou Asinus asinum fricat*; private performance, Berlin, ?1821 (first public performance, Berlin, 27 May 1962).

Die beiden Pädagogen was Mendelssohn's third operatic effort, although he was only 12 years old when he composed it. It was performed shortly after its completion before an audience of family and friends in the Mendelssohns' house in Berlin. The music is resourcefully matched to the requirements of the plot and contains some effective characterization.

Herr von Robert (bass), a wealthy landowner, insists that his young son Carl (tenor) should apply himself to his studies, though Carl is much more interested in his amorous feelings for his cousin Elise (soprano). Other characters include the gardener's girl, Hannchen (soprano), who has had an unhappy love affair in Vienna, and her uncle, the schoolmaster Kinderschreck (bass), whose name ('scare-child') suggests his educational approach. A terzetto between Carl, Elise and Hannchen shows Mendelssohn's familiarity with Mozart's technique of contrasting a unified pair of characters with a third whose vocal line is of a different nature. In an aria Kinderschreck relishes the sound of the cane. The Viennese professor engaged by Robert as tutor to his son is impersonated by the professor's servant, Luftig (bass); Hannchen, however, recognizes Luftig as her former lover and threatens to expose him unless he marries her. In an effective quartet, Luftig and Kinderschreck dispute the merits of Pestalozzi's and Basedow's educational theories, to the astonishment of Carl and his father. Luftig is eventually exposed, but the piece ends happily when Robert abandons his unrealistic plans and the two young couples are betrothed.

The libretto, long believed lost, was rediscovered in 1960 in the Bodleian Library, Oxford, by Karl-Heinz Köhler. CLIVE BROWN

Beiden Schützen, Die ('The Two Riflemen'). *Komische Oper* in three acts by ALBERT LORTZING to his own libretto after G. Cords's comedy *Die beiden Grenadiere*, in turn derived from Joseph Patrat's libretto for Grétry's *Les méprises par ressemblance* and Patrat's rearrangement of this as the comedy *Les deux grenadiers, ou Les quiproquos*; Leipzig, Stadttheater, 20 February 1837.

The plot, set in a German village at the turn of the 19th century, hinges on a rather improbable case of mistaken identity. The innkeeper Busch (bass), whose partial deafness makes him a comic figure, awaits the return of his son Gustav (tenor) from the army after many years. He expects a marriage between Gustav and Caroline (soprano), daughter of the local magistrate, Wall (bass). However, Busch mistakes another returning soldier, Wilhelm (baritone), Wall's son, for his own son. Wilhelm's comrade Schwarzbard (bass) encourages his friend to go along with the misconception for the fun of it. Wilhelm is at first reluctant, but agrees when he sees and falls for Busch's daughter Suschen (soprano). The second act begins with the magistrate's cousin Peter (tenor) complaining to his relative that he has been manhandled by a soldier (Wilhelm) at the inn. Gustav, who is portrayed in sharp contrast to the lusty Wilhelm, finally returns; he meets Caroline and they are attracted to one another. When he goes to the inn his father will not believe he is his son. Peter and Wall arrive, and Peter takes Gustav, wearing the same uniform as Wilhelm, for the soldier who mistreated him. Gustav is unable to prove his identity; they search Wilhelm's trunk and papers, believing they are Gustav's, but he sticks to his story even when they find a winning lottery ticket among the papers. The penultimate number of the opera, a septet which takes place in almost total darkness, provides the opportunity for further comic confusion as the two pairs of lovers and the other principal characters become mixed up. In the ensuing dialogue everything is resolved and a short finale concludes the work.

Die beiden Schützen was Lortzing's first significant success. Together with the even more successful *Zar und Zimmermann*, also mounted in 1837, it established him as the leading German composer of comic opera in his day. Here his extensive theatrical experience (he was particularly admired as a comic actor and sang Peter at the opera's première) enabled him to produce a genuinely amusing piece. The opera's success depended greatly on the adroitness with which he constructed the libretto. The music is unambitious and derivative but skilfully crafted, melodically attractive and eminently suited to its function. The ensembles are especially well devised to bring out the humour of each situation. Many of the solos too are aptly conceived, particularly the comic ones, such as Peter's complaints, accompanied by a Contretanz at the beginning of Act 2. The arias and duets, though charming, are rather obviously derived from examples in operas by Spohr and Weber.

CLIVE BROWN

Beijing. Chinese city; for a discussion of operatic activity there *see* CHINA.

Beilke, Irma (*b* Berlin, 24 Aug 1904; *d* Berlin, 29 Dec 1989). German soprano. She studied in Berlin, making her début in 1926 at the Städtische Oper as a Bridesmaid (*Der Freischütz*). After appearing at Leipzig, in 1936 she returned to Berlin, where she continued to sing until 1958. She also appeared in Vienna (1941–5) and sang Blonde at Glyndebourne (1936), Papagena, Marzelline and Sophie at Covent Garden (1938), the title role in the première of Weismann's *Pfiffige Magd* at Leipzig (1939), Blonde, Susanna and Pamina at Salzburg (1939–43), and Mimì and Violetta in Dublin (1950). Her roles included Rosina, Norina, Regina (*Mathis der Maler*), Nicolai's Mrs Ford, Aennchen, Butterfly, Zerbinetta and the Composer. In 1958 she took her farewell as Mimì, then taught at the Berlin Hochschule. A stylish singer with a light, flexible voice, she excelled at first in soubrette roles, later becoming a fine lyric soprano. ELIZABETH FORBES

Beirer, Hans (*b* Wiener Neustadt, 26 June 1911). Austrian tenor. He studied in Vienna, making his début in 1936 at Linz. After singing in Basle, St Gall and Hanover, he was engaged in 1943 at the Städtische Oper, Berlin, but sang only Nando (*Tiefland*) before the war closed all German theatres. In 1945 he reappeared in Berlin as Turiddu, later singing Babinski (*Svanda the Bagpiper*), Radames, Vasco da Gama, Don José and Bacchus. He also sang Parsifal in Rome (1949), Tannhäuser in Naples (1950), Walther in New York (1951), Siegmund and Tristan. He sang the Drum Major at Salzburg (1951); Siegfried at the Paris Opéra (1955); and Parsifal, Tristan and Tannhäuser at Bayreuth (1958–62). He created the Lord Mayor in Einem's *Der Besuch der alten Dame* (1971) at the Vienna Staatsoper, where in 1982 he made his farewell as Siegmund; in 1986 he sang Herod (*Salome*) in Berlin on his 75th birthday, and he appears as Aegisthus in the Götz Friedrich film of *Elektra*. He excelled in roles such as Tannhäuser, where he made up in dramatic intensity for any lack of tonal beauty in his voice. ELIZABETH FORBES

Bekker, (Max) Paul (Eugen) (*b* Berlin, 11 Sept 1882; *d* New York, 7 March 1937). German writer on opera and adminstrator. He studied music in Berlin and then joined the Berlin PO as a violinist. After conducting at Aschaffenburg and Görlitz he became music critic of the *Berliner neueste Nachrichten* in 1906, three years later taking a similar position on the *Berliner allgemeine Zeitung*. In 1911 he was appointed chief critic of the *Frankfurter Zeitung*; for 14 years he used this influential post to proselytize for contemporary music. He was Intendant at the theatre in Kassel, 1925–7, and at Wiesbaden, 1927–33. In 1934 he emigrated to New York to escape Nazi persecution.

Bekker championed a number of important 20th-century operatic composers, notably Schreker and Krenek, and also published controversial studies on such contrasting 19th-century figures as Offenbach and Wagner. His seasons as Intendant in Kassel and Wiesbaden showed considerable enterprise, with works by Schoenberg, Delius, Schreker, Stephan and Busoni in the repertory in addition to operas by Weber, Verdi and Berlioz. He was also responsible for the first performances of Krenek's one-act operas *Der Diktator*, *Das geheime Königreich* and *Schwergewicht, oder Die Ehre der Nation* (Wiesbaden, May 1928).

Das Musikdrama der Gegenwart (Stuttgart, 1909)
Jacques Offenbach (Berlin, 1911)
Franz Schreker (Berlin, 1919)
Kritische Zeitbilder (Stuttgart, 1921)
Klang und Eros (Stuttgart, 1923)
Richard Wagner (Stuttgart, 1924; Eng. trans., 1931)
Das Operntheater (Leipzig, 1931)
Wandlungen der Oper (Zürich, 1934, 2/1983; Eng. trans., 1936)

*

H. Mersmann: 'Paul Bekker und die zeitgenössischen Musiker', *Melos*, xi (1932), 400–03
G. Schubert: 'Aspekte der Bekkerschen Musiksoziologie', *IRMAS*, i (1970), 179–86
S. Grossmann-Vendrey: 'Das expressionistische Wagner-Bild Paul Bekkers', *SMz*, cxvii (1977), 1–3 ERIK LEVI

Bekku, Sadao (*b* Tokyo, 24 May 1922). Japanese composer. He studied physics and aesthetics at Tokyo University until 1950; he also studied composition privately with Tomojirō Ikenouchi after 1944. From 1951 to 1954 he was in Paris, where he was influenced by Milhaud, Rivier (both for their French neo-classicism) and Messiaen, his teachers at the Conservatoire. He was president of the Japanese branch of the ISCM for eight years.

His three operas are based on medieval Japanese stories and have all been successful. The comic opera *San-nin-no onna-no monogatari* ('A Story of Three Women'), after three *kyōgen* (comic theatre) plays, describes humorous relationships between men and women; it has been staged many times and broadcast in Europe. *Arima-no Miko* ('Prince Arima') deals with the tragic story of a 7th-century prince, who is also a famous poet. *Aoi-no-ue*, also a tragedy, concerns a medieval court lady, whose spirit kills the wife of her lover; it won a government prize for theatrical arts.

*

San-nin-no onna-no monogatari [A Story of Three Women] (comic op, 3, M. Suzuki, after *kyōgen* plays: *Hanako*, *Sumi-nuri* and *Hige-yagura*), Tokyo Bunka Kaikan, 9 March 1965, vs (Tokyo, n.d.)
Arima-no Miko [Prince Arima] (3, T. Matsubara, after T. Fukuda), Tokyo Bunka Kaikan, 13 March 1967
Aoi-no-ue (3, Suzuki, after Lady Murasaki: *The Tale of Genji* and 2 noh plays: *Aoi-no-ue* and *Nonomiya*), Tokyo, Shinjuku Bunka Centre, 14 July 1981 MASAKATA KANAZAWA

Belamarić, Miro (*b* Šibenik, Dalmatia, 9 Feb 1935). Croatian composer and conductor. He studied conducting with Milan Horvat and composition with Stjepan Šulek at the Zagreb Academy of Music. He continued his studies in conducting with Lovro von Matačić in Salzburg and Sergiu Celibidache in Siena. He has been active as a conductor since 1959, first with the symphony orchestra of Zagreb radio and television, later as chief conductor of the Komedija Theatre and, from 1978, as chief conductor of the Zagreb Opera. He was also assistant to Karajan at the Salzburg Festival (1965–8) and to Karl Böhm (1975–7). He has appeared as guest conductor in many prominent opera houses and at many festivals. As a composer Belamarić aims to combine modern stylistic features, intelligibility, and directness of musical expression, drawing on his considerable orchestral experience for the technical construction and use of sound colour in his scores. His first opera, the two-act *Ljubav don Perlimplina* ('The Love of Don Perlimplin'; Zagreb, 16 Nov 1975), after García Lorca's lyrical and tragic grotesque play, is neo-expressionist in style, with instrumental preludes based on classical forms and highly refined in sound, in the manner of Alban Berg. Belamarić won first prize in the 1983 Vienna State Opera competition with his second, three-act, opera, *Don Juan – ein Rebell für alle Zeiten*, based on a text by Tirso da Molina. KORALJKA KOS

Belarus'. For discussion of opera in Belarus' *see* MINSK.

Belasco, David (*b* San Francisco, 25 July 1853; *d* New York, 15 May 1931). American director and playwright of Portuguese Jewish origin. Born into a theatrical family who had emigrated from England to California at the time of the Gold Rush (*c*1850), he was educated by a Catholic priest, whose dress he affected all his life. At the age of 12 he had written his first play, *Jim Black, or The Regulator's Revenge*. From 1871 he was stage manager at various San Francisco theatres, adapting foreign plays and frequently appearing in them himself. In 1873 he met Dion Boucicault, for whom he acted for a time as secretary. He moved to New York in 1884 and achieved his first success as the author of *May Blossom*. Prolific in every genre from light comedy to historical melodrama, he specialized in plays with an exotic ambience, which he evoked with elaborate decor and cunningly devised lighting. *Adrea* (1904) is set on an Adriatic island in the 4th century; *Madame Butterfly* (1900) and *The Darling of the Gods* (1902, once considered his masterpiece) take place in Japan; and *The Girl I Left behind Me* (1893), *The Heart of Maryland* (1895) and *The Girl of the Golden West* (1905) are stage westerns. As a director Belasco could be called the Stanislavsky of his day, while the visual effects for which he was famous owe something to the early cinema (one of his last plays, *The Return of Peter Grimm*, 1911, was written in collaboration with Cecil B. De Mille). Indeed, in *Madame Butterfly* it was the scene of the heroine's silent vigil, during which the lighting portrays the passage of time from dusk to dawn, complete with bird-song, that first attracted Puccini to the drama. Belasco is remembered today as the writer who furnished Puccini with two operatic subjects.

*

D. Belasco: *The Theatre through the Stage Door* (New York, 1918)
W. Winter: *The Life of David Belasco* (New York, 1919)
JULIAN BUDDEN

Bel canto (It.: 'fine singing'). A term loosely used and open to a variety of interpretations, 'bel canto' is generally understood as indicating the elegant Italian vocal style of the 18th and early 19th centuries. It did not however enter the musical vocabulary until somewhat later, and does not appear, for example, in the treatises of P. F. Tosi (1723) or Giovanni Mancini (1774), the most important writings of the so-called golden age of bel canto. Musicians began using it only towards the middle of the 19th century, when a weightier vocal tone came to be prized and less emphasis was placed on a light, florid delivery.

In a conversation in Paris in 1858, Rossini is reported to have inveighed against the decline of the traditional Italian style of singing with the words 'Alas for us, we have lost our bel canto'. According to the same report, his concept of a bel canto singer involved three requirements: a naturally beautiful voice, even in tone throughout its range; careful training that encouraged effortless delivery of highly florid music; and a mastery of style that could not be taught but only assimilated from listening to the best Italian exponents.

The term 'bel canto' rapidly became a battle-cry in the vocabulary of Italian singing teachers (e.g. Ricci 1915), and the concept of bel canto became clouded by mystique and confused by a plethora of individual interpretations. Frequent use of the term in the jargon of the singing studio and the dilettante has led some to dismiss bel canto as a myth (Fuchs 1963); only rarely has the subject been treated with historical awareness (e.g. Duey 1951).

To complicate the matter further, German musicology in the early 20th century devised its own historical application for 'bel canto', using the term to refer to the simple lyricism that came to the fore in Venetian opera and the Roman cantata during the 1630s and 1640s (the era of Cavalli, Cesti, Carissimi and Luigi Rossi) as a reaction against the earlier, text-dominated *stile rappresentativo*. This anachronistic use was given wide circulation in Robert Haas's *Die Musik des Barocks* (Potsdam, 1928); its first important appearance in an English-language book was in Manfred Bukofzer's *Music in the Baroque Era* (1947, pp.118ff: a passage echoed in many subsequent musicological writings).

V. Ricci: *La crisi del bel canto* (Florence, 1915)
P. A. Duey: *Bel canto in its Golden Age* (New York, 1951)
V. Fuchs: *The Art of Singing* (London, 1963)
A. Michotte: 'An Evening chez Rossini, 1858', *Opera*, xviii (1967), 952–62
F. Thomas: *Bel canto: die Lehre des Kunstgesanges nach der Altitalienischen Schule* (Berlin, 1968)
D. Galliver: 'Cantare con affetto: Keynote of the bel canto', *SMA*, viii (1974), 1–7
R. Celletti: *La storia del belcanto* (Fiesole, 1983, 2/1986; Eng. trans., 1991)
OWEN JANDER

Belcourt, Emile (*b* Regina, Sask., 27 June 1926). Canadian tenor. After studying in Vienna he sang Purcell's Aeneas at Aix-en-Provence in 1961. The following year he made his British début at Covent Garden as Gonzalve (*L'heure espagnole*) and sang Pelléas for Scottish Opera. In 1963 he joined Sadler's Wells Opera (later ENO), with which he sang for over 20 years; he created Governor Sciocca in Williamson's *The Violins of Saint-Jacques* (1966), Hallam Matthews in Bennett's *A Penny for a Song* (1967), Hernando de Sota in Hamilton's *The Royal Hunt of the Sun* and Mars Plaisir in Blake's *Toussaint* (1977); he also sang Shuisky, Loge, Herod, Dr Suda (*Osud*) and operetta roles such as Eisenstein, Danilo, and Pluto (*Orphée aux enfers*). He created Bernard of Clairvaux (Charles Wilson's *Heloise and Abelard*) at Toronto (1973) and sang the Prince/Manservant/Marquis in *Lulu* (three-act version) at Covent Garden (1981) as well as Herod (1982), and Mark (*The Midsummer Marriage*) at San Francisco. A fine actor with an expressive voice and superb diction, he was specially effective as Loge (a role he also sang at Seattle) and as Tristan and Siegmund.

ELIZABETH FORBES

Belém. Brazilian city, capital of the state of Pará. It was founded in 1614. As early as 1775 an Italian architect was imported to supervise construction of a Casa da Ópera, where in 1794 Jommelli's *Ezio in Roma* and David Perez's *Zenobia* were presented. In 1821 the Teatro Providência was built to replace it, and this in turn was replaced by the sumptuous Teatro da Paz (1100 seats), inaugurated on 15 February 1878. As an outlet for local talent, the Teatro Chalet had been opened in 1873.

Carlos Gomes's *Il Guarany* was first given at the Teatro da Paz on 9 September 1880. The next year, Pará's own leading composer Henrique Eulálio Gurjão, who had studied with local teachers before becoming a pupil of Giovanni Pacini in Rome, had his *Idalia* given there by Tomaso Passini's visiting Companhia Lyrica Italiana. Gomes stayed in Belém in July and August 1882, during which *Salvator Rosa* was mounted four times; 17 other operas gave the 1882 season a brilliance never later surpassed. Occasionally local composers succeeded in having operas mounted at the Paz after this period. José Cândido da Gama Malcher, a pupil of Gurjão's before studying in Pennsylvania and at Milan, saw his *Bug-Jurgal* (17 September 1890) and *Iara* (20 March 1895) performed; Alipio César (1871–1925) his *Notte bizzarra* (7 September 1917); and Manuel Belarmino Costa (*b* 1907) his *A cabanagem* (10 March 1949). However, with the collapse in 1906 of the Amazon Valley rubber boom, grand opera disappeared in Belém. In 1953 an Italian impresario attempted a season, but admitted defeat after *La bohème*, *La traviata* and *Rigoletto* lost large sums.

L. H. Corrêa de Azevedo: *Relação das óperas de autores brasileiros* (Rio de Janeiro, 1938), 36, 53–4
V. Salles: *A música e o tempo no Grão Pará* (Belém, 1980)
R. Stevenson: Review of V. Salles: *A música e o tempo no Grão Pará*, *Inter-American Music Review*, vii/2 (1986), 104–16
ROBERT STEVENSON

Belfagor. Comic opera in a prologue, two acts and an epilogue by OTTORINO RESPIGHI to a libretto by CLAUDIO GUASTALLA after Ercole Luigi Morselli's play of the same name (*c*1919); Milan, Teatro alla Scala, 26 April 1923.

Only a tenuous thread links this opera to Machiavelli's pungently humorous tale with the same title: here too the devil Belfagor (baritone) has been sent into the world to find out why so many damned souls attribute their fall from grace to the evil influence of their wives. In Morselli's version (as further modified by Guastalla), he sets about this by marrying the idealistic Candida (soprano) against her wishes. She is totally devoted to the young sailor Baldo (tenor); yet Belfagor gets his way after bribing her father Mirocleto (bass). Having taken the human form of a rich merchant, the susceptible devil genuinely falls in love with the girl; but she stubbornly refuses to consummate the marriage, and the church bells, in sympathy with her, remain obstinately silent from the wedding day onwards. When Baldo returns after a period at sea, Candida escapes with him, helped by her mother Olimpia (mezzo-soprano). But Belfagor, now disguised as a tramp, arouses the sailor's jealousy by suggesting that Candida may, after all, have betrayed him during his absence. Her innocence is finally confirmed by the church bells, which suddenly and miraculously break their long silence.

Clearly this sentimental comedy – in which Belfagor's initial purpose in entering the world soon ceases to be the main point – pales in comparison with the witty, anarchic inventiveness of Machiavelli's story. Moreover, the rather uneven music hardly compensates for the libretto's weaknesses: it is scarcely surprising that the opera has seldom been revived. As usual in Respighi, however, there is much to admire in the picturesque orchestration; and the best of the love music is radiantly beautiful. The harmony is sometimes bold by his standards, especially in the devil music which repeatedly features superimposed 4ths, perfect and augmented. The relatively familiar *Belfagor* overture (a concert piece based on material from the opera) brings some of the best ideas together in a conveniently compact form.

JOHN C. G. WATERHOUSE

Belfast. Capital of Northern Ireland. From the middle of the 18th century, Belfast's single theatre had occasional performances of ballad and comic operas. From the late 1820s short seasons of Italian opera were occasionally presented by visiting companies, and these became increasingly popular; by the end of the century the scene was dominated by the annual visits of the Carl Rosa and D'Oyly Carte companies. The main venue was the Theatre Royal, but in 1895 a second was opened, the Grand Opera House (designed by Frank Matcham; cap. 2500). In succeeding years operatic activity declined; touring companies continued to be the mainstay of operatic life until the middle of the 20th century.

In 1950 Havelock Nelson founded the Studio Opera Group to perform chamber operas in English, using local singers whenever possible. For most of the next 30 years the company gave one or two seasons each year both in Belfast and on tour in Ireland; the repertory included five works by Britten each of which was given its Irish première by the company.

The Grand Opera Society of Northern Ireland (GOSNI) was formed in 1957 after the cessation of regular visits by the Carl Rosa company. After its first season, in spring 1958, the company relied on 'package deals', hiring Italian singers, director and conductor to work with the local amateur chorus and a freelance orchestra; in 1963 Luciano Pavarotti made his British début as Pinkerton in GOSNI's *Madama Butterfly*. The newly formed Ulster Orchestra played for GOSNI in 1967 but that year the Arts Council of Northern Ireland, concerned about falling standards and increasing subventions, created an expensive new company, Ulster Opera, for just seven performances of operas by Offenbach and Rossini. There was a drop in public support for GOSNI's 1968 season of three German operas with singers from Frankfurt. After a break of one year the company was restructured as the Northern Ireland Opera Trust (NIOT).

NIOT shared a professional administrator with the Studio Opera Group and both companies were able to use the Ulster Orchestra. During the successful 1970–71 seasons NIOT increasingly favoured young British singers; however, as civil disturbance in the city increased, the Grand Opera House, converted into a cinema in 1961, closed down and the annual opera seasons were given in less suitable cinemas and halls. In 1975 Alun Francis was appointed Artistic Director and the following year Patric Schmid was appointed Artistic Adviser. The restored Grand Opera House was opened in 1980 with a reduced seating capacity (1000) and an enlarged orchestra pit. In 1985 Opera Northern Ireland was created to replace NIOT and the Studio Opera Group. Kenneth Montgomery was appointed Artistic Director and the company now provides two Belfast seasons (seven performances of two operas each autumn and four performances of one opera each spring) and a touring production.

*

W. J. Lawrence: *The Annals of the Belfast Stage, 1731–1831* (unpubd typescript, 1897)

A. Fleischmann, ed.: *Music in Ireland* (Cork, 1952)

W. S. Clark: *The Irish Stage in the County Towns, 1720–1800* (Oxford, 1965)

N. McNeilly: *The Music Makers* (Belfast, 1976)

B. Walker, ed.: *Frank Matcham, Theatre Architect* (Belfast, 1980)

DAVID BYERS

Bel Geddes, Norman [Geddes, Norman] (*b* Adrian, MI, 27 April 1893; *d* New York, 8 May 1958). American stage designer. He studied briefly at the Cleveland School of Art, Chicago, but had no formal education after the age of 16. His first wife, Helen Belle Sneider, became his collaborator, and 'Norman-Bel-Geddes' was their *nom de plume* for articles on art and the theatre, until their divorce in 1932. Notable designs for Montemezzi's *La nave* for Chicago Opera (1919) and Henry Hadley's *Cleopatra's Night* for the Metropolitan (1920) attracted Broadway attention, and his innovative approach was soon recognized. At an early stage of his career he discarded the proscenium arch and planned open-stage projects, including Dante's *Divine Comedy* (never realized). For a commission in 1924 to design Vollmöller's morality play *The Miracle* with Humperdinck's music for Max Reinhardt, he converted the theatre into a Gothic cathedral. He designed films for Cecil B. De Mille and D. W. Griffith and circuses for Barnum and Bailey. His work for Broadway included Kurt Weill's *The Eternal Road* (1937), Gershwin's *Strike up the Band* (1927), Porter's *Fifty Million Frenchmen* (1929) and *The Seven Lively Arts* (1944, his last for Broadway): in all, he designed more than 200 theatrical productions. He later turned primarily to industrial design, in which world he became something of a giant, but he also had a pivotal influence on the development of American theatre. Inspired by the synthetic and plastic ideas of Adolphe Appia and Gordon Craig, he was a 'Renaissance' master – a craftsman who used steps, platforms and dramatic lighting (he invented lamps and lenses) to sculpture powerful theatrical images. He combined a tempestuous ego with implacable drive and imagination. His archives, designs and drawings were given to the University of Texas, Austin, in 1959.

For illustration *see* STAGE DESIGN, fig.24.

*

ES (L. Moore)

F. Bruguière: *The Divine Comedy* (New York, 1924)

N. Bel Geddes: *Horizons* (New York, 1932)

T. Komisarjevsky, T. Simonson and L. Simonson: *Settings and Costumes of the Modern Stage* (New York, 1933)

——: 'Design for a New Kind of Theatre', *New York Times* (30 Nov 1947)

——: *Miracle in the Evening* (New York, 1960)

D. Oenslager: *Stage Design: Four Centuries of Scenic Invention* (London, 1975)

DAVID J. HOUGH

Belgium. The *ballet de cour* (which had several precursors, such as a *divertissement* presented at Binche in 1549 by Marie of Hungary in honour of Charles V) was first evident in Brussels in 1634 with the *Balet des princes indiens*. Such works continued to appear for several decades, though it is impossible to say exactly what part local musicians played in them. Equally little is known of other spectacles combining theatre and music that were given in the 17th and 18th centuries in Jesuit colleges.

Appointed governor of the Low Countries in 1647, Archduke Léopold-Guillaume had a room intended for opera built in his palace in Brussels. In 1650 the first work performed there was *Ulisse all'isola di Circe*, composed by Gioseffo Zamponi, an Italian in the archduke's service. Besides the spectacles given occasionally at the governor's court, or at that of the Prince-Bishop of Liège, there were performances of foreign operas, both French and Italian, in several towns during the second half of the 17th century (Antwerp, 1673; Brussels, 1682). The genre enjoyed great success, and in about 1701 Antoine Claudinot, a Brussels bookseller, requested a music-printing privilege, specifying in his petition that he intended to print the operas of Lully (beginning with *Persée*). These were at the time being performed in Brussels with new prologues by P. A. Fiocco, the court's *maître de chapelle*, who also composed a *pastorale* in 1699, *Le retour du printemps*. (The privilege for the region was held by Aertssens in Antwerp, and Claudinot's request was rejected in 1702.)

In 1700 the Théâtre de la Monnaie was opened in Brussels. Its repertory up to 1745 consisted mostly of French works, except for the years 1727–30, when *opere serie* were given. During the French occupation (1745–7) the presence in Brussels of C.-S. Favart resulted in a shift towards vaudevilles, similar works by local composers also being presented. The repertory in the second half of the 18th century favoured *opéras comiques*, as is evident from the *Receuil* [*sic*] *des comédies nouvelles*, published in Brussels by J.-J. Boucherie in 1756. Local composers inevitably attempted the genre, notably Pierre van Maldere (*Le médecin de l'amour*, given in 1766) and Ignaz Vitzthumb, whose *Céphalide, ou Les autres mariages samnites* (1777) indicates how popular Grétry's music was at the time. Grétry's own career took him abroad, and the same was true of such composers as Gossec and A.-F. Gresnick. The most original composer in Liège was J.-N. Hamal, who modelled his four burlesques in local dialect (1756–8) on Neapolitan *opera buffa*. More recently, Sylvain Dupuis and Eugène Ysaÿe also wrote dialect operas.

Following the Brabant Revolution (1789–90), which prompted a number of works, notably by J.-E. Pauwels, the vogue for *opéra comique* was kept alive by Charles Borremans, M.-J. Mengal and F.-J. Fétis. From the 1820s a movement towards more serious subjects can be seen in the work of H. Messemaeckers and C.-L. Hanssens. Hanssens's *Alcibiade* (1829), a grand opera to a libretto by Scribe, shows the influence of Spontini. Opera attracted numerous composers steeped in French influence, but on the whole their works did not remain long in the repertory and were rarely performed abroad. Albert Grisar, who excelled in *opéra comique* (*Bonsoir, Monsieur Pantalon!*, staged in 1851), is the only real exception, since he spent most of his career in Paris. F.-A. Gevaert also had some success there (*Quentin Durward*, 1858), but his music lacks depth and stylistic cohesion. From the 1870s, Belgian composers became more eclectic: Fernand Le Borne, Nicolas Daneau and several others followed French models, while Emile Mathieu, F. M. Servais and Léon Du Bois (*Le mort*, 1894) were closer to Wagner. Eugène Samuel-Holeman's chamber opera *La jeune fille à la fenêtre* (1905) is distinguished by economy of means and novel harmonies.

During the 19th century several composers, such as Karel Miry, occasionally wrote operas to Flemish librettos. The establishment at Antwerp in 1893 of the Vlaamse Opera (from 1920 the Koninklijke Vlaamse (Royal Flemish) Opera) gave a boost to this repertory, originally dominated by followers of Peter Benoit. Of these, Jan Blockx (*Herbergprinses*, 1896) is notable for his effective dramatic scores, which frequently employ Flemish folk melodies. Edgar Tinel wrote religious dramas such as *Godelieve* (1897), which follow the German Romantic style of the mid-19th century. Paul Gilson, the most gifted Belgian composer of his generation, stayed faithful to the Wagnerian conception of music drama (*Prinses Zonneschijn*, 1903), although his brilliant orchestration betrays a Russian influence.

Among composers of the inter-war years, Albert Dupuis and Victor Vreuls were influenced by Franck, while Léon Jongen and Gaston Brenta sought vivid effects through colourful orchestration. Francis de Bourguignon and Marcel Poot (*Moretus*, composed in 1944, first performed at La Monnaie in 1950) show neo-classical influences, and Jean Absil has successfully turned towards *opéra bouffe* (*Fansou, ou Le chapeau chinois*, 1947).

Louis de Meester and Raymond Chevreuille mainly composed operas for radio, whose technical possibilities they exploited in their scores. In *Votre Faust* (1969), Henri Pousseur and Michel Butor created a work which involves the audience in its performance, and whose score is based on quotations from composers from Monteverdi to Webern. During the 1980s, the directors of La Monnaie at Brussels and of the Flanders Opera (resulting from the merging of the Ghent and Antwerp operas) commissioned operas from Philippe Boesmans (*La passion de Gilles*, 1983) and André Laporte (*Das Schloss*, 1986), both of whom reveal a debt to Berg, and from Willem Kersters (*Gansendonk*, 1984).

For further information on operatic life in the country's principal centres *see* ANTWERP; BRUSSELS; GHENT; and LIÈGE.

*

C. van den Borren: *Geschiedenis van de muziek in de Nederlanden*, ii (Antwerp, 1951)

R. Wangermée: *La musique belge contemporaine* (Brussels, 1959)

R. Wangermée and P. Mercier: *La musique en Wallonie et à Bruxelles*, ii (Brussels, 1982)

HENRI VANHULST

Belgrade (Serbo-Croat: Beograd). Capital of the former state of Yugoslavia. Before the foundation of the Belgrade Opera, opera was performed as part of the repertory of the National Theatre, founded in 1868. The 714-seat theatre, built in 1869, was reconstructed in 1922 with 944 seats; it was replaced in 1980 by a new building, with 660 seats (including 38 boxes). Performances in the 19th century were mainly of a type of Serbian Singspiel popularized by Davorin Jenko who, as composer-conductor for the National Theatre (1871–1902), provided incidental music for productions. The first all-sung opera staged there, in 1884, was Massé's *Les noces de Jeannette*, and the first Serbian opera Stanislav Binički's *Na uranku* ('At Dawn'), which received its première in 1903. Before 1914 not all the performances were fully professional, but between the two world wars standards rose to a high level, especially after the establishment of the Belgrade Opera in 1920 with Binički as director (succeeded by Stevan Hristić, 1925–35) and the arrival of many Russian singers, refugees from the revolution. By 1938–9 the number of performances each season had risen from the initial 58 or so to 164 with frequent inclusion of Italian and Russian works. Especially successful were performances conducted by Lovro von Matačić and directed by Erich Hetzel during the period from 1938.

The company became well known in Europe under Oskar Danon's directorship (1945–64). Operas performed during the company's guest appearances throughout Europe under Danon, Krešimir Baranović and others included *Boris Godunov*, *Khovanshchina*, *Don Quichotte*, *Kát'a Kabanová*, *Faust*, *The Love for Three Oranges*, *The Gambler* and *Yevgeny Onegin*. The company made complete recordings of *Prince Igor* (1955), *Yevgeny Onegin* and *A Life for the Tsar* (1956), and also *Don Quichotte*. Premières of works by Serbian composers include Hristić's *Suton* ('The Twilight'), Petar Konjović's *Knez od Zete* ('The Prince of Zeta') and Mihovil Logar's *Pokondirena tikva* ('The Stuck-up Woman').

*

ES (L. Salvini)

M. Djoković, ed.: *Jedan vek Narodnog pozorišta u Beogradu, 1868–1968* [A Century of the National Theatre in Belgrade] (Belgrade, 1968)

ROKSANDA PEJOVIĆ

Belhomme, Hypolite (*b* Paris, 1 Dec 1854; *d* Nice, 16 Jan 1923). French bass. He studied at the Paris Conservatoire and made his début as Baskir in Félicien David's *Lalla-Roukh* for the Opéra-Comique in 1879. He remained with the company until 1916, taking a wide variety of roles, some of them comic and comprimario such as the Sacristan in *Tosca* and Benoit in *La bohème*. He created Crespel in *Les contes d'Hoffmann*, appeared as Pistol in the Opéra-Comique's first *Falstaff* (1894) and was a noted Don Basilio in *Il barbiere di Siviglia*. He sang in other French towns, and in 1905 sang Kecal in the first French-language performance of *The Bartered Bride* at La Monnaie in Brussels, but otherwise had no international career. Recordings of his fine, sonorous voice show technical accomplishment not notably inferior to that of his contemporary, the renowned Pol Plançon. J. B. STEANE

Belisani [Bellisani, Belisana, Vellisani] **Buini** [Buina], **Cecilia** (*b* Bologna, *fl* 1716–67). Italian singer. She is referred to in some programmes as Ferrarese – perhaps through confusion with her father, the bass Francesco Belisani – but is the 'Belisania' mentioned in the celebrated frontispiece of Marcello's *Il teatro alla moda*. She sang in *opera seria* and pastoral dramas from 1716 (*Armida abbandonata*), mostly in works by the Bolognese composer G. M. Buini, whom she married in 1721, but parts were also written for her by Vivaldi (*Gli inganni per vendetta*, 1720), Chelleri, Orlandini, Brivio and others. From 1727 she styled herself *virtuosa* of the Prince of Hessen-Darmstadt, governor of Mantua.

*

G. F. Malipiero: *Antonio Vivaldi, il prete rosso* (Milan, 1958)

S. Durante: 'Alcune considerazioni sui cantanti di teatro del primo settecento e la loro formazione', *Antonio Vivaldi: teatro musicale, cultura e società: Venice 1981*, 427–82

E. Selfridge-Field: 'Marcello, Sant'Angelo and *Il teatro alla moda*', ibid, 533–46

R. Strohm: 'Vivaldi's Career as an Opera Producer', ibid, 11–66

FRANCO PIPERNO

Belisario. *Tragedia lirica* in three acts by GAETANO DONIZETTI to a libretto by SALVADORE CAMMARANO after Luigi Marchionni's adaptation of Eduard von Schenk's *Belisarius* (1820, Munich); Venice, Teatro La Fenice, 4 February 1836.

The action takes place in Byzantium and near the high mountain passes of Emo in the 6th century AD. While the public, including Belisarius's daughter Irene (mezzo-soprano), are eager to hail the victorious general on his return, his wife Antonina (soprano) tells the captain of the imperial guards, Eutropio (tenor), that she believes Belisarius responsible for the death of their son. After being greeted by Emperor Justinian (bass), Belisarius (baritone) frees his prisoners; but one, Alamiro (tenor), refuses to leave his side, revealing that he is a Greek, although raised by a barbarian along the shores of the Bosphorus. Belisarius accepts him as a replacement for the son he has lost. Their duet, 'Sul campo della gloria', is an early but arresting example of the friendship duet, a genre Verdi was to exploit. Entering, Eutropio demands Belisarius's sword, bidding him appear for trial; but Belisarius will yield his sword only to a brave man and hands it instead to Alamiro. On the basis of forged documents Belisarius is accused of plotting to seize the imperial throne; shown the evidence, Belisarius sees treasonable additions to his letters to Antonina. When he asks her to denounce the forgeries, she claims that the documents have not been altered and, further, publicly accuses him of filicide. Belisarius confesses to having ordered his son's death as the result of a dream that had told him that only by so doing could he save the Byzantine Empire from destruction. The universal shock is expressed in the slow section of the Act 1 finale.

Act 2 begins outside the prison where Belisarius is confined. His veterans reveal that his sentence has been commuted from death to blindness and exile. Alamiro, outraged at the barbarity of this judgment, vows revenge in an aria, 'Trema, Bisanzio!': a vigorous, triple-metre cabaletta whose forthright expression and formal economy presage 'Di quella pira' (*Il trovatore*). Irene prepares to lead her father into exile. At first he does not recognize her, but he is so moved by her concern that he wants to weep. The tenderness and intensity of their duet, 'Ah! se potessi piangere', prefigures another Verdi speciality, the father-daughter duet.

Act 3 begins as, far from home, the weary exiles withdraw into a cavern when they hear an approaching army, whose leaders include Alamiro and a young man, moving against Byzantium to avenge Belisarius's downfall. The blind man halts them and denounces Alamiro's action as treachery. By means of a cross around the young man's neck, Belisarius and Irene identify him as his son and her brother, Alessi, from whom they discover that the servant who was to have put him to death had abandoned him on the seashore. The invading army goes on its way, and Belisarius, aided by Irene and Alamiro, vows to defeat it.

After the battle, Antonina comes to Justinian's tent and confesses that she did indeed forge the evidence against her husband. Belisarius is carried in, fatally wounded, and dies proud that he is demonstrably neither a traitor to his Emperor nor a filicide. In a forceful aria, 'Egli è spento' (one of the great successes of Karoline Unger's career), Antonina expresses her anguish that he died before he could pardon her.

* * *

At the première the cast included Unger (Antonina), Celestino Salvatori (Belisarius) and Ignazio Pasini (Alamiro). Well and widely received during its first decade, *Belisario* was however overtaken by the vogue for *Lucia di Lammermoor*, which immediately precedes it in the Donizetti canon. That rarity, an opera without a romantic love interest, *Belisario* had problems sustaining its popularity because the prima donna's role is unsympathetic dramatically, in spite of her brilliant arias in the first and last acts. The plot is, in sum, an uneasy mixture of classical and Romantic elements; but considering the eloquence of the music it drew from Donizetti it is fair to say that *Belisario* does not deserve the neglect into which it has largely fallen.

WILLIAM ASHBROOK

Bell, W(illiam) H(enry) (*b* St Albans, 20 Aug 1873; *d* Gordon's Bay, Cape Province, 13 April 1946). English composer. He studied composition with Corder at the RAM, though for a short time Stanford (of the RCM) was his teacher in counterpoint. In 1893 he took an organist's post in St Albans and was a professor of harmony at the RAM from 1903 until 1912, when he became director of the South African College of Music, Cape Town. In 1919 he was appointed to the new chair of music at Cape Town University. Bell extended the college's activities by taking over the Little Theatre for ballet and opera; he resigned in 1935. Only one of his completed operas has been performed (MSS are held by Cape Town University Library). He also wrote five stage works based on Japanese noh plays, three of which were performed in Cape Town: *Tsuneyo of the Three Trees* (1926), *Hatsuyuki* (1934) and *The Pillow of Kantan* (1935).

Hippolytus, 1910–14 (music drama, 3, after Euripides), unperf.
Isabeau, 1924 (fantasia, 1), unperf.
The Mousetrap, 1928 (1, after R. L. Stevenson: *The Sire de Maletroits' Door*), unperf.
Doctor Love, 1930 (1, after Molière), unperf.
The Wandering Scholar (comedy, 1, C. Bax), Cape Town, Little, 28 Oct 1935
The Duenna, 1939 (comedy, 3, after R. B. Sheridan), unperf.
Romeo and Juliet, 1939 (inc.)

JAN BOUWS/R

Bella, Ján Levoslav [Johann Leopold] (*b* Liptovský Mikuláš, 4 Sept 1843; *d* Bratislava, 25 May 1936). Slovak composer. He was first taught music by his father, and although he pursued theology and was ordained priest in 1866, he nevertheless continued his musical studies, including composition with Sechter in Vienna (1863–5). From 1866 he was active in Banksá Bystrica and in 1869 became town and church music director in Kremnica. A scholarship in 1873 enabled him to study further in Germany and in Prague, where he met Smetana, Liszt and the influential music critic Ludevít Procházka. Besides writing songs in his native language and German, he also composed large-scale works. In 1877 he began an opera, *Jaroslav*, to a libretto by V. Pok Podebradský, but the work was never completed. He began to write a second opera in 1880, *Wieland der Schmied*, to a libretto by Oskar Schlemm after Wagner's prose scenario; it was finished ten years later and first performed at the National Theatre in Bratislava on 28 April 1926 as *Kováč Wieland*. After leaving the priesthood in 1881 Bella became organist at the Protestant church in Hermannstadt, Transylvania (now Sibiu, Romania); he also taught in schools, directed the local music society and worked as a conductor. He retired to Vienna in 1921 and settled in 1928 in Bratislava.

Bella dormente nel bosco, La ('The Sleeping Beauty in the Forest'). *Fiaba musicale* in three short acts by OTTORINO RESPIGHI to a libretto by Gian Bistolfi, after Charles Perrault's fairy-tale; original version (as *La bella addormentata nel bosco*) for puppets, Rome, Teatro dei Piccoli di Podrecca, Palazzo Odescalchi (Sala Verdi), 13 April 1922 (revised and reorchestrated for child mimes, Turin, Teatro di Torino, 9 April 1934; second revised version with new ending by Gian Luca Tocchi, RAI, 13 June 1967).

Bistolfi's adaptation of the familiar Perrault fairy-tale, though faithful to its broad outline, is full of naively whimsical details that must have suited the opera's original purpose admirably. For instance, the spindle on which the Princess (soprano) pricks her finger is itself a 'singing' role, and the spiders who weave the web around her as she sleeps likewise have voices that sing on their behalf. Moreover, in Bistolfi's version the long sleep lasts into the 20th century: the Prince (tenor) is first seen taking part in a paper chase, along with a rich American (Mr Dollar, speaking role) whose limited 'tourist' Italian leads him to misunderstand the nature of the 'sleeping beauty' completely.

There are ample opportunities for dancing, of a kind particularly appropriate for the child performers for whom the second version was designed. The final dance was updated in each successive revision – with distressingly banal results in the third version, in which Tocchi replaced Respighi's 1933 foxtrot with a twist. Respighi's own music, however, serves its simple purposes with a terse, elegantly colourful, freshly melodious perfection which none of his more ambitious operas can quite match. The many gently parodistic references range from late Baroque pomp through Wagner, Verdi's *Falstaff*, Massenet and Debussy to 20th-century popular music; yet the total effect is surprisingly unified, so manifestly sincere and apt is the composer's responsiveness to the details of the story.

The original version of *La bella* (composed during 1916–21) was performed by Vittorio Podrecca's puppet theatre all over the world for 20 years but was never published. The second version, though very successful at its première, remained unpublished until 1958. Even today the absence of a generally available printed vocal score is a serious obstacle to the wider currency which this winsome little opera, with its small orchestra and modest stage requirements, so richly deserves.

JOHN C. G. WATERHOUSE

Bella pescatrice, La ('The Beautiful Fishermaiden'). *Commedia per musica* in two acts by Pietro Alessandro Guglielmi (*see* GUGLIELMI family, (1)) to a libretto by FRANCESCO SAVERIO ZINI; Naples, Teatro Nuovo, October 1789.

Count Lumaca (bass) loves Dorinda (soprano), the daughter of a fisherman. His attempts to transform her into a gentlewoman are unsuccessful; she becomes arrogant and pretentious, and, what is worse, takes a male companion (*cicisbeo*), Celidoro (tenor). The opera ends happily when Lumaca renounces Dorinda and she returns to her true place in society. Don Alfonso (bass), who passes himself off as an itinerant dancing-master, enlivens the proceedings with *buffo* antics in Neapolitan dialect and contributes to the happy ending: he meets Dorinda at the seaside and they fall in love.

The Neapolitan librettist Zini seems to have maintained close ties with Guglielmi between 1788 and 1791, during which time they produced at least five operas together. *La bella pescatrice* was one of the most successful (it was also given under the titles *La villanella incivilita* and *La pescatrice*). Guglielmi's music fits Zini's light, cheerful libretto perfectly. Dorinda's aria 'Mi parea che sola, sola', vividly projecting her childlike innocence and her capacity for gentle mischief, is typical of the delicacy, simplicity and wit found throughout Guglielmi's score. JOHN A. RICE

Bellavite, Innocente (*b* Verona, 20 Dec 1691; *d* Verona, 9 June 1762). Italian stage designer. He studied painting first in Verona and then with the stage designer Alessandro Mauro in Venice. Between 1719 and 1721 he worked for the Teatro di S Giovanni Grisostomo in Venice, and in 1721 he moved to Turin, where he worked at the Teatro Carignano (designing the scenery for Gasparini's *Flavio Anicio Olibrio*, staged under the title *Ricimero*) and collaborated with Filippo Juvarra in celebratory displays. In 1723 he worked in Bergamo and Crema, then in Bohemia (1724–30), where he designed a small theatre – the Rasentheater – for Count Sporck at Guckuksbade; he also designed the scenery for operas performed there (including that for the première of Bioni's *Orlando furioso*, 1724) and at the count's other private theatre in Prague (Bioni's *Armida abbandonata*, 1725). After returning to Italy he designed a theatre for the Prince of Thurn und Taxis in Frankfurt in 1733, then worked in Stuttgart as architect and stage designer for the new court theatre. In 1739 he embarked on a period of intense activity in Italy as designer to the Regio Ducal Teatro in Milan and the Teatro Regio in Turin, and in Genoa. In 1745 he proposed, unsuccessfully, a design for a theatre to be built in Brescia. From 1746 to 1754 he was active in Berlin (his designs included scenery for the première of Graun's *Angelica e Medoro*, 1749); he then spent two years in Copenhagen (during which time he created the scenery for the first performance of Sarti's *Arianna e Teseo*), before returning to Verona in 1756, where he remained until his death.

Little pictorial evidence survives of Bellavite's extensive activity. Of particular interest are eight drawings (formerly in the possession of Lodovico Pogliaghi at Varese, but present whereabouts unknown) for scenery for Antonio Pollarolo's *Lucio Papirio dittatore* in the Teatro di S Giovanni Grisostomo, Venice (produced Carnival 1721; see illustration). They demonstrate how he sought both to improve on the traditional centre-focus perspective and to avoid the new 'angled vision' imposed by the Galli-Bibiena family, and instead to give greater importance to the pictorial and panoramic effects of the scenery. Bellavite had some influence on Bernardino and Fabrizio Galliari, who were his assistants, 1739–42, for the productions at the Regio Ducal Teatro, Milan, and the Teatro Regio, Turin; he collaborated with Bernadino on the first performance of Latilla's *Zenobia* at Turin in 1742.

DBI (R. Bossaglia); *ES* (M. Viale Ferrero)
C. Denina: *La Prusse littéraire sous Frédéric II*, iii (Berlin, 1791)
M. Viale Ferrero: 'Disegni inediti dello scenografo Innocente Bellavite', *Bollettino della Società Piemontese di Archeologia e di Belle Arti*, vi-vii (1952–3), 183–98
M. T. Muraro: 'Teatro di San Giovanni Grisostomo', *I teatri pubblici di Venezia (secoli XVII-XVIII)*, ed. L. Zorzi and others (Venice, 1971), 132–41 [exhibition catalogue]
M. Viale Ferrero: *La scenografia dalle origini al 1936*, Storia del Teatro Regio di Torino, iii (Turin, 1980)
P. Rigoli: 'Lettere di Innocente Bellavite e di altri scenografi per il teatro di Brescia (1745)', *Atti e memorie della Accademia di Agricoltura, Scienze e Lettere di Verona*, 6th ser., xxxvii (1985–6), 167–206 MERCEDES VIALE FERRERO

Belle Hélène, La ('The Fair Helen'). *Opéra bouffe* in three acts by JACQUES OFFENBACH to a libretto by HENRI MEILHAC and LUDOVIC HALÉVY, after classical mythology; Paris, Théâtre des Variétés, 17 December 1864.

La belle Hélène followed *Orphée aux enfers* of six years earlier as a satirical treatment of the classics, and

Stage design by Innocente Bellavite for A. Pollarolo's 'Lucio Papirio dittatore', Teatro di S Giovanni Grisostomo, Venice, 1721: drawing

Hortense Schneider as Helen in Offenbach's 'La belle Hélène', the role she created in the original production at the Théâtre des Variétés, Paris, 17 December 1864

Hélène [Helen] *Queen of Sparta*	soprano
Oreste [Orestes] *son of Agamemnon*	mezzo-soprano
Pâris [Paris] *son of King Priam of Troy*	tenor
Ménélas [Menelaus] *King of Sparta*	tenor *buffo*
Agamemnon *King of Kings*	baritone
Calchas *grand soothsayer to Jupiter*	baritone
Achille [Achilles] *King of Phtiotis*	tenor or baritone
Ajax I *King of Salamis*	tenor or baritone
Ajax II *King of the Locrians*	tenor or baritone
Bacchis *Helen's maid*	soprano

Guards, slaves, people, princes, princesses, mourners of Adonis, Helen's handmaidens

Setting Sparta and Nauplia, just before the Trojan Wars

as a very thinly disguised comment on many aspects of Second Empire society life. It was one of Offenbach's greatest successes. Above all others of his works, it was epitomized in the music he composed for Hortense Schneider in the role of Helen, and secondarily in that for José Dupuis in the role of Paris. Other members of Offenbach's standard company of the time were Grenier (Calchas), Couder (Agamemnon) and Kopp (Menelaus). Later famous Helens have included Maria Jeritza in 1911 at Salzburg, Jarmila Novotna in 1931 in Berlin (both productions by Max Reinhardt) and, in recent years, Jane Rhodes, while Jussi Björling's recording of Paris's 'Au mont Ida' has set the standard by which other versions are judged.

ACT 1 *A public square in Sparta, before the temple of Jupiter* Calchas, High Priest of Jupiter, is bemoaning the meagre sacrifices at his temple and the increase in popularity of Venus since she won the golden apple from the shepherd Paris and promised him the most beautiful maiden on earth. This is generally recognized to be Helen, wife of the somewhat dull King Menelaus, and she is excitedly contemplating what fate has in store for her ('Amours divins! Ardentes flammes!'). The shepherd Paris now arrives to claim his prize, describing how he judged the beauty contest ('Au mont Ida') and Calchas promises to help him. Helen is immediately drawn to the shepherd, but the Greek kings Achilles, Agamemnon and the two Ajaxes are busy assembling for a ceremonial contest ('Voici les rois de la Grèce!'). This takes the form of a game of charades which, to the kings' chagrin, Paris duly wins. He now reveals his identity as the son of King Priam – much to Helen's consternation ('L'homme à la pomme'). He is crowned winner by Helen, and Calchas declares that the gods have banned the reluctant Menelaus to Crete for a month ('Pars pour la Crète!').

ACT 2 *In Queen Helen's apartments* A month later the arrival of Paris at the palace is announced. Helen gazes at the wall painting of Leda and the Swan (her father and mother) and, contemplating her destiny, asks Venus what pleasure she finds in destroying her virtue ('On me nomme Hélène la blonde'). Paris insists that, after her month of dallying, she really must give herself as promised by Venus. She continues to prevaricate, and Paris vows to resort to subterfuge, as the four kings settle down to a board game, which Calchas wins by the use of loaded dice. Helen retires to her bed, asking Calchas to arrange that she at least dream of her shepherd. Seeing Paris hiding in the room dressed as a slave, Calchas decides to let matters take their course. Paris proceeds to make love to Helen, who is convinced that it is merely her dream ('Oui, c'est un rêve') until the illusion is shattered by the return of Menelaus and the hasty departure of Paris. The husband summons his fellow kings, as Helen seeks to put the blame on to him for returning from Crete without warning ('Un mari sage est en voyage'). The kings denounce Paris in incongruously seductive waltz tempo ('Un vile séducteur!').

ACT 3 *The beach at Nauplia* The whole court has come to Nauplia for the bathing season. Menelaus presses Helen to explain her action, but she is adamant that she is blameless ('Là! Vrai, je ne suis pas coupable'). Menelaus continues to express his indignation, but his fellow kings declare that it is the fault of Venus who, they claim, has turned Greece into one gigantic orgy ('Lorsque la Grèce est un champ de carnage'). Menelaus has demanded a visit from the High Priest of Venus, who now arrives yodelling a message from the goddess ('Je suis gai, soyez gais!'). He explains that he will take Helen to Cythera to sacrifice 100 white heifers to Venus. Only after the High Priest whispers in her ear is Helen finally persuaded to go, and after the boat has set sail the Priest throws off his disguise and reveals himself as Paris. He tells the people that he is taking Helen to Troy, and the kings vow they will go to war against Troy to avenge the affront to Menelaus.

* * *

As with most of Offenbach's greatest works, the creation of *La belle Hélène* seems to have been largely untroubled. With some of the composer's most shapely and expressive vocal writing in the music for Helen and Paris, some of his most beguiling waltz tunes, and with such outstanding numbers as the March of the Kings and the rousing patriotic chorus which brilliantly parodies that in Rossini's *Guillaume Tell*, the work's popularity was established from the first. There is a twinkle in the eye throughout, not least in bewitching parodies such as the mock-operatic ensemble 'L'homme à la pomme'. Offenbach composed alternative numbers for the Viennese production with Marie Geistinger, and the original German score, published by Bote & Bock in 1865, also contains the subsequently celebrated overture by an unknown arranger. ANDREW LAMB

Bellerophon. Libretto subject favoured in the 17th and 18th centuries.Bellerophon, who loves (and is loved by) Philonoë, rejects the advances of Stheneboea (or Anteia), wife of King Proteus of Argos; she causes a monster, the Chimaera, to be unleashed on the kingdom, but Bellerophon kills it, secures Philonoë's hand and turns out to be the son of Neptune.

The earliest setting is that of Sacrati, to a text by Vincenzo Nolfi, as *Bellerofonte* (1642, Venice). Lully set it for the Opéra in 1679, using a libretto by Thomas Corneille with Bernard le Bovier de Fontenelle (after Hesiod's *Theogony*); here the various magical incantations and other supernatural events provide an excuse for the extensive use of the chorus coupled with dramatic *symphonies*. Among later settings are one by Graupner to a text by Feind (1708, Hamburg), by Terradellas to a text by Vanneschi (1747, London), by Araia to a text by Bonecchi (1750, St Petersburg), by Sciroli (1760, Genoa), Mysliveček (1767, Naples), Ignazio Platania (1778, Naples) and Winter (1785, Munich). In his *Bellerofonte* Mysliveček introduced to Naples a new kind of opera, a Franco-Italian synthesis of the type being performed in Parma, Mannheim, Vienna and Stuttgart, in which an italianate libretto was infused with long-banished French spectacular elements: chorus, dance and machine effects, both natural (thunder and lightning) and unnatural (Minerva descending in a globe of clouds to kill the monster and, in the best French tradition, achieve a happy ending).

LOIS ROSOW, MARITA P. McCLYMONDS

Belletti, Giovanni Battista (*b* Sarzana, 17 Feb 1813; *d* Sarzana, 27 Dec 1890). Italian baritone. He studied with Pilotti in Bologna and made his début in Stockholm in 1838 as Figaro (*Il barbiere di Siviglia*); he then appeared there with Jenny Lind in *Robert le diable* (1839) and *Lucia di Lammermoor* (1840), both sung in Swedish. In 1848 he was engaged at Her Majesty's Theatre, singing in the first London performance of *Attila*, in *L'elisir d'amore* and *Don Pasquale*, and as Mozart's and Rossini's Figaro. He sang in Paris at the Théâtre Italien in *Semiramide*, *Fidelio* and Mercadante's *Il bravo*. In 1853 he appeared at Covent Garden, singing Silva (*Ernani*), Saint-Bris (*Les Huguenots*), Alphonse (*La favorite*), Don Giovanni and Tristan d'Acunha (Spohr's *Jessonda*). His beautiful voice and fine musicianship were much admired by his contemporaries. ELIZABETH FORBES

Bellezza, Vincenzo (*b* Bitonto, Bari, 17 Feb 1888; *d* Rome, 8 Feb 1964). Italian conductor. At the Naples Conservatory he studied with Alessandro Longo, Nicola d'Arienzo and Giuseppe Martucci. He made his début at the S Carlo with *Aida* in 1908, and as music director of the Caramba-Scognamiglio Operetta Company, 1912–16, he toured Italy. In 1917 he went to the Teatro Colón, Buenos Aires, and for some years alternated between South America and Europe. He first appeared at Covent Garden in 1926, conducting Boito's *Mefistofele* at Shalyapin's Covent Garden début and participating in Melba's farewell performance. From 1926 to 1930 he was a regular conductor of the Italian repertory at Covent Garden, during which time he conducted the British première of *Turandot* (1927) and the London débuts of Ponselle (1929) and Gigli (1930), and from 1926 to 1935 he was also guest conductor at the Metropolitan. In 1935 he returned to Covent Garden for a year, then worked almost entirely in Italy, chiefly at the Rome Opera. He reappeared in London at the independent Italian opera seasons at the Stoll Theatre in 1957 and Drury Lane the next year. A reliable and skilled conductor, he combined attention to detail with consideration for the singers, and achieved performances that were effective at the time rather than memorable in retrospect. PIERO RATTALINO

Belli, Domenico (*d* Florence, bur. 5 May 1627). Italian composer. He is first heard of in 1610–13, when he served as musical instructor at S Lorenzo, Florence. Between those dates and September 1619, when he became a musician at the Medici court, he established himself as an audacious composer of opera and solo song: his sole surviving theatrical work, *Orfeo dolente*, was performed and published in 1616, the year that his only known collection of accompanied song also appeared.

Orfeo dolente, a set of five *intermedi*, was presented between the acts of Tasso's *Aminta* during Carnival 1616 at the Palazzo della Gherardesca, the Rinaldi family residence, in Florence and published in Venice the same year (libretto reprinted in Solerti, 1905, pp.375–91; music ed. A. Tirabassi in *Torquato Tasso: Aminta*, ed. A. de Rudder, Brussels, 1927). In a series of brief *tableaux* Orpheus (tenor) grieves for Eurydice in lyrical interaction with his mother Calliope (soprano), Pluto (bass) and the Three Graces; they are joined by a chorus of Nymphs and Shepherds who try in vain to distract him with song and dance. In the fashion of other early librettos, the work ends with Orpheus' acceptance of his fate and his companions' apotheosis of his faithful love (though in Ovid's original ending Orpheus is punished for scorning love and women). The text is probably a reworking by Gabriello Chiabrera of his *Il pianto d'Orfeo*, a *favoletta da recitar cantando* published in 1615 but dating from the Florentine festivities of 1608.

Belli's musical style, noted for its striking chromaticism, places him among the most daring of monodists. According to Dahlhaus, his harmonic boldness results not from avant-garde harmonic practices but from the contrapuntal manipulation of chromatic lines in the service of textual expression. Caccini, describing a performance in 1618 of Belli's setting of *Andromeda* (now lost; text by Jacopo Cicognini), remarked that 'it had so much variety of invention and sweetness of harmony ... [that Belli] could exult in having demonstrated the effectiveness of the art of judiciously accompanied music' (Solerti, 128).

A. Solerti: *Musica, ballo e drammatica alla corte medicea dal 1600 al 1637* (Florence, 1905), 106, 127–8, 375–91

A. Tirabassi: 'The Oldest Opera: Belli's *Orfeo dolente*', *MQ*, xxv (1939), 26–33

C. Dahlhaus: 'Domenico Belli und der chromatische Kontrapunkt um 1600', *Mf*, xv (1962), 315–40

Y. Corboz: 'L'oeuvre de Domenico Belli: une contribution au "stile recitativo" et "rappresentativo" ', *SMz*, cxx (1980), 213–24

BARBARA R. HANNING

Bellincioni, Gemma (Cesira Matilda) (*b* Como, 18 Aug 1864; *d* Naples, 23 April 1950). Italian soprano. She was taught by her father, a professional bass, and later by the famous tenor Roberto Stagno, whom she first met in 1886 and subsequently married. Except in the role of Violetta (in which she was praised by Verdi), she was rarely at her best in the older type of opera, and came into her own, both as actress and as singer, with the arrival of the *verismo* school of opera; the great event of her life was her sensational portrayal of Santuzza in the première of *Cavalleria rusticana* (1890), with Stagno as Turiddu. Though very successful in the principal European opera houses and in South America, she failed to establish herself at Covent Garden, where she appeared in 1895 amidst a company that was exceptionally strong in soprano talent; even her Santuzza, like her Carmen, was overshadowed by the immense popularity of Calvé. She created many other roles in *verismo* operas, among them Giordano's Fedora, with the then unknown Caruso as Loris. The last phase of her career was dominated by *Salome*; she appeared in the first Italian performance of the opera (1906, Turin) under Strauss, who much admired her interpretation, and sang the role over 100 times. After World War I she spent some years as a teacher of singing in Holland, and in 1924 reappeared as Santuzza, Tosca and Carmen at The Hague, Rotterdam and Amsterdam. Her 14 early recordings (1903–5), though dramatic, lend support to the view that sheer voice was not her strongest suit.

GV (R. Celletti; R. Vegeto)
G. Bellincioni: *Io e il palcoscenico* (Milan, 1920/*R*1977 with discography)
B. Stagno Bellincioni: *Roberto Stagno e Gemma Bellincioni, intimi* (Florence, 1943)
J. B. Richards: 'Gemma Bellincioni', *Record Collector*, xvi (1964–6), 197–219 [with discography]; xviii (1968–9), 139–40

DESMOND SHAWE-TAYLOR

Bellini. Theatre in Naples, built in 1864, rebuilt in 1878 and used mainly for opera until 1908; it became a cinema in 1950. *See* NAPLES, §3.

Bellini, Vincenzo (*b* Catania, 3 Nov 1801; *d* Puteaux, nr Paris, 23 Sept 1835). Italian composer, a leading figure in early 19th-century opera, admired particularly for the graceful, expressive lines of his melodies.

1. EDUCATION AND EARLY CAREER (1801–26). Bellini was the eldest of seven children born to a family of musicians. His grandfather, Vincenzo Tobia Bellini, from the Abruzzi, had studied at a Naples conservatory and from 1767–8 had been an organist, composer and teacher in Catania. Bellini's father, Rosario, was also a composer, *maestro di cappella* and teacher. Vincenzo was given piano lessons by his father long before normal school age; a priest taught him the rudiments of school learning. According to a manuscript in the Museo Belliniano, Catania, he could play the piano marvellously at little more than five years of age; he also showed an excellent ear and memory. At six he wrote his first composition and at seven he was taught Latin, modern languages, rhetoric and philosophy. His principal composition teacher after his seventh year was his grandfather. Bellini was now writing much sacred music; soon it was not only in churches that his compositions were heard, but also in the salons of the aristocrats and patricians, for which he wrote his first ariettas and probably instrumental pieces.

Bellini went to Naples in June 1819 to study at the conservatory, where his first teacher was Giovanni Furno; Carlo Conti supervised him as a *maestrino*, and he learnt counterpoint, probably from 1821, with Giacomo Tritto. In 1822 he entered the class of the director, Niccolò Zingarelli, studying strict composition and solfège, the masters of the so-called Neapolitan school and the instrumental works of Haydn and Mozart.

It was a custom at the Naples Conservatory to introduce a composition student who had completed his studies to the public at large with a dramatic work, and in 1825 Bellini and a cast of male pupils of the conservatory performed *Adelson e Salvini*, his *opera semiseria*, in the conservatory theatre. Its success led to a commission for an opera for a gala evening at the Teatro S Carlo. *Bianca e Fernando* (renamed *Bianca e Gernando* out of consideration for the late king) met with good success in May 1826. His hopes for a performance at the Teatro del Fondo of his reworking of *Adelson e Salvini* came to nothing. He was also disappointed in his hope of marrying a Neapolitan girl, Maddelena Fumaroli. Thus his good fortune was all the more appreciable when he received from the impresario Barbaia a *scrittura* for an opera for La Scala, Milan.

2. OPERATIC SUCCESS (1827–33). In Milan, between May and October 1827, Bellini composed his third opera, *Il pirata*, which laid the foundation of his career. He achieved the kind of public success that came to Donizetti only after more than 30 operas (*Anna Bolena*, 1830). With *Il pirata* Bellini began his fruitful collaboration with the librettist Felice Romani, who was to write the librettos for six further operas – no other Italian opera composer of the time showed such attachment to a single librettist. This partnership was founded not only on Bellini's admiration for the sonorousness and elegance of the poet's verses, but also on the friendship that united the composer and Romani until their eventual estrangement over *Beatrice di Tenda*. 1827 also marked the beginning of his close working relationship with the tenor G. B. Rubini (who had appeared in *Bianca e Gernando* in 1826), an association which continued until *I puritani* (1835) and was as fruitful for the singer as for the composer. Later Bellini was to work just as closely with Giuditta Pasta (in *La sonnambula*, *Norma* and *Beatrice di Tenda*). Early in 1828 *Il pirata* was performed in Vienna: Bellini was already attracting attention abroad.

Between 1827 and 1833 Bellini lived mostly in Milan, where he quickly gained an his entrée into higher social circles. He made his living solely from opera commissions; unlike his colleagues Rossini, Donizetti, Pacini and Mercadante, he never held an official position at a conservatory or an opera house. He was able to ask a higher price for his works than had been usual in Italy. For months he lived at the country residences of his friends, the Cantù and Turina families, and until 1833 had a passionate love affair with Giuditta Turina, who was unhappily married (it began in April 1828 in Genoa, where the second version of *Bianca e Fernando* was enjoying a success as the opening production of the Teatro Carlo Felice). The second important landmark in his artistic career, after *Il pirata*, was *La straniera*, performed in February 1829, again at La Scala. Its success exceeded even that of *Il pirata*, but it also gave rise to critical debate (see Cambi 1943) about the work's genuinely novel style. In May 1829 Bellini opened the new Teatro Ducale in Parma. *Zaira* however was a failure, partly caused by ill-feeling (it was thought that Bellini showed too little enthusiasm for the undertaking). All the more marked, therefore, was the success, barely a year later, of *I Capuleti e i Montecchi* at the Fenice in Venice.

Bellini knew that he had reached his years of mastery. He wrote on 28 March 1830: 'My style is now heard in the most important theatres in the world ... and with the greatest enthusiasm'. Early in 1830 he had a violent attack of gastro-enteritis, the illness of which he was to die five years later; he spent the summer convalescing at Lake Como. In August he directed rehearsals of *La straniera* in Bergamo and in the autumn began to compose *Ernani*. Felice Romani had adapted part of Hugo's play as a libretto, but the project was abandoned because of fears of censorship difficulties. Instead he wrote *La sonnambula*, performed with enormous success at the Teatro Carcano in Milan in March 1831. *Norma*, which opened the 1831–2 carnival season at La Scala, did not at first fare as well: 'Fiasco, fiasco, solenne fiasco' reported Bellini. The public soon, however, began to understand the worth of this masterpiece. It was with an easy mind that he was able, on 5 January 1832, to set out for Naples and Sicily; the journey became a veritable triumphal procession when he reached his native island. Back in Milan at the end of May, he directed rehearsals of *Norma* in Bergamo and Venice. *Beatrice di Tenda*, the new opera for Venice, was a failure, but Bellini considered *Beatrice* 'not unworthy of her sisters'.

3. Final activity: London and Paris (1833–5). In April Bellini travelled to London. *Il pirata*, *Norma* and *I Capuleti e i Montecchi* (with Pasta as principal) were highly successful at the King's Theatre, as was *La sonnambula* (with Malibran in the title role) at Drury Lane. In August he went to Paris. Negotiations with the Opéra came to nothing, but he came to terms with the Théâtre Italien, where *Il pirata* and *I Capuleti e i Montecchi* were staged successfully in the autumn. Since negotiations over a new opera were long drawn out (only early in 1834 did he receive a definite commission), Bellini had time to devote himself to social life, for which he had also shown enthusiasm in London. He formed a closer acquaintance with Rossini, who became a fatherly friend, and got to know Chopin, Carafa, Paer and other musicians. In the salon of Princess Belgioioso, who had emigrated to Paris, he met Heinrich Heine. Of the musical impressions he received in Paris, the strongest was of performances of Beethoven at the Conservatoire: 'È bel comme la nature', Bellini cried to Ferdinand Hiller after the Sixth Symphony.

In April 1834 Bellini began work on *I puritani*, to a libretto by the Italian émigré Count Carlo Pepoli – 'after a year of real solid rest', as the composer put it. At about the same time as the commission from the Théâtre Italien, he received from Naples an invitation to write a new opera. He declined for reasons of time, but remained in touch with the directors of the Teatro S Carlo. The outcome of numerous proposals and counter-proposals was a second version of *I puritani*, adapted to the voices of Malibran, Duprez and Porto; this however was not performed, since the score did not arrive in Naples by the agreed deadline. With the Paris version of *I puritani*, the only one to be published, Bellini enjoyed a genuine triumph in January 1835, a few months after the success of *La sonnambula* in the same theatre. He was appointed a Chevalier of the Légion d'honneur. Bellini found he had arrived at the point to which his ambition had always led him, 'namely, second only to Rossini'. He decided to remain in Paris. During the early months of 1835, once again without a commission for an opera, project succeeded project in his head. These plans concerned a hoped-for marriage, his career in general and certain operas in particular. Negotiations with the Opéra and the Opéra-Comique dragged on, and none of the projects was accomplished. At the end of August he fell ill, and on 23 September he died, alone, at a country house in the Paris suburb of Puteaux, apparently in isolation because of suspected cholera. The post-mortem gave the true cause of death: 'It is clear that Bellini succumbed to an acute inflammation of the large intestine, complicated by an abscess of the liver'. The requiem was at the Church of the Invalides on 2 October. 'Paer, Cherubini, Carafa and Rossini each held a corner of the shroud', according to one report of the ceremony. He was buried in the Père Lachaise cemetery, but in 1876 his remains were moved to the cathedral of his native town, Catania.

4. Character. The most celebrated literary portrait of the composer is that by Heinrich Heine (*Florentinische Nächte*, 1837). His amusing portrayal lays bare only one side (at most) of Bellini, however: the somewhat dandyish aspect, probably characteristic of him at least during his Paris period. Even so, Heine noted that 'his character was thoroughly noble and good. His soul certainly remained pure and unsullied by anything hateful'. That Bellini retained an essential integrity is also testified to by other observers whom there is no reason to disbelieve. His lifelong friend Francesco Florimo spoke of an 'animo candido'. Rossini said to the painter Guglielmo De Sanctis: 'He had a most beautiful, exquisitely humane soul'. Ferdinand Hiller wrote: 'His personality was like his melodies – it was captivating – just as charming as it was sympathetic', and that 'his thinking was acute and his feelings animated ... He knew very well what he wanted, and was far from the kind of purely instinctive artist as which he is often portrayed'. This reflective side of Bellini's personality is much in evidence in a number of letters in which he wrote about his art.

'Animo candido', but not 'angelico': there were darker sides to Bellini's nature. Not infrequently he reacted to his fellow composers with mistrust, envy and even malevolence. Much of this may have been occasioned by the rivalries that were inevitably a feature of operatic life. But Bellini often went to needless lengths, as in his relationship with Donizetti. One need only compare his thoroughly spiteful derogation of *Marino Faliero* (letter of 1 April 1835) with Donizetti's ungrudging admiration of *Norma* (his letter of 31 December 1831). Negative aspects of his character are also unmistakable in his dealings with women. That he did not take his minor love affairs very seriously (their frequency has been exaggerated in popular literature) should bring reproaches only from strict moralists. But it is less easy to condone the fact that even when, as in his relationship with Giuditta Turina, he felt ardent passion, he was still capable of cold calculation (letter to Florimo, 27 September 1828); he did not emerge with much credit from his relationship with a woman seriously in love with him. His marriage plans of 1834–5 were as egotistical as they were vague; his letters mention no names, but speak much of a dowry.

Bellini was not a delicate, melancholy being without strong masculine qualities. Florimo described his character as not only 'sincere, amiable, appreciative, modest' but also 'passionate, inflammable, bold'; Giovanni Ricordi spoke of a 'volcanic character, quick to erupt'. In Parisian theatrical circles he was considered, as he himself wrote to Florimo in 1835, 'a little haughty and full of vanity'.

5. Sources of style. The first influences on Bellini were Rossini, the teaching of Zingarelli and the folk music of his native Sicily and of Naples. During his time at the conservatory, Florimo reported to Scherillo, Bellini enjoyed making music out of an 'anthology of Sicilian poetry'. The influence of Sicilian folk music may lie behind his preference for melodies that move in small intervals and compound metres. But long before 1825 Sicilian folk music had already affected art music generally. The influence of Neapolitan folk music is even more elusive though certain affinities are evident. Zingarelli will have stressed to him that melody is the central element of music and must be conceived in the simplest possible way. But he could not prevent Bellini from falling under the influence of Rossini, with his vital melodies and rhythms and his superabundance of coloratura, which went against all 'simplicity'. The Naples *Semiramide* of 1824 was a decisive experience in Bellini's student period.

Adelson e Salvini shows the young composer combining these tendencies and influences. There are echoes of Rossini in the score: in the crescendos of the *introduzione* and the first finale, in numerous orchestral motifs, in the part of the *buffo* character Bonifacio, but also in a number of cantilenas in the *parti serie* (such as the beginning of Adelson's entrance aria 'Obliarti! abbandonarti!'). But this first opera also presents evidence of an entirely independent cast of expression: a genuinely Romantic feeling for sound, evident in major–minor shifts and in the emphatic élan of certain melodies. Such exuberant effusions represented something new in Italian, indeed European, opera. It is misleading to relate Bellini's novel lyrical style to the 'Neapolitan school'; rather, it represented a sentimentalization and heightening of Rossinian lyricism. But this too neglects the spontaneity with which a new, profoundly Romantic form of expression sprang into being. In *Adelson*, and in the two versions of *Bianca e Fernando*, passages of strongly individual expression remain few by comparison with the operas of any respected Italian contemporary. In *Il pirata*, however, an original style is more apparent, and the work is more tightly and impressively integrated. Thereafter Bellini was one of Italy's most influential composers, particularly after Rossini's early decision to abandon opera. Quintessential features of Italian opera after Rossini can be traced back to Bellini; Donizetti and Pacini, Mercadante and Verdi all learnt from him.

6. Words and music. Foremost among the essentials of Bellini's music – the operas of 1827–35 will be discussed here synoptically rather than chronologically – is the close relationship between music and text (which impressed his contemporaries to the extent that they often called his music 'filosofica'). It even won Wagner's approval: 'Bellini's music comes from the heart, and it is intimately bound up with the text', he told Florimo in 1880. The new seriousness with which Bellini treated his text represented a reaction against Rossini's frequent nonchalance. In Bellini's melodies the text is precisely declaimed and the verbal and musical accents normally coincide. Moreover, each scene's intellectual content and mood are interpreted in the music. Bellini did not essay any pervasive and systematic musical delineation of character; like the generality of Italian operas of the period from about 1815 to 1850, his works present a sequence of scenes depicting particular emotions, not always psychologically connected. Whether a good or a bad character expressed these emotions was immaterial: villains (like Filippo in *Beatrice di Tenda*) used the same beautiful cantabile style as the purer souls. A love aria remains a love aria, whoever sings it. True musical characterization of individuals entered Italian opera only with middle- and late-period Verdi.

Associated with this new seriousness was a lessening in the number and the extent of coloratura passages. In *La straniera* he restricted them to a degree that led critics to speak of 'declamazione cantata, o canto declamato' (see ex. 1, from the cabaletta of the duet

Ex.1
Allegro moderato
Un ul - ti-mo ad-di - o ri - ce - vi, in-fe - li - ce, di
più non pos - s'i - o, di più non ti li - ce,

['Receive my last farewell, unhappy one, more I cannot do, more you are not allowed to do']

between Arturo and Alaide in Act 1). This radical approach was bound up with Bellini's efforts to break free from the Rossinian style, 'to introduce a new genre and a music which should express the text as closely as possible, making a unity of song and drama' (see Cicconetti). From *La sonnambula* on he gave somewhat more space to coloratura, but often integrated it thematically (as in ex.2, from the second Elvino–Amina

Ex.2
Andante assai sostenuto
Son ge - lo - so del ze - fi-ro er - ran - te che ti
abbandonandosi
a tempo
scher - za, che ti scher - za col cri - ne, col ve - lo

['I envy the roving breeze that plays with your hair, with your veil']

duet in Act 1 of *La sonnambula*, or Norma's 'Casta diva').

Bellini needed a good libretto and good verse to fire his imagination. A good libretto was one with thrilling situations and verses 'designed to portray the passions in the liveliest manner' (letter to Florimo, 4 August 1834); 'Opera, through singing, must make one weep, shudder, die' (letter to Count Pepoli, early 1834). In his demands for dramatically tense situations (he praised the far-fetched plot of *La straniera* as 'full of situations, all of them new and magnificent'; letter to Florimo, August

1828), Bellini resembled Verdi in his early and middle periods, but he was probably more fastidious than any Italian contemporary in his feeling for the poetic merits and deficiencies of verse. The fact that he was 'very fond of good words' (letter to Florimo, September 1828) led him to adhere faithfully to Romani, the best versifier of the time.

It is hard to believe in the authenticity of Bellini's alleged letter to Gallo, setting out his method of composition: study of the characters; declamation of the verses and attention to their 'speech melody'; translation of the speech melody into musical melody; trying-out on the piano. In fact, Bellini's melodies arose in varied ways: often, certainly, through the inspiration of a specific text, but equally frequently in 'daily exercises', which consisted in sketching out melodies at random. Several Bellini scenes are provisioned from stocks of such melodies (sketches are in the Museo Belliniano, Catania) and from parodies of earlier pieces (proportionally no fewer than they are in Rossini). It is not only in subsidiary scenes that Bellini used existing melodies but also in central ones – the worship scene in *Norma*, the duet of Adalgisa and Pollione, the first-act finale in *I Capuleti e i Montecchi*.

7. MELODY AND SONORITY. In a letter to Camille Bellaigue (2 May 1898), Verdi praised the broad curves of Bellini's melody: 'there are extremely long melodies as no-one else had made before'. This was indeed one of Bellini's greatest contributions, and the more remarkable in that these curves are built up of small (generally two-bar) units of the same rhythmic types used by his Italian contemporaries and corresponding to the various Italian verse forms. Bellini's works belong to that phase of Italian operatic music characterized by melodic correspondence and symmetry; there are very few metrically irregular melodies. Bellini employed a variety of techniques: for example, pitch climaxes in which the melody forces its way systematically upwards, as in 'Casta diva', the avoidance of accentuated harmonic cadences over long periods, as in Amina's 'Ah! non credea mirarti' (*La sonnambula*), or the combination of melodic gesture and dynamic intensification. In addition to the passages already mentioned, the Act 2 finale of *Norma* (particularly the E major section) and the Larghetto from the Act 2 quintet of *Beatrice di Tenda* are notable examples. In these passages, as in 'Casta diva', the melodic climax comes at the end – a striking innovation. Verdi was influenced by it: for example, in Leonora's *preghiera* 'Madre, pietosa Vergine' in the second act of *La forza del destino*.

A second new feature is the use of sonority to ecstatic effect. At the climax of 'Casta diva' Bellini luxuriates in sound in an unprecedented manner, and again, still more so, in the closing scene mentioned above. Here his tendency towards an ecstatic unfolding of sonorities reaches its highest expression. The way in which the sequential motif in the E major section screws itself up to the harmonically accented (tritone) climax over many bars is intoxicating in effect, new in 1831. These sequences also influenced Wagner, as in the mounting sequences of *Tristan*. The novelty of Bellini's climaxes lies in part in the treatment of dissonance. In the Act 2 finale of *Norma* the dissonances at the outset are resolved on notes of crotchet length, notably on weak beats of the bar (ex.3). But then Bellini gives the consonances less and less room: almost without exception they are only semiquaver passing notes. The tension is

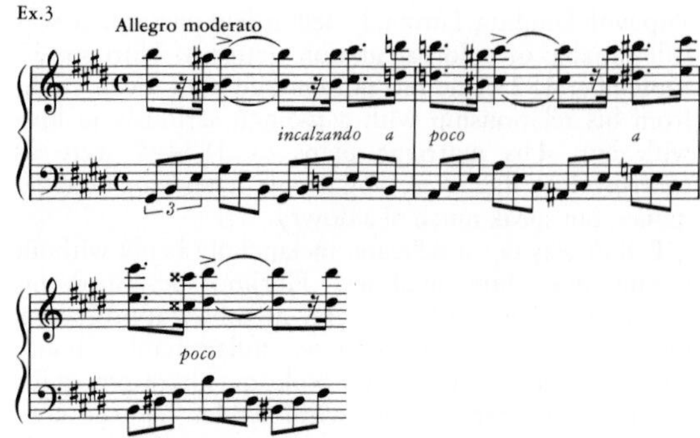
Ex.3
Allegro moderato
incalzando a
poco
a
poco

immensely strengthened, and finds its resolution in an E major chord on a strong beat.

The Romanticism of Bellini's music is grounded above all in his ecstasy of sound. A Romantic approach to sound is also apparent in his preference for small intervals. He favoured melodies that gain intensity and, frequently, a curious sweetness by sliding over semitone steps. Examples are, again, 'Casta diva', the first part of Isoletta's aria in Act 2 of *La straniera* and 'Prendi, l'anel ti dono' in the first duet between Amina and Elvino in *La sonnambula* (ex.4). Such melodies are wholly

Ex.4
Andante sostenuto
Pren - di, l'a - nel ti do - no che un
dì, che un dì re - ca - va al - l'a - - ra

['Take the ring I give you, which once she carried to the altar']

typical, though Bellini by no means abandoned writing melodies with large intervals (consider the wide pitch range of the final number of *La straniera*, the cabaletta 'Or sei pago, o ciel tremendo'). For Berlioz, and for Federico Ricci, Bellini's melodic style was characterized by the predominance of the third degree of the major scale. Neither realized that a predilection for the 3rd (often by way of an upwards leap of a 6th and associated with a suspended 4th) is a hallmark of the Romantic operatic style in general. But Bellini's melodies of this type are among the most convincing examples of that kind of Romantic exuberance. Even more typically Romantic are melodies characterized by a double leap, as in ex.5 (the cabaletta from Elvino's

Ex.5
Allegro moderato
Ah! per-chè non pos - so o - diar - ti

['Ah! why do I not hate you']

second-act aria in *La sonnambula*). The leap of a 6th to the 3rd above the bass is eclipsed by the emphasis in the following bar on the rise to the 6th above the bass, which functions as a suspension to the 5th: a fundamentally Romantic type of melody often found in Bellini's work.

Autograph score of the beginning of Act 2 of Bellini's 'Norma', composed in 1831; note the direction in bar 3 that the curtain should be raised, and the pause in bar 4 to allow time for this to happen before the new theme begins in bar 5

8. OTHER ASPECTS OF STYLE. Bellini's treatment of rhythm, like that of Donizetti and early Verdi, lacks the individuality of his melodic style. Certain formulae are all too frequent in the orchestral accompaniments. In the rhythmic construction of his vocal lines Bellini, again like Donizetti and early Verdi, inclined towards isorhythm: a model chosen for the first verse is readily retained for the whole piece or a large part of it. This is closely allied to the melodic hyperperiodicity mentioned above. On the others hand, those melodies in which he breaks through this hyperperiodicity merit attention; often they are those in which he strives for 'melodie lunghe lunghe lunghe' (Verdi). In Amina's 'Ah! non credea mirarti' none of the first 11 bars matches any of the others rhythmically.

With regard to Bellini's harmonic style, his fine treatment of dissonance should be mentioned again, as should the frequent interchange of major and minor. *La straniera* is rich in harmonic shifts into remote keys, and colourful modulations abound in *I puritani*. Bellini's orchestra, like Donizetti's, provides reticent, chordal accompaniments to markedly cantabile lines. Sometimes, however, as in the middle sections of arias, it comes vividly to the fore with motifs. In choruses and dialogues it may actually dominate, imparting unity and continuity to the scene through the use of a single motif. From 1831, the instrumentation sometimes becomes more highly coloured, notably in *I puritani*.

A composer who took a strong sensual delight in sound, and whose ecstatic sonorities betray the Romantic spirit *par excellence*, might be supposed to lack formal clarity or even to disregard it. In fact, Bellini's luxuriance in sound is combined with a strict economy of formal layout and occurs within confined limits. His favourite aria form is *A* (lines 1 and 2 of the first stanza), generally four bars in all; A^2 (lines 3 and 4 of the first stanza), again generally four bars; A' + coda (lines 3 and 4 of the second stanza), where a longer section is possible (this is also the place for coloratura passages). Such a concise form was not favoured by Rossini; even Donizetti inclined towards greater breadth.

In general, Bellini retained the standard Italian layout of scenes. Arias and ensembles are much subdivided, the arias being usually in two and the duets often in three sections or movements ('tempi'). The big finales (usually ending the first act) and *introduzioni* are even more subdivided. Following the model of Rossini and *opera buffa*, the main structural elements of the finale consist of a slow lyrical ensemble and the dramatic closing *allegro* with its stretta. The chorus plays an important part in these forms, even in the aria, sometimes with dramatic justification, sometimes merely to achieve a fuller body of sound or to create a contrast. Nowhere is the drama forgotten (as it often was in 18th-century arias); at most it is briefly suspended. The use of multipartite forms calling on varied performing forces enables the dramatic action to be propelled from one 'closed' (often not truly closed) form to the next; these are well suited to the Romantic spirit of the librettos with their rapidly changing situations. Bellini followed the general practice, but not without individual nuances and innovations. More than any other Italian composer of the time, he minimized the differences between aria and recitative, bringing together 'closed' and 'open' forms, mostly by introducing into his recitatives many cantabile, indeed aria-like, passages. What was new was the frequency and style (far beyond the traditional arioso) of such passages. Often the ear cannot distinguish the point where the actual aria begins. For example, at Riccardo's entry in *I puritani* one perceives the aria beginning at the start of the arioso 'O Elvira, o mio sospir', when in fact it begins only at 'Ah! per sempre io ti perdei'.

The notion that Bellini was able to express in a personal way only the more delicate, elegiac emotions – that he was fundamentally an 'elegist', a 'gentle Sicilian', as Wagner called him – is mistaken. It is true that many of his melodies are bathed in melancholy. But he was also well able to portray other emotions, as numerous examples show: Norma's songs of vengeance ('I romani a cento' and 'Già mi pasco' in the second-act duet with Pollione), the war chorus of the Gauls in the same opera, the belligerent melody 'Suoni la tromba' in the Act 2 finale of *I puritani*, the almost overflowing joy of the cabaletta 'A quel nome' in the duet for Elvira and Giorgio at the beginning of the same opera, and Alaide's defiant cabaletta at the conclusion of *La straniera*. The view that Bellini's style is 'delicate', 'elegiac' or simply 'lyrical' arises first from the strong impression created by his most powerfully elegiac melodies, but also from the stylistic developments subsequent to his work: the passion and the pathos of Verdi made Bellini's expression of the more violent emotions seem pale.

Bellini's music demands a style of singing that achieves a proper balance between bel canto and dramatic tension. It cannot be sung as pure bel canto. The soprano who as Norma reduces the dramatic features, which anticipate the manner of Verdi's heroines, merely to a mellifluous bel canto, falsifies Bellini much as the critic does who refers to him one-sidedly as 'delicate' and 'lyrical'.

Bellini's greatness is now accepted without question. His music struck a particular chord with audiences of the mid-19th century and went through a period of great popularity, inevitably to be followed by a reaction and severe neglect at the beginning of the 20th. A fairer balance has now been reached. Since about 1950 the number of performances has again increased; great singers, with Maria Callas and Joan Sutherland foremost among them, have rediscovered the techniques needed for his operas. Musicologists have produced reliable biographies and endeavoured to analyse Bellini's style. It is to be hoped that a critical edition of his major works will not be long delayed.

See also ADELSON E SALVINI; BEATRICE DI TENDA; BIANCA E FERNANDO; CAPULETI E I MONTECCHI, I; NORMA; PIRATA, IL; PURITANI, I; SONNAMBULA, LA; STRANIERA, LA; and ZAIRA.

title	*genre, acts*	*libretto*	*first performance*	*MS sources: printed scores*
Adelson e Salvini	op semiseria, 3	A. L. Tottola, after P. Delamarre	Naples, S. Sebastiano Conservatory, Feb 1825	*I-CATm**
2nd version	2		unperf. [rev. completed 1826 or 1828–9]	*GB-Lbl*, *I-Nc**, *Nc*, frags. *F-Pn**, *I-Baf**; vs (Paris, n.d.; Milan, 1903/*R*1985)
Bianca e Fernando	melodramma, 2	D. Gilardoni, after C. Roti		
1st version [as Bianca e Gernando]			Naples, S Carlo, 30 May 1826	*Nc**, *Nc*, frags. *CATm**; vs (Naples, 1826)
2nd version		rev. F. Romani	Genoa, Carlo Felice, 7 April 1828	frags. *Nc**, *Nc*, sketches *CATm**, *Gim**; excerpts (Milan, 1828; Naples, 1828), vs (Milan, 1837, 2/1903/*R*1985)
Il pirata	melodramma, 2	Romani, after I. J. S. Taylor: *Bertram, ou Le pirate*	Milan, Scala, 27 Oct 1827	*GB-Lbl*, *I-Nc** (*R*1983: ERO, i), *Vt* (with autograph markings), frags. *US-NYpm**; full score (Milan, *c*1960/*R*1978), vs (Milan, 1828)
La straniera	melodramma, 2	Romani, after V.-C. Prévôt	Milan, Scala, 14 Feb 1829	*GB-Ob*, *I-Mc* (with autograph markings; *R*1982: ERO, ii), *Mr**, *Nc*; vs (Milan, 1829)
Zaira	tragedia lirica, 2	Romani, after Voltaire	Parma, Ducale, 16 May 1829	*Nc**; full score (Catania, 1976), excerpts, vs (Milan, 1829; Milan, *c*1894)
I Capuleti e i Montecchi	tragedia lirica, 2	Romani, after L. Scevola: *Giulietta e Romeo*	Venice, Fenice, 11 March 1830	*CATm** (*R*1981: ERO, iii), *Mr* (with autograph markings), *Vt*; full score (Milan, *c*1955), vs (Milan, 1831)
La sonnambula	melodramma, 2	Romani, after E. Scribe and J.-P. Aumer	Milan, Carcano, 6 March 1831	*Mr** (*R*1934), *Nc*, sketches *CATm**, *US-NYpm**; full score (Milan, *c*1890), vs (Milan, 1831; London, 1849)
Norma	tragedia lirica, 2	Romani, after A. Soumet	Milan, Scala, 26 Dec 1831	*I-Rsc** (*R*1935; *R*1983: ERO, iv), sketches *CATm**; full score (Milan, 1898, 3/1915/*R*1975), vs (Milan, 1832; Paris, 1835; London, 1848, 2/1871/*R*1975)
Beatrice di Tenda	tragedia lirica, 2	Romani, after C. Tedaldi-Fores	Venice, Fenice, 16 March 1833	*I-Nc*, *Rsc**, *Vt*, sketches *CATm**; full score (Rome, *c*1840/*R*1980: ERO, v), vs (Milan, 1833)
I puritani	melodramma serio, 3	C. Pepoli, after J.-A. F.-P. Ancelot and Xavier [J. X. Boniface *dit* Saintine]: *Têtes Rondes et Cavaliers*	Paris, Italien, 24 Jan 1835	*PLcom** (*R*1983: ERO, vi), frags. *CATm**, *Mr**; full score (Milan, 1897, 2/*c*1960/*R*1978), vs (Milan, 1836)

title	genre, acts	libretto	first performance	MS sources: printed scores
(I puritani) 'Naples' version	2	Pepoli	London, Barbican, 14 Dec 1985	*CATm* (part autograph; *R*1983: ERO, vi)

Other: Ernani, Nov–Dec 1830 (Romani, after V. Hugo: *Hernani*), not completed, frags. *CATm**

LISTS OF WORKS

F. Pastura: 'Elenco delle opere', *Bellini secondo la storia* (Parma, 1959), 709–12
G. Pannain: 'Bellini: catalogo delle opere', *LaMusicaE*, 463–6
F. Lippmann: 'Bellinis Opern – Daten und Quellen', *Vincenzo Bellini und die italienische Opera seria seiner Zeit*, *AnMc*, no.6 (1969), 365–97; It. trans., rev., in M. Adamo and F. Lippmann: *Vincenzo Bellini* (Turin, 1981), 523–48
H. Weinstock: *Vincenzo Bellini: his Life and his Operas* (New York, 1971), 375–87

BIBLIOGRAPHIES

O. Viola: 'Bibliografia belliniana', *Omaggio a Bellini nel primo centenario dalla sua nascita*, ed. G. Giuliano (Catania, 1901), 336–84; pubd separately (Catania, 1902, 2/1923)
L. Ronga: 'Note sulla storia della critica belliniana', *Bollettino dei musicisti*, ii (1934), 70–74; repr. in L. Ronga: *Arte e gusto nella musica* (Milan and Naples, 1956)
A. Damerini: 'Bellini e la critica del suo tempo', *Vincenzo Bellini*, ed. I. Pizzetti (Milan, 1936), 215–50
S. Pugliatti: 'Problemi della critica belliniana', *Chopin e Bellini* (Messina, 1952), 93–113
H. Weinstock: *Vincenzo Bellini: his Life and his Operas* (New York, 1971), 549–54
W. Kümmel: 'Vincenzo Bellini nello specchio dell' "Allgemeine musikalische Zeitung" di Lipsia 1827–1846', *NRMI*, vii (1973), 186–205
R. Riehn: 'Auswahlbibliographie', *Vincenzo Bellini* (Munich, 1985), 109–16

DISCOGRAPHIES

A. Porter: 'Norma', *Opera on Record*, ed. A. Blyth, i (London, 1979), 154–72
G. Cataldo: *Il teatro di Bellini* (Bologna, 1980), 159–65
L. Bellingardi: 'Discografia', in M. Adamo and F. Lippmann: *Vincenzo Bellini* (Turin, 1981), 557–62
C. Marinelli: 'La sonnambula', *Opere in disco* (Fiesole, 1982), 136–47
R. Fairman: '"La sonnambula" and "I puritani"', *Opera on Record*, ed. A. Blyth, ii (London, 1983), 115–28

LETTERS

F. Florimo: *Bellini: memorie e lettere* (Florence, 1882)
A. Amore: *Vincenzo Bellini: vita: studi e ricerche* (Catania, 1894) [incl. letters addressed to Bellini]
L. Cambi, ed.: *Vincenzo Bellini: epistolario* (Verona, 1943)
F. Pastura: *Bellini seconda la storia* (Parma, 1959)
F. Walker: 'Lettere disperse e inedite di Vincenzo Bellini', *Rivista del Comune di Catania*, viii/4 (1960), 106–118
D. Musto: 'Vincenzo Bellini in due autografi inediti dell'Archivio di Stato di Napoli', *Rassegna degli Archivi di Stato*, xxi (1961), 351–60
L. Cambi: 'Bellini: un pacchetto di autografi', *Scritti in onore di Luigi Ronga* (Milan and Naples, 1973), 53–90
F. Lippmann: 'Belliniana: nuovi documenti', *Il melodramma italiano dell'ottocento: studi e ricerche per Massimo Mila* (Turin, 1977), 281–318

ICONOGRAPHY

Vincenzo Bellini: numero commemorativo a cura della Rivista del Comune di Catania (Catania, 1935) [incl. B. Condorelli: 'Il volto di Bellini', 18–24; O. Profeta: 'Dantan e la Parigi di Bellini', 77–82]
F. Pastura: *Bellini secondo la storia* (Parma, 1959)
H. Weinstock: *Vincenzo Bellini: his Life and his Operas* (New York, 1971)
R. Alajamo: 'Iconografia belliniana', *I teatri di Vincenzo Bellini* (Palermo, 1986), 159–223
C. Andò, D. de Meo and S. E. Failla, eds.: *Bellini: mostra di oggetti e documenti provenienti da collezioni pubbliche e private italiane* (Catania, 1988)

LIFE AND WORKS

ES (F. D'Amico); *FlorimoN*
P. Beltrame: 'Cav. Vincenzo Bellini', *Biografia degli italiani illustri nelle scienze, lettere ed arti*, ii (Venice, 1835), 451–61; repr. as *Biografia di Vincenzo Bellini* (Venice, 1836)
F. Gerardi: *Biografia di Vincenzo Bellini* (Rome, 1835)
G. Bürkli: *Biographie von Vincenz Bellini* (Zürich, 1841)
A. Pougin: *Bellini: sa vie, ses oeuvres* (Paris, 1868)
P. Voss: *Vincenzo Bellini* (Leipzig, 1901)
W. A. C. Lloyd: *Vincenzo Bellini, a Memoir* (London, 1909)
I. Pizzetti: 'Bellini, Vincenzo', *Enciclopedia italiana*, vi (Milan, 1930)
G. T. De Angelis: *Vincenzo Bellini: la vita, l'uomo, l'artista* (Brescia, 1935)
O. Tiby: *Vincenzo Bellini* (Turin, n.d.)
F. Pastura: *Bellini secondo la storia* (Parma, 1959)
L. Orrey: *Bellini* (London, 1969)
H. Weinstock: *Vincenzo Bellini: his Life and his Operas* (New York, 1971)
W. Oehlmann: *Vincenzo Bellini* (Zürich, 1974)
M. Adamo and F. Lippmann: *Vincenzo Bellini* (Turin, 1981)
P. Brunel: *Vincenzo Bellini* (Paris, 1981)
G. Tintori: *Bellini* (Milan, 1983)

BIOGRAPHICAL AND CHARACTER STUDIES

H. Heine: 'Florentinische Nächte', *Salon*, iii (Hamburg, 1837; Eng. trans., 1891), 1–144
F. Cicconetti: *Vita di Vincenzo Bellini* (Prato, 1859)
A. Amore: *Vincenzo Bellini: vita: studi e ricerche* (Catania, 1894)
A. Cametti: *Bellini a Roma: brevi appunti storici* (Rome, 1900)
G. de Gaetani: *Ipotesi sulla natura della malattia che condusse a morte Vincenzo Bellini* (Catania, 1931)
L. Cambi: *Bellini: la vita* (Milan, 1934)
G. Nataletti: '1819–1827: gli anni di Napoli', *Bollettino dei musicisti*, ii (1934), 45–9
F. Pastura: '1801–1819: a Catania', ibid, 41–4
A. Della Corte: 'L'animo', *Vincenzo Bellini*, ed. A. Della Corte and G. Pannain (Turin, 1935), 3–28
G. Policastro: *Vincenzo Bellini (1801–1819)* (Catania, 1935)
L. Cambi: 'La fanciullezza e l'adolescenza', *Vincenzo Bellini*, ed. I. Pizzetti (Milan, 1936), 11–38
J. Chantavoine: 'Bellini a Parigi', ibid, 191–214
E. J. Dent: 'Bellini in Inghilterra', ibid, 163–90
P. Cavazzuti: *Bellini a Londra* (Florence, 1945)
G. Roncaglia: 'Vincenzo Bellini: il musicista, quale appare dal suo epistolario', *RMI*, l (1948), 159–77
F. Walker: 'Amore e amori nelle lettere di Giuditta, Bellini e Florimo', *La Scala* (1959), no.112, pp.13–23; Eng. trans. as 'Giuditta Turina and Bellini', *ML*, xl (1959), 19–34
F. Lippmann: 'Belliniana: nuovi documenti', *Il melodramma italiano dell'ottocento: studi e ricerche per Massimo Mila* (Turin, 1977), 281–318
J. Rosselli: 'Vita e morte di Bellini a Parigi', *RIM*, xix (1984), 261–76

CRITICAL STUDIES

H. Berlioz: 'Bellini: notes nécrologiques', *Journal des débats* (16 July 1836); repr. in H. Berlioz: *Les musiciens et la musique* (Paris, 1903)
R. Wagner: 'Bellini: ein Wort zu seiner Zeit', *Zuschauer* (Riga, 7/19 Dec 1837); repr. in *Bayreuther Blätter* (Dec 1885); repr. in *Vincenzo Bellini*, ed. H.-K. Metzger and R. Riehn (Munich, 1985), 5–11; Eng. trans. in *Richard Wagner's Prose Works*, viii (1899)
C. Ritorni: *Ammaestramenti alla composizione d'ogni poema e d'ogni opera appartenente alla musica* (Milan, 1841)
J. C. Lobe: 'Bellini', *Fliegende Blätter für Musik: Wahrheit über Tonkunst und Tonkünstler* (Leipzig, 1855), 262–80; repr. in *Vincenzo Bellini*, ed. H.-K. Metzger and R. Riehn (Munich, 1985), 47–63
A. Basevi: *Studio sulle opere di Giuseppe Verdi* (Florence, 1859), 17–18

A. Amore: *Brevi cenni critici* (Catania, 1877)
F. Hiller: 'Vincenzo Bellini', *Künstlerleben* (Cologne, 1880), 144–59; repr. in *Vincenzo Bellini*, ed. H.-K. Metzger and R. Riehn (Munich, 1985), 95–108
F. Ricci: 'Una lettera di Federico Ricci su Bellini', in F. Florimo: *Bellini: memorie e lettere* (Florence, 1882), 140–48
M. Scherillo: *Vincenzo Bellini: note aneddotiche e critiche* (Ancona, 1882)
——: *Belliniana: nuove note* (Milan, n.d.)
A. Amore: *Vincenzo Bellini: arte: studi e ricerche* (Catania, 1892)
——: *Belliniana: errori e smentite* (Catania, 1902)
I. Pizzetti: 'La musica di Vincenzo Bellini', *La voce*, vii (1915), 149–228 [also pubd separately]; repr. in I. Pizzetti: *La musica italiana dell'800* (Turin, 1947)
C. Gray: 'Vincenzo Bellini', *ML*, vii (1926), 49–62; repr. in C. Gray: *Contingencies* (London, 1947)
F. Torrefranca: 'Il mio Bellini', *Bollettino dei musicisti*, ii (1934), 65–6
A. Della Corte: 'La formazione', *Vincenzo Bellini*, ed. A. Della Corte and G. Pannain (Turin, 1935), 29–48
D. de' Paoli: 'Bellini, musicien dramatique', *ReM*, no.156 (1935), 52–62
A. Einstein: 'Vincenzo Bellini', *ML*, xvi (1935), 325–32
G. Pannain: 'Saggio critico', *Vincenzo Bellini*, ed. A. Della Corte and G. Pannain (Turin, 1935), 77–123
——: 'Vincenzo Bellini', *RaM*, viii (1935), 1, 100, 174, 237; repr. in G. Pannain: *Ottocento musicale italiano* (Milan, 1952), 16–48
I. Pizzetti: 'Hommage à Bellini', *ReM*, no.156 (1935), 39–43
G. Gavazzeni: 'Spiriti e forme della lirica belliniana', *Vincenzo Bellini*, ed. I. Pizzetti (Milan, 1936), 81–131
M. Mila: 'Bellini cent'anni dopo', *Cent'anni di musica moderna* (Milan, 1944)
S. Pugliatti: 'Carattere dell'arte di Vincenzo Bellini', *Chopin e Bellini* (Messina, 1952), 115–30
I. Pizzetti: 'Spiriti e forme dell'arte belliniana', *Musica d'oggi*, new ser., i (1958), 346–50
F. Lippmann: *Vincenzo Bellini und die italienische Opera seria seiner Zeit*, *AnMc*, no.6 (1969); It. trans., rev., in M. Adamo and F. Lippmann: *Vincenzo Bellini* (Turin, 1981), 313–576
C. Brauner: *Vincenzo Bellini and the Aesthetics of Opera Seria in the First Third of the Nineteenth Century* (diss., Yale U., 1972)
F. Lippmann: 'Ein neuentdecktes Autograph Richard Wagners: Rezension der Königsberger "Norma"-Aufführung von 1837', *Musicae scientiae collectanea: Festschrift Karl Gustav Fellerer* (Cologne, 1973), 373–9
——: 'Donizetti und Bellini', *Studi musicali*, iv (1975), 193–243
E. J. Dent: *The Rise of Romantic Opera*, ed. W. Dean (Cambridge, 1976)
C. Greenspan: *The Operas of Vincenzo Bellini* (diss., U. of California, Berkeley, 1977)
G. Cataldo: *Il teatro di Bellini* (Bologna, 1980)
R. Alajamo, ed.: *I teatri di Vincenzo Bellini* (Palermo, 1986)

OPERAS: SPECIFIC ASPECTS

C. Di Ferrer: *Rossini e Bellini* (Cesena, 1843)
O. Viola: 'Saggio bibliografico delle più antiche edizioni dei libretti musicati da Vincenzo Bellini', appx to O. Viola: *Bibliografia belliniana* (Catania, 1902), 56–64
H. de Saussine: 'L'harmonie bellinienne', *RMI*, xxvii (1920), 477–82
A. Della Corte: 'Vicende degli stili del canto dal tempo di Gluck al novocento', *Canto e bel canto* (Turin, 1933), 229–79
L. Tonelli: 'I libretti di Bellini', *Bollettino dei musicisti*, ii (1934), 75–82
B. Condorelli: *Il Museo Belliniano: catalogo storico-iconografico* (Catania, 1935)
A. Della Corte: 'Il canto e i cantanti', *Vincenzo Bellini*, ed. A. Della Corte and G. Pannain (Turin, 1935), 49–64
H. de Saussine: 'Sur Bellini harmoniste', *ReM*, no.156 (1935), 63–4
F. Pastura: 'Due frammenti della "Beatrice di Tenda" di Bellini', *RaM*, viii (1935), 327–34
——: 'Rivelazioni degli autografi musicali belliniani: varianti e temi inediti', *Vincenzo Bellini: numero commemorativo a cura della Rivista del Comune di Catania* (1935), 25–34
——: 'Un'arietta inedita di Vincenzo Bellini', *Musica d'oggi*, xviii (1936), 115–17
G. Winternitz: 'I cimeli belliniani della R. Accademia Filarmonica di Bologna', *RMI*, xl (1936), 104–18
F. Schlitzer: 'Cimeli belliniani: "La sonnambula", "Norma"', *Tommaso Traetta, Leonardo Leo, Vincenzo Bellini: notizie e documenti*, Chigiana, ix (1952), 61–88
N. Gallini: 'Collana d'arie per Mademoiselle Carlier', *La Scala* (1953), no.49, pp.42–8
F. Schlitzer: 'Vincenzo Bellini', *Mondo teatrale dell'ottocento* (Naples, 1954)
M. Rinaldi: *Felice Romani* (Rome, 1965)
F. Lippmann: 'Verdi e Bellini', *I° congresso internazionale di studi verdiani: Venice 1966*, 184–96; Ger. trans. in *Beiträge zur Geschichte der Oper*, ed. H. Becker (Regensburg, 1969), 77–88
——: 'Pagine sconosciute de "I Capuleti e i Montecchi" e "Beatrice di Tenda" di Vincenzo Bellini', *RIM*, ii (1967), 140–51
——: 'Quellenkundliche Anmerkungen zu einigen Opern Vincenzo Bellinis', *AnMc*, no.4 (1967), 131–53
F. Cella: 'Indagini sulle fonti francesi dei libretti di Vincenzo Bellini', *Contributi dell'Istituto di filologia moderna, serie francese*, v (1968), 449–573
R. Celletti: 'Il vocalismo italiano da Rossini a Donizetti', *AnMc*, no.5 (1968), 267–94; no.7 (1969), 214–47
F. Lippmann: 'Wagner und Italien', *AnMc*, no.11 (1972), 200–47
——: 'Der italienische Vers und der musikalische Rhythmus', *AnMc*, no.12 (1973), 253–369; no.14 (1974), 324–410; no.15 (1975), 298–333; It. trans., rev., as *Versificazione italiana e ritmo musicale* (Naples, 1986)
A. Caswell: 'Mme. Cinti-Damoreau and the Embellishment of Italian Opera in Paris, 1820–1845', *JAMS*, xxviii (1975), 459–92
R. Dalmonte: 'La canzone nel melodramma italiana del primo ottocento: ricerche di metodo strutturale', *RIM*, xi (1976), 230–312
D. Goldin: 'Aspetti della librettistica italiana fra 1770 e 1830', *AnMc*, no.21 (1982), 128–91
Atti del convegno internationale di studi belliniani: Catania 1985 [incl. F. Giovale: '"Ah, tu perdoni. Quel pianto il dice": note sul tema del sacrificio e del perdono nei libretti belliniani di Felice Romani', 25–45; A. Nicastro: 'Il caso Pepoli e il libretto dei Puritani', 47–61; R. Meloncelli: 'La lirica vocale di Vincenzo Bellini nella produzione cameristica italiana dell'ottocento', 63–111; M. R. Adamo: 'Guarda che bianca luna: una "lettura" belliniana', 113–44; S. Maguire: 'On the Question of Analysis in Bellini', 145–56; G. Tintori: 'Lettere di Bellini e su Bellini al Museo Teatrale alla Scala', 157–74; R. Vlad: 'Modernità di Bellini', 175–85; F. A. Agostinelli: '"I Puritani" uno e due: la versioni napoletana', 187–93; S. E. Failla: 'La prima versione di Adelson e Salvini', 195–212; L. Arruga: 'Recitazione neoclassica: immedesimazione e drammaturgia', 213–20; J. Budden: 'La fortuna di Bellini in Inghilterra', 225–31; M. Conati: 'La "novella" belliniana', 241–60; D. Cranmer: 'A Portuguese Perspective', 261–88; P. Rattalino: 'I melodrammi di Bellini nelle parafrasi pianistiche coeve', 289–95; F. Lesure: 'Bellini et Berlioz', 297–304; R. Pagano: 'Vincenzo Tobia Bellini e le sue Toccate per clavicembalo', 305–29; 'L'attuale situazione degli studi belliniani', 331–61]
G. Tomlinson: 'Italian Romanticism and Italian Opera: an Essay in their Affinities', *19th Century Music*, x (1986–7), 43–60
S. Maguire: *Vincenzo Bellini and the Aesthetics of Early Nineteenth-Century Italian Opera* (New York and London, 1989)

INDIVIDUAL OPERAS

I Capuleti e i Montecchi

F. Schlitzer: *'I Capuleti e i Montecchi' di Vincenzo Bellini: l'autografo della partitura con note illustrative* (Florence, 1956)
W. Dean: 'Shakespeare and Opera', *Shakespeare in Music*, ed. P. Hartnoll (London, 1964), 89–175, esp. 148–50
F. Lippmann: 'Pagine sconosciute de "I Capuleti e i Montecchi" e "Beatrice di Tenda" di Vincenzo Bellini', *RIM*, ii (1967), 140–51
P. Gossett: Introduction to: *I Capuleti e i Montecchi*, ERO, iii (New York, 1981)
M. Collins: 'The Literary Background of Bellini's *I Capuleti ed i Montecchi*', *JAMS*, xxxv (1982), 532–8
L'avant-scène opéra, no.122 (1989) [*I Capuleti e i Montecchi* issue]

La sonnambula

F. Degrada: 'Prolegomeni a una lettura della Sonnambula', *Il melodramma italiano dell'ottocento: studi e ricerche per Massimo Mila* (Turin, 1977), 319–50
B. Cagli: 'Il risveglio magnetico e il sonno della ragione', *Studi musicali*, xiv (1985), 157–70

Norma

C. Ritorni: *Ammaestramenti* (Milan, 1841), 159–68
A. Damerini: *Vincenzo Bellini, 'Norma': guida attraverso il dramma e la musica* (Milan, 1923)
G. Pannain: 'La Norma', *ReM*, no.156 (1935), 44–51

——: '"Norma": cento anni', *Ottocento musicale italiano* (Milan, 1952), 49–51
R. Monterosso: 'Per un'edizione di "Norma"', *Scritti in onore di Luigi Ronga* (Milan and Naples, 1973), 415–510
C. S. Brauner: 'Textual Problems in Bellini's *Norma* and *Beatrice di Tenda*', *JAMS*, xxix (1976), 99–118
L'avant-scène opéra, no.29 (1980) [*Norma* issue]
Atti del simposio belliniano celebrato in occasione del 150º anniversario della 1º esecuzione di 'Norma': Catania 1981
P. Gossett: Introduction to: *Norma*, ERO, iv (New York, 1983)
J. Deathridge: 'Reminiscences of *Norma*', *Das musikalische Kunstwerk: Festschrift Carl Dahlhaus* (Laaber, 1988), 223–7

Beatrice di Tenda

F. Pastura: 'Due frammenti della "Beatrice di Tenda" di Bellini', *RaM*, viii (1935), 327
J. A. Boromé: 'Bellini and "Beatrice di Tenda"', *ML*, xlii (1961), 319–35
V. Gui: 'A proposito della mia revisione della *Beatrice di Tenda* di Bellini', *L'approdo musicale*, xix (1965), 207–14
F. Lippmann: 'Pagine sconosciute de "I Capuleti e i Montecchi" e "Beatrice di Tenda" di Vincenzo Bellini', *RIM*, ii (1967), 140–51
V. Gui: 'Beatrice di Tenda', *Musica d'oggi*, new ser., ii (1969), 194–7
C. S. Brauner: 'Textual Problems in Bellini's *Norma* and *Beatrice di Tenda*', *JAMS*, xxix (1976), 99–118
P. Gossett: Introduction to: *Beatrice di Tenda*, ERO, v (New York, 1980)

I puritani

P. Petrobelli: 'Note sulla poetica di Bellini: a proposito de *I puritani*', *MZ*, viii (1972), 99–118
L. Gherardi: 'Varianti ne "I puritani"', *Chigiana*, xxxiv (1977), 217–32
P. Petrobelli: 'Bellini e Paisiello: altri documenti sulla nascita dei Puritani', *Il melodramma italiano dell'ottocento: studi e ricerche per Massimo Mila* (Turin, 1977), 351–63
G. Spina: 'Origine de "I puritani"', *NRMI*, xii (1978), 29–33
R. Monterosso: 'Le due redazioni dei "Puritani"', *Letterature comparate, problemi e metodi: studi in onore di Ettore Paratore* (Bologna, 1981), 589–609
P. Gossett: Introduction to: *I puritani*, ERO, vi (New York, 1983)
G. Pugliese and R. Vlad: *I puritani ritrovati: la versione inedita dedicata a Maria Malibran* (Manduria, 1986)
L'avant-scène opéra, no.96 (1987) [*I puritani* issue]
M. Mauceri: 'Ancora su "I Puritani" per Napoli: un inedito', *NRMI*, xxiii (1989), 410–17
G. Spina: 'Scott-Ancelot-Pepoli-Bellini: genesi del libretto de "I Puritani"', *NRMI*, xxiii (1989), 79–97

others

P. Di Moiano: *Alcune osservazioni critiche intorno alla musica dell'opera 'La straniera' del sig Maestro Vincenzo Bellini* (Milan, 1830)
C. Alcari: 'La "Zaira" fu veramente fischiata?', *Musica d'oggi*, xvii (1935), 262–7
A. Della Corte: 'Le prime opere', *Vincenzo Bellini*, ed. I. Pizzetti (Milan, 1936), 39–80
F. Lippmann: 'Su "La straniera" di Bellini', *NRMI*, v (1971), 565–605
L. Orrey: 'The Literary Sources of Bellini's First Opera', *ML*, lv (1974), 24–9
Convegno di Studi sull'opera 'Bianca e Fernando' di Vincenzo Bellini: Genoa 1978
P. Gossett: Introduction to: *La straniera*, ERO, ii (New York, 1982)
——: Introduction to: *Il pirata*, ERO, i (New York, 1983)
S. E. Failla: 'Adelson e Salvini (prima versione)', *I teatri di Vincenzo Bellini*, ed. R. Alajamo (Palermo, 1986), 13–28
S. A. Willier: 'Madness, the Gothic and Bellini's *Il pirata*', *OQ*, vi (1989), 7–23

FRIEDRICH LIPPMANN (text), SIMON MAGUIRE (work-list, bibliography)

Belloc-Giorgi [Bellochi; née Trombetta], **(Maria) Teresa** (*b* S Benigno Canavese, nr Turin, 2 July 1784; *d* S Giorgio Canavese, 13 May 1855). Italian contralto. She made her début in 1801 at Turin. Engagements in Parma and Trieste followed and in 1803 she appeared in Paris, singing the title roles of Paisiello's *Nina* and Paer's *Griselda*. In the following year she sang Nina at La Scala, where she continued to appear during the next 20 years. From 1812, when she sang Isabella in the first performance of *L'inganno felice* in Venice, until her retirement in 1828, she specialized in Rossini roles. She created Ninetta, a soprano part, in *La gazza ladra* at La Scala (1817), but the contralto roles of Tancredi, Cenerentola and Isabella in *L'italiana in Algeri* were the most successful in her repertory. She appeared in London in 1819 under the name of Bellochi.

ELIZABETH FORBES

Belmont und Constanze (i) [*Belmont und Constanze, oder Die Entführung aus dem Serail* ('Belmont and Constanze, or The Abduction from the Seraglio')]. *Operette* in three acts by JOHANN ANDRÉ to a libretto by CHRISTOPH FRIEDRICH BRETZNER; Berlin, Theater in der Behrenstrasse (Döbbelin Company), 25 May 1781.

The libretto was later set by Christian Ludwig Dieter (1784, Stuttgart; *see* BELMONT UND CONSTANZE (ii)) and Anton Joseph Kuzzi (1796, St Petersburg); it was revised by Gottlieb Stephanie the younger for Mozart as *Die Entführung aus dem Serail* (1782, Vienna), a version also set by Joseph Heinrich Knecht (1787, Biberach).

Bretzner's story of attempted escape by Westerners in an exotic setting joined an extensive family tree of plays and operas with various traits in common (principally Dryden, *Don Sebastian*, 1689; Favart, *Soliman II*, 1761; Martinelli, *La schiava liberata*, 1768; Bickerstaffe, *The Captive*, 1769; and Grossmann, *Adelheit von Veltheim*, 1780). Except for the denouement, the plot was virtually unchanged by Stephanie (*see* DIE ENTFÜHRUNG AUS DEM SERAIL), who was interested mainly in enlarging the role Mozart's music was to play. Bretzner's Pasha Selim countermands his order to strangle the lovers only upon learning in the nick of time that Belmonte is his own son; Stephanie turned Selim's clemency into an act of high magnanimity by changing Belmonte to the son of Selim's worst enemy.

The libretto seems to have been written with André in mind; his name appears as composer in the printed libretto (Leipzig, 1781). André cast Osmin as a tenor and Pedrillo as a bass, reversed by Mozart. His janissary chorus (all male, rather than Mozart's SATB) provides the only attempt at exoticism ('Singt dem grossen Bassa Lieder'); he set Pedrillo's Romanze 'Im Mohrenland' in German lied style, a striking contrast to the haunting ambiguity of Mozart's rendering. But André's composition of the entire abduction scene in the style of an extensive *opera buffa* finale (with pantomime episode) was a remarkably advanced feature for north German opera in 1781.

THOMAS BAUMAN

Belmont und Constanze (ii) [*Belmont und Constanze, oder Die Entführung aus dem Serail* ('Belmont and Constanze, or The Abduction from the Seraglio')]. *Komische Oper* in three acts by CHRISTIAN LUDWIG DIETER to a libretto by CHRISTOPH FRIEDRICH BRETZNER; Stuttgart, Kleines Theater an der Planie (Herzogliche Nationale Schaubühne), 27 August 1784.

Dieter, who favoured texts by north German writers during the 1780s, set Bretzner's libretto exactly as he had written it (apparently for Johann André; *see* BELMONT UND CONSTANZE (i)). He treats the serious pair in coloratura style throughout, and with indifferent results. He uses a cheerful lied idiom for the comic pair and for Osmin (tenor; a very minor part in this version). Concertante winds, following Jommelli's practice, play a colouristic role throughout, and a viola d'amore appears in the extensive abduction sextet.

Like his other operas, Dieter's setting enjoyed great local popularity. Its cultivation at Stuttgart was apparently the reason why Mozart's *Die Entführung aus dem Serail* was not taken up there until 1795.

THOMAS BAUMAN

Belorussia. For discussion of opera in Belorussia *see* MINSK.

Bel'sky, Vladimir Nikolayevich (*b* 1866; *d* Belgrade, 28 Feb 1946). Russian librettist. In the summer of 1895, at Rimsky-Korsakov's request, he supplemented the libretto of *Sadko* with the text for Lyubasha's recitative and aria 'Vsyu noch' zhdala ego ya ponaprasnu' ('All night have I awaited him in vain'), which eventually became scene iii of the opera. He also revised the texts for the three songs of the foreign traders in scene iv. An outstanding connoisseur of Russian antiquities and folk literature (though professionally a political economist and statistician), Bel'sky wrote the librettos for Rimsky-Korsakov's three late fantasy operas *The Tale of Tsar Saltan* (1900), *The Legend of the Invisible City of Kitezh* (1907) and *The Golden Cockerel* (1909). At the time of his death, Rimsky-Korsakov was working on an opera-oratorio to a text by Bel'sky after Byron's *Heaven and Earth*. An unrealized scenario by Bel'sky for a historical opera on the revolt of Sten'ka Razin was published in the fifth volume of Andrey Rimsky-Korsakov's biography of his father.

Bel'sky also played godfather to the libretto of Stravinsky's *The Nightingale* after Andersen, of which the first draft was sketched (by Stravinsky and his collaborator, Stepan Mitusov) at Bel'sky's St Petersburg apartment on 22 March/4 April 1908. His influence may be detected in the use of Andersen's Fisherman as a framing character, who appears at the beginning and end of each scene (cf. the Astrologer in *The Golden Cockerel*). Having fled the Bolsheviks by way of Turkey in 1920, Bel'sky lived out his years in Yugoslavia.

*

N. Rimsky-Korsakov: *Letopis' moyey muzïkal'noy zhizni* [Chronicle of my Musical Life] (St Petersburg, 1909; Eng. trans., 4/1942)

A. Rimsky-Korsakov: *N. A. Rimsky-Korsakov: zhizn' i tvorchestvo* [Life and Works] (Moscow, 1933–46)

V. V. Yastrebtsev: *Nikolay Andreyevich Rimsky-Korsakov: vospominaniya* [Reminiscences], ed. A. Ossovsky (Leningrad, 1959–60; Eng. trans., abridged, 1985)

A. Orlova and V. Rimsky-Korsakov: *Stranitsï zhizni N. A. Rimskogo-Korsakova* [Pages from the Life of Rimsky-Korsakov] (Leningrad, 1969–72)

A. Orlova and V. Rimsky-Korsakov, eds.: '... "Strannaya Krasota i prichudlivaya simmetriya ...": iz perepiski N. A. Rimskogo-Korsakova s V. I. Bel'skim' [... A Strange Beauty and an Odd Symmetry ...: from Rimsky-Korsakov's Letters to Bel'sky], *SovM* (1976), no.2, pp.95–115; no.3, pp.99–114

RICHARD TARUSKIN

Beltrami, Luigi Guido (*b* Verona, *c*1753; *d* Verona, 23 Nov 1834). Italian composer. He was known primarily as a church composer and as an incomparable performer and teacher of the fortepiano and organ. A master at the Seminario Vescovile in Verona, he composed his four Metastasian operas and several cantatas (including *Ero e Leandro*, 1811) for the college with which the seminary was associated. His dramatic works were described by Sala as melodious and well-managed, reminiscent of Paisiello, Cimarosa and Gluck.

all first performed at the Collegio Vescovile, Verona

La clemenza di Tito (os, 3, P. Metastasio), 1779

Attilio Regolo (os, 3, Metastasio), 1780

Temistocle (os, 3, Metastasio), 1780

Siroe, rè di Persia (os, 3, Metastasio), 1783

*

A. Sala: *I musicisti veronesi (1500–1879)* (Verona and Padua, 1879), 17–23

ANITA HARDEMAN

Belval, Jules-Bernard (*b* La Fère, Aisne, 2 June 1819; *d* Paris, 13 Sept 1876). French bass. He studied at the Paris Conservatoire and made his début in 1846 at Antwerp. After singing in Toulouse, Lyons, the Hague, Ghent and Brussels, he was engaged at the Paris Opéra, making his début in 1855 as Marcel in *Les Huguenots*. His roles included Bertram (*Robert le diable*), Balthazar (*La favorite*), Walter Furst (*Guillaume Tell*) and Zaccharie (*Le prophète*). He took part in many premières and created Gargantua in Labarre's *Pantagruel* (1855), the Count of Poitou in Halévy's *La magicienne* (1858), Soloman in Gounod's *La reine de Saba* (1862), Archbishop Turpin in Mermet's *Roland à Roncevaux* (1864), Don Pédro in *L'Africaine* (1865) and King Claudius in Thomas' *Hamlet* (1868). His voice was a deep bass, ample in size and dark in tone. He made his last appearance at the Opéra in 1875 as Cardinal Brogni in *La Juive*, at the public inauguration of the Palais Garnier. On that occasion Princess Eudoxie was sung by his daughter Marie Belval (*b* Ghent, 1853), a soprano whose roles included Marguerite de Valois, Isabelle (*Robert le diable*) and Mathilde (*Guillaume Tell*).

ELIZABETH FORBES

Bemberg, Herman (*b* Paris or Buenos Aires, 29 March 1859 or 1861; *d* Berne, 21 July 1931). Composer of Franco-Argentine parentage. The son of a wealthy French banker and an Argentine mother, he studied in Paris with Franck and Massenet at the Conservatoire, won the Rossini prize in 1885 and gained recognition as a composer of elegant salon pieces. His first opera, *Le baiser du Suzon* (1888), was accepted by the Opéra-Comique before he had finished writing it, and in 1891 he completed what was to be his greatest success, the grand opera *Elaine*, based on the Arthurian poem by Tennyson. *Elaine* was first performed at Covent Garden in 1892 by a French company from Paris, and was given two years later at the Metropolitan, New York, with Melba and Jean and Edouard de Reszke among the cast. Reviews in the *New York Times* and *Tribune* were favourable, the critics remarking on the music's 'grace, flexibility, elegance and tenderness', the 'rich, sonorous and interesting' orchestral accompaniment and the composer's 'good taste and genuineness of feeling' as well as his evident facility (though a certain lack of power in heroic passages did not escape their notice). Among Bemberg's other operas, *Cleopatra* was announced in New York in 1894 and *Salomé* soon after in Paris at the Théâtre de la Renaissance. He also wrote piano pieces (some of which he performed in Buenos Aires early in his career), a cantata and songs.

Le baiser de Suzon (oc, 1, P. Barbier), Paris, OC (Favart), 4 June 1888

Elaine (légende, 4, P. Ferrier, after A. Tennyson), London, CG, 5 July 1892, vs (London, 1892)

Cleopatra, 1894

Salomé, 1894

Blessure d'amour (oc, 1, S. Bordèse), private perf., Paris, June 1902;? rev. as Après le rêve, *c*1907

Leïlah [Leila] (conte lyrique persan, 2, J. Bois), Monte Carlo, Opéra, March 1914, collab. E. de Lorey

*

Baker8; *StiegerO*

V. Gesualdo: *Historia de la música en la Argentina* (Buenos Aires, 1961), 480–86

P. E. Eisler: *The Metropolitan Opera: the First Twenty-Five Years, 1883–1908* (New York, 1984), 195–6

Bembo, Antonia (*b* Venice; *fl* Paris, 1690–1710). Italian composer and singer. She seems to have worked exclusively at the court of Louis XIV during the latter part of his reign. Her artistic output can be traced only through five manuscript volumes of her music that belonged to the king's library (now in *F-Pn*). The prefaces to her works reveal that between 1690 and 1695 she left Venice for France, to follow a companion who later abandoned her. Her reputation as a musician reached the king, who was so impressed with her singing that he awarded her a pension, enabling her to stay in France and devote herself to composing sacred and secular music, which she dedicated to the king and to other members of the royal family. As well as a collection of arias and cantatas, she wrote an opera, *Ercole amante* (1707, Paris; score in *F-Pn*), a tragedy in five acts, composed to the same libretto, by Francesco Buti, that Cavalli had set for the marriage of Louis XIV 45 years before. Though meeting the contemporary French requirements of dramatic form, its musical style is very much that of Italian composers at the end of the 17th century.

*

Y. Rokseth: 'Antonia Bembo, Composer to Louis XIV', *MQ*, xxiii (1937), 147–69

M. Laini: *Le produzioni armoniche di Antonia Bembo* (diss., U. of Pavia, 1988)

MARINELLA LAINI

Beňačková, Gabriela (*b* Bratislava, 25 March 1944). Czech soprano. She studied in Bratislava, making her début in 1970 at the National Theatre, Prague, as Natasha (*War and Peace*). In 1975 she sang Jenůfa, a role she has since repeated in many places, including Vienna, Munich, Geneva and San Francisco. She sang Kát'a in Amsterdam (1976) and at Carnegie Hall, New York, in 1979, the year she made her Covent Garden début as Tatyana. She has sung in Cologne, Stuttgart, Madrid, Barcelona and Los Angeles. Her repertory includes Leonore (*Fidelio*), which she sang at Salzburg in 1990, Desdemona, Maddalena (*Andrea Chénier*), Mařenka, Marguerite (*Faust*), Manon Lescaut, Aida, Rusalka and Smetana's Libuše, which she sang at the reopening of the National Theatre, Prague, in 1983. She made her Metropolitan début in 1991 as Kát'a. Her beautiful voice is used with great intelligence, especially in Czech music.

ELIZABETH FORBES

Benatzky, Ralph [Rudolf Josef František] (*b* Mährisch-Budweis, 5 June 1884; *d* Zürich, 16 Oct 1957). Austrian-Moravian composer. In 1890 his family moved to Vienna, where he took up a military career which injury forced him to abandon in 1907. He then studied in Vienna, Prague and Munich, gaining a doctorate in German philology in 1911 and studying music with Mottl. Benatzky began a musical career as a writer of song lyrics and as a conductor in Munich, before becoming director of a cabaret in Vienna. For the singer Josma Selim, whom he married in 1914, he wrote many songs, achieving particular success with 'Ich muss wieder einmal in Grinzing sein' (1915). He also composed over 20 stage works, before moving to Berlin in 1926 and providing music for spectacular operettas, including the Johann Strauss pastiche *Casanova* (1928) and *Im weissen Rössl* ('At the White Horse Inn', 1930). For the latter Benatzky wrote the bulk of the score including the title song, but some of the best-known numbers were by Robert Stolz, Robert Gilbert and Bruno Granichstaedten. Benatzky's first wife died in 1929, and in 1933 he left Germany, moving to Paris, Vienna, Hollywood (1940) and finally Zürich (1948). He was buried in St Wolfgang, the setting of *Im weissen Rössl*. Apart from his stage music Benatzky composed film scores, wrote librettos and a novel, and in all is estimated to have produced over 5000 songs.

See also IM WEISSEN RÖSSL.

selective list from about 50 operettas and revues

Casanova (3, R. Schanzer and E. Welisch), Berlin, Grosses Schauspielhaus, 1 Sept 1928 [arr. of music by J. Strauss]

Die drei Musketiere (2, Schanzer and Welisch, after A. Dumas *père*), Berlin, Grosses Schauspielhaus, 31 Aug 1929

Meine Schwester und ich (2, R. Blum and Benatzky, after G. Berr and L. Verneuil), Berlin, Komödienhaus, 29 March 1930

Im weissen Rössl (3, H. Müller and R. Gilbert, after O. Blumenthal and G. Kadelburg), Berlin, Grosses Schauspielhaus, 8 Nov 1930; incl. songs by Gilbert, R. Stolz and B. Granichstaedten

Bezauberndes Fräulein (4, Benatzky, after P. Gervault: *La petite chocolatière*), Vienna, Deutsches Volks, 24 May 1933

Deux sous de fleurs (P. Nivoix), Paris, Empire, 28 Sept 1933

Axel an der Himmelstür (3, P. Morgan, A. Schütz and H. Weigel), Vienna, An der Wien, 1 Sept 1936

*

MGG (F. Hadamowsky)

O. Schneidereit: *Operette von Abraham bis Ziehrer* (Berlin, 1966)

R. Traubner: *Operetta: a Theatrical History* (New York, 1983)

ANDREW LAMB

Benda. Bohemian family of composers, resident in Germany.

(1) **Georg** (**Anton**) [Jiří Antonín] **Benda** (*b* Staré Benátky, bap. 30 June 1722; *d* Köstritz, 6 Nov 1795). Trained by the Jesuits, he emigrated in 1742 to Prussia, where he served for eight years as violinist in Frederick the Great's court orchestra. On the death of G. H. Stölzel, in 1750 he was appointed, over the eminent J. F. Agricola, Kapellmeister to the court of Friedrich III of Saxe-Gotha. The duke chiefly demanded sacred music of him, but secular music grew in importance in an enlightened circle around Duchess Luise Dorothea. To celebrate her birthday in 1765 Benda composed his only *opera seria*, *Xindo riconnosciuto*, which helped induce Friedrich to grant him six months' paid leave to go to Italy. The court began cultivating Italian intermezzos at this time; Benda contributed two after his return. Theatrical activity however ceased on Luise Dorothea's death in 1767, and resumed only after Duke Ernst II succeeded his father in 1772.

The arrival of the eminent Seyler company after the burning of the court theatre at Weimar in 1774 brought both spoken drama and opera to Gotha. Benda immediately began writing three one-act works for the company, all produced in 1775 – the farce *Der Jahrmarkt* and the melodramas *Ariadne auf Naxos* and *Medea*. The troupe's music director, Anton Schweitzer, had already written the first German example of the MELODRAMA, a genre in which dramatic declamation is accompanied and intensified by orchestral music; Schweitzer's *Pygmalion* (1772) enjoyed only modest success, but Benda's two great works became almost at once the most admired and most performed examples of the genre. The text of *Ariadne* was written by J. C. Brandes for the affecting art of his wife Charlotte, and *Medea* for the more bone-chilling style of the troupe's other leading lady, Sophie Seyler.

Benda's friend and the librettist for *Der Jahrmarkt* and *Medea*, F. W. Gotter, also supplied the texts of his subsequent compositions for the Gotha court theatre, a court-sponsored enterprise that performed at the Schloss Friedenstein (1775–9). In 1776, with the one-act Singspiel *Walder* and especially the three-act adaptation of Shakespeare, *Romeo und Julie*, Benda and Gotter sought to create equivalents to Italian serious opera in terms of musical style and resources, but with the spoken dialogue and domestic tone characteristic of contemporary German and French drama. Both works earned widespread admiration.

In 1778 Benda resigned his post at Gotha, vexed with Schweitzer's control of the court theatre's musical offerings and anxious to promote his works and his children's singing careers. A year of travel brought him to Hamburg (where he conducted his works and wrote incidental music, now lost, for Shakespeare's *Macbeth*), to Mannheim and finally to Vienna, where he had hoped to secure the post of Kapellmeister to the Nationaltheater. Despite a successful concert and warm expectations kindled by his melodramas, his *Jahrmarkt* was coolly received and he returned to Gotha. For his third melodrama, Benda turned to *Pygmalion*; his setting of Rousseau's seminal text, given on the eve of the closing of the Gotha court theatre in 1779, continued the trend in his stage works, begun with the one-act comic opera *Der Holzhauer* (1778), towards a more conservative and dramatically attenuated style. This continued in his last two operas: *Das tartarische Gesetz*, written for Mannheim to an early libretto by Gotter, failed after a single performance, and the children's opera *Das Findelkind* was apparently never publicly performed.

Benda's significance for German opera rests squarely on the five works he completed for the Seyler company and Gotha court theatre in 1775 and 1776. In *Der Jahrmarkt*, librettist and composer still coordinate rather than collaborate: Gotter went beyond the stock-in-trade types of German comic opera with the likes of the recruiting sergeant Fickfack and his luckless victim Lukas, but Benda's attention remained centred on the heroine Bärbchen. The ensembles contain some fine strokes of musical characterization and the *recitativo accompagnato* and Bärbchen's main aria are individual features; but the work generally remains within the tradition established by Hiller (who himself added arias to the two-act version, renamed *Der Dorfjahrmarkt*).

Ariadne, on the other hand, impressed everyone as a work of astonishing novelty. Brandes's text found little favour, but critics universally praised Benda's music. The dithyrambic power of obbligato recitative's strongest accents combines with the sweep of a single tragic action to create an unprecedented sense of dramatic illusion, unity of tone and interest, and acceleration to catastrophe that won over many (including Reichardt and Mozart) who considered the very idea of the genre as nonsensical or theatrically ineffective. *Medea* is an even finer work (although to many 18th-century critics less engaging), intensifying the dramatic power already evident in *Ariadne* with the aid of a better text and a more compelling psychological portrait of the heroine. The web of motivic interconnections is more tightly spun, and the luxuriant tone painting of *Ariadne* has receded in favour of a stronger sectional structure often marked off by audacious harmonic jolts reminiscent of C. P. E. Bach. 'How everything is so new and still so true!', remarked C. G. Neefe of these two works, 'so varied and still so coherent!'.

Both *Walder* and *Romeo und Julie* combine serious elements derived from current Italian and French style with family-centred dramas of reconciliation already familiar on the German spoken stage. Only the principal roles are sung (owing to the small number of professional singers in the Gotha court theatre) and again primary musical attention rests on the female lead, with its elaborate recitative–aria scenes. Sophie Seyler, in *Walder*, also introduced one of Benda's most popular inspirations with the tender rondo 'Selbst die glücklichste von Ehen'. *Romeo und Julie* enriched and broadened the terrain already marked out by Schweitzer's *Alceste* (1773). F. W. Gotter's happy ending, an operatic necessity that nonetheless contrasts glaringly with the intense and unrelieved gloom of the rest of the drama, was adversely criticized even in its own day. In Benda's score, musical highlights include the obbligato recitatives (which show kinship with some of the finest and most daring passages in his melodramas), three prominent recitative–aria scenes and an impressive, Gluckian funeral chorus.

The impact of Benda's innovations was felt not only in northern and central Germany but also in Bavaria and Austria. Mozart, who was unimpressed with Schweitzer's music, wrote enthusiastically to his father about Benda's melodramas from Mannheim on 12 November 1778, where he had heard Sophie Seyler herself perform *Medea*. 'You know', he added, 'that Benda has always been my favourite among the Lutheran Kapellmeisters'. A year later Mozart's admiration found musical echoes in both his unfinished German opera *Zaide* K344/336*b* and the incidental music to Gebler's *Thamos, König in Ägypten* K345/336*a*. Northern composers, especially Neefe and Reichardt, stood even more strongly in Benda's debt in the late 1770s, as did Benda's son Friedrich Ludwig and his nephew Friedrich Wilhelm Heinrich. His operas and melodramas continued to enjoy occasional stagings throughout Germany well into the 19th century.

See also ARIADNE AUF NAXOS (i); JAHRMARKT, DER; MEDEA (i); ROMEO UND JULIE; and WALDER.

performances at Gotha in the theatre in Schloss Friedenstein

Xindo riconosciuto (os, 3, J. A. Galletti), Gotha, 11 Aug 1765, *D-Rtt*

Il buon marito (int, 2, Galletti), Gotha, 29 Oct 1766

Il maestro di capella (int, 2), Gotha, 25 April 1767

Ariadne auf Naxos (duodrama, 1, J. C. Brandes, after H. W. von Gerstenberg), Gotha, 27 Jan 1775, *B*, *Bds**, *Dlb*, vs (Leipzig, 1778), full score (Leipzig, 1781)

Der Jahrmarkt [Lukas und Bärbchen] (komische Oper, 1, F. W. Gotter, with J. J. Engel), Gotha, 10 Feb 1775, *A-Wn*, *D-B*, vs (Leipzig, 1786); rev. in 2 acts as Der Dorfjahrmarkt, Leipzig, Rannstädter Tor, 26 April 1775, *B*, *SWl* (2), *US-Wc*, vs (Leipzig, 1776)

Medea (melodrama, 1, Gotter, after Euripides), Leipzig, Rannstädter Tor, 1 May 1775, *D-B*, *Bds**, *Dlb*, vs (Leipzig, 1778)

Walder (ernsthafte Operette, 1, Gotter, after J. F. Marmontel: *Silvain*), Gotha, 23 Feb 1776, *B*, *Bds**, *Mbs*, *DS*, *SWl*, *US-Bp*, vs (Gotha, 1777)

Romeo und Julie (ernsthafte Oper, 3, Gotter, after W. Shakespeare and C. F. Weisse), Gotha, 25 Sept 1776, *A-Wn*, *D-B* (2 copies), *Dlb*, *DS*, *Mbs*, *Rtt*, *US-Wc*, vs (Leipzig, 1778)

Der Holzhauer, oder Die drey Wünsche (comische Operette, 1, Gotter and J. G. von Wulff, after Guichard and Castet: *Le bûcheron*), Gotha, 2 Jan 1778, *D-B*, *Dlb*, *US-Bp*, vs (Leipzig, 1777)

Theone [Philon und Theone; Almansor und Nadine], 1778 (melodrama, 1), unperf., *A-Wn** (2 copies, one with addl music not by Benda)

Pygmalion (monodrama, 1, J. J. Rousseau), Gotha, 20 Sept 1779, *D-B*, *Bds**, *Dlb*, vs (Leipzig, 1780)

Das tartarische Gesetz (Schauspiel mit Gesang, 3, Gotter, after C. Gozzi: *I pitocchi fortunati*), Mannheim, National, 4 March 1787, vs (Leipzig, 1787)

Das Findelkind, oder Unverhofft kömt oft (Operette, 1, Weisse), unperf., vs (Leipzig, 1787)

(2) **Friedrich (Wilhelm Heinrich) Benda** (*b* Potsdam, 15 July 1745; *d* Potsdam, 19 June 1814). He was a son of Franz (František) Benda (1709–86), who was the elder brother of (1) Georg Benda, and long active as a violinist and composer at the Prussian court in Potsdam. Friedrich, a Prussian court chamber musician, also took an active part in Berlin's concert life and was noted for his instrumental compositions. In 1785 and 1786 he completed two through- composed serious operas on traditional classical subjects, both intended for concert performance. *Orpheus*, on a libretto that originated in Dresden and was apparently intended for Naumann, is a frankly Gluckian work – formally diverse, rich in choruses and with arias largely in cavatina form, flowing directly into succeeding numbers. It found ardent adherents at Berlin among the anti-Italian camp and was revived in 1788 in pointed opposition to Bertoni's *Orfeo ed Euridice*. *Alceste*, now lost, appears to have been a revised three-act version of Wieland's famous libretto for Schweitzer of 1773 (coincidentally, the original five-act version was recomposed the same year by E. W. Wolf at Weimar).

See also ORPHEUS.

Orpheus (Spl, 3, G. F. von Lindemann), concert perf., Berlin, Corsika'scher Saal, 16 Jan 1785, vs (Berlin, 1787)
Alceste (Spl, 3, C. M. Wieland), concert perf., Berlin, Corsika'scher Saal, 15 Jan 1786
Das Blumenmädchen (Spl, 1, F. Rochlitz), Berlin, 16 July 1806, *D-B*

(3) **Friedrich Ludwig Benda** (*b* Gotha, bap. 4 Sept 1752; *d* Königsberg [now Kaliningrad], 20 or 27 March 1792). A son of (1) Georg Benda, he served from 1775 to 1779 as rehearsal violinist (répétiteur) in the troupe for which his father wrote his greatest works, the Seyler company. In 1776 at Leipzig he composed the opera for which he became best known in Germany, to G. F. W. Grossmann's adaptation of Beaumarchais' *Le barbier de Séville*.

When the Seyler company disbanded, Benda and his wife, the soprano Felicitas Rietz, served in the Berlin and Hamburg theatres and, in 1782–8, at the court of Duke Friedrich in Mecklenburg-Schwerin. In Königsberg in 1788 his wife divorced him, for drunkenness, adultery and prodigality; he remained there and composed three comic operas.

Benda's music to *Le barbier de Séville*, composed at Seyler's behest, enjoyed performances into the 19th century. It includes an overture, storm interlude and 13 vocal numbers, partly adaptations of Beaumarchais' own musical texts, partly additions by Grossmann. The arias are mostly rather lengthy italianate exercises tailored to the virtuosos in the company. By contrast, Benda's last two works, *Louise* (1791) and its sequel *Mariechen* (1792), achieved immense local popularity owing to an emphasis on pleasing, memorable tunes – a direct parallel with Hiller's success two decades earlier.

See also BARBIER VON SEVILLE, DER.

Der Barbier von Seville (komische Oper, 4, G. F. W. Grossmann, after P.-A. Beaumarchais), Leipzig, Rannstädter Tor, 7 May 1776, *D-B*, vs (Leipzig, 1779)
Die Verlobung (Spl, F. E. Jester), Königsberg, 1789
Louise (komische Operette, 3, Jester), Königsberg, 16 Jan 1791, vs (Königsberg, 1791)
Mariechen (komische Operette, 3, Jester), Königsberg, 1792, vs (Königsberg, 1792)

*

J. N. Forkel: *Musikalisch-kritische Bibliothek* (Gotha, 1778–9), ii, 230–74
J. F. Reichardt: Review of pubd vs of *Romeo and Julie*, *Allgemeine deutsche Bibliothek*, xl (1780), 129
G. Benda: 'Ueber das einfache Recitativ', *Magazin der Musik*, i (1783), 750–55
Der teutsche Merkur, ii (Sept 1785), cxlvii–cxlviii
K. F. Zelter: 'Ausstellung einer Szene aus dem musikalischen Drama *Romeo und Julie*, von Georg Benda', *Lyceum der schönen Künste*, i (1797), 132–44
F. Schlichtegroll: *Nekrolog auf das Jahr 1795* (Gotha, 1798), 290–336
R. Hodermann: *Georg Benda* (Coburg, 1895)
F. Brückner: 'Georg Benda und das deutsche Singspiel', *SIMG*, v (1903–4), 571–621
——: 'Zum Thema "Georg Benda und das Monodram"', *SIMG*, vi (1904–5), 496–500
E. Istel: 'Einiges über Georg Benda's "akkompagnierte" Monodramen', *SIMG*, vi (1904–5), 179–82
——: *Die Entstehung des deutschen Melodramas* (Berlin, 1906)
H. Güttler: *Königsbergs Musikkultur im 18. Jahrhundert* (Kassel, 1925)
J. Hutter and Z. Chalabala, eds.: *České umění dramatické*, ii: *Zpěvohra* [Czech Dramatic Art, ii: Opera] (Prague, 1941)
J. van der Veen: *Le mélodrame musical de Rousseau au romantisme* (The Hague, 1955)
Z. Pilková: 'Das Melodram Jiří Bendas im Zusammenhang mit der Mozartproblematik', *Internazionale Mozartkonferenz: Prague 1956*, 85–94
——: *Dramatická tvorba Jiřího Bendy* [The Dramatic Works of Jiří Benda] (Prague, 1960)
R. Pečman: 'Benda's "The Village Market" as a Precursor of "Fidelio"', *Sborník prací filosofické fakulty Brněnské University*, ser. H, ii (1967), 43–52
A. S. Winsor: *The Melodramas and Singspiels of Georg Benda* (diss., U. of Michigan, 1967)
E. V. Garrett: 'Georg Benda, the Pioneer of the Melodrama', *Studies in Eighteenth-Century Music: a Tribute to Karl Geiringer* (London, 1970), 236–42
F. Lorenz: *Die Musikerfamilie Benda: Georg Anton Benda* (Berlin and New York, 1971) [incl. H. Hagendorff: 'Friedrich Ludwig Benda', 115–29]
T. Bauman: 'Opera *versus* Drama: *Romeo and Juliet* in Eighteenth-Century Germany', *Eighteenth-Century Studies*, xi (1977–8), 186–203
——: 'Benda, the Germans, and Simple Recitative', *JAMS*, xxxiv (1981), 119–31
——: *North German Opera in the Age of Goethe* (Cambridge, 1985)

THOMAS BAUMAN

Bendall, Wilfred (Ellington) (*b* London, 22 April 1850; *d* London, 16 June 1920). English composer. He studied with Charles Lucas and Edouard Silas and in Leipzig. His chief dramatic compositions were one-act comic chamber operas performed in London. Some, including *Lovers' Knots* (C. Bridgman; St George's Hall, 5 May 1880), appeared among the German Reeds' entertainments; others, such as *Beef Tea* (H. Greenbank; Lyric, 22 Oct 1892), were companion pieces for longer musical works. Bendall's most popular work, *Quid Pro Quo* (R. Barrington and Bridgman; Opera Comique, 17 Oct 1881), appeared with Frederic Clay and W. S. Gilbert's comic opera *Princess Toto*. In 1894 Bendall was engaged as Sullivan's secretary, and in his last years Sullivan relied on him to copy and correct his works, and in some cases arrange them for publication.

FREDRIC WOODBRIDGE WILSON

Bendazzi, Luigia (*b* Ravenna, 1827 or 1828; *d* Nice, 5 March 1901). Italian soprano. She studied in Milan, then in Bologna, where her teacher was Federico Dallara. She made her début in 1850 in Venice as Elvira in Verdi's *Ernani*, after which her career developed rapidly. In 1857 she created Amelia in *Simon Boccanegra* in Venice. Her other Verdi roles included Hélène (*Vêpres*), Amelia (*Ballo*), Gilda and Violetta. Active at all the major Italian houses, she enjoyed particular success at La Scala, where she made her first appearance during the 1857–8 season. At the Liceo in Barcelona in 1869–70, in addition to the Verdi for which she was best known, she sang Valentine (*Les Huguenots*), Paolina (Donizetti's *Poliuto*) and the title role in Petrella's *Jone*. Her voice was a classic *soprano d'agilità*, but she evidently possessed sufficient reserves of power to make a convincing Lady Macbeth.

Bender, Paul (*b* Driedorf, nr Wetzlar, 28 July 1875; *d* Munich, 25 Nov 1947). German bass. A pupil of Louise Ress and Baptist Hoffmann, he made his début as Sarastro in 1900 at Breslau. In 1903 he was engaged by the Munich Opera and continued as their first bass for 30 years; his last performance, as Rossini's Don Basilio, took place only seven days before his death. Bender made his Covent Garden début in 1914 as Amfortas in the British stage première of *Parsifal*, singing also during this German winter season Hunding, Hans Sachs and Jacob in Méhul's *Joseph*. When German performances were resumed at Covent Garden in 1924 and 1927, Bender showed his outstanding gifts as a comedian in the parts of Osmin and Ochs, but was again much admired in his Wagner roles – which he sang also at the Metropolitan from 1922 to 1927. His great stature contributed to an imposing stage presence; but he became famous also as a lieder singer, especially in the songs and ballads of Carl Loewe. Among his many recordings, the most valuable are those of Loewe made in 1930 and 1933, which reveal a gripping dramatic power, a distinctness of enunciation and a quiet humour that are in sum entirely delightful.

*

J. Dennis: 'Paul Bender', *Record Collector*, xvii (1967–8), 245–56; xviii (1968), 46 [with discography] DESMOND SHAWE-TAYLOR

Bendl, Karel (*b* Prague, 16 April 1838; *d* Prague, 20 Sept 1897). Czech composer. He studied at the Prague Organ School, 1855–8. In 1864–5 he worked as a conductor and chorus master with opera companies in Brussels and Amsterdam and was later second conductor of the Czech opera at the Provisional Theatre in Prague for a single season, 1874–5. By inclination he was a vocal composer, and this is reflected in the predominance of songs and choral works in his output, which made him one of the most popular Czech composers of his time. His first stage work, the grand romantic opera *Lejla* (1868), was an immediate success and received 29 performances in Prague up to 1894. Based on the tragic fate of a Jewish adviser to the last Moorish king in Spain, it was regarded as a representative Czech grand opera and was the first Czech opera to be published in vocal score after Smetana's *The Bartered Bride*; a production was planned (though not realized) as part of the programme originally proposed for the International Exhibition of Music and Theatre in Vienna in 1892. Bendl's second historical opera, *Břetislav*, also followed the model of grand opera, this time taking patriotic subject matter from early Czech history, the Přemyslid feuds. Unlike that of *Lejla*, its libretto was not suited to the genre and the work failed, receiving only four performances.

In *Starý ženich* ('The Elderly Suitor', 1882), Bendl turned to comic opera, whose folklike Czech national character he tried to underline by quoting Czech folksongs; the work belongs to the group of Czech comic village operas by the librettist of *The Bartered Bride*, Karel Sabina. Although the opera was not staged until long after its composition, other Czech comic operas written at that time did not diminish its appeal: after its première in Chrudim in 1882 it received 23 performances in Prague, 1882–1902, and was later performed in Brno, Ostrava and Plzeň (1942) and revived in České Budějovice in 1974. Bendl next experimented with comic operas of other types in *Die Wunderblume*, a magic fairy-tale opera to a German text, and *Indická princezna* ('The Indian Princess'), which was the first Czech attempt at operetta and received 30 performances in Prague, 1877–1906.

Together with Fibich's *Blaník*, Bendl's next opera, *Černohorci* ('The Montenegrins', 1877), received a prize in the competition to mark the opening of the National Theatre in Prague in 1881. In it Bendl turned again to the concept of grand opera, making considerable use of southern Slav local colour, which was favoured in Bohemia at that time; 17 performances were staged up to 1886. The comic opera *Karel Škreta* won the prize for its libretto in the competition to mark the reopening in 1883 of the National Theatre after a fire. Bendl was at ease with the lyricism of Krásnohorská's libretto, which is based on the love story of the Czech Baroque painter; he used a leitmotif technique and wrote comic numbers for the secondary characters. The opera received ten performances up to 1885. Krásnohorská's serious-opera libretto *Dítě Tábora* ('The Child of Tábor') received a prize in the same competition; after being refused by Smetana, it was taken up by Bendl for his own historical tragic opera. The work deals with the Hussites at Naumburg and often uses a quotation from a 15th-century Hussite chorale. Bendl's attempt here to dissolve the traditional forms and set numbers is evidence of his conception of music drama. Although the opera was not a great success (it received only five performances in 1892), its reputation as a 'progressive' music drama contributed to the decision to revive it for the 30th anniversary of Bendl's death in 1927. Bendl's endeavour to respond to contemporary European trends can be traced also in his attempt at Italian *verismo* style in his one-act opera to a German text, *Mutter Mila* (1895, performed in Czech as *Máti Míla*); his unperformed *dramma lirico* to an Italian text, *Gina* (1884), represents an earlier attempt to respond to the impulses of Italian opera. By contrast, the folklike ballet *Česká svatba* ('The Czech Wedding', 1895) and the fairy-tale opera-ballet *Švanda dudák* ('Švanda the Bagpiper', 1895–6) show Bendl's orientation to the Czech ethnographic movement of the 1890s. Although Bendl's stage works still await evaluation from a musicological as well as a dramaturgical standpoint, the importance of his contribution to 19th-century Czech vocal music is undeniable.

first performed in Prague unless otherwise stated; all printed works published in Prague

Lejla (grand romantic op, 5, E. Krásnohorská, after E. Bulwer-Lytton: *Leila, or The Siege of Granada*), Provisional, 4 Jan 1868 [4-act version]; rev. (5), Provisional, 24 Sept 1874; *CS-Pnm**, *Pnd*, vs Acts 1 and 2 (1874), Acts 3–5 (1880)

Žena Vršovcova [Vršovec's Wife], 1868–74 (Krásnohorská), ?lost

Břetislav (historical op, 5, Krásnohorská), New Town, 18 Sept 1870, *Pnm**, 1 aria in Burghauser

Starý ženich [The Elderly Suitor], 1871–4 (folklike op, 3, K. Sabina,

rev. G. Eim and V. J. Novotný), Chrudim, 4 Feb 1882, *Pnd*, vs (1883)
Die Wunderblume, 1876 (komische Zauberoper, 3, E. Rüffer); Cz. excerpts (trans. M. Očadlík), Prague Radio, 30 Aug 1940, excerpts *Pr*
Indická princezna [The Indian Princess] (3, A. Pulda), New Czech, 26 Aug 1877, *Pnm** (Acts 2 and 3 only), *Pnd*
Černohorci [The Montenegrins], 1877 (3, J. O. Veselý), New Czech, 11 Sept 1881, *Pnm**
Karel Škreta (comic op, 3, Krásnohorská), National, 11 Dec 1883, *Pnm**
Gina, 1884 (dramma lirico, prol., 3, G. T. Cimino), unperf., vs *Pnd*
Dítě Tábora [The Child of Tábor], 1886–8 (tragic op, 3, Krásnohorská), National, 13 March 1892, *Pnd**
Mutter Mila, 1893–5 (1, A. Delmar), as Máti Míla (trans. Novotný), National, 25 June 1895, *Pnd**, lib. (n.d.)
Švanda dudák [Švanda the Bagpiper], 1895–6 (folk fairy-tale opera-ballet, 3, J. Vrchlický, after Cz. folk tale), National, 29 April 1907, vs *Pnd* [rev. version of cantata, 1880]

*

PEM (V. Vysloužilová)
V. J. Novotný: 'Černohorci', *Dalibor*, iii (1881), 211–13, 219–20, 229–30, 245–8
——: '"Starý ženich"', *Dalibor*, iv (1882), 65–7, 82–4, 122–4, 154–6, 161–3, 173–5
K. Stecker: 'Bendlův "Karel Škreta"', *Dalibor*, viii (1886), 2–4, 13–14, 21–2, 33–5, 41–2, 53–5, 61–3, 73–5, 81–3, 93–5, 101–4
E. Chvála: *Ein Vierteljahrhundert böhmischer Musik* (Prague, 1887)
K. Hda. [F. K. Hejda]: 'Dítě Tábora', *Dalibor*, xiv (1892), 105–5, 121–2, 140–42
V. A. J. Hornové: *Česká zpěvohra* [Czech Opera] (Prague, 1903)
L. Boháček: 'Karel Bendl a Národní divadlo' [Karel Bendl and the National Theatre], *Za hudebním vzděláním*, iii (1927), 24–7
Z. Nejedlý: *Dějiny Národního divadla*, iii: *Opera Národního divadla do roku 1900* [History of the National Theatre, iii: Opera at the National Theatre up to 1900] (Prague, 1935, 2/1949)
J. Bartoš: *Prozatímní divadlo a jeho opera* [The Provisional Theatre and its Opera] (Prague, 1938)
J. Polák: *Karel Bendl* (Prague, 1938)
F. Pala: 'Karel Bendl', *České umění dramatické*, ii: *Zpěvohra* [Czech Dramatic Art, ii: Opera], ed. J. Hutter and Z. Chalabala (Prague, 1941), 166–70
M. Pospíšil: 'Balada v české opeře 19. století' [The Ballad in Czech 19th-Century Opera], *HV*, xvi (1979), 3–25
M. Ottlová and M. Pospíšil; 'Opera "Crnogorci" od Karla Bendla', *Pobjeda*, xxxvii (1981), 12
J. Burghauser, ed.: *Národnímu divadlu: vklad zakladatelské generace* [Towards a National Theatre: the Investment by the Founding Generation] (Prague, 1983)
M. Ottlová: 'Die französische grand opéra in der Entwicklung der tschechischen Nationaloper', *2. Romantikkonferenz: Dresden 1982*, 82–90; Eng. summary in *Muzyka*, xxix (1984), 45–50
O. Hostinský: *Z hudebních bojů let sedmdesátých a osmdesátých: výbor z operních a koncertních kritik* [From the Musical Battles of the 1870s and 80s: a Selection of Opera and Concert Reviews], ed. E. Vítová (Prague, 1986)
J. Tyrrell: *Czech Opera* (Cambridge, 1988)

MARTA OTTLOVÁ, MILAN POSPÍŠIL

Bendler [Bendeler], **Salomon** (*b* Quedlinburg, 1683; *d* Brunswick, 1724). German bass. Son of the theorist J. P. Bendeler, who taught him, he is said to have enjoyed great success in north Italy and throughout Germany; he sang at Weissenfels (1708), Hamburg, Brunswick, Leipzig and Danzig. In 1712 he appeared in Handel's *Rinaldo* (as Argante) and Gasparini's *Ambleto* at the Queen's Theatre in London. Munchausen-like tales are told of the depth, power and resonance of his voice: that in London his E♭ below the bass staff drowned an orchestra of 50 playing *fortissimo* and on another occasion the full organ at St Paul's. WINTON DEAN

Bene, Adriana Ferrarese del. *See* FERRARESE, ADRIANA.

Benedetti, Michele (*b* Loreto, 17 Oct 1778; *d* after 1828). Italian bass. He made his début in 1805 and, after singing at Venice, Reggio Emilia and other cities, appeared in 1811 in Spontini's *La vestale* at S Carlo. There he created the following roles in operas by Rossini: Elmiro in *Otello* (1816); Idraote in *Armida* (1817); the title role in *Mosè in Egitto* and Ircano in *Ricciardo e Zoraide* (1818); Phoenicius in *Ermione* and Douglas in *La donna del lago* (1819); and Leucippo in *Zelmira* (1822). He also sang Atkins in the first performance of Donizetti's *Alfredo il grande* (1823), Clemente in the première of Bellini's *Bianca e Gernando* (1826) and the King in the first performance of Donizetti's *Gianni di Calais* (1828), the last named at the Teatro del Fondo. He visited London in 1822. Nothing is known of his later career or the circumstances of his death. ELIZABETH FORBES

Benedict, Sir **Julius** (*b* Stuttgart, 27 Nov or 24 Dec 1804; *d* London, 5 June 1885). English composer and conductor of German birth. His date of birth is usually given as 27 November 1804, but William Barclay Squire claimed that it 'is generally believed to have been on 24 Dec. of that year'. Benedict's father, a Stuttgart banker, placed him under J. C. L. Abeille for musical instruction; at 15 he went to Weimar to study with Hummel, who introduced him to Beethoven. In February 1821 he became Weber's first composition pupil at Dresden, and accompanied him to Vienna for the première of *Euryanthe* (25 October 1823). Weber introduced Benedict to the impresario Barbaia, who secured for him the post of conductor at the Kärntnertortheater from the summer of 1824. In 1825 he went with Barbaia to Naples, where he became conductor at the S Carlo and Fondo theatres. He composed three operas for Naples: the first, *Giacinta ed Ernesto* (1827), failed, apparently because it was written in the style of Weber. The second, *I portoghesi in Goa* (1830), succeeded, but subsequently failed at Stuttgart, having been modelled on Rossini.

In 1834 Benedict went to Paris. There he met Maria Malibran, who suggested that he visit London, which he did in 1835, remaining there until his death. In 1836 he was appointed conductor of the Opera Buffa at the Lyceum Theatre; his third Neapolitan work, *Un anno ed un giorno* (1836), was given there on 31 January 1837. From 1838 to 1848 he was musical director at Drury Lane, where he brought out three English operas of his own. None was particularly successful, though *The Crusaders* (1846), the most ambitious of them, eventually became quite popular in Germany. In 1848 he conducted Mendelssohn's *Elijah* at Exeter Hall, when Jenny Lind made her first appearance in oratorio. He accompanied her on her American tour in 1850, returning to London in 1852 to take up the post of conductor at Her Majesty's Theatre. He also conducted the Norwich Festival from 1845 to 1878. Benedict returned to the composition of opera with his masterpiece *The Lily of Killarney*, written for the Pyne-Harrison company and produced at Covent Garden in 1862. It was immediately successful and remained in the repertory until the 1930s. His last stage work, *The Bride of Song* (1864, Covent Garden), was a failure. He was knighted in 1871 and taught until his death in 1885.

Benedict's thorough German training is reflected in all his compositions, which are devoid of the amateurishness often found in his British operatic contemporaries. His technical accomplishments enabled him to master a succession of different styles, but it is consequently difficult to assign him a specific musical personality. His strongest vein, predictably, is German: founded on Weber, it progresses no further than slightly modernized

Mendelssohn (his oratorio *St Peter*, 1870, frequently recalls *Elijah*). Set against this are the Italian-orientated works, in which Rossini's influence predominates. This finds its purest expression in his second and third Neapolitan operas, but even *The Lily of Killarney* has a Rossinian rondo finale. As Benedict grew older, the two styles merged to produce a composite vocabulary, seen to advantage in pieces such as the cantata *The Legend of St Cecilia* (1866). He was thus supremely qualified to add Italian recitatives to Weber's *Oberon* for Her Majesty's Theatre in 1860. Viewed against this background, *The Lily of Killarney* cannot be accounted an entirely characteristic work. The opera owes its success to its melodic strength and thoroughly Irish idiom, though it should be remembered that Benedict had earlier mastered the English ballad-opera style in his three operas for Drury Lane in the 1840s.

See also LILY OF KILLARNEY, THE.

first performed in London unless otherwise stated; printed works are vocal scores published in London unless otherwise stated

Giacinta ed Ernesto (L. Ricciutti), Naples, Fondo, 31 March 1827

I portoghesi in Goa (2, V. Torelli), Naples, S Carlo, 28 June 1830, *I-Nc**

Un anno ed un giorno (operetta, 1, D. Andreotti), Naples, Fondo, 19 Oct 1836; (lib. rev. S. M. Maggioni), Lyceum, 31 Jan 1837, selections (1837)

The Gypsy's Warning (2, G. Linley and R. B. Peake), Drury Lane, 19 April 1838; pubd as Der Zigeunerin Warnung (Mainz, 1838); as Der Zigeunerin Weissagung, Berlin, 14 Oct 1840

The Brides of Venice (2, A. Bunn), Drury Lane, 22 April 1844 (1844); as Die Braüte von Venedig, Kassel, 20 Aug 1845

The Crusaders (3, Bunn, after J.-H. Vernoy de Saint-Georges), Drury Lane, 26 Feb 1846, selections (1846); as Der Alte vom Berge, Prague, May 1847

The Lily of Killarney (grand romantic op, 3, J. Oxenford and D. Boucicault, after Boucicault: *The Colleen Bawn, or The Brides of Garryowen* and G. Griffin: *The Collegians, or The Colleen Bawn*), CG, 10 Feb 1862 (1862)

The Bride of Song (operetta, 1, H. B. Farnie), CG, 3 Dec 1864 (1864)

Adaptation of Flotow: Alessandro Stradella, Drury Lane, 6 June 1846

It. recits. for Weber: Oberon, Her Majesty's, 3 July 1860, and for Mozart: Il seraglio, CG, 9 June 1881

*

DNB (W. B. Squire); *Kobbé10*; *LoewenbergA*; *PEM* (N. Temperley); *StiegerO*

AMZ, xxxiii (1831), 187–9

A. Bunn: *The Stage* (London, 1840)

The Times (8, 10, 11 Feb 1862)

J. Benedict: *Carl Maria von Weber* (London, 1881)

MT, xxvi (1885), 385–6

R. A. Streatfeild: *The Opera: a Sketch* (London, 1896), 364–5

J. F. Barnett: *Musical Reminiscences and Impressions* (London, 1906), 155–8

M. W. Disher: *Victorian Song* (London, 1955), 101

F. de Filippis: *Cronache del Teatro di S Carlo* (Naples, 1961)

M. Hurd: 'Opera: 1834–65', *Music in Britain: the Romantic Age, 1800–1914*, ed. N. Temperley (London, 1981), 314, 328

E. W. White: *A History of English Opera* (London, 1983)

——: *A Register of First Performances of English Operas and Semi-Operas* (London, 1983)

NIGEL BURTON

Benefit (Fr. *bénéfice*, *représentation à bénéfice*; Ger. *Benefizvorstellung*; It. *beneficiata, serata di beneficio*). A performance of which the proceeds are given in whole or part to one or more members of the cast, company or house servants, or donated to a specified charity or fund.

The practice evolved from the longstanding British custom of remunerating authors of plays with the profits of the third night of a new run, and often of each subsequent third night. The earliest reference to a performer benefit in British stage history is by Samuel Pepys, who on 28 September 1668 wrote that he had been told that 'the women's day at the playhouse is today, and that therefore I must be there to encrease their profit'. The first recorded benefit for an individual is stated by Colley Cibber to have been in the reign of James II (1685–8), the recipient being the actress Elizabeth Barry. From the 1695–6 season it became the London practice to award benefits to actors and, from 1697–8, to composers and singers, principally as a means of compensating them for low salaries. The first opera known to have been associated with a benefit was Daniel Purcell and Jeremiah Clarke's *The World in the Moon*, which was performed on 1 July 1697 'for the benefit of the Undertaker' (i.e. the company's owner, Christopher Rich). The first charity benefit of which we have a record was advertised in 1698.

Elsewhere in Europe the benefit system was slow to become established. The earliest recorded benefit in France was given in 1735 for the actress Mlle Gaussin, who had lost all her possessions in a fire; but it was not until later in the century that benefits became common practice in France and Italy. The earliest documented theatrical benefit in America took place on 16 October 1749, for the 'poor Debtors now under Confinement in

1. *Playbill for Wilhelmine Schröder-Devrient's benefit night at Covent Garden, London, 3 July 1833*

the Prison in New York'. Stage benefits for individuals are recorded at the Nassau Street Theatre in January 1751, given for the joint managers of the company: the ballad operas *The Devil to Pay* and *The Beggar's Opera* were included in the programmes, respectively on 8 January for Walter Murray and 14 January for Thomas Kean (who was also a singer and the leading actor).

Similar customs prevailed in the Viennese theatre during the late 18th century. At the Nationaltheater it was usual for authors of some new plays (and occasionally of translations) to receive the box-office receipts from the third performance, as a reward rather than a right; sometimes this was their only payment. Similar rewards were occasionally assigned, at the whim of Emperor Joseph II, to composers, singers or actors (though not to librettists); on one occasion box-office receipts were divided between the four principal singers (in Paisiello's *Il barbiere di Siviglia*).

The benefit became both a right demanded by artists and an inducement employed by managers to lure artists to their company – for beneficiaries could expect to reap considerable rewards from the occasion and indeed relied upon it for a substantial part of their income. The beneficiary was entitled to choose the programme and would call on the assistance of crowd-pulling colleagues, who would normally offer their services free; further, he or she would aim to swell receipts by selling tickets, often for more than the regular price, and by attracting wealthy patronage. Especially during the 19th century, benefit evenings tended to be lengthy affairs, often consisting of a succession of fragments of operas and dramas interspersed with miscellaneous singing and dancing.

Various types of benefit might be contracted, ranging from the 'clear' benefit, a rare occurrence in which the beneficiary took the entire gross takings, to less advantageous types, in which the expenses and sometimes even the profits would be shared with the management in an agreed proportion. During the second half of the 19th century the benefit system was gradually abandoned; in its place performers' salaries were raised and the royalty system was instituted. Occasional benefits for performers, often on their retirement, as well as for charities and good causes, have persisted up to the present day.

ES ('Beneficiata'; G. Brunacci); *LS*

C. Cibber: *An Apology for the Life of Mr. Colley Cibber* (London, 1740, 4/1756); new edn, with addns by R. W. Lowe (London, 1889), i, 161

'Benefiz', *Allgemeines Theater-Lexikon, Neue Ausgabe*, ed. G. K. R. Herlosssohn and H. Marggraff (Altenburg and Leipzig, 1846)

A. Pougin: *Dictionnaire historique et pittoresque du théâtre* (Paris, 1885), 95ff

A. Oppenheim and E. Gettke: 'Benefiz', *Deutsches Theater-Lexikon* (Leipzig, 1889)

T. A. Brown: *A History of the New York Stage from the First Performance in 1732 to 1901* (New York, 1903)

G. C. D. Odell: *Annals of the New York Stage* (New York, 1927–49)

'Benefit', *The Oxford Companion to the Theatre*, ed. P. Hartnoll (London, 1951, 4/1983)

V. C. Clinton-Baddeley: *All Right on the Night* (London, 1954), 149ff

D. E. McKenty: *The Benefit System in Augustan Drama* (diss., U. of Pennsylvania, 1966)

St V. Troubridge: *The Benefit System in the British Theatre* (London, 1967)

G. E. Bentley: *The Profession of Player in Shakespeare's Time 1590–1642* (Princeton, 1984)

R. D. Hume: 'The Origins of the Actor Benefit in London', *Theatre Research International*, ix (1984), 99–111

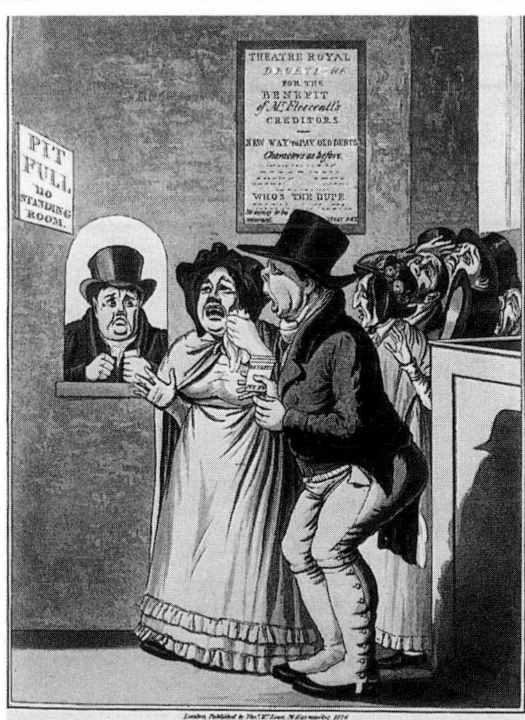

2. 'A BENE-FIT': *anonymous aquatint, 1826; at this period seats were generally unnumbered and it was common, especially at benefits, for there to be more tickets in circulation than there were seats in the theatre*

D. Edge: 'Mozart's Fee for *Così fan tutte*', *JRMA*, cxvi (1991), 211–35

RICHARD MACNUTT

Benelli, Antonio (Pellegrino) (*b* Forlì, 5 Sept 1771; *d* Börnichau, Saxony, 16 Aug 1830). Italian tenor, composer and singing teacher. He made his début as a singer in 1790 at Naples, where his own opera *Partenope* was produced eight years later. After appearing in London, he settled in Dresden in 1801 and sang there for over 20 years until his voice failed. He then taught singing in Berlin until 1829, when he was dismissed for publishing an attack on Spontini. Though not gifted with a large or brilliant voice, Benelli was a good teacher and composed many vocal pieces.

ELIZABETH FORBES

Benelli, Sem (*b* Filettole, nr Prato, 10 Aug 1877; *d* Zoagli, 18 Dec 1949). Italian dramatist. After working as a journalist, he wrote a successful comedy, *Tignola*, but thereafter turned to historical tragedies in hendecasyllabic verse set in the Italian Middle Ages and Renaissance, in the manner of D'Annunzio. *La cena della beffe* won international acclaim; it and five others were set as operas by Italian composers. After a period of adherence to Fascism (he sat in Parliament from 1921 until the murder of Matteotti in 1924) Benelli distanced himself from the regime and concentrated on writing plays with philosophical themes. He emigrated to Switzerland but returned to Italy after the end of World War II.

L'amore dei tre re, Montemezzi, 1913; *Il mantellaccio*, Setaccioli, comp. 1913, broadcast 1954; *La cena delle beffe*, Giordano,

1924; *Rosmunda*, E. Trentinaglia, 1929; *Gorgona*, L. Landi, comp. *c*1933; *Proserpina*, R. Bianchi, 1938 LUCA ZOPPELLI

Benelli, Ugo (*b* Genoa, 20 Jan 1935). Italian tenor. He studied in Milan, making his début at the Piccola Scala in 1960, then singing at La Scala, the Rome Opera and other Italian theatres. In 1966 he sang Auber's Fra Diavolo at Wexford. He first sang at Glyndebourne in 1967 as Nemorino (*L'elisir d'amore*), returning as Narciso (*Il turco in Italia*), Truffaldino (*The Love for Three Oranges*) and in 1984 Mozart's Don Basilio. He made his Covent Garden début in 1974 as Ernesto in *Don Pasquale*. His repertory included Rossini's Almaviva, Ramiro, Lindoro and Giannetto; Don Anchise (*La finta giardiniera*), Tonio, Elvino, Fenton, Nadir, Massenet's Des Grieux and Werther. An exuberant performer, he excelled in comic roles. ELIZABETH FORBES

Beneš, Juraj (*b* Trnava, Slovakia, 2 March 1940). Slovak composer. He studied the piano at the Bratislava Conservatory and composition with Cikker at the Bratislava Academy, where he was appointed lecturer in 1988. In his first opera, *Cisárove nové šaty* ('The Emperor's New Clothes'), orchestral passages, singing and verse merge to create a work that hovers between tragedy and farce, symbolism and a stylized reality, allegory and message-bearing. In *Skamenený* ('Turned to Stone') Beneš turned away from a universal to a uniquely Slovak musical language in which broadly conceived melodic lines are punctuated by forceful instrumental interjections. The text has a folk-ballad structure and consists of a montage of poems by the Slovak Romantic Janko Kráľ. Beneš's first full-length opera, *Hostina* ('The Feast'), is based on verse by the turn-of-the-century Slovak writer Pavol Országh-Hviezdoslav, particularly on the tragedy *Herodes a Herodias* ('Herod and Herodias'). The opera is one of the greatest achievements of Slovak musical drama. The composer here interweaves several chronological strands and borrows elements from oriental mask dramas; in the second part of the opera the fundamental dramatic motifs of the first are repeated, and the work ends with a tragic catharsis (the death of John the Baptist). Although this is a monumental work, even oratorio-like at times, it contains passages of great lyrical tenderness.

Cisárove nové šaty [The Emperor's New Clothes], 1965–6 (Beneš, after H. C. Andersen), Bratislava, Slovak National, 29 March 1969

Skamenený [Turned to Stone], 1974 (7 scenes, J. Kráľ), Bratislava, Academy of Music, 18 Feb 1978

Hostina [The Feast], 1979–80 (prol., 2, epilogue, Beneš, after P. Országh-Hviezdoslav), Bratislava, Slovak National, 13 April 1984

*

I. Vajda: *Slovenská opera* (Bratislava, 1988), 166-78, 241

IGOR VAJDA

Benigni, Domenico (*b* Cupramontana, 11 Jan 1596; *d* Rome, 16 Oct 1653). Italian librettist. After studying at the Collegio Romano he was active in Roman literary circles from the 1620s. He was secretary to Francesco Peretti (later Cardinal Montalto) by 1630 and to Camillo Pamphili (1644–7), before serving Pope Innocent X as *cameriere segreto*. Many of his poems were set to music. In 1627–8 he wrote the text of a *dramma per musica* for the marriage in Rome of Taddeo Barberini and Anna Colonna (Rome, 1629, copy in *I-Rvat*; music lost, composer unknown). It is entitled *Apollo* in Allacci's *Drammaturgia* (Rome, 1666). His *Sant'Agnese*, in three acts, with music by Mario Savioni (*Rdp*; libretto ed. F. Benigni, *Poesie*, Macerata, 1667), was commissioned by Pamphili for Carnival 1651 and includes arias that were written earlier (a manuscript libretto in *RIM* is wrongly attributed to Giulio Rospigliosi). MARGARET MURATA

Benigni [Benigno], **Pietro Paolo** (*fl* 1670–1707). Italian bass. His name appears first in 1670 in Milan, where he took the role of Giacco in *Ippolita reina delle amazzoni*, by Lodovico Busca, P. S. Agostini and P. A. Ziani. From 11 March 1678 until his dismissal on 15 January 1707 he was a virtuoso singer in the service of the dukes of Parma, Ranuccio II and Francesco I Farnese; he was also a musician of the church of the Madonna della Steccata, Parma, from 17 August 1678 until 1692, after which he took part only in major celebrations. During his long career he sang in various cities, especially in northern Italy and most frequently in Milan and Parma.

PAOLA BESUTTI

Benincori, Angelo Maria (*b* Brescia, 28 March 1779; *d* Belleville, nr Paris, 30 Dec 1821). Italian composer. He was something of a child prodigy, studying in Parma with Ghiretti (composition) and Alessandro Rolla (violin). He obtained the patronage of the Duke of Parma, and went on to study with Cimarosa. During a youthful musical tour with his brother, the ill luck that followed him made an early appearance: his brother died of a fever, and the family savings were lost to an unscrupulous lawyer.

Benincori's opera *Nitteti* was successfully produced, according to Fétis, in Italy and later in Vienna. On moving to Paris in about 1803 he had the operas *Galatée* and *Hésione* accepted at the Paris Opéra, but they were never staged. Embittered, he fell back on teaching. Much later, his three one-act works for the Opéra-Comique had limited success; the scores do not survive, as far as is known, although a draft MS libretto of *Les époux indiscrets* is held in Paris (*F-Pn*).

Benincori's greatest success came posthumously. Isouard died in 1818, leaving only two acts of the opera *Aladin* near completion. His friends and librettist asked Benincori to finish the work. He composed the last three acts, the march ending Act 1, and scenes ii and iv of Act 2. His death, six weeks before the première, was from a progressive illness. *Aladin* was clearly designed to be a showcase for the new gas lighting-system at the Opéra (just as Act 2 of Weber's *Oberon*, four years later, was conceived around a lighting effect at Covent Garden). In Act 4 scene iv 'the magic lamp lights up and throws brilliant illumination into the room', and at the end 'the scene changes to represent the palace of light'. It held the stage until 1830.

Nitteti (P. Metastasio), Italy, ?1797; Vienna, Hof, 1800

Les parents d'un jour (oc, 1, A. de Beauplan), Paris, OC (Feydeau), 7 Nov 1815

La promesse de mariage, ou Le retour au hameau (oc, 1, M. Dieulafoy and N. Gersin), Paris, OC (Feydeau), 14 May 1818

Les époux indiscrets, ou Le danger des confidences (oc, 1, Saint-Alme and C. de Saint-Just), Paris, OC (Feydeau), 16 Jan 1819

Aladin, ou La lampe merveilleuse (opéra-féerie, 5, C.-G. Etienne), Paris, Opéra, 6 Feb 1822, *F-Po* [Acts 1 and 2 mainly by Isouard]

Unperf.: Galatée, ou Le nouveau Pygmalion, *c*1804; Hésione, *c*1807 (tragédie lyrique)

*

FétisB

C.-G. Etienne: Preface to *Aladin, ou La lampe merveilleuse* (Paris, 5/1825)

T. de Lajarte: *Bibliothèque musicale du théâtre de l'Opéra* (Paris, 1876–8) DAVID CHARLTON

Benini, Anna (*fl* 1784–91). Italian soprano. She was *prima buffa* in the Italian opera company at the King's Theatre, London, in the 1786–7 season, when Burney found her singing 'extremely graceful and pleasing', and she substituted for Mara in Tarchi's serious opera *Virginia*. She had come from Naples with her husband, the tenor Mengozzi, but the London climate disagreed with him and they moved to Paris. She was singing at Venice in 1791. Richard Mount Mount Edgcumbe wrote that her voice lacked power but was of 'exquisite sweetness'.

BDA; *BurneyH*; *LS*
R. Mount Edgcumbe: *Musical Reminiscences* (London, 1824, 4/1834) OLIVE BALDWIN, THELMA WILSON

Benjamin, Arthur (*b* Sydney, 18 Sept 1893; *d* London, 10 April 1960). Australian-English composer and pianist. He began piano lessons at the age of nine while at school in Brisbane, and at 14 attended his first opera in Brussels during a visit to Europe with his parents. His first employment was as a demonstrator in a Brisbane piano store, but in 1911 he went to Britain to study at the RCM, working with Stanford for composition and Frederick Bridge for fugue. While at the RCM he wrote and sold two piano pieces for children, and after war service (Royal Flying Corps) he went back to Australia and a piano teaching appointment at the New South Wales State Conservatorium in Sydney.

In 1921 Benjamin returned to make his home in London, setting a pattern of composition interspersed with teaching and adjudicating as the basis of his subsequent career; much of this was focussed on the piano. He composed a large number of light piano works; *Jamaican Rumba* achieved a popular reputation worldwide unmatched by his other works, which included five operas.

His operas began with the comedy *The Devil Take Her*, the first performance of which, in 1931, was conducted by Beecham. It had a cast of 14 singers and no chorus, and was accounted a success. Two years later followed *Prima Donna*, another one-act comedy, for six singers and a small character-ballet, but such was the dearth of operatic opportunity in the 1930s that this waited until 1949 for a first production; it was revived at the RCM in 1968.

After spending World War II in Canada, as a teacher and conductor of the CBC Symphony Orchestra, Benjamin returned to London and composed a full-scale opera, *A Tale of Two Cities*. The work received three radio performances broadcast by the BBC Third Programme in 1953; its first stage production by the New Opera Company at Sadler's Wells Theatre in 1957 was followed by a performance on BBC Television the next year. Meanwhile the one-act *Mañana* was the first opera to be commissioned for television by the BBC; it was screened in 1956. *Tartuffe*, after Molière, was finished only in short score when Benjamin died; the orchestration was completed by Alan Boustead, who conducted the première in 1964, given by the New Opera Company at Sadler's Wells Theatre.

Benjamin's musical style in his operas, as in his other works, is melodically direct and harmonically uncomplicated, sustained by a keen rhythmic pulse sometimes inflected with the Latin-American rhythms of which he was notably fond. He acknowledged no distinction between 'light' and 'serious' music; his vocal writing is always understanding of technique and register. Its limitation is in a tendency to conform too closely to parlando speech rhythms instead of taking wing, so that his otherwise sure sense of theatre, in imagination and structure, misses too often the added dimension essential to operatic music.

See also DEVIL TAKE HER, THE; PRIMA DONNA; TALE OF TWO CITIES, A; and TARTUFFE.

all first performed in London

The Devil Take Her (prol., 1, A. Collard and J. B. Gordon), RCM, 1 Dec 1931, vs (London, 1932)

Prima Donna, 1933 (comedy op, 1, J. C. Cliffe), Fortune, 23 Feb 1949, vs (London, 1935)

A Tale of Two Cities, 1949–50 (6 scenes, Cliffe, after C. Dickens), BBC, 17 April 1953; stage, Sadler's Wells, 23 July 1957, vs (London, 1954)

Mañana (1, C. Brahms and G. Foa, after Brahms: *Under the Juniper Tree*), televised, BBC, 1 Feb 1956

Tartuffe, 1957–60 (2 and epilogue, Cliffe, after Molière), Sadler's Wells, 30 Nov 1964, orch completed A. Boustead

D. Arundell: 'Arthur Benjamin's Operas', *Tempo*, new ser., no.15 (1950), 15–18
R. M. Schafer: 'Arthur Benjamin', *British Composers in Interview* (London, 1963), 47–52
C. Cliffe: 'Benjamin's Tartuffe', *MT*, cv (1964), 819–20 NOËL GOODWIN

Bennelong. Puppet opera in 13 brief scenes by BARRY CONYNGHAM to a libretto by Murray Copland; Groningen, Netherlands, State Theatre, 21 April 1988.

Narrated by two soloists (soprano and tenor), who also supply voices for all the puppets, the opera traces, in the manner of a serio-comic 'conte philosophique', the well-intentioned attempt by Australia's first governor, Captain Phillip, to induct his mercurial aboriginal captive, Bennelong, into 'rational' European modes of behaviour. Accompanying Phillip to London, Bennelong finds British society rife, not with rationality, but with mystical fads and violent forms of sport – and ruled by a lunatic king. Disillusioned, Bennelong returns to Australia, only to find himself rejected as a stranger by his own people. In the moving final scene, drunk and hallucinating, he wanders through his native bush by night, to perish by a spear out of the darkness.

The vocal lines in *Bennelong* are mostly in parlando style; where melodic lines are used they are wide-intervalled, resembling inflected speech. The music is swift and direct, without much lyrical indulgence, and uses Conyngham's characteristic small metrical and rhythmic ostinato figures. THÉRÈSE RADIC

Bennett, Richard Rodney (*b* Broadstairs, 29 March 1936). English composer and pianist. He studied at the RAM with Lennox Berkeley and Howard Ferguson, and in Paris with Boulez. All Bennett's operatic works date from the decade following his return to London in 1958; these include the one-act opera *The Ledge*, three full-length operas (*The Mines of Sulphur*, *A Penny for a Song* and *Victory*) and one for children (*All the King's Men*); a further stage work (the ballet *Isadora*) was written following his move to New York in 1979.

Most of Bennett's distinguished output of non-operatic vocal music was to follow the composition of his operas, and not vice versa. The operas would, moreover, seem directly to have influenced the character of much of his orchestral and chamber music, especially that of his numerous concertos, as well as his stylistic evolution: from the 12-note writing of *The Ledge* and *The Mines of Sulphur*, through the freer harmonic idiom (not excluding suggestions of tonality) of *A Penny for a Song* and *Victory*, to the recognizably personal language, best described as a kind of serial tonality, of the 1980s. Throughout Bennett's career words, or literary images, have never been far from his mind even in his purely instrumental music, and extra-musical sources of various kinds – whether literary, pictorial or dramatic – have increasingly come to suggest either the form or the expressive impulse for larger works.

See also MINES OF SULPHUR, THE; PENNY FOR A SONG, A; and VICTORY.

The Ledge (1, A. Mitchell), London, Sadler's Wells, 12 Sept 1961 (Croydon, 1975)
The Mines of Sulphur (3, B. Cross), London, Sadler's Wells, 24 Feb 1965, vs (London, 1965)
A Penny for a Song (2, C. Graham, after J. Whiting), London, Sadler's Wells, 31 Oct 1967, vs (London, 1967)
All the King's Men (children's op, 1, Cross), Coventry, Technical College, 28 March 1969 (London, 1969)
Victory (3, Cross, after J. Conrad), London, CG, 13 April 1970, vs (London, 1970)

N. Goodwin: 'The Mines of Sulphur', *Opera*, xvi (1965), 85–8 [interview with Bennett]
S. Bradshaw: 'Victory', *MT*, cxi (1970), 370–72 [interview with Bennett] SUSAN BRADSHAW

Bennett, Robert Russell (*b* Kansas City, MO, 15 June 1894; *d* New York, 18 Aug 1981). American composer and orchestrator. He studied with Carl Busch in Kansas City (1912–15), with Nadia Boulanger in Paris (1926–31) and in Berlin and London. From the 1920s to the 1960s he was a leading orchestrator of Broadway musicals and Hollywood films. A prolific composer in his own right, Bennett wrote with special skill for orchestra and wind band. His concert works often treat American themes and incorporate popular idioms. In general they are distinguished by brilliant scoring rather than intrinsic musical quality.

Bennett's one-act opera-ballet *Endymion* (1927) is a minor work that owes much to French models, in particular its Debussian vocal lines and wordless choruses. The English libretto, after a poem by Bernard le Bovier de Fontenelle, tells of Endymion's unrequited love for the goddess Diana. The score calls for large orchestra and chorus and seven soloists. The Eastman School published a vocal score in 1934, and *Endymion* was produced there on 5 April 1935 under the direction of Howard Hanson. Another one-act opera from the same period, *An Hour of Delusion* to a libretto by Arthur Train jr, is lost.

Maria Malibran, Bennett's principal stage work, is more cosmopolitan in subject and style. The libretto by the music critic Robert A. Simon (with whom Bennett had collaborated on *Endymion*) freely recounts the famous singer's brief, unhappy sojourn in New York in the 1820s. Old-style dances and borrowed solos for Malibran, including 'Home, sweet home' and Rossini's 'Una voce poco fa', impart a period flavour that contrasts with the modernity of Bennett's harmonic language. Melody mattered less to him. 'I almost prefer a dull Reger to an inspired Puccini', he wrote at the time of the première on 8 April 1935 at the Juilliard School. Critical reaction was mixed, much of it focussing on Bennett's reliance on spoken dialogue rather than lyrical exposition to carry the story forward.

Bennett and Simon collaborated again on a radio opera, *The Enchanted Kiss*, based on a short story by O. Henry; it was broadcast on the Mutual network on 30 December 1945. In his last opera, *Crystal*, evidently completed in the early 1970s, Bennett conjured an idyllic community of cave-dwellers as a foil to the frenetic urbanity of modern American life. Despite several ingenious ensembles, including an improvised Dixieland jam session during a cocktail party, the two-act opera lacks sustained musical interest. It has never been published or performed; the vocal score, along with other materials relevant to Bennett's operatic activities, is at the Library of Congress, Washington, DC.

R. R. Bennett: 'From Composer of "Malibran"', *New York Times* (7 April 1935)
H. Taubman: '"Maria Malibran" Sung in Premiere', *New York Times* (9 April 1935)
O. Thompson: 'Maria Malibran has Premiere at Juilliard', *MusAm*, lv/8 (1935), 16, 33 HARRY HASKELL

Benois, Alexandre [Benua, Alexander Nikolayevich] (*b* St Petersburg, 21 April/3 May 1870; *d* Paris, 9 Feb 1960). Russian stage designer, director and art historian. He was one of a neo-Romantic group of St Petersburg artists (including Dyagilev, Bakst and Nuvel) associated with the journal *Mir iskusstvo* (1898–1905). After graduating in law he lived in France for a time. In his writings and as an artist, he tried to promote the understanding of both western European modernism and the national Russian cultural tradition. Thanks to his and Dyagilev's propagandist work, from 1899 the stage designs at the St Petersburg court theatres began to reflect trends in contemporary Russian painting, a process that Benois attempted to intensify and accelerate with his own designs (e.g. for *Götterdämmerung*, Mariinsky Theatre, 1902). He played an important part in the Russian opera and ballet guest season in Paris in 1908 (organized by the *Mir iskusstvo* group) and in Dyagilev's Ballets Russes seasons that followed, as artistic director (until 1911), librettist and designer, notably for *The Nightingale* (1914). Differences with Dyagilev led to a move to Stanislavsky's Moscow Arts Theatre, 1912–14. After the October Revolution he was director of the Hermitage painting collection and worked as designer for the Bol'shoy and Mariinsky theatres, including a production of *The Queen of Spades* (1921). In the 1920s he went to Paris, where he worked as an opera and ballet designer, notably for the Rubinstein Company (1923–34) and for the Opéra, as well as for La Scala and companies in Rome, Buenos Aires, Sydney and Monte Carlo. The main feature of his work was a desire to inject new life into the theatre of illusion by introducing the modernist style of painting of the turn of the century. His sets had a picturesque, fantastic quality, a fairy-tale atmosphere and attractive local colour. Among his writings may be mentioned *Russkaya shkola zhivopisi* ('The Russian School of Painting'; St Petersburg, 1904; Eng. trans., 1916), *Vozniknoveniye 'Mira iskusstva': Alexandr Benua* ('The Origins of *The World of Art*'; Leningrad, 1928) and a volume of memoirs, *Zhizn' khudozhnika: vospominaniya* (New York, 1955; Eng. trans., 1960).

M. G. Etkind: *Aleksandr Nikolayevich Benua 1870–1960* (Moscow, 1965)
M. Monteverdi, ed.: *Alexandre Benois: il classico della rivoluzione 1870–1960* (Milan, 1970) [exhibition catalogue]
E. Klimoff: 'Alexandre Benois and his Rôle in Russian Art', *Apollo*, xcviii (1973), 460–69
M. G. Etkind: *A. N. Benua i russkaya khudozhestvennya kultura kontsa XIX–nachala XX veka* [A. N. Benois and Russian Artistic Culture of the end of the 19th Century to the Start of the 20th Century] (Leningrad, 1989) MANFRED BOETZKES

Set design by Nicola Benois for a production of Musorgsky's 'Boris Godunov' at La Scala, Milan, 1952–3

Benois, Nicola [Benua, Nikolay Alexandrovich] (*b* Oranienbaum, 2/15 May 1901; *d* Switzerland, 30 March 1988). Russian painter and stage designer, son of Alexandre Benois. He was trained by his father, with whom he collaborated at the start of his career in the theatre. The family settled in Paris in 1923 and Benois rapidly established a reputation with his colourful, strongly characterized designs for Baliyev's Chauve-Souris company. Throughout his career, Russian opera and Russian subjects resulted in particularly successful productions, from his first engagements at La Scala – *Boris Godunov* (1926) and *Khovanshchina* (1927), undertaken at the invitation of Toscanini – to the folk-art inspired *Prince Igor* in Chicago in 1962. In 1936, having worked chiefly at the Rome Opera and the Teatro Colón, Buenos Aires, he was appointed resident designer at La Scala, where, until his retirement in 1977, he was responsible for over 300 productions and for the policy of encouraging younger, experimental designers in this erstwhile bastion of 19th-century realism.

A designer in the Romantic, painterly tradition of his father, whose influence he never entirely outgrew, Benois was not an innovator but modified and adapted new ideas skilfully. He was a master of the unified stage picture and of the technical means needed to achieve it, advising on problems of staging until his death.

*

C. E. Rava: *Nuovi orientamenti della scenografia* (Milan, 1965)
I giovani ottant'anni di Nicola Benois (Milan, 1981)

MARINA HENDERSON

Benoist, François (*b* Nantes, 10 Sept 1794; *d* Paris, 6 May 1878). French composer. He entered the Paris Conservatoire in 1811 as a pupil of Catel and in 1815 won the Prix de Rome. In 1819 he was appointed principal organist of the royal chapel and professor of organ at the Conservatoire; his pupils included Adolphe Adam, Alkan, Franck, Bizet, Dubois and Saint-Saëns. In 1840 he became *premier chef de chant* at the Opéra, with the additional task of revising the repertory for current use.

Benoist wrote two operas: the one-act *opéra comique, Léonore et Félix* (Saint-Marcelin; Paris, OC (Feydeau), 1821; Paris *c*1821), and the two-act *L'apparition* (G. Delavigne; Opéra, 16 June 1848), which had the misfortune to be staged just before all Paris theatres were closed by the 1848 disturbances, and was not revived. *L'apparition* concerns a Spanish girl, Clara, who pretends to be dead in order to haunt the French officer who has abandoned her. Benoist's music was praised for its effective instrumentation and for the ballets, but his style was considered too severe and learned for such material. He also wrote four ballets and sacred music.

*

FétisBS
C. Saint-Saëns: *Ecole buissonnière* (Paris, 1913)

HUGH MACDONALD

Benoit, Peter (Léonard Léopold) (*b* Harlebeke, 17 Aug 1834; *d* Antwerp, 8 March 1901). Belgian composer. A pupil at the Brussels Conservatory from 1851, he studied with Fétis; later he studied under K. L. Hanssens and in 1856 became conductor of the Théâtre Royal du Parc in Brussels. He won the Belgian Prix de Rome in 1857. After travelling in Germany, he became conductor of the Théâtre des Bouffes-Parisiens in 1862, but resigned in 1863 and returned to Belgium where he founded the Flemish Music School at Antwerp in 1867; this became the Royal Flemish Conservatory in 1898. In 1890 Benoit founded the Netherlands Lyric Theatre, which in 1893 became the Vlaamse Opera.

As a composer Benoit's chief aim was to bring Flemish musical life to the level of general European culture in conjunction with the movement for Flemish national consciousness. Stylistically, his works belong to 19th-century Romanticism. At first he was influenced by the French school as well as by Beethoven, Mendelssohn, Liszt, Chopin and Weber, but later he inclined towards Berlioz and Meyerbeer; at his peak he used bold, non-Classical harmony, with dramatic effects recalling Wagner.

Benoit was principally a composer of sacred and secular vocal music, with a striking mastery of large choral masses. The most original form that he employed was lyric drama, a play in which the actors speak in rhythm, accompanied orchestrally throughout. His aim was to be performed and understood by the Flemish people, to which end he deliberately simplified the style of his later works, searching for national traits in the melody and rhythm of traditional folk music and art music.

zpl – *zangspel*

all works published in Antwerp, no date, unless otherwise stated

Le règne du caprice (zpl), 1859
Le roi des aulnes (zpl, Castin), Brussels, Galeries, 2 Dec 1859, *B-Aa**, unpubd; rev. version, Paris, 1861
Le lutin d'Ascone (zpl), 1863, *Ac*
L'amour mendiant (zpl), 1863, *Ac**
Isa (zpl, 3, E. Hiel), Brussels, Cirque, 24 Feb 1867, *Aa**, excerpts pubd
Charlotte Corday (lyric drama, 4, Frenzel and E. Van der Ven), Antwerp, Vlaamse, 18 March 1876, *Aa**, *Ac*, excerpts (Brussels, 1877)
De pacificatie van Gent (lyric drama, E. Van Goethem), 3 Sept 1879, *Aa**, suite pubd
Karel van Gelderland (lyric drama, F. Gittens), Antwerp, Vlaamse, Sept 1892, *Aa*, unpubd
Het meilief (zpl, J. De Meester), Iseghem, 22 Oct 1893, *Aa*, vs (Ghent, 1895)
Pompéja, 1894–5 (lyric drama, P. Billiet, after E. Bulwer-Lytton), unperf.

Melodramas and other works: Madeleen, 1855, *Aa*; De noordster, 1855; Paljas, 1855; De belgische natie (J. Kats), Brussels, Parc, 27 July 1856, *Aa*; Het dorp in't gebergte (3, after A. von Kotzebue), Brussels, Parc, 14 Dec 1856, ov. *Ac*; Het gouden kruisbeeld, 1856; De dichter en zijn droombeeld (dramatic poem, H. Conscience), 1870; T'leven is liefde (monodrama, J. A. De Laet), 1874, *Ac*

*

A. Cornette: *De aesthetiek van het lyrisch drama* (Antwerp, 1895)
J. Sabbe: *Peter Benoit: zijn leven, zijne werken, zijne beteekenis* (Ghent and Antwerp, 1902)
M. Sabbe: *Peter Benoit: leven en work* (Antwerp, 1925)
C. van den Borren: *Peter Benoit* (Brussels, 1942)
A. Corbet: *Peter Benoit: leven, werk en beteekenis* (Antwerp, 1944)
P. Douliez: *Peter Benoit* (Haarlem and Antwerp, 1954)

MARIE-THÉRÈSE BUYSSENS

Benti [Bulgarelli], **Maria Anna** [Marianna] **(Garberini)** ['La Romanina'] (*b* Rome, ?1684; *d* Rome, 26 Feb 1734). Italian soprano. She first appeared in *opera seria* at Siena in Carnival 1704 (as Garberini Benti), first sang in Naples in 1706, Florence and Venice in 1707, and became one of the stars of the day. She apparently married Domenico (or Giuseppe) Bulgarelli near the beginning of 1715. Although she lacked brilliance of vocal technique (range approximately *c′* to *a″*) and was not beautiful, she maintained her position through her stage presence and action, reflecting a fascinating personality to which the young Metastasio succumbed. She encouraged his beginnings as an opera librettist, singing in the first settings of his works up to *Siroe*, and was particularly identified with his *Didone abbandonata* – of which she is said to have suggested certain dramatic elements – singing it in Naples, Venice and Reggio. She retired in 1727. DENNIS LIBBY

Bentoiu, Pascal (*b* Bucharest, 22 April 1927). Romanian composer. He studied composition and orchestration privately and from 1953 to 1956 was engaged in research at the Bucharest Folklore Institute. After writing music for plays by Aeschylus, Beaumarchais, Shakespeare, Rostand, Molière, Arbuzov, Vasile Alecsandri, Costel Popovici and Barbu Delavrancea between 1955 and 1964, he composed three operas. His works are conceived in large-scale symphonic terms (with such smaller, subsidiary forms as passacaglias, fugues and themes with variations), and include leitmotifs, which are built up into thematic patterns. *Hamlet* includes music for *a cappella* chorus and a fugal prelude for percussion.

Amorul doctor [Doctor Love] op.15, 1964 (comic op, 1, Bentoiu, after Molière: *L'amour médecin*), Bucharest, 23 Dec 1966
Jertfirea Iphigeniei [Iphigenia's Sacrifice] op.17 (radio op, A. Pop and Bentoiu, after Euripides), Bucharest, 20 Sept 1968
Hamlet op.18, 1969 (2, Bentoiu, after W. Shakespeare), Marseilles, 26 April 1974

*

O. L. Cosma: 'Dramaturgia operei contemporane româneşti: Hamlet – de Pascal Bentoiu', *Studii de muzicologie,* xvi (1981), 47–176

VIOREL COSMA

Bentzon, Niels Viggo (*b* Copenhagen, 24 Aug 1919). Danish composer. He studied piano and organ at the Copenhagen Conservatory, and toured widely as a pianist. From 1945 to 1949 he taught at the Århus Conservatory, thereafter at the Copenhagen Conservatory. In the post-Nielsen era he has become one of the best-known, most prolific and extensively performed Danish composers, having written in most genres (except liturgical music). His creative energies have also led him into visual art (he has produced many paintings and drawings) and he has worked as a writer and freelance music critic.

Bentzon's compositional style, which owes much to Hindemith, was well developed early in his career and has undergone relatively little evolution. His music is dissonant, though tonal in conception, free-flowing with an almost improvisatory character; frequent experiments with avant-garde procedures have not significantly altered his basic musical language. His interest in dramatic music, particularly opera, emerged later in his career. The three-act opera *Faust III* op.144 (K. Kroman, after Goethe, Kafka and Joyce) was first performed on 21 June 1964 at the Kiel Opera House and the première of his chamber opera *Automaten* op.328 (M. Leinert, after E. T. A. Hoffmann) was given in the same theatre on 3 May 1974. Both works show the influence of Berg.

*

K. Møllerhøj: *Niels Viggo Bentzons kompositioner* (Copenhagen, 1980)

WILLIAM H. REYNOLDS

Benucci, Francesco (*b c*1745; *d* Florence, 5 April 1824). Italian bass. He sang at Pistoia in 1769, then more widely in Italy, appearing as the leading character *buffo* in Venice (1778–9), and singing in Milan (1779–82) with great success and in Rome (1783–4). He first appeared in Vienna in 1783 and became the leading member of the celebrated company there, creating Tita in Martín y Soler's *Una cosa rara* and four Salieri roles including Trofonio and Axur. Described by Mozart as 'particularly good' (letter of 7 May 1783), he sang Figaro at the première of *Le nozze di Figaro* (1786), Leporello in the first Vienna performance of *Don Giovanni* (1788), when Mozart composed an extra duet for him, and Guglielmo in the première of *Così fan tutte* (1790). In 1789 he went to London where he sang Bartolo in Paisiello's *Il barbiere di Siviglia* and appeared in Gazzaniga's *La vendemmia* opposite Nancy Storace, with whom he had sung in Vienna. They introduced the first piece from any Mozart opera to be heard on the London stage, the duet 'Crudel! perchè finora' from *Figaro*. Benucci returned to Vienna later in 1789, remaining until 1795. His last great triumph was to create Count Robinson in Cimarosa's *Il matrimonio segreto* in 1792. He had a round, beautifully full voice, more bass than baritone; probably he was the finest artist for whom Mozart wrote, and as a *buffo* outshone his contemporaries as singer and actor.

CHRISTOPHER RAEBURN, DOROTHEA LINK

Benvenuti, Tomaso [Tommaso] (*b* Cavarzere, Veneto, 4 Feb 1838; *d* Rome, 26 Feb 1906). Italian composer. His first opera, *Valenza Candiano*, written when he was only 18, reached rehearsal stage, but not performance, at the Teatro Sociale, Mantua. Thereafter six of his works were performed in major centres in Italy, but after initial successes, none remained in the repertory or appears to have merited modern revival. Despite their somewhat workmanlike character, the most admired were *Adriana Lecouvreur*, *Guglielmo Shakespeare* and *Beatrice di Svevia*.

Valenza Candiano, 1856 (4), unperf.
Adriana Lecouvreur (L. Fortis), Milan, Canobbiana, 26 Nov 1857
Guglielmo Shakespeare (F. M. Piave), Parma, Regio, 14 Feb 1861
La stella di Toledo (A. Ghislanzoni), Milan, Canobbiana, 23 April 1864
Il falconiere (3), Venice, Rossini, 16 Feb 1878
Beatrice di Svevia (4), Venice, Rossini, 20 Feb 1890
Le baruffe chiozzotte (1, Benvenuti, after C. Goldoni), Florence, Pagliano, 30 Jan 1895
Tre milioni (Piave), unperf.

ES; *StiegerO* PATRICK O'CONNOR

Benvenuto Cellini. *Opéra semi-seria* in two acts by HECTOR BERLIOZ to a libretto by Léon de Wailly and AUGUSTE BARBIER, assisted by Alfred de Vigny, after the memoirs of Benvenuto Cellini; Paris, Opéra, 10 September 1838. Revised version, Weimar, Grossherzogliches Hoftheater, 20 March 1852; with further revision in three acts, 17 November 1852.

Design by Paul Lormier for the costume of Giacomo Balducci in the original production of 'Benvenuto Cellini' at the Paris Opéra (Salle Le Peletier), 10 September 1838

The opera is set in 16th-century Rome during the papacy of Clement VII. (Censorship in Paris did not allow a pope to be represented on stage so the part became that of Cardinal Salviati at the première and in all subsequent versions.) The overture, a triumph of rhythmic imagination, portends the general vivacity to follow; among the themes are allusions to the cardinal's arioso and to the lovely 'Ariette d'Arlequin' of the dumb show.

Act 1 tableau i opens on Shrove Monday in the home of the papal treasurer, Giacomo Balducci (bass). He is vexed that Clement VII has commissioned a bronze statue of Perseus from the libertine genius Cellini (tenor) instead of Fieramosca (baritone; tenor in 1838), the papal sculptor and suitor of Balducci's daughter Teresa (soprano). Passing maskers sing of the carnival and toss Teresa flowers, along with a billet-doux from Cellini. To be torn between love and duty, she complains in her cavatina 'Entre l'amour et le devoir', is no laughing matter; but at the age of 17 it would be a pity to behave. (This replaced an earlier cavatina, 'Ah, que l'amour une fois dans le coeur'.) Cellini comes to pay Teresa court, but their duet becomes a trio when Fieramosca tiptoes into the room and takes cover behind a door. (Berlioz re-used the melody of the duet 'O Teresa, vous que j'aime plus que ma vie' as the english horn solo in the overture *Le carnaval romain*; the other theme in the concert overture is the saltarello from the carnival scene.) Fieramosca overhears the lovers planning to elope to Florence (the trio 'Demain soir mardi gras'): the following evening, at the carnival, Cellini and his apprentice Ascanio will come disguised as monks to the Piazza Colonna, there to effect a rendezvous with Teresa. Balducci enters, surprised to find his daughter still awake; Cellini slips out of the open door. Teresa, stammering an explanation, says she has heard a prowler, and to her great surprise it is Fieramosca who is found in her room. Servants and neighbours are summoned to capture the seducer, but in the confusion he manages to get away. They chase him towards the public fountain.

Tableau ii begins at nightfall in the Piazza Colonna, with a tavern on one side and Cassandro's theatre, a place of lampoons, on the other. Cellini reflects that while glory was once his only goal, now Teresa alone rules his heart. The two ensemble scenes that follow – the goldsmiths' chorus ('Honneur aux maîtres ciseleurs') and the Roman carnival – are the musical high points of the opera, summarizing in orchestration, rhythm and organizational device the growth of Berlioz's style since his Italian sojourn. There is revealed, moreover, a bright sense of humour that until then had only been heard in the Abruzzi serenade from *Harold en Italie*. The smiths' apostrophe to their noble art, for example, is interrupted by the cross old innkeeper (tenor), who tallies a list of wine consumed and will deliver no more until the account is paid. Ascanio (mezzo-soprano; soprano in 1838) appears with money from the papal treasury, surrendering it only after Cellini's oath that the statue will be cast the next day. But the amount tendered by the parsimonious Balducci is scarcely enough to pay the innkeeper.

Cellini goes off to arrange an appropriate evening's entertainment with Cassandro, impresario of the adjoining theatre, as the goldsmiths' chorus is reprised. Fieramosca, beaten and bruised, has engaged a henchman, the swordsman Pompeo (baritone); they plan to appear at the carnival in habits identical to those of Cellini and Ascanio, in which dress they hope to succeed in abducting Teresa. Fieramosca practises his swordsmanship.

Trumpet fanfares summon the public to Cassandro's theatre, and the piazza begins to fill with revellers. Balducci and Teresa enter, then Cellini and Ascanio, in white and brown habits respectively; the conversation of the four intermingles in a *réunion des thèmes*. In the famous saltarello Cassandro's players attract the crowd ('Venez voir! venez voir!') as the women and children dance. The pantomime of King Midas, or The Donkey's Ears, begins: a papal treasurer unmistakably resembling Balducci remunerates Harlequin's lovely arietta and the buffoonery, with ophicleide and bass drum, of the donkey-eared Pasquarello (Polichinelle in 1838). A single coin goes to Harlequin, much as the pittance had gone to Cellini; the rest is paid to the ass. Balducci, recognizing himself, assaults the players; the rival friars converge on Teresa. During the confusion Cellini stabs Pompeo. Just as the crowd sees that a monk has been killed, the cannon of the fortress of Sant'Angelo sounds the end of the carnival and the beginning of Lent. The revellers extinguish their candles, and in the ensuing darkness Cellini escapes and Ascanio spirits Teresa away. Fieramosca, mistaken for Cellini, is arrested for murder.

The entr'acte is a sinister version of the 'Chant des ciseleurs' from the previous act, creating a sense of foreboding. Act 2 tableau iii opens in Cellini's studio at dawn on Ash Wednesday. A model of the statue of Perseus dominates the stage. Ascanio and Teresa pray for Cellini's safety as White Friars pass in the street chanting a litany to the Virgin. Cellini, still in his white habit, has been of their number. Reunited with Teresa, he describes his escape; the statue, they resolve, will be abandoned as they elope together. Ascanio tries to warn of the arrival of Balducci and Fieramosca, but it is too late. The principals encounter each other in a sextet, the centrepiece of the tableau; just as Balducci gives Teresa's hand to Fieramosca, the cardinal (bass) enters with his retinue. Finding the statue unfinished and Cellini accused of murder and kidnapping, the cardinal orders the casting to be done by someone else. Cellini, in audacious defiance, threatens to smash the plaster model. The gesture is impudent but effective: the cardinal has no choice but to return that evening. If by that time the Perseus is not cast, Cellini will hang.

Tableau iv opens later that afternoon, in Cellini's foundry in the Colosseum. Ascanio feigns optimism at the situation ('Tra-la-la ... mais qu'ai-je donc?'); Cellini pauses to long for a pastoral life far from the city's din ('Sur les monts les plus sauvages'). Off stage, the foundry workers sing symbolically of sailors at large on the sea. (Here there followed a 'scène et choeurs' including further reverses, excised by Berlioz before the first performance. The later Weimar version, sanctioned by the composer, conflates and reorders tableaux iii and iv for Act 3; for a letter from Berlioz to Liszt concerning later revisions, *see* BERLIOZ, HECTOR, fig.1.) Balducci and the cardinal return to observe the casting, but metal is in short supply and the meld begins to congeal. Cellini, on the verge of losing everything, orders his assistants to fetch all his artworks – gold, silver, copper, bronze – and throw them into the furnace. The crucible explodes and the molten metal flows through the trenches and into the mould. The statue is done, Cellini pardoned, Teresa's hand earned, and the reward of the *maîtres ciseleurs* is immortal glory.

The clumsy second act was the primary cause of the vicissitudes that befell *Benvenuto Cellini*. Not even the Weimar revisions could fully correct the confusions of the denouement. Berlioz behaved gracefully after each failure of *Benvenuto Cellini*, but 'I cannot help recognizing', he wrote in 1850 or so, 'that it contains a variety of ideas, an energy and exuberance and a brilliance of colour such as I may perhaps never find again, and which deserved a better fate'. D. KERN HOLOMAN

Beograd (Serbo-Croat). BELGRADE.

Berain, Jean (bap. Saint-Mihiel, Lorraine, 4 June 1640; *d* Paris, 24 Jan 1711). French designer. After beginning his career in Paris as an engraver, he was summoned to Versailles in 1674 to work on the festivities celebrating the conquest of the Franche-Comté. That year he was appointed Dessinateur de la Chambre et du Cabinet du Roi, succeeding Henry Gissey. Thereafter he was to provide all the models of costumes for the operas performed at the royal residences and on the operatic stage of Paris, replacing Carlo Vigarani as designer of the sets and stage effects there in 1680. Until at least 1707 he prepared designs at the Académie Royale de Musique for the works of Lully and his successors, Collasse, Marin Marais, Charpentier, Desmarets, Elisabeth-Claude Jacquet de la Guerre, Campra, Destouches and Jean-Féry Rebel.

Berain won fame in other areas as well, notably in naval decoration and 'grotesques' (styles of ornament widely diffused through engravings) and many of his designs for operatic performances have survived in collections in Paris, Stockholm and London. He drew inspiration for his scenery from the Italians Torelli, Grimaldi, Burnacini and Vigarani, although he was less of an innovator than the Galli-Bibienas; he continued to respect the principle of frontal representation, with regular and symmetrical disposition of the lateral frames, and never used the oblique perspective known as *per angolo* that was already in use in Italy. However, he brought operatic costume to a state of perfection unequalled in the Europe of the time.

While Berain sometimes turned to Gissey's models, he gave his costumes unusual refinement, striving for diversification in their cut and the details of their ornamentation. Like Gissey he attempted to make costumes appropriate to the roles, and was careful to give a good idea of the characters suggested in the librettos. When he was designing Lully's *Amadis*, with its subject taken from a chivalric romance, he did research of a kind unusual for the time to achieve historical authenticity, turning to the fashions of the Middle Ages and the Renaissance. Berain exerted great influence on his immediate successors at the Académie Royale de Musique – his sons Jean and Claude Gillot. The younger Jean is known to have worked there until his death in 1726.

For illustrations *see* *ALCESTE* (i); *AMADIS*; *ARMIDE* (i); COSTUME, fig.4; MACHINERY, fig.8; *MÉDÉE* (i); PARIS, fig.2; *ROLAND* (i); STAGE DESIGN, fig.3; and TRAGÉDIE EN MUSIQUE, fig.2.

*

R.-A. Weigert: *Jean I Berain: Dessinateur de la chambre et du cabinet du roi (1640–1711)* (Paris, 1937)

J. de La Gorce: *Berain, dessinateur du Roi Soleil* (Paris, 1986)

——: *Lully: un âge d'or de l'opéra français* (Paris, 1991)

JÉRÔME DE LA GORCE

Bérard, Christian(-Jacques) (*b* Paris, 20 Aug 1902; *d* Paris, 12 Feb 1949). French painter, designer and illustrator. He was a pupil of Maurice Denis, Edouard Vuillard and the Académie Julien; his considerable gifts as a painter were overshadowed by his genius for stage decor. Although he never worked in opera, Bérard was one of most influential designers of the mid-20th century, establishing an elegant style emulated by his contemporaries and plagiarized by the next generation. He reduced architectural and decorative elements to essentials, writing that he first visualized a full, realistic set and then eliminated ruthlessly: a historical epoch or psychological mood was created by the use of form, colour and light, and stage space was employed positively. The result was a modish charm which was inimitable. Sets for three of his productions have achieved classic status: those for Molière's *L'école des femmes* (staged by Jouvet in 1936), where the action flowed from scene to clearly visualized scene with minimum props and changes; Massine's ballet *Symphonie fantastique* (1936), where the blazing, restricted, sometimes dissonant use of colour was integral to the music and choreography; and Cocteau's film *La belle et la bête* (1946), where magic was created by the use of light, gauzes and sparse decorative details.

Paintings by Bérard are in the Centre Georges Pompidou, Paris, the Museum of Modern Art, New York, and the National Portrait Gallery, London. The Comédie Française and the Jouvet Foundation have collections of his designs.

*

B. Kochno: *Christian Bérard* (Paris, 1987)

MARINA HENDERSON

Bérard, Jean-Antoine (*b* Lunel, 1710; *d* Paris, 1 Dec 1772). French *haute-contre* and writer on singing. His début in 1733 at the Paris Opéra was in Collasse's *Thétis et Pélée*. After three years with the Italian troupe, performing *divertissements*, he returned to the Opéra and took minor roles in Rameau's works (1737–45), including *Castor et Pollux* (1737), *Dardanus* (1739), *Les fêtes d'Hébé* (1739) and *Les Indes galantes* (1743). In 1743 he sang the title role in the première of Boismortier's *Don Quichote chez la Duchesse*. He retired from opera in 1745 to teach and play the cello and became first cellist of the orchestra at the Comédie-Italienne in 1762, the year in which he married Mlle Deschamps, an actress at the Opéra-Comique.

In his treatise, *L'art du chant* (Paris, 1755), he discussed the physical and anatomical aspects of tone production and appended valuable examples from the works of Lully, Campra, Mondonville, Rameau and others, indicating the desired tone and appropriate ornaments. La Borde called Bérard a 'bon musicien' and recognized his treatise as a summation of vocal practice for the period from Lully to Rameau.

*

FétisB

J.-B. La Borde: *Essai sur la musique ancienne et moderne*, iii (Paris, 1780)

M. Cyr: 'Eighteenth-century French and Italian Singing: Rameau's Writing for the Voice', *ML*, lxi (1980), 318–37

MARY CYR

Berbié, Jane [Bergougne, Jeanne Marie Louise] (*b* Villefranche-de-Lauragais, nr Toulouse, 6 May 1934). French mezzo-soprano. She studied at the Toulouse Conservatory and in 1958 made her operatic début at La Scala in *L'enfant et les sortilèges* (Teapot, Squirrel). She appeared as the Second Lady in *Die Zauberflöte* at the Aix-en-Provence Festival in 1959, the year she joined the Opéra (her début was as Mercédès). Among the many parts she has played in Paris are Concepcion, Zerlina, Despina, Ascanio, Annina, Dorabella, Emilia (*Otello*), Aunt Lavinia (Damase's *L'héritière*), Grandmother Buryjovka, Auntie (*Peter Grimes*) and Marcellina (notably in the 1973 *Figaro* inaugurating Liebermann's administration). With a repertory ranging from Monteverdi to the 20th century, she is particularly delightful on stage in travesty, *ingénue* or soubrette roles. She sang Maffio Orsini in the Carnegie Hall concert performance of *Lucrezia Borgia* in which Caballé made her American début (1965). She first appeared at Glyndebourne in 1967 (as Mirinda in *L'Ormindo*), returning as Despina (1969, 1971, 1984); as the latter, and as Rosina at La Scala and Covent Garden (début, June 1971). She has also sung at Marseilles, Florence, Bologna, Cologne, Barcelona and Geneva where she created Oulita in Liebermann's *Le forêt* (1987). She sang La Marquise de Berkenfeld (*La fille du régiment*) in Lisbon (1990). Her rich-toned agile voice is combined with a warm personality and a very strong sense of humour.

ANDRÉ TUBEUF, ELIZABETH FORBES

Beregan [Berengani, Bergani], **Nicolò** (*b* Vicenza, 21 Feb 1627; *d* Venice, 17 Dec 1713). Italian lawyer, poet and librettist. He was one of the best-known lawyers in the Venice of his day and was widely respected as a literary figure and classical scholar. Between 1656 and 1660 he was exiled because of a personal vendetta against a German merchant. He was a member of three academies, the Dodonei in Venice, the Concordi in Ravenna and the Gelati in Bologna. During his period of activity as a librettist Beregan was in contact with the musically italianate imperial court and corresponded with Duke Johann Friedrich of Hanover, a principal military and musical supporter of the Venetians. Beregan's librettos, generally in a heroic vein, were set by some of the best-known composers of the time, or were revised or drawn upon by other librettists. *Genserico* was the source for the libretto of Handel's uncompleted opera of that name; and Handel also set Pariati's 1724 revision (for Rome) of Beregan's *Giustino*. Domenico Scarlatti wrote an opera based on *Giustino* to a text by G. Convò.

L'Annibale in Capua, P. A. Ziani, 1661 (Ger., G. C. Schürmann, 1726); *Il Tito*, Cesti, 1666; *Genserico*, probably Partenio, ? begun by Cesti, 1669; *L'Heraclio*, Ziani, 1671; *L'Ottaviano Cesare Augusto*, Legrenzi, 1682; *Giustino*, Legrenzi, 1683 (Ger., Schürmann, 1725)

*

DBI (G. E. Ferrari)

Obituary, *Giornale de' letterati d'Italia*, xviii (1714), 482

E. Rosand: *Opera in Seventeenth-Century Venice* (Berkeley and Los Angeles, 1991)

WILLIAM C. HOLMES

Berenice [*Berenice, regina d'Egitto*] ('Berenice, Queen of Egypt'). Opera in three acts by GEORGE FRIDERIC HANDEL to a libretto anonymously adapted from ANTONIO SALVI's *Berenice, regina d'Egitto* (1709, Pratolino); London, Covent Garden, 18 May 1737.

Handel composed *Berenice* between 18 December 1736 and 27 January 1737, during the last opera season in which his productions at Covent Garden contended with those of the rival 'Opera of the Nobility' at the King's Theatre. The title role is the historical character of Cleopatra Berenice, daughter of Ptolemy Lathyrus (Ptolemy IX Soter II), who succeeded to the Egyptian throne on her father's death in 81 BC. According to Appian (*Civil Wars*, i) she married her cousin Alexander

(Ptolemy XI Alexander II) by order of the Roman dictator Sulla the following year and was murdered by him shortly afterwards. The roles of Berenice (soprano) and Alessandro [Alexander] (soprano castrato) were originally sung by Anna Maria Strada del Pò and the castrato Gioacchino Conti ('Gizziello'); Selene (Berenice's sister, contralto) was sung by Francesca Bertolli, the royal prince Demetrio by the alto castrato Domenico Annibali, the vassal prince Arsace by the contralto Maria Caterina Negri, Berenice's captain and confidant Aristobolo by Henry Reinhold (bass) and the Roman ambassador Fabio by the tenor John Beard. (In Walsh's print *Berenice an Opera*, 1737, one of Fabio's arias is assigned to 'Savage'; this may be an error, or William Savage may have sung in some performances.) The plot is a complex one involving political marriages between the nominees of the Romans and their friends or enemies with Berenice and her sister; misunderstandings and the various proposed pairings arouse jealousy and anger, but all is resolved with the marriages of Alexander to Berenice and Demetrio to Selene. *Berenice* received only four performances near the end of the season and it is not clear whether Handel directed them or was even present in the theatre: four days before the first performance he was reported to be 'very much indispos'd' with 'a Paraletick Disorder, he having at present no Use of his Right Hand'. He never revived the opera. It was produced again at Brunswick in February 1743, in an arrangement by G. C. Schürmann, and then remained unheard until the production by students at the University of Keele, Staffordshire, on 26 April 1985.

Music and drama tend to be somewhat disengaged in *Berenice*: the best numbers are the lyrical major-key arias and duets (three of them with insinuating triplet figures in their accompaniments, in the style of Vivaldi), while the arias of distress and anger are tame by Handel's standards and have unusually thin orchestral textures. Berenice's reflection on fickle fortune in Act 3 ('Chi t'intende?') has the remarkable feature of an elaborate obbligato for solo oboe, vying with the voice for prominence. The opera seems to have been weakened by last-minute alterations, including the removal of a short but expressive aria for Berenice ('Avvertite mie pupille') before the final scene and the replacement of Demetrio's lofty C minor aria of defiance in Act 2 ('Sì, tra i ceppi') by a jaunty major-key setting using music originally written for different words. This latter setting of 'Sì, tra i ceppi' nevertheless became popular and remains a favourite recital piece today (usually sung by basses, though written for alto voice). The minuet of the fine overture is also well known.

ANTHONY HICKS

Bérénice*. Tragédie en musique* in three acts by ALBÉRIC MAGNARD to his own libretto after JEAN RACINE's tragedy; Paris, Opéra-Comique (Salle Favart), 15 December 1911.

In Act 1 Titus (baritone), heir to the Roman Empire, and Bérénice (soprano), Queen of Judaea, continue their love-affair at the latter's villa, though Titus's father is dying in Rome; in Act 2 Titus, now emperor, renounces their relationship; in Act 3, after farewells, Bérénice departs by sea, dedicating a lock of her hair and her lost youth to Venus.

Composed between 1905 and 1909, Magnard's last opera is the summation of his operatic ideals. Like Racine's tragedy, which is used more as a point of departure than a model, it concerns the (historical) relationship between Titus and Bérénice, but Magnard deliberately conflates the character of the Jewish Bérénice with the eponymous Alexandrian queen of three centuries earlier. Magnard considered his methods Wagnerian; certainly the score is saturated with leitmotifs, but the opera's ancestry also encompasses Gluck's tragic elevation and the Berlioz of *Les Troyens*.

Magnard clearly saw the story as an archetypal clash of classic and romantic impulses. Oriental passion struggles with Roman rationalism, and profound love with political expediency; in each case the latter triumphs, but at painful price. The conflicts are, however, essentially embodied in the music, in its counterpoise of masculine and feminine, Roman vigour and Eastern voluptuousness. Especially remarkable is Magnard's shaping of the drama, using instrumental forms to discipline Romantic feeling in a way that partly anticipates Berg's *Wozzeck*. The famous example is Titus's meditation in Act 2, constructed as a fugue. As Magnard himself observed, he employed 'the sweet harmony of canon at the octave in all the love scenes'; the duet that ends Act 1 he likened to a concertante episode, and elements of Act 3 corresponded for him to a sonata finale. These features probably puzzled *Bérénice*'s first audiences, and contributed to its notable lack of success; but among all French operas of the early 20th century it must now be the prime candidate for revival.

MALCOLM MACDONALD

Berens, (Johann) Hermann (*b* Hamburg, 7 April 1826; *d* Stockholm, 9 May 1880). Swedish composer of German origin. He studied music with his father and later with K. G. Reissiger in Dresden, and in 1847 he settled in Sweden. He was music director to the hussar regiment at Örebro from 1849 to 1860, then music director at the Little Theatre, Stockholm (Dramatic Theatre after 1863), and professor of composition at the Stockholm Conservatory from 1868. Berens's operas, which form only a small part of his output, use popular melodies and are sometimes sentimental in character. Some are based on librettos already set by French composers.

all first performed in Stockholm

Violetta (operetta, 3, J. Granberg), Royal, Jan or Feb 1855

En sommarnattsdröm (operetta, 2, F. Rosier and A. de Leuven), New, ?Oct 1856

Lully och Quinault (operetta, 2, L. Granberg, after Gaugiran-Nanteuil), Royal, 15 Nov 1859

En utflykt i det gröna (operetta), Little or New, ?Sept 1862

Riccardo (comic op, 3, F. Arlberg, after E. Scribe), Royal Grand, ?Feb 1869

Berenstadt, Gaetano (*b* ?Florence, *c*1690; *d* Florence, Jan or Feb 1735). German alto castrato. Born in Italy of German parents (his father was timpanist to the Grand Duke of Tuscany), he was probably a pupil of Pistocchi. He may have been the 'Gaet. Beynstetter' who sang in *La regina di Macedonia* by Francesco Gasparini and Giuseppe Vignola at Naples in 1708. In 1711 he sang at Bologna and in 1712 at Florence while in the employment of the Grand Duchess of Tuscany. In 1712–16 he was in the service of the Elector Palatine at Düsseldorf. After singing in London (1716–17) in revivals of Handel's *Rinaldo*, Haym's adaptation of Alessandro Scarlatti's *Pirro e Demetrio*, Ariosti's *Tito Manlio* and the pasticcio *Venceslao*, he was engaged for the autumn 1717 season at Dresden, and was described for some years as virtuoso of the King of Poland and Elector of Saxony. He sang in Bologna and Brescia (1719), Rome

(1719–20, in four operas by Gasparini), Milan (1720–21), Padua (1721) and Venice (1721). He returned to London in 1722 and remained with the Royal Academy for two seasons, during which he appeared in Handel's *Floridante*, and created roles in Handel's *Ottone*, *Flavio* and *Giulio Cesare*, Giovanni Bononcini's *Erminia*, *Farnace* and *Calpurnia*, and Ariosti's *Coriolano*, *Vespasiano* and *Aquilio Consolo*. He was a friend and strong partisan of Bononcini. Early in 1726 he sang again in Rome, and in the 1726–7 season in Naples in operas by Vinci, Hasse (two) and Domenico Sarro. While a member of the Neapolitan royal chapel (1727–34), he made frequent operatic appearances in Florence (1727–8, 1729–30, 1733–4), Livorno (1730–31) and Rome (1728–9, 1732). Later he traded in books, manuscripts and paintings in Florence; he was a passionate collector and also a publisher.

The parts Handel wrote for Berenstadt – Argante in *Rinaldo* (given new music in 1717), Adalberto in *Ottone*, the name part in *Flavio* and Ptolemy in *Giulio Cesare* – show that his voice had considerable flexibility and brilliance but not a wide compass (*g* to *e♭''*). Burney described him as an 'evirato of a huge unwieldy figure'. This made him unsuitable for young lovers; he generally played tyrants and disagreeable old men. He seems to have possessed the rare gift (for a castrato) of a sense of humour.

*

L. Lindgren: 'La carriera di Gaetano Berenstadt, contralto evirato (*ca.*1690–1735)', *RIM*, xix (1984), 45–112

W. Dean and J. M. Knapp: *Handel's Operas 1704–1726* (Oxford, 1987)

WINTON DEAN

Berezovsky, Maxim Sozontovich (*b* Glukhov, Ukraine, 16/27 Oct 1745; *d* St Petersburg, 24 March/4 April 1777). Russian (Ukrainian) composer. Though best known for his sacred music he was the earliest Russian composer of (Italian) opera. As a teenage soprano in the imperial court chapel choir under Galuppi he appeared at the Oranienbaum Palace in *Il finto Nino* and *Alessandro nell'Indie* by the recently departed Francesco Araia, who had introduced *opera seria* to the Russian court. Later, with the young Bortnyansky, he took part in a performance of Hermann Raupach's *Alceste* (to a Russian libretto by Sumarokov) at the court theatre in St Petersburg. A promising pupil of Galuppi, Berezovsky was sent abroad at crown expense in 1766, studied under Padre Martini (or under his assistant Stanislao Mattei) in Bologna, and was awarded the diploma of the Accademia Filarmonica in 1771. The climax of his Italian sojourn was the successful performance of his opera *Demofoonte* (to a libretto by Metastasio first set by Caldara some 40 years earlier) in Livorno during Carnival 1773. The castrato role of Timanthes was sung by Francesco Porri, who later made a brilliant career in St Petersburg. *Demofoonte* was repeated in Florence in November, but by that time the composer's stipend had run out and he had returned home (his arrival on 30 October 1773 is documented).

Berezovsky was then put in charge of the choir in which he had been trained. This was a position of some eminence; thus his celebrated suicide – unsupported by contemporary documents, but mentioned by all writers from the early 19th century onwards – cannot be imputed simply to 'insults and frustrations' (Rubets) experienced at the hands of the nobility or to resentment of the favoured treatment accorded foreign musicians at court. Recent scholarship has concentrated on personal factors (documents hint at debts and at the possible loss of his wife). Whatever their exact nature, the unhappy circumstances of Berezovsky's death at the age of 31 have inspired much literary embroidery, beginning in 1841 with a three-act play by the actor P. A. Smirnov with incidental music by I. N. Ushakov ('Departure for Bologna', 'Banishment', 'Victim') and the poet Nestor Kukol'nik's quasi-biographical novella (1844). More recently Andrey Tarkovsky's film *Nostalgia* (1983) portrayed a Russian musicologist in Italy researching the career of his *Doppelgänger*, an ill-fated composer fictionally rechristened Sosnovsky.

Demofoonte has not survived in its entirety (which prevented Dyagilev, always interested in Russo-Italian connections, from reviving it). All that remains is a copyist's score (in *I-Fc*) containing two arias apiece for Demophoön (tenor) and Timanthes (castrato soprano). They have been transcribed and published by V. Belyakov and M. Yurchenko (Kiev, 1988). Timanthes' arias, 'Misero pargoletto' (previously set by Mozart, K77/73*e*) and 'Prudente mi chiedi?', have elaborate da capo structures very much on the Jommellian model, with contrasting tempos and declamatory asides. Those for Demophoön, ruler of Thrace, are full of suitably regal bravura; 'Per lei fra l'arme dorme il guerriero' culminates in a dramatic downward leap of an 11th from *c''*.

*

N. Kukol'nik: 'Maxim Sozontovich Berezovsky', *Skazka za skazkoy*, iv (St Petersburg, 1844), 281–396; repr. in *Sochineniya*, ii (St Petersburg, 1852)

A. I. Rubets: *Biograficheskiy leksikon russkikh kompozitorov i muzïkal'nïkh deyateley* (St Petersburg, ?2/1886)

R.-A. Mooser: *Annales de la musique et des musiciens en Russie au XVIIIme siècle* (Geneva, 1948–51)

Yu. V. Keldïsh: 'Neizvestnaya opera russkogo kompozitora', *SovM* (1966), no.12, pp.39–50; repr. in *Ocherki i issledovaniya po istorii russkoy muzïki* (Moscow, 1978), 113–29, 486–94

S. L. Ginzburg: IRMO, i, 21–32

M. Rïtsareva: *Kompozitor M. S. Berezovsky* (Leningrad, 1983)

L. Fyodorovskaya: 'Neizvestnaya p'yesa o kompozitore Berezovskom', *Muzïkal'naya zhizn'* (1984), no.22, p.24

E. Levashov and A. Polekhin: 'M.S. Berezovsky', in Yu. V. Keldïsh and others: *Istoriya russkoy muzïki v desyati tomakh* [The History of Russian Music in Ten Volumes], iii (Moscow, 1985), 132–60

RICHARD TARUSKIN

Berg, Alban (Maria Johannes) (*b* Vienna, 9 Feb 1885; *d* Vienna, 24 Dec 1935). Austrian composer. Although he wrote a substantial amount of music in his late teens (most of it songs firmly fixed in the German lied tradition), he was almost entirely self-taught as a composer before he began studying with Schoenberg in October 1904. He had, however, already immersed himself thoroughly in the intellectual life of turn-of-the century Vienna, and the artistic friendships he had made at that impressionable age – with Zweig, Kraus, Altenberg, Loos, Klimt and Kokoschka – were to remain influential throughout his life. The works Berg composed during his formal studies with Schoenberg – from the Seven Early Songs (1905–8), to the String Quartet op.3 of 1910 – trace how the harmonic apparatus of late Romanticism was gradually replaced first with the kind of freely associative treatment of tonal relationships that Schoenberg himself was exploring in his works of the period, and finally with unfettered atonality.

In the works written immediately after leaving Schoenberg, Berg explored the possibilities of the miniaturized forms that his teacher and Webern had been employing at the same time. Yet perhaps already aware that his mode of expression was not naturally aphoristic, in 1912 he gave the first hint that he was contemplating an opera, considering a treatment of Strindberg's *Kammerspiele*. But after attending the Viennese première in May 1914 of Büchner's *Woyzeck* (then entitled *Wozzeck* because of a misreading of the manuscript) he fixed on that: 'Someone must set it to music', he is reported as saying after the performance. A draft of the libretto and the first musical sketches were made in 1914, while the Three Orchestral Pieces op.6 were being completed; material from the orchestral work, particularly from its final *Marsch*, was later to be incorporated into the opera. In May 1911 Berg had married Helene Nahowski; in the first months of their married life he earned a living making vocal scores of Schoenberg's *Gurrelieder* and Schreker's *Der ferne Klang* (the influence of the latter has been detected in the orchestration of *Wozzeck*).

Family pressures, the outbreak of World War I and Berg's subsequent conscription halted further work on *Wozzeck* (though his chronic asthma eventually ruled him out of active service), and he did not return to the score until 1917, by which time his military experiences had deepened his sense of identification with the central character of the tragedy. Progress was slow: in 1918 he had begun to manage the affairs of Schoenberg's newly formed Verein für Musikalische Privataufführungen, and he continued to write articles and polemics. The composition of *Wozzeck* was to occupy him until 1923, when he was able to arrange for the vocal score to be published privately; on Schoenberg's recommendation Universal Edition took over the work the following year. In an effort to secure a staging Berg prepared the *Drei Bruchstücke aus 'Wozzeck'*, which was introduced by Hermann Scherchen in Frankfurt in 1924; by then, however, Erich Kleiber had scheduled the première for the next season at the Berlin Staatsoper. The first performance, conducted by Kleiber on 14 December 1925, aroused much controversy, but a series of stagings across Europe in the following five years established its stature until the rise of the Nazis effectively proscribed it from German opera houses. *Wozzeck* marked the culmination of the first period of Berg's development and the beginning of its second phase. In its fusion of strict dramatic and musical schemes with a harmonic and melodic language of great richness and variety it recapitulated all the expressive possibilities of his previous works, while in its autobiographical references, arcane structural symmetries and number patterns it revealed for the first time a necessity to encode extra-musical meanings within the structures that would become a persistent and all-pervasive feature of his music.

In the works written immediately after the completion of *Wozzeck*, Berg moved rapidly towards systematizing his musical language by adopting Schoenberg's 12-note method of composition; his first strict 12-note music appeared in a short vocal setting and in three movements of the Lyric Suite for string quartet (1927). The undisclosed impulse behind the composition of the suite was Berg's covert love affair with Hanna Fuchs-Robettin, which was to continue until his death, and which also appears to have directed his search for the literary source for a second opera towards a subject through which he could explore both the life-enhancing and the destructive properties of erotic love. He considered first Gerhart Hauptmann's 'glassworks fairy tale' *Und Pippa tanzt*, and even made a few preliminary musical sketches, but was unable to reach a reasonable financial agreement with the author. Later the same year (1928) he turned instead to Wedekind's pair of Lulu plays, *Der Erdgeist* and *Die Büchse der Pandora*, which he had known since 1904; he began to combine them in a single libretto, even though his wife and Schoenberg both advised against taking on such an 'immoral' operatic subject.

The composition of *Lulu* occupied Berg for the rest of his life. It was interrupted twice to fulfil commissions: the concert aria for soprano *Der Wein* (1929), a setting of Baudelaire, became both a preliminary exploration of the *Lulu* sound-world and a study for the Lied der Lulu in Act 2 that provides its emotional centre of gravity, while the Violin Concerto, written in the last year of his life, was both an explicit requiem for Manon Gropius, daughter of Alma Mahler, and an implicit autobiographical memorial to himself. When Berg died from septicaemia in 1935, Acts 1 and 2 of *Lulu* were complete and fully scored; more than 200 bars of Act 3 were also complete, and all but a short passage of the remainder existed in short score. A further two sections had been orchestrated for the *Lulu* suite that Berg had prepared for performance by Kleiber in 1934. Acts 1 and 2 were staged for the first time in Zürich on 2 June 1937, but Helene Berg refused to allow anyone to attempt a completion of the rest. After her death in 1976 Friedrich Cerha completed the task he had begun covertly 14 years earlier, and the first performance of the three-act opera was given at the Paris Opéra on 24 February 1979, conducted by Pierre Boulez.

See also Lulu (ii) and Wozzeck.

*

GENERAL

A. Berg: 'Die Stimme in der Oper', *Gesang: Jb 1929 der UE*; repr. in Eng. trans. of Reich (1965)

W. Reich, ed.: *23*, nos.24–5 (1936) [special issue]

——: *Alban Berg: mit Bergs eigenen Schriften und Beiträgen von Theodor Wiesengrund-Adorno und Ernst Křenek* (Vienna, 1937)

H. Redlich: *Alban Berg: Versuch einer Würdigung* (Vienna, 1957; Eng. trans., abridged, as *Alban Berg: the Man and his Music*, 1957)

J. Russell: *Erich Kleiber* (London, 1957)

W. Reich: *Alban Berg: Bildnis im Wort* (Zürich, 1959)

——: *Alban Berg* (Zürich, 1963; Eng. trans., 1965)

H. Berg, ed.: *Alban Berg: Briefe an seiner Frau* (Munich, 1965; Eng. trans., 1971)

T. W. Adorno: *Alban Berg, der Meister des kleinsten Übergangs* (Vienna, 1968, 2/1978; Eng. trans., 1991)

International Alban Berg Society Newsletter (1968–)

M. Carner: *Alban Berg* (London, 1975)

V. Scherliess: *Alban Berg* (Reinbek bei Hamburg, 1975)

E. Barilier: *Alban Berg: essai d'interprétation* (Lausanne, 1978)

R. Hilmar: *Alban Berg: Leben und Wirken in Wien bis zu seinen ersten Erfolgen als Komponist* (Vienna, 1978)

D. Jarman: *The Music of Alban Berg* (London and Berkeley, 1979)

Alban Berg Symposion: Vienna 1980

D. Jarman, ed.: *The Berg Companion* (London, 1989) [incl. D. Puffett: 'Berg and German Opera', 197–219; C. Hailey: 'Between Instinct and Reflection: the Viennese Dichotomy', 221–34]

D. Goble and R. Morgan, eds.: *Alban Berg: Analytical and Historical Perspectives* (Oxford, 1991)

OPERAS

Wozzeck

H. Bieber: '*Wozzeck* und *Woyzeck*', *Literarisches Echo*, xvi (1914), 1188ff

F. H. Klein: 'Alban Bergs "Wozzeck" ', *Musikblätter des Anbruch*, v (1923), 216–19

E. Viebig: 'Alban Bergs "Wozzeck": ein Beitrag zum Opernproblem', *Die Musik*, xv (1923), 506–10

[A. Berg:] 'Alban Bergs "Wozzeck" und die Musikkritik', *Musikblätter des Anbruch*, viii (1926)

A. Berg: 'A Word about "Wozzeck" ', *MM*, v (1927–8), 22–4; repr. in Reich (1965)

——: Lecture on *Wozzeck*, 1929; Eng. trans. in Redlich (1957), 261–85
——: *Praktische Anweisung zur Einstudierung des 'Wozzeck'* (Vienna, 1930); repr. in Reich (1937); Eng. trans., in *MT*, cix (1968), 518–21
K. Blaukopf: 'New Light on "Wozzeck"', *Saturday Review* (26 Sept 1953), 62–3
——: 'Autobiographische Elemente in Alban Bergs "Wozzeck"', *ÖMz*, ix (1954), 155–8
F. Mahler: *Zu Alban Bergs 'Wozzeck': szenische und musikalische Übersicht* (Vienna, 1957; Eng. trans., as *Concerning Alban Berg's Opera Wozzeck*, 1965)
W. Martens: 'Der Barbier in Buchners "Woyzeck"', *Zeitschrift für deutsche Philologie*, xxix/1 (1960), 361–83
G. Perle: 'The Musical Language of *Wozzeck*', *Music Forum*, i (1967), 204–59
——: 'Three Views of *Wozzeck*', *Saturday Review* (2 Dec 1967), 54–5
——: '*Woyzeck* and *Wozzeck*', *MQ*, liii (1967), 206–19
——: '*Wozzeck*: ein zweiter Blick auf das Libretto', *NZM*, Jg./129 (1968), 218–21
G. Ploebsch: *Alban Bergs 'Wozzeck'* (Strasbourg, 1968)
G. Perle: 'Representation and Symbol in the Music of *Wozzeck*', *MR*, xxxiii (1971), 281–308
W. König: *Tonalitätsstruktur in Alban Bergs Oper 'Wozzeck'* (Tutzing, 1974)
E. Hilmar: *Wozzeck von Alban Berg: Entstehung–erste Erfolge–Repressionen (1914–1935)* (Vienna, 1975)
L. Treitler: '"Wozzeck" et l'Apocalypse', *SMz*, cvi (1976), 249; Eng. version in *Critical Inquiry*, iii (1976–7), 251–70, and *Opera II: Mozart and After*, ed. E. Rosand (New York, 1985), 307–26
S. Jareš: 'Inscenace Bergova Vojcka v Národním divadle roku 1926' [The staging of *Wozzeck* in the Prague National Theatre in 1926], *HV*, xiv (1977), 271–3
V. Lébl: 'Případ Vojcek' [The Fall of Wozzeck], *HV*, xiv (1977), 195–229 [with Ger. summary]
G. Schmidgall: 'Wozzeck', *Literature as Opera* (New York, 1977)
K. Vogelsand: *Dokumentation zur Oper 'Wozzeck' von Alban Berg: die Jahre des Durchbruchs 1925–1932* (Laaber, 1977)
O. Kolleritsch, ed.: *50 Jahre Wozzeck von Alban Berg: Vorgeschichte und Auswirkungen in der Opernästhetik* (Graz, 1978)
G. Perle: *The Operas of Alban Berg*, i: *Wozzeck* (Berkeley, 1980)
S. Mauser: *Das expressionistische Musiktheater der Wiener Schule: stilistische und entwicklungsgeschichtliche Untersuchen zu Arnold Schönbergs 'Erwartung', op.17, 'Die glückliche Hand', op.18, und Alban Bergs 'Wozzeck', op.7* (Regensburg, 1982)
C. Richter: 'Die Wirtshausszene aus Alban Bergs *Wozzeck*', *Musik und Bildung*, xiv (1982), 553–63
J. Schmalfeldt: *Berg's Wozzeck: Harmonic Language and Dramatic Design* (New Haven, 1983)
G. Rosenfeld, S. Matthus and P. Eckstein: 'Der epochale *Wozzeck*: zum 100. Geburtstag von Alban Berg', *Oper Heute*, vii (1984), 110–45
J. Ardoin: 'Apropos *Wozzeck*', *OQ*, iii/3 (1985), 68–74
A. Forte: 'Tonality, Symbol, and Structural Levels in Berg's *Wozzeck*', *MQ*, lxxi (1985), 474–99
P. Peterson: *Alban Berg, Wozzeck: eine semantische Analyse unter Einbeziehung der Skizzen und Dokumente aus dem Nachlass Bergs* (Munich, 1985)
S. Bruhn: *Die musikalische Darstellung psychologischer Wirklichkeit in Alban Bergs Wozzeck* (Frankfurt, 1986)
C. F. Mann: *A Comparison of Musical Settings of Georg Buchner's 'Woyzeck' by Alban Berg and Manfred Gurlitt* (diss., U. of Cincinnati, 1986)
D. P. Schroeder: 'Berg's *Wozzeck* and Strindberg's Musical Models', *Opera Journal*, xxi (1988), 2–12

Lulu

W. Reich: 'Alban Berg's *Lulu*', *MQ*, xxii (1936), 383–401
D. Mitchell: 'The Character of Lulu: Wedekind's and Berg's Conceptions Compared', *MR*, xv (1954), 268–74
G. Perle: 'The Music of *Lulu*: a New Analysis', *JAMS*, xii (1959), 185–200; see also xiv (1961), 96
R. Offergeld: 'Some Questions about *Lulu*', *HiFi/Stereo Review*, xiii/4 (1964), 58–60
G. Perle: 'The Character of Lulu: a Sequel', *MR*, xxv (1964), 311–19
——: '*Lulu*: the Formal Design', *JAMS*, xvii (1964), 179–92
——: 'A Note on Act III of *Lulu*', *PNM*, ii/2 (1964), 8–13
——: '*Lulu*: Thematic Material and Pitch Organization', *MR*, xxvi (1965), 269–302
W. Reich: 'Drei Notizblätter zu Alban Bergs Oper "Lulu"', *SMz*, cvi (1966), 336–9; cvii (1967), 165
G. Perle: 'Erwiderung auf Willi Reichs Aufsatz "Drei Notizblätter zu Alban Bergs *Lulu*"', *SMz*, cvii (1967), 163–5
——: 'Die Personen in Bergs *Lulu*', *AMw*, xxiv (1967), 283–90
——: 'Die Reihe als Symbol in Bergs *Lulu*', *ÖMz*, xxii (1967), 589–93
D. Jarman: 'Dr Schön's Five-Strophe Aria: some Notes on Tonality and Pitch Association in Berg's *Lulu*', *PNM*, viii/2 (1970), 23–48
——: 'Some Rhythmic and Metric Techniques in Alban Berg's *Lulu*', *MQ*, lvi (1970), 349–66
M. Reiter: *Die Zwölftontechnik in Alban Bergs Oper Lulu* (Regensburg, 1973)
V. Scherliess: 'Briefe Alban Bergs aus der Entstehungszeit der *Lulu*', *Melos/NZM*, ii (1976), 108–14
G. Perle: 'Inhaltliche und formale Strukturen in Alban Bergs Oper "Lulu"', *ÖMz*, xxxii (1977), 427–41
V. Scherliess: 'Alban Bergs analytische Tafeln zur Lulu-Reihe', *Mf*, xxx (1977), 452–64
W. Szmolyan: 'Zum III. Akt von Alban Bergs 'Lulu"', *ÖMz*, xxxii (1977), 396–401
D. Jarman: '*Lulu*: the Sketches', *International Alban Berg Society Newsletter*, no.6 (1978), 4–8
F. Herschkowitz: 'Some Thoughts on *Lulu*', ibid, no.7 (1978), 11
F. Cerha: *Arbeitsbericht zur Herstellung des 3. Akts der Oper Lulu von Alban Berg* (Vienna, 1979)
R. Holloway: 'The Complete *Lulu*', *Tempo*, no.129 (1979), 36–9
G. Perle: 'The Cerha Edition', *International Alban Berg Society Newsletter*, no.8 (1979), 5–7
——: 'The Complete "Lulu"', *MT*, cxx (1979), 115–20
D. Jarman: 'Countess Geschwitz's Series: a Controversy Resolved?', *PRMA*, cvii (1980–81), 111–18
——: 'Some Observations on Rhythm, Metre and Tempo in *Lulu*', *Alban Berg Symposion: Vienna 1980*, 20–30
F. Cerha: 'Zum III. Akt der Oper "Lulu"', *ÖMz*, xxxvi (1981), 541–50
D. Jarman: '*Lulu*: the Musical and Dramatic Structure', *Lulu* (London, Royal Opera House, Covent Garden, 1981) [programme notes]
R. Hilmar: 'Die Bedeutung der Textvorlagen für die Komposition der Oper *Lulu* von Alban Berg', *Festschrift Othmar Wessely* (Tutzing, 1982), 265–93
W. Gruhn: 'Alban Berg: *Lulu* – Mythos und Allegorie bei Wedekind und Berg: Gedanken zum dritten Akt der Oper', *Musiktheater heute: Darmstadt 1982*, 34–62
G. Perle: 'The Film Interlude of *Lulu*', *International Alban Berg Society Newsletter*, no.11 (1982), 3–8
M. Carner: 'Alban Berg's *Lulu* – a Reconsideration', *MT*, cxxiv (1983), 477–9
P. Hall: 'The Progress of a Method: Berg's Tone Rows for *Lulu*', *MQ*, lxxi (1985), 500–19
D. J. Headlam: *The Musical Language of the Symphonic Pieces from 'Lulu'* (diss., U. of Michigan, 1985)
G. Perle: 'An Introduction to *Lulu*', *OQ*, iii/3 (1985), 87–111
——: *The Operas of Alban Berg*, ii: *Lulu* (Berkeley, 1985)
D. Headlam: 'The Derivation of Rows in *Lulu*', *PNM*, xxiv/1 (1985–6), 198–223
T. F. Ertelt: '"Hereinspaziert ...": ein früher Entwurf des Prologs zu Alban Bergs *Lulu*', *ÖMz*, xli (1986), 15–25
D. Jarman: 'Alban Berg: the Origins of a Method', *Music Analysis*, vi (1987), 273–88
G. Perle: 'Die neue Ausgabe von "Lulu"', *ÖMz*, xlii (1987), 18–27
F. Cerha: 'Some Further Notes on my Realization of Act III of *Lulu*', *The Berg Companion*, ed. D. Jarman (London, 1989), 261–7
P. Hall: 'The Sketches for *Lulu*', ibid, 235–59
G. Perle: 'The First Four Notes of *Lulu*', ibid, 269–89
——: 'Some Thoughts on an Ideal Production of *Lulu*', *JM*, vii (1989), 244–53
A. Pople: Review of G. Perle: *The Operas of Alban Berg*, ii: *Lulu*, *JRMA*, cxiv (1989), 251–73 ANDREW CLEMENTS

Berg, Josef (*b* Brno, 8 March 1927; *d* Brno, 26 Feb 1971). Czech composer. From 1946 to 1950 he studied in Brno: composition at the conservatory with Vilém Petrželka and musicology with Jan Racek at the university. He worked as a music editor for Czech Radio in Brno, 1950–51, and then as a freelance composer and critic. Berg's formative influences at the start of the

1950s were Janáček and the folk music movement, but by the end of the decade he had begun to develop an interest in new compositional techniques such as collage and serialism; his approach became more individual and introspective and the influence of Brecht is particularly apparent.

Berg's versatility as an artist led him to take a keen interest in all aspects of writing for the theatre: incidental music, happenings, fully staged productions and acoustic theatre. This interest reached its peak in the 1960s with a series of unconventional avant-garde operas to his own librettos, in which he deliberately used very restricted resources and also included detailed instructions for staging and design. Berg intended his work to be a striking parody of conventional 'consumer' operas, although his musical pranks were never merely empty jokes, but vehicles by which to express something deeper. *Odyseeův návrat* ('The Return of Odysseus', 1963) for narrator, two singers, a dancer and five instruments, is the first of three chamber operas sharing the theme of protest against the inhumanity that results from narrow-mindedness; Odysseus, stripped of all heroic pathos, is here the symbol of the absurdity of war. *Evropská turistika* ('European Tourism', 1967) for six singers and seven instrumentalists, ostensibly the portrayal of a passion for sight-seeing, is a bitter and absurd parody of the Nazi campaign of conquest. *Eufrides před branami Tymén* ('Euphrides at the Gates of Tymen', 1967) parodies the heroes of antiquity and the conventions of grand opera: a garrulous general conquers a city without so much as a fight, to the accompaniment of an 'orchestra' consisting of a solo trumpet, alternating with appearances of a compère whose remarks are an ironic echo of the effusive outpourings of socialist cultural commentators.

His next work, *Snídaně na hradě Šlankenvaldě* ('Breakfast at Slankenvald Castle', 1969) for four narrators, baritone and six instruments, a semi-staged scene from an old marionette comedy, is a parody in miniature of Romantic opera, in which a farmer sings a German aria in praise of the Czech countryside. Berg's anti-illusional conception of theatre and his admiration for the supposedly declining art-form of the marionette theatre gave rise to the full-length opera *Johanes doktor Faust*, composed in 1966, in which there again occurs a naive debunking of the hero, now suddenly seen from a quite different angle. The composer also worked on, though did not complete, another quite distinct treatment of the Faust theme, *Provizorní předvedení opery Johanes doktor Faust* ('A Provisional Production of the Opera Johannes Doctor Faust'), a mini-opera for actor, two singers and three instruments. All the characteristics of irony, grotesquerie and the absurd, evident in the chamber operas, were further pursued in the 'happenings' which Berg wrote between 1965 and 1970.

librettos by the composer

Odysseův návrat [The Return of Odysseus], 1962 (chamber op, 10 pts, after Homer), concert perf., Brno, 8 March 1964; televised, CSTV, 28 Nov 1966; staged, Brno, Janáček Academy Opera Studio, 27 Nov 1967

Evropská turistika [European Tourism], 1963–4 (chamber op, 1), concert perf., Prague, Rudolfinum, 5 March 1967; staged, Brno, Janáček Academy, 27 Nov 1967

Eufrides před branami Tymén [Euphrides at the Gates of Tymen], 1964 (chamber op, 3), Brno, Janáček Academy, 27 Nov 1967

Snídaně na hradě Šlankenvaldě [Breakfast at Slankenvald Castle], 1966 (after an old marionette comedy by M. Kopecký), Prague, Rudolfinum, 6 March 1969

Johanes doktor Faust, 1966 (op, 1, after marionette play by Kopecký), Brno, Janáček, 19 June 1981 [orch completed by M. Štědroň and M. Ištvan]

Provizorní předvedení opery Johanes doktor Faust [A Provisional Production of the Opera Johannes Doctor Faust], 1970 (mini-op, 3), 2 acts completed, Brno, Reduta, 29 Sept 1971 [Act 1 only]

*

F. Hrabal: 'Odysseus v nás' [Odysseus to Us], *Divadlo* (1965), no.2, pp.41–50

——: *Eufrides před branami Tymén* (Supraphon: Prague, 1973) [record notes]

M. Štědroň: 'Johanes doktor Faust', *Opus musicum*, xii (1980), 204–9

L. Šip: *Česka opera a jeji tvurči* [Czech Opera and its Creators] (Prague, 1983), 336–41

'Sborník k nedožitým 60. narozeninam J. Berga' [Memorial Volume in Honour of the 60th Anniversary of the Birth of Josef Berg], *Opus musicum*, xix (1987), no.2 [whole issue]

HELENA HAVLIKOVÁ (with OLDŘICH PUKL)

Berg [Rexroth-Berg], **(Carl) Natanael** (*b* Stockholm, 9 Feb 1879; *d* Stockholm, 14 Oct 1957). Swedish composer. He was mainly self-taught in music. A patron offered him a large sum provided he also find himself non-musical work; Berg therefore studied to become a veterinary surgeon, and worked as such in the army (1902–39). He associated with Atterberg and Rangström in reaction against earlier Swedish music, but his style was sometimes bombastic, and heavier than the nationalist Romanticism of his colleagues. His orchestration was richly coloured and dramatic, sometimes melodramatic, giving his later operas the flavour of historical tableaux; although using one of his sympathetic Romantic subjects, *Birgitta* was cast in oratorio style. Around 1925 his technique grew more refined. His operas are central to his output; those to his original texts concern Engelbrekt, the 15th-century Swedish champion of liberty, and St Birgitta.

all to texts by the composer and first performed in Stockholm at the Kungliga Teatern

Leila, 1907–10 (4, after Byron: *The Giaour*), 29 Feb 1912

Engelbrekt, 1924–8 (4), 21 Sept 1929

Judith, 1931–5 (5, after F. Hebbel), 22 Feb 1936

Birgitta, 1940 (5), 10 Jan 1942

Genoveva, 1945 (4, after Hebbel), 25 Oct 1947

Fragments: Josua, 1914; Tre Konungar [Three Kings], 1950–57

*

A. Rundberg: *Svensk operakonst* (Stockholm, 1952)

ROLF HAGLUND

Bergamo. City in Lombardy, north Italy. The first public performance for which there is firm documentary evidence was that of *Ercole effeminato* (libretto by Almerico Passarelli, music by Maurizio Cazzati), performed in the Palazzo della Ragione on 8 January 1654. Until the end of the 18th century, operas were staged in wooden theatres or temporary structures, often erected in the Prato di S Alessandro in the lower city during the fair season. One wooden theatre, the Cerri, was active for a decade from 1797 in the Palazzo Vecchio. The city's first permanent opera house, the Teatro Riccardi, was completed by 1791, destroyed by fire in 1797 and rebuilt in 1801. The other large theatre in Bergamo, the Sociale (now in disuse), so called because it was founded by the Società dei Nobili Signori in the upper city, was inaugurated in 1807. Until 1824 it was directed by Simon Mayr, who had come to Bergamo in 1802 as *maestro di cappella*; Donizetti, a native of Bergamo, studied with Mayr from 1806 to 1815. Mayr's operas dominated the repertories of both the Sociale and the Riccardi during the first three decades of the 19th century. Throughout the century the two theatres maintained a stimulating rivalry, regularly staging works by Rossini, Bellini, Donizetti and Verdi. In 1897 the Riccardi was renovated and renamed the Teatro Donizetti to mark the centenary of the composer's birth.

The demand for opera in Bergamo during the late 19th century encouraged the construction of new opera houses which organized seasons of their own. The Rossi or Varietà, open from 1881 to 1894, was inaugurated with a strange performance of *Aida* using puppets. Other theatres opened during this period were the Politeama Givoli (1882), the Nuovo (1901), the Rubini (1907), inaugurated with *Poliuto* conducted by the elder Gino Marinuzzi, and the Duse (1926). Some of these theatres have since been demolished; others are now used for plays or as cinemas.

After World War I, performances at the Donizetti were among the most innovatory and stimulating in northern Italy. This tendency was institutionalized in the festival 'Teatro delle Novità' (under the management of Bindo Missiroli from 1931), whose purpose was announced as 'taking soundings among emerging musical personalities', offering three new operas by Italian composers each year together with a revival of one by Donizetti. In 1941 the festival was transferred to Parma for a year because of the war, but thereafter continued in Bergamo with some interruptions until 1973. Among the composers introduced were G. F. Ghedini (*Maria d'Alessandria*, 1937), Jacopo Napoli (*Un curioso accidente*, 1950), Vieri Tosatti (*Il sistema della dolcezza*, 1951), G. F. Malipiero (*Donna Urraca*, 1954), Luciano Chailly (*Ferrovia sopraelevata*, 1955), Giacomo Manzoni (*La sentenza*, 1960) and Roman Vlad (*Il sogno*, 1973). Since 1980 the city has sponsored an annual Donizetti festival in October.

Bergamo o sia Notizie patrie raccolte da Carlo Facchinetti (Bergamo, 1841–3) [annual almanac]

A. Bellotti: *Donizetti e i suoi contemporanei* (Bergamo, 1866)

F. Alborghetti and M. Galli: *Donizetti e Mayr* (Bergamo, 1875)

Biografie di scrittori e artisti bergamaschi nativi od oriundi, di Giovanni Simone Mayr raccolte e pubblicate con note (Bergamo, 1875)

Cenni biografici di Donizetti e Mayr raccolti dalla memoria di un vecchio ottuagenario (Bergamo, 1875)

E. Dolci: *Elenco degli spettacoli musicali nei teatri di Bergamo dal 1847 al 1893* (MS, *I-BGi*)

G. Gavazzeni: *Donizetti* (Milan, 1937)

Teatro delle Novità: Festival autunnale dell'opera lirica (Bergamo, Teatro Donizetti, 1950–61) [programme notes, criticism and documentation]

T. Torri: 'Lo scomparso teatro di S Cassiano in Bergamo Alta', *Atti dell'Ateneo di scienze, lettere ed arti di Bergamo*, xxix (1956), 113–28

L. Pelandi: 'Teatri scomparsi: il teatro di Cittadella e il teatro Cerri nel Palazzo della Ragione', *Gazzetta di Bergamo*, iii/7 (1959), 12–18

L. Pilon: 'Il teatro della Società di Bergamo alta', *Bergamo arte*, iv/14 (1973), 5–20

MARIA CARACI VELA

Berganza (Vargas), Teresa (*b* Madrid, 16 March 1935). Spanish mezzo-soprano. She studied in Madrid with Lola Rodriguez Aragon, a pupil of Elisabeth Schumann. She made her début in 1957 as Dorabella at Aix-en-Provence, returning as Rosina, Purcell's Dido, Cherubino, Octavia (*L'incoronazione di Poppea*) and Ruggiero (Alcina). In 1958 she sang Isolier (*Le comte Ory*) at the Piccola Scala and Cherubino at Glyndebourne, and made her American début at Dallas as Isabella (*L'italiana in Algeri*). She first appeared at Covent Garden in 1960 as Rosina, then sang Cherubino and, during La Scala's 1976 visit, the title role of *La Cenerentola*. She sang at Chicago, the Metropolitan (1967–8), Vienna, Paris and Salzburg; her roles included Cesti's Orontea, Mozart's Sextus and Cherubini's Neris (*Médée*). Her rich, creamy voice with its great agility, perfect for the Rossini mezzo-soprano roles, developed a heavier tone and a more dramatic style appropriate to Carmen, which she sang at Edinburgh (1977–8) and repeated at Hamburg (1980), San Francisco (1981) and Paris (1989); and to Charlotte, which she sang at Zürich (1979). She appeared as Zerlina in Joseph Losey's film of *Don Giovanni* (1979). In the 1980s she sang mainly in concerts. A volume of memoirs, *Flor de soledad y silencio: meditaciones de una cantante*, was published in Madrid in 1984.

K. Loveland: 'Teresa Berganza', *Audio & Record Review*, iii/5 (1963–4), 16–23 [with discography by F. F. Clough and G. J. Cuming]

J. B. Steane: *The Grand Tradition* (London, 1974)

HAROLD ROSENTHAL/R

Berger, Erna (*b* Cossebaude, nr Dresden, 19 Oct 1900; *d* Essen, 14 June 1990). German soprano. After studying in Dresden, she was engaged by the Dresden Staatsoper, making her début as First Boy (*Die Zauberflöte*) in 1925. She sang at Bayreuth (1929–33) as the Shepherd in *Tannhäuser*, the First Flowermaiden and the Woodbird. Her first Salzburg appearance (1932) was as Blonde, her last (1953–4) as Zerlina. She made her Covent Garden début in 1934 as Marzelline, returning in 1935 and 1938. She sang again in London in 1949, and in that year made her Metropolitan début as Sophie. She continued to appear in Germany and Austria until the end of the 1954–5 season. Berger's voice retained its youthful freshness throughout her career. At a time when dramatic coloratura sopranos were virtually non-existent her Queen of Night and Konstanze were considered peerless, and her purely sung, innocent Gilda was one of the best of its day.

K. Höcker: *Erna Berger, die singende Botschafterin* (Berlin, 1961)

HAROLD ROSENTHAL/R

Berger, Rudolf (*b* Brünn [now Brno], 17 April 1874; *d* New York, 27 Feb 1915). German baritone, later tenor. He was a pupil of Adolf Robinson, who also taught Leo Slezak and Joseph Schwarz. His début as Telramund in his native city in 1896 was followed by engagements at Olmütz (now Olomouc) and Berlin, where he remained as principal baritone for the next ten years. At Bayreuth, where he sang first in 1901, his roles were Gunther, Amfortas and Klingsor. As his early recordings show, he had a sturdy high baritone voice, useful in Verdi as well as Wagner, and when in 1909 he made the change to tenor he encompassed heroic roles such as Radames, Otello and Samson, though still specializing in Wagnerian heroes. It was for these that he was engaged in 1913 by the Metropolitan, where his début as Siegmund early in 1914 was described as 'manly, interesting and commendable' (W. J. Henderson). He went on to sing Walther, Tristan, Lohengrin, Parsifal and Siegfried, but contracted pleurisy and died at the height of his career.

J. B. STEANE

Bergersen, Baldwin (*b* Vienna, 20 Feb 1914). American composer. He was a pupil at the choir school of St John the Divine in New York City, but as a pianist and composer he was self-taught. From the mid-1930s he worked as a pianist and arranger in the theatre, and was soon composing dance music for Charles Weidman and Bill Robinson. His nine shows, produced in New York and London, include *Small Wonder* (1948) and *Rosa* (1980; ASCAP award for the best score of that year). *Carib Song* (1945), a critical success, might now be classified as an opera or a ballet-opera; its choreographer, Katherine Dunham, also sang and danced the leading role.

On 22 January 1948, the Ballet Society presented his one true opera, *Far Harbour*, a 'lyric drama', at Hunter College. The librettist was William Archibald, the conductor Leon Barzin. In this work the three levels of action, motion and dance were synchronized with the three levels of speech, recitative and aria. The music was highly praised, but the libretto dealt openly with sex and the production created a scandal. EDITH BORROFF

Berggeist, Der [*Der Berggeist, oder Schicksal und Treue*] ('The Spirit of the Mountain, or Destiny and Truth'). *Romantische Oper* in two acts by Franz Danzi (*see* DANZI family, (2)) to a libretto by Carl von Lohbauer; Karlsruhe, Hoftheater, 19 April 1813.

Der Berggeist, referred to in some sources as *Rübezahl*, is probably based on the Rübezahl stories in C. A. Musäus's collection, *Volksmärchen der Deutschen* (1782–7). Other adaptations of this subject, from a Silesian folktale, include works by Vincenc Tuček (1801), Vogler (1802), Weber (1805), Wilhelm Würfel (1824), Spohr (1825), Lindpaintner (1830) and C. G. Müller (1840). Danzi's innovatory setting blends a wide variety of arias, ensembles, choruses, melodrama and pantomime. The composer employed folk melodies for local colour and created a supernatural atmosphere with unusual harmonic effects, anticipating such later German operas as Weber's *Der Freischütz* and Marschner's *Hans Heiling*. PAUL CORNEILSON

Berghaus, Ruth (*b* Dresden, 2 July 1927). German director. She studied dance at the Palucca School in Dresden from 1947 to 1950. Her career as a choreographer began in 1964 with the Berliner Ensemble, of which she was later Intendant (1971–7), and she also staged productions of a strongly ideological character at the Deutsche Staatsoper, including a famous *Il barbiere di Siviglia* (in German) that remained in the repertory for 25 years. From 1980 to 1987 she worked under the Gielen-Zehelein regime at the Frankfurt Opera as one of a team of guest directors (which also included Alfred Kirchner, Christof Nel and Hans Neuenfels) who presented a series of challenging, radical stagings that put the house in the front rank of innovation.

In her production of *Die Entführung* (1981) the physical and psychological confinement of the harem was represented by an empty white, box-like set which at critical moments heaved and rolled. The staging was at once richly comic and a powerful theatrical realization of the notion that *Die Entführung* advocates freedom of choice for women as well as for men. Among Berghaus's other productions – which included *Die Zauberflöte* (1980), *The Makropulos Affair* (1982), *Parsifal* (1982) and *Les Troyens* (1983) – that of Wagner's last opera stood out as a bold attempt to address the 'regeneration' ideology that lies behind it. The Grail community was presented as a sinister gang of hoodlums with shaven heads and dark glasses, a depraved society in dire need of redemption. That process was aided by Kundry herself, who ultimately joined the knights in their apparently voluntary self-annihilation – a symbolic enactment of the passing away of the old, corrupt order.

The climax of Berghaus's work at Frankfurt came with her *Ring* (1985–7), a demythologized, deconstructionist production that could similarly be understood as a confrontation with the Wagnerian ethos and legacy. Her repertory of frequently shocking images and bizarre gestures makes a subliminal appeal to the imagination; her stage conventions owe something to the theories of Brecht and something to Beckett and the Theatre of the Absurd. Her *Don Giovanni* for the WNO (1984) was similarly notable for its arresting, if enigmatic, images and vibrant symbolism: crucifix-like swords shuddering in the ground fused the phallic with the religious. In a brilliant *coup de théâtre*, the swaddling-clothes caressed by Elvira unravelled to reveal that her baby was but a phantom; they then became a nun's headdress – a telling combination of erotic longing and religious fervour. Ottavio's isolation and frigidity were neatly represented by a snowfall.

Other notable productions have included *Lulu* at Brussels, *Tristan* at Hamburg and *Fierrabras* in Vienna (all 1988). Berghaus's surreal acting style, and even specific images, can be traced in the work of the next generation of directors.

*

S. Neef: *Das Theater der Ruth Berghaus* (Berlin, 1989)
K. Bertisch: *Ruth Berghaus* (Frankfurt, 1990)

BARRY MILLINGTON

Bergknappen, Die ('The Miners'). *Original-Singspiel* in one act by IGNAZ UMLAUF to a libretto by PAUL WEIDMANN; Vienna, Burgtheater, 17 February 1778.

Old Walcher (bass) opposes the suit of the young miner Fritz (tenor) for the hand of his ward Sophie (soprano), whom he secretly wishes to marry himself. After thwarting one rendezvous he ties Sophie to a tree. The gypsy Zelda (soprano) frees her and takes her place. When discovered, she reveals to Walcher that Sophie is his own daughter, stolen by gypsies. An attempt by Fritz to gain Walcher's consent miscarries but when a mine shaft caves in on Walcher, Fritz rescues him and earns his blessing.

Umlauf composed *Die Bergknappen* as a trial piece for the National Singspiel, the German opera company Joseph II hoped to create alongside the theatrical company (Nationaltheater) he had established in 1776. The opera enjoyed immediate success, ensuring a fair start for the enterprise with Umlauf as its music director. The work is notable for its musical portrayal of Walcher, for the brilliance of Sophie's part (written for Caterina Cavalieri, Mozart's original Konstanze in *Die Entführung*) and for the graphic portrayal of the mine's collapse.

For illustration *see* SINGSPIEL. THOMAS BAUMAN

Berglund, Joel (Ingemar) (*b* Torsåker, 4 June 1903; *d* 21 Jan 1985). Swedish bass-baritone. He studied at the Stockholm Conservatory with John Forsell, made his début at the Stockholm Royal Opera in 1929 as Monterone (*Rigoletto*) and continued to sing there for the next 30 years. In 1942 he sang the Dutchman at Bayreuth and in 1946 he made his Metropolitan début as Hans Sachs. Best known as a Wagner singer – his repertory also included Wotan, Kurwenal and Gurnemanz – he sang many other roles in French, Italian and German operas, among them Méphistophélès, Athanaël (*Thaïs*), Mozart's Figaro, Boccanegra, Philip II, Scarpia and John the Baptist (*Salome*). From 1949 to 1956 he was director of the Stockholm Opera. A fine actor and a versatile singer, he could portray the warm-hearted magnanimity of Hans Sachs or the sardonic diabolism of Méphistophélès with equal facility. ELIZABETH FORBES

Bergman, (Ernst) Ingmar (*b* Uppsala, 14 July 1918). Swedish stage and screen director and writer. Although he is generally regarded as one of the most distinguished and influential film-makers of the postwar period, Bergman's more constant sphere of activity has been the legitimate theatre, where he has concentrated his work since retiring from the cinema in 1982. He has described his musical limitations candidly, yet a lifelong love for opera drew him into staging *Die Dreigroschenoper* in Stockholm in 1950, *Die lustige Witwe* at Malmö in 1954 and *The Rake's Progress* at the Royal Opera, Stockholm, in 1961, which Stravinsky considered the perfect realization of his opera; a production of *Die Zauberflöte* planned for Hamburg in 1965 was cancelled because of Bergman's illness. Returning to the opera stage in 1991, he directed and collaborated in writing the libretto of a new work, *Backanterna* (after Euripides: *The Bacchae*), by the Swedish composer Daniel Börtz. The opera and, in particular, Bergman's stunning production were widely acclaimed.

Probably Bergman's best-known contribution to opera, however, is his film adaptation of *Die Zauberflöte* (*Tröllflöjten*), made in 1975 for the 50th anniversary of Swedish television; this was the culmination of a passion dating back to 1939, his time as an assistant at the Stockholm Opera, when he conversed with the conductor Issay Dobroven about a proper staging of the work: intimate, with simple scene changes, like the original production. The film, sung and vividly acted in Swedish, in part simulates a performance in the Drottningholm theatre, re-creating its stage, sets and machinery, with elegant, subdued lighting by the master cinematographer Sven Nykvist. A few excisions and slight reordering of numbers in the second act, though musically questionable, clarify the action. Characters and themes from earlier films by Bergman the Lutheran pastor's son – his obsession with morality and marriage, wisdom and strength made possible through harmony between man and woman – resonate in *Tröllflöjten*, illuminating the opera's own humanist preoccupations (for illustration *see* FILM, fig.6).

*

H. Sjögren: *Ingmar Bergman på teatern* (Stockholm, 1968)

R. Wood: *Ingmar Bergman* (London, 1969)

J. R. Taylor: 'Bergman, Ingmar', *Encyclopaedia Britannica* (Chicago, 15/1977), 1841

I. Bergman: *Laterna magica* (Stockholm, 1987; Eng. trans., 1988, as *The Magic Lantern*) [autobiography] RICHARD EVIDON

Bergonzi, Carlo (*b* Polisene, nr Parma, 13 July 1924). Italian tenor. He studied in Parma at the Boito Conservatory, making his début as a baritone at Lecce in 1948 as Rossini's Figaro. After studying the tenor repertory he made a second début as Chénier at Bari in 1951. He first sang at La Scala in 1953, creating the title role of Napoli's *Mas'Aniello*, and appeared there until the early 1970s. He made his London début at the Stoll Theatre in 1953 as Don Alvaro, the role in which he first appeared at Covent Garden (1962); he returned as Manrico, Riccardo, Radames, Cavaradossi, Nemorino, Rodolfo (*Luisa Miller*) and Edgardo, which he sang in 1985. He made his American début in Chicago in 1955 in a double bill as Luigi (*Il tabarro*) and Turiddu, and sang regularly at the Metropolitan from 1956 for 30 years, making his last appearance there in 1988 as Rodolfo (*Luisa Miller*). In addition to the Verdi tenor repertory Bergonzi sang more than 40 roles, including Pollione, Enzo, Boito's Faust, Des Grieux and Canio. His voice was of beautiful quality, well modulated and well defined. He used it with taste, discretion and an elegant sense of line.

*

GV (R. Celletti; R. Vegeto)

G. Gualerzi: 'Carlo Bergonzi', *Opera*, xxix (1978), 257–62

HAROLD ROSENTHAL/R

Bergsma, William (Laurence) (*b* Oakland, CA, 1 April 1921). American composer and teacher. His principal composition teachers were Howard Hanson and Bernard Rogers. His many awards include two Guggenheim fellowships (1946, 1951), an NEA Fellowship (1979) and the American Academy of Arts and Letters Award (1965). Between 1946 and 1963 he taught at the Juilliard School, and in 1963 he joined the school of music at the University of Washington, Seattle, where he later became Professor Emeritus.

His two operatic works are sharply distinct in character: one serious, the other comic. Both deal with realistic issues and provide vivid social commentary. *The Wife of Martin Guerre* (1956), an opera in three acts to a libretto by Janet Lewis, was first performed at the Juilliard School's Festival of American Music on 15 February 1956. The plot is based on a true story: the disappearance of a peasant in 16th-century France and his return eight years later. His wife accepts him back, but her suspicions that he is an impostor increase and she finally brings criminal charges against him. This action is central to the final act, in which the courtroom trial is played out. Musically the work is sombre, with tension in the drama heightened by a very dissonant harmonic language. The vocal lines are characterized by a new-found lyricism. Bergsma's musical style is supported by Lewis's stylish libretto, written in straightforward language.

The Murder of Comrade Sharik (1973) stands in vivid contrast to the first opera. It received its première on 10 April 1986 at Brooklyn College after winning the annual opera competition. The libretto, by Bergsma, is based on the novel *The Heart of a Dog* by Mikhail Afanas'evich Bulgakov. Set in Moscow in 1925, it focusses on a doctor whose experiments inadvertently transform a dog into a Soviet citizen. Divided into seven scenes and a prologue, the score quotes from *Carmen*, *La traviata* and *Don Giovanni* for comic effect. The voice of Stalin is portrayed by the orchestra. There is some use of aleatory techniques, the voices sometimes out of synchronization with the orchestra. The harmonic language is less dissonant than in *The Wife of Martin Guerre* and the vocal lines more linear and lyrically conceived.

*

Anderson2; *Baker7*; *VintonD*

R. F. Goldman: 'Current Chronicle', *MQ*, xlii (1956), 390–95

D. Stevens: 'Notes from Abroad', *MT*, xcvii (1956), 269–70

R. H. Kornick: *Recent American Opera: a Production Guide* (New York, 1991), 58–9 JAMES P. CASSARO

Bergt, (Christian Gottlob) August (*b* Oederan, Saxony, 17 June 1771; *d* Bautzen, 10 Feb 1837). German composer. After studying at the Dresden Kreuzschule and in Leipzig, he became a full-time organist of St Petri, Bautzen, where he was to remain all his life. In Bautzen he also taught, and founded a teachers' seminar and a Singverein. His *Briefwechsel eines alten und jungen Schulmeisters* (ed. C. G. Hering, Zittau and Leipzig, 1838), cast in the fashionable form of an exchange of letters, was a popular practical handbook for students and young church musicians; it includes a biography and list of works.

Bergt's stage works have been described as continuing the Singspiel tradition of J. A. Hiller but in a more sentimental, folklike idiom, his early Romantic style being coloured by Biedermeier tendencies (Härtwig). He also wrote a large quantity of church and instrumental music.

List gegen List (Spl, 1, C. F. Bretzner), Leipzig, 12 Sept 1797, vs (Leipzig, 1802)
Laura und Fernando (3, Bretzner), Leipzig, March 1801
Des Dichters Geburtstag (Liederspiel, 1, G. F. Treitschke), Leipzig, 1802
Das Ständchen (int, 1, C. Schulz), Leipzig, 1802
Die Wunderkur (3, Schmiedgen), Bautzen, 1803
Erwin und Elmire (int, 1, J. W. von Goethe), Bautzen, 1804
Jery und Bätely (Spl, Goethe), Bautzen, Stadt, 1804
Das Mitgefühl (Liederspiel, 1, Treitschke), Bautzen, 1807
Der Schulmeister (Spl)

*

MGG (D. Härtwig); *StiegerO* JOHN WARRACK

Bergwerk zu Falun, Das ('The Mine of Falun'). Opera in eight scenes by RUDOLF WAGNER-RÉGENY to his own libretto after HUGO VON HOFMANNSTHAL's play; Salzburg, Festspielhaus, 16 August 1961.

Hofmannsthal's play was based on a story, 'Die Bergwerke zu Falun', from E. T. A. Hoffmann's *Die Serapions-Brüder*. A fisherman's son lies unconscious after being hit by the yard of a sailing ship's mast. Elis Fröbom (baritone), a fisherman, comes home to find himself orphaned. Life holds no meaning for him now. An old man, Torbern (tenor), appears and offers him a way out: the earth under their feet opens and they go underground. There Fröbom meets the Mountain Queen (mezzo-soprano), to whom he is deeply attracted. She sends him back to the world: he is to take the place of the aging Torbern as the Mountain Queen's lover, but must first learn the ways of the mountains for himself. The only way to her domain seems to be through the mine of Falun; the fisherman's son mysteriously revives and transports Fröbom across the sea to the mine. Torbern takes Fröbom to the home of the mine owner Pehrson Dahlsjö (bass), where Fröbom is attracted to Dahlsjö's daughter Anna (soprano).

Some time later Dahlsjö offers Fröbom Anna's hand in marriage. The Mountain Queen entices Fröbom into the mine by magic, while Anna calls anxiously to him from above. Since he cannot decide between them, the mine collapses, blocking the gateway to the Mountain Queen's domain. Wedding arrangements are made for Fröbom and Anna, but he confides to her his secret fate. As Anna begs him to stay, Torbern reappears and urges him to join the Mountain Queen. On the wedding morning Fröbom leaves his bride and never returns. It is now Anna's life that is meaningless.

Wagner-Régeny's artistic leanings had always been opposed to the opulent operatic style of Strauss, but if his intentions in *Das Bergwerk* were to show how Hofmannsthal's ideas should be presented to a post-Strauss generation they were not fulfilled. The composer's tonally centred dodecaphonic idiom produced an austere style that made no musical distinction between the worlds above and below the mountain, and used the same components for quite different levels of the action. The opera thus retains the oratorio-like quality of the earlier *Prometheus*, but its many subdivisions of scenes mean that it does not share that work's statuesque dimension. *Das Bergwerk* is not easy to classify, and for that reason it does not fit comfortably into any repertory. On the one hand it seems more akin to *Wozzeck*, while on the other the recurrent B-A-C-H motif, richer in association than the rest of the 12-note row, and the plainchant *Media vita in morte sumus* reinforce the impression of an oratorio.

Rehearsals for the première coincided with the building of the Berlin Wall, and Wagner-Régeny's silence on that event adversely affected the opera's success. The East German authorities did nothing to reward the composer for returning to East Berlin and the only other production of the opera took place in the small Baltic town of Stralsund a few days before Wagner-Régeny's death in September 1969. TILO MEDEK

Berio, Luciano (*b* Oneglia, Imperia, 24 Oct 1925). Italian composer. He grew up among professional musicians: both his father and grandfather were church organists and composers. As a consequence, his musical training was early and thorough. Singing was all around him as a child, since his father gave lessons. He compounded this immediate, practical relationship with the voice during his studies (1945–51) at the Milan Conservatory, where he supported himself by working as an accompanist, and later as a conductor in provincial opera houses. One of the young singers with whom he worked in 1950 was Cathy Berberian, whom he married later that year.

Although he had originally aspired to be a pianist, Berio's years of study at the conservatory, and particularly with Ghedini, had reorientated him definitively towards composition. After a brief study trip to America, he joined the staff of the RAI in 1952. He immediately set about trying to organize resources for an electronic studio in Milan, a project in which he was subsequently joined by Bruno Maderna. The studio eventually opened under their dual direction in 1955, somewhat eccentrically designated by the RAI as the Studio di Fonologia Musicale. Work in the studio habituated Berio to thinking in terms of the co-existence of several layers of sound-material and thus to an exploratory, 'contrapuntal' mode of listening that was to be crucial to much of his subsequent work. The RAI afforded him many contacts, notably with the young Umberto Eco, with whom he developed a rich mix of enthusiasms. Together, in the late 1950s, they explored linguistics – particularly the phonetic components of language, and the borderline between sound and sense – and the work of Joyce. Eco was also working towards a theory of the 'open work' (*opera aperta*), in part springing from Joyce's example, in which a multiplicity of possible interpretative routes encourages the individual to synthesize his own meaning from each encounter with the work. Finally, at this crucial point in Berio's development Cathy Berberian was relaunching her singing career after a few years spent caring for their young daughter, Cristina. Prompted initially by John Cage's *Aria*, written for her in 1958, she launched into a brilliantly acrobatic exploration of the whole voice that offered Berio a vocal palette of singular richness and wit.

Berio thus had to hand the essential components of a theatre of the ear and mind that was realized either electronically (*Omaggio a Joyce*, *Visage*) or in the concert hall (*Circles*, *Sequenza III*), its dynamic deriving from the interplay of different types of vocal behaviour, or layers of meaning, or indeed meaning and its absence. Berberian's virtuosity set these into a virtual counterpoint, but other works, such as *Passaggio*, *Laborintus II*, *Sinfonia* or, later, *A-Ronne*, used multiple voices to make that counterpoint real. To place this 'theatre of the imagination' on stage was simply to add an extra dimension, but not essentially to change it. In consequence, the evolutions of Berio's theatre and of his work for the concert hall are intimately interlinked.

Granted the powerful role that the voice was to play in his work, there is a certain irony in Berio's first theatrical excursion: a mime piece, *Mimusique no.2/Tre modi per sopportare la vita* (1955), reworked with a new scenario by Italo Calvino in 1959 to form *Allez-Hop*. This 'mimed story', as the authors described it, was the last that Berio was to narrate on stage. In his first vocal work for the theatre, *Passaggio* (1961–2), Berio moved definitively into 'open' theatre: his collaborator in this and many future ventures was the poet Edoardo Sanguineti. The rich interplay of vocal layers that they conceived for *Passaggio* demanded a complementary visual austerity: a single woman crossing a stage and stopping at symbolical 'stations' that hint at (but are only retrospectively confirmed as) a skeletal narrative of arrest, torture and release. Contained within this frame is the real focus of theatrical tension: a constant interplay of the internal monologue pursued by the woman on stage, the singing chorus in the pit who comment on her plight and, most telling of all, speaking groups dispersed around the audience and giving voice to reactions that middle-class culture-lovers normally prefer to suppress.

Concurrently, Berio was exploring American experimental theatre. When in 1961 he left the RAI to take up the first of a series of teaching appointments in the USA, he took an interest in the work of Anne Halprin and the Dancers' Workshop of San Francisco, and subsequently brought them and Sanguineti together in *Esposizione*, a work for the 1963 Venice Biennale. This work abandoned narrative entirely. Instead, the whole theatrical space, auditorium included, was energized not merely by singers calling and responding across it but by a gradual invasion of every nook and cranny by Halprin's dancers, bearing with them a clutter of consumer durables, while voices launched themselves into analogous catalogues of our cultural stockpile. This frankly exploratory piece was subsequently withdrawn, but many of its materials were reworked in *Laborintus II*, an initially radiophonic homage to Dante that declares itself open to theatrical interpretation but is now usually performed in the concert hall.

The counterpointing of layers of material, until then a matter of detail, became the large-scale principle of Berio's first full-length theatre piece, *Opera* (composed 1969–70). Interweaving three radically different types of theatre, with a common theme of mortality, Berio sought to contain the tensions thus created within a coherent musical framework in which certain sections (such as 'Air') are repeatedly reworked, and the developmental flow from one movement is broken off, to be taken up at a later stage by another (a technique derived from the immediately preceding concert work *Sinfonia*). The failure of this brave but over-complex work caused Berio to examine his musico-dramatic resources carefully. His intensive investigation of evolving harmonic resources in the concert works of the 1970s allowed him to conceive *La vera storia* (composed 1977–81) as a cohesive structure proliferating from an eight-note pitch field. Only when he had established a musico-dramatic framework – separate numbers in the first half, outlining the skeleton of an 'operatic' scenario, which are then fused by massive reworking into a continuous flow in the second half as the same story is reworked in grimly contemporary terms – did he turn to Italo Calvino to find words for his music.

The same insistence on the primacy of musical structure is clear in *Un re in ascolto* (composed 1979–84). Although Calvino proposed a fully-fledged libretto, Berio, typically, fragmented and reworked the project until he had achieved a musically coherent whole, and only then did he search out a range of texts that would give focus to his vision. It is surely no accident that Berio's protagonist is a dying impresario who has imagined 'another theatre', realizing at the last that that is none other than 'the sea of music'.

See also OPERA; *PASSAGGIO*; *RE IN ASCOLTO, UN*; and *VERA STORIA, LA*.

Passaggio (messa in scena, 1, E. Sanguineti), Milan, Piccola Scala, 6 May 1963

Opera (3, Berio, after F. Colombo, U. Eco, A. Striggio, S. Yankowitz, with Open Theatre of New York), Santa Fe, 12 Aug 1970; rev., Florence, Comunale, 28 May 1977

La vera storia, 1977–81 (2, I. Calvino), Milan, La Scala, 9 March 1982

Un re in ascolto, 1979–84 (azione musicale, 2 pts, Berio, after Calvino, W. H. Auden, F. Einsiedel and F. W. Gotter), Salzburg, Kleines Festspielhaus, 7 Aug 1984

*

V. Puecher: 'Diario di un'esperienza', *Siparo* (Dec 1964), 45–6

M. Bortolotto: 'Luciano Berio o dei piaceri', *Fase seconda* (Turin, 1969), 141–3

R. Dalmonte: 'Luciano Berio', *Intervista sulla musica* (Bari, 1981); Eng. trans. in Osmond-Smith (1985) [interview]

R. Dalmonte and N. Lorenzini: 'Funzioni strutturanti nei rapporti musica-poesia: "Passaggio" e "Laborintus II" di Sanguineti-L. Berio', *Il gesto della forma: musica, poesia, teatro nell'opera di Luciano Berio*, ed. L. Azzaroni (Milan, 1981), 1–44

B. A. Varga: *Beszélgetések Luciano Berioval* [Conversations with Luciano Berio] (Budapest, 1981); excerpts from Eng. orig. in Osmond-Smith (1985)

P. Albèra and J. Demierre: 'Luciano Berio', *Contrechamps*, i (Lausanne, 1983), 64–6 [interview]

D. Osmond-Smith: *Two Interviews* (London, 1985)

I. Stoianova: *Luciano Berio: chemins en musique* (Paris, 1985)

L. Berio: 'Eco in ascolto', *Contemporary Music Review*, v (1989), 1–8

D. Osmond-Smith: 'Prospero's Peace: the Making of Berio's Opera *Un re in ascolto*', *The Listener*, cxxi (1989), 34–5

G. C. Taccani: 'Scena, musica, società', *Sonus*, ii/1 (1990), 82–7

D. Osmond-Smith: *Berio* (Oxford, 1991), 90–118

DAVID OSMOND-SMITH

Berkeley, Sir **Lennox** (**Randal Francis**) (*b* Boars Hill, nr Oxford, 12 May 1903; *d* London, 26 Dec 1989). English composer. Born into an aristocratic family (he was the 9th Earl of Berkeley *manqué*), he was educated at Gresham's School, Holt, and went up to Merton College, Oxford, in 1922. After taking a BA in modern languages in 1926, he studied with Nadia Boulanger in Paris until 1932. In 1936 he met Britten at the ISCM Festival in Barcelona, and for a time the two men shared a house in East Anglia. It was through Berkeley that Britten came to know Verdi's *Otello* while he was planning *Peter Grimes*. From 1942 to 1945 Berkeley was on the staff of the BBC, and from 1946 to 1968 he was a professor of composition at the RAM. He was made a CBE in 1957 and knighted in 1974.

His style remained basically tonal throughout his life, although he experimented with atonal elements from the mid-1950s onwards. His four operas embrace a diversity of genres: *Nelson* the heroic, *A Dinner Engagement* the comic, *Ruth* the biblical-pastoral and *Castaway* the classical. While none is perhaps flawless – in some cases a tougher line with his librettists would have been an advantage – Berkeley's sympathy for voices and for the English language is everywhere evident, and in *Nelson* especially there are passages of real dramatic power. A fifth opera, *Faldon Park*, remained unfinished at his death.

See also CASTAWAY; DINNER ENGAGEMENT, A; NELSON; and RUTH.

Nelson op.41, 1949–54 (3, A. Pryce-Jones), London, Sadler's Wells, 22 Sept 1954, *GB-Lbl**

A Dinner Engagement op.45 (2 scenes, P. Dehn), Aldeburgh, Jubilee Hall, 17 June 1954, *Lbl**, vs (London, 1955)

Ruth op.50 (3 scenes, E. Crozier), London, Scala, 2 Oct 1956, *Lbl**, vs (London, 1960)

Castaway op.68 (1, Dehn), Aldeburgh, Jubilee Hall, 3 June 1967, *Lbl**, vs (London, 1970)

Faldon Park op.100 (2, W. Dean) [only Act 1 composed]

*

D. Mitchell: 'Contemporary Chronicle: the Aldeburgh Festival', *MO*, lxxvii (1953–4), 645–6

W. Dean: 'Lennox Berkeley and Nelson', *The Listener* (16 Sept 1954), 461

P. Dehn: '*A Dinner Engagement*', *Opera*, v (1954), 335–8

A. Pryce-Jones: 'Some Notes on the Text of *Nelson*', *Opera*, v (1954), 595–8

P. Hamburger: 'Ruth: an Introduction', *Opera*, vii (1956), 590–94

P. Dickinson: *The Music of Lennox Berkeley* (London, 1989)

ROGER NICHOLS

Berkovec, Jiří (*b* Pilsen, 22 July 1922). Czech composer and musicologist. He studied at the Prague Conservatory (1941–8) and at Charles University (1945–8), then worked for Czech Radio (1945–65) and Supraphon (1965–76) before taking up a post at the Theatrical Institute (1976–82). His first opera was for children, *Pohádka o dvanácti měsíčkách* ('Fairy-Tale about Twelve Months', 1957); his second, *Krakatit*, a reaction to a possible outbreak of war, is a humanist's protest against the misuse of inventions to kill people. *Krakatit* tells of a peace-loving inventor of a dangerous explosive, forced to surrender it to warmongers and anarchists who want to take over the world with his help. Shocked, he identifies himself with an ordinary old man who suggests a helpful and harmless use of the invention. The text is articulated by means of a recitative-like parlando, supported by an elaborate, often polyphonic, orchestral texture. Berkovec's sense of humour is evident in *Hostinec U kamenného stolu* ('Inn at the Stone Table'), a satire set in a spa town, which unveils the pettiness underlying ostentatious snobbery in an intentionally naive way; and in *Epopej* ('The Epopee'), which concerns the lives of tramps and their fights with do-gooders.

Pohádka o dvanácti měsíčkách [Fairy-Tale about Twelve Months], 1957 (children's op, 3, J. Dolina), unperf.

Krakatit (2, Berkovec, after K. Čapek), Brno, Janáček, 10 March 1961

Hostinec U kamenného stolu [Inn at the Stone Table], 1961–2 (3, Berkovec, after K. Poláček), Opava, Z. Nejedlý, 18 March 1973

Epopej: Příběh z dýmu táborových ohňů aneb Nové pověsti české [The Epopee: Stories from the Camp-Fires, or New Czech Legends], 1973 ('tramp opera-parody', 2, Berkovec, after J. Žáček and V. Rada), unperf.

*

V. Lébl: 'Operní quo vadis', *Literární noviny*, x/11 (1961), 8

V. Šefl: 'Krakatit', *Divadelní noviny*, iv/20 (1961), 7

HELENA HAVLÍKOVÁ

Berkshire Music Center. Former name of the TANGLEWOOD Music Center.

Berlin. German city. Capital of the German Empire from 1871 to 1945, it has been an important centre for opera since the early 18th century. It was divided into sectors at the end of World War II and these were amalgamated into two, a west and an east, in 1961, the former allied to the Federal German Republic (with its capital at Bonn) and the latter the capital of the German Democratic Republic. After the removal of the wall separating the two sectors in November 1989, the subsequent reunification of the country and a popular referendum in 1991, Berlin was again designated the capital of a united Germany.

1. To 1806. 2. 1806–1914: (i) Königliche Schauspiele (ii) Other opera. 3. Since 1914: (i) Deutsche Staatsoper and Kroll Oper (ii) Charlottenburg / Städtische / Deutsche Oper (iii) Komische Oper (iv) Other opera.

1. TO 1806. During the 17th century there appears to have been little, if any, operatic activity in Berlin, and little demand for it. Italian singers appeared sporadically in court festivities involving music, singing and ballet. Towards the end of the century the wife of Elector Friedrich III (later Friedrich I, King of Prussia), Sophie Charlotte, fostered court productions of elaborate presentations called 'Wirtschaften'. Berlin's first opera was a lavish production, *La festa del Hymeneo*, mounted to celebrate the nuptials of the Crown Prince of Hesse-Kassel and Princess Louise Dorothea Sophie on 1 June 1700, with music by Attilio Ariosti and Karl Friedrich Rieck. It was performed in a specially built theatre above the royal riding stables which, as the Stallplatz Theater, remained in service into the 1780s.

Friedrich I had little personal interest in ballet or opera, and on the death of Sophie Charlotte (his first wife) in 1705 their cultivation slackened markedly. During the severe reign of his son Friedrich Wilhelm I there was no opera at all, and the Königliche Kapelle declined precipitously. In 1728 the elector and his young son, the crown prince Friedrich (later Friedrich II, known as Frederick the Great), visited Dresden, where the crown prince heard his first opera, Hasse's *Cleofide*, a decisive event in the formation of his taste and enthusiasm for opera. On this occasion he met not only Hasse but also the flautist J. J. Quantz, who soon became his teacher. The prince established his own Kapelle, to which Carl Heinrich Graun came in 1735 from Brunswick as a chamber singer.

When, in 1740, Frederick succeeded his father, one of his first acts was to order the building of an opera house; he also sent Graun, now Kapellmeister, to Italy to procure singers. A temporary theatre, the 'Comödiensaal auf dem Schlosse', was constructed in the royal palace; this was torn down in 1805. Here, upon Frederick's return from Silesia, Graun's *Rodelinda* was given on 13 December 1741, with an orchestra of 37, including two continuo players, strings (12–4–4–3), four each of flutes and oboes, two of bassoons and horns, a theorbo and a harp.

The new, spacious Königliches Opernhaus (Royal Opera House) was designed by Freiherr von

Knobelsdorff (see fig.3 below). On the site of the old Festungswerken on the present avenue Unter den Linden, it included a canal system for cascades and waterfalls that also provided fire protection. It stood until 1843, when it burnt down. Amid a heavy snowstorm, it was inaugurated on 7 December 1742 with Graun's *Cesare e Cleopatra*. Two years later Knobelsdorff completed the new Schlosstheater at Potsdam, in service until Friedrich Wilhelm III had it dismantled in 1800. Here travelling companies performed comic opera and spoken comedies for the court.

Frederick exercised unprecedented control over every aspect of operatic production. In 1743 he created an international incident by demanding that the dancer La Barbarina should honour her contract with Berlin despite her marriage to Lord Stuart Mackenzie. The king was always involved in the selection of librettos, and in 1749 began sketching opera plots himself, in French prose. He sent his outline for *Coriolan* to Count Algarotti, who with the court poet Villati worked up an Italian libretto, set by Graun. When Villati died in 1752 he was succeeded by Tagliazucchi, who put Frederick's best-known opera outline, *Montezuma* (1755; fig.1), into Italian verse for Graun. The king also supervised set and costume design, attended rehearsals, and insisted on a rather strict adherence to the written score by his singers. In 1751 Giuseppe Galli-Bibiena was hired as set designer; he died in 1757 and in 1765 his son Carlo was appointed head stage director, but soon returned to Italy.

The opera season ran from November to March, with performances twice a week. Admission, limited to members of the court, army officers and the higher strata of Berlin society, was free. A normal season included two new operas, usually by Graun, in addition to shorter works such as intermezzos, pastorales and serenatas; seldom was an opera given more than four times. In 1756 Graun mounted his last opera, *Merope*. During the Seven Years War (1756–63) nearly all the opera personnel were dismissed and the king contented himself with intermezzos at Potsdam. Graun died in 1759, and when the court opera was reorganized in 1764 Johann Friedrich Agricola succeeded him as Kapellmeister. His operas found little favour, and the opera turned more and more to older works by Graun and Hasse. In 1768 a theatre was included in the Neues Palais am Park at Sans Souci (fig.2).

1. Costume designed by Christian Gottlob Fechhelm for the title role of Graun's 'Montezuma', first performed at the Berlin Royal Opera, 6 January 1755

The decline of Italian opera after the war describes a counter-curve to the rising fortunes of German opera and German musicians in Berlin. In 1771 the famous singer Gertrud Elisabeth Mara ('La Mara') was engaged. Agricola died on 2 December 1774 and was replaced the following year by the young Johann Friedrich Reichardt. The War of the Bavarian Succession brought another halt to operatic activity at Berlin in 1778. In 1779 Mara was replaced by Juliane Koch, who died in 1783 at the age of 25. By 1785 the king was no longer attending the opera. Frederick died on 17 August 1786, and all theatres were closed until October.

His successor, Friedrich Wilhelm II, was a firm supporter of the German operatic and theatrical activities that Frederick had all but ignored. In 1743 the Schönemann company had presented the first German opera at Berlin, a translation of the English ballad opera *The Devil to Pay*. Sustained cultivation of comic opera in German came with the arrival of the company of H. G. Koch in 1771. Koch purchased from the widow of the impresario Franz Schuch the younger both his Prussian privilege and his theatre at Berlin in the Behrenstrasse. He confined his interest to the comic works of the Weisse-Hiller school, many of them written for his troupe while at Leipzig and Weimar. As crown prince, Friedrich Wilhelm visited his stage on 24 September 1771.

After Koch's death in 1775 C. T. Döbbelin obtained both privilege and theatre from his widow. His company had to compete with a French troupe that produced plays and *opéras comiques* under Frederick's protection. They performed at the (ineptly designed) new Theater am Gendarmenmarkt, which the king had built for them, from its inauguration on 22 April 1776 until 1778, when they were dismissed. Döbbelin improved on Koch's standards with a larger company (78 members by 1781, plus an orchestra of 20), better singers and newer works. His leading singer was the outstanding south German soprano Marie Sophie Niklas, who was later taken into the Italian Opera at Berlin. In July 1777 Döbbelin also hired as his music director Johann André, under whose leadership Berlin became a centre for the production of new German operas. The troupe played daily except for Fridays (when concerts took place in the innkeeper J. F. Corsica's hall, including serious operas on occasion) and for Sundays during summer. The theatre, which was small and narrow, included a royal box.

By 1784, when both André and Marie Niklas left Berlin, Döbbelin's fortunes were declining. On the accession of Friedrich Wilhelm II, however, his troupe was converted by the new king into the Berlin Nationaltheater. Döbbelin was given the French theatre at the Gendarmenmarkt (which seated about 1200), together with its decorations, a yearly subvention of 6000 thaler, and the right to borrow costumes from the Italian opera. But standards continued to slip, and old Döbbelin was soon replaced by J. J. Engel, who moved vigorously to improve both musical and dramatic offerings. The acquisition of new singers made possible the mounting of three Mozart operas, *Die Entführung aus dem Serail* (16 October 1788), *Le nozze di Figaro* (14 September 1790) and *Don Giovanni* (20 December 1790, given five times in ten days).

Despite fears that the new king's partiality for German opera might spell the end of his Italian company, support continued. The Royal Opera House was renovated in 1787, Reichardt was charged with acquiring new singers and the king himself sometimes played the cello in the orchestra during rehearsals. The house reopened with Reichardt's *Andromeda* on 11 January 1788. Perhaps Reichardt's greatest triumph was his *Brenno*, given on the queen's birthday, 16 October 1789. He was the centre of endless intrigues, took badly the failure of his *Olimpiade* in 1791 and fell from grace in 1793 owing to his outspoken republican sympathies.

In 1792 B. A. Weber came to the fore at the Nationaltheater as music director and composer. On 12 May 1794 the company mounted Mozart's *Die Zauberflöte*, given four times running, then twice weekly during the entire summer, when it was virtually the only work in the repertory. A production of Gluck's *Iphigénie en Tauride* on 24 February 1795 set the German company on an equal footing with the Italians. At the end of 1796 A. W. Iffland was named general director of the Nationaltheater, further enhancing the enterprise's prestige.

Friedrich Wilhelm II died on 16 November 1797, and there followed another period of mourning and uncertainty. Reichardt immediately ingratiated himself with Friedrich Wilhelm III, who allowed a concert performance early in 1798 of Reichardt's *Brenno*, given in German by members of the Nationaltheater on the birthday of Frederick the Great (24 January). Reichardt achieved a popular success later that year with *Die Geisterinsel* (6 July), but he was unable to obtain a fixed position within the new administration. The new king allowed both the Italian and the German theatres to continue, although he was personally uninterested in either.

The fortunes of the Italian opera company continued their steady decline. The Nationaltheater, by contrast, actually began showing a profit, thanks to a string of popular productions. Perhaps the most notable of them was Ferdinand Kauer's *Donauweibchen* which in 1801 was performed for four months to the exclusion of all other operas in the repertory. On 1 January 1802 the Nationaltheater moved into a new playhouse in the Gendarmenmarkt, next door to the old one which was torn down. Lurching towards its end, the Italian opera prepared a very poor production of Gluck's *Alceste* on royal orders in 1804; the next year the German company triumphed, in pointed opposition, with a production of Gluck's *Armide* (20 May). That year was the Italian opera's last. When French forces occupied Berlin in 1806 they found the opera house empty and used it as a storehouse for bread.

2. 1806–1914.

(i) Königliche Schauspiele. While the Royal Opera House remained closed during the two years of French occupation (1806–7), the Nationaltheater, no longer dependent on royal subsidy, continued its productions in the Schauspielhaus, the new house built by Carl

2. Auditorium of the theatre (1768) in the Neues Palais am Park, Sans Souci, Berlin, built for Frederick II by Johann Gottfried Büring and Heinrich Ludwig Manger

3. The Royal Opera House (designed by Georg Wenzeslaus von Knobelsdorff, 1741–43), Berlin, with St Hedwig's Cathedral (right)

Langhans, which it occupied from 1802. In 1807 the royal opera and the Nationaltheater companies merged as the Königliche Schauspiele, but maintained the distinction between the two repertories. All performances were open to the general public. Under Iffland's direction German opera was performed more frequently, though the opera house repertory was still entirely adapted to the king's wishes. Iffland supervised productions of Spontini's *La vestale* (1811) and *Fernand Cortez* (1814), Weber's *Silvana* (1812) and *Abu Hassan* (1813), and works by Méhul and Boieldieu. His successor Karl von Brühl was given the task of making the royal theatre the finest in Germany, and at first received enthusiastic support from Friedrich Wilhelm III. Scenery and costumes became more realistic and productions more dramatic. Brühl was responsible for the Berlin première of *Fidelio* (1815), the world première of E. T. A. Hoffmann's *Undine* (1816, with sets by Schinkel), as well as revivals of works by Gluck. In the decade 1815–25 Rossini's works became the most popular in Berlin.

Against the wishes of Brühl, who hoped to secure Weber as Kapellmeister, the king engaged Spontini as general music director in 1820. Only five weeks after the first performance of Spontini's *Olympia* Brühl produced the successful première of Weber's *Der Freischütz* (18 June 1821) under the composer's direction in the new Schauspielhaus designed by Schinkel (fig.4). Whereas the audience for Spontini's work consisted mostly of royalty and nobility, that for Weber's was largely made up of wealthy citizens, including Heinrich Heine, Hoffmann and Mendelssohn; this was a symptom of the rivalry between the two houses. Spontini's *Nurmahal* was produced in 1822 and his *Alcidor* in 1825; although the works satisfied court demands, neither was well received by the public. As Spontini's popularity decreased, Brühl had less trouble asserting his wishes at the Royal Opera House. Three years before his retirement in 1828 he arranged performances of Spohr's *Jessonda* and Weber's *Euryanthe*, each conducted by its composer.

Despite Spontini's opposition, Wilhelm von Redern, Brühl's innovatory successor, was able to expand the repertory in both sections of the Königliche Schauspiele, and included more operas by German composers. He was responsible for the successful Berlin premières of Spohr's *Faust* (1829) and Meyerbeer's *Robert le diable* (1832), as well as the world première of Marschner's *Hans Heiling* (1833). Works by Albert Lortzing, however, were first heard in this theatre some time after their first performance: *Zar und Zimmermann* in 1849 and *Hans Sachs* in 1851. Nevertheless, during the 1830s German works performed at the Royal Opera House remained in the minority, while those by the French (Auber and Méhul) and the Italians (Bellini, Donizetti and especially Rossini) took precedence.

On the accession of Friedrich Wilhelm IV in 1840, Spontini lost his support at court and was dismissed in 1841. Lortzing, Marschner and Mendelssohn were considered for the position, but after an impressive production of *Les Huguenots* in 1842 Meyerbeer was named Spontini's successor. Spontini had enlarged the opera orchestra from 78 to 94 members; Meyerbeer now secured greater financial benefits for the musicians. Also in 1842 Redern was appointed to the newly created position of general administrator of court music. The conservative K. T. von Küstner, who replaced him as director of the royal opera, was an administrator rather than a musician; he refused the world premières of *Der fliegende Holländer* and *Tannhäuser* and diminished the repertory during his nine years of service. However, this was partly because the audience now usually consisted less of royalty than of paying guests whom Küstner sought to please.

On 18 August 1843 the Royal Opera House burnt down, and performances were held in the Schauspielhaus during reconstruction. Lortzing's *Der Wildschütz* had its Berlin première there (1843), as did *Der fliegende Holländer* (1844), conducted by the composer (the first Wagner opera produced in Berlin). The new opera house, reconstructed, modernized (with gas lighting) and enlarged by the younger C. F. Langhans, opened on 7 December 1844 with Meyerbeer's *Ein Feldlager in Schlesien*.

Two years later *Rienzi* was given its first Berlin performance; however, neither it nor *Der fliegende Holländer* was successful and both were removed from the repertory until the late 1860s. After an absence from the

4. Interior of the Schauspielhaus on the Gendarmenmarkt, Berlin, designed by Karl Friedrich Schinkel (1817–21), showing his set and backcloth for the inauguration ceremony: from K. F. Schinkel, 'Sammlung Architektonischer Entwürfe', ii (Berlin, 1826)

city of three years, during which Wilhelm Taubert had acted as general music director, Meyerbeer was finally dismissed from that post by the king on 26 November 1848. In the same year Otto Nicolai had taken up the appointment of Kapellmeister at the opera; Nicolai died on 11 May 1849, two months after the première of his *Die lustigen Weiber von Windsor*, and was succeeded by Heinrich Dorn.

Under Botho von Hülsen, who replaced Küstner as director in 1851, the royal opera began to prosper even more. Meyerbeer's grand operas and works by Italian and French composers dominated the repertory for the next three decades. Hülsen assembled outstanding singers (Lilli Lehmann, Albert Niemann, Theodor Wachtel, Désirée Artôt and Adelina Patti), but performances suffered because of an inadequate orchestra until Carl Eckert replaced Dorn as Kapellmeister in 1869. As the operatic tastes of both court and public became more conservative, Hülsen grew more cautious, retaining only well-established works in the repertory.

The production of *Tannhäuser* (1856) was the first successful performance of a Wagner opera in Berlin, and the production of *Il trovatore* at the royal opera (1857) marked the first Berlin performance of an opera by Verdi. Although it was successful, later productions of Verdi's operas (*Rigoletto* and *La traviata*, 1860) were coolly received. In 1876, six years after a production of *Die Meistersinger von Nürnberg* had caused a scandal in the royal opera, Hülsen successfully staged the first Berlin performance of *Tristan und Isolde*. As comic opera became more popular, works by Offenbach came to be regarded as fit for the court opera, and his operas were added to those of Rossini in the repertory. During the 1870s Berlin's population approached one million; the demand for opera increased and daily performances were instituted.

After Eckert's death in 1879 there was a dearth of good conductors; neither Robert Radecke nor Heinrich Kahl adequately fulfilled the demands of the post, and Bülow referred to the royal operas as 'von Hülsen's circus'. When Bolko von Hochberg became director in 1886 he concentrated on improving this situation, and by the early 1890s the court opera had three good conductors, Felix Weingartner, Carl Muck and Josef Sucher. Under Hochberg Wagner's works became part of the standard repertory, partly as a result of the first performance by the royal opera of the *Ring* in 1888 (the Berlin première had taken place at the Viktoria Theater in 1881) and a spectacular production of ten Wagner operas from *Rienzi* to *Götterdämmerung* in chronological order in June 1889. Nevertheless the staple of Berlin opera was still provided by Ponchielli, Verdi and Mascagni.

For two decades after Weingartner left the royal opera in 1898, Richard Strauss served as general music director and added new works to the repertory. Hochberg and Emperor Wilhelm II had refused to mount the première of Strauss's *Feuersnot* in 1900, not realizing that Strauss was one of the most important composers of the day. Thereafter Strauss refused to allow a single first performance of his operas in Berlin. *Feuersnot* was presented in 1901, and *Salome* in 1906. As at its beginning under Frederick the Great, the last era of royal opera (1903–18) was characterized by the court's active participation in operatic administration. Wilhelm II took an interest in selecting the repertory and in stage design and, though the artistic quality of the productions occasionally suffered, stagings were always lavish and pompous. A result of this interest in opera was the commission of Leoncavallo's *Der Roland von Berlin*, first performed in 1904. In the previous year the emperor had welcomed the resignation of Hochberg and replaced him with Hülsen's son Georg von Hülsen-Haeseler, who remained until World War I disrupted operatic activity in the city. Under the new Intendant many older works were revived, while operas by Tchaikovsky, Puccini and Richard Strauss received their Berlin premières, including the successful production of *Der Rosenkavalier* in 1911.

(ii) Other opera. As well as the court and later municipal operas, Berlin has supported a number of theatres with varied artistic and financial success. In

1824 the Königstädtisches Theater opened, producing both popular drama and Italian and French opera, and soon became a serious rival to the court opera. The soprano Henriette Sontag made her Berlin début there before performing in the court opera. After the company closed in 1851 the theatre was used by visiting Italian opera companies.

In 1844 Josef Kroll opened a theatre which was to have an impressive role in early 20th-century Berlin opera. The first productions were of popular plays and puppet shows. Kroll's son Auguste was one of the leading Berlin impresarios in the 19th century. His theatre grew from the hostelry entertainment initially provided by his father at Krolls Etablissement. Later, the Kroll theatre became a popular musical theatre with revues, *Spielopern* (such as the works of the Biedermeier composer Albert Lortzing) and operettas. In the late 1850s, Offenbach's Bouffes Parisiens company gave 'Gasztspiele' with his one-act *opérettes Le mariage aux lanternes* and *Les deux aveugles*. Later still it was a receiving theatre for visiting companies such as that which hosted Lilli Lehmann and Francisco d'Andrade in Mozart's *Don Giovanni* in 1891. In 1894 the theatre came under the direction of the Königliche Schauspiele, and was later renamed the Neues Königliches Operettentheater.

F. W. Deichmann established in 1848 a small theatre where he produced plays with music. After two years this theatre became the Friedrich-Wilhelmstädtisches Theater where Lortzing was briefly conductor. During the 1850s it developed into the city's first operetta theatre and gradually specialized in the works of Offenbach, who established himself as Berlin's favourite composer in the next decade after he conducted the successful Berlin production of *Orphée aux enfers* in 1860.

The large Viktoria Theater was also constructed through private initiative in the three years before its opening in 1859 and equipped with modern stage machinery. As it was largely dependent on ticket sales, the theatre presented mostly familiar Italian operas and operettas by guest ensembles and with well-known singers. More recent works were occasionally staged, however, such as *Rigoletto* (in its Berlin première) in 1860. This theatre was let in May 1881 and ironically became the site of the first Berlin production of Wagner's complete *Ring* cycle (produced by Angelo Neumann and conducted by Anton Seidl), attended by both the composer and Liszt.

The Theater des Westens was founded in 1896 under the direction of Alvis Pasch and rapidly became distinguished through performances of guest singers, including Caruso in 1906. From 1903 to 1907 Pfitzner successfully conducted such performances as the Berlin première of Wolf-Ferrari's *Die neugierigen Frauen* (1904).

The Komische Oper, founded in 1905 by Hans Gregor, provided the most modern theatre in Berlin. Gregor presented comic opera, operetta and works from Mozart to Puccini, excluding Wagner, also arranging the Berlin premières of Wolf's *Der Corregidor* (1906) and Debussy's *Pelléas et Mélisande* (1908). He attempted a regeneration of theatre production, but as the theatre was unable to survive as a private enterprise it closed in 1911 (another Komische Oper was founded in 1947; *see* §3 (iii) below). It was succeeded by the Kurfürstenoper, which presented a similar repertory (until 1913) under Gregor's associate Viktor Moris.

Berlin's enthusiasm for the works of Dittersdorf and Rossini during the early 19th century was later transferred to the Parisian and Viennese operettas which then dominated the repertory of most Berlin opera houses. Offenbach's works were performed in almost all the city's theatres and even Johann Strauss was performed at the royal opera (*Die Fledermaus*, 1899, conducted by Richard Strauss). At the turn of the century Berlin developed its own style of musical comedy, created largely by Paul Lincke (*Frau Lune*, 1899) and Walter Kollo; works in this style were frequently produced at the Apollo-Theater where Lincke was conductor after 1892. The Metropoltheater (built 1898) subsequently became the chief theatre for popular operas and satirical revues, especially those of Viktor Holländer and Leon Jessel in which Fritzi Massary first attracted attention; it continues to be a centre for the performance of operetta.

3. Since 1914.

(i) Deutsche Staatsoper and Kroll Oper. During World War I performances continued at the Royal Opera House (though somewhat less frequently than before) largely through the efforts of Strauss, who assisted the new director, Droescher, during the 1918–19 season after Hülsen-Haeseler's resignation. Court opera in Berlin came to an end at the same time as the Prussian monarchy; in November 1919 it was placed under the administration of the Ministry of Culture and renamed the Staatsoper.

The modern golden age of the Staatsoper on Unter den Linden was unquestionably the period between the end of World War I and the rise of Hitler's National Socialist German Workers' Party in the early 1930s. Under the direction of the Generalintendant, Max von Schillings (the composer of the opera *Mona Lisa*), and conductors such as Erich Kleiber (who supervised the world première of Berg's *Wozzeck* at the Staatsoper on 14 December 1925), the Staatsoper gathered an ensemble of the finest German-speaking and Nordic singers including the great Wagnerians Frida Leider, Lauritz Melchior, Max Lorenz and Alexander Kipnis, and lyric singers such as Lotte Lehmann, Tiana Lemnitz, Richard Tauber and Gerhard Hüsch. Other works by leading contemporary composers were given their first performances during this period, including Franz Schreker's *Der singende Teufel* (1928), Milhaud's *Christophe Colomb* (1930) and Pfitzner's *Das Herz* (1931). Other conductors included George Szell and Ernst Praetorius.

The Nazis' suppression of political dissent and their systematic rooting out of Jews from the leading artistic institutions drove many of Berlin's star performers into exile or (as in Leider's case) premature retirement. Kleiber resigned in 1934, a year after Otto Klemperer, who had joined the Staatsoper's conducting roster in 1931 after a short-lived, but pioneering avant-garde experiment, the Kroll Opera.

Auguste Kroll had retired in 1894 when the directors of the Königliche Schauspiele assumed responsibility for his theatre and used it, despite poor acoustics, as an opera theatre (the Staatsoper, with only 1200 seats – the Kroll had 1600 – was considered too small to meet public demand). In 1924 the Kroll theatre (the Neues Königliches Operettentheater) was rebuilt and enlarged to a capacity of 2100, making it the largest opera theatre in Berlin, and, to the consternation of the Staatsoper management, it charged exceptionally low prices. In

1926 Klemperer signed a ten-year contract and the new Kroll opera company opened on 19 November 1927 with a highly controversial production of *Fidelio* (*see* PRODUCTION, fig.19), which was seen as a declaration of intent, a radical gauntlet thrown down to the operatic conservatives of the city. A sequence of bold re-interpretations of the classics ensued under Klemperer's direction in collaboration with Jürgen Fehling (*Der fliegende Holländer*) and the great German actor-director, Gustav Gründgens, then at the beginning of his career (*Le nozze di Figaro*, *Così fan tutte* and *Der Rosenkavalier*). Teo Otto, Ewald Dülberg and Caspar Neher were the Kroll's preferred stage designers during this period.

As well as the strikingly theatrical productions of standard works, the Kroll championed new works and Klemperer (or his colleagues Zemlinsky and Zweig) conducted the Berlin premières of Stravinsky's *Oedipus rex*, Janáček's *From the House of the Dead*, Hindemith's *Neues vom Tage* and *Cardillac*, and Schoenberg's *Erwartung* and *Die glückliche Hand* in a double bill. Inevitably with a programme such as this – and a predominantly hostile conservative press – the box office was badly hit as the German economic crisis deepened in 1930. The Kroll Oper was identified by right-wing politicians as a centre of leftist propaganda and 'Kulturbolschevismus' and on 25 March 1931 they determined to close it down. The last performance, of Mozart's *Figaro*, was given on 3 July of that year.

In 1926, the Staatsoper had also undergone a complete renovation and it reopened in late 1927, now under the stewardship of the Generalintendant, Heinz Tietjen, who was to take a leading role in Berlin's operatic life and that of the Bayreuth Festival until the end of World War II. By 1939, most of the Jewish and anti-Nazi artists had left – Friedelind Wagner, the anti-fascist granddaughter of the composer, left a moving eyewitness report of a *Zauberflöte* performance at the Staatsoper attended by Hitler, at which the departing Jewish conductor and Sarastro, Leo Blech and Alexander Kipnis, were given a heartfelt ovation – and the artistic fortunes of the Staatsoper remained in the hands of the determined but reluctant servant of the regime, Wilhelm Furtwängler, and the more enthusiastic, ambitious young maestro, Herbert von Karajan. It was in a review of a performance of *Tristan und Isolde* at the Staatsoper in 1938 that the critic Edwin van der Nüll dubbed the young Austrian conductor 'Das Wunder Karajan' ('the miraculous Karajan'), provoking a lifelong antagonism between the two most important conductors who chose to work in Germany under the Nazis.

Despite the depletion of the Staatsoper's ensemble during the Third Reich, Tietjen was still able to draw on the services of the finest 'Aryan' singers, including the sopranos Erna Berger, Maria Cebotari, Tiana Lemnitz and Viorica Ursuleac, the contralto Margarete Klose, the tenors Helge Rosvaenge, Max Lorenz and Franz Völker, the baritones Willi Domgraf-Fassbänder and Gerhard Hüsch and the bass-baritone Rudolf Bockelmann. An idea of the ensemble's strength (and weaknesses) can be gleaned from the recording Walter Legge made with Sir Thomas Beecham and a Goebbels-approved cast (no Tauber, no Kipnis) of *Die Zauberflöte* in 1937–8.

During the war, a veneer of normality was achieved – though both Frida Leider and Max Lorenz encountered difficulties because of their Jewish spouses – but the Staatsoper was bombed and destroyed on 9 April 1941. As the Reich's foremost theatre, it had to be rebuilt at once and the new Staatsoper opened on 7 December that year, when Furtwängler conducted *Die Meistersinger von Nürnberg* (Hitler's favourite opera), a performance which has survived (minus the great Act 3 quintet) in a recording. The opera house fell victim to further bombing on 3 February 1945 and it would take another ten years before the new house (reconstructed according to the original plans of Knobelsdorff's beautiful theatre of 1742) would rise from the rubble and ashes.

Under the direction of the Intendant Ernst Legal, the Staatsoper company re-formed for performances at the Admiralspalast – Gluck's *Orfeo ed Euridice*, starring Margarete Klose and Tiana Lemnitz, was the opening opera on 8 December 1945 – and continued there occasionally conducted by an aging and ailing Furtwängler, demoralized by the humiliation of his denazification trial. The growing tension between the administrations of the Soviet and Western Allies sectors of the city, and a deepening economic crisis in what was soon to become East Berlin, led to a migration of the best artists. Some outstanding singers – Lemnitz, Klose, the young Elisabeth Grümmer and Theo Adam – were still there when the restored Deutsche Staatsoper reopened (again with *Die Meistersinger*) on 4 September 1955, but by 13 August 1961, when the Berlin Wall was built overnight, the most prominent among them had already fled to the Deutsche Oper in West Berlin, successor of the Charlottenburg municipal opera. After 1949, when the communist German Democratic Republic (DDR) was declared, the direction of the Staatsoper company was increasingly put under ideological pressure. In 1951 it gave the world première of Paul Dessau's *Die Verurteilung des Lukullus* (based on a text by Bertolt Brecht); later, in the rebuilt Deutsche Staatsoper, Dessau's status as the new German socialist state's national composer was confirmed with premières of *Puntila* (based on Brecht's *Herr Puntila und sein Knecht Matti*; 1966) and *Einstein* (based on the life of Albert Einstein; 1974), which starred Theo Adam in the title role and was directed by Dessau's wife, the former choreographer and then director of the Berliner Ensemble, Ruth Berghaus. Among later first performances, Udo Zimmermann's *Die wundersame Schustersfrau* (1983, Berlin première) and Siegfried Matthus's *Graf Mirabeau* (1989) stand out.

In 1955, the Staatsoper had suffered the loss of its chief conductor, Erich Kleiber, who, after signing a contract, withdrew it, ostensibly on the grounds that the communist authorities had replaced the Latin Frederican inscription on the façade of the building with the words 'Deutsche Staatsoper'. He was succeeded by Franz Konwitschny, a worthy Kapellmeister but hardly a great conductor, who remained until his death in 1962. Under the Intendant Hans Pischner – a professional harpsichordist as well as musical administrator – the Deutsche Staatsoper became the flagship of the DDR's operatic enterprise, mounting productions with a strong ideological content by Berghaus and the resident producer, Erhard Fischer. The most memorable of these productions were probably Berghaus's famous all-white staging of Rossini's *Il barbiere di Siviglia* (in German) and of Weber's *Der Freischütz*, productions which remained in the repertory for 25 years. The major singers of this period of the Staatsoper's history were Theo Adam, Peter Schreier (an outstanding Mozart tenor and a moving Palestrina in Pfitzner's opera), Ludmila Dvořáková, Siegfried Vogel, Fritz Hübner and Ekkehard Wlaschiha, all of whom made international careers while remaining citizens of the DDR. With the demolition of the Berlin Wall in 1989, another period of uncertainty was ushered in as the Intendants who served the communist regime were removed from their posts. In 1991 the Berlin Senate appointed Daniel Barenboim as music director (from 1993), with a view to transforming the Staatsoper once again into a glittering international house employing the world's leading directors and singers, and with *Parsifal* as the inaugural work in a production by Harry Kupfer (chief producer of the Komische Oper; *see* (iii) below).

(ii) Charlottenburg/Städtische/Deutsche Oper. The Deutsches Opernhaus opened in Charlottenburg, then still independent but later integrated into Greater Berlin, with a performance of Beethoven's *Fidelio* on 7 November 1912. Unlike the royal opera house in Unter den Linden, the architect Heinrich Seeling's new theatre was envisaged as a 'people's opera', with a popular repertory. It could accommodate 2300 spectators in the auditorium, which had stalls and three circles. After the opening production, conducted by Ignaz Waghalter and staged by the new director Georg Hartmann, critics described the new building as 'inexpressibly bleak, dreary and commonplace'. However, success was not long in coming; in its second year the Deutsches Opernhaus had 11 000 subscribers and the repertory extended from *Die Meistersinger* to Puccini's *Manon Lescaut.* Two notable premières just before World War I should be mentioned: Puccini's *La fanciulla del West* had its first German performance there on 28 March 1913, and *Parsifal* was performed in Berlin for the first time on 1 January 1914.

The Charlottenburg opera found itself in great difficulties after the end of the war, as a result of revolution and the economic crisis. Many artists, including the director Hartmann, went to the USA. In 1923 the conductor Leo Blech succeeded Hartmann but stayed only a year, and there was then an interregnum. Finally the city of Berlin took over the theatre in 1925, renaming it the Städtische Oper. Bruno Walter, previously in charge of the Munich company, became musical director, with Heinz Tietjen (formerly of the Breslau theatre) as director. Walter opened the renovated theatre on 18 September 1925 with *Die Meistersinger.* He directed several major works in the repertory and had great ambitions for the theatre, bringing members of his former Munich company, including Maria Ivogün, to Berlin. Soon there was talk of the 'Walter miracle' and the Städtische Oper was regarded as a serious rival of the 'Linden-Oper'.

Besides operas by Wagner, Strauss and Mozart, less familiar works featured in the repertory, including Tchaikovsky's *The Queen of Spades*, Wolf's *Der Corregidor*, Verdi's *Falstaff* (rarely performed at the time on German stages) and Pfitzner's *Der arme Heinrich.* Mozart was at the heart of Walter's artistic achievement. New works conducted by Fritz Zweig were also given at the Städtische Oper, including Busoni's *Die Brautwahl*, Janáček's *Kát'a Kabanová*, Zemlinsky's *Der Zwerg*, Krenek's *Jonny spielt auf* in 1927, and Kurt Weill's *Der Protagonist* and *Der Zar lässt sich photographieren* in 1928. The Städtische Oper did not concentrate on modern composers as did the Kroll Oper, the city's experimental company, but it offered excellent casts, including such singers as Maria Müller, Lotte Schöne, Sigrid Onegin, Alexander Kipnis and Maria Ivogün.

In 1926 Heinz Tietjen took over the direction of the Staatsoper, but he remained director of the Städtische Oper. Increasing tension between Walter and Tietjen led to a crisis and in 1929 Walter left, with a farewell production of *Fidelio.* The next two years were an interim period, during which there were outstanding guest performances by La Scala under Toscanini (1929) and by the Dyagilev ballet. Leo Blech returned as a guest conductor and Wilhelm Furtwängler conducted *Tristan und Isolde*, *Don Giovanni* (designed by Max Slevogt) and *Lohengrin* (directed by Tietjen, with Emil Preetorius as stage designer).

In 1931 Carl Ebert, from Darmstadt, a successful man of the theatre, was appointed as the new director; his business manager, Rudolf Bing, accompanied him to Berlin. With his first production, Verdi's *Macbeth* conducted by Fritz Stiedry and designed by Caspar Neher, Ebert struck a theatrical note that was to be characteristic of his work. He also invited other famous directors, including Jürgen Fehling and Gustav Gründgens, to the theatre. Ebert himself directed the first performance of Kurt Weill's *Die Bürgschaft* (1932), among other works, and the same year saw the first performance of Franz Schreker's *Der Schmied von Gent.* Ebert's production of *Un ballo in maschera*, conducted by Fritz Busch and again with Caspar Neher as designer, was regarded as an artistic peak. In February 1933, after Hitler's seizure of power, Ebert directed *Der fliegende Holländer.* Soon afterwards he emigrated, and it was not long before the conductors Fritz Stiedry and Paul Breisach left the country, as well as Alexander Kipnis and many other singers.

The composer Max von Schillings took over the direction of the theatre in 1933. He died the same year, and was succeeded by Wilhelm Rode, who had been singing leading baritone roles at the Städtische Oper (now renamed Deutsches Opernhaus) since 1926. Under Nazi rule the high dramatic standards maintained by Ebert sank to the level of pleasing arrangements. However, the musical standard remained high, with singers such as Michael Bohnen, Walther Ludwig, Günther Treptow, Karl Schmitt-Walter and Irma Beilke.

In 1943 the conductor Hans Schmidt-Isserstedt succeeded Rode as opera director (and general director the following year). He recruited two young artists into his team: the director Günther Rennert and the conductor Leopold Ludwig. On 23 November 1943 the Deutsches Opernhaus was destroyed in a bombing raid. Productions continued, staged in the Admiralspalast, until the autumn of 1944, when all German theatres were closed.

After World War II the company resumed its activity, thanks to the initiative of Michael Bohnen, who had been a member of the ensemble since 1935. Reverting to the name of the Städtische Oper, it found new accommodation in the Theater des Westens, which had suffered little damage, and opened on 4 September 1945 with *Fidelio.* Bohnen retired from the post of director in 1947, and there was a transitional period, during which modern opera appeared in the repertory with Britten's *Peter Grimes.* On 1 August 1948 Tietjen returned as director of the Städtische Oper. In his first season he presented two outstanding artists in the company's première of Verdi's *Don Carlos*: the conductor Ferenc Fricsay, who was music director of the theatre until

1952, and Josef Greindl singing the part of Philip II. The young Dietrich Fischer-Dieskau, who had recently been engaged, sang Posa. After a ten-year break, Leo Blech returned in the 1949–50 season. On 23 September 1952 Boris Blacher's ballet-opera *Preussisches Märchen* was given its first performance. When Fricsay left, criticism of Tietjen's direction became increasingly open. He left his post and was succeeded in 1954 by Carl Ebert, who had been forced to emigrate in the 1930s by the Nazis. Ebert (who was still artistic director of the Glyndebourne Festival Opera), began his first Berlin season with a new production of Verdi's *Nabucco*. Mozart and Verdi were the mainstays of his repertory. He engaged Wilhelm Reinking as principal designer; other designers who worked with him were Caspar Neher, Jean-Pierre Ponnelle and Ita Maximovna. As well as guest conductors such as Karl Böhm, André Cluytens, Hermann Scherchen and Vittorio Gui, Ebert brought young artists into the company, including Silvio Varviso and Berislav Klobucar. One of Ebert's significant achievements was the founding of an opera studio to train young singers. Under his direction the Städtische Oper became the leading company in Berlin and soon had a leading position in international music. Among the most important artistic events of these years were the first performance of Henze's *König Hirsch*, under Hermann Scherchen, on 23 September 1956 and Gustav Rudolf Sellner's production of Schoenberg's *Moses und Aron* in 1959, also under the musical direction of Scherchen.

In 1961, the year when the wall that was to divide the city of Berlin until 1989 was built, the new opera house in the Bismarckstrasse (1885 seats; designed by Fritz Bornemann; *see* THEATRE ARCHITECTURE, fig.8) opened on 24 September with Mozart's *Don Giovanni*, and the company's occupation of the Theater des Westens came to an end. Carl Ebert directed the new production, with Fricsay as conductor and Dietrich Fischer-Dieskau in the title role. Sellner was appointed the new general director of the theatre, henceforth known as the Deutsche Oper Berlin, and held the post for 11 years, until 1972.

The opening production was followed by the première of Klebe's *Alkmene* on 25 September 1961. Wieland Wagner brought dramatic emphasis to his production of Verdi's *Aida*. Among outstanding premières given by the company in the Sellner years were those of Aribert Reimann's *Melusine* (1971; première at Schwetzingen in the same year), Henze's *Der junge Lord* (1965), Isang Yun's *Der Traum des Liu-Tung* (1965), Haubenstock-Ramati's *Amerika* (1966) and Blacher's *Zweihunderttausend Taler* (1969). Under Sellner the theatre consistently encouraged contemporary operatic writing.

Egon Seefehlner took over as general director for the 1972–3 season. On 23 October 1972, at the Berlin Festival, the Deutsche Oper gave the first performance of Fortner's *Elisabeth Tudor*, and following the first performance of Nabokov's *Love's Labour's Lost* in Brussels (1973) the Berlin company mounted its own production. In 1976 Egon Seefehlner moved to Vienna; his successor in Berlin was the cellist Siegfried Palm, an outstanding interpreter of new music. His appointment was controversial and the innovations he was expected to make did not materialize. This period saw the first performance of Dieter Siebert's *Der Untergang der Titanic* and a new production by Nikolaus Lehnhoff of Debussy's *La chute de la maison Usher*.

In 1981 the internationally famous director Götz Friedrich, a pupil of Walter Felsenstein, under whom he had worked at the Komische Oper in Berlin for many years, became general director of the Deutsche Oper. He described his approach as one of 'progressive cosmopolitanism', opening the repertory to a wide range of works and innovative stagings, and engaging singers of international repute. This cosmopolitanism bore fruit in the first performances of Antonio Bibalo's *Fräulein Julie* in the new instrumental version (1984), Wolfgang Rihm's *Oedipus* (1987) and Henze's *Das verratene Meer* (1990); in the revivals and first performances by the company of Korngold's *Die tote Stadt*, Rihm's *Jakob Lenz* and Bernd Alois Zimmermann's *Die Soldaten*; in the consistent attention paid to the operas of Janáček; and in the work of such directors as Günter Krämer, Hans Neuenfels, Jürgen Freyer and John Dew. Friedrich set a high standard in his theatre with his own productions, which included a *Ring* cycle.

Musical standards at the Deutsche Oper have always been determined by great conductors as well as by great singers. The names of Ferenc Fricsay, Karl Böhm, Eugen Jochum, Heinrich Hollreiser, Horst Stein, Lorin Maazel, Daniel Barenboim, Gerd Albrecht, Jesus López-Cobos (appointed music director by Friedrich 1981–90) are closely linked with the company. Friedrich appointed Giuseppe Sinopoli general music director in 1990, but because of contractual disagreements he did not take up the post. Guest conductors have included Claudio Abbado, Herbert von Karajan, Hermann Scherchen, Marek Janowski, Carlos Kleiber and Charles Mackerras. Walther Hagen-Groll, chorus master for many years, left his artistic mark on the company.

5. Poster for the first East Berlin production of the three-act version of Berg's 'Lulu' by the Komische Oper, directed by Joachim Herz in 1980

The Deutsche Oper has given guest performances in countries throughout the world, including Japan, Sweden, the USA, Greece, the Netherlands and Yugoslavia. Friedrich, as director, initiated close contacts with the Los Angeles Music Center. Following the peaceful revolution in East Germany and the demolition of the Berlin Wall, the Deutsche Oper has been affected by the political changes; its position in a city no longer divided is essentially unchanged, but is likely to alter as closer cooperation between the Berlin opera houses develops.

(iii) Komische Oper. The Komische Oper was founded in 1947 by the Austrian director Walter Felsenstein as a postwar realization of the aborted pre-war Kroll Oper experiment. Based in the flamboyant Metropoltheater (a pre-war venue for operetta, musicals and revues), the Komische Oper was to be a radical extension of the Volksoper concept, in which works of modest proportions (no big Wagner or Strauss operas) were to be treated as 'realistiches Musiktheater'. Although he had worked for the Nazis, Felsenstein found ideal working conditions in communist East Berlin, where manpower was no object and productions could be rehearsed and finely honed for months on end. Felsenstein's productions of *Die Zauberflöte*, Offenbach's *Les contes d'Hoffmann* and *Barbe-bleue*, *Otello*, *The Cunning Little Vixen* and Britten's *A Midsummer Night's Dream* won international attention for their highly theatrical and psychologically penetrating 'Personenregie'. Felsenstein created a 'school' of East German opera production, whose most celebrated alumni are Joachim Herz (Intendant of the Komische Oper, 1976–81, in succession to the founder-director), Götz Friedrich and Harry Kupfer, the Komische Oper's chief director, who succeeded Herz in 1981. The policy of the Komische Oper has remained true to the principles of Klemperer's Kroll Oper, with brilliantly acted – if moderately sung – performances of the medium-size classics and new works, among them Udo Zimmermann's *Der Schuhu und die fliegende Prinzessin* and Siegfried Matthus's *Judith* (1985).

(iv) Other opera. After World War I operetta, musical theatre and revue were all eagerly cultivated in Berlin and encouraged the rise of Berlin cabaret in the 1920s with a strong element of political satire set off by music with a sweet-sour flavour strongly influenced by jazz; its most lasting and influential product was Weill's *Die Dreigroschenoper*, performed at the Theater am Schiffbauerdamm in August 1928.

In 1922 the Theater des Westens was renamed the Grosse Volksoper and the repertory was expanded to include works by Handel and Russian composers. In the decade 1935–45, as the Institut der Arbeitsfront, it gave some notable performances conducted by Erich Orthmann. After serving as the house for the Städtische Oper between 1945 and 1961, the theatre has since been used for performances of plays, operettas and musicals by visiting ensembles.

*

[C. A. von Bertram]: *Ueber die Kochische Schauspielergesellschaft: aus Berlin an einen Freund* (Berlin and Leipzig, 1771)

C. M. Plümicke: *Entwurf einer Theatergeschichte von Berlin, nebst allgemeine Bemerkungen über den Geschmack, hiesige Theaterschriftsteller und Behandlung der Kunst, in den verschiedenen Epochen* (Berlin and Stettin, 1781)

L. Schneider: *Geschichte der Oper und des Königlichen Opernhauses in Berlin* (Berlin, 1852)

A. E. Brachvogel: *Geschichte des Königlichen Theaters zu Berlin* (Berlin, 1877–8)

A. Raeder: *Kroll: ein Beitrag zur Berliner Cultur- und Theatergeschichte* (Berlin, 1894)

O. Weddigen: *Geschichte der Berliner Theater* (Berlin, 1899)

W. Altmann: 'Zur Geschichte der Königlichen preussischen Hofkapelle', *Die Musik*, iii (1903), 1–227

C. Sachs: *Musikgeschichte der Stadt Berlin bis zum Jahre 1800* (Berlin, 1908)

——: *Musik und Oper am kurbrandenburgischen Hofe* (Berlin, 1910)

A. Weissmann: *Berlin als Musikstadt: Geschichte der Oper und des Konzerts 1740–1911* (Berlin and Leipzig, 1911)

G. Lenzewski: *Die Hohenzollern in der Musikgeschichte des 18. Jahrhunderts* (Berlin, 1926)

G. Born: *Die Gründung des Berliner Nationaltheaters und die Geschichte seines Personals, seines Spielplans und seiner Verwaltung bis zu Döbbelins Abgang (1786–1789)* (Borna-Leipzig, 1934)

H. Graf: *Das Repertoire der öffentichen Opern- und Singspielbühnen in Berlin seit dem Jahre 1771*, i (Berlin, 1934)

O. Schrenk: *Berlin und die Musik: 200 Jahre Musikleben einer Stadt 1740–1940* (Berlin, 1940)

A. Yorke-Long: 'Frederick the Great of Prussia', *Music at Court: Four Eighteenth Century Studies* (London, 1954), 97–147

H. Fetting: *Die Geschichte der Deutschen Staatsoper* (Berlin, 1955)

H. A. Frenzel: *Brandenburg-preussiche Schlosstheater: Spielorte und Spielformen vom 17. bis zum 19. Jahrhundert* (Berlin, 1959)

E. E. Helm: *Music at the Court of Frederick the Great* (Norman, OK, 1960)

W. Otto: *Geschichte der Deutschen Staatsoper Berlin: von der Gründung der Kapelle bis zur Gegenwart* (Berlin, 1961, 3/1969)

P. Heyworth: *Conversations with Klemperer* (London, 1973, 2/1985)

H. Curjel: *Experiment Krolloper*, ed. E. Kruttge (Munich, 1975)

H. Kühn, ed.: *Preussen – dein Spree-Athen: Beiträge zu Literatur, Theater und Musik in Berlin* (Reinbek, 1981) [exhibition brochure]

P. Heyworth: *Otto Klemperer: his Life and Times*, i (Cambridge, 1983)

G. Huwe, ed.: *Die Deutsche Oper Berlin* (Berlin, 1984)

T. Bauman: *North German Opera in the Age of Goethe* (Cambridge, 1985)

H. Becker: 'Friedrich der Grosse und die Musik', *Preussens grosse König*, ed. W. Treue (Freiburg, 1986), 150–61

25 Jahre Deutsche Oper Berlin: eine Dokumentation der Premieren von 1961 bis 1986 (Berlin, 1986)

J. H. Sutcliffe: '25 Jahre Deutsche Oper Berlin: Betrachtungen eines Zugereisten', *Deutsche Oper Berlin aktuell* (1986–7), passim [pubn of the Deutsche Oper]

W. Otto: 'Das Deutsche Opernhaus 1912–1925', ibid (1987–8), passim

R. Freydank: *Theater in Berlin (von den Anfängen bis 1945)* (Berlin, 1988)

THOMAS BAUMAN (1),
HEINZ BECKER, RICHARD D. GREEN (2, 3: iv),
HUGH CANNING (3: i, iii), IMRE FABIAN (3: ii)

Berlin, Irving [Baline, Israel] (*b* Mogilyov, 29 April/11 May 1888; *d* New York, 22 Sept 1989). American composer of Russian birth. The son of an impoverished Jewish cantor, he was taken to America at the age of five. His father died when he was 13, and a year later he ran away from home, rather than be a burden to his mother. He sang for pennies outside cabarets, became a chorus boy, a stooge in vaudeville, a song plugger and a singing waiter. Berlin had no formal musical training, but taught himself to play the piano, if only in one key, F♯. He began churning out songs, usually serving as his own lyricist, and finally caught America's ear with 'Alexander's Ragtime Band' in 1911.

Berlin's first complete stage work, *Watch your Step* (1914), purported to be the first musical written entirely in ragtime. Purists would argue that that was not strictly so, but cannot dispute that Berlin played a major role in making ragtime popular, just as the real genre was fading away. The show's hit was 'Simple melody'. Between *Watch your Step* and *Mr President* (1962) Berlin wrote all or most of the songs for 19 other Broadway shows. *Stop! Look! Listen!* (1915) included 'I love a piano' and 'The girl on the magazine cover' while *Yip, Yip, Yaphank*, performed by soldiers in 1918, gave us 'Mandy' and 'Oh, how I hate to get up in the morning'. His numerous contributions to several *Ziegfeld Follies* and *Music Box Revues* included 'All alone', 'Lady of the evening', 'A pretty girl is like a melody', 'Say it with music', 'Shaking the blues away', 'You'd be surprised' and 'What'll I do?'. *Face the Music* (1932) is remembered for 'Soft lights and sweet music', and *As Thousands Cheer* (1933) for 'Easter parade' and 'Heat wave'. 'It's a lovely day tomorrow' came from *Louisiana Purchase* (1940). In World War II, the all-soldier show *This is the Army* (1942) presented 'I left my heart at the stage door canteen' and 'This is the Army, Mr Jones'.

Berlin's most successful musical was *Annie Get your Gun* (1946). Based very freely on the life of Annie Oakley, the show was originally to have had music by Kern; he died while working on it, and Berlin replaced him. At the first performance Ethel Merman sang the title role and Ray Middleton played Frank. *Annie* has entered the repertory of opera companies in the USA, and the Vienna Volksoper. The hit of his last success, *Call me Madam* (1950), was 'You're just in love'. Berlin also created the music for many films. He always kept abreast of the latest in musical fashions and constantly composed memorable, musically inventive songs in the idiom of the moment.

Some detractors have suggested that his work was too often lacking in subtlety, but careful analysis of his seemingly simple tunes and lyrics usually shows a knowing, complex artistry hidden behind the deceptive façade. As an example, one could cite the marvellous harmonic modulations in 'A pretty girl is like a melody'. Berlin's remarkable ear and his often underrated inventiveness in the face of rapidly changing styles led his contemporary Jerome Kern to conclude: 'Irving Berlin has no *place* in American music; he *is* American music'.

musicals, for which Berlin wrote all or much of the score; lyrics by Berlin (names of librettists given in parentheses); dates are of first New York performance

Watch your Step (H. B. Smith), New Amsterdam, 8 Dec 1914
Stop! Look! Listen! (Smith), Globe, 25 Dec 1915
The Cocoanuts (G. S. Kaufman), Lyric, 8 Dec 1925
Face the Music (M. Hart), New Amsterdam, 17 Feb 1932
Louisiana Purchase (M. Ryskind), Imperial, 28 May 1940
Annie Get your Gun (H. Fields and D. Fields), Imperial, 16 May 1946
Miss Liberty (R. Sherwood), Imperial, 15 July 1949
Call me Madam (H. Lindsay and R. Crouse), Imperial, 12 Oct 1950
Mr President (Lindsay and Crouse), St James, 20 Oct 1962

*

A. Woollcott: *The Story of Irving Berlin* (New York, 1925)
D. Ewen: *The Story of Irving Berlin* (New York, 1950)
M. Freedland: *Irving Berlin* (New York, 1974)
L. Bergreen: *As Thousands Cheer* (New York, 1990)
R. H. Kornick: *Recent American Opera: a Production Guide* (New York, 1991)

GERALD BORDMAN

Berlioz, (Louis-)Hector (*b* La Côte-St-André, Isère, 11 Dec 1803; *d* Paris, 8 March 1869). French composer and writer on music. As essayist, coach and conductor he often found himself occupied with the central operatic repertory of his time; two of his three operatic masterpieces, however, demanded more in musicianship and staging than could be properly accommodated during his lifetime.

1. Life, 1803–40. 2. Life, 1841–51. 3. Life, 1852–69. 4. Literary and operatic achievements.

1. Life, 1803–40. Among Berlioz's earliest efforts in composition were guitar accompaniments to airs from popular *opéras comiques*, a repertory brought to La Côte-St-André primarily by a succession of municipal bandmasters. Berlioz eventually assembled some of his settings of Dalayrac, Catrufo, Boieldieu, Berton, Dellamaria and the like in a manuscript *Recueil de romances*. In November 1821 he went to Paris, where he spent two years as a reluctant and unsatisfactory medical student. Within days of his arrival in the capital he began his long and encyclopedic career of opera-going by attending productions of Salieri, Méhul, Dalayrac and, most significantly, Gluck; later his vivid memory of the vocal style of Mme Branchu, Dérivis, Nourrit and their colleagues helped shape his own Gluck productions as well as some of the characterizations in *Les Troyens*. The works of Gluck and Spontini, absorbed first by ear and then by diligent study of scores, formed his style well before the thunderstrokes of 1827 and 1828 – Shakespeare and Beethoven – that led to the *Symphonie fantastique*. In 1823 he gave up medicine for music, and found in Jean-François Le Sueur, his composition teacher, an accomplished exponent of opera from the Napoleonic era.

Throughout the 1820s projects for operas came and went: a 'Richard en Palestine' after Scott's *The Talisman*, a 'Robin Hood', an 'Atala' after Chateaubriand and so forth. In 1825–6 Berlioz composed the three-act *Les francs-juges* to a libretto by a friend, Humbert Ferrand. In neither its original form nor its revision of 1829 was it produced, and eventually Berlioz destroyed much of the score. But the overture, his first published orchestral composition, was widely performed and studied. The 'Marche au supplice' from the *Symphonie fantastique* is apparently based on a scene from *Les francs-juges*.

The Prix de Rome, which he won at his fourth attempt, took Berlioz to Italy (1831–2), where he was an avid but almost inevitably disappointed opera-goer. In Florence he heard Bellini's *I Capuleti e i Montecchi* and in a subsequent hostile review outlined an alternative treatment remarkably similar to the plan he later adopted for his own symphony *Roméo et Juliette*. In Naples he went to the Teatro S Carlo and Teatro del Fondo; on his journey back to France in May 1832 he heard *La sonnambula* in Florence, *L'elisir d'amore* in Milan and an unidentified work in Turin.

'Battering down the doors of the Opéra' was Berlioz's paramount goal upon returning to Paris in late 1832. This assault was delayed somewhat by his courtship of the actress Harriet Smithson, whom he married in October 1833, and by Paganini's commissioning of a viola concerto (the work that became *Harold en Italie*); but by spring 1834 Berlioz had begun to compose *Benvenuto Cellini*, a subject apparently suggested by Alfred de Vigny. *Cellini* was composed with comparative ease, even abandon, though opportunities to concentrate on it were limited by Berlioz's increasing activities as journalist and promoter of his own symphonic concerts.

The original libretto was declined by the Opéra-Comique; the acceptance of *Cellini* at the Opéra coincided with the alliance between Berlioz and the powerful Bertin family, his employers at the *Journal des débats*. Among his services to them was to supervise rehearsals at the Opéra for Louise Bertin's *Esmeralda*, an experience that stood him in good stead when *Cellini* reached production. (It was rumoured that his contribution to *Esmeralda* was substantial and that Quasimodo's bell song in Act 4 was his own; he admitted only to having suggested adjustments to its conclusion.) *Benvenuto Cellini* was completed by spring 1837 but waited for production until September 1838. In the interim the Requiem was composed and performed.

Cellini is, as Berlioz often held, a work of exceptional exuberance and verve, and warranted a better reception than it got. It was also, however, of surpassing technical difficulty. Moreover, Madame Dorus-Gras, the soprano, was due for a holiday shortly after the première; by the time she returned Duprez, the tenor, had resigned his role, finding Berlioz's 'gift', as he later put it, 'not precisely melodic'. *Cellini* had only four complete performances, three in September 1838 and one in January 1839.

2. LIFE, 1841–51. It is one of the ironies of Berlioz's career that his conquest of the Opéra was successful only with works of other composers. The first of these was Weber's *Der Freischütz*, produced as *Le Freyschutz* in 1841. Berlioz's contribution was to set the spoken dialogue as recitative and to provide the *ballet-divertissement*. For the ballet he chose excerpts from *Preciosa* and *Oberon* and orchestrated Weber's *Aufforderung zum Tanz*; this latter, as *L'invitation à la valse*, enjoyed great popularity in the concert hall. Wagner, writing from Paris to one of the Dresden papers, was hostile to the concept and its execution, but Berlioz was right in imagining that a less sympathetic hand would have agreed to it had he not undertaken the task. *Le Freyschutz* remained in the repertory for years, with the composer's royalties going to Berlioz – a source of supplementary income but, when he was told of the widow Weber's financial plight, of embarrassment as well.

As a symphonist Berlioz had enjoyed immense success with *Roméo et Juliette* in 1839; he had achieved prominence as a composer of music for national ceremony with the Requiem (1837) and the *Grande symphonie funèbre et triomphale* (1840); he was becoming a celebrated conductor. It was in the context of this growing national prestige that he was, at last, offered a libretto by Scribe. But the mediocre and for mulaic text of *La nonne sanglante* failed to stimulate his best thinking, and Scribe and Berlioz were never close

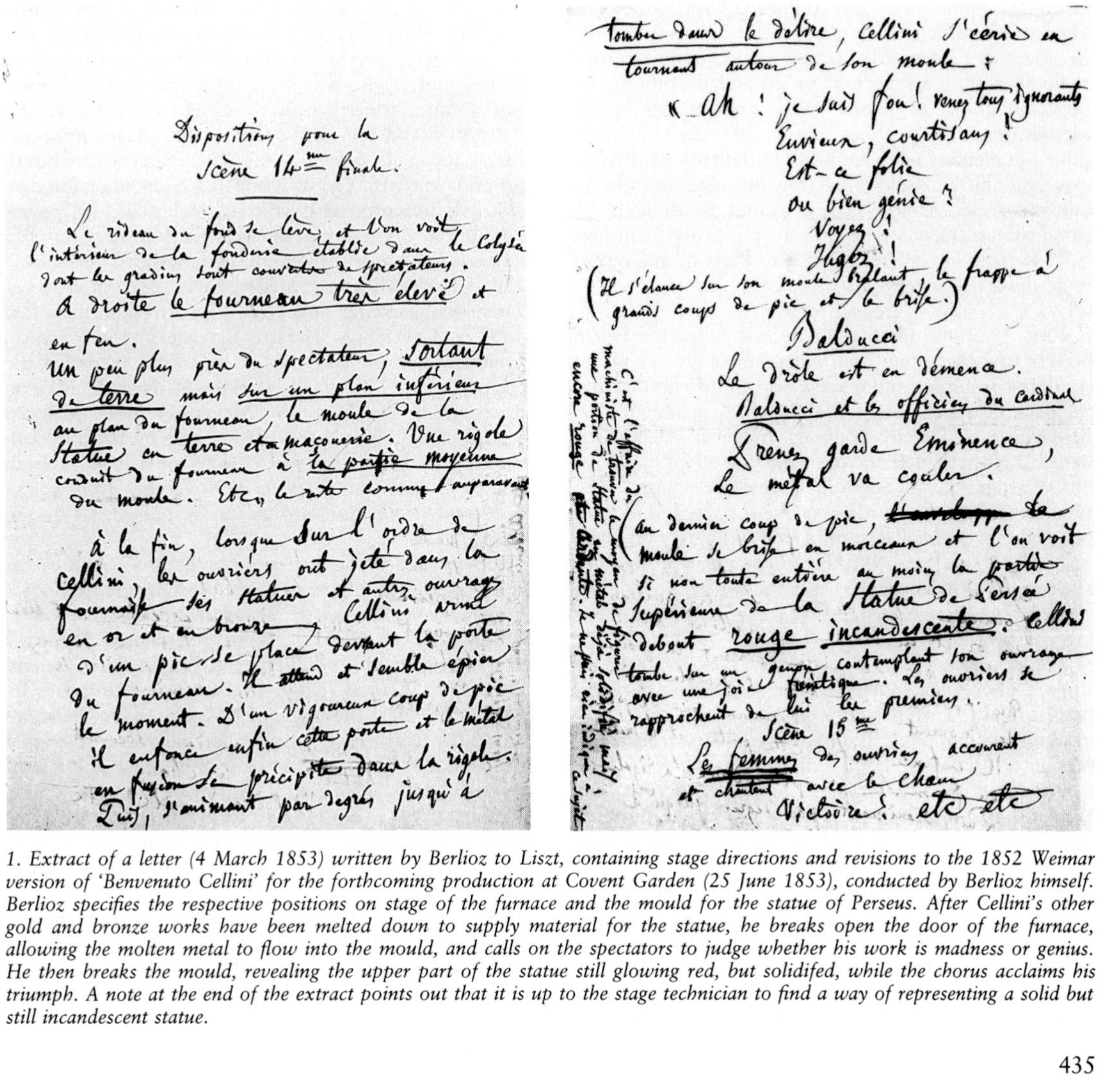

Dispositions pour la
Scène 14me finale.

Le rideau du fond se lève, et l'on voit l'intérieur de la fonderie établie dans le Colysée dont les gradins sont couverts de spectateurs. A droite le fourneau très élevé et en feu. Un peu plus près du spectateur, sortant de terre mais sur un plan inférieur au plan du fourneau, le moule de la Statue en terre et maçonnerie. Une rigole conduit du fourneau à la partie moyenne du moule. Etc, le reste comme auparavant.

à la fin, lorsque sur l'ordre de Cellini, les ouvriers ont jeté dans la fournaise ses statues et autres ouvrages en or et en bronze, Cellini armé d'un pic se place devant la porte du fourneau. Il attend et semble épier le moment. D'un vigoureux coup de pic il enfonce enfin cette porte et le métal en fusion se précipite dans la rigole, qu'il illumine par degrés jusqu'à

tomber dans le délire, Cellini s'écrie en tournant autour de son moule :
« Ah ! je suis fou ! venez tous ignorants
Envieux, courtisans !
Est-ce folie
ou bien génie ?
Voyez !
Jugez ! »
(Il s'élance sur son moule brûlant, le frappe à grands coups de pic, et le brise.)
Balducci
Le drôle est en démence.
Balducci et les officiers du Cardinal
Prenez garde Eminence,
Le métal va couler.
(au dernier coup de pic, le moule se brise en morceaux et l'on voit si non toute entière au moins la partie supérieure de la Statue de Persée rouge incandescente. Cellini debout tombe sur un genou contemplant son ouvrage avec une joie frénétique. Les ouvriers se rapprochent de lui les premiers.
Scène 15me
Les femmes des ouvriers accourent et chantent avec le chœur Victoire ! etc etc

C'est l'affaire du machiniste de trouver le moyen de figurer une portion de statue déjà solidifiée mais encore rouge [illegible]

1. *Extract of a letter (4 March 1853) written by Berlioz to Liszt, containing stage directions and revisions to the 1852 Weimar version of 'Benvenuto Cellini' for the forthcoming production at Covent Garden (25 June 1853), conducted by Berlioz himself. Berlioz specifies the respective positions on stage of the furnace and the mould for the statue of Perseus. After Cellini's other gold and bronze works have been melted down to supply material for the statue, he breaks open the door of the furnace, allowing the molten metal to flow into the mould, and calls on the spectators to judge whether his work is madness or genius. He then breaks the mould, revealing the upper part of the statue still glowing red, but solidifed, while the chorus acclaims his triumph. A note at the end of the extract points out that it is up to the stage technician to find a way of representing a solid but still incandescent statue.*

enough intellectually to encourage the resolution of their differences. (Afterwards, Berlioz fashioned his own librettos for parts of *La damnation de Faust* and all of *L'enfance du Christ*, *Les Troyens* and *Béatrice et Bénédict*.) Berlioz worked seriously at *La nonne sanglante* in late 1841 and dabbled at it occasionally thereafter, eventually completing several movements. Nothing was ever performed, however, and at his death the incomplete manuscript sat alongside the fragments of *Les francs-juges*, awaiting whatever re-use might have seemed appropriate. Scribe's libretto eventually passed to Gounod, whose *La nonne sanglante* was produced in 1854.

Berlioz's operatic misadventures reached their climax in 1847–8, shortly after the failure in December 1846 of the 'légende dramatique' *La damnation de Faust*. He was an obvious candidate to succeed Habeneck as chief conductor at the Opéra, but in the reorganization that followed the collapse of Léon Pillet's administration in 1847 Berlioz was offered nothing more than the menial job of chorus master. He declined, and instead accepted what appeared to be a lucrative contract as music director of Louis Jullien's new opera company at Drury Lane, London. He would reside in London for six months each year, to conduct operas and orchestral concerts and from time to time to compose a new opera. The London company opened in December 1847 with *Lucia di Lammermoor* and continued with Balfe's *The Maid of Honour*, Donizetti's *Linda di Chamounix* and *Le nozze di Figaro*. For his new opera Berlioz turned again to Scribe, asking him to expand the libretto of *La damnation de Faust* into a three-act opera, *Méphistophélès*. Nothing came of the initiative. Jullien's company went bankrupt and dissolved; Berlioz was paid little, if anything, for his nine months in England. The *Mémoires* were begun in these bleak circumstances, concurrent with the political disruptions of 1848. In mid-July he returned to Paris to attempt to re-establish his career.

3. Life, 1852–69. During the decade following *Faust*, Berlioz travelled often and widely through Europe to conduct concerts of his works; his rate of composition declined proportionately. Liszt's 1852 production of *Benvenuto Cellini* in Weimar, however, demanded Berlioz's participation and in turn focussed his compositional attention on operatic issues once more. The Weimar *Cellini* was a project of the Futurists, the result of a colloquy and collaboration that ultimately involved not just Berlioz, Liszt and the Weimar performers but Hans von Bülow, Cornelius, Raff and Richard Pohl as well. 'Honneur aux ciseleurs!' Liszt wrote of the opening, that March, to Berlioz in London: '[*Cellini*] is one of the strongest works I know'. By November 1852, when it was revived in the composer's presence during a Berlioz Week, *Cellini* had been recast into three acts from the original two acts and four tableaux of the Paris version. In London the following summer it fell victim to what amounted to widespread public impatience for authentic Italian bel canto. Berlioz withdrew it after a single performance, on 25 June 1853, interrupted at every turn by jeers from the audience.

In 1854 Harriet Smithson died, and seven months later Berlioz married the singer Marie Recio, who had been his mistress for some 12 years. His frequent visits to Weimar in the 1850s culminated in February 1856 in yet another revival of *Benvenuto Cellini* (the version preserved in the Choudens full score of 1886). There the Princess Carolyne Sayn-Wittgenstein slowly but deliberately brought Berlioz to the point of undertaking a new opera on a 'grandiose, magnificent and profoundly moving subject', Virgil's *Aeneid*. Berlioz began to allude to it after his visit of 1855; in 1856 the princess told him not to return if he shrank from the task.

Once begun, *Les Troyens* was accomplished with an intensity of purpose that, far from killing him (as Gounod had it), doubtless prolonged his life. By June he had fashioned a libretto. After yielding to the temptation of setting the Act 4 love duet, 'Nuit d'ivresse' (see fig.2), he went back to compose the long score number by number, act by act, more methodically than he had ever worked before. *Les Troyens* embraced not just Virgilian epic but other passions as well: the dialogue of Lorenzo and Jessica from Act 5 of *The Merchant of Venice* for the love duet; a scene based on a painting by Guérin for the tableau just preceding; thoughts of his mariner son, Louis, for the song of Hylas in Act 5, and of Harriet and Louis for the breathtaking mute appearance in Act 1 of Andromache and Astyanax, widow and son respectively of Berlioz's namesake, Hector. By April 1858, to all intents and purposes, his great undertaking was done.

In August 1859 Berlioz conducted excerpts from *Les Troyens* at his annual concert in Baden-Baden; the enthusiastic critical reception established a momentum that should have led to a production at the Opéra. But he was unsuccessful in attracting the patronage of Napoleon III, who was more interested in *Tannhäuser*. For a time, nevertheless, it seemed certain that *Les Troyens* would open at the Opéra, the only institution in France (said its director, Alphonse Royer) capable of properly staging 'a great work of a talented ... honourable and honoured man, who has on his side, moreover, both public opinion and the entire European press'. But this was to no avail. At length, with Berlioz's permission and assistance, the last three acts were excerpted as *Les Troyens à Carthage* and given 21 performances in late 1863 at Carvalho's Théâtre Lyrique in the Place du Châtelet. Berlioz was too ill to attend many of the performances but, much to his satisfaction, his son Louis went to them all. Meyerbeer saw a dozen performances. Ironically, Berlioz had meanwhile contributed to successful productions of Gluck at both houses in question: *Orphée* in November 1859 at the Théâtre Lyrique and *Alceste* in October 1861 at the Opéra.

Princess Carolyne had pressed Berlioz to return to Shakespeare for his next opera, perhaps a 'Roméo et Juliette' or a 'Cléopâtre'. Instead he ended his career with *Béatrice et Bénédict*, an operatic scherzo composed to inaugurate the new theatre in Baden-Baden, where since 1856 Berlioz had offered summer concerts. Its merriment and brevity made *Béatrice et Bénédict* successful from the first; after the première in August 1862, Richard Pohl presented it in Weimar and it was revived in Baden the following season. The performances in August 1863 were Berlioz's last conducting appearances anywhere near home and his farewell to a spirited holiday public that had always given him life.

The publisher Choudens chose to ignore specific provisions in Berlioz's will for the publication in full score of *Benvenuto Cellini* and *Les Troyens*. A lawsuit of the composer's heirs forced the firm to engrave and print the scores (*Les Troyens à Carthage*, 1885;

2. *Autograph drafts (July 1856) for the first and second versions (in D♭ and G♭) of the duet 'Nuit d'ivresse' in Act 4 of Berlioz's 'Les Troyens'*

Benvenuto Cellini, 1886; *La prise de Troie*, 1899), but *Les Troyens* was never offered for sale. Not until a century after Berlioz's death was a complete and properly ordered full score of his masterpiece made available, that of the New Berlioz Edition.

4. LITERARY AND OPERATIC ACHIEVEMENTS. Berlioz was a powerful critic of the lyric stage. Most of his thousand or so *feuilletons* treat new operatic productions, and his best criticism – apart from the great cycle on Beethoven's symphonies – concerns Gluck, Spontini, Weber and Meyerbeer, his pantheon of masters of the stage. He knew how to use his pen to political end, occasionally promoting his own work, the career of his mistress Marie Recio or the business enterprises of his friends Sax and Alexandre; but for the most part his

assessments are apt and wise, always withering where it came to the trivial but ever welcoming of novel or imaginative device. Above all he was passionate in his admiration of the successful fusion of music and poetry.

All six of his published volumes of prose, including the *Grand traité d'instrumentation* (1843) and the *Mémoires* (1870), consist primarily of material that had appeared previously in the press. *Les soirées de l'orchestre* (1852) are tales recounted in the opera pit while the typical meretricious fare of the day is underway above; only for *Der Freischütz*, *La vestale* and the like do the musicians cease their bantering. In *A travers chants* (1862) appear Berlioz's series on Beethoven, Gluck and Weber and the important, if retrogressive, article on Wagner and the Music of the Future. His last *feuilleton* was a notice on the première of Bizet's *Les pêcheurs de perles* in October 1863.

From the beginning Berlioz was acutely sensitive to fine poetry, the power of a vivid tableau, the human passions that lie at the heart of true drama; he was, moreover, a matchless melodist. These qualities promised a good career in opera, and until *Cellini* Berlioz assumed with all the others that becoming a great composer meant achieving long runs at the Opéra. Yet other truths of the opera house he was incapable of assimilating: the collaboration and compromise that were inevitable conditions of life there, and the need to rely on craft and formula when there was no time for his genius to run its full course. The compositional strategy that came most naturally to him involved perfecting his works by repeated experience of them in performances under his own baton, and this was impossible at the Opéra. Cultivating the new, hybrid genre of the *symphonie dramatique* came therefore to take precedence, and in some respects his most interesting solutions to issues of operatic style are to be found in *Roméo et Juliette* (Friar Laurence's scene and the superb finale which follows may be compared with the best in Meyerbeer) and *La damnation de Faust* (notably in the scene and ballet of Méphistophélès and the sylphs, and in Marguerite's two arias).

With neither *Benvenuto Cellini* nor *Les Troyens* did he have his final say. *Cellini* probably works best by combining the original act structure and some of the deleted Paris music with elements of the Weimar versions; the final scene of *Les Troyens* remains unwieldy. But it was with *Cellini* that he achieved a rhythmic and metric brio only adumbrated in *Harold en Italie*; it was in *Cellini*, too, that he made conspicuous advances in orchestration and other tactics of deploying a large force of singers and instrumentalists. This is apparent, especially, in the strettos of the Act 1 trio ('A demain, à demain'), the goldsmiths' tableau ('Honneur aux maîtres ciseleurs!') and the prayer of Teresa and Ascanio with the monks' litany outside. And the whole of the Roman carnival scene – the triple *réunion des thèmes* at the beginning, the famous saltarello, the 'harlequinades and pasquarelloisms' of the pantomime in Cassandro's theatre and the chaos at the end – rivals in genius, bar for bar, the many other sensations of that fertile decade. However disappointing its public reception, *Benvenuto Cellini* was a necessary prerequisite both for *Roméo et Juliette* and, ultimately, for *Les Troyens*.

Many of the most imaginative effects in *Les Troyens* – the grand processions, the evocations of antique wind and percussion instruments, the imaginary language of the Nubian slaves, the subtle transformation of motifs and themes and the panorama of vignette and tableau – in fact reiterate discoveries from Berlioz's past. What is new is the scale: the mastery of libretto, characterization (especially in the great mezzo-soprano roles, Cassandra and Dido) and musical coherence in a work about twice the length of *Faust*. The models for his stagecraft he found in Meyerbeer and, in particular, Spontini; but the panoply of musical and poetic images, mingling as it does the composer's vision of antiquity with elements of Shakespeare, high Romanticism and personal experience, is uniquely his own. In Act 4, after allusions to Gluck (Iopas as Orpheus) and to Guérin's painting of Aeneas recounting to Dido the misfortunes of Troy, comes the inspired paraphrase from *The Merchant of Venice*. Here Dido and Aeneas linger in the perfection of mythical romance of the sort Berlioz sought so long for himself but never found. Then destiny asserts itself, and Aeneas abandons his happiness for his calling. This, too, is autobiography.

See also BÉATRICE ET BÉNÉDICT; BENVENUTO CELLINI; DAMNATION DE FAUST, LA; and TROYENS, LES.

Editions: *H. Berlioz: Werke*, ed. C. Malherbe and F. Weingartner (Leipzig, 1900–10) [B&H]
New Berlioz Edition, general ed. H. Macdonald (Kassel, 1967–) [NBE]

title	*genre, acts*	*libretto*	*composed*	*first performance*	*sources*	*remarks*	*B&H; NBE*
Estelle et Némorin	opéra	H.-C. Gerono	1823			lost	
Les francs-juges	drame lyrique, 3	H. Ferrand	1825–6	unperf.	frags., *F-Pn**, lib. *Pc*, ov. (Paris, 1836)	rev. 1829; portions adopted for 1833 as *Le cri de guerre du Brisgaw* (I. T. Gounet); 5 complete movts extant	ov., iv; iv
Benvenuto Cellini	opéra semi-seria, 2	L. de Wailly, A. Barbier and A. de Vigny	1834–7	Paris, Opéra, 10 Sept 1838	*Pc**, excerpts (Paris, 1839), vs (Brunswick, 1856)	rev. version, Weimar, Grossherzogliches Hof, 20 March 1852; in 3 acts, Weimar, 17 Nov 1852	ov., v; i
La nonne sanglante	5	E. Scribe	1841–7	unperf.	frags. *Pn**	inc.	–; iv

title	genre, acts	libretto	composed	first performance	sources	remarks	B&H; NBE
La damnation de Faust	légende dramatique, 4 pts	Berlioz and A. Gandonnière, after G. de Nerval trans. of J. W. von Goethe: *Faust*	1845–6	concert perf., Paris, OC (Favart), 6 Dec 1846	*Pc** (Paris, 1854)	incorporating rev. versions of *Huit scènes de Faust* (1829); first staged, rev. Raoul Gunsbourg, 5 acts, Monte Carlo, Opéra, 18 Feb 1893	xi–xii; viii
Les Troyens	opéra, 5	Berlioz, after Virgil: *The Aeneid*	1856–8	Les Troyens à Carthage, Paris, Théâtre Lyrique, 4 Nov 1863; complete, Karlsruhe, 6 Dec 1890	*Pc**, vs (Paris, 1862)	divided into *La prise de Troie* and *Les Troyens à Carthage* (with prol.), 1863	–; ii
Béatrice et Bénédict	opéra or oc, 2	Berlioz, after W. Shakespeare: *Much Ado about Nothing*	1860–62	Baden-Baden, Stadt, 9 Aug 1862	*Pc**, vs (Paris, 1863)		xix–xx; iii

WRITINGS

(See Holoman 1987, pp.431–88, for more detailed bibliographical information)

Grand traité d'instrumentation et d'orchestration modernes (Paris, 1843, 2/1855; Eng. trans., 1855)
Voyage musical en Allemagne et en Italie (Paris, 1844)
Les soirées de l'orchestre (Paris, 1852; Eng. trans., 1956, 2/1973); ed. L. Guichard (Paris, 1968)
Le chef d'orchestre: théorie de son art (Paris, 1856; Eng. trans., 1917)
Les grotesques de la musique (Paris, 1859); ed. L. Guichard (Paris, 1969)
A travers chants (Paris, 1862; Eng. trans., 1913–18); ed. L. Guichard (Paris, 1971)
Mémoires de Hector Berlioz (Paris, 1870; ed. and Eng. trans. by D. Cairns, 1969, 2/1977); ed. P. Citron (Paris, 1969)
Les musiciens et la musique, ed. A. Hallays (Paris, 1903)
Hector Berlioz: cauchemars et passions, ed. G. Condé (Paris, 1981)

BIBLIOGRAPHY

BIBLIOGRAPHY AND CATALOGUE

C. Hopkinson: *A Bibliography of the Musical and Literary Works of Hector Berlioz 1803–1869* (Edinburgh, 1951; 2/1980, rev. R. Macnutt)
D. K. Holoman: *Catalogue of the Works of Hector Berlioz* (Kassel, 1987)

LIFE AND WORKS

J. Barzun: *Berlioz and the Romantic Century* (Boston, 1950; rev. and abridged as *Berlioz and his Century*, New York, 1956, 3/1969)
H. Macdonald: *Berlioz* (London, 1982)
D. Cairns: *Berlioz, i: 1803–1832: the Making of an Artist* (London, 1989)
D. K. Holoman: *Berlioz* (Cambridge, MA, and London, 1989)

INDIVIDUAL WORKS

Benvenuto Cellini

J. d'Ortigue: *De l'école musicale italienne et de l'administration de l'Académie royale de musique, à l'occasion de l'opéra de M. Hector Berlioz* (Paris, 1839)
H. von Bülow: 'Benvenuto Cellini', *NZM*, lxvi (1852), 156–9, 204–8; repr. in *Ausgewählte Schriften, 1850–92* (Leipzig, 1911), 61–78
A. Barbier: *Etudes dramatiques: Jules César, Benvenuto Cellini* (Paris, 1874)
J.-G. Prod'homme: 'Les deux "Benvenuto Cellini" de Berlioz', *SIMG*, xiv (1913–14), 449–60
H. Macdonald: 'The Original "Benvenuto Cellini"', *MT*, cvii (1966), 1042–5
——: 'Benvenuto Cellini', *RdM*, lxiii (1977), 107–45
T. K. La May: 'A New Look at the Weimar Versions of *Benvenuto Cellini*', *MQ*, lxv (1979), 559–72

Les Troyens

D. Cairns: 'Berlioz and Virgil: a Consideration of "Les Troyens" as a Virgilian Opera', *PRMA*, xcv (1968–9), 97–110; repr. as 'Les Troyens and the Aeneid', *Responses: Musical Essays and Reviews* (London, 1973), 88–110; abridged as 'Berlioz and Virgil', in Kemp (1988), 76–88
H. Macdonald: 'Les Troyens at the Théâtre-Lyrique', *MT*, cx (1969), 919–21
D. Cairns: 'Les Troyens et L'Enéide', *Romantisme*, xii (1976), 43–50
J. Langford: 'Berlioz, Cassandra, and the French Operatic Tradition', *ML*, lxii (1981), 310–17
J. Rushton: 'The Overture to *Les Troyens*', *Music Analysis*, iv (1985), 119–44
I. Kemp, ed.: *Hector Berlioz: Les Troyens* (Cambridge, 1988)
L'avant-scène opéra, nos.128–9 (1990) [*Les Troyens* issue]

Béatrice et Bénédict

A. Addison: 'Beatrice and Benedict: the German Edition', *Berlioz Society Bulletin* (1960), no.33
J. Rushton: 'Berlioz's Swan-Song: towards a Criticism of *Béatrice et Bénédict*', *PRMA*, cix (1982–3), 105–18

others

M. Brenet: 'Berlioz inédit: *Les francs-juges, La nonne sanglante*', *Guide musical*, xlii (1896), 63–7
H. Kling: 'Goethe et Berlioz', *RMI*, xi (1905), 714–32
J.-G. Prod'homme: 'Wagner, Berlioz and Monsieur Scribe: Two Collaborations that Miscarried', *MQ*, xii (1926), 359–75
M. Curtiss: 'Gounod before *Faust*', *MQ*, xxxviii (1952), 48–67
A. E. F. Dickinson: 'Berlioz's "Bleeding Nun"', *MT*, cvii (1966), 584–8
D. K. Holoman: 'Les fragments de l'opéra 'perdu' de Berlioz: *Les francs-juges*', *RdM*, lxiii (1977), 78–88
L'avant-scène opéra, no.22 (1979) [*La damnation de Faust* issue]
H. Hofer: 'Faust als Frédéric Moreau bei Hector Berlioz: der Text von *La Damnation de Faust*', *Oper als Text: romanistische Beiträge zur Libretto-Forschung*, ed. A. Gier (Heidelberg, 1986)

D. KERN HOLOMAN

Berman, Eugene [Yevgeny Gustavovich] (*b* St Petersburg, 4/16 Nov 1899; *d* Rome, 14 Dec 1972). Russian, later American, stage designer. He studied painting and architecture in St Petersburg until forced to flee in 1918. He settled in Paris in 1919 and remained there for 20 years, studying painting at the Académie Ranson until 1922. Along with Christian Bérard and Pavel Chelishchev (Tchelitchew), he was identified with neo-Romanticism and its preoccupation with architectural views of landscapes and the evocative use of perspective, twin features of his stage designs. In 1937 he designed a production of Weill's *Die Dreigroschenoper* at the Théâtre de l'Etoile, Paris, and then began a series of commissions for the Ballet Russe de Monte Carlo. He emigrated to the USA in 1940, became a naturalized citizen in 1944 and finally settled in Rome in 1957.

Berman attracted attention in 1952 with his designs for a television production (NBC) of Menotti's *Amahl and the Night Visitors* and for Pergolesi's *La serva padrona*, the inaugural production at the Ringling Museum of Art's Baroque theatre in Sarasota, Florida. From 1951 to 1957 he worked on productions at the Metropolitan Opera of *Rigoletto* (1951), *La forza del destino* (1952), *Il barbiere di Siviglia* (1954) and *Don Giovanni* (1957); he also designed *Così fan tutte* for La Scala in 1956. *Otello* (1963) was his last production for the Metropolitan.

Berman rejected the abstract impressions of Adolphe Appia and Edward Gordon Craig, describing them as 'gloomy, rigid and depressing in their puritanistic primness and intellectual intolerance'. His colourful and elegant designs were brilliant mannerist illustrations that evoked crumbling architectural fantasies of earlier times.

For illustration *see* AMAHL AND THE NIGHT VISITORS.

*

A. Delarue: 'The Stage and Ballet Designs of Eugene Berman', *Dance Index*, v/5 (1946), 4–24

G. Amberg: 'The Theatre of Eugene Berman', *The Theatre of Eugene Berman* (New York, 1947), 5–6 [catalogue, Museum of Modern Art]

J. Levy: *Eugene Berman* (London, 1948)

Eugene Berman (London, 1960) [catalogue, Lefevre Galleries]

DAVID J. HOUGH

Bern (Ger.). BERNE.

Bernabei, Giuseppe Antonio (*b* Rome, ?1649; *d* Munich, 9 March 1732). Italian composer. He was the elder son of Ercole Bernabei (*b* Caprarola, 1622; *d* Munich, 5 Dec 1687), court Kapellmeister to Elector Ferdinand Maria of Bavaria at Munich from 1674 and the composer of five operas there (the music is all lost but two librettos survive, from 1680 and 1686). Giuseppe Antonio, who studied with his father, followed him to Munich in 1677 as vice-Kapellmeister. In 1688 he succeeded to the post of Hofkapellmeister, which he held for the rest of his life. He composed most of his operas during the first decade of the reign of the art-loving Elector Max Emanuel (1680–1726). At that time his great rival in opera was Agostino Steffani, the chamber music director. The appointment of Max Emanuel as Statthalter of the Netherlands in 1691 led to the closing of the Munich court opera, and thereafter Bernabei devoted his creative talents to church music. Although his operas have been forgotten, some of his sacred works are still performed.

Bernabei, who like his father belonged to the Roman school influenced by Giacomo Carissimi, began his operatic career with *Alvilda in Abo* in 1678. He wrote his first festival opera, *Ermione* (1680), for Max Emanuel's 18th birthday and his accession to the title of Elector. The work is notable for its double-choral effects, both instrumental and vocal. The stage work *La fiera* (possibly written for the 22nd birthday of Electress Maria Antonia in 1691) is not entirely of a dramatic character, since it consists of arias and duets and dispenses entirely with recitative or dialogue. As a whole, Bernabei's operatic style is characterized by simple, cantabile lines rather than expansive theatrical gestures.

His brother Vincenzo Bernabei (*b* Rome, 1660; *d* Munich, 1732–6) was active in the production of operas during his early years in Rome; after 1684 he composed a number of pieces for operatic productions in Munich (one in *A-Wn*).

first performed in Munich

Alvilda in Abo (melodrama, 3, V. Terzago), 10 Feb 1678

Enea in Italia (Terzago), Jan 1679

Giulio Cesare ricovrato all'ombra (Terzago), 11 July 1680, lib. *D-Mbs, As, Sl*

L'Ermione (drama per musica, Terzago), Salvator, 14 July 1680, lib. *Mbs*

L'Ascanio in Alba (melodramma, 3, F. R. Sbarra), Salvator, 19 Feb 1686, *A-Wn* (*R*1982: IOB, lxvi), *D-Mbs*

La gloria festeggiante [Gli dei festeggianti] (introducimento dramatico musicale del torneo, L. Orlandi), 18 Jan 1688, *A-Wn*

Diana amante (componimento dramatico, 3, Orlandi), Georgi-Saal of the Residenz, 26 Feb 1688, *Wn*

Il trionfo d'Imeneo (festa, 5, ?Orlandi), 22 Nov 1688, *Wn*

L'Eraclio, 5 Feb 1690 [also attrib. Clementin, and V. Bernabei]

Il segreto d'Amore in petto del Savio (melodrama, Orlandi), 7 Feb 1690, *Wn, D-Mbs*

La fiera (trattenimento musicale), ? 18 Jan 1691, *A-Wn*; ed. R. Münster (Lottstetten, 1979)

Vaticinio di Apollo e Diana, Nov/Dec 1692, *Wn*

*

F. M. Rudhart: *Geschichte der Oper am Hofe zu München*, i: *Die italiänische Oper von 1654–1787* (Freising, 1865)

M. Zenger: *Geschichte der Münchener Oper* (Munich, 1923)

K. Forster: *Über das Leben und die kirchenmusikalischen Werke Giuseppe Antonio Bernabeis (1649–1732)* (diss., U. of Munich, 1933)

H. Bolongero-Crevenna: *L'arpa festante: die Münchner Oper 1651–1825* (Munich, 1963)

R. Münster: 'Die Musik am Hofe Max Emanuels', *Kurfürst Max Emanuel: Bayern und Europa um 1700*, i: *Zur Geschichte und Kunstgeschichte der Max-Emanuel-Zeit*, ed. H. Glaser (Munich, 1976), 295–316

JULIA LIEBSCHER

Bernacchi, Antonio Maria (*b* Bologna, 23 June 1685; *d* Bologna, 13 March 1756). Italian alto castrato. He was a pupil of Pistocchi and G. A. Ricieri, and studied counterpoint with G. A. Bernabei at Munich. He made his Italian operatic début at Genoa in 1703 and appeared in Vienna in 1709 and Venice in 1709–10, 1717–19, 1721–4, 1731–2 and 1735, singing in at least 22 operas there. During the same period he sang in many other Italian cities including Novara (1711), Bologna (1712–13, 1722, 1727, 1731), Florence (1712–15), Parma (1714, 1728–9, 1736), Pesaro (1719), Reggio (1719, in Gasparini's *Bajazet*), Milan (1719), Rome (1721, in the first performance of Alessandro Scarlatti's *Griselda*, and 1731), Turin (1726–7), Naples (1728–9) and Modena (1728–9, 1735–6). Following his success in Orlandini's *Carlo re d'Alemagna* at Parma in 1714, he was appointed virtuoso to Prince Antonio Farnese. His fame spread throughout Europe and he sang in operas by all the leading composers of the age, from Pallavicino and Alessandro Scarlatti to Hasse, Vinci and Leo. In 1720 he was engaged by the Elector of Bavaria for Munich and sang there frequently until 1727, remaining nominally in his service until 1735. In 1729 Swiney described him as 'the very best singer in the world'.

Bernacchi made his London début at the King's Theatre in Alessandro Scarlatti's *Pirro e Demetrio* in 1716 (when Handel composed three extra arias for him) and also sang in the pasticcio *Clearte*. In 1717 he appeared in Handel's *Rinaldo* and *Amadigi*. In 1729 Handel engaged him as leading man for the second Royal Academy and he sang in the first performances of *Lotario* (1729) and *Partenope* (1730), revivals of *Giulio*

Antonio Maria Bernacchi singing in Venice: caricature by A. M. Zanetti (the aria is from G. M. Capelli's 'Mitridate, re di Ponto', Venice, 1723)

Cesare and *Tolomeo* (1730), and the pasticcio *Ormisda*. Though English audiences preferred Senesino, Bernacchi was accepted on the score of his European reputation; Burney described him as 'past his meridian', but paid tribute to his taste and intelligence. He retired from the stage in 1736, apart from an unsuccessful reappearance in Florence, 1741–2, and founded a famous singing school at Bologna; among his many distinguished pupils were Guarducci, Raaff and Amadori.

The range of Bernacchi's voice was slightly higher than that of Senesino. The two parts Handel composed for Bernacchi – Lotario and Arsace (*Partenope*) – have a compass of *a* to *f''*. Though his natural musical gifts were not exceptional, he was renowned for technical virtuosity, especially in ornaments and cadenzas. He was accused, by Martinelli and Algarotti among others, of sacrificing expression to execution and adopting an instrumental style; his old master Pistocchi is said to have exclaimed: 'I taught you to sing, and you want to play'. Farinelli studied under him briefly in 1727.

*

L. Frati: 'Antonio Bernacchi e la sua scuola di canto', *RMI*, xxix (1922), 473–91

W. Dean and J. M. Knapp: *Handel's Operas 1704–1726* (Oxford, 1987)

WINTON DEAN

Bernal Jiménez, Miguel (*b* Morelia, Michoacán, 16 Feb 1910; *d* León, Guanajuato, 26 July 1956). Mexican composer. After early training in Morelia, he studied at the Pontificio Istituto di Musica Sacra in Rome, where one of his teachers was Refice. Graduating in 1933, he returned to Morelia and in 1936 became director of the Escuela Superior de Música Sagrada. He founded and edited the monthly periodical *Schola cantorum*, simultaneously touring widely as concert organist, choral conductor and lecturer. In 1943 the Mexican Academia de Ciencias y Artes Cinematográficas awarded him its annual prize in recognition of *La Virgen que forjó una patria*, one of four films for which he wrote music; he also composed two ballets. From 1954 to his death he was dean of the School of Music of Loyola University at New Orleans.

First performed at Pátzcuaro on 15 February 1941, the *drama sinfónico Tata Vasco* (5 scenes, M. Muñoz) was composed to celebrate the quatercentenary of the arrival at Pátzcuaro of Vasco de Quiroga (1470–1565), first bishop of Michoacán. Bernal Jiménez's command of a wide variety of musical styles enabled him in this opera to intersperse chant with imitations of aboriginal dance rhythms, battle music, fandango, scherzo, fugue and rondo. Permutations of four chief themes unify the heterogeneous musical forms. Scene 2 includes a friar singing a *serranilla* by the Marqués de Santillana, and in scene 3 Vasco de Quiroga (baritone) prepares to marry Princess Coyuva (soprano), daughter of the murdered Tarascan ruler, to Ticátame (tenor) amidst a choral *alabado* (hymn of praise). Scene 4 re-enacts the Tarascan festival after the marriage. The opera has been performed in Mexico City and Spain.

*

O. Mayer-Serra: 'Tata Vasco: a Mexican Opera', *The Commonwealth* (12 Sept 1941), 486–8

——: *Música y músicos de Latinoamérica* (Mexico City, 1947), i, 105–9 [incl. music excerpts]

R. Stevenson: *Music in Mexico* (New York, 1952), 262–4

A. E. Lemmon: 'Miguel Bernal Jiménez', *Heterofonía*, vii/4 (1974), 6–9

ROBERT STEVENSON

Bernard, Pierre-Joseph [Gentil-Bernard] (*b* Grenoble, 26 Aug 1708; *d* Paris, 1 Nov 1775). French poet and librettist. After working as an attorney's clerk he joined the army, distinguishing himself in the Italian campaigns of 1733–4. He soon gained the protection of the Comte de Coigny and Mme de Pompadour, who secured for him administrative posts in the army and at court that provided a substantial income and the leisure to indulge his epicurean tastes. In 1736 he was briefly involved with La Pouplinière's circle, where he probably met Rameau. He also participated in the Dîners du Caveau, a convivial literary society of which Rameau is said to have been a member.

Bernard's *Castor et Pollux* in its revised version (1754) has with some justification been described as the finest French libretto of the 18th century (Masson); in emphasizing brotherly rather than romantic love it was exceptional. The plot, which develops with pleasing logic, is rich in conflicts of sentiment and provides convincing pretexts for the all-important spectacle. While some of Bernard's phraseology was criticized, his text stands out as one of the most elegant of its period. Rameau originally set the text in 1737 and produced a revised version in 1754. As well as a later setting by Candeille (1791), there are three operas in Italian to (or after) a Frugoni libretto based on Bernard's text – by Traetta (as *I Tindaridi, o Castore e Polluce*, 1760), Bianchi (1779) and Vogler (1787).

His subsequent librettos, *Les surprises de l'Amour* and *Anacréon*, are more routine, though never less than competent. Both were set by Rameau: the first, written for Mme de Pompadour's amateur theatricals, as an *opéra-ballet* in 1748 (rev. 1757), and the second as an *acte de ballet* in 1757.

F. J. M. Fayolle, ed.: *Oeuvres de Bernard* (Paris, 1803)
M. Tourneux, ed.: *Correspondance littéraire, philosophique et critique par Grimm, Diderot, Raynal, Meister, etc* (Paris, 1877–82)
C. Malherbe: 'Commentaire bibliographique', *J.-P. Rameau: Oeuvres complètes* (Paris, 1895–1924), viii, pp.xv–cxix
M. Emmanuel and M. Ténéo: 'Commentaire bibliographique', ibid, xvii, pp.ix–clix
G. Cucuel: *La Pouplinière et la musique de chambre au XVIIIe siècle* (Paris, 1913)
P.-M. Masson: *L'opéra de Rameau* (Paris, 1930)
C. Girdlestone: *Jean-Philippe Rameau: his Life and Work* (London, 1957, 2/1969)
W. H. Kaehler: *The Operatic Repertoire of Madame de Pompadour's Théâtre des petits cabinets (1747–1753)* (diss., U. of Michigan, 1971)
C. Girdlestone: *La tragédie en musique (1673–1750) considérée comme genre littéraire* (Geneva, 1972) GRAHAM SADLER

Bernardi, Francesco. *See* SENESINO.

Bernardi, Mario (*b* Kirkland Lake, Ont., 30 Aug 1930). Canadian conductor. He studied at the Venice and Toronto conservatories and made his conducting début in *Hänsel und Gretel* with Canadian Opera in 1956. After moving to Britain he appeared in 1964 with Sadler's Wells Opera, of which he was later music director, 1966–9. There he conducted a varied repertory in which Mozart and Verdi featured prominently, and a notable recording in English of *Hänsel und Gretel* (1964). From 1967 he conducted at the San Francisco Opera, frequently at New York City Opera, 1970–86, and in 1984 at the Metropolitan, as well as further performances with the Canadian Opera. He was founder-conductor of the Ottawa National Arts Centre Orchestra, 1969–82, and is a Companion of the Order of Canada. His conducting favours transparent textures, judicious tempos and rhythmic crispness.

NOËL GOODWIN

Bernardini, Marcello [Marcello da Capua] (*b* ?Capua, 1730–40; *d* after 1799). Italian composer and librettist. There is evidence in the archives of the Collegio Nazareno in Rome that he may have been the son of Rinaldo di Capua. He reached Rome in about 1764, when his *La schiava astuta* and other intermezzos – *pantomime ed ariette in musica da recitare nel Teatro dei Signori Capranica* – were performed. In 1767 he held a civic office (*caporione*) in the Campitelli district and in 1769 he received an appointment at the Collegio Nazareno to write the music for the Nativity of the Virgin, an office he held until 1784. The fact that he had been preceded in this post by Rinaldo di Capua, who, according to Burney, had a 'graceless son', supports the theory of a close link between Rinaldo and Bernardini, especially since it was customary for composers to suggest their successors, usually a son or pupil.

In 1771 Bernardini wrote *Il vello di Gedeone* for the Oratory of S Girolamo, Rome, and later the same year he was in Naples, where his operas were performed at the Teatro del Fondo. From 1770 he also wrote librettos for himself and for other composers such as G. B. Borghi, Pietro Terziani and Martín y Soler. It is possible that he went to Turin and Munich when his operas were performed there. Some librettos from 1789 to 1799 designate him as being in the service of 'the Princess Lubomirski Czartoryska of Poland' (probably Elisabeth Helene Anna Czartoryska, Princess Lubomirski), whom he may have followed to Poland about 1795, after visiting Vienna for a performance of his cantata *Angelica placata*.

Of Bernardini's large output of nearly 40 operas only 13 survive, together with two cantatas and a few librettos. All but three of his operas are comic. Some, such as *La donna di spirito* (1770), *Li tre Orfei* (1784) and *Le donne bisbetiche* (1785) were highly successful and widely performed into the first decade of the 19th century. As a composer he was particularly appreciated for his comic writing and his skill in characterization. He wrote mainly comedies of intrigue; but instead of following rigid conventional formulae, they have lively innovations and a sharp line in caricature.

La schiava astuta (int, 2), Rome, Dame, carn. 1765
La pescatrice (farsetta), Rome, 1768
Il Don Chisciotte della Mancia (ob, ? G. B. Lorenzi), Turin, Carignano, aut. 1769
Il cavaliere errante (farsetta, 2, M. Bernardini), Rome, Capranica, carn. 1770
La donna di spirito (farsetta, 2, Bernardini, after C. Goldoni: *La vedova scaltra*), Rome, Capranica, carn. 1770, *A-Wgm*, *P-La* (as La donna bizzarra), *I-Fc* (as Le quattro stagioni)
La molinara astuta (int, 2), Rome, Valle, carn. 1770, *Mc*
Amore in musica (ob, 3), Rome, Valle, carn. 1773, vs *D-Dlb* (as L'amore della musica), *?H-Bn*
La contessina (ob, 3, M. Coltellini, after C. Goldoni), Rome, Dame, carn. 1773
La bella forestiera, o sia La viaggiatrice fortunata (farsetta, 2), Rome, Capranica, carn. 1776
La finta sposa olandese (farsetta, 2), Rome, Capranica, carn. 1777
L'isola incantata (int), Rome, Capranica, carn. 1778, *D-Dlb*, *P-La* (as L'isola d'Alcina)
L'ambizione delusa (int), Rome, Capranica, carn. 1779
Il bassà generoso (int, 2), Rome, Capranica, carn. 1780, *D-Dlb*, *I-Mc*
Il vecchio ringiovanito (int, 2), Rome, Tordinona, carn. 1781
Le vendette giocose, o sia Il conte pasticcio (int, 'F. C.'), Rome, Pace, carn. 1782
Il conte di bell'umore (int, 2), Florence, Palla a Corda, carn. 1783, *D-Wa*, *I-Mr*, *Tf*, *US-Wc*
La viaggiatrice fortunata (ob), Florence, 1783
La poetessa fanatica, o sieno Li due gemelli (ob, 2), Rome, Pace, carn. 1784
Li tre Orfei (int, 2), Rome, Palla a Corda, carn. 1784, *D-Rtt*, *I-Bc*, *Gl*, *Mr*, *P-La*
Le donne bisbetiche, o sia L'antiquario fanatico (farsetta, 2, Bernardini), Rome, Castel Gandolfo, aut. 1785; rev. as La finta Galatea, Naples, 1788, *D-B*, *F-Pn*, *I-Mc*, *Nc*, *US-Bp*
Li muti per amore, o sia La schiava fedele (farsetta, Bernardini), Florence, Palla a Corda, carn. 1786
Gli amanti confusi, o sia Il brutto fortunato (farsetta), Rome, Valle, spr. 1786
La fonte d'aqua gialla, o sia Il trionfo della pazzia (ob, 2, Bernardini), Rome, Valle, aut. 1786
Barone a forza, ossia Il trionfo di Bacco (ob), Florence, 1786, *D-Hs*
La fiera di Forlinpopoli (ob, 2), Rome, Valle, spr. 1789
Gl'incontri stravaganti (commedia, 2), Naples, Nuovo, carn. 1790
L'ultima che si perde è la speranza (commedia, 2, F. S. Zini), Naples, Fondo, 1 Aug 1790
Il pazzo glorioso (ob, 2, G. Bertati), Casalmaggiore, Communale, 1790
Pizzarro nell'Indie (dramma per musica, 2), Naples, S Carlo, 23 Jan 1791
L'allegria della campagna (commedia, 2), Naples, Nuovo, spr. 1791
L'amore per incanto (commedia), Naples, Fondo, aut. 1791, *Dlb* (as L'amore per magia)
La statua per puntiglio (ob, 2), Venice, S Moisè, carn. 1792, *B-Bc*
Il conte brillante, Varese, aut. 1792, collab. Uboldi
Le quattro nazioni (ob), Verona, Balbi, 1792
Li cinque pretendenti (ob), Trieste, carn. 1794
Achille in Sciro (dramma per musica, 3, P. Metastasio), Venice, Fenice, aut. 1794, *I-Mr*
La sposa polacca (dramma bernesco, 3, Bernardini), Rome, Nuovo Apollo, carn. 1796
Don Simoncino, ossia Furberia e puntiglio (farsa giocosa, 1, G. Foppa), Venice, S Moisè, 12 Sept 1798, *F-Pn*, *I-Fc*, *Gl*, *Mc*, *Mr*
Le tre orfanelle, o sia La scuola di musica (farsa, 1, Bertati), Venice, S Benedetto, 25 Nov 1798

Il muto per astuzia (farsa giocosa, 1, Foppa), Venice, S Moisè, carn. 1799

*

DBI (R. Meloncelli: 'Bernardini, Marcello'; A. Lanfranchi: 'Da Capua, Rinaldo')

F. F. de Daugnon: *Gli italiani in Polonia dal IX sec. al XVIII* (Crema, 1907)

G. Pavan: 'Il teatro Capranica (Catalogo cronologico delle opere rappresentate nel secolo XVIII)', *RMI*, xxix (1922), 425–44

A. Cametti: *Il teatro di Tordinona poi di Apollo* (Rome and Tivoli, 1938) RAOUL MELONCELLI (with MARITA P. McCLYMONDS)

Bernardon [Kurz-Bernardon]. *See* KURZ, JOSEPH FELIX VON.

Bernardoni, Pietro Antonio (*b* Vignola, nr Modena, 30 June 1672; *d* Bologna, 19 Jan 1714). Italian librettist. From his youth he was a close friend of the scholar Lodovico Muratori in Modena. He became a member of the Accademia dell'Arcadia in Rome in 1691, taking the name Cromiro Dianio; his later tragedies and musical dramas reflect many of the refining and purifying ideals of the Arcadians. In his twenties, he served various noblemen in northern Italy and in Paris, where he resided between June and September 1699. In July 1701 he was named to succeed Niccolò Minato as an imperial poet in Vienna, after Zeno had refused the honour. Here he served first Leopold I, together with the poet Donato Cupeda (*d* 1704), then Joseph I, together with Silvio Stampiglia. Muratori's letters reveal that Bernardoni returned to Italy when war ravaged Vienna in 1703–4, then again in 1706–7. He retired with an imperial pension in 1710.

The four opera librettos that Bernardoni wrote for Vienna presumably received splendid stagings, with magnificent sets (e.g. by L. O. Burnacini), ballets and combat scenes. Only two were revived. He also wrote texts for 34 oratorios, serenatas and similar works, set to music by composers at the imperial court; 30 of his texts were published in his *Poemi drammatici* (3 vols., Bologna, 1706–7, and Vienna, 1709).

drammi per musica unless otherwise stated

Il geloso di se medesimo (favola pastorale), *c*1690, unperf.; *Giulio Cesare in Torino*, 1699, unperf.; *L'amore vuol somiglianza*, C. A. Badia, 1702; *Meleagro*, M. Ziani, 1706 (Albinoni, 1718); *Amor tra nemici*, A. Ariosti, 1708 (1710, as Almahide); *Tigrane, re d'Armenia*, A. M. Bononcini, 1710; *Eraclio*, F. Gasparini and C. F. Pollarolo, 1712

*

DBI (S. Simonetti); *ES* (U. Rolandi and C. E. Tanfani)

A. von Weilen: 'Zur Wiener Theatergeschichte: die vom Jahre 1629 bis zum Jahre 1740 am Wiener Hofe zur Aufführung gelangten Werke theatralischen Charakters und Oratorien', *Mittheilungen des Österreichischer Vereins für Bibliothekswesen*, ii (1898), suppl.

M. Campori, ed.: *L. A. Muratori: Epistolario* (Modena, 1901–22)

M. L. Nava: 'P. A. Bernardoni e il melodramma', *Atti e memorie della Regia Deputazione di storia patria per le provincie modenesi*, 7th ser., v (1928), 88–138

F. Hadamowsky: 'Barocktheater am Wiener Kaiserhof: mit einen Spielplan (1625–1740)', *Jb der Gesellschaft für Wiener Theaterforschung 1951–52*, 7–117; pubd separately (Vienna, 1955)

J. H. van der Meer: *Johann Joseph Fux als Opernkomponist* (Bilthoven, 1961) LOWELL LINDGREN

Bernasconi, Andrea (*b* ? Marseilles, 1706; *d* Munich, 24 Jan 1784). Italian composer. Early sources state that he was born in 1712. His father, a French officer, settled in Parma after his withdrawal from military service. Little is known of Bernasconi's education. In the librettos of his early operas he is referred to as a Milanese dilettante (1737 and 1743) and as a Veronese (1742 and 1745), but mainly as a Milanese (1737, 1743–53). His first known position was as *maestro di cappella* at the Ospedale della Pietà in Venice (1744–53). In 1747 he married Maria Josepha Wagele (*c*1722–62) in Parma. He instructed his stepdaughter, Antonia, in music and helped launch her successful singing career. A decree of 24 November 1753 refers to his engagement as assistant Kapellmeister of vocal music in Munich from 1 August 1753; his appointment coincided with the opening of the Residenztheater. He was soon appointed electoral councillor. On 5 June 1754 he was named music teacher to the princesses Maria Anna Josepha (until July 1755) and Josepha Maria (until January 1765); Maximilian III Joseph, Elector of Bavaria, also received music lessons from him. Following the death of Giovanni Porta, Bernasconi was appointed to the post of Kapellmeister on 7 September 1755. In 1778 the new Elector, Carl Theodor, reconfirmed his official post, but he probably rendered no further service. His successor in 1784 was Franz Paul Grua.

As a composer, Bernasconi was a conservative working in the vein of Neapolitan *opera seria*, his music devoid of any attempts at reform. Most of his arias are in a modified da capo form with florid melodic writing; the recitatives are noteworthy for their fluent and vocally graceful declamation. He employs accompanied recitatives effectively, especially in the later operas. Gerber reports that Hasse's wife, the soprano Faustina Bordoni, liked Bernasconi's operas, and that his arias pleased her as much as those of her husband. His stage works performed in Munich, some being revisions of earlier works, were very popular. After 1772 he devoted his attention exclusively to church music. Although his music is rarely studied today, his scores provide insight into the operatic environment at Munich before the arrival of Carl Theodor and the musicians from Mannheim in 1778. Most of his operas for Munich are still extant (in *D-Mbs*).

opere serie in three acts unless otherwise stated

Flavio Anicio Olibrio (A. Zeno ?and P. Pariati), Vienna, carn. 1737, *A-Wn*

Alessandro Severo (Zeno), Venice, S Giovanni Grisostomo, 27 Dec 1738; rev. version, Palermo, S Cecilia, carn. 1746; rev. as Salustia, Venice, Vendramin, 31 May 1753

Temistocle (P. Metastasio), Padua, Obizzi, 6 June 1740, *I-PLcon*; rev. version, Lucca, 1741; rev. version, Venice, S Giovanni Grisostomo, aut. 1744; rev. version, Munich, Residenz, carn. 1754; rev. version, 1762; *D-B*, *Hs*, *Mbs*, *Wa*, *F-Pn*

Demofoonte (Metastasio), Rome, Dame, carn. 1741; rev. version, Munich, Residenz, carn. 1766, *D-Mbs*

Didone abbandonata (Metastasio), Venice, S Giovanni Grisostomo, carn. 1741; rev. version, Munich, Residenz, 26 Jan 1756, *Mbs*

Endimione (serenata, 2, Metastasio), Venice, 6 Feb 1742; rev. version, Munich, Residenz, 1756

Il Bajazet (A. Piovene), Venice, S Giovanni Grisostomo, aut. 1742; rev. version, Munich, Residenz, 12 Oct 1754; rev. version as Baiazet, Prague, 1762; arias *Mbs*

La ninfa Apollo (scherzo comico pastorale, 2, F. de Lemene), Venice, S Giovanni Grisostomo, 26 Feb 1743

Germanico (N. Coluzzi), Turin, Regio, carn. 1744, *A-Wgm*, *Wn*

Antigono (Metastasio), Venice, S Giovanni Grisostomo, carn. 1745; rev. version, Treviso, Delfino, carn. 1752

Artaserse (Metastasio), Vienna, 8 Oct 1746; rev. version, Munich, Residenz, 10 Jan 1763, *D-Mbs*, *F-Pn*

Ezio (Metastasio), Schönbrunn, 4 Oct 1749, *D- Mbs*

L'huomo (festa teatrale, 1, Wilhelmine of Bayreuth), Bayreuth, sum. 1754, *W*

Adriano in Siria (Metastasio), Munich, Residenz, 5 Jan 1755, *Mbs*, *F-Pn*

Il trionfo della costanza (festa teatrale, Honory, after Metastasio: *Il sogno di Scipione*), Nymphenburg, 20 July 1756

Agelmondo, Munich, carn. 1760, *D-Mbs*

Olimpiade (Metastasio), Munich, Residenz, 20 Jan 1764, *Mbs, F-Pn**
Semiramide riconosciuta (Metastasio), Munich, Residenz, 7 Jan 1765, *D-Mbs, F-Pn*
La clemenza di Tito (Metastasio), Munich, Residenz, Jan 1768, *D-Mbs, F-Pn** (*R*1982: IOB, lxxxviii)
Demetrio (Metastasio), Munich, Residenz, Jan 1772, *D-Mbs, F-Pn*

Music in: Didone abbandonata, 1743; Ixion, 1746; Andromeda, 1750; Euridice, 1750; Nerone, 1753; Issipile, 1763

*

GerberL; *GerberNL*
F. J. Lipowsky: *Baierisches Musiklexikon* (Munich, 1811)
F. M. Rudhart: *Geschichte der Oper am Hofe zu München*, i: *Die italiänische Oper von 1654–1787* (Freising, 1865)
E. J. Weiss: *Andrea Bernasconi als Opernkomponist* (diss., U. of Munich, 1923)
M. Zenger: *Geschichte der Münchener Oper* (Munich, 1923)
N. Pelicelli: 'Musicisti in Parma nel sec. XVIII', *NA*, xii (1935), 84–92
H. Bolongaro-Crevenna: *L'arpa festante: die Münchener Oper, 1651–1825* (Munich, 1963)
G. Zechmeister: *Die Wiener Theater nächst der Burg und nächst dem Kärntnerthor von 1747–1776* (Vienna, 1971)
E. Weimer: Preface to IOB, lxxxviii (New York, 1982)
H. Lühning: '"Titus"-Vertonungen im 18. Jahrhundert: Untersuchungen zur Tradition die Opera seria von Hasse bis Mozart', *AnMc*, no.20 (1983)

ROBERT MÜNSTER (with PAUL CORNEILSON)

Bernasconi [Wagele], **Antonia** (*b* Stuttgart, *c*1741; *d* ?Vienna, ?1803). German soprano. Taught singing by her stepfather Andrea Bernasconi, she made her début in his *Temistocle* (1762, Munich). In Vienna (from *c*1765) she performed in *opere buffe* by Piccinni and Sacchini and was highly successful as Alcestis in the première of Gluck's opera (1767). J. A. Hiller gave an account of her in the *Wochentlichen Nachrichten* of 24 October 1768. In 1770 she sang Aspasia in the première of Mozart's *Mitridate*; Ninetta in his *La finta semplice* was probably composed for her; his letters however are critical of her intonation and German declamation. She sang in Venice (1771–2), in Naples (1772–3 and 1774–5) and was a member of the Italian opera company at the King's Theatre, London (1778–80), returning to the Vienna Burgtheater in 1781. ROBERT MÜNSTER

Bernauer, Rudolf (*b* Vienna, 20 Jan 1880; *d* London, 27 Nov 1953). Austrian librettist. The son of a bank official, he was educated in Berlin and began a career in the theatre as a writer, actor and cabaret artist. He thereby became acquainted with Leo Fall and Oscar Straus, for whom he wrote some of his first operetta librettos, among them *Der tapfere Soldat* (popular in English as *The Chocolate Soldier*). In 1907 he became director of the Berliner Theater in association with Carl Meinhard, often acting as co-author of plays and operettas. He worked particularly closely with Max Reinhardt and was noted for his stagings of Strindberg and Wedekind. After the rise of Hitler he left Berlin for London and became a naturalized British citizen. He wrote an autobiography *Das Theater meines Lebens* (Berlin, 1955).

operettas unless otherwise stated

Schlumpeline Schlumebumbum [Hans der Raker] (Märchenspiel), B. Zepler, 1903; *Der Rebell* (with E. Welisch), L. Fall, 1905 (rev. as Der liebe Augustin, 1912); *Frau Lebedame* (with Pordes-Milo), A. Goetzel, 1907; *Der tapfere Soldat* [Der Praliné-Soldat] (with L. Jacobson), O. Straus, 1908; *Bummelstudenten* (Posse, with R. Schanzer), Zepler, 1910; *Grosse Rosinen* (Posse, with Schanzer), W. Bredschneider and others, 1911; *Die keusche Barbara* (with Jacobson), O. Nedbal, 1911; *Filmzauber* (Posse, with Schanzer), W. Kollo, 1912; *Wie einst im Mai* (Posse, with Schanzer), Kollo, 1913

Jung-England (with Welisch), Fall 1914 (rev. as Die Frau Ministerpräsident, 1920); *Wenn Zwei Hochzeit machen* (Scherzspiel, with Schanzer), Kollo and Bredschneider, 1915; *Auf Flügeln des Gesanges* (Lebensbild, with Schanzer), Kollo and Bredschneider, 1917; *Die tolle Comtesse* (Posse, with Schanzer), Kollo, 1917; *Blitzblaues Blut* (with Schanzer), Kollo, 1918; *Sterne, die wieder leuchten* (with Schanzer), Kollo, 1918; *Prinzessin Olala* (Operette-Vaudeville, with Schanzer), J. Gilbert, 1922; *Dolly* (Vaudeville-Operette, with H. Arnold and E. Bach), H. Hirsch, 1923; *Die Geliebte seiner Hoheit* (with R. Oesterreicher), Gilbert

ANDREW LAMB

Berne (Ger. Bern). Capital of Switzerland since 1848. Opera was first performed in the Ballenhaus, built in 1678. *Die Zauberflöte* was given there in 1796. The Hôtel de Musique, completed in 1770, was used for regular opera performances from 1799. Annual seasons of opera began in 1837, when the city began to subsidize performances. The following year the Theatersaal of the Hôtel de Musique was renovated, and *Tristan und Isolde* received its first Swiss performance there in 1889. The Stadttheater (cap. 830), situated on Kornhausplatz, opened on 25 September 1903 with *Tannhäuser*. Performances of the *Ring* were given in 1908, 1912 and 1930, and works by both Wagner and Strauss have played a prominent part in the repertory. Walter Oberer, director from 1960 to 1979, widened the range to include contemporary and neglected opera, including the first European performance of Rolf Liebermann's revised version of Fauré's *Pénélope* in 1971. The theatre, which was closed for renovation in 1982–4, has its own ensemble for opera, ballet and drama, and is open on most nights of the week from September to June. Each season there are up to six new opera productions and one revival. The theatre draws on the services of the Berne SO for opera performances.

*

Fünfzig Jahre Berner Theater (Berne, 1956)
Die Kunstendenkmäler des Kantons Bern (Basle, 1959)
P. Tschanz, ed.: *Stadttheater: unser Theater Bern* (Berne, 1984)

ANDREW CLARK

Berners, Lord [Tyrwhitt-Wilson, Sir Gerald Hugh, Baronet] (*b* Arley Park, nr Bridgnorth, 18 Sept 1883; *d* Faringdon House, Berks., 19 April 1950). English composer. In 1909 he joined the diplomatic service and was posted as honorary attaché to Constantinople, then (until 1920) Rome, where he was encouraged in his musical studies by Stravinsky and Casella. He succeeded an uncle as 14th Baron Berners in 1918. After 1920 he lived the life of an eccentric, wealthy English gentleman of cosmopolitan tastes, composing, writing and painting, and devising practical jokes and mystifications. Stravinsky described him as 'an amateur in the best – literal – sense'. In spheres where the amateur composer is at a disadvantage – ballet and film scores, for example, where the music has to fit other people's ideas precisely – Berners showed professional ability. He soon became notorious for short satirical songs and piano works, but behind the quizzical monocle there beat a tender heart. Like all good parodies these contain affection and, in the case of Berners, nostalgia for ways of life that were passing. The ambivalence found wider scope in five ballets (1926–46); the first was written for Dyagilev's Ballets Russes, the last three for Sadler's Wells. In the one-act comic opera *Le carrosse du Saint-Sacrement* (Paris, Trianon-Lyrique, 1923; vs London, 1923, 2/1925), a setting of a prose comedy by Prosper Mérimée about an 18th-century viceroy of Peru imprudent enough to lend his mistress his splendid new carriage, Berners handled the problem of accompanied arioso-recitative, sung in French at or near the speed of the spoken word, with a dexterity few of his English contemporaries could have matched. Two volumes of autobiography were published in London in 1934 and 1945. RONALD CRICHTON

Bernheimer, Martin (*b* Munich, 28 Sept 1936). American music critic. He studied at Brown University, the Hochschule für Musik in Munich (1958–9), and with Gustave Reese at New York University. He was on the music staff of the *New York Herald Tribune* (1959–62), assistant to Irving Kolodin at the *Saturday Review* (1962–5), music critic for the *New York Post* (1961–5) and from 1965 music critic of the *Los Angeles Times*. He won the Deems Taylor Award for music criticism in 1974 and 1978 and the Pulitzer Prize for criticism in 1982. Bernheimer is a widely respected and influential critic, who is particularly knowledgeable about opera and the voice. PATRICK J. SMITH

Bernicat, Firmin (*b* Lyons, 1843; *d* Paris, sum. 1883). French composer. He gained early experience of Parisian music theatre as an arranger and orchestrator (for Planquette, among others). In the early 1870s he supplied the music for several one-act *opérettes*, a formula from which he subsequently rarely strayed: they were performed at such venues as the Café Tertulia, the Folies-Bergère and the Eldorado. He attempted a few large-scale works, among them *Les beignets du roi* to a libretto by Paul Ferrier and Albert Carré, which brought him success at the Alcazar in Brussels. André Messager later provided extra music, at Carré's request, for Parisian performances in 1888, when the work appeared as *Les premières armes de Louis XV*. Bernicat was in the middle of a second major *opéra comique*, *François les bas-bleus*, when he died suddenly. The publisher Enoch commissioned Messager to complete the piece, which enjoyed great success at the Folies Dramatiques and firmly established Messager as a theatrical composer, Messager himself claimed in 1888 to have written 12 of the work's 25 numbers. A comic opera, *Vetah* (3, K. Santley), arranged from Bernicat's music with additions by Georges Jacobi, was given in England (Portsmouth) in 1886.

opérettes, first performed in Paris, unless otherwise stated

Ali pot-de-rhum (2, C. Gedhé), Brussels, Alcazar, 17 Dec 1869; M & Mme Véronique (saynète, Gedhé and L. Quentin), Brussels, Alcazar, 15 July 1872; Deux à deux (1, Quentin and ? G. Mancel), Café Tertulia, 14 Oct 1872; La queue du diable (1, Quentin and Gedhé), Café Tertulia, 15 Feb 1873; Ah c't Indien (1, Gedhé), Folies-Bergère, 1874; Par la fenêtre (1), Folies-Bergère, 1874; Les trois grand prix (1, A. G. M. Delilia and Lesenne), Salle Tailbout, 28 March 1875

Les deux Omar (1, Gedhé and W. Busnach), Fantaisies Oller, 4 March 1876; Le voyage du petit marquis (1, L. J. Péricaud and Villemer), Fantaisies-Parisiennes, 5 Oct 1876; La jeunesse de Béranger (1, Péricaud and Villemer), Eldorado, Jan 1877; La pâte empoisonnée (E. Frébault), Brussels, Alcazar, 22 Sept 1877; Fou-yo-po (pochade, E. Max), Brussels, Alcazar, 10 Oct 1877; La cornette (1, Péricaud, Villemer and L. Delormel), Eldorado, 1877; Les cadets de Gascoyne (1, G. Dorfeuil and C. Mey), Brussels, Alcazar, 25 Nov 1878

L'agence Raburdin (Dorfeuil), Eldorado, 17 Dec 1878; Une poule mouillée (1, Péricaud and Villemer), Concert du XIXe Siècle, 21 Dec 1878; Les barbières de village (1, F. Baumaine and Blondelet), Eldorado, 1878; On demande un Arlequin (1, Péricaud and Villemer), Eldorado, 1878; Le moulin des amours (1, Péricaud and Villemer), Eldorado, 1878; Le triomphe d'Arlequin (opérette-pantomime, A. Guyon), Eldorado, 1878; Les tziganes de Longjumeau (1, Dorfeuil), Brussels, Alcazar, 12 April 1879; Une aventure de Clairon (1, Péricaud and Villemer), *c*1879, ?unperf.

Les beignets du roi (oc, 3, A. Carré and P. Ferrier, after B. Antier), Brussels, Alcazar, 10 Feb 1882, rev. as Les premières armes de Louis XV, Menus-Plaisirs, 26 Feb 1888, collab. A. Messager; Le torchon (1, Dorfeuil and Mey), Gaîté-Montparnasse, 29 April 1882; Les premières armes de Parny (Péricaud and Delormel), Eldorado, 20 June 1882; François les bas-bleus (oc, 3, E. Dubreuil, E. Humbert and P. Burani), Folies-Dramatiques, 8 Nov 1883, completed by Messager; Le petit jeune homme (1, Péricaud and Delormel), Eldorado, 1892

FétisBS; *GänzlBMT*; *StiegerO*
C. Beaumont Wicks: *The Parisian Stage* (Alabama, 1950–79)
J. Wagstaff: *André Messager: a Bio-Bibliography* (Westport, CT, 1991)

Bernstein, Leonard (*b* Lawrence, MA, 25 Aug 1918; *d* New York, 14 Oct 1990). American composer and conductor. His musical education began with piano lessons when he was ten, and continued at Harvard University (1935–9), the Curtis Institute (1939–41) and the Berkshire Music Center (summers of 1940 and 1941), where he studied composition (with Walter Piston among others), orchestration (with Randall Thompson) and conducting (with Fritz Reiner and Sergey Koussevitzky). His activities in the following years typified the variety of his interests and talents: in addition to serving as Artur Rodzinski's assistant with the New York PO, he worked as a publisher's arranger and with a theatrical group called the Revuers. In 1943 he conducted one of the orchestra's concerts at short notice, successfully enough to make his name in the New York musical world. Appointed principal conductor in 1956, he directed the orchestra with distinction until 1966; during this time he also made himself familiar to American television audiences with the 'Young Peoples' Concerts' series, knowledgeably and effectively combining performance with explication. From the late 1960s his conducting career became even more illustrious, Vienna serving as an especially important centre for his work. His operatic conducting engagements were relatively few in number, but invariably noteworthy. Beginning auspiciously with the American première of *Peter Grimes* in 1946, they included engagements at La Scala (Cherubini's *Médée*, and *La sonnambula*, both with Callas), the Metropolitan Opera (*Falstaff*, *Cavalleria rusticana*, *Carmen*) and the Vienna Staatsoper (*Falstaff*, *Der Rosenkavalier*, *Fidelio*), as well as concert performances of Wagner, notably *Tristan und Isolde* in Munich (presented in instalments). Bernstein also conducted the first performance, in concert, of Marc Blitzstein's translation of *Die Dreigroschenoper* in 1952 (the mutual admiration between the two composers began in 1939 when Bernstein accompanied from memory, co-directed and performed roles in Blitzstein's *The Cradle will Rock* while still a senior at Harvard, and continued as a sometimes uneasy mentor-protégé relationship throughout Blitzstein's lifetime).

As a composer-conductor, Bernstein came closer than anyone since Mahler to achieving equal eminence in both spheres. Further, among American composers only Gershwin was more successful in gaining a high level of recognition in both serious and popular music. Bernstein quickly made a reputation as a composer in 1943, only months after his first conducting success, with the ballet *Fancy Free*, its breezy manner and offhand assurance showing his theatrical flair. Indeed all his music, including choral and vocal works, three symphonies and a variety of instrumental pieces, contains an unashamedly theatrical element in its extramusical inspiration and intended effect. As the composer himself accurately noted, everything he wrote, for whatever medium, was 'really theater music in some way'. His musical language varied through the years but never abandoned tonality, although in his later works he occasionally explored serial devices (most brilliantly in 'The Pennycandy Store beyond the El' from the 1977 *Songfest*). His command of musical dialects from late Romanticism to Broadway was sometimes criticized but in fact proved a strength, as he was able to fit each dramatic moment with the kind of music best suited for it. He was also one of the few Broadway composers capable of orchestrating his own music (although pressures on his time generally dictated some delegation).

Aside from incidental music for two Aristophanes plays composed for Harvard, Bernstein's first piece of sung theatre was a musical comedy, *On the Town*, written with his Revuers friends Betty Comden and Adolph Green. This successful excursion into the commercial theatre used the same basic idea as the ballet *Fancy Free* (with the same choreographer, Jerome Robbins) – three sailors on shore leave looking for fun in New York City – but the music and the plot details were freshly invented. A novel feature (though found in such predecessors as Rodgers's *On your Toes*) was the emphasis on self-contained dance sequences, written by the composer rather than a dance arranger. The songs, while partaking of the usual Broadway idiom, were enriched with canons, irregular phrase lengths and harmonic surprises. These adventures were extended in the next musical, *Wonderful Town*, in which several numbers are linked through shared musical material. This score also revealed Bernstein's skill at writing for particular performers (everything from high soprano to limited untrained voices) and at evoking past musical styles to simultaneously parodistic and sincere effect. These techniques continued to serve him well in his more ambitious theatre works.

Bernstein's belief in the possibility of developing an operatic repertory from the American musical was first put into action in the popular-flavoured *Trouble in Tahiti*, a one-act opera originally presented on a college campus. Further efforts to use the musical-comedy styles of the 1950s in a stage work that could carry the weight of a tragic theme resulted in *West Side Story*. During the years of its gestation the composer also turned out a European-flavoured operetta (a commercial failure but a cult, and ultimately a popular, success), *Candide*. In all three works he continued the idea of making musical links between numbers and ensuring motivic unity throughout most of a score, although the two later works retain spoken dialogue between musical sections.

West Side Story, an adaptation of the Romeo and Juliet story using youthful gang rivalry in New York City as the backdrop, finally gave Bernstein a satisfaction that had eluded him – the experience of hearing his songs widely performed and enjoyed, a genuine part of the popular culture. The musical was groundbreaking not only for its tragic tone, but for its full integration of dance and its unified musical material (based on the tritone). Bernstein's other theatrical works include incidental music for *Peter Pan* (1950) and Anouilh's *The Lark* (1955). Projects that never reached completion included *The Skin of our Teeth* (with Comden and Green, after Thornton Wilder's play; begun and abandoned in 1964, attempted briefly again in 1969) and *The Exception and the Rule* (lyrics by Sondheim, book by John Guare, after Brecht; abandoned in 1968). Success returned to the composer with the *sui generis* theatre piece *Mass*, which attracted extraordinary attention in its first years of existence. Its framework is the celebration of a Roman Catholic mass with vernacular interpolations (somewhat in the manner of Britten's *War Requiem*), its subject the nature of faith. With *Mass*, Bernstein produced his first full-length piece of musical theatre that was musically continuous throughout; the style is eclectic, and a recurrent musical motif is the minor 7th, generally as the sum of two perfect 4ths.

After an unsuccessful return to Broadway in 1976, Bernstein reaffirmed his dramatic skills with the opera *A Quiet Place*, which began as a sequel to *Trouble in Tahiti* and eventually incorporated it. Here he showed once again his ability to seize the potential of a scene and make it vivid through music that reveals what words cannot. His command of the possibilities of the stage, his structuring of scenes to be both formally satisfying and emotionally immediate, his feeling for the variety of texture and pace necessary to sustain a full-length work, and not least his melodic inventiveness are as evident in this opera as in his more familiar earlier works. These gifts confirm Leonard Bernstein's high place among American composers for the operatic stage.

See also CANDIDE; QUIET PLACE, A (incorporating *Trouble in Tahiti*); and *WEST SIDE STORY*.

On the Town (musical, 2, B. Comden, A. Green and Bernstein), orchd H. Kay, D. Walker, E. Jacoby, T. Royal and Bernstein, Boston, 13 Dec 1944, New York, Adelphi, 28 Dec 1944, *US-Wc*

Trouble in Tahiti (1, Bernstein), Waltham, MA, Brandeis U., 12 June 1952, *Wc*, vs (New York, 1953); incorporated in rev. of A Quiet Place, 1984

Wonderful Town (musical, 2, J. Fields and J. Chodorov, after their play *My Sister Eileen*; lyrics Comden and Green), orchd Walker, New Haven, 19 Jan 1953, New York, Winter Garden, 25 Feb 1953, *Wc*

Candide (comic operetta, 2, L. Hellman, after Voltaire; lyrics R. Wilbur, J. Latouche, D. Parker, Hellman and Bernstein), orchd Bernstein and Kay, Boston, 29 Oct 1956, New York, Martin Beck, 1 Dec 1956, vs (New York, 1958); rev. version in 1 act (H. Wheeler, after Voltaire; lyrics with S. Sondheim), orchd Kay, Brooklyn, New York, Chelsea Theatre Center, 20 Dec 1973, vs (New York, 1976), *Wc*; rev. version in 2 acts, orchd Bernstein, Kay and J. Mauceri, New York, City Opera, 13 Oct 1982; rev. version in 2 acts (lyrics with J. Wells), Glasgow, Royal, 19 May 1988

West Side Story (musical, 2, A. Laurents, after W. Shakespeare: *Romeo and Juliet*; lyrics Sondheim), orchd Bernstein, with S. Ramin and I. Kostal, Washington DC, 19 Aug 1957, New York, Winter Garden, 26 Sept 1957, *Wc*, vs (New York, 1959)

1600 Pennsylvania Avenue (musical, 2, A. J. Lerner), orchd Ramin and Kay, Philadelphia, 24 Feb 1976, New York, Hellinger, 4 May 1976

A Quiet Place (1, S. Wadsworth), Houston, Jones Hall, 17 June 1983; rev. version in 3 acts, incl. Trouble in Tahiti, Milan, Scala, 19 June 1984, vs (New York, 1988)

*

EwenD

P. Gradenwitz: 'Leonard Bernstein', *MR*, x (1949), 191–202

D. Drew: 'Leonard Bernstein: *Wonderful Town*', *Score*, no.12 (1955), 77–80

J. Briggs: *Leonard Bernstein: the Man, his Work, and his World* (Cleveland, 1961)

A. Holde: *Leonard Bernstein* (Berlin, 1961)

J. Gottlieb: *The Music of Leonard Bernstein: a Study of Melodic Manipulations* (diss., U. of Illinois, 1964)

M. Rhoads: *Leonard Bernstein's 'West Side Story'* (thesis, U. of Michigan, 1964)

J. Gruen: *The Private World of Leonard Bernstein* (New York, 1968)

M. Cone: *Leonard Bernstein* (New York, 1970)

G. Jackson: '*West Side Story*: Thema, Grundhaltung und Aussage', *Maske und Kothurn*, xvi (1970), 97–101

J. Gruen: 'In Love with the Stage', *ON*, xxxvii/3 (1972–3), 16–22

H. E. Phillips: *The Carmen Chronicle* (New York, 1973)

J. W. Weber: *Leonard Bernstein* (Utica, NY, 1975) [discography]

J. Gottlieb: *Leonard Bernstein: a Complete Catalogue of his Works* (New York, 1978)

L. Bernstein: *Findings* (New York, 1982)
P. Robinson: *Bernstein* (New York, 1982)
P. Gradenwitz: *Leonard Bernstein* (Zürich, 1984; Eng. trans., 1987)
O. L. Guernsey jr, ed.: *Broadway Song and Story* (New York, 1985)
J. A. Conrad: '*Candide*: the Most Confused of All Possible Worlds', *Opus*, iii/1 (1986), 23–25, 62
J. U. Wegner: 'Bald wieder Opernkomponist? Sinfonie, Musical, Oper – Leonard Bernstein im Gespräch', *NZM*, cxlvii/10 (1986), 29–31
M. Freedland: *Leonard Bernstein* (London, 1987)
P. Gradenwitz: 'Leonard Bernstein – dramatischer Sinfoniker und sinfonischer Opernkomponist: zum 70. Geburtstag des Musikers', *Das Orchester*, xxxvi (1988), 1006–11
R. Henderson: 'Bernstein: a Life full of Firsts', *Opera*, xxxix (1988), 279–82
A. von Heyl: 'Die *West Side Story* in Musikunterricht', *Musik und Bildung*, xx (1988), 110–16
S. Ledbetter, ed.: *Sennets and Tuckets: a Bernstein Celebration* (Boston, 1988)
J. P. Swain: *The Broadway Musical: a Critical and Musical Survey* (New York, 1990), 205–46
R. H. Kornick: *Recent American Opera: a Production Guide* (New York, 1991), 61–8

JON ALAN CONRAD

Berroa, Jorge (*b* Havana, 13 Dec 1938). Cuban composer. He studied in Havana at the Amadeo Roldán Conservatory (formerly the Conservatorio Municipal). His compositions include works for voice and instrumental groups (including some settings of poems by Nicolas Guillen), folksong arrangements and incidental music for the theatre and cinema. In 1979 he wrote the opera *Soyán* (Berroa and J. Massip; Havana, Nacional, 21 Jan 1980) for the first Havana theatre festival. Based on the Cuban folk legend *El limo des Alemandares* and some of Guillen's poetry, *Soyán* is a tale of love and betrayal culminating in murder. In addition to the four main roles a chorus of 11 voices takes on the nature of a fifth with a variety of functions. The African origin of the Cuban national character is acknowledged in the music, which includes elements of jazz, rumba, *son*, *guaguancó* and other contemporary styles.

*

J. A. González: *La composición operística en Cuba* (Havana, 1987)

JORGE ANTONIO GONZÁLEZ

Berry, Walter (*b* Vienna, 8 April 1929). Austrian bass-baritone. After study with Hermann Gallos at the Vienna Akadamie für Musik he joined the Staatsoper in 1950. His first big success was as Count Almaviva in *Figaro*, and in a very few years he built up a sizeable repertory and an enviable international reputation, appearing in the leading German houses and in North and South America, and making his Metropolitan début in 1966 as Barak (*Die Frau ohne Schatten*). From 1952 he was a regular soloist at the Salzburg Festival, creating roles in such modern operas as Liebermann's *Penelope*, Egk's *Irische Legende* and von Einem's *Der Prozess*, and singing the standard bass-baritone repertory. From 1957 to 1971 he was married to the mezzo-soprano Christa Ludwig. Apart from his Mozart roles (Masetto and Leporello, Guglielmo and Don Alfonso, Papageno, Count Almaviva and, more recently, Figaro) he has won acclaim in a wide variety of parts: Wozzeck, Ochs, Escamillo, Don Pizarro, Telramund, Barak (Covent Garden début, 1976), Wotan and Bartók's Duke Bluebeard. In 1986 he returned to Covent Garden as Waldner in *Arabella*. He has made numerous recordings.

*

P. Lorenz: *Christa Ludwig, Walter Berry* (Vienna, 1968)

PETER BRANSCOMBE

Bersa, Blagoje (*b* Dubrovnik, 21 Dec 1873; *d* Zagreb, 1 Jan 1934). Croatian composer. He studied at the conservatories in Zagreb and Vienna (1896–9). From 1903 to 1919 he worked in Vienna as a music teacher and orchestrator; from 1911 he was arranger and consultant for the publishing firm Doblinger. He was professor of composition at the Zagreb Academy of Music (formerly the conservatory) from 1922 until his death. Bersa was a typical *fin de siècle* composer who enriched the Romantic tradition with fresh nuances. Of his three operas the most important is *Der Eisenhammer* (1905–6), in which he drew on Wagnerian techniques as well as on the Italian *verismo* style to portray modern subject matter and the atmosphere of a factory; the 'music of the machines' in Act 3 is an example of musical futurism. He also composed 'melo-monodramas' and a film score. As both composer and teacher he laid the foundations of modern music in Croatia.

Jelka, 1901 (J. Bersa), unperf.
Der Eisenhammer, 1905–6 (A. M. Willner); in Croatian as Oganj [The Flame], Zagreb, 12 Jan 1911
Der Schuster von Delft, 1912 (comic op, J. Wilhelm and Willner); in Croatian as Postolar iz Delfta, Zagreb, 26 Jan 1914

*

M. Kuntarić: *Blagoje Bersa* (Zagreb, 1959)
K. Kovačević: *Hrvatski kompozitori i njihova djela* [Croatian Composers and their Works] (Zagreb, 1960), 32–40
J. Andreis: *Music in Croatia* (Zagreb, 1974)
B. Polić: 'Blagoje Bersa i "Postolar iz Delfta" u Beču 1918' [Blagoje Bersa and 'The Cobbler of Delft' in Vienna 1918], *Zvuk* (1980), no.1, pp.78–80

KORALJKA KOS

Berselli, Matteo (*fl* 1708–21). Italian soprano castrato. He was apparently Venetian; he sang in six operas in Venice (1708–9), including works by Gasparini and Albinoni, in Bologna (1712), Reggio (1713 and 1719), Rome (1714 in Gasparini's *Lucio Papirio* and 1716), Florence (1715), Milan (1715) and in three operas at Naples, including Alessandro Scarlatti's *La virtù trionfante* (1716). He was engaged at Dresden (1717–20) and appeared in Lotti's *Giove in Argo*, *Ascanio* and *Teofane* and Ristori's *Cleonice*. He sang for one season with the Royal Academy at the King's Theatre, making his début in Giovanni Bononcini's *Astarto* (1720) in a female role, and appearing in Handel's *Radamisto*, the pasticcios *Arsace* (*Amor e Maestà*) and *Ciro* (*Odio ed Amore*) and the composite *Muzio Scevola* (1721). Handel composed three new arias for him in *Radamisto* and a duet and aria in *Muzio Scevola*, of which Burney remarked that 'this singer must have been high in the composer's favour for taste, as he is left to himself in no less than six *ad libitums* and adagios, which he had to embellish'.

Berselli's voice was a high soprano with a compass from *e*′ to *b*″ in Handel, though according to Quantz, who thought his tone pleasing but rather thin, he could sing from *c*′ to *f*‴.

WINTON DEAN

Bertali [Bertalli, Berthali, Bartali, Barthali, Bartaldi], **Antonio** (*b* Verona, March 1605; *d* Vienna, 17 April 1669). Austrian composer of Italian birth. He received his early training in music from Stefano Bernardi, *maestro di cappella* of Verona Cathedral from 1611 to 1622. He then served Archduke Carl Joseph, Bishop of Breslau and Bressanone and brother of Emperor Ferdinand II, for two years before moving to Vienna to work at the imperial court. Although active there from 1624 and well respected as virtuoso violinist and composer of both sacred and secular music, it was not until after his appointment, on 1 October 1649, as Kapellmeister to Ferdinand III that Bertali began his career as a composer of operas. His authorship of ten of the 13 operas attributed to him has been clearly established although only three complete scores are extant. That he probably composed the two anonymous Mantuan works *Niobe* and *Theti* is indicated by the occasion of their performance, a visit of Archduke Ferdinand Karl to the Mantuan court; however, sources for the Vienna performance of *Theti* (1656) indicate that it was 'newly composed'. The lost intermezzo *Cibele ed Ati* (?1666), first attributed to Bertali by Köchel (without indication of evidence), may have been written for the festivities celebrating the first marriage of Leopold I.

As was customary at the Habsburg court, Bertali's operas were written for important official court functions – the Imperial Diet at Regensburg (*L'inganno d'amore*), Leopold I's first marriage (*La contesa dell'aria e dell'acqua*), birthdays of the emperor (*Theti* for Ferdinand III and *La magia delusa* and *Il Ciro crescente* for Leopold I) and the Empress Dowager Eleonora (*La Zenobia di Radamisto* and probably an untitled work, incipit 'Pazzo amor') – and for the carnival season. Members of the imperial household, including the emperor, frequently participated, particularly in the ballets. Most of Bertali's Vienna operas were produced in collaboration with the official court librettists (Aurelio Amalteo and Francesco Sbarra), theatre architects and stage directors (the Burnacini), choreographers (Santo Ventura) and composers of ballet music (Wolfgang Ebner and J. H. Schmelzer).

Some stylistic features of his early Viennese operas (*L'inganno d'amore*, *Theti* and *Il re Gelidoro*, extant only in librettos) can be ascertained from the structure and content of the texts. They contain an unusual number of solo ensembles (from two parts to eight) and choruses. Arias often have two or more strophes; a textual da capo is rarely indicated. *La magia delusa* exists, as does much of the Vienna repertory, only in partial score (continuo with occasional instrumental indications or incipits). This work and the two Vienna operas preserved in full score indicate Bertali's preference for a basic scoring of violins and two or more viols with continuo. Particularly noteworthy is the large number of arias scored for an ensemble of viols, without violins, in the untitled opera of 1664. The same score also indicates the use of *cornetti muti* and a bassoon. Arias are usually in 'seicento form' (*ABB* or *ABCC*). Generally, Bertali eschews elaborate vocal writing and concentrates on expressive settings of the text, notably in the frequent arioso endings of recitatives.

As capable administrator, versatile and prolific composer and trusted adviser to the two emperors he served, Bertali contributed in no small measure to the establishment of Italian operatic practices and styles at the imperial court in Vienna. His influence in sacred and instrumental music as well as opera can be seen throughout the reign of Leopold I.

L'inganno d'amore (prol., 3, B. Ferrari), Regensburg, 24 Feb 1653, pubd lib. *A-Wn*

Theti (favola dramatica, prol, 5, Diamante Gabrielli), Vienna, Hof, 13 July 1656, pubd lib. *Wn*

Il re Gelidoro (prol., 3, A. Amalteo), Vienna, Hof, 19 Feb 1659, pubd lib. *Wn*

La magia delusa (introduttione drammatica musicale ... avanti il balletto, prol., 1, Amalteo), Vienna, Favorita, 4 June 1660, *Wn*

Gli amori d'Apollo con Clizia (introdutione drammatica per musica per i balletti, prol., 1, Amalteo), Vienna, Hof, 1 March 1661, pubd lib. *Wn*

Il Ciro crescente (prol., 3 intermezzos, Amalteo), Vienna, Laxenburg, 14 June 1661, *Wn*

La Zenobia di Radamisto (prol., 3, C. de' Dottori), Vienna, Hof, 18 Nov 1662, Act 3 and pubd lib. *Wn*

Untitled opera [incipit: Pazzo amor] (prol., 1), Vienna, Hof, ?18 Nov 1664, *Wn*

L'Alcindo (prol., 3, A. Draghi), Vienna, Hof, 20 April 1665, prol., pubd lib. *Wn*

La contesa dell'aria e dell'acqua [vocal music] (festa a cavallo, F. Sbarra), Vienna, Hof, 24 Jan 1667, pubd lib. *Wn* [ballets by J. H. Schmelzer]

Doubtful: Niobe (introduttione alla barriera, 3, Gabrielli), Mantua, Ducale, 15 Feb 1652, pubd lib. *US-Wc*; Theti (favola dramatica, prol., 5, Gabrielli), Mantua, Ducale, 24 Feb 1652, pubd lib. *Wc* [relationship to Theti for Vienna, 1656, is unknown]; Cibele ed Ati (intermezzo), Vienna, ?Dec 1666

AllacciD

A. von Weilen: *Zur Wiener Theatergeschichte: die vom Jahre 1629 bis zum Jahre 1740 am Wiener Hofe zur Aufführung gelangten Werke theatralischen Charakters und Oratorien* (Vienna, 1901)

C. LaRoche: *Antonio Bertali als Opern- und Oratorienkomponist* (diss., U. of Vienna, 1919)

E. Wellesz: 'Die Opern und Oratorien in Wien, 1660–1708', *SMw*, vi (1919), 5–138

W. Senn: *Musik und Theater am Hof zu Innsbruck* (Innsbruck, 1954)

A. Bauer: *Opern und Operetten in Wien: Verzeichnis ihrer Erstaufführungen in der Zeit von 1629 bis zur Gegenwart* (Graz, 1955)

F. Hadamowsky: 'Barocktheater am Wiener Kaiserhof; mit einem Spielplan (1625–1740)', *Jb der Gesellschaft für Wiener Theaterforschung 1951–2*, 7–117; pubd separately (Vienna, 1955)

I. Bartels: *Die Instrumentalstücke in Oper und Oratorium der frühvenezianischen Zeit* (diss., U. of Vienna, 1970)

H. Haider-Pregler: 'Das Rossballett im Inneren Burghof zu Wien', *Maske und Kothurn*, xv (1970), 291–324

H. Seifert: 'Die Festlichkeiten zur ersten Hochzeit Kaiser Leopolds I', *ÖMz*, xxix (1974), 6–16

——: 'Die Entfaltung des Barock', *Österreichische Musikgeschichte*, ed. R. Flotzinger and G. Gruber, i (Vienna, 1977), 323–79

——: *Die Oper am Wiener Kaiserhof im 17. Jahrhundert* (Tutzing, 1985)

RUDOLF SCHNITZLER

Bertati, Giovanni (*b* Martellago, 10 July 1735; *d* Venice, *c*1815). Italian librettist. The son of a farm agent, he was sent by a local nobleman to study at the Treviso seminary, but showed more interest in the theatre. His libretto *La morte di Dimone, o sia L'innocenza vendicata*, a translation of a German play by the impresario J. F. von Kurz, was set by Antonio Tozzi and inaugurated the renovated Teatro S Cassiano in Venice in 1763. Thereafter he wrote almost exclusively comic librettos. He benefited from his association with Baldassare Galuppi, who took him to Vienna in 1770 and for whom he wrote two librettos. Bertati wrote over 70 librettos, at least 45 of them for the Teatro S Moisè in Venice, where he served as principal comic librettist from 1771 to 1791. Many of his works, set by Gazzaniga, Anfossi and other composers, achieved considerable success beyond Italy. In 1791, after several earlier visits to Vienna, he succeeded the ousted Da Ponte as chief poet to the imperial theatre, where his *Il matrimonio segreto* (music by Cimarosa) was an instant and long-lasting success. He returned to Venice in 1794, apparently by his own choice, having written five librettos for Vienna. After 1798 he largely gave up writing librettos and worked as a civil servant, later an archivist, at the arsenal in Venice.

Bertati's librettos reflect both the traditions of Italian comedy and the innovations of Carlo Goldoni, his leading predecessor in Venice. Most are dramas of domestic intrigue, populated by shrewd servants, vain or fatuous aristocrats and young lovers who have to outwit jealous, greedy or social-climbing guardians (as for example in *Il matrimonio segreto*). There are also librettos set in imaginary or distant lands, combining typical romantic intrigue with satirical observations about contemporary life and manners (for instance in *L'inimico delle donne* and *L'isola di Alcina*). Bertati relied heavily on the traditional mechanisms of Italian comedy: disguises and mistaken identities, magic incantations, and the other comic devices of the *commedia dell'arte*. He used to good advantage nonsense poetry, real or invented foreign languages, parodies of the elevated language of *opera seria*, and catalogue arias, which were a particular speciality. As with Goldoni, his intrigues involve rivalries both of class and of generation. Smith (1970) saw in Bertati's librettos 'a growing undertone of cynical protest at the license of the aristocrats' – a protest broader than in Goldoni's mocking of particular social customs (in particular in Bertati's *La villanella rapita* and *Don Giovanni*). But Bertati was no revolutionary; his works are light and entertaining, and for the most part conventional and unchallenging.

The widespread success of Bertati's librettos was due far more to their theatrical than to their poetic merits. Perhaps partly because of the haste in which he frequently had to work, his language is often coarse, lacking the grace of such librettists as Da Ponte or G. B. Casti. Moreover, as Goldin has shown, Bertati's poetry lacks the finesse and variety needed to distinguish characters from one another; the psychological subtlety of Da Ponte's librettos for Mozart is not to be found in Bertati's. His strength was his ability to 'order a story line with clarity and concision and stuff it with the requisite amount of plot intrigue and *commedia* business' (Smith 1970). Even Da Ponte, who had little that was positive to say about his rival, acknowledged that Bertati's librettos came across better on the stage than in reading.

Bertati's one-act libretto *Don Giovanni, o sia Il convitato di pietra* (set by Gazzaniga in 1787) served as the model for Da Ponte's *Don Giovanni* for Mozart. Da Ponte took over nearly complete the outlines of Bertati's work, adding to it the Act 1 finale and most of the second act. But Bertati's version, despite its strong characterization of Giovanni and its dramatic scenes of the duel and the final confrontation with the statue, has a less serious tone. It comprises the second act of a comedy, *Il capriccio drammatico*, depicting the woes of a touring opera company which out of desperation revives the old Don Juan story, even though the singers protest that the tale is fit for nothing but village fairs. This 'frame' thus presents Bertati's one-act *Don Giovanni* in an ironic light. Even more striking, its final scene (after Giovanni's descent to hell) is a frivolous comic ensemble in which the other characters imitate the sounds of musical instruments, with a variety of nonsense syllables.

La morte di Dimone, o sia L'innocenza vendicata (dramma serio, with J. F. von Kurz), A. Tozzi, 1763; *I creduti spiriti* (dg, with Kurz), J. G. Naumann and 2 others, 1764; *L'isola della fortuna* (dg), Lucchesi, 1765; *Il villano geloso* (dg), B. Galuppi, 1769 (Naumann, 1770; Sarti, 1785, as I finti eredi); *L'anello incantato* (dg), Bertoni, 1771; *Calandrano* (dg), Gazzaniga, 1771 (Sacchini, 1778, as L'avaro deluso o Don Calandrano); *L'inimico delle donne* (dg), Galuppi, 1771 (Gazzaniga, 1773, as Zon-Zon principe di Kibin-Kinka); *La locanda* (dg), Gazzaniga, 1771 (Paisiello, 1791); *L'isola di Alcina* (dg), Gazzaniga, 1772

I visionari (dg), Astarita, 1772 (Paisiello, 1779, as I filosofi immaginari); *La contessa di Bimbimpoli* (dg), Astarita, 1772; *La tomba di Merlino* (dg), Gazzaniga, 1772; *Armida* (os), Naumann, 1773 (Gazzaniga, 1773; Zumsteeg, 1786); *Mirandolina* (dg), P. A. Guglielmi, 1773 (Caruso, 1776, as Il padre della virtuosa; A. Franceschi or Franchini, 1776, as La virtuosa moderna; Fabrizi, 1786, as L'amore per interesse); *La villanella incostante* (dg), Naumann, 1773; *Il marito che non ha moglie* (dg), Astarita, 1774; *L'orfane svizzere* (dg), Bertoni, 1774; *Il geloso in cimento* (dg, after C. Goldoni: *La vedova scaltra*), Anfossi, 1774

Il principe ipocondriaco (dg), Astarita, 1774 (Naumann, 1776, as L'ipocondriaco); *L'avaro* (dg), Anfossi, 1775 (Astarita, 1776; V. Fioravanti, 1800; F. Orlandi, 1801; Bianchi, 1804); *L'amor bizzaro* (dg), Rust, 1775; *La novità* (dg), Alessandri, 1775; *Li sapienti ridicoli, ovvero Un pazzo ne fa cento* (dg), Astarita, 1775; *La donna instabile* (dg), Borghi, 1776; *Isabella e Rodrigo, o sia La costanza in amore* (dg), Anfossi, 1776; *Lo sposo disperato* (dg), Anfossi, 1777 (Nusco, 1808); *La forza delle donne* (dg), Anfossi, 1778 (? B. Ottani, 1784, as Le amazzoni; Winter, 1795, as Ogus, o Il trionfo del bel sesso; Nicolini, 1799); *La contessa di Novaluna* (dg), Gazzaniga, 1778 (Fabrizi, 1786)

Il cavaliero errante (dramma eroicomico), Traetta, 1778; *Le industrie amorose* (dg), Ottani, 1778 [? same lib. as that set by Anfossi, 1779, as Il matrimonio per inganno]; *La vendemmia* (op giocosa), Gazzaniga, 1778; *Azor re di Kibinga* (dg), Anfossi, 1779; *Le nozze in contrasto* (dg), G. Valentini, 1779; *Il più bel dono inutile* (dg), A. Rossetti, 1779; *I Quacqueri* (dg), Rossetti, 1779; *Li rivali ridicoli* (dg), Mortellari, 1780; *La statua matematica* (dg), Valentini, 1780 (Caruso, 1786, as L'antiquario burlato, ossia La statua matematica); *Le teste deboli* (dg), Salari, 1780 (various, 1794, as La donna di testa debole); *L'imbroglio delle tre spose* (dg), Anfossi, 1781 (Alessandri, 1784)

Il marito geloso (dg), Caruso, 1781 (? Alessandri, 1781 or 1784); *L'opera nuova* (dg), M. Rauzzini, 1781; *Lo sposalizio per dispetto* (dg), Monti, 1781; *Il vecchio geloso* (dg), Alessandri, 1781; *Gli amanti alla prova* (dg), Caruso, 1783 (Piticchio, 1784); *La villanella rapita* (dg), Bianchi, 1783 (Alessandri, 1784; Trento, 1797, as La fedeltà nelle selve; P. C. Guglielmi, 1805); *Le due sorelle incognite* (dg), Calegari, 1783; *Il serraglio di Osmano* (dg), Gazzaniga, 1784 (Ghinassi, 1787, as Osmanns Serail); *Le spose ricuperate* (dg), Caruso, 1785; *Le donne fanatiche* (dg), Gazzaniga, 1786; *L'amor costante* (int), Gazzaniga, 1787 (Dutillieu, 1792, as Nannerina e Pandolfino)

Don Giovanni, o sia Il convitato di pietra (dg), Gazzaniga, 1787 (Pacini, 1832, as Don Giovanni Tenorio); *Chi sta ben non si muova*, Robuschi, 1787; *L'orfanella americana* (commedia per musica), Anfossi, 1787 (Gestewitz, 1791); *Il curioso accidente* (dg), Astarita, 1789; *La fata capricciosa* (dg), Gardi, 1789; *Il pazzo glorioso*, Bernardini, 1790 (A. Brunetti, 1797); *Il matrimonio segreto* (dg, after G. Colman and D. Garrick: *The Clandestine Marriage*), Cimarosa, 1792 (Graffigna, 1883); *Amor rende sagace* (dg), Cimarosa, 1793; *La principessa d'Amalfi* (dg), J. Weigl, 1794 (B. Porta, 1780 [?same libretto]); *La bella Lauretta* (dg), Gardi, 1795

L'intrigo amoroso (dg), Paer, 1795; *Andromeda*, Zingarelli, 1796; *La donna innamorata* (dg), Nicolini, 1796; *La donna di genio volubile* (dg), Portugal, 1796 (Farinelli, 1808, as La sposa di genio volubile); *Amor l'astuzia insegna* (dg), Gardi, 1797; *Il medico di Lucca* (dg), Nasolini, 1797; *Melinda* (favola romanzesca), Nasolini, 1798; *La pace* (melodramma eroicomico), 'Giuseppe Pranzer', Mayr and Marinelli, 1798; *Le tre orfanelle, o sia La scuola di musica* (dg), Bernardini, 1798; *Gli umori contrarii* (dg), Nasolini, 1798; *Amore e dovere* (f), Mosca, 1800; *La bella selvaggia* (ob), Salieri, comp. 1802

Doubtful: *Stordilano, principe de Granata*, Traetta, 1760; *Il tamburo notturno* (commedia musicale, after G. Lorenzi: *Il tamburo*), Paisiello, 1773; Le finezze d'amore, o sia La farsa non si fa, ma si prova, ? Astarita, 1773; *Il curioso indiscreto* (dg), Anfossi, 1777 [lib. possibly by G. Petrosellini, acc. to Angermüller; ? same lib. as that set by Gherardeschi, 1764]; L'impresario in scompiglio, Astarita, ?1791

*

DBI (V. Frajese); *DEUMM* (F. Cella); *ES* (U. Rolandi)

L. Da Ponte: *Memorie di Lorenzo Da Ponte da Ceneda scritte da esso* (New York, 1823–7, rev., enlarged 2/1829–30; Eng. trans., 1929)

F. Fapanni: 'G. Bertati trivigiano poeta drammatico', *L'apatista*, i (1 Dec 1834)
G. Salvioli: *Intorno al poeta drammatico Giovanni Bertati: opuscolo per nozze Bertoja-centenari* (Venice, 1880)
A. Schatz: 'Giovanni Bertati', *VMw*, v (1889), 231–71
W. Dean: 'The Libretto of *The Secret Marriage*', *Music Survey*, iii (1950), 33–8
P. Smith: *The Tenth Muse: a Study of the Opera Libretto* (New York, 1970)
S. Kunze: *Don Giovanni vor Mozart: die Tradition der Don-Giovanni-Opern im italienischen Buffa-Theater des 18. Jahrhunderts* (Munich, 1972)
F. Cella: 'La premessa di Giovanni Bertati', *Storia dell'opera*, ed. A. Basso (Turin, 1977), iii/2, pp.143–51
D. Goldin: 'Un librettista da rivalutare', *Giovanni Bertati, 1735–1815* (Martellago, 1985), 23
——: *La vera fenice: librettisti e libretti tra sette e ottocento* (Turin, 1985)
M. G. Accorsi: 'Teoria e pratica della "variatio" nel dramma giocoso: a proposito della "Villanella rapita" di Giovanni Bertati', *I vicini di Mozart*, ed. M. T. Muraro and D. Bryant (Florence, 1989), 139–64
R. Angermüller: 'Die Wiener Fassung von Pasquale Anfossis "Il curioso indiscreto"', ibid, 35–98

JOHN PLATOFF

Berthélémy, Jean-Simon (*b* Laon, 5 March 1743; *d* Paris, 2 March 1811). French painter and costume designer. He won the Prix de Rome for painting in 1767, and his friendship with François-Guillaume Ménageot dates from this period. From 1770 to 1774 he was in Rome, at the Académie de France, and in September 1787 he joined the Opéra as Louis-René Boquet's assistant, taking over from Ménageot, who had just been appointed director of the Académie de France in Rome. In 1791 he succeeded Boquet and became official costume designer to the Opéra. He led an extremely active life until 1807, dividing his time between teaching at the Académie de Peinture, travelling in Italy (1796–8), his responsibilities at the Musée Central des Arts (now the Louvre museum) and his many commissions as a designer. On 29 December 1807 he tendered his resignation to the Opéra for health reasons, and returned the post to Ménageot. In a moving letter addressed to the theatre's administrative body, he recalled his zealous attention to his job for more than 20 years, despite the difficulties of the times: 'I have done all in my power to associate correctness of style in the costumes with the grace and dignity befitting this theatre'. After his death, his family gave the Opéra the sketches for the costumes he designed between 1791 and 1809. They were for a revival of Grétry's *La caravane du Caire*; Méhul's *Cora* (see illustration), P. J. Candeille's reworking of Rameau's *Castor et Pollux*, and Méreaux's *Oedipe et Jocaste* (all 1791); Mme Hippolyte de Vismes' *Praxitèle* (1800); François Charlemagne Lefebvre's *Les noces de Gamache* and Rodolphe Kreutzer's *Astyanax* (1801); Catel's *Sémiramis* and Winter's *Tamerlan* (1802); Paisiello's *Prosperine* (1803); Le Sueur's *Ossian*, Cherubini's ballet *Achille à Scyros* (1804); Blangini's *Nephtali* (1806); Persuis' *Le retour d'Ulysse* and Le Sueur's *Le triomphe de Trajan* (1807); and *Proserpine* (1809).

Designs by Jean-Simon Berthélémy for the costumes of Zilia (sung by Marie-Thérèse Davoux Maillard, left) and Cora (sung by Anne-Marie Jeanne Gavaudan) in the original production of Méhul's 'Cora' at the Paris Opéra, 15 February 1791

For further illustration *see* OSSIAN, OU LES BARDES and PRODUCTION, fig.11.

Registers of the Théâtre de l'Opéra (*F-Po*, AD 3, INV 13–14)
Archives Nationales, ser. AJ[13], 57, 75, 79, 106
N. Volle: *Jean-Simon Berthélémy (1743–1811): peintre d'histoire* (Paris, 1979)

NICOLE WILD

Berthelier, Jean-François (Philibert) (*b* Panissières, 14 Dec 1830; *d* Paris, 29 Sept 1888). French tenor. He made his début in Poitiers in 1849 as Fernand in Donizetti's *La favorite*, but when the theatre closed he took to singing in local *cafés-concerts*. In 1855 he was engaged by Offenbach to be a member of the first company at the Bouffes-Parisiens, and was a great success in the opening performance, Offenbach's *Les deux aveugles*; later he created several roles, including Paimpol in *Une nuit blanche* and Kokikako in *Ba-ta-clan*. He was then engaged for the Opéra-Comique where he created 12 roles, including those of Simplet in Gautier's *Le mariage extravagant*, Aignelet in Bazin's *Maître Pathelin* and Xailoun in Offenbach's *Barkouf*.

Berthelier was credited with the discovery of Hortense Schneider, who became Offenbach's greatest female interpreter, and with whom he appeared at the Palais-Royal in *Jeune poule et vieux coq* (1858). He later appeared at the Variétés, Renaissance, Nouveautés and Gaîté theatres in many roles, including Zappoli in *La tzigane*, one of the earliest French versions of Strauss's *Die Fledermaus*. Among his most famous numbers was 'Ah! Que c'est comme un bouquet de fleurs' from *Le petit ébéniste*, and his particular facility for wearing headgear led him to give a lecture on hats at the Variétés in 1874.

PATRICK O'CONNOR

Bertin, Louise(-Angélique) (*b* Bièvres, Essonne, 15 Jan [not Feb] 1805; *d* Paris, 26 April 1877). French composer. She was the only composer to collaborate directly with Victor Hugo on an opera, and the earliest French composer to write an opera based on Goethe's

Faust. Having received instruction from Antoine Reicha and F.-J. Fétis, she began writing operas in the mid-1820s with *Guy Mannering* (to her own libretto, after Scott's novel). This was performed by friends at her family's estate outside Paris in 1825, and was accepted by the Théâtre de l'Odéon, though not performed there because of a management change. After *Guy Mannering* she wrote *Le loup-garou*, first performed at the Opéra-Comique in March 1827. It received 24 performances that year, a moderate success, and enjoyed runs in several provincial towns.

As early as 1826, Bertin had begun work on a large-scale *opera semiseria*, in Italian, based on Goethe's *Faust*. In June 1826 she published the 'Ultima scena di Fausto', an arrangement of her opera's last scene. Thus she was in the vanguard of the Romantic Faust mania that swept France. By 1827, the Théâtre Italien accepted *Fausto* and scheduled it for performance in 1830. Maria Malibran was cast as Margarita, but the performance was postponed at the last minute, apparently because she refused to sing. *Fausto* finally reached the stage in 1831, with different singers, but received only three performances.

Victor Hugo and Louise Bertin became friends in the late 1820s and eventually agreed to collaborate on an opera. When Hugo wrote his novel *Notre-Dame de Paris*, he sketched an opera scenario on the same subject and it was accepted by the Opéra administration in late 1830 or early 1831. Ultimately known as *La Esmeralda*, the opera suffered a noisy reception in 1836; the audience was packed with *claqueurs*, especially those for and against the *Journal des débats*, the powerful newspaper run by Bertin's father, Louis-François Bertin *l'aîné*. Further cries of favouritism were fuelled by Louise's brother Armand's membership of the governmental commission overseeing the Opéra administration. A near-riot at the seventh performance prevented the continuation of the run, though a one-act reduction survived for three years. Bertin composed no further operas after 1836, but continued to write other music and poetry. Some works were performed publicly. Her *Six ballades* (1842) are especially worthy of revival. A published piano trio reworks themes from *Fausto* and *La Esmeralda*.

Bertin was a talented composer with an original voice. During her 11-year operatic career, she consistently saw beyond the conventions of her time. She was among the first to attempt a truly Romantic musical style to match her subject matter, uniting a German harmonic language (influenced by Mozart and Weber and her studies with Reicha) with her French sensitivity to the text. In her *opéras comiques*, she showed the influence of Rossini; in her serious operas, the Italian influence can be seen in some of the large forms, but these she also treated with a freedom guided by the dramatic situation. Her music is strongest when expressing gloom, sadness, anguish, rage and the supernatural. She shows originality in her delight in the unexpected: her adventurous sense of harmony, the sudden twists and turns of her melody. These are never gratuitous, however, but always dramatically or textually motivated. She uses the orchestra skilfully to provide the emotional setting, or to describe or comment on the action. Especially interesting is the extensive use of recurring melodic, harmonic and rhythmic motifs in *La Esmeralda*. Bertin's four operas are a remarkable achievement, and one can only speculate on what might have been her contribution had she not retired prematurely.

Design by Louis Boulanger for the costume of La Esmeralda (sung by Cornélie Falcon) in the original production of Louise Bertin's opera at the Paris Opéra, 14 November 1836

Guy Mannering (oc, 3, L. Bertin, after W. Scott), private perf., Bièvres, 25 Aug 1825, *US-Bp**

Le loup-garou (oc, 1, E. Scribe and E. Mazères), Paris, OC (Feydeau), 10 March 1827 (Paris, 1827)

Fausto (opera semiseria, 4, Bertin, after J. W. von Goethe), Paris, Favart, 7 March 1831, *F-Pn**, vs (Paris, 1831)

La Esmeralda (4, V. Hugo, after his *Notre-Dame de Paris*), Paris, Opéra, 14 Nov 1836, *F-Pn**, vs ed. F. Liszt (Paris, 1837)

PEM (A. Gerhard)

H. Berlioz: 'La Esmeralda', *Revue et gazette musicale de Paris*, iii (1836), 409

H. Blaze de Bury: 'La musique des femmes: Mlle Louise Bertin', *Revue des deux mondes*, 4th ser., viii (1836), 611–25

J.-J. Weiss, ed.: *V. Hugo: Lettres aux Bertin* (Paris, 1890)

M. Brenet: 'Quatre femmes musiciennes, 3: Mlle Bertin', *L'art*, 2nd ser., iv (1894), 177–83

A. Laster: '"La Esmeralda": Présentation', in V. Hugo: *Oeuvres complètes*, ed. J. Massin (Paris, 1967–9), v, 487–91

A. Gerhard: 'Die Machte der Fatalität: Victor Hugo als Librettist', *Perspektiven der Opernforschung I: Bad Homburg 1985*

D. Boneau: *Louise Bertin and Opera in Paris in the 1820s and 1830s* (diss., U. of Chicago, 1989)

A. Gerhard: *Der Verstädterung der Oper* (Stuttgart, 1992)

DENISE BONEAU

Bertin de la Doué, Toussaint (*b* Paris *c*1680; *d* Paris, 6 March 1743). French composer. Generally known incorrectly by the first name of Thomas, he was the son of a Parisian master carpenter, Jacques Ladoué; in 1705, the year of his marriage, he is recorded as teaching the harpsichord and 'other instruments'. The following year his first dramatic work, *Cassandre*, composed in collaboration with François Bouvard, was performed at the Opéra. He was to write two more *tragédies en musique*, *Diomède* (1710) and *Ajax* (1716), the latter enjoying particular success in the provincial theatres of

Lyons, Nantes and Bordeaux as well as in Paris, where it was revived in 1726, 1742 and 1770. He later composed a *pastorale-héroïque*, *Le jugement de Pâris* (1718), and an *opéra-ballet*, *Les plaisirs de la campagne* (1719). Between 1714 and 1734 he played the harpsichord for the continuo in the orchestra of the Opéra.

See also PLAISIRS DE LA CAMPAGNE, LES.

all first performed at the Paris Opéra; printed works published in reduced score in Paris, unless otherwise stated

Cassandre (tragédie en musique, prol., 5, F.-J. de Lagrange-Chancel), 22 June 1706, full score (1706), collab. F. Bouvard
Diomède (tragédie en musique, prol., 5, J.-L.-I. de La Serre), 28 April 1710 (1710)
Ajax (tragédie en musique, prol., 5, A. Menesson), 20 April 1716 (1716)
Le jugement de Pâris (pastorale-héroïque, prol., 3, M.-A. Barbier and S.-J. Pellegrin), 14 or 21 June 1718 (1718)
Les plaisirs de la campagne (opéra-ballet, prol., 3, Barbier and Pellegrin), 10 Aug 1719, *F-Po**, full score (1719)

Airs in: Lully: Atys, Dec 1709 (1709); Lully: Psyché, 22 June 1713 (1713)

*

ES (F. Lesure); *MGG* (G. Ferchault)
N. Boindin: *Lettres historiques sur tous les spectacles de Paris* (Paris, 1719)
F. Parfaict and C. Parfaict: *Histoire de l'Académie royale de musique depuis son établissement jusqu'à présent* (MS, ?1741, *F-Pn*)
G. Sadler: 'Rameau's Singers and Players at the Paris Opéra', *EMc*, xi (1983), 453–67
J. de La Gorce: 'L'orchestre de l'Opéra et son évolution de Campra à Rameau', *RdM*, lxxvi (1990), 23–43 JÉRÔME DE LA GORCE

Bertini, Gary (*b* Brichevo, Bessarabia [now Moldova], 1 May 1927). Israeli conductor of Russian birth. Taken to Palestine as a child, he later studied at the Milan and Paris conservatories, and with Nadia Boulanger, Chailley and others. He returned to Israel, and made his début as an orchestral conductor in 1955 with the Israel PO. From 1965 he was a frequent visitor to Britain and formed a close association with the Scottish National Orchestra and Scottish Opera, which he first conducted in 1971 (Rossini and Mozart). The same year he conducted the reconstructed version of Weill's *Royal Palace* at the Holland Festival and the première at Hamburg of Tal's *Ashmedai*. He also conducted the premières of Tal's *Masada 967* (1973, Jerusalem), and *Die Versuchung* (1977, Munich). His Paris Opéra début was in 1975 with Dukas' *Ariane et Barbe-bleue* and his Berlin début the next year with *Die Entführung*. In the decade that followed he was prominent on the Israeli musical scene (Jerusalem SO, Israel Festival) and in Germany. In 1987 he became general director at the Frankfurt Opera, where the opera house was destroyed by fire just as he began his intendancy with Gluck's two *Iphigénie* operas presented in tandem. He kept the ensemble performing in smaller theatres during rebuilding, but disputes involving the orchestra led to his contract being abruptly terminated before the reopening in April 1991. His recordings include the first recording of Weber's *Die drei Pintos* (1976). Bertini has shown himself a versatile and assiduous conductor, though on occasion lacking attack and dramatic impetus. He has composed theatre, ballet and concert music.

WILLIAM Y. ELIAS, NOËL GOODWIN

Bertinotti(-Radicati), Teresa (*b* Savigliano, Piedmont, 1776; *d* Bologna, 12 Feb 1854). Italian soprano. She studied under La Barbiera and sang at the Teatro Fiorentino, Naples, from 1788 (in works by Tritto, Guglielmi and others); she made her début at La Scala in 1794–5, in Tarchi's *Le Danaidi* and created the title role in Paer's *La Rossana*. By the time of her marriage to Felice Radicati in 1801 she was well known in Italy as a prima donna. From 1801 to 1818 she sang widely in Europe in operas by Mayr and others; a Munich reviewer praised her in Cimarosa's *Gli Orazi ed i Curiazi* (1806) as 'a sensitive, sweet singer with a voice not too strong or brilliant, but pleasant, clear and moving', and at the King's Theatre, London (1810–12), she enjoyed particular success in Mozart operas and was praised in W. T. Parke's *Musical Memoirs* (London, 1830). She later returned to Italy, retiring from the stage in 1820 and devoting herself to teaching. ALBERT MELL

Bertoli, Antonio Daniele (*b* Udine, 1678; *d* Vienna, 7 Dec 1743). Italian costume designer. He was engaged at the Viennese court theatre on 1 October 1707 as 'disegnatore da camera' at a salary of 1200 florins, and became drawing master to Empress Maria Theresa. The year after Metastasio became court poet, Bertoli was appointed Imperial Gallery Inspector (on 25 May 1731) and assumed responsibility for theatrical costumes. A master of the Rococo style, he probably designed costumes for the premières of 12 operas, by Caldara, Conti, Predieri and Hasse (all to librettos by Metastasio), between 1731 and 1743. Two folio volumes containing 283 costume drawings, known also as stage-figurines, in pencil, silver point, pen, *grisaille* and watercolour, are in the Österreichische Nationalbibliothek (C.P. Min 43).

For illustration *see* COSTUME, fig.5.

*

ES (J. Gregor)
J. Gregor, ed.: *Antoine Daniel Bertoli: desseins*, Monumenta scenica, iii (Vienna, 1925; Eng. trans., 1925), 10–13, pls.1–24

SIDNEY JACKSON JOWERS

Bertolli, Francesca (*b* Rome; *d* Bologna, 9 Jan 1767). Italian contralto. In 1728 she was in the service of the Grand Duchess of Tuscany and sang in two operas in Bologna and in Livorno. Handel engaged her for the second Royal Academy at the King's Theatre (1729–33); she appeared in 15 of his operas, in Ariosti's *Coriolano*, Leo's *Catone* and two pasticcios, and in Handel's first London oratorio performances. From 1733 to 1736 she sang with the 'Opera of the Nobility' in 11 operas, including five by Porpora, Veracini's *Adriano*, Giovanni Bononcini's *Astarto* and Handel's *Ottone*. She returned to Handel (1736–7) and sang in four of his operas, and in a pasticcio based on Vinci's *Didone*. She was in three operas at Venice (1740–41), but retired soon after.

No singer except Strada and Senesino appeared in so many of Handel's operas. The nine parts he composed for her, Idelberto in *Lotario*, Armindo in *Partenope*, Gandartes in *Poro*, Honoria in *Ezio*, Melo in *Sosarme*, Medoro in *Orlando*, Ramisa in *Arminio*, Leocasta in *Giustino* and Selene in *Berenice*, indicate a voice of limited range and capacity; her regular compass was *b*♭ to *e*″. She specialized in male roles, as the list above suggests. Mrs Pendarves, who was contemptuous of her voice, ear and manner, described her as 'a perfect beauty, quite a Cleopatra'. WINTON DEAN

Bertolo, Aldo (*b* Turin, 22 Oct 1949). Italian tenor. In 1978 he sang Ferrando (*Così fan tutte*) in Susa, then appeared at many Italian and other European cities. His repertory includes Don Ottavio, Pylades (Piccinni's *Iphigénie en Tauride*), the Fisherman (*Guillaume Tell*), Lindoro (*L'italiana in Algeri*), Narciso (*Il turco in Italia*), Adelberto (*Adelaide di Borgogna*), Ramiro, Elvino (*La sonnambula*), Arturo (*I puritani*), Edgardo (*Lucia di Lammermoor*), Tonio (*La fille du régiment*), Ernesto, Lorenzo (*Fra Diavolo)* and Alfredo. He has a light, flexible voice well adapted to Rossini and Bellini.

ELIZABETH FORBES

Berton. French family of composers and performers.

(1) **Pierre-Montan Berton** [Le Breton] (*b* Maubert-Fontaine, Ardennes, 7 Jan 1727; *d* Paris, 14 May 1780). Composer, conductor and arranger. He was a highly talented chorister at Senlis Cathedral (where motets he composed in his youth were performed), and after continued musical studies in Paris he joined the Opéra as a singer (*c*1744). In 1746 he moved to the Marseilles opera, and in 1748 to the opera in Bordeaux; here he became *maître de musique* and began the career of editing and arranging for which he is remembered. From about 1753 he was back in Paris, and in 1755 he was appointed *maître de musique* at the Opéra. From then on, honours accrued: master of the king's music (1760), joint director of the Opéra (with Jean-Claude Trial, 1767), then its general administrator (1775–6 and 1777–8). He was director of the Concert Spirituel from 1771 to 1773.

Berton's own works had only modest success, the most famous piece being a chaconne originally heard in the 1762 revival of *Iphigénie en Tauride* by Campra and Desmarets. However, he excelled in adapting older operas to suit contemporary taste: according to the 1782 obituary he treated almost all the earlier operas given after 1755. The process involved cuts, reorchestration, new recitatives, and insertion of new music (ballets, arias, choruses), often to new words; existing recitatives were sometimes modernized with string accompaniments. All the works that Berton arranged were performed at the Paris Opéra; some were published and MSS survive (in *F-Pc* and *Po*), but research has yet to determine the exact extent of these revisions and the dates on which they were definitely introduced (the list below gives the most likely dates). Berton, in addition, raised orchestral standards at the Opéra and assiduously looked for new talent; by updating performance techniques and facilitating the invitation to Paris of Gluck and Piccinni, he paved the way for those composers in France. Meude-Monpas described his conducting, and called him a 'sovereign master of the orchestra'.

printed works published in Paris

Deucalion et Pyrrha (opéra-ballet, 1, G.-F. P. de Saint-Foix and P. Morand), Paris, Opéra, 30 Sept 1755, *F-Po*, 1 duet *Pc*; (n.d.); collab. Giraud

Silvie (opéra, prol., 3, P. Laujon), Fontainebleau, 17 Oct 1765 (1767), collab. J.-C. Trial

Erosine (pastorale-héroïque, F.-A. Paradis de Moncrif), Fontainebleau, 9 Nov 1765 (1766) [3rd entrée of Moncrif: *Les fêtes lyriques*]

Théonis, ou Le toucher (pastorale-héroïque, A.-A.-H. Poinsinet), Paris, Opéra, 11 Oct 1767, *Pc*, *Po*, collab. Trial and Granier [2nd entrée of Poinsinet: *Fragments nouveaux*]

Adèle de Ponthieu (tragédie lyrique, 3, R. de Saint-Marc), Paris, Opéra, 1 Dec 1772, *Po*, frags. *Pn**, collab. J.-B. de La Borde; rev. in 5 acts, 1775

Linus, 1775 (opéra, La Bruère), inc., *Pn*, collab. Trial and Dauvergne

Addns and modifications to works by other composers: Royer: Zaïde, reine de Grenade, 1756 or 1770; Campra: Les festes vénitiennes, 1759; Campra: Camille, reine des Volsques, 1761; Campra and Desmarets: Iphigénie en Tauride, 1762; Campra: Tancrède, 1764; Rameau: Naïs, 1764; Rameau: Hippolyte et Aricie, 1767; Mouret: 'Apollon et Coronis' in Les Amours des dieux, 1767; La Borde: Amphion, 1767; Lalande and Destouches: 'Le feu' in Les élémens, 1767; Rameau: Dardanus, 1768; Collin de Blamont: 'Tibulle' in Les festes grecques et romaines, 1770; Destouches: Issé, 1770; La Borde: Ismène et Isménias, 1770; Rameau: Zoroastre, 1770; Lully: Amadis, 1771; Marais: Alcyone, 1771; Lully: Bellérophon, 1773; Destouches: Issé, 1773; Gluck: La Cythère assiégée, 1775; Lalande and Destouches: 'Vertumne et Pomone' [formerly 'La terre'] in Les élémens, 1776

Dates of first perf. unknown: Rameau: Castor et Pollux; Lully: Alceste

*

MGG (M. Briquet)

'Notice de la vie et des ouvrages de M. Berton', *Le nécrologe des hommes célèbres de France*, xvii (Paris, 1782), 43–56

J. J. O. de Meude-Monpas: *Dictionnaire de musique* (Paris, 1787), 91

T. de Lajarte: *Bibliothèque musicale du Théâtre de l'Opéra* (Paris, 1878)

M. Ténéo: 'Pierre Montan Berton d'après les "Souvenirs de famille historiques et artistiques" de son fils', *ReM*, vii (1908), 389–90, 416–7, 493–4

L. Rosow: 'From Destouches to Berton: Editorial Responsibility at the Paris Opéra', *JAMS*, xl (1987), 285–309

(2) **Henri-Montan Berton** (*b* Paris, 17 Sept 1767; *d* Paris, 22 April 1844). Composer, teacher and writer, son of (1) Pierre-Montan Berton. He was taught by J.-B. Rey, and later had some operatic tuition from Sacchini. After experience as a violinist at the Opéra, Berton composed a number of cantatas given at Parisian concerts, and was quickly accepted as a composer at the Comédie-Italienne. He had scant success before *Les rigueurs du cloître* (1790), which rose on a wave of popular anticlerical feeling (a young nun is saved from entombment at the hands of a corrupt mother superior).

Berton's output is striking for the large number of librettists with whom he collaborated. In 1797 he wrote his own libretto for *Ponce de Léon*, but the work made only a limited impression. His most original middle-period works were *Le délire* and *Montano et Stéphanie*. Both maintain the musical resources to match their high passions, and they held the stage for many years; but *Aline, reine de Golconde* was Berton's greatest international success. From 1807 to 1810 he was musical director at the Théâtre de l'Impératrice (Opera Buffa), moving afterwards to the Opéra as chorus master (1810–15). The chivalric *Françoise de Foix* featured marching-choruses. Berton attempted tragedy with *Virginie* (1823), which had an honourable 32 performances.

There are many streaks of originality in Berton's works, though not a persistent theatrical vision. His instrumentation, unified use of motifs and lyric gift were often noteworthy. He perpetuated the later 18th-century italianate melodic style, and opposed new idioms arising in the age of Spontini, Rossini and Berlioz.

all first performed in Paris; printed works published in Paris; genres are taken from librettos

PCI – *Comédie-Italienne (Salle Favart)* PO – *Opéra*
PFE – *Théâtre Feydeau* POC – *Opéra-Comique*

Le premier navigateur (cmda, 1, N.-F. Guillard), 1784, *F-Pn**

Les promesses de mariage, suite de L'épreuve villageoise (opéra bouffon, 2, Desforges [P.-J.-B. Choudard]), PCI, 4 July 1787 (n.d.)

L'amant à l'épreuve, ou La dame invisible (oc, 2, P.-L. Moline and C.-F. Fillette-Loraux, after P. Scarron: *Le roman comique*), PCI, 5 Dec 1787, *B-Bc**

Les brouilleries (comédie, 3, C.-J. L. d'Avrigny), PCI, 1 March 1790; rev. in 2 acts, 4 March 1790, *F-Pn**

Les rigueurs du cloître (cmda, 2, J. Fiévée), PCI, 23 Aug 1790 (1790)

Le nouveau d'Assas (trait civique mêlé de chants, 1, Dejaure [J.-E. Bédéno]), PCI, 15 Oct 1790 (1790)

Les deux sentinelles (1, F.-G.-J.-S. Andrieux), PCI, 27 March 1791, *Pn**

Les deux sous-lieutenants, ou Le concert interrompu (comédie, 1, E.-G.-F. de Favières), PCI, 19 May 1792, *Pn**; rev. version (with B.-J. Marsollier de Vivetières), POC (Feydeau), 31 May 1802 (1802)

Eugène, ou La piété filiale (3, d'Avrigny), PFE, 11 March 1793, *Pn**

Le congrès des rois (comédie, 3, Desmaillot [A. F. Eve]), POC (Favart), 26 Feb 1794, frag. by Berton *Pn**, collab. Dalayrac, Grétry, Méhul and 8 others

Agricol Viala, ou Le héros de la Durance (1, Fillette-Loraux), PFE, 9 Oct 1794, *Pn**

Bélisaire [Act 3] (opéra, 3, A. L. Bertin d'Antilly), POC (Favart), 3 Oct 1796 [Acts 1 and 2 by F.-A. D. Philidor]

Christophe et Jérôme, ou La femme hospitalière (comédie, 1, Favières), POC (Favart), 26 Oct 1796

Ponce de Léon (opéra bouffon, 3, H.-M. Berton), POC (Favart), 4 March 1797 (n.d.)

Le dénouement inattendu (1, Joigny), POC (Favart), 10 Nov 1797

Le rendez-vous supposé, ou Le souper de famille (comédie, 2, J.-B. Pujoulx), POC (Favart), 5 Aug 1798, *Pn**, excerpts, vs (n.d.)

Montano et Stéphanie (opéra, 3, Dejaure, after L. Ariosto: *Orlando furioso*), POC (Favart), 15 April 1799, *Pn** (1799); rev. with new Act 3 (G.-M.-J.-B. Legouvé), 4 May 1800, full score (*c*1800), vs (1841)

La nouvelle au camp, ou Le cri de vengeance (scène lyrique, 1), PO, 14 June 1799, *Po*

L'amour bizarre, ou Les projets dérangés (oc, 3, C.-L. Lesur), POC (Favart), 30 Aug 1799

Le délire, ou Les suites d'une erreur (comédie, 1, J.-A. de Révéroni Saint-Cyr), POC (Favart), 7 Dec 1799 (*c*1800)

Le grand deuil (opéra bouffon, 1, J.-B.-C. Vial and C.-G. Etienne), POC (Favart), 21 Jan 1801 (1801)

Aline, reine de Golconde (opéra, 3, Vial and Favières, after M.-J. Sedaine), POC (Feydeau), 3 Sept 1803, frag. *Pn**; (n.d.)

La romance (opéra, 1, Fillette-Loraux), POC (Favart), 26 Jan 1804 (1804)

Le vaisseau amiral [L'intrigue à bord, ou Forbin et Delville] (opéra, 1, Saint-Cyr), POC (Favart), 2 April 1805, *Pn**; (n.d.)

Délia et Verdikan (opéra, 1, P.-J.-B.-F. Elleviou), POC (Favart), 9 May 1805, frag. *Pn**; (n.d.)

Les maris garçons (cmda, 1, C. Gaugiran-Nanteuil), POC (Feydeau), 15 July 1806 (1806)

Le chevalier de Sénanges [Adèle de Sénanges] (3, A. J. P. Ségur and L. N. de Forbin), POC (Feydeau), 23 July 1808, *B-Bc**

Ninon chez Mme de Sévigné (comédie mêlée de chants, 1, Dupaty [L. E. F. C. Mercier]), POC (Feydeau), 26 Sept 1808, frag. *F-Pn**; (n.d.)

Françoise de Foix (opéra, 3, J.-N. Bouilly and Dupaty), POC (Feydeau), 28 Jan 1809, frag. *Pn*; (n.d.)

Le charme de la voix (oc, 1, Gaugiran-Nanteuil and Fillette-Loraux), POC (Feydeau), 24 Jan 1811, *Pn**

La victime des arts, ou La fête de famille (2, L.-M. d'Estourmel), POC (Feydeau), 27 Feb 1811, collab. Isouard and Solié

Valentin, ou Le paysan romanesque (oc, 3, L.-B. Picard and Fillette-Loraux), POC (Feydeau), 13 Sept 1813 (n.d.); rev. in 2 acts, 4 Dec 1819

L'oriflamme (opéra, 1, Etienne and L.-P.-M.-F. Baour-Lormian), PO, 1 Feb 1814, *Pn*, *Po*, *I-PAc*; (1814); collab. R. Kreutzer, Méhul and Paer

Les dieux rivaux, ou Les fêtes de Cythère (opéra-ballet, 1, Dieulafoy and Briffaut), PO, 21 June 1816, *F-Po*, collab. Kreutzer, Persuis and Spontini [for the wedding of the Duc de Berry]

Féodor, ou Le batelier du Don (oc, 1, Claparède), POC (Feydeau), 15 Oct 1816, *B-Bc*, *F-Pn**, vs (n.d.); as Une journée du Czar, Brussels, 26 Oct 1816

Roger de Sicile, ou Le roi troubadour (opéra, 3, J.-H. Guy), PO, 4 March 1817, *Po*; (n.d.)

Corisandre, ou La rose magique (oc, 3, J. A. P. F. Ancelot and Saintine [J. X. Boniface]), POC (Feydeau), 29 July 1820, *Pn*

Blanche de Provence, ou La cour des fées (opéra, 1 E.-G. Théaulon and De Rancé), Tuileries, 1 May 1821, PO, 5 May 1821, *Pc**, *Po*, collab. Boieldieu, Cherubini, Kreutzer and Paer

Virginie, ou Les décemvirs (tragédie-lyrique, 3, A. F. Désaugiers), PO, 11 June 1823, *Po*; (1823)

Les deux mousquetaires, ou La robe de chambre (oc, 1, Justin-Gensoul and Vial), POC (Feydeau), 22 Dec 1824 (n.d.)

Pharamond (opéra, 3, Ancelot, P.-M.-A. Guiraud and A. Soumet), PO, 10 June 1825, *Pn**, *Po*, *R(m)*, vs (n.d.), collab. Boieldieu and Kreutzer

Les créoles (drame lyrique, 3, P.-J.-L. de Lacour), POC (Feydeau), 14 Oct 1826, *Pn**; (n.d.)

Les petits appartements (oc, 1, J.-G. Ymbert, A. F. Varner and H. Dupin), POC (Feydeau), 9 July 1827, *Pn**; (n.d.)

La marquise de Brinvilliers (drame lyrique, 3, E. Scribe and Castil-Blaze [F.-H.-J. Blaze]), POC (Ventadour), 31 Oct 1831 (1831), collab. Auber, Batton, Blangini, A. Boieldieu, Carafa, Cherubini, Hérold and Paer

Unperf.: La fête du soleil (opéra, de la Touloubre), rehearsed at PO, 1789, *Pn* (partly autograph), *Po* [mentioned in Lajarte]; Tyrtée (2, Legouvé), rehearsed at PO, 1793 [mentioned in *FétisB* and Choron and Fayolle]; Vingt ans de constance [La mère et la fille] (3, Dupaty), *Pn**; Charles Deux [mentioned in Berton: *Traité d'harmonie*, 1815]

Arrangements: Gluck: Echo et Narcisse, reduced to 2 acts, PO, 25 March 1806; Le laboureur chinois (pasticcio), PO, 5 Feb 1813, music by Haydn and Mozart; Sacchini: Arvire et Evélina, reduced to 2 acts, PO, 13 Sept 1820; Grétry: Guillaume Tell, with new music, POC (Feydeau), 24 May 1828

*

FétisB; *FétisBS*; *PEM* (H. Schneider)

A. Choron and F. Fayolle: *Dictionnaire historique des musiciens* (Paris, 1810–11)

Etat du nombre de représentations de M. Berton depuis l'année 1787 jusqu'à 1826 (MS, *F-Pn** Rés 2715 (1–2))

H. Blanchard: *Henri-Montan Berton* (Paris, 1839)

P. Smith [pseud. of E. Monnais]: 'Histoire d'un chef-d'oeuvre', *Revue et gazette musicale de Paris*, viii (1841), 477–9, 485–7, 494–5

——: 'Appendice à l'histoire d'un chef-d'oeuvre', ibid, ix (1842), 121–2

A. Adam: 'Berton', *France musicale*, vii (1844), 129–30

P. Smith: 'Souvenirs anecdotiques sur Berton et plusieurs de ses ouvrages', *Revue et gazette musicale de Paris*, xi (1844), 173–5

D. Raoul-Rochette: 'Notice historique sur la vie et les ouvrages de M. Berton', *Académie royale des beaux-arts: séance publique annuelle du samedi 10 octobre 1846* (Paris, 1846), 21

A. Adam: *Derniers souvenirs d'un musicien* (Paris, 1859); Eng. trans., as 'Henri Berton: 1767–1844', *ML*, xxx (1949), 121–35

F. Halévy: *Derniers souvenirs et portraits* (Paris, 1863), 205ff

M. Tourneux, ed.: *Correspondance littéraire, philosophique et critique par Grimm, Diderot, Raynal, Meister, etc.* (Paris, 1877–82)

H. Cohen: 'Etudes sur Berton', *L'art musical*, xvii (1878), 73–114 passim

T. de Lajarte: *Bibliothèque musicale du Théâtre de l'Opéra* (Paris, 1878)

M. Dietz: *Geschichte des musikalischen Dramas in Frankreich während der Revolution bis zum Directorium* (Vienna, 2/1886)

A. Pougin: *L'Opéra-Comique pendant la Révolution de 1788 à 1801* (Paris, 1891)

J. Tiersot: *Lettres de musiciens écrites en français du XVe au XXe siècle*, i (Turin, 1924)

M. Pincherle, ed.: *Musiciens peints par eux-mêmes* (Paris, 1939)

R. M. Longyear: 'Notes on the Rescue Opera', *MQ*, xlv (1959), 49–66

B. Deane: 'The French Operatic Overture from Grétry to Berlioz', *PRMA*, xcix (1972–3), 67–80

M. D. Smith: *Antoine Joseph Reicha's Theories on the Composition of Dramatic Music* (diss., Rutgers U., 1979)

K. Pendle: '*A bas les couvents*: Anticlerical Sentiment in French Opera of the 1790s', *MR*, xlii (1981), 22–45

M. E. C. Bartlet: 'Opera as Patriotic Ceremony: the Case of *L'Oriflamme*', *La musique et le rite, sacré et profane: IMSCR*, xiii *Strasbourg 1986*, i, 327–39

C. J. Robison: *One-Act Opéra-Comique from 1800 to 1810: Contributions of Henri-Montan Berton and Nicolo Isouard* (diss., U. of Cincinnati, 1986)

M. Noiray: 'Les créations d'opéra à Paris de 1790 à 1794', *Orphée phrygien: Les musiques de la Révolution*, ed. J.-R. Julien and J.-C. Klein (Paris, 1989), 193–204

P. Taïeb: 'De la composition du *Délire* (1799) au pamphlet anti-dilettantes (1821): une étude des conceptions esthétiques de H.-M. Berton', *RdM*, lxxviii (1992), 67–107

P. Vendrix, ed.: *Grétry et l'Europe de l'opéra-comique* (Liège, 1992)

(3) **Henri** [François] **Berton** (*b* Paris, 3 May 1784; *d* Paris, 19 July 1832). Composer, son of (2) Henri-Montan Berton. After musical instruction by his father he entered the Paris Conservatoire in 1796. On leaving in 1804 he began to publish piano arrangements of operatic pieces (including his father's) and to compose. His first four stage works were produced in 1810 and 1811. *Ninette à la cour* displays fashionable levity with a predominance of lively movements in the major mode, but no melodic originality. In fact, the first finale borrows the principal subject of the first movement of Mozart's piano duet sonata K358/186*c*. From 1820 to 1 January 1828 he taught singing at the Conservatoire. His other works include *romances* and piano pieces. *Une heure d'absence* failed in 1827, but *Le château d'Urtuby*, produced posthumously, received some favourable comment. His son, Adolphe Berton (1817–57), was a tenor. He sang at the Opéra-Comique and the Théâtre de la Renaissance in Paris, and from 1843 in Nice and Algiers, where he died.

all opéras comiques, first performed in Paris

Le présent de noces, ou Le pari (1, R. A. P. A. de Chazet), OC (Feydeau), 2 Jan 1810

Monsieur Desbosquets (1, C.-A. Sewrin), OC (Feydeau), 6 March 1810

Jeune et vieille (1, Chazet and Dubois), OC (Feydeau), 12 Jan 1811, collab. L. B. Pradher

Ninette à la cour (oc, 2, C.-S. Favart and C. A. Creuzé de Lesser), OC (Feydeau), 21 Dec 1811 (Paris, n.d.)

Les casquets (1, Mme Riccoboni and J.-B.-C. Vial), OC (Feydeau), 19 Feb 1821

Une heure d'absence (1, C.-F. Fillette-Loraux, OC (Feydeau), 1827

Le château d'Urtuby (G. de Lurieu and Raoul), OC (Ventadour), 14 Jan 1834

*

M. Ténéo, ed.: H.-M. Berton: 'Souvenirs de famille de H. M. Berton', *BSIM*, vii (1911), no.1, p.1; no.3, p.41; no.6, p.42

DAVID CHARLTON (1 with GRAHAM SADLER; 2 with MICHEL NOIRAY and PATRICK TAÏEB)

Bertoni, Ferdinando (Gasparo) [Giuseppe] (*b* Salò, nr Brescia, 15 Aug 1725; *d* Desenzano, nr Lake Garda, 1 Dec 1813). Italian composer. He studied composition with Padre Martini in Bologna. His first opera was the successful pasticcio *La vedova accorta*, first performed in Florence in 1745. It was repeated in Venice (1746) and elsewhere in Europe. The Venetian libretto identifies Bertoni as the composer of 'La Musica de' recitativi, e delle [9] arie'. His first serious opera, *Il Cajetto*, was staged privately, with puppets, in 1746. He composed two more *opere serie* within the year for commercial theatres in Venice, but was more successful in the comic genre: *Le pescatrici* (1751), on a Goldoni libretto, had 14 productions in 17 years throughout Europe, including Dresden (1754), London (1761) and Madrid (1765) in a Spanish translation by Ramón de la Cruz. *La moda* (1754) contains his earliest extant cavatinas, and Bertoni may have been the first to introduce the cavatina to opera.

With his appointment as *primo organista* at St Mark's, Venice (1752), and *maestro* of the female chorus at the Ospedale de' Mendicanti (1753), Bertoni turned more to religious compositions and to serious opera, although his best comic opera, *L'anello incantato*, was written in 1771. In February of that year Mozart and his father may have heard Anna De Amicis sing in Bertoni's *Alessandro nell'Indie* (Venice, Teatro S Benedetto), and in 1778 Mozart requested a 'grand aria' by Bertoni, which Leopold sent to Mannheim. The Act 1 finale of *Alessandro* begins with accompanied recitative leading to a duet which includes a reprise of a cavatina and bravura aria from earlier scenes (sung now by opposite characters) and brilliant *passaggi* in thirds.

With the Bologna production of *L'olimpiade* (Carnival 1773), Bertoni began his professional association with the castrato Gasparo Pacchierotti, his former pupil in Venice. Following their triumphs in *Artaserse* (1776), *Medonte* (1777) and *Quinto Fabio* (1778), they travelled to London for the first of two visits with Bertoni as composer-in-residence and Pacchierotti as primo uomo at the King's Theatre. Of the seven operas Bertoni worked on during the first visit (1778–80), most were pasticcio versions of earlier works; only one new opera, *Il duca d'Atene*, was composed. He wrote music for two other pasticcios: *Demofoonte*, in which Pacchierotti sang 'Non temer bell' idol mio' which became a favourite song, and *La governante* whose rondo 'La virginella' became a popular salon song, translated into English and French and transcribed for various instruments, as well as inserted in other operas. During the second visit (1781–3), Bertoni composed two new operas, *Il convito* and *Cimene*. Pacchierotti sang in pasticcio verions of three other operas, and in a production of *Ifigenia in Aulide*. Bertoni returned to Italy with 'a bad portrait of Sacchini' and the Reynolds portrait of Burney for Padre Martini's collection.

Burney praised Bertoni's graceful and flowing melody and his 'clear and well arranged' harmony, and found his style 'natural, correct, and judicious; often pleasing, and sometimes happy', but had qualms about his inventiveness. Caffi described his style as 'natural, clear, the voice part agreeable; the orchestration graceful, and not exaggerated'. Bertoni's progressive tendencies show mostly in his use of more flexible aria forms such as the cavatina, some 40 of which are found in his operas, and large scene complexes with accompanied recitative and fuller orchestration, as in *Armida abbandonata*. He wrote only one 'reform' opera, *Orfeo ed Euridice* (1776), on Calzabigi's libretto, patterned after Gluck's music. It was highly successful and his only opera printed in full score during his lifetime. Gluckists have never forgiven him for the similarities, yet Gluck himself 'borrowed' several Bertoni arias without attribution for his operas.

Bertoni's success as an opera composer in Venice and admiration for his religious music led to his appointment as *maestro di cappella* of St Mark's in 1785, without opposition; he succeeded Galuppi, whose career he had emulated since their collaboration in *I bagni d'Abano* (1753). He composed only two new operas after this appointment and retired in 1808. Among his pupils in his last years in Venice were Mayr and Antonio Calegari.

See also ARISTO E TEMIRA; ORFEO ED EURIDICE (ii); PESCATRICI, LE (i); and QUINTO FABIO.

opere serie unless otherwise stated

LKH – *London, King's Theatre* TR – *Turin, Teatro Regio*
VB – *Venice, Teatro S Benedetto* VM – *Venice, Teatro S Moisè*

Il Cajetto (A. Gori), Venice, Palazzo Labia, carn. 1746

Orazio e Curiazio (S. A. Sografi), Venice, S Samuele, Ascension Fair 1746, aria *I-Vc*

Armida (B. Vitturi, after T. Tasso: *Gerusalemme liberata*), Venice, S Angelo, 26 Dec 1746, *D-Mbs*

Didone abbandonata (tragedia, P. Metastasio), Venice, Palazzo Labia, carn. 1748, aria *I-PAc*
Ipermestra (Metastasio), Genoa, Falcone, carn. 1748, arias in *B-Bc*, *I-Gl* and *Vnm*
Le pescatrici (dg, 3, C. Goldoni), Venice, S Samuele, 26 Dec 1751, *D-B*, *Dlb*, *Wa*, *F-Pc* (without recits.), *P-La*, Favourite Songs (London, *c*1761)
Antigono (Metastasio), VM, aut. 1752
I bagni d'Abano (dg, Goldoni), Venice, S Samuele, 10 Feb 1753, Act 2 *D-W* and *MGmi*, collab. Galuppi
Ginevra (A. Salvi, after L. Ariosto), Venice, S Samuele, aut. 1753
La moda (dg, D. Benedetti), VM, carn. 1754, *Dlb*
Sesostri (dramma, P. Pariati), TR, 26 Dec 1754, *Dlb*, *LEmi*
Antigona (G. Roccaforte), Genoa, Falcone, carn. 1756, *I-OS**, aria in Six Favourite Italian Songs Performed ... by Tenducci (London, 1778)
Lucio Vero (Zeno), TR, carn. 1757, *Vnm*, *P-La*
Il Vologeso (Zeno), Padua, Obizzi, carn. 1759, *D-MÜs*, *P-La*
Le vicende amorose (dg, D. Pallavicino), VM, aut. 1760, *A-Wn*, *P-La*
La bella Girometta (dg, P. Chiari), VM, aut. 1761, *La*
Ifigenia in Aulide (L. Serio or V. A. Cigna-Santi), TR, carn. 1762, *I-OS** (Act 2), *Tf*, *P-La*
Achille in Sciro (Metastasio), Venice, S Cassiano, carn. 1764, *I-OS**, *P-La*
L'ingannatore ingannato (dg, Chiari), Venice, S Cassiano, aut. 1764, *I-OS**
L'olimpiade (Metastasio), Venice, S Cassiano, carn. 1765, *D-Dlb*, *F-Pc*, *P-La*, Favourite Songs (London, *c*1779)
Il Bajazetto (J. A. Sanvitale, after A. Piovene), Parma, Regio Ducale, 3 May 1765, *I-OS**
Tancredi (Balbis, after Voltaire), TR, 26 Dec 1766, *F-Pn*, *I-OS** (Act 2), *P-La*, aria in Journal d'ariettes italiennes ... (Paris, 1779)
Ezio (Metastasio), VB, carn. 1767, *La*, Favourite Songs (London, *c*1781)
Semiramide riconosciuta (Metastasio), Naples, S Carlo, 3 May 1767, *La*
Scipione nelle Spagne (Zeno), Milan, Ducale, 30 Jan 1768, *I-Nc* (without recits), *P-La*
Alessandro nell'Indie (Metastasio), Genoa, Falcone, spr. 1769, *D-Bds* (Act 1), *P-La*
Il trionfo di Clelia (Metastasio), Padua, Nuovo, 10 June 1769, *I-OS**, *P-La*
L'anello incantato (dg, G. Bertati), VM, aut. 1771, *I-OS**
Andromaca (Salvi), VB, 26 Dec 1771, *OS** (Acts 1 and 2), *P-La* (Act 3)
L'orfane svizzere (dg, Bertati), Livorno, S Sebastiano, carn. 1774
Narbale (Metastasio: *L'eroe cinese*), VM, 25 May 1774, *I-OS** (Act 3), arias in *B-Bc*, *I-Gl* and *US-NYp*
Aristo e Temira (dramma per musica, 1, Conte de' Salvioli), VB, 3 Jan 1776, *D-Mbs*, *F-Pc* (inc.), parts *I-Pca*
Orfeo ed Euridice (dramma per musica, 3, R. de' Calzabigi), VB, 3 Jan 1776; *A-Wn*, *B-Bc*, *D-B* (with addns by Reichardt), *Dlb*, *DS*, *FS*, *WRl*, *F-Pn*, *GB-Lbl*, *H-Bn*, *I-BGc*, *BRq*, *CMbc*, *Gl*, *Mc*, *OS**(*R*1977: DMV, xxiii), *Pca*, *PAc*, *Tn*, *Vc*, *P-La*; (Venice, 1776, 2/1783)
Creonte (G. Roccaforte), Modena, Ducale, 27 Jan 1776
Artaserse (Metastasio), Forlì, Nuovo, spr. 1776, *I-Mc* (with addns by Generali), *P-La*; rev. version, Genoa, S Agostino, carn. 1788; arias in *A-Wgm*, *I-Gl*, *Mc*, *PAc*, *Rc* and *Tn*
Telemaco ed Eurice nell'isola di Calipso (G. Pindemonte), VB, 26 Dec 1776, *D-Bds*, *P-La*, arias in Recueil de romances et chansons (Paris, *c*1788)
Medonte re d'Epira (G. De Gamerra), TR, 26 Dec 1777, *I-Gl* (Act 1), *Tf*, *P-La*, Favourite Songs (London, 1782), ov. arr. hpd (London, *c*1783)
Quinto Fabio (3, Zeno: *I due dittatori*), Milan, Interinale, 31 Jan 1778, *I-Gl* (Act 1), *OS**, *Pl*, *Vc*, *P-La* (inc.), Favourite Songs (London, 1780)
Artaserse (Metastasio), LKH, 23 Jan 1779, Favourite Songs (London, *c*1779)
La governante, or The Duenna (dg, C. F. Badini, after R. B. Sheridan: *The Duenna*), LKH, 15 May 1779, arias in *I-Mc* and *Vnm*, Favourite Songs (London, 1779), arias (Edinburgh, Dublin and London, *c*1780)
Il duca d'Atene (dg, Badini), LKH, 9 May 1780
Armida abbandonata (Vitturi), VB, 26 Dec 1780, *B-Bc*, *D-Bds*, *I-Gl*, *P-La*
Cajo Mario (Roccaforte), VB, Ascension Fair 1781, *I-OS**, *P-La*
Il convito, or The Banquet (dg, A. Andrei, after F. Livigni), LKH, 2 Nov 1782, Favourite Songs (London, *c*1782)
Cimene, LKH, 7 Jan 1783, ov. arr. hpd (London, *c*1783)
Eumene (Zeno), VB, 26 Dec 1783, *P-La* (Act 1), arias in *B-Bc* and *I-Vc*
Nitteti (Metastasio), Venice, S Samuele, 6 Feb 1789, *B-Bc*, *I-OS*, ov. *B-Bc* and *I-Vc*
Angelica e Medoro (G. Sertor), VB, carn. 1791 [also attrib. G. Andreozzi]

Music in: La vedova accorta, 1745; Tigrane, 1755; Demetrio, 1757; Creso, 1758; Solimano, 1758; Cleonice, 1763; Gli orti esperidi, ?1764; The Summer's Tale, 1765; Le gelosie villane, 1776; Demofoonte, 1778; Il soldano generoso, 1779; Giulio Sabino, 1781; Il falegname, 1781; I viaggiatori felici, 1782; Giunio Bruto, 1782; The Castle of Andalusia, 1782; Robin Hood, 1784; Zemira e Azore, 1779; Richard Coeur de Lion, 1786; Der Fürst und sein Volk, 1791

Doubtful: Eurione (A. Papi), Udine, Sociale, Aug 1770; Decebalo (Papi), Treviso, Oneigo, Oct 1770

*

AllacciD; *BurneyH*; *CroceN*; *DBI* (F. Fano); *ES* (E. Zanetti); *LS*
C.-P. Coqueau: *Entretiens sur l'état actuel de l'Opéra de Paris, suite des entretiens sur l'état actuel de l'Opéra de Paris* (Paris, 1779); also in M. Tourneaux, ed.: *Correspondance littéraire, philosophique et critique par Grimm, Diderot, Raynal, Meister, etc.* (Paris, 1877–82), xii, 294–5, 305
M. Kelly: *Reminiscences of the King's Theatre* (London, 1826, 2/1826); ed. R. Fiske (London, 1975)
R. Mount Edgcumbe: *Musical Reminiscences, Containing an Account of the Italian Opera in England from 1773* (London, 1834)
G. Brunati: *Dizionarietto degli uomini illustri della riviera di Salò* (Milan, 1837)
M. Fürstenau: 'Ueber die Schluss-Arie des ersten Aktes aus Gluck's französ. *Orpheus*', *Berliner Musik-Zeitung Echo*, xix (1869), 261–5, 269–71
G. Desnoiresterres: *Gluck et Piccinni: 1774–1800* (Paris, 1872, 2/1875), 266ff
A. Valentini: *I musicisti bresciani ed il Teatro grande* (Brescia, 1897)
T. Wiel: *I teatri musicali veneziani nel settecento* (Venice, 1897)
G. Bustico: 'Un musicista salodiano del secolo XVIII: F. Bertoni', *Illustrazione bresciana* (1 Feb 1911)
——: *Per la storia del melodramma: F. Bertoni e Rubinelli* (Salò, 1913)
E. Anderson, ed.: *The Letters of Mozart and his Family* (London, 1938, 3/1985)
A. Loewenberg: 'Gluck's Orfeo on the Stage with some Notes on Other Orpheus Operas', *MQ*, xxvi (1940), 311–39, esp. 323
M. Gerosa: 'Il melodramma e la musica del salodiano Bertoni', *Il Benaco nei ricordi e nelle sovrane bellezze*, ii (Brescia, 1956)
H. Brofsky: 'Students of Padre Martini', *FAM*, xiii (1966), 159–60
G. T. Hollis: *Ferdinando Giuseppe Bertoni (1725–1813): a Study of his Operas and his Contribution to the Cavatina* (diss., U. of Southern California, 1973)
A. Schnoebelen: *Padre Martini's Collection of Letters in the Civico Museo Bibliografico Musicale in Bologna* (New York, 1979)

GEORGE TRUETT HOLLIS

Bertram, Theodor (*b* Stuttgart, 12 Feb 1869; *d* Bayreuth, 24 Nov 1907). German bass-baritone. He was trained by his father, Heinrich, who was a singer, as was his mother, Marie. In 1889 he made his début at Ulm as the Hermit in *Der Freischütz*, subsequently appearing in Hamburg, Berlin and Munich. At the Metropolitan he made a successful début in 1899 as Hans Sachs in *Die Meistersinger*, and sang most of the principal Wagnerian bass-baritone roles there and on tour. He sang at Covent Garden first in 1900 and at Vienna in 1902, but his artistic home was Bayreuth, where he sang from 1901 (when he took the title role in the first performance there of *Der fliegende Holländer*) to 1906. He was much admired by Cosima Wagner, though his few recordings suggest that his ample voice was used in the very ways for which singing at Bayreuth in those years was commonly criticized. He committed suicide, having become a victim of depression on the death of his wife in 1905. J. B. STEANE

Berutti, Arturo (*b* San Juan, 14 March 1858; *d* Buenos Aires, 3 Jan 1938). Argentine composer. He studied at the Leipzig Conservatory (1884–8) and in 1892 moved to Italy, where his first three operas, *Vendetta*, *Evangelina* and *Tarass Bulba*, had their premières (in 1892, 1893 and 1895 respectively). In 1895 he returned to Buenos Aires, and there he wrote five more operas which were all performed in Latin America.

Berutti's reputation as the first Argentine nationalist composer stems from works written between 1878 and 1909, a period which includes his entire operatic output. His operas, however, display a more international style. Most of them show, in both music and texts, the strong influence of Italian opera in Buenos Aires at the time. Even those on Latin American subjects, such as *Pampa* (on gauchos), *Yupanki* (on the Incas), *Horrida nox* (on local customs) and the epic *Gli eroi* (after V. F. López's *La loca de la guardia*), reflect the Italian style. *Yupanki* and *Gli eroi* also show the influence of Wagner in the heroic nature of their plots. Berutti devoted the years of his artistic and intellectual maturity exclusively to opera and was Argentina's most successful composer in the genre before the 1920s.

Vendetta, 1890 (opera lirica, 3, D. Crisafuli), Vercelli, Civico, 21 May 1892, vs (Milan and Buenos Aires, 1893)
Evangelina (idillio drammatico, 3, A. Cortella, after H. W. Longfellow: *Evangeline, a Tale of Acadie*), Milan, Alhambra, 19 Sept 1893, vs (Milan, 1893)
Tarass Bulba, 1892–3 (dramma lirico, 4, G. Godio, after N. V. Gogol), Turin, Regio, 9 March 1895, vs (Milan, n.d.)
Pampa (dramma lirico, 3, G. Borra, after E. Gutiérrez: *Juan Moreira*), Buenos Aires, Opera, 27 July 1897
Yupanki (3, E. Rodríguez Larreta, after V. F. López: *El hijo del sol*), Buenos Aires, Opera, 25 July 1899
Khrysé (ópera en cuatro partes, 4, J. Pacchierotti, after P. Louÿs: *Aphrodite*), Buenos Aires, Politeama, 20 June 1902
Horrida nox, 1904 (drama lírico, 1), Buenos Aires, Politeama, 7 July 1908
Gli eroi [Los héroes], 1906–9 (ópera lírica, 4, after López: *La loca de la guardia*), Buenos Aires, Colón, 23 Aug 1919
Facundo, *c*1909 (drama lírico, 3), unperf.

*

J. M. Veniard: *Arturo Berutti, un argentino en el mundo de la ópera* (Buenos Aires, 1988), 365ff JUAN MARÍA VENIARD

Berwald, Franz (Adolf) (*b* Stockholm, 23 July 1796; *d* Stockholm, 3 April 1868). Swedish composer. His formal education was negligible; he took violin lessons from his father, a violinist in the court orchestra, and probably studied composition with Edouard Du Puy, then conductor of the orchestra, whose ranks he joined in October 1812. As a young man Berwald must have played in operas by Mozart, Weber, Spontini, Spohr and Du Puy, and he cherished lively ambitions himself. By 1818 he had composed orchestral works, chamber music and songs, and in 1827 he embarked on his first opera, *Gustaf Wasa* – a bold undertaking since this was the subject of an extremely successful opera by J. G. Naumann (1786, Stockholm). Act 1 of *Gustaf Wasa* was performed the following year, when Berwald left the orchestra and applied for a scholarship abroad. He arrived in Berlin in June 1829 and occupied himself with numerous operatic plans (*Leonida*, *Der Verräter*, *Donna Isabella*, *Trubaduren* and *Cecilia*) which made scant progress. Berwald had hoped that *Der Verräter* would be produced in Stockholm; undeterred by its rejection he began work in 1841 on another opera, *Estrella de Soria*, returning to Sweden in April 1842. His operetta *Modehandlerskan* ('The Modiste'), composed in the following year, was a fiasco at its first performance at the Royal Opera in 1845.

From 1846 to 1849 Berwald travelled widely, staying in Paris, where he failed to interest the Opéra-Comique in performing his works, in Vienna, and in Salzburg, where he was made an honorary member of the Mozarteum. He returned to Sweden in 1849 and in 1850 became manager of a glass works in Sandö, Ångermanland, in north Sweden; he became part-owner of the firm in 1853, when he was also active in launching a sawmill. From about 1856 he published articles on a wide variety of social issues, showing a progressive vision and sympathy. He left the glass works in 1859. In 1862 the Royal Opera in Stockholm mounted a performance of a revised version of *Estrella de Soria* which scored a *succès d'estime*, but the attempt to secure for him a teaching post at the Swedish Royal Academy of Music proved abortive. Two years later he was made a fellow of the academy and that year completed his last opera, *Drottningen av Golconda* ('The Queen of Golconda').

During the 20th century, interest in his music gradually gathered momentum and the 150th anniversary of his birth in 1946 was celebrated by a revival of *Estrella de Soria* at the Royal Opera. Many of the earlier operas have disappeared, though some of their material may have been absorbed into *The Queen of Golconda*, which was finally produced in Stockholm in 1968, the centenary of his death. There is some delightful music in the operas, but Berwald's dramatic talent and his powers of musical characterization were limited, and it is unlikely that these works will ever gain more than a peripheral place in the repertory.

Franz Berwald's cousin Johan Fredrik Berwald (*b* Stockholm, 4 Dec 1787; *d* Stockholm, 26 Aug 1861) was Kapellmästare from 1822 to 1849 at Stockholm, where he wrote incidental music for a number of plays. His two-act operetta *L'héroine de l'amour filial* was composed in his youth during a visit to St Petersburg; it was performed there in 1811. The style of the opera is similar to that of Grétry and Dalayrac with colourful orchestration, lyrical but simple melodies and a more or less strict adherence to the *opéra comique* forms. Julie Mathilda Berwald (1822–77), Johan Fredrik's daughter, was a well-known opera singer.

See also DROTTNINGEN AV GOLCONDA.

Edition: *F. Berwald: Sämtliche Werke*, ed. N. Castegren and others, MMS, 2nd ser. (Kassel, 1966–) [BW]

first performed in Stockholm, Royal Theatre, unless otherwise stated
Gustaf Wasa (after J. H. Kellgren), inc., concert perf. of Act 1, 12 Feb 1828, scene and aria from Act 2, 18 Nov 1828; lost except Christjerns marsch, vs (Stockholm, 1828)
Cecilia, 1829, inc., lost
Leonida, 1829 (Curtius), lost except lib. and frags., Act 2 finale frag., BW ix
Der Verräter, 1830 (? M. G. Saphir), 1 chorus perf. 19 May 1842, lost
Donna Isabella, 1830, inc., lost except sketch frag.
Trubaduren, 1830 [? only projected] (B. von Beskow)
Estrella de Soria, 1841, 1848, rev. 1862 (3, O. Prechtler), 9 April 1862, vs (Stockholm, 1883), ov. (Stockholm, 1913); BW xvii
Jag går i kloster (operetta, 2, H. Sätherberg and F. Berwald), 2 Dec 1843, excerpts, vs (Stockholm, 1843); BW xix
Modehandlerskan [The Modiste], 1843 (operetta, 3, Berwald and others), 26 March 1845, excerpts, vs (Stockholm, 1845)
Slottet Lochleven [Maria Stuart], 1863 (5, after W. Scott: *The Abbot*), inc., lost

Drottningen av Golconda [The Queen of Golconda], 1864–5 (romantisk opera, 3, Berwald, after J.-B.-C. Vial and E.-G.-F. de Favières: *Aline, reine de Golconde*), 3 April 1968, BW xviii

*

A. Hillman: *Franz Berwald: en biografisk studie med kompositionsförteckning* (Stockholm, 1920)

E. Sundström: 'Till kännedomen om Franz Berwalds operaplaner', *STMf*, ix (1927), 195–200

——: 'Franz Berwalds operor', *STMf*, xxix (1947), 16–62

R. Layton: 'De ursprungliga hos Berwald' [Berwald's Originality], *Musikrevy*, ix (1954), 218–21

——: *Berwald* (Swed. trans., Stockholm, 1956; Eng. orig., 1959)

I. Andersson: *Franz Berwald* (Stockholm, 1970)

N. Castegren: 'Berwald, Franz', *Sohlmans musiklexikon* (Stockholm, 2/1975–9)

E. Lomnäs, I. Bengtsson and N. Castegren, eds.: *Franz Berwald: die Dokumente seines Lebens*, MMS, 2nd ser., suppl. (Kassel, 1979)

ROBERT LAYTON (with BERTIL H. VAN BOER)

Besanzoni, Gabriella (*b* Rome, 20 Sept 1888; *d* Rome, 8 July 1962). Italian mezzo-soprano. She studied in Rome and made her début in 1911 at Viterbo as Adalgisa (*Norma*). After further study she sang Ulrica (*Un ballo in maschera*) in Rome. She first sang at the Colón, Buenos Aires, in 1918 and was engaged at the Metropolitan in 1919–20, making her début as Amneris. She also sang Isabella (*L'italiana in Algeri*). In 1923–4 she sang Gluck's Orpheus at La Scala, where she also appeared as Mignon and Carmen, the role of her farewell performance in 1939 at the Baths of Caracalla, Rome. Her voice was full-toned and smoothly produced as well as flexible.

ELIZABETH FORBES

Besch, Anthony (John Elwyn) (*b* London, 5 Feb 1924). English director. During his period as an Oxford undergraduate he produced *Idomeneo* for the Oxford University Opera Club (1947); immediately afterwards he went to Glyndebourne, where he worked (1950–53) as an assistant to Moran Caplat and came under the influence of the producers Carl Ebert and Günther Rennert. Besch's first professional production was of Verdi's *Les vêpres siciliennes* (1953, WNO); thereafter he went on to produce operas at all the main British houses and festivals – he formed a particularly close link with Sadler's Wells Opera and the New Opera Company (of which he was a guiding figure) – and in most of the world's main operatic centres. Besch's skill in economically marshalling stage forces and his acute sense of style have very seldom failed him in the enormous number and wide variety of works tackled during a long career. He has been particularly associated with the operas of Rossini (his deft, elegantly witty Sadler's Wells stagings of *Le comte Ory* and *La gazza ladra* are well remembered by London audiences), and with a confident and freshly imaginative approach to the production of new and 'difficult' 20th-century operas – Szymanowski's *King Roger*, Shostakovich's *The Nose*, Dallapiccola's *Il prigioniero*, Birtwistle's *Punch and Judy* and Musgrave's *The Voice of Ariadne* prominent among them. He has held posts at several educational institutions including the London Opera Centre (1962–8), the University of Toronto (1969–70) and the GSM, London (1986–9).

MAX LOPPERT

Best, Matthew (*b* Farnborough, Kent, 6 Feb 1957). English bass. He studied at Cambridge, where his opera *Alice* was performed in 1979, and in London, then made his début at Aldeburgh in 1980 as Snout (*A Midsummer Night's Dream*). Engaged at Covent Garden (1980–86), he sang a wide variety of roles, including Timur, Colline, Fiorello, the Monk/Charles V (*Don Carlos*), Masetto, the Doctor (*Macbeth* and *Pelléas et Mélisande*), the Police Commissioner (*Lulu*), Hans Foltz (*Die Meistersinger*) and Lamoral (*Arabella*); he took part in the British première of Berio's *Un re in ascolto* (1989). For the WNO his roles have included Sparafucile, Count Ribbing and a Nazarene (*Salome*). He sang Don Fernando and King of Clubs (*The Love for Three Oranges*) for Glyndebourne Touring Opera and the Judge (*The English Cat*) at Frankfurt. For Opera North he has sung Narbal (*Les Troyens*), Polyphemus (*Acis and Galatea*), Raimondo, Des Grieux and Shchelkalov (*Boris Godunov*). A very musical singer, he has a fine, resonant voice.

ELIZABETH FORBES

Besuch der alten Dame, Der ('The Visit of the Old Lady'). Opera in three acts by GOTTFRIED VON EINEM to a libretto by Friedrich Dürrenmatt after his tragicomedy; Vienna, Staatsoper, 23 May 1971.

Dürrenmatt's play takes place in Güllen, a small dilapidated town somewhere in central Europe. Town dignitaries await the arrival at the station of Claire Zachanassian (mezzo-soprano), a multi-millionairess who has returned to her native town to buy revenge for the injustices of her youth, when she was deserted by her lover, Alfred Ill (high baritone), and cheated in the courts. Claire meets Ill and they reminisce. Ill tries to justify his action of having left her after she became pregnant. He bemoans his present situation and wishes to turn the clock back. At an official reception Claire promises the community a billion marks, but demands the murder of Ill in return. She summons up witnesses who claim that Ill had jilted her for a better match and had evaded the legal consequences of fatherhood by means of bribery. The citizens remain unconvinced of Ill's guilt at this stage. Nevertheless, the prospect of receiving vast sums of money encourages them to run up huge debts. Ill realizes to his dismay that he is being trapped. He seeks consolation from the Vicar (bass-baritone) and tries to escape. The citizens, however, prevent him from leaving Güllen. Claire, meanwhile, marries her ninth groom in the cathedral. The Doctor and the Teacher (both baritones) try to persuade her to change her mind about Ill, but she rejects their entreaties. The Lord Mayor (Heldentenor) visits Ill and suggests that the community would be saved if he committed suicide. However, Ill has now overcome his fear of death and demands that judgment should be given by his fellow citizens. Eventually the citizens congregate in the local theatre and decide, in the presence of the press, to accept Claire's money. Ill respects their decision and the judgment is carried out. Claire allows him to be put into the coffin which she has brought with her. She hands the mayor a cheque and the townspeople burst into an orgiastic dance.

Der Besuch der alten Dame is von Einem's fourth opera and was written in close collaboration with Dürrenmatt, who eliminated almost a quarter of the original material in the play but added the final gruesome dance of joy. The play is a biting critique of the amorality of wealth and the lust for money that engenders greed and corruption. Von Einem was strongly attracted to it, not least because Dürrenmatt's exploration of the ultimate betrayal of Alfred Ill provided him with further opportunity to develop a theme that runs through his previous operas. Two specific connections stand out: firstly, the citizens of Güllen who eventually decide Ill's fate seem to behave in much the same manner as the mob in DANTONS TOD. Second, Ill, like Danton and Josef K. (in DER PROZESS), seems condemned even before judgment has been passed. Yet it would be misleading to suggest that *Der Besuch der alten Dame* is simply a regurgitation of earlier ideas; the opera marks a considerable advance in both musical and dramatic terms. In particular, the characterization seems to be more defined than before. The composer strongly identifies with Alfred Ill, who is always portrayed in compassionate terms. Claire, on the other hand, represents the embodiment of the *femme fatale* that has dominated operatic history. Her music is vehement and intensely dramatic. As a foil to these central roles, the composer has produced brilliant thumb-nail sketches of the subsidiary characters. The musical idiom charts the course of the drama with great flexibility. While von Einem's harmonies are embedded in strong tonal centres, he does not shirk harsh dissonance if the occasion demands it. The orchestration, too, demonstrates great variety and effectively parallels the atmosphere on stage: the strings are featured at moments of reminiscence, the brass represent anger and rebellion and the percussion summons up the macabre elements of the action. The composer abandons the set-number form employed in *Dantons Tod* and conceives more symphonically integrated and extended structures which relate to the formal divisions of the play. At the same time, the ten brief instrumental preludes and interludes perform a vital function in galvanizing the action. They can be considered as musical chapter headings, but they also establish a direct relationship between the important undercurrents that run throughout the drama. Their significance reaches an inevitable climax in the scene where the sentence is executed, for, at the moment of truth, the 24 bars of the opera's introduction are repeated, albeit at a different pitch.

The conservative and accessible language of *Der Besuch der alten Dame* brought the opera before a wide public. During the 1970s the work was heard in many theatres after its triumphant première (with Christa Ludwig as Claire and Eberhard Wächter as Ill). Among the most notable were productions at Zürich (1971), Berlin (1972), Mannheim (1972), Glyndebourne (1973 and 1974), Munich (1975), San Francisco (1975) and Wiesbaden (1979). ERIK LEVI

Betly [*Betly, ossia La capanna svizzera* ('Betly, or The Swiss Chalet')]. *Dramma giocoso*, originally in one act, later revised in two, by GAETANO DONIZETTI to his own libretto after EUGÈNE SCRIBE and MÉLESVILLE'S [A.-H.-J. Duveyrier's] libretto for Adolphe Adam's *Le châlet*, ultimately derived from Goethe's Singspiel *Jery und Bätely* (1780); Naples, Teatro Nuovo, 21 August 1836 (revised version, Naples, probably Teatro del Fondo, 29 September 1837).

Daniele (tenor) arrives at Betly's chalet, delighted to have what purports to be a letter from her in which she agrees to marry him. In fact, village jokers wrote the letter, taking advantage of his simplicity; Betly (soprano) declares she knows nothing of it and asserts her independence (aria, 'In questo semplice modesto asilo'). Her brother, Max (baritone), a corporal who has not been home for years, decides not to tell Betly who he is, and, favourably impressed with Daniele, determines to assist him in his wooing of Betly. Max's plan involves lodging his troops in her house and provoking Daniele to a duel. This stratagem achieves the double purpose of causing Daniele to show some spirit and of persuading Betly that her independence has left her unprotected; she accepts Daniele in marriage (arias, 'Se crudele il cor mostraï' and 'Ah no! non posso esprimere').

Betly has a score full of unpretentious charm and a plot that works well on the stage. The role of Daniele is akin to that of Nemorino in *L'elisir d'amore*. The highlights of the score are Betly's solo moments: her *sortita* and her aria-finale, the former particularly for its local colour, with a yodel-like refrain. WILLIAM ASHBROOK

Betrothal in a Monastery [*Obrucheniye v monastïre*; *Duen'ya* ('The Duenna')]. 'Lyrico-comic' opera in four acts, op.86, by SERGEY PROKOFIEV to a libretto by the composer and MIRA ALEXANDROVNA MENDELSON (Prokof'yeva) after RICHARD BRINSLEY SHERIDAN's comic opera libretto *The Duenna, or The Double Elopement* (1775); Prague, National Opera Theatre, 5 May 1946 (Russian première, Leningrad, Kirov Theatre, 3 November 1946).

Sheridan's *The Duenna* is an extravagant parody of that venerable comic-opera genre in which a ward or daughter outsmarts her parent or guardian to marry the suitor of her choice. Its farrago of disguises, subterfuges and mistaken identities ends with no fewer than three couples finally matched correctly in defiance of the wishes of Don Jerome (tenor in Prokofiev's opera), a grandee of Seville, who had hoped to marry his headstrong daughter Louisa (soprano) off to Isaac Mendoza (bass), a rich old Portuguese Jew, who is accompanied on stage at all times by his friend Don Carlos (baritone). Mendoza ends up with Louisa's chaperone (contralto: the Duenna); Louisa with Don Antonio (tenor), her impoverished true love; and Don Jerome's son Ferdinand (baritone), assisted by his sister, succeeds in eloping with Donna Clara (mezzo-soprano), whose father had intended her for a convent. All of the weddings take place in a priory attached to the convent, the young lovers (and the duped Mendoza) having bribed an old toper of a friar to perform the ceremonies. When Sheridan's play was first performed at Covent Garden, its 27 musical numbers – mainly strophic songs, with an occasional ensemble – were set by the author's father-in-law and brother-in-law, both Thomas Linley, in collaboration (*see* LINLEY, THOMAS (i) and (ii)).

Prokofiev's opera owes its existence to Mira Mendelson, the composer's second (common-law) wife, whom in 1940 he had just met. She had been translating the piece in collaboration with a friend, and described it to the composer. Eager as he then was to retreat into politically innocuous terrain after the frustrations that had attended the production of his first Soviet opera, *Semyon Kotko*, Prokofiev immediately sensed its possibilities for innocent musical 'champagne à la Mozart or Rossini'.

Six of Sheridan's songs, translated into Russian verse by Mendelson, were retained: Antonio's 'The breath of morn bids hence the night' ('V Sevil'ye, spyashchey krepkim snom'); Jerome's 'If a daughter you have, it's the plague of your life' ('Esli est' u vas doch', eto, ver'te, chuma'); Clara's 'When sable night' ('Noch' bayukayet Sevil'yu'); Don Carlos's 'Gentle maid, ah! why suspect me?' ('Ne nado zhdat' vam ot lyudey'); the Duenna's 'When a tender maid is first essay'd' ('Kogda vokrug zelyonoy devochki'); and the friars' glee, 'This bottle's the sun of our table' ('Butïlka – solntse nashey zhizni'). For the rest, Prokofiev himself adapted Sheridan's prose quite elegantly into a very fast and pliant vehicle for continuous music.

Yet compared with his previous operas, *Betrothal in a Monastery* is anything but prosy. As his ad hoc generic designation for the opera suggests, the composer sought every opportunity for lyricism, giving primary emphasis to the romantic intrigue at the expense of the more grotesque elements he might have been inclined to underscore earlier in his career. (In particular, the character of Mendoza is considerably softened in Prokofiev's treatment, and Sheridan's blatant anti-Semitism is as far as possible erased; on the other hand, the play's peripheral anti-clerical and anti-mercantile satire is much exaggerated for the benefit of the Soviet audience.) A particularly happy invention was the casting of scene vi (corresponding to Sheridan's Act 3 scene i, the letter scene) against a background of domestic music-making: Don Jerome (on the clarinet) rehearsing a jaunty minuet with two onstage musicians (trumpet and bass drum).

Prokofiev's gift, virtually unparalleled among 20th-century composers, for writing distinctively original diatonic melodies is outstandingly in evidence in this appealing score, which in its tumble of racy minuscule numbers sooner recalls the manner of *Falstaff* or (particularly) *Gianni Schicchi* than the earlier models the composer advertised. RICHARD TARUSKIN

Betrug durch Aberglauben [*Betrug durch Aberglauben, oder Die Schatzgräber* ('Deception through Superstition, or The Treasure Seeker')]. *Komisches Singspiel* in two acts by CARL DITTERS VON DITTERSDORF to a libretto by Friedrich Eberl; Vienna, Kärntnertortheater, 3 October 1786.

Baron von Lindburg (bass) has been duped by his servant Kordula (soprano) and her crony, Magister Niklas (bass), into putting his daughter Luise (soprano) into a convent as a condition imposed by supernatural spirits for finding a buried treasure. Luise's lover, Count von Walldorf (tenor), also knows of the baron's superstitious nature and initiates a counter-stratagem. A mock apparition in the cellar (including a band of chimney-sweeps as the Furies) convinces the baron that he should give Luise to Walldorf in exchange for a crock filled with the Count's own ducats. Thereupon Niklas, his own scheme foiled, confesses and also exposes Kordula's embezzling from the household accounts.

Dittersdorf's second German comic opera for Vienna was only slightly less popular than his first, *Der Apotheker und der Doktor*, produced three months earlier. Ensembles loom larger here, and the chorus plays a more active role. The composer also took good advantage of opportunities for pictorial effects from the orchestra in the fire scene and windstorm in Act 1. In a send-up of the scene of the Furies in Gluck's *Orfeo ed Euridice*, Dittersdorf punctuates the confrontation between the Furies and the baron in the second finale with repeated calls of 'Nein' from the chorus.

THOMAS BAUMAN

Bettelstudent, Der (i) [*Der Bettelstudent, oder Das Donnerwetter* ('The Beggar Student, or The Thunderstorm')]. Singspiel in two acts by PETER WINTER to a libretto by PAUL WEIDMANN after MIGUEL DE CERVANTES's play *La cueva de Salamanca*; Munich, Nationaltheater, 2 February 1785.

One of Winter's earliest operas, this work was successful throughout Germany and Austria well into the 19th century. The plot revolves around the wandering student Wilhelm Mauser (tenor) and the residents of a small mill town. The central action, which includes a mock incantation recited by Wilhelm and a mill fire sparked off by lightning, takes place during a severe thunderstorm. In the process, Wilhelm helps persuade the miller Jakob (bass) to allow his daughter, Hannchen (soprano), to marry her true love, Brandheim (tenor). The music consists of square-cut strophic songs, lyrical arias and a smattering of modest ensembles. Winter successfully combines elements from *opéra comique*, *opera buffa* and the north German Singspiel.

LINDA TYLER

Bettelstudent, Der (ii) ('The Beggar Student'). *Komische Operette* in three acts by CARL MILLÖCKER to a libretto by F. ZELL and RICHARD GENÉE after EDWARD BULWER-LYTTON's *The Lady of Lyons* and VICTORIEN SARDOU's *Les noces de Fernande*; Vienna, Theater an der Wien, 6 December 1882.

The operetta is set in Kraków in 1704, when Poland is ruled by Friedrich-August II, Elector of Saxony. Colonel Ollendorf (bass-baritone), the Saxon governor of Kraków gaol, vows revenge on the Polish Countess Laura Nowalska (soprano), who slapped his face when he made advances to her at a ball. Laura's mother Palmatica (mezzo-soprano) insists that her daughter will marry only a Polish officer. Ollendorf therefore has two handsome, impoverished young rebel Polish students, Symon Rymanovicz (tenor) and Jan Janicki (baritone), brought from among the political prisoners in the gaol. He offers them money for Symon to pose as a Polish prince and Jan as his secretary. During a dinner at the spring holiday celebrations, Symon and Jan are presented to Laura and her sister Bronislawa (soubrette), and mutual attraction is immediate. When Symon realizes he really loves Laura, he feels unable to maintain the pretence, but Jan persuades him to do so as cover for his own activities in support of the exiled Polish King Stanislaus Leszczynski. Symon seeks to relieve his conscience in a letter to Laura, which is intercepted by Ollendorf, and assumes from her lack of reaction that she does not mind his pretence. The wedding duly takes place, but when Ollendorf marches in and triumphantly discloses Symon's real identity, the latter realizes that Laura had never received his letter. Chased from the house, Symon is in despair, but Jan proposes for him a dangerous role posing as the nephew of the exiled Polish king. The diversion thereby created permits the storming of the fortress of Kraków, the conquest of Saxon forces, and the reinstatement of Polish national rule. For his bravery Symon is made a Count, making him a fit husband for Laura, with Jan a no less suitable match for Bronislawa.

Millöcker's setting of a strong operetta libretto remains his most successful and widely performed work, demonstrating his fine sense of dramatic theatre allied to writing for soloists, chorus and orchestra of operatic quality. Originally produced with Alexander Girardi as Symon, Josef Joseffy as Jan, Caroline Finaly as Laura and Felix Schweighofer as Ollendorf, the principal numbers include Ollendorf's offended protestation that he merely kissed Laura on the shoulder, 'Ach ich hab' sie ja nur auf die Schulter geküsst', to a melody taken from Millöcker's early operetta *Der Dieb*, Symon's and Jan's lighthearted entrance duet, 'Die Welt hat das genialste Streben', Symon's song in praise of Polish womanhood,

'Ich knüpfte manche zarte Bande', and his tender duet with Laura, 'Ich setz den Fall'. ANDREW LAMB

Bettendorf, Emmy (*b* Frankfurt, 16 July 1895; *d* Berlin, 20 Oct 1963). German soprano. She made her début in 1914 at Frankfurt in Conradin Kreutzer's *Nachtlager in Granada*. After two years with the company at Schwerin and an appearance in Vienna as Agathe in *Freischütz* she joined the Berlin Staatsoper, where her roles included Eva, Elsa and Desdemona; she also sang Ariadne and the Marschallin in performances conducted by Strauss. During the 1920s she undertook much concert work and appeared in opera with an impressive German company touring Spain and the Netherlands. Increasingly important in her career were broadcasts and recordings, through which she became one of the most popular singers of her time. She retired in 1934, but toured the eastern front singing to troops in wartime, and from 1947 to 1952 taught at the Städtisches Konservatorium, Berlin. Recordings reveal her exceptionally pure and mellow voice, the style sometimes lacking in vitality but well suited to the quieter and more relaxed parts of her extensive repertory.

*

D. White: 'Emmy Bettendorf', *Record Collector*, xv (1963–4), 149–68 [with discography] J. B. STEANE

Betterton, Thomas (*b* London, 1635; *d* London, 28 April 1710). English actor, manager and opera director. Generally regarded as the greatest English actor before Garrick, Betterton played a key role in the invention of SEMI-OPERA. In 1668, on Sir William Davenant's death, he became co-manager of the Duke's Company. The company was already featuring plays with musical interludes, many of them by Matthew Locke. Under Betterton's guidance, productions became ever more musical, and in 1671 the troupe moved into the new Dorset Garden Theatre, specially equipped with the scenes and machines necessary for opera. Betterton had been to Paris to observe and study stagecraft and may have seen the famed *comédie-ballets* of Lully and Molière. Beginning in 1673 he produced a series of musical extravaganzas, including adaptations of *Macbeth* and *The Tempest*: these were the first semi-operas. In addition to coordinating production and devising the scenery, Betterton often acted the protagonists, roles which never required singing.

In September 1683 Charles II sent Betterton – now manager of the United Company, an amalgam of the former Duke's and King's companies – back to Paris to engage Lully and the Académie de Musique to produce a *tragédie lyrique* celebrating the 25th anniversary of the Restoration. When this proved impossible, Betterton instead brought out John Dryden and Luis Grabu's *ALBION AND ALBANIUS*, the first all-sung English opera since the furtive *Siege of Rhodes* (1656). But it failed, and no new major musical work was attempted in London until 1690, when Betterton adapted Philip Massinger and John Fletcher's *The Prophetess* (or *Dioclesian*). With music by Henry Purcell, it proved a great success and heralded the return of semi-opera. For *Dioclesian*, he cut and rewrote passages of the original play, provided new verses for Purcell, designed the machines and advised the choreographer Josias Priest on the dances. One may assume he performed a similar function for *The Fairy-Queen* (1692). In 1694 he was paid £50 to adapt and stage *The Indian Queen*, but any further involvement in Purcell's last semi-opera was prevented by the Actors' Rebellion: Betterton and a group of senior colleagues left the United Company at Drury Lane and set up a makeshift theatre in Lincoln's Inn Fields in spring 1695. Without Purcell, Betterton continued to produce musical plays, even an occasional semi-opera, and in 1700 staged the first professional production of *Dido and Aeneas* in conjunction with an adaptation of *Measure for Measure*.

*

J. Milhous: *Thomas Betterton and the Management of Lincoln's Inn Fields 1695–1708* (Carbondale, IL, 1979)
——: 'The Multi-Media Spectacular on the Restoration Stage', *British Theatre and the Other Arts 1660–1800*, ed. S. Kenny (Washington DC, 1984), 41–66
C. A. Price: *Henry Purcell and the London Stage* (Cambridge, 1984)
CURTIS PRICE

Bettinelli, Bruno (*b* Milan, 4 June 1913). Italian composer. A pupil of Bossi at the Milan Conservatory, where he himself later taught for many years, he has written much instrumental and vocal music. He came to opera in his maturity, after moving away from his early neo-classicism through the use of free chromaticism and contrapuntal techniques. His first work for the theatre was *Il pozzo e il pendolo* (1957–8), not performed until ten years after its composition. Based on Poe's famous story, it aims to create an agonizing build-up of tension. Soon afterwards, Bettinelli wrote the lighter piece *La smorfia*. His last opera, *Count Down* (1970), centres on the profound crisis experienced by a middle-aged man who kills himself because he thinks his world is crumbling about him. Stylistically the work belongs to an advanced phase of Bettinelli's development, but it remains unaffected by radical experimentation.

*

Il pozzo e il pendolo, 1957–8 (azione mimo-drammatica, 1, C. Crispolti, after E. A. Poe: *The Pit and the Pendulum*), Bergamo, Novità, 24 Oct 1967
La smorfia (atto buffo, 1, R. Bacchelli), Como, Villa Olmo, 30 Sept 1959
Count Down (A. Madau Diaz), Milan, Piccola Scala, 25 March 1970 PAOLO PETAZZI

Bettoni, Vincenzo (*b* Melegnano, nr Milan, 1 July 1881; *d* Melegnano, 4 Nov 1954). Italian bass. He made his début in 1902 at Pinerolo as Silva (*Ernani*) and first sang at La Scala in 1905 and at the Colón, Buenos Aires, in 1910. He sang Gurnemanz in the Spanish première of *Parsifal* (Barcelona, 1914). Changing to *buffo* roles in 1925, he appeared with Conchita Supervia in Rossini's *L'italiana in Algeri*, *La Cenerentola* and *Il barbiere di Siviglia*, in Turin, Paris, Florence and at Covent Garden (1935). In 1934 he sang Don Alfonso (*Così fan tutte*) in the opening season at Glyndebourne and took part in the first performance of Rocca's *Il dibuk* at La Scala, where as late as 1950 he sang in Wolf-Ferrari's *I quatro rusteghi*. He was a stylish singer, with a fine, flexible voice. ELIZABETH FORBES

Betz, Franz (*b* Mainz, 19 March 1835; *d* Berlin, 11 Aug 1900). German baritone. He studied in Karlsruhe and made his début at Hanover in 1856 as Heinrich (*Lohengrin*). In 1859 he sang Don Carlo (*Ernani*) at the Berlin Hofoper and was immediately engaged there, remaining a member of the company until his retirement in 1897. He sang Valentin in the first Berlin performance of Gounod's *Faust* (given as *Margarethe*) in 1863. At the Munich Hofoper he sang Telramund (1863), and Hans Sachs in the première of *Die Meistersinger* (1868), repeating the role in the first Berlin performance (1870).

He was also Berlin's first Amonasro (1874) and King Mark (1876).

Betz sang Wotan at Bayreuth in the first complete *Ring* cycle (1876). He took part in a gala performance of Spontini's *Olympie* in Berlin (1879). Returning to Bayreuth in 1889, he alternated as Kurwenal and King Mark, and also sang Hans Sachs. He made guest appearances in Vienna and other cities in Austria and Germany. His vast repertory included the Dutchman, Wolfram, Pizarro, Don Giovanni and Falstaff, which he sang at the first Berlin performance of Verdi's opera (1894), but his favourite role was Hans Sachs, which he sang over a hundred times in Berlin alone; it perfectly displayed the strength, evenness and warmth of his generous voice, and the humanity of his dramatic style.

E. Newman: *The Life of Richard Wagner* (London, 1933–47)
J. Kapp: *Geschichte der Staatsoper Berlin* (Berlin, 1937)
H. Fetting: *Die Geschichte der Deutschen Staatsoper* (Berlin, 1955)
H. Wagner: *200 Jahre Münchner Theaterchronik 1750–1950* (Munich, 1958)
G. Skelton: *Wagner at Bayreuth* (London, 1965)

ELIZABETH FORBES

Beuther, Friedrich Christian (*b* Cleeburg, nr Strasbourg, 22 April 1777; *d* Kassel, 21 April 1856). German stage designer. He appears to have received his early training in Frankfurt from the Italian theatre designer Giorgio Fuentes, then based at the court theatre. After engagements as an actor with several travelling troupes, Beuther worked as scene designer and painter in Darmstadt, Bamberg, Würzburg and Wiesbaden. In 1815 he was engaged by Goethe at Weimar, where he initiated a number of reforms, insisting that all objects within stage settings be integrated into an organic whole. These were endorsed by Goethe, who valued his work highly; in 1817 he wrote of Beuther in his diaries: 'through the art of the perspective, [he] was able to enlarge our small stage spaces endlessly; through characteristic architecture as well as taste and ornamentation he was able to multiply our spaces and to render them highly pleasing'. Designs for *Don Giovanni*, *La clemenza di Tito* (1815; see illustration) and *Die Zauberflöte* (1817) were among Beuther's more important works during his Weimar period. His style throughout his career followed the classical school of scenic design and adhered to the ideas of *scena per angolo*, in which a scene is viewed at an angular perspective.

In 1818 Beuther moved to the Brunswick court theatre, where he remained until 1824. The first of his theoretical writings, *Bemerkungen und Ansichten über Theatermalerei*, was published in the *Allgemeiner Theateralmanach* in 1822. From 1825 until his death he was in Kassel, where as chief scene designer at the court theatre he continued to refine and propagate his theories (some of which anticipated Wagner), with particular emphasis on the unity of the arts. Some of his designs were published (*Dekorationen für die Schaubühne*, 1816, 1824; *Neue Theater-Decorationen*, 1836); many original designs are in the Niessen Collection of the Theatermuseum, University of Cologne.

ES
U. Thieme and F. Becker, eds: *Lexikon der bildenden Künstler*, (Leipzig, 1907–50), iii, 555
F. Itzenplitz: *Friedrich Beuther und die Theaterdekoration des Klassizismus* (diss., U. of Göttingen, 1953)
O. Jung: *Der Theatermaler Friedrich Christian Beuther und seine Welt* (Emsdetten, 1963)
H. C. Wolff: *Oper: Szene und Darstellung von 1600 bis 1900* (Leipzig, 1968, 2/1979)
D. Oenslager: *Stage Design: Four Centuries of Scenic Invention* (New York, 1975), 153–6
E. Berckenhagen: *Bretter die die Welt bedeuten: Entwürfe zum Theaterdekor und zum Bühnenkostüm in fünf Jahrhunderten* (Berlin, 1978), 155–8

EVAN BAKER

Bevignani, Enrico (*b* Naples, 29 Sept 1841; *d* Naples, 29 Aug 1903). Italian conductor and composer. He studied in Naples, where his melodrama *Caterina Blum* (3, D. Bolognese; *I-Nc*) was produced with great success at S Carlo on 3 September 1863. The next year he was engaged by Mapleson for Her Majesty's Theatre, London, remaining there until he moved with Mapleson to Covent Garden in 1869. He stayed at Covent Garden with Gye from 1871 until the end of Gye's management in 1877; he returned later, leaving finally in 1896.

Beuther's design for the Capitol in Rome for Goethe's production of Mozart's 'La clemenza di Tito', Weimar court theatre, 1815

Bevignani conducted the first London performances of *Aida* (1876), *La Gioconda* (1883) and *Pagliacci* (1893). He was 'the most admirable of orchestral "accompanists"', according to Sir Dan Godfrey. He conducted several seasons of Italian opera in St Petersburg and Moscow (where he was decorated) and in New York (1893–5 and 1900). Tchaikovsky greatly admired him, and he conducted the first Bol'shoy performance of *Yevgeny Onegin* (1881). Shaw, however, considered his tempos to be too fast, and added: 'There are few persons whom I have less desire to see alive again than Costa; but there are moments when Bevignani makes me miss him.' 'Signor Bevignani's orchestra has ... no force; but it is polite and delicate.' Bevignani's compositions are full of unexpected harmonic twists which immediately distinguish them from those of his Italian contemporaries. He also composed piano pieces and songs.

*

DBI (A. Cammarano Lanfranchi); *ES* (E. Zanetti)
D. Godfrey: *Memories and Music* (London, 1924), 117
G. B. Shaw: *Music in London 1890–94* (London, 1932)
——: *London Music in 1888–89 as Heard by Corno di Bassetto* (London, 1937)
U. Manferrari: *Dizionario universale delle opere melodrammatiche*, i (Florence, 1954)
NIGEL BURTON, KEITH HORNER

Beyden Anton, Die. Singspiel by Benedikt Schack and F. X. Gerl; *see* DUMME GÄRTNER AUS DEM GEBIRGE, DER.

Beyron, Einar (Oscar) (*b* Malmö, 24 Feb 1901; *d* Stockholm, 29 March 1979). Swedish tenor. He studied in Copenhagen, Berlin and with John Forsell in Stockholm, where he made his début at the Royal Opera as Froh (*Rheingold*) in 1924 while still a student. Although he visited the other Scandinavian capitals and also the USA, he spent his career mainly in Stockholm. His huge repertory ranged from operetta roles to Wagner and included Cavaradossi, Sadko, Golitsïn (*Khovanshchina*), Jeník (*The Bartered Bride*), Števa (*Jenůfa*), Giosta (Zandonai's *Cavalieri di Ekebù*) and Matts (Rangström's *Kronbruden*). His finest role was Tristan, which he sang innumerable times with his wife, Brita Herzberg, as Isolde. He was also an impressive Parsifal. He used his powerful voice with style and musicality.
ELIZABETH FORBES

Bezanson, Philip (Thomas) (*b* Athol, MA, 6 Jan 1916; *d* Hadley, MA, 11 March 1975). American composer. He studied at Yale University and with Philip Clapp at the University of Iowa, where he joined the faculty in 1947 and succeeded Clapp as principal professor of composition in 1954. Ten years later he moved to the University of Massachusetts, Amherst, where he served as professor and head of the music department. Bezanson's honours include an award from the Fromm Foundation (1953) and a Guggenheim Fellowship (1971). His works fall within the mainstream of 20th-century music in the generation after Stravinsky, Bartók and Hindemith. The style is rooted in diatonicism but has frequently changing scales and tonal centres; shifting major and minor 3rds are common. Standard metres, often irregularly accented, predominate. Besides choral, orchestral and chamber music he composed two operas: *Western Child* (3, P. Engle), first performed at the State University of Iowa (Iowa City) on 28 July 1959 and later revised as *Golden Child* (NBC television, 16 Dec 1960); and *Stranger in Eden* (1963), a three-act work to a libretto by William Reardon (never performed).
FREDERICK CRANE

Béziers. Town in Hérault, southern France. It was important in the late 19th and early 20th centuries for its grand-scale open-air spectacles involving music. Although nearer to vastly inflated incidental music, the works given at these ventures bordered closely on opera, and several of the specially composed pieces were later rewritten for the confines of the conventional opera house. The town possesses the ruins of a Roman amphitheatre, but it was in the rebuilt modern amphitheatre that operas were mounted. The wooden *arènes*, used for bullfighting, were destroyed by fire in 1896 and replaced by a brick edifice the following year. At a time when several towns were experimenting with open-air spectacles involving the local people as well as the artistic élite (an idea promoted most notably by Romain Rolland) Saint-Saëns was invited to test the acoustic of the rebuilt *arènes* and was commissioned, together with Louis Gallet, to write a piece for performance there. The result was *Déjanire*, first mounted at Béziers in 1898 with a vast number of performers, including a massive chorus, drawn from the locality, and attracting huge audiences, some of whom travelled from Paris on special excursion trains (for illustration *see* SAINT-SAËNS, CAMILLE). A speciality of this and subsequent spectacles was the size of the orchestra necessitated by the open-air acoustic: the wind section was provided by massed military bands, there was a gigantic string orchestra, and Saint-Saëns referred to the 'curtain of harps'. When repeated indoors, operas composed for Béziers had to be entirely reorchestrated. Following the success of this first venture, Fauré was commissioned to write *Prométhée*: the two performances in 1900 drew more than 17 000 spectators and the work was repeated the following year. 1902 saw a new work by Saint-Saëns, *Parysatis*, as well as a revival of *Déjanire*. Later Gluck's *Armide* was presented (1904), followed by Levadé's *Les hérétiques* (1905), Rabaud's *Le premier glaive* (1908), Gailhard's *La fille du soleil*, Séverac's *Héliogabale* (1910) and Bousquet's *Zorriga* (1925).

*

J. Gachet: *Les représentations lyriques aux arènes de Béziers* (diss., U. of Paris IV, 1976)
L'opéra dans l'arène ou l'aventure de Fernand Castelbon (Béziers, 1989)
J.-M. Nectoux: 'Notes sur les spectacles musicaux aux arènes de Béziers, 1898–1910', *150 ans de musique française: Lyons, 1991*
RICHARD LANGHAM SMITH

Biaggi, Girolamo Alessandro (*b* Calcio, nr Bergamo, 2 Feb 1819; *d* Florence, 21 March 1897). Italian music critic and composer. He studied the violin in Milan, and was taught composition by Vaccai. While still a student he wrote a comic opera *Don Desiderio disperato per eccesso di buon cuore* (1839) and his later works include the opera *Martino della Scala* (1856, Messina), a requiem and other vocal music. He was for some time a conductor. In 1847 he founded *L'Italia musicale*, and (as Ippolito d'Albano) contributed to the *Gazzetta musicale di Milano* and other periodicals. From 1863 he taught at the Istituto Musicale in Florence and was critic of *La nazione*; he played a major role in the city's flourishing musical life.

Although Biaggi was a supporter of the German instrumental and chamber tradition, as an opera critic his standard was the Italian tradition that culminated in Rossini (he had met the composer in Paris), and he showed limited sympathy for opera of his own time. He did, however, adopt advanced ideas on Rossini, defending him against the formalistic criticism that categorized the composer as a mediocre dramatist. A large work on Rossini, the outgrowth of his essay 'Della vita e delle opere di Gioacchino Rossini' (*Atti dell'Accademia del R. Istituto musicale di Firenze*, 1869), was unfinished at Biaggi's death, as was his *Dizionario storico-critico della musica*.

*

L. Pinzauti: 'Un critico dell'ottocento: G. Alessandro Biaggi', *NRMI*, vii (1973), 388–40 SERGIO LATTES

Bialas, Günter (*b* Bielschowitz, Upper Silesia, 19 July 1907). German composer. In his childhood he absorbed musical influence through personal connections, since his father was business manager at the local German theatre. He was given private lessons in piano, organ and choral conducting. In 1925 he began formal studies at Breslau University and two years later moved to the Akademie für Kirchen- und Schulmusik, Berlin, where he remained until the advent of the Nazis. His first and principal composition teacher was Max Trapp whose masterclasses he attended at the Preussische Akademie für Künste from 1936 to 1938, although before this period he had become profoundly influenced by Fritz Jöde's work in the youth music movement. In 1940, he was appointed to teach music theory at Breslau University, but in the following year was called up for military service. After the war, he assumed the direction of the Bach-Verein in Munich for two years before being appointed composition teacher at the Weimar Musikhochschule in 1947. During the same year, he moved to Detmold where he taught composition and became director of the private music teachers' department at the Nordwestdeutsche Musikakademie. In 1959, he was appointed professor of composition at the Munich Staatliche Musikhochschule, a post he held until his retirement in 1974.

Although Bialas became thoroughly familiar with the mainstream operatic repertory during his youth, he avoided composing in the genre until he was nearly 60. In an interview published in 1984, he claimed that his three chamber operas, written between 1966 and 1975, follow the traditions of Stravinsky and Weill rather than those of Wagner, Strauss and Berg. Nevertheless in the first one, *Hero und Leander*, based on Grillparzer's *Des Meeres und der Liebe Wellen* and the *Epyllion* of Musaios, the influence of *Wozzeck* is evident despite the fact that the composer uses modest forces and employs an independent and versatile musical language. The work is through-composed with its principal structural procedures based upon recurring short motifs and sustained sonorities which tend towards atonality. Vocal lines are simple both in rhythm and intervallic patterns, inclining towards declamation rather than extended lyricism. The important role assigned to the chorus intensifies the feeling that the audience is witnessing the re-enactment of a Greek tragedy.

A different atmosphere pervades *Die Geschichte von Aucassin und Nicolette*, composed three years later. Here the familiar story of love overcoming all obstacles is presented not as a serious drama of human suffering but in the form of a fable full of improbable happenings. Consequently the musical idiom is ironic, with dance forms predominant, but at the same time there are more extended opportunities for lyrical writing. The style again suggests the influence of the Second Viennese School although the music is not organized serially. Bialas employs a chamber orchestra with a vast array of percussion instruments including a prepared piano.

A similar chamber-like instrumental complement underpins *Der gestiefelte Kater* (1975) which continues very much in the vein of the previous opera. Here Tieck's well-known fairy-tale is given a number of ironic twists with the introduction of many extra characters who carry out lengthy discussions on all aspects of contemporary music, including a dispute at the king's court over the relative health of modern opera. The score abounds in episodes of wit, irony and ambiguity, which are paralleled by the composer's parodistic use of many familiar compositional techniques, including those of Meyerbeer, Offenbach and the avant garde. Accordingly, Bialas employs all possibilities of vocal technique ranging from coloratura to spoken word while the stage action moves at an astonishing pace. Although all three of Bialas's operas were received with considerable acclaim by both critics and audiences after their first performances, they have failed so far to establish themselves securely in the German operatic repertory despite occasional revivals.

Hero und Leander (7 scenes, E. Spiess, after F. Grillparzer and Musaios), Mannheim, National, 8 Sept 1966 (Kassel, 1966)

Die Geschichte von Aucassin und Nicolette (13 scenes, T. Dorst), Munich, Cuvilliés, 12 Dec 1969 (Kassel, 1968)

Der gestiefelte Kater, oder Wie man das Spiel spielt (11 scenes, Dorst, after L. Tieck), Schwetzingen, Schloss, 19 May 1975 (Kassel, 1974)

*

G. Hausswald: 'Die erste Oper von Günter Bialas ("Hero und Leander"): Mannheim', *Musica*, xx (1966), 272–3

U. Stürzbecher: *Werkstattgespräche mit Komponisten* (Cologne, 1971, 2/1973)

G. Bialas: 'Eine Selbstdarstellung', *Zeitgenössische schlesische Komponisten*, ed. G. Pankalla and G. Speer (Dulmen, 1972)

K. D. Gräwe: 'Wie man den Kater spielt', *Programmheft und Jahrbuch der Hamburgischen Staatsoper* (Hamburg, 1975)

G. Speer and H. J. Winterhoff, eds.: *Meilensteine eines Komponistenlebens: Kleine Festschrift zum 70. Geburtstag von Günter Bialas* (Kassel, 1977)

A. L. Suder, ed.: *Günter Bialas* (Tutzing, 1984) ERIK LEVI

Bianca e Falliero [*Bianca e Falliero, ossia Il consiglio dei tre* ('Bianca and Falliero, or The Counsel of Three')]. *Melodramma* in two acts by GIOACHINO ROSSINI to a libretto by FELICE ROMANI after Antoine-Vincent Arnault's play *Les Vénitiens, ou Blanche et Montcassin*; Milan, Teatro alla Scala, 26 December 1819.

A conspiracy against Venice has been foiled and amid the general rejoicing Bianca's father Contareno (tenor) agrees to the healing of an old Venetian family feud by allowing Capellio (bass) Bianca's hand in marriage. Bianca (soprano) loves the young general Falliero (mezzo-soprano), erroneously reported to have died in the recent war, and expresses her love in her cavatina 'Della rosa il bel vermiglio'. News of her father's plan stuns her, driving Contareno into a towering rage in which he threatens to ruin Falliero and after that succumb to a mortal despair of his own. Bianca tells Falliero of her father's disapproval but not of the impending wedding. Act 1 ends with the wedding ceremony, Bianca's sudden refusal to sign the marriage certificate, and Falliero's equally sudden and angry eruption on to the scene. At the start of Act 2 Bianca reaffirms her love but Falliero has to flee at her father's approach. The wedding ceremony is resumed but again Bianca will not sign. Her father is furious; but then news comes that Falliero has been found hiding in the grounds of the Spanish Embassy, a treasonable action in the light of the Doge's decree against secret contacts with foreign powers. Falliero must now stand trial for his life before a Council of Three – Contareno, Capellio and Loredano – who will report to the Senate. In a highly dramatic scene, the demoralized Falliero refuses to defend himself but Bianca's intervention makes clear the context of Falliero's escape. Capellio is convinced by the sincerity of the two lovers and as the triumvirate's judgment cannot now be unanimous it is passed to the Senate. In Rossini's opera, though not in the original play, all ends happily.

The opera proved popular in Italy for more than a decade, after which it was slowly forgotten and dismembered, with only the great quartet from the trial scene, 'Cielo, il mio labbro ispira', surviving in various adapted forms. The score presents the three principals with formidable difficulties and was weakened by Rossini's re-use of the music of the rondo finale in the more successful *La donna del lago*. But the massiveness of the piece and the close gearing of the bel canto style to dramatic and psychological ends is, at times, awe-inspiring. Some of the love music has a latent eroticism rare in Rossini, and throughout there is an powerful preoccupation with states of emotional excess. Contareno's Act 1 confrontation with his daughter, 'Pensa che omai resistere', must be one of the nastiest set pieces ever penned for the tenor voice, by turns vindictive, suave and wilful. RICHARD OSBORNE

Bianca e Fernando ('Bianca and Fernando'). *Melodramma* in two acts by VINCENZO BELLINI to a libretto by DOMENICO GILARDONI after Carlo Roti's play *Bianca e Fernando alla tomba di Carlo IV duca di Agrigento*; Naples, S Carlo, 30 May 1826.

The opera was originally written for Adelaide Tosi and Giovanni Davide, the censor changing 'Fernando' to 'Gernando' to avoid similarity to the king's name, Ferdinando. The king then died, delaying the production, and Bellini had to recast the opera for Henriette Méric-Lalande and Giovanni Battista Rubini, with Luigi Lablache as Filippo. This version was also staged at the Teatro Carolino, Palermo, on 30 May 1829, when Filippo was sung by 'Guglielmo Balfe' – Michael William Balfe, the Irish composer. Meanwhile, in 1828 Bellini revised the score (and Felice Romani the libretto) for the opening of the Teatro Carlo Felice, Genoa, on 7 April, when the singers originally contracted in 1826 took the title roles and Antonio Tamburini sang Filippo.

In Act 1 Filippo (bass) has usurped the dukedom of Agrigento in Sicily, imprisoning its heir Carlo (bass) and announcing his death. He has banished Carlo's son, Fernando (tenor; Gernando in the first version), and is preparing to marry his daughter Bianca (soprano), a widow with a baby son. Fernando returns ('A tanto duol') and inveigles himself into Filippo's service as 'Adolfo', claiming to have seen Fernando die in battle. The celebrations for Bianca's marriage have begun when Filippo presents her to Fernando. Fernando recognizes her but assumes her to be Filippo's accomplice.

In Act 2 Filippo tells Fernando that Carlo is still alive, but that he must now be killed. In a *romanza a due voci*, 'Sorgi, o padre, e la figlia rimira', with Eloisa (soprano), Bianca reveals that she is marrying Filippo for the sake of her child. Fernando arrives to confront her, but they become reconciled; together they leave to seek out their father. Discovered in prison, Carlo is reunited with his son and daughter in a touching scene. Filippo arrives and threatens to kill Bianca's child. Her aria 'Deh non ferir, deh! sentimi' (which was added in the 1828 revision) evolves into a fine trio for Bianca, Fernando and Filippo, who is eventually overcome and disarmed. Although the cabaletta, for Bianca alone, is conventional, the finale as a whole contains the most dramatic music so far written by Bellini.

Bianco e Fernando is an unusual 'rescue opera' in which the theme of romantic love is avoided. Even in the revised version of 1828 the opera rarely creates the dramatic impact that the composer achieved in *Il pirata*. Nevertheless, the melodic originality of the earlier version, evident, for example, in 'Sorgi, o padre', is now enriched by the formal flexibility of the new 'aria finale' (clearly foreshadowing the finale to *Norma*).

SIMON MAGUIRE, ELIZABETH FORBES

Bianca und Giuseppe [*Bianca und Giuseppe, oder Die Franzosen vor Nizza* ('Bianca and Giuseppe, or The French before Nice')]. Opera in four acts by JAN BEDŘICH KITTL to a libretto by Richard Wagner (see WAGNER family, (1)) after Heinrich König's *Die hohe Braut*; Prague, Estates Theatre, 19 February 1848.

The opera is a tragic love story set in Nice in Savoy in 1793, at the time of the conquest of the town by the French Republican army. The first performance took place a few days before the beginning of the Prague Revolution of 1848. In Act 3 the French soldiers unfurled the tricolour on stage. Their march, adapted by Kittl from the French song *Ça ira*, became famous during the revolution; the original plan was to use the *Marseillaise*, but it was banned by the censor. The opera is in an early Romantic style and has self-contained musical numbers. JITKA LUDVOVÁ

Bianchi, Antonio (i) (*b* Venice, *c*1710; *d* Venice, ?1772). Italian poet and librettist. Although his early career as a gondolier implies a humble family background, the high quality of his writings clearly indicates a thorough education. His patron, Doge Pietro Grimani, was accused for a time of correcting his poetry or even writing it for him. Bianchi wrote several comic opera librettos: *Le villeggiatrici ridicole* (music by A. Boroni, performed 1765), *L'amore in ballo* (Paisiello, 1765) and *La buona figliuola supposta vedova* (G. Latilla, 1766). Musical settings of *Camma*, his *dramma per musica* dedicated to Carl Eugen of Württemberg (1767), and *L'Alcibiade*, a *tragi-commedia*, have not come to light. He also wrote oratorio texts (some are in *I-Vmc*) and provided occasional verse.

F. A. Zaccaria: *Storia letteraria d'Italia*, iii (Venice, 1752), 552; vii (1755), 120

G. M. Mazzuchelli: *Gli scrittori d'Italia*, ii (Brescia, 1760), 1130–31

E. A. Cicogna: *Delle inscrizioni veneziane*, v (Venice, 1842), 202ff, 659; vi (1853), 924ff

G. Ortolani, ed.: *Tutte le opere di Carlo Goldoni*, iv (Milan, 1945), 1003, 1272

SVEN HANSELL

Bianchi, Antonio (ii) (*b* Milan, 1758; *d* after 1817). Italian singer and composer. He began a career as a baritone in Milan and Genoa and may have sung in Paris in the 1780s. Touring Germany in the early 1790s, he became court singer to the Prince of Nassau Weilburg and sang at the Berlin Königliches Nationaltheater from 1792. His performances in German (including roles in Mozart's *Don Giovanni* and J. M. König's *Lilla, oder Die Gärtnerin*) were criticized, but those in Italian comic operas by Paisiello, Sarti, Cimarosa and Astarita were highly praised. On 16 February 1794 his own serious opera *Die Insel der Alcina* (2, G. Bertati; *D-SWl*) was staged at the Berlin Hoftheater, and in 1796 his pastoral intermezzo *Fileno e Clorinda* was given in Charlottenburg and Potsdam. Bianchi remained a member of the *opera buffa* company at the Prussian court until late 1797, when Friedrich Wilhelm II died. He then visited various German cities and became co-director with Krüger of an opera troupe touring Thuringia. After leaving Krüger's company in the late 1790s he sang in Hamburg. The last notice of him, dated 1817, is a petition to allow him and his family to perform briefly in Aachen. He may have performed in Paris about the turn of the 19th century. Bianchi's other compositions include ballets and many songs.

DBI (V. Frajese); *MGG* (J. Theurich) SVEN HANSELL

Bianchi, (Giuseppe) Francesco (*b* Cremona, *c*1752; *d* Hammersmith, London, 27 Nov 1810). Italian composer. A Cremonese priest financed his studies at a conservatory in Naples, where he studied with Cafaro and assisted Jommelli in exchange for instruction. In 1772 he returned to Cremona, where his first opera, *Giulio Sabino*, successfully launched his career. In the summer of 1775 he went to Paris, where he worked as harpsichordist and composer of comic operas for the Théâtre-Italien and where he tried unsuccessfully to establish a conservatory after the Neapolitan model. He was admitted to membership of the Accademia Filarmonica of Bologna in August 1776 but did not return to Italy until 1778. From 1782 until 28 February 1793 Bianchi served as vice-*maestro* at the Metropolitana, Milan. On 21 January 1785 he was named second organist of St Mark's, Venice. Except for a hiatus from 20 November 1791 to 20 February 1793, he remained there until the fall of the Venetian Republic in 1797.

In 1778 Bianchi began working with the progressive librettists De Gamerra and Sertor, and later also with Foppa, Botturini and Pepoli, Venetians moving away from the century-old *opera seria* conventions that were to prevail in Italy until the 1790s. Apparently influenced by Gluck and by Verazi's librettos for the opening of La Scala (1778–9), his *Erifile* contains one of the earliest action-ensemble finales in an *opera seria*, and his *Castore e Polluce* is replete with French-inspired choruses and dance; both were given in Florence during the reign of Archduke Leopold. In Venice 1780 his *Demetrio* acquired a final sextet, one of the earliest Italian examples of an extensive action-ensemble finale to conclude a Metastasian opera – not a finale in *buffa* style but a fluid, seamless ensemble spanning several abrupt changes of mood but without clear sectional delineations until an obbligato recitative breaks the continuity and paves the way for an extensive joyful conclusion.

Bianchi's collaboration with Sertor spanned 11 years, beginning in 1781, and yielded six new *opere serie*. Consequently, innovatory elements such as *introduzioni*, programmatic storms and battles, solos and ensembles with chorus, ensembles with increasing numbers of personnel and action-ensemble finales appear much more frequently and much earlier in Bianchi's works than in others. Perhaps the most influential of his collaborations with Sertor was *La morte di Cesare* (1788), which initiated a decade of 'morte' operas.

Bianchi was the first composer to work with Foppa. *Alonso e Cora* (1786) and *Calto* (1788) initiated a new era in Venetian opera, and their innovations soon became common operatic components. Both operas treat non-classical subjects, employ ballet and chorus along with a duet for two men with chorus (an early *giuramento*), and have extensive final scene complexes (one of which makes up the whole of the short Act 3 of *Alonso*). *Calto* contains a ghost scene in which the chorus takes part in the action and an aria with interjections from a second character. Also in *Calto* Bianchi introduced the clarinet to Venice, where it did not become a regular orchestral instrument for another five years.

By the early 1780s Bianchi was already bypassing the lengthy static solos that normally opened each ensemble and moving directly into animated musical diaglogue. Programmatic battle music replaces the *marcia*. Extensive stretches of obbligato recitative move freely among changing accompaniment patterns. Wind colour, chromaticism, excursions deep into the flat keys and occasional use of the *voce umana* heighten the terror of dungeons or ghost scenes (for example in *La Vendetta di Nino*, an opera with several innovatory features). Still, contemporary critics praised his 'lively, light and graceful music' and the 'softness and sweetness of his melodies'.

Bianchi took particular advantage of the wind instruments both as soloists and as a section, especially in his Neapolitan works. The bassoons have their own parts, and the violas often join with the upper strings or with the winds. In obbligato recitatives Bianchi employed a broad range of wind colour (oboe, bassoon, clarinet, horn and english horn) for expressive purposes. By the early 90s his orchestrations frequently combine the entire wind section. His accompaniments seldom adhere to a single figure throughout an aria. Often either the first violin or the voice states the melody, while the other provides embellishment or elaboration. The first violins may also join the seconds in maintaining rhythmic motifs, oscillating arpeggiation or tremolo. Wind instruments alone or with strings add musical commentary in caesuras and ritornellos, and solo winds answer each other, the strings and the voice. Wind instruments also reinforce dynamic contrasts and assist in building long crescendos.

Bianchi specialized in serious opera more than his contemporaries did, but he continued to write comic operas throughout his career. In a preface to the printed libretto of *Il disertore francese* (Venice, 1784), he defended its amalgam of serious and comic elements; nonetheless, audiences were shocked to see the castrato Pacchierotti singing the principal role in bourgeois dress.

Bianchi went to London in 1795 to direct a revival of *La vendetta di Nino*, performed 41 times in six seasons. Between 1795 and 1802 he prepared 14 other works for the King's Theatre – six of them in collaboration with Da Ponte, the poet there from 1793 to 1798. Between 1802 and 1807 Bianchi travelled between London and Paris, composing operas and directing revivals in both cities. For a time his works dominated the *opéra comique* productions at several Parisian theatres. The *Morning Chronicle* (29 November 1810) and the *Gentleman's Magazine* (December 1810) reported Bianchi's suicide at his home in Hammersmith. The *Daily Advertiser* aptly reviewed a revival of *Erifile* on 20 February 1805: 'Mr Bianchi's bent, in this, as in all his former musical efforts, is certainly directed toward the tender and pathetic, and if he does not ravish or surprise us by novelty and boldness of composition, he seldom fails pleasing us by the softness and sweetness of his melodies'. His operas enjoyed revivals for another 15 years.

See also Alonso e cora; Arbace; Calto; Castore e polluce (i); Morte di cesare, la; Seleuco, re di siria; Villanella rapita, la; and Zemira; *see further* Erifile.

FP – *Florence, Teatro della Pergola*
LK – *London, King's Theatre*
NC – *Naples, Teatro S Carlo*
PJE – *Paris, Jeunes-Elèves*
VB – *Venice, Teatro S Benedetto*
VM – *Venice, Teatro S Moisé*

Giulio Sabino (os), Cremona, 1772, cavatina (Vienna, n.d.)
Il gran Cidde (os, 3, G. Pizzi), FP, Jan 1773
Demetrio (os, 3, P. Metastasio), Cremona, carn. 1774, *F-Pn*, *P-La* (1780, Venice)
Eurione (os, 3, A. Papi), Pavia, Quattro Signori, 25 May 1775
La réduction de Paris (drame lyrique, 3, B. F. de Rosoi), Paris, Italien, 30 Sept 1775, unacc. arias (Paris, n.d.)
Le mort marié (oc, 2, M.-J. Sédaine), Fontainebleau, 25 Oct 1776
Erifile (os, 3, G. D. Gamerra), FP, Jan 1779, lost; Modena, 1781, *P-La* (Acts 2 and 3); Petrovich Sheremetev Collection, Moscow
L'innocenza perseguitata (ob, 3), Rome, Dame, carn. 1779
Castore e Polluce (os, 3, C. I. Frugoni), FP, 8 Sept 1779, *I-Pl*, *P-La* (1781, Padua)
Arbace (os, 3, G. Sertor), NC, 20 Jan 1781, *I-Nc*, *Tf* (Acts 2 and 3), *P-La*
Venere e Adone (azione teatrale, 2, F. Casorri), FP, 14 Sept 1781, *I-Fc*, *Tf*
La Zemira (os, 2, Sertor), NC, 4 Nov 1781, *Pi(l)* (1786, Padua), *P-La*
Olimpiade (os, 3, Metastasio), Milan, La Scala, 26 Dec 1781, *F-Pn*, *P-La*
Il trionfo della pace (festa teatrale, 2, C. Olivieri), Turin, Regio, spr. 1782, *I-Tf*, *P-La*
La Zulima (os, 3, C. Olivieri, after Voltaire), NC, 4 Nov 1782, *I-Nc*, *P-La*
L'astrologa (ob, 3, P. Chiari), Naples, Fondo, Dec 1782, *I-Tf*, *P-La*
Piramo e Tisbe (os, 3, Sertor), VB, Jan 1783, *GB-Lbl*, *I-Pca*, *P-La*
La villanella rapita (op giocosa, 2, G. Bertati), VM, aut. 1783; as Le gelosie di Pippo, Lisbon, 1796 (Paris, n.d.); *F-Pn*, *H-Bn*, *I-Gl* (Act 1), *Tf*, *P-La*, *PL-Kc*, Petrovich Sheremetev Collection, Moscow
Briseide (os, 3, F. S. Gambino), Turin, Regio, 26 Dec 1783, *P-La*
Aspardi, principe di Battriano (os, 3, Sertor), Rome, Dame, carn. 1784
Cajo Mario (os, 3, G. Roccaforte), NC, 30 May 1784, *I-Nc*, *P-La*
La finta principessa (ob, 2, F. Livigni), Bologna, Formagliari, aut. 1784
Il disertore francese (os, 3, B. Benincasa), VB, 26 Dec 1784, *D-Bds* (Act 3), *F-Pn*, *H-Bn*, *I-Bc*, *Mc*, *Tf*, *P-La*
Alessandro nell'Indie (os, 3, Metastasio), VB, 28 Jan 1785, *F-Pn* (1792 revival), *H-Bn*, *I-Bc*
Lo stravagante inglese (ob, 2, G. Greppi), VM, aut. 1785, *D-Wa*, *F-Pn*, *I-Bc*
Le villanelle astute (ob, 2, G. Foppa), Venice, S Samuele, carn. 1786
Alonso e Cora (os, 3, Foppa, after F. Moretti: *Idalide*), VB, 7 Feb 1786, *P-La*
Mesenzio, re d'Etruria (os, 2, F. Casorri), NC, 4 Nov 1786, *I-Nc*, *P-La*
L'orfano cinese (os, 3, after Voltaire), VB, 30 Jan 1787, *?D-Bds*, *F-Pn*, *I-Bc*, *P-La*
Artaserse (os, 3, Metastasio), Padua, Nuovo, 11 June 1787, *F-Pn* (as Arbace), *I-Pl*, *P-La*
Pizzarro (os, 3), Brescia, Accademia degli Erranti, sum. 1787, *D-Mbs*, *GB-Lbl*, *I-Nc* (2 copies), *P-La*
Scipione africano (os, 3, N. Minato), NC, 13 Aug 1787, *I-Fc*, *Nc*, *Rsc* (Act 1)
Il ritratto (ob, 2, F. S. Zini), Naples, Fondo, aut. 1787, *GB-Lbl*, *I-Nc* (2 copies), *Tf*
Calto (os, 3, Foppa, after Ossian), VB, 23 Jan 1788, *P-La*
La morte di Cesare (os, 3, Sertor), Venice, S Samuele, 27 Dec 1788, *B-Bc*
La fedeltà tra le selve (ob, 2, M. A. Prunetti), Rome, Capranica, carn. 1789, incl. 4 arias by Valentino Fioravanti
Nitteti (os, 3, Metastasio), Milan, La Scala, 20 April 1789, *P-La*
Daliso e Delmita (os, 2, De Gamerra), Padua, Nuovo, 12 June 1789, *F-Pn*, *GB-T*, *I-Pl*, *Vnm*
Il finto astrologo (ob, 2, A. Mariani), Rome, Capranica, carn. 1790, *F-Pn*, *GB-Lbl*, *I-BDG*, *P-La* (1792, Salvaterra)
L'Arminio (os, 3, F. Moretti), FP, aut. 1790
La vendetta di Nino, o sia Semiramide (os, 2, P. Giovannini, after Voltaire), NC, 12 Nov 1790, *D-Mbs*, *F-Pn*, *GB-Lbl*, *Lcm*, *T*, *I-Fc*, *Nc*
Caio Ostilio (os, 2, E. Manfredi), Rome, Argentina, carn. 1791, duet, trio in *D-MÜs*, *LB*, *I-Bc* and *Rsc*
La dama bizzarra (ob, 2, T. Mariani), Rome, Capranica, carn. 1791, *P-La*
Deifile (azione scenica, 2), Venice, Bruenner Palace, March 1791, *I-Fc*, *Vnm*
La sposa in equivoco (ob, 2, Zini), VM, aut. 1791, *F-Pn*, *I-Fc*
Seleuco, re di Siria (os, 3, M. Botturini), VB, 26 Dec 1791, *Bc*, *Fc* (1792, Bologna), *PAc*
Aci e Galatea (os, 2, Foppa), VB, 13 Oct 1792; as La vendetta di Polifemo, Palermo, 1793; ? new setting, London, 1795; arias in *Fc*, *Nc*
Tarara, o sia La virtù premiata (os, 3, Sertor), Venice, La Fenice, 26 Dec 1792, *F-Pn* (Act 1)
Il cinese in Italia (ob, 2, A. Pepoli), VM, aut. 1793; as L'olandese in Venezia, Turin, 1794; *GB-Lbl*, *I-Fc*
La secchia rapita (ob, 2, A. Anelli), Venice, S Samuele, 13 Feb 1794; rev. Milan, 1796, with new act by Zingarelli, *I-Mr**
Ines de Castro (os, 3, L. de Sanctis, after C. Giotti), NC, 30 May 1794, *Nc*, *Pl* (1798, Padua)
La capricciosa ravveduta (ob, 2, C. Mazzolà), VM, aut. 1794, *F-Pn*, *I-Mr* (?autograph)
Antigona (os, 2, Da Ponte), LK, 24 May 1796, *I-Fc* (1802, London)
Il consiglio imprudente (ob, 1, Da Ponte, after C. Goldoni: *Un curioso accidente*), LK, 20 Dec 1796, finale in vs (London, n.d.)
Merope (os, 2, Da Ponte, after Voltaire), LK, 10 June 1797, *GB-Lbl*, *I-T*
Cinna (os, 2, Da Ponte, ? after Anelli), LK, 20 Feb 1798, aria, trio (London, n.d.)
Alzira (os, 2, G. Rossi, after Voltaire), LK, 28 Feb 1801, *D-BFb*, *MÜs*, *GB-Ob*, *US-CA*, *Wc*
La morte di Cleopatra (os, 2, S. Bonaiuti), LK, 30 April 1801, aria (London, n.d.)
Armida (os, 2, Da Ponte, after T. Tasso: *Gerusalemme liberata*), LK, 1 June 1802, aria, duet (London, n.d.)
L'avaro (oc, 2, G. Bertati), Paris, Italien, 30 March 1804
Blaisot e Pasquin (oc, 1, Leroi, Francis and Martinelli), Paris, Montansier, 9 April 1804, duet (Paris, n.d.)
Le maître de chapelle (oc), Paris, Italien, 3 May 1804
Corali, ou La lanterne magique (oc, 1, A.-J. Grétry *neveu*), Paris, Molière, 7 July 1804, *S-St*, *US-Wc*; (Paris, n.d.)
L'eau et le leu, ou Le Gascon a l'épreuve (oc, 1, M. Gangiran-Nanteuil), Paris, Montansier, 10 Aug 1804
Le contrat signé d'avance, ou Laquelle est ma femme? (oc, 1, Ligier), Paris, Molière, 29 Sept 1804
Le gascon, gascon malgré lui (oc, 1, Guillet and E. Hus), Paris, Molière, 17 Nov 1804
Amour et coquetterie (oc, 1, Coffin-Rosny), PJE, 7 Jan 1806
Le livre des destins (oc, 1, F. Nogaret), PJE, 2 Feb 1806
La famille vénitienne, ou Le château d'Orseno (oc, 3, F. Dupetit-Méné), Paris, Jeunes Artistes, 7 May 1806
Monsieur Jugolo, ou Les chercheurs (oc, 1), PJE, 22 May 1806
Le château mystérieux ou Le crime commis et vengé (oc, 3, M. de Redon and C. R. Defresnoy), PJE, 12 July 1806
Le triomphe d'Alcide à Athènes (dramma eroico, 2, P. L. Moline and A. F. Pillon), Paris, Molière, Sept 1806
La soeur officieuse, ou Adresse et mensonge (oc, 1, Redon and Defresnoy), PJE, 18 Oct 1806
Almeria, ou L'Ecossaise fugitive (oc, 3, B. Hadot), PJE, 8 Dec 1806
Les illustres infortunés, ou La souveraine vindicative (oc, 3, Redon and Defresnoy), PJE, 8 Jan 1807
Le pied de boeuf et la queue du chat (oc, 3, P. J. Charrin and Redon), Paris, Jeunes Artistes, 9 June 1807

Music in: Medonte, 1782; L'ape musicale rinnuovata, 1791; Pirro, 1793

Doubtful: Mitridate, Genoa, 1781; Demofoonte, Venice, 1783; La caccia di Enrico IV, Venice, 1784; Il barone a forza, Rome, 1785; Li sponsi incommedia, Venice, 1785; Il nuovo Don Chischiotte, Voltri, 1788; Il gatto, Brescia, 1789; La calamità dei cuori, Padua, 1789; Il difensore, Vienna, 1793–4; Zenobia, London, 1797, *F-Pn*; La serva riconoscente, Lisbon, 1798, pasticcio; Telemaco,

Cremona, *c*1800; Vonima e Mitridate, Venice, 1803; Sofonisba, Venice; Cenobia; Don Pomponio; Eliodoro, *I-Mr*; Gara d'amore, *Mr*; Gengis-Kan

Miscellaneous arias and ensembles: *A-Wgm*, *B-Bc*, *CH-E*; *D-Bds*, *BFb*, *Dlb*, *DS*, *MÜs*, *W*; *F-Pn*, *GB-Lbl*; *I-BAcp*, *Bc*, *Bsf*, *Gl*, *Mc*, *MOe*, *Mr*, *OS*, *PAc*, *Pca*, *Vc*, *Vnm*; *P-La*, *US-Wc*

*

FlorimoN
B. F. de Rozoi: *Dissertation sur le drame lyrique* (The Hague, 1776)
L. Bachaumont: *Mémoires secrets* (London, 1777–8), viii, 227–8; x, 214
A. Choron and F. Fayolle: *Dictionnaire historique des musiciens* (Paris, 1810–11)
V. Lancetti: 'Bianchi', *Biografia cremonese* (Milan, 1820), ii, 218ff
L. da Ponte: *Memorie* (New York, 1823, 2/1829); ed. (Milan, 1960), 186ff, 190, 196
S. D.: 'Chronicles of the Italian Opera in England', *The Harmonicon*, viii (1830), 10, 70, 112, 196
T. Wiel: *I teatri musicali veneziani del settecento* (Venice, 1897), 385ff
A. Della Corte: *L'opera comica italiana nel '700* (Bari, 1923), ii, 81ff, 235ff
R.-A. Mooser: *Annales de la musique et des musiciens en Russie* (Geneva, 1948–51), ii, iii
M. McClymonds: '*La morte di Semiramide, ossia La vendetta di Nino* and the Restoration of Death and Tragedy to the Italian Operatic Stage in the 1780s and 1790s', *IMSCR*, xiv *Bologna 1987*, 285–92
R.-A. Mooser: 'The Venetian Role in the Transformation of Italian Opera Seria during the 1790s', *I vicini di Mozart: Venice 1987*, 221–40 MARITA P. McCLYMONDS

Bianchi, Giuseppe (*fl* 1637–63). Italian castrato. In 1637 his name was entered among the singers of the papal chapel in Rome; he then passed to the service of Taddeo Barberini, prefect of Rome. The Abate Elpidio Benedetti, who was commissioned by Cardinal Mazarin to recruit Italian singers for the French court, named him in 1643 as the best castrato in Rome, and as a result he took part in a private performance of an opera in the Palais Royal, Paris, during Carnival 1645. In 1646 he was back in the papal chapel in Rome, but subsequently was probably in Germany, in the service of several rulers. On 14 April 1654, under the name 'Giuseppe da Torino', he sang at the Petit-Bourbon in Paris in Carlo Caproli's opera *Le nozze di Peleo e di Theti*. He continued his career in the German-speaking states and in 1658 he sang in the Hofmusikkapelle in Vienna for at least several months. In 1662–3, and almost certainly earlier, he was among the chamber musicians of the court of Turin.

*

R. Casimiri: '"Disciplina musicae" e "Mastri di Capella" dopo il Concilio di Trento nei maggiori istituti ecclesiastici di Roma – Seminario romano – Collegio germanico – Collegio inglese – (sec. XVI–XVII)', *NA*, xix (1942), 103–29 PAOLA BESUTTI

Bianchi [Tozzi], **Marianna** (*b* ?Venice, *c*1735; *d* after 1790). Italian soprano. She made her *opera seria* début as *ultima parte* at Parma in 1753 and sang mostly secondary roles, sometimes appearing in *opera buffa*, before going to Vienna as prima donna in 1762, where she created Eurydice in Gluck's *Orfeo ed Euridice*. She then sang as prima donna in Italy and with her husband, the composer Antonio Tozzi, was engaged at Brunswick (1765–8) and Munich (1773–5); her Italian career then declined to secondary theatres and, after 1780, to *opera buffa*, ending in 1790. According to Burney, she had 'a sweet and elegant toned voice, always perfectly in tune, with an admirable *portamento*; I never heard any one sing with more ease, or in a manner so totally free from affectation'. DENNIS LIBBY

Biancolini(-Rodriguez), Marietta (*b* Fermo, Ascoli Piceno, 20 Sept 1846; *d* Florence, 31 May 1905). Italian mezzo-soprano. She made her début in 1864 as Bellini's Romeo at Novara, then appeared in Florence, Genoa, Naples, Lisbon, Buenos Aires and at La Scala, where she created Laura (*La Gioconda*) in 1876 and sang Fidès (*Le prophète*) in 1885. The flexibility of her voice enabled her to sing Rossini's coloratura mezzo-soprano and contralto roles, including Rosina, Angelina, Isabella and Arsace, with special success. ELIZABETH FORBES

Bianconi, Lorenzo (Gennaro) (*b* Minusio, Ticino, 14 Jan 1946). Swiss musicologist. He studied musicology at Heidelberg University and took the doctorate in 1974 with a dissertation on Cavalli and the diffusion of Venetian opera in Italy in the 17th century. In 1981 he was appointed professor of music history at the University of Siena in Arezzo and in 1983 of musical dramaturgy at the University of Bologna. He has produced far-reaching works in his chief fields of research, Italian opera of the 17th, 18th and 19th centuries, the libretto and musical dramaturgy. The six-volume history of Italian opera of which he is joint editor treats not only the text and music but also all aspects of production, design and socio-economic background.

Storia della musica, iv: *Il seicento* (Turin, 1982, 2/1991); Eng. trans., as *Music in the Seventeenth Century* (Cambridge, 1987)
with T. Walker: 'Production, Consumption and Political Function of Seventeenth-Century Opera', *Early Music History*, iv (1984), 209–96
ed.: *La drammaturgia musicale* (Bologna, 1986)
ed., with G. Pestelli: *Storia dell'opera italiana* (Turin, 1987–)
ed., with G. La Face Bianconi: *I libretti italiani di Georg Friedrich Händel e le loro fonti* (Florence, 1992–)
CAROLYN GIANTURCO

Bibalo, Antonio (*b* Trieste, 18 Jan 1922). Norwegian composer of Italian birth. He studied composition at the Trieste Conservatory, where he was taught by L. Gante and Giulio Viozzi, and in 1953 he became a pupil of Elisabeth Lutyens in London. He became internationally known when his Fantasia for violin and orchestra won a prize in the Wieniawski competition in Warsaw in 1955. Two years later he settled in Norway. His first stage work, the opera *Das Lächeln am Fusse der Leiter*, was enthusiastically received at its première (1965, Hamburg). It was followed by the ballets *Pinocchio*, *Nocturne for Apollo* and *Flammen* ('The Flame'). The chamber opera *Frøken Julie* ('Miss Julie'), which had its première in Århus in 1975, attracted widespread attention; it has subsequently been staged in several German cities and also in Oslo in 1976. There followed in 1977 the one-act *Askeladden* ('Numskull Jack') to a libretto by Hartvig Kiran based on Norwegian folklore, and then the dramatic operas *Ghosts* (based on Ibsen's play) in 1981 and *Macbeth* in 1990. In his music for the stage Bibalo has used a wide range of resources, from romantic harmonies to avant-garde techniques, to underline and add colour to the dramatic action. Besides operas and ballets, his important works include two symphonies, three concertos and some chamber and piano music.

Das Lächeln am Fusse der Leiter, 1958–62 (1, A. Bibalo after H. Miller: *The Smile at the Foot of the Ladder*), Hamburg, Staatsoper, 6 April 1965
Frøken Julie [Miss Julie] (chamber op, 3, A. Bibalo, after A. Strindberg), Århus, 8 Sept 1975
Askeladden [Numskull Jack] (childrens op, 1, H. Kiran), broadcast, Norwegian Radio, 26 Dec 1977

Gespenster [Ghosts] (3, A. Bibalo and G. Bibalo, after H. Ibsen), Kiel, 21 June 1981
Macbeth (3, A. Bibalo, after W. Shakespeare), Oslo, 29 Sept 1990

HAAKON NORDERVAL

Biber, Heinrich Ignaz Franz von (*b* Wartenberg, nr Reichenberg [now Liberec], Bohemia, bap. 12 Aug 1644; *d* Salzburg, 3 May 1704). Bohemian composer. An outstanding violin virtuoso of his day, he served Prince-Bishop Karl, Count Liechtenstein-Kastelkorn of Olomouc, at Kroměříž in central Moravia from 1668 or earlier to 1670. During the winter of 1670–71 he became a member of the Kapelle at the Salzburg court; he was promoted to vice-Kapellmeister in 1679, and in 1684 he became Kapellmeister. Though known primarily as a composer of sacred and instrumental music, he composed there at least two operas, a 'representation in three cantatas' and numerous school dramas with music.

Biber's three-act *dramma musicale*, *Chi la dura la vince*, is the only 17th-century Salzburg opera whose music has survived (*A-Sca*); the unique leather-bound copy is dedicated to Archbishop Thun and marked with the date of his accession to the episcopate in 1687. The librettist was most likely Francesco Maria Raffaelini, who provided the librettos for two other Salzburg operas: Biber's *Alessandro in Pietra* and Georg Muffat's *La fatale felicità di Plutone* (probably performed between 1688 and 1690). Dahms (1974) has shown that *Chi la dura la vince* was itself probably performed some time between 5 December 1690 and mid-1692. (There was a revival under the title *Arminius* at the Komische Oper, East Berlin, in 1981.) The story, loosely based on the account in Tacitus's *Annals* of the Germanic chieftain Arminio [Arminius], revolves primarily around the rescue by Arminius (bass) of his wife Segesta (soprano), a slave imprisoned by Germanico [Germanicus] (tenor). The plot also includes the love intrigues of Germanicus's two sons, Nerone [Nero] (tenor) and Calligda [Caligula] (alto), with Giulia [Julia] and Claudia (both sopranos), and there are additional comic scenes involving Julia's nurse, Climmia (tenor), and the court buffoon, Herchino [Herchinus] (tenor). Other characters include Tiberio [Tiberius] and Seiano [Seianus] (basses) and Vitellio [Vitellius] (alto).

The opera's set pieces include two choral numbers, five short duets (only in Act 3) and 49 arias. The arias are mostly of the 'Devisen-aria' type; 23 include separate ritornellos, mostly for two violins and continuo, though the ritornello in Act 2 scene vi is scored for four trumpets and timpani, and that in Act 2 scene xvi for four recorders. Each act is tonally centred: Act 1 on C (with emphasis on secondary flat keys), Act 2 on G (emphasis on secondary sharp keys) and Act 3 on C (equal emphasis on secondary flat and sharp keys). It is likely that Biber's other known Salzburg opera, *Alessandro in Pietra* (3; Jan or Feb 1689; lib. *A-Wn*, *KR*), was similar in musical style. Though more conservative than contemporary operas produced in Vienna, *Chi la dura la vince* demonstrates the same formal and tonal coherence found in Biber's better-known instrumental and sacred works.

Biber's school dramas belonged to a genre, produced mostly by students of the Benedictine University, in which musical set pieces alternated with dialogue. Based principally on classical models, Old Testament stories and saints' lives, they are known only from their Latin texts, which are extant for 13 works composed between 1684 and 1698 (most in *A-Su*; see Chafe, 250–53). The music of his representation, *Tratenimento musicale del'ossequio di Salisburgi* (February 1699, Salzburg), is also lost, though the libretto survives (*Sca*).

*

C. Schneider: 'Franz Heinrich von Biber als Opernkomponist', *AMw*, viii (1926), 281–347
T. Antonicek: 'Das Salzburger Ordensdrama', *ÖMz*, xxv (1970), 370–77
S. Dahms: 'Opern und Festkantaten des Salzburger Hochbarocks', ibid, 377–84
——: 'Neues zur Chronologie der Opern von Biber und Muffat', *ÖMz*, xxix (1974), 365–7
E. T. Chafe: *The Church Music of Heinrich Biber* (Ann Arbor, 1987)

CHARLES E. BREWER

Bibiena [Bibbiena]. *See* GALLI-BIBIENA family.

Bible. A collection of sacred books written over different periods in Hebrew, Aramaic and Greek. The 39 books of the Old Testament recount God's dealings with Israel as his chosen people. The historical period covered is some 1400 years, from Abraham to the rebuilding of Jerusalem after the Babylonian exile and the arrival of Ezra in Palestine in *c*400 BC during the reign of the Persian Artaxerxes II (404–358 BC). Innumerable oratorio texts have their basis in the Old Testament, but opera librettos are restricted to far fewer themes. First beginnings in *Genesis* were treated, if not always in fully operatic form, by Johann Theile in his *Adam und Eva* (1678), of which the music is lost. A vogue for biblical opera in France included, at the beginning of the 19th century, *La mort d'Adam* by Le Sueur, Rodolphe Kreutzer's *Abel* and *Joseph* by Méhul. The Cain and Abel story has also attracted more recent composers (d'Albert and Weingartner), and Wagner-Régeny composed a setting of the Esau and Jacob story. Moses and very different aspects of the Exodus have been treated by Rossini (*Mosè in Egitto*) and Schoenberg (*Moses und Aron*). The book of *Judges* has provided such effective stories as those of Jephtha (Montéclair, Meyerbeer), Samson and Delilah (Rameau, to a libretto by Voltaire, and Saint-Saëns) and Deborah (Pizzetti, J. B. Foerster). The first three kings of Israel have been often treated, if not always in fully operatic form: Saul most effectively by Nielsen, David by Honegger and Milhaud, and Solomon in association with the Queen of Sheba by Gounod and Goldmark. Nebuchadnezzar, responsible for the destruction of Jerusalem in 586 BC, is covered in *Ezekiel* and *Daniel*; Verdi is his best-known operatic interpreter (*Nabucco*). Racine's play of 1690 assisted the book of *Esther* towards both oratorio and opera (Mariotte; Nicolaus Strungk's *Esther* antedates Racine). The sufferings of Job, expressed in some of the Bible's finest poetry (probably 4th century BC), have been worked by Dallapiccola; the pastoral book of *Ruth* has provided a subject for Lennox Berkeley.

The book most highly favoured by opera librettists and composers comes from the *Apocrypha* and is one of the least historical in the Bible. The 14 books of the *Apocrypha* supplement the Old Testament and continue the Jewish story into the 2nd century BC, when the book of *Judith* was probably written. The author places the action in the 12th year of Nebuchadnezzar, but the military commander Holofernes is almost certainly the man sent against Phoenicia by Alexander Ochus in 350 BC. The steadfast courage of the widow Judith in the camp of Holofernes and her joyous return to Bethulia with the trophy of his head captured many imaginations from Peri to Matthus.

The 27 books of the New Testament, dealing with the life of Jesus and the spread of Christianity, have given less to opera. Christ's birth and early years were staged by Theile (*Die Geburth Christi*) and Vittadini (*Nazareth*). His teaching is represented by the story of the prodigal son in works by Auber (to Scribe's only biblical libretto) and Britten. His power of redemption was covered by Massenet in the staged oratorio *Marie-Magdeleine*. It is the disreputable characters who have attracted most operatic interest, such as Herod (Chaumet), Herodias (Massenet, based on Flaubert) and Salome (Strauss, to a translation of Oscar Wilde).

See also ORATORIO and SACRED OPERA. ROBERT ANDERSON

Bible, Frances (L.) (*b* Sackets Harbor, NY, 26 Jan 1927). American mezzo-soprano. After studying with Belle Julie Soudant and Queena Mario at the Juilliard School, she made her début as the Shepherd-boy (*Tosca*) in 1948 at the New York City Opera, where she remained a leading artist until 1977. She was particularly noted for her Cenerentola and her interpretations of trouser roles such as Cherubino, Hänsel, Nicklausse, Siébel and Octavian. In 1961 she created the role of Elizabeth Proctor in Robert Ward's *The Crucible*. She made her British début in 1955 at Glyndebourne as Cherubino, returning in 1962 as Monteverdi's Octavia. She sang Augusta Tabor in the second performance of Douglas Moore's *The Ballad of Baby Doe* (1956) at Central City, Colorado, and also appeared at San Francisco, Houston, Boston, Miami and other American cities, her repertory including Laura (*La Gioconda*), Cornelia (*Giulio Cesare*) and Marina (*Boris Godunov*). Bible's voice was warm, her technique assured; in her early career she was a lively and charming presence on stage, and later she excelled in roles demanding authority. Her qualities made her a prominent and well-loved figure in the American theatre. RICHARD DYER, ELIZABETH FORBES

Bickerstaff, Isaac (John) (*b* ?Dublin, 26 Sept 1733; *d* ?1808). English playwright of Irish birth. He served in the army before moving to London and drew on his military experience in his libretto for the patriotic afterpiece *Thomas and Sally* (1760). His successful Covent Garden piece *Love in a Village* (1762) started a new fashion in opera, as *The Beggar's Opera* had done decades earlier. He combined a witty, romantic plot in spoken dialogue with sophisticated music drawn from continental comic opera. The pasticcio score is derived mostly from Italian opera, from oratorio, and from the songs of Thomas Arne, but uses little traditional English music, which Bickerstaff despised. As in ballad opera, the songs help to advance the action, but they also demand well-trained singers and full orchestral accompaniment.

Bickerstaff's innovation spread quickly in the London theatre. He continued to vary the form: *The Maid of the Mill* (1765) had a strong continental flavour with its sentimental plot and borrowed French music; the farcical intrigue of *The Padlock* (1768), on the other hand, had a lively original score by Charles Dibdin. However, his successful career ended abruptly in 1772, when he fled from England rather than face charges of homosexuality. He probably died in 1808, the last year in which he received his military pension, although reports persisted for years that he was still alive. The genre of English comic opera that he pioneered eventually developed into the musical comedy.

Thomas and Sally, or The Sailor's Return (afterpiece), T. A. Arne, 1760; *Love in a Village* (comic op), Arne, compiled by Edward Toms, 1762; *The Maid of the Mill* (comic op), compiled by S. Arnold, 1765; *Daphne and Amintor* (comic op afterpiece), compiled by Bickerstaff, 1765; *Love in the City* (comic op), Dibdin, 1767 (shortened by T. Lloyd, 1771, as The Romp, or A Cure for the Spleen); *Lionel and Clarissa* (comic op), Dibdin, 1768 (rev. 1770 as A School for Fathers)

The Padlock (comic op afterpiece), Dibdin, 1768; *The Royal Garland* (interlude), Arnold, 1768; *The Ephesian Matron* (comic serenata), Dibdin, 1769; *The Captive* (comic op afterpiece), Dibdin, 1769; *The Maid the Mistress* (comic serenata, after Federico), Dibdin, 1770 (1771, as He Wou'd if he Could, or An Old Fool Worse than Any); *The Recruiting Sergeant* (comic serenata), Dibdin, 1770; *The Brickdust Man* (musical dialogue), Dibdin, 1772; *The Sultan: or, a Peep into the Seraglio* (play with songs, after C.-S. Favart), Dibdin, 1775

*

P. Tasch: *The Dramatic Cobbler: the Life and Works of Isaac Bickerstaff* (Lewisburg, PA, 1971)
R. Fahrner: 'David Garrick presents *The Padlock*: an Eighteenth-Century Hit', *Theatre Survey*, xiii (1972), 52–69
R. Fiske: *English Theatre Music in the Eighteenth Century* (London, 1973, 2/1986)
S. Hall: *English Dialogue Opera: 1762–1796* (diss., U. of Toronto, 1980)
P. Tasch, ed.: *The Plays of Isaac Bickerstaff* (New York, 1981)
L. Troost: *The Rise of English Comic Opera: 1762–1800* (diss., U. of Pennsylvania, 1985) LINDA V. TROOST

Bidera, Giovanni Emanuele (*b* Palermo, 4 Oct 1784; *d* Palermo, 8 April 1858). Italian librettist. He studied law in Naples but returned penniless to Sicily, to work as an actor and playwright. Back in Naples, he turned to librettos, altering Mercadante's *Gabriella di Vergy* for Genova (1832). He contributed the synopsis for Cammarano's *Ines de Castro* (Persiani, 1835), becoming involved in a year-long struggle with the censors, and provided Donizetti with *Marino Faliero*, which the Neapolitan censors considered a highly subversive text and which was also submitted as *Antonio Grimaldi* and *Il pascià di Scutari* to escape their notice. His best libretto, *Gemma di Vergy*, was also set by Donizetti (Felice Romani being unavailable); his later librettos, of variable quality, were for minor composers. Bidera's versification was better than his dramatic instinct, but he was willing to tackle 'strong' (notably Byronic) subjects. He was also the author of a popular book on travel around Naples and of one on declamation. He retired to Sicily in 1848.

I promessi sposi (melo-dramma semi-serio), L. Gervasi, 1834; *Gemma di Vergy* (tragedia lirica), Donizetti, 1834; *Marino Faliero* [Antonio Grimaldi; Il pascià di Scutari] (tragedia lirica), Donizetti, 1835; *Marfa* (melodramma), Coccia, 1835; *Lara* (tragedia lirica), H. de Ruolz, 1835; *Odda di Bernaver* (melodramma), Lillo, 1837; *La battaglia di Navarino* (dramma), N. Staffa, 1838; *Il coscritto*, D. Pagliani-Gagliardi, 1838; *Bianca Turenga* (melodramma), G. Balducci, 1838; *I pirati* [I pirati spagnuoli] (melodramma), E. Petrella, 1838 (A. Orsola Aspri, 1843)

Le due epoche [L'astuccio d'oro] (melodramma semi-serio), F. Falangola, 1839; *Ricciarda* (tragedia lirica), P. Selli, 1839; *Le miniere di Freinbergh* (melodramma), Petrella, 1843; *Adolfo di Gewal* [I montenari svedesi] (azione lirica romantica), A. Bruno, 1843; *Costanza d'Aragona* (azione romantica), S. Sarmiento, 1843; *Fenicia* (tragedia lirica), F. Chiaromonte, 1844; *Le nozze di Messina* (tragedia lirica), Chiaromonte, 1852; *Elena Castriotta* [La Saracena] (tragedia lirica), A. Butera, 1854; *Amalia di Carini* (tragedia lirica), L. Kyntherland, 1855; *Ericarda di Vargas*, M. Michieli, 1881

*

DBI (S. Sallusti)
L. Miragoli: *Il melodramma italiano nell'ottocento* (Rome, 1924)
W. Ashbrook: *Donizetti and his Operas* (Cambridge, 1982)
JOHN BLACK

Biego, Paolo (*fl* 1682–1714). Italian composer. A member of the clergy, he was player of one of the small organs at St Mark's, Venice, from 1687 to 1714, and *maestro di coro* at the Ospedale dei Derelitti from 1688 to 1698. At least two operas by him were staged in Venice: *Ottone il grande* (F. Silvani; SS Giovanni e Paolo, December 1682) and *La fortuna tra le disgratie* (3, R. Cialli; S Angelo, January 1688). *Il pertinace* (text wrongly attributed to P. d'Averara; Venice, S Salvatore, 1689), the libretto of which does not mention a composer, is given by Bonlini as Biego's. The music for all three works is lost, apart from a handful of arias from *Ottone* (in *I-Vqs*) and from *La fortuna tra le disgratie* (*GB-Ob*).

EitnerQ
C. Ivanovich: *Minerva al tavolino* (Venice, 1681)
G. C. Bonlini: *Le glorie della poesia e della musica* (Venice, 1730)
L. N. Galvani [pseud. of G. Salvioli]: *I teatri musicali di Venezia nel secolo XVII (1637–1700): memorie storiche e bibliografiche* (Milan, 1879), 46, 95, 113
F. Rossi: *Le opere musicali della Fondazione 'Querini-Stampalia' di Venezia* (Turin, 1984), 46
E. Selfridge-Field: *'Pallade Veneta': Writings on Music in Venetian Society, 1650–1750* (Venice, 1985) LORENZO BIANCONI

Bielefeld. City in western Germany, in North Rhine-Westphalia. The first theatrical productions were given in 1811 in the exercise hall of the riding school; the season ran from 16 November until 28 July, an unusually long period for a town then of only 6000. Operas were regularly performed until the 1850s, but with amateur orchestras or a piano. When the railway replaced post-horses the stables of the Spiegelscher Hof were converted into a theatre. Here the Eintracht company played from 1867 onwards, performing opera in collaboration with Detmold. In 1887 the first plans for an independent theatre were formed. The project had more support from citizens, even at this early stage, than comparable local buildings, and thirteen years later the town council finally decided to build the Stadttheater; it opened on 3 April 1904.

At first Bielefeld had no opera company of its own, but it did maintain an orchestra all year round. In 1907 the 'Opera Month' was introduced, a practice unique to Bielefeld by which another month specially for opera was added to an already full season of drama and operetta. Many works were given in a short space of time; in May 1912, for example, 21 operas were staged within 31 days. After World War I, opera had an established place in the regular seven-month season. During World War II bombs severely damaged the theatre. The first postwar season began on 14 October 1945, in the Oetkerhalle. The temporarily rebuilt theatre came back into use on 1 December 1947, and ten years later the building, extended to a capacity of 775 seats, was reopened. Among the high points of the postwar period were the new works of the Joachim Klaiber era (1958–63), including the stage première of Zillig's *Die Verlobung in St Domingo* and the première of Mihalovici's *Krapp* (both 1961), as well as the first performance in Germany of Martinů's *The Greek Passion* (1963).

Later years saw a production of *Lohengrin* by Friedelind Wagner and the première of Rudolf Mors's *Vineta* (both 1967–8). The Bielefeld company has achieved particular importance in the time that Heiner Bruns has been Intendant (appointed 1975); his willingness to experiment and to explore neglected works, notably with his chief theatrical director John Dew, has brought interesting new departures. Revivals of the last few years include Marschner's *Der Vampyr* (1980), Cherubini's *Médée* (1981), Brand's *Maschinist Hopkins* (1984), Leoncavallo's *La bohème* and Grétry's *Zémire et Azor* (1985), Meyerbeer's *Le prophète* (1986), Schreker's *Irrelohe* (1986) and *Der singende Teufel* (1989), Boito's *Nerone*, Rudi Stephan's *Die ersten Menschen* and Delius's *Fennimore and Gerda* (all 1987–8), Korngold's *Das Wunder der Heliane* (1988), Halévy's *La Juive* (1989), and modern works such as Thea Musgrave's *Mary, Queen of Scots* (first performance in Germany, 1984) and *Nixon in China* by John Adams (1989). The company has a strength of about 140, including the orchestra and dancers; the season runs from August to June. There are about 225 performances in the main theatre during the season, some 180 of them of opera. The Theater am Alten Markt puts on mainly plays and musicals.

P. Schütze, ed.: *75 Jahre Stadttheater Bielefeld 1904–1979* (Bielefeld, 1979) SABINE SONNTAG

Bierey, Gottlob Benedict (*b* Dresden, 25 July 1772; *d* Breslau [now Wrocław], 5 May 1840). German composer and conductor. He learnt singing, the oboe and violin at home and studied basso continuo and composition with the Kantor of the Kreuzschule, Christian Ehregott Weinlig. In 1788 he became musical director of the Voigt drama company, and in 1790 of the Döbbelin opera company. From 1791 to 1806 he held the same position in Joseph Seconda's company, which toured Dresden, Leipzig, Brunswick and Ballenstedt. He married the singer Sophie de Merell in 1794. Following the successful première of his opera *Wladimir, Fürst von Nowgorod*, commissioned for the Theater an der Wien by its director Prince Esterházy, Bierey became Kapellmeister and musical director of the Breslau Stadttheater in January 1808 and remained there for 20 years, much to the advantage of the city's musical and operatic life. He founded a choral society in 1812 and directed it until 1816. In January 1824 he took over the entire management of the theatre, of which he was also principal musical director, but after attacks from his enemies he resigned both posts in December 1828. Thereafter he divided his time between Leipzig, Weimar, Wiesbaden and Mainz, returning to Breslau in 1834.

Bierey was regarded as a 'skilful, conscientious and artistic conductor' (Mendel and Reissmann). He also won considerable renown as a prolific and versatile composer, and was even described as a 'favourite composer of Germany' (*AMZ*, 31 March 1840). His 30 or so operas and Singspiels, in particular, were popular during his lifetime, but the generally poor quality of their librettos prevented their having any lasting success. For serious opera, he admired and imitated Cherubini, whose influence is perceptible in, for instance, *Wladimir*. This and the delightful Singspiel *Rosette, das Schweizer Hirtenmädchen* are among Bierey's best works and, like most of his pieces, were performed on the leading German stages and in Budapest. Pleasing melodies, skilful ensemble writing and effective instrumentation are characteristic of his music, which unites Classical and early Romantic elements and was praised by contemporary critics for its 'fine ideas', 'artistic expression' and 'good sense of theatre'. His writings include *Mein Verhältnis zu Seconda* (Leipzig, 1804).

Der Schlaftrunk (os, 2, C. F. Bretzner), Ballenstedt, 1795
Das Blumenmädchen, oder besser Die Rosenkönigin (komische Oper, 1, F. Rochlitz), Leipzig, 1802
Clara, Herzogin von Bretannien (os, 3, Bretzner), Leipzig, 1803
Jery und Bätely (komische Oper, 1, J. W. von Goethe), Dresden, 1803
Der Mädchenmarkt (komische Oper, 1, C. A. Herklots), Vienna, 1805
Rosette, das Schweizer Hirtenmädchen (Spl, 2, Bretzner), Leipzig, 3 Feb 1806, *D-Dlb*
Wladimir, Fürst von Nowgorod (os, 3, M. Stegmayer), Vienna, Wien, 25 Nov 1807
Der Apfeldieb (komische Oper, 2, Bretzner), Breslau, 1809
Der Überfall (komische Oper, 1, Bretzner), Breslau, 1809
Elias Rips Raps (int, 1, W. Häser), Breslau, 1810
Die Gemsenjäger (2, S. G. Bürde), Breslau, 1811, *Dlb*
Pyramus und Thisbe, Breslau, 1811
Das unsichtbare Mädchen (Spl, A. von Kotzebue), Breslau, 1811
Liebesabentheuer, oder Wer zuletzt lacht, lacht am besten (komische Oper, 1, G. F. W. Grossmann), Breslau, 1817
Patriotenfreude (komische Oper, 2), Breslau, 1817
Die Opferung (komische Oper), Breslau, 1818
Almazinde, oder Die Höhle Sesam (komische Oper, 3), Vienna, 1823
Das Donauweibchen III. Teil (komisch-romantische Oper, 3, ?T. Berling) [pts 1 and 2 by F. Kauer]
Das Milchmädchen (4)
Das Alpenröslein (Operette)

*

ADB (A. von Dommer); *LoewenbergA*; *SeegerL*; *StiegerO*
C. J. A. Hoffmann: *Die Tonkünstler Schlesiens* (Breslau, 1830)
G. Schilling: *Encyclopädie der gesammten musikalischen Wissenschaften, oder Universal-Lexicon der Tonkunst* (Stuttgart, 1835–8, 2/1840–42)
Obituary, *AMZ*, xlii (1840), 506
Denkschrift zur Erinnerung an Bierey (Breslau, 1841)
K. Kossmaly and Carlo [C. H. Herzel]: *Schlesisches Tonkünstler-Lexikon* (Breslau, 1846–7)
H. Mendel and A. Reissmann: *Musicalisches Conversationslexikon* (Berlin, 1885)
DIETER HÄRTWIG

Bigari, Francesco (*fl* 1766–71). Italian stage designer. A native of Bologna, he was scene painter and machinist with his fellow townsman, Vincenzo Conti, at the King's Theatre in London (from 1766 to 1771), though Conti did not operate after 1767–8. The most important operas for which Bigari provided scenery were J. C. Bach's *Carattaco* (1767–8) and Gluck's *Orfeo ed Euridice* (1769–70). He was also scenographer for Piccinni's *La buona figliuola maritata* (1766) and *Le contadine bizzarre* (1768–9) and Guglielmi's *Ifigenia in Aulide* (1767–8) and *Le pazzie di Orlando* (1770–71) as well as other operas and pasticcios.

The only extant design is for the pasticcio *L'olimpiade* (1769). Described as 'The Temple of Olimpic Jove. A fire in the middle of the altar', it is reproduced in Allardyce Nicoll's *The Garrick Stage: Theatres and Audience in the Eighteenth Century* (Manchester, 1980). It depicts a Baroque hall with Corinthian side pillars ending in an arch, with the altar placed centrally on steps. Unfortunately it is not easy to break this print, by Walker after Gravelot, into its constituent elements. SYBIL ROSENFELD

Bigonzi, Giuseppe (*b* Rome; *fl* 1707–24). Italian alto castrato. He sang intermittently in Venice (1707–23), in five operas, including works by Albinoni and Michelangelo and Francesco Gasparini, and in Florence (1718–19) in Predieri's *Partenope*. He made his London début in Ariosti's *Vespasiano* at the King's Theatre in 1724, and sang small parts in Handel's *Giulio Cesare* and Giovanni Bononcini's *Calfurnia*, but made little mark. Another Bigonzi, Giovanni Battista, also an alto, sang at Sinigaglia in 1709. WINTON DEAN

Bigot, Eugène (*b* Rennes, 28 Feb 1888; *d* Paris, 17 July 1965). French conductor. After studying at the conservatories of Rennes and then Paris, where his teachers included Xavier Leroux, André Gédalge and Paul Vidal, he was appointed chorus master at the Théâtre des Champs Elysées in 1913. He returned as music director, 1925–7, though his most important appointments were as principal conductor of the Opéra-Comique (1936–47) and as a conductor for radio.

Bigot's repertory consisted largely of 19th-century works, especially Wagner and Russian and French composers, but he also gave many first performances of new music. He was a thoroughly competent and highly regarded conductor, faithful to the composer's score and eschewing all spectacular effects.

CHRISTIANE SPIETH-WEISSENBACHER

Bilash, Olexander Ivanovych (*b* Hraduzk, Poltavskaya region, 6 March 1931). Ukrainian composer. A graduate of the Kiev Conservatory, he made his name as a prolific writer of both concert and popular songs. He has written orchestral, vocal-instrumental and choral works, and music for plays and films; his output for the stage includes a mono-opera, *Balada viyny* ('Ballad of War'), and an operetta, *Chysta krynytsya* ('The Clear Well'). Bilash's operatic style conforms to the tradition of 'socialist realism' but with a national face: it is tuneful and melodramatic, with an orchestral style that owes much to the Russian school, and features clearly defined, if two-dimensional, characters. In 1989 he was elected head of the Composers Union of Ukraine.

Haydamaky, 1965 (after T. Shevchenko)
Balada viyny [Ballad of War], 1971 (I. Drach)
Chysta krynytsya [The Clear Well], 1975 (operetta)
Lehenda pro Kyïv [The Legend of Kiev] (operetta, V. Bykov and V. Neborachko), Kiev, State Operetta Theatre, 1983
Kolokola Rosiy [The Russian Bell] (operetta, Bïkov and Neborachko), Kiev, State Operetta Theatre, 1984
Praporonostsy [Standard-bearers] (B. Oliynyk, after O. Honchar), Kiev, Shevchenko Academic Theatre of Opera and Ballet, 1985

VIRKO BALEY

Bilbao. City in Spain, in the Basque country. In the mid-19th century opera was performed in the Teatro de la Villa until it was dismantled in 1886. Its 1860 season comprised, for example, 30 performances by Luis Bonoris's company, and later seasons included a visit by Julián Gayarre in 1882. Opera performances then moved to the Teatro Gayarre, where Petri Vicenzo's Italian company staged *La favorita* and *L'Africaine* in 1889. In 1890 a new theatre, the fine but small all-purpose Teatro Arriaga, was built on the site of the Teatro de la Villa. Named after Juan Crisóstomo Arriaga, who was born in Bilbao, the theatre opened with a season of Italian opera conducted by Giovanni (Juan) Goula (1843–1917). Tradition was broken with the visit of a French company in 1902, who staged Gounod's *Mireille* under the direction of R. Strakosch. An attempt to found a permanent opera company in Bilbao, under the direction of the Basque composer Nicolás Urién, failed in 1907.

Following a fire in 1914, the Arriaga reopened with *Don Carlos* on 5 June 1919. In the ensuing years the theatre was visited mainly by zarzuela and opera companies, although occasional opera performances were given, including a landmark season with Gigli in 1946. Since 1953, opera culture in Bilbao has been due mainly to the remarkable Asociación Bilbaina de

Amigos de la Opera, which promotes opera education, maintains an amateur chorus and from autumn to spring stages an opera season with world-class principals, the ABAO chorus and local or Eastern European orchestras. Its few ventures beyond the standard Italian repertory have included *Boris Godunov* with Nicola Rossi-Lemeni (1959) and *Die Walküre* with Siegfried Jerusalem (1991).

*

Asociación Bilbaina de Amigos de la Opera 1953–1978 (Bilbao, 1978)

M. Basas, C. Bacigalupe and A. Chapa: *Vida y miraglos del Teatro Arriaga, 1890–1990* (Bilbao, 1990)

BOB SUTCLIFFE

Bild (Ger.). *See* SCENE.

Billington [née Weichsel], **Elizabeth** (*b* 1765–8; *d* nr Venice, 25 Aug 1818). English soprano. On her death, the *Gentleman's Magazine* described her as 'the most celebrated vocal performer that England ever produced'. Her mother was a singer and her father an oboist; she was taught by him, J. C. Bach and J. S. Schroeter and as a child appeared as a pianist, generally with her violinist brother Charles, who often led the orchestra for her later operatic performances. In 1783 she married her singing teacher, James Billington, and they went to Dublin, where her début was as Eurydice in an adaptation of Gluck's *Orfeo ed Euridice*. Her first London stage appearance was as Rosetta in a royal command performance of *Love in a Village* (February 1786); she was an instant success, commanding high fees and playing only leading roles. She sang Clara in *The Duenna*, the title role in *Rosina* and Polly in *The Beggar's Opera*, and created parts in works by Shield and others. She continued to improve her technique, working with Mortellari, and with Sacchini in Paris in 1786. The accuracy of her intonation, the brilliance and taste of her ornaments and the high tessitura of her voice dazzled audiences and impressed the connoisseurs. Burney declared: 'nothing but envy or apathy can hear her without delight'.

The scandal following the publication of the scurrilous *Memoirs of Mrs Billington* in 1792 caused her to leave London and in 1794 the Billingtons travelled to the Continent. She sang in Italian opera, including works composed for her by Bianchi, Paer, Paisiello and Nasolini, with great success. James Billington died suddenly in 1794 and five years later she married a second husband who is reputed to have ill-treated her. She returned to London, where rivalry for her services resulted in her singing alternately at Drury Lane and Covent Garden in 1801–2. From January 1803 she starred in four seasons of Italian opera at the King's Theatre, where for her benefit in 1805 she revived J. C. Bach's *La clemenza di Scipione* and in her 1806 benefit sang Vitellia in *La clemenza di Tito*, the first Mozart opera to be given in London. She retired from the stage that year and from the concert platform in 1811. Mount Edgcumbe admitted that she was 'no actress' although she sang 'with the utmost delicacy and consummate skill' while Michael Kelly thought her 'an angel in beauty, and the Saint Cecilia of song'.

*

BDA; *BurneyH*; *DNB*; *LS*

A. Pasquin [pseud. of J. Williams]: *The Children of Thespis*, ii (London, 1787, 13/1792)

A. Seward: *Letters* (Edinburgh, 1811)

R. Mount Edgcumbe: *Musical Reminiscences* (London, 1824, 4/1834)

J. Sainsbury, ed.: *Dictionary of Musicians* (London, 2/1825)

M. Kelly: *Reminiscences of the King's Theatre* (London, 1826, 2/1826); ed. R. Fiske (London, 1975)

'Chronicles of the Italian Opera in England', *The Harmonicon* (1830), 10–13, 70–73

'Memoir of Mrs Billington', ibid, 93–7

T. J. Walsh: *Opera in Dublin 1705–1797* (Dublin, 1973)

OLIVE BALDWIN, THELMA WILSON

Billy Budd. Opera in two acts, op.50, by BENJAMIN BRITTEN to a libretto by E. M. FORSTER and ERIC CROZIER, after HERMAN MELVILLE's story; in four acts, London, Covent Garden, 1 December 1951 (revised in two acts, Covent Garden, 9 January 1964; previously broadcast, BBC, 13 November 1961).

Billy Budd *able seaman*	baritone
Edward Fairfax Vere *Captain of HMS Indomitable*	tenor
John Claggart *Master-at-arms*	bass
Mr Redburn *First Lieutenant*	baritone
Mr Flint *Sailing Master*	bass-baritone
Lieutenant Ratcliffe	bass
Red Whiskers *an impressed man*	tenor
Donald *a sailor*	baritone
Dansker *an old seaman*	bass
Novice	tenor
Squeak *a ship's corporal*	tenor
Bosun	baritone
First Mate	baritone
Second Mate	baritone
Maintop	tenor
Novice's friend	baritone
Arthur Jones *an impressed man*	baritone
Four Midshipmen	boys' voices
Cabin Boy	spoken

Officers, sailors, powder-monkeys, drummers, marines

Setting On board the *Indomitable*, a seventy-four, during the French wars of 1797, as she sails near enemy waters

Billy Budd was commissioned by the Arts Council of Great Britain for the Festival of Britain, 1951. Britten had discussed a possible opera on Melville's story with Crozier and Forster in late 1948 and early 1949, before the work was actually commissioned. The libretto evolved through four versions during 1949, and composition was begun in earnest during the summer of 1950. Originally planned in two acts, it was first performed in a four-act version, with Theodor Uppman in the title role, Peter Pears as Vere and Frederick Dalberg as Claggart, conducted by the composer. In 1960 Britten produced a two-act version, in which the main change was the excision of the original Act 1 finale where Captain Vere appears to general acclaim and addresses the crew. The revised version was first heard the next year under the composer's baton and has since remained the accepted version. The opera has not achieved the extensive international success of *Peter Grimes*, although the scenes televised in New York in 1952 were the 'first operatic music by Britten to be relayed by this medium' (Kennedy, 1981, p.60). Productions of *Billy Budd* by the WNO (1972), the Royal Opera (1979) and the ENO (1988) all featured Thomas Allen in the title role, and a video recording of the ENO production was issued in 1989. A complete gramophone recording, with Peter Glossop as Budd, Peter Pears as Vere and Michael Langdon as Claggart, conducted by Britten, was issued in 1968.

PROLOGUE *Captain Vere in old age* To music whose quiet oscillating motion and persistent harmonic clashes embody conflict and indecision, Captain Vere, long since retired, muses on the inseparability of good and evil. Neither, his experience tells him, is absolute. The conflict of 3rds (B♭/D♮, B♮/D♮) generates the opera's most pervasive melodic idea (the *Rights o' Man* motif), which is used for Vere's climactic self-questioning ('Oh what have I done?'), growing naturally out of the eloquent arioso which is the opera's principal formal feature. In old age Vere still cannot explain exactly what happened all those years ago, or why. The main action of the opera is therefore like a gigantic flashback in which Vere relives the decisive events of 1797 in the hope of finding illumination and peace, and it gives his character a dimension not found in Melville, where he dies on active service.

ACT 1.i *The main deck and quarterdeck of HMS Indomitable* Two parties of sailors are holystoning the main deck under the harsh instructions of their officers. They sing a shanty-like refrain, 'O heave, O heave away, heave!' to the opera's principal motif. In the mêlée a Novice accidentally bumps into the Bosun and is dragged away to be flogged. Meanwhile a guard-boat approaches, having been sent out to a passing merchant ship to pressgang the most likely-looking sailors for war service. The officers complain that the results of such forays are rarely satisfactory but in time of war they must take what they can get. As the three impressed men are brought forward the Master-at-arms John Claggart questions them in turn. The first, Red Whiskers, objects to being pressganged, and Claggart reveals his menacing side. Neither Red Whiskers nor Arthur Jones pleases the officers, but the third man is very different. He gives his name cheerfully as Billy Budd. He is an able, willing seaman and, although he reveals a stammer when trying to explain that he was a foundling child, he satisfies the officers and the Master-at-arms, who describes him as 'a find in a thousand'. Billy is overjoyed to be assigned to the foretop, and sings ecstatically of the joys of 'working aloft'. Then he cries out an eloquent farewell to his former ship, *The Rights o' Man* (the main motif reappears with emphasis here), and the officers, fearing the response of the other sailors, quickly call for the decks to be cleared. From that moment on Billy is regarded as a potential source of danger, able to use a ship's name as a rallying call for dissent.

Left alone, Claggart reveals his bitterness at existence on this 'accursed ship' and his disdain for the officers. He instructs the ship's corporal Squeak to put Budd to the test by taking every opportunity to annoy him. As Squeak runs off the Novice is helped in by a group of sailors. Claggart, moving away, regards him with contempt but, after a short ensemble in which the Novice sings of his despair and his comrades echo his lament ('We're all of us lost on the sea'), Billy appears and expresses his sympathy. Budd has been befriended by an old seaman, Dansker, and they join Red Whiskers and Donald in an ensemble expressing their reactions to the Novice's punishment. As the watch changes, Claggart returns. He is brusque with Billy, ordering him to remove a 'fancy neckerchief: this is a Man-o'-War'. Then, with sinister emphasis, he tells Billy to 'take a pride in yourself, Beauty, and you'll come to no harm'. Dansker warns Billy to avoid Claggart, and when the sailors begin to sing with enthusiasm of the captain, 'Starry Vere', Billy jubilantly expresses his desire to serve him.

1.ii *Captain Vere's cabin, a week later* Vere, who is reading Plutarch and finds parallels between present-day troubles and those of the Greeks and Romans, summons his senior officers for a glass of wine. They drink a toast to the king, and the officers, looking forward to action as they near enemy waters, express dislike of all things French – especially ideas of the kind that promoted the Revolution and which were held responsible for the recent naval mutinies, at Spithead and the Nore ('the floating republic', sung to the *Rights o' Man* motif). In his own reactions to these events, Vere reveals his fear of sedition, 'the infamous spirit of France'. The officers mention Budd as a potential source of trouble, but Vere disagrees: all Budd is guilty of is 'youthful high spirits'. As if to confirm the captain's optimism, the sound of the sailors singing a shanty becomes audible. As the officers leave, and Vere resumes his reading, an orchestral interlude based on the shanty culminates in a massive choral ensemble, simple yet powerful in Britten's finest vein.

1.iii *The berth-deck* Billy, with Donald and Red Whiskers, sings another lively shanty. Dansker refuses to join in and when Billy, to cheer him up, goes to his kitbag for some tobacco, he finds Squeak rifling his belongings. Anger brings on his stammer and the two men fight. In the uproar, Claggart appears, and after silencing Squeak, who tries to explain that he was only obeying Claggart's orders, he turns to Billy with a smile and words of praise. Left alone Claggart reveals that it is Billy's very 'handsomeness' and 'goodness' that attract his sadistic desire to destroy him. He instructs the Novice, willing to do anything to avoid further flogging, to carry out his plan; and the Novice, with great reluctance, agrees. Waking Billy, the Novice tries to tempt him with money provided by Claggart into leading a gang of dissidents who are plotting mutiny. Billy is initially attracted by the gold, but he grows angry, his stammer starts up, and the Novice runs off. Dansker appears and helps Billy calm down. Billy tells him of the mutiny plan and his resistance to it. Dansker warns him that Claggart is hostile to him, but Billy refuses to believe it. The two men sing together: Billy is enraptured at the prospect of promotion – he may even become captain of the mizzen top. But Dansker, to Claggart's own baleful motif, continues to warn him.

ACT 2.i *Main deck and quarterdeck some days later* Vere and the officers are on deck, while mist swirls round the ship. As Claggart approaches Vere and begins to tell him about the danger of mutiny, the mist lifts and a French ship is sighted. The whole crew swings rapidly into action. The *Indomitable* prepares her sails for pursuit and her guns for the assault in a complex and exciting ensemble for all the various groups of officers and seamen, including the treble powder-monkeys. Soon all is ready, but there is still only a light breeze. Despite the lack of progress, Vere orders a shot. To great excitement a cannon is fired, but the shot falls far short. The French ship is out of range, the wind dies and the mist closes in once more. Depressed, the crew disperses. Now Claggart approaches the captain again and this time he tells the full story, claiming that Budd offered gold to the Novice if he would join the

'Billy Budd' (Britten): Act 2 scene i (main deck and quarterdeck) of the original production at Covent Garden, London, 1 December 1951; the crew of the Indomitable prepares to fire on the French ship

mutineers. Vere reacts with anger and disbelief, but he agrees to interview Budd in Claggart's presence.

2.ii *The captain's cabin* In a state of great agitation, Vere asserts that Claggart is evil, Billy good. Claggart, he claims, will fail. But the florid music of this brief, hectic soliloquy has more of hysteria than confidence. Billy arrives, expecting news of his promotion, and sings fluently of his longing for action and his wish to be Vere's coxswain. But he makes no complaint when Vere explains that promotion is not the reason for this interview. Claggart is admitted and (to a variant of the *Rights o' Man* motif) accuses Billy of mutiny. As Vere urges him to defend himself, the stammer takes hold and is only broken when Billy strikes Claggart down with a single blow. When Vere discovers that Claggart is dead he sends Billy into a side cabin and summons the officers. In a short tormented monologue he blames his own lack of foresight for the catastrophe.

The officers hastily convene a drumhead court. Confronted with the charge of murder Billy can only explain that he was unable to answer Claggart's false accusation with words: 'I had to say it with a blow'. He cannot explain why Claggart should have wrongfully accused him, and when he and the officers turn to Vere for an explanation the captain refuses to respond. With Billy sent back to the side cabin, the death sentence is pronounced. After the officers have left, Vere is at first resolute in his acceptance of the sentence and the circumstances that make it just. Then, in a more turbulent phase, he sees himself doomed as well: he it is who must destroy handsomeness and goodness. As he enters the side cabin to tell Billy his fate the scene's orchestral coda unfolds a sequence of common chords, all harmonizing notes of the F major triad and expressing a mixture of resolution, compassion and resignation in a startlingly direct yet subtle manner.

2.iii *A bay of the gundeck, shortly before dawn the next day* Billy, only half awake, calmly contemplates his imminent death. Dansker brings him food and drink, and the news that the ship is now indeed close to mutiny, the sailors determined to prevent Billy's execution. Billy tells Dansker to stop them: fate decrees his death, just as it decreed Claggart's, and determined Vere's inability to save Billy. After Dansker has left, Billy sings an expansive farewell, affirming his acceptance of his fate to a reminiscence of the chord-sequence from the end of the previous scene.

2.iv *Main deck and quarterdeck, dawn* The ship's company assemble to martial music. Billy is brought in and the First Lieutenant reads from the Articles of War, ending with the sentence of death. In a last salutation, Billy sings out 'Starry Vere, God bless you!' and the entire ship's company, including the officers, echo his cry. Then he is marched off. At the moment of his death a wordless rumble of revolt begins among the sailors and wells up to a fierce climax. Vere remains motionless and silent; under the officers' orders the marines force the men to disperse.

EPILOGUE *Vere in old age* To the prologue's uneasily tranquil opening music, Vere describes how, after Billy's execution and burial at sea, the ship sailed on. He acknowledges that he could have saved Billy, but no longer seeks to explain why he did not do so. Instead, he explains that it is Billy, rather, who has saved him. To music echoing Billy's own farewell in Act 2 scene iii, Vere claims that he too has found contentment and the piled-up dissonances resolve into a radiant, powerfully reiterated B♭ major triad. As this chord dies away, Vere sings again the words that ended the prologue, to a vocal line whose descending pitches cast a shadow over the serenity of the harmonic resolution. Whether he has truly found peace, or whether he is doomed endlessly to relive the most powerful and traumatic event of his life, unable to find release even in death, is a question the opera leaves open.

* * *

Billy Budd, like *Peter Grimes* and *Gloriana*, demonstrates Britten's ability to create an opera in a distinctively 'grand manner' through the use of elaborate ensembles and unrestrained outpourings of emotion, often with richly orchestrated accompaniments. Its departures from Melville's original story, with Billy (in his song of farewell) achieving an unprecedented articulateness, and Vere, whose emotions are evidently intended to carry an element of sexual attraction, are fully justified by the power of the resulting music. In the way motivic and harmonic processes integrate the evolving drama into a flexible yet coherent form, *Billy Budd* is Britten's most richly worked operatic score, even though it lacks the purely technical progressiveness, with respect to 12-note features, of *The Turn of the Screw* and its successors. Of all Britten's operas, *Billy Budd* is the one in which the composer's instinct for tellingly simple musical ideas and his sense of how far such ideas could be extended and enriched to serve an ambivalent but never obscure dramatic theme is most impressively displayed. ARNOLD WHITTALL

Bilt, Peter van der (*b* Jakarta, 30 Aug 1936; *d* Amsterdam, 25 Sept 1983). Dutch bass-baritone. He studied at the Amsterdam Muzieklyceum, then with Hans Cleuver and Herman Schey. He made his début in 1960 in Amsterdam as Dulcamara, in 1963 in the USA at San Francisco as Rossini's Don Basilio and in 1973 at the Vienna Staatsoper as Beckmesser. In 1964 he became a principal bass-baritone at the Deutsche Oper am Rhein where he remained until his death. He had a wide repertory including Varlaam, Nick Shadow, Mozart's Figaro and Don Alfonso, Janáček's Šiškov, Forester and Baron Prus, Beckmesser, Don Quichotte and Bettler Akki (*Ein Engel kommt nach Babylon*). He created Wurm in Einem's *Kabale und Liebe* at the Vienna Staatsoper (1976), repeating the role in Florence (1977). As a guest artist he appeared in Europe, the USA, Russia and Japan. A fine Mozartian, he had a firm-toned voice, good diction and excellent musicianship, of special value in the 20th-century music in which he excelled. TRUUS DE LEUR, ELIZABETH FORBES

Bimboni, Alberto (*b* Florence, 24 Aug 1882; *d* New York, 18 June 1960). American composer of Italian birth. He studied at the Cherubini Conservatory in Florence and began his career there as a conductor. As an accompanist he later worked with Caruso, Eugene Ysaÿe and John McCormack. In 1911 he emigrated to the USA, where he toured as a conductor with the Henry Savage Opera Company; he also conducted the Century Opera Company and later appeared at the Havana Opera House. He taught at the Curtis Institute and at the University of Pennsylvania, and for 20 years was conductor of the Chautauqua Opera Association. For the last 26 years of his life he coached French and Italian at the Juilliard School. Bimboni composed six operas, of which the most important is *Winona*, first performed by the American Grand Opera Company in Portland in 1926. Basing the opera on a Sioux-Dakota legend, Bimboni incorporated melodies which he had either collected from Minnesota Indians or obtained from the Smithsonian collection; overall, however, the opera's music may be likened to the idealized 'Indian style' of his contemporary Charles Wakefield Cadman. Bimboni was awarded the David Bispham Memorial Medal when the opera was revived in Minneapolis in 1928. He also composed songs, including the collection *Songs of the American Indians* (1917).

Calandrino [The Fire Worshippers], 1902 (1, after Boccaccio), ?unperf.

Fiaschi?! Delitto perpetrato dagli studenti W. C. e Costanzo Arrigoni (operetta-ballo, 3), Florence, 1903, vs (Florence, 1909)

Winona (3, P. Williams), Portland, 11 Nov 1926, *US-Wc**

Karin, 1929–30 (3, C. W. Stork), unperf.

Il cancelleto d'oro [The Gilded Gate; There was a Gilded Gate] (1, A. Romano), New York, National Arts Club, 11 March 1936, vs *Wc**

In the Name of Culture (1, N. F. Stolzenbach), Rochester, Eastman School of Music, 9 May 1949 THOMAS WARBURTON

Binder, Carl (*b* Vienna, 29 Nov 1816; *d* Vienna, 5 Nov 1860). Austrian composer. He spent almost his entire career as a Kapellmeister at Viennese suburban theatres, writing a large number of scores for *Possen* (farces) and Singspiels, most of which did no more than satisfy the expectations of the audiences of his day. He did, however, achieve a few major successes, most notably in the scores to seven of Nestroy's plays written between 1851 and 1859, and in his instrumentation (from pirated vocal scores) of Offenbach's operettas which reached Vienna in the late 1850s. From 1840 to 1851 he wrote over 60 scores for the Theater in der Josefstadt, the most successful probably being that to J. Nikola's *Der letzte Zwanziger* (1850), which was performed first at the Hernals Arena and altogether 111 times. Of approximately 80 works written by Binder between 1849 and 1860, those most frequently performed at the Carltheater (formerly the Theater in der Leopoldstadt) included the scores to Nestroy's *Kampl* (1852) and *Umsonst* (1857), Kaiser's *Verrechnet* (1851) and the 'Charakterbild' *Die Frau Wirtin* (1856) and Kalisch's *Ein gebildeter Hausknecht* (1858). The only score truly to outlive its composer was for Nestroy's parody *Tannhäuser* (1857), which enjoyed 75 performances in the Carltheater between 1857 and 1860 and has been revived successfully in the 20th century (e.g. at the Theater an der Wien in 1927 and the Wiener Kammeroper in 1992). Contrary to some reports, Binder was not a Kapellmeister at the Theater an der Wien from 1837 to 1851; similar statements that he was engaged in Hamburg and Pressburg in 1847 require corroboration, as there are no marked gaps in the month-to-month record of his new works for Viennese theatres.

Possen unless otherwise stated; all first performed in Vienna

WC – *Carltheater (formerly Theater in der Leopoldstadt)*
WH – *Hernals, Arena* WJ – *Theater in der Josefstadt*

Agnes die Bräuerin, oder Biernigel unter den Wilden (Parodie, 2, Just, after A. Lewald), WJ, 6 Aug 1840; Der Wiener Schusterbub (3, J. Krautinger), WJ, 3 Oct 1840; Die drei Wittfrauen, oder Rot, braun und blond (3, J. Kupelwieser), WJ, 16 Jan 1841; Wahrheit und Täuschung, oder Die Nebelknappen (Märchen, 1, J. H. Mirani), WJ, 21 Sept 1841; Die Landpartie nach Kaltenleutgeben (3, K. Meisl), WJ, 18 Nov 1841; Der verhängnisvolle Mantel (2), WJ, 18 Jan 1842; Schwager Kreutzkopf, oder Der heimliche Handel (3, K. Elmar), WJ, 29 April 1843; Kapitän Charlotte (vaudeville, 2, Kupelwieser, after J. Bayard), WJ, 13 May 1843

Das verlorene Gedächtnis (Märchen, 3, Mirani), WJ, 13 June 1843; Der goldene Boden (2, A. Schmidl), WJ, 15 Sept 1843; Überdruss aus Überfluss (2, Kupelwieser), WJ, 9 April 1844; Der

Zauberschleier in Mirlsfeld (2, Arbesser), WJ, 1 June 1844; Der verwunschene Prinz (Schwank, 3, J. von Plötz), WJ, 14 Aug 1844; Die Königsbrüder, oder Ein Jahr im Wunderlande (Märchen, 3, Elmar), WJ, 4 Jan 1845; Postmeister und Verwalter (2, F. Blum and G. Schönstein), WJ, 21 Oct 1845; Nicht länger als 14 Tage (2, F. X. Told), WJ, 25 Oct 1845; Der fliegende Holländer (Märchen, 2, J. E. Gulden), WJ, 1 Nov 1845

Nur nobel!, oder Der verhängnisvolle Brief (3, K. Juin), WJ, 17 April 1846; Die Stiefschwestern (3, E. Breier), WJ, 8 May 1846; Drei Perlen (Zaubermärchen, 2, J. Nikola), WJ, 10 Oct 1846; Der Stock im Eisen (Volkssage, 3), WJ, 18 Dec 1846; Der Rock eines Glücklichen (Märchen, 3, A. Lödl), WJ, 6 March 1847; Das 4 Stock hohe Haus, oder Die Wette um ein Pferd (3, Nikola), WJ, 16 June 1847; Sanscravate (4, Wilson), 16 Nov 1848; Ein Wiener Früchtel (3, A. Langer), WJ, 13 Jan 1849; Zwei Zimmerherren, oder Die Bekanntschaft durch das Perspektiv (3, Schönstein), WJ, 3 March 1849; Das Parlament im Dorfe, oder Das alte Schloss (2, K. Haffner), WJ, 10 March 1849

Verschwender aus Geiz, oder Die Goldquelle (Zauberspiel, 3, Nikola), WJ, 28 April 1849; Das Kirchweihfest in Hernals, oder Die langen Gesichter (3, Schönstein), WH, 21 June 1849; Die Steinbrüderln, oder Der Traum vom Rittertum (Schwank, 3, Nikola), WH, 21 July 1849; Ein Sohn zweier Mütter (3, Schönstein), WJ, 20 Nov 1849; Krone und Herz (Zauberspiel, 3, Nikola), WJ, 8 Dec 1849; Doktor und Professor (3, W. Just), WJ, 28 Dec 1849; Glück und Glatteis (3, A. Blank), WJ, 16 Jan 1850; Der Stumme und sein Affe (Melodrame, 3, Rainoldi), WJ, 21 Feb 1850; Der alte Soldat, oder Der Goldfisch aus Californien (3, Haffner), WJ, 9 March 1850

Der Froschprophet, oder Der neue Robinson und sein Affe (Spektakelstück, 2), WJ, 15 March 1850; Student und Fabrikant (2), WH, 8 June 1850; Der Deserteur (Volksstück, 4, T. Megerle, after Szigligeti), WH, 20 June 1850; Tugend und Schönheit (3, J. Schönau), WH, 23 June 1850; Der Maler als Marquis (3), WH, 13 July 1850; Die Köchin mit 30 Millionen (2, Schönau), WH, 28 July 1850; Der letzte Zwanziger (Zauberposse, 3, Nikola), WH, 24 Aug 1850; Der daumenlange Hansel (2, Schönau), WJ, 1 Feb 1851; Rosenzauber (Zauberspiel, 3, Nikola), WJ, 6 March 1851; Verrechnet (3, F. Kaiser), WC, 5 June 1851

Naturmensch und Lebemann (3, Kaiser), WC, 4 Sept 1851; Der beste Kegelschieber (Volksstück, 2, E. Raupach), WC, 11 Oct 1851; Ein florentiner-Strohhut, oder Haserls Fatalitäten (3, Juin and Flerx), WC, 9 Nov 1851; Geist, Gemüt, Geld (Zauberspiel, 3, K. Allram and F. Fränkel), WJ, 13 Nov 1851; Der gemütige Teufel, oder Die Geschichte vom Bauer und der Bäuerin (Zauberspiel, 1, J. Nestroy), WC, 20 Dec 1851; Faschingsstückeln (2, Juin and Flerx), WC, 20 Feb 1852; Kampl (4, Nestroy), WC, 29 March 1852; Ein Lump (3, Kaiser), WC, 7 June 1852; Des Teufels Zopf (3, Juin and Flerx), WC, 11 Sept 1852

Ein armer Millionär (3, T. Flamm), WC, 25 Sept 1852; Ludwig Devrient (Schwank, 2, Gruner), WC, 8 Oct 1852; Spass und Ernst, oder Der Inspektor in 1000 Ängsten (3, J. A. Lang), WC, 24 Oct 1852; Fort! Fort! (2, after K. Gutzkow: *Liesli*), WC, 2 Nov 1852; Ein Schwur (3, K. Elwin), WC, 8 Nov 1852; Die Bürgermeisterwahl in Krähwinkel (1, Juin and Flerx), WC, 4 Dec 1852; Die Teufelsgaben: Mantel, Sack und Geige, oder Musikant und Waldbauer (Zauberspiel, 3), WC, 12 Dec 1852; Fiaker – Cab – Comfortabel (1), WC, 18 Dec 1852; Folgen einer Zimmervermietung (3, J. Doppler), WC, 9 Jan 1853; Heimliches Geld, heimliche Liebe (3, Nestroy), WC, 16 March 1853

Eine Feindin und ein Freund (3, Kaiser), WC, 2 April 1853; Von Zwirn und von der Feder (2, Kaiser), WC, 25 June 1853; Der Überspannte (2, Kaiser), WC, 6 Sept 1853; Im Dunkeln (3, Kaiser), WC, 8 Oct 1853; Der Kirchtag im Tipfelhausen, oder Die beiden Herren Brüder (3, C. F. Stix), WC, 5 Nov 1853; Ein Schatten (Volksstück, 3, after A. von Chamisso: *Peter Schlemihl*), WC, 12 Nov 1853; Harfenist und Wäschermädel (3, Kaiser), WC, 14 Jan 1854; Theaterg'schichten durch Liebe, Intrige, Geld und Dummheit (2, Nestroy), WC, 1 Feb 1854; Ein lediger Ehemann (3, Juin, after E. Scribe), WC, 10 March 1854

Ein Fuchs (3, Juin), WC, 18 March 1854; Die Schicksalsbrüder (4, L. Feldmann), WC, 20 April 1854; Kniffe und Pfiffe (2, Kaiser), WC, 6 May 1854; Der reisende Student, oder Das Donnerwetter (2, L. Schneider), WC, 17 June 1854; Der Dumme hat's Glück (3, A. Berla), WC, 18 Oct 1854, incl. music by Suppé; Spadifankerl, oder Brennrot, Kohlschwarz, Schneeweiss (1, Schönau), WC, 18 Aug 1855; Das Mädchen aus dem Fremdenblatt (3, T. Scheibe), WC, 20 Oct 1855; Das Auffinden der Zwerge (Skizzen aus dem Leben, 3, F. B.), WC, 3 Jan 1856

Das Grubernmännlein, oder Der Nörkelkönig und die Zwerge (Märchen, 1, Haffner), WC, 3 Jan 1856; Appel contra Schwiegersohn, oder Eine Ehe mit Hindernissen (3, A. Bahn), WC, 2 Aug 1856; Die Schnakerl-Noblesse (3, Bittner), WC, 3 Oct 1856; Der elektrische Telegraf (3, Morländer), WC, 11 Dec 1856; Der Herr Graf (3, Kaiser), WC, 27 Dec 1856; Domestikenstreiche (2, Bittner), WC, 24 Jan 1857; Eulenspiegel als Schnipfer (1, Bittner), WC, 21 Feb 1857; Umsonst (3 [later 1], Nestroy), WC, 7 March 1857; Die Rekrutierung in Krähwinkel (1, T. Flamm), WC, 21 March 1857; Ein Ecksitz im Parterre (3, Morländer), WC, 28 March 1857

Das Vorhängeschloss (1, Juin, after I. Bickerstaff), WC, 18 April 1857; Etwas Kleines (3, Kaiser), WC, 27 April 1857; Der 13 Mantel (1, Bittner), WC, 2 Oct 1857; Tannhäuser (Parodie, 3, Nestroy), WC, 31 Oct 1857, vs (Leipzig, 1904); Doktor Peschke (Schwank, 1, D. Kalisch), WC, 1857; Schöne Seelen finden sich (Schwank, 1, L. Julius), WC, 4 Jan 1858; Zimmer und Kabinett zu verlassen (1, A. Bittner), WC, 4 Jan 1858; Kling! Klang! (1, Morländer), WC, 5 Feb 1858; Eine Natur-Grille (Schwank, 2, Bittner and Morländer), WC, 18 March 1858; Der Eisstoss (1, Bittner), WC, 29 April 1858; Kathi, die schöne Kassierin (3, J. Doppler), WC, 15 May 1858; Herr Göd und Jungfer Godl (3, L. Gottsleben and Bittner), WC, 24 May 1858

Anna, Nina, Nannerl, Netti, oder Neu-Arkadien (2, after K. E. Grammerstötter), WC, 26 July 1858; Ein gebildeter Hausknecht, oder Verfehlte Prüfungen (1, D. Kalisch), WC, 11 Sept 1858; Adam und Eva (1, C. Arthur), WC, 25 Sept 1858; Jagdabenteuer (3, Kaiser), WC, 19 Feb 1859; Nur solid, oder Carnevalsabenteuer im Schlossergassel (1, L. Gottsleben), WC, 3 March 1859; Heerschau auf dem Felde der Parodie (3, Morländer), WC, 31 March 1859, with music by Krottenthaler for pantomime; Der Dreizehnte bei Tische (1, H. Salingré), WC, 19 May 1859; Nur einen tollen Streich (1, J. B. Poft), WC, 31 July 1859; Nur keine Protektion (2, Bittner), WC, 24 Sept 1859; An der Eisenbahn (1, Julius), WC, 14 Nov 1860

*c*40 further works described as Dramatische Gemälde, Lebensbild or Charakterbild

*

StiegerO

H. Mendel and A. Reissmann: *Musikalisches Conversations-Lexicon*, ii (Berlin, 1880)

F. Hadamowsky: *Das Theater in der Wiener Leopoldstadt*, Kataloge der Theatersammlung der Nationalbibliothek in Wien, iii (Vienna, 1934)

F. Hadamowsky and H. Otte: *Die Wiener Operette*, Klassiker der Wiener Kultur, ii, (Vienna, 1948)

A. Bauer: *Das Theater in der Josefstadt zu Wien* (Vienna, 1957)

PETER BRANSCOMBE

Bindernagel, Gertrud (*b* Magdeburg, 11 Jan 1894; *d* Berlin, 3 Nov 1932). German soprano. She studied at the Magdeburg Conservatory and the Berlin Musikhochschule. After engagements at Breslau and Regensburg she sang at the Berlin Staatsoper (1920–27). Powerful performances in the dramatic repertory took her to Barcelona, Munich, Hamburg, Mannheim and Vienna. She appeared at the Wagner festival at Zoppot (now Sopot) between 1926 and 1932. At the Berlin Städtische Oper in 1931 she was admired as Lady Macbeth but after a performance of *Siegfried* the following year she was shot by her jealous husband, a banker, and died of her wounds shortly after.

DAVID CUMMINGS

Bing, Sir **Rudolf** (*b* Vienna, 9 Jan 1902). British impresario of Austrian birth. The son of an iron and steel magnate, he began his career in a Viennese bookshop whose proprietor soon branched out as an impresario of artistic events. In the 1920s he worked in Berlin before becoming assistant to Carl Ebert at the Hessisches Staatstheater in Darmstadt (1928–30), assistant to the Intendant of the Charlottenburg Opera, Berlin (1930–33) and general manager of the Glyndebourne Opera (1936–49). In 1946 he took

British nationality and helped to found the Edinburgh Festival, of which he was artistic director from 1947 to 1949.

In 1950 he became general manager of the Metropolitan Opera, New York. His tenure (until 1972) was the second longest in its history. He had a great influence on both the company and American opera in the 1950s and 60s, particularly because of his autocratic attitudes. In the early years he improved standards of performance and direction. His emphasis on scenic design and imaginative direction reflected his European experience, and was new to the USA. Bing introduced a number of black singers and dancers and extended the season to fill the whole year; he also supervised the move to the Lincoln Center. In the later years, however, like his predecessor Gatti-Casazza, he failed to develop new ideas for coping with the economic and artistic climates of the period, although the house continued to have individual successes. In 1973 he was appointed Consultant for Special Projects by Columbia Artists Management. His *5000 Nights at the Opera* (London, 1972) and *A Knight at the Opera* (New York, 1981) relate some of the many vicissitudes of his career. He was knighted in 1971.

*

J. Higgins: 'Sir Rudolf Bing: a Lion in Winter', *HiFi/MusAm*, xxxii/11 (1982), 18–20
PATRICK J. SMITH

Binghamton. American town in New York State. The principal operatic activity is provided by the Tri-Cities Opera Company (also covering the nearby communities of Endicott and Johnson City). Founded in 1949 by Carmen Savoca and Peyton Hibbitt, the company became one of the first American companies outside New York City to receive government support for a world première – that of Myron Fink's *Jeremiah*, in 1962. It has produced two to four operas annually, giving a total of 15 to 20 performances between September and June, since production of its first fully staged undertaking, *Cavalleria rusticana*, on 24 May 1951. Tri-Cities Opera purchased its first permanent home and current administrative centre, a former Lithuanian meeting hall, in 1965.

By 1977 the company had developed a subscription season, and begun a touring education programme, whose object was to bring opera to schoolchildren. The programme, which features the singers of its Resident Artists Training Program, reached about 32 000 children in 1990. Although it generally produces operas of the standard repertory, Tri-Cities Opera presented the world première of Richard Brooks's *Rapunzel* in April 1971. In February 1979 it co-produced, with the State University of New York at Binghamton, the world première of *Galileo Galilei* by Ezra Laderman. In January 1986 it offered the world première of Fink's *Chinchilla.* Major productions are now presented in the publicly owned Broome Center for the Performing Arts (The Forum), the converted Binghamton Theatre, built in 1919 as a film theatre and vaudeville house and renovated to accommodate opera in the early 1970s. With a balcony and no boxes, the theatre seats 1519. About 14 000 people attend performances annually. The company uses almost exclusively singers who have gone through its training programme. The careers of the mezzo-soprano Cynthia Clarey and the young Placido Domingo were nurtured by Tri-Cities Opera.

ROBERT V. PALMER

Bini [Bifone], **Carlo** (*b* Naples, *c*1944). Italian tenor. He studied in Naples, making his début in 1969 at S Carlo as Pinkerton. He sang throughout Italy, including La Scala, where in 1977 he sang the Drum Major (*Wozzeck*), and Germany; he appeared in Paris, Brussels and at the Metropolitan Opera, where he made his début in 1978 as Rodolfo (*Luisa Miller*) and took over Enzo from Domingo after the first act of *La Gioconda* in 1982. His roles included not only the Duke, Alfredo, Don Carlos, Arvino (*I Lombardi*), Gabriele Adorno (which he sang at Covent Garden in 1981), Ernani, Henri (*Les vêpres siciliennes*), Manrico and Canio, but also Donello (*La fiamma*), Zandonai's Romeo, Avito (*L'amore dei tre re*), Don José, Laca (*Jenůfa*), Vakula the Smith and Prince Andrey (*Khovanshchina*). He had a strong, not always steady voice with ringing top notes.

ELIZABETH FORBES

Binički, Stanislav (*b* Jasika, nr Kruševac, 27 July 1872; *d* Belgrade, 15 Feb 1942). Serbian composer and conductor. After studying mathematics at Belgrade University he taught in a school, but in 1895 he went to Munich to study composition with Rheinberger. He was a founder of the Serbian School of Music in Belgrade and conducted the city's first regular symphonic concerts; he also conducted various choirs. He was the first director (from 1911) of the new Stanković Music School. With his wife, the singer Miroslava Binički (née Frieda Blanke; *b* Munich, 9 Oct 1876; *d* Belgrade, 5 Aug 1956), acting as répétiteur and choir trainer, he conducted the first operas at the National Theatre. During World War I he was a bandmaster in France. In 1920 he became the first director of the new permanent company at the National Theatre, resigning in favour of Stevan Hristić in 1924.

Most of Binički's music is theatrical, and includes much incidental music and the opera *Na uranku* ('At Dawn', 1903; B. Nušíc; Belgrade, 20 Dec 1903; vs, 1903). This was the first Serbian national opera, and, though based on the manner of Italian *verismo*, it makes significant use, to reflect the opera's subject of the conflict with the Turks, of Serbian folk music and of oriental melismas and augmented-interval scales. The opera was reorchestrated by Krešimir Baranović in 1968. Binički's output also includes choral works, religious music, songs and military marches.

Binički's brother Aleksandar (*b* Belgrade, 16 May 1885; *d* Zagreb, 7 Aug 1963) was a *buffo* tenor and administrator, who studied in Munich with Reger and Mottl. He was director of operetta in Zagreb; his own roles included Vašek (*The Bartered Bride*) and Beppe (*Pagliacci*).

JOHN WARRACK

Bioni, Antonio (*b* Venice, 1698; *d* after 1739). Italian composer, active mainly in Germany and Bohemia. The son of a tailor in the Rialto, he studied with Giovanni Porta. His first opera, *Climene*, was performed in 1721 in a provincial theatre in Chioggia, and in 1722 *Caio Mario* and *Mitridate* were staged in Ferrara. Not long afterwards Bioni joined an Italian opera company that performed *Orlando furioso* in the open-air theatre of the Bohemian Count Franz Anton von Sporck on his estate at Guckuksbade. Bioni's reputation was firmly established when the work was repeated at Whitsun 1725 to mark the opening of the Ballhaus Theater in Breslau. From then until 1734, the only period of Italian opera in Breslau, Bioni composed 21 of the 41 Italian operas produced at the Ballhaus. He served the theatre as impresario (1730–34) as well as composer and arranger of pasticcios. In 1731 he was named court composer to the Elector of Mainz, Franz Ludwig, Pfalzgraf of Neuburg (simultaneously Archbishop of Mainz, Breslau and Trier); but his career after 1734 is unknown. It is supposed that he visited Vienna in the late 1730s; Gerber claimed that his opera *Girita* was performed at the Hoftheater in 1738. Mattheson's *Ehren-Pforte* (1740) describes only Bioni's works for Breslau.

unless otherwise stated, first performed at Breslau, Ballhaus Theater
Climene (V. Cassani), Chioggia, Beregan, carn. 1721
Caio Mario, Ferrara, Bonacossi, spr. 1722, mentioned in *FétisB*
Mitridate (A. Zeno), Ferrara, Bonacossi, spr. 1722, mentioned in *FétisB*
Udine, Venice, 1722, mentioned in *FétisB*
Orlando furioso (G. Braccioli, after L. Ariosto), Guckuksbade, Bohemia, Rasentheater, spr. 1724
Armida abbandonata (F. Silvani, after T. Tasso: *Gerusalemme liberata*), Prague, private theatre of Count Sporck, Nov 1725
Armida al campo (Silvani, after Tasso: *Gerusalemme liberata*), June 1726
Endimione (pastoral op, F. Mazzarà), 7 Jan 1727
Lucio Vero (S. Burigotti), May 1727
Attalo ed Arsinoe (Braccioli), Nov 1727; ?rev. as Arsinoe, 1728
Artabano re dei Parti (A. Marchi), carn. 1728
Filindo (heroic pastoral), Breslau, Stadt, carn. 1728
La fede tradita e vendicata (Silvani), carn. 1729
Engelberta (Zeno), sum. 1729
Andromaco (Zeno), 1729/30
Ercole su'l Termodonte (Burigotti), spr. 1730
Adone, Prague, private theatre of Count Sporck, carn. 1731
Lucio Papirio (Salvi), carn. 1732
Silvia (E. Bissari), carn. 1732
Siroe (?Burigotti and P. Metastasio), carn. 1732
La verità conosciuta, spr. 1732
Demetrio, June 1732
Issipile (Metastasio), aut. 1732, *A-Wgm*
Alessandro Severo (Zeno), sum. 1733
Alessandro nell'Indie (?Metastasio), sum. 1733
L'odio placato (Silvani), sum. 1733
Artaserse, 1733
Girita, Vienna, Hof, 1738

Music in: Ariodante, 1727; Griselda, 1728; Merope, 1728; Il ritorno del figlio con l'abito più approvato, 1730

*

DBI (R. Meloncelli); *ES* (E. Zanetti); *FétisB*; *GerberNL*
J. Mattheson: *Grundlage einer Ehren-Pforte* (Hamburg, 1740), 374–8
H. Riemann: *Opern-Handbuch* (Leipzig, 1887)
H. H. Borcherdt: 'Geshichte der italienischen Oper in Breslau', *Zeitschrift des Vereins für Geschichte Schlesiens*, xliv (1910), 18
F. X. Seppelt: *Geschichte des Bistums Breslau* (Breslau, 1928)
R. Brockpähler: *Handbuch zur Geschichte der Barockoper in Deutschland* (Emsdetten, 1964) SVEN HANSELL

Birchill, Isabella. *See* VINCENT, ISABELLA.

Birds, The. Musical in two acts by LEJAREN HILLER to a libretto after ARISTOPHANES translated by Walter Kerr; Urbana, Illinois, University Theater, 12 March 1958.

The Athenians Pithetaerus (tenor) and Euelpides (spoken) come to the kingdom of the birds in search of an easier life. They convince Epops, king of the birds (tenor), his wife Procne (soprano) and their followers that they should fortify their airy kingdom and demand tribute from the gods in return for allowing the passage of sacrificial smoke from the mortals below. No sooner has the unbuilt city been christened ('Cloud Cuckoo-Land') than it begins to attract parasites: a Poet (tenor or baritone) and a Prophet, a Real Estate Man and a Lawyer (all spoken). Pithetaerus kicks them out, and the city is quickly built. The goddess Iris (spoken) inadvertently breaches the walls and is sent back to Olympus with word of the new order, while humans, flocking to the utopia, are fitted with wings so that they may participate in it. The gods, starving for lack of sacrificial food, send a delegation to negotiate. Pithetaerus, taking a hard line on the advice of Prometheus (spoken), demands the sceptre of Zeus and the hand of Iris in marriage, which the gods are forced to concede; the work ends with the combined coronation and wedding.

Kerr's translation preserves the numerous musical opportunities inherent in the ancient original, and it is these that Hiller set. Although influenced by the Broadway idiom, the result is unlike the usual musical; there are no 'big' songs among its 15 numbers and there is a preponderance of spoken dialogue; most of the singing is for the chorus. The work is peppered with dissonances (including some serial passages), palindromes, fughettas and Ivesian contrapuntal welter. The unorthodox musical dramaturgy and the use of an ancient Greek model alike betray the influence of Harry Partch, who was in residence at the University of Illinois at that time.

ANDREW STILLER

Birger Jarl och Mechtilde ('Birger Jarl and Mechtilde'). 'Drama with music' in three acts and a *divertissement* by FRANCESCO ANTONIO BALDASSARE UTTINI and HINRICH PHILIP JOHNSEN to a libretto by Gustaf Fredrik Gyllenborg after a plan by GUSTAVUS III; Stockholm, Rikssalen, 8 July 1774.

One of the earliest nationalist efforts of Gustavus III, the story concerns the founding of the Swedish royal line by the 14th-century knight Birger Jarl. Inside Bjelbo castle, the Danish king's widow Mathilde, disguised as Mechtilde (spoken), has sought to escape her husband's conqueror Birger Jarl (spoken), unaware that it is he who offers her sanctuary. In Act 1, Birger Jarl tells his lieutenant Sixten Sparre (spoken) that he loves Mechtilde, but his identity must never be revealed. Mechtilde tells her lady-in-waiting Christina that she is moved by the kindness of the anonymous Swedish knight, yet she feels guilty that her emotions should be aroused so soon after her husband's death. Christina persuades her to leave, but their flight is interrupted by Venus (soprano), who convinces Mechtilde that her love is sanctioned by the gods.

Act 2 opens with a pastoral scene in which Mechtilde confesses her love for the unknown knight. But when she asks for his identity, he refuses to answer. A group of Lapp prophets predict happiness for Birger Jarl and Mechtilde. As they are about to be united, a herald from the Danish army arrives and reveals Mechtilde's real name. When this fails to influence Birger Jarl, a challenge to battle is issued. As Act 3 opens, Mechtilde has had a vision in which her knight was killed. The horror vanishes when Christina tells her of his heroic defence of the castle. A herald announces that Birger Jarl has arrived at Bjelbo, and Sixten urges Mechtilde to set aside her hatred for him. Mechtilde is more concerned, however, about the safety of her knight. When he arrives she asks him to bring her Birger Jarl's sword, whereupon he finally reveals his identity.

Birger Jarl can be described more accurately as a play with sections of incidental music than as a pure opera, since none of the principal characters has a singing role. The music is concentrated in each of the acts into individual scenes, including a large final *divertissement*. The music of the first act, in which mythological figures interrupt the Nordic characters, is by Uttini, written in the Italian *seria* style. The second-act scene with Lapps and various seers is by Johnsen and contains exotic orchestrations and harmonies. The huge finale by both composers is characterized by the use of folk melodies arranged into more classical forms. As such, this represents the first attempt to infuse a Swedish opera with nationalist elements. The work was performed successfully for several years after its première in 1774 and was revived in 1792 as an afterpiece for *Gustaf Wasa.* BERTIL H. VAN BOER

Birmingham. City in the Midlands, second largest in England. Its musical traditions have favoured oratorio as the chief form of communal musical entertainment. It has never had a permanent repertory opera company; opera has always tended to come to Birmingham with touring companies, or has been provided by local groups on a more or less annual basis, without any conventional operatic seasons.

In the 18th century operas were staged at the city's main theatres, which included those in Moor Street (1740), King Street (*c*1750) and New Street (1774), and in the early 19th century the Theatre Royal (1807). Italian opera performed by touring companies was a regular feature of musical life in the 19th century, although the main theatres were given over largely to music hall and variety entertainments. The triennial festivals of the late 18th, 19th and early 20th centuries, based on a tradition of performing Handel, eschewed opera, except for overtures (in the 19th century). The possibility of introducing concert performances of opera into the festival led to the resignation in 1895 of the Festival Chorus's celebrated conductor W. C. Stockley; only a single performance was given (*Der fliegende Holländer*, 1896) before the demise of the triennial festival.

The Birmingham Repertory Theatre (founded in 1913) staged opera, including Boughton's *The Immortal Hour* in 1922 and the premières of Messager's *Monsieur Beaucaire* (7 April 1919), Smyth's *Fête galante* (4 June 1923) and Bantock's *The Seal-Woman* (27 September 1924). The new Repertory Theatre (1971) has favoured spoken theatre, although the School of Music staged its annual major production (*Contes d'Hoffmann*) there in 1986. The major source of opera in the city in the 20th century has been touring opera. Visiting companies have included Sadler's Wells (later the ENO), who brought *The Ring* in 1974, Scottish National Opera, Opera North and Glyndebourne Touring Opera. The touring company using the Hippodrome Theatre most frequently has been Welsh National Opera, who adopted Birmingham as their English 'home' in 1978.

The Midlands Arts Centre at Cannon Hill has provided an annual children's opera since 1973 and has originated major productions since 1976. An important addition to operatic resources was the establishment in 1987 of the City of Birmingham Touring Opera, which merged the combined forces of English Touring Opera and the Birmingham Music Theatre, under the direction of Graham Vick. The first production, *Falstaff* (Cocks Moors Woods Leisure Centre), established a twin aim of performing operas with reduced orchestral forces and in community venues. A climax of this endeavour was a two-night version of the *Ring* (1990), in a reduction by Jonathan Dove, performed at Stockland Green Leisure Centre. The company's policy of collaboration with the ethnic community of Birmingham led in 1989 to the première of Ravi Shankar's *Ghanashyam* ('A Broken Branch'; Stockland Green Leisure Centre). Since 1991 the Alexandra Theatre (1370 seats) has been the principal venue for the revived D'Oyly Carte company.

The Birmingham School of Music (since 1989 the Birmingham Conservatoire) began operatic performances in 1901 and has performed annually since then. From 1976 its endeavours have been focussed by the activities of a graduate opera school. After a series of unstaged Baroque operas, the Barber Institute of Fine Arts in the University of Birmingham (364 seats) began a series of annual (1959–72) and later (from 1974) more sporadically staged operas with professional casts. Under the directorship of Anthony Lewis (1959–68) and Ivor Keys (1969–85) the Barber Institute performances were known for their championship of Baroque opera, chiefly Handel.

In this century the most distinguished amateur operatic endeavour in Birmingham has been that of the Midlands Music Makers. Founded as a chapel choir in 1897, the group made its first operatic venture with a performance of excerpts from *The Pirates of Penzance* in 1931, which was followed by a fully staged *HMS Pinafore* (1933). Since 1946 the company has performed annually a mixture of familiar repertory and complete novelties to the British stage, including Berlioz's *Les Troyens* (1948) and Dvořák's *The Jacobin* (1967), many of them in the Crescent Theatre.

J. H. Langford: *A Century of Birmingham Life, 1741–1841* (London, 2/1870–71)
——: *Modern Birmingham, 1841–1871* (London, 1873–7)
W. C. Stockley: *Fifty Years of Music in Birmingham* (Birmingham, 1913)
J. Sutcliffe Smith: *The Story of Music in Birmingham* (Birmingham, 1945)
J. Stone: 'Music in Birmingham: a Concise History – Five Centuries', *HMYB*, ii (1946), 100
B. Pritchard and D. J. Reid: 'Some Festival Programmes of the Eighteenth and Nineteenth Centuries, iv: Birmingham', *RMARC*, viii (1970), 1, 5
E. W. White: *A History of English Opera* (London, 1983)
R. Fawkes: *Welsh National Opera* (London, 1986)

JAN SMACZNY

Birtwistle, Sir **Harrison** (*b* Accrington, 15 July 1934). English composer. He studied at the RMCM from 1952 to 1955, where his first study was the clarinet rather than composition; in 1953 he was a founder-member of the New Music Manchester Group with his fellow-students Alexander Goehr, Peter Maxwell Davies, John Ogdon and Elgar Howarth. Their performances of music of the Second Viennese School and the post-Webern avant garde gave Birtwistle a first grounding in modernism. After National Service he continued his clarinet studies at the RAM, but the impact of hearing recent scores by Boulez and Stockhausen in 1957 encouraged him to turn to composition. By the early 1960s, Birtwistle had established a distinctive musical style, which, though it owed something to the surface discontinuities of post-Webern serialism, employed none of its techniques. Two works composed while he was director of music at Cranborne Chase School, the dramatic cantata *The Mark of the Goat* (1965) and *The Visions of Francesco Petrarca* for baritone, mimes, and children's orchestra (1966, subsequently withdrawn), give the first direct expression to the abstract dramatic and ritual elements that had consistently been detectable in his works. The première in 1965 of *Tragoedia* for instrumental ensemble established Birtwistle's reputation as a leading British composer of the younger generation, and the following year he was awarded a Harkness Fellowship to study for two years in the USA, first at Princeton and then at the University of Colorado.

During these years he worked on his first opera, *Punch and Judy*, commissioned for the Aldeburgh Festival. On his return to Britain he formed the Pierrot Players with Maxwell Davies, with the specific purpose of exploring small-scale music theatre; for the group's début concert in London he composed *Monodrama*, but that and all but one of the other works he composed for the group have been withdrawn. The première of *Punch and Judy* in 1968 showed much more clearly the direction in which Birtwistle's own dramatic thoughts were leading, and the 'dramatic pastoral' *Down by the Greenwood Side* the following year confirmed his ability to reinvent dramatic forms and to construct musical rituals on the frameworks of received folk narratives: *Punch and Judy* contains the stylized violence of the traditional story within a severely formal structure of closed musical forms, while *Down by the Greenwood Side* interlocks elements of the Mummers Play and the ballad of the Cruel Mother, the former comic and spoken, the latter tragic and sung.

The works of the early 1970s began to reflect Birtwistle's desire to compose a large-scale opera on the Orpheus legend. Scores such as *Nenia: the Death of Orpheus* (1970), *Meridian* (1971) and *The Fields of Sorrow* (1971) began to explore the sound-world of the opera, as well as the layering of non-linear narrative time that characterizes *The Mask of Orpheus*. Work on the opera, to Peter Zinovieff's libretto, began in 1973 after a commission from the Royal Opera House, Covent Garden. By 1976 Birtwistle had completed the first act and the bulk of the second, while teaching in the USA, but the commission lapsed. The previous year he had been appointed music director of the National Theatre, and over the next eight years he wrote incidental music for 12 productions, including the score for Peter Hall's production of *The Oresteia* (1981), the dramatic techniques of which left their impression on *The Mask of Orpheus*. He also collaborated with Tony Harrison and the National Theatre Company on the theatre piece *Bow Down* in 1977, based on the Ballad of the Two Sisters, in which musicians and actors are integrated into a single chorus and the musical content is fashioned from a single pulse and three basic intervals.

In 1981 the ENO revived the commission for *The Mask of Orpheus*, and in the next three years Birtwistle completed the score. It was staged in 1986, and followed two months later by the première of *Yan Tan Tethera*, originally commissioned for television, in which Harrison's reworking of a northern folktale becomes the basis for a highly stylized dramatic treatment. For a commission from the Royal Opera House, however, Birtwistle returned to a subject that he had first tackled in a choral work in the early 1960s, in a musical style whose instrumental layering and dramatic grandeur owed much to his orchestral scores of the 1980s; *Gawain*, to a libretto by the poet and novelist David Harsent based on the Middle English *Sir Gawain and the Green Knight*, was staged at Covent Garden in May 1991. He received a knighthood in 1987.

See also GAWAIN; *MASK OF ORPHEUS, THE*; and *PUNCH AND JUDY*.

Monodrama (S. Pruslin), London, Queen Elizabeth Hall, 30 May 1967 (withdrawn)
Punch and Judy (tragicomedy or comitragedy, 1, Pruslin), Aldeburgh, Jubilee Hall, 8 June 1968
Down by the Greenwood Side (dramatic pastoral, 1, M. Nyman), Brighton, West Pier Pavilion, 8 May 1969
The Mask of Orpheus, 1973–5 (Acts 1 and 2), 1981–4 (Act 3) (lyric tragedy, 3, P. Zinovieff), London, Coliseum, 21 May 1986
Bow Down (music theatre, A. Harrison), London, Cottesloe, 4 July 1977
Yan Tan Tethera, 1984 (mechanical pastoral, 1, Harrison, after northern English folktale), London, Queen Elizabeth Hall, 7 Aug 1986
Gawain (2, D. Harsent, after *Sir Gawain and the Green Knight*), London, CG, 30 May 1991

*

G. Crosse: 'First Performances: Birtwistle's *Punch and Judy*', *Tempo*, no.85 (1968), 24–30
M. Chanan: 'Birtwistle's *Down by the Greenwood Side*', *Tempo*, no.89 (1969), 19–21
A. Clements: 'Harrison Birtwistle: a Progress Report at 50', *MT*, cxxv (1984), 136–9
M. Hall: *Harrison Birtwistle* (London, 1984)
A. Clements: 'Birtwistle Counts Sheep', *MT*, cxxvii (1986), 428–30
R. Samuel: 'The Mask of Orpheus', *Tempo*, no.158 (1986), 41–5
W. Mellers: *The Masks of Orpheus* (Manchester, 1987), 167
T. Morgan: 'Birtwistle's *The Mask of Orpheus*', *New Music 87* (Oxford, 1987), 76–8

ANDREW CLEMENTS

Bis, Hippolyte-Louis-Florent (*b* Douai, 29 Aug 1789; *d* Paris, 3 March 1855). French dramatist. While a clerk in the Droits Réunis in Lille he published pamphlets attacking the restored Bourbon monarchy, and was transferred to the Ministère des Finances in Paris. His first dramatic work, the tragedy *Lothaire*, written in collaboration with one F. Hay, was published in 1817 but not performed. *Attila*, a five-act verse tragedy, opened to acclaim at the Odéon, Paris, on 26 April 1822; its success, however, was probably due to Mlle George's acting and to some propaganda that led to the banning of the tragedy. *Blanche d'Aquitaine* (Comédie-Française, 29 October 1827) also had marked political leanings; this play was probably the source upon which Felice Romani based his libretto for Donizetti's *Ugo, conte di Parigi* (1832). Though not a particularly proficient playwright, Bis was called on to shorten Etienne de Jouy's version of Schiller's drama for Rossini's *Guillaume Tell* (1829); he largely recast Act 2, but the Three Cantons scene was later rewritten by Armand Marrast (H. Weinstock, *Rossini*, London, 1968) and Adolphe Crémieux, too, had a hand in the revisions. After the July Revolution Louis-Philippe rewarded Bis for his support with a promotion and made him a Chevalier of the Légion d'Honneur. His only other play, *Jeanne de Flandre* (1845), was a resounding failure.

CHRISTOPHER SMITH

Biscaccianti [née Ostinelli], **Eliza** (*b* Boston, 1824; *d* Paris, July 1896). American soprano. The daughter of a pianist mother and an Italian violinist, she was the granddaughter and niece respectively of the composers James Hewitt and John Hill Hewitt. In 1843 she and her father travelled to Italy; she studied first with Giuditta Pasta, then with Vaccai, Nani and Lamberti. Later she married a cellist. Her début (as Elvira in *Ernani*) was in 1847 in Milan; her American début, on 8 December 1847 (as Amina), was with the Astor Place Opera Company in New York. Her reception there was mixed, and she returned to Europe for further study in London and Paris. In 1852 she and her husband travelled to California, where she appeared with great success. The following year she went to Lima with the Lorini Opera Company, and in 1862 was performing in San Francisco with the Bianchi Company. Biscaccianti had a voice of great richness and beauty; she was one of the first

American-born singers to enjoy success abroad. She eventually returned to Europe and established herself as a teacher in Milan.

*

O. Thompson: *The American Singer* (New York, 1937)
P. Waddington: 'Musical Beginnings in the City of St. Francis', *Opera and Concert*, xii/9 (1947), 48–51, 59
V. Brodsky Lawrence: *Strong on Music: the New York Music Scene in the Days of George Templeton Strong, 1836–1874*, i: *Resonances, 1836–1850* (New York, 1988)
K. Preston: *Travelling Opera Troupes in the United States, 1825–1860* (diss., City U., New York, 1989)

KATHERINE K. PRESTON

Bishkek [Pishkek]. Capital of Kïrgïstan. Between 1926 and 1991 it was known as Frunze. A national theatre studio opened in 1926, concentrating at first on preserving the folk tradition; an important role was played by the conductor-composer P. F. Shubin, who arrived in 1928, and the composer Abdïlas Maldïbayev, who helped form a theatre studio in 1930, the Kirgizskiy Gosudarstvennïy Teatr (Kirghiz State Theatre). With the formation of the Kirghiz SSR in 1936, cultural activities were centrally directed, and the city theatre was reorganized as the Muzïkal'nïy-dramaticheskiy Teatr. For several years it concentrated on such new works as *Altïn kïz* ('Golden Girl') by Vlasov and V. G. Fere (1937), culminating in the first fully fledged Kirghiz national opera, *Aychurek* ('Lunar Beauty', 1939) by Vlasov, Maldïbayev and Fere. In 1942 the theatre was re-formed as the Kirgizskiy Teatr Operï i Baleta (Kirghiz Theatre of Opera and Ballet); performances are in Russian and Kirghiz. The company has presented premières of several works by Vlasov, Fere and Maldïbayev along with operas by M. Abdrayev, S. N. Ryauzov, Knipper and Kholminov. A new, 941-seat hall, completed in 1955, was renamed the Kirgizskiy Akademicheskiy Teatr Operï i Baleta imeni A. Maldïbayeva (Maldïbayev Kirghiz Academic Theatre) in 1978.

*

ME ('Frunze', V. V. Brailovsky; also 'Kirgizskiy teatr operï i baleta', B. Alagushov and A. Kaplan)
G. Bernandt: *Slovar' oper vpervïe postavlennïkh ili izdannïkh v dorevolyutsionnoy Rossii i vi SSSR 1736–1959* [Dictionary of Operas First Performed or Published in Pre-revolutionary Russia and in the USSR 1736–1959] (Moscow, 1962), 552–3
Yu. V. Keldïsh, ed.: *Istoriya muzïki narodov SSSR* [History of the Music of the Soviet Peoples], i–v (Moscow, 1970–74)
A. Saliyev, ed.: *Istoriya kirgizskogo iskusstva* [History of Kirghiz Art] (Frunze, 1971)
Kirgizskiy gosudarstvennïy ordena Lenina akademicheskiy teatr operï i baleta (Frunze, 1972)
B. Alagushov and A. Kaplan: *Kirgizskiye operï* (Frunze, 1973)

GREGORY SALMON

Bishop [née Riviere], **Anna** (*b* London, 9 Jan 1810; *d* New York, 18 March 1884). English soprano. She studied the piano with Moscheles and singing with Henry Bishop and made her début at the Antient Concerts on 20 April 1831, shortly before her marriage to Bishop. During the next few years she toured the provinces with her husband and the harpist Nicholas Bochsa. In 1839 she began to give 'dramatic concerts' with Bochsa in which she sang Italian opera excerpts; that summer she eloped with him and began a long concert tour of the Continent. In summer 1843 she arrived in Italy, where she was engaged for 27 months at S Carlo, appearing in 20 operas. Her many Italian admirers did not include Verdi, who had heard her in *I due Foscari*; despite a press campaign in her favour he refused to engage her for *Alzira* in 1845.

She returned to England in 1846, making her London début as Isoline in Balfe's *The Maid of Artois*. The next year she made her American début in *Linda di Chamounix* at the Park Theatre, New York (4 August). In New York she also appeared in the American premières of *The Maid of Artois*, at the Park Theatre (5 November 1847), and Flotow's *Martha*, which she produced, at Niblo's Garden (1 November 1852). After Bochsa's death in 1856 she toured in South America, returning in 1858 to New York, where she married a diamond merchant. Some 25 years of extensive touring followed; at one stage the couple were shipwrecked off an island in the Pacific. Bishop made her last public appearance in 1883 in New York. She was one of the most popular English singers of her generation. Her voice was brilliant, her technique masterly, her acting 'free, graceful and dramatic' according to a contemporary critic; but she lacked the expressive power of Jenny Lind or Clara Novello. Scrapbooks containing details of her concerts are in Boston Public Library and the Metropolitan Opera archives.

*

Travels of Anna Bishop in Mexico, 1849 (Philadelphia, 1852)
C. G. Foster: *Biography of Anna Bishop* (New York, 1853)
Obituaries: *MT*, xxv (1884), 212; *American Art Journal*, xl (1884), 356
R. Northcott: *The Life of Sir Henry Bishop* (London, 1920), 85ff
F. Schlitzer: 'Verdi's "Alzira" at Naples', *ML*, xxxv (1954), 125–7

NICHOLAS TEMPERLEY, JEAN BOWEN

Bishop, Sir **Henry R**(**owley**) (*b* London, 18 Nov 1786; *d* London, 30 April 1855). English composer. His father was a London watchmaker and later a haberdasher. Such education as Henry Bishop had was gained at Dr Barrow's Academy at 8 Soho Square. By the age of 13 he was already in business as a music seller, and his first songs and piano pieces were published by the firm in the years 1800–03. Later he studied harmony with Francesco Bianchi. He wrote the music for several ballets at the King's Theatre and Drury Lane Theatre before his first fully fledged opera, *The Circassian Bride*, was performed at Drury Lane on 23 February 1809; the score was destroyed when the theatre burnt down the following day, but the music had made an impact. Several notably successful works followed, including *The Maniac* (26 performances). As a result Bishop was offered the post of musical director at Covent Garden in 1810. There, in the next 14 years, he supervised the composition and performance of dramatic musical works of all kinds, from original operas to collections of songs interpolated in mangled versions of Shakespeare's plays. Despite the immense amount of musical hackwork which he was compelled to perform in this job, Bishop found time for several excursions to the Continent, for a season at the Dublin Theatre (1820), and for direction of many of the Lenten Oratorio concerts from 1819. In 1813 he was one of the founder-members of the Philharmonic Society, and he was also one of the original harmony professors at the RAM, though he did little teaching there.

In 1824 Bishop left Covent Garden because of a dispute over his salary, and became musical director at Drury Lane. His most ambitious opera, *Aladdin*, was put on there in 1826 in a futile attempt to steal the thunder of Weber's *Oberon* at the rival house. Shortly after this he was engaged to succeed Tom Cooke as 'director and composer' to Vauxhall Gardens, in an effort to revive the fading popularity of the resort; he continued to write theatre music on a regular basis until 1840. In 1841 he was elected to the Reid Professorship at Edinburgh University, but he resigned in 1843, having given a total of two lectures. He was knighted in 1842, and in 1848 he was appointed to the chair of music at Oxford. Bishop's second wife was the singer Anna Riviere (*see* BISHOP, ANNA). During his later years he almost ceased to compose, but he edited a number of works.

Bishop's reputation has altered more than that of almost any other composer. In 1820 he was considered 'one of the few modern composers whose writings will survive' (Hunt), and George Hogarth, writing in 1851, thought that the best of his operas 'are in many respects worthy of the greatest masters of the German school, and justify the title which was bestowed on him of "the English Mozart"'; but by 1902 Fuller Maitland was dismissing his 'so-called operas' in the following terms: 'the low taste of the public was pandered to in each and all of them'.

The list of Bishop's dramatic works suggests an almost incredible productivity, especially during the years 1813–20, but only one of his works, *Aladdin*, is anything like a full-length opera. Even this is not through-composed, for the autograph score contains cues indicating spoken dialogue. In the rest Bishop provided set pieces in what was essentially a spoken play, numbering anything from 25 (in *The Maniac*) to one. Many of his works are adaptations, or medleys of well-known airs; in some he collaborated with other composers. Corder boiled down the entire corpus of 70 published stage works to 48 overtures, 190 airs and ballads, 53 display songs, 73 duets and trios, 150 glees and ensemble pieces, and 340 melodramas, marches and ballet airs. Although these are often not apt in their dramatic context, Bishop could provide the musical part of an evening's entertainment in the theatre with considerable skill and taste, and occasionally with brilliance.

His mutilations of Mozart and Rossini have been condemned and ridiculed by critics from his day to ours; they are indeed abominable, but the 'blame' falls not so much on Bishop as on the managers who, sure of their public, tried in this way to snatch some of the takings of the Italian opera at the King's Theatre. His musical versions of Shakespeare (which, however, fall outside the scope of this dictionary) are more worthy of respect.

Bishop's most popular songs and glees were usually first associated with a dramatic work, but survived as separate numbers long after the show was forgotten. Examples are 'Lo, here the gentle lark' (from *The Comedy of Errors*, 1819), 'Bid me discourse' (*Twelfth Night*, 1820) and 'O well do I remember' (*Maid Marian*, 1822). Eclipsing all else in popularity is the ballad 'Home, Sweet Home', foreshadowed in *Who Wants a Wife?* (1816) and then used as the theme-song of *Clari* (1823), repeated in various transformations throughout the opera. Its fame was immediate, and spread quickly through Europe. It was used not only in the overture of Bishop's *Home, Sweet Home* (1829) but also in the mad scene in Donizetti's *Anna Bolena* (1830).

all first performed in London; all published in vocal score in London shortly after first performance

Descriptions of works, taken from original sources, often omit 'grand'. Unless otherwise stated, MSS at *GB-Lbl*; MS librettos of most works in *US-SM* (up to 1824) or *GB-Lbl*.

LCG – *Covent Garden* LDL – *Drury Lane*
LLH – *Little Theatre, Haymarket*
LVG – *Vauxhall Gardens*

† – *partly adapted* ‡ – *wholly adapted*

The Circassian Bride (3, C. Ward), LDL, 23 Feb 1809 [MS 'revised from memory by the composer']

The Vintagers (musical romance, 2, E. J. Eyre), LLH, 1 Aug 1809, 2 songs pubd

The Maniac, or The Swiss Banditti (serio-comic op, 3, S. J. Arnold), Lyceum, Drury Lane company, 13 March 1810

†The Knight of Snowdoun (musical drama, 3, T. Morton, after W. Scott: *The Lady of the Lake*), LCG, 5 Feb 1811

The Virgin of the Sun (operatic drama, 3, F. Reynolds, after A. von Kotzebue: *Die Spanier in Peru*), LCG, 31 Jan 1812, *US-Wc*

The Aethiop, or The Child of the Desert (romantic drama, 3, W. Dimond), LCG, 6 Oct 1812; rev. as *Haroun-al-Raschid (op, 3, Dimond), LCG, 11 Jan 1813

†The Lord of the Manor (3, J. Burgoyne), LCG, 24 Oct 1812, *GB-Lcm*, collab. Davy, J. C. Doyle, Reeve and T. Welsh; after Jackson

The Brazen Bust (melodrama, 2, C. Kemble), LCG, 29 May 1813

†Harry-le-Roy (heroic pastoral burletta, 1, I. Pocock, after R. Dodsley: *The King and the Miller of Mansfield*), LCG, 2 July 1813

†Artaxerxes (2, T. A. Arne, after P. Metastasio), LCG, 23 Sept 1813, *Lbl*, *Lcm*; after Arne

†Selima and Azor (2, G. Collier), LCG, 5 Oct 1813, collab. T. S. Cooke and Welsh; after T. Linley (i)

The Miller and his Men (melodrama, 2, Pocock), LCG, 21 Oct 1813

For England, Ho! (melodramatic op, 2, Pocock), LCG, 15 Dec 1813, collab. Welsh

†The Farmer's Wife (comic op, 3, C. Dibdin jr), LCG, 1 Feb 1814, collab. Davy, Reeve and others

The Wandering Boys, or The Castle of Olival (romantic drama, 2, Pocock, from the Fr.), LCG, 24 Feb 1814, MS lost

†Lionel and Clarissa (revived op, 3, I. Bickerstaff), LCG, 3 May 1814, MS lost; after Dibdin jr

The Dog of Montargis, or The Forest of Bondy (melodrama, 3, H. Harris, after R. C. G. de Pixérécourt), LCG, 30 Sept 1814, MS lost

†The Maid of the Mill (ballad op, 3, Bickerstaff), LCG, 18 Oct 1814, *Ge*; after S. Arnold

†John of Paris (comic op, 2, Pocock, from the Fr.), LCG, 12 Nov 1814, *US-Bp*; after Boieldieu: Jean de Paris

†Brother and Sister (musical entertainment, 2, Dimond, after J. Patrat: *L'heureuse erreur*), LCG, 1 Feb 1815, *GB-Lbl*, *Lcm*, collab. Reeve

The Noble Outlaw (comic op, 3, Mrs Opie, after J. Fletcher: *The Pilgrim*), LCG, 7 April 1815

†Comus (masque, 2, after J. Milton), LCG, 28 April 1815, *Ge*, *Lbl*, *Lcm*, unpubd; after Arne

†Telemachus (ballad op, 2, G. Graham), LCG, 7 June 1815, *Ge*, *Lbl*

†The Magpie or the Maid? (melodrama, 3, Pocock, after T. Badouin d'Aubigny and L.-C. Caigniez: *La pie voleuse*), LCG, 15 Sept 1815, *US-Bp*

John du Bart, or The Voyage to Poland (historical melodrama, 3, C. Farley and Pocock), LCG, 25 Oct 1815, MS lost

†Cymon (dramatic romance, 3, D. Garrick), LCG, 25 Nov 1815; after M. Arne

Who Wants a Wife? or The Law of the Land (musical drama, 3, Pocock), LCG, 16 April 1816

†Lodoiska (3, Kemble), LCG, 15 Oct 1816; after Storace

†The Slave (musical drama, 3, Morton), LCG, 12 Nov 1816

The Heir of Vironi, or Honesty the Best Policy (operatic piece, 2, Pocock), LCG, 27 Feb 1817; collab. J. Whitaker

‡The Libertine (operatic drama, 2, Pocock, after L. da Ponte and T. Shadwell), LCG, 20 May 1817, MS lost; after Mozart: Don Giovanni

The Father and his Children (melodrama, 2, Reynolds), LCG, 25 Oct 1817, unpubd

The Illustrious Traveller, or The Forges of Kanzel (melodrama, 2, Reynolds), LCG, 3 Feb 1818, unpubd

Zuma, or The Tree of Health (comic op, 3, Dibdin, after S. F. Genlis), LCG, 21 Feb 1818, collab. Braham

December and May (operatic farce, 2, Dimond, after B. Brittle), LCG, 16 May 1818, 1 song pubd

The Burgomaster of Saardam, or The Two Peters (musical drama, 2, Reynolds), LCG, 23 Sept 1818, *GB-Lcm*, unpubd

†The Barber of Seville (comic op, 3, J. Fawcett and D. Terry, after T. Holcroft and P.-A. Beaumarchais), LCG, 13 Oct 1818; after Rossini

†The Marriage of Figaro (comic op, 3, Bishop, after Holcroft and Beaumarchais), LCG, 6 March 1819; after Mozart
Fortunatus and his Sons, or The Magic Purse and Wishing Cap (melodramatic romance, 2, Farley, after T. Dekker), LCG, 12 April 1819
†A Roland for an Oliver (musical farce, 2, Morton), LCG, 29 April 1819
Swedish Patriotism, or The Signal Fire (melodrama, 2, W. Abbott), LCG, 19 May 1819, unpubd
†Henri Quatre, or Paris in the Olden Time (musical romance, 3, Morton), LCG, 22 April 1820
†Montrose, or The Children of the Mist (3, Pocock, after Scott: *The Legend of Montrose*), LCG, 14 Feb 1822, collab. Ware and Watson
†The Law of Java (musical drama, 3, G. Colman), LCG, 11 May 1822, *Lbl, Lcm*
Maid Marian, or The Huntress of Arlingford (op, 3, J. R. Planché, after T. L. Peacock, and Scott: *Ivanhoe*), LCG, 3 Dec 1822
Nigel, or The Crown Jewels (play, 5, Pocock, after Scott: *The Fortunes of Nigel*), LCG, 28 Jan 1823, *Lbl, Lcm*, unpubd
Clari, or The Maid of Milan (op, 3, J. H. Payne), LCG, 8 May 1823, *US-R*
Cortez, or The Conquest of Mexico (3, Planché, after Prescott), LCG, 5 Nov 1823, MS sold at Maggs Bros., Christmas 1927
†Native Land, or The Return from Slavery (3, Dimond, after G. Rossi: *Tancredi*), LCG, 10 Feb 1824; partly after Rossini: Tancredi
‡Der Freischütz (3, G. Soane, after F. Kind), LDL, 10 Nov 1824, MS lost; after Weber
The Fall of Algiers (3, C. E. Walker), LDL, 19 Jan 1825
Faustus (romantic drama, 3, Soane, Terry, after J. W. von Goethe), LDL, 16 May 1825, collab. Cooke, Horn
Aladdin (romantic fairy op, 3, Soane), LDL, 29 April 1826
Englishmen in India (comic op, 3, Dimond), LDL, 27 Jan 1827
The Rencontre, or Love will Find Out the Way (operatic comedy, 2, Planché), LLH, 12 July 1827
†Yelva, or The Orphan of Russia (musical drama, 2, Bishop, after E. Scribe), LCG, 5 Feb 1829, *B-Lc, GB-Lbl*
†Home, Sweet Home, or The Ranz des Vaches (operatic drama, 2, C. A. Somerset, from the Fr.), LCG, 19 March 1829, *Lbl, Lcm*
†The Night before the Wedding and the Wedding Night (comic op, 2, E. Fitzball), LCG, 17 Nov 1829, unpubd; after Boieldieu: Les deux nuits
‡Ninetta, or The Maid of Palaiseau (comic op, 3, Fitzball, after G. Gherardini), LCG, 4 Feb 1830, *US-Wc*, unpubd; after Rossini: La gazza ladra
‡Hofer, the Tell of the Tyrol (historical op, 3, Planché), LDL, 1 May 1830, *GB-Lcm*; after Rossini: Guillaume Tell
Under the Oak, or The London Shepherdess (vaudeville op, 1, Fitzball, after Burgoyne: *The Maid of the Oaks*), LVG, 25 June 1830, *Lcm*, unpubd
Adelaide, or The Royal William (nautical burletta, 1, Fitzball), LVG, 23 July 1830, *Lcm*, unpubd
The Romance of a Day (operatic drama, 2, Planché), LCG, 3 Feb 1831
‡The Love Charm, or The Village Coquette (comic op, 2, Planché, from the Fr.), LDL, 3 Nov 1831, MS lost, unpubd; after Auber: Le philtre
‡The Demon, or The Mystic Branch (romantic op, 3, Fitzball and J. B. Buckstone, after Scribe), LDL, 20 Feb 1832, *Lcm*, unpubd; after Meyerbeer: Robert le diable
‡Der Alchymist (romantic op, 3, Fitzball and T. H. Bayly, after W. Irving), LDL, 20 March 1832, MS lost, unpubd; after several Spohr operas
The Tyrolese Peasant (domestic op, 2, Payne), LDL, 8 May 1832, *Lcm*, 1 song pubd
The Magic Fan, or The Filip on the Nose (operetta, 1, Fitzball), LVG, 18 June 1832, *Lcm*, unpubd
†The Bottle of Champagne (operetta, 1, Fitzball), LVG, 27 July 1832, *Lcm*, unpubd
The Sedan Chair (operetta, 1, Fitzball), LVG, 27 Aug 1832, *Lcm*, unpubd
The Doom-Kiss (legendary operatic entertainment, 2, Pocock), LDL, 29 Oct 1832, unpubd
‡The Maid of Cashmere (ballet-op, 2, Fitzball, after Scribe), LDL, 16 March 1833, MS lost, 1 song pubd
‡La sonnambula (op, 2, S. Beazley), LDL, 1 May 1833, MS lost, vocal score pubd *c*1840; after Bellini
†Rural Felicity (comic op, 2, Buckstone), LLH, 9 June 1834, 1 duet pubd
†Manfred (dramatic poem, 3, Byron), LCG, 28 Oct 1834, unpubd
‡The Maid of Palaiseau (comic op, 2, Fitzball), LDL, 13 Oct 1838, MS lost, unpubd; after Rossini: La gazza ladra
‡Guillaume Tell (4, A. Bunn, after E. de Jouy, H.-L.-F. Bis and A. Marrast), LDL, 3 Dec 1838, *Lbl* [Dept of Printed Books: H.385.a], unpubd; after Rossini

*

DNB (W. B. Squire)
J. H. L. Hunt: Reviews in *The Examiner* (1 Oct 1820; 12 Nov 1820)
H. Bishop: *List of the Musical Compositions of Henry R. Bishop*, MS, 1841, lost; summarized and described in F. J. W. C.: 'Sir Henry R. Bishop', *MT*, xxxvi (1895), 662–6
G. Hogarth: *Memoirs of the Opera*, ii (London, 1851), 367ff
E. Fitzball: *Thirty-Five Years of a Dramatic Author's Life* (London, 1859)
'Henry Rowley Bishop', *MMR*, x (1880), 73, 88, 104
J. D. Brown and S. S. Stratton: *British Musical Biography* (London and Birmingham, 1897)
J. A. Fuller Maitland: *Music in the XIXth Century*, i: *English Music* (London, 1902), 103–4
H. Simpson: *A Century of Ballads 1810–1910* (London, 1910), 88ff
F. Corder: 'The Works of Sir Henry Bishop', *MQ*, iv (1918), 78–97
R. Northcott: *The Life of Sir Henry R. Bishop* (London, 1920) [incl. letters]
T. Fawcett: 'Bishop and Aladdin', *MT*, cxiii (1972), 1076–7
T. Fenner: *Leigh Hunt and Opera Criticism: the 'Examiner' Years, 1808–1821* (Lawrence, KS, 1972)
B. Carr: 'Theatre Music: 1800–1834', *Music in Britain: the Romantic Age, 1800–1914*, ed. N. Temperley (London, 1981), 288–306

NICHOLAS TEMPERLEY (text, bibliography)
BRUCE CARR (work-list)

Bispham, David (Scull) (*b* Philadelphia, 5 Jan 1857; *d* New York, 2 Oct 1921). American baritone. He studied in Milan (1886–9) with Vannuccini and Lamperti and in London with the tenor William Shakespeare, making his opera début in Messager's *La basoche* as Longueville at the English Opera House on 3 November 1891. The next year he sang Kurwenal at Drury Lane and soon afterwards sang at Covent Garden. He made his American début as Beckmesser at the Metropolitan Opera (18 November 1896), remaining there until 1903. There and at Covent Garden he sang most of the leading Wagnerian roles, considering Kurwenal and Beckmesser to be his best. His repertory also included Masetto, Pizarro, Escamillo, Alfio, Peter (*Hänsel und Gretel*), Iago, Falstaff and Urok in Paderewski's *Manru*. After 1902 Bispham devoted himself mainly to song recitals and teaching, and was an ardent promoter of the use of English in opera and song.

Bispham's voice was powerful and of fine quality, though with a tendency to excessive nasal resonance. He was a skilled actor and a forceful delineator of character. He published an autobiography, *A Quaker Singer's Recollections* (New York, 1921). His musical memorabilia are in the New York Public Library.

RICHARD ALDRICH, DEE BAILY

Bisquert (Prado), Próspero (*b* Santiago, 8 June 1881; *d* Santiago, 2 Aug 1959). Chilean composer. He was self-taught and, after a few years in Paris, became an able composer and a good orchestrator. In 1954 he received the National Award of Art, the highest award of this type in Chile. His works are written in a very personal, nationalistic style that shows the influence of French impressionism and expressionism. His short opera-ballet *Sayeda* (Santiago, Teatro Municipal, 20 September 1929) was considered 'a simple attempt to rejuvenate Chilean lyrical theater' (Salas). Bisquert's own libretto, based on *The Thousand and One Nights*, lacks any action or conflict. The cast includes three singers: Sayeda (soprano), Ishak de Mosul (tenor) and The Beggar (baritone). Ishak dreams that his beloved

Sayeda comes to his arms, houris dance for them and a blind beggar sings, but everything vanishes and Ishak's loneliness ends the plot.

*

V. Salas: *La creación musical en Chile, 1900–1951* (Santiago, [1951])

G. Becerra: 'Próspero Bisquert: Premio Nacional de Arte 1954', *Revista musical chilena*, ix/47 (1954), 18–29

SAMUEL CLARO-VALDÉS

Bittner, Julius (*b* Vienna, 9 April 1874; *d* Vienna, 9 or 10 Jan 1939). Austrian composer. He was essentially a self-taught musician, but received some formal instruction in composition from the Bruckner disciple Josef Labor. He composed mainly in his spare time while pursuing a career as a lawyer and judge in Wolkersdorf (from 1905) and Vienna (from 1908). After World War I, he was a counsel for the Ministry of Justice, 1920–22. Subsequently, he decided to give up his legal career and devote himself to music.

Although Bittner composed works in several genres, he was primarily interested in writing for the stage. His passion for opera was fuelled, according to his own account, by attending a performance of *Lohengrin* at the age of 12. Following the precedent set by Wagner, he wrote the librettos for 15 of his own operas. His early attempts failed to achieve public performance. Mahler rejected the 500-page score of *Hermann* written in 1897, pronouncing it impractical for the forces at the Vienna Opera. On the other hand, he recognized the considerable dramatic potential in the work and advised the younger composer to seek the counsel of his assistant Bruno Walter. Walter subsequently proved to be one of the composer's most devoted interpreters and was the dedicatee of *Der Abenteuer* (1913). Eventually Bittner's third opera, *Die rote Gred*, was performed in Frankfurt in 1907 and Mahler accepted the work for the following season in Vienna where it was given under Walter's direction. After this *Der Musikant*, produced in Vienna in 1910, scored a considerable success with its amiable portrait of the fictitious 18th-century Austrian court musician, Wolfgang Schönbichler. *Der Bergsee* (1911) proved to be more controversial because it was highly critical of the role of the Salzburg Bishopric in the 15th century. Neither this opera nor its successor, *Der Abenteuer*, pleased the public, although both works enjoyed the benefit of distinguished collaborators such as Walter, and the artist Koloman Moser who designed striking sets for *Der Bergsee*. With *Das höllisch Gold* (1916), however, the composer at last created a successful work that was performed extensively throughout German and Austrian theatres during the immediate postwar period. Here Bittner emulated his older compatriot Wilhelm Kienzl in attempting to merge the principles of German Singspiel with a post-Wagnerian harmonic language. *Der liebe Augustin* (1917) revealed a lighter touch with its irresistible use of Austrian dialects contained within simple closed forms.

After the break-up of the Austro-Hungarian Empire, Bittner's work ceased to arouse much interest. He was mercilessly attacked in the Viennese press for his dilettantism and lack of sophisticated musical technique, although the quality of his librettos never came under such scrutiny. His limitations were exposed when he attempted to set subjects of a tragic or demonic nature. *Die Kohlhaymerin* (1921), a romantic love story set in 19th-century Vienna, received only three performances before it was withdrawn, while *Mondnacht* (1928), heard at the Berlin Staatsoper under Walter, was regarded as stylistically anachronistic. The composer increasingly turned to operetta as a more appropriate vehicle for his musico-dramatic gifts. Unfortunately, his original works in this genre lacked the melodic memorabilty of those by Lehár and Kálmán. *Der unsterbliche Franz* (1928), a tasteful and affectionate portrait of the life of Schubert, failed to capitalize upon the enormous popularity of Harry Berté's 1916 operetta *Das Dreimäderlhaus* (which used Schubert's melodies). On the other hand *Walzer aus Wien* (1930), written in collaboration with Korngold and based on Strauss waltzes, secured many performances throughout Europe.

During the 1930s, Bittner completed three further operas of which only one, *Das Veilchen*, which appropriately includes a quotation of Mozart's well-known lied (K476), was given six performances at the Vienna Staatsoper under Clemens Krauss in 1934. After the Anschluss, his fortunes improved when the Nazis praised him for having resisted the influences of modernism. Nevertheless, the revival of some of his earlier works was short-lived.

librettos by Bittner unless otherwise stated

Hermann, 1897, unperf.

Alarich, 1899–1901, unperf.

Die rote Gred (3), Frankfurt, 26 Oct 1907, vs (Mainz, 1907)

Der Musikant (2), Vienna, Hofoper, 12 April 1910, vs (Mainz, 1909)

Der Bergsee (prelude, 2), Vienna, Hofoper, 2 Nov 1911 (Berlin, 1911); rev. 1938

Der Abenteuer (Spiel, 4), Cologne, 30 Oct 1913, vs (Berlin, 1913)

Das höllisch Gold (Spl, 1), Darmstadt, 15 Oct 1916 (Vienna, 1916)

Der liebe Augustin: Szenen aus dem Leben eines wienerischen Talents (4), Vienna, Volksoper, 11 June 1917, vs (Vienna, 1917)

Die Kohlhaymerin (3), Vienna, Staatsoper, 9 April 1921, vs (Vienna, 1920)

Lori, 1921 (Operette, prelude, 2), unperf.

Das Rosengärtlein (Legende, 3), Mannheim, 18 March 1923 (Vienna, 1922)

Die silberne Tänzerin (Operette, 3, L. Hirschfeld and P. Frank), Vienna, Carl, 1 Feb 1924 (Vienna, 1924)

Général d'amour (Operette, 3, J. Wilhelm and Frank), Vienna, Volksoper, 3 March 1926 (Vienna, 1926)

Der unsterbliche Franz (Operette, 4 scenes, E. Decsey), Vienna, Volksoper, 24 April 1928 (Vienna, 1928)

Mondnacht (3), Berlin, Staatsoper, 13 Nov 1928, vs (Vienna, 1928)

Der Maestro, 1931 (4), unperf.

Das Veilchen (3), Vienna, 8 Dec 1934, vs (Vienna, 1934)

Der blaue Diamant, 1937 (3), unperf.

Das Rosenkranzfest, 1937–8, inc.

Arrangement: Walzer aus Wien (Spl, 3, A. M. Willner, H. Reichert and E. Marischka), Vienna, Stadt, 30 Oct 1930, orch. Korngold, vs (Vienna, 1930) [based on music by J. Strauss father and son]

*

R. Specht: *Julius Bittner: eine Studie* (Munich, 1921)

J. Korngold: 'Julius Bittner: "Die rote Gred", "Der Musikant", "Der Bergsee", "Das höllisch Gold"', *Deutsches Opernschaffen der Gegenwart* (Vienna, 1922), 196–223

G. Renker: 'Julius Bittner, ein deutscher Musiker', *Die Musik*, xxviii (1936), 825–8

R. Mojsisovics: 'Julius Bittner', *ZfM*, cvi (1939), 175–6

K. Kobald: 'Julius Bittner und Franz Schreker', *ÖMz*, ix (1954), 78–81

H. Ullrich: *Julius Bittner* (Vienna, 1968)

W. Zauner: '"Meine tiefe und aufrichtige Verehrung für Ihre Person und Ihr Werk": Briefe an Julius Bittner', *ÖMz*, xliv (1989), 70–80

ERIK LEVI

Bizet, Georges (Alexandre César Léopold) (*b* Paris, 25 Oct 1838; *d* Bougival, nr Paris, 3 June 1875). French composer. His short career was very largely devoted to opera in various genres, reaching a remarkable climax in 1875 with the supremely well-crafted *Carmen*. This is one of the best-known of all operas, yet it followed a succession of complete, incomplete and projected works (a total of 30 in Winton Dean's listing in *The New Grove*) which had no great success in his lifetime. He planned many operas of which no trace remains; only six operas survive in a performable text.

1. Life and operas. 2. Bizet as opera composer.

1. LIFE AND OPERAS. Bizet's father was an amateur singer and composer, and his mother came from a musical family, being the sister of the famous singing teacher François Delsarte. His childhood was steeped in music, and he began to attend the Paris Conservatoire in October 1848, just before his tenth birthday. He developed extraordinary gifts as a pianist and score-reader and won prizes for both piano and organ playing. His teachers included Pierre-Joseph-Guillaume Zimmermann for piano and Fromental Halévy for composition, and he came strongly under the influence of Gounod at this time. For much of his career he worked as rehearsal pianist and score arranger, and he thus had an unrivalled familiarity with the current repertory of Parisian theatres.

Among his earliest works, from the mid-1850s, are piano pieces, the deft Symphony in C, composed after the example of Gounod, and his first attempt at opera. This is the one-act *opéra comique La maison du docteur*, which may have been intended for private performance at the Conservatoire; it survives only in vocal score. It is based on a libretto by Henri Boisseaux which was also set by Paul d'Ivry in 1855. Despite his proximity to Halévy and Gounod, tunefulness and a light style seem to have been his principal goals in this work, as they are also in his second opera, *Le Docteur Miracle*. This is a one-act operetta to a libretto by Léon Battu and Ludovic Halévy composed in 1856 for a competition offered by the Bouffes-Parisiens theatre in pursuance of Offenbach's determination to establish operetta as a more respectable genre. Out of 78 aspirants for the prize, two, Bizet and Lecocq, were awarded a shared first prize, with the result that both operettas were staged in April 1857, appearing on alternate nights with the same cast. It was invaluable operatic experience for Bizet, even though the work left little mark (it disappeared until long after his death and was not published until 1962). It shows Bizet in full command of the brisk, superficial style of French operetta and has been successfully revived.

Soon after the production of *Le Docteur Miracle* Bizet won the Prix de Rome. He went to Italy for about three years, during which he heard a fair quantity of Italian music and worked intermittently on operatic ideas. In February 1858 he wrote to his mother: 'I have chosen an Italian libretto, *Parisina*, a forgotten opera by Donizetti'. *Parisina* has a powerful and tragic plot, based on a poem by Byron, but Donizetti's piece had disappeared from the repertory by 1858. The idea may have been suggested by the librettist himself, Felice Romani, to whom Rossini had given Bizet a letter of introduction. Such serious stuff was probably not to Bizet's liking at this time, for nothing more was heard of it, and instead, two months later, he was discussing an *opéra comique* in collaboration with Edmond About. 'It is charming', wrote Bizet, 'but a little too comic for the Opéra-Comique. I don't regard it as anything more than an amusing occupation.' Perhaps none of this was written either.

By turning to Donizetti's lighter side as a model, Bizet found something he could succeed with. This was *Don Procopio*, an Italian comic libretto by Carlo Cambiaggio, which he found after he had gone through 'all the bookshops in Rome and read two hundred plays'. He compared it to Donizetti's *Don Pasquale* and finished it quickly. It is a brilliant, youthful work entirely in the Italian spirit, free, as he noted himself, of the influence of Gounod; he likened it to Cimarosa: 'On Italian words one must write Italian music', he affirmed. Submitted as an envoi to the Académie in 1859, it received warm but stiff praise. Bizet must have hoped it would be staged somewhere, but it was not heard of again in his lifetime and was not performed until 1906.

Even before *Don Procopio* was finished, new projects ran through Bizet's mind. He felt determined to raise his muse on to a more lofty level and to move more closely to what he regarded as a 'German' style. The first scheme was a grand opera on Hugo's *Notre-Dame de Paris*, using the libretto that Hugo had himself fashioned for Louise Bertin in 1836 under the title *Esmeralda*. He thought of writing an ode-symphony (after the model of Félicien David's *Le désert*) on a story of Circe and Ulysses. He told his mother how excited he was by E. T. A. Hoffmann's tale *Le tonnelier de Nuremberg* (*Meister Martin der Küfner*) with its singing contest, an idea which Wagner had already earmarked for his *Die Meistersinger*, unbeknown to Bizet, of course. He was attracted to some Voltaire stories. He wondered if *Don Quixote* would make a good opera. He considered *Hamlet* and *Macbeth*. The belief that Gounod was working on *Don Quixote* quelled one idea, the lack of a librettist hindered all. A marked uncertainty as to the direction his career was to go lies behind this string of abandoned ideas.

He tried writing his own libretto, an obvious resort in the circumstances. This was an adaptation of Molière's comedy *L'amour peintre*. But when a second, more disapproving report on *Don Procopio* arrived from the Académie, he lost heart and gave up. He returned to Paris in 1860, with two late envois still to be submitted to the Académie: the ode-symphony *Vasco de Gama* and an *opéra comique* in one act, *La guzla de l'émir*, on a libretto by Jules Barbier and Michel Carré, librettists of *Faust*. Probably composed in 1862, this work was put into rehearsal at the Opéra-Comique the following year, but Bizet withdrew it when he received a much more prestigious commission from the Théâtre Lyrique for *Les pêcheurs de perles*. No music for *La guzla de l'émir* survives, but the Académie report refers to 'a duet in which an elegant serenade is accompanied by a harp and a pretty design for flute', which suggests that the famous duet in Act 1 of *Les pêcheurs de perles* (and perhaps much else besides) was salvaged from it. The libretto, on a traditional Turkish theme, was later set by Dubois.

It is clear that *Les pêcheurs de perles* was a much more attractive proposition. The Ceylonese setting, for example, was much fresher than the Turkish one. The full three-act format allowed more scope for Bizet's gifts, and the prestige of a commission from the Théâtre Lyrique raised Bizet from student status to that of fully-fledged composer. The opera was composed at great speed in the summer of 1863 and given 18 performances that autumn. Although admired by many, including Berlioz, it was not well received, and it dropped out of the repertory until after Bizet's death. But it proved to Bizet himself that he was capable of writing an opera that combined an exotic background with strong dramatic conflicts, his most enduring gift as a composer. The opera public was for the first time made aware of

Bizet's autograph score of the closing pages of his one-act opéra comique, 'Djamileh', composed in 1871

his lyrical gifts, his harmonic audacity and his acute ear for orchestral sound.

Léon Carvalho, director of the Théâtre Lyrique, reaffirmed his faith in Bizet by offering him a further commission, for a grand opera on a libretto Gounod had abandoned, *Ivan IV*. This work may well have been begun as early as 1862, and the surviving autograph is complete except for a little orchestration. Owing to Carvalho's repeated postponements, Bizet in 1865 offered the work instead to the Opéra, where it was refused. Thereafter he gave up any attempt to have the work staged, and it was not played until long after his death. For all the effort that *Ivan IV* demanded, there were many projects that continued to take his fancy, whether or not any music was composed. Throughout the 1860s his standing as a composer was far from secure, and opportunities for rewarding work in the theatre fell far short of his potential. A tiny fragment survives of a piece called *La prêtresse*, of which nothing is known; he was reported by Edmond Galabert to have sketched a scene on a libretto by Ernest Dubreuil called *Nicolas Flamel* in May 1865. In July 1866 Bizet again signed a contract with Carvalho, despite the disappointment over *Ivan IV*. This was for a libretto by the experienced wordsmith J.-H. Vernoy de Saint-Georges with Jules Adenis on Scott's *The Fair Maid of Perth*. Bizet once again worked speedily, although he recognized the libretto's shortcomings and the necessity of fashioning the main soprano role for the flamboyant coloratura of Christine Nilsson (who in fact never sang it). *La jolie fille de Perth* was staged at the Théâtre Lyrique in December 1867 after a series of delays, and it received, like *Les pêcheurs de perles*, a run of 18 performances, insufficient to call the work a success or to ensure a revival in Paris in Bizet's lifetime (it was played in Brussels in 1868). It remains a brilliant series of operatic pieces rather than a convincing dramatic whole, and it still only hints at Bizet's potential as a musical dramatist.

Shortly before it opened, a four-act operetta was staged at the Théâtre de l'Athénée under the title *Malbrough s'en va-t-en guerre*. Bizet had contributed the first act, and although his name was supposed to have been kept a secret, the piece was a hit and his identity quickly leaked out; the other composers were Edouard Legouix, Emile Jonas and Delibes. Bizet's music has disappeared. He is also said to have composed music for a similar entertainment, *Sol-si-ré-pif-pan*, in 1872, although that has disappeared too.

In the five years that preceded the composition of *Carmen* Bizet was still without any settled means of support and, more significantly, still without any clear sense of direction as a composer; the continuing stream of unstarted and unfinished projects are testimony to this. But the flame of inspiration was unquestionably beginning to burn more brightly. In 1868 the Opéra urged him to set an unnamed libretto by Arthur Leroy and Thomas Sauvage, about which he was enthusiastic at first. This came to nothing; so did *Les templiers* (presumably based on Scott's *Ivanhoe*) on a libretto by Saint-Georges and Léon Halévy; so did *Vercingétorix*, about Caesar's Gallic wars; so did *Calendal*, an *opéra comique* on a Provençal tale by Mistral; so did *Rama*, a grand opera on the Indian epic *Ramayana*.

Of two projects there remain some tantalizing drafts. *Clarissa Harlowe*, after Richardson's novel, might have made a fine *opéra comique*. Bizet wrote one act at least, and four numbers survive in draft. *Grisélidis*, by Sardou, is a good deal more complete, consisting of drafts of ten numbers, two of which were to play an important part in later works: L'Innocent's theme in *L'arlésienne*, and Don José's Flower Song in *Carmen*. But the most tantalizing fragment from this period is *La coupe du roi de Thulé*, written in 1868–9 in response to a competition promoted by the Opéra. At first Bizet had supported his pupil Galabert's entry for the competition, then decided to set the libretto himself. His anxieties about the outcome were more than fully justified when the jury awarded the prize to an insignificant composer, Diaz. As was usual with his stranded scores, parts of it were transferred to later works. The autograph was further mishandled after his death, so that now only 15 fragments survive of what was evidently a superb example of Bizet's operatic craft, with a tragic story underlined by the compelling use of musical motifs.

In 1871, after the ordeal of the Siege and the Commune was over, the Opéra-Comique rejected *Grisélidis* but offered Bizet a one-act libretto by Louis Gallet, *Djamileh*, as compensation. Based on Alfred de Musset's Turkish story *Namouna*, this was performed in 1872, but without success. Its subtle qualities of colour and characterization were lost on the press and the public, but not on Bizet himself, who at last felt he was on the right path. Fortunately the Opéra-Comique continued to show faith in him and commissioned a full-length opera immediately afterwards. The librettists, Henri Meilhac and Ludovic Halévy, were specified, but the subject was not. Thus Bizet was able to suggest a story that had struck him as suitable, Mérimée's *Carmen*.

Before this became a reality, however, two more works intervened. Carvalho, one of Bizet's more persistent supporters, invited him to write incidental music and *mélodrames* for a production of Alphonse Daudet's *L'arlésienne* in October 1872. The unusual genre of *mélodrame* has made this work a rarity on the stage, although its intense sentiment and its delicate scoring for a small orchestra are both deeply impressive. Its vivid French provincial colouring is well known from the suite for larger orchestra that Bizet made soon afterwards. (A second *L'arlésienne* suite is the work of Guiraud.) In 1873 work on *Carmen* was interrupted – although it is hard to imagine that Bizet was happy to break off – by a scheme to set a libretto, *Don Rodrigue*, by Louis Gallet and Edouard Blau on *La jeunesse du Cid* (a Spanish version earlier than Pierre Corneille's) for the Opéra. He had a complete draft ready by October 1873, most of which survives. But the Opéra refused to proceed with the work, and it joined the now extensive collection of abandoned operas on Bizet's desk. Happily *Carmen* was soon finished, the first work to display on every page his immense talent for penetratingly original music in a highly coloured setting and to provide him with the scope for increasing dramatic tension in a full-length work. But its audaciously risqué character created problems at the Opéra-Comique from the first, and it only reached the stage on 3 March 1875 after considerable delays and many revisions to the score. Even before Bizet's death three months later *Carmen* had achieved more performances than any other of his works, but its uncomprehending reception angered him and perhaps contributed to his final illness. Its posthumous fame raised Bizet to a pinnacle of glory far higher than anything else he ever experienced in his lifetime.

2. Bizet as opera composer. Bizet's short career is bewildering in many ways. But for *Carmen* it would be reasonable to see his operas as illuminated here and there by great things but equally often marred by the mismatch of musician and text. It is hard to explain why he devoted such labour to unsuitable librettos, such as *Ivan IV* and *Don Rodrigue*, even *La jolie fille de Perth*, and yet was so half-hearted about *La coupe du roi de Thulé*, *Clarissa Harlowe* and the *Don Quixote* idea, all of which might have exhibited his talents at their best. He suffered nearly all his life from a profound uncertainty as to which way to move forward, aggravated by the capricious behaviour of theatre managements. Yet the repeated commissions from both the Théâtre Lyrique and the Opéra-Comique prove that he was not neglected; many composers would have given much for such opportunities. He came to maturity at a time when the traditional genres of French opera, both at the Opéra and at the Opéra-Comique, were falling into obsolescence. Despite Gounod's success and the enterprising activities of the Théâtre Lyrique, it was not clear to Bizet until he came to write *Carmen* how a new genre might evolve, while the powerful strains of Wagner's voice were constantly to be heard in the background. Bizet, like most advanced composers of the time, was repeatedly accused of Wagnerism. He was, it is true, a modernist in harmony and orchestration, but his brilliant touches of harmonic and orchestral colour owe nothing to Wagner; his whole spirit, not to mention his genius for the set piece, precludes such a charge.

Bizet's habit of self-borrowing is a further aspect of his uncertainty about the matching of music and text. From *Don Procopio* to *Carmen* he constantly pilfered his scores for pieces for re-use in later settings. The result is often a sense of strain in the declamation and word-setting (as in Don José's Flower Song). But Bizet's word-setting is often less than fastidious even in pieces that were not apparently self-borrowed; the Toreador Song is a famous example. He attached more importance to the sentiment and colour of words than to their metrical properties, and like Mozart, whom he admired enormously and whose career his own in some respects resembles, he had a wonderfully sure feeling for the human voice. He thought deeply about the problems of dramatic music, as his letters testify, and had trenchant opinions about contemporary composers.

He would surely have extended the list of masterpieces had he lived. Verdi, after all, found his true voice at about the same age as Bizet and lived into his 80s. Wagner, at 36, had still to write his seven greatest operas. No matter how satisfying we may find *Carmen*, its hint of yet finer unwritten operas to follow is inescapably dispiriting.

Equally dispiriting are the misrepresentations that Bizet's scores have suffered at the hands of his publishers. Although he supervised the Choudens vocal scores of *Les pêcheurs de perles*, *La jolie fille de Perth*, *L'arlésienne* and *Carmen*, all four works were subsequently issued in a variety of corrupt adaptations. *Les pêcheurs de perles* is the only vocal score to have been correctly restored in a recent edition. All the full scores are posthumous and unreliable; so too are the vocal scores of *Le Docteur Miracle*, *Don Procopio* and *Ivan IV*. The critical edition of *Carmen* prepared by Fritz Oeser in 1964 has been the subject of sustained controversy. So long as the lack of a dispassionate complete edition of his finished works and incomplete drafts prohibits the proper study of Bizet, no assessment of his achievement in the field of opera can be anything other than provisional.

See also Carmen; *Djamileh*; Docteur miracle, le; Don procopio; Ivan iv; *Jolie fille de perth, la*; and *Pêcheurs de perles, les.*

only works known to have been written are listed; works first performed and published in Paris unless otherwise stated

title	*genre, acts*	*libretto*	*first performance*	*composed*	*remarks, sources and publication*
La maison du docteur	oc, 1	H. Boisseaux	unperf.	*c*1855	autograph vs *F-Pn*
Le Docteur Miracle	opérette, 1	L. Battu and Ludovic Halévy, after R. B. Sheridan: *St Patrick's Day*	Bouffes-Parisiens, 9 April 1857	1856	*Pn**; vs (1962)
Don Procopio	ob, 2	C. Cambiaggio, after L. Prividali: *I pretendenti delusi*	Monte Carlo, 10 March 1906	1858–9	*Pn**; vs (1905), full score (1906)
La prêtresse	opérette, 1	P. Gille	unperf.	?1861	autograph sketch, private coll.
La guzla de l'émir	oc, 1	J. Barbier and M. Carré	unperf.	*c*1862	lost
Ivan IV	opéra, 5	F.-H. Leroy and H. Trianon	Württemberg, Mühringen Castle, 1946	?1862–5	Act 5 orchestration inc.; *Pn**; vs (1951)
Les pêcheurs de perles	opéra, 3	E. Cormon and Carré	Lyrique, 30 Sept 1863	1863	vs (1863), full score (n.d.)
La jolie fille de Perth	opéra, 4	J.-H. Vernoy de Saint-Georges and J. Adenis, after W. Scott: *The Fair Maid of Perth*	Lyrique, 26 Dec 1867	1866	*Pn**; vs (1868), full score (*c*1891)
Malbrough s'en va-t-en guerre	opérette, 4	P. Siraudin and W. Busnach	Athénée, 13 Dec 1867	1867	Act 1 by Bizet, lost; other acts by Legouix, Jonas and Delibes
La coupe du roi de Thulé	opéra, 3	L. Gallet and E. Blau	excerpts, BBC radio, 12 July 1955	1868–9	autograph frags. *Pn*, remainder lost
Noé	opéra, 3	Saint-Georges	Karlsruhe, 5 April 1885	1868–9	Bizet's completion of F. Halévy's last opera; vs (1885)
Clarissa Harlowe	oc, 3	Gille and A. Jaime, after S. Richardson: *Clarissa*	unperf.	1870–71	inc.; 4 nos. in draft *Pc*
Grisélidis	oc, 3	V. Sardou	unperf.	1870–71	inc.; 10 nos. in draft *Pc*
Djamileh	oc, 1	Gallet, after A. de Musset: *Namouna*	OC (Favart), 22 May 1872	1871	autograph, private coll.; vs (1872), full score (1892)
L'arlésienne	drame, 3	A. Daudet	Vaudeville, 1 Oct 1872	1872	incidental music and mélodrames; *Pn**; vs (1872)
Don Rodrigue	opéra, 5	Gallet and Blau, after G. de Castro y Bellvís: *Las mocedades del Cid*	unperf.	1873	inc. autograph draft *Pc*
Carmen	oc, 4	H. Meilhac and Ludovic Halévy, after P. Mérimée	OC (Favart), 3 March 1875	1873–4	*Pn**; vs (1875), full score (?1877)

SOURCE MATERIALS

Grove6 (W. Dean)

V. Wilder: Obituary, *Le ménestrel* (4–18 July 1875)

E. Galabert: *Georges Bizet: souvenirs et correspondance* (Paris, 1877)

A. Marmontel: *Symphonistes et virtuoses* (Paris, 1881)

L. Gallet: *Notes d'un librettiste* (Paris, 1891)

H. Imbert: *Portraits et études: lettres inédites de Georges Bizet* (Paris, 1894)

C. Gounod: 'Lettres à Georges Bizet', *Revue de Paris*, vi (1899), 677–703

A. and J. Charlot: 'A propos de la "millième" de "Carmen": coup-d'œuil retrospectif', *L'art du théâtre*, v (1905), 9–16

L. Halévy: 'La millième représentation de "Carmen"', *Le théâtre*, no.145 (1905), 5–14

G. Bizet: *Lettres*; *Impressions de Rome, 1857–60*; *La Commune, 1871*, ed. L. Ganderax (Paris, 1908)

——: *Lettres à un ami*, ed. E. Galabert (Paris, 1909)

Musica (June 1912) [Bizet issue]

G. Servières: 'Georges Bizet d'après les souvenirs de Pierre Berton', *Guide musical* (8–22 March 1914)

J. Chantavoine: 'Quelques inédits de Georges Bizet', *Le ménestrel*, xcv (1933), 316–73 passim

Exposition Georges Bizet au Théâtre national de l'Opéra (Paris, 1938) [illustrated catalogue]

RdM, xx (1938), 129–58 [Bizet issue]

M. Curtiss: 'Unpublished Letters by Georges Bizet', *MQ*, xxxvi (1950), 375–409

——: 'Bizet, Offenbach and Rossini', *MQ*, xl (1954), 350–59

G. Bizet: *Letters in the Nydahl Collection*, ed. L. A. Wright (Stockholm, 1988)

——: *Lettres*, ed. C. Glayman (Paris, 1989)

BIOGRAPHIES

C. Pigot: *Georges Bizet et son oeuvre* (Paris, 1886, 2/1911)

C. Bellaigue: *Georges Bizet: sa vie et son oeuvre* (Paris, 1891)

H. Imbert: *Georges Bizet* (Paris, 1899)

P. Landormy: *Bizet* (Paris, 1924, 2/1950)

J. Rabe: *Georges Bizet* (Stockholm, 1925)

D. C. Parker: *Georges Bizet* (London, 1926, 2/1951)

J. Tiersot: 'Bizet and Spanish Music', *MQ*, xiii (1927), 566–81

P. Laparra: *Bizet et l'Espagne* (Paris, 1935)

J. Chantavoine: 'Le centenaire de Georges Bizet', *Le ménestrel*, c (1938), 225–7, 233–5

M. Cooper: *Georges Bizet* (London, 1938)

W. Dean: *Georges Bizet: his Life and Work* (London, 1948, 3/1976)

——: *Introduction to the Music of Bizet* (London, 1950)

M. Cooper: 'Georges Bizet (1838–1875)', *The Heritage of Music*, ed. H. Foss, iii (London, 1951, 2/1969), 108–23

P. Stefan-Gruenfeldt: *Georges Bizet* (Zürich, 1952)

M. Curtiss: *Bizet and his World* (New York, 1958)

W. Dean: 'Bizet's Self-borrowings', *ML*, xli (1960), 238–44

F. Robert: *Georges Bizet* (Paris, 1965)

STUDIES OF OPERAS

F. Nietzsche: *Randglossen zu Bizets 'Carmen'*, ed. H. Daffner (Regensburg, 1912)

F. Hühne: *Die Oper 'Carmen' als ein Typus musikalischer Poetik* (Greifswald, 1915)

D. Imsan: *Carmen: Charakter-Entwicklung für die Bühne* (Darmstadt, 1917)
C. Gaudier: *Carmen de Bizet* (Paris, 1922)
E. Istel: *Bizet und Carmen* (Stuttgart, 1927)
M. Cooper: *Carmen* (London, 1947)
W. Dean: 'An Unfinished Opera by Bizet', *ML*, xxviii (1947), 347–63 [on *La coupe du roi de Thulé*]
——: *Carmen* (London, 1949)
J.-P. Changeur: Six articles on *Ivan IV*, *La vie bordelaise* (12 Oct–16 Nov 1951)
H. Malherbe: *Carmen* (Paris, 1951)
W. Dean: 'Bizet's Ivan IV', *Fanfare for Ernest Newman* (London, 1955), 58–85; repr., rev., in W. Dean: *Essays on Opera* (Oxford, 1990), 262–80
——: 'The True Carmen?', *MT*, cvi (1965), 846–55; repr., rev., ibid, 281–300
M. Poupet: 'Les infidélités posthumes des partitions lyriques de Georges Bizet: *Les pêcheurs de perles*', *RdM*, li (1965), 170–200
J. Westrup: 'Bizet's La Jolie Fille de Perth', *Essays Presented to Egon Wellesz* (Oxford, 1966), 157–70
W. Dean: 'The Corruption of Carmen: the Perils of Pseudomusicology', *Musical Newsletter*, iii/Oct (1973), 7–12, 20
R. Hahn: 'Comment interpréter et chanter Carmen', *Opéra*, cvi (1975), 55–62
M. Poupet: 'A propos de deux fragments de la partition originale de Carmen', *RdM*, lxii (1976), 139–43
——: 'Comptes rendus: Musique, *Les pêcheurs de perles*', *RdM*, lxii (1976), 343–9
L. A. Wright: 'A New Source for Carmen', *19th Century Music*, ii (1978–9), 61–9
L'avant-scène opéra, no.26 (1980) [*Carmen* issue]
T. J. Walsh: *Second Empire Opera: the Théâtre Lyrique Paris 1851–1870* (London, 1981)
L. A. Wright: *Bizet before Carmen* (diss., Princeton U., 1981)
N. John, ed.: *Carmen* (London, 1982) [ENO Opera Guide]
L. A. Wright: '*Les pêcheurs de perles*: Before the Première', *Studies in Music*, xx (1986), 27–45
L'avant-scène opéra, no.124 (1989) [*Les pêcheurs de perles* issue]
HUGH MACDONALD

Bjelinski, Bruno (*b* Trieste, 1 Nov 1909). Croatian composer. He first studied law at Zagreb University and later music at the Zagreb Academy, where his teachers included Blagoje Bersa. From 1945 to 1977 he was professor of counterpoint and fugue at the Zagreb Academy of Music. Bjelinski developed a vivid neoclassical style, notable for its complex rhythms, strong melodic appeal, inclination towards polyphony and sharply etched harmonic structure. His transparent, vivid and emotionally warm musical idiom, rich in contrasts and interwoven with dance rhythms and playful and sensitive lyrical episodes, has proved its charm and directness particularly in works for children, including several operas and ballets. Many of his stage works have achieved international success.

Pčelica Maja [Maya the Bee], 1952 (children's op, 2, M. Koletić, after W. Bonsels), Rijeka, 9 Feb 1963, vs (Vienna, 1957)
Heraklo, 1969 (comic youth chamber op, 1, Bjelinski), Osijek, 2 June 1971
Močvara [The Swamp], 1970 (1, Bjelinski), Osijek, 26 June 1972
Zvona [The Bells], 1972 (1, Bjelinski), Osijek, 7 Dec 1975
Orfej XX stoljeća [Orpheus of the 20th Century], 1978 (2, Bjelinski), Belgrade, 10 Oct 1981
Slavuj [The Nightingale], 1982 (3, epilogue, Bjelinski, after H. C. Andersen), Sarajevo, 15 Dec 1984

*

K. Kovačević: *Hrvatski kompozitori i njihova djela* [Croatian Composers and their Works] (Zagreb, 1960), 41–66
I. Supičić: 'Estetski pogledi u novijoj hrvatskoj muzici: pregled temeljnih gledanja četrnaestorice kompozitora' [Aesthetic Views in Contemporary Croatian Music: a Survey of the Basic Concepts of 14 Composers], *Arti musices*, i (1969), 23–61
——: 'Aesthetic Views in Contemporary Croatian Music: a Survey of the Basic Concepts of Nine Composers', *Arti musices* (1970) [special issue], 107–37
J. Andreis: *Music in Croatia* (Zagreb, 1974)
NIALL O'LOUGHLIN, KORALJKA KOS

Bjoner, Ingrid (*b* Kråkstad, 8 Nov 1927). Norwegian soprano. She studied at Oslo and Frankfurt. She made her stage début in Oslo as Donna Anna in 1957, and became a member of the Wuppertal Opera (1957–9), then of the Deutsche Oper am Rhein, Düsseldorf (1959–61). In 1960 she first appeared at Bayreuth, as Freia and Gutrune, and in 1961 she joined the Staatsoper in Munich. She sang at Covent Garden, La Scala, the Metropolitan, the Vienna Staatsoper, the Hamburg Staatsoper and Salzburg (Leonore, 1970). Her vibrant, dramatic soprano equipped her for all the major Wagner parts from Senta to Brünnhilde. She was also successful as Strauss's Marschallin, Ariadne and Empress; in the latter part of her career she concentrated particularly on Electra, both singing in and directing performances in Norway and Denmark (1986).
ALAN BLYTH

Björling, (Karl) Gösta (*b* Stora Tuna, Dalarna, 11 Sept 1912; *d* Stockholm, 10 Oct 1957). Swedish tenor. The younger brother of Jussi Björling, he studied with his father, David Björling, and made his début in 1937 at Göteborg. From 1940 until his death he was engaged at the Royal Opera, Stockholm, where he sang both lyric and character roles. His repertory included Don Ottavio, Pedrillo, Monostatos, Missail, David, the four comic tenor roles in *Les contes d'Hoffmann* and Bob Boles, which he sang in the first Swedish performance of *Peter Grimes* (1945). His finest part was Mime, evil in characterization, but sung with all the considerable sweetness of tone at his command. ELIZABETH FORBES

Björling, Jussi [Johan] (**Jonaton**) (*b* Stora Tuna, 5 Feb 1911; *d* Stockholm, 9 Sept 1960). Swedish tenor. He was first taught by his father, a professional tenor, with whom he, singing treble, and two brothers made many

Jussi Björling as Des Grieux in Puccini's 'Manon Lescaut'

tours in the Björling Male Quartet. In 1928 he entered the Stockholm Conservatory, studying with Joseph Hislop and John Forsell. In 1930 he became a member of the Royal Swedish Opera, where he made his recognized début on 20 August 1930 as Don Ottavio, and with which he always maintained a connection. Between 1937 and 1940 he made successful débuts at Chicago, New York, London and San Francisco. He did not appear at Covent Garden again until the last year of his life, but in America he became an indispensable favourite, returning regularly to the Metropolitan and other houses except during the war years of 1941–5, which he spent in Sweden. Although his repertory became almost wholly Italian, his appearances were infrequent in Italy itself.

His voice was a true tenor of velvety smoothness, though capable also of ringing high notes of considerable power; admirably schooled, it showed remarkable consistency from top to bottom of his register and throughout the 30 years of his career. Although he was well suited to the smooth legato required by Gounod's Faust and Romeo, the centre of his repertory consisted of Verdi's Duke, Manrico, Riccardo and Don Carlos and of Puccini's Rodolfo, Cavaradossi and Des Grieux (see illustration). Having a voice ideally adapted to the gramophone, he made many valuable recordings, including complete operas, among which his Rodolfo, in an unplanned and spontaneous Beecham set of *La bohème*, well illustrates the distinction of his tone and phrasing.

*

GV (G. Baldini; R. Vegeto)

E. S. Lund and H. Rosenberg: *Jussi Björling: a Record List* (Copenhagen, 1969)

J. W. Porter and H. Henrysson: *A Jussi Björling Discography* (Indianapolis, 1982)

A. Blyth: 'Jussi Björling', *Opera*, xxxvi (1985), 994–7

DESMOND SHAWE-TAYLOR

Björling, (Carl) Sigurd (*b* Stockholm, 2 Nov 1907; *d* Helsingborg, 8 April 1983). Swedish baritone. He studied in Stockholm, making his début there in 1934 as Billy Jack-rabbit (*La fanciulla del West*) at the Royal Opera, where he was engaged for nearly 40 years. He appeared in Vienna, Munich, Paris, Chicago, San Francisco and at La Scala. In 1951 he sang Kurwenal, Amfortas and Wotan at Covent Garden, and Wotan at the first Bayreuth festival after World War II. He made his Metropolitan début in 1952 as Kurwenal. Though renowned internationally as a particularly fine Wagner singer, he also sang Don Alfonso, Count Almaviva, Don Giovanni, Yevgeny Onegin, Amonasro, Iago, Tonio, Escamillo, Méphistophélès, Scarpia and John the Baptist, as well as the Dutchman, Wolfram and Hans Sachs. He sang Captain Balstrode in the first Swedish performance of *Peter Grimes* (1945). The title roles of Hindemith's *Mathis der Maler* and Peterson-Berger's *Arnljot* perfectly displayed the nobility of his voice and stage presence.

ELIZABETH FORBES

Björn, Didrik Gabriel (*b* Stockholm, 10 Aug 1757; *d* Vaxhälla, 17 March 1810). Swedish actor, singer and librettist. He made his début as an actor as Count Almaviva in Beaumarchais' play *Le barbier de Séville* in 1785 at the New Swedish Theatre, where he became well known for his comic roles and original opera librettos, mostly written for Carl Stenborg's comic opera. In 1790 he became an administrator at the Royal Dramatic Theatre, a position he held until after Gustavus III's assassination in 1792. In 1794 he turned to publishing in the provincial town of Linköping. During his career he supplied the texts for more than 65 one-act comedies with music, including the Singspiels *Födelsedagen* ('The Birthday', 1790), *Fricorpsen eller Dalkarlarne* ('The Free Corps or Men from Dalacarlia', 1788) and *Marknaden* ('The Market Place', 1792), all with music by Kraus. His tenor voice was considered expressive but fairly weak; his main talent as an actor lay in his satirical portrayals of figures such as Abbé Vogler in the first of the operas named above.

*

F. Dahlgren: *Anteckningar om Stockholms teatrar* (Stockholm, 1866)

B. van Boer: 'Joseph Martin Kraus's *Soliman den andra*: a Gustavian Turkish Opera', *STMf*, lxx (1988), 9–30

BERTIL H. VAN BOER

Blacher, Boris (*b* Niu-chang, China, 19 Jan 1903; *d* Berlin, 30 Jan 1975). German composer of Baltic descent. He went to Berlin in 1922 and after preliminary studies in architecture and mathematics became a composition pupil of Friedrich Ernst Koch at the Hochschule für Musik (1924–6). He also studied musicology at Berlin University (1927–31). During the 1930s, he worked in Berlin as a freelance composer before securing a post as director of a composition class at the Dresden Conservatory in 1938. He was forced to relinquish this position in the following year because the Nazis did not approve of his teaching methods. After World War II, he resumed his work as a composition teacher and from 1948 was a professor at the Berlin Hochschule für Musik, of which he was director from 1953 to 1970. In 1968 he was elected President of the West Berlin Academy of Arts.

Blacher's consuming interest in the theatre was manifested in several different areas including the writing of incidental music, numerous ballets, operas and librettos, these last for his pupil and friend Gottfried von Einem. The operas occupy an especially important position within his output. Not only do they span his entire creative career, from *Habemeajaja* of 1929 to *Das Geheimnis des entwendeten Briefes* of 1975, but they also share several common features in both musical and dramatic terms. In particular, the composer was attracted to characters and situations that exist outside the normal range of experience. Many of his operas inhabit a strange world that combines elements of the tragic with the grotesque. Often people are depicted in extreme situations, as if to imply a breakdown of social order. There is an almost surrealistic style in certain works, such as *Rosamunde Floris* (1960) and *Yvonne Prinzessin von Burgund* (1972); indeed, this element is already present in the early radio opera *Habemeajaja*, the piano score of which was discovered only after the composer's death. The plot concerns a group of European dignitaries who court Habemeajaja, the Prince of the North Pole, with the intention of exploiting the commercial potential of a new market. Their efforts fail when the Prince falls in love with the voice of a radio soprano and disappears. The music demonstrates Blacher's innate gift for dramatic representation in contrasting the deliberately archaic sounds of the Prince's music with the hectic dance forms of the modern world in which the influence of jazz is particularly evident.

During the 1930s, Blacher continued to cultivate this predominantly anti-Romantic style under the watchful eyes of the Nazis. The oppressive political climate probably dissuaded him from releasing his opera *Die Dame Kobold* for public performance, but in 1939 he began work on *Fürstin Tarakanova*. First performed in Wuppertal in 1941, it marks a considerable advance, particularly in its skilful juxtaposition of clearly delineated, closed forms with a more through-composed style that owes much to the models of *Der Rosenkavalier* and *Wozzeck*. Although the opera received a generally warm response, the fact that its text was based on a Russian subject ruled out further performances after the Nazis had invaded the Soviet Union. Recognizing that financial and production limitations would inevitably affect German opera houses during and after the war, Blacher concentrated on writing intimate stage works for which only a small complement of singers, musicians and stagehands was required. In 1943, he completed his first chamber opera, *Romeo und Julia*, which, like Stravinsky's *Histoire du soldat*, was initially conceived for performance by a travelling theatre group. Wartime conditions precluded performances of the work until 1947 when it was first given in a concert version. Blacher reduced Shakespeare's play to its principal scenes, and the spare instrumental accompaniment, dominated by obsessive repetitions and transformations of short, pithy motifs, provides a harsh antidote to the intensely romantic story. This style was further developed in *Die Flut* (1946), whose libretto is based on a short story by Maupassant. The opera, originally written for radio, involves four singers, a chamber choir and an instrumental accompaniment of ten players and lasts barely 35 minutes in performance. Its claustrophobic atmosphere reaches a particularly effective climax in a double duet in which the different interests of the protagonists are realized through strikingly contrasted vocal writing. Throughout the score, the choir plays a vital role in commenting upon the action, offering stage directives and delivering the final moralistic words, much in the manner of the Brechtian music theatre works of the 1920s and 30s.

Echoes of the music of Weill and Eisler can also be perceived in the opera-ballet *Preussisches Märchen* (1949), a brilliant satire upon the philistinism of Wilhelmine Germany with its blind worship of military bureaucracy. It was first performed at the Berlin Festival in 1952. The plot, based on Zuckmayer's play *Der Hauptmann von Köpenick*, describes how an ordinary civilian, Wilhelm Fadenkreutz, manages to buy the uniform of a Prussian captain, place himself at the head of a unit he finds marching down the street, and lead his men to the town hall where he confiscates tax payments with no authority other than his uniform. Blacher's effervescent score, with its extensive series of marches, galops and waltzes, parodies the operetta music of Paul Lincke but also recalls Stravinsky in its mixture of sparse polyphonic and polyrhythmic elements. As a number opera with few longer sustained sections, it effectively combines both fantasy and realism within individual episodes. A particularly impressive example of this process is the third scene, in which Wilhelm dreams of his future as a famous captain against the musical background of the incessant practising of a Czerny piano study.

Following the completion of *Preussisches Märchen*, the composer began to expand his compositional style in the wake of the experimental atmosphere of the early 1950s. In *Abstrakte Oper no. 1* (1953), he anticipated the music-theatre works of Kagel and Ligeti in setting an abstract text (by the composer Werner Egk) which has no specific plot but recreates human emotions through the use of arbitrary and often meaningless phonetics which are nonetheless capable of immediate association in the listener. The work is divided into seven titled sections, each of which is concerned with presenting a specific state of mind such as 'Fear', 'Love', 'Pain', 'Panic' and 'Negotiation'. It reaches the height of absurdity in 'Negotiation' where an incomprehensible conversation between a Russian and an American takes place against an instrumental background of particularly grotesque sonorities.

After writing *Rosamunde Floris* (1960), which, despite its more traditional plot, incorporates a wide range of contemporary techniques (serialism, variable metres, jazz and pointillistic orchestral colouring), Blacher further pursued his interest in experimental music theatre in his ninth opera, *Zwischenfälle bei einer Notlandung* (1965). Commissioned by the Hamburg Opera, this composition, described as a 'commentary in two phases and 14 situations', has an especially unusual structure in that the libretto dispenses with a conventional dramatic scenario and instead presents a series of film-like sequences showing the survivors of a crash-landing trying to escape from the nightmare of a strange, sinister and even murderous technical world. Electronic sounds play an important role in the score and reflect the continuing conflict between man and machine. As a contrast, the instrumental accompaniment is often reduced to short simple lines which oscillate between passages in unison, canonic imitation and note-clusters.

Such economy of means also characterizes Blacher's final operas, which generally return to more straightforward narratives, even if the choice of subject matter reflects an abundantly varied range of preoccupations. In *Zweihunderttausend Taler* (1969), Sholem Aleichem's short story is presented as a mixture of fable and social criticism. The vocal writing is mainly recitative-like and dominated by small melodic patterns that often suggest the influence of Jewish chant. A greater rhythmic energy underpins the orchestral accompaniment to *Yvonne, Prinzessin von Burgund* (1972), a reflection of the bitter and somewhat enigmatic scenario which culminates in a gruesome murder. In *Das Geheimnis des entwendeten Briefes* (1975), freely based on Poe's story *The Purloined Letter*, the composer recalls the chamber medium of his earlier operas in conceiving the work for modest forces which comprise seven singers, a speaker, nine instrumentalists and electronic tape, but somehow fails to achieve a similar level of dramatic intensity.

See also ABSTRAKTE OPER NO.1.

Habemeajaja, 1929 (Kammeroper, 1, Heggars), Berlin, Deutsche Oper, 30 Jan 1987

Die Dame Kobold, 1935 (after P. Calderón de la Barca: *La dama duende*), ? unperf.

Fürstin Tarakanowa op.19 (3, K. O. Koch), Wuppertal, Barmen, 5 Feb 1941 (Berlin, 1941)

Romeo und Julia op.22, 1943 (Kammeroper, 3, Blacher, after W. Shakespeare), broadcast, Berlin-Zehlendorf Radio, 1947; stage, Salzburg, 9 Aug 1950 (Vienna, 1971)

Die Flut op.24 (Kammeroper, 1, H. von Cramer, after G. de Maupassant), broadcast, Berlin Radio, 20 Dec 1946; stage, Dresden, Staatsoper, 4 March 1947 (Berlin, 1962)

Die Nachtschwalbe op.27, 1947 (dramatisches Notturno, 1, F. Wolf), Leipzig, 22 Feb 1948, vs (Berlin, 1947)

Preussisches Märchen op.30, 1949 (Ballett-Oper, 5 scenes, von Cramer, after C. Zuckmayer: *Der Hauptmann von Köpenick*), Berlin, Städtische Oper, 23 Sept 1952 (Berlin, 1950)
Abstrakte Oper no.1 op.43 (1, W. Egk), broadcast, Hesse Radio, 28 June 1953; stage, Mannheim, National, 17 Oct 1953, vs (Berlin, 1953), full score (Berlin, 1973)
Rosamunde Floris op.60 (2, G. von Westerman, after G. Kaiser), Berlin, 21 Sept 1960, vs (Berlin, 1960)
Zwischenfälle bei einer Notlandung, 1965 (Reportage, 2 phases and 14 situations, von Cramer), Hamburg, Staatsoper, 4 Feb 1966, vs (Berlin, 1965)
Zweihunderttausend Taler (3 scenes, Blacher, after S. Aleichem), Berlin, 25 Sept 1969, vs (London, 1970)
Yvonne, Prinzessin von Burgund (4, Blacher, after Gombrowicz), Wuppertal, 15 Sept 1973, vs (Berlin, 1973)
Das Geheimnis des entwendeten Briefes (Kammeroper, 7 scenes, H. Brauer, after E. A. Poe), Berlin, Hochschule für Musik, 14 Feb 1975 (Berlin, 1975)

*

K. H. Wörner: 'Boris Blachers Bühnenwerke', *SMz*, xciv (1954), 449–51
H. H. Stuckenschmidt: 'Kaiser plus Blacher: Uraufführung der Oper "Rosamunde Floris" bei den Berliner Festwochen', *Theater heute*, i/2 (1960), 7–9
——: *Boris Blacher* (Berlin, 1963)
H. Joachim: 'Boris Blacher's "Zwischenfälle bei einer Notlandung" ', *Opera*, xvii (1966), 280–82
H. H. Stuckenschmidt: 'Boris Blacher und die Bühne: Zum 65. Geburtstag am 19. Januar 1968', *Das Opernjournal*, v (1967–8), 12–14
W. E. von Lewinski: 'Musik ist eine instabile Kunst: Boris Blacher, ein Komponist unserer Zeit – Gedanken nach einem Gespräch', *Das Opernjournal*, ii (1969–70), 7–9
U. Stürzbecher: 'Boris Blacher', *Werkstattgespräche mit Komponisten* (Cologne, 1971), 9
Boris Blacher: Ausstellungskatalog der Akademie der Künste zu Boris Blachers 70. Geburtstag (Berlin, 1973)
H. H. Stuckenschmidt: *Boris Blacher* (Berlin, 1985)
S. Mahlke: 'Eine Berolinerie mit Wiederaufgefundenem: Boris Blachers "Habemeajaja" aus dem Jahre 1929 nun in Berlin uraufgeführt', *OW*, xxviii/3 (1987), 31–2

ERIK LEVI, JOSEF HÄUSLER

Blachut, Beno (*b* Ostrava-Vítkovice, 14 June 1913; *d* Prague, 10 Jan 1985). Czech tenor. He sang in the Ostrava opera chorus and studied at the Prague Conservatory under Louis Kadeřábek (1935–9), making his début as Jeník with the Olomouc Opera. After study under Karel Nedbal, he joined the Prague National Theatre in 1941 and was soon given Heldentenor roles; an excellent performance of *Dalibor* in 1945 established him as the leading Czech tenor, whose Smetana roles, Laca in *Jenůfa* and later Ondrei in Suchoň's *The Whirlpool* were regarded as models. Blachut's voice, balanced in all registers, did not lose its lyric character even in Heldentenor parts. He was noted for his beautiful cantilena, a brilliantly mastered *mezza voce*, exemplary enunciation and pleasant dark vocal colouring. He later took *buffo* roles, including Mr Brouček. He sang with the National Theatre on tours to Moscow, Berlin, Brussels and Edinburgh and as a guest in Vienna, Amsterdam and Helsinki.

*

V. Pospíšil: 'B. Blachut', *HRo*, v/1 (1952), 16
L. Šíp: *Pěvci před mikrofonem* [Singers before the Microphone] (Prague, 1960), 38ff
J. Brožovská: *Beno Blachut* (Prague, 1964) [incl. lists of operatic and concert repertory and discography]
E. Kopecký and V. Pospíšil: *Slavní pěvci Národního divadla* [Famous Singers of the National Theatre] (Prague, 1968), 189ff
Národní divadlo a jeho předchůdci [The National Theatre and its Predecessors] (Prague, 1988), 30ff [incl. list of operatic repertory and discography]

ALENA NĚMCOVÁ

Blackburn, Maurice (*b* Quebec City, 22 May 1914; *d* Montreal, 28 March 1988). Canadian composer. He studied at Laval University (1937–9), and privately in Montreal with Claude Champagne and Georges-Emile Tanguay. At the New England Conservatory in Boston (1939–41) he studied with Quincy Porter and Francis Findlay. Later he was a pupil of Nadia Boulanger in Paris (1946–8). Blackburn had a long career as a composer at the National Film Board of Canada between 1942 and 1978 and wrote music for more than a hundred films. In 1954–5 he returned to Paris to study composition and also worked with Pierre Schaeffer's Groupe de Recherches de Musique Concrète, at the RTF. He wrote his comic opera *Une mesure de silence* ('Silent Measures'; 1, M. Morisset-Blackburn) there in 1955. The plot, set in Montreal in about 1910, revolves around a wife's scheme to overcome her husband's stinginess. The opera, televised by the CBC on 21 April 1956, had its first stage performance at the Eaton Auditorium in Toronto on 17 November 1956. His second opera, *Pirouette* (1, Morisset-Blackburn), commissioned by Jeunesses Musicales du Canada, concerns the adventures of three Canadian music students who meet by chance in Rome; it was first performed at the Orford Art Centre in 1960, and given in a double bill with *Une mesure de silence* on a national tour. Blackburn has also written a ballet, *Rose latulippe* (1953), and incidental dramatic music. His music is spontaneous, with vibrant rhythm, colour and design, and shows the influence of early 20th-century French music, particularly that of Honegger and Poulenc.

*

EMC (D. Allaire)
J. Kraglund: 'Two Canadian Operas', *Canadian Music Journal*, i/2 (1956–7), 43–6

RUTH PINCOE

Blackham, Joyce (*b* Rotherham, 1 Jan 1934). English mezzo-soprano. She studied in London, making her début in 1955 with Sadler's Wells Opera as Olga (*Yevgeny Onegin*) and singing with the company until 1973, as Dorabella, Rosina, the Composer (*Ariadne auf Naxos*), Offenbach's Helen and Boulotte, Rosalind, which she created in *The Mines of Sulphur* (1965), Carmen and Preziosilla (which she also sang at the Deutsche Oper, Berlin). Her roles for the WNO included Cherubino, Rosina and Amneris. Having made her Covent Garden début in 1958 as Esmeralda (*The Bartered Bride*) she returned in 1974 as Maddalena (*Rigoletto*). Her rich-toned voice, especially powerful in the middle register, together with an attractive appearance, made her a magnificent interpreter of Carmen.

ELIZABETH FORBES

Black Patti. *See* JONES, SISSIERETTA.

Blackstone, Tsianina Redfeather [Evans, Florence] (*b* Oklahoma Indian Territory, ? 13 Dec 1882; *d* San Diego, 10 Jan 1985). American Indian (Cherokee/Creek) mezzo-soprano. After study (?1910–13) in Denver with Edward B. Fleck (piano) and John 'J. C.' Wilcox (voice), she embarked with Charles Wakefield Cadman on a 14-year series of immensely popular concert tours (about 400 concerts) devoted to American Indian music. Normally included were songs from Carlos Troyer's opera *Zuñiana* (yet to be performed in full) and several arrangements, which Cadman termed 'idealizations', of authentic melodies he had collected. During this same period, Blackstone sang leading roles in major productions of operas featuring music based on Native American melodies and librettos on related subjects, including the title role in Cadman's *Shanewis*, loosely based on her life story and in which she made her operatic début (5 December 1924, Denver), Wildflower in Cadman's *The Sunset Trail* (1924, Denver) and Wiwaste in S. Earle Blakeslee's *Legend of Wiwaste* (1927, Los Angeles, Hollywood Bowl). Thereafter, she retired from the stage to devote her life to improving American Indian education.

*

T. [Blackstone]: *Where Trails have Led Me* (Santa Fe, 2/1970)

A. D. Palmer: 'Tsianina Blackstone: a Chapter in the History of the American Indian in Opera', *Liberal Arts Review*, no.7 (1979), 40–51

A. DEAN PALMER

Blagoevgrad. Town in Bulgaria. The centre of a region rich in folklore, in recent decades it has become a cultural focal point in the south-western part of the country. Opera performances have been given since 1972 under the successive company names Mladezhka Opera (Youth Opera), Kamerna Mladezhka Opera (Chamber Youth Opera) and Mladezhka Opera za Vsichki (Youth Opera for All), with the local première of Haydn's *Lo speziale* in 1977 on the stage of the Blagoevgrad Dramatichen Teatar (Drama Theatre) marking the first maturity of opera in the town. Initially the soloists were amateurs and graduates of the state conservatory in Sofia; later they were more experienced singers. The staff's professionalism has been greatly aided by cooperation with the conductors Mihail Angelov, Emil Tabakov, Kamen Goleminov and Nevena Tomanova and the directors Mihail Hadjimishev, Nikolai Nikolov and others. The repertory consists almost exclusively of operas performed for the first time in Bulgaria, from works by Gluck, Haydn, Monteverdi, Purcell, Donizetti and Galuppi to some by Stravinsky, Alexander Holminov and Menotti.

*

R. Biks: *Bulgarski operen teatar*, ii (Sofia, 1985)

MAGDALENA MANOLOVA

Blaise, Adolphe Benoît (*d* ?Paris, 1772). French composer. He was a bassoonist at the Comédie-Italienne by 1737, when (according to the *Mercure de France*) he arranged music for Carolet's *Le petit maistre*. In 1743 he was *chef de l'orchestre* at the Foire St Laurent, and the next year he took a similar post at the Foire St Germain. Blaise continued as bassoonist for the Comédie-Italienne, composing and arranging *ariettes*, divertissements, vaudevilles and dances for altogether 44 parodies, ballet pantomimes, comic operas and a *spectacle à machines* presented there between 1737 and 1769. He was the orchestra's *maître de musique* (1753–60) and composer (1762–6). He retired in 1767.

The scoring of the popular *ariettes* for Favart's *Annette et Lubin*, first performed at a wedding in January 1762 and at the Comédie-Italienne the following month, is by Blaise; numerous 18th-century French song collections contain *ariettes* from the work. The version of Favart's *Isabelle et Gertrude*, published in 1765, with music by Blaise (except for three Gluck *airs*) was also successful. Some criticized Blaise's music as plain and weak, but others praised the way it fitted the verse and kept pace with the dialogue. The work played in Paris for more than 20 years; by 1767 there was a German adaptation using Blaise's music, and it was given as far afield as Moscow. Grimm wrote of *Isabelle et Gertrude*: 'There is nothing to be said about the music: it consists of chansons – little *airs* that do not merit that name; and as soon as M. Blaise attempts to raise himself above the poetry, the music becomes wretched'. Contemporary accounts in the *Mercure de France*, however, claimed Blaise was 'known for his other good works' and that his music was 'always distinctive'. The hundreds of performances at the Comédie-Italienne including music by him attest to his success. *Le feu de la ville*, a *cantatille*, was published in 1739, and another, *Le coucher du soleil*, without date; some of his songs and other items were included in contemporary anthologies.

first performed in Paris at the Comédie-Italienne (Hôtel de Bourgogne) unless otherwise stated

bp – *ballet pantomime* c – *comédie*
oc – *opéra comique* p – *parodie*
cmda – *comédie mêlée d'ariettes*

Annette et Lubin (cmda, 1, Favart, M.-J.-B. Favart and J.-B. Lourdet et Santerre), 15 Feb 1762 (Paris, 1763)

Isabelle et Gertrude, ou Les sylphes supposés (c, 1, C. S. Favart), 14 Aug 1765, excerpts with lib. (Paris, 1765)

Le trompeur trompé, ou La rencontre imprévue (oc, 1, J.-J. Vadé and N.-E. Freméry), 9 Aug 1767

La rosière de Salency (oc, 3, Favart), Fontainebleau, 25 Oct 1769, excerpts with lib. (Paris, 1769); collab. Duni, Philidor, Monsigny and van Swieten

Music by or attributed to Blaise in: Le petit maistre (p, D. Carolet), 9 Feb 1737; La conspiration manquée (p, 1, J.-A. Romagnesi and A. F. Riccoboni), 5 May 1738; Les filets de Vulcain (bp, Riccoboni), 5 May 1738; Orphée [from Les Muses] (bp, E. Morand and Riccoboni), 12 Dec 1738; L'amant Prothée (c, 3, J. de La Fond and Romagnesi), 5 March 1739; Les caprices du coeur et de l'esprit (c, 3, L.-F. Lisle de la Drevetiere), 25 June 1739, *F-Pn*; Les muses rivales (bp, Riccoboni), 17 Sept 1739; Talents à la mode (c, 3, L. de Boissy), 17 Sept 1739

Les rendez-vous nocturnes (bp, Riccoboni), 28 May 1740; Les jeunes mariés (oc, 1, C.-S. Favart and Parmentier), Paris, Foire St Laurent, 1 July 1740, collab. Rochar [rev. Foire St Germain, 16 March 1755]; Amadis (parodie mêlée des airs, 1, Romagnesi and Riccoboni), 19 Dec 1740, *Pn*; Alcyone (parodie mêlée des airs, 1, Romagnesi), 26 Oct 1741, *Pn*; Hippolyte et Aricie (p, 1, Favart), 11 Oct 1742; La ridicule supposée (c, 1, B.-C. Fagan), 12 Jan 1743, *Pn*; Le sylphe (c, 1, G.-F. Poullain de Saint-Foix), 5 Feb 1743

Les deux Basiles, ou Le Roman (c, 3, Riccoboni, J.-F. Deshayes [Dehesse] and M. Guyot de Merville), 22 May 1743; La déroute de Paméla (c, 1, C. Godard d'Aucort), 23 Dec 1743; Acajou (oc, 3, Favart), 18 March 1744, excerpts with lib. (Paris, 1763); Coraline magicienne (c), 2 July 1744; Le génie de la France, ou L'amour de la patrie (c, 1, Minet *fils* and Parvi), 21 Nov 1744; Le siège de Grenade (c, 5, M. J. Riccoboni and Chiavarelli), 2 Jan 1745; Thesée (p, 1, Favart), Foire St Germain, 17 Feb 1745, excerpts with lib. (Paris, 1745)

Compliment, ou Impromptu des acteurs (c, 1, C. F. Panard and A. F. Sticoti), 26 April 1745; La fille, la veuve et la femme (p, 3, P. Laujon and Parvi), 21 Aug 1745; Ariane abandonnée par Thesée et secourue par Bacchus (bp, 1, Dehesse), 25 Feb 1747; L'arcadie enchantée (c), 13 July 1747; Le pédant (bp, 1, Dehesse), Versailles, 5 Feb 1748; L'année merveilleuse (c, 1, P. Rousseau), 19 July 1748; Les fées rivales (c, Veronese), 18 Sept 1748; Le bal (bp, 1, Dehesse), 26 April 1749; La comète (c, 1, Boissy), 11 July 1749, *Pn*; Les savoyards, ou Les marmottes (bp, 1, Dehesse), 30 Aug 1749

Les quatre âges en récréation (divertissement, Dehesse), Versailles, 11 Dec 1749; Les berceaux (bp, 1, Dehesse), 30 July 1750; L'histoire des amours de Cupidon et de Psiche (spectacle à machines, 5, ?Bazin), 1751; La vallée de Montmorency, ou Les amours villageois (bp, 1, Favart), 25 Feb 1752; Les bergers de qualité (p, 1, Gondot), 5 June 1752; La frivolité (c, 1, Boissy), 23 Jan 1753, excerpts with lib. (Paris, 1753); Le Colin-Maillard (bp, 1, Dehesse and A. Pitrot), 16 June 1754; La caprice amoureux, ou Ninette à la cour [after V. Ciampi: Bertoldo in corte] (cmda, 3, Favart), 12 Feb 1755 (Paris, 1755) [rev. (2), 12 March 1756 (Paris, 1759)]

*

J.-A. J. Desboulmiers: *Histoire anecdotique et raisonnée du Théâtre italien, despuis son rétablissement en France jusqu'à l'année 1769* (Paris, 1769, repr. 1868)

A. d'Origny: *Annales du Théâtre italien despuis son origine jusqu'à ce jour* (Paris, 1788)

M. Tourneux, ed.: *Correspondance littéraire, philosophique et critique par Grimm, Diderot, Raynal, Meister, etc.* (Paris, 1877–82), vi
G. Cucuel: *Les créateurs de l'opéra-comique français* (Paris, 1914)
A. Iacuzzi: *The European Vogue of Favart: the Diffusion of the Opéra Comique* (New York, 1932)
C. D. Brenner: *A Bibliographical List of Plays in the French Language 1700–1789* (Berkeley, 1947)
——: *The Théâtre Italien: its Repertory 1716–1793* (Berkeley, 1961)
C. R. Barnes: *The Théâtre de la Foire (Paris, 1697–1762): its Music and Composers* (diss., U. of Southern California, 1965)
JEFFREY R. REHBACH

Blaise et Babet [*Blaise et Babet, ou La suite des trois fermiers* ('Blaise and Babet, or The Sequel to the Three Farmers')]. *Comédie mêlée d'ariettes* in two acts by NICOLAS DEZÈDE to a libretto by Jacques Marie Boutet de Monvel; Versailles, 4 April 1783 (Paris, Comédie-Italienne, Salle Favart, 30 June 1783).

After mutual accusations of disloyalty, the marriage between Blaise (tenor) and Babet (soprano) is called off by his father, Delorme (bass-baritone), and her mother, Alix (soprano). Mathurin (baritone) reads a letter from Belval (baritone) saying that he has unexpectedly won the trial mentioned in *LES TROIS FERMIERS* (1777), and that he would like to pay back the money which the farmers gave him. He also wishes to make a financial gift for the marriage of Blaise and Babet and other couples. Belval invites the villagers to his chateau. In talking to her father, Jacques (bass-baritone), Babet withdraws her accusations against Blaise. Belval discovers that the jealousy of the two lovers was a misunderstanding. He reconciles Blaise with Babet and the wedding can be celebrated together with Mathurin's birthday.

In comparison with *Les trois fermiers* Dezède's style has become much more dramatic, for example through a more conspicuous use of tremolos. The wind instruments are used much more often to give a fuller sound, and the employment of instruments and dynamics is often motivated either by the text or the action. The only proper dramatic scene set to music, the reconciliation of Blaise and Babet ('Avance un pas', Act 2 scene xi) appears to have played a crucial part in the success of the opera. This was partly due to the acting abilities of Louise Rosalie Dugazon, but Dezède's original development of thematic material in this scene must also have contributed to its favourable reception. *Blaise et Babet* was performed throughout Europe and it was given by the Opéra-Comique in Paris until 1827. MICHAEL FEND

Blaise le savetier ('Blaise the Cobbler'). *Opéra comique* in one act by FRANÇOIS-ANDRÉ DANICAN PHILIDOR to a libretto by MICHEL-JEAN SEDAINE after Jean de La Fontaine's story; Paris, Opéra-Comique (Théâtre de la Foire St Germain), 9 March 1759.

Blaise (tenor) and Blaisine (soprano) quarrel over his improvidence and their debts. He wants to go to Mathurin's where his cousin Nicaise is to be married; she wants him to work. Their argument continues while two bailiff's clerks take stock of their furniture; during a quintet the fury of the landlady, Mme Pince (soprano), unites the couple. Blaise is penitent and evolves a scheme. Hope of Blaisine's sexual favours induces M. Pince (tenor) to relinquish the IOU for the rent, but Blaise's entrance forces him to hide in the wardrobe, where he overhears Mme Pince making immoral overtures to Blaise. The older couple, each persuaded that the other has received the money, part in confusion. The printed score ends with the next duet, but the libretto includes scenes with dancing for the wedding of Nicaise.

Philidor's first complete *opéra comique* combines well-turned *ariettes* with his usual flair for ensemble writing, forming an excellent farce. Stylized laughter, sobbing and trembling anticipate later onomatopoeic effects, and the characterization, if simple, is already acute. JULIAN RUSHTON

Blake, David (Leonard) (*b* London, 2 Sept 1936). English composer. A formative influence on his development was his experience of Brechtian theatre with the Berlin Ensemble and of Felsenstein's productions at the Komische Oper when he was studying composition with Hanns Eisler in 1960. Although his first opera, *Toussaint* (3, A. Ward; London, Coliseum, 29 Sept 1977), was not completed until 16 years later, the East Berlin experience was clearly an important factor in determining its shape and character. One of the most ambitious works commissioned by the ENO, it is epic theatre in the sense that its subject is not so much an episode in the life of its titular hero as a decade of politics, revolution and war – with, moreover, an ironic commentator to address the audience directly and to effect the authentic alienation.

Having chosen to combine creative work with an academic career at York University, where he began teaching in 1963, Blake has not been prolific in any area of composition. As *Toussaint* demonstrates, however, his music is not limited in either expressive scope or stylistic variety. Always a lyric composer, he has been particularly successful in writing for voices and, as his melodic imagination and harmonic invention have freed themselves from serial restraints, his inspiration has become more spontaneous and more directly communicative.

If Blake's second opera, *The Plumber's Gift* (2; London, Coliseum, 25 May 1989), also commissioned by the ENO, proved disappointing in comparison with *Toussaint*, the fault is in the words rather than the music. Set in a seaside guest house, John Birtwhistle's libretto offers the composer little more than a television comedy situation together with a mannered and overlong pastoral interlude in the middle. Blake's talent for parody and pastiche (already abundantly evident in his school musical *It's a Small War* in 1962), his ear for the inflections of prosaic as well as poetic language, and even his considerable lyrical gift cannot redeem the librettist's clumsiness in construction, characterization and political comment.

See also TOUSSAINT.

G. Larner: 'Toussaint: David Blake Talks to Gerald Larner', *MT*, cxviii (1977), 721–3
GERALD LARNER

Blake, Rockwell (*b* Plattsburgh, NY, 10 Jan 1951). American tenor. While still at school he began his studies with Renata Carisio Booth, who remained his principal teacher. After apprenticeships with the Goldovsky and Wolf Trap opera companies, he made his début with the Washington Opera in 1976 as Lindoro in *L'italiana in Algeri*. In 1978 he was the first winner of the Richard Tucker Foundation Award. The following year he made his New York City Opera début in *Le comte Ory*, and he has subsequently sung widely in Europe and the USA. His Metropolitan Opera début was in 1981, again as Lindoro, and since 1983 he has appeared regularly at the Rossini Festival at Pesaro. His repertory includes some 30 roles, mostly by Bellini, Donizetti, Mozart and Rossini. Although the range (extending to *f″*) and prodigious flexibility of his voice are widely acknowledged, its penetrating timbre, and his unusually muscular approach to this repertory, have provoked controversy. CORI ELLISON

Blakeslee, S(amuel) Earle (*b* Oberlin, OH, 2 Nov 1883; *d* San Luis Obispo, CA, 9 March 1972). American composer. After completing basic studies in Oberlin and Denver, he received the bachelor's degree in music at Pomona College, Claremont, California, in 1908. In 1916 he joined the music faculty at Chaffey College, Ontario, California, where he remained until his retirement in 1954. Blakeslee's only opera, *The Legend of Wiwaste* [*Wewahste*], based on a Dakota Sioux legend dealing with tribal customs of betrothal and marriage before the coming of the white man, is cast in late 19th-century Romantic style and reflects in its large orchestral resources the influence of Puccini and Wagner. It also embodies many characteristics of American Indian music: Indian melodies, rhythmic figures inspired by Indian drumming patterns, choruses in parallel octaves, pentatonic scales and orchestral accompaniment in open 4ths and 5ths. First performed in Ontario, California, on 25 April 1924, the opera was revived in 1927 (Los Angeles, Hollywood Bowl), 1966 (as *Red Cloud*) and 1970. The best-known aria from this work is Wiwaste's 'Far Away in Northland'.

'Blakeslee's New Opera', *Pacific Coast Musician* (3 May 1924)
'Indians Dance to Blakeslee Opera Rhythms', *MusAm*, xlvi/8 (1927), 11 [on *The Legend of Wiwaste*]
A. D. Palmer: 'Tsianina Blackstone: a Chapter in the History of the American Indian in Opera', *Liberal Arts Review*, no.7 (1979), 40–51
A. DEAN PALMER

Blanc, Ernest (*b* Sanary-sur-Mer, 1 Nov 1923). French baritone. A student at the conservatories in Toulon and Paris, he made his début in Marseilles as Tonio (1950). At the Paris Opéra (1954–80) he sang a wide variety of roles including Rigoletto, Theogène (which he sang in the première of Barraud's *Numance*, 1955), Valentin, Amonasro, Germont, Renato, Wolfram, Enrico Ashton, Michele and Andrey Shchelkalov. His large, dark, sensuous voice established him from the start as outstanding. He was soon heard in Milan, Vienna and London, but the turning-point of his career came in 1958, when he sang a remarkable Telramund at Bayreuth. He made his American début in 1959 at Chicago as Escamillo (a role he recorded for Beecham) and his British début in 1960 as Riccardo at Glyndebourne, where he also sang Don Giovanni. He sang Rigoletto at Covent Garden (1961) and appeared in Milan, Vienna, Brussels and throughout France in a repertory that included Zurga, Scarpia, Luna, Massenet's Herod, Ourrias, the Father (*Louise*), Golaud, Bluebeard and the Count des Grieux. He could have had a longer international career, had he not preferred to stay in France. ANDRÉ TUBEUF

Blanc, Jonny (*b* Lessebo, 10 July 1939). Swedish tenor. He studied in Stockholm, making his début in 1962 as a baritone at Göteborg. He made his tenor début in 1967 as Grigory at the Royal Opera, Stockholm. He created Martin in Braein's *Anne Pedersdottor* (1971, Oslo) and the Narrator in Werle's *Tintomara* (1973, Stockholm). His repertory included Florestan, Siegmund, Don José, Hermann (*The Queen of Spades*), Cavaradossi and Števa (*Jenůfa*), which he sang at the 1974 Edinburgh Festival. The bright timbre of his voice enabled him to sing lyric as well as dramatic roles, while a compelling stage presence brought him success as Jimmy Mahoney in Weill's *Mahagonny*, Gustavus III in the Swedish version of *Un ballo in maschera* and the King in G. J. Vogler's *Gustaf Adolf och Ebba Brahe* (1973, Drottningholm). In 1986 he became artistic director of the Municipal Theatre of Malmö. ELIZABETH FORBES

Blanck, Hubert de. *See* DE BLANCK, HUBERT.

Bland [née Romanzini], **Maria Theresa** (*b c*1769; *d* London, 15 Jan 1838). English soprano of Italian Jewish descent. She sang in public from the age of four and appeared in Charles Dibdin's child company at the Royal Circus, at other London theatres and in Dublin and Liverpool. In 1786 she was a success at Sadler's Wells as La Petite Savoyarde in *The Gates of Calais* and that autumn began her long career at Drury Lane in Grétry's *Richard Coeur-de-lion*. She created roles in nearly all Storace's operas and Michael Kelly wrote of the 'great simplicity and truth' of her singing of 'A little bird sang on a spray' as the Welsh girl in *The Cherokee*. She was short and swarthy and so debarred from romantic opera roles, but Mount Edgcumbe admired her 'pure Italian taste' when she deputized for Banti in Italian opera in 1798. Her marriage in 1790 to the actor George Bland was short-lived and she had several illegitimate children. Her mental stability was affected by the death of a child and a year after her last stage appearance (June 1822) she suffered a complete breakdown. In 1825 Oxberry wrote: 'As a singer, we never heard her equal; she had all the requisites for a first-rate vocalist – compass, power, feeling, taste, flexibility, and sweetness'.

Her son James (1798–1861), a bass, sang in Planché's extravaganzas. Her son Charles (1802–after 1834), a tenor, had an unsuccessful stage career, making his début as Don Carlos in *The Duenna* in 1824; in 1826 he played the title role in the première of Weber's *Oberon*, but neither his singing nor his acting found favour.

BDA; *DNB* (W. B. Squire); *LS*
A. Pasquin [pseud. of J. Williams]: *The Children of Thespis*, i (London, 13/1792)
J. Roach: *Authentic Memoirs of the Green Room* (London, 1796)
The Thespian Dictionary (London, 1802, 2/1805)
C. H. Wilson: *The Myrtle and Vine* (London, 1802)
R. Mount Edgcumbe: *Musical Reminiscences* (London, 1824, 4/1834)
W. Oxberry: 'Memoir of Mrs. Bland', *Dramatic Biography*, i (1825), 161–7
The Harmonicon, iv (1826), 42, 108, 154
M. Kelly: *Reminiscences of the King's Theatre* (London, 1826, 2/1826); ed. R. Fiske (London, 1975)
W. Robson: *The Old Play-Goer* (London, 1846)
J. R. Planché: *Recollections and Reflections*, i (London, 1872)
J. Benedict: *Carl Maria von Weber* (London, 1881)
R. Fiske: *English Theatre Music in the Eighteenth Century* (London, 1973, 2/1986)
T. J. Walsh: *Opera in Dublin 1705–1797* (Dublin, 1973)
OLIVE BALDWIN, THELMA WILSON

Blangini, (Giuseppe Marco Maria) Felice (*b* Turin, 18 Nov 1781; *d* Paris, 18 Dec 1841). French composer, singing teacher and tenor of Italian birth. As a boy he sang in the Turin Cathedral choir and was a pupil of Bernardo Ottani. Arriving in Paris in 1799, he became fashionable as a singer, composer of salon music and singing teacher. He made his début as an opera composer at the Théâtre Feydeau in 1802 and at the

Opéra in 1806. In 1805 he became *maestro di cappella* to the Duke of Saxe-Coburg in Munich; he was also in the service of Pauline Borghese, Napoleon's sister, who had an affair with him. In 1809, Napoleon transferred him to Kassel, where he was director of the theatre, *maestro di cappella* and master of chamber music to the new King of Westphalia, Jérome Buonaparte, until the latter's fall. Back in Paris in 1814, he was superintendent of the royal chapel, court composer and professor of singing at the Conservatoire. He was a member of the Légion d'honneur and received an aristocratic title, became a French citizen and married a banker's daughter. After the Revolution of 1830 he lost his court appointments, and as a musician was overtaken by the rise of Romanticism. His autobiography, edited by Maxime de Villamorest, was published as *Souvenirs de Blangini* (Paris, 1834).

Blangini composed nearly 30 operas, mostly *opéras comiques*, as well as sacred works and vocal chamber music; he claimed, and has subsequently been credited with, the invention of the vocal nocturne. Many of his stage works were unsuccessful and received few performances. They are written in a light, almost banal, style, and although several *romances* are appealing, there is generally much artificiality in his harmonic language and formal structure.

opéras comiques unless otherwise stated

PFE – *Paris, Théâtre Feydeau*
PN – *Paris, Théâtre des Nouveautés*

La fausse duègne (3, G. Montcloux d'Epinay), PFE, 24 June 1802 [completion of Della-Maria's opera]
Zélie et Terville, ou Chimère et réalité (1, E. Aignan), PFE, 6 Jan 1803
Encore un tour de Calife (1), in Ger. as Noch ein Streich des Kalifen, Munich, 28 June 1805
Nephtali, ou Les ammonites (op, 3, Aignan), Paris, Opéra, 15 April 1806 (Paris, 1806)
Le sacrifice d'Abraham (op, 3, Col. Saint-Marcel), Kassel, Hof, 14 Nov 1810, excerpt, pf acc. (Leipzig, 1811), duet (Leipzig, 1811)
Les femmes vengées (1, M.-J. Sedaine), PFE, 22 Oct 1811, song (Paris, 1811)
L'amour philosophe (2, Aignan), Kassel, Hof, aut. 1811
Le naufrage comique (2, Sedaine), Kassel, Hof, spr. 1812
La fée Urgèle (2, ? C.-S. Favart), Kassel, Hof, sum. 1812, ariette (Paris, *c*1815)
La princesse de Cachemire (3, Sedaine), Kassel, Hof, aut. 1812
Trajano in Dacia (os, 2, G. Rossi), Munich, Hof, 14 July 1814
La sourde-muette (3, J. de Valmalette), PFE, 26 July 1815
La comtesse de Lamarck, ou Tout par amour (3, Saint-Cyr and Armand d'Artois), PFE, 16 April 1818
La fête des souvenirs (intermède, 2, T. M. Du Mersan), PFE, 16 April 1818
Le jeune oncle (1, H. A. Advenier-Fontenille), PFE, 10 April 1821, trio (Paris, 1821)
Le duc d'Aquitaine (1, Achille d'Artois, M. Théaulon and A.-J. Le Bouthillier Rancé), PFE, 1823, excerpts (Paris, *c*1825)
Le projet de pièce (1, Mély-Janin [J. M. Janin]), PFE, 4 Nov 1825
Le Saint-Henri (1, Advenier-Fontenille), Paris, Court, 1825
L'intendant (1, Mély-Janin), Paris, Court, 1826
Le coureur de veuves (2, M. J. Brisset), PN, 1 March 1827
Le jeu de cache-cache, ou La fiancée (2, Achille d'Artois), PN, 25 May 1827
Le morceau d'ensemble (1, Armand d'Artois), PN, 19 Nov 1827
L'anneau de la fiancée (3, Brisset), PN, 28 June 1828
Le chanteur de romances (2, Armand and Achille d'Artois), Paris, ?Variétés, 5 Nov 1830
La marquise de Brinvilliers [1 duet only] (drame lyrique, 3, E. Scribe and Castil-Blaze [F.-H.-J. Blaze]), Paris, OC (Ventadour), 31 Oct 1831 (Paris, 1831), collab. Auber, Batton, H.-M. Berton, A. Boieldieu, Carafa, Cherubini, Hérold and Paer
Un premier pas (1, E. Mennechet and J. F. Roger), Paris, OC (Bourse), 24 Nov 1832
Les gondoliers (2, E. Champeaux and A. Bréant de Fontenay), Paris, OC (Bourse), 19 April 1833

Music in: Figaro, ou Le jour des noces, 1827

Unperf.: Les fêtes lacédémoniennes, *c*1807; Inès de Castro, *c*1810; Marie Thérèse à Presbourg, ou La naissance du Duc de Bordeaux, 1820 (4, Berard), vs (Paris, 1820); Le vieux de la montagne (4), written for the Opéra

*

DBI; *FétisB*
Review of 'Le sacrifice d'Abraham', *AMZ*, xiii (1811), 137–42, 159–66
Review of 'Trajano in Dacia', *AMZ*, xvi (1814), 584
A. Houssaye: 'Blangini', *Revue de Paris*, new ser., i (1842), 37–52
M. Zenger: *Geschichte der Münchener Oper* (Munich, 1923), 85–6, 133, 135

EMILIA ZANETTI

Blank, Allan (*b* New York, 27 Dec 1925). American composer. He studied at the Juilliard School, New York University (BA 1948), University of Minnesota (MA in composition, 1950) and Columbia Teachers College (1954–7). He taught instrumental music in New York high schools between 1956 and 1965, and after further teaching posts became professor of Music at Virginia Commonwealth University in 1978. He has received numerous grants and awards for his work.

Blank has composed four operas, mixing comic and serious themes. In *Aria da capo*, a property dispute between two antagonists (read by Blank as an anti-war allegory) is framed by episodes of stylized, *commedia dell'arte* narration. *Excitement at the Circus* (1969), a children's opera, has been extensively performed in schools in New Jersey and Virginia. *The Magic Bonbons*, adapted by the composer from a short fantasy by L. Frank Baum, presents its protagonist with a sequence of magical talents leading to a career in vaudeville. *The Noise*, adapted from writings of Boris Vian, invokes existentialist themes in a surreal setting.

Aria da capo, 1958–60 (chamber op, E. St Vincent Millay), unperf.
Excitement at the Circus, 1968 (children's op, 1, I. A. Leitner), Patterson, NJ, spr. 1969
The Magic Bonbons, 1980–83 (8 scenes, A. Blank, after L. F. Baum), unperf.
The Noise, 1985 (chamber op, 2, G. C. Hopper, after B. Vian: *Les bâtisseurs d'empire*), Act 1, Richmond, Virginia Commonwealth U., April 1986

MARTIN BRODY

Blankenburg, Heinz Horst (*b* New York, 15 Oct 1931). American baritone. He made his début in 1955 as Moralès (*Carmen*) at San Francisco, where his later roles included Paolo (*Simon Boccanegra*), Ping, Fra Melitone, Beckmesser and Schaunard. At Glyndebourne (1957–70) he sang Papageno, Harlequin (*Ariadne auf Naxos*), the title role of Busoni's *Arlecchino*, Raimbaud (*Le comte Ory*), Mozart's Figaro and Pacuvio (*La pietra del paragone*). Engaged for many years at the Hamburg Staatsoper, in 1966 he took part in the first performance of Schuller's *The Visitation* there and in the British première of *Die Frau ohne Schatten* with the Hamburg company at Sadler's Wells. He sang at Los Angeles, Amsterdam and Vancouver; his repertory included Leporello, Don Giovanni and Sid (*Albert Herring*). An excellent comic actor, he used his light, flexible voice with considerable artistry.

ELIZABETH FORBES

Blankenheim, Toni (*b* Cologne, 12 Dec 1921). German bass-baritone. He studied in Stuttgart and Cologne, making his début in 1947 at Frankfurt as Mozart's Figaro. In 1950 he was engaged at the Hamburg Staatsoper, where he remained for over 30 years. At Bayreuth (1954–60) he sang Beckmesser, Kothner, Klingsor and Donner. He appeared in Vienna, Berlin, Munich, Milan, San Francisco, New York and London, where he sang Wozzeck and Dr Schön in the British première of *Lulu* with the Hamburg company at Sadler's Wells (1962). His other roles included Leporello, Don Alfonso, Pizarro, Alberich and John the Baptist (*Salome*). He took part in the first performances of Henze's *Der Prinz von Homburg* (1960), Krenek's *Der goldene Bock* and Einem's *Der Zerrissene* (1964), Goehr's *Arden must die* (1967), in which he sang Arden, Kelemen's *Der Belagerungszustand* (1970), and Constant's *Candide* (1971) at Hamburg, and Orff's *Prometheus* (1968) at Stuttgart. He sang Schigolch in the three-act *Lulu* (1979) at the Paris Opéra and Juhani Puntti in Kalevi Aho's monologue *The Birthday* at Hamburg Studio (1982). A powerful singing actor, he had a strong, dark-toned voice. ELIZABETH FORBES

Blankenship, Rebecca (*b* New York, 24 March 1954). American soprano, daughter of William Blankenship. She studied in New York, making her début in 1984 at Ulm as Idamantes, a mezzo role. She made her soprano début in 1986 as Katerina Izmaylova at Basle, where she also sang First Lady (*Die Zauberflöte*), Electra (*Idomeneo*), Leonora (*Il trovatore*) and the Female Chorus (*The Rape of Lucretia*). She has appeared in Berlin, Vienna, Liège, Stuttgart, Bregenz and Berne. Her repertory includes Leonore (*Fidelio*), Martha (*Tiefland*), Elsa, Senta (at the Bregenz Festival, 1989), Foreign Princess (*Rusalka*), Ariadne, and Marie (*Wozzeck*). She made her American début in 1990 at San Francisco as Sieglinde. She has a strong, vibrant voice, dramatic ability and a striking appearance. ELIZABETH FORBES

Blankenship, William (*b* Gatesville, TX, 7 March 1928). American tenor, father of Rebecca Blankenship. He studied at the Juilliard School and in Vienna, making his début in 1956 at Klagenfurt. He was engaged at Brunswick, Mannheim, Berne, Munich (from 1965) and the Vienna Volksoper and Staatsoper. He also sang at Aix-en-Provence (1967), San Diego (1968) and as Phoebus (Purcell's *The Fairy-Queen*) at Bregenz (1972). His repertory included Don Ottavio, Tamino, Belmonte, Ferrando, Edgardo, Ernesto, Lionel, the Duke, Lensky, Hoffmann, Henry (*Die schweigsame Frau*), Camille (*Dantons Tod*) and the Painter (*Lulu*). An excellent actor with a fine presence, he had a lyric voice especially suited to Mozart. ELIZABETH FORBES

Blasius [Blassius], **(Matthieu-)Frédéric** (*b* Lauterbourg, 24 April 1758; *d* Versailles, 1829). French conductor and composer. Like his contemporaries Chapelle, Chartrain and Vandenbroek, he made his Parisian début at the Concert Spirituel (in 1784). He was leader and conductor of the orchestra of the Opéra-Comique from 1790 to 1801 and from 1804 to 1818, but he also worked for the Théâtre de la Porte-Saint-Martin and the Gaîté, where in November 1801 he conducted the first performance in Paris of *Die Entführung* in the original language, given by Elmenreich's German company. He was appointed violin professor at the Paris Conservatoire in 1795 and held various other official posts during the Revolution and the Consulate. His first opera, *La paysanne supposée*, failed because of its libretto, but *L'amour hermite* was successful enough to be published. This work is a pastoral, conceived in the tradition of the Académie Royale de Musique, with a choreographic *divertissement* and a sleep scene both of which are typical of serious opera of the period.

all first performed in Paris

La paysanne supposée, ou La fête de la moisson (cmda, 3, C. Dubois), Italien, 28 Aug 1788

L'amour hermite (pièce anacréontique mêlée d'ariettes, 1, P. Desriaux), Beaujolais, 31 Jan 1789 (Paris, n.d.)

Le Pelletier de Saint-Fargeau, ou Le premier martyr de la République française (trait historique, 2, A.-L. Bertin d'Antilly), OC (Favart), 23 Feb 1793

Le congrès des rois (cmda, 3, Desmaillot [A. F. Eve]), OC (Favart), 26 Feb 1794, collab. Dalayrac, Grétry, Méhul and 8 others

Africo et Menzola (mélodrame), 1798

Don Pèdre et Zulika (mélodrame), Gaîté, 1802

Fernand, ou Les Maures (3, A.-J. Coffin-Rony), OC (Favart), 11 Feb 1805

Adelson et Salvini (mélodrame)

Doubtful: Les trois sultanes, ou Soliman Second (C.-S. Favart), OC (Favart), 25 Aug 1792

*

C. D. Brenner: *A Bibliographical List of Plays in the French Language, 1700–1789* (Ann Arbor, 1947)

C. L. McCormick: *Matthieu-Frédéric Blasius (1758–1829): a Biographical Sketch, Catalog of Works, and Critical Performance Edition of the 'Quatuor concertant' in F, op.1, no.1* (diss., Michigan State U., 1983)

N. Wild: *Dictionnaire des théâtres parisiens au XIXe siècle* (Paris, 1989) MICHEL NOIRAY

Blass, Robert (*b* New York, 27 Oct 1867; *d* Berlin, 3 Dec 1930). American bass of German parentage. He studied under Julius Stockhausen at Frankfurt, having been trained first as a violinist. His début in 1892 as King Henry in *Lohengrin* at Weimar led to engagements throughout Germany, and in 1900 to his first appearances at Covent Garden and the Metropolitan. In London, where he sang for four seasons, his roles included King Henry, Hagen, Pogner, Hunding and the Landgrave in *Tannhäuser*; he was also Dogberry in the première of Stanford's *Much Ado about Nothing* in 1901. At the Metropolitan he remained as a hard-working member of the company in every season until 1910, reappearing in 1920 to sing King Mark in English. His single Bayreuth season was in 1901, when he sang Gurnemanz and Hagen. From 1913 to 1919 he sang at the Deutsche Oper, Berlin, and taught there after his retirement. Although he appears not to have been highly rated at the Metropolitan ('stodgy' and 'thick-voiced' are descriptions quoted in Kolodin's history of the house), his few recordings show a voice of considerable beauty and a fine cello-like evenness of production.

J. B. STEANE

Blatný, Pavel (*b* Brno, 14 Sept 1931). Czech composer. He studied at the Brno Conservatory (1950–55) and with Bořkovec in Prague (1955–8), and in 1963 began work at Brno Television; in 1979 he was appointed to teach at the Janáček Academy of Musical Arts in Brno. His two mini-operas for children, known together as *Pohádky lesa* ('Fairy-Tales of the Wood'), composed for radio and television in a lucid neo-classical idiom with chamber-orchestra accompaniment, depict animals by witty melodic, rhythmic and instrumental means. The first, *Studánka* ('The Little Pool', composed 1959; Z. Malý), is a lyrical work about animals that save a forest pool from drying up; the second, *Domeček* ('The Little House', composed 1975; K. Bednář), is more dramatic and combines narration and singing. The vocal parts may be taken by either adults or children. *Fairy-Tales of the Wood* was broadcast on Czechoslovak Television in 1979. HELENA HAVLÍKOVÁ

Blau, Edouard [Stanislas-Viateur] (*b* Blois, 30 May 1836; *d* Paris, 7 Jan 1906). French librettist. He went to Paris at the age of 20 and began a career in the Assistance Publique administering social services; he finally gave it up in 1870, by which time he was making his name as a theatre journalist and a librettist. As was usual at that time he frequently collaborated with other writers, notably, in his early days, with Louis Gallet, a colleague in the Assistance Publique, and with his cousin Alfred Blau (the author, with Camille du Locle, of the text for Reyer's *Sigurd* of 1884 and, with Louis de Gramont, of Massenet's *Esclarmonde* of 1889). An adept versifier, Blau responded to a trend towards greater seriousness in opera, taking pains to devise librettos that could bear comparison with the major literary works on which they were based. For *Le Cid*, for instance, one of the acknowledged masterpieces of French classical drama, he drew on Guillén de Castro, the Spanish source to which Pierre Corneille had turned in the 17th century. Originally intended for Bizet, the libretto was set by Massenet, but did not find favour. Massenet's *Werther*, however, to a libretto after Goethe by Blau with P. Milliet and G. Hartmann, has remained in the repertory. In *Le roi d'Ys* and *Lancelot* Blau kept up with developments in taste by exploiting Celtic myth for operatic purposes.

selective list

Le chanteur florentin (opérette, with A. Blau), Duprato, 1866; *La chanson de l'étoile* (oc, with Blau), L. Gérôme, 1872; *La coupe du roi de Thulé* (with L. Gallet), Bizet, 1868–9 [unperf.] (E. Diaz, 1873); *Bathyle* (oc), W. Chaumet, 1877; *Belle lurette* (oc, with E. Blum and R. Toché), Offenbach, 1880; *Le chevalier Jean* (with Gallet), Joncières, 1885; *Le Cid* (with A. d'Ennery and Gallet), Massenet, 1885; *Le roi d'Ys*, Lalo, 1888; *Dante* (drame lyrique), Godard, 1890; *Zaïre* (with L. Besson), P. V. de la Nux, 1890; *Werther* (drame lyrique, with P. Milliet and G. Hartmann), Massenet, 1892; *La jacquerie* (with S. Arnaud), Lalo, completed by Coquard, 1895; *Beaucoup de bruit pour rien*, P. Puget, 1899; *Lancelot* (drame lyrique, with Gallet), Joncières, 1900

*

P. Dufay and others: *Un poète blasois: Edouard Blau (1836–1906)* (Blois, 1907)

CHRISTOPHER SMITH

Blavet, Michel (bap. Besançon, 13 March 1700; *d* Paris, 28 Oct 1768). French composer and flautist. The son of a turner, he taught himself several instruments, becoming accomplished on the bassoon and flute. Towards the end of 1723 he went to Paris in the entourage of Duke Charles-Eugène Lévis. Three years later he made his début at the Concert Spirituel, where he appeared (as a flautist) during the next 25 years more frequently than any other performer. About 1728 Blavet was in the service of the Prince of Carignan, and by 1731 he had transferred his allegiance to the Count of Clermont, with whom he maintained ties for the rest of his life. When he added to his other duties the posts of first flute in the Musique du Roi (1738) and at the Opéra (1740), Blavet's position in Parisian musical life was unrivalled.

Blavet's four stage works were written for the private theatre of the Count of Clermont's chateau at Berny; the pasticcio *Le jaloux corrigé* (1752) was also given six performances at the Paris Opéra on a double bill with Rousseau's *Le devin du village*. *Le jaloux corrigé* is made up of ten arias drawn from three intermezzos then popular in Paris: *La serva padrona*, *Il giocatore* and *Il maestro di musica*, all attributed to Pergolesi. The arias were parodied with new French texts, but only four were actually by Pergolesi; the others were by Orlandini, Buini, Caroli, Galuppi and Capelli. Blavet composed the italianate overture, the connecting recitatives and the French-style *divertissement* (seven dances and two vocal numbers). His innovation was to abandon for the first time the arioso recitative which the French had used since Lully. 'The recitative of this French intermezzo', reported the *Mercure de France*, 'is approximately in the style of Italian recitative, at least to the extent that the differences between the languages permitted it; and in spite of the almost universal bias of our nation against the Italian recitative, it did not appear that the spectators were extremely shocked by this first attempt'. Whatever the initial reception (Blavet's *divertissement* continued to be performed at the Opéra after the rest of the intermezzo had been dropped), *Le jaloux corrigé* and *Le devin du village* helped launch a new era of italianate music at the Opéra, and with it the Querelle des Bouffons.

Floriane, ou La grotte des spectacles (comédie-ballet), Chateau de Berny, 25 Aug 1752, *F-Pa*

Le jaloux corrigé (opéra bouffe with divertissement, 1, C. Collé), Chateau de Berny, 18 Nov 1752 (Paris, 1753), incl. music by Pergolesi, Galuppi, Orlandini, Buini, Caroli and Capelli

Les jeux olympiques (ballet héroïque, Henri-Charles, Count of Senneterre), Chateau de Berny, 25 Aug 1753, *Pa*

La fête de Cythère (1, A. de Laurès), Chateau de Berny, 19 Nov 1753, *Pa*

*

M. François de Neuf-Château: 'Eloge de M. Blavet', *Nécrologe des hommes célèbres* (Paris, 1770)

L. de La Laurencie: 'Deux imitateurs français des bouffons: Blavet et Dauvergne', *Année musicale*, ii (1912), 5–125

G. Migot: 'Un grand musicien bisontin, Michel Blavet', *Franche-Comté et Monts Jura*, xvii/197 (1935), 227

J. R. Anthony: *French Baroque Music from Beaujoyeulx to Rameau* (London, 1973, 2/1978)

D. Launay, ed.: *La querelle des bouffons* (Geneva, 1973) [a repr., with introduction and index, of more than 50 pamphlets pubd Paris, 1753–4]

NEAL ZASLAW

Blaze, François-Henri-Joseph. *See* CASTIL-BLAZE.

Blažek, Zdeněk (*b* Žarošice, Hodonín district, 24 May 1905). Czech composer. He studied with Vilém Petrželka and Vladimír Helfert in Brno and Josef Suk in Prague, and took the PhD at Brno (1933) with a dissertation on Smetana. His first appointment was with Czech Radio; he then taught at the Brno Conservatory and was later its director, and was professor of music theory at Brno University. His music, essentially homophonic in style, is faithful to the late Romantic, nationalist Suk-Novák tradition. Many of his works are vocal, and his songs and choruses achieve considerable expressiveness through harmonic subtlety. Blažek's *Verchovina* ('Highland'), a four-act opera to a libretto by Jaroslav Zatloukal, was composed in 1951 and first performed at the Brno State Theatre on 3 March 1956. Its theme is the working-class struggle during the 1930s in sub-Carpathian Russia (Ruthenia; the easternmost part of inter-war Czechoslovakia). Its style is traditional and accessible, incorporating realism, lyricism and effective choral scenes. Blažek's 1975 opera *R.U.R.* is based on Karel Čapek's futuristic play of the same name. He has also edited Janáček's writings on music theory (1968).

JAN TROJAN

Blech, Leo (*b* Aachen, 21 April 1871; *d* Berlin, 24 Aug 1958). German conductor and composer. In Berlin he studied the piano with Ernst Rudorff, and composition with Woldemar Bargiel and Humperdinck. He was conductor at the Stadttheater, Aachen (1893–9) and then at the Neues Deutsches Theater in Prague (1899–1906), where his reputation as a conductor and composer of opera became well established. In 1906 he was appointed conductor of the Berlin Hofoper, where he became Generalmusikdirektor in 1913. In 1923 he moved to the Deutsches Opernhaus, Berlin, as artistic director, and this was followed by a year at the Berlin Volksoper in 1924, and a year at the Vienna Volksoper in 1925. In 1926 he returned to Berlin as conductor of the Städtische Oper (formerly the Deutsches Opernhaus), and remained there, achieving great success, until, being Jewish, he found himself unable to return from a guest engagement at Riga in 1937. He stayed at Riga for four years; in 1941, when his safety was again threatened, he moved to Stockholm, securing a post at the Stockholm Royal Opera. In September 1949 he returned to Berlin as conductor at the Städtische Oper.

Blech's repertory was wide; he was especially renowned for his performances of Wagner and Verdi, and of *Carmen*, which he conducted about 600 times. His many recordings were made principally with the orchestra of the Berlin Staatsoper. During his lifetime he achieved considerable success with his own operas, particularly *Das war ich* (1902, Dresden), *Alpenkönig und Menschenfeind* (1903, Dresden), and, most popular of all, *Versiegelt* (1908, Hamburg). His stage works were said to show a deft lightness of touch in the tradition of Humperdinck.

Aglaja (1), Aachen, 4 Oct 1893
Cherubina (2), Aachen, 21 Dec 1894
Das war ich op.12 (komische Oper, 1, R. Batka, after J. Hutt), Dresden, Königlichsächsiches Hof, 6 Oct 1902
Alpenkönig und Menschenfeind op.14 (3, Batka, after F. Raimund), Dresden, Königlichsächsiches Hof, 1 Oct 1903; rev. as Rappelkopf, Berlin, Opernhaus, 2 Oct 1917
Aschenbrödel (3, Batka), Prague, Neues Deutsches, 26 Dec 1905
Versiegelt op.18 (1, komische Oper, Batka and A. S. Pordes-Milo, after S. Raupach), Hamburg, 1908
Die Strohwitwe (operetta, 3, A. Neidhardt), Hamburg, 16 June 1920

*

E. Rychnovsky: *Leo Blech* (Prague, 1905)
W. Jacob: *Leo Blech* (Hamburg, 1931)

J. A. FULLER MAITLAND, ROBERT PHILIP

Bledsoe, Jules [Julius] (*b* Waco, TX, 29 Dec 1898; *d* Hollywood, CA, 14 July 1943). American baritone. He studied at Central Texas College, Bishop and Virginia Union College, and then at Columbia University Medical School, but abandoned the idea of a career in medicine. He made his début at the Aeolian Hall, New York, in April 1924. He appeared in W. Frank Harling's hybrid opera *Deep River* and Gruenberg's *The Creation* and *In Abraham's Bosom*, and then in 1927 created the role of Joe in Kern's *Show Boat*, a role he also sang in the first film version in 1929. Later roles in opera included the Voodoo Man in Shirley Graham du Bois' *Tom-Tom* and Amonasro in *Aida*, and the title roles in *Boris Godunov* and Gruenberg's *The Emperor Jones*. He was one of the first African American singers to appear in opera in the USA. His final appearance was in the film *Drums of the Congo* in 1942.

*

SouthernB
M. C. Hare: *Negro Musicians and their Music* (Washington DC, 1936), 173, 332, 358

Blegen, Judith (*b* Missoula, MT, 27 April 1941). American soprano. She studied singing with Euphemia Gregory at the Curtis Institute from 1959. After an apprenticeship at the Santa Fe Festival (to which she later returned as a principal), she was engaged for concerts at Spoleto in 1963. She studied further in Italy and in 1964 went to Nuremberg, where during two years she sang such varied roles as Lucia, Susanna and Zerbinetta. Engagements followed in Vienna, Salzburg and the major American houses; her début role of Papagena at the Metropolitan (1970) led to performances as Marcellina, Mélisande, Ascanius and Sophie in *Werther*. She made her Covent Garden début in 1975, as Despina, and her début at the Opéra in 1977, as Sophie in *Der Rosenkavalier*. Her singing is notable for its charm, intelligence and polish; she avoids soubrette clichés and makes the most of a voice that is exceptionally pure and sweet if not particularly large or colourful. She has both sung and creditably played the violin in Menotti's *Help, Help, the Globolinks!* and *Die Fledermaus* (as Adele).

MARTIN BERNHEIMER

Blewitt, Jonathan (*b* London, 19 July 1782; *d* London, 4 Sept 1853). English composer. He studied with Battishill and with Haydn, and held various organ appointments in England and Ireland. In Dublin he was composer and music director to the Theatre Royal (Crow Street), succeeding Thomas Simpson Cooke in the latter post in June 1813. He soon became the foremost teacher in Dublin, and conducted the principal concerts there. Before 1825 Blewitt was again in London. He wrote music for Drury Lane productions in 1826–7, then in 1828 and 1829 was director of the music at Sadler's Wells. His stage pieces are mostly light works mixing song and speech; he was better known for his ballads in the Irish style.

first performed in London unless otherwise stated

DBCS – *Dublin, Theatre Royal, Crow Street*

The Corsair, or The Pirate's Isle (musical play, M. O'Sullivan), DBCS, 1814 (Dublin *c*1814)
The Forest of Bondy, or The Dog of Montargis (musical play, ?C. Dibdin, after G. de Pixérécourt), DBCS, 1814 (Dublin, *c*1814)
Egbert and Ethelinda (?Dibdin), DBCS, 1816
Actors al fresco (burletta, W. T. Moncrieff), Vauxhall Gardens, 1823, collab. T. S. Cooke and Horn
The Boy of Santillane, or Gil Blas and the Robbers of Asturia (musical play, G. Macfarren), Drury Lane, 16 April 1827, collab. Cooke
The Talisman, or The Genii of the Elements (musical play, Macfarren), Surrey, 7 April 1828
Auld Robin Grey (operetta, Macfarren), Surrey, 17 May 1828, collab. A. Lee
Black-eyed Susan, or All in the Downs (musical play, D. Jerrold), Surrey, 8 June 1829 (London, 1829)
Paul Clifford (musical drama, E. Fitzball, after E. L. Bulwer-Lytton), Covent Garden, 28 Oct 1835, collab. Rodwell
Rory O'More (burletta, S. Lover), Adelphi, 29 Sept 1837

Partly adapted: The Musician without Magic (operatic drama, W. H. Hamilton), DBCS, 1 March 1815 [Isouard: Le magicien sans magie]; My Old Woman (comic op, Macfarren, after E. Scribe and G. Delavigne: *La vieille*), Surrey, 14 Jan 1829 [Fétis: La vieille]

*

DNB (W. B. Squire); *NicollH*

Blind Beggars, The. Opera by Jacques Offenbach; *see* DEUX AVEUGLES, LES.

Bliss, Anthony A(ddison) (*b* New York, 19 April 1913; *d* Prince Edward Island, 10 Aug 1991). American administrator. After attending Harvard University (BA 1936), he studied at Columbia University (1936–8) and the University of Virginia (LLB 1940); he practised law in New York. In 1949 he became a member of the board of directors of the Metropolitan Opera Association and served as its president (1956–67), executive director (1974–81) and general manager (1981–5). Among the changes Bliss initiated, the expanding of the Metropolitan's season and the introduction of sounder financing were especially important. He regretted never having developed a creative space or small theatre more appropriate for Mozart and Rossini productions, or having organized a Metropolitan summer season or festival. He also held administrative or board positions with a number of arts organizations.

*

CBY 1979

J. Rockwell: 'Bliss Looks Back on Years at Met,' *New York Times* (29 July 1985), §C, p.11

WILLIAM McCLELLAN

Bliss, Sir **Arthur** (**Drummond**) (*b* London, 2 Aug 1891; *d* London, 27 March 1975). English composer of American descent. Educated at Rugby, Cambridge and the RCM, the young Bliss enjoyed prominence in the Anglo-French avant garde after World War I but matured to a more expansive, Romantic outlook in the 1930s and 40s when his film scores (especially *Things to Come*) and four major ballets proved him a durable composer for his times. He also undertook public and educational work as a visiting professor at Berkeley, California (1939–41), director of music at the BBC (1942–4) and Master of the Queen's Music (1953–75). His operas failed to achieve the success of his ballets, though *The Olympians* has not yet been given the chance of a second professional production and *Tobias and the Angel*, written for television, has never been staged. Both enjoy competent librettos, strong dramatic outlines and heartening music, though neither delves far into the contemporary psyche.

See also OLYMPIANS, THE.

The Olympians, 1945–9 (3, J. B. Priestley), London, CG, 29 Sept 1949, *GB-Cu**, vs (London, 1950)

Tobias and the Angel (television op, 2, C. Hassall, after the Apocryphal Book of Tobit), BBC, 19 May 1960, London, vs [stage version] (London, 1961)

*

N. Cardus, H. Rosenthal, A. Notcutt and R. Buckle: 'Four Opinions on "The Olympians" ', *Opera*, i (1950), 10–15

J. B. Priestley: 'Sir Arthur Bliss, 75th Birthday', *Composer*, xx (1960), 12

A. Bliss: *As I Remember* (London, 1970)

J. B. Priestley: 'My Friend Bliss', *MT*, cxii (1971), 740–41

E. Dent, N. Cardus and W. McNaught: 'Three Views of "The Olympians" ', *MT*, cxiii (1972), 145–7

L. Foreman, ed.: *Arthur Bliss: a Catalogue of the Complete Works* (London, 1980); *Supplement to Catalogue*, ed. G. Easterbrook and T. Bliss (London, 1982)

S. Craggs: *Arthur Bliss: a Bio-Bibliography* (Westport, CT, 1988)

STEPHEN BANFIELD

Blitzstein, Marc (*b* Philadelphia, 2 March 1905; *d* Fort-de-France, Martinique, 22 Jan 1964). American composer. He was the first to develop convincing music theatre reflecting American vernacular speech style. He studied the piano with Alexander Ziloti, attended the University of Pennsylvania and the Curtis Institute, then studied with Nadia Boulanger in Paris and with Schoenberg in Berlin. His early works were often angry, polytonal and experimental. Though he wrote vocal and instrumental music, and music for dance, radio, films and plays, he composed primarily for the musical theatre, mostly to his own librettos. His translation of Weill's *Dreigroschenoper* was performed off-Broadway for six years in the late 1950s and has become the standard version.

Blitzstein's first operas were all of short duration and in the avant-garde style. *Triple Sec* (composed 1928) is a dadaistic farce, which ran for 150 performances in a Broadway revue. *Parabola and Circula* (1929), set in a world of geometric abstraction, has French influences. *The Harpies* (1931) is a take-off of Stravinsky's neoclassicism. With *The Condemned* (1932), a choral opera loosely based on the Sacco and Vanzetti case of 1920, Blitzstein first approached the social themes which characterize most of his later work.

In the mid-1930s Blitzstein developed a pro-labour, anti-fascist stance, switching from a *beaux-arts* aesthetic to a populist, more strictly tonal language influenced by Kurt Weill and Hanns Eisler. The chief result of his new idiom was *The Cradle will Rock* (composed 1936), a proletarian 'play in music' in ten scenes, whose cartoon-like style comes largely from American vaudeville and popular music forms. Recorded three times and often revived, it is probably Blitzstein's best-known work. In *I've Got the Tune* (1937), a half-hour 'song-play' originally for radio but subsequently staged, he explored the dilemma of the modern composer in a set of inventive thematic variations. *No for an Answer* (composed 1936–40), a full-length opera about immigrant workers and their middle-class supporters, also draws on popular styles but treats its characters in depth.

After World War II service in London, where he composed the *Airborne Symphony*, Blitzstein set Lillian Hellman's drama *The Little Foxes* as the opera *Regina* (composed 1946–9). Exploiting a varied palette, Blitzstein depicted the musical world of Alabama in 1900, emphasizing the beginnings of jazz. In *Reuben Reuben* (1950–55), an allegory about contemporary society, he strove to create a Broadway opera; perhaps his most lush, ecstatic score, its uncommunicative book kept its message a mystery. *Juno* (1957–9), a musical based on Sean O'Casey's *Juno and the Paycock*, uses traditional Irish folk tunes dressed in rich, Britten-like harmonies that were too advanced for Broadway.

In the 1960s Blitzstein had a Ford Foundation – Metropolitan Opera commission to write *Sacco and Vanzetti*. Troubled by the complexities of finding the right forms for his text and music, he put it aside to work on two one-act operas based on stories by Bernard Malamud, *Idiots First* and *The Magic Barrel*. Of these last projects, only *Idiots First* was sufficiently advanced at the time of Blitzstein's death for another hand to complete it; Leonard J. Lehrman did so.

Blitzstein's legacy is a body of works reaffirming the artist's legitimate involvement in social issues. In an age when Broadway musicals and American opera both relied heavily on European models, there were few composers searching for an American voice who fused classical and popular styles, or who fitted to music the many accents of the American language, as well as Blitzstein. In these ways he influenced succeeding generations of composers and librettists for the American musical stage.

See also REGINA.

to librettos by Blitzstein unless otherwise stated; MSS at Madison, Wisconsin, State Historical Society of Wisconsin

Triple Sec (op-farce, 1, R. Jeans), Philadelphia, Bellevue-Stratford Ballroom, 6 May 1929, vs (Mainz and Leipzig, 1929)

Parabola and Circula, 1929 (1, G. Whitsett), unperf.

The Harpies, 1931 (1), New York, Manhattan School of Music, 25 May 1953
The Condemned, 1932 (1), unperf.
No for an Answer, 1936–40 (2), New York, Mecca Temple, 5 Jan 1941
The Cradle will Rock (10 scenes), New York, Venice, 16 June 1937
I've Got the Tune (radio song-play, 1), New York, CBS, 24 Oct 1937, vs (New York, 1938)
Regina (3, after L. Hellman: *The Little Foxes*), New York, 46th Street, 31 Oct 1949; rev. 1953, 1958; vs (New York, 1954)
Reuben Reuben (2), Boston, Shubert, 10 Oct 1955
Juno (2, J. Stein and Blitzstein, after S. O'Casey), New York, Winter Garden, 9 March 1959
Sacco and Vanzetti, 1959–64 (3), inc., unperf.
Idiots First, 1962–4 (1, after B. Malamud), Bloomington, IN, Monroe County Library, 14 March 1976, completed by L. J. Lehrman
The Magic Barrel, 1962–4 (1, after Malamud), inc.

*

P. M. Talley: *Social Criticism in the Original Theatre Librettos of Marc Blitzstein* (diss., U. of Wisconsin, 1965)
J. O. Hunter: 'Marc Blitzstein's "The Cradle will Rock" as a Document of America, 1937', *American Quarterly*, xviii (1966), 227–33
R. J. Dietz: 'Marc Blitzstein and the "Agit-Prop" Theatre of the 1930's', *Yearbook for Inter-American Musical Research*, vi (1970), 51–66
——: *The Operatic Style of Marc Blitzstein* (diss., U. of Iowa, 1970)
L. J. Lehrman: *A Musical Analysis of "Idiots First"* (thesis, Cornell U., 1975)
E. A. Gordon: *Mark the Music: the Life and Work of Marc Blitzstein* (New York, 1989)
R. H. Kornick: *Recent American Opera: a Production Guide* (New York, 1991), 68–70
ERIC A. GORDON

Bloch, André (*b* Wissembourg, Alsace, 18 Jan 1873; *d* Paris, 7 Aug 1960). French composer. Something of a child prodigy, Bloch won first prizes in both harmony and piano; he went on to study with Massenet and won the Prix de Rome at the age of 23. He took several teaching posts and composed mainly works for the stage. His first opera, *Maïda*, is set in Ceylon and depicts the life of a beautiful maiden before her marriage. Quasi-oriental modes and extended dances and choral scenes characterize the work. *Broceliande*, named after a fairy-tale forest, tells the story of the Sleeping Beauty. Amidst a shimmeringly orchestrated score, fairies and gnomes are charmingly evoked and choruses of frogs and toads sing with onomatopoeic noises suggested by Aristophanes but reminiscent of Ravel's *L'enfant et les sortilèges* whose première was a matter of months before. *Guignol* is based on the exploits of Punch and Judy and was given at a press gala in Lyons in 1936 before its public première at the Opéra-Comique. It is likely that Bloch, who is named by Raoul Gunsbourg as the orchestrator of part of Offenbach's *Les contes d'Hoffmann* for Monte Carlo in 1904, composed the septet normally included in that work and some of the ballet music.

Maïda (conte musical, 4, C. Réty-Darcours), Aix-les-Bains, Grand Cercle, 12 Aug 1909
La nuit de Noël (3), Liège, Royal, March 1922
Broceliande (conte bleu, 1, F. Gregh), Paris, 19 or 23 Nov 1925
Guignol (opéra bouffe, 3, H. Fabert and J. Godart), Paris, OC (Favart), 18 Jan 1949

*

P. Locard: 'Jean Nouguès, Ch. Silver, André Bloch, Francis Bousquet', *Le théâtre lyrique en France*, iii (Paris, 1939), 249–52
A. Lamb: 'Tales of a Monte Carlo "Hoffmann"', *Opera*, xlii (1991), 634–7 [also 880–82]
RICHARD LANGHAM SMITH

Bloch, Augustyn (Hipolit) (*b* Grudziądz, 13 Aug 1929). Polish composer. He studied composition with Tadeusz Szeligowski at the Warsaw Conservatory and in 1954 was appointed music consultant to the Polish Radio Theatre. After an essentially neo-classical phase his music became more experimental in the 1960s. His range covers most genres, including several ballet-pantomimes, the musical *Pan Zagłoba* ('Mr Zagłoba', 1971) and much music for children, notably the full-length musical *Bajka o skrzypcowej duszy* ('A Tale of the Violin Soul'; J. Kierst; Gliwice, State Operetta, 28 Dec 1978). Another stage work, *Z gwiazdą w cudobudzie* ('With the Star in the Stall of Wonder'; Warsaw, Wielki, 20 Jan 1975), re-creates the Christmas tradition, associated with performance by youngsters, of a Mazovian shepherds' nativity play. The title of *Bardzo śpiąca królewna* ('Very Sleeping Beauty'; 1, Bloch; Warsaw, Wielki, 29 Sept 1974) demonstrates the composer's keen sense of humour, and the work's typically Polish amalgam of opera, ballet and pantomime also reveals Bloch's ability to enter the unfettered world of a child's mind through invented language and vivid instrumental and vocal characterization. The religious aspect of Bloch's musical personality gave rise to his earliest stage piece, the short mystery opera *Ajelet, córka Jeftego* ('Ayelet, Jephtha's Daughter'; 1, J. Iwaszkiewicz; Warsaw, 22 Sept 1968). His concern in *Ajelet* with persecution down the ages is embodied in his use of Christian and Jewish music as the inspiration for a sombre mix of monodic chant and atonal heterophonic textures.

*

T. Marek: 'Ayelet: Mystery Opera', *Polish Music* (1968), no.3, pp.6–7
——: '"The Sleeping Princess": a Musical Fairy Tale for the Stage by Augustyn Bloch', *Polish Music* (1973), no.2, pp.23–7
ADRIAN THOMAS

Bloch, Ernest (*b* Geneva, 24 July 1880; *d* Portland, OR, 15 July 1959). American composer of Swiss origin. After studies in his native city with Louis Rey (violin) and Emile Jaques-Dalcroze (composition) during the 1890s, Bloch, with the encouragement of Marsick, went to study in Brussels with Eugène Ysaÿe (violin) and François Rasse (composition) from 1897 to 1899. A year in Frankfurt, where his principal teacher was Iwan Knorr, taught Bloch, as he later acknowledged, to think independently and to develop his own musical personality. Following periods in Munich (1901–3) with a few lessons from Ludwig Thuille, and Paris (1903–4), he returned to Geneva, married and began work in his father's clock business. Such time as he could spare was devoted to conducting, lecturing and composing. In 1916, Bloch went to the USA for the first time as conductor for the Maud Allan dance company. He taught at the David Mannes School of Music in New York (1917–20) and was then appointed the first director of the Cleveland Institute of Music (1920–25) and director of the San Francisco Conservatory of Music (1925–30). He became a citizen of the USA in 1924.

Although Bloch's fame as a composer still rests on his 'Jewish cycle', notably the cello rhapsody *Schelomo* (1915–16), he evinced an early interest in and aptitude for the stage. His only completed opera, *Macbeth* (1910), designated a lyric drama, synthesized elements drawn from Wagnerian music drama, from *Pelléas et Mélisande* and from *Boris Godunov* with Bloch's own evolving style. First and second publication proofs, with corrections, of the vocal score and the male chorus parts are housed in the Library of Congress, as are sketches and drafts for a second, unfinished, four-act opera,

Jézabel (1911–18), to a text by the librettist of *Macbeth*, Edmond Fleg.

During the 1930s, Bloch lived principally in Switzerland, but travelled to European capitals and to the USA to conduct his works. He returned to and resettled in the USA, and from 1940 until his retirement in 1952 taught summer courses at the University of California at Berkeley. After his death, an Ernest Bloch Society was founded in the USA, largely through the efforts of the composer's three children. During the later 1930s a London-based Bloch Society flourished through the efforts of Alex Cohen, who had translated the libretto of *Macbeth* into English.

See also MACBETH (iii).

*

P. Lalo: 'La musique', *Le temps* (31 Dec 1910)
I. Pizzetti: 'Ernest Bloch', *Musicisti contemporanei* (Milan, 1914), 193–210
G. Gatti: 'Ernest Bloch', *MQ*, vii (1921), 20–38
R. Sessions: 'Ernest Bloch', *MM*, v/1 (1927–8), 3–11
M. Tibaldi-Chiesa: *Ernest Bloch* (Turin, 1933)
R. Hall: 'The *Macbeth* of Bloch', *MM*, xv (1938), 209–15
A. Cohen: 'Ernest Bloch's *Macbeth*', *ML*, xix (1939), 142–8
R. Mariani: 'Bloch e il suo *Macbeth*', *La Scala* (Feb 1953), 29–33
D. Z. Kushner: 'The Revivals of Bloch's *Macbeth*', *Opera Journal*, iv/2 (1971), 9-12
F. Kinkaid: 'The Other *Macbeth*', *ON*, xxxvii/25 (1973), 10–11
R. Strassburg: *Ernest Bloch, Voice in the Wilderness* (Los Angeles, 1977)
D. Z. Kushner: 'Ernest Bloch: a Retrospective on the Centenary of his Birth', *College Music Symposium*, xx/2 (1980), 77–86
——: *Ernest Bloch: a Guide to Research* (New York, 1988)
P. Gradenwitz: 'Ernest Bloch (1880–1959)', *Swiss Composers in the 20th Century*, ed. A. Briner (Zürich, 1990), 15–20

DAVID Z. KUSHNER

Blochwitz, Hans Peter (*b* Garmisch-Partenkirchen, 28 Sept 1949). German tenor. He studied at Mainz and in Frankfurt, where he made his début in 1984 as Lensky. He has sung in Brussels, Geneva, Zürich, Aix-en-Provence, Vienna, Hamburg, Amsterdam and San Francisco. He made his Covent Garden début in 1989 as Ferrando and his Metropolitan début in 1990 as Don Ottavio. His repertory includes Monteverdi's Nero, Belmonte, Idamantes, Lucio Silla and Tamino. A stylish singer, he has a firm, lyrical voice heard to best advantage in Mozart.

ELIZABETH FORBES

Blockx, Jan (*b* Antwerp, 25 Jan 1851; *d* Kapellenbos, nr Antwerp, 26 May 1912). Belgian composer. He was a pupil of Peter Benoit at the Vlaamsche Muziekschool and in 1879 went to Leipzig, where he became a friend of Grieg and Sinding and attended Reinecke's classes at the conservatory. After travelling in Italy he succeeded Hendrik Waelput at the Vlaamsche Muziekschool in 1885; he was an outstanding teacher, his pupils including Lodewijk Mortelmans and Flor Alpaerts. In May 1901 he succeeded Benoit as director of the Koninklijk Vlaams Conservatorium. He was a member of the Académie Royale de Belgique and of a jury, set up by the publishers Sonzogno of Milan, for an international competition in opera composition.

Blockx's fame rests chiefly on the success enjoyed by his operas, and the first performance of *Herbergprinses* may be regarded as the beginning of Flemish opera. His work can be seen as a national variation of Romantic realism, influenced by the study of Flemish folksong; he knew instinctively how to underline the dramatic action with suitable musical effects and from Wagner he inherited certain principles in the use of leitmotif, recitative and symphonic commentary. His orchestration, usually conventional, is always polished and effective, and his melodies reveal a considerable lyric gift. He also wrote cantatas, orchestral works, chamber music, a ballet and a pantomime.

all publications in vocal score

VO – Vlaamse Opera

Iets vergeten (Spl, 1, V. de la Montagne), Antwerp, Koninklijke Harmonie, 19 Feb 1877
Maître Martin (4, E. Landoy, after E. T. A. Hoffmann: *Meister Martin, der Küfner, und seine Gesellen*), Brussels, Monnaie, 30 Nov 1892
Herbergprinses (3, N. de Tière), Antwerp, VO, 10 Oct 1896 (Paris, 1897)
Thijl Uilenspiegel (3, H. Cain and L. Solvay), Brussels, Monnaie, 12 Jan 1900 (Paris, 1900)
De Bruid der Zee (3, de Tière), Antwerp, VO, 30 Nov 1901 (Paris, 1902)
De Kapel (1, de Tière), Antwerp, VO, 7 Nov 1903 (Paris, 1903)
Baldie (3, de Tière), Antwerp, VO, 25 Jan 1908, rev. as Liefdelied, Antwerp, VO, 6 Jan 1912
Telamon en Myrtalee, 1910 (R. Verhulst)
Thijl Uylenspiegel II (3, Cain and Solvay), Brussels, Monnaie, 12 Nov 1920, completed by P. Gilson

*

L. Solvay: *Académie royale de Belgique: notice sur Jan Blockx* (Brussels, 1920)
F. Blockx: *Jan Blockx* (Brussels, 1943)

MARIE-THÉRÈSE BUYSSENS

Blodek, Vilém (*b* Prague, 3 Oct 1834; *d* Prague, 1 May 1874). Czech composer. After studying at the Prague Conservatory (1846–52) with Antonín Eiser (flute) and Jan Bedřich Kittl (composition), he taught music in Lubycza, Galicia (1853–5) and then in Prague. In 1860 he succeeded Eiser as professor of flute at the conservatory. He was also active as a composer of incidental music for both the German and the Czech theatres: from 1858 he wrote music for 60 plays and collaborated with Smetana on music for the *tableaux* for the Prague 1864 Shakespeare celebrations. In 1865 he married his pupil Marie Daublebská, despite opposition from her father, a rich lawyer. Overwork caused a nervous breakdown, and after a spell in a mental home in 1870 he returned there permanently in May 1871.

Blodek began composing at the age of 13 in a style that owed much to Kittl, Mendelssohn and the early German Romantics. His works include male-voice choruses, a tuneful symphony (1859) and a brilliant and attractive flute concerto (1862). His best-known work, however, is his one-act opera *V studni* ('In the Well', 1867). It shared not only the librettist (Karel Sabina) and folk milieu of Smetana's *The Bartered Bride*, but also its number-opera conventions and something of its musical idiom. It is the only Czech opera from this period to survive in the Czech repertory apart from those of Smetana.

Blodek completed only Act 1 and part of Act 2 of his next opera, *Zítek*, based on a comic intrigue from the 14th century. It was more ambitious both in musical vocabulary and structure, avoiding closed numbers and making greater use of arioso and a chorus more closely integrated into the action.

See also V STUDNI.

Clarissa, 1861, inc. [lib in Ger.]
V studni [In the Well] (comic op, 1, K. Sabina), Prague, Provisional, 17 Nov 1867, vs (Prague, 1878)
Zítek, 1868–9 (comic op, 3, Sabina), inc.; rev. F. X. Váňa, Prague, National, 3 Oct 1934; *CS-Pr, Pnd*

*

F. X. Váňa: *Vilém Blodek* (Prague, 1934)

——: 'Vilém Blodek a dopis Bedřicha Smetany' [Vilém Blodek and Bedřich Smetana's Letter], *Tempo – Listy Hudební matice*, xiv (1935), 33–42 [on *Zítek*]
——: 'Vilém Blodek', *České umění dramatické*, ii: *Zpěvohra* [Czech Dramatic Art, ii: Opera], ed. J. Hutter and Z. Chalabala (Prague, 1941), 159–65
R. Budiš: *Vilém Blodek* (Prague, 1964) [incl. earlier bibliography]
M. Ottlová and M. Pospíšil: 'K otázce českosti v hudbě 19. století' [The Question of Czechness in 19th-Century Music], *OM*, xi (1979), 101–3 [incl. discussion of contemporary reception of *In the Well*]
J. Tyrrell: *Czech Opera* (Cambridge, 1988), 80–81, 213

JOHN TYRRELL

Bloemfontein. City in the Republic of South Africa. The Miranda-Harper Company was the first to perform opera there, at the Raadzaal in 1869. Several other companies followed from England, America, Australia and later, Johannesburg, presenting a predominantly English repertory. Until the first town hall was built in 1883, their usual venues were the old Wesleyan chapel and the Raadzaal. Local companies such as the Bloemfontein Dramatic and Operatic Company and the Ramblers' Musical and Dramatic Society performed operettas by Gilbert and Sullivan during the 1880s and 1890s. The D'Oyly Carte Opera Company inaugurated the Grand Theatre in 1906 and grand opera was first performed in the city by the Quinlan Opera Company in 1912 with great success. Light opera and musicals continued to be regularly performed by local companies. The headquarters of the Performing Arts Council of the Orange Free State (PACOFS) were established there in 1963; the Council is responsible for opera and ballet performances in the province. Opera is performed in the 964-seat Sand du Plessis Theatre, which was opened in August 1985. Four or five seasons of opera are given each year, accompanied by the PACOFS SO. Musicals are also included.

*

J. P. Malan: 'Bloemfontein, Music in', *South African Music Encyclopedia* (Cape Town, 1979), 175–200

Blomdahl, Karl-Birger (*b* Växjö, 19 Oct 1916; *d* Kungsängen, nr Stockholm, 14 June 1968). Swedish composer. He began his musical studies in 1935 with Hilding Rosenberg, whose influence is obvious in his motivic work; later he studied at the Swedish Royal Academy of Music. In the 1940s he was active in the Monday Group, which discussed and analysed contemporary music. The beginning of the 1950s was marked by his collaboration with the poet Erik Lindegren and the choreographer Birgit Åkesson, resulting in such important works as the ballets *Sisyphos* (1957) and *Minotauros* (1958). During these years he became active as a teacher (he was a professor at the Swedish Royal Academy of Music, 1960–64); he also held administrative posts, eventually becoming director of the music department of Swedish Radio (1965–8).

In 1957–8 Blomdahl composed his best-known work, the space opera *Aniara* (2, Lindegren, after H. Martinson; Stockholm, Royal Opera, 31 May 1959, *S-Ssk**). He called it 'a revue about man in time and space', and the musical language moves abruptly between different idioms including jazz, sacred choral music, extensive vocalise, intense lyrical outbursts, mime and also electronic episodes (the 'Mima tapes'). The expansive architectonic climaxes and elegiac string writing are typical of his mature style. His second opera, *Herr von Hancken*, composed 1962–3 (3, Lindegren, after H. Bergman; *S-Ssr**), contrasts sharply with *Aniara*; an individualistic, psychological tragedy in the form of an *opera buffa*, it was coolly received and since the first performance (Stockholm, Royal Opera, 2 Sept 1965) has not been revived. It is set throughout in a recitative style, with very few arias and the orchestra generally following the dramatic flow rather than determining it, as in *Aniara*. One reason for this musical economy, which approaches asceticism, was the development of Blomdahl's own style, but he was also becoming increasingly occupied with electronic music and as a consequence was forced to question the function of music and concerts in a modern society where the means of communication are the record, tape and loudspeaker. The works that followed *Herr von Hancken*, including the unfinished opera *Sagan om den stora datamaskinen* ('The Tale of the Big Computer', after H. Alfvén), were purely electronic. In this light, *Herr von Hancken* is seen to reflect Blomdahl's paralysing doubts about means of artistic expression.

See also ANIARA.

*

R. Aiken: *Karl-Birger Blomdahl* (diss., U. of Cincinnati, 1968)
R. K. Inglefield: 'Karl-Birger Blomdahl: a Portrait', *MQ*, lviii (1972), 67–82
G. Bucht: 'Karl-Birger Blomdahl som musikdramatiker', *Operan 200 år*, ed. K. Ralf (Stockholm, 1973), 165–78
F. Sandgren: 'Erik Lindgren på Operans domäner', *Operan 200 år*, ed. K. Ralf (Stockholm, 1973), 156–64

ANDERS WIKLUND

Blood Wedding [*Vérnász*]. Opera in three acts (seven pictures) by SÁNDOR SZOKOLAY to his own libretto after FEDERICO GARCÍA LORCA's *Bodas de sangre*; Budapest, Hungarian State Opera House, 31 October 1964.

After a short introduction by the female chorus, the first act develops in concise, elliptical scenes. The Bridegroom (tenor) leaves for the family vineyard. His Mother (contralto), who has lost both husband and elder son as victims to village hostilities, follows his every step with foreboding. She learns from a neighbour (soprano) that the bride of her son has been engaged before to Leonardo from the family of Felix, responsible for her past tragedies. The mere mention of this family name sends her into a paroxysm of fear. The Wife (soprano) and Mother-in-law (contralto) of Leonardo sing a lullaby to his son. Leonardo (baritone) enters, but soon leaves as he is met with reproaches for having been seen 'at the other end of the plain' (where, we surmise, his former betrothed lives). The mother and the bridegroom come to ask for the hand of the Bride (soprano). After they leave, the Maid (soprano) tells the bride about Leonardo's nightly visits to the premises. The bride cannot conceal her ecstasy as she catches sight of him again through the window.

At the beginning of Act 2, the bride is getting dressed for the wedding when Leonardo arrives unexpectedly early. The old emotions of the two break out in an extended, passionate love duet. The guests arrive, and they all leave for the church (orchestral intermezzo). After their return, a brief scene follows between the bridegroom and the bride, who seeks his help against her own passions. She disappears, and the climax comes when the guests learn that she has eloped with Leonardo. In a furious finale (the chorus speaking and shouting rhythmically) the bridegroom and his male relatives prepare to follow the culprits and take revenge.

Act 3 is without real action, and introduces purely allegorical figures like the three Fellers (deep male voices), the Moon (tenor with female chorus), and Death, dressed as a beggar woman (contralto). In symbolic dialogue they prepare the human characters, who stray into a mysterious forest facing a dangerous future with possibly fatal consequences. The ensuing catastrophe itself (the two men kill each other) is not brought to the stage, but is told musically in an orchestral interlude with textless chorus. In the finale, which has an epilogue, Death comes to the village women waiting for the news, and tells them about the end of the duel. The bride goes to the mother and tries to explain the motive of her failing: love is more powerful than moral decisions. The chorus mourns for both men, and the mother quotes in a monologue the words of foreboding which she uttered in the first act.

Blood Wedding was perhaps the most successful opera by a Hungarian composer since Bartók's *Bluebeard*, and has been remarkably popular. In this, his first opera, Szokolay captures the emotional forces of the libretto in a concentrated musical form, with resourceful use of orchestral ostinatos and short, recurring motives in the voices. He eschews the temptations of exaggerated folklorism, and, through varied resources (folklore for the village life, operatic declamation for the dialogues, chromaticism for the surrealistic scenes), finds adequate musical expression for the various levels of Lorca's work.

Lorca's *Bodas de sangre* was also set by Wolfgang Fortner as *DIE BLUTHOCHZEIT*. TIBOR TALLIÁN

Bloomington. American town in Indiana. In 1948 Wilfred C. Bain, dean of Indiana University School of Music, initiated what was to become known as the Indiana University Opera Theater. Using faculty members as conductors, directors, designers and vocal coaches, this organization provided students with training opportunities in all phases of operatic production and performance. The first opera was *Les contes d'Hoffman* in a production with several innovatory features. All works were sung in English, with one or two exceptions from 1985–6.

The production that first caught national attention was *Parsifal*, performed on Palm Sunday 1949 and repeated on that day for the following 21 years at the University Auditorium (a theatre seating 3720 and able to accommodate the Met on its annual spring visit, 1946–61). Kurt Weill's *Down in the Valley* was broadcast nationally in the summer of 1948. Menotti's *Amahl and the Night Visitors* had its first stage performances in February 1952 after the televised version the previous Christmas Eve. *Billy Budd* was given its first American stage performance on 7 December 1953. Over the years 16 American operas have been given their premières. The regular presentation of both familiar and unfamiliar works to an audience with limited access to opera has always been a top priority.

In January 1972 the Indiana University Musical Arts Center (1400 seats) became the company's permanent home. It opened with a performance of *Heracles* by John Eaton, who has had five other works mounted in Bloomington, including *Myshkin* for television. His *Cry of Clytemnestra* was taken to Moscow in June 1990 as part of an exchange with the Moscow Conservatory, while the Russians brought Rakhmaninov's *Francesca da Rimini*.

The season consists of six different works during the autumn and spring semesters, performed three to six times, on Saturdays. Two additional productions (often including an operetta or a musical) are offered during the summer; there are also tours (the company gave *The Greek Passion* at the Met in May 1981).

The repertory ranges from Luigi Rossi's *Orfeo* to Wolfgang Rihm's *Jacob Lenz* and includes the standard works as well as Handel (*Belshazzar*, 1959; *Deidamia*, 1969; *Tamerlano*, 1983), Rimsky-Korsakov (*Christmas Eve*, *The Tale of Tsar Saltan*, *The Golden Cockerel*), Busoni (*Doktor Faust*, 1974; *Arlecchino*, 1980), Janáček (*Jenůfa*, 1972; *The Excursions of Mr Brouček*, 1981) and Henze (*Elegy for Young Lovers*, 1968).

Casting has been from among both the students and the faculty, and has included Margaret Harshaw, Walter Cassel, James King, Marko Rothmüller, Martha Lipton, Nicola Rossi-Lemeni and Charles Kullman, with Richard Stilwell, Pablo Elvira and Nancy Shade among the younger generation. ROSS C. ALLEN

Blow, John (*b* Newark, Notts., bap. 23 Feb 1649; *d* London, 1 Oct 1708). English composer and organist. In the first generation of boys recruited for the restored Chapel Royal Choir under Captain Henry Cook, Blow was a prolific composer of odes, anthems and secular songs. Appointed organist of Westminster Abbey in 1668, he resigned this prestigious post in 1679 in favour of his gifted pupil Henry Purcell, resuming it upon the younger man's death in 1695. Blow's works for the professional theatre are limited to a number of songs and dialogues for plays, mostly produced in the 1680s: Nahum Tate's *The Loyal General* (1680), Nathaniel Lee's *The Princess of Cleve* (*c*1680), Robert Howard's *The Committee* (undated revival), Aphra Behn's *The Lucky Chance* (1687) and Robert Gould's *The Rival Sisters* (1696). His most important stage work is, however, the privately performed court opera *Venus and Adonis* (*c*1683). Given its originality and dramatic intensity, one is surprised that Blow wrote no other opera; he was surely among the English composers who were reportedly chagrined at the choice of the foreigner Luis Grabu as composer of Dryden's royal opera *ALBION AND ALBANIUS* (1684–5). Blow's true métier was, however, the Anglican anthem, and his stage works, even *Venus and Adonis*, whose highly charged libretto drove him to invent unorthodox modes of expression, cannot be fully acquitted of Burney's charge of harmonic and contrapuntal crudity.

See also VENUS AND ADONIS (i).

*

E. J. Dent: *Foundations of English Opera* (London, 1928)
E. W. White: *A History of English Opera* (London, 1983)
C. A. Price: *Henry Purcell and the London Stage* (Cambridge, 1984)
R. Luckett: 'A New Source for "Venus and Adonis"', *MT*, cxxx (1989), 76–9 CURTIS PRICE

Bluebeard's Castle [*A Kékszakállú herceg vára* ('Duke Bluebeard's Castle')]. Opera in one act, op.11, by BÉLA BARTÓK to a libretto by BÉLA BALÁZS after a fairy-tale by Charles Perrault; Budapest, Opera, 24 May 1918.

Duke Bluebeard [A Kékszakállú herceg]	baritone
Judith [Judit] *his wife*	(mezzo-)soprano
Prologue	spoken
Bluebeard's three former wives	silent

Setting A hall in Bluebeard's castle in legendary times

Balázs belonged to the same generation as Bartók, and shared his determination to create an opera which was both Hungarian and modern. Thus where Bartók was influenced by the modality and rhythmic irregularity he found both in Transylvanian music and in Debussy, Balázs looked at once to folk ballads and to Maeterlinck. His immediate source was Maeterlinck's *Ariane et Barbe-bleue*, set by Dukas; but he changed the story significantly. Where Ariane's quest is for independence and escape from the castle/prison, Judith wants a relationship with Bluebeard which will make the castle a prison no longer. And where Ariane is by far the most important character, with Bluebeard present for only two brief, if critical, moments, Balázs's libretto is cast throughout for Judith and Bluebeard together, and alone. Moreover, the opening of the doors, which in Maeterlinck occupies only about a half of the first of the three acts, is now the main dramatic business. The two characters are on stage from the first, and all that happens, until the very end, is that doors are successively opened. As a result, *Bluebeard's Castle* is unusually successful as an opera for the ears alone, whether in concert performance or on record, and one might wonder whether Bartók the folksong-collector's familiarity with recording, with listening to disembodied voices, had some effect on the nature of the work. Even in a stage production the spoken prologue, if it is not omitted, alerts the audience to the fact that what they are to see is an interior drama, a mirror of a real action taking place iside the head of each spectator.

Balázs wrote the text for either Bartók or Kodály to set; Bartók wrote his version in 1911 and entered it in a national competition for one-act operas. It failed to win a prize, and the Budapest Opera was reluctant to produce it until after the success of the Bartók-Balázs ballet *The Wooden Prince* in 1917. It was in a double-bill with the ballet that the work had its first performance, sung by Oszkár Kálmán and Olga Haselbeck (fig.1), conducted by Egisto Tango and produced by Dezsó Zádor.

The libretto is cast almost exclusively in trochaic tetrameters, a constant reminder that this is the world of ballad, though Bartók's setting fluctuates around the basic model of quaver beats in 2/4 and 4/4. Bluebeard's part is centred on this plainest sort of declamation, while Judith's hazards more triple time and more rhythmic variety, seeming to want to loosen the rigidity in which she is contained; there is a parallel in the modal construction of the opera, Bluebeard preferring pentatonic expressions whereas Judith sings in richer modes. No doubt Bartóks word-setting, in what was his first important vocal work, owed much to what he had heard of folk music, but Debussy showed the way too, through the example of his own Maeterlinck opera. As in *Pelléas et Mélisande*, the setting is syllabic, the vocal lines follow speech patterns, and there are few occasions where they rise to self-contained melody or high register. The differences in vocal style in the two operas, which include a preponderance of falling phrases in *Bluebeard's Castle*, can be ascribed to differences between the languages: in this regard, as with the use of trochaic metre, the opera is locked into Magyar as securely as Bluebeard is locked into the castle which is his self.

1. Oszkár Kálmán as Bluebeard and Olga Haselbeck as Judith in the original production of Bartók's 'Bluebeard's Castle' at the Budapest Opera, 24 May 1918

After the prologue, the stage reveals a circular Gothic hall with seven great doors and, to the left, a smaller door through which Bluebeard and Judith enter. Their opening dialogue has Bluebeard introducing his new wife to his home but also inviting her to reconsider her decision to live with him (it seems a poignant and almost cruel admonitory gesture that Bartók should have dedicated the work to his own new wife, Márta, whom he had married two years earlier). Judith proclaims firmly that she has made up her mind, and there is then a passionate embrace, which brings forward for the first time nearly the whole of the large orchestra Bartók uses here, a larger ensemble than in anything else he wrote. Bluebeard calls for the door to be bolted, and the music returns to the austere pentatony with which it had begun, though now with D♯ rather than F♯ as tonic. This is the castle reasserting itself, and Judith notices that its walls are 'weeping' (symbolically, of course, they are the walls of Bluebeard's skull). Again she is offered the opportunity to go back; again she declines.

Next Bluebeard turns his attention to her motivation and suddenly asks her why she came, a question which she answers only indirectly, declaring that she will warm and dry his castle from him. But this is not what he wants. Nor does he want her to open the seven doors which she now notices, and when she violently insists, the castle itself answers for him in a sound effect described as 'a cavernous sighing, as when the night wind sighs down endless, gloomy labyrinths'. Perhaps in hope (his feelings are very often ambiguous) Bluebeard asks if she is frightened, but she is not, and recovers to repeat her request for the keys. Now, however, she does not demand but uses the argument of her love for him, and this he cannot resist. He gives her a key, and as she opens the first door the sigh is heard again. Xylophone

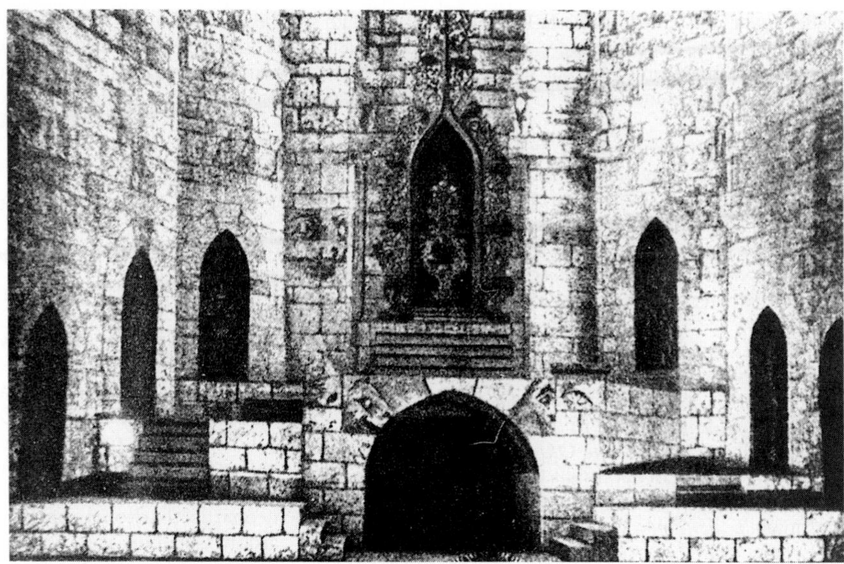

2. 'Bluebeard's Castle' (Bartók): set design for the original production at the Budapest Opera, 24 May 1918

and high woodwind, harshly rushing up and down scales through a tritone, present an image of the torture chamber that stands revealed: here, as when the other doors are unlocked, the graphic musical illustration recalls that, before Debussy, Strauss had been one of Bartók's chief enthusiasms. At the same time (and at very much the same time as Skryabin in *Prometheus* or Schoenberg in *Die glückliche Hand*) he uses lighting effects to intensify his harmonic resources. From within the torture chamber a beam of red light is thrown across the floor; the next three openings complete the spectrum in rays of yellowish-red, gold and bluish-green, and then the fifth doorway brings a flood of radiance, which the sixth withdraws, 'as though a shadow were passing over'. Gradually Judith assembles an image of Bluebeard's inner life, and when that image is complete it is taken from her.

The warnings, though, are present from the start. Not only is Judith first mesmerized and then horrified by the instruments of torture, she also sees blood on the castle walls: the motif of a minor second, here played shrilly by trumpets and oboes, recurs as a symbol of blood at each doorway. However, Judith reinterprets the redness as that of dawn, and confidently asks for the remaining keys. When she again gives love as her reason, Bluebeard capitulates and hands her the second key, which opens the door on his armoury (the music includes trumpet fanfares in E♭). Once more there is blood, and once more, even more resolutely, Judith turns to demand the rest of the keys. Bluebeard gently tries to warn her off, and when that does not work he rises to a rare lyricism, in warm C♯ major with solo horn. But she is adamant that she must know his secrets because she loves him, and he gives here three more keys.

If the first two doors had shown the force sustaining Bluebeard's power, the next three reveal the pleasures of that power. First there is the jewel house, glittering with harps and celesta in D major; then the gardens, evoked in a spacious E♭ major. In both cases Bluebeard offers everything to Judith, and in both cases she notices the blood as she had before. Now, though, she does not turn from anguished awareness to firm demand: instead it is Bluebeard who moves her on swiftly from one door to the next, so that they come with a rush to the fifth door, and a burst of C major, throughout the orchestra with organ, as it opens on the vista of Bluebeard's domain. Judith sees the blood again, but Bluebeard is concerned rather to praise the light she has brought to his castle: her work is now done, he suggests. But she cannot stop at this point. She has become obsessed with knowing Bluebeard's secrets, and obsessed too, the music suggests, with the blood she has seen everywhere: she gains the accompaniment of a *meto perpetuo* circling through minor seconds. Bluebeard gives in and hands her another key, which she turns, and as at the start there is a sigh, only this time it has come nearer and invaded the orchestra (a *glissando* in lower strings with bassoons).

As the light fades, a lake of tears is revealed, and there is a harmonic darkening a A minor. Hope is now gone. The first half of the work has brought the music round from the F♯ of Bluebeard's gloomy castle to the bright light of C major, by way notably of E♭/D♯: the A tonality now implies a completion of a circle of minor thirds back to the original F♯, and this is indeed what happens. The awesome prospect holds Judith in thrall. She is even for a moment compliant when Bluebeard says the last door must remain shut, and she joins him in a second passionate embrace. But her inquisitiveness only grows. She asks is Bluebeard really loves her; she asks whom he loved before; she asks how and how much he loved her predecessor. He tries to stop her questioning, but inevitably she arrives at the demand to know what lies behind the last door, and when he remains silent she leaps to the conclusion that the rumours were right: he has murdered all his former wives; hence the blood and the tears. There is now no point in holding back. Numbly Bluebeard hands over the final key.

As Judith opens the seventh door the fifth and sixth swing shut and it becomes much darker, with only the coloured beams from the first four doors and a silver ray of moonlight from the last. Three ex-wives silently step out, and in a second passage of elevated arioso Bluebeard addresses them as the loves of his dawns, noons and evenings. Through all this Judith can only give voice to her comparative unworthiness (it is perhaps some feeling of insecurity that has brought her thus far), but Bluebeard turns to her as the most beautiful of them all, destined to reign over his nights once she has taken her place, as she must, with the rest. The wives, all four, go back behind the seventh door, and Bluebeard is left alone, in the pentatonic F♯ of his solitary castle, with an addition only to his memories.

* * *

Bartók never attempted opera again: like *Fidelio*, that other work of marriage, *Bluebeard's Castle* is the unique operatic expression of a musical mentality that was essentially concerned with large-scale process and abstract form. Nor has the work gained any notable successors from other composers, remaining, like its central character, in its own world, alone.

PAUL GRIFFITHS

Blume, Heinrich (*b* Berlin, 25 April 1788; *d* Berlin, 2 Nov 1856). German bass-baritone. He studied in Berlin, where he made his début in 1808 at the Hofoper in Winter's *Das unterbrochene Opferfest*. He took part in the Berlin première of Spontini's *Olympie* (1821) and, at the Berlin Schauspielhaus, created Huldbrant in E. T. A. Hoffmann's *Undine* (1816) and Caspar in *Der Freischütz* (1821). A famous Don Giovanni, he also sang Masetto and the Commendatore. His powerful voice had a wide range and he was able to sing both baritone and bass roles. ELIZABETH FORBES

Blumenfeld, Felix (Mikhaylovich) (*b* Kovalyovka, South Ukraine, 7/19 April 1863; *d* Moscow, 21 Jan 1931). Russian conductor. He studied composition with Rimsky-Korsakov at the St Petersburg Conservatory, where he taught the piano for many years. From 1895 to 1911, as conductor at the Mariinsky Theatre in St Petersburg, he gave the premières of Rimsky-Korsakov's *Serviliya* (1902) and *Legend of the Invisible City of Kitezh* (1907) and the Russian première of *Tristan und Isolde* (1898). In 1908 he conducted the Russian seasons in Paris where he lived and worked in close contact with Anton Rubinstein, Rimsky-Korsakov, Glazunov, Rakhmaninov and Shalyapin. He achieved wide recognition as a conductor and pianist though his compositions did not outlive him. JOACHIM BRAUN

Blumenfeld, Harold (*b* Seattle, WA, 15 Oct 1923). American composer. He studied composition with Bernard Rogers at the Eastman School and with Hindemith at Yale, and in 1950 began teaching at Washington University, St Louis. He directed the Opera Theatre of St Louis (1962–6) and the Washington University Opera Studio (1960–71), offering an innovatory mixture of the standard repertory, Baroque opera and 20th-century works.

Blumenfeld developed his early compositional style while under the influence of Hindemith, but later adopted an approach similar to that of such composers as Berio, Crumb and Carter. About 1970 he began to relinquish his responsibilities as an opera director to concentrate on composing. His comic opera *Amphitryon 4* (3, after Molière; 1962) is a large-scale work requiring a huge cast: only the overture and orchestral excerpts have been performed. Blumenfeld's other dramatic works are *Fritzi* (1, C. Kondek; 1979), an 'opera-bagatelle' produced by Chicago Opera Theater (1988, Chicago); and *Fourscore: an Opera of Opposites* (2, Kondek, after J. Nestroy: *Haus der Temperamente*; 1981–5), produced by the University of Cincinnati (1989). Blumenfeld's two television operas, *Gentle Boy* (after Hawthorne; begun 1968) and *The Road to Salem* (1973), have never been completed. He began work in 1991 on a two-act opera, *Season in Hell: a Life of Rimbaud*. His style favours declaimed texts with subtle, often contrapuntal orchestration; chamber ensemble, piano and percussion are frequently used.

*

EwenD

S. Jenkins, jr: 'Waiting at the Gateway', *ON*, xxxii/26 (1967–8), 19–21

J. Wierzbicki: 'Blumenfeld's Music', *St. Louis Globe-Democrat* (3–4 Feb 1979) RICHARD S. JAMES

Blumer, Rodney. *See* MILNES, RODNEY.

Bluthochzeit, Die ('Blood Wedding'). Lyric tragedy in two acts by WOLFGANG FORTNER to a libretto by Enrique Beck after FEDERICO GARCÍA LORCA's play *Bodas de sangre*; Cologne, Städtische Oper, 8 June 1957.

Lorca's play concerns family intrigue set against the background of the Andalusian countryside: a Young Girl (soprano) runs away with her former fiancé, Leonardo (baritone), on her wedding day. The Bridegroom (speaking role) follows them into the forest and both men are killed in the ensuing fight. The Bridegroom's Mother (dramatic soprano) had already suffered premonitions of this event since her husband and elder son had been killed by the ex-fiancé's family years ago. She is now left alone again with her bitterness.

The original inspiration for Fortner's first full-length opera came from a commission by the Hamburg Staatstheater, in 1948, to write incidental music for a production of Lorca's play. Further material for the work was drawn from his dramatic scene *Der Wald* (first performed in 1954). The opera has been described as a performance of Lorca's play with extensive spoken dialogue that breaks into music only when the tension in the drama rises. In fact, the juxtaposition of speech and song is a deliberate process which emphasizes the play's stark divisions between the realistic and the mystical and between light and dark. Accordingly, Fortner's musical style, built around a strict permutation of a 12-note row, also incorporates Spanish folk music to enhance this contrast. ERIK LEVI

Blyma, Franz Xaver (*b* Austria or Bohemia, 1770; *d* Kiev, *c*1812). Russian composer and conductor of Czech birth. In 1799–1800 he was music director at the Petrovsky Theatre, Moscow. Later he entered the service of Count Komburley, provincial governor of Volhynia, where he spent the remainder of his life. In addition to violin music and a pair of symphonies, Blyma composed (in 1798) the score for *Starinnïye svyatki* ('The Old-Time Yuletide'; three acts, libretto by A. F. Malinovsky), one of the most popular Russian Singspiels of its day. First performed at the Petrovsky under the composer's direction on 3/14 February 1800, it remained in the repertory until the 1830s, epitomizing the sentimental approach to national subject matter that characterized the early Romantic style in Russia. The plot is simple to the point of virtual non-existence; the essence of the libretto, the work of a famous historian and connoisseur of antiquities, lay in its pageantry of old ceremonies, costumes, song and dance. A couple of maidens are seen telling their fortune according to the old yuletide custom. Their young men unexpectedly intrude, to the consternation of the old folks; but, the latter having been mollified, the couples are blessed and their betrothal is celebrated.

One of the divining songs (*podblyudnïye*) the maidens sing is 'Slava' ('Glory'), famous owing to its use in Musorgsky's *Boris Godunov*; in *The Old-Time Yuletide* it is heard (for the first time on stage) in its natural habitat, accompanying a domestic ritual (an excerpt, together with one from the overture, is printed in Findeyzen). During the Patriotic War of 1812, it became customary to insert the names of valorous officers into the 'Slava', turning it into an expression of civic sentiments. This direction was continued by Alexey Nikolayevich Titov in his patriotic opera of 1817, *Muzhestvo kievlyanina, ili Vot kakovïye russkiye* ('The Courage of a Kievian, or That's what Russians are Like'), where it serves as a climactic chorus in praise of the Great Prince Svyatoslav. Musorgsky's use of the song to epitomize a tsar's coronation may thus be seen as a further continuation along this line of transformation.

*

N. Findeyzen: *Ocherki po istorii muzïki v Rossii s drevneyshikh vremyon do kontsa XVIII vekayo* [Studies in the History of Music in Russia from Ancient Times to the End of the 18th Century], ii (Moscow and Leningrad, 1929)

R.-A. Mooser: *Annales de la musique et des musiciens en Russie au XVIIIme siècle*, iii (Geneva, 1951)

A. Gozenpud: *Muzïkal'nïy teatr v Rossii ot istokov do Glinki* [Music Theatre in Russia from its Origins to Glinka] (Leningrad, 1959)

Yu. V. Keldïsh and others: *Istoriya russkoy muzïki v desyati tomakh* [The History of Russian Music in Ten Volumes], iv (Moscow, 1986)

RICHARD TARUSKIN

Blyth, (Geoffrey) Alan (*b* London, 27 July 1929). English critic. Educated at Rugby and Oxford, he began writing criticism in *The Times* in the early 1960s and later in the *Listener* and *Gramophone*, and quickly made a mark as a sure judge of the human voice and performing style. He was an associate editor of *Opera* magazine, 1967–83, and worked as a staff critic for the *Daily Telegraph*, 1977–89. A prolific writer with wide experience, on singers and on opera from Mozart to the present day, Blyth has edited a valuable three-volume series *Opera on Record* (London, 1979, 1983, 1984) and has written an introduction to the *Ring* (London, 1984).

Boatswain's Mate, The [*Der gute Freund*]. Comedy in one act (two parts) by ETHEL SMYTH to her own libretto after William Wymark Jacobs's story; London, Shaftesbury Theatre, 28 January 1916.

Harry Benn (tenor), the ex-boatswain, is continually proposing to Mrs Waters (soprano), the attractive widowed landlady of 'The Beehive'. Having struck up company in the pub with the young ex-soldier Ned Travers (baritone), he enlists Travers in a plan to win Mrs Waters's hand: Travers will pretend nocturnal burglary and Benn will be on hand to tackle him, thus earning the landlady's gratitude. The plan misfires when Mrs Waters locks Travers in the wardrobe, discovers the plan and gets her revenge on Benn by pretending to shoot the burglar. Benn, terrified at the apparent murder, calls a policeman (bass), and once both have been sent packing Mrs Waters's attraction to Travers and its likely outcome become clear. The score, although interspersed with spoken dialogue in part i, is symphonically constructed around folksongs and Smyth's own *March of the Women*; its pacing and orchestration are adroitly managed. STEPHEN BANFIELD

Bobescu, Constantin (*b* Iaşi, 21 May 1899). Romanian composer. He studied in Iaşi (1908–12) with Eduard Caudella and in Craiova (1912–16) with Jean Bobescu, then at the Schola Cantorum in Paris (1920–24, 1926–7) with Nestor Lejeune (violin), d'Indy (composition) and Paul le Flem (harmony). After starting his career as a solo violinist he became professor of violin at the conservatories of Cernăuţi and Braşov. In 1936 he was appointed conductor of the Radio Symphony Orchestra in Bucharest where he remained until 1972. Bobescu's compositions range in theme from historical and biblical subjects to satirical comedy. Though post-Romantic in structure, his music has a pronounced lyrical character: the melodic writing is essentially Romanian but it is clothed in a traditional European harmonic language. His lively orchestration displays a perfect handling of timbres (especially of strings) used, in the operas, to achieve impressionistic shading.

librettos by the composer

Zobail (1, after G. Coşbuc), Cluj, Romanian Opera, 10 March 1930

Trandafirii roşii [Red Roses], 1934 (3, after Z. Bârsan), Cluj, Romanian Opera, 15 Jan 1937

Ioan Botezătorul [John the Baptist] (5, after H. Sudermann), broadcast, Bucharest radio, 1939 [Act 2 only]

Gaiţele [The Clackers], 1980 (3, after A. Kiriţescu), unperf.

*

V. Cosma: *Muzicieni din România* [Romanian Musicians] (Bucharest, 1989)

VIOREL COSMA

Boccabadati, Luigia (*b* Modena, 1800; *d* Turin, 12 Oct 1850). Italian soprano. She made her début in 1817 at Parma, then sang in Venice, Rome and at La Scala, where in 1826 she sang Vaccai's Giulietta and the title role in Meyerbeer's *Marguerite d'Anjou*. At Naples she sang in five Donizetti premières: Amelia in *Elisabetta, o Il castello di Kenilworth* (S Carlo) in 1829; Cristina in *I pazzi per progetto* (Fondo) and Sela in *Il diluvio universale* (S Carlo) in 1830; La Contessa in *Francesca di Foix* (S Carlo) and Chiarina in *La romanziera e l'uomo nero* (Fondo) in 1831. She sang the title role in Rossini's *Matilde di Shabran* at the Théâtre Italien, Paris (1832), and Angelina (*La Cenerentola*) at the King's Theatre, London (1833). Her other roles included Rosina, Bellini's Giulietta, Imogene, Elvira, Amina and Norma as well as Donizetti's Zoraide, Eleanora (*Il furioso all'isola di San Domingo*), and the title roles in *Maria di Rohan*, *Gemma di Vergy* and *Lucrezia Borgia*. She retired in 1844. Her powerful, flexible voice was perfectly suited to Semiramis, her finest role. Her daughter, the soprano Virginia Boccabadati (*b* 29 April 1828; *d* Turin, 6 Aug 1922), made her début in 1847 at Palermo as Linda di Chamounix, then sang at Florence, Rome, Bologna and Paris in a repertory including Amina, Norina, Gilda and Violetta. She took part in the first performance of Marchetti's *La demente* at Turin (1856). Her voice, lighter than her mother's, was equally flexible. ELIZABETH FORBES

Boccaccio. *Operette* in three acts by FRANZ SUPPÉ to a libretto by F. ZELL and RICHARD GENÉE after a play by J. F. A. Bayard, A. de Leuven, Brunswick and V. A. de Beauplan, itself based on G. Boccaccio: *Decameron*; Vienna, Carltheater, 1 February 1879.

As the people of 14th-century Florence go to mass at S Maria Novella, the novelist Boccaccio (mezzo-soprano) disguises himself as a beggar in order to get close to Fiametta (soprano), daughter of the Duke of Tuscany and foster-daughter of the grocer Lambertuccio (baritone). Boccaccio likes to base his stories of amorous intrigue on real life, and his exploits and writings understandably scandalize the men of Florence, who are commonly depicted as cuckolds. They determine to rid themselves of him but, unable to find him, have to settle for burning his books. In Act 2, disguised as a peasant, Boccaccio arrives with his student friends at the adjoining premises of Lambertuccio and the cooper Lotteringhi (baritone); he persuades Lambertuccio that one of his trees is magic and uses this as cover for his friends Leonello (baritone) and Pietro (tenor) to make love to Lambertuccio's and Lotteringhi's wives, Beatrice (soprano) and Isabella (contralto), while Boccaccio himself makes love to Fiametta. In Act 3 a reception takes place to celebrate Fiametta's forthcoming marriage to Pietro, who is really Prince of Palermo; Boccaccio has been commissioned to provide an entertainment. Fiametta is astonished to find the young man she loves is the notorious author, while the citizens of Florence are appalled at his presence. However, Boccaccio convinces them of the wit and humour of his writings, and the moral of his *commedia dell' arte* entertainment persuades Pietro that Fiametta should marry the man she really loves – Boccaccio.

In a rich score of genuine comic-opera proportions, the major numbers include Fiametta's tender expression of feelings towards Boccaccio ('Hab' ich nur deine Liebe'), Lotteringhi's comic description of how his barrel-making drowns the sound of his wife's nagging ('Tagtäglich zankt mein Weib') and the Act 3 waltz duet for Boccaccio and Fiametta, 'Florenz hat schöne Frauen'.

Antonie Link was the original Boccaccio, with Rosa Streitmann as Fiametta and Karl Blasel as Lambertuccio. ANDREW LAMB

Bocca chiusa (It.: 'mouth closed'; Fr. *bouche fermée*). Term used to indicate music to be sung with the mouth closed, i.e. hummed. Though wordless choruses and solo passages are not uncommon in 20th-century operas, *bocca chiusa* singing is rare, no doubt principally because it does not carry. Puccini's use of it in the Humming Chorus in *Madama Butterfly* shows that the effect can be magical, but he was careful to score the orchestral accompaniment sympathetically. There are further examples at the end of Act 1 of *La fanciulla del West* and more incidentally in *Turandot*. The last act of Prokofiev's *The Fiery Angel* opens with nuns singing 'en coulisse, bouche fermée', but here and elsewhere the general practice is to sing on a half-open vowel rather than with completely closed lips. Humming is also sometimes practised as a singing exercise to help the breathing and bring the tone forward without taxing the voice. J. B. STEANE

Boccardi [Boccardo], **Michelangelo** (*fl* 1724–35). Italian librettist. He was a curious kind of literary adventurer: his output was small, his propensity to borrow tacitly from others great, and his lack of respect for the truth staggering. His first libretto was *Amore e sdegno* (original title *Ottone amante*), performed at the Venetian theatre of S Cassiano in 1726 with music by Luigi Tavelli – but this is merely a new version of Silvani's *La moglie nemica*. His *Il regno galante* (Giovanni Reali) was given at S Moisè, Venice, in 1727. In 1730 Boccardi dedicated to the Elector of Bavaria the libretto of an *Adelaide* which he claimed (falsely) was to be performed at the Haymarket Theatre with music by Handel. His statements on the title-page that he was a member of the Roman Arcadia and a Fellow of the Royal Society of London were equally untrue, and one must view with suspicion his description of himself as a 'patrizio Torinese', particularly since other sources make Mazara in Sicily his birthplace. Continuing his deceptions, he dedicated to the Elector of Saxony a *tragedia per musica*, *Kandakaar, re dell'Indie*, that he claimed was intended for a production at the Venetian theatre of S Samuele in the spring of 1731. The pretence evidently worked, for later that year Boccardi had the task of revising Metastasio's *Alessandro nell'Indie*, produced at Dresden with music by Hasse under the new title of *Cleofide*. We last encounter him as the librettist of Zelenka's oratorio *Gesù al Calvario* (1735, Dresden). MICHAEL TALBOT

Boccherini, Giovanni Gastone (*b* Lucca, 5 Feb 1742; *d* after 1798). Italian librettist, dancer and choreographer. A brother of Luigi Boccherini, he made his début as a dancer in Venice in 1757, but his major successes were achieved in Vienna between 1759 and 1767 (for example, Noverre's revived *Médée et Jason*) and from 1769 to 1771. He used this success to begin a career as a librettist; he was a member of the Accademia dell'Arcadia (with the name of Argindo Bolimeo) and published a collection of sonnets. His libretto *Turno, re dei Rutoli*, a *dramma tragico* (Vienna, 1767), was never set to music, but reveals a progressive approach to drama; its commendation by Calzabigi, appended to the libretto, led to contact with Salieri, who set to music most of Boccherini's subsequent librettos. These reveal a talent for pantomime and choreography, and handle theatrical conventions with ease. From 1772 to 1775 he was artistic director of the Burgtheater; he was in Spain in 1781 and was librettist, choreographer and superintendant at the Caños del Peral theatre in Madrid from 1796 to 1798.

Le donne letterate (commedia per musica), Salieri, 1770; *L'amore innocente* (pastorale per musica), Salieri, 1770; *Don Chisciotte alla nozze di Gamace* (divertimento teatrale), Salieri, 1770; *La fiera di Venezia* (commedia per musica), Salieri, 1772; *I rovinati* (commedia per musica), Gassmann, 1772; *La secchia rapita* (dramma eroicomico), Salieri, 1772; *La casa di campagna*, Gassmann, 1773; *Cleopatra* (os); *L'ungarese innamorata* (operetta); *Le belle amiche* (operetta)

DBI (C. Mutini); *ES* (U. Rolandi)

E. Lazzareschi: 'Nota di documenti sulla famiglia Boccherini conservati nel R. Archivio di Stato in Lucca', *Lucca a Luigi Boccherini* (Lucca, 1927), 10–11

A. Della Corte: *Un italiano all'estero: Antonio Salieri* (Turin, 1936), 104–15

E. I. Luin: 'Italiani per il mondo: Giangastone Boccherini', *Rivista italiana del teatro*, vii (1943), 63–6

G. Arrighi: 'Giovan Gastone Boccherini', *Lucca: rassegna del Comune*, vi (1962), 13–23

G. de Rothschild: *Luigi Boccherini: sa vie, son oeuvre* (Paris, 1962; Eng. trans., 1965)

G. Biagi Ravenni: 'Calzabigi e dintorni: Boccherini, Angiolini, la Toscana e Vienna', *La figura e l'opera di Ranieri de' Calzabigi: Livorno 1987*, 29–71 GABRIELLA BIAGI RAVENNI

Boccherini, (Ridolfo) Luigi (*b* Lucca, 19 Feb 1743; *d* Madrid, 28 May 1805). Italian composer and cellist. He studied with his father, a professional musician, with Vanucci in Lucca and in Rome under Costanzi. As a young man he paid three visits as a cellist to Vienna, where his elder brother the librettist Giovanni Gastone Boccherini worked; he held a post in Lucca from 1764 and visited Paris in 1767–8. By 1769 he was in Madrid, where the following year he was appointed to the service of the Infante, Don Luis (as *virtuoso di camera e compositor di musica*), for whom he worked in Avila from 1776. After Don Luis's death in 1785 Boccherini worked, from Spain, as composer to Friedrich Wilhelm II, King of Prussia; he also enjoyed the patronage of Spanish noble families (notably the Benavente-Osuna family) and later of Lucien Bonaparte.

Boccherini was chiefly a composer of chamber music; he wrote over a hundred each of string quartets and quintets. Apart from a setting for soprano of a scene from *Ines de Castro* (G541, 1798), and possibly an aria for insertion in G. F. de Majo's opera *L'Almeria*, to a text by Coltellini (G542, *c*1770), he wrote only a single dramatic work, *La Clementina* (G540), described as a zarzuela in two acts; it was performed in Madrid in 1786 at the palace, the Puerta de la Vega, of the Countess of Benavente, who had commissioned the work, apparently for members of the family to take part in themselves. To a text by Ramón de la Cruz (published in *Teatro, o colecion de los saynetes*, v, Madrid, 1788), it is in two acts, with spoken dialogue, and includes six ensembles and 13 arias; the plot concerns the identity of the mysterious Clementina, supposed daughter of a rich widower. *La Clementina*, which survives in score (*D-B*) and parts (*E-Mm*), has been revived in Venice (1951) and Munich (1960) as well as in Spain.

*

D. De Paoli: 'La "Clementina" di Boccherini', *La Biennale di Venezia* (1951), 44–5

G. de Rothschild: *Luigi Boccherini: sa vie, son oeuvre* (Paris, 1962; Eng. trans., 1965)

Y. Gérard: *Thematic, Bibliographical, and Critical Catalogue of the Works of Luigi Boccherini* (London, 1969) STANLEY SADIE

Bochsa, (Robert) Nicholas Charles (*b* Montmédi, 9 Aug 1789; *d* Sydney, 6 Jan 1856). French composer. His father, a Czech oboist and composer, settled first in Lyons and from about 1806 was established as a music seller in Paris. Nicholas studied music with his father and was remarkably precocious as a performer on many instruments and as a composer. At the age of 16 he composed an opera *Trajan* in honour of Napoleon's visit to Lyons in 1805. When his family moved to Bordeaux soon afterwards, he began formal composition studies with Franz Beck. In 1806 he entered the Paris Conservatoire. He studied the harp, and finally decided to make it his principal instrument.

In 1813 he was appointed harpist to the emperor, and in 1816 to Louis XVIII. During this period he composed seven or more operas for the Opéra-Comique, one of which, *La lettre de change* (1815), had a long run and became known outside France. At the same time he developed a lucrative business as a forger, and in 1817 he was compelled to leave the country. He took refuge in London, where he soon achieved prominence as a harpist and conductor. But his forgeries became known and it was rumoured that he had contracted a bigamous marriage; in 1824 he was declared bankrupt. In 1826, however, through the influence of the king, he was appointed musical director at the King's Theatre, and he retained this post until 1830.

After eloping with ANNA BISHOP in 1839 Bochsa followed her around the world on her various tours; at Naples he was appointed musical director of the S Carlo theatre for two years. He arrived in Sydney from San Francisco late in 1855, became ill and died there.

opéras-comiques, first performed at the Opéra-Comique (Feydeau), Paris, unless otherwise stated; printed works published in Paris, unless otherwise stated

Le retour de Trajan, ou Rome triomphante (opéra, 2, St A. Despreaux), Lyons, 1805 (Bordeaux, 1807)

L'héritier de Paimpol (3, C.-A. Sewrin), 29 Dec 1813 (*c*1813)

Les héritiers Michau, ou Le moulin de Lieursaint (1, F. A. E. de Planard), 30 April 1814

Alphonse de Aragon (3, J. M. Souriguière), 19 Aug 1814

Le roi et la ligue, ou La ville assiégée (2, M. Théaulon and J. Dartois), 22 Aug 1815 (*c*1815)

Les noces de Gamache (3, Planard, after M. de Cervantes: *Don Quixote*), 16 Sept 1815

La lettre de change (1, Planard), 11 Dec 1815 (*c*1815); as The Promissory Note, London, English Opera House, 29 June 1820, lib. (London, 1820)

Un mari pour étrennes (1, Théaulon and Dartois), 1 Jan 1816, vs (*c*1816)

*

'Royal Academy of Music', *The Harmonicon*, i (1823), 21

Scrapbook of concerts by Bochsa and Anna Bishop, 1839–45 (MS, *US-Bp* 446. 109)

A. Pougin: 'Un musicien voleur, faussaire et bigame', *Le ménestrel*, lxxiii (1907), 19

R. Northcott: *The Life of Sir Henry R. Bishop* (London, 1920), 63ff, 89ff

B. R. Harvey: 'Nicholas Charles Bochsa', *Canon*, xi (1958), 174–6

NICHOLAS TEMPERLEY (text), BRUCE CARR (work-list)

Bock, Berta (*b* Sibiu, 15 March 1857; *d* Sibiu, 4 April 1945). Romanian composer. She studied in Sibiu with Rosa Pfaff (theory and piano), Wilhelm Weiss and Hermann Bönicke (composition). Active as a pianist and singer in Transylvania, Germany and Austria, she also composed vocal and piano music, songs and two ballets. Her most important work, *Die Pfingstkrone* op.16, a three-act popular opera to a libretto by Anna Schuller, was given its première on 28 April 1927 by the Männergesangverein in Sibiu; it has since been performed elsewhere in Romania (at Petreşti, Saeş, and Apoldul de Sus) as well as in the USA (1931, Cleveland). The opera portrays traditional Saxon customs in Transylvania using music in a popular style; its arias reflect the simplicity and rhythmic richness of Transylvanian folk melody, while its harmony is predominantly modal.

*

H. Tobie: 'Berta Bock: ein Leben für die Musik', *Karpatenrundschau*, nos. 21 and 22 (1974) VIOREL COSMA

Bock, Jerry [Jerrold] **(Lewis)** (*b* New Haven, CT, 23 Nov 1928). American composer. He studied at the University of Wisconsin and served an apprenticeship writing for college shows, summer-camp entertainments and television. Three of his songs were heard in the revue *Catch a Star* (1955) and he provided the score for *Mr Wonderful* (1956). He then entered into a collaboration with the lyricist Sheldon Harnick which made them the most popular and successful theatrical songwriters of the 1960s. Their most memorable efforts were *Fiorello!* (1959), a musical biography of the New York mayor Fiorello La Guardia; *She Loves Me* (1963), an exquisite, intimate musical derived from the Lubitsch film *The Shop around the Corner*; and their biggest hit, *Fiddler on the Roof* (1964), a musical version of Sholom Aleichem stories. Bock's music is noteworthy not merely for its sense of place and time but for its structural and harmonic invention, showing a remarkable melodic gift that stamped him as the logical heir to Jerome Kern and the superior melodists of Kern's generation. He chose to retire early, at the height of his career.

musicals; dates are of first New York performance

Mr Wonderful (J. Stein and W. Glickman; lyrics L. Holofcener and G. Weiss), Broadway, 22 March 1956; The Body Beautiful (Stein and Glickman; lyrics S. Harnick), Broadway, 23 Jan 1958; Fiorello! (G. Abbott and J. Weidman; lyrics Harnick), Broadhurst, 23 Nov 1959; Tenderloin (Abbot and Weidman; lyrics

Harnick), 46th Street, 17 Oct 1960; She Loves Me (J. Masteroff; lyrics Harnick), O'Neill, 23 April 1963; Fiddler on the Roof (J. Stein; lyrics Harnick), Imperial, 22 Sept 1964; The Apple Tree (Bock, Harnick and J. Coopersmith), Shubert, 18 Oct 1966; The Rothschilds (S. Yellen; lyrics Harnick), Lunt-Fontanne, 19 Oct 1970

*

D. Ewen: *Popular American Composers* (New York, 1962, suppl. 1972)
G. Bordman: *The American Musical Theatre* (New York, 1978, 2/1986)

GERALD BORDMAN

Bockelmann, Rudolf (August Louis Wilhelm) (*b* Bodenteich, nr Lüneburg, 2 April 1892; *d* Dresden, 9 Oct 1958). German bass-baritone. He studied with Oscar Lassner and Scheidemantel. Engaged at the Leipzig Opera, he made his début in 1921 as the Herald in *Lohengrin*; he was leading Heldenbariton at Hamburg (1926–32) and at the Berlin Staatsoper (1932–45). He sang regularly at Bayreuth from 1928, as the Dutchman, Gunther, Kurwenal, Sachs and Wotan; in 1930 he created the title role in Krenek's *Leben des Orest* in Leipzig. He sang at Covent Garden (1929, 1930 and 1934–8) and with the Chicago Civic Opera (1930–32). Bockelmann had a beautiful voice of sympathetic quality and sustained with ease the long Wagnerian roles. Although a dignified and authoritative Wotan, he could not encompass the moments of towering rage. Nevertheless, his warm, mellow voice, his feeling for poetry and his artistry made his interpretation of Hans Sachs one of the greatest of the century.

*

B. W. Wessling: *Verachtet mir die Meister nicht!* (Celle, 1963)

HAROLD ROSENTHAL/R

Böcklin von Böcklinsau, Franz Friedrich Siegmund August von, Reichsfreiherr zu Rust (*b* Strasbourg, 28 Sept 1745; *d* Ettenheim, 2 June 1813). German composer and writer. He studied composition with Jommelli and F. X. Richter. His operas are now lost, as are most of his other works including lieder and symphonies, but he left significant writings on music in which he stressed the importance of folksong, and anticipated the *Gesamtkunstwerk* by advocating the communion of music, poetry and the dance. His *Beyträge zur Geschichte der Musik besonders in Deutschland* (1790) provides valuable insight into musical events in various European cities and reveals an admiring contemporary's views of composers such as Mozart, Gluck and Salieri. However, Gerber (*Neues historisch-biographisches Lexikon*) cast serious doubts as to Böcklin's opinions (the latter reported by Christmann). In the absence of both substantial musical scores by Böcklin and references to Böcklin's music in 18th-century thematic catalogues, Gerber's assertions must now, prima facie, be accepted.

Der Amtmann von Kleefeld, *c*1780
Die Wilddiebe, *c*1780
Der Zauberer, *c*1780
Der Abend im Garten, *c*1783
Das Orakel (after Gellert), *c*1783
Hüon und Amande, *c*1790
Phädon und Naide (J. G. Jacobi), *c*1790

*

GerberL; *GerberNL*
J. F. Christmann: 'Reichsfreiherr Franz Friedrich Siegmund August von Boeklin von und zu Boeklinsau, Herr zu Rust und anderer Herrschaften, ...', *Musikalische Real-Zeitung* (1789), cols.151, 154
J. Müller-Blattau: 'Ein alemannischer Musikfreund zu Goethes Zeit', *Jb der Stadt Freiburg im Breisgau*, ii (1936), 156–72

SHELLEY DAVIS

Bockshorn, Samuel Friedrich. *See* CAPRICORNUS, SAMUEL FRIEDRICH.

Bodanzky, Artur (*b* Vienna, 16 Dec 1877; *d* New York, 23 Nov 1939). Austrian conductor. In 1900 he made his début conducting Jones's *The Geisha* with the 18-man orchestra in České Budějovice. In 1903 he went to the Vienna Opera as Mahler's assistant, also conducting in Vienna, Berlin, Prague and Mannheim. In 1914 he introduced *Die Fledermaus* to Paris and *Parsifal* to London, the latter making such an impression that he was invited to succeed Alfred Hertz at the Metropolitan Opera (American début with *Götterdämmerung*, 1915) where he remained until his death. Though best known as a Wagnerian, Bodanzky was anything but a narrow specialist. He was the conductor for Caruso's last Metropolitan evening (Halévy's *La Juive*), and his repertory in New York included Gluck, Richard Strauss, Tchaikovsky, Meyerbeer, Suppé and the American premières of Weinberger's *Švanda the Bagpiper* and Krenek's *Jonny spielt auf*. From 1921 to 1931 he conducted for the Society of the Friends of Music where his repertory ranged from *Dido and Aeneas* to Pizzetti and Zemlinsky, and included the American première of Honegger's *Le roi David*. The typical Bodanzky performance was fast, intense and heavily cut (however, he gave as well as taking away, composing recitatives and other additions for *Oberon*, *Der Freischütz*, *Die Zauberflöte* and *Fidelio*).

MICHAEL STEINBERG

Bode, Hannelore (*b* Berlin-Zehlendorf, 2 Aug 1941). German soprano. She studied in Berlin and in 1964 was engaged at Bonn. In 1967 she moved to Basle and then sang in Düsseldorf, Hanover, Mannheim and Berlin. At Bayreuth (1970–78) she sang the Woodbird, Woglinde, Freia, Eva, Sieglinde and Gutrune. She made her Covent Garden début in 1977 as Agathe (*Der Freischütz*), and sang Eva in San Francisco in 1981. Her repertory includes Elsa, Elisabeth and Micaëla. During the early years of her career, her voice was exceptionally pure and even, but the singing of heavy roles affected the beauty of its timbre.

ELIZABETH FORBES

Boeck, August de (*b* Merchtem, 9 May 1865; *d* Merchtem, 9 Oct 1937). Belgian composer. He studied at the Brussels Conservatory. De Boeck was influenced by the Five, especially by Rimsky-Korsakov, and helped to introduce musical impressionism into Belgium. He was organist of several churches and taught at the Royal Flemish Conservatory in Antwerp (1909–21) and at the Brussels Conservatory (until 1930), as well as being director of the Mechelen Conservatory. Besides operas, his output includes many songs and piano pieces. He is considered one of the most representative Belgian composers of his generation. His music is lyrical, spontaneous and spiced with a certain irony.

Théroigne de Mérincourt (2, Léonce de Catillon), Antwerp, Jan 1901
Winternachtsdroom (2, Léonce de Catillon), Amsterdam, Dec 1902
Rijndwergen [Rhine Dwarfs] (1, Pol de Mont), Antwerp, Oct 1906
Reinaert de Vos (comic op, R. Verhulst), Antwerp, 1 Jan 1909
Papa Poliet, 1914–18 (operetta)
La route d'emeraude (4), Ghent, Royal, Feb 1921
Totole (operetta), 1929

*

StiegerO
A. Corbet: 'In Memoriam August De Boeck', *De Vlaamse Gids* (Ghent, Nov 1937)
F. Rasse: *A. De Boeck* (Brussels, 1943)

CORNEEL MERTENS

Boehmer, Konrad (*b* Berlin, 24 May 1941). Dutch composer of German origin. He studied musicology, sociology and philosophy at Cologne University (1961–6) and was a scientific assistant at Utrecht University Institute of Sonology (electronic music) (1966–8) as well as music editor of *Vrij Nederland* (until 1973). Since 1971 he has taught at the Royal Conservatory in The Hague. As a journalist and critic working from a strongly left-wing perspective, he is widely known for his sharp and aggressive articles.

Boehmer's compositions were initially influenced by Gottfried Michael Koenig and Stockhausen, but he soon developed his own language, working within a broader concept of serialism, based on logical instead of permutational principles. He has written two operas, *Dr Faustus* (1980–83) and *Woutertje Pieterse* (1986–8). In *Dr Faustus* (2, H. Claus; Paris, Opéra, 20 February 1985) Boehmer and Claus depict Faust not as someone searching for Truth but as a charlatan who visits fairs with his black magic; for Boehmer this is a metaphor for the modern artist as outcast. *Woutertje Pieterse* (2, Boehmer, after Multatuli; Rotterdam, Stadsschouwburg, 4 June 1988) tells an ironical story about a little boy whose pure and dreamy character is ruined by the narrow-minded morality of his middle-class environment. The musical style of both operas is eclectic: Boehmer's atonal and post-serial language is combined with elements of entertainment music, musicals and pop music.

*

R. de Beer: 'Dr. Faustus, a Cynical Opera by Konrad Boehmer', *Key Notes*, xx (1984), 18–23
——: 'Dr. Faustus van Konrad Boehmer en Hugo Claus in Parijs in première', *Muziek & dans*, ix/2 (1985), 2–6
C. Pitt: 'Boehmer's Docteur Faustus', *Opera*, xxxvi (1985), 512–14
G. R. Koch: 'Die bösen alten Mächte haben wieder gesiegt', *Neue Musikzeitung*, xxxiv/2 (1985–6), 6

MICHAEL VAN EEKEREN

Boero, Felipe (*b* Buenos Aires, 1 May 1884; *d* Buenos Aires, 9 Aug 1958). Argentinian composer. After studies with Pablo Beruti he won the Europa Prize (1912) and studied in Paris with Vidal and Fauré. His professional career was as a teacher and choral director at the Mariano Acosta teacher-training college and of the Manuel Belgrano Training Institute, Buenos Aires. In 1915 he was one of the founders of the musical society that is now the Argentinian Composers' Association, and as a member of the National Fine Arts Committee he devoted himself to the promotion of Argentinian art music. He was an important native opera composer; beginning with his first opera *Tucumán* (1918), he always set Spanish librettos, usually on subjects based on Argentinian history or folk customs. His greatest success was *El matrero* (1929), a work in which the musical language is almost entirely based on folksongs and rhythms. For many years this work remained in the repertory of the Teatro Colón, Buenos Aires. With special emphasis on the style and melodic forms of traditional Argentinian folk music, his music retains links with late Romantic and early impressionist styles and also has some features of *verismo*.

See also MATRERO, EL.

first performed at the Teatro Colón, Buenos Aires

Tucumán (1, L. Diaz), 29 June 1918
Ariana y Dionysos (1, Diaz), 7 Aug 1920
Raquela (1, V. Mercante), 26 June 1923
Las Bacantes (after Euripides, trans. L. Longhi), 19 Sept 1925
El matrero (3, Y. Rodriguez), 12 July 1929, vs (Buenos Aires, n.d.)
Siripo (3, L. Bayón Herrera, after Labardén), 8 June 1937
Zincalí (3, A. Capdevila), 12 Nov 1954

*

P. W. Jacob: *El arte lírico: su historia y sus compositores* (Buenos Aires, 1944)
J. P. Franze: 'Recordando a Felipe Boero', *Revista confitería del Teatro Colón* (Buenos Aires, 1968)
M. E. Kuss: *Nativistic Strains in Argentine Operas Premiered at the Teatro Colón (1908–1972)* (diss., UCLA, 1976)
J. A. Sala: *Kommentar und Inhaltsangabe in Programmheften des Teatro Colón, Buenos Aires* (Buenos Aires, 1976) [programme notes]
C. Boero de Izeta: *Felipe Boero* (Buenos Aires, 1978)
R. Garcia Morillo: *Estudias sobre música argentina* (Buenos Aires, 1984)

JUAN PEDRO FRANZE

Boesmans, Philippe (*b* Tongeren, 17 May 1936). Belgian composer. He studied the piano at the Liège Conservatory and composition with Pousseur, Froidebise and Célestin Deliège. In 1961 he became a music producer for Belgian Radio; ten years later he was seconded to the Centre de Recherches Musicales de Wallonie. His first staged work, the monodrama *Attitude*, is experimental both in its use of a multilingual libretto (by Michèle Blondeel) and in the stark simplicity of its action, which is repeated 20 times. Scored for soprano, two pianos, synthesizer and percussion, *Attitude* also exists in a concert version. It was first performed in Brussels at La Monnaie on 2 March 1979.

Boesmans's interest in lyrical music increased with his appointment as composer-in-residence at La Monnaie in 1983. That year he composed *La passion de Gilles*, to a libretto by Pierre Mertens. Adopting more traditional operatic conventions, it tells the story of Gilles de Rais, Joan of Arc's companion, who was tried and burnt for sorcery and paedophilia in 1440. The opera received its première at La Monnaie on 18 October 1983. His third stage work is a 'realization' of Monteverdi's incomplete score of *L'incoronazione di Poppea*. First performed at La Monnaie on 16 May 1989, the work calls for a chamber ensemble comprising harpsichord, strings, wind, piano, synthesizer and prominent percussion. In each of these works Boesmans shows his predilection for using consonance as an intermittent foil to predominantly dissonant harmonies. He sometimes adopts an 'organic' approach towards composition, allowing larger musical structures to develop naturally from cell-like beginnings. His music is often sensuous and encompasses many moods.

*

C. Deliège, B. Foccroule and C. Ledoux: *Philippe Boesmans* (Paris and Brussels, 1983)

FERNAND LECLERCQ

Bogart, John-Paul (*b* New York, 17 Sept 1952). American bass. He studied at Juilliard and from 1974 appeared at the Santa Fe Opera, where he made his début as First Nazarene in *Salome*. He sang Rossini's Don Basilio at La Scala in 1980 and appeared at the Vienna Staatsoper from 1982, notably as Ramfis, Sarastro, Raimondo (*Lucia di Lammermoor*) and Count Walter in *Luisa Miller*. He has sung with the operas of Hamburg and Munich and at the Orange and Bregenz festivals. Returning to the USA, he sang Masetto in Chicago and Gremin in Baltimore. In 1989 he sang Gounod's Méphistophélès in Milwaukee and Montreal. Donizetti's *L'esule di Roma* is among his recordings.

DAVID CUMMINGS

Bogatïri ('The Heroic Warriors'). Opera-farce in five acts (often designated the 'first Russian operetta') by ALEXANDER PORFIR'YEVICH BORODIN to a libretto by VIKTOR ALEXANDROVICH KRÏLOV; Moscow, Bol'shoy Theatre, 6/18 November 1867.

The music, about one-quarter original and the rest pastiche, was orchestrated with the assistance of F. F. Büchner, the Bol'shoy's first flautist, and E. N. Merten, the assistant conductor, who conducted the first performance.

The libretto, by the Russian translator of *Orphée aux enfers*, is an Offenbachian send-up of Russian heroic legends and chronicles and their stereotyped operatic offshoots, chiefly Verstovsky's *Askold's Grave* and Serov's recent success *Rogneda* (but not even Glinka's *Ruslan and Lyudmila* was spared). The pastiche component of the music was drawn from a wide variety of sources: Offenbach (*Barbe-bleu*, *Les bavards*, *La belle Hélène*), Meyerbeer (*Robert le diable*, *Le prophète*), Rossini (*Il barbiere*, *Semiramide*), Verdi (*Ernani*), Hérold (*Zampa*) and others, plus a small amount of Russian folksong. The Russian school is represented by *Askold's Grave* and *Rogneda*. The quotations are presented either exactly as in the original – in which case they are wildly incongruous to the action – or in absurdly distorted form.

The Heroic Warriors was revived in Moscow twice: in 1886 (as a 'musico-dramatic chronicle') and in 1936, to a new text by the Stalinist poet-laureate Dem'yan Bednïy (for the tragicomical stage history of this production see Lloyd-Jones 1959). RICHARD TARUSKIN

Bogatïryov, Anatoly Vasil'yevich (*b* Vitebsk, 31 July/13 Aug 1913). Belorussian composer. He studied at the Minsk Music Technical College (1931–2) and at the Belorussian Conservatory (1932–7), where his teacher Zolotaryov stimulated his interest in Belorussian folk music. He was chairman of the board of the Belorussian Composers' Union (1938–41, 1942–9) and was pro-rector of the Sverdlovsk (now Yekatarinburg) Conservatory (1941–2). He also taught at the Belorussian Conservatory from 1948, becoming head of the composition department in 1962. He has received numerous state awards and was made People's Artist of the Belorussian SSR in 1968. Vocal music (including choral songs and 'cantata-oratorios') has been at the centre of his output. In 1939 he wrote one of the earliest Belorussian operas, *V pushchakh Poles'ya* ('In the Virgin Forests of the Poles'ye'; E. Romanovich, after Ya. Kolos: *Tryasina* ['Quagmire']), based on the republic's indigenous folk music; it was first performed in Minsk on 28 August 1939. His second opera, *Nadezhda Durova (1812)*, was written in 1946 to a libretto by I. Keller, and received its première, again in Minsk, on 22 December 1956.

*

S. Nisnevich: *Opera 'V pushchakh Poles'ya'* (Minsk, 1957)

L. M. BUTIR/STEPHEN JOHNSON

Bogdanov-Berezovsky, Valerian Mikhaylovich (*b* Starozhilovka, nr St Petersburg, 4/17 July 1903; *d* Moscow, 13 May 1971). Russian critic and composer. In 1919 he entered the Petrograd Conservatory, where he was influenced by a circle of fellow young composers that included his friend Shostakovich. At this time he also established himself as one of the city's leading music critics. After graduating in 1927 he was a propagandist for contemporary music, both Western and Soviet, working closely with Asaf'yev and others. In 1940 he published his *Opernoye i baletnoye tvorchestvo Chaykovskogo* and *Sovetskaya opera* (both Leningrad and Moscow) and was appointed principal teacher of the history of Soviet music at the Leningrad Conservatory. Outstanding compositions of this period include the opera *Granitsa* ('The Frontier').

Bogdanov-Berezovsky remained in Leningrad during World War II; he devoted himself to administrative and mass-cultural work, and wrote the opera *Leningradtsï* ('The Leningraders') during the blockade. After the war he collaborated in the Leningrad Institute for Scholarship and Research in the Theatre and Music (from 1946); in 1947 he obtained the degree of *kandidat* of arts. He directed the repertory division of the Leningrad Malïy theatre, 1951–61, and the music-theatre section of the Leningrad branch of the Composers' Union, later heading its musicology and criticism section. During this time his book *Teatr operï i baleta im. Kirova* (Leningrad, 1959) was published. In the 1960s he adopted a new, more dramatic style in his compositions, but he did not follow the new trends of that decade.

Granitsa [The Frontier]/Doch' Barmaka [Barmak's Daughter] op.20, 1938–9 (Bogdanov-Berezovsky), 1941
Leningradtsï [The Leningraders] op.29, 1944–64 (V. Ketlinskaya), unperf.
Nastas'ya Filippovna op.50, 1964 (Bogdanov-Berezovsky, after F. M. Dostoyevsky: *The Idiot*), concert perf., 1968
Gorod Lenina [Lenin's City] (Ketlinskaya), inc.

*

I. Gusin: *Valerian Mikhaylovich Bogdanov-Berezovsky* (Moscow and Leningrad, 1966)
G. B. Bernandt and I. M. Yampol'sky: *Kto pisal o muzïke* [Writers on Music], i (Moscow, 1971) [incl. list of writings] L. M. BUTIR

Boggio, Giandomenico (*b* San Giorgio Canavese, 15 April 1738; *d* San Giorgio Canavese, 25 Nov 1816). Italian librettist. He abandoned a medical education for a literary one and had already provided several librettos for the Teatro Regio of Turin when, in 1786, the Società di Cavalieri named him official theatre poet. He continued to provide librettos for that theatre even when it became the Teatro Nazionale after the establishment of the republic in the mid-1790s. Except for one comic opera, *L'amante democratico*, all were *opere serie* and *feste teatrali*. Two of his operas enjoyed performances outside Turin: *Argea* (1797, Florence) and *Teodolinda* (1790, Venice).

Typically for *opere serie* at Turin in the latter half of the 18th century, Boggio's librettos are frequently based on historical accounts in other than the usual antique sources. Often they have an exotic aspect and always an emphasis on spectacle, both natural and human. *La conquista del vello d'oro* shows strong French influences – a dance of the infernal spirits, a fire-breathing dragon and a mid-air appearance of Jove's Palace of the Sun.

Argea (os), Alessandri, 1773 (V. Fiocchi, 1797; Andreozzi, 1799; Curcio, 1799); *L'Aurora* (festa teatrale), G. Pugnani, 1775; *Volodimiro* (os), Cimarosa, 1787; *Teodolinda* (os), Andreozzi, 1789 (Gardi, 1790); *Demetrio a Rodi* (festa teatrale), G. Pugnani, 1789; *La conquista del vello d'oro* (os), Isola, 1790; *La disfatta de' Mori* (os), Gazzaniga, 1791; *I veri amici repubblicani* (os), Zingarelli, 1799; *L'amante democratico* (dg), S. Cristiani, 1799; *Ildegarta*, various composers, 1801; *Hoanga*, V. Lavigna, 1807; *La conquista delle Indie orientali* (os), Federici, 1808

*

ES (E. Zanetti) MARITA P. McCLYMONDS

Bogianckino, Massimo (*b* Rome, 10 Nov 1922). Italian administrator and musicologist. He studied the piano and composition in Rome and Paris, and after performing widely in Europe and the USA taught at the Carnegie Institute, Pittsburgh (1948–51), the Pesaro Conservatory (1951–7), the Rome Conservatory (1957–67), and Perugia University (1967–8, 1989–), where he founded the journal *Esercizi: arte, musica, spettacolo*. In addition to serving as director of *Enciclopedia dello spettacolo* (1957–62) he has held a number of administrative positions as artistic director, of the Accademia Filarmonica Romana (1960–63), the Teatro dell'Opera, Rome (1963–8), the Spoleto Festival of Two Worlds (1968–71) and the Accademia di S Cecilia concerts at La Scala (1972–4); he was also general manager of the Teatro Comunale, Florence (1975–81), and of the Paris Opéra (1982–5). Among his writings are *Aspetti del teatro musicale in Italia e in Francia nell'età barocca* (Rome, 1968) and *L'interpretazione scenografica nel teatro musicale* (Perugia, 1979). He was mayor of Florence, 1986–9, and from 1991 he has been Sovrintendente of the Teatro Comunale, Florence.

CAROLYN GIANTURCO

Bogotá. Capital of Colombia. Between 1848 and 1978 it had visits by 13 touring companies who mounted some 72 operas by 35 composers. The venues were the Coliseo Maldonado, from 1840, and then the Teatro de Colón, inaugurated on 24 March 1885.

In 1848 Francisco Villalba (*d* 1868) brought a company that included the Venezuelans Atanasio Bello Montero, as conductor, and Román Isaza. After presenting *Il barbiere di Siviglia* in February, it remained that spring to offer *L'italiana in Algeri*, *La Cenerentola*, *Lucia* and Boïeldieu's *Le calife de Bagdad*, all in Spanish. A few years later the Rossina Olivieri de Luisia troupe arrived; its patron was Lorenzo María Lleras, the doctor who in 1853 had founded the first local Compañía Dramática Nacional. In the summer of 1856 the Rossina company gave versions of Bellini's *I Capuleti e i Montecchi* (libretto translated by Lleras) and *Norma*; Donizetti's *Lucrezia Borgia*, *La fille du régiment*, *Maria de Rohan*, *Lucia* and *Marino Faliero*; Verdi's *Ernani*, *Attila* and *Macbeth*; and Auber's *Le domino noir*. The tenor with this troupe, Enrique Rossi Guerra, remained in Bogotá – a precedent soon followed by Oreste Sindici (1837–1904), who on 20 July 1865 sang the Duke in the local première of *Rigoletto* with the Egisto Petrilli troupe; after the 1865 season Sindici married, residing thenceforth in Colombia, and in 1887 he composed the Colombian national anthem.

Among other important local premières at Bogotá were *Aida* and Carlos Gomes's *Il Guarany* (both 1890), given by the Zenardo company, *La forza del destino* (1891) by the Augusto Azzali (1868–1907) troupe, *Otello* (1893) by the Azzali company, *Lohengrin*, in Italian (1916), by the Mancini company and *Don Giovanni* (1978) by the Colcultura troupe. The first composer of Colombian operas was José María Ponce de León (1846–82), who on 2 July 1874 heard his biblical opera *Ester* sung in Italian by Virginia Florellini de Balma's troupe. His *Florinda* was first performed on 22 November 1880. Sung in Italian by a troupe headed by Emilia Benic, Adolfo Cochi and Guillermo Comoletti, *Florinda* earned Ponce de León a gold medal and ecstatic approval by his fellow townspeople. Operas by Luis Antonio Escobar, in 1958 and 1961, and Guillermo Uribe Holguín, in 1962, were given concert performances in the city.

J. V. Ortega Ricaurte: *Historia crítica del teatro en Bogotá* (Bogotá, 1927)
J. Calcedo Rojas: *Recuerdos y apuntamientos* (Bogotá, 1950)
H. H. Orjuela: *Bibliografía del teatro colombiano* (Bogotá, 1974) [incl. information on zarzuelas presented at Bogotá]
J. I. Perdomo Escobar: *La ópera en Colombia* (Bogotá, 1979)
L. A. Escobar: *Hoja de vida y catálogo de sus obras* (Bogotá, 1982)

ROBERT STEVENSON

Bogusławski, Edward (*b* Chorzów, 22 Sept 1940). Polish composer. He studied with Bolesław Szabelski at the Katowice Conservatory, where he later taught. His music is primarily instrumental and draws on post-serial and aleatory techniques. His one opera is a particularly powerful example of many contemporary Polish composers' fascination with the grotesque black comedies and philosophical writings of Stanisław Ignacy Witkiewicz [Witkacy]. *Sonata Belzebuba*, to a libretto by the composer after the play by Witkiewicz, was first performed by the Wrocław State Opera on 19 November 1977. The Faust legend is given musical weight by being threaded through the story of a possessed musician's suicide (Witkiewicz himself committed suicide in 1939). Bogusławski's musical ideas are developed symphonically, largely avoiding operatic conventions such as arias, ensembles or orchestral commentaries.

ADRIAN THOMAS

Bogusławski, Wojciech (*b* Glinno, nr Poznań, 9 April 1757; *d* Warsaw, 23 July 1829). Polish impresario, librettist and singer. He was a central figure in the history of the Polish theatre. In 1778 he became an actor at the National Theatre in Warsaw; later, under his direction (1799–1814), the theatre reached a peak in its development. He was director of theatres in various Polish towns from 1783. He wrote and translated plays, thus creating a rich theatre repertory, and he was particularly interested in opera. Often the first Polish performance of an opera followed soon after its première in Italy or Germany: *Die Entführung* was given in Warsaw in Bogusławski's translation on 23 November 1783, 16 months after its première in Vienna.

His first dramatic work was the libretto (after Franciszek Bohomelec) to the first Polish opera, Maciej Kamieński's *Nędza uszczęśliwiona* ('Misery made Happy'), which was given in Warsaw on 11 July 1778; this work also marked Bogusławski's début as an opera singer. Perhaps his best libretto was *Cud mniemany czyli Krakowiacy i Górale* ('The Pretended Miracle, or The Krakowians and the Highlanders', 1794; music by Jan Stefani), a national story dealing with events from Polish folktales. His other librettos (set by Józef Elsner) are *Herminia, czyli Amazonki* ('Herminie, or The Amazons'; Lwów, 1797), *Izkahar, król Guaxary* ('Iskahar, King of Guaxara'; Lwów, 1797) and *Sydney i Zuma, czyli Moc kochania czarnej niewiasty* ('Sidney and Zuma, or The Power of a Black Woman's Love'; Lwów, 1798). He translated many Italian, French and German operas for Warsaw and other Polish towns. In operas translated from Italian he often created the *buffo caricato* roles. He organized the first Polish school of drama in Warsaw (1811). His writings include a history of the National Theatre (Warsaw, 1820).

*

PSB (L. Simon); *SMP*
Z. Raszewski: *Bogusławski* (Warsaw, 1972)

ALINA NOWAK-ROMANOWICZ

Boháč, Josef (*b* Vienna, 25 March 1929). Czech composer and impresario. He studied composition with Vilém Petrželka in Brno from 1955 to 1959, and went on to hold such important positions as head of music broadcasting at Czechoslovak Television and director of the music publishing house Panton, as well as other cultural and political posts. He has written six operas, many revolving around themes glorifying socialism. His first opera, *Námluvy* ('The Courtship'), is a comic story of unrequited love between a shy boy and a farmer's daughter. A 30-minute television opera, *Oči* ('Eyes'), tells of an American soldier haunted by the eyes of a Vietnamese woman he was ordered to kill. *Goya* is a dynamic, animated work based on a simplified story of the artist's life when he was an opponent of the Inquisition and royal power. *Zvířátka a Petrovští* ('The Little Animals and Petrovští') is a short opera for children, and the comic opera *Zlatá svatba* ('The Golden Wedding') is a pseudo-folktale set in a contemporary Czech village. *Rumcajs* contrasts a good robber with the conceited nobility. Boháč's music is noted for its use of attractive themes illustrating dramatic situations, melodic recitatives and compact instrumentation.

Námluvy [The Courtship], 1967 (comic op, 1, Boháč, after A. P. Chekhov: *The Proposal*), Prague, Academy of the Performing Arts Opera Studio, 18 Mar 1971
Oči [Eyes] (television op, 1, Boháč, after M. Lane and R. Hlaváč), Prague, Czechoslovak TV, 1974
Goya (2, Boháč and D. Makovička, after L. Feuchtwanger), Ostrava, Nejedlý, 30 Sept 1978
Zvířátka a Petrovští [The Little Animals and Petrovští], 1980, unperf.
Zlatá svatba [The Golden Wedding], 1981 (comic op, 2, Boháč, after J. Mach), unperf.
Rumcajs, 1985 (2, V. Březa, after V. Čtvrtek), unperf.

*

J. Bajer: 'Čechovovské aktovky' [Chekhov's One-Acters], *HRo*, xxxi (1978), 209–11
E. Herrmannová: 'Jihočeský Goya' [The South Bohemian *Goya*], *Tvorba* (1980), no.26, p.18
V. Pospíšil: 'Boháčův Goya podruhé' [Boháč's *Goya* for the Second Time], *HRo*, xxxiii (1980), 321
J. Pávek: 'Významný úspěch soudobé české opery' [The Significant Success of Contemporary Czech Opera], *Gramorevue*, xviii/7 (1982), 2
L. Šíp: *Česká opera a její tvůrci* [Czech Opera and its Composers] (Prague, 1983), 342–7

HELENA HAVLÍKOVÁ

Bohdan Khmel'nyts'ky. Opera in four acts by KOSTYANTYN FEDOROVYCH DAN'KEVYCH to a libretto by V. Vasylevska after Olexander Korniychuk's play; Kiev, Shevchenko Academic Theatre of Opera and Ballet, 29 January 1951.

The opera (composed 1948–50) was conceived both to bring attention to the 'heroic struggle' of Ukrainian peasants against the Polish aristocracy in the 17th century and to show the eternal union and 'friendship of the Ukrainian and Russian peoples' through the historical figure Het'man Bohdan Khmel'nyts'ky (baritone); it was based on the well-known play by Korniychuk, at that time one of the most popular playwrights of the Soviet Union. However, the end of World War II did not bring about the hoped-for lessening of political pressures on opera composers in the Soviet Union, and *Bohdan Khmel'nyts'ky*, after its première, was heavily criticized for being formalistic and too nationalistic (in part for not stressing enough the 'eternal friendship' aspect). Musically and dramatically, the work is modelled on Mykola Lysensko's *Taras Bulba*, considered a classic in Ukraine. The style can be described as eclectic, relying heavily on 19th-century Russian models, especially *Boris Godunov*, yet with touches of more 'contemporary' colour and rhythmic drive; in substance, it is not unlike the music of Aram Khachaturyan.

Dan'kevych produced a revised version of *Bohdan Khmel'nyts'ky*, which was staged in 1953 to great approval and went on to achieve international recognition; not yet satisfied, he wrote a third version in 1977, first performed at Dnipropetrovs'k in 1978.

VIRKO BALEY

Bohème, La (i) ('Bohemian Life'). Opera in four acts by GIACOMO PUCCINI to a libretto by GIUSEPPE GIACOSA and LUIGI ILLICA after HENRY MURGER's novel *Scènes de la vie de bohème*; Turin, Teatro Regio, 1 February 1896.

Rodolfo *a poet*	tenor
Mimì *a seamstress*	soprano
Marcello *a painter*	baritone
Schaunard *a musician*	baritone
Colline *a philosopher*	bass
Musetta *a singer*	soprano
Benoit *their landlord*	bass
Alcindoro *a state councillor*	bass
Parpignol *a toy vendor*	tenor
A customs official	bass

Students, working girls, townsfolk, shopkeepers, street-vendors, soldiers, waiters and children

Setting Paris, about 1830

Puccini's intention to base an opera on Murger's picaresque novel appears to date from the winter of 1892–3, shortly before the première of *Manon Lescaut*. Almost at once it involved him in a controversy in print with Leoncavallo, who in the columns of his publisher's periodical *Il secolo* (20 March 1893) claimed precedence in the subject, maintaining that he had already approached the artists whom he had in mind and that Puccini knew this perfectly well. Puccini rebutted the accusation in a letter (dated the following day) to *Il corriere della sera* and at the same time welcomed the prospect of competing with his rival and allowing the public to judge the winner.

Scènes de la vie de bohème existed both as a novel, originally published in serial form, and as a play written in collaboration with Théodore Parrière. There were good reasons why neither Puccini nor Leoncavallo should have availed themselves of the latter, whose plot in places runs uncomfortably close to that of *La traviata* (Mimì is persuaded to leave Rodolfo by her lover's wealthy uncle, who uses the same arguments as Verdi's Germont). As the novel was in the public domain Ricordi's attempt to secure exclusive rights to it on Puccini's behalf were unsuccessful. Work proceeded slowly, partly because Puccini had not yet definitely renounced his idea of an opera based on Giovanni Verga's *La lupa* and partly because he spent much of the next two years travelling abroad to supervise performances of *Manon Lescaut* in various European cities. By June 1893 Illica had already completed a prose scenario of which Giacosa, who was given the task of putting it into verse, entirely approved. Here the drama was articulated in four acts and five scenes: the Bohemians' garret and the Café Momus (Act 1), the Barrière d'Enfer (Act 2), the courtyard of Musetta's house (Act 3) and Mimì's death in the garret (Act 4).

1. 'La bohème' (Puccini), Act 2 (a crossroads with the Café Momus to one side): design by Riccardo Salvadori for the original production at the Teatro Regio, Turin, 1 February 1896

Giacosa completed the versification by the end of June and submitted it to Puccini and Ricordi, who felt sufficiently confident to announce in the columns of the *Gazzetta musicale di Milano* that the libretto was ready for setting to music. He was premature. Giacosa was required to revise the courtyard and Barrière scenes, a labour which he found so uncongenial that in October he offered – not for the last time – to withdraw from the project; however, he was persuaded by Ricordi to remain.

At a conference with his publisher and the librettists during the winter of 1893–4, Puccini insisted on jettisoning the courtyard scene and with it Mimì's desertion of Rodolfo for a rich 'Viscontino' only to return to the poet in the final act. The librettists strongly objected, but Illica finally proposed a solution whereby the last act, instead of opening with Mimì already on her deathbed as originally planned, would begin with a scene for the four Bohemians similar to that of Act 1, while Mimì's absence would be the subject of an aria by Rodolfo. The aria became a duet, but otherwise Illica's scheme was adopted in all essentials. Other revisions outlined by Illica and filled out by Giacosa during 1894 included the 'two self-descriptions of Rodolfo and Mimì' in Act 1 and their duet 'O soave fanciulla'. At the time the Café Momus scene was still envisaged as a 'concertato finale' to Act 1; nor is it clear precisely when it was made into a separate act. At one point Illica wished to eliminate it altogether, but Puccini stoutly defended the Latin quarter 'the way I described it ... with Musetta's scene which *I* invented'. His own doubts, curiously, concerned the Barrière d'Enfer, a scene that owes nothing to Murger and which the composer felt gave insufficient scope for musical development. His suggestion that they replace it with another episode from the novel was curtly refused by Illica.

Having finally decided to abandon *La lupa* in the summer of 1894 Puccini began the composition of *La bohème*. From then on the librettists' work consisted mostly of elimination, extending even to details on whose inclusion Puccini had originally insisted, such as a drinking song and a diatribe against women, both allocated to Schaunard. The score was finished on 10 December 1895.

Since La Scala was now under the management of the publisher Edoardo Sonzogno, who made a point of excluding all Ricordi scores from the repertory, the première was fixed for the Teatro Regio, Turin (where *Manon Lescaut* had received its première in 1893). The principals were Cesira Ferrani (Mimì), Camilla Pasini (Musetta), Evan Gorga (Rodolfo), Michele Mazzini (Colline) and Antonio Pini-Corsi (Schaunard); the conductor was Toscanini. The public response was mixed: favourable to Acts 1 and 4, less so to the others. Most of the critics saw in the opera a falling-off from *Manon Lescaut* in the direction of triviality. But nothing could stop its rapid circulation. A performance at the Teatro Argentina, Rome, under Edoardo Mascheroni (23 February) introduced Rosina Storchio as Musetta, a role in which she later excelled. A revival at the Politeama Garibaldi, Palermo (24 April) under Leopoldo Mugnone included for the first time the Act 2 episode where Mimì shows off her bonnet. On this occasion Rodolfo and Mimì were played by Edoardo Garbin and Adelina Stehle (the original young lovers of Verdi's *Falstaff*), who did much to make *La bohème* popular in southern Italy in the years that followed. Outside Italy most premières of *La bohème* were given in smaller theatres and in the vernacular of the country. In Paris it was first given in 1898 by the Opéra-Comique, as *La vie de bohème*, and achieved its 1000th performance there in 1951. After a performance at Covent Garden by the visiting Carl Rosa company in 1897 *La bohème* first established itself in the repertory of the Royal Italian Opera on 1 July 1899 with a cast that included Nellie Melba (Mimì), Zélie de Lussan (Musetta), Alessandro Bonci (Rodolfo), Mario Ancona (Marcello) and Marcel Journet (Colline). From then on its fortunes in Britain and America were largely associated with Melba, who was partnered, among others, by Fernando de Lucia, John McCormack, Giovanni Martinelli and, most memorably of all, Enrico Caruso. Today *La bohème* remains, with *Tosca* and *Madama Butterfly*, one of the central pillars of the Italian repertory.

ACT 1 *A garret overlooking the snow-covered roofs of Paris; Christmas eve* The act opens in a conversational style based on two motifs, one instrumental, the other vocal. The first, taken from the central section of Puccini's *Capriccio sinfonico* (1883), is associated with Marcello and the Bohemians generally; the second, to the words 'Nei cieli bigi', derives from sketches for *La lupa* and belongs to Rodolfo (ex.1). Both men are

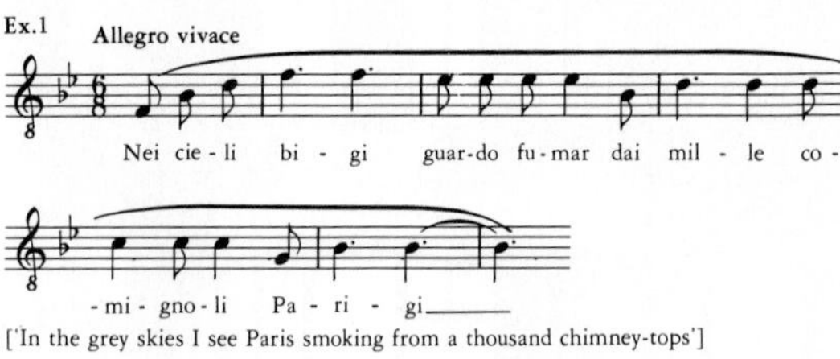
Ex.1
Allegro vivace
Nei cie - li bi - gi guar-do fu-mar dai mil - le co -
- mi - gno - li Pa - ri - gi
['In the grey skies I see Paris smoking from a thousand chimney-tops']

chafing at the cold. Marcello suggests chopping up a chair for firewood; but Rodolfo prefers to burn the five-act drama on which he has been working. Colline enters to find the hearth ablaze. Just as the fire is about to die a brisk orchestral theme (ex.2) heralds the arrival of

Ex.2
Allegro
deciso
f
ff

Schaunard accompanied by two boys carrying logs and victuals. While his three friends take charge of their disposal Schaunard explains his sudden wealth. He had been employed by a rich milord to play to a neighbour's noisy parrot until it dropped dead. He charmed the chambermaid into giving him some parsley which he fed to the parrot, who promptly died; hence his own reward. The Bohemians decide to celebrate by dining out in the Latin Quarter (and here the orchestra adumbrates a motif of parallel triads which will connote the Café Momus), when there is a knock at the door. It is their landlord, Benoit, come to demand the rent. They receive him cordially and ply him with wine together with much flattery regarding his amorous exploits; when he waxes indiscreet over his wife's ugliness and ill-nature they pretend to be shocked and throw him out. They depart for the Café Momus, leaving Rodolfo to finish writing an article before joining them. Soon there is another, more timid knock on the door. It is Mimì, their neighbour, whose candle has gone out. Rodolfo ushers her into a chair as she is clearly ailing and revives her with a glass of wine. She is about to leave when she discovers that she has dropped her key. Together they look for it. Rodolfo finds it and slips it into his pocket; then his hand touches Mimì's, prompting his aria 'Che gelida manina' ('Your tiny hand is frozen'), which incorporates a reminiscence of his own motif. Mimì replies with a modest story of her life, 'Mi chiamano Mimì', whose opening strain will serve as her own identifying motif (ex.3). The voices of the

Ex.3
Andante lento
con semplicità
Mi chia-ma-no Mi - mì
['They call me Mimì']

Bohemians are heard below urging Rodolfo to make haste. He replies that he is not alone. He then turns to see Mimì bathed in a shaft of moonlight and the act concludes with their duet 'O soave fanciulla', which is partly a reprise of 'Che gelida manina'.

ACT 2 *A crossroads with the Café Momus to one side* Tables are set out on the pavement, between which waiters hurry to and fro. To the 'Momus' motif, resplendent on brass, vendors from nearby shops hawk their wares. Schaunard disputes with a shopkeeper, Rodolfo takes Mimì to buy a bonnet, Colline exults over the purchase of a book and Marcello ogles the passing girls. He, Colline and Schaunard carry out a table from the café and sit down at it, to the annoyance of other clients, and Rodolfo presents Mimì to his friends. Mimì expresses delight in her new bonnet. To a vigorous theme in 9/8, one of whose phrases will be associated with her throughout the opera (ex.4), Musetta makes a

Ex.4
Allegro moderato
p

spectacular entrance, followed by her latest 'protector', the state councillor Alcindoro. Seeing Marcello, the lover to whom she always returns, she stages a scene for his benefit. She torments Alcindoro by complaining about the service, smashing a plate and then bursting into song ('Quando me'n vo'), a shameless piece of exhibitionism which forms the musical basis of an ensemble. Finally, she gets rid of her escort by pretending that her shoes are hurting and sending him off to buy another pair. Then she falls into Marcello's arms, to the delight of the bystanders. The waiter arrives to settle accounts. As a military tattoo passes by Musetta tells the Bohemians to add their bill to hers. They leave as Alcindoro returns with the shoes and is presented with the bill.

ACT 3 *The Barrière d'Enfer* A descending motif of parallel 5ths on flute and harp evokes a cold winter's dawn. From the nearby tavern come the sounds of revelry. The toll-gate keepers admit street cleaners and then milkmaids. Mimì enters to a reminiscence of her motif, broken off by a fit of coughing. She inquires for Marcello and when he appears pours out her heart to him. Rodolfo has ruined their life together with his unreasonable jealousy. As Marcello attempts to comfort her Rodolfo comes out of the inn. Mimì hides and overhears him telling Marcello that he intends to leave her because she is a flirt; then under pressure from Marcello he admits the real reason for their separation; she is dying of consumption and he is unable to provide for her. This revelation is couched in an elegiac terzettino which forms the dramatic crux of the act. Here Puccini uses for the first time a device that served him in the future to depict painful situations: an insistent alternation of minor chords and dissonances over which the voice declaims in monotones (ex.5). Mimì reveals her presence. Marcello, hearing Musetta's brazen laugh, hurries into the tavern, and Mimì takes a sad farewell of her lover in an arietta interwoven with musical reminiscences ('Donde lieta usci'). In a final quartet, whose melody is taken directly from Puccini's song 'Sole e amore' (1888), Mimi and Rodolfo decide to remain together until the spring, and Musetta and Marcello quarrel furiously.

[Rodolfo: 'Mimì is so ill. Every day she grows weaker. The poor little one is condemned!' Mimì: 'What do you mean?']

ACT 4 *The garret, several weeks later* Rodolfo and Marcello are once more at their work, but their thoughts stray to their absent sweethearts ('Ah, Mimì, tu più non torni'). They are joined by Schaunard and Colline bearing meagre provisions. There follows a scene of forced high spirits and horseplay, interrupted by the arrival of Musetta with the dying Mimì. Rodolfo assists her to the bed; Musetta gives her earrings to Marcello, telling him to buy medicine and to send for a doctor; she herself will buy a muff for Mimì's cold hands. Colline bids a mournful farewell to his overcoat which he intends to pawn so as to help the dying girl, in an arietta ('Vecchia zimarra'); he then leaves with Schaunard. Alone with Mimì, Rodolfo declares that she is as beautiful as the dawn, in an exchange that seems about to introduce a lyrical outburst (ex.6), but instead,

2. 'La bohème' (Puccini), Act 3 (the Barrière d'Enfer), in the original production at the Teatro Regio, Turin, 1 February 1896: from 'L'illustrazione italiana' (23 February 1896)

Ex.6
Ah! Mi - mì, mia bel - la Mi - mì!
['Ah! Mimì, my lovely Mimì!']

to appropriate musical quotations, the lovers recall their first meeting. The others return, Musetta bringing the muff, pretending that Rodolfo has paid for it. Mimì sinks calmly into death; and Rodolfo falls on her lifeless body to a thunderous orchestral peroration, ending with the final bars of 'Vecchia zimarra'.

* * *

In their preface to the printed libretto Giacosa and Illica claimed to have made their heroine a composite of Murger's Mimì and Francine. In fact she is based almost entirely on Francine, a marginal character in the novel who appears with her lover, the sculptor Jacques, in one chapter only ('Francine's muff') in total isolation from the other Bohemians. Unlike his pert, wilful Mimì, Murger conceived Francine in purely romantic terms – all innocence and fragility. By taking Francine as a model for their Mimì the librettists allowed Puccini not only to distinguish her musically from Musetta, as Leoncavallo was never able to do, but also to achieve that perfect balance of realism and romanticism, of comedy and pathos which makes *La bohème*, on its own level, one of the most satisfying works in the operatic repertory.

There is a retreat here both from the 'symphonism' that marked Act 1 of *Manon Lescaut* as well as from the unrestrained emotionalism of its last two acts. Mimì, an archetypal Puccinian heroine, tugs at the heart-strings mostly by a subdued pathos; only once in Act 3 does she burst out in an agony of soul ('O buon Marcello, aiuto!'). *La bohème* establishes a first-act design, already outlined in *Manon Lescaut*, which served Puccini for all the operas of his middle period, namely a lively opening with much variety of incident that eventually broadens out into a calm love-duet. Throughout, the harmonic idiom is bolder yet more subtle than in Puccini's previous operas (the triads of the Café Momus theme would not disgrace the Stravinsky of 15 years later). His ability to conjure up a particular ambience is nowhere shown to better advantage than at the start of Act 3, with its suggestion of falling snowflakes conveyed by a succession of open 5ths on flutes and harp over a cello pedal. Debussy, who disliked the works of the 'giovane scuola', is reported to have said to Falla that he knew of no one who had described the Paris of that time better than Puccini. JULIAN BUDDEN

Bohème, La (ii) ('Bohemian Life'). *Commedia lirica* in four acts by RUGGERO LEONCAVALLO to his own libretto after HENRY MURGER's novel *Scènes de la vie de bohème*; Venice, Teatro La Fenice, 6 May 1897 (revised version, *Mimì Pinson*, Palermo, Teatro Massimo, 14 April 1913).

On Christmas eve a group of artists – Marcello, a painter (tenor), Rodolfo, a poet (baritone), Schaunard, a musician (baritone), and Gustavo Colline, a philosopher (baritone) – meet in the Café Momus, but the proprietor Gaudenzio (tenor) is uneasy about their presence. Musetta (mezzo-soprano) and Mimì (soprano) arrive, and Musetta is introduced by Mimì's waltz aria 'Musetta svaria sulla bocca viva'; later, Musetta answers with the waltz 'Mimì Pinson, la biondinetta'. The friends are unable to pay their bill, and a quarrel with the café staff ensues. Barbemuche (bass) offers to help the artists, and honour is satisfied by a game of billiards. In Act 2, some months later, Musetta's lover discovers the attachment she has formed to Marcello,

'La bohème' (Leoncavallo), scene from Act 2 of the original production at La Fenice, Venice, 6 May 1897: drawing by A. Beltrame from 'L'illustrazione italiana' (May 1897)

'The Bohemian Girl' (Balfe), scene from the original production at Drury Lane, London, 27 November 1843: engraving from 'The Illustrated London News' (23 December 1843)

and she is forced to leave her house. Guests arriving for a party remain in the courtyard, and their chorus 'Inno della bohème', along with Marcello's cantata 'L'influenza del bleu sulle arti' and Musetta's aria 'Da quel suon soavemente', bring angry reactions from neighbours. In the ensuing fight the Viscount Paolo (baritone) leaves with Rodolfo's girlfriend Mimì. In Act 3, set in Marcello's garret the following autumn, Mimì returns to Rodolfo in an attempt at reconciliation; there she meets Musetta, who is about to leave Marcello. Marcello reacts violently, especially when he realizes that Mimì is present. Rodolfo is summoned and angrily tells Mimì to leave. Marcello's desperate aria 'Musette! O gioia della mia dimora' ends the act. In the final act Rodolfo is writing a poem ('Scuoti o vento fra i sibili') when Marcello and Schaunard arrive. Mimì returns to see Rodolfo for the last time, homeless after her separation from the viscount, and dies of tuberculosis to the sound of Christmas choruses offstage.

Recent evidence has shown that Leoncavallo wrote his *Bohème* in direct competition with Puccini, and that the scenario on which both operas are based was probably Leoncavallo's. Since the two works were written at the same time, a mutual influence was exercised by the assumptions each composer made about his adversary's libretto and musical style. The deletion of the 'atto del cortile' from Puccini's opera may be seen as a direct consequence of his aquaintance with Leoncavallo's libretto, whereas Leoncavallo, in the later version of his opera entitled *Mimì Pinson*, tried to adopt the inverse order of vocal roles which by that time had been accepted by Puccini's public.

After the successful première of Leoncavallo's *Bohème* both works coexisted for a decade or so, but Leoncavallo's proved less attractive to a broader public. A comparison of both works – highly interesting on dramatic as well as musical grounds – reveals a closer adherence to Murger's novel by Leoncavallo as well as a peculiar technique of literary and musical quotations which permeate his libretto and score. On the other hand, the impact of Puccini's musico-dramatic vision and the superiority of his musical invention eventually made history decide against Leoncavallo.

Despite the overwhelming predominance of Puccini's *Bohème* in the repertory of the world's opera houses, Leoncavallo's has retained a degree of importance, especially in Italy. Memorable stagings include a production in 1957 at the S Carlo, Naples, and another in 1990 at La Fenice. JÜRGEN MAEHDER

Bohemian Girl, The. Grand opera in three acts by MICHAEL WILLIAM BALFE to a libretto by ALFRED BUNN after Joseph Mazilier's and JULES-HENRI VERNOY DE SAINT-GEORGES' ballet pantomime *La gypsy*, based on MIGUEL DE CERVANTES's short story *La gitanilla*; London, Drury Lane, 27 November 1843.

The setting is Pressburg (Bratislava), Austria, in the 18th century (not Poland, as is often stated). In Act 1 Thaddeus, a rebel Polish nobleman (tenor), has taken refuge with a band of gypsies led by Devilshoof (bass) to avoid detection. He saves the life of the six-year-old Arline (soprano), daughter of Count Arnheim, Governor of Pressburg (baritone). The delighted Count invites Thaddeus and Devilshoof to a banquet at his castle; they go, but refuse to drink a toast to the Emperor's health. Devilshoof is imprisoned; Thaddeus is released because he saved the child. Devilshoof soon escapes, however, and to revenge himself on the Count he steals Arline and hides her among the gypsies.

Act 2 takes place 12 years later. Arline has grown to womanhood, and she and Thaddeus have fallen in love. The Queen of the Gypsies (soprano), who also loves Thaddeus, is forced to 'marry' the lovers according to gypsy custom, but seeks Arline's downfall. She contrives to make it appear that Arline has stolen a medallion belonging to Florestein (tenor), the Count's nephew, but at Arline's trial the Count discovers that she is his long-lost daughter.

In Act 3, Arline remains faithful to Thaddeus, despite her high station. They appeal to the Count, who refuses to permit his daughter to marry a gypsy. Thaddeus then reveals his true identity, which entirely changes the situation. Devilshoof and the Queen plan to shoot Arline at the wedding-feast, but the bullet ricochets and kills the Queen instead.

The Bohemian Girl was Balfe's greatest triumph and the only 19th-century British opera to gain widespread international recognition. Some of the music was composed before Balfe's departure for Paris in the summer of 1841, and other numbers were probably written there to French words by Saint-Georges, 1841–3, with a French première in mind. Denis Arundell, who edited the version conducted by Beecham at the Festival of Britain in 1951, points out that the opera's clumsy word-setting disappears when the English score is joined to the words of the (apparently later) French version. Before it was produced at Drury Lane in November 1843, however, Balfe was forced to revise the score, since he had used some of its original music in *Le puits d'amour*, performed in Paris in April that year. The main roles were sung by William Harrison and Elizabeth Rainforth, with a younger actress as Arline in Act 1.

The critics were harsh, even claiming that 'Mr Balfe has no vein of original melody' (*Musical World*). The public ignored them, intuitively recognizing *The Bohemian Girl* as the classic English ballad opera par excellence. Arline's famous aria 'I dreamt that I dwelt in marble halls' raised the early Victorian ballad to the level of art song by means of its carefully notated off-beat accents and unusual melodic spirals, and in Thaddeus's 'When other lips', Balfe's subtle use of accented passing notes perfectly expresses the genuine pathos of Bunn's lyrics. Balfe is often justly accused of over-hasty workmanship, yet he set this song six or seven times before composing the final version (and was rewarded when it sold more than 80 000 copies within a year). The initially charming chorus 'In the Gypsy's life you read', on the other hand, recurs too frequently to be effective. Like much of Balfe's music, the score is heavily indebted to Rossini.

The opera was performed in New York and Philadelphia in 1844, in Madrid in 1845, in Hamburg and Vienna in 1846, in Munich and Berlin in 1850 and in Zürich and Bologna in 1854. On 6 February 1858 it was given in Italian with recitatives, as *La Zingara*, at Her Majesty's and on 30 December 1869 as *La bohémienne* (text by Saint-Georges) at the Théâtre Lyrique, Paris. It remained in the repertories of British touring companies until the 1930s and was revived in 1932 at Sadler's Wells. Today it is seldom heard outside Ireland.

NIGEL BURTON

Bohemios ('Bohemians'). Zarzuela in one act by AMADEO VIVES to a libretto by Guillermo Perrín and Miguel de Palacios; Madrid, Teatro de la Zarzuela, 24 March 1904.

Like Murger's *Scènes de la vie de bohème*, the action takes place in the Latin Quarter of Paris about 1830. In a garret live two penniless young artists – the composer Roberto (tenor) and the poet Victor (baritone), who are writing an opera together. In a neighbouring attic lives Cossette (soprano), who is preparing for an audition at the Opéra-Comique: Roberto has never seen her, but her singing distracts him, particularly as she echoes the music she hears him writing at the piano, which has caused her to fall in love with him. When they finally see each other he is immediately captivated by her beauty. At her audition, to which Roberto and Victor have been invited by the would-be impresario Girard (bass), she insists on singing a love duet from their opera, in which Roberto enthusiastically partners her. The future of all three seems assured.

This zarzuela enjoyed an enormous vogue, often being performed simultaneously in several theatres by different companies. With the composer's consent, Conrado del Campo converted *Bohemios* into an opera, which was produced at the Teatro Real, Madrid, on 26 February 1920; but this failed owing to the differences in style between the work of the two musicians. A further attempt, in 1965, by Rafael Ferrer with the librettist José López Rubio, to expand the work into a three-act zarzuela was even less successful.

LIONEL SALTER

Böhm, Johann(es Heinrich) (*b* ? Moravia or Upper Austria, ?1740s; *d* Aachen, bur. 7 Aug 1792). Austrian theatre manager, actor and singer. He was engaged at Brünn (now Brno) in 1770, from the autumn of that year as director of the troupe. For long periods he toured in Austria, southern Germany and the Rhineland. In early summer 1776 he directed an opera season at the Kärntnertortheater, Vienna, in collaboration with Noverre: 14 works were given, almost all of them Singspiel adaptations of French operettas, many of which later became standard fare in Vienna. He was Joseph II's original choice as producer for the new National Singspiel company, but his appointment was frustrated. However, he and his wife (Maria Anna [Marianne]; née Jacobs) appeared in his translation of the Sedaine-Monsigny *Rose et Colas* at the Burgtheater on 9 May 1778 and were with the company for the remainder of the season; their daughters appeared in minor roles.

Böhm then formed a new touring company, giving performances in Salzburg (where he got to know the Mozarts) and, in summer 1779 and 1780, in Augsburg; the intervening winter was passed in Salzburg. From autumn 1780 he established his company at Frankfurt am Main, though they also gave seasons at Mainz, Cologne, Düsseldorf and Aachen. From 1787 he was director of the Elector of Trier's theatre at Koblenz, but he continued his association with Frankfurt, where Mozart met him again (they stayed at the same house) in September 1790. When Böhm died his wife succeeded him as director of the company.

The Böhms did much to further interest in Mozart's works. They revived *La finta giardiniera* in German (1779) and frequently performed it in southern Germany; Mozart wrote of composing an 'aria for Böhm' in a letter to his cousin (24 April 1780) and in other letters there are references to Böhm and members of his troupe. *Zaide* may have been started with a production by Böhm's company in mind; certainly he used parts of Mozart's *König Thamos* music for performances of Plümicke's play *Lanassa*; and Böhm chose *Die Entführung* to open the new theatre in Koblenz in 1787. Early performances of *Don Giovanni* and *Figaro* in the Rhineland were given by his company, and of *Die Zauberflöte* after his death. The repertory included many operas, ballets and plays. At a time when distinguished sedentary theatre companies were becoming established (Vienna, Hamburg, Mannheim), Böhm maintained a decent standard of touring performance in a valuable repertory over large areas of Germany and Austria.

NDB (W. Kunze)
H. G. Fellmann: *Die Böhmsche Theatertruppe und ihre Zeit* (Leipzig, 1928)
H. F. Deininger: 'Die deutsche Schauspielergesellschaft unter der Direktion von Johann Heinrich Böhm, einem Freunde der Familie Mozart, in Augsburg in den Jahren 1779 und 1780', *Augsburger Mozartbuch* (Augsburg, 1942–3), 299
O. Michtner: *Das alte Burgtheater als Opernbühne* (Vienna, 1970)
E. Mies: *Prinzipale zur Genealogie des deutschsprachigen Berufstheaters von 17. bis 19. Jahrhundert* (Ratingen, 1973), 57

PETER BRANSCOMBE

Böhm, Karl (*b* Graz, 28 Aug 1894; *d* Salzburg, 14 Aug 1981). Austrian conductor. He studied with Eusebius Mandyczewski and Guido Adler in Vienna, then pursued law studies at Graz, where he coached singers at the Opera before making his début as conductor there in Nessler's *Der Trompeter von Säckingen* in 1917. Carl Muck and Bruno Walter, who invited Böhm to the Munich Staatsoper in 1921, were strong influences on his approach to Wagner and Mozart operas. He left Munich after six years and in 1927 became Generalmusikdirector at Darmstadt, where he frequently conducted modern operas, including *Wozzeck* in 1931, a work he introduced to several musical centres. He moved to Hamburg in 1931, succeeding Egon Pollak. In 1933 Böhm first conducted the Vienna PO in an opera, and his initial success with *Tristan und Isolde* established a musical partnership that matured gradually over the following decades. Equally successful in his début at Dresden, Böhm accepted the invitation to succeed Fritz Busch as director of the Staatsoper in 1934.

He made his London début in 1936 conducting the Sächsische Staatsoper and Orchestra at Covent Garden and the Queen's Hall. His nine years at Dresden represent a golden era. He established a close friendship with Richard Strauss, whose devoted and inspired interpreter he remained throughout his career, and he conducted the premières of *Die schweigsame Frau* (1935) and *Daphne* (1938), the latter dedicated to him.

Two periods as director of the Vienna Staatsoper (1943–5 and 1954–6), and his artistic responsibility for the German seasons at the Teatro Colón, Buenos Aires, from 1950 to 1953, were his last administrative commitments. He opened the rebuilt Vienna Staatsoper in 1955 with *Fidelio*, which he called his 'Schicksalsoper'. He rapidly won a worldwide reputation as a freelance conductor, appearing regularly at Salzburg, where he gave the première of von Einem's *Der Prozess* in 1953, Bayreuth, Vienna, Berlin, Munich, Hamburg, Milan and Paris. He made his Metropolitan début in 1957 with *Don Giovanni* and last appeared there in 1979. Böhm recorded almost every major piece by his favourite composers, including three versions of *Così fan tutte*. His many honours included the exclusive title Austrian Generalmusikdirektor. His musical approach, expressed in strictly functional gestures, was direct, fresh, energetic and authoritative, avoiding touches of romantic sentimentality or self-indulgent virtuoso mannerisms. His skilful balance and blend of sound, his feeling for a stable tempo and his sense of dramatic tension made Böhm one of the outstanding conductors of the century.

*

K. Böhm: *Begegnung mit Richard Strauss*, ed. F. E. Dostal (Vienna, 1964) [incl. Böhm's own discography and repertory listings]
M. Roemer: *Karl Böhm* (Berlin, 1966) [with discography]
K. Böhm: *Ich erinnere mich ganz genau*, ed. H. Weigel (Zürich, 1968; Eng. trans., 1992)
T. Heinitz: 'Eighty Years On: Karl Böhm Talks to Thomas Heinitz on the Occasion of his Eightieth Birthday', *Records and Recording*, xvii/12 (1973–4), 24–6 [with suppl. discography by M. Ashman, ibid, xviii/5 (1974–5), 7–8]
J. Wechsberg: 'Karl Böhm', *Opera*, xxviii (1977), 1118–26
F. Endler: *Karl Böhm: ein Dirigentleben* (Hamburg, 1981)
H. Hoyer: *Karl Böhm an der Wiener Staatsoper (1933–1981): eine Dokumentation* (Vienna, 1981)

GERHARD BRUNNER

Böhme, Kurt (*b* Dresden, 5 May 1908; *d* nr Munich, 20 Dec 1989). German bass. He studied with Kluge at the Dresden Conservatory, and made his début in 1929 as Caspar at Bautzen. He sang at the Dresden Staatsoper (1930–50), and in 1950 joined the Bayerische Staatsoper in Munich. In Dresden he created Vanuzzi in *Die schweigsame Frau* (in which he later became a famous interpreter of Sir Morosus), Capulet in Sutermeister's *Romeo und Julia* (1940) and Prospero in his *Die Zauberinsel* (1942). At Salzburg he created Ulysses in Liebermann's *Penelope* (1954) and Aleel in Egk's *Irische Legende* (1955).

Böhme first sang at Covent Garden with the Dresden company in 1936, and then regularly (1956–60) as Hunding, Hagen and Ochs; he last appeared there in 1972 with the Munich Opera as Sir Morosus. He also sang at the Metropolitan (making his debut in 1954 as Pogner), Bayreuth and La Scala. His most famous role was Ochs, which he first sang in 1942, and in which his rich voice and even richer sense of humour had full play.

HAROLD ROSENTHAL/R

Bohnen, Michael (*b* Cologne, 2 May 1887; *d* Berlin, 26 April 1965). German bass-baritone. He studied at the Cologne Conservatory and made his début at Düsseldorf in 1910 as Caspar. Engagements followed at Wiesbaden (1912–13), the Berlin Hofoper (1914–18), the Metropolitan (1923–32) and the Deutsche Opernhaus, Berlin (1933–45). In 1914 he sang Hunding and Daland at Bayreuth, Ochs and Sarastro in the Beecham season at Drury Lane, and King Henry (his sole appearance) at Covent Garden. He created the title role of Rezniček's *Holofernes* in 1923 in Berlin, and sang Caspar at Salzburg in 1939.

Bohnen had a large voice of extensive range which enabled him to take both bass and baritone parts. He was as much at home as Scarpia and Amonasro as he was singing Ochs and Méphistophélès. He was attracted by parts outside the standard repertory, and at the Metropolitan sang Francesco in the American première of Schillings's *Mona Lisa* and the title role in *Jonny spielt auf*. From 1945 to 1947 he was Intendant of the Städtische Oper, Berlin, where in 1951 he made his farewell as Hans Sachs.

*

GSL; *GV* (F. Zanetti)

HAROLD ROSENTHAL/R

Boieldieu, (François-)Adrien (*b* Rouen, 16 Dec 1775; *d* Jarcy, nr Paris, 8 Oct 1834). French composer. He was the most important composer of *opéras comiques* in the first quarter of the 19th century.

1. LIFE. Boieldieu's father was clerk to the archbishop's secretary at Rouen, where the young Adrien studied with the cathedral organist, Charles Broche. He began to compose at an early age and his first stage work, the two-act *opéra comique La fille coupable*, was produced at the Théâtre des Arts, Rouen, in 1793, when he was only 18. Two years later the three-act *Rosalie et Myrza*

was performed at the same theatre; the texts for both these operas were by the composer's father.

In 1796 Boieldieu moved to Paris, where his great natural talent was immediately recognized. After three one-act pieces had been produced by the Opéra-Comique, *Zoraïme et Zulnar*, in three acts, was performed by the same company in 1798. Boieldieu scored a popular triumph in 1800 with *Le calife de Bagdad*, but when Cherubini asked if he was not ashamed of such an undeserved success, he enrolled as a pupil with the Italian master. His next opera, *Ma tante Aurore* (1803), displayed greater technical skill as well as more originality.

Having two years previously contracted an unsuccessful marriage with Clotilde Malfleurai, the dancer known as Mlle Clotilde, in 1804 Boieldieu went to St Petersburg as court composer to Tsar Alexander I. He made his Russian début with *Aline, reine de Golconde* to a libretto by Vial and Favières which H.-M. Berton had set the year before. Boieldieu composed eight other comic operas, as well as incidental music to Racine's tragedy *Athalie*, during the years he spent in Russia. In 1811 he came back to Paris on leave and, because of the deteriorating political situation between France and Russia, never returned to his post in St Petersburg.

Boieldieu spent the remainder of his comparatively short career in Paris. He was welcomed back to the Opéra-Comique in 1812 with his greatest success to date, *Jean de Paris*, and he continued to compose for that company, either on his own or in collaboration with other musicians such as Hérold, Berton, Auber, Catel and Cherubini. He also collaborated on two works for the Opéra: *Blanche de Provence* (with Berton, Rodolphe Kreutzer, Paer and Cherubini) in 1821 and *Pharamond* (with Berton and Kreutzer) in 1825, the year that *La dame blanche* started its triumphal and long-lasting reign at the Opéra-Comique.

With *La dame blanche*, one of the most popular French operas ever written, Boieldieu reached the apogee of his career (for illustration *see* OPÉRA COMIQUE, fig.2). After it he completed only one more work, *Les deux nuits* (1829), on his own and one, *La marquise de Brinvilliers* (1831), in collaboration. Then the tuberculosis which he had contracted in Russia became much worse. Before his departure for Russia Boieldieu had taught piano at the Conservatoire. In 1817 he succeeded Méhul as a member of the Académie des Beaux-Arts, and in 1820 he became professor of composition at the Conservatoire, where his pupils included Adolphe Adam and Boieldieu's illegitimate son, Adrien Louis Victor (1815–83), whose *Marguerite* was successfully performed by the Opéra-Comique in 1838. His son was also a composer (*see* BOIELDIEU, LOUIS).

2. WORKS. During the early years of his career Boieldieu was victim to his own extraordinary facility; music gushed from his pen, tuneful and stylish but unoriginal. After Cherubini's implied criticism of *Le calife de Bagdad* (an unpretentious and wholly delightful piece), which Boieldieu evidently took to heart, he could never again be accused of lack of originality, while his technique certainly improved. The works he wrote in Russia were mainly pot-boilers, but *Aline, reine de Golconde* (1804), with Jeannette Philis (sister of Boieldieu's second wife and one of his favourite interpreters) in the title role, was well received, and *Les voitures versées* (1808) was adapted for the Opéra-Comique at the Théâtre Feydeau in 1822. Berlioz heard it there and apparently enjoyed it, though his *Mémoires* contain the somewhat jaundiced comment that Boieldieu 'expressed surprise at any combination of harmonies outside the three chords with which he had trifled all his life'.

With *Jean de Paris* (1812) Boieldieu attained his maturity, displaying to the full the lyrical profusion and orchestral mastery so greatly admired by his contemporaries. He also began to show much deeper insight into character and a growing sense of drama in his subsequent operas. *Le nouveau seigneur de village* (1813), a feather-light one-act entertainment, and *La fête du village voisin* (1816), a more substantial piece, were both highly praised on their initial productions, but neither remained for long in the Opéra-Comique repertory. With reference to the latter, Félix Clément wrote that 'no other composer can better express in music the elegance, the sweet and subtle humour, the flirtatiousness and the gracious frivolity of the gentle sex' than Boieldieu can. It was not only attractive young women that he could draw with sympathy; as early as 1803 *Ma tante Aurore* offered a splendid protrait of an elderly female eccentric, while Rose, heroine of *La jeune femme colère* (1805), created by Jeannette Philis in Russia, is a termagant with a heart of gold.

In *Le petit chaperon rouge* (1818), a version of *Little Red Riding Hood* for adults with a wicked baron as villain in place of the wolf, Boieldieu paid tribute to Méhul, who had died the previous year and whose seat in the Academy he had inherited. It was generally noted that the orchestration in this work was considerably richer and more varied than in earlier operas. For his contribution to *Blanche de Provence* (1821), a *pièce d'occasion* commissioned by the Opéra to celebrate the birth of the Duc de Bordeaux, posthumous son of the Duc de Berry, Boieldieu was awarded the cross of the Légion d'honneur; he was also attached to the household of the Duchesse de Berry in the capacity of honorary composer.

With *La dame blanche* (1825) Boieldieu achieved fame not only in Paris but throughout Europe. The opera was admired by Weber, whose music had had a strong influence on the French composer, and also by Wagner; Clément allowed that the chief male characters, George Brown, Dickson and, in particular, Gaveston the villainous steward, were this time as well drawn as the female ones. The score of *La dame blanche* brims over with gorgeous melodic invention, but it is a significant advance in dramatic power that singles out this work from the rest of Boieldieu's oeuvre and which gives rise to speculation about the operas that he might have composed had his health not given out when it did.

Les deux nuits (1829) was not a success, being saddled with a poor libretto and a complicated plot, but it contains much fine music, including one scene almost as dramatic as that of the auction in *La dame blanche* and a chorus, 'La belle nuit', which provided Wagner with a source for the Bridal March in *Lohengrin*. Boieldieu's final operatic composition, his small contribution to *La marquise de Brinvilliers* (1831) – there were nine collaborators in all – was of minor importance. The subject of the opera, a murderess who kills her husband and several other people as well, was considered unsuitable for the family audiences of the Opéra-Comique, which continued to flock to *La dame blanche* whenever it was revived till the end of the 19th century.

Boieldieu's influence on French composers of *opéra comique* throughout the century was considerable. Hérold and Adam were the immediate inheritors of his style; Auber, though four years older than Boieldieu, was also influenced by him, as was Thomas in his earlier comic works. Boieldieu's sure touch in character-drawing is to be found in Gounod and subsequently in Bizet, but the elegance and wit of the composer of *Jean de Paris* are most nearly approached and most strongly displayed by Delibes and Chabrier.

See also CALIFE DE BAGDAD, LE; DAME BLANCHE, LA; and JEAN DE PARIS.

printed works published in Paris unless otherwise stated
POC – *Paris, Opéra-Comique* SPH – *St Petersburg, Hermitage*

title	*genre, acts*	*libretto*	*first performance(s)*	*sources; remarks*
La fille coupable	oc, 2	J. F. A. Boieldieu	Rouen, Arts, 2 Nov 1793	*F-R(m)*
Rosalie et Myrza	oc, 3	Boieldieu	Rouen, Arts, 28 Oct 1795	lost
La famille suisse	oc, 1	C. de Saint-Just [G. d'Aucourt]	POC (Feydeau), 11 Feb 1797	vs (1797)
L'heureuse nouvelle	oc, 1	Saint-Just and C. de Longchamps	POC (Feydeau), 7 Nov 1797	lost
Le pari, ou Mombreuil et Merville	oc, 1	Longchamps	POC (Favart), 15 Dec 1797	lost
Zoraïme et Zulnar	oc, 3	Saint-Just	POC (Favart), 10 May 1798	vs (1798)
La dot de Suzette	oc, 1	J. Dejaure, after J. Fiévée	POC (Favart), 5 Sept 1798	vs (1798)
Les méprises espagnoles	oc, 1	Saint-Just	POC (Feydeau), 18 April 1799	lost
Emma, ou La prisonnière	oc, 1	V. de Jouy, Saint-Just and Longchamps	Paris, Montansier, 12 Sept 1799	frag. *R(m)*; collab. Cherubini
Béniowski, ou Les exilés du Kamtchatka	oc, 3	A. Duval, after A. F. F. von Kotzebue	POC (Favart), 8 June 1800	vs (1800); rev. version, POC (Feydeau), 20 July 1824, vs (1824)
Le calife de Bagdad	oc, 1	Saint-Just	POC (Favart), 16 Sept 1800	vs (1800)
Ma tante Aurore, ou Le roman impromptu	oc, 2	Longchamps	POC (Feydeau), 13 Jan 1803	vs (1803)
Le baiser et la quittance, ou Une aventure de garnison	oc, 3	L. B. Picard, M. Dieulafoy and Longchamps	POC (Feydeau), 18 June 1803	*B-Bc*, *F-Pn*; collab. Kreutzer, Méhul and Isouard
Aline, reine de Golconde	oc, 3	J. Vial and E. de Favières	SPH, 5/17 March 1804	*Pn*
La jeune femme colère	oc, 1	Claparède, after C.-G. Etienne	SPH, 18/30 April 1805; POC (Feydeau), 12 Oct 1812	vs (1805)
Abderkan	oc, 1	Dégligny	St Petersburg, Peterhof Palace, 26 July/7 Aug 1805	*R(m)*
Un tour de soubrette	oc, 1	N. Gersin	St Petersburg, 16/28 April 1806	*RU-SPtob*
Télémaque	oc, 3	P. Dercy	SPH, 16/28 Dec 1806	vs (St Petersburg, 1807)
Amour et Mystère, ou Lequel est mon cousin?	oc, 1	J. Pain	St Petersburg, 1807	lost
Les voitures versées	oc, 2	E. Dupaty	SPH, 4/16 April 1808	*F-R(m)*
Rien de trop, ou Les deux paravents	oc, 1	Pain	SPH, 25 Dec 1810/6 Jan 1811; POC (Feydeau), 19 April 1811	vs (1811)
Jean de Paris	oc, 2	Saint-Just	POC (Feydeau), 4 April 1812	vs (1812)
Le nouveau seigneur de village	oc, 1	A. F. Creuzé de Lesser and J. F. Roger	POC (Feydeau), 29 June 1813	vs (1813)
Bayard à Mézières, ou Le siège de Mézières	oc, 1	A. R. P. Allisan de Chazet and Dupaty	POC (Feydeau), 12 Feb 1814	vs (1814); collab. Catel, Cherubini and Isouard
Le béarnais, ou Henri IV en voyage	oc, 1	C. Sewrin	POC (Feydeau), 21 May 1814	lost; collab. Kreutzer
Angéla, ou L'atelier de Jean Cousin	oc, 1	C. Montcloux d'Epinay	POC (Feydeau), 11 or 13 June 1814	*Pn*; collab. Gail
La fête du village voisin	oc, 3	Sewrin	POC (Feydeau), 5 March 1816	vs (1816)
Charles de France, ou Amour et Gloire [Act 1]	oc, 2	M. E. G. M. Théaulon de Lambert and F. V. A. d'Artois de Bournonville	POC (Feydeau), 18 June 1816	vs (1816); Act 2 by Hérold
Le petit chaperon rouge	oc, 3	Théaulon de Lambert	POC (Feydeau), 30 June 1818	vs (1818)
Blanche de Provence, ou La cour des fées	opéra, 1	Théaulon de Lambert and de Rancé	Paris, Tuileries, 1 May 1821	*Po*; collab. H.-M. Berton, Cherubini, Kreutzer and Paer
Les arts rivaux	scène lyrique, 1	R. A. P. de Chazet	Paris, Hôtel de Ville, 2 May 1821	lost; collab. Berton
La France et l'Espagne	scène lyrique, 1	Chazet	Paris, Hôtel de Ville, 15 Dec 1823	lost
Les trois genres	scène lyrique, 1	E. Scribe, Dupaty and M. Pichat	Paris, Odéon, 27 April 1824	frag. *R(m)*; collab. Auber

title	genre, acts	libretto	first performance(s)	sources; remarks
Pharamond	opéra, 3	F. Ancelot, P.-M.-A. Guiraud and L. A. Soumet	Paris, Opéra, 10 June 1825	*Pn**, *Po*, *R(m)*, vs (Paris, n.d.); collab. Berton and Kreutzer
La dame blanche	oc, 3	Scribe, after W. Scott	POC (Feydeau), 10 Dec 1825	vs (1825)
Les deux nuits	oc, 3	Scribe, after J.-N. Bouilly	POC (Ventadour), 20 May 1829	vs (1829)
Marguerite	oc, 3	Scribe		*R(m)*; inc., Act 1 sketched 1830
La marquise de Brinvilliers	drame lyrique, 3	Castil-Blaze [F.-H.-J. Blaze] and Scribe	POC (Ventadour), 31 Oct 1831	vs (1831); collab. Auber, Batton, Berton, Blangini, Carafa, Cherubini, Hérold and Paer
Les jeux floraux				frag. *R(m)*; inc.

A. L. V. Boieldieu: *Relation de mon voyage en Italie* (MS, *F-Rm*, 1832–3)
H. Berlioz: 'Boieldieu', *Le rénovateur* (14 Oct 1834)
Quatremère de Quincy: *Notice historique sur la vie et les ouvrages de M. Boieldieu* (Paris, 1837)
J.-A. Réfuville: *Boieldieu: sa vie, ses oeuvres* (Rouen, 1851)
A. Adam: *Souvenirs d'un musicien* (Paris, 1857)
G. Héquet: *A. Boieldieu: sa vie et ses oeuvres* (Paris, 1864)
H. Berlioz: *Mémoires* (Paris, 1870; Eng. trans., 1969)
A. Adam: *Derniers souvenirs d'un musicien* (Paris, 1871)
J. Carlez: *Notices sur quelques musiciens rouennais* (Caen, 1885)
P.-L. Robert: 'Lettres de Boieldieu (1830–1834)', *BSIM*, v (1909), 899–918, 996–1007
——: 'Correspondance de Boieldieu', *RMI*, xix (1912), 75–107; xxii (1915), 520–59,
——: Lettres inédites d'Adrien Boieldieu', *ReM*, vii/4 (1925–6), 111–30
A. Schaeffner: 'A propos de *La dame blanche*', ibid, 97–101
R.-A. Mooser: *L'opéra-comique français en Russie au XVIIIe siècle* (Geneva, 1932)
G. Favre: 'Quelques lettres inédites de Boieldieu', *ReM* (1938), no.185, pp.1–10
——: 'La danseuse Clotilde Malfleurai: première femme d'Adrien Boieldieu', *ReM* (1940), no.195, pp.1–11
——: *Boieldieu, sa vie, son oeuvre* (Paris, 1944–5) [with complete bibliography]
——: 'L'amitié de deux musiciens: Boieldieu et Cherubini', *ReM* (1946), no.201, pp.217–25
D. Charlton: *Orchestration and Orchestral Practice in Paris, 1789–1810* (diss., U. of Cambridge, 1973)
J.-M. Bailbé: '*La dame blanche, ou Le fantastique galant* (Boieldieu et Nodier)', *Etudes normandes*, ii (1984), 6–16
C. Goubault: 'Adrien Boieldieu (1815–1883), compositeur d'*opéras comiques*: l'ombre de son père', *Etudes normandes*, ii (1984), 42–56

ELIZABETH FORBES

Boieldieu, (Adrien) Louis (Victor) (*b* Paris, 3 Nov 1815; *d* Quincy, 9 July 1883). French composer. The illegitimate son of Adrien Boieldieu and Thérèse Regnault, a singer at the Opéra-Comique, he was served both ill and well by his father's fame. Following the death of his father in 1834 the French government allocated him an annual pension of 1200 francs. His début as a stage composer came with *Marguerite*, a work left incomplete by his father which Louis hastened to finish, only to be met with resounding failure at the box office. None of his subsequent works achieved more than ephemeral notice in contrast to the triumphs of the elder Boieldieu.

In *La fille invisible*, the heroine plays the role of a phantom, an echo of *La dame blanche* that did not find favour with the public; a waltz chorus is used to provide local colour for the German setting in the first two acts, five years before Gounod's use of the same topos in the second act of *Faust*. The work is representative of Boieldieu's mature writing: it shows thorough acquaintance with the style of Donizetti – particularly in parlante passages – liberal use of modulations through thirds, but undistinguished melodies. *L'opéra à la cour*, initially intended for the inauguration of a new building for the Opéra-Comique, is of interest as a particularly elaborate example in the tradition of 19th-century French operatic pastiches. It includes musical materials from such diverse sources as Weber's *Der Freischütz*, Rossini's *Bianca e Falliero* and 'God Save the Queen'.

first performed in Paris unless otherwise stated

Marguerite (oc, 3, E. Scribe and F. de Planard), OC (Bourse), 18 June 1838 (Paris, *c*1838), collab. A. Boieldieu
L'opéra à la cour (oc, 4, Scribe and J.-H. Vernoy de Saint-Georges), OC (Favart), 16 July 1840, collab. Grisar
L'aïeule (oc, 1, Saint-Georges), OC (Favart), 27 Aug 1841
Le bouquet de l'infante (oc, 3, Planard and A. de Leuven), OC (Favart), 27 April 1847, vs (Paris, *c*1847)
La butte des moulins (oc, 3, J. Gabriel and P. Desforges), Lyrique, 6 Jan 1852, vs (Paris, *c*1852)
La fille invisible (oc, 3, Saint-Georges and H. Dupin), Lyrique, 6 Feb 1854, vs (Paris, *c*1854)
Le moulin du roi (oc, 2, de Leuven), Baden Baden, 15 July 1858
Le chevalier Lubin (oc, 1, M. Carré and V. Perrot), Fantaisies-Parisiennes, 23 May 1866, vs (Paris, *c*1867)
La fête des nations (à-propos allégorique, 1, A. Pougin), Fantaisies-Parisiennes, 27 April 1867
La halte du roi (oc, 2, C.-L.-E. Nuitter), Rouen, Arts, 16 Dec 1875
Alain Blanchard (opéra, 3, J. Réfuveille), unperf.
Phryné, unperf.

STEVEN HUEBNER

Boismortier, Joseph Bodin de (*b* Thionville, 23 Dec 1689; *d* Roissy-en-Brie, 28 Oct 1755). French composer. After spending his early life in Metz and Perpignan, he moved to Paris in about 1722 and quickly established a reputation as a composer of cantatas and instrumental music. His output in these genres was prolific, in contrast to his operatic works, of which there are four (including two sung ballets). He is known to have been *chef d'orchestre* at the Foire St Laurent in 1744, having served as *sous-chef* the year before, and in 1745 he also assumed the same position at the Foire St Germain. His first stage work, the picturesque ballet *Les voyages de l'Amour* (1736), contains episodic vignettes of love in rustic, urban and courtly settings, linked by the travels of Amour [Cupid] in search of constancy. *Daphnis et Chloé*, similar in tone and based on a pastoral romance by Longus, followed in 1747. Portraying innocent *amour champêtre* in a continuous but loosely woven plot, its most notable features are an oracle, announced by a *symphonie mystérieuse* in E minor with widely spaced obbligatos for flutes, violins and bassoons, and a dream sequence preceding the reunion of the two lovers. A revival in 1752 gave rise to P. T. Gondot's parody *Les bergers de qualité* at the Comédie-Italienne.

Boismortier had meanwhile composed his most important operatic work, the *ballet-comique Don Quichote chez la duchesse* (1743), significant historically as the first of C.-S. Favart's librettos to be set entirely to music. Its source was the second volume of Cervantes's work – Don Quichote and his squire are made welcome at the castle in Spain of an anonymous duke and duchess, and there follows a series of spectacular practical jokes – although this scenario provided ample scope for further elaboration by Favart. The first performance featured Marie Fel as Altisidore (who, as a self-styled Queen of Japan, dressed in oriental costume for a Japanese *divertissement*), the dancers Camargo and Louis Dupré and a chorus of 32. The work, like its companion piece, Mouret's *comédie-lyrique Les amours de Ragonde* (first heard in 1742), was influential in pointing the way to a lighter form of lyric comedy in contrast to the *opéras-ballets* previously staged at the Opéra, and in some measure prepared the ground for the later emergence of the *opéra comique*. Boismortier's music contains many italianate figurations and elaborate, inventive instrumental effects, particularly in the *ariettes*, although the recitatives and *airs* follow French stylistic models. His stage works, in general, are characterized by a clear prosody, and if the vocal writing lacks at times a strong sense of invention and development, it is nonetheless enlivened by its delicacy and charm, and by much elegant dance music.

first performed and published in Paris unless otherwise stated

Les voyages de l'Amour op.60 (ballet, 4, C.-A. Le Clerc de La Bruère), Opéra, 26 April 1736 (1736)

Don Quichote chez la duchesse op.97 (ballet-comique, 3, C.-S. Favart), Opéra, 12 Feb 1743, *F-Po*; (1743); ed. R. Blanchard (1971)

Daphnis et Chloé op.102 (opéra, 4. P. Laujon), Opéra, 28 Sept 1747 (1747)

Unperf.: Daphné (tragédie-lyrique, Pigné)

*

ES (E. Zanetti); *MGG* (F. Raugel)

Mercure de France (May 1736), 977–87; (June 1736), 1443–7; (October 1747), 128–34; (June 1752), 164

F. Parfaict and C. Parfaict: *Histoire de L'Académie royale de musique* (MS, 1741, *F-Pn*), ff.80f

——: *Dictionnaire des théâtres de Paris* (Paris, 1756), ii, 249–50

J.-B. de La Borde: *Essai sur la musique ancienne et moderne* (Paris, 1780)

H. Tribout de Morembert: 'Bodin de Boismortier: notes sur un musicien lorrain', *RdM*, liii (1967), 41–52

R. Blanchard: Preface to Joseph Bodin de Boismortier: *Don Quichote chez la duchesse* (Paris, 1971)

ELISABETH COOK, PHILIP WELLER

Boito, Arrigo [Enrico] (*b* Padua, 24 Feb 1842; *d* Milan, 10 June 1918). Italian librettist, composer, poet and critic. He is best remembered for his one completed opera, *Mefistofele*, and for his collaborations as librettist with Verdi.

1. Life. 2. Librettos. 3. Operas.

1. Life. The son of a painter of miniatures and a Polish countess, he was brought up in Venice after his father deserted his wife and two sons. Between the ages of five and ten he received his first musical instruction from Luigi Plet and the brothers Antonio and Giovanni Buzzolla. There being no conservatory at Venice (one would be founded in 1866), he enrolled at the Milan Conservatory in 1853; after 1854 his course was subsidized by a grant. At first his teachers found him eccentric and lackadaisical, but when he began his lifelong friendship with another student, Franco Faccio, admitted in 1855, Boito's progress became marked. In September 1860 their joint cantata, *Il quattro giugno*, was performed at the conservatory. The title referred to 4 June 1859, the date of the battle of Magenta in which one of their schoolmates was killed. Boito supplied the text and composed half of the music, and the work earned a notable success in the Risorgimental fervour of those days. In their graduation year, 1861, he and Faccio presented a second cantata, *Le sorelle d'Italia*, celebrating European peoples still under foreign domination.

Boito's principal teacher and advocate at the conservatory was Alberto Mazzucato, an opera composer and, from 1859 to 1868, principal conductor at La Scala. On the strength of Mazzucato's support and that of the Countess Maffei, Boito and Faccio were awarded grants for a year's travel abroad. In March 1862 they arrived in Paris, where they met Rossini and Verdi. There Boito wrote the text for Verdi's *Inno delle nazioni*, performed at Her Majesty's Theatre, London, on 24 May 1862. Boito was already at work on an opera on the Faust subject, which he had begun, according to Alberto Mazzucato's son Gian Andrea, while he was still a student. He was also planning another opera, *Nerone*, which he would never complete. In summer 1862 he visited relatives in Poland, orchestrating part of what would become *Mefistofele* and writing the libretto of *Amleto* for Faccio. He was back in Milan at the end of the year.

At a banquet following the première of Faccio's opera *I profughi fiamminghi* at La Scala on 11 November 1863, Boito declaimed his notorious ode *All'arte italiana*, wherein he advocated cleansing the altars of Italian art that had been stained like the external walls of a brothel, a sentiment that gravely offended Verdi. This was the period when Boito was associated with the Scapigliatura ('the Unkempt Ones'), an iconoclastic and bohemian group dedicated to ridding the arts in Italy of their besetting provincialism. The conservatives of the day found the group's jaunty satire and propensity for derision offensive. At the première of *Amleto* in Genoa on 30 May 1865 the self-congratulatory antics of the *scapigliati* aroused antagonism, and the reviews made sardonic references to 'the music of the future', then a favourite cliché of disapproval. Boito's affinity for the Scapigliatura can be most clearly observed in the poems of 1862–5 (published in 1877 as the *Libro de' versi*) and in his fantastic fable *Re Orso*. Here in abundance are his ironical wit, his passion for exotic words and clever rhymes and, particularly in his poem *Dualismo*, the underlying ideas that he would later elaborate.

Boito's work on his own opera was delayed by the enthusiastic reception of Gounod's *Faust* at La Scala on 11 November 1862. According to Leone Fortis, Boito had first determined upon a pair of operas, *Margherita* and *Elena*, derived from the two parts of Goethe's poetic drama (see P. Nardi: *Vita di Arrigo Boito*, p.237). When he returned from service as a volunteer in Garibaldi's campaign of 1866 his friends urged him to take up his project again, and it was at this point that he decided to fuse the two parts into a single grandiose work. During 1867 he laboured over *Mefistofele*, which went into rehearsal in January 1868. Although he had originally designed the role of Faust for a tenor, he was persuaded for budgetary reasons to revise it for a baritone. This opera was the first at La Scala for which a composer was his own librettist, and Boito unprecedentedly circulated his printed libretto some weeks before the première. Late in the rehearsal period Mazzucato insisted upon making some cuts and withdrew when Boito refused to countenance them, leaving the inexperienced composer to conduct his own work.

The première of *Mefistofele* on 5 March 1868 was a historic fiasco, lasting until well past midnight with the opposing factions in the audience vociferously sustaining their positions; the only part to be well received was the prologue. A second performance was given, this time divided between two evenings, each prefaced by the prologue and completed by Dall'Argine's ballet *Brahma*. Both parts of the opera were scorned, but the ballet was much applauded. Boito withdrew his score, his self-confidence deeply shaken.

During the next few years Boito (frequently using the anagrammatic pseudonym 'Tobia Gorrio') devoted himself to writing articles, including many on opera (see Nardi, ed.: *Tutti gli scritti di Arrigo Boito*), and to supplying Italian translations of German lieder, among them Wagner's *Wesendonk-Lieder*. He began work, too, on a libretto, *Ero e Leandro*, and started to compose it, but then consigned it first to Bottesini and then to Luigi Mancinelli. The idea of salvaging *Mefistofele* was prompted by a successful performance of the prologue at Trieste in 1871. He shortened the work, restoring the role of Faust as a tenor part, and also made a few additions; he submitted his amended orchestration to Cesare Dominiceti, whose suggestions he heeded. The revised *Mefistofele* was performed with a strong cast on 4 October 1875 at the Teatro Comunale, Bologna, a town more hospitable to novelty than Milan. Further material was added to the Prison Scene the following year at Venice. In this form *Mefistofele* made its way, particularly after its revival at Milan in 1881.

To the 1870s belongs most of Boito's activity as librettist of a number of all but forgotten operas, the single exception being Ponchielli's *La Gioconda* (1876, La Scala). His translation of *Rienzi* was given in 1874. Giulio Ricordi, a supporter of Boito from the mid-1860s, having learned that Verdi was interested in the subject of *Nerone*, suggested that Boito relinquish his libretto to the elder composer, but Verdi, still smouldering over Boito's ode, refused it. After this episode Boito returned to the subject, working desultorily on *Nerone*, and to this period belongs the first level of music for it. In 1879, through the offices of Ricordi and Faccio, came the rapprochement with Verdi and the idea of a possible collaboration on *Otello*.

Before the end of 1879 Boito submitted a complete libretto, rather different in some respects from the final version, but Verdi was impressed with its quality. It was arranged that, as a trial, Boito would revise Piave's libretto for *Simon Boccanegra*. This *rifacimento* was successful, particularly the new scene in the council chamber. Verdi then agreed to start on *Otello*, but the work progressed fitfully, and only Boito's patience and his readiness to modify his text kept the project afloat. The triumphant first performance, on 5 February 1887, set the seal upon Boito's friendship with Verdi, a relationship he regarded as the climax of his artistic life.

Their collaboration on *Falstaff* proceeded more smoothly, except for the tragic parenthesis when Boito assumed the directorship of the Parma Conservatory for his friend Faccio, so that he, confined to an institution with paralytic syphilis, might continue to receive his salary. After the successful introduction of *Falstaff* in 1893 Boito started to sketch a libretto for a *Re Lear* for Verdi, but the composer realized he was too old to undertake this challenge. Boito continued a frequent visitor to Verdi's home and was present when he died.

In May 1891 Boito had read his libretto of *Nerone* to Verdi, who urged him to get on with his own career. Within a month of Verdi's death, Boito published his five-act libretto, which was received as a major literary event. Giulio Ricordi urged Boito to complete the score so that the opera could be given at La Scala in 1904 with Tamagno. Increasingly reluctant to confront the public, Boito began an extensive study of classical metres and the musical ethos of the ancients, as well as a detailed study of harmony, as his notebooks of the period testify. Persuaded by Ricordi to discard the fifth act, Boito continued to fiddle indecisively with the score until his death, from heart disease. The incomplete score was extensively revised by a committee consisting of Toscanini, Antonio Smareglia and Vincenzo Tommasini. *Nerone*, which had engaged Boito's attention irregularly for nearly 60 years, was finally brought out six years after his death.

2. LIBRETTOS. The literary quality of Boito's librettos follows an ascending scale from those he wrote for composers other than Verdi, through *Otello* and *Falstaff*, to those he supplied for himself. It was consistent with his belief that a libretto should be notable as drama that his first effort, *Amleto*, for Faccio, was drawn from Shakespeare. Boito's strengths and weaknesses are already evident: his ability to simplify a complicated plot and the variety of his poetic language, as well as his penchant for obscure polysyllables, his faulty sense of overall proportion, and his tendency to overstress contrasts of good and evil. *Ero e Leandro*, originally intended for himself, experiments with classical metres and embodies considerable antiquarian lore. *Semira*, for Luigi San Germano, was withdrawn in rehearsal and never performed. *Basi e bote*, a comedy in Venetian dialect, dates from 1887, but was not set until 1927, by Pick-Mangiagalli. *Iràm* was intended for Dominiceti, who did not set it; it is a pithy comedy with foreshadowings of *Falstaff* (e.g. 'Il mondo è un trillo'). *Pier Luigi Farnese*, for Costantino Palumbo (1843–1928), is more intense and more vividly characterized than the other librettos in this group. The best-known of Boito's texts for composers other than Verdi is that for Ponchielli's *La Gioconda*, loosely derived from Hugo's *Angelo*. Boito changed the setting to Venice and introduced a good deal of local colour, and the flamboyant melodramatic tone faithfully mirrors Hugo's style. The characterization is anything but subtle.

Otello, the first of Boito's completed librettos for Verdi, has perhaps been overpraised. While undeniably a formidable achievement, the reduction of Shakespeare's text to operatic proportions was not as skilful as is usually maintained. Boito drastically altered Iago's motivation; Rodrigo's participation in the plot is inadequately developed; and the decisive fact of Cassio's survival is glossed over. That the libretto is finely proportioned is due more to Verdi's influence than to Boito. Nor was Boito's treatment as Shakespearean as is sometimes claimed. (Francis Hueffer's translation in the Ricordi scores has deceived more than one critic.) Laws of heresy in Shakespeare's day forbade specific Christian references on stage, yet many of Boito's changes and additions (the 'Credo' and the 'Ave Maria') insert these once-proscribed references. Boito's *Falstaff* is more extraordinary, perhaps because he was working from a lesser play. His fondness for word-play, his knack for hitting upon an epigrammatic phrase and his mordant irony all found full scope. He seems less strained than in *Otello*, and the result is exhilarating and beautifully paced.

The 1868 libretto of *Mefistofele* is more interesting as a literary document than as a potential text for music. The condensed version of 1875 sheds most of its novel features but is full of verbal felicities. The prologue, common to both versions, is without precedent in Italian operatic dramaturgy for its metrical variety and grandiose scope. *Nerone* exists in two versions: in five acts, as in the printed libretto of 1901, and in four acts, as in the printed score. The excised fifth act, for which Boito sketched music, presents Nero playing Aeschylus's Orestes while Rome burns. The four-act version ends with the death of the Christian convert Rubria. All in all, *Nerone* possesses great originality, vividly contrasting pagan magic, imperial corruption and Christian *caritas*. It is arguably Boito's finest achievement.

3. Operas. It is impossible to reconstruct the original *Mefistofele* because the revisions were made in the autograph score and the excised pages removed. The 1875 revision reveals Boito's uncertainty as a composer and his difficulty in spinning out musical ideas. Although the music contains some allusions to Beethoven, the dominant influence is that of Meyerbeer, particularly in the arias of Mephistopheles. Two episodes keep the work on the fringes of the modern repertory: the prologue and the Prison Scene.

Boito's sketches and preparatory notebooks for *Nerone* survive; they bear eloquent witness to his extraordinary capacity for taking pains, but also reveal an increasing incapacity to come to practical grips with the opera. The peculiar eclecticism of *Nerone* arouses morbid fascination, but for all its grandiose spectacle and erudition the music contains little to move an audience, except in the scene of Rubria's death in the Spoliarium. In the lifelong struggle between literature and music that represents the true dualism of Boito's career, it was literature that proved supreme and in the end stifled his talent for composition.

See also Mefistofele and Nerone (ii).

Mefistofele (prol., 5, epilogue, Boito, after J. W. von Goethe: *Faust*), Milan, Scala, 5 March 1868, excerpts (Milan, 1868); rev. version (prol., 4), Bologna, Comunale, 4 Oct 1875; rev. version, Venice, Rossini, 13 May 1876, *I-Mr**, vs (Milan, 1876), full score (Milan, *c*1895)

Nerone, 1877–1915 (tragedia, 5, Boito), inc., completed V. Tommasini, A. Smareglia and A. Toscanini, Milan, Scala, 1 May 1924 (Milan, 1925)

Librettos: *Amleto* (tragedia lirica), Faccio, 1865; *Mefistofele*, Boito, 1868; *Un tramonto* (egloga, with E. Praga), G. Coronaro, 1873; *La falce* (egloga orientale), Catalani, 1875; *La Gioconda* (melodramma), Ponchielli, 1876; *Ero e Leandro* (tragedia lirica), Bottesini, 1879 (Mancinelli, 1896); *Semira* (tragedia lirica), unperf.; *Pier Luigi Farnese* (dramma lirico), C. Palumbo, 1891; *Iràm* (commedia lirica), unperf.; *Simon Boccanegra* (melodramma, after Piave), Verdi, 1881; *Basi e bote* (commedia lirica), Pick-Mangiagalli, 1927; *Otello* (dramma lirico), Verdi, 1887; *Falstaff* (commedia lirica), Verdi, 1893; *Nerone* (tragedia), Boito, 1924

*

LETTERS

R. de Rensis, ed.: *Lettere di Arrigo Boito* (Rome, 1932)

A. Luzio, ed.: *Carteggi verdiani*, ii (Rome, 1935) [Boito's letters to Verdi]

Arrigo Boito nel trentennio della morte (Naples, 1950) [incl. previously unpubd letters]

F. Walker, ed.: *Arrigo Boito: lettere inedite e poesie giovanili* (Siena, 1959)

M. Morini: 'Lettere inedite di Arrigo Boito', *La Scala* (1969), Aug–Sept, 26

BIOGRAPHY AND CRITICISM

DBI (E. Giachery)

A. Luzio: *I copialettere di Giuseppe Verdi* (Milan, 1913)

B. Croce: *La letteratura della nuova Italia*, i (Bari, 1914, 6/1956), 257ff

I. Pizzetti: *Musicisti contemporanei* (Milan, 1914)

C. Bellaigue: 'Arrigo Boito: lettres et souvenirs', *Revue des deux mondes*, xliii/4 (1918), 900–15

C. Ricci: *Arrigo Boito* (Milan, 1919, 2/1924)

P. Nardi: *Scapigliatura da Rovani a Dossi* (Bologna, 1924, 2/1969)

L. Pagano [pseud. of Romualdo Giani]: *La fionda di David* (Turin, 1928)

F. Ballo: *Arrigo Boito* (Turin, 1939)

W. Pöschl: *Arrigo Boito: ein Vertreter der italienischen Spätromantik* (Berlin, 1939)

R. de Rensis: *Arrigo Boito: anedotti e bizzarrie poetiche musicali* (Rome, 1942)

——: *Arrigo Boito: capitoli biografici* (Florence, 1942)

P. Nardi, ed.: *Tutti gli scritti di Arrigo Boito* (Milan, 1942) [incl. all libs. and writings]

P. Nardi: *Vita di Arrigo Boito* (Milan, 1942, 2/1944)

——: *Arrigo Boito: scritti e documenti* (Milan, 1948)

F. Walker: *The Man Verdi* (London, 1962)

G. Mariani: *Storia della Scapigliatura* (Rome, 1967)

C. Orselli: 'Arrigo Boito: un riesame', *Chigiana*, xxv (1968), 197–214

G. Mariani: *Arrigo Boito* (Parma, 1973)

G. Scarsi: *Rapporto poesia-musica in Arrigo Boito* (Rome, 1973)

G. Salvetti: 'La Scapigliatura milanese e il teatro d'opera', *Il melodramma italiano dell'ottocento: studi e ricerche per Massimo Mila* (Turin, 1977), 567–604

G. Tintori, ed.: *Arrigo Boito: musicista e letterato* (Milan, 1986)

T. G. Kaufman: 'Arrigo Boito', *Verdi and his Major Contemporaries* (New York and London, 1990), 13–25

INDIVIDUAL OPERAS

Mefistofele

F. Filippi: 'Il "Mefistofele" di Arrigo Boito', *La perseveranza* (9, 16 March 1868)

G. Ricordi: 'Analisi musicale del "Mefistofele" di Boito', *Gazzetta musicale di Milano*, xxiii (1868), 81

J. Huneker: 'Verdi and Boïto', *Overtones: a Book of Temperaments* (New York, 1904), 256–76

M. Risolo: *Il primo 'Mefistofele' di Arrigo Boito* (Naples, 1916) [incl. 1st version of lib.]

A. Bonaventura: *Mefistofele di Arrigo Boito: guida attraverso il poema e la musica* (Milan, 1924)

S. Vittadini: *Il primo libretto del 'Mefistofele' di Arrigo Boito* (Milan, 1938)

A. Borriello: *Mito poesia e musica nel 'Mefistofele' di Arrigo Boito* (Naples, 1950)

J. Nicolaisen: 'The First *Mefistofele*', *19th Century Music*, i (1978), 221–32

W. Ashbrook: 'Boito and the 1868 *Mefistofele* Libretto as a Reform Text', *Reading Opera*, ed. R. Parker and A. Groos (Princeton, 1988), 268–87

Nerone

R. Giani: *Il 'Nerone' di Arrigo Boito* (Milan, 1901); repr. in *RMI*, xxxi (1924), 235–392

G. Borelli: *Linee dello spirito e del volto di Arrigo Boito* (Milan, 1924) [on *Nerone*]

G. Forzano: 'La preparazione scenica del "Nerone"', *Lettura* (1924), March

V. Gui: *Nerone di Arrigo Boito* (Milan, 1924)

others

R. de Rensis: *L'Amleto di A. Boito* (Ancona, 1927)

D. Bianchi: 'Intorno a "La Gioconda" di Arrigo Boito', *Studia ghisleriana*, 2nd ser., i (1950), 81

WILLIAM ASHBROOK

Bokor, Margit (*b* Budapest, 1905; *d* New York, 9 Nov 1949). Hungarian soprano. She studied in Vienna and in Budapest, where she made her début in 1928. Two years later she appeared in Berlin and then joined the Dresden Staatsoper, singing Zdenka in the world première of *Arabella* in 1933. She also sang this role the following year in the London première and, according to Richard Capell, 'could hardly have been better' (*Daily Telegraph*, May 1934). In the same year she sang in the première of Léhar's *Giuditta* in Vienna. At Salzburg her parts included Octavian in *Der Rosenkavalier* and

Zerlina in *Don Giovanni*. In 1939 she left Europe for the USA and appeared in Chicago, San Francisco and elsewhere, usually in light roles such as Susanna, Sophie and Adele in *Die Fledermaus*. She was engaged by the New York City Opera in 1947 but died within two years. Recordings preserve her voice in a duet from *Arabella* with Viorica Ursuleac, and a transcript of *Don Giovanni*, broadcast from Salzburg, reveals the charm and accomplishment of her Zerlina. J. B. STEANE

Bolcom, William (Elden) (*b* Seattle, WA, 26 May 1938). American composer. He began composition studies at an early age with John Verrall at the University of Washington and went on to study with Milhaud at Mills College (1958–61) and with Leland Smith at Stanford University (1961–4). He worked with Milhaud and Messiaen in Paris, where in 1960 he began work on his first music-theatre piece, *Dynamite Tonite*, a cross-genre cabaret opera that was the first of many collaborations with the librettist Arnold Weinstein. In 1965 it received the Marc Blitzstein Award from the American Academy of Arts and Letters. His second stage work, *Greatshot*, describes an incident in the life of William Burroughs. Bolcom cites Charles Ives as his earliest and strongest influence; from the 1970s he made a conscious effort to avoid an emphasis on European styles. He is fluent in a wide range of classical and American popular idioms, blending elements of jazz, rock, pop and traditional Americana. *Casino Paradise*, the first work commissioned by the American Music Theater Festival, is an accessible, cabaret-like opera that calls to mind the populist styles of Kurt Weill. Bolcom's newest stage work, *McTeague*, based on the novel by Frank Norris, is the first commission of an American composer by the Chicago Lyric Opera. The score is broadly defined by its composer as 'an eclectic mix, from simple to complex, atonal to tonal'. The two-act piece is the composer's most traditional opera to date and features a Heldentenor in the title role. Over the years his music has grown increasingly tonal and American-sounding, yet its accessibility never overshadows its integrity of craft or intent. Bolcom was active in the ragtime revival of the 1960s and 70s. He wrote *Reminiscing with Sissle and Blake* (New York, 1973) with Robert Kimball, and edited the writings of George Rochberg in *The Aesthetics of Survival: a Composer's View of 20th-Century Music* (1984).

Theatre of the Absurd, 1960 (paraphrase, Bolcom), San Francisco, Conservatory of Music, 4 March 1979
Dynamite Tonite (actors' op, 2, A. Weinstein), New York, Actors Studio, 21 Dec 1963
Greatshot, 1966 (cabaret op, 2, Weinstein), New Haven, Yale, 15 May 1969
The Beggar's Opera (J. Gay), Minneapolis, Tyrone Guthrie, 31 Jan 1979 [completion of adaptation begun by Milhaud, 1937]
Casino Paradise (op for singing actors, 2, Weinstein), Philadelphia, Play and Players, 4 April 1990
McTeague (2, Weinstein and R. Altman, after F. Norris), Chicago, Lyric, 31 Oct 1992

*

N. Malitz: 'Michigan's Crack Composer', *Detroit News* (13 April 1986)
R. Dyer: 'Pop (and Mom) Songs', *Connoisseur* (Jan 1987), 114–17
J. Rockwell: 'Music, Every Which Way', *New York Times Magazine* (16 Aug 1987), 32–3, 49–54 SUSAN ELLIOTT

Boldemann, Laci (*b* Helsinki, 24 April 1921; *d* Munich, 18 Aug 1969). Swedish composer of Finnish birth. He studied conducting with Henry Wood in London, and the piano at the RAM; in 1939 he moved to Sweden where he took piano lessons with de Frumerie. Forced to join the German army in 1942, he later deserted to join the partisans in the Abruzzi. After two years in an American prison camp he returned to Sweden in 1947. During the 1950s he supported himself as a timber measurer, and in the next decade he worked in music teaching and administration. As a composer he aimed at simplicity, purity and expressiveness, finding vocal music his ideal medium, and projecting a message of humanity, especially in his operas. He felt musically isolated in the Sweden of the 1950s, but his work achieved recognition in Germany. In later years he became increasingly concerned with composing for children; his children's opera *Svart är vitt, sa kejsaren* op.20 ('Black is White, said the Emperor'; prelude, 2, L. Hellsing, after K. Boldemann) had its première at the Royal Theatre in Stockholm on 1 January 1965. The comic opera *Dårskapens timme* op.21 ('The Hour of Folly'; 3, epilogue, K. Boldemann, after A. Bonacci; Malmö, Stads, 22 March 1968), constructed from 20 leitmotifs, has a self-ironic tone, and Boldemann's music is generally cheerful, direct and tuneful.

ROLF HAGLUND

Bologna. Italian city. It has maintained a practically uninterrupted outstanding musical tradition. Its central geographic position allowed easy contact with other musical centres in Italy, and as a trading and economic hub, it remained for centuries a thriving commercial centre whose wealthy classes could patronize the arts.

The city's operatic history is marked by a predisposition to accept and assimilate prevailing theatrical fashions, stimulated by and often in competition with the major operatic centres in Italy. Until the mid-17th century, opera at Bologna was characterized by a heterogeneity of performances organized and subsidized mainly by prominent aristocratic intellectuals: Nicolò Zoppio Turchi, Virgilio Malvezzi, Carlo Bentivoglio, Paolo Emilio Fantuzzi and Cornelio Malvasia, who depended mostly either on singers from nearby Modena or on Venetian itinerant companies. At the peak of its splendour in the 18th century the city had four major theatres, and operas were produced privately in palaces and suburban villas, convents, monasteries and boarding-schools, subsidized by such aristocratic families as the Bentivoglio, Marescotti, Pepoli, Orsi and Albergati. During this period the city acquired a wide reputation as a training-ground for the opera singers who for many years dominated the major Italian and European theatres. The most important treatise on singing of the 18th century, P. F. Tosi's *Opinioni de' cantori antichi e moderni*, was published at Bologna in 1723. At that time the city also had a remarkable concentration of conductors, scenographers, costumiers, theatrical agents and impresarios. Significantly, operatic activity proceeded without interruption (except in 1750) from 1634 to 1792. As Bologna was not ruled by a court or potentate, public opinion played an important role in governing its theatrical life. In the 19th century the Bolognese public was exposed to the newest currents in European opera, welcoming first the grand operas of Meyerbeer and then enthusiastically accepting, for the first time in Italy, Wagner's music dramas. Important music periodicals published in the city contributed to this openness.

The Teatro del Pubblico (also known as the Teatro della Sala or Sala del Pallone), in the Palazzo del Podestà on the Piazza Maggiore, designed by A. Chenda, was

Section of the Teatro Comunale, Bologna: wooden model (1755) built by G. B. Martorelli and A. Gambarini after Antonio Galli-Bibiena's designs

used for public spectacles from 1547. Opera performances were mounted from 1610, beginning with Giacobbi's *L'Andromeda* (music lost). On 17 December 1623 it burnt down; it was replaced by a wooden structure in 1624. The Teatro del Pubblico, like all Chenda's theatrical buildings, was arranged in superimposed rows of boxes rather than graded seating (a design later imitated in most Italian theatres), making it accessible not only to the nobility but also to the bourgeois paying public. Later in the century important opera productions were mounted elsewhere and entertainment for lower social classes prevailed; the theatre was demolished as a dangerous structure in 1767.

Formally opened in 1636, the Teatro Formagliari was also called Guastavillani and dei Casali until about 1660; in the last quarter of the 18th century it was also known as Teatro Zagnoni. In January 1636 members of the Accademia dei Riaccesi rented the palace of the Formagliari family to stage operatic performances and comedies. Soon afterwards Marchese Filippo Guastavillani commissioned the architect Sighizzi to renovate the small hall with ranges of boxes sloping down and projecting towards the stage, so that the entire audience had an excellent view. Privately managed by Guastavillani, it was frequented by the nobility and devoted mainly to serious opera. In 1640 the singer, composer and impresario Francesco Manelli introduced such works of the fashionable Venetian repertory as his own *Delia* and Monteverdi's *Il ritorno d'Ulisse in patria* in this theatre. Subsequently and well into the 18th century, composers previously heard in Venice dominated its stage (Cavalli, Pallavicino, M. A. and P. A. Ziani). During the 18th century its two or three seasons favoured a diversified repertory that included numerous *opere buffe* as well as serious operas. It was renovated in 1776 by Francesco Tadolini, but burnt down in 1802; the Teatro del Corso was built on the same site in 1805.

The Teatro Malvezzi opened on 27 March 1653, built on a site bought in 1651 by Marchese Francesco Pirro Malvezzi. It was restored several times between 1681 and 1691 and enlarged and repainted by the Galli-Bibiena brothers in 1697. Although it staged fewer works, it replaced the Teatro Formagliari as the theatre favoured by the Bolognese aristocracy. Its repertory included works by the best Bolognese composers (D. Gabrielli, Ariosti, Aldrovandini, G. M. Orlandini and particularly Perti), performed by eminent singers (M. M. Musi, M. Scarabelli and Pistocchi), often using sets designed by members of the Galli-Bibiena family. It burnt down on 19 February 1745 and its leading position was taken over by the new Teatro Comunale.

The Marchese Silvio Marsigli-Rossi-Lombardi bought a large warehouse in 1709 and remodelled it to accommodate opera performances. As the Teatro Marsigli-Rossi it opened on 28 October 1710 with L. A. Predieri's *La Partenope*, and after it was enlarged in spring 1711, it reopened on 28 October that year with Predieri's *Griselda*. It remained a theatre of modest size in the shape of an open bell, with three tiers of boxes and an upper gallery running as far as the proscenium. In keeping with the size of the theatre, performances of *opere buffe* and comedies, particularly by local writers such as G. M. Buini, were favoured, especially in the years 1722–36. During the French occupation it was renamed Teatro Civico, but it was found to be a dangerous structure in 1821 and was demolished in 1825.

As a result of the destruction of the Teatro Malvezzi, a group of noblemen proposed in 1750 that a new theatre, the Teatro Comunale, be constructed. Financed by the papal government and the Bolognese senate, the building (designed and built by Antonio Galli-Bibiena) was completed in 1757 (see illustration). The first season was delayed by financial difficulties, but the theatre eventually opened on 14 May 1763 with Gluck's *Il trionfo di Clelia*, given its première under the composer's supervision. It became the leading operatic institution in the city, giving up to three seasons annually. Nevertheless, its activity was at times interrupted for several years (no record of operatic performances has survived for the years 1780–87). During the French occupation it was renamed Teatro Nazionale and from 1820 the administration granted use of the theatre to impresarios on a deposit of 5000 scudi. From 1820 to 1860 the repertory included works of the major Italian composers of the time (Morlacchi, Mercadante, Rossini from 1814, Donizetti from 1823, Bellini from 1830 and Verdi from 1843); there were usually three seasons a year, each comprising up to four new productions that were often repeated 30 to 40 times. The theatre was renovated in 1818–20, 1853–4 and 1859.

Angelo Mariani's appointment as 'maestro concertatore e direttore delle musiche' in autumn 1860 inaugurated a splendid period for the Teatro Comunale, and his authority established a new status for the modern Italian orchestral conductor. Under his leadership, which lasted until 1872, the quality of the orchestra was greatly improved and the repertory notably revitalized with performances of operas by Meyerbeer, Verdi and Wagner; these included the Italian premières of *L'Africaine* (4 November 1865), *Don Carlos* (27 October 1867), *Lohengrin* (1 November 1871) and *Tannhäuser* (7 November 1872). Mariani's successors (Marino Mancinelli, Franco Faccio, Luigi Mancinelli and Giuseppe Martucci) also expanded the repertory of the theatre by channelling it within the mainstream of European musical life (for example Martucci directed the Italian première of *Tristan und Isolde*, 2 June 1888). At the beginning of the 20th century the theatre still featured performances of German operas and gave the Italian première of *Parsifal* (1 January 1914, simultaneously with Rome), conducted by Ferrari; it has maintained a keen interest in the Wagnerian repertory. From 1931 to 1935 the Teatro Comunale was closed, following a fire that destroyed the stage. After it reopened it established a regular opera season and continued to be one of the main centres of Italian musical life, organized as an autonomous institution with its own orchestra and chorus.

In June 1980 the theatre was closed because of an infestation of woodworm. A total and scrupulous restoration, which strengthened the original structure and renovated Bibiena's characteristic white and gold decoration, enabled the theatre to reopen on 5 December 1981 with *Aida*. Contemporary works are given as well as the traditional repertory. Among world premières have been Giacomo Manzoni's *Per Massimiliano Robespierre* (17 April 1975) and Adriano Guarnieri's *Trionfo della notte* (3 February 1987); Italian premières include Ligeti's *Le Grand Macabre* (5 May 1979) and Henze's *The English Cat* (20 April 1986). From January 1986 the principal conductor was Riccardo Chailly. During its season, lasting from about December to mid-June, the company takes its performances also to other cities in Emilia and Romagna.

Designed by the architects Santini and Gasparini, the Teatro del Corso opened on 19 May 1805 with Ferdinando Paer's *Sofonisba*, in the presence of Napoleon and with Rossini singing a minor role. The theatre was used for concerts (Paganini in 1818, Malibran in 1835), opera productions and plays. The first performance of Rossini's *L'equivoco stravagante* was given there (26 October 1811), as was, many years later, the Italian première of *Les contes d'Hoffmann* (28 September 1903). The theatre's status declined during the second half of the 19th century because of the strong competition of the Teatro Comunale; it was destroyed during the war, in 1944.

The Teatro Contavalli, constructed by Marinetti and Nadi on the site of the S Martino convent, opened on 3 October 1814 with Carlo Coccia's *La Matilde*. From 1815 to 1826, in 1840 and in 1843 Rossini supervised numerous performances of his works there. Operas by Donizetti (from 1830) and Verdi (from 1854) were among the most frequently performed. In 1938 the theatre was transformed into a film theatre.

*

ES (G. Pardieri and R. Morara)
[A. Machiavelli]: *Serie cronologica dei drammi recitati sù de' pubblici teatri di Bologna dall'anno di nostra salute 1600 sino al corrente 1737* (Bologna, 1737)
G. Giordani: *Intorno al gran Teatro del comune e ad altri minori in Bologna* (Bologna, 1855)
L. Bignami: *Cronologia di tutti gli spettacoli rappresentati nel gran Teatro comunale di Bologna dalla solenne sua apertura 14 maggio 1763 a tutto l'autunno del 1880* (Bologna, 1880)
C. Ricci: *I teatri di Bologna nei secoli XVII e XVIII: storia aneddotica* (Bologna, 1888)
G. Cosentino: *Un teatro bolognese del secolo XVIII: il Teatro Marsigli-Rossi* (Bologna, 1900)
F. Bosdari: 'La vita musicale a Bologna nel periodo napoleonico', *L'archiginnasio*, ix (1914), 213
L. Frati: 'Musicisti e cantanti bolognesi del settecento: notizie e lettere', *RMI*, xxi (1914), 189–202
O. Trebbi: *Il Teatro Contavalli (1814–1914)* (Bologna, 1914)
F. Vatielli: *Cinquant'anni di vita musicale a Bologna (1850–1900)* (Bologna, 1921)
L. Frati: 'Antonio Bernacchi e la sua scuola di canto', *RMI*, xxix (1922), 473–91
F. Vatielli: *Arte e vita musicale a Bologna* (Bologna, 1927)
O. Trebbi: 'Cronache del Teatro Comunale: Giuditta Pasta', *Strenna storica bolognese*, i (1928), 63–72
W. Osthoff: 'Zur Bologneser Aufführung von Monteverdis "Ritorno di Ulisse" im Jahre 1640', *Anzeiger der Österreichischen Akademie der Wissenschaften, philosophisch-historische Klasse*, xcv (1958), 155–60
R. Giacomelli: *Il Teatro comunale di Bologna* (Bologna, 1965)
L. Trezzini and R. Verti, eds.: *Due secoli di vita musicale: storia del Teatro comunale di Bologna* (Bologna, 1966–87)
S. Ingegno Guidi: 'Per la storia del teatro francese in Italia: L. A. Muratori, G. G. Orsi e P. J. Martello', *Rassegna della letteratura italiana*, 7th ser. (1974), no.78, pp.64–94
U. Jung: *Die Wagner Rezeption in Italien* (Regensburg, 1974)
T. Walker and L. Bianconi: 'Dalla *Finta pazza* alla *Veremonda*: storie di Febiarmonici', *RIM*, x (1975), 379–454
M. Sergardi: 'Bologna teatrale nel periodo giacobino', *Chigiana*, xxxiii (1979), 265–81
C. Vitali: 'Un fondo di musiche operistiche settecentesche presso l'Archivio di stato di Bologna (Fondo Malvezzi-Campeggi)', *NRMI*, xiii (1979), 371–84
P. Mioli: 'La scuola di canto bolognese nel Settecento', *Quadrivium*, xxii (1981), 5–59
M. Conati and M. Pavarani, eds.: *Orchestre in Emilia-Romagna nell'ottocento e novecento* (Parma, 1982), 325–92
J. Rosselli: 'Agenti teatrali nel mondo dell'opera lirica italiana dell'ottocento', *RIM*, xvii (1982), 134–54
G. Rostirolla, ed.: *Wagner in Italia* (Turin, 1982)
M. Sergardi: 'Momenti del teatro d'avanguardia a Bologna (1920–1930)', *Chigiana*, xxxv (1982), 163–84
E. Surian: 'Organizzazione, gestione, politica teatrale e repertori operistici a Napoli e in Italia, 1800–1820', *Musica e cultura a Napoli dal XV al XIX secolo*, ed. L. Bianconi and R. Bossa (Florence, 1983), 317–68
R. Verti: 'La presenza della musica nei periodici bolognesi dal 1800 al 1830', *Periodica musica*, i (1983), 6–9
J. Rosselli: *The Opera Industry in Italy from Cimarosa to Verdi: the Role of the Impresario* (Cambridge, 1984)
P. Weiss: 'La diffusione del repertorio operistico nell'Italia del settecento: il caso dell'opera buffa', *Civiltà teatrale e settecento emiliano: Reggio Emilia 1985*
SOI, iv–vi (1987–8) GRAZIANO BALLERINI, ELVIDIO SURIAN

Bolognese, Domenico (*b* Naples, 11 Feb 1819; *d* Naples, 2 Jan 1881). Italian librettist. He published poetry and literary criticism before he was 20, and began to write for the theatre in 1841. Income from these sources being insufficient to support his family, he turned to writing librettos. Following Cammarano's death in 1852, he was appointed *poeta e concertatore* to the royal theatres, a post he held until 1860. Thereafter he confined himself to writing plays and to literary studies. His librettos were conventional but lacking in dramatic tension, and he did nothing to halt the continuing impoverishment of verse-form and language which was so marked a feature of the period. His best work was probably for Errico Petrella, including *Elnava* (1856). He was also a noted exponent of Neapolitan dialect poetry.

dl – *dramma lirico* melss – *melodramma semiserio*
melt – *melodramma tragico* tl – *tragedia lirica*

Il carceriere di 1793 (melss), M. de F. Delfico, 1845; *Rodolfo da Brienza* (melss), A. Pistilli, 1846; *Il ritorno di un vagabondo* (melss), G. Giaquinto, 1850; *Il muratore di Napoli* (melss), Aspa, 1850; *Ermelinda* (dl), V. Battista, 1851; *Mudarra* (tl), Battista, 1852; *Elena di Tolosa* (dl), E. Petrella, 1852; *Guido Colmar* (tl), De Giosa, 1852; *Statira* (tl), Mercadante, 1853; *Il corsaro della Guadalupa* (melss), Battista, 1853; *Marco Visconti* (melt), Petrella, 1854; *Ettore Fieramosca* (tl), De Giosa, 1855

Margherita Pusterla (melt), G. Pacini, 1856; *Elnava* (melt), Petrella, 1856; *Matilde d'Ostan* (dl), Pistilli, 1856; *Evelina* (melss), E. Viceconte, 1856; *Diana di Vitry* (dl), M. Ruta, 1859; *Ruggiero di Sangineto* (melodramma), M. Sansone, 1859; *Morosina* (melt), Petrella, 1860; *Il folletto di Gresy* (commedia lirica), Petrella, 1860; *Virginia* (tl), Petrella, 1861; *Luisa Strozzi*, Viceconte, 1862; *Giovanna di Castiglia*, Battista, 1863; *Caterina Blum* (dl), Bevignani, 1863; *Celinda* (melt), Petrella, 1865; *La figlia di Domenico*, C. Alberti, 1873

*

DBI (A. Palermo)
V. Viviani: 'Libretti e librettisti', *Cento anni di vita del Teatro S. Carlo, 1848–1948*, ed. F. de Filippis (Naples, 1948), 29–39

JOHN BLACK

Bolognese, Il. *See* GRIMALDI, GIOVANNI FRANCESCO.

Bol'shakov, Nikolay (Arkad'yevich) (*b* Khar'kov, 10/23 Nov 1874; *d* Leningrad [now St Petersburg], 20 Jan 1958). Russian tenor. He studied in St Petersburg with Ippolit Pryanishnikov. He made his début with the Khar'kov Company in 1899 at St Petersburg, and sang with the Mariinsky Company there (1906–29). Although he visited Paris and London with Dyagilev in 1913, and sang in Barcelona and Berlin, most of his career was spent in Russia. Among his best roles were Hermann, Lensky, Vaudémont in *Iolanta*, Finn in *Ruslan and Lyudmila* and parts in operas by Rimsky-Korsakov. In the standard repertory he was admired as Faust, Don José, Rienzi and Pinkerton. He taught at the Leningrad Conservatory from 1923, becoming a professor in 1935. DAVID CUMMINGS

Bol'shoy (i). Theatre in MOSCOW, completed in 1825, the leading opera house in Russia.

Bol'shoy (ii). Theatre in ST PETERSBURG built in 1783; it served as the main opera house until the 1860s.

Bolzano (Ger. Bozen). City in the South Tyrol, northern Italy. Performance licences furnish sporadic evidence that operatic entertainments were staged during the Bolzano fairs in the 17th and 18th centuries by travelling companies. For 15 years from 1784 a wealthy merchant family, the von Menz, organized Carnival seasons in the Palazzo Mercantile of Italian (usually comic) opera given in German, mainly by local artists. Translations were made on the spot from librettos and scores originating mostly in Vienna, Naples and Venice. To this period belong Franz Bühler's Singspiels *Die falschen Verdachte* (Carnival 1796) and *Der tiroler Landsturm in franzosen Kriege* (Carnival 1798). Travelling Italian-speaking companies came for the summer–autumn season, but did so less often in the following century.

The city's first theatre was the Kaiserkrone, built in 1805 by public subscription in the Piazza della Mostra and inaugurated with Generali's *Pamela nubile*. The theatre was designed by Andrea Caminada with 800 seats, two tiers of 33 boxes and a gallery. Changing economic circumstances led to a break in the initially annual performances, which had been given mostly by Austrian companies or local amateurs. Although playbills indicate that Italian and French works were produced, most of the operas performed were those in vogue in German-speaking areas. The Kaiserkrone was closed in 1904.

The construction of a new theatre opposite the railway station (1913–18, designed by Max Littmann) coincided with the transfer of the city from Austrian to Italian possession, which hindered the traditional contacts with the German cultural area. The aggressive italianization of the Fascist era ensured that the theatre, renamed the Verdi in 1937, was restricted to presenting the Italian 19th- and 20th-century repertory. It was destroyed by bombing in 1943. After World War II productions were held mainly in the summer season, in a wide variety of venues, and from 1967 regularly in operatic seasons organized by the Südtiroler Kulturinstitut in the Casa della Cultura theatre, mostly with Austro-German companies. A new theatre was commissioned from Marco Zanuso in 1985.

*

L. Onestinghel: 'L'inaugurazione del teatro vecchio di Bolzano nel 1805', *Archivio per l'Alto Adige con Ampezzo e Livinallongo*, ix (1914), 297–303
A. Dörrer: 'Komödianten auf den Bozner Märkten vom 1684 bis 1764', *Der Schlern*, x (1929), 223–32
K. T. Hoeniger: 'Das Bozner Stadttheater', *Altbozner Bilderbuch* (Bolzano, 1933), 179–86
G. Canali: 'Storia del primo teatro di Bolzano', *Atesia augusta*, ii/10 (1943), 42–4
J. Sydow: 'Vom Bozner Theater am Ende des 18. Jahrhunderts', *Der Schlern*, xxx (1956), 181–2
E. Schneider: 'Das Bozner Stadttheater im Bahnhofspark', *Bozen, Stadt im Umbruch* (Bolzano, 1973), 393–409
G. Tonini: 'Il teatro musicale a Bolzano', *Il cristallo*, xxiv (1982), 23–54
T. Chini and G. Tonini: 'Introduzione', *La raccolta di manoscritti e stampe musicali 'Toggenburg' di Bolzano (secc. XVIII–XIX)* (Turin, 1986), pp.ix–xxxii
G. Tonini: 'La fortuna di Bellini nelle stagioni operistiche a Bolzano nell'ottocento e nel novecento', *Il cristallo*, xxix (1987), 85–92
H. Romen: *L'opera a Bolzano alla fine del settecento: il Teatro von Menz* (diss., U. of Bologna, 1987–8)
M. A. Marongiu: *Metamorfosi operistiche a Bolzano alla fine del sec. XVIII* (diss., U. of Trent, 1988–9)
G. Tonini: 'Bellina "pazza per amore": le ragioni di un successo mancato', *Domenico Cimarosa: 'Amor rende sagace'* (Bolzano, 1991), 26–9

ALESSANDRO ROCCATAGLIATI, GIULIANO TONINI

Bolzoni, Giovanni (*b* Parma, 15 May 1841; *d* Turin, 21 Feb 1919). Italian conductor and composer. He studied composition, with Giovanni Rossi, and the violin at the music school in Parma, graduating in 1859. He was leader and assistant conductor at Reggio Emilia (1864–6) and at the Teatro Comunale Cremona, where he collaborated with Ponchielli as conductor during the carnival of 1866–7. He worked in Savona (1867–74); his *melodramma La stella delle Alpi* was given its première there in 1871. He was then director of the music school and conductor at the municipal theatre in Perugia; from 1876 he held similar posts in Piacenza, where his opera *Jella* was produced in 1881. Recommended by Verdi, he conducted at the Teatro Regio in Turin from 1884 to 1889. A strict and gifted teacher, he was director and professor of composition at the Turin Conservatory (1887–1916), which he began to reorganize with less emphasis on its operatic tradition. As a composer he had technical ability and inventiveness, but in a period dominated by opera he wrote mostly chamber and symphonic music.

Giulia da Gazzuolo, 1869 (os, V. Meinis), unperf.
Il matrimonio civile (comic op, 1, G. Schianelli), Parma, Regio, 11 Oct 1870
La stella delle Alpi (melodramma, 4, Schianelli), Savona, Chiabrera, carn. 1871
Jella (os, 4, Schianelli), Piacenza, Comunale, 3 July 1881
Venezia in Vienna (scena lirica), Vienna, 1899

*

DBI (C. Frajese)
G. Fino: *Il maestro G. Bolzoni: commemorazione* (Turin, 1923)
A. Basso: *Storia del Teatro Regio di Torino*, ii (Turin, 1976), 413ff

ANDREA LANZA

Bomarzo. Opera in two acts, op.34, by ALBERTO GINASTERA to a libretto by Manuel Mujica Láinez after his own novel *Bomarzo*; Washington, DC, Lisner Auditorium, 19 May 1967.

Pier Francesco Orsini, Duke of Bomarzo	tenor
Gian Conrado Orsini *his father*	bass
Diana Orsini *his grandmother*	contralto
Girolamo *his elder brother*	baritone
Maerbale *his younger brother*	baritone
Julia Farnese *his wife*	soprano
Abul *his slave*	mime
Nicolas *his nephew, Maerbale's son*	contralto or tenor
Silvio de Narni *an astrologer*	baritone
Pantasilea *a Florentine courtesan*	mezzo-soprano
A Shepherd Boy	treble

Boys, prelates, courtiers, pages and servants

Setting Bomarzo, Florence and Rome in the 16th century

The central character of the work is Pier Francesco, a member of the great Orsini family, who created not far from his palace (near Viterbo) a garden of bizarre and nightmarish grotesques (*grotteschi*) carved from the volcanic rock. This stirred the imagination of the Argentine writer Mujica Láinez, who interpreted the place as the extension of a tormented Renaissance figure, twisted in body and mind, in the form of timeless monuments through which he sought his own immortality and the reflection of himself. The result was the novel *Bomarzo* (1962), which became a best-seller and won several prizes. In 1964 Mujica Láinez provided the text for the *Cantata Bomarzo*, and when a year later Hobart Spalding commissioned a stage work for the Opera Society of Washington, Ginastera returned to the same subject. At its première, which was conducted by Julius Rudel and directed by Tito Capobianco, the opera caused a sensation and was hailed as a triumph, but its explicit eroticism caused it to be banned in Buenos Aires by the repressive regime of President Onganía; it was not given there until 1972. An instrumental suite, with substitutions for the vocal parts, received its first performance in 1970.

The two acts of the opera are divided into 15 scenes (each consisting of the classic Greek infrastructure of exposition, crisis and resolution) linked by orchestral interludes. The action takes place as a series of recollections of Pier Francesco's inner life, reenacted at overlapping levels of reality, dream and oneiric fantasy in the mind of the dying Duke, seen in the first and last scenes. The orchestra includes harpsichord, mandolin, viola d'amore and a huge array of 68 percussion instruments, and the chorus (employing techniques including hissing, humming, cries and choral speaking) operates from the orchestra pit: in the Prelude it sings on isolated consonants to suggest the ghostly whispering of the stone statues.

ACT 1.i A shepherd boy is heard singing (to the melody of the 14th-century Lamento di Tristano) that, poor as he is, he would not change places with the Duke, who is carrying in his hump the burden of his sins. Standing by one of his stone carvings, which represents the 'Mouth of Hell', the Duke is persuaded to drink a magic potion that he has been promised will bring him immortality. Instead, he finds that he has been poisoned; and the flashbacks begin.

1.ii As a child, Pier Francesco is bedevilled by his brothers, who torment him by dressing him up as a girl. His stern father, mocking his weakness, shows him a secret panel where he sees the reclining figure of a skeleton; in his fantasy the skeleton dances, filling him with an abject terror that is to haunt him all his life.

1.iii Now a young man, he is fearful that his father will put him to death. But his astrologer predicts immortality for him and by black magic invokes demons to protect him; as peacocks foretelling tragedy are heard in the garden, a messenger announces that the old Duke has been mortally wounded in the siege of Florence.

1.iv To deride his virility, the wounded Duke has sent him to Pantasilea; her sensuality and voluptuous beauty stand in contrast with his impotence and deformity, reflected in mirrors all about him. 'Break the mirror you are carrying within yourself', says Pantasilea as she taunts him with aphrodisiacs.

1.v The Duke's impending death brings Pier Francesco no comfort, for his brother Girolamo, heir to the title, hates him too. As Girolamo, about to bathe in the Tiber, boasts about his strength he loses his foothold, hitting his head on a rock. Pier Francesco tries to save him but Diana Orsini holds him back protectively: 'Come with me ... Now you are Duke of Bomarzo, forever'.

1.vi In a magnificent ceremony Pier Francesco is proclaimed Duke (to the sound of the Gregorian melody *O rex gloriae*). His grandmother introduces him to the lovely Julia Farnese, pointing out the advantages of alliance with her powerful family; but Maerbale leads Julia away, and Pier Francesco is haunted by his father's ghost.

1.vii At the celebratory ball Maerbale dances with Julia. In a soliloquy Pier Francesco identifies with the yet uncarved and enigmatic stones, his dream of possessing Bomarzo fulfilled. His fancy conjures up a ballet in which an idealized form of himself dances with Julia, Pantasilea and his slave Abul while they struggle to possess him.

1.viii Returning from fighting against Charles V in Picardy, he admires the portrait of an anonymous nobleman by Lorenzo Lotto, the idealized image of himself. When he uncovers an adjacent mirror the reflection becomes an image of the 'Mouth of Hell'; in a frenzy he smashes the mirror.

ACT 2.ix Pier Francesco becomes insanely jealous watching Maerbale at Julia's feet as she sings a madrigal. He bursts in on them and spills red wine on her dress; the stains are seen as an omen.

2.x He has married Julia, but in the bridal chamber he sees demonic faces invisible to her.

2.xi Unable to possess Julia, he has visions of the still uncarved *grotteschi*. In the erotic ballet that follows, disembodied figures of himself and Julia lose themselves in a forest of intertwined couples, the chorus murmuring

Ming Cho Lee's design for the 'Mouth of Hell' (modelled on one of Pier Francesco Orsini's grotteschi) for the original production of Ginastera's 'Bomarzo' by the Opera Society of Washington in 1967

the word 'love' in more than 30 languages. In his dream he possesses her.

2.xii In the gallery of the palace he embraces a statue of the Minotaur. As his ambiguous sexuality has alienated him from his ancestors, he identifies with the fate and alienation of the mythical creature.

2.xiii Crazed by jealousy and frustration, he orders the astrologer to entice Maerbale into Julia's bedchamber; Abul is then to stab him.

2.xiv Now carved, each of the *grotteschi* in Bomarzo's garden symbolizes an episode in his puzzling existence. The astrologer mixes the potion that carries the promise of immortality made to Pier Francesco in his horoscope, as figures of alchemists of the past dance like furies around him warning him that Pier Francesco has challenged the supreme powers. Nicolas, Maerbale's son, poisons the potion to avenge his father's murder.

2.xv As in Act 1 scene i, he lies dying below the 'Mouth of Hell', his promised immortality transferred to the permanence of the carvings. The shepherd boy approaches the lifeless Duke and kisses his face. The final quote from the 'Lamento di Tristano' restores innocence and timeless peace to Bomarzo.

* * *

Ginastera's musical language here is based on 12-note procedures and also makes use of microtones, aleatory procedures and chord clusters. The idea of permanence is associated with the basic 12-note series, a chromatically contracting all-interval row which, presented as a static cluster, provides a musical analogue for the timelessness of the rocks. (This cluster also closes Ginastera's *Don Rodrigo*, intentionally beginning the second opera where the first ends.) Reproducing the circular direction of the tableaux, the opera begins and ends with this cluster on C: Act 2 begins with it on G, maintaining between the acts a relationship of a perfect 5th which also appears between the static lyricism of the shepherd boy's song (Act 1.i) and Julia's madrigal (Act 2.ix). Just as permanence contains a set of opposite modalities – innocence and guilt, dream and reality, love and rejection, beauty and deformity – so the basic series contains subordinate and derived 12-note rows associated with dream (Act 1.vii) and death (the Villanella of Interlude xii), with transposition points respectively on F♯ and C, the last and first pitches of the basic series. The circle closes when permanence subsumes dream and death in the Elegy that forms Interlude xiv. The dramaturgy of *Bomarzo* might be defined in terms that have been applied to the place of Antonio Gaudí in architecture: 'A chance encounter of genius with medieval revival, art nouveau, savagely erotic shapes and Spanish religiosity' (R. McCullen, *Horizon*, 1968, 29–44).

MALENA KUSS, LIONEL SALTER

Bombaciari [Bombasari], **Anna.** *See* FABBRI, ANNA MARIA and FABRI, ANNIBALE PIO.

Bon, Rosa Ruvinetti. *See* RUVINETTI BON, ROSA.

Bonaventura, Arnaldo (*b* Livorno, 28 July 1862; *d* Florence, 7 Oct 1952). Italian musicologist. He first studied law, then turned to music and joined the staff of the Biblioteca Nazionale Centrale, Florence. He became successively professor of music history, assistant director and finally director and librarian of the Istituto Musicale (Reale Accademia di Musica Luigi Cherubini), Florence, retiring in 1932. His numerous writings (over 900) include regular contributions to newspapers and periodicals, among them the *Gazzetta musicale di Milano*, *La critica musicale* and the *Rivista musicale italiana*.

Saggio storico sul teatro musicale italiano (Livorno, 1913)
La figura e l'arte di G. Verdi (Livorno, 1919)
Bernardo Pasquini (Ascoli Piceno, 1923)
Verdi (Paris, 1923)
Mefistofele di Arrigo Boito (Milan, 1924)
G. Puccini: l'uomo e l'artista (Livorno, 1925)
L'opera italiana (Florence, 1928)
Rossini (Florence, 1934)

Publicazioni di Arnaldo Bonaventura nel cinquantenario, 1880–1930 (Florence, 1930)
B. Becherini: 'Ricordi di Arnaldo Bonaventura (1862–1952)', *RMI*, liv (1952), 329–31

Bonci, Alessandro (*b* Cesena, nr Rimini, 10 Feb 1870; *d* Viserba, nr Rimini, 9 Aug 1940). Italian tenor. After study with Pedrotti and Felice Coen in Pesaro, and with Delle Sedie in Paris, he made his début in Parma (1896) as Fenton in *Falstaff*. In the early years of the new century he was for some time regarded as Caruso's only serious rival, excelling in roles demanding lightness, agility and elegance rather than the heavier and more dramatic parts. After some appearances at Covent Garden, he scored a great success in New York in 1906, singing in *I puritani* at the opening of Hammerstein's new Manhattan Opera House; but for the next three seasons he transferred his activities to the Metropolitan, where he sang 65 performances of 14 roles. In World War I he served with the Italian Air Force; he made only sporadic appearances thereafter, devoting most of his time to teaching in Milan. In the older repertory, he excelled by virtue of the sweetness of his tone and the finish of his phrasing: qualities that are especially evident in his earlier recordings.

*

GV (R. Celletti; R. Vegeto)
T. Hutchinson: 'Alessandro Bonci', *Record Collector*, xi (1957), 149–62 [with discography]

DESMOND SHAWE-TAYLOR

Boncompagni, Elio (*b* Caprese Michelangelo, Arezzo, 8 May 1933). Italian conductor. He studied the violin and composition in Florence and Padua, and conducting in Perugia and Hilversum, winning a prize in the 1961 Italian Radio international competition which brought him to the attention of Tullio Serafin. His début was at Bologna in 1962 replacing Serafin for *Don Carlos*. He won a further prize in the 1967 Mitropoulos Competition, New York, and developed a busy career in leading European opera houses, with a spell as resident conductor at La Monnaie, Brussels, from 1974. He continued freelance engagements in the USA and Canada as well as in Europe, and made his British début in 1983, replacing Abbado in a concert performance of Cherubini's *Médée* at the Barbican Hall given as a memorial tribute to Maria Callas.

ELVIDIO SURIAN, NOËL GOODWIN

Bond, Edward (*b* London, 18 July 1934). English dramatist and librettist. He first achieved success and some notoriety on the London stage with *Saved* (1965); with his subsequent plays, including *Lear* (1972) and *Bingo* (1974), he became established as one of the most trenchant of contemporary British dramatists, offering a consistent Marxist critique of capitalist society and often using imagery of extreme violence. He first collaborated with Henze on the 'actions for music' *We Come to the River* (1976, London), subsequently providing the scenario for the ballet *Orpheus* (1979) and the libretto for *The English Cat* (1983, Schwetzingen), 'a story for singers and instrumentalists'.

ANDREW CLEMENTS

Bondeville, Emmanuel (Pierre Georges) (*b* Rouen, 29 Oct 1898; *d* Paris, 26 Nov 1987). French composer. He studied the organ at Rouen Cathedral, taking his master's place at the age of ten. Losing his parents at 16, he studied subsequently at the Paris Conservatoire. Dupré was also a friend and adviser. In the 1930s Bondeville produced orchestral pieces and his first opera, *L'école des maris*. After working for French radio he held operatic appointments at Monte Carlo (1945), at the Paris Opéra-Comique (1949) and at the Opéra (1952–70); he was well known for his administrative capabilities as well as for his compositions. Admired by many critics for its sure-handed craftsmanship, *Madame Bovary* was first performed while Bondeville was director at the Opéra-Comique and successfully revived there in 1961. It is at times Fauréan in its harmony and uses all the forms of traditional 19th-century opera, alternating recitative sections with unashamedly lyrical melodies. *Antoine et Cléopâtre* was well received at its first production at the Opéra-Comique. It is divided into many short scenes, into which the set pieces of traditional *opéra comique* are introduced.

L'école des maris (oc, 3, J. Laurent, after Molière), Paris, OC (Favart), 15 June 1935
Madame Bovary (drame lyrique, 3, R. Fauchois, after G. Flaubert), Paris, OC (Favart), 1 June 1951
Antoine et Cléopâtre (3, Bondeville, after W. Shakespeare), Rouen, Théâtre des Arts, 8 March 1974

*

L. Aubert: 'P.-O. Ferroud, Marcel Delannoy, Henri Tomasi, E. Bondeville', *Le théâtre lyrique en France* (Paris, 1937–9) [pubn of Poste National/Radio-Paris], iii, 266–74
P. Landormy: *La musique française après Debussy* (Paris, 1943)
A. Machabey: *Portraits de trente musiciens français* (Paris, 1949)

RICHARD LANGHAM SMITH

Bondi, Michele Neri. *See* NERI BONDI, MICHELE.

Bondini, Pasquale (*b* ?Bonn, ?1737; *d* Bruneck, Tyrol, 30 or 31 Oct 1789). Italian impresario. He is first mentioned as a *buffo* bass in Cajetan Molinari's opera company at Prague in the 1762–3 season. He was later a prominent member of Bustelli's company in Prague and Dresden. In 1777 he became director of the Elector of Saxony's new company at Dresden; he also assumed responsibility for Leipzig. The company's repertory also included plays by Shakespeare, Lessing and Schiller. Operas performed included works by virtually all the leading Italian composers of the day. In 1781 Bondini also took over direction of the theatre at Count Thun's palace in Prague and shortly afterwards Count Nostitz's theatre. His company performed at Leipzig mainly in the summer and gave *Die Entführung* there at Michaelmas 1783 and at Dresden on 12 January 1785. But because he and his personnel were so heavily extended by his many activities Bondini was obliged to engage other troupes and managers. His most important assistant was Domenico Guardasoni, who in 1787 became his co-director and in 1788 or 1789 his successor as impresario of the operatic side of his companies. Johann Joseph Strobach became musical director in 1785, and though the opera ensemble was small, it was highly regarded and very popular.

In December 1786 Bondini mounted *Figaro*, and in January he invited Mozart and his wife to Prague to share in the triumph the opera was enjoying; during his stay Mozart conducted a performance. Before returning to Vienna in February he had been commissioned by Bondini to write *Don Giovanni*; after delays due to illness in the company, the work was first performed on 29 October 1787 with Mozart conducting. His letter to Gottfried von Jacquin of 15–25 October contains valuable but tantalizingly brief comments on Bondini's ensemble and on the preparations for the work. Within a year of the première Bondini's fortunes had waned; ill-health led him to make Franz Seconda responsible for the drama company, and in summer 1789 he handed over his remaining assets before setting off for a visit to Italy. He died at Bruneck on the way.

Bondini's wife Caterina was a popular soprano in her husband's company in the mid 1780s. She sang Susanna in the first Prague production of *Figaro* in early December 1786, and on 14 December a performance was given for her benefit; her praises were sung in poems distributed in the theatre. She created the role of Zerlina in *Don Giovanni*; from the rehearsals dates the anecdote that Mozart taught her to scream effectively during the abduction scene in the finale of Act 1 by grabbing her unexpectedly round the waist.

The Bondinis' daughter Marianna (1780–1813) sang Susanna in the French première of *Figaro* and often appeared with her husband, the bass Luigi Barilli, who was later manager of the Théâtre de l'Odéon in Paris.

*

ČSHS; *ES* (F. D'Amico); *NDB* (K. Richter)

O. Teuber: *Geschichte des Prager Theaters*, i (Prague, 1883), 354ff; ii (Prague, 1885), 127ff

R. Prochazka: *Mozart in Prag* (Prague, 1892, 4/1938, ed. P. Nettl as *Mozart in Böhmen*)

O. E. Deutsch: *Mozart: die Dokumente seines Lebens* (Kassel, 1961; Eng. trans., 1965)

E. Devrient: *Geschichte der deutschen Schauspielkunst* (Berlin, 1967)

PETER BRANSCOMBE

Bondon, Jacques (Laurent Jules Désiré) (*b* Boulbon, Bouches du Rhône, 6 Dec 1927). French composer. He studied at the Ecole César Franck and at the Paris Conservatoire, where his teachers included Charles Koechlin, Milhaud and Rivier. A prolific composer, he has composed five operas, and many orchestral and chamber works; he has drawn on a wide range of tonal precedents, and also on ideas from science fiction. *La nuit foudroyée* is the story of a diurnal man and a nocturnal woman who disintegrates in his arms at the coming of dawn, and *Ana et l'albatros* is based on a Celtic legend telling how sea-captains are transformed into albatrosses. *1-330* is set in the 30th century in a world inhabited by computers.

La nuit foudroyée, 1961–3 (opéra, 4, Y. Mauffret), concert perf., Paris, 26 Nov 1964; stage, Metz, 10 Feb 1968

Les arbres (opéra de chambre, 1, Mauffret), ORTF, 6 March 1965

Mélusine au rocher (opéra, 1, A. Lanoux), Radio Luxembourg, 14 Nov 1968; ORTF, 30 Nov 1969

Ana et l'albatros (opéra, 4, Mauffret), Metz, 21 Nov 1970

1-330 (opéra, 4, J. Goury, after E. Zamiatine), Nantes, 20 May 1975

*

J. Roy: *Présences contemporaines: musique française* (Paris, 1962), 471–83

P. Ancelin: 'Entretien avec Jacques Bondon', *Lettres françaises* (1964), no.1050

M.-J. Chauvin: 'Entretien avec Jacques Bondon', *Courrier musical* (1970), no.29, pp.3–13

PAUL GRIFFITHS, RICHARD LANGHAM SMITH

Bondy, Luc (*b* Zürich, 1948). Swiss director. He studied at Jacques Lecocq's Ecole de Pantomime in Paris and made his début directing at the Théâtre Universitaire International de Paris. In 1969 he was appointed a production assistant at the Thalia Theater, Hamburg, and from 1971 staged his own productions of a series of important plays – Genet's *Les bonnes* (1971, Hamburg), Ionesco's *Les chaises* (1972, Nuremberg), Shakespeare's *As you like it* (1973, Wuppertal) and Goethe's *Stella* (1973, Darmstadt). Between 1974 and 1976 he was a resident director at the Frankfurt Städtische Bühne. From the early 1980s, Bondy worked in Cologne and during this period made his first forays into opera with *Lulu* and *Wozzeck* for the Hamburg Staatsoper and *Così fan tutte* and *L'incoronazione di Poppea* at La Monnaie. In 1985 he succeeded Peter Stein as artistic director of the Schaubühne, Berlin. Since 1987 he has divided his activities as a freelance director between opera and the theatre. His opera productions are marked by a surrealistic representationalism in scenic design and acting of great emotional intensity. His production of *Salome* was part of Gerard Mortier's inaugural programme as director of the Salzburg Festival in 1992.

HUGH CANNING

Bonelli [Bunn], **Richard** (*b* Port Byron, NY, 6 Feb 1887; *d* Los Angeles, 7 June 1980). American baritone. He studied at Syracuse University and later in Paris under Jean de Reszke. He made his début as Valentin at the Brooklyn Academy in 1915 and joined the San Carlo Opera Company in 1922. He made his European début at Modena in 1923 in Catalani's *Dejanice*, then sang at Monte Carlo (1924). Performances in Chicago and San Francisco were followed in 1932 by his Metropolitan début as Germont with Ponselle. Although he was considered a Verdi specialist, the roles he sang most often were Valentin, Tonio and Sharpless; his few performances as Wolfram were highly praised. His recordings show a lyric voice with an excellent legato but no great power.

RICHARD LeSUEUR

Bonesi, Barnaba (*b* Bergamo, 1745–6; *d* Paris, 25 Oct 1824). Italian composer. His first name has sometimes mistakenly been given as Benedetto. After studying singing and composition, he went in about 1778 to Paris, where he lived as a music teacher and composer (there is no evidence for Gerber's statement that he was *maître de chant* at the Comédie-Italienne). He composed several operas of which *Le rosier* had a good success at the Théâtre des Beaujolais in April 1788, but he is best known for his theoretical writings.

Pigmalion (drame lyrique, 1, B. F. de Rosoi), Paris, Comédie-Italienne, 16 Dec 1780, arias (Paris, *c*1781)

Le rosier (oc, 2), Paris, Beaujolais, 14 April 1788, *GB-Lbl* (Paris, *c*1788)

Amasis (3, N. Bricaire de La Dixmerie), 1788, unperf.

Le prince de Brunswick (drame lyrique), *D-Bds**

Doubtful: La magie à la mode, ou La sorcière de village (oc, 2, Bricaire de La Dixmerie), Paris, Beaujolais, 28 Aug 1787; also attrib. P. F. Bonnay

Bonetti, Lucia (*b* Bologna; *fl* 1688–1719). Italian singer. She is first mentioned in 1688, when she sang Alvilda in Carlo Pallavicino's *L'amazone corsara, ovvero L'Alvilda regina de' Goti* and Lesbia in Giovanni Legrenzi's *Lisimaco riamato da Alessandro*. She appeared with singers such as Margherita Salicola, Maria Maddalena Musi and Domenico Cecchi, and sang in many Italian cities, including Reggio Emilia, Modena, Ferrara, Parma, Milan, Naples, Casale, Udine, Venice, Verona, Genoa and Pesaro. She was still active in 1719, singing in *intermezzi comici musicali* and perhaps in G. M. Orlandini's *Griselda* in Florence.

*

S. Durante: 'Alcune considerazioni sui cantanti di teatro del primo settecento e la loro formazione', *Antonio Vivaldi: teatro musicale, cultura e società: Venice 1981*, ii, 427–81

PAOLA BESUTTI

Boninsegna, Celestina (*b* Reggio Emilia, 26 Feb 1877; *d* Milan, 14 Feb 1947). Italian soprano. She studied first with Mattioli at Reggio Emilia (where she sang Norina in *Don Pasquale* when she was 15), then with Virginia Boccabadati at the Pesaro conservatory, and in 1897 made her début at Bari in *Faust*. Subsequently she sang in the first Rome performance of Mascagni's *Le maschere* (Rosaura), at the Teatro Costanzi, and made her first appearances, as Aida, at Covent Garden (1904), La Scala (1904–5) and the Metropolitan (1906–7). She also appeared in Boston (1909–10), Barcelona (1912) and St Petersburg (1913), but until her retirement from the stage (1920) sang mostly in less important theatres.

Her rich, resonant voice with its wide compass was particularly suited to Verdi, as were her smooth delivery, and the dignity and refinement of her vocal line; she excelled as Aida and as Leonora in both *Il trovatore* and *La forza del destino*. In an era of dynamic and passionate singing actresses (Bellincioni, Burzio, Carelli, Destinn, Kruscenisky), her primitive acting and unfamiliarity with the *verismo* repertory, except for *Cavalleria rusticana* and *Tosca*, prejudiced her career. However, she scored a great success on records, being one of the first dramatic sopranos whose voice recorded well.

*

W. R. Moran: 'Boninsegna in the United States', *Record Collector*, xii (1958–60), 267–83

C. Williams and J. B. Richards: 'Celestina Boninsegna', *Record Collector*, xii (1958–60), 5–33 [with discography]

RODOLFO CELLETTI

Bonis, Novello (*b* Venice; *fl* 1675–81). Italian librettist. His first libretto was for the Teatro ai Saloni, a small Venetian theatre used by academics for plays and only intermittently for opera. On the title-page, he styles himself the somnolent follower of Tasso ('sonnolento tassista'); in his letter to the reader, he emphasizes that he is not a professional. His two other librettos were for successive seasons at the Teatro S Angelo. In all three works the emphasis is on lively, often comic, stage interaction, with plots loosely based on history. *Odoacre*, for example, mixes matters of war, love and succession and illustrates the havoc wrought by the tyrant Odoacer, conqueror of Rome. Set by Giovanni Varischino, *Odoacre* proved to be one of the most popular operas of the 1680s. Because of its modest staging requirements it could be easily mounted, even on provincial stages, and within seven years of its Venetian première it was produced in nine other towns. The last production under the original title was in Naples (1694), for which Alessandro Scarlatti provided additional arias, carefully distinguishing his own contribution from the original, which he misattributed to Legrenzi.

Dario ravvivato, various, 1675; *Odoacre*, G. Varischino, 1680 (Perti, 1697, as Fausta restituita all'impero); *Flora*, A. Sartorio and M. A. Ziani, 1681

*

AllacciD

C. Ivanovich: *Minerva al tavolino* (Venice, 1681, 2/1688)

G. Bonlini: *Le glorie della poesia e della musica* (Venice, 1730)

HARRIS S. SAUNDERS

Bonisolli, Franco (*b* Rovereto, 25 May 1937). Italian tenor. He won first prize in a competition at Spoleto in 1961 and made his début at the festival there in 1962 as Ruggero (*La rondine*), later singing the Prince in *The Love for Three Oranges*. Further engagements for leading roles in Verdi and the *verismo* repertory quickly followed. He made his Vienna Staatsoper début in 1968 and his American début as Alfredo at San Francisco in 1969; later he appeared at the Metropolitan Opera as Almaviva (1971). He was first heard at Covent Garden in 1981 as Vasco de Gama (*L'Africaine*); this was followed by Calaf, a role which, together with Don José, he also sang on the Royal Opera's Far East tour in 1986. At Verona (1988–9) he has sung Enzo and Radames. His recordings include Leoncavallo's *La bohème*, Bizet's *Djamileh* and Gluck's *Iphigénie en Tauride* and *Paride ed Elena*; he also appeared in a film of *La traviata*. Bonisolli is a *tenore robusto* whose performance may be excitingly dramatic but also ill-disciplined in vocal style. NOËL GOODWIN

Boniventi [Bonaventura, Boneventi, Bonaventi, Beneventi], **Giuseppe** (*b* Venice, ?1670–73; *d* Venice, after 1727). Italian composer. He is credited with writing 12 operas for various Venetian theatres between 1690 and 1727, usually those of the second rank (the S Angelo, S Moisè and S Cassiano), as well as an opera for Turin and part of another for Ferrara. He studied under Legrenzi at St Mark's, where he may have been employed as a singer, and wrote his first opera, for the autumn 1690 season, when he was no more than 20 years old. The libretto of *Armida al campo* (1708) refers to him as *maestro di cappella della camera* of the Duke of Mantua, Ferdinando Carlo Gonzaga, who resided in Venice at the time; it is unclear when the appointment began, but it must have ended with the duke's death in July 1708. There are frequent gaps in Boniventi's activity as an opera composer in Venice. From 1712, he served as *maestro di cappella* to Margrave Charles III William of Baden-Durlach. Court records show that he left Durlach some time before 15 May 1718. He had presumably returned to Venice by then, since his *La virtù tra nemici* was performed there during Carnival of that year. The libretto to *Filippo re di Macedonia* (1720) still refers to him as the Margrave's *maestro di cappella*. In Durlach, he conducted an average of six operas annually, only one of them his own: *Armida al campo*. This was one of only two operas performed there in Italian, both in 1717, despite the presence of Boniventi and Italian singers at the court in Durlach from 1712 to 1717.

drammi per musica in 3 acts and first performed in Venice unless otherwise stated

Il gran Macedone (G. Pancieri), S Cassiano, aut. 1690, arias *GB-Lbl*, *I-Rvat*

Almerinda (Pancieri), S Cassiano, carn. 1691

Almira (Pancieri), SS Giovanni e Paolo, aut. 1691

La vittoria nella costanza (F. Passarini), S Angelo, carn. 1702

Armida al campo (F. Silvani, after T. Tasso: *Gerusalemme liberata*), S Angelo, week before 28 Jan 1708

La Partenope (S. Stampiglia), Ferrara, Bonacossi, Ascension 1709, collab. A. Caldara

Endimione (tragicommedia, F. Mazzari), S Angelo, aut. 1709

Circe delusa (G. A. Falier), S Angelo, 29 Jan 1711

La virtù tra nemici (G. B. Abbati), S Moisè, carn. 1718

Arianna abbandonata (A. Schietti), S Moisè, aut. 1719, arias formerly *D-Dlb*

Venceslao (A. Zeno), Turin, Carignano, 26 Dec 1720

Filippo re di Macedonia (D. Lalli), S Angelo, 27 Dec 1720 [Act 3 by Vivaldi]

L'inganno fortunato (B. Pavieri, after G. B. Sara), S Moisè, aut. 1721

Bertarido re dei longobardi (after A. Salvi: *Rodelinda*), S Cassiano, aut. 1727

*

R. Brockpähler: *Handbuch zur Geschichte der Barockoper in Deutschland* (Emsdetten, 1964)

R. Freeman: 'The Travels of Partenope', *Studies in Music History: Essays for Oliver Strunk* (Princeton, 1968), 336–85

HARRIS S. SAUNDERS

Bonlini, Giovanni Carlo (*b* Venice, 7 Aug 1673; *d* Venice, 20 Jan 1731). Italian writer. He published anonymously in Venice in 1730 a detailed catalogue of the operas performed in the city to that time: *Le glorie della poesia e della musica contenute nell'estatta notizia de' Teatri della città di Venezia, e nel catalogo purgatissimo dei drammi quivi sin'hora rappresentati, con gl'auttori della poesia e della musica e con le annotazioni ai suoi luoghi propri*. Drawing on earlier works by Leone Allacci and Cristoforo Ivanovich, Bonlini provided valuable information about the history of Venetian opera, and particularly about the works of Monteverdi and Cavalli. His work was continued by the Venetian Antonio Groppo, who published in about 1745 a *Catalogo di tutti drammi per musica recitati ne' teatri di Venezia dall'anno 1637 ... fin all'anno presente 1745*.

*

Novelle della Repubblica delle lettere dell'anno M.D. CCXXXI, publicate sotto gli auspizi dell'Illustrissimo Signor Agostino Tilli (Venice, 1732)

G. M. Mazzuchelli: *Gli scrittori d'Italia cioè notizie storiche e critiche intorno alle vite, e agli scritti dei letterati italiani*, ii/3 (Brescia, 1762), 1669

P. Ryom: 'Les catalogues de Bonlini et de Groppo', *Informazioni e studi vivaldiani*, ii (1981), 3–30

——: 'Deux catalogues d'opéras', ibid, iii (1982), 13–44

Bonn. City in western Germany, formerly the capital of the German Federal Republic (1949–90). Its significance for music began after 1257, when it became the seat of the Archbishop of Cologne, who played a prominent part in German political life as elector. Under the electors, opera was performed by touring companies from outside Bonn – in 1745 Pietro Mingotti's company from Hamburg, with G. B. Locatelli, and in 1757 and 1764 Angelo Mingotti's company. The repertory consisted mainly of Italian *opera buffa*. In 1767–71 Beethoven's father, Johann, was active in promoting the performance of Italian operas including Pergolesi's *La serva padrona*.

The Bonner Theater was opened on 26 November 1778, and the next year the Grossmann company with Christian G. Neefe visited Bonn. Neefe produced Singspiel and *opéra comique* as well as *opera buffa*; he also staged operas by Mozart in Bonn for the first time. The theatre closed after the death of Elector Max Friedrich in 1784.

Although a new theatre was built by the citizens of Bonn in 1826, no one company was responsible for opera productions and there was not an unbroken tradition of performances. In 1844 the theatre was demolished; a new one was built in 1848 and used for opera until it was destroyed in World War II. The Cologne company also visited Bonn from time to time during the 19th century. After World War I operatic activity was suspended for lack of a suitable orchestra; it was not resumed until 1934.

In 1965 the Theater der Stadt Bonn, a tripartite concern, constructed a new building with 896 seats. Although Bonn was now the seat of government its opera company was scarcely known outside the region. The musical directors of the 1960s and 70s were Hans Zender and Ralf Weikert. In 1980 the city appointed Jean-Claude Riber Generalintendant, with the task of raising the opera's reputation to an international level. Riber introduced a stagione system, in a season running from August to June, with world-famous guest artists, and provided fine casts, equal in all respects to those of the principal opera houses of Europe. Riber's 'theatre of stars' – a term not entirely justified, as it does not include all the prominent directors who have also worked regularly in Bonn – was subjected to bitter attacks in the local and provincial press. The American conductor Dennis Russell Davies became general musical director in 1987. That year Riber appointed the composer Udo Zimmermann director of the Werkstattbühne, opened in 1972, a studio theatre concentrating on contemporary opera. The theatre director Giancarlo del Monaco was appointed to succeed Riber in 1992.

IMRE FABIAN

Bonney, Barbara (*b* Montclair, NJ, April 1956). American soprano. She studied at Salzburg and in 1979 joined the Darmstadt Opera, making her début as Anna in *Die lustigen Weiber von Windsor*. She also sang Blonde, Cherubino, Adina, Gretel, Gilda, Lauretta, Massenet's Manon and Natalie (Henze's *Der Prinz von Homburg*). She has appeared at Munich, Frankfurt, Hamburg, Vienna, Geneva, Zürich and Covent Garden, where she made her début in 1984 as Sophie and returned as Nannetta. She sang Pamina at La Scala (1985), Adele at Chicago (1989) and Sophie at the Metropolitan (1991). Her other roles include Norina, Adina, Lucieta (*I quatro rusteghi*), Thibault (*Don Carlos*) and Susanna. She has a beautiful voice and a charming stage personality.

ELIZABETH FORBES

Bonno, Giuseppe [Bon, Josephus Johannes Baptizta; Bono, Josef] (*b* Vienna, 29 Jan 1711; *d* Vienna, 15 April 1788). Austrian composer of Italian origin. The son of an imperial footman from Brescia, he received his first musical instruction from the court composer and Kapellmeister of St Stephen's, J. G. Reinhardt. In 1726 Charles VI sent Bonno to Naples, where he remained for ten years, studying composition (primarily of church music) with Francesco Durante and dramatic composition with Leonardo Leo; he also had singing lessons. In 1732 he made his début as a composer with the pastorale *Nigella e Nise* (text by G. C. Pasquini).

In February or March 1736 Bonno returned to Vienna. On 26 July of that year his *festa di camera* in one act, *L'amore insuperabile*, was performed to celebrate the name-day of the Archduchess Maria Anna, and on 1 October *Trajano* was performed, the first of several stage works written for the birthday of Charles VI. In 1737 he became 'court scholar in composition', and in 1739 court composer. From about 1749 to 1761 Bonno was Kapellmeister to the household of Field Marshal Joseph Friedrich, Prince of Sachsen-Hildburghausen, in Schlosshof and Mannersdorf, where his fellow musicians included Gluck (1754–6) and Dittersdorf (1751–61). He withdrew from the operatic stage in 1763.

In 1774 Bonno succeeded F. L. Gassmann as Kapellmeister to the imperial court in recognition of his particular talent 'in the composition of chamber music and stage works'. He was later assisted in this position by Antonio Salieri, his eventual successor, who conducted the Italian opera when Bonno was unable to do so. For several years Bonno was also conductor of the Tonkünstlersocietät, the benevolent society for musicians' dependants. He retired from his court duties in 1788.

Bonno was a highly esteemed figure in Viennese musical life. He collaborated closely with Metastasio, composing the first settings of the poet's *Il natale di*

Giove, *Il vero omaggio*, *Il re pastore*, *L'eroe cinese*, *L'isola disabitata* and *L'Atenaide, ovvero Gli affetti più generosi*. As a teacher he was particularly successful; his pupils included Dittersdorf (composition) and Therese Teyber and Karl Frieberth (singing). Stylistically he stands between the late Venetian Baroque style that survived in Vienna with Fux and Caldara and the Classicism of Gluck and Haydn. True to his Neapolitan training, he was not a reformer like Gluck; he thoroughly mastered the difficulties of opera and was generally content to work within the conventions of his time, though a growing concern for greater dramatic realism occasionally affected the melodic and rhythmic style of his recitative. His orchestration rises above the routine, showing a taste for colourful instrumentation and picturesque effects. Especially in his later operas he synthesized the Neapolitan style of his early training with the late Venetian style in Vienna; the arias have mellifluous Neapolitan melodies as well as contrapuntal forms. He also composed oratorios and much church music.

unless otherwise stated, first performed in Vienna at the Burgtheater, MSS in A-Wn; catalogue in Breitner 1961

L'amore insuperabile (festa di camera, 1, G. C. Pasquini), 26 July 1736
Trajano (festa di camera, 1, Pasquini), 1 Oct 1736
La gara del genio con Giunone (serenata, 1, Pasquini), Laxenburg, 13 May 1737
Alessandro Severo (festa di camera, 1, Pasquini), 1 Oct 1737
La generosità di Artaserse (serenata, Pasquini), 4 Nov 1737
La pace richiamata (festa di camera , Pasquini), 26 July 1738
La pietà di Numa (festa di camera, 1, Pasquini), 1 Oct 1738
La vera nobilita (festa di camera, Pasquini), 26 July 1739
Il natale di Numa Pompilio (festa di camera, 1, Pasquini), 1 Oct 1739
Il nume d'Atene (festa di camera), 19 Nov 1739
La generosa Spartana (serenata, 1, Pasquini), Laxenburg, 13 May 1740
Il natale di Giove (azione teatrale, 1, P. Metastasio), Vienna, Favorita, 1 Oct 1740
Il vero omaggio (componimento drammatico, 1, Metastasio), Vienna, Schönbrunn, 13 March 1743
Danae, 1744, ?unperf., lost
Ezio, 1749, ?unperf., lost
Il rè pastore (dramma per musica, 3, Metastasio), Vienna, Schönbrunn, 27 Oct 1751
L'eroe cinese (dramma per musica, 3, Metastasio), Vienna, Schönbrunn, 13 May 1752
L'isola disabitata, 1752 (azione teatrale, 1, Metastasio), 23 Sept 1754
Didone abbandonata, 1752 (Metastasio), unperf., lost
L'Atenaide, ovvero Gli affetti più generosi, 1762 (azione teatrale, 2, Metastasio), unperf.
Il sogno di Scipione, 1763 (Metastasio), unperf.

Music in: Catone in Utica, 1742; L'Armida placata, 1750

*

C. D. von Dittersdorf: *Lebensbeschreibung* (Leipzig, 1801); Eng. trans., 1896; ed. N. Miller (Munich, 1967)
L. von Köchel: *Die kaiserliche Hof-Musikkapelle in Wien von 1543–1867* (Vienna, 1869)
E. Wellesz: 'Giuseppe Bonno (1710–1788): sein Leben und seine dramatischen Werke', *SIMG*, xi (1909–10), 395–442
W. Vetter: 'Zur Entwicklungsgeschichte der Opera seria um 1750 in Wien', *ZMw*, xiv (1931–2), 2–28
H. Kunz: 'Der Wiener Theaterspielplan 1741–1765', *Jb der Gesellschaft für Wiener Theaterforschung 1953–4*, 72–113
F. Hadamowsky: 'Leitung, Verwaltung und ausübende Künstler ... am Burgtheater (französisches Theater) und am Kärntnertortheater (deutsches Theater) in Wien 1754–1764', *Jb der Gesellschaft für Wiener Theaterforschung*, xxi (1960), 113–33
K. Breitner: *Giuseppe Bonno und sein Oratorienwerk* (diss., U. of Vienna, 1961) [with extensive bibliography]
W. Vetter: 'Italiens Musik im Lichte von Dichtung und bildender Kunst', *DJbM*, viii (1963), 54–95 RUDOLPH ANGERMÜLLER

Bononcini, Antonio Maria (*b* Modena, 18 June 1677; *d* Modena, 8 July 1726). Italian composer. During the first 35 years of his life he worked alongside his more famous elder brother, Giovanni, who was likewise a composer and cellist. By 1686 both were students of G. P. Colonna at Bologna. When Cardinal Pamphili was papal legate there in 1690–93 both played in his orchestra. Afterwards they worked in Rome, where Antonio wrote one quasi-dramatic work, *La fama eroica* (1698) for two allegorical characters, based on a text by G. B. Andriani.

Around 1700 Antonio joined his brother in Vienna, and Telemann heard them perform in Berlin in summer 1702. Antonio was first commissioned to compose for the Viennese court in 1705, the year in which Joseph I became emperor. During Joseph's reign, the emperor's great favour for Giovanni Bononcini extended to Antonio, who provided the court with 13 richly accompanied cantatas, six festive serenatas, four two-part oratorios and one three-act opera. Scores survive for all except the oratorio of 1705; the music is distinguished by intricate textures that incorporate contrapuntal artifice and extensive sequential development, underscored by the rapid harmonic movement characteristic of Corelli. Arias are mainly in minor keys, and they often feature dotted rhythms, angular melodic lines and chromatic harmonies that convey great pathos. Perhaps mainly on the basis of these works, Geminiani judged Antonio to be 'much beyond his brother in point of depth and knowledge'. Joseph I must have appreciated their rich detail, for in 1710 he named Antonio a 'composer to the emperor', made the appointment retroactive to the beginning of 1707, provided a lucrative salary (equivalent to that of his own Kapellmeister, Marc'Antonio Ziani) and commissioned Antonio's first opera, *Tigrane*. A year later Joseph died of smallpox, and his successor, Charles VI, did not retain the Bononcinis.

Antonio may have accompanied his brother to Rome when the two returned to Italy in 1713, but he settled in Modena, where his wife, Eleonora Suterin, bore him four sons and a daughter between 1715 and 1722. He subsequently achieved a modicum of fame throughout Italy with his settings of ten operas for various cities. In these works his style is Vivaldian rather than Corellian, featuring tuneful rather than angular lines, enticing syncopations rather than excruciating dotted notes, and doublings of voices rather than contrapuntal accompaniments for the treble instruments. He also 'directed' (i.e. perhaps compiled the music for) *L'enigma disciolto* and *Lucio Vero* at Modena in October 1716 and *Mitridate Eupatore* at Reggio Emilia in January 1723, and he may likewise have 'directed' other Modenese productions of 1717–21.

During the last five years of his life Bononcini became *maestro di cappella* at the Modenese court, and this appointment presumably terminated his need to compose operas in order to earn a living. He probably wrote his extant mass and *Stabat mater* during his final years, and the contrapuntal complexities in the latter were largely (and perhaps wholly) responsible for Padre Martini's judgment of his style: 'so elevated, lively, artful and delightful, that he is distinguished above most early 18th-century composers'.

See also GRISELDA (i).

three-act drammi per musica unless otherwise stated

Tigrane, re d'Armenia (P. Bernardoni), Vienna, Favorita, 25 July 1710, *A-Wgm*, *D-MEIr*

I veri amici (F. Silvani and D. Lalli, after P. Corneille: *Héraclius empereur d'Orient*), Naples, S Bartolomeo, 26 Nov or 26 Dec 1715, music lost

Il tiranno eroe (drama, 3, V. Cassani), Milan, Regio Ducal, 26 Dec 1715, arias *Dlb*

Sesostri, re di Egitto (drama, 3, P. Pariati), Milan, Regio Ducal, 2 Feb 1716, *Dlb*

La conquista del vello d'oro (drama, 3, F. Parisetti), Reggio Emilia, Pubblico, 29 April 1717, *A-Wn*

Astianatte (A. Salvi), Venice, S Giovanni Grisostomo, carn. 1718, arias *D-W*

Griselda (drama, 3, Zeno), Milan, Regio Ducal, 26 Dec 1718, *A-Wgm*, *D-B* (*R*1977: IOB, xxi)

Nino [Act 3] (3, I. Zanelli), Reggio Emilia, Pubblico, May Fair 1720, arias *F-Pc* [Act 1 by Capelli, Act 2 by F. Gasparini]

Merope (Zeno), Rome, Pace, carn. 1721, arias *Pn*

Endimione (pastorale in musica, 3, F. de Lemene), Naples, S Bartolomeo, 14 May 1721, arias Milan, private library of Natale Gallini

Rosiclea in Dania (melodrama, 3, Silvani: *L'oracolo in sogno*), Naples, royal palace, 1 Oct 1721; S Bartolomeo, 4 Oct 1721, *I-MC*

*

DBI (C. Frajese)

E. Wellesz: 'Die Opern und Oratorien in Wien von 1660–1708', *SMw*, vi (1919), 75–9

G. Roncaglia: 'Di insigni musicisti modenesi (documenti inediti), ii: Su la famiglia dei Bononcini', *Atti e memorie della R. Deputazione di storia patria per le provincie modenesi*, 7th ser., vi (1930), 14–16

——: 'Antonio Maria Bononcini e il suo *Stabat mater*', *Musicisti lombardi ed emiliani*, Chigiana, xv (1958), 117–25

L. Lindgren: *A Bibliographic Scrutiny of Dramatic Works set by Giovanni and his Brother Antonio Maria Bononcini* (Ann Arbor, 1974)

R. Strohm: *Die italienische Oper im 18. Jahrhundert* (Wilhelmshaven, 1979), esp. 73–94 [on *Griselda*]

L. Bennett: *The Italian Cantata in Vienna, c.1700–c.1711* (Ann Arbor, 1980)

L. Lindgren: 'Antonio Maria Bononcini e *La conquista del vello d'oro* (Reggio Emilia 1717)', *Civiltà teatrale e settecento emiliano* (Bologna, 1986), 309–28

E. Careri: 'The Correspondence between Burney and Twining about Corelli and Geminiani', *ML*, lxxii (1991), 38–47

LOWELL LINDGREN

Bononcini, Giovanni (*b* Modena, 18 July 1670; *d* Vienna, 9 July 1747). Italian composer, son of the composer, theorist and violinist Giovanni Maria Bononcini. He was renowned internationally after the unprecedented success of his opera *Il trionfo di Camilla* (1696).

1. LIFE. Bononcini moved to Bologna when his father's death made him an orphan at the age of eight. He studied with G. P. Colonna at S Petronio, then, at the age of 15, published three instrumental collections and was accepted into the Accademia Filarmonica (on 30 May 1686). During the next two years he published three further collections, was engaged at S Petronio as a string player and singer, composed two oratorios (performed in both Bologna and Modena) and succeeded G. F. Tosi as *maestro di cappella* at S Giovanni in Monte. For this church he wrote four double-choir masses. He composed a new oratorio for his native city in 1690, and in 1691 dedicated his op.8, consisting of well-wrought cantatas for two voices, to the emperor and played in the orchestra of the papal legate, Cardinal Benedetto Pamphili.

By 1692 Bononcini was in Rome, where he entered the service of Filippo Colonna, his wife Lorenza and her brother Luigi della Cerda. The librettist Silvio Stampiglia had served the Colonnas since the 1680s, and from 1692 to 1696 his collaboration with Bononcini resulted in at least six serenatas, five operas and one oratorio. The last of these works, *Il trionfo di Camilla*, was produced at Naples after della Cerda became its Spanish viceroy. According to Geminiani, it 'astonished the musical world by its departure from the dry, flat melody to which their ears had until then been accustomed'. By 1710 its great success had led to productions in 19 other Italian cities and in London. All of them were apparently based on Bononcini's setting (see Lindgren 1974, 1977, 1980 and 1990), which should thus be regarded as a touchstone of Italian taste around 1700. Many of its brief da capo arias feature the tunefulness that characterizes his works of the 1690s.

A few months after the death of his Roman patron, Lorenza Colonna, in August 1697 Bononcini was accepted into the service of Leopold I in Vienna. There he earned the unusually large salary of 5000 florins a year from 1698 to 1712. Between 1698 and 1705 Leopold's heir, Joseph I, paid two-fifths of this salary, and Bononcini was clearly Joseph's favourite composer: six of his ten dramatic works performed at the court during Leopold's reign were dedicated to the heir or his wife. In 1702, because the War of the Spanish Succession had caused an interruption of musical activities in Vienna, Bononcini led a group of musicians to Sophie Charlotte's court in Berlin. There he became the centre of the queen's daily musical life and composed two dramatic 'bagatelles', *Cefalo* and *Polifemo*. He apparently went to Italy during the year of mourning for Leopold's death (May 1705 to June 1706); his only opera composed for Venice was produced during Carnival 1706.

By 1706 Bononcini was famous throughout Europe. Raguenet, who had seen the 1698 production of *Camilla* in Rome, declared in 1705 that more than 200 cantatas as well as entire operas by Bononcini were known in Paris, where he was the 'modèle pour le gracieux'. In London 63 performances of *Camilla* were given between 1706 and 1709, an attempt was made to attract Bononcini himself in 1707, and arias from his works were inserted into eight pasticcios produced in 1707–11. Gasparini ended his 1708 treatise with praise for the '*bizzaria*, beauty, harmony, artful study and fanciful invention' in Bononcini's cantatas, about 300 of which are extant today. According to Benedetto Marcello (*c*1720), the standard cantata for singers' auditions was Bononcini's *Impara a non dar fede*.

During Joseph's reign (1705–11) Bononcini set seven operas and five shorter dramatic works. His great favour probably prompted Joseph to engage his brother Antonio and his former librettist, Stampiglia. These three were not retained by Joseph's successor, Charles VI, though Stampiglia and Giovanni did write the serenata that welcomed the new empress at Milan in 1713. Giovanni then entered the service of the Viennese ambassador in Rome, Johann Wenzel, Count Gallas. His service began with a serenata in 1714 and an opera in 1715, both written in collaboration with Paolo Rolli, and he remained musical director at the embassy until the count's death in July 1719.

In summer 1719 the Earl of Burlington was on his second trip to Italy, and he was chiefly responsible for obtaining Bononcini as a composer for the Royal Academy of Music in London. Bononcini went there in October 1720, and his first two seasons were outstandingly successful: five of his works (including Act 2 of *Muzio Scevola*) accounted for 82 of the 120 performances given by the Royal Academy; his *Cantate e duetti* were engraved with a list of no fewer than 237 subscribers; and his *Divertimenti da camera* appeared in two editions. At the end of his second season he was commissioned by Francis Atterbury, Dean of Westminster, to write the anthem for Marlborough's funeral and by the Duchess of Buckingham to set the choruses that ended the acts of her late husband's play, *Marcus Brutus*.

The duchess was a notorious Jacobite, and Atterbury was imprisoned for treasonous Jacobite activities in August 1722. Mainly because of his Jacobite acquaintances and Italian Catholic heritage, Bononcini soon saw his London success ruined. Even though his operas had led the Royal Academy to its only profitable season in 1721–2, the directors apparently did not re-engage him in autumn 1722. His *Erminia* was produced in March 1723, but it seems to have been written mainly for a projected Parisian production with singers from the Royal Academy in July 1723. Although this was cancelled, Bononcini and at least Anastasia Robinson performed in Paris during the summer. The Royal Academy did re-engage him for 1723–4, but cabals against him were strong. He planned to leave London at the end of the season in order to accept a position offered him by the mistress of the Regent of France. Together with several of the academy's singers (including Cuzzoni), he did spend the summer of 1724 performing in France, but then he returned to England.

His return had been ensured by an offer of £500 a year for life, made by Henrietta, the young Duchess of Marlborough, on 14 May 1724. In return for this stipend he was to direct only performances of his own music at her private concerts, which he did until 1731. His only academy opera during these years was *Astianatte* (1727), the performances of which are infamous because of fighting between the partisans of Cuzzoni and Faustina. Although it was produced 20 years before his death, it virtually ended his career as a dramatic composer.

Bononcini was an active member of the Academy of Ancient Musick from 1726, and it was in 1727 or 1728 that his friend Maurice Greene introduced an unsigned manuscript of *In una siepe ombrosa*, which was performed at a meeting. Bononcini apparently claimed to be the composer of this madrigal until, at the meeting on 14 January 1731, Bernard Gates directed a performance of the same work drawn from Antonio Lotti's *Duetti, terzetti e madrigali* (Venice, 1705). An unusually flagrant example of the ubiquitous custom of unacknowledged borrowing had been uncovered, and the Ancient Musick's directors made a great noise about it in order to discredit Bononcini and Greene. By means of this and other ill-advised moves, Bononcini was indeed discredited by 1732, when he attempted to produce a 'pastoral entertainment' at the opera house. The projected work was a serenata, but it may have been replaced by some miscellaneous music, because the prima donna, Anna Maria Strada del Pò, refused to sing for Bononcini.

The composer, then aged 62, went to Paris, where he wrote vocal works for the Concert Spirituel on 7 February and 2 April 1733 and published a *Laudate pueri*. He proceeded to Madrid in December 1733 and then to Lisbon, where he apparently stayed until 1736; in both cities he performed and wrote music, but nothing for the stage. In mid-1736 he returned to Vienna, where he composed two operas and an oratorio for productions of 1737. The Empress Maria Theresa granted him a small pension and increased it from 1 October 1742 to an amount which allowed him to spend his final five years in comfortable frugality. It is not known if his wife Margherita Balletti (who was in London between 1736 and 1738) was with him in Vienna during his last years, but their 22-year-old daughter died there on 10 May 1743.

2. WORKS. Plaintive tunefulness (such as that of 'Per la gloria d'adorarvi' from *Griselda*, 1722) was always a primary attraction in Bononcini's dramatic works. Hawkins aptly found that 'Bononcini's genius was adapted to the expression of tender and pathetic sentiments. His melodies, the richest and sweetest that we know of, are in a style peculiarly his own; his harmonies are original, and at the same time natural'. In the decades after 1700, however, when Bononcini's arias became markedly longer and more fully accompanied, their Handelian proportions were infrequently supported by the musical substance and inner propulsion which justifies such length in Handel's works or by the neutral, concerto-like figuration which maintains the momentum in Vivaldi's or Vinci's. Thus Burney (1819–20) was less complimentary in his assessment of Bononcini: 'his melody was, perhaps, more polished and vocal, though not so new as that of his powerful Saxon rival'. It may indeed have seemed antiquated to partisans of new stars such as Faustina and Farinelli, whose agility was astounding.

A secondary attraction was Bononcini's superb text setting, which the librettist Rolli lauded in 1724 as indescribably expressive of human passions. Such expressiveness was undoubtedly encouraged by his extensive work with noted Arcadian librettists, especially Stampiglia and Rolli. In his recitatives, according to Hawkins, 'those manifold inflexions of the voice, which accompany common speech, with the several interjections, exclamations and pauses proper thereto, are marked with great exactness and propriety'. Burney (1819–20) concurred by stating that his recitative 'was universally allowed to be the best of the time, and in the true genius of the Italian language'. Such expressiveness is best judged by Italian connoisseurs, and much of it must have passed unnoticed in Vienna and London, the cities for which Bononcini produced most of his dramatic works between 1699 and 1737.

Since Arcadian writers favoured the pastoral realm, it is not surprising that Bononcini's works typically feature sighing emotions and tender moods, which James Ralph (1728) contrasted with Handel's heroic emotions and tyrannical rage. In 1716 J. E. Galliard had termed Bononcini's style 'agreeable and easie', but by the late 1720s it was found to be lulling rather than exciting, and was derided by some 'very fine Gentlemen for its too great Simplicity' (*Craftsman*, 10 June 1727). If we hear this 'simplicity' as both the final stage of 17th-century bel canto and the precursor of *galant* and pre-classical melodies, it aptly becomes the touchstone of taste at the turning-point around 1700.

See also ALMAHIDE; ASTARTO; ASTIANATTE; CRISPO; GRISELDA (iii); MUZIO SCEVOLA; TRIONFO DI CAMILLA, REGINA DE' VOLSCI, IL; and XERSE (ii).

three-act drammi per musica unless otherwise stated

Edition: A. Ford: *Giovanni Bononcini: [12] Arias for the Vienna Operas* (London, 1971) [F]

Eraclea, ovvero Il ratto delle Sabbine (? S. Stampiglia, after N. Minato), Rome, Tordinona, 12 Jan 1692, arias in *B-Bc*, *D-MÜs*, *I-Rsc* and *Rvat* [pasticcio with at least 20 arias by Bononcini]
Xerse (Stampiglia, after Minato), Rome, Tordinona, 25 Jan 1694, *D-MÜs*, *GB-Lbl* (*R*1986: HS, viii)
Tullo Ostilio (Stampiglia, after A. Morselli), Rome, Tordinona, *c*10 Feb 1694, arias in *B-Bc*, *D-MÜs*, *F-Pn*, *I-Rvat* and *Tn*
Muzio Scevola (Stampiglia, after Minato), Rome, Tordinona, 5 Feb 1695, arias in *D-Müs*, *I-Bc*, *Mc*, *Rc*, *Rli*, *Rvat*, *REm* and *US-NYlibin*; rev. version, Naples, S Bartolomeo, carn. 1698, comic scenes *D-Dlb*, arias in *F-Pn*, *I-Nc* and *PAVu*; rev. as Mutio Scevola, Vienna, Hof, 30 June 1710, *A-Wn*, 5 arias in F
L'amore eroico fra pastori [Act 3] (favola pastorale for puppets, 3, P. Ottoboni), Rome, Palazzo della Cancelleria, Feb 1696 [Act 1 by C. F. Cesarini, Act 2 by G. L. Lulier]; as La pastorella, with addns to Act 3 by A. Scarlatti, Rome, Venetian Embassy, 5 Feb 1705, arias *GB-Lbl*; rev. P. A. Motteux and V. Urbani as Love's Triumph, London, Queen's, 26 Feb 1708, arias (London, 1708)
Il trionfo di Camilla, regina de' Volsci (Stampiglia), Naples, S Bartolomeo, 27 Dec 1696, *D-B*, *Dlb*, *MÜs*, *F-Pc* [Act 3], *GB-AB* (*R*1978: IOB, xvii), *Lbl* [2 copies], *I-MOe*, *Nc*, *US-AUS*, *Wc*, comic scenes *D-Dlb*; as La rinovata Camilla, Rome, Capranica, 18 Jan 1698, *A-Wgm*, *GB-Cfm*, *CDp*, Acts 2, 3 and intermedio after Act 2 *Lbl*
La clemenza d'Augusto [Act 3] (C. S. Capece), Rome, Tordinona, 4 Feb 1697, *E-Mn* [Act 1 by S. De Luca, Act 2 by C. F. Pollarolo]
Temistocle in bando [Act 3] (Morselli), Rome, Capranica, Feb 1698, arias *B-Br*, *F-Pn*, *GB-Lam*, *Lbl*, *Lcm*, *Ob*, *I-Bc* and *REm* [Act 1 by Lulier, Act 2 ? by M. A. Ziani]
La fede publica (D. Cupeda), Vienna, Hof, 18 Jan 1699, Acts 1 and 3 *A-Wn*
Gli affetti più grandi, vinti dal più giusto (Cupeda), Vienna, Favorita, 30 Aug 1701, *A-Wgm*, *Wn*
Cefalo [Pastorella] (1, A. Guidi), Litzenbourg [now Charlottenburg], spr. 1702, *D-WD*, *GB-Lbl*
Polifemo (1, A. Ariosti), Litzenbourg, sum. 1702, *D-B*; adapted with Ger. trans. G. Kärnbach (Berlin, 1938)
[Feraspe], Vienna, ?*c*1702, Acts 2 and 3 *Wn*
La regina creduta re (M. Noris), Venice, S Angelo, carn. 1706; as Semiramide, Brunswick, 1708, arias *D-Bds*, *SWl* and *GB-Lcm*
Endimione (favola per musica, ?Stampiglia, after F. de Lemene), Vienna, Palazzo di Belfonte, 6 July 1706, *A-Wn*, 2 arias in F
Etearco (Stampiglia), Vienna, Hof, carn. 1707, *Wgm*, *Wn*, *D-WD*, *GB-Cfm* [Act 1], 14 arias (London, 1711), 1 aria in F; rev. version, Rome, Pace, carn. 1719, arias *B-Bc* and *F-Pc*
Turno Aricino (Stampiglia), Vienna, Favorita, 26 July 1707, *A-Wn*, *D-MEIr*, *GB-Lbl* [2 copies]; ov., 6 arias in pasticcio Almahide, London, Queen's, 10 Jan 1710
Mario fuggitivo (Stampiglia), Vienna, Hof, 8 Feb 1708, *A-Wgm*, *Wn*, *D-Dlb*, *MEIr*, *W*; 11 arias in pasticcio Almahide, London, Queen's, 10 Jan 1710
Abdolomino (Stampiglia), Vienna, Hof, 3 Feb 1709, *A-Wn*, 4 arias in F; rev. version with addns by F. Mancini, Naples, S Bartolomeo, 1 Oct 1711
Caio Gracco (Stampiglia), Vienna, Hof, 16 Feb 1710, *D-W*
Astarto (P. A. Rolli, after A. Zeno and P. Pariati), Rome, Capranica, Jan 1715, *D-MÜs*; rev. version, London, King's, 19 Nov 1720, arias *GB-Lcm*, ov., sym., 33 arias (London, 1721/*R*1984: BMB, section 4, xx)
Erminia (favola pastorale, 5, 'd'un accademico Quirino' [? D. O. Petrosellini]), Rome, Pace, carn. 1719, arias in *F-Pc*, *I-Rc* and *US-Wc*; rev. version (favola boschereccia, 3, Rolli), London, King's, 30 March 1723, arias in *GB-Lbl*, 5 arias (London, 1723)
Crispo (drama, 3, G. Lemer), Rome, Capranica, carn. 1721, arias *B-Bc*, *D-MÜs*, *F-Pc* and *I-Rc*; rev. version (Rolli, after Lemer), London, King's, 10 Jan 1722, arias *EIRE-Dam*; 10 arias (London, 1722); 4 arias in Favourite Songs ... in Cyrus (London, 1722) [see L'odio e l'amore]
Muzio Scevola [Act 2] (drama, 3, Rolli, after Stampiglia), London, King's, 15 April 1721, *GB-Lbl*, ov., 4 arias (London, 1721) [Act 1 by F. Amadei, Act 3 by Handel]
L'odio e l'amore [Ciro; Cyrus, or Odio ed amore] (drama, 3, Rolli, after Noris), London, King's, 20 May 1721, arias *EIRE-Dam*, *US-SFsc* and *Wc*, 2 arias in Favourite Songs ... in Cyrus (London, 1722)
Griselda (drama, 3, Rolli, after Zeno), London, King's, 22 Feb 1722, ov., 29 arias (London, 1722)
Farnace (drama, 3, L. Morari), London, King's, 27 Nov 1723, *D-WD*, 10 arias (London, 1724)
Calfurnia [Calphurnia] (drama, 3, N. Haym, after G. Braccioli), London, King's, 18 April 1724, arias *GB-ABu*, 11 arias (London, 1724)
Astianatte (drama, 3, Haym, after A. Salvi, after J. Racine), London, King's, 6 May 1727, arias *US-Wc*, 7 arias, minuet (London, 1727), 1 aria in Hawkins
Alessandro in Sidone (tragicommedia per musica, 5, after Zeno and Pariati), Vienna, Kleines Hof, 6 Feb 1737, *A-Wgm*, *Wn*
Zenobia (P. Metastasio), Vienna, Favorita, 28 Aug 1737

*

HawkinsH
F. Raguenet: *Paralèle des italiens et des françois, en ce qui regarde la musique et les opéra* (Paris, 1702; Eng. trans., enlarged, 1709)
——: *Défense du Parallèle des italiens et des françois* (Paris, 1705)
F. Gasparini: *L'armonico pratico al cimbalo* (Venice, 1708; Eng. trans., 1968)
J. E. Galliard: 'To the Lovers of Musick', *Six English Cantatas after the Italian Manner* (London, 1716)
B. Marcello: *Il teatro alla moda* (Venice, *c*1720); Eng. trans., *MQ*, xxxiv (1948), 371–403; xxxv (1949), 85–105
P. A. Rolli, ed. and trans.: *Gli amanti interni: commedia inglese del Cavaliere Riccardo Steele* (London, 1724)
A. Primcock [pseud. of J. Ralph]: *The Touchstone* (London, 1728)
C. Burney: 'Bononcini, Giovanni', *Rees's Cyclopaedia* (1819–20)
L. von Köchel: *Johann Josef Fux* (Vienna, 1872)
E. Sola: 'Curiosità storico-artistico-letterarie tratte dal carteggio dell'inviato estense Giuseppe Riva con Lodovico Antonio Muratori', *Atti e memorie della R. Deputazione di storia patria per le provincie modenesi e parmensi*, 3rd ser., iv (1887), 197–392
E. Dent: *Alessandro Scarlatti* (London, 1905), 65
R. Doebner, ed.: *Briefe der Königin Sophie Charlotte von Preussen* (Leipzig, 1905)
C. Sachs: *Musik und Oper am kurbrandenburgischen Hof* (Berlin, 1910)
E. Dent: 'Italian Chamber Cantatas', *MA*, ii (1910–11), 185–99, esp.193
A. Koczirz: 'Exzerpte aus den Hofmusikakten des Wiener Hofkammerarchivs', *SMw*, i (1913), 278–303
G. Roncaglia: 'L. A. Muratori, la musica e il maggior compositore modenese del suo tempo', *Atti e memorie della R. Deputazione di storia patria per le provincie modenesi*, 7th ser., viii (1933), 277–318
X. de Courville: *Luigi Riccoboni dit Lélio* (Paris, 1943–5)
W. C. Smith: *A Bibliography of the Musical Works Published by John Walsh During the Years 1695–1720* (London, 1948)
K. Hueber: 'Gli ultimi anni di Giovanni Bononcini: notizie e documenti inediti', *Atti e memorie dell'Accademia di scienze, lettere e arti di Modena*, 5th ser., xii (1954), 153–71
O. E. Deutsch: *Handel: a Documentary Biography* (London, 1955)
K. Hueber: *Die Wiener Opern Giovanni Bononcinis von 1697 bis 1710* (diss., U. of Vienna, 1955)
E. O. Downes: 'The Neapolitan Tradition in Opera', *IMSCR*, viii *New York 1961*, i, 277–84; ii, 132–4
H. S. Powers: 'Il Serse trasformato', *MQ*, xlvii (1961), 481–92; xlviii (1962), 73–92
G. E. Dorris: *Paolo Rolli and the Italian Circle in London, 1715–1744* (The Hague, 1967)
W. C. Smith and C. Humphries: *A Bibliography of the Musical Works Published by the Firm of John Walsh During the Years 1721–1766* (London, 1968)
H. S. Powers: 'Il *Mutio* tramutato, i: Sources and Libretto', *Venezia e il melodramma nel seicento: Venice 1972*, 227–58
A. Ford: 'Music and Drama in the Operas of Giovanni Bononcini', *PRMA*, ci (1974–5), 107–20
L. Lindgren: *A Bibliographic Scrutiny of Dramatic Works Set by Giovanni and his Brother Antonio Maria Bononcini* (Ann Arbor, 1974)
——: 'The Three Great Noises "Fatal to the Interests of Bononcini"', *MQ*, lxi (1975), 560–83
——: 'I trionfi di Camilla', *Studi musicali*, vi (1977), 89–159
——: 'Parisian Patronage of Performers from the Royal Academy of Musick (1719–28)', *ML*, lviii (1977), 4–28
——: '*Camilla* and *The Beggar's Opera*', *Philological Quarterly*, lix (1980), 44–61
S. Franchi: *Drammaturgia romana: repertorio bibliografico cronologico dei testi drammatici pubblicati a Roma e nel Lazio, secolo XVII* (Rome, 1988)
L. Lindgren: Preface to Giovanni Bononcini, *Camilla*, MLE, E1 (1990)
E. Careri: 'The Correspondence between Burney and Twining about Corelli and Geminiani', *ML*, lxxii (1991), 38–47

L. Lindgren: 'Musicians and Librettists in the Correspondence of Gio. Giacomo Zamboni (Oxford, Bodleian Library, MSS Rawlinson Letters 116–138)', *RMARC*, no.24 (1991)

LOWELL LINDGREN

Bontempi [Angelini, Angelini-Bontempi], **Giovanni Andrea** (*b* Perugia, 21 Feb 1625; *d* Brufa, Torgiano, nr Perugia, 1 July 1705). Italian composer, librettist and theatre architect. Born Angelini, he studied under Sozio Sozi at S Filippo, Perugia, in 1635, continuing in Rome as a protégé of Cesare Bontempi (a nobleman whose surname he adopted). There he studied singing under Virgilio Mazzocchi and won the patronage of Cardinal Francesco Barberini. He was in Florence in 1641 and in 1643 became a singer at St Mark's, Venice, under Monteverdi, Rovetta and Cavalli. In 1651 he entered the service of the Elector Johann Georg I in Dresden and after the elector's death in 1656 he was joint Kapellmeister with Heinrich Schütz and Vincenzo Albrici. The favour that Albrici enjoyed with Johann Georg II and the arrival in 1667 of Carlo Pallavicino were given by Bontempi as reasons why he turned his attention away from music. In 1671 he returned to Dresden and was appointed designer and master of the machines at the court theatres. When Johann Georg II died in 1680 his musicians left Dresden, and Bontempi returned to Italy, retiring to his villa at Brufa. He was often invited to sing and compose for S Maria Maggiore, Spello, and was briefly *maestro di cappella* there in 1682, but he devoted most of his time to his studies. His *Historia musica* (1695) was the first history of music in Italian. He was elected to the Accademia degli Insensati, Perugia, in 1697.

His *Il Paride* (1662), the first opera in Italian to be performed in Dresden, was given at the castle on the marriage of Erdmunde Sophia, the daughter of the elector of Saxony, and Christian Ernst, Margrave of Brandenburg. The scenery was by Giacomo Torelli and the performance lasted from nine in the evening to two in the morning. The staging of the opera and the publication of the printed full score in celebration, a practice by then abandoned in Italy, suggest that Dresden was attempting to reproduce the atmosphere of the festive early Italian court operas. The action is in five acts and 39 scenes, with many minor roles and episodes revolving around the central plot. Stylistically it shows Venetian influence, of Monteverdi, Cavalli and Cesti, and it is characterized by a predominance of *arioso*. In the text, however, 25 passages of 'Rede' (recitative) and 'Lied' (aria) are clearly indicated. Each act ends with a dance, the music of which does not appear in the score; there is only one chorus, of minor gods, but there are many numbers for two and three voices. *Il Paride* has often been cited as a forerunner of Cesti's *Il pomo d'oro*, performed in Vienna six years later. They are on similar subjects and both are more lyrical than dramatic, showing a taste for Italian bel canto which in Bontempi is accentuated by the modest instrumentation (two violins and continuo). Ermilio's lament in Act 5, on a chromatic bass descending by a 4th, is an important example of a 17th-century operatic lament, although its comic context (the character wrongly believes he is wounded) modifies the dramatic tension, which is also affected by an interruption. *Il Paride* represents, along with Loreto Vittori's *Galatea*, a rare instance of a 17th-century opera for which the composer had sufficient classical background to be able to write his own libretto. Bontempi described the work as neither comedy, tragedy, tragicomedy nor drama but 'erotopegnio musicale'.

Dafne (1671) and *Jupiter und Io* (1673), both in German, were written with the literary and possibly the musical collaboration of M. G. Peranda. *Dafne* was inspired by early Florentine opera, borrowing directly from Rinuccini's libretto which had been translated by Martin Opitz in 1627 for Schütz. *Jupiter und Io*, of which only the libretto survives, has many comic and grotesque moments deriving from the contrast between the ideal world of the gods and the humble condition of the peasants. The model appears to be A. M. Abbatini's *Ione*.

Il Paride (erotopegnio musicale, 5, Bontempi), Dresden, Riesensaal, 3 Nov 1662 (Dresden, 1662/*R*1970); 1 recit. and aria ed. in *BurneyH*; 1 aria ed. in R. Rolland: 'Les origines de l'opéra allemande', *EMDC*, I/ii (1921), 914–15

Dafne (5, Bontempi, ? with D. Schirmer and D. E. Heidenreich, after O. Rinuccini), Dresden, 3 Sept 1671, collab. Peranda, *D-Dlb*; 1 aria ed. in H. Riemann: *Musikgeschichte in Beispielen* (Leipzig, 1912, 2/1921), 197

Jupiter und Io (Bontempi or C. C. Dedekind), Dresden, 16 Jan 1673, music lost, collab. Peranda

Doubtful: Teseo (5, G. A. Moniglia), Dresden, 27 Jan 1667

*

J. Mattheson: *Critica musica*, i (Hamburg, 1722), 339
M. Fürstenau: *Beiträge zur Geschichte der Königlich sächsischen musikalischen Kapelle* (Dresden, 1849)
——: *Zur Geschichte der Musik und des Theaters am Hofe zu Dresden*, i (Dresden, 1861)
G. B. Rossi Scotti: *Di G. A. Bontempi di Perugia ricordo storico* (Perugia, 1878)
H. Kretzschmar: *Geschichte der Oper* (Leipzig, 1919), 86, 101, 137
R. Engländer: 'Il "Paride" in musica (1662) di G. A. Bontempi', *NA*, xvii (1940), 39–53
——: 'Zur Frage der "Dafne" (1671) von G. A. Bontempi und M. G. Peranda', *AcM*, xiii (1941), 59–77
F. Briganti: *Gio. Andrea Angelini-Bontempi (1624–1705), musicista, letterato, architetto: Perugia-Dresda* (Florence, 1956)
R. Engländer: 'Die erste italienische Oper in Dresden: Bontempis Il Paride in musica (1662)', *STMf*, xliii (1961), 119–34
Y. F.-A. Giraud: *La fable de Daphné* (Geneva, 1968), 459ff
L. Bianconi: *Il seicento* (Turin, 1982), 63, 133
W. Jahns: 'Il Paride von Giovanni Andrea Bontempi (1662), die erste italienische Oper in Dresden', *Schriftenreihe der Hochschule für Musik 'Karl Maria von Weber' Dresden*, no.9 (1985), 87–95

BIANCAMARIA BRUMANA, COLIN TIMMS

Bonynge, Richard (**Alan**) (*b* Sydney, 29 Sept 1930). Australian conductor. He studied the piano at the New South Wales Conservatorium (Sydney) with Lindley Evans, formerly Melba's accompanist, and in London with Herbert Fryer, and developed a special interest in vocal technique. Having known the soprano Joan Sutherland in Australia, he became her adviser in London and decisively influenced the direction of her vocal and artistic development; they were married in 1954. Although not formally trained as a conductor, he began to conduct many of his wife's operatic performances, beginning with Gounod's *Faust* in Vancouver and *La sonnambula* in San Francisco, both in 1963. His Covent Garden début was in 1964 with *I puritani*. In 1965 he and Sutherland returned to Australia, he as artistic director and chief conductor of the specially formed Sutherland-Williamson International Grand Opera Company. He made his Metropolitan Opera début in 1966 conducting *Lucia di Lammermoor*. He was artistic director of Vancouver Opera, 1974–8, and music director of Australian Opera, 1975–86.

On records, as in the theatre, Bonynge cultivated the revival of vocal ornamentation as it had flourished in the

18th and early 19th centuries, and wrote cadenzas for Sutherland and other singers. His ornamentation may have been excessive in some Handel and other Baroque works, but the alliance of his and his wife's artistry helped to promote the public's new acceptance of ornamentation as an expressive vocal art. Bonynge made an intense study of Bellini and his period, and of French operas of the mid- and late 19th century. His recordings of more than 30 operas, mostly with Sutherland, include several previously unfamiliar works by Delibes, Graun, Massenet, Shield and others, and 19th-century ballet scores. He conducted Sutherland's 'farewell' performances in the USA, Britain and Australia during 1990. Bonynge was made a CBE in 1977, and received the Order of Australia in 1983 and the French Ordre des Arts et Lettres in 1989.

ARTHUR JACOBS, NOËL GOODWIN

Boor, The. *Opera buffa* in one act by DOMINICK ARGENTO to a libretto by John Olon (pseudonym of John Scrymgeour) after ANTON PAVLOVICH CHEKHOV's play *The Bear*; Rochester, New York, Eastman School of Music, 6 May 1957.

A young Widow (soprano) has been mourning the death of her husband for exactly one year. A neighbour, the Boor (bass-baritone), arrives to collect a debt owed by the deceased, only to be rebuked for his indelicacy at making such a request on this anniversary. A lengthy argument ensues and a duel is proposed. In the heat of the moment, it comes out that the widow harboured no real fondness for her faithless, neglectful husband, and in the wake of these revelations, a new passion is kindled.

This work is Argento's earliest well-known opera, composed while he was completing his studies at the Eastman School. The tonal score with motivic unification employs vocally gracious lines and demonstrates exceptional sensitivity to comic and dramatic flow, features which have remained hallmarks of his operatic style. The opera's modest theatrical requirements and small cast (the Servant, a tenor, is the only other character) have made it a popular piece for workshop presentations, and it remains the composer's most frequently performed opera.

VIRGINIA SAYA

Boquet, Louis-René (*b* Paris, 1717; *d* Paris, 7 Dec 1814). French painter and stage designer. In 1741 he was a painter of scenes on ladies' fans. His earliest known work at the Opéra was the costume designs for Rameau's ballet *Pygmalion* (1748). After 1751 Boquet's name appears in the registers of the Opéra and the Menus-Plaisirs du Roi as costumier and director of a team of stage designers responsible for providing decor and dress at Fontainebleau, Versailles, Choisy and Paris. He designed the costumes for Jean-Georges Noverre's famous *Les fêtes chinoises* at the Opéra-Comique (1754); at the invitation of David Garrick, it was subsequently staged at Drury Lane Theatre, London (1755). Boquet became *Dessinateur en chef des habits du roi pour fêtes, spectacles et cérémonies* in 1764, and about 1770 was appointed *Inspecteur général des Menus-Plaisirs* (with a stipend of 1200 livres), posts he held until 1792.

Records survive for costumes and machines for Lully's *Thésée* (1763) and Rameau's *Castor et Pollux* (1765), costumes and scenery for Philidor's *Ernelinde, princesse de Norvège* (1767), and costumes and probably some scenery for Rameau's *Dardanus* (1768), Vachon's *Hippomène et Atalante* (1769), Rameau's *Zoroastre* (1770), Trial's *La fête de Flore* (1771), *Callirhoé* (Destouches and Dauvergne) and Marmontel's *Roland* (1778). The inauguration of the Grand Théâtre de Versailles in 1770 included notable productions of Lully's *Persée* (with additions by Dauvergne, Francoeur, Rebel and Blaze de Bury), *La tour enchantée* (Dauvergne) and a revival of *Tancrède* (probably by Campra). In 1771 Boquet decorated the gallery built for the *fête chinoise* and the ballroom adjoining the Petit Théâtre at Versailles; then, in 1778, he was entrusted with the decoration of the Petit Théâtre at the Trianon.

The collaboration with Noverre meant that his stage designs were seen outside France at the Württemberg court, Stuttgart, as well as at the courts of Vienna, Turin and Milan and on the London stage; his designs were also sent to opera houses in Stockholm and Lisbon. Boquet worked mainly in pen and watercolour (over pencil or crayon occasionally) in two distinct styles: the early period ('Louis XV' Boquet), shared with Boucher, is delicate and precise; after about 1770 his painting changes to freer, flamboyant strokes ('Louis XVI' Boquet). Major collections of Boquet's original costume designs are in the Bibliothèque Nationale, Paris (Cabinet des Estampes and Opéra archives), and in two manuscripts sent by Noverre to prospective patrons. The earlier one (*PL-Wu*, Royal Collection no. 802; microfilm in *US-NYp*) includes ballet scenarios and 445 designs sent to the Polish king in 1766; the other (*S-Sk*, Cod. holm S 254: 1–2) includes 20 ballet scenarios accompanied by 147 paintings of figures sent to the King of Sweden in 1791.

For illustration *see* COSTUME, fig.6; *DARDANUS* (i), fig.1; and *ERNELINDE, PRINCESSE DE NORVÈGE*.

*

J.-G. Noverre: *Lettres sur la danse et sur les ballets* (Lyons, 1760); as *Lettres sur la danse et sur les ballets, précédées d'une Vie de l'auteur par André Levinson* (Paris, 1927)

A. Tessier: 'Les habits d'opéra au XVIII siècle: Louis Boquet, dessinateur et inspecteur général des Menus-Plaisirs', *Revue de l'art ancien et moderne*, xlix (1926), 15–26, 89–100, 173–84

C. Fischer: *Les costumes de l'opéra* (Paris, 1931)

C. W. Beaumont: *Ballet Design Past & Present* (London, 1946)

D. Lynham: *The Chevalier Noverre: Father of Modern Ballet* (London, 1950)

F. van Thienen: 'Louis René Boquet', *Miscellanea I. Q. van Regteren Altena* (Amsterdam, 1969), 198–203, figs. 376–8

Deux siècles d'opéra français (Paris, 1972) [exhibition catalogue]

B. Labat-Poussin: *Archives du Théâtre National de l'Opéra (AJ 13 1 à 1466)* (Paris, 1977)

SIDNEY JACKSON JOWERS

Bordeaux. City in the Gironde, western France. It was the capital of Aquitaine and seat of English rule in France in the Middle Ages, and centre of the wine trade. Opera was first given in the second half of the 17th century. In 1735 an opera house was built in the municipal gardens (today the Cours Victor Hugo), which in 1752 became the Académie Royale de Musique. This theatre was destroyed by fire in 1756, and a temporary one set up near the Palais Rohan. The Duke of Richelieu, Governor of Aquitaine, decided that the flourishing city-port needed a new opera house and himself chose the site, overlooking the harbour, and appointed the architect, Victor Louis, architect of the Comédie-Française in Paris, in the teeth of opposition from the city fathers. Thus was built between 1773 and 1780 the Grand Théâtre, Place de la Comédie, one of the finest of French opera houses (see illustration, overleaf). The exterior, with its imposing colonnaded façade

Auditorium of the Grand Théâtre, Bordeaux (1773–80), designed by Victor Louis: engraving by Poulleau

surmounted by statues of goddesses and the Muses, and the peristyle surrounding the rest of the building, are neo-classical; the italianate auditorium (seating 1136 in stalls and three balconies) is, like the stage, built entirely of wood. Although this structure is much as it was originally, the decoration, apart from Robin's ceiling – an allegory of the town of Bordeaux with its ships and wine and slave trades – has been changed many times. What is today the Grand Foyer was originally a concert hall holding 700 (Mozart performed there); it was rebuilt as a ballroom in the 19th century. During the Franco-Prussian War, when the French government withdrew to Bordeaux in 1870, the National Assembly sat in the Grand Théâtre and the Third Republic was proclaimed there in 1871. The original candle lighting was superseded in 1793 by fish-oil lamps, in 1827 by hydrogen, in 1853 by gas and in 1889 by electricity. The theatre was run in the 18th and 19th centuries by impresarios who invited not only the stars of the Paris opera companies but often the entire companies. It had a particularly splendid period before 1939 under the administration of Chauvet and Maurice Lafage, and subsequently, through the efforts of Vanni-Marcoux (1948–51), Roger Lalande (1954–70) and Gérard Boireau (1971–90), productions have been opulently staged with high musical standards. World premières have included Henri Tomasi's *Sampiero Corso* (1956), Pierre Capdevielle's *Fille de l'homme* (1967) and Jean-Michel Damase's *Colombe* (1961) and *Eurydice* (1972). Bordeaux has also seen the first performances in France of *Dantons Tod* (1965), *Die Verlobung in San Domingo* and *Gloriana* (1967), *Die Bluthochzeit* (1968) and Salieri's *Falstaff* (1987). The stage has modern equipment, though the hall, very beautiful in itself, is uncomfortable and too small. The season currently runs from October to June, with four or five performances each of some five operas and six operettas (Friday evenings and Sunday matinée, with occasional midweek performances). There are also performances by the ballet company and concerts by the Orchestre National Bordeaux-Aquitaine, which plays for the operas. The annual festival known as Mai Musicale was founded in 1950; it includes opera performances in the Grand Théâtre, and sometimes chamber operas presented in the local chateaux, during May and June.

A. Detchverry: *Histoire des théâtres de Bordeaux* (Bordeaux, 1860)

J. Latreyte: *Le Grand Théâtre de Bordeaux* (Bordeaux, 1977)

L. J. Brote: 'A propos du répertoire lyrique des théâtres français', *Le théâtre lyrique français 1945–1985*, ed. D. Pistone (Paris, 1987), 51–73

CHARLES PITT

Bordman, Gerald (Martin) (*b* Philadelphia, 18 Sept 1931). American writer. He studied at Lafayette College and the University of Pennsylvania (PhD 1958). He is a prolific and spirited writer on the lighter forms of musical theatre in the USA.

The American Musical Theater: a Chronicle (New York, 1978, 2/1986)

Jerome Kern: his Life and Music (New York, 1980)

American Operetta from H.M.S. Pinafore to Sweeney Todd (New York, 1981)

Days to be Happy, Years to be Sad: the Life and Music of Vincent Youmans (New York, 1982)

The Oxford Companion to American Theatre (New York, 1984)

Bordogni, Giulio (Marco) (*b* Gazzaniga, nr Bergamo, 23 Jan 1789; *d* Paris, 31 July 1856). Italian tenor. He studied with Simone Mayr in Bergamo and made his début in 1813 at the Teatro Re, Milan, as Argirio (*Tancredi*), a role he also sang at La Scala (1817) and other theatres. Engaged at the Théâtre Italien, he sang in the Paris premières of Paer's *Agnese* (1819), Mercadante's *Elisa e Claudio* (1823) and of ten Rossini operas: *L'inganno felice* (1819); *Otello* and *La gazza ladra* (1821); *Elisabetta, regina d'Inghilterra*, *La Cenerentola* and *Mosè in Egitto* (1822); *Ricciardo e Zoraide* and *La donna del Lago* (1824); *Semiramide* and *Zelmira* (1826). He created the role of Libenskof in *Il viaggio a Reims* (1825). He retired in 1833 and taught singing in Paris; his pupils included Sontag, Giovanni Mario and Cinti-Damoreau. His voice was small, though perfectly placed, while he sang with great elegance and style though his acting ability was restricted. He published a singing method and several collections of exercises.

ELIZABETH FORBES

Bordoni [Hasse; Bordon Hasse], **Faustina** (*b* Venice, 30 March 1697; *d* Venice, 4 Nov 1781). Italian mezzo-soprano. She was brought up under the protection of the brothers Alessandro and Benedetto Marcello and taught by M. Gasparini. For many years she was in the service of the Elector Palatine. She made her début in 1716 in C. F. Pollarolo's *Ariodante* in Venice, where she sang until 1725, in operas by Albinoni, Lotti, M. and F. Gasparini, C. F. and A. Pollarolo, Orlandini, Giacomelli, Vinci and others. She appeared at Reggio in 1717, 1719 (F. Gasparini's *Bajazet*) and 1720, Modena in 1720, Bologna in 1721–2, Naples in 1721–3 (seven operas, including Leo's *Bajazete*), Florence (1723) and Parma (1724–5, including Vinci's *Il trionfo di Camilla*). She made her German début in 1723 at Munich in Torri's *Griselda*, and enjoyed great success there during the 1720s; she was also a favourite at Vienna (1725–6), appearing in operas by Caldara, Fux and others.

Faustina (as she was commonly known) made her London début as Roxana in Handel's *Alessandro* at the King's Theatre in 1726, with Cuzzoni and Senesino in the other leading roles. In the next two seasons (1727–8) she created four other Handel parts – Alcestis in *Admeto*, Pulcheria in *Riccardo Primo*, Emira in *Siroe* and Elisa in *Tolomeo* – and sang in Ariosti's *Lucio Vero* and *Teuzzone*, Giovanni Bononcini's *Astianatte* and Handel's *Radamisto*. Her rivalry with Cuzzoni, professional and personal, was notorious, and culminated in an exchange of blows on stage at a performance of *Astianatte* (6 June 1727), but despite this scandal they were both engaged for the following season. She sang at Florence, Parma, Turin, Milan, Rome and frequently at Venice in 1728–32; the operas included Orlandini's *Adelaide*, two by Giacomelli, and Hasse's *Dalisa*, *Arminio*, *Demetrio* and *Euristeo*. From her marriage to JOHANN ADOLF HASSE in 1730 she was associated chiefly with his music, and in 1731 both were summoned to the Saxon court at Dresden, where she enjoyed great success in his *Cleofide*. Hasse was Kapellmeister there for more than 30 years and Faustina sang in at least 15 of his numerous operas between *Caio Fabricio* (1734) and *Ciro riconosciuto* (1751), but also paid many long visits to Italy, singing in Naples, Venice and other cities in operas by Vinci, Pergolesi and Porpora as well as Hasse. In all she sang in more than 30 operas in Venice. After retiring from the theatre in 1751 she kept her salary and her rank as *virtuosa da camera* until 1763. She and Hasse lived in Vienna until 1773, then in Venice; their two daughters were both trained as singers.

Faustina Bordoni as Attilia in the costume designed by Francesco Ponte for the original production of Hasse's 'Attilio Regolo' at the Dresden Hoftheater, 12 January 1750

Faustina was universally ranked among the greatest singers of her age. Quantz described her voice as a mezzo-soprano, 'less clear than penetrating', with a compass of *b♭* to *g″* (about a tone lower than Cuzzoni's range). In her Handel parts it is *c′* to *a″*. She was a very dramatic singer, with equal power and flexibility, and a fine actress. Arteaga spoke of 'a matchless facility and rapidity in her execution ... exquisite shake [and] new and brilliant passages of embellishment'. Tosi contrasted her pre-eminence in lively arias with Cuzzoni's gift for the pathetic, and considered the virtues of the two complementary. An observer in 1721 remarked that Faustina 'always sang the first part of an aria exactly as the composer had written it but at the da capo repeat introduced all kinds of *doublements* and *maniere* without taking the smallest liberties with the rhythm of the accompaniment'. Burney emphasized her perfect intonation and exceptional breath control. His statement that 'E was a remarkably powerful note in this singer's voice, and we find most of her capital songs in sharp keys', is confirmed by the fact that half the arias Handel composed for her are in A or E, major or minor. Quantz (translated by Burney) gives perhaps the clearest account of Faustina's quality:

> Her execution was articulate and brilliant. She had a fluent tongue for pronouncing words rapidly and distinctly, and a flexible throat for divisions, with so beautiful and quick a shake, that she could put it in motion upon short notice, just when she would. The passages might be smooth, or by leaps, or consist of iterations of the same tone, their execution was equally easy to her ... She sung *adagios* with great passion and expression, but not equally well, if such deep sorrow were to be impressed on the hearer, as might require dragging, sliding, or notes of syncopation and *tempo rubato*. She had a very happy memory, in arbitrary changes and embellishments, and a clear and quick judgment in giving to words their full power and expression. In her action she was very happy; and as she perfectly possessed that flexibility of muscles and features, which constitutes face-playing, she succeeded equally well in furious, amorous, and tender parts; in short, she was born for singing and for acting.

Metastasio described her and Hasse in 1744 as 'truly an exquisite couple'.

BurneyH; *HawkinsH*

P. F. Tosi: *Opinioni de' cantore antichi e moderni* (Bologna, 1723; Eng. trans., 1742, 2/1743 as *Observations on the Florid Song*)

A. Niggli: *Faustina Bordoni-Hasse* (Leipzig, 1880)

M. Högg: *Die Gesangskunst der Faustina Hasse und das Sängerinnenwesen ihrer Zeit in Deutschland* (Berlin, 1931)

G. J. Buelow: 'A Lesson in Operatic Performance Practice by Madame Faustina Bordoni', *A Musical Offering: Essays in Honor of Martin Bernstein* (New York, 1977), 79–96

E. Gibson: *The Royal Academy of Music 1719–1728: the Institution and its Directors* (New York, 1989)

G. Vio: 'Documenti inediti relativi alla biografia di Faustina Bordon Hasse', *Venezia arti*, iii (1989), 170

K. Vlaardingerbroek: 'Faustina Bordoni Applauds Jan Alensoon: a Dutch Music-Lover in Italy and France, 1723–4', *ML*, lxxii (1991), 536–51

WINTON DEAN

Boréades, Les [*Abaris*] ('The Descendants of Boreas'). *Tragédie en musique* in five acts by JEAN-PHILIPPE RAMEAU to a libretto attributed to LOUIS DE CAHUSAC; no known date of performance in Rameau's lifetime.

Alphise *Queen of Bactria*	soprano
Sémire *her confidante*	soprano
Borilée } *a descendant of Boreas*	baritone
Calisis } *a descendant of Boreas*	haute-contre
Abaris	haute-contre
Adamas *high priest of Apollo*	baritone
A Nymph	soprano
L'Amour [Cupid]	soprano
Polymnie [Polyhymnia]	soprano
Boréas [Boreas] *God of the North Wind*	bass
Apollon [Apollo] *God of Light*	baritone

Pleasures and Graces, Apollo's priests, Bactrian people, Seasons, zephyrs, Subterranean Winds

Setting The ancient kingdom of Bactria

Until recently *Les Boréades* was believed to have been in rehearsal at the Paris Opéra at the time of Rameau's death but for some reason abandoned. Research now shows that the work was rehearsed more than a year earlier, in April 1763, and that it was probably intended for private performance before the court at Choisy. There is no clear evidence as to why this remarkable opera should have been discarded, though the reasons may have to do with changing tastes, with the fact that the music presents formidable difficulties, with the opposition of court factions, with the presence in the plot of elements that could be construed as politically subversive, or even with the burning down of the Opéra in the same month as the rehearsals.

ACT 1 *A forest near Alphise's palace* During a hunt (suggested by the overture's horn-calls, which continue intermittently during the opening scenes), Alphise reveals her troubled mind: although she must by tradition marry a Boread – a descendant of Boreas, God of the North Wind – her heart yearns for Abaris, a young foreigner. When two such Boreads, Borilée and Calisis, woo her in turn, she procrastinates. In a charming *divertissement* Pleasures and Graces try vainly to divert her. The queen, urged to undertake marriage, expresses disquiet: her virtuoso aria 'Un horizon serein' compares marriage with a deceptive calm interrupted by squalls (in depicting these, the simile aria anticipates events in Act 3).

ACT 2 *The entrance to Apollo's temple; in the background an altar* In a soliloquy ('Charmes trop dangereux'), Abaris tries to banish thoughts of hopeless love. Preoccupied, he does not overhear Adamas recalling that the youth was entrusted to him as a child by Apollo to be raised in ignorance of his origins. Abaris confesses to Adamas his love for Alphise and his frustration at not knowing his lineage. The priest replies that Abaris can discover the latter only through glorious deeds. Adamas leaves, placing Apollo's priests under Abaris's authority. Alphise arrives in agitation and reveals how Boreas, in a ghastly vision, had shown how he would avenge her impiety; her narration, 'Ministres saints, le trouble, l'épouvante', is a pungent accompanied recitative, the vocal line full of plunging intervals. Horrified, Abaris inadvertently reveals his love. Alphise, taken aback, nevertheless hints at her own feelings, acknowledging them as hopeless. Calisis, Borilée and Alphise's subjects arrive to pay homage to Apollo. Their celebrations include a *ballet figuré* reenacting Boreas's abduction of Oritheia – another anticipation of Act 3 – in which a lively rigaudon is rudely interrupted by rushing scales, interspersed with plaintive cries from the flutes. The light grows intense and the people expect Apollo, but it is Cupid who descends. The god presents Alphise with a magic arrow; though condoning her love, he nevertheless confirms that the new Bactrian king must be a Boread.

ACT 3 *A pleasant countryside* Alone, the queen tries to exorcise her vision ('Songe affreux'). Abaris appears and the two reaffirm their love. Calisis and Borilée, accompanied by the Bactrian people, continue their wooing. Adamas announces that Alphise's subjects and Apollo himself are impatient for the queen to make a decision. Rather than lose Abaris by marrying one of these suitors, Alphise abdicates; as her subjects express consternation, she gives Abaris the magic arrow as a token of their love. When Calisis and Borilée make rival claims to the throne, the people beseech Alphise to remain queen and marry Abaris. At this, the indignant claimants call on Boreas to punish Alphise's impiety. A violent storm arises and Aquilons (North Winds) appear; despite Abaris's efforts, Alphise is carried off in a storm that continues during the entr'acte, or 'Suite des vents'.

ACT 4 *A storm-ravaged landscape* The terrified people can be heard in the distance as Borilée enters; he gloats over Alphise's fate and the havoc wreaked by Boreas. After Borilée departs, Abaris appears and bewails the destruction ('Lieux désolés'), his desolation conveyed in a vocal line broken by frequent rests and an accompaniment of brief sighing figures. Adamas enters and instructs Abaris to rescue his beloved, even if that means self-sacrifice. Overcome with despair, Abaris tries to kill himself with Cupid's arrow; but Adamas prevents him, revealing that the arrow has the power to lead him to Alphise's captors. When Abaris beseeches Apollo's aid, Polyhymnia descends with the Muses and other divinities, who prepare him for his mission. Their dances include a delightful evocation of a clock (the 'Gavotte pour les heures').

ACT 5 *Boreas's domain* A bizarre tone-painting without parallel in Rameau's output depicts the impotent gasps of the Subterranean Winds. Boreas urges them to continue their devastation, but they reply that the voice of a mortal forces them into submission. Alphise is led in and given an ultimatum: reign with one of the Boread suitors or live in slavery. When she remains defiant, Boreas commands the winds to torture her. But as they begin, Abaris appears. In a chorus and ensemble thematically linked to those accompanying Alphise's torture ('Qu'elle gémisse'), the Boreads threaten him. But he produces his arrow, to the astonishment of all, including the god; touching them with it, he calms their fury. Apollo descends and reveals that Abaris is his son by a nymph-daughter of Boreas and may thus marry Alphise with impunity. Mollified, Boreas unites the lovers. As darkness gives way to light, Apollo causes Boreas's sombre domain to glow with a new beauty. Alphise and Abaris sing of their love ('Que ces moments sont doux'). The lively final *divertissement* includes another simile aria ('Que l'Amour embellit la vie') and a succession of ever more vigorous dances.

* * *

Although the libretto is ascribed posthumously to Cahusac by two independent 18th-century writers, there are problems in accepting the attribution unreservedly. The work takes uncharacteristic liberties with such little classical source material as it uses, while compared with *Zoroastre* its masonic elements – the initiatory voyage, the magic talisman, the various Apolline symbols – are undeveloped. Furthermore, the hymns and *ballets figurés* which normally feature prominently in Cahusac's work are each represented here by only a single, perfunctory example; at the same time, the simile arias have no parallel in his other work, though such arias may occasionally be found in other librettos of this date. It is possible that the text was among Cahusac's papers at the time of his death (1759) and that the perceived anomalies result from subsequent reworking. Against that, there is some evidence that composition may have begun before 1759.

Whoever its author, the libretto is among the more serviceable of those Rameau set. Despite its abuse of the supernatural and reduction of the hero and heroine to the level of pawns in a battle between superior forces, it is constructed in such a way that the all-important ballet and spectacle nowhere interfere with, and often contribute to, the development of the action. More important, successive stages of the plot generate increasing dramatic momentum – particularly so from the moment of Alphise's unexpected abdication in Act 3, through the tempest that dominates the rest of that act and most of the next, to the torture scenes in Act 5. Rameau fully exploits this to produce a work with greater forward drive than any of his others, exemplified by the way his fearsome storm continues without interruption from the middle of Act 3 well into Act 4 (and, less innovatory, his overture into the first scene). Most astonishing, given that Rameau was by now in his late 70s, is the sheer vigour of so much of the music. Many of the ballet movements have an almost pagan intensity and lack of inhibition.

Although not known to have been performed complete in Rameau's lifetime, *Les Boréades* was probably given a concert performance at Lille in the 1770s. It was taken up in Paris in 1896 by Louis Diémer and the Société des Instruments Anciens, who presented extensive excerpts with accompaniments arranged for 'clavecin, viole d'amour, viole de gambe et vielle' (score and parts in *US-Bp*). The work was broadcast by the ORTF on 16 September 1964 as part of the Rameau bicentenary, and its first stage production, at the Aix-en-Provence Festival in July 1982, generated the stylish and committed recording for Erato (1982) by John Eliot Gardiner. GRAHAM SADLER

Boretti, Giovanni Antonio (*b* Rome, *c*1640; *d* Venice, 29 Dec 1672). Italian composer and singer. Most of the information concerning his brief career, spent primarily in Venice, derives from prefaces to librettos of operas he wrote in the late 1660s and early 1670s. The preface to *Alessandro amante* (dated 1667) cites him as the composer of the opera and also as interpreter of one of the leading roles. His singing career had in fact begun somewhat earlier, since his name appears in the cast-list of an opera performed in Turin in 1662, *Le fortune di Rodope e Damira* by P. A. Ziani. But he is not the Guid'Antonio Boretti from Gubbio who was listed in the cast of *La maga fulminata* (1638, Venice) and who was a singer in the papal chapel (1619–46). The preface to a later libretto, *Claudio Cesare* (1672), mentions his recent appointment as *maestro di cappella* to the Duke of Parma; he had actually been appointed vice-*maestro* in April 1672, just eight months before his death, which occurred while he was in Venice for the production of his last two operas.

Except for the earliest known one, *La Zenobia*, possibly first performed in Vienna on 18 November 1662, all Boretti's operas received their premières in Venice, many of them appearing subsequently in other Italian cities. His musical language is richly varied and dramatically flexible, moving easily between recitative, arioso and aria. Yet the frequency and elaboration of the arias in several of his operas reflect the growing tendency to abandon the realistic musico-dramatic flow characteristic of early opera in Venice, notably Cavalli's, in favour of the more static, hedonistic vocal exhibitionism demanded by Venetian audiences from about the mid-17th century onwards. His most attractive arias include laments accompanied by strings and pieces in which a running bass participates in communicating the emotions of the text.

See also ERCOLE IN TEBE.

La Zenobia (drama per musica, 3, M. Noris), Venice, S Cassiano, ded. 10 Jan 1666, possibly already perf. Vienna, 1662 [Act 3 of a Zenobia opera in *A-Wn* may be Boretti's]

Eliogabalo (drama per musica, 3, A. Aureli), Venice, SS Giovanni e Paolo, ded. 10 Jan 1667 [=1668], *I-Vnm*, 3 arias ed. in Rosand

Alessandro amante (drama per musica, 3, anon. reworking of G. A. Cicognini: *Gli amori di Alessandro Magno e di Rossane*, 1651), Venice, S Moisè, ded. 28 Jan 1667 [=1668]

Ercole in Tebe (drama per musica, 3, Aureli, after G. A. Moniglia), Venice, SS Giovanni e Paolo, ded. 12 Dec 1670, *GB-Lbl* (*R*1977: IOB, vi), *I-Vnm*, 1 aria ed. M. Zanon (Milan, 1914), 2 arias ed. in Rosand

Marcello in Siracusa (drama per musica, 3, Noris), Venice, SS Giovanni e Paolo, 1670, *Vnm*, 1 aria ed. M. Zanon, *Raccolta di 24 arie di vari autori del secolo XVII* (Milan, 1914)

Dario in Babilonia (drama per musica, 3, F. Beverini), Venice, S Salvatore, ded. 24 Jan 1671

Claudio Cesare (drama per musica, 3, Aureli), Venice, S Salvatore, ded. 27 Dec 1672 [or 1671], *Nc*, *Vnm*, 1 aria ed. in Worsthorne, 1 aria ed. M. Zanon (Milan, 1914)

Domitiano (drama [per musica], 3, Noris), Venice, SS Giovanni e Paolo, ded. 27 Dec 1672

*

J. J. Maier: *Die musikalischen Handschriften der K. Hof- und Staatsbibliothek in Muenchen* (Munich, 1879)

T. Wiel: *I codici musicali contariniani del secolo XVII nella R. Biblioteca di San Marco di Venezia* (Venice, 1888)

A Belloni: *Storia letteraria d'Italia: il seicento* (Milan, 1899)

A. Cametti: *Il teatro di Tordinona, poi di Apollo* (Tivoli, 1938)

S. T. Worsthorne: *Venetian Opera in the Seventeenth Century* (Oxford, 1954)

L. Bianconi: '"L'Ercole in Rialto"', *Venezia e il melodramma nel seicento: Venice 1972*, 259–72

M. Viale Ferrero: 'Repliche a Torino di alcuni melodrammi veneziani e loro caratteristiche', *Venezia e il melodramma nel seicento: Venice 1972*, 145–72

V. Kastner: *Herakles: a Character Study in Two Seventeenth-Century Operas* (thesis, Rutgers U., 1982)

E. Rosand: *Opera in Seventeenth-Century Venice: the Creation of a Genre* (Berkeley, 1991) ELLEN ROSAND, BETH L. GLIXON

Borg, Kim (*b* Helsinki, 7 Aug 1919). Finnish bass-baritone. He studied at the Sibelius Academy, Helsinki, and later in several cities abroad including Vienna, Rome and New York. He confined himself to concert work for three years and then made his operatic début in 1951 at Århus, Denmark, as Colline in *La bohème*. An international career opened up in 1956 when he sang at Salzburg and Glyndebourne, his roles there being Don Giovanni, Pizarro (1958) and Prince Gremin in *Yevgeny Onegin* (1968). He made his Metropolitan début in 1959 as Count Almaviva. From 1960 he was a member of the Stockholm opera, also singing regularly in

Hamburg where in 1966 he appeared in the world première of Schuller's *The Visitation.* His repertory included Boris and Pimen (sung in 1977 at Tel Aviv), Baron Ochs, Méphistophélès and Osmin; he also sang Fafner and Hagen in the 1971 Stockholm *Ring*. In 1972 he was appointed Professor of Singing at the Copenhagen Academy. A fine linguist and a cultivated musician, he can be heard in many recordings from the 1950s when his firm, full-bodied voice was in its prime.

J. B. STEANE

Borgatti, Giuseppe (*b* Cento, 17 March 1871; *d* Reno, Lago Maggiore, 18 Oct 1950). Italian tenor. The pupil of Alessandro Busi at Bologna, he made his début at Castelfranco Veneto in 1892 (*Faust*), then sang in Madrid (1894–5), and St Petersburg (1895); at La Scala in 1896, he took the part of Chénier with great success in the opera's first performance. Performances in the leading Italian, Spanish and Argentinian theatres followed, as Puccini's Des Grieux and Cavaradossi. He then devoted himself to Wagner (having already sung Siegfried and Tristan at La Scala in 1899 and 1900 under Toscanini) with exceptional results. In 1914, after appearing in *Parsifal* at La Scala, he was forced by glaucoma to retire from the stage.

Borgatti's voice was large, robust and of beautiful timbre; he could also, especially in his early years, sing with delicacy and sweetness. He was the first tenor to introduce into the performance of *verismo* operas a forcefully emphatic delivery and an incisive, vehement declamatory manner, in contrast to the lyrical approach and virtuosity of the preceding generation of tenors, such as Stagno and De Lucia. These qualities, together with a strong physique, vigorous and lively acting, and remarkable insight into character, made him an exceptional Wagner tenor.

*

GV (E. Gara and R. Celletti; R. Vegeto)

G. Borgatti: *La mia vita d'artista* (Bologna, 1927)

E. Gara: 'Il San Paolo dei wagneriani, Giuseppe Borgatti', *La lettura* (Milan, 1938)

RODOLFO CELLETTI

Borghese [Borghesi, Borghesy], **Antonio D. R.** (*fl* late 18th century). French composer. He may have been born in Rome and seems to have travelled widely. A performance of his comic opera *The Fair Venetian* at Crow Street, Dublin, on 18 March 1776, and the publication of some sonatas in London suggest he was in the British Isles at that time. By 1780 he apparently was teaching in St Petersburg. His name next appears in connection with a performance of his operetta *Der unvermuthete glückliche Augenblick* (2, Borghese) in the Städtisches Theater, Riga, on 21 June 1783. By 1785 he was in Paris, where he received a privilege to publish his treatise *L'art musical ramené à ses vrais principes ... traduites de l'Italien*, and in 1786 (31 October) his *opéra comique* [*Le roi de*] *La basoche* (1, ? E. A. Bignon) was performed at the Théâtre des Beaujolais.

English editions of *L'art musical* appeared in London (1790, 1795), indicating that Borghese may have emigrated to escape the Revolution. In 1799 he was back in Paris, performing in a concert with his wife, Agathe-Elisabeth-Henriette Larrivée (the younger daughter of the singers Henri and Marie-Jeanne Larrivée). Apart from his three operas (all lost) and his treatise, Borghese wrote only a few minor instrumental and vocal pieces.

KENNETH LANGEVIN

Borghi, Giovanni Battista (*b* Camerino, Macerata, 25 Aug 1738; *d* Loreto, 25 Feb 1796). Italian composer. Early accounts often confuse him with the violinist Luigi Borghi and the harpsichordist Giovanni (or Giuseppe) Borghi. He studied at the Conservatorio della Pietà dei Turchini, Naples, from 1757 to 1759. He served first as *maestro di cappella* at Macerata Cathedral from 1759 to 1778 and then at the Santa Casa of Loreto until his death, taking frequent leave to produce operas throughout Italy, principally in Venice, Florence and Rome.

During the first 15 years of his career he wrote an equal number of *opere buffe* and *opere serie*. Typical of the 1770s, his serious operas have arias of extreme length, short third acts, multiple exits following individual arias, long ballets as entr'actes, trios and duets concluding the first two acts and aria-length cavatinas late in Act 3. The comic operas open with short static *introduzioni*, proceed with a succession of recitatives and arias and conclude with finales with increasing numbers of personnel. *Il filosofo amante* stands out for its many short ensembles, including a quartet, a quintet and a trio involving some action.

After 1777 Borghi turned exclusively to *opera seria*. His operas of the 1780s show innovatory traits common in the works of the librettist Sertor, such as the ensemble that increases from duet to trio in *Piramo e Tisbe*. In his setting of Metastasio's *Olimpiade* (1784) violence appears on the stage, and he carved a multi-sectional finale from the final scene of Metastasio's text. Accompanied recitative becomes more prevalent; such scenes may encompass cavatinas and employ wind instruments for 'ghost scenes' and other special effects.

Borghi's arias show extreme textural contrasts: a thin string accompaniment sometimes follows the voice and sometimes provides rhythmic background, thickening abruptly with the addition of wind instruments and obbligato commentary during vocal caesuras and ritornellos. Nevertheless, his accompaniments are often denser than those of many of his contemporaries and his forms less clearly sectional. Though he was judicious in his use of wind, his harmonic vocabulary was at times chromatic, his orchestration programmatic and his ornamental vocal style virtuoso.

In the two operas of the 1790s the amount of accompanied recitative increases significantly to encompass entire scenes, particularly near the end of each act. The *introduzione* becomes a component of serious opera, and the chorus assumes a more important role, participating in ensembles and concluding arias. Arias incur commentary from other characters, the chorus and even a full military wind band. Borghi's most successful work, *La morte di Semiramide*, proved to be a herald of the decade. In this early example of the new Venetian style, pioneered by the librettist Sografi, the traditional stark delineations of form disappear in great scene complexes of continuous music moving seamlessly among the textural options of accompanied recitative, aria, ensemble and chorus. There are only 11 arias, and some are interrupted or overlaid with choral or solo interpolations; in one of Semiramide's a military wind quartet is heard, and public comments restore her tranquillity. There are extended continuous scenes as each act draws to its climactic conclusion: the ghost scene in Act 1, the mother–son confrontation in Act 2 and the tomb and death scene in Act 3. Other features of this opera soon to become common are the *introduzione* for duo and chorus, the *giuramento* for quartet and chorus and the *nottorno* for duo.

dm – *dramma per musica* os – *opera seria*

Adriano in Siria (os, 3, P. Metastasio), Turin, carn. 1759, *P-La*
Il tutore deluso (intermezzo, 2, A. Gatta), Lucca, Pubblico, carn. 1762
Le nozze disturbate (farsetta, Gatta), Florence, Pallacorda, 1762
Merope (dm, A. Zeno), Rome, Dame, carn. 1768, *La*
Alessandro in Armenia (dm, 3, C. Doriano), Venice, S Benedetto, 26 Nov 1768, *La*
La schiava amorosa (farsetta, 2, M. Bernardini), Rome, Capranica, carn. 1770
L'amore in campagna [Le villanelle innamorate] (farsetta, P. Chiari), Rome, Capranica, 2 Jan 1771, *D-Dlb*, *I-Rdp*
Siroe (dm, 3, Metastasio), Venice, S Benedetto, Jan 1771, *P-La*
Le avventure di Laurina (intermezzo, 2), Rome, Capranica, carn. 1772
Il trionfo di Clelia (dm, 3, Metastasio), Naples, S Carlo, 30 May 1773, *I-Fc*, *Nc*, *P-La*
Ricimero (dm, 3, F. Silvani), Venice, S Benedetto, aut. 1773
Il filosofo amante (farsetta), Rome, Valle, carn. 1774, *La*
Artaserse (dm, 3, Metastasio), Venice, S Benedetto, 26 Dec 1775, *La*
La donna instabile (dramma giocoso, 3, G. Bertati), Venice, S Moisè, carn. 1776, *F-Pn*, *I-MOe*
Gli tre pretendenti (dramma giocoso, 3, M. Rossi), Bologna, Rossi, May 1777
Creso, re di Lidia (dm, 3, G. Pizzi), Florence, Pergola, aut. 1777, *Fc*; rev. carn. 1784, mostly by Borghi
Eumene (os, 3, Zeno), Venice, S Benedetto, 27 Dec 1777, *D-B*, *?Bds*, *P-La*
Tito Manlio (dm, after G. Roccaforte), Rome, Argentina, carn. 1780
Quinto Fabio (dm, after Zeno: *Lucio Papirio dittatore*), Florence, Pergola, carn. 1781
Arbace (dm, 3, G. Sertor), Venice, S Benedetto, carn. 1782, *F-Pn*
Piramo e Tisbe (dm, Sertor), Florence, Pergola, aut. 1783, *I-Fc*
Olimpiade (os, Metastasio), Modena, Rongoni, 26 Dec 1784, *Fc*
La morte di Semiramide (tragedia, 3, A. S. Sografi, after P. Giovannini), Milan, Scala, 9 Feb 1791, *Bc*
Egilina (os, 3, A. Anelli), Milan, Scala, 26 Jan 1793, *Mr*

Arias in *US-Wc*

*

StiegerO
J. B. de La Borde: *Essai sur la musique ancienne et moderne* (Paris, 1780)
M. McClymonds: '"La morte di Semiramide ossia La vendetta di Nino" and the Restoration of Death and Tragedy to the Italian Operatic Stage in the 1780s and 90s', *IMSCR*, xiv *Bologna 1987*, 285–92
——: 'The Venetian Role in the Transformation of Italian Opera Seria during the 1790s', *I vicini di Mozart*, i, ed. M. T. Muraro (Florence, 1989), 221–40
MARITA P. McCLYMONDS

Borghi-Mamo [née Borghi], **Adelaide** (*b* Bologna, 9 Aug 1826; *d* Bologna, 29 Sept 1901). Italian mezzo-soprano. She studied in Milan and made her début in 1843 at Urbino in Mercadante's *Il giuramento*. She sang in Italy and Vienna, then appeared in Paris at the Théâtre Italien as Azucena in the first performance in France of *Il trovatore* (1854) and at the Opéra as Léonore in *La favorite* (1856). She made her London début in 1860 at Her Majesty's Theatre, in the same two roles. She had a full-toned, vibrant voice and a passionate temperament. Her daughter Erminia Borghi-Mamo (1855–1941), a soprano, sang Margherita and Helen of Troy in Bologna in the successful revised version of Boito's *Mefistofele* (1875). ELIZABETH FORBES

Borgioli, Armando (*b* Florence, 19 March 1898; *d* Codogno, nr Modena, 20 Jan 1945). Italian baritone. He made his début in 1923 and came to prominence in 1927 when he sang for the first time at La Scala, and then in *Il trovatore* in London. He became popular in Italy and South America, but at Covent Garden and the Metropolitan, where he appeared first in 1931, he made little enduring impression though he was re-engaged in both houses. He sang throughout World War II, travelling to Germany and the Netherlands, and was killed in an air attack on his way to an engagement at Bologna. He can most readily be heard as Scarpia in a recording made in 1938 with Gigli as Cavaradossi. J. B. STEANE

Borgioli, Dino (*b* Florence, 15 Feb 1891; *d* Florence, 12 Sept 1960). Italian tenor. He studied with Eugenio Giachetti, and made his début as Arturo in *I puritani* at the Teatro Corso, Milan, in 1914, followed by a more significant appearance, in 1917, under Serafin as Fernand in *La favorite* at the Teatro Dal Verme, Milan. He was soon in demand for the lighter roles in other Italian theatres, and in 1918 began a long association with La Scala. His voice, of clear timbre but limited volume, was highly trained and well produced, and his elegant style made him a favourite in England, where he sang in distinguished casts at Covent Garden in *Lucia*, *Il barbiere di Siviglia* and *Rigoletto* (1925), and as Don Ramiro to the Cenerentola of Conchita Supervia (1934–5); also in pre-war Glyndebourne seasons as Don Ottavio and as Ernesto in *Don Pasquale*. Borgioli also made some appearances in the USA, but settled in London as a teacher of singing; he was later artistic director and adviser to the Jay Pomeroy seasons of 1946–8 at the Cambridge Theatre. His gramophone recordings, which include complete versions of *Il barbiere* and *Rigoletto*, support his claim to be considered the best light tenor of his day after Schipa.

*

GV (R. Celletti; R. Vegeto) DESMOND SHAWE-TAYLOR

Bori, Lucrezia [Borja y Gonzales de Riancho, Lucrecia] (*b* Valencia, 24 Dec 1887; *d* New York, 14 May 1960). Spanish soprano. She studied first in Spain and then in Milan with M. Vidal. She made her début in 1908 at the Teatro Adriano, Rome, as Micaëla. In 1910 she appeared at the Metropolitan Opera's first Paris visit as Puccini's Manon, which she repeated two years later at her official Metropolitan début in New York.

Meanwhile she had sung Octavian in the first Italian performance of *Der Rosenkavalier* at La Scala, and at the Colón. She sang at the Metropolitan until 1936, except in 1916–20, when she underwent a number of operations to remedy vocal problems. Among her important roles were Norina, Juliet and Montemezzi's Fiora (*L'amore dei tre re*). Endowed with a voice of modest size, rather limited in the upper register, Bori used its clear and delicate timbre to draw characters of pathetic fragility (Mimì, Manon); she imbued them with intense and passionate feeling and, in the comic repertory, with gentle and stylized charm.

*

J. B. Richards: 'Lucrezia Bori', *Record Collector*, iv (1949), 5–12, 98–9; ix (1954), 105–23; xxi (1973–4), 147–68, 169–74 [with discography by H. M. Barnes and J. B. Richards]
R. Celletti: 'Con un'espressione stilizzata e trasparente: Lucrezia Bori plasmava l'interpretazione dei suoi personaggi', *Musica e dischi*, no.107 (1955), 10 [with discography by R. Vegeto]
'Lucrezia Bori', *Record Advertiser*, i/2 (1970–71), 3–15 [with discography]
RODOLFO CELLETTI

Borisenko, Vera (*b* Bol'shaya Nemka, 16 Jan 1918). Russian mezzo-soprano. She studied in Gomel with Saizewa and at the Minsk Conservatory, and continued her training in Kiev with Evtushenko and in Moscow and Sverdlovsk. After engagements in Sverdlovsk and Kiev she sang at the Bol'shoy from 1946. She was most admired in operas by Rimsky-Korsakov: *Sadko* (as Lyubava), *The Tsar's Bride* (as Lyubasha) and *The Snow Maiden* (as Bonny Spring). Other roles included

Marfa (*Khovanshchina*) and Carmen. She made guest appearances in Italy and England. Late in her career she appeared as a concert artist. DAVID CUMMINGS

Boris Godunov. Opera in seven scenes, or a prologue and four acts, by MODEST PETROVICH MUSORGSKY to his own libretto, adapted from the historical tragedy by ALEXANDER SERGEYEVICH PUSHKIN, and supplemented (in the revised version) by material partly derived from historical works by NIKOLAY MIKHAYLOVICH KARAMZIN and others; St Petersburg, Mariinsky Theatre, 27 January/8 February 1874 (revised version; original version, Leningrad, State Academic Theatre of Opera and Ballet, 16 February 1928; first Rimsky-Korsakov version, concert performance, St Petersburg, Great Hall of the Conservatory, 28 November/10 December 1896, staged Moscow, Solodovnikov Theatre, Savva Mamontov's Private Russian Opera, 7/19 December 1898; 'standard' version, with additional music by Rimsky-Korsakov, Paris, Opéra, 19 May 1908).

Boris Godunov	baritone or bass
Xenia *his daughter*	soprano
Fyodor *his son*	mezzo-soprano
Pretender *known as* Grigory *(under Pimen's tutelage)* ['False Dmitry']	tenor
†Pimen *hermit chronicler*	bass
Prince Vasily Ivanovich Shuysky	tenor
Andrey Shchelkalov *secretary to the Boyars' Council*	baritone
†Varlaam } *tramps*	bass
†Missail } *tramps*	tenor
*Marina Mniszek *daughter of the Sandomierz commander*	mezzo- or dramatic soprano
*Rangoni *covert Jesuit*	bass
Innkeeper	mezzo-soprano
Yurodiviy ('Fool-in-God') [Holy Fool]	tenor
Xenia's [former] wet-nurse	low mezzo-soprano
Nikitich *police officer*	bass
Mityukha *a peasant*	bass
Boyar-in-attendance	tenor
*Boyar Khrushchyov	tenor
*Lewicki } *Jesuits*	bass
*Czernikowski } *Jesuits*	bass
Voices from the crowd *peasants*	tenor, soprano, mezzo-soprano

Boyars, their children, musketeers, royal bodyguards, police officers, *Polish lords and ladies, *maidens of Sandomierz, blind pilgrims (and the boys who guide them), inhabitants of Moscow

Setting Russia (Moscow and its environs, an inn near the Lithuanian border, Sokol'niki-on-the-Dnepr) and Sandomierz, Poland; 1598–1605

*role only in the revised version
†Pimen, Varlaam and Missail are monks in the Pushkin play and in Musorgsky's adaptation; but owing to a censorship regulation that forbade the portrayal of Orthodox clergy on the stage, their identity had to be concealed in the original published score and libretto.

The original version of *Boris Godunov*, composed between October 1868 and 15/27 December 1869, consists of seven scenes grouped into four 'parts' (acts). The revised version, accomplished between February 1871 and 23 June/5 July 1872, consists of nine scenes (six of the original, more or less radically altered, plus three newly composed) grouped into a prologue and four acts; this was the first version to be heard, with Eduard Nápravník conducting, Ivan Mel'nikov in the title role (fig.1), Yuliya Platonova as Marina, Fyodor Komissarzhevsky as the Pretender, Osip Petrov as Varlaam, Antonina Abarinova as the Innkeeper and Pavel Bulakhov as the Holy Fool. A vocal score of the revised version was published in 1874; both versions are in the complete edition of Musorgsky's works, edited by Pavel Lamm (1928).

1. Ivan Mel'nikov in the title role of Musorgsky's 'Boris Godunov', which he created at the Mariinsky Theatre, St Petersburg, 27 January/8 February 1874

For many years, beginning in 1896, the opera was performed exclusively in a re-orchestrated revision by Rimsky-Korsakov (he himself conducted the première, with Fyodor Stravinsky as Varlaam), which itself exists in two versions (published in 1896 and 1908) of which the more complete second ('standard version' in list of premières above) is the one that first achieved international repertory status; its Paris première was produced by Sergey Dyagilev and directed by Alexander Sanin, with Felix Blumenfeld conducting, Fyodor Shalyapin as Boris and Dmitry Smirnov as the Pretender. Of other performing versions two should be mentioned: by Shostakovich (1939–40, an orchestration of the vocal score in the complete edition), used mainly at the Kirov Theatre since 1960; and by Karol Rathaus, commissioned by the Metropolitan Opera, New York, and used there for two decades from 1952. Since the mid-1970s

Musorgsky's own versions have gradually been displacing those of Rimsky-Korsakov and others on the world's stages. A critical edition by David Lloyd-Jones, published in 1975, has been used increasingly since that date. The title role has been a great vehicle for Russian and Russian-style basses: Mark Reyzen sang in the première of the 1869 version, and other noted interpreters have included, besides Shalyapin, Vanni-Marcoux, Alexander Kipnis, Nicola Rossi-Lemeni, Boris Christoff, George London, Nicolai Ghiaurov and Martti Talvela. In recordings, some singers have taken both Boris's role and that of Pimen or Varlaam; both Reyzen and Christoff made recordings in which they sang all three.

* * *

Boris Godunov is the pre-eminent representative of the historical genre in Russian opera and the sole survivor of its type in the permanent international repertory (the increasingly standard *Khovanshchina* by the same composer being its only possible rival). It owes its position primarily, if not exclusively, to the extraordinary portrayal of the title character – one of the great bass/baritone roles, offering tremendous scope to a charismatic singing actor (it was the chief vehicle for Shalyapin's world acclaim), clearly the creation of a musical psychologist of genius.

Boris Godunov was composed at a time when historical drama was the dominant Russian theatrical genre, musical or otherwise, reflecting the widespread conviction that art had a civic obligation – an attitude that tends to flourish in states where open discussion of public policy is not permitted. In 19th-century Russia, such discussion took place mainly in the 'Aesopian' guise of historiography and literary criticism – and on the stage itself, where dramatists strove to invest their work with content 'worthy of the attention of a thinking man', to quote Nikolay Chernïshevsky, the most influential radical critic of the 1860s.

Musorgsky, influenced in this by a number of friends and mentors, including the historian Vladimir Nikol'sky and the arts publicist Vladimir Stasov, took these principles more seriously than any other Russian musician. He was also much preoccupied with the actual mechanics of musical representation. At first his model was Dargomïzhsky's opera *The Stone Guest*, a direct setting of a short verse play by Pushkin that sought in the name of realism to bypass the artificialities of the conventional libretto. Later Musorgsky adopted (from Aristotle by way of the German literary historian Georg Gervinus) a radically positivistic theory of emotional expression and character portrayal in music by means of meticulously objective imitation of 'natural' conversational speech. During the late 1860s Musorgsky systematically applied this technique in a series of avowedly experimental vocal works culminating in *Marriage*, a recitative opera based on the unaltered prose text of a comedy by Gogol, on which he worked during summer 1868, producing one act in vocal score.

So when in the autumn of that year Nikol'sky suggested as an operatic subject Pushkin's famous drama of Boris Godunov and his troubled reign (the acknowledged prototype for the historical spectacles that were lately so fashionable), the composer immediately recognized it as the natural and necessary field for the full deployment of his talents. The play, which had been finally cleared by the censor for stage performances in 1866, had everything: an important historical theme; a 'Shakespearean' mixture of poetry and prose, tragedy and comedy, which would vouchsafe the opportunity to combine the approaches of *The Stone Guest* and *Marriage* and so evade the monotony of style that had plagued both works; a wide range of character types from boyar to beggar, to be portrayed naturalistically through declamation; and a large role for the crowd that would enable the composer to project his ideas of formal realism and naturalistic declamation on a large canvas. Perhaps not least, owing to the 'predominance of politics' in it and the absence of romance, *Boris Godunov* had been pronounced unfit for (conventional) operatic treatment by Alexander Serov, the chief musical pundit of the day, to whom The Five or 'mighty kuchka' felt particularly hostile. Selecting Pushkin's play as a subject was thus an act of typical 'kuchkist'-cum-realist bravado.

As to actual text, the libretto of the original version of the opera was almost entirely drawn from Pushkin. With the sole exception of Boris's hallucination in scene 5 (suggested, ironically enough, by Holofernes' hallucination in *Judith*, an opera by Serov) there is nothing in the action of Musorgsky's drama that was not in Pushkin. The scene in Pimen's cell and the scene at the Lithuanian border were verbatim settings of scenes from the original play (the former in verse à la *Stone Guest* and the latter in prose à la *Marriage*). Musorgsky boiled the rest of Pushkin's play down to a length suitable for musical setting by a very simple expedient: he threw out every scene in which the title character failed to appear, leaving a total of six scenes (out of 23) from which to fashion the five remaining scenes of his libretto (two of Pushkin's scenes being conflated to provide the text for the long one in which Musorgsky's Boris sings his big soliloquies). The result was a characteristic canvas for what Musorgsky called *opéra dialogué* – i.e. a 'sung play' in recitative dialogue (the genre to which *Pelléas*, *Salome* and *Wozzeck* also belong).

Its method may have been dictated by practical necessity, but Musorgsky's radical condensation of Pushkin's play had the effect of casting the title character into much greater prominence than the poet had accorded him. This, of course, worked very much to the opera's advantage, since it provided a heroic role at the centre of the drama. It was an advantage the composer was uniquely equipped to exploit, though the role achieved its full stature only in the revised version of 1872.

The concomitant disadvantage of the original libretto was the elimination of the 'Polish' scenes and, with them, of the only major feminine role in Pushkin's play, that of Marina Mniszek. This deficiency, subsequent legends notwithstanding, was the sole reason for the opera's rejection by the selection committee of the Imperial Theatres Directorate in February 1871, which (theatre being at the time a state monopoly in Russia) precluded its performance. The composer was forced to revise the opera, a task he undertook almost immediately upon receiving news of the rejection and completed at the beginning of the summer of 1872.

To meet the directorate's demands all Musorgsky would have had to do was reinstate the love scene for Marina and the Pretender, a scene which (according to Vladimir Stasov) he had originally intended to include, and even sketched, when he first embarked on the opera. In fact, he went so much further than that in revising the opera that it is impossible to regard the second version as anything less than a total re-conception, now very much at variance with Pushkin, implying not only an entirely different reading of Russian history, but an entirely different view of the nature of musical drama. The revision of *Boris Godunov* was motivated by considerations of historiographical ideology, dramatic tone, and consistency in the deployment of leitmotifs. At this point it will be well to give a résumé and a parallel synopsis of the two versions, on the basis of which an interpretation of their differences may be essayed (the format follows Oldani 1978); see Résumé below.

The revised *Boris* was no longer an *opéra dialogué*. In part this change was dictated by practical necessity, since Pushkin's Polish scenes did not include the ingredients from which Musorgsky fashioned his Act 3. Musorgsky had to write the text for Marina's aria, for the big love duet and for the scenes with Rangoni, a character absent in Pushkin, who embodied a xenophobic anti-Catholicism that was entirely the composer's. He now freely paraphrased Pushkin even where it was possible to quote him directly. His melodies became rounder, more lyrically self-sufficient, and underwent a more conventional sort of development.

But if this conventionalizing turn could be indirectly attributed to the demands of the Imperial Theatres Directorate, Musorgsky bears sole responsibility for the decision he made, on completing the 'Polish Act', to go back and refashion the central Terem scene (the old Part 3, now Act 2) as well. He happily de-Pushkinized its text, and, as he put it in a letter to Stasov, 'perpetrated an arioso' for the title character, very much along the more thematically generalized, lyrical lines of the love duet. At the same time he removed from the opera a

RÉSUMÉ (INCORPORATING THE EVENTS OF BOTH VERSIONS)

The Tsarevich Dmitry, the nine-year-old son of Ivan the Terrible, and next in line (after his feeble-minded half-brother Fyodor) to the Russian throne, is murdered in the town of Uglich in 1591, at the instigation of the boyar Boris Godunov, Ivan's brother-in-law and regent under Fyodor (modern historians do not subscribe to the theory of Boris's guilt, but Ivan Karamzin, the official Russian historian of the early 19th century, asserted it, and Pushkin and Musorgsky accepted it as the basis for their dramas). On Fyodor's death in 1598, Boris is elected tsar and, after a show of reluctance, accepts and is crowned. He reigns wisely and in peace for several years and is portrayed by the dramatists as a loving father, devoted in particular to grooming his son Fyodor to succeed him and establish a dynasty.

In spite of his good intentions and wise policies, Russia is visited by famines, which those who know of Boris's crime attribute to divine judgment. Among his enemies is an old soldier who witnessed the murder. He has become a monk and taken the name Pimen. He records Boris's crime in a chronicle, which he shows to his ward, the novice Grigory Otrep'yev, who is exactly the same age as the slain tsarevich. Grigory vows to pose as the tsarevich risen from death and claim the throne. With two vagabond monks, Varlaam and Missail, who do not know his plan, he sets out for Poland/Lithuania, Russia's hostile Roman Catholic neighbour to the west, to enlist support. In an inn near the border he is recognized by a patrol and narrowly escapes capture. Reaching Sandomierz, he falls in love with Marina, the daughter of the local governor, who is induced by the Jesuit Rangoni to feign love in return, so to coopt the Pretender's campaign on behalf of the Church.

Boris is informed of the Pretender's rise, and his formidable Polish support, by Prince Vasily Shuysky, a powerful but treacherous courtier. The news sends Boris into a paroxysm of fear, accompanied by hallucinations. He orders a church service so as to pronounce an anathema on the Pretender. On his way out he is accosted by a Holy Fool, who complains to Boris that some boys have stolen a penny from him, and that the tsar should have them killed, the way he had had the tsarevich killed. Boris asks the holy man to pray for him but is rebuffed. Shuysky now conspires with Pimen. The latter visits the court and frightens Boris with a false tale of the slain tsarevich, now a miracle-working saint, who, Pimen says, has cured him of blindness. At this Boris has a seizure and, after a last farewell to his son, whom he points out to the assembled boyars as their new tsar, expires. The Pretender, meanwhile, makes his way through the countryside, accompanied by a retinue of Jesuits and mercenaries (including Varlaam and Missail), plus an ever-increasing mob of peasants and local gentry who believe him to be the risen tsarevich. The Holy Fool, witnessing the credulous procession, laments the fate of unhappy Russia.

Original version, 1869 (underlined matter exclusive to this version)	Revised version, 1872 (underlined matter exclusive to this version)
1 PART 1.i *Courtyard of the Novodevichiy Monastery, Moscow*	1 PROLOGUE.i *Courtyard of the Novodevichiy Monastery, Moscow*
a After an orchestral introduction, a policeman is seen ordering the crowd on its knees to beg Boris to accept the throne; chorus of supplication; the policeman returns; the crowd banter with him; ordered to beg again they uncomprehendingly comply; Shchelkalov, secretary of the Boyars' Council, exhorts the crowd with a gloomy arioso about Boris's feigned implacability and its consequences; a group of blind pilgrims arrives to add their voices to the crowd entreating Boris.	*a* as *a* opposite
b The crowd again express their incomprehension, particularly of the pilgrims. They agree to come the next day to resume their entreaties, but cynically.	

2 PART 1.ii *Square in the Moscow Kremlin* Boris is crowned. Processions before and after. The new tsar expresses humility and invites all to a feast. The forced praises of the crowd are sung to the words and tune of an old Russian fortune-telling song from the L'viv-Pratsch anthology (2/1806) chosen because it happens to include the word 'Glory!' as a refrain.	2 PROLOGUE.ii *as opposite*
3 PART 2.i *Cell in the Chudov Monastery*	3 ACT 1.i *Cell in the Chudov Monastery*
a Pimen's monologue, on finishing his chronicle but for one last tale	*a* as *a* opposite
	b Chorus of monks behind the scenes
b Grigory wakes	*c* Grigory wakes (different music)
	d Second chorus of monks behind the scenes
c Grigory recounts a dream of being exalted, then dashed	*e* as *c* opposite
d Pimen recalls Ivan the Terrible's visit to the monastery and the saintliness of the late Tsar Fyodor	*f* as *d* opposite
e Pimen's narrative of the murder of the Tsarevich Dmitry	
f Grigory's question about the tsarevich's age; chorus of monks behind the scenes; Grigory's vow	*g* as *f* opposite
4 PART 2.ii *Inn on the Lithuanian Border*	4 ACT 1.ii *Inn on the Lithuanian Border*
a Orchestral introduction	*g* as *a* opposite
	b Innkeeper sings a song about a drake as she darns an old padded jacket
b Arrival of Grigory, Varlaam, Missail	*c* as *b* opposite
c Varlaam's first song ('Song about Kazan') [Pushkin quotes the first line of the song ('Oh, 'twas in Kazan town') in his play; it is a *khorovod* song, about a monk who renounces the cowl for a gayer life with women. Stasov, mistaking this reference, assumed Pushkin meant a historical song about Ivan the Terrible's conquest of the Tatar capital in 1552. He found the text Musorgsky used in an anthology edited by Ivan Khudyakov in 1860. After his little by-play with Grigory, Pushkin's Varlaam resumes his song with the second line, also supplied by the poet. Not knowing the original reference, Musorgsky assumed Varlaam was now singing a different song, and adapted a tune he had learnt from Rimsky-Korsakov to his own words.]	*d* as *c* opposite
d Varlaam waves Grigory aside and strikes up another song; while he sings, Grigory learns the way to Lithuania from the innkeeper; the police come; Grigory tries to convince them that Varlaam is the Pretender, but Varlaam, laboriously making out the warrant, exposes him; he makes a fenestral exit.	*e* as *d* opposite, but for the music that accompanies Grigory's escape at the very end
5 PART 3 *The Tsar's Quarters (Terem) in the Kremlin*	5 ACT 2 *The Tsar's Quarters (Terem) in the Kremlin* [both words and music of this scene were rewritten in 1871–2; even items that conform to the old scenario are in fact new]
a Xenia laments her lost bridegroom	*a* as *a* opposite
b Fyodor sings at his map	*b* The children with the chiming clock
c Nurse comforts Xenia	*c* as *c* opposite
	d Song of the Gnat
	e Handclapping game (text conflated from eight different children's songs in P. V. Sheyn's anthology of Russian folklore, 1870; music original)
d Boris's entrance; he comforts Xenia and sends her away	*f* as *d* opposite
e Boris and Fyodor at the map	*g* as *e* opposite
f The opening portion of the title character's great soliloquy on kingship and conscience, 'Dostig ya vïsshey vlasti' ('I have attained the highest power'), set almost verbatim from Pushkin in the form of a lengthy scena in melodic recitative over an orchestral tissue of leitmotifs, most of them derived from music written earlier for *Salammbô*	*h* Boris's monologue, recast as an aria to a heavily adapted text that refers much more openly than Pushkin's had done to Boris's crime and the popular discontent it has brought about. The main lyric theme, broadly developed in the vocal part as well as the orchestra, is also a derivation from *Salammbô*
	i Tumult of nurses' voices offstage.
g The boyar-in-attendance announces Shuysky's arrival and denounces his treachery.	*j* as *g* opposite

h Boris curses Shuysky; Shuysky delivers the news of the False Dmitry; Boris obtains Shuysky's assurance that the tsarevich was truly dead in Uglich
i Boris's hallucination, preceded by the concluding portion of the soliloquy begun in section *f* above.

k Fyodor explains the disturbance offstage with his 'Song of the Parrot'; Boris praises his narrative and encourages him to continue improving his mind
l as *h* opposite

m Boris's soliloquy concluded, culminating in

n The hallucination with the chiming clock

6 Act 3.i *Marina's Boudoir in Sandomierz Castle*
a Chorus of Polish maidens serenade Marina as she dresses
b Marina's aria (in mazurka style), expressing her haughtiness, her boredom, her ambition and her determination to use the Pretender as her path to queenhood
c Rangoni overpowers Marina and obtains her vow to help him convert the Pretender and, through him, all of Russia

7 Act 3.ii *Garden by the Fountain*
a Dmitry awaits Marina; Rangoni appears and fans his passion
b Polonaise for the 'Pans and Pannas' (Polish nobles)
c Marina appears; love duet

6 Part 4.i *Square before St Basil's*
a Crowd uncomprehendingly discuss the anathema service
b Boys steal a penny from a Holy Fool
c Boris and his retinue leave the church; the crowd beseech him for bread
d The Holy Fool confronts Boris with his crime and refuses to pray for him
e The Holy Fool laments the fate of Russia

7 Part 4.ii *Granovitaya Palace, the Kremlin*
a Orchestral introduction (adapted from *Salammbô* music)
b Shchelkalov reads Boris's ukase convening the meeting of the Boyars' Council to consider means of halting the Pretender's advance
c The boyars discuss the matter, sense futility, express annoyance at Shuysky's absence
d Shuysky arrives and describes Boris's hallucination
e Boris enters in grip of hallucination
f Pimen's narrative about the wonder-working Dmitry
g Boris's farewell to his son
h Death of Boris.

8 Act 4.i *Granovitaya Palace, the Kremlin*
a as *a* opposite

b as *c* opposite

c as *d* opposite, with some small cuts (28 bars)
d as *e* opposite
e as *f* opposite, less six bars
f as *g* opposite, with some small cuts (13 bars)
g as *h* opposite

9 Act 4.ii *A forest glade near Kromï*
a Orchestral introduction, entrance of the crowd with the captive boyar Khrushchyov
b Mocking 'glorification' of Khrushchyov (based on a folksong Musorgsky learnt from Balakirev)
c Boys steal a penny from a Holy Fool (transferred from Part 4.i, 6*b* opposite)
d Entrance of Varlaam and Missail: their song is based on an ancient epic song Musorgsky had transcribed from the singing of the famous bard Trofim Ryabinin
e 'Revolutionary' chorus in da capo form: the middle section based on a song from Balakirev's anthology of 1866
f The False Dmitry's (Pretender's) procession, including Jesuit hymns; Dmitry's proclamation and the crowd's glorification of him (procession music adapted from *Salammbô*)
g The Holy Fool laments the fate of Russia (from the end of Part 4.i, 6*e* opposite).

2. *'Boris Godunov' (Musorgsky): set design by Mikhail Il'yich Bocharov for the coronation scene (Prologue, scene ii) in the first production of the revised version at the Mariïnsky Theatre, St Petersburg, 27 January/8 February 1874*

great deal that was especially characteristic of his earlier manner. This applies particularly to the St Basil's scene and the closing section of the very first scene, which in its original conception had been the boldest dramaturgical stroke: a scene of naturalistic prose recitative for the chorus. Clearly we are dealing with a retrenchment.

Its motivation may be located in a letter from Musorgsky to Rimsky-Korsakov, written during the year in which the original version was in limbo between completion and rejection (23 July/4 August 1870), following a party at which the composer had run through his opera before a handpicked audience. 'As regards the peasants in *Boris*', he wrote with bemusement, 'some found them to be *bouffe* (!), while others saw tragedy'. In other words, it became evident to the composer that his naturalistic methods carried ineluctable associations with comedy, their traditional medium. From this experience, perhaps, rather than the subsequent rejection, dated Musorgsky's first impulse to revise his opera, born of a wish to clarify its genre – that is, to elevate its tone unambiguously to the level of tragedy.

Accordingly, to restore the title character to full tragic dimension, it was necessary not only to 'perpetrate an arioso' for him but to surround the arioso with a profusion of trivial genre pieces. (The new Terem scene was modelled, in fact, on the second act of Cui's *William Ratcliff*: in both, a lengthy *divertissement* full of songs and games is suddenly interrupted by the entrance of the stern baritone protagonist, who, having dispersed the revellers, proceeds to sing a crucial and self-revealing monologue.) The formally petty methods of naturalism are replaced by larger structural entities, and the subtle expressive vagaries of recitative are replaced by sustained moods, their succession calculated for maximum contrast. As a result, to quote Abram Gozenpud, the foremost Soviet historian of the Russian operatic stage, 'though much of poetic enjoyment and beauty was lost, [Musorgsky] undeniably achieved a rough and gaudy theatricality that had been lacking in Pushkin'. It seems clear, moreover, that he took the formerly despised Verdi – and particularly *Don Carlos*, which had its Russian première during the gestation of *Boris Godunov* – as an important model in achieving the dramatic scale he needed.

The new historiographical conception embodied in the revised *Boris* can best be viewed by comparing the Kromï Forest scene with the scene it replaced (St Basil's). That Musorgsky never meant the two of them to be performed side by side (as has become a 20th-century tradition, originally fostered by the Moscow Bol'shoy Theatre, which in 1925 commissioned Mikhail Ippolitov-Ivanov to make an orchestration of the scene suitable for insertion into the standard Rimsky-Korsakov edition) is clear from the fact that Musorgsky transferred two sections from the one to the other – physically ripped them out of the earlier score, in fact. The earlier scene portrayed the crowd (following Pushkin) as cowed and submissive to the tsar. The Holy Fool, who challenges and insults Boris, is the embodiment of nemesis, which in the first version of the opera took the form of the 'Tsar-Herod's' conscience.

In the revised opera, that overriding theme was replaced by another, timelier one: that of Tsar *v.* People, the latter viewed as the real driving force in history. It was a view that accorded with the social outlook of the 1860s and 70s, deriving not from Pushkin (still less from Pushkin's historical source, the 'Caesaristic' Karamzin), but from the writings of Ivan Kostomarov, a populist historian. In Kromï, the crowd is viewed in active revolt against the criminal tsar. At the same time, and almost paradoxically, their music is far less 'radical' than the crowd music in the earlier version. Instead of mass recitative, it is now a series of vast choral numbers in strophic, or (especially telling) da capo form. In making the crowd a tragic protagonist (literally so, in Aristotelian terms: though powerful and just in its righteous condemnation of Boris, they have a tragic flaw, namely the credulousness that causes them to accept the claims of the Pretender), Musorgsky subjected their music to the same kind of formal 'elevation' as he had the music of their antagonist in Act 2.

A similar concern for formal unity (expressed through symmetry) governs the whole of the revised *Boris*, quite belying the frequent complaint (true enough if applied to the radically 'realist' first version) that the opera is an 'inorganic' assemblage of disconnected scenes. The three

focal characters in the revised scenario – Tsar, Pretender, Crowd – are balanced in a palindromic equilibrium, with the people, seen from two radically differing points of view, as the alpha and omega:

Prologue	1. Novodevichiy	Crowd
	2. Coronation	Boris
Act 1	3. Monastery cell	Pretender
	4. Inn	
Act 2	5. Terem	Boris
Act 3	6. Marina's boudoir	Pretender
	7. Fountain	
Act 4	8. Death of Boris	Boris
	9. Kromï Forest	Crowd

The final perspective from which to view the revised *Boris Godunov* as a total musico-dramatic conception pertains to the use of leitmotifs. On the face of it, their importance is much diminished. The earlier version of the opera was saturated with identifying and recalling themes, with every character, however insignificant, so equipped; with Boris given a complex of as many as half a dozen leitmotifs; and with the theme alternately associated with the Pretender and the dead tsarevich harped upon to the point where it becomes (as Oldani has put it) the opera's *idée fixe*. In the three newly composed scenes of the revised version, the role of leitmotifs (except for the Pretender's) is minimal. In the revised Terem scene, they are much attenuated, particularly with reference to the title character and his central monologue. The role of the Pretender's leitmotif, however, is both expanded and refined, in a way that affects not only his portrayal, but Boris's as well. Where in the earlier version the leitmotif could refer either to the 'real' or the False Dmitry, their confusion (especially in Boris's mind) being the whole point of its deployment, in the new version its treatment is stricter, to magnificently ironic effect. It now refers only to the Pretender – except in Boris's deranged mind, where just as unwaveringly it refers to the slain infant heir. The consistency with which otherwise inexplicable alterations (particularly deletions) realize this change leaves no doubt as to Musorgsky's intention. It accounts not only for the removal of Pimen's narrative of the murder from the Cell scene, it also makes plain the rationale for certain mysterious small cuts in the Death scene. One of the items cut there, for example, is a line from Boris's farewell to his son that contains the warning 'Silyon zloy Samozvanets!' ('the evil Pretender is strong'), set to the leitmotif that otherwise (for Boris) links up only with his victim, not his punisher.

Ex.2
(a) Musorgsky
Andante
pp
I v lgu - tom go - re, nis - po - slan-nom bo - gom, Za
tyazh - kiy nash grekh v is - pï - tan' - ye
['And in cruel sorrow, sent down by God as punishment for our grievous sin']
(b) Rimsky-Korsakov
I v lyu - tom go - re, nis - po - slan-nom bo - gom, Za
tyazh - kiy nash grekh v is - pï - tan' - ye

From the dual perspective of ideological updating and elevation of tone it is possible to explain virtually all aspects of the *Boris Godunov* revision. The one cut that Musorgsky seems to have made primarily in the interests of dramatic pacing is Shchelkalov's reading of the ukase in the Death scene, which merely recapitulates information already well known to the audience. It was deleted from the original version before submission to the theatre.

Rimsky-Korsakov's version still has its adherents. Its virtues, besides the surefire orchestration that made such an overwhelming impression in Paris, can be gauged from a trio of comparative examples drawn from the title role. In ex.1, the beginning of the central Act 2 aria, Rimsky expertly inserted a single chord to effect a polished modulation. In ex.2, from the climax of the aria, Rimsky transposed the second half of the melody to give the singer (now definitely a baritone) a more

Ex.3
(a) Musorgsky
Allegretto
BORIS
Stoy na stra - zhe bor-tsom za ve - ru pra - vu - yu, svya - to chti svya-tïkh u - god - ni - kov Bo - zh'ikh.
['Stand guard, a soldier for the true faith, revere the holy servants of God']
(b) Rimsky-Korsakov
Allegro moderato
BORIS
Stoy na stra - zhe bor-tsom za ve - ru pra - vu - yu svya - to chti svya-tïkh u - god - ni - kov Bo - zh'ikh.
mf sempre

felicitous tessitura. In ex.3, from the Act 4 farewell, Musorgsky's organum-like archaisms were replaced by a more grateful, Balakirevesque 'modality' that skirts forbidden parallels. Stravinsky may have been unfair to accuse his former teacher of having perpetrated a 'Meyerbeerization' of Musorgsky's work; the original, too, owed a heavy debt to Meyerbeer (as what 19th-century historical opera did not?). But Rimsky did conventionalize it in ways that may have facilitated its early acceptance, but now seem gratuitously to soften the harsh and hopeless impression Musorgsky calculated his opera to produce. The composer's revised version, it now seems clear, is a work not of raw genius alone but of a fastidious dramatist in sure command of his materials. It possesses an integrity of structure, of style and of purport – in short, of sullen historical vision – no other version, least of all the ad hoc conflations that have increasingly become the rule, can match.

RICHARD TARUSKIN

Borkh, Inge [Simon, Ingeborg] (*b* Mannheim, 26 May 1917). Swiss soprano. She began her career as an actress, before studying singing in Milan and making her début in 1940 at Lucerne as Czipra (*Der Zigeunerbaron*), followed by Agathe. She appeared in Zürich, Munich, Berlin, Stuttgart, Vienna and Basle, where she sang Magda in the first German-language performance of *The Consul* (1951). She sang Freia and Sieglinde at Bayreuth (1952) and made her American début in 1953 at San Francisco as Electra, returning for Verdi's Lady Macbeth. In 1954 she sang Eglantine (*Euryanthe*) at Florence and in 1955 created Cathleen in Egk's *Irische Legende* at Salzburg. She took part in the American première of Britten's *Gloriana* (1956, Cincinnati) and made her débuts at the Metropolitan (1958) and at Covent Garden (1959) as Salome. A notable exponent of 20th-century opera, she counted Turandot, Orff's Antigone and Bloch's Lady Macbeth among her roles, as well as the Dyer's Wife. Her voice, bright and incisive, was capable of great dramatic intensity. In 1977 she returned to straight acting.

*

GV (E. Stadler; R. Vegeto)

ALAN BLYTH

Bořkovec, Pavel (*b* Prague, 10 June 1894; *d* Prague, 22 July 1972). Czech composer. He studied composition with Křička and J. B. Foerster, and was later a member of the left-wing avant-garde music group Mánes (1933–7). He was a highly esteemed professor of composition at the Academy of Musical Arts in Prague, 1946–64. A leading neo-classicist, noted for the precision of his style, he was interested mainly in orchestral and chamber music. His two operas and his ballet *Krysař* ('Pied Piper') have in common the wartime themes of freedom and independence. *Satyr* (1937–8; 5, J. W. von Goethe, trans. O. Fischer; Prague, National, 8 Oct 1942) vividly portrays a cruel dictator who claims godlike power and gains fanatical support but whose character is eventually revealed. The grotesqueness of the story is reflected in a dynamic, elaborate succession of ariosos, dialogues, scherzo-like ensembles and choruses. *Paleček* ('Tom Thumb', 1945–7; 5, F. Kubka; Prague, Smetana, 17 Dec 1958) is set in the Prague student community of the late 15th century, and was written for the 600th anniversary of Charles University. Composed in a lighthearted and polished style, it concerns a scholar who tries to attack injustice.

*

ČSHS

I. Krejčí: 'Pavel Bořkovec', *České umění dramatické*, ii: *Zpěvohra* [Czech Dramatic Art: Opera], ed. J. Hutter and Z. Chalabala (Prague, 1941), 366–7

P. Blatný: *Scénická díla Pavel Bořkovce* [Bořkovec's Stage Works] (diss., U. of Brno, 1958)

J. Brožovská: 'O současné opeře dvakrát' [Twice About a Contemporary Opera], *Kultura*, iii/3 (1959), 5

J. Hach: 'Dvě operní novinky' [Two New Operas], *Divadlo*, x (1959), 222–5

K. Šrom: 'Konečně Paleček' [*Tom Thumb* at Last], *Divadelní noviny*, ii/12 (1959), 5

V. Holzknecht: 'Profil Pavla Bořkovce', *HRo*, xvii (1964), 451–3

J. Kasan and others: *Pavel Bořkovec: osobnost a dílo* [Pavel Bořkovec: the Personality and his Work] (Prague, 1964)

HELENA HAVLÍKOVÁ

Born, Claire (*b* Vienna, 1898). Austrian soprano. She studied in Vienna, where she was engaged at the Staatsoper (1920–26). Her roles included Countess Almaviva, Pamina, Agathe, Gutrune and Ariadne. At Salzburg (1922–7) she sang Countess Almaviva, Donna

Elvira and Ariadne; at Bayreuth (1924), Eva and Gutrune. She created the Daughter in Hindemith's *Cardillac* (1926) at the Dresden Staatsoper, where she was engaged from 1929 until she left Germany in 1933. She then taught in London. A stylish and subtle artist, she had a smooth, pure-toned voice. ELIZABETH FORBES

Borodin, Alexander Porfir'yevich (*b* St Petersburg, 31 Oct/12 Nov 1833; *d* St Petersburg, 15/27 Feb 1887). Russian composer, by profession a chemist. His operatic reputation is entirely posthumous: during his lifetime a single (insignificant) stage work that was partly his achieved a solitary (disastrous) performance in the (unidentified) composer's absence.

The illegitimate son of a Caucasian nobleman named Gedianishvili, the future composer was registered at birth as the son of Porfiry Borodin, one of his father's serfs. Brought up, like almost all the Russian composers of his generation, in genteel surroundings, he had an extraordinary education, was fluent in German, French, English and Italian, learnt to play the flute and cello as well as the piano, and dabbled in composition from his teens. His formative musical experiences included playing the German classics in piano duet arrangements and taking the second cello part in Boccherini quintets. His mother, Avdot'ya Konstantinovna Antonova, married a retired army doctor named Kleinecke. Borodin trained at first for a career in his stepfather's footsteps before becoming interested in chemistry, studying in western Europe, 1859–62, chiefly in Heidelberg, where he met his future wife, a young Russian pianist named Yekaterina Protopopova, whom he married in 1863.

From the time of his return to St Petersburg in 1862 to his death 25 years later, Borodin's life revolved around two poles. His distinguished scientific and educational career was spent chiefly at the Medico-Surgical Academy, where he was professor from 1864 and where from 1872 he administered a medical curriculum for women. It was his hobby, however, that won him immortality. Having met Balakirev soon after his return from western Europe, he became a member of the circle now known as The Five or the Mighty Kuchka. Few outside the circle were aware of him as a composer during his lifetime. His only publicly performed works were two symphonies and a tone poem (*In Central Asia*) in addition to a couple of numbers from his opera eternally in progress; these, plus one of his two string quartets, a few songs and a handful of salonish piano pieces were all he published. His world reputation is due partly to the efforts of Liszt, whom he met in Weimar and who recognized his extraordinary talent, and above all to Rimsky-Korsakov, who with Glazunov rescued *Prince Igor* from oblivion after Borodin's sudden death.

As an opera composer Borodin stood somewhat aloof from the ideals of the circle to which he nominally belonged – ideals that received their most extensive theoretical formulation in the critical writings of César Cui, and their most thoroughgoing practical application in the operas of Musorgsky (towards which Borodin remained rather cool). His earliest venture for the stage, an 'opera-farce' à la Offenbach entitled *Bogatïri* ('The Heroic Warriors'), was not only a spoof of the stereotyped 'style russe' and the trivial portrayal of Russian antiquities by such composers as Verstovsky and Serov, whose operas always seemed to revolve around a damsel's abduction and her rescue by a heroic warrior (*bogatïr'*). It also lampooned the pretensions to realism that by the late 1860s had captured the imaginations of more progressive musical thinkers. 'When, oh when will our authors stop dragging out this idiotic Russian *terem* [retreat] with its mamushkas and babushkas and captive maidens, its cherries and berries, its currants and raisins, its stupid fairy-tales and songs that drive you to distraction?!', exclaims one of the characters. But she also directs another character, who is about to sing a song, 'See particularly that it answers to all the requirements of contemporary music, that in it you strictly observe the laws of musical truth: if you are going to sing about a wolf, then growl like a wolf; if about a frog, then croak like a frog'.

The Heroic Warriors, in which only about a quarter of the music was original, the rest being derived by pastiche or direct appropriation from Offenbach, Meyerbeer, Verdi and others, was performed once only, at the Moscow Bol'shoy Theatre, on 6/18 November 1867. The composer, unidentified on the programme, remained in St Petersburg; he planned to catch the piece later in the run, but there was no run. Later in life he apparently kept its existence a secret even from his musical *confrères*. The unpublished score, part autograph, part in arrangers' hands, is preserved (*RU-SPtob*; the numbers that parody the work of Serov and Verstovsky are printed, with their models, in Taruskin 1981).

Borodin gave more serious and positive voice to what Cui considered his 'outmoded' operatic ideal in a long letter to a singer friend, Lyubov' Karmalina, of 1/13 June 1876:

> The purely recitative style has always gone against my grain and my character. I am drawn to singing, to cantilena, and not to recitative, although, to judge by the reactions of those who know, I am not too bad at the latter. Moreover, I am drawn to forms that are more closed, more rounded, more ample ... In my opinion, in the opera itself, just as in the sets, petty forms, details, tinycraft should have no place; everything must be painted in broad strokes, clearly, vividly and as practicably as possible, both for the voices and for the orchestra. The voices must be in the foreground, the orchestra in the background.

This description fits to perfection the opera around which Borodin's whole mature creative period revolved: *Prince Igor*, to the composer's libretto after a scenario by Stasov largely based on the 12th-century epic, *Slovo o polku Igoreve* ('The Lay of the Host of Igor'), Russia's earliest literary classic (unless it is, as some still contend, an 18th-century forgery). 'To the extent that I succeed in realizing my goals', Borodin wrote to Karmalina, 'my opera will tend more in the direction of [Glinka's] *Ruslan* than [Dargomïzhsky's] *The Stone Guest*', the latter being the much-touted type of the recitative-dialogue opera on which the rest of the Balakirev circle had set its sights. *Prince Igor* was indeed a second *Ruslan*, in all that pertains to 'epic' amplitude of musical form and colourfully contrasting national idioms, but also as regards dramatic incoherence and statuesque immobility of scenic action.

Borodin worked sporadically on this score from 1869 until his death, leaving it far from finished. Music from two other operatic projects – *Tsarskaya nevesta* ('The Tsar's Bride'), after Lev Mey's pseudo-historical drama, for which Borodin made sketches in 1867–8 (the subject was later used by Rimsky-Korsakov), and *Mlada*, an opera-ballet on which the whole Balakirev circle except Balakirev worked in 1872, each composer writing an act (Borodin's was the fourth) – was mostly absorbed into

Igor, the music for which kept accumulating without much plan or purpose, making for severe editorial problems when it came to fashioning a performing version after the composer's demise. (The standard one was prepared by Rimsky-Korsakov and Glazunov in 1887–8.)

While inevitably something of a dramaturgical fiasco (whether or not one subscribes to the notion, put forth by Dahlhaus, that its 'dialectic of heroic honor' was inherently 'nonviable' for opera), Borodin's magnum opus is an extraordinary musical accomplishment. Above all, it abstracted from precedents in Glinka and Balakirev, and epitomized, a Russian 'oriental' idiom that found a host of imitators both at home – the 19-year-old Rakhmaninov's popular 'Georgian Song' on Pushkin's *Ne poy, krasavitsa, pri mne* ('Sing not to me, O beauty'), composed shortly after *Igor's* première, is a veritable parody of its manner – and (after Dyagilev stunned Paris with a truncated balletic version of Act 2 in 1909) abroad as well. There are also many echoes of Musorgsky: the portrayal of the conflict-ridden Prince Igor recalls the guilty Tsar Boris (in the revised version of Musorgsky's opera, itself influenced by the title role in Cui's *William Ratcliff*), and the comic roles (especially the pair of minstrels, Skula and Yeroshka) deftly ape Musorgsky's naturalistic recitatives. Finally, there is no better stylization of Russian folksong than the Chorus for the villagers in Act 4, an exquisite evocation of the mournful 'drawn-out' peasant song (*protyazhnaya*) that was the pre-eminent model for the Russian national school in its early days. For all these reasons, Borodin may be looked on as the great (belated) summarizer of the aims and methods of the Mighty Kuchka when it was in fact a united faction on the Russian musical scene. In this sense, for all its fresh colour and allure, the opera was stylistically retrospective, even nostalgic.

See also BOGATÏRI; MLADA (i); and PRINCE IGOR.

title	*genre, acts*	*libretto*	*composition*	*first performance*	*sources*	*remarks*
Bogatïri [The Heroic Warriors]	opera-farce, 5	V. A. Krïlov	1867	Moscow, Bol'shoy, 6/18 Nov 1867	*RU-SPtob, US-STu*	about one-quarter by Borodin; the rest loosely based on excerpts from operas by Rossini, Meyerbeer, Offenbach, Serov, Verdi, Hérold and others; largely orchd by E. N. Merten; 2 choral excerpts ed. A. Nefedov (Moscow, 1977)
Tsarskaya nevesta [The Tsar's Bride]	opera	Borodin, after L. A. Mey	1867–8			sketches only; lost
Mlada	opera-ballet, 4	Krïlov, after scenario by S. A. Gedeonov	1872		*RU-Mcm, SPil, SPsc*	Act 4 by Borodin; other 3 acts by Rimsky-Korsakov, Cui and Musorgsky; finale (nos. 5–7) arr. and orchd Rimsky-Korsakov (Leipzig, 1892); choral excerpt from finale ed. A. Nefedov (Moscow, 1977)
Knyaz' Igor' [Prince Igor]	opera, prol., 4	Borodin, after scenario by V. V. Stasov	1869–70, 1874–87	St Petersburg, Mariinsky, 23 Oct/4 Nov 1890	*Mcm, SPsc*; Leipzig, 1889	unfinished; completed and partly orchd by Rimsky-Korsakov and Glazunov; 4 choral excerpts, not in orig. vocal score, ed. A. Nefedov (Moscow, 1977)

V. Stasov: *Aleksandr Porfir'yevich Borodin: ego zhizn', perepiska i muzïkal'nïye stat'i* [Life, Correspondence and Articles on Music] (St Petersburg, 1889); biographical section repr. in *Izbrannïye sochineniya*, iii (Moscow, 1952)

A. Glazunov: 'Zapiski o redaktsii "Knyazya Igorya" Borodina' [Notes on the Editing of Borodin's *Prince Igor*], *RMG*, iii (1896), 155–7; Eng. trans. in Abraham (1939)

C. Cui: '"Knyaz' Igor'" (Moskovskaya chastnaya opera)', *Novosti i birzhevaya gazeta*, no. 81 (1899)

I. Glebov [B. V. Asaf'yev]: 'Iz zabïtïkh stranits russkoy muzïki' [From the Forgotten Pages of Russian Music], *Muzïkal'naya letopis'*, i (1922), 14–19

P. Lamm and S. Popov: '"Bogatïri"', *SovM* (1934), no.1, pp.87–94

P. Kerzhentsev: 'Fal'sifikatsiya narodnogo proshlogo' [A Falsification of National History], *SovM* (1936), no.12, pp.11–14; repr. from *Pravda* (15 Nov 1936)

'O p'yese "Bogatïri" Dem'yana Bednogo' [On Dem'yan Bednïy's libretto *Bogatïri*], *Pravda* (14 Nov 1936)

G. Abraham: 'The History of "Prince Igor"', *On Russian Music* (London, 1939), 147–68

A. Dmitriyev: 'K istorii sozdaniya operï A. P. Borodina "Knyaz' Igor'"' [The History of the Composition of *Prince Igor*], *SovM* (1950), no.11, pp.82–8 [with musical suppl. giving the 1875 version of Igor's aria in vocal score]

N. A. Listova: 'Iz istorii sozdaniya operï "Knyaz' Igor'"' [The History of the Composition of *Prince Igor*], *Soobshcheniya instituta istorii iskusstv AN SSSR*, xv (1959), 36–75 [incl. fullest pubd edn of Stasov's original scenario]

D. Lloyd-Jones: '"The Bogatyrs": Russia's First Operetta', *MMR*, lxxxix (1959), 123–30

S. Dianin: *Borodin* (Moscow, 1960; Eng. trans., 1963)

V. Kiselyov: 'Stsenicheskaya istoriya pervoy postanovki "Knyazya Igorya" Borodina' [The History of the First Production of *Prince Igor*], *Muzïkal'noye nasledstvo*, iii, ed. M. P. Alexeyev and others (Moscow, 1970), 284–352

A. Gozenpud: *Russkiy opernïy teatr na rubezhe XIX–XX vekov i F. I. Shalyapin* [Russian Operatic Theatre at the Turn of the 20th Century and Shalyapin] (Leningrad, 1974), 23–53

A. Sokhor: '"Knyaz' Igor'" – izvestnïy i ne izvestnïy' [*Prince Igor* – the Known and the Unknown], *SovM* (1976), no.1, pp.63–9

A. Kandinsky: 'Opït rekonstruktsii' [An Attempt at Reconstruction], *SovM* (1977), no.3, pp.63–70

G. Miller: 'Slovo za teatrami' [The Theatres' Turn to Speak], *SovM* (1977), no.3, pp.70–73

R. Taruskin: *Opera and Drama in Russia as Preached and Practiced in the 1860s* (Ann Arbor, 1981) [three numbers from *Bogatïri*, plus their sources in appx]

M. Bobéth: *Borodin und seine Oper 'Fürst Igor'* (Munich and Salzburg, 1982)

I. Vïzgo-Ivanova and A. Ivanov-Ekhvet: 'Yeshchyo raz ob istokakh "Knyazya Igorya"' [Once More on the Sources of *Prince Igor*], *SovM* (1982), no.4, pp.89–95

P. Lamm: 'K podlinnomu tekstu "Knyazya Igorya"' [Toward the Authentic Text of *Prince Igor*], *SovM* (1983), no.12, pp.104–7

G. Abraham: *Essays on Russian and East European Music* (Oxford, 1985)
Yu. Levashov: 'O zagadkakh operï Borodina i "Slova o polku Igoreve"' [On the Riddle of Borodin's Opera and *The Lay of the Host of Igor*], *Muzïkal'naya zhizn'* (1985), no.13, pp.15–17; no.14, pp.15–17; no.15, pp.15–17
K. Bumpass and G. B. Kauffman: 'Nationalism and Realism in Nineteenth-century Russian Music: "The Five" and Borodin's *Prince Igor*', *MR*, xlviii (1988), 43–51
C. Dahlhaus: *Nineteenth-Century Music* (Berkeley and Los Angeles, 1989)
S. Neef: *Handbuch der russischen und sowjetischen Oper* (Kassel and Basle, 1989) RICHARD TARUSKIN

Boronat, Olimpia (*b* Genoa, 1867; *d* Warsaw, 1934). Italian soprano. She is believed to have studied with Franco Leoni in Milan and to have begun her operatic career in Italian provincial theatres, later singing in Spain, Portugal and Latin America. She was engaged at the Imperial Opera in St Petersburg from 1890 to 1893, when she married and left the stage. In 1901 she resumed her operatic career and sang in Russia and Poland until 1914. Her voice was exceptional for its crystalline purity and flexibility, ideally displayed in her repertory of lyric soprano roles, which included Thomas' Ophelia, Rosina, Violetta and Bellini's Elvira.

*

L. Witten: 'Olimpia Boronat Discography', *Record Collector*, xx (1971–2), 160–63 HAROLD BARNES

Boroni [Baroni, Borroni, Buroni, Burroni], **Antonio** (*b* Rome, 1738; *d* Rome, 21 Dec 1792). Italian composer. After studies with Martini in Bologna and Abos in Naples, in 1758 he returned to Rome where he gave music lessons to Clementi, to whom he was related. In 1761 his first comic opera, *La moda*, was performed at Turin (revived Venice, 1769) and he wrote the recitatives and some of the arias for *Demofoonte*, performed in Sinigal in the same year. After producing six operas at Venice (1763–6) he went to Prague with the Bustelli opera company; two new operas by him were put on there (1767–8), and in 1768 the company went to Dresden, where his next opera was performed in 1769 (revived Venice, Carnival 1770). In 1770 Boroni arrived in Stuttgart, where he succeeded Jommelli as Kapellmeister. A revision of his earlier comic opera *L'amore in musica* was staged there that year, but the Italian opera in Stuttgart was deteriorating, and while there he composed only *opéras comiques* and perhaps a setting of Metastasio's *L'isola disabitata* (the evidence for this is a score in *D-Bds* dated 31 December 1775). At the end of 1777 he returned to Rome, where his last opera was staged. He became *maestro di cappella* at St Peter's in 1778 and later gained posts at other Roman churches, writing a large amount of sacred music.

Boroni's career as an opera composer was relatively short and unprolific, but his comic operas were mostly very successful, particularly *L'amore in musica*, which was widely performed. Through a mistake in Gerber's *Lexicon* several operas by G. B. Borghi (*Alessandro in Armenia*, *Ricimero*, *La donna instabile*, *Eumene*) have frequently been ascribed to Boroni; because of their dates the second and third of these are sometimes stated to have been composed at Stuttgart.

Demofoonte (os, P. Metastasio), Sinigal, 1761 [incl. music not by Boroni]
La moda (dg, P. Cipretti), Turin, 1761, rev. Venice, 1769; *D-Dlb*, *I-MOe*
L'amore in musica (dg, ? F. Griselini, after his La Reginella, o La virtuosa di musica), Venice, S Moisè, 15 Oct 1763, *A-Wn*, *D-Dlb*, *Wa*, *F-Pn*, *I-Fc*, *MOe*, *Nc*, *P-La*
La pupilla rapita (dg), Venice, S Moisè, aut. 1763, collab. S. Laurenti
Sofonisba (dramma per musica, M. Verazzi), Venice, S Salvatore, Ascension 1764, *D-Dlb*, *P-La*
Siroe (dramma per musica, Metastasio), Venice, S Salvatore, 1764, *D-Dlb*
Le villeggiatrici ridicole (dramma comico, A. Bianchi), Venice, S Cassiano, aut. 1765
La notte critica (dg, C. Goldoni), Venice, S Cassiano, carn. 1766, *D-Dlb*, *P-La*
Artaserse (dramma per musica, Metastasio), Prague, Kotzen, Jan 1767, *D-Dlb*
Didone (dramma per musica, Metastasio), Prague, Kotzen, carn. 1768, *Dlb*
Il carnovale (dg, P. Chiari), Dresden, Hof, 1769, *D-Dlb*, *P-La*
Le orfane svizzere (dg, Chiari), Venice, S Moisè, aut. 1770, *D-Dlb*, *F-Pn*
Le contadine furlane (dg, Chiari), Venice, S Moisè, carn. 1771, *Dlb*
Le déserteur; L'amour fraternel; Zémire et Azor (opéras comiques), Stuttgart, 1774–5
L'isola disabitata (int, Metastasio), ?Stuttgart, 31 Dec 1775, *D-B*, *Mbs*, *Rtt*
Enea ne Lazio (dramma per musica, V. A. Cigna-Santi), Rome, Argentina, carn. 1778, ov. *D-Hs*, *I-Rdp*

*

DBI (S. Simonetti); *GerberL*
J. Sittard: *Zur Geschichte der Musik und des Theaters am Württembergischen Hofe* (Stuttgart, 1890–91)
DENNIS LIBBY, JAMES L. JACKMAN

Borosini, Antonio (*b* Venice or Modena, *c*1655; *d* Vienna, after 1721). Italian tenor. He sang at St Mark's, Venice, 1679–87, then moved to the ducal chapel at Modena, singing in oratorios and at the Teatro Fontanelli (1690, Legrenzi's *Eteocle e Polinice*) and in Parma and Reggio Emilia. In 1688 he was released at the request of the Elector of Hanover to sing in the première of Steffani's *Henrico Leone* (30 Jan 1689); he returned to Hanover for Carnival 1696. He was appointed to the imperial court at Vienna in 1692 and retired in 1711 (or 1721, according to J. G. Walther's *Musicalisches Lexicon*, Leipzig, 1732). He sang at the San Bartolomeo, Naples (1700, 1706–7), in Turin (1698, 1702), in Venice (1704–7, in serenatas and operas by C. F. Pollarolo and Caldara), in Genoa (1691, 1705, Caldara's *Arminio*) and at Pratolino (1707, Parti's *Dionisio*). His last theatrical appearance may have been in Vienna, in Conti's *Alba Cornelia* (1714). He was generally cast in heroic and solemn characters such as kings or military leaders. He was also a composer; some arias are extant (in *I-MOe*).

CARLO VITALI

Borosini, Francesco (*b* Modena, *c*1690; *d* after 1747). Italian tenor, son of Antonio Borosini. A pupil of his father, he sang in Reggio in Ballarotti's *Ottaviano in Sicilia* (1692), and probably made his true début in Lotti's *Il vincitor generoso* at Venice (1708). He was engaged for the imperial court at Vienna from 1712 to 1731, and sang there in oratorios and a number of operas by Fux, the first (*Orfeo ed Euridice*) in 1715, and Conti. He was in the famous production of Fux's *Costanza e fortezza* in Prague (1723), and was for a time co-director of the Kärntnertortheater in Vienna. He sang the title role in Gasparini's *Bajazet* (1719, Reggio), and appeared at Modena (1720) and Parma (1729). He made his London début as Bajazet in Handel's *Tamerlano* at the King's Theatre (1724); it has been suggested that he collaborated in Handel's treatment of this subject. Borosini sang Sextus (a soprano part rewritten with new music) in *Giulio Cesare* and was the original Grimoaldo in *Rodelinda* (1725); he also appeared in Ariosti's *Artaserse* and *Dario* and the Vinci-Orlandini *Elpidia*. He returned in 1747 to sing in Paradies's *Fetonte* and Terradellas's *Bellerofonte*.

Borosini was the first great Italian tenor to sing in London. Quantz called him a splendid singer and a fine actor, with a voice 'ausserordentlich biegsam und lebhaft'. The parts Handel composed for him were of exceptional quality and prominence, especially Bajazet, which has a compass of two octaves (*A* to *a'*) and requires a wide range of expression and dramatic power. Gasparini's extend down to *G*; Fux's parts for him are notated in the bass clef. He excelled in a forceful style of singing, with wide leaps and energetic declamation.

His wife Rosa Borosini, née d'Ambreville (*b* Modena, *c*1693; *d* after 1740), a soprano, sang in opera at Modena (1713–14, 1717, 1720), Venice (1715–16), Mantua (1718), Turin (1719) and in Fux's *Costanza e fortezza* in Prague. She was engaged at Vienna, 1721–40, as was her sister Anna (wife of the cellist Giovanni Perroni), who also sang at Bologna (1711), Modena (1713), Venice (1714, 1726) and Milan (1728). Both singers sang in Vivaldi's operatic undertakings in Venice and Mantua. Eleonora Borosini, a singer active at Innsbruck, Düsseldorf and Mannheim (1714–23), was not related to Rosa or Anna but may have been related to Antonio.

*

E. J. Luin: 'Antonio e Francesco Borosini, due celebri cantanti del XVIIo secolo', *RMI*, xxxix (1932), 41–5
R. Strohm: 'Francesco Gasparini, le sue opere tarde e G. F. Händel', *Francesco Gasparini (1661–1727): Camaiore 1978*, 71–83; Eng. trans. in *Essays on Handel and Italian Opera* (Cambridge, 1985), 80–92
WINTON DEAN

Børresen, (Aksel Ejnar) Hakon (*b* Copenhagen, 2 June 1876; *d* Copenhagen, 6 Oct 1954). Danish composer. He was a pupil of Johan Svendsen, who greatly influenced him; he also studied in Germany and France. His confident sense of musical form and balanced orchestration eventually made him the principal Danish successor of Svendsen. A lyrical, eclectic approach marked most of his later instrumental music as well as his stage works. Partly influenced by the one-act operas of Strauss and of the *verismo* composers, his conversational opera *Den kongelige gaest* (S. Leopold, after H. Pontoppidan; Copenhagen, Kongelige Teater, 1919) has a secure scenic layout, vocally idiomatic declamation and an accompaniment that constantly carries the work forwards – qualities which made the piece an immediate success and have established it as one of the most frequently performed Danish operas of the century. His second opera, *Kaddara* (C. M. Normann-Hansen; Copenhagen, Kongelige Teater, 1921), on a theme from Greenland, did not achieve the same popularity; the rest of his dramatic compositions are less substantial.

*

G. Hetsch: 'Den kongelige gaest', *Musik* (1919), 163–5
G. Hauch: 'En opera om Grønland og eskimoerne', *Ord och bild* (1921), 381–4
NIELS MARTIN JENSEN

Borri, Carlo. *See* BORZIO, CARLO.

Bortnyansky, Dmitry Stepanovich (*b* Glukhov, Ukraine, 1751; *d* St Petersburg, 28 Sept/10 Oct 1825). Russian composer. He was best known for his *a cappella* church music. His career as an opera composer fell into two distinct phases. The earlier pertained to his apprentice period in Italy (1769–79), where he was sent after distinguishing himself as a boy member of the court chapel choir (then directed by Galuppi, with whom he must have studied). Of his three Italian *opere serie*, all produced between 1776 and 1778, *Creonte* (set to a revision of Coltellini's *Antigone*, first set by Traetta for St Petersburg) is lost and only *Alcide* has been published. The libretto of *Alcide* is an anonymously revised and expanded version of Metastasio's *Alcide al bivio* (1760, first set by Hasse), originally a one-act *festa teatrale*. Even in its three-act *opera seria* form this moralizing fable of choice between pleasure and duty retains the character of a pageant with an abundance of choruses. Bortnyansky's third Italian opera, *Quinto Fabio*, is set to a revision of a libretto by Zeno drawn from the history of the Samnite Wars. The score, faithful to the older tradition of *opera seria*, consists almost entirely of arias (the only ensembles are two duets), with occasional accompanied recitatives.

On his return to Russia Bortnyansky entered the service of the Crown Prince Paul, who as Paul I promoted him to the directorship of the imperial court chapel choir in 1796. His second group of operas consists of three *opéras comiques*, performed (by casts of willing courtiers) within a single year at Prince Paul's suburban residences at Gatchina and Pavlovsk. The non-professional circumstances decreed a simple style: these are 'little operas with airs and couplets', as one of the participants, Prince Ivan Dolgorukov, described them in his memoirs (published posthumously, 1916). Indeed, the earliest of them, *La fête du seigneur*, according to its title-page a *comédie mêlée d'aires et des balets* performed in the summer of 1786 on the prince's name-day, was nothing but an adaptation by Count G. I. Chernïshev, one of the prince's retainers, of the prototype of the genre, Charles Favart's *Annette et Lubin*. The rest were written to original French librettos by the prince's Swiss secretary and tutor François-Hermann Lafermière, who was in charge of entertainments at the so-called 'little court'.

The subject of *Le faucon* was adapted from Boccaccio via Sedaine; that of *Le fils-rival, ou La moderne Stratonice* is a sentimental love-triangle inspired by the story of Don Carlos (tenor in the opera), who loved the consort of his father, Philip II of Spain (Don Pedro in the opera; bass). (This has given rise to some bibliographical confusion over a phantom 'lost' opera by Bortnyansky called *Don Carlos*.) Within the constraints of the genre, Bortnyansky managed some very affecting music, particularly Don Carlos's Act 1 aria, 'O nuit, redouble tes ombres' (ed. in Ginzburg 1968), with atmospheric clarinet obbligato. Tchaikovsky, who edited Bortnyansky's sacred music, quoted the overture to *Le fils-rival* in his neo-classical *divertissement* in *The Queen of Spades*.

See also FAUCON, LE.

Creonte (dramma per musica, 2, after M. Coltellini: *Antigone*), Venice, S Benedetto, 26 Nov 1776
Quinto Fabio (dramma serio, 3, after A. Zeno: *Lucio vero*), Modena, Ducal, 26 Dec 1778, *RU-Mcm*
Alcide (dramma per musica, 3, after P. Metastasio: *Alcide al bivio*), Venice, 1778, *GB-Lbl*; ed. M. Berdennikov (Kiev, 1985)
La fête du seigneur (comédie mêlée d'aires et des balets, 1, G. I. Chernïshev, after C.-S. Favart: *Annette et Lubin*), Pavlovsk Palace, sum. 1786, *SPia*; 12 nos. in *Muzïkal'noye nasledstvo*, iii (Moscow, 1970), 411–57 [music suppl.]
Le faucon (oc, 3, F.-H. Lafermière, after M.-J. Sedaine), Gatchina

Palace, 11/22 Oct 1786, *GB-Lbl*, *RU-SPit*, *SPtob*; ed. A. Rozanov (Moscow, 1975); excerpts in Ginzburg (1968)
Le fils-rival, ou La moderne Stratonice (oc, 3, Lafermière), Pavlovsk Palace, 11/22 Oct 1787, *GB-Lbl*, *RU-SPit*, *SPtob*; excerpts in Ginzburg (1968)

*

A. S. Rabinovich: *Russkaya opera do Glinki* [Russian Opera Before Glinka] (Moscow, 1948)
R.-A. Mooser: *Annales de la musique et des musiciens en Russie au XVIIIme siècle*, ii (Geneva, 1951)
D. Lehmann: *Russlands Oper und Singspiel in der zweiten Hälfte des 18. Jahrhunderts* (Leipzig, 1958)
G. R. Seaman: 'D. S. Bortnyansky (1751–1825)', *MR*, xxi (1960), 106–13
S. L. Ginzburg: *Istoriya russkoy muzïki v notnïkh obraztsakh* [History of Russian Music in Examples], i (Moscow, 2/1968), 194–232, 489–90
A. Rozanov: '"Prazdnestvo sen'yora", opera D. S. Bortnyanskogo' [Bortnyansky's Opera *La fête du seigneur*], *Muzïkal'noye nasledstvo*, iii (Moscow, 1970), 9–27
——: Commentary to *Le faucon*, Pamyatniki russkogo muzïkal'nogo iskusstva [Monuments of Russian Art Music], v (Moscow, 1975)
——: 'Frants German Laferm'yer, librettist D. S. Bortnyanskogo', *Muzïkal'noye nasledstvo*, iv (Moscow, 1976)
——: *Muzïkal'nïy Pavlovsk* (Leningrad, 1978)
M. Rïtsareva: *Kompozitor D. Bortnyansky: zhizn' i tvorchestvo* (Leningrad, 1979)
Yu. Keldïsh: 'D. S. Bortnyansky', *Istoriya russkoy muzïki v desyati tomakh* [The History of Russian Music in Ten Volumes], iii (Moscow, 1985), 161–93 RICHARD TARUSKIN

Bortolotti, Mauro (*b* Narni, Terni, 26 Nov 1926). Italian composer. He studied at the Conservatorio S Cecilia, Rome, where Petrassi was his composition teacher. He also attended courses at Darmstadt (1957–68), which aroused his interest in avant-garde composition. He was one of the founders of the Nuova Consonanza association in Rome in 1960, and from 1968 he worked with Pietro Grossi at the electronic music studios in Florence.

Neither of Bortolotti's theatrical works is a straightforward opera. The first, *E tu?* (1971–3; 1, A. Giuliani, S. Mallarmé and A. Porta; unperf., unpubd), for soprano and chamber orchestra, is a 'non-drama', with no action, centred on a single female character who lives in total, endured solitude. The second is the one-act 'letturazione' *Berryman* to words by the American poet John Berryman, for soprano, bass, two speakers, female dancer, chamber ensemble and tape (Rome, Spaziozero, 3 April 1981; unpubd). The texts centre on three themes: the poet's vitality, his rebellion and his profound resentment of his father's suicide (paradoxically, since the poet also eventually killed himself); his relationship with music is expressed in his 'Beethoven Triumphant', in which he addresses the composer in an imaginary dialogue. In both these works Bortolotti shows his links with the language of the postwar theatrical and musical avant garde, which place him among the many post-Darmstadt composers.

*

G. Zaccaro: 'Profilo di giovani musicisti: Mauro Bortolotti', *Avanti!* (8 March 1962)
A. M. Bonisconti: '*Contre 2* di Mauro Bortolotti', *Il Veltro*, xi (1967), 320–3
S. Ragni: 'Incontro con Mauro Bortolotti', *La Nazione* [Perugia] (21 Dec 1974)
M. Bortolotti and E. Valente: record notes, *Gli archi di Mauro Bortolotti* (Edipan PAN PRC S20, 1986) RAFFAELE POZZI

Börtz, Daniel (*b* Hässleholm, 8 Aug 1943). Swedish composer. He studied composition privately with Hilding Rosenberg and with Karl-Birger Blomdahl and Ingvar Lidholm at the Stockholm Musikhögslkolan, as well as electronic music at the University of Utrecht. During the 1970s he composed two church operas (the second written for the 600th anniversary of St Bridget at Lund Cathedral) and a chamber opera, written for choir and double orchestra for university performance; but it was not until 1991 that he won a substantial success on the operatic stage when his two-act opera *Backanterna*, after Euripides, was given at the Stockholm Opera, with Ingmar Bergman as director. This opera, the story of the misfortune of the last great matriarchy, was written on Bergman's initiative, and designed to show the foolishness of all kinds of fundamentalism.

Muren–Vägen–Ordet [The Wall, the Way, the Word], 1971–2 (church op, 3, B. V. Wall), unperf.
Den heliga Birgittas död och mottagande i himlen [The Death of St Bridget and her Acceptance in Heaven] (church op, 2, Wall), Lund, 7 Oct 1973
Landskab med flod [Landscape with a River] (chamber op, 2, J. Ljungdahl, after H. Hesse: *Siddharta*), U. of Århus, 1974
Backanterna [The Bacchantes] (2, J. Stolpe and G. O. Eriksson, after Euripides), Stockholm, Kungliga, 2 Nov 1991 ROLF HAGLUND

Borzio [Bortio, Borri], **Carlo** (*b* Lodi, nr Milan; *fl* *c*1656–76). Italian composer. He was a member of the clergy and *maestro di cappella* at Lodi. He collaborated with Paolo Magni on *Gratitudine umana*, to a libretto by Carlo Maria Maggi, which was first given at the private theatre of Count Vitaliano Borromeo on Isola Bella, Lake Maggiore, in December 1670; it was then performed at the Teatro Regio, Milan, in 1675 as *Affari ed amori*. Fragments of the music survive (*I-IBborromeo*), as does the complete libretto (*Gu*, *Mb*, *Mc*, *Rn*). Borzio composed for Lodi a *favola boschereccia*, *Il Narciso* (scores in *IBborromeo*, *Rvat*, *Vnm*), to a libretto by the classicist poet Francesco de Lemene, who was also from Lodi; it was given on 29 September 1676. Borzio was a friend of Lemene and about 1656 had taken part (in the role of a maidservant) in the performance of improvised comedies in the poet's house. *Il Narciso* was also given a successful performance in the circle of Queen Christina of Sweden (Rome, March 1679), and was later revived at Pietra Bianca near Naples (?February 1682) and at the Teatro Rangoni in Cremona (12 February 1683). The music includes a wealth of short, rhythmically regular arioso passages and a remarkable number of arias, justified by the opera's pastoral theme. Borzio also composed oratorios for the Philippine Congregation and a *Dialogo pastorale* to texts by Lemene.

*

F. de Lemene: *Poesie diverse* (Milan and Parma, 1698–9), i, 2ff, 174ff; ii
C. M. Maggi: *Rime varie* (Milan, 1700), iv, 311ff; v, 41
F. S. Quadrio: *Della storia, e della ragione d'ogni poesia*, iii/2 (Milan, 1744), 512
C. Vignati: 'Francesco de Lemene e il suo epistolario inedito', *Archivio storico lombardo*, xix (1892), 345–76, 629–70, esp.357, 635
G. Barblan: 'Il teatro musicale a Milano nei secoli XVII e XVIII', *Storia di Milano*, xii (Milan, 1959), 947 LORENZO BIANCONI

Bosabalian, Luisa (*b* Marseilles, 24 March 1936). Armenian soprano. She studied in Milan, making her début in 1964 at Brussels as Micaëla. A member of the Hamburg Staatsoper (1965–73), she appeared with the company at the Metropolitan Opera in 1966 as Jenůfa. In 1967 she made her Covent Garden début as Alice Ford and sang Mimì for Scottish Opera, with whom she also sang Desdemona and Donna Elvira. She appeared at Vienna, Montreal, Düsseldorf, Munich and Aix-en-

Provence, where in 1972 she sang Countess Almaviva. Her repertory included Phaedra (*Hippolyte et Aricie*), Donna Anna, Butterfly, Manon Lescaut, Antonia and Giulietta (*Les contes d'Hoffmann*), Amelia (*Ballo*) and Ursula (*Mathis der Maler*). Her vibrant, expressive voice and acting ability were best displayed as Jenůfa, her finest role.

ELIZABETH FORBES

Boschi, Francesca. *See* VANINI, FRANCESCA.

Boschi, Giuseppe Maria (*b* ?Mantua; *fl* 1698–1744). Italian bass. He probably made his operatic début at Genoa in 1705, appeared in Venice in four operas by Gasparini and two by Lotti in 1707 and was re-engaged there in 1708–9 and 1713–14, singing in five further operas by Lotti and others by Caldara, Handel (*Agrippina*, 1709) and C. F. Pollarolo. He sang at Vicenza in 1707, Ferrara and Vienna in 1708, Bologna in 1709 and 1719, and Genoa again in 1717. He made his London début with the Queen's Theatre company in Mancini's *Idaspe fedele* (1710), sang in Giovanni Bononcini's *Etearco* and created Argante in Handel's *Rinaldo* (1711). From 1714 he was a member of the choir at St Mark's, Venice, but was allowed frequent leave of absence. He was at Dresden from 1717 to 1720, singing in Lotti's *Giove in Argo* (1717), *Ascanio* (1718) and *Teofane* (1719). Handel engaged him from 1720 to 1728 in London where he sang in all 32 operas produced by the Royal Academy, including 13 by Handel and seven each by Bononcini and Ariosti. He reappeared in Venice in 1728–9 in three operas, two by Porpora, and was still living there in 1744.

Boschi's voice had a compass of *G* to *g′* and the tessitura of a high baritone. James Miller's line 'And Boschi-like be always in a rage' points to the style in which he excelled. He generally played villains or tyrants, and the power and agility of his voice encouraged Handel to accompany many of his arias with energetic counterpoint, though the voice is often doubled by the instrumental bass. In 15 operas, Handel scarcely ever allowed him a slow aria. Lotti wrote very similarly for him in *Teofane*. He was married, probably about 1698, to the contralto Francesca Vanini.

WINTON DEAN

Bose, Hans-Jürgen von (*b* Munich, 24 Dec 1953). German composer. He studied with Hans Ulrich Engelmann at the Frankfurt Musikhochschule from 1972 and received the Berlin Arts Prize in 1977 and a Villa-Massimo scholarship in 1980. He became a member of the Berlin Akademie der Künste in 1986 and of the Bavarian Academy of Arts three years later. During his years of study he produced his first stage works: *Blutbund* (composed 1974), derived from a shadow play, and *Das Diplom* (composed 1975), after Pirandello. The premières established Bose in Germany as a young composer with distinct theatrical flair; the ballet *Die Nacht aus Blei* (1981) further increased his dramatic range. In these scores and all the vocal and instrumental music leading up to his first full-length opera, *Die Leiden des jungen Werthers* (composed 1984), Bose established an individual, highly crafted style, commanding a wide vocal and expressive range and, as with the music of his contemporary Rihm, owing no obvious allegiance to any distinct school of composition. In his operatic version of James Purdy's novel *63: Dream Palace* for the 1990 Munich Biennale, however, Bose's style became much more heterogeneous, and showed the influence of rock and jazz styles. While the matrix of his music retained its expressive potency, and continued to serve as the dramatic anchor for the opera, the forays into music-hall numbers and pop routines gave its surface a much busier and perhaps less coherent texture. In the early 1990s Bose began work on a treatment of the Medea story.

Blutbund, 1974 (1, W. Boehlich, after R. del Valle-Inclan), Hamburg, Staatsoper, 8 June 1977

Das Diplom, 1975 (comic op, 1, G. Richert, after L. Pirandello), Ulm, Ulmer, 26 Nov 1976

Die Leiden des jungen Werthers, 1984 (lyric scenes, 2 pts, int, F. Sanjust and Bose, after J. W. von Goethe), Schwetzingen, 30 April 1986

Chimäre (musical scenes, after F. García Lorca), Aachen, Städtische Bühnen, 11 June 1986

63: Dream Palace (11 scenes, Bose, after J. Purdy), Munich, Carl-Orff-Saal, 6 May 1990

*

W. Burde: 'Young Composers in the Federal Republic of Germany: the Search for a New Identity', *CMc*, nos.37–8 (1984), 177–82

ANDREW CLEMENTS

Bosello, Anna. *See* MORICHELLI, ANNA.

Bosetti [von Flick], **Hermine** (*b* Vienna, 28 Sept 1875; *d* Hohenrain, Upper Bavaria, 1 May 1936). Austrian soprano. She studied in Vienna, making her début in 1898 in Wiesbaden as Aennchen (*Der Freischütz*). She sang in the première of Wolf-Ferrari's *I quattro rusteghi* (1906) at the Munich Hofoper, where she was engaged from 1901 until her retirement in 1924. She first sang at Covent Garden in 1905 as Rosina and Norina, returning in 1907 for Mařenka, Eva, both Aennchen and Agathe, and in 1913 for Octavian. A stylish singer with a phenomenal coloratura technique, she excelled in roles such as Marie (*La fille du régiment*) and Zerbinetta, which she sang in the first London performance of *Ariadne auf Naxos*, at Her Majesty's Theatre (1913).

ELIZABETH FORBES

Bosio, Angiolina (*b* Turin, 22 Aug 1830; *d* St Petersburg, 1/13 April 1859). Italian soprano. She studied in Milan, making her début there in 1846 as Lucrezia in *I due Foscari*. Two years later she appeared for the first time in Paris, again as Lucrezia, and then went on an extended tour of North America. She made her London début in 1852 at Covent Garden as Adina (*L'elisir d'amore*). The following year she sang Gilda in the first London performance of *Rigoletto*. Other Verdi operas in which she appeared were *Ernani*, *Luisa Miller*, *Il trovatore* and *La traviata*. Engaged for the winter season of 1855–6 in St Petersburg at a salary of 100 000 francs, she died suddenly in Russia at the age of 28.

ELIZABETH FORBES

Boskovsky, Willi (*b* Vienna, 16 June 1909; *d* Visp, Switzerland, 21 April 1991). Austrian conductor and violinist. He studied at the Vienna Academy and in 1932 joined the Vienna PO. Appointed one of four leaders in 1939, he remained at the front desk of this and the Vienna Staatsoper orchestra until 1971, as well as leading his own chamber groups. He conducted the annual Vienna New Year's Day concert, 1954–79, as well as the Vienna Strauss Orchestra, which he formed in 1969. He was unsurpassed in his intuitive feeling for the music of Johann Strauss and his contemporaries, and was also much admired in Mozart, whose complete dance music he recorded. He made distinctive operetta recordings including *Die Fledermaus* (1973), Zeller's *Der Vogelhändler* (1975) and Lehár's *Paganini* (1978). He received the Mozart Medal from both Salzburg and Vienna, and the Austrian Ehrenkreuz.

LESLIE EAST, NOËL GOODWIN

Bosnia and Hercegovina. Part of the former republic of Yugoslavia. For discussion of operatic activity *see* SARAJEVO.

Bossi, (Rinaldo) Renzo (*b* Como, 9 April 1883; *d* Milan, 2 April 1965). Italian composer. After studying in Leipzig (1902–4) he became an opera conductor, later teaching composition in Parma, Milan and Venice. When young he associated himself with progressive trends: in 1911 he was a member of Bastianelli's short-lived pressure group known as I Cinque Italiani, and in some works he rejected thematicism in favour of an instinctive, free-ranging succession of musical images. But his modernity seldom went beyond the free use of 9th and 11th chords, progressions derived from the whole-tone scale, frequent unrelated triads and 7ths and occasional excursions into simple bitonality. At his best he could use such resources with pungent wit, reinforced by vivid, kaleidoscopic instrumentation.

None of Bossi's theatre works won as lasting a success as, for example, his amusing tone poem *Pinocchio* (1921–2, revised 1935), and his longer operas have been largely ignored, even in Italy. *Nell'anno mille* (to a libretto drafted but not completed by Pascoli) nevertheless has a striking and unusual subject, the widely held belief that the world was about to end in AD 1000. Bossi achieved greater public recognition with his one-act operas, initially with the luridly 'veristic' *Passa la ronda!*, and more notably with *Volpino il calderaio*. This most successful of his stage works parallels Wolf-Ferrari's *Sly* in using a free adaptation of the Induction to Shakespeare's *The Taming of the Shrew* as the starting-point for a very different story. But whereas Wolf-Ferrari's opera ends in grim tragedy, Bossi's is a comedy full of lively caricatural touches, in a musical idiom which shares some of the best qualities of *Pinocchio*.

Bossi's father, Marco Enrico Bossi (1861–1925), was an organist and composer, whose few completed operas were but a minor branch of his large output; his *Il veggente* (1, G. Macchi, Milan, Dal Verme, 4 June 1890; rev. 1906 as *Il viandante*) is in effect a religious-dramatic cantata to which stage presentation adds little.

Rosa rossa op.18, 1910 (1, Bossi, after O. Wilde: *The Nightingale and the Rose*), Italian Radio, 9 Aug 1938; staged Parma, Regio, 9 Jan 1940

Passa la ronda! op.20, 1913 (1, L. Orsini, after R. Francheville), Milan, Lirico, 3 March 1919

Nell'anno mille op.25, 1915–16, later rev. (prol., 3 scenes, G. Pascoli and Orsini), RAI, 1956

Volpino il calderaio op.32, 1923 (1, Orsini, after W. Shakespeare: *The Taming of the Shrew*), Milan, Carcano, 13 Nov 1925

I commedianti alla corte di Francia op.37, 1930 (3, G. Adami), unperf.

Il principe felice op.52, 1950 (radio op, 1, Bossi, after Wilde: *The Happy Prince*), RAI, 11 Oct 1951

La crociata degli innocenti op.53, ?early 1950s (poema francescano in 3 sequenze e 4 quadri, E. Possenti, after G. d'Annunzio's film scenario), RAI, 1962

*

B. Hogarth: 'A Composer of Young Italy: Renzo Bossi', *Scottish Music Magazine*, xii (1930–31), 42–3

A. Ferloni: *Note biografico-critiche su Renzo Bossi: guida alla commedia lirica 'Volpino il calderaio'* (Milan, 1933)

S. Pintacuda: *Renzo Bossi* (Milan, 1955)

A. Cataldo: 'Un dramma musicale di Pascoli e Renzo Bossi', *La Scala*, no.78 (May 1956), pp.56–8 [on *Nell'anno mille*]

JOHN C. G. WATERHOUSE

Bostel, Lucas von (*b* Hamburg, 11 Oct 1649; *d* Hamburg, 15 July 1716). German librettist. He studied law at Heidelberg and Leiden and in 1674 undertook an educational tour of Europe lasting five years. On his return to Hamburg he became connected with the newly founded opera, where his first libretto, *Vespasianus*, was performed in 1681 with music by J. W. Franck, for whom he wrote another four texts; he also provided texts for operas by Förtsch and Strungk. In 1687 he became Syndicus to Hamburg, on whose behalf he took part in a number of diplomatic missions. In 1709 he was elected mayor of Hamburg.

Bostel was the most important poet in the early years of the Hamburg opera: his texts are superior in every way to the librettos of C. Richter, Elmenhorst and Förtsch. *Cara Mustapha* is a landmark in the first decade of the Hamburg opera; in it Bostel realized an effective, clear development of the plot through highly imaginative language. He had a preference for the alexandrines typical of 17th-century French poetry and employed dramatic nuances of language, especially in the frequent alterations of rhythm contributing to the dramatic climaxes of many scenes. *Crösus* retained its popularity longer than almost any other libretto written during the first decades of the Hamburg opera: as well as the initial setting by Förtsch there are two by Keiser (the second as late as 1730) and an adaptation for the Brunswick court opera with music by Schürmann.

Vespasianus, J. W. Franck, 1681; *Attila*, Franck, 1682; *Diocletianus*, Franck, 1682; *Theseus*, Strungk, 1683; *Crösus*, Förtsch, 1684 (Keiser, 1710, 1730); *Das unmöglichste Ding*, Förtsch, 1684; *Der glückliche Gross-Verzier Cara Mustapha*, Franck, 1686; *Der unglückliche Cara Mustapha*, Franck, 1686

*

H. C. Wolff: *Die Barockoper in Hamburg (1678–1738)* (Wolfenbüttel, 1957)

W. Braun: *Vom Remter zum Gänsemarkt: aus der Frühgeschichte der alten Hamburger Oper (1677–1697)* (Saarbrücken, 1987)

——: *Johann Wolfgang Franck, Hamburger Opernarien im szenischen Kontext* (Saarbrücken, 1988) GEORGE J. BUELOW

Boston. American city, capital of Massachusetts, founded in 1630. Opera first came to Boston in the late 18th century. A Puritanical 'Act to Prevent Stage Plays and Other Theatrical Entertainments' was law between 1750 and 1799, so performances were restricted to 'readings' of ballad operas. Perhaps the first of these was a one-man performance of *The Beggar's Opera* in 1769 in which James Juhan sang all the airs and impersonated all the characters.

By 1830 Boston, like most other major American cities, regularly received touring companies from Italy and Germany and was a prominent stopping-place for travelling celebrities; in 1854 Grisi and Mario presented a season of eight operas conducted by Arditi. In 1883 the Metropolitan company made its first visit to Boston, a tradition that continued, with occasional interruptions, for the next century. Other regular visitors were the Mapleson, Savage and Hammerstein companies.

The city's first important resident company was the ambitious Boston Opera Company, founded by Henry Russell and funded by the department-store magnate Eben D. Jordan jr; the original plan was for it to share productions and singers with the Metropolitan and companies in Chicago and Philadelphia. For the new company Jordan built the Boston Opera House, a 2700-seat theatre with 54 boxes designed by Parkman B. Haven, with acoustical advice from Wallace Clement Sabine, who had been responsible for the success of Symphony Hall.

The Boston Opera's first season opened on 8 November 1909, when Lillian Nordica appeared in the title role of *La Gioconda*. During its six seasons the company performed six nights a week between early November and the end of March, and in the first year there was also an extensive touring schedule (Pittsburgh, Chicago, St Louis, Indianapolis, Cincinnati, Springfield, Providence and New Haven); in 1914 it travelled to Paris for two months, an adventure that precipitated its bankruptcy. Felix Weingartner was the most importantt of the company's conductors, and among the singers who appeared were Alda, Baklanov, Boninsegna, Bori, Clément, Constantino, Dalmorès, Destinn, Eames, Fremstad, Hempel, Lipkowska, Matzenauer, Melba, Mardones, Slezak, Tetrazzini, Urlus and Zenatello, a mainstay of the house. Garden and Vanni-Marcoux ran foul of the mayor and the vice squad because of the enthusiastic realism of their performance of the second act of *Tosca*. After many vicissitudes the company declared bankruptcy in 1915, although the impresario Max Rabinoff was able to mount two brief seasons of a successor, the Boston Grand Opera Company, in 1916 and 1917. Thereafter there were annual tour seasons by the Chicago Opera between 1917 and 1932, and in this period and later Fortune Gallo's touring San Carlo Opera and Salmaggi's Popular Opera Company were also regular visitors; the final visit of the San Carlo was in 1963.

The next important attempt to found a resident company was made by Boris Goldovsky in 1946; the New England Opera Theater was an outgrowth of his educational activities at the New England Conservatory and at Tanglewood. Perhaps its most impressive achievement was the American première of *Les Troyens* in 1955. Goldovsky's successor was his former student Sarah Caldwell, whose prodigious personality dominated the operatic scene in Boston for over 30 years, beginning in 1958, the year that the Boston Opera House was demolished. Since then the city has had no proper facility for operatic performance.

Caldwell began on the Boston Common with an outdoor production of Offenbach's *Le voyage dans la lune* and then moved into a cinema for *La bohème*. Over the decades her Boston Opera Group and its successor, the Opera Company of Boston, performed in a variety of plausible and implausible spaces, including the gymnasium of Tufts University and the field house at the Massachusetts Institute of Technology; in 1978 the company purchased the old B. F. Keith Memorial Theater, a vaudeville palace seating 2604 now known as the Opera House (it had been built in 1925 on the site of the Boston Theater, where Mahler had conducted *Don Giovanni* and Ternina had sung Tosca). The stage is only 13 metres deep, though a tiled room remains in place beneath it for the comfort of trained seals.

Caldwell's company survived many financial and administrative perils to present the world premières of works by Gunther Schuller and others and the American premières of operas by Nono, Prokofiev, Rameau, Schoenberg, Sessions, Tippett and Zimmermann. In 1987 there was also a three-week festival of 'Making Music Together' with Soviet musicians that included the American première of Shchedrin's *Dead Souls*. The artistic standards of the Caldwell era fluctuated wildly, often within the same performance, but there was never a dull moment. Caldwell herself usually both conducted and staged the works in a flamboyant style, and she was far in advance of others in America in preferring to perform operas uncut, in the composers' original versions, or in musicologically significant variants (the American première of the original orchestration of *Boris Godunov*, the full *Don Carlos* in French, the alternative third-act finale in *Otello*, the original version of *Madama Butterfly*). While Caldwell was most famous for her adventurous and exploratory work, she also excelled in her detailed and loving re-examination of the traditional repertory.

From 1962 until her retirement Beverly Sills was the undisputed diva of the company, singing many roles in Boston for the first time, with the bass Donald Gramm as a frequent colleague and partner. In later years Shirley Verrett often appeared with the company, although Caldwell also began promoting younger American singers. Among the internationally prominent singers who appeared with the company were Barstow, Crespin, Los Angeles, Domingo, Ewing, Hendricks, Horne, McCracken, Tebaldi, Schoeffler, Sutherland and Vinay.

In 1975 a number of the city's smaller companies joined to form the Boston Lyric Opera, the initial purpose of which was to provide early performance opportunities for resident singers, many of whom had been trained at local conservatories and universities. Under the direction of John Balme, the Lyric in 1982 gave the city its first *Ring* cycle in 40 years and built up an ambitious but erratic artistic record. In 1989 it acquired a new director, Justin Moss, and artistic adviser, Richard Gaddes, who with a view to dominating the local scene formulated a new and more professionalized agenda for its new home in the Majestic Theater, a repertory theatre building recently purchased and renovated by Emerson College.

Meanwhile some of the most significant operatic work in the city was being undertaken by the director Peter Sellars and the conductor Craig Smith, working largely with locally based singers. Their first collaboration was on Handel's *Saul* in 1981; it continued with an unprecedented 40-performance run of *Orlando* at the American Repertory Theater. Their most important work in the 1980s came in highly controversial, vividly politicized and emotionally immediate updated productions of Handel's *Giulio Cesare in Egitto* and the cycle of Mozart-Da Ponte operas. (These were initially rehearsed in Boston but the performances took place under the auspices of the Pepsico Summerfare festival in Purchase, New York.) After the productions toured Europe, where they were taped for international television distribution, the Boston Opera Theater was formed by some former allies of Caldwell's to present their own and others' innovatory work; the company opened in 1991 in the central Colonial Theater, a house best known for pre-Broadway productions, with a revival of *Le nozze di Figaro*.

*

E. Tompkins: *History of the Boston Theatre* (Boston and New York, 1908)

F. W. Jackson: *Monograph of the Boston Opera House* (Boston, 1909)

Q. Eaton: *The Boston Opera Company* (Boston, 1965)

RICHARD DYER

Boteler [Botoler], **Charlotte.** *See* BUTLER, CHARLOTTE.

Bottacchiari, Ugo (*b* Castelraimondo, Macerata, 10 March 1879; *d* Como, 17 March 1944). Italian composer. He studied at the Pesaro Conservatory for four years with Mascagni, who considered him his favourite student. When he was 20 years old he wrote his first opera, *L'ombra*, adapted from a Bavarian legend. It tells the story of a young girl, Margherita, who has been buried in a foreign land. Her ghost returns to her lover, Wolfgang, at night in the form of a shadow. Margherita reminds Wolfgang that the only worthy thing to look for is love, but when he tries to embrace her the shadow vanishes into the night as an invisible children's chorus chants Margherita's warning, 'Un'ora è spesso tutto'. This haunting *verismo* opera achieved overnight fame for Bottacchiari at its première, and became a perennial favourite with the Italian critics and public; he continued to follow the *verismo* school in his other operas. In 1935 his last opera, *L'uragano*, was awarded first prize in a national opera competition sponsored by the Acadamy of Italy.

L'ombra (1, C. Giorgieri-Conti), Macerata, Lauro Rossi, 12 Nov 1899
Il paradiso della signore (3, A. Lanzoni), Figline Valdarno, Garibaldi, 21 Dec 1920
Severo Torelli (4, C. Zangarini), Como, Sociale, 24 Feb 1924
Le beffe dell'amore (3, A. Rossato), Como, Sociale, 6 June 1933
L'uragano (4, A. Testoni), Como, Sociale, 31 Dec 1935

MARTIN S. LIPPMAN

Bottarelli [Botarelli], **Giovanni Gualberto** (*fl* 1762–79). Italian librettist. He was house poet at the King's Theatre in London in the 1760s and 70s and author or adapter of more than 25 opera texts. A poet of the same name wrote librettos set by Graun at Berlin in the early 1740s, but whether this is the same person is doubtful. The London Bottarelli was chiefly employed in piecing together pasticcios based on frequently revived works of Goldoni, Calzabigi, Petrosellini, Pizzi and others. He also provided new librettos for J. C. Bach, including *Orione* (1763), *Zanaida* (1763), and probably *Carattaco* (1767) and *La clemenza di Scipione* (1778), as well as *Leucippo* (1764) for Mattia Vento. Among Bottarelli's more important adaptations are *Orfeo ed Euridice* (1770), based on Gluck with additional music by Bach, and a reworking of Galuppi's *Li tre amanti ridicoli* as *Il filosofo di campagna* (1768). His wife was a singer, and his son F. Bottarelli also worked at the King's Theatre as translator. CURTIS PRICE

Bottega da caffè, La. Opera by G. F. Malipiero; *see* TRE COMMEDIE GOLDONIANE.

Bottesini, Giovanni (*b* Crema, 22 Dec 1821; *d* Parma, 7 July 1889). Italian conductor and composer. His father taught him the rudiments of music at a very early age. Before he was 11 he studied the violin and appeared in public, singing in choirs and playing the timpani. In 1835, within a few weeks, he learnt enough about the double bass to obtain one of two remaining scholarships (the other was for bassoon) to study at the Milan Conservatory. His teachers there included Vaccai and Basili; he left in 1839 with a prize for solo playing. His highly successful concert début in Crema in 1849 led to many engagements in Italy and in Vienna. He was appointed principal double bass at the Teatro S Benedetto, Venice, where he met Verdi. In 1846 he went to Havana with his colleague Arditi; he was principal double bass at the Teatro Tacón, where he also conducted the première of his first opera, *Cristoforo Colombo*. Concert engagements followed, taking him to New Orleans, New York, London and Europe. He went to Mexico and St Petersburg and directed the Italian Opera in Paris in 1855 and 1857. He was musical director of the Teatro Bellini, Palermo, during the period 1861–3, and held similar appointments in Barcelona and Madrid and in Portugal.

Bottesini soon devoted an increasingly large part of his life to composing and conducting. His compositions include many virtuoso pieces for the double bass, sacred music and orchestral and chamber works. In 1870 his opera *Vinciguerra* ran for 40 performances in Paris and in January 1871 his comic opera *Alì Babà* was presented at the Lyceum Theatre, London, where he was musical director for the season. On 24 December 1871 he was in Cairo to direct the first performance of *Aida*, which was being given in honour of the opening of the Suez Canal. 1879 saw the production of his opera *Ero e Leandro* (libretto by Boito, who had intended it for his own use). Critics who thought *Ero e Leandro* a 'charming work' were less impressed by *La regina di Nepal* in 1880. The opera, they said, did not meet 'with anything like an enthusiastic reception'. However, it was not so much the music as the libretto that caused disappointment.

On 20 January 1889, after a proposal by Verdi, Bottesini was nominated director of the Parma Conservatory. He is best remembered for his contribution to the technique of the double bass.

Cristoforo Colombo (R. de Palma), Havana, Tacón, 31 Jan 1848
L'assedio di Firenze (4, F. Manetta and C. Corghi), Paris, Italien, 21 Feb 1856, vs (Milan, 1860)
Il diavolo della notte (4, L. Scalchi), Milan, S Radegonda, 18 Dec 1858, vs (Milan, 1859)
Marion Delorme (A. Ghislanzoni, after V. Hugo), Palermo, Bellini, 10 Jan 1862
Vinciguerra il bandito (1, E. Hugot and P. Renard), Monte Carlo, Casino, 22 Feb 1870, vs (Paris, 1870)
Alì Babà (comic op, 4, E. Taddei), London, Lyceum, 18 Jan 1871, vs (London, 1871)
Ero e Leandro (3, A. Boito), Turin, Regio, 11 Jan 1879, vs (Milan, 1879)
Cedar, completed Naples, 2 Oct 1880
La regina di Nepal (B. Tommassi), Turin, Regio, 26 Dec 1880

Unperf.: Azeale; Graziella; La torre de Babele; La figlia dell Angelo

*

DBI (A. Pironti)
T. G. Kaufman: *Verdi and his Major Contemporaries* (New York and London, 1990), 27–30 RODNEY SLATFORD

Bottone, Bonaventura (*b* London, 19 Sept 1950). English tenor. After studying at the RAM, he toured with Phoenix Opera (1975); he sang Arturo (*Lucia*) in Belfast, a Servant (*Capriccio*) at Glyndebourne, Bardolph for Glyndebourne Touring Opera (1976) and Auber's Masaniello at Nottingham (1977). At Wexford (1977–9) he appeared in *The Two Widows* (Smetana), *Crispino e la comare* (F. and L. Ricci) and *L'amore dei tre re*. His roles for the ENO include Cassio, Brighella, Janek and Gregor (*The Makropulos Affair*), David (*Die Meistersinger*), the Duke, Beppe and Truffaldino (*Love for Three Oranges*). His Scottish Opera roles include Jack (*The Midsummer Marriage*), Loge and Narraboth. With Opera North he has sung Váňa (*Káťa Kabanová*), Nemorino and Pedrillo, the role of his American début at Houston in 1987. That year he made his Covent Garden début as the Italian Singer (*Der Rosenkavalier*), returning as Alfred (*Die Fledermaus*) and the Italian Tenor (*Capriccio*). He sang Count Ory for the WNO in 1991. A superb actor with a strong, lyrical voice, he excels in comic roles such as Nanki-Poo (*Mikado*) and Mercury (*Orphée aux enfers*), while making a magnificent Loge. ELIZABETH FORBES

Botturini, Mattia (*b* Salò, 26 Feb 1752; *d* 1797 or later). Italian librettist. He joined those who were producing innovatory *opera seria* librettos for Venetian theatres in the 1790s. His handful of works represents a wide range of subject matter including plots taking their inspiration from earlier librettos (*Seleuco, rè di Siria* and *Merope*) and plots with exotic settings (*Gl'indiani* and *Zaira*). His *Bianca de' Rossi* is an early example of an opera based on contemporary subject matter dealing with ordinary citizens, rather than historical figures or the nobility. Both Zaira and Bianca die tragically – Zaira at the hands of her lover, who then kills himself, and Bianca in the tomb of her husband, where she has buried herself. Such tragedies mark the end of a tradition more than a century old that proscribed unhappy endings and death on stage.

Botturini's librettos contain multiple choruses, ensembles, scene-complexes and even dance (*Seleuco*) and combine vocal textures within the fluid constructions that Sografi pioneered in Venice early in the decade. Botturini carried Sografi's concept to its inevitable conclusion in *Merope*, where he combined the action ensemble with Sografi's freely alternating textures to build enormous freely constructed action pieces incorporating chorus and involving changing personnel.

all opere serie

L'apoteosi d'Ercole, Tarchi, 1790; *Seleuco, rè di Siria*, Bianchi, 1791; *Gl'indiani*, Nasolini, 1796; *Merope*, Nasolini, 1796; *Zaira*, Nasolini, 1797; *Bianca de' Rossi*, Trento, 1797

*

M. P. McClymonds: 'The Venetian Role in the Transformation of Italian Opera Seria during the 1790s', *I vicini di Mozart: Florence 1987*, 221–40 MARITA P. McCLYMONDS

Boucicault [Bourcicault, Bourciquot], **Dion** [Dionysus Lardner] (*b* Dublin, 26 Dec 1820 or 1822; *d* New York, 18 Sept 1890). Irish dramatist. Known primarily as an actor, he played regularly in New York and London from the 1850s, excelling in his depictions of Irish heroes. Though nearly all his dramatic works were adaptations, they were often brilliantly constructed. His most successful pieces were *London Assurance* (1841, produced under the pseudonym Lee Morton); *The Colleen Bawn, or The Brides of Garryowen* (1860, after G. Griffin: *The Collegians, or The Colleen Bawn*), later adapted by Boucicault and John Oxenford as the libretto for Benedict's opera *The Lily of Killarney* (1862); and *Arrah-na-Pogue* (1865). With B. N. Webster Boucicault adapted an *opéra comique* by Ambroise Thomas, *Le panier fleuri*, for London, as *The Fox and the Goose, or The Widow's Husband* (1844, Adelphi Theatre).

*

DNB (J. Knight)
J. W. Cole: *The Life and Theatrical Times of Charles Kean, F.S.A.* (London, 1860), ii, 119–32
C. E. Pascoe, ed.: 'Boucicault, Dion', *The Dramatic List* (London, 1879), 39–49
D. Cook: *Nights at the Play* (London, 1883)
'Boucicault, Dion', *Men of the Time* (London, 12/1887)
Obituary, *The Athenaeum* (27 Sept 1890)
C. V. Stanford: *Pages from an Unwritten Diary* (London, 1914), 73
M. W. Disher: *Victorian Song* (London, 1955), 100–01, 155–6
NIGEL BURTON

Boudousquié, Charles (*b* New Orleans, LA, 29 Feb 1814; *d* New Orleans, 23 Aug 1866). American impresario. He was the third and last director of the Théâtre d'Orléans, succeeding Pierre Davis, son of the theatre's founder, in about 1853. He did much to create the reputation of the theatre, which was important for its promotion of opera. In 1858 he married the French soprano Julie Calvé, who had been prima donna at the theatre (1837–46). In 1859 he left the Théâtre d'Orléans to build the French Opera House, which was formally opened on 1 December that year with Rossini's *Guillaume Tell*, in French. Under Boudousquié's brief but vigorous directorship, which saw the American première of Meyerbeer's *Dinorah* (1861, with Adelina Patti in the title role), the French Opera House quickly eclipsed the Théâtre d'Orléans as New Orleans's leading opera house. JOHN JOYCE

Bouffar [Boufflar], **Zulma (Madeleine)** (*b* Nérac, 23 May 1841; *d* Couilly-St Germain, 20 Jan 1909). French soprano. After a number of years performing in provincial France, Germany and Scandinavia, she was seen at Hamburg by Offenbach who brought her to Paris for a début at the Bouffes-Parisiens in his *Lischen et Fritzchen* (1864). Soon becoming a public favourite, over the next 12 years she created many leading roles for Offenbach (with whom she was discreetly linked amorously), including Gabrielle in *La vie parisienne* (1866) and boy roles in *Les brigands* (1869) and *Le voyage dans la lune* (1875). She created roles in the French versions of Strauss's *Indigo* (1875) and *Die Fledermaus* (1877), and in Lecocq's *Kosiki* (1876) and *La Camargo* (1878). For two years from 1891 she managed the Théâtre Ambigu-Comique. In spite of plain features, Bouffar triumphed among the saucy queens of *opéra bouffe* through dynamism, sex appeal and a strong, true singing voice. KURT GÄNZL

Bouffes-Parisiens. Company founded by Jacques Offenbach in 1855, staging light opera in Paris until 1879; *see* PARIS, §4 (vii).

Boughton, Rutland (*b* Aylesbury, 23 Jan 1878; *d* London, 25 Jan 1960). English composer and writer. He left school at 14, was apprenticed to a London concert agency, and remained musically self-taught except for a brief period with Stanford and Walford Davies at the RCM (1900–01). A desperate Grub Street existence ensued until Bantock offered him a teaching post at the Birmingham and Midland Institute (1905–11). While there he imbibed the socialism of Morris and the theories of Wagner, beginning a cycle of Arthurian music dramas with a central role for the chorus ('I … intended somehow or other to relate dramatic art to the indigenous choral art of England', he later wrote) and with the poet Reginald Buckley and the artist Christina Walshe (with whom he was living) planning a provincial festival, run as an artists' commune, to mount them. This may not have been what Bernard Shaw envisaged in *The Perfect Wagnerite*, but he could not ignore Boughton and supported him generously over the years, admitting that 'the very desperation of the enterprise has been its salvation'.

Desperate it was. Performances were given in a small hall, the Assembly Rooms, Glastonbury, with piano accompaniment, beginning in August 1914. Friends, pupils, amateurs and professionals, locals and Londoners were all involved. Boughton's own works were interspersed with revivals of operas by Gluck, Purcell, Blow and others, and around 350 performances took place before the Glastonbury Festival was wound up in 1927, partly as a result of Boughton's extramarital affairs and what was seen as the imposition of active support for the General Strike of 1926 (he was by now a member of the Communist Party). Further festivals took place during the next decade, at Stroud and Bath, but were less successful, and Boughton, who had moved to Gloucestershire, took up farming while continuing to write music and books.

The Arthurian cycle never became the core of the festival, for its last three dramas were written many years later; rather, it was *The Immortal Hour*, the centrepiece of the first festival, which made Boughton's name. His simple treatment of Celtic myth, telling a universal parable of lost love, appealed to a wide audience when Barry Jackson produced it in 1921 at the Birmingham Repertory Theatre and the following year in London, where it ran non-stop for 216 performances. Revivals in 1923, 1926 and 1932 increased this number to over 500, setting an operatic record.

Boughton is not easy to assess. His musical technique was limited and his style homespun in the extreme; yet it found resonances in his audience much as Lloyd Webber does today, for similar reasons, connected with its folk inflections, which cannot be overlooked. And if his style of community production now seems hopelessly quaint, it has to be remembered that it helped set a new model (or, as with his nativity play *Bethlehem*, revive an ancient one) without which the later achievements of Britten, Maxwell Davies and countless schoolteachers and church musicians might not have been possible.

See also IMMORTAL HOUR, THE.

first performed at Glastonbury, Assembly Rooms, unless otherwise stated

Eolf, 1901–3 (3, Boughton), unorchd, unperf.

The Chapel in Lyonesse, 1904 (dramatic scene, Boughton, after W. Morris), Aug 1914, *GB-Lbl**; later used in Galahad

The Birth of Arthur [Uther and Igraine], 1908–9 (choral drama, 2, R. Buckley and Boughton), 16 Aug 1920, *Lbl** [no.1 of the Arthurian cycle]

The Immortal Hour (music drama, 2, after F. Macleod), 26 Aug 1914, *Lbl**, vs (London, 1920)

Bethlehem (choral drama, 2, Boughton, after Coventry Nativity Play and traditional carols), Street, Crispin Hall, 28 Dec 1915, *Lbl**, vs (London, 1920)

The Round Table (music drama, prol., 3, Buckley and Boughton), 14 Aug 1916, *Lbl** [no.2 of the Arthurian cycle]

Agincourt, 1918 (dramatic scene, after W. Shakespeare: *Henry V*), 26 Aug 1924, *Lbl**, vs (London, 1926)

The Moon Maiden (choral dance, 1, after Jap. noh play, trans. M. Stopes), 23 April 1919, *Lbl**, vs (London, 1926)

Alkestis (music drama, 2, Boughton, after G. Murray's trans. of Euripides), 26 Aug 1922, *Lbl**, vs (London, 1923)

The Seraphic Vision (dramatic scene, L. Housman), 20 Aug 1924, *Lbl**

The Queen of Cornwall (music drama, 2, Boughton, after T. Hardy), 21 Aug 1924, *Lbl**, vs (London, 1926)

The Ever Young, 1928–9 (music drama, 5 scenes, Boughton), Bath, Pavilion, 9 Sept 1935, *Lbl**

The Lily Maid (music drama, 3, Boughton), Stroud, Church Room, 10 Sept 1934, *Lbl** [no.3 of the Arthurian cycle]

Galahad, 1943–4 (music drama, 4 scenes, Boughton), unperf., *Lbl** [no.4 of the Arthurian cycle]; scene ii consists of The Chapel in Lyonesse

Avalon, 1944–5 (music drama, 2, Boughton), unperf., *Lbl** [no.5 of the Arthurian cycle]

WRITINGS

Music Drama of the Future (London, 1911)
The Self-Advertisement of Rutland Boughton (London, 1911)
The Death and Resurrection of the Music Festival (London, 1913)
The Glastonbury Festival (London, 1917)
The Glastonbury Festival Movement (London, 1922)
'Festivalediction – III', *The Sackbut*, xi/5 (1930), 135–40
'The Immortal Hour', *Philharmonic Post*, iv/10 (1949), 6–10

*

Kobbé10

R. Buckley: '"The Arthurian Cycle": Notes on the Drama', *Music Student*, ix/2 (1916), 56

P. Scholes: 'Music Drama in Somerset: the Glastonbury Pilgrimage Revived', ibid, 55–6

——: 'A Talk with George Bernard Shaw', ibid, 57–60

M. Hurd: *Immortal Hour: the Life and Period of Rutland Boughton* (London, 1962)

——: 'The Glastonbury Festivals: 1914–1926', *Theatre Notebook*, xvii/2 (1963), 51–61

——: 'The Queen of Cornwall', *MT*, civ (1963), 700–01

D. H. Laurence, ed.: *George Bernard Shaw: Collected Letters* (London, 1965–88)

M. Hurd: 'Rutland Boughton, 1878–1960', *MT*, cxix (1978), 31–3

E. W. White: *A History of English Opera* (London, 1983), 392–402

M. Hurd: 'Rutland Boughton', *British Opera in Retrospect* (n.p., 1986) [pubn of the British Music Society], 85–8

STEPHEN BANFIELD

Bouhy, Jacques(-Joseph-André) (*b* Pepinster, 18 June 1848; *d* Paris, 29 Jan 1929). Belgian baritone. He studied at the Liège Conservatory and in Paris, where he made his début at the Opéra in 1871 as Méphistophélès (*Faust*). At the Opéra-Comique, where he was first heard as Mozart's Figaro (1872), he created the title role of Massenet's *Don César de Bazan* (1872) and sang Hoël in Meyerbeer's *Le pardon de Ploërmel* (1874) and Escamillo at the première of *Carmen* (1875). At the Théâtre Lyrique he took part in Massé's *Paul et Virginie* (1876) and Salvayre's *Le bravo* (1877), both first performances. In 1880 at St Petersburg he sang Méphistophélès in Gounod's *Faust* and the title role in Boito's *Mefistofele*, and in 1882 he appeared at Covent Garden in *Faust* and *Carmen*. After some years in the USA he returned to Paris to sing the High Priest in the first staged performance there of Saint-Saëns' *Samson et Dalila* (1890, Eden-Théâtre). His voice was praised by Massenet, and his rendering of the Toreador's Song always evoked the warmest applause, even at the first, unsuccessful performance of *Carmen*.

*

S. Wolff: *Un demi-siècle d'opéra-comique, 1900–1950* (Paris, 1953)

——: *L'Opéra au Palais Garnier (1875–1962)* (Paris, 1962)

ELIZABETH FORBES

Bouilly, Jean-Nicolas (*b* La Coudraye, nr Tours, 23/24 Jan 1763; *d* Paris, 25 April 1842). French librettist. He was born shortly after his father's death, but was lovingly raised by his mother and his stepfather, a lawyer and professor of natural philosophy. Though aware of the boy's talent for writing, the stepfather recommended law and Bouilly was duly presented at the bar of the Paris Parlément in 1787. The outbreak of the Revolution caused him to return to Tours, where he practised law and began to write theatre pieces. His first libretto, *Pierre le Grand*, found favour with the administration of the Opéra-Comique and with Mme Dugazon, a leading singer, who helped persuade Grétry to set it. Though the work had a successful première, its royalist sentiments later caused its banishment from the stage. Bouilly became engaged to Grétry's daughter, Antoinette, but she died of tuberculosis before the wedding could take place.

At the period of the Terror, Bouilly returned to Tours, where he became head of the Military Commission. In the course of his duties he was involved in the supposedly true incidents that formed the bases of his best-known librettos, *Léonore, ou L'amour conjugal* (set by Gaveaux, later transformed into Beethoven's *Fidelio*) and *Les deux journées* (Cherubini). In 1795 he returned to Paris, where he worked for the Committee of Public Instruction but left after three years to devote himself to writing. He began to branch out from *opéra comique*, producing several plays and vaudevilles (most successful was *Fanchon la vielleuse*, 1801, a collaboration with Joseph Pain). Two collections of moral tales for children were often reprinted, and his memoirs, *Mes récapitulations*, provide an interesting if idealized picture of his life and times.

Sedaine recognized in Bouilly a kindred spirit and referred to the younger man as his successor. Indeed *Pierre le Grand*, Bouilly's first libretto, is already marked by the kind of dramatic truth and realism that made Sedaine the leading 18th-century French librettist. The cast presents a cross-section of society, characterized not only by their actions and costumes but also by their manners of speaking. Bouilly's writing is always clear in its moral purpose and sentimental enough to have earned him the title *poète lachrymal*. *Pierre* teaches that a king need not have riches to be happy, while *Léonore* is a tale of virtue rewarded and *Les deux journées* a picture of the simple goodness of working people. Bouilly could also produce delightful comedy, as *Une folie* demonstrates, and his qualities were sought out by leading composers. Though his manner of *sensibilité* went out of style by the second decade of the 19th century, he was nevertheless respected as a skilled writer and a sure dramatic craftsman.

Pierre le Grand (oc), Grétry, 1790; *La famille américaine* (oc), Dalayrac, 1796; *Le jeune Henri* (oc), Méhul, 1797; *La mort de Turenne* (pièce historique, with J. V. A. Cuvellier), G. J. Navoigille, 1797; *Léonore, ou L'amour conjugal* (fait historique), Gaveaux, 1798 (It., Paer, 1804; It. Mayr, 1805; Ger., Beethoven, 1805, as Fidelio, rev. 1806, 1814); *Les deux journées, ou Le porteur d'eau* (comédie lyrique), Cherubini, 1800 (It., Mayr, 1801); *Teniers* (comédie, with M. J. Pain), 1800 (A.-P. M. G. Peellaert, 1826); *Zoé ou La pauvre petite* (comédie), Plantade, 1800; *La haine aux femmes* (vaudeville, with Pain), J. D. Doche and others, 1800; *Une folie* (comédie), Méhul, 1802 (Du Puy, 1806)

Fanchon la vielleuse (vaudeville, with Pain), Doche and others, 1803; *Héléna* (oc), Méhul, 1803; *Le désastre de Lisbonne* (drame), L. A. Piccinni, 1804; *L'intrigue aux fenêtres* (opéra-bouffe, with L. E. F. C. M. Dupaty), Isouard, 1805; *Cimarosa* (oc), Isouard, 1808; *Françoise de Foix* (oc, with Dupaty), Berton, 1809; *La belle au bois dormant* (féerie, with T. M. Dumersan), Doche, 1811; *Le séjour militaire* (oc, with Dupaty), Auber, 1813; *Les jeux floraux*, P. L. F. Aimon, 1818; *Valentine de Milan* (drame lyrique), Méhul, completed Daussoigne, 1822; *Jenny la bouquetière* (with Pain), Kreubé and Pradher, 1823; *Agnes Sorel* (comédie, with Dupaty), Peellaert, 1823; *Les deux nuits* (oc, with E. Scribe), Boieldieu, 1829

*

J. N. Bouilly: *Mes recapitulations* (Paris, 1836–7)
J.-X. Carré de Busserolle: *Bouilly (Jean-Nicolas)* (Tours, 1875) [with list of writings]
M. Ruhnke: 'Die Librettisten des Fidelio', *Opernstudien: Anna Amalie Abert zum 65. Geburtstag* (Tutzing, 1975), 121–40
D. Galliver: 'Jean-Nicolas Bouilly (1763–1842), Successor of Sedaine', *SMA*, xiii (1979), 16–33
J. Warrack: 'Bouilly and his "fauvette"', *Opera*, xxxiv (1983), 595–8
D. Charlton: *Grétry and the Growth of Opéra-Comique* (Cambridge, 1986)

KARIN PENDLE (text)
KRISTIN M. KNITTEL (work-list)

Boukouras. Theatre inaugurated in 1840 and in use until 1897; *see* ATHENS.

Boulevard Solitude. *Lyrisches Drama* in seven scenes by HANS WERNER HENZE to a libretto by Grete Weil after Walter Jockisch's *Boulevard Solitude*, itself based on ANTOINE-FRANÇOIS PRÉVOST's *Manon Lescaut*; Hanover, Landestheater, 17 February 1952.

Manon Lescaut	high soprano
Armand des Grieux *a student*	lyric tenor
Lescaut *Manon's brother*	baritone
Francis *Armand's friend*	baritone
Lilaque *père, a rich old gentleman*	high buffo tenor
Lilaque *fils*	baritone
A Prostitute	dancer
Servant to Lilaque *fils*	mime
Two Drug Addicts	dancers
A Cigarette Boy	dancer

Newspaper sellers, beggars, whores, police, students, travellers

Setting Paris, after the end of World War II

Henze's first fully fledged opera (after the 1949 'opera for actors' *Das Wundertheater*, and the radio opera after Kafka, *Ein Landarzt*, 1951) was composed in 1950 and 1951. Its updating of the Manon Lescaut story, transferring the focus of attention from Manon to Armand des Grieux, as well as its carefully regulated mixture of idioms, ensured immediate success. The first performance was conducted by Johannes Schüler, with a cast led by Sigrid Klaus and Walter Buckow; it was staged twice in Italy in 1954 (in Naples, conducted by Ionel Perlea, and Rome, conducted by Nino Sanzogno). The British première took place in London (at Sadler's Wells) in 1962 where the cast included April Cantelo, John Carolan and Peter Glossop.

i *A railway-station waiting-room in a large French town* After a brief introduction built up from percussion ostinatos, Francis is seen bidding farewell to Armand. Manon enters with her brother Lescaut, and they sit at Armand's table. While Lescaut goes to get a drink, Manon and Armand begin to talk; she is going to finishing school in Lausanne, he is returning to life as a student in Paris. His self-pitying account of his loneliness there is interrupted by Manon who provides it with a happier ending; the couple leave the waiting-room together.

ii *An attic room in Paris* Armand and Manon are together. Lying in bed they sing a bittersweet duet. Armand has stopped his studies, and his father has withdrawn his allowance; they have no money. When Armand leaves, Lescaut appears, to tell Manon that he has found her a new admirer, an old man but very rich. After Armand has returned briefly, Lescaut comments sarcastically in an extravagant aria that the more cruelly Manon treats her lovers the more successful she will become; he gives her five minutes to decide where her future lies.

iii *An elegant boudoir in the house of Lilaque père* Manon writes to Armand assuring him that she is happy and well treated. Her only disappointment is that she cannot see him, and she suggests a subterfuge. Lescaut interrupts her, furious that she should be writing to Armand rather than paying attention to her sugar-daddy. He tears up the letter; when Manon protests that he is killing the one thing she values, his

'Boulevard Solitude' (Henze): set by Jean-Pierre Ponnelle for scene iv (a university library) of the original production at the Landestheater, Hanover, 17 February 1952

response is brutal: she is his source of income and he needs more money. He steals money from a strong box and the two are joined by Lilaque. In a highly expressive trio Lilaque's initial warmth (couched in tenor lines of very high tessitura) turns to rage when he discovers the robbery; he throws out both of them.

iv *A university library* The students, Armand and Francis among them, are studying Catullus. While their choral murmurings form a backdrop to the scene, Armand confesses that still he can think only of Manon. He does not believe Francis when he is told that she has robbed Lilaque, and when Francis leaves indignant, Manon appears. The couple read a love poem that mirrors their own predicament and builds into a passionate duet.

v *A dive* Manon and Armand have parted again, and he has resorted to drugs. Against a background of dance music, he sings of his attempts to forget the past. Lescaut arrives with Lilaque's son, his new client for Manon. He demands to know where she is, but Armand wants only more cocaine which Lescaut supplies. When Manon arrives to join her brother and Lilaque *fils*, Armand is enraged, threatening Lilaque. Manon tries to calm him, and they leave. A girl enters with a letter for Armand. Manon's voice is heard asking Armand to meet her the following night, and in the meantime she will arrange for him to spend the night with one of the most beautiful girls in Paris. Armand cannot absorb it all.

vi *The apartment of Lilaque fils* Manon and Armand are together at dawn. Though Manon is pleased with her upward mobility, Armand reminds her that once they were always together. Lescaut has watched them, and arrives to warn Armand to leave before the servants see him; he notices a modern painting on the wall and takes it from its frame. They hear the voice of Lilaque *père* and Manon hides both men. Despite her efforts the old man insists on entering the room and discovers the theft. All the old suspicions return, and he calls to the servant to fetch the police. Lescaut shoots him, forces the revolver into Manon's hand and escapes; Manon and Armand are discovered, by Lilaque *fils*, standing over the body.

vii *Outside a prison* In the depths of winter Armand waits to catch a final sight of Manon before she goes off to prison. His pathetic aria ends when Manon and the prisoners are taken away without any chance for the lovers to talk, and the action dissolves into a fast-moving 'revue' over a rumba rhythm in which images from their life together flood back, and a children's choir sings 'Jubilate exultate'.

* * *

Though everything in the opera derives from a single 12-note row, Henze's breadth of style is considerable. Several aspects of the opera recall Berg, not only in the use of dance music as an image of degradation (in scene v) which evokes the Tavern scene in *Wozzeck*, but in the surreal exits and entrances throughout the opera, which recall the similar farcical elements of *Lulu*. Yet Henze casts his net wider still; the seven scenes and the orchestral intermezzos between them move between tonality and atonality with total freedom, while the closed vocal forms, recitative, aria and ensemble, hark back to 18th- and 19th-century usages.

ANDREW CLEMENTS

Boulez, Pierre (*b* Montbrison, 25 March 1925). French composer and conductor. He studied in Paris with Messiaen and Leibowitz. In 1948 he acted as conductor and composer for Jean-Louis Barrault's theatre company. He conducted an admired performance of *Wozzeck* in 1963, a work he later recorded. The following year he conducted a concert performance of *Hippolyte et Aricie* for the Rameau bicentenary celebrations in Paris. His next major operatic engagement was at Bayreuth – the first French-born conductor to appear there – where he gave a controversial account of *Parsifal* in 1966, notable for its fast tempos and objective approach. In 1969 he was much praised for his conducting of *Pelléas et Mélisande* at Covent Garden, another production that was recorded. He returned to Bayreuth in 1976 to conduct the centenary production of the *Ring* (produced by Patrice Chéreau as a modern allegory); the cycle was recorded both in sound and vision. Again his conducting was swift, clear and for the most part unromantic, though it was certainly faithful to the scores. Perhaps his most important conducting assignment in the theatre and on record was Berg's *Lulu* in its completed form at the Paris Opéra in 1979.

Boulez's performances have been noted primarily for their analytical precision and textural clarity. His consistent fidelity to the written note banished traditional slovenliness, even if on occasion it led to an absence of emotional involvement. In the 1960s he shocked conventional opinion by declaring that all opera houses should be blown up. It was not, one imagines, meant literally but simply to shake bourgeois attitudes. However it gained him a reputation as an *enfant terrible* that was never entirely justified. In any case, though a leading proponent of the music of the second quarter of the 20th century, with its sometimes arid procedures, he was quite able to immerse himself with appreciable success in the very different ethos of Wagner.

ALAN BLYTH

Boult, Sir **Adrian (Cedric)** (*b* Chester, 8 April 1889; *d* London, 22 Feb 1983). English conductor. He studied at Oxford and the Leipzig Conservatory before joining the music staff at Covent Garden in 1914. In 1919 he joined the teaching staff of the RCM (where he remained until 1930), and was chief conductor for the autumn season of Dyagilev's Ballets Russes. Operatic experience embraced performances with the British National Opera Company (including *Parsifal*), a further spell in 1926 at Covent Garden as assistant musical director, and chamber opera in Bristol, Birmingham and London. He relinquished his six-year directorship of the CBSO in 1930 to train and conduct the newly formed BBC SO (until 1942 he was also director of music for the BBC). As well as appearing with various orchestras in Europe and the USA he conducted *Die Walküre* during the 1931 English season at Covent Garden and *Fidelio* at Sadler's Wells in 1939. On reaching official retiring age in 1950, he left the BBC but continued to appear at home, in Europe and the USA, occasionally taking charge of the Covent Garden Orchestra for Royal Ballet performances of *Job* and other works. He returned to the RCM to teach from 1962 to 1966.

Of the leading British conductors of his time, Boult was the least flamboyant but not the least remarkable. He expressed himself with trenchancy, and his gentlemanly self-control was said to be ruffled by occasional fierce storms. He learnt from Arthur Nikisch how to concentrate on essentials in rehearsal, conjuring the essence of the music with the point of his stick. At his best Boult displayed true loyalty to the composer, and an ability to see the music as a whole. On less inspired, low vitality evenings, his performances never lacked care or fidelity. Though his interpretations of the classics and, in particular, of British music were of high quality, in his BBC days he introduced much new music to London, with concert performances of *Wozzeck* (1934) and Busoni's *Doktor Faust* (1937). In addition to an autobiography, *My own Trumpet* (London, 1973), he wrote two valuable handbooks on conducting technique. He was knighted in 1937 and made a Companion of Honour in 1969.

*

M. Kennedy: *Adrian Boult* (London, 1987) RONALD CRICHTON

Bourcicault, Dion. *See* BOUCICAULT, DION.

Bourdin, Roger (*b* Lavallois, 14 June 1900; *d* Paris, 14 Sept 1973). French baritone. After studying at the Paris Conservatoire he made his début in 1922 at the Opéra-Comique as Lescaut (*Manon*) and sang there regularly until the mid-1960s in a wide range of roles, creating parts in operas by Pierné, Ibert and Bertrand. He made his Opéra début in 1942 as Mârouf, and created the title role in Milhaud's *Bolivar* there in 1950. His only appearance at Covent Garden was as Pelléas to Teyte's Mélisande (1930). He was a notable interpreter of non-French parts, including Beckmesser, Scarpia and Mozart's Figaro. He also sang Athanaël (*Thaïs*) and Ourrias (*Mireille*) with his wife, the soprano Geori Boué, in the title role. His voice was a warm, mellifluous, typically French baritone, as can be heard on his many recordings.

ALAN BLYTH

Bourgault-Ducoudray [Bourgault], **Louis (Albert)** (*b* Nantes, 2 Feb 1840; *d* Vernouillet, Yvelines, 4 July 1910). French composer. He prepared for a career in law, but entered Ambroise Thomas' class at the Conservatoire in 1859, a year after his comic opera *L'atelier de Prague* had been performed in Nantes. He won the Prix de Rome in 1862, and during his visit to Italy developed an interest in both the music of Palestrina's time and folk music. In 1868 he moved to Paris and in 1871 was one of the founders of the Société Nationale de Musique. He was appointed professor of aesthetics and music history at the Conservatoire in 1878 (a position he held until 1909), and in September the same year he lectured at the Exposition Universelle on Greek music. This, together with the music of Russia and Brittany, remained a lifelong interest, and it was Bourgault-Ducoudray's compositional response to these influences that led Calvocoressi to credit him with laying the groundwork for the new direction taken by French music in the late 19th and early 20th centuries.

Although Bourgault-Ducoudray's compositions are numerous, his lectures and writings had more influence on his contemporaries than his music. Nevertheless, according to Léon Vallas in his biography of Debussy (1932), that composer had a high regard for *Thamara*, because of its use of oriental scales and its contempt for harmonic convention. In this connection it may be significant that Bourgault-Ducoudray was responsible for bringing about the first Parisian performance of Balakirev's symphonic poem *Tamara*.

Bourgault-Ducoudray's *Thamara* is set in the besieged Russian city of Baku. The people are in despair, and deaf to appeals for continued resistance. A Priest (bass) appears with Thamara (soprano), who declares herself ready to go to the camp of the invading leader, Nour-Eddin (tenor), and kill him; this inspires the people to renew the fighting. At the opening of the second tableau, Nour-Eddin awakes from a dream in which he has seen a beautiful woman who brought both love and death. His soldiers arrive, and report new resistance from Baku, whereupon Nour-Eddin orders the city's destruction. Scarcely has he done this when Thamara arrives, asking for shelter. Nour-Eddin quickly succumbs to her charms, although recognizing her as the woman in his dream. She is equally affected by him, and the pair become lovers. This places Thamara in a terrible dilemma, as she must now kill the man she loves or betray her people. She hears the voices of Baku's people and sees the ghosts of its dead, and finally delivers the fatal blow. The final tableau begins in triumph with Thamara hailed as saviour of the city. Realizing she cannot live without Nour-Eddin, and seeing his ghost, she stabs herself and dies.

Both *Thamara* and the Arthurian epic *Myrdhin*, which deals with the struggle between paganism and Christianity, are conceived on a grand scale, and probably reflect Bourgault-Ducoudray's attitude to dramatic music more than his early *opéras comiques*. He was highly regarded by contemporaries: subscribers to *La conjuration des fleurs* included Duparc, Gounod and Pauline Viardot, while Pierné, Ropartz and Camille Chevillard put their names to the subscription list for *Myrdhin*.

L'atelier de Prague (oc, 1, G. Derrien), Nantes, Grand, 29 Dec 1858, vs (Paris, ?1860)
La conjuration des fleurs ('petit drame satirique', 2 tableaux), concert perf., Paris, Salle Herz, 27 Jan 1883
Michel Colomb (oc, 1, L. Gallet and E. Bonnemère), Brussels, Turkish Embassy, 7 May 1887
Thamara (4 tableaux, Gallet), Paris, Opéra, 28 Dec 1891, vs (Paris, 1892); rev. version, Opéra, 23 Jan 1907
Anne de Bretagne (4, Bourgault-Ducoudray), Nantes, Société Musicale Concordia, Dec 1892, unpubd
Le songe de Vasco de Gama, 1898 (scène, S. Arnaud), unperf., unpubd
Myrdhin, 1905 (légende dramatique, 4, Arnaud), Nantes, Grand, 28 March 1912, vs (Paris, 1919)

Recits. for Méhul's *Joseph* (Paris, 1899)

*

Gringoire [? pseud. of M. Lemée]: *L'oeuvre de L.-A. Bourgault-Ducoudray* (Nantes, 1898) [incl. worklist]
M. Emmanuel: *Eloge funèbre de Bourgault-Ducoudray* (Paris, 1911)
M. D. Calvocoressi: 'Bourgault-Ducoudray: a Memoir', *MMR*, liii (1923), 37–8; abridged version in *Musicians Gallery: Music and Ballet in Paris and London* (London, 1933, 2/1934 as *Music and Ballet*)
M. Poté: 'Bourgault-Ducoudray', *Bulletin de la Société Archéologique et Historique de Nantes* (1965)
ELAINE BRODY/JOHN WAGSTAFF

Bourgeois, Thomas-Louis(-Joseph) (bap. Fontaine-l'Evêque, 24 Oct 1676; *d* Paris, Jan 1750 or 1751). French composer and singer. After publishing two collections of *Pièces en trios* in 1701 and holding posts as *maître de chapelle* at Toul and Strasbourg cathedrals, he went to Paris, where he gained a post as a singer with the Opéra in 1707. As a *haute-contre*, he appears in several cast-lists of librettos, including those of his own two *opéras-ballets*, *Les amours déguisés* (1713) and *Les plaisirs de la paix* (1715). After the death of Louis XIV he continued his career in the Netherlands, where in 1725 he was conducting the Opéra of The Hague. In his works for the stage he excelled at the pastoral and rococo scenes so popular in France in the early 18th century.

See also AMOURS DÉGUISÉS, LES.

Les amours déguisés (opéra-ballet, prol., 3, L. Fuzelier), Paris, Opéra, 22 Aug 1713 (Paris, 1713)
Le comte de Gabalis et les peuples élémentaires (divertissement, 2, P.-F. G. de Beauchamps), Sceaux, Château de Sceaux, Oct 1714
Les plaisirs de la paix (opéra-ballet, prol., 3, A. Menesson), Paris, Opéra, 29 April 1715 (Paris, 1715)
Diane (divertissement, A. Danchet), Chantilly, 8 Sept 1721 (Paris, 1721) [vocal music only]; sym. by J. Aubert
Les peines et les plaisirs de l'amour, 1730 (ballet-héroïque, prol., 3, P. de Morand), unperf.

*

E. Titon du Tillet: *Le Parnasse françois*, suppl.ii (Paris, 1755)
L.-F. Beffara: *Dictionnaire alphabétique des auteurs* (MS, *F-Po*, rés.602)
C. Lyon: 'Thomas-Louis-Joseph Bourgeois', *L'éducation populaire* (Charleroi, 1882), 1–6
J. Fransen: *Les comédiens français en Hollande* (Paris, 1925)
M. Rambaud: *Documents du Minutier Central concernant l'histoire de l'art* (Paris, 1964)
JÉRÔME DE LA GORCE

Bourgogne, Hôtel de. Theatre used by the Comédie-Italienne, and later the Opéra-Comique, Paris, from 1716 to 1783; *see* PARIS, §§2 (iii) and 3 (i).

Bourguignon, Francis de (*b* St Gilles, Brussels, 29 May 1890; *d* Brussels, 11 April 1961). Belgian composer. He studied at the Brussels Conservatory, where he won a first prize for piano. Wounded in World War I, he was evacuated to England and then moved to Australia, where he became Melba's accompanist. After several international tours he settled in Brussels in 1925; he studied composition and joined the 'Synthétiste' group, and at the same time began to write music criticism. Until 1955 he taught at the Brussels Conservatory. A fluent composer, he began with works describing his memories of travel. His works for the theatre include three operas: the unfinished *drame lyrique* in two acts, *Tradimento* op.35 (composed 1929; E. Van Damme), the one-act chamber opera *Le mauvais pari* op.51 (composed 1937; R. Avermaete, after a Renaissance farce), and the one-act *opéra comique*, *Floris l'incomparable* op.110 (composed 1959; F. Walder); none of the operas was ever staged. Both of the completed works are set during the Renaissance. *Le mauvais pari* was composed during Bourguignon's transition to a neo-classical style evident in works written after 1937, in which he often wrote fugually though retaining a lyrical quality. *Floris l'incomparable* has a light orchestration, often limited to the strings.

*

D. von Volborth-Danys: *CeBeDeM and its Affiliated Composers* (Brussels, 1977–80)
HENRI VANHULST

Bournonville, Auguste (Antoine) (*b* Copenhagen, 21 Aug 1805; *d* Copenhagen, 30 Nov 1879). Danish dancer and choreographer, deeply influenced by French romantic ballet. He studied with his father and Auguste Vestris before dancing at the Paris Opéra (1820, 1823–30), where he became Marie Taglioni's favourite partner. In 1829 he returned to Denmark and was ballet-master and principal dancer at the Royal Theatre in Copenhagen until his retirement in 1877 (he held brief appointments at the Viennese court theatre, 1855–6, and the Swedish Opera, 1861–4). Bournonville choreographed many ballets and *divertissements* for Copenhagen as well as original dances for 51 operas, including Auber's *La muette de Portici* and *Le dieu et la bayadère* and Mozart's *Don Giovanni*, *Die Entführung*, *Figaro* and *Die Zauberflöte*. He also choreographed dances for performances of Gluck's *Orfeo* and Iphigenia operas, Donizetti's *Lucia di Lammermoor* and *Lucrezia Borgia*, Meyerbeer's *Robert le diable* and *Les Huguenots* and Verdi's *Il trovatore*.

Bournonville was eager to comply with composers' intentions. When he was assigned to choreograph *L'étoile du nord* in Vienna in 1855 Meyerbeer played him the ballet music with correct tempos and suggested suitable places to insert dances or military manoeuvres. Later, in Sweden, Bournonville choreographed an entirely new cloister scene for *Robert le diable*, which, he claimed, helped to revive interest in an opera long out of fashion. As stage director at the Royal Theatre, he introduced Wagner to the Danish stage with his production of *Lohengrin* in 1870, having earlier visited the composer in Munich to attend rehearsals and performances of the opera. Bournonville invariably censored the erotic dimension from portrayals of love in his ballets, and he confessed in his autobiography to difficulty in staging the orgiastic Venusberg scenes in

Tannhäuser, though admiring the 'superbly thrilling moments' of its music.

A great Danish patriot, Bournonville delighted in working with local composers, such as J. P. E. Hartmann, and employed Nordic legends and characters in some of his most popular ballets. Hans Christian Andersen called him 'the poet of the ballet'. The Royal Danish Ballet in Copenhagen has preserved much of his choreography.

*

A. Bournonville: *Mit theaterliv* (Copenhagen, 1847–77; Eng. trans., 1979)

——: *Efterladte Skrifter*, ed. C. Bournonville (Copenhagen, 1891)

S. Kragh-Jacobsen: *The Royal Danish Ballet* (Copenhagen, 1955)

E. Aschengreen: 'The Beautiful Danger: Facets of the Romantic Ballet', *Dance Perspectives*, lviii (1974), 2–52

K. Jurgensen: *The Bournonville Ballets: a Photographic Record, 1844–1933* (London, 1987)

MAUREEN NEEDHAM COSTONIS

Bousquet, Francis (*b* Marseilles, 9 Sept 1890; *d* Roubaix, Nord, 22 Dec 1942). French composer. After winning the Prix de Rome in 1923, he became director of the Conservatoire in Roubaix. His first opera, *Zorriga* (1925), was one of several written for and performed in the amphitheatre at Béziers. It is set in a Moroccan harem and like *Sarati-le-terrible* (1928), also set in North Africa, employs surface elements of Arabic music. It is a large-scale work dealing with the exploits of an Arab tyrant and the struggle between Christians and Moslems. *Mon oncle Benjamin* (1942) is also a full-length work with a large cast. Based on an 18th-century novel, it recounts the fortunes of a country doctor in the time of Louis XV. Bousquet's work is traditional in its harmonic language and motivic construction but adds vivid elements of local colour.

Zorriga (drame lyrique, 5, J. Camp and P. Vedert), Béziers, Arena, 1925

Sarati-le-terrible (drame lyrique, 4, J. Vignaud), Paris, OC (Favart), 9 May 1928

Mon oncle Benjamin (comédie musicale, 3, G. Ricou, after C. Tillier), Paris, OC (Favart), 10 March 1942

*

P. Locard: 'Jean Nouguès, Ch. Silver, André Bloch, Francis Bousquet', *Le théâtre lyrique en France* (Paris, 1937–9) [pubn of Poste National/Radio-Paris], iii, 252–6

RICHARD LANGHAM SMITH

Bouvard, François (*b* Lyons, *c*1683–4; *d* Paris, 2 March 1760). French composer. Parisian by early adoption, as a boy he sang female roles at the Opéra until his exceptionally wide-ranging soprano voice broke. He composed a book of violin sonatas (1723) but was known mainly as a composer of vocal music.

After he had studied in Rome, two of his operas were given at the Paris Opéra, *Médus* (1702) and *Cassandre* (1706), both to serious librettos of high literary quality by Racine's pupil Lagrange-Chancel. Neither was revived, both were published by Ballard, and in each is found an original if flawed solution to the problem of giving opera authentic 'Hellenic' tragic intensity. In *Médus*, Medea (soprano; created by Maupin) returns to Colchis – after the episodes at Corinth and Athens – still full of demonic power. The dramatic reversal (*péripétie*) at the denouement is a mutual recognition scene for Medea and her estranged son Médus (*basse-taille*; Thévénard), who is about to be sacrificed. There is political tension in the plot, as there is in *Cassandre*, which was written in collaboration with Bertin de La Doué (the division of labour is given in the published score). Of *Cassandre*, Bouvard himself wrote: 'le sujet sérieux, et les louanges de l'Hymen aux depens de l'Amour, ne plurent point aux dames. Cependant le 5e acte, qui est de moi en entier, fut fort goûté'. Act 5 indeed contains both a prophetic frenzy and a passionate lament ('Restes du nom Troyen') for Cassandra (soprano; Desmatins), who then dies on stage in the penultimate scene. Throughout, love is treated as a 'passion funeste' rather than as erotic 'galanterie', and pathos is generated through the tableaux. Bouvard's declamation is – unsurprisingly for a singer – vividly inflected, and his accompaniments are seriously worked, in the manner of Lully.

all printed works published in Paris

Médus, roi des Mèdes (tragédie en musique, prol., 5, F.-J. de Lagrange-Chancel), Paris, Opéra, 23 July 1702 (1702)

Cassandre (tragédie en musique, prol., 5, Lagrange-Chancel, after C. Boyer: *Agamemnon*), Paris, Opéra, 22 June 1706 (1706), collab. Bertin de La Doué

Ariane et Bacchus (opéra), Versailles, 1729

Other stage works: L'école de Mars (divertissement, 1, P. de Morand), lib. pubd (2/1728); Le triomphe de l'hymen et de l'amour (divertissement, 1, L. R. de Saint-Jorry), lib. pubd (1729); Diane et l'Amour (idylle héroïque, 1, de Morand), lib. pubd (*c*1743)

*

F. Parfaict and C. Parfaict: *Histoire de l'Académie royale de musique* (MS, 1741, *F-Pn*), ff.102ff, 115

——: *Dictionnaire des théâtres de Paris* (Paris, 1756), i, 489ff; ii, 59ff; iii, 370ff

C. Girdlestone: *La tragédie en musique* (Geneva, 1972), 158–63

PHILIP WELLER

Bouvier, Hélène (*b* Paris, 20 June 1905; *d* Paris, 11 March 1978). French mezzo-soprano. She studied in Paris and made her début in 1930 at Nantes as Gluck's Orpheus. She first sang at the Paris Opéra in 1939 as Delilah; her repertory there included Amneris, Margared (*Le roi d'Ys*), Honegger's Antigone, Emilia (*Otello*), the Innkeeper (*Boris Godunov*), Massenet's Hérodiade, Roussel's Padmâvatî, Fricka, Brangäne and Ortrud. In 1950 she created Précipitation in Milhaud's *Bolivar* and in 1952 took part in Rameau's *Les Indes galantes*. She also sang with the Opéra-Comique, making her début in 1939 as Charlotte (*Werther*) and singing Santuzza, Carmen and the Mother (*Louise*). She had a rich, warm-toned voice and a fine stage appearance.

ELIZABETH FORBES

Bovier de Fontenelle, Bernard le. *See* FONTENELLE, BERNARD LE BOVIER DE.

Bovy, Vina [Van Overberghe, Malvina Johanna Pauline Félicité] (*b* Ghent, 22 May 1900; *d* Ghent, 16 May 1983). Belgian soprano. She studied in Ghent and made her début there in 1918 as Argentine in Poise's *Les deux billets*. After three seasons at the Monnaie, in 1925 she made her Paris début at the Opéra-Comique as Manon. She sang at the Opéra from 1935 to 1947, as Gilda, Lucia, Thaïs and the Queen of Shemakha, and at the Metropolitan (1936–8), where her roles included Violetta, Lakmé, Gounod's Juliet and the four soprano parts in *Les contes d'Hoffmann*. In 1947 she became director of the Vlaamse Opera, where she sang the title role of *L'aiglon* and Katiusha in Alfano's *Risurrezione*. She retired in 1955. Bovy had a well-schooled voice, typically French in timbre, with a fine coloratura technique.

*

J. Deleersnyder: *Vina Bovy* (Ghent, 1965)

HAROLD ROSENTHAL/R

Bowles, Paul (*b* Jamaica, NY, 30 Dec 1910). American composer. In the late 1920s and early 30s he studied with Copland, Thomson and Boulanger, and lived in Europe and North Africa. Between 1936 and 1963 he occasionally wrote music for the New York theatre, being associated with Orson Welles, William Saroyan and Tennessee Williams. In 1938 he completed his first opera, *Denmark Vesey* (3, C. H. Ford), of which the first act had had its première in 1937. He received a Guggenheim Fellowship in 1941 to compose the one-act zarzuela *The Wind Remains*, to a libretto after Federico García Lorca; it was completed in 1943 and given later that year in New York with Leonard Bernstein conducting. In 1948 Bowles returned to Tangier where he wrote a third opera, *Yerma* (after García Lorca; completed 1955), for the singer Libby Holman; it was first performed at the University of Denver on 29 July 1958. From 1949 he was more active as a writer and translator than as a composer. His music, which also includes ballets, film scores, chamber works and songs, is nostalgic and witty, evocative in its use of American jazz, Mexican dance and Moroccan rhythm, and exclusively in short forms – the operas are constructed as suites of songs.

EwenD
P. Glanville-Hicks: 'Paul Bowles: American Composer', *ML*, xxvi (1945), 88–96
NED ROREM

Bowman, James (Thomas) (*b* Oxford, 6 Nov 1941). English countertenor. He studied at Oxford and made his début in 1967 with the English Opera Group in Paris and Aldeburgh as Britten's Oberon, a role he sang at Covent Garden, Strasbourg, Sydney, with the WNO and at Glyndebourne, where he made his début in 1970 as Endymion in Cavalli's *Calisto*. He created the Priest-Confessor in Maxwell Davies's *Taverner* (1972), his Covent Garden début; voice of Apollo in *Death in Venice* (1973, Aldeburgh Festival); Astron (with Anne Wilkens) in Tippett's *The Ice Break* (1977, Covent Garden); and sang Ridout's *Phaeton* for BBC Radio. For the Handel Opera Society he sang Otho, Scipio, Xerxes and Justinian, as well as Polinesso (*Ariodante*) which he repeated at Geneva and Buxton. His other Handel roles include Julius Caesar (Barber Institute), Ptolemy (San Francisco and ENO), Goffredo in *Rinaldo* (Reggio Emilia and Paris) and Orlando (Scottish Opera). He has also sung Lidio in Cavalli's *Egisto* at Santa Fe and Ruggiero in Vivaldi's *Orlando furioso* at Verona and Dallas; Herod in Fux's *La fede sacrilega* in Vienna, Theramene in Cavalli's *Eritrea* at Camden and Monteverdi's Otho at Spitalfields. In 1988 he took part in Jommelli's *Fetonte* at La Scala. He has been partly responsible for the present wide acceptance of the countertenor voice in modern and Baroque opera. His voice is individual in timbre and he uses it to highly dramatic effect. ALAN BLYTH

Bowman, John (*b* *c*1660; *d* London, 23 March 1739). English bass and actor. He entered the Duke's Company as a boy and was a member of the Royal Private Musick from 1684. Cibber related that as a youth 'fam'd for his Voice' he sang before Charles II at Nell Gwynn's lodgings. Bowman was Purcell's principal stage bass from 1680 when he sang as Atticus in *Theodosius* (a part he last played in 1733). He took the important acting and singing role of Grimbald in *King Arthur* (1691) and played Cardenio in *Don Quixote* (1694) with the famous mad song 'Let the dreadful engines'. He sang in the Eccles music for *Macbeth* and was Mars in *The Loves of Mars and Venus* (1696). He remained on stage until a few months before his death, when the *London Magazine* described him as the oldest actor and singer in England, erroneously giving his age as 87.

In August 1692 he married Betterton's adopted daughter, Elizabeth Watson (*d* 1707), a popular actress and singer who was Pallas in *The Judgment of Paris* (1701) and Diana in Fedeli's *The Temple of Love* (1706).

BDA; *LS*
C. Cibber: *An Apology for the Life of Mr. Colley Cibber* (London, 1740)
C. A. Price: *Henry Purcell and the London Stage* (Cambridge, 1984)
OLIVE BALDWIN, THELMA WILSON

Boxberg, Christian Ludwig (*b* Sondershausen, 24 April 1670; *d* Görlitz, 1 Dec 1729). German composer and librettist. He studied at the Leipzig Thomasschule (1682–6), and was organist in Grossenhain, north of Dresden, from 1692 until 1702. However, his early career was centred on Leipzig, where he was active as librettist, singer and opera composer.

He was a pupil of Nikolaus A. Strungk, director of the Leipzig Opera, 1688–92, whose opera *Amyntas und Phyllis*, now lost, was completed after his death by Boxberg and given at Leipzig in 1700. Boxberg wrote at least five librettos for operas by Strungk and sang in performances of those works. He seems also to have been active at the court of Ansbach, 1697–8, where his most important operas (for which he also wrote the librettos) were first performed: *Orion*, *Die verschwiegene Treue* and *Sardanapalus*. Only the last score is extant (*D-AN*). In 1702 he gave up his operatic career to become organist at the church of SS Peter and Paul in Görlitz.

A soprano, Christina Charlotta Buxberg (*b* 1681), who studied in Dresden and sang with the Hamburg Opera, 1695–7, may have been related to Boxberg.

H. Mersmann: *Christian Ludwig Boxberg und seine Oper 'Sardanapalus', Ansbach, 1698* (diss., U. of Berlin, 1916)
GEORGE J. BUELOW

Box office (Fr. *bureau de location*; Ger. *Theaterkasse*; It. *biglietteria*). The place in or near an opera house where tickets are reserved, sold and distributed. Any theatre that charges admission needs an audience control system of some kind – at the simplest a secured entrance, a pay box – where the management can collect an entrance fee or tickets from patrons. The system becomes more complicated if the house is scaled, with different sections having different prices. Box-office attendants not only have a heavy responsibility in accounting; they are among the first theatre people that patrons encounter and consequently serve an important public relations function.

The term seems to have derived both from the container (box) in which tickets or money were deposited and the office (the pay box) where transactions for seats (in the boxes) were made. British documents from as early as 1760 at Covent Garden (see *GB-Lbl* Egerton MS 2271) use the term box office and refer also to pit and gallery offices. London theatres began calling house servants who waited upon box patrons 'box book-keepers' in 1737 (*London Daily Post*, 18 April), so there were probably box offices by that date. Box or special seating goes back to the ancients.

Today the term box office (and its comparable names in other languages) means the ticket office generally, where employees handle seating for all parts of the house. From the term have come box-office intendant, manager, attendant; box-office appeal, draw, poison, flop; box-office window, plan, receipts; etc.

EDWARD A. LANGHANS

Boyarïnya Vera Sheloga ('The Noblewoman Vera Sheloga'). Opera in one act by NIKOLAY ANDREYEVICH RIMSKY-KORSAKOV to his own libretto after Lev Alexandrovich Mey's drama; Moscow, Solodovnikov Theatre, 15/27 December 1898; it was given as prologue to *THE MAID OF PSKOV* in 1901.

Boyce, William (*b* London, Sept 1711; *d* Kensington, London, 7 Feb 1779). English composer. After serving as a choirboy at St Paul's Cathedral he became articled to the cathedral organist, Maurice Greene. His first appointment, in 1734, was as a church organist, and not until 1768 did he relinquish his last such post. Shortly after the performance in 1736 of his oratorio *David's Lamentation over Saul and Jonathan*, Boyce was appointed a composer to the Chapel Royal. In 1755 he succeeded Greene as Master of the King's Musick, and he became an organist of the Chapel Royal in 1758. In his later years he devoted himself to the completion of the monumental collection of English church music of the 16th, 17th and 18th centuries initiated by Greene and published as *Cathedral Music* (1760–73). Though Boyce contributed about 65 anthems of his own to the repertory, none was printed in his lifetime. The first of his major works to be published, the serenata *Solomon* (1743), achieved lasting success.

The extent of Boyce's contribution to theatre music has only recently been fully appreciated. His earliest dramatic works, *Peleus and Thetis* and *The Secular Masque*, were masques based on librettos from the beginning of the 18th century. The former had started life as an interpolation into Act 2 of *The Jew of Venice* (1701), Granville's adaptation of Shakespeare's *The Merchant of Venice*, while the latter was written by Dryden in 1700 as an afterpiece to Vanburgh's adaptation of Fletcher's *The Pilgrim.* Both were conceived by Boyce as independent works and given concert performances, but *The Secular Masque*, evidence for the existence of which dates from 1746, did reach the stage at Drury Lane in 1750 when it took its original place in revivals of *The Pilgrim. The Secular Masque* contains some of Boyce's most attractive music, in particular the song of Diana (alto/tenor), 'With horns and with hounds', and that of Momus (tenor) to Mars, 'Thy sword within the scabbard keep', sung respectively by Kitty Clive and John Beard at the Drury Lane performances, which became highly popular; the work has been successfully staged in modern times. However, Dryden's satirical allegory on 17th-century English politics was written specifically for its day and age and exerted little appeal 50 years later. As Cross, the Drury Lane prompter recorded: 'Play not much lik'd, and ye masque greatly dislik'd'. Boyce's first direct theatrical commission, the dirge in *Cymbeline*, 'Fear no more the scorching sun', came from John Rich of Covent Garden in 1746. Though Boyce's music is carefully crafted and apt in expression, Rich appears not to have solicited further work from him. It was David Garrick, the great actor-manager at Drury Lane from 1747 to 1776, who provided Boyce with the opportunity to make his mark as a theatre composer.

The leading dramatic composer of the time, despite his inconsistencies, was Thomas Arne. When Burney wrote that 'Mr. Arne and Mr. Boyce were frequently concurrents at the theatres and in each other's way, particularly at Drury Lane', he must have had the years 1749–51 in mind, for it was only then that Boyce composed regularly for the theatre. Garrick may have turned to Boyce in the wake of the cool reception afforded to Arne's masque *The Triumph of Peace* (February 1749), which probably exacerbated their perennially strained relationship. (The complete failure of Arne's 'musical entertainment' *Don Saverio* in February 1750 only served to lend weight to Garrick's judgment.) Garrick's first major commission to Boyce was to set *The Chaplet* by Moses Mendez, a writer who had already had considerable success with the ballad opera *The Double Disappointment* (1746). Boyce's setting (1749), an all-sung pastoral afterpiece, proved to be the pinnacle of his theatrical career. Boyce also provided new settings for two of the songs in Garrick's first play, *Lethe* (1740), which he revived early in 1749, but exactly when Boyce's settings were included in the new production has yet to be established.

Early in 1750 Boyce provided an extended 'pastoral interlude' for a new burlesque, *The Rehearsal*, which satirized contemporary Italian comic opera. Its author, Kitty Clive, was a leading actress-singer in Garrick's company for whom the part of Pastora in *The Chaplet* had been written. The turbulent and impassioned air in G minor for Marcella (soprano), 'Rise, rise, tempest rise', sung after Corydon (tenor), whom she loves, has spurned her, demonstrates Boyce's capacity to respond to a dramatic situation when it fired him. In autumn 1750 Boyce and Arne became inadvertently embroiled in the culminating event in the longstanding competition between the two patent theatres. Both theatres announced new productions of *Romeo and Juliet* to open on 28 September. Covent Garden stole a march on its rival by inserting 'an additional scene ... representing the funeral procession of Juliet ... accompanied by a solemn dirge' for which Arne provided the music. Garrick felt impelled to respond in kind, and three days later Drury Lane heard Boyce's setting of Garrick's hastily penned dirge 'Rise, rise, heart-breaking sighs'. The similarity of instrumentation in the two pieces suggests that Arne's evocative scoring, employing trumpets, drums and a tolling bell, had been communicated to Boyce, but where Arne's music is inclined to be bland, Boyce's is the more deeply felt.

After the lukewarm response to *The Shepherd's Lottery* (1751), Boyce's second pastoral afterpiece in conjunction with Mendez, he wrote only intermittently for the theatre. His subsequent work ranged from single songs, such as the carefully wrought solo air 'When Damon languished at my feet' for Edward Moore's *The Gamester* (1753), to two extensive odes for soloists and chorus which formed an integral part of John Home's tragedy *Agis* (1758). Boyce contributed further to Shakespearean productions with an attractive vocal trio, 'Get you hence', and some effective music for animating the statue of Hermione in *Florizel and Perdita* (1756), Garrick's adaptation of *The Winter's Tale*, and a short, rather insubstantial masque in Act 4 of *The Tempest.* Finally, Boyce's setting of Garrick's 'Heart of oak', included in his pantomime *Harlequin's Invasion* (1759) to celebrate British naval victories that 'wonderful year', exceeded even *The Chaplet* in popular acclaim and lasting fame. Notwithstanding the national response to 'Heart of oak', by this time Boyce may well have become disenchanted with the theatre; in any case, his extensive commitments elsewhere must have been all-consuming.

A survey of Boyce's contribution to the theatre would be incomplete without reference to his trio sonatas (London, 1747), which are known to have been regularly played as act tunes in the theatres from the late 1740s to the early 1760s; his arrangement of the music for *Macbeth* (London, 1770), attributed by Boyce to Matthew Locke (but now thought to be by Richard Leveridge); and his settings of two Shakespearean odes, 'Titles and ermine fall behind' (1756), written by William Havard, an actor in the Drury Lane company, and 'Arise, arise, immortal Shakespeare' (*c*1759), by Garrick himself.

See also CHAPLET, THE; PELEUS AND THETIS; and SHEPHERD'S LOTTERY, THE.

all performed in London
LDL – *Drury Lane*

Peleus and Thetis (masque, G. Granville, Lord Lansdowne), by 1740, *GB-Ob**, ov. in MB, xiii (1957)
The Secular Masque (J. Dryden), *c*1746, *Lcm*, *Ob*, ov. (London, 1770)
The Chaplet (musical entertainment, 2 pts, M. Mendez), LDL, 2 Dec 1749, *Lbl*; (London [1750]), MLE (in preparation)
The Shepherd's Lottery (musical entertainment, 2 pts, Mendez), LDL, 19 Nov 1751, 2 songs *Ob**; (London, 1751/*R*1990: MLE, C4)
The Tempest (masque, D. Garrick, after W. Shakespeare), LDL, 20 Oct 1757, *Lcm*, *Ob**
Harlequin's Invasion, or A Christmas Gambol (pantomime, Garrick), LDL, 31 Dec 1759, 2 songs pubd (London, n.d.), collab. M. Arne and T. Aylward

*

BurneyH; *LS*
J[ohn] H[awkins]: 'Memoirs of Dr. William Boyce', *Cathedral Music*, i (London, 2/1788), p.ix; repr. with introduction and notes by G. Beechey, *MQ*, lvii (1971), 87–106
E. Taylor: 'William Boyce and the Theatre', *MR*, xiv (1953), 275–87
G. Finzi: Preface to *William Boyce: Overtures*, MB, xiii (1957)
C. Cudworth: 'Boyce and Arne: the Generation of 1710', *ML*, xli (1960), 136–45
C. Haywood: 'William Boyce's "Solemn Dirge" in Garrick's *Romeo and Juliet* Production of 1750', *Shakespeare Quarterly*, xi (1960), 173–85
C. Cudworth: 'Songs and Part-song Settings of Shakespeare's Lyrics, 1660–1960', *Shakespeare in Music*, ed. P. Hartnoll (London, 1964), 51–87
R. Fiske: 'The Macbeth Music', *ML*, xlv (1964), 114–25
——: 'Boyce's Operas', *MT*, cxi (1970), 1217–18
——: *English Theatre Music in the Eighteenth Century* (London, 1973, 2/1986)
T. J. Walsh: *Opera in Dublin 1705–1797* (Dublin, 1973)
R. J. Bruce: 'William Boyce: some Manuscript Recoveries', *ML*, lv (1974), 437–43
——: Introduction to *The Shepherd's Lottery*, MLE, C4 (London, 1990)

IAN BARTLETT

Boyer, Claude (*b* Albi, 1618; *d* Paris, 22 July 1688). French dramatist. Over a period of 50 years he wrote 23 plays, 14 of them tragedies, the rest machine-plays and comedies. He wrote the libretto for one opera, *Méduse* (C. H. Gervais, 1697); mainly in alexandrine verse, its plot revolves around Medusa's love for Perseus and her jealous reaction to his love for Ismene. Boyer viewed *Méduse* as a tragedy set to music – a play to which *intermèdes* were added and in which spectacle was an important element. There are similarities with Metastasian drama in his plays *Artaxerce*, *Porus, ou La générosité d'Alexandre* and *La mort de Démétrius*; the last is echoed in Metastasio's *Antigono* rather than *Demetrio*. Boyer's *Agamemnon* was the source for the opera *Cassandre* (1706, Paris; music by Bouvard and Bertin de la Doué, libretto by Lagrange-Chancel), and *Ulysse* shows parallels with Rebel's opera of the same name (1703, Paris).

*

H. C. Lancaster: *A History of French Dramatic Literature in the Seventeenth Century* (Baltimore, 1929–42)
C. Brody: *The Works of Claude Boyer* (New York, 1947)
C. Girdlestone: *La tragédie en musique (1673–1750) considérée comme genre littéraire* (Geneva, 1972)

ALISON STONEHOUSE

Bozay, Attila (*b* Balatonfüzfő, 11 Aug 1939). Hungarian composer. He studied with Ferenc Farkas at the Budapest Academy of Music, graduating in 1962. In 1962–3 he taught music theory at the Szeged Conservatory, then became a music producer for Hungarian Radio until 1966. A UNESCO scholarship took him to Paris in 1967 for six months. He then returned to Hungary, and worked as a freelance composer until 1979, when he was appointed to teach composition at the Budapest Academy of Music. In 1990 he was made director of the Hungarian National Philharmonia.

From 1957 Bozay adopted 12-note methods. After his studies in Paris his style was enriched by new resources including aleatory techniques and the exploitation of unusual timbres. His later music shows a return to Hungarian national and folk traditions. A good example is the three-act opera *Csongor és Tünde* ('Csongor and Tünde', after the play by the Hungarian romantic poet Mihály Vörösmarty, adapted by the composer), written for the centenary of the Hungarian State Opera House in Budapest and first performed there on 20 January 1985. The subject is the love between the immortal fairy Tünde and the mortal hero Csongor, and their victory over the intrigues of the witch Mirigy; it is essentially a story of initiation. The introspective, static nature of the play, with its almost total lack of propulsive dialogue, results in a musical structure with expansive, homogeneous surfaces of lyrical character, rhythmically free, melodically ornamented and chromatic, with contrasting scherzando sections in a clearly folk-derived and pantomimic vein. The lovers' victory is expressed in music of rich diatonicism. *Csongor* was preceded by a one-act opera on Sándor Weöres's verse tale, *Küngisz királynője* ('Queen Küngis'), composed in 1968–9 but never performed; it was later rejected by the composer.

TIBOR TALLIÁN

Bozen (Ger.). BOLZANO.

Božič, Darijan (*b* Slavonski brod, Croatia, 29 April 1933). Slovene composer. He studied composition (1958) and conducting (1961) at the Ljubljana Academy of Music. After further studies in Paris and London (1967), he worked in Ljubljana, becoming conductor and director of studies at the Slovene Opera (1968–70) and conductor and artistic director of the Slovene Philharmonic (1970–74). He was appointed professor at the University of Maribor in 1988. Božič is the only modern Slovene composer to have tackled new and individual techniques of composition effectively and with determination. He describes his stage works variously as operas, musical dramas and projects, farces and happenings. While his first opera, *La bohème 57*, is traditional in form, his second, *La putain respectueuse*, uses serial techniques, the work being constructed entirely on fugal principles. Different again is the musical drama *Ares-Eros*, which is composed according to the technique of *collage sonore*.

La bohème 57, 1958 (3, B. Dolinar, after R. Dorgeles: *Love in Montmartre*), unperf.
La putain respectueuse, 1960 (1, Dolinar, after J. P. Sartre), ov. perf. Ljubljana, 1970–71 season
Jago, 1968 (happening for 8 performers and tape, Božič, after W. Shakespeare: *Othello* and W. Heinrich: *Gottes zweite Garnitur*), Ljubljana, 20 April 1970
Ares-Eros, 1970 (musical drama, Božič, after Aristophanes: *Lysistrata* and other classical texts), Ljubljana, 12 May 1971
Lizistrata 75, 1975 (operatic farce, 2, S. Rozman, after Aristophanes: *Lysistrata*), Maribor, 14 Nov 1980
Kralj Lear [King Lear], 1985 (musico-dramatic project, Božič, after Shakespeare), Maribor, 20 June 1986
Telmah, 1990 (musico-dramatic project, montage by Božič of texts from Shakespeare plays and sonnets and R. Bolt: *A Man for All Seasons*), Opatija, 5 Nov 1990 [abridged version]; Ljubljana TV, 15 June 1991 [complete]

MANICA ŠPENDAL

Bozza, Eugène (*b* Nice, 4 April 1905). French composer. He studied at the Paris Conservatoire, where his teachers included Büsser and Rabaud, and won *premiers prix* for the violin, conducting and composition, and also the Prix de Rome with *La légende de Roukmâni*, a dramatic cantata for three singers whose luxuriously orchestrated score is reminiscent of Roussel's *Padmâvatî* and whose libretto is similarly based on an Indian legend. From 1939 to 1948 he conducted the Opéra-Comique in Paris and in 1951 was appointed director of the Ecole Nationale de Musique, Valenciennes. He was made a Chevalier of the Légion d'honneur in 1956. Though his large-scale works have been successfully performed in France, his international reputation rests on his chamber music for wind. His most recent opera, *La duchesse de Langeais*, is set in 1818 under the reign of Louis XVIII. Antoinette, the duchess (soprano), ends up in a convent and rejects her former lover, Montriveau (tenor), remaining faithful to her vows of chastity.

La légende de Roukmâni (fantaisie lyrique, 1, C. Orly), Paris, Institut de France, 30 June 1934, *F-Pn*
Beppo, ou Le mort dont personne ne voulait (ob, 1, J. Bruyr), Lille, Opéra, 1963
La duchesse de Langeais (drame lyrique, F. Forté, after H. de Balzac), Lille, Opéra, 27 April 1967

*

P. Bertrand: *Le monde de la musique* (Geneva, 1947)
A. Machabey: *Portraits de trente musiciens français* (Paris, 1949)

PAUL GRIFFITHS, RICHARD LANGHAM SMITH

Bracale, Adolfo (*b* Naples, 1873; *d* Bogotà, 28 Aug 1935). Italian impresario and cellist. He joined the orchestra of an Italian opera company touring the Balkans in 1890, and also performed in Egypt, but decided to try his hand as an impresario in 1895, giving performances in Alexandria (Alhambra Theatre) during August and September and in Cairo (Ezbekieh Gardens) for the next two months. The company was joined in Cairo by the young and not yet famous Enrico Caruso, who sang in five operas. Bracale was again impresario in Cairo, but at the much more important khedivial theatre from 1908 to 1912; here he continued his practice of hiring outstanding young singers (Amelita Galli-Curci, Hipolito Lazaro) before they became famous. Salomea Krusceniski, Eugenia Burzio, Carmen Melis, Antonio Magini-Coletti and Eugenio Giraldoni also sang for him during these years. In 1912 he put on *Aida* at the Pyramids.

Bracale's Latin-American activities began in 1915 with a tour of South America, including Buenos Aires (the Teatro Coliseo), Santiago and Valparaìso. In January 1916 his company performed *Aida* with Tina Poli-Randaccio in Havana, the city that was to be his future base of operations. For most of the next eight years he toured the Caribbean basin and the northern half of South America. In addition to his ten or so seasons in Havana, he also provided operatic entertainment to San Juan (four seasons), Caracas (six seasons), Bogotà (three seasons), Panama City, San José, Lima (four seasons), Quito and Guayaquil as well as many smaller cities. His companies featured many of the greatest singers of the period, among them Amelita Galli-Curci, Maria Barrientos, Carmen Melis, Elvira de Hidalgo, Tito Schipa and Giuseppe De Luca, and could probably have competed with any in the world. Enrico Caruso sang with him again in Havana in May 1920, followed by a tour of Cuba, but is reported to have turned down a lucrative contract to go on to Lima. Bracale returned to Egypt (Alexandria and Cairo) for the 1925–6 season, with Pietro Mascagni as principal conductor and Hipolito Lazaro as his star tenor.

He started another Caribbean tour in Havana in May 1927, revisiting among other places San Juan, Caracas, Bogotà, Panama City and San José, and venturing for the first time to Cali (the first opera season there), Managua, San Salvador and Guatemala City. By now the calibre of his singers was lower, only Lazaro and the mezzo Aurora Buades being well known. Several more tours followed, one of which featured Miguel Fleta. His centre of operations began to shift south to Venezuela and Colombia in the 1930s.

*

A. Bracale: *Mis memorias* (Caracas and Bogotà, 1931)
J. I. Perdomo Escobar: *La opera en Colombia* (Bogotà, 1979)

TOM KAUFMAN

Braccioli, Grazio (*b* Ferrara, 1682; *d* Ferrara, 26 July 1752). Italian librettist. By profession he was a lawyer; most of his activity as a librettist took place during a period of residence in Venice around 1710–15. His earliest libretto was *Crisippo*, set by Floriano Arresti in 1710. The next year saw the appearance of his *Armida in Damasco* (G. Rampini), the first of nine librettos exclusively for the Venetian theatre of S Angelo. The best known of these are *Orlando furioso* and *Orlando finto pazzo* (both set by Vivaldi). The last of his librettos was *Alessandro fra le Amazoni*. After his return to Ferrara Braccioli ended his involvement with opera but remained active in other literary fields. He was a member of the Roman Arcadia under the name of Nigello Preteo. In his adaptation for the operatic stage of episodes from the epics of Ariosti, Boiardo and Tasso he showed imagination and ingenuity, managing to preserve something of the liveliness of his sources amid a 'reforming' literary climate quite alien in spirit.

Crisippo, Arresti, 1710; *Armida in Damasco*, Rampini, 1711; *La gloria trionfante d'amore*, Rampini, 1712; *Arsinoe vendicata*, Ruggieri, 1712; *La costanza in cimento con la crudeltà*, Arresti, 1712; *Orlando furioso*, Ristori, 1713 (Vivaldi, 1714, rev. 1727 as Orlando; Schürmann, 1722; Bioni, 1724; O. Pollarolo, 1725; various later pasticcios); *Calfurnia*, Heinichen, 1713; *Orlando finto pazzo*, Vivaldi, 1714; *Rodomonte sdegnato*, Gasparini, 1714; *Alessandro fra le Amazoni*, Chelleri, 1715

*

G. M. Mazzuchelli: *Gli scrittori d'Italia*, ii/4 (Brescia, 1763), 1954–6
B. Brizi: 'Gli *Orlandi* di Vivaldi attraverso i libretti', *Antonio Vivaldi: teatro musicale, cultura e società: Venice 1981*, 315–30

A. L. Bellina, B. Brizi and M. G. Pensa: *I libretti vivaldiani* (Florence, 1982), 85–96
J. W. Hill: 'Vivaldi's *Orlando*: Sources and Contributing Factors', *Opera and Vivaldi*, ed. M. Collins and E. K. Kirk (Austin, 1984), 327–46
MICHAEL TALBOT

Bracegirdle, Anne (*b* Northampton, bap. 15 Nov 1671; *d* London, 12 Sept 1748). English actress and soprano. She was brought up in the family of Thomas Betterton and was London's leading actress from 1688 until her retirement in 1707. Her roles often included songs by John Eccles and verses in praise of her performance of his mad song 'I burn' in *Don Quixote* were set by both Purcell and Finger. Dryden described her singing with Dogget in *The Richmond Heiress* (1693) as 'wonderfully good' and Congreve wrote that she performed Venus in Eccles's setting of his *Judgment of Paris* (1701) 'to a miracle'. She was the second female lead in Fedeli's all-sung opera in the Italian style, *The Temple of Love* (1706). She is buried in the east cloisters of Westminster Abbey.

*

BDA; *DNB* (J. Knight); *LS*
J. Downes: *Roscius Anglicanus* (London, 1708); ed. J. Milhous and R. D. Hume (London, 1987)
C. Cibber: *An Apology for the Life of Mr. Colley Cibber* (London, 1740)
J. H. Wilson: *All the King's Ladies* (Chicago, 1958)
C. A. Price: *Henry Purcell and the London Stage* (Cambridge, 1984)
OLIVE BALDWIN, THELMA WILSON

Braein, Edvard Fliflet (*b* Kristiansund, 23 Aug 1924; *d* Oslo, 30 April 1976). Norwegian composer. He had composition and conducting lessons with Bjarne Brustad and Odd Grüner-Hegge, and was a composition pupil of Rivier at the Paris Conservatoire (1950–51). His music may be characterized as humorous, gay and tuneful; it includes many vocal works, among them the operas *Anne Pedersdottor* (4, H. Kristiansen, after H. Wiers-Jenssen; Oslo, 16 April 1971) and *Den stundeslöse* (3, Kristiansen, after L. Holberg; Oslo, 8 Sept 1975). PETER ANDREAS KJELDSBERG

Braga, (Antônio) Francisco (*b* Rio de Janeiro, 15 April 1868; *d* Rio de Janeiro, 14 March 1945). Brazilian composer. After studying the clarinet and composition at the Imperial Conservatory of Music, he was awarded a government scholarship in 1890 for further study in Europe. At the Paris Conservatoire for four years, he was a pupil of Massenet, who exerted a lasting influence on him. In 1896 he moved to Dresden; he attended the Bayreuth Festival twice, soon becoming a Wagnerian in attitude and technique. Although Braga was primarily a symphonic composer, he wrote the one-act opera *Jupira* to a libretto by Escragnolle Doria; the libretto was translated into Italian and, later, into German. The work was given its première at the Rio Teatro Lirico on 7 October 1900, by an Italian troupe (under the Milan conductor Sanzone) participating in the celebration of the quatercentenary of the discovery of Brazil. It was revived at the Rio Teatro Municipal in 1923 by the Italian Giuseppe Marinuzzi. Although Braga later said he had wanted the subject of his opera 'to be national, but without Indians', Jupira (soprano) is an Indian woman who seeks revenge on her faithless lover. The composer worked for ten years (1912–22) on another opera, the four-act *Anita Garibaldi*, to a libretto by Osório Duque Estrada, but he never completed it.
GERARD BÉHAGUE

Braga, Gaetano (*b* Giulianova, nr Teramo, 9 June 1829; *d* Milan, 21 Nov 1907). Italian composer. He entered the Naples Conservatory in 1841 to study singing, but instead chose the cello, soon adding to this composition studies with Mercadante. He left in 1852 with the title 'Maestrino di violoncello' and made many concert tours of Europe and the USA until late in life.

In 1853 his first opera, *Alina*, was produced at Naples. The rejection in 1868 by La Scala, however, of his *Ruy Blas* in favour of Franchetti's work on the same subject coloured his decision to move to Paris, where he remained for some 30 years. He maintained a lifelong interest in opera but his early promise as a composer was not fulfilled, and none of his stage works remained in the repertory.

As a voice teacher Braga was much sought after; he coached Erminia Frezzolini, towards the end of her career, and Adelaide Borghi-Mamo, for whom he also wrote salon works. His other compositions, mainly unremarkable, include orchestral, chamber and vocal music, fantasias on well-known operatic themes, and salon pieces that enjoyed popularity during his lifetime.

Alina, o La Spregiata (L. E. Bardare), Naples, Fondo, 28 July 1853
Estella di San Germano (A. de Lauzières), Vienna, Hofoper, 29 May 1857
Il ritratto (de Lauzières), Naples, private theatre of the Count of Syracuse, 6 March 1858
Margherita la mendicante (F. M. Piave), Paris, Italien, 28 Dec 1859
Mormile (Piave), Milan, Scala, 4 Feb 1862
Ruy Blas, 1865 (G. Peruzzini), unperf.
Gli avventurieri (A. Ghislanzoni), Milan, S Radegonda, 30 Oct 1867
Reginella (Ghislanzoni), Lecco, Sociale, 16 Sept 1871
Caligola (Ghislanzoni), Lisbon, S Carlos, 22 Jan 1873
LYNDA MACGREGOR

Braga Santos, (José Manuel) Joly. *See* SANTOS, JOLY BRAGA.

Braham, John (*b* London, 20 March 1774; *d* London, 17 Feb 1856). English tenor and composer. As a boy at a London synagogue, he was heard by the singer Leoni (Leoni Meyer), who trained him and introduced him to Covent Garden as a boy soprano (1787). Later he studied at Bath with Rauzzini and in 1796 was engaged by Rauzzini's pupil Nancy Storace to sing in Stephen Storace's opera *Mahmoud*. With Storace he made a successful tour of the Continent. Back in London, he made his adult début at Covent Garden (1801). In 1806 he sang in the first complete performance of a Mozart opera in London (*La clemenza di Tito*). He began to write the music for his own part in composite operas, composing song melodies which were then harmonized and orchestrated by others. His ballads and patriotic songs, especially *The Death of Nelson*, won great popularity, and Weber wrote the role of Sir Huon in *Oberon* for him (1826, Covent Garden). He returned to the stage after a brief retirement, singing baritone parts at Drury Lane (*Guillaume Tell*, 1838; *Don Giovanni*, 1839) and subsequently touring America. He continued to sing in England until 1852. Walter Scott declared Braham to be 'a beast of an actor but an angel of a singer'. After his liaison with Storace ended, in 1816, he married Frances Elisabeth Bolton; their daughter, Frances, Countess Waldegrave, was a leading hostess of the Victorian era.

all first performed in London

Music in: The Cabinet (comic op, T. J. Dibdin), CG, 1802, vs (London, 1802); Family Quarrels (comic op, Dibdin), CG, 1802, vs (London, *c*1802); The English Fleet in 1342 (comic op,

Dibdin), CG, 1803, pf score (London, 1803); Thirty Thousand, or Who's the Richest? (Dibdin, after M. Edgeworth), CG, 1804, vs (London, 1805); Out of Place, or The Lake of Lausanne (G. N. F. Reynolds and Dibdin), 1805; False Alarms, or My Cousin (comic op, 3, J. Kenney), Drury Lane, 1807, excerpts (London, ?1817); Kais, or The Love in a Desert (4, Brandon), Drury Lane, 1808

The Americans (comic op, 3, S. J. Arnold), Lyceum, 1812, *GB-Lcm*, vs pubd; Narensky, or The Road to Yaroslav (Brown), CG, 1814, excerpts (London, 1814); Zuma, or The Tree of Health (comic op, 3, Dibdin, after S. F. Genlis), CG, 1818, songs (London, 1821); Isidore de Merida, or The Devil's Creek (W. Dimond), Drury Lane, 1827; The Taming of the Shrew (operatic farce), Drury Lane, 1828 RONALD CRICHTON

Braithwaite, Nicholas (Paul Dallon) (*b* London, 26 Aug 1939). English conductor, son of Warwick Braithwaite. He studied conducting with Maurice Miles at the RAM (1957–61), with Hans Swarowsky in Vienna (1961–3), and at the Bayreuth masterclasses. His professional début was with the WNO in *Don Pasquale* (1966), and after an auspicious début with Sadler's Wells Opera in a new production of *Les contes d'Hoffmann* (1970) he was appointed resident conductor with the company (1971–2) and associate principal conductor (1972–4). During that time he was much admired for his well-paced and expressive conducting of Bizet, Puccini and Verdi, and for the British première of Penderecki's *The Devils of Loudun* (1973), shortly after his Covent Garden début with *Tannhäuser*. He was music director for Glyndebourne Touring Opera, 1976–80, and for Stora Teater Opera, Göteborg, 1981–4. In the mid-1980s he began to be active in Australia, where he became chief conductor of the Adelaide SO in 1987 and conducted the first 'Opera in the Park' (*Tosca*) at Adelaide in 1990. NOËL GOODWIN

Braithwaite, (Henry) Warwick (*b* Dunedin, 9 Jan 1896; *d* London, 18 Jan 1971). New Zealand conductor. After study at the RAM from 1916, he joined the O'Mara Opera Company (a British touring company) as a conductor in 1919, and thereafter was associated with opera for most of his career. After a period at the BBC's West Region he became a regular conductor of the Vic-Wells (later Sadler's Wells) Opera from 1932 to 1940, conducting the company's first productions of such works as *Fra Diavolo*, *Die Meistersinger* and *Don Carlos*. He moved to Covent Garden as conductor of ballet and later (1950–53) of opera and was artistic director of the Australian National Opera in its 1954 and 1955 seasons. From 1956 to 1960 he was musical director of the expanding WNO (conducting Rimsky-Korsakov's *May Night* and Boito's *Mefistofele*, among other works), and then rejoined Sadler's Wells Opera, retiring in 1968. Although not achieving major renown he made a steady contribution to British operatic life. He wrote *The Conductor's Art* (London, 1952).
ARTHUR JACOBS

Brambilla. Italian family of singers.

(1) **Marietta Brambilla** (*b* Cassano d'Adda, 6 June 1807; *d* Milan, 6 Nov 1875). Contralto. After studying at the Milan Conservatory with Secchi, she made her début in 1827 at the King's Theatre, London, as Arsace in Rossini's *Semiramide*. During the season she sang two more travesty roles, Adriano (Meyerbeer's *Il crociato*) and Romeo (Zingarelli's *Romeo e Giulietta*), becoming a specialist in such parts. She sang Paolo at the first performance of Generali's *Francesca di Rimini* in 1828 at La Fenice. Donizetti composed two male roles for her, Maffio Orsini in *Lucrezia Borgia*, first given at La Scala in 1833, and Pierotto in *Linda di Chamounix*, which had its première at the Kärntnertortheater, Vienna, in 1842. He also adapted the second tenor role of Armando di Gondi in *Maria di Rohan* for her, adding an extra number, when the opera was performed at the Théâtre Italien in Paris (1843). She also sang Pippo in *La gazza ladra* and Smeton in *Anna Bolena*. In 1848 she retired. Her voice, a true contralto, ranged from *g* to *g''*.

(2) **Teresa Brambilla** (*b* Cassano d'Adda, 23 Oct 1813; *d* Milan, 15 July 1895). Soprano. A sister of (1) Marietta, she made her début in Milan in 1831. She sang throughout Italy with great success for 15 years. In 1846 she appeared in Paris as Abigaille in *Nabucco*. She sang Gilda at the first performance of *Rigoletto* at La Fenice (1851), while other Verdi operas in which she appeared included *Luisa Miller* and *Ernani*.

(3) **Giuseppina Brambilla** (*b* Cassano d'Adda, 1819; *d* Milan, 1903). Contralto. A sister of (1) Marietta and (2) Teresa, she made her début in Trieste in 1841. She sang in Rome, Milan and Barcelona; then in 1846 she was engaged at Her Majesty's Theatre, London, where she appeared as Maffio Orsini, the part created by her eldest sister.

(4) **Teresa** [Teresina] **Brambilla-Ponchielli** (*b* Cassano d'Adda, 15 April 1845; *d* Vercelli, 1 July 1921). Soprano. She studied with her aunts (1) Marietta and (2) Teresa. She made her début in 1863 as Adalgisa at Odessa, afterwards singing in Lisbon, Madrid, Paris, St Petersburg and Italy. In 1872 she sang in the revised version of Ponchielli's *I promessi sposi* at the Teatro dal Verme, Milan, and two years later married the composer. She was a famous interpreter of the title role of *La Gioconda*, and sang Paolina in a revival of Donizetti's *Poliuto* at the Teatro Costanzi, Rome (1883). Other roles that she sang included Leonora (*Il trovatore* and *La forza del destino*), Aida and Elsa (*Lohengrin*). She retired in 1889. ELIZABETH FORBES

Brammer, Julius (*b* Schraditz-Mähren, 9 March 1877; *d* Juan les Pins, 18 April 1943 or 18 March 1944). Austrian librettist. Originally an actor and a member of the company of the Theater an der Wien, he took minor operetta roles such as Pritschitsch at the première of Lehár's *Die lustige Witwe*. Later he turned to writing, collaborating with Robert Bodanzky (1879–1923) on straight comedies and with Alfred Grünwald on operetta librettos. The latter partnership produced some of the most noteworthy operettas of the decade after World War I, above all Fall's *Die Rose von Stambul* (1916), Straus's *Der letzte Walzer* (1920), Kálmán's *Gräfin Mariza* (1924) and Eysler's *Die gold'ne Meisterin* (1927). In these well-constructed librettos a modern social touch was successfully integrated into the traditional framework of the Viennese operetta. Brammer left Austria on the rise of the Nazis.

Operetten, written with A. Grünwald, unless otherwise stated

Fräulein Sherlock Holmes (Posse mit Gesang), G. Criketown, 1907; *Die grüne Redoute* (Vaudeville-Operette), L. Ascher, 1908; *Die lustigen Weiber von Wien*, R. Stolz, 1908; *Die kleine Manikure* (Operette), Ascher, 1908; *Elektra* (Parodie-Operette), B. Laszky, 1909; *Georgette*, Laszky, 1910; *Vindobona, du herrliche Stadt* (Operette-Burleske), Ascher, 1910, rev. as *Hoheit tanzt Walzer*, 1912; *Das goldene Strumpfband*, Ascher, 1911; *Die Dame in Rot*, R. Winterberg, 1911; *Das Damenparadies*, R. Fall, 1911; *The Dancing Viennese* [Eine vom Ballett] (Operette), Straus,

1912; *Die ideale Gattin*, Lehár, 1913, rev. as Die Tangokönigin, 1921; *Der lachende Ehemann*, Eysler, 1913
Die schöne Schwedin, Winterberg, 1915; *Die Kaiserin* [*Fürstenliebe*], L. Fall, 1916; *Die Rose von Stambul*, Fall, 1916; *Bruder Leichtsinn*, Ascher, 1917; *Dichterliebe* (Spl), E. Stern, after Mendelssohn, 1919; *Der letzte Walzer*, Straus, 1920; *Die Bajadere*, Kálmán, 1921; *Die Perlen der Cleopatra*, Straus, 1923; *Gräfin Mariza*, Kálmán, 1924; *Die Zirkusprinzessin*, Kálmán, 1926; *Die gold'ne Meisterin*, Eysler, 1927; *Die Herzogin von Chicago*, Kálmán, 1928; *Das Veilchen vom Montmartre*, Kálmán, 1930; *Der Bauerngeneral* (with G. Beer), Straus, 1931; *Donauliebchen* (with E. Marboth), Eysler, 1932; *Die Dame mit dem Regenbogen* (with Beer), J. Gilbert, 1933; *Božena* (Operette), Straus, 1952 ANDREW LAMB

Branchu, Alexandrine Caroline (*b* Cap Françaix, Haiti, 2 Nov 1780; *d* Passy, nr Paris, 14 Oct 1850). French soprano. She studied at the Paris Conservatoire and made her début in 1799 at the Théâtre Feydeau. From 1801 to 1826 she was engaged at the Opéra, where she created roles in Cherubini's *Anacréon* (1803) and *Les Abencérages* (1813) as well as the title role in Spontini's *La vestale* (1807), Amazilly in *Fernand Cortez* (1809) and *Olympia* (1819). Her statuesque presence and noble, declamatory style made her a fine interpreter of Gluck's Alcestis, Armide and Iphigenia (*Tauride*), and Piccinni's Dido. She retired in 1826.

For illustration *see* VESTALE, LA (i). ELIZABETH FORBES

Brand, Max (*b* Lemberg [L'viv], 26 April 1896; *d* Langenzersdorf, nr Vienna, 5 April 1980). Austrian, later American, composer. He studied with Schreker in Vienna in 1919, and in 1920 followed him (as did Krenek) to Berlin, where he also had lessons from Alois Hába and Erwin Stein. His earliest works were vocal, notably *Fünf Balladen nach Gedichten von Else Lasker-Schüler* (1927), one of the earliest dodecaphonic works produced outside Schoenberg's circle. In 1929 his first opera, *Maschinist Hopkins* op.11, was an overnight success: it combined a sensuously humanistic *fin-de-siècle* lyricism with a powerfully rhythmic, mechanistic precision, characteristic of Brand's own, industrial age. It also mixed a broadly atonal idiom with the 'jazzy' tonal dance-music fashionable at the time. The work was felt to be a late expressionistic flowering yet also a hit, following soon after Krenek's *Jonny spielt auf*. However, the rising fascist force in German politics felt threatened by the way the opera's popularity aroused too great an interest in controversial contemporary social questions and, although the Nazis could have interpreted the plot in such a way as to exploit the work for their own ends, its success was short-lived. Because Brand was Jewish, not only *Maschinist Hopkins* but also the composer went rapidly out of favour and his second opera, the appropriately named *Requiem*, was banned before its première in 1933. Even though further operatic works stood little chance of being staged, Brand nevertheless completed *Kleopatra* and *Die Chronik* by 1938, before Vienna (where he had returned to live) also fell under Nazi domination. He had more luck with other dramatic compositions, largely because he created his own opportunities, and his ballet pantomime *Tragödietta* (1927) was staged at several German opera houses. He sustained his interest in the relationship between technology and the arts, both initiating and participating in avant-garde projects: he founded the Mimoplastisches Theater für Ballett and was co-director of the Raimund Theatre, forming the 'Wiener Opernproduktion' company which was inaugurated in 1931 with a condensed version of Weill's *Mahagonny* – its first performance in Austria. His involvement with experimental film production (working in a studio alongside Eisler) earned him a prize for film music at the Venice festival in 1933. His writings include articles on opera published in *Musikblätter des Anbruch* and *Blätter der Staatsoper* (Berlin).

Forced out of Austria in 1938, Brand went to Brazil and finally settled in the USA in 1940. A performance of his theosophically inspired scenic oratorio *The Gate* was staged at the Metropolitan in 1944, the year he took American citizenship. He directed the Music and Theatre Wing, Caravan of East and West in New York City for many years, during which time he composed a sixth operatic work, *Stormy Interlude* (1955). In about 1958 he began experimenting again, this time with electronics, entering a sound-world which fascinated him up to his death. His stage work *The Astronauts: an Epic in Electronics* (1962) is, like *Maschinist Hopkins*, a utopian work demonstrating his faith in technological progress. In 1975 he retired to live near Vienna. His electronic studio there has been preserved as part of the Max-Brand-Archiv.

See also MASCHINIST HOPKINS.

Maschinist Hopkins op.11 (prol., 3, Brand), Duisburg, Stadt, 13 April 1929 (Vienna and Leipzig, 1928)
Kleopatra, *c*1932–8 (1, Brand)
Requiem (1, Brand), Berlin, Staatsoper, 1933, MS ?lost
Die Chronik, 1938 (scenic cantata, Brand)
The Gate (scenic oratorio, 2, Brand, M. A. Sohrab and J. Chanler), New York, Metropolitan, 23 May 1944
Stormy Interlude, 1955 (1, Brand)

*

E. L. Stahl, ed.: *Das Prisma: Blätter der Vereinigten Stadttheater Duisburg-Bochum*, no.23, Jg.5 (1929) [whole issue; incl. M. Brand: '"Mechanische" Musik und das Problem der Oper', 296–9, and 'Die bewegte Opernbühne', 299–303]
M. Giesing, T. Girshausen and H. Walther: 'Fetisch "Technik" – Die Gesellschaft auf dem Theater der "Neusachlichkeit": Max Brand's "Maschinist Hopkins" als Beispiel', *Weimarer Republik* (Berlin, 1977), 783–8 [pubn of Kunstamt Kreuzberg and the Institut für Theaterwissenschaft der Universität Köln]
M. Wagner: 'Max Brand zum Gedenken', *ÖMz*, xxxv (1980), 302–4
C. Bennett: 'Maschinist Hopkins: a Father for Lulu?', *MT*, cxxvii (1986), 481–4
W. Mann: 'Radio 3's Weimar Season: Hopkins Redivivus', *Opera*, xxxvii (1986), 394–7
J. Warren: 'Ernst Krenek and Max Brand: Two Austrians at the "Court" of Weimar', *German Life and Letters*, xli (1987–8), 467–78
T. Brezinka: 'Max Brand: Sein Leben und sein Werk', *Arbeit der Hochschule für Musik und darstellende Kunst in Wien im Rahmen des Ergänzungsstudiums* (Vienna, 1989)
H. Schwarzjirg: 'Max Brand (1896–1980), Komponist zwischen Spätromantik und Elektroakustik', *Rund um den Bisamberg*, v (Vienna, 1989) CHARLOTTE PURKIS

Brand, Michael. *See* MOSONYI, MIHÁLY.

Brandenburgers in Bohemia, The [*Braniboři v Čechách*]. Opera in three acts by BEDŘICH SMETANA to a libretto by KAREL SABINA; Prague, Provisional Theatre, 5 January 1866.

Smetana's first opera was written for the opera competition sponsored by Count Jan Harrach to provide the recently-instituted Czech Provisional Theatre with new Czech operatic repertory. Since no entries were received by the deadline of 30 September 1862 it was extended by a year, thus allowing Smetana, who had returned from Sweden in 1861, to enter. The libretto that he acquired from Karel Sabina in February

Volfram Olbramovič *mayor of Prague*		bass
Ludiše	*Volfram's daughters*	soprano
Vlčenka		soprano
Děčana		contralto
Oldřich Rokycanský *knight*		baritone
Junoš	*young citizens of Prague*	tenor
Jan Tausendmark		baritone
Varneman *a Brandenburg captain*		tenor
Jíra *a vagrant*		tenor
Elder		bass
Constable		bass

Knights and squires, Volfram's retainers, country folk, the Brandenburg army, deserters, Prague beggars, judges

Setting Prague, and the countryside near Prague in 1279

1862 was in two acts and had to be revised to suit the three-act format stipulated by Harrach. Smetana completed the full score of Act 1 by 8 January 1863, Act 2 by 16 February and Act 3 by 23 April. The judges took three years to reach a decision about the four entries submitted, thus denying the opera a public showing in the theatre until January 1866, when a production was finally conceded. Three months later, on 25 March 1866, the judges awarded Smetana first prize, despite their reservations about the libretto. The opera was a great success in its first season, much more so than its successor a few months later, *The Bartered Bride.*

Following the death in 1278 of the Czech king Přemysl Otakar II, his seven-year-old son Václav II was taken from Prague in February 1279 and imprisoned by his guardian Otto of Brandenburg in an attempt to gain control of the Czech kingdom. The opera's subject is the public reaction to the interregnum following the Brandenburg invasion and the driving out of the Brandenburgers from Bohemia – historical events which in reality spread over several years.

ACT 1.i *Volfram's estate, a garden in front of his house* The opera begins unconventionally. There is no overture; 30 bars of orchestral turbulence lead into a recitative discussion between Oldřich and Volfram about the unhappy state of the country and what should be done. When Junoš arrives with news of the abduction of the young king and his mother, all three (and the male chorus) set off for Prague. Ludiše, Volfram's daughter and Junoš's beloved, is left. After her recitative and *adagio* aria her other admirer (the German Jan Tausendmark) finds her, but she angrily rejects his advances: their confrontation culminates in a cabaletta-like Allegro agitato. The cut of the opera becomes increasingly imitative of European models when Ludiše, joined by her two sisters and with antiphonal choral support, invokes God's help in an *andante religioso* Prière. They go off and the scene ends with Tausendmark leading Brandenburgers on to the farm, against the sound of cries and alarm bells.

1.ii *An open place in Prague, midnight* The poor of Prague are seen looting, and celebrating their new-found freedom. This genre scene is elaborated in a series of set pieces: a chorus; a song (with choral support) for the mob's leader Jíra; a 'ballet' characterized by syncopations and abrupt major-minor juxtapositions; and finally a 'revolutionary' chorus 'Uhodila naše hodina' ('Our hour has come'), in whose middle section Jíra is crowned king. Suddenly Ludiše runs on begging help against Tausendmark, who soon appears, sword in hand, with Brandenburg soldiers guarding her sisters. Their arrival marks the beginning of the finale: a substantial slow concertato for chorus and the six soloists. At its close Jíra manages to seize Tausendmark's sword, but in the confusion the Brandenburgers take off all three girls – just before the arrival of Volfram and the others. Tausendmark accuses Jíra (still with Tausendmark's sword) of abducting the girls and is believed: Jíra is arrested and the act ends with an *allegro con fuoco* ensemble – the stretta conclusion to the concertato.

ACT 2.i *A village green* A village Elder leads his people antiphonally in a 'chorale', 'Pane, v prachu se kloníme' ('Lord, we kneel in the dust'), as they prepare to leave their village for the safety of the forest. Varneman, a Brandenburg captain, arrives demanding food for his forces and his captives (Volfram's three daughters), but he is overtaken by events – a constable announces a decree from Otto of Brandenburg (the king's guardian) that foreign forces must withdraw from Bohemia within three days. The people celebrate and Varneman instructs the Elder to seek out Volfram to ransom his daughters.

2.ii *A court house in Prague* At his trial (a scene conducted in declamatory recitative) Jíra puts up a spirited defence but Tausendmark's false witness is believed and Jíra is condemned to death despite Junoš's late news that Volfram's daughters are safe, awaiting ransom.

2.iii *A garden overgrown by trees* A new atmosphere is created in a series of set pieces: a long, contemplative prelude which leads into an aria for Děčana, then a trio for the three sisters, lamenting their captivity. Left alone, Ludiše sings a strophic song, 'Byl to krásný sen' ('It was a beautiful dream'). Junoš, who has crept in unnoticed, supplies the third verse. The folklike suggestions of this number are emphasized by its contrast to the next: a formal cantabile-cabaletta duet for Ludiše and Junoš at the end of which Junoš hides again. He overhears Varneman declare that since he has received no ransom, he will take the women back to Brandenburg with him the next day. Ludiše is defiant and she and her sisters proclaim the belief that they will be released.

ACT 3 *The same garden, evening* The action of this act is confused and its dramatic impact weakened by two insert arias canvassed by the original singers. Tausendmark's aria, 'Tvůj obraz, dívko' ('Your picture, my girl'), is a response to Varneman's refusal to take him and the girls back to Brandenburg. Later the Elder is similarly granted a lyrical aria. In the dark the company assemble: the Elder, naively following Tausendmark's instructions to send the girls in different directions; Varneman, attracted by the commotion; a male chorus (with an extended homophonic celebration of night); Junoš; and Jíra, now released from prison by Junoš. Varneman reveals Tausendmark's plan and the girls are sought and quickly found. So is Tausendmark, who is led away for trial. In an elaborate concertato Junoš, the sisters and the chorus beg Jíra to return to Prague with them (he declines). Volfram arrives, asks Jíra's forgiveness for believing Tausendmark and offers him shelter. The opera concludes with a brief stretta ensemble.

* * *

The initial popularity of *The Brandenburgers in Bohemia* owes something to local enthusiasm for the attempts of Czech composers such as Smetana and Sebor to compete in the hitherto alien medium of opera. *The Brandenburgers* is Smetana's most derivative opera, in its plot, conception, choice of vocal types and musical forms; its melodic freshness is not enough to disguise the weaknesses of its libretto, in particular the sheer muddle of the final act. Its less ambitious successor, *The Bartered Bride*, was able to build on more obviously Czech roots and thus it, rather than Smetana's first opera, established itself as the quintessential Czech opera. JOHN TYRRELL

Brandes, Johann Christian (*b* Stettin [now Szczecin], 15 Nov 1735; *d* Berlin, 10 Nov 1799). German playwright. He fled his family business at the age of 18 and eventually joined an itinerant theatrical company. He was an indifferent actor but won considerable popularity as a playwright. In May 1772 he and his actress wife Charlotte, then both with the Seyler company in Weimar, saw the first German melodrama, Anton Schweitzer's setting (now lost) of Rousseau's *Pygmalion*, in translation. Using H. W. von Gerstenberg's tragic cantata *Ariadne auf Naxos* as a model, Brandes prepared a dramatic scene in the new genre to display Charlotte's abilities. Schweitzer temporized in setting Brandes's text, and after the troupe moved to Gotha it was given to the court Kapellmeister there, Georg Benda. The première of *Ariadne auf Naxos* on 27 January 1775 was a resounding success, mainly because of Benda's music and Charlotte's acting. Brandes wrote a second melodrama for his wife while he was theatrical director at Dresden in 1779. J. F. Reichardt had given him the score of his melodrama *Cephalus und Prokris* on condition that Brandes write him a new text; the result, *Ino*, was first performed in Leipzig on 4 August 1779. THOMAS BAUMAN

Brandram, Rosina (Moult) (*b* Southwark, London, 2 July 1845; *d* Southend, 28 Feb 1907). English contralto. She was engaged by Richard D'Oyly Carte as an understudy for Isabella Howard Paul in the original production of Gilbert and Sullivan's *The Sorcerer* (1877, London) and filled her place towards the end of the run. She played Kate in the New York première of *The Pirates of Penzance* (1879), and assumed the principal contralto parts in Carte's London company, beginning with Lady Blanche in *Princess Ida* (1884). Brandram was intimately connected with the Gilbert and Sullivan operas, remaining with D'Oyly Carte for well over 20 years. She created Katisha in *The Mikado* (1885) and the Duchess of Plaza-Toro in *The Gondoliers* (1889) and also took principal roles in Sullivan's later comic works, including *The Rose of Persia* (1900), and in Edward German's Savoy operas.

She performed only in comic opera, nearly always in roles written for her, and seldom appeared outside London. Although typecast in matronly, sometimes unsympathetic roles, Brandram was not at all unattractive and was less massive than her predecessor, Alice Barnett. Her deep, rich voice was characterized by Gilbert (in a speech to the O. P. Club, 30 December 1906) as 'full-bodied burgundy'.

FREDRIC WOODBRIDGE WILSON

Brandstetter, John (*b* Wayne, NE, 2 Oct 1949). American baritone. He studied with Richard Grace at the University of Nebraska and with Richard Hughes in New York. In 1976 he made his début as Ben in Conrad Susa's *Black River* with Minnesota Opera, where he was a member of the training studio. His flexible, lyrical voice and sharp dramatic and musical skills brought him to the attention of several contemporary composers: he has created roles in *A Quiet Place*, *Jōruri*, Oliver's *Beauty and the Beast* and Argento's *The Voyage of Edgar Allan Poe*. His repertory includes Count Almaviva, Danilo, Falke, Figaro, Germont, Papageno and Silvio. He has also appeared in Chicago, Düsseldorf, Miami, New York (City Opera), Philadelphia, St Louis and Seattle. CORI ELLISON

Brandt, Aleksander. *See* BANDROWSKI-SAS, ALEKSANDER.

Brandt, Marianne [Bischoff, Marie] (*b* Vienna, 12 Sept 1842; *d* Vienna, 9 July 1921). Austrian mezzo-soprano. She studied in Vienna and in Baden-Baden with Viardot, making her début at Olmütz in 1867 as Rachel (*La Juive*). She first appeared in Berlin in 1868 as Azucena, and was engaged there until 1882. After making her London début at Covent Garden in *Fidelio* (1872), she sang Amneris in the first Berlin performance of *Aida* (1874) and Waltraute in *Götterdämmerung* during the first Bayreuth Festival (1876). At Bayreuth she also sang Kundry at the second performance of *Parsifal* (1882). Her other Wagner roles included Brangäne, which she sang at the first Berlin (1876), London (1882) and New York (1886) performances of *Tristan und Isolde*, Ortrud, Fricka (*Die Walküre*), Magdalene, Adriano (*Rienzi*) and Erda (*Siegfried*). The extensive compass (*g* to *d'''*) of her large and well-projected voice enabled her to sing both soprano and mezzo-soprano parts, and at the Metropolitan, where she appeared from 1884 to 1888, her roles included Leonore, Fidès (*Le prophète*), Siébel (*Faust*) and Eglantine, which she sang at the first American performance of Weber's *Euryanthe* (1887).

A. Ehrlich: *Berühmte Sängerinnen der Vergangenheit und Gegenwart* (Leipzig, 1895)
J. Kapp: *Geschichte der Staatsoper Berlin* (Berlin, 1937)
W. H. Seltsam: *Metropolitan Opera Annals* (New York, 1949)
H. Fetting: *Die Geschichte der Deutschen Staatsoper* (Berlin, 1955)
G. Skelton: *Wagner at Bayreuth* (London, 1965)

ELIZABETH FORBES

Brandt-Forster, Ellen (*b* Vienna, 11 Oct 1866; *d* Vienna, July 1921). Austrian soprano. She studied in Vienna with Dustmann, making her début in 1885 at Danzig as Marguerite in Gounod's *Faust*. In 1886 she appeared as a flowermaiden at Bayreuth and in 1887 joined the Hofoper, Vienna, where she remained until her retirement in 1909. She sang Clarissa in *Die drei Pintos* (1889) and Lola in *Cavalleria rusticana* (1891), both first Vienna performances, and created Sophie in *Werther* (1892). A stylish singer with a pure-toned, flexible voice, she made a charming Adele in the first performance at the Hofoper of *Die Fledermaus* (1894).

ELIZABETH FORBES

Braniboři v Čechách. Opera by Bedřich Smetana; *see* *BRANDENBURGERS IN BOHEMIA, THE*.

Brannigan, Owen (*b* Annitsford, Northumberland, 10 March 1908; *d* Newcastle upon Tyne, 9 May 1973). English bass. He studied part-time at the GSM and won its gold medal in 1942; he made his début the next year with Sadler's Wells as Sarastro, remaining with the company from 1943 to 1948 and returning later (1952–8). As well as specializing in Mozart and *buffo* characters, including Handel's Polyphemus, he created Britten's Swallow, Collatinus and Superintendent Budd (*Albert Herring*); Britten later composed Noye and Bottom for him. Brannigan also created roles in operas by John Gardner (*The Moon and Sixpence*, 1957) and Malcolm Williamson (*Our Man in Havana*, 1963; *English Eccentrics*, 1964; *The Violins of Saint-Jacques*, 1966). He performed at Glyndebourne from 1946 (his roles included Leporello) and at Covent Garden from 1948. He had a voice of expressive tone and ripe verbal inflection. NOËL GOODWIN

Branscombe, Peter (John) (*b* Sittingbourne, 7 Dec 1929). English musicologist. He studied at Oxford, where he was influenced by Jack Westrup and Egon Wellesz. He later took the PhD at London University with a dissertation *The Connexions between Drama and Music in the Viennese Popular Theatre, 1781–1855* (1976). Since 1959 he has taught German at the University of St Andrews, becoming Professor of Austrian Studies in 1979. Branscombe's work, in studies of the Classical period and of the German Romantics, has a strong literary basis, but he is also a perceptive and judicious critic, especially of opera and of singing generally. He has written particularly valuably on *Die Zauberflöte*, in a number of studies of its literary and theatrical context as well as its music, culminating in a Cambridge Opera Guide (1991); Haydn, Strauss and Wagner are among the composers on whom he has worked, as well as Schubert – he co-edited *Schubert Studies* (Cambridge, 1982) with Eva Badura-Skoda, contributing a chapter on the melodrama. Branscombe has written many articles and chapters for collective works and dictionaries, chiefly on German and Italian opera of the Classical period.

Branzell, Karin (Maria) (*b* Stockholm, 24 Sept 1891; *d* Altadena, CA, 14 Dec 1974). Swedish contralto. She studied in Stockholm and sang with the Stockholm Royal Opera (1912–18), then the Berlin Staatsoper (1918–23), where she was the Nurse in the Berlin première of *Die Frau ohne Schatten* under Strauss. She sang Kundry in Vienna, and made her American début at the Metropolitan as Fricka in *Die Walküre* (1924), singing major contralto roles there, including Amneris and Delilah, until 1942 and returning in 1951–2; her range was such that she could also sing the *Walküre* Brünnhilde. She sang at Bayreuth in 1930 and 1931 and at Covent Garden under Beecham in 1935, 1937 and 1938, and made other guest appearances at leading houses. After retiring from the stage she taught in New York and later California. Branzell's was one of the great voices of her day, rich, sumptuous, voluminous, and her tall figure with its aura of the grand manner fitted her signally for the big Wagnerian roles.

*

GV [with discography by L. Riemens] MAX DE SCHAUENSEE/R

Brânzeu, Nicolae (*b* Piteşti, 28 Dec 1907; *d* Arad, 7 March 1983). Romanian composer and conductor. He studied at the Bucharest Conservatory (1920–26) and then with Marcel Labey (conducting) and others at the Schola Cantorum in Paris (1931–4). He also graduated in law. Later he worked as a piano accompanist and conductor to the Romanian Opera in Bucharest (1937–47) and at the Opera in Sibiu (1948), and thereafter as a conductor in Arad. He was also a professor at the Bucharest Conservatory and at the university in Arad. He wrote several operas and other works for the theatre and the puppet theatre. In his operas elements of Romanian folk music are thoroughly transformed into a traditional dramatic style, demonstrating his mastery of symphonic language.

Monna Vanna, 1934 (dramatic scene, after M. Maeterlinck)
Săptămîna luminată [Illuminated Week] (musical drama, 1, C. Pavel), Bucharest, 29 April 1943
Cruciada copiilor [Children's Crusade], 1961 (musical drama, 3, Brânzeu, after L. Blaga)
Dragostea triumfă [Love Triumphant] (comic op, 3, G. Haiduc), concert perf., Arad, 6 June 1968

*

O. L. Cosma: *Opera românească* [The Romanian Opera] (Bucharest, 1962) VIOREL COSMA

Braşov (Ger. Kronstadt; Hung. Brassó). Town in central Romania, on the southern edge of the Carpathians, and the main town of southern Transylvania. It was founded in 1235 as Corona and has had several subsequent names; Kronstadt was officially used up to 1918, when the town became Romanian. It was an outstanding printing centre in the 16th century as well as an artistic and cultural centre. Gheorghe Dima and Franz Lehár worked here, as did Ciprian Porumbescu (1853–83), the composer of the two-act operetta *Crai nou* ('Morning Star'), first performed in Braşov in 1882.

There have been performances of opera and operetta since 1812, but the Teatrul Muzical (State Musical Theatre) was not founded until 1955. As well as the standard repertory it has presented works by Sabin Drăgoi, Norbert Petri, Tudor Jarda, Teodor Bratu and Doru Popovici. Prominent singers who have been associated with the town's theatres include Angelica Catalani, Nicolae Popovici, Gheorghe Folescu, Lucia Cosma, Ludovic Spiess, Florin Farcaş, Carmen Hanganu, Ion Gonţea, Mariana Nicolesco and Felicia Filip; among the well-known conductors are Gheorghe Dima, Norbert Petri, Dinu Niculescu, Ilarion Ionescu-Galaţi and Lucian Gropşianu. VIOREL COSMA

Brassac, René de Béarn, Marquis [Chevalier] de (*fl* Paris, 1733–50). French composer. He pursued a military career, but was praised by Voltaire for daring, as an aristocrat, to present his own compositions. He wrote two stage works. The first, a *ballet-héroïque L'empire de l'Amour* (prol., 3, F.-A. P. de Moncrif), given at the Opéra on 14 April 1733, was revised even during the opening run and restaged on 31 May; a letter by Moncrif to the *Mercure* (May 1733) details the changes. The programme of the work, announced in the prologue on Naxos, was to show Love's universal sovereign power. Three domains were chosen: Crete (with its mortals Phaedra, Ariadne and Theseus), Paphos (with the gods Cupid and Psyche) and the kingdom of Zélindor, king of the fire spirits. The last entrée should have come second, but a complicated scene change was required for the sumptuous 'décoration si éclatante qu'à peine en peut-on soutenir la vue'. This was the vast interior of a richly decorated, galleried, domed and arcaded palace, the unprecedented effect of which was judged 'particulier et bizarre' (*Mercure*, April 1733), but riveting. When the work was revived in 1741, another entrée ('Les demi-dieux', showing Linus, son of Apollo, courting in Egypt) was substituted for the second.

Brassac's *tragédie lyrique Léandre et Héro* (prol., 5, J. J. Le Franc de Pompignan) was staged at the Opéra on 5 May 1750; it was engraved and printed but never revived. Marie Fel sang Hero, and Jélyotte Leander. Writing for an orchestra with horns, giving typical care to bassoon writing, and using some italianate figuration, Brassac shows a perfectly competent French technique.

*

ES (J.-F. Paillard)
Mercure de France (April 1733), 793–811; (May 1733), 998; (June 1741), 1430–36
F. Parfaict and C. Parfaict: *Histoire de l'Académie royale de musique* (MS, 1741, *F-Pn*), ff. 65ff
——: *Dictionnaire des théâtres de Paris* (Paris, 1756), iii, 267ff
C. Girdlestone: *La tragédie en musique* (Geneva, 1972), 296ff

PHILIP WELLER

Bratislava (Hung. Pozsony; Ger. Pressburg). Capital of Slovakia and of the former kingdom of Hungary, 1563–1853. The earliest opera performances were given by visiting Italian companies to celebrate coronations and other national events, the first known production being of Sances's *I trionfi d'Amore* in 1648. From the mid-18th century German troupes also appeared. Operas were at first staged in inns until the building, in a private house in 1764, of a small theatre known as the Grüner Stüble; it was replaced in 1776 by the imposing four-storey Városi Színház (Town Theatre), financed by Count György Csáky, on the site of the present Slovenské Narodné Divadlo (Slovak National Theatre). The theatre was leased to German companies, whose performances were open to the public. The Hungarian archbishop Count József Batthyány (1727–99) occasionally invited visiting companies, particularly that of Hubert Kumpf, to present German operas at his palace and country houses, to which nobility and public were admitted. Following Batthyány, Count János Erdődy established a private theatre, 1785–9, also engaging Kumpf's company, which in 1785 gave the first performance in Hungary of a Mozart opera, *Die Entführung aus dem Serail*; the repertory consisted mainly of Italian operas sung in German and works by Haydn and Dittersdorf.

In the early 19th century the traditions of Viennese classicism were continued in the operas and Singspiels of János Fusz (*Pyramus és Thisbe*, *c*1801; *Watwort*, 1806) and his older contemporary Franz Tost (1755–1829). As orchestral conductor at the Grassalkovich palace, 1817–21, Marschner was well placed to have his opera *Saidar und Zulima* (1818) performed in Pozsony. German spoken drama dominated the repertory at the Town Theatre for most of the century, a rare exception being during the directorship of Ferenc (or János) Pokorny, 1830–44: Pokorny mounted an eight-month opera season each year, with guest performers from the Kärntnertortheater and the Városi Színház (Municipal Theatre) in Pest, as well as open-air performances in summer; in 1844 the National Theatre of Pest presented the first Hungarian operas heard in Pozsony, Erkel's *Bátori Mária* and *Hunyadi László*, and shortly after the middle of the century József Szabó's company staged *Hunyadi László* and Franz Doppler's *Ilka* as well as numerous examples of the *népszinmü* (native Singspiel) by Erkel and Doppler. From the establishment in 1867 of the Austro-Hungarian monarchy, the pattern of a main season presented by Hungarian companies followed by a shorter one of light opera and operetta given by a German troupe persisted until the end of World War I and the creation of the Czechoslovak Republic.

The first opera performed in Slovak, *The Bartered Bride*, was given in Bratislava in 1919, but the staging of *The Kiss* the following year marked the true beginning of the Slovak National Opera; the opera and ballet companies, state-run since 1938, are based at the former Municipal Theatre, built in 1886 to replace the Town Theatre (which had been demolished in 1884) and renovated between 1969 and 1972. Until 1945 the company also put on operettas, now given at the Nová Scéna. During the inter-war period, the National Opera was directed by the Czech conductors Milan Zuna (1920–23), Oskar Nedbal (1923–30) and his nephew Karel Nedbal (1930–38). Zuna set the company on the path to professional status, notably with performances of *Tannhäuser* (1922), *Aida* (1923) and *Kát'a Kabanová* (1923, one year after its première). Oskar Nedbal first took the company abroad, to Spain in 1924, and in 1926 he gave the première (in Slovak) of Ján Levoslav Bella's *Wieland der Schmied*. He invited Mascagni and Strauss as guest conductors, and Shalyapin to sing. Under Karel Nedbal's directorship the repertory included *Figaro* (1932), *Don Giovanni* (1933), *Tristan* (1934), *Parsifal* (1935) and *Lady Macbeth of the Mtsensk District* (1935; the first performance outside the Soviet Union).

During the Slovak Republic (1939–45), Josef Vincourek was head of the National Opera and Štefan Hoza its Dramaturg. The repertory was translated into Slovak (until 1939 most works had been sung in Czech); Ladislav Holoubek (répétiteur and conductor, 1933–52) conducted his first three operas, *Stella* (1939), *Svitanie* ('Dawn', 1941) and *Túžba* ('Aspiration', 1944); and the Slovak première of Egk's *Peer Gynt* took place (1941).

After the reconstruction of Czechoslovakia the company's work grew in quality, despite disruptions, under the successive direction of Krešimir Baranović, Zuna, Zdeněk Chalabala, Tibor Frešo, Šimon Jurovský, Frešo again, Pavol Bagin, Marián Jurík and (from 1989) Juraj Hrubant. The National Opera has given the first performances of most Slovak operas, including Suchoň's *Krútnava* ('The Whirlpool', 1949), and has presented many other 20th-century operas – Egk's *Der Revisor* (1959), *Die Verurteilung des Lukullus* (1962), *Cardillac* (revised version, 1964), *Albert Herring* (1966), *The Consul* (1967), *The Greek Passion* (1969), *The Makropulos Affair* (1973), *Porgy and Bess* (1974), *Salome* (1976), *Elektra* (1980), *The Rake's Progress* (1982) and *Wozzeck* (1986) – as well as the standard repertory. The golden age was Zdeněk Košler's tenure as chief conductor (1971–6). The Bratislava Festival (founded 1965), which takes place in September and October, has included opera productions given by the National Opera as well as by visiting companies, notably the première in 1979 of Jan Cikker's *Rozsudok* ('The Sentence').

Composers associated with the city are Oto Ferenczy and Tadeáš Salva, whose *Margita a Besná* (1976) was the first Slovak television opera.

*

A. Heppner: *A Pozsonyi német színészet története a XVIII. században* [History of German Theatre in Pozsony in the 18th Century] (Pozsony, 1910)
K. Benyovszky: *Das alte Theater: Kulturgeschichte aus Pressburgs Vergangenheit* (Bratislava, 1926)
——: *A Pozsonyi magyar színészet története 1867–ig* [History of Hungarian Theatre in Pozsony since 1867] (Bratislava, 1928)

Š. Hoza: 'Koncerty a divadlá v Grassalkovičovom paláci v Bratislave' [Concerts and Theatres in the Grassalkovich Palace in Bratislava], *Kultura* (1939), 249–51
——: *Opera na Slovensku* (Martin, 1953–4)
Pamätnica Slovenského národného divadlá [Slovak National Theatre Memorial Volume] (Bratislava, 1960)
DEZSŐ LEGÁNY, IGOR VAJDA

Bratři Karamazovi ('The Brothers Karamazov'). Opera in three acts by OTAKAR JEREMIÁŠ to a libretto by the composer and Jaroslav Maria after FYODOR MIKHAYLOVICH DOSTOYEVSKY's novel; Prague, National Theatre, 8 October 1928.

The oppressive life of the land-owning Karamazovs is portrayed in Act 1; the main character is Mitya (tenor), not Alyosha (tenor) as in the novel. Mitya, in love with Grushenka (soprano), kills his father Fyodor (*basso buffo*) because he cannot bear the thought of his father's buying Grushenka's love. The relationship between Mitya and Grushenka develops in Act 2, though not without difficulties, and Mitya is eventually found out and arrested for his crime. In the court scene in Act 3 Mitya's brother Ivan (baritone) voluntarily takes the blame for the patricide, but Mitya is finally proven guilty by his former mistress, Katya (contralto), now Ivan's mistress. Expecting to be sentenced to exile in Siberia, Mitya is visited in his cell by Grushenka, Katya and Ivan, who have arranged his escape. The opera ends with the theme of redemption through love and pain, and the gates of a new life are opened.

In *Bratři Karamazovi* Jeremiáš combined the influences of Smetana and Fibich with those of impressionism and expressionism. The prose libretto allows for wide-ranging tonality and free structural format; the striking orchestration highlights both the action and the characters; and the use of leitmotif reflects a Wagnerian influence. The style of writing approaches that of Richard Strauss. JIŘÍ VYSLOUŽIL

Bratu, Teodor (*b* Drăghiceanu-Gogoşari, Giurgiu, 20 Jan 1922). Romanian composer. He studied at the Bucharest Conservatory (1950–57) with Alfred Mendelsohn (composition), Paul Constantinescu (harmony) and Marţian Negrea (counterpoint). Later he became secretary of the Musical Fund of the Union of Composers in Bucharest and music adviser to the Ministry of Culture (1958–82). His earlier works (mostly vocal) display a preference for historical subjects. His musical language relies on traditional harmonic and polyphonic styles; avoiding orchestral brilliance, it shows his remarkable mastery of choral and vocal writing, rooted in popular melody.

librettos by the composer unless otherwise stated

Stejarul din Borzeşti [The Oak Tree from Borzeşti] (musical drama, 4 scenes, after a legend), Iaşi, State Opera, 15 April 1969 (Bucharest, 1978)
Punguţa cu doi bani [The Bag with Two Coins] (children's op, 4 scenes, after I. Creangă), Iaşi, State Opera, 1971
Dreptul la dragoste [Right for Love] (3 acts and 7 tableaux, E. Lazăr and Bratu, after Lazăr), Bucharest, Romanian Opera, 1975 (Bucharest, 1981)
Vremuri de vitejie [Times of Bravery] (lyric-dramatic 'fresco', 9 scenes), Braşov, Muzical, 6 April 1977
Din vremea Unirii [From the Time of the Union] (lyric-dramatic 'fresco', 3, S. Popescu and C. Ghinea), Iaşi, State Opera, 24 Jan 1979
Tudor din Vladimiri [Tudor of Vladimiri] (3 acts and 6 tableaux), Craiova, Liric, 1983

*

V. Cosma: *Muzicieni din România* [Romanian Musicians] (Bucharest, 1989)
VIOREL COSMA

Braun [Brauns], Madame (*fl c*1725). German soprano. She sang in Dresden before going to the Hamburg Gänsemarkt Opera in 1724. She made frequent appearances at the Hamburg Opera until 1726, under Telemann's direction; her roles included Arethusa in Keiser's *Cupido* (1724), Ursel in Keiser's *Der Hamburger Jahrmarkt* (1725) and Columbina in Telemann's *Il Capitano* (1726).

*

K. Zelm: 'Die Sänger der Hamburger Gänsemarkt-Oper', *HJbMw*, iii (1978), 35–73, esp. 46–7
HANS JOACHIM MARX

Braun, Monsieur (*b* before 1700; *d* after 1735). German bass. The singer described as 'Ms. Braun' in the libretto of the Hamburg Gänsemarkt Opera (not to be confused with the Hamburg town musician Friedrich Nicolas Braun) appeared as a guest artist in 1722. Telemann, the new director of the Gänsemarkt Opera, probably engaged him in Brunswick. He is known to have sung in three operas in Hamburg that year, by Orlandini, Telemann and Keiser. He seems to have returned to the Brunswick Opera, where he is recorded in 1725.

*

G.-F. Schmidt: *Die frühdeutsche Oper und die musikdramatische Kunst Georg Caspar Schürmanns*, i (Regensburg, 1934), 127, 129, 131
K. Zelm: 'Die Sänger der Hamburger Gänsemarkt-Oper', *HJbMw*, iii (1978), 35–73, esp. 47–8
HANS JOACHIM MARX

Braun, Carl (*b* Meisenheim, 2 June 1886; *d* Hamburg, 24 March or April 1960). German bass-baritone. He studied first at Kreuznach and was accepted as a student singer at the Berlin Hofoper at 18. After further study he joined the Wiesbaden Opera in 1906, moving to Vienna in 1911. The following year brought his début at the Metropolitan where he remained, singing mostly in the Wagnerian repertory until 1917. He was by this time recognized internationally as a leading exponent of such roles as Gurnemanz, Hagen and Pogner, all of which he sang regularly at Bayreuth from 1906 to 1931. He also became a noted Wotan, singing the role at Bayreuth in 1924. At Covent Garden he sang the *Rheingold* Wotan and Kurwenal in *Tristan und Isolde* (1906). He was also heard in South America and throughout Europe. In 1935 he became director for a season at the Berlin Volksoper, and in 1937 set up a concert agency. His voice on records is deep, firm and strong, heavily Germanic in quality and method, but also expressively used, with a feeling for words and drama. J. B. STEANE

Braun, Helena (*b* Düsseldorf, 20 March 1903; *d* Sonthofen, 2 Sept 1990). German soprano. She made her début in 1929 at Koblenz, initially as a contralto, but taking soprano roles from 1934; after engagements at Bielefeld, Wuppertal and Wiesbaden, she joined the Bayerische Staatsoper, Munich, remaining there from 1940 until her retirement. She appeared at Berlin, Hamburg and Salzburg (1941–2), where she sang Donna Anna and Countess Almaviva. She sang Brünnhilde (*Götterdämmerung*) in the last performance at the Vienna Staatsoper before its destruction in 1944. After the war she sang Brünnhilde in *Ring* cycles at La Scala and in 1949 gave one performance of *Die Walküre* at the Metropolitan, with her husband Ferdinand Frantz as Wotan. In 1952 she sang Isolde at Covent Garden; her repertory also included Leonore, Elektra, the Feldmarschallin and Ortrud, the role of her farewell at Munich in 1959. She had a strong, sweet, vibrant voice with a warm stage personality. ELIZABETH FORBES

Braun, Victor (Conrad) (*b* Windsor, Ont., 4 Aug 1935). Canadian baritone. He studied with Lilian Watson and at the Royal Conservatory of Music, Toronto. He joined the Canadian Opera Company in 1961, making his début as Escamillo. In 1963 he joined the Frankfurt Opera and in 1968 the Staatsoper in Munich. He made his Covent Garden début in 1969 as Hamlet in the first London performance of Searle's opera and also sang there as Count Almaviva and Yevgeny Onegin and in several Verdi roles. At Santa Fe he has sung Jupiter in *Die Liebe der Danae* (1982), Mandryka in *Arabella* (1983), the General in *We Come to the River* (1984) and Holofernes in the American première of Matthus's *Judith*. His repertory also includes Wolfram, which he has sung at La Scala and at the Metropolitan, as well as Hans Sachs, which he first sang in Nice (1986) and repeated at the opening of the Essen opera house, and Wozzeck, which he sang in Chicago (1988). His soft-grained voice has developed considerable power without losing its beautiful lyric quality. During 1989 he sang Pizarro at Brussels, Golaud at Florence and Dr Schön in San Francisco. HAROLD ROSENTHAL/R

Braunfels, Walter (*b* Frankfurt, 19 Dec 1882; *d* Cologne, 19 March 1954). German composer. He studied the piano with Leschetizky in Vienna and composition with Thuille in Munich, and was later director of the Staatliche Hochschule für Musik in Cologne from 1925 to 1933, when he was dismissed by the Nazis. He spent the rest of the 1930s and the war years in self-imposed retirement at Bad Godesberg and then on Lake Constance, returning to Cologne after 1945 to resume his work at the Hochschule. He was made professor emeritus in 1950.

In both style and subject matter, Braunfels's operas mirror his overall compositional development, from the sparkling exuberance of his early period to the introspective spiritual austerity of his later years. His first fully staged opera, *Prinzessin Brambilla* (1909), much admired by Busoni, demonstrated the influence of the post-Wagnerian fairy-tale opera as cultivated by Ritter, Humperdinck, Klose and Pfitzner, as well as an instrumental virtuosity inherited from Berlioz. These trends were continued in his subsequent stage works, especially *Die Vögel* (1920), which with its mixture of brilliant characterization, effortless melodiousness and subtle formal control remained the most often performed of his operas, and the musical comedy *Don Gil von den grünen Hosen* (1924), a skilfully conceived sequence of through-composed ensemble scenes coloured with elements of Spanish folklore.

During the mid-1920s Braunfels's musical style assumed a more ascetic character. He became increasingly drawn to religious and mystical subjects and in works such as the choral opera *Verkündigung*, on which he collaborated with the poet Paul Claudel during the first years of the Nazi regime, the formal structure is more closely related to oratorio. A number of these late compositions were first performed after the composer's rehabilitation in the years immediately following the end of the war, but they failed to make much impact and were never revived.

Falada op.3, 1905 (Feerie, K. Wolfskehl), unperf.

Der goldene Topf op.6, 1906 (after E. T. A. Hoffmann), inc., unperf.

Prinzessin Brambilla op.12 (heitere Oper, 2, Braunfels, after Hoffmann), Stuttgart, 25 March 1909 (Munich, 1908); rev. Hanover, 10 Sept 1931

Ulenspiegel op.23 (3, C. de Coster), Stuttgart, 4 Nov 1913

Die Vögel op.30 (lyrisch-phantastisches Spiel, 2, Braunfels, after Aristophanes), Munich, National, 30 Nov 1920, vs (Vienna, 1920)

Don Gil von den grünen Hosen op.35 (musikalische Komödie, 3, Braunfels, after Tirso de Molina), Munich, National, 15 Nov 1924, vs (Vienna, 1923)

Der gläserne Berg op.39 (Weihnachtsmärchen, Elsner-Örtel), Krefeld, 1928

Galathea op.40 ('griechisches Märchen', 3, Braunfels, after S. Baltus), Cologne, 26 Jan 1930, vs (Vienna, 1929)

Verkündigung op.50, 1933–5 ('Mysterium', 4, P. Claudel), Cologne, 4 April 1948

Der Traum ein Leben op.51, 1934–7 (3, Braunfels, after F. Grillparzer), Frankfurt, Hessische Rundfunk, 22 March 1950

Scenen aus dem Leben der heiligen Johanna op.57, 1939–43 (Braunfels), unperf.

Das Spiel von der Auferstehung des Herrn op. 72, 1938–54 (Alsfeld Passion Play, after H. Reinhart), Cologne, Westdeutsche Rundfunk, 1954

*

PEM (M. Schwarz)

J. Kapp: 'Walter Braunfels', *Blätter der Staatsoper Berlin*, iv/4 (1921), 8–10

H. Schnackenburg: 'Walter Braunfels zum seinem 50. Geburtstag am 19 Dezember 1932', *Musikblätter des Anbruch*, xiv (1932), 195–7

W. Reich: 'Prinzessin Brambilla – ein musikalisches Phantasiestücke in Callots Manier', *Die Tribune*, xxiii/12 (1953–4), 133–7

M. Braunfels: 'Braunfels, Walter', *Rheinische Musiker*, i, ed. K. G. Fellerer (Cologne, 1960), 24–8

U. Jung: *Walter Braunfels (1882–1954)* (Regensburg, 1980)

ERIK LEVI

Braunschweig (Ger.). BRUNSWICK (ii).

Brautwahl, Die ('The Bridal Choice'). *Musikalisch-fantastisches Komödie* in three acts and an epilogue by FERRUCCIO BUSONI to his own libretto after E. T. A. HOFFMANN's *Die Brautwahl*; Hamburg, Stadttheater, 13 April 1912.

Edmund Lehsen (tenor), a young painter, falls in love with Albertine (soprano), daughter of Voswinkel, a wealthy Berlin merchant (baritone). Their romance is cause for concern on the part of Leonhard the goldsmith (baritone), a powerful 'white' magician, for he takes a guardian interest in the promising young painter. His adversary is the Jew Manasse (bass) who, like Leonhard, is over three hundred years old. Further rivals for Albertine's hand are Manasse's son Baron Bensch (tenor) and Thusman (tenor *buffo*), a pedantic minor official. The bridal choice is eventually decided, as in *The Merchant of Venice*, by a trial with three caskets. Manasse is disgraced; Edmund wins Albertine and immediately sets off, at Leonhard's command, to study in Rome.

E. T. A. Hoffmann's short story, published in *Die Serapionsbrüder* (1820), is an unlikely choice for an opera; the plot is complex, the language verbose and the ending inconclusive. Busoni, a connoisseur of Hoffmann, appears to have overlooked the difficulties of adapting such a work for the stage. He wrote the libretto in 1905–6, first publishing it (together with his *Entwurf einer neuen Ästhetik der Tonkunst*) the following year. The short score was begun in 1906 and finished in December 1908; the orchestration was completed in October 1911.

Busoni's brilliant score is almost overburdened with *buffo* scenes but also includes 'Serapiontic' moments, episodes in which reality gives way to a realm of pure fantasy. The vision of Albertine at a tower window (1.ii) and the climactic church vision of Edmund painting a great altarpiece (3.ii) are the finest instances. A distinguishing feature is Busoni's subtle integration of diverse foreign elements into the score (phrases of Carissimi or Rossini, folk music, synagogal chant etc.).

The work attracted considerable interest, and Busoni launched his project with a de luxe second edition of the libretto (Berlin, 1912), illustrated with hand-coloured designs by Karl Walser. The lavish presentation of *Der Rosenkavalier* by Strauss and Roller may have influenced him here, for the two works are almost exactly contemporaneous. At its première *Die Brautwahl* was poorly received and occasional revivals have not yet succeeded in rousing enthusiasm for it. Nevertheless, the score possesses sterling qualities and deserves to be better known. ANTONY BEAUMONT

Bravničar, Matija (*b* Tolmin, Slovenia, 24 Feb 1897; *d* Ljubljana, 25 Nov 1977). Slovene composer. He studied in Gorizia and later with Kogoj and Osterc at the Ljubljana Conservatory (1932). He was active in Ljubljana as a member of the opera orchestra (1919–45), a composition teacher at the academy of music (until 1968) and co-editor of the *Slovenska glasbena revija*. Although he made use of Slovene folk elements, his music is fundamentally expressionist, with some application of 12-note techniques. The operatic farce *Pohujšanje v dolini Šentflorjanski* ('Scandal in the Valley of St Florian', 3, Bravničar, after I. Cankar; Ljubljana, 11 May 1930) reveals Bravničar's rich musical inventiveness. Composed in a partly atonal idiom, it is naturalistic, concise and Janáčekian in style; it focusses mostly on recitative, with a colourful orchestral part supporting the drama. Bravničar based his 'opera of the masses' *Hlapec Jernej in njegova pravica* ('Bartholomew the Farmhand and his Rights', 2, F. Delak; Ljubljana, 25 Jan 1941) on a dramatization of Cankar's *Hlapec Jernej*, a monumental parable on the sufferings of a social outcast. The work is the only known example of a Slovene opera-oratorio: the chorus follows and comments on the plot, while the soloists sing in recitative. The instrumentation is transparent, and the textures are mainly homophonic. Bravničar also composed orchestral pieces. ANDREJ RIJAVEC

Bravo, Il [*Il Bravo, ossia La veneziana* ('The Bravo, or The Venetian Woman')]. *Melodramma* in three acts by SAVERIO MERCADANTE to a libretto by GAETANO ROSSI and Marco Marcelliano Marcello after James Fenimore Cooper's novel *The Bravo* and Auguste Anicet Bourgeois' play *La Vénitienne*; Milan, Teatro alla Scala, 9 March 1839.

The dark and complex plot, set in 16th-century Venice, is reminiscent in atmosphere of the *Gioconda* subject which Mercadante had already used in *Il Giuramento* two years earlier. The Bravo (tenor) of the title is a tormented character who long ago killed his wife in a fit of jealousy; unjustly accused of plotting against the state, he has been forced by the Council of Ten to become their secret hired assassin, while his father is held as hostage to compel his obedience. The story also involves Pisani (tenor), a young man under sentence of banishment, in love with a girl whom he believes to be immured in Venice; Violetta (soprano), the girl in question, who has been under the protection of the Bravo since the murder of her guardian by a would-be abductor; and Teodora (soprano), a wealthy foreigner living in Venice, who turns out to be not only Violetta's mother but also the Bravo's wife, whom he had not killed after all. To compound these complications the Bravo, moved by Pisani's predicament, allows him to borrow the mask and dagger of his office and impersonate the official assassin for two days. In this capacity Teodora employs him to rescue her daughter from the stranger who has apparently abducted her (that is, the Bravo himself). At the end of Act 2 Teodora, in the middle of a brilliant ball, sets fire to her own palace; the last act is largely concerned with the revealing of identities and the unravelling of family knots and, although Violetta and Pisani escape to freedom, Teodora is convicted of arson, and her death at her own hand cheats the Bravo of his last hope of happiness.

Il Bravo is one of Mercadante's most interesting and successful operas. The musical structures show a real attempt to fuse the varied elements of early 19th-century Italian opera into a more continuous dramatic texture. It had a prodigious success at La Scala at the time when the young Verdi had just arrived in Milan, and anyone interested in Mercadante's influence on his great successor can hardly miss the overtones of Sparafucile, and indeed Rigoletto, in the chief character.

MICHAEL ROSE

Bray, John (*b* England, 19 June 1782; *d* Leeds, 19 June 1822). American composer of English birth, active in Philadelphia, New York and Boston from 1805 to 1822. He went to Philadelphia from England in 1805 as a member of Warren and Reinagle's theatre company. In 1815 he moved to Boston, where he worked until the onset of his final illness, when he returned to England.

Most of Bray's compositions are songs for the stage, patriotic songs and sacred works. His most important surviving work is the 'Operatic Melo Drame' *The Indian Princess, or La belle sauvage* (3, J. N. Barker; Philadelphia, 6 April 1808), based on the story of Captain John Smith and Pocahontas; this was issued in 1808 in a vocal score which, besides songs and choruses, included the overture and instrumental background pieces for the scenes in melodrama – an unusually complete publication for the period (for illustration *see* PHILADELPHIA). Bray's musical style is less polished than that of his American contemporaries Reinagle, Graupner and Raynor Taylor, but his melodies are graceful and full of rhythmic variety. His output included seven other operas and pantomimes, and five melodramas, all now lost (listed in Parker).

J. R. Parker: 'Mr Bray', *Euterpeiad, or Musical Intelligencer*, i/3 (1820), 11 [incl. list of stage works]
H. W. Hitchcock: 'An Early American Melodrama: The Indian Princess', *Notes*, xii (1954–5), 375–88
R. Wolfe: *Secular Music in America, 1801–1825: a Bibliography* (New York, 1964)
V. F. Yellin: Record notes, *Two Early American Musical Plays* (New World 232, 1978)
A. D. Shapiro: 'Action Music', *American Music*, ii (1984), 49–71

ANNE DHU SHAPIRO

Brazil. The first opera houses in Brazil were established in the north-eastern coastal city of Salvador, Bahia, in the early 18th century. The short-lived Teatro da Câmara Municipal (1728) was followed by the Casa da Opera da Praia (1760) and the Teatro do Guadalupe. During the first half of the 19th century the Teatro S João (inaugurated in 1812) became the most important centre for visiting artists and lyric companies. The province of Minas Gerais made a modest start in the 1760s and 70s at the Casa da Opera of Vila Rica (now Ouro Prêto), mainly with productions of Italian operas. Church music had a much higher priority in colonial Brazil, but chapelmasters and other church composers provided music for opera and lesser lyric genres on special occasions. In 1786, for example, the municipal council of Vila Rica commissioned three operas for the festivities in celebration of the engagement of the royal infantas of Portugal and Spain; the church composer Marcos Coelho Netto is mentioned as the musical director and a Francisco Furtado da Silveira as the composer. Local opera troupes consisting of black and mulatto performers are reported not only in Bahia and Rio de Janeiro but also in places as remote from the coast as Cuiabá, Mato Grosso, where in 1790 an opera, *Ezio in Roma* (probably by Jommelli), was produced by an all-mulatto cast.

The earliest known lyric theatre at Rio de Janeiro was the Opera Velha (1767–70); the Opera Nova opened in about 1776 under the direction of Manuel Luiz Ferreira. With the transfer to Rio of the Portuguese royal court in 1808, opera and the theatre were greatly stimulated. The future king of Portugal, João VI, founded the Teatro Régio where the opera *Le due gemelle* by José Maurício Nunes García was produced in 1809. The presence in Rio from 1811 of the most famous Portuguese opera composer of the period, Marcos Portugal, added prestige to the operatic life of the city. At the court-subsidized Real Teatro de S João (a replica of the Teatro S Carlos at Lisbon), founded in 1813 and renamed the Imperial Teatro de S Pedro de Alcântara in 1824, several of his operas were performed, as well as numerous Italian operas of the period (sung in Italian). Rossini dominated the repertory until 1832, and Bellini and Donizetti after 1844.

As the seat of the Brazilian Empire from 1822 to 1889 and then the administrative centre of the federal government until 1960, Rio de Janeiro remained the chief centre for operatic activities in the 19th and 20th centuries. The reign of Emperor Pedro II (1831–89) was characterized by the cultivation and official protection of Italian opera; Bellini's *Norma* in particular was frequently performed, and Verdi's *Ernani* was first given in 1846, only two years after its world première. The Teatro Provisório, renamed the Teatro Lírico Fluminense in 1854, presented the most important opera seasons in the country until the end of the 19th century. Francisco Manuel da Silva, remembered today as the composer of the national anthem, attempted to stimulate the use of the vernacular in the operatic repertory. In 1857, under the auspices of the emperor, the Imperial Academia de Música e Opera Nacional was created with that aim and the additional goal of producing at least once a year a new opera by a Brazilian composer. In 1860 the Academy was replaced by a new organization called the Opera Lírica Nacional which immediately produced the first opera to deal with a local subject written by a Brazilian-born composer: Elías Álvares Lôbo's *A noite de São João*. Another composer in evidence in the 1860s was Henrique Alves de Mesquita, but opera in this period was dominated by the works of Carlos Gomes, the most successful opera composer of the Americas, whose international fame was established with the première of *Il Guarany* at La Scala, Milan, in 1870.

Numerous composers active at the turn of the 20th century, including Francisco Braga, Leopoldo Miguéz, Henrique Oswald and Alberto Nepomuceno, tried their hands at opera with varying success. The demand for opera in Rio de Janeiro and São Paulo remained quite high. Native operas followed either late 19th-century Italian and French models or Wagnerian music drama. In the 20th century Brazilian composers have been less creative in opera than in other vocal genres, despite a continued demand for opera in the major cities. Several new theatres were built at the turn of the century, including the Teatro Amazonas de Manaus in 1896 (remodelled in 1990), but only Rio and São Paulo continued to support regular opera seasons. The Rio Teatro Municipal (inaugurated in 1909) has been the main Brazilian stage where the great opera singers, conductors and ballet dancers have performed, including Toscanini, Weingartner, Ruffo, Caruso, Gigli, Muzio, Vallin, Pons, Del Monaco, Callas, Tebaldi, Schwarzkopf, Pavarotti and Domingo. The Teatro Municipal de São Paulo opened in 1911, and since then most of the great European companies and singers have followed the same itinerary: Buenos Aires, Rio de Janeiro and São Paulo.

Brazilian theatres have presented a mainly standard repertory, with only occasional 20th-century and native operas. The nationalist composers Camargo Guarnieri, Francisco Mignone and José Siqueira wrote some important works, and Villa-Lobos's early involvement with opera was renewed with *Yerma* (1955–6). Opera has not attracted the regular attention of more recent composers, perhaps because they have perceived grand opera as a genre which inhibits experimentation and one that is too complex and demanding for the usually inadequate local conditions of production. Among those that have been produced are Lindembergue Cardoso's *A Lenda do Bicho Turuna* (1974), Jorge Antunes's *Qorpo Santo* (1979) and Cirlei de Hollanda's *Judas em Sábado de Aleluia* (1989). In the last decade of the 20th century traditional opera seasons have continued in a few cities, supported primarily by the upper social classes, but opera as a compositional genre appears somewhat anachronistic to the majority of Brazilian composers.

For further information on operatic life in the country's principal centres *see* BELÉM; MANAUS; RIO DE JANEIRO; SALVADOR; and SÃO PAULO.

*

L. H. Corrêa de Azevedo: *Relação das óperas de autores brasileiros* (Rio de Janeiro, 1938) GERARD BÉHAGUE

Brecher, Gustav (*b* Eichwald [now Dubí, Czech Republic], nr Teplitz [now Teplice], 5 Feb 1879; *d* Ostend, May 1940). German conductor. He was a protégé of Richard Strauss, who gave the first performance of his pupil's symphonic poem *Rosmersholm* (op.1) in Leipzig in 1896 (and, later on, other works). Brecher began his conducting career as corépétiteur at the Leipzig Stadttheater. In 1901–2 he was a colleague of Mahler at the Vienna Hofoper, and the next season he was Kapellmeister at Olomouc. He was musical director at the Hamburg Stadttheater, 1903–11, giving the first performances of operas by Siegfried Wagner, d'Albert and Franckenstein, and in 1912 of Busoni's *Die Brautwahl* (dedicated to him). From 1911 to 1916 he was chief Kapellmeister at the Cologne opera house, and from 1916 to 1920 at the Frankfurt Opera. He became general music director and opera director at the Leipzig Opera in 1923, where he conducted the first performances of Krenek's *Jonny spielt auf* in 1927 and *Leben des Orest* in 1930 and of Weill's *Aufstieg und*

Fall der Stadt Mahagonny in 1930. Nazi persecution forced him to abandon his career, and eventually drove him and his wife to suicide.

Brecher was a brilliant and spirited conductor of opera. He endeavoured always to provide a faithful rendering of the work, and sought to transcend the routine artistic practices of his time by intensive musical and dramatic rehearsal. His *Opernübersetzungen* (Berlin, 1911) and his own translations of operas by Verdi (*Otello*), Gounod (*Faust*), Bizet and Puccini (*Tosca*) served the same ends. He was a particularly fine conductor of Wagner and Strauss, and a noted interpreter of Romantic and modern operas.

*

K. Driesch: 'Erinnerung an G. Brecher', *Neue Musikzeitschrift*, iv (1950), 318–20
H.-J. Irmen: *Gustav Brecher*, Beiträge zur rheinischen Musikgeschichte, lxxx (Cologne, 1969), 27ff
J. Schebera: 'Die Ära Brecher/Brügmann an der Leipziger Oper 1923–1932', *Theater der Zeit*, ii (1989), 49–52
——: *Gustav Brecher und die Leipziger Oper 1923–1933* (Leipzig, 1990) [incl. H. Creutzburg: 'Erinnerungen an Gustav Brecher']

DIETER HÄRTWIG

Brecht, Bertolt (Eugen Friedrich) (*b* Augsburg, 10 Feb 1898; *d* Berlin, 14 Aug 1956). German librettist and playwright. His career divides into three periods. The first is the pre-Marxist period, whose two landmarks were the premières of his play *Trommeln in die Nacht* (1922), which made his name generally known in literary circles, and of his and Weill's *Die Dreigroschenoper* (1928), which was and remains an outstanding popular success. The second period began in 1930 with his wholehearted commitment to Marxism. It included 16 years of exile and relative obscurity, and saw the creation of most of his finest plays. The third period began with his return to East Berlin in 1949 and culminated in the triumphs of 1954 and 1955, when his company, the Berliner Ensemble, was acclaimed as one of the world's greatest, and he was recognized internationally as a major figure in 20th-century theatre. Since then his international reputation, like his influence, has far outstripped that of any other writer of his generation.

Brecht's relationship to music is twofold. As a poetic source for composers and as a theatrical innovator whose ideas inevitably influence librettists, he is in the same position as any major poet-dramatist before him. But he was also directly involved with music through his collaborations with composers, notably Weill, Hindemith, Eisler and Dessau. His relationship to music was prompted at first by a natural musicality and from then on by his own creative interests and requirements. In the first and most celebrated of his musical collaborations (with KURT WEILL, 1927–30), he had no experience of working with a composer and consequently found himself perilously close to performing the normal functions of a librettist, which was all that Weill wanted from him. The need to assert himself led him in 1930 to publish the dogmatic and ill-considered tract 'Anmerkungen zur Oper "Aufstieg und Fall der Stadt Mahagonny"' as a means of dissociating himself from Weill's ideas about opera in general and *Mahagonny* in particular. In his subsequent collaborations, apart from the brief and doomed one with Hindemith, he was in a much stronger position. By far the most important was the one with HANNS EISLER, which lasted from 1930 until the end of his life. Their first collaboration, *Die Massnahme* (a *Lehrstück*), was definitive in two related aspects: the text is the first dramatic masterpiece of Brecht's maturity; and the music is its strictly subordinate though highly effective partner. The scores written for Brecht's post-1930 plays and for everything produced by the Berliner Ensemble during his lifetime constitute the most distinctive and coherent body of theatre music in the 20th century. But the ideas about the uses of music which he formulated in occasional articles and notes have little or no value to musicians who are not involved in, and committed to, his own kind of theatre. It is significant that the most powerful setting of any mature Brecht drama, Sessions's opera *The Trial of Lucullus*, ignores these ideas completely; on the other hand the opera *Die Verurteilung des Lukullus* by Paul Dessau is perhaps the most nearly perfect embodiment of them.

LIBRETTOS

Die Dreigroschenoper (with E. Hauptmann), Weill, 1928; *Lehrstück*, Hindemith, 1929; *Happy End* (with Hauptmann), Weill, 1929; *Aufstieg und Fall der Stadt Mahagonny*, Weill, 1930; *Die Massnahme*, Eisler, 1930; *Der Jasager* (with Hauptmann), Weill, 1930; *Die sieben Todsünden*, Weill, 1933; *Die Reisen des Glücksgotts*, Dessau, begun 1945, inc.

PLAYS ON WHICH OPERAS HAVE BEEN BASED

Baal (1922): Wagner-Régeny, 1963, as Persische Episode; Cerha, 1981
Die Gewehre der Frau Carrar (1937): Forest, 1971, as Eine Fahne hab' ich zerrissen
Das Verhör des Lukullus (radio play, 1939): Sessions, 1947, as the Trial of Lucullus; Dessau, 1951
Der gute Mensch von Sezuan (1943): Pironkov, 1972, as Dobriyat chovek ot Sechuan
Herr Puntila und sein Knecht Matti (1948): Dessau, 1966, as Puntila
Der kaukasische Kreidekreis (1948): Hayashi, 1978, as Hakuboku no wa

*

G. Hartung: 'Zur epischen Oper Brechts und Weills', *Wissenschaftliche Zeitschrift der Martin-Luther-Universität*, viii (1958–9), 659
F. Hennenberg: *Dessau-Brecht: musikalische Arbeiten* (East Berlin, 1963)
E. Hauptmann, ed.: *B. Brecht: Gesammelte Werke* (Frankfurt, 1967) [plays in vols. i–vii, essays on theatre in vols. xv–xvii]
H. Eisler: *Musik und Politik* (Leipzig, 1973)
P. Dessau: *Aus Gesprächen* (Leipzig, 1974)
G. Wagner: *Weill und Brecht: das musikalische Zeittheater* (Munich, 1977)
K. Kowalke, ed.: *A New Orpheus: Essays on Kurt Weill* (New Haven, CT, *c*1986)
D. Drew: *Kurt Weill: a Handbook* (London, 1987)

DAVID DREW

Brecknock, John (*b* Long Eaton, Derbys., 29 Nov 1937). English tenor. After studies at the Birmingham School of Music, he joined the Sadler's Wells Opera chorus in 1966 and began singing principal roles the next year, first as Alfred (*Die Fledermaus*). He remained with Sadler's Wells (later ENO) for more than a decade; his flexible, lyric tenor with a touch of brilliance brought him particular success as Tamino and Don Ottavio, and Almaviva and Count Ory, as well as Alfredo and Anatol (*War and Peace*). He created the title role in Gordon Crosse's *Story of Vasco* (1974) and made his Covent Garden début the same year as Fenton. He has also sung at Houston Grand Opera and at Ottawa, and his personable appearance helped to bring him leading roles in BBC television productions including *Rigoletto*, *La traviata* and *Lucia di Lammermoor*. NOËL GOODWIN

Bredemeyer, Reiner (*b* Velez, Colombia, 2 Jan 1929). German composer. In 1931 his family moved to Breslau [now Wrocław]. He learnt the piano and the violin and in 1949 began studying composition with Karl Höller at the Akademie für Tonkunst, Munich. More important were his encounters with Karl Amadeus Hartmann, whose works he analysed and whose Musica Viva concerts he attended, and with Paul Dessau, whom he met in 1951 after the production of Brecht's *Mutter Courage und ihre Kinder* in Munich. He moved to East Berlin in 1954, where he studied at the Akademie der Künste with Rudolf Wagner-Régeny and became music director of the Theater der Freundschaft (1957) and (from 1961) of the Deutsches Theater. In 1978 he became a member of the German Democratic Republic Akademie der Künste (since 1990 the Akademie der Künste zu Berlin).

Since leaving Munich Bredemeyer has composed in a variety of media. His works for the stage in the widest sense have included the 'Schulopernszene' *Leben der Andrea* (1971), after Brecht's *Leben des Galilei*; *Der neue Mendoza* (1973), a sketch to a fragmentary libretto by Thomas Körner after Jakob Lenz; *Galoschenoper*, an adaptation by Heinz Kahlau of Brecht and Weill's *Dreigroschenoper*; and the operas *Candide* (1981–2), to a libretto by Gerhard Müller after Voltaire's story, and *Der Neinsager* (1990, unperformed).

Candide – a 'speculative philosophical parable' – consists of five acts comprising 17 brief scenes with three connecting interludes, beginning with a women's chorus and ending with a 'song and dance of the people'. Voltaire's tale can be interpreted as playful criticism of the compulsory optimism imposed on the narrowly provincial society of the DDR. However, it loses none of its genuinely illuminating charm and wit in this context. With four principal and 15 supporting roles, chorus and orchestra, the work calls for large forces, but they are economically employed to elucidate the text. The composer follows no hard and fast rules, but uses 12-note techniques and pitch sets, with a few quotations (e.g. from Handel's *Music for the Royal Fireworks* and Dessau's *Spanienlied*). The work is remarkably light and cheerful, and strong on characterization. At the première (Halle, Landestheater, 12 January 1986, directed by Andreas Baumann and conducted by Christian Kluttig), the interludes were performed with mime, choreography and film. *Candide* is one of the finest German-language works of music drama of the 1980s.

*

R. Oehlschlägel: '"Wir müssen unseren Garten bestellen": Zu Reiner Bredemeyers und Gerhard Müllers "Candide"', *MusikTexte*, 13 (1986), 61

D. Reinhold: 'Opernkomödie aus Distanz: *Candide* von Gerhard Müller und Reiner Bredemeyer in Halle', *Musik und Gesellschaft*, xxxvi (1986), 146–7

REINHARD OEHLSCHLÄGEL

Brediceanu, Tiberiu (*b* Lugoj, 20 March 1877; *d* Bucharest, 19 Dec 1968). Romanian composer. His teachers included Mureşianu in Blaj and Paul Richter in Braşov. Extremely active in the musical life of Romania, he was partly responsible for the foundation of the Romanian Opera, the Romanian National Theatre (1919), the Romanian Composers' Society (1920) and the conservatories at Cluj (1920) and Braşov (1928); during this period he directed the opera houses in Cluj and Bucharest. He collected more than 2000 folksongs, recorded on 214 cylinders. All of his music remained close to folksong: his operas *La şezătoare* ('At a Village Sitting', 1908), *Seara mare* ('Great Evening', 1924) and *La seceriş* ('Harvest', 1936) explore the life of the Romanian villages in music of simple, moving tunes and a supple orchestration which sometimes approaches that of a gypsy band.

La şezătoare [At a Village Sitting] (1, C. S. Aldea and I. Borcea), Sibiu, 15 June 1908

Seara mare [Great Evening] (3, Brediceanu, after A. Maniu), Cluj, 26 Dec 1924

La seceriş [Harvest] (1, Brediceanu, after N. I. Moldoveanu), Blaj, 20 Sept 1936

VIOREL COSMA

Breeches part [trouser role] (Fr. *travesti*; Ger. *Hosenrolle*; It. *travestito*). A male role played by a female singer (the French and Italian terms apply equally to the converse; *see* TRAVESTY). In 18th-century *opera seria* most heroic male roles were written for high voices and were sung by a castrato or, alternatively, by a woman (never by a male alto). Handel roles written for women include Goffredo (*Rinaldo*, 1711), Dardano (*Amadigi*, 1715) and the title part in *Radamisto* (1720). In early Neapolitan *opera buffa* the hero was normally a soprano. In Mozart's *La clemenza di Tito* (1791) the secondary male part was created by the soprano Carolina Perini. As the castrato gradually disappeared, his mantle fell initially on the prima donna contralto (more rarely soprano) who inherited his title of 'musico'; hence the existence of a number of singers during the early and middle 19th century who specialized in masculine roles, among them Rosamunda Pisaroni, Carolina Vietti and Marietta Alboni. Several of Rossini's operas feature heroes *en travesti*, for example the title role of *Tancredi* (1813), Malcolm (*La donna del lago*, 1819), Calbo (*Maometto II*, 1820) and Arsace (*Semiramide*, 1823). The last Italian breeches part of real importance is Bellini's Romeo (*I Capuleti e i Montecchi*, 1830); written for the soprano Giuditta Grisi, its attractions for the star singer (Maria Malibran, Giuseppina Ronzi De Begnis, Wilhelmine Schröder-Devrient) kept the opera in the repertory for over 30 years. The advent of the romantic tenor pushed the 'musico' into a more marginal place, for example Donizetti's Louis V (*Ugo, conte di Parigi*, 1832) and Maffio Orsini (*Lucrezia Borgia*, 1833), and Federico Ricci's Stefano Rolla (*Luigi Rolla*, 1841); a rare exception is Aurelio, hero of Donizetti's *L'assedio di Calais* (1836). By 1850 the adult breeches role had vanished from Italian opera, though for his planned *Re Lear* Verdi intended to cast the Fool as a contralto.

From early on, however, boys and 'beardless youths', especially pages, were often conceived as breeches parts. Examples include Telemachus (*Il ritorno d'Ulisse in patria*, Monteverdi, 1640), Sextus (*Giulio Cesare*, Handel, 1724 – though the part was revised for tenor), Cherubino (*Le nozze di Figaro*, Mozart, 1786), Pierotto (*Linda di Chamounix*, Donizetti, 1842), Oscar (*Un ballo in maschera*, Verdi, 1859), Beppe (*L'amico Fritz*, Mascagni, 1891), Walter (*La Wally*, Catalani, 1892) and the title role of Mascagni's *Zanetto* (1896).

Outside Italy breeches parts are mostly confined to pre-adult characters. Examples from French opera include Cupid (l'Amour) in many French Baroque works, Urbain (*Les Huguenots*, Meyerbeer, 1836), Ascanio (*Benvenuto Cellini*, Berlioz, 1838), Siébel (*Faust*, Gounod, 1859), Nicklausse (*Les contes d'Hoffmann*, Offenbach, 1881) and the title role of Massenet's *Chérubin* (1905); from English opera, Puck (*Oberon*, Weber, 1826) and Lazarillo (*Maritana*, Wallace, 1845); from Russian, Fyodor (*Boris Godunov*, Musorgsky, comp. 1868–9); from Czech, the kitchen boy (*Rusalka*, Dvořák, 1901) and Aljeja (*From the House of the Dead*,

A scene from Mozart's 'Die Zauberflöte' at the Bregenz Festival, 1985

Janáček, 1930). German opera features four trouser roles of considerable importance: Adriano (*Rienzi*, Wagner, 1842), Hänsel (Humperdinck, 1893) and Strauss's Octavian (*Der Rosenkavalier*, 1911) and the Composer (*Ariadne auf Naxos*, 1916) – the last two being the outcome of Strauss's self-confessed love-affair with the female voice.

Breeches parts are often found in French and German operetta: Valentin (*La chanson de Fortunio*, Offenbach, 1861), Orlofsky (*Die Fledermaus*, Johann Strauss, 1874) and the hero of Suppé's *Fatinitza* (1876). Occasionally they stray into *opéra comique* (e.g. Man Friday, *Robinson Crusoé*, Offenbach, 1867, and the juvenile lead of Chabrier's *L'étoile*, 1877). It is harder to account for the presence of a female Prince Charming in Massenet's *Cendrillon* (1899) except as a nod in the direction of pantomime.

Modern opera eschews the breeches role. In the works of Britten one can always be certain that boys will be boys.

For illustration *see* ALBONI, MARIETTA; *ATTILIO REGOLO*; *CENDRILLON* (ii); *FLEDERMAUS, DIE*; *ROSENKAVALIER, DER*; and SCHRÖDER-DEVRIENT, WILHELMINE.

JULIAN BUDDEN

Bregenz. Town in the Vorarlberg, western Austria, on Lake Constance (Bodensee). It is the site of the annual Bregenz Festival, which takes place in summer. The festival centres around the spectacular lakeside theatre. In 1945 a 'Spiel auf dem See' was first improvised on a large boat on the lake, and in 1947 *Die Entführung* was performed on the shore. The first production given on a stage on the lake took place in 1948, *Eine Nacht in Venedig* by Johann Strauss (ii). Since then classical Viennese operetta, including works by Suppé, Millöcker, Zeller and later Lehár and Offenbach, has dominated the lake productions.

The present lakeside theatre (4379 seats) was opened in 1979 and has an area of 3600 square metres, consisting of island stages, movable platforms and the surrounding stretches of water, making it the largest stage of its kind anywhere. Over the last few years in particular, the productions have given scope for the blending of natural surroundings and theatrical machinery. Special lighting and acoustic installations control and coordinate the performers, who are sometimes 300 metres away from the audience.

Operas have also been performed on the lake: works by Rossini, Lortzing and Smetana were followed by *Porgy and Bess* (1971), *Der fliegende Holländer* (1973, 1989, 1990), *Carmen* (1974, 1991), *Les contes d'Hoffmann* (1976, 1987, 1988), *Oberon* (1977) and *Turandot* (1979). Between 1955 and 1979 a complementary programme ran at the Theater am Kornmarkt (630 seats), offering mainly the less frequently heard Italian operas. The Neues Festspielhaus (1753 seats; designed by Willi Braun) opened with *Falstaff* in 1980 and gave *Otello* the next year, both with star casts. Subsequent productions have included works by Donizetti, Bellini, Verdi, Saint-Saëns and Catalani.

After the death of Ernst Baer, the festival's longstanding artistic director, Alfred Wopmann was appointed to the post in 1983. The engagement of Jerome Savary as producer led to hugely successful lake performances of *Die Zauberflöte* (1985), *Les contes d'Hoffmann* (1987) and *Carmen* (1991). The festival offers a total of some 70 performances during five weeks in July and August; the orchestra is the Vienna SO.

HARALD GOERTZ

Brehme, Hans (Ludwig Wilhelm) (*b* Potsdam, 10 March 1904; *d* Stuttgart, 10 Nov 1957). German composer. After studying piano and composition in Berlin, he taught at the Stuttgart Hochschule für Musik (professor of composition, 1940). His works stand squarely in the German Romantic mainstream: while his harmony and rhythm show the influence of modern currents, his pieces depend essentially on older models. His first opera to be produced, *Der Uhrmacher von Strassburg*, is clearly modelled on Wagner's *Die Meistersinger*.

Der Tor und der Tod op.14, 1928 (Kammeroper, after H. von Hofmannsthal), unperf.

Der Uhrmacher von Strassburg op.36 (3, P. Ginthum), Kassel, 1941 (Mainz, 1941)

Liebe ist teuer op.39 (heitere Oper, 3, F. Clemmens and K. E. Jaroscheck, after E. Raupach), Münster, 1950 (Mainz, 1949)

*

MGG (E. Klemm)

K. Laux: *Musik und Musiker der Gegenwart*, i (Essen, 1949), 43ff

E. Klemm: 'Hans Brehme zum Gedächtnis', *Mitteilungen an die Freunde der Staatlichen Hochschule für Musik in Stuttgart*, vii (1958), 9 [with list of works] WILLIAM D. GUDGER

Breil, Joseph Carl (*b* Pittsburgh, 29 June 1870; *d* Los Angeles, 23 Jan 1926). American composer and singer. While a law student in Leipzig he decided to pursue a career in music. He first studied singing there with Ewald and then in Philadelphia with Giuseppe del Puente. In 1891 he was appointed principal tenor of the Emma Juch Opera Company. He returned to Pittsburgh in 1892, and from 1897 to 1903 worked for a variety of theatre companies. Breil composed incidental music, some 15 of the earliest film scores and five operas, which are lyrical in style and at times sentimental.

Love Laughs at Locksmiths (comic op, 1, Breil), Kingston, NY, 26 Oct 1910
Professor Tattle (comic op, Breil), New York, 1913
The Seventh Chord (comic op, 4, Breil and A. Miller), Chicago, 1913, songs (New York, 1913)
The Legend (1, J. Byrne), New York, Met, 12 March 1919, vs (London, 1919)
The Asra (1, Breil, after Heine), Los Angeles, Gamut Club, 24 Nov 1925

*

D. J. Teall: 'Mr Breil's "Legend" Embodies his Theories of Practical Democracy', *MusAm*, xxviii/22 (1918), 5
E. E. Hipsher: 'Joseph Carl Breil', *American Opera and its Composers* (Philadelphia, 1927), 87–90

Bréjean-Silver [Bréjean-Gravière], **Georgette** [née Sisout, Georgette-Amélie] (*b* Paris, 22 Sept 1870; *d* after 1951). French soprano. She studied at the Conservatoire and made her début at Bordeaux in 1890. She joined the Opéra-Comique in 1894, making a strong impression as Manon, which remained a favourite role; Massenet wrote the 'Fabliau' (as an alternative to the gavotte in Act 3) for her to sing at a performance in Brussels. She appeared in *Manon* and *Lakmé* at Monte Carlo the following season, adding *Les pêcheurs de perles* and *Guillaume Tell* a year later. At this time she sang under the name Bréjean-Gravière, changing it on her marriage to the composer Charles Silver, whose opera *La belle au bois dormant* provided her with another leading part. She also appeared as the Fairy Godmother in the première (1899) of Massenet's *Cendrillon*. On retirement she taught in Paris, having made some recordings in 1905 and 1906. Though a trifle shrill, they show exceptional accomplishments and hint at the possession of a charming manner. J. B. STEANE

Brema, Marie [Fehrman, Minny] (*b* Liverpool, 28 Feb 1856; *d* Manchester, 22 March 1925). English mezzo-soprano of German-American parentage. She studied with Henschel and made her début in 1891 as Lola in the English première of *Cavalleria rusticana* at the Shaftesbury Theatre, London. In 1894 she became the first British-born singer to appear at Bayreuth, singing Ortrud in the first Bayreuth *Lohengrin* and Kundry. She returned to sing Fricka and Kundry during the 1896–7 season. After touring the USA with the Damrosch company (1894–5), singing Ortrud, Brangäne and the *Walküre* Brünnhilde, she joined the Metropolitan for the 1895–6 season, when in addition to the Wagner repertory, she sang Amneris and Orpheus. In 1893 she made her Covent Garden début as Siébel, returning several times until 1907 and creating Beatrice in Stanford's *Much Ado about Nothing* (1901). She sang Brangäne in French in the first Paris *Tristan* (1899, Nouveau Théâtre). In 1910 Brema organized a season of opera in English at the Savoy Theatre, London, singing Orpheus and the title role in the English première of Emanuel Moor's *La Pompadour*. She had an imposing stage presence, and contemporary critics praised her expansive singing and committed acting.
HAROLD ROSENTHAL/R

Bremen. City and port on the River Weser in northern Germany. Its first operatic performances were given in about 1695. Regular performances did not begin until about 1790, when the Komödienhaus auf dem Reithof was used, followed by the Schauspielhaus. Up to this time opera generally took second place to concert-giving in the city's musical life because of the Lutheran church's reservations about the theatre, but a civic theatre was built in 1843. After the destruction a century later of the Schauspielhaus – at which the première of Manfred Gurlitt's *Wozzeck* had been given in 1926 – the Theater am Goetheplatz (989 seats) was opened on 27 August 1950. Montserrat Caballé sang her first Violetta and Tatiana there in 1959. In the 1960s Bremen became a centre of modern operatic and dramatic productions. Between 1964 and 1968 Götz Friedrich produced *Ariadne auf Naxos*, *La forza del destino*, *Carmen*, *Don Giovanni*, *La bohème*, *Salome* and *Le nozze di Figaro* in Bremen. Each season normally includes at least one rarely performed work, such as *Jephtha* by Handel (1981–2 in the production by Herbert Wernicke), *L'italiana in Londra* by Cimarosa (1983–4), *La Wally* by Catalani (1985–6), *King Roger* by Szymanowski (1987–8) and *Der Traumgörge* by Zemlinsky (1988–9). Premières in recent years have included *Der Garten der Lüste* by Wolf Vostell (1981–2) and *Der Turm* by Detlef Heusinger, after Peter Weiss (1988–9). During the season, from August to July, the Bremer Oper stages approximately 245 music-theatre and dance performances. In 1985 Pinchas Steinberg was appointed musical director; in 1990 he was succeeded by Marcello Viotti. SABINE SONNTAG

Bremerhaven. City and port in northern Germany. The first operatic performances were given from 1867 in the Volksgarten und Stadttheater Bremerhaven. A new Stadttheater, in the *art nouveau* style, opened in 1911; the first opera presented there was *Der Freischütz*. Before the advent of air transport, until the 1930s, Bremerhaven was the starting-point for many singers on their way to make guest appearances in the USA. The first administrator of the theatre succeeded in persuading such artists to appear in the city on the eve of their departure. Since 1911, therefore, Bremerhaven has seen guest appearances by the greatest artists of their time, including Richard Strauss (conducting *Salome*), Leo Blech, Maria Ivogün and Lauritz Melchior. The theatre was destroyed in 1944, and theatrical productions were resumed in temporary premises in the Bürgerhaus in 1947. On 12 April 1952 the present Stadttheater, which consists of the Grosses Haus (722 seats) and the Kleines Haus (122 seats), opened with *Don Giovanni*. Of particular interest in recent years have been the German-language premières of the original version of Verdi's *I due Foscari* (1989–90) and the seldom-performed operas by Tchaikovsky, *Mazeppa* (1980–81) and *Cherevichki* (1985–6). The Stadttheater presents five operas, two operettas, two musicals and one ballet in each season, which comprises some 145 music-theatre performances. The season runs throughout the year from August to August.

F. Ernst: *Das Bremerhavener Theater: ein Beitrag zu seiner Geschichte von den Anfangen bis zur Wiedererrichtung nach dem Zweiten Weltkrieg* (Bremerhaven, 1981) SABINE SONNTAG

Brendel, Karl Franz (*b* Stolberg, 26 Nov 1811; *d* Leipzig, 25 Nov 1868). German music historian and critic. He studied Hegelian aesthetics with C. H. Weisse at Leipzig from 1832, then studied in Berlin and Freiburg. He returned to Leipzig, and in 1845 took over the editorship of the *Neue Zeitschrift für Musik* from Schumann, a post which he retained until his death. In his series of articles 'Vergangenheit, Gegenwart und Zukunft der Oper' (*NZM*, xxii, 1845, pp.33ff; xxiii, 1846, pp.57–60, 61–4) he proposed the creation of a national style of German opera, with set numbers replaced by larger scenic units, less emphasis on vocal virtuosity, and the elimination of spoken dialogue; these ideas foreshadowed Wagner's writings, as did his suggestion of the Nibelung legend as a suitable subject for opera. Soon after Liszt settled in Weimar (1848) Brendel's journal became the champion of 'New Weimar'. Its columns were filled by, or on behalf of, Wagner, Berlioz and Liszt with revolutionary political, musical, theatrical and social ideas that were of pressing urgency in Germany before its unification. In June 1859 Brendel coined the term Neudeutsche Schule (New German School) to embrace the progressive music associated with Weimar, and in 1861 he founded the Allgemeiner Deutscher Musikverein, in whose annual festivals new music was featured. His other writings include a history of music in Italy, Germany and France, and *Die Musik der Gegenwart und die Gesamtkunst der Zukunft* (Leipzig, 1854). DEREK WATSON

Brendel, Wolfgang (*b* Munich, 20 Oct 1947). German baritone. He studied at Wiesbaden, making his début at Kaiserslautern in 1969 as Guglielmo (*Così fan tutte*). In 1971 he joined the Bavarian State Opera, Munich. He also sang at Hamburg, Berlin, Düsseldorf, Cologne, Vienna, La Scala and the Metropolitan, where he made his début in 1975 as Count Almaviva. In 1985 he sang Wolfram at Bayreuth and Luna at Covent Garden. His wide repertory includes Papageno, Don Giovanni, Pelléas, Yevgeny Onegin, Peter the Great (*Zar und Zimmermann*), Germont, Don Carlo (*La forza del destino*), Marcello, Mandryka and the Barber (*Die schweigsame Frau*). His voice is full and warm, German in timbre, but agile enough for Italian roles such as Enrico Ashton. ELIZABETH FORBES

Brendler, (Frans Fredric) Eduard (*b* Dresden, 4 Nov 1800; *d* Stockholm, 16 Aug 1831). Swedish composer. He was taught by his father, Johann Franz Brendler, a flautist at the Royal Opera in Stockholm. He does not appear to have composed any music before 1827, but in the last three years of his life he was very active, particularly in Stockholm. In 1828 he turned from his career in business to devote himself seriously to music, and in 1830 wrote two successful melodramas, *Edmond och Clara* and *Spastaras död*. The libretto of his opera *Ryno* was by Bernhard von Beskow (director of the Royal Opera from 1831), and may have been inspired by a short story by Ludvig Tieck. The three acts comprise 14 numbers: Brendler composed eight and orchestrated six before his sudden death; his friend Prince Oscar completed the remaining six numbers, and J. F. Berwald the rest of the orchestration (which is preserved in *S-Skma*). It was performed at the Royal Opera, Stockholm, to great acclaim in May 1834 and was revived 20 times in the following four years. Brendler's work is unique in Swedish musical history as he was the only exponent there of central European early Romantic opera. He exploited the connection between lyric intensity and dramatic characterization, and the drama flows through use of free declamation. In form and harmony the influence of Weber, Marschner and particularly Spohr is apparent, but he also used colourful orchestration and a more individual and advanced harmonic style, including a refined use of 'Tristan chords'.

SBL (T. Norlind)
A. Wiklund: *Eduard Brendlers opera Ryno: Källkritik–analys–edition* (diss., U. of Göteborg, 1991) ANDERS WIKLUND

Brenna, Guglielmo (*b* ?1806–7; *d* after 1882). Italian opera house official. An accountant by training, he was from 1843 to 1882 (with a break in 1859–67) secretary to the management committee of the largely aristocratic society that owned La Fenice, Venice, one of the three leading Italian opera houses in the 1840s and 50s. A committee member arranged the opera seasons, conducting much of the business himself, but as the post changed hands fairly often it was the secretary who provided continuity and acted as permanent manager. Brenna behaved in some ways like an impresario-agent, for example, by taking a cut on artists' agency fees; he even tried unsuccessfully to take a cut on the baritone Felice Varesi's fee when no outside agent was involved. His letters, written mainly on his superiors' behalf, are impersonal. He appears to have been trusted: he negotiated with Verdi over the librettos of *Ernani*, *Rigoletto* and *Simon Boccanegra*, and was twice dispatched to Verdi's country home, once to dissuade him from cancelling *La traviata*. In Habsburg-ruled Venice Brenna was an Italian nationalist; during the 1859 war of independence he was arrested and taken to a fortress in Bohemia, but soon released. Fearing further trouble (or perhaps aware that his superiors did not propose to reopen La Fenice), he took refuge in Florence until Venice was united with Italy in 1866.

Correspondence: *I-Vt*, Fondazione Levi [esp. 'Spettacoli' ser.]
S. Dalla Libera: 'La presidenza del Teatro La Fenice' (typescript, *Vt*), 35
J. Budden: *The Operas of Verdi* (London, 1973–81)
M. Conati: *La bottega della musica: Verdi e la Fenice* (Milan, 1983)
JOHN ROSSELLI

Brenneis, Gerd (*b* Ostseebad Nienhagen, 3 Jan 1936). German tenor. Engaged in 1965 at Augsburg, he sang Lensky, Dimitri, Gabriele Adorno, Lionel (*Martha*), Idomeneus, Manrico, Chénier, Puccini's Des Grieux and Max. At Bayreuth (1973–4) he sang Siegmund and Walther. In 1974 he was engaged at the Deutsche Oper, Berlin, where his repertory over 25 years has included Huon, Florestan, Tristan, Parsifal, Erik, Tannhäuser, Lohengrin, the Emperor (*Die Frau ohne Schatten*) and Bacchus. He made his Metropolitan début in 1976 as Walther and has appeared at Düsseldorf, Cologne, Vienna, Milan, Florence and Turin, where he sang Siegfried (1987). A reliable singer, he has a powerful voice suitable for Wagnerian roles. ELIZABETH FORBES

Brenno ('Brennus'). *Opera seria* ('Dramma con cori e balli analoghi') in three acts by JOHANN FRIEDRICH

REICHARDT to a libretto by Antonio de' Filistri da Caramondani; Berlin, Königliches Theater, 16 October 1789.

Under the leadership of Egisto (soprano), the Gauls successfully storm the walls of Rome. The Roman noblewoman Ostilia (soprano) is brought before Brennus (bass), King of the Gauls, who immediately falls in love with her. She, however, loves the Roman consul Fabio (castrato). They determine to flee. To their surprise, they are offered the aid of Egisto, who is actually the Teutonic maid Zelinda in disguise, formerly the beloved of Brennus. Twice the lovers attempt escape, and twice they are intercepted. To win Ostilia, Brennus threatens to put Fabio to death and simultaneously initiates a bloody sack of Rome. But then Egisto discloses her true identity to him, reproves him for his infidelity and reminds him of the promise of the gods that he will found a new nation in the North. Brennus takes stock, calls an end to the hostilities, returns Ostilia to Fabio, and, reunited with Zelinda, turns his steps northward.

Filistri's contrived ending turned on the dubious legend that the historical Brennus, who never entered Italy, had founded the Mark Brandenburg (Brennabor). The opera was first given on the birthday of Friedrich Wilhelm III but, as one reviewer put it, as a historical compliment it was neither historical nor a compliment. It was visually spectacular, nonetheless, with ballet and chorus integrated into the finales. Despite the poor libretto, Reichardt's music ensured a triumph. The overture remained a favourite at Berlin well into the next century. Another musical high point, Ostilia's two-tempo rondò 'Dei di Roma', includes obbligato parts for solo horn, bassoon and cello. Reichardt tailored the opera's title role to the voice of Ludwig Fischer, culminating in his aria 'Dirai che di pace'. Fischer sang the part the following season and in a German concert version in 1798, as well as in an 1802 revival, for which Reichardt wrote new ballet music. THOMAS BAUMAN

Brent, Charlotte (*d* London, 10 April 1802). English soprano, whose father was a fencing-master and alto singer. A pupil of Arne, she made her stage début in his *Eliza* at Smock Alley Theatre, Dublin, on 29 November 1755. In 1756 she sang with Frasi in *Eliza* at Drury Lane. Unable to agree with Garrick, Arne offered his pupil to Covent Garden where, with John Beard, she triumphed in *The Beggar's Opera* (1759), *The Jovial Crew* (1760), with new music by Arne, and, in the same year, his *Thomas and Sally*. In 1762 she had a double success in his opera *Artaxerxes*, in which he wrote her a specially florid part, and his pasticcio *Love in a Village*, both works holding the stage for many years. She created the role of Patty in *The Maid of the Mill* (arranged by Arnold) in 1765.

She married the violinist Thomas Pinto in 1766. As Mrs Pinto, she repeated her Covent Garden triumph in *Artaxerxes*, eclipsing Arne's rival production at Drury Lane, but Pinto's debts as a result of his part in the management of Marylebone Gardens in 1769 led to her singing mainly outside London after the 1769–70 season. She appeared in Edinburgh and later in Dublin, where in 1773 she sang in Michael Arne's *Cymon*. Pinto died in 1783. Charlotte appeared at the Haymarket in March 1785 as Polly in a benefit organized for her. Her only post-1771 performance at Covent Garden was in 1785, in Arne's *Comus*.

JULIAN HERBAGE/OLIVE BALDWIN, THELMA WILSON

Brenta, Gaston (*b* Schaarbeek, Brussels, 10 June 1902; *d* Schaarbeek, 30 May 1969). Belgian composer. He was a founder of the group of Synthétistes in 1925, and worked for Belgian radio from 1931; he was made a member of the Belgian Royal Academy in 1966. Brenta was a romantic composer, giving pride of place to amply developed and expressive melodic line. Concentrating mainly on orchestral works, he usually employed conventional forms, but his tonal harmony included unexpected use of dissonance. As well as a consummate mastery of orchestration, he displayed a taste for the exotic, notably in his two-act *comédie lyrique Le khâdi dupé*, for which he wrote his own libretto after *The Thousand and One Nights* (Brussels, Monnaie, 16 Dec 1929).

*

D. von Volborth-Danys: *CeBeDeM and its Affiliated Composers* (Brussels, 1977–80) HENRI VANHULST

Brentano, Clemens (Wenzeslaus Maria) (*b* Ehrenbreitstein, 9 Sept 1778; *d* Aschaffenburg, 28 July 1842). German poet. One of the leading figures of the younger Romantic generation, he was a versatile writer whose modern reputation rests mainly on his lyric poetry and the collection of folk poetry which he edited with Achim von Arnim under the title *Des Knaben Wunderhorn* (i, 1805). His rich imagination was matched by a melodiousness of expression which led Nietzsche to call him the most musical of German poets; he could also demonstrate a purely verbal ingenuity and wit of a high order.

In 1803 Brentano wrote a Singspiel, *Die lustigen Musikanten*, which was set to music by E. T. A. Hoffmann (1805, Warsaw), though it had little success. In 1814 he attempted to write a libretto for Weber on the Tannhäuser theme (after Tieck), but the work was never completed and remains unpublished. He sketched a plan for a second opera, *Phaon et Sappho* (1815–16), the manuscript of which contains a detailed description of the overture, and he is said to have toyed with the idea of an opera on the story of Cinderella.

*

P. H. Gehly: 'Ein romantisches Singspiel E. T. A. Hoffmanns', *ZfM*, c (1933)
W. Pfeiffer-Belli: *Clemens Brentano: ein romantisches Dichterleben* (Freiburg, 1947), 154–5 [two opera sketches]
J. F. Fetzer: *Music in the Life and Works of Clemens Brentano* (diss., U. of California, Berkeley, 1965) CEDRIC WILLIAMS

Brescia. North Italian city, part of the Venetian Republic from 1428 to 1797. Known as a centre of violin making, organ building and music printing, it also has a long operatic history. In 1664 the Accademia degli Erranti built the city's first public theatre designed primarily for opera. The first impresario was Antonio Barzino; in 1670 Giacomo Ruffoni entered a five-year contract. The small building was replaced twice (1711, 1742) by a larger structure with three rows of boxes for the noble families to rent, a gallery for the commoners, and a stalls section with collapsible seats for the middle-class citizens. At one time called the Teatro Nuovo, this theatre was described by Burney as smaller than that in Milan but with a more spacious stalls section. Further improvements were made, including the addition of a splendid staircase (1789), until the Accademia came to an end along with the Venetian Republic.

During the Napoleonic regime the theatre was renamed the Teatro Nazionale; in 1810, enlarged to 108 boxes in five tiers, it became the Teatro Grande. It was again restored and redecorated in 1863; located on the Corso Zanardelli, near the cathedral, it retains its 18th-century elegance. Another theatre, built in 1851 and known as the Teatro Guillaume until 1905, is now the Teatro Sociale, used for operettas and variety shows. In earlier centuries theatrical works in genres related to opera (*azione sacra*, *tragedia*, *pastorale*) were also performed in the theatres of the Collegio dei Nobili di S Antonio Viennese (from 1658) and the Oratorio di S Filippo Neri (Congregazione della Pace) and in churches.

Throughout the 17th and 18th centuries there were two regular opera seasons: Carnival, which lasted from 26 December to Ash Wednesday, and the August Fair. Even as late as 1871 the *Statuto del Teatro* designated these seasons for opera, defining the fair as the period from the first week of August to the first Sunday in September. In the 18th century one to three operas were usually presented each season, ranging from works already performed in one of the larger operatic centres, such as Venice or Naples, to those by minor or local composers. The patterns of operatic production reflected those of Italian opera generally; in the 17th century and early 18th the *dramma per musica* dominated, but in the second half of the 18th century comic opera, usually called *dramma giocoso* in extant librettos, gained popularity (51 of 77 operas were comic), with a resurgence of *opera seria* in the 1790s. Likewise, danced interludes, or balli, became more frequent than comic intermezzos, especially in the 1780s. Composers represented in Brescia reflect the gradual shift from Venetian to Neapolitan predominance in the later 18th century.

The first opera produced at the Teatro dell' illustrissima Accademia degli Erranti was Cavalli's *Eritrea* (1665). In subsequent years Cavalli, Cesti, Legrenzi, and M. A. Ziani represented Venice, but among Brescian composers the most active for the stage was C. F. Pollarolo, whose first opera had its première at the same theatre in 1678 (*Venere travestita*), followed by others such as *I delirii per amore* (1685) and *Antonino e Pompeiano* (1689). Other important productions included Galuppi's comic operas *La serva astuta* (August Fair 1755, a restaging of his *Il povero superbo*) and *L'avventuriera* (Carnival 1758, a restaging of *La diavolessa*). This composer was one of the dominating figures in the later 18th century, whereas his rival Ferdinando Bertoni (born at nearby Salò) had surprisingly few Brescian performances (Bettoni mentions an *Artaserse* said to be by Bertoni given at Brescia in the 1751–2 season). Among the Neapolitans were Niccolò Piccinni (*Le contadine bizzarre*, August 1764), Giuseppe Gazzaniga (*L'isola d'Alcina*, August 1772) and Luigi Caruso (première of *La caffettiera di spirito*, Carnival 1777).

The theatre was reopened as the Grande in 1811 with Simon Mayr's *Il sacrifizio di Ifigenia*, and his *Egeria* had its première there in 1816. Productions of standard Italian and French repertory as well as some obscure works continued throughout the 19th century. Ponchielli revised his *Marion Delorme* for Brescia in 1885, and its initial failure at La Scala was converted into success. Franco Faccio conducted the world première of Verdi's *Otello* at La Scala in 1887 and repeated it at Brescia in the same year. Puccini brought a revised three-act version of *Butterfly* to Brescia only slightly over three months after the fiasco at its première in Milan (May 1904). Brescia was also among the earliest Italian cities to produce Wagner's *Parsifal* (1914).

BurneyFI
F. Odorici: *Del teatro di Brescia dalle sue origini* (Brescia, 1863)
F. Bettoni: *Brescia nel secolo passato* (Brescia, 1875)
A. Valentini: *I musicisti bresciani ed il Teatro Grande* (Brescia, 1894)
F. Glissenti: *Il Teatro Grande di Brescia* (Brescia, 1895)
P. Treves Sartori: 'Il Teatro Grande', *La lettura* (1914), Aug
P. Guerrini: 'Per la storia della musica a Brescia', *NA*, xi (1934), 1–28
O. Foffa: 'Il Teatro Grande di Brescia', *Curiosità storiche di Brescia* (Brescia, 1936)
C. Sartori: 'Franco Faccio e 20 anni di spettacoli di fiera al Teatro Grande', *RMI*, xlii (1938), 64–77, 188–203, 350–62
F. Lechi: 'Il nostro teatro: cinque sale in trecento anni', *Il Teatro Grande dal 1800 al 1927* (Brescia, 1968)
U. Vaglia: 'Un salotto bresciano fra il settecento e l'ottocento', *Studi in onore di Alberto Chiari* (Brescia, 1973), 1341–57
M. T. R. Barezzani: 'L'Opera in musica', *La musica a Brescia nel settecento* (Brescia, 1981), 17–56
——: 'L'organizzazione e la produzione della cultura musicale', *Brescia nel settecento* (Brescia, 1985), 163–80 OLGA TERMINI

Bresgen, Cesar (*b* Florence, 16 Oct 1913; *d* Salzburg, 7 April 1988). Austrian composer of German origin. He studied composition, the organ, piano and conducting at the Munich Akademie für Musik, 1930–36, where his teachers included Emmanuel Gatscher, Gottfried Rüdinger and Josef Haas. In 1936 he was awarded the Felix Mottl Prize for composition and subsequently was employed in the music division of Bavarian Radio. In 1939, he settled in Salzburg where he founded a youth music school and was invited by Clemens Krauss to teach composition at the Mozarteum. After military service during the last years of the war, he became a church organist and choir director at Mittersill before resuming his career as professor in composition in Salzburg from 1947. He received many awards including the Austrian State Music Prize (1974).

Bresgen's interest in writing music for the stage was stimulated by three important formative influences. First, his work as a répétiteur with the Mary Wigman Dance School, 1932–4, gave him an unrivalled experience in the art of theatrical improvisation, as well as a deep understanding for dance forms. Secondly, his studies in folksong and early acquaintance with pre-classical German music provided the basis for a flexible musical style. Finally, his intensive association with youth music movements which initially included active participation in the Hitler Youth resulted in a lifelong commitment to writing worthwhile *Gebrauchsmusik*. This versatility was already manifested in his early theatrical compositions of which the Singspiel *Dornröschen*, first performed under Hans Rosbaud in Strasbourg, was the most successful. During the same period, he attempted more ambitious projects including an adaptation (which remained incomplete) of the old Bavarian legend *Goggolore* and a full-length opera *Paracelsus* commissioned by the Dresden Staatsoper. The latter work, announced for production in 1943, was never performed because an air raid destroyed all performance materials. After the war, the composer produced a steady stream of stage works of which the children's operas *Der Igel als Bräutigam* (1948, rev. 1951) and *Der Mann im Mond* (composed 1959), both written in collaboration with the publisher Ludwig Andersen, remained especially popular in West Germany and latterly in the German Democratic Republic. *Der Igel als Bräutigam*, written at the instigation of Fritz Jöde, exemplifies an ability to juxtapose various levels of scenic representation within one work including descriptive music, spoken text, dance and pantomime. This polymorphous approach resulted in a number of compositions including scenic cantatas and oratorios which can be performed either in the concert hall or in the opera house. The major work in this genre is the *Visiones amantis* (*Der Wolkensteiner*) based on the texts and melodies of the 15th-century Tyrolean Minnesinger Oswald von Wolkenstein, written in 1951 but not performed on the stage until 20 years later. Bresgen described it as a scenic oratorio with dance and pantomime projections. During the 1970s, he returned to the more conventional form of grand opera in his adaptation of Leo Perutz's *Der Engel von Prag* (composed 1974–5), based on a story of the 16th-century Austrian Emperor Rudolf II who neglected the government of his country in pursuit of his love for Esther, the wife of Prague's richest Jew. This love appears to be more traumatic than real when Esther dies of the plague and thereby atones for their imagined adultery. The work is constructed in a series of dialogues and soliloquies and is conceived on the largest scale. Musically, the idiom, with its skilful exploitation of Hebrew chant, is reminiscent of Orff and Stravinsky, both of whose influences can be felt throughout Bresgen's compositions.

Der Goggolore, 1937–9 (Spl, 5 scenes, O. Reuther), inc.
Dornröschen (Spl, 4, Reuther), Strasbourg, 15 April 1942 (Potsdam, 1941)
Paracelsus, 1942–3 (5, Bresgen, after Paracelsus), unperf. (Mainz, 1943)
Das Urteil des Paris (komisches Spl, 1, Reuther), Göttingen, 31 Jan 1943 (Mainz, 1943)
Der Igel als Bräutigam (Kinderoper, 5 scenes, Bresgen and L. Andersen), Esslingen, Stadt, 3 Nov 1948; rev. version, Nuremberg, Städtische Bühnen, Opernhaus, 13 Nov 1951, vs (Mainz, 1952)
Visiones amantis [Der Wolkensteiner], 1951 (Ludus tragicus, 6 scenes, E. Gärtner, after O. von Wolkenstein), Radio Bremen, 17 Feb 1964; stage, Innsbruck, 20 Dec 1971 (Frankfurt, 1962)
Niño fliegt mit Niña (Insektkomödie für Kinder, 5 scenes, Bresgen), Munich, 14 May 1953
Brüderlein Hund (Kinderoper, 3 scenes, Andersen), Nuremberg, 12 Nov 1953 (Mainz, 1953)
Der ewige Arzt (Mysterienspiel, 6 scenes, P. Kamer, after Grimm), Schwyz, 10 Feb 1956 (Frankfurt, *c*1956)
Ercole (H. H. Vogl), Hamburg Radio, 1956
Der Mann im Mond (musikalisches Märchenspiel, 6 scenes, Andersen), Nuremberg, 22 May 1960, vs (Mainz, 1959)
Die alte Lokomotive (szenische kantate, 1, Bresgen and Gärtner), Munich, 7 Oct 1960, vs (Mainz, 1960)
Die Schattendiebe [Ali und der Bilderdiebe] (Spl für Kinder, 5 scenes, K. Kraska), Vienna, 13 April 1962
Bastian der Faulpelz (musikalische Pantomime, after H. Hoffmann), Hamburg, 1966
Trubloff, 1970 (Spl, 3, E. Dittrich, after J. Burningham)
Der Engel von Prag (3, after L. Perutz), Salzburg, Kleines Festspielhaus, 25 Dec 1978 (Cologne, 1978); rev. 1985 (Wiesbaden, 1986)
Pilatus (G. Fussenegger), Villach, 2 Aug 1980
Krabat, 1982 (Spl, O. Preussler) (Hamburg, *c*1982)
Albolina, oder Der Kampf der Geister um die Morgenrote (Musikmärchen, after F. Wolff), Villach, 12 July 1987

*

E. Valentin: 'Cesar Bresgen', *ZfM*, cv (1938), 841–7
C. Niessen: *Die deutsche Oper der Gegenwart* (Regensburg, 1944)
H. Braun: *Untersuchungen zur Typologie der zeitgenössischen Schul- und Jugendoper* (Regensburg, 1963)
D. Larese: *Cesar Bresgen: eine Lebensskizze* (Amriswil, 1968)
R. Lück: 'Gespräche mit Cesar Bresgen', *Musik und Bildung*, v (1973), 682–5
——: *Cesar Bresgen* (Vienna, 1974)
H. K. Smith: *Selected Chamber Operas of Cesar Bresgen Adapted for Use in American Schools* (diss., U. of Arizona, Tucson, 1974)
C. Bresgen: 'Cesar Bresgen aus eigener Sicht', *ÖMz*, xxxiv (1979), 362–4
——: *Musikalische Dokumentation* (Vienna, 1982)

ERIK LEVI

Breslau (Ger.). Wrocław.

Bressand, Friedrich Christian (*b* Durlach, *c*1670; *d* 4 April 1699). German poet and librettist. After the early death of his parents he was sent to the court of Brunswick-Wolfenbüttel, where his literary talents were encouraged and he became a secretary to Duke Anton Ulrich. From 1690 until his death he was overall director of festive entertainments as well as stage director. During his brief career he wrote most of the librettos for operas performed there, supplying texts for such distinguished composers as Kusser, Keiser, J. P. Krieger, Schürmann, Mattheson, Erlebach and Georg Bronner. Many of these operas were repeated at Hamburg; he also wrote a few librettos specifically for Hamburg. His literary taste was determined to some degree by the French dramatists, and he was among the first to introduce to Germany through his own translations the masterpieces of Corneille and Racine. His librettos show a preference for the French alexandrine, which many Hamburg librettists had already discarded as unsuitable for opera, and also for exceedingly long recitatives. Nevertheless they are fine works, with dramatic, affect-laden arias and splendid ballet scenes. Like his more famous contemporary Postel, Bressand was an imaginative craftsman of considerable sensitivity who worked within the conventions of German Baroque poetry. He contributed manifestly to the remarkable growth of opera in north Germany during its richest period.

selective list

Ariadne, Kusser, 1692; *Jason* (Spl), Kusser, 1692; *Die Plejades, oder Das Siebengestirne* (Spl), Erlebach, 1693 (Mattheson, 1699; Schürmann, 1716); *Echo und Narcissus*, Bronner, 1693; *Herkules unter den Amazonen* (Spl), J. P. Krieger, 1693; *Porus* (Spl), Kusser, 1693; *Der Wettstreit der Treue* (Schäferspiel), Krieger, 1693; *Erindo, oder Die unsträfliche Liebe* (Schäferspiel), Kusser, 1694; *Basilius*, Keiser, 1694; *Procris und Cephalus* (Spl), Keiser, 1694 (Schürmann, 1714)
Die wiedergefundenen Verliebten (Schäferspiel), Keiser, 1695; *Circe, oder Des Ulysses erster Theil* (Spl), Keiser, 1696; *Penelope, oder Des Ulysses ander Theil*, Keiser, 1696; *Orpheus* (Spl), Keiser, 1698 (Keiser, 1699, as Die sterbende Eurydice, oder Orpheus erster Theil and Orpheus ander Theil); *Die Wiederkehr der güldnen Zeit*, Keiser, 1699; *La forza della virtù, oder Die Macht der Tugend*, Keiser, 1700; *Der edelmüthige Porsenna*, Mattheson, 1702 (Schürmann, 1718, as Porsenna [Clelia])

Doubtful: *Julia*, Kusser, 1690; *Cleopatra* (Spl), Kusser, 1690

*

H. C. Wolff: *Die Barockoper in Hamburg (1678–1738)* (Wolfenbüttel, 1957)
D. I. Lindberg: *Literary Aspects of German Baroque Opera: History, Theory and Practice (Christian H. Postel and Barthold Feind)* (diss., U. of California, Los Angeles, 1964)
W. Braun: *Vom Remter zum Gänsemarkt: aus der Frühgeschichte der alten Hamburger Oper (1677–1697)* (Saarbrücken, 1987)

GEORGE J. BUELOW

Bretan, Nicolae (*b* Năsăud, 25 March 1887; *d* Cluj, 1 Dec 1968). Romanian composer, singer, director and conductor. He began formal studies in Năsăud and continued in the early 1900s at the Conservatory of Music in Cluj. In 1908 he entered the Vienna Academy, studying with Gustav Geiringer and Julius Meixner. After a temporary disruption he enrolled at the Royal National Hungarian Academy of Music in Budapest, where he studied singing with József Sik. He graduated in 1912, having also earned his licentiate in law from the University of Cluj in 1910. His first opera, *Luceafărul* ('The Evening Star'), was composed in 1921 to a libretto adapted by the composer from Minai Eminescu's celebrated poem of the same name. Four operas followed, all with librettos by the composer: *Golem Lázadása* ('The Revolt of the Golem', 1924); *Eroii de la Rovine* ('The Heroes of Rovine', 1934); *Horia* (1937); and *Arald* (1942).

Bretan's compositional activity paralleled a prominent and successful operatic career that began with a role with the Bratislava Opera in 1913, followed by a position at the Oradea Opera. In 1917 Bretan settled permanently in Cluj, where he fulfilled numerous responsibilities as singer, stage director and even briefly Director-General (Romanian Opera, 1944–5), for the various resident Hungarian and Romanian opera companies there. In 1948 he was forced to retire for political reasons.

Bretan's operas retain a predominantly 19th-century idiom. The harmonic language and its orchestral realization are essentially pre-Wagnerian. Contrapuntal interest remains minimal and instrumental groups are most often employed in blocks; colouristic combinations rarely emerge. Thus the orchestra merely provides enhanced harmonic support for the melody. For Bretan the singer and the voice retained the prominent role in his compositions, which are still little known outside Romania.

Material relating to Bretan is available at the Indiana University Music Library at Bloomington.

Luceafărul [The Evening Star] (1, Bretan, after M. Eminescu), Cluj, Romanian Opera, 2 Feb 1921

Golem Lásadása [The Revolt of the Golem] (music drama, 1, Bretan, after I. Kaczér), Cluj, Hungarian, 23 Dec 1924

Eroii de la Rovine [The Heroes of Rovine] (1, Bretan, after Eminescu: *Scrisoarea III* [The Third Letter]), Cluj, Romanian Opera, 24 Jan 1935

Horia (3, Bretan, after G. Popp), Cluj, Romanian Opera, 24 Jan 1937

Arald, 1942 (1, Bretan, after Eminescu: *Strigoii* [The Ghosts]), Iaşi, State Opera House, 1982

*

V. Cosma: *Muzicieni din Romania: lexicon* (Bucharest, 1989)

D. GRIFFIOEN

Bretón (y Hernández), Tomás (*b* Salamanca, 29 Dec 1850; *d* Madrid, 2 Dec 1923). Spanish composer and conductor. At the age of 12 he was earning his living as a violinist in his native city. He then moved to Madrid, where he studied the violin at the conservatory and took part in zarzuela and circus orchestras. While appearing as a conductor and instrumentalist in Madrid and elsewhere in Spain, he pursued composition studies under Arrieta at the Madrid Conservatory, where he took the first prize for composition in 1872. He also studied in Rome, Milan, Vienna and Paris. Back in Spain he founded and conducted the Unión Artístico-Musical, which performed a large number of new Spanish and foreign works. In 1891 his friend Albéniz took him to London and there he conducted two successful concerts of Spanish music. Later he was a teacher and director at the Madrid Conservatory and conductor of the Sociedad de Conciertos and of the Madrid SO in its early years. He was a member of the Royal Academy of S Fernando and a recipient of the crosses of Carlos III and Alfonso XII.

Bretón struggled tirelessly for the establishment of a sophisticated Spanish lyric drama, but his own operas met with little favour. *Los amantes de Teruel* was an ephemeral *succès de scandale*; it was taken as an act of youthful rebellion against Spanish music, and Bretón's music continued to be attacked for a lack of Spanish character. Nonetheless, the cheerful tunes of Aragón enrich *La Dolores*, which was the most successful of his operas and was staged in Madrid, Barcelona, Milan, Vienna and Prague. He found still greater popularity with the lively farce *La verbena de la paloma*, where the street atmosphere of Madrid is painted in vivid colours.

See also DOLORES, LA and VERBENA DE LA PALOMA, LA.

zarzuelas unless otherwise stated

El alma en un hilo (2, C. Coello and C. Arana), Madrid, Zarzuela, 22 May 1874; Los dos caminos (1, C. Navarro), Madrid, Prado, 1 Aug 1874; El viaje de Europa (2, J. Feliú y Codina), Madrid, Bolsa, 1874, collab. Valverde *padre*; El inválido (1, Navarro), Madrid, Romea, 11 Sept 1875; El 93 (1), Madrid, 1875; Guzmán el bueno (ópera, 1, A. Arnao), Madrid, Apolo, 25 Nov 1876; Un chaparrón de maridos (1), 1876; Maria (2), 1876; Vista y sentencia (1), Madrid, 1876 or 1886; Cuidado con los estudiantes (1), 1877; Los dos leones (2), 1877

El campanero de Begoña (3, M. Pina), Madrid, Zarzuela, 18 Oct 1878; El bautizo de Pepín (2), 1878, collab. F. Chueca and Valverde; Bonito pais (2), 1878; Corona contra corona (3, Navarro), Madrid, Zarzuela, 5 Nov 1879; El barberillo de Orán (3), 1879; Los amores de un príncipe (3, J. Siguer), Madrid, Apolo, Feb 1881; Las señoritas de Conil (1), 1881; El grito en el cielo (1), 1886; Los amantes de Teruel (ópera, 5, Bretón), Madrid, Real, 12 Feb 1889; Garín, l'eremita di Montserrat (ópera, 4, C. Fereal), Barcelona, Liceo, 14 May 1892

La verbena de la paloma, ó El boticario y las chulapas (sainete lírico, 1, R. de la Vega), Madrid, Apolo, 17 Feb 1894; El domingo de Ramos (1, M. Echegaray), Madrid, 31 Jan 1895; La Dolores (ópera, 3, Bretón, after Feliú y Codina), Madrid, Zarzuela, 16 March 1895; Al fin se casa la Nieves (1, Vega), Madrid, 1895; El guardia del corps (1), Madrid, Comedia, 9 Nov 1897; El reloj de curo (1, M. Labra and Agusa), Madrid, Apolo, 29 Jan 1898; El puente del diablo (1), Madrid, Zarzuela, 18 May 1898; El clavel rojo (3, G. Perrín and M. de Palacios), Madrid, Price, 1 April 1899

Ya se van los quintos madre (Alfaro), Barcelona, 19 June 1899; La cariñosa (1, J. Jackson Veyan), Madrid, Zarzuela, 15 Dec 1899; Raquel (ópera, 4, Bretón, after F. Grillparzer: *Die Jüdin von Toledo*), Madrid, Real, 20 Jan 1900; Covadonga (3, E. Sierra and M. Zapata), Madrid, Price, 22 Jan 1901; Farinelli (ópera, 4, J. A. Cavestany), Madrid, Lírico, spr. 1901 or June 1902; El caballo de señorita (1, Vega), Madrid, 29 Dec 1901; Botín de guerra (1, Sierra), Madrid, Zarzuela, 29 Oct 1902; La bien planta (1, Vela y Servet), Madrid, Eslava, Oct 1902

El certamen de Cremona (ópera, 1, C. Fernández Shaw), Madrid, Zarzuela, 2 Nov 1906; La generosa (1), 1909; Piel de oso (1), 1909; Al alcance de la mano (1, J. & J. de la Cueva), Madrid, Apolo, 1911; Las percheleras (1), 1911; Tabaré (ópera, 3, Bertón, after J. Zorilla de San Martín), Madrid, Real, 26 Feb or March 1913; Don Gil (ópera, 3, T. Luceño), Barcelona, Tivoli, 31 July 1914; Los húsares del czar (1), 1914; Salamanca (ópera), Salamanca, Príncipal, Oct 1916; Las cortes de amor (3), 1916; La guitarra del amor, 1916, collab. J. Giménez

*

'Bretón y Hernández (Tomás)', *Enciclopedia universal ilustrada europeoamericana* (Barcelona, 1907–30)

A. Sánchez Salcedo: *Tomás Bretón: su vida y sus obras* (Córdoba, 1924)

E. Cotarelo y Mori: 'Ensayo histórico sobre la zarzuela, ó sea el drama lirico español desde su origen a fines del siglo XIX', *Boletín de la Real academia española*, xix–xxiii (1932–6); pubd separately as *Historia de la zarzuela, o sea el drama lírico* (Madrid, 1934)

J. Deleito y Piñuela: *Origén y apogeo del 'género chico'* (Madrid, 1949)

J. de Montillana: *Bretón* (Salamanca, 1952)

A. Fernández-Cid: *Cien años de teatro musical en España (1875–1975)* (Madrid, 1975)

J. Arnau and C. M. Gomez: *Historia de la zarzuela* (Madrid, 1979)

R. Alier and others: *El libro de la zarzuela* (Barcelona, 1982, rev. 1986 as *Diccionario de la zarzuela*)

C. Gómez Amat: *Historia de la música española: el siglo xix* (Madrid, 1984, 2/1988)

CARLOS GÓMEZ AMAT, ANDREW LAMB

Brett, Charles (*b* Maidenhead, 27 Oct 1941). English countertenor. He began his career as a choral scholar at King's College, Cambridge, and he has become a leading specialist in the Baroque repertory. His operatic début was at Graz in 1984, in a revival of *Angelica vincitrice di Alcina* by J. J. Fux. At the Ludwigsburg Festival he sang Athamas in a German language version of *Semele*. He toured France with Gluck's *La clemenza di Tito* under Jean-Claude Malgoire, and sang Britten's Oberon in 1987 at Aachen. DAVID CUMMINGS

Bretzner, Christoph Friedrich (*b* Leipzig, 10 Dec 1748; *d* Leipzig, 31 Aug 1807). German playwright and librettist. He spent his entire life as a businessman in Leipzig, and began writing plays in 1771. A set of four comic opera texts printed in 1779 quickly established him as a fashionable librettist in Germany. More colourful and exotic than those of C. F. Weisse, they also offer somewhat greater scope for music. Viennese as well as northern composers greeted them warmly. Bretzner is best remembered as the author of *Belmont und Constanze*, written for the Berlin composer Johann André in 1780 and subsequently adapted by Stephanie the younger for Mozart as *Die Entführung aus dem Serail*. (The much-quoted 'protest' against Mozart of 1782 is a fabrication, although in 1783 Bretzner did publicly denigrate Stephanie's poetic additions.) A second set of librettos, issued in 1796, shows Bretzner's facility at imitating *opera buffa* in German. In addition to writing original opera texts and one melodrama, he translated several Italian texts for the German stage, including Mozart's *Così fan tutte* (as *Weibertreu, oder Die Mädchen sind von Flandern*, 1794) and Salieri's *La scuola de' gelosi* (*Die Schule der Eifersüchtigen*, 1794).

Adrast und Isidore (komische Oper), F. Preu, 1779; *Der Irrwisch* (Operette), Preu, 1779; *Das wütende Heer, oder Das Mädchen im Thurme* (Operette), André, 1780 (Kaffka, 1782); *Der Äpfeldieb, oder Der Schatzgraber* (Operette), Kaffka, 1780; *Belmont und Constanze, oder Die Entführung aus dem Serail* (Operette), André, 1781; *Rosemund* (Melodram), Kaffka, 1782; *Die Luftbälle, oder Der Liebhaber à la Montgolfier* (Posse), Fränzl, 1787

Der Talisman, oder Der seltene Spiegel (Spl), Kaffka, 1789; *List gegen List* (Operette), Bergt, 1797; *Schattenspiel an der Wand* (Spl), G. E. G. Kallenbach, 1797; *Der Schlaftrunk* (komisches Spl), Bierey, 1797 (J. P. S. Schmidt, 1797; F. Teyber, 1801); *Die Opera buffa* (komisches Spl), Kallenbach, 1798 (Dittersdorf, 1798); *Laura und Fernando* (Spl), Bergt, 1801; *Clara, Herzogin von Bretannien* (os), Bierey, 1803; *Rosette, das schweizer Hirtenmädchen* (Spl), Bierey, 1806 THOMAS BAUMAN

Breuer, Hans (*b* Cologne, 27 April 1868; *d* Vienna, 11 Oct 1929). German tenor. He began his studies in Cologne and continued with Cosima Wagner and Julius Kniese in Bayreuth, where he sang small parts in the season of 1894, gaining a special success as Mime in 1896. This was to be his principal role for many years, and he continued to sing it at Bayreuth until 1914. It was as the *Rheingold* Mime that he made his Covent Garden début in 1898, with further performances in 1900 when his roles also included Jaquino in *Fidelio* and David in *Die Meistersinger*. His reputation as a clever *buffo* tenor took him to the Metropolitan in 1898 and to Salzburg for the seasons of 1910, 1922 and 1925. For many years his career centred on the Vienna Staatsoper, where he sang up to the time of his death. At Covent Garden he was described as a 'gabbling' Mime; his 1904 recordings show him giving full value to most notes, with little regard for steadiness of tone. J. B. STEANE

Breuning, Stephan von (*b* Bonn, 17 Aug 1774; *d* Vienna, 4 June 1827). German poet. He had some musical training as a young man and went on to study law at Bonn and Göttingen. Settling in Vienna around 1800, he was appointed to the war council and in 1818 became a court councillor. When in 1805–6 Beethoven needed help in revising his opera *Fidelio* he turned to his childhood friend; von Breuning 'remodelled the whole book for him, quickening and enlivening the action' by reducing the opera to two acts and reordering events in Act 1. Although some of his ministrations were crude, he did much to remedy one of the major failings in the libretto: its slow, uneventful first act. Von Breuning died shortly after Beethoven; his son, Gerhard (1813–92), Beethoven's constant companion during his final illness, published a memoir, *Aus dem Schwarzspanierhause* (Vienna, 1874), which remains the best account of the composer's last months.

M. Unger: 'Zur Entstehungs- und Aufführungsgeschichte von Beethovens Oper "Leonore"', *ZfM*, cv (1938), 130–39

W. Hess: *Beethovens Oper Fidelio und ihre drei Fassungen* (Zürich, 1953); enlarged as *Das Fidelio-Buch* (Winterthur, 1986)

——, ed.: *Leonore. Oper in zwei Aufzügen: zweite Bearbeitung (1806)*, L. von Beethoven: Supplemente zur Gesamtausgabe, xiii/3 (Wiesbaden, 1970) [complete 1806 lib.]

M. Ruhnke: 'Die Librettisten des Fidelio', *Opernstudien: Anna Amalie Abert zum 65. Geburtstag* (Tutzing, 1975), 121–40

KRISTIN M. KNITTEL

Bréval, Lucienne [née Schilling, Berthe] (*b* Mannendorf, nr Zürich, 4 Nov 1869; *d* Neuilly-sur-Seine, 15 Aug 1935). Swiss soprano. She studied the piano at Lausanne, then singing at the Conservatoire in Paris, where she made her début as Sélika in *L'Africaine* in 1892. She remained as principal soprano at the Opéra until 1919, during which time she sang in many world premières including those of Massenet's *Grisélidis*, Dukas' *Ariane et Barbe-bleu* and Février's *Mona Vanna*. She was also Kundry in the first French performance of *Parsifal*. In 1901 she made her début at the Metropolitan in *Le Cid*, singing also in *Die Walküre* and the American première of Reyer's *Salammbô*. Her only appearances at Covent Garden were as Gluck's Armide in 1906. In 1910 she sang Lady Macbeth in the première of Bloch's *Macbeth*, which he dedicated to her, at the Opéra-Comique in Paris. At Monte Carlo in 1913 she created the title role in Fauré's *Pénélope*; her other roles there had been Amy Robsart in De Lara's opera and Carmen.

Despite her great reputation in France she had limited success elsewhere: the New York critics found her acting 'semaphoric' and her singing lacking in polish. Her only recordings are the primitive cylinders made during a performance of *L'Africaine* with Jean de Reszke, where the high notes are impressive.

For illustration *see* COSTUME, fig.23*b* and PÉNÉLOPE.

J. B. STEANE

Bréville, Pierre (Eugène Onfroy) de (*b* Bar-le-Duc, 21 Feb 1861; *d* Paris, 24 Sept 1949). French composer. Having trained as a diplomat, he decided in favour of music and after studying with Théodore Dubois at the Conservatoire, he left to become a pupil of Franck. He attended the première of *Parsifal*, met Bruckner and Liszt at Wahnfried, and Fauré and Debussy at the 1888 Bayreuth Festival. He visited Grieg during his Scandinavian tour in 1889 and travelled to Constantinople in 1894, a journey which was reflected in his music. He taught at the Schola Cantorum, 1898–1902, at the Conservatoire, 1917–19, and devoted much time to the Société Nationale de Musique. He was also active as a music critic, especially for the *Mercure de France*. In 1905 Bréville wrote his only opera, the *conte lyrique Eros vainqueur* (3, J. Lorrain; vs, Paris, 1909), which he considered one of his most important works. It had been commissioned in 1900 by the Opéra-Comique, but was not given there until 1932; its première was at the Monnaie, Brussels, on 7 March 1910, with Claire Croiza in the title role. Ravel praised the orchestration, and other critics lauded the work's melodic inventiveness, meticulous prosody and the sensitive evocation of an enchanted dream. Bréville also worked on another opera, *St François d'Assise*, but the work was never completed. His songs were particularly admired; he also wrote incidental dramatic music and chamber works.

*

O. Maus: 'Eros vainqueur', *L'art moderne*, xxx (1910), 81–3
C. Van den Borren: 'Théâtre Royal de la Monnaie: première représentation de *Eros vainqueur*', *Courrier musical*, xiii (1910), 219–22
M. Ravel: 'Le mois – Concert Lamoureux', *SIM Revue musicale*, viii (1912), 62–3
R. Kemp: 'De Bréville, Witkowski, Savard', *Le théâtre lyrique en France* (Paris, 1937–9) [pubn of Poste National/Radio-Paris], iii, 209–13
M. S. Daitz: 'Pierre de Bréville', *19th Century Music*, v (1981–2), 35
MIMI SEGAL DAITZ

Brewer, Bruce (*b* San Antonio, TX, 12 Oct 1944). American tenor. He studied in Austin and made his début in 1970 at San Antonio as Don Ottavio. His career has mostly been spent in Europe. He sang Roberto (*Torquato Tasso*) at the 1974 Camden Festival. In 1975 he first appeared at Aix-en-Provence, as Orpheus in Campra's *Le carnaval de Venise*; he has specialized in *haute-contre* roles and sang at Covent Garden (1977) in the English Bach Festival production of Rameau's *La princesse de Navarre*. He has sung Renaud (Gluck's *Armide*), Pharnaspes (Pergolesi's *Adriano in Siria*) and Rameau's Plataea (1988, Spoleto). His phenomenal range allows him to sing Rossini's and Bellini's high tenor roles, such as Rodrigo (*Otello*), Giannetto, Elvino and Arturo, in their original keys. He sang Mr Brouček at Lyons and Lord Puff (Henze's *English Cat*) in Paris, where he has created roles in Ballif's *Dracula* (1984), Denisov's *L'écume des jours* (1986) and Ohana's *Célestine* (1988). He sang Fatty (*Mahagonny*) in Florence in 1991. ELIZABETH FORBES

Brewster-Jones, (Josiah) Hooper (*b* Orroroo, S. Australia, 29 June 1887; *d* Adelaide, 8 July 1949). Australian composer. He studied at the Elder Conservatorium, University of Adelaide, and subsequently at the RCM, London, where his teachers included Stanford. He returned to South Australia, where he identified himself with the major forward-looking movements of pre-1914 Europe.

Brewster-Jones's output in the period 1915–25 was mainly operas and music dramas, but most works survive only in short score or as extended sketches. The most substantial is for the opera *Deirdre of the Sorrows*, after J. M. Synge's unfinished tragedy. It comprises 477 pages and dates from 1915–16; it shows dramatic use of motifs, harmony and instrumentation, and if completed it would have been the most advanced through-composed opera written in Australia up to that time. His other operatic projects, *Ondine (*1918–23) and *The Nightingale and the Rose* (1927, of which only an orchestral suite survives), show a response to literary influences as diverse as E. T. A. Hoffmann, Fouqué and Oscar Wilde. Other dramatic works (all incomplete) include the opera-ballet *The Call of France* (1917), *Sweet Doll of Haddon Hall* and *The Belle of Cairo* (both 1921), and *Dagobert the Jester* (1925).

*

E. Wood: *Australian Opera 1842–1970* (diss., U. of Adelaide, 1979)
A. D. McCredie: 'Creative Challenges and Models: Composition in South Australia', *From Colonel Light into the Footlights: the Performing Arts in South Australia from 1836 to the Present* (Adelaide, 1988), 252–3
——: 'Hooper Brewster-Jones: a Post Centennial Tribute', *MMA*, xvi (1989), 13–34
ANDREW D. McCREDIE

Brian, Havergal (*b* Dresden, Staffs., 29 Jan 1876; *d* Shoreham, 28 Nov 1972). English composer. At school he displayed talent as a chorister, though his formal education ceased at 12. Despite the support of Elgar, Henry Wood and Granville Bantock, he did not consolidate the success of his early compositions. On moving to London in 1913 he began his first opera, *The Tigers*, but failed to secure performances for his increasingly ambitious works. He continued to compose while working as assistant editor at *Musical Opinion* (1927–40) and in the Civil Service (until 1948).

An extraordinary late flowering of creativity then produced four operas (the last two in German) and 27 symphonies, before he ceased composing at the age of 92. The only opera performed in his lifetime was his last, *Agamemnon* (1957), conceived as 'a curtain-raiser to Strauss's *Elektra*'; *Agamemnon*, *The Tigers* and the prologue to *Faust* have been broadcast, largely due to the efforts of composer and BBC producer Robert Simpson.

Though interest has concentrated on Brian's 32 symphonies, many of his early works are vocal or choral, and he frequently declared his real ambition was to write opera. The contemporary satire in his libretto for *The Tigers* aligns it with his earlier music rather than his later, where his preference was to adapt classic tragedy. This avoided the necessity of copyright permission, refusal of which blocked his long-standing desire to set the work of J. M. Synge. At various times Brian projected treatments of *Riders to the Sea* (pre-empting Vaughan Williams) and *The Tinker's Wedding* as well as Shakespeare's *The Tempest* and Sophocles' *Antigone*. He began an opera based on Synge's *Deirdre of the Sorrows* (its prelude became his Symphony no.6, *Sinfonia tragica*) and in 1967 he started sketching *Oedipus at Colonus*, after Sophocles (its material was probably subsumed into his Symphony no.30). The four-hour 'lyric drama' *Prometheus Unbound* (1937–44), after Shelley, also has strong operatic elements, though it was clearly intended for concert performance.

Brian's operas take opulent, late Romantic orchestral certainties and subject them to an ironic undercutting of muscular neo-Baroque polyphony and to startling juxtapositions of mood and texture. Despite his Straussian roots he avoided leitmotif technique in favour of continuous, allusive development. Whether any of his operas are true stage works has yet to be demonstrated, but the visionary ballet sequences of *The Tigers*, the overwhelming pathos of Cassandra (mezzo soprano) in her scene in *Agamemnon* and the monumental prologue and Cathedral Scene of *Faust* create maximum dramatic impact in the theatre of the mind.

See also TIGERS, THE.

The Maiden and the Flower-Garden, 1914 (children's operetta, G. Cumberland), vv, pf, lost
The Tigers, 1917–19 (burlesque op, prol., 3, Brian), concert perf., London, St John's, Smith Square, 1976; BBC, 3 May 1983, vs (1932)
Turandot, Prinzessin von China, 1949–51 (tragikomisches Märchen, 3, F. von Schiller, after C. Gozzi), unperf.
The Cenci, 1951–2 (8 scenes, P. B. Shelley), unperf.
Faust, 1954–6 (prol., 4, J. W. von Goethe), BBC, 31 March 1979 [prol. only]
Agamemnon, 1957 (1, Brian, after Aeschylus, trans. J. S. Blackie), London, St John's, Smith Square, 28 Jan 1971

MALCOLM MACDONALD

Briani, Francesco (*b* Venice; *fl* 1709–10). Italian librettist. Briani wrote only two librettos, both for the Teatro S Giovanni Grisostomo, the most prestigious Venetian opera house of his day. They are in the elevated, serious style cultivated at this theatre, and their subjects are closely suited to Briani's illustrious dedicatees. Both were set by Lotti. *Il vincitor generoso* (1709) is dedicated to King Frederick IV of Denmark, who visited Venice from 29 December 1708 until 9 March 1709. Although not based on history, it is set in and around Warsaw, which was neutral (as was Denmark during the War of the Spanish Succession). *Isacio tiranno* (1710), dedicated to a hero of that war, John Churchill, Duke of Marlborough, is loosely based on an episode involving Richard I as he passed through Cyprus on his way to the Holy Land. Although neither work was ever restaged in Italy, Paolo Rolli used *Isacio tiranno* as the basis for *Riccardo I, rè d'Inghilterra*, which Handel set for London in 1727.

*

AllacciD
G. Bonlini: *Le glorie della poesia e della musica* (Venice, 1730)
A. Groppo: *Catalogo di tutti i drammi per musica recitati ne' teatri di Venezia* (Venice, 1745)
J. M. Knapp: 'The Autograph of Handel's *Riccardo Primo*', *Studies in Renaissance and Baroque Music in Honor of Arthur Mendel* (Kassel and Hackensack, NJ, 1974), 331–58
R. Strohm: 'Händel und seine italienischen Operntexte', *HJb*, xxi–xxii (1975–6), 101–59; rev. and trans. in *Essays on Handel and Italian Opera* (Cambridge, 1985), 34–79
E. Selfridge-Field: *Pallade veneta: Writings on Music in Venetian Society, 1650–1750* (Venice, 1985)
C. Sartori: *I libretti italiani a stampa dalle origini al 1800* (Cuneo, 1990–)

HARRIS S. SAUNDERS

Brice, Carol (Lovette Hawkins) (*b* Sedalia, NC, 16 April 1918; *d* Norman, OK, 15 Feb 1985). American contralto. She studied at Talladega College, Alabama, and the Juilliard School (1939–43), where she trained under Francis Rogers. While still a student, she appeared in *The Hot Mikado* at the New York World's Fair in 1939, and in 1943 she became the first black American to win the Naumburg Award. Her stage performances included the role of the Voodoo Princess in Clarence Cameron White's *Ouanga* (independently given at the Metropolitan in 1956 and at Carnegie Hall), Addie in Blitzstein's *Regina*, Kakou in Arlen's *Saratoga*, Queenie in Kern's *Showboat* and Maria in *Porgy and Bess* (1961, 1976); she appeared at the Vienna Volksoper, 1967–71, in *Porgy and Bess*, *Showboat* and *Carousel*. In 1974 she and her husband, the baritone Thomas Carey, established the Cimarron Circuit Opera Company.

SouthernB
P. Turner: *Afro-American Singers* (Minneapolis, 1977)

DOMINIQUE-RENÉ DE LERMA

Bride of Messina, The. Opera by Zdeněk Fibich; *see* NEVĚSTA MESSINSKÁ.

Bridge, Frank (*b* Brighton, 26 Feb 1879; *d* Friston, Sussex, 10 Jan 1941). English composer and conductor. His style developed from its Brahmsian foundations inculcated by Stanford at the RCM to a progressive seriousness in some ways comparable to the Second Viennese School. This lost him his English following, and he was further neglected after his death. Now he is regarded as the most far-reaching British composer between Vaughan Williams and Britten, who was his only pupil. Elizabeth Sprague Coolidge was Bridge's patron; she enabled him to continue concentrating on his preferred medium of chamber music, and his experience as a player and conductor ensured absolute professionalism when he turned to other genres. He conducted opera early in his career but composed only a nativity 'mystery', *The Christmas Rose*, which was sketched in 1919, completed and orchestrated in 1929 and first performed at the RCM on 8 December 1931 (MS (copy) *GB-Lcm*; vs London, 1931); the work shows his faultless handling of feeling and resources.

See also CHRISTMAS ROSE, THE.

*

A. Payne, L. Foreman and J. Bishop: *The Music of Frank Bridge* (London, 1976)
P. Hindmarsh: *Frank Bridge: a Thematic Catalogue* (London, 1983)
A. Payne: *Frank Bridge: Radical and Conservative* (London, 1984)
L. Foreman: 'British Opera Comes of Age: 1916–61', *British Opera in Retrospect* (n.p., 1986) [pubn of the British Music Society], 106

STEPHEN BANFIELD

Briegel, Wolfgang Carl (*b* Königsberg, nr Coburg, May 1626; *d* Darmstadt, 19 Nov 1712). German composer. He was educated in Nuremberg, where he was strongly influenced by S. T. Staden. After studying at Altdorf University he became an organist in Schweinfurt. In 1650 Duke Ernst the Pious appointed him court cantor at Gotha; he rose gradually to the post of Kapellmeister and had several ballets performed there. From 1671 until his death he was Kapellmeister at Darmstadt, where he produced several stage works, including operas, ballets and incidental music. None of the music has survived, but his dramatic dialogues and lively *Tafelkonfekt*, with their clear and eloquent melodies, possibly give an idea of what some of it was like. Briegel also wrote many church cantatas, other sacred works and various instrumental pieces. His music enjoyed an extraordinarily wide circulation throughout Germany.

all first performed at Darmstadt; only librettos extant

Triumphierendes Siegespiel der wahren Liebe (comédie, 1, J. Mylius), 8 June 1673
Das verliebte Gespenst, 1673
Das verbesserte Parisurteil (opera-ballet), 6 Jan 1674
Die beglückwünschte Majorennität des Fürsten, 22 June 1676
Das Band der beständigen Freundschaft (Spl), 8 May 1683
Die wahre Seelenruhe, oder Gekrönte Eustathia (tragi-comedy), May 1686
Die triumphierende Tugend (opera-ballet), 29 July 1686
L'enchantement de Medée, 11 Nov 1688

*

E. Pasqué: *Geschichte der Musik und des Theaters am Hofe zu Darmstadt* (Darmstadt, 1853–4)
K. F. Hirschmann: *Wolfgang Carl Briegel* (Marburg, 1934)
H. Kaiser: *Barocktheater in Darmstadt* (Darmstadt, 1951)

E. Noack: *Wolfgang Carl Briegel: ein Barockkomponist in seiner Zeit* (Berlin, 1963) ELISABETH NOACK/R

Brigands, Les ('The Brigands'). *Opéra bouffe* in three acts by JACQUES OFFENBACH to a libretto by HENRI MEILHAC and LUDOVIC HALÉVY; Paris, Théâtre des Variétés, 10 December 1869.

The action takes place on and around the mountainous border between the Italian province of Mantua and the Spanish province of Granada. On the Italian side a band of brigands led by Falsacappa (tenor) captures a young landowner Fragoletto (soprano). The latter seeks to marry Falsacappa's daughter Fiorella (soprano), but Falsacappa insists that Fragoletto prove himself in the business of brigandry. He earns his initiation into the band by capturing a courier with a diplomatic bag carrying a portrait of the Princess of Granada, together with plans for her marriage to the Prince of Mantua. Attracted by the dowry, Falsacappa substitutes Fiorella's portrait and sends the courier on his way. In Act 2 the brigands take over an inn on the border and capture the wedding delegations, disguising themselves to hilarious effect. By the time Falsacappa is unmasked, the local *carabinieri* have rendered themselves incapable through having sampled the wine stocks in the cellar. In Act 3 Falsacappa arrives at the Mantuan court with Fiorella disguised as the Princess of Granada, only to find that the Granada coffers have been emptied by the treasurer Antonio (baritone) to support his amorous adventures. When the genuine wedding delegations finally arrive, Fiorella earns Falsacappa a pardon for having helped the Prince when he got lost in the mountains. Falsacappa agrees to lead a blameless life and gives Fragoletto his daughter's hand.

Offenbach's last big Second Empire success, *Les brigands* featured José Dupuis as Falsacappa and Zulma Bouffar as Fragoletto. Its principal numbers include Fiorella's rondò 'Après avoir pris à droite', Fragoletto's saltarello 'Falsacappa voici ma prise', the canonic chorus 'Soyez pitoyables' and Antonio's 'O mes amours, ô mes maîtresses'. The work is noted for the comic *carabinieri* who always arrive too late to capture their prey, and for witty political comment such as Antonio's declaration that 'one should steal according to the position one occupies in Society'. ANDREW LAMB

Briganti, I ('The Brigands'). *Melodramma* in three acts by SAVERIO MERCADANTE to a libretto by Jacopo Crescini after FRIEDRICH VON SCHILLER's play *Die Räuber*; Paris, Théâtre Italien, 22 March 1836.

Crescini's libretto is conventional, with none of the power of Schiller's original, or indeed of the more substantial treatment of the same subject that Maffei later provided for Verdi's *I masnadieri*. It concerns the mutual hatred of the rival sons of Massimiliano, Count Moor (bass), both of whom aspire to the hand of Amelia (soprano), the count's niece. Corrado (bass), the younger, imprisons his father and announces that he is dead. He assumes control of the family estates and makes ready to marry Amelia. The elder, Ermanno (tenor), who has become a brigand leader, rallies his men and delivers his father from the tower in which he has been immured, in so doing precipitating the death of his brother, who takes his own life in an access of guilt and remorse.

I briganti was the only opera Mercadante wrote for Paris. It was not a success. Clément and Larousse (*Dictionnaire lyrique*, 1867–9) commented that 'the forms of Mercadante's music are too developed and too classical to associate well with such wild and brusque situations', and even the singing of Grisi, Rubini, Tamburini and Lablache was unable to save the day – though one is tempted to wonder whether the role of an old man starving to death was an ideal one for Lablache. MICHAEL ROSE

Brighton. English seaside resort on the south coast. It had short-lived oratorio and choral festivals in the late 19th and early 20th centuries, but the present Brighton Festival, held each May, dates from 1967. Several experimental works by Alexander Goehr were staged by his Music Theatre Ensemble, 1968–71, and classical opera has formed part of most festivals since 1971. Productions are usually by British companies but have included foreign ones, notably Drottningholm (1972, 1987), Ludwigsburg (1976) and the Warsaw Chamber Opera (1984), which brought music-theatre works by Elżbieta Sikora (*Ariadna*) and Bernadetta Matuszczak (*Diary of a Madman*), and Moniuszko's *Halka* as well as standard repertory operas. In 1990 the Polish State Opera of Poznań brought Penderecki's *Die schwarze Maske*. New Sussex Opera, formed in 1978, has often contributed ad hoc productions of large-scale works such as *Aida*, *Benvenuto Cellini* and *Boris Godunov*, performed by young professional soloists with chorus singers from local choirs, with an orchestra of student professionals from the National Centre for Orchestral Studies, London. In 1991 the company gave the first European performances of Weill's *Lost in the Stars*.

*

A. Dale: *The Theatre Royal Brighton* (Stocksfield, 1980) NOËL GOODWIN

Brilioth, Helge (*b* Växjö, 7 May 1931). Swedish tenor. He studied in Stockholm, Rome and Salzburg, and made his début as a baritone at Drottningholm in 1960 as Paisiello's Bartolo. He sang at Bielefeld (1962–4), then returned to Stockholm, making his tenor début, after further study, in 1965 as Don José. At Bayreuth he sang Siegmund (1969–71) and Tristan (1974). In 1970 he sang Siegfried at the Salzburg Easter Festival, and made his Covent Garden début as Siegmund and his Metropolitan début as Parsifal. In 1971 he sang Bacchus at Glyndebourne. His roles in Stockholm included Verdi's Otello, the Emperor (*Die Frau ohne Schatten*) and Jean (Bibalo's *Frøken Julie*) which he sang in 1977. In the late 1970s he appeared in character roles such as Leonard (*Maskarade*) and Mozart's Don Basilio. He took part in the première of Gefors's *Christina* at Stockholm in 1986. Although his voice was not of true Heldentenor proportions, his musical, intelligent singing and his notable stage presence were much admired, especially in Wagner. HAROLD ROSENTHAL/R

Brindisi (It.; from Sp. *brindis*, a corruption of Ger. *bring dir's*). A drinking song in which a solo singer raises a toast and all present follow suit with the same words and melody. Another soloist may intervene, as in 'Libiamo ne' lieti calici' (*La traviata*, Verdi, 1853). The action may continue between verses or repetitions, as in 'Si colmi il calice' (*Macbeth*, Verdi, 1847) and 'Il segreto di esser felice' (*Lucrezia Borgia*, Donizetti, 1833). A particularly elaborate instance is 'S'innaffia l'ugola' (*Otello*, Verdi, 1887) which develops into an affray. In 'Viva il vino spumeggiante' (*Cavalleria rusticana*,

Mascagni, 1890) the choral response follows at some distance from the solo.

Drinking songs in French and German opera show greater freedom in form, using different words and music for the choral refrain, e.g. 'Versez, que tout respire' (*Le prophète*, Meyerbeer, 1849), 'Oh vin, dissipe la tristesse' (*Hamlet*, Thomas, 1868) and 'Lasst mich Euch fragen' (*Martha*, Flotow, 1847).

JULIAN BUDDEN

Brioschi. Italian (later Austrian) family of stage designers. Their designs, particularly those before 1900, had a significant influence on set design in central Europe and their works were highly praised. Many of the family's original drawings, sketches, plans and personal papers are in the Österreichisches Theatermuseum, Vienna.

(1) **Giuseppe Brioschi** (*b* Trezzano, 1802; *d* Vienna, 1858). He was a pupil of Alessandro Sanquirico, the chief stage designer at La Scala, Milan. In 1838 he went to Vienna, where he established a studio which served the Hofoper at the Kärntnertortheater.

(2) **Carlo Brioschi** (*b* Milan, 24 June 1826; *d* Vienna, 12 Nov 1895). Son of (1) Giuseppe Brioschi. After training at the Akademie der Bildenden Künste, Vienna, he took over the direction of his father's studio in 1854 and remained there until his retirement in 1886. He initiated many reforms and improvements in the scenic arts and in theatrical production, among them the incorporation of panoramas, walls, staircases, steps and platforms into the design and into the stage action. He supervised the construction and installation of the backstage machinery and technical apparatus at the new opera house in Vienna in 1869, at the same time repainting and creating new sets for the larger space. A consortium with Theodore Jachimovitz, Hermann Burghart and Johann Kautsky was founded in 1874 through which the studio created designs and sets for other theatres, notably those in the Austro-Hungarian empire.

(3) **Anton Brioschi** (*b* Vienna, 30 Nov 1855; *d* Vienna, 20 Aug 1920). Son of (2) Carlo Brioschi. After apprenticeship in Munich, he moved to the Hanover court theatre in 1883. In 1885 he joined the Vienna studio and became director on his father's retirement the following year. He continued to refine the art of stage design and created new works for the Vienna Hofoper, as well as contributing designs to the Burgtheater. These reflect the influence of the flowering 'Makart' style in the use of realist scenes imbued with historical accuracy, along with numerous decorative elements and liberal amounts of rich and luminous colours. Although Brioschi's responsibilities were permanently reduced when Heinrich Lefler and Alfred Roller were chief designers of the Hofoper in the early 1900s, he remained as the chief scenic artist there until his death.

For illustration *see* KÖNIGIN VON SABA, DIE and LIBUŠE.

*

ES (J. Gregor)

A. Martinez: *Wiener Ateliers* (Vienna, 1893), i, 5–11

U. Thieme and F. Becker, eds.: *Lexikon der bildenden Künstler* (Leipzig, 1907–50), v, 21–2

E. Greisenegger-Georgila: *Naturmotiv in Angebot eines Theaterdekorationsateliers des 19. Jahrhunderts: das Atelier Brioschi und seine Tradition in der K.u.K. Hofoper in Wien* (diss., U. of Vienna, 1985)

W. Greisenegger: 'Set Designs and Costumes', *The Vienna Opera*, ed. A. Seebohm (New York, 1987), 188–9

EVAN BAKER

Brisbane. Australian city, capital of Queensland. Like other Australian state capitals, it relied in the early days on visiting companies: W. S. Lyster's in 1865, Martin Simonsen's in 1887, George Musgrove's and J. C. Williamson's in 1901 and 1949, the Gonsalez in 1916 and 1928 and the Sutherland-Williamson in 1965. From 1952 to 1954 the New South Wales National Opera Company presented short seasons in Her Majesty's Theatre (built in 1888 as Her Majesty's Opera House), since demolished. Locally based efforts, starting with a touring company organized by the composer Colin Brumby and his wife, led to the formation of the Queensland Opera Company, which gave Brisbane seasons from 1970 to 1980, when it was disbanded. It also gave performances in the State Government Insurance Office Theatre (now the Suncorp Theatre). Its successor, the Lyric Opera of Queensland, was founded in 1982 and presents three operas a year in the Lyric Theatre of the new Queensland Performing Arts Complex (cap. 1000, 1500 or 2000), opened in 1985. The Australian Opera has performed in Brisbane intermittently since 1956.

A. I. GYGER

Bristow, George Frederick (*b* Brooklyn, New York, 19 Dec 1825; *d* New York, 13 Dec 1898). American composer. He began his professional career at 13, as a violinist in the orchestra of the Olympic Theatre. In addition to his 36 years (1843–79) as a member of the New York PO, he led the violin section in Jullien's orchestra (1853–4) and the ensembles that accompanied Jenny Lind (1850–51) and Marietta Alboni (1852). He held posts as choir director and organist in several New York churches, and from 1854 until his death he contributed significantly to school music education. He was an outspoken proponent of American music, and himself wrote orchestral, keyboard and chamber pieces as well as choral music and songs. Bristow completed only one opera, *Rip Van Winkle*; he left an unfinished work *King of the Mountains* (M. A. Cooney; 1894) and plans for an opera *Columbus* ended when the librettist, William E. Burton, died before work had really started, though Bristow did compose an overture (op.32, 1866).

Bristow's fame as a composer has largely been based on the claim that *Rip Van Winkle* op.22 was the first American opera on an American subject, though this statement overlooks earlier works in the tradition of the ballad opera or English opera style. The three-act libretto by Jonathan Wainwright is based on Washington Irving's famous tale. Bristow completed the score in 1853 and the work was finally scheduled for production in autumn 1855, when the composer was hired as conductor for the Pyne and Harrison opera troupe's New York season; the first performance took place at Niblo's Garden on 27 September. As late as 1890, Max Maretzek called *Rip Van Winkle* one of the best American operas of the century and insisted that if it had been first performed in Paris or London it 'would have been imported to America with a flourish of trumpets'. Maretzek himself planned a lavish 1865 revival at the New York Academy of Music, to be sung in Italian with Clara Louise Kellogg in the principal soprano role, but before it could open, the theatre, sets and costumes were all destroyed by fire. The work was then revived in 1870, receiving three performances at Niblo's Garden in New York and one at the Academy of

Music in Philadelphia between 9 and 21 November. This revival was given in English; the original 1855 libretto was reprinted for the occasion.

In 1878 J. W. Shannon revised the libretto, completely rewriting the spoken dialogue, though retaining most of the lyrics except in the second act, where he changed the plot considerably. Bristow also reworked the score, replacing the original overture with a short dramatic prelude and writing new music for the new lyrics. The autograph score at the New York Public Library contains both the full original score and inserts in his hand for the revisions. In 1882 the revision was published in vocal score (as a 'Grand romantic opera'); there is no record of a stage performance.

In the original version, the first and third acts are closely drawn from Washington Irving's story. The second act – invented, according to Wainwright, with Irving's approval – depicts incidents connected with the American Revolution that take place during Rip's 20-year nap, introducing a love story between Rip's daughter and an American officer. Shannon's revision retains most of the material drawn from Irving, but changes the added sub-plot considerably.

In the first act, set in 1763, Rip (baritone) quarrels with his shrewish wife and leaves to hunt in the mountains, where he encounters the ghosts of Hendrik Hudson and his crew. Rip drinks and plays ninepins with them, at the end of the act falling into a sleep which, the chorus warns, will last 20 years. The second act (1777) takes place during the war. Rip's daughter Alice (soprano) loves an American captain, Edward Gardinier (tenor), but is pursued by Herman van Slaus, Tory son of the Burgomaster who had persuaded Rip, on the day of his disappearance, to sign a contract of marriage between their children. Herman attempts to assassinate Edward, but Alice warns him in time and the plot is foiled. The third act takes place in autumn 1783, immediately after the American victory at Yorktown. Rip awakens and returns home, but he recognizes no one (aria, 'Alas, alas they know me not'), and learns that most of his old friends have died. As the suspicious villagers threaten to attack him, Alice suddenly rushes out to protect the unknown old man. Herman arrives with a judge to enforce the provisions of the wedding contract: Alice can marry Edward if she insists, but Herman will receive her inheritance. Rip immediately steps forward to annul the contract, obtained fraudulently, then produces its counterpart from his own pocket to prove his identity. Alice and the villagers rejoice in Bellinian coloratura ('List, the merry bells are ringing').

Despite the description 'Grand romantic opera' in the published vocal score, *Rip Van Winkle* resembles most English operas of its day in having spoken dialogue, and much of the score consists of solo songs, with relatively little ensemble music. It draws on diverse musical traditions, from the parlour ballad and Protestant hymn to vocal styles and dramatic gestures common to the works of Donizetti, Bellini, Balfe and others popular in America in the middle of the century.

*

DAB (C. N. Boyd)

W. M. Thoms: 'George F. Bristow', *American Art Journal*, xxxvii (1882), 241

M. Maretzek: *Sharps and Flats* (New York, 1890)

G. H. Curtis: 'G. F. Bristow', *Music*, iii (1893), 547–64

W. Rieck: 'When Bristow's Rip was Sung at Niblo's Garden', *MusAm*, xliii/7 (1925), 3, 19

'Bristow, George Frederick', *The National Cyclopedia of American Biography*, xxiii (New York, 1933)

D. D. Rogers: *Nineteenth-Century Music in New York City as Reflected in the Career of George Frederick Bristow* (diss., U. of Michigan, 1967)

K. E. Gombert: *'Leonora' by William Henry Fry and 'Rip Van Winkle' by George Frederick Bristow: Examples of Mid-Nineteenth-Century American Opera* (diss., Ball State U., 1977)

V. B. Lawrence: 'William Henry Fry's Messianic Leanings', *American Music*, vii (1989), 382–411

S. Ledbetter: Introduction to George Frederick Bristow: *Rip Van Winkle*, Earlier American Music, xxv (New York, 1990) [facs. of the 1882 vs, incl. 1st edn of the rev. lib.] STEVEN LEDBETTER

Britain, Radie (*b* Silverton, TX, 17 March 1903). American composer. After graduating from the American Conservatory, Chicago, she studied composition in Munich with Albert Noelte and the organ in Paris with Marcel Dupré. She returned from Europe in 1926 and continued to work with Noelte, then at the Chicago Conservatory. Between 1930 and 1960 she taught in Chicago and Hollywood. Over 50 of her compositions, mostly orchestral and choral and chamber works, have received national or international awards. Although she experimented with atonal and serial techniques in some of her later works, Britain's primary concerns have been lyric expression and the creation of atmosphere in music. For the stage she has written a musical drama, two operas and two children's operettas.

Ubiquity, 1937 (musical drama, L. Luther)

Happyland, 1946 (children's operetta, A. Greenfield)

Carillon, 1952 (3, R. Hughs)

The Spider and the Butterfly, 1953 (children's operetta, 3, L. P. Hasselberg)

Kuthara (chamber op, 3, Luther), Santa Barbara, 1961

*

EwenD

W. B. Bailey and N. G. Bailey: *Radie Britain: a Bio-bibliography* (Westport, CT, 1990) KATHERINE K. PRESTON

British National Opera Company. An organization set up in 1922 by leading singers and musicians of the Beecham Opera Company (*see* LONDON, §II, 1). Its board of directors included Allin, Buesst, Hyde, Pitt, Radford and Agnes Nicholls. Pitt was the company's first artistic director and was succeeded by Frederic Austin in 1924. The company first performed in Bradford on 6 February 1922 with a production of *Aida*; it gave its first Covent Garden season in May and June that year. Three further Covent Garden seasons were given until the spring of 1924, after which its London seasons were at His Majesty's Theatre. The company toured widely in the provinces and in Scotland, and performed a number of British operas, including Holst's *At the Boar's Head* and *The Perfect Fool*, Vaughan Williams's *Hugh the Drover* and Ethel Smyth's *Fête galante*. It also staged the *Ring*, *Tristan und Isolde*, *Parsifal* and a notable production in English of *Pelléas et Mélisande* with Maggie Teyte. Distinguished guest artists who appeared with the company during its London seasons included Melba, Joseph Hislop, Edward Johnson and Dinh Gilly. A new generation of British singers and conductors began their careers with the company, including Heddle Nash, Dennis Noble, Barbirolli, Sargent and Clarence Raybould. The first broadcast in England of a complete opera was of the company's matinée performance of *Hänsel und Gretel* at Covent Garden on 6 January 1923. By 1928 the company was in serious financial difficulties and went into voluntary liquidation. It was taken over by the Royal Opera House, and survived as

Benjamin Britten (at the piano) with Peter Pears singing an aria from 'Billy Budd' for Ronald Duncan (centre) and Arthur Oldham during the early stages of the opera's composition in 1949

the Covent Garden English Opera Company for three more years. HAROLD ROSENTHAL

Britten, (Edward) Benjamin (*b* Lowestoft, 22 Nov 1913; *d* Aldeburgh, 4 Dec 1976). English composer. His operas are the most important British contribution to the genre in the 20th century, yet in some respects he had an uneasy relationship with the operatic medium. He hated the backbiting and posturing of the theatre world and much preferred country to city life; his compositions up to the age of 30, while often strongly dramatic in character, showed a special gift for imaginative settings of fine poetry (Seven Sonnets of Michelangelo, Serenade) and for substantial instrumental forms (Violin Concerto, *Sinfonia da Requiem*). Nevertheless, after completing his studies at the RCM in 1933, and then settling in London, his main means of making a living was by writing incidental music for theatre, film and radio – an excellent apprenticeship for opera. In addition, two of his most significant relationships played crucial roles in launching his operatic career. W. H. Auden encouraged his interest in the theatre and provided the libretto for his first stage work, the operetta *Paul Bunyan* (1941), while Peter Pears helped with the drafting of a synopsis and early versions of the libretto of Britten's first opera, *Peter Grimes* (1944–5). On their return to England from America during World War II, Pears became a prominent member of the Sadler's Wells Opera, where *Grimes* was first performed.

The public and critical success of *Peter Grimes* combined with a degree of purely creative satisfaction to encourage Britten to contemplate further operas. Yet the hostility of many in the Sadler's Wells company to the work left him suspicious of the operatic establishment and the attitudes of large companies. He was soon involved with the more flexible, smaller-scale organization suitable for chamber opera at Glyndebourne: *The Rape of Lucretia* and *Albert Herring* were first performed there, in 1946 and 1947. There were problems at Glyndebourne too, however, and by the time of the *Herring* première Britten had decided, in company with Pears, Eric Crozier (who had produced the original *Grimes*) and others, to establish a new, independent organization, the English Opera Group. This became in effect the house company for the Aldeburgh Festival from its inception in 1948, and was involved in the premières of all Britten's later operas apart from *Billy Budd* and *Gloriana*.

Billy Budd, a Festival of Britain commission (1950–51) and *Gloriana*, a coronation commission (1952–3), were Britten's only large-scale operas after *Peter Grimes*, and in later years projects likely to require substantial forces, such as *Anna Karenina* and *King Lear*, were contemplated but abandoned. Between *Herring* and *Budd*, Britten's versions of *The Beggar's Opera* (1948) and *Dido and Aeneas* (1951), as well as his young people's entertainment *The Little Sweep (Let's Make an Opera)* (1949), were all relatively small-scale, and after *Gloriana* the chamber opera *The Turn of the Screw*, a Venice Biennale commission (1954), powerfully confirmed his ability to create a strong and highly personal dramatic effect with severely restricted means. Thereafter all his operatic works – *Noye's Fludde* (1957), *A Midsummer Night's Dream* (1959–60), the three parables for church performance (*Curlew River*, 1964; *The Burning Fiery Furnace*, 1966; *The Prodigal Son*, 1968), *Owen Wingrave* (1969–70), *Death in Venice* (1971–3) and the revised *Paul Bunyan* (1976) – were first performed in Suffolk, at the Jubilee Hall in Aldeburgh, the Snape Maltings or Orford Church. (*Owen Wingrave*, written for television, was filmed at Snape and later staged at Covent Garden.)

After *Grimes* and *Lucretia*, Britten worked with a small number of librettists receptive to his own needs and initiatives as the operas took shape. These were Eric Crozier, who collaborated with E. M. Forster on *Billy Budd* and wrote *Albert Herring* and *The Little Sweep*, William Plomer (*Gloriana* and the church parables) and Myfanwy Piper (*The Turn of the Screw*, *Owen Wingrave* and *Death in Venice*).

Britten's creative life after *Peter Grimes* was dominated by opera, and other large-scale compositions – the *Spring Symphony*, the ballet *The Prince of the Pagodas*, the *War Requiem*, the Cello Symphony – are relatively few. He always worked under pressure, and composition was itself complemented by activity as a performer, not least as conductor of his own operas. Only with the onset of serious illness in 1973 did he abandon this aspect of his career.

Britten's attitude to operatic composition can be deduced from two comments he made in a note about *Peter Grimes*. One of his main aims was 'to try to restore to the musical setting of the English language a brilliance, freedom and vitality that have been curiously rare since Purcell'. On its own, this could have served as the manifesto for an exclusive concern with the non-operatic setting of great poetry. Yet he was also 'especially interested in the general architectural and formal problems of opera' – meaning, in essence, how to preserve 'the classical practice of separate numbers that crystallize and hold the emotion of a dramatic situation at chosen moments'. That 'classical practice' was found at its finest in Mozart, and Britten's declaration is on the face of it highly conservative, representing his resistance (despite his youthful enthusiasm for Berg's *Wozzeck*) to post-Wagnerian through-composition, whole-hearted atonality and expressionist textural fragmentation. At the same time, however, Britten did not regard opera as mere entertainment. He never lost the belief, nurtured in the 1930s, that art (especially if it shunned pretension and needless complexity) could convey fundamental truths, for example by confronting social majorities (heterosexual, anti-pacifist) with evidence of their intolerance and insensitivity. Having heard *Wozzeck* in 1934, Britten had tried to arrange lessons with Berg. Nothing came of that plan, but it seems clear that Berg's unsparing yet compassionate attitude to his central character, unable to escape from his low-life existence yet sensitive enough to sense something of his own predicament, suggested to Britten the type of subject (though not the kind of music) that he was able to approach with conviction.

Britten's commitment to 'classical practice' did not, in the event, promote a sequence of neo-classical number operas. Relatively small-scale, self-contained formal units from arias to choruses and orchestral interludes, with strophic, ternary or other independent forms like the chaconne and passacaglia, are consistently evident but do not preclude the kind of pervasive motivic and harmonic relations appropriate to through-composition. He also retained tonal harmonic elements even when, from *The Turn of the Screw* onwards, he made use of certain features of 12-note technique. Britten's harmony may have a higher level of dissonance than that of Verdi, or even Janáček, but the capacity of dissonance to resolve on to consonance remains a property of his language, as does the distinction between relatively explicit (diatonic) and relatively ambiguous (chromatic) tonal tendencies. In the church operas, in particular, which are performed without conductor, Britten made use of heterophonic and freely aligned contrapuntal textures that owe much to his experience of Balinese and Japanese music. These features further loosened the grip of traditional functional harmony without destroying the ultimate significance of tonality itself.

There is a high degree of consistency in the subject-matter that Britten's operas adapt from diverse sources. What connects stories by Henry James, Guy de Maupassant and Thomas Mann, a poem by Crabbe and a historical biography by Lytton Strachey, plays by Shakespeare and André Obey, a noh play and certain

stories from the Bible is a concern for the 'outsider', the innocent, vulnerable misfit, exposed to corruption, temptation or (in the least extreme case) the mystery of night in a wood near Athens. There is nevertheless more than mere consistency in Britten's operatic world. While *Peter Grimes*, *Billy Budd*, *Gloriana*, *The Turn of the Screw*, *Owen Wingrave* and *Death in Venice* represent that principal theme at its clearest, *The Rape of Lucretia* and the church operas admit the kind of resolution consequent on a Christian orientation, and the happy endings of *Paul Bunyan*, *Albert Herring* and *A Midsummer Night's Dream* are much more than perfunctory acknowledgments of an acceptable alternative to tragic dissolution. (In the case of *Billy Budd* it is possible to differ over whether the ending is 'happy' or not: whether the aged Vere is positively experiencing or pathetically imagining a state of serenity.)

There is a no less significant variety in the ways the diverse types of subject-matter are dramatically and musically presented. What tends to distinguish Britten's outsider-protagonists (and their sympathizers) is their greater sensitivity, and it follows that harshness and coarseness, lending themselves to musical realization through parody or even caricature, will be a prime feature of their opponents. The ironically pointed collision between these opposed characteristics is powerfully presented in Act 1 scene ii of *Peter Grimes*, where the fisherman's disturbed yet poetic flight of fancy provokes jaunty, aggressive incomprehension in the others. The conflicting states are portrayed with equal musical conviction – Grimes's short aria 'Now the Great Bear and Pleiades', the round 'Old Joe has gone fishing' – and the whole opera is ultimately a resourceful, extended working-out of degrees of interaction and confrontation between personal needs and collective convictions.

Many of the operas trace the ways in which this conflict of individual instinct and social convention produces first a moment of self-realization – Grimes's 'So be it, and God have mercy upon me!', Aschenbach's 'I love you!' – then the failure of the discovery to save the protagonist from the consequences of that conflict. Britten seems to have been drawn especially to schizoid characters – notably Grimes, Vere, and the Governess in *The Turn of the Screw* – whose acts and thoughts are persistently at odds. The results may not always be naturalistically plausible, but they are psychologically convincing, and this explains why, even though Britten's music may not aspire to the full-blooded intensity and moments of overwhelming rhetorical power found in Berg or Janáček, the effect can be both gripping and moving. Britten's operas survive primarily because their ambivalent psychological atmosphere is projected by wholly appropriate musical techniques. The literary source of that atmosphere is in the confusion of public and private motives and imperatives the central characters often embody. Its fundamental musical source is a combination of economy and ambiguity, where instantly memorable ideas and tonally refined contexts fuse to generate high levels of expressive tension. Even if, in comparison with Tippett, for example, Britten seems to avoid the transcendent in his operatic themes, he represents states of heightened consciousness in masterly fashion.

Music and plot work together most effectively in Britten's operas at the level of psychological motivation, and nowhere is this more evident than in the final opera, *Death in Venice*. This work is concerned less with pederasty, or even weakened creativity, than with their causes and consequences: guilt, self-doubt, masochistic resignation. With Aschenbach, thoughts and acts are more complementary than conflicting. His death is as much resolution as dissolution, hence the extraordinarily ambivalent mixture of fulfilment and loss we experience in the opera's final moments. Although it might have appeared that, after 1960, Britten was being overtaken by more progressive contemporaries, from the older Tippett to the younger Birtwistle and Maxwell Davies, *Death in Venice* shows that he never ceased to evolve within the constraints he could accept as personally relevant. Increasing economy of means and increasing enrichment of the musical language enhance the highly personal eloquence of the later operas, an eloquence the more intense for so rarely raising its voice to a shout. Its ultimate distillation is the brief 'Phaedrus' monologue in *Death in Venice* (scene xvi), a passage of surpassing poignancy which only the most disciplined and sensitive artist could have conceived (ex.1). With it Britten set the seal on a career that raised him into the company of the major operatic masters.

See also *Albert Herring*; *Billy Budd*; *Burning fiery furnace, The*; *Curlew river*; *Death in venice*; *Gloriana*; *Little sweep, The*; *Midsummer night's dream, A*; *Noye's fludde*; *Owen wingrave*; *Paul bunyan*; *Peter grimes*; *Prodigal son, The*; *Rape of Lucretia, The*; and *Turn of the screw, The*.

Autograph full scores in GB-ALb unless otherwise stated; all music published in London; dates are of first publications; earlier printed rehearsal editions are in ALb and Lbl

op.	*title*	*genre, acts*	*libretto*	*first performance*	*publication; autograph*
17	Paul Bunyan	operetta, prol., 2	W. H. Auden	New York, Brander Matthews Hall, 5 May 1941, cond. H. Ross; withdrawn	
	rev. version			BBC, 1 Feb 1976; stage, Snape, Maltings, 4 June 1976, cond. S. Bedford	vs 1978, full score ov. 1980
33	Peter Grimes	prol., 3	M. Slater, after G. Crabbe: *The Borough*	London, Sadler's Wells, 7 June 1945, cond. R. Goodall	vs 1945, full score 1963; *US-Wc*
37	The Rape of Lucretia	2	R. Duncan, after A. Obey: *Le viol de Lucrèce*	Glyndebourne, 12 July 1946, cond. E. Ansermet	vs 1946, vs 1947 (rev. edn), full score 1958
39	Albert Herring	comic op, 3	E. Crozier, after G. de Maupassant: *Le rosier de Madame Husson*	Glyndebourne, 20 June 1947, cond. Britten	vs 1948, full score 1969
—	The Little Sweep [Act 3 of Let's Make an Opera op.45]	'an entertainment for young people'	Crozier	Aldeburgh, Jubilee Hall, 14 June 1949, cond. N. Del Mar	vs 1950, full score 1965
50	Billy Budd	4	E. M. Forster and Crozier, after H. Melville	London, CG, 1 Dec 1951, cond. Britten	vs 1952
	rev. version	2		BBC, 13 Nov 1960, cond. Britten; stage, London, CG, 9 Jan 1964, cond. G. Solti	vs 1961, full score 1985
53	Gloriana	3	W. Plomer	London, CG, 8 June 1953, cond. J. Pritchard	vs 1953, full score 1990; *GB-Lbl*
54	The Turn of the Screw	prol., 2	M. Piper, after H. James	Venice, Fenice, 14 Sept 1954, cond. Britten	vs 1955, full score 1966

op.	title	genre, acts	libretto	first performance	publication; autograph
59	Noye's Fludde	1	Chester miracle play	Orford Church, 18 June 1958, cond. C. Mackerras	1959
64	A Midsummer Night's Dream	3	Britten and P. Pears, after W. Shakespeare	Aldeburgh, Jubilee Hall, 11 June 1960, cond. Britten	1961
71	Curlew River	church parable, 1	Plomer	Orford Church, 12 June 1964, dir. Britten	rehearsal score 1965, full score 1983
77	The Burning Fiery Furnace	church parable, 1	Plomer	Orford Church, 9 June 1966, dir. Britten	rehearsal score 1968, full score 1983
78	The Golden Vanity	vaudeville for boys' voices and pf	C. Graham, after old English ballad	Snape, Maltings, Vienna Boys' Choir, 3 June 1967	1967
81	The Prodigal Son	church parable, 1	Plomer	Orford Church, 10 June 1968, dir. Britten	rehearsal score 1971
85	Owen Wingrave	2	Piper, after James	BBC TV, 16 May 1971, cond. Britten; stage, London, CG, 10 May 1973, cond. Bedford	vs 1973
88	Death in Venice	2	Piper, after T. Mann	Snape, Maltings, 16 June 1973, cond. Bedford	vs 1975, full score 1979

Realizations: The Beggar's Opera, op.43 [after J. Gay] (3, ballad op), Cambridge, Arts, 24 May 1948, cond. Britten, MS full score (inc.), vs (1949); Dido and Aeneas [after H. Purcell] (3, N. Tate), Hammersmith, Lyric, 1 May 1951, cond. Britten (1961), collab. I. Holst

E. Crozier, ed.: *Peter Grimes* (London, 1945)
H. Keller: *The Rape of Lucretia; Albert Herring* (London, 1947)
E. Crozier, ed.: *The Rape of Lucretia: a Symposium* (London, 1948)
E. Stein: 'Benjamin Britten's Operas', *Opera*, i (1950), 16–21
Tempo, new ser., no.21 (1951) [Britten issue on *Billy Budd*]
D. Mitchell: 'More off than on "Billy Budd"', *Music Survey*, iv (1951–2), 86–108; repr. in *Music Survey: New Series, 1949–52*, ed. D. Mitchell and H. Keller (London, 1981), 386–408
D. Mitchell and H. Keller, eds.: *Benjamin Britten: a Commentary on his Works from a Group of Specialists* (London, 1952)
A. Porter: 'Britten's "Billy Budd"', *ML*, xxxiii (1952), 111–18
Tempo, new ser., no.28 (1953) [Britten issue on *Gloriana*]
J. Klein: 'Reflections on "Gloriana"', *Tempo*, new ser., no.29 (1953), 16–21
A. Porter: 'Britten's "Gloriana"', *ML*, xxxiv (1953), 277–87
E. Stein: '"The Turn of the Screw" and its Musical Idiom', *Tempo*, new ser., no.34 (1955), 6–14
E. Roseberry: 'The Music of "Noye's Fludde"', *Tempo*, new ser., no.49 (1958), 2–11
J. W. Garbutt: 'Music and Motive in "Peter Grimes"', *ML*, xliv (1963), 334–42
A. Gishford, ed.: *Tribute to Benjamin Britten on his Fiftieth Birthday* (London, 1963)
R. M. Schafer: 'Benjamin Britten', *British Composers in Interview* (London, 1963), 113–24
P. Howard: *The Operas of Benjamin Britten* (London, 1969)
E. W. White: *Benjamin Britten: his Life and Operas* (London, 1970)
G. Schmidgall: *Literature as Opera* (New York, 1977)
P. Evans: *The Music of Benjamin Britten* (London, 1979)
R. Duncan: *Working with Britten: a Personal Memoir* (Bideford, 1981)
M. Kennedy: *Britten* (London, 1981)
L'avant-scène opéra, no.31 (1981) [*Peter Grimes* issue]
A. Whittall: *The Music of Britten and Tippett* (Cambridge, 1982, 2/1990)
P. Brett, ed.: *Peter Grimes* (Cambridge, 1983)
W. T. Flynn: 'Britten the Progressive', *MR*, xliv (1983), 44–52
N. John, ed.: *Peter Grimes; Gloriana* (London, 1983)
C. Palmer, ed.: *The Britten Companion* (London, 1984)
J. Evans: 'Britten's Venice Workshop', pt i: 'The Sketchbook', *Soundings*, xii (1984–5), 7–24; pt ii: 'The Revisions', xiii (1985), 51–77
P. Howard, ed.: *The Turn of the Screw* (Cambridge, 1985)
Peter Pears: a Tribute on his 75th Birthday (London, 1985)
P. F. Alexander: 'The Process of Composition of the Libretto of Britten's "Gloriana"', *ML*, lxvii (1986), 147–58
P. Brett: 'Character and Caricature in "Albert Herring"', *MT*, cxxvii (1986), 545–7
E. Crozier: 'The Writing of "Billy Budd"', *OQ*, iv (1986), 11–27
S. Corse: *Opera and the Uses of Language: Mozart, Verdi and Britten* (Cranbury, NJ, 1987)
J. Evans, P. Reed and P. Wilson: *A Britten Source Book* (Aldeburgh and Winchester, 1987)
D. Mitchell, ed.: *Death in Venice* (Cambridge, 1987)
R. Travis: 'The Recurrent Figure in the Britten/Piper Opera "Death in Venice"', *Music Forum*, vi (1987), 129–246
P. F. Alexander: 'A Study of the Origins of Britten's "Curlew River"', *ML*, lxix (1988), 229–43
W. H. Auden: *Paul Bunyan, the Libretto of the Operetta: with an Essay by D. Mitchell* (London, 1988)
M. Cooke: 'Britten and the shō', *MT*, cxxix (1988), 231–3
——: 'Britten and Bali', *Journal of Musicological Research*, vii (1988), 307–39
P. Reed: 'A Rejected Love Song from "Paul Bunyan"', *MT*, cxxix (1988), 283–8
S. Corse and L. Corse: 'Britten's "Death in Venice": Literary and Musical Structures', *MQ*, lxxiii (1989), 344–63
C. Hindley: 'Love and Salvation in Britten's "Billy Budd"', *ML*, lxx (1989), 363–81
——: 'Contemplation and Reality: a Study in Britten's "Death in Venice"', *ML*, lxxi (1990), 511–23
——: 'Why does Miles Die? A Study of Britten's "The Turn of the Screw"', *MQ*, lxxiv (1990), 1–17
A. Whittall: '"Twisted Relations": Method and Meaning in Britten's "Billy Budd"', *Cambridge Opera Journal*, ii (1990), 145–71
D. Mitchell and P. Reed, eds.: *Letters from a Life. Selected Letters and Diaries of Benjamin Britten* (London, 1991)

ARNOLD WHITTALL

Brivio, Giuseppe Ferdinando (*b* Milan, ? end of the 17th century; *d* Milan, ?*c*1758). Italian composer and singing teacher, possibly also an impresario. 18th-century sources (e.g. La Borde, Burney and Gerber) blur the distinction between two or more musicians active in Milan by failing to give first names. Only the revised edition of Mancini (1779) supplies Giuseppe Ferdinando as the composer's first names and describes him as a prominent Milanese singing teacher without identifying him with the violinist, composer and impresario also active in Milan.

In fact a family of Brivios could be involved, including an older singing teacher, Carlo Francesco Brivio, who appeared in Milanese operas of 1696, *Teodolinda* and *L'Etna festante*, the librettos for which call him 'musico di S. E. il Castellano' (the castle commander's musician). Suggested (by Martinotti) as Giuseppe Ferdinando's father, this Carlo Francesco may have been the bass employed in the ducal court chapel until 1737 and then as a substitute singer until 1749. Relying on Gerber (1812, but based on La Borde), recent sources credit Carlo Francesco with having taught Giuseppe Appiani and Salimbeni. Since Mancini (1779) stated that Giuseppe Ferdinando taught Caterina Visconti and Giovanna Astrua, both Brivios may have taught singing at about the same time.

In 1720 the orchestra of the ducal theatre in Milan included two performers named Giuseppe Ferdinando Brivio, a first violinist and a trumpeter; only the latter, however, was cited in a list of June 1711 naming the Milanese players in Novara for the festival of S Gaudenzio. Although the ducal theatre orchestra did not include any player named Giuseppe Ferdinando Brivio in 1748 or 1765, a Gaetano Brivio played second violin in both years. It is generally assumed that the violinist Giuseppe Ferdinando Brivio also composed operas and symphonies and served as impresario in Milan. Archival documents indicate that he was in charge of the ducal theatre for a relatively long time: 26 February 1727 to 13 October 1732. Contrary to reports in modern encyclopedias, Brivio did not assist Giuseppe Milesio or any other of his predecessors, and his successor, G. A. Rozio, was forbidden to use him as partner.

Perhaps because some of Brivio's arias were used in pasticcios at the King's Theatre, London, or because Brivio's pupils Frasi (according to Burney) and Visconti sang in these pasticcios, Loewenberg and others have been led to suppose that Brivio was in London about 1742–5; no document proving a visit has come to light, however. Even though certain arias were published by Walsh, the pasticcios *Gianguir*, *Mandane* (both 1742) and *L'incostanza delusa* (1745; with music from Brivio's earlier opera of that name) were not especially popular with London audiences.

Archival papers of the ducal theatre at Milan indicate that Giuseppe Ferdinando Brivio was reimbursed for lodging Leonardo Leo (1740), the choreographer François Sauveterre (1748) and the prima donnas A. Conti (1753) and Columba Mattei (1754) at his residence in Milan. No known documents, however, verify his death in 1758, and no evidence has been found to link unequivocally some of the instrumental music published at Paris and London (1730–63) under the name Brivio with Giuseppe Ferdinando.

Ipermestra (3, A. Salvi), Milan, Regio Ducal, 26 Dec 1727 [probably a pasticcio arr. Brivio]
Olimpiade (3, P. Metastasio), Turin, Regio, 5 March 1737 [for wedding of King Carlo Emanuele III of Savoy and Princess Elisabetta Teresa of Lorraine]
Demofoonte (3, Metastasio), Turin, Regio, carn. 1738, *A-Wgm* (attrib. Carlo Francesco Brivio), arias, *F-Pc*
Artaserse (3, Metastasio), Padua, Obizzi, 2 June 1738 [for visit of Maria Amalia, Queen of the Two Sicilies]
Merope (3, A. Zeno), Milan, Regio Ducal, 26 Dec 1738
Didone abbandonata (3, Metastasio), Milan, Regio Ducal, Jan 1739 [sometimes attrib. A. Bernasconi]
La Germania trionfante in Arminio, Milan, Regio Ducal, 2 May 1739 [for visit of Maria Teresa as Archduchess of Austria]
L'incostanza delusa (2), Milan, Regio Ducal, ? sum. 1739, 2 arias (London, 1745)
Alessandro nell'Indie (3, Metastasio), Milan, Regio Ducal, Jan 1742, aria *Pc*

Music in: Gianguir, 1742; Mandane, 1742; L'incostanza delusa, 1745

Unidentified arias and duet in *A-Wn*, *I-Gl*

BurneyH; *DBI* (S. Martinotti); *GerberL*; *GerberNL*; *Grove5* (A. Loewenberg)
G. B. Mancini: *Pensieri e riflessioni pratiche sopra il canto figurato* (Vienna, 1774, 2/1779; Eng. trans., 1967, as *Practical Reflections on Figured Singing*)
J.-B. de La Borde: *Essai sur la musique ancienne et moderne*, iii (Paris, 1780), 173
M. Brenet: 'La librairie musicale en France de 1653 à 1790', *SIMG*, viii (1906–7), 437, 440, 446, 449
C. Cesari: 'G. Giulini musicista', *RMI*, xxiv (1917), 25–6
V. Fedeli: *Le cappelle musicali di Novara dal secolo XVI ai primordi dell'ottocento*, IMi, iii (1939), 30
C. A. Vianello: *Teatri spettacoli musiche a Milano* (Milan, 1941), 276, 365, 372
G. Barblan: 'Il teatro musicale in Milano nei secoli XVII e XVIII', *Storia di Milano*, xii (1958), 973–5
C. Sartori: 'G. B. Sammartini e la sua corte', *Musica d'oggi*, new ser., iii (1960), 108, 117
G. Barblan: 'La musica strumentale e cameristica a Milano nel '700', *Storia di Milano*, xvi (1962), 620, 623, 626, 651, 657

SVEN HANSELL

Brkanović, Ivan (*b* Škaljari, Boka Kotorska, 27 Dec 1906; *d* Zagreb, 20 Feb 1987). Croatian composer. He studied at the Zagreb Academy with Blagoje Bersa (composition) and others, graduating in 1935, and then at the Schola Cantorum in Paris in 1939. Between 1935 and 1951 he taught in Zagreb schools, and was made opera dramaturg to the Croatian National Theatre in Zagreb in 1951 and director of the Zagreb PO in 1954. He was also a prolific writer of music criticism during the period 1932–41. Brkanović was one of the most prominent representatives of the so-called national style in Croatian music. Using traditional musical means, he blended elements of Croatian folk music with his own strong artistic ideas, and in an attempt to evoke folk art in all its aspects, he drew on traditional rites, particularly on their most primitive features. His musical style is characterized by innovative formal and harmonic procedures, and dense polyphonic textures. Brkanović's feeling for dramatic tension and powerful emotions made him an ideal operatic composer. His first opera, *Ekvinocij* ('Equinox'), is a realistic musical drama, while the opera-oratorio *Škrinja svetog Šimuna* ('St Simon's Shrine'), inspired by scenes from a 14th-century shrine in Zadar, is strongly archaic. Two other stage works are oratorio-like in style: *Heloti* ('The Helots') and *Hod po mukah Ambroza Matije Gupca, zvanog Beg* ('The Passion of Ambroz Matija Gubec, called Beg').

Ekvinocij ['Equinox'], 1945 (musical drama, 3, T. Prpić, after I. Vojnović), Zagreb, 4 Oct 1950
Škrinja svetog Šimuna [St Simon's Shrine] (opera-oratorio, 3, D. Robić); as Zlato Zadra [The Gold of Zadar], Zagreb, 15 April 1955
Heloti [The Helots], 1960 (ballet-oratorio, prol., 2, Pio Mlakar and Pina Mlakar, after Robić), Zagreb, 17 March 1963
Hod po mukah Ambroza Matije Gupca, zvanog Beg [The Passion of Ambroz Matija Gubec, called Beg], 1972 (scenic oratorio, Robić), Zagreb, 13 Dec 1974
Fedra, 1975 (musical tragedy, 2 pts, Brkanović, after J. Racine), unperf.

*

I. Kirigin: 'Ekvinocij I. Brkanovića', *Muzička revija* (1950), 270–83
N. Turkalj: 'Zlato Zadra', *Teatar* (1955), 34–5
K. Kovačević: *Hrvatski kompozitori i njihova djela* [Croatian Composers and their Works] (Zagreb, 1960), 76–90
I. Supičić: 'Estetski pogledi u novijoj hrvatskoj muzici: pregled temeljnih gledanja četrnaestorice kompozitora' [Aesthetic Approaches in Contemporary Croatian Music: a Survey of the Basic Views of 14 Composers], *Arti musices*, i (1969), 23–61
J. Andreis: *Music in Croatia* (Zagreb, 1974)
Ivan Brkanović 1906–1987, Spomenica [Ivan Brkanović 1906–1987, Memorial] (Zagreb, 1989) [pubn of the Yugoslav

Academy of Arts and Sciences: with list of works and bibliography]

KORALJKA KOS, NIALL O'LOUGHLIN

Brno (Ger. Brünn). City in the Czech republic, capital of Moravia. Until the creation of an independent Czechoslovakia in 1918, German speakers preponderated and wielded a decisive influence over the city's cultural institutions. Brno's geographical position meant that its cultural development was closely connected with that of Vienna and the aristocratic estates of Moravia. Until the end of World War II theatrical life developed along parallel lines, Czech and German, a state of affairs mirrored in opera, which, after an Italian phase and a period dominated by opera sung in German, was divided between two fiercely rival theatres.

The first stirrings of operatic activity in Moravia were evident in the 1720s, when performances were given in Italian at the castle in JAROMĚŘICE NAD ROKYTNOU and on the estates of the Bishop of Olomouc at Vyškov and Kroměříž. Productions at František Antonín Rottal's castle at Holešov (1733–9) were directly tied to the Brno seasons managed by the Italian impresario Angelo Mingotti, whose singers would join Rottal's family in private performances. On 17 October 1732 Mingotti acquired permission from the city council to stage Italian operas in a temporary theatre by the Špilberk fortress. His company gave three public performances a week for four winter seasons, held in the Reduta from 1734, in which year Galuppi's *Argenide*, Eustachio Bambini's *La pravità castigata* and *Arianna e Teseo* (probably by Porpora) were presented.

By the 1770s German stage works had begun to predominate, and when Johann Böhm's troupe performed before Joseph II in Vienna it made such a favourable impression that the emperor recommended the imperial theatre in Vienna be modelled on the Brno ensemble. Böhm's successor Roman Weizhofer (1777–84) continued to put on successful Singspiels, adding operas by local composers (Zehenmark's *Was erhält die Männertreue* and Holzbauer's highly popular *Günther von Schwarzburg*); he also gave the first performance in Brno of Gluck's *Orfeo ed Euridice*. On 14 August 1786 Joseph II issued a decree granting the city a theatrical privilege, which ensured stability and permanence. By the turn of the century Mozart's operas had begun to appear (though the composer failed to achieve in Brno the popularity he had enjoyed in Prague), as well as those of Cherubini and Dittersdorf. Heinrich Schmidt (director 1815–25, 1831–7) succeeded in establishing a permanent opera chorus and enlarging the orchestra, so that he was then able to build up the repertory, staging *Fidelio* (1817), *Der Freischütz* (1822) and Rossini's operas. Anton Zöllner (1860–66) introduced the earlier operas of Wagner (*Tannhäuser*, 1861; *Lohengrin*, 1864).

In 1881, when the municipal theatre company had already been playing for ten years in the temporary Interimstheater, work began on the construction of a new theatre designed by Ferdinand Fellner and Hermann Helmer. The most up-to-date lighting system was installed, and the ceremonial opening of the new Stadttheater (the 'Neues Haus') took place on 14 November 1882. Until 1919 all performances were in German. The building was used for opera, operetta and plays (after 1965 for plays only). From independence it was known as the Národní Divadlo (National Theatre) or sometimes the Divadlo na Hradbách (Theatre on the Ramparts); after 1945 it became the Janáčkovo Divadlo (Janáček Theatre) and in 1965 the Mahenovo Divadlo (Mahen Theatre). It was reconstructed in 1971, the original seating capacity of 1195 being reduced to 572 (excluding the upper balcony, usually closed).

Between 1882 and 1905 there were over 300 Wagner performances at the German Stadttheater, the Wagner fever culminating in the Brno première of *Parsifal* in 1914; but for many years the Czech opera companies' resources were inadequate to tackle Wagner, and his nationalism was seen as symbolic of the less acceptable aspects of the German character. The theatre had an artistically strong ensemble with a good basic repertory, systematically augmented by the addition of new works. Close contacts with other German theatres in the area made possible the exchange of soloists and frequent guest appearances, the most important regular visitors including Leo Slezak (who began his career in Brno in 1896–8) and Maria Jeritza, a native of the city.

Czech opera began inconspicuously on 11 January 1767, when a performance of Jan Tuček's opera-pantomime *Der verliebte Nachtwächter*, with arias in Czech, was given by a company of German actors from Baden, probably in the Reduta. Another Czech work, the Singspiel *Strašidlo ve mlejně* ('The Ghost in the Mill') with music by Karel František Rafael, was heard in the Reduta in 1814. The Czech folk plays of the 1830s derived from this performance, and Anton Emil Titl's opera *Die Burgfrau auf dem Schlosse Pernstein*, though sung in German, was easily understood by a lowly audience as a reworking of the local legend of the White Lady. By the end of the 1830s excerpts from *Il barbiere di Siviglia* and *Die Zauberflöte* were being sung in Czech, and in 1839 the first performance of a complete opera in translation took place: Méhul's *Joseph*. The first period of Czech opera performances ended with František Škroup's *Dráteník* ('The Tinker', 1840) and with an original opera on a subject from Czech history, František Bedřich Kott's *Žižkův dub* ('Žižka's Oak', performed in 1841 in German and in 1842 in Czech). A new phase began in the 1870s with Czech companies putting on operas, operettas and plays in Czech. From 1874, visiting companies appeared in the new Czech social centre, the Besední Dům (Meeting House), where Jan Pištěk's company gave the Brno premières of *The Bartered Bride* (1879), *The Kiss* (1881) and other operas.

In 1881 a movement aimed at establishing a permanent, independent Czech theatre in Brno began to gather pace; the resulting Družstvo Českého Národního Divadla (Society for a Czech National Theatre) bought a house in Veveří Street, which, after basic repairs, opened on 6 December 1884. For ten years it was called the Prozatímní Divadlo (Provisional Theatre); after further work, which increased the seating capacity from 771 to 1150, it acquired the exaggeratedly grand title Národní Divadlo (National Theatre), becoming generally known from 1918 as the Staré Divadlo (Old Theatre). This inadequate and unattractive building was for 37 years the only Czech stage, and from 1919 to 1940 it functioned as a playhouse. In 1943–4 the České Lidové Divadlo (Czech People's Theatre), a stop-gap professional company, resumed performances there in all the traditional forms, including opera. In the last phase of its existence the theatre was again a playhouse, known as the Mahenovo Divadlo (Mahen Theatre); despite war damage the building remained open until its demolition in 1952.

During the first phase of the professional Czech

theatre's history (until 1919), works from the standard Czech and international repertories (Smetana, Dvořák, Fibich, Verdi, Bizet, Gounod) were presented, and on 21 January 1904 the première of *Jenůfa* was enthusiastically received. Czech opera did not, however, reach a full flowering until after 1919, when the company moved into the superior Stadttheater building. Central to this development was František Neumann, who the same year, on Janáček's recommendation, became director of the opera company and from 1925 managing director of the theatre. Neumann reorganized the entire company and embarked on a systematic building of the repertory, taking in new works by Novák, Ostrčil, Martinů and especially Janáček (all of whose operas from *Kát'a Kabanová* onwards had their premières at the Theatre on the Ramparts). During the 1930s, the conductors Milan Sachs (1932–8) and Rafael Kubelík (1939–41) carried on the work begun by Neumann.

The outstanding figure of the postwar period was the conductor František Jílek (1948–78; artistic director from 1952), who created a superb team of soloists (Vilém Přibyl, Hana Janků, Naděžda Kniplová, Richard Novák). With the director Miloš Wasserbauer and the designer František Tröster, he staged revelatory productions of *From the House of the Dead* and *The Fiery Angel* and in 1958 mounted the première of *Osud*. Among the company's most commendable postwar endeavours were the staging of the complete Janáček operas at the 1958 festival and the gradual introduction of the complete Martinů operas. A solution to the problem of Brno's theatre buildings was finally found in 1965, when the new Janáček Theatre opened on 2 October with a gala performance of *The Cunning Little Vixen*. The theatre, seating 1400, is used mainly for opera.

The Janáček Academy of Musical Arts administers an experimental studio, the Miloš Wasserbauer Chamber Opera, for the training of opera singers, directors and conductors, which since 1957 has given two to three opera premières each year. The Reduta (388 seats), in use as a theatre periodically since the 17th century, is today used for operetta and occasionally also for chamber performances of operas.

*

A. Rille: *Geschichte des Brünner Stadttheaters 1734–1884* (Brno, 1885)

G. Bondi: *Fünfundzwanzig Jahre Eigenregie: Geschichte des Brünner Stadttheaters 1882–1907* (Brno, 1907)

M. Hýsek: 'Dějiny českého divadla v Brně' [History of Czech Theatre in Brno], *Hlídka*, xxiv/8 (1907)

J. Helfert: *Národní divadlo v Brně* [The National Theatre in Brno] (Prague, 1919)

G. Bondi: *Geschichte des Brünner deutschen Theaters 1600–1925* (Brno, 1929)

Zlatá kniha Družstva českého Národního divadla [The Golden Book of the Society for a Czech National Theatre] (Brno, 1934)

J. Racek: 'Brněnská opera a její význam v moravské hudební kultuře' [The Brno Opera and its Importance in Moravian Musical Culture], *Divadelní list* (1934–5), 221

L. Firkušný: *Leoš Janáček a brněnské divadlo* [Leoš Janáček and the Brno Theatre] (Brno, 1939)

J. Telcová: 'Divadlo na Veveří ulici a jeho budova' [The Theatre in Veveří Street and its Building], *ČMm*, xlv (1960), 199–214

A. Němcová and S. Přibáňová: 'Příspěvek k dějinám opery Národního divadla v Brně 1884–1919' [Notes on the History of Opera at the National Theatre in Brno 1884–1919], *ČMm*, xlviii (1963), 261–82

F. Černý, ed.: *Dějiny českého divadla* [History of Czech Theatre] (Prague, 1968–9)

J. Suchomelová, ed.: *Divadlo je divadlo* [The Theatre is Theatre] (Brno, 1969)

J. Dřímal and V. Peša, eds.: *Dějiny města Brna* [History of the City of Brno] (Brno, 1969–73)

Budova Státního divadla v Brně [The Building of the Brno State Theatre] (Brno, 1971)

Almanach Státního divadla v Brně 1884–1974 [Almanac of the Brno State Theatre 1884–1974] (Brno, 1974) [vol.ii incl. operatic repertory]

J. Sehnal: 'Počátky opery na Moravě' [The Beginnings of Opera in Moravia], *O divadle na Moravě*, ed. E. Petrů and J. Stýskal (Prague, 1974), 55–77

Hudba v českých dějinách: od středověku do nové doby [Music in Czech History: from the Middle Ages to Modern Times] (Prague, 1983)

E. Dufková, ed.: *Putování múzy Thálie: sto let stálého českého divadla v Brně 1884–1984* [Thalia's Pilgrimage: 100 Years of a Permanent Czech Theatre in Brno 1884–1984] (Brno, 1984)

E. Dufková and B. Srba, eds.: *Postavy brněnského jeviště* [Personalities of the Brno Stage] (Brno, 1984–9)

J. Tyrrell: *Czech Opera* (Cambridge, 1988), 56–9

M. Wurmová: *Repertoár brnenského divadla v letech 1777–1848* [Repertory of the Brno Theatre 1777–1848] (Brno, 1990)

ALENA NĚMCOVÁ

Brocchi, Giovanni Battista (*fl* 1776–1807). Italian bass. He was a singer of *buffo* parts. His first known appearances were in Venice (1776–7), Reggio Emilia (1779) and Warsaw (1780–81). In 1782–4 he was in St Petersburg, where he created Figaro in *Il barbiere di Siviglia* and Ernesto in *Il mondo della luna*, both by Paisiello. After further appearances in Warsaw (1785) and Bologna (1786) he sang at Naples in 1787–8 in Cimarosa's *Il fanatico burlato* and Valentino Fioravanti's *Gl'inganni fortunati*. He performed at Genoa in 1789–90, 1793 (Cimarosa's *Il matrimonio segreto*) and 1796, and in 1793–1800 appeared at Venice in 40 operas, including new works by Mayr and Paer. In 1802 he sang at La Scala (Lavigna's *La muta per amore*), in summer 1807 at Piacenza, and in autumn 1807 again at Milan, as Don Alfonso in *Così fan tutte*.

COLIN TIMMS

Bröcheler, John (*b* Vaals, 21 Feb 1945). Dutch baritone. He studied in Maastricht and Paris. At Amsterdam he sang Talbot in *Maria Stuarda* (1977), Don Giovanni, Marcello and Germont and created the title role in the posthumous première of Jan van Gilse's *Thijl* (1980). At San Diego he created Felipe/Ferdinand/Carlos in Menotti's *La loca* (1979), then repeated the opera at the New York City Opera. He has appeared at Geneva, Frankfurt, Toronto, Paris and Glyndebourne, where he sang Mandryka (1984). His repertory includes Gluck's Agamemnon, the title role of *Nabucco*, Ford, Tebaldo (Zandonai's *Giulietta e Romeo*), Tomsky, Amfortas, Kurwenal, Wolfram, John the Baptist, Orestes, Thomas' Hamlet and Golaud, which he sang at La Scala (1986) and the Vienna Staatsoper (1988). At Munich (1990) he sang the title roles of *Mathis der Maler* and *Dantons Tod*. A powerful actor with a fine presence, he has a firm, warm-toned voice. ELIZABETH FORBES

Brod, Max (*b* Prague, 27 May 1884; *d* Tel-Aviv, 20 Dec 1968). German-Israeli writer, translator and librettist of Czech birth. He studied law and worked in Prague for a time as a state employee. He was a fine pianist and a composer (mostly of songs); his first published volume of verse (1907) earned the approval of Rilke, his first novel (1909) brought him notoriety. Thoughts on music are woven into his novels and poetry: his final book (1962) was a novelistic defence of Karel Sabina, librettist of Smetana's *The Bartered Bride*, who was discovered to be a police informer. Brod was a friend of other German-Jewish writers in Prague such as Kafka and Werfel, and did much to promote their careers, becoming Kafka's biographer and literary executor. His own talents and wide sympathies enabled him to become a prominent music and theatre critic for the *Prager Abendblatt* and *Prager Tagblatt*), the translator of some of Novák's operas into German and the author of a few original librettos: (for Gurlitt (*Nana*), W. Kaufman (after Gogol's story *Nos*) and Lavry (*Dan Hashomer*).

Alerted by Josef Suk to the Prague production of *Jenůfa*, Brod wrote an enthusiastic review in *Die Schaubühne* (1916), on the basis of which Janáček begged him to translate the opera into German. Brod did so, initiating a friendship with the composer and a series of translations of most of the subsequent operas. Brod's suggestions as he translated resulted in some additions to *Káťa Kabanová* and a free reinterpretation of *The Cunning Little Vixen*, but Janáček made Brod withdraw most of his changes to *The Makropulos Affair*. Brod also wrote the first substantial biography of Janáček, a valuable source relying on information drawn directly from the composer. Other Czech opera texts which Brod translated included that of Weinberger's *Švanda dudák* ('Švanda the Bagpiper'), where he rewrote the first act and made Weinberger change the music accordingly. In 1939 Brod left Czechoslovakia and settled in Palestine, leading an active life as a composer and writer on Israeli music.

WRITINGS

Sternenhimmel: Musik- und Theatererlebnisse (Prague and Munich, 1923, enlarged as *Prager Sternenhimmel: Musik- und Theatererlebnisse aus den zwanziger Jahren*, 1966; Cz. trans., 1969) [incl. 'Tschechisches Opernglück', first pubd 1916]
Leoš Janáček: život a dílo [Life and Works] (Prague, 1924; Ger. orig., 1925, 2/1956)
Streitbares Leben (Munich, 1960; Cz. trans., 1966)
Die verkaufte Braut: der abenteuerliche Lebensroman des Textdichters Karel Sabina (Munich, 1962)

*

J. Racek and A. Rektorys, eds.: *Korespondence Leoše Janáčka s Maxem Brodem* (Prague, 1953)
R. Cígler: 'Janáčkovo libreto a Brodův překlad Lišky Bystrouška' [Janáček's Libretto and Brod's Translation of *The Cunning Little Vixen*], *HRo*, x (1957), 746–51
B. Jičínský: 'Das Brodsche Paradox', *Operní dílo Leoše Janáčka: Brno 1965*, 105–8; see also 'K Brodově interpretaci Janáčkových operních textů' [Brod's Interpretation of Janáček's Operatic Texts'], *Sborník Janáčkovy akademie múzických umění*, v (1965), 81–8
J. Procházka: 'Brods Übersetzung des Librettos der *Jenůfa* und die Korrekturen Franz Kafkas', *Operní dílo Leoše Janáčka: Brno 1965*, 109–13; repr. in *Leoš Janáček – Materialen*, ed. J. Knaus (Zürich, 1982), 30–38
H. Gold, ed.: *Max Brod: ein Gedenkbuch, 1884–1968* (Tel-Aviv, 1969)
B. W. Wessling: *Max Brod: ein Portrait* (Stuttgart, 1969)
J. Tyrrell: *Leoš Janáček: Káťa Kabanová* (Cambridge, 1982), 61–9 [trans. of Brod's correspondence with Janáček]
C. Susskind: *Janáček and Brod* (Newhaven and London, 1985)
J. Tyrrell: *Janáček's Operas: a Documentary Account* (London, 1992)

JOHN TYRRELL

Brogi [Pertici], **Caterina** (*b* Florence, *fl* 1737–58). Italian mezzo-soprano. Initially a singer of intermezzos, in 1742 she married the bass Pietro Pertici, with whom she performed *commedie per musica*; as members of companies specializing in *opera buffa* the two contributed significantly to the wide success of the genre. Brogi took soubrette and leading juvenile roles in the highly successful comic operas of Auletta, Chinzer, Latilla and others. She worked mainly in Tuscany but also sang in Venice, Milan, Turin, Brescia, Mantua, Genoa and Bologna; outside Italy she appeared in comic opera in London (1748–9) and Brussels (1749) and in Metastasian opera in Barcelona (1753–4).

*

P. Weiss: 'La diffusione del repertorio operistico nell'Italia del settecento: il caso dell'opera buffa', *Civiltà teatrale e settecento emiliano*, ed. S. Davoli (Bologna, 1986), 241–56

FRANCO PIPERNO

Bromberg (Ger.). BYDGOSZCZ.

Bronhill [Gough], **June** (*b* Broken Hill, NSW, June 1930). Australian soprano. After winning two competitions in the early 1950s, she went to England to study. At the beginning of her career she assumed the name Bronhill (derived from her birthplace, Broken Hill). She made her début at Sadler's Wells (1954), where her roles included Gilda, Norina, Zerbinetta, and Lucy in Menotti's *The Telephone*. She sang the title role in the first performance in the UK of Janáček's *The Cunning Little Vixen* (1961), in which her performance was praised for its 'clear and straightforward' singing and 'telling and authentic gestures'. She followed Joan Sutherland in Donizetti's *Lucia* on the Covent Garden tour in 1959. During the early seasons of Australian Opera at the Sydney Opera House she sang Blonde in *Die Entführung* and Adele in *Die Fledermaus*; she had special success at Sadler's Wells in operettas by Offenbach, Johann Strauss and Lehár; she sang Hanna in *Die lustige Witwe* more than two hundred times. She returned to London in 1974 to sing Hanna once again at the Coliseum as well as Magda in Puccini's *La rondine* with the English Opera Group. Her vibrant personality and her voice, clear and true with exemplary diction, easily filled the largest theatres, despite her small stature. She was awarded an OBE in 1976.

*

B. Mackenzie and F. Mackenzie: *Singers of Australia* (Melbourne, 1967)

PATRICK O'CONNOR

Bronner, Georg [Jürgen] (*b* Hamburg, bap. 17 Feb 1667; *d* Hamburg, bur. 8 March 1720). German composer. He was an organist in Hamburg and the only one there to have connections with the Hamburg opera. He was co-director of the company in 1699 and composed for it a series of works (some in collaboration with Mattheson and Schieferdecker) between 1693 and 1702. These operas, which received Mattheson's critical approval, are lost, as are most of his other works, including two oratorios and some church music.

all first performed in Hamburg

Echo und Narcissus (3, F. C. Bressand), 1693
Venus, oder Die siegende Liebe (H. Hinsch or J. Kremberg), 1694
Philippus Herzog von Mailand (3, Hinsch), 1701, ? collab. Mattheson; as Beatrix, 1702
Procris und Cephalus (3, Bressand), 1701
Berenice (Hinsch, after J. Racine), 1702
Der Tod des grossen Pans (Hinsch), 1702, ? collab. Mattheson
Victor [Viktor] Herzog der Normannen [Act 3] (3, Hinsch), 1702 [Act 1 by J. C. Schieferdecker, Act 2 by Mattheson]

*

WaltherML
J. Mattheson: *Der musicalische Patriot* (Hamburg, 1728)
——: *Grundlage einer Ehren-Pforte* (Hamburg, 1740); ed. M. Schneider (Berlin, 1910)
F. Chrysander: 'Matthesons Verzeichniss Hamburgischer Opern von 1678 bis 1728', *AMZ*, new ser., xii (1877), 198–282 passim
H. C. Wolff: *Die Barockoper in Hamburg* (Wolfenbüttel, 1957)

FRIEDHELM KRUMMACHER

Bronsart [née Starck], **Ingeborg (Lena) von** (*b* St Petersburg, 12/24 Aug 1840; *d* Munich, 17 June 1913).

German composer of Swedish parentage. She studied the piano and composition with Henselt in St Petersburg (1855–7) and Liszt in Weimar (1858–9). Between 1858 and 1867 she developed a very successful career as a concert pianist, often performing with her husband, the pianist, conductor and composer Hans Bronsart von Schellendorf. She had to give up her performing career in 1867, when Hans was appointed Intendant of the Hoftheater in Hanover. There as well as later in Weimar (after 1887), she devoted herself to composition. She had already written the opera *Die Göttin von Sais*, performed in 1867 for the crown prince in Berlin. A second opera, *Jery und Bätely*, established her reputation as opera composer: it received acclaim at the première in Weimar (1873) and at performances in ten other German cities. The text for her third opera, *Hiarne*, was written by Hans during the early 1860s and later revised by Friedrich Bodenstedt; she worked on the score during the 1870s and 80s. Despite a successful première at the royal opera in Berlin in 1891, the work did not enter the repertory. The Bronsarts retired in 1895 to Munich, where Ingeborg composed her final opera *Die Sühne*. It received only two performances, in Dessau in 1909.

Bronsart's four operas, spanning more than 40 years, are so individual in style that they almost defy treatment as a unified body of work. *Die Göttin von Sais*, a Greek idyll, was described by Liszt as 'learned and inspired'; the one-act *Jery und Bätely* adopts a very simple style appropriate to Goethe's Singspiel; *Hiarne*, with its use of leitmotifs and arioso vocal writing, approaches a Wagnerian style; *Die Sühne* adds to those Wagnerian traits colourful orchestration, continuity of music and pervasive chromaticism. Despite the later operas' indebtedness to Wagner, something the composer herself vehemently denied (she once described *Hiarne* as 'not in a Wagnerian but rather a modern Gluckian style'), Bronsart's music generally features vocally derived melodies, simple forms and moderately chromatic harmonies. With the exception of *Jery und Bätely*, the operas tend to suffer from weak librettos that above all lack dramatic tension. The literature of the period emphasized Bronsart as the first major female composer of opera in Germany. Whether this is true or not, her operas *Jery und Bätely* and *Hiarne* were favourably received and widely disseminated within Germany at a time when operas by women were infrequently staged in the country's theatres.

Hans Bronsart (*b* Berlin, 11 Feb 1830; *d* Munich, 3 Nov 1913) wrote a dramatic tone poem in five scenes, *Manfred* (Weimar, Court Theatre, 1 December 1901), that is largely operatic in conception. However, the text, based on Byron, is more descriptive than dramatic, and this probably contributed to the work's failure. The music reveals various influences, recalling Wagner in declamatory passages and resembling Schumann at other times, especially in the choruses.

Die Göttin von Sais, oder Linas und Liane (idyllische Oper, 3, Meyer), Berlin, Kronprinzliches Palais, 1867, lost, lib. (Berlin, 1866)
Jery und Bätely (Operette, 1, J. W. von Goethe), Weimar, Hof, 26 April 1873, *D-B*, *Mbn*, *WRdn*, *US-NYp**; (Leipzig, 1876)
Hiarne, *c*1870–90 (prol., 3, H. von Bronsart and F. Bodenstedt), Berlin, Kgl, 14 Feb 1891, *D-WRdn**
Die Sühne (Tragödie, 1, after T. Körner), Dessau, Hof, 12 April 1909, *DEl**

*

R. Pohl: 'Die 14. Tonkünstler-Versammlung des Allgemeinen Deutschen Musikvereins', *NZM*, xliv (1877), 233–4 [*Jery und Bätely*]
E. Polko: 'Ingeborg von Bronsart: biographisches Skizzenblatt', *Neue Musik-Zeitung*, ix (1888), 142–3
'Sangkönig Hiarne', *NZM*, lvii (1890), 37–9
P. Simon: 'Hiarne', ibid, 553–5
——: 'Die erste Aufführung der Oper Hiarne von Frau Ingeborg von Bronsart im Königl. Opernhause zu Berlin', *NZM*, lviii (1891), 87
G. Crusen: 'Ingeborg von Bronsart's *Hiarne* im Königlichen Hoftheater zu Hannover', *NZM*, lix (1892), 85–6
W. Asmus: 'Ingeborg von Bronsart', *NZM*, lxv (1898), 193–5
La Mara [M. Lipsius]: 'Ingeborg von Bronsart', *Die Frauen im Tonleben der Gegenwart*, Musikalische Studienköpfe, v (Leipzig, 1902), 35–53
E. Hamann: 'Kritische Rundschau: Dessau', *Neue Musik-Zeitung*, xxx (1909), 326 [*Die Sühne*]
A. Spanuth: '*Die Sühne*', *Signale*, lxvii (1909), 550–52
A. Morsch: 'Ingeborg von Bronsart', *Gesangspädagogische Blätter*, iv (1910), 100–02
F. Stieger: 'Opernkomponistinnen', *Die Musik*, xiii (1913–14), 270–72

JAMES A. DEAVILLE

Bronsgeest, Cornelis (*b* Leiden, 24 July 1878; *d* Berlin, 22 Sept 1957). Dutch baritone. He studied with Julius Stockhausen in Frankfurt and made his début in Hamburg in 1901 (*Das Nachtlager in Granada* by Kreutzer). After five years in Hamburg he moved to the Berlin Hofoper, where his most notable roles were Amonasro, Amfortas, Posa and Telramund. His only English appearance was as Papageno at Drury Lane (1914) conducted by Beecham. He directed his own touring opera company from 1922 to 1924 and took such roles as Don Giovanni and Count Almaviva. From 1924 until the rise of the Nazis he directed operas for Berlin Radio and was founder of the Berlin Radio Orchestra and Chorus; he gave up his position as director in 1933 for political reasons. He helped to organize the first opera performances in postwar Berlin. DAVID CUMMINGS

Bronskaya, Eugenia (*b* St Petersburg, 20 Jan/1 Feb 1882; *d* Leningrad, 12 Dec 1953). Russian soprano. She studied first with her mother in Russia and later with Teresa Arkel in Milan. After her début at Tbilisi in 1901 she sang for three years in Kiev and from 1905 to 1907 in Moscow. Returning to Italy she performed Tatyana in the Venice première of *Yevgeny Onegin*. She toured widely until 1909, when she joined the Boston Opera Company, making her début there as Micaëla in *Carmen*. Other roles included Marguerite de Valois in *Les Huguenots*, Gilda in *Rigoletto* and on one occasion the title role in *Lucia di Lammermoor*, which she undertook for an indisposed colleague as the curtain was about to rise, knowing no more than the Sextet and Mad Scene. At this period she also became well known as a recording artist, and on her return to Russia in 1911 was engaged at the Mariinsky and Bol'shoy theatres. From 1923 to 1950 she taught at the Leningrad Conservatory. Recordings show a bright voice, sometimes hardening on the high notes but used with exceptional skill, especially in staccato passages. J. B. STEANE

Brook, Peter (Stephan Paul) (*b* London, 21 March 1925). English director. He studied at Oxford, where his theatrical skills first became apparent. His main work has been in the spoken theatre, but between 1948 and 1950 he caused several sensations at Covent Garden with his avant-garde stagings. These included a highly idiosyncratic *Boris Godunov* designed by George Wakhévitch (1948), and an outrageous (for its time) *Salome* (1949), with decor by Dalí, which was abandoned after six controversial performances. He also staged the première of Bliss's *The Olympians* at

Covent Garden (1949). Brook was regarded as an *enfant terrible*: he was determined to rehearse operas as he would plays, and was not prepared to tolerate good singers who were bad actors. In 1953 he filmed Gay's *The Beggar's Opera* with Laurence Olivier. His *Faust* at the Metropolitan in 1953 caused something of a furore, but his *Yevgeny Onegin* there in 1957 was by comparison more conventional. After that Brook gave up directing opera, concluding that the public for that art was not yet ready for his advanced ideas. He returned to the fray with his own company, producing *La tragédie de Carmen* at the Bouffes du Nord in Paris in the 1981–2 season. This was a reduction of the piece, both dramatically and musically, to fit into a tiny venue. The results were arresting and typically unconventional yet faithful to the Mérimée–Bizet ethos. The staging travelled to various centres and was filmed for television. He was made a CBE in 1965. ALAN BLYTH

Brooks, Patricia (*b* New York, 7 Nov 1937). American soprano. She studied at the Manhattan School, and after working as a dancer and an actress joined the New York City Opera in 1960, singing Marianne in *Der Rosenkavalier*. She soon graduated to Sophie, to a leading role in Robert Ward's *The Crucible*, Violetta, Massenet's Manon, Nedda, Gilda, Lucia and, perhaps most memorably, Mélisande. She made her Covent Garden début as the Queen of Shemakha in *The Golden Cockerel* in 1969, and has appeared at Chicago, San Francisco, Toronto and Santiago (Chile). In 1974 she played Berg's Lulu at Santa Fe and later at Houston. Brooks is a highly individual actress, and her performances are more often notable for theatrical impact than vocal perfection. MARTIN BERNHEIMER

Broschi, Carlo. *See* FARINELLI.

Broschi [Brosca], **Riccardo** (*b* Naples, *c*1698; *d* Madrid, 1756). Italian composer, brother of Farinelli. He was probably trained in Naples, where he presented his one and only comic opera, *La vecchia sorda*, at the Fiorentini theatre in 1725. His heroic operas all date from between 1728 and 1735, and in several his famous younger brother, the castrato Carlo Broschi, called Farinelli, sang. It is just possible that Riccardo accompanied his brother to London in 1734 when the latter made his début on the English stage in the pasticcio *Artaserse* (King's Theatre, 29 October); for this pasticcio, with music primarily by Hasse and Porpora, Broschi wrote the bravura aria 'Son qual nave' which became one of Farinelli's most famous showpieces and was published in *Favourite Songs* (London, 1734). In 1736 Duke Carl Alexander of Württemberg appointed Broschi his *compositore di musica*, and the Italian opera company then in the duke's employ at Stuttgart performed *Adriano in Siria* (composed 1735) at the beginning of 1737. However, following the duke's death in March 1737 the company was disbanded and Broschi lost his post. It seems that he made his way to Naples, where he was asked to compose a few arias for a new opera, *Demetrio* (music primarily by Leo), but failed to gain other significant commissions. During the 1740s he joined his brother in Madrid, but nothing is known about his musical activities during his final years in Spain.

all in three acts; opere serie unless otherwise stated

La vecchia sorda (ob, S. Saddumene), Naples, Fiorentini, aut. 1725
L'isola d'Alcina (A. Fanzaglia), Rome, Tordinona, 1728; as Bradamante nell'isola d'Alcina, Parma, carn. 1729
Idaspe (G. P. Candi), Venice, S Giovanni Grisostomo, carn. 1730, *A-Wn*
Ezio (P. Metastasio), Turin, Regio, carn. 1731
Arianna e Teseo (P. Pariati), Milan, Regio Ducal, 28 Aug 1731
Merope (A. Zeno), Turin, Regio, carn. 1732, *Wgm*
Anagilda (M. A. Gigli), ?1735, *A-Wgm*
Adriano in Siria (Metastasio), Milan, Regio Ducal, carn. 1736

Arias in Demetrio (Metastasio), Naples, S Carlo, 30 June 1738, music by L. Leo and others
Miscellaneous arias in *GB-Cfm*, *I-Bc*, *Nc*

*

FlorimoN
F. Häbock: *Die Gesangkunst der Kastraten* (Vienna, 1923)

MICHAEL F. ROBINSON

Brough, William Francis (*b* Wexford, 1798; *d* at sea, 21 May 1867). English bass and operatic manager. After several years' acting at the Haymarket Theatre, he accompanied Joseph and Mary Anne Paton Wood to the USA in 1833 and 1840; his American début (as Dandini in M. R. Lacy's adaptation of *Cenerentola*) was in New York on 4 September 1835. He sang intermittently with the Park Theatre company in New York, and made several extended tours that included performances in Savannah, Mobile and New Orleans. In 1839 he performed with Jane Shirreff and John Wilson on their North American tour. After the mid-1840s he concentrated on the business side of music, working as manager for the Anna Bishop, Brough-Delcy and Manvers opera companies; during the mid-1850s he managed an extensive tour by the Pyne-Harrison English Opera Company. He died aboard ship while returning to England and was buried in Brooklyn in February 1868.

*

F. Boase: *Modern English Biography* (London, 1892)
G. C. D. Odell: *Annals of the New York Stage* (New York, 1927–31)
V. Lawrence: *Strong on Music: The New York Music Scene in the Days of George Templeton Strong, 1836–1875*, i: *Resonances: 1836–1850* (New York, 1988)
K. K. Preston: *Travelling Opera Troupes in the United States, 1825–1860* (diss., City U., New York, 1989)

KATHERINE K. PRESTON

Brouwenstijn, Gré [Gerda Demphina] (*b* Den Helder, 26 Aug 1915). Dutch soprano. She studied in Amsterdam and made her début there in 1940 as one of the Ladies in *Die Zauberflöte*. In 1946 she joined the newly formed Netherlands Opera, where her first successes were as Tosca and Santuzza. She made her Covent Garden début in 1951 as Aida and sang there regularly until 1964, notably as Elisabeth de Valois in Visconti's production of *Don Carlos* (1958; see illustration, overleaf) and as Desdemona. She appeared at Bayreuth (1954–6) as Elsa, Elisabeth, Sieglinde, Gutrune and Eva; she also sang in Vienna and Stuttgart, where she took the title role in Wieland Wagner's production of *Fidelio* (1956). She sang Jenůfa at Chicago (1959) and Amelia in *Un ballo in maschera* at San Francisco (1961). She appeared at Glyndebourne as Leonore (1959, 1961, 1963) and made her farewell in that role with Netherlands Opera in 1971. She possessed a beautiful voice, allied to natural musical intelligence and an attractive stage presence.

*

GV (F. Serpa; R. Vegeto)
H. Rosenthal: 'Gré Brouwenstijn', *Opera*, vii (1959), 440–44
A. Natan: 'Brouwenstijn, Gré', *Prima donna* (Basle, 1962) [with discography]
D. Cairns: *Responses* (London, 1973), 140ff

HAROLD ROSENTHAL/R

Gré Brouwenstijn as Elisabeth de Valois in Visconti's production of Verdi's 'Don Carlos' at Covent Garden, London, in 1958

Brown, Ann [Mrs Cargill] (*b* London, *c*1759; *d* off Scilly Isles, Feb or March 1784). English soprano and actress. She made her début as a child in Arne's *The Fairy Prince* (November 1771) and appeared regularly on the London stage from autumn 1772. She created the roles of Clara in *The Duenna*, Mrs Townly in Hook's *The Lady of the Manor* and Marinetta in Linley's *The Carnival of Venice*. She was a captivating Macheath in Coleman's travesty *Beggar's Opera* in 1781. Her private life was unsettled, both before and after her marriage, and in 1782 she went to India, reputedly with a lover. There she 'played all her favourite opera characters at immense prices, and likewise attempted tragedy with considerable applause'. On her return journey she drowned with a child in her arms when the packet *Nancy* sank.

BDA; *DNB* (J. Knight); *LS*
A. Pasquin [pseud. of J. Williams]: *The Children of Thespis*, ii (London, 13/1792)
The Thespian Dictionary (London, 1802, 2/1805)
J. Adolphus: *Memoirs of John Bannister, Comedian* (London, 1839)
R. Fiske: *English Theatre Music in the Eighteenth Century* (London, 1973, 2/1986) OLIVE BALDWIN, THELMA WILSON

Brown, Howard Mayer (*b* Los Angeles, 13 April 1930). American musicologist and editor. He studied at Harvard, receiving the PhD in 1959 for his dissertation *Music in the French Secular Theatre, 1400–1550* (Cambridge, MA, 1963); he also studied conducting privately in Vienna. In 1960 he joined the music department at the University of Chicago, becoming its chairman in 1970. He was appointed King Edward Professor of Music at King's College, University of London (1972–4), then returned to Chicago, where he was made Ferdinand Schevill Distinguished Service Professor in 1976. In 1987 he was awarded the Galileo Galilei Prize by the University of Pisa for his contribution to the study of Italian culture. Though known primarily for his work on early instrumental music, Brown has made a significant contribution to the study of opera in his editing of the 60-volume facsimile series, *Italian Opera, 1640–1770* (New York, 1977–83). His edition of Peri's *Euridice* was published in 1981. H. COLIN SLIM

Browne, Marmaduke E(dmonstone) (*b* 1843–4; *d* ?1917). English translator. He was a scholar of Oriel College, Oxford (BA 1866), and was ordained in the Church of England in 1868. He was choirmaster and organist of Christ Church, Marylebone, London, from 1878 to 1882.

For the production of *Così fan tutte* (at that time rarely staged) by the Royal College of Music at the Savoy Theatre in 1890, he wrote an amusing and elegant English version, 'translated and adapted from the original Italian and the German paraphrase', in a style Richard Brinsley Sheridan would not have disdained. It was published in vocal score by Novello, with the characters Fiordiligi and Guglielmo renamed Isidora and Gratiano, presumably for the convenience of English tongues. The long survival of this version, with modifications, extended to the ENO production of 1990. Browne also translated Cornelius's *Der Barbier von Bagdad* (RCM, Savoy, 1891) and Hermann Goetz's *Francesca da Rimini* (RCM, Her Majesty's, 1908), as well as *Fidelio* (published 1891). ARTHUR JACOBS

Browne, Sandra (*b* Point Fortin, Trinidad, 22 July 1947). Trinidad mezzo-soprano. She studied in New York, Brussels and Manchester, making her début in 1972 as Fenena (*Nabucco*) with the WNO. She created Uma in Hoddinott's *Beach of Falesá* (1974, WNO), then sang Carmen in 1975 for the ENO, repeating the role in Toulouse, San Francisco, Marseilles, Nancy and Florence. Her repertory includes Dorabella, Idamantes, Monteverdi's Poppaea, Purcell's Dido, Rossini's Andromache (*Ermione*), Clarice (*Pietra del paragone*) and Neocle (*Le siège de Corinthe*) and Handel's Radamisto. She sang Pharnaces in Mozart's *Mitridate* at Schwetzingen and Aix-en-Provence (1983). With a handsome stage presence and a vibrant voice, she makes a fine Octavian. ELIZABETH FORBES

Browning, Jean. *See* MADEIRA, JEAN.

Brownlee, John (Donald Mackenzie) (*b* Geelong, 7 Jan 1901; *d* New York, 10 Jan 1969). Australian baritone. He first studied in Melbourne, then with Dinh Gilly in Paris, and was introduced to Covent Garden by his countrywoman Dame Nellie Melba, at whose farewell concert (8 June 1926) he made his London début as Marcello in the last two acts of *La bohème*. In the following February he made his first appearance at the Paris Opéra, remaining as a prominent member of the company until 1936. At Covent Garden he sang Golaud in the 1930 revival of *Pelléas et Mélisande* and was also successful in Verdi roles such as Renato and Amonasro. Brownlee was among the earliest singers at Glyndebourne, singing Don Alfonso in 1935 and Don Giovanni in 1936. In 1937 he began a long association with the Metropolitan Opera, making his début as Rigoletto on 17 February 1937, and remaining for 21 seasons, during which he sang 348 performances of 33 roles. He also appeared widely elsewhere in North and South America, and became the director (1956) and president (1966) of the Manhattan School of Music, New York. His singing, while neither so rich nor so resonant as to place him among the greatest baritones, was admirably schooled and distinguished in style.

*

GV (H. D. Rosenthal and W. Weaver; R. Vegeto)
D. Franklin: 'John Brownlee', *Opera*, xx (1969), 209–10

DESMOND SHAWE-TAYLOR

Brú (Albiñana), Enrique (*b* Valencia, 9 April 1873; *d* ?Madrid, 4 May 1951). Spanish composer. He pursued a musical career in Madrid, where he combined teaching (his pupils included Luis Sagi-Vela) with the composition of numerous zarzuelas, often in collaboration with other composers. Of these, *La chula de Pontevedra* has been recorded, under the direction of Ataulfo Argenta.

selective list; all zarzuelas, first performed in Madrid

El primer amor (1), Feb 1909; El rata primero, Sept 1913, collab. C. Vela; La faraona (1), Novedades, Feb 1914, collab. Vela; Arriba la liga!, Novedades, Sept 1914, collab. Vela; Los matafires (1), Novedades, 1915, collab. Vela; Chiribitas (1, J. Jiménez and E. Paradas), Novedades, 7 March 1919, collab. Vela; La madrina (sainete lírico, 2, Jiménez and Paradas), Apolo, 25 Sept 1919, collab. Vela; A quince el metro (pasatiempo, Jiménez and Paradas), Martín, 28 Nov 1919; Voluntarios a Melitta, Novedades, Nov 1921, collab. M. Quislant; La chula de Pontevedra (sainete, 2, Jiménez and Paradas), Apolo, 27 Jan or 27 Feb 1928, collab. Luna; El viaje del amor (revue); La villa de los gatos (revue)

*

StiegerO
R. Alier and others: *El libro de la zarzuela* (Barcelona, 1982, 2/1986 as *Diccionario de la zarzuela*)

ANDREW LAMB

Brú, Isabel (*b* Valencia, *c*1870). Spanish soprano. The daughter of actors, she was a zarzuela chorister from an early age and at 12 deputized in Chueca and Valverde's *Cádiz*. She progressed through zarzuela and operetta roles to become a member of the company of the Teatro Eslava in Madrid, where she created the title role in Chapí's *El tambor de Granaderos* (1894). From 1896 she was a member of the company of the Teatro Apolo, where she created the leading soprano roles in Giménez's *Las mujeres* (1896), Chapí's *Las bravías* (1896), *La revoltosa* (1897) and *El puñao de rosas* (1902), Chueca's *Agua, azucarillos y aguardiente* (1897), López Torregrosa's *La fiesta de San Antón* (1898) and Serrano and Valverde's *El perro chico* (1905). She was noted as a versatile interpreter with a fine soprano voice.

*

E. Zamacois: *Memorias intimas del teatro: Isabel Brú* (Madrid, 1905)

ANDREW LAMB

Bruce, (Frank) Neely (*b* Memphis, 21 Jan 1944). American composer and conductor. He studied the piano with Roy McAllister at the University of Alabama, and composition with Ben Johnston and the piano with Soulima Stravinsky at the University of Illinois. He has taught at the University of Illinois and at Wesleyan University in Connecticut (appointed 1974). In 1978 he founded the American Music/Theater Group, a professional ensemble of singers and instrumentalists who specialize in performing American music, and in 1982 he directed scenes from American operas at the Holland Festival. A prolific composer, his style evolved from the use of serial techniques and information theory (1962–72), through a juxtaposition of widely contrasting, almost incompatible styles (1971–6), to an assimilation of the entire American music tradition, including hymn tunes, marches, ragtime and rock.

Bruce has completed three operas. *Pyramus and Thisbe* (1965) is a chamber opera in one scene especially designed for college opera workshop productions. *The Trials of Psyche* (1971) requires three conductors; the première production was designed by Wolf Sigfried Wagner. *Americana, or A New Tale of the Genii* is based on an anonymous 18th-century allegorical masque of the American Revolution and deals with the political history of the USA as mythology; its 1985 première was a semi-staged concert version by the American Music/Theater Group.

Pyramus and Thisbe (chamber op, 1 scene, Bruce, after W. Shakespeare: *A Midsummer Night's Dream*), Tuscaloosa, U. of Alabama, spr. 1965
The Trials of Psyche (1, J. Orr, after L. Apuleius), Urbana-Champaign, U. of Illinois, 1971
Americana, or A New Tale of the Genii, 1978–83 (4, T. Connor), Hartford, CT, Wadsworth Atheneum, June 1985

WILLIAM DUCKWORTH

Bruch, Max (Christian Friedrich) (*b* Cologne, 6 Jan 1838; *d* Berlin, 2 Oct 1920). German composer. His early training with Ferdinand Hiller ensured that he adhered to the classical tradition inherited from Mendelssohn and Schumann. He remained implacably opposed to the New German School of Wagner and Liszt, and placed greater emphasis on the beauty of melody (particularly when derived from folksong) than on experimenting with harmony. His hundred published works cover all forms, though he was most admired during his lifetime as a composer of secular oratorios and works for violin and orchestra. He spent much of his life as a conductor to courts (Koblenz, Sondershausen) or cities (Liverpool, Breslau), and finally as a respected teacher in Berlin.

Bruch wrote three operas; the first (op.1), in one act for just three singers, is based on Goethe's *Scherz, List und Rache*. It was produced at Cologne on 14 January 1858. The score and orchestral parts were subsequently lost in a fire at the opera house but a published piano score (Leipzig, ?1858) remains. Bruch's second opera was *Die Loreley* op.16 (grosse romantische Oper, 4), produced at Mannheim on 14 June 1863; the full score was published at Breslau in 1862. The story is based on the Rhine legend of a jilted girl who sells her soul to the river spirits in exchange for the power to exact revenge on her lover. The libretto, by Emanuel Geibel, had originally been intended for Mendelssohn, who completed only three numbers before his early death in 1847. Bruch had to convince Geibel of the worth of his composition, since the poet, despite publishing the libretto, had banned any attempt by composers (including Marschner) to set it. The première was a success and did much for Bruch's reputation; performances took place in many German cities and elsewhere for a few years, after which the opera disappeared from the repertory. In 1887 it was revived in Leipzig, where the director asked for many alterations (including cuts and changes in the order of the music); the conductor was Mahler. In 1916 Pfitzner (whose music Bruch despised) was the unlikely champion of a revival of *Die Loreley* in Strasbourg, and in 1986 it received its British première by University College Opera, London.

Bruch's final opera was *Hermione* op.41, which he wrote in 1871 during a three-year period in Berlin as a freelance composer; it was produced and the full score published there in 1872. This four-act opera is based on Shakespeare's *The Winter's Tale*, though the omission of several characters and incidents from the play created serious weaknesses in the libretto, by Emil Hopffer. The opera received negative critical reactions in Berlin, and only a handful of performances were given elsewhere. Thereafter Bruch resolved never to write for the stage again. His operas failed mainly because of poor librettos, a weak sense of drama and his antipathy to contemporary developments in musical form and harmony, but the beautiful melodies in *Die Loreley* deserve admiration.

See also LORELEY, DIE.

*

H. Pfitzner: *Meine Beziehungen zu Max Bruch: persönliche Erinnerungen an den Komponisten, Originalbriefe von diesem, Bericht über meine Aufführungen von dessen Oper 'Die Loreley' sowie Gedanken über die romantische Oper überhaupt* (Munich, 1938)

D. Kämper, ed.: *Max Bruch-Studien: zum 50. Todestag des Komponisten*, Beiträge zur rheinischen Musikgeschichte, lxxxvii (Cologne, 1970) [15 essays on life, works and relation to important contemporaries, with comprehensive bibliography]

K. G. Fellerer: *Max Bruch* (Cologne, 1974)

C. Fifield: *Max Bruch: his Life and Works* (London, 1988)

CHRISTOPHER FIFIELD

Bruči, Rudolf (*b* Zagreb, 30 March 1917). Croatian composer. He studied at the Belgrade Academy of Music and with Alfred Uhl at the Vienna Academy, and was later director of the opera house in Novi Sad (1962–5). He was also a professor and one of the founders of the Academy of Art there. In 1965 he won the Grand Prix at the Brussels competition for composition. Bruči's dramatic output includes several ballets, among them *Demon zlata* ('Demon of Gold', 1965), *Kirka* ('Circe', 1967) and *Katarina Izmailova* (1977), and the opera *Gilgamesh* (3, A. Milošević; Novi Sad, 2 November 1986). Dealing with the Sumerian-Babylonian epic, the story brings to life Gilgamesh's exciting adventures and the fantastic world of Ishtar's temple. The composer described it as 'pure in form, with music anyone can understand even when it comes in sharply contrasted blocks', and it displays spontaneity of invention and strong emotions. Its main features are the archaic character of the choral writing and the richness of the orchestration, which includes a synthesizer. The melodic language comprises declamation as well as wide-ranging lines and polyphonic textures.

*

S. Đuric-Klajn: 'Rudolf Bruči', *Muzička enciklopedija* (Zagreb, 2/1971)

ROKSANDA PEJOVIĆ

Bruck, Charles (*b* Timişoara, 2 May 1911). French conductor of Romanian birth. He studied in Vienna and Paris, attended Monteux's conducting classes and in 1936 won a Paris SO competition to become assistant conductor, making his American début the same year. After 1945 he worked in French music administration and conducted casino orchestras in Cannes and Deauville, then the Netherlands Opera, 1950–54. In 1954 he conducted the first complete performance of Prokofiev's *The Fiery Angel* at a Paris concert, and later the first recording of it. He also gave the first performances in France of Dallapiccola's *Ulisse* and *Il prigioniero* and Janáček's *The Makropulos Affair*, and worked mainly with French orchestras until he became head of the Pierre Monteux Conducting School in Hancock, Maine, in 1970. His skill in analysis, and fine technique acquired in radio work, helped to make him a reliable interpreter of contemporary works.

CHRISTIANE SPIETH-WEISSENBACHER, NOËL GOODWIN

Brüggemann, Kurt (*b* Berlin, 30 March 1908). German composer. A composition pupil of Paul Graener, he was awarded the first state prize for composition in 1935 and later taught at the Staatliche Hochschule für Musikerziehung in Berlin-Charlottenburg. From 1932 he served as composer, conductor and choral director for German, Austrian and Swiss radio stations. Although he has composed in all genres, Brüggemann's particular contribution has been in music for children, including operas; he has also written Singspiels and other works for radio, film scores, a dramatic cantata and a ballet.

De Fischer un syne Fru (Schuloper), Berlin, 1935

Das kalte Herz (Schuloper), Berlin, 1937

Neun Landsknechte im Himmel (Jugendspiel, after H. Sachs), Berlin, 1937

Das Schachspiel von Bagdad (komische Oper, B. Nadolny, after folk legend), Salzburg, 1948

Birnbaum und Hollerstauden, Munich, Deutsches, 1951

40 radio Singspiels

CHARLOTTE ERWIN

Bruja, La ('The Witch'). Zarzuela in three acts by RUPERTO CHAPÍ to a libretto by MIGUEL RAMOS CARRIÓN and (Act 3) Vital Aza; Madrid, Teatro de la Zarzuela, 10 December 1887.

In Navarra in the 1690s, Rosalía's mother has refused to let her marry young Tomillo (tenor) unless he can produce 100 gold coins like the one he was given by a mysterious woman, regarded in the village as a witch, for assisting her to cross a swollen river. As she has, in gratitude, also promised him her help at any time, he explains his predicament to her and, swearing him to secrecy, she gives him the money he needs. She is in fact Blanca (mezzo-soprano), a noble lady who is under an evil spell and can recover her beauty only if a suitor will perform feats of valour on her behalf. Tomillo's friend Leonardo (tenor), who, not knowing who she is, has fallen in love with her on seeing her bathing in the river, promptly goes off to prove himself as a soldier in Italy. He returns two years later as an honoured captain to claim her hand, only to find the Inquisition seizing her as a witch, despite the good deeds she has performed for all the village. Leonardo, Tomillo and Rosalía (soprano) dress up as demonic witches, frighten the nuns in the convent in which she is incarcerated, and rescue her; as they celebrate, news arrives of the death of the deranged Carlos II, which means the end of the Inquisition's stranglehold. The most famous number in a distinguished and inventive setting is the *jota* that ends Act 1.

LIONEL SALTER

Brüll, Ignaz (*b* Prossnitz [now Prostejov], 7 Nov 1846; *d* Vienna, 17 Sept 1907). Austrian composer. He studied the piano and composition in Vienna and made several successful tours as a concert pianist, appearing in London in 1878. He taught the piano in Vienna (1872–8) and was a close friend of Brahms, for and with whom he often played. His first opera was written in 1864; nine others followed, of which *Das goldene Kreuz* (1875) was the most successful. The operas are always enjoyable if not profound. He excels in devising rhythmically varied melodies (much admired by Brahms) which are grateful to the voice and linger in the memory.

See also GOLDENE KREUZ, DAS.

Die Bettler von Samarkand (O. Prechtler), Vienna, 1874

Das goldene Kreuz (romantische Oper, 2, S. H. Mosenthal, after

A. H. J. Mélesville and N. Brazier: *Catherine*), Berlin, Kgl, 22 Dec 1875 (Berlin, 1876)
Der Landfriede (3, Mosenthal, after E. von Bauernfeld), Vienna, Hof, 4 Oct 1877 (Berlin and Posen, 1877)
Bianca (romantisch-komische Oper, 3, A. Schirmer), Dresden, 25 Nov 1879
Königin Mariette (komische Oper, 3, F. Zell and G. Genée, after E. Scribe: *La reine d'un jour*), Munich, Kgl, 16 June 1883 (Berlin and Posen, 1883)
Gloria (3, G. Menasci), Hamburg, 15 Oct 1886
Das steinerne Herz (Märchenoper, 3, V. Widmann), Prague, 19 Dec 1888, vs (Leipzig, 1888)
Gringoire (1, V. Léon, after T. de Banville), Munich, Kgl, 19 March 1892 (Leipzig, *c*1892)
Schach dem König (komische Oper, 3, Léon), Munich, Kgl, 24 Nov 1893, vs (Leipzig, 1893)
Der Husar (komische Oper, 1, Léon, after Scribe: *Broskovano*), Vienna, Wien, 2 March 1898 (Leipzig, 1897)

*

NDB (W. Bollert); *StiegerO*
E. Hanslick: *Die moderne Oper*, vii (Berlin, 1896), 56ff
E. von Komorzynski: Obituary, *Die Musik*, vii (1907–8), 229
R. Specht: 'Ignaz Brüll', *Biographisches Jb und deutscher Nekrolog*, xii (Berlin, 1909), 221
K. Goldmark: *Erinnerungen aus meinem Leben* (Vienna, 1922)
H. Schwarz: *Ignaz Brüll und sein Freundeskreis* (Vienna, 1922)
JOHN A. PARKINSON

Brumagne, Fernand (Maximilien Napoléon) (*b* Namur, 11 Nov 1887; *d* Brussels, 17 March 1939). Belgian composer. After studying at the Brussels Conservatory, where he worked with Léon Du Bois, he completed his training at the Schola Cantorum in Paris, and was awarded a second Belgian Prix de Rome in 1913. From 1925 he was on the administrative staff of the Théâtre Royal de la Monnaie in Brussels. The composer of several *mélodies*, Brumagne is principally known for his music dramas. Of these *Le marchand de Venise*, sometimes compared to Rabaud's *Marouf*, is considered his most successful composition. Wagnerian influence is perceptible in both the vocal style and the orchestration, although the composer varies the leitmotifs. Brumagne has a genuine sense of the theatre: he takes pains to provide variety and accuracy of expression, and skilfully underlines the course of the action. His art seeks dramatic effect, but lacks originality.

autographs in B-Bc

L'invasion (drame lyrique, 4, R. Ronvaux-Harroy and P. Max), Brussels, Monnaie, 20 Oct 1919
Le miracle de Saint Antoine (farce, 2, M. Maeterlinck), Brussels, Monnaie, 10 March 1927
Le joyau de la mitre (5, P. Desachy, after M. des Ombiaux), unperf.
Le marchand de Venise (comédie lyrique, 5, P. Spaak, after W. Shakespeare), Brussels, Monnaie, 30 Jan 1933

*

C. van den Borren: *Geschiedenis van de muziek in de Nederlanden*, ii (Antwerp, 1951), 260
HENRI VANHULST

Brumby, Colin (James) (*b* Melbourne, 18 June 1933). Australian composer. He graduated from the Melbourne University Conservatorium of Music in 1957. He then studied composition in Spain with Philipp Jarnach and in England with Alexander Goehr, returning in 1964 to a position at the University of Queensland. Following the award of his DMus from Melbourne University in 1971, he undertook further advanced compositional studies in Rome. Since 1976 Brumby has been an associate professor in music at the University of Queensland.

In 1968 he founded the Vocal Arts Ensemble which toured operas throughout Queensland and became the Queensland Opera Company in 1970. While he was the company's musical director, Brumby composed seven one-act operettas for young audiences and two operas for adults, *The Seven Deadly Sins* (1970) and *The Marriage Machine* (1972). In addition he conducted what were probably the first Australian performances of Bizet's *Le docteur miracle* (as *Dr Miracle*, 1969), and Haydn's *L'infedeltà delusa* (as *The Sting of the Wasp*, 1970). It was not until 1985 that he found an opportunity to return to opera. He orchestrated *The Marriage Machine*, which had originally been set for solo voices, piano and pre-recorded tape effects, for performance in Sydney. Also for Sydney, he composed the three-act *Lorenzaccio* (1985–6), set in Renaissance Florence, and a one-act work in contemporary setting, *La Donna* (1986).

Stylistically, *The Marriage Machine*, *La Donna* and his operettas for children are melodic and tonal. *The Seven Deadly Sins* employs devices ranging from modes to electronic effects; *Lorenzaccio* and *Fire on the Wind* (1991), while vocally idiomatic, are underpinned by late-Romantic chromaticism. *Summer Carol* (1991), also Romantic in idiom, includes choral arrangements of lesser-known Christmas carols.

librettos by the composer unless otherwise stated

Rita and Dita (children's operetta, 1, after J. L. and W. C. Grimm: *Hänsel und Gretel*), Brisbane, 13 May 1968
The Wise Shoemaker (children's operetta, 1), Brisbane, 13 May 1968
Rita and Dita and the Pirate (children's operetta, 1), Brisbane, 24 Feb 1969
The Prince Who Couldn't Laugh (children's operetta, 1), Brisbane, 24 Feb 1969
Rita and Dita in Toyland (children's operetta, 1), Rockhampton, 23 Feb 1970
The Two Suitors (children's operetta, 1), Rockhampton, 23 Feb 1970
The Seven Deadly Sins (2, T. Shapcott), Brisbane, State Government Insurance Office Theatre, 12 Sept 1970
Rita and Dita and the Jolly Swagman (children's operetta, 1, after A. B. 'Banjo' Paterson: *Waltzing Matilda*), Brisbane, 15 Feb 1971
The Marriage Machine (1), Sydney, Teachers' College, 28 Jan 1972; orchd 1985, Sydney, Cell Block Theatre, 4 Sept 1985
Lorenzaccio (3, after A. de Musset), 2 scenes, Sydney, Broadwalk Studio, Sydney Opera House, 29 Oct 1986
La Donna (1, D. Goddard), workshop perf., Sydney, Opera Centre, 2 July 1988
Summer Carol (1, T. Shapcott), Canberra, Llewellyn Hall, 10 Aug 1991
Fire on the Wind (2, after A. Coburn), excerpts, workshop perf., Brisbane, Lyric Opera of Queensland Studios, 25 Sept 1991

*

J. Villaume: 'Building an Audience for Opera: a Queensland Experiment', *Australian Journal of Music Education*, iv (1969), 3–5
C. Brumby: 'Touring in the Outback', *ON*, xxxiv/11 (1969–70), 13
P. Bracanin: 'Colin Brumby', *Australian Composition in the Twentieth Century*, ed. F. Callaway and D. Tunley (Melbourne, 1976)
P. K. BRACANIN

Bruneau, (Louis Charles Bonaventure) Alfred (*b* Paris, 3 March 1857; *d* Paris, 15 June 1934). French composer. He began his musical studies as a cellist, winning a *premier prix* on the instrument and in his twenties playing in the Pasdeloup orchestra. From 1879 to 1881 he studied composition with Massenet, who left an indelible impression on his musical style. A cantata, *Geneviève*, won him a second prize in the Prix de Rome and in 1887 his first opera, *Kérim*, was successful enough to convince him that he should devote himself largely to opera.

Kérim, like a number of Bruneau's operas, directly incorporates folk melodies (in this case of oriental origin), and these are clearly indicated in the score. Although they are blended with more conventional elements of contemporary French operatic style, following Massenet and Gounod, Bruneau attempts to present the oriental elements in an unconventional way, using harmonies derived from the melodies themselves as well as highly coloured orchestration. The story is taken from the 'legend of tears' and concerns an Emir who falls in love with a girl, Zaïdé, who demands a necklace of tears as a condition of returning his love. Already Bruneau underlines a moral theme: 'you may have my body', she protests when he tries to seduce her, 'but you will not have my soul'. At the end of the opera heartfelt tears overcome him and turn to pearls. Love has triumphed: Bruneau rounds off the opera with an aria for the two protagonists using the stock-in-trade technique of unison singing, finally accompanied by the stage chorus.

It is easy to dismiss the central period of Bruneau's output, dominated by his collaborations with Emile Zola, as one of realism, naturalism or French *verismo*. Yet despite his close identification with Zola's works, strong elements of fantasy, symbolism and extravagant musical effects are found in his many operatic transformations of Zola's tales. The first, *Le rêve*, to a Zola adaptation by Louis Gallet, has as its central character an *ange-femme*, Angélique, a pallid Pre-Raphaelite damsel who passes her time reading *The Golden Legend* and doing embroidery. Her medieval dreams are partly pious and partly concerned with her conviction that a prince charming will suddenly enter her life. This happens when she meets Félicien, a worker in stained glass. Angélique is strongly characterized in Gallet's libretto and Bruneau responds extravagantly, with an unseen choir and orchestra for the hidden virgin voices which she frequently hears. The opera, whose blend of eroticism and religiosity caused it to enjoy considerable success after its première in 1891, was precisely in tune with artistic tastes in the 1890s, although these soon went out of favour, causing such works to fall into neglect. But Bruneau's fundamental achievement should not be overlooked: namely, in the words of Georges Pioch, who attended the première, 'to have introduced on to the stage of an opera house [in 1891] singers dressed in 1891 costumes'. Among those who wrote to congratulate him was Chabrier: 'c'est un début de maître, absolument'.

In *L'attaque du moulin* Bruneau repeated the formula of setting a Gallet adaptation of Zola, again with considerable success, but this time more dependent on the pace and realism of the story than on special effects. Its theme is the effects of war on a miller's family and a stranger who has fallen in love with the miller's daughter. Bruneau provides two possible endings.

From this time onwards, Zola himself supplied Bruneau with librettos. *Messidor* (1897) was the first fruit of this collaboration. Although initially successful, it was produced at the height of the Dreyfus affair, in which Bruneau actively followed Zola's support of Dreyfus. This led to a marked fall in his popularity and for some years his works were less than welcome in Paris.

Within the limits of Bruneau's musical response, *L'ouragan* (1901) is an opera in which libretto and music are particularly closely wedded. The hurricane of the title not only provides an opportunity for descriptive music but also mirrors the increasing conflict between the two pairs of brothers and sisters on whom the story centres. Richard saves Jeannine from his loutish brother Landry. Landry is eventually murdered by Jeannine's sister, leaving Richard and Jeannine free to indulge their love, which began before her marriage to Landry. As a magic tree (common in the Celtic mythology on which this opera is based) sings to the lovers, Bruneau employs an orchestra behind the scenes. But the lovers cannot find happiness in the fishing village that was their home and Richard runs away with Lulu, a young orphan whom he adopted when she was 12. Lulu, strongly characterized as Richard's spiritual guide, is linked with the 'bay of grace', a garden of Eden in which Lulu promises renewal. The cast-list is unusual in giving the exact age of each character, and the opera successfully portrays the power of innocent youth over corrupt experience.

Bruneau's final direct collaboration with Zola was *L'enfant roi*, a *comédie lyrique* set in a Parisian bakery. Here the composer introduces extended passages evoking Parisian street life: children singing nursery rhymes in the Tuileries, the cries of flower sellers in a street market and scenes in the patisserie. François, the baker, is happily married to Madeleine but is told that she meets a lover in the afternoons. In fact she is meeting her own illegitimate son, but François is still jealous, demanding that she choose between her son and her husband. The opera ends happily when he realizes the hopelessness of his demand; instead of parting, the couple accept the son and their marriage is renewed.

After Zola's death in 1902, Bruneau continued his allegiance by fashioning his own librettos from the author's work. In *Naïs Micoulin* (1906), the first of these, Bruneau's libretto is curiously lacking in drama, although its extended dialogues are faithful to Zola in their inclusion of poignant physical detail. Set near Marseilles, the town of 'dirty pleasures', it concerns Naïs, a girl of 20, 'sauvage et travailleuse'; Frédéric, her suitor, who despite his experience of more sophisticated town girls loves Naïs for her 'smell of the earth'; Toine, her hunchback friend; and Micoulin, her overprotective father. Frédéric and Naïs are passionately in love. Toine, her guardian and 'bon chien fidèle', is jealous but faithful. Her father tries to kill Frédéric but is constantly thwarted by Toine. Everyone is killed at the end, swallowed up by falling cliffs, but it is Toine and Naïs who are heard singing ecstatically together from the abyss.

Les quatre journées is an opera concerned with a family before, during and after a war. It is a naively sentimental work recounting the fortunes of a couple brought up on the banks of the river Durance. Each act represents one of the seasons. In spring the couple are full of optimism. Some years later, in summer, they are at war, the hero Jean saving the life of an Alsatian soldier. Here Bruneau plays to the contemporary audience with some appropriately jingoistic choruses. Autumn, after the war, brings riches from the land, while in winter, with the couple now old, the river floods. The inconclusive ending sees the family floating away on the flood waters on a makeshift raft.

Henceforth Bruneau turned away from contemporary realism, *Le jardin du paradis* being the first of his works to take such a step. Based on a Hans Christian Andersen fairy-tale, the work has as its centrepiece an oriental paradise garden, with appropriately stylized music. To attain paradise the Prince Assur must vow purity but he is tempted by his beloved Arabella. His taste of paradise, conjured up by a sorceress and the four winds, has strengthened the couple's love. A final chorus 'On earth or in heaven, the only paradise is that of love' rounds off the opera, which is characterized by more static, scenic music than found elsewhere in Bruneau's output.

Le roi Candaule and *Virginie* are both much lighter in tone. The former, set in 687 BC, is a mixture of ribald comedy and oriental sensuality concerning a king who allows a friend to delight in the pleasures of his naked wife. She calls his bluff by making love to the friend so that the king can see. 'Two people may think themselves alone', remarks the king, 'but there are always three'. *Virginie* recounts the adventures of a vivacious artist's model when a rich new pupil arrives.

In *Angelo*, set in the 17th century, Bruneau uses authentic dances and ground basses to create pastiche background music for drama; music more akin to his usual realistic style is used to characterize the Tyrant of Padua, who forces his wife to drink poison when he discovers that she has a lover, even though he himself is at least as culpable.

Bruneau's writings on music include important memoirs of Zola (Paris, 1932), a book on Massenet (Paris, 1935), essays outlining his own theory of opera (notably in *Le Figaro* and *Rivista musicale italiana* in 1897), and perceptive comments on other operas in reviews and articles.

See also ATTAQUE DU MOULIN, L' and MESSIDOR.

unless otherwise stated, drames lyriques, first performed in Paris; all printed works published in Paris

Kérim (opéra, 3, P. Milliet and H. Lavedan), Château d'Eau, 9 June 1887, *F-Pn*; (1887)
Le rêve (4, L. Gallet, after E. Zola), OC (Favart), 18 June 1891, *Pn*; (1892)
L'attaque du moulin (4, Gallet, after Zola), OC (Favart), 23 Nov 1893, *Pn*; (1893)
Messidor (4, Zola), Opéra, 19 Feb 1897, *Pn*; (1897)
L'ouragan (4, Zola), OC (Favart), 29 April 1901 (1901)
L'enfant roi, 1902 (comédie lyrique, 5, Zola), OC (Favart), 3 March 1905 (1905)
Lazare, 1902 (1, Zola), Radio France, 20 May 1954, *Pn*
Naïs Micoulin (2, Bruneau, after Zola: *La douleur de Toine*), Monte Carlo, 2 Feb 1907, *Pn*; (1907)
Les quatre journées (conte lyrique, 4, Bruneau, after Zola), OC (Favart), 25 Dec 1916, *Pn*; (1916)
Le jardin du paradis, 1913–21 (conte lyrique, 4, R. de Flers and G.-A. de Caillavet, after H. C. Andersen), Opéra, 31 Oct 1923, *Pn*; (1924)
Le roi Candaule, 1917–19 (comédie lyrique, 4 acts and 5 tableaux, M. Donnay), OC (Favart), 1 Dec 1920, *Pn*; (1922)
Angelo, tyran de Padoue, 1923–5 (5, C. Méré, after V. Hugo), OC (Favart), 16 Jan 1928, *Pn*; (1928)
Virginie, 1928–30 (comédie lyrique, 3, H. Duvernois), Opéra, 7 Jan 1931, *Pn*; (1930)

Undated: Vercingétorix, vs frag. *Pn*

*

E. Zola: 'Le drame lyrique', *Le Journal* (22 Nov 1893)
E. Destranges: Thematic guides to A. Bruneau operas (Paris): *Le rêve* (1896); *Messidor* (1897); *L'attaque du moulin* (1901); *L'ouragan* (1902); *Naïs Micoulin* (1907)
A. Bruneau and E. Zola: 'Messidor expliqué par les auteurs', *Le Figaro* (20 Feb 1897)
E. Zola: 'A propos du Messidor', *Le Gaulois* (23 Feb 1897)
A. Jullien: 'L'ouragan', *Le théâtre*, no.60 (1901), 3–13
——: 'L'enfant roi', *Le théâtre*, no.152 (1905), 8–14
A. Hervey: *Alfred Bruneau* (London, 1907)
A. Boschot: *La vie et les oeuvres de Alfred Bruneau* (Paris, 1937)
G. Pioch: 'Alfred Bruneau', *Le théâtre lyrique en France* (Paris, 1937–9) [pubn of Poste National/Radio-Paris], ii, 214–23; iii, 37
S. Wallon: 'Chronologie des oeuvres d'Alfred Bruneau', *RdM*, xxix (1947), 25–62
R. Dumesnil: 'Réalistes et naturalistes', *Histoire de la musique*, iv (Paris, 1958)
J.-M. Guieu: 'Lazarus, a musical comedy by Emile Zola', *French American Review*, ii/3 (1978), 135
D. Pistone: *La musique en France de la Révolution à 1900* (Paris, 1979)
R. M. Longyear: 'Political and Social Criticism in French Opera 1827–1920', *Essays on the Music of J. S. Bach and Other Divers Subjects: a Tribute to Gerhard Herz* (Louisville, 1981), 245–54
F. Nicolodi: 'Parigi e l'opera verista: dibattiti, riflessioni, polemiche', *NRMI*, xv (1981), 577–623
G. Favre: *Musique et naturalisme: Alfred Bruneau et Émile Zola* (Paris, 1982)
D. Pistone: 'Souvenirs inédits d'Alfred Bruneau', *RIMF*, vii (1982), 9
J.-M. Guieu: *Le théâtre lyrique d'Emile Zola* (Paris, 1983)
M. Kelkel: *Naturalisme, vérisme et réalisme dans l'opéra d'1890 à 1930* (Paris, 1984)
B. H. Bakker, ed.: *Correspondance d'Emile Zola* (Montreal, 1985)

RICHARD LANGHAM SMITH

Brunetti, Antonio (*b* ?1767; *d* ? after 1845). Italian composer, grandson of G. G. Brunetti. He is frequently called a Pisan in contemporary sources, but may have been born elsewhere. In 1786 he composed an opera for Bologna; he wrote a further six during the next six years (the *Demofoonte* performed in Venice in 1791 and ascribed to him by Gerber has no composer's name on the libretto and was perhaps a pasticcio) and another five followed intermittently until 1815. Meanwhile he was *maestro di cappella* at the cathedrals in Chieti (1790–1800), Urbino (1810–16), Macerata (1816–26) and Imola. In 1837 he was reported in the *Allgemeine musikalische Zeitung* (xxxix, col.423) as living in Bologna as a theatrical agent and later that year (col.730) as having been the impresario of an unsuccessful opera season in Imola. He wrote a large amount of church music and was a member of the Bologna Accademia Filarmonica.

Lo sposo di tre e marito de nessuna (dg, F. Livigni), Bologna, Zagnoni, aut. 1786
Le stravaganze in campagna (dg, 2), Venice, S Cassiano, aut. 1787
Il Bertoldo (dg, 2, L. da Ponte), Florence, Pergola, carn. 1788, *F-Pn* [attrib. G. G. Brunetti], *I-Fc*
Vologeso re de' Parti (os, 3, A. Zeno), Florence, Intrepidi, spr. 1789
La serva alla moda (dg, 2), 1789
Fatima (2), Brescia, Accademia degli Erranti, sum. 1791
Le nozze per invito, ossia Gli amanti capricciosi (dg, 2), Rome, Valle, 1791
Li contrasti per amore (dg), Rome, Dame, aut. 1792
Il pazzo glorioso (dg, 2, G. Bertati), Rome, Tordinona, carn. 1797
Il libretto alla moda (2), Naples, Fiorentini, carn. 1808, *Nc*
La colomba contrastata, ossia La bella carbonara, Rimini, Comunale, carn. 1813
Amore e fedeltà alla prova (2), Bologna, Corso, May 1814
La fedeltà coniugale (G. Rossi), Parma, Ducale, 30 Jan 1815 [possibly same work as the preceding]

FRANCO BAGGIANI

Brunetti, Giovan Gualberto (*b* Pistoia, 24 April 1706; *d* Pisa, 20 May 1787). Italian composer. He studied counterpoint with Clari in Pisa, and then trained for five years as a tenor in Naples. He remained there as a church singer, and in 1733 had a comic opera performed. As *maestro di cappella* to the Duke of Monte Nero, he composed a serenata for the arrival of Charles III in Messina in 1735 and two comic operas to librettos by Pietro Trinchera. Brunetti taught at the Turchini Conservatory (1744–54) and then succeeded Clari as *maestro di cappella* in Pisa, composing three more operas, occasional cantatas and a large amount of liturgical music. He was a member of the Bologna Accademia Filarmonica, and in 1763 became a priest.

Amore imbratta il senno (3), Naples, Fiorentini, 1733
Don Pasquino (chelleta, 3, P. Trinchera), Naples, Pace, aut. 1735
Lo corrivo (pazzia, Trinchera), Naples, Pace, 1736
Ortensio (commedia per musica, G. Federico), Naples, Fiorentini, carn. 1739
Alessandro nell'Indie (os, P. Metastasio), Pisa, Publico, carn. 1763

Arminio (T. Reghini), Lucca, Giglio, 1763, collab. G. Puccini
Temistocle (os, Metastasio), Lucca, Publico, aut. 1776

FRANCO BAGGIANI

Bruni, Antonio Bartolomeo (*b* Cuneo, 28 Jan 1757; *d* Cuneo, 6 Aug 1821). Italian composer. According to Fétis he studied the violin with Pugnani in Turin and composition with Speziani in Novara. He made his début in Paris in 1780 at the Concert Spirituel performing one of his own violin concertos. Between 1789 and 1806 he held various positions, including those of first violinist and director of the orchestra at the Théâtre de Monsieur, the Montansier, the Opéra-Comique and the Théâtre Italien. His output consists mainly of some 20 *opéras comiques* composed between 1785 and 1801. He returned to Cuneo in 1806 but was back in Paris in 1814–15, when two new *opéras comiques* were performed. The failure of these works and his earlier support for the Revolution obliged him to retire to Cuneo after the restoration of the Bourbons in 1816.

Apart from the mythological subject of *L'isle enchantée* and the oriental plot of his late opera *Le règne de douze heures*, the core of Bruni's stage works shows the civic life of revolutionary France with a mixture of sentimentality and realism. Both *Claudine* and *Le major Palmer*, for example, tell of young, distressed mothers hiding their illegitimate children until the return of the repentant fathers. The sensational plot of *Toberne* includes the heroine Gernance's leap into a lake to escape from a villainous suitor who turns out to be the nephew of a Swedish king. Gernance prefers to marry the good-hearted fisherman Toberne instead. While in *Claudine* and *Le major Palmer* the law of nature is presented as the driving force behind the fathers' return (a clear reference to the reign of terror), the elderly Loffield in *Toberne* appeals to his fellow countrymen to obey civic law as the only means to achieve happiness rather than seek to avenge themselves on the villain.

Bruni shared with contemporary Italian composers a penchant for the insistent repetition of certain phrases, octave leaps and a quick-paced recitation on the same pitch. But the brevity of many song-like arias, the syllabic text-setting without repetitions, and vaudevilles at the ends of operas such as *Claudine* and *La rencontre en voyage* reveal his reliance on the French style. His stage works can be divided between small-scale, one-act operas suitable for the various theatrical entertainments of revolutionary France and extensive two- or three-act works such as *Toberne* and *Le major Palmer*. In these two operas he used a much larger wind section (including piccolos, four horns, two trumpets and trombones) and created a much livelier interplay between the instruments. He concealed his basically homophonic writing by means of ornamental accompaniments and displayed a much greater variety of rhythm and articulation. But he still remained faithful to small aria forms: in *Le major Palmer* Amelia's 'Cruel auteur' consists of nine bars of recitative and an aria of 36 bars. Some pieces incorporate sonata-form elements. In the overtures of *Le major Palmer* and *Toberne*, for example, a second theme appears in the main key in the recapitulation while the first theme is not repeated; moreover, a development section can be discerned in central passages of harmonic instability, although its motifs are unrelated to the exposition. A similar technique is employed in the aria 'Le désespoir qui m'accable' in *Claudine*. This opera also incorporates local colour in the form of a Savoyard song, which effectively brings about Claudine's recognition of her former lover Floreville, and a direct reference to the revolutionary song *Ah! Ça ira*.

first performed in Paris unless otherwise stated; printed works published in Paris

Coradin (comédie lyrique, 3, Magnitot or Tacusset), Fontainebleau, 15 Nov 1785, OC (Favart), 19 Jan 1786
Célestine (comédie lyrique mêlée d'ariettes, 3, Magnitot), OC (Favart), 15 Oct 1787 (1788)
L'isle enchantée (opéra bouffon, 3, J.-F. Sedaine de Sarcy), Monsieur, 3 Aug 1789 (n.d.)
Le mort imaginaire (oc, 2, Ponteuil), Montansier, 27 April 1790
Spinette et Marini, ou La leçon conjugale (1, ?Bodard de Tezay), Montansier, 21 June 1790, *F–Mc*, ov. (n.d.)
Cadichon, ou Les bohémiennes (opéra-vaudeville, 1, J.-B. Pujoulx), Feydeau, 12 March 1792, *Pc**
L'officier de fortune, ou Les deux militaires (cmda, 2, J. Patrat), Feydeau, 24 Sept 1792, *A*, *Pc*, excerpts (n.d.)
Claudine, ou Le petit commissionnaire (1, J. M. Deschamps, after Florian), Feydeau, 6 March 1794, *A*, *Pc*, (n.d.)
Le mariage de Jean-Jacques Rousseau (intermède, 1, Baunier and Blanvillain), Egalité, 25 Oct 1794
Galatée (mélodrame, F.-M. Poultier d'Elmotte), République, 1 Feb 1795
Toberne, ou Le pêcheur suédois (comédie mêlée de morceaux de musique, 2, Patrat), Feydeau, 2 Dec 1795, *Pn* (inc.), excerpts (n.d.)
Les sabotiers (oc, 1, C. Pigault-Lebrun), Feydeau, 23 June 1796 (n.d.)
Le major Palmer (drame, 3, Pigault-Lebrun), Feydeau, 26 Jan 1797 (n.d.)
La rencontre en voyage (comédie, 1, Pujoulx), Feydeau, 28 April 1798, *Pc* (n.d.)
L'auteur dans son ménage (oc, 1, E. Gosse), Feydeau, 28 March 1799, *Pc* (n.d.)
L'esclave (1, Gosse), Feydeau, 16 March 1800
Augustine et Benjamin, ou Le Sargines de village (oc, 1, Bernard-Valville and E. Hus), OC (Favart), 4 Nov 1800
La bonne soeur (comédie lyrique, 1, Petit *aîné* and L. Philipon de la Madeleine), Feydeau, 21 Jan 1801
Le règne de douze heures (oc, 2, E. de Planard, after Mme de Genlis), OC (Feydeau), 8 Dec 1814, *Pc* (n.d.)
Le mariage par commission, ou Le seigneur allemand (oc, 1, J. B. Simonnin), OC (Feydeau), 4 Dec 1815, *Po*

Doubtful: L'époux déguisé (1, Gosse), 1800; Théodore l'Auvergnat (2, Hus)

*

FétisB
C. Pierre: *Les hymnes et chansons de la Révolution* (Paris, 1904)
G. Cesari, L. de La Laurencie and others: *Antonio Bartolomeo Bruni, musicista cuneese (1761–1821)* (Turin, 1931)
L. de La Laurencie: 'Un musicien italien en France à la fin du XVIIIe siècle', *RdM*, xv (1931), 268–77
A. Marfini and O. Masoero: 'Contributi alla biografia di A. B. Bruni', *NRMI*, v (1971), 861–6
G. Pestelli: '"Claudine ou Le petit commissionnaire" di Antonio Bartolomeo Bruni (1794)', *Quadrivium*, xiv (1973), 217–34

MICHAEL FEND (text, bibliography), MICHEL NOIRAY (work-list)

Bruni, Domenico Luigi (*b* Fratta [now Umbertide], 28 Feb 1758; *d* Fratta, 17 Jan 1821). Italian castrato soprano. He studied in Fratta and then in Urbania with Francesco Paciotti. His début was in Fratta in 1772 playing female roles and he first sang as primo uomo in Treviso in 1780. He sang also in Rome, Florence, Bologna, Milan, Naples and other important Italian towns. From 1787 to 1790 he was in St Petersburg as primo uomo of the Italian Theatre, at a salary of 4000 roubles. In 1793 he sang in London and in the same year Ercole III d'Este appointed him *virtuoso da camera* in Modena. His last performance was in Bologna in 1796. The reporter of the *Morning Herald* (6 February 1793) said about him: 'Bruni, the new man, is the best singer of his kind within our remembrance, being distinguished from the rest by uniting to their softness and clearness of tone greater strength than they were master of'.

G. Perugini: *Biografia del cantante Domenico Bruni di Umbertide* (Umbertide, 1884)
N. Lucarelli: *Domenico Bruni (1758–1821): biografia di un cantante evirato* (Umbertide, 1990) NICOLA LUCARELLI

Brünn (Ger.). BRNO.

Brunsvic. *See* PARIS, NICOLA.

Brunswick (i) [Lévy, Léon; Lhérie, Léon] (*b* Paris, 20 April 1805; *d* Le Havre, 29 July 1859). French librettist. The name Brunswick was a pseudonym; his original name was Léon Lévy, but to his acquaintances he was known as Léon Lhérie (under which he also wrote). Educated in Paris, he worked as a journalist during the Restoration, turning to the theatre after the July Revolution. For over 20 years he was a prolific author of *comédies-vaudevilles*, often topical or satirical and sometimes with elements of literary parody. They combine prose dialogue with songs, generally performed to existing tunes. Brunswick wrote mostly in collaboration, notably (from 1834) with Adolphe de Leuven, who was for a while co-director of the Opéra-Comique. Of their librettos the most notable were *Le panier fleuri*, for Ambroise Thomas, and *Le postillon de Lonjumeau*, *Le brasseur de Preston*, *Le roi d'Yvetot* and *Le roi des Halles*, all for Adolphe Adam.

opéras comiques and collaborations with A. de Leuven unless otherwise stated

Le postillon de Lonjumeau, A. Adam, 1836; *Le brasseur de Preston*, Adam, 1838; *Un conte d'autrefois*, Monpou, 1838; *Eva*, N. Girard, 1839; Le panier fleuri, A. Thomas, 1839; *Carline*, Thomas, 1840; *La reine Jeanne*, L. Bordèse and Monpou, 1840; *Les deux voleurs*, Girard, 1841; *Mademoiselle de Mérange*, H. H. Potier, 1841; *Les dix*, Girard, 1842; *Le roi d'Yvetot*, Adam, 1842; *Les quatre fils Aymon*, Balfe, 1844; *Gibby la cornemuse*, Clapisson, 1846

Les deux bambins, Bordèse, 1848; *Il Signor Pascarello*, Potier, 1848; *Bonsoir, voisin* (with A. de Beauplan), Poise, 1853; *Elisabeth, ou La fille du proscrit* (drame lyrique), U. Fontana, 1853, after D. Gilardoni: *Otto mesi in due ore*; *Le roi des Halles*, Adam, 1853; *Le billet de Marguerite*, Gevaert, 1854; *Dans les vignes* (with de Beauplan), Clapisson, 1854; *La promise*, Clapisson, 1854; *Mam'zelle Geneviève* (with de Beauplan), Adam, 1856 CHRISTOPHER SMITH

Brunswick (ii) (Ger. Braunschweig). City in Lower Saxony, northern Germany. Its operatic development in the 17th century was largely due to Duke Anton Ulrich, who was respected for his literary and artistic proclivities. His extant libretto for J. J. Loewe's *Amelinde, oder Dy triumphirende Seele* (1657) shows a preference for a type of drama closer to Singspiel than to the Italian opera of the period. Brunswick was a leading centre of music during the Baroque era, reaching a peak under Duke Anton Ulrich the younger (1704–14). Renowned 17th-century Kapellmeisters were Schütz (non-resident, but often in Brunswick), Rosenmüller, Theile and, from 1682 to 1694, Sigismund Johann Kusser, the teacher of Reinhard Keiser. Hasse and C. H. Graun also briefly held the post of Kapellmeister, and Schürmann was very active. Kusser, Erlebach, Keiser, D. G. Treu, Schürmann, Hasse and Graun all wrote operas for Brunswick.

The first commercial opera house was opened in April 1690 with a performance of *Cleopatra* by Kusser; this theatre, the Rathaus, was entirely renovated in 1818, and given the status of a national theatre. The new Hoftheater was opened in 1861. About this time Franz Abt was active as a conductor in the city; he was principally responsible for introducing Wagner's operas to Brunswick. The Hoftheater was renamed the Landestheater in 1919; it remained in use until destroyed in World War II. After rebuilding, the theatre was reopened in 1948 as the Staatstheater with a production of *Don Giovanni*.

The auditorium and stage were completely renovated in 1983–4 and 1989–90 respectively. The Brunswick Staatstheater (900 seats) presents about 150 performances of opera and operetta and about 35 of ballets every season in the Grosses Haus. The theatre is owned by the state of Lower Saxony. It has an orchestra of 84 and a chorus of 40. Of particular importance in recent years have been the company's *Ring* cycle, the West German première of Cikker's *Earthquake in Chile* and a production of Reimann's *Lear*.

*

F. Chrysander: 'Geschichte der Braunschweigisch-Wolfenbüttelschen Oper vom 16. bis zum 18. Jahrhundert', *Jb für musikalische Wissenschaft*, i (1863), 147–286
E. Rosendahl: *Geschichte der Hoftheater in Hanover und Braunschweig* (Hanover, 1927)
G. F. Schmidt: *Neue Beiträge zur Geschichte der Musik und des Theaters am Herzoglichen Hofe zu Braunschweig-Wolfenbüttel* (Munich, 1929)
——: *Die frühdeutsche Oper und die musikdramatische Kunst Georg Caspar Schürmanns* (Regensburg, 1933–4)
250 Jahre Braunschweigische Staatstheater (Brunswick, 1941)
Generalintentendanz des Staatstheaters Braunschweig: *275 Jahre Theater in Braunschweig: Geschichte und Wirkung* (Brunswick, 1965)
I. Büttenbender: *Braunschweiger Theaterleben von 1690 bis heute* (Brunswick, 1988) SABINE SONNTAG

Brusa, (Giovanni) Francesco (*b* Venice, *c*1700; *d* after 1768). Italian composer. Because his known works fall into two groups 30 years apart, some writers have postulated the existence of an older and a younger composer of that name; the theory cannot be wholly dismissed on the sparse evidence available. Brusa's name first appears in connection with his four operas of 1724–6, and in 1726–40 he was an organist at St Mark's, Venice. He re-emerged as an operatic composer in 1756, as the impresario of his own travelling company (which included his wife, son and two daughters) in 1758 and finally as a choirmaster at the Ospedale degli Incurabili from at least 1766 to 1768. He may have been in Barcelona in 1761. Of the extant operas, only *Le statue* has been critically appraised in modern times (by Della Corte). Many sacred works by him also survive.

opere serie unless otherwise stated

Il trionfo della virtù (3, P. d'Averara), Venice, S Giovanni Grisostomo, aut. 1724, 25 arias *I-Vnm*
L'amore eroico (3, A. Zeno and P. Pariati), Venice, S Samuele, Ascension 1725
Arsace (3, A. Salvi), Milan, Ducale, 28 Aug 1725
Semiramide riconosciuta (3, P. Metastasio), Venice, S Benedetto, Feb 1756
Medea e Giasone (3, G. Palazzi), Venice, S Angelo, 26 Dec 1726
Adriano in Siria (3, Metastasio), Venice, S Benedetto, Jan 1757
Le statue (dg, 1, G. B. Brusa), Venice, S Samuele, 27 Dec 1757, selections *D-B*, *F-Pn*, *I-Fc*
La cascina (dg, 3, C. Goldoni), Pesaro, Sole, carn. 1758; as La quesera, Barcelona, 1761 [perf. with Scolari's setting]
La ritornata da Londra (dg, 3, Goldoni), Forlì, Pubblico, carn. 1759
L'olimpiade [Act 3] (3, Metastasio), Venice, S Benedetto, 1766, *P-La* [Act 1 by P. A. Guglielmi, Act 2 by A. G. Pampani]

*

BurneyH; *DBI* (E. Carone); *MGG* (E. Simonetti)
A. Della Corte: *L'opera comica italiana nel '700: studi ed appunti* (Bari, 1923)
C. Goldoni: *Tutte le opere*, i (Milan, 1935), 680

PIERO WEISS

Bruscantini, Sesto (*b* Porto Civitanova, Macerata, 10 Dec 1919). Italian bass-baritone. He studied with Luigi Ricci in Rome and made his début at Civitanova in 1946 as Colline. He first sang at La Scala in 1949 as Geronimo (*Il matrimonio segreto*). In 1951 he made his Glyndebourne début as Don Alfonso (*Così fan tutte*) and returned there regularly until 1956, as Guglielmo, Dandini, Figaro (both Rossini's and Mozart's), Raimbaud (*Le comte Ory*), and then in 1960 as Ford and Leporello and in 1961 as Rossini's Figaro. He sang Malatesta in Salzburg (1953) and made his American début in 1961 in Chicago.

After 1962 he added the more dramatic Verdi roles to his repertory – Rigoletto, Renato and Iago. A particularly fine Germont, he sang Falstaff for the first time in 1976 with Scottish Opera. He made his Covent Garden début in 1971 as Rossini's Figaro, returning in 1974 as Malatesta. He has appeared several times at Wexford, notably in Ricci's *Crispino e la comare* (1979) and *Un giorno di regno* (1981), which he also directed. In 1988 he sang Don Alfonso at Los Angeles and in 1989 Michonnet at Rome. His versatility (he has sung over 130 roles), musicality, sense of style and dramatic ability make him one of the finest Italian singers of the second half of this century.

*

E. Forbes: 'Sesto Bruscantini', *Opera*, vi (1971), 491–6

HAROLD ROSENTHAL/R

Brusilovsky, Yevgeny Grigor'yevich (*b* Rostov-na-Donu, 30 Oct/12 Nov 1905; *d* Moscow, 9 May 1981). Russian composer. He developed a serious interest in music while serving in the Red Army, which he left in 1922 to spend a year at the Moscow Conservatory; in 1926 he entered the Leningrad Conservatory, where he studied with Maximilian Shteynberg, graduating in 1931. He settled in Alma-Ata (1933), where he began work in the research department of the Kazakh Music and Drama Technical College, studying Kazakh folksongs; his folksong arrangements provided material for later compositions. He began to teach at the Alma-Ata Conservatory in 1934 and was made professor there in 1955. From 1934 to 1938 he was artistic director of the Kazakh Music and Drama Theatre (later the Abay Opera and Ballet Theatre), for which he composed works that laid the foundations of Kazakh national opera. In addition, he created the first Uzbek national ballet, *Gulyandom* (1940). Brusilovsky was an organizer and the first chairman of the Kazakhstan Composers' Union (1939–59). He was awarded the State Prize of the USSR (1948), the Order of Lenin (1959) and other honours.

Brusilovsky was trained in Russian classical traditions, and his works represent an interesting attempt to introduce the characteristic vocal monophony and distinctive instrumental harmonies of Kazakh music into the standard European genres, but without any superficial orientalism. His path led from arrangements in quartal and quintal harmonies to the introduction of these arrangements into operas as separate numbers – the operas of the 1930s were, in their first versions, essentially conversational dramas with aria-songs and instrumental dance episodes – and then (from about 1940) to the harmonic enriching of folk melodies and their more or less organic development into large-scale sonata-symphonic forms.

all first performed in Alma-Ata

Kïz-Zhibek (G. Musrenov), 7 Nov 1934
Zhalbïr (B. Maylin), 1935; rev. 1938; rev. 1946
Er-Targïn (S. Kamalolov), 1936; rev. 1954
Ayman-Sholpan (M. Auezov), 1938
Zolotoye zerno [Golden Grain]/Altïn stïk (S. Mukhanov), 1940
Gvardiya, vperyod! [Forward, Guard!]/Gvardiya, alga! (Mukhanov), 1942
Amangel'dï (Musrenov), 1945, collab. M. Tulebayev
Dudaray (A. Khangel'dïn), 1953
Nasledniki [The Heirs] (A. Anov and M. Balïkin), ?1962

L. M. BUTIR

Bruson, Renato (*b* Este, nr Padua, 13 Jan 1936). Italian baritone. He studied at Padua and made his début in 1961 at Spoleto as Luna. After singing in many of the major Italian theatres, in 1969 he made his Metropolitan début as Enrico Ashton, returning as Luna, Germont, Don Carlo (*Forza*) and Posa. In 1972 he made his début at La Scala as Antonio (*Linda di Chamounix*) and sang Ezio (*Attila*) in Edinburgh with Palermo Opera. He made his Covent Garden début in 1976 as Anckarstroem (*Ballo*), returning for Macbeth, Boccanegra, Miller and Iago. He has also appeared in Vienna, Berlin, Munich, Chicago, San Francisco and Los Angeles, where he sang Falstaff (1982) under Giulini. A specialist in Donizetti as well as Verdi, he has sung in revivals of *Belisario*, *Gemma di Vergy*, *Les martyrs*, *Le duc d'Albe*, *Torquato Tasso*, *Caterina Cornaro* and *La favorite*. Well-focussed tone and eloquent phrasing make him an ideal exponent of noble characters such as Boccanegra and Posa, but he is also effective as Scarpia and Don Giovanni. He has recorded many of his best roles, including Rigoletto and Falstaff.

*

G. Gualerzi: 'Renato Bruson', *Opera*, xxx (1979), 214–8

ALAN BLYTH

Brussels (Fr. Bruxelles; Flem. Brussel). Capital of Belgium since 1830. *Ulisse all'isola di Circe* by Gioseffo Zamponi was the first opera produced in the city, marking the wedding of Philip IV of Spain and Maria Anna of Austria in 1650. In 1694 Gian Paolo Bombarda, treasurer to the governor, Max Emanuel, opened the first public opera house, in a disused building that became the Opéra du Quai aux Foins. After the theatre was destroyed in 1695, Bombarda obtained the right to build a theatre on the site of the Hôtel d'Ostrevent, the former mint; the new theatre thus became the Théâtre de la Monnaie. Built between 1696 and 1699 by the architect Bezzi, with five tiers of boxes seating 1200, it opened in 1700, probably with Lully's *Atys*. The foyer was heated but not the auditorium. The repertory was the typical French one of the period – Lully, Campra, Mouret, Destouches. When the French entered Brussels in 1745, Maréchal de Saxe imposed Favart as director. Works by Gluck, Rameau, Philidor, Blaise, Monsigny, Duni, Gossec and Grétry were performed during the 18th century, when the theatre was also used for plays.

In 1817 it was decided to build a new theatre on a site just behind the old one; the architect was Damesne. Again called La Monnaie, this opened on 25 May 1819 with Grétry's *La caravane du Caire*. Auber's *La muette de Portici* was given in 1829, the year after its Paris première, in the presence of William I, King of the Low Countries; there were no problems then, but the work was later banned. The ban was lifted and the work performed anew on 25 August 1830; the riots that followed led to the Revolution of that year which gave rise to the modern state of Belgium. La Monnaie reopened on 12 September with a benefit concert for the wounded. *La muette* became almost a fetish, being given

Riot following the performance of Auber's 'La muette de Portici' at the Théâtre de la Monnaie, Brussels (25 August 1830), which sparked off the Revolution leading to Belgium's independence: engraving

every year until 1906. It marked the reopening of the theatre after World War I; 22 performances celebrated the centenary of the revolution in 1930, and 14 performances the reopening after World War II.

Rossini, Bellini, Donizetti and Verdi were played in this theatre, often for the first time in French, together with the works of Meyerbeer, Halévy, Berton, Adam and Belgian composers including Grisar and Fétis. On 21 January 1855 the theatre was largely destroyed by fire, only the outer walls and Damesne's famous peristyle remaining. The architect Joseph Poelaert rebuilt the theatre within the remaining walls, with four tiers seating 1700. His red and gold auditorium with its famous caryatids, considered one of the most beautiful in Europe, remains today much as he designed it. It was inaugurated on 23 March 1856 with Halévy's *Jaguarita l'indienne*. Soon all the important works created in Paris were given there only several months later; sometimes French versions of foreign works such as *Rigoletto* (1858) were given there before Paris saw them. A splendid period in the theatre's history occurred between 1875 and the early 20th century, under Stoumon (1875–85), Lapissida (1886–9), Calabresi (1899–1900) and Kufferath and Guidé (1900–14), when the world premières were given of Massenet's *Hérodiade* (1881), Reyer's *Sigurd* (1884) and *Salammbô* (1890), Chabrier's *Gwendoline* (1886), Godard's *Jocelyn* (1888), d'Indy's *Fervaal* (1897), *L'étranger* (1903) and *Le chant de la cloche* (1912) and Chausson's *Le roi Arthus* (1903). There too, and before Paris, the first performances in French were seen of *Lohengrin* (1870), *Der fliegende Holländer* (1872), *Walküre* (1887), *Siegfried* (1891), *Tristan* (1894), *Salome* (1907), *Elektra* (1910), *Mefistofele* (1883) and *Pagliacci* (1895). *Samson et Dalila* was tried out in concert form in 1878. Among the singers were Calvé, Litvinne and Melba. During World War I the occupying Germans put on seasons by German ensembles including performances of *Rosenkavalier*, conducted by the composer and sung by the original sopranos, and the *Ring*. From 1918 to 1953 La Monnaie was directed by the pianist and conductor Corneil de Thoran. During this period world premières were given of Milhaud's *Les malheurs d'Orphée* (1926), Honegger's *Antigone* (1927) and Prokofiev's *The Gambler* (1929), as well as many first performances in French, *Prince Igor*, *The Golden Cockerel*, *Turandot*, *Ariadne auf Naxos*, *I quatro rusteghi* (Wolf-Ferrari), *Wozzeck*, *The Rape of Lucretia* and *The Rake's Progress* among them. Singers included Vina Bovy, Fernand Ansseau, André d'Arkor, John Charles Thomas, Rita Gorr, Gabriel Bacquier, Huc-Santana and Joseph Rogachevsky (director, 1953–9).

In 1959 a new policy was instituted under the director Maurice Huisman, who instead of maintaining a permanent company invited foreign troupes to perform, with Belgian and French singers appearing in certain works. André Vandernoot was the chief conductor. Huisman founded the Opera Studio to help train young singers. In 1963 La Monnaie, until then a municipal theatre, was taken over by the state and became the national opera under the title Théâtre Royal de la Monnaie/Koninklijke Muntschouwburg, marking the fact that the population of Brussels was now a delicately balanced mixture of Walloons and Flemings. Huisman invited the choreographer Maurice Béjart to direct the ballet; this led to the creation of the Ballet du XXe Siècle, which with its school became the most vital element at La Monnaie. In these conditions the opera and the orchestra rapidly declined.

In 1981 Huisman retired and the Flemish administrator Gérard Mortier (*b* 1944), previously director of planning at Düsseldorf, Frankfurt (with Dohnányi), Hamburg and Paris (with Liebermann), took over the direction of La Monnaie and set about turning it into a centre of operatic excellence. He immediately improved the orchestra (brought up to 96 players) and chorus by appointing John Pritchard and Sylvain Cambreling musical directors, with Dohnányi as music adviser. World-famous directors such as Patrice Chéreau, Peter Stein, Karl-Ernst Hermann, Ruth Berghaus and Luc Bondy, together with the Belgians Gilbert Deflo, Philippe Sireuil and André Delvaux, were engaged and given long rehearsal periods, enabling them to pay meticulous attention to intelligent, well-thought-out productions. Peter Sellars added a little American wackiness. There is no permanent ensemble, although there is a kernel of 30 to 40 youngish singers from whom casts are made up as required. The *stagione* system prevails and ten or 12 operas are performed each season (September–June). Up to 90% of the seats are sold by subscription. A policy of commissioning new works has been followed, with Philippe Boesmans's *La passion de Gilles* (1983), André Laporte's *Das Schloss*, after Kafka (1986) and John Adams's *The Death of Klinghoffer* (1991), a co-production with Glyndebourne, Lyons, Houston, the Brooklyn Academy, Los Angeles and San Francisco. The performance of Schreker's *Der ferne Klang* given in 1988 was the first in Belgium.

During the 1985–6 season the stage of the theatre was rebuilt to a high technical specification and a new fly tower and rehearsal room were built on the roof. While not improving the exterior architecture, this has made La Monnaie into a superbly equipped modern theatre. During the rebuilding the company performed in the Cirque Royal, where in 1867 Benoit's *Isa*, one of the earliest Flemish operas, had been produced. During the 1987–8 season Gluck's *Orfeo ed Euridice* was presented in the Halles de Schaerbeek, the old covered market offering an ideal space.

Chéreau's production of *Lucio Silla* (part of the Monnaie Mozart cycle) was a co-production with La Scala and Chéreau's own Théâtre des Amandiers in Paris. The Monnaie presented *Wozzeck*, *Capriccio* and *Kát'a Kabanová* with great success at the Châtelet in Paris in 1982 and 1985. The Monnaie productions of *Così* and *La finta giardiniera* were shown at the Wiener Festwochen in 1986, and the latter was also given at the Brooklyn Academy of Music in 1989. During Mortier's regime all productions were broadcast on Belgian Radio and most on television, making them accessible to a wide public. In 1992 Mortier was succeeded by Bernard Fouccroulle.

Although the greater part of operatic activity in Brussels has always been at La Monnaie, in 1872 several of Lecocq's works, including *Les cent vierges* and *La fille de Madame Angot*, were presented in the Théâtre des Fantaisies-Parisiennes and operetta seasons were given in the Théâtre Molière.

*

J. Isnardon: *Le Théâtre de la Monnaie depuis sa fondation jusqu'à nos jours* (Brussels, 1890)

A. de Gers: *Théâtre royal de la Monnaie 1856–1926* (Brussels, 1926)

L. Renieu: *Histoire du théâtre à Bruxelles* (Paris, 1928)

R. Wangermée: *La musique belge contemporaine* (Brussels, 1959)

C. Mertens: *Hedendaagse muziek in België* (Brussels, 1967)

J. Salès: *Théâtre royal de la Monnaie, 1856–1970* (Nivelles, 1971)

CHARLES PITT

Bruyr, José (*b* Aiseau, 18 March 1889; *d* 1980). French writer and librettist of Belgian birth. He studied technical subjects at Liège University while also studying musicology and then settled in Paris (1919), where he became friendly with Honegger. He was attached to the Paris office of the Liège daily *La meuse*, 1931–9, and from 1950 to 1972 took part in the Parisian weekly radio programme 'La tribune des critiques de disques'.

He wrote the librettos for Le Flem's *La magicienne de la mer* (1954, Paris), Chailley's *Thyl de Flandre* (1954, Brussels), Fornerod's *Geneviève* (1954, Lausanne) and Sancan's *Ondine, fille de la forêt* (1966, Bordeaux). His many articles and studies, written in a fluent and spirited style, include *Grétry* (Paris, 1931), *Honegger et son oeuvre* (Paris, 1947), *Maurice Ravel ou Le lyrisme et les sortilèges* (Paris, 1950), *Massenet* (Lyons, 1964) and *L'opérette* (Paris, 1962).

CHRISTIANE SPIETH-WEISSENBACHER

Bruzdowicz, Joanna (*b* Warsaw, 17 May 1943). Polish composer. Between 1968 and 1970 she studied with Messiaen, Boulanger and Pierre Schaeffer in Paris; there she was closely involved in electro-acoustic music until 1975, when she moved to Belgium. Her three works for the stage all involve tape and speaking roles. In *Les Troyennes* (1972) she interweaves the modern (atonal techniques) with the ancient (African and Asian instrumental sources on tape), as well as making use of a modern version of the Greek theatre's thunder machine, the bronteon. *Bramy raju* ('The Gates of Paradise', 1982), about a 13th-century children's crusade, opens with a 30-minute taped overture played in the foyer; it experiments further with traditional approaches by allowing for the structural interchange of certain sections and by using both a singer and an actor to represent each character.

Kolonia karna [The Penal Colony], 1968 (musical tragedy, 1, J. Simonides, after F. Kafka), Tours, Grand, 12 Feb 1972 (Paris, 1975)

Les Troyennes (musical tragedy, 17 scenes, J. Luccioni, after Euripides), Paris, Théâtre Gérard Philippe, 29 March 1973 (Paris, 1974)

Bramy raju [The Gates of Paradise], 1982 (musical drama, 1, J. Lisowski and Bruzdowicz, after J. Andrzejewski), Warsaw, Wielki, 15 Nov 1987

*

L. Erhardt: 'Joanna Bruzdowicz about her New Opera', *Polish Music* (1986), nos.1–2, pp.11–17

ADRIAN THOMAS

Bryars, Gavin (*b* Goole, 16 Jan 1943). English composer. He studied philosophy at Sheffield University and music privately; since 1970 he has lectured at Leicester Polytechnic. He has worked as a jazz musician (playing double bass), and his interest in improvisation and indeterminism led him to be identified with the British experimental composers of the 1960s and 70s. His multi-media piece *The Sinking of the Titanic* (1969) became arguably the best-known work of that movement. Subsequently his music was influenced as much by Satie and Berners as by Cage, in its use of large-scale harmonic and melodic structures built from the repetition of small diatonic units. At the same time a background of philosophical and literary theories, especially those of Raymond Roussel, has continued to inform many of his works.

Bryars contributed to Robert Wilson's *The Civil Wars* (1984, Los Angeles), and afterwards collaborated with Wilson on the opera *Medea* (Lyons, Opéra, 23 October 1984). It is an extensive three-act treatment of the myth, which sets Euripides' tragedy in classical Greek with sections of English texts interpolated (translated into French for the first production); Bryars's scoring replaces violins with tuned percussion and oboes with saxophones, and dispenses with trumpets altogether. Subsequently he has worked on three smaller-scale operatic projects, *Bouvard et Pécuchet* (to a libretto by Conrad Cork after Gustave Flaubert), *The Last Days of Immanuel Kant* (to a libretto by Andrew Hugill Thomson based in part on De Quincey), and *Doctor Ox's Experiment* (to a libretto by Blake Morrison after Jules Verne), the final scene of which was performed in concert at the Queen Elizabeth Hall, London, on 18 November 1988.

*

R. Bernas: 'Three Works by Gavin Bryars', *New Music 87* (Oxford, 1987), 34–46

A. H. Thomson: 'The Apprentice in the Sun: An Introduction to the Music of Gavin Bryars', *MT*, cxxx (1989), 724–8

ANDREW CLEMENTS

Brzowski, Jósef (*b* Warsaw, 1803; *d* Warsaw, 3 Dec 1888). Polish composer. He studied music in Warsaw, where his teachers included Karol Kurpiński and Václav Würfel. From 1824 to 1832 he was successively cellist, coach and conductor of the ballet at the Warsaw Opera. He made several tours abroad and from 1861 until his death, taught at the Warsaw Institute of Music. In 1877 he received the Spanish Order of Isabella the Catholic. His sister Zofia (1799–1879) was an opera singer and the wife of Karol Kurpiński.

Brzowski composed two operas, unoriginal in style: the comic opera *Hrabia Weseliński* ('Count Merrymaker'; 1, L. Dmuszewski; *PL-Kj*), first performed in Warsaw on 24 November 1833, and *Rejent z Flandrii czyli Piwowar z Gandawy* ('The Regent of Flanders, or The Brewer of Ghent'; 4, J. Jasiński; *Kj*), written in 1886 but unperformed. His writings include 'Słów kilka o operze' ('A Few Words on Opera'), in *Świat dramatyczny* (Warsaw, 1838).

ALINA NOWAK-ROMANOWICZ

Bucceleni [Bucelleni], **Giovanni.** *See* BUZZOLENI, GIOVANNI.

Bucchi, Valentino (*b* Florence, 29 Nov 1916; *d* Rome, 9 May 1976). Italian composer. He graduated in philosophy at Florence University in 1940 and studied music at the Florence Conservatory under Vito Frazzi, Corrado Barbieri and Dallapiccola, obtaining a diploma in composition in 1944. From 1945 he taught at the conservatories of Florence, Venice and Perugia, and he was artistic director of the Accademia Filarmonica Romana (1958–60) and the Teatro Comunale, Bologna (1963–7). He was active as music critic for various newspapers, including *La Nazione* (1938–44) and *Avanti!* (1966–7).

Bucchi's interest in the theatre is apparent in his earliest works. The first version of his one-act *Il giuoco del barone*, conceived in 1937 but orchestrated and completed two years later, contains archaisms typical of madrigal writing and reveals the influence of Stravinsky (as noted by Abbiati 1939). The action centres on an old Tuscan dice game which governs the actions of the baron, who is a traditional Tuscan figure: the less than successful adventurer. Bucchi's next work for the theatre was the one-act 'grottesco' *Il contrabbasso* (1954), after a story by Chekhov. The central figure is a double-bass player whose artistic dedication condemns him to solitude. Bucchi treats the pathos and humour of the libretto in a spare, lucid musical language and with biting irony, which were to become characteristic.

Bucchi returned to the theatre in 1960 with the 'cantafavola' *Una notte in paradiso*, from Italo Calvino's Italian fairy-tales, about two friends who swear to be each other's best man wherever they may be when the weddings take place. The opera brings out another of the components of Bucchi's poetic world, an interest in the life of ordinary people, especially in Tuscany; this is evident in the way he combines elements from popular song and jazz with stylistic features from 'serious' music. His next opera (and the last completed), *Il coccodrillo* (1970), is based on the novella by Dostoyevsky about a man who discovers fulfilment and his real relationship with other people by living inside a crocodile; it combines music, recitation, film projection and dance in a sequence of 32 episodes, and is evidently a metaphor for the stressful situation of contemporary man. Bucchi also reworked Adam de La Halle's *Li gieus de Robin et de Marion* and Monteverdi's *Orfeo*. His unfinished, unpublished and unperformed work *Il tumulto dei Ciompi* (1972), to a libretto by Massimo Dursi, was intended to be a popular outdoor entertainment.

Characteristic of Bucchi's theatre works is a taste for irony, for the grotesque and for popular culture, combined with an essentially poetic style defined by D'Amico as 'del minimo mezzo' and producing a personal amalgam which is equally distant from conservatism and the avant garde.

See also COCCODRILLO, IL and CONTRABBASSO, IL.

printed works are vocal scores published in Milan

Il giuoco del barone (1, A. Parronchi), Florence, Sperimentale, 20 Dec 1939; rev. 1955, Spoleto, 26 June 1958; (1953)
Il contrabbasso (grottesco, 1, M. Mattolini and M. Pezzati, after A. P. Chekhov: *Roman s kontrabasom*), Florence, Comunale, 20 June 1954 (1954)
Una notte in paradiso (cantafavola, 1, L. Bazzoni, after I. Calvino: *Le fiabe italiane*), Florence, Comunale, 11 May 1960 (1960)
Il coccodrillo (4, in 2 pts, Bucchi and Pezzati, after F. M. Dostoyevsky: *Krokodil*), Florence, Pergola, 9 May 1970 (1970)
Il tumulto dei Ciompi, begun 1972 (M. Dursi), unperf., unpubd

*

DBI (L. Pannella and S. Ragni)
F. Abbiati: 'Il giuoco del Barone di Valentino Bucchi allo Sperimentale di Firenze', *Corriere della sera* (21 Dec 1939)
F. D'Amico: 'Romanzo del Contrabbasso', *Il contemporaneo* (29 May 1954); repr. in F. D'Amico: *I casi della musica* (Milan, 1962), 30–33
M. Mila: 'Maggio Musicale: i fantasmi dell'opera', *L'espresso* (29 May 1960)
M. Messinis: 'Prima assoluta al Maggio Musicale: "Il Coccodrillo" di Bucchi metafora del mondo moderno', *Il gazzettino* (10 May 1970)
L. Pannella: *Valentino Bucchi: anticonformismo e politica musicale italiana* (Florence, 1976)

RAFFAELE POZZI

Bucci, Mark (*b* New York, 26 Feb 1924). American composer. He studied in New York with Serly (1942–5) and at the Juilliard School with Frederick Jacobi and Vittorio Giannini; subsequently he was a pupil of Copland at the Berkshire Music Center. The majority of Bucci's works are for the stage; in addition to operas, he has composed musicals, film scores and incidental music. His one-act opera *Tale for a Deaf Ear* was commissioned for performance at the Berkshire Music Festival in 1957. In 1966 he was named co-winner of the Prix Italia, an international television award, for *The Hero*, an opera that had been commissioned by the Lincoln Center Fund and broadcast from New York the previous year. He has also written several plays and the book and lyrics for a pop opera, *Myron, its Deep Down Here* (1972). An admirer of Puccini, Bucci writes in a modern yet lyric style, using marked rhythms and catchy harmonies and melodies.

first performed in New York unless otherwise stated

The Boor (1, E. Haun, after A. P. Chekhov: *The Bear*), 29 Dec 1949
The Beggar's Opera (after J. Gay), 1950
The Dress (1, Bucci), 8 Dec 1953
Sweet Betsy from Pike (op satire, 1, Bucci), 8 Dec 1953
Tale for a Deaf Ear (1, after E. Enright), Tanglewood, 5 Aug 1957
The Hero (television op, after F. D. Gilroy: *Far Rockaway*), televised, New York, 24 Sept 1965
The Square One (jazz op, T. Brown), unperf.
Myron, its Deep Down Here, 1972 (pop op, Bucci), unperf.
Midas, 1981 (H. Hackaday), unperf.

KATHERINE K. PRESTON

Buchan, Cynthia (*b* Edinburgh, 1 July 1949). Scottish mezzo-soprano. She studied at the Royal Scottish Academy of Music and Drama and made her début in 1968 with Scottish Opera in Monteverdi's *Il ballo delle ingrate*. A Richard Tauber Memorial Award took her to Vienna for further study, and she has since sung a range of leading roles with British companies, notably Cherubino, Dorabella, Charlotte (*Werther*), Olga (*Yevgeny Onegin*), Orlofsky and Rosina. She sang in three operas during her first Glyndebourne season (1974) and made her Royal Opera début in 1980 as a flowermaiden in *Parsifal*. Her repertory extends from Handel and Vivaldi (*Griselda*) to Britten and Ligeti (*Le Grand Macabre*), winning her praise for versatility of dramatic character as well as full-toned and flexible singing. NOËL GOODWIN

Buchanan, Isobel (*b* Glasgow, 15 March 1954). Scottish soprano. She studied at the Royal Scottish Academy of Music and Drama. In 1975 she joined the Australian Opera on a three-year contract, making her début as Pamina and also singing Countess Almaviva, Micaëla and Gilda. Her British début was at Glyndebourne in 1978 as Pamina; in the same year she made her Vienna Staatsoper début as Micaëla under Kleiber, in a Zeffirelli production with Domingo. She first appeared at Covent Garden in 1979 as Sophie (*Werther*) and with Scottish Opera as Mimì. Her first American appearance was at Santa Fe as Pamina and Mimì in 1979, and she has also appeared in Chicago, Munich, Paris and elsewhere. A lyric soprano with a firm mezzo-soprano range, she is admired for her brightness of tone and vitality of character. NOËL GOODWIN

Buchardo, Carlos López. *See* LOPEZ BUCHARDO, CARLOS.

Bucharest (Rom. Bucureşti). Capital of Romania, on the Dîmbovita river in the south of the country. The town is first mentioned in documents of 1459; it became the capital of Wallachia in 1539 and of Romania in 1861. Opera troupes, principally Italian, performed in Bucharest on their way to Russia, beginning with Livio Cinti's company in 1771–3. The Theatrum Vlahicum Bucharestini was built in the city in 1814, and the Cişmeaua Roşie theatre in 1818. At the same time as European companies were arriving, the lyric troupe of Johann Gerger – actor, singer and manager from Braşov – was also performing locally, specializing in Mozart and Rossini. In 1820–21 a tour by the Angelica Catalani troupe proved a great success, though it was interrupted by the outbreak of the 1821 revolution. The repertory included works by Rossini, Carlo Guglielmi, Vincenzo Pucitta (the MS of his *Aristodemo*, written in 1814 in London, is now in the library of the Academy of Music) and Pietro Generali. After 1830 opera ensembles from Timişoara (Theodor Müller), Sibiu, Braşov (Eduard Krebig) and Iaşi (Joseph Foureaux) performed in Bucharest, using Romanian singers and orchestral players. The composer Ion Wachmann (1807–63), conductor of the Timişoara troupe, had several of his operas and vaudevilles produced, including *Braconierul* ('The Poachers', 1833), *Zamfira* (1834), *Triumful amorului* ('Love's Triumph', 1835) and *Mihai Bravul în ajunul bătăliei de la Călugăreni* ('Michael the Brave on the Eve of the Battle at Călugăreni', 1848). In 1843 the Italian opera company was founded, representing the first permanent lyric theatre in Romania. Meanwhile the Momulo-Slătineanu theatre had been built in 1833, and the Bossel theatre in 1848. After the Teatrul Naţional (National Theatre) opened in 1852, foreign and Romanian troupes alternated in performance.

Opera Română (Romanian Opera), endowed by the composer and conductor George Stephănescu, was formed in 1877. Its repertory included works by Eduard Caudella, Constantin Dimitrescu, George Stephănescu and Alexandru Flechtenmacher. The first Romanian opera singers to appear in Bucharest were Eufrosina Popescu-Vlasto, Cornelia Creţu, Gheorghe Brătianu, Elena Teodorini, Grigore Gabrielescu, Dimitrie Popovici-Bayreuth, Hariclea Darclée and Nuovina and Zina de Nori. The première of Caudella's *Petru Rareş* in 1900 was an event of national importance. Foreign stars such as Patti, Stagno, Van Dyck and Bellincioni in the 19th century were followed by Titta Ruffo, Leo Slezak, Shalyapin, Toti Dal Monte, Tito Gobbi, Giuseppe Di Stefano, Nicolai Ghiaurov, Anton Dermota and Grace Bumbry in the 20th. In 1921 the Romanian Opera was taken over by the state, the opening performance, *Lohengrin* on 8 December, conducted by George Enescu. Alongside the state ensemble other lyric troupes also performed in the capital, including those of Constantin Grigoriu, Grigore Gabrielescu and Stefănescu Spira, the Cărăbuş music hall and the Alhambra operetta theatre. After World War II the national Opera (whose present building was inaugurated in 1953), the State Operetta Theatre, the Constantin Tănase music hall and the opera studio of the Academy of Music resumed their activities in the city. Besides works ranging from Pergolesi, Vivaldi and Telemann to Britten, Khachaturian and Falla, many premières of Romanian works have been given, by Gheorghe Dumitrescu, Pascal Bentoiu, Paul Constantinescu, Cornel Trăilescu, Matei Socor, Doru Popovici, Paul Urmuzescu and others. The International George Enescu Festival, founded in 1958 and held every three years, includes opera and ballet performances by eminent visiting artists.

*

D. C. Ollănescu: *Teatrul la români* (Bucharest, 1897)

I. Dumitrescu: *Muzica în Bucurestiul de ieri şi de azi* [Music of Yesterday's and Today's Bucharest] (Bucharest, 1959)

V. Cosma: *România Muzicală* (Bucharest, 1980)

VIOREL COSMA

Bucharoff [Buchalter], **Simon** (*b* Berdichev, Ukraine, 8/20 April 1881; *d* Chicago, 24 Nov 1955). American composer and pianist of Russian birth. He studied the piano in New York with Paolo Gallico and Leopold Kramer and in Vienna with Julius Epstein and Stefan Stocker. He held various teaching posts in the USA and was, from 1937 to his death, a music editor and orchestrator at Warner Brothers studios in Hollywood. Bucharoff composed in various genres, but is best remembered for his operas, for which he received the David Bispham Memorial Medal in 1925. *A Lover's Knot* (vs, London, *c*1916), a light opera in one act to a libretto by Cora Bennett-Stephenson, was first performed in Chicago on 15 January 1916 and was revived in the same city in 1923. Bucharoff's second opera, *Sakahra* (vs, Leipzig, 1923), a three-act grand opera to a libretto by Isabel Buckingham (German translation by Rudolf Lothar), was first performed at the opera house in Frankfurt on 8 November 1924. The plot deals with a brother and sister who, separated at birth, fall innocently into an incestuous union which leads to tragedy when the truth becomes known. The music is neo-romantic in style. Bucharoff left five other operas: *Jewel*, *Addio*, *Wastrel*, *Soul of Israel* and *Indestructible Man*, the last two of which he completed shortly before his death.

*

E. E. Hipsher: *American Opera and its Composers* (Philadelphia, 1927), 86–90 BRADFORD R. DEVOS

Buchhöfer, Monsieur (*fl c*1725). German tenor. He sang comic roles, such as servants or peasants, at the Hamburg Gänsemarkt Opera, 1722–8; he was also a dancer in opera performances. In 1722, under the composer's musical direction, he sang Sancio in Telemann's *Don Quichotte der Löwenritter*, and in 1725 he danced in Kunzen's Singspiel *Critique des hamburgischen Schauplatzes*. In the succeeding years he appeared in operas by Telemann and Keiser; nothing is known of him after 1728. A soprano of the same name who sang at Hamburg in 1722 was probably related to him.

*

K. Zelm: 'Die Sänger der Hamburger Gänsemarkt-Oper', *HJbMw*, iii (1978), 35–73, esp. 48–9 HANS JOACHIM MARX

Büchner, Eberhart (*b* Dresden, 6 Nov 1939). German tenor. He studied in Dresden, making his début in 1964 at Schwerin as Tamino. In 1966 he joined the Dresden Staatsoper and in 1968 the Berlin Staatsoper, where for a decade he sang lyrical roles: Ferrando, Sextus (*Giulio Cesare*), Ernesto, Oberon, Faust, Henry (*Die schweigsame Frau*), Fra Diavolo, Gluck's Achilles and Loge. In 1979 he sang the Dancing Master (*Ariadne auf Naxos*) at Salzburg and in 1982 Admetus (*Alceste*) at Brussels. He made his Covent Garden début in 1983 as Don Ottavio and sang Flamand (*Capriccio*) at Brussels and J. C. Bach's Amadis at Hamburg. Turning to heavier roles, he sang Lohengrin at Copenhagen (1986), Düsseldorf (1987) and Covent Garden, then Erik at La Scala and Parsifal in Dresden (1988). His voice is not large but it is well projected. ELIZABETH FORBES

Büchner, Georg (*b* Goddelau, nr Darmstadt, 17 Oct 1813; *d* Zürich, 19 Feb 1837). German dramatist. The son of a doctor, he studied medicine in Strasbourg and Giessen before settling in Switzerland, where he began a promising career as a lecturer in comparative anatomy. He left Germany in 1835 after publication of the pamphlet *Der hessische Landbote*, which was born of the same desire to effect social justice and relieve the sufferings of the poor that informs his best-known drama, *Woyzeck*. His first drama, *Dantons Tod*, was his only work to be published in his lifetime; indeed, despite the advocacy of Hebbel and Gutzkow, his works were hardly performed until the 20th century. Danton, sickened by the Terror and his involvement in the September Massacres, makes no effort to save his own life; indeed, his denunciation of Robespierre hastens his end. The only positive message is of the invincibility of the human spirit. The play was turned into an opera by von Einem, to a libretto by Blacher, and was first heard at the Salzburg Festival in 1947. In 1929 Eisler wrote incidental music for a production of the play in Berlin.

The best-known work based on Büchner is Berg's *Wozzeck* (1925, Berlin) which sets almost verbatim Büchner's text as edited by K. E. Franzos (1879), but in a revised ordering of scenes. Other composers who have written music for *Woyzeck* are Gurlitt (1926) and Gerhard (1961, for BBC radio). Not surprisingly, Büchner's brilliant and disturbing comedy *Leonce und Lena* (1836–7) has been most often taken up by musicians, though none of the resulting works has established itself. Robert Müller-Hartmann wrote incidental music for a production in 1923, and a year later Weismann set it as an opera to a text by himself and W. Calé (1925, Freiburg); it was set as *Valerio* by Hans Simon, to a libretto by Theodor Ginster in 1931. Will Eisenmann wrote an opera based on the story in 1943, and Svend Erik Tarp in 1955; in 1972 Peter Maxwell Davies used the play for his masque *Blind Man's Buff*. Paul Dessau's last opera (1979) was a setting of *Leonce und Lena*. Wagner-Régeny's *Der Günstling* (1935), to a libretto by Caspar Neher, was based on Büchner's translation of Victor Hugo's *Marie Tudor*. Büchner's unfinished prose work *Lenz* (published 1839), a narrative depiction of an episode in the life of the 18th-century dramatist Jakob Lenz, formed the basis of operas by Larry Sitsky (1974) and Wolfgang Rihm (1979).

*

Dantons Tod (play, written 1835): von Einem, 1947
Lenz (prose work, written 1835–6, inc.): Sitsky, 1974; Rihm, 1979
Leonce und Lena (play, written 1836): Weismann, 1925; H. Simon, 1931, as Valerio; S. E. Tarp, 1955; Schwaen, 1961; P. M. Davies, 1972, as Blind Man's Buff; Dessau, 1979
Woyzeck (play, written 1836, inc.): Berg, 1925; Gurlitt, 1926

PETER BRANSCOMBE

Buck, Dudley (*b* Hartford, CT, 10 March 1839; *d* West Orange, NJ, 6 Oct 1909). American composer and organist. After two years at Trinity College, Hartford, he went to Europe and studied music in Leipzig, Dresden and Paris. Returning in 1862, he held posts as organist in Hartford and Chicago before moving to Boston in 1871 where he was organist for the Music Hall Association and was also on the faculty of the New England Conservatory. In 1875 Buck went to New York to be assistant conductor of the Theodore Thomas Orchestra. He lived in Brooklyn, where he held positions as organist and choirmaster until his retirement in 1903.

Buck's major works include a large amount of church music and several secular cantatas. His first operatic composition was a comic opera, *Deseret, or A Saint's Affliction*, described as 'An American Opera in Three Acts'. The first performance was on 11 October 1880 at Haverley's Fourteenth Street Theatre, New York; the work was subsequently given in Baltimore and Cincinnati but never performed thereafter. It was soundly condemned by the critics for its subject, libretto and music. The libretto, written by the journalist William Augustus Croffut and based on sensational and distorted stories of Mormon polygamy, was seriously flawed and judged offensive. Buck's compositional talents were considered unsuited to the genre. Selections from *Deseret* were published in New York in 1880.

For his second and last operatic effort Buck chose a religious subject, wrote his own text (in English and German), and cast the work in the form of grand opera. *Serapis*, which tells of the triumph of Christianity over the cult of Serapis in ancient Alexandria, was completed in about 1888 but was never performed or published (MS full score, *US-Wc*; vocal score, *Bp*).

*

W. Gallo: *The Life and Church Music of Dudley Buck* (diss., Catholic U. of America, 1968) ELLEN KNIGHT

Buckman, Rosina (*b* Blenheim, New Zealand, 16 March 1881; *d* London, 31 Dec 1948). New Zealand soprano. She studied in England, at the Birmingham and Midland School of Music, and made her début in Wellington (1905) as La Zara in Alfred Hill's *A Moorish Maid*. She first appeared in Australia with the Melba Grand Opera Company in 1911. At Covent Garden she was a flower-maiden in the first English stage performance of *Parsifal* on 2 February 1914, then sang Musetta in *Bohème* with Melba and Martinelli. Throughout the war she was a leading member of the Beecham Opera Company, her Isolde being particularly admired; she also appeared with great success as Butterfly, Mimì and Aida. At Covent Garden in 1919 she sang the title role of De

Lara's *Naïl*; in 1923 she sang in the only performances there of Smyth's *The Boatswain's Mate*. Her last Covent Garden appearance was in a benefit concert for Emma Albani in 1925. Her clear, generous voice is heard on many records that enjoyed considerable popularity, notably a complete English-language *Butterfly* under Goossens.

*

A. Simpson and P. Downes: *Southern Voices: International Opera Singers of New Zealand* (Auckland, 1992), 24–37 J. B. STEANE

Buczynski, Walter (*b* Toronto, 13 Dec 1933). Canadian composer. He studied at the Toronto Conservatory with Earle Moss (piano) and Godfrey Ridout. Later he studied with Milhaud (1956) and Nadia Boulanger (1960–61), and continued his piano studies in New York (1958–9) and Warsaw (1959–60). In his early career he was active as a pianist. He taught at the Toronto Conservatory, 1962–72, and from 1969 at Toronto University, where he became a professor of music theory and composition.

Much of Buczynski's music is characterized by theatrical devices and humorous high spirits. In *From the Buczynski Book of the Living* he combined the eastern mystic text of Murray Schafer's choral work *From the Tibetan Book of the Dead* with other words, reducing the entire message to nonsense. The opera includes a deathbed scene in which the singer is revived, and a scene satirizing the contemporary technique of using meaningless words for their evocative value.

Mr Rhinoceros and his Musicians, 1957 (children's op, 1, L. Barnes), CBC, 25 Dec 1965

Do Re Mi (children's op, 1, Barnes), CBC, 13 Dec 1967

From the Buczynski Book of the Living, 1972 (chamber op, 8 scenes, Buczynski), CBC, 11 July 1975

Naked at the Opera (chamber op, 1, T. Hendry), Toronto, Royal Ontario Museum, 23 Oct 1979 RUTH PINCOE

Budai, Livia (*b* Esztergom, 23 June 1950). Hungarian mezzo-soprano. She studied in Budapest, where she made her début as Mamma Lucia in 1973, the year she first sang Carmen in Sofia. In 1977 she was engaged at Gelsenkirchen, making her début as Eboli, a role she has sung in San Francisco, Savonlinna, Brussels and at Covent Garden, where she was first heard (1978) as Azucena, also the role of her Metropolitan début (1987). She has sung at Florence, Munich, Hamburg, Geneva, Berlin and the Paris Opéra, where she sang Ada in Berio's *Vera storia* (1985). Her repertory includes Brangäne, Venus, Fricka, Elizabeth (*Maria Stuarda*), Preziosilla, Amneris, Laura (*La Gioconda*), Delilah, Cassandra, Adalgisa, Santuzza and Mistress Quickly, which she sang at Aix-en-Provence (1987). She sang Ortrud at La Monnaie, Brussels, in 1990. She has a strong, warm voice which is not always subject to perfect control. ELIZABETH FORBES

Budapest. Capital of Hungary. It was created in 1873 by the unification of three towns: Buda, on the right bank of the Danube, which with its great castle served as the royal seat of the kingdom from the 13th century; Óbuda, north of Buda on the right bank, which as Aquincum was the capital of the province of Pannonia, part of the Roman Empire from AD 100 to 400; and Pest, opposite Buda on the left bank.

The first theatre in Pest, the Rondella, was built in 1773–4 inside one of the bastions of the city wall. Kumpf's troupe from Count Erdődy's theatre in Pozsony (now Bratislava) was the first to perform an opera there, Salieri's *La scuola de' gelosi*, in 1784. In 1787 another theatre, the Várszínház (Castle Theatre), was built in the former Carmelite Church in Buda. It is now Budapest's oldest theatre. At first all the companies were German. Henrik Bulla's troupe gave regular performances of operas by Benda, Dittersdorf, Grétry, Mozart (*Die Entführung*, 1788), Paisiello, Salieri and Sarti in both theatres. After Count Erdődy's death in 1789 Kumpf's troupe took up residence for eight months, and by its high standard of performance firmly established opera in Buda and Pest. The two companies alternated, with operas by Dittersdorf, Mozart (*Die Zauberflöte*, 1793; *Figaro*, 1795; *Così fan tutte*, *Don Giovanni* and *La clemenza di Tito*, 1797), Paisiello, Joseph Weigl, Salieri and Winter forming the backbone of the repertory until 1800. The conductor and singer Alois Czibulka then hired the theatres and introduced new works, by Cherubini (*Les deux journées*, 1804), Grétry, Dalayrac, Méhul and Boieldieu (*Le calif de Bagdad*, 1810). The Rondella was small, so in 1812 the Városi Színház (Town Theatre) was built in Pest; it opened with two of Beethoven's overtures, *König Stephan* and *Die Ruinen von Athen*. This theatre, however, was too large (cap. 3500) for a town with 35 000 inhabitants, and it was a financial disaster; its size was also a problem for the singers. Its conductors – Czibulka, Vincenc Tuček, Schindelmeisser, Urbany, and Erkel in the 1836–7 season – and companies, sometimes with famous guest artists such as Wild (1835–6), Schröder-Devrient (1835) and Fanny Elssler (1846), excelled in the performance of contemporary operas, chiefly those of Auber, Bellini (*I Capuleti e i Montecchi*, 1833; *I puritani*, 1836), Donizetti (*Anna Bolena*, 1833), Halévy (*La Juive*, 1836) and Meyerbeer. However, after the theatre burnt down in 1847, seasons of German opera in Pest took place only occasionally, as for example those under the direction of C. E. Barbieri (1862–7); in addition to operettas there were guest performances by companies such as the Viennese Komische Oper and Morini's Italian troupe in 1877, and by Angelo Neumann's company touring the *Ring* in 1883.

Performances of Hungarian opera began with the acting company of László Kelemen (1760–1814), which in 1793 gave a performance of the first Hungarian Singspiel, *Pikkó Hertzeg és Jutka Perzsi*, by the company's conductor József Chudy, formerly of Count Erdődy's theatre. It worked in difficult circumstances, often on the verge of financial collapse, despite the enthusiastic participation of the two important *verbunkos* composers János Lavotta and (briefly) A. G. Csermák, as well as the Singspiel composer András Szerelemhegyi (1762–1826); besides their works an opera by Paisiello, *Socrate immaginario*, was performed in Hungarian in 1793. The company could not compete with the German troupes at the two theatres and finally failed in 1796. A second Hungarian company, from Kolozsvár (now Cluj-Napoca, Romania), performed in the Rondella from 1807 to 1815. Its conductor Gáspár Pacha (1776–1811) wrote Hungarian Singspiels, and the first outstanding Hungarian opera singer, Róza Déry (1793–1872), began her career with this company. Operas given in Hungarian included works by Pacha, Benda (*Ariadne auf Naxos*), Dittersdorf (*Doktor und Apotheker*), Méhul and J. B. Schenk. When Pacha's company was forced to move to Miskolc, there were only occasional visits by Hungarian companies to Buda and Pest for nearly two decades. Dávid Kilényi's touring company arrived in Pest in 1822; its programme is not known, but Róza Déry was among the singers. The group returned with her as the Transylvanian Company, giving operas by Cherubini and Rossini at the Town Theatre from October 1827 until February 1828. The Miskolc company also returned in 1826 and 1827 and performed in the Castle Theatre; the opening work was a new Hungarian opera by József Ruzitska, *Béla futása* ('Béla's Escape').

A new epoch began in 1833 when part of the Kassa (now Košice, Slovakia) National Opera and Theatrical Troupe arrived and was given the Castle Theatre in Buda in which to establish a Hungarian company. This new company staged comedies, Hungarian ballets and light operas; in April 1835 it was joined by the rest of the troupe, then in Kolozsvár, and in the first season, under the conductor Ferenc Erkel, 22 performances were given of works by Rossini, Dalayrac, Auber, Boieldieu, Cherubini, Hérold, Mercadante, Ruzitska and Weber. From that time Hungarian opera was regularly performed in Buda and Pest. The combined company found a home at the Magyar Színház (Hungarian Theatre) when it opened in Pest in 1837, three years later becoming the Nemzeti Színház (National Theatre). The opera section moved into the new Magyar Királyi Operaház (Royal Hungarian Opera House) in 1884.

At the National Theatre (cap. 1460) the leading conductors were Ferenc Erkel (1838–74), Hans Richter (1871–5) and Sándor Erkel (1874–1900). In addition to *Fidelio*, *Don Giovanni* and Hungarian operas, under Ferenc Erkel the company quickly formed a repertory of contemporary Italian and French works. For decades the trend was to mount the operas one to four years after their premières, from *La fille du régiment* and *Linda di Chamounix* in 1844 to Thomas' *Hamlet* in 1870 and *Mignon* in 1873. The aim was to have a broad repertory of about 45 to 50 operas and to give about 130 performances annually, as well as ballets. The season always began on 1 April, though the theatre was closed in July. In 1864 the stage lighting was changed from gas to electric; and from that time also the orchestra played at the pitch favoured in Paris, nearly a semitone lower than before. Verdi remained the favourite composer, but many French works were also given, including *Carmen* in 1876. In 1883 the most financially successful operas were *Bánk bán* and *Hunyadi László* (Erkel), *Lohengrin*, *Les Huguenots*, *Lucrezia Borgia* and *Aida*. The company's development at this time was partly due to the building of two bridges that connected the towns (in 1849 and 1875), and to a rapid increase in the population – 370 000 by 1880. More fundamentally, however, it was due to the excellence of the orchestra under Ferenc Erkel, and to the quality of such opera singers as Róza Schodel, Kornélia Hollósy, Ilka Markovits, Ida Benza and David Ney, who became nationally known, and Ferenc Stéger, Lajos Bignio, Vilma Voggenhuber, Zsigmond Hajós and Etelka Gerster, who gained international recognition. Operas were given in Hungarian, but guest artists could perform in their own or the original language. Some guests became permanent members of the company.

The National Theatre company gave a weekly performance in the Castle Theatre from 1874. In 1875 the Pesti Népszínház (Pest People's Theatre) was opened (demolished in 1965) and operettas and musicals were transferred to it from the National Theatre. Its greatest star was Lujza Blaha. Sometimes foreign companies gave opera performances as well; Patti appeared there in the 1870s. When the Fővárosi Operettszínház (Capital Operetta Theatre) was opened in 1893, the People's Theatre lost its audience, and ceased to exist in 1907; the theatre company of the National Theatre moved into the building in 1908.

The second great chapter in the history of permanent Hungarian opera in Budapest began when the Royal Hungarian Opera House (cap. 1310) was opened in 1884; from then until World War II the outstanding conductors were Sándor Erkel (until 1888), Mahler (1888–91), Nikisch (1893–5), Rezső Máder (1895–1907), István Kerner (1896–1915), Dezső Márkus (1903–11), Egisto Tango (1913–19), Nándor Rékai (1912–27), Antal Fleischer (1920–39), Sergio Failoni (1928–44) and János Ferencsik (1931–47). At the beginning there were 34 soloists, 81 chorus members and 75 orchestral players. The best soloists of earlier years were in decline by the 1880s, and others returned from abroad only years later; few were of the highest level. A new generation emerged after some 20 years: Elza Szamosi, Erzsi Sándor, Béla Venczell, Béla Környei, Anna Medek and Ferenc Székelyhidy. To maintain a wide repertory – *Otello*, *Fidelio*, *Il barbiere*, *Bánk bán*, *Hunyadi László*, *Carmen*, *Faust* and *Die Königin von Saba* were permanently featured – it was necessary to invite guest artists to perform; some of them (Italia Vasquez, Carl Burrian) settled in Budapest. Of Ferenc Erkel's operas, only the last, *István király* ('King Steven', 1885), was first produced in the Opera House rather than in the National Theatre; nearly all of them retained their attraction until recently. The once popular operas of Doppler and F. G. Császár have disappeared. For some decades after 1890 Wagner's works were dominant. Their great triumph was a little overshadowed nevertheless by the new French or Italian operas of Bizet (*Les pêcheurs de perles*, 1883), Delibes (*Lakmé*, 1887), Mascagni (*Cavalleria rusticana*, 1890), Saint-Saëns (*Samson et Dalila*, 1892) and Leoncavallo (*Pagliacci*, 1893), but the real challenge came with the operas of Puccini (*Tosca*, 1903; *La bohème*, 1905; *Butterfly*, 1906) and to some extent Strauss (*Elektra*, 1910; *Der Rosenkavalier*, 1911). For the most part, Hungarian composers between 1885 and 1910 (Mihalovich, Aggházy, Ö. Farkas, Zichy) did not compete successfully; only Hubay's *A cremonai hegedüs* ('The Cremona Lutenist', 1894) and Poldini's *Vagabund und Prinzessin* (1903) had any popularity.

In 1911 the Népopera (People's Opera) was opened (cap. 3000), whose low prices and varying companies attracted part of the Royal Hungarian Opera House's audience. It underwent frequent changes of name and function, for a time becoming the Városi Színház (City Theatre) where Shalyapin and other stars performed. Since 1953, under the name Erkel Színház (Erkel Theatre), it has been the second home of the Opera House company. Meanwhile, however, the Opera House maintained its pre-eminence by inviting Dyagilev's Ballets Russes in 1912, and putting on Musorgsky's *Boris Godunov* (1913) and Bartók's *The Wooden Prince* (1917) and *Bluebeard's Castle* (1918).

After World War I Hungary lost two-thirds of its territory and inhabitants. The population of Budapest grew from 930 000 in 1920 to 1 500 000 in 1938. A new generation of famous singers appeared, including Mária Basilides, Imre Palló, Kálmán Pataky, Mária Németh and Mihály Székely. In 1925, a golden age began at the Opera House under its artistic director

Miklós Radnai with the conductors Failoni, Ferencsik and Solti and the singers Endre Rösler, Lujza Szabó, Sándor Svéd, Júlia Orosz, Júlia Osváth, Anna Báthy and Mária Gyurkovics. Guest conductors included Kleiber, Dobroven, Beecham, Krauss, Walter, Weingartner and Karajan, and guest singers, Battistini, Jeritza, Lauri-Volpi, Rosvaenge, Maria Müller, Gigli, Svanholm and Kiepura. In 1938 an open-air theatre (cap. 3300) was built on Margaret Island. The repertory of the Opera House gradually widened: as well as Mozart, Verdi and Wagner it embraced Puccini (*Il trittico*, 1922; *Turandot*, 1927), Debussy (*Pelléas et Mélisande*, 1925), Stravinsky (*Oedipus rex*, 1928), Falla (*El sombrero de tres picos*, 1928), Malipiero (*Il finto Arlecchino*, 1931), Milhaud (*Trois opéra-minutes*, 1932), Strauss (*Die äegyptische Helena*, 1932; *Arabella*, 1934) and Respighi (*La fiamma*, 1935). Among Hungarian composers, lasting success was achieved by Dohnányi (*Der Schleier der Pierrette*, 1910; *A vajda tornya* ('The Vaivode's Tower'), 1922; *Der Tenor*, 1929), Hubay (*Anna Karenina*, 1923), Poldini (*Hochzeit im Fasching*, 1924) and Kodály (*Háry János*, 1926; *Székely fonó* ('The Transylvanian Spinning Room'), 1932). Bartók's *Miraculous Mandarin*, first performed in Cologne in 1926, was not given in Budapest until 1945.

After World War II the city lay in ruins. The Royal Hungarian Opera House, now called Magyar Állami Operaház (Hungarian State Opera House), was damaged, and the theatre on Margaret Island destroyed. After the latter was rebuilt in 1951, it became the venue for spectacular performances by the opera house and national theatre companies. Since 1966 it has been independent. From 1947 to 1955 the State Opera House had a touring company, Gördülő Opera, conducted by P. Mura and later A. Németh, for which the state railway provided the orchestra and a special train. With a repertory of eleven 19th-century operas, it gave 100 performances annually in 61 towns and villages all over the country. To replace this service the People's Theatre organized an opera company in the early 1970s.

The state monopoly of power that followed the war induced some members of the Opera House company to flee to western countries, including the conductors Failoni, Fricsay, Ferencsik, Klemperer (chief conductor from 1947) and Kertész; Ferencsik returned in 1950. After him the most important Hungarian conductors were Miklós Lukács, András Kóródi, Ádám Medveczky, Miklós Erdélyi and Ervin Lukács. From 1950 Hungarian soloists were not permitted to perform in the West. Eventually the country lost many excellent singers – Sándor Kónya, Dezső Ernster, Magda Tiszay, Magda László, Eva Marton, Sylvia Geszty, Julia Hamari and Sylvia Sass – though later some of them returned as guests. Among those who stayed and became famous were József Simándy, György Melis, Róbert Ilosfalvy, Ilona Tokody and László Polgár. Though Molinari-Pradelli conducted in Budapest in 1956 for the first time, generally there were no contacts with western European countries until 1960. Gardelli often visited, as did Patanè and others. Guest singers have included many internationally famous names.

From 1962 the company toured, to Helsinki (1962, 1964, 1980), Edinburgh (1963, 1973, 1983), Paris (1963, 1969, 1980), Stockholm (1964), Monte Carlo (1965, 1978), Vienna (1967, 1979) and many other cities. Among 20th-century works to be performed are *Albert Herring* (1960), *Wozzeck* (1964) and *Lulu* (1973), *Katerina Izmaylova* (1965) and *The Nose* (1978), and *The Rake's Progress* (1980). New Hungarian operas include works by Emil Petrovics (*C'est la guerre*, 1962; *Bűn és bűnhődés* ('Crime and Punishment'), 1969), Sándor Szokolay (*'Blood Wedding'*, 1964; *Hamlet*, 1968; *Samson*, 1974; *Ecce homo*, 1987), Zsolt Durkó (*Moses*, 1977), Sándor Balassa (*Az ajtón kívül* ('Out of Doors'), 1978), Attila Bozay (*Csongor és Tünde*, 1985). Of these, Szokolay's *Blood Wedding* has been the most successful at home and abroad; it was translated into 10 languages and performed in 13 countries between 1965 and 1988.

The State Opera House underwent major refurbishment in 1980–84, in which the capacity was reduced to 1261 seats; during this time the company performed in the Erkel Theatre.

*

F. Schams: *Vollständige Beschreibung der königl. Freystadt Pest* (Pest, 1821)

J. Patacsich: *Szabad királyi Pest városának leirása* [Description of the Royal Borough of Pest] (Pest, 1831)

J. Pardoe: *The City of the Magyar, or Hungary and her Institutions in 1839–40* (London, 1840)

I. Palugyay: *Buda-Pest szabad királyi városok leírása* [Description of the Royal Borough of Buda-Pest] (Pest, 1852)

J. Kádár: *A budai és pesti német színészet története 1812-ig* [History of the German Stage in Buda and Pest to 1812] (Budapest, 1914)

——: *A pesti és budai német színészet története 1812–1847* [History of the German Stage in Pest and Buda 1812–47] (Budapest, 1923)

K. Isoz: *Buda és Pest zenei művelődése (1686–1873)*, i: *A 18-ik század* [The Musical Life of Buda and Pest (1686–1873), i: The 18th Century] (Budapest, 1926)

A Magyar királyi operaház évkönyve 50 éves fennállása alkalmából (1884–1934) [Yearbook of the Hungarian Royal Opera House on its 50th Anniversary] (Budapest, 1935)

J. Pukánszkyné Kádár: *A Nemzeti színház százéves története* [100 Years of the National Theatre] (Budapest, 1940)

I. Balassa, ed.: *A hetvenötéves Állami operaház* [75 Years of the State Opera House] (Budapest, 1959)

D. Legány: *A magyar zene krónikája: Zenei művelődésünk ezer éve dokumentumokban* [A Chronicle of Hungarian Music: 1000 Years of Music History in Documents] (Budapest, 1962)

J. Breuer: *Harminc év magyar zenekúltúrája* [30 Years of Hungarian Musical Culture] (Budapest, 1975)

E. Gábor: 'The Reopening of the Budapest Opera House', *New Hungarian Quarterly*, xxv/wint. (1984), 189–94

G. Staud, ed.: *A Budapesti operaház 100 éve* [100 Years of the Budapest Opera House] (Budapest, 1984)

G. Staud: 'One Hundred Years of the Budapest Opera House', *New Hungarian Quarterly*, xxv/wint. (1984), 194–206; xxvi/spr. (1985), 194–200

DEZSŐ LEGÁNY

Budden, Julian (**Medforth**) (*b* Hoylake, Cheshire, 9 April 1924). English musicologist. He studied classics at Oxford, then went to the RCM, London. In 1951 he joined the BBC, becoming music producer (1956), chief producer of radio opera (1970–76) and external services music organizer (1976–83). In his research he has concentrated on 19th-century Italian opera, Verdi in particular: he has published several articles as well as a three-volume study *The Operas of Verdi* (London, 1973–81), widely acknowledged as the standard authoritative study of these works, and *Verdi* for the Master Musicians series (London, 1985); he has also worked extensively on Donizetti and Puccini.

Budweis (Ger.). ČESKÉ BUDĚJOVICE.

Buelow, George J(**ohn**) (*b* Chicago, 31 March 1929). American musicologist. He studied in Chicago and at New York University (PhD 1961) and has taught at the University of California at Riverside, Rutgers University and at Indiana University, where he was appointed professor of musicology in 1977. He specializes in German Baroque music, with emphasis on performing practice, theory and opera, but he is also interested in 19th-century German opera, particularly Wagner and Richard Strauss; he is co-author (with Donald G. Daviau) of *The 'Ariadne auf Naxos' of Hugo von Hofmannsthal and Richard Strauss* (Chapel Hill, 1975). His studies of operas by Mattheson include an edition of *Cleopatra* (EDM, 1st ser., lxix, 1975). PAULA MORGAN

Buenos Aires. Capital of Argentina. The city was permanently established in 1580 and had a population of 12 000 by 1750. In that year the flautist D. M. Saccomano of Bari, Italy, arrived and in 1756 petitioned the governor for the right to show 'óperas y comedias' – the operas to be given in a covered courtyard by women singers brought from Brazil. In September 1757 he opened a tiny Casa de Operas y Comedias. The next year his business partner Pedro Aguiar signed a contract with the composer Bartolomé Mazza (*b* Novi, Italy, 1721; *d* Lima, 1799) and the cathedral *maestro de capilla* Francisco Vendemer before leaving for Spain to engage singers. With these imported artists Mazza's opera *Las variedades de Proteo* (libretto by António José da Silva) was given several times in November 1760.

In 1776 Buenos Aires became capital of a newly created viceroyalty. Musical spectacles, chiefly of the *tonadilla* type, were given in the wooden Teatro de la Ranchería, from 1783 until it burnt down on the night of 13 August 1792. An inventory dated 14 June 1792 mentions scores valued at 517 pesos for *tonadillas* and other music. The Santander-born composer Antonio Aranaz conducted the ten-member house orchestra from 1787 to 1792.

In the Coliseo, opened in 1804, the Italian Pietro Angelelli sang excerpts from popular Italian operas in a series from November 1810 to June 1811. The first complete Italian opera performance, on 27 September 1825, was of *Il barbiere di Siviglia*, inaugurating the first regular opera season. During the next three years further operas by Rossini were given: *La Cenerentola*, *L'inganno felice*, *L'italiana in Algeri*, *Otello*, *Armida*, *Tancredi* and *La gazza ladra*. *La vestale* by Pucitta was performed in 1825, *Romeo e Giulietta* by Zingarelli in 1826, *Don Giovanni* on 9 February 1827, and Dalayrac's *La maison à vendre* and *Adolphe et Clara*, translated into Spanish, in 1826 and 1827. Mariano Pablo Rosquellas sang the chief tenor roles not only in Rossini's operas, but also in Boïeldieu's *Le calife de Bagdad*, which had its première on 21 November 1827 in the Coliseo 'before an elegant audience' (*British Packet*, 29 December 1827). In 1831 Rosquellas organized his own company, which opened at the new Teatro del Parque Argentino (constructed in 1828 by James Wilde) with Mercadante's *Elisa e Claudio*. Mounting political pressures caused Rosquellas and his talented family to leave Buenos Aires in April 1833.

During the reign of the xenophobic dictator Juan Manuel Rosas (1829–52) opera languished. Only in his last years did such operas as *Lucia*, *L'elisir d'amore*, *Beatrice di Tenda*, *Norma* and *Ernani* gain a first hearing. In the 1852–4 seasons, a company of French singers with Prosper Fleuriet as orchestral director shuttled back and forth across the estuary from Montevideo, giving *porteños* their first exposure to 13 operas by Adam, Auber, Boïeldieu, Donizetti (the original French versions of *La favorite* and *La fille du régiment*), Hérold, Isouard and Thomas, and of another 16 by Auber, Bazin, Fleuriet (*Le 14 juillet*), Halévy, Meyerbeer and Rossini (*Guillaume Tell*). The venues for these were the Teatro de la Victoria (inaugurated in 1838, abandoned in 1882) and the Teatro Argentino (formerly the Coliseo, renamed in 1838). In the 1854 season, up to then the most brilliant in Argentine operatic annals, 30 first performances were given by two visiting companies. The Italian Pestalardo company occupied the Argentino, giving *Luisa Miller*, *Giovanna d'Arco*, *Macbeth*, *Roberto Devereux*, *Maria di Rudenz*, *Anna Bolena* and other works. Fleuriet's French company occupied the Victoria. In 1855 the Pestalardo company gave the local premières of *Il trovatore* and *Rigoletto*; in the following year the Lorini company mounted the first performance of *La traviata*, at the Victoria. In 1856 Buenos Aires also first heard a season of zarzuelas (*El duende*, *Jugar con fuego*, *El valle de Andorra*).

The need for a new opera house to satisfy a more demanding public resulted in the building of the first Teatro Colón, inaugurated with *La traviata* on 25 April 1857 (for which the Lorini company enrolled Enrico Tamberlik). Seating 2500, with 80 boxes in three balconies, it also had a *cazuela* (gallery for single women) and a *paraíso* (men's gallery, with a separate entrance). Fronting the Plaza de Mayo, the first Colón was also the first theatre to be lit by gas, and in every other respect it enjoyed all the most advanced equipment of the day. The last production there was the local première of *Otello*, on 13 September 1889; the reconstruction of the building to house the Banco de la Nación Argentina had begun on 10 October 1887. During its last years it had experienced mounting competition from the Teatro de la Opera, opened in 1872. Both theatres concentrated on Italian and French operas; the German repertory had to wait for *Der Freischütz*, first sung in Italian at the Colón on 4 September 1864 (a production brought from Rio de Janeiro by the Pestalardo company), and *Lohengrin*, also in Italian at the Colón, on 17 June 1883. The Opera gave the Buenos Aires premières of *Don Carlos* (17 June 1873) and Gomes's *Il Guarany* (27 June 1874), and predated the Colón with premières of operas by such lesser lights as Petrella (1878), Bottesini (1879) and Usiglio (1884). Towards the end of the century it also proved more receptive to works by native Argentines.

The first indigenous composer to see his own stage work produced in a local theatre was Francisco Hargreaves, whose one-act *La gatta bianca* was sung after two acts of *Rigoletto* at the Victoria on 11 January 1877. Arturo Berutti's *Pampa* was first heard in 1897 at the Opera and Héctor Panizza's *Il fidanzato del mare*, given there in the same year, was followed by his *Medioevo latino* in 1901 with Toscanini conducting.

On 1 August 1901 Toscanini conducted at the Opera the Buenos Aires première of *Tristan und Isolde*, sung in Italian. The first opera he conducted there was *Tosca* on 19 May 1901 (with Enrico Caruso and Hariclea Darclée); his last was *Götterdämmerung* on 28 August 1912. The only time that he conducted *Der Freischütz* anywhere was on 6 August 1904 at the Opera, when, as with everything else during his five operatic seasons in Buenos Aires (1901, 1903, 1904, 1906, 1912), Italian was the language.

Caruso, who was first heard at the Opera in *Fedora* on 14 May 1899, created the title role in Berutti's pseudo-Inca story *Yupanki* that same year. But although

Teatro Colón, Buenos Aires, inaugurated on 25 May 1908

he returned to Buenos Aires repeatedly until 1917, this was the only opera by a composer from the Americas in which he sang. Puccini visited the city during the 1905 season, when *Edgar* was added to his four previously heard operas. In 1911 Mascagni's *Isabeau* was given, conducted by the composer.

The present Teatro Colón (built with 2500 seats, now enlarged to a capacity of some 4000 spectators) opened on 25 May 1908 with *Aida*, conducted by Luigi Mancinelli. In that year five other theatres offered operatic seasons: the Opera (giving the local premières of Massenet's *Thaïs* and *Ariane*), the Politeama Argentino, the San Martín, the Coliseo and the Marconi. From World War I the Colón eclipsed all competition, but as late as 1911 the Opera still offered important Buenos Aires premières (among them Debussy's *Pelléas et Mélisande*, in French).

No other New World opera house has been so open to local composers as the Colón. A total of 23 composers born or naturalized in Argentina have had operas mounted at the Colón between 1908 and 1970, from Berutti, Boero and Castro to Panizza, Sciammarella and Ugarte. Despite grave difficulties during the Perón epoch (1946–55) the Colón continued to present the first South American performances of such operas as *Jenůfa* (30 June 1950), *Wozzeck* (14 October 1952), *Christophe Colomb* (21 July 1953), *Il prigioniero* (24 November 1954) and Pizzetti's *La figlia di Iorio* (3 June 1955). Schoenberg's *Erwartung* occupied a double bill with Dallapiccola's *Volo di notte* (26 June 1959); Britten's *A Midsummer Night's Dream* (25 July 1962), conducted by Meredith Davies, was the novelty of its season. The complete Catalan version of Falla's *Atlántida* was given on 3 May 1963, and the South American premières of *Idomeneo* (24 September 1963), *Les Troyens* (5 May 1964) and *Dialogues des Carmélites* (18 May 1965) were highlights. The Argentine première of Ginastera's *Bomarzo* announced for 8 August 1967 was cancelled by order of a retired colonel who was mayor of the municipality (the city had owned the Teatro Colón since 1931). To recover some prestige, Enzo Valenti Ferro (who became director-general in 1965) added extra works at both ends of the season (14 new productions in an April to December season). The outstanding event of the 1969 season was *La clemenza di Tito* with Teresa Berganza. Opening on 11 July, it was repeated five times in ten days to full houses.

Jon Vickers in *Tristan* capped the 1971 season. The disastrous 1972 season closed prematurely. Bruno Jacovella, appointed general director in 1973, then began by cancelling contracts with foreign artists engaged for the season; on 14 July he was publicly denounced at the third performance of *Rigoletto*. During a later *Traviata*, performed by local singers, eggs were thrown onto stage for the first time in the Colón's history, after which a new management team led by Elvio H. Romeo was appointed. Local singers remained the norm in the 1975 and 1976 seasons. Sung in English by imported and local singers, *Peter Grimes* opened the 1979 season on 8 May. *I due Foscari*, another first at the Colón, followed on 10 and 17 July. Placido Domingo sang in *La fanciulla del West* in July 1979, and in 1980 *Pelléas* with Thomas Allen was the event of the season.

Donizetti's *Belisario* (not heard in Buenos Aires since 1954) was revived on 26 May 1981, the year a new *Ring* cycle was begun; Szymanowski's ill-received *King Roger* ended the season. Despite a lavish mounting on 8 June 1982, Pedro Saenz's realization of Juan Hidalgo's *Celos aun del aire matan* (1660, libretto by Calderón) failed to generate any enthusiasm. On the other hand, the first South American performance of Berlioz's *Benvenuto Cellini* (20 August) reaped an ovation, and the season ended on 9 December with a rapturously applauded *Doña Francisquita* by Amadeo Vives. Preceded by publicity not known since Caruso's heyday, Pavarotti sang Rodolfo (without a high C) in *La bohème* on 16 August 1987. The 1988 season was cancelled for stage repairs, but the short 1989 season closed on 17 December with a double bill that included the premières of *Escorial*, by the Buenos Aires-born composer Mario Perusso (*b* 1936), and *Adonais* by Alejandro Pinto (*b* 1922).

*

ES (J. A. Sala and A. E. Giménez)

M. G. Bosch: *Historia de la ópera en Buenos Aires* (Buenos Aires, 1905)

V. Gesualdo: *Historia de la música en la Argentina* (Buenos Aires, 1961)

——: *Pablo Rosquellas y los orígenes de la ópera en Buenos Aires* (Buenos Aires, 1962)

J. D'Urbano: *Música en Buenos Aires* (Buenos Aires, 1966)

R. Caamaño, ed.: *La historia del Teatro Colón (1908–1968)* (Buenos Aires, 1969)
M. E. Kuss: *Nativistic Strains in Argentine Operas Premiered in the Teatro Colón (1908–1972)* (diss., UCLA, 1976)
R. Stevenson, ed.: *La púrpura de la rosa* (Lima, 1976), 120ff
E. Valenti-Ferro: *Las voces Teatro Colón 1908–1982* (Buenos Aires, 1983) ROBERT STEVENSON

Buen Retiro [Coliseo del Buen Retiro]. Theatre in the Buen Retiro royal palace, Madrid, staging opera performances from 1629; *see* MADRID, §§1–2.

Buesst, Aylmer (*b* Melbourne, 28 Jan 1883; *d* St Albans, 25 Jan 1970). Australian conductor. He studied in London with August Wilhelmj and in Leipzig with Arthur Nikisch. After engagements in Breslau and Görlitz he settled in England and was engaged by the Moody-Manners Opera Company (1914–16) and the Beecham Opera Company (1916–17 and 1919–20). When the latter went into liquidation in 1920, Buesst was one of the prime movers in establishing the British National Opera Company, which he conducted from 1922 to 1928; at Covent Garden in January 1923 he conducted the company's performance of *Hänsel und Gretel*, one of the first opera broadcasts. He also conducted the first London performance of Boughton's *Alkestis* in 1924. In 1933 he was appointed assistant music director of the BBC and he later taught at the three main London music colleges. He wrote the excellent analysis *Richard Wagner: the Nibelung's Ring: an Act by Act Guide to the Plot and Music* (London, 1932, 2/1952).

HAROLD ROSENTHAL

Buffo [buffo caricato] (It.: 'comedian [tricked comedian]'). Term used for a singer who specializes in comic roles; it is the same word as in 'opera buffa', and has links with 'buffoon', which in turn derives from the Italian *buffa*, 'a jest', and the verb *buffare*, 'to puff'. The type of singer and role is almost as old as opera itself, with Irus, the stuttering drunkard of Monteverdi's *Il ritorno d'Ulisse in patria* and Nero's bibulous crony Lucan in *L'incoronazione di Poppea* as early examples. These are commonly sung by a tenor, but from the 18th century onwards it became more customary for the principal *buffo* parts to go to a bass or a low baritone (*see* BASSO BUFFO). He was frequently the 'buffo caricato' or 'tricked' *buffo*, an elderly, foolish and often wealthy character with designs on the heroine and eventually to be thwarted by the tricks of the young lovers or their witty assistant. Well-known examples are Dr Bartolo in *Il barbiere di Siviglia* and Don Pasquale in the opera by Donizetti. Earlier, a variant of the type can be seen in the gullible employer of Serpina in Pergolesi's *La serva padrona*. Francesco Benucci (*c*1745–1824), Mozart's original Figaro and first Viennese Leporello, was a *buffo* bass, and, partly because of the vivid portraits of him, Luigi Lablache (1794–1858), the first Don Pasquale, remains the archetype, with Salvatore Baccaloni (1900–69) as his nearest counterpart in modern times.

A capacity for rapid articulation is a prerequisite in many *buffo* roles. Curiously, Falstaff himself, the greatest jester of the operatic stage, is not normally considered a *buffo* role, though it has been taken by some (Geraint Evans and Fernando Corena, for instance) who would also undertake roles such as Don Pasquale. In German opera, Osmin in *Die Entführung* and Ochs in *Der Rosenkavalier* are prime examples of roles in which the skills of the *buffo* need to be combined with considerable resources of vocal power and range. The Germans recognize the *Bass-buffo* as a category (or *Fach*), and parts such as Beckmesser in *Die Meistersinger* would come within its scope or perhaps be assigned to the sub-*Fach* of 'Spielbass', applicable to 'character' parts, but in practice Osmin and Ochs are most often taken by a heavy bass who will also sing the 'black' or 'serious' Wagnerian roles. The tenor *buffo* is confined to relatively small parts such as Goro in *Madama Butterfly* or Sellem the auctioneer in *The Rake's Progress*. Comic female roles are also relatively few and secondary, the servant Berta in *Il barbiere di Siviglia* being an example.

J. B. STEANE

Bugarinović, Melanija [Melanie; Melka; Milada] (*b* Bela Crkva, 29 June 1905; *d* Belgrade, 8 May 1986). Serbian mezzo-soprano. Educated in Timişoara and at the Belgrade Conservatory, she made her début in 1930 with the Belgrade Opera and appeared there regularly until 1937. She sang at the Vienna Staatsoper, 1938–44, and was Herodias in their production of *Salome* conducted by Richard Strauss (1942). She returned to the Belgrade company in 1946, singing there until 1961, and in 1952–3 appeared at Bayreuth. Her best roles included Marfa (*Khovanshchina*), Azucena (*Trovatore*), Ulrica (*Ballo*), Tchaikovsky's Countess (*Queen of Spades*) and the Wagnerian parts of Fricka, Erda, Brangäne and Ortrud. Bugarinović had an exceptional voice, dark in timbre and unusually beautiful. She made several recordings of Russian works with the Belgrade Opera.

ROKSANDA PEJOVIĆ

Buini, Cecilia Belisani. *See* BELISANI BUINI, CECILIA.

Buini [Bovina, Buina], **Giuseppe Maria** (*b* Bologna, 2 Feb 1687; *d* Alessandria, 13 May 1739). Italian composer, librettist and impresario. In 1719 he was active as an impresario at Lugo di Romagna with G. M. Alberti, and in 1721 he married Cecilia, daughter of the famous *buffo* singer Francesco Belisani. He was admitted to the Accademia Filarmonica of Bologna as an organist on 11 December 1721 and later (21 May 1722) as a composer, presenting a *Laudate Dominum* for three choirs in 12 parts. In 1723–4 he became impresario, again with Alberti, at the Teatro Formagliari in Bologna, and with his wife he was in the service of the court of Mantua from 1729. He was elected *principe* of the Accademia Filarmonica in 1730 and 1735, and he also held minor offices. Penna records a period of activity in Vienna, but documentary evidence of this has not been found.

In the context of Italian opera in the first decades of the 18th century Buini is an interesting and exceptional figure: he combined the roles of librettist, composer and impresario, and took an interest in a type of *opera buffa* independent of the Naples tradition. Nearly all his music is lost; his numerous librettos show facility but rarely elegance in the writing, perhaps as a result of his being largely self-taught. His works in the *buffa* genre have links with a tradition of farce in the Po valley that exploits a taste for unconventional theatre and satire. As to his musical language, one can only make hypotheses based on a few secondary sources. Penna relates that 'a rare eccentricity and invention, and an excellent natural aptitude for composing won him universal esteem', while a contemporary satire characterized Buini's stage music by his use of 'tarantella airs easy to the ear' (the same source suggests also that many of the operas for which he composed music were actually pasticcios, which would partly explain the rare survival of scores). Such comments would suggest the frequent use of simple song structures and an attractive, catchy and effective idiom. It is probable that Tosi's polemic against composers of 'canzonette' was aimed at Buini, among others. In such a context his presentation of a difficult and erudite composition for admission to the Accademia Filarmonica could be interpreted as an attempt to silence possible accusations of incompetence.

drammi per musica in three acts, unless otherwise stated

BF – *Bologna, Teatro Formagliari*
BMR – *Bologna, Teatro Marsigli-Rossi*
VM – *Venice, Teatro S Moisè*

Armida abbandonata (F. Silvani), BF, 16 Aug 1716
L'ipocondriaco (G. C. Villafranca), BF, carn. 1718
Il mago deluso della magia (divertimento per musica, A. Zaniboni), BF, carn. 1718
La pace per amore (A. Schietti), VM, carn. 1719, collab. F. Chelleri; rev. as Il nemico amante, VM, carn. 1724
La caduta di Gelone (F. Rossi), Venice, S Angelo, aut. 1719
Armida delusa (G. M. Buini), Venice, S Angelo, carn. 1720
Gl'inganni fortunati (pastorale per musica, 3, B. Valeriani), VM, May 1720
Apollo geloso (pastorale per musica, 3, P. J. Martello), Lugo, Aug 1720
Il filindo (pastorale eroica, 3, P. d'Averara), VM, 19 Oct 1720
Cleofile (Zaniboni), VM, carn. 1721
Amore e maestà (A. Salvi), BMR, 26 Dec 1721
Pithonessa sul Monte Olimpo, BMR, carn. 1722
Gl'inganni felici (A. Zeno), VM, aut. 1722
La fede ne' tradimenti (G. Gigli), Faenza, Accademia de' Remoti, 21 June 1723
Amor non vuol rispetti, BMR, carn. 1724
La ninfa riconosciuta (Silvani), BF, carn. 1724
Il Tolomeo re d'Egitto (Silvani), Verona, dell'Accademia, carn. 1724
La vendetta disarmata dall'amore (A. Passerini), BF, carn. 1724
L'Agrippa tetrarca de Gerusalemme, Milan, Regio Ducal, 1724
La Cleonice, BF, carn. 1725
Li sdegni cangiati in amore (Silvani, rev. ?Buini), VM, carn. 1725
L'Adelaide (Salvi), BF, spr. 1725
Il savio delirante (divertimento comico per musica, 3, Buini), BF, carn. 1726; as Le frenesie d'amore, VM, May 1726
Albumazar (Buini), BF, carn. 1727
Il Malmocor (dramma tragichissimo per musica, 3, Buini), BMR, carn. 1728; as Artaganamennone, VM, Ascension 1731
La forza del sangue (?Buini), BMR, spr. 1728
Teodorico (Salvi), BF, aut. 1728
Chi non fa non falla (divertimento comico per musica, 3, Buini), BMR, carn. 1729
I diporti d'amore in villa (scherzo drammatico, 3, A. M. Monti), BMR, carn. 1729
Amore e gelosia (dramma pastorale per musica, 3, A. Aureli), S Giovanni in Persiceto, Accademia dei Candidi Uniti, aut. 1729
La maschera levata al vizio (Silvani), BMR, carn. 1730; as Il filosofo ipocrita, BF, carn. 1735
Il podestà di Colognole (G. A. Moniglia), BF, 1730
Fidarsi è bene, ma non fidarsi è meglio (divertimento comico per musica, 3, Buini), VM, Ascension 1731
Gli amici (pastorale per musica, 3, P. J. Martello), Bologna, spr. 1734
La Zanina maga per amore (dramma comico per musica, 3, Buini), S Giovanni in Persiceto, Accademia dei Candidi Uniti, aut. 1737

*

Nel teatro dell'amara rimembranza (MS, *I-Bc* I.45, 11)
O. Penna: *Catalogo degli aggregati della Academia Filarmonica di Bologna* (MS, *I-Baf*, 1736/*R*1971) [sometimes attrib. G. B. Martini]
E. J. Dent: 'Giuseppe Maria Buini', *SIMG*, xiii (1911–12), 329–36
G. Rossi: *Varietà letterarie* (Bologna, 1912), 165–86 [on *Malmocor*]
L. Frati: 'Musicisti e cantanti bolognesi del settecento', *RMI*, xxi (1914), 189–202
F. Vatielli: 'Operisti librettisti dei sec. XVII e XVIII', *RMI*, xliii (1939), 605–21
A. Della Corte: *Satire e grotteschi* (Turin, 1946), 365
M. G. Accorsi: *Dialetto e dialettalità* (Bologna, 1982)

SERGIO DURANTE

Buini, Matteo (*fl* Bologna, 1748–9). Italian singer and composer. This minor figure in 18th-century comic opera is noted here mainly to distinguish him from his more illustrious predecessor, Giuseppe Maria Buini, to whom he is not known to have been related. He sang in the 1748 production of Cocchi's *La maestra* in Modena. For Carnival 1749 he reset the recitatives and 'almost all' of the arias in *La virtuosa corteggiata da tre cicisbei ridicolo* (Bologna, Formagliari); the original opera was Natale Resta's *Li tre cicisbei ridicoli* (C. A. Vasini; carn. 1748, Bologna). The following autumn he did the same for Parma with *Lo scolaro alla moda* (apparently from the original A. Palomba-Latilla-Pergolesi work *Orazio*, 1738, Rome). He did not sing in either of these productions, the music of which has been lost. The attribution sometimes made to Matteo Buini of *Il protettore alla moda* (1747, Venice) is mistaken: it was a whole or partial resetting by Galuppi of G. M. Buini's *Chi non fa non falla* (1729, Bologna).

*

A. Gandini: *Cronistoria dei teatri di Modena dal 1539 al 1871* (Modena, 1873), i, 61
P. E. Ferrari: *Spettacoli drammatico-musicali e coreografici in Parma dall'anno 1638 all'anno 1883* (Parma, 1884), 338
U. Sesini: *Catalogo della biblioteca del Liceo musicale di Bologna*, v/1 (Bologna, 1943), 75–6

JAMES L. JACKMAN

Bukša, Mykolas (*b* Vilnius, 16 April 1869; *d* Vilnius, 7 March 1953). Lithuanian conductor and composer. He studied the piano, composition and conducting at the St Petersburg conservatory with Rimsky-Korsakov, Lyadov and Glazunov, graduating in 1900. His début as an opera conductor took place in Gor'kiy (now Nizhny-Novgorod) in 1899; later he worked in Moscow (at the Mamontov Theatre), Tbilisi, Kiev, Kharkiv, Vladicaucasus, Smolensk and Perm'. Battistini, Ruffo, Shalyapin and Sobinov were among those who sang under him. From 1927 Bukša conducted in Kaunas, making his début with Rubinstein's *Demon*; he directed some 30 local premières there, among them works by Borodin, Musorgsky, Nápravník, Wolf-Ferrari, d'Albert and Lithuanian composers. In 1948 he moved (with the theatre and conservatory) to Vilnius.

*

R. Geniušas: *Dirigavimas ir Lietuvos dirigentai* [Conducting and Lithuanian Conductors] (Vilnius, 1973), 58–72

ADEODATAS TAURAGIS

Bulakhov, Pavel Petrovich (*b* Moscow, 15/27 March 1824; *d* St Petersburg, 15/27 Oct 1875). Russian tenor. He was a member of a distinguished musical family: his father, Pyotr Alexandrovich Bulakhov (?1793–1835) and elder brother, Pyotr Petrovich Bulakhov (1822–85) were both tenors, and the younger Pyotr's daughter, Yevgeniya Zbruyeva, achieved fame as the leading operatic contralto of her day. Following his operatic début in St Petersburg in 1849, Pavel Bulakhov embarked on a versatile career that embraced the spoken theatre as well as Russian and Italian opera. His principal roles included Almaviva, Lyonel (*Martha*), Sobinin (*A Life for the Tsar*) and Finn (*Ruslan and Lyudmila*). In 1856 he created the role of the Prince in Dargomïzhsky's *Rusalka*, partnered by his wife Anis'ya Alexandrovna Bulakhova (*née* Lavrova, 1831–1920) in the role of Natasha. Like her husband, Bulakhova was particularly noted for her appearances in Glinka's operas: apart from their creators, Mariya Stepanova (1815–1903) and Yekaterina Semyonova (1821–1906), she was the sole interpreter of the roles of Antonida and Lyudmila during the composer's lifetime.

BORIS SEMEONOFF

Bulgakov, Mikhail Afanas'yevich (*b* Kiev, 14 May 1891; *d* Moscow, 10 March 1940). Soviet novelist. He graduated in medicine from Kiev University in 1916 but soon abandoned that career to work as a writer, travelling throughout Russia before settling in Moscow in 1921. His first success was in 1926, with the play *Dni Turbinykh* ('The Day of the Turbinykh'), a dramatization of his own novel *Belaya gvardiya* ('The White Guard'). The play was later suppressed; in fact all his work was banned by Stalin from 1929. Bulgakov's masterpiece, *Master i Margarita* ('The Master and Margarita', 1938), an allegorical novel about the Stalinist terrors, remained unpublished until 1966. Its exotic mixture of fantasy and satire – the devil incarnated in Moscow interwoven with a retelling of the Crucifixion from the viewpoint of Pontius Pilate – prefigured 'magic realism'; its operatic potential has attracted several composers, including Slonimsky (1989, concert perf.), Rainer Kunad (1986) and York Höller (1989); both Nicholas Maw and Nigel Osborne have drafted librettos based on the novel. William Bergsma has composed an opera, *The Murder of Comrade Sharik* (1973), to his own libretto, based on Bulgakov's novel *Sobach'ye serdtse* ('The Heart of a Dog', 1925).

ANDREW CLEMENTS

Bulgarelli-Benti, Maria Anna. *See* BENTI, MARIA ANNA.

Bulgaria. The beginnings of Bulgarian opera date from the end of the 19th century only, probably as a result of the absence, owing to historical circumstances, of significant musical developments in the country in earlier centuries when national operatic styles were becoming established elsewhere in Europe. The earliest operas were directly influenced by National Revival theatre, at that time one of the principal manifestations of an awakened national consciousness. Considerable impetus also came from the Czech bandmasters who set up orchestras in Bulgaria immediately after the liberation of the country from the Turks in 1878, as well as from performances in the 1880s and 90s by touring opera companies (nine Italian and two Russian). The subjects and plots were largely drawn from contemporary Bulgarian literary classics and from national history; but foreign operas performed in the country also influenced the development of musical theatre. The first Bulgarian opera, *Siromachkinya* ('The Poor Woman', 1900) by Emanuil Manolov, despite the immaturity of its style, shows how the musical and theatrical forms common in the National Revival period were transformed into a new national genre. The transformation was complete by the time the works of Georgi Atanasov began to appear. His operas follow the genre-specific pattern typical of the new school of operatic writing: a mixture of the everyday and the fantastic (*Gergana*, 1917), the historical (*Borislav*, 1911) and the legendary (*Kosara*, 1926). *Gergana* was particularly significant to the development of Bulgarian opera: its succession of colourful local scenes combined with spontaneous folklike music attracted large and enthusiastic audiences.

By the end of the 1920s there was a move away from folk styles towards various modern European musical and theatrical traditions, involving an increasingly professional approach. One important development was the adoption of the principles of Wagner's music dramas, as can be heard, for example, in Atanasor's last two operas, *Kossara* and *Altzec* (1930). In the 1930s a new generation of composers animated Bulgarian musical life. Educated in countries with rich, sophisticated musical traditions, these composers, with their broader cultural horizons and their professionalism, opened up new paths, especially in opera, and helped establish a true national identity and international recognition for their country's music. Pancho Vladigerov and Veselin Stoyanov responded in particular to the Austro-German tradition: Vladigerov collaborated with Max Reinhard, the stage director at the Deutsche Theater, Berlin; Vladigerov's keen receptivity to Wagner's orchestration and to the music of Strauss can readily be heard in his opera *Tsar Kaloyan* (1936). The latter harks back to the traditions and spectacle of grand Romantic opera, with its elaborate plot, impressive crowd scenes and choruses, majestic processions and ballet episodes. Akin to it in style is Stoyanov's *Salambo* (1940), again displaying the full splendour and lavishness of late Romantic opera.

In the same period there appeared a work which, because of its artistic merits and unique character, was as significant for Bulgaria as Debussy's *Pelléas et Mélisande* was for France: Lyubomir Pipkov's *Yaninite devet bratya* ('Yana's Nine Brothers', 1937). The dramatic nature of this opera (comparable in style to Janáček's *Jenůfa* and Shostakovich's *Lady Macbeth*) is consistent with that of its subject-matter, the Turkish invasion of Bulgaria, and reveals expressionist and symbolist qualities. The emphasis on folk tradition – peasant songs and native verse – finds a parallel in Musorgsky's works.

The development of Bulgarian opera after the 1944 socialist revolution reflected a new social and cultural environment, in that the customary freedom of treatment of the two most frequently encountered genres associated with the Romantic aesthetic – the heroic-historical opera and the comic opera based on everyday life – was now strictly proscribed. Compared with operas of the 1930s, the musical language was much simplified: the works were pervaded by the tunes of mass revolutionary and urbanized peasant songs. The best-known operas from this period are Pipkov's *Momchil* (1948), *Ivaylo* by Marin Goleminov and *Lud Gidiya* ('The Madcap') by Parashkev Hadjiev (both 1959).

The early 1960s witnessed a move away from the inertia of rigid aesthetic norms and formal stereotypes. In contrast to the heroic and epic pseudo-Romantic operas of the 1940s and 50s, composers began to explore the more intimate psychological dimensions of drama, as in Hadjiev's *Maistori* ('The Masters', 1966), *Yula* by Krasimir Kyurkchiski (1969) and Goleminov's *Zakhary Zografat* ('The Icon Painter Zakhary', 1972). The opera genre came to be regarded as a means whereby composers, through the use of self-parody, cinematic and Brechtian alienation techniques, could transcend the human and artistic limitations imposed on them by a totalitarian regime. In Pipkov's *Antigona 43* (1963), the force of the drama is conveyed in the static, oratorio-like choral episodes, the more dynamic orchestral interludes acting as musical commentary. A free interplay of elements of opera, cantata and virtuoso instrumental ensemble music is evident in Lazar Nikolov's *Prikovaniyat Prometey* ('Prometheus Unbound', 1972), whose theme of ethical stoicism becomes a symbol of artistic dissidence under government dictatorship. The idea of distance achieved through irony or the grotesque was the underlying principle governing many works of the next two decades, including Simeon Pironkov's *Dobriyat chovek ot Sechuan* ('The Good Person of Szechuan', 1969) and *Pastrata ptiza* ('The Coloured Bird', 1980), Dimiter Hristov's *Igra* ('A Game', 1977) and *Slatnata ribka* ('The Golden Fish', 1982), and Bozhidar Spasov's *Omag yaosaniyat* ('The Bewitched', 1975).

There are currently ten opera theatres in Bulgaria: in Sofia, Plovdiv, Stara Zagora, Russe, Varna, Bourgas, Pleven, Blagoevgrad, Sliven and Schumen. Their repertory draws mainly on standard Bulgarian and 19th-century Russian and Italian works, with a limited selection of 20th-century operas.

*

I. Kamburov: *Operno iskustvo* [Operatic Art] (Sofia, 1926)
D. Kasakov: *Materiali po istoriyata na narodniya teatar i opera* (Sofia, 1929)
A. Khristov: *Opera i savremennost* [Opera and Modern Times] (Sofia, 1969)
L. Sagayev: *Savremennoto balgarsko operno tvortschestvo* [Contemporary Bulgarian Operas] (Sofia, 1974)
V. Krastev: *Ochertsi po istoriyata na balgarskata musikay* [An Outline History of Bulgarian Music] (Sofia, 1977)

MARIA KOSTAKEVA

Bullant [Bulant], **Antoine** (*b* ? nr Amiens, ?*c*1750; *d* St Petersburg, 13/25 June 1821). French composer. He should not be confused with a phantom Czech musician named Bullandt, evidently the creation of the lexicographer Dlabacz (see *The New Grove Dictionary of Music and Musicians*, 1980) and accepted by Mooser, thence by many other authorities. A bassoonist and instrument dealer, he had several instrumental works published in Paris before going to St Petersburg (by December 1780), where he was engaged as a bassoonist at the court of Catherine II in 1783. His chief claim to fame, and his only stage work for which the music survives, was the enormously successful comic opera *Sbiten'shchik* ('The Hot-Mead Vendor'; score in *RU-SPtob*, excerpts in Ginzburg, Findeyzen and Rabinovich). The three-act libretto was modelled on Molière (*L'école des femmes*), Sedaine (*On ne s'avise jamais de tout*) and Beaumarchais (*Le barbier de Séville*) by Yakov Knyazhnin, who realized 'that all these three works about the escape of a sheltered young ward from the tutelage of her elderly guardian were variations on the same theme' (Karlinsky). Another Russian comic opera in the same tradition was *Skupoy* ('The Miser'), also to a text by Knyazhnin, with music by Pashkevich; Paisiello's *Il barbiere di Siviglia*, produced at Catherine II's court in 1782, was doubtless also in the background.

The title character Stepan (bass), Beaumarchais' Figaro or Molière's Scapin reincarnated, is an outdoor vendor of *sbiten'*, a hot drink consisting of honey and spices dissolved in boiling water. Like Figaro, Stepan helps young Izved (tenor; corresponding to Lindoro) steal from old Voldïryov (bass; Bartolo) his ward Pasha (soprano; Rosina), on whom the guardian had his own designs. First performed at the court theatre in St Petersburg in 1784, *The Hot-Mead Vendor* was remounted in the capital as late as 1851 and was still playing in the provinces long after the middle of the 19th century. It spawned a host of imitations and sequels, of which the most popular was *Svad'ba gospodina Voldïryova* ('Mr Voldïryov's Wedding'), by Kerzelli and Levshin. Numbers from Bullant's opera proliferated in popular songbooks and found their way into oral tradition. The opening aria (quoted complete in Ginzburg) is, by the standards of its day, a naturalistic portrayal of the title character hawking his wares, though he sings it at dawn in an empty street.

Bullant's other works for the stage include a prologue with choruses and ballets to open the festivities in honour of Catherine II's silver jubilee (1787) and at least one other comic opera: *Vinetta, ili Taras v ul'ye* ('Vinetta, or Taras in the Beehive'; 2, K. Damsky; 1799). Half a dozen other attributions to him are regarded by Russian specialists as doubtful.

*

Grove6 (B. Brook, R. Viano)
N. F. Findeyzen: *Ocherki po istorii muzïki v Rossii s drevneyshikh vremyon do kontsa XVIII veka* [Studies in the History of Music in Russia from Ancient Times to the End of the 18th Century], ii (Moscow and Leningrad, 1929)
A. S. Rabinovich: *Russkaya opera do Glinki* [Russian Opera Before Glinka] (Moscow, 1948)
R.-A. Mooser: *Annales de la musique et des musiciens en Russie au XVIIIme siècle*, ii (Geneva, 1951)
A. A. Gozenpud: *Muzïkal'nïy teatr v Rossii ot istokov do Glinki: ocherk* [The Music Theatre in Russia from its Origins to Glinka: a Study] (Leningrad, 1959)
Yu. V. Keldïsh: *Russkaya muzïka XVIII veka* [Russian Music of the 18th Century] (Moscow, 1965)
S. L. Ginzburg: *Istoriya russkoy muzïki v notnïkh obraztsakh* [History of Russian Music in Examples], i (Moscow, 2/1968), 461–8
S. Karlinsky: *Russian Drama from its Beginnings to the Age of Pushkin* (Berkeley and Los Angeles, 1985)
Yu. V. Keldïsh and others: *Istoriya russkoy muzïki v desyati tomakh* [The History of Russian Music in Ten Volumes], iii (Moscow, 1985)

RICHARD TARUSKIN

Buller, John (*b* London, 7 Feb 1927). English composer. He trained as an architectural surveyor before studying with Anthony Milner and taking a BMus at London University in 1964. Among his works are notable settings of James Joyce. His opera *The Bacchae/Bakxai*, commissioned by English National Opera, was first performed on 5 May 1992. Dionysus (tenor), son of Zeus and Semele, returns to his birthplace, Thebes, disguised as a mortal. When Semele's sisters refuse to acknowledge his divinity, he drives them mad and they retreat to Mount Cythera as Bacchae. Pentheus (tenor), King of Thebes, vows to destroy them; but when he disguises himself as a bacchante to watch their rites the women tear him to pieces.

Buller, following Euripides closely, wrote his own libretto in Greek. English is used only in the prologue, in which Dionysus speaks as a god, and by the Shadow of Euripides (spoken), which provides occasional commentary on the action. After the opening monologue, the text is set syllabically, the main characters never singing in ensemble. The impassioned, recitative-like dialogue of the soloists contrasts powerfully with the more formal and predominantly homophonic choruses for nine women's voices. The orchestra plays mainly a supportive role.

HUGO COLE

Bülow, Hans (**Guido**) Freiherr **von** (*b* Dresden, 8 Jan 1830; *d* Cairo, 12 Feb 1894). German conductor. After hearing Wagner conduct in Dresden in 1849 and the première of *Lohengrin* under Liszt at Weimar in 1850, he abandoned the law career chosen for him by his mother. He sought advice from Liszt and practical help from Wagner, now in Zürich, who arranged for him to conduct Donizetti's *La fille du régiment*. Bülow's lack of tact soon led to his dismissal from Zürich, however, and he moved as musical director to the small opera house in St Gall, where he began with *Der Freischütz*. It was well received, not least because he conducted it without the score, a feature of his working method that was to become renowned.

His conducting work was then interrupted by Liszt, who accepted him as a piano pupil. After teaching in Berlin (1855–64) and undertaking concert tours as a pianist, Bülow began an important phase in his career when he was appointed Hofkapellmeister in Munich. Here he gave the premières of *Tristan und Isolde* (1865) and *Die Meistersinger von Nürnberg* (1868). In his meticulous preparation and rehearsal from memory of both operas (for five years he had been preparing a piano score of *Tristan*), Bülow virtually developed the procedure by which operas have since come to be staged in Germany and elsewhere. He began with individual coaching of his répétiteurs so that they in turn could prepare the singers to his satisfaction. He would then rehearse the singers both singly and in ensembles before they began production rehearsals with piano. This schedule of preparation was also used for the orchestra, with sectional and then full orchestral rehearsals before combining players and singers in *Sitzproben* and stage rehearsals (there were 11 pre-dress rehearsals for *Tristan* before the final dress rehearsal).

In 1869 Bülow resigned from Munich, unable to cope when his wife, Liszt's daughter Cosima, left him for Wagner, and when he foresaw the problems of staging the première of *Rheingold* according to demands made by King Ludwig against the composer's wishes. After more concert tours, he spent the years 1878–80 as Hofkapellmeister in Hanover, but resigned after a quarrel with the tenor Anton Schott (whom he had described during *Lohengrin* as a Knight of the Swine rather than of the Swan). Bülow moved on to Meiningen as Hofmusikdirektor, where from 1880 to 1885 he moulded the orchestra into one of Germany's finest, insisting that they play standing up and from memory. His last years were spent touring, teaching or guest conducting at the Berlin or Hamburg opera houses.

Bülow was a musician of formidable ability, with absolute self-command and an acute intellectual power of interpretation, notably of new German works. But he also possessed an irascible nature; he was quarrelsome, nervous, passionate and given to extremes of mood. Weingartner thought he lacked the necessary instinct for working in opera and that by devoting his entire attention to the orchestra he ignored his singers; Bülow's 1887 performance of *Carmen* in Hamburg horrified Weingartner with its musical aberrations and excessive rubato. Yet Richard Strauss, a Bülow protégé, had the highest regard for his intellect, analysis of phrasing and grasp of the psychological content of the music of Beethoven and Wagner. CHRISTOPHER FIFIELD

Bulwer-Lytton, Edward (George Earle Lytton), 1st Baron Lytton (*b* London, 25 May 1803; *d* Torquay, 18 Jan 1873). English writer. The son of General Bulwer and Elizabeth Lytton, he was born into a comfortable family background, but from the age of 22 was obliged to earn his living from writing. Having produced a volume of poetry at the age of 17, he went on to write a vast number of novels, plays, poems and journalistic articles. He also had a distinguished career in politics, entering the House of Commons as a Whig in 1831 but defecting to the Tory Party for whom he served as Colonial Secretary (1858–9) before being made a peer in 1866. On inheriting Knebworth from his mother in 1843 he took the additional name -Lytton, although he was still known as Bulwer and generally published under the name Bulwer Lytton; in 1866 he was created Baron Lytton of Knebworth.

Bulwer's novel *Rienzi, the Last of the Tribunes* (1835; later *Rienzi: the Last of the Roman Tribunes*), the story of the 14th-century Roman who delivers the city from corruption and lawlessness, was the chief source for Wagner's opera (1842). Bulwer's tendentiously idealized view of Rienzi was taken over in part by Wagner, although the opera libretto does show a greater awareness of political ambition and opportunism than the novel. Other settings based on Bulwer-Lytton's work include operas by Giuseppe Apolloni, Yury Arnold, Bantock, Bendl, Cowen, W. H. Fry, Kashperov, Marziano Perosi, Petrella and Rodwell.

*

E. R. B. Lytton, ed.: *The Life, Letters and Literary Remains of Edward Bulwer, Lord Lytton* (London, 1883)

A. Warncke: *Miss Mitfords und Bulwers englische Rienzibearbeitung* (diss., U. of Rostock, 1904)

K. Burdach: *Briefwechsel des Cola di Rienzo* (Berlin, 1913–29)

J. Deathridge: *Wagner's 'Rienzi': a Reappraisal Based on a Study of the Sketches and Drafts* (Oxford, 1977) BARRY MILLINGTON

Bumbry, Grace (Melzia Ann) (*b* St Louis, MO, 4 Jan 1937). American mezzo-soprano and soprano. She studied at Boston and with Lotte Lehmann in Santa Barbara. A joint winner in 1958 of the Metropolitan Opera auditions, she made her début in 1960 at the Paris Opéra as Amneris, then joined Basle Opera for four seasons. In 1961 she sang Venus at Bayreuth, the first black artist to appear there. She made her Covent Garden (1963) and Metropolitan (1965) débuts as Eboli. At Salzburg she sang Lady Macbeth (1964) and Carmen. Her roles included Azucena, Ulrica, Delilah, Fricka, Gluck's Orpheus and Santuzza, which she sang at the Vienna Staatsoper (1966). Taking on soprano roles, she sang Salome, Sélika (*L'Africaine*), Adalgisa and Norma at Covent Garden, while adding Tosca, La Gioconda, Leonora (*Trovatore* and *La forza*) and Gershwin's Bess to her Metropolitan repertory. She sang Jenůfa at La Scala (1974), Dukas' Ariane in Paris (1975) and continued to sing mezzo roles. Her voice, particularly in the middle and lower registers, is warm and voluminous and she has a commanding presence on stage. In 1990 she sang Cassandra (*Prise de Troie*) at the opening of the Bastille Opera in Paris.

*

A. Blyth: 'Grace Bumbry', *Opera*, xxi (1970), 506–10

ALAN BLYTH

Bungert, (Friedrich) August (*b* Mülheim an der Ruhr, 14 March 1845; *d* Leutesdorf, 26 Oct 1915). German composer. After studies at the Cologne Conservatory he went to Paris in 1866, sponsored by the first of several benefactors. The most significant was Queen Elizabeth of Romania, whose friendship and support later ensured his security and might have financed a planned Bayreuth-style theatre at Godesberg to house his *Homerische Welt* cycle; his songs include many settings of poems written by her under the name of Carmen Sylva. He returned to Germany in 1868, subsequently working as music director in Kreuznach, where he conceived and wrote the text for his play *Hutten und Sickingen*. From 1874 he studied with Friedrich Kiel in Berlin, and four years later visited Italy, where he became interested in Greek mythology and Homer. He met Nietzsche in

Genoa in 1883, having begun work on *Die Homerische Welt* (whose completed parts comprise the cycle *Die Odyssee*). Only in 1896 however did *Odysseus' Heimkehr* receive its première in Dresden, achieving some success and inspiring debate about Bungert's status as either a true or an apostate Wagnerian. Dismissed by critical historians such as Louis and Niemann, Bungert was most enthusiastically championed by Max Chop, a founder member of the 'Bungert Bund' and editor of its journal, *Der Bund*, who hailed Bungert as an exemplary idealist in times of decadent and directionless modernism (1915).

Although *Odysseus' Heimkehr*, given 16 times in Berlin in 1898, established Bungert's prominence there during the 1890s, none of the other four operas of the cycle moved far from Dresden. Bungert retired to his Wahnfried-like house in Leutesdorf and was rapidly forgotten, save as the composer of songs favoured by Lilli Lehmann.

See also ODYSSEE, DIE.

librettos by the composer

Die Studenten von Salamanka (Musiklustspiel, 3), Leipzig, Stadt, 1884; rev. as Aurora [Liebe Siegerin]

Die Odyssee (Musik-Tragödie, 4 pts, after Homer) Dresden, Hof
Kirke (prol., 3), 24 Jan 1898
Nausikaa (prol., 3), 20 March 1901
Odysseus' Heimkehr (prol., 3), 12 Dec 1896 (Leipzig, 1896)
Odysseus' Tod (prol., 3), 30 Oct 1903

*

M. Chop: *August Bungert: ein deutscher Dichterkomponist* (Leipzig, 1903)
F. A. Geissler: 'August Bungert', *Die Musik*, vii (1907–8), 259–73
F. Nietzsche: *Briefe an Peter Gast* (Leipzig, 1908)
R. Louis: *Die deutsche Musik der Gegenwart* (Munich and Leipzig, 1909)
W. Niemann: *Die Musik seit Richard Wagner* (Berlin and Leipzig, 1913)
M. Chop: *August Bungert* (Berlin, 1915)
R. Sietz: 'Friedrich August Bungert', *Rheinische Musiker*, ed. K. G. Fellerer, iii, (Cologne, 1964), 14 PETER FRANKLIN

Bunlet, Marcelle (*b* Fontenay-le-Comte, Vendée, 9 Oct 1900; *d* Paris, 13 Dec 1991). French soprano. She made her début in 1928 at the Paris Opéra as Brünnhilde (*Götterdämmerung*) and was then engaged at the Théâtre de la Monnaie, Brussels. At Bayreuth she sang Kundry in *Parsifal* conducted by Toscanini in 1931, but was then offered only minor roles. She sang Arabella in the French-language première of Strauss's opera at Monte Carlo in 1934. Returning to the Opéra (1934–8) she sang Salome, Brünnhilde (*Siegfried* and *Die Walküre*), Isolde, Dukas' Ariane, Valentine (*Les Huguenots*) and Boito's Margherita. She ended her career in Strasbourg, teaching at the conservatory. An intelligent singer with a magnificent dramatic soprano voice, she excelled in Wagner and Strauss. ELIZABETH FORBES

Bunn, Alfred (*b* London, 8 April *c*1797; *d* Boulogne, 20 Dec 1860). English librettist and theatre manager. He became stage manager at Drury Lane in 1823 and manager of the Theatre Royal, Birmingham, in 1826. In 1833 circumstances combined to make him joint manager at Drury Lane and Covent Garden, and from 1835 onwards he attempted to establish English opera, relying heavily on the popularity of Balfe's works. As early as 1816 he had published an anthology of verse. His highly stylized librettos, set mainly by Balfe and Benedict, catered for middle-class tastes in a manner that unintentionally parodied continental Romanticism: 'As in her smile, where beauty play'd,/She bade me place my trust,/A ball from yonder coppice laid/My courser in the dust' (*The Enchantress*). In lyrics such as 'The light of other days' (*Maid of Artois*) and 'When other lips' (*Bohemian Girl*) there is no doubt, however, that Bunn unerringly touched on a vein of plaintive nostalgia which lies at the heart of early Victorian opera.

As a manager Bunn has been accused of 'cheeseparing methods' (Rosenthal) because the artists he engaged (principals, chorus and *corps de ballet*) often found themselves appearing at both his theatres on the same evening. Yet he was a shrewd and energetic businessman who did not stint to pay an artist of Malibran's calibre £125 a night. He made enemies by winning his literary and theatrical battles: he successfully petitioned the House of Lords to throw out Bulwer-Lytton's bill to abolish the patent theatres; when assaulted by Macready after a performance of *Richard III* he was subsequently awarded £150 damages; and when *Punch* lampooned his literary efforts, deriding him as 'the Poet Bunn', he turned the tables on the journal in *A Word with Punch* (London, 1847), ridiculing its staff. Declared bankrupt in 1840, he had extricated himself by 1843, and in 1848 retired from the management of Drury Lane.

The Maid of Artois, Balfe, 1836; *Guillaume Tell*, Bishop, 1838; *The Bohemian Girl*, Balfe, 1843; *The Brides of Venice*, Benedict, 1844; *The Daughter of St Mark* (drama), Balfe, 1844; *The Enchantress*, Balfe, 1845; *The Crusaders*, Benedict, 1846; *Loretta, a Tale of Seville* (drama), L. H. Lavenu, 1846; *The Bondman*, Balfe, 1846; *Matilda of Hungary*, Wallace, 1847; *The Sicilian Bride*, Balfe, 1852; *The Devil's In It*, Balfe, 1852

*

DNB (J. Knight); *LoewenbergA*; *NicollH*
A. Bunn: *The Stage* (London, 1840)
C. Forsyth: *Music and Nationalism* (London, 1911)
E. W. White: *The Rise of English Opera* (London, 1951)
H. D. Rosenthal: *Two Centuries of Opera at Covent Garden* (London, 1958)
M. Hurd: 'Opera: 1834–1865', *Music in Britain: the Romantic Age, 1800–1914*, ed. N. Temperley (London, 1981), 307–29
E. W. White: *A History of English Opera* (London, 1983)
——: *A Register of First Performances of English Operas and Semi-operas* (London, 1983) NIGEL BURTON

Bunnell, Jane (*b* Dover, DE, 19 Dec 1952). American mezzo-soprano. After attending Indiana University, she won the Metropolitan Opera Auditions and made her operatic début as Suzuki in *Madama Butterfly* with Connecticut Grand Opera in 1979. She made her European début at the Spoleto Festival in 1983, and has since sung at the Vienna Volksoper and the Schwetzingen Festival and in Cologne and Toulouse. With the New York City Opera she sang roles including Cherubino, Rosina (*Il barbiere di Siviglia*) and Suzuki, 1985–9; she also performed with other American companies. In 1991 she made her Metropolitan Opera début as Annius in *La clemenza di Tito*, and she has since appeared there as Dorabella in *Così fan tutte* and Thibault in *Don Carlos*. The warmth, suppleness and legato line of her voice, coupled with elegant musicianship and an ingratiating stage presence, promise to make her a leading interpreter of Mozart and the *bel canto* repertory. CORI ELLISON

Buona figliuola, La [*La Cecchina, ossia La buona figliuola* ('Cecchina, or The Accomplish'd Maid')]. *Opera buffa* in three acts by Niccolò Piccinni (*see* PICCINNI family, (1)) to a libretto by CARLO GOLDONI; Rome, Teatro delle Dame, 6 February 1760.

'La buona figliuola': engraving from the 'Opere teatrali' of Carlo Goldoni (Venice: Zatta, 1788–95)

The most immediate source for this libretto is Samuel Richardson's immensely popular novel *Pamela, or Virtue Rewarded* (1740); like Richardson's novel, it also bears some structural similarity to the quasi-folktale of the patient Griselda. It is peripherally related to the increasingly popular genre of the *comédie larmoyante*; operas on this theme are characterized by the sentimental treatment of the heroine and by her minimal interest in the material advantages of marrying into a higher social class. Goldoni adapted Richardson's novel as a play, *Pamela nubile* (1750), and then adapted this as a libretto, *La buona figliuola*, first set by Duni and performed in Parma in 1756. That opera was not a notable success, receiving only about four productions up to 1761. Goldoni's libretto was set again in 1760 by Piccinni, and was first performed to great acclaim by an all-male cast in Rome. *La buona figliuola* took Europe by storm: by 1790 it had received more than 70 different productions, appearing in all the major European cities and often for more than one season. The opera was also given as *La baronessa riconosciuta*, *La Cecchina zitella* and *Cecchina nubile*; it was translated and performed in English as *The Accomplish'd Maid*, in French as *La bonne fille* and in German as *Das gute Mädchen*.

The kernel of the plot resembles that of Richardson's novel: a nobleman, the Marchese della Conchiglia (tenor), loves a young woman far below his station, Cecchina (soprano). His sister, the Marchesa Lucinda (soprano), strenuously objects to the match; in the novel she is simply concerned for her family's reputation, whereas in the opera her lover, the Cavaliere Armidoro (tenor), has said he cannot marry her if her brother stains the family honour by marrying a common garden maid. The opera's remaining characters are not directly derived from the novel: Sandrina and Paoluccia (sopranos) are two spiteful maidservants who envy Cecchina's good fortune in love; Mengotto (bass) is a poor bumpkin who also loves Cecchina to no avail; and Tagliaferro (bass) is a comic German soldier who supplies the piece of information that allows the story to end happily.

The ending of the opera differs significantly from that of the novel. While the point of Richardson's novel is that Pamela's virtue (her refusal to be seduced by Mr B. without benefit of wedlock) is finally rewarded by her elevation in social status, the point of both Goldoni's play and his libretto is that circumstances can sometimes allow natural love to be fulfilled in marriage. In Goldoni's adaptations Cecchina turns out to be the daughter of a German baron (this is the information provided by Tagliaferro), so her union with the marquis disrupts no social norms. Goldoni in fact, in the preface to his play, specifically noted the difficulty of Richardson's denouement: 'The reward of virtue is the aim of the English author; such a purpose would please me greatly, but I would not want the propriety of the family to be sacrificed to the merit of virtue'.

The novelty, variety and sweetness of Piccinni's music for this opera has often been discussed. The two finales (in Acts 1 and 2) are of the 'chain' type, with successive sections vividly illustrating the characters and situations. By Mozartean standards the finales are modest in size and tonal range. Both remain within the tonic, dominant, subdominant and their related minor key areas; with one exception, all sections within finales begin and end in the tonic. Each finale has a long, modulating opening section, held together by a small number of repeated motifs, followed by a series of shorter sections in contrasting tempos and metres; sometimes motifs are repeated in other sections. In addition to allowing considerable continuity and fluidity of action, these finales also achieve vivid and immediate dramatic effects; two examples are the recurring alternation between tonic minor and major as Cecchina pleads unsuccessfully for sympathy at the end of the first finale, and the wonderfully malicious chattering of Sandrina and Paoluccia at the beginning of the second. Cecchina's music is especially lovely, often including active accompaniments which enrich the gestural or affective content of the vocal line. Particularly striking are the nervous second violin demisemiquaver figure that accompanies and illustrates the heroine's halting melody in 'Una povera ragazza' (1.xii) and the soporific triplet accompaniment in her invocation to sleep (2.xiii).

Goldoni's libretto was also set by Salvatore Perillo in 1760 and by Achille Graffigna in 1886; neither of these settings achieved any significant success. A number of other operas in the late 18th century used the archetype of *La buona figliuola*. One of these, *L'incognita perseguitata* (libretto by Petrosellini), was also set by Piccinni (1764, Venice). His music is attractive and economical, but neither as sharply characterized nor as original as that for *La buona figliuola*. Piccinni's setting was only moderately successful and was eclipsed by Anfossi's setting of the same text (1774, Rome). Anfossi's music is more modern than Piccinni's, with more sharply distinguished (but also more conventional) characterizations and longer arias; this opera was extremely popular throughout Europe until the early 1780s.

Another related subject is Francesco Puttini's libretto *La vera costanza*, set by Anfossi (1776) and Haydn (1779). Sacchini's *La contadina in corte* (1766, Rome) also belongs to the same subgenre of *opera buffa*. Paisiello's celebrated opera *Nina, o sia La pazza per amore* owes much to the traditions established by Piccinni in *La buona figliuola* and continued by Anfossi and others. Piccinni himself returned to a grander version of this archetype when he set *Griselda* (1793), a libretto probably by Angelo Anelli, but it achieved only minor success. MARY HUNTER

Buona figliuola maritata, La ('The Accomplish'd Maid Married'). *Opera buffa* in three acts by Niccolò Piccinni (*see* PICCINNI family, (1)) to a libretto by CARLO GOLDONI; Bologna, Teatro dei Formagliari, May 1761.

Piccinni and Goldoni capitalized on the success of *La buona figliuola* by writing a sequel, *La buona figliuola maritata*. Also known as *La baronessa riconosciuta e maritata*, *La buona figliuola puta* and *La buona moglie*, this libretto uses essentially the same cast as the earlier work. Cecchina's name was changed to the Marchesa Marianna (soprano), while Cecchina's beer-swilling and carnivorous German father (bass) makes an appearance. The plot more or less replays the conflicts of the earlier libretto: the Marchesa Lucinda (soprano) and Sandrina (soprano) suspect the authenticity of Cecchina's lineage, and the Cavaliere Armidoro (tenor) supports Cecchina, thus arousing the predictable jealousies of her husband, the Marchese della Conchiglia (tenor). The Marquis couches some of his suspicions of Cecchina as 'tests' of her fidelity in ways that are reminiscent of the Griselda story; and there is a scene in which Cecchina is forced to change out of her finery back into her garden clothes, which recalls not only the Griselda story but also a famous scene in Richardson's novel *Pamela*. Marianna's solo scene of misery in the garden also echoes Cecchina's scene of escape and oblivion in *La buona figliuola*. The music of this opera is generally less inspired than that of *La buona figliuola*; Marianna's music in particular does not sustain the lyric sweetness that so strongly characterizes her role in the earlier opera. Although the sequel had considerable success in its first few years (at least 20 productions between 1761 and 1765), it had less staying power than the original, fading from the repertory in the late 1770s.

MARY HUNTER

Buon soldato Svejk, Il ('The Good Soldier Svejk'). Opera in two acts by GUIDO TURCHI to a libretto by Gerardo Guerrieri after Jaroslav Hasek's novel; Milan, Teatro alla Scala, 5 April 1962.

Turchi began work on the opera in 1953, conceiving it independently of Brecht's *Schweyk im zweiten Weltkrieg* (written in 1943 but not performed in Germany until 1959 and in Italy until 1961). Its 1962 première was conducted by Nino Sanzogno, and Rolando Panerai sang the title role. Turchi and Guerrieri provided their own ending, making Svejk (baritone) volunteer for a risky wartime exploit in which he dies. Turchi was not very interested in the political and social aspects of Svejk's adventures, and in stressing the picaresque side he alternates grotesque caricatural and dramatic touches. Although there are pages of melody in a style reminiscent of Kurt Weill, the vocal line depends heavily on recitation. In addition to the influence of Hindemith and *Wozzeck*, other methods of composition including dodecaphony are used for dramatic purposes; for this reason the opera has been considered a work of intelligent eclecticism.

PAOLO PETAZZI

Buontalenti, Bernardo [Timante, Bernardo delle Girandole] (*b* Florence, 15 Dec 1531; *d* Florence, 6 June 1608). Italian architect, stage designer, engineer and painter. He studied with Vasari and in 1574 succeeded him as director of productions at the Florentine court; the theatre that he built in 1585 in the Uffizi became the centre of all such festivities. For the Medici he designed palaces, villas, fortresses, canals and harbour installations in Florence and Tuscany.

Buontalenti had worked for the court before his appointment as director, designing costumes and special machines for transformation scenes in *intermedi* directed by Vasari in 1565 and Lanci in 1569. He gave the new theatre in the Uffizi an advanced system of *periaktoi* (revolving prisms) that were a great improvement on the clumsy machinery of his predecessors, enabling the scenery to be changed virtually as often as was required. The capabilities of the stage were demonstrated by the productions of the comedies *L'amico fido* (1586) and *La pellegrina* (1589), each accompanied by six *intermedi* and involving respectively six and seven different sets, changed in front of the audience. The purpose of these court festivities was to glorify the prince by ostentation and splendour, and Buontalenti created a form of production that was equal to the task. Visual splendour based on machinery became obligatory in later musico-dramatic enterprises at every court in Europe, especially in opera, the new musical genre that evolved in Florence. The earliest productions at the Florentine court, for which Buontalenti was still at hand to design the sets (e.g. Caccini's *Il rapimento di Cefalo*, 1600), not only took advantage of the mechanics of stage transformation but also retained the cycle of mythological settings (Helicon, the Underworld, pastoral scenery, the sea, etc.) developed in the *intermedi* of 1586 and 1589, which were to set their seal on the visual conventions of opera for decades.

See also STAGE DESIGN, §3(i). For illustration *see* COSTUME, fig.1; ORCHESTRA, fig.1; PRODUCTION, fig.2 and STAGE DESIGN, fig.1.

*

DBI (I. M. Botto); *ES* (P. Turchetti)
B. de'Rossi: *Descrizione del magnificentiss. apparato e de'*

maraviglioso intermedi fatti per la commedia rappresentata in Firenze ... l'anno MDLXXXV (Florence, 1586)
——: *Descrizione dell'apparato, e degl'intermedi, fatti per la commedia rappresentata in Firenze* (Florence, 1589)
M. Buonarroti: *Descrizione delle felicissime nozze della Cristianissima Maestà di Madama Maria Medici Regina di Francia e di Navarra* (Florence, 1600)
A. Warburg: 'I costumi teatrali per gli intermedii del 1589', *Atti dell'Accademia del R. Istituto musicale di Firenze*, xxxiii (Florence, 1895), 103–46
J. Laver: 'Stage Designs for the Florentine Intermezzi of 1589', *Burlington Magazine*, lx (1932), 294–300
J. Jacquot: 'Les fêtes de Florence (1589): quelques aspects de leur mise en scène', *Theatre Research*, iii (1961), 157–76
A. M. Nagler: *Theatre Festivals of the Medici* (New Haven, CT, 1964), 58–100
G. G. Bertelà and A. Petrioli Tofani: *Feste e apparati medicei da Cosimo I a Cosimo II* (Florence, 1969) [illustrated catalogue]
A. R. Blumenthal: *Italian Renaissance Festival Designs* (Madison, WI, 1973) [exhibition catalogue]
M. Fabbri, E. Zorzi and A. M. P. Tofani, eds.: *Il luogo teatrale a Firenze – Brunelleschi, Vasario, Buontalenti, Parigi* (Milan, 1975)
A. Fara: *Buontalenti, architettura e teatro* (Florence, 1979)
A. R. Blumenthal: *Theater Art of the Medici* (Hanover, NH, 1980) [exhibition catalogue]
L. Zorzi: 'La scenotecnica brunelleschiana: problemi filologici e interpretativi', *Filippo Brunelleschi: la sua opera e il suo tempo* (Florence, 1980), 161–71
E. Povoledo: 'Origins and Aspects of Italian Scenography', in N. Pirotta and E. Povoledo: *Music and Theatre from Poliziano to Monteverdi* (Cambridge, 1982), 281–383
A. Fara: *Bernardo Buontalenti* (Genova, 1988)

MANFRED BOETZKES

Buranello, Il. *See* GALUPPI, BALDASSARE.

Burchell, Isabella. *See* VINCENT, ISABELLA.

Burchinal, Frederick (*b* Wichita, KS, 7 Dec 1948). American baritone. He studied with H. John Lennon at Emporia State University, Daniel Ferro at the Juilliard School, and privately with Joshua Hecht. He was a member of the Metropolitan Opera Studio. His repertory centres on the dramatic Verdi and *verismo* roles, although he has also sung Enrico (*Lucia*), Rossini's Figaro, Nick Shadow, Horace Tabor (*The Ballad of Baby Doe*) and Valentin. Since his 1976 European début in Amsterdam in Floyd's *Of Mice and Men*, he has appeared in Berlin, Cologne, Düsseldorf, Frankfurt, London and Zürich. He has also performed with leading American companies, including New York City Opera and San Francisco Opera. In 1979 Burchinal sang Scrooge in the première of Musgrave's *A Christmas Carol* at Virginia Opera and also appeared on Broadway as Tony in Loesser's *The Most Happy Fella.* He made his Metropolitan Opera début in 1988 as Macbeth and has also sung Rigoletto there.

CORI ELLISON

Burchuladze, Paata (*b* Tbilisi, 12 Feb 1951). Georgian bass. He studied in Tbilisi and Milan, making his début in 1976 at Tbilisi, where he sang Leporello, Gounod's Méphistophélès, Prince Gremin and René (*Iolanta*). He made his Covent Garden début in 1984 as Ramfis, returning as Don Basilio (1987), Khan Konchak (1990) and Boris (1991). At La Scala he sang Banquo, Pagano (*I Lombardi*), Count Walter (*Luisa Miller*) and Zaccaria (*Nabucco*). He has appeared in Moscow, Paris, Munich, Vienna and Salzburg. He made his American début at Philadelphia as Boris (1987) and sang Don Basilio at the Metropolitan (1989). His roles include Don Ruy Gomez (*Ernani*), Fiesco (*Simon Boccanegra*), Boito's Mefistofele and Dosifey (*Khovanshchina*). His magnificent dark-toned voice and imposing stature make him an ideal Boris or Konchak.

ELIZABETH FORBES

Bürde, Samuel Gottlieb (*b* Breslau, 7 Dec 1753; *d* Berlin, 28 April 1831). German writer. After studies at Halle he worked as a teacher and private secretary. His literary endeavours, warmly supported by Wieland, included poetry, plays, librettos and copious translations from the French and English. *Don Sylvio von Rosalva*, his first and most popular opera text, is based on Wieland's fashionable novel *Der Sieg der Natur über die Schwärmerei* (1764).

Don Sylvio von Rosalva (komische Oper), O. C. F. Phanty, 1796 (Sander, 1797; G. Bachman, 1797; K. W. Müller, 1799); *Die Regata zu Venedig*, Sander, 1796 (J. B. Fliess, 1798); *Rübezahl*, V. Tuček, 1801; *Der Nachtwächter* (Spl), Ebell, 1808; *Der Taucher* (grosse Oper), Reichardt, 1811 (C. Kreutzer, 1813); *Die Gemsenjäger* (Operette), Bierey, 1811

THOMAS BAUMAN

Bürde-Ney, Jenny. *See* NEY, JENNY.

Burg [Bartl], **Robert** (*b* Prague, 29 March 1890; *d* Dresden, 9 Feb 1946). Czech baritone. He studied in Prague, where he made his début in 1915. After a season at Augsburg, he joined the company at Dresden and remained there from 1916 to the time of his death. He took the title role in two important premières: Busoni's *Doktor Faust* (1925) and Hindemith's *Cardillac* (1926). He was also involved in the 'Verdi renaissance' of those years, under Fritz Busch, singing such roles as Count di Luna in *Il trovatore*, Renato in *Un ballo in maschera* and Amonasro in *Aida*. At Bayreuth he appeared first in 1933, singing Kothner in *Die Meistersinger* and Klingsor in *Parsifal* and gaining highest praise for his Alberich. A guest artist in many other German cities, he also made some appearances in Austria, Hungary and Switzerland. Whatever his best qualities, they are not well represented on records, where the voice sounds ungainly and the style often faulty: his acting ability and carrying power created a more favourable impression in the theatre.

J. B. STEANE

Burgas. The second largest city in Bulgaria, on the Black Sea coast. The first evidence of opera performances in the city dates from 1901. In 1954 a permanent opera company, Burgaska Samodeyna Opera (Burgas Amateur Opera), was formed, consisting predominantly of instrumentalists from the State Symphony Orchestra and singers from the Naroden Khor (Folk Choir) and the Rodna Pesen (Homeland Song) choir. Its first production, *La traviata*, in 1955 was followed mainly by Italian operas and operas by Mozart and by Bulgarian composers. The Burgas Amateur Opera became the State (National) Opera on 2 March 1972 when it opened with Krasimir Kyurkchiiski's *Yula*. Its notable conductors have included Nevin Mikhalev, Ivan Vulpe, Stojan Kralev and Romeo Raichev, and it has engaged Dragan Kardjiev and Nikolaji Nikolov (as guest directors) and the baritone Stojan Popov. The opera's repertory is influenced by the summer resort character of the city and by the opportunities offered by the open-air stage at the Sunny Beach resort. Until the early 1980s the opera performed in the 670-seat hall of the Culture Club of a petrochemical plant; since 1983 a new building, the Burgas Opera House (800 seats), intended for drama, opera and ballet, has been used for two or three opera performances a week.

R. Biks: *Balgarski operen teatar* (Sofia, 1985), ii
MAGDALENA MANOLOVA

Bürger von Calais, Die ('The Burghers of Calais'). Opera in three acts by RUDOLF WAGNER-RÉGENY to a libretto by CASPAR NEHER after Jean Froissart's *Chronicles*; Berlin, Deutsche Staatsoper, 28 January 1939.

It is 1347 and Calais has been under siege for months. The people defend it bravely, but the governor Johann von Wien (bass) decides to surrender. His wife Cornelia (soprano) asks the Queen of England (soprano) to show mercy to Calais. She receives a sympathetic but vague response. It turns out that the condition for sparing the city is that it must surrender six victims. The six burghers willing to sacrifice themselves are pardoned, and there is a final reconciliation.

Die Bürger von Calais was a success, although it incurred some suspicion of pandering to dictatorship, and the subject ran counter to the kind of art officially approved in the Third Reich. After its Berlin première it was performed in Breslau, Darmstadt and Stuttgart, and there were 20 productions in East Germany between 1959 and 1989. Stylistically it mixes the epic music theatre of Brecht and Weill with the 'sweetness' of the Italian Bellini-Verdi tradition; Wagner-Régeny himself thought it the best of his operas. TILO MEDEK

Burgess, Anthony (*b* Manchester, 25 Feb 1917). English composer and translator. He is best known as a writer, but has remained close to the musical stage throughout his career, writing incidental music for plays and being in demand for the translation of opera and oratorio librettos. His translation of *Carmen* has been performed by the ENO, and in 1972 his translation of *Oedipus Rex* was set as a dramatic cantata by Stanley Silverman. In 1985 Burgess was commissioned by Scottish Opera to rescue Weber's *Oberon* (1826) from J. R. Planché's stilted text; his version sets the story in the contemporary Middle East, with hijackers and hostages. For the James Joyce centenary in 1982 Burgess composed a musical version of *Ulysses* entitled *The Blooms of Dublin*, broadcast by BBC radio: it incurred the displeasure of critics who, according to Burgess, 'expected opera, not a Broadway musical'. He has reworked his controversial novel *A Clockwork Orange* into 'a play with music' (1987), and his translation of Edmond Rostand's play *Cyrano de Bergerac* evolved into a Broadway musical (1972). At the end of his autobiography, *You've had your Time* (London, 1990), Burgess describes work in progress on an opera about Sigmund Freud. ANTHONY PARR

Burgess, Sally (*b* Durban, 9 Oct 1953). English mezzo-soprano. She studied in London at the RCM, where she sang Adriana Lecouvreur in 1977. The same year she joined the ENO as a soprano, singing Pamina, Martinů's Julietta, Jenny (Bennett's *The Mines of Sulphur*) and Mimì. Becoming a mezzo-soprano in 1981, she sang Charlotte, Octavian, the Composer, Nicklausse, Orlofsky, Sextus (*Giulio Cesare*), Carmen, Nefertiti in the British première of *Akhnaten* (1985), Laura in the British première of *The Stone Guest* (1987), Pauline (*The Gambler*) and Judith (*Bluebeard's Castle*, 1991). In 1983 she sang Siébel (*Faust*) at Covent Garden and Smeraldina (*Love for Three Oranges*) at Glyndebourne. For Opera North she has sung Amneris, Dido (*Les Troyens*) and Carmen, dramatic roles which suit her temperament and vibrant voice particularly well; for Scottish Opera she has sung Fricka (1991).

E. Forbes: 'Sally Burgess', *Opera*, xlii (1991), 16–21
ELIZABETH FORBES

Burghauser, Jarmil (*b* Písek, 21 Oct 1921). Czech composer and musicologist. He studied at the Prague Conservatory, where his teachers included Křička (1933–7), Jeremiáš (1937–40) and Talich (1940–46), and at the University of Prague (1945–8). He held various appointments, including Dramaturg for chamber opera (1943–4) and choirmaster and conductor (1946–53) at the Prague National Theatre. From 1953 he worked as a freelance. He served as adviser for a film on Smetana and a cinematic version of *Dalibor*, and is on the editorial boards of the complete editions of Dvořák, Fibich and Janáček.

The stimulus for Burghauser's extensive creative work (which includes orchestral and chamber music, songs and many film scores) came first from the music of Dvořák and Novák, and at the same time he made considerable use of stylized Czech folk music. He moved towards neo-classicism in the opera *Lakomec* ('The Miser', 1950), with its expressive dramatic flow and melodious arias and ensembles, and later in *Karolinka a lhář* ('Caroline and the Liar', 1955) which, in closed musical numbers, tells the story of a frivolous young man who finds the meaning of life in true love. At the beginning of the 1960s Burghauser began to seek an original expression within the post-Webernian mainstream. His principal interests include serialism, aleatory music and unconventional colour combinations, all features which he gradually synthesized in his work. His 'anti-opera' *Most* ('The Bridge', 1967) combines aleatory and serial procedures in two separate sequences of events which are chronologically remote from each other: it explores both the fate of Czech emigrants in the wake of the Battle of the White Mountain, and the plight of those who left the country after the communist coup of February 1948.

Lakomec [The Miser] (3, L. Mandaus, after Molière), Liberec, North Bohemian, 20 May 1950
Karolinka a Lhář [Caroline and the Liar] (lyrical comedy, 3, Mandaus, after C. Goldoni), Olomouc, Great, 13 March 1955
Most [The Bridge] (anti-opera, 2, J. Pávek), Prague, National, 31 March 1967 OLDŘICH PUKL, HELENA HAVLÍKOVÁ

Burghersh, Lord [later 11th Earl of Westmorland; Fane, John] (*b* London, 3 Feb 1784; *d* Wansford, Northants., 16 Oct 1859). English amateur musician. He was educated at Harrow and at Trinity College, Cambridge (MA 1808), where he studied music under Professor Hague. His career was political, military and diplomatic. He was MP for Lyme Regis (1806–16), served in the Napoleonic wars and held diplomatic posts in Florence, Berlin and Vienna. He received many British and foreign decorations and distinctions, and succeeded to the earldom in 1841.

Burghersh devoted most of his leisure hours to music: wherever his career took him, he brought together local professional musicians and profited from their instruction and entertainment. He was a good violinist and a prolific composer: this fact helped to improve the standing of the profession in England. But (like many aristocrats) he regarded Italy as the only source of good music. His compositions, including seven full-length operas, are in the older Italian style and show no trace of individuality. It is their existence, rather than their quality, that is remarkable.

His most important achievement was the foundation of the Royal Academy of Music in 1822. As president for 37 years he took far more interest in its administration than was expected of a gentleman amateur. His rule was autocratic and he kept control of the RAM concerts, insisting on programmes of Italian operatic music and allowing no English compositions but his own.

first performed at Burghersh's residence in Florence

Bajazette, 1821, *GB-Lbl*, (Berlin, *c*1845)

Fedra (os), 17 Nov 1824, vs (Berlin, 1848)

Il torneo (os), carn. 1829; London, St James's, 18 July 1835, *Lbl*, vs (London, 1839)

L'eroe di Lancastro (dramma serio, 2. G. Rossi), 13 June 1829, *Lbl*, vs (Berlin, *c*1845)

Lo scompilio teatrale (melodramma giocoso), carn. 1830, *Lbl*, vs (Berlin, 1849)

L'assedio di Belgrado (3), 15 April 1830; as Catherine, or The Austrian Captive (after Cobb: *The Siege of Belgrade*), London, RAM, Oct 1830, *Lbl*, vs (London, 1830)

Il ratto di Proserpina, unperf., *Lbl*, vs (Berlin, 1846)

*

Review of *Catherine*, *Harmonicon*, viii (1830), 525–6

NICHOLAS TEMPERLEY

Burgoyne, John (*b* London, 4 Feb 1723; *d* London, 4 Aug 1792). English dramatist. 'Gentleman Johnny' Burgoyne, the English general forced to surrender to the Americans at Saratoga (1777), was the librettist of William Jackson's only successful opera, *The Lord of the Manor* (1780), in the preface to which he advocated English 'musical comedy'. Garrick's staging of his first dramatic piece, *The Maid of the Oaks* (1774, with music by François Barthélemon), had spectacular scenery by Loutherbourg and was very popular; 12 years later Burgoyne's translation of Sedaine's libretto, *Richard Coeur-de-lion*, with music arranged by Thomas Linley (i), proved a great success at Drury Lane.

*

J. Burgoyne: *The Dramatic and Poetical Works* (London, 1808)

G. B. Shaw: *The Devil's Disciple* (in *Three Plays for Puritans*) (London, 1901)

J. Lunt: *John Burgoyne of Saratoga* (London, 1976)

OLIVE BALDWIN, THELMA WILSON

Bürgschaft, Die ('The Pledge'). Opera in three acts by KURT WEILL to a libretto by CASPAR NEHER after Johann Gottfried Herder's tale *Der afrikanische Rechtspruch*; Berlin, Städtische Oper, 10 March 1932.

In the mythical land of Urb, a cattle dealer, Johann Mattes (high baritone), having lost all his money through gambling, is being pursued by creditors. His wife Anna (mezzo-soprano) persuades him to seek help from a grain dealer, David Orth (bass), who lives across the lake. 'He [her husband] has always been like that since I've known him', she muses, 'and will never change.' The chorus intones a chorale-like passage, reiterated throughout the opera: 'It's not man that changes merely, it's social relations that change his attitude.' Orth is prepared to make a pledge on behalf of his 'best customer'. The creditors, about to dispossess Mattes, accept. The chorus concludes the narration: Mattes repays his debts.

Six years later, Mattes buys two sacks of grain from Orth. Orth's son Jakob (tenor) subsequently points out that the sacks were in fact a hiding-place for his father's savings. Orth is sanguine: Mattes will return the money. Mattes is mugged by three Highwaymen (basses) on his way home, but they take only his purse. Mattes decides that Orth does not know about the contents of the sacks either. Three Blackmailers (baritones) discover the secret and threaten to reveal it to Orth. Mattes races them across the lake and confesses to Orth, whose reaction is surprising. Although he considers Mattes's confession 'too late', he also questions his own right to the money: the judge in the city shall decide.

The Judge (tenor) decrees that the money belongs neither to Mattes nor to Orth: it shall be set aside for the former's son and the latter's daughter when they are older. An announcement is made that the Great Power, which has seized control of Urb, is to send its Commissar (tenor). Henceforth a new law is to prevail, the law of money and power. The Commissar, eager to assert his authority as a 'warning and a sign of discipline', forces the Blackmailers, under threat of execution, into assisting him, then retries Mattes and Orth. Declaring both parties criminals, he will release them only if they, like all civil servants, actively support the regime. Meanwhile Anna bemoans the temporary loss of her husband and of her daughter Luise (soprano), who has left for the big city.

A further six years elapse. As the chorus reports, times have changed; man has not. Under the new rule, the rich have become richer, the poor poorer. As if in a pageant, the inhabitants of Urb have to pass through four gates: War, Inflation, Hunger and Disease. But thanks to the war, Mattes and Orth have come into money. Although Anna wishes to leave, Mattes, seized by greed, wishes to stay. The aftermath of the war brings inflation, followed by hunger. Mattes and Orth exploit these for their own gain, but Anna falls victim to disease. As she is dying, Luise can be seen in a dance hall in the city, pursued by suitors. The people of Urb rise up in anger against Mattes who, contrary to his expectation, fails to receive support from the Commissar, or from Orth, who is no longer willing to help his friend. Instead they fight, and Orth leaves Mattes, blinded by blood, to be finished off by the crowd. Orth reiterates the maxim: 'Everything happens according to a law, the law of money, the law of power.'

After increasing alienation from Brecht during work on *Aufstieg und Fall der Stadt Mahagonny*, Weill turned to Caspar Neher, his stage designer on a number of previous productions, for his next libretto. *Die Bürgschaft* (composed August to October 1931) represents the summation of Weill's career as an opera composer in Europe. It is his most ambitious work for the operatic stage – and his most sombre. Parallels to the political climate of the time are unmistakable. Yet *Die Bürgschaft* is no mere 'Zeitoper'. It bears every sign of having been built to endure. The work's dramatic centre is the double chorus, which delivers its terse commentary in the bare, lapidary style already used in *DER JASAGER*. On the surface a number opera with occasional spoken dialogue, *Die Bürgschaft* is organized into expanded structural units such as are found in late Verdi. Its neoclassical style largely eschews the irony of *Mahagonny*, except for a number of passages which equate dance idioms with corruption. As 'epic theatre' it is more consistently radical than any of Weill's collaborations with Brecht. Taking its cue from the Herder parable, which promotes a pre-industrial, almost pre-lapsarian ideal of humanity, the piece owes an obvious debt to Stravinsky's *Oedipus rex* in its unemotional objectivity, as also to Handelian oratorio. Neher's libretto, his first, is not without flaws, of which the composer was no doubt aware when he contemplated post-première

'Die Bürgschaft' (Weill): scene from Carl Ebert's revival at the Städtische Oper, Berlin, 1957, with the double chorus seated at the sides of the stage

revisions of the second act. Weill is also reported to have expressed concern about the bleakness of the ending. Otherwise sympathetically disposed, the drama critic Bernhard Diebold objected to the unswerving, rather naive didacticism of the reiterated motto, which presents man as the puppet of epic forces rather than as an active agent in the drama of life. This certainly detracts from the work's effectiveness on stage as conventional opera, while adding to its impact as a powerful statement on the tragedy of modern civilization. As Weill wrote in response to a review of the première, 'the job of opera today consists in reaching out beyond the fate of private individuals towards universality'. It was through universals that he sought to reflect the topical. Indeed the topicality of the piece was felt to be such that its original producer, Carl Ebert, made a number of revisions for the only staged revival, given in Berlin in 1957 (see illustration). STEPHEN HINTON

Burgstaller, Alois (*b* Holzkirchen, Upper Bavaria, 27 Sept 1871; *d* Gmund, 19 April 1945). German tenor. He studied in Frankfurt and with Kniese at Bayreuth, where he made his début in 1894, singing the First Knight of the Grail (*Parsifal*) and Heinrich der Schreiber (*Tannhäuser*). The same year he sang Siegfried at Nuremberg and in 1896 he sang Froh and Siegfried at Bayreuth, adding Siegmund, Erik and Parsifal over the next few years. In 1903 he made his New York début at the Metropolitan as Siegfried and then earned the displeasure of the Wagner family by singing Parsifal there. In 1906 he appeared at Covent Garden, as Tristan and Erik. Two years later he made up his quarrel with the Bayreuth Festspielhaus and returned there to sing Siegfried. He retired prematurely, his voice exhausted from singing such heavy roles too early in his career.

ELIZABETH FORBES

Burgtheater. Theatre in Vienna. Originally a tennis court, it was refurbished as a theatre in 1741 and used for opera for the next 70 years. It was one of the bases of the Hofoper until 1810. *See* VIENNA, §§2, 3 and 4(i).

Burian, Emil František (*b* Plzeň, 11 April 1904; *d* Prague, 9 Aug 1959). Czech composer and director. His father and his uncle (Carl Burran) were outstanding singers, and his mother taught singing. He studied at the Prague Conservatory, graduating from Foerster's composition masterclasses in 1927. Before completing his studies he was active in the Prague avant-garde theatre as director, dramatist, actor and musician. From 1920 he organized with his mother concerts of new works, and in 1924 founded a society of contemporary music. He was employed as a director in Brno and Olomouc from 1929 to 1932. Back in Prague he worked as a jazz band leader, vocalist, composer and director, and in 1933 established his own theatre, D 34, where he was able to concentrate his musical and dramatic efforts. He worked again as a director in Brno (1945–6) and at the musical theatre Karlín in Prague (1946). He also became active politically.

Despite the variety of Burian's interests, composition remained the foundation of his creative work. He began to write in a Straussian style, shown in his first operas *Alladine a Palomid*, composed in 1923, and *Před slunce východem* ('Before Sunrise') in 1924, but he was soon influenced by jazz, Les Six and dadaism. The ballet *Fagot a flétna* ('The Bassoon and the Flute', 1925) and the parody opera buffa *Mastičkář* ('The Quack'), written in 1925, document this new orientation. At about the same time he became interested in folk music. This interest developed, and his enthusiastic use of fair songs, urban music and national songs culminated in the folk play with songs and dances *Vojna* ('The War', 1935), influenced by Janáček and, in particular, by Stravinsky's *The Wedding*. An important aspect of Burian's activity was his work for the Voice Band, a choral group (founded by him in 1927) whose material stressed speech sounds, with onomatopoeic effects and non-verbal vocal utterances.

A major work is the opera *Maryša* (1939), for which Burian was composer, dramatist and director. Continuing Janáček's melodic style, the vocal parts often take a middle position between singing and excited speech. The naturalist approach is furthered in the stark harmony, the violent interjections and the generally expressive quality of the orchestral writing, but the promise of the work was never fully developed. After World War II Burian adopted the precepts of socialist realism, composing political and work songs and a few orchestral pieces. His best work had been completed in the inter-war period, when he was a leader of the Czech avant garde. Although he lacked strong individuality, he knew how to weave the techniques of others into clever, grotesque or amusing music. His writings include biographies of his father (1947) and his uncle (1948), and *Pražská dramaturgie* (1938) and *Divadlo za našich dnů* ('The Theatre of our Days', 1962).

Alladine a Palomid, 1923 (after M. Maeterlinck); rev. and completed version, Prague, 14 Oct 1959
Před slunce východem [Before Sunrise] (1, B. Bělohlávek), Prague, 24 Nov 1925
Bubu z Montparnassu [Bubu from Montparnasse], 1927 (jazz lyric op, after C.-L. Philippe)
Mastičkář [The Quack] (parody ob, V. Lacina and J. Trojan), Prague, 23 May 1928; rev. with new lib. by R. Krátký, 1955
Milenci z kiosku [The Lovers from the Market Stall] (vaudeville, after V. Nezval), Prague, 13 Nov 1935
Maryša op.81 (5 scenes, Burian, after A. and V. Mrštík), Brno, Provincial, 16 April 1940 (Prague, 1964)
Opera z pouti [Country Fair Scenes], Prague, 28 Jan 1956
Račte odpusdit [Please Forgive me] (Krátký), 13 Oct 1956

*

J. Volek: 'Na okraj Burianovy Maryši' [On the Margin of Burian's *Maryša*], *Rytmus*, x (1945–6), no.8, pp.13–15
K. Bundálek: 'Působení J. Honzla a E. F. Buriana v brněnském divadle na počátku třicátých let' [Honzl and Burian's Work in the Brno Theatre at the Beginning of the 1930s], *Sborník Janáčkovy akademie múzických umění*, ii (1960), 77–104
B. Karásek: 'Velké dílo moderní české opery' [A Great Work of Modern Czech Opera], *HRo*, xiii (1960), 622, 672–6
——: 'Emil František Burian – skladetel' [Emil František Burian – Composer], *HV*, v (1968), 522–47
J. Bajer: 'Vztah vyjadřovacích prostředků hudby, poezie a divadla v Burianově tvorbě dvacátých a třicátých let' [The Relationship of the Expressive Means of Music, Poetry and Theatre on Burian's Works of the 1920s and 1930s], *HV*, viii (1971), 287–97 [with Eng. summary]
B. Srba: *Poetické divadlo E. F. Buriana* [The Poetic Theatre of E. F. Burian] (Prague, 1971)
J. Kladiva: *E. F. Burian* (Prague, 1982)
L. Šíp: *Česka opera e její tvůrci* [Czech Opera and its Creators] (Prague, 1983), 229–34

JOSEF BEK

Burke, Edmund (Arbrickle) (*b* Toronto, 12 July 1876; *d* Pasadena, CA, 19 Feb 1970). Canadian bass. He studied at the RCM and in Paris with Duvernoy, and made his début at Montpellier in 1905 as Cardinal Brogni in *La Juive*. After appearances in Nice and The Hague he was engaged in 1910 for Covent Garden, where he appeared between 1911 and 1920 in roles including Nilakantha (*Lakmé*), Méphistophélès and Pogner. He sang for one season at the Metropolitan Opera, 1922–3, making his début as the King in *Aida*. HAROLD ROSENTHAL/R

Burke, Thomas [Tom] **(Aspinall)** (*b* Leigh, Lancs., 2 March 1890; *d* Sutton, Surrey, 13 Sept 1969). English tenor. He studied at the Manchester College of Music and the RAM, and in Italy with Ernesto Colli and De Lucia. He made his début at the Teatro Dal Verme, Milan, in 1917 as the Duke in *Rigoletto*. He first sang at Covent Garden in 1919 as Rodolfo, returning in 1920 as Rinuccio and Luigi in the English premières of *Gianni Schicchi* and *Il tabarro*. Puccini said of him: 'I have never heard my music sung so beautifully'. He returned to Covent Garden in 1927 and 1928, when he sang Turiddu.

S. Winstanley: 'Thomas Burke', *78 rpm* (1969), no.8, pp.31–4 [with discography]

HAROLD ROSENTHAL/R

Burkhard, Willy (*b* Evilard, nr Biel, 17 April 1900; *d* Zürich, 18 June 1955). Swiss composer. He studied in Berne, Leipzig, Munich and Paris; from 1924 he taught at the Berne Conservatory. He became internationally known for his oratorio *Das Gesicht Jesajas* (1933–5) and his Fantasy for string orchestra (1934). Burkhard's early style followed the Renaissance masters (including Ockeghem, Dufay and Josquin) and Bach; he was influenced by Bartók, Hindemith and Stravinsky. He later turned to the 12-note technique. His harmony is based on modal structures; his style, at first strongly contrapuntal, became more relaxed only in his mature works. From the 1940s Burkhard was regarded as one of the outstanding Swiss composers of his generation. He composed mainly choral and church music; his two-act opera, *Die schwarze Spinne* op.80, was commissioned by the Fondation Pro Helvetia and was first performed in Zürich in 1949. The libretto, by Robert Faesi and Georgette Boner, is based on a story by Jeremias Gotthelf, widely read in Switzerland, about a pact with the devil. The use of a background story (mainly in spoken dialogue), with a storyteller conveying the course of the action, brings the work close to such dramatic oratorios as those of Honegger and Frank Martin. Burkhard's lively choruses in particular are the strength of this work; the solo voices take a less prominent part. As contemporary critics wrote, this is a 'borderline case of music drama'. Burkhard revised the work in 1954.

*

E. Mohr: 'Betrachtungen zum Stil Willy Burkhards', *SMz*, lxxxvii (1947), 1–8
W. Burkhard: 'Zu meiner Oper *Die schwarze Spinne*', *SMz*, lxxxix (1949), 187–90; also in *Musica*, iii (1949), 126–8
E. Mohr: *Willy Burkhard: Leben und Werk* (Zürich, 1957)
K. Gudewill: 'Das Lebenswerk Willy Burkhards', *Sagittarius*, i (1966), 66–77

WULF KONOLD

Burlesque (Fr.; It. *burlesca*; Ger. *Burleske*). A humorous piece involving parody and grotesque exaggeration; in particular, a genre of light theatrical entertainment with music, common on the English stage especially in the 19th century. It involved the treatment of a familiar and usually serious subject in which the general spirit of the model was retained but distorted for comic effect, reducing historical, legendary or classical character and situation to the level of commonplace modern life.

Burlesque was related to and in part derived from the PANTOMIME and may be considered an extension of the introductory section of pantomime with the addition of gags and 'turns' such as traditionally accompanied a transformation scene. But whereas pantomime most often took its subject matter from stories familiar to children – fairy-tale (e.g. Jack and the Beanstalk, Cinderella), nursery rhyme (Jack and Jill, Cock Robin), folk story (Dick Whittington), familiar fiction (*Robinson Crusoe*) or exotic tales (Ali Baba, *The Thousand and One Nights*) – burlesque tended to employ more elevated and serious models: mythology (e.g. Dido and Aeneas, Pygmalion, Orpheus and Eurydice), classical or historical legend (Medea, Ivanhoe), literature (*Don Quixote*, *Hudibras*), Shakespearean drama and history (Guy Fawkes, Lucrezia Borgia). Among the objects of ridicule were the conventions of serious theatre and melodrama. Burlesques followed the appearance of virtually every major opera, as for example J. Halford's *Faust and Marguerite* (1853) after Gounod's *Faust*.

Like the pantomime, burlesque became a largely seasonal entertainment, appearing in legitimate theatres at Christmas and Easter in place of more serious bills. Occasionally a burlesque appeared as a companion piece to other works. Whereas pantomime entertained all classes and all ages, the burlesque and extravaganza tended to appeal to a relatively educated and sophisticated audience. In both genres dialogue was cast in rhymed couplets of iambic pentameter verse (less often in blank verse). Music was an essential if often a minor feature, consisting chiefly of arrangements of songs and incidental music to underscore the action or for comic effect. In operatic burlesques, numbers were appropriated from the model, with new words and often with humorous touches; additional numbers were interpolated from a variety of familiar sources (such as music hall and minstrel songs). Rarely was there any attempt at musical parody.

The heyday of burlesque began with Lucia Elizabeth Vestris's production of *Olympic Revels, or Prometheus and Pandora* by JAMES ROBINSON PLANCHÉ (Olympic Theatre, 1831), written with Charles Dance with music by John Barnett. Planché virtually invented this style of burlesque and for a generation he dominated the genre. A master of refined, delicate effect, he deplored the absurdity, inconsistency and broader physical and verbal foolery found in the works of later and lesser dramatists, among whom the most important were Henry J. Byron, Robert and William Brough, F. C. Burnand and Robert Reece. The appearance of W. S. Gilbert (1836–1911) signalled the last important phase of burlesque. His first dramatic work, *Dulcamara, or The Little Duck and the Great Quack* (St James's Theatre, 1866) was a successful burlesque on Donizetti's *L'elisir d'amore*. Gilbert's five operatic burlesques (all announced as extravaganzas) led to the evolution of the genre into the more sophisticated Savoy-style comic opera, characterized by original stories, absurdity regulated by internal consistency, satire in place of parody, the absence of travesty and clowning, close directorial supervision and highly developed musical scores.

Although the works of such as Planché and Gilbert had literary merit, with sophisticated word-play and current and historical allusions, works of lesser providers, however successful on the stage, seldom seem satisfactory on the printed page. Their success may be explained by their eccentric and often lavish staging, with interpolated physical humour and sometimes extraneous displays of skill and spectacle, as distinct from their broad and sometimes forced verbal humour, with an emphasis on punning and often inept verse. Although an almost indispensable element of burlesque was the display of attractive women dressed in tights, often in travesty roles, the plays themselves did not normally tend to indecency.

A special, highly developed species of burlesque was the EXTRAVAGANZA. The various genre terms were always applied freely, however, often in combination with such other equivocal terms as BURLETTA; by the 1860s their use had become arbitrary and capricious.

In the USA, burlesque followed the English form until the 1860s. From the late 1830s William Mitchell presented burlesques of operas and romantic plays at the Olympic Theatre, New York, and the English immigrant John Brougham wrote and acted in numerous burlesques from 1842 to 1879. Brougham's *Po-ca-hon-tas* (1855, after Longfellow's narrative poem) is peopled with 'Salvages', its dialogue is a string of *doubles entendres* and its songs were selected from such popular tunes as 'Widow Machree' and 'Rosin the Bow' and Tyrolean melodies. Several minstrel troupes presented such satires; in the 1860s the Kelly & Leon Negro Minstrels performed burlesques of Offenbach (*La Belle L. N.*, *Grand Dutch S.*) throughout the north-eastern states, and Sanford's Minstrel Burlesque Opera Troupe advertised a 'change of programme every night'. From about 1860 burlesque often provided the framework for elaborate spectacles, beginning with those produced in New York by Laura Keene, who employed ballet troupes of women whose costumes exposed their legs; nearly all New York theatres presented shows that relied less for their effect on dramatic elements, wit or satire than on female beauty, and the term gradually shifted in meaning from the ridicule of stage conventions to an emphasis on women in various degrees of undress, with striptease elements prominent by the 1920s. The burlesque was banned in New York in 1937.

T. F. Dillon Croker and S. Tucker, eds.: *The Extravaganzas of J. R. Planché, Esq. (Somerset Herald, 1827–1871)* (London, 1879)
W. Davenport Adams: *A Book of Burlesque* (London, 1891)
I. Goldberg, ed.: *New and Original Extravaganzas by W. S. Gilbert, Esq.* (Boston, 1931)
H. Granville-Barker: 'Exit Planché – Enter Gilbert', *The Eighteen-Sixties*, ed. J. Drinkwater (Cambridge, 1932), 102–48
V. C. Clinton-Baddely: *The Burlesque Tradition in the English Theatre after 1660* (London, 1952)
M. R. Booth, ed.: *English Plays of the Nineteenth Century* (Oxford, 1969–76), v
G. Rowell: *The Victorian Theatre, 1792–1914* (Cambridge, 2/1978)

FREDRIC WOODBRIDGE WILSON
(with DEANE L. ROOT)

Burletta. A type of English operatic comedy that flourished in the late 18th century and the early 19th. The term was one of several used for Italian comic operas of the light intermezzo variety: for instance Pergolesi's *La serva padrona* was so described at its first London performance in 1750. Several Italian burlettas were successfully played at Dublin in the 1750s and Lord Mornington commissioned Kane O'Hara to write an English imitation of one; the result was *Midas*, the first English burletta, performed privately near Belfast in 1760 and publicly at Dublin in 1762 and at Covent Garden in 1764. It was a burlesque on classical mythology; the music was a pasticcio, partly folksongs and partly tunes from Italian and English operas, with recitative. Its compiler is unknown.

Midas was a great success and was imitated both in Dublin and in the London patent theatres. These early burlettas, in verse throughout and all-sung, satirized the mythological and historical conventions of *opera seria*, though the music rarely participated in the joke. Prominent examples were *The Judgment of Paris* (Barthélemon, 1768), *The Portrait* (Samuel Arnold, 1770), *The Golden Pippin* (Fisher, 1773) and *Poor Vulcan* (Dibdin, 1778).

The decline of the burletta began with an adaptation of the burlesque tragedy *Tom Thumb*, revived at Covent Garden in 1780, a spoken play with added songs from various sources, compiled by J. Markordt. According to George Colman the younger, it was 'inadvertently announced by the managers ... as a burletta', thus giving the minor theatres a precedent for the evasion of the Licensing Act (1737), which had conferred a monopoly in legitimate drama on the two patent theatres, Covent Garden and Drury Lane. Comedies of all sorts, often with no burlesque element, were now put on at the minor theatres under the general title 'burletta' and departed increasingly from the original model. The orchestra was reduced to a harpsichord or piano. Songs became shorter and scarcer. The dialogue was still supposed to be in rhyme and sung in recitative: in 1812, according to the *Theatrical Inquisitor*, 'the tinkling of the piano and the jingling of the rhyme' were still the distinctive marks of the burletta. But by degrees the recitative became indistinguishable from spoken dialogue. In 1824 Colman told the Lord Chamberlain that a burletta must have at least five or six songs 'where the songs make a natural part of the piece, *and not forced into an acting piece*, to qualify it as a burletta'. Even this was an optimistic description. In some of John Barnett's early stage pieces, the few songs, though often highly successful in themselves, were mere 'music-shop ballads', introduced irrelevantly into a spoken play for subsequent sale as sheet music.

The term 'burletta' did not long survive the repeal of the Licensing Act in 1843, although it was occasionally used later in the century in the USA as a synonym for BURLESQUE.

*

R. B. Peake: *Memoirs of the Colman Family* (London, 1841), ii, 397ff
E. W. White: *The Rise of English Opera* (London, 1951)
E. B. Watson: *Sheridan to Robertson* (New York, 1963), 38ff
A. Nicoll: *A History of English Drama 1660–1900*, iv–v (Cambridge, 2/1966–7)
J. Donohue: 'Burletta and the Early Nineteenth-Century English Theatre', *Nineteenth Century Theatre Research* (1973), 29–51
R. Fiske: *English Theatre Music in the Eighteenth Century* (London, 1973, 2/1986)

NICHOLAS TEMPERLEY

Burmeister, Annelies (*b* Ludwigslust, Mecklenburg, 1930; *d* Berlin, 16 June 1988). German mezzo-soprano. She studied in Weimar, making her début in 1956 as Nicklausse at Erfurt. Engagements followed at Weimar and Dresden, and in 1962 she joined the Berlin Staatsoper. At Bayreuth she sang Fricka in 1966 and Second Norn in 1967. She made guest appearances in Hamburg, Vienna, Paris and other cities in western Europe. Her repertory included Orpheus, Dorabella, Azucena, Ulrica, Mistress Quickly, Brangäne, the Witch (*Rusalka*), Gaea (*Daphne*) and the Fishwife (*Die Verurteilung des Lukullus*). She had a rich, vibrant voice of ample volume.

HAROLD ROSENTHAL/R

Burnacini, Giovanni (*b* ?Cesena, *c*1605; *d* Vienna, 21 July 1655). Italian stage designer and architect. His first known works as an artist were the tournament theatre and stage designs for Marazzoli's *Le pretensioni del Tebro e del Po* (1642, Ferrara). These show the influence of Alfonso Rivarola ('il Chenda'), whose pupil he may have been and whom he may have succeeded as stage designer and engineer at the Teatro SS Giovanni e Paolo, Venice, about 1640, where he probably staged operas by Monteverdi. He was active there in 1643 and 1651 and may have built the small Teatro SS Apostoli (opened 1648), for which he directed and designed until 1651. With his brother Marc'Antonio he was summoned to Vienna by Ferdinand III in 1651, and until his death, assisted by his son Ludovico Ottavio, he was responsible for the decor of the operatic and festive productions at the imperial court.

In the librettos of *La finta savia* (1643, music by Ferrari and others) and Lucio's *Gl'amori di Alessandro magno e di Rossane* (1651) Burnacini was hailed as the true pioneer of Venetian theatrical machinery. His stage designs, preserved in a number of engravings (A. Bertali: *La gara*, 1652, and *L'inganno d'amore*, 1653), confirm this high estimate and show that in both technical and artistic respects he was the equal of his better-known rival Giacomo Torelli.

*

ES (E. Povoledo)
F. Torrefranca: 'Il primo scenografo del popolo, Giovanni Burnacini', *Scenario*, iii (1934), 191
P. Bjurström: *Giacomo Torelli and Baroque Stage Design* (Stockholm, 1961, rev. 2/1962)

For further bibliography *see* BURNACINI, LUDOVICO OTTAVIO.

MANFRED BOETZKES

Burnacini, Ludovico Ottavio (*b* ?Mantua, 1636; *d* Vienna, 12 Dec 1707). Italian stage designer and architect, son of Giovanni Burnacini. He went to Vienna in 1651 as his father's assistant and pupil. After his father's death (1655) he at first succeeded him as stage designer at the imperial court, but on 30 June 1657 he was dismissed by the new emperor, Leopold I, in favour of G. B. Angelini. Re-engaged from 1 January 1659, for nearly five decades he designed all the stage sets, machines and costumes for the theatrical performances, *sacre rappresentazioni*, festivals and memorial ceremonies of the Viennese court. He also did architectural work, including the building of the new court theatres, 1666–8.

Burnacini's unique scenic imagination stamped Viennese opera in the 17th century – the works of Bertali, Cesti, Draghi and the Zianis – with an unmistakable imprint. Surpassing even the masterly theatrical machinery of his father, he developed a spectacular style of courtly stage design, particularly in the great 'homage operas' of the 1660s and 1670s (e.g. Cesti's *Il pomo d'oro*, 1668, and Draghi's *La monarchia latina trionfante*, 1678). This style satisfied most effectively his employer's demands for supreme strength, both at an emotional level, by virtue of its ostentatious splendour, and at a didactic one, through a stringent symbolism. His unparalleled richness of invention raised his stage designs above those of many theatrical artists of his day yet without going beyond the limits of court convention. His costumes, notably for masquerades, ventured into the grotesque. He also trod new paths with his stage designs for comic operas and with the stage presentation of religious works.

See also STAGE DESIGN, §3(ii). For illustration *see* DRAGHI, ANTONIO; *POMO D'ORO, IL*; STAGE DESIGN, fig.4 and VIENNA, fig.2.

*

DBI (A. Barigozzi-Brini); *ES* (J. Gregor)
J. Gregor: *Wiener szenische Kunst: Die Theaterdekoration der letzten drei Jahrhunderte nach Stilprinzipien dargestellt* (Vienna, 1924)
——, ed.: *L. O. Burnacini: maschere* (Munich, 1925; Eng. trans., 1925)
F. Biach-Schiffmann: *Giovanni und Ludovico Burnacini: Theater und Feste am Wiener Hof* (Vienna, 1931) [incl. list of works]
F. Hadamowsky: 'Das Hoftheater Leopolds I. und das Kostümwerk des L. O. Burnacini', *Die Österreichische Nationalbibliothek: Festschrift Josef Bick* (Vienna, 1948), 397ff
——: 'Barocktheater am Wiener Kaiserhof: mit einem Spielplan 1625–1740', *Jb der Gesellschaft für Wiener Theaterforschung 1951/1952*, 7–117, esp.33, 45, 70
P. Fleischacker: *Rekonstruktionsversuch des Opernhauses und des Bühnenapparates in dem Theater des L. O. Burnacini* (diss., U. of Vienna, 1960)

H. Berger: *Die Grotesken Kostümentwürfe Lodovico Ottavio Burnacinis* (diss., U. of Vienna, 1962)
M. Baur-Heinold: *Theater des Barock: festliches Bühnenspiel im 17. und 18. Jahrhundert* (Munich, 1966; Eng. trans., 1966)
D. Hahn Shock: 'Costuming for "Il pomo d'oro"', *Gazette des beaux arts*, 6th ser., lxix (1967), 251–6
S. Solf: *Festdekoration und Groteske: der Wiener Bühnenbildner Lodovico Ottavio Burnacini: Inszenierung barocker Kunstvorstellung* (Baden-Baden, 1975)
W. Greisenegger: 'Set Designs and Costumes', *The Vienna Opera*, ed. A. Seebohm (New York, 1987), 177–82

MANFRED BOETZKES

Burnand, Sir **F(rancis) C(owley)** (*b* London, 29 Nov 1836; *d* Ramsgate, 21 April 1917). English librettist and dramatist. Educated at Eton and Cambridge, where he founded the Amateur Dramatic Club, he studied for the church and later read law and was admitted to the bar. But he soon abandoned these pursuits for the London stage, becoming a prolific writer of farce, pantomime, burlesque and extravaganza. In the 1860s he was a chief provider of burlesque for the Royalty Theatre, where his first marked success was *Black Eyed Susan* (1869). Meanwhile he began to write humorous prose and verse, notably for *Punch*, of which he was editor, 1880–1906. He was knighted in 1902.

Burnand, one of the most popular of Victorian dramatists, was a facile and slapdash writer. False rhymes and awkward rhythms occur frequently in his verse, and his favourite devices included puns, topical references and slang. His only piece to hold the stage was *Cox and Box* (1866), adapted from J. Maddison Morton's 1847 farce *Box and Cox* and set as a one-act operetta by Sullivan. He had already written nearly 20 pieces for the German Reeds' entertainments. It was Reed who brought Burnand and Sullivan together again for *The Contrabandista, or The Law of the Ladrones* (St George's Hall, 1867), later expanded as *The Chieftain* (Savoy Theatre, 1894). Among Burnand's other collaborators in comic opera were Alexander Mackenzie, Alfred Cellier, Edward Solomon, J. L. Molloy and German Reed himself. He also provided translations for London productions of operas by French composers, including Audran, Lecocq and Planquette.

FREDRIC WOODBRIDGE WILSON

Burney, Charles (*b* Shrewsbury, 7 April 1726; *d* Chelsea, London, 12 April 1814). English music historian and composer. As a youth in Shrewsbury and Chester, he studied the organ and violin. In Chester he met many of the prominent musicians travelling between London and Dublin. Among these was Thomas Augustine Arne, who took Burney to London as an apprentice in 1744. Burney lived with Arne for about two years, working under his direction at the playhouses and pleasure gardens and meeting leading musicians including Handel, in whose orchestra he occasionally performed on the violin or viola. In 1746 a young aristocrat, Fulke Greville, purchased from Arne Burney's services as a music master. Released from his apprenticeship in 1749, Burney became a Freeman of the Musicians' Company and established himself as a performer, music teacher and organist at St Dionis's Backchurch. He also wrote accompaniments and served as editorial assistant for the music publisher James Oswald.

Information about Burney's career as a theatre composer is confused because of his involvement with the Society of the Temple of Apollo, a group whose 'members' were Oswald, Burney and perhaps others (the evidence is disputed and contradictory). Burney provided music for three productions under the guise of the Society. The first, *Robin Hood*, written by Moses Mendez, was given on 13 December 1750 as an afterpiece to *The Alchemist*. The work was moderately successful, but had 'little more than musical merit to recommend it'. The highly successful *Queen Mab*, written by Henry Woodward and directed by David Garrick, was first performed on 26 December 1750 at Drury Lane and resulted in several publications by the Society. David Mallet's revision of *The Masque of Alfred*, for which Burney provided most of the music, had its première at Drury Lane on 23 February 1751. It was moderately successful and provoked a heated response from Arne – composer of the music for the original staging – who disavowed the production and indignantly claimed ownership of the two songs of his that were retained.

In 1751 ill-health forced Burney to leave London for King's Lynn, where he spent nine years as organist of St Margaret's Church. In addition to teaching, composing and presenting concerts, he began developing his literary interests. He was particularly drawn to the French writers on music and began translations of several works, including Rousseau's *intermède Le devin du village*, which he started to adapt as an English opera. Returning to London in 1760, he re-established himself as a fashionable private teacher. In 1766 Garrick prompted Burney to resume his preparation of an English version of *Le devin du village*. Burney's adaptation, *The Cunning Man*, was quite successful and his most important contribution to dramatic music.

In 1769 he took the degree of DMus at Oxford. He increasingly turned his attention to writing a history of music. Publication of the two journals from his continental travels of 1770 and 1772 launched the literary career that was to be his primary occupation during the rest of his life and for which he is justly famed. He continued to teach but composed no further music for the theatre. In 1773 Burney became organist of Oxford Chapel (now St Peter's, Vere Street), and in 1783 he was appointed organist of Chelsea College, where he lived until his death.

Among his writings, the continental tours contain many insights into the contemporary musical theatre. His important *General History of Music* (1776–89) has several large chapters on opera, and Handel's operas are treated at length. His biography of Metastasio (1796) offers thoughtful views on the librettist's activities. His final great literary contribution consists of hundreds of articles on music for Abraham Rees's *Cyclopaedia* (1802–19); though largely derived from earlier writings, these do contain important new material. As a critic, Burney often seems insensitive to opera as a dramatic form. His remark that opera is the 'completest concert' has often been cited. He was, however, well versed in the writings of important continental critics. He regarded as the 'nonage' of opera the period preceding the reforms advocated by Apostolo Zeno and Metastasio, who 'purified and sublimed the libretto', and condemns the substitution of arias and the pasticcio form of opera which, he says, inclines 'the good people of England to imagine the words of an opera to be all nonsense'. Burney himself explains the contradiction by observing that in England, where the poetry of an opera had little to do with success, 'it is generally upon *singing* that its favour entirely depends'; whereas 'in France and Italy, on the contrary, where operas are performed in the language of each country, the poetry and conduct of the drama are of infinite consequences to its success'. Burney's extensive history of Italian opera in England, with its curious plates showing divisions and ornaments introduced by notable singers, is that history which Burney considered relevant to his English readership; this approach does not, however, represent the whole of his own understanding of the genre.

Burney steadfastly defended Metastasian opera to the end of his life and measured all opera against its ideals. His critical insights were limited by his inflexible adherence to an aesthetic derived from Rousseau's *Lettre sur la musique française* and *Dictionnaire de musique*. In fastening so firmly on this aesthetic, important changes in dramatic music pass unnoticed or largely unappreciated. His lively literary style and his advocacy of the most modern and innovatory instrumental music mask his relative conservatism about dramatic music.

See also CUNNING MAN, THE.

Journal of Burney's travels in France and Italy (MS, 1771, *GB-Lbl*) [see Poole 1969]

The Present State of Music in France and Italy: or the Journal of a Tour through those Countries, undertaken to collect Materials for a General History of Music (London, 1771, 2/1773) [based on Journal, 1771; see Scholes 1959 and Poole 1969]

The Present State of Music in Germany, the Netherlands and the United Provinces, or the Journal of a Tour through these Countries, undertaken to collect Materials for a General History of Music (London, 1773, 2/1775) [see Scholes 1959]

A General History of Music from the Earliest Ages to the Present Period, to which is prefixed, a Dissertation on the Music of the Ancients, i (London, 1776, 2/1789), ii (1782, repr. 1811–12), iii-iv (1789); ed. F. Mercer in 2 vols. with the 1789 text of the orig. vol. i (London, 1935)

Memoirs of the Life and Writings of the Abate Metastasio (London, 1796)

Memoirs (MS, *US-NH*, Mellon Library, Osborne collection) [see F. Burney 1832 and Scholes 1959]

*

[F. Burney]: *Memoirs of Doctor Burney ... by Madame d'Arblay* (London, 1832)

P. Scholes: *The Great Dr Burney* (Oxford, 1948)

——, ed.: *Dr Burney's Musical Tours in Europe* (Oxford, 1959) [i, *An Eighteenth-Century Musical Tour in France and Italy*, based on Memoirs, n.d., and *The Present State of Music in France and Italy*, 2/1773; ii, *An Eighteenth-Century Musical Tour in Central Europe and the Netherlands*, based on *The Present State of Music in Germany, the Netherlands, and the United Provinces*, 2/1775]

R. Lonsdale: *Dr Charles Burney: a Literary Biography* (Oxford, 1965)

H. E. Poole, ed.: *Music, Men and Manners in France and Italy, 1770: Being a Journal Written During a Tour through these Countries* (London, 1969) [based on Journal, 1771, and *The Present State of Music in France and Italy*, 2/1773]

K. Grant: *Dr Charles Burney as Critic and Historian of Music* (Ann Arbor, 1983)

S. Klima, G. Bowers and K. Grant, eds.: *The Memoirs of Dr Charles Burney* (Lincoln, NE, 1987)

A. Ribeiro, ed.: *The Letters of Charles Burney* (Oxford, 1991–)

KERRY S. GRANT

Burning Fiery Furnace, The. Second parable for church performance by BENJAMIN BRITTEN to a libretto by WILLIAM PLOMER; Orford Church, Suffolk, 9 June 1966.

Like *CURLEW RIVER* and *The Prodigal Son*, Britten's second church parable is laid out for a small group of singers and instrumentalists, dressed as monks and acolytes and performing without a conductor. *The Burning Fiery Furnace* begins with the processional hymn 'Salus aeterna'; then the Abbot (bass) explains that the company will enact the Old Testament story of the three young Israelites whose faith was tested by the heathen Babylonians. After the ceremonial robing and masking of the main actors, a Herald (baritone) pronounces the Babylonian declaration of the feast in honour of the visiting Israelites, an alto trombone pungently evoking the brazen splendour of the court. King Nebuchadnezzar (tenor) appears, proclaiming his belief in magic, and the feast begins, but the Israelites (tenor, baritone and bass) refuse to participate, as the laws of Israel forbid it. The King is angry, and an Astrologer (bass) further disturbs him by suggesting that the King has endangered his kingdom by ignoring the warning in the stars. In anger, Nebuchadnezzar decrees that an image of the great god Merodak be set up, and as this is done the instrumentalists process in a march dominated by the pagan brayings of the alto trombone. The Israelites refuse to bow before the image, and as the King grows increasingly disturbed they are cast into the furnace, from where, miraculously unharmed, and joined by an Angel (treble), they sing a solemn *Benedicite*. Amazed and duly repentant, Nebuchadnezzar and his followers join in its final stages. After the Abbot points the moral the company moves away from the acting area, recapitulating the processional hymn, and the parable ends with a benediction.

The Burning Fiery Furnace is no less resourceful than its predecessor, *Curlew River*, in its striking melodic characterization (the blunt Herald, the volatile King, the calm, confident Israelites) and in the way it builds powerful vocal and instrumental ensembles from the contrapuntal combination of chant-derived lines. Reflecting its subject, it is much brighter in instrumental colour than the other parables, and the result, for all its stylization, is a vivid presentation of the confrontation between idolatry and monotheism. ARNOLD WHITTALL

Burnson [Burnstein], **George.** *See* LONDON, GEORGE.

Burrian, Carl [Burian, Karel] (*b* Rousinov, 12 Jan 1870; *d* Senomaty, nr Prague, 25 Sept 1924). Bohemian tenor. He made his first appearance at Brno on 28 March 1891 as Jeník in Smetana's *The Bartered Bride*; after singing the title role in the same composer's *Dalibor* the next day, he was offered a contract. By 1899 he had reached the National Theatre in Prague, but he did not remain for long with that company, having by then become a *Heldentenor* much in demand in Germany. For over a decade before World War I Burrian was a leading and much-admired tenor at the Dresden Opera, where he made a powerful impression in the première (1905) of Strauss's *Salome* as Herod, repeating this role in the first productions of the opera in both New York and Paris in 1907. Wagner was the mainstay of his international repertory; as well as singing Tristan in the Hungarian première of *Tristan und Isolde*, he sang several of the chief Wagner roles at Covent Garden in four seasons between 1904 and 1914, and virtually all of them (*Die Meistersinger* excepted) during seven seasons at the Metropolitan. He appeared in *Parsifal* at Bayreuth in 1908. In Burrian's numerous but somewhat primitive recordings, the penetrating clarity of his tone is more in evidence than the golden quality for which he was also praised. Reminiscences of Mahler and Toscanini are included in his memoirs, *Z mých pameti* (Prague, 1913).

For illustration *see* SALOME.

ČSHS [incl. list of writings and extensive bibliography]; *GV* (J. Dostal and R. Celletti; T. Kaufmann)
J. Dennis: 'Karel Burian', *Record Collector*, xviii (1968–9), 149–65 [with discography by D. Brew and G. Sova]

DESMOND SHAWE-TAYLOR

Burrowes, Norma (*b* Bangor, Co. Down, 24 April 1944). British soprano. She studied in London at the RAM, singing Thérèse (*Les mamelles de Tirésias*), Monteverdi's Poppaea and Puccini's Magda (*La rondine*) while still a student. In 1970 she made her professional début with Glyndebourne Touring Opera as Zerlina, sang Philidel in Purcell's *King Arthur* with the English Opera Group and made her Covent Garden début as the Fiakermilli (*Arabella*). In 1971 she appeared at Salzburg as Blonde, a part she also sang with the ENO, Netherlands Opera, at the Paris Opéra and for her Metropolitan début in 1979. At Glyndebourne (1970–81) she sang Papagena, the Vixen, Pamina and Susanna. Other roles in her repertory included Fiorilla (*Il turco in Italia*), Oscar, Zerbinetta and Sophie. She combined a delightful appearance with a pure, bright voice and secure coloratura technique. She retired in 1982. ELIZABETH FORBES

Burrows, (James) Stuart (*b* Cilfynydd, nr Pontypridd, 7 Feb 1933). Welsh tenor. A schoolteacher before winning the tenor solo competition at the Royal National Eisteddfod in 1959, he studied at Carmarthen. He made his début in 1963 with the WNO as Ismaele (*Nabucco*), also singing Rodolfo, Macduff, Jeník, the Duke and Ernesto (*Don Pasquale*). At Athens in 1965 he sang the title role in *Oedipus Rex* under Stravinsky. He made his Covent Garden début in 1967 as Beppe (*Pagliacci*), returning for 22 seasons as Fenton, Elvino, Faust, Lensky, Jack (*The Midsummer Marriage*), and in Mozart roles. He made his San Francisco (1967) and Vienna Staatsoper (1970) débuts as Tamino and sang Don Ottavio at Salzburg (1970) and for his Metropolitan début (1971), returning there as Belmonte, Des Grieux (*Manon*) and Alfredo. He also sang in Aix-en-Provence and Santa Fe. A notable exponent of Idomeneus and Titus, he had a sweet-toned voice of great flexibility which was ideally suited to Mozart and which he used with skill. He recorded many of his best roles, including Hoffmann, a part he never sang on stage. ALAN BLYTH

Burt, Francis (*b* London, 28 April 1926). English composer and teacher resident in Vienna. He studied with Howard Ferguson at the RAM, with Boris Blacher at the Berlin Hochschule für Musik (1951–4) and with Dallapiccola in Italy. In 1973 he became professor of composition at the Vienna Hochschule. Several of his earlier orchestral works performed in England proved him to be a resourceful composer working confidently within a tonal framework. His first opera, *Volpone* (4, Burt, after B. Johnson; vs, Vienna, 1962), written at the suggestion of Blacher, was well received at Stuttgart (Staatsoper, 2 June 1960) and at Oldenburg, where it was given in a revised and simplified version in 1963. *Barnstable* (1, Burt, after J. Saunders; Kassel, Staatstheater, 30 November 1970) is based on a radio play of 1960 and deals lightheartedly with the havoc caused by a ghostly presence in an English country house.

See also VOLPONE. HUGO COLE

Burton, Stephen Douglas (*b* Whittier, CA, 24 Feb 1943). American composer. He was educated at the Oberlin and Peabody conservatories (MM 1974), and at the Salzburg Mozarteum with Hans Werner Henze. He is professor of music at George Mason University in Fairfax, Virginia. He has received commissions from major orchestras, including the Berlin Philharmonic, the Chicago Symphony and the Orchestre National de France. His many awards include a Guggenheim Fellowship and grants from the National Opera Institute and the Coolidge Foundation.

Burton's compositional aesthetic centres around the voice, for which he writes artfully and colourfully, and his music is challenging to the singer in its requirements of both range and expression. His considerable gift for melody is supported by an ample palette of harmonies. He uses an extensive spate of idioms, from the popular to the avant-garde, in the service of the text, and his choice of stories demonstrates a sophisticated literary sense as well as a bold concept of dramaturgy. He makes use of all the resources of the modern orchestra and has a discriminating ear for dramatic mood. The première of his three-act opera *The Duchess of Malfi* (1978) was hailed as 'the birth of a masterpiece' by the *Washington Post*.

*

No Trifling with Love (1, Burton, after A. de Musset), 1970
An American Triptych, 1975 (trilogy, Burton), Alexandria, VA, Athanaeum, 29 July 1989
The Duchess of Malfi (3, C. Keene, after J. Webster), Vienna, VA, Wolf Trap Filene Center, 18 Aug 1978
Dr Heidigger's Experiment (1, after N. Hawthorne), 1988
Maggie (1, after S. Crane: *Maggie, a Girl of the Streets*)
Benito Cereno (1, after H. Melville) SAM DI BONAVENTURA

Bury [Buri], **Bernard de** (*b* Versailles, 20 Aug 1720; *d* Versailles, 19 Nov 1795). French composer. He came from a musical family, many of whom held court appointments, and was a pupil of his father, Jean-Louis de Bury, and Collin de Blamont. When he was 19 he composed a three-act ballet produced by the Duke of Tremouille, and in 1743 he wrote the *opéra-ballet Les caractères de la Folie* for the Paris Opéra. The third entrée ('Les caprices de l'Amour') was admired most, chiefly for the writing for Eucharis which was made to measure for Lemaure's vocal and dramatic *pathétique*. In 1745, to celebrate the victorious Louis XV's return from Fontenay, Bury wrote (with Collin de Blamont) an obviously allegorical tragedy, *Jupiter, vainqueur des Titans*. Two years later the overture to his new dense and elaborately allegorical prologue for Lully's *Persée* was identified as being 'dans le goût moderne' (*Mercure*, March 1747). He later collaborated on a revival of *Persée*, performed in 1770 at court for the second marriage of the dauphin.

For the 1762 revival of *Les caractères*, Bury added a new pastoral entrée ('Hylas et Zélis'); it was extravagantly praised in the *Mercure* as an example of 'le grand genre et la science de l'art', which combined 'l'essence du goût italien mariée avec un délicatesse admirable au goût français' in 'plusieurs morceaux transcendants'. While Bury's italianate vein might have been easily assimilable at Versailles, its (recognized) appearance at the Opéra is surprising. From 1779 Bury received a royal pension; he was enobled by Louis XVI in 1785, just months before his death.

Since Bury was essentially a court composer, his works received limited coverage from the *Mercure* and the Parfaicts. The single act of *Titon et l'Aurore* (1750,

Peter Hall rehearsing the cast in the use of John Bury's machines for Monteverdi's 'Il ritorno d'Ulisse', Glyndebourne, 1972

Versailles; 1751, Opéra) was little appreciated in its day because of the eccentric liberties taken with the well-known story. The music moves easily in keys ranging from three flats to four sharps. The picturesque and expressive use of instruments in graceful *airs* is often French in cut. But the passage-work, figuration and the contour of the harmonic bass are frequently italianate. The declamation is in the unreformed French tradition.

all printed works published in Paris

Les caractères de la Folie (opéra-ballet, prol., 3, C.-P. Duclos), Paris, Opéra, 20 Aug 1743 (1743), *F-Pn*; with new entrée, Hylas et Zélie, Opéra, 6 July 1762

Jupiter, vainqueur des Titans (tragédie lyrique), Versailles, 11 Dec 1745, lib. *Pc*, music ?lost, collab. Collin de Blamont

La nymphe de Versailles (divertissement, Mlle de Lussan), Versailles, 19 March 1746

Les fêtes de Thétis (ballet-héroïque, prol., 2, P.-C. Roy), Versailles, 14 Jan 1750, *Pn*, collab. Collin de Blamont

Titon et l'Aurore (pastorale-héroïque, prol., 1, Abbé de la Marre and A. H. de Lamotte), Versailles, Théâtre des Petits Appartements, 14 Jan 1750 (1750)

La parque vaincue (divertissement, 1, A. Tanevot), 'sur la convalescence de Mgr le duc de Fronsac', Versailles, Hôtel de Richelieu, 1751, ?lost

Palmyre (ballet-héroïque, S.-R.-N. Chamfort), Fontainebleau, 24 Oct 1765, *Pc*

Zénis et Almasie (ballet-héroïque, 1, Chamfort and Duke of Vallière), Fontainebleau, 2 Nov 1765 (1765), collab. J. B. de La Borde, ?lost

Prol. for Lully: Persée, 1747; adds. to Persée, Versailles, 17 May 1770, lib. *Pc*, collab. Dauvergne, Francoeur and Rebel

Doubtful: La nymphe de la Seine (divertissement), 1746; Les bergers de Sceaux (divertissement), for Duke of Maine [both cited by Fétis]

*

FétisB

Mercure de France (Sept 1743), 2066–79; (March 1747), 127–33, 177; (April 1751), 160ff; (July 1762), 124–32

C. Parfaict and F. Parfaict: *Dictionnaire des théâtres de Paris* (Paris, 1756), ii,43

J. B. de La Borde: *Essai sur la musique ancienne et moderne* (Paris, 1780), iii, 398–9

PHILIP WELLER

Bury, John (*b* Aberystwyth, 27 Jan 1925). British designer. Bury, who studied chemistry at London University, had no formal training but graduated from stage carpenter to designer with Joan Littlewood's Theatre Workshop, designing some of her most successful productions (*The Quare Fellow*; *Oh, What a Lovely War!*). From 1964 to 1973 he was head of design at the Royal Shakespeare Company (RSC) and from 1973 to 1986 at the National Theatre.

Bury's distinctive style was established early on: an emphasis on textures, the realistic use of materials, simplicity, ingenuity in achieving dramatic effects with minimal means (even the Baroque 'machines' in *Il ritorno d'Ulisse*, 1972, Glyndebourne; see illustration). It was perhaps most uncompromisingly demonstrated in the RSC's steely *Wars of the Roses* cycle (1962–4) and the monumental *Moses und Aron* (1965, Covent Garden), his first operatic collaboration with Peter Hall, for whom he has done virtually all his opera work, including the swiftly moving, sombre *Don Giovanni* (1978, Glyndebourne) and the sinister *Salome* (1987, Los Angeles). Bury lights all his own productions.

MARINA HENDERSON

Burzio, Eugenia (*b* Turin, 20 June 1872; *d* Milan, 18 May 1922). Italian soprano. She appeared first as a violinist, then studied singing at the Milan Conservatory, making her début in 1899 at Turin in *Cavalleria rusticana*. Specializing in the new *verismo* school, she sang throughout Italy, in South America and at St Petersburg. Among her many appearances at La Scala were admired performances in Gluck's *Armide* and Bellini's *Norma*. For a while she was one of the leading dramatic sopranos in Italy, but suffered from nerves and ill-health. She made her final appearance in 1919 in Ponchielli's *Marion Delorme*. Her recordings show a vibrant voice and a passionate style, which was imaginative and exciting at best but open to many criticisms.

GV (R. Celletti; R. Vegeto)
M. Scott: *The Record of Singing* (London, 1977) J. B. STEANE

Busby, Thomas (*b* Westminster, Dec 1755; *d* London, 28 May 1838). English composer and writer. After an early career as a singer at Vauxhall Gardens, he was apprenticed to Jonathan Battishill and became organist at two churches; he received the MusB from Cambridge University (1801). He was noted for his journalistic work in music and his *General History of Music* (London, 1819), as well as for his music for the theatre and for his oratorios and other vocal music. He composed incidental music to Kenrick's *The Man the Master* (*c*1778), Cumberland's *Joanna of Montfoucon* (Covent Garden, 16 January 1800), Lewis's *Rugantino, or the Bravo of Venice* (Covent Garden, ?18 October 1802) and Porter's *The Fair Fugitives* (Covent Garden, ?16 May 1803).

His most famous and most significant music, however, is that for the first melodrama in English, *A Tale of Mystery* by Thomas Holcroft, after Pixérécourt's *Coelina*. Its première was as an afterpiece on 13 November 1802 at Covent Garden, where it ran until the Christmas pantomime took over, reappearing in February for 15 performances. It was revived frequently in London and travelled to Ireland, provincial playhouses and America. Busby's music includes a three-movement overture, opening dances, a song and over 30 'melos' (short lengths of music underlying speech or action). While passages illustrating happy emotions tend towards the sentimental conventions of the *galant* style, with long chains of 3rds over simple harmonies, the music for the darker emotions and actions is reminiscent of the turbulent parts of a Haydn development section, with quick changes of mood and key-centre and skilful use of augmented 6ths and diminished 7ths. Busby's rather light orchestration may be seen in the song from *A Tale of Mystery* published in the score (London, 1802).

*

A. D. Shapiro: 'Action Music', *American Music*, ii (1984), 49–71
ANNE DHU SHAPIRO

Busca, Lodovico (*b* Turin; *fl* 1670–88). Italian composer. He was a monk in Milan; earlier he had probably been in the service of the court of Savoy. The music of his operas is mostly lost, but the librettos of three presented at the Teatro Regio Ducal, Milan, survive: *La regina Floridea* (P. Manni; ?1669; collab. P. S. Agostini and F. Rossi), *Ippolita reina delle amazzoni* (? C. M. Maggi; 1670; *I-Nc*; collab. Agostini and P. A. Ziani) and *Amor tra l'armi, overo Corbulone in Armenia* (Maggi; 1672–3).

*

G. Barblan: 'Il teatro musicale a Milano nei secoli XVII e XVIII', *Storia di Milano*, xii (Milan, 1959), 947 SERGIO LATTES

Busch, Fritz (*b* Siegen, Westphalia, 13 March 1890; *d* London, 14 Sept 1951). German conductor. After studying in Steinbach's conducting class at the Cologne Conservatory, he began his career in 1909 with a season as conductor at the Deutsches Theater, Riga, and in 1912 was appointed municipal music director at Aachen. In 1918 he moved to Stuttgart as music director of the Opera, where he brought a fresh mind to broadening the repertory and encouraging new artistic developments: for instance, with premières of the young Hindemith's one-act operas *Mörder, Hoffnung der Frauen* and *Nusch-Nuschi*; by the inclusion of five Verdi operas and three by Pfitzner; and in the choice of Appia's designs for *Das Rheingold*.

From 1922 to 1933 he was music director of the Dresden Staatsoper, and during this time he also made guest appearances which included conducting *Die Meistersinger* for the reopening of Bayreuth in 1924 and visits to New York (1927, 1928) and London (1929). At first he was criticized for not doing enough German repertory, but Busch and his Intendant Alfred Reucker between them brought the Staatsoper to high renown. Busch conducted the premières of Strauss's *Intermezzo* (1924) and *Die ägyptische Helena* (1928), Busoni's *Doktor Faust* (1925), Weill's *Der Protagonist* (1926) and Hindemith's *Cardillac* (1926). In 1932 Busch found a congenial spirit in Carl Ebert, and the two worked harmoniously on Mozart's *Die Entführung* for that year's Salzburg Festival and on Verdi's *Ballo* at the Städtische Oper, Berlin. Busch held the latter production to mark the culmination of his work in Germany; soon he began openly to express dislike of the Nazis, and he was dismissed from Dresden in March 1933. He refused to take the place of his friend Toscanini at Bayreuth after the latter had severed his connection wth the Festival.

After a spell at the Colón, Buenos Aires, and radio and concert work in Denmark and Sweden, Busch was invited to become music director of the private opera house John Christie had recently built at Glyndebourne. He accepted, on condition that Ebert was made artistic director. There, from 1934 to 1939, with a carefully chosen and rehearsed ensemble and a repertory based mainly on Mozart, Busch was 'able to build up an opera production in the smallest detail and with ... complete respect for the work'. He conducted three more seasons in Buenos Aires and in 1945 appeared with the Metropolitan Opera, subsequently touring with them for four seasons; he was never entirely at ease in New York, however, where one concert promoter complained that 'he was not a showman'. Busch resumed work in Scandinavia in 1949 and appeared as a guest conductor at the Vienna Staatsoper in 1950. At Glyndebourne in 1951 he conducted four Mozart operas including *Idomeneo*. The Glyndebourne *Don Giovanni* was repeated at the Edinburgh Festival, where he also included Verdi's *La forza del destino*.

Busch was the soundest type of German musician, not markedly original or spectacular, but thorough, strong-minded, decisive in intention and execution, with idealism and practical sense nicely balanced. Recordings of three Mozart operas remain as testimony of his work at Glyndebourne. A volume of memoirs, *Aus dem Leben eines Musikers*, was published in Zürich in 1949 (Eng. trans. as *Pages from a Musician's Life*, 1953).

*

A. Christie: 'Fritz Busch: an Appreciation', *Opera*, ii (1950–51), 697
J. Strachey: 'Fritz Busch 1890–1951', *Glyndebourne Festival 1952* [programme book]
S. Hughes: *Glyndebourne: a History of the Festival Opera, 1934–1964* (London, 1965)
G. Busch: *Fritz Busch, Dirigent* (Frankfurt, 1970) [with discography]
B. Dopheide: *Fritz Busch* (Tutzing, 1970)
R. Bing: *5000 Nights at the Opera* (London, 1972)
RONALD CRICHTON

Busenello [Businello], **Giovanni** [Gian] **Francesco** (*b* Venice, 24 Sept 1598; *d* Legnaro, nr Padua, 27 Oct 1659). Italian librettist. He probably studied at the University of Padua. He was a member of several academies: the Delfici, the Umoristi, the Imperfetti and most notably the Accademia degli Incogniti, a circle of libertines and sceptics who dominated the literary, and to some extent the commercial, side of Venetian public opera in its first years.

Busenello wrote five librettos for Venice; these were set to music by Cavalli and probably Monteverdi and published collectively in *Delle hore ociose* (Venice, 1656). As one of Venice's earlier librettists he was a participant in the transformation of opera from court spectacle to bourgeois entertainment. The succession of his dramas exemplifies an instability of type characteristic of the search for successful formulae. The preface to *Gli amori d'Apollo e di Dafne*, a work faithful to the tradition of the *favola pastorale*, cites Guarini's *Il pastor fido* as a precedent for its multiple love affairs. *La Didone* capriciously treats a portion of Virgil's *Aeneid*, discarding the Aristotelian unities of time and place after the Spanish manner. *L'incoronazione di Poppea* is today among the best known of all early operas, largely because of Monteverdi's strong setting, although in its own day it had no greater currency than Busenello's other works. The fact that it was one of the earliest operas based on historical events has received more attention than it deserves, for in 17th-century Italy historical and mythological plot sources were generally used indiscriminately. Specially striking features of *L'incoronazione di Poppea* are the variety of character types portrayed and the fullness of relationships between them. The moral choice expressed in its conclusion – in which Nero exiles his wife Octavia and marries his mistress Poppaea – violates the nascent Venetian tradition: a rejected spouse would nearly always have been re-embraced at the last. The work shares with Busenello's other dramas a language rich in erotic expression in keeping with his place in the Marinist tradition. *La prosperità infelice di Giulio Cesare dittatore* (supposedly performed in 1646 with music by Cavalli but perhaps never even composed) resembles *L'incoronazione di Poppea* in its historical origin and wealth of character type. Like Badoaro's *L'Ulisse errante* it is in five acts (instead of the more normal three) separated by time and place, each a discrete episode with largely different characters. The decade between *La prosperità infelice di Giulio Cesare dittatore* and *La Statira* (1655) saw the rise of a drama of intrigue to which Giovanni Faustini and G. A. Cicognini were principal contributors. Although *La Statira* obeys some of the superficial conventions of this type, such as disguise and the pairing of lovers, it is curiously static, lacking all real conflict of love interest. Its main event is an offstage war in which the entire cast is on the same side. Busenello's connection with the development of the opera libretto extended only to the mid-1640s, although he may have revised the text of *L'incoronazione di Poppea* for the Naples performance of 1651. A sixth drama, *La discesa d'Enea all'inferno*, survives in manuscript but was apparently not set to music.

Gli amori d'Apollo e di Dafne, Cavalli, 1640; *La Didone*, Cavalli, 1641; *L'incoronazione di Poppea* (opera musicale), Monteverdi, 1643; *La prosperità infelice di Giulio Cesare dittatore* (opera musicale), ? Cavalli, 1646; *La Statira* (dramma per musica), Cavalli, 1655 [?1656]

*

C. Ivanovich: *Minerva al tavolino* (Venice, 1681, 2/1688)

G. M. Mazzuchelli: *Gli scrittori d'Italia*, ii/4 (Brescia, 1763)

A. Livingston: *Una scappatella di Polo Vendramino e un sonetto di Gian Francesco Busenello* (Rome, 1911)

——: *La vita veneziana nelle opere di Gian Francesco Busenello* (Venice, 1913) [incl. list of sources]

G. Spini: *Ricerca dei libertini* (Rome, 1950)

A. A. Abert: *Claudio Monteverdi und das musikalische Drama* (Lippstadt, 1954)

W. Osthoff: 'Die venezianische und neapolitanische Fassung von Monteverdis "Incoronazione di Poppea"', *AcM*, xxvi (1954), 88–113, esp. 96

——: 'Neue Beobachtungen zu Quellen und Geschichte von Monteverdis "Incoronazione di Poppea"', *Mf*, xi (1958), 129–38, esp. 135

——: *Das dramatische Spätwerk Claudio Monteverdis* (Tutzing, 1960)

F. Degrada: 'Gian Francesco Busenello e il libretto della *Incoronazione di Poppea*', *Congresso internazionale sul tema Claudio Monteverdi e il suo tempo: Venice, Mantua and Cremona 1968*, 81–108

K. von Fischer: 'Eine wenig beachtete Quelle zu Busenellos *L'incoronazione di Poppea*', ibid, 75–80

P. J. Smith: *The Tenth Muse* (London, 1971)

A. Chiarelli: '*L'incoronazione di Poppea o Il Nerone:* problemi di filologia', *RIM*, ix (1974), 117–51

L. Bianconi and T. Walker: 'Dalla *Finta pazza* alla *Veremonda*: storie di Febiarmonici', *RIM*, x (1975), 379–454

THOMAS WALKER

Bush, Alan (Dudley) (*b* London, 22 Dec 1900). English composer. He studied at the RAM, where he taught from 1925 until 1978, with a break for war service. He composed copiously in many genres, his works being distinguished by clear tonality, close thematic working, athletic vigour and contrapuntal mastery. From 1925 onwards he took an active part in the working-class movement, joining the Communist Party in 1935. Thereafter, as explained in his essays (1980), Marxism has been for him a guide to action 'as a musician and as a man', the challenge being most clearly taken up in the four full-length operas. The librettos of all but the last of these were written by his wife Nancy.

Before the composition of *Wat Tyler* Bush served his dramatic apprenticeship writing music for masques and pageants for left-wing organizations, and composed *The Press Gang*, the first of three children's operas. *Wat Tyler*, his first full-length opera, was a prize-winner in the Arts Council Competition of 1951, but the first production, at Leipzig, did not take place until 1953. Bush's three subsequent operas were also first produced in (East) Germany, *Wat Tyler* alone receiving a professional stage production in England, more than 20 years after its Leipzig première.

In his operas Bush makes free use of popular song or of original material inspired by music of the locality, and the chorus, always identified with the workers, plays a vital role. E. J. Dent found in the choruses of *Wat Tyler* an aggressive ruthlessness allied to breadth and simplicity which suggested a line of descent from Musorgsky rather than from Verdi or Wagner. Word-setting is generally syllabic and closely based on the intonation patterns of spoken English. Big ensemble scenes are planned on a grand architectural scale, with the orchestra supplying an independent commentary. All four operas depict the workers' struggle against the oppression of rulers or employers, clearly defined forces of good and evil striving for mastery, as in medieval mystery plays.

Because Bush is essentially a sober and optimistic composer, lacking Weill's ability to portray wicked or debauched characters, the battle between good and evil is never fought on equal terms. Historical issues are often oversimplified and characterization is generally conventional, determined by the need to transmit a political message in plain and unambiguous form. His later operas have more dramatic and psychological plausibility; the almost Verdian monologue for the mine manager, Fletcher, in *Men of Blackmoor* is a fine piece of character-painting, while *The Sugar Reapers* makes fruitful use of Guyanan rhythms and timbres. Working with a new librettist in *Joe Hill*, he combined the more deliberate processes of the number opera with cinematic techniques of rapid cross-cutting which heighten dramatic tension as the opera moves towards its close.

See also SUGAR REAPERS, THE, and WAT TYLER.

The Press Gang [The Enraged Apprentice] (children's op, N. Bush), Letchworth, St Christopher School, 7 March 1947, vs (Saale, 1953)
Wat Tyler (prol., 2, N. Bush), Leipzig, Staats, 6 Sept 1953, vs (London, 1959)
The Spell Unbound (operetta for girls, N. Bush), Bournemouth School for Girls, 6 March 1955, vs (London, 1954)
Men of Blackmoor (3, N. Bush), Weimar, National, 18 Nov 1956, vs (London 1959)
The Ferryman's Daughter, 1961 (op for schools, N. Bush), Letchworth, St Christopher School, 6 March 1964, vs (London, 1963)
The Sugar Reapers [Guyana Johnny] (2, N. Bush), Leipzig, Opernhaus, 11 Dec 1966, vs (Berlin, 1965)
Joe Hill: the Man who Never Died, 1965–7 (2, B. Stavis), Berlin, Staatsoper, 29 Sept 1970, *GB-Lmic**

*

A. Bush: 'The Problems of Music', *Music*, i/11 (1952), 19–21; repr. as 'Problems of Opera', *In my Eighth Decade and Other Essays* (London, 1980), 32–7
E. J. Dent: 'Wat Tyler, a New Opera by Alan Bush', *MO* (Jan 1952), 231
H. Ottaway: 'Alan Bush's Wat Tyler', *MT*, xcvii (1956), 633–6

HUGO COLE

Bush, Geoffrey (*b* London, 23 March 1920). English composer. He was educated at Balliol College, Oxford, where he took the MA in classics and the DMus, both in 1946; he was largely self-taught as a composer. He became extra-mural music lecturer at Oxford University (1946) and London University, and from 1969 was visiting professor at King's College, London. Though Bush has written works in every genre, his lyrical and approachable music, which is firmly rooted in tonality, stems mainly from the British vocal tradition. His operas, like Britten's, are practically planned and economical in their use of resources. All are scored for small chamber ensembles and have been aptly devised for particular contexts and for certain types of performer. *The Blind Beggar's Daughter* (1954), a ballad opera for young people, makes use of folktunes and of folksong-like material; *If the Cap Fits* (1956) and *Lord Arthur Savile's Crime* (1972) are more sophisticated entertainment pieces written respectively for the three-strong Intimate Opera Company and for the students of the GSM, the latter work revealing a talent for parody and epigram which match the mood and manner of Wilde's short story. *The Equation* (1967), which was commissioned by the Sacred Music-Drama Society and performed in London at All Saints, Margaret Street, treats a serious pacifist theme: two pairs of friends are on opposite sides in the Roman-Jewish war of AD 70; in each case, one friend dies at the hands of one of the opposing pair, and the futile equation is completed. *The Cat who Went to Heaven* (1976) is a music-theatre work based on a Buddhist story, with dialogue, and scenes linked by a narrator.

librettos by Bush unless otherwise stated

The Blind Beggar's Daughter (ballad op for young people, 3 scenes, S. Bathurst), Farnham, 21 Jan 1954; rev. version, 1964
If the Cap Fits (1, after Molière: *Les précieuses ridicules*), Cheltenham, 12 July 1956
The Equation (1, after J. Drinkwater), London, 11 Jan 1968
Lord Arthur Savile's Crime (1, after O. Wilde), London, GSM, 5 Dec 1972
The Cat who Went to Heaven (1, after E. Coatsworth), Croydon, 9 Dec 1976
Love's Labour's Lost, 1988 (2, after W. Shakespeare), unperf.

HUGO COLE

Busoni, Ferruccio (Dante Michelangelo Benvenuto) (*b* Empoli, 1 April 1866; *d* Berlin, 27 July 1924). German-Italian composer.

1. Life. 2. Stage works. 3. Stylistic features.

1. LIFE. He was the son of professional musicians, Ferdinando Busoni, a clarinet virtuoso, and Anna Weiss, a pianist. The family moved to Trieste when he was a few months old, transplanting him into a cosmopolitan, German-orientated environment. His first compositions date from 1873, and his career as virtuoso pianist was inaugurated in the same year. Opera and theatre were a mainstay of his early education: a visit to a *teatro meccanico* with automated puppets remained unforgettable, while his first experience of opera was a performance in Trieste of Ricci's *Crispino e la comare*.

Thanks to patronage, the nine-year-old Busoni was able to spend two years at the conservatory in Vienna. From 1881 he studied composition and counterpoint with Wilhelm Mayer (W. A. Rémy) in Graz. A period of further study in Leipzig under Carl Reinecke began in 1885. Three years later Busoni took a post as piano professor at the Helsinki Musikinstitut. Two years in Finland were followed by a season at the conservatory in Moscow (where he married Gerda Sjöstrand, the daughter of a Swedish sculptor), then by two years in Boston and New York. In 1894 he settled in Berlin. He accepted the directorship of the Liceo Musicale in Bologna in 1913, and from 1915 to 1920 he lived in Zürich, but he considered Berlin his home and, although he was a travelling virtuoso, remained resident there for the rest of his life.

In 1920 he was appointed professor of composition at the Akademie der Künste, where his most distinguished pupils were Kurt Weill and Vladimir Vogel. Ill health prevented his appearing as concert pianist after 1922 and caused his relatively early death two years later.

Busoni enjoyed no regular schooling and matured very early. A specialist knowledge of Bach and Liszt, adoration of Mozart and growing antipathy towards Wagner were accompanied by sympathy for Schoenberg and lively interest in all contemporary developments. Versatility was his hallmark: he made light of his stupendous abilities as a pianist, preferring to consider himself a composer, conductor and writer. He was also a bibliophile and linguist, a talented draughtsman and a *bon vivant*.

2. STAGE WORKS. Busoni's first theatre project, a one-act opera based on Henrik Hertz's *King René's Daughter*, dates from 1883. A Trieste poet, Michele Buono, was the intended librettist, but he failed to deliver and the project came to nothing. (Tchaikovsky's *Iolanta*, composed in 1892, used the same literary source.) In 1884 Busoni negotiated with J. V. Widmann for a libretto on Gottfried Keller's *Romeo und Julia auf dem Dorfe*. Widmann declined and countered by offering the text for *Manuel Venegas*, which Busoni rejected (it was set by Richard Heuberger, a fellow pupil of Rémy, in 1889).

During the Leipzig years Busoni began to compose his first opera, *Sigune, oder Das stille Dorf*. A complete short score is preserved (in *D-Bds*) but only the prelude to Act 1 was orchestrated before the project was abandoned in 1889. Some of the music from *Sigune* was salvaged in the Konzertstück op.31*a* for piano and orchestra, written for the Rubinstein Competition (St Petersburg, 1890). A further *Sigune* theme, the motif of a master builder admiring a new cathedral, appears in two unpublished works for solo piano (dating from 1883 and 1898) before finding its eventual place in the *pezzo serioso* of the monumental Piano Concerto op.39 (1904). The concerto closes with a chorus of off-stage male voices, to a text from Adam Oehlenschlaeger's play *Aladdin*. This too is the remainder of a theatrical plan, a setting of *Aladdin*, 'not as an opera but as a *Gesamtkunstwerk* with drama, music, dance [and] magic'.

The last decade of the 19th century was a period of consolidation for Busoni, during which he composed relatively little, expending much energy on perfecting his piano technique and widening his repertory (above all to include the major piano works of Liszt). The première of Verdi's *Falstaff* in 1893 revived his belief in the future of Italian music and influenced his developing style. During this period he worked on the libretto for an opera about the Wandering Jew, *Ahasver*. Although he later abandoned the plan, he was to vary the central theme – the intellectual outsider who strives for immortality – in several subsequent operatic projects, arriving at a definitive version in his final masterpiece, *Doktor Faust*. Variants of the same idea are to be found in his *Der mächtige Zauberer* (based on a short story by Gobineau), *Leonardo da Vinci* and *Dante*. Librettos or sketches for these have survived; many further plans for opera librettos are mentioned in Busoni's copious correspondence.

In 1905 Busoni composed incidental music for Carlo Gozzi's *Turandot*. The first production to use his music was not staged until 1911, but the *Turandot* suite op.41 rapidly established itself as an effective concert piece, one of whose earliest advocates was Gustav Mahler.

Although Busoni made sporadic approaches to such writers as Shaw, D'Annunzio and Hofmannsthal, he ultimately decided to write his opera texts himself, in German. In 1907 he published the controversial, thought-provoking *Entwurf einer neuen Ästhetik der Tonkunst*, flanking it with two new original librettos, *Der mächtige Zauberer* and *Die Brautwahl*, the latter an intricate adaptation of E. T. A. Hoffmann's short story of the same name. Busoni worked on the score of *Die Brautwahl* from 1906 to 1908, spending three further years on the orchestration. The première was unsuccessful and the opera was withdrawn after four further performances. A radically shortened version (1913, Mannheim) also failed. Despite these setbacks, Busoni remained convinced that opera was the 'universal domain' of contemporary music and that his own musical language was intrinsically theatrical.

In the revised edition of the *Entwurf* (1916) Busoni elaborates on his idea of opera as a multi-media spectacle which should 'rely on the incredible, untrue or unlikely'. The opera of the future, he believed, should use music only where it is indispensable, particularly for the portrayal of the supernatural or the unnatural, hence as a magic mirror (*opera seria*) or a distorting mirror (*opera buffa*). These theories, coupled with his earliest memories of Italian puppet theatre, form the dramaturgical foundation of his three remaining operas, *Arlecchino*, a one-act 'theatrical caprice', its companion piece *Turandot* (both 1917), and *Doktor Faust*. *Turandot* and *Arlecchino* are grouped together as 'La nuova commedia dell'arte', while *Doktor Faust* is based largely on the early German puppet play of *Faust*.

3. Stylistic features. *Die Brautwahl*, written soon after publication of the *Entwurf*, marks a significant turning-point in Busoni's musical development. Tonality is at no point abandoned, but the harmony is exploratory, frequently employing modes or unusual scales. In weaker moments, the musical language seems contrived and lacks convincing melodic invention; at its best, it 'floats', occasioning that sense of *Auflösung* (dissolution, liberation) which Edward J. Dent, his first biographer, valued so highly. As Paul Bekker commented, the score is weighed down by a surfeit of *giocoso* passages. Yet there is also a speculative, mystical element in the music, which was to exercise considerable influence on Busoni's later style.

During the years immediately preceding World War I Busoni came into contact with progressive artists in various fields – the Viennese Secessionists, the Italian Futurists, D'Annunzio, Rilke, Schoenberg and Varèse, to name but a few – and himself entered on a new period of experiment. The earliest studies for *Doktor Faust*, the *Sonatina seconda* for piano and *Nocturne symphonique* op.43 for orchestra, date from this time. Apart from their dense, brooding textures, these works are notable for a new harmonic and rhythmic boldness and a distinctive instrumental chiaroscuro.

The war effected a gradual change of direction, which finally led Busoni in 1918 to proclaim 'Junge Klassizität' as his artistic aim. 'Many experiments have been made in this young century. Now ... it is time to form something *durable* again'. The one-act opera *Arlecchino* (composed in 1914 and 1916) was his first, brilliant essay in the new style. Musically it appears to fall between two stools: a bold and liberal spirit of experiment is applied to a parodistic vocabulary of operatic cliché. Yet fine musical balance and turbulent dramatic pacing unify the score, while apt quotations (of Mozart, Beethoven, Donizetti etc.) are wittily integrated. The opera *Turandot*, adapted in just three months from the incidental music to the play, is less convincing and lacks the cogency of *Arlecchino*.

'Junge Klassizität' is a concept which embraces many styles and, in theory, excludes none. Busoni believed that the achievements of past generations could be combined with all new developments, and that a full flowering of Western music would hence lie in the distant future. The libretto of *Doktor Faust* expresses this belief in allegorical form and can be interpreted as an autobiographical statement. Busoni worked on this ambitious project from 1910, when he first drafted the libretto, until his death; indeed he considered the work to be the culmination of all his artistic endeavours. Helen of Troy appears before Faust as 'the unattainable ideal of absolute beauty'; Faust's death symbolizes the continuing search for perfection. When Busoni died, the Helen scene and Faust's closing monologue were unfinished. Nevertheless, *Doktor Faust* is widely accepted as one of the outstanding operas of the 20th century.

See also Arlecchino; Brautwahl, die; Doktor Faust (ii); and Turandot (i).

Sigune, oder Das stille Dorf (L. Soyaux and F. Schanz), 1889, inc., *D-Bds*

Die Brautwahl (musikalisch-fantastische Komödie, 3, Busoni, after E. T. A. Hoffmann), Hamburg, Stadt, 13 April 1912 (Berlin, 1914)
Arlecchino, oder Die Fenster op.50 (theatralisches Capriccio, 1, Busoni), Zürich, Stadt, 11 May 1917 (Leipzig, 1918)
Turandot (chinesisches Fabel, 2, Busoni, after C. Gozzi), Zürich, Stadt, 11 May 1917, vs (Leipzig, 1917); 'Diese Zeichen von Trauer', addn to Turandot, 1921, *Bds*, *WIbh*
Doktor Faust, 1916–24 (prol., 6 scenes, Busoni, after 16th-century puppet plays), completed P. Jarnach, Dresden, Sächsisches Staats, 21 May 1925, vs (Leipzig, 1925); completed A. Beaumont, Bologna, 2 April 1985, vs (Wiesbaden, 1984)

Other librettos: *Der mächtige Zauberer* (after J. A. Gobineau), 1905 (Trieste, 1907); *Aladdin* (after A. Oehlenschlaeger), 1906, *Bds*; *Leonardo da Vinci*, 1908, frag., *Bds*; *Frau Potiphar*, 1909, *Bds*; *Das Geheimnis* (after V. de l'Isle-Adam), ?1912, pubd in *Blätter der Staatsoper* [Berlin] (Nov 1924); *Die Götterbraut*, 1912, unpubd, set by L. Gruenberg as The Bride of the Gods; *Die Wunderbühne* (after M. de Cervantes), 1917, *Bds*; *Arlecchino II. Teil*, 1918, *B*, *Bds*; *Das Wandbild*, 1918 (Leipzig, 1920), set by O. Schoeck, 1921

*

F. Busoni: *Über die Möglichkeiten der Oper und über die Partitur des 'Doktor Faust'* (Leipzig, 1926)
E. J. Dent: *Ferruccio Busoni* (London, 1933, 2/1974)
F. Schnapp, ed.: *Busoni: Briefe an seine Frau* (Zürich and Leipzig, 1935; Eng. trans., 1938)
E. J. Dent: 'Busoni and his Operas', *Opera*, v (1954), 391–7
R. Stevenson: 'Busoni's *Arlecchino*', *MT*, xcv (1954), 307–8
K. Weill: *Ausgewählte Schriften*, ed. D. Drew (Frankfurt, 1975)
V. Vogel: *Schriften und Aufzeichnungen über Musik*, ed. W. Labhart (Zürich, 1977)
J. Kindermann: *Thematisch-chronologisches Verzeichnis der Werke von Ferruccio Busoni* (Regensburg, 1980)
P. op de Coul: *Doktor Faust, opera van Ferruccio Busoni* (diss., Groningen U., 1983)
A. Beaumont: *Busoni the Composer* (London and Boston, 1985)
——: 'Busoni and the Theatre', *Opera*, xxxvii (1986), 384–91
——: 'Busoni's "Doctor Faust": a Reconstruction and its Problems', *MT*, cxxvii (1986), 196–9
——, ed.: *Ferruccio Busoni: Selected Letters* (London and Boston, 1987)

ANTONY BEAUMONT

Bussani [née Sardi], **Dorothea** (*b* Vienna, 1763; *d* after 1810). Austrian soprano. On 20 March 1786 she married the Italian bass Francesco Bussani. She specialized in *opera buffa* and made her début creating Cherubino in *Le nozze di Figaro* (1786); she also created Ghita in Martín y Soler's *Una cosa rara* (1786), Despina in *Così fan tutte* (1790) and Fidalma in Cimarosa's *Il matrimonio segreto* (1792). She always pleased the public, and a contemporary wrote that he had never heard such a beautiful and charming chest voice nor one used with such humour and so mischievously (*Grundsätze zur Theaterkritik*, 1790). Da Ponte, on the other hand, wrote: 'though awkward and of little merit, by dint of grimaces and clowning and perhaps by means even more theatrical, she built up a large following among cooks, grooms, servants, lackeys and wigmakers, and in consequence was considered a gem' (*Memorie*, 1823–7).

In 1795 she went to Florence and sang in Italy during the next decade. She appeared in Lisbon, 1807–9, and at the King's Theatre, London; Parke later described her as having 'plenty of voice, but whose person and age were not calculated to fascinate an English audience' (*Musical Memoirs*, 1830).

CHRISTOPHER RAEBURN

Bussani, Francesco (*b* Rome, 1743; *d* after 1807). Italian bass. He started his career as a tenor, appearing in Rome in 1763 in Guglielmi's *Le contadine bizzare*. He sang in Venice, Milan and Rome for the next 15 years and first appeared in Vienna in 1771. In 1777 he was described in Florence as singing *primo buffo* and *mezzo carattere* roles; by this time his voice was a bass-baritone. He appeared in Venice from 1779 and in 1783 was invited to Vienna where he remained until 1794. With 20 years' experience of the theatre, he was engaged not only as a singer but also as manager of scenery and costumes; he also arranged pieces and in 1784 adapted Goldoni's *Il mercato di Malmantile* as a libretto for music by Barta. He appeared regularly in the Italian repertory and sang Pippo in Bianchi's *La villanella rapita*, for which Mozart wrote the quartet 'Dite almeno' K479 (28 November 1785); he doubled the roles of Bartolo and Antonio in the première of *Le nozze di Figaro* (1 May 1786). He was an active member of the Italian faction in Vienna during the 1780s and according to Da Ponte (*Memorie*, 1823–7) intrigued against him and Mozart when *Figaro* was in rehearsal. Da Ponte described Bussani as knowing something of every profession except that of a gentleman.

Bussani sang the Commendatore and Masetto in the first Vienna performance of *Don Giovanni* (1788) and created Don Alfonso in *Così fan tutte* (26 January 1790). According to Da Ponte, Bussani found little favour with the new emperor, Leopold II. He achieved only moderate success as he was always in the shadow of Benucci, who had the stronger stage personality and was the public's favourite. In 1795 he sang in Florence, in 1799 in Rome, and in 1800–01 in Naples and Palermo. He remained active in Italy and went with his wife, Dorothea, to Lisbon in 1807.

CHRISTOPHER RAEBURN

Bussani [Bussano], **Giacomo** [Giovanni] **Francesco** (*b* Cremona; *fl* 1673–80). Italian librettist. He was a canon regular of the Lateran Congregation at the Carità in Venice. He wrote seven librettos for Venetian theatres from 1673 to 1680; five were for the Teatro S Salvatore and were set to music by Antonio Sartorio. The other two were for theatres owned by the Grimani brothers Giovanni Carlo and Vincenzo. The Teatro SS Giovanni e Paolo provided the stage for *Enea in Italia* set to music by Carlo Pallavicino in 1675. The Teatro S Giovanni Grisostomo, which the Grimani brothers had recently opened in 1678, was the location for *Il ratto delle Sabine* set by P. S. Agostini in 1680.

Except for *Enea in Italia* and *Ercole sul Termodonte*, Bussani's works are loosely based on history enlivened with complications arising from added love interests. The *Mercure galant* (August 1677) briefly mentions his two works of 1677. Most of his works were restaged in several Italian cities within two decades of their Venetian premières. Sartorio's associations with Hanover (he served Duke Johann Friedrich of Brunswick-Luneburg as Kapellmeister) and Bussani's own connection (*Antonino e Pompeiano* was dedicated to the same duke) may have played some part in bringing Bussani's *Giulio Cesare in Egitto* to Handel's notice. In 1724, Nicola Haym's adaptation of this work formed the basis for one of Handel's greatest operas. It is more surprising that native Italian composers also drew upon such an old-fashioned work, including L. A. Predieri (1728, Rome), Giacomelli (1735, Milan and Venice), A. Colombo (1744, Venice), Jommelli (1751, Rome and Strasbourg) and Sarti (aut. 1763, Copenhagen).

Massenzio, A. Sartorio, 1673; *Enea in Italia*, C. Pallavicino, 1675 (J. W. Franck, 1680, as Aeneas); *Giulio Cesare in Egitto*, Sartorio, 1676 (Kusser, 1690, as Cleopatra; Handel, 1724; L. A. Predieri, 1728, as Cesare in Egitto; G. Giacomelli, 1735, as Cesare in

Egitto; Jommelli, 1751, as César en Egipte; G. Sarti, 1763); *Antonino e Pompeiano*, Sartorio, 1677 (Keiser, 1717, as Julia; comp. unknown, Padua, Obizzi, 1721, as La tirannide punita); *Anacreonte tiranno*, Sartorio, 1677 (A. Scarlatti, 1689; F. de Castris, M. Bitti and A. Scarlatti, 1698, as Anacreonte); *Ercole sul Termodonte*, Sartorio, 1678; *Il ratto delle Sabine*, P. S. Agostini, 1680

*

AllacciD; *ES* (U. Rolandi)
Mercure galant (August 1677)
C. Ivanovich: *Minerva al tavolino* (Venice, 1681, 2/1688)
G. Bonlini: *Le glorie della poesia e della musica* (Venice, [1730])
F. Arisi: *Cremona literata*, iii (Cremona, 1741), 145
A. Groppo: *Catalogo di tutti i drammi per musica recitati ne' teatri di Venezia* (Venice, 1745)
G. M. Mazzuchelli: *Gli scrittori d'Italia*, vol. 2/iv (Brescia, 1763), 2459
H. C. Wolff: *Die venezianische Oper in der zweiten Hälfte des 17. Jahrhunderts; ein Beitrag zur Geschichte der Musik und des Theaters im Zeitalter des Barocks* (Berlin, 1937)
J. M. Knapp: 'Handel's *Giulio Cesare in Egitto*', *Studies in Music History: Essays for Oliver Strunk* (Princeton, 1968), 389–403
R. Strohm: 'Händel und seine italienischen Operntexte', *HJb*, xxi–xxii (1975–6), 101–59; rev. and trans. in *Essays on Handel and Italian Opera* (Cambridge, 1985), 34–79
M. Viale Ferrero: 'Antonio e Pietro Ottoboni e alcuni melodrammi da loro ideati o promossi a Roma', *Venezia e il melodramma nel settecento*, Studi di musica veneta 5, ed. M. T. Muraro (Florence, 1976), 271–94
C. Monson: '*Giulio Cesare in Egitto*: from Sartorio (1677) to Handel (1724)', *ML*, lxvi (1985), 313–43
— —, ed.: A. Sartorio: *Giulio Cesare in Egitto*, Collegium musicum, 2nd ser., xii (Madison, WI, 1991) [incl. trans. of lib.]
E. Rosand: *Opera in Seventeenth-Century Venice: the Creation of a Genre* (Berkeley, 1991)
L. Bianconi, ed.: *I libretti italiani di Georg Friedrich Händel e le loro fonti*, i (Florence, 1992) HARRIS S. SAUNDERS

Busse, Barry (Lee) (*b* Gloversville, NY, 18 Aug 1946). American tenor. He studied at Oberlin College and the Manhattan School of Music; his teachers included Ellen Repp, Marlena Malas and Ted Taylor. After singing as a baritone, he made his début as a tenor in Floyd's *Of Mice and Men* in Houston in 1977. In 1980 he sang at the New York City Opera as Bothwell in *Mary, Queen of Scots*, a role he had sung for Virginia Opera in 1978. His European début was in 1982 as Don José at the Netherlands Opera, and he has since sung in Florence, Geneva and Toulouse. His career has chiefly been with American regional opera companies, including Miami, San Francisco, Santa Fe and Seattle. In 1990 he sang Agrippa and Mephistopheles (*The Fiery Angel*) at the Holland Festival. His repertory includes Canio, Cavaradossi, Florestan, Quint and Siegmund.

CORI ELLISON

Büsser [Busser], **(Paul-)Henri** (*b* Toulouse, 16 Jan 1872; *d* Paris, 30 Dec 1973). French composer and conductor. He showed a prodigious musical talent as a boy and was taken to Paris to study; in 1889 he entered the Conservatoire, where he studied the organ with Franck and composition with Guiraud. He received valuable advice from Gounod, who arranged his appointment as organist of St-Cloud, near Paris, in 1892. In the following year he won the Prix de Rome, and after his return to Paris he began his career as a conductor. He conducted at the Théâtre du Château d'Eau from 1900, and the Opéra-Comique in 1902; there, at the request of Debussy, he stood in for Messager (who had to leave for London) for the fourth and subsequent performances of *Pelléas*. In 1905 he was appointed conductor at the Opéra. He also taught at the Conservatoire (from 1931 as professor of composition), and was elected to the Académie in 1938.

The most important of his works were those for the stage: *Colomba*, which is set in Corsica, met with great success at its première (1921). *Le carrosse du Saint-Sacrement* is set in Peru and recounts a farcical situation in which a carriage is given to the church after brushing against another carriage on the way to a wedding. *Diafoirus 60* is a modernization of Molière's *Le malade imaginaire*. His compositions are sophisticated in orchestration and accomplished in craftsmanship; although there is sometimes an indebtedness to Debussy, Büsser remained faithful to the French 19th-century tradition.

vocal scores published in Paris

Hélène, ? before 1890 (drame lyrique, 1, E. Blau), inc., *F-Pn*
Les accordailles, 1890 (opéra comique, 1, A. Noël), ?unperf., *Pn*
Les Marivaudages, 1891 (pantomime, 1, Noël), ?unperf., *Pn*
Daphnis et Chloé, before 1896 (scenic pastorale, 1, C. Raffalli), Paris, OC (Lyrique), 14 Dec 1897, vs (1897)
Le miracle des perles, 1898 (drame lyrique, 3, J. Dieulafoy and L. Gallet), ?unperf., *Pn*
Blanc et noir (pantomime, 1, V. Capoul), Paris, Palais de Luxembourg, 1900, *Pn*
Colomba, *c*1910 (drame lyrique, prol., 3, Büsser, after P. Mérimée), Nice, Casino Municipal, 4 Feb 1921, *Po*; (?1921)
Les noces corinthiennes, 1916–18 (tragédie lyrique, 3, A. France), Paris, OC (Favart), 10 May 1922, vs (1922)
La pie borgne op.76 (comédie lyrique, 1, R. Benjamin), Aix-les-Bains, Grand Cercle, 5 Aug 1927, vs (1929)
Le carrosse du Saint-Sacrement (comédie lyrique, 1, Büsser, after Mérimée), Paris, OC (Favart), 2 June 1948, *Pn*, vs (1948)
Roxelane (comédie lyrique, 3, Büsser, after C.-S. Favart), Mulhouse, Municipal, 31 Jan 1948, *Pn*; (?1948)
Diafoirus 60 (farce musicale, 1), Lille, Opéra, 4 April 1963, *Pn*; (?1963)
La Vénus d'Ille (drame lyrique, 2, Büsser, after Mérimée), Lille, Grand, 15 April 1964, *Pn*, vs (1961)
Hélène (drame lyrique, 1, E. Blau), inc., *Pn*

ARTHUR HOÉRÉE/RICHARD LANGHAM SMITH

Busseto. Small town in northern Italy. Verdi was born nearby, at Roncole, and later bought a villa at Sant'Agata, about 4 km north of Busseto, settling there in 1857. Now open to visitors, Villa Verdi holds materials relevant to the study of the composer (but not however generally available to scholars). The summer festival Busseto per Verdi was founded in 1991.

Bussoleni, Giovanni. *See* BUZZOLENI, GIOVANNI.

Bussotti, Sylvano (*b* Florence, 1 Oct 1931). Italian composer, stage designer and director. Born into a Tuscan-Venetian family with strong artistic tendencies he entered the Florence Conservatory in 1940, where he studied the violin with Maglioni and the piano with Dallapiccola. In 1944 he interrupted his studies in order to dedicate himself to composition, which he studied independently in Florence and later in Paris. More important for his development than formal academic training in composition were encounters with Max Deutsch, John Cage (Darmstadt, 1958), Pierre Boulez and Heinz-Klaus Metzger. From the late 1960s he began to develop a highly successful career as a stage designer in Italian opera houses, with productions of the standard Italian repertory in Turin, Florence, Bergamo and Venice during the 1970s. After the impressive première of his first full-scale opera *Lorenzaccio* at the Venetian Biennale (1972) Bussotti was appointed artistic director of the Teatro La Fenice in Venice in 1975. In 1982 he became the director of the Festival Pucciniano at Torre del Lago (Viareggio); his open-air staging of *Turandot* in 1982 marked one of the artistic highlights of the Puccini Festival. After his resignation in 1983 Bussotti dedicated more time to the composition of operas, to opera staging and to the foundation of his own opera festival 'Bussottioperaballet' in 1984. Unlike most composers of his generation Bussotti has always maintained a close link with the operatic tradition of the 19th century; his tendencies to create a post-Wagnerian, decadent form of *Gesamtkunstwerk* are obvious. His compositions and activities as director and designer are firmly rooted in the musical life of present-day Italy, where the radically decadent, egocentric aestheticism of his productions has won general acclaim.

Following a general tendency of the musical avant garde of the 1950s Bussotti did not at first show much interest in opera composition, but theatrical elements began to acquire more presence within his concert works. The only genuine stage work of this period, *La passion selon Sade* (1969), marked the end of Bussotti's dedication to the experimental music theatre of the 1960s; his *Rara Requiem* (1970) opened a new path that eventually led to the composition of *Lorenzaccio* (1972) which incorporates the *Requiem* as its fourth and fifth acts. Bussotti's increasing contact with the everyday practice of opera staging inspired his wish to recreate the grand opera of the 19th century using the techniques of his own musical and dramatic language. Through the character of Alfred de Musset who views his own drama onstage, Bussotti reveals the gradual identification of his creative self with the characters of de Musset's drama, followed by a prolonged farewell to the characters of his imagination, which is musically represented by the *Rara Requiem.*

Bussotti's musical style underwent major changes between *La Passion selon Sade* and *Lorenzaccio*, incorporating a variety of musical quotations from other composers as well as a continuous stream of self-quotations from his earlier works, which often possess a hidden cohesion with the new score. *Lorenzaccio* blends various dramatic genres into one whole: spoken melodrama, ballet, film, offstage events and the continuous display of lavish costumes contrast with pieces such as Maria's aria (Act 2) which seem like an ironic revival of the traditions of 19th-century opera. Bussotti's main technique for the appropriation of a dramatic subject, namely the identification of a character on stage with the author of the text, was extended in his subsequent operas through a mirror-like technique of dramatic construction which blends two plots into one. His score for *Nottetempo* (1976) begins with a chorus of martyrs and partisans which quotes Tallis's 40-part motet *Spem in alium*, to which Bussotti added 40 dissonant instrumental parts in order to create a dense texture of great beauty. The opera's central character, Michelangelo Buonarrotti, the incarnation of the creative artist, becomes identified with Philoctetes as the symbol of human endurance.

At the end of the 1970s Bussotti started to work on two ambitious projects which occupied most of his activities during the next decade: a cycle of symphonic movements for orchestra with or without solo instruments, called *Il catalogo è questo* in obvious reference to Leporello's aria from *Don Giovanni*; and a series of operas which centre around the character of Racine's *Phèdre*. In his chamber opera *Le Racine* (1980) Bussotti imitated the artificial situation of stage rehearsals with singers and piano; again an author (Jean Racine on stage) appears as the object of the composer's self-identification. *Fedra* (1988), an extended transformation of *Le Racine* on a larger scale and with the three acts set respectively in ancient Greece, Paris in 1677 and Paris in 1931, and *L'ispirazione* (1988), a treatment of the subject of artistic creation in which an old composer has a new opera performed in the year 2031, show Bussotti as an opera composer in full command of his dramaturgical and musical means.

See also ISPIRAZIONE, L'; LORENZACCIO; NOTTETEMPO; PASSION SELON SADE, LA; and RACINE, LE.

La passion selon Sade (mystère de chambre, 1, Bussotti, after L. Labé), partial perf., Palermo, Biondo, 5 Sept 1965; complete perf., Stockholm, Opera, 1 Nov 1968; *I-Mr*

Lorenzaccio (melodramma romantico danzato, 5, Bussotti and F. Philippe, after A. de Musset), Venice, Fenice, 7 Sept 1972, *Mr*

Nottetempo (dramma lirico, 1, Bussotti and R. Amidei), Milan, Lirico, 7 April 1976, *Mr*

Le rarità, potente (rappresentazioni liriche, 1, Amidei), Treviso, Comunale, 12 Oct 1979, *Mr*

Le Racine (op balletto, 3, Bussotti, after J. Racine), Milan, Piccola Scala, 9 Dec 1980, *Mr*

Fedra (tragedia lirica, 3, Bussotti, after Racine), Rome, Opera, 19 April 1988, *Mr* [reworking of Le Racine]

L'ispirazione (melodramma, 3, Bussotti, after E. Bloch: *Die gutmachende Muse*), Florence, Comunale, 26 May 1988, *Mr*

WRITINGS

Antonio Veretti: i sette peccati: mistero musicale e coreografico: schema generale di allestimento scenico e regia (Milan, 1968)

I miei teatri (Palermo, 1982)

with J. Maehder: *Turandot* (Pisa, 1983)

Letterati ignoranti (Siena, 1986)

*

C. Annibaldi: 'Musica gestuale e nuovo teatro: ritorno alla teatralità', *Musica moderna*, iii/6 (1969), 145

M. Bortolotto: 'Le cinque tentazioni di Bussotti', *Fase seconda* (Turin, 1969), 201

L. Pinzauti: 'A colloquio con Sylvano Bussotti', *NRMI*, iv (1970), 898–909

G. La Face: *Eros, grafia e musica nell'opera di Sylvano Bussotti* (diss., U. of Messina, 1970–71); extract pubd as 'Teatro, eros e segno nell'opera di Sylvano Bussotti', *RIM*, ix (1974), 250–68

F. Degrada, ed.: *Bussottioperaballet: Sylvano Bussotti e il suo teatro: Oggetto amato-Nottetempo* (Milan, 1976)

I. Stoïanova: *Geste – texte – musique* (Paris, 1978)

J. Maehder: 'Bussottioperaballet: sviluppi della drammaturgia musicale bussottiana', *NRMI*, xviii (1984), 441–68

L. Morini: *Moda e musica nei costumi di Sylvano Bussotti* (Milan, 1984)

Fedra di Sylvano Bussotti (Milan, 1988) [with contribs. by F. Orlando, G. Malvezzi and Bussotti]

A. Lucioli: *Sylvano Bussotti* (Milan, 1988)

La lunga litania dei nostri affetti: omaggio a Sylvano Bussotti (Milan, 1991)

J. Maehder: 'Auf der Suche nach der verlorenen Oper – Mozarts Musiktheater und sein Einfluss auf Luciano Berio und Sylvano Bussotti', *Mozart in der Musik des 20. Jahrhunderts: Formen ästhetischer und kompositionstechnischer Rezeption*, ed. S. Mauser [forthcoming] JÜRGEN MAEHDER

Bustelli, Giuseppe (*d* Vienna, before 10 April 1781). Italian impresario active in Bohemia and Germany. He was a merchant in Brno. On 13 January 1764 he applied to lease the theatre in the Old Town of Prague; his opera company opened at the theatre on 4 October 1764 with *Vologeso, re de Parti* (with Pietro DeMezzo in the title role) by the musical director, Domenico Fischietti. He later introduced *opere buffe*, by Galuppi, Pietro Guglielmi, Gassmann, Hasse, Borono, Piccinni, Righini, Paisiello and others, which gradually came to dominate the repertory. Each summer the company was at Carlsbad (now Karlový Vary); they also visited Laibach (now Ljubljana) (Carnival 1769), Hamburg (1770) and Leipzig (1773). From 1765 Bustelli had a company at Dresden where, in 1770, 1776 and 1778, he negotiated contracts and subsidies from the electoral court.

Between 1765 and 1778 the Prague and Dresden companies shared musical directors, repertory and singers. But at the same time Bustelli paid regard to local interests; in Prague he introduced works by the Czech composers Mysliveček and J. A. Kozeluch and in Dresden works by J. G. Naumann. His successor was Pasquale Bondini, a member of his company. Some opera scores from his estate were bought for Haydn's ensemble at Eszterháza.

O. Teuber: *Geschichte des Prager Theaters*, i–ii (Prague, 1883–5)

R. Haas: 'Beitrag zur Geschichte der Oper in Prag und Dresden', *Neues Archiv für sächsische Geschichte und Altertumskunde*, xxxvii (1916), 68

P. Kneidl: 'Libreta italské opery v Praze v 18. stoletì' [Italian Opera Librettos in Prague in the 18th Century], *Strahovska knihovna*, ii (1967), 115

TOMISLAV VOLEK

Buti, Francesco (*b* ?Narni, 1604; *d* Rome, 15 June 1682). Italian librettist. Trained in church and civil law, he pursued a career in Rome before 1645, serving prelates of the curia. He must have belonged to a circle of literati by the early 1630s; his poems were set to music by Kapsberger (Rome, 1632), Carissimi, Marazzoli and others. The success of his political and theatrical career in France in the decade after 1645 depended on the intense activity of Cardinal Mazarin, prime minister to the queen regent, and of Cardinal Antonio Barberini, ex-papal nephew in exile in Paris. Buti would have known both men from Rome. In his three operas for Paris he mixed elements of contemporary Italian opera and courtly machine spectacle with the French traditions of ballet and spectacle. As a result none is typical of opera as it was being staged in Italy at the time. After the death of his protector Mazarin (in 1661) Buti fell into obscurity.

Buti wrote two comedies for music. *Il Capriccio, overo Il giuditio della Ragione tra la Beltà e l'Affetto* (also known as *La Bellezza amata*) is a moral allegory in the form of a situation comedy: Ragione [Reason] tries to persuade Belezza [Beauty] to turn back to Vero Amore [True Love] and abandon her difficult courtship with Capriccio [Caprice]. Short rhyming lines convey the quips and puppet-like speech of the all-soprano cast; the performance, in private, with music by Marazzoli, was commended for being brief, novel and well acted. Buti's second comedy, the three-act *Il giusto inganno*, is more conventional. Set in Argos, it treats the return in disguise of the first wife of the Prefect of the Peloponnese, after he has re-married, and offers a large number of arias; it is not known who might have set it to music.

Two outstanding Roman composers set Buti's first two librettos for Mazarin – Luigi Rossi (*Orfeo*) and Carlo Caproli (*Le nozze di Peleo e di Theti*); the latter was called an 'Italian comedy entwined with a ballet on the same subject'. The mythological subjects and extensive use of choruses were by mid-century uncommon in Rome. Caproli's score is lost, but Rossi's is peppered with *ariette*, arias and canzonettas. Both librettos have simple main plots surrounded by secondary, related scenes. In *Orfeo* Venus tries to help a rival lover displace Orpheus in Eurydice's affections; in *Peleo* the mortal Peleus's quest for the nymph Thetis is a loose framework for spectacular tableaux dramatizing Neptune and Jupiter's rival declarations of love.

Ercole amante, set by Cavalli, unfolds the story of true love between Hercules' son Hyllus and Iole (daughter of a king slain by Hercules) and recounts Hercules' death indirectly at the hands of his wife Deianira. Commissioned in 1659 by Mazarin for Paris (though not performed until 1662), the opera developed out of plans for a new theatre and ambitious new stage machines and sets designed by Gaspare Vigarani. Each of the five acts thus centres on some spectacular 'marvel', such as Juno's rage in Act 1 or Hyllus's shipwreck and rescue by Neptune in Act 4. The element of spectacle, the large cast of 17 characters and the numerous choruses (of rivers, priests, damned souls etc.), together with Cavalli's music, all tend to overshadow Buti's text, which has attracted little attention. Prunières judged that the poetry at best was 'fluent and singable'. Despite Buti's consistently unpredictable mixture of metres and of rhymed and unrhymed lines, a short-breathed, sing-song uniformity emanates from all the characters, belying the story's latent passion and tragedy. Festive lyricism is further emphasized by short airs and numerous arioso passages. Buti's three Paris operas, with the three ballets with music by Lully (1656, 1657 and 1662), belong in effect more to the history of court spectacle than that of musical drama.

Il Capriccio, overo Il giuditio della Ragione tra la Beltà e l'Affetto (dramma ideale), M. Marazzoli, 1643; *Orfeo* (tragicommedia per musica), L. Rossi, 1647; *Le nozze di Peleo e di Theti* (commedia), C. Caproli, 1654; *Ercole amante* (tragedia), F. Cavalli, 1662; *Il giusto inganno* (commedia per musica), n.d.

C.-F. Ménestrier: *Des représentations en musique anciennes et modernes* (Paris, 1681), 195–206

P. Mandosio: *Bibliotheca romana* (Rome, 1692), i, 45

A. Ademollo: *I primi fasti della musica italiana a Parigi 1645–1662* (Milan, 1884)

H. Goldschmidt: *Studien zur Geschichte der italienischen Oper im 17. Jahrhundert* (Leipzig, 1901), i, 78–86

R. Rolland: *Musiciens d'autrefois* (Paris, 1908; Eng. trans., 1915)

H. Prunières: *L'opéra italien en France avant Lulli* (Paris, 1913)

F. Liuzzi: 'I musicisti italiani in Francia', *L'opera del genio italiano all'estero* (Rome, 1946), i, 171, 177, 182

P. Bjurström: *Giacomo Torelli and Baroque Stage Design* (Stockholm, 1962)

M.-F. Christout: ' "Les noces de Pelée et Thétis": comédie italienne en musique entremêlée d'un ballet dansé par le Roi (1654)', *Actes des journées internationales d'étude du Baroque: Montauban 1970*, pubd in *Baroque*, v (1972), 59–62

T. E. Lawrenson: 'Les "Noces de Pelée" et la guerre des bouffons', *Venezia e il melodramma nel Seicento: Venice 1972*, 121–9

S. Franchi: *Drammaturgia romana: repertorio bibliografico cronologico dei testi drammatici pubblicati a Roma e nel Lazio, secolo XVII* (Rome, 1988)

N. Zaslaw: 'The First Opera in Paris: a Study in the Politics of Art', *Jean-Baptiste Lully and the Music of the French Baroque: Essays in Honour of James R. Anthony* (Cambridge, 1989), 7–23

MARGARET MURATA

Butler [Boteler, Botoler], **Charlotte** (*b* c1660; *d* after 1692). English soprano and actress. She sang in Crowne's masque *Calisto* at Court in 1675 and may have appeared on the public stage before then. Cibber wrote that she was 'not only a good Actress, but was allow'd, in those Days, to sing and dance to great Perfection. In the Dramatick Opera's of *Dioclesian*, and that of *King Arthur*, she was a capital, and admired Performer'. In Purcell's *King Arthur* she took the role of the airy spirit Philidel and was Cupid in the Frost Scene. She had dark eyes and a lively personality and was attacked in satires as a mercenary whore. After singing in *The Fairy-Queen* in 1692 she was tempted to the Smock Alley Theatre in Dublin by a higher salary, but nothing is known about her career there.

BDA; *LS*
C. Cibber: *An Apology for the Life of Mr. Colley Cibber* (London, 1740)
J. H. Wilson: *All the King's Ladies* (Chicago, 1958)
J. Wilson, ed.: *Roger North on Music* (London, 1959)
O. Baldwin and T. Wilson: 'Purcell's Sopranos', *MT*, cxxiii (1982), 602–9
C. A. Price: *Henry Purcell and the London Stage* (Cambridge, 1984)
OLIVE BALDWIN, THELMA WILSON

Butsko, Yury Markovich (*b* Lubny, 21 May 1938). Russian composer. He studied composition with Sergey Balasanian at the Moscow Conservatory, where he completed his graduate work in 1968. The melos of archaic Russian music – its modes and its distinctive liturgical and folk styles – have been formative in his music. Likewise, the subjects of his three operas are taken from quintessentially Russian sources.

Zapiski sumasshedshego [The Diary of a Madman], 1964 (mono-opera, 2, Butsko, after N. V. Gogol), concert perf., Moscow, 1971
Beliye nochi [White Nights], 1967 (1, Butsko, after F. Dostoyevsky), première, broadcast, USSR; stage, as Weisse Nächte, Dresden, Staatsoper, 15 Sept 1973
Iz pisem khudozhnika (muzïkal'nïye povesti) [From the Letters of an Artist (Musical Tales)], 1974 (mono-opera, after K. Korovin), concert perf., Moscow, All-Union House of Composers, 29 Oct 1979

*

W. Lange: '"Weisse Nächte" von Juri Buzko', *Theater der Zeit*, xi (1973), p.45–6
A. Selitsky: 'Bespodobnïy tip operï' [An Incomparable Type of Opera], *SovM* (1978), no.1, pp.24–9
LAUREL E. FAY

Butt, Dame **Clara (Ellen)** (*b* Steyning, Sussex, 1 Feb 1872; *d* North Stoke, Oxon., 23 Jan 1936). English contralto. She studied with Daniel Rootham in Bristol and in 1890 gained a scholarship at the RCM with J. H. Blower. She sang Orpheus in the RCM production of Gluck's opera at the Lyceum Theatre in 1892, and from then on her success was assured, although it was almost entirely a success of the concert platform. She made a reappearance on the operatic stage only in 1920, singing Orpheus at Covent Garden under Beecham. In the same year she was created DBE for her charitable services during the war. She was a tall woman, standing 6′ 2″; her voice was exceptionally powerful, with a trombone-like boom in the lower register. She made many recordings.

*

W. Ponder: *Clara Butt: her Life-Story* (London, 1928)
'Clara Butt Discography', *Record Advertiser*, ii/1 (1971–2), 2–8; ii/2 (1971–2), 2–9

Buxton. English town in the Peak District of Derbyshire. It was famous from Roman times for its natural springs and was popular as a spa town in the late 19th century, largely through the patronage of the Dukes of Devonshire. The Buxton Opera House, built by Frank Matcham on the edge of the Pavilion Gardens, opened on 1 June 1903. A few visiting opera companies appeared there, but it was mostly used for plays and latterly as a cinema, before its restoration in 1978–9 by Derek Sugden on the initiative of the founders of the Buxton Festival. The town had a theatre festival in 1937–42 and one based around the Hallé Orchestra in 1959–65. Neither was as ambitious as that which opened in 1979 directed by the producer Malcolm Fraser (until 1987) and the conductor Anthony Hose. Although the festival (in late July and early August) includes plays, exhibitions, concerts and lectures, it has normally been built around the presentation of two little-known operas. Among these have been three works by Cimarosa, three by Donizetti and operas of Galuppi, Piccinni and Francesco Conti.

*

R. McCoola: *Theatre in the Hills: Two Centuries of Theatre in Buxton* (Chapel-en-le-Frith, 1984)
M. Kennedy: *Buxton Festival 1979–1988: the First Ten Years* (Buxton, 1989)
DAVID FALLOWS

Buzzoleni [Buzoleni, Bussoleni, Bucceleni, Bucelleni, Bozzdeni], **Giovanni** (*b* Brescia; *fl* 1682–1722). Italian tenor. He was in the service of Ferdinando Carlo Gonzaga, Duke of Mantua, and sang Herenio, Cibele, Pescatore and Neptune in Giovanni Legrenzi's *Ottaviano Cesare Augusto* in 1682; he was among the 'virtuosi' of the court of Mantua at least until 1690 and again in 1700. He is named in three librettos in Naples between 1697 and 1698: in *Aiace* (C. A. Lonati, Paolo Magni and Francesco Ballarotti), Alessandro Scarlatti's *La caduta de' Decemviri* and G. C. Bononcini's *Muzio Scevola*; he is also named in one in Parma in 1700, as a musician of the emperor. He sang in many other Italian cities as well, including Milan and Venice. In the collection of Duke Francesco II d'Este he appears as the composer of a cantata for solo voice, *Clorinda idolo mio* (in *I-MOe*), and was noted for singing cantatas by Ballarotti.

*

S. Durante: 'Alcune considerazioni sui cantanti di teatro del primo settecento e la loro formazione', *Antonio Vivaldi: teatro musicale cultura e società: Venice 1981*, ii, 427–81
PAOLA BESUTTI

Buzzolla, Antonio (*b* Adria, nr Rovigo, 2 March 1815; *d* Venice, 20 March 1871). Italian composer and conductor. He studied with his father and in Venice. In 1831 he joined the orchestra of La Fenice as flautist and then as violinist. His first opera, *Il Ferramondo*, was performed successfully at the Teatro S Benedetto in 1836. He completed his studies at the Naples Conservatory (1837–9) under Donizetti and Mercadante. On his return to Venice another two operas were performed, *Gli avventurieri* (1842) and *Mastino I della Scala* (1841), though with only moderate success.

In 1843 he went to Berlin as conductor of the Italian Opera and later toured Poland and Russia. In 1847 he was conductor of the Théâtre Italien in Paris. He returned to Venice, where two more operas were performed at La Fenice: *Amleto* (1848) and *Elisabetta di Valois* (1850). He became *maestro di cappella* at St Mark's and he helped found the Società dei Concerti Benedetto Marcello, which later became the conservatory. His many songs in Venetian dialect won him greater acclaim than his operas and can still be considered masterpieces of the genre. Buzzolla left one incomplete opera, *La puta onorata*, also in the Venetian dialect, and some fine church music.

first performed in Venice unless otherwise stated
Il Ferramondo (os, 2), S Benedetto, 3 Dec 1836
Mastino I della Scala (G. Fontebasso), S Benedetto, 31 May 1841
Gli avventurieri (ob, 2, F. Romani), Fenice, 14 May 1842
Amleto (os, G. Peruzzini, after W. Shakespeare), Fenice, 24 Feb 1848
Elisabetta di Valois (F. M. Piave), Fenice, 16 Feb 1850
La puta onorata, inc.
GIOVANNI CARLI BALLOLA

Bydgoszcz (Ger. Bromberg). Polish town in Pomerania, from 1772 to 1918 under Prussian rule. During the 17th and 18th centuries theatrical works were performed in the Jesuit College. From 1788 visiting German and Polish companies and local amateur troupes occasionally gave light musical works such as Jan Stefani's *Cud mniemany* ('The Supposed Miracle', 1812) and Kauer's *Donauweibchen* (1815). In 1824 a new Stadttheater was built and regular guest appearances by the German company from Poznań were organized; *Tannhäuser* and Halévy's *Die Jüdin* were given in 1853. Later the theatre established its own company, while various German, Polish or mixed amateur troupes – Opernverein, Czytelnia Polska, Towarzystwo Przemysłowe (the latter two from 1870) – continued to appear. In 1871 a professional Polish company from Poznań, under M. Sztengel, performed Moniuszko's *Jawnuta*, Kurpiński's *Krakowiacy i górale* ('Krakovians and Mountaineers') and other operettas. From 1885 to 1902 highly successful summer seasons were given almost every year by the Teatr Polski from Poznań, presenting among other works Moniuszko's *Halka* (1892) and many Polish folk pieces; these were forbidden by the German authorities in 1902. After a fire in 1890, the Stadttheater (780 seats) was reconstructed in 1896 by C. H. Seeling; it remained open until 1945. A second, 500-seat summer theatre had been built in 1882, the Victoria (from 1892 the Elysium), where until 1920 mostly operettas were given.

After Poland regained independence, the municipal theatre was taken over on 22 January 1920 by a Polish company as the Teatr Polski. Its vast repertory included Moniuszko's *Verbum nobile* (1920) and *Halka* (1925), Kurpiński's *Zamek na Czorszytnie* ('The Castle of Czorsztyn', 1920) and *Krakovians and Mountaineers* (1920, 1930), and operas by Verdi, Bizet and Puccini as well as classical and modern operettas and many folk pieces. Between the wars there was also a German amateur company, the Deutsche Bühne; from 1921 until 1935 it gave regular performances of over 20 operettas and musical comedies by Schubert, J. Strauss, Lehár and Künnecke, and several operas by Weber, Lortzing, Nicolai and others. After World War II operatic activity was first started by the Studio Operowe at the Musical Society. On 3 March 1956 it established the Teatr Muzyczny Opery i Operetki (Music Theatre of Opera and Operetta), which became state owned in 1960. In 1980 it was renamed the Państwowa Opera (State Opera House) and has been directed since then by Alicja Weber. Its ambitious range includes works from the current international repertory as well as new operas by Polish composers. Performances take place in the Teatr Polski, but the company's own 1000-seat building is to be opened in 1992.

*

Z. Raszewski: *Z tradycji teatralnych Pomorz, Wielkopolski i Śląska* [Theatrical Traditions in Pomerania, Great Poland and Silesia] (Wrocław, 1955)

Aus Brombergs Vergangenheit (Wilhelmshaven, 1973)

J. Formanowicz: *Historia Teatru Polskiego w Bydgoszczy w latach 1920–1939* [History of the Teatr Polski in Bydgoszcz] (Warsaw and Poznań, 1978)

W. Kotowski: *Teatry 'Deutsche Bühne' w Wielkopolsce i na Pomorzu 1919–1939* [The 'Deutsche Bühne' Theatres in Great Poland and Pomerania] (Warsaw and Poznań, 1985)

S. Michalski, ed.: *Bydgoszcz wczoraj i dzisiaj* [Bydgoszcz Yesterday and Today] (Warsaw and Poznań, 1988)

KORNEL MICHAŁOWSKI

Byrding, Holger (*b* Mariager, 28 Dec 1891; *d* Copenhagen, 13 June 1980). Danish bass-baritone. He studied in Copenhagen, where he made his début in 1911 as Prince Gremin in *Yevgeny Onegin*. Developing a wide repertory, he became one of the most valued members of the Danish Opera, the resident Wotan, Sachs, Iago and Falstaff, and retired in 1964. He made guest appearances in Stockholm, and later taught there and in Copenhagen. His recordings include some made 'live' in the 1930s, showing fine, full-bodied tone and even production. He was also a good actor with an impressive stage presence. J. B. STEANE

Byron, Lord [6th Baron; Byron, George Gordon (Noel)] (*b* London, 22 Jan 1788; *d* Missolonghi [now Mesolóngion], 19 April 1824). English poet. The success of the first two cantos of *Childe Harold's Pilgrimage* (1812) brought him immediate fame, and even greater success followed *The Giaour* (1813), *The Bride of Abydos* (1813) and *The Corsair* (1814). Their cultivation of wild emotions, of exotic settings and of a disdainful gloom won him a European reputation; and the irregularity of his private life (which included an affair with his half-sister Augusta Leigh) did nothing to diminish his appeal to his generation as a Romantic outsider, ruled by his passions and tinged with doom. That this is a very incomplete view of him as a poet mattered little to European artists, who, further excited by his death fighting for the liberation of Greece, hailed him as an essential Romantic. The Byronic hero was widely imitated – notably by Pushkin in *Yevgeny Onegin* – and stimulated composers to base works on his poems, however loosely. Byron's reputation was particularly longlasting in Russia. His writings have inspired more than 40 operas; among the composers to project operas based on his works were Schumann (*Der Corsair*, 1844) and Massenet (*Manfred*, *c*1869). There are also three operas about Byron himself, including Virgil Thomson's *Lord Byron* (1972).

The Bride of Abydos (poem, 1813): Poniatowski, 1845; A. Fell, 1853; F. Sand, 1858; T. Dubois, 1864; A. Barthe, 1865; P. Lebrun, 1897

The Giaour (poem, 1813): J. Bovery, 1840; A. Hermann, 1866; N. Berg, 1912, as Leila; M. Delmas, 1928

The Corsair (poem, 1814): W. Reeve, 1814; L. Arditi, 1847; Verdi, 1848; A. Marracino, 1900, as Corrado

Lara (poem, 1814): H. Ruolz-Fontenay, 1835; M. Salvi, 1843; A. Maillart, 1864; A. Marsick, 1929

Parisina (poem, 1816): Donizetti, 1833; T. Giribaldi, 1878; E. Keurvels, 1890; V. Veneziani, 1901; G. Orefice, 1915, as Ugo e Parisina

The Siege of Corinth (poem, 1816): A. Cahen, 1890, as Le vénitien

Manfred (play, 1817): H. Bronsart von Schellendorf, 1901; A. B. Bogatïryov, 1926

Cain (play, 1821): C. Delvincourt, 1948, as Lucifer; Schmodtmann, 1952; F. Lattuada, 1957

Marino Faliero (play, 1821): F. von Holstein, 1881; W. Freudenberg, 1889

Sardanapalus (play, 1821): D. Litta, 1844; G. Alary, 1852; V. Joncières, 1867; Mme Baronne de Maître, 1870; A. S. Famintsïn, 1875; G. Libani, 1880; V. Duvernoy, 1882; J.-J. Grunenwald, 1961

The Two Foscari (play, 1821): Verdi, 1844; Bogatïryov, 1940

Heaven and Earth (play, 1823): Donizetti, 1830, as Il diluvio universale; R. Glier, 1900

Don Juan (poem, unfinished, cantos i–xvi pubd 1819–24): J. Polignac, 1877; Z. Fibich, 1896, as Hedy

*

P. G. Trueblood, ed.: *Byron's Political and Cultural Influence in Nineteenth-Century Europe* (London, 1981)

JOHN WARRACK

C

Cabaletta (It.). A term probably of Spanish derivation, first encountered during the second decade of the 19th century, and defined in Pietro Lichtenthal's *Dizionario* (1826): it denotes the second, usually fast movement of a double aria in an Italian opera, consisting of a melodic period of two stanzas which is repeated with decorations added by the singer after an orchestral ritornello, often accompanied by choral or solo PERTICHINI and followed by a matching coda designed to stimulate applause (e.g. 'Non più mesta': *La Cenerentola*, Rossini, 1817). Only rarely does a cabaletta occur in isolation, without a preceding 'cantabile'; one is 'Non fù sogno' (*I Lombardi*, Verdi, 1843). In early examples such as 'Io sono docile' (*Il barbiere di Siviglia*, Rossini, 1816) only the second half of the period is repeated, a procedure found as late as 'No, non udrai rimproveri' (*La traviata*, Verdi, 1853). In certain cases there is a brilliant coda for the voice, e.g. 'Vien diletto, è in ciel la luna' (*I puritani*, Bellini, 1835). In Romantic opera, cabalettas in moderate time with no element of display become increasingly frequent, for example 'Meco tu vien, o misera' (*La straniera*, Bellini, 1829), 'Tu che a Dio spiegasti l'ali' (*Lucia di Lammermoor*, Donizetti, 1835) and 'Pondo è letal, martiro' (*Giovanna d'Arco*, Verdi, 1845); the term thus comes to designate the piece's form rather than its character. After 1860 the solo cabaletta rapidly declined, becoming virtually extinct about 1870. As the practice of embellishment died out, it became customary in revivals of repertory works to omit the cabaletta repeat, a habit that modern scholarship tends to deplore on structural grounds. Verdi, however, sanctioned it for a late revival of his own *I masnadieri* (1847).

The term 'cabaletta' is also used to describe the final movement of a duet. Here the same formula is elaborated, the melody being sung successively by each singer and a third time, after an orchestral ritornello, by both voices in unison, harmony or more rarely in dialogue, as in 'Vieni a Roma' (*Norma*, Bellini, 1831). A classic instance is 'Verranno a te sull'aure' (*Lucia di Lammermoor*). Where the voice-types are unequal (soprano-baritone, contralto-tenor) the singers may enter in different keys, as in 'Veglia, o donna, questo fior' (*Rigoletto*, Verdi, 1851), or even be assigned different melodies, as in 'Ah te bada, a te stesso pon mente' (*Lucrezia Borgia*, Donizetti, 1833), before joining in the initial one. The duet cabaletta outlived its solo counterpart for more than a decade. Verdi uses it several times for lovers who outstay their own safety; but triple repetition became increasingly rare. A late instance of the form is 'Sì, pel ciel marmoreo giuro!' (*Otello*, Verdi, 1887).

See also ARIA.

D. Rosen and C. Rosen: 'A Musicological Word Study: It. *cabaletta*', *Romance Philology*, xx (1966), 168–76

F. Noske: 'The Notorious Cabaletta', *The Signifier and the Signified: Studies in the Operas of Mozart and Verdi* (London and The Hague, 1977), 271–93

A. B. Caswell, ed.: *Embellished Opera Arias* (Madison, WI, 1989)

JULIAN BUDDEN

Caballé, Montserrat (*b* Barcelona, 12 April 1933). Spanish soprano. She studied for 12 years at the Barcelona Liceo, with (among others) Eugenia Kemmeny and Napoleone Annovazzi, winning the 1954 Liceo gold medal. She joined the Basle Opera in 1956; in three years she built up an impressive repertory, including Pamina, Tosca, Aida, Marta in d'Albert's *Tiefland*, and Strauss's Arabella, Chrysothemis and Salome. In 1959 she sang her first Violetta and Tatyana, at Bremen, and the heroines of Dvořák's *Armida* and *Rusalka*. At La Scala the next year she first appeared as one of Klingsor's flowermaidens (*Parsifal*); a gradually widening international career took her to Vienna, back to Barcelona, to Lisbon and, in 1964, Mexico City (as Massenet's Manon). In 1965 she replaced Horne at short notice in a New York concert *Lucrezia Borgia*, and achieved overnight stardom. After that many Donizetti operas were revived for her (notably *Roberto Devereux*, *Maria Stuarda*, *Parisina* and *Gemma di Vergy*). In 1965 she also made débuts at Glyndebourne (Marschallin and Mozart's Countess) and the Metropolitan (Marguerite). At La Scala she has played Lucrezia Borgia, Mary Stuart, Norma and Amelia (*Ballo*) and at Covent Garden Violetta (début, 1972), Norma, Leonora (*Il trovatore*), Amelia (*Ballo*) and Aida. In 1987 she sang Saffo (Pacini) and, in 1989, Isolde, at the Liceo, Barcelona. Other roles include Spontini's Agnes, Rossini's Ermione and Madama Cortese (*Il viaggio a Reims*), which she sang in Vienna (1988).

Regarded by many as Callas's successor, Caballé was for a time the leading Verdi and Donizetti soprano of the day, able to spin effortless long legato phrases and noted for her floated *pianissimo* high notes. She is an actress of refinement and dignity, but no great dramatic intensity. Her many recordings include roles (in Puccini and Strauss operas) which she sang more frequently in earlier years, and others, such as Lucia and Fiordiligi, which she has never sung on stage. In the 1980s and early 90s she became a notable recitalist, especially successful in Spanish song. She married the tenor Bernabé Marti in 1964.

*

A. Blyth: 'Montserrat Caballé Talks', *Gramophone*, li (1973–4), 174

J. B. Steane: *The Grand Tradition* (London, 1974), 537ff

F. G. Barker: 'Montserrat Caballé', *Opera*, xxvi (1975), 342–8

ALAN BLYTH

Caballero, Manuel Fernández [Fernández Caballero, Manuel] (*b* Murcia, 14 March 1835; *d* Madrid, 26 Feb 1906). Spanish composer and conductor. He received tuition in piano, violin and flute from the age of five, notably from his violinist brother-in-law Julian Gil. In addition he studied with the composer José Calvo and with Indalecio Soriano Fuertes. In 1850 he entered the Madrid Conservatory, where he was a pupil of Hilarión Eslava and others, and in 1856 he obtained first prize in composition. After playing the violin in the orchestra of the Teatro Real he became successively conductor at the Variedades, Lope de Vega, Circo and Español theatres, composing large numbers of songs, choruses and dances and, in 1854, his first zarzuelas, *La vergonzosa en palacio* (not performed until 1855) and (under the pseudonym of 'Florentino Burillo') *Tres madres para una hija*. In 1853 he had been prevented on account of his youth from taking up a position as conductor in Santiago, Cuba, which he had won in a competition, but in 1864 he went to Cuba as conductor of a zarzuela troupe, and he also organized and conducted concerts there. Returning to Madrid in 1871, he devoted himself successfully to the prolific composition of zarzuelas. A habanera from the now forgotten *La gallina ciega* (1873) was used by Pablo de Sarasate for the second of his *Danzas españolas* (op.21 no.2), but it was *La Marsellesa* (1874), set in revolutionary Paris, that firmly established his melodic style, with the dance rhythms and lyric patterns of continental operetta intermingled with more specifically Spanish touches. In 1884 Caballero went to Lisbon and in 1885 to South America, conducting his works with great success. He was elected to the Academy of Fine Arts in 1891, though pressure of work and failing eyesight delayed presentation of the necessary written discourse until 1902. After the composition of *El dúo de la africana* (1893) his eyesight forced him to use as amanuenses Mariano Hermoso and his own son Mario, until he was operated on for cataracts in 1899 and 1902. The scores written during these blind years include two of his greatest successes, *La viejecita* (1897) and *Gigantes y cabezudos* (1898). These and his other enduring successes display his rich gift of melody, rhythmic élan and good humour.

zarzuelas, published in Madrid in vocal score at about the time of production

MDC – *Madrid, Teatro del Circo*

MDZ – *Madrid, Teatro de la Zarzuela*

Tres madres para una hija (2, A. Alverá), Madrid, Lope de Vega, 24 Dec 1854; La vergonzosa en palacio (1, L. Eguílaz), MDC, 9 May 1855; Mentir á tiempo (1, A. M. Decarrete), MDC, 23 March 1856; Cuando ahorcaron á Quevedo (3, Eguílaz), MDZ, 1856; Juan Lanas (1, F. Camprodón), MDZ, 1856; La jardinera (3, Camprodón), MDZ, 1857; El vizconde de Letorière (3, J. M. García), MDC, 1858; Un cocinero (1, Camprodón), MDZ, 1858; Frasquito (1, R. de la Vega), MDZ, April 1859; La guerra de los sombreros (1, J. Picón), MDZ, June 1859; Una emoción (1, L. Bremon), MDZ, 12 Sept 1859; Un zapatero (1, F. Castellón), MDZ, 1859; El gran bandido (2, Camprodón), MDZ, 23 Dec 1860, collab. C. Oudrid; Los dos primos (1, Vega), MDZ, 1860

La red de flores (1, Pedrosa), MDZ, 3 April 1861; El caballo blanco (1, C. Frontaura), MDZ, 12 June 1861, collab. Oudrid; Llegar y besar el santo (1, E. Inza), MDZ, 15 June 1861, collab. Oudrid; Un embargo (1, Inza), El Escorial, 1861; La reina Topacio (3, E. Alvarez), MDZ, 11 Sept 1861; El loco de la guardilla (1, N. Serra), MDZ, 9 Oct 1861; Roquelaure (3, J. Belza), MDZ, 17 March 1862, collab. Oudrid and J. Rogel; Equilibrios del amor (1, Pedrosa), MDZ, 20 April 1862, collab. Oudrid; Juegos de azár (2, M. Pina), MDZ, 30 Oct 1862; La campanilla del boticario (1, Pina), MDC, 2 Dec 1862, collab. Campos; Los dos mellizos (1, Camprodón), MDZ, 7 Dec 1862; Las suicidas (1, Camprodón), MDZ, Dec 1862; Aventuras de un jóven honesto (3, Pina), MDC, 24 Dec 1862

El hijo de Lavapiés (1, Belza and Macía), MDZ, 1864; Tres para dos (1, E. Zafra), Havana, Tacon, 1 Feb 1865; Luz y sombra (2, Serra), MDZ, 18 Oct 1867; El criado de mi suegro, MDC, *c*1868, collab. Rogel and I. Hernández; El primer día feliz (3, D. Céspedes, after A. P. d'Ennery and E. Cormon: *Le premier jour de bonheur*), MDZ, 31 Jan 1872; El atrevido en la corte (3, L. M. de Larra), MDZ, 19 Oct 1872; La gallina ciega (2, M. Ramos Carrión), MDZ, 3 Oct 1873; El sargento Bailén (2, Artea), MDZ, 3 Nov 1873; Las hijas de Fulano (1, Larra), MDZ, 4 March 1874; El velo de encaje (3, Puente y Brañas), MDZ, 3 Oct 1874; El año del diablo (1, S. M. Granés), MDZ, 3 March 1875, collab. M. Nieto; Este jóven me conviene (1, Granés), MDZ, 3 March 1875, collab. J. Casares; El trono de Escocia (3, Puente y Brañas), MDZ, 28 March 1875, collab. R. Aceves; La clave (2, Ramos Carrión and Arana), Madrid, Circo de Rivas, 26 June 1875; Las nueve de la noche (3, Trigo y Bermejo), MDZ, 19 Oct 1875, collab. Casares; Entre el alcalde y el rey (3, Nuñez de Arco), MDZ, 23 Dec 1875, collab. P. E. Arrieta

La Marsellesa (3, Ramos Carrión), MDZ, 2 Feb 1876; El siglo que viene (3, Ramos Carrión and C. Coello), Madrid, Circo de Rivas, 3 July 1876; La jaula de locos (1, Vega), Madrid, Buen Retiro, July 1876; Blancas y azules (3, J. M. Nogués and R. M. Liern), Madrid, Apolo, 22 Dec 1876, collab. Oudrid and Casares; Los sobrinos del capitán Grant (4, Ramos Carrión, after Verne), Madrid, Circo de Rivas, 25 Aug 1877; La aurora de un reinado (3, F. Godino), MDZ, 16 Jan 1878, collab. Casares; El salto del pasiego (3, Eguílaz), MDZ, 17 March 1878; Los negros catedráticos [probably by Caballero]; La banda del rey (3, Alvarez), MDZ, 4 Oct 1878, collab. Casares; Las dos princesas (3, Ramos Carrión and Pina), MDZ, 15 Jan 1879; El lucero del alba (1, Pina), Madrid, Apolo, 15 April 1879; La jota aragonesa (1, C. Navarro), Zaragoza, Pignatelli, 30 June 1879; Amor que empieza y amor que acaba (1, R. Dalmau), MDZ, 25 Oct 1879; El cepillo de las ánimas (3, Alvarez), MDZ, 28 Nov 1879; El corpus de sangre (3, Larra), MDZ, 24 Dec 1879

Las hazañas de Hércules (3, Alvarez), Madrid, Circo de Rivas, 13 June 1880; Al polo (1, Navarro), Madrid, Buen Retiro, 22 Aug 1880, collab. F. Espino; El asesino de Arganda (1, Pina), Madrid, Alhambra, 25 Nov 1880, collab. Espino; Los feos (1, P. Gil), Madrid, Eslava, 1880; Mata moros (1, Navarro), Madrid, Váriedades, 6 Dec 1880; El sacristán de San Justo (3, L. Blanc and Navarro), Madrid, Apolo, 24 Dec 1880, collab. Nieto; Mantos y capas (3, J. Santero), Madrid, Apolo, 16 May 1881, collab. Nieto; La niña bonita (3, Larra), MDZ, 7 Dec 1881; De verano (2, Pina), Madrid, Eslava, Dec 1881, collab. Rubio; Contaduría (1, Blanc and Navarro), Madrid, Eslava, 1881; Los bonitos (1, Gil), Madrid, Eslava, 1881; Las mil y una noches (3, Santero), Madrid, Circo de Rivas, 21 June 1882, collab. Rubio; Dar la castaña (1, Navarro), Madrid, Recoletos, 6 July 1882; El gran Tamorlán de Persia (3, Santero [and Cabidas or Cabridos?]), MDC, Sept 1882, collab. Nieto

Curriya (1, Andrade), Madrid, Martín, 12 Nov 1883; El capitán Centellas (3, J. J. Herranz), Madrid, Apolo, 15 Dec 1883, collab. A. Almagro; Trabajo perdido (1, S. Lastra), Madrid, Variedades, 3 Jan 1884; Para casa de los padres (1, Pina), Madrid, Eslava, 10 March 1884; La farsanta (3, Pina), Madrid, Apolo, 16 April 1884, collab. Rubio; Los bandos de Villafrita (E. Navarro Gonzalvo), Madrid, Recoletos, 5 Aug 1884; El hermano Baltasar; Las grandes figuras; El guerrillero (3, F. Muñoz), Madrid, Apolo, Jan 1885, collab. Arrieta and R. Chapí; La mejor receta (Gascón), MDZ, June 1885; Una noche en Loreto (A. Menchaca), Buenos Aires, Aug 1885; Los dioses se van; El oro de la reacción; Locos de amor (1), Madrid, Maravillas, July 1886; Ciclón XXII (1), Madrid, Maravillas, 30 July 1886; Somatén

Las mujeres que matan (1, Coello), Madrid, Princesa, Jan 1887; La doctora; El merendero del tuerto; La viña del Señor; Lorita real; La revolución; ¿Vamos a ver eso?; El bazar H (Navarro), Madrid, Recoletos, 8 Aug 1887; Por sacar la cara; Lista de compañía; Chateau Margaux (1, J. Jackson Veyán), Madrid, Variedades, 5 Oct 1887; Cubra libre (drama, F. Jacques and Aguado), Madrid, Apolo, Nov 1887; La chiclanera; Aguas azotados (Pina), Madrid, Apolo, 7 Jan 1888; La noche del 31; Don Manuel Ruiz; La riojana (Navarro Gonzalvo), Madrid, Felipe, 15 June 1888; El golpe de gracia (S. E. Sena), Madrid, Recoletos, 23 July 1888; De Madrid á Siberia; El alcalde de Amurrio; Septiembre, Eslava y Compañía; El pasmo de Cecilia; El lavadero del Mico; Las manías; La hija de la mascota

Los zangolotinos (1, Jackson Veyán), Madrid, Apolo, 1889; A Roma por todo; Los Isidros; A ti suspiramos (Liern and Granés), Madrid, Maravillas, June 1889; Don Jaime el Conquistador; A dos luces; Muerte, juicio, infierno y gloria; Buñuelos; Pedidos á cuenta; Garibaldi; ¡Olé Sevilla! (1, Jackson Veyán), Madrid, 1889; España (Palencia), Barcelona, 25 April 1890, rev. 1893; ¿A que no puedo casarme?; Concierto europeo; Hace falta un caballero; El día de la Asención; La choza del diablo (R. Ramirez Cumbreras), Madrid, 1891; Las cuatro estaciones; El fantasma de fuego (M. Gullón and L. de Larra), Madrid, Price, Dec 1891; La una y la otra; Antón Perulero

Los aparecidos (C. Arniches and C. Lucio), Madrid, Apolo, 23 Feb 1892; La casa encantada; De Herodes á Pilatos; La revista; La venta del hambre; Los extranjeros; Triple Alianza (1, Jackson Veyán), Madrid, Eslava, March 1893; El dúo de la africana (1, M. Echegaray), Madrid, Apolo, 13 May 1893; La vispera de la fiesta; Un punto filipino; Los dineros del sacristán (1, L. de Larra and Gullón), Madrid, Eslava, 24 March 1894; Los africanistas (G. Merino, E. López Marín), Madrid, Romea, 5 April 1894; Campanero y sacristán (1, E. Ayuso and M. de Labra), Madrid, Príncipe Alfonso, Aug 1894; El cabo primero (1, Arniches and Lucio), Barcelona, Eldorado, Oct 1895; El domador de leones; La rueda de la fortuna (L. de Larra and Gullón), MDZ, Jan 1896; Tortilla al ron (Merino), Madrid, 4 April 1896; El saboyano (G. Perrín and M. de Palacios), MDZ, Aug 1896, collab. Chalons; La expulsion de los judios 1493 (Arniches and Lucio), MDZ, Sept/Oct 1896; El padrino del Nene [Todo por el arte] (1, J. Romea), MDZ, Sept or 28 Nov 1896

La viejecita (1, Echegaray), MDZ, 29/30 April 1897; San Gil de las afueras; El señor Joaquín (1, Romea), MDZ, 18 Feb 1898; Aun hay patria, Veremundo (Navarro Gonzalvo), Madrid, 10 May 1898; La magia negra (opereta-revista, Gullón), MDZ, 24 Sept 1898, collab. Valverde *hijo*; El traje de luces (J. Alvarez Quintero and S. Alvarez Quintero), MDZ, 28 Nov 1898; Gigantes y cabezudos (1, Echegaray), MDZ, 29 Nov 1898; El testamento del siglo; La virgen del puerto (M. Caballero), MDZ, 17 Jan/March 1899; ¡Citrato, de ver será! (parodía-opereta, Merino and Lucio), Madrid, 24 March 1899, collab. Valverde *hijo*; Los estudiantes (Echegaray), MDZ, 28 Nov 1899; El rey de los aires (Labra), Madrid, Cómico, Nov 1900; La barcarola (E. Sellés), MDZ, 18 Dec 1900

La tribu salvaje (E. Gaspar), MDZ, June 1901; La diligencia (Echegaray), Madrid, Eldorado, 5 July 1901; Los figurines; El trapera (2, L. de Larra), Madrid, Cómico, 28 Jan 1902; El favorito del duque (1), Madrid, Eslava, Jan 1902; La manta zamorana (1, Perrín and Palacios), MDZ, March 1902; La señá Justa (Echegaray), Madrid, Apolo, Nov 1902; Mundo, demonio y carne; El Dios grande (M. Caballero), MDZ, Feb 1903; La guerrilla del fraile; La mariposa negra; Tolete; La inclusera (1, L. de Larra), Madrid, 19 Nov 1903, collab. Valverde *hijo*; El pícaro mundo (1), collab. Lleó; La faena; Las bellas artes; El día de San Eugenio; El aouelito; Rusia y Japán (González Rendón), Madrid, Cómico, 21/22 Feb 1905; Los huertanos (1, Olete), Madrid, Apolo, May 1905; La silla de manos, 1905, collab. T. Barrera; María Luisa (1), Madrid, Apolo; La cacharrera (1), MDZ; El lego de San Pablo (M. Fernández de la Puente), Madrid, 22 Dec 1906

*

A. Peña y Goñi: *La ópera española y la música dramática en España en el siglo XIX* (Madrid, 1881; abridged E. Rincón as *España desde la ópera a la zarzuela*, 1967) [with list of works to 1884]

'Fernández Caballero (Manuel)', *Enciclopedia universal ilustrada europeo-americana* (Barcelona, 1907–30), xxiii, 770–71

E. Cotarelo y Mori: *Historia de la zarzuela, ó sea el drama lírico* (Madrid, 1934)

J. Deleito y Piñuela: *Origen y apogeo del 'género chico'* (Madrid, 1949)

A. Fernández-Cid: *Cien años de teatro musical en España (1875–1975)* (Madrid, 1975)

J. Arnau and C. M. Gomez: *Historia de la zarzuela* (Madrid, 1979)

R. Alier and others: *El libro de la zarzuela* (Barcelona, 1982, 2/1986 as *Diccionario de la zarzuela*)

ANDREW LAMB

Caballone [Cabalone, Gabbalone, Gabellone], **Michele** (*b* Naples, 1692; *d* Naples, 19 Jan 1740). Italian composer. He was the son of Vito Cesare and Antonia Ricca Caballone. His life and works are sometimes confused with those of his son Gaspare, who later spelt his name 'Gabellone'; in addition some sources mistakenly claim that he was the teacher of Faustina Bordoni, who in fact studied with Michelangelo Gasparini. Caballone is not known to have held any regular position, and he died in poverty. Towards the end of his life he became a novice in the confraternity of the Congregazione dei Musici in Naples.

During his late thirties Caballone wrote a number of comic operas, mostly for the Teatro dei Fiorentini, including Act 1 of *La Cantarina*; *La Ciulla, o puro Chi ha freuma arriva a tutto*; *La fenta schiava*; and *Ammore vò speranza*. The production of *Ammore vò speranza* gave rise to a notorious scandal: the two leading ladies, Rosa Albertini and Francesca Grieco, quarrelled so violently because of rivalry both on the stage and in love that Grieco had to retire with injuries, and the Viceroy of Naples felt obliged to intervene. Shortly afterwards Albertini was assassinated by a youth named Giulio Lerro. The lady had no relatives whereas those of Lerro were in high positions, and the court dismissed Lerro with only a fine. Caballone also wrote church music and a counterpoint manual.

opere buffe unless otherwise stated

La Cantarina [Act 1] (?A. Piscopo), Naples, Fiorentini, 1728; Acts 2 and 3 by C. Roberto

La Ciulla, o puro Chi ha freuma arriva a tutto (C. de Palma), Naples, Fiorentini, 1728

La fenta schiava (D. Senialbo), Naples, Fiorentini, 1728, *I-Rn*

Ammore vò speranza, Naples, Fiorentini, 1729

Adone re di Cipro (F. Vanstryp), Rome, Capranica, 28 Dec 1730

Li dispiette amoruse (?A. Palomba), Naples, Nuovo, aut. 1731, aria *Rc*, selection *Rsc*

Doubtful: Cecilia, Naples, Fiorentini, 1728; Adriano in Siria (os, P. Metastasio), Naples, 1740, *F-Pn*; Alessandro nell'Indie (os, Metastasio), Naples, *c*1740, *Pn*

*

CroceN; *FlorimoN*

M. Scherillo: *L'opera buffa napoletana durante il settecento: studia letteraria* (Naples, 1883, 2/1917), 175–6

U. Prota-Giurleo: *Nicola Logroscino: 'il dio dell'opera buffa'* (Naples, 1927), 54–6

G. Hardie: 'Neapolitan Comic Opera, 1707–1750: Some Addenda and Corrigenda for *The New Grove*', *JAMS*, xxxvi (1983), 126

JAMES L. JACKMAN

Cabel [née Dreulette], **Marie(-Josèphe)** (*b* Liège, 31 Jan 1827; *d* Maisons-Laffitte, 23 May 1885). Belgian soprano. She studied in Liège and in Brussels with L. J. Cabel. She continued her studies at the Paris Conservatoire and made her début at the Opéra-Comique (1849) in Halévy's *Val d'Andorre*, then accepted a three-year engagement in Brussels. In 1853 she returned to Paris (Théâtre Lyrique) as Toinon in Adam's *Le bijou perdu*. She repeated the role the next year at the St James's Theatre, London, where she also sang Marie in *La fille du régiment*. Returning to the Opéra-Comique, she created the title role of Auber's *Manon Lescaut* (1856), Dinorah in *Le pardon de Ploërmel* (1859) and Philine in Thomas' *Mignon* (1866). She had a supple, silvery voice, and the bravura parts written for her by Auber, Meyerbeer and Thomas attest to her virtuosity.

Cabrillo Music Festival. Annual summer festival held near SANTA CRUZ.

Caccini. Italian family of musicians.

(1) **Giulio Caccini** [Giulio Romano] (*b* Rome or ?Tivoli, 8 Oct 1551; *d* Florence, bur. 10 Dec 1618). Composer, instrumentalist, singer and singing teacher, a pioneer in the Florentine monodic and representational styles of the early Baroque era. Of humble origins, he was trained in singing by Giovanni Animuccia, choirmaster of the Cappella Giulia in Rome, where he was noticed by the Florentine ambassador. He probably made his début at the Medici court in 1565, singing the solo-voice lament of Psyche in the *intermedi* that were part of the wedding entertainments for Prince Francesco and Joanna of Austria. Once in Florence he received further training from the singer Scipione delle Palle, which must have included composition and vocal improvisation of strophic poetry. He probably became a salaried court musician in the 1570s and certainly participated prominently in all subsequent wedding festivities at the Medici court until his death.

During the 1570s and 80s Caccini's reputation was enhanced by his association with the Camerata of Giovanni de' Bardi, who became his lifelong mentor and patron. Caccini claimed to have learnt more from Bardi's circle than from 'more than 30 years of counterpoint'. In 1589 he composed and sang one of the solo songs in the spectacular *intermedi* for the comedy *La pellegrina*, devised by Bardi to celebrate the marriage of Ferdinando I to Christine of Lorraine. His work was not included in the music printed in 1591, perhaps because Caccini and Bardi had fallen out of favour with Ferdinando when he succeeded his brother as grand duke in 1587 and brought his own entourage of musicians from Rome. When Bardi moved to Rome in 1592 Caccini followed, probably as his secretary. In October of that year he also visited Ferrara, where he coached the famous Ferrarese sopranos in the Florentine style of ornamentation.

In Florence in the 1580s Caccini had trained and directed the female vocal ensemble established to rival the one in Ferrara. With his first wife, Lucia, who was probably one of his pupils, and their daughter Francesca, he formed the nucleus of his own family consort, which eventually included his second wife, Margherita, and their children Settimia and Pompeo. When he was formally dismissed from Duke Ferdinando's service in July 1593, Caccini contemplated moving to Rome permanently but eventually decided to settle in Genoa, where he went in 1595 hoping to begin a more lucrative career as a virtuoso performer and teacher.

By 1600 he was back in Florence, having been commissioned to write the music for Chiabrera's *intermedio*-like drama, *Il rapimento di Cefalo*, the production of which was the main theatrical event of the celebrations in October for Maria de' Medici's wedding to Henri IV of France. Although reinstated at court, Caccini was still subject to the rivalries and jealousies that had marked his earlier years. For the modest production of Rinuccini and Peri's opera *Euridice*, which took place a few days before *Il rapimento*, Caccini refused to allow his singers to perform Peri's music and substituted his own for certain sections of the work. Anxious to be able to claim priority as the 'inventor' of the new recitative style, Caccini then completed his setting of Rinuccini's libretto and rushed it into print before Peri's score was published. Caccini's uncommissioned *Euridice* was not performed in its entirety until 1602, however, and of the music for *Il rapimento*, also a collaborative effort, only a few excerpts were published (in *Le nuove musiche*). In fact, Caccini's reputation as a composer rests principally on his two collections of solo madrigals and airs published in 1601/2 and 1614, *Le nuove musiche* and *Nuove musiche e nuova maniera di scriverle*. It is unlikely that he ever composed music for Rinuccini's *Dafne* libretto, as he claimed in his 1614 preface.

As performer and teacher Caccini continued to win acclaim. In 1603 and again during the winter and spring of 1604–5 he visited Paris, where his family was invited to perform at the court of Maria de' Medici. He trained the virtuoso singer Francesco Rasi, who created the title role of Monteverdi's *Orfeo* in Mantua in 1607, as well as Giovanni Gualberto Magli. In Florence Caccini and Bardi supervised the musical productions for Prince Cosimo's wedding in 1608; rather than a new opera, six extravagant *intermedi* with music mainly by Caccini were presented in the manner of the 1589 festivities. In 1609, however, Cosimo succeeded Ferdinando as grand duke, and the young Florentine composer Marco da Gagliano was appointed to the most important musical post in the city. This marked the beginning of Caccini's semi-retirement. In 1614 he became choirmaster at Ss Annunziata, where he was buried a few years later.

Caccini's claims to priority in the invention of recitative are based on his early adoption of Bardi's humanistic concern for clarity of text setting, which in turn prompted him to reject counterpoint and 'introduce a kind of music in which one could almost speak in tones'. The results of his experiments in song reform were the solo madrigals and airs with simple harmonic accompaniment and judiciously regulated ornamentation that he performed for Bardi's Camerata in the 1580s and 90s and finally published in 1602. But Caccini did not apply this new compositional style to the stage until 1600, after several successful performances of Rinuccini and Peri's first opera *Dafne*. Moreover, there was a qualitative difference; Pirrotta coined the phrase 'cantar recitando' (song modified by speaking) to characterize Caccini's more lyrical style as opposed to Peri's more realistic 'recitar cantando' (speech modified by singing).

Although more difficult to document, Caccini's most important contributions to the field of opera seem to have been in the area of performance rather than composition. In teaching that ornamentation was the key to moving the affections, Caccini redefined the concept of virtuosity and attempted to limit its role to that of enhancing the impact of the words themselves. He also advocated 'a certain *sprezzatura*', or studied effortlessness on the part of the singer, a quality that resembled the polished grace of Castiglione's courtiers and lent an air of spontaneity to their calculated demeanour and actions. Through the didactic prefaces to his song collections and by his influence and example in musical circles at court, Caccini instructed the first opera singers in the art of captivating and moving their audiences.

See also EURIDICE (ii) and *RAPIMENTO DI CEFALO, IL*.

Il rapimento di Cefalo (prol., 5 scenes, epilogue, G. Chiabrera), Florence, Palazzo Uffizi, 9 Oct 1600, excerpts (Florence, 1601/2/*R*1934); incl. choruses by S. Venturi del Nibbio, P. Strozzi and L. Bati
Euridice (prol., 5 scenes, O. Rinuccini), Florence, Palazzo Pitti, 5 Dec 1602 (Florence, 1600/01 and 1615/*R*1976)

Arias and choruses in Peri: Euridice, 1600

*

A. M. Nagler: *Theatre Festivals of the Medici, 1539–1637* (New Haven, CT, 1964), 93–115
N. Pirrotta and E. Povoledo: *Li due Orfei: da Poliziano a Monteverdi* (Turin, 1969, 2/1975; Eng. trans., 1982)
H. W. Hitchcock: Introduction and translation of Caccini's preface to *Le nuove musiche*, RRMBE, ix (1970)
D. Galliver: 'Giulio Caccini – per canto famoso', *MMA*, x (1979), 38–46
M. A. Bacherini Bartoli: 'Giulio Caccini: nuovi fonti biografiche e lettere inedite', *Studi musicali*, ix (1980), 59–72
B. R. Hanning: *Of Poetry and Music's Power: Humanism and the Creation of Opera* (Ann Arbor, 1980)
H. M. Brown: 'The Geography of Florentine Monody: Caccini at Home and Abroad', *EMc*, ix (1981), 147–68
R. Giazotto: *Le due patrie di Giulio Caccini* (Florence, 1984)
T. Carter: 'Giulio Caccini (1551–1618): New Facts, New Music', *Studi musicali*, xvi (1987), 13–31

(2) **Francesca Caccini** [Francesca Caccini Signorini; 'La Cecchina'; Francesca Raffaelli] (*b* Florence, 18 Sept 1587; *d* after 1637). Composer and singer, elder daughter of (1) Giulio Caccini. The first woman to compose opera, she worked for the Medici family from 1600 to 1627 and again from 1634 to 1637, modelling her career on that of her well-known father and teacher. She made her début as a *virtuosa* singer with his family ensemble in the entertainments for the wedding of Maria de' Medici and Henri IV of France in 1600. In 1607 she married a fellow-singer, Giovanni Battista Signorini, and formally entered the service of Grand Duke Cosimo II, working as a teacher, singer and composer in Florence, and in Rome in the circle of Virginio Orsini and Cardinal Montalto. From 1622 until 1627 she was the highest-paid musician on the staff of Grand Duke Ferdinando II. Widowed in late 1626, by January 1628 she had married the Lucchese patron and amateur singer Tomaso Raffaelli and entered the service of the banker-diplomat Vincentio Buonvisi in Lucca. By 1634, widowed again, she had returned to Florence, where she was in the service of the dowager Grand Duchess Christine of Lorraine and the new Grand Duchess Vittoria della Rovere until at least 1637. Although Caccini was a prolific composer of songs, incidental entertainments and music for the theatre, little of her work survives. 26 extant letters reveal her as an astute judge of patrons' tastes, and of her own gifts as a teacher and composer.

Only one opera by Caccini survives, *La liberazione di Ruggiero dall'isola d'Alcina*, first performed in Florence for the visit of Prince Władisław of Poland during Carnival 1625. (A performance in Warsaw in 1628 has been incorrectly considered the first known operatic production outside Italy.) A setting of the gynocentric, feminist libretto by Ferdinando Saracinelli, the opera was praised by contemporary listeners for the beauty of its siren's song, its chorus of enchanted plants and its ensemble writing for women's voices and recorder trio. Caccini's approach to serious passages resembles that of Jacopo Peri in that she constructs dramatic speeches as an unfolding variation on an opening musico-rhetorical gesture. Prunières thought her style was influenced by Monteverdi; but while she shares with him tonal clarity and a mastery over the affective use of dissonance, she is far more faithful to the Florentine ideal of matching musical to poetic structures. Two features of *La liberazione* set it apart from contemporary works. First, it uses tonal contrast to reflect gender: Alcina and her women attendants sing in flat keys, Ruggiero and lesser men sing in sharp keys, and the androgynous sorceress Melissa sings mainly in C major. Women and men are portrayed as experiencing the action from different points of view, while juxtapositions of gender-identified key areas are frequent and striking enough to create a musical subtext exploring the relationship between social status and cross-gender behaviour. Second, Caccini's intense, chromatic setting of Alcina's long complaint to the unfaithful Ruggiero gradually dissolves the union between poetic and musical form as the woman retreats from the treachery behind Ruggiero's courtly promises. This formal disjunction combines with Alcina's retreat to the furthest reaches of the flat keys to create a haunting image of an abandoned woman whose grief turns to unreconciled anger. Lingering memory of this scene undermines the moralizing at the conclusion of the opera and challenges the stereotypical treatment of the lamenting woman in most early opera. *La liberazione* so pleased the Polish prince that he commissioned two new operas from Caccini in 1626, one on the subject of St Sigismund, the other on a subject of her choice. *Rinaldo innamorato*, known to Giuseppe Baini and now lost, was possibly composed in partial fulfilment of this commission.

La stiava (balletto, M. Buonarroti the younger), Pisa, 26 Feb 1607
Il ballo delle Zingane (balletto, F. Saracinelli), Florence, Palazzo Pitti, 24 Feb 1615
La fiera (5 intermedi, Buonarroti), Florence, Palazzo Pitti, 11 Feb 1619
Il martirio di Sant'Agata (J. Cicognini), Florence, Compagnia di S Giorgio in Costa, 23 Jan 1622, collab. G. B. da Gagliano [roles of S Agata and Eternità and minor women's parts by Caccini]
La liberazione di Ruggiero dall'isola d'Alcina (prol., 4 scenes, Saracinelli, after L. Ariosto), Florence, Villa Poggio Imperiale, 3 Feb 1625 (Florence, 1625), ed. D. Silbert, SCMA, vii (1945)
Rinaldo innamorato, ?commissioned 1626, MS, formerly owned by G. Baini, lost
S Sigismondo, ?commissioned 1626

Music in: La mascherata delle ninfe di Senna, 1611; La Tancia, 1611; Il passatempo, 1614; La serpe, 1620

*

A. Solerti: *Musica, ballo e drammatica alla corte medicea dal 1600 al 1637* (Florence, 1905)
M. G. Masera: 'Alcune lettere inedite di Francesca Caccini', *RaM*, xiii (1940), 173–82
——: 'Una musicista fiorentina del seicento: Francesca Caccini', *RaM*, xiv (1941), 181–207, 237–51; xv (1942), 249–66
M. Gliński: *La prima stagione lirica italiana all'estero* (Siena, 1943)
D. Silbert: 'Francesca Caccini, called La Cecchina', *MQ*, xxxii (1946), 50–62
S. G. Cusick: 'Of Women, Music and Power: a Model from Seicento Florence', *Musicology and Difference*, ed. R. Solie (Berkeley, CA, forthcoming)

(3) **Settimia Caccini** (*b* Florence, 6 Oct 1591; *d* Florence, *c*1660). Soprano, younger daughter of (1) Giulio Caccini. According to Severo Bonini, she established 'an immortal reputation', having 'mastered to perfection the art of singing'. She was taught to sing and compose by her father, and by 1602 was performing at the Florentine court. Two years later, at the invitation of Maria de' Medici, the Caccini family spent six months in Paris. It was once thought that Settimia went to Mantua in 1608 to sing in Monteverdi's *L'Arianna* but it is now known that the singer was another Florentine woman. In 1609 she married Alessandro Ghivizzani; both remained in Medici service until the following

year. In 1613 Duke Ferdinando Gonzaga recruited them in Lucca, and Settimia soon became one of the highest-paid musicians at the Mantuan court. After six years there, the couple returned to Lucca, and in 1622 they settled in Parma, where Settimia sang Aurora in Monteverdi's *Mercurio e Marte* (1628). After the death of her husband she returned to Florence. She is recorded on the Medici payroll in December 1636, and a few months later sang in Giovanni Carlo Coppola's *Le nozze degli dei*. Of her own compositions only five songs are extant, but four of these are also attributed to Nicola Parma or Ghivizzani.

*

S. Bonini: *Discorsi e regole sovra la musica et il contrappunto* (MS, c1649–50); ed. and Eng. trans. M. Bonino (Salt Lake City, 1979), 148–9

A. Solerti: *Musica, ballo e drammatica alla corte medicea dal 1600 al 1637* (Florence, 1905)

F. Hammond: 'Musicians at the Medici Court in the Mid-Seventeenth Century', *AnMc*, no.14 (1974), 157, 159

S. Parisi: *Ducal Patronage of Music in Mantua, 1587–1627: an Archival Study* (diss., U. of Illinois, 1989), 418–22

BARBARA R. HANNING (1), SUZANNE G. CUSICK (2), SUSAN PARISI (3)

Caddy, Ian (Graham) (*b* Southampton, 1 March 1947). English bass-baritone. He studied at the RAM where he won the President's Prize (1970). Later, his teachers included Otakar Kraus. He made his début as Schaunard in *La bohème* with the Glyndebourne Touring Opera in 1973. Though he has appeared in a wide variety of operas with Kent Opera, the ENO, Scottish Opera, the WNO and at Covent Garden and Glyndebourne, he is best known for his Baroque roles, particularly those he has sung for the English Bach Festival: Rameau's Theseus (*Hippolyte et Aricie*), Pollux, Telenus (*Naïs*) and others. On stage his attention to historical authenticity of movement and gesture is as notable as is his clear diction and resonant voice. His sound recordings include Rameau's *Naïs* and *La princesse de Navarre* and his video recordings include *Macbeth, The Beggar's Opera, La fanciulla del West* and *Intermezzo*.

NICHOLAS ANDERSON

Cadenza (from It.: 'cadence'). A virtuoso passage inserted near the end of an aria (or of a section of an aria), usually indicated by a fermata over an inconclusive chord.

1. Up to 1750. 2. 1750–1800. 3. Since 1800.

1. UP TO 1750. The metrical stress commonly occurring on the penultimate syllable of a line of Italian verse prompted early 17th-century monodists such as Caccini to favour this moment, the cadence, for a melisma. Little is known about the cultivation of the cadenza during the mid-17th century, but the increasing popularity of virtuoso singing during the late 17th and early 18th centuries led to the greater importance of improvised embellishment, in which the cadenza, invented by the singer at a place indicated by the composer, formed a conspicuous feature. Whereas ornamentation in the rest of an aria had to adhere to the pulse of the music, at the cadenza the singer was metrically free, since the accompanying instruments had a pause, either on a rest or on a chord. The commonest places for a cadenza were just before the final vocal cadence in the principal section and the middle section of a da capo aria (in the case of the former the intention may have been that a cadenza should be inserted only at the da capo). It was normally indicated by a pause on a rest or by a verbal rubric such as 'ad arbitrio'; there are examples of both in the autograph portions (Acts 1 and 3) of Alessandro Scarlatti's *Griselda* (1721). Handel's indication was a fermata and/or the marking 'Adagio'.

In referring to three cadenzas per aria, Tosi is not condoning such 'excess' (in his view), let alone the extravagance cultivated by certain singers:

> Every *Air* has (at least) three *Cadences*, that are all three final. Generally speaking, the Study of the Singers of the present Times consists in terminating the *Cadence* of the first Part with an overflowing of *Passages* and *Divisions* at Pleasure, and the *Orchestre* waits; in that of the second the Dose is encreased, and the *Orchestre* grows tired; but on the last *Cadence*, the Throat is set a going, like a Weather-cock in a Whirlwind, and the *Orchestre* yawns.

The ornamentation (attributed to Faustina Bordoni) of the aria 'Sciolta dal lido' from Vignati's *Ambleto* (1719) contains a modest cadenza at the end of the principal section, of which Tosi would probably have approved (ex.1). He would certainly not have approved of the

Ex.1 Vignati: *Ambleto* (1719), 'Sciolta dal lido', bars 81–4

la na - vi - cel la al scoglio va.
la na - vi - cel la al sco - glio va.

['The boat heads towards the rock.']

seven cadenzas that Farinelli incorporated in the aria 'Quell'usignolo' from Giacomelli's *Merope* (1734); ex.2

Ex.2 Giacomelli: *Merope* (1734), 'Quell'usignolo'

appears at the end of the first vocal entry (i.e. halfway through the principal section).

2. 1750–1800. The final cadenza, symbolized by a fermata on the tonic, a trill on the supertonic and a final resolution on the tonic, was inserted between the first two – that is, begun on the tonic and concluded with the written supertonic trill and its resolution. Most theorists agree that cadenzas should be sung on a single breath. However, the rule is often stated together with an observation that infringements are frequent (raising the question of balance between conservative and liberal, or theoretical and theatrical, practice); and singers of the period, especially castratos, were trained to execute in a single breath passages that far exceed the capacity of most vocalists today. A singer who wishes to perform 'authentically' may have to decide between authenticity of process (proceeding only as far as his breath span will permit) and of results (executing cadenzas of typical duration even though he may have to take extra breaths to do so). Mancini (3/1777) recommended the former approach to students. Ex.3 gives cadenzas from several sources.

A number of principles may be observed in the surviving Classical cadenzas:

(a) The initial tonic is generally taken in the register shown in the score, though taking it in a different octave is not unknown; beginning the cadenza on a note other than the tonic is rare.

(b) The inserted passage-work is not confined to the tonic 6-4 chord over which it appears but describes a modulatory gesture or sequence, generally emphasizing a subdominant just before the final trill. Of the hundreds of surviving cadenzas from the period 1750–1800, only a tiny minority lack chromatic inflection.

(c) The passage-work is formulaic but varied, and tends to include notes of more than one rhythmic denomination. Mancini (1774) seems to envisage basing the cadenza on a motif from the aria, but this procedure is rarely described elsewhere and is not encountered in notated cadenzas that have come to light. More often it is urged that the spirit or character of the cadenza should suit that of the piece. Wide leaps in long notes were much favoured alongside rapid figuration.

(d) The final trill is taken in the register shown in the score, though here too octave displacement is not unknown.

(e) Resolution of the final trill was not limited to a simple turn but included, increasingly as the period progressed, brief dominant 7th roulades of varying prominence (usually eight semiquavers in Corri's examples) and compass (rising as high as the submediant or even, in a few instances, the leading note); these sometimes included subsidiary trills and were forerunners of the dominant-founded cadenza popular early in the 19th century.

The two- or multi-part aria (or rondò) generally lacked the formal cadenza of the earlier da capo or dal segno type, but contained other fermatas (or 'punti coronati') where the accompaniment was suspended while a flourish was interpolated (ex.4). The most important type appeared at the end of a section in or on the dominant key where after a pause the music would resume in the tonic. The flourish might occur on the dominant chord or on the preceding harmony; or there could be a full-scale cadenza. A fermata on a dominant preparation would always be elaborated; one on the dominant itself might be, either with a flourish rounded off on dominant harmony (if the music resumes with instruments alone, as in ex.4*a*), or with a dominant 7th or 9th (if the voice resumes, ex.4*b*). The latter type, the 'lead-in' (Fr. *rentrée*, *conduit*; Ger. *Eingang*, *Eintritt*; It. *conducimento*, *cadenza di ripresa*), is often encountered. Occasionally the lead-in may be from a key other than the dominant, as in ex.4*c* and *d*.

Towards the end of the Classical period, the full cadenza in the tonic may appear to conclude the cantabile segment of a two-part aria; the 6-4 chord is usually prepared by a subdominant-based harmony, with vocal flourishes on the 6-4 chord and possibly also on the preparatory chord.

3. SINCE 1800. The fermatas of Classical arias are still found often in bel canto opera; even after they fell out of use, the modulations and structural joins continued to be marked by rallentando and embellishment, often facilitated by the suspension of the accompaniment. Ex.5 shows several versions of the preparation ('deh, tu premia') and cadence in the dominant ('la mia fè') immediately preceding the reprise of 'Di piacer mi balza il cor' (Rossini, *La gazza ladra*). Internal cadential points were often embellished even when no fermata appears in the score.

The final cadenza of the *andante* air underwent several mutations before vanishing in most music composed after about 1875. Early in the Romantic period (and occasionally earlier) its two parts became more independent, and the *andante* ended with a full close, occasionally in the dominant up to the early 1820s but later in the tonic. The usual cadenza form in the first quarter of the century consisted of two fermatas for successive elaboration: one on the tonic 6-4 and one (generally brief) on the dominant. The burden of figuration gradually shifted from the former to the latter.

In German music the tonic 6-4 was often prepared by a secondary dominant (or sometimes a diminished 7th chord), a descendant of the Classical procedure, and the voice often began the cadenza by sustaining the tonic. The tenor aria from Weber's *Freischütz* gives an example (ex.6*a*); two typical realizations for such a cadence are shown from Peter Winter's *Vollständige Singschule*, published in 1825 (four years after *Freischütz*; ex.6*b*). In ex.6*c*, in contrast, Winter starts the voice on the dominant. Sometimes the preparatory chord as well as the tonic 6-4 and the dominant chord was embellished. Typically these cadenzas were sung on

one or two words, and resolved to the tonic in a middle or low vocal range. Some theorists continue to require that the cadenza be sung in one breath, but Rossini and others acknowledged tacitly that this was no longer the rule. More typical seems to have been a breath between the tonic 6-4 figuration (if there was any) and the dominant 7th, with another breath possible before the final resolution. Garcia advised singers to reserve a word or syllable for this final resolution, singing the melisma on 'ah' if necessary. Ex.7 gives two examples from the Rossinian period in which all three chords are present. Velluti (ex.7*a*) embellishes the tonic 6-4 and follows the rule about a single breath. Rossini's own cadenza for 'Il braccio mio' (ex.7*b*) is over the dominant chord, though the rising figure could be heard as either tonic or dominant; Adelaide Kemble's is on the dominant, with a breath and brief ornament at the end.

In the 1830s, elaboration on the 6-4 fell from use; Donizetti rarely gives occasion for it, but Bellini retains it more often, as in ex.8, which illustrates the practice of passing it by undecorated. The concentration was by then on the dominant chord. By the time of early Verdi this process was complete; the supertonic 6th and the tonic 6-4 do not appear in most of his codas. These dominant cadenzas gradually came to be sung in two parts, as the portion after the breath became freer and more elaborate. The cadenzas attributed to Pisaroni and Rubini in ex.9*a* and that by Verdi in ex.9*b* are typical.

Concurrently, there were changes in the vocal style of the cadenzas. Florid passage-work gradually becomes less demanding after about 1835; declamatory exclamation, sometimes involving a whole line of text, supplements or even supplants the melisma. (This kind of cadenza, wrote Garcia, 'is the recourse of comic singers and singers lacking flexibility'.) Upward resolution – taking the tonic in an upper-middle part of the range – gradually began to appear, especially in Verdi, though this remained relatively rare. Ex.10 gives a typical concluding portion of a cadenza from *Ernani* in this new style. This migration of the cadenza did not end with its settlement on the dominant 7th chord. Verdi, in his

Ex.7

(a) Rossini: *Aureliano in Palmira*, cadenza by Velluti for Arsace's solo in the duet 'Mille sospiri e lagrime' (published by Mechetti in Vienna, n.d.)

Velluti

se a te mi ren - de a - mor

original

se a te mi ren - - de a - mor

(b) Nicolini: 'Il braccio mio' (insert aria for Rossini's *La donna del lago*)

Rossini (autograph in *F-Pn*)

bel cor del tu-o del tuo bel

Kemble (from her notebook, private coll.)

bel cor del tuo del tuo bel

original

bel cor del tu-o bel

ii$^6_5$ preparation I$^6_4$ V^7

Ex.8 Bellini: *La sonnambula*

García, 1847 (after Malibran?)

a - mor la co - lo - rò, ah a - mor

ii$^6_5$ I$^6_4$

Cinti-Damoreau (notebook in *US-BLl*)

a - mor la co - lo - rò, a - - - - - - - - mor

ii$^6_5$ I$^6_4$

original

a - mor la co - lo - rò, a - - - - - - - - - mor

ii$^6_5$ I$^6_4$

con brio

a - mor del mio di - let - to

(V^7)

a - - - - - - - mo - re del mio di - let - to

(I$^6_4$) V^7

ossia del mio di -

a - - - - - - - - - mor del mio di - let - to

(I$^6_4$) V^7

Ex.9

(a) Two attributed cadenzas from Duprez: *L'art du chant*

Pisaroni

Rubini

Ha

mature operas, often concludes arias with vocal figuration or arpeggios on the final tonic (see for instance 'O patria mia', 'O ma chère compagne', 'Il lacerato spirito'; the device was developed in ensemble numbers, where it occurs frequently).

In France it was a widespread practice to print final cadenzas and other 'points d'orgue' in vocal scores of the operas of Halévy, Auber, Thomas, Meyerbeer and others. They were shown in small print, marked 'variante', while on the main staff would appear a simple closing formula. These variants generally correspond to the earlier and more conservative Italian cadenzas, with a single roulade and downward resolution. The cadenzas of several French singers, especially the renowned vocal improviser Laure Cinti-Damoreau, tend towards the later Italian practice of inserting a second, freer roulade (but not a syllabic sequence) after a breath.

For primary sources and bibliography *see* ORNAMENTATION.

ANDREW V. JONES (1), WILL CRUTCHFIELD (2, 3)

Cadi dupé, Le ('The Duped Judge'). *Opéra comique* in one act by CHRISTOPH WILLIBALD GLUCK to a libretto after Pierre-René Lemonnier; Vienna, Burgtheater, 8 December 1761.

Gluck's music for *Le cadi dupé*, the first of his two 'Turkish' *opéras comiques*, replaced that of Monsigny, first performed at the Paris Foire St-Germain on 4 February 1761. The Cadi, or judge (baritone), wishes to divorce his wife Fatime in favour of the young Zelmire (both sopranos). As she refuses him, he seeks revenge by promising her to someone he believes to be an unknown pauper, but who is actually Zelmire's lover Nouradin (*haute-contre*). They seek revenge for this by inciting the Cadi to betroth himself to the hideous dyer's daughter Ali (tenor, played by a male singer), on the basis of false reports of her beauty. She and the veiled Zelmire (who had undertaken the seduction) reveal their identities at the end of the opera, whereupon the Cadi repents his folly.

Janissary music and instruments colour much of this opera, depicting both the Cadi's joy and his rage (triangle, tremolo strings), and characterizing (with 'biffero' [fife], Turkish drum and cymbals) the philosophic dyer Omar (baritone) and Fatime ('salterio', or dulcimer). Two other musical strains are prominent: tender lyricism for the lovers (with some melismatic writing for Zelmire) and grotesque clumsiness for the misshapen Ali. Fatime's complaint about men's mistreatment of women (moved to the start of the opera in the Viennese arrangement) is of universal appeal.

BRUCE ALAN BROWN

Cádiz. City and provincial capital in south-west Spain. The Teatro de Comedias was built in 1608 by a doctor who donated it to the Hospital de Misericordia as a source of revenue. In June 1739 the impresario Luis Armesto de Troya undertook to construct a Teatro de Opera for performances by Joseph (or Giuseppe) Jordan's company, but the hospital opposed the project and Armesto de Troya was obliged to stop work on his theatre and to use instead the Teatro de Comedias. On 15 June 1740 José Peiro's zarzuela *El jardín de Falerina* was performed in honour of the Duke of Medina Sidonia.

From 1761 an Italian opera company directed by the dancer Antonio Ribaltó performed at the Teatro Italiano, built for the purpose by the impresario Giuseppe Darbricio. The theatre was used regularly by a succession of companies until about 1773. Important singers (some later connected with Setaro), including Filippo Elisi, appeared there and in other Andalusian cities (Córdoba, Jerez de la Frontera, Málaga and Seville) as well as in the public theatres of Lisbon and Oporto. In 1768 the hospital began a legal battle which years later obliged the Italians to abandon their theatre and use the Teatro Español, built in 1772 by Manuel Fernández de Morales and considerably improved in 1781.

In 1768 Jacques Constantin tried to build a Teatro Francés for comedies, tragedies and opera, but it lasted only a single season. 1792 saw the arrival from Madrid of Charles-Auguste Favier's ballet company, which also performed operas (especially those of Cimarosa). The troupe settled in Cádiz until 1797, when it was expelled (having taken refuge in Seville from the English siege of Cádiz) after a protest at the pro-French version of a ballet by Favier.

Throughout the 19th century the Cádiz theatres were extremely active, giving predominantly Italian opera, especially when Mercadante was there in autumn 1829 to present two comic works. This activity intensified with the development of the zarzuela, following on from the success of the *tonadilla escénica* in the last years of the 18th century; Manuel García was one of the earliest practitioners in the genre, which was hugely successful in the city. In the second half of the century there was progressive acceptance of French and German opera. The destruction by fire of the Teatro Italiano in 1881 represented a great setback for opera, and it was not until 1910 that the Gran Teatro de Cádiz (now Gran Teatro Falla) was inaugurated with a performance of *La bohème*. The use of the theatre as a cinema resulted in the gradual disappearance of operatic performances.

*

E. Cotarelo y Mori: *Orígenes y establecimiento de la opera en España hasta 1800* (Madrid, 1917)
R. Solís: *El Cádiz de las Cortes* (Esplugas de Llobregat, 1978)
C. Greppi: *'Virtuose': viaggi e stagioni nell'ultimo decennio del settecento* (Madrid, 1979)
X. M. Carreira: 'Orígenes de la opera en Cádiz: un informe de 1768 sobre el Coliseo de Operas', *RdMc*, x (1987), 581–99
C. M. Fernández-Fernández: 'Espectáculos, opera y hospitales en España', *RdM*, xii (1989), 569–89 XOÁN M. CARREIRA

Cadman, Charles Wakefield (*b* Johnstown, PA, 24 Dec 1881; *d* Los Angeles, 30 Dec 1946). American composer. He was largely self-taught; having seen a production of De Koven's operetta *Robin Hood* when he was 14, he composed three operettas by the age of 20. His most famous work, the song 'At Dawning', which was inspired by American Indian tribal songs, was written before he was 25. Cadman made his livelihood from royalties, piano concerts, music journalism, film scores, and lecture tours of the USA and Europe, which included a celebrated talk on American Indian music. Two of his operas were based on American Indian tales and songs, developed after research into their culture. One of Cadman's main interests was to 'idealize' American Indian music by adding conservative 19th-century harmonies to the native melodies, a treatment that the musicologist John Comfort Fillmore claimed the American Indians themselves approved. While his opera *Shanewis*, based on the life of the Creek Indian Tsianina Redfeather, was the most successful and lasting of his opera ventures, his dramatic works also include cycles for vocal quartet with piano, one of which, *The Full Moon*, was intended to be staged. His radio opera *The Willow Tree* was likewise originally conceived for a vocal quartet. He saw productions of all but his first opera *Daoma* ('The Land of Misty Water'), which he continued to revise until late in his life under the title *Ramala*. While he considered his 'serious' compositions, particularly the operas, to be his most significant works, it was for his shorter novelties that he was best known.

See also SHANEWIS.

Daoma [The Land of Misty Water], 1909–12 (3, N. R. Eberhart), unperf., rev. as Ramala, 1939 (4), unperf.
The Garden of Mystery, 1915 (1, Eberhart, after N. Hawthorne: *Rappaccini's Daughter*), concert perf. New York, Carnegie Hall, 20 March 1925, vs (New York, 1925)
Shanewis (1, Eberhart), New York, Metropolitan, 23 March 1918, vs as The Robin Woman: Shanewis (New York, 1918)
A Witch of Salem, 1922 (2, Eberhart), Chicago, Auditorium, 8 Dec 1926, vs (Boston, 1925)
The Willow Tree (radio op, 1, Eberhart), NBC, 26 April 1932

THOMAS WARBURTON

Cadmus et Hermione ('Cadmus and Hermione'). *Tragédie en musique* in a prologue and five acts by Jean-Baptiste Lully (see LULLY family, (1)) to a libretto by PHILIPPE QUINAULT after OVID's *Metamorphoses*; Paris, Jeu de paume de Béquet, 27 April 1673.

The prologue tells the mythological tale of Apollo (symbolic of Louis XIV, who attended the première) slaying the serpent Python – a reference to an ongoing war against the Dutch. The tragedy, set in ancient Greece, concerns the prince Cadmus (baritone; immediately afterwards Lully established the *haute-contre* as the usual voice type for leading male lovers) and Hermione (soprano), daughter of Mars (baritone) and Vénus [Venus] (soprano). They love each other, but Mars has betrothed Hermione to the giant Draco (baritone). To win Hermione's hand, Cadmus proves his bravery to Mars by killing a dragon, sowing the dragon's teeth and vanquishing the soldiers who spring forth from them; he then defeats Draco.

Cadmus, however, is merely a pawn of the gods, who descend on spectacularly decorated machinery. He relies on his personal strength to kill the dragon, but his other victories are achieved only with the help of L'Amour [Cupid] (soprano) – responding to an invocation by Hermione – and Pallas (soprano), both acting on Jupiter's behalf (Cupid was sung by a foreign castrato in performances at the French court in 1677–8). The final complication and resolution are carried out by the gods alone, with no pretence of involvement by Cadmus: Junon [Juno] (soprano) abducts Hermione and, as Cadmus laments this in the monologue *air* 'Belle Hermione, Hélas', Pallas descends to announce that Cupid has brought about a reconciliation between Juno and Jupiter, thus eliminating Juno's opposition to the marriage. All ends happily.

This was Lully's first tragedy and established the essential traits of the genre. Of the ballet *divertissements*, the most impressive are the grandiose sacrificial rite honouring Mars (Act 3) and the massive chaconne (Act 1). The moving farewell scene between the lovers (2.iv) prefigures Lully's more mature dialogues of this type. Comedy – a feature that Lully borrowed from Venetian and Roman opera, and later avoided – is provided by an interlude with a love triangle among the servants, including an old nurse played by a man (haute-contre), and by the cowardice and clumsy posturing of Cadmus's confidant, Arbas (bass). The opera was revived in Paris up to 1737. LOIS ROSOW

Caesar, Julius. *See* JULIUS CAESAR.

Cafaro, Pasquale (*b* S Pietro in Galatina, nr Lecce, 8 Feb 1716; *d* Naples, 25 Oct 1787). Italian composer. According to some sources he was born in 1706, but a statement that he made in 1735 places his birthdate in 1715 or 1716. He studied in Naples at the Conservatorio di S Maria della Pietà dei Turchini, with Nicola Fago and Leo, and thereafter remained in Naples all his life. Between 1745 and 1771 he established himself as a respected composer of oratorios, operas, cantatas and church music, and his appointments included *secondo maestro* of the conservatory in 1759, *primo maestro* of the royal chapel in 1771 and music master to Queen Maria Carolina. Between 1763 and 1766 he conducted operas by Hasse and Traetta, among others, at the Teatro S Carlo.

Although Cafaro never composed an *opera buffa*, certain stylistic tendencies associated with this genre (simplicity of harmonic structure, texture and orchestration) are reflected in his serious works. In them the dramatic pathos of earlier composers gave way to Classicist abstraction, expert use of Neapolitan formulae and accepted modes of expression. As a result his music was praised by his contemporaries for 'grace and purity of style' and later criticized for 'poverty of invention'. In the Neapolitan tradition Cafaro was one of the essential links between the generation of Leo and Durante and that of Cimarosa and Paisiello.

all staged at S Carlo, Naples

La disfatta di Dario (3, A. Morbilli), 20 Jan 1756, *F-Pc**, *I-Mc*, *Nc*, *P-La*, *US-Wc*

L'incendio di Troia (3, Morbilli), 20 Jan 1757, *A-Wn*, *F-Pc**, *P-La*, *US-Wc*

Ipermestra (3, P. Metastasio), 26 Dec 1761, *F-Pc**, *I-Vnm*, *P-La*

Arianna e Teseo (3, P. Pariati), 20 Jan 1766, *F-Pc**, *I-Nc*, *P-La*

Creso, ultimo rè della Lidia (3, G. G. Pizzi), Turin, Regio, spr. 1768, *F-Pc** (dated 1777), *P-La*

L'olimpiade (3, Metastasio), 12 Jan 1769, *F-Pc**, *I-Nc*, *P-La*, *US-Wc*

Antigono (3, Metastasio), 13 Aug 1770, *F-Pc**, *I-Nc*, *P-La*, rev. 1774

*

FlorimoN

G. de' Silva dei Marchesi della Banditella: *Elogio di Pasquale Cafaro* (Naples, 1788)

G. De Napoli: *Una triade melodrammatica altamura* (Rome, 1925)

U. Prota-Giurleo: *La grande orchestra del R. Teatro San Carlo nel settecento* (Naples, 1927) HANNS-BERTOLD DIETZ

Caffarelli [Cafariello, Cafarellino, Gaffarello] [Majorano, Gaetano] (*b* Bitonto, 12 April 1710; *d* Naples, 31 Jan 1783). Italian mezzo-soprano castrato. After studying under Porpora at Naples, he made his début at Rome in 1726, in a female part in Sarro's *Valdemaro*. His success was rapid: he sang in Venice, Turin, Milan and Florence before returning to Rome (1730) as chamber virtuoso to the Grand Duke of Tuscany. He enjoyed a triumph in Hasse's *Cajo Fabricio* and Porpora's *Germanico in Germania* in 1732. After singing in Venice, Milan and Bologna (1730–32), he made his Naples début in Leo's *Il castello d'Atlante* (1734), and settled there in a post in the royal chapel. Over the next 20 years he appeared at Naples in operas by Pergolesi, Porpora, Hasse, Perez, Leo, Latilla, Sarro, Vinci, Cocchi, Abos and others, and latterly (1751–3) Traetta's *Farnace*, Gioacchino Conti's *Attalo rè di Bitinia*, Gluck's *La clemenza di Tito* and Lampugnani's *Didone*.

He appeared frequently elsewhere, in Rome again in 1735, Milan in 1736 and London in 1737–8, when he made his début at the King's Theatre in the pasticcio *Arsace* and created the title roles in Handel's *Faramondo* and *Serse*. He also appeared in Madrid by royal invitation in 1739, and in the late 1740s and early 1750s in Florence (where Horace Mann thought he sang 'most divinely well' in Caldara's *Caio Marzio*), Genoa, Rome, Vienna (where his performance in Jommelli's *Achille in Sciro* was the subject of barbed criticism from Metastasio in letters to Farinelli), Turin, Venice, Lucca and Modena. In 1753 Louis XV invited him to Versailles and he remained in France until 1754, singing in several works by Hasse, but left under a cloud after seriously wounding a poet in a duel.

Caffarelli made his last Italian operatic appearances at Rome and Naples in 1754. In 1755 he was engaged for Lisbon, where he sang in four operas, three of them by Perez. He visited Madrid in 1756 and spent some time with Farinelli, before returning to Naples and retiring from the stage. In 1763 he refused an invitation to manage the S Carlo theatre. He was a favourite with royal families everywhere and amassed a substantial fortune, with which he bought himself a dukedom, an estate in Calabria and a palace in Naples. In 1770 Burney recognized signs 'of his having been an amazing fine singer'.

Caffarelli's voice was a high mezzo-soprano. The compass in the two parts Handel wrote for him is *b* to *a''*. By many judges he was ranked second only to Farinelli, and by some above him. According to Burney 'Porpora, who hated him for his insolence, used to say, that he was the greatest singer Italy had ever produced'.

Grimm reported from Paris:

> It would be difficult to give any idea of the degree of perfection to which this singer has brought his art. All the charms and love that can make up the idea of an angelic voice, and which form the character of his, added to the finest execution, and to surprising facility and precision, exercise an enchantment over the senses and the heart, which even those least sensible to music would find it hard to resist.

Caffarelli's principal enemy was his own temperament; he was notorious for overbearing arrogance both to fellow artists and to the public. He had spells under house arrest and in prison, for assault, misconduct at a performance (of Latilla's *Olimpia nell'isola d'Ebuda*, 1741), when he indulged in indecent gestures and mimicry of other singers, and for humiliating a prima donna in Hasse's *Antigono* (1745). He was constantly late for concerts and rehearsals, and sometimes failed to turn up. He is said to have mellowed in old age and given large sums to charity; Burney was charmed by his politeness.

*

J. G. Prod'homme: 'Un chanteur italien à Paris – le voyage de Caffarelli en 1753', *BSIM*, vi-vii (1911)

E. Faustini-Fasini: 'Gli astri maggiori del bel canto napoletano: Gaetano Majorano detto "Caffarelli"', *NA*, xv (1938), 121–8, 157–70, 258–70 WINTON DEAN

Cage, John (Milton, jr) (*b* Los Angeles, 5 Sept 1912; *d* New York, 12 Aug 1992). American composer and philosopher. The son of an inventor, he became one of the most influential figures in 20th-century music. He dropped out of Pomona College, Claremont, but later studied with Richard Buhlig, Henry Cowell, at the New School for Social Research (1933), and Adolph Weiss. Under the tutelage of Schoenberg (1944) he adopted the 12-note system, with characteristic freedom, but, soon finding Schoenberg's authoritarian and dogmatic teaching methods uncongenial, he began to base his compositions on unusual rhythms and innovatory instrumentation. In Los Angeles, Seattle, San Francisco, Chicago and New York he served as accompanist and composer for a number of dance companies, creating for them a body of works for percussion ensemble or solo prepared piano. His appearance in New York with this material created a sensation and he was never again out of the public eye. Cage's subsequent career has pivoted around a long-term collaboration with the dancer-choreographer Merce Cunningham, whom he met in Seattle; from 1944 to 1966 he was music director of Cunningham's company, and the collaboration continued. In addition, Cage taught intermittently at the New School and held short-term academic residencies at Black Mountain College and Center for Advanced Studies at Wesleyan University, Middletown, Connecticut.

Cage's music underwent a dramatic change of style in 1951, when, influenced by Eastern philosophies and Zen Buddhism, he began to introduce chance procedures into his works. Compositional decisions were made by flipping coins or by tossing yarrow stalks in the fashion prescribed for obtaining *I Ching* oracles, and many performance decisions were left to the performer. He proposed that music is not something a musician produces, but something a listener perceives: any sounds can be music, provided they are heard as such.

For more than a decade Cage's indeterminate music met a wall of hostile incomprehension from musicians, press and public, though his notoriety made him a celebrity, increasingly in demand for lectures and performances. A small body of disciples (Morton Feldman, Earle Brown, Christian Wolff and David Tudor) collected around him, forming a distinct 'New York School' of avant-gardists. The publication of his ideas in *Silence* (Middletown, 1961) increased his influence, but broad acceptance of his work came only in the wake of a major American cultural shift in the 1960s. His aesthetic stance led him increasingly in the direction of social and political anarchy, climaxing in a crisis of conscience in 1967. Most of his subsequent works had an underlying socio-political subtext, often embodying social structures based on freedom and cooperation – the anarchist ideal. At the same time, he became less doctrinaire in his indeterminancy, and his late works displayed a broader variety of technical means than previously. He also branched out into poetry and graphics.

Cage's influence on opera stems from his music-theatre work, a genre in which he was a pioneer as well as a prolific contributor. Under the influence of Lejaren Hiller, his collaborator on *HPSCHD* (1967–9), his theatre pieces took the form of large-scale multi-media spectacles which he called 'musicircuses'; the first, *Musicircus* (1967), was simply an invitation to a large variety of performers to appear in one place at one time. It is to this tradition that *Europeras 1 & 2* (1987) belongs. Though it includes every diagnostic feature of opera, and was called an opera by its creator, the work is best understood – and most readily enjoyed – as an extended multi-media meditation on opera as a European social institution, employing its materials but viewing it from outside with an almost anthropological detachment. *Europeras 3 & 4* (1990) employs less lavish materials, but to the same end. An element of nostalgia is introduced through the use, alongside live singers, of antique gramophones playing recordings of great singers of the past. Both these works, as well as *Europera 5* (1991), are deliberately randomized phantasmagorias of European opera fragments performed with sets, costumes, props, scenery, lighting, movement and scenarios all also chosen at random and without reference to each other. *Europeras 1 & 2* requires a cast of 31, plus full orchestra, while *Europeras 3 & 4* needs only six singers and two pianists. In *Europera 5* a small cast is accompanied by a chamber ensemble, a television set and a radio.

Cage's style and techniques have also been adapted to opera by other composers including Stockhausen, Berio, Peter Maxwell Davies, R. Murray Schafer and, less obviously, Philip Glass.

See also EUROPERAS 1 & 2.

Europeras 1 & 2, Frankfurt, Schauspielhaus, 12 Dec 1987
Europeras 3 & 4, London, Almeida, 17 June 1990
Europera 5, Buffalo, 18 April 1991

P. Griffiths: *Cage* (London, 1980)
D. Charles, ed.: 'John Cage', *Revue d'esthétique*, new ser., no.13–15 (1987–8) [whole issue]
A. Porter: 'Musical Events: Festival Fare', *New Yorker* (8 Aug 1988)
F. Reininghaus: 'Ein wohlabgeschmecktes Opern-Ragout', *NZM*, cxlix/3 (1988), 34–6
M. Swed: 'Celebration of Chaos', *ON*, liii/1 (1988–9), 30–31
P. Driver: 'Europeras 3 & 4', *Opera*, xli (1990), 994–5
D. Campana: 'Europera 5', *John Cage Now*, 10 [festival programme book, Evanston and Chicago, IL, March 1992]

ANDREW STILLER

Cagli, Augusto (*fl* 1865–85). Italian impresario. He gave an extended season of Italian opera in Calcutta in the spring and summer of 1866 and tried to establish a regular opera company there by presenting autumn and winter seasons up to 1871. That year he joined forces with Giovanni Pompei, in Melbourne, but Pompei returned to India and Cagli, after a disastrous attempt at solo management, entered into partnership with W. S. Lyster, touring in Australia and New Zealand. He then returned to Italy. In 1875 he put on the first Italian opera to be heard in Cape Town (*Il trovatore*, 15 November 1875), and gave seasons there up to 1877. The next year he embarked on an extended Asian tour, to Bombay, Allahabad, Calcutta, Madras, Singapore, Batavia (followed by a Javan tour), Hong Kong and, in 1880, Shanghai, where he gave the city's first Italian opera season. In further tours he visited Yokohama in 1880–81 and Java in 1881–2, and then Australia, where his company broke up in 1883. After that he travelled with the tenor Lodovico Balzofiore.

H. Love: *The Golden Age of Australian Opera: W. S. Lyster and his Companies, 1861–1880* (Sydney, 1981)
A. Gyger: *Opera for the Antipodes: Opera in Australia 1881–1939* (Sydney, 1990)

TOM KAUFMAN

Cagli, Bruno (*b* Narni, 2 June 1942). Italian administrator, writer on music and librettist. He studied at Rome University and at first worked as a writer for theatre, radio and television, also writing criticism in journals and newspapers. He also wrote librettos for two operas by Renosto (*L'ombra di Banquo*, 1976, Spoleto; *Le campanule*, 1981, Casale Monferrato). In 1971 he became director of the Fondazione Rossini, Pesaro, where he did much to initiate the new critical edition of Rossini. The posts he has held include the artistic directorship of the Teatro dell'Opera at Rome (1987–90), where he did much to broaden the repertory. Cagli has also taught at universities in Naples and Urbino and at conservatories in Rome and Naples. A prolific writer in many different areas, he has published a number of musicological works including studies of aspects of Donizetti and Verdi as well as several of Rossini (among them essays on the literary sources of his librettos as well as iconographical and editorial work); his books include *Storia del San Carlo* (Naples, 1989) and *Lettere e documenti di G. Rossini* (Urbino, 1992).

Cagliari. Italian city, the capital of Sardinia. It is the home of one of the 13 Italian Enti Lirici (opera syndicates). The history of opera in Cagliari concerns mainly the Teatro Civico and the Politeama Regina Margherita. The former was originally the 18th-century Teatro Regio of the Marchesi Zapata di Las Passas, acquired by the municipality in 1831, rebuilt to the designs of Cominotti and Cima and reopened on 2 October 1836, with either Donizetti's *Belisario* (De Francesco 1900) or *Anna Bolena* (Ruggieri 1989, based on contemporary press notices). The latter, designed by Costa and built on the site of the old Teatro Cerruti in the viale Regina Margherita, was inaugurated on 25 December 1897 with Meyerbeer's *L'Africaine*. Performances of secondary provincial standard were given sporadically in the small and aristocratic Teatro Civico (seating 900) and the larger Politeama (seating 2000), patronized mainly by the middle classes. During World War II the Politeama was destroyed by fire and the Civico in a heavy bombing raid. After the war there were opera seasons at the Massimo film theatre and, in the summer, at the Arena Giardino. From 1977, during the building of the new Teatro Civico, opera was performed in the auditorium of the conservatory, and from 1986 there were summer seasons in the Roman amphitheatre, where between 1956 and 1966 there was a series of superb productions that drew audiences of over 6000.

*

G. Giacomelli: *Ricerche storiche sulla musica in Sardegna* (Cagliari, 1896)
F. Corona: *Il Politeama Regina Margherita* (Cagliari, 1898)
G. De Francesco: *Il Teatro Civico di Cagliari: centotrent'anni di cronaca cagliaritana* (Cagliari, 1900)
Diorama della musica in Sardegna (Cagliari, 1937)
Auditorium, i–xiii (1966–78)
S. Muscas: *La lirica in Sardegna* (Cagliari, 1983)
M. Satta Mognorani: *Lo spettacolo nella Cagliari turistica* (Cagliari, 1988)
F. Ruggieri: 'In serata d'onore due casizzolus per il bel soprano', *Esse come Sardegna*, i/1 (1989), 159–62
——: 'Notizie sul Teatro Regio di Cagliari nel periodo della residenza della Corte Sabanda in Sardegna', *Bollettino bibliografico e rassegna archivistica e di studi storici della Sardegna*, vi/11–12 (1989), 79–88
ANTONIO TRUDU

Cagnoni, Antonio (*b* Godiasco, nr Voghera, 8 Feb 1828; *d* Bergamo, 30 April 1896). Italian composer. He began his musical studies in Voghera under Felice Moretti, then from March 1842 to September 1847 he was at the Milan Conservatory. While there, he composed three operas, of which *Don Bucefalo*, given at the conservatory in 1847, proved a lasting success, since more than one *basso buffo* chose it as his warhorse. Written to the same plot as Valentino Fioravanti's *Le cantatrici villane* and owing much to Donizetti, it shows melodic inventiveness and a gift for elegant foolery (including an unmistakable dig at Verdi's early manner). In 1865 the famous *buffo* Alessandro Bottero sang it at the Théâtre Italien in Paris, where it was coolly received.

In the early 1850s Cagnoni continued to write for north Italian theatres works that never roused the public to enthusiasm, but earned him respectful notices. In 1856 he was appointed *maestro di cappella* at Vigevano and in 1863 succeeded Coccia as director of the Istituto Musicale of Novara. In 1886 he was made a commander of the Order of the Corona and in the same year became *maestro di cappella* of S Maria Maggiore, Bergamo, on the death of Ponchielli. Although increasingly occupied with religious composition, he was slow to abandon the stage entirely. His *Michele Perrin* (1864, Milan), produced when Wagner's ideas were beginning to be known in Italy, was hailed by Alberto Mazzucato as 'music of the future'. However, *Claudia* (1866, Milan), a blend of early *verismo* and sentimental Romantic melodrama, was judged to be laboured and unoriginal. Cagnoni's last four operas, in which he collaborated with Ghislanzoni, the librettist of *Aida*, were better received. *Papà Martin* (1871, Genoa) was given by Carl Rosa in 1875 at the Lyceum Theatre, London, in an English version entitled *The Porter of Havre*, which was much praised by the young Bernard Shaw. *Francesca da Rimini* (1878, Turin), which enjoyed a genuine *succès d'estime*, was Cagnoni's farewell to the theatre, though until his death he cherished a project of producing *Re Lear*. Of his religious works the most important is a Requiem Mass (1888); an earlier tribute to his skill in that field was the commission to contribute a movement to the Rossini Requiem of 1869. He also wrote a *Romanza* for the album of songs published at Verdi's suggestion for the benefit of the librettist Piave, then paralysed by a stroke (Cagnoni had been one of Piave's last collaborators).

Writing at a time when the post-Rossinian tradition was breaking down, Cagnoni, like most of his generation, was forced to experiment with results that are often both ugly and unsure. But if he never recaptured the ease and fluency of *Don Bucefalo*, in his later serious operas he evolved a characteristic slow-paced melody of wide intervals and mildly dissonant harmonies that pointed forward to Leoncavallo. *Claudia* and, more particularly, *Francesca da Rimini* show a use of leitmotifs far beyond anything attempted by Verdi, while Alberigo, the villain of *Francesca*, with his credo of evil and his jaunty 6/8 rondo of *fausse bonhomie*, intimates Verdi's Iago.

mel – *melodramma*

Rosalia di S Miniato (mel, 2, C. Bassi), Milan, Conservatory, 28 Feb 1845, *I-Mc*
I due Savoiardi (mel, 2, L. Tarantini), Milan, Conservatory, 15 June 1846, *Mc*
Don Bucefalo (dg, 3, Bassi), Milan, Conservatory, 28 June 1847, *Mr*, vs (Milan, 1848; Paris, 1865)
Il testamento di Figaro (mel comico, 2, Bassi), Milan, Re, 26 Feb 1848, *Mr*, excerpts (Milan, 1848)
Amori e trappole (mel giocoso, 3, F. Romani), Genoa, Carlo Felice, 27 April 1850, excerpts (Milan, 1850); rev., Rome, 1867, *Mr**, vs (Milan, 1865)
Il sindaco babbeo (op comica, 3, G. Giachetti), Milan, S Radegonda, 3 March 1851, collab. C. Marcora, Ponchielli and A. Cunio
La valle d'Andorra (mel, 2, Giachetti), Milan, Cannobiana, 7 June 1851, *Mr**, vs (Milan, n.d.)
Giralda (dg, 3, Giachetti and R. Berninzone), Milan, S Radegonda, 8 May 1852, *Mr*, vs (Milan, n.d.)
La fioraia (mel giocoso, 3, Giachetti), Turin, Nazionale, 24 Nov 1853, *Mr*, vs (Milan, 1854)
La figlia di Don Liborio (ob, 3, F. Guidi), Genoa, Carlo Felice, 18 Oct 1856
Il vecchio della montagna, ossia L'Emiro (tragedia lirica, 4, Guidi), Turin, Carignano, 5 Sept 1860
Michele Perrin (op comica, 3, M. M. Marcello), Milan, S Radegonda, 7 May 1864, *Mr*, vs (Milan, 1864)
Claudia (dramma lirico, 4, Marcello), Milan, Cannobiana, 20 May 1866, vs (Turin, n.d.)
La tombola (commedia lirica, 3, F. M. Piave), Rome, Argentina, 30 Jan 1868, *Mr*, vs (Milan, ?1868)
Un capriccio di donna (mel serio, prol., 3, A. Ghislanzoni), Genoa, Carlo Felice, 10 March 1870, *Mr*, vs (Milan, 1873)
Gli amori di Cleopatra, *c*1870 (Marcello), unperf.
Papà Martin (op semiseria, 3, Ghislanzoni), Genoa, Nazionale, 4 March 1871, *Mr*, vs (Milan, ?1871); as The Porter of Havre, London, Lyceum, 1875, vs (London and New York, 1875/6)
Il duca di Tapigliano (op comica, prol., 2, Ghislanzoni, Lecco, Sociale, 10 Oct 1874, *Mr*, vs (Milan, ?1876)
Francesca da Rimini (tragedia lirica, 4, Ghislanzoni, after Dante: *Commedia*), Turin, Regio, 19 Feb 1878, vs (Turin, ?1878)
Re Lear, *c*1883 (tragedia lirica, 4, Ghislanzoni, after W. Shakespeare), unperf., vs (Turin, n.d.)

Music in: La vergine di Kermo (1870)

*

A. C. Sangiorgi: 'Antonio Cagnoni', *Gazzetta musicale di Milano*, xxiii (1868), 298
G. Tebaldini: 'Antonio Cagnoni', *Gazzetta musicale di Milano*, li (1896), 317–9
JULIAN BUDDEN

Cahen, Albert [Cahen d'Anvers] (*b* Antwerp, 8 Jan 1846; *d* Cap d'Ail, nr Monte Carlo, 27 Feb 1903). French composer. In the mid-1860s he became one of Franck's first pupils. Songs on poems by Musset date from this period; his first important work, the 'biblical drama' *Jean le Précurseur*, was given in 1874. After the poor reception of his *poème mythologique Endymion* (1875), he turned to the stage, making his début in 1880 with *Le bois*; a *féerie*, *La belle au bois dormant*, followed in 1886 and his best-known work, the opera *Le vénitien*, was staged in Rouen and Paris in 1890. After Franck's death Cahen's relationship with Franck's 'circle' – and with d'Indy in particular – became cooler and he grew disillusioned when his last stage work, *La femme de Claude*, achieved little success. His works reflect the influence of Franck; de Romain, in writing about *Endymion*, commented that Cahen's music was melodically rich but suffered from dull orchestral writing. None of his uneven operas held the stage into the 20th century.

Le bois (oc, 1, A. Glatigny), Paris, OC (Favart), 11 Oct 1880, vs (Paris, n.d.)
La belle au bois dormant (opéra féerie), Geneva, Grand, 1886
Le vénitien (3, L. Gallet), Rouen, Nouveau Lyrique, 14 April 1890, vs (Paris, ?1890)
La femme de Claude (drame lyrique, 3, Gallet, after Dumas *fils*), Paris, OC (Lyrique), 23 June 1896, excerpts, vs (Paris, n.d.)

*

L. de Romain: *Essais de critique musicale* (Paris, 1890)
M. Boucher: *L'école de César Franck* (Paris, 1917)
L. Davies: *César Franck and his Circle* (London, 1970)

JOHN TREVITT, ROBERT ORLEDGE

Cahier, Mme **Charles** [née Layton Walker, Sarah (Jane); Charles-Cahier, Sarah; Black, Mrs Morris] (*b* Nashville, TN, 8 Jan 1870; *d* Manhattan Beach, CA, 15 April 1951). American contralto. Her teachers included Jean de Reszke in Paris, Gustav Walter in Vienna and Amalie Joachim in Berlin. Two years after her operatic début in Nice (1904), she was engaged by Mahler at the Vienna Hofoper, where for six seasons she sang roles that included Carmen and several in Wagner operas. She made her Metropolitan début in 1912 as Azucena and during the next two years sang Amneris and Fricka with the company; elsewhere her most famous role was Carmen. Her concert work, however, was more significant, and in 1911 Bruno Walter chose her for the posthumous première of *Das Lied von der Erde* in Munich. The few recordings that she made document an imposing voice, if somewhat uncentred in tone, and a stately style.

RICHARD DYER

Cahill, Teresa (*b* Maidenhead, 30 July 1944). English soprano. She studied in London, making her début in 1967 as Rosina with Phoenix Opera. Engaged at Covent Garden (1970–77), she sang Barbarina, Zerlina, Sophie, the First Niece (*Peter Grimes*) and Woglinde, and took part in the première of Henze's *We Come to the River* (1976). At Glyndebourne (1970–80) her roles included Alice Ford. She created Pauline Leclerc in Blake's *Toussaint l'ouverture* (1977) for the ENO. Her other roles have included Donna Elvira, Pamina, Micaëla, Antonia (*Les contes d'Hoffmann*), Blanche (*Dialogues des Carmélites*), Semele, Miss Wordsworth (*Albert Herring*) and Tchaikovsky's Iolanta. Her warm, lyrical voice was heard to best advantage in Mozart, although in the 1990s she took on heavier roles, including Daphne and Arabella (in concert performances).

ELIZABETH FORBES

Cahusac, (Jean-)Louis de (*b* Montauban, Tarn-et-Garonne, 6 April 1706; *d* Paris, 22 June 1759). French librettist and playwright. After embarking on a legal career, he moved to Paris in 1733 to oversee the staging of his tragedy *Pharamond*. In 1739 he was appointed secretary to the Count of Clermont, grand master of the French grand masonic lodge, by which time he himself was almost certainly a freemason. Although he enjoyed some success at the Comédie-Française, notably with *Zénéaïde* (1743), Cahusac soon turned exclusively to opera, and was Rameau's principal collaborator from 1745 until his death.

Though widely criticized in contemporary literary circles, Cahusac possessed certain strengths as a librettist. His choice of subject matter was adventurous. He was among the first to exploit 'la féerie' – the enchanted world of Middle Eastern myth, with its genies and other fantastical aerial beings. This is most fully developed in *Zaïs* (1748), though Cahusac had explored it in the entrée 'La féerie' from *Les fêtes de Polymnie* (1745) and was to incorporate elements of it in *Zoroastre* (1749). *Zoroastre* itself is derived from ancient Persian religious sources, which provided Cahusac with the pretext to introduce various masonic symbols (also found in some of his other librettos, though never so prominently). The religion of ancient Egypt furnishes the subject matter of *Les fêtes de l'Hymen et de l'Amour, ou Les dieux d'Egypte* (1747) and *La naissance d'Osiris* (1754). Even where he derived his material from the more conventional classical Greek sources, Cahusac showed the same interest in spectacle that was both unusual and lent itself to elaborate musical treatment (as in *Naïs*, 1749, with its battle between Titans and Gods, its representation of the Isthmian Games and its birdsong oracle).

Cahusac's skill in introducing such spectacle in a dramatically convincing way was conceded even by his most vociferous critics. Of all Rameau's librettists, he was the most consistently successful in making the obligatory *divertissement* seem not only appropriate to the action but essential to it. Keen that the all-important ballet should be more effectively integrated with the drama than it had formerly been, he devised numerous opportunities for pantomime, of which there existed two broad (if to some extent overlapping) categories: *danses en action*, in which the dancers' mimed movements were indispensable to the plot (e.g. where they performed some ceremonial function); and *ballets figurés*, in which a group of dancers mimed an action related to, or analogous with, the main plot but usually independent of it. Though neither was an innovation, Cahusac made more extensive use of both than any predecessor; moreover, the degree of detail in his stage directions for such ballets was unprecedented.

Cahusac is often criticized for his overuse of the supernatural – *le merveilleux*. From his various writings, which between them constitute one of the earliest coherent theories of French lyric theatre, it becomes clear that for Cahusac *le merveilleux* was not a weakness, in opera at least, but a source of strength: through its use all the arts could more easily combine to astonish and bewitch the spectator, which for Cahusac were among the principal functions of opera. His interest in *le merveilleux* extended to aspects of its staging. He did, however, disavow a statement in the *Mercure de France* that he had invented the principal machines for *Naïs* and for the representation of the overflowing Nile in *Les fêtes de l'Hymen et de l'Amour*. For the revival of *Zoroastre* in 1756 he tried with only partial success to introduce costume designs based on historical models.

In addition to his librettos, Cahusac is known for an important treatise, *La danse ancienne et moderne* (1754), and for the articles on music and dance that he contributed to Diderot and D'Alembert's *Encyclopédie* (1751–65).

Les fêtes de Polymnie (opéra-ballet), Rameau, 1745; *Les fêtes de l'Hymen et de l'Amour, ou Les dieux d'Egypte* (opéra-ballet), Rameau, 1747; *Zaïs* (pastorale-héroïque), Rameau, 1748; *Naïs* (pastorale-héroïque), Rameau, 1749; *Zoroastre* (tragédie), Rameau, 1749, rev. 1756; *La naissance d'Osiris* (acte de ballet), Rameau, 1754; *Anacréon* (acte de ballet), Rameau, 1754

Attrib. Cahusac: *Les Boréades* (tragédie), Rameau, n.d.; possibly by Cahusac: *Io* (acte de ballet), Rameau, n.d.

*

C. Malherbe: 'Commentaire bibliographique', *J.-P. Rameau: Oeuvres complètes* (Paris, 1895–1924), xiii, xv, xvi, xviii
A. R. Oliver: *The Encyclopedists as Critics of Music* (New York, 1947)
C. Girdlestone: *La tragédie en musique (1673–1750) considérée comme genre littéraire* (Geneva, 1972)
C. Kintzler: *Jean-Philippe Rameau: splendeur et naufrage de l'esthétique du plaisir à l'âge classique* (Paris, 1983, 2/1988)
F. A. Kafker and S. L. Kafker: 'The Encyclopedists as Individuals: a Biographical Dictionary of the Authors of the *Encyclopédie*', *Studies on Voltaire and the Eighteenth Century*, no.257 (1988) [whole issue]
P. Russo: 'Les incertitudes de la tragédie lyrique: *Zoroastre* de Louis de Cahusac', *RdM*, lxxv (1989), 47–64
G. Sadler: 'A Re-examination of Rameau's Self-borrowings', *Jean-Baptiste Lully and the Music of the French Baroque: Essays in Honor of James R. Anthony* (Cambridge, 1989), 259–89
C. Kintzler: *Poétique de l'opéra français de Corneille à Rousseau* (Paris, 1991)

GRAHAM SADLER

Cain, Henri (*b* Paris, 1859; *d* Paris, 21 Nov 1937). French writer and librettist. A son of the sculptor Auguste-Nicolas Cain and brother of the painter Georges Cain, he was a man of many talents, in the visual as well as the literary arts. He won some renown as a painter in the first half of his life, initially for his historical canvases and then for his portraits; subsequently he became a prolific writer, with many novels, essays, plays and some 40 librettos, written over more than four decades, to his name. As a librettist he is mainly remembered for his association with Massenet, which began in 1894 with *La Navarraise*; this was Cain's second libretto, written in collaboration with Jules Claretie, the author of the story on which it is based. Portraying violence and heightened emotions in the Spanish Carlist Wars, with realistic military detail, *La Navarraise* was designed for a *verismo* opera (Massenet's setting shows the influence not only of Mascagni's *Cavalleria rusticana* but also of *L'attaque du moulin* (1892–3) by Massenet's pupil, Alfred Bruneau). The highly successful *Sapho*, written three years later, is a love story after Alphonse Daudet, set in Provence and with a pronounced folk element. In *Cendrillon* (1899), however, Cain and Massenet reverted to a far less realistic manner for their interpretation of one of Charles Perrault's best-loved fairytales. *Chérubin* (1905) is one of the numerous French 19th-century attempts to imagine what might have befallen the Chérubin of Beaumarchais' *Mariage de Figaro* in later life, and *Don Quichotte* (1910) is notable for its role created for Shalyapin. Massenet also composed scores for Cain's ballet scenarios *Cigale* (1894) and *Une aventure de la Guimard* (1902).

La Navarraise (épisode lyrique, with J. Claretie), Massenet, 1895; *Sapho* (pièce lyrique, with A. Bernède, after A. Daudet), Massenet, 1897; *Cendrillon* (opéra féerique), Massenet, 1899; *Le Juif polonais* (with P.-B. Gheusi), 1900; *La cabrera*, Dupont, 1904; *Chérubin* (comédie chantée, with F. de Croisset), Massenet, 1905; *Les pêcheurs de Saint-Jean*, Widor, 1905; *Marcella* (with J. Adenis), Giordano, 1907; *Don Quichotte* (comédie-héroïque), Massenet, 1910; *Roma* (opéra tragique), Massenet, 1912; *Sangre y sol* (drame lyrique, with M. Star), A. Georges, 1912; *La mégère apprivoisée* (comédie lyrique, with E. Adenis), C. Silver, 1922; *La victoire* (tragédie antique), A. Dupuis, 1923; *Un drame sous Philippe II* (drame lyrique), Dupuis, 1926; *Quatre-vingt-treize* (épopée lyrique), Silver, 1935; *Cyrano de Bergerac* (after E. Rostand), Alfano, 1936; *L'aiglon* (drame musical, after Rostand), Honegger, 1937

CHRISTOPHER SMITH

Caio Mario ('Gaius Marius'). Libretto by GAETANO ROCCAFORTE, first set by Niccolò Jommelli (1746, Rome); the title also appears as *Cajo Mario* and *Caio Marzio*.

Roccaforte, typically, drew his subject matter from Roman history, in this case from Titus Livius, book 62.64, and Plutarch's *Lives*. When Jugurtha invades a neighbouring kingdom, the Roman Senate sends the Consul, Gaius Marius, against him, accompanied by Annio [Annius], his future son-in-law, and Lucio [Lucius], his first lieutenant. Jugurtha is defeated in battle, and the only member of his family to survive is his daughter, Princess Rodope, with whom Lucius falls in love. She, however, loves Annius and wants to kill Marius's daughter Marzia. Marius dreams that he has sacrificed his daughter to the gods; to discover the meaning of the dream he secretly sends Lucius to the oracle at Delso with instructions to follow his party to Rome. Lucius confides his mission to Rodope, who suggests that he falsify the oracle, and he agrees; he persuades her to meet him in Rome.

The opera begins with the triumphant return of Marius to Rome from Numidia; Rodope has been received into his house and Marzia has offered to help her regain her kingdom. Lucius arrives shortly afterwards with the false oracle, saying that the gods require Marzia's death. Marius agonizes alone over this dilemma throughout Act 1; he reveals it to his daughter at the beginning of Act 2, and the others struggle with it as well. The tragedy is narrowly averted in the final scene when Lucius and Rodope are forced to confess. Marius, however, pardons them and joins them in marriage.

For a list of settings *see* ROCCAFORTE, GAETANO.

DOROTHEA LINK

Cairns, David (Adam) (*b* Loughton, Essex, 8 June 1926). English writer on music. He studied at Trinity College, Oxford (where he read history, 1945–8), and Princeton (1950–51). In 1950, with Stephen Gray, he founded the Chelsea Opera Group. He has held various appointments as music critic, notably on the *Financial Times* and the *Sunday Times*. From 1967 to 1972 he took part in planning several substantial recordings by Philips Records, among them works by Mozart, Berlioz and Tippett. These composers, especially Berlioz, are at the centre of his interests: he wrote an introduction and notes to a translation of Berlioz's *Les soirées de l'orchestre* (1963), translated and edited his memoirs (London, 1969, 2/1977) and is author of a substantial biography (London, 1989–). *Responses* (London, 1973, 2/1980), a collection of his writings, includes essays on operas and conductors.

STANLEY SADIE

Cairns, Janice (*b* Ashington, Northumberland, 1954). English soprano. She studied at the Royal Scottish Academy of Music and Drama and with Tito Gobbi, making her début while still a student at Salonica (Thessaloniki) as Desdemona. In 1980 she sang Alice Ford with Kent Opera. Since her ENO début (1982) as Musetta she has sung Ariadne, Eva, Butterfly, Maria (*Mazepa*), Aida, Lisa (*The Queen of Spades*, 1987),

Tosca and Amelia (*Simon Boccanegra* and *Un ballo in maschera*) with the company. For Scottish Opera she has sung Reiza and Leonora (*Il trovatore*). Her roles also include Donna Anna, Leonore, Odabella, Leonora (*La forza del destino*), Maddalena (*Andrea Chénier*) and Hélène, which she sang in the British stage première of Verdi's *Jérusalem* (1990, Opera North). A powerful actress, she has a vibrant, flexible voice well suited to both Verdi and Puccini. ELIZABETH FORBES

Cairo. Capital of Egypt, the largest city in Africa. Opera came to Egypt in 1841, when an Italian touring company presented a season in Alexandria. Subsequently opera was given in Cairo; in the 1860s Adelina Patti sang there. In 1869 the khedive decided to build a new opera house in the city to mark the opening of the Suez Canal; the theatre, designed by Italian architects (seating 850 in three tiers of boxes, stalls and top gallery), opened later the same year, not with *Aida*, as is often stated, but with *Rigoletto*. Delays were caused by the Franco-Prussian War: the costumes and scenery for *Aida* were blocked in Paris, and the opera was not performed until the end of the second season in 1871, since when it has become a favourite, with revivals almost every season. (In 1912 it received its first presentation at the foot of the Pyramids.) From 1869 to 1876–7 seven seasons of Italian and French operas (and *Lohengrin*), all in Italian, were given in Cairo and Alexandria, until the company went bankrupt. There were no more official productions until 1879, when the Italian impresario L. Gianoli took control, but various unofficial touring companies performed in Cairo and in Alexandria. In 1895 one of these, organized by Adolfo Bracale, included the young Caruso. Besides his normal repertory he sang two roles for the first time, Enzo in *La Gioconda* and Des Grieux in *Manon Lescaut*. In 1907 the French impresario Marius Poncet organized a season of Italian and French operas (and the ever popular *Lohengrin*), all sung in French. But the Opera House, with its limited capacity, was never profitable, and in 1923, after the failure of another French season, the organization of opera was left to the Italians, and spoken drama to the French. In 1922, with the break-up of the Ottoman empire, the Cairo Opera and the Zizinia Theatre in Alexandria became the Théâtres Royaux, French being the official language of the court. By now operas were being given in Arabic at the Garden Theatre, alongside works by native composers such as Sayed Darwish (1892–1923). (Other prominent Egyptian composers of opera and other vocal music are Mohammed Abdul Wahab, Hassan Rasheed, Abu Bakr Khayrat and Aziz El-Shawan.) The 1927 season at the Opera (which included the first performance in Egypt – in Italian – of *Pelléas et Mélisande*), though an artistic success, only avoided financial disaster when the Italian government stepped in. Thereafter this subsidy became almost annual. (The last season under a French impresario, Clément Fichefet, was given in 1934.) Italian companies came most years up until World War II; in 1935 a company with Rosa Raisa as leading soprano gave 16 operas. Many of the postwar seasons were under the musical direction of Vincenzo Bellazza. At that time performances in Cairo were usually repeated in Alexandria, first at the Zizinia Theatre, then at the Alhambra Theatre, and later at the Mohammed Ali Theatre (now the Sayed Darwish Theatre). Neither the fall of the monarchy in 1952 nor the Suez crisis in 1956 held up performances at the Opera for long. Many famous Italian singers and conductors of the day appeared, but Egyptian singers, usually trained in Italy, gradually took their place, first as understudies then as principals.

The Cairo Opera Company was formed by the Egyptian Ministry of Culture in 1964. Its inaugural performance, at the Opera, was *La traviata* (in Arabic) with Nabila Erian and Hassan Kamy. Kamy later became a popular Radames (the first Egyptian to sing the role). In 1968 Gluck's *Orfeo* was presented with the first all-Egyptian cast. Ratiba el Hefni, later the interim director of the new Opera House, sang Orpheus. The Berlin Staatsoper gave a season in 1969 during the festivities to mark the millennium of the city. In 1971 the theatre caught fire, apparently because of an electrical fault. Projects to rebuild came and went until 1983, when during the president's visit to Japan the Japanese government announced the gift of a new opera house as part of the national cultural centre donated to the Egyptian people. The new building, designed by Kuashiro Shikeda in his own 'modern Islamic' style and completed in 1988, is sited beside the Nile on the old exhibition site of Gezira. It includes a main auditorium of 1300 seats, a smaller hall of 500, an open-air theatre and many well-equipped practice rooms. The house was inaugurated in 1988 with a concert of specially commissioned music followed by three performances of kabuki theatre. In 1989 the Cairo Opera Company and the artistic groups attached to it were affiliated to the National Cultural Centre Organization (NCC), an independent body. Since then the opera company, with the opera chorus and the Cairo SO, have presented works from the standard repertory, including *Il trovatore*, *La traviata*, *Aida*, *La bohème*, *Tosca* and *Butterfly*, and new works have been commissioned. In 1991 the 'Opera in Arabic' movement marked the Mozart bicentenary with the first ever production in Arabic of *Le nozze di Figaro* and *Don Giovanni* – to a largely Arabic-speaking audience and with great success – under the musical direction of Thomas Christian David.

Visits have been made by opera companies from abroad, including the Chinese Opera of Singapore and the Houston Grand Opera, and by members of the Varna and Sofia companies. The Cairo Opera Ballet Company was revived by the NCC and has presented new Egyptian works as well as participating in opera productions.

*

C. Pitt: 'L'Opéra du Caire', *Opéra international*, no 155 (1992), 25–7 CHARLES PITT, TAREK H. A. HASSAN

Calandra [Calandria, Calandro], **Nicola** (*b* ?Frasso Tebesino, Benevento; *fl* 1747–59). Italian composer. Lack of biographical information makes him appear an obscure minor figure, but the distribution of some sacred and instrumental manuscripts north of the Alps suggests a certain popularity outside Italy. His birthplace is inferred from his nickname, 'Frascia'. He may have studied in Naples and was perhaps a *maestro di cappella* in Rome. He appears to have worked in Naples at the small Teatro della Pace from about 1747 to 1749, continuing the tradition of dialect *opera buffa*; to judge from performance records, he had moved by 1756 to northern Italy, where he styled himself 'virtuoso della Casa Orsini d'Aragona'. He contributed five arias for a revival of Galuppi's *La diavolessa* (1759, Bologna).

all opere buffe

Lo Barone Landolfo (G. d'Arno [G. D'Avino]), Naples, Pace, carn. 1747 [not 1767]

La mogliera traduta (A. Palomba), Naples, Pace, spr. 1747

Li dispiette d'ammore [sinfonia and Act 3] (Palomba), Naples, Pace, carn. 1748 [Acts 1 and 2 by N. Logroscino]

Il tutore 'nnamorato (P. Trinchera), Naples, Pace, carn. 1749

I tre matrimoni (?C. Gozzi), Venice, S Samuele, aut. 1756

La pugna amorosa, o sia Amor cagion del tutto (int), Rome, Valle, carn. 1757

Lo stordito deluso (int), Bologna, Pubblico della Sala, carn. 1758

La schiava per amore (int), Città di Castello, Terra della Fratta, 1772

Aria in *F-Pn*

*

CroceN

M. Scherillo: *L'opera buffa napoletana durante il settecento: storia letteraria* (Naples, 1883, 2/1917), 258–9

U. Prota-Giurleo: *Nicola Logroscino: 'il dio dell'opera buffa'* (Naples, 1927), 39

——: 'Musicisti sanniti', *Samnium*, i (1928) JAMES L. JACKMAN

Caldara, Antonio (*b* Venice, *c*1670; *d* Vienna, 28 Dec 1736). Italian composer. He was one of the most prolific composers of his generation, and the quantity and style of his operatic works reflect the varied circumstances of his career.

Caldara was a choirboy at St Mark's, Venice, where he may have studied with the *maestro di cappella* Giovanni Legrenzi. His earliest operas, written for Venetian houses and no doubt for immediate public recognition, are the chief products of his fledgling years, when from 1688 to 1699 he was engaged as a cellist at St Mark's. Publication of two sets of trio sonatas (opp.1 and 2, 1693 and 1699) and 12 chamber cantatas (op.3, 1699) preceded Caldara's first important appointment, as *maestro di cappella* at Mantua to the last Gonzaga duke, Ferdinando Carlo, from May 1699 to late 1707. With his opera-loving patron's indulgence hampered by the north Italian conflicts of the War of the Spanish Succession, Caldara could fulfil only a spasmodic demand for operas, and of these as many were produced beyond Mantua (in Genoa, Casale and Venice) as in the city itself. At Rome, more secure as *maestro* to the Marquis Francesco Maria Ruspoli from 1709 to mid-1716, Caldara's activities centred on oratorios and cantatas. The handful of dramatic works, very much occasional pieces, includes two large outdoor serenatas (1709) and two operas (one of which, *L'Anagilda*, contains Caldara's earliest extant intermezzo) for Ruspoli's private theatre in January 1711. This entire Italian corpus, however, was rapidly overtaken by the immense outpouring of Caldara's Viennese years.

Between 1716 and 1736, as vice-Kapellmeister to the Emperor Charles VI in Vienna, Caldara produced more than 35 dramatic works in response to the strict ceremonial requirements of the Habsburg court; a *dramma per musica* or a single-act *festa da camera* or *festa teatrale* (spectacular exhibitions of the opulent artistic resources of the court) was mandatory for the principal secular feasts, the birthdays and name-days of the emperor and empress. Probably Charles himself chose Caldara to provide an almost unbroken stream of operas for his name-day (4 November) and many for his birthday (1 October). From the late 1720s Caldara frequently relieved the ailing Kapellmeister, J. J. Fux, of responsibility for operas for the empress's feast days, and after 1728 he supplied several of the annual carnival operas in place of the ill court composer, Francesco Conti. The customary practice at the Viennese court was

1. Account submitted by Tarquinio Lanciani (one of Ruspoli's principal copyists), countersigned by Caldara, for the preparation of the score and parts for Caldara's 'L'Anagilda' and the intermezzo 'Lisetta ed Astrobolo' (probably by F. Gasparini); performances took place in Ruspoli's Palazzo Bonelli, Rome, between 4 January and 5 February 1711

to have a single opera during carnival, performed once a week for three or four weeks. In addition, there were occasional operas for Habsburg wedding festivities, as well as small semi-dramatic celebratory pieces (such as *Ghirlanda di fiori*, 1726). From the late 1720s there were also the *componimenti* given privately (some, at least, in costumed presentations) by the young duchesses before the imperial family. Beyond Vienna, Caldara provided a series of operas between 1716 and 1727 for the archiepiscopal court at Salzburg.

Despite the wealth of extant source material, especially in Viennese archives, Caldara's operas have been seldom studied and rarely revived. After the death in 1740 of Charles VI, for whose conservative tastes he catered exclusively, Caldara's pre-eminence in the repertory at court faded rapidly, his works thrust aside by others in the emerging Viennese pre-Classical style. In modern times he has been remembered mainly as the first composer to have set a substantial proportion of the 'reform' librettos of Apostolo Zeno and Pietro Metastasio.

Caldara's Venetian and Roman works stand in a tradition of operas characterized by large numbers of arias variously placed within the scenes. His arias are particularly diverse in length and formal design. Although da capo structures (in which the *A* and *B* sections are well contrasted) predominate, strophic and through-composed arias are not uncommon. Ritornello construction, the foundation of all Caldara arias, is imaginatively and extensively explored. This, allied with a wealth of instrumental textures (continuo alone, unison strings, strings in three, four and five parts and in concertino-ripieno groupings, and voice and upper strings in unison), obvious dance influences (especially of corrente, gigue, saraband and siciliana) and a fascination with the instrumental style of the concerto, produces a kaleidoscope of stylistic resource.

In Vienna Caldara set librettos quite different in character and less lavishly endowed with aria texts. The almost invariable *ABA* verse structure and end-of-scene placings curbed variety in formal design as well as diversity in the scope and scale of the aria settings. Gone, too, was the stimulus of satisfying diverse tastes in public and semi-public performances; after 1716 Caldara had to secure the approval of a single patron. His response was realistic and pragmatic rather than richly artistic. Every opportunity for a formal musical number was deliberately exploited, whatever the dramatic situation. Arias uniformly, even unnecessarily, lengthy and elaborately accompanied (with three- and four-part strings busy in contrapuntal endeavour) were the norm; the relief and variety brought by continuo arias and single-line accompaniments in upper strings all but vanished. Charles VI's penchant for 'long and serious' operas was accommodated in streams of regular da capo structures almost weighed down by ritornellos whose motifs and counterpoints intertwined in textures as delightful to the eyes as to the ears. Concentrated bravura writing, frequently based on rigid rhythmic patterns, seldom inspired by word or affect and typically inserted towards the end of each main section of the aria, demonstrated the prowess of the court's soloists and confirmed the ceremonial and propagandist roles of imperial opera. Overall, refined and polished handling of instruments and voice, and of tonality, harmony and melody, replaced the rough-hewn vigour of the earlier works. Nowhere is this more apparent than in slow, 'pathetic' arias. Chromatic harmonies and pungent suspensions enrich accompaniments, while singers proceed in broken affective phrases in 4/4 largos (e.g. 'Se tutti i mali miei' in *Demofoonte*, 2.vi) or spin effortless bel cantos in 12/8 sicilianas (e.g. 'Numi, se giuste siete' in *Adriano in Siria*, 1.ii). Nevertheless, such high points seldom disguise the emotional uniformity of many ceremonial operas, an enervating tendency towards superficial depiction of both characters and moods through stereotyped gestures (especially of heroic and bellicose sentiments) and motifs too often sharing common devices.

Caldara's carnival operas and those for Salzburg are much livelier. Possibly he found the librettos (especially those of G. C. Pasquini) more congenial; certainly, the hand of ceremony weighs less heavily. Aria scorings are lighter, structures are more varied, textures emphasize melody-bass polarity, while the melodies themselves are fresh and seldom burdened with extended bravura. Both *L'Etearco* (1726, Salzburg) and *I disingannati* (1729, Vienna) indicate the direction in which the early galant style of *L'Anagilda* (1711, Rome) might have developed had not substantial financial rewards suggested an alternative.

The treatment of the voice in recitatives undergoes little stylistic change throughout Caldara's career. Short phrases (rarely more than two bars in length) that sometimes force the text to unnecessary halts characterize his *secco* writing. The setting is syllabic, the unremarkable vocal lines occasionally enlivened by affective intervals. The obvious difference between the early operas and much of Caldara's Viennese output is the immense increase in monologue or dialogue setting demanded by the librettos of Zeno and Metastasio. In response Caldara curtailed the vibrant and rapid harmonic shifts typical of his early writing – obviously less effective for the marathon Viennese recitatives – and instead relied on frequent and extensive pedals (above which tonic harmonies moved to supertonic and dominant chords and back) to support large portions of text. Interrupted cadences, in which the dominant bass note rises by a semitone to become the 3rd of a new dominant chord, and the inconclusive inversions of perfect closes maintained flow across a character's sentences and paragraphs. Character changes above, rather than after, a cadence and a restrained use of the formal *cadenza tronca* secured overall momentum. The pithier recitatives and rapid exchanges of the carnival and Salzburg operas, reminiscent of pre-1716 librettos, were accorded a speedier harmonic flow; anchoring pedal points became fewer.

Recitativo accompagnato is found in the ceremonial operas. Caldara always employed it sparingly, usually reserving it for the closing scenes of the final act. There its homophonic four-part string writing in sustained notes or reiterated semiquavers and its chromatic harmonies intensify that emotional climax (usually of despair or remorse) in a principal character which heralds the unfolding of the *lieto fine*.

Caldara's ensembles, rarely significant in his operatic output, typically involve two characters. His standard techniques comprise the strophic aria *a* 2 (framed with ritornellos) and the imitative duet (usually da capo) in which the vocal phrases, heard first in succession, gradually overlap in stretto fashion to climax in sustained two-part writing. Paired characters, for example lovers (whether agreeing or disagreeing), share the same motifs and ultimately unite in parallel 3rds and 6ths; 'independent' characters express their differing sentiments in a counterpoint of melodically and rhythmically contrasted motifs and rather less duet writing. Traits of the *allegro* patter duets of the intermezzo characters, with their vehement altercations (for example in 'Non ti vo' from *L'Anagilda*, 3.xi), occasionally surface in the Viennese carnival operas; one instance is 'Pupille vezzose' in *I disingannati*, 1.xii. Less common is the 'dialogue aria' of some pre-1716 operas; numerous natural exchanges between two characters create a single continuous melodic line (e.g. 'Un sospiro' in *L'Anagilda*, 2.vi) in the guise of a continuo or unison aria. Still more exceptional is the terzetto 'Scopri, infedel' (*I disingannati*, 3.viii); the presentation of three contrasted emotional states in well-characterized motifs foreshadows the 'psychological' ensemble of later 18th-century operas.

The extensive and lavishly accompanied choral finales of several non-dramatic *feste* (some with concertante parts for soloists) are far removed from the perfunctory choruses (moralistic, congratulatory or celebratory) rounding off the majority of Caldara's operas. The homophonic binary chorus (8 + 8 bars, each section repeated), with its syllabic setting for SATB and *colla parte* accompaniment, that concludes *L'ingratitudine gastigata*, probably typifies Caldara's early settings. Through-composed structures are favoured in the Viennese finales, together with independent accompaniments (as in *Andromaca*) and minute preludes and/or postludes (as in *Demofoonte*).

2. Opening of the violin and continuo part of Act 1 scene ii (the aria 'Perchè troppo') of Caldara's 'Sancio Pansa'; these parts, prepared for a projected performance in 1730 (postponed until 1733) bear modified style and tempo indications probably suggested by the composer (the words 'ed il Bargello' close the preceding recitative, serving as a cue)

More important are the choruses that begin an opera or occur within an act. Through corporate expressions of jubilation, loyalty, happiness etc. by the soldiers, servants and rustics, and by the *numi* and *geni* who populate the Zeno and Metastasio texts, choral writing is integrated into the operatic texture. Caldara's style remains unadventurous, but when these choruses are placed in sequence and varied by metre and tonality, or repeated after intervening recitatives and arias (as in *Adriano in Siria*, 1.i), or, again, when juxtaposed in the manner of a concerto grosso with ensembles for the principals (for example in *Achille in Sciro*, 1.i), their impact is considerable. The Viennese carnival and Salzburg operas do not share this expanded role of the chorus; few librettos call for crowd scenes. Caldara reverts to choral closes little removed from pre-1716 examples and which, as in *I disingannati*, may be taken by the soloists.

Each *introduzione* is independent of the opera it precedes. No thematic connections exist; no anticipatory mood is created; even the instrumental resources of the overture may not reappear in the ensuing accompaniments. Among the Salzburg and Viennese operas and *feste* only the half-dozen overtures whose third movement is converted into the opening aria or chorus of the first act are neither detachable nor interchangeable. The lavish scoring for two trumpet choirs, each consisting of two clarini, two *trombe* and timpani, in seven overtures is a hallmark of the Emperor's name-day operas, a musical allusion to the two 'pillars' of Charles's personal motto, 'Fortitudine & Constantia'.

Excepting the single-movement introduction to *Caio Marzio Coriolano* and some 16 two-movement pieces, Caldara's overtures to both pre- and post-1716 operas follow a fast-slow-fast plan. There is a marked emphasis on the first allegro, always the longest movement. These range from pieces modelled on the concerto grosso (*L'ingratitudine gastigata*), through substantial fugal structures (*Scipione Africano*), to ternary designs in which expositions display obvious first- and second-subject areas in contrasted tonalities (*I disingannati* and *Don Chisciotte*). Transitional slow movements of seldom more than a dozen bars serve as links to lightweight binary finales, usually Neapolitan minuets (as in *Mitridate* and *Enone*) but not infrequently vigorous march-like 'arias' (as in *Gianguir* and *Ciro riconosciuto*).

See also ADRIANO IN SIRIA (i); ANAGILDA; DISINGANNATI, I; and OLIMPIADE, L' (i).

drammi per musica, in three acts, unless otherwise stated

WF – *Vienna, Teatro della Favorita*
WG – *Vienna, Hoftheater (Teatro Grande)*

L'Argene (trattenimento per musica, 3, P. E. Badi), Venice, Accademia ai Saloni, aut. 1689, lib. *I-Bc*

Il Tirsi [Act 2] (drama pastorale, 5, A. Zeno), Venice, S Salvatore, aut. 1696, lib. *Bc* [Act 1 by A. Lotti, Act 3 by A. Ariosti; composers of Acts 4 and 5 unidentified]

La promessa serbata al primo (various authors), Venice, SS Giovanni e Paolo, spr. 1697, lib. *Bc*
L'ingratitudine gastigata (F. Silvani), Venice, ?1698, *D-MÜs*
L'oracolo in sogno [Act 1] (Silvani), Mantua, Teatro di Mantova, 6 June 1699, pubd lib. *I-Bc* [Act 2 by A. Quintavalle, Act 3 by C. F. Pollarolo]
La Partenope (S. Stampiglia), ? Mantua, Teatro di Mantova, May 1701; rev., Ferrara, Bonacossi, May 1709, lib. *Bc*, collab. G. Boniventi [Caldara named only in 1709; earlier version probably by Caldara]
Opera pastorale (3), Mantua, ? Teatro di Mantova, 1701, *A-Wgm**; rev. as La costanza in amor vince l'inganno (drama pastorale), Rome, Palazzo Bonelli, 9 Feb 1711, Act 1 *D-MÜs*, lib. *I-MAC* [2 copies; one with T. Albinoni: Vespetta e Pimpinone (int, first part only of 3); other with Lisetto ed Astrobolo (int, first part only; by ? F. Gasparini)]
Farnace (L. Morari), Venice, S Angelo, aut. 1703, lib. *Bc*
Gli equivoci del sembiante (? D. F. Contini), Casale, Novo, 1703 (? carn.), lib. *Bc*
Paride sull'Ida, overo Gl'amori di Paride con Enone (favola pastorale), Mantua, ? Teatro di Mantova, spr. 1704, lib. *Bc*, collab. Quintavalle
L'Arminio (A. Salvi), Genoa, S Agostino, carn. 1705, lib. *Bc*
Il selvaggio eroe (tragicomedia eroico-pastorale, 5, G. Frigimelica Roberti), Venice, S Giovanni Grisostomo, 20 Nov 1707, arias *D-MÜs*, lib. *I-Bc*
Il più bel nome (componimento da camera, 1, P. Pariati), Barcelona, Llotja de Mar, 2 Aug 1708, *B-Bc*
Sofonisba (Silvani), Venice, S Giovanni Grisostomo, aut. 1708, arias *D-MÜs*, lib. *I-Bc*
L'inimico generoso, Bologna, Malvezzi, 11 May 1709, *A-Wn*
Il nome più glorioso (componimento da camera, 1, Pariati), Barcelona, 4 Nov 1709, *Wn*
L'Atenaide [Act 2] (Zeno), ? Barcelona, Milan or Vienna, 1709, *Wn* [Act 1 by A. S. Fiorè, Act 3 by Gasparini]; as Teodosio ed Eudossa (os), Brunswick, 12 Sept 1716, lib. *D-W*, collab. Fux and Gasparini; as Teodosio, Hamburg, ded. 14 Nov 1718, collab. Fux and Gasparini
L'Anagilda, o vero La fede ne' tradimenti (G. Gigli), Rome, Palazzo Bonelli, 4 Jan 1711, *MÜs*; perf. with Dorina e Grullo (int, 2, Gigli), *MÜs*
Giunio Bruto, overo La caduta de' Tarquinii [Act 2], 1711 (? G. Sinibaldi), unperf., *A-Wn* [Act 1 by C. F. Cesarini, Act 3 by A. Scarlatti]
Tito e Berenice (C. S. Capece), Rome, Capranica, carn. 1714, lib. *I-Bc*
L'Atenaide [Act 3] (Zeno), WG, 19 Nov 1714, *A-Wn*, *D-W* [Act 1 by M. A. Ziani, Act 2 by A. Negri, int and licenza by F. Conti]
Il giubilo della salza (festa, R. M. Rossi), Salzburg, 1716 (?sum.)
Il maggior grande (componimento per musica da camera, 1, Pariati), Vienna, court, 1 Oct 1716, *MEIr*
Pipa e Barlafuso (int, 3, F. R. Cantù), WG, 19 Nov 1716, *A-Wn*; perf. with Lotti and J. J. Fux: Il Constantino
Caio Marzio Coriolano (Pariati), WF, 28 Aug 1717, *Wgm**, *Wn*
Il Tiridate, overo La verità nell'inganno (Silvani), Vienna, Hof (Teatrino), 11 Nov 1717, *Wgm**, *Wn* [includes int Lisetta ed Astrobolo (3), attrib. Caldara]
Ifigenia in Aulide (Zeno), WG, 5 Nov 1718, *Wgm**, *Wn*
Sirita (Zeno), WF, 21 Aug 1719, *Wgm**, *Wn*
Dafne (dramma pastorale, 3, G. Biavi), Salzburg, 1719 (? 4 Oct), *Wgm**; ed. in DTÖ, xci (1955)
Lucio Papirio dittatore (Zeno), WG, 4 Nov 1719, *Wgm**, *Wn*
[Zaira], ? Vienna or Salzburg, ?1719, *Wgm**
Apollo in cielo (componimento da camera, 1, Pariati), Vienna, court, 4 Nov 1720, *Wn*
Psiche (componimento da camera, 1, Zeno), Vienna, court, 19 Nov 1720, *Wn*, collab. Fux
Gli eccessi dell'infedeltà (?3, D. Lalli), Salzburg, 1720
L'inganno tradito dall'amore (A. M. Lucchini), Salzburg, Fürstbischöfliche Palast, 1720, *Wgm**; perf. with Atomo huomo vecchio e Palancha giovine (int, 2, ?Lucchini), *Wgm**
Il germanico Marte, Salzburg, 4 Oct 1721, *Wgm**; perf. with Grespilla e Fanfarone (int, 3), *Wgm**
Ormisda, re di Persia (Zeno), WG, 4 Nov 1721, *Wgm**, *Wn*; 1 aria ed. in DTÖ, lxxxiv (1942)
Nitocri (Zeno), WF, 30 Aug 1722, *Wgm**, *Wn*
Camaide, imperatore della China, overo Li figliuoli rivali del padre (Lalli), Salzburg, 1722 (? 4 Oct), *Wgm**; perf. with La marchesina di Nanchin (int, 2, Lalli), *Wgm**
Scipione nelle Spagne (Zeno), WG, 4 Nov 1722, *Wgm**, *Wn*
La contesa de' numi (servigio di camera, 2, G. Prescimono), Prague, Hradcin, 1 Oct 1723, *Wgm**, *Wn*
La concordia de' pianetti (componimento teatrale, 1, Pariati), Znojmo [outdoor perf.], 19 Nov 1723, *Wn*
Euristeo (Zeno), Vienna, court, 16 May 1724, *Wn* [sometimes incorrectly listed as Aglatido ed Ismene]
Andromaca (5, Zeno), WF, 28 Aug 1724, *Wn*, *D-Bds**; ? perf. with Madama ed il cuoco (int, 2, Trotti), *A-Wn*, ? attrib. Caldara
Gianguir, imperatore del Mogol (5, Zeno), WG, 4 Nov 1724, *Wgm**, *Wn*
Il finto Policare (tragicommedia per musica, 3, Pariati), Salzburg, 1724, *Wgm**
Semiramide in Ascalone (5, Zeno), WF [outdoor perf.], 28 Aug 1725, *Wgm**, *Wn*
Astarto (Zeno and Pariati), Salzburg, 4 Oct 1725, *Wgm**; perf. with Lidia ed Ircano (int, 2, ?Pariati), *Wgm**
Il Venceslao (5, Zeno), WG, 4 Nov 1725, *Wgm**, *Wn*
Amalasunta (N. Blinoni), ? Jaroměřice, Schloss Questenberg, aut. 1726, *Wgm**
I due dittatori (5, Zeno), WG, 4 Nov 1726, *Wgm**, *Wn*
L'Etearco (?Stampiglia), Salzburg, 1726, *S-St**
Don Chisciotte in corte della duchessa (opera serioridicola, 5, G. C. Pasquini, after M. de Cervantes), Vienna, Hof (Teatrino), 6 Feb 1727, *A-Wgm**, *Wn*
Imeneo (pastorale, 3, Zeno), WF [outdoor perf.], 28 Aug 1727, *Wgm**, *Wn*
Ornospade (Zeno), WG, 4 Nov 1727, *Wgm**, *Wn*
La verità nell'inganno, ossia Arsinoe (Silvani), Salzburg, 15 Nov 1727, *Wgm**; perf. with Lisetta ed Astrobolo (int, 3, ?Silvani), *Wgm** [different from 1717 settings]
La forza dell'amicizia, ovvero Pilade ed Oreste [Acts 2 and 3] (Pasquini), Graz [outdoor perf.], 17 Aug 1728, *Wgm**, *Wn* [Act 1 by G. Reutter]; perf. with Alisca e Bleso (int, 2, ?Pasquini), *Wgm**, *Wn*
Amor non ha legge (favola pastorale, 3, Blinoni), Jaroměřice, Schloss Questenberg, aut. 1728, *Wgm**
Mitridate (5, Zeno), WG, 4 Nov 1728, *Wgm**, *Wn*
I disingannati (commedia per musica, 3, Pasquini, after Molière: *Le misanthrope*), Vienna, Hof (Teatrino), 8 Feb 1729, *Wgm**, *Wn*
Enone, 14–30 July 1729 (pastorale, 5, Zeno), WF, 28 Aug 1734, *Wgm**, *Wn*
Caio Fabbrizio (Zeno), WG, 13 Nov 1729, *Wgm**, *Wn*
Sancio Pansa, governatore dell'isola Barattaria, completed 27 Jan 1730 (commedia per musica, 3, Pasquini, after Cervantes: *Don Quixote*); rev., Vienna, Hof (Teatrino), 27 Jan 1733, *Wgm**, *Wn*
La pazienza di Socrate con due mogli [Act 1 scenes i–v and Act 3] (scherzo drammatico, 3, N. Minato), Vienna, Hof (Teatrino), 17 Jan 1731, *Wgm**, *Wn*, collab. Reutter
Il Demetrio (P. Metastasio), WG, 4 Nov 1731, *Wgm**, *Wn*
Livia (festa teatrale, 1, Pasquini), Vienna, ?WG, 19 Nov 1731, *Wn*
L'asilo d'amore (festa teatrale, 1, Metastasio), Linz [outdoor perf.], 28 Aug 1732, *Wgm**, *Wn*
Adriano in Siria (Metastasio), WG, 9 Nov 1732, *Wgm**, *Wn*
L'olimpiade (Metastasio), WF [outdoor perf.], 30 Aug 1733, *Wn*(R1979: IOB, xxxii), *D-Bds**
Demofoonte (Metastasio), WG, 4 Nov 1733, *A-Wgm**, *Wn*
La clemenza di Tito (Metastasio), WG, 4 Nov 1734, *Wgm**, *Wn*
Le cinesi (componimento drammatico, 1, Metastasio), Vienna, court, carn. 1735, *Wgm** [preceded a 'ballo cinese' by Reutter]
Il natale di Minerva Tritonia (festa per musica, 1, Pasquini), WF [outdoor perf.], 28 Aug 1735, *Wgm**, *Wn*
Scipione Africano il maggiore (festa di camera, 1, Pasquini), Vienna, ?WG, 4 Nov 1735, *Wgm**, *Wn*
Achille in Sciro (Metastasio), WG, 13 Feb 1736, *Wn*, *D-Bds**
Ciro riconosciuto (Metastasio), WF, 28 Aug 1736, *A-Wgm**, *Wn*
Il Temistocle (Metastasio), WG, 4 Nov 1736, *Wgm**, *Wn*

dramatic works possibly presented as operas

Chi s'arma di virtù (serenata, 2, A. Fezzoneo [J. Buonaccorsi]), Rome, Palazzo Bonelli [outdoor perf.], 27 Aug 1709, *D-MÜs*
Il trionfo d'amore (cantata, F. Fozio), WF, 6 Oct 1722, *A-Wgm**
Ghirlanda di fiori (?festa, 1), Vienna, 1726, *Wgm**
[Melibeo e Tirsi] (servigio di camera, 2), ?Vienna, before 1728, *Wgm**
Festa di camera per introduzione al ballo ('Vieni o compagna') (Pasquini), Vienna, Hof, carn. 1728, *D-MEIr*
La corona d'Imeneo (festa, 2, Pasquini), Vienna, ?Hof, 13 March 1728, *A-Wgm**

Cantata pastorale eroica ('Andiam sorella'), WF, 1729 (? 15 Oct), *Wgm**, *Wn*
Dialogo tra la vera disciplina ed il genio (festa di camera, 1, Pasquini), WF, 15 Oct 1730, *Wgm**; rev., 15 Oct 1735, *Wn*
Il natale d'Augusto (festa da camera, 1, ?Pasquini, after Ovid: *Metamorphoses*, book 15), WF, 1 Oct 1733, *Wgm**, *Wn*
Il giuoco di quadriglio (cantata), Vienna, Hof, ?carn. 1734, *Wgm**, *Wn*
Le lodi d'Augusto (festa di camera, 1, Pasquini), WF, 1 Oct 1734, *Wgm**, *Wn*
Le grazie vendicate (festa di camera, 1, Metastasio), Vienna, ?WF, ?28 Aug 1735, *Wgm**, *Wn*

Doubtful (all lost): La libertà nelle catene, Rome, Palazzo Zagarolo, 1690; L'onestà nelli amori (?Contini), Genoa, 1705, lib. *I-Pci*; L'Atenaide [Act 1] (Zeno), Rome, Argentina, carn. 1711, collab. with composers unknown; La selva illustrata del merito (Biavi), Salzburg, 4 Oct ?1717, lib. *A-KR*

*

DBI (U. Kirkendale and W. Kirkendale)
U. Kirkendale: 'The War of the Spanish Succession Reflected in the Works of Antonio Caldara', *AcM*, xxxvi (1964), 221–33
R. S. Freeman: 'The Travels of "Partenope"', *Studies in Music History: Essays for Oliver Strunk* (Princeton, 1968), 356–85
——: 'La verità nella ripetizione', *MQ*, liv (1968), 208–27
U. Kirkendale: 'Antonio Caldara: la vita', *Chigiana*, xxvi–xxvii (1971), 223–346
C. E. Troy: *The Comic Intermezzo: a Study in the History of Eighteenth-Century Opera* (Ann Arbor, 1979)
R. S. Freeman: *Opera Without Drama: Currents of Change in Italian Opera, 1675–1725* (Ann Arbor, 1981)
B. W. Pritchard: 'Caldara's *Adriano in Siria*', *MT*, cxxvii (1986), 379–82
A. P. Brown: 'Caldara's Trumpet Music for the Imperial Celebrations of Charles VI and Elisabeth Christine', *Antonio Caldara: Essays on his Life and Times*, ed. B. W. Pritchard (Aldershot, 1987), 3–48
H. Serizawa: 'The Overtures to Caldara's Secular Dramatic Compositions, 1716–1736: a Survey and Thematic Index', ibid, 79–113
P. Besutti: *La corte musicale di Ferdinando Carlo Gonzaga ultimo duca di Mantova: Musici, cantanti e teatro d'opera tra il 1665 e il 1707* (Mantua, 1989)

BRIAN W. PRITCHARD

Calderara, Giacinto (*b* Casale Monferrato, 1730; *d* 1757 or later). Italian composer. He studied in Naples, then served as *maestro di cappella* for the cathedral at Asti from 1750 to 1753 and in 1757. He composed two three-act *opere serie*: *Alessandro nell'Indie* (1752, Alexandria), a setting of Metastasio, and the *dramma per musica Ricimero*, which was first performed at the Teatro Regio, Turin, on 26 December 1755 (sinfonia and arias *I-Tf*).
MARITA P. McCLYMONDS

Calderón de la Barca, Pedro (*b* Viveda, nr Santander, 17 Jan 1600; *d* Madrid, 25 May 1681). Spanish writer and librettist. One of the three leading dramatists and the leading librettist of the Spanish 17th century, he was celebrated as much for his central role in founding the zarzuela as for his authority as an exponent of Christian drama. He studied in Madrid from 1609 to 1614, at the University of Alcalá in 1614 and at the University of Salamanca from 1615 to 1619 or 1620. After taking Franciscan holy orders in 1651, he gave up writing for the secular public theatre and concentrated on sacred drama (allegorical *autos sacramentales* for Corpus Christi, commissioned by the municipality) and secular plays, often spectacular music drama, commanded by the court.

Throughout his career Calderón showed a thoughtful awareness of the dramatic function of music, and from about 1652 his texts included passages designed to be set to recitative-style music. When, in 1659, the court perceived the political need (as Calderón himself averred) to vie with other nations in producing spectacular opera, Calderón was the obvious choice for librettist, as was Juan Hidalgo for composer, of the two pioneering Spanish operas of 1660, though it is not certain that Hidalgo was Calderón's collaborator for the first. (*La selva sin amor* of 1627, with music by the Italians F. B. Piccinini and B. M. Monanni to a libretto by Lope de Vega, was an apparently unsuccessful precursor.) *La púrpura de la rosa*, in one act, was performed after a number of hitches in rehearsal in the Coliseo of the Buen Retiro Palace just outside Madrid on 17 January 1660. Calderón, in the prologue (*loa*) to this opera, along with his comment on the political context noted above, voiced his fears that the Spanish temperament would prove impatient of the rigorous demands made on the audience by wholly sung opera. Whether out of diplomatic expediency or artistic taste, less than a year later the second opera, *Celos aun del aire matan*, in three acts, was commanded of Calderón and Hidalgo and, once more after a number of hitches in rehearsal, presented in the Salón of the Royal Palace on 5 December 1660, probably again in 1661 and certainly in 1679 and 1684. Nevertheless, Calderón's fears were well grounded in so far as wholly sung native opera has never thrived in Spain as much as the partly sung zarzuela has. And, although the zarzuela that developed in Spain from the 18th century to the 20th became more plebeian than the aristocratic *fiesta de zarzuela* fostered by Calderón from the 1650s, he played the main part in giving it a name, characteristic form and lasting impetus. His works have also been the basis of operas by later composers, including B. H. Romberg (*Ulysses und Circe*, 1807), Raff (*Dame Kobold*, 1870) and Weingartner (*Dame Kobold*, 1916).

Librettos: *El jardín de Falerina* (fiesta … de la zar), by 1649 (J. Peyró, ? early 18th century); *Darlo todo y no dar todo* (comedia), 1651 (later setting, ? late 17th century); *La fiera, el rayo y la piedra* (fiesta), 1652; *Fortunas de Andrómeda y Perseo* (fábula), 1653; *El golfo de las sirenas* (fiesta de la zar, égloga piscatoria), 1657; *El laurel de Apolo* (fiesta de la zar), Hidalgo, 1657; *Los tres afectos de amor* (fiesta), 1658; *La púrpura de la rosa* (fiesta de la zar), ? Hidalgo, 1660 (Torrejón y Velasco, 1701); *Celos aun del aire matan* (fiesta … cantada, comedia), Hidalgo, 1660; *Eco y Narciso* (zar), 1661; *Ni amor se libra de amor* (zar), Hidalgo, 1662; *El Faetonte* [*El hijo del sol Faetón*] (comedia), 1662; *Fieras afemina amor* (zar), 1670; *La estatua de Prometeo* (fiesta, comedia), Hidalgo, *c*1670–75; *Hado y divisa de Leonido y de Marfisa* (fiesta, comedia), Hidalgo, 1680

*

ES (C. Vian)
F. Pedrell: *Teatro lírico español anterior al siglo XIX*, iii–v (La Coruña, 1897–8)
J. Subirá: *Celos aun del aire matan: ópera del siglo xvii* (Barcelona, 1933)
A. Farinelli: 'Wagner e Calderón', *Nuova antologia*, no.371 (1934), 193–212
J. Subirá: 'Calderón de la Barca, libretista de ópera: consideraciones literario-musicales', *AnM*, xx (1965), 59–73
——: 'Músicos al servicio de Calderón y de Comella', *AnM*, xxii (1967), 197–208
R. L. Pitts: *Don Juan Hidalgo, Seventeenth-Century Spanish Composer* (diss., George Peabody College for Teachers, Nashville, TN, 1968)
J. Sage: 'Texto y realización de *La estatua de Prometeo* y otros dramas musicales de Calderón', *Hacia Calderón: coloquio anglogermano: Exeter 1969*, 37–52
——: 'The Function of Music in the Theatre of Calderón', in P. Calderón de la Barca: *Comedias*, xix: *Critical Studies of Calderón's Comedias*, ed. J. E. Varey (London, 1973)
M. Querol: *La música en el teatro de Calderón* (Barcelona, 1981)
J. Sage: 'Music as an *Instrumentum Regni* in Spanish Seventeenth-Century Drama', *Bulletin of Hispanic Studies*, lxi (1984), 384–90

L. K. Stein: '*La plática de los dioses*: Music and the Calderonian Court Play, with a Transcription of the Songs from *La estatua de Prometeo*', in P. Calderón de la Barca: *La estatua de Prometeo*, ed. M. R. Greer (Kassel, 1986)
A. Cardona, D. Cruickshank and M. Cunningham, eds.: *P. Calderón de la Barca and T. de Torrejón y Velasco: La púrpura de la rosa* (Kassel, 1990)
L. Gentili: *Mito e spettacolo nel teatro cortigiano di Calderón de la Barca ('Fortunas de Andromeda y Perseo')* (Rome, 1991)
L. K. Stein: 'Opera and the Spanish Political Agenda', *AcM*, lxiii (1991), 125–66 JACK SAGE

Caldesi, Vincenzo. *See* CALVESI, VINCENZO.

Caldwell, Sarah (*b* Maryville, MO, 6 March 1924). American impresario, conductor and director. After studies at Arkansas, she studied the violin at the New England Conservatory in Boston. In 1946 she was a violist at the Berkshire Music Center at Tanglewood, where she staged Vaughan Williams's *Riders to the Sea* in 1947. She studied with Boris Goldovsky. From 1952 to 1960 she was head of the Boston University opera workshop; in 1958 she founded what was to become the Opera Company of Boston, and served as its musical and administrative director.

Caldwell developed an enthusiastic following, partly through her determination to overcome the conditions in which she had to work (there was no opera house in Boston), but more for her interest in contemporary or little-known operas. She soon established a reputation throughout the USA as a conductor and innovatory stage director; in 1976 she was the first woman conductor at the Metropolitan Opera (*La traviata*). She conducted the American premières of Prokofiev's *War and Peace*, Nono's *Intolleranza 1960*, Roger Sessions's *Montezuma*, Zimmermann's *Die Soldaten*, Peter Maxwell Davies's *Taverner* and Rodion Shchedrin's *Dead Souls*, as well as the world première of Robert Di Domenica's *The Balcony*. She has also directed the original version of *Boris Godunov*, the uncut, five-act French version of *Don Carlos*, the original version of *Madama Butterfly* and the American première of Schoenberg's *Moses und Aron*.

Despite its many successes, the Opera Company of Boston suffered financial problems, partly as a result of combining the roles of musical and administrative director. Plans for the company to develop opera in the Philippines in 1982 were abandoned, and the following year Caldwell was appointed artistic director of the New Opera Company of Israel. By the late 1980s the Boston company had reached a nadir, although Caldwell organized a Soviet-American musical exchange in 1988 and 1991, involving several hundred Soviet and American musicians in chamber and orchestral programmes, ballet and opera.

As a director Caldwell has been considered a follower of Walter Felsenstein, but her approach to opera is wholly her own; at her best she is regarded as one of the most influential opera directors in the USA.

*

'Caldwell, Sarah', *CBY 1973*

STEVEN LEDBETTER, PATRICK J. SMITH

Calegari. Italian family of musicians.

(1) **Giuseppe Calegari** [Callegari] (*b* Padua, *c*1750; *d* Padua, 1812). Impresario and composer. A cellist in Padua, he had his first dramatic work, a setting of Metastasio's *azione teatrale L'isola disabitata*, performed privately there in 1770. Between 1777 and 1782 three of his operas were performed at leading houses in Venice and Modena. He served Padua's Teatro Nuovo as impresario intermittently from 1787 until 1801. In August 1792 the Venetian administration prohibited the Teatro Nuovo from functioning during Carnival and spring (when Padua's Teatro Obizzi gave comedies), but by choosing his repertory carefully, however much it reflected a local taste for comic opera, Calegari was able to keep his theatre in a leading position. He also composed cantatas and sacred music.

L'isola disabitata (azione teatrale, 1, P. Metastasio), Padua, private academy, 1770
Il convitato di pietra (dg, 2, P. Pariati), Venice, S Cassiano, carn. 1777, *F-Pn*
La Zenobia in Palmira (os, 3), Modena, court, Jan 1779
Artemisia (os, 3, G. A. Migliavacca), Venice, S Benedetto, Ascension 1782, *P-La*
Il natal d'Apollo (os, 3, S. Mattei), Padua, private academy, 1783, *I-Pca*
L'ape musicale, ossia Il poeta impresario (pasticcio), Trieste, 1792

(2) **Antonio Calegari** [Callegari] (*b* Padua, 17 Feb 1757; *d* Padua, 22 or 28 July 1828). Composer, brother of (1) Giuseppe Calegari. He was often called 'Il seniore' to distinguish him from his nephew (3) Luigi Antonio. He studied in Venice with Ferdinando Bertoni, and conducted the first performance in Padua of Bertoni's short opera *Orfeo ed Euridice* on 2 May 1776 at the Teatro Obizzi. His *Deucalione e Pirra* (1781, Padua), a *festa teatrale*, initiated a series of stage works that established him for several decades as the most popular and respected composer among Paduans. One notable failure, however, was his serious opera *Telemaco in Sicilia*, lavishly staged in 1792 at the Teatro Nuovo. He was music director at the Nuovo from about 1790 until 1796 or later, while his brother Giuseppe was impresario there. Latterly he served as organist and then as *maestro di cappella* at the basilica of S Antonio in Padua, for which he wrote many sacred works. A respected composition teacher and theorist, he numbered among his pupils his nephew (3) Luigi Antonio Calegari. He was awarded membership in the Bologna Accademia Filarmonica in 1791. His *Modi generali del canto* (Milan, 1836), a method for teaching elaborate vocal ornamentation, was based on the practices of his close friend, the singer Pacchiarotti. Showing the ornamentation encountered in Antonio's dramatic scores, it is the most valuable description known of the highly decorated vocal style that was disappearing at the beginning of the 19th century.

Alessandro nell'Indie (dramma per musica, 3, P. Metastasio), Verona, Filarmonico, carn. 1779
Deucalione e Pirra (festa teatrale, G. Sertor), Padua, private academy, 1781, *I-Pca*
Le due sorelle incognite (dg, 2, G. Bertati), Venice, S Moisè, carn. 1783
Il fanatico per gli antichi romani (dg, G. Palomba), ?Padua, 4 July 1792
Telemaco in Sicilia (dramma per musica, 4, S. Sografi), Padua, Nuovo, 4 July 1792, arias *A-Wgm*, *I-Vc*, *Vnm*
La conversazione, ossia La farsa in casa (dg, A. Calegari), Padua, Casa Santorini a Pontecorvo, 1806

Doubtful: Il matrimonio scoperto, Venice, 1789 [probably by Luigi Calegari]; La serenata (farsa giocosa, 1), Padua, Nuovo, ? aut. 1806 [probably by Luigi Calegari]

(3) **Luigi Antonio Calegari** (*b* Padua, *c*1780; *d* Venice, 1849). Composer, nephew and pupil of (2) Antonio

Calegari and possibly a son of (1) Giuseppe Calegari, with whom he is also said to have studied. His first opera, *Il matrimonio scoperto*, was staged with considerable success in both Padua and Venice in 1804. It was followed by seven others produced in those cities, Parma and Rome. *Amor soldato* of 1807, his most successful comic opera, was revived in Padua (1809), Trieste (1812) and Venice (1812), where, according to the *Allgemeine musikalische Zeitung* (xiv, 1812, col.61), it was received with enthusiasm. Of much greater interest is his setting of Alfieri's tragedy *Saul*, performed privately in Venice in 1821. Its accompaniment consisted of two pianos, one of which was a 'forte piano organistico'. The composer played this instrument as he conducted the five solo singers (including Nicola Vaccai) and a large chorus. His other works include ballet music and cantatas. He is later said to have retired from music for a government post in Milan.

Il matrimonio scoperto, ossia Le polpette (farsa giocosa, 1, G. Artusi), Padua, Nuovo, aut. 1804, *D-Hs* (1804, Venice), *I-Mr*, *Pl*, arias *Vnm*
Erminia (farsa giocosa, 1, L. G. Buonavoglia, after T. Tasso: *Gerusalemme liberata*), Venice, S Moisè, aut. 1805
La serenata (farsa giocosa, 1), Padua, Nuovo, aut. 1806
Amor soldato (dramma giocosa, 2, G. Rossi, after N. Tassi), Padua, Obizzi, April 1807, *Mr*, sinfonia *Pca*
Irene e Filandro (dramma sentimentale, 2), Venice, S Giovanni Grisostomo, carn. 1808
Raoul di Crequi (dramma semiserio, 2, Artusi), Parma, Imperiale, 2 Feb 1808
La giardiniera (burletta, 2), Rome, Capranica, aut. 1808
Il prigioniero (farsa giocosa, 1, G. D. Camagna), Venice, S Moisè, 2 Oct 1810
Omaggio del cuore (componimento drammatico, S. Sografi), Piacenza, 1815
Saul (tragedia per musica, after V. Alfieri), Venice, private academy, 1821

SVEN HANSELL

Calife de Bagdad, Le ('The Caliph of Baghdad'). *Opéra comique* in one act by ADRIEN BOIELDIEU to a libretto by Claude de Saint-Just [Godart d'Aucourt]; Paris, Opéra-Comique (Salle Favart), 16 September 1800.

Isaoun (tenor), Caliph of Baghdad, wishes to be loved for himself, not for his wealth and position; consequently he pays court to Zétulbe (soprano) in disguise. When Isaoun is mistaken for a notorious local brigand of extreme ferocity Zémaïde (mezzo-soprano), Zétulbe's mother, is terrified, but Zétulbe remains faithful to the man she has grown to love.

With *Le calife de Bagdad*, which was given more than 800 performances by the Opéra-Comique by mid-century, Boieldieu scored his first major operatic success. The subject may be farcical but it is handled with wit, while the music, as in all the composer's best works, is beautifully fabricated and elegantly finished. Boieldieu did not attempt to introduce any so-called orientalisms into his music, but his use of orchestral colour does suggest the East – or rather the East as seen by Western eyes and heard by Western ears.

The cast at the first performance was particularly strong, with Jean Elleviou (who later created the title role of *Jean de Paris*) as the Caliph, Alexandrine Gavaudan as Zétulbe and, as Zémaïde, the great Louise Dugazon, who sang the role again at her farewell performance in 1804. Since then the high spirits and freshness of the opera have made it especially popular with students and young artists. ELIZABETH FORBES

Calisto ('Callisto'). *Drama per musica* in a prologue and three acts by FRANCESCO CAVALLI to a libretto by GIOVANNI FAUSTINI after OVID's *Metamorphoses* (book 2); Venice, Teatro S Apollinare, 28 November 1651.

Giove [Jupiter] (bass) has descended from Olympus to re-establish the world after the devastation of recent war. He quickly forgets his noble mission when he sees the nymph Callisto (soprano) and falls in love with her. But Callisto, a follower of the goddess Diana (soprano), has taken a vow of chastity. She is determined to resist Jupiter's advances. Mercurio [Mercury] (tenor) persuades Jupiter to transform himself into Diana. Thus Jupiter succeeds in luring the naive and foolish Callisto into his arms instead of those of her adored goddess. Meanwhile Diana longs for the shepherd Endimione [Endymion] (contralto). Callisto approaches and implores Diana for more kisses. The goddess becomes incensed at this betrayal of her chaste ideals and expels Callisto from her charmed circle. With self-righteous nonchalance, Diana resumes her intensive dalliance with Endymion.

Giunone [Juno] (soprano) has learnt that her husband is pursuing a new conquest. Always suspicious of Jupiter and wearied by his amorous adventures, Juno realizes that she must again rectify the mistakes caused by his excessive ardour. As she undertakes her mission, the first earthly soul she encounters is Callisto, weeping at her rejection by Diana. Juno recognizes that Jupiter is to blame for Callisto's plight and takes her revenge at his duplicity by invoking the Furies (sopranos), who turn Callisto into a bear. Jupiter is swift to overcome Juno's mischievous magic. He changes Callisto back to her human form and, by doing so, at last attains her loving and compliant surrender. He places her among the stars of the constellation Ursa Minor, where she will revel in the joys of 'celestial harmony' and eternal life.

Calisto is the ninth of 11 operas that Cavalli composed during the 1640s and early 1650s with the librettist Giovanni Faustini; its initial run was from 28 November to 31 December 1651. As experienced and skilful collaborators, they understood that short and incisive *mezz'arie* quicken and tighten the action. The brevity of the concerted arias as well as the swift tempos cogently set off the personalities of both serious and comic characters. Composer and librettist sympathetically illustrate the myth of Callisto and Jupiter, a tale of human frailty injured by the arrogant insensitivity of the gods. Two gentle humans, Callisto and Endymion, earn our respect through their unwavering loyalty to the goddess Diana. On the other hand, the quarrelling Jupiter and Juno deserve the ridicule hurled at them by two comic figures, the ancient nymph Linfea (soprano) and a young satyr. Despite such scorn, Juno and Jupiter emerge individually successful: she at the mid-point of the opera and he at the triumphant finale.

A modern realization, by Raymond Leppard, was given at Glyndebourne in 1970.

MARTHA NOVAK CLINKSCALE

Callas [Kalogeropoulou], **(Cecilia Sophia Anna) Maria** (*b* New York, 2 Dec 1923; *d* Paris, 16 Sept 1977). Greek soprano. She was American by birth and early upbringing, and Italian by career and by marriage to G. B. Meneghini, whose surname she incorporated with her own during the period of her marriage (1949–59). In 1937 she left the USA for Greece and in 1940 became a pupil of the well-known soprano Elvira de Hidalgo at the Athens Conservatory. Two years later she sang

Tosca in Athens (27 August 1942), and went on to appear, in 1944, as Santuzza, Marta (in d'Albert's *Tiefland*), and Leonore (*Fidelio*). Returning to New York with her parents in 1945, she was heard by Giovanni Zenatello, who engaged her for Ponchielli's *La Gioconda* in Verona. This successful appearance (2 August 1947) under Serafin was the start of her real career, and she was soon in demand in Italian theatres for such heavy roles as Aida, Turandot, Isolde, Kundry and Brünnhilde. A rare versatility was shown in Venice in 1949 when, only three days after singing a *Walküre* Brünnhilde, she deputized for an indisposed colleague in the florid bel canto role of Elvira in Bellini's *I puritani*. Thereafter, under the guidance of Serafin, she gradually relinquished her heavier roles in order to concentrate on the earlier Italian operas. Besides adding to her repertory Bellini's Amina, Donizetti's Lucia and Verdi's Leonora (*Il trovatore*), Violetta and Gilda, she was in constant demand whenever rare and vocally taxing operas of the older school were produced, such as Haydn's *L'anima del filosofo*, Gluck's *Alceste* and *Iphigénie en Tauride*, Cherubini's *Médée*, Spontini's *La vestale*, Rossini's *Armida* and *Il turco in Italia*, Donizetti's *Anna Bolena* and *Poliuto*, and Bellini's *Il pirata*. Her greatest triumphs were won as Norma, Medea, Anne Boleyn, Lucia, Verdi's Lady Macbeth and Violetta, and Tosca (for illustration *see* COSTUME, fig.19*b*). Many of these roles she repeated in the major opera houses of the world, where her fame reached a level that recalled the careers of Enrico Caruso and Shalyapin.

Callas first appeared at La Scala as Aida (12 April 1950); her débuts at Covent Garden (8 November 1952), the Lyric Theatre of Chicago (1 November 1954) and at the Metropolitan (29 October 1956), were as Norma. Her relations with the Bing regime at the Metropolitan were uneasy, and the same could unfortunately be said, in latter days, of those with the Rome Opera and La Scala. Nevertheless, sensational publicity suggesting that she was a difficult and jealous colleague was an accusation resented by many of those who worked with her most closely. The truth was probably that an exacting, self-critical temperament coupled with recurrent vocal troubles often forced her into a difficult choice between withdrawal from contractual engagements and singing below her best form. Whether her vocal troubles (inequality of registers, harshness in the middle voice and tremolo on sustained high notes) were mainly due to inadequate training or to some physical intractability remains uncertain.

Of Callas's artistic pre-eminence there can be no doubt. Among her contemporaries she had the deepest comprehension of the Classical Italian style, the most musical instincts and the most intelligent approach. There was authority in all that she did on the stage and in every phrase that she uttered. During the 1960s growing vocal troubles led to her gradual withdrawal from the stage; after her last operatic appearance (at Covent Garden, as Tosca, on 5 July 1965) she made only sporadic returns to the concert stage (in 1973–4) and organized some masterclasses. Fortunately, numerous recordings, including many complete operas, remain to show that her technical defects were outweighed by her genius.

*

GV (R. Celletti, R. Vegeto)

E. Callas: *My Daughter – Maria Callas*, transcr. L. G. Blochman (New York, 1960, enlarged 2/1967)

G. Jellinek: *Callas: Portrait of a Prima Donna* (New York, 1960)

L. Riemens: *Maria Callas* (Utrecht, Netherlands, 1960)

F. Herzfeld: *La Callas* (Berlin, 2/1962)

J. Ardoin and G. Fitzgerald: *Callas* (New York, 1974)

D. Hamilton: 'The Recordings of Maria Callas', *HiFi/MusAm*, xxiv/3 (1974), 40–46 [with discography]

H. Wisneski: *Maria Callas: the Art behind the Music* (New York, 1975) [with performance annals 1947–74, and discography of private recordings by A. Germond]

J. Ardoin: *The Callas Legacy* (New York, 1977, 2/1982) [a critical discography]

P.-J. Rémy: *Callas: une vie* (Paris, 1978)

——: *Maria Callas: a Tribute* (New York, 1978)

S. Segalini: *Callas: les images d'une voix* (Paris, 1979; Eng. trans., 1981)

S. Linakis: *Diva: the Life and Death of Maria Callas* (Englewood Cliffs, NJ, 1980)

C. Verga: *Maria Callas: mito e malinconia* (Rome, 1980)

C. G. Chiarelli: *Maria Callas: vita, immagini, parole, musica* (Venice, 1981)

G. B. Meneghini: *Maria Callas mia moglie* (Milan, 1981; Eng. trans., 1982, as *My Wife Maria Callas*)

A. Stassinopoulos: *Maria Callas: the Woman behind the Legend* (New York, 1981)

L'avant-scène opéra, no.44 (1982) [whole issue]

L. Rasponi: 'Maria Callas', *The Last Prima Donnas* (New York, 1982), 577–86

P. Marchand: *Maria Callas* (Athens, 1983)

J. Ardoin: 'Maria Callas: the Early Years', *OQ*, iii (1983), 6–13

D. A. Lowe: *Callas as They Saw Her* (London, 1987)

J. Ardoin: *Callas at Juilliard: the Master Classes* (London, 1988)

N. Stancioff: *Callas Remembered* (London, 1988)

J. Callas: *Sisters* (London, 1989) [with appx listing early performances 1938–45]

M. Scott: *Maria Meneghini Callas* (London, 1991)

DESMOND SHAWE-TAYLOR

Calleja, Rafael (Gómez) (*b* Burgos, 23 Dec 1874; *d* Madrid, 11/12 Feb 1938). Spanish composer. He pursued his musical education in Burgos, where at six he became a cathedral choirboy and studied the violin and piano. He completed his musical education at the Madrid Conservatory, studying the piano, organ and harmony, as well as composition with Emilio Arrieta y Corera. At 18 he began his career as a conductor of various zarzuela companies in Spain, Portugal and Latin America. He composed a symphonic suite *Escenas Montañesas* and also made important studies of Spanish folk music, publishing collections of songs from Santander, Asturias and Galicia. However, his major activity was as a prolific composer of some 300 lightweight zarzuelas and revues.

selective list; zarzuelas and revues unless otherwise stated, most in one act

Alta mar, 1893; La mujer del saco, 1893; Paso de ataque, 1893; Se suplica la asistencia (revista, Chicote, Leira and Manini), Madrid, Martín, March 1895; El coche nº 13, 1895; El año del bólido, 1896; Lion d'or, Madrid, Romea, March 1897; De noche a dos (E. Navarro Gonzalvo), Madrid, Eslava, 14 Oct 1897; El segundo aviso, 1897; Los remiendos (Navarro Gonzalvo), Madrid, Cómico, 5 March 1898; Sandalio el posadero (Viñas), Valladolid, Lope de Vega, 20 April 1899; Concurso universal (E. García Alvarez, A. Paso and A. López Monis), Madrid, Maravillas, 3 June 1899, collab. J. Valverde *hijo*; El estado de sitio (Soriano and Falcado), Madrid, Maravillas, 20 June 1899, collab. V. Lleó; Los presupuestos de Villapierde (operetta revista, S. M. Granés, García Alvarez and Paso), Madrid, Maravillas, 15 July 1899, collab. Lleó, rev. 1900; Venus Salón (revista, F. Limendoux and López Marín), Madrid, Romea, 14 Dec 1899; collab. Lleó, rev. as Venus Kursaal, Madrid, 31 Oct 1906

A cuarto y a dos (parodía, G. Merino and C. Lucio), Madrid, 26 Jan 1900, collab. Barrera; La cara de dios (parodía, Merino and Lucio), Madrid, Oct 1900, collab. Barrera; Sandías y melones, 1900; La maestra (Navarro Gonzalvo and J. López Silva), Madrid, Eslava, 19 Jan 1901, collab. Lleó and Barrera; Los monigotes del chico (Navarro Gonzalvo), Madrid, Moderne, June 1901, collab. Barrera; El jilguero chico (J. C. de Luna), Madrid,

Cómico, Oct 1901, collab. Lleó; El dios Apolo (Limendoux), Madrid, Apolo, 19 Oct 1901, collab. Lleó; Don César de Bazán, 1901; Subasta nacional (fantasia-lírica, Navarro Gonzalvo), Madrid, Apolo, Jan 1902, collab. Lleó; La boda (A. Casero), Madrid, Eslava, March 1902, collab. García Alvarez; El respetable publica (revista, Paso, Gabaldon and Canevas), Madrid, Eslava, Oct 1902, collab. Lleó; Gazpacho andaluz, 1902; Inés de Castro, ó Reinar despues de morir (op, 3, Paris and J. J. Cadenas), Madrid, Lírico, 1903, collab. Lleó; Arlequin Rey (op), Madrid, 1903, collab. Lleó; Copite de nieve, Madrid, 1903, collab. Lleó; El famoso Colirón, 1903, collab. Lleó; El mozo crúo (E. Prieto), Madrid, Sept 1903, collab. Lleó

La vendimia (J. Prieto and J. Guerra), Madrid, Cómico, 12 March 1904, collab. A. Vives; El serrano, Madrid, Zarzuela, 18 April 1904, collab. Viniegra; Gloria pura (Paso and Cruselles), Madrid, Zarzuela, 24 May 1904, collab. Lleó; Hulé (intermedio, Arias and Arroyo), Madrid, Zarzuela, 14 June 1904, collab. Lleó; Las de Capirote, 1904; El rey de valor (1), Madrid, Cómico, Aug 1904, collab. Lleó; M'hacéis de reir, Don Gonzalo, 1904; El cabo López, 1904; Frou-Frou, Madrid, Jan 1905; Music-hall (revista), Madrid, Eslava, 18 Feb 1905, collab. Lleó; El iluso Cañizares (C. Arniches, García Alvarez and Casero), Madrid, Apolo, Dec 1905, collab. Valverde *hijo*; ¿Quo vadis, Montero?, Madrid, Zarzuela, 8 July 1905, collab. Lleó; La mulata, 1905; Emigrantes, 1905, collab. Barrera; La ola verde, 1906, collab. Valverde *hijo*; El ratón (intermedio, García Alvarez) Madrid, Cómico, 24 April 1906; La manzana de oro, 1906, collab. Barrera; El señor Embajador, 1906; El hijo de Budha, 1906

El corse de Venus (intermedio), Madrid, Price, 10 Jan 1907; A la piñata, ó la verdadera machicha, 1907; La diosa del placer, Madrid, Feb 1907; La brocha gorda (revista, J. Capella and J. González Pastor), Madrid, Gran, 1907, collab. T. L. Torregrosa; El chato del Albaicín (Ontiveros), Madrid, Cómico, May 1907; Fenisa la comedianta, 1907; El señorito, 1907; Los niños de Tetuán (A. Rámos Martín), Madrid, Apolo, April 1908, collab. Torregrosa; Los ojos negros (Paso), Madrid, June 1908/9; El banco del Retiro, 1908; La canción á la vida, 1908, collab. Barrera; Las bribonas (A. Viérgol), Madrid, June 1908; La golfa de Manzanares (Soler and Eustachio), Madrid, 1908, collab. Lleó; La ilustra fegona (S. Delgado), Madrid, Zarzuela, Dec 1908; El arbol de Bertoldo (J. Jackson Veyán), Madrid, Apolo, Dec 1908

El 'cine' de Embajadores (Viérgol), Madrid, 1909; El dios exito (revista), Madrid, Novedades, Jan 1910; El poeta de la vida, Madrid, Apolo, April 1910; La luna del amor, Madrid, Martín, April 1910, collab. Barrera; La perla del harem, Madrid, Apolo, May 1910; Mano de Santo, Madrid, Apolo, May 1910; El amo de la calle (Arniches and López Silva), Madrid, Apolo, May 1910, collab. García Alvarez; El país de las hadas (revista, G. Perrín and M. de Palacios), Madrid, Gran, May 1910; Los holgazanes, Madrid, Jan 1911; Por poteneras, Madrid, 1911; La tierra del sol (Perrín and Palacios), Madrid, May 1911; El chico del cafetín (A. Asenjo and A. Torres del Alamo), Madrid, Apolo, May 1911; Sangre y arena (E. González del Castillo, after V. Blasco Ibáñez), Madrid, Apolo, 1911, collab. P. Marquina; La suerte de Isabelita (1, M. Sierra), 1911, collab. J. Giménez

S. M. El couplet (Viérgol), Madrid, Price, Feb 1912; El nuevo testamento (Lapina and Planiol), Madrid, Apolo, April 1913; La socorito (A. Caamaño), Madrid, Novedades, Jan 1914, collab. Barrera; La piedra azul, Madrid, Cómico, Feb 1914; El statua quo, Madrid, Feb 1914; Las llaves del cielo, Madrid, Cómico, Feb 1914; Los dioses del día, Madrid, Gran, Feb 1914; La romantica, Madrid, Martín, Feb 1914; La hija del guarda, Madrid, Martín, 1914; El chic parisien, Madrid, Apolo, Dec 1914; Las dos reinas, 1914, collab. Barrera; La estrella del Olympia (Arniches and López Silva, after G. de Maupassant: *Boule de suif*), Madrid, Apolo, Dec 1915; El entierro de la sardina (A. Ramos Martín), 1915; El Rajah de Bengala (2), Madrid, Apolo, Dec 1915

Los cortigéros (1, Caamaño), Madrid, Novedades, May 1919; La flor del barrio (sainete lírico, 1, Arniches), Madrid, Apolo, May 1919, collab. L. Foglietti; El as (vaudeville, 3, Sánchez Pastor), Madrid, Reina Victoria, 13 Nov 1919; La liga matrimonial (Viérgol and F. Gíl Asensio), Madrid, Novedades, 21 Nov 1919; El conde de Lavapicó (sainete), Madrid, Apolo, June 1920, collab. J. Estremera; Los mariscalas (J. Tellaeche), Madrid, Zarzuela, 1923; La ventera de Alcalá (J. M. Granada and D. San José), Madrid, Zarzuela, 1928/9, collab. P. Luna; El himno de Briviesca (J. J. Pérez de Urbiel), 1929

Date unknown: El abanico de la Pompadur; Aires nacionales; Las alondras; La arana azul; El genio de Velázquez; Hasta la vuelta; Los hijos del mar, collab. Lleó; La maja desnuda; Maese Figaro; El premio de honor, collab. Lleó; El reloj de arena; El viajante en cueros (Paso and Estremera), collab. E. Rosillo

*

StiegerO

Enciclopedia universal ilustrada europeo-americana (Barcelona, 1907–30) x, 999–1000; appx ii (1930), 897

A. Fernández-Cid: *Cien años de teatro musical en España (1875–1975)* (Madrid, 1975)

ANDREW LAMB

Callirhoé ('Callirhoë'). *Tragédie en musique* in a prologue and five acts by ANDRÉ CARDINAL DESTOUCHES to a libretto by PIERRE-CHARLES ROY after Pausanias and Antoine d'Aubigny de la Fosse; Paris, Opéra, 27 December 1712.

The high priest of Bacchus at Calydon, Coresus (bass), loves Callirhoë (soprano), and when he is rejected by her in favour of Agenor (*haute-contre*) demands vengeance from the god. This comes in the form of a dionysiac frenzy which turns the people on one another. An oracle tells Coresus that he can save his people only by sacrificing either Callirhoë or someone who will offer to take her place. In order to spare Callirhoë, Coresus takes his own life.

The score illustrates Destouches' ability to integrate a wider range of instrumental colour into the solo vocal music than had been the case with Lully and his pupils: for example flutes alternating with violins in 'O nuit' (Act 1 scene i); oboes in 'Regnez amour' (1.v), and 'petites flûtes' in 'Que les mortels' (3.iii).

CAROLINE WOOD

Calliroe ('Callirhoë'). Libretto by MATTIA VERAZI, first set by Antonio Sacchini (1770, Ludwigsburg).

Agricane has conquered Assyria to avenge his sister, Bicestre, whom the Assyrian heir Tarsile has scorned, and to prevent Tarsile's marriage to Callirhoë. Believing Tarsile dead, Callirhoë poisons herself. When Tarsile appears with an army, Callirhoë's father Arsace and brother Sidonio join him in seeking vengeance. Callirhoë wakes – she had taken only a sleeping potion – and restores peace. The author credits Giacommelli's Italian translation of Greek stories and Lopez de Vega's *Giulietta, e Roselo* as his sources. (Destouches' opera *Callirhoé* of 1712 is unrelated to Verazi's plot.)

Calliroe was Verazi's last libretto for the Duke of Württemberg's new French theatre at Ludwigsburg. Sacchini set it because the former resident composer, Jommelli, had returned to Italy. Typically of Verazi's librettos, *Calliroe* contains lavish spectacle with chorus and pantomime, and the entr'acte ballets and the opening sinfonia are related to the opera. The initial Allegro of the programmatic sinfonia accompanies the besieging of a city wall; the Andante is a victorious march and the final Allegro, a duet with chorus, functions also as *introduzione* and opening scene of the opera.

Also typical is the large number of ensembles, four duets, a trio, a quartet and a quintet. The quartet (concluding Act 1) and the quintet (in Act 2) are notable as ensembles whose forces gradually diminish, over several scenes, leaving one singer alone: a Verazi invention. The opera closes with an action ensemble that expands from a quintet to an octet in comic finale style. Verazi's constructions anticipate by 17 years both the internal action ensembles found in Mozart's *Don Giovanni* and the finales in comic opera style found in De Gamerra's *Pirro* for Paisiello.

This libretto enjoyed more Italian productions than any other of Verazi's librettos for Germany: Giacomo Rust (1776, Padua), Mysliveček (1778, Naples; 1779,

Pisa), Felice Alessandri (1778, Milan) and Sebastiano Nasolini (1792, Florence). All show extensive revision. Mysliveček's is an 'aria' opera with a duet closing Act 2, and retains only the battle scene in Act 3. Rust's and Nasolini's versions retain the sinfonia-*introduzione* and the concluding action finale. Alessandri and Rust move the 'death' trio from Act 3 to the end of Act 2. The Florentine version is modernized, with only two acts, lavish choruses and arias with solo and choral interpretations, and multi-sectional finales with chorus and dance.

For a list of settings *see* VERAZI, MATTIA.

MARITA P. McCLYMONDS

Calliroe **(i)** ('Callirhoë'). *Opera seria* by ANTONIO SACCHINI to a libretto by MATTIA VERAZI (*see* CALLIROE above); Ludwigsburg, Schlosstheater, 11 February 1770.

Sacchini responded to Verazi's libretto with highly dramatic music. Strong orchestral gestures, sweeps, scales, arpeggiation, long crescendos and *forte–piano* contrasts amplify the passion and violence in the aria and recitative texts, and the obbligato recitatives employ accompagnato, tremolo and measured string accompaniments as well as vocal arioso. In both style and frequency, Sacchini's obbligato recitatives anticipate those in Mozart's *Idomeneo* and Italian opera of the 1780s; the many ensembles and finales look forward to Mozart's *Il rè pastore* and Italian opera of the 1790s. Following Italian practice, Sacchini confines obbligato accompaniments mainly to passionate static monologues, though an armed exchange between Arsace (tenor) and Tarsile (soprano castrato) takes place in obbligato recitative in Act 2 scenes ii and iii. His melodies are strong, simple, triadic and little ornamented, but have ample melismatic display (e.g. for Sidonio, soprano castrato, in Act 2 scene i). His repetitious accompaniments extend for entire sections before giving way to thicker, more active textures and tremolo as he builds long crescendos. Recitative invades his arias (Agricane, contralto castrato: 2.xi). Winds play only once in the obbligato recitative (Callirhoë, mezzo-soprano: 2.xiii) and tend to drop out when the voice enters, unless featured as soloists (Tarsile: 2.vii; Callirhoë: 2.xiii) or used for special effect (Dorisia, mezzo-soprano: 1.iii). The strings are often reduced to two treble parts and continuo, though they sometimes maintain true four-part textures (Bicestre, soprano: 1.v). Sacchini writes through-composed ternary arias and sets Verazi's action ensembles straight through, without textual repetition. MARITA P. McCLYMONDS

Calliroe **(ii)** ('Callirhoë'). *Opera seria* in three acts by FELICE ALESSANDRI to a libretto by MATTIA VERAZI (*see* CALLIROE above); Milan, Teatro alla Scala, 26 December 1778.

Responding to outrage at the departures from convention in his first three librettos for the opening season of La Scala, Verazi revised his earlier libretto for *Calliroe* (first written for Ludwigsburg, 1770), removing the spectacle, the chorus, the ballet and many of the innovatory formal features of the 1770 version. The two pairs of principals are still given equal billing, which was unusual, but except for the quintet and the finale all the ensembles take conventional forms. Tarsile and Agricane are soprano castrato roles, Arsace and Sidonio are tenors, and Callirhoë and Dorisia are sopranos. Alessandri enhanced Verazi's text with stunning coloratura, vivid programmatic effects, astonishing chromaticism and a large variety of melodic and accompaniment styles. Dynamic ensembles and an assortment of aria forms, half in two tempos, are set within a carefully designed tonal plan. MARITA P. McCLYMONDS

Calori, Angiola (*b* Milan, 1732; *d* c1790). Italian soprano. She sang at Venice in 1756 in Cocchi's *Emira* and Galuppi's *Le nozze di Paride*. Cocchi was doubtless responsible for her engagement in London when he was appointed composer to the King's Theatre in 1757. She made her début in the pasticcio *Demetrio, rè di Siria* and remained a member of the company, first as seconda donna and eventually as 'serious woman' (Burney), until 1761, returning in 1765–6. She appeared in many operas, including Cocchi's *Ciro riconosciuto*, *La clemenza di Tito*, *Erginda* and *Tito Manlio*, Perez's *Farnace* and *Didone abbandonata*, Jommelli's *L'isola disabitata*, Galuppi's *Attalo*, *Il mondo della luna* and *Il filosofo di campagna* and Bertoni's *La pesca*, often in male parts. She sang again at Venice in 1765 in Bertoni's *L'olimpiade* and Traetta's *Semiramide*, and at Dresden in 1772, when Burney heard her in Salieri's *L'amore innocente*. He was not impressed, but admitted that earlier in London she 'wanted only spirit to make her an excellent performer; for then her voice, shake, and execution, were good'. She continued to appear in opera in Italy until 1783. WINTON DEAN

Calto. *Opera seria* in three acts by FRANCESCO BIANCHI to a libretto by GIUSEPPE MARIA FOPPA after the poems of Ossian; Venice, Teatro S Benedetto, 23 January 1788.

Duntalmo (tenor) has killed the father and brothers of Calto (soprano castrato) and usurped the throne. Calto, as the adopted son of Sinveno (soprano castrato), has secretly married Duntalmo's daughter Corimba (soprano) and fathered two children. During the opera Calto learns of Duntalmo's deed. Corimba faces an arranged marriage, and Duntalmo uncovers a plot against his throne, as well as discovering the secret marriage and the two children. When Duntalmo is deposed and Calto restored to the throne, Corimba secures a pardon for her father.

In this early *dramma serio*, Bianchi used extraordinary means to intensify the horrifying aspects of the plot. He made lavish use of wind instruments and particularly of the clarinet (a novelty in Venice), composed many complete scenes in obbligato recitative and freely departed from traditional formal procedures. In Act 1 he set the confrontational duet between daughter and father as an aria for Corimba with angry interruptions from Duntalmo. Later, Calto's encounter with his father's ghost occasions a dialogue in obbligato recitative between Calto and a chorus of ghosts; here Bianchi used flat keys, fluctuating modes, chromatic dissonances and an unusually wide range of wind timbres (oboe, bassoon, clarinet, horn, and english horn) for maximum dramatic effect. In Act 2 there is a through-composed scene complex with choruses, dancing, recitative, duet and aria, which takes place in subterranean tombs. In the fluid trio finale, Duntalmo seizes the children, threatening to kill them. Act 3 closes with an aria for Calto, interrupted by a brief comment from his beloved Corimba and followed by a joyful concluding chorus. MARITA P. McCLYMONDS

Emma Calvé as Santuzza in Mascagni's 'Cavalleria rusticana'

Calvé [Calvet] **(de Roquer), (Rosa-Noémie) Emma** (*b* Decazeville, 15 Aug 1858; *d* Millau, 6 Jan 1942). French soprano. A pupil of Jules Puget, Mathilde Marchesi and Rosina Laborde, she made her début as Marguerite in *Faust* at the Théâtre de la Monnaie, Brussels, on 23 September 1881, and three years later appeared in Paris, mainly at the Opéra-Comique. Soon afterwards she had great successes in Italy, as Santuzza and as Suzel in the première of Mascagni's *L'amico Fritz* (1891, Rome). These were repeated at Covent Garden and at the Metropolitan; at both houses, however, as elsewhere, her Carmen soon came to dominate her repertory – although Massenet wrote two roles for her, the heroines of *La navarraise* and of *Sapho*, and she created the title role in Hahn's *La carmélite* at the Opéra-Comique in 1902. In 1904, having taken part in the thousandth performance of *Carmen* at the Opéra-Comique, she announced her intention of leaving the stage, and did not thereafter reappear at either the Metropolitan or Covent Garden; but she sang at Oscar Hammerstein's Manhattan Opera House in 1907 and 1908, and continued to give concerts in the USA until 1927. Her voice – a luscious, finely trained soprano with the addition of strong chest-notes and some very pure high notes – derived a peculiar charm from its combination of absolute steadiness with rich colour. As an interpreter she was intensely dramatic and impulsive, to the point of capriciousness in later life. Her recordings, though disappointingly limited in repertory, are nonetheless fascinating.

*

E. Calvé: *My Life* (New York, 1922)
——: *Sous tous les ciels j'ai chanté* (Paris, 1940)
D. Shawe-Taylor: 'Emma Calvé', *Opera*, vi (1955), 220–23
H. Barnes and W. Moran: 'Emma Calvé: a Discography', *Recorded Sound* (1975), no.59, pp.450–52
G. Girard: *Emma Calvé* (Millau, 1983) [with discography]
J. Contrucci: *Emma Calvé, la Diva du siècle* (Paris, 1988)
J. B. Steane: 'Singers of the Century, 2: Emma Calvé', *Opera Now* (1991), July, 65–7
DESMOND SHAWE-TAYLOR

Calvesi [Caldesi], **Vincenzo** (*b* ?Faenza; *fl* 1780–94). Italian tenor. After successful appearances in Verona (as Count Bandiera in Salieri's *La scuola de' gelosi*, 1780) and Venice, he made his Vienna début in 1785 as Sandrino in Paisiello's *Il re Teodoro* and remained there until 1788. He went to Naples but returned to Vienna in 1789 and stayed until 1794 with occasional absences (he sang in Moscow in 1790). As the leading Italian lyric tenor in Vienna, he created Prince Giovanni in *Una cosa rara* (1786) and Endymion in *L'arbore di Diana* (1787), both by Martín y Soler, as well as roles in operas by Storace (*Gli sposi malcontenti* and *Gli equivoci*) and Salieri (*La grotta di Trofonio* and *Axur, re d'Ormus*). In 1785 he sang the Count in the quartet 'Dite almeno, in che mancai' K479 and the trio 'Mandina amabile' K480 written by Mozart for Bianchi's *La villanella rapita*. He created Eufemio of Syracuse in Storace's *Gli equivoci* (1786), and Ferrando in *Così fan tutte* (1790). He was described in *Grundsätze zur Theaterkritik* (1790) as 'one of the best tenors from Italy ... with a voice naturally sweet, pleasant and sonorous'. Calvesi also acted as impresario, at Faenza (apparently his native city) in 1788, and later in Rome (*c*1800–04).

*

A. Messeri and A. Calzi: *Faenza nella storia e nell'arte* (Faenza, 1909), 89, 273
CHRISTOPHER RAEBURN, DOROTHEA LINK

Calvocoressi, Michel-Dimitri (*b* Marseilles, 2 Oct 1877; *d* London, 1 Feb 1944). Translator and musicologist of Greek parentage, French birth and English adoption. A friend of Ravel, a man of wide musical interests and a gifted linguist, he was the leading champion in western Europe of the original version of Musorgsky's *Boris Godunov* (as distinct from the Rimsky-Korsakov edition used for most performances at that time). His English translation was printed in Pavel Lamm's edition (1928) and was used for the opera's first performance in England in its original musical version (1935, Sadler's Wells).

He translated Kodály's *The Transylvanian Spinning-Room* (1933) and Shostakovich's *Lady Macbeth of the Mtsensk District* (1936), both for first performances in Britain. He was also author of the first French translations of Stravinsky's *The Nightingale* (1926, Metropolitan) and Rimsky-Korsakov's *The Golden Cockerel* (1927, Opéra). Among his books are three studies of Musorgsky (published 1908, 1946 and 1956) and one on Glinka (Paris, 1911) as well as *A Survey of Russian Music* (Harmondsworth, 1944).

ARTHUR JACOBS

Calypso and Telemachus. Opera in three acts by JOHN ERNEST GALLIARD to a libretto by JOHN HUGHES after François Fénelon's *Les aventures de Télémaque* (1699); London, Queen's Theatre in the Haymarket, 17 May 1712.

The subject of the opera has a Homeric and mythological background. In Act 1, Telemachus (contralto), Grecian prince and son of Ulysses, comes to the island of Ogygia, accompanied by his friend Mentor (soprano), who is really Minerva in disguise. On the island, Telemachus meets the goddess Calypso (soprano) and her chief nymph, Eucharis (soprano), with whom he promptly falls in love. Calypso is attracted to Telemachus. In addition, Proteus (bass), son of Neptune and Tethys, who has the power to transform himself into all manner of shapes, is in love with Eucharis but is scorned by her. Mentor warns Telemachus about the illusions of Calypso's charms and urges him to leave the island and continue his search for Ulysses and his homeland. In Act 2, Telemachus and Eucharis go hunting. Mentor warns Telemachus that it holds hidden dangers for him. Calypso learns of the tryst and is deliberately made jealous by Mentor. She calls upon Proteus for help in parting the pair. He takes the form of Eucharis during the chase and changes himself into a tree and then a fire, both of which disappear. The real Eucharis, finally reunited with Telemachus, explains that Proteus is trying to thwart their love. In Act 3, Calypso promises Eucharis to Proteus for his service and says she will charm Telemachus herself. When she finds Telemachus asleep, her scorn and anger nearly impel her to strike him a fatal blow with his spear. On his awakening, she relents but banishes him from her sight when he asks for Eucharis. Proteus stalks Telemachus and seizes him, but Mentor as Minerva rescues him in a cloud machine and bears him away to safety. Calypso, Proteus and Eucharis are left helpless on the shore. The traditional happy ending of contemporary *opera seria* is thus negated, but at least no tragedy ensues.

One of the distinguishing features of the opera is the cohesive, intelligent and lyrical English libretto by John Hughes. His blank verse is logical and fluent, and his recitative flows along without any distractions. It leads convincingly to the airs, generally couplets and quatrains of rhymed poetry, which are pleasing and mellifluous. Galliard's music also shows quality and substance with a fine sense of musical variety in the airs (no recitative or incidental instrumental music survives; only the overture, songs and three duets were printed by Walsh). J. MERRILL KNAPP

Calzabigi [Calsabigi], **Ranieri (Simone Francesco Maria) de'** [de, da] (*b* Livorno, 23 Dec 1714; *d* Naples, ?31 July 1795). Italian writer and librettist. He was the librettist who most successfully and persistently challenged the Metastasian form of serious opera, in both librettos and polemical prose writings. He adopted the form 'de' Calsabigi' while in France, probably conforming to mispronunciations he frequently heard there, but his family name in Italian has always been simply 'Calzabigi'.

1. Early career. 2. Vienna, 1761–73. 3. Later career.

1. EARLY CAREER. The first-born son of a merchant family in the port city of Livorno, he was educated at the Jesuit College of Prato between 1722 and 1729; in 1733 he took charge of the correspondence (largely French) of the family business, at the same time assembling a fine private library. His supposed involvement in a poisoning, previously assumed to be the cause of his departure from Naples in 1750, has been shown by Masini (1987) to be connected with earlier difficulties in the management of his family's firm. His first literary productions date from the late 1730s; by 1740 he had become a member of the Arcadian Academy (as 'Liburno Drepanio'), and of the more classically orientated Etruscan Academy of Cortona.

In 1741 Calzabigi moved to Naples, partly because of declining patronage of the arts in Tuscany following the demise of the Medici. He gained a post under the French ambassador to the Kingdom of the Two Sicilies, the Marquis de l'Hôpital, whom he followed to Paris in 1750. He also kept up literary contacts with Tuscany, even selling copies of a Florentine literary gazette in the public square. His first poems for music, both called 'componimenti drammatici', honoured the marriage of the French dauphin with Maria Teresa of Spain; only the second was performed, changing political circumstances having made the first out of date. He produced a similar piece, *Il sogno d'Olimpia*, for the birth of a son to Carlo III in 1747. This and other early works won praise from Metastasio (indeed they are largely dependent on his style), but also his criticism of their exaggerated naturalism and lack of artifice.

Relatively little is known of Calzabigi's sojourn in Paris (1750–*c*1759) beyond the portrait Casanova provides in describing the lottery scheme they devised (along with Calzabigi's younger brother Anton Maria) in 1757–8. His time in the French capital was nevertheless crucial to his developing conception of theatrical spectacles. The most important product of his stay was the 'Dissertazione sulle poesie drammatiche del Sig. Abate Pietro Metastasio', which accompanied the first volume (1755) of his complete edition of the works of Vienna's imperial poet. He had received a royal privilege to publish in December 1752, and was in close consultation with Metastasio throughout the editorial process. In his 'Dissertazione' Calzabigi defends the poet against certain Italian detractors, combining high praise for Metastasio's diction and characterization with indirect criticism of his general approach. Despite harsh words for *tragédie lyrique* as it was usually practised, he closed with the suggestion that the Metastasian plan could be improved through judicious use of the French spectacle's 'numerous chorus, ballet, [and] scenery masterfully united with the poetry and the music'. In later years, answering the charge that in his 'Dissertazione' he had sought mainly to flatter the *poeta cesareo*, Calzabigi pointed specifically to this passage as evidence to the contrary. (His epic poem 'La Lulliade', begun in 1754, which documents the famous Querelle des Bouffons, likewise makes clear his basic hostility to French and Metastasian serious opera.) Excerpts of the 'Dissertazione' in the *Journal étranger* were cited as the inspiration for an anonymous writer's more openly critical *Lettre sur le méchanisme de l'opéra italien* (?Paris, 1756).

2. VIENNA, 1761–73. For reasons possibly connected with the lottery, Calzabigi was exiled from French territory and about 1760 made his way to Brussels, in the Austrian Netherlands (possibly also to England, according to Herta Michel, 1918). By February 1761 he was in Vienna, working in the Netherlands Finance Ministry and as secretary to Chancellor Kaunitz. (Casanova, visiting Calzabigi during this Viennese period, portrays the poet as 'always speaking ill of Metastasio, who despised him'.) Calzabigi quickly came to the attention of the theatre director Count Giacomo Durazzo, another Kaunitz protégé. In a June 1761 memorandum to the count, Calzabigi recommended advertising in newspapers as a means of recruiting French actors. Also during that year he apparently helped draft the programme essay for GASPARO ANGIOLINI and CHRISTOPH WILLIBALD GLUCK's first major pantomime ballet, *Le festin de pierre, ou Don Juan*; though Angiolini signed the essay, Calzabigi in

1784 claimed it as his own. His role in drafting the unsigned *Dissertation sur les ballets pantomimes des anciens*, which accompanied Angiolini and Gluck's ballet *Sémiramis* of 1765, is better established.

During 1762 the same group collaborated to produce the first of the so-called Viennese reform operas, *Orfeo ed Euridice*. Though not entirely free of Metastasian features (there are reminiscences of both *L'olimpiade* and *Alcide al bivio*), Calzabigi's poem is essentially a rebuke of both Metastasio's system and his language. It largely dispenses with similes and exit and da capo arias, taking inspiration instead from the large-scale tableaux and integral ballets of *tragédie lyrique*, and even the *romance* of *opéra comique*. The remarkable directness of Calzabigi's language was noted by Lablet de Morambert, who in the 'Réflexions' accompanying his French translation of the libretto stated that 'his works seem like extracts of pieces; the beauties are more indicated than developed; but it must be noted that the words of an opera are not made to be read'.

Early in 1764 Calzabigi welcomed to Vienna another progressive Tuscan poet, Marco Coltellini, who had already impressed the court with his libretto for Traetta's *Ifigenia in Tauride* of 1763. (Coltellini's next work, *Telemaco*, was for Gluck, and librettos for Giuseppe Scarlatti and Gassmann followed.) Calzabigi himself did not write another libretto until *Alceste* (1767), which celebrated Empress Maria Theresa's devotion to her recently deceased husband, Francis of Lorraine. *Alceste* was viewed by many, including its author, as the purest embodiment of opera reformed along the lines of ancient tragedy. Rousseau and others criticized its uniformity of sentiment, but this and the opera's architectural monumentality Calzabigi defended as virtues. In the dedication of the score published two years later he wrote, in Gluck's name, a forceful manifesto on opera reform; his authorship is confirmed in a letter of 12 December 1768 to Antonio Greppi. As *Alceste* was being composed, Calzabigi sought assurances concerning its proper casting, and at the same time vented his scorn for Metastasio's subjects and his manner of treating them, in an extraordinary letter to Kaunitz (published by Helfert in 1938), who following Durazzo's dismissal served as protector of the reform. In 1769 Calzabigi penned a different sort of critique of traditional *drammi per musica* and their performers, a satirical libretto entitled *La critica teatrale* (set by Gassmann as *L'opera seria*). His next (and last) text for Gluck, *Paride ed Elena* of 1770, he himself acknowledged as a failure, saying that the commission for a festive opera excluded strong passions of the sort he had brought into play in *Alceste* – although in 1762 such considerations had not prevented *Orfeo*'s being given for the Emperor's name-day. In 1772 Calzabigi wrote a *dramma per musica* for Giuseppe Scarlatti, *Amiti e Ontario, o I selvaggi* (of which only the libretto survives), which shows the influence of the *drame* and of newer, more serious *opéras comiques* (such as Grétry's *Le Huron*, recently performed in the Burgtheater).

With Gluck turning towards Paris, and *opera seria* in Vienna threatened by drastic economies in the theatres, Calzabigi began to contemplate leaving the Habsburg capital. (Around this time he encouraged Giovanni Gastone Boccherini in his career as a librettist, but there are no grounds on which to assume the two collaborated.) At the moment of his departure – in 1773, according to a letter of Metastasio – he was embroiled in polemics between Angiolini and his successor Jean-Georges Noverre, supporting his former colleague though later he would shift his sympathies somewhat. In 1774 he published in Livorno a fine edition of his works, dedicated to Kaunitz, which included besides librettos various poems, translations from the English and his 1755 'Dissertazione'.

3. Later career. By 1775 Calzabigi had established residence in Pisa; there he composed two tragic librettos, which in 1778 he offered to Gluck: a *Semiramide* (now lost), and an *Ipermestra, o Le danaidi*, meant as a critique of Metastasio's *Ipermestra*. The composer declined to set either work but passed *Le danaidi* on to his protégé Salieri; in 1784 it was presented in Paris, translated and much reworked, and at first passed off as a work by Gluck. News of the production caused Calzabigi (since 1780 back in Naples) to publish his original libretto immediately and to commission a partial setting by the castrato Giuseppe Millico. He also sent an indignant letter of protest to the *Mercure de France*, in which he claimed principal credit for the reform of opera and stated that he had had to teach Gluck how properly to set Italian declamation in *Orfeo*; he was more generous towards the composer in his 1790 *Risposta* to Esteban de Arteaga. Also about this time Calzabigi stated, in a footnote to his *Lettera … al Sig. Conte Vittorio Alfieri*, that he had written both programme essays for Angiolini, and even (contradicting the essays themselves) that Noverre's *ballets en action* for Stuttgart had preceded those of Angiolini and himself for Vienna. This note was suppressed in subsequent editions of the *Lettera*.

During his later years Calzabigi continued sporadically to compose opera texts. For Senigallia in 1780 he wrote a *componimento drammatico per musica*, *Comala*, after Ossian, set by Pietro Morandi. In the early 1790s he wrote two librettos for Paisiello; *Elfrida* (1792), like *Comala*, was on a medieval subject. Between these works he was largely occupied with critical writings and the completion of his epic 'La Lulliade'. In 1790 he replied anonymously, but transparently, to attacks on his reform in Arteaga's *Le rivoluzioni del teatro musicale italiano*; his *Risposta* contains a hyperbolic yet revealing account of the Viennese reform and of Gluck's character and capabilities, as well as a somewhat revisionist gloss on his 'Dissertazione' on Metastasio.

Calzabigi's reform librettos, though few in number, stand as landmarks in the history of opera. Rarely have aesthetic idealism and a classicizing spirit (in his case, founded on a profound knowledge of ancient literature) been realized so successfully in the theatre. This success was due in large part to his having found in Gluck a composer temperamentally better equipped to portray powerful passions and 'theatrical tumult' than the decorous comparisons and maxims found in Metastasio. The unique theatrical situation in Vienna in the 1760s was likewise crucial, as was demonstrated by later misguided performances of *Orfeo* and *Alceste* in impresarial theatres.

EDITIONS

Poesie di Ranieri de' Calsabigi (Livorno, 1774)
Poesie e prose diverse di Ranieri de' Calsabigi (Naples, 1793)

LIBRETTOS

La gara fra l'Amore e la Virtù (componimento drammatico), planned for 1745, unperf.; *L'impero dell'universo diviso con Giove* (componimento drammatico), G. Manna, 1745; *Il sogno d'Olimpia* (festa teatrale), G. de Majo, 1747; *Orfeo ed Euridice* (azione teatrale per musica), Gluck, 1762; *Alceste* (tragedia per musica), Gluck, 1767; *La critica teatrale* (dramma giocoso per musica), F. L. Gassmann, 1769, as L'opera seria; *Paride ed Elena* (dramma per musica), Gluck, 1770; *Amiti e Ontario, o I selvaggi* (dramma per musica), G. Scarlatti, 1772; *Semiramide*, by 1778; *Comala* (componimento drammatico per musica), P. Morandi, 1780; *Ipermestra, o Le danaidi*, G. Millico, 1784 (A. Salieri, 1784, as Les Danaides); *Elfrida* (dramma per musica), Paisiello, 1792; *Elvira* (tragedia per musica), Paisiello, 1794

Spurious: *Le donne letterate* (commedia per musica), Salieri, 1770 [actually by G. G. Boccherini]; *L'amore innocente* (pastorale per musica), Salieri, 1770 [by G. G. Boccherini]; *La contessina* (dg), Gassmann, 1770 [by M. Coltellini, after C. Goldoni]; *La finta giardiniera* (dg), Anfossi, 1774 [possibly by G. Petrosellini]; *Cook, o sia Gli inglesi in Othaiti*, 1785 [attrib. to Paisiello and Calzabigi by Faustini-Fasini]

WRITINGS

'Dissertazione sulle poesie drammatiche del Sig. Abate Pietro Metastasio', *Poesie del Signor ... Metastasio*, ed. Calzabigi, i (Paris, 1755)

'Lettre au rédacteur du Mercure de France' (signed 25 June 1784), *Mercure de France* (21 Aug 1784) [mentions *Semiramide*]

Lettera di Ranieri De' Calsabigi al Sig. Conte Vittorio Alfieri sulle quattro sue prime tragedie (n.p., 1784); ed. M. Pagliai, *Tutte le opere di Vittorio Alfieri*, xxxv (Asti, 1978), 171–213

'La Lulliade o I buffi scacciati di Parigi' (poema eroicomico, MS, 1789); ed. G. Muresu, *La ragione dei 'buffoni' (La Lulliade di Ranieri de' Calzabigi)* (Rome, 1977)

Risposta che ritrovò casualmente nella gran città di Napoli il licenziato Don Santigliano di Gilblas, y Guzman, y Tonnes, y Alfarace. Discendente per linea paterna, e materna da tutti quegli insigni personaggi delle Spagne alla critica ragionatissima delle poesie drammatiche del C. de' Calsabigi, fatta dal baccelliere D. Stefano Arteaga suo illustre compatriotto (Venice, 1790)

Lettera del consigliere de' Calsabigi a S. E. il sig. Conte Alessandro Pepoli ... nel trasmettergli la sua nuova tragedia intitolata Elfrida (Naples, 1792)

*

DBI (C. Gabanizza)

[A. J. Lablet de Morambert]: *Orphée et Eurydice, tragédie-opéra par M. Calsabigi, traduite de l'italien ... avec des réflexions sur cette pièce* (Paris, 1764)

A. Planelli: *Dell'opera in musica* (Naples, 1772); ed. F. Degrada (Fiesole, 1981)

J.-J. Rousseau: 'Fragments d'observations sur l'*Alceste* italien de M. le Chevalier Gluck', *Projet concernant de nouveaux signes pour la musique* (Geneva, 1781); repr. in *Oeuvres complètes* (Paris, 1857), iv, 453

S. Arteaga: *Le rivoluzioni del teatro musicale italiano* (Bologna, 1783–8)

C. Ricci: *I teatri di Bologna nei secoli XVII e XVIII* (Bologna, 1888), 631–40 [5 letters to A. Montefani, 1778]

G. Lazzeri: *La vita e l'opera letteraria di Ranieri Calzabigi* (Città di Castello, 1907)

A. Einstein: 'Calzabigis "Erwiderung" von 1790', *Gluck-Jb*, ii (1915), 56–102; iii (1917), 25–50 [trans. of excerpts from *Risposta*]

——: 'Ein unbekannter Operntext Calzabigis', *Gluck-Jb*, ii (1915), 103–5

J. G. Prod'homme: 'Deux collaborateurs italiens de Gluck', *RMI*, xxiii (1916), 33–65

H. Michel: 'Ranieri Calzabigi als Dichter von Musikdramen und als Kritiker', *Gluck-Jb*, iv (1918), 99–171

V. Helfert: 'Dosud Neznámý Dopis Ran. Calsabigiho z r. 1767', *Musikologie*, i (1938), 114–22 [letter to W. Kaunitz of 6 March 1767]

E. Faustini-Fasini: *Opere teatrali, oratori e cantate di Giovanni Paisiello (1764–1808)* (Bari, 1940)

G. Casanova: *Histoire de ma vie*, ed. F. A. Brockhaus (Wiesbaden and Paris, 1960–62)

M. Fubini and E. Bonora: 'L'opera per musica dopo Metastasio', *Pietro Metastasio: Opere*, ed. M. Fubini (Milan and Naples, 1968)

H. Hammelmann and M. Rose: 'New Light on Calzabigi and Gluck', *MT*, cx (1969), 609–11 [trans. of letter in Helfert 1938]

G. Carli Ballola: '"Paride ed Elena"', *Chigiana*, ix–x (1972–3), 465–72

——: 'L'ultimo Calzabigi, Paisiello e l'*Elfrida*', *Chigiana*, ix–x (1972–3), 357–68

D. Heartz: '"Orfeo ed Euridice": Some Criticisms, Revisions, and Stage-realizations during Gluck's Lifetime', *Chigiana*, ix–x (1972–3), 383–94

M. Donà: 'Dagli archivi milanesi: lettere di Ranieri de Calzabigi e di Antonia Bernasconi', *AnMc*, no.14 (1974), 268–300 [26 letters to A. Greppi and P. Frisi]

J. Joly: *Les fêtes théâtrales de Métastase à la cour de Vienne (1731–1767)* (Clermont-Ferrand, 1978)

A. L. Bellina: 'Ranieri Calzabigi: teoria e prassi melodrammatica tra Parigi e Vienna', *Lettere italiane* (1984), 25–36

M. Noiray: 'Genèse de l'oeuvre', *L'avant-scène opéra*, no.73 (1985), 7–11 [*Alceste* issue]

M. Hager: 'Die Opernprobe als Theateraufführung: eine Studie zum Libretto im Wien des 18. Jahrhunderts', *Oper als Text: romanistische Beiträge zur Libretto-Forschung*, ed. A. Gier (Heidelberg, 1986), 101–24

F. Marri, ed.: *La figura e l'opera di Ranieri de' Calzabigi: Livorno 1987* [incl. P. Gallarati: 'Ranieri de' Calzabigi e la teoria della "musica di declamazione"', 5–13; G. B. Ravenni: 'Calzabigi e dintorni: Boccherini, Angiolini, La Toscana e Vienna', 29–71; F. Tariffi: 'La formazione intellettuale di Ranieri Calzabigi dalla Toscana all'Europa', 73–105; A. L. Bellina: 'I gesti parlanti ovvero il recitar danzando: *Le festin de pierre* e *Sémiramis*', 107–17; B. Brizi: 'Uno spunto polemico Calzabigiano: *Ipermestra o le Danaidi*', 119–45; E. Masini: 'La famiglia Calzabigi in documenti inediti livornesi', 147–201] BRUCE ALAN BROWN

Camargo, Marie-Anne de Cupis de ['La Camargo'] (*b* Brussels, bap. 15 April 1710; *d* Paris, 28 April 1770). Franco-Flemish dancer. She was engaged as first dancer at the Brussels opera house, after studying in Paris with François Prévost in about 1720. Her Paris Opéra début in Rebel's ballet *Les caractères de la danse* (1726) was so sensational that Prévost jealously refused to teach her any longer, and Camargo subsequently studied with Dumoulin and Blondy; it is said that she shortened her skirts to demonstrate her mastery of rapid beating steps and jumps, modelled on those of the male dancers with whom she studied. A fierce rivalry broke out between her and Marie Sallé, which Voltaire characterized as a competition between opposing qualities of lively brilliance and expressive gracefulness. Camargo danced in 79 operas and ballets at the Paris Opéra from 1726 to 1751 (she was absent from the company, 1734–41). Known for her exquisite performance in Rameau's *Les fêtes d'Hébé*, she specialized in noble dances in Rameau's operas and ballets, including revivals of *Les Indes galantes*, *Dardanus* and *Hippolyte et Aricie*, and premières of *Les fêtes de Polymnie* (1745), *Le temple de la gloire* (1745), *Les fêtes de l'Hymen et de l'Amour* (1747), *Zaïs* (1748), *Naïs* (1749) and *Zoroastre* (1749), and revivals of nine Lully operas. She also appeared in the premières of Lacoste's *Orion* (1728) and *Biblis* (1732), and Francoeur and Rebel's *Tarsis et Zélie* (1728), Royer's *Pyrrhus* (1730), Collin de Blamont's *Diane et Endymion* (1731), Montéclair's *Jephté* (1732), Mondonville's *Isbé* (1742), Leclair's *Scylla et Glaucus* (1746), Boismortier's *Daphnis et Chloé* (1747) and Brassac's *Léandre et Héro* (1750). Camargo's fame was long-lived; two 19th-century operas (by Enrico de Leva and Charles Lecocq) were named after her.

*

'Eloge historique de Mademoiselle de Camargo', *Almanach des spectacles de Paris* (Paris, 1771), 17–23

G. Letanturier-Fradin: *La Camargo, 1710–1770* (Paris, 1908)

P. Migel: *The Ballerinas from the Court of Louis XIV to Pavlova* (New York, 1972) MAUREEN NEEDHAM COSTONIS

Cambert, Robert (*b* Paris, *c*1628; *d* London, Feb or March 1677). French composer and co-founder of French opera. He was appointed organist at St Honoré in Paris in 1652 and by 1657 was setting poems by PIERRE PERRIN. In 1658 he composed *La muette ingratte*, an elegy for three voices in dialogue (librettist unknown; music lost), which he claimed was the outcome of his 'longstanding desire to introduce into France *comédies en musique* like those found in Italy'. A substantial piece lasting at least 45 minutes, it was performed in concerts and, according to Cambert, inspired Perrin to write the libretto for his first stage work. The resultant *Pastorale* was Cambert and Perrin's first major collaboration. It was billed by Perrin as the 'première comédie françoise en musique' (a somewhat dubious claim) and required three sopranos, an *haute-contre*, tenor, baritone and bass. It was staged eight or ten times in the house of M. de la Haye at Issy early in April 1659; later it became known as the *Pastorale d'Issy*.

As Perrin was in prison at the time, Cambert had to organize the entire enterprise. Although the music is lost, it is known that each act opened and closed with an instrumental *symphonie* and that short *ritournelles* linked the scenes. The five acts were relatively short, and the piece lasted an hour and a half. Perhaps because of its modest length, the *Pastorale* was a great success with the French, who had hitherto been subjected to overlong Italian operas, the words of which few could understand. Jean Loret (*La muze historique*, Paris, 1659) claimed that about 300 people attended each performance and he singled out the singing of Mlle Sercamanan (Anne Fronteux) in the role of Diane.

After a special royal command performance in late April or early May at Vincennes, the opera-loving Cardinal Mazarin suggested to Cambert that a second *pastorale* be composed. Cambert and Perrin accordingly produced *Ariane, ou Le mariage de Bacchus*. No music survives, but it is clear from the libretto that Cambert attempted a more ambitious score, with a chorus of Corybantes as well as eight solo roles, four entr'actes, each comprising two entrées, percussion instruments (cymbals and tambourines) on stage, and trumpets and woodwinds in certain instrumental items. In spite of public rehearsals in Paris, *c*1660–61, the work was not formally performed, and Mazarin's death in 1661 effectively put an end to Cambert and Perrin's experiments. In 1662 Cambert became *maître de musique* to the Queen Mother, Anne of Austria. During the next six years his sole stage piece appears to have been the *trio-bouffe* for tenor, baritone and bass, *Bondi Cariselli*, which he wrote for Brécourt's play, *Le jaloux invisible* (Paris, 20 August 1666).

In March 1669, when the royal privilege to establish 'Académies d'Opéra' in France was in the offing, Cambert and Perrin resumed their partnership and began to rehearse *Ariane* once more. The official privilege was awarded to Perrin on 28 June and shortly afterwards he and Cambert started to set up a proper company. By April 1670 four or five singers had been recruited from churches in Languedoc and brought to Paris, where Cambert began the long process of training them. Plans to perform *Ariane* were abandoned at about this time and a new collaboration, *Pomone*, was taken into rehearsal.

Pomone finally opened at the theatre at the Jeu de Paume de la Bouteille on 3 March 1671. Considered by modern scholars to be the first true French opera, it involved ballets (danced by male dancers under the direction of Pierre Beauchamps and Des Brosses), spectacle and elaborate machine effects (designed by the Marquis de Sourdéac). It was a great success with audiences and performances continued to be given for seven or eight months. The poet Charles Robinet (*Lettres en vers à Monsieur*, 18 April 1671; repr. in Nuitter and Thoinan) marvelled at the many aural and visual delights in verse:

> Je l'ai vû cet opéra-là
> Et je pensais n'avoir pas là
> Suffisamment d'yeux et d'oreilles,
> Pour toutes les rares merveilles
> Que l'on y peut ouir et voir,
> Et qu'à peine on peut concevoir.

But behind the scenes all was not well: none of the company was paid – including Cambert, who had been promised a salary of 250 livres per month – because of the machinations of Perrin's business associates, Sourdéac and Champeron; and in June 1671 Perrin was imprisoned for debt. Cambert subsequently collaborated with the playwright Gabriel Gilbert on a second opera, *Les peines et les plaisirs de l'amour*, which received its première in February or March 1672. Saint-Evremond judged it a better work than *Pomone*, and it looked set to enjoy a long run. Performances were brought to an abrupt end, however, on 1 April 1672, when the Académies were closed by royal edict, Lully having seized control of the privilege.

Cambert's career as a composer of dramatic music was thus suddenly curtailed, and the following year he began a self-imposed exile in England. He settled in London, where his fellow countryman Luis Grabu was Master of the King's Musick, and became attached to Charles II's court. Early in 1674 his *Ballet et musique pour le divertissement du roy de la Grande-Bretagne* was performed at court in celebration of the recent marriage of James, Duke of York, and Mary of Modena. Then followed (30 March) the inauguration of a French-style Royal Academy of Musick with a production of a revised and enlarged *Ariane*. The libretto had been expanded before Cambert left Paris and was on a similar scale to that of *Pomone*. A new prologue with an English royalist slant was added in London (for illustration *see* ARIANE (i)). Grabu was deeply involved in the production and is thought to have collaborated with Cambert, writing some, if not all, of the extra music. The enterprise was unsuccessful, and Cambert appears thereafter to have kept a relatively low profile. No contemporary evidence firmly indicates that either *Pomone* or *Les peines et les plaisirs* was performed in England.

Cambert is remembered primarily for having written the music for the first French opera. His achievement as a composer of dramatic music is difficult to assess, since very little of his output is extant. In 1671 Christophe Ballard began to print the scores of *Pomone* and *Les peines et les plaisirs* but, due perhaps to the escalation of affairs at the Académies, did not finish them. *Pomone* breaks off during the fifth scene of Act 2 and *Les peines et les plaisirs* preserves only the overture, prologue and Act 1. No contemporary manuscripts survive.

Cambert's operas were essentially mixtures of *airs*, *récits*, ensembles, dances and spectacle. Each began with an overture and a laudatory prologue to the monarch. The overtures to *Pomone* and *Les peines et les plaisirs* are scored for four-part string band (Lully at the time used a five-part ensemble) and often favour three-part textures; in each a slow introduction gives way to faster, contrasting sections of dance-like music. Wind instruments are specified in *ritournelles* of individual numbers or as accompaniments to *airs*. Several bass *airs* are in the 'double continuo' style, in which the bass melody is doubled by the continuo beneath two accompanying treble instruments. Cambert is said to have been particularly skilled at composing expressive melody and recitative. This is not surprising, since the librettos he set were designed primarily to express characters' developing emotions. Saint-Evremond wrote that 'the laments in *Ariane* were equal to Lully's finest music' and praised the funereal 'tombeau de Climène' in *Les peines et les plaisirs*. Although both passages are lost, there are good examples of affective word-setting in surviving recitatives.

Providing music for dance and spectacle was an important part of Cambert's brief. He wrote numerous entrées for insertion in or between acts and may have intended certain choral ensembles – those imbued with triple-metre dance rhythms – to accompany the dancing and spectacle beloved of the French.

See also ARIANE (i); PEINES ET LES PLAISIRS DE L'AMOUR, LES; and POMONE.

Pastorale d'Issy (pastorale en musique, 5, P. Perrin), Issy, house of M. de la Haye, early April 1659, lib. *F-Pn*

Ariane, ou Le mariage de Bacchus, 1659 (comédie en musique, prol., 5, Perrin), unperf., lib. *Pn*; rev. version (opéra), London, Drury Lane, 30 March 1674, collab. L. Grabu, lib. in Fr. and Eng. (London, 1674)

Pomone (pastorale, prol., 5, Perrin), Paris, Jeu de Paume de la Bouteille, 3 March 1671, ov., prol., Act 1, pt of Act 2 (Paris, 1671/*R*1980), ed. J.-B. Weckerlin, Chefs-d'oeuvre classiques de l'opéra français, ii (Paris, 1881)

Les peines et les plaisirs de l'amour (pastorale-héroïque, prol., 5, G. Gilbert), Paris, Jeu de Paume de la Bouteille, Feb or March 1672, ov., prol., Act 1 (Paris, 1671/*R*1980), ed. J.-B. Weckerlin, Chefs-d'oeuvre classiques de l'opéra français, iii (Paris, *c*1882)

Ballet et musique pour le divertissement du roy de la Grande-Bretagne (S. Brémond), London, at court, late Jan or early Feb 1674, lib. (London, 1674)

*

C. de Saint-Evremond: 'Les opera: comedie', *Oeuvres meslées*, xi (Paris, 1684; Eng. trans., 1728)

A. de Boislisle: *Les débuts de l'opéra français* (Paris, 1875)

A. Pougin: *Les vrais créateurs de l'opéra français* (Paris, 1881)

C. Nuitter and E. Thoinan: *Les origines de l'opéra français* (Paris, 1886)

H. Prunières: 'Lully and the Académie de musique et de danse', *MQ*, xi (1925), 528–46

W. H. Grattan Flood: 'Quelques précisions nouvelles sur Cambert et Grabu à Londres', *ReM*, ix (1927–8), 351–61

A. Tessier: 'Robert Cambert à Londres', *ReM*, ix (1927–8), 101–22

P. H. Kennedy: 'The First French Opera', *RMFC*, viii (1968), 77–88

J. Anthony: *French Baroque Music from Beaujoyeulx to Rameau* (London, 1973, 2/1978)

R. Isherwood: *Music in the Service of the King: France in the Seventeenth Century* (Ithaca, NY, 1973)

S. Pitou: *The Paris Opéra: an Encyclopedia of Operas, Ballets, Composers, and Performers*, i: *Genesis and Glory, 1671–1715* (Westport, CT, 1983)

P. Danchin: 'The Foundation of the Royal Academy of Music in 1674 and Pierre Perrin's *Ariane*', *Theatre Survey*, xxv/1 (1984), 53–67

C. Bashford: 'Perrin and Cambert's "Ariane, ou Le Mariage de Bacchus" Re-examined', *ML*, lxxii (1991), 1–26

CHRISTINA BASHFORD

Cambiaggio, Carlo (*b* Milan, 12 Dec 1798; *d* Milan, 13 April 1880). Italian bass, librettist, composer and impresario. His father traded in silk and he himself was in trade until he made his début in 1829 at the small Piedmontese town of Varallo, in Mercadante's *Elisa e Claudio*. For the following 30 years he combined singing with acting as impresario of comic opera seasons; he was one of the last to work the 18th-century system of moving about with the core of a permanent company. In 1832–3 and again in 1834 he managed the Teatro Carcano, Milan, putting on two new operas by Michael Balfe (a member of his company) and himself achieving success as Dulcamara in *L'elisir d'amore*, for which he composed a duet in Milanese dialect. In 1837–8 he unsuccessfully ran seasons in Lisbon and Oporto. He developed a theatrical agency on which he concentrated in later life, in addition to acting as Milan representative for leading impresarios. When he was praised as a singer it was for his comic verve and acting ability: in a one-act opera (to his own libretto), Frondoni's *Un terno al lotto*, he sang all the parts. His son Giorgio Cambiaggio was an impresario in Mantua and Cremona in the 1880s.

*

ES (C. Sartori)

Correspondence: *I-Fn*, Carteggi Vari 351 [also comments on him in 364/153, 365/34–5]; *Mt*, Spettacoli Pubblici 109, 112/1; *Ms*

JOHN ROSSELLI

Cambiale di matrimonio, La ('The Bill of Marriage'). *Farsa comica* in one act by GIOACHINO ROSSINI to a libretto by GAETANO ROSSI after the play by Camillo Federici (1791) and Giuseppe Checcherini's libretto for Carlo Coccia's *Il matrimonio per lettera di cambio* (1807); Venice, Teatro S Moisè, 3 November 1810.

The English merchant Tobias Mill (bass) receives a blank matrimonial bill of exchange from an eccentric Canadian businessman Mr Slook (bass). Though suitably taken aback, Mill announces to his servants Norton (bass) and Clarina (mezzo-soprano) that he is minded to accept the document on behalf of his daughter Fanny (soprano). When news of this reaches Fanny and her charming but penniless lover Edward Milfort (tenor), Milfort vows to fight to save the situation. Slook arrives, a rather ratty man in bizarre attire, and is surprised both by the elaborate nature of his reception and by Mill's prompt desire to enact the bill. Slook addresses Fanny in a duet which soon expands as Milfort joins in what is the opera's pivotal ensemble; Milfort's message is that if Slook values his safety he should take the first boat home. Deciding that he has landed among a bunch of backwoodsmen stranger than any he has met in Canada, Slook offers to pull out of the contract, whereupon Mill challenges him to a duel. This is too much for Slook who prepares to leave at once, though not before he has settled the marriage bill by making Milfort his heir and signing Fanny over to him. Fanny sings an eloquent aria of thanks, 'Vorrei spiegarvi il giubilo', that includes phrases Rossini was later to use for Rosina in *Il barbiere di Siviglia*. During the uproarious finale, Slook urbanely smokes a pipe of peace while Mill, who does not yet know of the settlement, rages belligerently about the house before all is revealed and Rossini's military burlesque turns into a joyous matrimonial romp.

La cambiale di matrimonio was Rossini's first professional opera, written when he was 18. Already it reveals a tolerable technique, a vivid sense of invention, a sharp ear and a fine sense of pace. More astonishingly, it reveals a precocious mastery of the long single-act structure, with eight carefully marshalled numbers including a multi-movement introduction and finale and a carefully placed central ensemble of crisis and confusion.

RICHARD OSBORNE

Cambini, Giuseppe Maria (Gioacchino) (*b* Livorno, ? 13 Feb 1746; *d* ? Paris, 1825). Italian composer. The date of his birth and the place and date of his death are taken from Fétis, who incorrectly gives his forenames as Giovanni Giuseppe (Jean-Joseph). Nothing is known for certain about his musical training or his years in Italy. He went to Paris in about 1770, and played the violin at the Concert Spirituel on 20 May 1773, his only public appearance as a violinist. Thereafter he devoted himself to composition, proving extraordinarily successful and prolific, particularly in the field of instrumental music. Between 1773 and 1789 hundreds of his works were published in Paris.

It is difficult to assess Cambini's operas as a whole. Of his 14 stage works, only two, *La statue* and *Le tuteur avare*, have been preserved complete with orchestral scores, while the music to three others survives in fragmentary form. The librettos of four more works are preserved, but the remaining five are known only by title. For his only work performed at the Paris Opéra, *Les romans* (1776), Cambini turned to Bonneval's libretto (previously set to music by J.-B. Niel in 1736), suppressing the prologue and the fourth entrée. The work, which is in the French *opéra-ballet* tradition, had only three or four performances. With *Rose et Carloman* (1779) he turned definitively to *opéra comique*. Judging by contemporary comments, the main reason for this work's failure was the weakness of the libretto. The piece was revived, with no greater success, in 1789.

Despite these failures, Cambini was to play an important part in the theatrical life of Paris during a crucial and highly eventful period. From 1787 or 1788 he conducted the orchestra of the popular Théâtre des Beaujolais, opened in 1785, and wrote seven new *opéras comiques* for this establishment within two years (1788–90). When the theatre closed in March 1791, he took up a similar post at the Théâtre Louvois, which opened in August 1791 and was directed by the same team. He also had to scrutinize new works and recruit singers and instrumentalists. This heavy workload, which he must have carried until 1794, probably explains the small number of his own works having their premières at the Théâtre Louvois. Cambini's importance in opera derives far more from his involvement in Parisian theatrical life before and during the early years of the Revolution than from his own operatic works, which do not seem to have been as successful as his instrumental compositions.

all first performed in Paris; music lost unless otherwise indicated

Les romans (ballet-héroïque, 3, L.-C.-M. de Bonneval), Opéra (Palais-Royal), 2 Aug 1776, 1st entrée *F-Po**

Rose et Carloman (comédie-héroïque, 3, A. D. Dubreuil), Comédie-Italienne (Bourgogne), 24 April 1779; lib. as Rose d'amour (Paris, n.d.)

La statue (comédie, 2, M.-R. de Montalembert), Hôtel de Montalembert, ?2 Aug 1784, *Pn*

La bergère de qualité (comédie, 3, Montalembert), Hôtel de Montalembert, 24 Jan 1786

Le tuteur avare (opéra bouffon, 3, J.-L. Gabiot de Salins), Beaujolais, 1 March 1788 (Paris, *c*1789) [ov., nos.12–17 and part of no.11 by Cambini, the rest from P. Anfossi: L'avaro]

La croisée (comédie, 2), Beaujolais, 26 April 1788, 14 airs (Paris, *c*1789)

Colas et Colette (opéra bouffon, 1), Beaujolais, 20 June 1788, 2 airs in *Journal hebdomadaire, composé d'airs d'opéra*, xxiii (Paris, 1788)

Le bon père (opéra bouffon, 1, J.-F. Le Pitre), Beaujolais, 18 Oct 1788, air arr. Fournier for 2 vn in *Douze petits airs pour deux violons* (Paris, 1789)

La prêtresse du soleil (drame, 3, Gabiot de Salins), Beaujolais, 26 March 1789; also as Cora, ou La prêtresse du soleil

La revanche, ou Les deux frères (comédie, 3, P. U. Dubuisson), Beaujolais, 12 July 1790; also as Les deux frères

Adèle et Edwin (opéra, 3), Beaujolais, ?1790; rev. (1), Louvois, 19 Aug 1791

Nantilde et Dagobert (opéra, 3, P.-A.-A. de Piis), Louvois, 1 Oct 1791

Les trois Gascons (opéra, 1, Cambini, ?after N. Boindin), Louvois, 1 July 1793

Encore un tuteur dupé (comédie, 1, P.-J.-A. Roussel), Montansier, 22 Feb 1798

Doubtful: Alcméon (tragédie lyrique, 3, Dubreuil), Opéra (Porte-St-Martin), 13 July 1782 [cited by Goizet; according to Fétis, unperf.; does not appear in the records of the Opéra]; Alcide, 1782 (opéra, 3, Dubreuil), unperf. [cited by Goizet]; L'Amour et la peur, ou L'amant forcé d'être fidèle (oc, 4, Cambini), Jeunes Artistes, 20 Oct 1795 [cited by Goizet]; contribs. [cited by Fétis] to Campra's Les fêtes vénitiennes, 1789, to Armide and to 4 pantomimes

Spurious: Les fourberies de Mathurin (oc, 1, B. Davesne), Beaujolais, 5 Aug 1786 [actually by F. Bambini]

*

FétisB; *StiegerO*

Calendrier musical universel pour l'année 1789 (Paris, 1788), 129–30

Almanach général de tous les spectacles (Paris, 1792), 158, 171

L. A. Beffroy de Reigny: *Dictionnaire néologique des hommes et des choses de la révolution* (Paris, 1800), i, 35; ii, 70

H. Duval: *Dictionnaire des ouvrages dramatiques* (MS, *c*1850, *F-Pn*)

J. Goizet: *Dictionnaire universel du théâtre en France* (Paris, 1867)

M. Tourneux, ed.: *Correspondence littéraire, philosophique et critique par Grimm, Diderot, Raynal, Meister …* (Paris, 1877–82), xi, 312

C. D. Brenner: *A Bibliographical List of Plays in the French Language, 1700–1789* (Berkeley, 1947, 2/1979)

——: *The Théâtre Italien: its Repertory, 1716–1793* (Berkeley and Los Angeles, 1961)

M. Noiray: 'Les créations d'opéra à Paris de 1790 à 1794: chronologie et sources parisiennes', *Orphée phrygien: les musiques de la révolution*, ed. J.-R. Julien and J.-C. Klein (Paris, 1989), 193–203

JEAN GRIBENSKI

Cambon, Charles-Antoine (*b* Paris, 1802; *d* Paris, 20 Oct 1875). French set designer and scene painter. A pupil of Carlo Ciceri, he was one of the longest-serving designers at the Paris Opéra, 1833–73. At a time when productions were among the most elaborate and spectacular ever mounted at the Opéra, and up to seven designers were employed for one production, Cambon specialized in architectural settings. From 1847 to 1849 he worked at the Gran Teatre del Liceu, Barcelona, where, with his frequent collaborator, Humanité-René Philastre, he promoted the French school of Romantic design in Spain. On his return to Paris, he established a scene-painting studio where many designers were trained. He was a skilled painter, a considerable technician and a pioneer in the use of electric light (in Meyerbeer's *Le prophète*, 1849). While working strictly within the contemporary idiom, he was an imaginative designer, reproducing on stage the interior of the Opéra, in meticulously painted detail, in the last scene of Auber's *Gustave III* (1833; see illustration overleaf). Among many other Opéra productions he designed or contributed to were the premières of Auber's *L'enfant prodigue* (1850) and Meyerbeer's *L'Africaine* (1865) and the Opéra première of Gounod's *Faust* (1869).

For further illustrations *see* DON CARLOS and HAMLET (i).

*

ES (B. Horowicz)

I. Guest: *The Ballet of the Second Empire* (London, 1953)

——: *The Romantic Ballet in Paris* (London, 1980)

MARINA HENDERSON

Cambreling, Sylvain (*b* Amiens, 2 July 1948). French conductor. He studied at Amiens and with Pierre Dervaux in Paris, and won the 1974 conductors' competition at Besançon. He became assistant to Serge Baudo at Lyons in 1975, making his operatic début there in the same year with *La Cenerentola*, soon followed by *The Rake's Progress* at the Opéra-

Charles-Antoine Cambon's design for the original production of Auber's 'Gustave III' (Act 5, the ballroom scene) at the Paris Opéra in 1833: pen, ink and gouache

Comique. From 1976 he worked with Boulez and the Ensemble InterContemporain and in 1980 conducted the Chéreau production of *Les contes d'Hoffmann* at the Opéra. In 1981 he was at Glyndebourne for *Il barbiere* and conducted *Louise* for the ENO. The same year he succeeded John Pritchard as music director at the Théâtre Royal de la Monnaie, Brussels, where his observant detail, spirited performances and clarity of purpose significantly broadened the repertory and developed the company's reputation. He first conducted at La Scala in 1984 (Mozart's *Lucio Silla*, again with Chéreau), at the Metropolitan in 1985 with *Roméo et Juliette* and at the Salzburg Festival in 1986 with Debussy's *Le martyre de St Sébastien*. NOËL GOODWIN

Cambridge. English university city. Until 1894 the university authorities licensed theatrical performances out of term, normally only during the Stourbridge Fair (18 September to 10 October). Of the earliest theatrical booths near the fair no trace remains and few records survive, though a wooden structure (the Stirbitch Theatre) seems to have been constructed in 1784 and improved in 1789. In 1808 a small Theatre Royal opened at Barnwell, served by actors from Norwich; it was replaced in 1816 by another, designed by Wilkie, which continued until 1878 when it became a mission hall. The repertory reflected that of London, including afterpieces and the occasional operatic piece such as *The Padlock* (1765), *The Beggar's Opera* (1778), *No Song, No Supper* (1793) or *The Siege of Belgrade* (1810). The earliest foreign operas arrived in versions by Henry Bishop (*The Barber of Seville* and *The Marriage of Figaro*, both 1825); an English version of *Der Freischütz* was first done in 1828.

In 1882 W. B. Redfern converted St Andrew's Hall into a theatre, also called the Theatre Royal; in 1896 it was rebuilt with 1400 seats, as the New Theatre (closed 1956). The Arts Theatre (1936) is now the only large theatre in the city. None of these supported a resident opera company, though all have received visits from the D'Oyly Carte, Carl Rosa, Sadler's Wells, Kent Opera and other groups.

The formation of a Greek Play Committee in 1882 led to a remarkable tradition of triennial undergraduate performances of a Greek play in the original, with the choruses sung to specially commissioned music from composers associated with the university. The first was Sophocles' *Ajax*, with music by Macfarren. Stanford, Wood, Hadley and Orr contributed to this special form of theatre music; the most notable setting is that of Aristophanes' *Wasps* by Vaughan Williams (1909).

Under the guidance of E. J. Dent, Mozart's *Die Zauberflöte* was produced in 1911, when the opera was little known. *The Fairy-Queen* was proposed for 1914 but World War I enforced postponement until 1920. The 1920s, 30s and 40s saw several operatic ventures by the Cambridge University Musical Society under Cyril Rootham and Boris Ord. In particular, Purcell's *King Arthur* (1928) and stagings of Handel oratorios (*Semele*, 1925; *Jephtha*, 1934; *Saul*, 1937; and *Solomon*, 1947) did much to influence the understanding of these men as dramatic composers. There were also premières and early performances of new works, including Rootham's *Two Sisters* (1922), Honegger's *Le roi David* (1929), and Vaughan Williams's *The Poisoned Kiss* (1936) and *The Pilgrim's Progress* (1954). Since 1950 the management of opera within the university has been mostly in student hands. Significant productions have included Peter Tranchell's *The Mayor of Casterbridge* (1951) and Stravinsky's *The Rake's Progress* (1956) and Vaughan Williams's *Sir John in Love* (1956), produced by Brian Trowell and the conductor Leon Lovett (who formed the University Opera Society in the 1950s, and was subsequently to found the influential New Opera Company). Innovation continued with the premières of Liebermann's *School for Wives* (1958) and Copland's *The Tender Land* (1962), under Philip Ledger. Nicholas Snowman and David Atherton produced the first version of Strauss's *Ariadne auf Naxos* (1966) and Weber's *Oberon* and Berlioz's *Beatrice and Benedict* (both

1967). In the 1980s several Handel operas were revived by Andrew Jones in the University Music School with period staging.

W. B. Redfern: 'The Stage in Cambridge', *Cambridge Magazine*, ii (1912), 34
S. Rosenfeld: 'The Players in Cambridge, 1662–1800', *Studies in English Theatre History* (London, 1952), 24–37
F. Knight: *Cambridge Music* (Cambridge, 1980)
H. C. Porter: 'The Players Well Bestowed? Stourbridge and Barnwell Theatres, 1740–1814', *Cambridge Review* (1984), 214–18
Playbills, programmes etc., *GB-Ccl, Cpl, Cu*

RICHARD ANDREWES

Camerata (It.). A term meaning 'club' or 'society', first used by Giulio Caccini in the dedication of his opera *Euridice* (20 December 1600), which has traditionally been used to define a group who met at the palace of Count GIOVANNI DE' BARDI in Florence between about 1573 and 1587. It consisted of musicians and intellectuals (several of the latter being musical amateurs) who, in the manner of the academies of the day, conducted learned investigations into numerous subjects, much the most fruitful of which were on the theory and philosophy of music. They promoted research into Greek music and its supposed forms, the two most influential writers on which – the one within the Camerata, the other associated with it – were Vincenzo Galilei and Girolamo Mei. Important writings emerged from the group's deliberations, and the most significant practical outcome was their experimentation with accompanied solo song or monody (as opposed to the then ubiquitous polyphony): solo vocal music, recitative as well as song, was the predominant musical feature of the earliest operas.

The term 'Camerata' has recently been extended to include a further group of Florentine literati and practical musicians around JACOPO CORSI in the 1590s, whose main concern was the development of dramatic music, arising out of the study of the relationship between music and dramatic poetry, and in fact it was out of their activities that the new medium of opera was born. Yet, as Palisca says (1989, p.3):

> it is no longer possible to give a simple explanation of why opera began in Florence in the last years of the sixteenth century, and the luster of Giovanni Bardi's reputation and that of his camerata have faded as we have had to fit more facts and personalities into the picture.

Even so, the texts and music of the earliest operas – whatever their other antecedents, such as *intermedi*, or the influence on them of other Florentine academies – were written by men from the groups round Bardi and Corsi: *Dafne* by Corsi and Jacopo Peri and the *Euridice* settings by Caccini and Peri, all to words by Ottavio Rinuccini and all seen in Florence by 1600.

O. Strunk: *Source Readings in Music History* (New York, 1950), 363–415
N. Pirrotta: 'Temperaments and Tendencies in the Florentine Camerata', *MQ*, xl (1954), 169–89
N. Pirrotta and E. Povoledo: *Li due Orfei* (Turin, 1969; Eng. trans., 1982)
C. V. Palisca: 'The "Camerata fiorentina": a Reappraisal', *Studi musicali*, i (1972), 203–36
B. R. Hanning: *Of Poetry and Music's Power: Humanism and the Creation of Opera* (Ann Arbor, 1980)
C. V. Palisca: *Humanism in Italian Renaissance Musical Thought* (New Haven, CT, and London, 1985)
R. Katz: *Divining the Power of Music: Aesthetic Theory and the Origins of Opera* (New York, 1986)
G. Tomlinson: *Monteverdi and the End of the Renaissance* (Berkeley, 1987)
C. V. Palisca: *The Florentine Camerata: Documentary Studies and Translations* (New Haven, CT, and London, 1989)

NIGEL FORTUNE

Camilla, ossia Il sotterraneo ('Camilla, or The Underground Vault'). *Dramma semiserio* in three acts by FERDINANDO PAER to a libretto by GIUSEPPE CARPANI after BENOÎT-JOSEPH MARSOLLIER DES VIVETIÈRES' libretto *Camille, ou Le souterrain*; Vienna, Kärntnertortheater, 28 February 1799.

In its concentration of macabre settings, abnormal behaviour and grotesque juxtapositions of comic and serious elements, *Camilla* is the most shocking of Paer's semi-serious operas. Camilla (soprano) has been imprisoned for seven years in the underground vaults of a remote ruined castle owned by the Neapolitan Duke Uberto (bass), her husband by a secret marriage, because she has refused to reveal the identity of a man who once abducted her and attempted unsuccessfully to seduce her. Uberto's nephew Loredano (tenor) and his servant Cola (bass) arrive accidentally at the castle – without realizing at first who owns it – shortly before Uberto enters in disguise with his son Adolfo (soprano), who has been kept from Camilla during her captivity. Uberto attempts to use the boy to force a confession, but is arrested for murdering his wife and son before she can name Loredano as the culprit, and they are left imprisoned without food or water. Almost too late, Uberto realizes their predicament, disclosing their whereabouts to Loredano and Cola and allowing them to rescue Camilla and Adolfo. Eventually Loredano confesses his transgressions, and Camilla and Uberto are reconciled. Comic relief is provided by the cowardly Cola, the melodramatic gardener Gennaro (bass) and his fiancée Ghitta (soprano). SCOTT L. BALTHAZAR

Cammarano, Salvadore [Salvatore] (*b* Naples, 19 March 1801; *d* Naples, 17 July 1852). Italian librettist and playwright. His family, Sicilian in origin, settled in Naples in the 1760s and immediately established itself in the theatrical and artistic life of the city. He himself was first trained as a painter and sculptor, not without success, before turning to the theatre. In the 1820s he wrote a number of plays for Neapolitan theatres, many of them comedies but all showing a vein of melancholy. His first venture into librettos, in 1832, failed when Domenico Barbaia rejected his *Belisario* (later revised and set by Donizetti). Within a year or two he was established as poet and stage director at the royal theatres, a post which combined writing and revising librettos with responsibility for seeing operas on to the stage. His early training in art clearly influenced his work as a stage director. Surviving notes and sketches, and the detailed stage directions in his librettos, show that he had constantly in mind a picture of what was happening on the stage.

Cammarano's first major task, for which Giovanni Emanuele Bidera wrote the plot outline, was *Ines de Castro* for Persiani (1835, though it had involved a year-long struggle with the censors), but after *Lucia di Lammermoor* (Donizetti, 1835) he never looked back. Until Donizetti left Naples for Paris in 1838 he used no other librettist. Cammarano remained on the staff of the royal theatres for the rest of his life, writing for all the important (and many of the unimportant) composers of the period, among them Mercadante (eight librettos, including *La vestale*, one of Cammarano's best), Pacini (six, starting with *Saffo*, the text considered his best, against which his later output was judged) and finally

Verdi (four, culminating in *Il trovatore*, which he finished on his deathbed, though Verdi later required a number of changes).

Cammarano was the most important, and the most fully professional, of the operatic poets in the generation following Felice Romani. Many of his working papers have survived, and show meticulous craftsmanship. His mellifluous verses were achieved only by careful polishing, and he had an evident concern for the sound of his lines. Composers like Donizetti, Pacini and Verdi often made wholesale changes to the texts they set, but Cammarano's seem to have been largely unaltered. He was a conscientious, if slow, writer, lavishing as much care on texts for lesser composers as on those for the likes of Donizetti or Verdi. He can be faulted only for his stilted language and his reliance on librettists' stock-in-trade of expressions and constructions. His writing broke no new ground, although he did develop the use of the longer 'double' lines.

His librettos drew on a wide variety of sources, mostly plays and ballets performed in Naples; none were original. There is an emphasis on the long-suffering, ill-used heroine, whose death provides a pathetic final curtain. Few of Cammarano's texts have a male protagonist, and even fewer are heroic. He was not wedded to conventional themes, and himself pointed out that he was quite prepared to do without a love interest. He had a highly developed sense of dramatic structure and was adept at moulding his plots into arias, ensembles and other components. With the exception of one hurried commission (Pacini's *Stella di Napoli*) he did not need to write explanatory prefaces, as his librettos were self-sufficient. When called on to experiment (as in *Il trovatore*) he was willing to cooperate, although the essential form of his librettos remained unchanged over the whole canon. Nevertheless he held surprisingly advanced views on the relationship of words and music in opera, considering that, ideally, both should come from the same hand. Inevitably he fell foul of the censors from time to time, but he was held in high regard and relations were generally smooth. He showed remarkable sensitivity in presenting his plots in ways which did not offend, and to pilot a libretto based on Victor Hugo's *Ruy Blas* through the Neapolitan censors, not once but twice, was a tour de force.

The composers he worked with invariably treated Cammarano with respect. He remained on friendly terms with Donizetti, who insisted on using him also for his Venetian operas. Verdi began by treating him warily, accepting with only a mild comment an inferior libretto (*Alzira*) previously rejected by Pacini. He never bullied him, although, like other composers, he complained constantly about delays. His distress at Cammarano's death was genuine, even if his first thoughts were to retrieve the draft libretto for *Re Lear*.

The physical and financial conditions of Cammarano's life were wretched, but he remained devoted to the theatre. Much of his work disappeared quickly, being tied to poor music, in the ephemeral ambience in which he worked. But it was no mean achievement to go down in the history of opera as the poet of *Lucia di Lammermoor* or *Il trovatore*; nor, as his contemporaries would have added, *La vestale* or *Saffo*.

La sposa (dramma per musica), E. Vignozzi, 1834 (G. Miceli, 1858, as La fidanzata); *Ines de Castro* (tragedia lirica), Persiani, 1835 (Fabio Marchetti, 1840; P. A. Coppola, 1841; Luigi Gibelli, 1849, as Don Pedro di Portogallo; G. Pacini, 1851, as Malvina di Scozia; R. Drigo, 1868, as Don Pedro di Portogallo); *Un matrimonio per ragione* (melodramma), G. Staffa, 1835; *Lucia di Lammermoor* (dramma tragico), Donizetti, 1835; *Belisario* (tragedia lirica), Donizetti, 1836; *L'assedio di Calais* (dramma lirico), Donizetti, 1836; *Pia de' Tolomei* (tragedia lirica), Donizetti, 1837; *Roberto Devereux* (tragedia lirica), Donizetti, 1837; *Maria de Rudenz* (dramma tragico), Donizetti, 1838; *Elena da Feltre* (dramma tragico), Mercadante, 1839; *I ciarlatani* (scherzo melodrammatico), L. Cammarano, 1839

Il conte di Chalais (melodramma tragico), Lillo, 1839 (Donizetti, 1843, as Maria di Rohan); *La vestale* [Emilia] (tragedia lirica), Mercadante, 1840; *Cristina di Svezia* (tragedia lirica, Act 3 by G. Sacchèro), Nini, 1840 (Lillo, 1841, Act 3 by Cammarano; P. Fabrizi, 1844); *Saffo* (tragedia lirica), Pacini, 1840; *Luigi Rolla* (melodramma tragico), Federico Ricci, 1841; *Il proscritto* (melodramma tragico), Mercadante, 1842; *La fidanzata corsa* (melodramma tragico), Pacini, 1842 (Andreu, 1846, as La desposada corsa); *Il reggente* (tragedia lirica), Mercadante, 1843; *Ester d'Engaddi* (dramma tragico), A. Peri, 1843; *Il ravvedimento* (melodramma), L. Cammarano, 1843; *Il Vascello de Gama* (melodramma romantico), Mercadante, 1845

Bondelmonte (tragedia lirica), Pacini, 1845; *Alzira* (tragedia lirica), Verdi, 1845; *Stella di Napoli* (dramma lirico), Pacini, 1845; *Orazi e Curiazi* (tragedia lirica), Mercadante, 1846; *Eleonora Dori* (melodramma tragico), V. Battista, 1847; *Merope* (tragedia lirica), Pacini, 1847 (L. Zandomeneghi, 1871); *Poliuto* (tragedia lirica), Donizetti, 1848; *La battaglia di Legnano* [L'assedio di Arlem] (tragedia lirica), Verdi, 1849; *Luisa Miller* (melodramma tragico), Verdi, 1849; *Non v'è fumo senza fuoco* (farsa), L. Cammarano, 1850 (Lauro Rossi, 1867, as Lo zigaro rivale); *Folco d'Arles* (melodramma tragico), De Giosa, 1851; *Medea* (tragedia lirica), Mercadante, 1851; *Il trovatore* (dramma), Verdi, 1853; *Virginia* (tragedia lirica), Mercadante, 1866

*

DBI (A. Lanfranchi)

C. T. Dalbono: 'Salvatore Cammarano', *Poliorama pittoresco* (1853)

S. Di Giacomo: 'Salvatore Cammarano, il libretto del "Trovatore" e Giuseppe Verdi', *Musica e musicisti*, lix (1904), 81–92

E. Checchi: 'Librettisti e libretti di Giuseppe Verdi', *Nuova antologia*, ccli (1913), 529–40

J. Black: *The Italian Romantic Libretto: a Study of Salvadore Cammarano* (Edinburgh, 1984)

JOHN BLACK

Camp, Maria Theresa de. *See* DE CAMP, MARIA THERESA.

Campa, Gustavo E(milio) (*b* Mexico City, 8 Sept 1863; *d* Mexico City, 29 Oct 1934). Mexican composer. After three years' study at the Mexico City conservatory (1880–83) with Melesio Morales, a composer of italianate operas, Campa took the lead in a 'Group of Six' – young composers in revolt against Morales's aesthetic. From 1896 to 1914 he expounded his views (favouring French rather than Italian models) in a periodical, *Gaceta musical*, that he edited for the Mexico City publishers Wagner & Levien.

After his return from a trip to Paris in 1900 he succeeded in obtaining a single performance of his one-act opera *Le roi poète* at the Teatro Principal (9 November 1901), as a special event in honour of the Congress of Americanists' meeting. Written to a libretto by the local journalist Alberto Michel, the opera romanticizes the amours of Nezahualcóyotl, the 15th-century poet-king of Texcuco. Although the highest government officials attended, it was produced without adequate rehearsal by the López-Pizzorni Italian opera touring company. Unfortunately, the tenor in the title role, Emanuel Izquierdo, rendered his part so wretchedly that Campa's supporters made 'an infernal racket denouncing him' for having ruined the opera (*El universal*, 17 November 1901). Only Ricardo Castro, Campa's former colleague at the conservatory, was able to see beyond the defects of the single presentation, when he categorized the music as 'impassioned, frequently inspired, clothed in beautiful harmonies, colourfully instrumented, and worthy of all praise'.

Campa lived until long after the lavish epoch of Porfirio Díaz's rule, when opera was a Mexican's highest artistic ideal, and subsequently taught at and directed the conservatory.

*

E. de Olavarría y Ferrari: *Reseña histórica del teatro en México*, iii (Mexico City, 1961), 2162–9
G. Orta Velázquez: *Breve historia de la música en México* (Mexico City, 1970), 411–12
G. Carmona: *Periodo de la independencia a la revolución (1810 a 1910)*, La música de México: Historia, iii (Mexico City, 1984), 155–6 ROBERT STEVENSON

Campagnolo, Francesco (*b* Mantua, ? 2 Feb 1584; *d* Innsbruck, 7 Oct 1630). Italian tenor. As an adolescent he served at the Mantuan court (he was a godson of Duke Vincenzo Gonzaga), where he lived briefly with Claudio Monteverdi's family. He undoubtedly played roles in entertainments of this period, including Monteverdi's *Orfeo* and *Arianna* and Gagliano's *Dafne*. In 1607 he was sent by Vincenzo to Rome for further vocal training. Campagnolo was frequently sought as a performer and sang in the wedding entertainments for Cosimo de' Medici and Maria Magdalena of Austria in Florence in 1608. In 1609–10 he travelled in the Low Countries, to England and to the courts of Lorraine and Munich. He briefly served Cardinal Ferdinando Gonzaga in Rome in 1612. Four years later he sang in the restaging of Peri's *Euridice* in Bologna and visited the Salzburg court. The Accademia Filarmonica of Verona extended membership to him in 1617.

After a longer stay in Salzburg, he was back in Mantua in 1619. There, according to Monteverdi, he was among the best-rewarded employees of the court; the title of Cavaliere was also bestowed on him. In 1622 he travelled in Hungary. In 1624 in Florence he sang in Gagliano's *Regina Sant'Orsola*, and in 1627 he visited Monteverdi in Venice. During the war over Mantua's succession he became theatre Kapellmeister at the imperial court in Innsbruck.

*

A. Bertolotti: *La musica in Mantova: musici alla corte dei Gonzaga dal secolo XV al XVIII* (Milan, 1891), 98, 101
W. Senn: *Musik und Theater am Hof zu Innsbruck* (Innsbruck, 1954)
H. Seifert: 'Beiträge zur Frühgeschichte der Monodie in Österreich', *SMw*, xxxi (1980), 14–26
S. Parisi: *Ducal Patronage of Music in Mantua, 1587–1627: an Archival Study* (diss., U. of Illinois, 1989), 422–8 SUSAN PARISI

Campana, Fabio (*b* Livorno, 14 Jan 1819; *d* London, 2 Feb 1882). Italian composer and singing teacher. He studied at the Liceo Musicale of Bologna, and his first opera was produced at Livorno while he was still a student. According to Fétis, the productions of his early operas in Italy were not very successful. In 1850 he moved to London, where he became well known as a singing teacher and composer of Italian songs. His opera *Almina* was given on 26 April 1860 at Her Majesty's Theatre with the soprano Marietta Piccolomini; his *Esmeralda* (1869, St Petersburg) was produced in London (Covent Garden) in 1870 with Patti in the title role.

Caterina di Guisa (3, F. Romani), Livorno, Avvalorati, sum. 1838
Giulio d'Este [Il postiglione di Longjumeau] (3, C. A. Monteverdi), Livorno, 1841, vs (Milan, 1850)
Vannina d'Ornano (F. Guidi), Florence, Pergola, 1 April 1842
Luisa di Francia (Guidi), Rome, Argentina, spr. 1844
La Duchessa de La Vallière (Guidi), Livorno, Rossini, sum. 1849
Mazeppa (A. de Lauzières), Bologna, Comunale, 6 Nov 1850
Almina (de Lauzières), London, Her Majesty's, 26 April 1860
Esmeralda (4, G. T. Cimino, after V. Hugo), St Petersburg, Italian, 20 Dec 1869, excerpts (London, 1870)

*

FétisB ('Campana, Fabrice') ELIZABETH FORBES

Campanari, Giuseppe (*b* Venice, 17 Nov 1855; *d* Milan, 31 May 1927). Italian baritone. After a premature operatic début at the Dal Verme in Milan he became a cellist, playing first at La Scala and from 1884 with the Boston SO. In 1893 he returned successfully to singing, appearing first with Gustav Hinrichs's company in Philadelphia and making his début at the Metropolitan the following year as Luna. His first conspicuous success was as Ford in the American première of *Falstaff* (1895). He was also a popular Figaro in Mozart and Rossini. He made over 200 appearances at the house and on tour, retiring in 1912. He then taught in New York and Milan, where his daughter Marina became a noted soprano. His voice took well to early recording conditions and his performances are both stylish and characterful. J. B. STEANE

Campana sommersa, La ('The Sunken Bell'). Opera in four acts by OTTORINO RESPIGHI to a libretto by CLAUDIO GUASTALLA after Gerhart Hauptmann's play *Die versunkene Glocke*; Hamburg, Stadttheater, 18 November 1927.

At the surface level, Hauptmann's famous symbolist fantasy drama (followed closely, though with omissions, in the libretto) depicts the impossibility of a stable relationship between the fairy realm and the world of mortals. It can also be seen as an elaborate metaphor for conflicts that arise in the creative process, between the needs of inspiration and those of ordinary domesticity.

Enrico (tenor, Heinrich in the play) is a skilled bell-maker whose finest creation is caused to fall to the bottom of a lake when he inadvertently takes it into fairy territory. He is injured when this happens, but after being brought home he is miraculously restored to health by the elf Rautendelein (soprano), who has fallen in love with him and followed him into the world of mankind. The cure is effected when she kisses his eyes: as a result, the invalid leaps to his feet, inspired by a sudden vision which makes his home life seem humdrum by comparison. He deserts his wife Magda (soprano) and plunges with renewed energy into his work, which with Rautendelein's help (in a magic work-shop on the mountain) reaches levels he could never have achieved on his own. But the bell tolls at the bottom of the lake as news arrives of Magda's suicide. Racked with guilt, Enrico rejects Rautendelein, but her enchantment still haunts him and he cannot live without her. Although now married to the King of the Frogs (Ondino, baritone), she is allowed to rejoin Enrico and comfort him as he dies.

Respighi is only intermittently at his best in this opera; but he responded vividly to the fantasy elements in the story. The first act, set in the realm of the fairies, contains music whose kaleidoscopic colourfulness can fully match that in his best tone poems. Haunting, too, are the various chiming, tolling effects that reverberate through the score (and not only at the opera's climax). The music associated with human passions is less distinctive or memorable: here Respighi tends to lapse into a sub-Puccinian lingua franca which is expressive enough in its way but lacks real individuality. This is perhaps the main reason why the big initial success of *La campana sommersa* on both sides of the Atlantic has not proved lasting; yet the work's positive qualities are more than sufficient to justify its occasional revivals.

JOHN C. G. WATERHOUSE

Campanello di notte, Il ('The Night Bell'). *Melodramma giocoso* in one act by GAETANO DONIZETTI to a text by the composer after a French vaudeville, *La sonnette de nuit*, by Brunswick, Mathieu-Barthélemy Troin and Victor Lhérie; Naples, Teatro Nuovo, 1 June 1836.

An elderly pharmacist, Don Annibale Pistacchio (*buffo* bass), is celebrating his marriage to Serafina (soprano). Attending the party is Enrico (baritone), who has been in love with Serafina himself and plots to discomfit Don Annibale on his wedding night. Relying on the legal requirement that a pharmacist must answer his bell at any hour of the night, Enrico proceeds to assume a series of disguises to keep Don Annibale otherwise occupied. First he comes as a French dandy, then as an opera singer out of voice, and last as a querulous old man with an endless prescription. Rid of this patient at last, Annibale starts upstairs, only to set off the fireworks that Enrico had obligingly planted. The ensuing uproar brings out the partygoers, now gathered to speed Annibale on his way to Rome, where he must see about an inheritance. Enrico wishes him a lifetime of nights as happy as the one just past, a sentiment enthusiastically endorsed by all but Don Annibale.

Enrico's role (created by Giorgio Ronconi) is fitted with all sorts of musical and dramatic opportunities. His encounters with Annibale develop in musical ingenuity. Particularly effective are the episode of the hoarse singer, replete with musical allusions to other scores by Donizetti and by Rossini, and the encounter over the prescription which develops into something with even more bizarre medical terms than Dr Dulcamara's aria in *Elisir*, and with more frantic parlando than the Don Pasquale-Malatesta duet. WILLIAM ASHBROOK

Campanini, Cleofonte (*b* Parma, 1 Sept 1860; *d* Chicago, 19 Dec 1919). Italian conductor and violinist. He studied in Parma where in 1880 he made his conducting début at the Teatro Reinach, and in 1882 he conducted *Carmen* at the Teatro Regio with great success. After assisting at the Metropolitan Opera in its inaugural season (1883–4) he returned to Italy, conducting the premières of *Flora mirabilis* by Samaras (1886), *Adriana Lecouvreur* (1902), Giordano's *Siberia* (1903), and *Madama Butterfly* (1904) in Milan. He was on the rostrum for the première of *Les pêcheurs de perles* in Rome and for the American première of *Otello* (1888, New York) when his wife, Eva, sang Desdemona. His extensive travels took him to Nice, Buenos Aires, Montevideo, Rio de Janeiro, Barcelona, Madrid and Lisbon. From 1906 to 1909 he was principal conductor of Oscar Hammerstein's Manhattan Opera Company, where he conducted the American première of *Pelléas et Mélisande* (1908) before moving to the Chicago Grand Opera Company in 1910. For the Verdi centenary in 1913 he staged (at his own expense) and conducted a cycle of Verdi operas at Parma. In 1914 at the Parma Conservatory, with funds given by the American Edith MacCormick, he founded the Campanini-MacCormick competition for an opera composed by an Italian.

ES (G. Graziosi)
M. Ferrarini: *Parma teatrale ottocentesca* (Parma, 1946)

SERGIO LATTES, R. ALLEN LOTT

Campanini, Italo (*b* Parma, 30 June 1845; *d* Corcagno, nr Parma, 22 Nov 1896). Italian tenor. He studied with Griffini in Parma, making his début there in 1864 as Vitellozzo in *Lucrezia Borgia*. Engaged to sing in *Il trovatore* in Russia, he stayed there for three years, returning to Italy for further study with Lamperti in Milan. After appearing at La Scala, he sang Lohengrin at Bologna (1871), the first Italian performance of Wagner's opera. He made his London début at Drury Lane (1872) as Gennaro (*Lucrezia Borgia*) and in 1874 sang Kenneth in the première of Balfe's *Il talismano*. He appeared as Faust in Boito's *Mefistofele* at Bologna (1875) and as Don José in the first London (Her Majesty's Theatre) and New York (Academy of Music) performances of *Carmen* (1878). He sang in Gounod's *Faust* at the opening of the Metropolitan (1883) and in Berlioz's *La damnation de Faust* at the Albert Hall in 1894, the year he retired. His voice was reportedly neither large nor perfectly even, but was sweet, flexible, brilliant on top and used with intuitive musicality.

ES (R. Celletti) ELIZABETH FORBES

Campaspe, La. *See* SARDELLI, ANNA MARIA.

Campbell, Ian David (*b* Brisbane, 21 Dec 1945). Australian director and administrator. He studied singing in Sydney and received the BA at the University of Sydney in 1967. After singing tenor roles with the Elizabethan Trust Opera Company (later the Australian Opera) from 1967 to 1974, he became senior music officer with the Australia Council, overseeing federal grants to opera companies and orchestras. In 1976 he was named general manager of New Opera of South Australia (later the State Opera of South Australia) in Adelaide. He became assistant artistic administrator at the Metropolitan Opera in 1982. At San Diego, Campbell expanded the company's production of 20th-century opera, presenting regional premières of Britten's *The Rape of Lucretia*, Floyd's *The Passion of Jonathan Wade* and Peter Maxwell Davies's *The Lighthouse*.

NANCY MALITZ

Campiello, Il ('The Small Venetian Square'). *Commedia lirica* in three acts by ERMANNO WOLF-FERRARI to a libretto by Mario Ghisalberti after CARLO GOLDONI's play of the same name (1756); Milan, Teatro alla Scala, 12 February 1936.

Although unaccountably ignored in English-speaking countries, this last of Wolf-Ferrari's five operas based on Goldoni comedies is undoubtedly one of the two best: some Germans and Italians have rated it even higher than *I quatro rusteghi* (1906). After the tormented state of mind that evidently underlay *Sly* (1927), *Il campiello* shows signs – in an altogether deeper way than the relatively slight *La vedova scaltra* (1931) – of a new inner calm. To some extent this transformation may reflect the composer's long-delayed breakthrough to full acceptance by the Italian musical world.

The libretto of *Il campiello* follows Goldoni closely, despite inevitable cuts: as in the case of *I quatro rusteghi*, both the play and the opera are mainly in Venetian dialect, and this time Goldoni's text is itself in verse. The plot as such is even slenderer than in *I quatro rusteghi*, being mainly a pretext for a delightful, richly satirical kaleidoscope of interacting characters – all in the unchanging setting of the small Venetian square to which the title refers. The frequenters of this square are mostly members of a close-knit working-class community, which is nevertheless repeatedly torn by short-lived strife. Again as in *I quatro rusteghi*, the locals are contrasted with an aristocratic 'outsider' who uses standard Italian; but Cavaliere Astolfi (baritone) no longer has riches commensurate with his rank – which does not prevent him from inviting everyone to meals, and from courting Gasparina (soprano), a prim young lady with a lisp whom he eventually takes back to Naples with him. Other important characters include Lucieta and Gnese (sopranos), who also get their share of the Cavaliere's attentions, despite their commitments to local boyfriends Anzoleto (bass) and Zorzeto (tenor). Older women include the grotesque travesty roles of Dona Cate Panciana and Dona Pasqua Polegana (tenors), who themselves try – somewhat improbably – to win success in the maze of love affairs.

Most of the best musical and dramatic qualities of *I quatro rusteghi* are again present in *Il campiello*. Moreover there are signs, in the ferocious quarrel scene that explodes in Act 3, that Wolf-Ferrari was willing, if and when the dramatic situation warranted it, to use tougher 20th-century dissonances than one normally associates with him. The pervading atmosphere, however – between the moments of strife, and only superficially disturbed by them – is of a profound yet childlike serenity: 'Quanta pace dà questa musica!', a listener is said to have exclaimed when the work was in rehearsal, and many who know this radiantly charming opera would echo his words. JOHN C. G. WATERHOUSE

Campioli [Gualandi, Antonio] (*fl* 1703–38). Italian alto castrato. Born in Germany of Italian parents, he was trained in Italy. He sang in Stuttgart (before 1704), Berlin (1708–13), Darmstadt (1718), Hamburg (1719) and Brunswick (1720–22), appearing in operas by Schürmann, Caldara and Francesco Conti. He then joined the Hamburg opera (1722–8), where he sang the title role in Handel's *Giulio Cesare*. In 1728 he went to Venice to train singers for Dresden. He sang in Hasse's *Cleofide* (1731, Dresden), but the part of Poro had to be cut down for him. Handel engaged him for the London season of 1731–2, and he sang in revivals of *Poro*, *Admeto* and *Flavio*, Ariosti's *Coriolano*, the pasticcio *Lucio Papirio dittatore*, and as Argone in the first performance of Handel's *Sosarme* (1732). Handel, who evidently thought little of him, gave him a meagre part without an aria in *Sosarme* (compass *a* to *c''*) and severely cut his parts in *Admeto* and *Flavio*. Campioli was still attached to the Dresden court in 1738, when he returned to Italy on a pension. Margherita Gualandi detta la Campioli, who appeared in 12 operas in Venice between 1709 and 1726, in Mantua (1719), Milan (1721), Florence (1725–6) and Ancona (1738), and from 1728 to 1735 was engaged at Prague, may have been his sister.

*

D. E. Freeman: 'An 18th-Century Singer's Commission of "Baggage" Arias', *EMc*, xx (1992), 427–33 WINTON DEAN

Campistron, Jean Galbert de (*b* Toulouse, 1656; *d* Toulouse, 11 May 1723). French librettist. He approached the operatic stage having already had success with conventional tragedy (he had adopted Racine as his mentor on arriving in Paris). For the Duc de Vendôme he wrote the *pastorale Acis et Galatée*, which was set to music by Lully and first performed at the Chateau d'Anet. The duke rewarded him with a sinecure and pensions. *Achille et Polyxène*, in the more conventional form of the *tragédie en musique*, was commissioned by Lully, whose regular librettist Quinault had retired from the scene. Lully wrote only one act before he died, but the work was completed by Collasse. Campistron had continued success with his *tragédies* and was admitted to the Académie Française in 1701, though he made only one more foray into opera before returning to the provinces. His style reflects his theatrical roots: the spectacular and decorative trappings of opera are grafted on to verses fashioned more for spoken declamation than for singing.

Acis et Galatée (pastorale-héroïque), Lully, 1686; *Achille et Polyxène* (tragédie en musique), Collasse [Act 1 by Lully], 1687; *Alcide, ou Le triomphe d'Hercule* (tragédie en musique), L. Lully and Marais, 1693 CAROLINE WOOD

Campo (y Zabaleta), Conrado del (*b* Madrid, 28 Oct 1878; *d* Madrid, 17 March 1953). Spanish composer. He studied composition with Emilio Serrano at the Madrid Conservatory and later with Chapí. Supported by a scholarship, he also spent a period in Berlin. He was appointed professor of harmony at the conservatory in 1915, and eight years later succeeded Bretón as professor of composition. In his 30-year tenure of this post he became one of the most influential figures in Spanish musical life, teaching most of the leading musicians of the next generation. He was one of the founders of the Orquesta Sinfónica de Madrid and later of the orchestra of the Radio Nacional, of which he was conductor from 1947 to 1951. A man of wide culture and ceaseless interest in all aspects of music and music-making, he drove himself with tireless energy and enthusiasm to the end.

Besides large quantities of chamber and orchestral music he composed some 40 operas and zarzuelas and converted Vives's zarzuela *Bohemios* into an opera. Many of his stage pieces were never performed, and he often had to contend with theatrical cabals against him which, in the case of one of his greatest successes, *El Avapiés* (1919), resulted in the orchestra's having to read the whole of one act at sight at the first performance.

In his works he was at first influenced by Franck, but later (in contrast to his contemporaries Falla and Turina, who were influenced by French impressionism) he fell under the spell of Wagner and, more particularly, Richard Strauss, whose Romantic idiom and rich orchestral texture he wholeheartedly adopted. Consequently much of his music is characterized by over-ripe orchestration and a spirit of *Sturm und Drang*, though in his operas these Germanic tendencies were to some extent tempered by his choice of Spanish subjects. *El final de Don Alvaro* (1911), for example, is based on the same play as Verdi's *La forza del destino*; and in lighter vein *El Avapiés* is set against the Goyesque background of 18th-century Madrid.

El final de Don Alvaro (1, C. Fernández Shaw and A. de Saavedra, after Rivas: *Don Alvaro o la fuerza del sino*), Madrid, Real, 4 March 1911; La dama desconocida (3, T. Borrás), 1911; La tragedia del beso (2, C. Fernández Shaw), Madrid, Real, 18 May 1915; Los amantes de Verona (Romeo y Julieta) (4, F. de Iracheta), 1916; Dies irae (3, Iracheta), 1917; El Avapiés (3, Borrás), Madrid, Real, 18 March 1919, collab. A. Barrios; Fantochines (1, Borrás), Madrid, Comedia, 1924; Leonor Telles (M. Mesquita) [Port. text], 1927; El árbol de los ojos (1, Borrás),

1931; Lola la piconera (3, J. M. Pemán), Barcelona, Liceo, 14 Nov 1950; El pájaro de dos colores (Borrás), 1951; Figaro (Borrás); La hija de Jefté; Irene de Otranto; La malquerida (J. Benavente, F. Romero and G. Fernández Shaw); Paolo y Francesca

Zarzuelas (3, unless otherwise stated): Aires de la Sierra (1, A. Osete), Madrid, Noviciado, 4 Feb 1909, collab. G. Baudot-Puente; Alondra (Ballester), collab. Ruiz de Luna; El bachiller Medina; La boda de Montseny; El burlador de Toledo (T. Borrás and Ferraz Revenga), Madrid, Zarzuela, 1965, collab. E. Rosillo; Los crepúsculos; La culpa, collab. A. Barrios; Una dama se vende a quien la quiere (D. San José); El demonio de Isabela (R. Fernández Shaw and G. Fernández Shaw); La flor del agua (V. S. Armesto), Madrid, Zarzuela, 1915; La flor del pazo, collab. J. Forns; El hombre más guapo del mundo (Borrás); Juan Moncada; Lady Godiva; Los maestros cantores de Ortuña (H. Catá); La niña (F. Oliver), collab. Barrios; La noche blanca (E. M. de Acevedo); Una noche en Pedraza (C. Fernández Shaw); La pandereta rota; Pepe María; El rey trovador; La romería, 1917, collab. Barrios; Teatro del peón de música; La máscara (3, L. Domínguez and G. M. Sierra), 1917, collab. Barrios; Una vieja (F. Camprodón)

Sainete: El mirar de sus ojos (1, C. Arniches)

*

H. Collet: *L'essor de la musique espagnole au XXe siècle* (Paris, 1929), 135ff
J. Subirá: *Historia y anecdotario del Teatro Real* (Madrid, 1949), 638–9, 710–11
T. Borrás: *Conrado del Campo* (Madrid, 1954)
A. Fernández-Cid: *Músicos que fueron nuestros amigos* (Madrid, 1967), 59–71
——: *Cien años de teatro musical en España* (Madrid, 1975)

LIONEL SALTER

Campobasso d'Alessandro, Vincenzo (*b* Naples, 1760; *d* after 1788). Italian composer. He set the second of only two librettos by Marco Coltellini ever performed in Milan, *Antigona* (La Scala, 26 December 1788). The opera's shocking introductory scene, which freely combines pantomime, dance, chorus and recitative, focusses on a brutal battle to the death between two brothers whose bodies lie on stage during the coronation that follows. Choruses, which were just beginning to appear regularly in opera during the latter years of the decade, figure prominently in several other scenes, either alone or in combination with ensemble.

MARITA P. McCLYMONDS

Campora, Giuseppe (*b* Tortona, 30 Sept 1923). Italian tenor. He studied in Genoa and Milan and made his début at Bari in 1949 as Rodolfo in *La bohème*. He appeared first at La Scala in 1952 as Boris in the première of Rocca's *L'uragano*; roles in subsequent seasons included Rodolfo, Maurizio in *Adriana Lecouvreur* and Orombello in *Beatrice di Tenda*. Abroad, he made a successful début at the Colón in 1952 and from 1955 to 1965 sang frequently at the Metropolitan in a lyric repertory ranging from Edgardo in *Lucia di Lammermoor* to the title role in *Les contes d'Hoffmann*. His active and durable career took him to most of the leading Italian houses, and he travelled widely throughout Europe and the USA. In later years he appeared also in operettas such as *Die Fledermaus* and *Das Land des Lächelns*. His recordings, which include several complete operas, show a style that is reliable rather than imaginative and a serviceable voice, not very distinctive in timbre but of pleasing quality. J. B. STEANE

Camporese, Violante (*b* Rome, 1785; *d* Rome, 1839). Italian soprano. She studied with Crescentini in Paris and made her début there in 1815. She made her London début at the King's Theatre in 1817, in the title role of Cimarosa's *Penelope*, later singing Donna Anna in the first London performance of *Don Giovanni*, as well as three other Mozart roles, Susanna, Dorabella and Sextus (*La clemenza di Tito*). She also appeared in Paer's *Agnese*. In 1818 she sang in the first performances of Morlacchi's *Gianni di Parigi*, Gyrowetz's *Il finto Stanislao* and Pacini's *Il barone di Dolsheim* at La Scala.

After singing Bianca at the première of *Bianca e Falliero* (1819, La Scala), she returned to London and appeared in several other Rossini operas. She sang Ninetta in *La gazza ladra* in 1821 (the first London performance) and the following year took part in *Pietro l'eremita* (*Mosè in Egitto*) at the King's Theatre. The same season she sang Desdemona (*Otello*), and in 1823 took her farewell of the London stage in *Ricciardo e Zoraide*. Her voice was of wide compass and even throughout the scale, while technical mastery and style made her a particularly fine interpreter of Mozart.

ELIZABETH FORBES

Campos, Carlos de (*b* Campinas, 6 Aug 1866; *d* São Paulo, 27 April 1927). Brazilian composer. Trained as a lawyer, he rose to become director of the São Paulo newspaper *Comércio paulistano* and president of São Paulo state (1924–7). His musical instructors were Carlos Gomes and Luís Provesi, the latter of whom orchestrated his opera *A bela adormecida*. In two acts, with a prologue and intermezzo, to a libretto by João Kopke after the Sleeping Beauty story, this work was first given at the Teatro Municipal in São Paulo on 28 April 1924 and repeated in Rio de Janeiro in November that year. A second opera, *Um caso singular*, in three acts to a libretto by P. A. Gomes Cardim, is set in 17th-century Brazil and concerns a Portuguese rebel's daughter in man's disguise. It was given its first professional performance, conducted by Edoardo Vitale, in Rio on 30 July 1926, and it was staged by local singers, at the Teatro Municipal, São Paulo, in August the same year.

*

L. H. Corrêa de Azevedo: *Relação das óperas de autores brasileiros* (Rio de Janeiro, 1938), 63–4
Enciclopédia da música brasileira (São Paulo, 1977), i, 134

ROBERT STEVENSON

Campra, André (*b* Aix-en-Provence, bap. 4 Dec 1660; *d* Versailles, 29 June 1744). French composer. He was a leading figure in French theatrical and sacred music in the early 18th century.

1. LIFE. Campra's father and first music teacher was Jean-François Campra, a surgeon and violinist from Graglia near Turin; his mother was Louise Fabry of Aix. In 1674 he became a choirboy at St Sauveur under Guillaume Poitevin. Nothing supports La Borde's claim that Campra was *maître de musique* at Toulon in 1679. He was still at Aix in 1681 when he was threatened with dismissal for unauthorized participation in theatrical performances. Despite this offence he was made a chaplain on 27 May 1681.

Campra left Aix on 7 August 1681 to become *maître de musique* at Ste Trophime, Arles, where he remained until May 1683. In June he became *maître de musique* at St Etienne, Toulouse. On 8 January 1694 he received four months' leave in Paris 'to render himself more capable of giving service'. He never returned to Toulouse and his position there was declared open in August 1694. On 21 June 1694 he succeeded Jean Mignon as *maître de musique* at Notre Dame, Paris. He could not have replaced Charpentier at the Jesuit College soon after arriving in the city, as Titon du Tillet alleged, for Charpentier remained there until 1698, when he accepted the post of *maître de musique* at the Sainte-Chapelle. Campra's name does appear on programmes at the Jesuit College from 1698 to 1737 as a composer of music for Latin tragedies, and the *Mercure de France* referred to him in August 1721 as 'maître de musique du Collège Louis-le-Grand'. Campra received a canonicate at St Jean-le-Rond in May 1696.

The lure of the secular stage soon disturbed his execution of ecclesiastical duties. In 1697 two works of his were performed: a *divertissement*, commissioned by the Duke of Sully in honour of the Duke of Chartres, and *L'Europe galante*, the first *opéra-ballet*. The question of authors' royalties was resolved at the time of the latter's première. Campra and the librettist, Lamotte, refused the paltry fees offered them by an administration bent on economy. An agreement was worked out whereby composer and librettist would each receive 100 livres for each of the first ten performances and 50 livres for each of the next ten.

The first three Paris editions of *L'Europe galante* (1697, 1698 and 1699) appeared anonymously, as did the 1698 edition of Campra's *divertissement Vénus, feste galante*. *Le carnaval de Venise* (1699) and seven *airs* from Ballard's collections of 1698 and 1700 carry the legend 'par M. Campra le Cadet', a reference to André's younger brother. A chanson of 1697 shows that this subterfuge fooled no one:

Quand nôtre Archevesque sçaura
L'Auteur du nouvel Opéra,
De sa Cathédrale Campra
Décampera.

Encouraged by the success of *L'Europe galante* and secured by royal patrons, Campra left Notre Dame on 13 October 1700. The Ballard score of his first *tragédie en musique*, *Hésione*, bore his correct name in time for its première that December. *Tancrède*, his masterpiece in the genre of lyric tragedy, was performed in 1702 at the Paris Opéra where he was a 'batteur de mesure'. A quarrel with the royal printer, J.-B.-C. Ballard, forced Campra to seek a royal privilege to bypass Ballard's monopoly. A 12-year privilege was granted him on 9 May 1704 to 'engrave, print, sell and distribute anywhere in our Realm, all pieces of music of his composition'. It was renewed on 7 September 1720 and 23 November 1736, long after his differences with Ballard were resolved.

The regency of Philip of Orléans found Campra at his zenith as a stage composer. Le Cerf de la Viéville placed him first among post-Lully composers of operas. His *opéras-ballets* and earlier *tragédies en musique* enjoyed many revivals. His first two books of *cantates françoises* and his first four books of *petits motets* were in print. His *airs* graced the pages of *recueils d'airs sérieux et à boire*. It comes as no surprise, then, that the young Louis XV (undoubtedly at the urging of the regent) granted Campra an annual pension of 500 livres on 15 December 1718 'in recognition of his talents as a composer of stage works for the Académie Royale [de Musique] and as an incentive to continue such composition'. In 1722 Campra became director of music for the Prince of Conti, for whom he composed several *divertissements* (the music of which is lost). Campra composed his last *opéra-ballet*, *Les âges*, in 1718. It was moderately well received. His late *tragédies* (*Télèphe*, 1713; *Camille, reine des volsques*, 1717; and *Achille et Déidamie*, 1735) were all failures.

Campra returned to the composition of sacred music in 1720 with his fifth book of *petits motets*. When Lalande gave up three-quarters of his work at the royal chapel, the 'regent's men' quickly filled in. In January 1723 Campra, Nicolas Bernier and Charles-Hubert Gervais were appointed *sous-maîtres* without the usual competitive examinations. After the deaths of Lalande (1726) and Bernier (1734), Campra and Gervais divided the work into two six-month periods until 1738, when they were joined by Esprit Blanchard and Henri Madin.

Campra replaced Destouches as Inspector General at the Académie in 1730 at a salary of 1500 livres. His health was deteriorating after years of double allegiance to chapel and stage. The *Mémoires* of Cardinal de Fleury describe an André Campra in 1741 'with little control over his affairs, burdened by years and by debts'. Still, Campra produced two books of psalms (1737 and 1738) and he left many *grands motets* in manuscript. In 1742 he relinquished the royal chapel and the training of its boy sopranos to his successor, Mondonville. He spent his last years in a small Versailles apartment, sustained mainly by his pensions. On his death at the age of 84 he left the little money he possessed to two faithful servants.

2. WORKS. Campra's main contribution to the French lyric stage was the creation of the *opéra-ballet*. In this genre, simply designated 'ballet' in the period of first performance, but called *opéra-ballet* by the late 18th century, each act (or entrée) contains its own characters and plot that relate in a general way to a collective idea expressed in the work's title. Although structural models for the *opéra-ballet* did exist (e.g. Collasse's *Ballet des saisons*, 1695), it remained for Campra and his librettists to replace the shopworn deities of the *tragédie lyrique* with lively *petits-maîtres*, amorous ladies and flirtatious soubrettes in recognizable contemporary settings. Such innovation was not lost upon audiences of the time. Cahusac likened the *opéra-ballet* to 'pretty Watteaus'; for the librettist P. C. Roy the *opéra-ballet* 'pleases by its variety and sympathizes with French impatience'.

The flexible format of the *opéra-ballet* allowed for innovation. Campra and his librettists could substitute new entrées for those that lacked audience appeal. In 'L'opéra' (*Les fêtes vénitiennes*, third entrée) Campra exploited the device of a play within a play which he had first tried out in the lyric comedy *Le carnaval de Venise* (1699). In the *avertissement* to the 1714 edition of *Les fêtes vénitiennes* Campra said that he had included 'several melodies and symphonies by our most skilful composers'. We find easily recognizable extracts from operas by Lully, Destouches and Marais within the dramatic context of the work's fourth entrée, 'Le bal'.

Experimentation was not confined to *opéra-ballet*. Campra broke with French operatic tradition in lyric tragedy by using only low voices for the main male roles in *Tancrède* and by scoring the role of Clorinde for alto (although the range is practically identical to that of the main soprano role). Musical frescoes of nature in turmoil are found in *Hésione*, *Tancrède* and *Idomenée*. The last named includes an offstage chorus that anticipates Rameau's use of the same device in *Zoroastre* 37 years later.

Campra's musical style is seen at its best in his four *opéras-ballets*. The syllabic *airs*, with their short asymmetrical phrases and expressive vocal ornamentation, are characteristically French, as is the five-part texture inherited from Lully. The complex vocalises of the *ariettes* and da capo *airs*, the concerto-like rhythms of certain *ritournelles* and the use of rapid modulations all come from Italy. Mellers observed that Campra was 'perhaps the most enchanting of dance composers'. This is borne out by the gestic directness of the minuets, by their triadic melodies that bring Haydn to mind, by the carefree humour of the rigaudons in *Les âges*, whose unabashed parallel 5ths suggest rustic dances of Campra's meridional homeland, and by the kinetic energy of the contredanses and *forlane*, which have an extra bar thrown in here and there to avoid symmetrical phrase groupings.

With his delicate sense of orchestral colour, the kaleidoscopic brilliance with which he used the dance, his gift for melody and his sensitivity to the expressive possibilities of harmony, Campra greatly expanded the musical vocabulary of Lully. Through his *opéras-ballets* he introduced a degree of verisimilitude to the French lyric stage. On his limited scale and at his best, he was a poet who, like Watteau, created a world half real, half fantasy. Campra's awareness of the primary role of the musician in opera was not shared by most French aestheticians of the period, but it enabled him to turn to the Prince of Conti after the first performances of Rameau's *Hippolyte et Aricie* in 1733 and prophesy, 'There is enough music in this opera for ten operas: this man will eclipse us all'.

See also CARNAVAL DE VENISE, LE; EUROPE GALANTE, L'; FÊTES VÉNITIENNES, LES; IDOMENÉE; and TANCRÈDE.

Editions: *Chefs-d'oeuvre classiques de l'opéra français*, ed. J. B. Weckerlin and others (Leipzig, *c*1882) [W]
André Campra, ed. G. Sadler, The Baroque Operatic Arias, ii (London, 1973) [S]

first performed at Paris Opéra unless otherwise stated; printed works published in Paris unless otherwise stated

title	*genre, acts/entrées*	*librettist*	*first performance*	*remarks; sources; publications*
[Divertissement]	1		Paris, hôtel of Duke of Sully, 1697	commissioned by Duke of Sully in honour of Duke of Chartres; MS (private collection)
L'Europe galante	opéra-ballet, prol., 4	A. H. de Lamotte	24 Oct 1697	entrées: La France, L'Espagne, L'Italie and La Turquie; short score (1697), full score (1724/*R*1967), ed. T. Lajarte in W iv, 1 air in S
Vénus, feste galante	divertissement, prol., 1	A. Danchet	Paris, home of the Duchesse de la Ferté, 27 Jan 1698	for 2nd version see Les fragments de Monsieur de Lully, for 3rd version see Les amours de Vénus et de Mars, for 4th version see Les nopces de Vénus; short score (1698)
Le carnaval de Venise	comédie lyrique, prol., 3	J.-F. Regnard	20 Jan 1699	*F-Pn* (*R*1990: FO, xvii), short score (1699)
Hésione	tragédie en musique, prol., 5	Danchet	21 Dec 1700	short score (1700)
Aréthuse, ou La vengeance de L'Amour	ballet, prol., 3	Danchet	14 July 1701	short score (1701)
Les fragments de Monsieur de Lully	prol., 5	Danchet	10 Sept 1702	arr. from Lully (Les fêtes de l'Amour et de Bacchus, Le bourgeois gentilhomme, Les jeux pythiens, Les amours déguisés, Ballet des muses, La naissance de Vénus, La princesse d'Elide, La fête de Versailles, Les amours déguisés and Alcidiane). Later perfs. with 4 new entrées by Campra: Le triomphe de Vénus [2nd version of Vénus, feste galante], La sérénade vénitienne, Le bal interrompu and Le jaloux trompé [2nd version of La sérénade vénitienne]; *Pn*; (1731)
Tancrède	tragédie en musique, prol., 5	Danchet, after T. Tasso	7 Nov 1702	short score (1702); *Pn* based on 1737 edn, ed. A. Guilmant in W iv, ed. R. Blanchard (Paris, 1973)
Les muses	opéra-ballet, prol., 4	Danchet	28 Oct 1703	entrées: La pastorale (in later perfs. Amarillis), La satire, La tragédie, La comédie; *Pn* (pts); short score (1703)
Iphigénie en Tauride	tragédie en musique, prol., 5	J.-F. Duché de Vancy and Danchet	6 May 1704	unfinished work by Desmarets for which Campra composed prol., 5 scenes and several airs; short score (1711)
Télémaque, ou Les fragments des modernes	tragédie en musique, prol., 5	Danchet	11 Nov 1704	extracts from operas by Campra, Charpentier, Collasse, Desmarets, Marais and Rebel, arr. Campra; *Pn*, *Po*
Alcine	tragédie en musique, prol., 5	Danchet, after L. Ariosto	15 Jan 1705	short score (1705)
Le triomphe de l'Amour	opéra-ballet, prol., 4	Danchet, after P. Quinault	11 Sept 1705	rev. of ballet by Lully; music lost
Hippodamie	tragédie en musique, prol., 5	P.-C. Roy	6 March 1708	short score (1708), 3 airs in S

title	genre, acts/entrées	librettist	first performance	remarks; sources; publications
Les fêtes vénitiennes	opéra-ballet, prol., 5 [orig. 3]	Danchet	17 June 1710	orig. prol. (Le triomphe de la Folie sur la Raison) and 3 entrées (La feste des baquerolles, Les sérénades et les joueurs, L'amour saltimbanque); short score (1710). New entrées: La fête marine, Le bal, ou Le maître à danser, Le carnaval dans Venise [2nd version of orig. prol.], Les devins de la place St-Marc, L'opéra, ou Le maître à chanter, Le triomphe de la folie; *Po*; short score of some items (1710), ed. A. Pougin in W v, ed. M. Lütolf [based on *Po* MS, 1737] (Paris, 1971)
Idomenée	tragédie en musique, prol., 5	Danchet, after P. J. Crébillon	12 Jan 1712	*Pn* [1731]; short score (1712), 2 airs in S
Les amours de Vénus et de Mars	ballet, prol., 3	Danchet	6 Sept 1712	3rd version of Vénus, feste galante; prol. (1712) [with Le triomphe de la folie]
Télèphe	tragédie en musique, prol., 5	Danchet	28 Nov 1713	*Po* (pts); short score (1713), 2 airs in S
Enée et Didon	divertissement, 1		Marseilles, 29 Oct 1714	in honour of Queen of Spain; *Pa*; pubd in Cantates françoises ... livre second (1714)
Camille, reine des volsques	tragédie en musique, prol., 5	Danchet	9 Nov 1717	*Po* (pts); short score (1717), 1 air in S
Ballet représenté à Lion devant M. le marquis d'Harlincourt	ballet	F. Gacon	Lyons, 17 May 1718	music lost
Les âges	opéra-ballet, prol., 3	L. Fuzelier	9 Oct 1718	entrées: La jeunesse, ou L'amour ingénu, L'âge viril, ou L'amour coquet, La vieillesse, ou L'amour enjoué; *Pc*; excerpts (1718), 1 air in S. New entrée: Les âges rivaux, *Pn*
La feste de l'Isle-Adam	divertissement, 1		1722	music lost
Les muses rassemblées par l'Amour	divertissement	Danchet	Aix, Académie, Feb 1724	music lost
Les sauvages	divertissement, 1		Paris, Concert Spirituel, 14 Sept 1729	music lost
Achille et Déidamie	tragédie en musique, prol., 5	Danchet	24 Feb 1735	*Po* (pts); short score (1735)
Les nopces de Vénus	divertissement, prol., 3	Danchet		4th version of Vénus, feste galante; (1740), 2 airs in S

Intermèdes, pastorales or ballets, all lost, for Latin and French plays performed at the Collège Louis-le-Grand, Paris: intermèdes in Philochrysus, ou L'avare (P. Lejay), 15 Dec 1698; Les songes (ballet, Lejay), 12 Aug 1699; Abdolomine (Lejay), 26 March 1700; Timandre, pastorale in Cresus (Lejay), 22 Dec 1700; Adulatores, intermède in Joseph vendu par ses frères (Lejay), 27 Feb 1704; L'art de vivre heureux, ballet in Hermenegilde (P. Porée), 3 Aug 1718; intermèdes in Annibal jurant ad aras (Du Val), 11 Jan 1719; intermèdes in Agapitus (Porée), 20 March 1722; Les couronnes, ballet in Mauritius Imperator (Porée), 15 Aug 1722; intermèdes in Euloge, ou Le danger des richesses (J.-A. Du Cerceau), 16 May 1725; prol. and vaudeville for Le fils indocile (P. de la Sante), 19 Feb 1727; intermèdes in Le génie françois exilé du Théâtre latin (Porée), 5 March 1728; La curiosité, ballet moral (Porée), 4 Aug 1737

ES (N. Pirrotta); *MGG* (R. Girardon)

J. N. de Francini and others, eds.: *Recueil général des opéra* (Paris, 1703–45)

J.-L. Le Cerf de la Viéville: *Comparaison de la musique italienne et de la musique françoise* (Brussels, 1704–6)

N. Boindin: *Lettres historiques sur tous les spectacles de Paris* (Paris, 1719)

C. Parfaict and F. Parfaict: *Histoire de l'Académie royale de musique* (MS, 1741, *F-Pn* n. a. fr. 6532)

L. de Cahusac: *La dance ancienne et moderne* (The Hague, 1754)

E. Titon du Tillet: *Le Parnasse françois*, suppl.ii (Paris, 1755)

A. de Leris: *Dictionnaire portatif historique et littéraire des théâtres* (Paris, 2/1763)

P. J. B. Nougaret: *De l'art du théâtre en général* (Paris, 1769)

L.-A. B. Fontenay: *Dictionnaire des artistes* (Paris, 1776)

J.-B. de La Borde: *Essai sur la musique ancienne et moderne* (Paris, 1780)

L.-F. Beffara: *Dictionnaire de l'Académie royale de musique* (MS, 1783–4, *F-Po* [rés. 602])

A. Pougin: 'André Campra', *Revue et gazette musicale de Paris* (1861), 299–323

A. Jal: *Dictionnaire critique de biographie et d'histoire* (Paris, 1872)

T. de Lajarte: *Bibliothèque musicale du théâtre de l'Opéra: catalogue historique, chronologique, anecdotique* (Paris, 1878)

A. Pougin: 'André Campra', *Le ménestrel*, xlvii (1881), 176–261

C. Pierre: 'L'editeur Ballard contre Campra', *Art musical* (Dec 1893), 105–6, 113–24

E. Marbot: *Gilles, Cabassol et Campra* (Aix, 1903)

L. de La Laurencie: 'Notes sur la jeunesse d'André Campra', *SIMG*, x (1908–9), 159–258

——: 'André Campra, musicien profane', *Année musicale*, iii (1913), 153–205

——: '*Orfeo nell'inferni* d'André Campra', *RdM*, ix (1928), 129–33

P.-M. Masson: *L'opéra de Rameau* (Paris, 1930)

——: '*Les fêtes vénitiennes* de Campra', *RdM*, xiii (1932), 127–46, 214–26

P. Mélèse: *Le théâtre et le public à Paris sous Louis XIV 1659–1715* (Paris, 1934)

A. Gastoué: 'Les notes inédites du Marquis de Paulmy sur les oeuvres lyriques françaises (1655–1775)', *RdM*, xxv (1943), 1–7

W. Mellers: *François Couperin and the French Classical Tradition* (London, 1950, 2/1987)

M. Barthélemy: 'L'orchestre et l'orchestration des oeuvres de Campra', *ReM*, no.226 (1955), 97–103

——: *André Campra* (Paris, 1957)

——: 'Le premier divertissement connu d'André Campra', *RBM*, xi (1957), 51–3

J. R. Anthony: *The Opera Ballets of André Campra: a Study of the First Period French Opera Ballet* (diss., U. of S. California, 1964)

——: 'The French Opera Ballet in the Early 18th Century: Problems of Definition and Classification', *JAMS*, xviii (1965), 197–206

——: 'Thematic Repetition in the Opera Ballets of André Campra', *MQ*, lii (1966), 209–20
——: 'Some Uses of the Dance in the French Opera Ballet', *RMFC*, ix (1969), 75–90
P. Fortassier: 'Aspects de la mise en scène dans quelques ouvrages lyriques français du XVIIIe siècle', *Cahiers de l'Association internationale des études françaises*, no.21 (1969), 105–22
D. Heartz: 'The Genesis of Mozart's *Idomeneo*', *MQ*, lv (1969), 1–19
J. R. Anthony: 'Printed Editions of André Campra's *L'Europe galante*', *MQ*, lvi (1970), 54–73
A. Ducrot: 'Les représentations de l'Académie royale de musique au temps de Louis XIV', *RMFC*, x (1970), 19–55
P. Fortassier: 'Musique et paroles dans les opéras de Campra', *Centre aixois d'études et de recherches sur le dix-huitième siècle: La régence* (Paris, 1970), 31–43
M. Benoit: *Versailles et les musiciens du roi, 1661–1733* (Paris, 1971)
C. Girdlestone: *La tragédie en musique considérée comme genre littéraire (1673–1750)* (Geneva, 1972)
H. Lagrave: *Le théâtre et le public à Paris de 1715 à 1750* (Paris, 1972)
A. McConnell: *The Opera-Ballet: Opera as Literature* (diss., U. of Arizona, 1972)
J. R. Anthony: *French Baroque Music from Beaujoyeulx to Rameau* (London, 1973, 2/1978, Fr. trans., 1981)
G. E. Barksdale: *The Chorus in French Baroque Opera* (diss., U. of Utah, 1973)
C. Girdlestone: 'Idomenée ... Idomeneo: transformations d'un thème 1699–1781', *RMFC*, xiii (1973), 102–32
R. M. Isherwood: *Music in the Service of the King: France in the Seventeenth Century* (Ithaca, NY, and London, 1973)
P.-M. Masson: 'French Opera from Lully to Rameau', NOHM, v (London, 1975), 206–66
E. Lemaître: *L'orchestre dans le théâtre lyrique français chez les continuateurs de Lully, 1687–1715* (diss., Conservatoire National Supérieur de Musique, Paris, 1977)
L. E. Brown: *The Tragédie Lyrique of André Campra and his Contemporaries* (diss., U. of North Carolina, 1978)
J. de La Gorce: *L'opéra sous le règne de Louis XIV: le merveilleux ou les puissances surnaturelles, 1671–1715* (diss., U. of Paris-Sorbonne, 1978)
R. P. Wolf: 'Metrical Relationships in French Recitative of the Seventeenth and Eighteenth Centuries', *RMFC*, xvii (1978), 29–49
J. de La Gorce: 'L'Académie royale de musique en 1704, d'après des documents inédits conservés dans les archives notariales', *RdM*, lxv (1979), 160–91
L. E. Brown: 'Oratorical Thought and the Tragédie-Lyrique: a Consideration of Musical-Rhetorical Figures', *Symposium*, xx (1980), 99–116
G. Sadler: 'The Role of the Keyboard Continuo in French Opera, 1673–1776', *EMc*, viii (1980), 148–57
C. Wood: *Jean-Baptiste Lully and his Successors: Music and Drama in the tragédie en musique* (diss., U. of Hull, 1981)
——: 'Orchestra and Spectacle in the *tragédie en musique*, 1673–1715: Oracle, *Sommeil* and *Tempête*', *PRMA*, cviii (1981–2), 25–46
M. Cyr: '*Basses* and *basse continue* in the Orchestra of the Paris Opera, 1700–1764', *EMc*, x (1982), 155–70
R. Fajon: 'Le préramisme dans le repertoire de l'Opéra', *Jean-Philippe Rameau: Dijon 1983*, 307–29
S. Pitou: *The Paris Opera: an Encyclopedia of Operas, Ballets, Composers and Performers* (Westport, CT, 1983)
L. Rosow: 'French Baroque Recitative as an Expression of Tragic Declamation', *EMc*, xi (1983), 468–79
J. Boyer: 'Nouveaux documents sur la jeunesse d'André Campra et la vie musicale à Aix-en-Provence au XVIIe siècle', *RMFC*, xxii (1984), 79–88
L. E. Brown: 'Departure from Lullian Convention in the *tragédie lyrique* of the *préramiste* Era', *RMFC*, xxii (1984), 59–78
——: 'The *récit* in the Eighteenth-Century *tragédie en musique*', *MR*, xlv (1984), 96–111
R. Fajon: *L'opéra à Paris du Roi-Soleil à Louis le Bien-aimé* (Geneva, 1984)
E. Lemaître: 'L'orchestre dans le théâtre lyrique français chez les continuateurs de Lully, 1687–1715', *RMFC*, xxiv (1986), 107–27
L. Rosow: 'From Destouches to Berton: Editorial Responsibility at the Paris Opera', *JAMS*, xl (1987), 285–309
C. Smith: *André Campra's Idomenée: a Study of its Structural Components and a Critical Edition of the Work* (diss., U. of Kentucky, 1988)
A. L. Banducci: *'Tancrède' by Antoine Danchet and André Campra: Performance History and Reception (1702–1764)* (diss., Washington U., 1990)
M. Barthélemy: *Métamorphoses de l'opéra français au siècle des lumières* (Arles, 1990)
J. de La Gorce: 'L'orchestre de l'Opéra et son évolution de Campra à Rameau', *RdM*, lxxvi (1990), 23–43
C. Kintzler: *Poétique de l'opéra français de Corneille à Rousseau* (Paris, 1991)

JAMES R. ANTHONY

Canada. Opera started relatively late in Canada. Once established in the 18th century, it followed a variable course before eventually settling down as a mainstream and indigenous activity. Before the 18th century, the earliest documented predecessor of opera was Marc Lescarbot's masque *Le théâtre de Neptune en la Nouvelle-France*, a musico-dramatic work performed from small boats in the harbour of Port-Royal (now Annapolis Royal, Nova Scotia) on 14 November 1606. Although the performance was an isolated occurrence, it was contemporaneous with the first French settlements in Canada. Port-Royal, established in 1605, was where Samuel de Champlain, recognized as the founder of New France, organized the first social club in north America and this first theatre event in Canadian history. It predates Champlain's founding of Quebec in 1608.

Operatic performances proper began in Canada only in the late 18th century when travelling theatrical companies from abroad appeared in Montreal, Quebec City and Halifax. The fare was comic operas of English and French provenance, such as Charles Dibdin's *The Padlock* (1768; performed in Quebec City in 1783 and Montreal in 1786), *The Duenna, or The Double Elopement* by the two Thomas Linleys, father and son (1775; performed in Halifax in 1790 and St John's in 1820), or E. R. Duni's *Les deux chasseurs et la laitière* (1763; performed in Montreal in 1789). The first known Canadian work was Joseph Quesnel's *Colas et Colinette, ou Le bailli dupé*, given in Montreal in 1790. At the time of Quesnel's work, it was usual for an opera to be heard as an 'afterpiece' to an evening's entertainment, which might consist of a play, a song and a dance or recitation, before the opera. Such was the case with *Colas et Colinette*, produced as an afterpiece to Molière's *Le médecin malgré lui*. Usually the operas had musical numbers alternating with spoken dialogue, as in the English ballad opera or French *opéra comique*. From about the 1790s to 1830, the repertory favourites were Arnold, Arne, Dibdin, Duni, Linley, Shield and Storace. There was also the occasional work by Paisiello or Grétry, who was noticeably more familiar to Quesnel than Mozart. The earliest operas performed in Toronto were C. E. Horn's *The Devil's Bridge*, Coleman's *The Mountaineers* and Stephen Storace's afterpiece *No Song, No Supper*, in 1825.

The political unrest and cholera epidemics of the 1830s provided one of the interruptions in operatic performance in the 19th century. The history of opera in Canada during this period, however, is linked with the improvements in transport, especially the railways. The revival of opera in the 1840s and 50s was due to the appearances of small visiting companies who expanded the repertory to include more exacting works, by Auber, Bellini, Boieldieu, Donizetti, Rossini and Verdi. Gradually, international vocal stars such as John Braham, Jenny Lind, Henriette Sontag and Adelina Patti came to visit Canadian cities, particularly Montreal, Quebec and Toronto, to give recitals of operatic excerpts. Numerous itinerant companies from the USA led by American manager-entrepreneurs and prima donnas visited Montreal and Toronto. One such prima donna was the expatriate Canadian soprano Emma Albani, who crossed Canada and the USA by rail between 1889 and 1891, appearing in Quebec City, Ottawa, Toronto, Hamilton and London in 1889.

By the turn of the century, the repertory included Meyerbeer, Wagner, Gounod and Puccini. The absence of Mozart is still noticeable. During the 1850s, 60s and 70s, indigenous operatic production was aided by the formation of resident opera associations in Montreal and Toronto. These included the Holman English Opera Troupe and the Cooper English Opera Troupe, to be followed by the Société d'Opéra Français (1893–6) and the Montreal Opera Company (1910–13). But it remained the foreign companies that were responsible for most of the performances. Because of this, Montreal and Toronto had more opera than ever before. After World War I, Montreal was home to over 30 opera associations and Toronto to about a dozen. The Canadian Opera Company, known as the Opera Festival Association when it was founded in 1950, has continued to be the most successful and resilient. The Théâtre Lyrique de Nouvelle-France was founded in 1961, changed its name in 1966 to the Théâtre Lyrique de Québec and ceased activities in 1970. Quebec's co-operative company producing opera in Montreal and Quebec from 1971 to 1975, originally called L'Opéra de Québec, was resurrected as L'Opéra de Montréal in 1980. Canada's major opera companies spread across the country from Vancouver, Calgary, Edmonton, Winnipeg, Hamilton, Toronto, to Montreal and Quebec. The associations in Vancouver, Edmonton, Manitoba and Southern Alberta Opera (Calgary) amalgamated as Opera West in 1973.

The mainstays of operatic promotion in Canada have been the Canadian Broadcasting Corporation and Radio Canada. The radio programmes since the 1940s and 50s in addition to television transmissions of opera performances from 1953 onwards have established modern standards. The CBC Opera Company, active 1948–58, which grew out of the Opera School of the Royal Conservatory of Music in Toronto, was particularly influential and gave opportunities to many promising singers. The CBC has commissioned operas from Healey Willan, John Beckwith, Kelsey Jones, Ben McPeek, Murray Adaskin, Godfrey Ridout, Maurice Blackburn, Raymond Pannell, Robert Turner, István Anhalt and others. Radio Canada commissions include John Rea's *Le petit livre des 'Ravelet'*. Although the CBC has been the main disseminator of opera, various festivals such as the Stratford Festival, Guelph Spring Festival, Vancouver International Festival and (until 1983) Festival Ottawa have had an important impact on the growth of opera audiences and have introduced premières of new Canadian works. The Banff Centre School of Fine Arts and various university music departments, including the Opera Division at the University of Toronto, have not only trained singers but also put on productions of a wide variety of works including Canadian and world premières.

Due to heavy costs, opera companies rarely tour. The Metropolitan Opera of New York appeared from time to time in Montreal and Toronto between 1899 and 1952, when the regular Met spring tours started to include Toronto. Increasing costs brought these to an end in 1961 except for a one-week visit in 1984 to the Toronto International Festival. Several international companies (La Scala, the Royal Swedish Opera and the Vienna Staatsoper) performed in Montreal during Expo 67. The Canadian Opera Company no longer tours, its last important tour being to Washington, DC, in 1976 for the USA centennial celebration with Somers's *Louis Riel*. The Canadian Opera Company ensemble, its resident group of young singers, has since toured in its stead, taking productions to the east and west coasts as well as Ontario.

Canadian operatic composition has followed a rather spasmodic course from the première of Quesnel's *Colas et Colinette*. 19th-century works include Oscar Ferdinand Telgmann's *Leo, the Royal Cadet* (1889), Calixa Lavallée's three light operas of the 1870s and 80s, Charles A. E. Harriss's *Torquil* (1900) and Susie Frances Harrison's *Pipandor* of the late 1880s. Calixa Lavallée, who wrote the Canadian national anthem, composed four light operas between 1865 and 1886, using a genre little known in Canada at that time. His *The Widow* was performed in Hamilton in 1882. There have been more Canadian operas written in the 20th century, stimulated largely, since the 1940s, by the CBC, which commissioned many one-act operas in the 1950s and 60s. A number of composers, including for example Eugène Lapierre in the 1940s and Barbara Pentland in the 1950s, have been inspired to use Canadian subjects. The most successful among them is Harry Somers, whose three-act *Louis Riel* (1967) was commissioned by the Canadian Opera Company for Canada's Centennial Year. Somers must be regarded as Canada's most successful opera composer. During the 1960s and 70s short operas for small orchestra were increasingly popular with composers, including Gabriel Charpentier, Quenten Doolittle, Charles Wilson, Tibor Polgar, Norman Symonds, Paul McIntyre and Barrie Cabena as well as those already noted. Large-scale operas have become increasingly rare in the last two decades because of production costs, though Wilson's *Heloise and Abelard*, commissioned by the Canadian Opera Company in 1973, is a notable exception. Derek Healey's *Seabird Island*, given by the Guelph Spring Festival in 1977, uses full orchestra except in that the string parts are for string quartet and double bass. One of the most individual voices is that of R. Murray Schafer, whose *Ra*, commissioned by the Toronto Comus Music Theatre in 1983, is an experimental musico-dramatic work of vast dimensions, using Schafer's idea of the audience as pilgrims as well as observers. Celebrations such as those for the Canadian centennial year (1967) or the International Year of Canadian Music (1986) have stimulated new commissions and performances; among the events of 1986 István Anhalt's *Winthrop* for six soloists and two choirs and the Kitchener Waterloo SO stands out.

Works of the 1980s include chamber operas and multimedia events which incorporate musical theatre (and, often, dance). Composers include Ruth Watson Henderson, Henry Kucharzyk and Elizabeth Raum, in addition to Schafer. Canadian contributions to opera reflect the individuality of the country's composers and the diversity of their inspiration, whether it be Rudolf Komorous in western Canada, Bengt Hambraeus in Montreal or the late Claude Vivier. Composers rarely adhere to any particular school or have a distinctly Canadian or Québecois sound, though it is possible to distinguish some Quebec composers by their coloured sonorities and dense textures as opposed to the more astringent music of many Anglo-Canadian composers.

For further information on operatic life in the country's principal centres, *see* BANFF; EDMONTON; GUELPH; MONTREAL; OTTAWA; QUEBEC; TORONTO; VANCOUVER; and WINNIPEG.

*

H. Charlesworth: 'Grand Opera in Canada', *Canadian Courier* (12 Oct 1912) [issue on music in Canada]
Arts and Letters Club [compiler]: *The Year Book of Canadian Art 1913* (Toronto, 1913)
A. Walter: 'The Present State of Opera in Canada', *Royal Conservatory of Music of Toronto Monthly Bulletin* (Feb 1950)
J. Beraud: *350 Ans de théâtre au Canada français* (Montreal, 1958)
H. Kallmann: *A History of Music in Canada 1534–1914* (Toronto, 1960–69)
——: 'History of Opera in Canada', *OC*, v/3 (1964), 10–12, 78
'Salute to Canada', *ON*, xxxi/26 (1966–7) [Canadian issue]
C. Morey: 'Pre-Confederation Opera in Toronto', *OC*, x/3 (1969), 13–15
R. Mercer: 'A 150-Year History', OC, xiv/3 (1973), 43–61
W. Amtmann: *Music in Canada 1600–1800* (Montreal, 1975, enlarged, as *La musique au Québec 1600–1875*, 1976)
Q. Eaton: *Opera Caravan: Adventures of the Metropolitan Opera on Tour 1883–1956* (New York, 1978)
G. Potvin: 'A Short History of Opera in Canada', *Musicanada*, (1980), no.44, pp.4–6
C. A. Lussier: 'L'Opéra a-t-il un avenir?' *OC*, xxii/1 (1981), 10–13
D. R. Cooper: *Opera in Montreal and Toronto: a Study of Performance Traditions and Repertoire 1783–1980* (diss., U. of Toronto, 1984)
E. Keillor: '1986: The International Year of Canadian Music', *Queen's Quarterly*, xcvi (1987), 173–86 GAYNOR G. JONES

Canadian Opera Company. Company formed during the 1950s, based in TORONTO.

Canary Islands. Group of islands off the coast of northwest Africa. For a discussion of operatic activity *see* LAS PALMAS and SANTA CRUZ DE TENERIFE.

Canberra. Capital of Australia. It was founded in 1927 as a neutral answer to the rivalry between Sydney and Melbourne. Touring productions of the Australian Opera (founded 1956) are now less frequent in Canberra than in earlier years for economic reasons. Local amateur and semi-amateur activity in the later 1960s led to the founding in 1970 of the Canberra Opera Society, which changed its name to Canberra Opera in 1975 and moved from the Playhouse, the smaller of the two auditoriums in the Canberra theatre complex, to the main theatre at the same time. Productions, which were staged occasionally and for short runs, included *The Turn of the Screw* (1972), *L'elisir d'amore* (1973), *Die lustigen Weiber von Windsor* (1974), *La traviata* and *Madama Butterfly* (both 1975) and *The Pilgrim's Progress* (1980), and a large-scale open-air *Aida* (1983) performed at a major sports ground. Canberra Opera was forced to close down after a scandal about the disappearance of its funds (1983–4), and its successor, Opera ACT (Australian Capital Territory), has continued to present occasional productions since the 1984–5 season, including *Il barbiere di Siviglia* (1990). Operas have also been staged from time to time on the initiative of professionally experienced staff of the Canberra School of Music. ROGER COVELL

Candeille, (Amélie-) [Emilie] **Julie** [Simons, Julie] (*b* Paris, 31 July 1767; *d* Paris, 4 Feb 1834). French singer, actress, composer and playwright. The daughter of Pierre Joseph Candeille, she was primarily educated by her father and was a 'joli monstre de talents' (E. de Goncourt and J. de Goncourt, 353). By 1780 she had already appeared in public as a pianist and composer. In 1782 she sang the title role in Gluck's *Iphigénie en Aulide*, and a year later Sangaride in Piccinni's *Atys*. In 1785 she became an actress at the Comédie-Française, playing Hermione in Racine's *Andromaque* and Roxane in his *Bajazet*. Her greatest success was as singer and actress in *Catherine, ou La belle fermière*, a *comédie en prose, mêlée de chant* created in Paris at the Théâtre de la République on 27 November 1792; it received 154 consecutive performances and was revived many times over the next 35 years. She had written both the text and the three songs (Paris, 1793). According to Jourdin, the plot was based on Marmontel's *La bergère des Alpes*. Subsequent comedies, partly interspersed with songs, were failures: *Bathilde, ou Le duc* (République, 16 September 1793), *Le commissionnaire* (1794), *La bayadère, ou Le Français à Surate* (24 February 1795) and *Louise, ou La réconciliation* (14 December 1808). Musically, her most important work for the stage was the two-act *opéra comique Ida, ou L'orpheline de Berlin*, given at the Salle Feydeau on 15 May 1807. According to Fétis, the work was hissed, and performed only five or six times. Candeille (married to Jean Simons, 1798–1821) also wrote six novels, partly on historical subjects, and composed instrumental music mostly for the piano. For Fétis she had 'la carrière d'une femme qui par ses talents, aurait pu en espérer une meilleure'.

*

ES (R. Averini and A. Sorel-Nitzberg); *FétisB*
A. J. Candeille: *Notice biographique sur Anne-Louise Girodet et Amélie-Julie Candeille, pour mettre en tête de leur correspondance secrète* (MS, *F-Pn*)
E. de Goncourt and J. de Goncourt: *Histoire de la Société Française pendant le Directoire* (Paris, 1855)
A. Pougin: 'Une charmeuse: Julie Candeille', *Le ménestrel*, xlix (1883), 356, 365, 372, 380, 388, 403, 413
C. Jourdin: *Essai historique sur Estaires ... augmenté d'une étude sur la famille des musiciens estairois Candeille* (Paris, 1958)
MICHAEL FEND

Candeille, Pierre Joseph (*b* Estaires, 8 Dec 1744; *d* Chantilly, 24 April 1827). French composer, father of Julie Candeille. He was educated at St Pierre, Lille. He joined the chorus of the Paris Opéra as a *basse-taille* in 1767, and that of the Concert Spirituel in 1769, holding both places until 1781. From 1777 Candeille had ballets and divertissements performed at various theatres including that of the Duke of Orléans, the Comédie Française and the Opéra. Between 1784 and 1800 he devoted himself almost entirely to composition, rejoining the Opéra as choirmaster (1800–02, 1804–5) before retiring to Chantilly. Candeille's first major stage work was *Laure et Pétrarque* (1778), which failed partly because of Moline's text. Of his operas only *Castor et Pollux*, which received 130 performances between 1791 and 1800, achieved real success. In it Candeille used a few selected passages from Rameau's original, rescoring it to provide some consistency of texture with his own, far larger, contribution. At a time when heroic opera was hardly fashionable, its success was outstanding.

Candeille was an eclectic composer who conformed easily to prevailing fashions, and showed more dramatic and scenic sense than musical originality. He drew his operas from mythical, historical, exotic, revolutionary (*Brutus*) and contemporary subjects; but even the *Marseillaise* could not rescue *L'apothéose de*

Beaurepaire, which was at least performed, if only twice. Usually his operas passed the preliminary stage of acceptance but were rejected after the music had been written because of their poor librettos; Candeille's extensive revisions bore no fruit. One of his few major works to be performed, *Pizarre*, was accepted three years before its first presentation in 1785. It is a spectacular and rather cumbersome opera, more effective in scenes, choruses and dances than in formal arias. The attractive instrumentation includes use of castanets for the Spaniards, and of two horns in different keys (Act 4). The impressive dream narration of Act 1 was probably modelled on that of Gluck's *Iphigénie en Tauride*. The recitative was considered dull, however, and *Pizarre* had only nine performances.

Candeille also composed religious music and four symphonies.

first performed in Paris unless otherwise stated

Les saturnales, ou Tibulle et Délie (ballet entrée, L. Fuzelier), Duc d'Orléans, 1777 [new music to a ballet by C. de Blamont]

Les curieux indiscrets (divertissement, J.-G. Noverre), Comédie Française, 1778

Les deux comtesses (divertissement, Noverre), Comédie Française, 1778

La Provençale (ballet entrée, 1, J. de La Font), Opéra, 8 Nov 1778, *F-Po* [new vocal music to an opera by J. J. Mouret]

Laure et Pétrarque (pastorale-héroïque, 1, P. L. Moline), Marly, Royal, 1778; rev. version, Opéra, 1780, *Po*

Pizarre, ou La conquête du Pérou (tragédie lyrique, 5, C. P. Duplessis, after Voltaire: *Alzire, ou Les américains*), Opéra, 3 May 1785; rev. version, 1791, *Po*, excerpts pubd

Castor et Pollux (opéra, 5, P. J. J. Bernard), Opéra, 14 June 1791, *Po*, excerpt (Paris, n.d.) [rev. of Rameau's opera]

La patrie reconnaissante, ou L'apothéose de Beaurepaire (opéra, 1, [?J.-J.] Lebouef), Opéra, 3 Feb 1793, *Po*

Unperf.: Les fêtes lupercales, 1777 (pastorale-héroïque); L'Amour et Psyché, Bacchus et Erigone, 1780 (opéra) [rev. of Acts 2–3 of Mondonville: Fêtes de Paphos]; Thémire, *c*1781 (opéra); Lausus et Lydie, 1786 (opéra); Les jeux olympiques, 1788 (opéra); Ladislas et Adélaide, 1791 (opéra); Roxane et Statira, ou Les veuves d'Alexandre, *c*1792 (tragédie lyrique); Brutus, 1793 (opéra); Danaé, *c*1796 (opéra); Tithon et l'Aurore, *c*1796 (opéra); Ragonde, *c*1798 (pastorale-héroïque); Pithys (pastorale-héroïque); other airs de ballet

*

ES (A. Sorel-Nitzburg)

F. J. Fétis: Obituary, *Revue musicale*, ii/April (1827), 310–11

A. Rabbe, C. A. Vieilh de Boisjolin and Saint-Preuve, eds.: *Biographie universelle et portative des contemporains* (Paris, 1830, 2/1834)

T. de Lajarte: *Bibliothèque musicale de théâtre de l'Opéra* (Paris, 1878)

L. Aillaud: 'Julie Candeille', *Chronique mondaine, littéraire et artistique* (Nîmes, 27 Oct 1923–12 Jan 1924) [incl. excerpts from A. J. Candeille's unpubd memoirs]

M. Pincherle: *Musiciens peints par eux-mêmes* (Paris, 1939)

JULIAN RUSHTON

Candi, Giovanni Pietro (*b* Padua; *fl* 1703). Italian librettist. He is known to have written only one libretto, *Gli amanti generosi* (Vinaccesi, 1703). He originally conceived the work as a spoken tragedy and adapted it for the operatic stage later, lightening the serious tone and inserting arias, often outside their proper niche. Although two characters (Artaxerxes I and his son Darius II) are historical, the plot is fictional. The castrato Nicolo Grimaldi ('Nicolini'), who sang Hydaspes in all restagings of the work, probably witnessed the original production. G. Convò and Stampiglia revised *Gli amanti generosi* for the Teatro S Bartolomeo, Naples, in 1705, with music by Francesco Mancini, and Nicolini revised this setting for a production in 1710 at the Haymarket, London, as *Idaspe fedele* or *Hydaspes*. The work was last performed in 1730 as *Idaspe* at the Teatro S Giovanni Grisostomo with music by Riccardo Broschi.

Giovanni Pietro should not be confused with Giovanni Battista [Giambattista] Candi, also from Padua, who may have been his brother. He likewise wrote only one libretto, as it happens, for the same Venetian theatre: *Il tradimento premiato* (favola pastorale, 3, Polani; S Angelo, 3 November 1709).

*

AllacciD; *LS*

G. Bonlini: *Le glorie della poesia e della musica* (Venice, 1730)

A. Groppo: *Catalogo di tutti i drammi per musica recitati ne' teatri di Venezia* (Venice, 1745)

Herrn Zacharias Conrad von Uffenbachs merkwürdige Reisen (Ulm and Memmingen, 1753–4); trans. and ed. W. H. Quarrell and M. Mare as *London in 1710* (London, 1934)

E. Selfridge-Field: *Pallade veneta: Writings on Music in Venetian Society, 1650–1750* (Venice, 1985)

C. Sartori: *I libretti italiani a stampa dalle origini al 1800* (Cuneo, 1990–)

HARRIS S. SAUNDERS

Candide. Comic operetta in two acts by LEONARD BERNSTEIN to a libretto by Lillian Hellman after VOLTAIRE, with lyrics by Richard Wilbur, John Latouche, Dorothy Parker, Hellman and Bernstein, orchestrated by Bernstein and Hershy Kay; Boston, 29 October 1956 (New York, Martin Beck Theatre, 1 December 1956; revised in one act to a libretto by HUGH CALLINGHAM WHEELER, with lyrics by Wilbur, Latouche, Bernstein and STEPHEN SONDHEIM, orchestrated by Kay, Brooklyn, New York, Chelsea Theater Center, 20 December 1973).

Candide (tenor), a Westphalian youth who believes fervently in the teaching of his tutor, Pangloss (baritone), that everything that happens must be for the best, plunges into travel and experiences an endless series of disasters, including the apparent death of the woman he loves, Cunegonde (soprano), and the execution of Pangloss in the Spanish Inquisition. Candide's travels take him to the New World in the company of an Old Lady (mezzo-soprano) and the miraculously saved Cunegonde, to the fabled land of Eldorado, back to Europe surviving a shipwreck and eventually back to Westphalia. Here Candide finally repudiates Pangloss's philosophy and resolves to try and build a good, honest life for himself and his companions.

This general description applies to all versions of *Candide*, although the details vary enormously in the several revisions that were undertaken. Most notable of these is the version staged by Harold Prince in 1973, to a new libretto by Hugh Wheeler (Hellman having withdrawn permission to use her words). Wheeler provided a new selection of scenes, some from Voltaire and others newly invented. Martin, a pessimistic counterpart to Pangloss played by the same actor, disappeared in this version, but in compensation the Pangloss also played Voltaire as narrator, as well as the Latin American Governor. The maid Paquette (mezzo-soprano) and Cunegonde's brother Maximilian (baritone), minor parts in the first version, became moderately important in the new one. The zany vaudeville atmosphere and irreverent tone of this production proved far more acceptable to audiences than the statelier format of the original; unfortunately, the score itself suffered severely, with five songs omitted and the rest rescored for a tiny ensemble (some new songs were added as well). A version made for the New York City Opera (and recorded in slightly fuller form) attempted to restore the missing music from 1956 within Wheeler's framework. A 1988 Scottish Opera production (supervised, like the previous two editions, by John Mauceri) made in consultation with the composer returned for the most part to Hellman's sequence of scenes while retaining some of Wheeler's additions, with revisions in libretto and lyrics by John Wells. A 1989 concert performance conducted by Bernstein in London (and the recording made at that time) used this edition as the 'final revised version', the last form of the work to which he gave his approval. To the 1956 score, it adds material from the 1973 edition, music discarded before the initial production, and numbers written for revivals in 1958 and 1971.

The more familiar excerpts from the work remain common to all versions: the sparkling overture, no mere potpourri but a sonata form concluding with a Rossinian crescendo, and Cunegonde's aria 'Glitter and Be Gay', a caricature of coloratura jewel songs. Throughout the score, a sprightly manner prevails, with pastiche styles (waltz, schottische, tango, gavotte) clearly labelled. The work also contains a unifying theme, associated primarily with Candide's optimism: an octave rise followed by two falling steps. Variants among the several versions are numerous and complex; alternative lyrics exist for many numbers, and some of the original music has been used elsewhere. One early idea was to end the opera with a wedding scene, a love duet followed by a chorale prelude on its theme; when this plan was discarded, the duet was used as 'One Hand, One Heart' in *West Side Story*. Not only delightful as music, and for the most part blessed with exceptional lyrics, *Candide* serves the needs of Voltaire's narrative in the way it both sends up the operatic framework and finds genuine humanity and power in it.

JON ALAN CONRAD

Čangalović [Changalovitch, Changalovich], **Miroslav** (*b* Glamoč, 3 March 1921).Yugoslav bass. He was trained in Belgrade (début in 1946 as Pimen in *Boris Godunov*), and remained there throughout his career. His repertory included Sarastro and Leporello, Philip II and Méphistophélès in *Faust*; he also specialized in the Russian operas, singing Boris in Basle, Zürich and Geneva. Čangalović scored a personal success as Don Quichotte (Massenet) at the opening of the Théâtre des Nations in Paris in 1957. He also sang in Germany, Poland, Italy and Egypt, and at the Edinburgh Festival of 1962. Many of his principal roles can be heard on the Belgrade company's recordings, made mostly in the 1950s. If not notable for refinement, they nevertheless present a powerful, full-bodied voice and sincere characterization.

J. B. STEANE

Caniglia, Maria (*b* Naples, 5 May 1905; *d* Rome, 16 April 1979). Italian soprano. She studied at the Conservatory S Pietro a Maiella, Naples, and made her début at Turin in 1930 as Chrysothemis in *Elektra*. That year she made her first appearance at La Scala as Maria in Pizzetti's *Lo straniero*; she sang there regularly until 1943, and again from 1948 to 1951. She appeared at Covent Garden in 1937, 1939 and, with the Scala company, 1950; she sang at the Metropolitan during the 1938–9 season. Among the roles she created were Manuela in Montemezzi's *La notte di Zoraima* (1931, Milan), Roxane in Alfano's *Cyrano de Bergerac* (1936, Rome) and the title role in Respighi's *Lucrezia* (1937, Milan).

Caniglia sang most of Verdi's lyric-dramatic soprano roles, from Leonora in his first opera, *Oberto*, produced during the Verdi year (1951) at La Scala, to Alice in *Falstaff* (1935, Salzburg). She was much admired as Tosca, Adriana Lecouvreur and Fedora. Although by no means a perfect singer or a great actress, she brought a warm human quality and dramatic excitement to her performances.

GV (R. Celletti; R. Vegeto)

G. Lauri-Volpi: 'Le grandi voci della lirica contemporanea: Maria Caniglia', *Musica e dischi*, no.278 (1969), p.38

HAROLD ROSENTHAL/R

Cannabich, (Johann) Christian (Innocenz Bonaventura) (*b* Mannheim, bap. 28 Dec 1731; *d* Frankfurt, 20 Jan 1798). German composer. He was a pupil of Johann Stamitz and became a violinist in the Mannheim orchestra at the age of 12. The Elector Carl Theodor sent him to study in Italy, and in autumn 1750, at the earliest, he began tuition with Jommelli in Rome, where he remained until July 1753. Cannabich then accompanied his teacher to Stuttgart, but returned to Italy (Milan) in 1754. By 1758 he had succeeded Stamitz in Mannheim. In the following years he brought about a flowering of dramatic ballet at the court, composing more than 30 works for performance between the acts of operas (some were published in versions for keyboard and string quartet). He is credited with a Singspiel, *Azakia* (1778, Mannheim; lib. *D-MHrm*, *US-Wc*), although no music survives and no performances are documented, and a 'musikalische Declamation', *Electra* (Mannheim, Nationaltheater, 4 Sept 1781; *D-DS*/ *R*1986: GOB, x), to a libretto by Wolfgang Heribert von Dalberg. This monodrama follows in the tradition of the works of Benda and marks, with works by Winter, Vogler and Danzi, the summit of the melodrama in south and west Germany.

In 1774 Cannabich became sole conductor and trainer of the Mannheim orchestra. In 1778 he moved with the court to Munich. His *galant*, melodious style found fitting expression in the ballet and symphony.

BurneyGN

F. Walter: *Geschichte des Theaters und der Musik am kurpfälzischen Hofe* (Leipzig, 1898)

——: *Archiv und Bibliothek des Grossherzoglichen Hof- und Nationaltheaters in Mannheim 1779–1839* (Leipzig, 1899)

R. Kloiber: *Die dramatische Ballette von Christian Cannabich* (Munich, 1928)

T. Bauman: Introduction to C. Cannabich: *Electra*, GOB, x (1986)

PAUL CORNEILSON, ROLAND WÜRTZ

Canne-Meijer, Cora (*b* Amsterdam, 11 Aug 1929). Dutch mezzo-soprano. She studied with Jan Keizer, and then in Vienna and Paris. In 1951 she joined the Netherlands Opera, playing the title role in Ambroise Thomas' *Mignon*, Cherubino (which she sang at Glyndebourne in 1956), Dorabella, Rosina, Concepcion, Carmela, La Frugola, Preziosilla, Clairon, the Composer and Baba the Turk; she remained there for 25 years. She has appeared at Salzburg (Haydn's *Il mondo della luna*, 1959) and Marseilles – in the French première of Bennett's *The Mines of Sulphur* (1968) and in the title role of Louis Sauger's *Maria Pineda* at its première (1970). She sang Isolier in the Glyndebourne recording of *Le comte Ory*. Her warm, flexible voice was not large but well projected, and her musicianship and dramatic ability were especially valuable in modern roles.

TRUUS DE LEUR, ELIZABETH FORBES

Cannetti, Linda (*b* nr Verona, 8 Nov 1878; *d* Milan, 14 March 1960). Italian soprano. She studied with Melchiorre Vidal in Vienna and made her début at Fossombrone in *Faust* in 1899. Later that year she sang in *Lohengrin* with the tenor Francesco Bravi, whom she subsequently married. His early death brought her career to a temporary halt, but on its resumption in 1909 she achieved her greatest success to date as Chrysothemis in the Italian première of *Elektra*, at La Scala. In 1913 she appeared in another Strauss première in Italy, that of *Feuersnot*, and at Turin sang the title role in the world première of Zandonai's *Francesca da Rimini* (1914). Other notable events included commemorative performances of Boito's *Mefistofele* under Toscanini and a personal triumph in Buenos Aires in Montemezzi's *L'amore dei tre re*. She retired in 1928. Her recordings show warmth of voice and emotion, with a quick, somewhat uneven vibrato, probably more acceptable then than it is now. J. B. STEANE

Cannobiana [Canobbiana]. Theatre in MILAN, inaugurated in 1779. In 1894 it was renamed the Teatro Lirico Internazionale, and later known as the Teatro Lirico.

Canobbio, Carlo (*b* ?Venice, 1741; *d* St Petersburg, 23 Feb/7 March 1822). Italian composer. After working for a while in Spain he returned to Italy, where he led the orchestra at the Teatro S Samuele in Venice (1773–5). From 1779 to 1795 he served at the Imperial Theatres in St Petersburg, combining his activities as a composer with duties as first violin in the orchestra (from 1789) and deputy to Paisiello, the director of the Italian opera. In 1783–5 he again travelled in Italy, and from 1796 led the performances of the Astarita company in Russia. He is best known for his contribution to the 'historical spectacle' *Nachal'noye upravleniye Olega* ('The Early Reign of Oleg', 5, Catherine II; St Petersburg, Hermitage, 15/26 Oct 1790, score pubd St Petersburg, 1791), in which he collaborated with V. A. Pashkevich and Sarti. He also wrote a *dramma giocoso, L'amore artigiano* (3, C. Goldoni, St Petersburg, 1785), as well as ballets and instrumental music. GEOFFREY NORRIS

Canon. The device of canon – where one voice imitates another, in some more or less exact way – is relatively unusual in opera. Many duets of the Baroque period begin canonically, or embody short examples of canonic writing. A more extended use of canon established itself in operatic ensembles towards the end of the 18th century, chiefly in Vienna, whence it passed during the following century to Italy, where it was usually termed 'falso canone', since it never proceeds beyond the entry of the last voice.

The device was much favoured by Vicente Martín y Soler, who included three-voice canons in *In amor ci vuol destrezza* (1784, Venice) and in his Viennese operas *Una cosa rara* (1786) and *L'arbore di Diana* (1787). His example was followed by Storace in *Gli equivoci* (1786) and by Salieri in *La cifra* (1789) – which features a canon 9 in 3 – and *Falstaff* (1799). In Mozart's *Così fan tutte* (1790) the wedding toast in the Act 2 finale is canonic, but as the opening strain lies at an unsuitable pitch for the fourth voice, the singer enters with a new countersubject that expresses his anger at the situation. Other instances are to be found in Paer's *Camilla* (1799), Beethoven's *Fidelio* (1805, 'Mir ist so wunderbar', the most famous example), Cherubini's *Faniska* (1806), Spohr's *Alruna* (composed 1808) and C. Kreutzer's *Der Taucher* (1813).

In later Italian opera the device is often used for the slow movement of an ensemble, whether the cantabile of a trio, quartet or quintet or the *pezzo concertato* of a finale. A familiar case is 'Freddo ed immobile' from the Act 1 finale of Rossini's *Il barbiere di Siviglia* (1816); and there is a particularly elaborate specimen in the *quintetto dell'introduzione* 'Mi manca la voce' from his *Mosè in Egitto* (1818), as also in the canon 'Di gioia, di pace' from Meyerbeer's *Emma di Resburgo* (1819). Examples from Mercadante include the terzettino 'Dopo due lustri, ahi, misero' from *Caritea, regina di Spagna* (1826). With Bellini the contrapuntal aspect is always subordinated to the melodic, as in 'Oh di qual sei tu vittima' from the Act 1 finale of *Norma* (1831), where the continuations amount to no more than harmony notes. In his early operas Verdi twice uses the 'falso canone': in the trio 'Su quella fronte impresa' in *Oberto, conte di San Bonifacio* (1839) and in the Act 2 finale of *Nabucco* (1842), where the final entry is assigned to the chorus. Imitative writing also characterizes the priests in *Aida* (1871), while the opening dialogue between Radames and Ramfis is delivered over a loose three-part canon played by divided cellos. Canonic technique is present in the preghiera from Puccini's *Le villi* (1884). Britten's *Peter Grimes* (1945) contains a canon in the stylized form of a popular round ('Old Joe has gone fishing').

*

D. Link: 'The Viennese Operatic Canon and Mozart's "Così fan tutte"', *Mitteilungen der Internationalen Stiftung Mozarteum*, xxxviii (1990), 111–21 JULIAN BUDDEN, STANLEY SADIE

Caños del Peral. Theatre in Madrid, open to opera performances from 1716; it closed in 1810 and was demolished in 1817, the site later being used for the Teatro Real (inaugurated 1850). *See* MADRID, §§2, 3.

Cantabile (It.: 'singable'). As an adjective, it is used for a line to be performed in a singing style (particularly of instrumental music). It was used as a noun by 19th-century Italian composers to denote the first, slow movement of a double aria (*see* ARIA and CAVATINA). Occasionally it was applied to a single movement entrusted to a secondary singer, e.g. 'Infelice, e tuo credevi' in Verdi's *Ernani* (1844), before the addition of a cabaletta ('Infin che un brando vindice') conferred principal status on the singer's role. JULIAN BUDDEN

Cantatrici villane, Le ('The Country Singers'). *Commedia per musica* in two acts by VALENTINO FIORAVANTI to a libretto by GIUSEPPE PALOMBA; Naples, Teatro dei Fiorentini, January 1799.

Three local women live on the village square: Rosa, Agata (who runs an inn) and Giannetta (all sopranos). A newcomer, Don Bucefalo Zibaldone (*buffo* bass), hears them singing; a pompous musician, he offers to teach them. Rosa (whose husband has fled the country because of an illegal duel and is believed dead) welcomes the lessons, to be given at her home; this annoys the other ladies. The stupid Don Marco Mbomma (*buffo* bass), a wealthy local dilettante suffering from gout, becomes a rival for Rosa's affections. Into the scene of music lessons enters Carlino (tenor), Rosa's husband, now bearded and masquerading for safety's sake as a soldier. He seeks his wife and, while unrecognized, is furious to discover her enjoying the attentions of others. In the Act 1 finale he invades Rosa's house, forcing the two frightened gentlemen to hide in a giant cask. All is lost when the other ladies maliciously ask Rosa where the men are.

Act 2 is concerned with putting on an opera (Metastasio's *Ezio*) with Don Marco as the impresario. There are the usual backstage jokes of rehearsal, poor musicians and so on; in addition, Carlino's armed presence creates havoc. Soldiers arrive to subdue him; he reveals himself to Rosa and all is forgiven.

The libretto of *Le cantatrici villane* was frequently revised. In a version by G. M. Foppa as *Le virtuose ridicole* (1801, Venice), the village of Casoria became Frascati, and one of the minor characters, the baker woman Nunziella, was turned into Giansimone, a male waiter working for Agata. Two performances (as *Die Sängerinnen auf dem Lande*) were given in Weimar on 10 and 13 April 1813 under the direction of Goethe. A modern edition of 1951 cuts some of the first act and introduces a chorus. MARVIN TARTAK

Cantelli, Guido (*b* Novara, 27 April 1920; *d* Paris, 24 Nov 1956). Italian conductor. He studied at the Milan Conservatory and became conductor and artistic director at the Teatro Coccia, Novara, in 1943. His concert work with the orchestra of La Scala was warmly praised by Toscanini, for he was a conductor of characteristic italianate verve, tempered by a sensibility to expressive nuance and balance of timbre. He had just begun to interest himself in opera in 1956 when he produced and conducted *Così fan tutte* at the Piccola Scala. His appointment as principal conductor at La Scala from 1957 was announced a few days before he was killed in an air accident. NOËL GOODWIN

Cantelo, April (Rosemary) (*b* Purbrook, Hants., 2 April 1928). English soprano. She studied in London and, after singing in the Glyndebourne chorus, made her début in 1950 with the company at Edinburgh as Barbarina and Echo. At Glyndebourne she also sang Blonde (1953) and Marzelline (1963). With the English Opera Group she created Helena in Britten's *A Midsummer Night's Dream* (1960) and sang Emmeline in Purcell's *King Arthur* (1970). In Williamson's operas she created Beatrice (*Our Man in Havana*, 1963), Swallow (*The Happy Prince*, 1965), Ann (*Julius Caesar Jones*, 1966) and Berthe (*The Violins of St Jacques*, 1966). She was a very gifted singing actress, demonstrating her skill as Manon Lescaut in Henze's *Boulevard Solitude*, and Jenny in Weill's *Aufstieg und Fall der Stadt Mahagonny* (both first British productions). She directed a production of Purcell's *The Fairy-Queen* in New Zealand in 1972. Her voice was a pure, clear lyrical soprano, not large, but capable of flexibility and variety of expression. ALAN BLYTH

Canteloube (de Malaret), (Marie) Joseph (*b* Annonay, 21 Oct 1879; *d* Paris, 4 Nov 1957). French composer. Born into an old Auvergnois family, he studied with d'Indy at the Schola Cantorum from 1901 and soon established himself as a composer of nature music, music descriptive of the landscape of his native region. From about the turn of the century he sought stimulus in folksong, and for the rest of his life he travelled through France, collecting songs and making arrangements of them, some of which have proved enduringly popular. His original works by contrast have been neglected; they include two operas. His first was *Le mas* (the Provençal word for a farmstead), composed 1910–13 (to his own libretto), which won the lucrative Prix Heugel in 1925. It evidently impressed the jury more for its musical than for its theatrical potential and it was only after pressure from Canteloube's publishers that it was reluctantly accepted for performance at the Opéra in 1929 (27 March). It was never revived and the composer's second opera *Vercingétorix*, dealing with Caesar's victory over Gaul (libretto by E. Clémental and J. Louwyck; in 4 acts), suffered the same fate. Given its first performance on 22 June 1933, at the Opéra, it was criticized for its lack of theatricality, despite a substantial presence of supportive compatriots from the Auvergne. This was the first opera to use ondes martenot in the orchestra.

*

L. G. Boursiac: *Canteloube* (Toulouse, 1941)

P. Bertrand: *Le monde de la musique* (Geneva, 1947)

F. Cougnaud-Reginel: *Joseph Canteloube: chantre de la terre 1879–1957* (Béziers, 1988) RICHARD LANGHAM SMITH

Canterina, La ('The Singer'). *Intermezzo in musica* in two acts by JOSEPH HAYDN to a libretto, possibly by CARL FRIBERTH, after that of Piccinni's *L'Origille* (1760) with additions (nos. 2 and 3) from Zeno's *Lucio Vero*; Pressburg (now Bratislava), 16 February 1767 (also given in 1766, possibly at Eisenstadt, before 11 September).

This intermezzo, clearly derived from the traditional italianate pattern, is Haydn's earliest extant comic opera. The plot is simple yet effective: Gasparina (soprano; sung by Maria Anna Weigl) and her pretended mother Apollonia (soprano; originally taken by Leopold Dichtler) live in the house of the *maestro di cappella* Don Pelagio (tenor; sung by Carl Friberth), who gives the girl singing lessons and hopes to persuade her to marry him. She however prefers the attentions of the wealthy, young Don Ettore (soprano; written for Barbara Dichtler), who after various setbacks secures her hand.

Haydn's work consists of two arias for the *maestro di cappella* and one each for Apollonia and Gasparina, recitatives both simple and accompanied, at times embodied in the lyrical numbers, and two quartet finales, the second a substantial piece in three sections. The scoring is restricted – pairs of oboes (replaced in one number by flutes and in another by english horns), horns and strings – but the music is never less than delightful. In Don Pelagio's accompanied recitative and aria, 'Io sposar l'empio tiranno?', Haydn amusingly parodies *opera seria* practice (perhaps the taxing horn-writing was inspired by the 12-times-repeated invocation, 'misero cor'), while in Gasparina's C minor aria, 'Non v'è chi mi aiuta', the music conveys a tension and passion that again wittily suggest a potentially tragic situation. PETER BRANSCOMBE

Canto fiorito (It.: 'flowery song'). A style of vocal writing characterized by abundant melismatic ornamentation and chiefly associated with Rossini and his followers during the 1820s, e.g. 'Bel raggio lusinghier' (*Semiramide*, Rossini, 1823). Examples can be found in the early works of Donizetti and Mercadante. From 1830, under the influence of Bellini, there was a steady move towards a more syllabic manner of verse-setting in which moments of *fioritura* take on a more expressive, less hedonistic character. Later in the century 'canto fiorito' is found only as parody, as in 'Ah fiera scadenza' (*La bohème*, Leoncavallo, 1897). JULIAN BUDDEN

Canuti, Giovanni Antonio (*b* Lucca, *c*1680; *d* Lucca, April 1739). Italian composer. He was a priest and a *maestro di cappella* in Lucca. He composed one opera, *Rodelinda*, to a text by Antonio Salvi, and at least five serenatas for the *Tasche* (three days of elections for the town magistrates), all performed in Lucca. Although these works are lost, his surviving cantatas and oratorios show him as an able contemporary of Alessandro Scarlatti and Giovanni Bononcini.

serenatas for the Tasche unless otherwise stated; all performed in Lucca

Muzio Scevola, 13 Dec 1723
Rodelinda (dm, 3, A. Salvi), Pubblico, carn. 1724
Codro re d'Atene (N. de' Nobili), 9 Dec 1726
Timoleonte cittadino di Corinto (S. Mansi), 12 Dec 1729
Dione Siracusano (D. Sesti), 11 Dec 1732
Lucio Giunio Bruto, primo console di Roma (?F. Marchini), 12 Dec 1735

*

G. Biagi-Ravenni and C. Gianturco: 'The *Tasche* of Lucca: 150 Years of Political Serenatas', *PRMA*, cxi (1984–5), 45–65

CAROLYN GIANTURCO

Canzone (It.: 'song'). The Italian word for a poetic or lyric expression. It is used in opera primarily for items presented as songs sung outside the dramatic action, for example Count Almaviva's serenade 'Io son Lindoro' in Paisiello's *Il barbiere di Siviglia* (1782) or Cherubino's 'Voi, che sapete' in *Le nozze di Figaro* (1786) – although Mozart in fact called it simply 'arietta'. In some editions of *Don Giovanni* (1787) the serenade 'Deh vieni alla finestra' is described as a 'canzonetta'. Rossini used the term for 'Nessun maggior dolore' in *Otello* (1816); Verdi applied it to 'La donna è mobile' in *Rigoletto* (1851), two arias ('Di' tu se fedele' and 'Saper vorreste') in *Un ballo in maschera* (1859) and the Willow Song in *Otello* (1887).

Canzonetta. (It.). Diminutive of CANZONE.

Capdevielle, Pierre (*b* Paris, 1 Feb 1906; *d* Bordeaux, 9 July 1969). French composer. He studied at the Paris Conservatoire, where he later taught, and also benefited from private lessons from d'Indy and the guidance of Maurice Emmanuel. He worked for the RTF and was president of the French section of the ISCM (1948) and founder-president of the Centre de Documentation de Musique International (1949). He also worked as a conductor, and in 1961 was made a Chevalier of the Légion d'honneur. His works for the theatre include the *mythe lyrique Les amants captifs*, composed 1947–58 (2, P. Guth; Bordeaux, Grand, 20 May 1960), and the *tragédie lyrique Fille de l'homme*, composed 1960–66 (3, J. de Beer; ORTF, 9 Nov 1964; stage, Bordeaux, Grand, 1 Dec 1967). Capdevielle's music is the expression of a stormy, romantic temperament, moderated somewhat in the manner of Roussel. The characters of *Les amants captifs* are planets and mythical gods, while *Fille de l'homme*, set in Southern Italy during World War II, is the story of a girl ordered by a resistance leader to murder her lover, who is suspected of treachery; the drama of the plot is matched by tense harmonic language.

*

P. Landormy: *La musique française après Debussy* (Paris, 1943)
A. Machabey: *Portraits de trente musiciens français* (Paris, 1949)

PAUL GRIFFITHS, RICHARD LANGHAM SMITH

Capecchi, Renato (*b* Cairo, 6 Nov 1923). Italian baritone. Trained in Lausanne and Milan, he was first heard as a prizewinner on Italian radio. His stage début was as Amonasro at Reggio Emilia (1949) and he has since sung over three hundred roles. At the Metropolitan he first appeared in *La traviata* (1952), but he has become associated most closely throughout Europe and the USA with such comic parts as Bartolo, Gianni Schicchi and Melitone, in which he made his Covent Garden début (1962). Widely appreciated as a singer of unusual intelligence, clever timing and clear enunciation, he has taken part in many premières, including operas by Malipiero and Ghedini, and in the Italian première of Shostakovich's *The Nose* (1964, Florence). His career has continued energetically, 1986 bringing his first Sharpless (Philadelphia), 1987 his début in Montreal, and 1988 the role of the Maestro di Cappella in the première of Bussotti's *L'ispirazione* (Florence). He has also taught in many opera schools in Europe and the USA, where his productions have included *Don Giovanni* (1987, Milwaukee). Several of his best roles, such as Dulcamara, Bartolo and Melitone, have been recorded, but he is an artist whose value is best represented on the stage.

J. B. STEANE

Capece [Capeci], **Carlo Sigismondo** (*b* Rome, 21 June 1652; *d* Polistena, Calabria, 12 March 1728). Italian librettist. After studying philosophy and law in Spain, he became a doctor of jurisprudence in Rome, practised as a judge for some years and later became governor of Terni, Cascia and Assisi. He returned to Rome in about 1700 as poet to Maria Casimira, widow of John Sobieski, King of Poland; he rewrote for her his earlier opera libretto *Il figlio delle selve* (1687), as well as seven new librettos, all set by Domenico Scarlatti; Filippo Juvarra provided sets for the last five and for Caldara's setting of *Tito e Berenice*, performed at the Teatro Capranica. In addition to his opera librettos, he wrote the texts for two oratorios and a number of serenatas, but after Maria Casimira left Rome in June 1714, he wrote mainly prose plays.

Capece's first two operas, written for performance at his father's home, deal with ordinary characters' attempts to disentangle misunderstandings over love relationships. The second, *Il figlio delle selve*, was by far his most popular. His later, serious opera librettos draw on Euripides, Ovid, Ariosto, Corneille and Racine, and treat both pastoral characters and regal heroes with Arcadian propriety. Capece became a member of the Accademia dell'Arcadia in 1692, taking the name Metisto Olbiano, and belonged to several other academies as well. A portrait of him is included in Gimma (1703).

drammi per musica unless otherwise stated

L'amor vince fortuna, F. Colonnese, 1686; *Il figlio delle selve*, C. Bani, 1687 (Eng., Legnani, 1701; ?A. Scarlatti, 1709; I. Holzbauer, 1753; C. Sala, 1756); *I giochi Troiani*, B. Pasquini, 1688; *La clemenza d'Augusto*, S. De Luca, C. F. Pollarolo and G. Bononcini, 1697; *Silvia* (drama pastorale), D. Scarlatti, 1710; *Tolomeo et Alessandro, overo La corona disprezzata*, D. Scarlatti, 1711 (Handel, 1728, as Tolomeo, rè di Egitto); *Orlando, overo La gelosa pazzia*, D. Scarlatti, 1711 (Handel, 1733); *Tetide in Sciro*, D. Scarlatti, 1712 (Pollarolo, 1715); *Ifigenia in Aulide*, D. Scarlatti, 1713; *Ifigenia in Tauri*, D. Scarlatti, 1713; *Tito e Berenice*, A. Caldara, 1714; *Amor d'un ombra e gelosia d'un aura*, D. Scarlatti, 1714 (1720, rev. T. Roseingrave as Narciso; G. Sellitto, 1725); *Telemaco*, A. Scarlatti, 1718 (Gluck, 1765, as Telemaco, o sia L'isola di Circe)

DBI (A. Lanfranchi); ES (E. Zanetti)
G. Gimma: *Elogi accademici della Società degli Spensierati di Rossano* (Naples, 1703), ii, 93–100
G. Amati: *Bibliografia romana: notizie della vita e delle opere degli scrittori romani dal secolo XI fino ai nostri giorni*, i (Rome, 1880), 69–71
I. Carini: *L'Arcadia dal 1690 al 1890: memorie istoriche*, i: *Contributo alla storia letteraria d'Italia del secolo XVII e de' principii del XVIII* (Rome, 1891), 470
A. Cametti: 'Carlo Sigismondo Capeci (1652–1728), Alessandro e Domenico Scarlatti e la Regina di Polonia in Roma', *Musica d'oggi*, xiii (1931), 55–64
R. Kirkpatrick: *Domenico Scarlatti* (New York, 1953)
L. E. Lindgren and C. B. Schmidt: 'A Collection of 137 Broadsides Concerning Theatre in Late Seventeenth-Century Italy: an Annotated Catalogue', *Harvard Library Bulletin*, xxviii (1980), 204–7
M. Viale Ferrero: 'Juvarra tra i due Scarlatti', *Händel e gli Scarlatti a Roma: Rome 1985*, 175–89
M. Boyd: *Domenico Scarlatti* (London, 1986)
S. Franchi: *Drammaturgia romana: repertorio bibliografico cronologico dei testi drammatici pubblicati a Roma e nel Lazio, secolo XVII* (Rome, 1988)
L. Bianconi and G. La Face Bianconi, eds.: *I libretti italiani di Georg Friedrich Händel e le loro fonti* (Bologna, 1992–)

LOWELL LINDGREN

Čapek, Karel (*b* Malé Svatoňovice, nr Trutnov, 9 Jan 1890; *d* Prague, 25 Dec 1938). Czech writer and dramatist. He was the best-known Czech writer between the two world wars, with works widely published in many languages. Although his final novel, incomplete at his death, was about a charlatan composer, and his detective story about the conductor Kalina may have had Janáček in mind (Fischmann, 146), he had no close relationship to music and took no hand in the adaptation of his works into operas apart from Zdeněk Folprecht's one-act opera *Lásky hra osudná* ('The Fatal Game of Love'), for which he wrote the libretto (1922) with his brother Josef.

Ze života hmyzu [From the Life of the Insects] (play, with J. Čapek, 1922): Kalmanoff, 1977, as Insect Comedy; Cikker, 1987
Věc Makropulos [The Makropulos Affair] (play, 1922): Janáček, 1926
Krakatit [invented word, from 'Krakatoa'] (novel, 1924): Berkovec, 1961; Kašlík, 1961
Jako za starých časů [As in Days of Yore] and *Romeo a Julie* (short stories, 1926, 1932): Poděšť, 1959 (1st and 3rd of his three *Apokryfy*)
Balada o Juraji Čupovi [The Ballad of Juraj Čup] (tale, 1929): J. Ceremuga, 1981, as Juraj Čup
Svatá noc [Holy Night] (short story, 1930): Poděšť, 1959 (2nd of his three *Apokryfy*)
Pohádka pošťácká [A Postman's Fairy-tale] (fairy-tale, 1931): Křička, 1943, as Psaníčko na cestách [A Little Note from One's Travels]; J. Feld, 1968, as Pošťácká pohádka
Zpověď Dona Juana [The Confession of Don Juan] (short story, 1932): G. Auer, 1983, as Spoveď Dona Juana
Válka s mloky [War with the Newts] (novel, 1936): V. Uspensky, 1968, as Voyna s salamandrami
Bílá nemoc [The White Plague] (play, 1937): T. Andrašovan, 1967, as Biela nemoc

*

H. Čapková: *Moji milí bratři* [My Dear Brothers] (Prague, 1962, 3/1986)
M. Halík: *Karel Čapek: Život a dílo v datech* [Life and Work in Dates] (Prague, 1983)
V. Forst, ed.: *Lexikon české literatury*, i (Prague, 1985) [incl. further bibliography]
Z. E. Fischmann: *Janáček-Newmarch Correspondence* (Rockville, MD, 1986)
I. Vajda: *Slovenská opera* [Slovak Opera] (Bratislava, 1988)
B. Mědílek and others: *Bibliografie Karla Čapka* (Prague, 1990)
J. Tyrrell: *Janáček's Operas: a Documentary Account* (London, 1992), chap. 8

JOHN TYRRELL

Capelli, David August von. *See* APELL, DAVID AUGUST VON.

Capelli [Capello, Cappelli, Capella], **Giovanni Maria** (*b* Parma, 7 Dec 1648; *d* Parma, 16 Oct 1726). Italian composer. He became *maestro di cappella* at Parma Cathedral in 1700, and was also an organist and priest. Surviving copies of the librettos of his operas describe him as 'Maestro di Capella del Ser.mo Principe Antonio Farnese'.

I rivali generosi [Act 3] (A. Zeno), Reggio Emilia, 1710 [Act 1 by C. Monari, Act 2 by F. A. Pistocchi]
L'amore politico e generoso della regina Ermengarda, Mantua, 1713, collab. F. Gasparini
L'Eudamia (favola pastorale, V. Piazza), Colorno and Parma, 1718
Nino [Act 1] (os, 3, I. Zanelli), Reggio Emilia, Pubblico, May Fair, 1720 [Act 2 by Gasparini, Act 3 by A. M. Bononcini]
Giulio Flavio Crispo (tragedia, 5, B. Pasqualigo), Venice, S Giovanni Grisostomo, carn. 1722
Mitridate re di Ponto vincitor de se stesso (3, Pasqualigo, after J. Racine: *Mitridate*), Venice, S Giovanni Grisostomo, carn. 1723
Il Venceslao (Zeno), Parma, 1724
I fratelli riconosciuti (O. Frugoni, after F. Silvani: *La verità nell'inganno*), Parma, 1726, *GB-CDp*
Erginia mascherata (after A. Marchi: *Rosalinda*), Rovigo, 1727

*

ES (N. Pirrotta)
A. Pezzana: *Memorie degli scrittori parmigiani* (Parma, 1827–33)
P. E. Ferrari: *Spettacoli drammatico-musicali e coreografici in Parma dal 1628 al 1883* (Parma, 1884)
N. Pelicelli: *Storia della musica in Parma dal 1500 al 1860* (Rome, 1936)

Cape Town (Afrikaans Kaapstad). Chief city and legislative capital of South Africa. Its first theatre, the African Theatre, opened in 1800. The building is now used as a church. In the early years of the 19th century many performances of *opéras comiques* were given by amateurs and visiting musicians. The first serious opera production was given by an amateur company, All the World's a Stage, in 1831 when they performed *Der Freischütz* in English.

Although Cape Town remained the operatic centre of South Africa well into the 20th century, it had to rely mainly on touring companies for performances. Under the direction of Erik Chisholm and Gregorio Fiasconaro, the University of Cape Town Opera Company staged many operas from the standard repertory. This company regularly toured throughout southern Africa. Notable premières include Chisholm's *The Pardoner's Tale* (1961) and Joubert's *Silas Marner* (1961). In a London season (1956–7) the company presented the first staged performance of Bartók's *Bluebeard's Castle* in England.

The Eoan Group, an amateur company of Coloured singers, under the musical direction of Joseph Manca, produced a number of operettas up to 1956 and then a series of operas, mainly from the Italian repertory.

Since the formation of provincial arts councils in 1963, opera has been presented mainly by the Cape Performing Arts Board (CAPAB), which has its headquarters in Cape Town. CAPAB at first performed at a number of venues in Cape Town with the assistance of the University Opera Company. The Nico Malan Theatre complex opened in 1971, since when opera and ballet have been given in its 1204-seat opera house. At first the theatre was open only to whites, and although this apartheid measure was dropped some years later, many black patrons still boycott performances there.

The CAPAB orchestra plays for opera and ballet performances. Roughly seven operas are given during the year and two musicals are performed. These alternate with ballet presentations. Emphasis is on the standard Italian and German repertory. The works are generally sung in the original language; only rarely are they given in English or Afrikaans.

*

J. Bouws: *Die musieklewe van Kaapstad* (Cape Town, 1966)
D. Talbot: *For the Love of Singing: 50 Years of Opera at UCT* (Cape Town, 1978) JAMES MAY

Capobianco, Tito (*b* La Plata, Argentina, 28 Aug 1931). American director and administrator of Argentine birth. He studied law and philosophy at La Plata and music at the University of Buenos Aires; he made his début as a producer at the Teatro Argentino in his native town with *Pagliacci* in 1953. He became technical director of the Teatro Colón in Buenos Aires (1958–62), and general director at the Teatro Argentino (1959–61). He first attracted serious notice in the USA in 1966 with his stagings for the New York City Opera during its first year at Lincoln Center; Ginastera's *Don Rodrigo* was presented in a hieratic manner, and the singers in Handel's *Giulio Cesare* were directed to move like 'incorrigible courtiers'. The première of Ginastera's *Bomarzo*, given by the Opera Society of Washington, followed in 1967. Capobianco then became resident stage director for the New York City Opera, where he brought his broad, almost balletic sense of style to bear on works as dissimilar as Boito's *Mefistofele* and Donizetti's three 'Tudor queen' operas for Beverly Sills. He has also designed operas, and has worked in Europe, Australia and the Canary Islands, where he established the Las Palmas Festival in 1975. He was artistic director of the Cincinnati Opera Festival (1961–5) and the Cincinnati Opera (1962–5) and in 1975 was appointed to the same position at the San Diego Opera (general director from 1977). In July 1983 he became vice-president and general director of the Pittsburgh Opera. Capobianco's wife, the choreographer Elena Denda, has worked with him on some of his most celebrated productions. Capobianco was professor of acting and interpretation at the Academy of Vocal Arts, Philadelphia (1962–8), founded and directed the American Opera Center at the Juilliard School of Music (1967–9), and was appointed director of opera studies and festival stage director at the Music Academy of the West, Santa Barbara, in 1983. In the same year he became professor of acting, staging and interpretation at the Graduate School of Music, Yale University. FRANK MERKLING

Capotorti, Luigi (*b* Molfetta, 1767; *d* San Severo, Foggia, 17 Nov 1842). Italian composer. He studied in Naples at the Conservatorio di S Onofrio, 1778–96, although his presence there is documented only between 1783 and 1794. He was a successful *maestro di cappella* in various Neapolitan churches, and taught composition and singing (Pavesi and Mercadante were among his pupils). After some successes in minor theatres due to the support of his teacher Niccolò Piccinni, *Enea in Cartagine* and *Gli Orazi e i Curiazi* were performed at the S Carlo, Naples, in 1800.

Outstanding among his operas is *Ciro*, performed in 1805 for the birthday of Ferdinand IV, in which the 'magnanimous' Ferdinand is represented by the character of Cyrus the Younger. The unusual plot is freely translated from Xenophon's *Anabasis*. It marks a transition from a late 18th-century style to a rich symphonic and choral texture, and *Marco Curzio* (1813) is reminiscent of the late operas of Cimarosa and of Spontini's *La vestale*. Capotorti was admired by the French and was admitted to the Académie de Musique in 1827. He composed chamber and sacred music, and left some modest theoretical writings.

all performed in Naples

Gli sposi in rissa (ob, 2, G. M. Diodati), Nuovo, 1796
Nice (2), 1796, lib. *I-Nc*
Enea in Cartagine (os, G. M. d'Orange), S Carlo, 1800
Gli Orazi e i Curiazi (os, 3, A. Sografi), S Carlo, 1800
Le nozze per impegno, ovvero L'impegno superato (ob, 2, L. Tottola), Fiorentini, sum. 1802, lib. *Nc*
Obeide e Atamare (os, 2, Tottola), S Carlo, 4 Nov 1803, *Nc*
Ciro (os, 2, trans. G. Imbimbo, from Xenophon: *Anabasis*), S Carlo, 12 Jan 1805, *Nc*
Bref il sordo (ob, G. Palomba), Fiorentini, 1805
Marco Curzio (os, 2, Giovanni Schmidt), S Carlo, 15 Aug 1813, *Nc*
Ernesta e Carlino, ovvero I due Savoiardi (op semiseria, 2, Tottola), Fiorentini, 1815, *Nc*

*

A. Ceri: 'Nel mondo dei dimenticati: Luigi Capotorti', *Gazzetta di Puglia* (3 Jan 1924)
F. Peruzzi: *Maestri compositori e musicisti molfettesi* (Molfetta, 1931), 35–51
N. Pastina: 'Passerà inosservato il bicentenario di Capotorti?', *La gazzetta del mezzogiorno* (9 Nov 1967)
M. Caraci Vela: 'Un omaggio a Ferdinando IV di Capotorti e Imbimbo: il *Ciro* (1805)', *Francesco Florimo e la musica nel suo tempo: Morcone 1990* MARIA CARACI VELA

Capoul, (Joseph) Victor (Amadée) (*b* Toulouse, 27 Feb 1839; *d* Pujaudran-du-Gers, 18 Feb 1924). French tenor. He studied at the Conservatoire where he won a *premier prix*, making his début with the Opéra-Comique in 1861 as Daniel (Adam's *Le chalet*). Engaged by J. H. Mapleson in London, he appeared first in *Faust* at Drury Lane in 1871. He made his Covent Garden début as Fra Diavolo in 1877. His roles there included Almaviva, Ernesto, Elvino, and Paul in Massé's *Paul et Virginie*, which he had created in Paris (1876). In the USA he made his début at the Academy of Music, New York, in 1871, and appeared in the opening season at the Metropolitan in 1883–4 as Wilhelm Meister and Alfredo; there he had to renounce the title role in *Roméo et Juliette*, in which he excelled, to Jean de Reszke and play Tybalt instead. Back in Paris he became director of the Opéra, lost his fortune through speculation and died in poverty. His single recording, made at the age of 66, is of the lullaby in Godard's *Jocelyn*, which he sang in the opera's première at the Opéra-Comique in 1888. An eloquent lyric singer, he was particularly admired as Méhul's Joseph.

ELIZABETH FORBES, J. B. STEANE

Cappelli [Capello, Capella], **Giovanni Maria.** *See* CAPELLI, GIOVANNI MARIA.

Cappello di paglia di Firenze, Il ('The Florentine Straw Hat'). *Farsa musicale* in four acts by NINO ROTA to a libretto by Nino and Ernesta Rota after Eugène Labiche and Marc Antoine Amédée Michel's vaudeville *Un chapeau de paille d'Italie*; Palermo, Teatro Massimo, 21 April 1955.

Preparations are being made at the Parisian home of Fadinard (tenor) for his wedding to Elena (soprano), the daughter of Nonancourt (bass). While he is out a hatbox arrives among the wedding presents; on his return he recounts an odd thing that has just happened to him: his horse ate a hat belonging to a lady on her way to an assignation. She is Anaide (contralto), wife of the jealous Beaupertuis (bass), and without revealing her identity she arrives at Fadinard's house with her lover, Lieutenant Emilio (tenor), and demands another identical hat, threatening Fadinard that otherwise Emilio will challenge him to a duel. Fadinard sets off in search of the hat, without explanation to the guests, Nonancourt or his bride, who all follow him intent upon the wedding. He goes first to a hat shop, and then to the home of Baroness di Champigny (soprano), where a party is in preparation; Fadinard is taken for Minard, a celebrated violinist, and he asks for the hat in payment, but, while his guests tuck into the banquet which they assume was prepared for them, the baroness realizes that she has lent her hat to her niece, Mme Beaupertuis.

Fadinard, still followed by the guests, who assume they are going to the couple's new home, rushes off to Beaupertuis and tells him the story, unaware that he is talking to the husband of Anaide. The affair now seems to be discovered and the dismayed Fadinard returns home, pursued by a furious Beaupertuis armed with a pistol. In the general turmoil Fadinard at last discovers that there is an identical hat among the wedding presents, and the situation is resolved at the last moment with no harm done.

Il cappello di paglia was composed in 1945 and completed in full score in 1955 when the Teatro Massimo decided to produce it. The music is related in style to vaudeville and 19th-century *opera buffa*, and is completely tonal, with occasional audible quotations from operas such as Rossini's *Il barbiere di Siviglia* and especially from Rota's own film scores, including those for Matarazzo's *Il birichino di papà*, Soldati's *Le miserie del signor Travet* and Fellini's *Lo sceicco bianco*. Among the stock operatic items cleverly used by the composer are some ensembles reminiscent of Rossini (especially the Act 3 finale, 'Io casco dalle nuvole'), some elegant flirtations with bel canto and a Puccinian sentimental style, the characteristic verse forms of vaudeville and recitative passages in the French tradition. Of immediate appeal and with a rare balance of musical and dramatic elements, it is Rota's best-known and most frequently performed work for the theatre.

GIORDANO MONTECCHI

Cappuccilli, Piero (*b* Trieste, 9 Nov 1929). Italian baritone. He studied singing under Donaggio at the Teatro Giuseppe Verdi, Trieste, where he appeared in small parts. His official début was at the Teatro Nuovo, Milan, as Tonio in *Pagliacci* (1957). In 1960 he was chosen by Walter Legge to sing Enrico in a recording of *Lucia di Lammermoor* with Maria Callas, and in the same year he sang Germont in *La traviata* at the Metropolitan. His début (as Enrico) at La Scala in 1964 confirmed his position, strengthened in many subsequent seasons there, as one of Italy's foremost baritones. He appeared at Covent Garden first in *La traviata* (1967) and crowned a worthy career in that house by singing in *Cavalleria rusticana* and *Pagliacci* the same evenings at the age of 60. He has sung in most other leading European opera houses as well as in South Africa and South America, and in 1969 he made the first of many successful appearances at Chicago. His performances in *Don Carlos* under Karajan (1975, Salzburg) and *Simon Boccanegra* under Abbado (La Scala and Covent Garden, 1976) showed a development of interpretative powers and technique, a remarkable feature of which has been his breath control. His warm, ample voice can be heard in many important recordings.

J. B. STEANE

Capranica. A noble Italian family of theatre builders and managers, who built and ran two theatres in Rome, important in the history of opera: *see* ROME, §§2 and 3 (i)–(ii). The Teatro Capranica, opened in 1692, was used for opera regularly until 1756 and on occasion afterwards. Its history has never been systematically studied, but in its first half-century it was a leading opera house, where new works (e.g. three by Alessandro Scarlatti) were performed in some style. In the 1720s the family built the smaller Teatro Valle, which it ran, as it did the Capranica, through a subordinate impresario. The Valle at first specialized in comic opera and plays. The ambitious policy of Marquis Bartolomeo Capranica (1788–1865) led him, from 1809, to engage leading singers (Giovanni David, Giuseppina Ronzi, Maria Malibran, Giorgio Ronconi) and to commission not only the usual comic operas but more venturesome serious and 'semi-serious' ones as well; the latter type included Rossini's *Torvaldo e Dorliska* and Donizetti's *Torquato Tasso* and *Il furioso all'isola di San Domingo*. This was more than the Valle's limited capacity could sustain; in 1845 it reverted to a straight dramatic theatre, which it still is. Marquis Bartolomeo also had a share in the management of two other leading Rome opera houses (*c*1830), and members of his family acted as informants on opera seasons elsewhere. The Capranica family papers are in the Biblioteca Teatrale del Burcardo and the Archivio Storico Capitolino, Rome.

*

B. M. Antolini: 'La musica a Napoli nell'ottocento nel carteggio dei Marchesi Capranica', *Francesco Florimo e la musica nel suo tempo: Morcone 1990*

——: 'Cronache teatrali veneziane: 1842–1849', *Musica senza aggettivi: studi per Fedele d'Amico* (Florence, 1991), 297–322

JOHN ROSSELLI

Capranica [Capranico], **Matteo** (*b* ?Amatrice, Rieti, 26 Aug 1708; *d* ?Naples, after 1776). Italian composer. Not to be confused with Domenico Capranica (1791–1870), he is said to have studied in Naples with Nicola Porpora, Ignazio Prota and Francesco Feo. He then worked as *maestro di cappella* in various Neapolitan churches and produced a number of operas, beginning, as was customary with young composers in the city, with a comedy in 1738. In 1744 he completed the score of *La finta frascatana*, left unfinished by Leonardo Leo at his death.

Il Carlo (ob, A. Palomba), Naples, Nuovo, 1736, lib. *I-Nn*
L'amante impazzito (ob, P. Trinchera), Naples, Nuovo, wint. 1738
L'Eugenia (ob, Palomba), Naples, Fiorentini, wint. 1745, lib. *Nn*
Alcibiade (os, G. Roccaforte), Rome, Argentina, 1746
L'Emilia (ob, Trinchera, after F. Oliva: *Lo castiello sacchejato*), Naples, Fiorentini, 1747
L'Aurelio (ob, Trinchera, after G. A. Federico: *Alidoro*), Naples, Nuovo, spr. 1748
Merope (os, A. Zeno), Rome, Argentina, 1751
La schiava amante (ob, Palomba), Naples, Fiorentini, aut. 1753, *Mc* (?autograph), lib. *Nn*
L'Olindo (ob, Palomba), Naples, Fiorentini, 1753; collab. N. Conti

Doubtful: Aristodemo, Rome, 1746 (possibly a misattribution of Domenico Capranica's Aristodemo, Rome, 1831, *Mr*)

*

M. Scherillo: *L'opera buffa napoletana durante il settecento: storia letteraria* (Naples, 1883, 2/1917), 177–8, 256, 257

JAMES L. JACKMAN

Capricci di Callot, I ('The Caprices of Callot'). *Commedia* in a prologue and three acts by GIAN FRANCESCO MALIPIERO to his own libretto freely based on parts of E. T. A. HOFFMANN's 'Capriccio nach Jakob Callot' *Prinzessin Brambilla*; Rome, Teatro Reale dell'Opera, 24 October 1942.

This winsomely inconsequential *jeu d'esprit* (composed in 1941–2) represents a partial return of Malipiero's more quirkily experimental side, after an interlude (1934–41) during which he had reverted to relatively safe, traditional operatic methods. E. T. A. Hoffmann's highly individual world of freakish fantasy clearly struck a sympathetic chord in him, releasing once again that zest for anarchic nonconformity which had been so conspicuous a feature of his stage works of 1917–29.

The resultant libretto is bafflingly discontinuous, both in plot and in musico-dramatic methods. Vocal sections alternate capriciously with long stretches of orchestrally accompanied dance and mime, and some sequences of events seem no less 'surrealistic' than those in the outer panels of the triptych *L'Orfeide* (composed 1918–22). Malipiero's use of material derived from Hoffmann is highly selective (straying right away from him in the final scene); and although attempts have been made to find a deeper symbolic meaning in the libretto, Ferdinando Ballo was probably right when he suggested that Malipiero's text, 'precisely because of its lack of logical substance, gives rise to a very free flowering of episodes, details, gestures, which find their justification only in the musical imagery which seemingly comments on them'. Certainly it is the vividness of the music as such, particularly in the purely orchestral sections, that makes the work so memorable. Some passages which in the opera are scored for strings alone were subsequently brought together to form the composer's ebulliently neo-madrigalian Fifth String Quartet (1950).

JOHN C. G. WATERHOUSE

Capriccio. Konversationsstück für Musik in one act by RICHARD STRAUSS to a libretto by the composer and CLEMENS KRAUSS; Munich, Staatsoper, 28 October 1942.

Countess Madeleine *a young widow*	soprano
The Count *her brother*	baritone
Flamand *a composer*	tenor
Olivier *a poet*	baritone
La Roche *a theatre director*	bass
Clairon *an actress*	contralto
Monsieur Taupe *a prompter*	tenor
Two Italian Singers	soprano and tenor
The Major-Domo	bass
Eight Servants	four tenors, four basses

A young ballerina, three onstage musicians

Setting A drawing-room in the Countess's chateau near Paris; May 1777

The conception of *Capriccio*, Strauss's 15th and last opera, arose from Stefan Zweig's research in the British Museum, where in 1934 he came upon a short comedy by GIOVANNI BATTISTA CASTI, a rival of Mozart's librettist Da Ponte. *Prima la musica e poi le parole* ('First the music, then the words') had in fact been set to music by Mozart's own rival Salieri, and shared its Schönbrunn première with *Der Schauspieldirektor* (text by the *Entführung* librettist Stephanie, not Da Ponte). Mozart's little comedy was about opera as a practical business, but Casti and Salieri also represented the words-versus-music tension built into opera itself by including as characters a composer and his poet. The idea, though not the trivial plot, seized Zweig's imagination, and Strauss liked it too; even before the première of their *Die schweigsame Frau*, the writer had enlisted Joseph Gregor's collaboration on a libretto. The Jewish Zweig knew that his days in Nazi Germany were numbered, and hoped that his 'Aryan' friend might take his literary place at the composer's side. So Gregor did, for Strauss's next three operas – but his 1935 draft for a neo-Casti piece found no favour, nor did his later attempt when Strauss's interest was rekindled in 1939 (with *Die Liebe der Danae* still in progress).

What the composer really wanted was nothing much like a story, but a 'theoretical comedy' or 'theatrical discussion': a wry, self-illustrating debate about the nature of Opera. That was beyond Gregor's range. Eventually it was the conductor Clemens Krauss (who had prompted substantial changes in Gregor's *Daphne* scenario) and Strauss himself who devised the 'conversation-piece' he needed, with the eventual label *Capriccio* to mark its status as a *jeu d'esprit*. At one time he imagined it as a curtain-raiser for *Daphne*, which would then count as the opera created by the personnel of *Capriccio* – or rather of 'Prima le parole, dopo la musica', an interim title. Soon it outgrew that modest scale, and Strauss allowed himself a generous orchestra. Yet he took unprecedented care to make (nearly) all the words audible, for the dramatic contest would otherwise have been a fake from the start. Knowing that the opera was unlikely to work in a 'big house', he hoped for a small-house Salzburg Festival première; instead, Krauss arranged a grand Strauss Festival in Munich, with *Capriccio* as its centrepiece in the Staatsoper and his wife Viorica Ursuleac as the Countess. Hotter sang Olivier, Horst Taubmann the Composer, Georg Hann La Roche (a loving caricature of the great Max Reinhardt).

The prologue-sextet had already had its first performance at the home of the Nazi Gauleiter and arts-lover Baldur von Schirach, who helped Strauss to secure his Belvedere home in Vienna at a difficult time. In 1943 the Staatsoper was bombed out, but while the war continued *Capriccio* was performed in Darmstadt, Dresden and Vienna, and in Zürich under Karl Böhm. The opera has made its way slowly but steadily into the international repertory – chiefly because of its marvellous soprano-finale, and then the charms of the sextet and the 'moonlight interlude'; but much else is regularly lost. For full appreciation, old Strauss's subtle even-handedness with words-versus-music throughout requires not only an intimate performing scale, but delivery in the language of the audience.

Before the curtain rises on *Capriccio* we hear a sextet, played by first-desk strings in the pit. It is the composer Flamand's latest piece, sweetly serene in F at start and finish – with a theatrical eruption of passion in the middle, soon mollified (it fixes perfectly the urbane, nothing-too-serious manner of the whole opera). In a garden salon in early afternoon Flamand watches the Countess Madeleine's reaction to his sextet, continuing now in the next room – and so does Olivier, his rival for her affections, and the dozing theatre director La Roche. They exchange banter about words, music and modern

'Capriccio' (Richard Strauss): scene from the original production at the Staatsoper, Munich, 28 October 1942

productions, and slip off to prepare the private theatre as the Countess-Muse enters with her talented amateur brother. La Roche has come to direct the poet's new play, with the Count and the famous actress Clairon, once the poet's mistress, as hero and heroine. Count and Countess tease each other about their 'artistic' partialities (this becomes a lively duet); then the others return, still arguing, and Clairon makes a dashing entrance. She and the Count read through a fraught scene from the play, culminating in his passionate sonnet ('Kein Andres, das mir so im Herzen loht': Ronsard, freely and elegantly translated by the conductor Hans Swarowsky). When La Roche leads them away to rehearse, Olivier recites the sonnet again as an intimate declaration to Madeleine – inspiring Flamand to rush off and compose it. The poet seizes the chance to press his ardent suit, in E♭, but the Countess still hesitates to choose between poetry and music.

Flamand returns triumphantly (wrenching the key up to F♯); he has set the sonnet, and forthwith sings the result to his own harpsichord accompaniment. Muted divided strings shadow his voice, which stays within the compass of a major 9th. Strauss rose superbly to the occasion with this song, which is of course to haunt the rest of the score. At 'Leben ... oder Tod', the close of the 'octave' verses, it drops theatrically and briefly into D minor; but its subtle life lies in continual rhythmic displacements, such as only a master of lied prosody could devise. (In an earlier, higher-lying draft of the sonnet, which has been published, there are fascinating variants.) Without missing a beat, the song is now recycled as a glowing trio: Flamand strums the chords and repeats the phrases that please him most, the Countess effuses over this higher synthesis of words and notes, Olivier – like Mozart's Guglielmo in the *Così* wedding-quartet – emits cross-grained complaints (he has been moved, but thinks the composer has wrecked his scansion). Now La Roche comes to demand a cut in Olivier's script, and as they go off to discuss it Flamand seizes the chance to bare his own heart to Madeleine (in E, more shyly and sweetly than the lusty poet, with thematic echoes of *Ariadne*'s young Composer). Having extracted her promise to make a final choice by 11 o'clock next morning, he flees in rapt confusion. Rehearsal noises are heard again, and the Countess orders chocolate in the salon for everybody. (In the two-act version often used now, her spoken line ends Act 1.)

Her brother returns first, professing his entrancement by Clairon, while Madeleine reports her suitors' protestations and her inability to decide between them. They mock each other's plights. The others join them for the refreshments, with a *divertissement* arranged by La Roche – an Italian soprano-and-tenor duo, preceded by a young *danseuse*. For her three dances Strauss wrote pastiches of Rameau and Couperin. During her Passepied the director regales the Count with predictions of a golden future for her, in royal beds as well as the ballet; her Gigue accompanies Olivier's peace overtures to Clairon (smartly rebuffed); only her Gavotte earns courteous general attention. Ever susceptible, the Count exclaims that music is after all only an adjunct to dance, thus cueing the 'theatrical fugue' which Strauss had always imagined as his centrepiece (surely with Verdi's final *Falstaff* fugue in mind). Starting in plain C, the subject – 'Tanz und Musik/steh'n im Bann des Rhythmus' ('Dance and music stem from rhythm') – generates a long and lively debate over what the fundamental, instinctive art must be: rhythmic movement, or human speech, or the ordering of tones? In midstream the Count reflects that 'Eine Oper ist ein absurdes Ding', to an expansive tune borrowed from Strauss's old *Krämerspiegel* song cycle.

The preening Italians' operatic duet makes a diversion, but also shows that the debate has been too narrow. What about the direct *Affekt* of the singing voice? – even in banal words, and the crudest musical routine? (Easy parody here: Strauss caricatures the vocal gestures of Italian opera over a stolid *Biergarten* pulse, and the singers invariably make a contest of upstaging each other.) Now La Roche announces the grand spectacle he plans for Madeleine's birthday: fake-mythological, hugely epic. Unable to contain themselves, his junior colleagues begin an elaborate 'Laughing Ensemble'; as tempers rise it becomes a 'Strife Ensemble', topped by the tipsy Italian soprano. Deeply wounded, the theatre director mounts a towering defence – 'Hola! ihr Streiter in Apoll!' – of his own art, devoted to rescuing the thin-blooded efforts of modern composers and librettists. (The *Feuersnot* hero's diatribe against Munich philistines, 40 years earlier, makes a touching parallel.) Everyone relents graciously, and La Roche joins his fellow artists in a rhetorical 'Homage Quartet' to himself. But a new birthday plan has emerged: what he must direct is a new opera by Olivier and Flamand. Possible subjects are discussed, including those of earlier Strauss operas, which the orchestra duly quotes; but the outcome is that the competing swains will write an opera, *Intermezzo*-like, on the events of this day, the very opera that we are hearing. The ending has yet to be decided by Madeleine.

Twilight falls as the guests depart for Paris, escorted by the Count. Coming to tidy the salon, a servants' octet assesses the situation: everyone is playing Theatre, and 'the Countess is in love but doesn't know with whom'. In the darkness Monsieur Taupe emerges like a mole, having fallen asleep in his prompt box, and the patient Major-Domo hears out his dreamy claim that the show really depends upon *him*, before arranging his transport home. The moon rises; a solo horn begins an ecstatic A♭ interlude (on the *Krämerspiegel* song) while the Countess reappears, pensive in a new evening-gown. The Major-Domo reminds her that a decision is expected by 11 tomorrow morning. Crying 'Morgen mittag um elf!', she interrogates her own heart, and then her mirror-image – with no clearer result. This rich operatic epiphany (in D♭, of course) is Strauss's last, and Madeleine concludes her soliloquy with a wry question: 'Is there any ending that isn't trivial?' – 'Supper is served', says the Major-Domo; both Flamand's and Olivier's themes peep in before the silvery, uncommitted closing cadences.

* * *

The musical idiom of *Capriccio* lies close to Strauss's 1946 Oboe Concerto: artfully serene and warmly tonal, with the merest chromatic squalls *en passant*. The Countess is a gift to seasoned Strauss sopranos (tactfully, we are not told which birthday it is that she will be celebrating); Flamand is one of Strauss's rarely gentle, lyrical tenors. Clever singer-actors can make even the seemingly under-composed roles of the Count, Olivier and Clairon blossom, and the quarrel-ensembles are brilliantly transparent. Though the action is selfconsciously contrived to the point of frank 'deconstruction', Strauss manages, like his 'Italian' duo, to command gut reactions from his audience, with the ironic blessing of Krauss's arch, know-all text. DAVID MURRAY

Caprices d'Oxane, Les. Opera by P. I. Tchaikovsky; *see* CHEREVICHKI.

Capricornus [Bockshorn], **Samuel Friedrich** (*b* Schertitz [now Zerčiče, nr Mladá Boleslav], 21 Dec 1628; *d* Stuttgart, 10 Nov 1665). German composer of Bohemian birth. His family fled to Hungary to escape religious persecution. He worked at the imperial court in Vienna, as a teacher and (from 1651) as director of music to the churches in Pressburg (now Bratislava), and became Kapellmeister to the Württemberg court at Stuttgart in 1657.

Although Capricornus's works were widely distributed, his stage works, like most of his other secular compositions, are now lost. Among them was *Raptus Proserpinae, in einem singenden Schaw-Spiel vorgestellt*, of which the published libretto survives (Stuttgart, 1662); a second work (18 May 1665) was a comedy. Capricornus also wrote a ballet, much sacred music and some instrumental pieces.

*

J. Sittard: *Zur Geschichte der Musik und des Theaters am Württembergischen Hofe*, i (Stuttgart, 1890)
H. Buchner: *Samuel Friedrich Capricornus* (diss., U. of Munich, 1922)
R. Rybarič: 'Samuel Capricornus in Bratislava/Pressburg', *Musica antiqua Europae orientalis III: Bydgoszcz 1972*, 107–26
KERALA JOHNSON SNYDER

Caproli [Caprioli, Del Violino], **Carlo** (*b* Rome, 1615–20; *d* probably in Rome, 1692–5). Italian composer. He was first an organist at the German College, Rome (1643–5), and later a violinist at S Luigi dei Francesi (1649–70). By 1653 he was also in the service of Prince Ludovisio Pamphili, nephew of Pope Innocent X, and his reputation as a composer must have become well established by then through his many fine cantatas. Evidently he was known to the poet Francesco Buti and to Cardinal Antonio Barberini, for it was through them that he received Cardinal Mazarin's invitation to compose an opera for the French court. After his sojourn at the French court, from January to June 1654, he entered Barberini's musical household where he was employed until about 1664.

Caproli's opera *Le nozze di Peleo e di Theti*, a *commedia* to a libretto by Buti, was first given at the Petit Bourbon on 14 April 1654. It received some eight more performances, the last two of which were attended by the general public at the king's invitation. The opera – the music of which is lost – was well received. The title of *maître de la musique du cabinet du Roy* granted by Louis XIV suggests that Caproli may have directed the performances. The young king himself participated in the ballets that followed each scene of the opera.

*

A. Berardi: *Ragionamenti musicali* (Bologna, 1681)
H. Prunières: *L'opéra italien en France avant Lulli* (Paris, 1913)
A. Tessier: 'Giacomo Torelli a Parigi e la messa in scena delle *Nozze di Peleo* di Carlo Caproli', *RaM*, i (1928), 573–90
F. Liuzzi: *I musicisti in Francia* (Rome, 1946)
ELEANOR CALUORI

Capsir, Mercedes [Mercè] (*b* Barcelona, *c*1895; *d* Suzzara, 13 March 1969). Spanish soprano. She studied in Barcelona and Italy, making her début in 1914 at Barcelona in *Rigoletto*; she sang in Spain and Portugal until 1918, and in 1916 at the Teatro Colón. In 1919 she began her Italian career at Bologna and Florence, appearing frequently at Naples, Turin and Rome until 1943. She also sang at La Scala (1924–34), taking part in the posthumous première of Leoncavallo's *Il re* (1929), returned often to Spain, and was heard in Berlin (1924), at Covent Garden (*Il barbiere di Siviglia*, 1926) and in Vienna (1935). Her last appearance was in 1949 at Barcelona. A coloratura soprano with a pure and well-focussed voice of wide range, she was famous for her Rosina, Lucia, Gilda and Violetta.

*

GV (R. Celletti; R. Vegeto) RODOLFO CELLETTI

Captive in the Caucasus, The. Opera by C. A. Cui; *see* KAVKAZSKIY PLENNIK.

Capua, Marcello da. *See* BERNARDINI, MARCELLO.

Capua, Rinaldo di. *See* RINALDO DI CAPUA.

Capuana, Franco (*b* Fano, 29 Sept 1894; *d* Naples, 10 Dec 1969). Italian conductor. He studied composition at the Naples Conservatory and during the 1920s conducted in Italian provincial theatres including at Genoa, where he gave the première of Lattuada's *Sandha* in 1924. He was engaged at the S Carlo (1930–37), and at La Scala (1937–40), where he conducted premières of operas by Bianchi, Refice and Sonzogno, as well as Ghedini's *La pulce d'oro* (1940) at Genoa. After touring abroad to Spain and South America, he was in charge of the S Carlo company which brought the first visiting postwar opera to Covent Garden in 1946. He returned to La Scala the next year, becoming musical director there (1949–52) and sharing the Milan company's Covent Garden visit in 1950 with De Sabata. He also conducted the resident company at Covent Garden in 1951 and 1952. Though he preferred Italian *verismo* opera his repertory included Wagner, Strauss, Borodin, Granados, Meyerbeer and Janáček, whose *Jenůfa* he introduced to the Italian stage at Venice in 1941. He explored some of the early 19th-century operas, in advance of their wider revival, including Bellini's *I Capuleti* and Verdi's *Alzira*. His performances were in the Toscanini tradition of rhythmic vitality and bold effects. He composed an operetta, *La piccola irredenta* (1915, Naples). CLAUDIO CASINI

Capuana, Maria (*b* Fano, 1891; *d* Cagliari, 22 Feb 1955). Italian mezzo-soprano, sister of Franco Capuana. She studied singing and the piano at the Naples Conservatory and made her début at the S Carlo theatre in 1913. Her roles there, where she remained a favourite for more than 20 years, included Amneris, Azucena, Léonor (*La favorite*) and Rubria (Boito's *Nerone*). She also had great success in the German repertory as Fricka (*Die Walküre*), Brangäne (*Tristan und Isolde*) and, at La Scala, Ortrud (*Lohengrin*) and Herodias (*Salome*). In 1925 she appeared at the Colón in Buenos Aires and was later heard in Spain, Egypt and South Africa. Her recordings include a complete *Aida*, in which her opulent voice and imposing manner make Amneris a particularly dominant figure. J. B. STEANE

Capuleti e i Montecchi, I ('The Capuleti and the Montecchi'). *Tragedia lirica* in two acts by VINCENZO BELLINI to a libretto by FELICE ROMANI; Venice, Teatro La Fenice, 11 March 1830.

Tebaldo *betrothed to Giulietta*	tenor
Capellio *chief of the Capuleti, father of Giulietta*	bass
Lorenzo *doctor and retainer of the Capuleti*	tenor or bass
Romeo *head of the Montecchi*	mezzo-soprano
Giulietta *in love with Romeo*	soprano

Capuleti, Montecchi, maidens, soldiers, guards

Setting Verona in the 13th century

Behind the libretto stand many Italian, ultimately Renaissance, sources rather than Shakespeare's *Romeo and Juliet* (Collins 1982). Romani rewrote for Bellini the *Giulietta e Romeo* he had written originally for Vaccai (1825, Milan), which drew on a play *Giulietta e Romeo* of 1818 by Luigi Scevola, and which had also been set by E. Torriani (1828, Vicenza). The theme was very popular in Italy: there were earlier librettos by Luzzi for Marescalchi (1785, Venice), Foppa for Zingarelli (1796, Milan), and Buonaiuti for P. C. Guglielmi (1810, London). The first Italian libretto explicitly based on Shakespeare's play was by M. M. Marcello, for Marchetti's *Romeo e Giulietta* (1865, Trieste).

In Venice to prepare the local première of *Il pirata* with Giuditta Grisi as Imogene, Bellini wrote *I Capuleti* in a month and a half (starting about 20 January) after the Teatro La Fenice had been let down by Giovanni Pacini. He wrote the part of Romeo for Grisi (whose presence, together with a relatively weak male company, may have conditioned the choice of subject); it rarely descends below *c′*. Giulietta was sung by Maria Caradori-Allan, Tebaldo by Lorenzo Bonfigli and Lorenzo by Ranieri Pocchini Cavalieri. Bellini had intended the part of Lorenzo for a bass, but in Act 1 of the autograph score he transposed it for tenor, and in Act 2 the part is written in the tenor clef throughout. Although these changes were possibly for Senigallia (summer 1830), Cavalieri, the singer at the première, appears to have been a tenor. (Published scores and most performances assign the role to a bass.)

Bellini thoroughly reworked ten melodies from his unsuccessful *Zaira* (1829, Parma) into *I Capuleti e i Montecchi*: he explained that '*Zaira*, hissed at Parma, was avenged by *I Capuleti*' (letter of 21 March 1833). Giulietta's 'Oh quante volte' in Act 1 uses Nelly's *romanza* 'Dopo l'oscuro nembo' from *Adelson e Salvini* (1825, Naples). Bellini prepared a version for La Scala (26 December 1830), lowering Giulietta's part for the mezzo-soprano Amalia Schütz-Oldosi. Early librettos divide the opera into four parts; at Bologna in 1832 Maria Malibran replaced the last part with the tomb scene from Vaccai's final act, a tradition followed by contralto Romeos such as Alboni (Vaccai's scene is included as an appendix to Ricordi's vocal score). This version was performed at Paris and London with Pasta as Romeo in 1833, but in Florence the following year Giuseppina Ronzi de Begnis restored Bellini's ending. Wilhelmine Schröder-Devrient's singing as Romeo in Leipzig (1834) and Magdeburg (1835) created a profound impression on the young Wagner. *I Capuleti* was revived in 1935, the centenary of Bellini's death, at Catania and in 1954 at Palermo, with Giulietta Simionato as Romeo and Rosanna Carteri as Giulietta. In 1966 Claudio Abbado prepared a version for La Scala in which Romeo was sung by a tenor, Giacomo Aragall; the cast included Renata Scotto as Giulietta and Luciano Pavarotti as Tebaldo. This version was also performed in Amsterdam, Rome and Philadelphia and at the 1967 Edinburgh Festival but is no longer used.

The opening sinfonia uses themes from the following *introduzione* and Giulietta's 'Ah! non poss'io partire'.

ACT 1.i ('Parte prima') *A gallery in the Capuleti palace* The Guelph followers of Capellio gather, fearing an attack from their Ghibelline rivals, the Montecchi. Capellio and Tebaldo warn them that the Ghibelline chief, Romeo, whom they have never seen and who has recently killed Capellio's son, is sending an envoy urging peace. Tebaldo swears to take vengeance on Romeo himself to mark his forthcoming marriage to Giulietta. His military cavatina, 'È serbata a questo acciaro', uses a thoroughly reworked version of

Corasmino's opening cavatina in *Zaira*, while the Allegro 'L'amo tanto, e m'è si cara' is new. Romeo enters unrecognized, posing as his own envoy, and expresses regret for the accidental death of Capellio's son in the cavatina 'Se Romeo t'uccise un figlio' (adapted from Nerestano's rondò from *Zaira*, Act 2). He offers to seal peace through the union of Romeo and Giulietta but is told that she is betrothed to Tebaldo. The Capuleti reject Romeo's offer of peace and he warns of future bloodshed in 'La tremenda ultrice spada' (from Zaira's aria in Act 2).

1.ii *A room in Giulietta's apartment* A horn solo introduces Giulietta's *romanza* 'Oh! quante volte, oh! quante' (adapted from *Adelson e Salvini*); there is a contrast between her festive raiment and her unfulfilled longing for Romeo. Lorenzo then leads in Romeo, who urges Giulietta to flee with him in the duet 'Sì, fuggire: a noi non resta' (derived in part from the duet in *Zaira*, finale to Act 1). Giulietta resists all his pleading and begs him to cause her no more torment.

1.iii ('Parte seconda') *A courtyard in Capellio's palace* The Capuleti prepare for Giulietta's wedding to Tebaldo. Lorenzo finds Romeo disguised as a Guelph and awaiting the help of his friends to abduct Giulietta. The Montecchi launch their attack on the Capuleti and during the commotion Giulietta meets Romeo who again urges her to flee with him, but they are discovered by Capellio and Tebaldo, who recognize Romeo as the enemy ambassador. He reveals his true identity, introducing the finale, 'Soccorso, sostegno'. The Montecchi arrive and the act ends with Romeo and Giulietta separated by their respective factions. Bellini contrasts their high voices, in unison, with those of their antagonists in 'Se ogni speme è a noi rapita' (taken from the trio 'Non si pianga, si nasconda' in *Zaira*, Act 1).

ACT 2.i ('Parte terza') *An apartment in Capellio's palace* An arioso for cello introduces Giulietta, who wonders what has happened to Romeo. Lorenzo enters, offering her a sleeping potion that will counterfeit death, and assuring her that Romeo will be with her when she wakes. Her aria 'Morte io non temo, il sai' (revised from Zaira's Act 2 aria) expresses her fear that she will never wake, despite Lorenzo's interpolated protestations. Probably for the production in Milan, Bellini added an unpublished ensemble passage, 'Morir dovessi ancora', as Giulietta takes the potion. Capellio enters and she begs his forgiveness as she feels herself growing weaker ('Ah! non poss'io partire', taken directly from Nerestano's aria in *Zaira*, Act 2). Capellio is left anxious but suspicious, and has Lorenzo watched.

2.ii *A deserted place near Capellio's palace* Alone, Romeo complains that Lorenzo has not made contact with him. He comes face to face with Tebaldo and their furious duet, 'Stolto! a un sol mio grido', is about to lead to a duel when they hear an offstage chorus of lament ('Pace alla tua bell'anima', taken directly from *Zaira*, Act 2). When they learn that it is Giulietta's cortège the two antagonists end the scene, united in their grief.

2.iii ('Parte quarta') *At the tombs of the Capuleti* The Montecchi have come to mourn Giulietta. Romeo appears and approaches her tomb, which his followers force open for him. Romeo makes his farewell to Giulietta in 'Deh! tu, bell'anima' (the melody is from Zaira's Act 1 aria celebrating her forthcoming marriage), after which he takes poison himself. A phrase for clarinet and flute in octaves marks Giulietta's revival and she tells an incredulous Romeo about Lorenzo's potion. Their increasingly agitated exchanges are mirrored in the accompaniment as Romeo admits that he has taken poison. His strength quickly ebbs. When he expires, Giulietta falls dead upon his body, to the horror of the Capuleti and Montecchi who rush in. This entire scene, a continuous alternation of chorus, recitative, arioso and ensemble, is, emotionally and dramatically, the most powerfully effective yet written by Bellini.

* * *

In *I Capuleti e i Montecchi* (particularly the final scene) Bellini further establishes the melodic *morbidezza* evident in the earlier *Bianca e Fernando*, and something of the formal unconventionality found in the works of his maturity. The concentration of the action on the two principal characters is notably successful. The opera is

'I Capuleti e i Montecchi' (Bellini), Act 2 scene iii (at the tombs of the Capuleti): design by Francesco Bagnara for the original production at La Fenice, Venice, 11 March 1830

primarily a work of reclamation, in which previously written material is skilfully adapted to its new context. Admittedly the haste with which it was put together is reflected in a certain schematicism and lack of rhythmic variety in the closed numbers. On the other hand the subject of star-crossed lovers enabled Bellini to play from strength as a purveyor of tender, elegiac melody. Here, as in *Zaira*, he infused the simple, syllabic vocal writing of *La straniera* with melismatic bravura, preparing the way for that perfect synthesis of expression and virtuosity he attained in *La sonnambula*. As the last important opera with a breeches-part hero, *I Capuleti* survived throughout the century as a favourite warhorse for star sopranos such as Wilhelmine Schröder-Devrient and Johanna Wagner, despite the hostility of progressives such as Liszt, who dismissed it as intolerably old-fashioned, and the ambivalence of Wagner, who loved its melodies while deploring its dramatic conception. Berlioz was no less contemptuous, though he singled out the unison cantilena for the lovers in the Act 1 finale for special praise.

SIMON MAGUIRE, ELIZABETH FORBES, JULIAN BUDDEN

Capuzzi [Capucci], **Giuseppe Antonio** (*b* Breno, Brescia, 1 Aug 1755; *d* Bergamo, 28 March 1818). Italian composer. He studied the violin with Nazari, a pupil of Tartini, and composition with Bertoni. For some years after 1780 he was active in Venice as a performer in theatres and in St Mark's. He visited London in 1796, and settled in Bergamo in 1805, leading the orchestra at the Teatro Riccardi. He was highly regarded both as teacher and performer, and was equally proficient as a composer of theatrical and of chamber music.

Cefalo e Procri (favola in prosa con musica, A. Pepoli), Padua, 1792
Eco e Narciso (favola, 1, Pepoli), Venice, carn. 1793
I bagni d'Abano, ossia La forza delle prime impressioni (commedia, 2, A. S. Sografi, after C. Goldoni), Venice, S Benedetto, carn. 1794
Sopra l'ingannator cade l'inganno, ovvero I due granatieri (farsa giocosa, 2, G. Foppa), Venice, S Moisè, 14 Jan 1801
La casa da vendere (farsa giocosa, 1, G. D. Camagna), Venice, S Angelo, 4 Jan 1804, arias *I-Nc*
Arias in *GB-Lbl*, *I-Nc*, *PLcon*

Caracas. Capital of Venezuela. The first theatre in the city was built in 1783, on the corner of El Conde and Las Carmelitas streets; it seated 1500 and was destroyed in an earthquake in 1812. The first recorded opera performances, of P. J. Candeille's *Pizarre, ou La conquête de Pérou* and excerpts from *Don Giovanni* and *Die Zauberflöte*, were given there in 1808 by a visiting French company under Jeanne Faucompré. An Italian company visited the city in 1843, giving nine operas, five of them by Donizetti, at the Coliseo. A new theatre seating 1200, the Teatro Caracas, opened in 1854 with *Ernani*. Annual seasons of the most popular Italian works were given there up to 1862 by visiting Italian troupes; but attendance flagged and a later season (in 1866) could be given only with government subsidy.

The first full-scale opera by a Venezuelan has traditionally been taken to be José Angel Montero's *Virginia*, given at the Teatro Caracas in 1873 (it was revived in 1969 at the Teatro Municipal); Montero also composed zarzuelas, given at the Teatro Caracas and the Teatro de la Zarzuela. But it has recently been claimed that José María Osorio's *El maestro Rufo Zapatero* of 1847 should take precedence, although the circumstances of its first performance remain obscure (see Peñín 1985). The noted Venezuelan pianist Teresa Carreño (1853–1917) was also active in opera, bringing a 48-member troupe to the Teatro Guzmán Blanco in Caracas in 1886–7, chiefly in works by Verdi. She herself conducted some of these, becoming the first woman opera conductor in the western hemisphere. Opera seasons were given in the city between 1917 and 1932 by the Adolfo Bracale organization, in French and German repertory as well as Italian; later visitors included companies from New York (notably, in 1948, a section of the Metropolitan Opera, with Flagstad in *Tristan und Isolde*) and France. Seasons continued in the 1960s and 70s; memorable events have included the premières of Carolyne Lloyd's *Doña Barbara* (23 July 1967), based on a local subject, and of *El caballero de Ledesma* (18 May 1979) by Eric Colón, a Belgian resident in Venezuela, as well as a visit in 1975 by Plácido Domingo (when, with support from the Teresa Carreño Foundation, 12 operas were performed). In 1981 five standard works were given at the Teatro Municipal and six others by Opera Metropolitana; two years later a fine new theatre, named after Carreño, was opened, with Justino Díaz in *Aida*.

*

M. Milinowski: *Teresa Carreño* (New Haven, CT, 1940), 162–8
C. Salas and E. Feo Calcaño: *Sesquicentenario de la ópera en Caracas* (Caracas, 1960)
R. Stevenson: 'National Library Publications in Brazil, Peru, and Venezuela', *Inter-American Music Review*, iii (1980–81), 41–2
L. Noguera Messuti: *30 años de historia gráfica de la ópera en Caracas* (Caracas, 1985)
J. Peñín: *José María Osorio: autor de la primera ópera venezolana* (Caracas, 1985)
M. J. Brito Stelling: 'El teatro lírico en Caracas', *Revista musical de Venezuela*, viii/19 (1986), 25–49
M. Milanca Guzmán: *Teresa Carreño, gira caraqueña y evocación (1885–1887)* (Caracas, 1988)
E. Feo Cesas: 'Los teatros de Caracas y la ópera', pt 3, *Revista nacional de la cultura*, no.282 (1991), 162–71

ROBERT STEVENSON

Caradori-Allan [née de Munck], **Maria (Caterina Rosalbina)** (*b* Milan, 1800; *d* Surbiton, 15 Oct 1865). Alsatian soprano of Italian birth. She was taught by her mother, and made her début at the King's Theatre, London, in 1822 as Cherubino. She also appeared in Italy, and was engaged at Venice for the carnival season of 1830, when she created Giulietta in Bellini's *I Capuleti e i Montecchi*. Her other roles included Emilia (Rossini's *Otello*), Rosina, Zerlina and Amina (*La sonnambula*), but it was as a concert and oratorio singer that she became best known. Chorley, writing about her stage performances, considered her 'one of those first-class singers of the second class, with whom it would be hard to find a fault, save want of fire'.

*

Lord Mount Edgcumbe: *Musical Reminiscences of an Old Amateur* (London, 1827)
H. F. Chorley: *Thirty Years' Musical Recollections* (London, 1862)

ELIZABETH FORBES

Carafa (de Colobrano), Michele [Michel] **(Enrico-Francesco-Vincenzo-Aloisio-Paolo)** (*b* Naples, 17 Nov 1787; *d* Paris, 26 July 1872). Italian composer. The second son of Giovanni, Prince of Colobrano and Duke of Alvita, he was intended for a career in the army, but was permitted to acquire a musical training beforehand, first in Naples and then in Paris (1806) with Cherubini and Kalkbrenner. Returning to Naples in 1808, he continued his studies with Fenaroli and entered the army. He served as aide to Joachim Murat, King of Naples, and took part in various campaigns, including the Russian expedition of 1812; he was awarded the Order of the Two Sicilies and the Légion d'honneur for conspicuous gallantry. On the restoration of the Bourbons he left the army to devote himself to music.

As a student he had shown promise with cantatas and an opera for amateurs, *Il fantasma* (1805, Naples). From 1814 he developed into one of the most prolific opera composers of his day; his first big success was *Gabriella di Vergy* (1816, Naples). He began a lifelong friendship with Rossini, contributing to *Adelaide di Borgogna* (1817) and providing Pharaoh's first aria in *Mosè in Egitto* (1818). In 1821 he gained a foothold at the Opéra-Comique, Paris, with *Jeanne d'Arc à Orléans*, dedicated to Cherubini. Although he continued to produce operas in Italy and outside (*Abufar*, 1823, by which he set great store, was a failure in Vienna), it was in Paris that his works prospered most. Outstanding successes there included *Le solitaire* (1822), *Le valet de chambre* (1823) and above all *Masaniello* (1827), generally considered the highpoint of his career. Later works that held the stage for a while were *Le nozze di Lammermoor* (1829), *La prison d'Edimbourg* (1833) and *Thérèse* (1838), his last work for the theatre, apart from *airs* contributed to Adam's *Les premiers pas* (1847) and the ballet music commissioned by Rossini for the French version of his *Semiramide* (*Sémiramis*; 1860).

Carafa took French citizenship in 1834 and in 1837 succeeded Jean-François Le Sueur as a member of the Académie Française. He was appointed director of the Gymnase de Musique Militaire (1838), but resigned soon afterwards, and was professor of counterpoint at the Conservatoire from 1840 to 1870, although his activity there ended in 1858. During the 1860s he was one of the most faithful members of Rossini's circle. Unlike most 19th-century musical noblemen Carafa was a true professional, and as such enjoyed the unqualified approval of even the exacting Cherubini. His music, however, has not lasted. Rossini was one of the important influences in the formation of Carafa's style. His presence can be felt chiefly in the overtures, strictly patterned after Rossini's except for occasional variations in the tonal scheme, and in the later Italian operas such as *Le nozze di Lammermoor*. Even here, as in *Gabriella di Vergy*, groundings in an older, more classical tradition are apparent. For his French operas the chief model is Cherubini, and at their best they have a supple rhythmic strength, combined with delicacy of craftsmanship, not unworthy of him. The more contemporary styles of Auber, Boieldieu and Weber also left their mark. Carafa's chief limitation lay in his melody, which varies from the agreeably fluent to the devastatingly banal. For this as much as for any other reason his most popular pieces were superseded by others on the same subjects – *Masaniello* by Auber, *Le nozze di Lammermoor* by Donizetti and *La prison d'Edimbourg* by Federico Ricci. Nor did his music grow in individuality over the years. The ballet music for *Sémiramis* is on the lowest level of professional hackwork. Carafa gave his manuscripts to the Naples Conservatory library.

POC – *Paris, Opéra-Comique*
dl – *drame lyrique* oss – *opera semiseria*

Il fantasma (oss, 2), Naples, private theatre of the Prince of Caramanico, 1805, *I-Nc* [cantata, according to lib.]

Il prigioniero (oss), Naples, 1805, *Nc**

La musicomania (op comica, 1, anon., after R. C. G. de Pixérécourt), Paris, 1806, *Nc**

Il vascello l'occidente (melodramma, 2, A. L. Tottola), Naples, Fondo, 14 June 1814, *Nc**

La gelosia corretta (commedia per musica, 1, Tottola), Naples, Fiorentini, carn. 1815, *Nc**; as Mariti, aprite gli occhi, *Nc**

Gabriella di Vergy (os, 2, Tottola), Naples, Fondo, 3 July 1816, *Nc**, copies *Bc*, *Fc*, vs (Vienna, *c*1820); rev. version *Mr*

Ifigenia in Tauride (melodramma serio, 2), Naples, S Carlo, 19 June 1817, *Nc*

Adele di Lusignano (melodramma serio, 2, F. Romani), Milan, Scala, 27 Sept 1817, *Mc*, *Mr*, *Nc*, excerpts (Paris, 1817; Milan, 1818; Florence, n.d.)

Berenice in Siria (azione tragica, 2, Tottola), Naples, S Carlo, 29 July 1818, *Nc**, excerpts (Milan, n.d.; Naples, n.d.)

Elisabetta in Derbyshire, ossia Il castello di Fotheringhay (azione eroica, 2, A. Peracchi), Venice, Fenice, 26 Dec 1818, *Nc**, excerpts (Paris, Naples, Rome, Milan, London)

Il sacrifizio d'Epito (dramma, 2, D. Tindario [G. Kreglianovich]), Venice, Fenice, 26 Dec 1819, *Nc*, excerpts (Milan, 1820); as Aristodemo, Naples, 1821, *Mr*

I due Figaro, o sia Il soggetto di una commedia (dramma buffo, 2, Romani, after Martelly), Milan, Scala, 6 June 1820, *Mr**

La festa di Bussone (farsa, 2, ?S. Pellico), Milan, Re, 28 June 1820

Jeanne d'Arc à Orléans (dl, 3, E. G. Théaulon de Lambert and F. V. A. d'Artois de Bournonville), POC (Feydeau), 10 March 1821, *Nc** (Paris, ?1821)

La capricciosa ed il soldato, o sia Un momento di lezione (melodramma giocoso, 2, J. Ferretti), Rome, Apollo, 26 Dec 1821, *Nc**, excerpts (Rome, n.d.)

Le solitaire (oc, 3, F. A. E. de Planard), POC (Feydeau), 22 Aug 1822, *Nc** (Paris, ?1822)

Eufemio di Messina (melodramma eroico, 2, Ferretti), Rome, Argentina, 26 Dec 1822, excerpts *Bsf*, *Mc*, *Nc*, *Rsc*, *Rvat*, excerpts (Paris, Milan, Rome, Florence)

Abufar, ossia La famiglia araba (melodramma eroico, 2, Romani), Vienna, Kärntnertor, 28 June 1823, *Nc*, excerpts (Paris, London, Naples)

Le valet de chambre (oc, 1, E. Scribe and Mélesville [A. H. J. Duveyrier]), POC (Feydeau), 16 Sept 1823, *Nc** (Paris, ?1823)

Tamerlano (os, 3, Ferretti), written for Naples, S Carlo, 1823–4, unperf.

L'auberge supposée (oc, 3, Planard), POC (Feydeau), 26 April 1824, *Nc**

Il sonnambulo (oss, 2, Romani), Milan, Scala, 13 Nov 1824, *Mr*, *Nc*

La belle au bois dormant (opéra féerie, 3, Planard), Paris, Opéra, 2 March 1825, *Nc**

Gl'italici e gl'indiani (melodramma, 3, ?Tottola), Naples, S Carlo, 4 Oct 1825, *Nc**

Il paria (melodramma tragico, 2, G. Rossi), Venice, Fenice, 4 Feb 1826

Sangarido (oc, 1, Planard and J. B. Pellissier de Laqueyrie), POC (Feydeau), 19 May 1827, *Nc**

Les deux Figaro (oc, 3, V. Tirpenne), Paris, Odéon, 22 Aug 1827, collab. Leborne

Masaniello, ou Le pêcheur napolitain (dl, 4, C. F. J. B. Moreau de Commagny and A. M. Lafortelle), POC (Feydeau), 27 Dec 1827, *Nc** (Paris, ?1828)

La violette (oc, 3, Planard, after Comte de Tressan: *Gérard de Nevers*), POC (Feydeau), 7 Oct 1828, *Nc** (Paris, ?1828) [finales to Acts 1 and 2 by Leborne]

Jenny (oc, 3, J.-H. Vernoy de Saint-Georges), POC (Ventadour), 26 Sept 1829, *Nc**

Le nozze di Lammermoor (oss, 2, L. Balocchi, after W. Scott), Paris, Italien, 12 Dec 1829, *Nc**, vs (Paris, ?1829)

L'auberge d'Auray (oc, 1, Moreau de Commagny and J.-B. V. d'Epagny), POC (Ventadour), 11 May 1830 (1830); collab. F. Hérold

Le lure de l'hermite (oc, 2, Planard and P. Duport), POC (Ventadour), 11 Aug 1831, *Nc**

La marquise de Brinvilliers [ov., Act 2 finale only] (dl, 3, Scribe and Castil-Blaze [F.-H.-J. Blaze]), POC (Ventadour), 31 Oct 1831, (Paris, 1831), ov. (Berlin, n.d.); collab. Auber, Batton, H.-M. Berton, Blangini, A. Boieldieu, Cherubini, Hérold and Paer

L'orgie (ballet-pantomime, Scribe and Coralli), 1831

La prison d'Edimbourg (oc, 3, Scribe and Planard, after Scott: *The Heart of Midlothian*), POC (Bourse), 20 July 1833, *Nc** (Paris, ?1833)

La maison du rempart, ou Une journée de la Fronde (oc, 3, Mélesville), POC (Bourse), 7 Nov 1833, *Nc**

La grande duchesse (dl, 4, Mélesville and P. F. C. Merville and [P. F. Camus]), POC (Bourse), 16 Nov 1835, *Nc**

Thérèse (oc, 2, Planard and A. de Leuven), POC (Bourse), 26 Sept 1838, *Nc**
Les premiers pas [recit., aria only] (scène-prologue), Paris, Opéra-National, 15 Nov 1847, *Nc**; collab. A. Adam, Auber, F. Halévy

*

FlorimoN JULIAN BUDDEN

Caravane du Caire, La ('The Cairo Caravan'). *Opéra-ballet* in three acts by ANDRÉ-ERNEST-MODESTE GRÉTRY to a libretto by Etienne Morel de Chédeville; Fontainebleau, 30 October 1783.

By the river Nile a slave caravan has stopped on its way to Cairo. Slaves lament their misfortune. Among them are Saint-Phar (tenor), son of a French officer named Florestan (bass), and Zélime (soprano), daughter of an Indian chief. They declare their undying love. Husca (baritone), leader of the caravan, assures them that fate will separate them. Suddenly there is an alarm: the caravan is attacked by Arabs. Saint-Phar is released by Husca so that he may assist in beating off the attackers, who are in due course repulsed. Husca awards Saint-Phar his freedom, but refuses to release Zélime.

The first scene of Act 2 is set in the Pasha's palace at Cairo. One of his ships has been saved by Florestan. The Pasha (bass) praises the virtues of the French ('Oui, oui, toujours'). Almaïde (soprano), the most favoured of his harem, sings of her devotion to her master who is, however, bored with her. After a short *divertissement* the eunuch Tamorin (high tenor) introduces Husca, and the men leave for the bazaar. Scene ii depicts the bazaar; after dances, a march announces the Pasha, who then watches women from different countries singing and dancing. He buys Zélime, and Saint-Phar is left to vent his anger ('Va, va, cruel').

Act 3, in the Pasha's palace, opens with Florestan discussing his son's disappearance ('Ah! si pour la patrie'). Almaïde expresses her jealousy to Osmin (bass), a harem slave. But the Pasha is wholly absorbed by Zélime ('C'est en vain qu'Almaïde encore'). In a public room, a celebration begins for Florestan and French officers. News arrives of Zélime's abduction by an unknown Frenchman. She is captured, and confesses her desire to escape with one Saint-Phar. He is arraigned, his father is obliged to plead for him and the Pasha is compelled to free the lovers.

La caravane du Caire was the most successful of Grétry's lighter large-scale works, being seen at the Paris Opéra frequently up to 1829, in more than 500 performances. Grétry's melodic and orchestral skills were heard to advantage in the dances; the score also contains important chorus music, including double choruses with contrasted motifs, and a variety of ensembles. Instrumental forces include a triangle and a harp. Tradition has it that the libretto was partially written by the Count of Provence, later Louis XVIII.

DAVID CHARLTON

Carcani [Carcano], **Giuseppe** [Gioseffo] (*b* Crema, 1703; *d* Piacenza, 17 Dec 1778). Italian composer. He succeeded Hasse in 1739 as *maestro di cappella* of the Incurabili in Venice, and in 1744 became *maestro di cappella* of Piacenza Cathedral, where he remained until his death. He also held other ecclesiastical posts in Piacenza, and became a leading light at the Bourbon court of the dukes of Piacenza and Parma. Seven operas by him are known, as well as cantatas, oratorios and instrumental music. Although famous in his day, Carcani does not now appear to have possessed strikingly individual gifts. His operatic arias and duets follow obsequiously the style of Hasse's without possessing their purely musical qualities.

all opere serie; in three acts unless otherwise stated

Demetrio (P. Metastasio), Crema, Civico, 23 Sept 1742, duet *GB-Lbl*
Ambleto (A. Zeno and P. Pariati), Venice, S Angelo, wint. 1742, duet *Lbl, I-Fc*
Alcibiade (A. Aureli), Venice, S Cassiano, aut. 1746
Artaserse (Metastasio), Piacenza, Ducale, carn. 1748, aria *I-MOe*
Alcuni avvenimenti di Telemaco figliuolo di Ulisse, re d'Itaca (G. Riviera), Piacenza, Ducale, Feb 1749; ? as Telemaco, Milan, Regio Ducale, 1749 [acc. to Manferrari]
Il Tigrane (2, C. Goldoni), Milan, Regio Ducale, Feb 1750, aria *Mc*
Olimpiade (Metastasio), Mantua, Vecchio, 1757, aria *MAav*
Arianna e Teseo (Pariati), Verona, Filarmonico, carn. 1759

Arias in *A-Wn, I-MOe, Nc*

*

G. Carpani: *Le Haydine* (Milan, 1812)
F. Bussi: *Alcuni maestri di cappella e organisti della cattedrale di Piacenza* (Piacenza, 1956) FRANCESCO BUSSI

Carcano. Theatre in MILAN, opened in 1803. It was the venue of the premières of Donizetti's *Anna Bolena* (1830) and Bellini's *La sonnambula* (1831), but its importance gradually declined and by 1900 it was no longer used for music.

Card, June (*b* Dunkirk, NY, 10 April 1942). American soprano. She made her début in 1966 with the Central City Opera in Colorado as Elvira (*L'italiana in Algeri*). Engaged at the Theater am Gärntnerplatz, Munich, she sang the title role in Janáček's *Cunning Little Vixen* (1967) and created Una in Lothar's *Der widerspenstige Heilige* (1968). She joined Frankfurt Opera in 1969, and has also sung in Vienna and Barcelona and at Wexford as Magda in *La rondine* (1971). At the 1978 Edinburgh Festival she took part in the British première of Luigi Nono's *Al gran sole carico d'amore*. Her repertory includes Donna Elvira, Senta, Nedda, Chrysothemis, Zdenka (*Arabella*), Minnie, and Janáček's Jenůfa, Kát'a and Emilia Marty; she has also appeared in Henze's *Der junge Lord* and *The Bassarids*, Schreker's *Die Gezeichneten*, Shostakovich's *Katerina Izmaylova*, Stravinsky's *The Rake's Progress*, Zimmermann's *Die Soldaten* and other contemporary operas, where the security of her singing and the intensity of her interpretation are of especial value. ELIZABETH FORBES

Carden, Joan (*b* Richmond, Melbourne, 9 Oct 1937). Australian soprano. She studied in Melbourne, then in London, making her début at Sadler's Wells (1963) as the Water-Melon Seller in Malcolm Williamson's *Our Man in Havana*. A technically capable Gilda for the Australian Opera led to her Covent Garden début in the same part in 1974. She sang Donna Anna at Glyndebourne (1977) and for the touring Metropolitan Opera (1978), and Konstanze for Scottish Opera (1978). Her Australian Opera roles include Ellen Orford, Tatyana (*Yevgeny Onegin*), the title roles in *Lakmé* and *Alcina*, two Leonoras (*Il trovatore* and *La forza del destino*), several Mozart roles and the four heroines in *Les contes d'Hoffmann*. She gradually moved away from the coloratura to the lyric-dramatic repertory, singing Tosca at Adelaide in 1990. Her Butterfly was much admired for its well-focussed, graceful singing. ROGER COVELL

Cardiff. Capital of Wales. The country had little of an operatic tradition before the 20th century, and until World War II opera performances in Cardiff were given either by visiting companies or by amateur, and usually short-lived, local societies. The Welsh National Opera Company, as it was first called, also began as an amateur venture, and its first one-week season (*Pagliacci, Cavalleria rusticana* and Gounod's *Faust*) at the Prince of Wales Theatre in 1946 included only one professional, the tenor Tudor Davies; the casts were completed by members of the chorus. The company's first Musical Director was Idloes Owen, and all three operas were directed by Norman Jones. Together with the business manager (later chairman) William ('Bill') Smith, they guided the company through its difficult early years.

In 1952 the company transferred its Cardiff performances to the Sophia Gardens Pavilion and in 1954 to the New Theatre, its regular base ever since (though its offices, workshops and rehearsal studios are situated elsewhere in Cardiff). From there it toured to other Welsh, and later English, centres, gradually acquiring greater professionalism in all departments. Its wider reputation was built in the 1950s largely on a series of Verdi operas, which included several early and little-known works and capitalized on the strength of the company's still amateur chorus. Verdi, together with Mozart, Rossini and Puccini, continued to provide the staple fare during the 1960s, with John Moody as Director of Productions, but the end of the decade saw many changes in the WNO's organization and aspirations. In 1968 the amateur chorus was joined, and in 1973 replaced, by a smaller, professional body, and in 1970 the company established its own orchestra, known at first as the Welsh Philharmonia; previously orchestras from England had been engaged for its productions.

The WNO was now a fully professional opera company, and one to which its administrators (notably Albert Francis, executive chairman 1968–75, and Brian McMaster, general administrator 1976–91) were able to impart a corporate identity, often in the face of financial and other difficulties. The productions of the 1970s were largely shaped by Michael Geliot, who succeeded Moody in 1969 and who became Artistic Director in 1974. Unpredictable and often controversial as a director, Geliot was responsible for the first *Lulu* by a British company (1971) – a milestone in the WNO's history; the excellent production was conducted by James Lockhart, Musical Director, 1968–73. Lockhart's successor, Richard Armstrong, extended the company's reputation in 20th-century opera, and works by the Welsh composers Alun Hoddinott and John Metcalf were commissioned. Another notable achievement was the staging of five Janáček works directed by David Pountney with designs by Maria Björnson. Sir Charles Mackerras became Musical Director in 1986, but Geliot had not been replaced when he resigned his post in 1978. McMaster's policy was to engage innovatory directors for particular projects, including several from eastern Europe. Harry Kupfer's *Elektra* (1978), Andrei Serban's *Yevgeny Onegin* (1980) and Göran Järvefelt's *Ring* cycle (1983–5) have been among the most notable successes; others, such as Lucian Pintilie's *Carmen* (1983) and Ruth Berghaus's *Don Giovanni* (1984), have divided both audiences and critics.

*

R. Fawkes: *Welsh National Opera* (London, 1986)

MALCOLM BOYD

Cardillac. Opera in three acts, op.39, by PAUL HINDEMITH to a libretto by Ferdinand Lion after E. T. A. HOFFMANN's story *Das Fräulein von Scuderi*; Dresden, Staatsoper, 9 November 1926; revised in four acts to a libretto by Hindemith after Lion, Zürich, Stadttheater, 20 June 1952.

In the original version, the action takes place in 17th-century Paris. The streets are in uproar, murderers are at large. A Cavalier (tenor) explains to a Lady (soprano) that whoever buys a trinket from the goldsmith Cardillac is immediately stabbed to death and robbed. The Lady bids the Cavalier, if he wishes her favour, to bring her 'the finest object Cardillac ever made'. Accepting the challenge, the Cavalier brings to her bedroom a golden belt. While he is receiving his reward, a masked figure breaks in, kills him and escapes with the belt. Act 2 reveals Cardillac (baritone) in his workroom, so

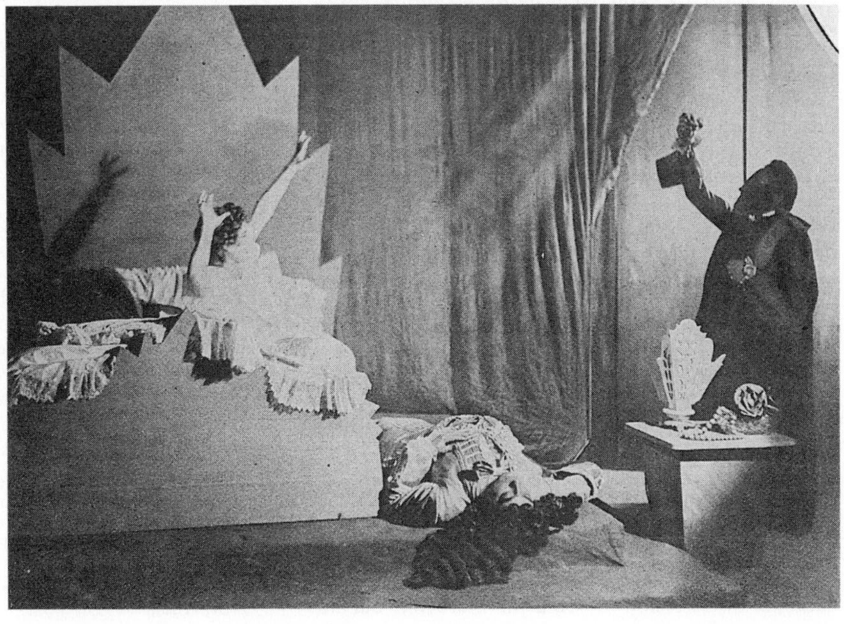

'Cardillac' (Hindemith), Act 1: scene from the original production at the Staatsoper, Dresden, 9 November 1926, with (from left to right) Grete Merrem-Nikisch as the Lady, Eybisch as the Cavalier and Robert Burg as Cardillac

possessive of his work that he resents even a visit by the King (silent role) and refuses to sell him anything. Cardillac's Daughter (soprano), torn between her father and her lover, an Officer (tenor), is indifferently told to marry him if she wants; as he informs the Officer, his work is more important to him than his daughter. The Officer, perceiving Cardillac's weak point and anxious to break his power over his daughter, insists on buying a gold chain, despite the risk to himself. Cardillac, unable to bear its loss, follows him in disguise. Act 3 takes place outside a tavern, where Cardillac overtakes the Officer and stabs him. A Gold Dealer (bass) witnesses the deed and recognizes the attacker, denouncing him to the crowd. However, the wounded Officer protects him out of pity for his daughter, accusing the Gold Dealer of being the unknown murderer's accomplice. Cardillac, unwilling to be indebted to anyone, reveals himself as the murderer, and the enraged crowd kill him.

Despite the romantic nature of the subject, Hindemith chose a demonstratively anti-romantic line for his music, modelling it on Handelian opera, then enjoying a revival in Germany. The music begins and ends with extended polyphonic choral numbers (depicting the crowd's unrest over the murders and their determination to find and punish the murderer); between these are 15 musical sections, each identified by name (aria, arioso and duet, scena and quartet, etc.). The action, however, is continuous, moving forward with a minimum of recitative. A tight control of length, combined with rhythmic variety, ensures that there is no sense of the drama being held up by the demands of musical form. Hindemith nevertheless finds room for dramatic devices of a distinctly Verdian hue, as in the accompaniment to the Cavalier's Act 1 aria, where he is torn between temptation and the fear of death, and the Lady's aria, full of restless erotic desire. The anticipated love duet is replaced by a 'pantomime' for two flutes in which, to a minuet rhythm, Cavalier and Lady silently admire the belt the Cavalier has brought. Traces of Verdi are also apparent in the innocent Daughter's vacillation between father and lover in the second act, and in Cardillac's aria as he wrestles with his conscience before setting out to murder his daughter's lover.

In the revised version, Hindemith's main object was to humanize his hero in order to shed further light on the question of the artist's responsibility to society, the subject of both *Mathis der Maler* and *Die Harmonie der Welt*. In bringing the story closer to Hoffmann's original, he rewrote the text but fitted his words to the existing music, altering the order of some numbers and at times changing the vocal line. The Lady becomes the Opera Singer (soprano) and the Daughter's lover is Cardillac's Journeyman (tenor). In Act 1 a new duet between Cardillac and the Cavalier replaces the Cavalier's solo: here Cardillac behaves in a kindly way until the Cavalier insists on buying a diadem for the Opera Singer, when his mood darkens. The Opera Singer is seen bidding farewell to a Marquis (silent role) before the Cavalier arrives, and her intervening solo (to the same music) tells of her disillusionment with, rather than her desire for, men. However, the outcome is the same. In Act 2 the King's visit is replaced with a visit by the Marquis and the opera company who have come, in Cardillac's absence, to buy a crown for the Opera Singer to wear on stage. She recognizes the diadem stolen from her, but accepts it without revealing her suspicions. The naive Journeyman is arrested by a Police Officer (bass-baritone) on suspicion of being the murderer, but he escapes and begs Cardillac to allow his daughter to flee with him. Cardillac refuses, and the Journeyman, though hinting that he knows Cardillac to be the murderer, is thrown out. Cardillac sets off in pursuit of the missing diadem. The new third act consists of three numbers, the first being a stage performance of scenes from Lully's opera *Phaëton*. Against this, in a juxtaposition of music and action, the Journeyman comes to warn the Opera Singer (wearing the diadem as Theo in Lully's opera), followed by the Police Officer and Cardillac. After the opera has ended, the Opera Singer dismisses the other singers and returns the diadem to Cardillac. A duet hints at his redemption through her understanding and sympathy, but, finding the diadem gone yet again (the Police Officer has surreptitiously taken it), Cardillac relapses and goes off in pursuit. In Act 4 it is the Police Officer whom Cardillac wounds and the Journeyman, attempting to intervene, whom the crowd accuse of being the murderer. The Police Officer protects him, and the opera ends as before, with Cardillac revealing and defending his own murderous deeds, whereupon the enraged crowd kill him.

Hindemith's revised text is stronger in motivation than the original, but its argumentative tone is less suited to the form of the music, and the interpolated third act, however ingenious, lessens the dramatic tension. It has not proved as popular as its forerunner.

GEOFFREY SKELTON

Cardonne, Jean-Baptiste [Philibert] (*b* Versailles, 26 June 1730; *d* after Aug 1792). French composer. A child prodigy, he began his career as a royal page, receiving music instruction from Collin de Blamont. He held various posts in royal service, including singer and harpsichordist from 1745 and *sous-maître* of pages and harpsichordists from 1761. He was also a choir member at the Marquise de Pompadour's theatre during the 1750s; while there he wrote the pastorale *Amaryllis*. However, it was not until after his retirement as a former *officier de la dauphine* that he composed his first opera. He chose for his subject Lamotte's tragedy *Omphale*, which had been severely attacked when it was revived with Destouches' music in 1752. Grimm had been particularly harsh in his criticism, and Cardonne, while following Grimm's principles, attempted to bring together the ideas of both factions in the Querelle des Bouffons. Rather than achieving a compromise, he found himself caught in an argument that went beyond the merits of his work, however attractive its melodies and serious its intentions. He next wrote a one-act ballet, *Ovide et Julie*, as part of a work entitled *Fragments héroïques*, the other two sections being revivals of works by Destouches ('Feu' from *Les éléments*) and Rameau ('Sauvage' from *Les Indes galantes*). Once again he met with mixed reaction and little public success. After failing to have his opera *Epaphus* produced he returned to the court and composed chamber music. In 1780 he became *maître de la musique du roi*, and from 1781 he was *surintendant honoraire*. He maintained his position as *maître* at least until August 1792, but with the fall of the monarchy in September of that year public notices of him ceased.

Amaryllis (pastorale, 3), Compiègne, 17 July 1752, lost

Omphale (tragédie, 5, A. H. de Lamotte), Paris, Opéra, 2 May 1769, *F-Po*

Epaphus [? et Memphis] (opéra, P. Laujon), unperf. [cited by La Borde]

L'amant jaloux persécuté (comédie, 1) [cited in *Spectacles de Paris* (1781, 1782)]

J.-B. de La Borde: *Essai sur la musique ancienne et moderne*, iii (Paris, 1780), 402
A. Pougin: *Histoire du théâtre de Mme de Pompadour* (Paris, 1874)
M. Tourneux, ed.: *Correspondence littéraire, philosophique et critique par Grimm, Diderot, Raynal, Meister, etc.* (Paris, 1877–82) DEANNE ARKUS KLEIN

Carelli, Emma (*b* Naples, 12 May 1877; *d* nr Rome, 17 Aug 1928). Italian soprano. She was born into a musical family, and in 1895 made her début in the title role of Mercadante's *La vestale* during the centenary celebrations at Altamura. After appearances in Naples and at the Dal Verme in Milan, she went to La Scala, singing Desdemona to Tamagno's Otello and, in 1900, Tatyana in the Italian première of *Yevgeny Onegin*. A spectacular tour of South America was followed by her greatest success, as Zazà in the opera by Leoncavallo. In 1898 she married the left-wing politician Walter Mocchi, who later became a theatrical impresario and acquired the Costanzi in Rome. Carelli took over the management in 1912, her first season including the Rome première of Strauss's *Elektra* in which she sang the title role to great acclaim, having coped with a fire in the theatre earlier that evening. She ran the theatre for 15 years, maintaining an enterprising repertory with distinguished casts and despite serious financial losses. She died in a car accident in 1928. Her few and rare recordings are not attractive as pure singing but have plenty of energy and temperament.

GV (R. Celletti; R. Vegeto)
A. Carelli: *Emma Carelli: trenti anni di vita del teatro lirico* (Rome, 1932)
K. Hardwick: 'Emma Carelli', *Record Collector*, xi (1957), 173–83; xii (1958–60), 36–7 [with discography] J. B. STEANE

Carena, Maria (*b* Turin, 1891; *d* Turin, 9 Oct 1966). Italian soprano. She studied with Virginia Ferni-Germano in Turin and made her début there in 1917, as the *Trovatore* Leonora. After appearances in Rome, Naples, Buenos Aires and Lisbon she made her La Scala début as Suor Angelica in 1922. She sang in Milan until 1932, notably as Asteria in the première of Boito's *Nerone* and as Amelia in *Ballo*. Her dramatic temperament was admired in the role of Julia in *La vestale* by Spontini (1932, Rome). She retired at the outbreak of World War II. DAVID CUMMINGS

Carestini, Giovanni [Cusanino] (*b* Filottrano, nr Ancona, *c*1704; *d* ?Filottrano, *c*1760). Italian soprano, later alto, castrato. He was taken to Milan at the age of 12 under the protection of the Cusani family, and first performed there in Vignati's *Porsena* in 1719. Several northern appearances preceded his Roman début in 1721 (Scarlatti's *La Griselda*), where he sang alongside Bernacchi, his teacher. He remained for two years and then graced the Viennese court in 1723–4, appearing in Fux's *Costanza e fortezza* in Prague. He was at Venice in 1724–6, 1729 and 1731, singing in operas by Vinci and Porpora, and in Rome in 1727–30, where he appeared in works by Vinci and Feo; he also sang in operas by Hasse and others in Naples, 1728–9. He crossed the Alps in 1731 and entered the service of the Duke of Bavaria in Munich, returning to Italy before following Handel to London in 1733. There he created the principal male roles in Handel's *Arianna in Creta*, *Parnasso in festa*, *Terpsichore*, *Ariodante* and *Alcina*, also singing in revivals and pasticcios. Back in Naples in 1735, his salary was higher than Caffarelli's. During a second London engagement, for six months ending in May 1740, he enjoyed little success. In the 1740s he appeared in Italy, was in Maria Theresa's employ by 1744 and sang under Hasse in Dresden, 1747–9. Brief Italian appearances preceded a Berlin engagement, 1750–54; he then moved to St Petersburg under Araia until 1756. His career declined rapidly; a Naples audience was hostile in 1758.

Carestini was at first 'a powerful and clear soprano' (Burney), with a compass of *b* to *c‴*; later he had 'the fullest, finest, and deepest counter-tenor that has perhaps ever been heard'. Handel's roles for him call for a two-octave compass, *a* to *a″*; Hasse's *Demofoonte* (1748) requires *e♭* to *g′*. His reputation was enormous. Hasse remarked: 'He who has not heard Carestini is not acquainted with the most perfect style of singing'; Quantz added: 'He had extraordinary virtuosity in brilliant passages, which he sang in chest voice, conforming to the principles of the school of Bernacchi and the manner of Farinelli'. Others, including Burney, commented on his superb acting, and his handsome and majestic profile. DALE E. MONSON

Carey, (Francis) Clive (Savill) (*b* Sible Hedingham, 30 May 1883; *d* London, 30 April 1968). English baritone and director. He studied at Cambridge and in London and with Jean de Reszke in Paris and Nice. He directed *Die Zauberflöte* and sang Papageno at Cambridge University in 1911 when Edward J. Dent's English translation was first used. Engaged at the Old Vic opera company (1920–24) as singer and director, he appeared in *Le nozze di Figaro*, *Don Giovanni* and *Die Zauberflöte*. He taught in Australia at Adelaide (1924–7), where he also worked in the straight theatre, and in 1928 he toured North America in *The Beggar's Opera*, singing Captain Macheath. In the 1930s he worked at Sadler's Wells Opera, where he was director in 1945–6, after a further period of teaching in Adelaide and also Melbourne (1939–45). A stylish performer, particularly of Mozart roles, and an accomplished actor, he was an imaginative director, much concerned with the elimination of accumulated tradition and returning to composers' intentions, and a fine teacher.

ELIZABETH FORBES

Carey, Henry (*b* ?Yorkshire, 1687; *d* London, 4 Oct 1743). English dramatist and composer. His background has been the subject of much controversy, but it is clear that he had a strong connection with Yorkshire. Although his first excursion into print was in poetry, he showed an early interest in and involvement with music and musicians. Soon after he settled in London (*c*1711) he became a pupil of the organist John Reading (himself a pupil of Blow) and later of Roseingrave. Pepusch was a neighbour, and it is possible that he too was influential. Although Carey the poet was always ebulliently active throughout his career, it is impossible not to form the opinion that Carey the composer was always jealously struggling to achieve supremacy. Hawkins was far less kind to him than Burney, who went so far as to say of Carey that 'popular strains at least, if not learned and elegant Music may be produced by the writer of a dramatic poem'.

In the 1720s Carey acted as one of Drury Lane's house composers, but his operatic achievement was always propelled by an intense patriotism and a thorough-going dislike of the foibles of Italian singers and those who idolized them. In 1729 he demonstrated his flair for writing a well-structured libretto enhanced by thoroughly amiable music by revising his farce of 1715, *The Contrivances*, to provide a version whose memorable songs and catchy tunes showed a mastery of the ballad style as well as good understanding of the Italian idiom (there are ten da capo arias), although he was unable completely to disguise his inability to develop his material sufficiently. His use of spoken dialogue with operatic arias allows *The Contrivances* to defend a claim to be the first English comic opera, predating, as it does, Bickerstaffe's *Love in a Village* by more than 30 years. Carey shows greater sensitivity in his handling of the transition between dialogue and verse than do most of his contemporaries.

In spring 1732 Carey, Lampe, Arne, J. C. Smith and others made a concerted attempt to establish English opera on the London stage with works that were not ballad operas but operas 'after the Italian manner'. Carey contributed two librettos: *Amelia* (set by Lampe) and *Teraminta*, the setting of which has been attributed to J. C. Smith despite strong indications that it may be by John Stanley. Later that year Arne led a splinter group away from Lampe and the Little Theatre to set up in John Rich's old theatre in Lincoln's Inn Fields. His first production there was *Teraminta*, but diversification and disagreement among the company in 1733 as well as upheavals in the management, together with the lack of any real success with *Britannia* (Lampe), *Rosamond* (Arne) and *Ulysses* (J. C. Smith), culminated in the only modest success of *The Opera of Operas* (Lampe, with contributions by Arne) and the campaign for English national opera collapsed. However, solid achievements had been made in that a number of new works of unquestionable musical and literary value had been produced, and many new English singers had made their débuts. The English revival movement may just have prompted Handel to explore the possibilities of oratorio using English singers for this purpose; whatever the reason, the timing is certainly suggestive.

In 1734 Carey, using his pseudonym Benjamin Bounce, showed the full possibilities of musical burlesque, with Italian *opera seria* the butt of his humour, in his *Chrononhotonthologus*. The songs 'in the Italian style' have not survived, but we know that there was a splendid burlesque of the *deus ex machina* as well as an ensemble with the singers singing at one another and 'rough' music demanding the use of marrowbones, cleavers, saltboxes and the like. In 1737, under his other pseudonym of Signor Carini, Carey wrote the libretto for *The Dragon of Wantley* (Lampe) and dealt Handel a crushing blow by cashing in on the more absurd aspects of operatic convention while utilizing Lampe's deep understanding of the Italian style to sharpen the point of the parody. The work quickly became a rallying point for anti-Italian sentiment with the support of the impresario John Rich, who showed his racehorse-owner's knack of successfully backing an outsider in the same way as he had done for *The Beggar's Opera*. *The Dragon* ran for 69 nights, seven more than *The Beggar's Opera* in its first season, although a sequel, *Margery, or A Worse Plague than the Dragon*, was less successful. The setting for *The Dragon* was Yorkshire, which Carey had used before in both *Hanging and Marriage* (1722) and *The Honest Yorkshireman* (1735). In the latter the hero is given regional speech, rarely used at this time, with lines such as 'I'll toss'n in, and you after'n'.

Carey's most original piece was *Nancy* (1739), which began life as an interlude and was expanded to contain not only the most delightful music he ever wrote but also an entirely satisfying and unusual libretto highlighting a contemporary social injustice. Each setting is characterized well. There are crackling melismas, instrumental preludes and postludes and even a Purcellian five-part chorus. In its expanded all-sung form it remained popular throughout the 18th century as *True Blue, or The Press Gang*. In this, his final work, Carey shows signs of breaking away from Italian influences and developing a more thorough-going English style. However, the English revival had by now lost its impetus and Carey's freshness of approach after *Nancy* became faded. Debt was inevitable and suicide the most frequent solution of the age.

all performed in London; all printed works published in London

LCG – *Covent Garden* LDL – *Drury Lane*
LLH – *Little Theatre in the Haymarket*
bal – *ballad opera*

The Quaker's Opera (bal, T. Walker), Southwark Fair, 24 Sept 1728, songs arr. Carey
Love in a Riddle (bal, C. Cibber), LDL, 7 Jan 1729, songs arr. Carey
The Contrivances (op with dialogue, Carey), LDL, 20 June 1729, songs pubd
The Generous Freemason (bal, W. R. Chetwood), Bartholomew Fair, 20 Aug 1730, songs arr. Carey
Betty, or The Country Bumpkins (bal, Carey), LDL, 1 Dec 1732, only song words pubd
Chrononhotonthologus (burlesque op, Carey), LLH, 22 Feb 1734, tunes in lib.
The Honest Yorkshireman (bal, Carey), LLH, 15 July 1735, songs pubd
The Coffee House (J. Miller), LDL, 26 Jan 1738, songs pubd
Nancy, or The Parting Lovers (all-sung afterpiece, Carey), LCG, 1 Dec 1739, rev. *c*1765; also as True Blue, or The Press Gang

Librettos: *Amelia* (Eng. op), J. F. Lampe, 1732; *Teraminta* (Eng. op), J. C. Smith, 1732, and J. Stanley, *c*1750–55; *The Dragon of Wantley* (burlesque op), Lampe, 1737; *Margery, or a Worse Plague than the Dragon* (burlesque op), Lampe, 1738

*

BUCEM; *BurneyH*; *HawkinsH*
G. Hogarth: *Memoirs of the Musical Drama* (London, 1838)
F. T. Wood: Preface to *Poems of Henry Carey* (London, 1930)
J. Trevithick: *The Dramatic Work of Henry Carey* (diss., Yale U., 1939)
H. J. Dane: *The Life and Works of Henry Carey* (diss., U. of Pennsylvania, 1967)
J. Burke and C. Caldwell, eds.: *Hogarth: the Complete Engravings* (London, 1968)
E. L. Oldfield: *The Achievement of Henry Carey* (diss., U. of Washington, 1969)
S. J. Trussler, ed.: *Burlesque Plays of the Eighteenth Century* (London, 1969)
R. Fiske: *English Theatre Music in the Eighteenth Century* (London, 1973, 2/1986)
C. G. Chapman: *English Pantomime and its Music 1700–1730* (diss., U. of London, 1981)
J. N. Gillespie: *The Life and Works of Henry Carey, 1687–1743* (diss., U. of London, 1982)
CLIVE CHAPMAN

Cargill, Mrs. *See* BROWN, ANN.

Carignano. Theatre in TURIN, inaugurated in 1715 by the princes of Carignano; since 1945 it has been used solely for plays.

Carinthian Summer. Summer festival held in OSSIACH, in Carinthia, southern Austria, since 1969.

Carlani, Carlo (*fl* 1743–65). Italian tenor. Little is known of his life; librettos refer to him only as 'bolognese'. He first sang in a revival of Buini's *Le* *frenesie d'amore* in Bologna in 1736, then appeared in Rimini two years later. After 1743 he was regularly engaged as *tenore* in Venice, Lucca, Rome, Bologna, Naples, Ferrara and Siena. In 1749–51 he appeared in Madrid, where he created the title role for Galuppi's first setting of *Demofoonte*, a part he later repeated for Bologna. He spent 1755–6 in Vienna and returned for four more operas in 1760–61. His last known engagements were in Venice in 1764–5. Carlani's voice was lyric, and his music often marked by profound pathos. Hasse's new setting of *Artaserse* for Naples in 1760 shows that he had an extraordinarily wide range of nearly three octaves, from *F* to *d''*. He was capable of extended coloratura, including large leaps in fast tempos, repeated notes and frequent scale passages. In his later years, when his voice was in decline, he increasingly accepted secondo uomo roles. DALE E. MONSON

Carl [Karl] **Eugen,** Duke of Württemberg (*b* Stuttgart, 11 Feb 1728; *d* ?Stuttgart, 1793). German patron of music. Educated at the court of Frederick the Great, the young duke began his reign in 1744, emulating the Potsdam court at his own residence in Stuttgart. The court theatre was rebuilt in 1750, and in November 1753 Jommelli was appointed Ober-Kapellmeister. For the next 16 years he wrote and supervised virtually all operas at the court, and during that time assembled one of the best orchestras in Europe. Carl Eugen authorized extensive renovations to the court theatre in Stuttgart between 1756 and 1758, and after being forced to move to Ludwigsburg he built a new Schlosstheater (1765–6). His tastes in opera favoured French-inspired spectacle and dance; Noverre served as his ballet-master from 1760 until 1767, when a mounting deficit forced drastic reductions in personnel. Jommelli left two years later, after the departure of a number of singers including the castrato Giuseppe Aprile. Sacchini was engaged to write an opera in 1770, but performances at the court theatres were given much less frequently than in former times. In 1769 Carl Eugen established a school of the arts, reorganized in 1775 as the Carlsschule. A famous libertine, he could also be a tyrant: the soprano Marianne Pirker was imprisoned for eight years, and the organist and writer Schubart was also banished and subsequently jailed after insulting the duke's mistresses. Burney compared him to Nero for indulging in his own pleasure at the expense of his people.

BurneyGN
C. F. D. Schubart: *Ideen zu einer Aesthetik der Tonkunst* (Vienna, 1806)
J. Sittard: *Zur Geschichte der Musik und des Theaters am Württembergischen Hofe* (Stuttgart, 1890)
H. Abert and others: *Herzog Karl Eugen von Württemberg und seine Zeit* (Esslingen, 1905–9)
A. Yorke-Long: *Music at Court: Four Eighteenth Century Studies* (London, 1954)
A. L. Tolkoff: *The Stuttgart Operas of Niccolo Jommelli* (diss., Yale U., 1974)
M. McClymonds: 'Mattia Verazi and the Opera at Mannheim, Stuttgart and Ludwigsburg', *Studies in Music from the University of Western Ontario*, vii (1982), 99–136 PAUL CORNEILSON

Carli, Antonio Francesco (*fl* 1698–1723). Italian bass. There were two singers of this name, a tenor who sang in at least five Venetian operas between 1689 and 1699 and who may have been the father of his namesake, and a bass. The latter sang in Giovanni Bononcini's *Camilla* at Piacenza in 1698, at Genoa in 1706 and 1715, Bologna in 1708, Rome in 1717 (as Bajazet in F. Gasparini's *Il Trace in Catena*), Florence (where he was a virtuoso of the Tuscan court) in 1708 and 1719–20, and regularly in Venetian theatres, 1706–18 and 1722–3. He appeared there in 28 operas, including works by C. F. Pollarolo, Caldara, Lotti, Albinoni and Gasparini, and Handel's *Agrippina* (1709), as the original Claudius. The tessitura and compass of this part (*C* to *e'*) point to a singer of exceptional powers, capable of sudden leaps and changes of register.

WINTON DEAN

Carlino di Ratta, Il. *See* ZANARDI, CARLO ANTONIO.

Carlo Felice. Theatre in GENOA, opened in 1828, damaged in 1943 and renovated in 1991.

Carl Rosa Opera Company. Company founded in 1875 by Karl August Nikolaus Rose (later Carl Rosa). It opened at the Gaiety Theatre, Dublin, on 29 March 1875; its first London season began on 11 September 1875, at the Princess's Theatre, with *Le nozze di Figaro*. Rosa had organized the Parepa-Rosa Grand English Opera which toured the USA from 1867 to 1871; his wife, Euphrosyne Parepa, was the leading soprano. The company also included Rose Hersee, Jennie van Zandt, Karl Formes, Charles Santley and Theodor Wachtel. In September 1873 the company opened a British tour in Manchester, and a London season was planned for 1874, but was cancelled when Rosa's wife died in January. Rosa established a Parepa-Rosa Scholarship at the RAM and went to the USA. He soon decided to devote the rest of his life to promoting opera in English and returned to Great Britain to establish the Carl Rosa Company.

The repertory of the first London season included the first performance in England of Cagnoni's *Papà Martin* (in English, as *The Porter of Havre*), a revival of Cherubini's *Les deux journées* (*The Water Carrier*), as well as *Le nozze di Figaro*, *Faust*, *Fra Diavolo*, *Il trovatore*, *The Bohemian Girl* and *The Siege of Rochelle*. From 1876 to 1882 the company gave seasons at the King's Theatre and by 1882 had given the first performances in English (or in England) of *Der fliegende Holländer*, *Rienzi*, *Tannhäuser*, *Carmen*, *Lohengrin*, *Mignon*, *Aida* and Goetz's *Der widerspenstigen Zähmung*, at the Lyceum, Adelphi and Her Majesty's Theatres.

From 1883 until his death Rosa had an association with Augustus Harris, which resulted in the company's London seasons being given at the Theatre Royal, Drury Lane. Rosa commissioned a number of works from British composers including Mackenzie's *Colomba* and *The Troubadour*, Stanford's *The Canterbury Pilgrims* and Corder's *Nordisa*. The company also gave the first production in England of Massenet's *Manon* (1885, Liverpool). An important development at this time was the turning of the Carl Rosa Opera into a limited liability company.

Harris's growing involvement with Covent Garden meant a loss of interest in the fortunes of Rosa's company. By 1889, the year of Carl Rosa's death, a Light Opera Company had also been established, which gave a season at the Prince of Wales Theatre. Harris became the owner of the company, and in 1891 sold it to T. H. Friend and H. Bruce, the company's managers. In the same year three Carl Rosa touring companies were set up. In 1893 the company was commanded by Queen Victoria to perform at Balmoral, and the title

'Royal' was granted by the queen. In 1894 the company presented the first performances in England of *Hänsel und Gretel* at Daly's Theatre and in 1897, during the Manchester season, the British première of *La bohème*. In 1899 the company had severe artistic and financial difficulties after which a 'Commonwealth' of artists took over the management from August 1899 to May 1900. The Carl Rosa Opera then passed into the joint management of Alfred and Walter van Noorden.

During the 1890s the company's repertory was increased by the first performances in English of *Roméo et Juliette*, *Cavalleria rusticana*, *L'amico Fritz*, *Djamileh*, *Otello*, *Pagliacci*, *La damnation de Faust*, *Die Meistersinger* and *Tristan und Isolde*. Among the singers were Alice Esty, Zélie de Lussan, Louise Kirkby Lunn and Charles Manners. From 1900 to 1914 it gave the first performances in England of *Andrea Chénier* and *Die Königin von Saba*, and the first performances in English of *Siegfried*, *La Gioconda*, *La forza del destino* and *I gioielli della Madonna*.

During World War I the touring companies continued to perform throughout Great Britain. In 1918 H. Barrett Brandret became general manager, and the companies took over a number of touring opera groups including the Harrison-Frewin Company, the H. B. Phillips Company, the Cynlais-Gibbs Company and the Flintoff-Moore Company. Two companies were set up, the first touring between 1918 and 1923 and based on the existing Carl Rosa Company, and the second on an amalgamation of the H. B. Phillips and the Harrison-Frewin companies. The first appeared at Covent Garden in autumn 1921 with a repertory of 23 operas. In autumn 1924 H. B. Phillips took over the company and reorganized it. Until 1930 its singers included Eva Turner and Audrey Mildmay.

Between 1930 and 1940 the company performed most of the opera heard outside London – it was particularly active in the large industrial cities, such as Birmingham, Leeds, Liverpool and Manchester – and gave occasional seasons in London, at the Lyceum Theatre, the King's, Hammersmith, and the People's Palace. During World War II it continued to tour and gave seasons at the Winter Garden Theatre and in the London suburbs. Charles Webber, one of its conductors from 1924 to 1930, carried on as musical director; the repertory was mostly popular, and until 1940 included much Wagner. Up to 1945 artists included the singers Howell Glynne, Gwen Catley, Joan Hammond, Norman Allin, Tudor Davies, Heddle Nash, Otakar Kraus and Parry Jones, and the conductors Peter Gellhorn, Arthur Hammond, Walter Susskind and Vilem Tausky.

With the establishment of the Arts Council after World War II, and the new Covent Garden Opera and Sadler's Wells, the Carl Rosa began to run into financial and artistic difficulties. Nonetheless, in 1948 it gave the first stage performance in England of Smetana's *The Kiss*, and in 1951 the première of George Lloyd's *John Socman* in Bristol, as its contribution to the Festival of Britain. Phillips died in 1950, and his widow carried on as director of the company, with Hammond as her musical director. In 1953 the Arts Council made an initial grant of £20 000, which was increased in stages to £61 000 for the 1957–8 season; it also provided additional funds for the purchase of the company by the Carl Rosa Trust from Mrs Phillips, who resigned in September 1957. Humphrey Proctor-Gregg was appointed director, but resigned after what he termed 'ten months of relentless animosity'. A proposed merger with Sadler's Wells Opera led to resignations in both organizations, which resulted in the Arts Council's withdrawing its grant. At the end of 1958 Sadler's Wells took over some of the company's personnel and the short-lived 'Touring Opera 1958' was formed.

The Carl Rosa Trust promoted, unsuccessfully, a month's season at the Prince's Theatre, London, in summer 1960. The company's existence came to an end with a performance of *Don Giovanni* on 17 September 1960.

HAROLD ROSENTHAL

Carlson, Lenus (*b* Jamestown, ND, 11 Feb 1945). American baritone. He studied at the Juilliard School, New York, taking part in the Callas masterclasses. He made his début in 1967 at Minneapolis as Demetrius in Britten's *A Midsummer Night's Dream*. In 1974 he sang Andrey in the American première of *War and Peace* at Boston, and made his Metropolitan début as Silvio, later singing Yevgeny Onegin, Escamillo, Guglielmo, Lescaut and Billy Budd. He created Archie in Orr's *Hermiston* (Scottish Opera, 1975) and made his Covent Garden début as Valentin (1976). At the Deutsche Oper, Berlin, he has sung Marcello, Wozzeck, Gunther and Fritz (*Die tote Stadt*) and created the Messenger in Rihm's *Oedipus* (1987). His other roles include Nick Shadow, Papageno, the Count (*Capriccio*), Count Almaviva and Don Giovanni. He has a strong, well-managed voice.

ELIZABETH FORBES

Carltheater. Theatre in Vienna, built in 1847 and used for operetta until it was damaged in World War II. *See* VIENNA, §4(ii).

Carl [Karl] **Theodor,** Elector Palatine, later Elector of Bavaria (*b* Drogenbusch, nr Brussels, 11 Dec 1724; *d* Munich, 16 Feb 1799). German patron of music. He was educated by the Jesuits, gaining an appreciation for the arts and sciences. At the age of 18 he succeeded his uncle, Carl Philipp, as Elector Palatine; on 17 January 1742 his wedding to Elisabeth Auguste had been celebrated with the opening of the Hoftheater at Mannheim. Carl Theodor studied the flute with Johann Baptist Wendling, and he performed occasionally at court concerts. Burney and Schubart praised his musical skills, and the variety and high quality of musical performances at his court. In addition to operas written by his Kapellmeister, Ignaz Holzbauer, he commissioned operas by Jommelli, Traetta, G. F. de Majo, J. C. Bach and Anton Schweitzer. From 1753 intermezzos and *feste teatrali* were also performed at the rococo theatre at Schwetzingen. Voltaire, Lessing and C. M. Wieland, among other distinguished guests, enjoyed the elector's hospitality. In 1778, following the death of Maximilian III Joseph, Carl Theodor became Elector of Bavaria and moved his court to Munich. Mozart's *Idomeneo* (1781) is the most famous opera in a series of sumptuous works written to satisfy the tastes of the elector. Although Carl Theodor banned the performance of Italian opera at the court theatre in 1787, he continued to maintain theatres at Mannheim and Munich.

BurneyGN

C. F. D. Schubart: *Ideen zu einer Aesthetik der Tonkunst* (Vienna, 1806)

F. Walter: *Geschichte des Theaters und der Musik am kurpfälzischen Hof* (Leipzig, 1898)

S. Pflicht: *Kurfürst Carl Theodor von der Pfalz und seine Bedeutung für die Entwicklung des deutschen Theaters* (Reichling, 1976)

G. Ebersold: *Rokoko, Reform und Revolution: Ein politisches Lebensbild des Kurfürsten Karl Theodor* (Frankfurt, 1985)
PAUL CORNEILSON

Carlyle, Joan (*b* Upton-on-the-Wirral, 6 April 1931). English soprano. She studied privately, making her début in 1955 at Covent Garden as Frasquita (*Carmen*), remaining a member of the company until 1969 and continuing to sing there until 1976. Her repertory included Nedda, Micaëla, Pamina, Sophie, Mimì, Oscar, Ascanius (*Les Troyens*), Dirce (*Médée*), Angelica, Lauretta, Madame Lidoine (*Dialogues des Carmélites*), Donna Anna, Desdemona and Titania. In 1964 she sang Zdenka in the first Covent Garden *Arabella*, before taking on the title role in 1967. Her last appearance was as Freia. She sang Countess Almaviva at Glyndebourne (1965) and appeared in Vienna, Munich and Buenos Aires. For the BBC she sang Rusalka (1968), Reiza (1970) and Adriana Lecouvreur (1972). She was a stylish singer and actress with an appealing, soft-grained voice. She recorded two of her best roles, Jenifer in Tippett's *The Midsummer Marriage* and Nedda with Karajan.
ALAN BLYTH

Carmel. Coastal town in California. Since the 1960s the Carmel Bach Festival under its music director Sandor Salgo has given a summer season including operas and oratorios, with the emphasis on Handel until the mid-1970s and thereafter Mozart. Its first opera production, at Sunset Theater, was Monteverdi's *Orfeo* (1965). Other notable choices, typically semi-staged, have been Purcell's *Fairy-Queen* (1969) and *Dido and Aeneas* (1976), Blow's *Venus and Adonis* (1971), Telemann's *Pimpinone* (1974), the pasticcio *Il maestro di musica* by Pergolesi and others (1975), Haydn's *Orlando paladino* (1984) and Handel's *Imeneo* (1985). Meanwhile in Carmel Valley the imaginative but intermittent Hidden Valley Opera, under Peter Meckel, has produced the works of composers such as Samuel Barber (*A Hand of Bridge*), Conrad Susa (*Black River*, *Transformations*) and Malcolm Seagrave (*The Birthday of the Infanta*, world première, 1977). It commissioned Henry Mollicone's *Hotel Eden* and produced a wide range of works starting in 1975, including Pasatieri's *Signor Deluso*, Britten's *Albert Herring* and *The Turn of the Screw*, Menotti's *The Unicorn, the Gorgon and the Manticore* and Carlisle Floyd's *Of Mice and Men*. Performers have included Neil Rosenshein, while Elisabeth Schwarzkopf has given masterclasses.
PAUL HERTELENDY

Carmen. *Opéra comique* in four acts by GEORGES BIZET to a libretto by HENRI MEILHAC and LUDOVIC HALÉVY after PROSPER MÉRIMÉE's novel; Paris, Opéra-Comique (Salle Favart), 3 March 1875.

Carmen *a gypsy*	mezzo-soprano
Don José *a corporal*	tenor
Escamillo *a bullfighter*	bass/baritone
Micaëla *a country girl*	soprano
Zuniga *a lieutenant*	bass
Moralès *a corporal*	baritone
Frasquita } *gypsies*	soprano
Mercédès } *gypsies*	soprano
Lillas Pastia *an innkeeper*	spoken
Andrès *a lieutenant*	tenor
Le Dancaïre } *smugglers*	tenor/baritone
Le Remendado } *smugglers*	tenor
A Gypsy	bass
A Guide	spoken
An Orange-Seller	contralto
A Soldier	spoken
The Alcalde	silent

Soldiers, young men, cigarette factory girls, Escamillo's supporters, gypsies, merchants and orange-sellers, police, bullfighters, people, urchins

Setting Seville around 1830

Despite the failure of *Djamileh* in 1872, the Opéra-Comique directors, Du Locle and De Leuven, invited Bizet to compose an opera in three acts. Meilhac and Halévy were named as librettists and various subjects suggested. It was Bizet himself who put forward Mérimée's novel *Carmen* as a subject. The librettists were enthusiastic, but De Leuven was alarmed at the thought of Carmen being killed on stage and other elements unsuitable in what he regarded as a family opera house. He soon resigned, while the project went ahead. Bizet worked on the score in 1873, interrupted by the never completed *Don Rodrigue*, and at the end of that year Galli-Marié was engaged to sing the role of Carmen. The opera was orchestrated in the summer of 1874, and rehearsals began in September. During the unusually long rehearsal period Bizet had to contend with objections from both the orchestra, who found Bizet's forthright style of scoring beyond their reach, and the chorus, who were expected to act convincingly as individuals rather than respond in unison as a group. He also encountered the ill-will of Du Locle, who publicly expressed his incomprehension, calling the score 'Cochin-Chinese' music, and urged Bizet to tone down the realistic force of the opera. Fortunately Bizet was firmly supported by Galli-Marié and his Don José, Lhérie, so that few compromises had to be made. The most shocking features of the opera were Carmen's blatant sexuality and her readiness to discard men like picked flowers; also the rowdy women's chorus who both fight and smoke on stage. To have Carmen murdered on stage at the final curtain was too strong for many tastes.

The opera eventually opened on 3 March 1875, and a vocal score was issued by Choudens at the same time. Despite the notorious response of the press and the evident outrage of many in the audience, *Carmen* was not truly a failure. It ran for 45 performances in 1875 with three more in 1876, sustained partly by its reputation as a shocker and by the appalling misfortune of Bizet's death on the night of the 33rd performance, 3 June 1875. Discerning musicians, such as Saint-Saëns and Tchaikovsky, recognized its force and originality from the first. Parisian managements, however, kept clear of the work until 1883, by which time it already enjoyed world success. This grew from a production in Vienna in October 1875 in a version for which Guiraud adapted the dialogue as recitative. The opera quickly spread to many cities all over Europe and beyond, often with Galli-Marié in the title role. Both Brahms and Wagner expressed admiration, and Nietzsche issued his famous assertion that it was the perfect antidote to Wagnerian neurosis.

Carmen has remained one of the most frequently performed operas in the entire repertory. Many great singers have been associated with its leading roles. The

'Carmen' (Bizet), Act 1 (a public square in Seville): lithograph by Auguste Lamy after a design for the original production at the Opéra-Comique (Salle Favart), 3 March 1875

orchestral suite drawn from the opera is often played, and in 1954 it extended its currency in a film version, *Carmen Jones*. For three-quarters of a century it was regularly played not as an *opéra comique* with dialogue, as Bizet wrote it, but with the Guiraud recitatives. It is now played almost everywhere in *opéra comique* format, although the edition on which modern performances rely, that of Fritz Oeser published in 1964, has aroused bitter controversy since it includes a quantity of music that Bizet himself rejected in his own edition of the vocal score published in 1875. That first edition, published by Choudens, is exceedingly rare, for it was replaced at an early stage by the first of many corrupt editions from the same house.

The prelude to Act 1 introduces three themes from the opera: the energetic *corrida* from Act 4 makes a noisy, vigorous opening in A major. This switches directly to the famous Toreador Song, from Act 2, in F. A fuller reprise of this melody has an ingenious modulation back to A for a return of the opening music. The prelude has a separate second part which introduces a strong note of tragedy with the chromatic motif associated both with fate and with Carmen throughout the opera. This links directly to the first scene on a strong diminished 7th.

ACT 1 *A public square in Seville; a tobacco factory on the right faces a guardroom on the left with a covered gallery in front* Some soldiers watch people coming and going in the square ('Sur la place, Chacun passe'). Micaëla shyly enters, looking for a corporal by the name of Don José. Moralès, a sergeant, tells her that he belongs to a different company but begs her to wait with them with the assurance that she will be in safe hands. She evades their entreaties and runs away. This introductory scene begins and ends according to convention with the same music, a picturesque chorus with an inner dominant pedal. In between, Bizet moves swiftly through many keys and with many nuggets of melody, including the playful military tune for 'Il y sera', a tune which Micaëla shares with the soldiers. Moralès then sings some *couplets*, 'Attention! Chut! Taisons-nous!', which were retained for 30 performances in 1875, then dropped. They serve to fill the space between Micaëla's exit and Don José's arrival, for a trumpet-call is heard, announcing the changing of the guard. Two piccolos and a chorus of urchins ('Avec la garde montante') provide accompaniment. A solo violin and solo cello in canon provide background for the *mélodrame* in which Moralès tells José that a girl was asking after him. The guard moves off, leaving José with Zuniga, the lieutenant.

In dialogue José tells Zuniga about the cigarette girls who will shortly return to the factory after lunch; he also explains that he is from Navarre and that Micaëla, a 17-year-old orphan, has been brought up by his widowed mother. The factory bell rings and a crowd gathers to watch the girls go by ('La cloche a sonné'). José shows no interest. The girls' chorus is placid and seductive. But when La Carmencita (Carmen) arrives with a flower in her mouth and a following of admirers the music takes a more angular turn, echoing the theme of fate already heard at the end of the prelude. In some *couplets* (the famous Habanera, 'L'amour est un oiseau rebelle'), Carmen expounds her view of love as something to be seized when it passes: 'If I love you, take care!'. Bizet borrowed the melody from a song by Iradier but transformed it with his inimitable harmonic style and the haunting habanera rhythm. The fate theme is forcefully heard as Carmen breaks out of the throng and approaches José, who has remained apart from the others, busy with his rifle primer. She throws a flower at his feet. He is transfixed by this provocative gesture. The girls go into the factory and the crowd disperses, leaving José alone. He picks up the flower but hides it hurriedly when Micaëla comes up. She has brought a letter and some money from his mother and, as she shows in a deeply affecting duet, a kiss. José asks her to return the kiss. The duet's enchanting stream of melody is interrupted in the middle by his sudden fear of a 'demon' whose meaning Micaëla does not grasp. His mother's letter urges him to marry Micaëla, who leaves while he is reading it to run some errands for his mother.

Suddenly there is an uproar in the factory. The girls rush out to tell Zuniga of a fight between Carmen and another girl. Zuniga sends José into the factory to restore order; with two soldiers he brings her out (this very lively scene was somewhat shortened by Bizet, removing a contrapuntal combination of José's theme with Carmen's fate theme). In dialogue José reports the fight to Zuniga, who challenges Carmen to respond. She does so by nonchalantly humming a few tra-la-las. Zuniga gives orders for her to be led off to prison and instructs José to conduct her. Left alone with José she attempts to suborn him, assuring him that he will do what she wants 'because you love me'. She knows he has kept the flower she threw him. In the seguidilla which follows ('Près des remparts de Séville') she sings of her friend Lillas Pastia's tavern and of her taste for free living and loving. The music and Carmen's behaviour are so seductive that José quickly yields to temptation, especially since she has said that if he loves her, she will love him. In the brief finale which follows at once, Zuniga arrives with the order for her arrest, so José and the soldiers lead her off. She whispers to José to fall when she pushes him. He does so, and in the noisy confusion Carmen escapes.

ACT 2 *Lillas Pastia's tavern* The entr'acte, based on Don José's offstage song in the coming act, is a perfectly crafted *divertissement* alternating minor and major. The curtain rises on Carmen, Frasquita and Mercédès who are sitting with some officers, including Zuniga and Moralès. Gypsy girls are dancing and Carmen suddenly rises to sing 'Les tringles des sistres tintaient' to tambourine accompaniment. The others girls join in and the piece works up to a frenzy of noise and movement. The landlord is preparing to close, so the officers invite the girls to the theatre. They refuse. Carmen learns from Zuniga that José was stripped to the ranks and sent to prison for a month for allowing her to escape. He was released the day before.

Outside, voices are heard applauding the famous toreador Escamillo. Zuniga invites them in and persuades Pastia to keep serving drinks. To the sound of triumphant C major fanfares Escamillo appears and immediately launches into his *couplets*, the famous Toreador Song 'Votre toast, je peux vous le rendre', the main melody of which has already been heard in the prelude. Everyone joins in the refrains. Escamillo finds himself next to Carmen, but she rebuffs him saying that for the moment she is not available. The soldiers leave, although Zuniga tells Carmen that he will be back in an hour. The three gypsy girls are left with Pastia, who reveals that the smugglers Le Dancaïre and Le Remendado have arrived. Pastia calls them in and they unveil their plan in a brisk quintet ('Nous avons en tête une affaire'), whose pace and lightness are breathtaking, especially since the two smugglers are stock comic figures from *opéra comique* in a scene of intrinsic comedy. But Carmen tells the others that she cannot join them on their smuggling expedition since she is in love. She has no sooner told them that she is awaiting the soldier who went to prison for setting her free than José's voice is heard.

They leave Carmen, urging her to bring José to join them the next day. Before their duet begins, Carmen orders food and drink, and even tests José's jealousy by telling him that she was dancing with Zuniga not long before. José quickly declares his love, while Carmen promises to repay her indebtedness to him. The duet begins with Carmen taking her castanets (in the first text she breaks a plate and simulates castanets with the pieces) and singing another of her seductive Spanish songs, dancing now to make up to José. The song, entirely diatonic, also serves as foreground to offstage bugles sounding the retreat, a compelling dramatic moment since José is torn between Carmen's alluring humming and his military duties. When he says he has to go, Carmen taunts him, saying he does not love her. To prove her wrong he draws the crumpled flower from his uniform and sings the Flower Song ('La fleur que tu m'avais jetée'), an ecstatic, beautifully scored outpouring of love. But instead of the duet ending conventionally as a climax of shared passion, Carmen continues to doubt and test José's love by urging him to join her and her friends in the mountains. José refuses, and bids her a final farewell.

Suddenly there is a knock; Zuniga bursts in. He taunts José and orders him to leave. José stands firm and a clash of swords is only avoided by Carmen's summons to the smugglers who suddenly appear and disarm Zuniga. He is led away by some of the gypsies while Carmen turns to José to ask if he is now prepared to join them. José has no choice, and as they pick up Carmen's earlier song about the thrills of mountain life and the lure of liberty, he joins in with gusto. There is no turning back.

ACT 3 *A rocky place near Seville at night* The entr'acte is an exquisite solo for flute and harp, with other wind and strings joining in. It suggests a Grecian pastoral or perhaps a virginal idyll, quite remote from the hot tempers and fiery passions of Carmen's Spain. There is no evidence to support the widely repeated supposition that it was originally intended for *L'arlésienne*, yet its purpose at this point is far from clear.

The curtain rises. To a stealthy march there appear a number of smugglers, heavily laden. Among them are Carmen, Frasquita, Mercédès, Le Remendado, Le Dancaïre and Don José. In comic-opera style (almost entirely homophonic) they sing about the perils of the smuggler's trade: the rewards are fabulous when nothing goes wrong. Bizet offers a breathtaking series of descending chromatic chords on 'Prends garde de faire un faux pas!' Le Remendado and Le Dancaïre go off to reconnoitre, while Carmen and José resume what has evidently been a quarrel. She admits her love is already fading, and when José mentions his mother she suggests he would be better off if he left them now. Carmen says the cards have been telling her that they would 'end up together'. José seems to be threatening her if she were to betray him. There follows a trio in which Frasquita and Mercédès rather frivolously hope to read their fortunes in the cards.

When Carmen joins them the tone of the music darkens and the fate theme is heard. She immediately turns up cards that foretell the deaths of herself and then Don José, and sings a tragic cantilena ('En vain pour éviter les réponses amères') asserting that the cards never lie. Somewhat artificially the others girls resume their light-hearted song, with doomladen interjections from Carmen. The smugglers decide to proceed into the city since the three girls can take care of the three guards on duty (José smarts with jealousy at this suggestion). José is posted nearby to guard their things. To a rousing ensemble in jaunty style, with some effective and very characteristic harmonic twists, the smugglers set off for the city.

Micaëla now arrives at the deserted encampment, led by a guide who seems more frightened than she is. She sings an air ('Je dis que rien ne m'épouvante') with prominent parts for four horns which is in essence a prayer for strength. Its sweet sentiment in the outer sections encloses a more dramatic middle section. She espies José and calls out to him, at which he fires his rifle, thinking she is an intruder. She dives for cover, and at that very moment, against all probability, Escamillo enters, hat in hand. The bullet narrowly missed him.

José appears and challenges him. In the duet that follows, Escamillo at once reveals that he has come to find Carmen, with whom he is in love. José, enraged, draws his knife. A fight ensues in which at first Escamillo has José on the ground but spares his life. They resume, and this time Escamillo is floored by José, who is about to strike when Carmen and Le Dancaïre appear on the scene. (Bizet shortened the fight considerably in 1875.) Carmen thus saves Escamillo's life. The toreador invites them all to his next bullfight in Seville, while José can barely restrain himself. Escamillo leaves to a ravishing version of the Toreador Song in D♭ major scored for four cellos. The smugglers are about to set off when Le Remendado discovers Micaëla hiding. She immediately resumes her great melody from Act 1, imploring José to return to his mother. Carmen too suggests he should go, whereupon in a thrilling burst of defiance José, insane with jealousy, declares he will stay with Carmen, even if it costs him his life. Micaëla then reveals that his mother is in fact dying. This changes his mind. As Escamillo's voice is again heard in the distance, José and Micaëla rush off.

ACT 4 *Outside the bullring in Seville* The entr'acte, based on some Spanish songs compiled by Manuel García, is a lively Spanish dance which sets the tone for the final scene. Street sellers are busy calling their wares to the crowd. In the dialogue, Frasquita learns from Zuniga that an order for José's arrest has been issued but that he has not been found. Frasquita is alarmed for Carmen's safety. To the lively music that began the prelude a procession begins, culminating in the arrival of Escamillo, acclaimed by all. He and Carmen exchange a brief sentimental duet in which she declares her love for him. The Alcalde takes his place at the head of the procession. Frasquita warns Carmen that José is there in the crowd, but Carmen affects not to be afraid and even waits outside while everyone else enters the bullring. She confronts José boldly, and although he implores her, gently at first, to make a new life with him, she insists that she cannot be untrue to herself and that all is over between them. Although she knows her life is in danger, she never wavers. José's passionate pleas are in vain. Cries of victory are heard from the bullring. As Carmen moves towards the entrance, José bars her way, and even in the face of such danger she affirms her love for Escamillo. The fate theme is heard ever more menacingly. She throws down the ring José had given her, triggering José's rage. He stabs her and she falls dead. The Toreador Song is heard off stage. As the screen opens and a triumphant Escamillo appears with the crowd, José stands over Carmen's body and gives himself up.

* * *

Carmen's success may be attributed to its felicitous inclusion of conventionally comic and sentimental scenes alongside stark realism and a tale of risqué morality. Its exoticism is due to more than just the Spanish setting, for if a tavern and a smugglers' hide-out were familiar operatic settings, the atmosphere of the bullring and the outrageous behaviour of the cigarette girls brought a new dimension to the operatic stage. Yet much of the opera is not Spanish at all. It belongs to the tradition of French *opéra comique*, as we can tell both from the dialogue and from the two-verse songs which give the singer an opportunity to present himself to his listeners on both sides of the footlights. Carmen's Habanera in Act 1 and Escamillo's *couplets*, the Toreador Song, are of this kind, both crowned by rousing choral refrains. The depiction of the two smugglers Le Dancaïre and Le Remendado as comic figures belongs to the same tradition. There is also a strong strain of French lyricism derived from Gounod, Bizet's devoted mentor; Gounod jokingly said that Micaëla's Air in Act 3, 'Je dis que rien ne m'épouvante', was stolen from him. It faithfully echoes his style in such works as *Roméo et Juliette* (on which Bizet had worked as pianist and assistant). So too does José's Flower Song, which is miraculously touched by Bizet's genius; Gounod would never have incorporated so fine a solo within an extended duet, as Bizet does. Also derived from Gounod is the character of Escamillo, a first cousin of Ourrias, the braggart cowherd from the Camargue in *Mireille*, which Bizet also knew well.

Neither Micaëla nor Escamillo is of any importance in Mérimée's novel. They were introduced by the librettists as balancing characters to make the story convincingly operatic. Micaëla's devotion to Don José, her purity and her attachment to his dying mother, make Carmen's personality all the more brazen, although the contrast is not simply one of goodness and badness. Escamillo is the irresistible lure that entices Carmen from Don José, although the bullfighter, unlike the soldier, would never shed a tear over her infidelity.

Above all, Bizet had reached the peak of his inventive powers, bestowing on this score such melodic, harmonic and orchestral richness that every number seems to be shaped to perfection. He had never before had such a strong libretto, and never before did he have such a consistent stream of inspiration at his command. The impact of *Carmen* was probably felt less in France than in Italy, where demonstrations of jealous passion as violent as Don José's were a commonplace of the *verismo* school. French opera never produced another *femme* as *fatale* as Carmen, although her capacity to seduce and bewitch her lovers may be traced in some of Massenet's exotic heroines, Esclarmonde and Thaïs especially. Strauss's Salome and Berg's Lulu may be seen

Frontispiece to the first edition of the short score of Campra's 'Le carnaval de Venise' (Paris: Ballard, 1699)

as distant degenerate descendants of Bizet's temptress.

The memorability of Bizet's tunes will keep the music of *Carmen* alive in perpetuity, and the title role will always be a challenge for great singing actresses. No other French opera has ever achieved the same status as a popular classic.

For further illustration *see* GALLI-MARIÉ, CÉLESTINE and OPÉRA COMIQUE, fig.3.

HUGH MACDONALD

Carmina burana ('Songs of Beuren'). 'Cantiones profanae cantoribus et choris comitantibus instrumentis atque imaginibus magicus' in three scenes by CARL ORFF to 13th-century Latin and German poems by the monks of Benediktbeuern; Frankfurt, Städtische Bühnen, 8 June 1937.

Orff's best-known composition is more frequently encountered in the concert hall than in the opera house, but it was originally conceived for the stage. The work, divided into three main sections which deal with nature, the tavern and love, is framed by an imposing opening and concluding chorus in praise of Fortune, the goddess of fate. In the first section entitled 'Im Frühling' and 'Uf dem Anger' the awakening of spring is depicted in a simple rising unison melody in the chorus, and the ensuing baritone solo praises the overwhelming power of love. There follows a series of dances and short choral movements set in medieval German evoking a peasant spring feast. In the second section, 'In taberna', the theatrical element of the work is manifested in a series of parodies – a baritone solo of exaggerated pathos in which the drunkard seems oblivious of the perilous condition of his soul, the grotesque falsetto singing of a Swan (tenor) which is being roasted, the inebriated psalmody of the Abbot (baritone) from Fool's paradise and an orgiastic hymn to earthly enjoyment sung by the male chorus. The final section, 'Cour d'Amours' and 'Blanziflor et Helena', provides a dramatic contrast in extolling the pleasures of refined courtly love. Individual numbers include a baritone solo in which the lover seeks to make his wooing more seductive by indulging in a brilliant coloratura vocal line, a coquettish song for soprano which seeks to kindle a young man's desire, a wooing song for double chorus and finally a chorus of Dionysiac intensity in praise of Venus.

Carmina burana received a wide variety of representations in German theatres from cosmological music drama and epic world-theatre to allegorical medieval mystery play. Later the work formed the first part of Orff's theatrical triptych *Trionfi* which also includes *Catulli carmina* and *Trionfo di Afrodite*. Its simple primitive musical language owes much to Stravinsky and has a freshness of invention that eluded the composer in much of his later work.

ERIK LEVI

Carnaval de Venise, Le ('The Venetian Carnival'). *Comédie lyrique* in a prologue and three acts by ANDRÉ CAMPRA to a libretto by Jean-François Regnard; Paris, Opéra, 20 January 1699.

Le carnaval de Venise is a romantic comedy concerning a double rivalry: that of Léonore (soprano) and Isabelle (soprano) for Léandre (bass), and that of Léandre and Rodolphe (bass) for Isabelle. It may be viewed in part as a study for Campra's and Danchet's *LES FÊTES VÉNITIENNES* (1710). 'La place St-Marc' is the location for Act 1 of *Le carnaval de Venise* and for the first and second entrées of *Les fêtes vénitiennes*. Both operas use the device of a play within a play. Part of the concluding *divertissement* of Act 3 of *Le carnaval* is an autonomous one-act Italian opera, *Orfeo nell'inferni*, introduced by its own sinfonia. Other innovations are the strikingly realistic *divertissement* of Act 3 scene iv, which celebrates the victory of the 'Castellani' over their rival street gang, the 'Nicolotti'; the realistic stage directions, rare in a 17th-century mythological prologue, that describe workers' preparation of a theatrical event in a room 'filled with pieces of wood and unfinished stage sets'; and the use of a trio of basses ('Joignons nos voix') in the prologue to the first version of the opera. Campra anticipated his *Tancrède* by three years in scoring the main roles of Léandre and Rodolphe for bass voice.

Campra's younger brother, Joseph, was named as the composer on the short score (1699), in a futile attempt by the publisher Ballard to disguise authorship because of Campra's position as *maître de musique* at Notre Dame.

JAMES R. ANTHONY

Carner, Mosco (*b* Vienna, 15 Nov 1904; *d* Stratton, nr Bude, 3 Aug 1985). British writer on music of Austrian birth. He studied at the Neues Konservatorium, Vienna, and with Adler at Vienna University, taking the doctorate in 1928. He then took posts as opera conductor at Opava, Czechoslovakia (1929–30), and Danzig (1930–33). In 1933 he settled in London, first as music correspondent for continental publications, then as critic of *Time and Tide* (1949–62) and the *Evening News* (1957–61). He wrote frequently for *The Times* and the *Daily Telegraph* and contributed to periodicals and symposia. His writings cover a wide range of music but he wrote with special perception and authority on early 20th-century Viennese music (notably that of Berg) and Puccini, on whom his critical biography stands as the most important book in English, marked by the sharp psychological insight that informs his discussion of both life and music.

Puccini: a Critical Biography (London, 1958, 2/1974)
rev.: G. Adami, ed.: *Letters of Giacomo Puccini* (London, 1974)
Alban Berg: the Man and his Work (London, 1975)
Madam Butterfly (London, 1979)
Giacomo Puccini: Tosca (Cambridge, 1985)

STANLEY SADIE

Carnevale di Venezia, Il [*Il carnevale di Venezia, ossia Le precauzioni* ('The Carnival of Venice, or The Precautions')]. *Opera buffa* in three acts by ERRICO PETRELLA to a libretto by MARCO D'ARIENZO; Naples, Teatro Nuovo, 20 May 1851.

The scene is set in Venice, during the last days of Carnival, though the characters derive clearly from traditional Neapolitan prototypes. The action revolves round Muzio (*buffo*), a merchant, and his two young and attractive daughters, Albina (soprano) and Romilla (soprano), whom he keeps locked up and permanently at work in the house to protect them from the attentions of undesirable young men. Under this heading come Oreste (tenor) and Pilade (baritone), two Venetian ladykillers who have already seen the girls and are determined to make their closer acquaintance, with the assistance of the Conte Bietola (bass).

Muzio, having to go away on business, leaves the keys of his house with Cola (*buffo*; aptly described on the cast list as a 'servo sciocco'), with strict instructions to let no one in or out. Within the space of a single ensemble the daughters, encouraged by Muzio's plain sister, Mimosa (contralto), enlist Cola's muddle-headed sympathy and secure their own liberty. Once in the streets of Venice, they meet Oreste and Pilade and go with them to a nearby café. To the same café, by chance, come Cola and Mimosa. Muzio unexpectedly reappears. He too is drawn to the café, and the stage is set for a second-act finale of the best 'perplexity' type.

The third act resolves the situation. The two lovers get into Muzio's house by climbing over the wall, refuse to take no for an answer, and virtually force Muzio to accept their dual offer of marriage. Bietola, entering by a more conventional route, requests the hand of Mimosa: he recoils briefly when he sees her face, but is quickly reassured by her wealth and all ends in merriment.

Petrella treats this tenuous plot with great vivacity and humour but little melodic charm. His score is famous for its extensive use of 'parlanti' (vocal declamation over orchestral music), but the other side of the coin was expressed by Verdi when he compared *Le precauzioni* with Ricci's comedies, and commented: 'In these operas Ricci doesn't progress the action with "parlanti", but with good tunes. The characters are clear and the opera exists. Not so *Le precauzioni*'.

MICHAEL ROSE

Carnicer (y Batlle), Ramón (*b* Tárrega, nr Lérida, 24 Oct 1789; *d* Madrid, 17 March 1855). Spanish composer. He was a chorister in Seo de Urgel Cathedral from 1799 to 1806, when he moved to Barcelona, where he studied with the cathedral *maestro de capilla* Francisco Queralt and organist Carlos Baguer. Driven from Barcelona in 1808 by the French occupation, he spent the next five years teaching the piano and singing in Mahón (Minorca) and became closely associated with Charles Ernest Cook, who advertised himself as a pupil of Mozart. In 1814 he returned to Barcelona, but continued political unrest forced him to seek refuge in London late that year. On returning to Barcelona, in 1816 he was entrusted by the Duke of Bailén with the recruitment in Italy of an opera troupe for the Teatre de la S Creu. In 1818 he became director of the Liceu theatre orchestra, and his first dramatic works, substitute cavatinas and overtures, were written for the Barcelona premières of Paer's *Agnese* (14 October 1816) and Rossini's *La Cenerentola* (15 April 1818) and *Il barbiere di Siviglia* (10 July 1818); these were followed by three of his own Italian *opere semiserie*, *Adele di Lusignano* (1819), *Elena e Costantino* (1821) and *Don Giovanni Tenorio* (1822). The première of the first of these – timed to coincide with the arrival of Luisa Carlota, the bride of Fernando VII's brother – was followed by 19 further performances in the same season. The second, no less successful, was revived at Madrid in 1827. But the third failed, although Carnicer considered it the best of the three. According to the Barcelona journal *El vapor* (7 June 1824), it displeased because its harmonies seemed to belong to the 'German school'. From then on he wrote no more operas for Barcelona, though he continued during 1823 to write inserts for other composers' operas, among them Pacini's *Adelaide e Comingio*, *Il falegname di Livonia* and *La schiava di Bagdad*. In 1823–4 Carnicer conducted opera for the first time at Madrid. But in 1824 political changes forced him to emigrate again, this time with his family briefly to Paris and then for two years to London, where he taught and had several of his short works published. His fame led the Chilean minister in London to commission from him the music for the Chilean national anthem.

On royal order dated 24 February 1827 Carnicer moved to Madrid, where he succeeded Mercadante as conductor of Italian opera at the Cruz and Príncipe theatres. Among the reforms he instituted in his first year was the replacement of those chorus singers who could not read music by ones who could; he also increased the size of the chorus from 20 singers to 28. To improve the orchestra he brought from Italy valve trumpet and ophicleide players. The seven opera seasons during which he was in sole control lasted from 1828–9 to 1844–5, with interruptions in 1830–31 (shared with Mercadante), 1833–4 to 1835–6 and 1838–9 to 1843–4. In addition to the revival of his own *Elena e Costantino* (1827, Príncipe) he conducted at Madrid the premières of his *Elena e Malvina* (1829), *Cristoforo Colombo* (1831), one of his most important works, and *Eufemio di Messina* (1832) at the Teatro del Príncipe, and *Ismalia* (1838) at the Teatro de la Cruz.

In 1830 he was appointed one of the 16 founder-professors of the Spanish national conservatory, which opened on 1 January 1831; he held the post until his death. His pupils included Barbieri and Saldoni. His funeral was the most sumptuous yet given a Spanish musician. Though now out of fashion because of changes in taste, Carnicer's stage and religious music ranks as the best produced in Spain during the early Romantic period.

Adele di Lusignano (melodramma semiserio, 2, F. Romani), Barcelona, S Creu, 15 May 1819, *I-Mr*, excerpt *E-Bc*
Elena e Costantino (opera semiseria, 2, A. L. Tottola), Barcelona, S Creu, 16 July 1821, lib. (Madrid, 1827)
Don Giovanni Tenorio, ossia Il convitato di pietra (opera semiseria, 2, G. Bertati), Barcelona, S Creu, 20 June 1822
Elena e Malvina (melodramma semiserio, 2, Romani), Madrid, Príncipe, 11 Feb 1829, *Mn*
Cristoforo Colombo (melodramma serio, 2, Romani), Madrid, Príncipe, 12 Jan 1831
Eufemio di Messina, ó Los sarracenos en Sicilia (melodramma serio, 2, Romani), Madrid, Príncipe, 14 Dec 1832, lib. (Madrid, 1832)
Ismalia, ossia Morte ed amore (melodramma, 2, Romani), Madrid, Cruz, 12 March 1838
Ipermestra (dramma, 3, P. Metastasio), Saragossa, Liceo, early 1843 [perf. mentioned in *AMZ*, xlv (1843), 483]

Contrib. to: Los enredos de un curioso (melodrama lírico, 1), Madrid, Conservatorio, 6 May 1832

*

L. Carmena y Millán: *Crónica de la ópera italiana en Madrid desde el año 1738 hasta nuestros días* (Madrid, 1878)
B. Saldoni: *Diccionario biográfico bibliográfico de músicos españoles* (Madrid, 1880)
A. Peña y Goñi: *La ópera española y la música dramática en España en el siglio XIX* (Madrid, 1881; abridged E. Rincón, as *España desde la ópera a la zarzuela*, 1967), 144–57
F. V.: 'Ramón Carnicer y Batlle', *Ilustración musical hispano-americano*, i/1 (20 Jan 1888), 3–6 [incl. biographical data from Carnicer's niece]
F. Pedrell: *Diccionario biográfico y bibliográfico de músicos y escritores de música españoles, portugueses e hispano-americanos* (Barcelona, 1894–7)
R. Mitjana y Gordón: 'La musique en Espagne', *EMDC*, I/iv (1920), 2309–13
E. Pereira Salas: *Los origenes del arte musical en Chile* (Santiago, 1941), 84, 93–4
J. Subirá: *La ópera en los teatros de Barcelona*, i (Barcelona, 1946), 79ff
V. Salas Viu: 'Ramón Carnicer, músico y liberal', *Revista musical chilena*, x/Jan (1955), 8–14
J. Subirá: 'En el centenario de un gran musico, Ramón Carnicer', *Revista de la Biblioteca, Archivo y Museo del Ayuntamiento de Madrid*, lxix (1958), 39–73
Seminario de Bibliografia Hispánica de la Facultad de Filosofía y Letras de Madrid: *Cartelera teatral madrileña*, i: *Años 1830–1839* (Madrid, 1961), items 76, 428, 445, 489
F. Asenjo Barbieri: *Biografías y documentos sobre música y músicos españoles (Legado Barbieri)*, ed. E. Casares (Madrid, 1986), 118–25
——: *Documentos sobre música española y epistolario (Legado Barbieri)*, ed. E. Casares (Madrid, 1988)
A. Ruiz Tarazona: 'En el centenario de Ramón Carnicer (1789–1855)', *Revista de musicologia*, xii/1 (1989), 331–47

ROBERT STEVENSON

Carnival (Fr. *carnaval*; Ger. *Fasching*; It. *carnevale*). The carnival season – the period between Christmas and Lent – was traditionally the principal and most fashionable season for opera, both in Italy and in other parts of Catholic Europe. The term first appears in an operatic context on the title-pages of the librettos for Agazzari's *Eumelio* (1606) and Monteverdi's *Orfeo* (1607). Carnival seasons generally began on 26 December and ended on the following Shrove Tuesday (in February or early March); in many opera houses it opened with a serious opera, to be followed by either a serious or a comic one (which might be a revival). The operatic significance of the carnival season began to decline in the late 18th century.

The usage 'Carnival 1730' signified the entire carnival season; an opera so dated might have had its première on 26 December 1729. (Calendar conventions were however subject to local variation; for dating *more veneto*, *see* VENICE, §2.)

See also SEASON.

Caroli, Angelo Antonio (*b* Bologna, 13 June 1701; *d* Bologna, 26 June 1778). Italian composer. He was admitted to the Accademia Filarmonica as an organist in 1726 and promoted to the rank of composer in 1728; six times he served as *principe*. He held a series of ecclesiastical posts in the city, becoming director at the Cathedral of S Pietro in 1753. As well as church music and oratorios, he wrote several operas which are now known only through citations of their librettos (catalogue, *I-Bc*): *Amor nato tra l'ombre* (A. Zaniboni; Bologna, Marsigli Rossi, carn. 1723), *Il dolor di Cerere nel ratto di Proserpina* (P. F. Donadi; 1735), *L'Andromaca* and *Il Demetrio re della Siria (*Bologna, Formagliari, carn. 1742), and *S Marino sul monte Titano* (G. Manfredi; Bologna, Madonna di Galiera).

Burney's judgment of Caroli's music, based on a performance heard during his visit to Bologna in 1770, is harsh: 'there was ... neither learning, taste, or novelty to recommend the music'. Certainly Caroli's extant music is very ordinary, in the concertato style well established by other Bolognese composers of the period.

*

BurneyFI
Inventario della musica del Sig.r Angelo Caroli (MS, *I-Bc* H/61, ff.83–91)
G. Gaspari: *Miscellanea musicale I, II* (MS, *I-Bc* UU/12)

ANNE SCHNOEBELEN

Caron, Rose [Meuniez, Lucille] (*b* Mondeville, 17 Nov 1857; *d* Paris, 9 April 1930). French soprano. She studied at the Paris Conservatoire and then with Marie Sass. She made her concert début in 1880 and three years later appeared for the first time in opera, as Alice in *Robert le diable* at Brussels. Here in 1884 she created the role of Brunehild in the première of Reyer's *Sigurd*; other world premières included those of Godard's *Jocelyn* (1888) and Reyer's *Salammbô* (1890); see illustration overleaf. From 1885 she became closely associated with the Paris Opéra, rivalling Lucienne Bréval as the reigning prima donna, and winning the respect of musicians for her avoidance of showy effects or violent emotions, cultivating instead 'un art sobre, propre à la rêverie et à la douceur'. She was Paris's first Desdemona in Verdi's *Otello* and Sieglinde in *Die Walküre*. At the Opéra-Comique she sang in the first performances there of *Fidelio* and *Iphigénie en Tauride*, and was also a noted exponent of Gluck's Orpheus. She also sang in the stage première of *La damnation de Faust* at Monte Carlo in 1893. After 1895 her appearances became less frequent, and from 1902 she was Professor of Singing at the Conservatoire, nevertheless preserving her voice so well that she was still singing to great acclaim as late as 1923. Her recordings date from 1903 and 1904; they are few and of extreme rarity but include an excerpt from *Sigurd* which gives some hint of the qualities so greatly admired by the composer.

*

E. de Solenière: *Rose Caron* (Paris, 1896)
H. de Curzon: *Croquis d'artistes* (Paris, 1898)

J. B. STEANE

Carosio, Margherita (*b* Genoa, 7 June 1908). Italian soprano. She studied at the Paganini Conservatory, Genoa, and made her début at nearby Novi Ligure in 1924 at the age of 16 in the title role of *Lucia di Lammermoor*. In 1928 she sang Musetta, and Fyodor in

Rose Caron in the title role of Reyer's 'Salammbô' (which she created at the Théâtre de la Monnaie, Brussels, 10 February 1890) with Albert Saléza who sang the role of Mathô at the first Paris performance (Opéra, 16 May 1892)

Boris Godunov with Shalyapin, at Covent Garden. The next year she made her début at La Scala and from 1931 to 1939, and 1946 until 1952, never missed a season there. At La Scala she created Gnese in Wolf-Ferrari's *Il campiello* and Egloge in Mascagni's *Nerone* and sang Aminta in the first Italian performance of Strauss's *Die schweigsame Frau*. She returned to London in 1946 as Violetta with the San Carlo company, and in 1950 to La Scala as Adina in *L'elisir d'amore*, a role for which her piquant charm, exquisite phrasing and fine musicianship admirably suited her.

*

GV (R. Celletti; R. Vegeto)

HAROLD ROSENTHAL

Carpani, Giuseppe (*b* Vill'Albese, Como, 28 Jan 1752; *d* Vienna, 21/2 Jan 1825). Italian librettist and writer on music. He received a Jesuit education in Milan, then studied law in Pavia, during which time he wrote poetry and drama, some in Milanese dialect. His libretto for Rust, *Gli antiquari in Palmira* (1780), won approval and resulted in many librettos for the country residence at Monza of the Milanese court. There the repertory consisted of contemporary French works which Carpani translated and revised for musical production, some appearing under his own name. From 1792 to 1796 Carpani was editor of the *Gazzetta di Milano*, but his anti-French sentiments forced him to move to Vienna during the French occupation of Lombardy. He remained there until his death despite his nomination at some time after 1797 as censor, with directive responsibilities, of the Venetian theatres. Pensioned by the Viennese court, he enjoyed imperial favour as a librettist and writer on music. In 1822 he may have visited Beethoven with Rossini.

Carpani is best remembered for the controversy surrounding his somewhat fictionalized biographies of Haydn and Rossini, the former, *Le Haydine* (1812), boldly plagiarized by Stendhal. His writings on Rossini include a *Lettera all'anonimo autore* (1818) regarding an article on *Tancredi* and *Le rossiniane ossia Lettere musico-teatrali* (1824). In a lively public exchange of letters Carpani called Stendhal 'a literary cuckoo who does not lay his egg in another's nest but warms eggs he has not laid'. Most of his librettos are Italian translations of *opéras comiques* for Monza, by such composers as Grétry, Dalayrac and R. Kreutzer. *Nina ossia La pazza per amore*, originally set by Dalayrac, was taken up by Paisiello (with additions by Lorenzi); Tarchi set *Lo spazzacamino principe*, a translation of *Le ramoneur prince*; and *Rinaldo d'Aste* was set many times.

Gli antiquari in Palmira, G. Rust, 1780; *Il principe invisibile*, L. Caruso, 1802; *L'uniforme* (eroicommedia), Weigl, 1805

Settings unknown: *Amore vince pregiudizio* (commedia); *L'amore alla persiana* (dramma); *L'allievo dell'orsa* (dramma); *Pilade e Oreste* (dramma); *La lezion d'on dì* (commedia, in Milanese dialect); *La figlia del sole* (dramma); *Didone in America* (dramma buffo); *Formosa* (dramma buffo); *La scuola della maldicenza* (after Sheridan)

*

ES (E. Zanetti)

G. B. Corniani: *I secoli della letteratura italiana dopo il suo risorgimento* (Turin, 1854–6)

D. Kerner: 'Carpanis Verteidigung Salieris', *NZM*, Jg.127 (1966), 479; repr. in *Das Orchester*, xv (1967), 3

G. Pestelli: 'Giuseppe Carpani e il neoclassicismo musicale della vecchia Italia', *QRaM*, iv (1968), 105

R. N. Coe: Foreword to Stendhal: *Lives of Haydn, Mozart and Metastasio* (London, 1970), xi–xvii

G. Brosche: 'Ein Opernstreit auf Wiener Boden', *ÖMz*, xxviii (1973), 500–03

M. Sergardi: 'Le Rossiniane, lettere musico-teatrali di Giuseppe Carpani, ed altri scritti epistolari', *Rossini, edizioni critiche e prassi esecutiva: Siena 1977*, 53–67

H. Jacobs: *Literatur, Musik und Gesellschaft in Italien und Österreich in der Epoche Napoleons und der Restauration* (Frankfurt, 1988)

M. Spada: 'Elisabetta, regina d'Inghilterra: Literary Sources and Musical Self-Borrowing', *NRMI*, xxiv (1990), 147–82

PATRICIA LEWY GIDWITZ

Carpentras. Town in the Rhône valley, southern France. Although the annual festival was founded in 1967, opera has been a part of it only since 1978, when Jean-Marie Grenier took over the artistic direction and presented *Mireille*. One or two productions are mounted in the open-air theatre (cap. 1534) that is erected each year against the apse of the cathedral of St Siffren; normally two performances of each are given in July or early August. Smaller-scale productions are given in the Cour de la Charité (cap. 350). The French repertory predominates (*Tosca* in 1980 with Gwyneth Jones was an exception). From 1985 the festival was given over to the works of Offenbach, though in 1990 under a new director, Henri Maier, the main production was Purcell's *Dido and Aeneas*. CHARLES PITT

Carr, Benjamin (*b* London, 12 Sept 1768; *d* Philadelphia, 24 May 1831). American composer of English birth. He operated a musical repository in London and was a principal tenor, harpsichordist and conductor at the Academy of Ancient Music. Foremost among his London compositions was his first opera,

Philander and Silvia, or Love Crown'd at Last (Sadler's Wells, 16 Oct 1792). He emigrated to the USA in 1793, settled in Philadelphia, and established music shops and publishing businesses there and in New York. He made his American stage début in 1794 and pursued a concert career as a singer and pianist until about 1800. Thereafter, his main activities were as church organist, teacher, composer and music editor.

In America Carr's output for the stage was prodigious up to about 1800. His catalogue lists five operas, music for seven pantomimes, four overtures, accompaniments to 14 operas by other composers and incidental music. The operas were in the English comic opera tradition, in which spoken dialogue was interspersed with songs, choruses, dances and short instrumental numbers. His most successful opera, *The Archers, or Mountaineers of Switzerland* (New York, John Street, 18 April 1796), and *The Patriot, or Liberty Obtained* (Philadelphia, Chesnut Street, 16 May 1796) were both based on the William Tell legend. The libretto of *The Archers* (by William Dunlap) was published and survives, but the music is lost, except for two songs, a march, and a rondo from the overture (available in modern editions or reprints). Also lost are *The Patriot* and two other operas, *Bourville Castle, or The Gallic Orphans* (New York, 16 January 1797) and *American Soldier.*

*

W. Dunlap: *A History of the American Theater* (New York, 1832)
O. G. T. Sonneck: *Early Opera in America* (New York, 1915)
J. Mates: *The American Musical Stage before 1800* (New Brunswick, NJ, 1962)
C. A. Sprenkle: *The Life and Works of Benjamin Carr* (diss., Peabody Conservatory, 1970)
J. Mates, ed.: *The Musical Works of William Dunlap* (Delmar, NY, 1980)
E. R. Meyer, ed.: *B. Carr: Selected Secular and Sacred Songs*, RRAM, xv (Madison, 1986) EVE R. MEYER

Carrara, Agata (*fl* 1772–88). Italian soprano. She was married to Antonio Carrara, a Venetian employed by David Garrick. By 1772 she had begun to sing in London concerts and was seconda donna at the Italian Opera in 1772–3, described by Walpole as 'the prettiest creature upon earth', but by Burney as having a 'voice ... naturally drowsy, childish, and insipid'; however, after lessons from Millico she sang with him as prima donna at Florence in 1775, then in leading Italian houses up to 1784 (and at La Scala in 1788). Her written music suggests a technically competent singer with no great expressive gifts, and her acting and figure seem to have been more admired. DENNIS LIBBY

Carré, Albert (*b* Strasbourg, 22 June 1852; *d* Paris, 12 Dec 1938). French theatre and opera director, actor and librettist. Always modest about his understanding of the technical side of music, Carré had studied drama at the Paris Conservatoire and had a successful career as an actor before becoming co-director of various Paris theatres: first the Vaudeville, and later the Théâtre Libre and the Comédie-Française. He soon left the Vaudeville to become director of the theatre in Nancy. Carré's main contribution to operatic history was made as director of the Opéra-Comique, a post which he held from 1898 to 1914. He worked hard to raise the musical standards of this institution and was responsible for the premières of major operas by French composers: he commissioned Debussy's *Pelléas*, Charpentier's *Louise* and Dukas' *Ariane et Barbe-bleue*, and works by Hahn, Bruneau and Hüe. He gave the first French performances of several Italian operas, including *Tosca* and *Madama Butterfly*, and many important new productions, including Bizet's *Carmen*. After World War I he was persuaded by his wife, the singer Marguerite Carré, and others to give up his directorship of the Théâtre Français to return to the Opéra-Comique. He retired in 1936 and wrote his memoirs, *Souvenirs de théâtre* (Paris, 1950).

André Messager was a lifelong friend and collaborated on his most important projects. Carré's librettos include those of Messager's *La Basoche* (1890) and Elsa Barraine's *Le roi bossu* (1932).

*

E. Genest: *L'Opéra-Comique connu et inconnu* (Paris, 1925)
S. Wolff: *Un demi-siècle d'Opéra-Comique* (Paris, 1953)
H. R. Cohen and M. O. Gigou: 'Les livrets de mise en scène dans la Bibliothèque de l'Association de la Régie Théatrale', *RdM*, lxiv (1978), 253–67 RICHARD LANGHAM SMITH

Carré, Marguerite [Giraud, Marthe] (*b* Cabourg, 16 Aug 1880; *d* Paris, 26 Dec 1947). French soprano. She studied in Bordeaux and Paris, making her début at Nantes in 1899, as Mimì. In 1902 she first appeared in Paris, at the Opéra-Comique, and married its director, Albert Carré, being known thereafter as Marguerite Carré. She created 15 roles at the Opéra-Comique; she was also the first French Butterfly (1906) and Salud (*La vida breve*), and a famous interpreter of Manon, Louise and Mélisande. At the Opéra she sang Zina in the Paris première of Gunsbourg's *Le vieil aigle* in 1909 and Thaïs in 1916. She continued to sing in Paris until 1923. HAROLD ROSENTHAL/R

Carré, Michel(-Florentin) (*b* Besançon, 21 Oct 1822; *d* Paris, 27 June 1872). French librettist. He arrived in Paris in 1840, entering the studio of Paul Delaroche with the intention of training as a painter, but soon turned to writing. His first literary work was a collection of verse, *Les folles rimes et poèmes* (1842), and then he found a more congenial outlet for his talents in the theatre. His early plays include the one-act verse drama *La jeunesse de Luther* (1843, Odéon) and a verse translation of Terence's *Eunuchus*. It was not long, however, before he began working with collaborators, as was the practice in Paris at the time, on plays of various sorts and librettos for *opéras-comiques* and operas. Though he did write the libretto for Gounod's *Mireille* (1864), after Mistral, on his own, and that for Bizet's *Les pêcheurs de perles* with Eugène Cormon, it was in association with Jules Barbier that he made his most significant contribution to opera as he devised a succession of adaptations of acknowledged literary masterpieces for the major French composers of the day. These include *Faust* (Gounod, 1859), *Roméo et Juliette* (Gounod, 1867), *Hamlet* (Thomas, 1868), *Paul et Virginie*, after Jacques Henri Bernardin de Saint-Pierre (Massé, 1876), *Graziella* and *Les contes d'Hoffmann* (Offenbach, 1881) (for a list, *see* BARBIER, JULES). His son, Michel-Antoine (*b* 7 Feb 1865; *d* 11 Aug 1945), wrote many librettos for light operas, *opérettes* and revues, including works with Messager, Lecocq, Pierné, Vincent Scotto and Charles Cuvillier (*Afgar*, 1909), and later directed silent films. CHRISTOPHER SMITH

Carrer [Carreris], **Pavlos** (*b* Zákinthos, 12 May 1829; *d* Zákinthos, 7 June 1896). Greek composer. He is perhaps the most important opera composer of the early Ionian School and was particularly noted for his operas on historical figures and on events of the revolt against

Turkish rule (1821). Biographical information on him derives mainly from his incomplete and unpublished memoirs dating from about 1887: he studied in Zákinthos with Giuseppe Cricca and Francesco Mirangini and, after moving to Milan in 1850, with Raimondo Bosserone, Tassistri and Winter. His first operas were performed at the Teatro Carcano, Milan, in the early 1850s. In 1857 he returned to Zákinthos, where he secured further performances of his *Isabella d'Aspeno* and *La rediviva* with the title roles sung by the soprano Isavélla Yatra whom he married two years later. In 1858 excerpts from his most famous work, *Marcos Botsaris*, were performed in Athens before King Otto; it proved difficult to stage the opera, however, since in the Ionian Islands (then under British rule) the subject matter – the Greek war of independence – seemed set to kindle a desire for union with Greece, while on the mainland the patriotic sentiments might compromise Greece's relations with other powers. *Marcos* was eventually performed in Patras in 1861 and enjoyed immense popularity, not least for the song incorporated into Act 1, 'O Yéro Demos' ('Old Demos'), a heartbreaking farewell to life sung by an old *klepht*.

Carrer emerges as a monumental figure in Greek music, perhaps the most popular and widely performed composer in 19th-century Greece before Spyridon Samaras. Because of his training he invites comparison with Italian composers, although his style seems closer in origin to early Verdi rather than Bellini or Donizetti. Melody, 'spontaneously conceived' in terms of the stage, is rich, fluent, and with a direct dramatic appeal. His gift for atmosphere, if not drama, is equally evident in his songs. Carrer may be the most important of the older generation of Ionian composers who began, timidly, to abandon the Italian musical heritage and turn towards the cultural and historical background of the Hellenic mainland.

all extant MSS at the Dionyssios Solomos and Eminent Zakynthians Museum, Zákinthos

Il pellegrino di Castiglia, *c*1848–50 (1, G. Laguidaras), lost

Dante e Beatrice (Bice) (3, S. Torelli), Milan, Carcano, ?1852, lost

Isabella d'Aspeno, ?1853 (3, 'R. G. S.'), Milan, Carcano, ?1853 [première, Corfu, San Giacomo, carn. 1854, according to pubd lib. (Corfu, 1853)]

La rediviva (tragedia lirica, prol., 3, I. Sapios), Milan, Carcano, ?1854, lost; lib. pubd (Milan, 1856)

Marcos Botsaris, 1857–8 (4, G. Caccialupi and A. Valaoritis), Athens, 26 April 1858 (excerpts); Patras, 30 April 1861 (complete)

Fior di Maria, ovvero I misteri di Parigi (4, Caccialupi, after E. Sue), Corfu, Jan 1868

I kyra Frossyni [Lady Frossyni] (4, E. Martinéngos and after Valaoritis), Zákinthos, 16 Nov 1868, lost; lib. pubd (Zákinthos, 1882)

Maria Antoinetta, 1873–4 (4, G. Romas), Zákinthos, carn. 1884; lib. pubd (Zákinthos, 1884)

Déspo, i iroïs tou Souliou [Déspo, heroine of Souli] (1, A. Manoussos), Patras, Apollo, 25 Dec 1882; lib. pubd (Zákinthos, 1882)

Marathon – Salamis, 1886 (4, A. Martzokis and A. Kapsokéfalos), unperf.

O konte Spourghitis i Lipothymies ke nevrika [Count Sparrow, or Faintings and Nervous Strains], ?1888 (comic op, 1, I. Tsakassianos); duet pubd in *Asty* [City], Athens (18 Dec 1888), lost

Projected operas, both ? after 1886, both lost: Don Pigna (Don Piña); O Lambros (? after D. Solomos)

*

E. Legrand: *Bibliographie ionienne ... du quinzième siècle à l'année 1900*, ed. H. Pernot, iii (Paris, 1910)

N. Varvianis: 'Pávlos Carréris', *Ellinikí Dhimiourghía* [Hellenic Creation], viii/85 (1951), 276–80

S. Motsenigos: *Neoellinikí moussikí, symvolí is tin istorían tis* [Modern Greek Music: a Contribution to its History] (Athens, 1958), 70, 196, 241–7

D. Conomos: 'Anékdota apomnimonévmata tou Pávlou Carrér' [Unpublished Memoirs of Pavlos Carrer], *Filologikí Protochroniá* [The Literary New Year's Day] (Athens, 1962), 239–77

N. Varvianis: *To ekpolitistikó moussikó érgo tis Eptanísou ke o Zakynthinós moussourgós Pávlos Carréris* [The Musical Civilization of the Ionian Islands and the Zákinthian Composer Pavlos Carréris] (Zákinthos, 1975)

G. Leotsakos: 'Carrér, Pavlos', *Pangósmio viografikó lexikó* [Universal Biographical Dictionary], iv (Athens, 1985), 322–3

GEORGE LEOTSAKOS

Carreras, José [Josep] (*b* Barcelona, 5 Dec 1946). Spanish tenor. He studied with Jaime Francisco Puig. After graduating from the Barcelona Conservatory he made his operatic début in Barcelona as Ismaele (*Nabucco*). Winning the Giuseppe Verdi Competition, he appeared in various Italian cities and in Paris; his American début was with the New York City Opera as Pinkerton in 1972. He subsequently appeared at the Hollywood Bowl (Duke) and the San Francisco Opera (Rodolfo, 1973) and he made his débuts at the Metropolitan (Cavaradossi) and Covent Garden (Alfredo) in 1974. He has also sung at Salzburg (Don Carlos, 1976), Chicago, Tokyo and Buenos Aires. In 1987, at the peak of his career, he contracted leukaemia but after extensive treatment he returned to the stage and to a demanding mixture of operatic roles and appearances for charity; he was able to sing Saint-Saëns' Samson at Covent Garden in 1991. The sweetness of timbre and purity of phrasing that typify his singing have made him one of the most popular lyric tenors of his generation, winning special repute from a recording made with Domingo and Pavarotti. He has been tempted on occasion to essay roles heavier than ideal for his resources, or to follow an over-taxing schedule. Nevertheless, at his best, he has justified comparisons with Björling and the young Di Stefano. His recorded repertory is varied, ranging from *Aida* to *West Side Story*. He published an autobiography, *El placer de cantar*, in 1989.

*

N. Goodwin: 'José Carreras', *Opera*, xxxviii (1987), 507–12

MARTIN BERNHEIMER

Carrillo(-Trujillo), Julián (Antonio) (*b* Ahualulco, San Luis Potosí, 28 Jan 1875; *d* San Angel, 9 Sept 1965). Mexican composer and theorist. Of Indian extraction, he was born during the period of tumultuous social change (the 'Porfirato', 1872–1911) under the rule of Porfirio Díaz. As a student he was influenced by one of Mexico's intellectual élites, Justo Sierra, who supported the education of Mexico's Indians by exposing them to European ideas and who, as Secretary of Education, later commissioned Carrillo's opera *Matilde*. Carrillo became conductor of the National Symphony Orchestra and was twice director of the National Conservatory (1913–14, 1918–24). These appointments should have made it possible for him to obtain performances of his three operas, which, however, were never produced (although they were rehearsed for concert performance). From 1924 he devoted his career to experimenting and composing with microtones.

All three operas deal with love as the influential force for Mexicans in their struggle for political and social liberation from Spain. *La princesse Oïna*, also known as *Ossian* (1, H. Albert; 1902), is set in the third century and concerns love that is doomed because of royal heritage and family feuding. In the *opera trágica Matilde*, alternatively known as *México en 1810* (4, L. Viramontes; 1909), Carrillo depicts a Spanish woman's attempt to conquer the patriotic spirit of Leon, who rejects her and the Spanish church for love of Mexico and its new independence. Mexico's new spirit of Indianism in the 1920s and a neo-classical revival of its Aztec past were the inspiration for *Xulitl* (3, C. d'Erzel; 1921). The theme centres around the love and self-sacrifice of an Indian couple in opposition to the betrayal of their people to the Spanish conqueror. In *Oïna* and in *Matilde* (which was under revision at the time of Carrillo's death), the composer uses an ultra-chromatic harmonic idiom and declamatory vocal style reminiscent of late Verdi, while in the Indian and priestly choruses he combines Rossinian crescendos and italianate tonal progressions inherited from his teacher Melesio Morales with a contrapuntal texture that may show the influence of Salomon Jadassohn, with whom he studied in Germany. In *Xulitl* (which was revised in 1947), Carrillo uses thematic material also found in his first microtonal piece, *Preludio a Colón* (1922); thus the tonal idiom has become increasingly atonal, tinged with impressionistic orchestration. The manuscripts are in the Carrillo home (now a museum) in San Angel, Mexico.

*

J. Velasco-Urda: *Julián Carrillo: su vida y su obra* (Mexico, 1945) [autobiography in form of Socratic dialogue]

R. Stevenson: 'The Operatic Nineteenth Century', *Music in Mexico* (New York, 1952), 172–223

G. R. Benjamin: 'Julián Carrillo and "sonido trece"', *Yearbook, Inter-American Institute for Musical Research*, iii (1967), 33–68

B. E. Burns: 'Cultures in Conflict: the Implication of Modernization in Nineteenth-Century Latin America', *Elites, Masses, and Modernization in Latin America*, ed. V. Bernhard (London, 1979), 27ff

G. R. Benjamin: 'Una deuda cultural saldada: la contribucion de Julián Carrillo a la música del futuro', *Revista musical chilena*, no.158 (1982), 60–71

GERALD R. BENJAMIN

Carroli, Silvano (*b* Venice, 22 Feb 1939). Italian baritone. He studied at the opera school of La Fenice and with Marcello and Mario del Monaco, making his début at Venice in 1963 as Schaunard. His career took him to leading Italian centres including La Scala, with whose company he toured to Washington, DC (1976), and Japan (1981). His American début was at Dallas in 1972 as Tonio, followed by engagements at Chicago Lyric Opera and the Metropolitan. He has sung at leading European centres including Vienna, Munich, West Berlin and Paris, and first appeared at Covent Garden in 1977 as Jack Rance (*La fanciulla del West*), followed by Iago, and Nélusko in *L'Africaine*, in which he was much praised for his commanding stage presence and sonorous, smoothly produced vocal line. He has concentrated on the Italian repertory with occasional performances of Mozart (Don Giovanni) and Wagner (Telramund).

NOËL GOODWIN

Carron [Cox], **Arthur** (*b* Swindon, 12 Dec 1900; *d* Swindon, 10 May 1967). English tenor. He made his début in 1929 at the Old Vic, London, where his first major role was Tannhäuser. When the company moved to the Sadler's Wells Theatre in 1931, Carron became its leading tenor. His repertory included Fra Diavolo, Manrico, Radames, Cavaradossi and Otello. In 1936 he won the Metropolitan Opera Auditions of the Air and made his New York début as Canio at the Metropolitan, where he remained until 1946, creating Nolan in Damrosch's *The Man without a Country* (1937); his roles included Siegmund, Tristan, Florestan and Herod. Carron also sang in Chicago and Buenos Aires. In 1947 he returned to England, singing at Covent Garden (1947–8) and retiring in 1952. He possessed a powerful, dramatic voice and sang with effective diction.

HAROLD ROSENTHAL/R

Carte, Richard D'Oyly (*b* Soho, London, 3 May 1844; *d* London, 3 April 1901). English impresario and composer. The son of the flautist Richard Carte, he was educated at the University of London. Initially he determined to become a composer, but several unsuccessful essays in light opera, notably *Dr Ambrosius*, convinced him that his talents lay elsewhere. In 1870 he established an agency for musical and dramatic artists and lecturers. Among his early clients were Adelina Patti, G. M. Mario and Gounod; later, in 1881, he was to organize Oscar Wilde's American lecture tour. Carte's first undertaking in theatre management took place in 1874, when he mounted *opéra bouffe* by Serpette and Lecocq, as well as English comic opera, at the Opera Comique Theatre in London. The following year, as manager of the Royalty Theatre for Selina Dolaro, he commissioned *Trial by Jury* from Gilbert and Sullivan as an afterpiece for *La Périchole*. On the basis of its success Carte incorporated a syndicate of investors as the Comedy Opera Company in 1877. He hired the Opera Comique and in November produced *The Sorcerer*, which was immediately recognized as a novel and promising form of musical theatre. *H.M.S. Pinafore* followed in May 1878; when Carte's agreement with the syndicate expired in July 1879 he succeeded in gaining control of the production, whereupon the Comedy Opera Company was dissolved. Thereafter 'Mr R. D'Oyly Carte's Opera Company', as it was known during his lifetime, was inseparable from the names of Gilbert and Sullivan.

At the Opera Comique Carte produced *The Pirates of Penzance* (1880 after the New York première) and *Patience* (1881). On 10 October 1881 *Patience* was transferred to the new Savoy Theatre, which Carte had constructed on a site in the Strand next to his offices in Beaufort Buildings. Here the remaining Gilbert and Sullivan operas (the 'Savoy operas') were profitably produced under his auspices. He commissioned operas from other composers, including Edward Solomon, Alfred Cellier, Alexander Mackenzie and André Messager, but they were not as successful as the Gilbert and Sullivan operas and none of them were revived. Carte also maintained touring companies that travelled throughout the provinces, to Europe and across North America.

Having established a home, and cultivated a demand, for English comic opera, Carte sought to do the same for native grand opera. To this end he built the Royal English Opera House in Cambridge Circus, which opened on 31 January 1891 with Sullivan's *Ivanhoe*, commissioned for the purpose. Other composers were also enlisted, but they failed to provide further operas and the plan collapsed (although *Ivanhoe* ran for half a year). The magnificent building (now the Palace Theatre) was sold soon afterwards, and for many years it was used as a variety theatre.

Carte was known as a masterful promoter, a meticulous organizer, a man of refined tastes and high principles, and a generous but firm employer. He initiated a number of theatrical reforms – the Savoy was the first public building in London to be lit entirely by electricity – and his success helped to create an environment favourable to the development of English opera in the next century. In 1871 he married Blanche Julia Prowse; in 1888, three years after her death, he married Helen Lenoir (*nom de théâtre* of Susan Couper-Black, 1852–1913), his capable and devoted assistant. From 1915 the D'Oyly Carte Opera Company, revived by Carte's son Rupert (1876–1948), achieved new popularity through its London seasons, provincial and American tours and recordings of the Gilbert and Sullivan operas (*see* LONDON, §II, 1). On Rupert D'Oyly Carte's death his daughter Bridget D'Oyly Carte supervised the company until its closing in 1982. In 1988 a revival of the company was made possible largely through her bequests.

selective list

Dr Ambrosius – His Secret (opera di camera, 2, after T. H. Bayly: *Tom Noddy's Secret*), London, St George's Hall, 8 Aug 1868

Marie (operetta, 1), London, Opera Comique, 26 Aug 1871

Happy Hampstead (musical pastoral, 1, F. Desprez), tour perf., 3 July 1876; London, Royalty, 13 Jan 1877

*

F. Cellier and C. Bridgman: *Gilbert, Sullivan and D'Oyly Carte* (London, 1927)

A. Williamson: *Gilbert and Sullivan Opera* (London, 1953)

A. Jacobs: *Arthur Sullivan: a Victorian Musician* (Oxford, 1984, 3/1992)

FREDRIC WOODBRIDGE WILSON

Carter, Ernest Trow (*b* Orange, NJ, 3 Sept 1866; *d* Stamford, CT, 21 June 1953). American composer. He studied the piano, horn and organ and after graduating from Princeton University in 1888 went to Berlin. There he took lessons in composition with Wilhelm Freudenberg (1894–8) and Otis Boise (1895–7) before returning to the USA and further studies at Columbia University (1899). Employed as organist and choirmaster of Princeton from 1899 to 1901, he then moved to New York, where he worked as an arranger, conductor and composer.

His first opera, *The White Bird* (to a libretto by B. Hooker), is set in the Adirondack lake area during the early 19th century and is a story about the love between a forester and his employer's wife. The forester is tricked into shooting the wife by mistaking her white scarf for a gull that had been haunting the camp. Carter conducted a concert version of his work at the Carnegie Chamber Music Hall in New York on 23 May 1922 and it was first staged at the Studebaker Theater in Chicago on 6 March 1924. The European première was at the Städtisches Theater, Osnabrück, on 15 November 1927; it was the first American opera presented there. *The White Bird* won the David Bispham Medal in 1924.

The Blonde Donna, an 'opera comique' in three acts, concerns an uprising of Mission Indians in Santa Barbara, California, in 1824, in which the Padres, with the help of the Blonde Donna, persuade the rebel Indians to give up their insurrection. A concert performance of this work took place in 1912 but it was subsequently revised and offered again in New York in February 1931 at the Century Theater; it was staged at the Little Theater, Brooklyn, on 8 December 1931. The vocal score was published in New York in 1936.

*

E. E. Hipsher: *American Opera and its Composers* (Philadelphia, 1927)

N. Slonimsky: *Music Since 1900* (New York, 1937, 4/1971)

BRADLEY H. SHORT

Caruso, Enrico (*b* Naples, 25 Feb 1873; *d* Naples, 2 Aug 1921). Italian tenor. Born of poor parents, he first sang as a child in churches. He studied with Guglielmo Vergine and made his début in Morelli's *L'amico francesco* at the Teatro Nuovo, Naples (1894). He continued to sing, not always successfully, in small theatres in southern Italy, and to study under Vincenzo Lombardi until 1897. In May that year he achieved his first real success at Palermo in *La Gioconda*. The foundations of his career were laid at appearances in Milan (Teatro Lirico), which included the premières of Cilea's *L'arlesiana* (1897) and *Adriana Lecouvreur* (1902) and Giordano's *Fedora* (1898); at his Buenos Aires début in 1899; his Rome début in Mascagni's *Iris*, also in 1899; and finally, during the 1900–01 season, when a relatively unsuccessful appearance in *La bohème* at La Scala was followed by a triumph in *L'elisir d'amore*. Caruso sang in *L'elisir* at the S Carlo, Naples, also in 1901, but after his controversial reception he resolved never to sing again in Naples.

On 14 May 1902 Caruso made his début in *Rigoletto* with great success at Covent Garden, where he subsequently appeared from 1904 to 1907 and in 1913 and 1914. He also sang in Spain, Germany, Austria and France. But the theatre where he most often sang was the Metropolitan, where he made his début in *Rigoletto* on 23 November 1903. Over the next decade he performed there periodically, creating Dick Johnson in *La fanciulla del West* in 1910; from 1912 he sang there continuously (*Pagliacci*, *Bohème*, *Tosca*, *Aida*, *Traviata*, *Ballo*). He repeated Dick Johnson in 1911 at his only appearance with the Chicago Grand Opera Company. In Italy he made only two other appearances, in benefit performances of *Pagliacci* in Rome (1914, Costanzi) and Milan (1915, Verme). He sang several times in Latin America (Havana, Mexico City, São Paulo) in 1917–20. His last public appearance was in Halévy's *La Juive*, at the Metropolitan on 24 December 1920. He died of a lung ailment.

Because of his incomplete and irregular training, Caruso began his career with certain technical deficiencies. In his early years he was ill at ease in the upper register, often using falsetto or transposing. He did not achieve security in his high notes, at least up to the high B, until about 1902. In his early years, too, his dark tone gave rise to ambiguities; his voice was often regarded as almost a baritone. This, however, became one of Caruso's resources, once he had mastered production. The exceptional appeal of his voice was, in fact, based on the fusion of a baritone's full, burnished timbre with a tenor's smooth, silken finish, by turns brilliant and affecting. This enabled him in the middle range to achieve melting sensuality, now in caressing and elegiac tones, now in outbursts of fiery, impetuous passion. The clarion brilliance of his high notes, his steadiness, his exceptional breath control and his impeccable intonation, formed a unique instrument.

The winning quality of the sound, the tender *mezza voce* (particularly in the early years) and his phrasing, based on a rare mastery of legato and portamento, enabled Caruso to sing the French and Italian lyric repertory (particularly *Faust*, *Les pêcheurs de perles*, *Manon*, *Manon Lescaut*, *Bohème* and *Tosca*), as well as such lighter operas as *L'elisir* and *Martha*. In addition, his noble, incisive declamation, his broad, high-mettled phrasing, and his vigour in dramatic outbursts, made Caruso a notable interpreter of Verdi and the *grand opéra* (*Rigoletto*, *Ballo*, *Forza*, *Aida*, *La Juive*,

Enrico Caruso as Canio in Leoncavallo's 'Pagliacci'

L'Africaine, *Samson et Dalila*). In this repertory, too, his performances were characterized by the irresistible erotic appeal of his timbre. But the legend of Caruso, considered the greatest tenor of the century, was also due to a temperament as warm and vehement as his voice. His numerous recordings not only made him universally famous; they also did much to encourage the acceptance of recording as a medium for opera.

J. H. Wagenmann: *Caruso und das Problem der Stimmbildung* (Altenburg, 1911)
M. H. Flint: *Caruso and his Art* (New York, 1917)
S. Fucito and B. J. Beyer: *Caruso and the Art of Singing* (New York, 1922)
P. V. R. Key and B. Zirato: *Enrico Caruso: a Biography* (Boston, 1922; Ger. trans., 1924)
P. M. Marafioti: *Caruso's Method of Voice Production* (London, 1925)
D. Caruso: *Wings of Song* (London, 1928)
——: *Enrico Caruso: his Life and Death* (New York, 1945)
H. Steen: *Caruso: eine Stimme erobert die Welt* (Essen, 1946)
E. Gara: *Caruso: storia di un emigrante* (Milan, 1947)
T. R. Ybarra: *Caruso: the Man of Naples and the Voice of Gold* (New York, 1953)
F. Robinson: *Caruso: his Life in Pictures* (New York, 1957)
J. Freestone and H. J. Drummond: *Enrico Caruso: his Recorded Legacy* (London, 1960)
A. Favia-Artsay: *Caruso on Records* (Valhalla, NY, 1965)
J. P. Mouchon: *Enrico Caruso: sa vie et sa voix* (Langres, 1966)
'A Century of Caruso', *ON*, xxxvii/16 (1972–3) [whole issue]
J. R. Bolig: *The Recordings of Enrico Caruso* (Dover, DE, 1973)
H. Greenfield: *Caruso* (New York, 1983)
P. Gargano and G. Cesarini: *Caruso* (Milan, 1990) [with discography by M. Aspinall and Cesarini]
E. Caruso jr and A. Farkas: *My Father and my Family* (Portland, OR, 1991)

RODOLFO CELLETTI

Caruso [Carusio], **Luigi** [Lodovico] (*b* Naples, 25 Sept 1754; *d* Perugia, 15 Nov 1823). Italian composer. He first studied with his father, Giuseppe, and then with Nicola Sala at the Conservatorio della Pietà dei Turchini, Naples. He began composing operas at an early age, achieving success both in Italy and abroad, where his works were performed almost every year. According to Gervasoni, his first opera was *Il barone di Trocchia* (Naples, Carnival 1773), but that is not certain because a work with that title by Giuseppe Gazzaniga was performed in the same year. His first opera for which there is documentary evidence was *Artaserse* (London, 1774). From 15 March 1788 he was *maestro di cappella* of Perugia Cathedral (and for several years also of the S Filippo Neri oratory), a position he held until his death, except for a brief period of leave from 16 March 1801 to 31 July 1802. The suggestion that from 1808 to 1810 he was *maestro di cappella* at Urbino, after serving at Cingoli and Fabriano, arises from confusion with his brother Salvatore, who was dismissed after several disagreements with the chapter there. Caruso founded and directed a public music school in Perugia, where his pupils included Francesco Morlacchi. He had a profound knowledge of vocal technique and contributed, along with Guglielmi, Nicolini and Zingarelli, to Anna Maria Pellegrini Celoni's *Grammatica o siano Regole di ben cantare* (Rome, 1810, 2/1817). He travelled in Italy and to Portugal, France and Germany to supervise productions of his operas, and six were performed in Perugia. Stricken with paralysis, he was partly disabled during the last years of his life.

Caruso wrote many operas; his comic operas were sometimes reworked under different titles to satisfy the constant demand of the theatres. Their comedy always has a touch of pathos and intimacy, typical of 18th-century Neapolitan opera. Orchestral numbers and excerpts were widely distributed in contemporary manuscripts and were published in Florence, London, Paris and Rome. The librettos he set, whether by illustrious poets (Metastasio, Bertati, Rossi) or little-known writers, were always of high quality. He is notable for his extended melodies (often reminiscent of Paisiello) and for their formal construction. Although he continued to compose into the 19th century, he was unwilling to accept the innovations of Romanticism, remaining firmly linked to the older Neapolitan style.

d – *dramma*   g – *giocosa*

Il barone di Trocchia (F. Cerlone), Naples, carn. 1773
L'innocente fortunata (g), Livorno, S Sebastiano, spr. 1774, collab. Paisiello
Artaserse (d, 3, P. Metastasio), London, 1774; rev. Florence, Intrepidi, spr. 1780, *I-Bc*
La lavandaia astuta (g, P. Chiari), Livorno, S Sebastiano, carn. 1775, *MOe*; rev. as Il marchese Tulipano, Reggio Emilia, Pubblico, 1777
Il padre della virtuosa (g, G. Bertati), Trieste, S Pietro, carn. 1776; rev. as La virtuosa alla moda, Bologna, Marsigli-Rossi, 19 Oct 1776; rev. as Li due amanti rivali, Venice, S Samuele, aut. 1779
La caffettiera di spirito (g), Brescia, Accademia degli Erranti, carn. 1777
Il cavaliere Magnifico (g, N. Tassi), Florence, Cocomero, Sept 1777, Act 2 finale *F-Pn*
La creduta pastorella (g, 2), Rome, Dame, carn. 1778, *I-Fc*
L'americana in Italia (Frediano), Rome, 1778
Il tutore burlato [balordo], Bologna, 1778
L'amore volubile (S. Bellini), Bologna, Zagnoni, carn. 1779
Scipione in Cartagena (d, Bellini), Venice, S Samuele, aut. 1779, Rome, Argentina, carn. 1781, *I-PS*, *Rc*, *Rsc*
L'albergatrice vivace (g, 2, G. Palomba), Venice, S Samuele, carn. 1780, *B-Bc*, *D-Bds*, *Wa*, *F-Pn*, *H-Bn*

L'arrivo del burchiello da Padova a Venezia (2, G. Fiorio), Venice, S Giovanni Grisostomo, carn. 1780
La locanda in scompiglio (g), Florence, Pallacorda, aut. 1780
Il fanatico per la musica (g), Rome, Dame, 10 Feb 1781, *D-Rtt*, collab. C. Spontone
L'albergatrice rivale, Milan, Scala, 25 July 1781
Il marito geloso (g, 2, Bertati), Venice, S Moisè, aut. 1781, *F-Pn*, *GB-Lbl*, *I-Fc*, *Tf*
Il matrimonio in commedia (g, Palomba), Rome, Capranica, 29 Dec 1781, Milan, Scala, spr. 1782, *F-Pn*; as Gli sposi in commedia, Venice, S Samuele, carn. 1786
L'inganno (commedia, G. Gilberti), Naples, Fondo, spr. 1782
La gelosia (g), Rome, Capranica, carn. 1783
Il vecchio burlato (g, Palomba), Venice, S Samuele, aut. 1783, *Pn*
Gli amanti alla prova (g, 2, Bertati), Venice, S Moisè, 26 Dec 1783, *B-Bc*, *I-Gl*; rev. as Gli amanti dispettosi, Naples, Fondo, 1787; rev. as Il vecchio collerico, Genoa, S Agostino, spr. 1787
Gli scherzi della Fortuna (int), Rome, Capranica, carn. 1784
Le quattro stagioni (commedia, Palomba), Naples, Fondo, June 1784
Puntigli e gelosie tra moglie e marito (commedia, Palomba), Naples, Nuovo, aut. 1784
Giunio Bruto, Rome, Dame, carn. 1785
I tre amanti burlati, Ancona, Fenice, carn. 1785
Le parentele riconosciute (g), Florence, Intrepidi, aut. 1785
Le spose ricuperate (g, Bertati), Venice, S Samuele, aut. 1785, *F-Pn*; rev. as I campi Elisi ossia Le spose ricuperate, Milan, Scala, spr. 1788
Il poeta melodrammatico in Parnaso (eroicomico), Verona, Accademia Filarmonica, carn. 1786, *I-Fc*
Le rivali in puntiglio (g, F. Livigni), Venice, S Moisè, carn. 1786
Il poeta di villa (farsetta, 2), Rome, Pallacorda, spr. 1786, *OS*
Lo studente di Bologna, Rome, Pallacorda, sum. 1786
L'impresario fallito, Palermo, S Cecilia, aut. 1786
Il servo astuto, Gallarate, Borgo, aut. 1786
L'antiquario burlato, ossia La statua matematica (Bertati), Pesaro, 1786
Alessandro nelle Indie (d, 3, Metastasio), Rome, Dame, carn. 1787, *B-Bc*
La convulsione [confusione] (Palomba), Naples, Fiorentini, carn. 1787
Il maledico confuso (g), Rome, Valle, spr. 1787
Gli amanti disperati, Naples, aut. 1787
Antigono (d, 3, Metastasio), Rome, Dame, carn. 1788, rev. 1794, *F-Pn*, *I-Mr*
Il calabrese fortunato, Cento, Sampieri, sum. 1788
La sposa volubile, ossia L'amante imprudente (int), Rome, Capranica, 7 Feb 1789, rev. Florence, 1790, *F-Pn*
Le due spose in contrasto (g), Rome, Valle, aut. 1789
La disfatta di Duntalmo, re di Theuta [Duntalamo] (d), Rome, Argentina, 1789, ov. *I-Mc*, arias *Mc*, *PAc*, *Rc*, *Rsc*
Amleto (d, F. Dorsene Aborigeno, after Ducis), Florence, Pergola, carn. 1790, aria *Rsc*
Attalo re di Bitinia (d, A. Salvi), Rome, Argentina, carn. 1790
Demetrio (Metastasio), Venice, spr. 1790
I due fanatici per la poesia (int), Florence, Intrepidi, carn. 1791, *Gl*, *PEsp*, *PS*
La locandiera astuta (G. Rossi), Rome, carn. 1792
Gli amanti ridicoli, Rome, carn. 1793
Oro non compra amore, ossia Il barone di Moscabianca (2, A. Anelli, after Bertati), Venice, S Benedetto, 26 Nov 1794, *F-Pn*, *GB-Lcm*
Il giocatore del lotto, Rome, carn. 1795
La Lodoiska (d, F. G. Ferrari), Rome, Argentina, carn. 1798
La tempesta, Naples, spr. 1798
La donna bizzarra (A. Bernardini), Rome, Valle, carn. 1799
Due nozze in un sol marito (g), Livorno, Avvalorati, spr. 1800
Le spose disperate, Rome, Valle, carn. 1801
Il trionfo di Azemiro, Rome, Dame, carn. 1802
Il principe invisibile (Carpani), St Petersburg, Imperial, spr. 1802
La ballerina raggiratrice (B. Mezzanotte), Rome, Apollo, 7 Jan 1805, *I-Rc*
L'inganno felice (G. Ciliberti), Venice, 1807, *Gl*
La fuga, Rome, 1809
Così si fa alle donne, ossia L'avviso ai maritati, Florence, Pergola, 23 April 1810, *Mr*
La villanella rapita

Miscellaneous arias and ensembles: *F-Pn*, *I-BAc*, *Bc*, *BZtoggenburg*, *Fa*, *Fc*, *FEM*, *Gl*, *Mc*, *Nc*, *PAc*, *PEsp*, *PS*, *Rc*, *Ria*, *Rsc*, *Rvat*, *SPE*, *Vc*, *Vs*

DEUMM (B. Brumana); *Grove6* (D. Libby and J. L. Jackman)
C. Gervasoni: *Nuova teoria di musica* (Parma, 1812)
B. Brumana: 'Alcune precisazioni biografiche sul musicista Luigi Caruso', *Annali della Facoltà di Lettere e Filosofia dell' Università di Perugia*, xiv (1976–7), 619–28
——: 'Luigi Caruso e la cappella musicale del duomo di Perugia dal 1788 al 1823', *NRMI*, xi (1977), 380–405
——: *Il fondo musicale dell'archivio di S. Pietro a Perugia* (Perugia, 1986)
B. M. Antolini: 'Editori, copisti, commercio della musica in Italia: 1770–1800', *Studi musicali*, xviii (1989), 282–375

GALLIANO CILIBERTI (work-list with MARITA P. McCLYMONDS)

Carvalho, João de Sousa (*b* Estremoz, 22 Feb 1745; *d* Alentejo, 1798). Portuguese composer and teacher. As a child he studied at the Colégio dos Santos Reis in Vila Viçosa. In 1761 he went to Italy where he studied at the Conservatorio di S Onofrio, Naples, with Carlo Cotumacci and Nicola Porpora. Five years later his opera *La Nitteti* was performed in Rome. Returning to Lisbon, in 1767 Carvalho joined the Irmandade de S Cecília, a union to which all Lisbon musicians belonged. He was appointed teacher of counterpoint at the Seminário da Patriarcal and in 1773 *mestre de capela* of the same institution. While there he taught many of the greatest Portuguese musicians of the late 1700s, including António Leal Moreira, João Domingos Bomtempo, João José Baldi and Marcos António Portugal. Later he succeeded David Perez as music teacher to the royal family (1778). He retired to his properties in Alentejo, where he died in 1798.

Carvalho wrote much sacred music and some keyboard *tocatas*. His religious music was influenced by the theatrical works that constitute the most important part of his output. In these he followed the conventions of contemporary Italian *opera seria*: *secco* and accompanied recitative followed by arias, normally da capo with a modified repeat. The principal roles, all taken by castratos (public performance by women was banned at the Portuguese court), demand great virtuosity. Three of the operas have enjoyed modern revivals: *L'amore industrioso* (1967), *Penelope* (1970) and *Testoride* (1987). They confirm him as the most important Portuguese composer of the second half of the 18th century and reveal the possible influence of Jommelli.

first performed in Lisbon unless otherwise stated; all surviving scores in P-La

La Nitteti (3, P. Metastasio), Rome, Dame, carn. 1766, lost
L'amore industrioso (dg, 3, F. Casorri), Ajuda Palace, 31 March 1769; ov. ed. in PM, ser. B, ii (1960)
L'Eumene (dramma serio per musica, 3, A. Zeno), Ajuda Palace, 6 June 1773; ov. ed. A. de Almeida, *L'offrande musicale*, xix (Paris, 1965)
L'Angelica (serenata, 2, Metastasio, after L. Ariosto: *Orlando furioso*), Queluz Palace, 25 July 1778
Perseo (dramma per musica, G. Martinelli), Queluz Palace, 5 July 1779
Testoride argonauta (dramma, 2, Martinelli), Queluz Palace, 5 July 1780
Seleuco, re di Siria (dramma per musica, 1, Martinelli), Queluz Palace, 5 July 1781
Everardo II re di Lituania (dramma per musica, Martinelli), Queluz Palace, 5 July 1782
Penelope nella partenza da Sparta (dramma per musica, 1, Martinelli), Ajuda Palace, 17 Dec 1782
L'Endimione (dramma per musica, 1, Metastasio), Queluz Palace, 25 July 1783
Tomiri amazzone guerriera (dramma per musica, 1, Martinelli), Ajuda Palace, 17 Dec 1783
Adrasto rè degli Argivi (dramma per musica, 1, Martinelli), Queluz Palace, 5 July 1784

Nettuno ed Eglé (favola pastorale, 2, G. Sertor), Ajuda Palace, 9 June 1785
Alcione (dramma per musica, 1, Martinelli), Ajuda Palace, 25 July 1787
Numa Pompilio II re de Romani (dramma per musica, Martinelli), Ribeira Palace, 24 June 1789

*

DBP (E. Vieira)
M. Sampayo Ribeiro: *A música em Portugal nos séculos XVIII e XIX* (Lisbon, 1938)
J. Scherpereel: *A orquestra e os instrumentistas da Real Câmara de Lisboa 1764–1834* (Lisbon, 1985)
M. C. de Brito: *Opera in Portugal in the Eighteenth Century* (Cambridge, 1989)
LUISA CYMBRON

Carvalho [Carvaille], **Léon** (*b* Mauritius, 1825; *d* Paris, 29 Dec 1897). French theatre director. He moved to Paris at an early age and studied singing at the Conservatoire. After 1848 he assumed small baritone roles at the Opéra-Comique; there he met the soprano Marie Miolan, whom he married in 1853. She was hired by the Théâtre Lyrique in 1855, and a year later Carvalho assumed the directorship of that house – with the financial advantage that his leading singer was also his wife. Carvalho brought the Théâtre Lyrique from a rather tenuous existence to a position of prominence on the Parisian operatic scene: the most memorable works of the Second Empire, including Gounod's *Faust* and *Roméo et Juliette*, Bizet's *Les pêcheurs de perles* and Berlioz's *Les Troyens*, were first performed there. Overextending himself, he also took responsibility for a fledgling operatic enterprise called the Théâtre de la Renaissance, and was forced into bankruptcy in 1868. Following a brief period as director of the Théâtre du Vaudeville, when he commissioned Bizet for the incidental music to Daudet's *L'arlésienne*, Carvalho returned to opera as director of the Opéra-Comique from 1876 to 1887, during which time Delibes' *Lakmé* and Massenet's *Manon* had their premières. He was made to shoulder legal responsibility for a fire at the Salle Favart in May 1887, and following his resignation was sentenced to imprisonment and fined. On appeal he was acquitted, and in 1891 reinstated as director of the Opéra-Comique. STEVEN HUEBNER

Carvalho [Miolan, Miolan-Carvalho; née Félix-Miolan], **Marie Caroline** (*b* Marseilles, 31 Dec 1827; *d* Château-Puys, nr Dieppe, 10 July 1895). French soprano. She studied first with her father and then with the tenor Duprez at the Paris Conservatoire. She made her début in a benefit performance for Duprez at the Opéra in 1849, singing in the first act of *Lucia di Lammermoor* and the trio from the second act of *La Juive*. She was immediately engaged for the Opéra-Comique. In 1853 she married Léon Carvalho. From 1856 until 1867 she sang at the Théâtre-Lyrique, creating four roles by Gounod: Marguerite (1859), Baucis in *Philémon et Baucis* (1860), Mireille (1864) and Juliet (1867). Her other roles there included Zerlina, Cherubino and Pamina.

She first appeared at Covent Garden in 1859, singing Dinorah in the first London performance of *Le pardon de Ploërmel*. She returned to London each year until 1864 and again in 1871–2, singing Gilda, Mathilde (*Guillaume Tell*), Marguerite de Valois and Countess Almaviva, among other roles. She also appeared in Berlin and St Petersburg and in 1885 made her farewell appearance at the Opéra-Comique as Marguerite.

H. Morley: *The Journal of a London Playgoer from 1851–66* (London, 1866)
E. Accoyer-Spoll: *Mme Carvalho: notes et souvenirs* (Paris, 1885)
H. de Curzon: *Croquis d'artistes* (Paris, 1897)
HAROLD ROSENTHAL/R

Cary, Annie Louise (*b* Wayne, ME, 22 Oct 1841; *d* Norwalk, CT, 3 April 1921). American contralto. She studied in Milan with Giovanni Corsi and made her début as Azucena in Copenhagen in 1867. For two seasons she sang in Scandinavia, studying between engagements with Viardot at Baden-Baden. After appearances at Hamburg, Stockholm, Brussels and London, she returned in August 1870 to the USA, where on 26 November 1873 she sang Amneris in the American première of *Aida* in New York. She was constantly in demand throughout the USA, until she retired after marrying Charles Monson Raymond in 1882. In 1877 she became the first American woman to sing a Wagner role (Ortrud) in the USA. Her voice had wide range and great beauty.

*

O. Thompson: *The American Singer* (New York, 1937), 79
H. E. KREHBIEL, DEE BAILY

Casablanca. City in Morocco. The country was a French Protectorate from 1912 until 1956. In 1922 Casablanca, which had become an important port and holiday resort, decided on the construction of the Théâtre Municipal. Built in four months and seating 1200, it was inaugurated on 22 December 1922 with a performance of Delibes' *Lakmé* in the presence of Maréchal Lyautey, the French Resident. The opening season also included performances of *Faust*, *Manon*, *La traviata*, *Il barbiere di Siviglia* and *Madama Butterfly*, with Germaine Revel singing all the prima donna roles. From then until the French left Morocco there were usually annual opera seasons at the theatre, run by impresarios bringing companies from France with a municipal government subsidy. The theatre was demolished in 1982. CHARLES PITT

Casaccia. Italian family of singers. They were among the greatest exponents of Neapolitan *opera buffa* from the mid-18th century to the late 19th.

(1) **Giuseppe Casaccia** (*b* Naples, 1714; *d* Naples, 1783). Baritone. He made his début as Don Bastiano in Latilla's *La celia* at the Teatro dei Fiorentini, Naples, in 1749 and sang in nearly all the comic operas at that theatre until 1779. He went to Rome in 1757 and returned as Mengotto in Piccinni's *La buona figliuola* at the Teatro delle Dame in 1760, but otherwise spent his life in Naples. Also in 1760 he scored a notable success as Don Flaminio in Piccinni's *La furba burlata* – first at the Fiorentini, where it was performed 80 times, then at the Teatro Nuovo, where it ran from Easter to autumn and where he then appeared regularly until 1782. In 1767 he created Tuberone in Paisiello's *L'idolo cinese*, the first comic opera performed in the court theatre at Caserta (1768). His last appearance was in P. A. Guglielmi's *La donna amante di tutti e fedele a nessuno* at the Teatro del Fondo in autumn 1783.

(2) **Antonio Casaccia** ['Casacciello'; 'Il grande Casaccia'] (*b* Naples; *d* Naples, 1793). Baritone. Some say he was the son of (1) Giuseppe Casaccia and that he died in November 1793; others that he was Giuseppe's brother (*b* 1719; *d* 22 Feb 1793). It may be, however, that there were two Antonios; for though he was

described as 'short, sturdy, fat and bald', the portrait of him in the Museo S Martino at Naples does not entirely bear this out.

He made his début at the Fiorentini in 1758, in Sacchini's *Olimpia tradita*, and at the Nuovo in 1762, in Piccinni's *La furba burlata*, appearing alongside Giuseppe, his regular partner at the Nuovo for many years. He returned to the Fiorentini in 1770 and was *primo buffo* from 1775. Burney saw one of them there in Piccinni's *Gelosia per gelosia* in 1770:

> This opera had nothing else but the merit and reputation of the composer to support it, as both the drama and singing were bad. There was, however, a comic character performed by Signor Casaccia, a man of infinite humour; the whole house was in a roar the instant he appeared; and the pleasantry of this actor did not consist in buffoonery, nor was it local, which in Italy, and, indeed, elsewhere, is often the case; but was of that original and general sort as would excite laughter at all times and in all places.

Antonio sang again at the Nuovo, 1779–84, and in 1783 appeared in two operas at the Fondo. According to a contemporary letter to the composer, the great success of a 1780 performance of Paisiello's *Socrate immaginario* (Nuovo) was due largely to the fact that the title role was taken by Casaccia. He returned to the Fiorentini in 1788, appearing in Paisiello's *Nina* in 1790, and last performed in public during Carnival 1793. His repertory included operas by all the leading Neapolitan composers of the period, but he never sang outside his native city.

A younger Antonio (or Antonino) Casaccia took a boy's role in Mayr's *Elena* at the Fiorentini in 1814.

(3) **Filippo Casaccia** (*b* Naples, 1751; *d* after 1781). Baritone, son of (1) Giuseppe or (2) Antonio Casaccia; he enjoyed a brief career alongside both. He made his début in Masi's *I tre amanti burlati* at the Fiorentini in 1766 and appeared there regularly, 1770–72. In 1780–81 he sang at the Fondo.

(4) **Carlo Casaccia** ['Casacciello'] (*b* Naples, 26 Feb 1768; *d* after 1826). Baritone, son of (2) Antonio Casaccia. He made his début in P. A. Guglielmi's *La finta zingara* at the Fiorentini in 1785 and appeared in nearly all the comic operas performed there between 1791 and the mid-1820s, including works by Paisiello, Cimarosa and Rossini. He also sang regularly at the Fondo, in 1793–7 and from 1816, appearing in *La Cenerentola* (1818) and in operas by Mayr and Mercadante, and at the Nuovo, in 1798–1801 (two works by Spontini) and in the 1820s (Donizetti and Mercadante). His last appearance was in Generali's *Chiara di Rosemberg* at the Fondo in 1826. After the first performance of Rossini's *La gazzetta* in 1816, the critic of the *Giornale delle due Sicilie* described Casaccia as 'always full of naturalness and truth'. Stendhal, who saw him in P. C. Guglielmi's *Paolo e Virginia* in 1817, was much impressed with his comic acting, though he added that he had 'a nasal voice, like a Capuchin'. Nevertheless it is clear that Casaccia was immensely popular.

(5) **Raffaelle Casaccia** (*d* Naples, 1852). Baritone, son of (4) Carlo Casaccia. According to the unpublished memoirs of his son (6) Ferdinando, he was at first a 'maestro di contrappunto'. In 1810 he was engaged as 'maestro di cembalo' at the Fiorentini, but his voice and comic figure (very short and very fat) made him the natural heir to the family tradition. He made his début in 1818 in Rossini's *Torvaldo e Dorliska* at the Nuovo, where he worked alongside his father for seven years and then as *primo buffo*. He also sang at the Fondo in 1826 (in Generali's *Chiara di Rosemberg*) and in 1845–7. The high point of his career was his performance in the title role of De Giosa's *Don Checco* (1850), allegedly one of the greatest successes in the history of opera in Naples. His death marked the end of a glittering period in Neapolitan *opera buffa*.

(6) **Ferdinando Casaccia** (*d* Naples, 1894). Baritone, son and pupil of (5) Raffaelle and pupil of (4) Carlo Casaccia. Much of the information on his life comes from his unpublished memoirs (*I-Nlp*). He made his début in 1852 at the monastery of Monte Oliveto in Naples. Shortly afterwards he appeared at the Nuovo in Mario Aspa's *Muratore di Napoli*, in which the Act 2 cavatina was written especially for him. Although he also performed outside Naples (*Don Checco* in Trani, in Capua, Santa Maria and Caserta), the Nuovo was his base until 1861. He then appeared in other Neapolitan theatres, including the Giardino d'inverno (1862), the Bellini Vecchio (1866), the Fenice (1867) and the Rossini (1873). His last appearance was in *Don Checco* at the Nuovo on 20 May 1888. With his death six years later, in poverty and oblivion, the Casaccia dynasty came to an end.

*

BurneyFI; *DBI* (A. Ascarelli); *DEUMM*; *ES* (F. Schlitzer); *GSL*

COLIN TIMMS

Casali, Giovanni Battista (*b* Rome, *c*1715; *d* Rome, 6 July 1792). Italian composer. In 1740 he was admitted to the Bologna Accademia Filarmonica. He was *maestro di cappella* at St John Lateran, Rome (from 1759), and at S Maria in Vallicella (1761–at least 1773). Grétry was his pupil for two years. Though principally a composer of sacred music, Casali wrote at least nine stage works.

Candaspe [Campaspe] regina de' Sciti (dramma per musica, ?B. Vitturi), Venice, S Angelo, carn. 1740
La costanza vincitrice (dramma per musica), S Giovanni in Persiceto, Sept 1740, collab. others
Il Bajazette (A. Piovene), Rimini, 1741
La lavandarina (int, A. Lungi), Rome, Valle, 1746
Le furbarie di Bruscolo Trasteverino (int), Rome, Pace, carn. 1747
L'impazzito (int, G. Aureli), Rome, Valle, carn. 1748
Antigona (dramma per musica, G. Roccaforte), Turin, Regio, carn. 1752
La finta tedesca (int), Rome, Tordinona, carn. 1753
Arianna e Teseo, n.d.

Casalmaggiore. Town on the river Po in northern Italy, near Parma. The earliest date for theatrical presentations with music is 1737, when one of the rooms in the Palazzo della Comunità was arranged as a theatre. Its small capacity led a group of 12 citizens to form an association to build a new theatre, the design of which was entrusted to Andrea Mones under the supervision of Giuseppe Piermarini. Work was begun in 1782 on a site in the Contrada della Posta (now via Cairoli) and completed in the following year: the U-shaped Teatro della Società had three rows of boxes with a gallery above. It was inaugurated in autumn 1783, with Anna Morichelli, Gasparo de Filippis and Matteo Babbini in Sarti's *Medonte*. The next year Anfossi's *Tito nelle Gallie* was performed with Giovanni Ansani, and the theatre continued in use on the contract system until at least 1795 with performances of *opere buffe* by Paisiello, Cimarosa, Sarti and Guglielmi. In the 19th century operas by Rossini, Bellini, Donizetti and Verdi predominated; generally two operas were staged each year during the autumn fair, and orchestra and chorus were supplied by the local Società Filarmonica. Towards the end of the century the system of private management by a society ran into financial difficulties, but the staging of opera seasons and, after 1908, operetta continued until World War I; even between the wars there were regular autumn seasons when two or three operas were performed with well-known singers. In 1931 the box holders could no longer meet the costs of the necessary restoration work and sold their shares to the Comune, when the name of the theatre was changed to 'Comunale'. The last operatic performances took place in 1952, after which the theatre was occasionally used as a cinema until it closed in 1957. It was restored and reopened in 1989 as a concert venue.

*

Il teatro di Casalmaggiore: storia e restauro (Cremona, 1990)

CLAUDIO TOSCANI

Casanova's Homecoming. *Opera buffa* in three acts by DOMINICK ARGENTO to his own libretto based on Jacques Casanova's *L'histoire de ma vie*; St Paul, Minnesota, Ordway Music Theater, 12 April 1985.

In writing his own text for this theatrically vivid opera – the music of which consists of borrowings from Jommelli's 1770 revision of his *opera seria Demofoonte*, coloured by Argento's more pungent style – Argento embellished the facts of Casanova's life with what he termed 'accidenti verissimi', small fictional liberties historically characteristic of Venetian librettos. The opera is set in 1774, when Casanova was 49 years old and recently returned to Venice after 18 years of exile. Casanova (baritone), in middle age a reputed master of the occult arts, carefully swindles the gullible Madame d'Urfé (contralto) in order to obtain a dowry for his godchild Barbara (soprano), who in the final scene is revealed to be his daughter. Other characters include Abbé Lorenzo (baritone), meant to depict Lorenzo da Ponte, whose relationship with Casanova actually began in the year *L'histoire* was abandoned, and Terese (mezzo-soprano), a female singer who disguises herself as a castrato (and whose affair with Casanova is borne out in the memoirs).

The opera has a narrative plot, clear character development and many surprising turns, all in keeping with the work's *opera buffa* inspiration. Here Argento turned completely from 12-note writing, favouring a rich, post-romantic harmonic idiom and arching, expressive vocal lines. Written into the score are large-scale scene changes, often accomplished with little mechanical assistance. Act 1 scene ii, set at an opera house during a performance, has been cited as a musical and dramatic tour de force. VIRGINIA SAYA

Casapietra, Celestina (*b* Genoa, 23 Aug 1939). Italian soprano. She studied with Gina Cigna in Milan, where she made her début in 1963 at the Teatro Nuovo in Giordano's *Mese Mariano*. After singing in various Italian theatres, from 1965 she spent 20 years with the Berlin Staatsoper, also appearing elsewhere in Europe and in the USA. Her wide repertory includes Handel's Cleopatra, Konstanze, Vitellia and Fiordiligi as well as Reiza (*Oberon*), Agathe, Tatyana, Marguerite, Maddalena (*Andrea Chénier*), and Mimì, which she sang with the WNO. She has also sung Wagner's Elisabeth, Elsa and Eva, and Strauss's Marschallin and Daphne. At Hamburg in 1983 (and Amsterdam in 1989) she sang Yü-Pei in Zemlinsky's *Der Kreidekreis*. She has a strong, vibrant voice and an attractive stage personality. ELIZABETH FORBES

Casarini, Domenica (*b* Venice; *fl* 1743–58). Italian soprano. She made her début in Venice in Lampugnani's *Ezio* (1743). She was engaged for the King's Theatre, London (1746–8), appearing in operas by Terradellas and Paradies, and a version of Handel's *Alessandro* under the title *Rossane* (in which she took the title role), and (1747–8) in the Handel pasticcio *Lucio Vero*, Galuppi's *Enrico* and Hasse's *Didone* and *Semiramide riconosciuta*. The two parts Handel composed for her in the oratorios *Joshua* and *Alexander Balus* are long and rewarding, but narrow in compass (*d'* to *g*♯'').

Casarini sang again at Venice in the 1750s in operas by Jommelli, Cocchi, Latilla (whom she married about 1752) and others, at Turin in 1751, when she was imprisoned for sending emissaries to assault a rival singer, and at the S Carlo, Naples, in 1751–2 in operas by Traetta, Cafaro and G. Conti. The impresario Tufarelli described her as well proportioned, with a good soprano voice and sufficient skill in music and acting. She sang at Padua in 1753 (in Latilla's *Siroe*) and at Genoa (1755). In 1758 she was engaged for Madrid, but was taken ill on arrival in April and eight days later gave birth to a daughter in Farinelli's house; this did not prevent her singing in Conforto's *La forza del genio* at Aranjuez on 30 May. WINTON DEAN

Casavola, Franco (*b* Modugno, Bari, 13 July 1891; *d* Bari, 7 July 1955). Italian composer and critic. He studied in Bari, in Milan and with Respighi in Rome. In 1920 he became involved in the futurist movement, in connection with which during the next seven years he wrote (or contributed to) several manifestos, a 'novel', dramatic sketches and music employing Luigi Russolo's 'noise machines' (*intonarumori*). His most ambitious futurist scores were ballets, all later repudiated, among which *La danza dell'elica* (with parts for wind machine and internal combustion engine) and *Il cabaret epilettico* had scenarios by Marinetti. At the same time Casavola showed a marked interest in mixed-media experiments. After 1927 he reverted to a more traditional outlook, winning his biggest public success (abroad as well as in Italy) with the gently parodistic, mildly exotic *Il gobbo del califfo*, in which the after-effects of his futurist experience are perceptible in a restrained yet insistent piquancy in the harmony. From 1936 much of his energy was directed into film music: the side effects are all too apparent in his last opera, *Salammbô*.

Don Cesare di Bazan, 1921 (C. Giardini, after A.-P. Dennery), unperf.

Il gobbo del califfo (1, A. Rossato, after *The Thousand and One Nights*), Rome, Opera, 4 May 1929

Astuzie d'amore (3 scenes, Rossato), Bari, Petruzzelli, 1936

Salammbô (4, E. Mucci, after G. Flaubert), Rome, Opera, 1948

*

DBI (C. Strinati)

A. Giovine: 'Franco Casavola', *Musicisti e cantanti di terra di Bari* (Bari, 1968), 11–14 JOHN C. G. WATERHOUSE

Casazza [née Mari], **Elvira** (*b* Ferrara, 15 Nov 1887; *d* Milan, 26 Jan 1965). Italian mezzo-soprano. She studied in Milan, making her début at Varese in 1909. In 1911 she toured the USA with the Lombardi Opera Company and in 1916 appeared at the Teatro Colón, as Amneris, Ulrica and Mistress Quickly, which became her finest role. She first appeared at La Scala as Amneris in 1916 and also sang Ortrud, Clytemnestra, and the Nurse in *Ariane et Barbe-bleue* there, as well as creating Deborah in Pizzetti's *Debora e Jaele* (1922) and La Comandante in Zandonai's *I cavalieri di Ekebù* (1925). She sang Mistress Quickly and other roles at Covent Garden in 1926 and 1931. After her last Scala performance, as the Witch in *Hänsel und Gretel* in 1942, she sang occasionally until 1948 in *I quatro rusteghi*. It was the fully finished quality of her stage peformances that made her one of the finest and most versatile singing actresses in Italy in the inter-war years.

HAROLD ROSENTHAL/R

Cascina, La ('The Farmhouse'). *Dramma giocoso* in three acts by GIUSEPPE SCOLARI to a libretto by CARLO GOLDONI; Venice, S Samuele, 26 December 1755.

Essentially *La cascina* is a pastoral with seven characters. There are two pairs of peasant lovers – Cecca (soprano) and Berto (tenor), and Lena (alto) and Pippo (bass) – and a triangle of noble lovers: Lavinia (soprano), the widowed owner of a wine-and-cheese producing *cascina*, and two suitors, Costanzo (alto), who is disguised at first as a peasant with the pastoral name Silvio, and Conte Ripoli (bass), a pompous nobleman. The last, after causing a goodly number of lovers' quarrels by his indiscriminate flirtations, is the odd man out at the end.

The work had considerable success; its popularity rested upon Scolari's skill in composing simple, tuneful arias and ensembles in major keys. Only Lavinia's arias require a modest *fioritura*, though Ripoli's contain some mock virtuosity. The opera was heard at least nine times in the north Italian cities between 1756 and 1760, and was transported to Barcelona, Berlin, Warsaw, Lisbon, London and Dresden over the next two years. The last performance took place in Parma in 1772.

ROBERT LAMAR WEAVER

Case, Anna (*b* Clinton, NJ, 29 Oct 1889; *d* New York, 7 Jan 1984). American soprano. Her teacher in New York was Mme Ohrström-Renard. Singing at the Metropolitan from 1909 in small parts, she made a favourable impression as Fyodor in the first American production of *Boris Godunov* in 1913. The same year brought her a greater opportunity in the first performance there of *Der Rosenkavalier*; she was not in best voice, however, and the critic W. J. Henderson concluded that the role of Sophie was 'outrageously written'. Other parts with the company included Micaëla and Papagena. She retired from opera in 1920 but continued her extensive concert career until her marriage in 1931; in England her elegant style and her middle and lower notes were admired. She was a favourite with Thomas Edison, and her clear, bright tone can be heard in about a hundred of his recordings.

J. B. STEANE

Casella, Alfredo (*b* Turin, 25 July 1883; *d* Rome, 5 March 1947). Italian composer, organizer and conductor, the most influential figure in Italian music between the two world wars. After studying with his mother, he showed precocious promise as a pianist and in 1896 went to study at the Paris Conservatoire. The musical and cultural life of the French capital, his base for the next 19 years, had a lasting influence on him. In 1900–01 he attended Fauré's composition classes. His friends included Enescu and Ravel, and he developed enthusiasms for the music of Debussy, the Russian nationalists, Strauss, Mahler and later for Bartók, Schoenberg and Stravinsky. Revolutionary trends in the visual arts (cubism, futurism, 'pittura metafisica') also affected him strongly. His taste and culture thus became both adventurous and cosmopolitan. In 1915 he returned to Italy, as professor of piano at the Liceo di S Cecilia, Rome, and began to introduce new music to the Italian public. He gathered around him a group of young composers, including G. F. Malipiero, Pizzetti and Respighi, who collaborated with him (in varying degrees) in the modern music societies that he founded.

In 1922 he resigned his post at the S Cecilia, though he returned to direct the advanced class from 1932. At the same time he became a leading light in the Venice Festival of Contemporary Music. Like many other Italians of otherwise good judgment, Casella fell under the spell of fascism: his opera *Il deserto tentato* was written in praise of Mussolini's Ethiopian campaign. But his fascism was of the 'innocent' kind, reflecting nothing worse than gullibility and lack of political understanding. Nor did it seriously undermine his interest in contemporary musical developments: indeed, on his initiative, the 1937 Venice Festival prominently featured the music of Schoenberg. In 1939 he helped to found the Settimane Senesi at the Accademia Chigiana, Siena. Three years later he suffered the first attack of the illness which was to kill him, but he continued to compose until 1944 and remained active as a conductor and accompanist until shortly before his death.

In Italy Casella's creative career is customarily divided into three 'manners' (up to 1913, 1913–20 and 1920–44), but this is no more than a useful oversimplification. The period of his 'first manner' was an eclectic formative phase. Then, in 1913–14, he confounded predictions by leaping into the extreme avant garde: influences of Stravinsky, Bartók and even Schoenberg, as well as the later Debussy, invaded his music. About 1920, however, this 'second manner' almost as suddenly disappeared. Elements of it persisted as a harmonic 'stiffening' in his third-period style, yet his approach changed drastically: tense, involuted chromaticism gave place to crisply dissonant diatonicism with chromatic excursions; harmonic experiment gave place to linear textures underpinned by driving motor rhythms; sardonic humour tended to resolve itself into easy-going bonhomie; Italian folk-music influences, sometimes prominent before 1913, returned in force in the ballet *La giara* (1924); and for the first time Casella showed marked signs of responding creatively to pre-19th-century Italian music. The more ponderous aspects of his neo-classical style are epitomized in the *Concerto romano* (1926), and much of his music of the 1930s follows in that concerto's wake. But his only full-length opera, *La donna serpente*, though imperfect, exemplifies many of the best qualities of the 'third manner'. The one-act opera *La favola di Orfeo* is slighter and less convincing but has been relatively often performed, whereas *Il deserto tentato*, though musically not without interest, has for obvious reasons never been revived since the fall of fascism.

See also DONNA SERPENTE, LA and FAVOLA DI ORFEO, LA.

La donna serpente op.50, 1928–31 (op fiaba, prol., 3, C. V. Lodovici, after C. Gozzi), Rome, Opera, 17 March 1932

La favola di Orfeo op.51 (chamber op, 1, C. Pavolini, after A. Poliziano), Venice, Goldoni, 6 Sept 1932

Il deserto tentato op.60 (mistero, 1, Pavolini), Florence, Comunale, 19 May 1937

M. Castelnuovo-Tedesco: 'Casella operista', *Pegaso* [Florence], iv/1 (1932), 481–8
L. Colacicchi: 'La donna serpente di Alfredo Casella', *RaM*, v (1932), 126–8
F. D'Amico: 'Casella e La donna serpente', *L'Italia letteraria* [Rome], iv/13 (1932), 5
F. Liuzzi: 'Casella e il teatro musicale', *Nuova antologia*, no.360 (1932), 529–34
L. Cortese: *Alfredo Casella* (Genoa, 1936), esp. 63–77
D. de' Paoli: *La crisi musicale italiana* (Milan, 1939), esp. 255–8
A. Gasco: 'Alle prese con *La donna serpente*', *Da Cimarosa a Strawinsky* (Rome, 1939), 414–21
A. Casella: *I segreti della giara* (Florence, 1941), esp. 242–4, 249, 251–7, 266, 283–4, 286–9, 293 (Eng. trans., slightly abridged, 1955, as *Music in my Time*) [autobiography]
M. Mila: *La donna serpente di Alfredo Casella* (Milan, 1942)
F. D'Amico and G. M. Gatti, eds.: *Alfredo Casella* (Milan, 1958) [incl. G. Gavazzeni: 'Il teatro', 71–86]
J. C. G. Waterhouse: 'Casella and Opera', *The Listener* (10 March 1966), 362
——: *The Emergence of Modern Italian Music (up to 1940)* (diss., U. of Oxford, 1968), esp. 361–9, 376–7
F. D'Amico and others: *La donna serpente di Alfredo Casella* (Palermo, Teatro Massimo, 1982) [programme book]
A. Bassi: *Alfredo Casella, l'anticipatore* (Poggibonsi, 1983), esp. 127–40 JOHN C. G. WATERHOUSE

Casella, Enrique Mario (*b* Montevideo, 1 Aug 1891; *d* Tucumán, 1948). Argentine composer. His father was an Italian musician. From the age of five he lived in Argentina, which he came to consider his country. He studied in Buenos Aires, then in Bologna, Brussels and Paris. In 1921 he settled in the inland city of Tucumán, where he came into contact with the literary and musical traditions of north-west Argentina. Like many of his contemporaries he made use of the tritonic and pentatonic scales of the Incas and the traditional music of the region to give character to his compositions, a kind of Andean musical nationalism that became known as 'americanismo musical'.

His first work to be performed was *Corimayo*, given in Tucumán in 1926 under his own direction and later the same year in Buenos Aires. In the 1930s he set the Inca poem by Ataliva Herrera, *Las vírgenes del sol*, which had also been offered to Alfredo Schiuma. Both composed an opera, but only Schiuma's was performed. In 1934 Casella's lyric drama *La tapera* was given in Buenos Aires. The title refers to the abandoned and ruined houses of the gauchos. *Leyendas líricas* (*Chasca*, *El irupé* and *El crespín*) is a triptych of legends from three different regions of Argentina. In a preliminary study Casella proposed the basis for a new Argentinian lyric theatre, and set out musical, literary and visual aims. He attempted to put his ideas into practice in the triptych, but only *Chasca* (with an Inca setting) was performed.

In 1942 *La vidala* – the title refers to a type of traditional lyric of central Argentina – was awarded a major national prize, but in spite of this was not considered of sufficient merit to have its première at the Colón. This so frustrated the composer that he did not seek performance for two other operas, *El país del ensueño* and *La venganza del sol*. Nevertheless, Casella's large output and his proposal for a national lyric theatre make him one of the most significant composers of Argentine musical nationalism.

unperformed unless otherwise stated

Corimayo (3, L. Pascarella), Tucumán, July 1926
Las vírgenes del sol, *c*1930 (3, A. Herrera)
La tapera (drama lírico, 3, E. Casella), Buenos Aires, Cervantes, 1934
Leyendas líricas, 1936–9 (tríptico, Casella): Chasca (1), Tucumán, Alberdi, 1939; El irupé (1); El crespín (1)
La vidala, 1942
Dates of composition unknown: El maleficio de la luna (2); El embrujo de la copla (3); El país del ensueño; La venganza del sol (leyenda lírica)

*

J. M. Veniard: *La música nacional argentina: Influencia de la música criolla tradicional en la música académica argentina: relevamiento de datos históricos para su estudio* (Buenos Aires, 1986), 88, 102–4, 114 JUAN MARÍA VENIARD

Casellato-Lamberti, Giorgio. *See* LAMBERTI, GIORGIO.

Caserío, El ('The Farmstead'). *Zarzuela vasca* in three acts by JESÚS GURIDI to a libretto by FEDERICO ROMERO and GUILLERMO FERNÁNDEZ SHAW; Madrid, Teatro de la Zarzuela, 11 November 1926.

In the Basque countryside the well-to-do, middle-aged Santi (baritone) loves his farmhouse and the estate he has built up over the years by his labours, and, being a bachelor, would like to hand them on to two young relations, Ana Mari (soprano) and José Miguel (tenor), who he hopes will marry. The young man however thinks of nothing but playing pelota and has no wish to settle down. Only when Santi, to spur him on, proposes marrying Ana Mari himself does José realize that he in fact returns her love.

The lyrical score introduces the Basque folk pipe, the *txistu*, and also makes use of the characteristic 5/8 rhythm of the *zortziko* dance. One of the highlights of the work is the sword dance in Act 2. LIONEL SALTER

Casken, John (Arthur) (*b* Barnsley, 15 July 1949). English composer. He studied at Birmingham University, where his teachers included John Joubert and Peter Dickinson, and later in Poland with Andrzej Dobrowolski. He was lecturer in music at the universities of Birmingham (1973–9) and Durham (1981–92) and fellow in composition at Huddersfield Polytechnic (1980–81); in 1992 he became professor of music at Manchester University.

Casken's works of the 1970s showed the influence of Lutosławski, with whom he had begun an association during his period in Warsaw, but though Lutosławski's fastidious working methods have remained an important stimulus, Casken's own music moved in a very different direction. The landscape and literature of the north of England played an increasingly important part in the music he wrote in the 1980s, while the vocal *Firewhirl* (1979–80) and the dramatic schemes of several subsequent instrumental works began the development towards his first stage work. *Golem*, an operatic treatment of the Jewish legend to a text by the composer in collaboration with Pierre Audi, was first performed at the Almeida Theatre, London, in 1989. It uses a variety of musical styles and techniques, folk music references, freely synchronized passages and pre-recorded tape to mediate between the worlds of the community in which the main action of the opera is located and a timeless mythic past.

See also GOLEM. ANDREW CLEMENTS

Casona, Alejandro [Álvarez, Alejandro Rodríguez] (*b* Besullo, 23 March 1903; *d* Madrid, 17 Sept 1965). Spanish dramatist and librettist. He studied in Murcia and Madrid. Between 1928 and the outbreak of the Spanish Civil War in 1936, he pursued drama and pedagogy. His first successful play was *La sirena varada*

(1929); his *Nuestra Natacha* ran for 500 performances in Madrid in 1936 and was produced simultaneously in Barcelona. Casona was abroad in political exile for 23 years, settling in Buenos Aires in 1939 and remaining in La Reina del Plata until 1962. His only opera libretto, for Ginastera's *Don Rodrigo*, was written in close collaboration with the composer. Except for the text for Teudiselo's aria at the close of scene viii ('Oh, Rodrigo, Entre los pastos verdes son charcos de amapolas los heridos'), added for the bass Víctor de Narké and composed on a metric pattern to which Casona adapted the poetry in Madrid, the libretto was written in Buenos Aires before Casona's departure in 1962.

Essentially poetic and ultimately didactic, Casona's theatre reconciles levels of illusion subordinated to reality in the treatment of universal themes, including death, the redeeming power of love, and dreams as mirrors of the subconscious. Casona's use of the poetic imagination to reveal internal conflicts places him next to Federico García Lorca in revitalizing the Spanish theatre. In his *Don Rodrigo* libretto Casona subsumes imagery and substance from the long literary progeny of one of Spain's richest epics. MALENA KUSS

Casorri, Ferdinando (*b* Tuscany, *c*1730; *d* after 1792). Italian librettist and stage director. He was one of two poets at the Teatro del Cocomero in Florence around 1755, a position requiring him to alter and add to librettos by other authors, notably Goldoni. His *I matrimoni in maschera* (1763) and *L'amore industrioso* (1765), comic operas composed by G. M. Rutini, established the reputations of both men in Italy and can be regarded as Casorri's masterpieces. He was an active translator into Italian of French farces, the most successful being *Il disertore*, originally by L. S. Mercier and set to music by Giuseppe Gazzaniga, which probably owed its popularity to its unswerving morality and optimism. Casorri wrote two *opera seria* librettos, *Attalo, re di Bitinia* (1780) and *Mesenzio, re d'Etruria*, the latter set by the young Cherubini in 1782; both are solemn and noble, though conventional. In the 1790s Casorri directed a Tuscan prose company which performed in the Palla a Corda and the Piazza Vecchia theatres. His principal composer there was Neri Bondi; Casorri wrote and translated intermezzos and farces for the company to perform.

I matrimoni in maschera (dg), Rutini, 1763; *L'amore industrioso* (dg), Rutini, 1765 (J. de S. Carvalho, 1769; ? B. Ottani, ? 1769 or 1774; Andreozzi, 1783); *Il disertore* (dg, after L. S. Mercier), G. Gazzaniga, 1779 (M. Portogallo, 1800); *Attalo, re di Bitinia* (dramma per musica), Alessandri, 1780 (Sarti, 1783; F. Robuschi, 1788; Caruso, 1790; Marinelli, 1793); *Venere, e Adone* (azione teatrale), F. Bianchi, 1781; *I due fratelli sciocchi* (dg, after F. S. Zini: *La villanella ingentilita*), P. Guglielmi, 1782; *Mesenzio, re d'Etruria* (dramma per musica), Cherubini, 1782 (Bianchi, 1786); *Le serve in contesa* (int), Neri Bondi, 1783; *Ogni disugualianza amore agguaglia* (int), Neri Bondi, 1784; *Il ripiego improvviso, ovvero Quel che l'occhio non vede, il cor non crede* (int), Neri Bondi, 1784; *I mietitori, ovvero L'amante dispettosa* (int), Neri Bondi, 1785; *L'amor rusticale* (int), Neri Bondi, 1785; *Tizio, e Sempronio* (int), Neri Bondi, 1787; *La villa* (farsa), Neri Bondi, 1790; *Il vecchio speziale deluso in amore* (farsa), Neri Bondi, 1790; *L'amor comico* (farsa), L. Barbieri, 1792

*

M. de Angelis: *La felicità in Etruria* (Florence, 1990)
——: *Melodramma spettacoli e musica nella Firenze dei Lorena* (Florence, 1991)
R. L. Weaver and N. Weaver: *A Chronology of Music in the Florentine Theater 1751–1800* (Warren, MI, 1992)
ROBERT LAMAR WEAVER

Cassani, Giuseppe (*b* Bologna; *fl* 1700–28). Italian alto castrato. A church singer at Bologna about 1700, he made his London début at the Queen's Theatre in a revival of Haym's adaptation of Giovanni Bononcini's *Camilla* in 1708, but was severely hissed and forced to withdraw after two performances. Returning in 1710, he sang in *Almahide*, Mancini's *Idaspe fedele*, Bononcini's *Etearco*, Handel's *Rinaldo* and Gasparini's *Antioco* and *Ambleto*. Handel composed the part of the Mago in *Rinaldo* for him; its narrow compass (*b* to *c''*) and absence of coloratura suggest that his powers were limited. He sang in two operas in Florence, 1717–18.
WINTON DEAN

Cassani, Vincenzo (*b* Venice, ?1677; *fl* Venice, 1710–32). Italian librettist. He wrote five librettos for various Venetian theatres between 1710 and 1727, and one for Chioggia (*Climene*) in 1721. Three were for Albinoni, for whom he also provided a text celebrating Charles VI's name-day, *Il nome glorioso in terra, santificato in cielo* (1724). He also provided Marcello with the texts for two dramatic works performed outside the context of the opera house, *Arianna* and *Psiche*. *Il tiranno eroe* deals with the same Roman dictator as Handel's *Silla* (1713, London), but Cassani's libretto did not provide a direct model for that work. Cassani conforms to the elevated libretto style of his day, carefully distinguishing between historical elements and his own invention. He criticized the necessity of bowing to the demands of impresarios and singers.

Il tiranno eroe, Albinoni, 1710 (A. M. Bononcini, 1715); *Cleomene*, Albinoni, carn. 1718; *Climene*, Bioni, carn. 1721; *Plautilla*, A. Pollarolo, 1721; *Romolo e Tazio*, C. L. P. Grua, 1722; *L'incostanza schernita* (dramma comico-pastorale), Albinoni, 1727, as Filandro, carn. 1729 (Porpora, 1747, as Filandro-Philander); *Nino* (after I. Zanelli), F. Courcelle, 1732

*

AllacciD; *ES* (U. Rolandi)
G. Bonlini: *Le glorie della poesia e della musica* (Venice, 1730)
G. Tintori: *'L'Arianna' di Benedetto Marcello* (Milan, 1951)
E. Selfridge-Field: *Pallade veneta: Writings on Music in Venetian Society, 1650–1750* (Venice, 1985)
M. Talbot: *Tomaso Albinoni: the Venetian Composer and his World* (Oxford, 1990)
HARRIS S. SAUNDERS

Cassel, (John) Walter (*b* Council Bluffs, IA, 15 May 1910). American baritone. He studied with Frank La Forge and made his début in 1942 as Brétigny in Massenet's *Manon* at the Metropolitan but left the company in 1945, dissatisfied with its casting policy. He ventured into musical comedy but continued to appear in opera with various companies, including those at Philadelphia, Pittsburgh, Cincinnati, New Orleans and San Antonio. After World War II he sang at the Vienna Staatsoper and in Düsseldorf before appearing with the New York City Opera between 1948 and 1960, making his début as Escamillo. In 1955 he rejoined the Metropolitan, remaining until 1974. He created the roles of Horace Tabor in Douglas Moore's *The Ballad of Baby Doe* (1956, Central City, Colorado) and Petruccio in Vittorio Giannini's *The Taming of the Shrew* (1958, New York City Opera). From 1970 to 1972 he sang the role of Johann Strauss sr in Korngold's *The Great Waltz* in London, then performed in Italy and Spain. His well-modulated, resonant voice was suited to the works of Wagner (Telramund, the Dutchman, Kurwenal) and Richard Strauss (John the Baptist, Orestes, the Music Master). CHARLES JAHANT

Cassilly, Richard (*b* Washington DC, 14 Dec 1927). American tenor. He studied in Baltimore and New York, making his début in 1955 as Michele in Menotti's *The Saint of Bleecker Street* on Broadway. In 1956 he joined New York City Opera, singing Vakula in *Cherevichki* (the revised version of Tchaikovsky's *Vakula the Smith*). He first sang at Chicago in 1959 as Laca (*Jenůfa*) and at San Francisco in 1964 as Max, returning in 1972 as the Lord Mayor in Einem's *Besuch der alten Dame* (American première). He made his European début in 1965 at Geneva as Sutermeister's Raskolnikoff, then joined the Hamburg Staatsoper in 1966. He made his Covent Garden début as Laca (1968), returning for Siegmund, Tannhäuser, Otello, Florestan and Peter Grimes, which he had already sung for Scottish Opera (1970, Edinburgh). He appeared at the Vienna Staatsoper, La Scala and the Paris Opéra. At the Metropolitan he sang over 100 performances, making his début in 1973 as Radames, and returning for Canio, Tristan, Saint-Saëns' Samson, Captain Vere (*Billy Budd*), the Drum Major (*Wozzeck*), Herod and Jimmy Mahoney (*Aufstieg und Fall der Stadt Mahagonny*), which he also sang for Scottish Opera in 1986. He sang Schoenberg's Aaron at Hamburg in 1974, and recorded the role under Boulez. He had a powerful, vibrant voice of heroic proportions and superb diction, and acted with authority. ALAN BLYTH

Cassirer, Fritz (*b* Breslau, 29 March 1871; *d* Berlin, 26 Nov 1926). German conductor. After studying in Munich, and in Berlin with Pfitzner and Gustav Holländer, he was successively conductor at the opera houses of Lübeck, Posen, Saarbrücken and Elberfeld (1903–5). At the latter he became particularly interested in Delius, whose music had already been played there by Cassirer's predecessor, Hans Haym. According to Beecham, Cassirer had naturally good if slightly fastidious taste, and he attached himself to Delius with great devotion; he conducted the première of *Koanga* at Elberfeld in 1904 and helped bring about the première of *A Village Romeo and Juliet* at the new Berlin Komische Oper in 1907. He accompanied the Komische Oper company to London (where it played only Offenbach) and stayed for a time. Having refused an offer from the Manhattan Opera House, New York, he retired to Munich, devoting himself to philosophical and literary studies. ALAN BLYTH

Castagna, Bruna (*b* Bari, 15 Oct 1905; *d* Pinamar, Argentina, 10 July 1983). Italian mezzo-soprano. She studied in Milan and made her début in 1925 at the Teatro Soziale, Mantua, as Marina in *Boris Godunov*. In the same year she made her first appearance at La Scala and remained there till 1928. She also sang at the Colón, Buenos Aires, taking part in the South American première of *Sadko*. In 1930 she returned on Toscanini's invitation to La Scala, where in 1933 she had a great success in *L'italiana in Algeri*. Opera and recital work took her to Australia and Egypt and then to the USA, where for a decade she was a leading mezzo at the Metropolitan. She made her début there in 1936 as Amneris, after which Lawrence Gilman wrote of her 'remarkable voice, sensuously beautiful, voluptuous, richly expressive'. Her Carmen was considered the best for many years; she retired in this role in the 1949–50 season at Philadelphia. She then taught in Milan. She can be heard in a few recordings of live performances from the Metropolitan. J. B. STEANE

Castaway. Opera in one act, op.68, by LENNOX BERKELEY to a libretto by PAUL DEHN after HOMER's *Odyssey* (book 6); Aldeburgh, Jubilee Hall, 3 June 1967.

The sea god Poseidon has taken revenge on Odysseus (baritone), for blinding his son Polyphemus, by sending a storm which wrecks him on the island of Scheria. Odysseus is found on the beach by Princess Nausicaa (soprano), who is delighted to come across this handsome, if bedraggled, stranger. She directs him to the palace, with the unwittingly prophetic words 'May the Gods guide you safely on your way!'

In the banqueting hall of the palace, the blind minstrel Demodocus (tenor), learning that the stranger fought at Troy, sings of Odysseus and the wooden horse. Nausicaa asks the stranger why he is weeping and he admits that he is Odysseus and that he is on his way home to his wife Penelope (Berkeley underlines musically the identity of stress and syllables in the names Penelope and Nausicaa – a dramatically potent idea, even if its precise relevance is hard to pin down). As he leaves the island, Nausicaa weeps and again offers up the prayer 'May the Gods guide you safely on your way!', this time without accompaniment as its earlier, hidden force is now revealed.

The musical language throughout the opera is varied, though inclining to the sparse rather than the lush, and bears out Berkeley's willingness to use traditional harmony 'when the feeling I want to convey in a particular piece seems to demand it ... at the risk of being accused of eclecticism by the critics'.

ROGER NICHOLS

Castel, José (*fl* 1761–81). Spanish composer. His works are prominent in an inventory of the *tonadillas* performed by the Manuel Martínez company in Madrid, especially before 1778. More than 50 of Castel's tonadillas are extant. A rare use of chorus is seen in his *La gitanilla en el coliseo* (ed. in Subirá 1928–30, iii). Three of his four *sainetes*, the comedy *Ifigenia en Tauride* and the zarzuela *El amor en la aldea* are to texts by Ramon de la Cruz. His works found their way to the Americas: a *tonadilla* was performed in Montevideo in 1830.

Sainetes: El caballero de Medina de Pomar (R. de la Cruz), 1766; El careo de los majos (de la Cruz), 1766; Los hombres con juicio (de la Cruz); Suene, suene el pandero

Zarzuelas: El amor en la aldea (2, A. Vázquez), 1766; La fontana del placer

Comedias: Ifigenia en Tauride (de la Cruz); El principe Don Carlos

*

LaborD

J. Subirá: *La tonadilla escénica* (Madrid, 1928–30), i, 150, 329–40; iii/4, 104–16; iii/5, 65–9

——: *Tonadillas teatrales inéditas* (Madrid, 1932), 88–92, 173–4, 176–8, 190–92

——: *La tonadilla escénica: sus obras y sus autores* (Barcelona, 1933)

——: *El teatro del Real palacio (1849–1851)* (Madrid, 1950), 76

ELEANOR RUSSELL

Castellan, Jeanne Anaïs (*b* Beaujeu, Rhône, 26 Oct 1819; *d* after 1858). French soprano. She studied in Paris with Bordogni, Nourrit and Cinti-Damoreau, and began her stage career at Varese in 1837, appearing later at Turin, Bergamo, Rome, Milan and Florence. In winter 1843–4 she sang in New York and Boston, then (1844–7) appeared in Italian opera alternately in St Petersburg and at Her Majesty's Theatre, London, as

Lucia (1 April 1845), repeating that role for her débuts at the Théâtre Italien, Paris (1847), and Covent Garden (1848). She sang Berthe in the première of *Le prophète* (1849, Opéra) and then continued to appear at Covent Garden until 1853. She was said to possess considerable agility and an extensive range, remarkably unified in tone quality; but several critics found fault with her intonation and considered her ornamentation over-ambitious or inappropriate.

*

H. F. Chorley: *Thirty Years' Musical Reminiscences* (London, 1862)

PHILIP ROBINSON

Castellano, Francesco (*fl* 1898–1918). Italian impresario. By 1899 he had spent four years in Egypt and the Balkans, and, starting in Odessa, had headed the first extended tour of the Russian provinces by an Italian company. Early that year, he reached Samarkand, later visiting Baku, Astrakhan and Saratov. He frequently visited Vilnius, Minsk and Riga during the early years of the century. He returned to the Balkans and Egypt in 1903–4. During 1905 he toured North Africa and then went through France into the Low Countries. On 26 April 1909 he opened a season at the Coronet Theatre in London, following it by several extended tours of the British Isles which lasted until around 1915. His was the first tour of Great Britain and Ireland presenting opera in Italian since Augustus Harris in the late summer and autumn of 1894. During lengthy portions of this period he split his company into two, one group singing in the British Isles while the other would perform in Warsaw, Odessa, the Baltic countries and the Balkans. Some of the better-known singers he engaged included Mattia Battistini, Maria Galvany, Antonio Magini-Coletti and Aida Gonzaga. He also introduced London audiences to Leoncavallo's *Zazà* on 30 April 1909. TOM KAUFMAN

Castelli, Ottaviano (*b* Spoleto, ? 1602–3; *d* Rome, 14 May 1642). Italian librettist and composer. A professor of medicine, he was one of the most original dramatists in the early history of opera. He had a daring, experimental approach to his theatrical projects, most of which combine eclectic literary theory, gentlemen's academy humour and his own readiness to exploit theatre fever in any potential noble patron. Above all, he attempted to be original in style, subject and plot. In his Italian verse he exploited uncommon metres, including French alexandrines and Spanish *romance* and *redondilla* metres; he also used ridiculous alliterations, unusual characters and roles spoken in dialect or with speech defects. He justified many of these devices by citing models from ancient comedy, in particular Aristophanes.

Probably active as a dramatist in Rome from about 1630, Castelli is first heard of in 1635 with three texts dedicated to the Barberini: a comic pastoral romance in four acts set by Angelo Cecchini, a poem commemorating the Barberini opera *Didimo e Teodora* and a festive cantata set by Stefano Landi. Castelli's most widely known work, *La Sincerità trionfante, overo L'Erculeo ardire*, was produced in December 1638 for the celebrations for Louis XIV's birth given by the French ambassador in Rome (see illustration). This event began Castelli's association with the pro-French faction in Rome, leading to a steady correspondence with Mazarin in Paris and, ultimately, to the honour 'mastro delle poste di Francia in Roma' with a pension from the crown. His second opera for the French, *Il favorito del principe* (1640, Rome), launched Filiberto Laurenzi and the soprano Anna Renzi on their operatic careers. This dark and dramatic, well-plotted and strongly psychological *opera regia* anticipates trends of the 1640s. Castelli himself set his last two librettos to music. His 1641 pastoral reportedly employed equal temperament as well as the ancient genera and modes. The music to all his librettos is lost.

Primavera urbana col trionfo d'Amor pudico (dramma boscareccio), Cecchini, 1635; *Il trionfo dell'autunno* (dramma ditirambico), Cecchini, 1636; *L'intemperie d'Apollo* (dramma boscareccio), Cecchini, 1638; *La Sincerità trionfante, overo L'Erculeo ardire* (favola boscareccia), Cecchini, 1638; *L'età dell'oro* (dramma musicale), ? before 1640; *Il favorito del principe* (dramma musicale boscareccio), Laurenzi, 1640; Untitled 'drametto in musica', Castelli, Rome, carn. 1641; *Mi feci quel che non ero per*

Set design by Giovanni Francesco Grimaldi for 'La Sincerità trionfante, overo L'Erculeo ardire' by Ottaviano Castelli, performed in Rome, 1638: engraving from the libretto (Rome, 1640), showing the Ile de la Cité in Paris illuminated by fireworks

esser quel che sono (dramma boscareccio musicale), Castelli, Rome, carn. 1642

*

Grove6 (L. Bianconi)

J. N. Erythraeus [pseud. of G. V. Rossi]: *Pinacotheca imaginum illustrium ... virorum* (Cologne, 1645), i, 293

H. Prunières: *L'opéra italien en France avant Lulli* (Paris, 1913)

H. Becker and others, eds.: *Quellentexte zur konzeption der europäischen Oper im 17. Jahrhundert* (Kassel, 1981), 51–7 [incl. excerpts from Castelli's 'Dialogo sopra la poesia dramatica']

S. Franchi: *Drammaturgia romana: repertorio cronologico dei testi drammatici pubblicati a Roma e nel Lazio, secolo XVII* (Rome, 1988)

P. Fabbri: *Il secolo cantante: Per una storia del libretto d'opera nel seicento* (Bologna, 1990) MARGARET MURATA

Castelmary [de Castan], **Armand** (*b* Toulouse, 16 Aug 1834; *d* New York, 10 Feb 1897). French bass. From 1863 to 1870 he sang at the Paris Opéra, where he created Don Diégo in *L'Africaine* (1865), a Monk (Charles V) in *Don Carlos* (1867) and Horatio in Thomas' *Hamlet* (1868). He also sang Gounod's Méphistophélès, Leporello, Oberthal (*Le prophète*) and Ferrando (*Il trovatore*). He sang with the French Opera Company, New Orleans (1870), and toured the USA with the Max Strakosch English Opera Company (1879). At Monte Carlo (1884) he sang Balthazar (*La favorite*), Giacomo (*Fra Diavolo*), Ramfis and Claudius (*Hamlet*). From 1889 to 1896 he sang at Covent Garden, as King Henry (*Lohengrin*), Giacomo (Mascagni's *I Rantzau*, 1893), Remigio (*La Navarraise*), the Bailli (*Werther*), Sparafucile, Sartorio (Cowen's *Signa*), Vulcan (*Philémon et Baucis*) and Hunding. He was engaged at the Metropolitan from 1893, making his début as Vulcan and singing Mephistopheles (Boito's as well as Gounod's) and Fafner. He died on stage during a performance of *Martha*, in which he was singing Lord Tristan.

ELIZABETH FORBES

Castelnuovo-Tedesco, Mario (*b* Florence, 3 April 1895; *d* Los Angeles, 17 March 1968). Italian composer. After attending the Florence Conservatory he studied the piano with Edoardo del Valle and composition with Pizzetti. With the help of Alfredo Casella, Castelnuovo-Tedesco's works soon reached an international audience. His first opera, *La mandragola* (1920–23), won first prize – a performance at La Fenice – at the first Concorso Lirico Nazionale in 1925. Emil Hertzka, director of Universal Edition, encouraged him to shorten its three acts to two; to complement the new version Castelnuovo-Tedesco wrote the one-act *ditiramo Bacco in Toscana* (1925–6), a cantata-like setting of Francesco Redi's poem (1685) for two soloists, chorus, mimers and large orchestra. Discouraged by the reception of these two works, however, he turned to writing concert overtures and incidental music before returning to opera with *Aucassin et Nicolette* (1938), a marionette opera scored for mezzo-soprano and chamber orchestra.

World War II and Italy's anti-semitism forced the Castelnuovo-Tedesco family to flee the country in 1939; assisted by Toscanini and Heifetz they moved to the USA, settling in Beverly Hills. The composer and his wife became US citizens in 1946. In addition to film scores, orchestral music and many works for classical guitar, he composed a number of scenic oratorios on biblical texts: *The Song of Songs* (1954–5, subtitled 'A Rustic Wedding Idyll') received its première in 1963 in Hollywood; *Tobias and the Angel* (1964–5), was first staged in New York in 1975. Two operas to texts by Shakespeare followed: *All's Well that Ends Well* (retitled in his later version as *Giglietta di Narbona*; 1955–8), and *The Merchant of Venice* (1956), which won first place in the Concorso Campari Internazionale sponsored by La Scala. His final opera was a musically sophisticated comedy based on *The Importance of Being Earnest* (1961–2); he devised a libretto in Italian metrical verse, adopting a title which preserves the play on words of Wilde's original – *L'importanza di esser Franco*. His writings on music include *Under the Sign of Orpheus*, a series of lectures on opera (MS at Castelnuovo-Tedesco Estate).

Castelnuovo-Tedesco's vocal writing suggests a post-*verismo* lyricism and his orchestral writing a post-impressionistic harmony. The inherent weakness of his operas is their librettos, which he crafted through cutting and pasting together the literary texts. Not wishing to add his own phrases, or text from other sources, he produced collages which lack, for the most part, true arias and ensembles to relieve the dialogue.

See also IMPORTANCE OF BEING EARNEST, THE; MANDRAGOLA, LA; and MERCHANT OF VENICE, THE.

librettos by the composer

La mandragola op.20, 1920–23 (commedia musicale fiorentino, prol., 2, after N. Machiavelli), Venice, Fenice, May 1926 (Vienna, 1926); rev., 2 acts, in Ger., Wiesbaden, Staatsoper, 1928

Bacco in Toscana op.39, 1925–6 (ditirambo, 1, after F. Redi), Milan, Scala, 1931 (Vienna, 1930)

Aucassin et Nicolette op.98, 1938 (chant-fable for Mez, 10 insts, marionettes, after 12th-century Fr.), Florence, Piccolo, 2 June 1952; rev. for S and Bar, in Eng., Beverly Hills, High School Auditorium, 8 March 1964

The Song of Songs op.172, 1954–5 (rustic wedding idyll, the Bible), Hollywood, High School Auditorium, 7 Aug 1963

All's Well that Ends Well op.182, 1955–8 (3, after W. Shakespeare); It. trans., as Giglietta di Narbona, unperf.

The Merchant of Venice op.181, 1956 (3, after Shakespeare), as Il mercante di Venezia, Florence, Comunale, 25 May 1961 (Milan, 1961); in orig. Eng. version, Los Angeles, Shrine Auditorium, 13 April 1966

Saul op.191, 1958–60 (3, after V. Alfieri), unperf.

The Importance of Being Earnest op.198, 1961–2 (comic op, 3, after O. Wilde), New York, La Guardia, 22 Feb 1975; in It., as L'importanza di esser Franco, Florence, Chiostro delle Donne, 30 June 1984

Tobias and the Angel op.204, 1964–5 (scenic oratorio, Apocrypha), New York, La Guardia, 2 Feb 1975

*

A. Lualdi: '"La mandragola" di M. Castelnuovo-Tedesco alla Fenice di Venezia', *Serate musicali* (Milan, 1928), 262–5

G. Pugliese: 'Florence (ii): Aucassin et Nicolette', *Opera*, iii (1952), 470–72

A. Damerini: '"Il mercante di venezia" di Mario Castelnuovo-Tedesco: novità assoluta al XXIV Magio Musicale Fiorentino', *Musica d'oggi*, new ser., iv (1961), 114–17

M. Rinaldi: 'Castelnuovo-Tedesco and The Merchant of Venice', *Ricordiana*, vi/4 (1961), 1–3

N. Rossi: 'A Tale of Two Countries: the Operas of Mario Castelnuovo-Tedesco', *OQ*, vii/3 (1990), 89–121 NICK ROSSI

Casti, Giovanni Battista [Giambattista] (*b* Acquapendente, 29 Aug 1724; *d* Paris, 6 or 7 Feb 1803). Italian librettist. He studied at the seminary of Montefiascone from 1734 to 1744, becoming a cathedral canon in 1747. However, he spent much of his time in Rome, where he settled in 1761. In the following decades his constant travels took him to all the important courts of Europe. He went in 1765 to Florence, where he received from Archduke Leopold in 1769 the title of court poet. In 1772 he visited Vienna for the first time; in the same year he went with Count

Kaunitz to Berlin, where he dedicated sonnets to Frederick the Great. In 1773 he met Casanova in Trieste. From 1776 to 1779 he journeyed to northern European capitals, including Stockholm, Copenhagen and St Petersburg, where in 1778 he wrote his first libretto, an inferior *opera buffa* called *Lo sposo burlato*, for Paisiello. After travelling to Madrid, Lisbon and Milan he returned to Vienna in 1783, partly in the hope of becoming imperial poet, in succession to Metastasio. In the following year he wrote what he called his first libretto, the highly successful *Il re Teodoro in Venezia*, again for Paisiello.

With *La grotta di Trofonio* (1785) Casti began a fruitful association with Salieri, for whom he wrote his most important librettos. His *Prima la musica, poi le parole*, a *divertimento teatrale* set by Salieri, was performed at Schönbrunn on 7 February 1786 in a double bill with Mozart's *Der Schauspieldirektor*; it both satirized contemporary Italian operatic fashions and attacked Lorenzo da Ponte, Casti's rival in Vienna. *Il poema tartaro* (1786), a literary satire on the Russian court, offended Joseph II, and Casti was obliged temporarily to leave Vienna. The librettos *Cublai, gran Kan de' tartari*, based on *Il poema*, and the satirical *Catilina* were also set by Salieri, but neither was performed. Late in 1792 Casti was made court poet by Francis II, but in 1796 he left Vienna permanently. He spent 1797 in Italy, and lived in Paris from 1798 until his death.

While Casti's librettos represent only a small part of his poetic output, they demonstrate an unusual degree of originality and personality. According to Goldin, he varied the typical locations and themes of the *buffo* genre by ideas drawn from his own background in literature. The resulting enrichment encompasses not only references to and reminiscences of earlier poets and librettists, but a new fusion of many heterogeneous elements, theatrical and other. Casti's basic sensibility was literary rather than dramatic – Goldin pointed to the length of his recitatives in comparison with his lyric movements – and he created characters with an eye to variety, letting each present a different expressive style. Of course, many such characters derive directly from the stereotypes of *opera buffa*, but others, such as King Theodore in *Il re Teodoro in Venezia*, reveal considerable complexity and individuality (*Il re Teodoro* is frequently cited as an important source of influence on Mozart and Da Ponte in the creation of *Figaro*). King Theodore's unhappy fate – the final scene of the opera finds him in a debtors' prison – exemplifies the unusually acerbic or pessimistic point of view found frequently in Casti's librettos. Several works are more or less openly satirical, taking their substance from contemporary, above all political, events, and in fact the political satire in *Cublai, gran Kan de' tartari* prevented the opera from being performed.

Casti's librettos are also noteworthy for the high quality of their poetry. His writing shows an ease and a gracefulness of language rivalled in its time only by the librettos of Da Ponte, whose work was far less original in content. Casti's works were influential, drawing praise of such figures as Stendhal. Richard Strauss was particularly impressed by *Prima la musica* and used it as a basis for his opera *Capriccio*.

Lo sposo burlato (ob), Paisiello, 1778; *Il re Teodoro in Venezia* (dramma eroicomico, after Voltaire: *Candide*), Paisiello, 1784; *La grotta di Trofonio* (dg), Salieri, 1785; *Prima la musica, poi le parole* (divertimento teatrale), Salieri, 1786; *Cublai, gran Kan de' tartari, imperador de' mogolli* (dramma eroicomico, after Casti: *Il poema tartaro*), Salieri, comp. *c*1786–8; *Catilina* (dramma tragicomico, after Voltaire), Salieri, comp. 1792 (De Ferrari, comp. 1852)

Librettos not set to music: *Il re Teodoro in Corsica* (dramma); *Li dormienti* (dramma); *Orlando furioso* (dramma eroicomico); *Rosamunda* (dramma tragicomico); *Bertoldo* (dramma)

*

DBI (S. Nigro); *DEUMM* (A. Lanfranchi)

L. Pistorelli: 'I melodrammi giocosi di Giovanni Battista Casti', *RMI*, ii (1895), 36–56, 449–76

——: 'I melodrammi giocosi inediti di Giovanni Battista Casti', *RMI*, iv (1897), 631–71

R. Benaglia-Sangiorgi: 'I melodrammi giocosi dell'abate Casti, poeta cesareo', *Italica*, xxxvi (1959), 101–26

A. Heriot: 'Casti as a Librettist', *Opera*, xiii (1962), 716–19

E. E. Swenson: '"Prima la musica e poi le parole": an Eighteenth-century Satire', *AnMc*, no.9 (1970), 112–29

A. Fallico: 'Notizie e appunti sulla vita e l'operosità di Giovanni Battista Casti negli anni 1776–90 (con documenti inediti)', *Italianistica*, i (1972), 520–38

G. Muresu: *Le occasioni di un libertino (G. B. Casti)* (Messina and Florence, 1973)

R. Angermüller: 'Die entpolitisierte Opera am Wiener und am Fürstlich Esterházyschen Hof', *HayJb 1978*, 5–22

G. Muresu: *La parola cantata: studi sul melodramma italiano del settecento* (Rome, 1982)

D. Goldin: *La vera fenice: librettisti e libretti tra sette e ottocento* (Turin, 1985)

M. Hager: 'Die Opernprobe als Theateraufführung, Eine Studie zum Libretto im Wien des 18. Jahrhunderts', *Oper als Text: Romanistische Beiträge zur Libretto-Forschung*, ed. A. Gier (Heidelberg, 1986), 101–24

G. Loubinoux: 'L'impasse castiana: un tentativo problematico di rinnovamento del libretto', *I vicini di Mozart: Venice 1987*, i, 173–84

RUDOLPH ANGERMÜLLER, JOHN PLATOFF

Castiglioni, Niccolò (*b* Milan, 17 July 1932). Italian composer. After studying at the Milan Conservatory, where his teachers included Ghedini and Margola, he attended courses in piano and composition at the Salzburg Mozarteum given by Gulda, Zecchi and Blacher. Courses at Darmstadt from 1958 and contact with Berio and Maderna in Milan during the 1950s turned him towards the post-Webern avant garde, filtered through a liking for decoration and neo-impressionist tone colour which reached its apogee in *Consonante* (1962). His next creative phase showed a tendency towards an eclectic tonal idiom without, however, any abandonment of his personal feeling for timbre. After teaching composition at various American universities between 1966 and 1971, Castiglioni returned to Italy; he has taught at the Milan Conservatory.

Among Castiglioni's works for the theatre – which include some which the composer considers to be failures: *Uomini e no* (1955), *Jabberwocky* (1962), *Sweet* and *Three Miracle Plays* (both 1968) – is the radio opera *Attraverso lo specchio*, based on Lewis Carroll's *Alice in Wonderland* and *Through the Looking Glass*, which won the Italia Prize in 1961. This introduced a fairy-tale dimension in which the composer's experiments with timbre had ample play, and a sense of magic is also dominant in *Oberon, the Fairy Prince* and *The Lords' Masque*. These two one-act operas, first performed at the International Festival of Contemporary Music in Venice on 9 October 1981, are based on post-Elizabethan works by Ben Jonson and Thomas Campion. Their style reflects Castiglioni's return to tonality and tradition (a kind of camouflage, according to the composer) and reveals a tendency to pastiche which was already evident in *Attraverso lo specchio*.

Grove6 (C. Annibaldi)
M. Mila: 'Troppe Biancanevi in musica', *L'espresso* (1 Oct 1961)
G. M. Gatti: 'Un mondo irreale', *Tempo* (14 Oct 1961)
G. Zaccaro: 'Tre misteri e un postludio', *Lo spettatore musicale*, iii/10–11 (Bologna, 1968), 16–17
M. Bortolotto: 'Le capriole di Niccolò', *Fase seconda: Studi sulla nuova musica* (Turin, 1969), 149–69
R. Cresti: *Linguaggio musicale di Niccolò Castiglioni* (Milan, 1991)

RAFFAELE POZZI

Castil-Blaze [Blaze, François-Henri-Joseph] (*b* Cavaillon, Vaucluse, 1 Dec 1784; *d* Paris, 11 Dec 1857). French critic, librettist, translator and arranger. His early studies in music were directed by his father. In 1799, after moving to Paris nominally to study law, he enrolled at the Conservatoire. Returning to the Vaucluse, he became Inspecteur de la Librairie but left his post in 1820 and began anew on a musical career in Paris. Success came early with widespread acclaim for *De l'opéra en France* (1820), in which he sketched out many of the positions he was to adopt and develop in the next 30 years. That work and the two-volume *Dictionnaire de musique moderne* (1821) were largely responsible for the invitation he received to become music critic for the *Journal des débats*. From this vantage point he was able to survey musical and theatrical trends in Paris throughout the 1820s. He moved to *Le constitutionnel* in 1832, and wrote for most of the main specialist and non-specialist journals in Paris during his long career.

Castil-Blaze claimed to have founded French music criticism. The precise technical writing about music that he developed at the *Débats* in the 1820s differed in many respects from that of his predecessors and many of his contemporaries. His articles in the *Débats* and elsewhere, signed 'XXX', were generally well received (though sometimes controversial), and were highly influential. He was no less important as an opera historian. In the 1850s he wrote histories of the three principal operatic institutions in Paris, the Académie Royale de Musique, the Théâtre Italien and the Opéra-Comique; only the first two were published in his lifetime. All are still used but the information must be carefully sifted to separate anecdote, review and polemic from the genuine scholarly component. Castil-Blaze was the first to use, in these histories, the unpublished material bequeathed to the Bibliothèque Nationale by Louis-François Beffara. Throughout his publishing career Castil-Blaze kept up a crusade against inept uses of French verse (which he called rhymed prose) for librettos.

Castil-Blaze's original stage works, *Belzébuth, ou Les jeux du roi René* (*mélodrame*, 4; Montpellier, 15 April 1841; Paris, 1841) and *Le pigeon volé, ou La colombe* (*mélodrame*, 3; Paris, OC (Favart), 12 Aug 1843; Paris, ?1843), for which he wrote the librettos as well as the music, were not well received. A third work, *Choriste et liquoriste* (mentioned by Fétis), appears not to have been performed or published. This lack of success, coupled with what he saw as his exclusion from important venues for musical performance, was a constant source of disappointment to him, and his bitterness is reflected constantly in his writings. More important was the role he played in the reception of Italian and German opera in France after 1820, when he was responsible for translations and arrangements and for the production of pasticcios largely based on Italian and German models. He adapted the libretto to the requirements of opera with dialogue and translated the texts. With Scribe, he wrote the libretto for the three-act *drame lyrique La marquise de Brinvilliers* (1831), set by Auber, Cherubini and others.

In his pasticcios, Castil-Blaze reset fragments of Mozart, Rossini and Meyerbeer in the context of *opéra comique* or *opéra bouffon*, giving the borrowed music new texts. Some of the inclusions were innovatory: the overture to *La fausse Agnès* (1824), for example, was the first music by Meyerbeer heard in Paris, predating the production of *Il crociato in Egitto* by over a year.

Castil-Blaze's translations and arrangements of entire operas by Mozart, Cimarosa, Rossini and Weber were of great significance for their reception and dissemination in France. His collaboration with the publisher Charles Laffillé resulted in the publication, 1821–3, of a series of translations that had been used for performances between 1817 and 1822: *Le nozze di Figaro*, *Don Giovanni*, *Il matrimonio segreto*, *Il barbiere di Siviglia* and *La gazza ladra*. A sixth, of *Die Zauberflöte*, was never finished. Most were first performed under Alexis Singier in Nîmes or Lyons; Paris premières were generally at the Théâtre de l'Odéon (1824–8). Castil-Blaze translated more Rossini (*Otello* specifically for the Odéon) and *Der Freischütz* (as *Robin des bois*). Two of his pasticcios were written for the Odéon, and a further two were revived there. Later translations were sometimes for publication only, not for immediate production. An exception was that of *Euryanthe*, given at the Opéra in April 1831, but resources were appropriated for *Robert le diable* and it had little success.

Castil-Blaze's skilful reworking of German and Italian material for the French stage played an important role in the absorption of foreign opera in Paris and the French provinces.

WRITINGS

De l'opéra en France (Paris, 1820, 2/1826)
Dictionnaire de musique moderne (Paris, 1821, 2/1825)
Mémorial du Grand-Opéra, épilogue de l'Académie royale de musique: histoire littéraire, musicale, chorégraphique, pittoresque, morale, critique, facétieuse, politique et galante de ce théâtre, de 1645 à 1847 (Paris, 1847)
Molière musicien: notes sur les oeuvres de cet illustre maître et sur les drames de Corneille … Beaumarchais, etc, où se mêlent des considérations sur l'harmonie de la langue française (Paris, 1852)
Théâtres lyriques de Paris, [i]: *L'Académie impériale de musique de 1645 à 1855: histoire littéraire, musicale, chorégraphique, pittoresque, morale, critique, facétieuse, politique et galante de ce théâtre* (Paris, 1855)
Théâtres lyriques de Paris, [ii]: *L'Opéra-Italien de 1548 à 1856* (Paris, 1856)
Sur l'opéra français: vérités dures mais utiles (Paris, 1856) [Prélude and Cadence finale of *L'Opéra-Italien de 1548 à 1856*]
Théâtres lyriques de Paris, [iii]: *L'Opéra-Comique* (MS, 1857, *F-Po*)
L'art des vers lyriques (Paris, 1858)

ARRANGEMENTS

Les folies amoureuses (opéra bouffon, 3, after J.-F. Regnard), Lyons, Grand, 1 March 1823; incl. music by Rossini, Paer, Mozart, Cimarosa, Pavesi, Steibelt, Generali
La fausse Agnès (oc, 3, after P. Néricault-Destouches), Paris, Gymnase Dramatique, 6 July 1824; incl. music by Mozart, Cimarosa, Rossini, Meyerbeer, Pucitta
La forêt de Senart (oc, 3, after C. Collé), Paris, Odéon, 14 Jan 1826; incl. music by Weber, Beethoven, Mosca, Mozart, Meyerbeer, Lully, Rossini, Generali, Thibaut de Champagne
Monsieur de Porceaugnac (opéra bouffon, 3, after Molière), Paris, Odéon, 24 Feb 1827; incl. music by Rossini
Bernabo, 1856 (opéra bouffon, 1, after Molière); incl. music by Cimarosa, Paisiello, Guglielmi, Salieri, Farinelli, Grétry

*

ES (J. Liegner); *FétisB; Grove6* (C. Nazloglou)
'Blaze (Fr.-Henri-Joseph, dit Castil)', *Grand dictionnaire universel du XIXe siècle*, ed. P. Larousse (Paris, 1867)

S. Henze-Döhring: 'E. T. A. Hoffmann-"Kult" und "Don Giovanni"-Rezeption im Paris des 19. Jahrhunderts: Castil-Blazes "Don Juan" im Théâtre de l'Académie royale de musique am 10. März 1834', *MJb 1984–5*, 39–51

M. Everist: 'Lindoro in Lyon: Rossini's *Le barbier de Séville*', *AcM*, liv (1992)

MARK EVERIST

Casting. The selecting of singers to perform in an opera.

1. Definition and history. 2. Composers and conductors. 3. Particular factors.

1. DEFINITION AND HISTORY. The concept of casting is relatively young. It presupposes the existence of a pool of singers available for selection by an opera-house casting director, and also a priority of artistic factors to a degree that the musical and dramatic requirements of an opera enjoy paramountcy over other considerations. Accordingly, until about the middle of the 19th century the concept of casting scarcely existed; it was recognized that it was a part of the composer's task (or the task of those acting in his stead, normally the opera-house musical director) to write or rewrite an opera in such a way as to make it effective for the available singers. Handel engaged the best singers from the European mainland to come to London to sing in his operas, and wrote his roles to fit their specific abilities, in terms of their compass, their qualities of tone and phrasing and their capacities for different types of decorative writing; when an existing role was to be taken by a different singer it was often rewritten, in whole or in part. At many public theatres during the 18th century operas were radically adapted for the available singers; at court theatres it was more usual for the composer to write for a resident company. Leopold Mozart comments in a letter (17 November 1770) on his son's writing arias for the voices 'so as to fit the costume to the figure', to make them effective for the singers, as indeed the singers expected – often they would be asked to approve their music at an early stage of rehearsal, with the understanding that it might be modified or rewritten to suit them better, or indeed that substitute arias might be introduced. This applied even as late as *Idomeneo* (1781). By that time the impresario who controlled a theatre would engage a company at least as much to seduce public taste and increase his audience and his receipts as to perform the operas planned for the season. In Italy during the first half of the 19th century this was still the case and a composer invited to write for a particular opera house would take care to suit his music to the powers and the abilities of the singers engaged for the season. Moreover, the nature and style of operatic writing, even up to the time of Verdi's maturity, was sufficiently standardized as to ensure that the right kinds of singer for almost any role written within a French or Italian idiom during the previous 25 years would be to hand.

The choice of 1860 as a rough watershed has therefore some significance, since by the last four decades of the century great composers such as Verdi and Wagner were already demanding specific singers for specific roles, and without those singers the operas could not be suitably cast. As the concept of a company evolved from an assemblage for a particular season to become a team which persisted, with changes, from year to year in a particular theatre, the notion of the ensemble as an artistic force started to grow and the largest and best-equipped theatres would be able to cast from strength almost any opera they wanted to perform. Occasionally, a less than wholly appropriate singer from the ensemble would take over a particular role and the element of unsuitability (perhaps as compared with a previous performer in that role) would be commented on and explained as caused by understandably limited versatility within a company.

For nearly a hundred years, between the later 19th century and the mid-20th, it was within the context of an opera company, either permanent or engaged for a season, that decisions on casting were taken, and they affected the public's enjoyment, its perception of individual operas and the careers of the singers. To some extent, however, Italy remains outside this generalization. There during much of the 19th century an impresario would engage his troupe for the season; but during the 20th a different pattern emerged. Apart from those contracted to the Metropolitan Opera in New York, Italian singers tended to be engaged for the major theatres at relatively short notice, with patterns evolving over the years so that some names came to be particularly associated with certain theatres although few had long-term contracts. Nonetheless, the clannish nature of the Italian operatic scene allowed ensembles to develop even without a specific company system.

Responsibility for casting passed over the years from composers and impresarios to conductors and directors, with the 'visual' side perceptibly gaining ground as the 20th century moves towards its end. Dominant figures have tended to develop teams of trusted performers with whom they have done their best work and outside which they prefer not to venture. In the later 20th century, the influence of artists' managements has grown as far as international opera is concerned; such organizations sometimes assemble a 'package' of conductor-singers-director, leading to commercial factors overriding the artistic control that properly belongs with opera-house managements. Similar factors, involving the difficulty of putting teams together, may compel opera-house managers to engage singers four or five years ahead, by which time their voices may have changed or personal factors may oblige them to cancel, so that an opera house may be left with no appropriate singer for a role that cannot readily be cast. It is here that rapid air travel – which can be so damaging to the development of a singer by providing opportunities to sing too many roles in too short a time or at too early a stage of his or her career – can help a casting director through a crisis. Another factor involved in 'ensemble' casts is that of recording, where the cost of rehearsing a complex opera may be shared between the opera house and a recording company ready to take a performance more or less as it stands.

Voices and the use made of them have of course changed over the centuries as composers and audiences made different demands. From the perspective of the late 20th century we think of the highly trained singers of the past as virtuosos; we tend, correctly, to equate that virtuosity with agility and flexibility and, incorrectly, with high notes, mainly because the most obvious vocal virtuosos of our own time and the recent past, known at least through gramophone recordings, have been coloratura sopranos. But there is small doubt that Monteverdi wrote for highly-trained singers without asking them for stratospheric display (for example Orpheus's pleading with Charon) and no doubt at all that Handel did so; neither placed any emphasis on top notes. The power, control and flexibility and above all the expressiveness of the castrato voice (as described by contemporaries) suggest the characteristics of Handel's writing, and this highlights a problem of modern casting. Because of octave transposition and the consequent upset to instrumental colouring, it is now unacceptable to have Handel's Julius Caesar sung by a baritone, as happened in revivals of the 1920s and later. On the other hand, are we nearer to doing justice to music written for a male soprano by assigning it to a female contralto or to a male countertenor? The one may lack power and virility, the other tends to be short of contrast and colour and usually sounds best at less than full heroic throttle. Nonetheless, the operas of Handel are still there to be cast – and with singers who are necessarily virtuoso.

2. COMPOSERS AND CONDUCTORS. In the Paris première of *Iphigénie en Tauride*, Gluck cast a lyric tenor and a high baritone for Pylades and Orestes, but in Vienna the availability of Adamberger (later Mozart's Belmonte) suggested a limited rewriting of Orestes for tenor. With Caterina Cavalieri available for Donna Elvira at the Viennese première of *Don Giovanni*, Mozart wrote for her voice and talents 'Mi tradì', a new aria of such splendour that, in spite of its slender dramatic relevance, it nowadays takes a bold spirit to omit it. At the same première he substituted for 'Il mio tesoro' a less taxing aria to accommodate a tenor not so flexible as the one he had had in Prague. So available casting affected the new music.

As we have seen, it was specifically for his original singers that Mozart wrote his music, and the personalities of the singers no doubt fitted their roles to perfection. A by-product of initial casting in *Così* is that the tessitura of Guglielmo's music is that of a lyric bass-baritone, whereas the music of the older Don Alfonso suits a baritone. Nowadays, that vocal casting is not infrequently reversed and the youthful baritone with the right looks for Guglielmo sings the lower tessitura, while the higher-lying Don Alfonso is allotted to a senior character bass-baritone – which is musically incorrect. At Glyndebourne in the 1930s, Mariano Stabile sang Figaro with John Brownlee as Count Almaviva, but in the ensembles Brownlee took over the lower line Mozart wrote for Figaro, which was ill-suited to the higher-based voice of Stabile, although the personalities involved were in other respects admirably cast. There is precedent for this in Mozart's own time; early texts show the composer interchanging Susanna and the Countess Almaviva in the C major trio and the finale of Act 2 to allow whichever of the sopranos was more comfortable with high music to sing the upper line. A purist might object, but find his position hard to maintain when reminded that Mozart himself composed the role of Fiordiligi for a singer who had lately sung Susanna. Theoretically, we now accept that the two roles are written for quite different vocal types; nonetheless, in Vienna in the period 1945–55, Irmgard Seefried, a member of what was by general consent the last great Mozart ensemble, was regularly cast as Susanna and Fiordiligi in the same season and came to be accepted as a model in the roles.

Verdi customarily tailored the music of his earlier operas to fit the singers engaged by the impresario who had commissioned him, but we know how he protested the engagement of Tadolini (a fine soprano he knew well) for a performance of *Macbeth* in Naples some months after the première: 'Tadolini has a beautiful and attractive appearance, and I would like Lady Macbeth to be ugly and evil ... Tadolini has a stupendous voice, clear, limpid and powerful; and I would like the Lady to have a harsh, stifled and hollow voice'. Tadolini sang, but whether Verdi maintained his point of view or not, we see how keenly he, like other composers, was involved in casting.

More recently, Benjamin Britten wrote *Peter Grimes* with members of the wartime Sadler's Wells company in mind and a year after its première founded the English Opera Group, whose hand-picked personnel, *mutatis mutandis*, provided basic casting for his operas over the next 30 years. In all this time, in every one of his 13 operas after *Peter Grimes*, the prodigious and individual talents of Peter Pears governed Britten's writing for tenor voice, something which has presented problems to anyone casting the operas and to many later interpreters unable to cope either with the low-lying tessitura which came easily to Pears, or with the soft, high singing where he found some of his most expressive moments. When in its second year Britten revised both words and music of *The Rape of Lucretia*, he took the opportunity to add an arietta to suit Margaret Ritchie, whose talents he had particularly admired in the initial run of performances. For the title role of *Gloriana*, from the outset he envisaged Joan Cross, then in the last phase of a notable career, and for her he wrote music which lies well for mature soprano voice but soars only once (and then unclimactically) to B♭. For this opera, the deep understanding a distinguished performer would bring to the role compensated for a restricted vocal range.

Among conductors, Mahler was one of the earliest consciously to develop a regular ensemble, and on it he relied for what Viennese operagoers of the early years of the 20th century have testified were some of the most revelatory and innovatory of opera performances. From a position of high artistic conviction he took risks, casting for instance as Mozart's Figaro the young Richard Mayr, hitherto known for Hagen, Hunding and King Mark, and thus encouraging a new lightness of touch in a heavyweight bass later to become world-famous as Ochs; and scandalizing the more conservative by pressing the great italianate baritone of the ensemble, Leopold Demuth, into service as Hans Sachs, where the rolling grandeur of his vocal endowment almost compensated for his lesser dramatic powers.

Toscanini, particularly in his last period at the head of La Scala in the 1920s, built up a comparable ensemble, preferring the greater intensity and dedicated musicianship of a tenor like Aureliano Pertile to the vocal splendours of a Gigli or a Lauri-Volpi and moulding singers such as Mariano Stabile and Gilda dalla Rizza into artists who commanded the stage as they were never able to command the gramophone (a comment, incidentally, on modern casting in the international field, which has too often been dictated by the popular renown of microphone-friendly voices). Toscanini seems to have been acutely aware that, when casting a role like Falstaff, singing was not the only factor; anyone but a considerable artist would be lost and a moderate actor would get nowhere. But he would not have fallen into the trap of casting a character baritone in this role; it should be remembered that the original Falstaff, Victor Maurel, had been chosen for the remodelled Boccanegra in 1881 (a great singing role) and for Iago in 1887, and that Toscanini's own preferred singers for Falstaff, Scotti (over the period 1899–1913) and Stabile (1921–37), were noted respectively for Don Giovanni and Hans Sachs, Iago and Scarpia.

3. PARTICULAR FACTORS. Successful casting often involves physical compatibility. It is not hard to imagine vocal casting which might be ideal for the gramophone or radio but would on stage reverse the physical types concerned. Wagner's giants and dwarfs present a perennial problem; a small Alberich rearing himself up to 5′4″ to deliver the Curse provides great drama, whereas a 5′10″ dwarf who must crouch until that moment arrives risks the effect disappearing altogether. In Rossini's *Il barbiere di Siviglia* the tall, smooth-voiced Ezio Pinza and the rotund, eruptive Salvatore Baccaloni made an irresistible combination during the 1930s as Don Basilio and Dr Bartolo. Opera-house managements and their audiences still seem to accept that, if a singer's vocal abilities are sufficiently sensational, any physical incongruity or lack of dramatic ability will be overlooked. The opposite is also true though to a lesser extent: where histrionic excellence is concerned many people are prepared to overlook vocal insufficiency.

Decisions on casting may be taken for a variety of reasons: on vocal and dramatic suitability (Tosca must dominate, Mimì need not); on the balance between voices and appearance in a cast (Arabella and Zdenka must provide a vocal blend, with the one patently maturer than the other); on sympathy, even compatibility, between individual singers (a young Belcore in *L'elisir d'amore* opposite an aging Nemorino is an example of a solecism to be avoided); on whether the knowledgeable singing of a middle-aged Otello will be upstaged by a fresh-voiced ingénue of a Desdemona. If the most promising soprano in an ensemble needs a regular challenge, should it be Sieglinde in a revival now, or will Wagner's less precise, non-bel canto style detract from her scheduled Leonora in next year's new production of *Il trovatore*? Will the company be able to hold the promising young bass to the Grand Inquisitor or must a risk be taken of mortifying a senior singer by depriving him of Philip II in the interests of the future?

Opera houses in Handel's, Mozart's or Beethoven's time were smaller than those in Europe today and much smaller than those in the great operatic centres of the USA. The same was true of orchestras, so that originally to back up the flexibility expected of any singer, a robust projection was needed rather than vocalism on a heroic scale. 20th-century casting of Reiza and Huon in Weber's *Oberon*, of Leonore and Florestan in *Fidelio*, of Valentine and Raoul in Meyerbeer's *Les Huguenots*, of Medea in Cherubini's opera or Alcestis in Gluck's, postulates not only flexibility but an emphasis on volume of sound the composers would never have dreamed of. Such singers are only rarely around to help solve the problems of the casting office.

Other problems are less intractable. To cast a Mozart opera adequately requires singers with technique and beauty of sound, but intelligence and taste are just as vital. When setting up *Così fan tutte*, which is perhaps closer to a wind serenade than a piano concerto, it is as essential to find voices which blend in ensemble as those which have the high profile for 'Come scoglio' or 'Un'aura amorosa', whereas in *Don Giovanni* contrast and personality are as much at a premium as they would be in the more individualist music of Wagner, Verdi or Puccini. Curiously, a matching ensemble is almost as important in *La bohème* as it is in *Così*; in Mozart it might be expected but in Puccini it is less obvious – though an undercast Schaunard spoils the balance of the ensemble as much as an inadequate Dorabella.

Expectations can dominate casting rather than the objective standards which should more properly prevail. The Metropolitan Opera in New York, subconsciously perhaps still mindful of the celebrated 'Nights of the Seven Stars' in *Les Huguenots* in the 1880s and 90s, has traditionally been thought of as a temple of opera-singing, with casts packed with great voices and the expectations of audiences and critics so geared to grandiose vocalism that lighter-weight casting is hard for them to accept. Italian audiences, not short of generosity where foreign opera is concerned, see themselves as uncompromising when it comes to accepting a non-Italian in Verdi or Puccini, so that even a singer of Leonard Warren's calibre at La Scala made little success as Rigoletto, a role for which the rest of the world would have thought him vocally ideal.

Casting, then, may be done with an eye to the national characteristics of the audience as well as to the music's needs; to suit the short-term scale of a festival and the highly-pitched expectations of its audience or to develop the long-term capacity of a permanent ensemble; to fit a 'stagione' calendar with several performances within a short period, or that of a company playing in repertory with performances sprinkled over ten months. When casting is discussed, it may be the music director who has first as well as last word, a visiting conductor or even the production director whose voice is most audible – or it may be a consensus of some or all of them and the Intendant. What is quite certain is that, however priorities may seem to change, decisions on casting will continue to affect operatic performance, both positively and negatively: an unimaginative actor cast in a role which perfectly suits his or her vocal potential may be transformed into a puissant stage figure, while a fine actor faced with music he cannot sing may overcompensate and forfeit his trump card. No stressing of any of the factors which influence the casting of an opera – artistic, economic, personal – will of itself guarantee success or lead to certain failure, but each will continue to affect the company's budget, the singers' morale, and the individual opera's success. There is no magic formula – and ultimately no chance of appeal against the audience's verdict. HAREWOOD

Castle of Andalusia, The. Comic opera, op.20, in three acts by SAMUEL ARNOLD to a libretto by JOHN O'KEEFFE; London, Covent Garden, 2 November 1782.

Don Caesar (bass), the banished son of Don Scipio (baritone), lives in the forest as Ramirez, captain of the banditti. Alphonso (mezzo-soprano) comes to Don Scipio's castle to prosecute his suit of Lorenza (soprano). He is captured by the banditti, but set at liberty by the exiled Ramirez who is also in love with Lorenza; Alphonso later surrenders his claim. Fernando (tenor), in love with Victoria (soprano), saves the life of Don Scipio, who is attacked by Sanguino (spoken role), one of the banditti. Don Scipio's life is saved again, this time by Ramirez, who is repatriated. Fernando marries Victoria. Although the plot now seems artificial, its farrago of gothic sentimentality and wild romantic action was a novelty in its day.

This pastiche opera originally failed as *The Banditti*, written for Thomas Harris, the Covent Garden manager, in 1781. In its revised form, however, it rivalled the Linleys' *The Duenna* (1775) in popularity and stayed in the repertory for at least half a century – though, according to Haydn, with no benefit to the composer. Act 1 is nearly all Arnold's work while the rest consists chiefly of folktunes and popular Italian arias. The finest parts of Arnold's score are the overture, a remarkable example of the composer's orchestral skill, and Victoria's G major aria 'Ah solitude', with obbligato flute. ROBERT HOSKINS

Castles, Amy (*b* Melbourne, 25 July 1880; *d* Melbourne, 19 Nov 1951). Australian soprano. Although she was fêted throughout much of her career, her subsequent obscurity has been attributed by her partisans to the dominance of Melba. She received generous support in her late teens for study overseas, first with Mathilde Marchesi (who dismayed her by wishing to turn her into a contralto), then with Jacques Bouhy. She made her début, after further study, at Cologne (1907) in Thomas' *Hamlet*, followed by other appearances as Gounod's Marguerite and Juliet. Her 1909–10 Australian tour included her alternation with the French soprano Bel Sorel in the Australian first performances of *Madama Butterfly*. A four-year contract awarded her by the Hofoper in Vienna in 1912 was cut short by World War I. She returned to Australia for the Rigo-J. C. Williamson opera season of 1919. Diabetes contributed to her loss of enthusiasm for an international operatic career and her subsequent concentration on concert work. Her singing of the mad scene in *Hamlet* was described by Ernest Newman as having 'a lustrous quality of tone ... with scintillating, clearness [and a] ... complete absence of effort', qualities still evident in the best of her surviving recordings (which have been collected on CD).

*

A. Gyger: *Opera for the Antipodes* (Sydney, 1990)

ROGER COVELL

Cast-list. A list of the cast of an opera is normally available in the house before the performance, either included in the programme (or, earlier, in the libretto) or handed out to patrons as they enter. *See* PROGRAMME.

Castore e Polluce **(i)** ('Castor and Pollux'). *Opera seria* in three acts by FRANCESCO BIANCHI to a libretto by CARLO INNOCENZO FRUGONI after PIERRE-JOSEPH BERNARD's *Castor et Pollux*; Florence, Teatro della Pergola, 8 September 1779.

Newly returned from four years in Paris, Bianchi must have seemed particularly well-qualified to compose a new setting of Frugoni's translation originally prepared for a revival of Rameau's opera for Parma in 1758 and set in 1760 by Traetta: *see* TINDARIDI, I. French-inspired pieces were seldom done in Italy, and Bianchi's was the first such production in Florence since a revival of Traetta's opera ten years earlier. The plot centres on twin magnanimous deeds: Pollux (soprano castrato) replaces his dead half-brother Castor (soprano castrato) in the underworld so that Castor can be reunited with Telaira (soprano), a union Febe [Phoebe] (soprano) plans to disrupt; after a tender meeting, Castor asks to return so that Pollux may be freed, and Jupiter (tenor) rewards all three by reuniting them in heaven. *Castore* contains all the elements that had been purged from Italian serious opera before the turn of the century: gods appearing in machines, miraculous scene changes, arias without exit, much use of chorus, and an infernal scene in the underworld with dancing.

MARITA P. McCLYMONDS

Castore e Polluce **(ii)** ('Castor and Pollux'). *Tragedia lirica* in three acts by GEORG JOSEPH VOGLER to a libretto adapted from one by CARLO INNOCENZO FRUGONI after PIERRE-JOSEPH BERNARD's *Castor et Pollux*; Munich, Residenztheater, 12 January 1787.

Written for the court of Elector Carl Theodor, *Castore e Polluce*, like Mozart's *Idomeneo*, is modelled on a French *tragédie lyrique*. Vogler compressed the original five-act play into three acts, reduced the dialogue and made minor changes for the singers. But the opera retains much of the original spectacle, combining lavish scenes of dancing and choral singing with lyrical scenas and arias typical of *opera seria*. In order to maintain musical and dramatic continuity, Vogler set most of the dialogue as obbligato recitative. Self-contained numbers alternate freely with ensembles and choruses.

The first production featured Michael Bologna (soprano castrato, Pollux), Vincenzo dal Prato (soprano castrato, Castor), Teresa Buschietti (Phoebe), Margarethe Marchand (soprano, Telaira), J. B. Zonca (bass, Jupiter) and Franz Hartig (tenor, Mercury). Vogler took advantage of the virtuoso musicians at Munich by writing a dynamic orchestral score. It became a local custom for his chorus of Furies to be incorporated into the damnation scene of Mozart's *Don Giovanni*. PAUL CORNEILSON

Castor et Pollux ('Castor and Pollux'). *Tragédie en musique* in a prologue and five acts by JEAN-PHILIPPE RAMEAU to a libretto by PIERRE-JOSEPH BERNARD; Paris, Opéra, 24 October 1737.

Minèrve [Minerva]	soprano
L'Amour [Cupid]	haute-contre (or soprano)
Mars	baritone
Vénus [Venus]	soprano
Phébé [Phoebe] *a Spartan princess*	soprano
Télaïre [Telaira] *daughter of the Sun*	soprano
Pollux *son of Jupiter and Leda*	bass
Two Athletes	haute-contre, bass
The High Priest of Jupiter	tenor
A Follower of Hébé [Hebe]	soprano
Castor *son of Tyndareus [and Leda]*	haute-contre
A Blessed Spirit	soprano
Jupiter	bass
A Planet	soprano
Cléone *Phoebe's confidante* [revised version only]	soprano

Arts and Pleasures, Spartans, athletes, priests of Jupiter, Celestial Pleasures, Hebe's attendants, demons, Blessed Spirits, stars

Setting Sparta; the Elysian Fields

At its first appearance, Rameau's third opera was only moderately successful. Audiences compared it unfavourably with *Hippolyte et Aricie* and *Les Indes galantes* which, though initially controversial, had by now gained support among open-minded operagoers. This cool reception explains the brevity of *Castor*'s first run – 21 performances compared with about 40 for *Hippolyte* and 64 for *Les Indes* – despite a distinguished cast including Tribou (Castor), Chassé de Chinais (Pollux), Pélissier (Telaira) and the dancers Sallé and Dupré.

Exceptionally, *Castor* had to wait 18 years for a revival: it reappeared in June 1754, at the height of the

Querelle des Bouffons. This time the opera was ecstatically received: it was widely seen (with *Platée*, revived earlier that year) as a more effective counterblast to the Bouffonistes than any of the pro-French pamphlets. By the time it was revived again in 1764, equally triumphantly, *Castor* had come to be seen as Rameau's crowning achievement. Among the cast was the young Sophie Arnould as Telaira, a role eventually regarded as one of her finest. The work, increasingly disfigured by cuts and additions, remained in the repertory until 1785 – longer than any of Rameau's others; some of the music was still performed at the Opéra as late as 1817. The first modern revival, organized by Charles Bordes, took place at Montpellier on 23 January 1908 and the work was presented in a concert performance at the Schola Cantorum, Paris, six days later.

PROLOGUE *Ruined buildings and mutilated statues; in the distance, military camps* Minerva implores Venus and Cupid to subdue Mars with the power of love. During a *symphonie* contrasting trumpet and flute, Mars and Venus descend: the symbols of war disappear and those of the Arts and Pleasures are restored. Mars, his heart softened, announces the return of peace. The ensuing *divertissement* is rich in graceful and varied airs and dances, among them a tambourin, later re-used in the *Pièces de clavecin en concerts* (1741), and a menuet from the *Nouvelles suites de pièces de clavecin* (*c*1729–30).

ACT 1 *The Spartan kings' burial place* Castor, mortal twin of the immortal Pollux, has been slain by Lyncaeus. As they prepare for Castor's funeral, the Spartans mourn. Their chorus 'Que tout gémisse', from which the opening chorus of Gluck's *Orfeo* is descended, is notable for its chromatic ritornellos and quasi-religious character. (At Rameau's own memorial services it was indeed adapted as a Kyrie.) Alone with Phoebe, Telaira is disconsolate: what compensation is vengeance for the loss of one's dearest love? She renounces the light of day now that Castor can no longer experience it; in her monologue 'Tristes apprêts' Rameau eschews chromatic extremes and the minor mode, capturing the dignity of Telaira's sorrow by means of simple but telling harmony and a sombre bassoon obbligato. Pollux enters with athletes and soldiers bearing Lyncaeus's body. Their victory chorus 'Que l'Enfer applaudisse' is interspersed with recollections of Castor's fate. The athletes' dances re-enact the battle. After they have left, Pollux offers Telaira his love as a substitute for Castor's. Telaira is taken aback but exploits this revelation, persuading Pollux to ask his father Jupiter to restore Castor to life.

ACT 2 *The vestibule of Jupiter's temple, prepared for a sacrifice* In 'Nature, Amour, qui partage mon coeur', a elegiac soliloquy characterized by drooping scales of paired quavers, Pollux resignedly debates the implications of Telaira's request. When she arrives, Pollux compares his fate unfavourably with his brother's: Castor's life was short, but at least he had the satisfaction of pleasing Telaira. Jupiter descends. At first he refuses Pollux's request, but eventually he reveals the price his son must pay: if Castor is restored to life, Pollux must take his place. Pollux selflessly agrees. Jupiter commands Hebe, goddess of eternal youth, to remind Pollux of what he would sacrifice by renouncing immortality. In a series of exquisitely sensual airs and dances, Hebe's Celestial Pleasures reveal a vision of eternal bliss. Pollux is unmoved: breaking the garlands which bind him, he departs.

ACT 3 *The fiery cavern at the entrance to Hades, guarded by monsters* The spurned Phoebe exhorts the Spartans to bar their king from hell. When Pollux brushes her aside, she resolves to end her life by following him to the underworld. Phoebe's despair increases when she learns of his love for Telaira. As Pollux prepares to enter the cavern he, Telaira and Phoebe sing a short trio in which each reflects on the outcome of the mission. Demons emerge from hell. In the tersely contrapuntal trio 'Sortez de l'esclavage', Pollux and Telaira fend them off while Phoebe encourages them. The demons threaten Pollux, their chorus 'Brisons tous nos fers' menacingly unmelodic. Mercury descends, strikes the demons with his caduceus and disappears with Pollux into Hades.

ACT 4 *The Elysian Fields* Castor has found no happiness in Elysium. His nostalgic soliloquy 'Séjour de l'éternelle paix', dominated by plaintive dotted rhythms for flutes and strings, captures the heartache of separation. In a sequence of ethereal choruses and airs, the Blessed Spirits vainly try to divert him. When Pollux appears, the brothers greet each other ecstatically. Castor is overjoyed that he will again see the light of day but disconcerted by Pollux's confession of love for Telaira. When he learns the price of freedom – Pollux's own life – Castor refuses. He eventually agrees to return to Telaira, but for a single day: afterwards he will go back to Elysium and let Pollux regain his life and love. Mercury appears as Castor's escort, while the Blessed Spirits implore him to return.

ACT 5 *A pleasant prospect in Sparta* Having seen the lovers reunited, Phoebe expresses impotent rage ('Soulevons tous les Dieux'). When Telaira, alone with Castor, realizes that his return is temporary she is incredulous; but Castor holds to his promise, despite her pleas and taunts. Thunder is heard and Jupiter descends. Declaring Destiny satisfied, he absolves Castor of his oath and grants him immortality. As the twins are reunited, Pollux renounces his love for Telaira: he has been so moved by Castor's selflessness that he can let nothing cloud his happiness. The only victim, he reveals, is Phoebe, who is now in Hades. Jupiter commands the skies to open, revealing the Zodiac with the Sun crossing it and gods assembled around Olympia's temple. During a Festival of the Universe, the Heavenly Twins take their places in the Zodiac, while Telaira is granted a place in the firmament. A Planet sings an *ariette*, 'Brillez, astres nouveaux', the orchestral parts characteristically more elaborate than the vocal line. Of the dances, the finest is the lengthy chaconne. Another, the 'Entrée des Astres', is a reworking of part of the overture, a device Rameau was to develop extensively.

* * *

For the 1754 revival, Bernard and Rameau made substantial changes. The dramatically irrelevant prologue was omitted: in commemorating the Peace of Vienna (1736) it was no longer topical. (Besides, most French operas after 1749 were given without prologues.) A new expository act was inserted before Act 1. Here, Telaira is to marry Pollux although she loves Castor. As she prepares for the wedding, Castor discloses his own feelings but, to her distress, plans self-imposed exile rather than be forever reminded of his hopeless love. Pollux, overhearing this conversation, vetoes his brother's plan. To

Revival of Rameau's 'Castor et Pollux' (1754 version) by the English Bach Festival in 1981

their astonishment, he encourages Castor to marry Telaira, since he cannot bear to see the unhappiness of the two he values most. The Spartans congratulate the lovers and praise Pollux's magnanimity. Their *divertissement* is curtailed by news that Lyncaeus is attacking the palace in an attempt to abduct Telaira. The brothers take up arms. Sounds of battle are interrupted by sudden silence, whereupon an offstage voice announces Castor's death. The Spartans call for vengeance. During the entr'acte (an adaptation of a *bruit de guerre* from the 1744 *Dardanus*) the noise of battle continues.

To compensate for this new material, the original Acts 1 and 2 now became 2 and 3 respectively while the former Acts 3 and 4 were combined. In the process, many details were changed. Mercury was now played by a singer (*haute-contre*) rather than a dancer. The role of Phoebe was expanded, though not improved, by the assignment to her of magic powers, and she now has a confidante, Cléone (soprano). Moreover, the libretto was pruned by well over a quarter, a compression achieved largely by cutting recitative.

As with most of Rameau's revisions, dramatic gains involved musical pruning. In the case of *Castor* this is comparatively slight. True, the outstandingly beautiful but irrelevant prologue was omitted, but several of the best pieces were moved to the Act 4 *divertissement.* Almost all the most memorable movements remain, including the *tombeau* 'Que tout gémisse', Telaira's 'Tristes apprêts' and Castor's 'Séjour de l'éternelle paix'. One exception is Pollux's soliloquy 'Nature, Amour'; yet his new air, 'Présent des dieux', is a hymn to friendship as affecting as the piece it replaces. Of three fine new *ariettes*, 'Tendre Amour, qu'il est doux' (Act 5 scene v) must be one of the most purely beautiful of its kind. Rameau here resists the temptation to end with brilliant display; instead he provides Castor with an air of exquisite tenderness, enriched in the final section by the unexpected but beguiling entry of the semi-chorus. Among the ballet movements there are many substitutions, seldom for the worse. Much of the new music is orchestrated in the more varied style which Rameau had developed by the 1750s. Even so, the 1754 orchestra is less colourful than that in several of his then recent operas.

In its emphasis on brotherly love *Castor* was unusual, since French opera of the period reserved a central role for the romantic kind. Bernard's libretto has many virtues: not only does it provide convincing pretexts for ballet and spectacle, but it develops logically; especially in the revised version, it is arguably the tautest, best constructed and most elegant of any that Rameau set. *Castor* may lack the elements of pure tragedy that make *Hippolyte et Aricie* such a powerful if flawed masterpiece, but it compensates for this with an abundance of conflicts of sentiment: the struggle between Pollux's inclination and duty, the complication of his love for Telaira, Phoebe's jealousy, the conflict provoked by the twins' mutual affection where neither can bear to benefit at the other's expense. Despite this, the opera has an evenness of tone unique among Rameau's *tragédies.* Much of the music is characterized by an ethereal, nostalgic beauty, while the lean, athletic style adopted in the more energetic episodes seems a deliberate evocation of the conventional image of Lycurgus's Sparta, anachronistic though that is to the Castor myth.

GRAHAM SADLER

Castori [Castoreo; 'Castorino'], **Castore Antonio** (*b* Gubbio, *c*1700; *d* after 1740). Italian soprano castrato. He probably studied in Rome. When he made his first appearances (1717–22), in minor theatres in Ancona, Pesaro and Rome, he was called 'virtuoso di casa Vallemani'. His first roles (some female) were minor, in operas by Venetian masters such as Lotti, Pallavicino and C. F. Pollarolo. He was in the service of the Este and the Farnese, 1725–31, also singing in Milan, Genoa, Turin, Florence, Perugia and Rome, in operas by Albinoni, Sarro and Vinci among others. In Venice he sang at the S Moisè in 1722, then in the 1729–30 season in cameo roles at the S Giovanni Grisostomo (in casts which included Nicolino Grimaldi, Cuzzoni and the young Farinelli) in fashionable works by Hasse, Giai and Riccardo Broschi. The peak of his career was between 1731 and 1736, when he was secondo uomo in Fano, Milan, Naples and again in Venice, mostly in works by Hasse, but also in Albinoni, Araia, Pergolesi, Galuppi, Leo and Vinci operas. Castori's final appearances (1738–40) were in such provincial theatres as Mantua and Macerata. The characters he portrayed included predominantly kings, tyrants and barbaric heroes, appropriate to his vigorous singing style and imposing presence.

*

C. Vitali: 'Vivaldi e il conte bolognese Sicinio Pepoli: nuovi documenti sulle stagioni vivaldiane al Filarmonico di Verona', *Informazioni e studi vivaldiani*, x (1989), 25–56

——: 'I fratelli Pepoli contro Vivaldi e Anna Girò: le ragioni di un'assenza', ibid, xii (1991), 14–33 CARLO VITALI

Castrato (It.). A type of high-voiced male singer, brought about by castrating young boys with promising voices before they reached puberty, that was central to Italian opera in the 17th and 18th centuries, and that disappeared from opera (though not from church music) by 1830. At the height of their popularity, leading castratos were among the most famous and most highly paid musicians in Europe, and their virtuoso singing method had considerable influence on the development of opera. The term 'musico' was commonly used in the 18th century as a euphemism for castrato.

The practice of castration for musical purposes was confined almost wholly to Italy, though it may have originated in Spain and was occasionally adopted in the southern German states. The first documented castrato singers appeared in Ferrara and Rome, about 1550–60. Then, and at all times up to their eventual disappearance (as late as the 1920s), most castratos were church singers; some undertook no other work, while others also performed as chamber singers in the service of noble or royal patrons or appeared in occasional, often local and minor, opera seasons on the side. The whole practice appears to have been bound up not with the rise of opera (which it antedated) but with the profound and lasting economic crisis that struck Italy about the turn of the 16th and 17th centuries, and with the accompanying surge in the numbers of those joining the monastic orders. There is evidence to suggest that in 17th-century Italy castration for musical purposes was regarded as a specialized form of the celibacy imposed by a monastic vocation and, for the boy's family, one more likely to bring financial security. It did not then attract the obloquy that was visited upon it in the late 18th century; operations were carried out with only perfunctory concealment, and were sometimes paid for by the ruler of a princely state or by the governing body of a leading church.

The taste for castrato voices arose mainly because in Italy women's voices were not allowed in church. Of the available substitutes, choirboys were no sooner trained than lost. Falsettists came to seem unsatisfying compared with castratos, particularly in soprano parts; the use of falsettists in alto parts went on side by side with castratos, to whom they were regarded, however, as inferior – for, odd though it now seems, castrato voices were referred to as 'natural' and 'true' (*sincere*) while falsettists' voices were artificial. The quality of castrato voices cannot now be recaptured; the gramophone records made in 1902–3 by Alessandro Moreschi, a leading soprano in the Sistine Chapel choir, give only a faint notion. Contemporary accounts speak of uncommon brilliance allied with power, a wide range, a breathing capacity beyond the reach of most normal voices, and sometimes an unearthly timbre (not at all like that of falsettists). This was true of the best castratos; many turned out to be mediocre or poor singers, and had none or few of these merits.

This quality of voice was accounted for in part by physiology, in part by training. The operation ensured that the thoracic cavity developed greatly, sometimes disproportionately (leading to a form of gigantism), while the larynx and the vocal cords developed much more slowly and had considerable power brought to bear on them. Training was not interrupted by puberty as in normal males; since the whole point of the operation was to produce a professional singer a young castrato would as a rule undergo regular training from an early age, often in instrumental music and in theory as well as in singing. Castratos were therefore often more accomplished musicians than were most normal singers, especially women, whose chances of a thorough professional training were limited. This intensive and continuous training (whether with a private teacher or in one of the many schools attached to churches, orphanages and other religious institutions throughout Italy) made possible the cultivation of the elaborately florid singing for which the best of the castratos became famous. In this sense it was the castratos, rather than (as popular fancy has it) the stars of early 19th-century Romantic opera, who were identified with bel canto: it is no accident that two of them, PIER FRANCESCO TOSI and GIOVANNI BATTISTA MANCINI, wrote the most influential 18th-century treatises on singing.

Within the new genre of opera in the early 17th century, castratos were not predominant as they were to become later on. In Monteverdi's *Orfeo* (1607) the castrato Giovanni Gualberto Magli sang three parts, episodic but significant, and was much appreciated; the all-important title part, however, was sung by a tenor. In Venetian opera through most of the century women were at least as dominant as castratos, because of the stress on eroticism. Though we know little about detailed casting it seems that leading male parts were assigned to castratos or to normal voices according to which singers were available rather than on any set plan: compare the dominance of normal male voices in Monteverdi's *Il ritorno d'Ulisse in patria* of 1640 with the castrato leads – Nero and Otho – in his *L'incoronazione di Poppea* of two years later. In Rome about the same time, a few leading castratos who were mainly church singers appeared in occasional operas put on by the cardinal who patronized them; while in Naples in 1675 similar artists were reluctant to appear in opera on grounds of status and respectability (the prima donna being a notorious courtesan). A peculiarity of Rome and other towns in the Papal States (Bologna and its neighbouring towns excepted) was that women were not supposed to appear on stage: the pope sometimes allowed women to sing in operas put on by a great personage in the semi-privacy of his own palace, but the rule, enforced until 1798, was for the women's parts in opera to be sung by young castratos. Many famous singers made their débuts in this way, generally in their teens.

From about 1680 the expectation, eventually the rule, was that the leading male part in a serious opera (primo uomo) should be sung by a castrato; there might be a less important secondo uomo part, also for a castrato, with tenors singing the parts of kings and old men. This was also the period when, from having been an occasional entertainment (but for Venice in the carnival season with its six or seven semi-commercial opera houses), Italian opera came to be given fairly regularly both in Italy and in those parts of Europe under Italian musical influence – in the German-speaking countries and the Iberian peninsula, from about 1710 in London, from the 1730s in St Petersburg. The best castratos therefore became international stars, welcomed and highly paid in all the leading courts and capital cities, with the notable exception of Paris (where, after Cardinal Mazarin's attempts at importation in the mid-17th century, they were not allowed to appear in opera; some leading castratos gave concerts when they were passing through, and some much more modest ones remained on the king's musical establishment as church singers until the Revolution).

The reasons for this new dominance of the castrato voice are interrelated. Italian composers of the period 1680–1720, under the patronage of princes, the most influential of whom was the Grand Prince Ferdinand, heir to the throne of Tuscany, began to write operas calling for more technically demanding coloratura singing; the range expected of leading singers widened, and the tessitura generally rose, as it was to go on doing (for both men and women) through most of the 18th century. Since, however, operas were composed with specific singers in mind, this is another way of saying that virtuoso castratos were now available in numbers in the service of princes who promoted frequent opera seasons: GIOVANNI FRANCESCO GROSSI ('Siface') and FRANCESCO ANTONIO MASSIMILIANO PISTOCCHI were only the most prominent among a new group of star singers. It was still possible at this time for a famous castrato not to sing in opera at all or, like Matteo Sassano ('Matteuccio'), whose career lasted from 1684 to 1711, to do so only occasionally. But from then on a famous castrato was in the first place an opera singer. A wider shift of taste may explain the early 18th-century liking for a prevalence of high voices; it may be related to the preference then shown for a light palette in the visual arts (e.g. in Tiepolo's frescoes and in Rococo architecture and interior decoration) and for elegance rather than massiveness in literature. Finally, the neo-classical aesthetic movement known in Italy as the Arcadia encouraged a hiving off of comic, grotesque and extravagant elements into the new genre of comic opera, while serious opera now dwelt on elevated sentiments uttered by high personages drawn in the main from ancient history. Castratos occasionally appeared in comic opera, but (outside Rome) normal voices were there the rule. In the newly refined genre of serious opera, on the other hand, the castrato voice with its special brilliance appears to have struck contemporaries as the right medium to convey nobility and heroism. Objections, when they came, were to the incongruity of castratos in general – or, on moral grounds, to their singing of women's parts – rather than to their appearance as heroes or lovers.

Serious opera in the first two-thirds or so of the 18th century was dominated by a succession of famous castratos, of whom Nicolo Grimaldi ('NICOLINI'), ANTONIO MARIA BERNACCHI, Francesco Bernardi ('SENESINO'), Carlo Broschi ('FARINELLI'), GIOVANNI CARESTINI, Gaetano Majorano ('CAFFARELLI') and GAETANO GUADAGNI are only the best known. These and others were the 18th-century equivalents of pop stars; the story of the woman in a London opera audience who cried out 'one God, one Farinelli!' may not be authentic, but it sums up a widely shared craze. Such artists could command engagements in one European capital after another at unprecedented fees – in Turin the primo uomo's fee for the carnival season was sometimes equal to the annual salary of the prime minister – while they also kept, as insurance, permanent appointments in a monarch's chapel choir.

Their achievements are now difficult to gauge, not only because we no longer hear such voices but also because the operas they sang have nearly all dropped out of the repertory, with the exception of some by Handel, Gluck and Mozart that are themselves untypical. (The best – indirect – guide for a modern ear may be the voice of Marilyn Horne at the height of her powers, e.g. in a recorded version of Vivaldi's *Orlando*; it suggests why the best castratos were described as astounding.) Their command of vocal agility – of trills, runs and ornamentation, especially in the da capo section of an aria – was clearly central to their success. So, at least for some, was a phenomenally wide range: Farinelli is said to have commanded more than three octaves (from *c* to *d'''*), others more than two, though, like some modern sopranos and tenors, they were apt to lose the upper part of their range as their careers wore on. It would, however, be a mistake to regard leading castratos as vocal acrobats and no more. Command of 'pathetic' singing – soft, laden with emotion, powered by controlled devices such as *messa di voce* – was highly regarded: it was, for instance, central to the reputation of GASPARO PACCHIEROTTI. Nor was acting ability ignored: Guadagni's performance as Gluck's original Orpheus was thought deeply affecting. The issue is clouded by the habit of commentators through most of the 18th century of bemoaning the supposed decadence of opera through an excessive cult of vocalism and ornamentation. This was in part a literary convention. The cult flourished, and was in practice forwarded by some of those who decried it.

Another contemporary habit that needs to be guarded against is that of mocking the castratos as grotesque, extravagant, inordinately vain near-monsters. This was in part a nervous reaction against a phenomenon experienced as sexually threatening twice over: the fact of castration was disconcerting in itself, yet according to legend (persistent though held by modern medical opinion to be baseless) castratos could perform sexually all the better for the loss of generative power. In part the mockery visited upon castratos was roused by highly paid star singers in general, among whom they were the most prominent. The 'caprices' of castratos were often no more than the (in part justified) susceptibility of artists who gave highly exposed performances dependent on their own physical and emotional powers. Though Grossi was vainglorious and Caffarelli was a boor on and off stage, Farinelli was notably tactful and GIOACCHINO CONTI ('Gizziello') was gentle and modest; most other castratos seem to have been of at least average conscientiousness. Because of their musical education they often did well as teachers; some who had also had a general education acted in retirement, or even during their singing careers, as antiquarian booksellers, diplomats, or officials in royal households.

From about 1740, if not earlier, the number of castratos, which may have reached several hundred at any one time in the middle decades of the 17th century, began to fall, and the practice of castration for musical purposes came under increasing attack even in Italy. The reasons for the general decline – which to begin with affected the Church more obviously than the operatic stage – are probably to be sought in relative economic improvement during the 18th century, and in the simultaneous decline in the kind of Christian asceticism that had held up celibacy as an unmixed good. (The cause once assigned, the ban imposed by the Jacobins after Napoleon's invasion of Italy in 1796, postdated the decline and was anyhow temporary.) *Opera seria*, the genre with which the castratos were identified, was itself in decline from mid-century and was little attended to when not performed by one of the last star castratos such as LUIGI MARCHESI or GIROLAMO CRESCENTINI. The very last, GIOVANNI BATTISTA VELLUTI, still had parts written for him by leading composers – in Rossini's *Aureliano in Palmira* (1813) and Meyerbeer's *Il crociato in Egitto* (1824) – but he was isolated and on his retirement in 1830 no more castratos were heard in opera. The habit of entrusting a leading male part to a high voice went on in Italy for another decade, with the castrato replaced, as he largely had been since early in the century, by the female contralto in breeches (*contralto musico*). It then gave way under the impact of Verdi, bequeathing as a final vestige the principal boy in English pantomime.

*

BurneyFI; *BurneyH*; *ES* (F. D'Amico); *Grove6* (T. Walker)
P. Della Valle: *Della musica dell'età nostra* (1640; repr. in A. Solerti: *Le origini del melodramma*, Turin, 1903), 163–6
C. d'Ollincan [C. Ancillon]: *Traité des eunuques* (Berlin, 1707; Eng. trans., as *Eunuchism Displayed*, 1709)
[J.-J. Le François de Lalande]: *Voyage d'un françois en Italie* (Venice and Paris, 1769), vi, 345–9
Stendhal: *Rome, Naples et Florence* (Paris, 1826); repr., ed. V. del Litto (1960), 294
F. Haböck: *Die Kastraten und ihre Gesangskunst* (Stuttgart, 1927)
P. Browe: *Zur Geschichte der Entmannung* (Breslau, 1936)
H. B. Bowman: *A Study of the Castrati Singers and their Music* (diss., Indiana U., 1952)
A. Heriot: *The Castrati in Opera* (London, 1956)
A. G. Bragaglia: 'Degli "evirati cantori": contributo alla storia del teatro', *Amor di libro*, v (1957), 67–76, 163–72, 229–36; vi (1958), 41–8, 103–8, 155–62, 237–44; vii (1959), 45–50, 78–83
A. Milner: 'The Sacred Capons', *MT*, cxiv (1973), 250–53
P. Stella: 'Strategie familiari e celibato sacro tra seicento e settecento', *Salesianum*, xli (Turin, 1979), 73–109
R. Strohm: 'Aspetti sociali dell'opera italiana del primo settecento', *Musica/Realtà*, ii (1981), 117–41
R. Celletti: *Storia del belcanto* (Fiesole, 1983; Eng. trans., 1991)
S. Durante: 'Il cantante', *SOI*, iv (1987), 347–415
C. Pampaloni: 'Giovani castrati nell'Assisi del settecento', *Musica/Realtà*, viii (1987), 133–53
J. Rosselli: 'The Castrati as a Professional Group and a Social Phenomenon, 1550–1850', *AcM*, lx (1988), 143–79

JOHN ROSSELLI

Castris, Francesco de. *See* DE CASTRIS, FRANCESCO.

Castro, Juan José (*b* Avellaneda, Buenos Aires province, 7 March 1895; *d* Buenos Aires, 3 Sept 1968). Argentinian composer and conductor. A member of a distinguished family of musicians with Spanish roots, he received his early training in Buenos Aires from Manuel Posadas, Constantino Gaito and Eduardo Fornarini. In 1916 he won the Europa Prize but the war delayed his departure for Paris until 1920, by which time the finance had been withdrawn; he had to work as a café musician, while studying composition with d'Indy at the Schola Cantorum and piano with Edouard Risler. He returned to Buenos Aires in 1925 and in 1928 began a brilliant international conducting career which lasted for 35 years; among the many 20th-century works he conducted were the Buenos Aires premières, at the Teatro Colón, of Ravel's *L'heure espagnole* (1932), the staged version of Falla's *El retablo de maese Pedro* (1942) and in 1963 the posthumous world première of Falla's *Atlántida*, complete and in the original Catalan (following Falla's explicit wishes). In 1941 Toscanini invited him to conduct the NBC Orchestra in New York. During nine years of self-imposed political exile Castro was conductor of the Havana PO (1947), the SODRE Orchestra, Montevideo (1949–51) and the Victoria SO in Melbourne (1952–3); he toured Europe and the USA until his return to Argentina after the overthrow of Perón's first regime in 1955, when he became permanent conductor of the Orquesta Sinfónica Nacional in Buenos Aires. He directed the Puerto Rico Conservatory, 1959–64.

As a composer Castro's cultural allegiance was both to his Spanish ancestry and to Argentinian urban popular tradition. Of his four operas *La zapatera prodigiosa* (1949) and *Bodas de sangre* (1956) reflect the stronger hold of his Spanish roots, while the *milonga* (predecessor of the urban tango) is adopted in *Proserpina y el extranjero* (1952; Act 1, Marfa's *milonga*), the only opera which incorporates elements from the urban popular tradition. While a Lorquian obsession with death links three of his four operas, there is a sharp stylistic breach between the allegorical *Proserpina y el extranjero*, with its complex manipulation of eclectic material, and the more episodic *La zapatera prodigiosa* and *Bodas de sangre*. *Proserpina* attracted international attention when it was awarded the Verdi Prize in 1951. Whereas the material for *Proserpina* is generated from motivic cells developed organically through varied repetition, the Lorca operas favour the use of recomposed elements from the Spanish vernacular. *Bodas de sangre* is based on incidental music that Castro wrote for a production of Lorca's play in 1937; in *La zapatera prodigiosa* one of Lorca's songs forms the pivotal chorus that ends the opera. Closer to the symbolic style of *Proserpina* than to the Lorca operas is Castro's fourth dramatic work, *La cosecha negra*; a statement of self-determination against political dogmas that disregard the rights of individuals, it nonetheless shows Lorca's influence in its matriarchal theme and imagery of death. Following Castro's express wishes, the orchestration was completed after Castro's death by the Argentinian composer Eduardo Ogando.

See also PROSERPINA Y EL EXTRANJERO.

La zapatera prodigiosa (2, J. J. Castro, after F. García Lorca), Montevideo, SODRE, 22 Oct 1949
Proserpina y el extranjero (3, O. del Carlo), Milan, Scala, 17 March 1952, as Proserpina e lo straniero; vs (Milan, 1953)
Bodas de sangre (3, Castro, after García Lorca), Buenos Aires, Colón, 9 Aug 1956
La cosecha negra, 1961 (3, Castro), unperf.

*

PEM; *VintonD* (R. Arizaga)
Composers of the Americas, iv (Washington DC, 1958)
R. Arizaga: *Juan José Castro* (Buenos Aires, 1963)
I. Schlagman, ed.: *ARS dedicado a Juan José Castro*, xxix/109 (1969) [incl. J. P. Franze: 'Juan José Castro, compositor dramático']
R. Arizaga: 'Castro, Juan José', *Enciclopedia de la música argentina* (Buenos Aires, 1971)
M. Kuss: *Nativistic Strains in Argentine Operas Premiered at the Teatro Colón (1908–1972)* (diss., U. of California, Los Angeles, 1976), 284–318, 484–92

MALENA KUSS

Castro Alberty, Margarita (*b* San Sebastian, 18 Oct 1947). Puerto Rican soprano. She studied in San Juan and Rome, and at the Juilliard School, New York. In 1978 she sang in Santiago, Chile, and in 1980 at the Teatro Colón, Buenos Aires. She made her European début at Madrid as Salud (*La vida breve*) in 1980 and her Metropolitan début as Amelia (*Un ballo in maschera*) in 1982. She has sung in Lyons, Marseilles, Venice, Rome, Orange, Nancy and Avignon. Her roles include Donna Anna, Lucrezia Borgia, Aida, Elisabeth de Valois (*Don Carlos*), Leonora (*Il trovatore*), Amelia (*Simon Boccanegra*), Lucrezia (*I due Foscari*), Nedda, Butterfly and Magda (*La rondine*). She has a fine voice but not a great deal of dramatic feeling.

ELIZABETH FORBES

Castro Herrera, Ricardo (*b* Nazas, Durango State, 7 Feb 1864; *d* Mexico City, 28 Nov 1907). Mexican composer. He studied the piano at Durango City with Pedro H. Ceniceros (1870–77), then entered the Conservatorio Nacional at Mexico City where he studied the piano, and theory and composition with Melesio Morales. He graduated in May 1883. In 1885 he started his first opera, *Giovanni d'Austria*, but left it unfinished because the craze for Italian opera was subsiding, to be succeeded by worship of French models.

By 1889 he had become so much a musical cynosure that Felipe Pedrell devoted a dense article to him, listing his published works. After a decade of instrumental works, in 1899 he began his three-act lyric drama *Atzimba* (Mexico City, Renacimiento, 9 Nov 1900; Mexico City, 1900), to a libretto by the local journalist Alberto Michel (1867–1947). Mounted by the Sieni-Pizzioni-López troupe, the opera is set in Pátzcuaro, Michoacán, in 1522, and recounts the love of an invading Spanish captain, Jorge de Villadiego, for a Tarascan princess. Music from it was heard at a concert in Antwerp on 28 December 1904 in Castro's presence; a review in *La fédération artistique* (1 January 1905, quoted in Campa) judged the closing scene 'a deeply moving experience'.

In September 1906 Castro returned to Mexico with the score of a new opera to a French text by Henri Brody, *La légende de Rudel* op.27 (*poème lyrique en trois parties*; Mexico City, Arbeu, 1 Nov 1906; vs, Leipzig, 1906). Divided into three 'episodes', the story concerns the 12th-century Provençal troubadour Jaufré Rudel (tenor) who deserts Ségolaine (soprano) in search of a more perfect beauty. After being shipwrecked en route to Syria, he is carried into the presence of the paragon of beauty, the Countess of Tripoli (contralto), at whose feet he expires, whereupon a chorus of her attendants wafts his spirit heavenward. The opera had to be sung in Italian to meet the whims of the season's visiting Italian opera company. According to Campa, no other previous Mexican lyric work was 'so replete with poetic sentiment, so competently written, and so continuously inspired'.

*

F. Pedrell: 'Artistas mexicanos: Ricardo Castro', *Ilustración musical hispano-americana*, ii/31 (1889), 57–8

G. E. Campa: *Críticas musicales* (Paris, 1911), 311–12, 348

R. Stevenson: *Music in Mexico: a Historical Survey* (New York, 1952), 211–14, 224–6

F. Moncada-García: *Pequeñas biografías de grandes músicos mexicanos* (Mexico City, 1966), 75–80

R. Stevenson: 'Latin America in *Ilustración musical hispano-americana*', *Inter-American Music Review*, iii (1980–81), 153–4

ROBERT STEVENSON

Castrovillari, Daniele da [di] (*fl* Venice, 1660–62). Italian composer. La Borde described him as a Franciscan monk and a theorist; according to Nicola Papini (see Sparacio) he was for many years an organist at Ferrara Cathedral, but local studies have not yet confirmed this. He may have taught G. B. Bassani. Three operas written for Venice are attributed to him: *Gl'avvenimenti d'Orinda* (Pietro Angelo Zaguci; Teatro SS Giovanni e Paolo, 1660), *La Pasife* (Giuseppe Artale; Teatro S Salvatore, 1661) and *La Cleopatra* (Giacomo dall'Angelo; Teatro S Salvatore, 1662). Only the last survives (in *I-Vnm*). It places Castrovillari in the generation after Cavalli, close in style to P. A. Ziani. The score includes many concerted arias, some of them requiring considerable vocal agility, and a lament of unusually large dimensions. The music is not of high quality and in places is rather awkward.

*

J.-B. de La Borde: *Essai sur la musique* (Paris, 1780)

D. Sparacio: 'Musicisti minori conventuali', *Miscellanea francescana*, xxv (1925), 34

THOMAS WALKER

Catalani, Alfredo (*b* Lucca, 19 June 1854; *d* Milan, 7 Aug 1893). Italian composer. His operas were among the most important of those in the period immediately preceding the rise of the *verismo* school.

1. Life. The musical families of Lucca include the Catalani as well as the Boccherini and the Puccini. Alfredo was introduced to music by his father, and after achieving the necessary scholastic qualifications studied composition at the Istituto Pacini in Lucca under Fortunato Magi, the uncle and first teacher of Giacomo Puccini, graduating in 1872 with a prize for composition. He proceeded to the Paris Conservatoire, where he attended classes by Marmontel (piano) and Bazin (composition) and also suffered the first attacks of haemoptysis, a condition that was to overshadow his future career. At the end of 1873 he went to the Milan Conservatory to study with Bazzini. His diploma piece and first contribution to stage music was the one-act *La falce* (1875) to a libretto by Arrigo Boito, whom Catalani had met in Milan, together with Franco Faccio and Marco Praga, at the salon of Clarina Maffei. He strengthened his ties with the Milanese followers of the Scapigliatura movement, taking part in discussions of contemporary topics and sharing their interest in innovations in drama and opera, above all the aesthetics of Wagner, whose works were then frequently performed in some Italian opera houses.

Giovannina Lucca, the publisher involved at first hand in the publication of Wagner's music, commissioned from Catalani a new large-scale dramatic work, *Elda*. The libretto, by the translator Carlo d'Ormeville, was based on the legend of the Lorelei as narrated by Heine and others. The score was completed in 1876 and revised in 1877, but the work was staged at the Teatro Regio, Turin, only in 1880, through the efforts of the conductor Carlo Pedrotti and the music critic Giuseppe Depanis, who became a devoted friend.

The libretto for Catalani's next opera, *Dejanice*, was provided by another translator, Angelo Zanardini, but it was a weak neo-classical drama, coldly received at La Scala in 1883. Boito inspired the programme of Catalani's most important orchestral composition, the symphonic poem *Ero e Leandro*; it was conducted in 1885 by Faccio, who in the following February also conducted *Edmea* at La Scala. This, Catalani's fourth opera, a collaboration with Ghislanzoni, had a moderate success, repeated at the Carignano in Turin later in the same year; the conductor was Arturo Toscanini, then under 20, who was later to make Catalani's work widely known.

With only small earnings from theatrical work, Catalani applied for the post of composition professor at the Milan Conservatory left vacant by the death of Ponchielli in 1886. Although he was the outstanding candidate, his appointment was not made official until April 1888 because of doubts about his health. In the same year he lost the support of Lucca, whose firm was taken over by Ricordi. Depanis secured a successful production of the revised *Elda*, now called *Loreley*, at Turin in 1890, after a reworking of the libretto by Zanardini with help from Giuseppe Giacosa and Luigi Illica. Catalani then asked Illica to produce a libretto for *La Wally*, and when the new opera was completed he offered it to Ricordi. The publisher appreciated its qualities but stipulated a contract in which payment was to be made in three instalments, the last to be due on the 60th performance.

In spite of the successful first performance at La Scala in 1892, the opera was not often staged, while the slow but progressive worsening of Catalani's illness had intensified the persecution complex from which he suffered: he interpreted the success of other composers, more favoured by Ricordi, as a threat to his own work. He was wounded by Verdi's recommendation of Franchetti to the Genoese authorities to compose *Cristoforo Colombo*, and by the triumph of *Manon Lescaut* that marked Puccini as the legitimate successor to Verdi. His complaints at Ricordi's high-handed treatment of *La Wally* were not without justification, although criticisms he made of Puccini's music in letters were perhaps understandably unfavourable. Catalani never received the third and final instalment guaranteed by his publisher; he died on 7 August 1893 after a series of attacks of haemoptysis.

2. Operas. Almost all Catalani's work reflects his preference for the sort of theme favoured by the Scapigliatura, characterized by a Nordic setting in which natural elements play an important part, with suggestions of the supernatural and echoes of legend, and love romantically linked with death. *La falce*, his first and only collaboration with Boito (the most influential member of the group), cannot be called a success. Opening with an atmospheric symphonic prologue typical of the time (as in Boito's *Mefistofele* and the interlude in Puccini's *Le Villi*), the opera has an oriental flavour generically akin to that of Félicien David's *Le désert*. The plot is contrived, with a heroine morbidly attracted to a reaper who is believed to be the incarnation of Death but who instead reveals himself to be a real flesh-and-blood man. The denouement results in an unintentional, somewhat grotesque trivialization of the love-death equation, and the setting and characters are not adequately realized in the music.

When Boito refused to continue to collaborate with him, Catalani formed a partnership with d'Ormeville, who condensed the best features of the Rhinegold mythology into the text of *Elda*. The failure of the production, however, meant that Catalani's originality, his avoidance of excessive realistic contrasts by immersing the action in an atmosphere of suffused timbres and original harmonic textures, was not appreciated.

His next work, *Dejanice*, a bombastic historical drama, represented a distinct setback in his career. Zanardini was predominantly a translator of grand operas and of Wagner's works. He provided the composer with verses composed lightheartedly and with dramatic situations constituting a collection of the most famous operatic commonplaces of the day, from the neo-classical setting of *Norma* to the chorus of priestesses with dances as in *Aida*; there are also echoes of *Un ballo in maschera*, *Luisa Miller* and *L'Africaine*. The dramatic situation and its final solution are those of *La Gioconda* – a conflict between a woman who is loved (Argelia/Laura), and a loving woman (Dejanira/La Gioconda) who sacrifices herself to secure the happiness of her rival and the man she loves (Admeto/Enzo). This plot, with the variation that the voluntary victim is a man (Ulmo), was used again in *Edmea*, a more interesting opera musically because Catalani had matured considerably as a composer, and more successful, though Ghislanzoni was no better a librettist. The melodic line is more original, the Bohemian setting represented with realistic vivacity and the love drama that drives the heroine to madness happily resolved in the end.

Because of its lively dramatic style, *Edmea* pleased the public more than Catalani's other operas, and this made him realize that its formula was better suited to his abilities. On the advice of Depanis, he decided to apply this further by revising *Elda*. He restored the original names and places, wrote new passages and improved the musical quality of the existing score. The plot of the new *Loreley*, sketched out by Depanis and elaborated by Zanardini and d'Ormeville (who were helped by Illica and Giacosa, later to write librettos for Puccini), gained considerably in liveliness and interest.

Loreley was a worthy forerunner to *La Wally*, indisputedly Catalani's most successful opera. His liberation from the traditional structure of self-contained numbers, largely observed in his previous works, was mainly the result of a new conception of characterization and of atmospheric orchestral writing to act as connective tissue in the drama. If many lyrical passages, vocal and orchestral, anticipate features of *verismo*, and the harmonic organization shows that he had learnt from Wagner, Catalani's real achievement in *La Wally* is the fusion of these heterogeneous factors into a unified and original whole. He was perhaps the most authoritative musical representative of the ideals of the Scapigliatura, although he inclined equally to a decadent and twilight world, providing a glimmer of refined if anaemic originality in Italian opera as it moved away from the domination of Verdi towards *verismo* conformity. Unfortunately Catalani could not aspire to the leading role in Italian and European opera assumed by Puccini, who had greater musical gifts and outstanding dramatic talent. But though on a lower level, his works are the fruit of a similar sensitivity and permeated with a similar restlessness.

See also Loreley and Wally, la.

La falce (egloga orientale, 1, A. Boito), Milan, Conservatory, 19 July 1875, vs (Milan, 1875)

Elda (dramma fantastico, 4, C. d'Ormeville, after the Lorelei legend), Turin, Regio, 31 Jan 1880, vs (Milan, 1876, 2/1877); rev. as Loreley (azione romantica, 3, A. Zanardini and others, after d'Ormeville), Turin, Regio, 16 Feb 1890, *I-Mr**, vs (Milan, 1889)

Dejanice (dramma lirico, 4, Zanardini), Milan, Scala, 17 March 1883, *Mr**, vs (Milan, 1883)

Edmea (3, A. Ghislanzoni, after Newsky [A. Dumas *fils* and P. de Corvin Kroukowsky]: *Les Danicheff*), Milan, La Scala, 27 Feb 1886, *Mr**, (Milan, 1886)

La Wally (dramma musicale, 4, L. Illica, after W. von Hillern: *Die Geyer-Wally*), Milan, La Scala, 20 Jan 1892, *Mr** (Milan, 1892)

*

G. Depanis: *Alfredo Catalani: appunti, ricordi* (Turin, 1893)

F. R. Pfohl: 'Der Verismus und sein Gefolge', *Die moderne Oper* (Leipzig, 1894), 190–315

C. Paladini: 'Un maestro di musica e due poeti da teatro: alcune lettere inedite di Alfredo Catalani', *Musica e musicisti*, lviii (1903), 1041–7
G. Depanis: *I concerti popolari e il Teatro regio di Torino*, ii (Turin, 1915)
G. B. Nappi: 'In memoria di Alfredo Catalani', *La perseveranza* (Sept 1918)
G. Adami: *G. Ricordi e i suoi musicisti* (Milan, 1933)
D. L. Pardini: *Alfredo Catalani: Quaderno di ricordi lucchesi* (Lucca, 1935)
J. W. Klein: 'Alfredo Catalani', *MQ*, xxiii (1937), 287–94
A. Bonaccorsi: *Alfredo Catalani* (Turin, 1942)
C. Gatti, ed.: *Lettere di Alfredo Catalani a Giuseppe Depanis* (Milan, 1946)
A. Luzio: 'Verdi e Catalani', *Carteggi verdiani*, iv (Rome, 1947), 91–107
L. Lun: *Loreley* (Florence, 1949)
C. Gatti: *Alfredo Catalani: la vita e le opere* (Milan, 1953)
G. Barblan: 'Presagio di gloria e ombre di mestizia ne *La falce* di Alfredo Catalani', *Accademia musicale Chigiana, Musicisti toscani*, xi (1954), 65–71
R. Cortopassi: *Il dramma di Alfredo Catalani* (Florence, 1954)
G. Gavazzeni: 'Disegno di un saggio sul Catalani', *La rassegna* [Pisa] (1954), June–Aug
J. W. Klein: 'Alfredo Catalani 1854–1893', *ML*, xxxv (1954), 40–44
Nel centenario della nascita di Alfredo Catalani (Lucca, 1954)
S. Pagani: *Alfredo Catalani: ombre e luci nella sua vita e nella sua arte* (Milan, 1957)
J. W. Klein: 'Catalani and his Operas', *MMR*, lxxxviii (1958), 67ff, 101–7
F. Walker: 'Verdian Forgeries: Letters Hostile to Catalani', *MR*, xix (1958), 273, xx (1959), 28
J. W. Klein: 'Verdian Forgeries: a Summing-up', *MR*, xx (1959), 244
G. Gavazzeni: 'Catalani e Puccini', *I nemici della musica* (Milan, 1965), 17–41
M. Morini: 'Carteggio Catalani–Illica', *L'opera* (1966)
A. Bonaccorsi: *Maestri di Lucca* (Florence, 1967)
J. W. Klein: 'Toscanini and Catalani: a Unique Friendship', *ML*, xlviii (1967), 213–28
G. Gavazzeni: 'L'esperienza della *Loreley* di Catalani', *Non eseguire Beethoven* (Milan, 1974), 117–28
R. Mariani: *Verismo in musica e altri studi* (Florence, 1976)
J. R. Nicolaisen: *Italian Opera in Transition, 1871–1893* (Ann Arbor, 1977)
M. Zurletti: *Catalani* (Turin, 1982)
——: 'Catalani e la Scapigliatura', *Musica/Realtà*, iii/8 (1982), 117–28
T. G. Kaufman: 'Alfredo Catalani', *Verdi and his Major Contemporaries* (New York and London, 1990), 31–44

MICHELE GIRARDI

Catalani, Angelica (*b* Sinigaglia, 10 May 1780; *d* Paris, 12 June 1849). Italian soprano. She received very little formal musical instruction and made her début at La Fenice at the age of 17 in Mayr's *La Lodoiska*. In 1800 she sang in Cimarosa's *Gli Orazi ed i Curiazi* in Trieste, and the following season in the same composer's *Clitennestra* at La Scala. After appearances in Florence and Rome, in 1804 she went to Lisbon, and in 1806 she made her London début at the King's Theatre in M. A. Portugal's *Semiramide*, also singing in Portugal's *Il ritorno di Serse* and *La morte di Mitridate*, Mayr's *Che originali* (*Il fanatico per la musica*) and Nasolini's *La morte di Cleopatra*.

Between 1808 and 1814 at the King's she appeared in Paisiello's *La frascatana* and *Didone*, sang Sesostris in Nasolini's *La festa d'Iside*, and sang in Pucitta's *La vestale*, *Le tre sultane* and *La caccia di Enrico IV*, Piccinni's *La buona figliuola* and Paer's *Camilla*. She also sang Vitellia (*La clemenza di Tito*) and Susanna in the first London performance of *Le nozze di Figaro* (1812; see illustration). Moving to Paris, she took over the direction of the Théâtre Italien in 1814, continuing to sing in operas written for her by Pucitta and Portugal.

Angelica Catalani as Susanna and Giuseppe Naldi as Figaro in Mozart's 'Le nozze di Figaro' at the King's Theatre, London, 1812: anonymous drawing

In 1817 she embarked on an extended tour of Europe, returning to London in 1824 for a few performances of *Che originali* (*Il fanatico per la musica*); then she gave up the stage. A beautiful woman with a superb, perfectly controlled voice, and a fine actress, she lacked the taste or education to make the most of her gifts.

ELIZABETH FORBES

Catania. Italian city, capital of Sicily. An eruption of Etna in 1664 and the earthquake which devastated eastern Sicily in 1693 largely destroyed whatever records of earlier musical activity may have existed, and surviving 18th-century librettos and programmes give little hint of the intense operatic activity suggested by other sources. Bibliographical records list various *drammi per musica*, either manuscript or printed in the second half of the 17th century, but the first certain reference is to *L'esaltazione di Sergio Galba nella caduta di Claudio Nero* by Giuseppe Parisi, *maestro di cappella* of the cathedral, performed in 1689 according to the libretto. Another theatre, in the university, called Teatro della Sapienza, was 'adorned with an abundance of scenery and enriched with all the most ingenious devices necessary for a stage'. There were probably minor theatres also in the palaces of the wealthy aristocracy: a century later those of the princes of S Domenica and of the Baron of S Demetrio were in use, but especially the one with three tiers of boxes created by the Prince of Biscari from some of the spacious storehouses of his fine palace. The Comte de Borch, a traveller who was not easily satisfied, noted in the late 1770s that actors with good voices performed Italian operas almost every night with danced intermezzos. By then Bellini's grandfather, also named Vincenzo, was in the prince's service, having moved to Sicily in 1767. Only one opera by him is known, *La figlia dello Svevo Adolfo*, but he may have written or reworked music for other performances. The librettos of *La contadina in corte*, a comedy with intermezzos of the type described by Borch, refers to the 'Catania carnival theatre' – probably that of the Palazzo Biscari, which continued in use at least until 1832. In 1819 a royal decree prohibited performances in the minor theatres; that of the Baron of S Demetrio had already ceased to function.

In 1812 work began on the construction of a large Teatro Comunale in the piazza Nuovaluce, but when it became obvious that municipal funds were insufficient to complete it a more appropriate solution presented itself: the conversion of a large naval warehouse into a provisional Teatro Comunale. But 69 years were to pass between the inauguration of the 'Provvisorio' (9 June 1821, with Rossini's *Aureliano in Palmira*) and the opening of the Teatro Massimo Bellini (31 May 1890, with *Norma*). This theatre, commissioned in 1839, opened in 1866 as the Arena Nuovaluce (renamed Pacini in 1869) with a disastrous performance of *Macbeth*. In 1872 the idea of building a large-scale theatre on the site was proposed, and after various vicissitudes the Arena Pacini was transformed into the Teatro Massimo Bellini, plans for which were drawn up in 1879 by Carlo Sada. The Arena Pacini's concession had not been renewed, and its managing syndicate built next to the city hall a *politeama*, also named after Pacini, where productions included operatic performances fairly regularly from 1878 to 1932. Other theatres (the Politeama Castagnola and the Nazionale, Sangiorgi and Principe di Napoli theatres, to mention only the most important) staged opera seasons from 1880 to 1948 with singers of high calibre: Tito Schipa at the Sangiorgi in autumn 1911, and Toti Dal Monte in *Il barbiere di Siviglia*, which on 27 May 1922 inaugurated the Anfiteatro of the impresario Gangi, where Basiola, De Muro and Dino Borgioli also appeared.

No theatre, however, could match the attractions of the Massimo Bellini, which Gigli described in his memoirs as 'the most beautiful and most acoustically perfect in the world'. Such a verdict justifies the regular visits there of celebrated conductors and singers, from Borgioli, Galeffi, Arangi-Lombardi, Stabile, Pampanini, Capsir, Pagliughi, Schipa and Cigna to Callas, Tebaldi, Corelli and Pavarotti; only Caruso refused to add his name to the distinguished list because of a dispute with the Catania management. The low standard of performance in some seasons, and occasional periods of closure (due to dubious political strategies rather than to operating difficulties), cannot detract from the brilliant tradition of the Massimo Bellini over the hundred years of its existence. The high level of musical, particularly operatic, awareness (at least until just after World War II) of the inhabitants of the native city of Bellini, Pacini, Platania and many illustrious singers meant that the theatre became a symbol of civic unity; its designation as the Ente Lirico Regionale has ensured the availability of the financial resources necessary to support its status. An important annual festival, founded in 1989, is dedicated to Bellini, and the theatre arranges concerts throughout eastern Sicily.

*

F. Ferrara: *Storia di Catania sino alla fine del secolo XVIII* (Catania, 1829)

V. Cordaro-Clarenza: *Osservazioni sopra la storia di Catania* (Catania, 1833–4)

F. Paternò-Castello di Carcaci: *Descrizione di Catania e delle cose notevoli intorno ad essa* (Catania, 1847)

E. Serravalle: *Sul nuovo teatro da costruirsi in Catania* (Catania, 1870)

L. Vigo: *Cenno dell'arte drammatica e del teatro in Sicilia* (Catania, 1885)

G. Lanza di Trabia: *La Sicilia filarmonica* (Palermo, 1922)

E. Fischetti: *Vicende storiche d'un teatro* (Catania, 1948)

G. Policastro: *Catania nel settecento* (Catania, 1950)

——: 'I teatri del '600 a Catania', *RMI*, liv (1952), 207–17, 316–28

——: 'Musica e teatro nel seicento nella provincia di Catania', *RMI*, lv (1953), 109–48

F. Pastura: *Secoli di musica catanese* (Catania, 1968)

D. Danzuso and G. Idonea: *Musica, musicisti e teatri a Catania* (Palermo, 1985)

ROBERTO PAGANO

Catarina Cornaro, Königin von Cypern ('Catarina Cornaro, Queen of Cyprus'). *Grosse tragische Oper* in four acts by FRANZ PAUL LACHNER to a libretto by JULES-HENRI VERNOY DE SAINT-GEORGES, translated by Alois Büssel; Munich, Hofoper, 3 December 1841.

The initial success within Germany of this, Lachner's third opera, was due partly to his generally acknowledged good vocal style, but chiefly to the opera's appearance of being in the same class as the great French operas of Meyerbeer, Halévy and Hérold. Lachner's contemporaries felt the work, whose libretto was expressly imported from Paris (where it formed the basis of Halévy's *La reine de Chypre*), counteracted the dramatic failings of the libretto by amalgamating the historical theatrical styles of pomp and effect with Germanic sincerity and profundity, and possessed an originality comparable with the grandiose successes of the period, such as Auber's *La muette de Portici*, Meyerbeer's *Robert le diable* and Weber's *Der Freischütz*. For 40 years the work survived on the German stage, on the strength of its arias (above all those for the lead soprano) and its ensembles. In time, however, the failings of the plot – the same as that of Donizetti's *CATERINA CORNARO* – began to obtrude, as did the general lack of drama and characterization and an inclination to unvaried musical treatment; as one critic maintained, the bandits sang in the same lively march tempo as the knights with no noticeable difference in musical style. Lachner did improve the finale, which originally faded away quietly – an unforgivable lapse of instinct in relation to the requirements of grand opera. But after his death the work, which had been prematurely celebrated as the great national hope, and which had never been as controversial as the Wagnerian music dramas, did not endure. HORST LEUCHTMANN

Catel, Charles-Simon (*b* Laigle, Normandy, 10 June 1773; *d* Paris, 29 Nov 1830). French composer. He studied with Gossec before joining the band of the Garde National de Paris, for which he supplied new music and later taught. He was also répétiteur at the Opéra, a post he held until 1803, and in 1795 was appointed professor at the new Conservatoire. Between 1792 and 1797 he composed many Revolutionary hymns, marches and military symphonies, and during the late 1790s wrote chamber music. His influential monograph, *Traité d'harmonie*, was published in 1803. In the same year, he turned his attention to the stage. By

Interior of the Paris Opéra (Salle Le Peletier) during the inaugural performance of Catel's 'Les bayadères', 16 April 1821: painting by Du Locle

1819 had written ten works in the various operatic genres currently in vogue. In 1810 he won two honourable mentions for his *Sémiramis* and *L'Auberge de Bagnères* from the special jury awarding the decennial prize for the best musical dramas. He was appointed inspector at the Conservatoire in 1810 but resigned in 1816; in 1817 he was accepted into the Académie des Beaux Arts. After the failure of his last two operas in 1818 and 1819 he stopped composing altogether.

Catel's works for the Académie de Musique (Opéra) exemplify the approach of his generation to operatic composition. *Sémiramis* (1802) demonstrates Catel's acceptance and understanding of the conventions of the *tragédie lyrique* of the preceding century. With *Les bayadères* (1810), a *tragi-comédie* set in India, Catel acknowledged the latest trends in operatic dramaturgy in a style (similar to Spontini's in *La Vestale*, 1807) which marks the transition from the older tradition to that of 19th-century grand opera. This spectacular and grandiloquent work typifies the *style empire* approved by Napoleon. Finally, *Zirphile et Fleur de Myrte* (1818), an *opéra féerie*, illustrated Catel's desire to experiment, being a work unique at the Académie both in its *opéra comique* subject matter and in its musical style.

Of Catel's *opéras comiques* all but one, *Wallace, ou Le ménestrel écossais* (1817), are lighthearted farces, in which the plots, structures and musical styles – in particular the ensembles and finales – are indebted to late 18th-century Italian *opera buffa*. These were remote from the dramatic 'rescue' and 'horror' operas of the 1790s that were also called *opéras comiques*. In *Wallace* Catel aspired to a more serious style; it is one of the first musical works with a Romantic Gothic and Scottish plot and evocations of the Scottish landscape. He also wrote a dramatic *ballet d'action*, *Alexandre chez Apelles* (1808).

Catel was neither a visionary nor an innovator. He was limited also by banal librettos, and the musical and dramatic interest of his works is never sustained. But he was a capable craftsman with an expert approach to details and a sense of a work as an entity; he created unity by such relatively new techniques as the recurring theme. He sought consistency in his portrayal of individual characters and endeavoured to relate musical expression to the immediate dramatic context. In his first works Catel favoured the control and balance of the musical forms of 18th-century opera, but gradually he wearied of the inflexibility of the number opera and began to compose extended scene complexes (e.g. the end of Act 2 of *Les bayadères*), heightening dramatic continuity by a carefully structured tonal scheme, a recurrence of musical motifs, and a systematic piling up of impressive climaxes. There is an absence of rhythmic diversity; similar patterns tend to dominate a work such as *Les bayadères*. On the other hand, the technical proficiency of the music, the sweeping melodic lines, the rich and often eloquent harmonic language, the symphonic developmental procedures and the skilful handling of instrumental tone colour all reveal an imaginative and articulate composer. Moreover, all the large-scale works afford scope for the theatrical spectacle dear to French opera audiences and manifest the variety and opulence of the *style empire*. Although he was not a dramatist of the first order, Catel composed music that is often moving, with passages that could stand beside the finest contributions of his age.

all first performed in Paris; published in Paris in year of first performance, unless otherwise stated; MSS in F-Pn, Po

Sémiramis (tragédie lyrique, 3, P. Desriaux, after Voltaire), Opéra, 4 May 1802

Les artistes par occasion (opéra bouffon, 1, A. Duval), OC (Feydeau), 22 Jan 1807

L'Auberge de Bagnères (opéra bouffon, 3, C. Jalabert), OC (Feydeau), 23 April 1807

Les bayadères (opéra, 3, E. Jouy), Opéra, 8 Aug 1810
Les aubergistes de qualité (oc, 3, Jouy), OC (Feydeau), 11 June 1812
Bayard à Mézières (oc, 1, Chazet and Dupaty), OC (Feydeau), 12 Feb 1814; collab. Boieldieu, Cherubini, Isouard
Le premier en date (oc, 1, M. A. Desaugiers), OC (Feydeau), 3 Nov 1814
Wallace, ou Le ménestrel écossais (opéra héroïque, 3, Saint-Marcellin), OC (Feydeau), 24 March 1817
Zirphile et Fleur de Myrte, ou Cent ans en un jour (opéra féerie, 2, Jouy and N. Lefebvre), Opéra, 29 June 1818
L'officier enlevé (oc, 1, Duval), OC (Feydeau), 4 May 1819

*

J. A. Carlez: *Catel: étude biographique et critique* (Caen, 1894)
F. Hellouin and J. Picard: *Un musicien oublié: Catel* (Paris, 1911)
S. Suskin: *The Music of Charles-Simon Catel for the Paris Opéra* (diss., Yale U., 1972)
G. Buschmeier: *Die Entwicklung von Arie und Szene in der französischen Oper von Gluck bis Spontini* (Tutzing, 1991)

SYLVAN SUSKIN

Catelani, Angelo (*b* Guastalla, 30 March 1811; *d* S Martino di Mugnano, Modena, 5 [not 15] Sept 1866). Italian composer and musicologist. He studied music in Modena, then at the Naples Conservatory for six months; he continued as a private pupil of Zingarelli and Crescentini. In 1833 the Teatro Nuovo in Naples commissioned Catelani to write an opera, *Il diavolo immaginario, o L'ossesso per supposizione* (G. Checcherini), but no performances were given. He also had lessons from Donizetti, who secured him a contract for the 1835–6 season as composer and conductor at the theatre in Messina. He wrote *Beatrice di Tolosa* (A. Peretti) for Modena in 1840, but because of the death of the duchess it was not performed. He took this score and the libretto of a new opera, *Caràttaco*, to Bologna in 1841 for Rossini's criticism. *Caràttaco* was successful in Modena in 1842, but on hearing Verdi's *Nabucco* Catelani abandoned writing for the stage. He was *maestro di cappella* at Reggio Emilia (1837–9) and then at Modena. From 1841 he wrote critical articles for periodicals and after 1850 published a series of biographical and bibliographical works, among them studies of Italian music of the 16th and 17th centuries and collections of letters, that constitute his most important work. BRUNO CAGLI

Catena d'Adone, La ('The Chain of Adonis'). *Favola boscareccia* in a prologue and five acts by DOMENICO MAZZOCCHI to a libretto by OTTAVIO TRONSARELLI after G. B. Marino's *Adone*; Rome, Palazzo Conti, 12 February 1626.

The sorceress Falsirena (soprano) attempts to seduce Adonis (alto); but she can hold him prisoner only by a magic chain forged by the cyclops at the order of Apollo (tenor) in the prologue. Rejected by Adonis and desperate, she conjures up Plutone [Pluto] (bass) from the underworld to learn that her rival is Venere [Venus] (soprano) and resolves to transform her own appearance into that of the goddess of love. Adonis is rescued from the false Venus just in time by the descent of the true goddess.

Less than a year after the death of the poet Marino, the Aldobrandini family, his former patrons, had an episode from his famous poem turned into a pastoral drama of seduction and trial; focussed in plot and elaborate in presentation, it was the first early opera to bear the hallmarks of later musical drama in Rome. Falsirena's machinations to win Adonis were realized by the scenic designer Francesco de Cuppis. (The same designs were re-used for a spoken comedy written to fit them and described by M. Pagani in 1626.) Six triangular *periaktoi*, three in a row on each side of the stage, rotated to make swift and noiseless scene changes. Vulcan's grotto formed the setting of the prologue; a horrid wood turned into an idyllic garden; this opened up into a golden palace, with a flight of endless rooms and Adonis chained in a bed; in Act 4 hell disgorged Pluto, and all was framed by a false proscenium bearing the arms of the Conti. The stage was raked, and an orchestra of 30, including two harpsichords, was seated out of view of the audience.

The scene changes denote Falsirena's power, but when she finally alters herself, she is defeated. The nuances of her psychological state are effectively conveyed by harmonic (and often chromatic) shifts and contrasts in and between recitatives. Mazzocchi avoids illustrating single words or musically forcing the expression. Each act has only three to four short scenes, the last always a classically derived choral response of intertwining solos, polyphony and dancing to mark each new stage in the plot. The movement through recitative to aria, or to choral and instrumental polyphony, is thoughtfully crafted and paced, though the recitative itself lacks melodic and rhythmic variety. Mazzocchi tried to articulate the recitative with what he called *mezz'arie*. These are single phrases or brief passages in song style that were at the time also labelled 'in aria', 'alla battuta' or even 'ariette', and now usually 'arioso'. Pirrotta cites Mazzocchi's *mezz'arie* as the ancestors of the later introspective cavatina.

In addition to the printed score (Venice, 1626), six editions of the libretto appeared, three Roman (all 1626) and three Venetian (1626 and 1627). Two further publications indicate that later performances took place in Bologna (1648, but heavily altered) and Piacenza (1650). MARGARET MURATA

Caterina Cornaro. *Tragedia lirica* in a prologue and two acts by GAETANO DONIZETTI to a libretto by GIACOMO SACCHÈRO after JULES-HENRI VERNOY DE SAINT-GEORGES' libretto for Halévy's *La reine de Chypre* (1841); Naples, Teatro S Carlo, 18 January 1844.

In Venice, the approaching marriage between Caterina (soprano) and Gerardo (tenor), a young Frenchman, is suspended when Mocenigo (bass) announces that she has been selected the bride of Lusignano (baritone), King of Cyprus. Gerardo hopes to persuade her to run off with him, but she refuses, having been told that her beloved will be slain if they attempt an elopement. In Cyprus, Mocenigo, now the Venetian ambassador, plots a rebellion to overthrow Lusignano and win the island for Venice. Gerardo's life is saved by Lusignano in the resulting mêlée. Ironically, the former is unaware that his rescuer is the man on whom he has sworn vengeance, while the king does not know that this is the man for whom Caterina has been pining. When they realize they both love Caterina, they sing a duet of friendship ('Sì, dell'ardir degl'empi'). When next Caterina and Gerardo meet, she is Queen of Cyprus and he is enrolled in the Knights Hospitaler, come to defend Lusignano, who is being poisoned by his enemies. Hearing of Gerardo's victory, the dying Lusignano confides the Cypriots to Caterina's care.

Donizetti revised the ending of the opera for a production in Parma in February 1845. This version concludes with Lusignano telling Caterina that Gerardo has been killed in his defence of Cyprus and that she must rule the island alone.

Caterina Cornaro was partly composed in 1842, just before *Don Pasquale*, and completed during the following summer. It was the last of Donizetti's operas to have its première during his lifetime; in the cast were Fanny Goldberg (Caterina), Gaetano Fraschani (Gerardo) and Filippo Coletti (Lusignano). This dark, vigorous score is notable for its use of surprisingly restless harmonies to create dramatic tension; yet it also contains passages of gratifying lyricism, notably in Lusignano's Act 1 aria 'Ah! non turbarti' and Caterina's 'Non più affanni' in Act 2. WILLIAM ASHBROOK

Caterina di Guisa ('Catherine of Guise'). *Melodramma* in two acts by CARLO COCCIA to a libretto by FELICE ROMANI after ALEXANDRE DUMAS (i)'s play *Henri III et sa cour* (1829, Paris); Milan, Teatro alla Scala, 14 February 1833.

The action takes place in Paris in 1578 and concerns the feud between Enrico, Duke of Guisa (tenor), and the Count of San Megrino (tenor) and their love for Enrico's wife Caterina (soprano). Enrico forces Caterina to write a shaming letter (Act 1 finale), inviting San Megrino to her room. He is finally killed by Enrico's followers.

Coccia revised the opera (Turin, Teatro Carignano, 1836), rewriting Enrico's part for a bass and lowering San Megrino's part. Caterina's cousin, Arturo, is a *musichetto* role (contralto), similar to Smeton in *Anna Bolena*; he sings a sonnet by Ronsard to Caterina. This *romanza*, 'Deh! non pensar che spegnero', is notable for its use of contrasting major and minor keys, a Bellinian trait which can also be seen in Caterina's final aria. The finale to Act 1 is a remarkable duet featuring obbligato violin and much use of appoggiaturas. It was greatly tamed in the revised version for Turin. SIMON MAGUIRE

Cathcart, Allen (*b* Baltimore, 2 Aug 1938). American tenor. He studied in Los Angeles and New York, making his début in 1961 as a baritone at the Metropolitan Opera Studio singing Guglielmo (*Così fan tutte*). He sang Sharpless in Syracuse, New York (1967), then in the early seventies became a tenor. He sang in Brussels, Frankfurt, Zürich, Rome, Paris and San Francisco and with the WNO and Scottish Opera. His repertory includes Florestan, Don José, Hoffmann, Cavaradossi, the Emperor (*Die Frau ohne Schatten*), Hermann (*Queen of Spades*), Jeník, Laca (*Jenůfa*), Otello, Walther, Bacchus and Don Juan (*The Stone Guest*). ELIZABETH FORBES

Catherine [Yekaterina] **II** [née Sophie Auguste Fredericke von Anhalt-Zerbst] (*b* Stettin [now Szczecin], 21 April/2 May 1729; *d* Tsarskoye Selo, 6/17 Nov 1796). Empress of Russia. She acceded in 1762 following a palace coup against her husband Peter III, and became known as 'Catherine the Great'. Continuing the policy of her predecessors, the empresses Anna (reigned 1730–40) and Elizabeth (1741–61), she maintained a court opera theatre staffed by Italians, personally patronizing Cimarosa, Paisiello, Galuppi and Sarti, as well as her special favourite, the italianized Spaniard Martín y Soler. She also patronized comic opera in the vernacular and encouraged native talent to apply itself to this genre. Among the talents she nurtured was her own very modest one as a dramatist, which she exercised, as she put it to a friend, for the sake of relaxation and distraction from affairs of state. With the assistance of two literary secretaries, Ivan Yelagin and Alexander Khrapovitsky, she wrote three volumes of Russian plays and a fourth in French.

Between 1786 and 1790 Catherine wrote librettos for five comic operas and one historical pageant. The operas, based on fairy-tales and meant as moral instruction for her grandsons, the future tsars Alexander I and Nicholas I, were *Fevey* (1786, music by Pashkevich), *Novgorodskiy bogatïr' Boyeslavich* ('Boyeslavich, Champion of Novgorod'; 1786, music by Fomin), *Khrabroy i smeloy vityaz' Akhrideich* ('The Brave and Bold Knight Akhrideich'; 1787, music by Vančura), *Gorebogatïr Kosometovich* ('The Sorrowful Hero Kosometovich'; 1789, music by Martín y Soler) and *Fedul s det'mi* ('Fedul and his Children'; 1791, music by Pashkevich and Martín y Soler). The historical pageant was *Nachal'noye upravleniye Olega* ('The Early Reign of Oleg', 1790), for which Pashkevich harmonized folksongs for a bride's party (*devichnik*) scene, Carlo Canobbio (a ballet composer) furnished an overture and entr'actes, and Sarti composed some curious choruses in the 'Greek' modes. Published in 1791 in honour of the empress, it was the first full score ever printed in Russia.

*

J. Grot, ed.: *Lettres de Grimm à l'impératrice Catherine II* (St Petersburg, 2/1866)

A. Rabinovich: *Russkaya opera do Glinki* [Russian Opera Before Glinka] (Moscow, 1948)

R.-A. Mooser: *Annales de la musique et des musiciens en Russie au XVIIIme siècle*, ii (Geneva, 1951)

M. Whaples: 'Eighteenth-century Russian Opera in the Light of Soviet Scholarship', *Indiana Slavic Studies*, ii (1958), 113–34

S. Karlinsky: *Russian Drama from its Beginnings to the Age of Pushkin* (Berkeley and Los Angeles, 1985), chap. 5

RICHARD TARUSKIN

Catiline Conspiracy, The. Opera in two acts by IAIN HAMILTON to his own libretto after BEN JONSON; Stirling, MacRobert Centre, 16 March 1974.

The action is set between 64 and 62 BC, in the last years of the Roman Republic. Catiline (baritone), failing in his attempt to gain election as consul, plots to seize power. The courtesan Fulvia (soprano) and her lover Quintus (tenor) reveal his plans to Cicero (tenor), who denounces Catiline in the Senate. Caesar (baritone) plays an equivocal part. Fulvia and Quintus are killed by Catiline's wife Aurelia (soprano) and the patrician Sempronia (mezzo-soprano). Catiline raises a rebellion but is defeated by Cicero, the 'man of peace'. Dying, he declares that Caesar will triumph where he has failed.

The most substantial of the nine short scenes is that in which Cicero denounces Catiline. There are no formal arias or ensembles, the vocal line for the most part following the inflections of natural speech, while the orchestra supplies a continuous commentary, carrying the action forward rapidly and with sure dramatic sense. The chorus play an important role. The opera was well received by public and critics, and laid the foundations of Hamilton's operatic reputation. HUGO COLE

Catley, Anne (*b* London, 1745; *d* nr Brentford, 14 Oct 1789). English soprano. The daughter of a hackney coachman and a washerwoman, she was apprenticed to William Bates about 1760. She sang at Vauxhall and Covent Garden in 1762–3 and then went to Dublin after the scandal arising from a payment of £200 by her lover to end her apprenticeship. There she played Polly and later a 'rakish, joyous Macheath'; the ladies had their hair 'Catleyfied' and she earned enormous sums. She sang at Covent Garden from 1770, making her mark as Rosetta in the pasticcio *Love in a Village*, Rachel in the ballad opera *The Jovial Crew* and a scandalously impudent Juno in O'Hara's burletta *The Golden Pippin*, a part designed for her. An intelligent woman and fine singer, she settled down with Colonel Lascelles after her notorious youth, and her will provided for their eight surviving children. She was ill in the later part of her career (she died of tuberculosis), but retained on stage the 'bold, volatile, audacious' manner which captivated audiences.

*

BDA; *DNB* (J. Humphreys); *LS*
'Memoirs of Colonel Las-lles and Miss C-tl-y', *The Town and Country Magazine*, ii (1770), 569–72
Miss Ambross: *The Life and Memoirs of the Late Miss Ann Catley* (London, *c*1790)
The Thespian Dictionary (London, 1802, 2/1805)
M. J. Young: *Memoirs of Mrs Crouch*, ii (London, 1806)
J. O'Keeffe: *Recollections* (London, 1826)
J. Boaden: *Memoirs of Mrs Siddons* (London, 1827)
——: *The Life of Mrs Jordan*, i (London, 1831)
R. Fiske: *English Theatre Music in the Eighteenth Century* (London, 1973, 2/1986)
T. J. Walsh: *Opera in Dublin 1705–1797* (Dublin, 1973)

OLIVE BALDWIN, THELMA WILSON

Catone in Utica ('Cato in Utica'). Libretto by PIETRO METASTASIO, first set by Leonardo Vinci (1728, Rome).

ACT 1 Cesare [Caesar] is preparing to attack Utica. Cato, ruler of Utica and Caesar's last opponent after the murder of Pompey, wants his daughter, Marzia [Marcia], to marry his ally, Arbace [Arbaces], Prince of Numidia. Marcia, secretly in love with Caesar, persuades Arbaces not to mention the subject of marriage. Cato receives Caesar and Fulvio [Fulvius] who arrive unarmed with a bid for peace. Emilia, Pompey's widow, suspects treachery and rails against Caesar. Fulvius, Caesar's ally, expresses his love for Emilia, who demands that he murder Caesar before speaking to her of love. Caesar, at first spurned by Marcia, convinces her of his honourable intentions. Emilia is quick to counter such notions, suspecting Marcia's feelings for Caesar.

ACT 2 Cato rejects a demand from the Senate for a reconciliation with Caesar, but agrees to meet him. Caesar offers to divide the empire with Cato, but the latter, unmoved, insists that Caesar surrender his dictatorial powers. Caesar refuses, and Marcia's pleas are unable to subdue his impulse for war, while her confession to Cato of her love for Caesar only heightens her father's anger. Arbaces feels his love for Marcia betrayed, and Emilia seizes this opportunity to try to lure him into an assassination attempt on Caesar.

ACT 3 Fulvius is led to believe that Emilia will make an attempt on Caesar's life as he leaves by the city gate. He therefore advises departure by a secret path – only to discover that Emilia has used him to deliver Caesar into the hands of her followers.

[1st version] Marcia, planning to flee Utica, comes upon the secret pathway before the others. She thwarts Emilia's attempt on Caesar's life, and Emilia accuses her of an attempted assignation with the general just as Cato arrives. Fulvius then interrupts Cato's threats and accusations to announce the victory of Caesar's armies in Utica. Cato stabs himself and grants forgiveness to Marcia on condition that she swear loyalty to Arbaces and hatred towards Caesar. She yields, and, still unreconciled with Caesar, Cato dies, claiming that the freedom of Rome dies with him.

[2nd version] Caesar is rescued, however, by the timely arrival of Cato, who condemns Emilia then challenges Caesar to a private contest. News that a battle has

'Catone in Utica', Act 3 scene xii (CATO: *'And swear eternal contempt for the base oppressor of our country and of the world'); engraving from the 'Opere' of Pietro Metastasio (Paris: Hérissant, 1780–82)*

already broken out averts this duel, and when Caesar's armies prevail, Marcia and Arbaces are forced to struggle with Cato to prevent him taking his own life. To Marcia's petition for his forgiveness, Cato responds with a demand for her hatred of Caesar and loyalty to Arbaces. Caesar, victorious, pronounces a general pardon, but Marcia enters to announce Cato's suicide and her pledged hatred towards the victor.

* * *

The most detailed classical account of Cato's final confrontation with Caesar is recorded in Plutarch's *Vitae* (Cato the Younger). Other sources include the *Vitae* (Caesar), Appian's *Historia* (Civil Wars, book 2) and Cassio Dio's *Historiarum* (book 43). The closeness of Metastasio's plot to those of Joseph Addison's *Cato* (1713) and François Deschamps' *Caton d'Utique* (1715) suggests that these works served as contemporary models. There are also parallels with Jacques Auger's *La mort de Caton* (1648). Two dramas of Pierre Corneille also contain similar situations: Cornelia, Pompey's widow (Metastasio's Emilia), confronts Caesar in *La mort de Pompée* (1643) and two Roman leaders (Pompey and Sertorius) contend in *Sertorius* (1662). Further, the conflict between Cato and Caesar underlies *Catone Uticense*, a libretto by Matteo Noris set by C. F. Pollarolo for Venice (1701), and allusions to Cato's actions and eventual suicide occur throughout Dominique de Colonia's drama *Juba* (1718), although Cato never appears on stage.

Catone in Utica was Metastasio's first opera for Rome, and although audiences in Naples had previously accepted Dido's disappearance among the flames during the last spectacular moments of *Didone abbandonata*,

Roman critics took exception to the mortally wounded Cato's slowly expiring across two entire scenes at the end of *Catone in Utica*. Objections were also raised to the secret pathway scene being played in a disused sewer. Ever sensitive to critical opinion, Metastasio altered the second half of his third act. In the second version, first set by Leo for Venice (1729), Cato's death is simply reported, and all that remains of the *acquedotti antichi* of the secret pathway scene is the entrance, to which a fountain of Isis and its surrounding trees create a visual diversion. Metastasio clearly regarded both versions of this drama as authentic, although most composers preferred the revision. In a setting by Giovanni Ferrandini, *Catone in Utica* opened the Cuvilliés theatre in Munich in 1753, and for J. C. Bach his setting for Naples (1761) was to become his most widely performed opera.

For a list of settings *see* METASTASIO, PIETRO. DON NEVILLE

Catone in Utica (i) ('Cato in Utica'). *Tragedia per musica* in three acts by LEONARDO LEO to a libretto by PIETRO METASTASIO; Venice, Teatro di S Giovanni Grisostomo, Carnival 1729.

Leo was the first composer to set the revised version of Metastasio's libretto (*see* CATONE IN UTICA above); his setting includes some additional arias by an unknown Venetian (possibly Lalli). *Catone in Utica* was his third opera for Venice and his first setting of a Metastasian libretto. Leo's style is generally more complex, with thicker textures, than that of his contemporaries; notable are the increasingly periodic phrase structure, slower harmonic rhythm, sophisticated orchestration and the lack of simple continuo arias. The singers in the first production were the soprano castrato Nicolini (Catone [Cato]), the soprano castrato Domenico Gizzi (Cesare [Caesar]), the soprano Lucia Facchinelli (Marzia [Marcia]), the soprano Antonia Negri (Emilia), the soprano castrato Farinelli (Arbace [Arbaces]) in his Venetian début, and the bass Giuseppe Maria Boschi (Fulvio [Fulvius]). The opera was also performed in London in the form of *Catone*, a pasticcio arranged by Handel, at the King's Theatre in the Haymarket on 4 November 1732, for which the libretto was 'Done into English by Mr. Humphreys'. It has been suggested by scholars that at least two arias and the opening sinfonia of Leo's original version may be spurious (see Brown 1983). STEPHEN SHEARON

Catone in Utica (ii) ('Cato in Utica'). *Opera seria* in three acts by JOHANN CHRISTIAN BACH to a libretto by PIETRO METASTASIO; Naples, Teatro di S Carlo, 4 November 1761.

Catone in Utica was Bach's most successful and widely performed opera. After its initial run in Naples, it was performed in Milan (Regio Ducal, summer 1762), Pavia (Omodeo, Carnival 1763), Perugia (Paone, Carnival 1763), Parma (Regio Ducal, spring 1763, where it was seen by Gluck and Dittersdorf), Naples again (S Carlo, 26 December 1764), Brunswick (Fürstliches, 1 August 1768) and again in Pavia (Omodeo, Carnival 1772). A MS copy of the score (*F-Pn*) which corresponds to none of the known librettos suggests that there was probably also a ninth production.

Bach's second opera sets Metastasio's revised version of the text (*see* CATONE IN UTICA above), with a number of cuts and additions. All the arias, except the first and last in Act 3, are of the *dal segno* type. The orchestra of flutes, oboes, bassoons, horns, trumpets and strings is the normal one of the time. However, what ensured the opera's success within this conservative framework was the high quality of Bach's melodic invention. This is attested by the large number of contemporary manuscript copies of arias such as 'Confusa smarrita' and 'Per darvi alcun pegno' which still survive. Bach himself drew freely on the score for pasticcios in London. ERNEST WARBURTON

Catone in Utica (iii) ('Cato in Utica'). *Dramma per musica* in three acts by Niccolò Piccinni (*see* PICCINNI family, (1)) to a libretto by PIETRO METASTASIO; Mannheim, Hoftheater, 5 November 1770.

Piccinni's setting follows the second version of Metastasio's text (*see* CATONE IN UTICA above), in which the suicide of Cato (tenor) takes place offstage. The opera may have been written for Naples, but no libretto has survived, and Burney, who visited Piccinni in October 1770, did not mention a performance of the work. Anton Raaff apparently took a manuscript score with him to Mannheim, where he sang the title role in his local début. The autograph score (in *D-Mbs*) includes several changes in the hands of Mannheim copyists, the most significant being an alternative aria by Sacchini, 'Ovunque m'aggiri sol veggio perigli' (2.ix). Piccinni set 16 of Metastasio's 26 original aria texts, along with four additional arias, possibly provided by Verazi, the Mannheim court poet. Some of the textual changes follow J. C. Bach's setting (1761, Naples), in which Raaff also sang the role of Cato. The quartet in Act 3 was omitted, but a new trio, 'Fra cento squadre, e cento', was added to conclude Act 2. PAUL CORNEILSON

Catrufo, Gioseffo [Giuseppe] (*b* Naples, 19 April 1771; *d* London, 19 Aug 1851). Italian composer. A student at the Conservatorio della Pietà dei Turchini, Naples, he was known under the name 'Spagnoletto' as a singer of comic roles. At the end of 1791 he went to Malta, where he made a reputation as an opera composer: his *opere buffe Il Corriere* and *Cajacciello disertore* were given at the Teatro Manoel in 1792. Possibly involved in the Naples Revolution of 1799, he emigrated to France in the same year and followed a military career until 1804. He then returned to Italy to resume his theatrical activities, settling in Geneva. In 1810 he moved to Paris, working in particular at the Théâtre Feydeau; ten of his operas were given their premières at the theatre between 1813 and 1832. In 1835 he moved to London and taught singing there for the rest of his career. Known chiefly for his stage works (his output included songs and piano pieces), Catrufo followed closely in the footsteps of the *opéra comique* composers of the beginning of the 19th century. He possessed a fresh melodic inspiration and a spontaneous, simple style.

first performed in Paris, Théâtre Feydeau by the Opéra-Comique, unless otherwise stated

Il Corriere (ob, 2), Malta, Manoel, spr. 1792
Cajacciello disertore (ob, 1), Malta, Manoel, 1792
Il liabattino ingentilito (ob, 2, L. Tottola), Arezzo, Petrarca, 26 Dec 1798; rev. as Il furbo contra il furbo, Pavia, Homodei, Oct 1799
La fée Urgèle (oc, 3, C.-S. Favart), 1805
Clarisse (oc, 2), Geneva, Grand, spr. 1806
L'amant alchimiste (oc, 3), Geneva, Grand, 1808 [according to Manferrari, spr. 1812]
Les aveugles de Franconville (oc, 1), Geneva, Grand, aut. 1809
L'aventurier (oc, 3, C. Leber), 13 Nov 1813
Félicie, ou La jeune fille romanesque (oc, 3, E. Mercier-Dupaty), 28 Feb 1815, vs (Paris, *c*1815)

Une matinée de Frontin (oc, 1, Leber), 17 Aug 1815, vs (Paris, *c*1815)
La boucle de cheveux (oc, 1, F.-B. Hoffman), spr. 1816
La bataille de Denain (oc, 3, F. V. A. Dartois de Bournonville, M. E. G. M. Théaulon de Lambert and J. D. Fulgence de Bury), 26 Aug 1816, vs (Paris, *c*1816)
Le caprice d'une jolie femme (oc, 1), 29 May 1817 [according to Manferrari, 1832]
Zadig (oc, 1, after Voltaire), carn. 1818
Der Diener aller Welt (1), Munich, Isartor, 17 Oct 1818, *D-Mbs*
L'intrigue au château (oc, 3, M. A. J. Gensoul), 14 June 1823
Le voyage à la cour (oc, 2, Marville [P. E. Létang]), 20 Aug 1825
Les rencontres (oc, 3, J. B. C. Vial and Mélesville [A.-H.-J. Duveyrier]), 11 June 1828, *F-Pn*, collab. J. F. A. Lemière de Corvey
Le passage du régiment (oc, 1, C. A. B. Sevrin), 5 Nov 1832 [according to Manferrari, 15 Nov 1828]

Unperf.: Blanche et Olivier (2); Don Raphaël (3); Clotaire (3)

*

ES (E. Zanetti)
U. Manferrari: *Dizionario universale delle opera melodrammatiche* (Florence, 1954–5) FRANCESCO BUSSI

Cattani, Lorenzo (*b* Massa Carrara; *d* Pisa, 1713). Italian composer. An Augustinian monk, he was an organist and *maestro di cappella* at Livorno, 1670–1713. According to the libretto of *Il Conte di Cutro*, he was *maestro di cappella* to the Grand Duke of Tuscany. He composed a number of operas for the Florentine court, all to librettos by Moniglia, but none of the music is known to survive (see G. A. Moniglia: *Delle poesie drammatiche*, Florence, 1689–90).

Quinto Lucrezio proscritto, 12 Nov 1681; Il Conte di Cutro, 12 Nov 1682; Il pellegrino, 1685; Gneo Marzio Coriolano, 25 May 1686; La pietà di Sabina, comp. before 1690, unperf.

*

P. Raddichi: *Giovanni Lorenzo Cattani* (Pisa, 1980)

Catulli carmina ('Songs of Catullus'). *Ludi scaenici* in three acts by CARL ORFF after poems by Catullus; Leipzig, Städtische Bühnen, 6 November 1943.

Three groups of people (young girls, young boys and old men) fill the stage. The young people make love to each other but are interrupted by the old men (basses) who declare that love is ridiculous because it is fleeting and cannot resist the corroding power of time. The men then tell the story of Catullus (tenor) and Lesbia (soprano) which unfolds in a series of three acts: in Act 1 Catullus declares his love for Lesbia. He falls asleep in her arms, but she abandons him to dance in the tavern. Catullus awakens and expresses his despair over her behaviour. In Act 2 Catullus is once more asleep outside Lesbia's cottage, troubled by dreams depicting her in the embrace of his friend Caelus. In Act 3 Catullus espies the beautiful courtesan Ipsitilla at a nearby window and writes her a declaration of love. But the ugly Ameana offers herself to him instead. Catullus rebuffs her and seeks Lesbia among the throng of harlots and their customers, but having found her he decides to break the relationship. Lesbia, suffering under a flood of reproaches, runs home. The narrative is then interrupted by the young people, who seem to have ignored its message. Their erotic games become even wilder than before, and the work ends with an exhortation to light up the flames of love-making.

Catulli carmina is the second in the trilogy *Trionfi*, in which Orff attempted to re-create the spirit of the allegorical Renaissance court masque. The work, better known in the concert hall, demonstrates the unmistakable influence of Stravinsky's *The Wedding* in its instrumentation and rhythm. ERIK LEVI

Caturla, Alejandro García (*b* Remedios, 7 March 1906; *d* Remedios, 12 Nov 1940). Cuban composer. He studied law in Havana and pursued his training in harmony and counterpoint with Pedro Sanjuán. In 1928 he studied with Nadia Boulanger in Paris. A district judge by profession, he was assassinated at the age of 34 outside his home by a convict awaiting sentence. The circumstances of his untimely death, his marriage to a black woman and his exuberant, uncompromising yet sheltered nature have cast an aura of fascination around him. With Amadeo Roldán (1900–39), Caturla was one of the first exponents of Afro-Cubanism in symphonic and dramatic genres. He left theatre and music criticism, essays on jurisprudence and more than 150 compositions in a powerful language that blends folk melodies with unorthodox harmonic procedures and complex rhythmic structures. In 1946 Alejo Carpentier characterized him as 'the richest musical talent to have emerged from the island'. The text for Caturla's only dramatic work, the puppet opera *Manita en el suelo* (1934–7, first performed 1985), was written in 1931 by Carpentier, whose poetry Caturla had previously set.

Manita en el suelo, a 'misterio bufo afro-cubano' for puppets and one actor, brings together characters from Christian legend and Afro-Cuban rituals practised by brotherhoods on the outskirts of Havana. Caturla's style combines a harmonic language rooted in octatonicism with diatonic interaction with complex rhythmic polyphony and the melodic simplicity of popular tunes. These are unified by a generative motif. He differentiates the characters' traditions by applying metric and rhythmic patterns associated with each, while the Virgin Patron of Cuba, who protects all races, sings a Cuban *son*, the most syncretic exponent of national identity. Only the ballad, the overture (a *danzón*) and the interlude were orchestrated before the composer's death, but his short score specified the orchestration for the remaining numbers. A reconstruction with dancers instead of puppets was given in Havana on 15 February 1985, at the Gran Teatro García Lorca.

*

A. G. Caturla: 'The Development of Cuban Music', *American Composers on American Music*, ed. H. Cowell (Stanford, CA, 1933), 173–4
A. Salazar: 'La obra musical de Alejandro García Caturla', *Revista cubana* (Jan 1938), 5–43
N. Slonimsky: 'Caturla of Cuba', *MM*, xvii (1939–40), 76–80
A. Carpentier: *La música en Cuba* (Mexico City, 1946), 235–53
J. J. Arrom: 'La Virgen del Cobre: historia, leyenda y símbolo sincrético', *Certidumbre de América* (Madrid, 1971), 184–214
A. Carpentier: 'Manita en el Suelo', *Signos* [Santa Clara, Cuba] (1978), 83–97
M. A. Henríquez, ed.: *Alejandro García Caturla: correspondencia* (Havana, 1978)
M. Kuss: 'The Confluence of Historical Coordinates in the Carpentier-Caturla Puppet Opera *Manita en el Suelo* (1934)', *Musical Repercussions of 1492: Encounters in Text and Performance*, ed. C. Robertson (Washington DC, 1992)
MALENA KUSS

Caudella, Eduard (*b* Iaşi, 22 May 1842; *d* Iaşi, April 1924). Romanian composer. After studying the violin in Berlin with Hubert Ries, in Frankfurt with Vieuxtemps and in Paris with Massart and Alard, he became a leading figure in the musical life of 19th-century Iaşi: he taught at and directed the Conservatory (1861–1901) and conducted at the National Theatre (1861–75) and the Italian Opera (1870–73). He was a prolific composer, writing in a wide range of genres including music for the theatre such as vaudevilles, operettas, comic operas and incidental music. Using subjects from Romanian history, he may be considered the father of Romanian national opera. In *Petru Rareş* he successfully fused Romanian folklore and international musical language. Caudella was a master of form and orchestration, and though eclectic traits are evident in his music it is nevertheless distinguished by a certain melodic accessibility, doinas and Romanian folk dances appearing harmonized according to traditional Western rules.

Olteanca [The Girl from Olt] (comic op, 3, G. Bengescu-Dabija), Iaşi, National, 8 March 1880
Hatmanul Baltag [Commandant Baltag], 1882 (ob, 3, I. Negruzzi and I. L. Caragiale, after N. Gane), Bucharest, National, 1 March 1884
Petru Rareş, 1889 (3, T. Rehbaum, after Gane), Bucharest, National, 2 Nov 1900
Traian and Dochia, 1917 (lyrical legend, 1, N. A. Bogdan)

*

O. L. Cosma: *Opera românească* [Romanian Opera] (Bucharest, 1962)
G. Constantinescu, G. Constantinescu, D. Caraman and I. Sava: *Ghid de operă* [Opera Guide] (Bucharest, 1971)

VIOREL COSMA

Cavalieri [Cavallieri], **Caterina** [Kavalier, Franziska Helena Appolonia] (*b* Vienna, 19 Feb 1760; *d* Vienna, 30 June 1801). Austrian soprano. During a versatile career, confined almost exclusively to Vienna, she appeared with equal success in comic and serious roles in both the Italian and German repertories. In her early career Cavalieri possessed an impressive upper range, to *d'''*. An extraordinary stamina and flexibility are reflected in consistently large-scale bravura arias. Of her début in Vienna (19 June 1775 at the Kärntnertortheater), as Sandrina in Anfossi's *La finta giardiniera*, Count Khevenhüller wrote that she possessed a very strong chest voice and met with 'well-deserved approbation'. In 1776–7 she belonged to a troupe of Italian singers. In 1778 she sang Sophie in Umlauf's *Die Bergknappen*, the inaugural production of the National Singspiel, and went on to sing 18 leading roles in the company including Nannette in Salieri's *Der Rauchfangkehrer* (1781) and Konstanze in Mozart's *Die Entführung* (1782). Of the challenging *fioriture* in 'Ach ich liebte', Mozart wrote to his father (26 September 1781): 'I have sacrificed Konstanze's aria a little to the flexible throat of Mlle Cavallieri'; this and another bravura showcase in the same act, 'Martern aller Arten', came willingly from the astute Mozart, eager to ingratiate himself with Cavalieri and her protector, the court composer Salieri. When Joseph II inaugurated *opera buffa* at the Burgtheater, Cavalieri was put to use both as a serious and comic lead. Her hard-hitting bravura is evident in rewritten or new solo numbers in works by Salieri and Cimarosa.

Cavalieri is best known through Mozart's music for her. Her aria as Mme Silberklang in *Der Schauspieldirektor* (1786) has muscular tunes, with driving, vigorous two-note phrases and quaver scales. For her appearance as Donna Elvira in the first Vienna production of *Don Giovanni* (1788), Mozart composed a large-scale aria ('Mi tradì') for her; she clearly no longer commanded her earlier high notes. For the revival of *Le nozze di Figaro* (1789), in which Cavalieri sang the Countess, Mozart rewrote 'Dove sono', eliminating the repeat of the intimate, restrained initial material and adding *fioriture* in the faster section.

Early in her career, Cavalieri was said to want 'animation and accuracy, and a firmer assurance', and criticized for almost 'unintelligible' speech (M. A. Schmitt, *Meine Empfindungen im Theater*, 1781). The Viennese dramatist Gebler, writing in 1780–81, said she had 'eine starke und angenehme Stimme, mit tiefen und hohen Tönen, die man selten beysammen antrift, singt ebenfalls die schwehrsten Passagen' ('a strong and pleasant voice, in both the high and the low notes, a combination which one seldom encounters, [she] sings equally well the most difficult passages'). Zinzendorf noted that in a duet in Sarti's *Giulio Sabino* 'Cavalieri drowned Marchesini's voice with her shouts' (4 August 1785), but two days later recorded that 'she screamed less'.

For illustration *see* GIULIO SABINO.

*

R. M. Werner: *Aus dem Josephinischen Wien: Geblers und Nicolais Briefwechsel während der Jahre 1771–1786* (Berlin, 1888)
O. Michtner: *Das alte Burgtheater als Opernbühne* (Vienna, 1970)
A. Tyson: *Mozart: Studies of the Autograph Scores* (Cambridge, MA, 1987)
P. Lewy Gidwitz: *Vocal Profiles of Four Mozart Sopranos* (diss., U. of California, Berkeley, 1991)

PATRICIA LEWY GIDWITZ

Cavalieri, Emilio de' (*b* Rome, *c*1550; *d* Rome, 11 March 1602). Italian composer. He was an important contributor to the pre-operatic genres of *intermedio* and pastorale, and composed the music of the first surviving opera, *Rappresentatione di Anima, et di Corpo … per recitar cantando* (prol., 3, A. Manni), produced in Rome in February 1600; its score, published later that year, was the earliest printed one with a figured bass (Rome, 1600; facs. Wolfenbüttel and Zürich, 1976).

Cavalieri was born into a noble Roman family. He held various civic administrative posts in Rome, and was associated there with Cardinal Ferdinando de' Medici. When Ferdinando succeeded his brother Francesco in 1587 as Grand Duke of Tuscany, Cavalieri moved to Florence as superintendent of the court's artists, craftsmen and musicians. He oversaw the festivities in 1589 for the marriage of Ferdinando and Christine of Lorraine, contributing at least two numbers to the extraordinarily lavish *intermedi* for the play *La Pellegrina*, a pseudo-monodic solo ('Godi turba mortal') and the culminating ballo ('O che nuovo miracolo'). In the latter, a chorus of nymphs and shepherds alternates with a trio of female soloists who not only sing but dance and play instruments; the bass of the ballo – called the 'Aria di Fiorenza' or 'Ballo del Gran Duca' – served as the basis for many improvisatory compositions by later composers.

In 1590 Cavalieri turned to the newer genre of the pastorale. In that year he produced Tasso's *Aminta*, with sets and machines by Bernardo Buontalenti and perhaps some music by himself, as well as his own pastorales (to texts by the poet Laura Guidiccioni), *Il Satiro* and *La disperazione di Fileno*. In 1595 he set to music an adaptation by Guidiccioni of the 'Giuoco della cieca' from Guarini's *Il pastor fido*, for the first stage production based on that celebrated pastorale; Guarini was also the author of *La contesa fra Giunone e Minerva*, which Cavalieri set in October 1600 for the marriage of Maria de' Medici and Henri IV of France. None of the music for these survives, which is unfortunate since they must have represented the first application to drama of the new Florentine monody, judging by the report of Alessandro Guidotti (in the preface to the

Rappresentatione) that Cavalieri's music 'renewed' that of the ancients and moved listeners both to tears and laughter; and by Jacopo Peri's generous deferral to Cavalieri (in the preface to his *Euridice*, dated 6 February 1601) as the first to make use of 'our kind of music on the stage'.

Although Cavalieri's *Rappresentatione di Anima, et di Corpo* had roots in the traditions of the *sacra rappresentazione* and the *lauda*, was produced in the Oratorio di S Maria in Vallicella in Rome and is considered 'of primary importance to the history of the oratorio' (Smither 1977), it was in fact a fully staged sacred opera (in a spoken prologue and three acts entirely set to music), the first of a genre which was to be favoured in 17th-century Rome.

See also RAPPRESENTATIONE DI ANIMA, ET DI CORPO.

*

A. Solerti: 'Laura Guidiccioni ed Emilio del Cavaliere', *RMI*, ix (1902), 797–829

——: *Le origini del melodramma* (Turin, 1903)

——: *Gli albori del melodramma* (Milan, 1905)

——: *Musica, ballo e drammatica alla corte medicea dal 1600 al 1637* (Florence, 1905)

D. Alaleona: *Studi su la storia dell'oratorio in Italia* (Turin, 1908, 2/1945 as *Storia dell'oratorio musicale in Italia*)

N. Pirrotta: 'Temperaments and Tendencies in the Florentine Camerata', *MQ*, xl (1954), 169–89

F. Ghisi and D. P. Walker: Introductory essays in *Musique des intermèdes de 'La Pellegrina'* (Paris, 1963)

C. V. Palisca: 'Musical Asides in the Diplomatic Correspondence of Emilio de' Cavalieri', *MQ*, xlix (1963), 339–55

T. C. Read: *A Critical Study and Performance Edition of Emilio di Cavalieri's 'Rappresentazione di Anima e di Corpo'* (diss., U. of Southern California, 1969)

W. Kirkendale: 'Emilio de' Cavalieri, a Roman Gentleman at the Florentine Court', *Quadrivium*, xii/2 (1971), 9–21

——: *L'aria di Fiorenza, id est Il ballo del Gran Duca* (Florence, 1972)

H. M. Brown: *Sixteenth Century Instrumentation: the Music for the Florentine Intermedii* (Rome, 1973)

H. E. Smither: *A History of the Oratorio*, i: *The Oratorio in the Baroque Era: Italy, Vienna, Paris* (Chapel Hill, NC, 1977), 79–91

H. WILEY HITCHCOCK

Cavalieri, Lina (*b* Viterbo, 25 Dec 1874; *d* Florence, 7 Feb 1944). Italian soprano. Of humble origins, she began her career singing in cafés and soon became celebrated for her exceptional beauty. She studied with Maddelena Mariani-Masi and made her début in 1900 at the Teatro S Carlos, Lisbon, in *Pagliacci* and appeared soon after at the S Carlo, Naples, in *La bohème*. Although mostly engaged in Paris, Monte Carlo and, above all, St Petersburg, she also sang in New York (Metropolitan and Manhattan Opera, 1906–10), and in London (Covent Garden, 1908, and London Opera House, 1911). With an agreeable though limited voice, she was an elegant, natural actress and preferred roles which allowed her to display her attractive figure in splendid jewels and spectacular costumes: Violetta, both Manons, Thaïs, Fedora and Tosca. One of her four husbands was the tenor Lucien Muratore (1913–27). Between 1914 and 1921 she made several films.

*

GV (R. Celletti; R. Vegeto)

L. Cavalieri: *Le mie verità* (Rome, 1936) [autobiography]

RODOLFO CELLETTI

Cavalieri di Ekebù, I ('The Knights of Ekeby'). *Dramma lirico* in four acts by RICCARDO ZANDONAI to a libretto by ARTURO ROSSATO after *Gösta Berlings saga* by Selma Lagerlöf; Milan, Teatro alla Scala, 7 March 1925.

The main characters are Giosta (tenor), a young and dissolute Lutheran pastor driven from the church at Bro, in western Sweden; Anna (soprano), daughter of the demoniacal Sintram (bass), loved by Giosta; La Comandante (mezzo-soprano), owner of the ironworks of Ekeby, with a stormy past but a good heart. A work of the composer's maturity, the opera combines *verismo*-style vocal writing with skilful instrumentation and a poetic handling of the choruses and the Nordic atmosphere. Among the best-known arias are those of Giosta ('Bro: la chiesetta triste') and Anna ('Vivevo umile e sola'); there is some striking writing for theatre band in Act 2, with parallel dissonances somewhat in the manner of Puccini's *Turandot*. RENATO CHIESA

Cavalleria rusticana (i) ('Rustic Chivalry'). *Melodramma* in one act by PIETRO MASCAGNI to a libretto by Giovanni Targioni-Tozzetti and Guido Menasci after GIOVANNI VERGA's play based on his story; Rome, Teatro Costanzi, 17 May 1890.

Santuzza *a young peasant woman*	soprano
Turiddu *a young peasant*	tenor
Lucia *his mother, an innkeeper*	contralto
Alfio *a carrier*	baritone
Lola *Alfio's wife*	mezzo-soprano

Villagers

Setting A village in Sicily on Easter Sunday 1880

Verga's play *Cavalleria rusticana* received its first performance in the Teatro Carignano, Turin, on 14 January 1884 with Eleanora Duse as Santuzza. Mascagni saw it less than a month later in Milan but did not think of making it into an opera until June 1888, when he read in *Il secolo* that the publisher Sonzogno had announced the second competition for a one-act opera (Puccini had unsuccessfully submitted *Le villi* for the first). Mascagni commissioned the libretto from his fellow-citizen Targioni-Tozzetti who, worried about his ability to satisfy the precise terms of the competition, enlisted the help of another Livornese writer, Menasci. The libretto was ready in December 1888, the opera in May 1889; part of it was sent to Puccini and he in turn sent it to the publisher Giulio Ricordi, who failed to realize its worth, thus losing a golden opportunity. Needless to say, the opera won the competition and made a fortune for the publishing firm of Edoardo Sonzogno, who had arranged that the short season of the Teatro Costanzi in Rome would include the operas of the three finalists. Mascagni's masterpiece, interpreted by Gemma Bellincioni and Roberto Stagno and conducted by Leopoldo Mugnone, was a resounding success and within a few months had been rapturously received in all the principal cities of Europe and America. For over a century it has found a place in the repertory of leading singers and conductors from Mahler, who conducted it in Budapest and included it in the programmes of the Vienna Staatsoper, through Levi and Weingartner and on to Karajan, among more recent performers. Today *Cavalleria* is usually paired with Leoncavallo's *Pagliacci*, a work of similar concision from which it has become virtually inseparable.

The plot can be briefly summarized. On Easter morning, Turiddu sings of his love for Lola. Among the people on their way to church is Santuzza, who had been seduced by the young peasant before he returned to his former love, now married to Alfio. Santuzza reproaches him, with entreaties and finally with curses, and tells Alfio of his wife's infidelity. Alfio insults Turiddu, and finally challenges him to a duel. Turiddu charges his mother to look after Santuzza, and is killed in the fight.

It has often been said that Verga's *Cavalleria* inaugurated the *verismo* period in Italian theatre. Mascagni stressed his adherence to the play as his source, insisting that it was Verga's treatment of the subject which had spurred him to set it and rejecting the idea of a close affinity between his opera and Bizet's *Carmen*. But *Cavalleria* is as closely linked to the French opera, which, as the box-office hit of the day, was widely admired and imitated, as it is to Verga's text, which was performed everywhere and so available to any composer in need of a good subject. It was used by Gastaldon for his *La mala Pasqua!*, which was withdrawn from the competition won by Mascagni so that it could be performed at the Costanzi some weeks before the winning entries.

Carmen was in reality a decisive model for the dramatic composition of *Cavalleria*, not only because jealousy is in both cases the driving force of the action and its bloody outcome (presented more realistically on stage in the French work), but above all because Bizet had chosen a subject set not in the remote East as was then fashionable but under more familiar Mediterranean skies, clearly indicating a shift in stylistic influence. Mascagni sketched in the local background from the beginning, including an example of the dialect siciliana within the prelude before the curtain rises, so providing a true prologue to the action in his use of a formal element that breaks with tradition but is consonant with the rustic code of honour of the melodrama. The voice of Turiddu, accompanied by offstage harps, at once places Sicily at the core of the action, in which it reappears several times evoked with a descriptive capacity arguably even greater than Bizet's prelude and the *chanson bohémienne*.

The entire structure of *Cavalleria*, in which almost all the action occurs while the Easter Mass is taking place in the church, mirrors Act 4 of *Carmen*, where the enthusiasm of the spectators at the bullfight serves as background to the murder of the Spanish gypsy. But here too Mascagni outdoes his model, in which collective pleasure is contrasted with individual tragedy and the new lover with the old, because the church that dominates the square, and the popular devotion expressed in the Easter hymn, symbolize the violated innocence of Santuzza, the more dishonoured by Alfio's accusation.

All the tragic elements of the story are concentrated in a musical framework calculated to convey maximum immediacy. In this Mascagni followed a line of logical adherence to the traditional plan of 19th-century opera, returning to the closed numbers already abandoned by Verdi, a regressive step compared with *Otello* (1887). Mascagni's aim was to provide himself with a traditional channel of communication, but he treated his material with an originality first seen in the prelude, before the curtain rises: although it appears at first to be typical in its exposition of the principal melodies of the work, the way in which they are later recalled re-evokes its entire structure in the listener's memory, with the orchestral crescendo of the prelude interrupted by the siciliana and resumed more strongly when the voice behind the curtain ceases. In the continuation of the duet between Santuzza and Turiddu, the central point of the drama, the reprise of the prelude is in the orchestra only, intensifying the emotion of the concluding *appassionato* section. Mascagni attained his aim of creating an opera realistically dominated by sentiment by using formal means more effective in their subtlety than openly veristic and impassioned ones, of which there are indeed few. Conscious of the need to write an 'Italian' work, he made use above all of the special qualities of the closed number and its interaction with recitative. The melody on the lower strings that accompanies Santuzza's entrance is in effect a leitmotif, reminiscent of the theme that concludes the overture to *Carmen*. In using it in proximity to the song of Alfio, Turiddu's executioner, which immediately follows, Mascagni links him with Santuzza as different facets of a common destiny, the motif itself being linked not so much to Santuzza as to the deadly destiny she brings. It reappears at all the high points of the drama, from the *romanza* to the 'Mala Pasqua' she tragically hurls at Turiddu, before concluding the opera and so revealing itself as the musical symbol of the tragic ending. This sense of conclusion is reinforced by the use of the key of F at crucial moments, from the prelude (in the major) to the central series of numbers and the Intermezzo, and to the final statement, in the minor, of the 'tragedy' motif.

Mascagni's instinct was thus primarily to create, through a series of continuous scenes, a fluid background to the individual passions. In the first scene, devoted to the Sicilian peasants, the atmosphere of an important religious feast is conveyed by an attractive orchestral waltz, a barrel-organ piece above which the chorus is heard and which reappears when the church service is over. Turiddu's entrance is delayed until interest in him has been aroused by the siciliana ('O Lola ch'hai di latti la cammisa'). Meanwhile Santuzza's dramatic dialogue with Mamma Lucia, giving the background to the story, precedes the arrival of Alfio; she then leads the chorus of peasants in the powerful prayer ('Inneggiamo, il Signor non è morto') that follows the *Regina coeli* of the offstage chorus. The tripartite Romanza e Scena rounds out her portrait in a generous and sensuous but elegant vocal line that remains within the traditional stylized limits: the middle section is skilfully crafted from variants of the tragedy motif, and the number ends with a final reference to the prelude.

Alfio makes his entrance with a character-piece ('Il cavallo scalpita') in which, like Bizet's toreador, he boasts about his occupation, accompanied by the chorus; but there is in his song an element of ambiguity arising from the syncopation and the sinister nature of the melody and harmony in the middle section, which give the lie without a trace of irony to Alfio's words ('Mi aspetta a casa Lola, che m'ama e mi consola').

The song becomes agitated on Turiddu's entrance: the beginning of his duet with Santuzza ('Tu qui, Santuzza?'), the first of four sections, takes the form of a recitative interspersed with brief arioso passages. The tension approaches a climax but is frozen for a few moments by the simple stornello, 'Fior di gaggiolo', which Lola begins to sing offstage; it explodes with renewed force in the continuation of the duet after she has gone into the church and her melody is recalled on the flute. The situation is resolved in the melodic impulse of the vocal line, with high *appassionato* phrases in the first violins doubled at various octaves by

'Cavalleria rusticana' (Mascagni): final scene in the first Milan production (La Scala, 3 January 1891) with sets by Giovanni Zuccarelli; engraving (1891) by A. Bonamore

the orchestra, and in the contrast between sonorities and dynamics: the marking *quasi parlato* is placed only on 'Mala Pasqua', though it is often disregarded by the singer. The duet that follows concludes with a fiery cabaletta in F minor for Alfio and Santuzza ('Ad essi non perdono').

All the tension that has accumulated up to this point is channelled into the Intermezzo, a hymn in F based on the melody of the *Regina coeli* with which the service began, metrically varied and doubled by the violins with a simple chorale-like harmonization. Played with the curtain up, it marks the end of the Easter ceremony, but the story continues to unfold, the serenity of village life being contrasted with the passions devouring the main characters.

After the orchestral reprise of the waltz heard at the beginning, mingling with the sound of bells and followed by the chorus, the tonality is raised to G for Turiddu's brindisi, 'Viva il vino spumeggiante', one of the most brilliant drinking-songs in all opera. It conveys well the atmosphere of nervous excitement surrounding Turiddu and Alfio at the moment of the challenge and prepares the tragic ending. The anxious whispering of divided violins accompanies the fragmented recitative in which Turiddu addresses his mother before taking his leave of her ('Mamma, quel vino è generoso') in an impassioned progression towards the top note, a last *cri de coeur* before the cries of the women offstage and the tragedy motif bring the opera to an end.

* * *

Evaluation of *Cavalleria rusticana* by present-day criteria necessitates examination of the reasons for its continuing unqualified success. The work achieved a perfect balance between all its components, the dominant feature still being stylization in the 19th-century sense. Even such possible defects as the conventional orchestration and academic harmony have their place in the dramatic characterization, combined with felicitous melodic invention and an original way of handling the standard formal operatic situations so as to please both the traditional Italian opera-going public and that of foreign theatres in a nostalgic frame of mind. Mascagni's masterpiece hastened the end of an epoch by exhausting its possibilities, leaving to Puccini the task of representing Italy in the context of international opera and the fin-de-siècle crisis. It was soon evident that this national path led nowhere, and the spirit of his unrepeatable masterpiece haunted its composer for the rest of his life.

MICHELE GIRARDI

Cavalleria rusticana (ii) ('Rustic Chivalry'). *Dramma lirico* in one act with prologue by DOMENICO MONLEONE to a libretto by Giovanni Monleone from the story and play of the same title by GIOVANNI VERGA; Amsterdam, Paleis voor Volksvlyt, 5 February 1907.

The opera followed in the wake of Mascagni's version (1890) and retains his vocal roles (Turiddu's mother is here called Nunzia). In the nocturnal prologue, after the serenade for Turiddu (tenor), Lola (soprano) leaves the house and joins him in a short love scene; in the single act the sequence of events is the same as in Mascagni, except for the extra development given to the comic figure of Zio Brasi (bass): when he arrives on the scene Alfio (baritone) describes how he routed the brigands who had attacked him. The lyrical passages show melodic invention which is often entrusted to the orchestra, as in the narrative of Santuzza (soprano) and Nunzia (mezzo-soprano), and the dramatic passages use simple leitmotifs. The choral parts are important, particularly the hymn over which Santuzza and Alfio sing their duet. LUCA ZOPPELLI

Cavalletti, Giulio Maria [Giulietto] (*b* Rome, *c*1668; *d* Rome, 19 Feb 1755). Italian soprano castrato and composer. He was already a member of the Congregazione dei Musici di Roma in 1683, and in 1684 was in the *cappella* of St Mark's, Venice; in the 1683–4 season he appeared at the Teatro di S Bartolomeo, Naples. He studied with Colonna (and possibly Pistocchi) in Bologna and in 1688 joined the Accademia Filarmonica and the *cappella* of S Petronio. Between 1683 and 1692 he was among the singers of S Maria Maggiore, Rome. In 1696 he took part in Perti's *Penelope la casta* and *Furio Camillo* in Rome. During the following two years Cavalletti sang in Florence and Pratolino, and between 1698 and 1703 he was *virtuoso di camera* to the Duchess of Laurenzano. During this period he was granted leave to sing in Naples; at the Teatro di S Bartolomeo he performed in Scarlatti's *La caduta de' Decemviri*, *Tito Sempronio Gracco* and *Tiberio imperatore d'Oriente*. During 1705–7, in the service of Grand Prince Ferdinando in Florence, he sang the title role in Gasparini's *Ambleto* and Spiridate in Orlandini's *Artaserse*. He was summoned to Barcelona by Charles III in 1707, and in October was appointed *primo musico di camera* and assistant *maestro de capilla* to the king. In the former capacity he supervised the opera seasons at the Teatro de la Lonja. After 1707, nothing is known about his career as a theatrical singer. In 1720 he was a member of the imperial chapel in Vienna (as a tenor). He was pensioned in 1723 and returned to Rome. Penna, in the *Catalogo degli aggregati della Accademia Filarmonica di Bologna* ascribed to Padre Martini (*I-Baf*/*R*1971), calls him 'one of the most famous singers of his time in church and theatre'; known as a soprano capable of singing alto parts, Cavalletti had a range of more than two octaves from *e*.

*

A. Ademollo: *I teatri di Roma nel secolo decimosettimo* (Rome, 1888)
R. L. Weaver and N. W. Weaver: *A Chronology of Music in the Florentine Theater 1590–1750* (Detroit, 1978)
R. Pagano: *Scarlatti Alessandro e Domenico: due vite in una* (Milan, 1985)
C. Vitali: Introduction to C. F. Pollarolo: *Il Faramondo*, DMV, ix (1987) CARLO VITALI (with JULIANE RIEPE)

Cavalli [Caletti, Caletto, Bruni, Caletti-Bruni, Caletto Bruni], (**Pietro** [Pier]) **Francesco** (*b* Crema, 14 Feb 1602; *d* Venice, 14 Jan 1676). Italian composer. He was the most performed, and perhaps the most representative, composer of opera in the quarter-century after Monteverdi and was a leading figure, as both composer and performer, in Venetian musical life.

1. Life. 2. Reputation. 3. Operas.

1. Life. Cavalli received his first instruction in music from his father, Giovanni Battista Caletti, *maestro di cappella* of Crema Cathedral, and probably sang in the cathedral choir. His sweetness of voice and musical accomplishment brought him to the notice of Federico Cavalli, Venetian governor of Crema from July 1614 to March 1616, who persuaded Caletti to let him take the boy to Venice at the end of his term of office. Francesco entered the *cappella* of St Mark's, Venice, on 18 December 1616, as a soprano. His voice must have broken almost at once, but he is not mentioned as a tenor until 1 February 1627 (as F. Caletto).

During the first quarter-century of Cavalli's activity at St Mark's the music was directed by Monteverdi, with whom he clearly enjoyed a close association. On 18 May 1620 he was appointed organist at the church of SS Giovanni e Paolo, a position he held until 4 November 1630. Earlier in 1630, on 7 January, he had married Maria Sozomeno, niece of the Bishop of Pula and widow of a well-to-do Venetian. This advantageous marriage gave Cavalli some degree of financial independence and may explain his disinclination to travel and his early willingness to invest in operatic ventures. Also from about this time he began to use the name of his first patron; but in official documents the distinction between his real and assumed names was nearly always made as 'Francesco Caletti detto il Cavalli'.

Cavalli won the competition for the post of second organist at St Mark's on 23 January 1639. Despite the appointment of Massimiliano Neri as first organist in 1644, he seems to have been the principal organist during the following years. His début as an opera composer was in 1639, only two seasons after the introduction to Venice of musical theatre for paying audiences. At first his role was that of investor and organizer as well as composer. He was co-signatory, along with the librettist Orazio Persiani, the singer Felicità Uga and the dancing-master Giovanni Battista Balbi, of an agreement to produce 'accademie in musica' at the Teatro S Cassiano, Venice's first opera house. The first fruit of this collaboration was the 'opera scenica' *Le nozze di Teti e di Peleo*. Although the arrangement was soon disrupted by financial difficulties, Cavalli wrote eight more operas for S Cassiano during the next decade. Most of his operas during the 1640s were settings of librettos by Giovanni Faustini, beginning with *La virtù de' strali d'Amore* (1642) and *Egisto* (1643). *Egisto* enjoyed wide success as part of the repertory of travelling companies, which were instrumental in the spread of opera throughout Italy; it was even performed in Paris (1646) and possibly in Vienna. More successful still was Cavalli's setting of G. A. Cicognini's libretto *Giasone* (1649), with *Orontea* (also to a text by Cicognini, music by Cesti) the most enduringly popular opera in 17th-century Italy.

Cavalli's activity in the 1650s reflects the many facets of the development of public opera more than any individual initiative. When Faustini took an interest in the Teatro S Apollinare in 1650, he followed him there, composing four operas in two years. After Faustini's death in December 1651, he worked for the Teatro SS Giovanni e Paolo, partly in association with the librettist Nicolò Minato. In 1658–9 both were at the Teatro S Cassiano, which had been taken over by Marco Faustini, Giovanni's elder brother. With Balbi, Cavalli contributed to the installation of a stable opera at Naples, where in 1650 and 1651 *Didone*, *Giasone* and *Egisto* were staged. In general Cavalli's works (above all *Egisto*, *Giasone*, *Xerse* and *Erismena*) were a mainstay of the repertory as opera gained a firm footing even in many smaller Italian towns during the 1650s and 1660s.

Cavalli's wife died in 1652; they had no children. By her will, probated on 16 September, she left nearly all her property to him. Most of the operas that he composed specifically for other cities date from the next period, and he may have considered seeking employment away from Venice. In 1653 *Orione* was given at Milan to celebrate the election of Ferdinand IV, King of the Romans. *Hipermestra* was composed for Florence at the instance of Cardinal Giovanni Carlo de' Medici and used to celebrate the birth of the Spanish infante in 1658.

Following the Treaty of the Pyrenees between France and Spain (1659), the French prime minister, Cardinal Mazarin, laid plans for the celebration of the marriage of Louis XIV to Maria Theresa, daughter of the King of Spain. Cavalli was asked to compose an Italian opera for the occasion, but he reacted with some hesitation. His objections were overcome by March 1660, and he left for France in April or May with an entourage of five. After visits to Innsbruck and perhaps Munich, they arrived in Paris in July to find the theatre – newly commissioned from the well-known Italian architect Gaspare Vigarani and his sons for the Tuileries – far from ready.

Cavalli spent nearly two years in Paris while the theatre was being finished. As an interim measure, beginning on 22 November 1660, another of his operas, *Xerse*, was performed in a temporary theatre built in the great picture gallery of the Louvre. The original three acts were redistributed into five and supplied with *entrées de ballet* by Lully. Cavalli probably composed the celebratory opera, *Ercole amante*, on a libretto by the superintendent of Italian artists Francesco Buti, during his first year in France. Mazarin's death on 9 March 1661 spelt the beginning of the end of Italian cultural prominence at the court, and the opera might not have been performed at all had not so much money already been spent on it. A supposed conspiracy against the Italian artists may have sabotaged Vigarani's machinery; but if Cavalli's music was not appreciated when *Ercole amante* was first performed on 7 February 1662, it was because no one could hear it, owing to the theatre's bad acoustics. The spectacle lasted six hours and again included ballets by Lully, in which the king, queen and others of the court danced.

The last performance of *Ercole amante* took place on 6 May 1662, and by the summer Cavalli was again in Venice. He had left behind an unfulfilled contract for operas with Marco Faustini, but in a letter of 8 August he declared that he had left France resolved never to work for the theatre again.

In the event, Cavalli set three more librettos by Minato, the first for Faustini at the Teatro SS Giovanni e Paolo, the others for the Teatro S Salvatore. Two further operas composed for Venice were never performed: *Eliogabalo*, intended for Carnival 1668, and *Massenzio*, composed for Carnival 1673, were scrapped during rehearsals, the former possibly and the latter certainly because Cavalli's arias were not liked. *Coriolano*, his last new opera to be performed, was again a celebratory piece, written for the Farnese theatre at Piacenza (1669). On 20 November 1668 he succeeded Rovetta as *maestro di cappella* of St Mark's and remained in the post until his death. His will and property inventory show that he was assiduous, if conservative, in building an estate. A most important item was his collection of opera scores, which he gave to his pupil and assistant Giovanni Caliari: shortly afterwards it passed to the Contarini collection (*see* CONTARINI, MARCO), which now includes all of his surviving operas.

2. REPUTATION. Cavalli's growing fame in later life and after his death was in contrast to his waning effectiveness as an opera composer. Publication of the first chronology of Venetian opera by his erstwhile collaborator Cristoforo Ivanovich made him seem an even more central figure than he was, for Ivanovich attributed to him most of the anonymous works from the first 15 years of public opera, many of which were taken up in later chronicles (Walker 1972). Critical study and performance of Cavalli's music has largely followed on that of Monteverdi. *Didone* was performed in Florence in 1952 on the 350th anniversary of his birth. A seminal stage in the revival of his operas was the series of popular and controversial reconstructions (of *Ormindo*, *Calisto*, *Egisto* and *Orione*) by Raymond Leppard from 1967, the first two initially for Glyndebourne.

3. OPERAS. Cavalli produced music for the theatre during most of his working life. He composed nearly 30 operas for Venetian houses, and they run from the tentative beginnings of public opera to the establishment of Venice as a centre whose operas were imitated by, and exported to, cities throughout Italy. His works are central to that process of dissemination and as few operas by other composers survive from before the late 1650s, his works offer the only continuous view of musical style in Venetian opera over two decades. The absence of a development in his musical language has sometimes been overstated, but stability weighs more heavily than change. Since Cavalli was first and foremost an evaluator and inventive translator of the affective moment, even differences of musical mood between operas (the lugubriousness of *Didone*, the rustic playfulness of *Calisto*) can be traced to the poetry.

Most free verse is set as recitative. However inventive, it rarely shows a clear melodic form. It usually consists of a succession of phrases, each ending in a clearly formulated and carefully approached cadence. Another common technique of organization in the early operas is a long, slowly descending bass, over which any amount of melodic thread can be spun (e.g. *Gli amori d'Apollo e di Dafne*, Act 1 scene iii). The categories of gesture in Cavalli's recitative are by and large those of Monteverdi. If there are standard reactions to excited exclamation (rapid note values, word repetition) and to pathos (slow, descending lines, chromatic writing, usually in the bass), the details are always worked out afresh. His rhetoric is also responsive to syntax (questions, paragraphs) and sensitive and resourceful in the face of surprise. A casual madrigalism and symbolism of idea inform many passages (see ex.1).

In the later operas, rapid dialogue accounts for much of the poetry. This is particularly visible in the faster cadence formulae of the recitative. Lively argument is sometimes supported by a chain of 5ths in the harmony (e.g. *Scipione affricano*, Act 3 scene xviii). Nearly all the recitative is 'semplice', accompanied only by continuo. Exceptional moments, rarely more than one per opera, may be underscored by string accompaniment in sustained chords.

In *Le nozze di Teti e di Peleo*, *Didone* and *Gli amori d'Apollo e di Dafne*, arioso passages – that is, recitative verse set lyrically – are infrequent. These passages usually involve either a shift to triple metre or a 'walking' bass in crotchets. From *La virtù de' strali d'Amore* onwards, arioso plays a much larger part and lends greater fluidity to the later operas. Many ariosos are settings of aphoristic final lines or couplets, others are madrigalesque in impulse, still others reflect outbursts, festive or pathetic. The gestural content of arioso is similar to that of aria. Most arioso passages are short

Ex.1 *Gli amori d'Apollo e di Dafne*, Act 3 scene iv

['I wished to give her my tears to drink from the cup of a kiss. Disdainful she quickly fled from me. I followed her, pleading, and she, in order to scorn me and rob my kisses of her mouth's sweetest treasure, changed from a nymph into a laurel.']

Ex.2

Giasone, Act 1 scene ii

De - li - tie e con - ten - ti che l'al - ma be - a - te

Calisto, Act 1 scene vii

Se - re - na-ti o co - re, a quel - le bel - lez - ze

Oristeo Act 1 scene v

Di - vi - no pe - nel - lo l'i - dea quì del bel - lo

Xerse, Act 2 scene i

Spe - ran - ze fer - ma - te, si to - sto fug - gi - te

['Delights and pleasures that make the soul happy'
'Be calm, o heart, to those beauties'
'Divine paintbrush, the idea here of the beautiful . . .
'Cease, o hopes, quickly flee']

and simple, though melismatic writing and text repetition are part of the equipment, and emphasis may be given by an instrumental sinfonia.

Most poetry other than recitative verse in Cavalli's librettos is strophic, and it is this kind of verse on which most pieces that the sources call arias are based. The first three operas have a great quantity of such verse (between 20 and 25 poems). A majority of these poems use the same metres as recitative (lines of seven and 11 syllables); they may have up to nine strophes. They are always set as some sort of musical unit. All of the earliest operas include recitative settings of strophic poems, usually with the melody, but not the bass line, varied between the strophes. Strophic recitative is an old-fashioned procedure, and examples in Cavalli's later operas are rare. It is significant that as early as *Ormindo* such pieces are uttered by gods (Destiny, Fortune).

Most of Cavalli's arias are in triple metre. This is particularly true of the first operas, for example *Gli amori d'Apollo e di Dafne*, which has only three arias in duple time. Brief recitative interruptions are frequent, however; sometimes they prepare the triple-time settings of a gnomic final line or couplet, as in the last strophe of 'Giovanetta che tiene' (*Gli amori d'Apollo e di Dafne*, Act 1 scene i). As with arioso, the other most common feature of aria-writing is the 'walking' bass.

There is less plain strophic poetry in Faustini's librettos than in most others that Cavalli set before or after. By way of compensation they have many groups of lines of distinct poetic metre (four, five, six or eight syllables), which are generally composed in arioso fashion. These librettos also abound in refrains. Cavalli usually set the refrains as large and highly articulated aria forms, complete with ritornello and sometimes with contrasts of musical metre, for example 'D'haver un consorte io son risoluta' (*Calisto*, Act 2 scene xiv). Other examples of dramatically or textually motivated structures larger and more elaborate than the simple aria are the several alternating pairs of strophes in *Egisto*; the prison scene in *Ormindo* Act 3 (also used in *Erismena*: see Rosand 1975); and the double varied strophic setting of *capitoli sdruccioli* at the beginning of Act 3 of *Veremonda l'amazzone di Aragona* ('Né meste più, né più dolenti siano'), whose concluding duet is freely based on both sets of strophes.

Cavalli's aria style, while essentially syllabic, makes use of melismatic flourishes; these are more often than not madrigalesque image portrayals, but their real function is increasingly that of 'bel canto' writing. Aria poems are set one or two lines at a time, with some kind of cadence but not necessarily a rhythmic hiatus at the end of each unit. Phrases tend to be asymmetrical and do not in general correspond to preconceived patterns. The relationship of musical rhythm to poetic metre is highly variable. It is least predictable in settings of *versi sciolti* (lines of seven and 11 syllables), whereas it is almost tediously regular in the six-syllable verse much used by Faustini (see ex.2). A related special case are the five-syllable *sdruccioli* (lines with antepenultimate accent), widely used for rage, terror or invocation in 17th-century opera. The best-known example is Medea's incantation scene 'Dell'antro magico' (*Giasone*, Act 1 scene xv).

The operatic lament has its principal model in Monteverdi's *Arianna*; another model for Cavalli was the intervening lament repertory using stepwise descending ostinatos. Nearly all his operas include at least one lament, almost invariably in triple metre and the minor mode. Some are ostinato pieces, either chromatic ('Piangete, occhi dolenti', *Egisto*, Act 2 scene vi)

Autograph of Cavalli's 'Xerse', Act 2 scene xviii (the beginning of Adelanta's 'Et e pur vero, o core'), first performed at the Teatro SS Giovanni e Paolo, Venice, 1655

Ex.3 *Eritrea*, Act 3 scene v

['The woman always shrieks and screams at her husband, and while she adorns and beautifies herself to be coveted, she wants him to remain chaste and alone to quiet the children's crying.']

or diatonic ('Al carro trionfale', *Statira principessa di Persia*, Act 3 scene iv). Several have recitative interruptions ('Con infocati teli', *Doriclea*, Act 2 scene ii) or else dissolve into recitative ('Rivolgo altrove il piede', *Didone*, Act 2 scene ii). Pathetic chromaticism expressed either harmonically or melodically, rhythmically eccentric outbursts of passion and a sense of resignation conveyed by regularly cadencing phrases and descending lines are the common coin of his laments. Simple use of ostinato technique apart from the lament, such as in 'Vieni, vieni in questo seno' (*Rosinda*, Act 3 scene vi), is rare.

Cavalli responded less consistently to comedy than to pathos. Arias by comic characters may make their point by assertive repetition, as in 'Pazze voi che sdegnate' (*Egisto*, Act 1 scene vi), or, as in 'Che città' (*Ormindo*, Act 1 scene iii), by jagged rhythms taken over in the ritornello. Trivial melodies of regular phrase length, and jaunty use of the 'walking' bass (e.g. 'O sagace chi sa', *Ormindo*, Act 2 scene vi), are also associated with humorous contexts. Occasionally he used intentionally bizarre gestures, as in the image-motivated cross-rhythms of 'Sempre garisce e grida' (*Eritrea*, Act 3 scene v: see ex.3).

'Sempre garisce e grida' is representative of a formal expansion and increase in range of gesture that mark Cavalli's aria style from the early 1650s. Arias in duple metre (though still a minority) are more numerous than before, and they use means other than the 'walking' bass. In line with more modern taste are the motto openings of 'Bel sembiante' (*Rosinda*, Act 3 scene xi) and particularly 'Bella fede, over sei gita' (*Veremonda*, Act 1 scene xi). The fleet vocality of 'La bellezza è un don fugace' (*Xerse*, Act 2 scene ix) is indicative of the increase in passage-work; less ostentatious but equally characteristic is the aria in triple metre 'Zeffiretti placidetti' from *Artemisia* (Act 1 scene xiii). *Artemisia* also includes the only example in Cavalli of an 'aria in eco' ('Fortunato, chi piegato', Act 2 scene vi), a double reducing echo added (after the fact) to phrase endings.

The librettos of Cavalli's later operas contain large numbers of two-strophe aria poems (*Scipione affricano*, for example, has 35), and they mostly fall into a few metrical patterns. They are usually set as *ABB′* forms or as *ABA* (elementary da capo arias). In many of his arias from the last three dramas by Minato the musical rhythm rests directly on that of the poetry. At the same time most of them are less obviously dance-like than those of some younger composers.

The amount of duet writing varies greatly from opera to opera, according to the structure of the libretto; it is concentrated in the dramas by Faustini. Most duets are in triple metre and in a lightly imitative style. A standard procedure is to spin out the imitations over a bass line that moves predominantly in dotted semibreves, as in 'Noi tempriamo' or 'Nel gran regno' from *Egisto* (Act 1, scenes ii and viii respectively).

Choral writing in most operas is brief and incidental, for instance the shout of 'Viva' that greets Pompeo in Act 2 scene vi of *Pompeo magno*. For obvious reasons of circumstance it is very much more extensive in *Ercole amante*, which includes 'Dall'occaso' (Act 5), a genuine four-part continuo madrigal. The choruses of the earliest operas, such as 'Al cinghiale' in *Didone* (Act 3 scene ii), are probably best seen in the light of an earlier concertato tradition.

The principal function of Cavalli's orchestra is to provide ritornellos before and/or after the strophes of arias. The music of the ritornello is nearly always related to that of the aria. Ritornellos may have one, two or three phrases; the commonest type has two of roughly equal length, each based on a point of imitation and often using sequence. In nearly all the operas (*Orimonte* is an exception) some arias have more elaborate accompaniment, either phrase by phrase in antiphonal fashion, over the voice throughout (particularly in laments and pieces of related mood), or some combination of the two.

Sinfonias also form part of all the operas. Those at the beginnings of operas or acts most commonly are in duple metre with a *grave* minim movement, though some have more than one movement and use triple metre as well. More descriptive orchestral music, usually of an extremely simple and rhythmic character, is provided by the 'sinfonia navale' of *Didone*, the 'sinfonia in battaglia' of *La virtù de' strali d'Amore* (one of several battle pieces in Cavalli's operas), the 'infernale' of *Ercole amante* and, much more striking, the 'ballo de' tori' of *Veremonda*. There are also elements of *stile concitato* in several works. Apart from an occasional corrente (*Le nozze di Teti e di Peleo, Gli amori d'Apollo e di Dafne*, *La virtù de' strali d'Amore*) and a few balli, the dance music called for by the librettos is either notated for continuo alone or missing altogether from the scores. The orchestra is laid out in five, less often four, parts in nearly all full fair-copy scores, but the musical skeleton consists of two violins and bass, the combination found in all Cavalli's autographs. Wind instruments may have been used in the very first operas and *Ercole amante*; otherwise his orchestra certainly consisted of (solo) strings and continuo (lutes, theorbos, harpsichords), though one piece in *Elena* seems to call for trumpets in A.

See also CALISTO; DIDONE; EGISTO (ii); ERCOLE AMANTE; ERISMENA; GIASONE; NOZZE DI TETI E DI PELEO, LE; ORISTEO; ORMINDO; POMPEO MAGNO; SCIPIONE AFFRICANO; and XERSE (i).

Dates are generally those of the printed librettos; arias in MS are indicative rather than exhaustive; performed in Venice unless otherwise stated

title	*genre, acts*	*libretto*	*performance*	*sources, remarks*
Le nozze di Teti e di Peleo	opera scenica/festa teatrale, prol., 3	O. Persiani	S Cassiano, 24 Jan 1639	*I-Vnm*
Gli amori d'Apollo e di Dafne	opera, prol., 3	G. F. Busenello	S Cassiano, 1640	*Vnm* (*R*1978: IOB, i), lib. first published 1656 in Busenello's works
Didone	opera, prol., 3	Busenello	S Cassiano, 1641	*Vnm*, lib. first published 1656 in Busenello's works
Amore innamorato	favola, prol., 3	plot by G. F. Loredan, poetry P. Michiel, rev. G. B. Fusconi	S Moisè, 1 Jan 1642	music lost
La virtù de' strali d'Amore	tragicomica musicale, prol., 3	G. Faustini	S Cassiano, 1642	*Vnm*
Egisto	favola dramatica musicale, prol., 3	Faustini	S Cassiano, 1643	*A-Wn*, *I-Vnm*; ed. R. Leppard (London, 1977)
Ormindo	favola regia per musica, prol., 3	Faustini	S Cassiano, 1644	*Vnm*; ed. R. Leppard (London, 1969)
Doriclea	dramma musicale, prol., 3	Faustini	S Cassiano, 1645	*Vnm*
Titone	drama per musica, prol., 3	Faustini	S Cassiano, 1645	music lost, probably by Cavalli
Giasone	drama musicale, prol., 3	G. A. Cicognini, after Apollonius: *Argonautica*	S Cassiano, 5 Jan 1648 [=1649]	*A-Wn*, *B-Bc* (2 modern copies), *GB-Ouf*, *I-Fn*, *MOe*, *Nc*, *Rvat* Chigi, *Sc*, *Vnm*, *P-La*; part ed. in PÄMw, xi (1883)
Euripo	drama per musica, prol., 3	Faustini	? S Moisè, 1649	music lost, possibly not by Cavalli
Orimonte	drama per musica, prol., 3	Faustini	S Cassiano, 20 Feb 1650	*Vnm*
Oristeo	drama per musica, prol., 3	Faustini	S Apollinare, 1651	*Vnm* (*R*1982: IOB, lxii)
Rosinda	drama per musica, prol., 3	Faustini	S Apollinare, 1651	*Vnm*

title	genre, acts	libretto	performance	sources, remarks
Calisto	drama per musica, prol., 3	Faustini, after Ovid: *Metamorphoses*	S Apollinare, 28 Nov 1651	*Vnm*; ed. R. Leppard (London, 1975)
Eritrea	drama, prol., 3	Faustini	S Apollinare, 17 Jan 1652	
Veremonda, l'amazzone di Aragona	drama, prol., 3	rev. by L. Zorzisto [G. Strozzi] of G. A. Cicognini: *Celio* (1646, Florence)	Naples, Palazzo Reale, 21 Dec 1652; Venice, SS Giovanni e Paolo, 28 Jan 1652 [=1653]	*Vnm*
Orione	dramma, prol., 3	F. Melosio	Milan, June 1653	*Vnm*, private collection R. Leppard
Ciro	drama per musica, prol., 3	G. C. Sorrentino, rev. ?A. Aureli	orig. perf. Naples with music by Francesco Provenzale; Cavalli composed changes for perf. at Venice, SS Giovanni e Paolo, 30 Jan 1653 [=1654]	*MOe*, *Vnm* (1665 version with addl music by Mattioli)
Xerse	drama per musica, prol., 3	N. Minato	SS Giovanni e Paolo, 12 Jan 1654 [=1655]	*F-Pn*, *I-Rvat* Chigi, *Vnm*
Statira principessa di Persia	drama per musica, prol., 3	Busenello	SS Giovanni e Paolo, 18 Jan 1655 [?=1656]	*Mc*, *Vnm*, arias *Nc*
Erismena	drama per musica, prol., 3	A. Aureli	S Apollinare, 30 Dec 1655	*Vnm* (2 versions); score in T. Bever's private collection (according to Burney), score with Eng. text in J. S. Cox's private collection (White 1966)
Artemisia	drama per musica, prol., 3	Minato	SS Giovanni e Paolo, 10 Jan 1656 [=1657]	*Vnm*
Hipermestra	festa teatrale, prol., 3	G. A. Moniglia	Florence, Immobili, 12 June 1658	*Vnm*; composed 1654
Antioco	drama per musica, prol., 3	Minato	S Cassiano, 25 Jan 1658 [=1659]	music lost
Elena	drama per musica, prol., 3	Faustini, completed Minato	S Cassiano, ded. 26 Dec 1659	*Vnm*
Ercole amante	opera, prol., 5	F. Buti, after Ovid: *Metamorphoses*	Paris, Tuileries, 7 Feb 1662	*Vnm*
Scipione affricano	drama per musica, prol., 3	Minato	SS Giovanni e Paolo, 9 Feb 1664	*Rvat* Chigi, *Sc*, *Vnm* (*R*1978: IOB, v), *P-La* (Act 3)
Mutio Scevola	drama per musica, prol., 3	Minato	S Salvatore, 26 Jan 1665	*I-Vnm*
Pompeo magno	drama per musica, prol., 3	Minato	S Salvatore, 20 Feb 1666	*D-AN*, *I-Vnm*
Eliogabalo	dramma per musica, 3	anon., completed Aureli	composed for SS Giovanni e Paolo, 1668, but not perf.	*Vnm*
Coriolano	dramma, 3	C. Ivanovich	Piacenza, Ducale, 27 May 1669	music lost
Massenzio	drama per musica, 3	G. F. Bussani	composed for S Salvatore, 1673, but not perf.	music lost
		doubtful: attrib. Cavalli by Ivanovich unless otherwise stated; music lost		
Narciso et Ecco immortalati	opera drammatica, prol., 3	Persiani	SS Giovanni e Paolo, 30 Jan 1642	by M. Marazzoli and F. Vitali (see *ES*, ix, 1725)
Deidamia	poema drammatica/opera musicale, prol., 3	S. Herrico	Novissimo, 5 Jan 1644	
Il Romolo e 'l Remo	dramma, prol., 3	G. Strozzi	SS Giovanni e Paolo, 5 Feb 1645	by ? B. Strozzi
La prosperità infelice di Giulio Cesare dittatore	opera musicale, prol., 5	Busenello	intended for SS Giovanni e Paolo but possibly not perf.	lib. pubd 1656 in Busenello's works
Torilda	dramma, prol., 3	P. P. Bissari	SS Giovanni e Paolo, 1648 [?1649]	
Bradamante	dramma per musica, prol., 3	Bissari	SS Giovanni e Paolo, 1650	
Armidoro	dramma per musica, prol., 3	B. Castoreo	S Cassiano, 20 Jan 1651	attrib. Cavalli by Bonlini (1730), attrib. G. Sartorio by Ivanovich
Helena rapita da Theseo	dramma musicale, prol., 3	?G. Badoaro	SS Giovanni e Paolo, 1653	
La pazzia in trono, overo Caligola delirante	opera di stile recitativo, prol., 3	D. Gisberti	S Apollinare, 1660	lib. pubd 1675 in Gisberti: *Talia*, spoken drama with a little music, attrib. Cavalli by A. Groppo (1745)

AllacciD; *BurneyH*; *DBI* ('Caletti, Pietro Francesco, detto Cavalli'; L. Bianconi); *ES* (N. Pirrotta)
C. Ivanovich: *Minerva al tavolino* (Venice, 1681, 2/1688)
G. C. Bonlini: *Le glorie della poesia e della musica* (Venice, 1730)
A. Groppo: *Catalogo di tutti i drammi per musica recitati ne' teatri di Venezia dall'anno 1637 ... sin all'anno presente 1745* (Venice, 1745)
A. W. Ambros: 'Francesco Cavalli', *NZM*, lxv (1869), 313, 321
L. N. Galvani [pseud. of G. Salvioli]: *I teatri musicali di Venezia nel secolo XVII (1637–1700): memorie storiche e bibliografiche* (Milan, 1879)
A. Ademollo: *I primi fasti della musica italiana a Parigi (1645–1662)* (Milan, 1884)
——: *I primi fasti del Teatro di Via della Pergola in Firenze (1657–1661)* (Milan, 1885)
T. Wiel: *I codici musicali contariniani del secolo XVII nella R. Biblioteca di San Marco in Venezia* (Venice, 1888)
H. Kretzschmar: 'Die venetianische Oper und die Werke Cavallis und Cestis', *VMw*, viii (1892), 1–76
H. Goldschmidt: 'Cavalli als dramatischer Komponist', *MMg*, xxv (1893), 45–8, 53–8, 61–111
——: *Studien zur Geschichte der italienischen Oper im 17. Jahrhundert*, i (Leipzig, 1901)
A. Heuss: 'Die venetianischen Opern-Sinfonien', *SIMG*, iv (1902–3), 404–77
R. Rolland: 'L'opéra populaire à Venise: Francesco Cavalli', *Mercure musical*, ii/1 (1906), 60–70, 151–60
H. Kretzschmar: 'Beiträge zur Geschichte der venetianischen Oper', *JbMP 1907*, 71–81
H. Prunières: *L'opéra italien en France avant Lulli* (Paris, 1913)
E. Wellesz: 'Cavalli und der Stil der venetianischen Oper von 1640–1660', *SMw*, i (1913), 1–103
T. Wiel: 'Francesco Cavalli (1602–1676) e la sua musica scenica', *Nuovo archivio veneto*, 3rd ser., xviii (1914), 106–50; partial Eng. trans., *MA*, iv (1912–13), 1–19
H. Prunières: 'Notes sur une partition faussement attribuée à Cavalli: "L'Eritrea" (1686), *RMI*, xxvii (1920), 267–73
——: *Cavalli et l'opéra vénitien au XVIIe siècle* (Paris, 1931)
——: 'Les opéras de Francesco Cavalli', *ReM*, nos.111–12 (1931), 1–16, 125–47
H. C. Wolff: *Die venezianische Oper in der zweiten Hälfte des 17. Jahrhunderts* (Berlin, 1937, 2/1975)
U. Rolandi: 'Le opere teatrali di Francesco Cavalli', *La scuola veneziana (secoli XVI–XVIII): note e documenti*, Chigiana, iii (1941), 15–18
B. Hjelmborg: 'Une partition de Cavalli: quelques remarques complémentaires aux recherches cavalliennes', *AcM*, xvi–xvii (1944–5), 39–54
'Cavalli Opera Restored', *Musical Courier*, clxvi (1952), 5
A. A. Abert: *Claudio Monteverdi und das musikalische Drama* (Lippstadt, 1954)
S. T. Worsthorne: *Venetian Opera in the Seventeenth Century* (Oxford, 1954)
W. Osthoff: 'Neue Beobachtungen zu Quellen und Geschichte von Monteverdis "Incoronazione di Poppea"', *Mf*, xi (1958), 129–38
——: 'Antonio Cestis "Alessandro vincitor di se stesso"', *SMw*, xxiv (1960), 13–
H. S. Powers: '*Il Serse trasformato*', *MQ*, xlvii (1961), 481–92; xlviii (1962), 73–92
B. Hjelmborg: 'Aspects of the Aria in the Early Operas of Francesco Cavalli', *Natalicia musicologica Knud Jeppesen* (Copenhagen, 1962), 173–98
W. Osthoff: 'Maske und Musik: die Gestaltwerdung der Opera in Venedig', *Castrum peregrini*, lxv (1964), 10–49; It. trans., *NRMI*, i (1967), 16–44
B. Hjelmborg: 'Om den venezianske arie indtil 1650', *DAM*, iv (1964–5), 91–112
D. Arnold: 'Francesco Cavalli: some Recently Discovered Documents', *ML*, xlvi (1965), 50–55
N. Pirrotta: 'Il caval zoppo e il vetturino: cronache di Parnaso 1642', *CHM*, iv (1966), 215–26
E. W. White: 'English Opera Research', *Theatre Notebook*, xxi (1966), 32–7 [incl. repr. of page from English *Erismena* MS]
R. Leppard: 'Cavalli's Operas', *PRMA*, xciii (1966–7), 67–76
G. F. Crain: 'Francesco Cavalli and the Venetian Opera', *Opera*, xviii (1967), 446–51
N. Pirrotta: 'Early Opera and Aria', *New Looks at Italian Opera: Essays in Honor of Donald J. Grout* (Ithaca, NY, 1968), 39–107; repr., rev., in N. Pirrotta and E. Povoledo: *Music and Theatre from Poliziano to Monteverdi* (Cambridge, 1982), 237–80
H. S. Powers: '*L'Erismena travestita*', *Studies in Music History: Essays for Oliver Strunk* (Princeton, 1968), 259–324
D. Swale: 'Cavalli: the "Erismena" of 1655', *MMA*, iii (1968), 258–85
J. Noble: 'Cavalli's "Ormindo"', *MT*, cx (1969), 830–32 [review of the performing edn. by Raymond Leppard and a recording]
N. Pirrotta: 'Early Venetian Libretti at Los Angeles', *Essays in Musicology in Honor of Dragan Plamenac* (Pittsburgh, 1969), 233–43
I. Bartels: 'Zum Problem des Instrumentalstückes in der frühvenezianischen Oper', *GfMKB, Bonn 1970*, 336–8
M. N. Clinkscale: *Pier Francesco Cavalli's 'Xerse'* (diss., U. of Minnesota, 1970)
A. Hicks: 'Cavalli and "La Calisto"', *MT*, cxi (1970), 486–9
E. Rosand: *Aria in the Early Operas of Francesco Cavalli* (diss., New York U., 1971)
G. Morelli and T. R. Walker: 'Tre controversie intorno al San Cassiano', *Venezia e il melodramma nel seicento: Venice 1972*, 97–120
H. S. Powers: 'Il "Mutio" tramutato, i: Sources and Libretto', ibid, 227–58
E. Rosand: 'Aria as Drama in the Early Operas of Francesco Cavalli', ibid, 75–96
T. Walker: 'Gli errori di "Minerva al tavolino": osservazioni sulla cronologia delle prime opere veneziane', ibid, 7–20
J. Glover: 'Cavalli and "Rosinda"', *MT*, cxiv (1973), 133–5
L. Bianconi and T. Walker: 'Dalla *Finta pazza* alla *Veremonda*: storie di Febiarmonici', *RIM*, x (1975), 379–454
J. A. Glover: *The Teatro Sant'Appollinare and the Development of Seventeenth-Century Venetian Opera* (diss., U. of Oxford, 1975)
E. Rosand: '"Ormindo travestito" in *Erismena*', *JAMS*, xxviii (1975), 268–91
J. Glover: 'Aria and Closed Form in the Operas of Francesco Cavalli', *Consort*, xxxii (1976), 167–75
E. Rosand: 'Comic Contrast and Dramatic Continuity: Observations on the Form and Function of Aria in the Operas of Francesco Cavalli', *MR*, xxxvii (1976), 92–105
R. Donington: 'Cavalli in the Opera House', *MT*, cxix (1978), 327–9
J. Glover: *Cavalli* (London, 1978)
G. Yans: 'Poésie et musique: l' "Hipermestra" de Moniglia-Cavalli', *Quadrivium*, (1978), 129–83
E. Rosand: 'Francesco Cavalli in Modern Edition', *CMc*, no.27 (1979), 73–83
E. R. Rutschman: 'Minato and the Venetian Opera Libretto', *CMc*, no.27 (1979), 84–91
——: *The Minato-Cavalli Operas: the Search for Structure in Libretto and Solo Scene* (diss., U. of Washington, 1979)
P. G. Jeffery: *The Autograph Manuscripts of Francesco Cavalli* (diss., Princeton U., 1980)
G. Morelli: *Scompiglio e lamento (simmetrie dell'incostanza e incostanza delle simmetrie): L'Egisto di Faustini e Cavalli (1643)* (Venice, 1982)
E. Rosand: *Opera in Seventeenth-Century Venice: the Creation of a Genre* (Berkeley and Los Angeles, 1991)
B. L. Glixon and J. E. Glixon: 'Marco Faustini and Venetian Opera Production in the 1650s: Recent Archival Discoveries', *JM*, x (1992), 48–73

THOMAS WALKER

Cavana, Giovanni Battista (*b* Mantua, *fl* 1684–1732). Italian bass. He was the most important *buffo* singer of his time, possessing a masterly technique and an outstanding aptitude for expressive acting without theatricality. 18 *buffo* scenes composed for him in Naples between 1696 and 1702 by Alessandro Scarlatti, Aldrovandini, Giovanni Bononcini and others have survived in a Dresden manuscript. From 1706 he was active at the Teatro S Cassiano, Venice, where he formed a close professional partnership with Santa Marchesini and collaborated with Pariati, Francesco Gasparini, Lotti and Albinoni in launching the first independent intermezzos. The production of this repertory at the Teatro S Cassiano was intimately connected with the presence of Cavana in Venice and came to an end only one season after his departure for Naples with Marchesini in spring 1709. He was famous throughout Italy, praised by the poet P. A. Rolli, and often highly paid for his performances. At the end of his career he was elected to the Accademia dei Geniali of Padua.

*

P. Rolli: *De' poetici componimenti* (Venice, 1761)
C. E. Troy: *The Comic Intermezzo* (Ann Arbor, 1979)
F. Piperno: 'Appunti sulla configurazione sociale e professionale delle "parti buffe"', *Antonio Vivaldi: teatro musicale, cultura e società: Venice 1981*, 483–97
——: 'Buffe e buffi', *RIM*, xviii (1982), 240–84
R. Strohm: 'P. Pariati librettista comico', in G. Gronda: *La carriera di un librettista* (Bologna, 1990) FRANCO PIPERNO

Cavata (It.: 'excavated'). (1) In the 17th and early 18th centuries a setting in aria style ('arioso') of the last line or couplet of a recitative text – i.e. an aria 'excavated' from recitative. The words normally sum up the sentiment of the passage, and the setting underlines their significance. This kind of cavata, which is described by Salvadori, Neumeister, Walther and Quadrio, is found in most forms of Baroque vocal music, including opera, though the most characteristic examples occur in Italian chamber cantatas, *c*1670–1720. It may take one of a variety of forms (e.g. *AA′*, *AABB*), normally exhibits a contrapuntal texture between voice and basso continuo, and is often the tonal complement of the preceding recitative. The earliest cavata is the six-bar phrase 'La Ragion perde dov'il Senso abbonda' in Domenico Mazzocchi's opera *La catena d'Adone* (1626, Rome), while some of the latest appear in the church cantatas of Bach (e.g. BWV76 and 117).

(2) In the first half of the 18th century a substantial and carefully composed aria, with instrumental accompaniment, set to blank or rhymed verse but not in da capo form. This definition, derived from Mattheson, could apply to many cavatas of the standard type (1), but it also seems to refer to the kind of non-da capo aria, increasingly common in 18th-century opera, that came to be known as the CAVATINA. By 1751 and 1760 Traetta could use the words 'cavata' and 'cavatina' apparently without distinction.

*

G. G. Salvadori: *Poetica toscana all'uso* (Naples, 1691), 74–5
E. Neumeister: *Die allerneueste Art, zur reinen und galanten Poesie zu erlangen* (Hamburg, 1706), 228
J. Mattheson: *Das neu-eröffnete Orchestre* (Hamburg, 1713), 183
J. G. Walther: *Musicalisches Lexicon* (Leipzig, 1732), 150
J. Mattheson: *Der vollkommene Capellmeister* (Hamburg, 1739), 213
F. S. Quadrio: *Della storia e della ragione d'ogni poesia*, ii (Milan, 1741), 335
C. G. Krause: *Von der musikalischen Poesie: Mit einem Register vermehrt* (Berlin, 1753), 128–9
N. Pirrotta: 'Falsirena e la più antica delle cavatine', *CHM*, ii (1957), 355–66, Eng. trans. in *Music and Culture in Italy from the Middle Ages to the Baroque* (1984), 335–42, 464
W. Osthoff: 'Mozarts Cavatinen und ihre Tradition', *Helmuth Osthoff zu seinem siebzigsten Geburtstag* (Tutzing, 1969), 139–77
P. Fabbri: 'Recitativo e cavate', *SOI*, vi (1988), 180–85
C. Timms: 'The Cavata at the time of Vivaldi', *Nuovi studi vivaldiani: edizione e cronologia critica delle opere* (Florence, 1988), i, 451–77 COLIN TIMMS

Cavatina (It.; Fr. *cavatine*; Ger. *Kavatine*). In 18th-century opera the term, the diminutive of CAVATA, signifies a short ARIA, without da capo; it may occur as an independent piece or as an interpolation in a recitative. Many such arias, though not necessarily described as cavatinas, occur in the operas of Handel, Keiser and their contemporaries. Graun's *Montezuma* (1755) has an unusually large number of cavatinas, apparently at the prompting of Frederick the Great, who wrote the original libretto. Mozart used the term three times in *Le nozze di Figaro* (1786), for Figaro's 'Se vuol ballare', the Countess's 'Porgi amor' and Barbarina's 'L'ho perduta'. The tradition was maintained in the 19th century by Rossini, as in 'Ah! che scordar non so' in *Tancredi* (1813), Weber in 'Und ob die Wolke' in *Der Freischütz* (1821) and 'Glöcklein im Thale' in *Euryanthe* (1823), and by French composers, e.g. 'Salut! demeure chaste et pure' in Gounod's *Faust* (1859) and the Duke's 'Comme un rayon charmant' in Bizet's *La jolie fille de Perth* (1867). While the French and German terms retained their meaning, by 1820 the Italian one was regularly applied to a principal singer's opening aria, whether in one movement or two; but it could also serve for an elaborate aria demanding considerable virtuosity, e.g. Rosina's 'Una voce poco fa' in Rossini's *Il barbiere di Siviglia* (1816) or Lady Macbeth's 'Vieni! t'affretta' in Verdi's *Macbeth* (1847, rev. 1865). Modern writers frequently employ it to describe the slow first movement (more often called 'cantabile') of a double aria; this has no basis in 19th-century usage.

For bibliography *see* ARIA and CAVATA.

Caverne, La ('The Cavern'). *Drame lyrique* in three acts by JEAN-FRANÇOIS LE SUEUR to a libretto by Palat (known as P. Dercy) after Alain-René Le Sage's novel *Gil Blas de Santillane* (book 1, chapters 4–12); Paris, Opéra-Comique (Théâtre Feydeau), 16 February 1793.

Gil Blas (tenor), imprisoned by brigands in an underground cave, escapes with a noble Spanish lady, Séraphine (soprano). Her husband Don Alphonse (*haute-contre*) comes to save her from the hands of the brigand chief Rolando (bass), who turns out at the end to be the heroine's own brother. The violent action (shots are fired on stage at one point) arises from the brigand story that was very fashionable in France about 1785 (Schiller's *Die Räuber* had just been translated into French). The work also celebrates married love, another subject frequently found in operas at the end of the 18th century and the beginning of the 19th, the masterpiece being Beethoven's *Fidelio*. *La caverne* embodies the typical dramatic pattern of the type that has sometimes been called 'rescue opera'.

The striking feature of this opera is its novelty at the strictly formal level: it shows how the distinctions between separate dramatic genres were beginning to crumble during the last years of the 18th century. Grand tragic scenes are presented in a new way in *La caverne*. In the opening of the second act, in which Séraphine protests her distress, a long obbligato recitative is followed by an aria in two parts, an Andante grazioso in the major and an Allegro agitato in the minor. This division into two sections, slow and fast, widely used in Italy in the 1780s (the so-called rondò), was new in French opera at the time and would occur again, as early as 1791, in Cherubini's *Lodoïska*; subsequently it became a major development in Romantic opera.

Side by side with these highly dramatic scenes, however, are little *ariettes*, sometimes quite *risqué*, particularly those sung by Léonarde (soprano), the brigands' old serving woman. Like the use of spoken dialogue instead of recitative, forbidden at the Théâtre Feydeau, these *ariettes* derive from the *opéra comique* tradition. Also noteworthy is the remarkable

Title-page of the full score of Le Sueur's 'La caverne' (Paris: J.-H. Naderman, 1793)

prominence given to the choruses (the brigands' chorus employs three different types of male voices), and the development of the finales, using a double chorus. In *La caverne*, Le Sueur's melodies seldom flow smoothly; rugged and expressive, his writing contains jarring harmonies fully in accord with the sombre nature of the subject. This opera, unlike anything that had existed before, was a triumphant success at the time of the Revolution. Translated into several languages, it was still being performed in a number of foreign theatres at the beginning of the 19th century. JEAN MONGRÉDIEN

Cavos, Catterino Al'bertovich (*b* Venice, 30 Oct 1775; *d* St Petersburg, 28 April/10 May 1840). Russian composer and conductor of Italian birth. The son of the ballet-master at the Teatro La Fenice and a pupil of Francesco Bianchi, he went to Russia in 1799 to conduct the superannuated Italian opera troupe, then under the direction of a fellow Venetian, Ferdinando Antonolini. He was almost immediately put to work composing music to accompany French vaudevilles. With the bureaucratic reorganization of the Imperial Theatres in 1803, Cavos was officially named director of the Italian troupe. The latter folded the next year, but by then he had scored a signal success with some additional numbers he composed for Ferdinand Kauer's immensely popular Singspiel *Das Donauweibchen* in Nikolay Krasnopol'sky's translation, *Dneprovskaya rusalka* ('The Dnepr Water-Nymph'). He was offered a contract to replace Stepan Davïdov as conductor of the Russian Opera, a post he held until his death. At the same time he became the chief musical pedagogue at the St Petersburg theatre school, training the cadres of singers and conductors who staffed the city's stages. He thus became one of that redoubtable pleiad of foreigners – along with the ballet-master Charles Didelot (with whom he collaborated) and the designer Pietro Gonzaga – who created the modern Russian musical theatre. He was a consummate routinier in all that pertained to the musical stage, its art and its business. His main literary collaborator was his employer, Prince Alexander Shakhovskoy (1777–1846), the first Intendant of the Imperial Theatres.

The libretto of Cavos's first Russian opera, *Knyaz' nevidimka* ('The Invisible Prince', 1805), was, as was typical at the time, an adaptation by a staff theatrical translator of a French original. By contrast, *Il'ya bogatïr'* ('Ilya the Hero', 1806/7) continued the line of Russian magic and romantic operas on subjects drawn from national legends and antiquities – a line that had originated with Catherine the Great's librettos of the 1780s and extended through *Ruslan and Lyudmila* to *Prince Igor*. The book, by the great fabulist Ivan Krïlov, is based on episodes from the bardic songs or epics known as *bïlinï*, the collection and publication of which, spurred by the nationalistic upsurge which followed the early Napoleonic wars, marked the beginning of the Romantic movement in Russia. *Dobrïnya Nikitich* (1818), written in collaboration with Antonolini, continued the folk-legendary line.

Cavos's early collaborations with Shakhovskoy resulted in one-act comic operas (or 'opera-vaudevilles' as they were called in Russia), among which *Kazak stikhotvorets* ('The Cossack Poet'), about Semyon Klimovsky, a valorous Ukrainian soldier-poet of the 18th century, is noteworthy. Like most theatrical spectacles on the eve of the Patriotic War of 1812, it was a vehicle for national sentiment. Cavos accordingly based several numbers on Ukrainian folksongs, also citing popular soldiers' tunes and marches.

The peak of post-Napoleonic patriotic fervour was reached with *Ivan Susanin* (1815), a celebration of civic heroism concerning the semi-legendary peasant who in 1612 sacrificed his life to protect Mikhail Romanov, sire of the last Russian dynasty, from Polish invaders. In Shakhovskoy's treatment the title character, instead of dying his historical death, is spared by the timely intervention of Russian troops. Cavos's score is a veritable chip off Cherubini's famous rescue opera *Les deux journées* (known in Russia as *Vodovoz*, from its subtitle, *Le porteur d'eau*). His most grandly executed opera (and his most popular one, remaining in the repertory until 1854), it contains a number of elaborate choruses on themes drawn from folksongs. Although, curiously, the title character has no solo number, he is represented by a leitmotif of recognizable popular-military cast.

Cavos's operas include several – for example *Vavilonskiye razvalinï* ('Babylonian Ruins', 1818) and *Zhar-ptitsa* ('The Firebird', 1822, with Antonolini) – that reflect the nascent vogue for 'oriental' (i.e. Middle Eastern) motifs that followed on Russia's military expansion into the Caucasus and Central Asia. As conductor, he was responsible for the Russian premières of many important European operas, including *Der Freischütz*. He also supervised and conducted the epochal first production of Glinka's *A Life for the Tsar* (1836), based, like his own opera of 1815, on the legend of Ivan Susanin.

all first performed in St Petersburg; MSS mainly in RU-SPtob

Dneprovskaya rusalka [The Dnepr Water-Nymph] (magical-comical op, 3, N. Kras'nopolsky), Bol'shoy, 5/17 May 1804;

music by F. Kauer from Das Donauweibchen, with addl numbers by Cavos

Knyaz' nevidimka, ili Licharda-volshebnik [The Invisible Prince, or Richard the Magician] (magical-comical op, 4, Y. Lifanov, after the *opéra comique* Le prince invisible, ou Arlequin Prothée by M. Hapdé), Bol'shoy, 5/17 May 1805

Lyubovnaya pochta [The Lovers' Post] (comic op, 1, A. Shakhovskoy), Bol'shoy, 21 Jan/3 Feb 1806

Beglets ot svoyey nevestï [He Deserted his Bride] (comic op, 1, Shakhovskoy), Bol'shoy, 18/30 April 1806

Il'ya bogatïr' [Ilya the Hero] (grand magical-comical op, 4, I. Krïlov), Bol'shoy, 31 Dec 1806/12 Jan 1807

Tri brata gorbunï [The Three Hunchbacked Brothers] (comic op, 1, A. Luknitsky, after Cavos: Les trois bossus), Bol'shoy, 15/27 April 1808

Kazak stikhotvorets [The Cossack Poet] (anecdotal opera-vaudeville, 1, Shakhovskoy), Winter Palace, 15/27 May 1812

Mnimïy nevidimka, ili Sumatokha v traktivz [The Imaginary Invisible Man, or Commotion in a Tavern] (comic op, 1, Scheller, from the Ger.), German Theatre, 26 May/7 June 1813

Soliman vtoroy, ili Tri sultanshi [Suleiman II, or The Three Sultanesses] (comic op, 1, A. Scheller, from the Fr.), German Theatre, 26 May/7 June 1813

Otkupshchik Brazhkin, ili Prodazha sela [Brazhkin the Tax-Farmer, or The Village is Sold] (comic op, 1, Shakhovskoy), Malïy, 17 Feb/1 March 1815

Ivan Susanin (2, Shakhovskoy), Malïy, 19/31 October 1815

Vavilonskiye razvalinï, ili Torzhestvo i padeniye Giafara Barmesida [Babylonian Ruins, or The Triumph and Fall of Giafar Barmecides] (historical op, 3, from the Fr.), Bol'shoy, 6/18 Nov 1818

Dobrïnya Nikitich, ili Strashnïy zamok [Dobrïnya Nikitich, or The Haunted Castle] (magic op, 3), Bol'shoy, 25 Nov/7 Dec 1818, with F. Antonolini

Volshebnïy baraban, ili Blagodetel'nïy dervish [The Magic Drum, or The Beneficent Dervish] (magical-comical op, 3, E. Schikaneder, trans. Kunyayev), Pashkov's Theatre, 31 Oct/12 Nov 1819, with Antonolini and Schneider

Novaya sumatokha, ili Zhenikhi chuzhikh nevest [A New Commotion, or The Grooms Take the Wrong Brides] (comic op, 1, Shakhovskoy), Bol'shoy, 22 Sept/4 Oct 1820, partly after Rossini

Zhar-ptitsa, ili Priklyucheniya Lesvila-Tsarevicha [The Firebird, or The Adventures of Tsarevich Lesvil] (magic op, 3, M. Lebedev, after S. Andreyev), Bol'shoy, 6/18 Nov 1822, with Antonolini

Svetlana, ili Sto let v odin den' [Svetlana, or A Hundred Years in One Day] (2, A. Veshnyakov, after V. A. Zhukovsky), Bol'shoy, 29 Dec 1822/10 Jan 1823, music adapted from C. S. Catel with addl numbers by Cavos

Geniy Itrubiyel', ili Tïsyacha let v dvukh dnyakh Vizirya Garuna [The Genie Itrubiel, or The Vizier Harun's Thousand Years in Two Days] (3, R. Zotov), 5/17 Nov 1823, with Antonolini; incl. music by Méhul and Isouard

P'yemontskiye gorï, ili Vzorvaniye chortova mosta [The Mountains of Piedmont, or The Devil's Bridge is Blown up] (3, Scheller, from the Fr.), Bol'shoy, 16/28 Oct 1825, with I. Lengard

One-act comic ops, in Fr.: L'alchimiste; L'intrigue dans les ruines; Le mariage d'Aubigny; Les trois bossus

*

R. Zotov: 'Biografiya kapel'meystera Kavosa', *Repertuar russkogo i Panteon vsekh yevropeyskikh teatrov*, xii (1840), no.10

G. Blokh: 'K. A. Kavos', *Yezhegodnik imperatorskikh teatrov*, ii (1896–7), suppl. (1898)

A. Rabinovich: *Russkaya opera do Glinki* [Russian Opera Before Glinka] (Moscow, 1948)

R.-A. Mooser: *Annales de la musique et des musiciens en Russie au XVIIIme siècle*, iii (Geneva, 1951)

P. V. Grachyov: 'K. A. Kavos', *Ocherki po istorii russkoy muziki 1790–1825*, ed. M. Druskin and Yu. V. Keldïsh (Leningrad, 1956), 283–305

A. Gozenpud: *Muzïkal'nïy teatr v Rossii* (Leningrad, 1959)

S. L. Ginzburg: IRMO, ii [excerpts from *Ilya the Hero, The Cossack Poet, Ivan Susanin, The Firebird*]

R.-A. Mooser: 'Un musicista veneziano in Russia: Calterizo [*sic*] Cavos', *NRMI*, iii (1969), 13–26

S. Karlinsky: *Russian Drama from its Beginnings to the Age of Pushkin* (Berkeley and Los Angeles, 1985)

Yu. V. Keldïsh: 'K. A. Kavos i russkaya opera', *Istoriya russkoy muzïki*, iv (Moscow, 1986), 123–44 RICHARD TARUSKIN

Cazette, Louis (*b* 1887; *d* Paris, 1922). French tenor. He sang first as a baritone, later studying the lyric tenor repertory with Albert Saleza and winning a *premier prix* at the Paris Conservatoire in 1914. His début at the Opéra-Comique had to be delayed until 1919, when he sang such roles as Des Grieux in *Manon*, Ferrando in *Così fan tutte* and, his greatest success, Don Ottavio in *Don Giovanni*. His reputation, supported by his few recordings, suggests that he would have become the leading French lyric tenor of his generation. His sudden death was announced as resulting from blood-poisoning in a finger cut while mending a bicycle puncture; but it appears he was fatally wounded in a rehearsal of the duel in Gounod's *Mireille*. J. B. STEANE

Cazzati, Maurizio (*b* Lucera, duchy of Guastalla, nr Reggio Emilia, *c*1620; *d* Mantua, 1677). Italian composer. After his ordination he became *maestro di cappella* and organist in Mantua (1641) and had charge of music at the court of the Duke of Sabioneta at Bozzolo (1647–8). He was *maestro di cappella* in Ferrara, probably 1648–53. In 1657, after a period at Bergamo, he was elected *maestro* at S Petronio, Bologna, a post he held until 1671. He successfully reformed the musical establishment there, but his career was marked by personal and professional difficulties; there were bitter polemics over his weakness in contrapuntal writing.

As a composer, Cazzati made his most influential contribution in instrumental music, especially sonatas for trumpet and strings, but he was more prolific in sacred vocal music, including solo motets in bel canto style. Gaspari cited five operas by him: *I gridi di Cerere* and *Il carnevale esigliato* (both 1652, Ferrara), *Ercole effeminato* (1654, Bergamo), *Le gare de' fiumi* (1658, Bologna) and *Le gare d'Amore e di Marte* (1662, Bologna); none is known to survive.

*

G. Gaspari: *Catalogo della Biblioteca del Liceo musicale di Bologna*, i–iv (Bologna, 1890–1905); v, ed. U. Sesini (Bologna, 1943) ANNE SCHNOEBELEN

Cebotari, Maria (*b* Kishineu, 10/23 Feb 1910; *d* Vienna, 9 June 1949). Austrian soprano of Russian birth. She studied with Oskar Daniel in Berlin and made her début at the Dresden Staatsoper in 1931 as Mimì, remaining there until 1936; in 1935 she created Aminta in *Die schweigsame Frau*. She sang at the Berlin Staatsoper (1936–44) and at the Vienna Staatsoper (1946–9). She first appeared at Covent Garden with the Dresden company in 1936 as Susanna, Zerlina and Sophie, and returned there in 1947 with the Vienna Staatsoper as Countess Almaviva, Donna Anna and Salome. She appeared regularly in Salzburg in Mozart roles, and there created Lucile in *Dantons Tod* (1947). Her repertory also included Butterfly, Violetta, Tatyana, Arabella and Turandot. In 1934 she was made a *Kammersängerin*. Cebotari was a sensitive artist and a fine actress, with a beautiful fresh voice and a charming stage presence.

*

A. Mingotti: *Maria Cebotari: das Leben einer Sängerin* (Salzburg, 1950) HAROLD ROSENTHAL/R

Ceccarelli, Francesco (*b* Foligno, 1752; *d* Dresden, 21 Sept 1814). Italian soprano castrato. He sang mainly in the German-speaking countries and was thought better suited to church and concert music than to opera. Despite Fétis, his known opera performances are few.

He sang in Venice theatres: at S Samuele (1775) and at S Benedetto, in Pio's *Nettuno ed Egle* (1783) and as the second man in P. A. Guglielmi's *Tomiri* (1795). His most notable engagement was as court singer at Salzburg (1777–88), where he became a friend of the Mozart family; Mozart wrote a mass, K275/272*b*, and a rondò, K374, for him. Later he held posts at Mainz (1788–92) and in Italy, and in decline he served the Elector of Saxony in Dresden from 1800. He was said in 1790 to have 'grace and a perfect method'.

*

R. Engländer: 'Zur Musikgeschichte Dresdens gegen 1800', *ZMw*, iv (1922), 199–241

E. Anderson, ed.: *The Letters of Mozart and his Family* (London, 1938, 3/1985)

JOHN ROSSELLI

Ceccarelli, Odoardo (*b* Bevagna, nr Perugia; *d* Rome, 7 March 1668). Italian singer. He is described as both tenor and bass from the beginning of his career in Rome (at S Spirito in Sassia in 1620 and at the Collegio Germanico from 1622). He sang in the Sistine chapel choir from 1628 and was a priest by 1641. Later he was active at the Oratorio del Crocifisso. His theatrical career was entirely in court opera. He was among the Roman singers called for the Farnese-Medici wedding spectacles of 1628 (presumably to appear in da Gagliano's *La Flora* and Monteverdi's Parmesan *intermedi* and *torneo*). He sang in the Barberini productions of Michelangelo Rossi's *Erminia sul Giordano* and Luigi Rossi's *Il palazzo incantato* (1633–42) as well as in *La Sincerità trionfante* (text by O. Castelli, music by A. Cecchini), given at the French embassy in Rome in the 1638–9 winter season. His last known performance was in *Il ratto di Proserpina* in 1645 for Pompeo Colonna. In modern terms, Ceccarelli would probably be classed as a baritone. His role of Orlando in *Il palazzo incantato* extends from *B*♭ to *g'*, with *d* to *d'* the central octave; it calls for expressive singing in recitative and lyric pathos in his duets and trios.

MARGARET MURATA

Ceccato, Aldo (*b* Milan, 18 Feb 1934). Italian conductor. He studied at the Milan Conservatory and at the Berlin Hochschule für Musik, where he conducted a student performance of *Otello*. He made his professional début with *Don Giovanni* at the Teatro Nuovo, Milan, in 1964, and in 1966 he conducted Busoni's *Die Brautwahl* at the Maggio Musicale, Florence. His performance of Rossini's *L'equivoco stravagante* at the Wexford Festival in 1968 was widely admired, and in 1969 he conducted *Il signor Bruschino* and *Gianni Schicchi* at the Edinburgh Festival. The same year he made his American début with *I puritani* at the Chicago Lyric Opera. He appeared for the first time at Covent Garden in 1970, conducting *La traviata*, and at Glyndebourne in 1971 with *Ariadne auf Naxos*. He made his Paris Opéra début in 1973 with *La bohème*, and since 1975 has worked mainly in Germany. Ceccato recorded *La traviata* and *Maria Stuarda*, both in 1971 with Beverly Sills. His interpretations have been noted particularly for his care over detail. ALAN BLYTH

Ceccherelli, Chiara. *See* CICCERELLI, CHIARA.

Cecchi, Anna Maria Torri. *See* TORRI, ANNA MARIA.

Cecchi, Domenico ['Il Cortona'] (*b* Cortona, *c*1650–55; *d* Cortona or Vienna, 1717–18). Italian soprano castrato. He studied singing with Placido Basili, *maestro di cappella* at Cortona Cathedral, and probably made his operatic début in Basili's *La forza per amore*. In 1673 he appeared at Bologna (Teatro Formagliari). He first appeared in Venice in Antonio Sartorio's *I duo tiranni al soglio* in 1679, and returned in 1681–2 and 1682–4. In 1685 he sang at Modena and again at Venice; he was in the Duke of Mantua's service by 1687. In the late 1680s he appeared at Turin and Munich, and in 1689 he made his début in Milan (Teatro Ducale), where he appeared in at least eight operas in the next ten years. On 25 May 1690 he sang the lead in the sumptuous production of Sabadini's *Il favore degli dei*, mounted for a royal marriage in Parma; the 25 principals included G. F. Grossi ('Siface') and Pistocchi.

The 1690s were the summit of his career. In 1691 he sang in Rome (Tordinona) in Cardinal Ottoboni's extravagant fiasco *Il Colombo, ovvero l'India scoperta*. Cecchi alone was applauded, and his role (Fernando) was enlarged. Further appearances followed in Genoa, Mantua, Bologna and Reggio before he was engaged, in autumn 1696, at the Teatro S Bartolomeo in Naples, where he scored a tremendous success (Scarlatti's *Comodo Antonino*).

Less is known of his last 20 years. At Christmas 1697 he sang at St Mark's, Venice; he is also said to have appeared in Venice in operas by C. F. Pollarolo in 1698 and 1703, and certainly performed in Scarlatti's *Turno Aricino* at Pratolino in 1704. After singing in Dresden, Vienna and Venice (the last in works by Albinoni, Pollarolo, Gasparini and Lotti), he returned to Vienna and was music master to the archduchesses until the death of Emperor Joseph I in 1711. He may have died, friendless and miserable, in the Viennese fever hospital. According to other accounts, however, he enjoyed a luxurious retirement in Cortona. Algarotti considered him on a par with Siface and Buzzoleni, 'the memory of whom is not extinct although their voices are heard no more', and said that he was outstanding 'nelle parti tenere e appassionate'.

*

DBI (E. Gentile); *DEUMM* (A. Basso); *ES* (N. Pirrotta)

F. Algarotti: *Saggio sopra l'opera in musica* (Livorno, 1755)

A. Yorke-Long: *Music at Court: Four Eighteenth-Century Studies* (London, 1954)

A. Heriot: *The Castrati in Opera* (London, 1956)

O. Termini: 'Singers at San Marco in Venice: the Competition Between Church and Theatre (*c*1675–*c*1725)', *RMARC*, no.17 (1981), 65–96

E. Selfridge-Field: *Pallade Veneta: Writings on Music in Venetian Society 1650–1750* (Venice, 1985)

COLIN TIMMS

Cecchina, La. *See* CACCINI family, (2).

Cecchina, La. Opera by Niccolò Piccinni; *see* BUONA FIGLIUOLA, LA.

Cecchini, Angelo (*fl* Rome, 1619–39). Italian composer. He is first heard of in 1619, as *maestro di cappella* at S Maria della Consolazione, Rome, but is principally known from the librettos of his collaborator OTTAVIANO CASTELLI in which he is identified variously as 'gentilhuomo', 'famigliare', 'compositore' or 'musico' of the Duke of Bracciano, Paolo Giordano Orsini. All his music is lost.

librettos by Ottaviano Castelli

Primavera urbana col trionfo d'Amor pudico (dramma boscareccio, 4), Rome, carn. 1635, lib. *I-Rvat*

Il trionfo dell'autunno (dramma ditirambico, 3), ? Castel Gandolfo, 28 Oct 1636, lib. *Rvat*

L'intemperie d'Apollo (dramma boscareccio, 3), Rome, carn. 1638, lib. *Rc, US-CA*

La Sincerità trionfante overo L'Erculeo ardire (favola boscareccia, 5), Rome, Palazzo del Ceuli (French Embassy), ?12 or 14 Dec 1638, lib. (Rome, 1639, 2/1640)

*

S. Reiner: 'Collaboration in "Chi soffre speri"', *MR*, xxii (1961), 265–82

A. Ziino: 'Pietro della Valle e la "musica erudita": nuovi documenti', *AnMc*, no. 4 (1967), 97–111

M. Murata: 'The Recitative Soliloquy', *JAMS*, xxxvi (1979), 45–73

——: 'Classical Tragedy in the History of Early Opera in Rome', *Early Music History*, iv (1984), 101–34 MARGARET MURATA

Cecere, Carlo (*b* Naples, 7 Nov 1706; *d* Naples, 15 Feb 1761). Italian composer. He is principally known for having written the music for a satiric comic opera, *La tavernola abentorosa* (libretto by Pietro Trinchera), which, by its alleged impiety, offended both church and state authorities. This work illustrates a special chapter in the history of *opera buffa*, for it was a carnival entertainment written not for a public but for a monastic audience (a Neapolitan custom of the time). Records discovered by Prota-Giurleo show that *La tavernola* was performed in February 1741 at the monastery of Monteoliveto and then at SS Demetrio e Bonifacio. The plot dealt with the machinations of a hypocritical rogue disguised as a monk who, after gulling some humble Neapolitans, finally converts them all to the monastic life. Ecclesiastical dignitaries were not amused and, after an inquiry, the king ordered the arrest of both the poet and his publisher and suppression of copies of the libretto (which had not been authorized by the public censor). Trinchera took sanctuary in the church of the Carmine and eventually suffered at least a month's actual imprisonment, but no official blame for *La tavernola* fell on the composer. For the Teatro Nuovo, Naples, Cecere also composed the comic opera *Lo secretista* (Trinchera; spr. 1738) and the sinfonia to *La Rosmonda* (A. Palomba; carn. 1755), a comic pasticcio with contributions by Logroscino, Pietro Comes and Traetta. In his own time, however, his reputation rested on his instrumental music, which is characteristic of Italian chamber music of about 1740–60.

*

CroceN

P. Napoli-Signorelli: *Vicende della cultura nelle due Sicilie* (Naples, 1810–11), iv, 322–3

——: 'Ricerche sul sistema melodrammatico: lette a' Soci Pontaniani da Pietro Napoli-Signorelli nelle adunanze de' mesi di novembre e dicembre del 1812', *Atti della Società Pontaniana*, iv (Naples, 1847), 66

M. Scherillo: *L'opera buffa napoletana durante il settecento: storia letteraria* (Naples, 1883, 2/1917), 239ff, 264ff

U. Prota-Giurleo: *Nicola Logroscino: 'il dio dell'opera buffa'* (Naples, 1927), 67ff

V. Viviani: *Storia del teatro napoletano* (Naples, 1969), 320ff, 335ff

JAMES L. JACKMAN

Čech, Svatopluk (*b* Ostředek, nr Benešov, 21 Feb 1846; *d* Troja [now in Prague], 23 Feb 1908). Czech poet and writer. One of the most substantial Czech literary figures of the 19th century, he completed law school and worked until 1878 in a lawyer's office; thereafter he devoted himself to literature. He is best known for his patriotic poetry, much of it set by Czech composers, for which he is sometimes described as the 'last poet of the Czech Revival'. His satirical tales about the Prague landlord Mr Brouček have also lasted well and were the basis for several musical settings – incidental music by Karel Kovařovic (1894) and a pantomime by J. E. Zelinka (1942), but most notably Janáček's opera *The Excursions of Mr Brouček*.

Malířský nápad [A Painter's Idea] (story, 1875): O. Zich, 1908

Václav z Michalovic (verse epic, 1880): J. Bartovský, 1927

Lešetínský kovář [The Blacksmith from Lešetín] (novel in verse, 1883): S. Suda, 1903; Dvořák, planned opera, 1901, inc.; K. Weis, 1920

Dagmar (verse epic, 1883–4): A. Jiránek, 1908

Pravý výlet pana Broučka do Měsíce [The True Excursion of Mr Brouček to the Moon] (story, 1888): K. Moor, 1910; L. Janáček, 1920, as pt 1 of Výlety páně Broučkovy [The Excursions of Mr Brouček], 1920

Nový epochální výlet pana Broučka, tentokráte do patnáctého století [The New Epoch-Making Journey of Mr Brouček, this Time to the 15th Century] (story, 1889): Janáček, as pt 2 of Výlety páně Broučkovy, 1920

*

ČSHS [lists texts used for other musical settings]

F. Strejček: *O Svatopluku Čechovi* (Prague, 1908)

R. Šťastný: *Čeští spisovatelé deseti století* [Czech Writers of Ten Centuries] (Prague, 1974)

V. Forst, ed.: *Lexikon České literatury*, i (Prague, 1985) [incl. extensive list of writings and further bibliography]

J. Tyrrell: *Czech Opera* (Cambridge, 1988)

——: *Janáček's Operas: a Documentary Account* (London, 1992)

JOHN TYRRELL

Cecil, Winifred (*b* Staten Island, NY, 31 Aug 1907; *d* New York, 13 Sept 1985). American soprano. She studied at the Curtis Institute as well as privately with Sembrich and Elena Gerhardt. Having declined a contract with the Metropolitan, she went to Italy in 1937 and made her opera début at the S Carlo in the title role of Respighi's *Maria Egiziaca*. Engagements followed in Prague and Vienna, and at La Scala her roles included Aida, Tosca, Maddalena (*Andrea Chénier*), Fiora (*L'amore dei tre re*), Elsa, Elisabeth (*Tannhäuser*), Donna Anna and Countess Almaviva. She lived in retirement in Italy during World War II, doing unofficial diplomatic work, and returned in 1950 to New York, where she taught. PHILIP LIESON MILLER

Cecilia. *Azione sacra* in a prologue and three episodes by LICINIO REFICE to a libretto by Emidio Mucci; Rome, Teatro Reale dell'Opera, 15 February 1934.

An angel (soprano) introduces the opera, based on the story of the patron saint of music, in the prologue. In the first episode the Valerii await the arrival of Cecilia (soprano), the betrothed of Valeriano (tenor). After the marriage ceremony Cecilia, who is already a Christian, asks Valeriano to respect her virginity but he is ardent; he is prevented from using violence by the appearance of an angel (silent role). In the second episode Valeriano is taken by Cecilia to the catacombs where the Christians are at prayer, led by the bishop Urbano (bass); the appearance of the apostle Paul (silent role) marks the conversion of Valeriano. In the third episode the prefect Amachio (baritone) gives orders for Cecilia to be put to death; after her martyrdom, she appears as a saint in glory. The chorus is present (as servants, handmaidens, congregation), and supernatural apparitions in tableaux create spectacular scenic effects. The music has many Gregorian echoes but also veristic features, notably in the more passionate moments (such as the duet between Cecilia and Valeriano in the first episode).

LUCA ZOPPELLI

Cehanovsky, George (*b* St Petersburg, 2/14 April 1892; *d* Yorktown Heights, NY, 25 March 1986). Russian baritone. He made his début in St Petersburg where he sang Yevgeny Onegin and Valentin in *Faust*, fleeing to Constantinople after the Revolution and then to the USA. After a period with the Baltimore Civic Opera he joined the Metropolitan in 1926. During his 40 seasons there he sang 97 roles (mostly comprimario) in over 2000 performances in New York and on tour, remaining as Russian coach until he was over 90. His first wife was the soprano Elisabeth Rethberg. Though his serviceable voice is heard on many Metropolitan recordings, he is probably best remembered as one of those whose vitality and goodwill help to make all who work in a great international house feel that they belong to a company. J. B. STEANE

Célestine, La. Lyric tragicomedy in two acts (11 tableaux) by MAURICE OHANA to a libretto by Ohana and Odile Marcel after Fernando de Rojas's dialogue novel *La Celestina: tragicomedia de Calisto y Melibea*; Paris, Opéra, 13 June 1988.

Commissioned by Radio France and the Paris Opéra, *La Célestine* was written between autumn 1982 and April 1987. Calyx (baritone) falls in love with Mélibée (soprano) and, following the advice of his dishonest servants, Tristan (tenor) and Sosie (tenor), seeks the go-between and procuress Célestine (contralto) to arrange a lovers' assignation for the payment of 100 gold coins. Through invocations to the supernatural powers of witchcraft, Célestine brings the lovers together in the symbolic Garden of Delights. On refusing to share her payment, Célestine is murdered by Tristan and Sosie in the presence of the prostitutes Elys (soprano) and Aréis (soprano). Following a setting of the *Dies irae*, a client, Ruffian (bass), presents a grotesque and comic elegy to Célestine's memory. After a second meeting with Mélibée, Calyx falls from the wall of the Garden of Delights to his death. Mélibée commits suicide, and her father (bass-baritone) mourns her death in a setting of King Lear's lament for Cordelia.

The opera is enclosed by two historical tableaux depicting events contemporaneous with the Rojas play: *Le camp des rois catholiques à Santa Fé*, which depicts the persecution of Jews and Arabs to the accompaniment of the *Te Deum*, and *Triomphe de Christophe Colombe à Seville*. Ohana includes characters additional to the Rojas original: a narrator, Illuminé, representing Rojas, introduces and explains the action throughout; the Sibyl (two sopranos) stands outside the action and pronounces three prophecies; the female chorus of Parques ('Parcae' or 'Fates') comments on the action as a Greek chorus and is associated with a Fate motif. The opera makes use of French, Spanish, Italian, English and Latin text as well as Ohana's characteristic wordless declamation in phonemes, and incorporates vocal ensemble writing for trios, quartets, quintets and a septet. Within a closed form Ohana uses aleatory counterpoint and allusions to techniques from African and Spanish folk music. To a standard orchestra of double woodwind is added a solo harpsichord and a large percussion section. CAROLINE A. RAE

Celletti, Rodolfo (*b* Rome, 13 June 1917). Italian music critic. He took a degree in law from the University of Rome but was self-taught in music. He has written for various journals, including *La Scala* (1953–63), *Discoteca* (1963–82), *Epoca* (1974–84) and more recently *Musica viva*, *Musica* and *C D Classica*, his main interest being the voice, and the style and interpretation of Italian operatic vocal music. After overseeing the section on singers for the *Enciclopedia dello spettacolo* (vols. v–x, 1958–66), he showed his wide knowledge of vocal styles and techniques in his dictionary *Le grandi voci* (1964), the most complete biographical and critical source on the subject at the time; he has since updated some of its material, most notably in 'La vocalità' (1977) and *Il canto* (1989). He has written many articles on Italian opera for *Musica d'oggi*, *L'opera* and *Nuova rivista musicale italiana*, concentrating on Baroque and 19th-century singing. In 1980 he became artistic director of the festival of Valle d'Itria, and in 1984 consultant to the Teatro Comunale of Bologna.

Le grandi voci: dizionario critico-biografico dei cantanti (Rome, 1964)
Il teatro d'opera in disco (Milan, 1976, 3/1989)
'La vocalità', *Storia dell'opera*, ed. A. Basso and G. Barblan, iii/1 (Turin, 1977), 3–317
Storia del belcanto (Fiesole, 1983, 2/1986; Eng. trans., 1991)
Memorie d'un ascoltatore (Milan, 1985)
Il canto (Milan, 1989)
Voce di tenore (Milan, 1989) CAROLYN GIANTURCO

Celli [Standing], **Frank H.** (*b* London, 1842; *d* London, 27 Dec 1904). English bass-baritone. In 1862 he sang Matt of the Mint in *The Beggar's Opera* at the Marylebone Theatre, London. In 1871 he joined Mapleson's provincial touring company, making his operatic début as Valentin. He was a member of the Carl Rosa company for several years, singing Gounod's Méphistophélès on the second night of the company's first London season (1875) and taking part in first performances of many new English works. His voice retained its freshness and charm throughout his career. HAROLD ROSENTHAL/R

Cellier, Alfred (*b* London, 1 Dec 1844; *d* London, 28 Dec 1891). English composer and conductor. A school-friend of Sullivan, he followed the same path as a conductor and composer, his first one-act opera, *Charity Begins at Home* (1872), being successfully staged by Thomas German Reed, who had produced Sullivan's early works. After a period as musical director at the Court Theatre, he took up a similar post under Charles Calvert, at the Prince's Theatre, Manchester, and his first full-length comic opera, *The Sultan of Mocha* (1874), was played there for several seasons before being taken to London in 1876; a revised version was given in London in 1887.

His next three full-length works were all produced in Manchester, *Tower of London* (1875), *Nell Gwynne* (1876) and *Belladonna* (1878), but meanwhile Cellier had returned to London, where he provided music for a range of theatres, from Reed's Gallery of Illustration to the pantomime at Covent Garden. He succeeded G. B. Allen as conductor of *The Sorcerer* at the Opera Comique, and subsequently took charge of Richard D'Oyly Carte's productions in Britain, the USA and Australia on a number of occasions, including the first performances of *HMS Pinafore* and *Ivanhoe*. He also conducted and supplied a series of one-act forepieces for the Savoy operas, before his brother François (*d* 1914) took over the position of company musical director (which he retained until Carte's death in 1901).

Cellier's major success as a composer came in 1886, at the Gaiety, when George Edwardes produced his comedy opera *Dorothy*, a revision of the *Nell Gwynne* music to a new libretto by B. C. Stephenson. *Dorothy* became the longest-running musical show of its time, and the baritone serenade, 'Queen of my Heart', sung by Hayden Coffin, the biggest song hit of the era. This success resulted in a new London production of *The Sultan of Mocha*. There followed a new version of *Tower of London*, by Stephenson, as *Doris* (1889) and a collaboration with W. S. Gilbert on *The Mountebanks* (1892), which was completed by Ivan Caryll when Cellier died. Elegant and infallibly musical, Cellier's work has a refinement and a pretty, somewhat dignified melodiousness, lacking only the sense of humour and burlesque gaiety of which Sullivan was capable.

first performed in London unless otherwise stated

Charity Begins at Home (musical proverb, 1, B. Rowe [B. C. Stephenson]), Gallery of Illustration, 7 Feb 1872
Dora's Dream (operetta, 1, A. Cecil), Gallery of Illustration, 3 July 1873
Topsyturveydom (2 scenes, W. S. Gilbert), Criterion, 21 March 1874
The Sultan of Mocha (comic op, 3, ? A. Jarret), Manchester, Prince's, 16 Nov 1874; rev., lib. rev. W. Lestocq, Strand, 21 Sept 1887
Tower of London (comic op, 3), Manchester, Prince's, 4 Oct 1875; rev. as Doris, 1889
Nell Gwynne (3, H. B. Farnie, after W. G. T. Moncrieff: *Rochester*), Manchester, Prince's, 17 Oct 1876; rev. as Dorothy, 1886
Two Foster Brothers (operetta, 1, G. a'Beckett), St George's Hall, 12 March 1877
The Spectre Knight (fanciful operetta, 1, J. Albery), Opera Comique, 9 Feb 1878
Belladonna, or The Little Beauty and the Great Beast (3, A. Thompson), Manchester, Prince's, 27 April 1878
After All (vaudeville, 1, F. Desprez), Opera Comique, 23 Dec 1878
In the Sulks (vaudeville, 1, Desprez), Opera Comique, 21 Feb 1880
The Carp (whimsicality, 1, Desprez), Savoy, 13 Feb 1886
Dorothy (comedy op, 3, B. C. Stephenson), Gaiety, 25 Sept 1886; rev. of Nell Gwynne
Mrs Jarramie's Genie (operetta, 1, Desprez), Savoy, 14 Feb 1888, collab. F. Cellier
Doris (comedy op, 3, Stephenson), Lyric, 20 April 1889; rev. of Tower of London
The Mountebanks (comic op, 2, Gilbert), Lyric, 4 Jan 1892; completed by I. Caryll

Music in: Les manteaux noirs, 1882; Little Jack Sheppard, 1885; The Water Babies, 1902 KURT GÄNZL

Celoniati [Celoniatti, Celoniat, Celonieti, Celonietto], **Ignazio** (*b* Turin, *c*1731; *d* Turin, 22 Dec 1784). Italian composer. He was a violinist in the royal service at Turin and also at the Teatro Regio, under Pugnani. Between 1778 and 1780 he was impresario for performances of comic opera at the Teatro Carignano with Giuseppe Boroni. Among the most successful of his operas was *Ecuba*, given 22 times in its first run. He also composed instrumental works and some sacred music.

Il caffé di campagna (ob, 3, P. Chiari), Turin, Carignano, 18 Nov 1762
Ecuba (os, 3, J. Durandi), Turin, Regio, 14 Jan 1769, *I-Tf*
Didone abbandonata (os, 3, P. Metastasio), Milan, Regio Ducal, 26 Dec 1769, *F-Pn*, *I-Tf*, *P-La*
Il nemico audace (os, 3), 1769

*

M.-T. Bouquet: *Musique et musiciens à Turin de 1648 à 1775* (Turin, 1968)
——: *Storia del Teatro Regio di Torino: il Teatro di Corte dalle origini al 1778* (Turin, 1976)
——: *Turin et les musiciens de la cour 1619–1775* (diss., Paris-Sorbonne, 1987)
R. Moffa: *Storia della regia cappella di Torino dal 1775 al 1870* (Turin, 1990) MARIE-THÉRÈSE BOUQUET-BOYER

Celos aun del aire matan ('Jealousy, Even of the Air, Kills'). Opera in three acts by JUAN HIDALGO to a libretto by PEDRO CALDERÓN DE LA BARCA; Madrid, Salón of the Palacio Real, ? 5 December 1660.

The earliest Spanish opera whose music is preserved, it was commissioned for the Spanish celebration of the marriage of the Infanta María Teresa and Louis XIV of France. Dramatist and composer based the opera on the myth of Cephalus and Procris, modifying and interpreting the myth as it was known in their day to suit contemporary political events. The choice of fully sung opera, unusual in 17th-century Spain, was motivated by the importance of the celebrations and by rivalry with the French court, where Mazarin was planning Italian operas. *Celos aun del aire matan* complemented Hidalgo's one-act *La púrpura de la rosa* produced some months earlier.

In keeping with Spanish theatrical conventions, all the roles except for one (the comic Rústico) were sung by women, the principal roles being those for the goddess Diana, the nymph Aura, Céfalo, Pocris and Eróstrato. The roles of Rústico, Clarín and Floreta are comic in the tradition of the *gracioso*. Hidalgo's extant music demonstrates his adaptation of Spanish conventions from semi-operas and zarzuelas to the genre of fully sung opera. The action and interaction of the plot unfold largely through strophic airs (some in popular Spanish forms such as seguidilla and *jácara*) for narrative and dialogue, with recitatives reserved for highly dramatic exclamations and monologues in which supernatural power is manifest. Hidalgo's recitative, which differs considerably from Italian paradigms, is associated especially with the goddess Diana. The opera was revived at the Madrid court several times before the end of the 17th century and may have been performed at the Spanish court in Naples in 1682. LOUISE K. STEIN

Celos hacen estrellas, Los ('Jealousy Produces Stars'). Zarzuela in two acts by JUAN HIDALGO to a libretto by Juan Vélez de Guevara; Madrid, Alcázar Palace, 22 December 1672.

Written to celebrate the birthday of Queen Mariana, this is the earliest zarzuela for which nearly all of the sung numbers are preserved: songs by Hidalgo survive in loose scores and performing parts (part of the music has been ascribed to Francisco Garau). The text is based on an episode from the story of Jupiter and Io as transmitted through Spanish versions of Ovid. As was typical of late 17th-century zarzuelas, the production begins with an allegorical *loa* or prologue in praise of the occasion, bringing the attention of the spectators from the everyday world of the court and the palace to the imaginary world to be represented on stage. During the two acts of the zarzuela proper, the songs and choruses are set pieces only loosely integrated into the spoken context, although each musical number has a reasonable dramatic justification. The zarzuela does not include sung dialogue, even for the principal deities (Jupiter, Juno, Mercury and Cupid), largely because it takes place on earth in a rustic-pastoral setting and the divine characters are burlesqued, interacting on the level of common mortals as in a standard Spanish spoken play. With its comic *entremés* performed between the acts of the zarzuela proper, and a nonsensical, somewhat spicy *fin de fiesta* at the end, this zarzuela is a good example of the short, humorous and uncomplicated musical plays that dominated the court stages of the later 17th century. It also includes some typical musical numbers: a stunning lament-like song of enchantment, a comic *pregón* and four-part choruses for the rustics and for celestial voices. Hidalgo's songs offer fine examples of his compositional style, especially his consistently original text painting and restrained, focussed approach to affective expression.

For illustration *see* MADRID, fig.1. LOUISE K. STEIN

Cena delle beffe, La ('The Supper of Jests'). *Poema drammatico* in four acts by UMBERTO GIORDANO to a libretto by SEM BENELLI after his play of the same title; Milan, Teatro alla Scala, 20 December 1924.

The action takes place in Florence at the time of Lorenzo il Magnifico. Act 1 opens in the palace of Tornaquinci (bass), who is giving a supper that is intended to reconcile Giannetto Malaspini (tenor) with Neri Chiaramantesi (baritone) and Neri's brother Gabriello (tenor), who, Giannetto recounts, have beaten him up, ducked him in the Arno and then stabbed him ('Calato in Arno e pugnalato poi'). Also present is Ginevra (soprano), Neri's mistress and the object of their feud. Giannetto's hints that Gabriello is likewise in love with Ginevra cause the young man to leave, embarrassed. Having made Neri drunk, Giannetto dares him to go to a dangerous quarter of the city clad in a suit of white armour and equipped with a bill-hook. Neri accepts the challenge. When he has left Giannetto spreads word that he has lost his wits. Act 2 begins in Ginevra's house next morning, when the news is brought to her of Neri's supposed madness. This she emphatically denies; for has not Neri spent the night with her? But it is Giannetto, not Neri, who appears from her bedroom, where he has lain at her side disguised in Neri's scarlet cloak. They are interrupted by the arrival of Neri himself, who threatens vengeance before being overpowered by Lorenzo's men and taken into custody. In Act 3, set in the Medici palace, Neri is subjected at a doctor's orders to mockery by his previous victims as a means of restoring his sanity. One of them, Lisabetta (soprano), who genuinely loves him, persuades him to feign total idiocy, so that he may be released as mad but harmless. Giannetto then proposes a test; he will return that night to Ginevra's arms. If Neri is really mad he will not attempt to follow him. In Act 4 Neri, duly released, arrives at Ginevra's house intending to catch the lovers *in flagrante delicto* and murder Giannetto. But the man he kills is his own brother disguised in Giannetto's cloak. Now his insanity is real enough.

Giordano's last full-length opera, *La cena delle beffe* was first performed under Toscanini with Carmen Melis (Ginevra), Hipolito Lazaro (Giannetto) and Benvenuto Franci (Neri). Though less well known than *Andrea Chénier* and *Fedora* it has been revived in recent years with some success. Here, as usual, Giordano made sparing use of thematic recall, the most memorable instance being an expansive lyrical phrase that accompanies Ginevra's words 'Perchè la donna ama vedendo altri amare' and later forms the basis of her solo in Act 1 ('Sempre così sul margine del sogno'). Local colour is provided by a Tuscan *stornello* ('Tornato è maggio dopo lungo viaggio') sung by a minstrel behind the scenes just before the shocking denouement.

JULIAN BUDDEN

Cendrillon (i) ('Cinderella'). *Opéra-féerie* in three acts by NICOLAS ISOUARD to a libretto by Charles-Guillaume Etienne after Charles Perrault's fairy-tale of the same title (published in *Contes de ma mère l'oye*, 1698); Paris, Opéra-Comique (Salle Feydeau), 22 February 1810.

Isouard emphasizes the simplicity of character of Cendrillon (soprano) by never allowing her to outshine musically her stepsisters, Clorinde and Tisbe (sopranos). In this opera the coloratura style conveys negative associations as it is employed only by the sisters. At the ball given by Prince Ramir (tenor), Clorinde competes with Cendrillon in an aria (no.12) based on a bolero rhythm, one of the earliest instances of a bolero in opera. (Isouard wrote an alternative aria, published separately as 'Nouvel air chanté dans l'opéra de Cendrillon', which contains even more coloratura.) Similarly, Tisbe is given an elaborate three-part aria with *strette* (no.13) at the beginning of Act 3. By contrast Cendrillon presents herself in the Act 2 finale with a three-stanza *romance*, which Weber thought possessed 'nothing to make an effect on an audience'. The arias of Tisbe and Clorinda are the only pieces of any musical substance; otherwise *romances* and ensembles prevail. The musical simplicity of the role of Cendrillon may have been due in part to the limited talents of Alexandrine Saint-Aubin, whose brief, celebrated career started with this role. Weber also complained about 'the routine nature of practically every piece' in the opera and its 'clumsy instrumentation'. Similar criticism was raised in the *Tablettes de Polymnie* (i, 1810, pp.5–10) without preventing the opera's quick rise to fame. It was performed throughout Europe and was only gradually superseded by Rossini's *La Cenerentola* after 1817.

MICHAEL FEND

Cendrillon (ii) ('Cinderella'). *Conte de fées* in four acts by JULES MASSENET to a libretto by HENRI CAIN after Charles Perrault's fairy-tale of the same title (published in *Contes de ma mère l'oye*, 1698); Paris, Opéra-Comique (Salle Favart), 24 May 1899.

Cendrillon	soprano
Madame de la Haltière *her stepmother*	mezzo-soprano
Le Prince Charmant (Prince Charming)	soprano ('Falcon')
La Fée (Fairy Godmother)	coloratura soprano
Noémie } *Cendrillon's stepsisters*	soprano
Dorothée } *Cendrillon's stepsisters*	mezzo-soprano
Pandolfe *her father*	bass
Le Roi (The King)	baritone
Le Doyen de la Faculté	tenor
Le Surintendant des plaisirs	baritone
Le Premier Ministre	bass

Fairies, servants, courtiers, doctors, ministers

Preliminary plans for *Cendrillon* were apparently laid at the Cavendish Hotel, Jermyn Street (later made famous by its flamboyant proprietress Rosa Lewis), when Massenet and Cain were in London for the première of *La Navarraise* in 1894. The score was completed in 1896, but the première planned for the following year was postponed owing to the urgency of mounting *Sapho* before the imminent death of Alphonse Daudet and while Emma Calvé was available to sing it. *Cendrillon* followed in 1899 and was one of the first important premières in the regime of Albert Carré, who was appointed director of the Opéra-Comique after the death of Léon Carvalho in December 1897. (Before the dress rehearsal Carré persuaded Massenet to cut a Prologue in which the characters introduce themselves

'Cendrillon' (Massenet), Act 3 (a magic landscape around a great oak tree) in the original production at the Opéra-Comique (Salle Favart), Paris, 24 May 1899, with Julia Guiraudon (Cendrillon, left), Georgette Bréjean-Gravière (Fairy Godmother, in the oak tree) and Mlle Emelan (Prince Charming): photograph from 'Le théâtre' (July 1899)

to the audience, but a brief epilogue in which they step out of character survives.)

The lavish production as well as the quality of the music ensured an immediate success for *Cendrillon*: there were 50 performances before the end of 1899. The title role was sung by Julia Guiraudon, an Opéra-Comique Micaëla and Mimì who later married Cain, the Fairy Godmother by Georgette Bréjean-Gravière (later Bréjean-Silver) and Pandolfe by Lucien Fugère. The conductor was Alexandre Luigini, composer of the infamous *Ballet egyptien*. The charm of the work conquered even the habitual sarcasm – when writing about Massenet – of 'Willy' (Henri Gauthier Villars). *Cendrillon* was staged frequently on both sides of the Atlantic in the first 15 years of its existence; there was a notable production in Chicago in 1911 with Maggie Teyte in the title role and Mary Garden as the Prince. Lord Berners was responsible for the British stage première in Swindon in 1939. The work has never entirely lapsed from the repertory, and has enjoyed frequent revivals in recent years. There is a considerable complete recording with Frederica von Stade, alas with a tenor in the travesty role of the Prince: there is neither authority nor tradition for this reprehensible practice.

ACT 1 *A state room in Madame de la Haltière's town house, with a large chimney-piece* Servants bustle to prepare for the ball. The henpecked Pandolfe wonders why he ever left his country estate to remarry an overbearing countess with two daughters ('Ai-je quitté ma ferme et nos grands bois!') and pities the lot of his own child Lucette (Cendrillon). He leaves as his wife enters to instruct her daughters on strategy ('Le bal est un champ de bataille') and supervise a troupe of milliners, tailors and hairdressers. Pandolfe, late for departure, is not allowed to say goodnight to his child. Cendrillon enters and, in a quasi-folksong not dissimilar to Rossini's in the parallel situation, sits by the fire to regret her lot ('Reste au foyer, petit grillon') before falling asleep. Her Fairy Godmother appears in a flurry of coloratura and to a graceful waltz orders her attendants to dress Cendrillon for the ball ('Pour en faire un tissu'). She warns her charge to leave before midnight, and tells her that the glass slippers are a talisman to prevent her being recognized by her family.

ACT 2 *The royal palace* A gaggle of courtiers and a stage band of glass flute, lute and viola d'amore fail to alleviate the melancholy that the Prince shares with his counterpart in Gozzi's (and Prokofiev's) *L'amore delle tre melarance* ('Coeur sans amour, printemps sans roses'). The King orders him to marry. Eligible princesses arrive in five danced entrées. The unknown beauty appears to a Rossinian unaccompanied concertato of general amazement, and the Prince launches a rapturous love-at-first-sight duet ('Toi qui m'es apparue'). She responds with a phrase of characteristic Massenetian simplicity, repeated in later acts, 'Vous êtes mon Prince Charmant'. As midnight strikes she hurries away.

ACT 3.i *As in Act 1* Cendrillon relives the glamour of the ball and the terror of her precipitate nocturnal flight before singing once more of the *petit grillon*. The family returns. Madame de la Haltière reminds Pandolfe of her greatly superior ancestry (including a Doge, a dozen bishops, six abbesses and 'two or three royal mistresses') before disputing his account of the ball. According to her, the Prince and the courtiers decisively rejected the bold intruder. Pandolfe notices that Cendrillon is about to faint, finally loses his temper and brusquely orders the women from the room. In a duet of great tenderness he promises that he and Cendrillon will return to his country seat ('Viens, nous quitterons cette ville'). When he exits to prepare for the journey, Cendrillon gives way to despair: rather than allow her father to share her pain, she decides to run away and die on her own ('Adieu, mes souvenirs de joie').

3.ii *A magic landscape around a great oak tree* Fairies and will-o'-the-wisps interrupt their dance as Cendrillon and the Prince approach separately, and the Fairy Godmother conjures up a magic arbour so that they may hear but not see each other. After praying to be released from their misery, they recognize each other's voices and reaffirm their love in a mystical ceremony. The Prince hangs his bleeding heart on the oak, and both fall into an enchanted sleep.

ACT 4.i *A terrace* Pandolfe watches over his sleeping daughter. Months have passed since she was found by a stream half dead with cold. In her delirium she has been singing about the ball, the mysterious oak, the bleeding heart and the missing slipper. None of this ever happened, her father assures her, and she resigns herself to having dreamt it all. They celebrate her recovery by greeting the spring ('Printemps revient'). Madame de la Haltière enters with the news of a grand assembly of princesses (from as far away as Japan, Norway and the banks of the Thames) to try on the missing slipper, and Cendrillon joyfully realizes that her dream was true. To the glittering 'Marche des Princesses' (a favourite concert item) the scene changes.

4.ii *The palace* Cendrillon steps forward ('Vous êtes mon Prince Charmant'), and the opera ends amid general rejoicing.

* * *

Cendrillon is the Massenet opera most readily approachable by those with reservations about his idiom. His musical sense of humour, all too seldom given full rein, is here at its frothiest, and liberally spiced with dry Gallic wit. Variety is assured by the four distinct soundworlds conjured up to tell the fairy-tale: the vigour and pomp of the court music, with Massenet's best dance numbers apart from *Le Cid* and affectionate pastiche of classical forms from the ages of Lully and Rameau; the music for the fairy world, which has the airiness and harmonic savour of Mendelssohn crossed with Richard Strauss, both in their E major mode; the writing for Cendrillon and Pandolfe, showing Massenet at his most artlessly economical to match the simple virtues they represent; and the love music, which in its heavily perfumed chromaticism reminds one constantly how well Massenet knew his Wagner (as a student he may have played percussion in the Opéra orchestra at the famous *Tannhäuser* fiasco of 1861, and there are distinct echoes of the Bacchanale in Act 2 of *Cendrillon*). The mystical marriage of Act 3 is one of the composer's most succulent love scenes.

The characteristic motifs – 'Vous êtes mon Prince Charmant', or the phrase associated with Cendrillon's dream – are recalled with more discretion than is often the case with this composer; indeed, *Cendrillon* could almost be subtitled 'the art of reminiscence'. All these elements serve to present through music a wide range of characters, with the broad comedy of Madame de la Haltière in neat counterpoint to the gentler Pandolfe, whose humour is tinged with overwhelming melancholy. The way the latter role is written helps, like that of the Devil in *Grisélidis*, one to imagine the appeal of Fugère, for whom both were written. The treatment of Cendrillon and the Prince as lost, desperate children reinforces the musical reasons for never countenancing the casting of a tenor as the Prince. The whole character of the relationship is changed thereby from innocence to mere operatic sentiment. RODNEY MILNES

Cenerentola, La [*La Cenerentola, ossia La bontà in trionfo* ('Cinderella, or Goodness Triumphant')]. *Dramma giocoso* in two acts by GIOACHINO ROSSINI to a libretto by JACOPO FERRETTI after Charles Perrault's *Cendrillon* and librettos by Charles-Guillaume Etienne for Nicolas Isouard's *Cendrillon* (1810, Paris) and Francesco Fiorini for Stefano Pavesi's *Agatina, o La virtù premiata* (1814, Milan); Rome, Teatro Valle, 25 January 1817.

Cenerentola (Angelina) *Don Magnifico's step-daughter*	contralto
Don Ramiro *Prince of Salerno*	tenor
Dandini *valet to Don Ramiro*	bass
Don Magnifico *Baron of Monte Fiascone*	baritone
Clorinda } *his daughters*	soprano
Tisbe } *his daughters*	mezzo-soprano
Alidoro *a philosopher, tutor to Don Ramiro*	bass

Ladies and gentlemen of the Prince's court

Setting Don Magnifico's mansion and the court of Don Ramiro

Rossini wrote *La Cenerentola* in a little over three weeks in January 1817. As with two earlier comic masterpieces, *L'italiana in Algeri* and *Il barbiere di Siviglia*, Rossini and his librettist had important precedents with which to work, enabling a text to be assembled and musical and dramatic perspectives to be calculated in the shortest possible time. The *prima* was noisily received by the Roman audience but the fiasco of the first night of *Il barbiere di Siviglia* was not repeated. Rossini's Rosina in that production, Geltrude Righetti Giorgi, sang Cenerentola, Giacomo Guglielmi sang Don Ramiro and Giuseppe de Begnis, Dandini. The Don Magnifico, Andrea Verni, had sung the same role at La Scala on 10 April 1814 in the *prima* of Pavesi's Cinderella opera.

Rossini's opera quickly proved to be enormously popular in Italy and abroad. It was performed in Barcelona in April 1818, in London at the King's Theatre, Haymarket, in January 1820, and in Vienna, in German, the following August. Performances followed in Paris (1822), Berlin (1825), Moscow (1825), Buenos Aires (1826) and New York (1826), where it was given by Manuel García's company. In February 1844 it became the first opera to be performed in Australia. Distinguished interpreters of the title role in Rossini's time included Laure Cinti-Damoreau, Henriette Sontag, Maria Malibran, Pauline Viardot and Marietta Alboni, who appeared with the Royal Italian Opera at Covent Garden in 1848; Antonio Tamburini sang Dandini and Michael Costa conducted. Like many Rossini operas, *La Cenerentola* was performed only intermittently in the years following the composer's death in 1868, but it began to return to the repertory in the 1920s and early 1930s. The Spanish mezzo-soprano Conchita Supervia was the outstanding Cenerentola of those years. In June 1934, Covent Garden staged the opera for the first time since 1848 with Supervia and a cast that included Dino Borgioli as Don Ramiro and Ezio Pinza as Don Magnifico; for this production ballet was added, choreographed by Ninette de Valois. The opera has received a number of distinguished revivals at the Glyndebourne Festival beginning in 1950 with Carl Ebert's production, to designs by Oliver Messel, conducted by the incomparable Vittorio Gui. Marina de Gabarain sang Cenerentola, Juan Oncina Don Ramiro, and Sesto Bruscantini Dandini. The EMI recording of the production remains one of the most charmingly idiomatic accounts of the opera on record. However, the 1973 La Scala revival, conducted by Claudio Abbado and also recorded, had the advantage of a new performing edition by Alberto Zedda; the production was by Jean-Pierre Ponnelle and the Cenerentola was Lucia Valentini-Terrani. On record, and at some later revivals, the role was sung by Teresa Berganza, one of the leading Rossini interpreters of her generation.

The recitatives and three of the 16 numbers performed at the *prima* are not by Rossini and were not subsequently replaced by him. They are Alidoro's aria 'Vasto teatro è il mondo', the chorus 'Ah, della bella incognita', and Clorinda's aria 'Sventurata! Me credea'; according to Ferretti, these and the recitatives are the work of the Roman composer Luca Agolini. When the opera was revived at the Teatro Apollo, Rome, in December 1820 Rossini composed a new grand aria for Alidoro, 'Là del ciel nell'arcano profondo'; the text is also Ferretti's. The rondo that concludes the opera is an adaptation of Almaviva's final aria from *Il barbiere di Siviglia*. No overture was composed for *La Cenerentola*; instead Rossini used the overture to *La gazzetta*, the *opera buffa* which had had its *prima* in Naples in September 1816.

ACT 1.i *A room in the tumbledown castle of the Baron, Don Magnifico* Clorinda and Tisbe, the two ugly sisters, are locked in one of their habitual disputes while Cenerentola quietly goes about her household chores. As she works, she sings her favourite song 'Una volta c'era un re': the tale of a king who, bored by being alone, chooses a bride not for her ostentation or her wealth but for her innocence and her goodness. Rossini's sad, minor-key 'folk tune', which crops up several times during the opera, paints to perfection Cenerentola's solitary and expiatory mood. He also keeps sentimentality at bay as the song is cruelly mocked by the ugly sisters at its first reprise, the obsessive, bird-like tones of the two sopranos set, here and elsewhere, in stark contrast to Cenerentola's velvety contralto. A knock is heard at the door and Don Ramiro's tutor, Alidoro, appears disguised as a beggar. The sisters spurn him with disgust but Cenerentola manages surreptitiously to give him bread and a mug of coffee. The sisters' mood changes when courtiers announce the imminent arrival of Prince Ramiro, who proposes to escort Don Magnifico's daughters to his palace where festivities are to be held during which the Prince will choose a bride. The sisters immediately goad the servants into action, remorselessly chivvying the endlessly harassed Cenerentola in a brilliant stretta during which Alidoro and the courtiers look wryly on.

The hubbub arouses Don Magnifico who proceeds, in his cavatina 'Miei rampolli femminini', to relate the contents of a bizarre dream he has just had; the dream, he suggests somewhat improbably, presages royal connections for Clorinda, Tisbe and himself. When the prince, Don Ramiro, arrives disguised as his valet Dandini, the room is deserted. Alidoro has alerted him to the presence in the household of a woman worthy of his hand and he is determined to pursue the matter further. Cenerentola is so shocked to see the stranger that she drops a cup and saucer. The duet 'Un soave non so che', full of tenderness and shy, hesitant affection, reveals the mature Rossini's ability to point psychological detail within a long, evolving dramatic movement. For Cenerentola's gabbled and nonsensical 'Quel ch'è padre, non è padre' ('My father's not my father'), Rossini uses comic patter and a sinking tonality to convey to us Cenerentola's pathetically confused state of mind; he further intensifies the tension by the brilliant use of minatory offstage calls from the ugly sisters.

The 'Prince', actually Dandini, finally makes his entrance with an absurdly grandiloquent cavatina in which he is joined by the chorus and Magnifico's sycophantic household. The sisters leave for the ball but Ramiro and Dandini overhear Cenerentola's request that she may go too (quintet, 'Signor, una parola'). Magnifico refuses, ruthlessly insulting the girl while at the same time trying to make himself agreeable to Ramiro and Dandini. Unhappily for him, Alidoro now chooses to re-enter with information about a third daughter in the household. Magnifico blusters briefly and then, with Cenerentola standing beside him, he announces that the third daughter is in fact dead. In a naive aside, Cenerentola denies the story but Magnifico, warming to his morbid lie, repeats it with a chilling assumption of sincerity as the orchestra judders to one of opera's most shocked silences. Having reduced the audience to numbed disbelief, Rossini launches into one of those ensembles in which the characters attempt to work out with dispassionate concern who is duping whom. Alidoro, disguised once more as the beggar, returns to take Cenerentola to the ball. In the scena and aria added by Rossini for the 1820 Rome revival, 'Là del ciel nell'arcano profondo', Alidoro tells her of the Lord of Creation who will not allow innocence to be crushed.

1.ii *A room in Don Ramiro's country house* 'Prince' Dandini offers Don Magnifico the position of court vintner on the strength of his having sampled 30 barrels without signs of undue staggering. Newly installed, Magnifico passes a decree forbidding the adulteration of wine. The Act 1 finale begins with one of Rossini's finest conspiratorial duets, 'Zitto, zitto, piano, piano', as the Prince and Dandini briefly compare notes on their impressions so far of the Magnifico family. They are mystified by Alidoro's idea of one of the daughters' suitability. When Clorinda and Tisbe track the 'Prince' down he offers his servant Dandini as a possible husband. They are suitably outraged, but outrage turns to bemusement when a girl strangely resembling Cenerentola appears at the ball in the company of Alidoro. Confusion reigns but Dandini, in his role as enterprising puppet-master, announces a feast, and the entire company takes off to dinner in a whirlwind stretta in which, not for the first time in a Rossini finale, the characters rue the fact that they no longer appear to be in touch with reality.

ACT 2.i *A room in Don Ramiro's country house* The banquet is over but Don Magnifico harbours doubts about the progress he and his daughters are making. In the aria 'Sia qualunque delle figlie' he reassures himself that he will eventually be the Prince's father-in-law. Tired of being pursued by 'Prince' Dandini, Cenerentola tells him that she prefers his servant. This is overheard by the Prince and Alidoro; overjoyed, the Prince reveals himself, but Cenerentola forbids him to follow her: if he truly loves her, she insists, he must search her out once she has left the court. She gives him a bracelet that matches one she always wears. In the bravura aria 'Sì, ritrovarla io giuro', the Prince resolves to find and win the mysterious girl. Meanwhile, Dandini is confronted by Magnifico demanding a decision on whom he is going to marry. Dandini launches a superb comic duet,

'Un segreto d'importanza', by counselling patience; then, choosing his moment carefully, he reveals to Magnifico that he is in fact the servant, which throws Magnifico into bewilderment and fury.

2.ii *A room in Don Magnifico's castle* Cenerentola, once more dressed in rags, is singing 'Una volta c'era un re'. Magnifico and his daughters return, remarking again on the similarity between Cenerentola and the guest at the ball. A storm breaks during which Alidoro ensures that the Prince's carriage comes to grief right outside Don Magnifico's castle. Safely inside, the Prince soon recognizes Cenerentola, to the mingled joy and consternation of the various parties. They gradually unpick 'the snarled knot, the tangled web' in the great sextet 'Siete voi?' The magnificent 357-bar movement has its apogee in Cenerentola's great plea to the Prince that Magnifico and his daughters be forgiven, 'Ah, signor, s'è ver che in petto'. It is a moment that marks the final transformation of Cenerentola from mouse-like skivvy to a mature woman capable of real passion.

2.iii *The throne room in Don Ramiro's palace* The fairy-tale transformation of Cenerentola is completed in the final scene into which she enters in triumph to sing the showpiece scena and rondo finale 'Nacqui all'affanno e al pianto'. Here music originally drafted for Almaviva in the final scene of *Il barbiere di Siviglia* finds its proper voice and dramatic resting-place. In particular, a note of pathos and longing is struck amid the vocal triumphalism, making it a worthy conclusion to a score that is less purely comic than is sometimes supposed. Brilliantly entertaining as much of *La Cenerentola* is, it also reveals Rossini's unnervingly dispassionate gaze and, at times, his almost morbid sensitivity to the crueller and more venal aspects of human affairs. RICHARD OSBORNE

Censorship. Censorship has been applied to opera at most times and in most countries. Governments have regarded the theatre, with its direct appeal to a large public gathering, as a potential fount of sedition or disorder. If opera has been censored less than the spoken theatre, it is partly because music is hard to pin down to a set of political or ethical rules, and partly because the opera form itself cannot with ease carry a great deal of specific information.

The actual music of opera has not as a rule been subject to detailed censorship, though music-loving rulers and theatre owners have at times laid down requirements for the kind of operas they would countenance, like Frederick the Great of Prussia with his immutable series of operas by Graun. Totalitarian regimes in modern times have, however, banned whole categories of music (as of other arts). The Nazi regime in Germany forbade performances of 'degenerate art', which it defined to include a number of operas created under the preceding Weimar Republic, among them Berg's *Wozzeck*. Stalin's regime in the Soviet Union in effect banned Shostakovich's *Lady Macbeth of the Mtsensk District* in 1936, two years after its initial production, by mounting a blistering attack in the Communist party paper *Pravda*. In 1948 an official resolution of the party central committee condemned 'formalism' in music. It was preceded by a conference at which Andrey Zhdanov, a leading member of the Politburo, raked up the old insults directed at *Lady Macbeth*, and followed by a campaign of persecution of composers held to have deviated from the party line, among them Shostakovich and Prokofiev: they could get no commissions unless for works of the approved melodic simplicity and patriotic uplift. All this took place in a pervasive climate of fear: rather than specifically censored, Prokofiev's opera *War and Peace* was shaped by the composer's repeated efforts to make both the libretto and the musical style acceptable to the authorities.

Sung words move more slowly than spoken ones, and are less easy to grasp. An opera libretto is therefore much shorter than a play; it cannot readily impart complex information, short of intensive preliminary study (such as used to be given the librettos of Wagner's operas) or, nowadays, surtitles. Hence an opera has at times been allowed by the censor when the play it was based on was forbidden. The best-known example is Mozart's *Le nozze di Figaro*, based on Beaumarchais' then highly topical play, which was banned in Vienna. Lorenzo da Ponte's preface to his libretto, explaining why he has made an 'adaptation' of or 'extract' from the play, mentions, first, the requirements of the opera form, and secondly 'some other prudent considerations and exigencies imposed by morality, place and spectators'. The first point is a valid one. No opera of that date could possibly have carried the freight of information in Figaro's long soliloquy in the play (the censor's chief bugbear), in which he attacks the Count – the representative of the aristocracy – for having 'merely taken the trouble to be born', and acts as spokesman for the discontented commoners who were about to make the French Revolution. On the other hand Da Ponte did not just simplify; in place of the soliloquy he introduced a conventional diatribe against women. In Britain, the mid-Victorian censor banned Dumas *fils*'s play *La dame aux camélias* but allowed its operatic version, *La traviata*, on the grounds that in a musical version 'the story is ... subsidiary to the music and singing'. Again, Strauss's *Salome* was allowed in London in 1910 (with some adaptation of the text and business) while the play it was based on remained banned until 1931. (The point sometimes made that the British censor was more indulgent to works in incomprehensible foreign languages seems invalid here: there were English-language *Traviatas*, and Wilde's *Salomé* was banned in the original French as well as in English.)

Censorship of opera, then, has almost always confined itself to the libretto and the stage action. Though there are glaring examples of such censorship, opera has in the first place been subject for much of its history to self-censorship. But for some uncharacteristic episodes, due to special circumstances, it has been on the side of the ruling order – whatever that was.

The reasons for this are largely economic. Opera is expensive; it has generally required a subsidy, or at least the chance to appeal to a sizable, well-off public. Opera as the voice of an embattled minority is almost a contradiction in terms. It originated in the courts of would-be absolute rulers and in the households of great nobles, whose standing it was meant to enhance. Such patrons or their successors were for many years to go on providing subsidies as well as the most conspicuous part of the audience, even when operas started being given in public theatres rather than in the ruler's or nobleman's own palace. Librettists met such patrons' expectations. Even in our own century, some of the ultra-rich people who owned the Metropolitan Opera in New York (J. P. Morgan's daughter prominent among them) could make their taste prevail: they forced the withdrawal of Strauss's *Salome* after a single performance in 1907.

In the Europe of the 17th and 18th centuries censorship was merely one among many aspects of control over theatres and theatre people, which was vested in a royal official or a board: in England, in the Lord Chamberlain (or, at first, in his subordinate the Master of the Revels); in the German states, in a series of similar court dignitaries; in Naples, in an official who was in the first place responsible for the army, supported by a board. Such control generally carried with it the licensing of theatres and, sometimes, exclusive jurisdiction over the theatrical profession in court cases; the officials in charge had the power to send singers, musicians etc. to gaol for indeterminate but short periods as a disciplinary measure for misbehaviour in the course of their work. In England, exceptionally, these powers fell into disuse in the late 17th century; repeated satirical attacks on the prime minister, Sir Robert Walpole, led to the banning in 1728 of a stage performance of John Gay's ballad opera *Polly* (its publication could not be stopped) and to the 1737 Act which reasserted the Lord Chamberlain's power to license theatres, plays and operas without, however, bringing back his old detailed disciplinary powers. In France, the 1789 revolution ended the old monopoly of opera but not the censorship. In the German and Italian states the old arrangements were maintained; little changed until the granting of liberal constitutions in 1848. These constitutions, as they were restored or extended (after a further period of reaction) about 1860, did not abolish stage censorship, but the new climate of opinion greatly limited its scope.

In most of these countries, censorship until about 1860 (in Britain until 1969) was the job of a subordinate official or officials under the royal dignitary in charge; this subordinate was often a minor literary man who might have notions about propriety of language, and, at the extreme, might try to substitute a virtual libretto of his own for one that was deemed objectionable (as with *Un ballo in maschera*). The normal course, however, was for librettist and manager to avoid subjects likely to raise difficulties, and to meet without too much fuss the censor's requests for detailed changes.

In the early days of opera self-censorship was the norm. Lully's operas for Paris and Versailles, the work of a court official, were vehicles of monarchical propaganda. The operas on religious themes given in mid-17th-century Rome embodied the values of the Counter-Reformation. Even opera of the Venetian type, intended for public theatres, gave its largely aristocratic hearers a version of court life as they liked to imagine it. Metastasio's librettos, which dominated serious opera (outside France) for most of the 18th century, in their more refined way endorsed the virtues of rulers as arbiters of conflict, upholders of law and promoters of the public good.

Comic opera, when it developed in the early 18th century, was more of a problem to censors: it was not at first patronized by courts, it poked fun at people or groups – some of whom might resent it – and it often included rapid improvised gesture in the tradition of *commedia dell'arte*, which did not lend itself to previous censorship and which might be obscene or imitate well-known individuals. All this might cause disorder. These difficulties may explain why such banning of Neapolitan comic operas as we know of took place after the first performances: the librettist Pietro Trinchera, some of whose works lampooned hypocritical monks and nuns (under a pretence of attacking 'false' religion), had to go into hiding after *La tavernola abentorosa* (1741), apparently because he drew attention to it by printing it; G. B. Lorenzi's *Socrate immaginario* (1775, Naples; music by Paisiello) was forbidden after six performances because it made fun of a well-known local scholar. Otherwise, comic opera, which in the early years of the century – especially in Naples – had often used dialect and given a realistic picture of lower-class life, became more and more anodyne in its subject matter and less concrete in its sense of place. Its reliance on stereotypes like the comic foreigner, the temperamental prima donna, or the elderly guardian set on marrying his pretty ward – all that easily makes it look inane today – shows the self-censorship that had to be worked as the genre came more under the official eye.

Even in the French Revolution period, when opera began to deal, though indirectly, with themes inspired by recent experience, self-censorship intervened. The 'rescue operas' of the late 1790s and the 1800s were mostly set in distant times (like Cherubini's *Les deux journées*) or distant places (Poland, the Great St Bernard Pass) or both (Beethoven's *Fidelio*). It did not prevent them from expressing enlightened sentiments in favour of liberty and humanity. When these were missing, as in Méhul's *Mélidore et Phrosine* (1794, a sensitive year), the censor got the librettist to put them in – a mirror image of the contortions which the censors of the old Italian states were to impose, some 40-odd years later, on the libretto of Rossini's Paris opera *Guillaume Tell*: there, not only did the word 'liberty' have to disappear, but likewise 'chains', 'oppressor', even 'freely' used in a non-political sense.

The onset of the Romantic movement nonetheless brought a period of uncommon trouble, in Italian opera especially: it coincided with Europe-wide political reaction after Waterloo and with deepening concern for respectable manners and morals.

Religion was a main stumbling-block. Romantic art was often drawn to it in its picturesque and historical aspects. British censors, however, would not allow biblical characters on stage: Rossini's *Mosè in Egitto* had to be adapted to deal with Peter the Hermit, while Verdi's *Nabucco* was renamed *Nino* and set in a non-biblical period of Babylonian history. The censorship did not relax this general ban until 1909, when *Samson et Dalila* (previously given in 1893 but only in a concert performance) was allowed on stage; though *Salome* in the following year had to disguise the identity of John the Baptist the ban was in effect at an end. In Lutheran Hamburg on the other hand, opera in its earliest days was required to be on biblical subjects. Roman Catholic countries were untroubled by Old Testament subject matter, anyhow by the late 18th century; there had been an attempt to stop biblical opera in Venice in 1703. They were however much exercised by any attempt to represent the clergy or (in a reversal of Counter-Reformation values) saints. Pope Leo, who intervenes in Verdi's *Attila* to save Rome, had to be described as 'an ancient Roman'. Nicolai's *Il templario* was allowed in Milan only on condition that the Grand Master of the Knights Templar and his followers should not appear with the insignia of their order, 'all the more because he has to act the part of a guilty monk'. More damagingly, the Protestant minister in Verdi's *Stiffelio*, whose cloth is central to the story, was not allowed to be a minister at all. The Vienna censor would not at first let a devil appear in *Der Freischütz* or permit Wagner's *Rienzi* to be given at all, as it dealt with a revolution in papal Rome. In Russia, a prohibition on showing Orthodox clergy was the only one that Musorgsky had seriously to heed in *Boris Godunov*; it was met by calling Pimen a 'hermit' and the two rascally monks 'vagrants'. On the whole, just because Romantic artists' interest was in the incidentals of religion rather than in faith, they could often be accommodated by such expedients; when Donizetti however wrote *Poliuto*, based on Corneille's *Polyeucte*, a classical work that does deal with faith, the King of Naples overruled his own censor and banned it, saying 'Let's leave the saints in the calendar and not put them on the stage'.

Kings and their officials felt much the same about putting fellow monarchs on the stage, especially if they were to be conspired against, deposed or assassinated (but not only then: in 1907 *The Mikado* was temporarily banned in Britain on the occasion of a visit by the Japanese Crown Prince). Romantic art took a deep interest in critical and violent moments of history. Where even the British writer Mary Russell Mitford could not in the 1820s get her play about Charles I past the Lord Chamberlain, it is not surprising that Donizetti and Verdi should have run into deep trouble from the suspicious Italian states; the problem was at its worst in the decade of reaction after the 1848 revolutions (notably affecting *Maria Stuarda*, *Rigoletto* and *Un ballo in maschera*).

But although this is the best-known aspect of operatic censorship, it mattered less than the steady drizzle of demands for the avoidance of the personal, the indecorous and the specific. In Italy especially, persistent neo-classical ideals of elevated diction came together with fear of scandal and with 19th-century prudery. When the Rome and Naples censors of the 1850s faced *Rigoletto* with its deliberate justification of the 'low' and the grotesque they hacked out so much that in the end there was no longer a hunchback, a buffoon, a curse, an assignation or a sack; the work was given under three other titles. Suicide, multiple murder and public execution, all staples of Romantic drama, likewise made censors nervous; some operatic characters therefore died without visible cause (for example in *I Capuleti e i Montecchi* and *Maria Padilla*).

In Germany there were far fewer difficulties, probably because German Romanticism was 'folkish', nostalgic and often socially and politically conservative. French censorship under Napoleon III was sensitive to possible diplomatic repercussions (as with *La Grande-Duchesse de Gérolstein*). Russian composers had less trouble than might have been expected. Putting a monarch of the reigning dynasty on the stage, forbidden by an 1837 decree, caused Tchaikovsky (in *Cherevichki*) and Rimsky-Korsakov (*Christmas Eve*) some difficulties. The one glaring case was Rimsky-Korsakov's *The Golden Cockerel*, which the censor rightly spotted as a bitter satire on autocracy and accordingly held up for two years, past the composer's death. Though not quite thought through as an allegory, *The Golden Cockerel* seems to be an almost unique example of an opera that was not only politically subversive but was meant to be. Since then, with the very considerable exceptions of the Nazi and Stalinist tyrannies, censorship of opera has not been a serious problem.

*

'Esecutori contro la bestemmia', Ruling of 29 Nov 1703 (*I-Vas* b.60 reg.99 c.5)

Memorandum: I. R. Direzione Generale della Polizia, to Direzione, I. R. Teatri, Milan, 22 May 1840 (*PAi* xerox 26/3)

V. Hallays-Dabot: *Histoire de la censure théâtrale en France* (Paris, 1862)

L. Quicherat: *Adolphe Nourrit* (Paris, 1867), i, 389–90

F. Chrysander: 'Ueber die Unsittlichkeiten in unseren Operntexten', *AMZ*, xiv (1889), 257–9, 273–4, 305–8

L. C. Borghi: *La polizia sugli spettacoli nella Repubblica veneziana* (Venice, 1898), 21–4

W. H. Cummings: 'The Lord Chamberlain and Opera in London, 1700 to 1741', *PMA*, xl (1913–14), 37–72

L. Bourquin: 'La controverse sur la comédie', 'La querelle du théâtre', *Revue d'histoire littéraire de la France* (Paris, 1919–21)

'Sumbur vmesto muzïki; ob opere "Ledi Makbet Mtsenskogo Uyezda" D. Shostakovicha' [Muddle instead of Music: on Shostakovich's Opera *Lady Macbeth of the Mtsensk District*], *Pravda* (28 Jan 1936); *SovM* (1936), no.2, pp.4ff

E. Newman: *The Life of Richard Wagner* (London and New York, 1937), i, 374

E. Monti: 'Contributo ad uno studio sui "libretti d'opera" in Lombardia e sulla censura teatrale in Milano nell' Ottocento', *Archivio storico lombardo* (July–Dec 1939), 306–66

W. H. Rubsamen: 'Political and Ideological Censorship of Opera', *PAMS* (1946), 30–42

A. Werth: *Musical Uproar in Moscow* (London, 1949)

C. Di Stefano: *La censura teatrale in Italia (1600–1962)* (Bologna, 1964)

R. Findlater: *Banned! A Review of Theatrical Censorship in Britain* (London, 1967)

I. Kolodin: *The Metropolitan Opera 1883–1966* (New York, 1967), 185–7

V. Monaco: *G. B. Lorenzi e la commedia per musica* (Naples, 1968), 122–5

G. Abraham: 'Satire and Symbolism in *The Golden Cockerel*', *ML*, lii (1971), 45–54

P. Schmid: '*Maria Stuarda* and *Buondelmonte*', *Opera*, xxiv (1973), 1060–66

J. Commons: 'Un contributo ad uno studio su Donizetti e la censura napoletana', *1° Convegno internazionale di studi donizettiani: Bergamo 1975*, 65–106

——: '*Maria Stuarda* and the Neapolitan Censorship', *Journal of the Donizetti Society*, iii (1977), 151–67

F. Degrada: *'L'opera napoletana', Storia dell'opera*, ed. G. Barblan and A. Basso (Turin, 1977), i, 267

R. W. Oldani: '*Boris Godunov* and the Censor', *19th Century Music*, ii (1978–9), 245–53

M. Lavagetto: *Un caso di censura: il 'Rigoletto'* (Milan, 1979)

C. Maurer-Zenck: 'Unbewältigte Vergangenheit: Kreneks "Karl V" in Wien: zur nicht bevorstehenden Wiener Erstaufführung', *Mf*, xxxii (1979), 273–88

N. Tschulik: 'Die verhinderte Uraufführung von Kreneks Karl V', *ÖMz*, xxiv (1979), 122–9

M. Viale Ferrero: '*Guillaume Tell* a Torino (1839–40) ovvero una "procella" scenografica', *RIM*, xiv (1979), 378–94

B. Brévan: *Les changements de la vie musicale parisienne de 1774 à 1799* (Paris, 1980), 117

E. Sala di Felice: *Metastasio: ideologia, drammaturgia, spettacolo* (Milan, 1983)

M. E. C. Bartlet: 'Politics and the Fate of *Roger et Olivier*, a Newly Recovered Opera by Grétry', *JAMS*, xxxvii (1984), 98–138

J. Black: 'Code of Instructions for the Censorship of Theatrical Works: Naples, 1849', *Journal of the Donizetti Society*, v (1984), 147–50

——: *The Italian Romantic Libretto: a Study of Salvadore Cammarano* (Edinburgh, 1984)

J. Rosselli: *The Opera Industry in Italy from Cimarosa to Verdi* (Cambridge, 1984)

C. Maurer-Zenck: 'The Ship Loaded with Faith and Hope: Krenek's *Karl V* and the Viennese Politics of the Thirties', *MQ*, lxxi (1985), 116–34

R. M. Isherwood: *Farce and Fantasy: Popular Entertainment in Eighteenth-Century Paris* (New York and Oxford, 1986)

M. E. C. Bartlet: 'On the Freedom of the Theatre and Censorship: the *Adrien* Debate (1792)', *Musique, histoire, démocratie: Paris 1989*

I. D. Glikman: 'Kazn' "Ledi Makbet"' [The Execution of Lady Macbeth], *Sovetskaya kul'tura* (23 Sept 1989)

R. J. Goldstein: *Political Censorship of the Arts and the Press in Nineteenth-Century Europe* (London, 1989)

M. Spada: '"Ernani" e la censura napoletana', *Studi verdiani*, v (1989), 11–34

R. Taruskin: 'The Opera and the Dictator: the peculiar martyrdom of Dmitri Shostakovich', *New Republic* (20 March 1989), 34–40

JOHN ROSSELLI

Central City. American town in Colorado, near Denver. The Central City Opera, founded as a summer festival in 1932, performs in an 800-seat stone Victorian structure completed in 1878 (shortly before the end of the Colorado gold rush), at which opera, operetta and drama were performed before 1900. The current company, largely the inspiration of Anne Evans, daughter of Colorado's second territorial governor, was conceived first of all as a Mozart ensemble because of the ideal dimensions of the house. Early seasons included both opera and drama; indeed, the opening performance featured Lillian Gish in *Camille*. Singers heard there early in their careers include Beverly Sills (her only Aida was sung there), James McCracken, Regina Resnik and Norman Treigle; Samuel Ramey had his first live opera experience there as a chorus member in 1963 in *Don Giovanni*. The company closed during World War II, and financial problems prevented performances for the whole of 1982. It was successfully restructured and now presents a seven-week festival season each summer that includes two operas from the standard repertory and one classical operetta, on which special affection is focussed. Douglas Moore's *The Ballad of Baby Doe*, a story that exploits local history, was commissioned for the company and had its première in 1956. All performances are in English. Members of the apprentice programme are active in the Denver region throughout the winter, where they perform at times with the Colorado SO. Recent seasons have witnessed vast improvements in the house itself in efforts to restore it to its original brilliance. WES BLOMSTER

Central Opera Service. An organization founded in 1954 by Eleanor Belmont and sponsored by the Metropolitan Opera National Council, with headquarters in New York. Its 2000 members included opera companies and workshops, professionals involved with opera and interested individuals. It provided information about performing material and repertory and offered a wide range of services including advising on organization, public relations and fund-raising techniques. From 1959 it published a bulletin (quarterly from 1971–2), several complete issues of which consist of important directories: *Opera Companies and Workshops in the United States and Canada* (annually from 1962), *Directory of American Contemporary Operas* (1967 and supplements), *Directory of English Opera Translations* (3/1974 and supplements), *Directory of Operas and Publishers* (1976), *Career Guide for the Young American Singer* (3/1978 and quarterly addenda), and *Directory of Sets and Costumes for Rent: Operas – Operettas – Musicals* (3/1979 and annual addenda). The service ceased operations in October 1990; its information and research functions are continued by OPERA AMERICA. JOHN SHEPARD

Cerha, Friedrich (*b* Vienna, 17 Feb 1926). Austrian composer. He studied at the Vienna Academy of Music, and became one of the central figures of Austrian avant-garde music after 1945. He heard the first production of Berg's *Lulu* in Vienna in 1949 and studied analysis with Joseph Polnauer, a former pupil of Schoenberg. In 1958 he co-founded the Vienna chamber ensemble Die Reihe. His work on *Lulu*, of which he eventually completed Act 3, was crucial to his musical development and consequently to his own operas, even though for a long time he composed mainly instrumental music. Traditional opera exerted little influence on Cerha's first dramatic works: instead of setting a drama, he developed the stage action from the musical structures. In the seven-part composition *Spiegel* (1960–61) for orchestra, tape and silent actors, first given complete at the ISCM Festival at Graz in 1972, he created blocks of subtly changing sound, while eliminating traditional rhythmic, melodic and harmonic structures. His interest in visual elements is reflected in the graphic notation of the score. The composer indicated a particular stage action, but suggested that this was only one possibility among several; indeed, concert performances proved that the music could stand alone without the work having necessarily to be staged. In *Netzwerk* (1962–80) for two voices, six speakers, silent actors and orchestra, Cerha's first composition specifically for the stage, music is again the starting-point for the action. There is no continuous plot and singers and speakers use non-semantic language made up of 57 sounds of the phonetic alphabet. The scenes show societal groups and the place of the individual within them; especially remarkable are the short intermediate sections (*Regresse*) that use, for dramatic purposes, a more conventional musical idiom.

Baal, Cerha's first opera in the traditional sense, was begun in 1974 and given its première at the Salzburg Festival in 1981; in it the composer dissociated himself from his earlier experiments. In a number of loosely connected scenes Brecht's play tells the story of the poet Baal, a man of both rudeness and artistic sophistication. In some respects Baal is a victim of society; on the other hand, he is himself extremely brutal. (It seems ironic that by setting a play that focusses on a man who does not wish to be integrated into society, Cerha became part of the élitist world of the *Literaturoper*.) Whereas in Brecht's play Baal's inhumanity can be clearly seen (Brecht's reinterpretation of the play in 1954 has to be understood as a strategic political move demanded by the time), Cerha's music makes him a victim rather than a criminal. The composer himself drew the obvious parallel with the protagonists in Berg's operas. The large orchestra, the rich chromatic polyphony and the almost symphonic orchestral interludes all try to make the audience understand and sympathize with Baal. Other compositional devices, such as the twisted *Volkston* of the stage music, the integration of traditional forms and the undogmatic use of serial techniques, can also be traced back to Berg's music.

In *Der Rattenfänger* (1984–7), a joint commission from the Styrian Autumn Festival, the Graz Opera and the Vienna Staatsoper, Cerha goes a step further in his social criticism while preserving the more or less retrospective musical language of *Baal*. In some parts, the musical language is simplified, and the songs function as traditional arias, interrupting the action and explaining the background of the singer. In his play Carl Zuckmayer rewrote the old German legend of the Pied Piper of Hamelin by adding many references to the present. At times the plot seems overloaded with episodes too obvious in their social criticism; but the colourful music and Cerha's masterful orchestration keep the opera from falling apart in spite of its duration of more than three hours.

Despite several successful productions of his own operas, Cerha is best known internationally for his completion of Act 3 of Berg's *Lulu*, which he began in 1962 at the request of Universal Edition. It had its first performance at the Opéra, Paris, on 24 February 1979, and Cerha's *Arbeitsbericht zur Herstellung des 3. Akts der Oper 'Lulu' von Alban Berg* was published in Vienna the same year. He obtained access to Berg's sketches for *Lulu* only after this production, however, which led to some minor revisions to the score.

See also LULU (ii).

Spiegel, 1960–68 (cycle, 7 pts, Cerha), Graz, Stadt, 1972
Netzwerk, 1962–80 (Cerha), Vienna, Wien, 31 May 1981
Baal, 1974–81 (2 pts, Cerha, after B. Brecht), Salzburg, Festspielhaus, 16 Aug 1981, vs (Vienna, 1981)
Der Rattenfänger, 1984–7 (2 pts, Cerha, after C. Zuckmayer), Graz, Stadt, 26 Sept 1987

*

PEM (S. Weismann)
F. Cerha: *Arbeitsbericht zur Herstellung des 3. Aktes der Oper 'Lulu' von Alban Berg* (Vienna, 1979)
G. Perle: 'The Cerha-Edition', *International Alban Berg Society Newsletter*, no.8 (1979), 5–7
W. Szmolyan: 'Der Komponist Friedrich Cerha', *ÖMz*, xxxiv (1979), 148–52
F. Cerha: 'Zu meinem Musiktheater', *ÖMz*, xxxv (1980), 278–82
——: 'Von "Exercises" zu "Netzwerk"', *ÖMz*, xxxvi (1981), 318–22
K. Ager: 'Friedrich Cerha: *Spiegel*', *Melos*, xlviii/3 (1986), 2–39
F. Cerha: 'Some Further Notes on my Realization of Act III of *Lulu*', *The Berg Companion*, ed. D. Jarman (London, 1989), 261–7

WERNER GRÜNZWEIG

Cerilli, Francesco. *See* CIRILLO, FRANCESCO.

Cerlone, Francesco (*b* Naples, 25 March 1722; *d* Naples, *c*1812). Italian playwright and librettist. Little is known of his formative years except that he followed family tradition and worked as an embroiderer. He probably did not have a formal education but learnt of the theatre through the improvised performances of *commedia dell'arte* troupes that appeared regularly in the piazzas of Naples. He followed a troupe to Rome about 1750, and by the early 1760s his own efforts as a playwright in Naples had come to the attention of the critics. Throughout his writing career, Cerlone was criticized for a lack of sophistication. Yet his work was well received by Neapolitan audiences and he was commissioned to write librettos for such celebrated composers as Paisiello, Piccinni and Cimarosa; his work was staged in both the Neapolitan theatres devoted to comic opera: the Teatro Nuovo (11 librettos, 1764–80) and the Teatro dei Fiorentini (3, 1768–83). In addition to 56 plays, 17 librettos are extant, many showing a talent for popular comedy and, in some cases, for fantasy.

cm – *commedia per musica* dg – *dramma giocoso* int – *intermezzo*

La fedeltà in amore (cm), G. Tritto, 1764; *La pittrice* (int), C. Franchi, 1768; *Il barone di Trocchia* (int), G. Gazzaniga, 1768; *L'osteria di Marechiaro* (cm), Paisiello, 1768 (G. Insanguine, 1768); *Li napoletani in America* (cm), N. Piccinni, 1768; *La Zelmira* (cm), Paisiello, 1770; *Le trame per amore* (cm), Paisiello, 1770; *La Mergellina* (cm), F. Corbisieri, 1771; *I scherzi d'amore e di fortuna* (cm), Paisiello, 1771; *La Dardané* (cm), Paisiello, 1772; *La finta parigina* (cm), Cimarosa, 1773; *L'osteria di Pausilippo* (cm), Corbisieri, 1775; *Le astuzie amorose* (cm), Paisiello, 1775 (M. Mortellari, 1775); *La marinella* (farsetta), Tritto, 1780; *Il principe riconosciuto* (cm), Tritto, 1780; *La Bellinda* (cm), Tritto, 1781; *La creduta infedele* (cm), Gazzaniga, 1783

WILLIAM R. BOWEN

Cernay [Pointu], **Germaine** (*b* Le Havre, 1900; *d* Paris, 1943). French mezzo-soprano. At the Paris Opéra in 1925 she sang Eurycleia in Fauré's *Pénélope* but for most of her career was at the Opéra-Comique, where she made her début in Alfano's *Risurrezione* with Mary Garden in 1927. She appeared there in the French stage première of Pierre de Bréville's *Eros vainqueur* (1932) and also sang Charlotte in *Werther*, Mignon and Carmen as well as many secondary parts such as Suzuki in *Madama Butterfly* and Mallika in *Lakmé*. She enjoyed some success at the Monnaie in Brussels and had a special reputation as a singer of Bach. Her strong, bright-toned voice and forthright rather than subtle style are heard in recordings, which include the roles of Mignon and Geneviève (*Pelléas et Mélisande*).

J. B. STEANE

Cerquetti, Anita (*b* Montecorsaro-Macerata, 13 April 1931). Italian soprano. She studied in Perugia, making her début in 1951 at Spoleto as Aida. She appeared in Verona, Florence, Chicago and at La Scala, where she sang Abigaille (*Nabucco*) in 1958. Her roles included Norma (which she took over from Maria Callas during a performance at Rome), Mathilde (*Guillaume Tell*) and La Gioconda, but her magnificent, vibrant voice and fiery temperament were displayed to best advantage in Verdi: as Elvira (*Ernani*), Leonora (*Il trovatore*), Amelia (*Ballo*), Hélène (*Les vêpres siciliennes*) and Elisabeth de Valois (*Don Carlos*). In 1960, after a career of less than ten years, she was forced to retire because of ill health.

ELIZABETH FORBES

Čert a Káča. Opera by Antonín Dvořák; *see* *DEVIL AND KATE, THE*.

Čertova stěna. Opera by Bedřich Smetana; *see* *DEVIL'S WALL, THE*.

Cervantes (Saavedra), Miguel de (*b* Alcalá de Henares, ?29 Sept 1547; *d* Madrid, 22 April 1616). Spanish writer. He was brought up in Valladolid, Seville and Madrid, and in about 1569 went to Rome in the service of Cardinal Acquaviva. He distinguished himself as a soldier and was wounded at the Battle of Lepanto in 1571. Captured by corsairs in 1575 and taken as a slave to Algiers, he was held captive by the Moors until 1580. After his return to Spain he made an unhappy marriage, fell frequently into trouble with the law and was several times imprisoned. Despite the success of *Don Quixote* (1605–15) he lived in straitened circumstances to the end of his life.

Cervantes's works and life have stimulated many composers from the 17th century onwards. *Don Quixote* alone has served as the basis for more than 100 pieces; the first opera was probably *Il Don Chisciot della Mancia* by Carlo Sajon (1680, Venice). This was followed by J. P. Förtsch's opera *Der irrende Ritter Don Quixotte de la Mancia* (1690, Hamburg), the engaging *Comical History of Don Quixote*, a play by Thomas D'Urfey with music by Purcell and others (1694–6, London), and Henry Fielding's witty ballad opera *Don Quixote in England* (1734, London), which in turn served as a model for Arne's rumbustious burletta *Squire Badger* (1772). The first Spanish opera was *Las bodas de Camacho* (1784) by Pablo Esteve y Grimau. The best-known treatment is Massenet's (1910). Other writings by Cervantes that have inspired several operatic works include the short story *La gitanilla* from the *Novelas ejemplares* (1613), the basis of Balfe's *The Bohemian Girl*, and the farce *La cueva de Salamanca* from *Ocho comedias y ocho entremeses nuevos* (1615). Cervantes himself was the subject of stage works by C. G. Foignet (1793), E. Lassen (on his capture by the Moors; 1865), R. Aceves y Lozano (on his role in the

Battle of Lepanto; 1867) and Johann Strauss (*Das Spitzentuch der Königin*, 1880); the last is almost wholly invented.

El ingenioso hidalgo Don Quixote de la Mancha (novel, pt 1, 1605), *Segunda parte del ingenioso cavallero Don Quixote de la Mancha* (pt 2, 1615): C. Sajon, 1680, as Il Don Chisciot della Mancia; J. P. Förtsch, 1690, Der irrende Ritter Don Quixotte de la Mancia; H. Purcell, collab. Eccles and others, 1694–5, The Comical History of Don Quixote; A. d'Eve, 1700, Het Gouvernement von Sancho Pança; F. B. Conti, 1719, Don Chisciotte in Sierra Morena; Caldara, 1727; Ristori, 1727, Un pazzo ne fà cento, ovvero Don Chisciotte; Treu, 1727; [composer unknown], Portugal, 1733, Vida do grande Don Quixotte e do gordo Sancho Pança; Caldara, 1733, Sancio Pansa, governatore dell'isola Barattaria; A. J. Da Silva, 1733; Fielding, 1734, Don Quixote in England (rev. T. A. Arne, 1772, Squire Badger); C. F. Panard, 1734; J. Ayres, 1741, Sancho at Court, or The Mock Governor; Leo, 1743, Il fantastico; G. B. Martini, 1746; Holzbauer, 1755; N. Piccinni, carn. ?1755–6, Il curioso del suo proprio danno; Telemann, 1761; F.-A. D. Philidor, 1762, Sancho Pança dans son isle; Gherardeschi, 1764, Il curioso indiscreto; Bernardini, 1769; Paisiello, 1769; N. Piccinni, 1770; Salieri, 1770; S. Arnold, 1774; Anfossi, 1777, Il curioso indiscreto; Beecke, 1784; Esteve y Grimau, 1784, Las bodas de Camacho; ?F. Bianchi, 1788, Il nuovo Don Chischiotte; Champein, 1789, Le nouveau Don Quichotte; Hubaček, 1791; Tarchi, 1791; A.-E.-M. Grétry, 1792, Basile, ou A trompeur, trompeur et demi; Arnold, 1793, The Mountaineers; Dittersdorf, 1795, Don Quixote der Zweyte; W. Müller, 1802; Generali, 1805; A. de Miari, 1810; F. L. Seidel, 1811; M. García, ?1814–17; Bochsa, 1815, Les noces de Camache; ? Mercadante, 1825, Les noces de Camache; Mendelssohn, 1827, Die Hochzeit des Camacho; Mercadante, carn. 1829–30; Donizetti, 1833, Il furioso all'isola di San Domingo; Rodwell, 1833; Mazzucato, 1836; Macfarren, 1846; Clapisson, 1847; Hervé, 1848; Moniuszko, 1849, Nowy Don Quichot; A. Reparaz, 1859, La venta encantada; C. Rispo, 1859; M. F. Caballero, 1861, El loco de la guardilla; Hochberg, 1861, Der neue Don Quixote; P. E. Arrieta, 1864, La ínsula Barataria; E. Lassen, 1865, Le captif; A. Reparaz, 1866, Las Bodas de Camacho; E. H. A. Boulanger, 1869; A. Müller, 1874; Pessard, 1874; Clay, 1876; F. Ricci, comp. 1876 (inc.); E. Planas, 1877; Rohl, collab. Weinzierte, 1877; Neuendorff, 1882; L. de Larra, 1887, En un lugar de La Mancha; Roth, 1888; R. De Koven, 1889; Santonja, 1896; Jaques-Dalcroze, 1897, Sancho Pança; G. W. Rauchenecker, 1897; Kienzl, 1898; Jarecki, comp. 1901, Nowy Don Kiszot; Chapí, 1902, La venta de Don Quijote; P. E. de Ferrán, 1903, Las bodas de Camacho; W. G. Kaufmann, 1903; Legouix, 1903, Le gouvernement de Sancho Pança; Teodoro San José, 1905; T. Barrera, 1907, El carro de las cortes de la muerte; Beer-Walbrunn, 1908; T. J. Hervitt, 1909; R. Heuberger, 1910; Massenet, 1910; E. Ábrányi, 1917; M. de Falla, 1923, El retablo de maese Pedro; E. Lévy, 1930; R. Halffter, comp. 1934–6, Clavileño; A. José, 1934; R. Rodríguez Albert, 1948; Frazzi, 1952; Frazzi, 1953, Le nozze di Camaccio; C. Halffter, 1970

Novelas ejemplares (short stories, 1613):
- *El casamiento engañoso*: Anfossi, 1779, as Il matrimonio per inganno
- *La fuerza de la sangre*: Auber, 1824, as Léocadie
- *La gitanilla [Preciosa]*: C. G. Neefe, 1777, as Die Zigeuner; Kaffka, 1778, as Die Zigeuner; Balfe, 1843, as The Bohemian Girl; A. Reparaz, 1861; E. García, 1890; A. Vives, 1901, as La buenaventura; Gabrielson, 1934, as Gipsy Blonde
- *El celoso extremeño*: C. Dibdin, 1768, as The Padlock; T. Barrera, 1908
- *Rinconete y Cortadillo*: Doncel, 1850, as La Picaresca
- *La ilustre fregona*: J. Guerrero, 1926, as El huésped del sevillano; Laparra, 1931

Ocho comedias y ocho entremeses nuevos (plays, 1615):
- *La cueva de Salamanca*: Winter, 1785, as Der Bettelstudent, oder Das Donnerwetter; E. Istel, 1906, as Der fahrende Schüler; J. Gay, 1908; M. Giró, as L'étudiant de Salamanque (unperf.); Paumgartner, 1923, as Die Höhle von Salamanca; R. Mojsisovics, 1926, as Der Zauberer; F. Lattuada, 1938, as La caverna di Salamanca; J. Bach, 1980, as The Student from Salamanca
- *La guarda cuidadosa*: H. Haug, 1966, as Le gardien vigilant
- *Los habladores*: Offenbach, 1862, as Les bavards
- *El retablo de las maravillas*: F. Mannino, 1963, as Il quadro delle meraviglie
- *El viejo celoso*: Petrassi, 1949, as Il cordovano; H. Aitken, 1980, as Felipe

*

V. Espinós: *Las realizaciones musicales del 'Quijote'* (Madrid, 1933)
——: *El 'Quijote' en la música* (Barcelona, 1947)
C. Haywood: 'Musical Settings to Cervantes Texts', *Cervantes Across the Centuries*, ed. A. Flores and M. J. Bernardete (New York, 1947, 2/1969), 264–73
M. Querol Gavaldá: *La música en las obras de Cervantes* (Barcelona, 1948)
G. Diego: 'Cervantes y la música', *Anales Cervantinos*, i (1951), 5–40
S. Kunze: 'Die Entstehung eines Buffo-Librettos: Don Quijote-Bearbeitungen', *DJbM*, xii (1967), 79–95
J. B. Avalle-Arce and E. C. Riley, eds.: *Suma Cervantina* (London, 1973)
M. McKendrick: *Cervantes* (Boston, 1980) JACK SAGE

Cervená, Sona (*b* Prague, 9 Sept 1925). Czech mezzo-soprano. She studied in Prague and first joined an operetta ensemble there before making her début in 1954 at Brno, where her success as Octavian in 1957 took her to the Prague National Theatre and thence to the Staatsoper, East Berlin, 1958–61. After this she became a resident principal at Frankfurt, where she made her home. She sang in a wide variety of performances, including the première of Wagner-Régeny's *Das Bergwerk zu Falun* (1961) at the Salzburg Festival, and made appearances at leading opera houses including Dresden, Hamburg and Vienna as well as at Bayreuth. Later roles in her career include Kabanicha (1983, Brussels) and several in operetta. NOËL GOODWIN

Červinková-Riegrová, Marie (*b* Prague, 9 Aug 1854; *d* Prague, 19 Jan 1895). Czech librettist. She was a daughter of the prominent *Staročech* politician F. L. Rieger and received a comprehensive private education. Her first libretto was written originally for her husband Václav Červinka, but was set ultimately by Šebor, as a conservative response to *The Bartered Bride*, though it failed to win favour with the public. *Dimitrij* was written expressly for Šebor, but he proved so dilatory that both this and *Jakobín* ('The Jacobin') were set by Dvořák. Červinková-Riegrová complied conscientiously with Dvořák's many requests for modifications; after his daughter's death Rieger himself supplied extra material for Dvořák's revision of *The Jacobin*.

Zmařená svatba [The Frustrated Wedding], Šebor, 1879 (orig. for V. Červinka); *Dimitrij*, Dvořák, 1882, rev. 1894 (orig. for Šebor but not set by him); *Jakobín* [The Jacobin], Dvořák, 1889, rev. 1898; *Dal si hádat* [He was Made to Argue], Červinka, 1892

*

ČSHS [incl. further bibliography]
L. Bráfová: *Rieger, Smetana, Dvořak* (Prague, 1913) [reminiscences by Červinková-Riegrová's sister]
J. Burghauser, ed.: *Marie Červinková-Riegrová: Dimitrij* (Prague, 1961) [critical edn with biographical introduction]
V. Forst, ed.: *Lexikon české literatury*, i (Prague, 1985) [incl. further bibliography]
J. Tyrrell: *Czech Opera* (Cambridge, 1988), 116–17, 164, 236

For further bibliography *see* DVOŘÁK, ANTONÍN. JOHN TYRRELL

Cesarini, Carlo Francesco (*b* San Martino [Urbino], 1666; *d* after 1741). Italian composer. Well known as a violinist, he also wrote dramatic works including at least nine oratorios, one act for each of four operas, and three serenatas for Christmas eve performances at the Vatican. He also set various cantatas to texts by Cardinal Benedetto Pamphili, including one in May 1688 to celebrate the birth of the Prince of Wales. In

1690 Cesarini succeeded Lulier as the manager of Pamphili's musical establishment in Bologna. He became *maestro di cappella* for the church of Il Gesù on 1 September 1704. His work for Roman churches and families (including the Ruspoli and Borghese as well as the Pamphili) made him a wealthy man. When he retired from Il Gesù on 31 August 1741, the prefect of the church requested copies of all of his compositions, because their excellence was 'rarely matched by composers of the present day'. He was a gifted composer in the tuneful yet contrapuntal 'Corellian' style of the late 17th century. His compositions were almost all for the church or for private performances; indeed, only the first of his four operatic ventures was written for a public theatre.

Il Clearco in Negroponte [Act 3] (dramma, 3, after A. Arcoleo), Rome, Capranica, 18 Jan 1695, arias *D-MÜs*, *I-Rc*, *Rmalvezzi*, *US-NYlibin* [Act 1 by B. Gaffi, Act 2 by G. Lulier]

L'amore eroico fra pastori [Act 1] (favola pastorale, 3, P. Ottoboni), Rome, Palazzo della Cancelleria, Feb 1696 [Act 2 by G. Lulier, Act 3 by G. Bononcini]; rev. A. Scarlatti, as La pastorella, Rome, Venetian embassy, 5 Feb 1705, arias *GB-Lbl*; rev. P. A. Motteux and V. Urbani, as Love's Triumph, London, Queen's, 26 Feb 1708, arias (London, 1708)

Giunio Bruto, overo La caduta de Tarquinii [Act 1], 1711 (dramma, 3, ?G. Sinibaldi), unperf., *A-Wn* [Act 2 by A. Caldara, Act 3 by A. Scarlatti]

La finta rapita [Act 3] (favola boscareccia, 3, D. Renda), Cisterna, Principe di Caserta, Jan 1714 [Act 1 by Giuseppe Valentini, Act 2 by N. Romaldi]

*

H. J. Marx: 'Die "Giustificazioni della Casa Pamphilij" als musikgeschichtliche Quelle', *Studi musicali*, xii (1983), 124, 133, 161–84

E. Careri: 'Giuseppe Valentini (1681–1753): Documenti inediti', *NA*, new ser., v (1987), 91, 95

S. Franchi: *Drammaturgia romana: Repertorio bibliografico cronologico dei testi drammatici pubblicati a Roma e nel Lazio, secolo xvii* (Rome, 1988) LOWELL LINDGREN

České Budějovice (Ger. Budweis). City in the Jihočeský region of Czechoslovakia. Its first theatre, built in 1764 in the oldest part of town, was replaced by the Městské Divadlo (Town Theatre), constructed 1817–19. Although the theatre was originally German, touring Czech companies staged opera in May and June. In 1919, the year after Czechoslovakia gained its independence, the Jihočeské Národní Divadlo (South Bohemian National Theatre) opened with Smetana's *The Bartered Bride* and *Dalibor*. Over the next ten years its professional company performed 70 operas, including 24 by Czech composers, and toured northern Bohemia, visiting the industrial regions of towns such as Most and Ústí nad Labem. From 1929 to 1940 only operettas and Czech plays were staged, while during the occupation only German theatre was performed. Despite war damage, the theatre was restored and it reopened in 1946. It underwent organizational changes under the management of the Regional National Committee and in 1955 became known as the Jihočeské Divadlo (South Bohemian Theatre). Opera was reintroduced in 1954 and became a regular feature in 1959.

The company is particularly noted for its chamber productions, including works by Haydn, Paisiello, Vranický, Rossini, Mozart, Otmar Mácha and Evžen Zámečník. From 1971 it also played in the Baroque theatre (built 1682) in the castle nearby in Český Krumlov. After reconstruction work, the South Bohemian Theatre reopened in 1990 with Mozart's *Don Giovanni*.

K. Padrta and others: 'Hudba' [Music], *Jihočeská vlastivěda* (České Budějovice, 1989)

Z. Kazilová and others: *Jihočeské divadlo* [South Bohemian Theatre], (České Budějovice, 1990) EVA HERRMANNOVÁ

Cesti, Antonio [Pietro] (*b* Arezzo, bap. 5 Aug 1623; *d* Florence, 14 Oct 1669). Italian composer and singer. He was the most celebrated Italian musician of his generation.

1. LIFE. Cesti's baptismal name was Pietro; he took the name Antonio on joining the Franciscan order. (The name 'Marc'Antonio' is incorrect.) Though often associated with Venice, where several of his operas were highly successful, his musical training apparently began in Arezzo. Baini and Coradini claimed that Cesti was a pupil of Abbatini in Città di Castello, Caffi that he studied with Carissimi; no known document supports either claim.

Cesti's early training as a singer came through service as a choirboy at Arezzo. In 1637, he joined the Franciscan order at Volterra and entered the monastery of S Francesco of Arezzo. On 10 September 1643 he was elected organist at Volterra, and by 8 March 1644 organist at S Croce in Florence. From 27 February 1645 until September 1649 his activities again centred in Volterra, and he began to enjoy Medici patronage. In 1647 he sang in an opera inaugurating Prince Matthias's new theatre in Siena and asked the prince to support his (unsuccessful) application to become *maestro di cappella* of Pisa Cathedral in 1648. He was a favourite of Cardinal Giovanni Carlo de' Medici and the Grand Duke of Tuscany Ferdinando II (see Cinelli Calvoli). He must have become acquainted with members of a Florentine literary circle later known as the Accademia dei Percossi; one member, Giulio Maffei, owned property near Volterra, where he was visited by others, including G. A. Cicognini and G. F. Apolloni, who both later supplied Cesti with librettos. The painter and writer Salvator Rosa, the circle's most distinguished member, became Cesti's close friend; from 27 March 1649 his letters provide significant biographical information.

Cesti's career as an opera composer is generally dated from the supposed production of *Orontea* at the Teatro di SS Apostoli, Venice, in 1649. This assertion, made by Ivanovich in the late 17th century, has been seriously challenged by Bianconi and Walker (1975). Evidence now suggests that Cesti composed his *Orontea* for Innsbruck in 1656. Although details about his activities before *Alessandro vincitor di se stesso* (Carnival 1651, Venice) are sketchy, he may have sung in the Florentine première of Cavalli's *Giasone* (dedication 15 May 1650); Bianconi suggests that Cesti, a tenor, sang either Aegeus or Demo. In several letters Rosa mentioned Cesti, calling him 'the glory and splendour of the secular stage' (3 July 1650). On 24 August 1650, Rosa wrote to Maffei alluding to an affair between Cesti and a certain Signora Anna Maria; this was Anna Maria Sardelli, who sang the part of Campaspe in Cesti's *Alessandro*. Cesti probably sang with touring opera companies at this time; on 30 October 1650 the superior-general of his order addressed an official rebuke to his monastery at Arezzo, citing him for his 'dishonourable and irregular life' and referring to a stage performance at Lucca. During this period Cesti met Francesco Sbarra ('gentiluomo lucchese'), who became his most frequent librettist.

Rosa, in his satire on music (*La musica*), deplored the easy and ample success that a musician could achieve in his time. Italians had in fact established musical hegemony over Europe in a period of serious economic decline. Cesti's career affords an ideal instance. After his first opera, *Alessandro*, Rosa reported to Maffei: 'I have news of our Father Cesti, who has become immortal in Venice and is esteemed first among composers of our day' (30 November 1652). In a letter to G. B. Ricciardi, Rosa also wrote that Cesti had begged him 'to compose the verses for a *drammetto musicale* to be performed in that city next year' (12 May 1651). When Rosa refused, Cesti set *Il Cesare amante*, a scenario by M. Bisaccioni versified by D. Varotari. Although the libretto is dated 1651 the opera was probably performed early in 1652 (*more veneto*).

In 1652 Cesti secured a regular position at the court of Archduke Ferdinand Karl at Innsbruck and remained there until 1657. The position, especially created for him, included supervision of a select group of musicians, some of whom were surely recruited on Cesti's occasional journeys to Italy. Precisely when Cesti arrived at court is unknown. During 1654 a new Komödienhaus was completed at Innsbruck and inaugurated with *Cleopatra*, Apolloni's refurbishment of Cesti's *Cesare amante*, with a new prologue and ballets to conclude each act. More important, however, was Cesti's *Argia*, performed on 4 and 7 November 1655 to celebrate a visit of the recently abdicated Queen Christina of Sweden, then on her way to Rome. Accounts indicate that the opera lasted more than six hours and that 'her Majesty ... beheld it with great pleasures, and attention'. Whether or not Cesti wrote the music for *Marte placata*, a 'componimento scenico per musica' given on 3 November 1655, is uncertain. However, Cesti's next two operas, *Orontea* (1656) and *Dori* (1657), are among the most famous of the 17th century, each having revivals into the 1680s. This setting of *Orontea* was the third adaptation of Cicognini's libretto, after those of Francesco Lucio (1649) and the Neapolitan Francesco Cirillo (1654).

By 4 January 1658 Cesti was in Rome with the apparent intention of securing release from his monastic vows. He seems to have achieved this by ingratiating himself with Pope Alexander VII, as reported in Rosa's letters of 1659; according to a letter of 1 March, Cesti had just been released from his vows and would remain a secular priest. By the end of that year he secured a position in the papal choir, but spent most of 1661 in Florence on leave from Rome in connection with festivities for the wedding of the future Grand Duke Cosimo III and Marguerite Louise d'Orléans. Cesti must already have left for Tuscany by 8 April because on 12 July he sang the title role in Jacopo Melani's *Ercole in Tebe*. He probably sang Alidoro in six performances of his own *Orontea* at the Cocomero theatre, between 5 and 24 October, presented to Cosimo by Archduke Ferdinand Karl's musicians; he may also have sung in his *Dori*, performed by the same group beginning on 25 October. Towards the end of 1661, Cesti broke faith with the pope and, despite threatened excommunication, returned to Innsbruck to Ferdinand Karl, who had earlier rewarded him with the title 'Cavaliere di S Spirito in Sassia'. That Cesti's failure to return to Rome greatly angered papal authorities can be ascertained from Rosa's letters of November. Only the combined influence of Ferdinand Karl, Cosimo III and Emperor Leopold I secured Cesti's official release from the papal choir in late 1661 or early 1662.

Cesti returned to Innsbruck with the archduke during early February 1662, after which he must have immediately composed *La magnanimità d'Alessandro*, honouring Christina of Sweden. The opera was performed on 4 and 11 June when Christina stopped in Innsbruck while returning to Rome from her father's funeral in Sweden. Since Apolloni was unavailable in Italy, Cesti turned again to Sbarra, who was to become his sole librettist in Vienna. Before the archduke's death in December 1662, Cesti was handsomely rewarded with property and other monetary considerations.

Cesti's musical activities during 1663–4 are virtually unknown. He set *Semiramis, ossia La schiava fortunata*, a libretto commissioned by the 'Serenissimo Principe Leopoldo di Toscana' from the Florentine court poet G. A. Moniglia, but plans to mount it in celebration of the new archduke's marriage were cancelled when the archduke died in June 1665. With the last Tyrolese Habsburg now deceased, the archduke's musical establishment – including Cesti's most trusted Italian singers Pompeo Sabbatini, Antonio Pancotti, Giuseppe Maria Donati and Giulio Cesare Donati – was transferred to Vienna. Before moving, Cesti began a lengthy correspondence with the Venetian impresario Marco Faustini and the librettist Nicolò Beregan (11 March 1665 to 5 September 1666), showing that his ties with that theatrical city remained strong.

Cesti arrived in Vienna on 22 April 1666 as 'Honorary chaplain and director of the theatrical music'. Once settled he began a period of intense operatic activity. On 9 June Cesti sang in P. A. Ziani's *L'onore trionfante* and on 12 July his own *Nettunno e Flora festeggianti* was performed. On 27 June Cesti told Faustini that he was writing an 'Opera Grande', none other than *Il pomo d'oro*, for the marriage of Leopold I to the Infanta Margherita of Spain. Although Cesti apparently completed most of the lengthy score in 1666, numerous problems postponed performances until mid-1668. In the interim he composed *Le disgrazie d'Amore*, performed 19 February 1667, and resurrected *Semirami* (never mounted in Innsbruck) for the emperor's birthday on 9 June 1667. Just over a month later, on 13 July, the equestrian ballet *La Germania esultante*, with ballet music by J. H. Schmelzer and vocal music by Cesti, was performed for Margherita's birthday. *Il pomo d'oro* was finally given the following year, divided between July 12 and 14, and accounts of this work, the most spectacular of Cesti's creations, were published or sent by courier throughout Europe. Pressure from such heightened activity took its toll on Cesti, who had already served notice in late 1667 of his intention to leave the imperial court. According to Rosa, in a letter of 15 September 1668, Cesti was in the process of going to Venice; in November he was in Florence where court records indicate he was granted an annual sum of 25 scudi. Apparently his last activity connected with opera took place in Siena where *Argia* was performed in 1669 'with his continued assistance' (see Bianconi, *DBI*). Cesti also planned to compose several other operas: *Ermengarda regina de' Longobardi*, intended for performance as the first opera during Carnival 1670 at the SS Teatro di Giovanni e Paolo; and *Genserico*, which he apparently began, but which was completed by G. D. Partenio and produced at the SS Giovanni e Paolo in 1669. Cesti also asked Prince Mattias of Tuscany for permission to set G. A. Moniglia's *Giocasta*, but he probably did not write any music for it. Cesti, just 46, died on 14 October at Florence, at the height of his career. Farulli stated that he was 'poisoned by his rivals', but his earliest biographer, Cinelli Calvoli, does not refer to a violent death.

2. Operas. Cesti's first Venetian opera represented significant competition for Cavalli, who had virtually ruled the stage since Monteverdi's death. Cesti excelled at setting comic situations to music; he was at his best dealing with servants such as Gelone in *Orontea*, Bleso in *Alessandro*, Golo in *Dori*, Gobbo in *La magnanimità d'Alessandro* and Momus or Filaura in *Il pomo d'oro*. Gelone, for example, has entire scenes to himself, and his arias are among the best in the opera. While *Alessandro* represents no significant stylistic departure from mid-century operas by Cavalli and was not nearly as popular, Cesti's Innsbruck opera *Argia* is, like *Il pomo d'oro* more than a decade later, a stylistic anomaly. Written as a private entertainment, it depends heavily on stage machinery, many supernumeraries and four separate ballet groups. Vocal ensembles for five to eight voices occur in prominent places, and there are many strophic arias in *ABA'* or *ABB'* form, where the *A'* or *B'* portion is much shortened. Most strophic arias change metre at least once and generally several times, and some attain the considerable length of 80 or more bars per strophe.

Orontea and *Dori* exhibit the fast-developing contrast between aria and arioso, used for moments of reflection, and declamatory recitative, used for narrative action. Each includes more continuo arias than accompanied arias, and the forms are more developed. Cesti's melodies are increasingly graceful; duets make frequent use of fluid parallel 3rds and 6ths but are only occasionally imitative. Accompanied recitative, still rare, is restricted to significant dramatic events such as the ghost scene in *Dori* (Act 3 scene xii). Instrumental pieces are consistently scored for two violins and continuo, and ritornellos are musically linked to arias, a progressive trait that Cesti developed further in later operas and that was to be particularly prominent in such works as Antonio Sartorio's *Orfeo* (1672, Venice). Cesti generally avoided descending chromatic ostinato bass lines, so effectively employed by Cavalli in his earlier operas. He reserved chromaticism for emotionally charged words and scenes. Examples involving three-part parallel movement and leaps of a diminished 3rd, 4th or 5th occur, for example, in *Orontea* (Act 1 scene xiv) and in *Alessandro* (Act 1 scenes vi and xii). Arias in triple metre, with lyrical flowing melodies, appear with increasing frequency. They are often interrupted by hemiola cadential figures using third inversion dominant 7th chords.

Cesti's Viennese operas display great variety, but generally differ from his earlier ones in treating allegorical or mythological plots rather than historical ones and in exploiting the large forces available at Emperor Leopold's court. *Nettunno e Flora*, the sung prologue to a ballet, is an allegory about Margherita's journey from Spain to become Leopold's wife. It contains an unusually large amount of concerted vocal music, particularly duets and double choruses, and is scored for five instrumental parts. There is a remarkable bass role (Proteus) with a very low tessitura. *Le disgrazie d'Amore*, dating from a year later, contains some of Cesti's finest music, especially the more contrapuntally conceived instrumental sections. *Il pomo d'oro*, the *non plus ultra* of Baroque court operas, is exceptional in many ways. It has a lengthy prologue plus five acts instead of the normal three, uses an extremely large cast including many supernumeraries, and is scored for a greatly enlarged orchestra – much in the allegorical tradition of Monteverdi's *Orfeo*. Its 23 stage sets, designed by Ludovico Burnacini, were published in various editions of the libretto, engraved by Matthäus Küsel. Cesti showed a strong interest in the individual abilities of his singers, whom he jealously protected (see Schmidt 1978), and *Il pomo d'oro* gave them ample opportunity to display their virtuosity.

Most of Cesti's operas, including *Argia*, *Orontea*, *Dori*, *Tito*, *Semirami* and *Il pomo d'oro*, have been revived since the late 1960s, often to considerable critical acclaim. These performances, directed by William Holmes, Alan Curtis, René Jacobs, Gerhard Kramer and others, have convincingly laid to rest claims by Wellesz (1914 and 1950) that 20th-century aesthetics differ too significantly from those of the 17th century to permit successful revivals.

See also Dori; Orontea; Pomo d'oro, il; and Tito.

drammi musicali in a prologue and three acts unless otherwise stated

Alessandro vincitor di se stesso (F. Sbarra), Venice, SS Giovanni e Paolo, ded. 20 Jan 1651, *I-Rvat*; Lucca, 1654, with some music by M. Bigongiari

Il Cesare amante (A. Rivarota [D. Varotari], after M. Bisaccioni), Venice, SS Giovanni e Paolo, 1651–2, lib. and 2 arias *Vmc*, 1 aria *US-SFsc*; rev. as La Cleopatra (Varotari, with addns by G. F. Apolloni), Innsbruck, Komödienhaus, 5 July 1654

L'Argia (Apolloni), Innsbruck, 4 Nov 1655, *Nc* (2 copies), *Vlevi*, *Vnm* (*R*1978: IOB, iii)

Orontea (G. A. Cicognini, rev. Apolloni), Innsbruck, Sala, 19 Feb 1656, *GB-CMc*, *I-PAc*, *Rsc*, *Rvat*; ed. W. Holmes, WE, xi (1973)

La Dori (Apolloni), Innsbruck, 'Hof-Saales', 1657, *A-Wn* (*R*1981: IOB, lxiii), *D-MÜs*, *GB-Lbl*, *I-MOe*, *Vnm*; excerpts in PÄMw, xii, Jg.xi (1883), 86–177; edn in Schmidt 1973

La magnanimità d'Alessandro (Sbarra), Innsbruck, 4 and 11 June 1662, *A-Wn*, excerpts in PÄMw, xii, Jg.xi (1883), 195–206

Il Tito (melodramma, prol., 3, N. Beregan), Venice, SS Giovanni e Paolo, ded. 13 Feb 1666, *I-Nc*, *Rvat*, *Vnm*; 3 arias (Amsterdam, 1691)

Nettunno e Flora festeggianti (dramma musicale per introduttione al gran balletto, Sbarra), Vienna, 12 July 1666, *A-Wn* [aria beginning Act 2.iii by Leopold I; ballet music by J. H. Schmelzer in *CS-KRa*, edn in DTÖ, lvi, Jg.xxviii/2 (1921)]

Le disgrazie d'Amore (dramma giocosomorale, prol., 3, Sbarra), Vienna, 19 Feb 1667, *A-Wn*; excerpts in PÄMw, xii, Jg.xi (1883), 178–87; inst music by Schmelzer; music for *licenza* by Leopold I

La Semirami (drama musicale, 3, G. A. Moniglia, rev. ?Sbarra), Vienna, Nuovo Teatro nella gran Sala di Palazzo, 9 June 1667, *Wn* [ballet music by Schmelzer in *Wn*]; as La schiava fortunata, Modena, 1674; with addl music by P. A. Ziani, Venice, S Moisè, 1674, *I-MOe*, *Vnm*; excerpts in PÄMw, xii, Jg.xi (1883), 188–95

La Germania esultante (festa a cavallo, Sbarra), Vienna, Imperial giardino della Favorita, 13 July 1667; ballet music by Schmelzer in *A-Wn*

Il pomo d'oro (festa teatrale, prol., 5, Sbarra), Vienna, Hoftheater auf der Cortina, 12 and 14 July 1668, *Wn* (prol., Acts 1, 2 and 4 only), arias *I-MOe*; edn in DTÖ, vi, Jg.iii/2 (1896); ix, Jg.iv/2 (1897); extant music for Acts 3 and 5 ed. C. B. Schmidt in RRMBE, xlii (1982) [Acts 2.ix and 5.v by Leopold I; ballet music by Schmelzer in *A-Wn*, *CS-KRa*, edn of ballets for Acts 1 and 5 in DTÖ, lvi, Jg.xxviii/2 (1921)]

Doubtful: Marte placata [Marte und Adonis] (componimento scenico per musica, Apolloni), Innsbruck, 3 Nov 1655, lib. *Rn*; Venere cacciatrice (Sbarra), Innsbruck, Maggiore d'Insprugg, 27 Feb 1659, lib. *A-Imf*, *US-Wc*; Genserico, Venice, SS Giovanni e Paolo, 1669, *I-MOe*, *Vm* (contains some music by Cesti, completed by G. D. Partenio)

*

DBI (L. Bianconi); *PEM* (W. Osthoff)

C. Ivanovich: *Minerva al tavolino* (Venice, 1681, 2/1688)

G. Cinelli Calvoli: *La Toscana letterata, ovvero Istoria degli scrittori toscani* (MS, before 1688, *I-Fn* Magl.IX.68) [biographical entry on Cesti, reproduced in Hill 1976]

P. Farulli: *Annali, overo Notizie istoriche dell'antica, nobile, e valorosa citta di Arezzo* (Foligno, 1717)
G. A. Cesareo: *Poesie e lettere edite e inedite di Salvator Rosa* (Naples, 1892)
H. Kretzschmar: 'Die venetianische Oper und die Werke Cavallis und Cestis', *VMw*, viii (1892), 1–76
A. Stanley: 'Cesti's *Il Pomo d'Oro*', *Studies in Musical Education, History and Aesthetics*, Papers and Proceedings of the Music Teachers' National Association, i (Oberlin, OH, 1906), 139–49
L. Schiedermair: *Bayreuther Festspiele im Zeitalter der Absolutismus* (Leipzig, 1908)
E. Wellesz: 'Zwei Studien zur Geschichte der Oper im XVII. Jahrhundert', *SIMG*, xv (1913–14), 124–54
——: 'Ein Bühnenfestspiel aus dem siebzehnten Jahrhundert', *Die Musik*, xiii/4 (1913–14), 191–217
A. Sandberger: 'Beziehungen der Königin Christine von Schweden, zur italienischen Oper und Musik, insbesondere zu ... Cesti. Mit einem Anhang über Cestis Innsbrucker Aufenthalt', *Bulletin de la Société 'Union musicologique'*, v (1925), 121–73
P. Nettl: 'Ein verschollenes Tournierballett von M. A. Cesti', *ZMw*, viii (1925–6), 411–18
A. Tessier: L'Orontée de Lorenzani et l'Orontea du Padre Cesti', *ReM*, ix/8 (1927–8), 169–86
A. de Rinaldis, ed.: *Lettere inedite di Salvator Rosa a G. B. Ricciardi* (Rome, 1939)
F. Walker: 'Salvator Rosa and Music', *MMR*, lxxix (1949), 199–205; lxxx (1950), 13–16, 32–6
U. Limentani, ed.: *Poesie e lettere inedite di Salvator Rosa* (Florence, 1950)
E. Wellesz: *Essays on Opera* (London, 1950)
F. Hadamowsky: 'Barocktheater am wiener Kaiserhof mit einem Spielplan (1625–1740)', *Jb der Gesellschaft für wiener Theaterforschung, 1951–2* (Vienna, 1955), 7–117
N. Pirrotta: 'Tre capitoli su Cesti', *La scuola romana: G. Carissimi – A. Cesti – M. Marazzoli*, Chigiana, x (1953), 27–79
F. Schlitzer: 'Fortuna dell' "Orontea"', ibid, 81–92
——: 'Una lettera inedita di A. Cesti e un frammento di lettera inedita di Salvator Rosa', ibid, 93–8
N. Pirrotta: 'Le prime opere di Antonio Cesti', *L'orchestra*, ed. P. Castiglia (Florence, 1954), 153–79
W. Senn: *Musik und Theater am Hof zu Innsbruck* (Innsbruck, 1954)
N. Burt: 'Opera in Arcadia', *MQ*, xli (1955), 145–70
F. Schlitzer: *Intorno alla 'Dori' di Antonio Cesti* (Florence, 1957)
W. Osthoff: 'Antonio Cestis "Alessandro vincitor di se stesso"', *SMw*, xxiv (1960), 13–43
F. Schlitzer: *'L'Orontea' di Antonio Cesti: storia e bibliografia* (Florence, 1960)
J. V. Crowther: *The Operas of Pietro Antonio Cesti* (diss., U. of Durham, 1961)
D. Burrows: 'Antonio Cesti on Music', *MQ*, li (1965), 518–29
M. Dietrich, ed.: *Der guldene Apfel* (Vienna, 1965)
D. H. Shock: 'Costuming for "Il pomo d'oro"', *Gazette des beaux-arts*, lxix (1967), 251–6
N. Burt: 'Plus ça change: or, the Progress of Reform in Seventeenth- and Eighteenth-century Opera as Illustrated in the Books of Three Operas', *Studies in Music History: Essays for Oliver Strunk* (Princeton, 1968), 325–39
M. Dietrich: 'Le livret d'opéra et ses aspects sociaux à la cour de Léopold 1er', *Dramaturgie et société: rapports entre l'oeuvre théâtrale, son interprétation et son public aux XVIe et XVIIe siècles*, ed. J. Jacquot (Paris, 1968), 203–10
W. C. Holmes: 'Comedy–Opera–Comic Opera', *AnMc*, no.5 (1968), 92–103
——: 'Giacinto Andrea Cicognini's and Antonio Cesti's Orontea (1649)', *New Looks at Italian Opera: Essays in Honor of Donald J. Grout* (Ithaca, NY, 1968), 108–32
——: *'Orontea': a Study of Change and Development in the Libretto and the Music of Mid-Seventeenth Century Italian Opera* (diss., Columbia U., 1968)
——: *'Orontea Regina d'Egitto'* (Ithaca, NY, 1968) [Eng. trans.]
T. Antonicek: 'Zum 300. Todestag Antonio Cestis', *ÖMz*, xxiv (1969), 573–7
R. Giazotto: 'Nel CCC anno della morte di Antonio Cesti: ventidue lettere ritrovate nell'Archivio di Stato di Venezia', *NRMI*, iii (1969), 496–512
W. C. Holmes: 'Cesti's "L'Argia": an Entertainment for a Royal Convert', *Chigiana*, xxvi–xxviii (1969–70), 35–52
T. Antonicek: 'Antonio Cesti alla corte di Vienna', *NRMI*, iv (1970), 307–19
I. Bartels: *Die Instrumentalstücke in Oper und Oratorium der frühvenezianischen Zeit: dargestellt an Werken von Cavalli, Bertali, P. A. Ziani und Cesti anhand der Bestande der Österreichischen Nationalbibliothek in Wien* (diss., U. of Vienna, 1970)
J. V. Crowther: 'The Operas of Cesti', *MR*, xxxi (1970), 93–113
W. C. Holmes: 'The Stage Sets for Cesti's l'Argia, 1655', *Memorie e contributi alla musica dal medioevo all'età moderna offerti a F. Ghisi nel settantesimo compleanno (1901–1971)* (Bologna, 1971), 109–28
W. C. Holmes: 'Yet Another "Orontea": Further Rapport Between Venice and Vienna', *Venezia e il melodramma nel seicento: Venice 1972*, 199–225
T. Walker: 'Gli errori di "Minerva al tavolino": osservazioni sulla cronologia delle prime opere veneziane', *Venezia e il melodramma nel seicento: Venice 1972*, 7–16
C. B. Schmidt: *The Operas of Antonio Cesti* (diss., Harvard U., 1973) [incl. complete transcr. of *La Dori*]
H. Seifert: 'Die Festlichkeiten zur ersten Hochzeit Kaiser Leopolds I.', *ÖMz*, xxix (1974), 6–16
L. Bianconi and T. Walker: 'Dalla *Finta pazza* alla *Veremonda*: storie di Febiarmonici', *RIM*, x (1975), 379–454
C. B. Schmidt: 'Antonio Cesti's *La Dori*: a Study of Sources, Performance Traditions and Musical Style', *RIM*, x (1975), 455–98
J. W. Hill: 'Le relazioni di Antonio Cesti con la corte e i teatri di Firenze', *RIM*, xi (1976), 27–47
C. B. Schmidt: 'Antonio Cesti's *Il pomo d'oro*: a Reexamination of a Famous Hapsburg Court Spectacle', *JAMS*, xxix (1976), 381–412
——: '"La Dori" di Antonio Cesti: sussidi bibliografici', *RIM*, xi (1976), 197–229
D. Frosini: 'Antonio Cesti da Volterra a Pisa nel 1649', *RIM*, xiii (1978), 104–17
C. B. Schmidt: 'An Episode in the History of Venetian Opera: the *Tito* Commission (1665–66)', *JAMS*, xxxi (1978), 442–66
H.-J. Bauer: *Barockoper in Bayreuth* (Bayreuth, 1982)
L. Bianconi: record notes, *Orontea* (HM 1100–2, 1982) [incl. lib. in It., Fr., Eng. and Ger.]
Festwoche der alten Musik in Innsbruck 21–27.8.1983 [articles on *Il Tito*, with facs. and Ger. trans. of lib.]
L. Bianconi and T. Walker: 'Production, Consumption and Political Function of Seventeenth-Century Opera', *Early Music History*, iv (Cambridge, 1984), 209–96
H. Seifert: *Die Oper am wiener Kaiserhof im 17. Jahrhundert* (Tutzing, 1985)
G. Morelli and T. Walker: 'Migliori plettri', DMV, iv (Milan, 1986), ix–lvii, cxxxi–clxiv
F. E. Dostal: '"Il pomo d'oro" – die berühmste unbekannte Oper der Weltliteratur', *Spectaculum 89* (Vienna, 1989), 10–12 [programme notes for *Il pomo d'oro*]
E. Rosand: *Opera in Seventeenth-Century Venice* (Berkeley, 1991) [incl. musical excerpts]

CARL B. SCHMIDT (with DAVID L. BURROWS)

Cesti, Remigio (*b* Arezzo, *c*1635; *d* Florence, between 1710 and 1717). Italian composer, nephew of Antonio Cesti. He entered the Dominican order in 1649 and is consistently referred to in subsequent documents as 'Don Remigio'. In 1663 he was organist to the Knights of St Stephen at Pisa, but no dates are known for other musical positions he held: *maestro di cappella* at Pisa, Volterra, Arezzo and Faenza. He was with his uncle in Florence in 1661 for the musical events attendant on the wedding of Prince Cosimo de' Medici (the future Grand Duke Cosimo III) and Marguerite Louise d'Orléans. His association with the Medici family may have been quite close, for ten years later he wrote several pieces in commemoration of the death of Ferdinand II. The high point of his musical career came in 1665 with the performance in Innsbruck of his opera *Il principe generoso*, presumably under his uncle's sponsorship. If he experienced any of the conflict between the claims of music and the Church such as troubled his uncle's career, he resolved it very differently, for after 1671 the known dates in his biography all relate to ecclesiastical administration. Gregorio Farulli (1710) referred to him in the present tense, Pietro Farulli (1717) in the past. At his death he was titular abbot at the Monastero degli Angeli, Florence.

The action of *Il principe generoso* (MS libretto and score in *A-Wn*) is set on the island of Crete and involves 11 characters. To judge by the music, Cesti was more progressive than his uncle in the degree of emphasis he placed on instrumental writing and in the relative importance he gave to the aria and to closed scenes.

*

G. Farulli: *Istoria cronologica del nobile, ed antico Monastero degli Angeli di Firenze* (Lucca, 1710)

P. Farulli: *Annali, overo Notizie istoriche dell'antica, nobile, e valorosa città di Arezzo* (Foligno, 1717)

Poligrafo Gargani (MS, *I-Fn*) [slip catalogue of information on Tuscan personalities]

E. Wellesz: 'Zwei Studien zur Geschichte der Oper im XVII. Jahrhundert', *SIMG*, xv (1913–14), 124–54

DAVID L. BURROWS, CARL B. SCHMIDT

C'est la guerre ('That's War'). Opera in one act by EMIL PETROVICS to a libretto by Miklós Hubay; Budapest, Opera, 11 March 1962 (previously broadcast, Hungarian Broadcasting Corporation, 27 August 1961).

The scene is the flat of a middle-class family in Budapest during the German occupation in summer 1944. The Husband (baritone), an engineer in a war factory, and the Wife (soprano) hide their friend, the Deserter (tenor), in their home. In the short prologue the Janitress (mezzo-soprano) and Vizavi ('vis-à-vis'; tenor) are engaged in a conversation: they know almost everything about the tenants. Vizavi is an invalid in a wheelchair who uses his binoculars to peep into the tenants' homes while the Janitress, whose husband and sons fell in the war, harbours a fanatical hatred towards everybody who is young and alive.

A conversation between the couple and the Deserter is interrupted by three Officers from the war factory (tenor, baritone and bass). They take the Husband to the factory, so that the Third Officer, a brutal man, may be alone with the Wife, to whom he has taken a fancy. The Wife fends off his attempt at courtship by letting his dispatch case fall from the balcony. The Officer leaves and the Deserter emerges from the inner room. A love duet between him and the Wife is interrupted by the appearance of the Janitress; the suspicious old woman returns with a picklock, catches the lovers kissing and calls the patrol. Meanwhile the Husband arrives home with the Officers. To save the situation he accuses his friend of being his Wife's lover and orders him to leave their home. Everything goes well until the Janitress appears with the Deserter's uniform. The patrol leads away the Husband and the Deserter and soon after the sound of a salvo is heard. The Third Officer remarks 'C'est la guerre' while the Wife jumps from the balcony. In the epilogue, Vizavi and the Janitress search for new victims.

The musical style of Petrovics's first opera combines freely treated dodecaphony, a broad melodiousness reminiscent of Puccini and an essentially Puccinian dramaturgy. Powerful character contrasts contribute to the dramatic qualities of the work, which represented the first decisive step taken towards a new era of Hungarian opera. After its Budapest staging in 1962 it was produced in several opera houses in Europe, and was recorded in 1965. PÉTER P. VÁRNAI

Chabanon, Michel-Paul-Guy de (*b* Santo Domingo, West Indies, 1729–30; *d* Paris, 10 July 1792). French writer on music. Educated in Paris, he was one of the most perspicacious theorists of music and opera in the period before the French Revolution, and certainly among the most well read and broad-minded. A staunch defender of French musical tradition and of opera in French, he raised the level of discussion above the egregious polemics of the Querelle des Bouffons (1752–4) and the disputations of Gluckistes and Piccinnistes in the next generation. Chabanon rejected some of Rousseau's early notions, including the impossibility of French opera because of the 'unmusicality' of the language, and upheld the need for music to 'sing' (not only in the vocal line) and to dominate in opera.

In a country where the librettist still vied in importance with the composer, Chabanon received praise in both roles: as the youthful composer and librettist of *Sémélé* (unperformed) and as the mature prize-winning librettist of a *tragédie lyrique* in four acts, *La toison d'or* (admired by Voltaire but never set to music). He also wrote the libretto for Gossec's *tragédie lyrique Sabinus*, given at the Opéra in 1773. (Gossec's librettos for *Philémon et Baucis* and *Alexis et Daphné* were by Chabanon's brother, Chabanon de Maugris.) Through his first-hand knowledge of violin playing and instrumental composition, as also his expertise in ancient music and drama, Chabanon was well equipped to be the proponent of music's status as an autonomous art, whether in the opera house or the concert room. His *Eloge* (1764) for his friend and mentor Rameau, and subsequently the 'Observation' (1772), heightened French society's consciousness of its musical patrimony and of Rameau's enormous achievements, both theoretical and operatic. In the 'Lettre' of 1773, Chabanon's bold assertion of music's independence from language and from rhetorical laws of accent and versification allowed him to propound its supremacy over other operatic elements. The idea was expanded and developed in the *Observations* (1779) and in *De la musique* (1785), along with key theories such as the use of motif to form the foundation of musical character and the existence of four general characteristic types of music (*tendre*, *gracieuse*, *gaie* and *vive*) representing intrinsic musical expressivity. He thus contributed to the contemporary European tendency seen in Lessing's *Laocoön* (1766) to stress the different powers of the various means of artistic communication to create beauty: music must be distinguished from literature must be distinguished from painting.

Chabanon propounded theories capable of justifying Gluck's accomplishments, identifying in Gluck the importance that he himself (influenced by Rameau's theories) gave to melody and harmony. His later theory dissociates music altogether from language and the aesthetic of the imitation of nature. Chabanon's scholarship and pragmatic musical philosophy allowed him to do what Rousseau's vision and limited musical taste had prevented: to play a role appropriate to the man of letters of promoting, among a cultivated public, music's autonomy and prestige and thus the composer's legitimate dominance in any opera-making team. He did not live to see the worst excesses of the French Revolution, but its need for simple music, national hymns and propagandist drama temporarily drowned out his advocacy of a developed and sophisticated music for the opera. Only relatively recently has his historical neglect begun to be rectified.

Eloge de M. Rameau (Paris, 1764)
'Observation sur la musique à propos de Castor', *Mercure de France* (April 1772)
'Lettre de M. de Chabanon sur les propriétés musicales de la langue française', *Mercure de France* (Jan (i) 1773), 171–91 [also pubd separately]
Réponse à la critique de l'opéra de Castor; & Observations sur la musique ([?Paris], 1773)
Observations sur la musique et principalement sur la métaphysique de l'art (Paris, 1779); ed. and trans. J. Hiller (Leipzig, 1781)
De la musique considérée en elle-même et dans ses rapports avec la parole, les langues, la poésie et le théâtre (Paris, 1785)
'Essai sur le théâtre lyrique', *Oeuvres de théâtre et autres poésies* (Paris, 1788) [in verse]

*

Grove6 (R. Cotte); *MGG* (A. Sorel-Nitzberg)
M. Lussy: 'Chabanon, précurseur de Hanslick', *Gazette musicale de la Suisse romande* (7 May 1896)
H. Goldschmidt: *Die Musikaesthetik des 18. Jahrhunderts* (Zürich and Leipzig, 1915)
W. Serauky: *Die musikalische Nachahmungsästhetik* (Münster, 1929)
M. R. Maniates: '"Sonate, que me veux-tu?": the Enigma of French Musical Aesthetics in the 18th Century', *CMc*, no.9 (1969), 117–40
I. Supičić: 'Expression and Meaning in Music', *IRASM*, ii (1971), 193–211
O. F. Saloman: 'Chabanon and Chastellux on Music and Language, 1764–1773', *IRASM*, xx (1989), 109–20
——: 'French Revolutionary Perspectives on Chabanon's *De la musique* of 1785', *Music and the French Revolution*, ed. M. Boyd (Cambridge, 1992), 211–20

PHILIP E. J. ROBINSON, ORA FRISHBERG SALOMAN

Chabrier, (Alexis-)Emmanuel (*b* Ambert, Puy-de-Dôme, 18 Jan 1841; *d* Paris, 13 Sept 1894). French composer. At the age of six he had his first piano lessons from Manuel Zaporta. As he was intended for the legal profession, the family moved in 1851 to Clermont-Ferrand to further his education; there he studied music with Tarnowski, a Polish violinist. He wanted to devote himself to music, but in 1856 his father moved the family to Paris to prepare his son for law school. During this period he studied composition with T. E. Semet and Aristide Hignard, as well as the piano and the violin, and spent all his spare time analysing scores. In 1858 he entered law school, and on graduating in 1861 took a post in the Ministry of the Interior. He had fulfilled his father's intention, but continued to compose and offer his works to publishers.

Chabrier was as interested in poetry and painting as in music, and made the acquaintance of Jean Richepin, José Maria de Heredia, Catulle Mendès and Villiers de l'Isle Adam, to whom he taught the rudiments of music. His friendship with Verlaine, also from this period, resulted in his embarking on two operettas, *Fisch-Ton-Kan* (1863–4) and *Vaucochard et fils Ler* (1864) to Verlaine librettos; neither was completed. Other friends from the Parisian salons included Fauré, Duparc, Chausson and d'Indy. Large-scale projects of this period include the opera *Jean Hunyade* (libretto by Henri Fouquier, 1867), which remained unfinished, though Chabrier used fragments from it in later operas, *Gwendoline* and *Briséïs*.

Chabrier had to leave Paris during the Franco-Prussian War (1870–71). In December 1873 he married Marie Alice Dejean, by whom he had two sons. His innate feeling for the comic was developing and manifested itself in two light stage works, *L'étoile* (1877) and *Une éducation manquée* (1879). In both buffoonery, vivacity, melodic spontaneity and tenderness are combined with a free use of harmonic dissonance. *L'étoile* had 48 performances but *Une éducation manquée* was presented only once at a private performance.

During this period the Chabriers had frequent gatherings at their home, where they received Saint-Saëns, Massenet, Lecocq and Messager as well as older friends. His closest associates at this time included Duparc, who was determined to make Chabrier share his admiration for Wagner. Chabrier already knew some of Wagner's music, but the profound impression made by *Tristan und Isolde* when he first heard it in Munich convinced Chabrier that his real calling was composition, and in November 1880 he resigned from his government post. The conductor Charles Lamoureux employed him as chorus director and secretary for the newly founded Nouveaux Concerts in 1881, and from 1877 the firm of Enoch & Costallat published his works.

From 1883 Chabrier spent much of his time in the village of La Membrolle-sur-Choisille, Touraine, where he wrote the opera *Gwendoline*, to a libretto by Mendès. The setting, Britain in the Middle Ages, provided occasion for colourful battle scenes and contrasting tender love duets. It was first performed in 1886 at the Monnaie, Brussels, where it was favourably received, but was withdrawn after two performances when the director of the theatre became insolvent. From this time comes the quadrille for piano (four hands) on themes from *Tristan und Isolde*, the apparent breeziness of which masks an unabated fervour for Wagner. In 1884, Chabrier helped Lamoureux with a concert performance of Act 1 of *Tristan*, and during the 1880s he belonged to a small group of musicians known as 'Le petit Bayreuth' who studied Wagner's scores.

Chabrier was also working on a new *opéra comique*, *Le roi malgré lui*. The libretto, involving the accession to the Polish throne in 1573 of the French Prince Henri III, is somewhat obscure but it is illumined by the grace and gaiety of Chabrier's music. It was very successful at its first performance in 1887 (at the Opéra-Comique), but after the third a fire destroyed the theatre and performances were suspended for several months. This work made Chabrier better known abroad, particularly in Germany, where, through his friendship with the tenor Ernest Van Dyck and the conductor Felix Mottl, *Gwendoline* and *Le roi malgré lui* were staged in various cities, including Munich and Leipzig from 1889. As a result, Chabrier made several visits to Germany, which included an enjoyable stay at Bayreuth.

In his last years, Chabrier was embittered by illness, anxious about the future, pressed by financial need and disheartened by the small success of his stage works in France. Yet the first act of *Briséïs*, the only completed portion of an opera which preoccupied him to the point of obsession for several years, still shows a lively imagination supported by skilful orchestration. From 1892 his health failed rapidly; the Paris première of *Gwendoline* in December 1893 came too late to give him much satisfaction and during his last year he suffered from general paralysis.

In assessing Chabrier's position in French music, the elements of his music which derive from his ambitions as a dramatic composer should be distinguished from those which reflect his natural and original talent for the lyric and the comic and for creating varied moods and colours. His fervent Wagnerism prompted him to attempt a Wagnerian sense of drama in his serious stage works, and *Gwendoline* and *Briséïs* show his assimilation of some of Wagner's vocabulary. He made obvious use of the leitmotif in *Gwendoline*; he handled harmonic complexities with as much ease, if not as much continuity, as Wagner and used the unprepared 9th chord as freely. But he refused to follow Wagner's habitual practice in the resolution of leading notes or the declamatory aspects of his melodic style. Chabrier's concentrated melodic writing allowed him to retain traditional operatic construction (using *airs*, duets, choruses and ensembles), which was still popular in Paris.

See also EDUCATION MANQUÉE, UNE; ETOILE, L'; GWENDOLINE; and ROI MALGRÉ LUI, LE.

all printed works published in Paris

Fisch-Ton-Kan, 1863–4 (operetta, P. Verlaine), inc., Paris, Salle de l'Ancien Conservatoire, 22 April 1941

Vaucochard et fils Ler, 1864 (operetta, Verlaine and L. Viotti), inc., Paris, Salle de l'Ancien Conservatoire, 22 April 1941

Jean Hunyade, 1867 (opéra, H. Fouquier), inc.

L'étoile (opéra bouffe, 3, E. Leterrier and A. Vanloo), Paris, Bouffes-Parisiens, 28 Nov 1877 (1877)

Le Sabbat, 1877 (oc, 1, A. Silvestre), inc.

Une éducation manquée (operetta, 1, Leterrier and Vanloo), Paris, Cercle de la Presse, 1 May 1879 [with pf]; Paris, Arts, 9 Jan 1913 (1879)

Les muscadins, 1880 (opéra, 4, J. Clarétie and Silvestre), inc.

Gwendoline (opéra, 3, C. Mendès), 1885, Brussels, Monnaie, 10 April 1886 (1886)

Le roi malgré lui (oc, 3, E. de Najac and P. Burani, rev. J. Richepin, after A. Ancelot and M. Ancelot), Paris, OC (Favart), 18 May 1887 (1887); lib. rev. A. Carré, OC (Favart), 6 Nov 1929

Briséïs, ou Les amants de Corinthe, 1888–91 (drame lyrique, 3, Mendès and E. Mikhaël, after J. W. von Goethe: *Die Braut von Korinth*), 1 act, Paris, Concerts Lamoureux, 31 Jan 1897 [concert perf.]; Berlin, Royal Opera, 14 Jan 1899 (1897)

*

R. Brussel: 'Emmanuel Chabrier et le rire musical', *Revue d'art dramatique*, viii (1899), Oct–Dec, 55, 81

J. Desaymard: *Un artiste auvergnat: Emmanuel Chabrier* (Paris, 1908)

R. Martineau: *Emmanuel Chabrier* (Paris, 1910)

A. Legrand and M. Chabrier: 'En hommage à Emmanuel Chabrier', *BSIM*, vii/4 (1911), 1–13

J. Desaymard and others: *Emmanuel Chabrier: in Memoriam* (Paris, 1912)

G. Servières: *Emmanuel Chabrier 1841–1894* (Paris, 1912)

E. Blom: 'The Tragedy of a Comic Opera', *Stepchildren of Music* (London, 1925), 173–9 [*Le roi malgré lui*]

R. Gorer: 'Emmanuel Chabrier', *MR*, ii (1941), 132–42

A. Besch: 'Chabrier and "Une éducation manquée"', *Opera*, xii (1961), 166–7, 206

F. Poulenc: *Emmanuel Chabrier* (Paris, 1961; Eng. trans., 1981)

R. Delage: 'Emmanuel Chabrier', *Histoire de la musique*, ii, ed. Roland-Manuel (Paris, 1963), 831–40

—: 'Emmanuel Chabrier in Germany', *MQ*, xlix (1963), 75–84

Y. Tienot: *Chabrier* (Paris and Brussels, 1964)

R. Myers: *Emmanuel Chabrier and his Circle* (London, 1969)

F. Robert: *Emmanuel Chabrier: l'homme et son oeuvre* (Paris, 1969)

T. Hirsbrunner: *Claude Debussy und seine Zeit* (Laaber, 1981)

R. Delage: *Emmanuel Chabrier* (Geneva, 1982)

N. A. Gisbrecht: *Wagnerian Elements in Six French Operas* (diss., U. of Southern California, 1985) [*Gwendoline*]

MYRIAM SOUMAGNAC

Chaconne (Fr.). A dance in triple metre and moderate tempo which in the Baroque period was usually built over a recurring bass pattern. In French opera of the 17th and 18th centuries, as the longest and most impressive piece in a *divertissement*, it was conventionally placed at the end and could involve vocal soloists and chorus; it also appears in some Italian operas, particularly those subject to French influence. For the French, contrasts between major and tonic minor, variation of material and variety of mood within a consistent tempo were more telling characteristics than the bass pattern. Lully's 'Chantons tous en ce jour' (*Amadis*, 1684) is an excellent example of a chaconne where repetition of instrumental sections, *grand choeur* and *petit choeur* result in a rondeau-like structure. In his chaconnes, Rameau often treated the recurring bass line very freely and achieved contrast through orchestration and dynamics (see, for example, that in *Dardanus*, 1739). By the mid-18th century, as theorists pointed out, composers no longer felt obliged to keep to a bass pattern at all. Gluck's chaconne in *Alceste* belongs to this later tradition; while he used motivic developmental techniques of the symphony, he continued to emphasize contrast between sections by thematic definition and modulations to the dominant and relative minor; the same applies to Mozart's in *Idomeneo* (1781). As late as 1791, Ginguené recommended the chaconne as the best way of ending an opera; however, by then composers were more often concluding *divertissements* with a lively dance. With the fall of the monarchy chaconnes virtually disappeared; one of the last examples is that in Méhul's *Adrien*, 1799.

*

Grove6 (R. Hudson)

R.-A. Feuillet: *Chorégraphie, ou L'art d'écrire la dance, par caractères, figures et signes démonstratifs* (Paris, 1700; Eng. trans., 1906, as *Orchesography*)

J. Lacombe: *Dictionnaire portatif des beaux-arts* (Paris, 1752, enlarged 5/1766)

J.-J. Rousseau: *Dictionnaire de musique* (Paris, 1768)

N. E. Framery and P. L. Ginguené: *Encyclopédie méthodique: musique*, i (Paris, 1791)

M. ELIZABETH C. BARTLET

Chadwick, George W(hitefield) (*b* Lowell, MA, 13 Nov 1854; *d* Boston, 4 April 1931). American composer. His father approved of music in church but decidedly not in the theatre. Chadwick's first musical instruction came from his elder brother, who took him secretly to his first theatrical performance, a Christmas 1870 musical extravaganza. In 1873 his brother took him to hear his first opera, *Faust*, followed by *Don Giovanni*. He continued to frequent all types of theatrical performance, from light entertainments to opera. When studying in Leipzig (1877–9) and Munich (1879–80), and on return visits to Europe, he missed no opportunity to familiarize himself with the operatic scene. Returning to Boston, Chadwick entered fully into the city's musical life as composer, conductor, organist and teacher, and his music was often performed. From 1897 he was director of the New England Conservatory; his innovations included the establishment of an opera workshop.

Chadwick's first work for the theatre, *The Peer and the Pauper*, was an imitation of the Gilbert and Sullivan operas, then enjoying a remarkable success in the USA; but it was never produced. He wrote his next stage work, *A Quiet Lodging*, in 1892 for an April Fool's evening at a private Boston club. A satire on local musical life, with lampoons of local critics, it was composed and put on the stage within a month.

The following summer he was invited to write the music for a 'burlesque opera', *Tabasco*, for the Boston Cadets. Chadwick and his librettist nevertheless conceived it with an eye to professional production later. The limited original run in 1894 was a success (particularly the 'March of the Pasha's Guard', which was published separately and sold 100 000 copies). The comedian Thomas Q. Seabrooke adapted it for his company; his production opened in Boston on 9 April, moved to New York and toured the country for most of the next year. The plot of *Tabasco* involves the search by the Bey of Tangier for the ultimate in gastronomic excitement. An Irish-American drifter introduces him to a potent new sauce, Tabasco, and wins the post of 'French' chef in his house. The music offers a veritable anthology of popular styles, including a 'Plantation Ballad', a Spanish 'Bolero', an Irish 'Ditty' and a French 'Rigaudon', most of them designed as set pieces to show off the talents of the first performers. But Chadwick also composed complex musical numbers that advance the plot and demonstrate his command of the extended finale as employed by Sullivan.

Though his next dramatic work, *Judith* (based on the Apocryphal story of Judith and Holofernes), has been performed only in concert, Chadwick wanted it to be staged. The principal American opera companies were not open to American composers in 1900, so he wrote *Judith*, his largest score, for the Worcester choral festival, of which he was the director, 1898–1901; he called it a 'lyric drama'. The first reviewers found the choral passages to have the 'nobler' music and the long central duet, a scene of seduction and murder, to be disturbing in the context of a choral festival. At a 1919 revival Olin Downes hailed the seduction scene in particular and lamented the lack of encouragement given in the USA to aspiring opera composers. Chadwick himself worked out the basic scenario of *Judith* from the biblical text, adapting the prose narrative with a sure sense of theatrical effect; Saint-Saëns' *Samson et Dalila* was its principal structural and expressive model.

Chadwick's most important opera, *The Padrone*, proved his greatest disappointment. Composed in 1912 and never produced, it was extraordinarily original for its place and time. Other American composers of the day favoured exotic subjects – Parker's *Mona* with its druids and Roman soldiers, Converse's *The Pipe of Desire* with its air of fantasy, or Herbert's *Natoma* with its California Indians and Spaniards – but Chadwick chose to treat a contemporary American social problem: the *padrone* system through which poor Italian immigrants were brought to America with the financial support of a 'padrone' who then held them in a kind of indentured service until they paid off the debt. The story concerns four main characters involved in a web of lust, jealousy, deceit, revenge and murder, clearly similar to that of recent *verismo* operas; Chadwick found his approach in Verdi's last works, Mascagni, Leoncavallo and Puccini. *The Padrone* unfolds rapidly in a continuous, orchestrally supported melodic recitative that broadens, when appropriate, into lyric moments. Yet despite this strong influence, Chadwick's score is American in character, especially in its natural treatment of the rhythms of the English language.

In 1912, he sent the vocal score of *The Padrone* to the Metropolitan Opera, where Giulio Gatti-Casazza had begun introducing American operas; but it was deemed 'unsuitable for production at their establishment' and Gatti-Casazza 'disliked the book because it was a drama of life among the humble Italians – and probably too true to life' (Chadwick's diary).

Chadwick wrote only one more stage work, a slight piece for school use with either mixed or treble voices. *Love's Sacrifice* is an Arcadian pastoral equivalent of O. Henry's famous short story *The Gift of the Magi*. It had only one professional production, in Chicago in 1923 under the auspices of Opera in Our Language.

Renowned in his day as a composer of symphonies, choral works and chamber music, Chadwick never achieved the same kind of recognition for his theatre music. This lack of acclaim arose less from defects in the works themselves than from the state of American operatic life at the time they were written.

The Peer and the Pauper, 1883–4 (comic operetta, 2, R. Grant), unperf., *US-Bc* (inc.)
A Quiet Lodging (operetta, 2, A. Bates), Boston, 1 April 1892, lib. *Bc*, 1 song *NYyellin*
Tabasco (burlesque op, 2, R. A. Barnet), Boston, 29 Jan 1894, *Bc*, vs (Boston, 1894); uses material from The Peer and the Pauper
Judith (lyric drama, 3, W. C. Langdon, after scenario by Chadwick), Worcester, MA, 23 Sept 1901 (concert perf.), *Wc*, vs (New York, 1901)
The Padrone, 1912 (2, D. K. Stevens, after scenario by Chadwick), unperf., *Bc*
Love's Sacrifice, 1916–17 (pastoral op, 1, Stevens), Chicago, 1 Feb 1923, *Bc*, vs (Boston, 1917); partly orchd by Chadwick's students

*

F. O. Jones: 'Chadwick, George W.', *A Handbook of American Music and Musicians* (Canaseraga, NY, 1886)
C. Engel: 'George W. Chadwick', *MQ*, x (1924), 438–57
A. L. Langley: 'Chadwick and the New England Conservatory of Music', *MQ*, xxi (1935), 39–52
V. F. Yellin: *The Life and Operatic Works of George Whitefield Chadwick* (diss., Harvard U., 1957)
——: 'Chadwick, American Realist', *MQ*, lxi (1975), 77–97
S. Ledbetter: 'George W. Chadwick: a Sourcebook' (1984, MS, *US-Bc*)
——: 'Two Seductresses: Saint-Saëns's Delilah and Chadwick's Judith', *A Celebration of American Music: Words and Music in Honor of H. Wiley Hitchcock* (Ann Arbor, 1990), 281–301
V. F. Yellin: *Chadwick, Yankee Composer* (Washington DC, 1990)

STEVEN LEDBETTER

Chailley, Jacques (*b* Paris, 24 March 1910). French composer and musicologist. He studied composition with Boulanger (1925–7), Delvincourt (1933–5) and Büsser (at the Conservatoire, 1933–5) and conducting with Monteux (1936–7); he also studied musicology and the history of medieval French literature (doctorat d'Etat, 1952). A wide-ranging scholar, he has taught at several institutions and served in various capacities at the Conservatoire (1936–53) and at the University of Paris. Among his many writings are *Tristan et Isolde de Wagner* (Paris, 1963, 2/1972) and *'La flûte enchantée', opéra maçonnique: essai d'explication du livret et de la musique* (Paris, 1968; Eng. trans., 1972).

As a composer Chailley progressed from a modal style permeated with elements of Gregorian chant and French folk music to a harmonic language based on the assimilation of the first 13 harmonics. Although he is hostile towards serialism, he has sometimes used dodecaphonic technique, usually for satire. He was one of the first composers to use the ondes martenot (1934) and to write unaccompanied monody (incidental music to Aeschylus's *Les perses*, 1936). In his second opera, *Thyl de Flandre*, composed 1949–54 (4, J. Bruyr, after C. de Coster; Brussels, Monnaie, 1954), these tendencies are synthesized. Chailley's other compositions include the *comédie lyrique Pan et la Syrinx* (J. Laforgue; broadcast, 1946, stage, Paris, 1962).

CHRISTIANE SPIETH-WEISSENBACHER/R

Chailly, Luciano (*b* Ferrara, 19 Jan 1920). Italian composer. He studied the violin in Ferrara, then composition with Renzo Bossi in Milan, and finally conducting with Antonino Votto, taking an advanced course with Hindemith in Salzburg (1948); he also received a degree in literature from the University of Bologna. From 1951 to 1967 he was music consultant to the RAI, then artistic director and consultant at La Scala (1968–71), the Teatro Regio, Turin (1973–5), the

Angelicum in Milan, the Arena in Verona and the Opera in Genoa. From 1968 he taught composition at the Milan Conservatory.

Theatre music played a leading role in Chailly's work and stylistic development, his first opera being *Ferrovia sopraelevata* (1955) to a libretto by Dino Buzzati, an important partnership for the composer, who returned to Buzzati's surrealist fantasies in his later works for the stage, of 1959–63 – *Procedura penale*, *Il mantello*, *Era proibito* – and was influenced by his poetic vision. While his point of departure was neo-classical and owed something to Hindemith, he used the 12-note system (though without total commitment) later. Then he evolved an eclectic style which absorbed some avant-garde experiments and which he liked to define as 'de-formalized', having as its aim the conveying of 'sound hallucination'. This new atmosphere was appropriately first exploited in *Sogno (ma forse no)* (1975), based on Pirandello, and confirmed Chailly's tendency to a form of expression characterized by suspension between reality and hallucination, related to the poetic world of Buzzati which provided him with his strongest stimulus to compose.

See also DOMANDA DI MATRIMONIO, UNA and IDIOTA, L'.

printed works published in vocal score in Milan in year of first performance unless otherwise stated

Ferrovia sopraelevata (1, D. Buzzati), Bergamo, Donizetti, 1 Oct 1955, unpubd

Una domanda di matrimonio (op lirica, 1, C. Fino and S. Vertone, after A. P. Chekhov: *The Proposal*), Milan, Piccola Scala, 22 May 1957

Il canto del cigno (scena lirica, 1, R. Chailly, after Chekhov: *Swan Song*), Bologna, Comunale, 16 Nov 1957

La riva delle Sirti (op lirica, 4, R. Prinzhofer, after J. Gracq), Monte Carlo, Opéra, 1 March 1959, unpubd

Procedura penale (ob, Buzzati), Como, Villa Olmo, 30 Sept 1959

Il mantello (op lirica, 1, Buzzati), Florence, Pergola, 11 May 1960

Era proibito (op lirica, 1, Buzzati), Milan, Piccola Scala, 5 March 1963

L'idiota, 1966–7 (op lirica, 3, G. Loverso, after F. M. Dostoyevsky), Rome, Opera, 18 Feb 1970

Vassiliev (op lirica, 1, R. Chailly, after Chekhov), Genoa, Comunale, 16 March 1967

Markheim (op lirica, 1, Prinzhofer, after R. L. Stevenson), Spoleto, 14 July 1967

Sogno (ma forse no) (op lirica, 1, Prinzhofer, after L. Pirandello), Trieste, Comunale, 28 Jan 1975

Il libro dei reclami (op lirica, 1, Prinzhofer, after Chekhov), Vienna, Kammeroper, 29 May 1975

La cantatrice calva (chamber op, 1, R. Chailly, after E. Ionesco), Vienna, Kammeroper, 8 Nov 1986

*

P. Santi: 'Luciano Chailly', *Diapason*, ii (1951), 14–16

M. Mila: 'Le opere possibili di Luciano Chailly', *Cronache musicali 1955–1959* (Turin, 1959), 197–206

F. D'Amico: 'Lupi, Chailly, Bucchi', *I casi della musica* (Milan, 1962), 362–5

R. Vlad: *Era proibito* (Milan, Piccola Scala, 1963) [programme notes]

RAFFAELE POZZI

Chailly, Riccardo (*b* Milan, 20 Feb 1953). Italian conductor. Son of the composer Luciano Chailly, with whom he studied composition, he attended the conservatories in Milan and Perugia, where he turned to conducting with Piero Guarino and later Franco Caracciolo and Franco Ferrara. He was a drummer in a rhythm-and-blues band before joining La Scala as assistant conductor, learning the repertory under Abbado and making his début with *Werther*. His American début was at the Chicago Lyric Opera in 1974 with *Madama Butterfly*; débuts followed at Covent Garden (*Don Pasquale*, 1979), the Metropolitan (*Les contes d'Hoffmann*, 1982) and Salzburg Festival (*Macbeth*, 1984). In 1986 he became music director at the Teatro Comunale, Bologna, with whose forces he made several recordings, and in 1988 he was appointed artistic director of the Royal Concertgebouw Orchestra, Amsterdam. His opera recordings include *Guillaume Tell* and *Andrea Chénier* (both with Pavarotti) and *The Rake's Progress*. Visually energetic in performance, he is not indulgent to singers, his sensitive approach stressing musical dynamics and originality of detail.

NOËL GOODWIN

Chalabala, Zdeněk (*b* Uherské Hradiště, Moravia, 18 April 1899; *d* Prague, 4 March 1962). Czech conductor. At the Brno Conservatory he studied with František Neumann (1919–22) and attended Janáček's masterclasses. From 1925 he conducted the Brno Opera and from 1930 was its production adviser, his preference for Czech and Slavonic works determining the company's choice of operas. His most successful productions were *Prince Igor*, *Boris Godunov*, *Khovanshchina*, operas by Rimsky-Korsakov, J. B. Foerster and Novák, and Schulhoff's *Plameny* ('The Flames'). In 1936 he moved to the Prague National Theatre, subsequently becoming head of opera in Ostrava, Brno and Bratislava before returning to Prague in 1953 as first conductor of the National Theatre. He toured successfully with the company to Moscow in 1955 and Berlin in 1956, and in 1956 was engaged for three seasons at Moscow's Bol'shoy Theatre, conducting *Boris*, *The Bartered Bride*, *Jenůfa* and Shebalin's *Ukroshcheniye stroptivoy* ('The Taming of the Shrew'). He gave the Prague premières of Suchoň's *Svätopluk* and Prokofiev's *Story of a Real Man*.

Chalabala was an expressive artist who worked out every phrase in detail; he had an outstanding baton technique and a sensitive feeling for dramatic expression and the capabilities of the voice. His recordings include *Rusalka*, *Svätopluk* and Fibich's *Šárka*.

*

ČSHS

V. Šefl: 'Umělec v plné tvůrči zralosti' [An Artist in Full Creative Maturity], *HRo*, xii (1959), 276

E. Suchoň: 'Rozlúčka s majstrom taktovky' [Farewell to a Master of the Baton], *HRo*, xv (1962), 228 [obituary]

J. Burghauser: *Slavní čeští dirigenti* [Famous Czech Conductors] (Prague, 1963), 95ff [with discography]

ALENA NĚMCOVÁ

Chalaça, O ('The Tricksy Jester'). Opera in two acts by FRANCISCO MIGNONE to a libretto by Humberto Mello Nóbrega; Rio de Janeiro, Sala Cecília Meireles, 27 November 1976.

The story concerns the Portuguese Francisco Gomes da Silva (baritone), an ambitious servant at the court of the Brazilian Emperor Pedro I (reigned 1822–31), who nicknamed him 'Chalaça' for his reputation as an intriguer. The libretto stresses the malice of court life in such a way as to give the work the character of a lyric comedy. In the mansion of the Emperor's mistress, Dona Domitila (soprano), Chalaça brings to Lieutenant Felicio (tenor), Domitila's husband, an imperial order for his transfer from the court. Later, at an evening party, an Afro-Brazilian dance is heard; the guests comment on the music of the Black people and Chalaça criticizes Portugal for having instituted the slave trade in Brazil and other colonies. Domitila asks Chalaça to entertain the guests, which he does by singing a sentimental love song. Plácido (tenor), the Emperor's valet, brings a present from the Emperor to Domitila, provoking curiosity and disdain. The orchestra plays a hymn, taken up by Chalaça and the Marquis (bass) with chorus. The arrival of the Emperor is announced. The guests form lines and bow in reverence; outside, fireworks light up the sky. The opening of the Hymn of Independence (written by Pedro himself) is played. The figure of the Emperor appears at the entrance and remains immobile, while the curtain falls.

In this well written and amusing work, composed in 1973, Mignone's nationalist stance is seen (as it is not in his operas of the 1920s) in his combination of Luso-Brazilian serenading music with Afro-Brazilian traditional music (he even refers to a historical composition of Pedro I in homage to Brazilian independence). For its well-balanced dramatic structure, its melodic fluency, and its instrumental substance, the opera is regarded in Brazil as one of the best in the national repertory.

GERARD BÉHAGUE

Chalet, Le. *Opéra comique* in one act by ADOLPHE ADAM to a libretto by EUGÈNE SCRIBE and MÉLESVILLE [A.-H.-J.-Duveyrier] after JOHANN WOLFGANG VON GOETHE's Singspiel *Jery und Bätely*; Paris, Opéra-Comique (Salle de la Bourse), 25 September 1834.

Adam's first major success, *Le chalet* was performed more than a thousand times by the Opéra-Comique during its first 40 years. Bettly (soprano), the Swiss owner of the chalet, refuses to marry Daniel (tenor), who loves her. When Max (bass), an ex-soldier, takes a hand in the proceedings, he causes her such annoyance that she changes her mind and accepts Daniel. The score, partly derived from a cantata, *Ariane à Naxos*, composed by Adam for the 1825 Prix de Rome, is fresh and melodious but without the originality of his later operas.

ELIZABETH FORBES

Chaliapin, Fyodor. *See* SHALYAPIN, FYODOR.

Chalmeau-Damonte [née Damonte], **Magali** (*b* Marseilles, 30 June 1960). French mezzo-soprano. She studied in Marseilles, where she made her début in 1978 as Zulma (*L'italiana in Algeri*) and sang Taven (*Mireille*). In 1980 she sang Iphise (*Dardanus*) at the Paris Opéra. At Aix-en-Provence (1981–4) she sang Isaura (*Tancredi*), Cenerentola and Rosina. She has appeared at Pesaro, Lyons, Lausanne and the Edinburgh Festival, where she sang Aloes in *L'étoile* (1985). Her repertory includes Ragonde (*Le comte Ory*), Marie (*Moïse*), Isabella (*L'italiana*), Dorabella and Fidalma (*Il matrimonio segreto*) and in 1991 she sang Carmen at Monte Carlo. Her warm, flexible voice is particularly well suited to Rossini's mezzo-soprano coloratura roles.

ELIZABETH FORBES

Chamber opera. A term used to designate 20th-century operas of small and relatively intimate proportions using a chamber orchestra. Examples include Strauss's *Ariadne auf Naxos* (1916), Hindemith's *Hin und zurück* (1927), Stravinsky's *The Rake's Progress* (1951) and Britten's *The Turn of the Screw* (1954). The term has also been applied, retrospectively, to small-scale 18th-century works such as Pergolesi's *La serva padrona* (1733).

Chamlee, Mario [Cholmondeley, Archer] (*b* Los Angeles, 29 May 1892; *d* Los Angeles, 13 Nov 1966). American tenor. He studied with Achille Alberti in Los Angeles, making his début there as Edgardo in 1916, and then in New York. Scotti secured his début at the Metropolitan (*Tosca*, 1920), where he sang in 1927–8 and 1935–7, his roles including Faust, Turiddu and Rossini's Almaviva, as well as the title role in the première of Hageman's *Caponsacchi* (1937) and the Lover in Menotti's *Amelia al ballo*. He also sang in Europe and in San Francisco (Lohengrin and Walther). He retired in 1939. Chamlee was admired for his legato and his rich, dark timbre, well represented in his recordings, which show limitations in the upper range and in his sense of style.

J. B. STEANE

Champein, Stanislas (*b* Marseilles, 19 Nov 1753; *d* Paris, 19 Sept 1830). French composer. By the age of 13 he was music master for the collegiate church at Pignon, Provence, where he composed some religious music. In 1776 he went to Paris and three years later, having gained a reputation as a church composer, wrote the first of his 69 known operas, many of which remained unperformed. He entered politics in 1793 when he was appointed president of the Rhin-et-Moselle département at Koblenz. On his return to Paris in 1804, he adapted old operas and composed new ones but with little success. At the Restoration he lost his pension of 6000F granted to him by Napoleon, and his ensuing poverty was not relieved until a committee of authors (among them Fétis, Scribe, Boieldieu and Catel) secured him an annual pension of 1200F which was supplemented by a state pension in the last two years of his life.

Champein's career spanned more than 40 years. His early works emulate the style of Grétry and Dalayrac, whereas his later works are contemporaneous with those by Méhul, Isouard and Boieldieu (with whom he was unfavourably compared). His greatest success, the farcical *La mélomanie* (1781), was performed all over Europe and given at the Opéra-Comique until 1829. In contrast with some other early works, such as *Le poète supposé* (1782) and the very successful *Les dettes* (1787), where the orchestral accompaniment is rather stiff and schematic, *La mélomanie* excels through the inventiveness of its motifs and a more individual treatment of wind instruments. Its parody of music and musicians has the freshness of an *opera buffa* mingled with accompanied recitatives reminiscent of classical French opera, and the poetic metre is observed closely. However, as in another successful work, *Le nouveau Don Quichotte* (1789), the music is not always inspired by dramatic situations: moments of high drama are treated in a conventional musical language that avoids any unusual modulation. Although in his later career Champein failed to recapture the lightheartedness of his early works, he adopted at times a more experimental approach. *Menzikoff et Foedor* (1808), for example, shows a new dramatic structure with most solo songs being woven into ensembles or choruses: the heroine has no individual number at all. It also includes a backstage wind ensemble that creates a spatial effect, and certain numbers contain strong musical contrasts such as rhythmical irregularities and the interspersing of recitative passages in arias or *romances*. These do not, however, result in an original operatic style and the improbability of the libretto renders the opera melodramatic.

first performed in Paris unless otherwise stated; printed works published in Paris

PCI – *Comédie-Italienne* POC – *Opéra-Comique*

Le soldat françois (scènes lyriques mêlées de chant, 2), Petits Comédiens du Bois de Boulogne, 1 June 1779, collab. A. Albanese

Mina (cmda, 3, E. Grenier), PCI (Bourgogne), 26 Jan 1780
La mélomanie (opéra comique mêlé d'ariettes, 1, Grenier), Versailles, 23 Jan 1781, *F-Pc**; rev. 1799, frag. *Po*; (1783)
Léonore, ou L'heureuse épreuve (2, H. M. N. Duveyrier), PCI (Bourgogne), 7 July 1781
Le baiser, ou La bonne fée (comédie mêlée de musique, 3, J.-P.-C. de Florian), PCI (Bourgogne), 26 Nov 1781, *Pc**; (1784)
Le poète supposé, ou Les préparatifs de fête (cmda et de vaudevilles, 3, P. Laujon), PCI (Bourgogne), 25 April 1782, *Pc**; (n.d.)
Isabelle et Fernand, ou L'alcade de Zalaméa (cmda, 3, L.-F. Faur, after P. Calderón), PCI (Bourgogne), 9 Jan 1783, *Pn*; (n.d.)
Colombine et Cassandre le pleureur [Les amours de Colombine; Columbine douairière] (parade mêlée d'ariettes, 2, Faur or J. L. Brousse-Desfaucherets), PCI (Favart), 3 Feb 1785
Les amours de Bayard, ou Le chevalier sans peur et sans reproche [Bayard en Bresse] (comédie-héroïque mêlée d'intermèdes, 4, J.-M. Boutet de Monvel), Comédie-Française, 24 Aug 1786
Les fausses nouvelles (cmda, 2, N. Fallet), PCI, 26 Aug 1786 [rev. as Les noces cauchoises, Montansier, 11 Aug 1790]
Le manteau, ou Les nièces rivales (opéra bouffon, 1, A.-L.-B. Beaunoir), Beaujolais, 2 Sept 1786, *Pc**; excerpt (n.d.)
Les dettes (comédie lyrique, 2, N.-J. Forgeot), Versailles, 8 Jan 1787, *Pc**; rev. 1803–4; (1787)
Florette et Colin (opéra bouffon, 3, Le Bas), Beaujolais, 7 July 1787, *Pc** (in 1 act)
Lanval et Viviane, ou Les fées et les chevaliers (comédie héroï-féerie, 5, P.-N. André-Murville), Comédie-Française, 13 Sept 1788, *Pc**; excerpts (n.d.)
Le nouveau Don Quichotte (opéra bouffon, 2, T.-C.-G. Boissel de Monville, after M. de Cervantes), Monsieur, 25 May 1789, *A*; (n.d.)
Les déguisements amoureux (opéra bouffon, 2, Mayeur de St-Paul, after J. Patrat), Beaujolais, 8 Aug 1789, *Pc**; rev. 1803–4
Les ruses de Frontin (2, Marchand), Monsieur, 8 March 1790, *Pc**
Le portrait, ou La divinité du sauvage (comédie lyrique, 2, Saulnier), Opéra, 22 Oct 1790, *Pc**
Bayard dans Bresse [Créqui et Clémentine] (cmda, 4, J. Rouget de Lisle), PCI (Favart), 21 Feb 1791, *Pc**
Les espiègleries de garnison (cmda, 3, E.-G.-F. de Favières), PCI (Favart), 21 Sept 1791; rev. as Les trois hussards (comédie lyrique, 2), POC (Favart), 26 July 1804, *A*, *Pc**, *Pc*
Les deux prisonniers, ou La fameuse journée (drame lyrique, 3, J. Martin), Rouen, 10 Feb 1794, *Pc**
Les épreuves du républicain, ou L'amour de la patrie (essai patriotique, 3, Laugier), POC (Favart), 4 Aug 1794, *Pc**
Le cannonnier convalescent (fait historique en vaudevilles, 1, J.-B. Radet), Vaudeville, 1794, air (n.d.)
Menzikoff et Foedor, ou Le fou de Bérézoff (drame, 3, J.-H.-F. Lamartelière), POC (Feydeau), 30 Jan 1808, *Pc**; (n.d.)
La ferme du Mont-Cenis (3, Lamartelière), POC (Feydeau), 20 May 1809, *Pc**
Les rivaux d'un moment (1, Corsange), POC (Feydeau), 30 June 1812, *Pc**
Le mariage extravagant (comédie vaudeville, 1, M.-N.-A. Désaugiers, Gentil and Valory-Mourier, after Mimaut: *Les épouseurs*), Vaudeville, 8 Sept 1812, *Pc**
Les hussards en cantonnement (oc, 3, Sainte-Elme), POC (Feydeau), 28 June 1817, *Pc**

Undated: L'amoureux goutteux (1, M.-J. Sedaine), rev. 1807, *Pc**; L'avare amoureux, ou La chaise à porteurs (2), theatre of Prince of Condé, Chantilly, *Pc**; Les deux seigneurs, ou L'alchimiste en société (2, Anson and Hérissant)

Unperformed (autographs in *Pc*): Abbas et Shory (frag.); L'aubergiste de campagne (oc, 1); Le barbier de Bagdad (3); Bellérophon (tragédie, 5, T. Corneille); Béniovsky (3, A. V. P. Duval); Béranger (2); Camille, ou Les Gaulois dans Rome (2); Diane et Endymion (3); L'échelle (1); L'éducation de l'amour (3, Laujon); Les Egyptiens par amour (3); Electre (5, M. F. S. Champein); Gustave Wasa (Lamartelière), inc.; Hassan; L'inconnue (1, Duval); Isis (5, P. Quinault); Issé (5, pastorale-héroïque, A. H. de Lamotte); Laurette (1, Pein), 1807; Le magicien et le revenant (comédie mêlée de musique, 3); Les métamorphoses, ou les parfaits amants (4), excerpt (n.d.); Le noyer, ou Les ruses villageoises, ou Le marchand dupé et battu (1), rev. 1806; Pandore (5, Voltaire); Paolo et Bianca [Bianca Capello]; La paternité recouvrée (oc, 3, Gohier); Pazzarello, ou Le Figaro vénitien (3), inc.; Le père adolescent, ou L'adoption (1, Laugier), 1804–5; Psyché (tragédie, 4, Corneille); Samson (opéra biblique, 5, Voltaire); Les surprises; Le temple de l'Hymen (allégorie lyrique); Le trésor retrouvé (1), rev. 1804–5; Le triomphe de Camille (2); Valmier, ou Le soldat du roi (comédie-héroïque, 3, Verment-Mariton); Vénus et Adonis (tragédie, 5, J.-B. Rousseau); Vichnou (2, Lassalle)

*

S. Champein: *Lettres et documents autographes* (MS, *F-Pn*)
A. Choron and F. Fayolle: *Dictionnaire historique des musiciens* (Paris, 1810–11)
J.-D. Martine: *De la musique dramatique en France* (Paris, 1813)
M. Tourneux, ed.: *Correspondance littéraire, philosophique et critique par Grimm, Diderot, Raynal, Meister, etc.* (Paris, 1877–82)
A. Pougin: *Monsigny et son temps* (Paris, 1908)
J. Tiersot: *Lettres de musiciens*, i (Turin, 1924), 237–48

MICHAEL FEND (text, bibliography), MICHEL NOIRAY (work-list)

Chance, Michael (*b* Penn, Bucks., 7 March 1955). English countertenor. He studied at King's College, Cambridge, where he was a choral scholar, and quickly established a reputation. He made his British operatic début as Apollo in Cavalli's *Giasone* (1983, Buxton Festival) and his European début as Andronicus in Handel's *Tamerlano* (1985, Opéra de Lyon). Other roles have included Otho, in Monteverdi's *L'incoronazione di Poppea* and in Handel's *Agrippina*, and Ptolemy in Handel's *Giulio Cesare*. He sang with Kent Opera as the Military Governor in the première of Judith Weir's *A Night at the Chinese Opera* (1987, Cheltenham Festival) and in 1988 achieved a notable success in the title role of *Giasone* at Innsbruck Early Music Week. In 1989 he appeared at Glyndebourne as Oberon in Britten's *A Midsummer Night's Dream* and as Apollo in *Death in Venice* with the Glyndebourne Touring Opera; in 1990 he sang with the Netherlands Opera as Human Frailty and as Amphinomus in Monteverdi's *Il ritorno d'Ulisse in patria*. His recordings include *Tamerlano* (1985), *Orfeo* (Monteverdi, 1987; Gluck, 1992) and *Giasone* (1988). Chance's secure technique and natural-sounding, unstrained vocal projection have made him much in demand in both opera and oratorio. NICHOLAS ANDERSON

Chancel, François-Joseph de. *See* LAGRANGE-CHANCEL, FRANÇOIS-JOSEPH DE.

Changalovich [Changalovitch], **Miroslav.** *See* ČANGALOVIĆ, MIROSLAV.

Chapelle, Pierre-David-Augustin (*b* Rouen, 18 Aug 1756; *d* Paris, 1821). French composer. He made his début in 1780 as a violinist at the Concert Spirituel, and in the same period became leader of the orchestra at the Théâtre Italien. His first operas were staged at the Théâtre des Beaujolais, where *L'heureux dépit* was one of the works most frequently performed; its score was printed, unusually for an opera in the repertory of such a small theatre. Chapelle's most important work is *La vieillesse d'Annette et Lubin* (1789), even though he did not write all its numbers; the social tensions of the time are apparent in a violent finale, in which peasants armed with their tools face the representatives of the seigneurial order. Chapelle continued his career at the Théâtre du Vaudeville as an arranger of vaudevilles and a violinist.

all first performed in Paris; printed works published in Paris
PB – *Théâtre des Beaujolais*

La rose, PB, 1785
L'heureux dépit, ou Les enfantillages de l'amour (comédie lyrique, 1, Rauquil-Lieutaud), PB, 16 Nov 1785 (1786)

Le bailli bienfaisant, ou Le triomphe de la nature (cmda, 1, Gabiot de Salins or Théo [T. Burette]), PB, 15 May 1786; vaudeville (n.d.)
Le double mariage (opéra bouffon, 1, Duserre or Théo), PB, 11 Nov 1786
Les deux jardiniers (1, Duserre), PB, 1787
La vieillesse d'Annette et Lubin (cmda, 1, A.-L. Bertin d'Antilly), Italien, 1 Aug 1789, *F-A*; (1790)
La famille réunie (cmda, 2, C.-N. Favart, after J. de La Fontaine: *Le laboureur et ses enfants*), Italien, 6 Dec 1790 (1792)
La huche, ou le médecin dupé (1, Mayeur de Saint-Paul), Cité, 9 Feb 1793
La ruse villageoise (oc, 1, C. A. Sewrin), Louvois, 2 July 1793
Le mannequin (cmda, 1, Rauquil-Lieutaud), Louvois, 6 July 1793
La nouvelle Zélandaise (1), Ambigu-Comique, 1793
Goanna et Jennuy (P. de Lamontagne), Ambigu-Comique, May or June 1795

*

ES (F. Lesure); *StiegerO*
A. Choron and F. Fayolle: *Dictionnaire historique des musiciens* (Paris, 1810)
L. Péricaud: *Théâtre des Petits Comédiens de S. A. S. Monseigneur le comte de Beaujolais* (Paris, 1909)
C. D. Brenner: *A Bibliographical List of Plays in the French Language, 1700–1789* (Ann Arbor, 1947) MICHEL NOIRAY

Chapí (y Lorente), Ruperto (*b* Villena, nr Alicante, 27 March 1851; *d* Madrid, 25 March 1909). Spanish composer. The son of a village barber with an enthusiasm for music, he played in the local band and, in his early teens, became its conductor. At 16 he went to Madrid, entered the Conservatory and (with Bretón as a fellow-pupil) studied composition under Arrieta. After graduating, he lived in extreme poverty, eking out a living by teaching and by playing the cornet in the Circo de Price orchestra, until in 1872 he competed successfully for the post of conductor of the artillery regimental band. This he held for two years, giving concerts in the Salón del Prado and writing *La corte de Granada*, a 'Moorish fantasy' which became very popular. He had previously tried his hand at a zarzuela, *Abel y Cain*, but in 1874 his one-act opera *Las naves de Cortés*, performed at the Teatro Real, won him a grant from the Academy of Fine Arts to spend three years in Rome. From there he sent back various proofs of his industry, including a monograph on works by Spanish composers in the Sistine Chapel, a symphonic poem, a motet for seven voices, two one-act operas and the three-act *Roger de Flor*. The production of two acts of this at a gala celebrating the wedding of Alfonso XII led to his grant being extended by a year for him to go to Paris. Musical styles there greatly influenced an oratorio, *Los ángeles*, and the stage works he wrote after his return to Madrid.

The necessity of earning a living and supporting a young family, and the failure of another one-act opera, turned Chapí's thoughts to writing zarzuelas, then enjoying a renaissance, and he became the most prolific composer of the genre. After a few one-acters like *Música clásica* (1880), he shot to fame with the triumph of his three-act melodrama *La tempestad* (1882), and followed this up with other notable successes such as *La bruja* (1887) and *El rey que rabió* (1891). In 30 years he was to compose some 160 stage works, many of which ran for more than 100 consecutive nights. A quarrel with theatre impresarios and publishers in 1893 over money matters moved him to devote much of his time to organizing protection for the rights of authors and composers (which was to blossom in 1901 into the Society of Authors); after this hiatus he concentrated almost entirely on the *género chico* (the one-act type of zarzuela). Among his greatest successes in this genre were *El tambor de granaderos* (1894), *Las bravías* (1896), *La revoltosa* (1897) and *El puñao de rosas* (1902). Chapí was gifted with great melodic facility and rhythmic vivacity and was a skilful orchestrator, but was less effective in dramatic characterization.

See also BRUJA, LA; REVOLTOSA, LA; REY QUE RABIÓ, EL; TAMBOR DE GRANADEROS, EL; and TEMPESTAD, LA.

all first performed in Madrid; MSS in E-Mn

Las naves de Cortés (1, A. Arnao), Real, 19 April 1874
La hija de Jefté (1, Arnao), Real, 11 May 1876
Roger de Flor (3, M. Capdepón), Real, 25 Jan 1878
La muerte de Garcilaso (1), 7 Feb 1878
La serenata (1, J. Estremera), Apolo, 5 Nov 1881
Circe (3, M. Ramos Carrión, after P. Calderón de la Barca: *El mayor encanto amor*), Lírico, 7 May 1902
Margarita la tornera (3, C. Fernández Shaw, after J. Zorrilla), Real, 24 Feb 1909

ZARZUELAS

Abel y Cain (2, S. M. Granés and M. Pastorfido), Rivas, 14 May 1873; Las niñas desenvueltas (1, E. Arago), 1878, collab. J. Giménez; Los dos huérfanos (3, P. Dominguez), Jan 1880; Música clásica (1, Estremera), Comedia, 20 Sept 1880; La calle de carretas (3, R. Santisteban), Nov 1880; La calandria (1, Ramos Carrión and V. Aza), Alhambra, 24 Dec 1880; La serenata (1, Estremera), Apolo, 5 Nov 1881; Nada entre dos platos (1, Estremera), Comedia, 1881

La tempestad (3, Ramos Carrión, after Erckmann-Chatrian: *Le juif polonais*), Zarzuela, 11 March 1882; El milagro de la Virgen (3, Dominguez), Apolo, Oct 1884; La flor de lis (1, Estremera), Eslava, 13 Dec 1884; El guerillero (3, F. Muñoz), Apolo, Jan 1885, collab. P. E. Arrieta and M. F. Caballero; El país del abanico (1, F. Serrano de la Pedrosa), Martin, 14 Sept 1885; Término medio (1, R. de Marsal), Martin, Oct 1885; Los quintos de mi pueblo (1, P. Buisco), Eslava, Dec 1885

¡Ya pican! (1, E. Prieto and J. Barbera), 1885; El domingo gordo [Las tres damas curiosas] (2, R. de la Vega), Variedades, Jan 1886; El figón de las desdichas (1, A. Llanos), Eslava, Feb 1887; Los lobos marinos (2, Ramos Carrión and Aza), Apolo, 17 May 1887; El fantasma de los aires (2), Variedades, May 1887; La bruja (3, Ramos Carrión and Aza), Zarzuela, 10 Dec 1887; Playeras (1, Llanos), 1887; Ortografía (1, C. Arniches and G. Cantó), Eslava, 31 Dec 1888; Las hijas del Zebedeo (2, Estremera), Maravillas, 9 July 1889

El cocodrillo (1, Dominguez), Príncipe Alfonso, 11 July 1889; A casarse tocan (1, Vega), Sept 1889; Todo por ella (2, P. Novo), Alhambra, April 1890; Las doce y media y sereno (1, F. Manzano), Apolo, 7 May 1890; Los nuestros (1, Estremera), Tivoli, July 1890; Las tentaciones de San Antonio (1, A. Ruesga and Prieto), Felipe, 20 Aug 1890; La leyenda del monje (1, Arniches and Cantó), Apolo, 6 Dec 1890; Nocturno (1, F. Campano), Maravillas, 1890; Los trabajadores (1, J. Jackson Veyán), Apolo, 10 Jan 1891

La bala del rifle (3, Jackson Veyán), Zarzuela, Jan 1891; El rey que rabió (3, Ramos Carrión and Aza), Zarzuela, 20 April 1891; El mismo demonio (2, Manzano), Felipe, 7 Nov 1891; Los alojados (1, E. Sánchez Pastor), 1891; Las campanadas (1, Arniches and Cantó), Apolo, 13 May 1892; La czarina (1, Estremera), Apolo, 8 Oct 1892; El organista (1, Estremera), Apolo, 20 Dec 1892; Via libre (1, Arniches and C. Lucio), Apolo, 25 April 1893; Los gendarmes, Apolo, Oct 1893; El reclamo (1, Arniches and Lucio), Apolo, 25 Nov 1893

El duque de Gandía (3, J. Dicenta), Zarzuela, 17 March 1894, collab. E. Llanos; El tambor de granaderos (1, Sánchez Pastor), Eslava, 16 June 1894; El moro Muza (1, F. Jacques), Eslava, Oct 1894; Los mostenses (3, Arniches, Cantó and Lucio), 1894; Mujer y reina (1, Dominguez), Zarzuela, Jan 1895; El cura del regimiento (1, Sánchez Pastor), Eslava, March 1895; El bajo de arriba (3, Sánchez Pastor), Eslava, 1895; El señor corregidor (1, F. Iráyzoz), Eslava, 1895

El cortejo de la Irene (1, Fernández Shaw), Eslava, Feb 1896; La gitanilla (1), 1 May 1896; Los golfos (1, Sánchez Pastor), Apolo, 24 Sept 1896; Las bravías (1, Fernández Shaw and J. López Silva, after W. Shakespeare: *The Taming of the Shrew*), Apolo, 12 Dec 1896; Las peluconas (1), 1896; ¡Viva el rey! (1), 1896; El segundo de ligeros (1, Labra and Ayuso), Feb 1897; La niña del estanquero

(1, T. Luceño), 13 June 1897; La revoltosa (1, López Silva and Fernández Shaw), Apolo, 25 Nov 1897; Los hijos del batallón (3, Fernández Shaw, after V. Hugo: *Quatre-vingt-treize*), Parish, 17 Dec 1897

La piel del diablo, Comedia, Dec 1897; Pepe Gallardo (1, G. Perrin and V. Palacios), Apolo, 7 July 1898; La chavala (1, López Silva and Fernández Shaw), Apolo, 28 Oct 1898; Curro Vargas (3, Dicenta and M. Paso), Parish, 10 Dec 1898; La afrancesada (1, A. Más and Zurrón), Parish, 3 March 1899; El fonógrafo ambulante (1, J. Gonzáles), Apolo, 24 April 1899; La cara de Dios (3, Arniches), Parish, 28 Nov 1899; La seña Frasquita (1, Perrin and Palacios), Apolo, 7 Dec 1899

Los buenos mozos (1, López Silva and Fernández Shaw), Apolo, 21 Dec 1899; El baile del casino (1, Arniches and Fernández Shaw), Apolo, 1899; El galope de los siglos (1, S. Delgado), Apolo, 5 Jan 1900; La cortijera (1, Dicenta and Paso), Parish, March 1900; Maria de los Angeles (1, Arniches and Lucio), Apolo, 12 May 1900; El gatito negro (1, López Silva and Fernández Shaw), Apolo, May 1900; Mississippi (1, Paso and G. Alvares), Eldorado, 23 June 1900; El estreno (1, S. Alvarez Quintero and J. Alvarez Quintero), Apolo, 19 July 1900

El barquillero (1, López Silva and Jackson Veyán), Eldorado, 21 July 1900; Blasones y talegas (2, J. M. de Pereda and E. Sierra), Apolo, 21 March 1901; ¿Quo vadis? (1, Delgado), Apolo, 28 Dec 1901; El sombrero de plumas (1, M. Echegaray), Apolo, 1 Jan 1902; Plus ultra (1, Delgado), Apolo, June 1902; El tío Juan (1, Fernández Shaw), Zarzuela, July 1902, collab. Morera; El puñao de rosas (1, Arniches and Más), Apolo, 30 Oct 1902; La venta de don Quijote (1, Fernández Shaw, after M. de Cervantes), Apolo, 19 Dec 1902

Don Juan de Austria (1, J. de la Parra and Servet), Lírico, Jan 1903; La chica del maestro (1, López Silva and Jackson Veyán), 1903; Cuadros vivos (1), Zarzuela, 1903; El equipaje del rey José (1), 1903; Mam'zelle Margot (1, Más and Fernández Shaw), Zarzuela, 1903, collab. J. Valverde; El rey mago (1, Delgado), 1903; La cuna (1, Perrin), Moderno, 5 May 1904; La tragedía del Pierrot (1, J. Cadenas and Más), Zarzuela, 20 Oct 1904; La puñalada (1, Fernández Shaw), Apolo, Oct 1904; Juan Francisco (1, Dicenta), Príncipe, 22 Dec 1904; La guardia de honor (1, E. Sellés), Zarzuela, 17 Feb 1905

Miss Full (1, A. Viergol), March 1905; El amor en solfa (1, S. Alvarez Quintero and J. Alvarez Quintero), 16 April 1905, collab. E. Serrano; El alma del pueblo (1, López Silva and Fernández Shaw), Apolo, 21 April 1905; El seductor (1, Dominguez), Zarzuela, 30 May 1905; El hijo de Doña Urraca (1), Zarzuela, 13 Oct 1905; La reina (1, Perrin and Palacios), Zarzuela, 14 Dec 1905; Alma gitana (1), 1905; El género chico (1), 1905, collab. Valverde; La leyenda dorada (1, Delgado), 1905; La sobresaliente (1, J. Benavente), 1905; La joroba (1, Ramos Carrión and R. Martin), Apolo, 14 Feb 1906; El maldito dinero (1, Arniches and Fernández Shaw), Apolo, 8 May 1906

El triunfo de Vénus (1, Fernández Shaw and M. Seca), Gran, 5 June 1906; La pesadilla (1, L. Boada and M. de Castro Tieda), Gran, 22 Dec 1906; El rey del petróleo (1), 1906; El pino del norte (1, V. Casanova), Apolo, 27 Feb 1907; Niñón (1, F. de la Puente and C. Allen-Perkins), Zarzuela, 13 May 1907; La Puerta del Sol (1, C. Lucio and M. Fernández Palomero), Gran, July 1907; Los veteranos (1, M. Labra), Zarzuela, Sept 1907; La patria chica (1, S. Alvarez Quintero and J. Alvarez Quintero), Zarzuela, 15 Oct 1907; Los bárbaros del norte (1, Delgado), Apolo, 1907, collab. Valverde

El hijo merendero de la alegría (Donde hay faldas hay jaleo) (1, A. Casero and A. Larrubiera), Eslava, 24 April 1908; La doña roja (1, J. B. Pont and Sotillo), Apolo, April 1908; Los Madrileños (1, Perrin and Palacios), Apolo, June 1908; Las mil maravillas (1, Fernández Shaw), June 1908; Las calderas de Pedro Botero (1, Delgado), Zarzuela, Dec 1908; La carabina de Ambrosio (1), 1908; La eterna revista (Más and J. Capella), 1908, collab. Giménez; Aquí hace falta un hombre (1), Jan 1909; El diablo con faldas (1, Delgado), 1909; Entre rocas (1, Dicenta), 1909; La magia de la vida (1), Apolo, Jan 1910

*

ES (J. Subirá)

A. S. Salcedo: *Ruperto Chapí: su vida y sus obras* (Córdoba, 1929)

J. Deleito y Piñuela: *Origén y apogeo del género chico* (Madrid, 1949)

J. Subirá: *Historia y anecdotario del Teatro Real* (Madrid, 1949)

'Chispero': *El teatro Apolo* (Madrid, 1953)

J. de D. Aguilar Gómez: *Ruperto Chapí y su obra lírica* (Alicante, 1973)

LIONEL SALTER

Chapin, Schuyler G(arrison) (*b* New Yor[k] ... 1923). American impresario and music admin[istrator]. He attended the Longy School in Camb[ridge], Massachusetts (1940–41), where he was a pupi[l of] Boulanger, and then worked for NBC (1941–51). H[e] has held administrative or board appointments with several organizations. He was vice-president in charge of programming at Lincoln Center (from 1963) and general manager of the Metropolitan Opera (1972–5). At the Metropolitan he appointed James Levine music director and John Dexter director of production. He brought new works into the repertory, including Britten's *Death in Venice* and Berlioz's *Les Troyens*. In 1983 he was appointed to the President's Committee on the Arts and the Humanities. His autobiography *Musical Chairs: a Life in the Arts* was published in 1977.

*

CBY 1974

S. E. Rubin: 'A Met Understudy Makes it to the Top', *New York Times Magazine* (23 Sept 1973), 36ff

ELLEN HIGHSTEIN

Chaplet, The. Musical entertainment in two parts by WILLIAM BOYCE to a libretto by Moses Mendez; London, Drury Lane, 2 December 1749.

The libretto of *The Chaplet* is based on a conventional pastoral plot in which stock Arcadian characters pursue their amorous inclinations. An 'eternal triangle' involving the shepherd Damon (tenor) and two shepherdesses, Laura (soprano) and Pastora (mezzo-soprano), is eventually resolved. The scene is a grove. The young and innocent Laura loves Damon but is distressed by his inconstancy. The more worldly-wise Pastora is abandoned by her youthful lover Palaemon (treble). Though Pastora sees Damon as an attractive proposition, she thwarts his advances by insisting on marriage. In Part 2 Laura and Pastora in turn lament their apparent failure to capture Damon. He resolves first to tease Pastora, whom he knows to have compromised her avowed principles with Palaemon, and then to offer his hand to Laura. The happy couple finally rejoice in the prospect of their future life together.

The Chaplet was one of the most widely acclaimed musical afterpieces of the 18th century. In its first season at Drury Lane it received 31 performances, and a further 86 were given in the succeeding decade. From 1758 it was also given occasionally at Covent Garden. It reached Dublin as early as February 1750 and America by 1767, and survived on the London stage until at least 1785. This remarkable success should be seen in the light of the continuing vogue for the pastoral and the essential function of the afterpiece in the 18th-century theatre as a lightweight, inconsequential and above all entertaining foil to the main dramatic fare of the evening. The songs in *The Chaplet* are rooted in the popular style so effectively utilized in *The Beggar's Opera* (1728), which was sustained in the many ballad operas that succeeded it and enjoyed by the crowds from all classes who thronged to the London pleasure gardens.

Beyond a natural fecundity of melodic invention, Boyce reveals a lightness of touch and a keen responsiveness to the mood and character of Mendez's verses. If there are *longueurs* in Part 1, they are mainly due to the extensive recitative and the conventional strophic treatment of the airs rather than to a lack of inspiration on Boyce's part. Part 2 is undoubtedly strengthened by the one through-composed air, Laura's affective lament in G minor, 'How unhappy's the nymph', scored for strings and obbligato flute, which is strategically placed at its centre and transcends stylistic expectations with its persistent sigh motifs and sustained dissonances. Such is the impact of Laura's outpouring that Damon is persuaded to face up to the inevitability of marriage.

The early performances of *The Chaplet* benefited from a strong cast with John Beard as Damon, Kitty Clive as Pastora and Miss Norris as Laura. The casting of a boy treble, George Mattocks, as a young lover such as Palaemon was not uncommon at the time, though in later performances tenors undertook the role. Individual songs from *The Chaplet* were widely disseminated and some were included in pasticcio operas. The overture in C was included in Boyce's *Eight Symphonys* (London, 1760). *The Chaplet* was revived by the Arts Theatre Club in London in 1936. IAN BARTLETT

Chapuis, Auguste (Paul Jean-Baptiste) (*b* Dampierre sur Salon, 20 April 1858; *d* Paris, 6 Dec 1933). French composer. He studied at the Paris Conservatoire with Massenet and Franck, winning *premiers prix* for harmony and for organ as well as the Rossini Prize (1885). Besides his activities as an organist and educationist in Paris, Chapuis was professor of harmony at the Conservatoire from 1894 until 1923. He edited Rameau's *Castor et Pollux* for the *Oeuvres complètes* (1903) and published a variety of vocal and instrumental works, though his operas were unsuccessful. *Enguerrande*, set in 'a chimerical Sicily, at an imaginary time', is heavily influenced by the style of later Wagner. Its chromatic harmony cadences more regularly, however, and in *Les demoiselles de Saint-Cyr* the style was thinned out to allow for the conversational exchanges, which exposed the lack of individuality in Chapuis' music.

Enguerrande (drame lyrique, 4, V. Wilder, after E. Bergerat), Paris, OC (Lyrique), 9 May 1892, vs (1892)
Les demoiselles de Saint-Cyr (comédie musicale, 4, A. Lénéka, after A. Dumas, *père*), Monte Carlo, 19 April 1921 (Paris, 1921)
Yannel (3) DAVID CHARLTON

Chard, Geoffrey (William) (*b* Sydney, 9 Aug 1930). Australian baritone. He studied in Sydney, making his début there in 1951 as Le Dancaïre. Moving to England, at Aldeburgh he created the roles of Odysseus in Berkeley's *Castaway* (1967) and Choregos in Birtwistle's *Punch and Judy* (1968). Joining Sadler's Wells (later the ENO), he created Peter in Williamson's *Lucky Peter's Journey* (1969), Pizarro in Hamilton's *Royal Hunt of the Sun*, Dessalines in Blake's *Toussaint* (1977) and Karenin in Hamilton's *Anna Karenina* (1981). He sang Grandier in *The Devils of Loudun* (1973), Silvio de Narni in *Bomarzo* (1976) and Nekrotzar in *Le Grand Macabre* (1982), all British premières. His repertory includes Mozart's Count Almaviva and Don Giovanni, Rossini's Dr Bartolo, Escamillo, Marcello, Germont, Scarpia, Szymanowski's King Roger, the four villains in *Les contes d'Hoffmann*, Gunther, Kurwenal and several Janáček roles. A fine actor and musician, he excels in 20th-century works. ELIZABETH FORBES

Chardiny [Chardine, Chardini], **Louis-Claude-Armand** (*b* Fécamp, 1755 or 1758; *d* Paris, 1 Oct 1793). French composer and singer. Italianizing his name to increase his chances of success, he joined the Académie Royale de Musique as a *basse-taille* in 1780, although judging by his most successful part, that of Theseus in Sacchini's *Oedipe à Colonne*, his voice was a tenor rather than a baritone. His taste was for serious opera (he was a fervent admirer of Gluck), but his only contribution to the repertory of the Opéra was to write the recitatives and some cavatinas for a French adaptation of Paisiello's *Le roi Théodore à Venise* (1787). *La ruse d'amour*, produced at the Théâtre des Beaujolais, brought that small theatre its first real success ten months after it had opened. In this work, as in *Le pouvoir de la nature*, the other of his operas available in score, Chardiny sought to compete with the *opéras comiques* produced at the Comédie-Italienne. Later he was employed as an arranger for the Théâtre du Vaudeville (from January 1792). Beffroy de Reigny wrote that 'Chardiny hated the revolutionaries', but he was nonetheless captain of a section of the National Guard at the time of his death.

all first performed in Paris; printed works published in Paris

PB – *Paris, Théâtre des Beaujolais*

Les deux porteurs de chaise (comédie parade en vaudevilles, 1, P. A. A. de Piis and P. Y. Barré), Trianon, 26 July 1781, pts (n.d.)
Le diable boiteux, ou La chose impossible (divertissement mêlé de vaudevilles, 1, C.-N. Favart), Comédie-Italienne (Bourgogne), 27 Sept 1782, pts (n.d.)
L'oiseau perdu et retrouvé, ou La coupe des foins (oc en vaudevilles, 1, Piis and Barré), Comédie-Italienne (Bourgogne), 5 Nov 1782, *F-A*, pts (n.d.)
La ruse d'amour, ou L'épreuve (cmda, 1, Maillé de Marencour, after G. Colman the elder: *The Deuce is in Him*), PB, 25 Aug 1785 (1785)
Annette et Basile (mélodrame comique, 1, C. J. Guillemain), PB, 17 Oct 1785
Honoré, ou L'homme célèbre (L.-A. Beffroy de Reigny), 1786, unperf.
Le pouvoir de la nature, ou La suite de la ruse d'amour (cmda, 2, Maillé de Marencour), PB, 4 March 1786 (1786)
Le clavecin (cmda, 2), PB, 21 Feb 1787
Clitandre et Céphise (opéra bouffon, 1), PB, 19 May 1788
L'anneau perdu et retrouvé (oc, 2, M.-J. Sedaine), Comédie-Italienne (Favart), 11 Sept 1788, chanson (n.d.)
L'amant sculpteur (oc, 1, F. P. A. Léger), Français Comique et Lyrique, 15 Sept 1790; rev. as Les parents réunis, 19 Nov 1790
L'histoire universelle (comédie mêlée de vaudevilles et d'airs nouveaux, 2, Beffroy de Reigny), Monsieur, 16 Dec 1790; collab. Beffroy de Reigny; 1 air by Gaveaux, 1 air by J.-P.-E. Martini
Le petit sacristain, ou Le départ des novices (comédie en vaudevilles, 1, Demautort), Vaudeville, 13 March 1792

Doubtful: La papesse Jeanne (Flins), Vaudeville, 5 Feb 1793

*

ES (F. Lesure)
Journal des spectacles (3 Oct 1793)
Les spectacles de Paris (1794), 56–7
L.-A. Beffroy de Reigny: *Dictionnaire néologique des hommes et des choses de la Révolution* (Paris, 1800), iii, 195–6
C. D. Brenner: *A Bibliographical List of Plays in the French Language, 1700–1789* (Berkeley, 1947, 2/1979)
MICHEL NOIRAY

Charleston. American city in the state of South Carolina. The cultural centre of the Southeast until the Civil War, it was the site of the first recorded operatic performance in the American colonies. On 18 February 1735 the ballad opera *Flora; or, Hob in the Well* was performed in the Courtroom above Shepheard's Tavern. Theatrical performances of all kinds were intermittent throughout the colonial period, but by the mid-1790s there were two theatres, one with a resident company of French comedians. Mattfeld lists over 20 Charleston performances of English ballad operas and French operas before 1800 as American premières. From 1817 to 1822 Charles Gilfert, a composer of several ballad operas, included short seasons in Charleston on his circuit as a theatre manager and conductor.

With the advent of better transport in the 1840s and 50s, the busy port city had visits from many small touring opera troupes based in New York, New Orleans and Havana. Performances of the popular works of Auber, Balfe, Bellini, Donizetti, Rossini and Verdi were given; *Trovatore* was heard with two different casts in 1858 alone. Jenny Lind sang in Charleston in 1850 and Adelina Patti in 1861. Little operatic activity other than concerts by touring singers can be documented for the next hundred years. In 1934 George Gershwin visited Charleston and the surrounding area to absorb local musical colour while working on *Porgy and Bess*. Set in the city's 'Catfish Row' (Cabbage Row) and on nearby 'Kittiwah' (Kiawah) Island, *Porgy* uses street vendors' cries and builds on the vivid music of the Lowcountry blacks. The opera was not produced in Charleston until 1970 (designed by Emmett Robinson), with revivals in 1985 and 1990. The Charleston Opera Company, founded by Vernon W. Weston, presented standard repertory operas (as well as a revival of *Flora*) from 1965 to 1988. Since 1977 Charleston has been the site of the annual Spoleto Festival USA, the American branch of Menotti's Festival of Two Worlds. Operatic productions of an international calibre are presented during May and June, though there have been no significant first performances.

*

O. G. T. Sonneck: *Early Opera in America* (Boston, 1915)
E. Willis: *The Charleston Stage in the XVIII Century* (New York, 1933)
W. S. Hoole: *The Ante-Bellum Charleston Theatre* (Tuscaloosa, AL, 1946)
E. Robinson: *The Dock Street Theatre: a Guide and a Brief Resume of the Theatres in Charleston, S.C., from 1730* (Charleston, SC, 1954, 2/1975)
J. Mattfeld: *A Handbook of American Operatic Premieres 1731–1962* (Detroit, 1963)
M. J. Curtis: *The Early Charleston Stage: 1703–1798* (diss., Indiana U., 1968)
N. L. Stephenson: *The Charleston Theatre Management of Charles Gilfert, 1817–1822* (diss., U. of Nebraska, 1988)

WILLIAM D. GUDGER

Charles VI, Emperor (*b* Vienna, 1 Oct 1685; *d* Vienna, 20 Oct 1740). Austrian patron, Holy Roman Emperor. The younger son of the Habsburg Emperor Leopold I, he was declared King of Spain in 1703 in opposition to Philip V, who was already reigning in Madrid. Charles had his residence in Barcelona, where he also maintained a musical establishment. Several operas with texts by Pariati and Zeno and music by Caldara, Albinoni, Gasparini and others were performed there, beginning in 1708 on Charles's marriage. He became emperor upon his brother Joseph's death in 1711 and soon adopted the rich italianate operatic life of his predecessors in Vienna. He engaged Pariati, Zeno and Caldara, who joined J. J. Fux and F. B. Conti (whom he had taken over from his brother). From the 1720s they were supported or replaced by the poets Metastasio and G. C. Pasquini and the composers Giuseppe Porsile, Georg Reutter jr and Giuseppe Bonno. Members of the Galli-Bibiena family were responsible for the stage designs.

The most spectacular performance of Charles's reign was of *Costanza e fortezza* by Fux, given in 1723 in Prague during the festivities for his coronation as King of Bohemia. Charles was a composer as well as a patron, but, unlike his father, not of operas. He directed several performances from the harpsichord, including Caldara's *Euristeo* in 1724. None of his own works survives. After his death the tradition of Italian court opera ceased.

*

F. Hadamowsky: 'Barocktheater am Wiener Kaiserhof, mit einem Spielplan (1625–1740)', *Jb der Gesellschaft für Wiener Theaterforschung 1951–52*, 7–96
H. Seifert: 'Die Aufführungen der Opern und Serenate mit Musik von Johann Joseph Fux', *SMw*, xxix (1978), 14–27
T. Antonicek: 'Die Vollendung des Barock im Zeitalter der höfischen Repräsentation', *Musikgeschichte Österreichs*, ii (Graz, 1979), 17–33, 50–55
G. Gronda: *La carriera di un librettista: Pietro Pariati di Reggio di Lombardia, da Venezia a Vienna* (Bologna, 1990)

HERBERT SEIFERT

Charles VI. Opéra in five acts by FROMENTAL HALÉVY to a libretto by Casimir and GERMAIN DELAVIGNE; Paris, Opéra, 15 March 1843.

Set in the 15th century, following the defeat of Agincourt, *Charles VI* strikes a strong note of French patriotism, recounting French efforts to repulse the English invaders. The Delavigne brothers had both worked with Scribe and here produced a libretto on the Scribe model that contrasts the country wisdom of Odette (mezzo-soprano) and her father Raymond (bass) with the refined Isabelle of Bavaria (soprano) and the Duke of Bedford (tenor). The role of Charles VI (baritone) calls for special gifts since the king hovers on the edge of madness, which Halévy portrayed with considerable imagination. In Act 4 the king is confronted by a series of ghosts, and the short second scene of Act 5 is set in the abbey of Saint-Denis, where the English are overwhelmed to cries of 'Guerre aux tyrans! Jamais en France l'Anglais ne règnera!' while the king expires in the arms of his son. The principal roles were written for the Opéra's leading singers of the day: Barroilhet, Duprez, Dorus-Gras and Stoltz. HUGH MACDONALD

Charlotte. American city, in North Carolina. It is the home of Opera Carolina, the oldest opera company in the state. The company began as the Charlotte Opera Association in 1948, a project of the Charlotte Music Club, with a budget of $125. North Carolina Opera was founded in May 1978 as the touring and educational branch of the association. In 1986 the two merged, creating Opera Carolina. The 1989–90 season featured four operas with two performances of each, produced from an annual budget of $1.3 million. The company's educational programme, Opera Carolina Theatre, presents an average of 200 performances annually in schools and communities throughout the south-eastern states. The world première of Robert Ward's opera *Abelard and Heloise* was given by the company in 1982.

NATALIE SHELPUK

Charlton, David (*b* London, 20 June 1946). British musicologist. He studied at Nottingham University and at Cambridge with Hugh Macdonald (PhD 1970) and in 1970 was appointed a lecturer at the University of East Anglia (Reader, 1991). His work has centred on French opera, especially *opéra comique*, of the late 18th and early 19th centuries, as well as French Revolutionary music and its instruments. Among his writings are an important study, *Grétry and the Growth of Opéra-Comique* (Cambridge, 1986); the chapters on French opera in the 19th century in the *New Oxford History of Music*, ix (1990); an edition of E. T. A. Hoffmann's musical writings (Cambridge, 1989); and many articles in periodicals and reference works.

Charodeyka. Opera by P. I. Tchaikovsky; *see* ENCHANTRESS, THE.

Charpentier, Gabriel (*b* Richmond, Quebec, 13 Sept 1925). Canadian composer. His teachers included Jean Papineau-Couture in Montreal and Nadia Boulanger, Annette Dieudonné and Andrée Bonneville in France. On his return to Canada in 1953 he worked for the CBC in Montreal and as a teacher and theatre musician. A consultant to the Shakespeare Festival at Stratford, Ontario, for many years, he wrote incidental scores for the company (1963–73); his short opera *An English Lesson* was first given at Stratford on 3 August 1968. His music is structurally clear and shows an openness to new trends, notably in his works on the Orpheus myth. *Orphée I*, commissioned by the Canada Council for the opening festival at the National Arts Centre, Ottawa (1969), is a stage piece without scenery, involving actors, musicians and audience in a quasi-liturgical manner, comparable with medieval religious drama or with the noh theatre; the libretto, like those of most of his operas, is his own. For the 1972 Stratford Festival Charpentier produced a revised, English-language version of the work, *Orpheus II*. The three works given in 1979 are on a modest scale, between 15 and 25 minutes long and for small ensembles; they belong, with *An English Lesson* and *A Tea Symphony*, to a projected series to be called 'A Night at the Opera'.

librettos by the composer unless otherwise stated

An English Lesson ('opera-happening', 1), Stratford, Ont., 3 Aug 1968

Orphée I ('liturgy', 7 pts), Ottawa, National Arts Centre, 10 June 1969; rev. as Orpheus II, Stratford, July 1972

A Tea Symphony or The Perils of Clara ('kitsch-opera in 9 drinks'), Banff, 6 May 1972

Clara et les philosophes, 1976 ('opera-cocktail', B. Char), Montreal, La Salle de l'Association des vétérans de guerre polonais, 9 Feb 1979

La ballade du fils de l'homme ('opera seria'), Toronto, Walter Hall, 31 March 1979

Clarabelle-Clarimage ('une opération', Char), Toronto, Walter Hall, 31 March 1979

*

EMC (F. Malouin-Gélinas; also 'An English Lesson', B. J. Edwards)

'Un petit opéra from Stratford', *CBC Times* (3–9 Aug 1968)

P. W. Desjardins: 'Orphée', *Vie des arts*, lvii (1969–70), 59

JACQUES THÉRIAULT/R

Charpentier, Gustave (*b* Dieuze, Lorraine, 25 June 1860; *d* Paris, 18 Feb 1956). French composer. The son of a baker with an amateur interest in music, he moved with his family to Tourcoing, near the Belgian border, in 1870 to escape the advance of the Prussian army. Aided by a rich patron there, he studied the violin at the Lille Conservatoire, winning a *prix d'honneur*. In 1881 he registered at the Paris Conservatoire, supported by a scholarship from the townspeople of Tourcoing, studying the violin and later composition, but he aroused the displeasure of several of his teachers for incorporating jokes or popular music into his student exercises. It was at this time that he took up residence in Montmartre, which became his adopted home for the rest of his life and the inspiration and subject matter of his operas *Louise* and *Julien*.

His official studies in composition began with Hector Pessard, and in 1885 he entered Massenet's class. Massenet remembered him as a pupil 'who always wanted to shock', and he advised him to be more natural. In 1887 he won the Prix de Rome with a cantata, *Didon*, but was at first so reluctant to leave his beloved Montmartre that he went three times to the station without being able to face catching the train to Rome for the prizewinner's obligatory sojourn at the Villa Medici.

It was in Rome that he wrote or began his most successful works: the orchestral *Impressions d'Italie* (admired by Debussy), the symphony-drama *La vie du poète* and *Louise*. On his return to Paris he organized several performances of his works in streets and gardens, notably *Le couronnement de la muse* (1897), which was incorporated into *Louise*. It was *Louise* above all that made him famous, for when, after long delays, it was performed at the Opéra-Comique reactions were on the whole favourable. Although the style of the music clearly derives from Gounod and Massenet, the subject matter, with its up-to-date social realism and controversial theme, has ensured it a secure place in the repertory; it is widely regarded as the chief representative of *verismo* in France. Not surprisingly, Gounod and Massenet admired the work, but there was praise from other quarters: Strauss, who attended a performance with Romain Rolland, was delighted with parts of it, licking his lips at the titbits he particularly admired, and finding a realistic portrayal of the French. 'Each nation has its defects', he remarked, 'and those are yours.' More important, he admired *Louise* for its originality.

In 1900 Charpentier founded an institution, named after Mimi Pinson, the working-girl heroine of a tale by Alfred de Musset, dedicated to giving free seats at the opera to working-class Parisians. In 1902 this was extended when he founded the Conservatoire Populaire de Mimi Pinson, providing free courses in music and dance. He popularized this institution by promoting festivals of his music, often in the open air, throughout France.

He planned several sequels to *Louise* but completed only *Julien*. Among incomplete or discarded ideas were *L'amour au faubourg*, *Comédiante*, *Tragédiante*, *Marie* (about Louise's daughter) and *Orphée*. In 1936 he was involved in a film version of *Louise*.

See also JULIEN and LOUISE.

Louise, *c*1889–96 (roman musical, 4, Charpentier, ? or P. Roux), Paris, OC (Favart), 2 Feb 1900, vs (Paris, 1900), full score (Paris, 1905)

Julien, ou La vie du poète (poème lyrique, prol., 4, Charpentier), Paris, OC (Favart), 4 June 1913, vs (Paris, 1913) [incl. material from the symphony-drama La vie du poète]

L'amour au faubourg (drame lyrique, 2, Charpentier), *c*1913, unpubd

Orphée (légende lyrique, 4, Charpentier), 2 acts believed completed

*

A. Bruneau: *Musiques d'hier et de demain* (Paris, 1900, 173–9)

A. Jullien: 'Louise', *Le théâtre*, no.33 (1900), 3–10

L. Laloy: 'Le drame musical moderne III: les véristes français: Gustave Charpentier', *Mercure musical*, i (1905), 169–77

G. Fauré: 'Charpentier: Quelle merveille!' *Figaro* (4 June 1913); repr. in *Opinions musicales* (Paris, 1930), 27–30

A. Himonet: *'Louise' de G. Charpentier* (Paris, 1922)

M. Delmas: *Gustave Charpentier et le lyrisme français* (Paris, 1931)

K. O'Donnell Hoover: 'Gustave Charpentier', *MQ*, xxv (1939), 334–50

P. Landormy: *La musique française après Debussy* (Paris, 1943)

Richard Strauss et Romain Rolland: correspondance, fragments de journal (Paris, 1950; Eng. trans., 1968)

R. Dumesnil: 'Réalistes et naturalistes', *Histoire de la musique*, iv (Paris, 1958)

D. Egbert: *Social Radicalism and the Arts: Western Europe: a Cultural History from the French Revolution to 1968* (New York, 1970)

R. M. Longyear: 'Political and Social Criticism in French Opera, 1827–1920', *Essays on the Music of J. S. Bach and Other Divers Subjects: a Tribute to Gerhard Herz* (Louisville, KY, 1981), 245–54

F. Andrieux, ed.: *Gustave Charpentier: Lettres inédites à ses parents: la vie quotidienne d'un élève du Conservatoire 1879–1887* (Paris, 1984)

M. Kelkel: *Naturalisme, vérisme et réalisme dans l'opéra d'1890 à 1930* (Paris, 1984) RICHARD LANGHAM SMITH

Charpentier, Marc-Antoine (*b* Paris, 1643; *d* Paris, 24 Feb 1704). French composer. Between 1662 and 1667 he studied with Carissimi in Rome (for three years, according to the *Mercure galant*, February 1681), and his earliest music reveals an assimilation of Italian styles and forms. According to Sébastien de Brossard, Charpentier imported the music of his Italian contemporaries: copies of Carissimi's oratorio *Jephte* and of Francesco Beretta's unpublished *Missa mirabiles elationes maris* for four choirs are found among his autograph manuscripts. Charpentier himself wrote cantatas and pastorales to Italian texts, as well as settings of 'Superbo amore' and 'Il mondo così và' from Cicognini's opera libretto *Orontea* (best known in Cesti's setting). The Italian song and chorus of Love's captives in his 1693 opera *Médée* (Act 2. vii) is another reminder of Charpentier's Italian training.

On his return to Paris (around 1670), Charpentier was employed by Marie de Lorraine, the Duchess of Guise. A cousin of Louis XIV, she employed in her *hôtel*, in the Marais district of Paris, a dozen singers (including Charpentier himself, who sang *haute-contre*) and instrumentalists (two treble viols, bass viol, harpsichord, theorbo, recorder and transverse flute). The *Mercure galant* (March 1688) judged her musical establishment to be 'so fine, that it can be said that those of several great sovereigns could not rival it'. For her private concerts (until the mid-1680s) Charpentier wrote allegorical and pastoral chamber operas (*La descente d'Orphée aux enfers*, *Actéon*, *Les arts florissants*, *La couronne de fleurs* and *Il faut rire et chanter: dispute de bergers*) and other secular dramatic works for which the names of singers employed by the Duchess of Guise appear in the margins of Charpentier's autograph manuscripts.

At about the same time Charpentier began his long association with the Troupe du Roy (which in 1680 became the Comédie-Française) and his collaboration with Molière. In 1672 Molière's association with Lully ended when Lully obtained from the king a monopoly on opera composition together with the rights to found the Académie Royale de Musique. Molière thereupon approached Charpentier to compose new music for his plays (*Les fâcheux*, *La comtesse d'Escarbagnas*, *Le mariage forcé*) to replace the overtures, dances, songs and vocal ensembles written earlier for these plays by Lully (for which Lully owned the performing rights). Charpentier also composed the prologue and entr'acte *intermèdes* for the première of Molière's last play, *Le malade imaginaire* (1673). While Molière's premature death put an end to their collaboration, Charpentier continued to write music for the company until 1686. During these 14 years Charpentier twice revised his score to *Le malade imaginaire* to conform to the restrictive terms of various royal ordinances obtained by Lully limiting the players' use of musicians, and he replaced earlier music for plays by Molière and others with his own musical settings; in addition, Charpentier composed new music for the first runs of stage works by Thomas Corneille, Poisson, Brécourt, Baron, Dancourt and Donneau de Visé. This incidental music ranges from simple entr'acte songs and dances to performances-within-the-play (often presented as entertainments for the play's characters) and full-scale operatic *divertissements*, complete with their own dramatic action and cast of characters.

In the early 1680s Charpentier was named musical director to the dauphin, for whom he probably composed two one-act theatre works on courtly subjects (*Les plaisirs de Versailles* and *La fête de Rueil*). Some years later he was appointed music teacher to Philippe, Duke of Chartres (named Duke of Orléans in 1701 and Regent of France from 1715 to 1723). According to Titon du Tillet, the two collaborated on an opera, *Philomèle* (now lost), 'which was sung three times in the Palais-Royal'. Perhaps it was the royal backing of Philippe that enabled Charpentier in 1693 to have his opera *Médée* performed at the Académie Royale de Musique.

From the mid-1680s until 1698 Charpentier apparently served as composer and *maître de musique* at the principal Jesuit church in Paris, St Louis (later named St Paul-St Louis). For the Jesuits Charpentier composed an immense number of sacred works, including dramatic oratorios modelled after those of his teacher Carissimi. The Jesuit colleges also commissioned him to write musical interludes for religious dramas, such as *Polieucte* (1680) for the Collège d'Harcourt, and *Celse Martyr* (1687) and *David et Jonathas* (1688) for the Collège de Louis-le-Grand. His only *tragédie en musique* was *Médée*, to a libretto by Thomas Corneille (younger brother of the playwright Pierre Corneille). It received its première at the Académie Royale de Musique on 4 December 1693 and was considered by many to be the most noteworthy opera produced there in the decade following Lully's death. Titon du Tillet proclaimed it a great success, and Brossard referred to it as 'the one opera without exception in which one can learn the things most essential to good composition'. In June 1698 Charpentier succeeded François Chaperon as *maître de musique* of the Sainte-Chapelle, and his last years were devoted mainly to sacred composition.

As Hitchcock has remarked, Charpentier's dramatic works show extraordinary diversity in length, performing forces, compositional techniques, musical forms and styles. Charpentier brought élan and *esprit gaulois* to the incidental music he wrote for the Comédie-Française. For the Jesuit church and the Académie Royale de Musique he wrote operas of unsurpassed emotional depth and psychological penetration that in many ways transcend the conventions of the genre. Charpentier drew his musical inspiration from both Italian and French music of the time. His overtures are suitably ceremonial and follow Lully's design, while his dance airs are light in texture, exuberant, and full of delicate nuances of chromaticism and rhythmic interplay between the parts. His vocal music embraces both the heightened manner of French declamation and warm italianate lyricism and is occasionally spiced with piquant touches of chromaticism and suspension dissonances. Hitchcock mentions how contemporaries remarked upon his rich harmonic palette, some with admiration and others with disdain. His textures are contrapuntal and linear, and the audacious false relations (both simultaneous and successive), Corelli clashes, and suspensions (single and double) that often result between the parts create an extraordinary degree of harmonic tension. Because of Charpentier's delight in diverse orchestral colours and textures, his scores reveal exceptional attention to details of instrumentation, tempo and dynamics (he was master of the dramatic pause). By means of these seemingly inexhaustible resources of lyric melody, poignant harmony, affective key relationships and imaginative orchestrations – all directed by his innate sense of musical drama – Charpentier personalized and vividly portrayed the texts he set.

See also ACTÉON; ARTS FLORISSANTS, LES; DAVID ET JONATHAS; and MÉDÉE (i).

roman numerals refer to volumes of Charpentier's autographs in F-Pn Rés.Vm[1] 259 (28 vols)

Petite pastorale (pastorale), mid-1670s, *F-Pn* ii
Les amours d'Acis et de Galatée (pastorale), 1678
Les plaisirs de Versailles (divertissement), early 1680s, *Pn* xi
Orphée descendant aux enfers (dramatic cantata), 1683, *Pn* vi, ed. J. S. Powell, RRMBE, xlviii (1986)
Actéon (pastorale en musique, 6 scenes), 1683–5, *Pn* xxi
Actéon changé en biche (pastorale), 1683–5, *Pn* xxi
Il faut rire et chanter: dispute de bergers (pastorale), 1684–5, *Pn* xxi
La couronne de fleurs (pastorale, 3 scenes), 1685, *Pn* vii, ed. H. Büsser (Paris, 1907)
La fête de Rueil (pastorale, 7 scenes), 1685, *Pn* xxii, *Pn* Vm[6] 17
La descente d'Orphée aux enfers (opéra, 2), 1685–6, *Pn* xiii
Les arts florissants (opéra, 5 scenes), 1685–6, *Pn* vii, *Pn* Vm[6] 18
Idyle sur le retour de la santé du roi (divertissement), 1686–7, *Pn* viii
David et Jonathas (sacred op, 5, F. Bretonneau), Paris, Collège de Louis-le-Grand, 28 Feb 1688, *Pc*; ed. J. Duron (Paris, 1981)
Médée (tragédie en musique, 5, T. Corneille), Paris, Opéra, 4 Dec 1693 (Paris, 1694); ed. E. Lemaître (Paris, 1987)
Philomèle (opéra), Paris, Palais Royal, ?1694; collab. Philippe de Bourbon
Apothéose de Laodamus à la mémoire de M le Maréchal duc de Luxembourg (divertissement, P. de Longemare), 1695–6

Music in: Télémaque, ou Les fragmens des modernes (tragédie en musique, prol., 5, A. Danchet), Paris, Opéra, 11 Nov 1704, *Pn*; arr. A. Campra

*

Grove6 (Hitchcock)
[S. de Brossard]: *Catalogue des livres de musique* (MS, *F-Pn* Rés. Vm[8] 21)
E. Titon du Tillet: *Description du Parnasse françois* (Paris, 1727), 144ff
——: *Le Parnasse françois* (Paris, 1732), 490–91
J. Bonnassies: *La musique à la Comédie-Française* (Paris, 1874)
J. Tiersot: *La musique dans la comédie de Molière* (Paris, 1922)
J. De Froberville: 'L'Actéon de Marc-Antoine Charpentier', *RdM*, xxvi (1928), 75–6
L. de La Laurencie: 'Un opéra inédit de M.-A. Charpentier: La descente d'Orphée aux enfers', *RdM*, xiii (1932), 184-93
C. Crussard: *Un musicien français oublié: Marc-Antoine Charpentier, 1634–1704* (Paris, 1945)
A. R. Oliver: 'Molière's Contribution to the Lyric Stage', *MQ*, xxxiii (1947), 350–64
E. Borrel: 'La vie musicale de M.-A. Charpentier d'après le Mercure galant (1678–1704)', *XVIIe siècle*, xxi–xxii (1954), 433–41
R. Lowe: *Marc-Antoine Charpentier et l'opéra de collège* (Paris, 1966)
H. W. Hitchcock: 'Marc-Antoine Charpentier and the Comédie-Française', *JAMS*, xxiv (1971), 255–81
——: 'Problèmes d'édition de la musique de Marc-Antoine Charpentier pour Le malade imaginaire', *RdM*, lviii (1972), 3–15
J. R. Anthony: *French Baroque Music from Beaujoyeulx to Rameau* (London, 1973, 2/1978)
H. W. Hitchcock: *Les oeuvres de Marc-Antoine Charpentier: catalogue raisonné* (Paris, 1982)
J. S. Powell: *Music in the Theater of Molière* (diss., U. of Washington, 1982)
C. Grand: *Un opéra jésuite: David et Jonathas de Marc-Antoine Charpentier* (Paris, 1983)
S. Pitou: *The Paris Opéra: an Encyclopedia of Operas, Ballets, Composers, and Performers* (Westport, CT, 1983–5)
L'avant-scène opéra, no.68 (1984) [*Médée* issue]
J. Burke: *The Early Works of Marc-Antoine Charpentier* (diss., U. of Oxford, 1985)
E. Lemaître: 'L'orchestre dans le théâtre lyrique français chez les continuateurs de Lully, 1687–1713', *Recherches sur la musique française classique*, xxiv (1986), 107–27
J. S. Powell: Charpentier's Music for Molière's *Le malade imaginaire* and its Revisions', *JAMS*, xxxiv (1986), 87–142
——: Preface to *Marc-Antoine Charpentier: Vocal Chamber Music*, RRMBE, xlviii (1986)
C. Cessac: *Marc-Antoine Charpentier* (Paris, 1988)
A. Parmley: *The 'Pastorales', 'Intermèdes' and Incidental Music of Marc-Antoine Charpentier* (diss., U. of London, 1988)
H. W. Hitchcock: *Marc-Antoine Charpentier* (Oxford, 1990)
J. S. Powell: Preface to *Marc-Antoine Charpentier: Music for Molière's Comedies*, RRMBE, lxii (1990)

JOHN S. POWELL

Charton-Demeur [de Meur; née Charton], **Anne** [Arsène] (*b* Saujon, Charente Maritime, 5 March 1824; *d* Paris, 30 Nov 1892). French mezzo-soprano. She studied at Bordeaux, where she made her début in 1842 as Lucia. On 18 July 1846 she made her London début at Drury Lane, singing Madeleine in *Le postillon de Lonjumeau*; she later sang Angèle in *Le domino noir*. In 1849–50 she was the leading female singer with Mitchell's French Company at St James's Theatre, London. She sang her first Italian role (Amina) at Her Majesty's Theatre on 27 July 1852. Her performances at the Opéra-Comique in 1849 and 1853 were not well received, but she was acclaimed in St Petersburg, Vienna, the Americas and in Paris at the Théâtre Italien, where in 1862 she sang Rossini's Desdemona. In the same year she created Berlioz's Beatrice at Baden-Baden; the composer praised her 'warmth, delicacy, great energy, and rare beauty of style' in his *Mémoires*, and chose her for Dido in the first performances of *Les Troyens à Carthage* at the Théâtre Lyrique in 1863. She retired about 1869 but appeared occasionally in concerts of Berlioz's music.

THOMASIN LA MAY

Chartrain [Chartrin; ? Nicolas-Joseph] (*b* ? Liège, 1740; *d* ? Paris, 1793). South Netherlands composer. Recent investigations show that most of the biographical data on Chartrain given in musical dictionaries are merely conjecture (including his first name). The one certainty is that he was successful from 1772 to 1783 at the Concert Spirituel as a violinist and a composer of concertos and symphonies. His preferred field was instrumental music, as can be seen from his published works. The music of his first opera, *Le lord supposé*, seems to have met with approval despite a mediocre libretto. *L'avocat Patelin* was a success.

Le lord supposé (cmda, 3, Oisemont), Paris, Comédie-Italienne (Bourgogne), 22 Feb 1776, excerpts (n.d.)
L'avocat Patelin (oc, 2, J. Patrat, after D.-A. de Brueys), Paris, Montansier, 21 Jan 1792, *F-A*
Alcione (tragédie lyrique, 5, A. H. de Lamotte), unperf., *Pc*

MICHEL NOIRAY

Chassé (de Chinais), Claude Louis Dominique [de] (*b* Rennes, 1699; *d* Paris, 25 Oct 1786). French bass. Born into an untitled and impoverished branch of a family of the lesser Breton nobility, he made his début at the Paris Opéra as Léandre in the 1721 revival of Campra's *Les fêtes vénitiennes*; this was followed by Saturn in Lully's *Phaëton* (1721 revival). Though he was highly, even disproportionately, appreciated in minor parts, he did not sing principal roles until the retirement of Thévenard in 1729. He created the title role in Montéclair's *Jephté* in 1732, the first biblical opera staged at the Opéra. For

Rameau he created Theseus (*Hippolyte et Aricie*, 1733), Huascar (*Les Indes galantes*, 1735) and Pollux (1737). He also took the leading *basse-taille* roles in revivals of works by Lully, Campra, Destouches and Desmarets. He withdrew from the stage between 1738 and 1742, to try to recover his *titres de noblesse* and re-establish his fortune. His place in the company was taken by Le Page, but he returned to the Opéra in 1742 as Hylas in a revival of Destouches' *Issé*. He created leading roles in Rameau's *Naïs*, *Zoroastre* and *Acante et Céphise*, and sang all the principal *basse-taille* parts in the continuing revivals of the staple 17th- and early 18th-century repertory. He retired in 1757.

His intensity and intelligence in declamation and action made him arguably the greatest male singing actor of the 18th century in Paris, who could stand comparison at the highest level with the members of the Comédie-Française. Voltaire envisaged him as the ideal protagonist for his biblical tragedy *Samson*, predicting that he would be as dramatically effective as the leading actor Quinault-Dufresne. His sonorous voice was of great power and beauty, though subject to harsh attack (*saccades*) and to *chevrotement*, according to Collé.

*

ES (B. Horowicz)
J.-J. Rousseau: 'Acteur', 'Chevroter', *Dictionnaire de musique* (Paris, 1768)
J.-B. La Borde: *Essai sur la musique ancienne et moderne* (Paris, 1780), iii, 500–01
J. F. Marmontel: 'Déclamation', *Eléments de littérature* (Paris, 1822)
H. Bonhomme, ed.: *Journal et mémoires de Charles Collé* (Paris, 1868), i, 52–3, 395
T. Besterman, ed.: *The Complete Works of Voltaire*, lxxxv–cxxxv: *Correspondence and Related Documents* (Geneva, 1968–77)
PHILIP WELLER

Chastellux [Châtellux], **François-Jean,** Marquis [Chevalier] de (*b* Paris, 5 May 1734; *d* Paris, 24 Oct 1788). French writer on music. A soldier and administrator by profession, he consorted with artists and philosophers (he was one of the celebrated circle of Mlle de Lespinasse) and was elected to the Académie Française in 1775. In 1765 he published anonymously his *Essai sur l'union de la poésie et de la musique*, a vigorous polemic in favour of Metastasian *opera seria* with its taut, concise dialogue and rounded, periodic aria texts set to music in the international, 'Neapolitan' style of Hasse. However, his aim was not the wholesale importation of *opera seria* performed in the original Italian, but the reform of serious opera in French. He approved in principle the integration of the chorus in the French manner, but was much more concerned to advocate periodic phrasing for aria music than to discuss dramaturgy. He wished to see a bel canto style properly set in relief by the restriction of the orchestral accompaniment to simple patterns with largely homogenous instrumentation. The place for contrast and volatility was in the accompanied recitatives.

The *Essai*, for which Chastellux obtained the written approval of Metastasio himself, is probably best seen as a polemical prolongation of the Querelle des Bouffons and as a plea for the italianization of French opera at a time when the Opéra was financially and artistically almost bankrupt. In 1772 Chastellux published, again anonymously, his *Observations*, in response to the challenge of LAURENT GARCIN's *Traité du mélodrame*; here he simply restated his position (claiming incidentally that Philidor's *Ernelinde* (1767) had been composed in accordance with the guiding principles of his *Essai*). In 1773 he published a translation of Algarotti's *Saggio sopra l'opera in musica* as *Essai sur l'opéra ... suivi d''Iphigénie en Aulide', opéra par le traducteur*. The text shows differences from that published (anonymously) in the *Mercure de France* in 1757, itself possibly the work of the young Chastellux. His claimed authorship of the text to *Aulide* should be treated with caution, though this text is not identical with the French libretto written by Algarotti to conclude his *Saggio*. Known for most of his life as the Chevalier de Chastellux, he became marquis on his brother's death in 1786.

*

A. R. Oliver: *The Encyclopedists as Critics of Music* (New York, 1947)
B. Brunelli, ed.: *Tutte le opere di Pietro Metastasio*, iii (Milan, 1951)
PHILIP WELLER

Chatrian, Alexandre. *See* ERCKMANN-CHATRIAN.

Chaumel, Adèle. *See* COMELLI-RUBINI, ADELAIDE.

Chausson, (Amédée-)Ernest (*b* Paris, 20 Jan 1855; *d* Limay, nr Mantes, Yvelines, 10 June 1899). French composer. Brought up in a protective family environment and educated by a private tutor, he became acquainted not only with music but also with literature and art at an early age. By his late teens he had gained entry to several prestigious Parisian salons where he came into contact with such artists as the painters Fantin-Latour and Odilon Redon, musicians such as d'Indy and several important literary figures. It was in literature, for which he displayed a considerable talent, that he first considered a career, but he was persuaded by his parents to study law. He was sworn in as a barrister but never entered practice, and in the late 1870s resolutely turned to music. He attended classes given by Franck and Massenet and in the early 1880s succumbed to the spell of Wagner, several times visiting Bayreuth.

Although Chausson composed in virtually every genre, much of his music draws its inspiration from literature: his songs and vocal music include settings of Parnassian poets such as Leconte de Lisle and Banville as well as of symbolists such as Maeterlinck and Verlaine. He was also well versed in Shakespeare and wrote both songs and incidental music for Shakespeare's plays. One of his first completed works with a dramatic element was the *scène lyrique Jeanne d'Arc*, begun before 1880. There followed two unfinished projects: *Les caprices de Marianne*, based on a story by Alfred de Musset, and a *drame lyrique*, *Hélène*, to a verse play by Leconte de Lisle. One of his most enduring works has been the *Poème de l'amour et la mer*, a setting for voice (originally tenor) and orchestra of a poem by Maurice Bouchor. This piece, in which he developed a fine sense of vocal writing and of orchestral accompaniment, together with his overture *Viviane*, based on a Celtic legend, were eventually to lead him to his one mature opera, *Le roi Arthus*, written between 1885 and 1895 and first given in Brussels in 1903.

His own list of projected dramatic works reveals that had Chausson not met a premature death in a cycling accident, he might well have contributed further to the operatic repertory. It includes operas to be based on Pushkin, Schiller, Shakespeare, Cervantes and Thomas Moore, among others. His single completed opera, the *drame lyrique Le roi Arthus*, to his own libretto, reflects his self-confessed struggle to find a musical language that was entirely personal, a quest which he regarded as retarded by his admiration for Wagner and his absorption of Wagner's techniques and style. In the light of his plans for future works it is an open question as to whether he would have ultimately been able to shed the influence of Wagner when confronted with operatic subjects less obviously Wagnerian in nature.

See also ROI ARTHUS, LE.

Les caprices de Marianne op.4, 1882–4 (comédie lyrique, after A. de Musset), inc.

Hélène op.7, 1883–4 (drame lyrique, 2, after Leconte de Lisle), inc., excerpts (Paris, ?1895)

Le roi Arthus op.23, 1885–95 (drame lyrique, 3, Chausson), Brussels, Monnaie, 30 Nov 1903, vs (Paris, 1900)

*

M. D. Calvocoressi: 'Le roi Arthus d'Ernest Chausson', *Le guide musical*, no.49 (18 Oct 1903), 703–8

G. Fauré: 'Chausson, *Le roi Arthus*', *Le Figaro* (1 Dec 1903); repr. in *Opinions musicales* (Paris, 1930)

C. Joly: '*Le roi Arthus* à la Monnaie', *Le théâtre*, no.122 (1904), 8–14

ReM, i/2 (1 Dec 1925) [whole issue]

C. Oulmont: *Musique de l'amour* (Paris, 1935)

G. Samazeuilh: 'Ernest Chausson', *Musiciens de mon temps* (Paris, 1947), 81

Y. Gérard: 'Lettres de Henri Duparc à Ernest Chausson', *RdM*, xxxviii (1956), 125–46

J. Gallois: *Ernest Chausson: l'homme et l'oeuvre* (Paris, 1967)

R. S. Grover: *Ernest Chausson: the Man and his Music* (Lewisburg and London, 1980)

RICHARD LANGHAM SMITH

Chautauqua. A group of institutions that in the late 19th century and the early 20th brought music to mostly rural and small-town North American audiences in its summer assemblies; it organizes festivals, in which opera plays a part.

Taking its name from the Chautauqua Institution, founded in 1874 on the shore of Chautauqua Lake, New York, the movement offered programmes of education and entertainment by local and touring performers. Opera and (more often) light opera were among the offerings. In many cases the companies toured with a single work at a time; in others they presented scenes and selections from several operas. The works, invariably in English, were normally abridged and reduced in scope: a typical company was a mixed quartet with a pianist. Balfe's *The Bohemian Girl* and Flotow's *Martha* were often taken on the road, while there were occasional tours of *Carmen*, *Faust*, *Il trovatore*, *Rigoletto*, *Il barbiere di Siviglia* and *Cavalleria rusticana*. Among light operas, Gilbert and Sullivan works were frequently performed.

The Chautauqua Institution itself, one of the few Chautauquas still in existence, has a particularly distinguished record of operatic activity. A summer festival season is now held, each June to August, in which three operas and an operetta are given; there is also training for young singers, children's opera and puppet opera.

*

R. H. Cowden: *The Chautauqua Opera Association, 1929–1958: an Interpretative History* (n.p., 1974)

FREDERICK CRANE

Chauvet, Guy (*b* Pau, 2 Oct 1933). French tenor. He made his début at the Paris Opéra in January 1959 as an Armed Man in *Die Zauberflöte*. The shortage of genuine French tenor voices led to his undertaking, perhaps too early, roles as demanding as Florestan, Ulysses (in Fauré's *Pénélope*) and Jason (in Cherubini's *Médée*). At the Opéra his performances as Berlioz's Faust and Aeneas were vocally resplendent if dramatically somewhat immature. But he strengthened his acting techniques and musicianship, and consolidated the gifts of a brilliant upper register, broad declamation and natural energy. He continued to sing Aeneas for the next 20 years in Europe and America. Other roles at the Opéra included Dmitry, Don Carlos, Pylades and Laca (1980). In 1963 he made his Covent Garden début as Cavaradossi and his American début in Chicago as Gounod's Faust. During the next 15 years he sang Don José, Siegmund and Parsifal at La Monnaie; Ratan-Sen (Roussel's *Padmâvatî*) and his first Otello at Strasbourg; and Lohengrin and Kratos (Fauré's *Prométhée*) at Lyons. In San Francisco he sang Radames, Don José, Lohengrin and Samson, the last in 1983. He sang Don José at La Scala and Calaf in Geneva in 1972; the following year in Marseilles he sang the Drum Major. He made his Metropolitan début in 1977 as Samson and returned in 1979 as John of Leyden. His roles include Reyer's Sigurd and John the Baptist (*Hérodiade*), which he sang at Avignon in 1982.

*

A. Chédorge: 'Guy Chauvet', *Opéra*, no. 108 (1975), p.14

ANDRÉ TUBEUF, ELIZABETH FORBES

Chávez (y Ramírez), Carlos (Antonio de Padua) (*b* Mexico City, 13 June 1899; *d* Mexico City, 2 Aug 1978). Mexican composer. Mexico's most renowned 20th-century composer belonged to the stratum of society that, during the first century of the nation's independence, regarded opera as a Mexican composer's highest aspiration. Nevertheless, ill success attended Chávez's longest work, his 135-minute three-act opera on a libretto by Chester Kallman originally entitled *The Tuscan Players*. The result of four years' writing (1953–6), the opera was first performed in New York at the Brander Matthews Theater, Columbia University, on 9 May 1957, under the title *Panfilo and Lauretta*. It was so poorly rehearsed that the conductor Howard Shanet had to halt the performance in the third act; nevertheless, nine performances were given between 9 and 18 May.

Drawing on Boccaccio, the plot concerns four 14th-century Florentine nobles taking refuge in a villa outside the city to escape the plague. To amuse themselves, they enact playlets dealing with Cupid and Psyche, a Roman centurion rapist, and Adam and Eve. Howard Taubman, the *New York Times* reviewer, concluded (19 May 1957) that 'it does not hang together as a whole; it is too dense verbally and musically; there are too many passages where the vocal writing is unyielding in its harshness and heaviness'.

Chávez made three later efforts to salvage his opera, in productions in Mexico City; the first (28 and 30 October 1959) was in the original English with the New York cast, but with the title *Love Propitiated*; an abridged, Spanish translation by Noel Lindsay and Eduardo Hernández Moncada, *El amor propiciado*, was given on 21 and 25 May 1963, but despite a month of rehearsals and a professional cast the Mexican public 'deserted the hall after the first performance'. Chávez's next attempt (26 July 1968), under the title *Los visitantes* and with a new Lauretta (Angeles Chamorro), was also unsuccessful. In a last effort to gain acceptance for the work that 'cost him more pains and more energy than anything else he wrote' (Parker), Chávez conducted unstaged excerpts with the title *The Visitors* at the 1973 Cabrillo Music Festival (Aptos, California). He continued revising and reorchestrating the opera until his death.

H. Taubman: Reviews of 'Panfilo and Lauretta', *New York Times* (10 and 19 May 1957)
C. Díaz Du-Pond: *Cincuenta años de ópera en México* (Mexico City, 1978), 222, 248, 279–80
R. Stevenson: 'Carlos Chávez's United States Press Coverage', *Inter-American Music Review*, iii/2 (1981), 130
——: 'Cincuenta años de ópera', *Inter-American Music Review*, v/2 (1982), 118–21 [review]
R. L. Parker: *Carlos Chávez, Mexico's Modern-day Orpheus* (Boston, 1983), 118–20 [with music excerpt]

ROBERT STEVENSON

Chaykovsky, Alexander Vladimirovich (*b* Moscow, 19 Feb 1946). Russian composer. After finishing piano studies under Lev Naumov at the Moscow Conservatory in 1970, he completed the composition course there under Tikhon Khrennikov in 1972 and finished his graduate studies in 1975. In addition to teaching at the Moscow Conservatory, he is a leading administrator of the Union of Soviet Composers.

As a composer he is best known for a series of instrumental concertos and for two ballets, but his innately theatrical sensibility has also found an outlet in his operatic works. The musical language of *Dedushka smeyotsya* ('Grandfather Laughs') suggests the influence of early Shostakovich and operetta.

Dedushka smeyotsya [Grandfather Laughs] (eccentric op, 2, after I. A. Krïlov), Moscow, Chamber Music, 31 Dec 1976
Vtoroye aprelya [The Second of April] (children's op, 3, N. Sats, after I. Zverev), Moscow, Children's Music, 6 July 1984
Vernost' [Loyalty] (after T. Zumakulova), Nal'chik, Musical Theatre of Kabardino-Balkar ASSR, 5 April 1985

LAUREL E. FAY

Chaykovsky, Modest Il'ich. *See* TCHAIKOVSKY, MODEST IL'YICH.

Chaykovsky, Pyotr Il'ich. *See* TCHAIKOVSKY, PYOTR IL'YICH.

Chekhov, Anton Pavlovich (*b* Taganrog, 17/29 Jan 1860; *d* Badenweiler, 2/15 July 1904). Russian dramatist and short-story writer. Along with Leo Tolstoy and Maxim Gorky he represented the flower of Russian writing at the end of the 19th century. A planned collaboration on an opera with Tchaikovsky came to nothing, but his one-act farcical comedy for three characters, *Medved'* ('The Bear', 1888, which he denigrated as 'a piffling little Frenchified vaudeville'), gave rise to several mid-20th-century operas, notably Argento's *The Boor* (1957) and Walton's *The Bear* (1967). The short story *Roman s kontrabasom* (1886) was the basis of Dubensky's American opera *Romance with Double Bass* (1916), Sauguet's *La contrebasse* (1932) and Bucchi's *Il contrabbasso* (1954). Another short story, *Ved'ma* ('The Witch', 1886), is the source of Hoiby's *The Scarf* (1958). In one of Chekhov's last and most celebrated stories, *Dama s sobachkoy* ('The Lady with the Little Dog'), there is an allusion to a provincial Russian performance of Sidney Jones's operetta *The Geisha* (1896).

Shvedskaya spichka [The Phosphorus Match] (short story, 1882): Banshchikov, 1976, as Smert'Korneta Klyauzova [The Death of Cornet Klyauzov]
Khirurgiya [Surgery] (play, 1884): Ferroud, 1928, as Chirurgie
Na bol'shoy doroge [On the High Road] (play, 1885): Nottara, 1934, as La drumul mare
Aptekarsha [The Chemist's Wife] (short story, 1886): Guaccero, 1956, as La farmacista
Van'ka (short story, 1886): Kholminov, 1984
Proizvedeniye iskusstva [The Objet d'art] (short story, 1886): I. Dibák, 1977, as Svietnik [The Candelabra]
Roman s kontrabasom [Romance with a Double Bass] (short story, 1886): A. Dubensky, 1916; Sauguet, 1930, as La contrebasse; Bucchi, 1954, as Il contrabbasso; Poser, 1964, as Die Bassgeige; Kounadis, 1979, as Die Bassgeige
Ved'ma [The Witch] (short story, 1886): Yanovsky, 1916; Hoiby, 1958, as The Scarf; Vlasov, 1961
Potseluy [The Kiss] (short story, 1887): Oliver, comp. 1973
Lebedinaya pesnya [Swan Song] (play, 1888): L. Chailly, 1957, as Il canto del cigno; Pauer, 1974, as Labutí píseň; Kobekin, 1980
Medved' [The Bear] (play, 1888): A. Walbrunn, 1914, as Der Ungeheuer; Dobronić, comp. 1947, as Medvjed; Bucci, 1949, as The Boor; Fink, 1955, as The Boor; Argento, 1957, as The Boor; Semyonov, pubd *c*1958, as L'ours; Moss, 1961, as The Brute; E. Dressel, 1963, as Der Bär; L. Hrabovsky, 1963; Jirásek, 1965; Walton, 1967; Kay, 1968, as The Boor
Predlozheniye [The Proposal] (play, 1889): Chailly, 1957, as Una domanda di matrimonio; Röttger, 1961, as Der Heiratsantrag; Hrabovsky, 1964; J. Wagner, 1965; Boháč, 1971, as Námluvy [The Courtship]
Svad'ba [The Wedding] (play, 1889): V. G. Ehrenberg, 1916; Kholminov, 1984
Skripka Rotshil'da [Rothschild's Violin] (story, 1894): Fleyshman, 1960
Chayka [The Seagull] (play, 1896): Vlad, 1968, as Il gabbiano; Pasatieri, 1974
Dyadya Vanya [Uncle Vanya] (play, 1899): K. Fribec, 1972, as Ujak Vanja
Tri sestrï [The Three Sisters] (play, 1901): Pasatieri, 1986
O vrede tobaka [The Harmfulness of Tobacco] (play, 1903): Argento, 1977, as A Water Bird Talk; Kalmanoff, 1979
Vishnovïy sad [The Cherry Orchard] (play, 1904): Kelterborn, 1984, as Der Kirschgarten

*

D. Rigotti: 'Checov librettista mancato', *La Scala*, no.129–30 (1960), 26–7
A. Balabanovich: *Chekhov i Chaykovsky* (Moscow, 1962)

ARTHUR JACOBS

Chelard [Chélard], **Hippolyte-André(-Jean)-Baptiste** (*b* Paris, 1 Feb 1789; *d* Weimar, 12 Feb 1861). French composer. He studied with Fétis before entering, in 1803, the Paris Conservatoire, where he studied with Rodolphe Kreutzer, Gossec and probably Méhul and Cherubini. He won the Prix de Rome in 1811 and during the subsequent trip to Italy studied with Zingarelli and Paisiello. His *commedia per musica*, *La casa da vendere* (1815), was quite successful in Naples. In 1816 he returned to Paris, playing the violin at the Opéra and teaching, and by 1821 had opened a publishing establishment.

In 1827 Chelard's opera *Macbeth* was given at the Opéra, but despite a brilliant cast it failed and was withdrawn after five performances. Chelard submitted the reworked score to the court theatre in Munich, where it was repeatedly and successfully performed between August 1828 and March 1829. His comic opera *La table et le logement* was performed in Paris in December 1829, but this also was unsuccessful. By 1830 he had made his home in Germany.

In June 1831 Chelard staged his second serious opera, *Mitternacht*, in Munich (written as *Minuit* for the Salle Ventadour, but never performed there); although well received, it never achieved the success of *Macbeth*. In February 1832 *Der Student*, a largely rewritten version of *La table et le logement*, was an overwhelming success. In 1832 and 1833 he successfuly directed the German Opera's season in London, during which time his *Macbeth* was given twice at Covent Garden and *Der Student* (translated by Planché as *The Students of Jena*) was performed at Drury Lane. Neither was a great success despite the contributions of the singers Malibran and Templeton.

In September 1835 Chelard's most significant work, the five-act opera *Die Hermannsschlacht*, achieved great success in Munich. In 1836 he was active in Augsburg and in 1840 was appointed Kapellmeister at Weimar, where his opera *Die Seekadetten* was performed in 1844. In 1843 he had given help and encouragement to his friend Berlioz during the latter's visit to Weimar. Liszt's appointment to Weimar overshadowed Chelard's position there, and he returned to Paris in 1852; but he returned to Weimar in 1854.

Chelard's compositional style varies: whereas *Macbeth* is in the Gluck-Cherubini-Spontini tradition, *Mitternacht* inclines more to the German Romantic school. In both there is an attempt to create local colour by rhythmic and harmonic means but in neither is this wholly convincing. These operas, however, exerted considerable influence, and keyboard arrangements of his 'Marche hongroise' and of the ballet from *Macbeth* were popular. His activities in the opera house were criticized for their supposed extravagance, though as an opera conductor and general music director he was known to be first-rate. His urge to compose was not matched by his powers of imaginative invention and his works, though competent and intelligently made, lack real excitement. He prepared southern Germany for the music of Berlioz and Liszt, whose orchestral and melodic characteristics he sometimes palely foreshadowed.

La casa da vendere (commedia per musica, 1, A. L. Tottola), Naples, Fiorentini, 1815, excerpts pubd separately

Macbeth (opéra, 3, C. J. Rouget de Lisle and A. Hix), Paris, Opéra, 29 June 1827, *F-Po*; rev., Munich, Hof, 25 Aug 1828, vs (Munich, ?1828), excerpts pubd separately

La table et le logement (oc, 1, J. J. Gabriel and T. M. Dumersan), Paris, OC (Ventadour), 24 Dec 1829; rev. as Der Student, Munich, Hof, 19 Feb 1832

Mitternacht (opéra, 3), Munich, Hof, 19 June 1831, ov. in concert version (Berlin, 1846)

Die Hermannsschlacht (opéra, 5, K. Weichselbaumer), Munich, Hof, 12 Sept 1835, ov. pubd in many arrs.

Die Seekadetten, oder Die Emancipation der Frauen [Nieder mit den Männern] (komische Oper, 2, P. Sondershausen), Weimar, Hof, ?April 1844

Le aquile romane (opéra, 3, M. Marcello, after P. E. A. Du Casse), Milan, Scala, 10 March 1864

*

ES (W. Boetticher); *FétisB*

W. Schwinger: *Das Opernschaffen A.-H. Chelard* (diss., Berlin U., 1954)

——: 'Schumann und Chelard', *Robert Schumann: aus Anlass seines 100. Todestages* (Leipzig, 1956), 73ff BRIAN PRIMMER

Cheliabinsk. CHELYABINSK.

Chelleri [Kelleri, Keller, Cheler], **Fortunato** (*b* Parma, 1686–90; *d* Kassel, 11 Dec 1757). Italian composer. His father, a German emigrant and amateur musician, died when Fortunato was 12, his mother three years later; her brother, a priest and *maestro di cappella* at Piacenza Cathedral, cared for him and gave him a thorough musical education. Although Chelleri's name appears in lists of choirboys of churches in Parma (1700–03), the fact that his first opera, *La Griselda*, was performed at Piacenza in 1707 suggests influential contacts there. After writing another opera for Cremona (1708), he visited Barcelona, where his *Zenobia in Palmira* was performed in 1709. Its revival in Milan the next year established his reputation in Italy. During the following 12 years he composed operas for several north Italian cities; on the librettos of the period between 1715 and 1719 he is described as *maestro di cappella della camera* of Johann Wilhelm, the Elector Palatine (1658–1716). One of his operas for Ferrara, *La caccia in Etolia* (1715), uses a text by Valeriani later set by Handel in 1736 as *Atalanta*. Its plot differs from Zeno's, which Chelleri had already set in 1713.

In 1722 Chelleri went to Germany as Hofkapellmeister to the Prince-Bishop Johann Philipp Franz von Schönborn at Würzburg. Soon after the bishop's death in 1724 Chelleri became Kapellmeister to the Landgrave of Hesse in Kassel, where, except for spells in London and Stockholm, he remained for the rest of his life. Although he composed no new operas in Germany, he revived several of his Italian works. *L'innocenza difesa*, for example, was refurbished for Kassel (1726) and then taken to Brunswick and Wolfenbüttel (1731). As *Judith, Gemahlin Kayser Ludewige des Frommen*, and with new recitatives (in German) by Telemann and six arias (in Italian) by Telemann and Handel, it was performed in Hamburg between 1732 and 1737. On the death in 1730 of his patron, Chelleri entered the service of his son Friedrich, who was both Landgrave of Hesse and King of Sweden. He served as musical director to Friedrich in Stockholm for two years but returned to Kassel in 1734 as Hofrat to Friedrich's brother Wilhelm.

Although ignored by modern scholars and performers, Chelleri's music represents the best by those Italian-trained musicians who served the smaller German courts. 50 years after his death the *Gallerie der vorzüglichsten Tonkünstler … in Cassel* voiced a lingering, if exaggerated, admiration for his art: 'numerous parts of this opera [*L'innocenza difesa*] are so gracefully written that even now, after 80 years, they could be inserted without incongruity into a modern opera'. Chelleri was in London from autumn 1726 to summer 1727, when he was connected with the Royal Academy of Music and had a collection of arias and cantatas published.

drammi per musica unless otherwise indicated

La Griselda (A. Zeno), Piacenza, Ducale, 1707

Alessandro il grande (3, Zeno), Cremona, Nobile Società, 1708

Zenobia in Palmira (3, Zeno and P. Pariati), Barcelona, casa Lonja, 1709

L'innocenza giustificata (2, F. Silvani), Milan, Provvisorio, 1711; rev. as L'innocenza difesa dai numi (Silvani), Venice, S Angelo, carn. 1722 [adapted as Judith, Gemahlin Kayser Ludewige des Frommen, oder Die siegende Unschuld (pasticcio), Hamburg, 1732, with 6 arias by Handel and Telemann and Ger. recits. by Telemann]; *D-B* according to Eitner, *Hs*, *Kl*, *I-MOe*

Atalanta (3, Zeno), Ferrara, Bonacossi, carn. 1713

La caccia in Etolia (favola pastorale, B. Valeriani), Ferrara, Bonacossi, 28 May 1715

Ircano innamorato (int, Valeriani), Ferrara, Bonacossi, 28 May 1715

Alessandro fra gli Amazzoni (3, O. Braccioli), Venice, S Angelo, aut. 1715

Penelope la casta (3, M. Noris), Venice, S Angelo, carn. 1716

Alessandro severo (Zeno), Florence, Infuocati, carn. 1718

Amalassunta, regina di Goti (3, G. Gabrieli), Venice, S Angelo, 26 Dec 1718; perf. with Il marito giocatore (int, Salvi), ? by G. M. Orlandini; 24 arias *I-Vc*

La pace per amore (3, A. Schietti), Venice, S Moisè, carn. 1719, collab. G. M. Buini; rev. as Il nemico amante, Venice, S Moisè, carn. 1724

Tamerlano (3, A. Piovene), Treviso, Dolfin, carn. 1720

Arsacide (3, A. Zaniboni), Venice, S Moisè, carn. 1721, perf. with Petronio e Dorise (int), ? by Chelleri; 7 arias *D-Mbs*

Il Temistocle (3, Zeno), Padua, Obizzi, June 1721

L'amore della patria superiore ad ogni altro (? comic op, F. Sbarra, rev. D. Lalli), Venice, 1722

L'amor tirannico (3, Lalli), Venice, S Samuele, May 1722; Acts 1 and 3 by Chelleri, Act 2 by G. Porta

Zenobia e Radamisto (? Noris), Venice, S Angelo, 1722

N. Pelicelli: 'Musicisti in Parma', *NA*, xi (1934), 49–51
F. Bussi: *Alcuni maestri di cappella e organisti della cattedrale di Piacenza* (Piacenza, 1956), 8–10
B. S. Brook, ed.: *The Breitkopf Thematic Catalogue, 1762–1787* (New York, 1966)
C. E. Troy: *The Comic Intermezzo in 18th-century Italian Opera Seria* (diss., Harvard U., 1971)
I. Mamczarz: *Les intermèdes comiques italiens au XVIIIe siècle en France et en Italie* (Paris, 1972), 69, 113, 126, 217
J. Jaenecke: *Die Musikbibliothek des Ludwig Freiherrn von Pretlack (1716–81)* (Wiesbaden, 1973), 195–7
C. Pierre: *Histoire du Concert spirituel, 1725–1790* (Paris, 1975), 423 SVEN HANSELL

Chelsea Opera Group. A group formed in 1950 by Colin Davis, David Cairns and Stephen Gray, with the principal aim of giving concert performances of Mozart's operas. It first appeared at the Holywell Music Room, Oxford, in a performance of *Don Giovanni* so successful that it was soon repeated in Oxford and Cambridge. The group first appeared in London at St Pancras Town Hall in 1953, with *Fidelio*; the next year one of its rare staged productions, a double bill comprising *The Telephone* and *Der Schauspieldirektor*, was also given there. Other works performed in Oxford, Cambridge and London included *Falstaff*, *Les Troyens*, *Benvenuto Cellini*, *Guillaume Tell*, *Der Freischütz*, *Euryanthe*, *Simon Boccanegra*, *Macbeth*, *Don Carlos*, *Iphigénie en Tauride* and *Khovanshchina*. It proved an excellent training ground for young British conductors including Colin Davis, John Matheson, Nicholas Braithwaite and John Eliot Gardiner. Several singers who appeared regularly at Covent Garden and with English National Opera tried out new roles with the group. Operas performed during the 1970s and 80s included *Les vêpres siciliennes*, *Feuersnot*, *Mazepa*, *Béatrice et Bénédict*, *Oberon*, *Lady Macbeth of the Mtsensk District*, *Friedenstag*, *Turandot*, *The Snow Maiden*, Bizet's *Ivan IV*, *La Gioconda* and Berkeley's *Nelson*. HAROLD ROSENTHAL/R

Cheltenham. English spa town. Since 1945 it has been the home of the Cheltenham Festival, the first postwar 'shop-window' for new British music, held each July (renamed Cheltenham International Festival in 1974). Opera has made sporadic appearances, in the early years with productions by the English Opera Group (1948–51 and 1974) and the Intimate Opera Company (1955–6 and 1959). Premières given at the Everyman Theatre include Gordon Crosse's *Purgatory* and Phyllis Tate's *The What D'ye Call It*, in a double bill by the New Opera Company (1966), and Judith Weir's *A Night at the Chinese Opera* by Kent Opera (1987). An ad hoc 'Festival Opera' ensemble was formed in 1983 to give *Ruth* by the festival's then president, Sir Lennox Berkeley, and *What the Old Man does is Always Right* during Alun Hoddinott's year as composer-in-residence (1989). Other productions have been staged by the Singers' Company (1980), the WNO (1981), Warsaw Chamber Opera (1982), Opera Stage, Los Angeles (1985), Thameside Opera (1988), Opera North (1989) and Music Theatre Wales and British Youth Festival Opera (1990). NOËL GOODWIN

Chelyabinsk [Cheliabinsk]. City in Russia, on the eastern flank of the Ural Mountains. A 1205-seat hall, designed by the architect N. P. Kurenna and built in 1954, became the home for the Chelyabinskiy Teatr Operï i Baleta imeni M. I. Glinki (Glinka Chelyabinsk Theatre of Opera and Ballet) on its official opening in 1956. Early in its history the theatre featured works by G. M. Shantïr, giving the première of his *Gorod yunosti* ('City of Youth') on 19 October 1957; the repertory today is a mixture of Russian and European classics with contemporary Russian operas.

*

ME ('Chelyabinskiy teatr operï i baleta'; E. I. Margina)
I. Dzerzhinsky: 'Pis'ma puteshestvuyushchego muzïkanta, v: Chelyabinske' [Letters of a Travelling Musician: Chelyabinsk], *SovM* (1956), no.11, pp.88–93
G. Dmitrin and K. Antonova: *Chelyabinskiy opernïy (1956–1966)* (Chelyabinsk, 1967)
E. I. Margina: *Chelyabinskomu teatru operï i baleta im. M. I. Glinki 25 let.* [25 Years of the Glinka Chelyabinsk Opera and Ballet Theatre] (Chelyabinsk, 1981) GREGORY SALMON

Chementi, Margherita. *See* CHIMENTI, MARGHERITA.

Chemin-Petit, Hans (Helmuth) (*b* Potsdam, 24 July 1902; *d* Berlin, 12 April 1981). German composer and conductor. He was born into a musical family and studied the cello with Becker and composition with Juon and Trapp at the Berlin Hochschule für Musik. In 1929 he became theory teacher at the Staatliche Akademie für Kirchen- und Schulmusik in Berlin and assistant to the musicologist H. J. Moser who provided the libretto for his unperformed chamber opera *Lady Monika*. His career changed direction ten years later when he took charge of musical life in the state of Memel and was appointed director of the Magdeburg Cathedral choir. In 1944, he became director of the Berlin Philharmonic Choir in succession to Günter Ramin. After the war, he remained in Berlin where he continued to teach theory at the Hochschule für Musik, where he was acting director 1965–9. From 1963 he was a member of the Berlin Akademie für Künste and head of its music division from 1968. He was awarded the Berlin Arts Prize in 1964.

Although Chemin-Petit's output is dominated by a substantial series of choral and orchestral compositions, he maintained a lifelong interest in writing operas with the result that works in this genre appeared during the early and late periods of his career. His first opera, *Der gefangene Vogel*, scored a considerable success after its performance at the Duisburg Opernfestwoche in 1929 and was broadcast during the Nazi era by Bavarian Radio. Later, the composer consciously distanced himself from the neo-classical tendencies of this chamber work and his next opera, *König Nicolo*, written more than 30 years later, assumes a very different and more ambitious range of emotions. Based on a play by Wedekind, *König Nicolo* invites comparison with Berg's *Lulu*, especially as the work opens with a prologue in which the main characters, Nicolo and Alma, are represented by the figures of the Fool and Pierrot, accompanied by sharply defined and somewhat ironic trumpet fanfares. The final scene, which incorporates Nicolo's monologue, is constructed in the form of a powerful passacaglia, demonstrating the composer's predilection for Baroque forms and complex polyphony, handled in masterly fashion (this section was subsequently extracted from the opera to form a separate orchestral piece, *Intrada e Passacaglia*, 1963).

After *König Nicolo*, the composer planned to write an opera based on Thornton Wilder's novel *The Ides of March*, but opposition from the American author prevented its realization. Some of the music found its way into the very different surroundings of *Die Komödiantin* (composed 1965), a burlesque set in Spain during the time of the Napoleonic wars. In this work, the atmosphere is predominantly lighthearted, with the orchestral forces displaying many touches of contrapuntal ingenuity and the characterization enhanced by the effective use of arioso and accompanied recitative. Two further theatre compositions, *Die Rivalinnen* (1969), a comedy set in 18th-century Venice, and *Die Klage der Ariadne* (1971), were intended to form an operatic evening, although neither work had been heard in the opera house by 1990. In *Die Rivalinnen*, the composer continues to exploit the carefree atmosphere of *Die Komödiantin* and the score is notable for its witty incorporation of quotations from the works of Domenico Scarlatti. By contrast, *Die Klage der Ariadne* is a dramatic monologue underpinned by passionate, intoxicating orchestral sonorities.

Der gefangene Vogel (Kammeroper, 1 scene, K. Höcker), Berlin, Renaissance, 1927; rev. Duisburg, 21 Feb 1929
Lady Monika, 1929 (Kammeroper, H. J. Moser), unperf.
König Nicolo, 1959 (3, Chemin-Petit, after F. Wedekind), Aachen, 23 April 1962 (Berlin, 1962)
Die Komödiantin, 1965 (3, Chemin-Petit, after H. Coubier), Coburg, 7 June 1970
Die Rivalinnen, 1969 (Kammeroper, 1, W. Poch and Chemin-Petit, after Loredano), unperf.
Die Klage der Ariadne, 1971 (dramatische Szene, 1, Chemin-Petit, after Nietzsche), concert perf., Berlin, 15 Sept 1973

*

W. Oehlmann: *Hans Chemin-Petit: Dirigent, Lehrer, Komponist* (Berlin, 1971)
——: 'Hans Chemin-Petit als Opernkomponist', *Hans Chemin-Petit: Betrachtung eines Lebensleistung*, ed. M. Buder and D. Gonschorek (Berlin, 1977), 69–71

ERIK LEVI

Chenda, Alfonso ['Il Chenda', 'Il Chendi']. *See* RIVAROLA, ALFONSO.

Chéreau, Patrice (*b* Lézigné, Maine-et-Loire, 2 Nov 1944). French director. The early part of his career was spent almost entirely in the spoken theatre. He was administrator of the theatre in Sartrouville, 1966–9, artistic co-director of the Théâtre de la Cité Villeurbanne, Lyons, from 1971, co-director of the Théâtre National Populaire, Paris, from 1972 to 1981, and co-director with Richard Peduzzi of the Théâtre des Amandiers, Nanterre, from 1982.

His first excursions into opera were with productions of *L'italiana in Algeri* in Spoleto (1969) and *Les contes d'Hoffmann* at the Paris Opéra (1974). But it was with his centenary production of the *Ring* at Bayreuth (1976) that he made his international reputation. His *Lulu* at the Paris Opéra in 1979 was the first staging of the complete, three-act version made by Friedrich Cerha. Other productions have included Mozart's *Lucio Silla* at La Scala in 1984, later repeated at Nanterre and Brussels; and *Wozzeck* in Paris in 1992, conducted by Barenboim.

Chéreau's deconstructionist *Ring*, though following in the wake of radical productions by Herz and Melchinger, has already taken its place as one of the most important and influential in the history not only of Bayreuth but also of opera production generally. His conviction that the mythological setting of the *Ring* heightens rather than diminishes the social and historical dimensions of the work led him to locate the action in a chronological continuum extending from the mid-19th century to the present day. His starting-point was the context of the 19th-century industrial revolution. Thus the flowing waters of the Rhine became a hydro-electric dam, and Siegfried's forge housed a mechanical steam-hammer (*see* PRODUCTION, fig.24). The trappings of pit-wheel, power station, privileged bourgeoisie and oppressed proletariat emphasized the extent to which the work was conceived as a political allegory, but the deliberate mixing of periods, as with the costumes and weapons, betokened an attempt to integrate the contemporary and mythological spheres.

A caged woodbird and the moving of trees by conspicuous stagehands emphasized the necessary artificiality of the stage representation of nature. These and other Brechtian alienation techniques, together with a strong element of parody (as in the pantomime dragon), gave rise to an unprecedented level of humour in the staging. Indeed, it was its theatricality and the physical realization of intense emotion, ranging from the tender embraces of lovers to the brutal violence of tyrants (including Wotan), that struck home most forcibly. Gesture, posture, facial expression and movement formed an integral part of the staging and were executed with an immediacy then rare on the operatic stage.

*

C. Schmid, P. Boulez and P. Chéreau: 'Mythologie et idéologie', *Bayreuther Festspiele, Programmheft IV: Das Rheingold* (Bayreuth, 1977; Eng. trans.), 1–23, 104–10
J.-J. Nattiez: *Tétralogies – Wagner, Boulez, Chéreau: essai sur l'infidélité* (Paris, 1983)
N. Ely and S. Jaeger, eds.: *Regie heute: Musiktheater in unserer Zeit* (Berlin, 1984), 47–64
M. Ewans: 'The Bayreuth Centenary *Ring*', *The Richard Wagner Centenary in Australia*, ed. P. Dennison (Adelaide, 1985), 167–73
J.-J. Nattiez: 'The Centenary *Ring* and the Judgement of Fidelity', *Wagner in Performance*, ed. B. Millington and S. Spencer (New Haven, CT, 1992), 75–98

BARRY MILLINGTON

Cherepnin, Alexander. *See* TCHEREPNIN, ALEXANDER.

Cherepnin, Nikolay. *See* TCHEREPNIN, NIKOLAY.

Cherevichki ('The Slippers'; 'The Empress's Slippers'; 'The Golden Slippers'; 'The Little Slippers'; 'The Little Shoes'; 'Les caprices d'Oxane'). Comic-fantastic opera in four acts by PYOTR IL'YICH TCHAIKOVSKY (1885; a revision of *Vakula the Smith*, 1876) to a libretto by Yakov Polonsky, amplified by Nikolay Chayev and the composer after NIKOLAY VASIL'YEVICH GOGOL's story *Noch' pered rozhdestvom* ('Christmas Eve'); Moscow, Bol'shoy Theatre, 19/31 January 1887.

Vakula *a blacksmith*		tenor
Solokha *Vakula's mother, a witch*		mezzo-soprano
A Devil from the Stove *fantastic character*		baritone
Chub *an elderly Cossack*		bass
Oxana *Chub's daughter*		soprano
Pan Golova *the village head*	*Chub's chums*	bass
Panas	*Chub's chums*	tenor
Deacon	*Chub's chums*	character tenor
His Highness		bass-baritone
Master of Ceremonies		bass
Sentry		tenor
An Old Zaporozhian Cossack		bass
Forest Sprite [Leshiy] *an offstage voice*		baritone

Peasant lads and lasses, old men and women, kobza players, echoes, spirits, courtiers and ladies, Zaporozhian Cossacks etc.

Setting Dikanka (a Ukrainian village) and St Petersburg at the close of the 18th century

The libretto to Tchaikovsky's only comic opera was originally commissioned by the Grand Duchess Yelena Pavlovna on behalf of the Russian Music Society for setting by Alexander Serov, who died unexpectedly in 1871 having only just begun to sketch the opera. (A suite for piano based on these sketches, *Noch' pod rozhdestvo*, was published by the composer's widow in 1879.) As a memorial, the society sponsored a contest for the best setting of the libretto, the winner to be awarded a cash prize and a Mariinsky Theatre production. Tchaikovsky entered, having first made sure that neither Anton Rubinstein nor Rimsky-Korsakov would be competing, and completed the opera in short score during the summer months of 1874, the unusual speed of work being attributable not only to happy inspiration but also to his misapprehension that the deadline for submission of the full score was 1 January, rather than 1 August, 1875. Posthumously published correspondence with Rimsky-Korsakov, one of the contest judges, shows that Tchaikovsky lobbied outrageously on behalf of his supposedly blind submission not only with the jury but with the theatre staff. Yet the outcome was never in doubt: except for Nikolay Solov'yov, whose *Vakula kuznets* was eventually given a non-professional performance in 1880, the field otherwise consisted of amateurs.

Contrary to expectations of friend and foe (e.g. Cui) alike, the opera did not succeed. Possibly influenced by his critics (including Eduard Nápravník, who conducted the première), Tchaikovsky came to believe that the fault lay in an excessively elaborate 'symphonic' texture at the expense of vocal melody. Because he believed so strongly in the opera's potential, he subjected it to the most painstaking revision he was ever to accord any of his works. More than 500 bars were either pruned away (e.g. the highly contrapuntal development section in the overture) or replaced with simpler counterparts (e.g. the duettino for Chub and Panas in Act 1 scene i, in which declamation over some impressively developed chromatic storm music became a sparsely accompanied diatonic recitative). In addition, a slew of small rounded vocal numbers was interpolated at various strategic spots, enhancing the predominance of lyric melody over declamatory writing and further emphasizing the theme of young love over the farcical and fantastic elements that Gogol, and the original libretto, had stressed. (Items unique to the revised version of the opera are indicated in the following synopsis by the use of italics.) The changes were sufficient to warrant a changed title, and the composer asked his younger brother Modest to supply one: Modest came up with *Cherevichki*, after the prop that motivates the fantastic flight to St Petersburg. (Though usually mistranslated 'slippers', *cherevichki* are actually high-heeled, narrow-toed women's holiday boots.) This title was in its modest way the Tchaikovsky brothers' first musico-literary collaboration.

The singers at the première of the original version, in 1876, included Fyodor Komissarzhevsky (Vakula), Ivan Mel'nikov (the Devil), Osip Petrov (Chub) and Fyodor Stravinsky (His Highness), under Nápravník; Tchaikovsky himself conducted the première of the revised version.

ACT 1.i *Outside Solokha's hut* The widow Solokha comes out of her hut singing of the lovely moonlit evening and her longing for a lover. The Devil steals up on her; they flirt, eventually breaking into the first of the opera's several hopaks; Solokha agrees to help the Devil steal the moon. Using a *buffo parlante* style modelled on that of Farlaf in Glinka's *Ruslan and Lyudmila*, the Devil spells out his plan: he is angry with Solokha's son Vakula, who has painted an icon that caricatured him; to prevent Vakula from paying court to Oxana, his beloved, he will stir up a snowstorm and hide the moon, which will keep Oxana's father Chub from going out to drink with the Deacon (this character was changed to a schoolmaster by the censor). The Devil summons up a chorus of spirits who set the winds rushing; Solokha rides up into the sky and takes the moon. Chub and his pal Panas are seen groping their way to the Deacon's in the dark; they lose their way in the storm.

1.ii *Inside Chub's hut* The beautiful Oxana, the village coquette, is feeling lonely because her father has left her at home alone. In an ingenious folkish adaptation of the classical Italian aria, she goes through a series of moods mirrored by accelerating tempos; the last is ushered in when she picks up a mirror and begins admiring her deep dark eyes and long white neck. Vakula enters and watches Oxana delight in herself. Finally noticing him, all she can do is tease; he protests his love in an arioso. Chub stumbles in, not realizing he is home; Vakula, not recognizing him, chases him out with blows. Oxana realizes what has happened, cruelly upbraids Vakula, and turns him out, *rebuffing his entreaties and reducing him to a state of utter misery. Some village youths and maidens come round singing Ukrainian Christmas carols and invite Oxana to join them; but she has reflected on her cruelty to Vakula and, in a reprise of her aria, realizes that she loves him.*

ACT 2.i *Inside Solokha's hut* Solokha and the Devil have returned from their moon-stealing jaunt and, as prelude to lovemaking, dance another hopak. There is a knock at the door; Solokha hides the Devil in a sack. The village head appears, having been diverted from the Deacon's house by the storm; Solokha gives him some brandy and he becomes amorous. There is a knock at the door; Solokha hides him in another sack. Now it is the Deacon ('schoolteacher') himself who appears at Solokha's door and tries to seduce her. *He sings her a song he has composed in her honour* ('Baba k besu privyazalas': 'A woman did once consort with a devil'). There is a knock at the door; Solokha hides the Deacon in yet another sack, which she has to empty of coal. Chub comes in and Solokha receives him sweetly; now Vakula knocks at the door and Chub makes straight for the sack containing the Deacon. *All the men in sacks now begin to complain, in a brief, bizarre ensemble, while the Devil mocks the lot of them.* Solokha lets Vakula in, whereupon the smith begins brooding on his frustrations; he complains that he is so worn out by woe that he cannot even lift the three sacks cluttering up the room; but he summons his strength and carries them out.

2.ii *Outside Solokha's hut* Three groups of carollers contend. Oxana and her friend Odarka enter in a sleigh. Oxana spies Vakula and holds him up to mockery, then complains that she has no-one to bring her fancy boots like Odarka's. Vakula promises to get them for her, whereupon Oxana compulsively derides his offer, promising to marry him only if he will bring her the tsaritsa's own boots. The chorus joins her as she taunts him. He runs off in despair, threatening suicide, leaving two of his sacks by the side of the road. The carollers untie them, expecting to find victuals inside; instead out step the village head, the Deacon and Chub, who claims to be playing a practical joke.

ACT 3.i *The banks of the Dnepr* A Forest Sprite warns the water nymphs that a peasant lad is headed their way and seems determined to throw himself into their realm. Enter Vakula with the smallest sack, lamenting *(aria, words by Chayev:* 'Slïshit li, devitsa, serdtse tvoyo lyutoye': 'Does your cruel heart not hear, O maiden'; *this last interpolation was added in 1886 between the printing of the vocal score and the première).* The Devil jumps out of the sack and offers Oxana in return for Vakula's soul, but Vakula pins him to the ground and forces the Devil to carry him on his back to the tsaritsa's court in St Petersburg.

3.ii *Palace reception hall* The Devil deposits Vakula and disappears into the fireplace. A group of Cossacks enter on their way to an audience with the tsaritsa. With the unseen Devil's help, Vakula persuades them to take him along.

3.iii *Hall of columns* Against a polonaise, the chorus sing the tsaritsa's praises and the Master of Ceremonies arranges the Cossacks' audience. *Abetted by choral acclamations, an ode to the Russian victories against the Turks is sung by the chief minister His Highness* (this character, putatively modelled on Potyomkin, otherwise sings lines assigned by Gogol to Catherine the Great, who could not be shown on the operatic stage). To the strains of a courtly minuet, Vakula makes his strange request for the tsaritsa's boots. The plea, found amusing, is granted. His Highness calls for entertainment; Russian and Cossack dances ensue. As a neoclassical comedy gets under way, the Devil reappears and, having diverted all eyes, flies off with Vakula.

ACT 4 *Bright Christmas morning in the town square* Thinking Vakula drowned, Solokha and Oxana mourn him together. The villagers emerge from church and invite Oxana to the Christmas feast, but she goes off weeping. The young lads merrily make off for the inn, singing a hopak. Suddenly Vakula is back. He asks Chub for forgiveness and then for Oxana's hand. She runs on stage; he shows her the tsaritsa's boots but she waves them aside, admitting it is Vakula she wants, not the preposterous present. Chub calls upon the village *kobzari* (lutenists) to lead the nuptial rejoicing.

* * *

In its revised form the opera has weakly held the Russian and the Soviet stage; but Tchaikovsky never returned to the comic genre. Indeed, by assimilating some of the folkloristic music in *Vakula the Smith* to the sentimental romance style he had worked out for *Yevgeny Onegin*, he not only attenuated the opera's peasant idiom, but also thinned its humoristic vein considerably. Despite the fact that its main theme is an authentic folk tune, Vakula's aria ad libitum in Act 3 is heavily redolent of Lensky's similarly placed aria in the popular 'lyric scenes after Pushkin' and may even have been inspired by it. But Vakula's aggravated weepiness in *Cherevichki*, which some have found incongruous in a comic opera, has its counterpart in the monstrously overstated (and at least equally unfunny) portrayal there of Oxana's cruelty, which is hard not to associate with the composer's misogyny. RICHARD TARUSKIN

Cherici [Chierici, Clerici], **Sebastiano** (*b* Pistoia, 1647; *d* Pistoia, Dec 1703). Italian composer. He spent his formative years at Bologna as a pupil of G. P. Colonna and at Ferrara. Except for a visit to Dresden in 1675–6 he resided until 1695 at Ferrara, where he was *maestro di cappella* of the cathedral (1670–79) and of the Accademia dello Spirito Santo (from at least 1672). In 1685 he was elected to the Bolognese Accademia Filarmonica and in 1695 he became *maestro di cappella* of Pistoia Cathedral. Mainly a composer of sacred music, Cherici also wrote several operas, now lost.

Il mondo mascherato (esercizio cavalleresco, F. Berni), Ferrara, 1672
Amor, piaga ogni core (A. Donati), Ferrara, 1691
Ildegarde (Mellini), Pistoia, 1697
Il conte di Bacheville (F. Frosini), Pistoia, 1699
L'Egelinda, Pistoia, 1699

*

N. Bennati: *Musicisti ferraresi: notizie biografiche* (Ferrara, 1901), 17–18
A. Chiappelli: *Storia del teatro in Pistoia dalle origini alla fine del secolo XVIII* (Pistoia, 1913), 78, 114–15, 205–6
ELVIDIO SURIAN

Chérubin. *Comédie chantée* in three acts by JULES MASSENET to a libretto by HENRI CAIN and Francis de Croisset after the latter's play; Monte Carlo, Opéra, 14 February 1905.

Croisset's boulevard comedy is one of the less substantial of the countless sequels to Beaumarchais' Figaro plays. The opera based closely upon it is set on Chérubin's 17th birthday; although well past puberty, the amorous and active page (now infantry officer) is still played by a soprano *en travestie*, despite the playwright's objections. Among the women with whom he is involved are L'Ensoleillad (coloratura soprano), dancer, royal mistress and main attraction at the birthday celebrations; Nina (soprano), the 'girl next door'; a Baroness (mezzo-soprano); and a Countess (soprano). Chérubin's tutor, named Le Philosophe (bass), tries only vaguely to exert a restraining influence on his charge.

In the first act a compromising letter from Chérubin to the Countess nearly causes a duel with her husband but Nina, secretly in love with him, claims that it was intended for her and saves the situation. In the second act Chérubin steals an hour of love with L'Ensoleillad while also receiving compromising tokens of love from the Countess and the Baroness, and in the third multiple duels are prevented by his tryst with the dancer being made public. The noblewomen are outraged and their husbands placated. When L'Ensoleillad returns regretfully to her duties at court, Chérubin decides that he loves Nina after all, and they run off together. 'C'est Don Juan', remarks one of the subsidiary characters, to an appropriate quote from *Don Giovanni*; 'C'est Elvire,' answers Le Philosophe as the curtain falls.

The description 'comédie chantée' is as apt as the date of the première: *Chérubin* is short on melody and memorable set numbers, and long on deftly set dialogue that approaches Straussian fluency and ease. The fact that the dialogue in question aspires to a level no higher than that of standard boulevard fare may account for the work's failure with the public (it ran for only 14 performances at the Opéra-Comique). But it was conceived as a vehicle for a star singer – Mary Garden – and Massenet plainly had Lucien Fugère in mind for Le Philosophe; and when stars of equal lustre are available the piece can afford an evening's stylish and pleasing entertainment, as has been proved by Frederica von Stade both on stage and in the recording studio.

RODNEY MILNES

Cherubini, (Maria) Luigi (Carlo Zanobi Salvadore) [(Marie-)Louis(-Charles-Zénobi-Salvador)] (*b* Florence, ?8 Sept 1760; *d* Paris, 15 March 1842). Italian composer belonging to the French school. For half a century he was a dominant figure in French musical life, not only on account of his operas but also as a teacher and administrator. His contribution to French and German operatic history was substantial.

1. Life. 2. Operas. 3. Historical position.

1. LIFE. Although the exact date of Cherubini's birth is uncertain, evidence from baptismal records and from Cherubini himself suggests that 8 September is more likely than the 14th, as sometimes given. The strongest argument is his first name: 8 September is the feast-day of the Nativity of the Virgin. The original Italian form of his name has been retained here, although after moving to France Cherubini adopted the French version, which is found in all extant documents dating from 1790 onwards that show his full name.

Cherubini first learnt music from the age of six with his father, Bartolomeo, *maestro al cembalo* at the Teatro della Pergola in Florence. Something of a child prodigy, he received a solid training in counterpoint and Italian-style dramatic music. According to his autobiographical notes (see the catalogue of his works reproduced in Bottée de Toulmon), he studied with Bartolomeo Felici and his son Alessandro until their deaths and continued with Pietro Bizzarri and Giuseppe Castrucci. In 1778 he was awarded a scholarship by Grand Duke Leopold of Tuscany (later Emperor Leopold II) to study with Sarti in Bologna and Milan. All five of Cherubini's teachers were advocates of the old school of musical education: learn thoroughly the time-honoured rules, then see if you can improve on them. He thus received a complete grounding in the *a cappella* style, Palestrinian counterpoint, sight-singing, figured-bass accompaniment, and keyboard and string instruments, and he never lost his admiration for the older masters and their techniques. One of the ways in which he trained himself was by making copies of their music, examples of which are extant in London and Paris.

Cherubini's works from this period are mainly sacred, apart from two intermezzos and a few arias; but he must have been a frequent spectator at the local opera house where his father played, and his choice of Sarti, a renowned composer of *opera seria*, as his teacher would seem to indicate a preference for dramatic music. Although most of the compositions dating from his first two years with Sarti are religious, in 1779 his first *opera seria*, *Il Quinto Fabio*, was performed in Alessandria; he frequently contributed arias to his teacher's operas as part of the learning process; and within the next two years his output became almost completely operatic. Thus his studies with Sarti, while putting the finishing polish on his musical techniques, added another dimension to his education: the new school of Italian dramatic music as espoused by Jommelli, Traetta and Sacchini, as well as Sarti. Cherubini followed in their footsteps with works such as *Armida abbandonata* (1782, Florence), *Adriano in Siria* (1782, Livorno) and *Mesenzio, re d'Etruria* (1782, Florence) on librettos by Jacopo Durandi, Metastasio and Ferdinando Casorri. In 1781 he left Sarti and returned to Florence.

By 1783 he was not only ready to work on his own but was finding the currently popular *opera seria* form restricting. In that year he wrote his first *opera buffa*, *Lo sposo di tre e marito di nessuna* (Venice). Although he returned to *opera seria* in 1784 with *L'Alessandro nell'Indie* (Mantua) and *L'Idalide* (Florence), he was already experimenting with the form. He was also feeling stifled in his native country and decided to travel, going first to London, where the *opera buffa La finta principessa* (1785) and the *opera seria Il Giulio Sabino* (1786) were presented at the King's Theatre. In summer 1785 he visited Paris, where he met his compatriot G. B. Viotti, who presented him to Marie-Antoinette and introduced him to Parisian intellectual society. Except for a visit to London at the end of 1785 and one to Italy for the performance of his *opera seria Ifigenia in Aulide* in 1788, he spent the rest of his life in France.

Through Viotti, Cherubini became music director of the Théâtre de Monsieur, which opened in the Tuileries on 26 January 1789 – an opportunity he welcomed, with good reason: in 1786 he had accepted a commission to write an opera for the Académie Royale de Musique (the Opéra) on a libretto by Marmontel, and despite his lack of experience in setting French metrical texts, he made his début in Paris with *Démophon* on 2 December 1788. The results were neither disastrous nor reassuring, but the critics admitted that Cherubini did not yet possess the necessary technique to set a French text properly, and the work was dropped from the repertory after eight performances. Viotti's offer thus provided him with a job while he familiarized himself with the French language and acquired a name among French music lovers. In his capacity as music director he was obliged to add arias and ensembles in a style currently in vogue to the mediocre and sometimes outdated Italian operas presented by the company, and to rehearse and conduct performances. With the arrival in Paris of the royal family because of the political situation, the company had to find new quarters as the Tuileries was hastily reconverted into a royal residence. It reopened temporarily on 10 January 1790 in the Salle des Variétés of the Foire St Germain, but a permanent home was not established until it settled in the rue Feydeau with a gala performance on 6 January 1791.

Several events of the early 1790s were to influence the rest of Cherubini's life. In 1792 he signed a new contract with the Théâtre de la rue Feydeau which paid him 6000 livres a year for continuing his duties, plus 2000 for the first two completely new operas produced by him each year and another 4000 for each additional opera. This provided Cherubini with a series of librettos from which he could choose those that best met his demands. The result was a ten-year period of creativity which produced the following works: *Lodoïska* (1791), *Elisa, ou Le voyage aux glaciers du Mont St-Bernard* (1794), *Médée* (1797), *L'hôtellerie portugaise* (1798), *La punition* (1799) and *Les deux journées* (1800), as well as *La prisonnière* (1799) for the Théâtre Montansier. Cherubini also began work in 1790 on *Marguerite d'Anjou*, in 1793 on *Koukourgi* and in 1794 on *Sélico*. Of these, only the music for *Koukourgi* was re-used and completed, as *Ali-Baba, ou Les quarante voleurs* (1833). In essence, the Feydeau gave Cherubini financial stability and a stage which he used to experiment with the *opéra comique* form. This security allowed him to make changes in his personal life. Deciding that he could now assume the responsibilities of a family, in 1792 he became engaged to Anne Cécile Tourette, the daughter of a former countertenor in the royal chapel. The couple were married in 1794; the first of their three children was born the following year.

During this period Cherubini started an association with a new institution which was to last until his death. In summer 1794 he joined the staff of the Ecole de Musique de la Garde Nationale, formed on 9 June 1792. It was renamed the Institut National de Musique in 1793, and Cherubini was appointed to the provisional administration on 1 November 1794. The National Convention made a final change on 3 August 1795, decreeing that the Institut should be known thenceforth as the Conservatoire National de Musique. Cherubini was appointed an inspector with a salary of 5000F and free lodging. He was employed continuously by the Conservatoire (except between 1814 and 1816 when the institution was dissolved owing to the change from an imperial to a royalist government), first as teacher and inspector and then as director from April 1822 until 4 February 1842.

Finally, French politics began to play a substantial role in Cherubini's life in the 1790s and continued to do so until his death. The Revolution forced him to hide his royalist sympathies and to undertake engagements for the provisional government in order to distance himself from his aristocratic connections. The first of these was occasioned by the death of the Count of Mirabeau in 1791; Cherubini contributed three choruses to the spectacle *Mirabeau à son lit de mort* at the Théâtre de Monsieur. He was represented by at least one nationalistic piece at most important celebrations until the end of the decade, when Napoleon assumed power. Despite the mythology of the last 150 years concerning Napoleon's dislike of Cherubini (whose music, admittedly, was not the simple italianate confection which pleased the emperor), there were numerous commissions during the First Empire. These included a brief appointment as Napoleon's director of music in Vienna from late 1805 until early 1806; the composition of the *dramma lirico Pimmalione*, presented at the Tuileries on 30 November 1809; and an *Ode pour le mariage de l'empereur* written in May 1810. Napoleon was even present at the première of *Les abencérages, ou L'étendard de Grenade*, a remarkable event considering that he departed the next day for the Eastern campaign, the beginning of the end of his brilliant military and political career. With the return of the monarchy, Cherubini was named *surintendant* of the royal chapel in December 1814, a post he occupied until the fall of the Bourbon dynasty in summer 1830. During this time he wrote a considerable number of sacred works.

Although Cherubini was successful as a composer of *opéras comiques* (even if the French were lukewarm in their praise, these works were performed and respected in Germany and Austria), he was continually expanding the limits of the genre; in truth he wished to be known as a creator of great *tragédies lyriques*. He was twice represented on the stage of the Académie Impériale de Musique, by *Anacréon, ou L'amour fugitif* in 1803 and *Les abencérages* in 1813. Neither was well received, and that, together with his appointment to the royal chapel, turned him from dramatic music; after 1813 he composed mainly chamber and religious music. There were three exceptions: contributions to two political commissions, *Blanche de Provence, ou La cour des fées* (1821) and *La marquise de Brinvilliers* (1831), and a final attempt at recognition at the Académie Royale de Musique with *Ali-Baba, ou Les quarante voleurs* (1833). The last was a *succès d'estime* for Cherubini but never equalled the importance of *Les deux journées* (1800) or even *Médée*. In the last 25 years of his life, Cherubini contributed six string quartets to chamber music literature and two Requiem masses (1816, 1836) to the new style of opera-inspired sacred compositions. Many of the theoretical treatises which he wrote alone (*Cours de contrepoint et de fugue*, *Marches d'harmonie*, *Solfèges* etc.) or with others were used at the Conservatoire throughout the 19th century. He was honoured by the French for his contributions to musical life: in 1814 he was made a member of the Institut and a Chevalier of the Légion d'honneur, and in 1841 he was appointed Commander of the Légion d'honneur, the first musician to hold that office.

2. OPERAS. In an era when the freer, more liberalizing forms of *opera buffa* and *opéra comique* were coming to the fore, Cherubini seemed more interested in *opera seria* and *tragédie lyrique*. It is difficult to assess his contribution to *opera seria* because of the present inaccessibility of the original scores, but a brief look at what is available and reference to contemporary criticism indicate that Cherubini belonged to the 'reform' school. As early as *Il Quinto Fabio* he was showing signs of original use of orchestral colour through imaginative instrumentation, and in *Armida abbandonata* the orchestration serves to heighten dramatic moments, even to the detriment of the vocal line. The instrumentation of *Adriano in Siria* is unusual in its use of flutes, oboes, bassoons, french horns, trumpets and kettle drums in addition to the strings, a feature also found in *Mesenzio, re d'Etruria*. Cherubini first used the 'recall motif' in *L'Alessandro nell'Indie*, to underline those points in the text where the poet has characters refer to previous events or feelings; here too the instrumentation is interesting: flutes, oboes, english horn, bassoons, trumpets and four french horns. Cherubini also made use of the recapitulation aria, but not necessarily with the progression tonic-dominant-tonic. In *L'Idalide* he again employed recall motifs. His next serious opera, *Il Giulio Sabino*, was a fiasco. The critics blamed the disaster on the singers' inadequacy, but the fault was also Cherubini's, as he was still experimenting with *opera seria* and unsure of the direction he wished to take.

Cherubini's contribution to *opera seria* culminated in *Ifigenia in Aulide*. The single most important element differentiating this work from its predecessors was Cherubini's use of music to delineate character, arising perhaps from his thorough grounding in counterpoint; or perhaps it was a personal trait that led him to empathize more fully with a libretto whose text called for development through music. Whatever the reason, his most successful operas were always those requiring the revelation of character through dramatic, out-of-the-ordinary situations. We may assume that the demands of *opera seria* were more congenial to Cherubini, and that he preferred the classical plots typical of the genre, or perhaps historical subjects in general, to more mundane situations.

With his move to France, the logical continuation of Cherubini's development of *opera seria* would be in the exploitation of *tragédie lyrique*. To his chagrin, however, he was unable to break into the clique which ruled the tastes of the Académie Royale (or Impériale, depending on the government) de Musique, and his three works in the form, *Anacréon*, *Les abencérages* and *Ali-Baba*, were never successful, either in France or elsewhere. Nor was Cherubini able to meet two of the requirements of *tragédie lyrique*: the use of recitative and the need for ballet, even if it did not fit into the plot. Consequently his most important contributions to 19th-century opera were made within the framework of *opéra comique*. Forms lost their importance before the demands of the drama; vocal lines were ornamented no more than was required by their meaning, as long as the orchestra brought out the true emotions that the character was experiencing; individual solos gave way to ensembles and to choral and instrumental numbers which more effectively advanced and clarified the dramatic situation. Almost half a century before Wagner, in fact, Cherubini evolved a style which was criticized for being unsingable and unmelodic, for putting emphasis on the orchestra and making it play loudly, and for creating long musical numbers which slowed down the action even if they did underline the emotions and actions of the protagonists. The two most successful examples of this new style were *Médée* and *Les deux journées*.

Although Cherubini virtually stopped composing for the stage after 1813, his dramatic sense was evident in other musical forms: the symphony he composed for the Royal Philharmonic Society of London in 1815 has been described as a play without words; his numerous masses continued the operatic tradition begun by Mozart; and his two requiems established a new style for the form which culminated in Verdi's setting. The intrigues of the world of French opera defeated Cherubini but did not stifle the dramatic qualities of his creativity.

3. Historical position. In an era that has witnessed the revival of unknown compositions by many Baroque and Classical composers, renewed enthusiasm for Cherubini's music has yet to be generated. He spanned the years from the Classical era to the Romantic; he was trained in the old system of Palestrinian counterpoint and Italian bel canto singing and spent the first half of his creative life as an opera composer; his earliest works are unmistakably tied to his Italian ancestry, but his thirst for new ideas took him to France, where he studied Handel and Haydn, then Beethoven and Mozart, in an effort to improve his technique and to encourage similar advances in the composers around him.

Many books and dictionaries have implied, erroneously, that Cherubini had no effect on later schools of composition. The names of his pupils, friends and visitors read like a 19th-century musical who's who: Bellini, Berlioz, Chopin, Donizetti, Fétis, Halévy, Hérold, Liszt, Mendelssohn, Meyerbeer, Rossini and Schumann, to mention only the most illustrious. But his influence extended beyond the circle of his acquaintances. His developments in *opéra comique* were continued by Halévy and Hérold and culminated in Bizet's *Carmen*; in Germany, Weber examined every work of Cherubini's that he could find, and the new style of Singspiel, of which *Der Freischütz* is the first definitive example, owed its origin in some measure to the French master. In *tragédie lyrique* Spontini copied most of what his colleague Cherubini had done, and thus, starting with Rossini and Meyerbeer, a direct link with Romantic grand opera, which pervaded the French stage during the mid-19th century, was established. Later musicians who studied Cherubini included Brahms, Bruckner, Bülow and Wagner. The genesis of German music drama as epitomized by Wagner's works can also be traced directly to Cherubini.

There are good reasons why Cherubini's works disappeared from European stages after his death, despite their affinity with the Romantic era: his *opéras comiques* were soon surpassed by those of his pupils and admirers, and his *tragédies lyriques* were too tedious to excite interest, especially after the subsequent reforms of Rossini and Meyerbeer. More important, Cherubini was unfortunate in his librettists, and the music of most of his lyric works outclasses their texts. However, it is impossible to study operatic developments in the 19th century without acknowledging his place. Judicious editing of many of his stage compositions would render them palatable to contemporary taste and ensure Cherubini's rightful survival as one of the principal architects of Romantic opera.

See also Deux journées, les; Elisa; Lodoïska; and Médée (ii).

printed works published in Paris unless otherwise stated

title	*genre, acts*	*libretto*	*first performance*	*publication*	*remarks and sources*
Amore artigiano	int		Fiesole, S Domenico, 22 Oct 1773		lost
Il giocatore	int		Florence, 1775	vs (Florence, 1980)	*F-Pn*
untitled int			Florence, Serviti, 16 Feb 1778		not listed in autograph catalogue
Il Quinto Fabio	os, 3	A. Zeno	Alessandria, Paglia, aut. 1779		lost; reworked 1783, see below
Armida abbandonata	os, 3	B. Vitturi, after J. Durandi, F. De Rogatis and T. Tasso: *Gerusalemme liberata*	Florence, Pergola, 25 Jan 1782		*B-Bc*, *F-Pc*, *I-Fc*, ?*PL-Kj**
Adriano in Siria	os, 3	P. Metastasio	Livorno, Armeni, 16 April 1782		?*Kj**
Mesenzio, re d'Etruria	os, 3	F. Casorri	Florence, Pergola, 6 Sept 1782		*B-Bc* (final chorus missing), *I-Fc*, ?*PL-Kj**
Il Quinto Fabio	os, 3	Zeno	Rome, Argentina, Jan 1783	aria, 1v, orch, *Journal d'ariettes italiennes* (1786)	reworking of 1779 setting; ?*Kj**
Lo sposo di tre e marito di nessuna	ob, 2	F. Livigni	Venice, S Samuele, Nov 1783		*F-Pn*, ?*PL-Kj**

title	genre, acts	libretto	first performance	publication	remarks and sources
Olimpiade	os, 3	Metastasio	1783		*B-Bc* (inc.), *I-Fc*
L'Alessandro nell'Indie	os, 2	Metastasio	Mantua, Regio, April 1784	aria, *Journal d'ariettes italiennes* (1794)	?*PL-Kj**
L'Idalide	os, 2	F. Moretti	Florence, Pergola, 26 Dec 1784		?*Kj**
Demetrio		Metastasio	London, King's, 1785		4 pieces by Cherubini; ?*Kj**
La finta principessa	ob, 2	Livigni	London, King's, 2 April 1785		?*Kj**
Il Giulio Sabino	os, 2		London, King's, 30 March 1786		*I-Fc, Mc*, ?*PL-Kj**
Ifigenia in Aulide	os, 3	Moretti	Turin, Regio, 12 Jan 1788	aria, S, orch (London, 1789)	*B-Bc, D-Dlb, F-Pc, I-Nc*, ?*PL-Kj**
Démophon	tragédie lyrique, 3	J. F. Marmontel, after Metastasio	Paris, Opéra, 2 Dec 1788	(1788/*R*1978: ERO, xxxii)	*F-Po*, ?*PL-Kj**
Lodoïska	comédie-héroïque, 3	C.-F. Fillette-Loraux, after J.-B. Louvet de Couvrai: *Les amours du chevalier Faublas*	Paris, Feydeau, 18 July 1791	(1791/*R*1978: ERO, xxxiii)	2 entr'actes, 1 aria, added for Vienna, 1805; *D-Bds**, ?*PL-Kj**
Le congrès des rois	cmda, 3	Desmaillot [A. F. Eve]	Paris, OC (Favart), 26 Feb 1794		collab. Dalayrac, Grétry, Méhul and 8 others; lost
Elisa, ou Le voyage aux glaciers du Mont St-Bernard	oc, 2	J.-A. R. de Saint-Cyr	Paris, Feydeau, 13 Dec 1794	(1794/*R*1979: ERO, xxxiv)	?*Kj**
Médée	oc, 3	F.-B. Hoffman	Paris, Feydeau, 13 March 1797	(1797)	*A-Wn, D-Bds, I-Mc, US-NYcu, STu**; copy of 1st edn, with autograph changes and addns to ov. and Act 2 finale, *B-Bc*
L'hôtellerie portugaise	oc, 1	E. Saint-Aignan	Paris, Feydeau, 25 July 1798	vs (Leipzig, 1798)	*A-Wn, D-Bds** (incl. copy), *I-Fc, US-Wc*
La punition	oc, 1	J.-L. B. Desfaucherets	Paris, Feydeau, 23 Feb 1799		*D-Bds**
La prisonnière	oc, 1	E. de Jouy, C. de Longchamps and C. G. d'A. de Saint-Just	Paris, Montansier, 12 Sept 1799	ov. (?1799)	collab. Boieldieu; ov. and nos. 1, 2, 5, 8 by Cherubini; *B-Bc, D-Bds** (incl. copy), *F-Pn, R(m), US-Bp*
Les deux journées	comédie lyrique, 3	J. N. Bouilly	Paris, Feydeau, 16 Jan 1800	(1800/*R*1980: ERO, xxxv)	*A-Wn, D-Bds** (incl. copy), *F-Pn, Po, R(m), I-Fc*
Epicure	oc, 3 [later 2]	C. A. Demoustier	Paris, OC (Favart), 14 March 1800	arr. pf (1800)	collab. Méhul; ov., Act 1, Act 3 [2] nos. 8 and 10 by Cherubini; *D-Bds**
Anacréon, ou L'amour fugitif	opéra-ballet, 2	R. Mendouze	Paris, Opéra, 4 Oct 1803	(1803)	*A-Wn, D-Bds**, *F-Po*
Faniska	oc, 3	J. von Sonnleithner, after R. C. G. de Pixérécourt: *Les mines de Pologne*	Vienna, Kärntnertor, 25 Feb 1806	vs (Leipzig, 1806), full score (1845)	*A-Wgm, Wn, B-Bc, C-Lu, D-Bds** (incl. copy), *F-Pn, I-Mc*
Pimmalione	dramma lirico, 1	S. Vestris, after J.-J. Rousseau and A. S. Sografi	Paris, Tuileries, 30 Nov 1809	vs (Florence, 1970)	*B-Bc, D-Bds**, *F-Pc, Pn, GB-Lbl, I-Fc, PAc*
Le crescendo	opéra bouffon, 1	C. A. Sewrin [C. A. de Bassompierre]	Paris, OC (Feydeau), 1 Sept 1810		*D-Bds** (except ov.), ov. *F-Pn**
Les abencérages, ou L'étendard de Grenade	tragédie lyrique, 3 [later 2]	Jouy, after J.-P. C. de Florian: *Gonzalve de Cordoue*	Paris, Opéra, 6 April 1813	vs (?1813)	*B-Bc, D-Bds** (incl. copy), *F-Pn, Po*
Bayard à Mézières	oc, 1	E. Dupaty and R. A. de Chazet	Paris, OC (Feydeau), 12 Feb 1814	vs (1814)	collab. Boieldieu, Catel and Isouard; 3 pieces by Cherubini; lost
Blanche de Provence, ou La cour de fées	1	M. E. G. M. Théaulon and de Rancé	Paris, Tuileries, 1 May 1821		collab. H.-M. Berton, Boieldieu, Kreutzer and Paer; pt 3 by Cherubini, *D-Bds**, *F-Po*

title	genre, acts	libretto	first performance	publication	remarks and sources
La marquise de Brinvilliers	drame lyrique, 3	E. Scribe and Castil-Blaze [F.-H.-J. Blaze]	Paris, OC (Ventadour), 31 Oct 1831	full score (Paris, 1831)	collab. Auber, Batton, H.-M. Berton, Blangini, Boieldieu, Carafa, Hérold and Paer; Act 1 introduction by Cherubini; lost
Ali-Baba, ou Les quarante voleurs	tragédie lyrique, prol., 4	Mélesville [A.-H.-J. Duveyrier] and E. Scribe	Paris, Opéra, 22 July 1833	vs (Leipzig, 1834)	4 pieces taken from unfinished op Koukourgi, lib. largely reworking of that of Koukourgi; *D-Bds**, *F-Pn*, *Po*

Uncompleted: untitled op, 1781, ?*PL-Kj**; Marguerite d'Anjou, 1790, ?*Kj**; Koukourgi, 1793, ?*Kj**; Sélico, 1794, *D-Bds**; untitled oc, 1802, *Bds**; Les arrêts, 1804, *Bds**; La petite guerre, 1807, *Bds**

Addl pieces (no. in parentheses) for new productions of: untitled op, 1781 (5), ?*Pl-Kj**; Semiramide, 1782 (1), ?*Kj**; Cimarosa, Giannina e Bernardone, 1786 (2), *F-Pn**; Paisiello, Il marchese Tulipano, 1786 (6), ?*PL-Kj**; La molinarella, parody of Paisiello, La molinara, 1789 (9), ?*Kj**; Cimarosa, Il fanatico burlato, 1789 (1), lost; P. A. Guglielmi, La pastorella nobile, 1789 (1), ?*Kj**; Sarti, Le gelosie villane, 1790 (1), lost; Paisiello, La grotta di Trofonio, 1790 (2), ?*Kj**; Désaugiers, Les deux jumelles, 1790 (2), *F-Pn**; Paisiello, La frascatana, 1790 (2), ?*Pl-Kj**; ?Anfossi, I viaggiatori felici, 1790 (3), ?*Kj**; Cimarosa, L'italiana in Londra, 1790 (6), 2 *F-Pn*, 1 *Po*, ?*PL-Kj**; Paisiello, Il tamburo notturno, 1791 (2), ?*Kj**; Martín y Soler, Il burbero di buon cuore, 1791 (1), ?*Kj**; ?Gazzaniga, Le vendemmie, 1791 (1), ?*Kj**; Paisiello, La pazza per amore, 1791 (2), 1 *B-Bc**, ?*Pl-Kj**; Gazzaniga, Don Giovanni, 1792 (1), ?*Kj**; Martín y Soler, Una cosa rara, 1792 (1), *F-Pn**; Salieri, La locandiera scaltra, 1792 (5), 1 *Pn**

I. T. F. C. Arnold: *Luigi Cherubini: seine kurze Biographie und ästhetische Darstellung seiner Werke* (Erfurt, 1810)
Castil-Blaze: 'Cherubini', *Revue de Paris*, lii (1833), 86–108, 165–80
A. Bottée de Toulmon, ed.: *Notice des manuscrits autographes de la musique composée par feu M.-L.-C.-Z.-S. Cherubini* (Paris, 1842)
E. F. A. M. Miel: *Notice sur la vie et les ouvrages de Cherubini* (Paris, 1842)
C. Place: *Essai sur la composition musicale, bibliographie et analyse phrénologique de Cherubini* (Paris, 1842)
L. Picchianti: *Notizie sulla vita e sulle opere di Luigi Cherubini* (Milan, 1843)
D. Raoul-Rochette: *Notice historique sur la vie et les ouvrages de M. Cherubini* (Paris, 1843)
C. A. Gambini: *Hommage à Cherubini* (Paris, 1844)
'Un homme de rien' [L. de Loménie]: *Cherubini* (Paris, 1847)
W. Neumann: *Luigi Cherubini: eine Biographie* (Kassel, 1854)
R. D. Denne-Baron: *Mémoires historiques d'un musicien: Cherubini, sa vie, ses travaux, leur influence sur l'art* (Paris, 1862)
E. Cianchi: 'Cenno analitico sopra *Le due giornate*, opera teatrale di Luigi Cherubini', *Atti dell'Accademia del Regio Istituto Musicale de Firenze*, i (1863), 31–40
T. E. X. N. Torfs [T. Nisard]: *Cherubini* (Le Mans, 1867)
B. Gamucci: *Intorno alla vita ed alle opere di Luigi Cherubini* (Florence, 1869)
E. Bellasis: *Cherubini: Memorials Illustrative of his Life and Work* (London, 1874, enlarged 2/1905, 3/1912; Ger. trans., 1876, 2/1972 ed. H.-J. Irmen)
A. Pougin: 'Cherubini: sa vie, ses oeuvres, son rôle artistique', *Le ménestrel*, xlvii–xlix (1880–83)
La Mara [pseud. of M. Lipsius]: *Musikalische Studienköpfe* (Leipzig, 1881–8)
J. Bennett: *Luigi Cherubini* (London, 1884)
F. J. Crowest: *Cherubini* (London, 1890)
M. E. Wittmann: *Cherubini* (Leipzig, 1895)
J. Carreras y Bulbena: *Luigi Cherubini: estudio musical* (Barcelona, 1896)
E. O. Nodnagel: *Der Wasserträger, textlich und musikalisch erläutert* (Leipzig, 1900)
E. Prout: 'Some Forgotten Operas, IV: Cherubini's *Medea*', *MMR*, xxxv (1905), 21–5, 41–6, 62–5
H. Kretzschmar: 'Über die Bedeutung von Cherubinis Ouvertüren und Hauptopern für die Gegenwart', *JbMP 1906*, 75–91
A. Lega: *Cherubini e l'opera 'Medea': cenno biografico con brani musicale* (Milan, 1909)
R. H. Hohenemser: *Luigi Cherubini: sein Leben und seine Werke* (Leipzig, 1913)
M. Quatrelles [pseud. of E.-L.-V.-J. L'Epine]: *Cherubini (1760–1842): notes et documents inédits* (Lille, 1913)
R. H. Hohenemser: 'Cherubinis *Wasserträger*', *Die Musik*, xiii (1913–14), 131–46
L. Schemann: 'Cherubinis dramatisches Erstlingsschaffen', *Die Musik*, xvii (1924–5), 641–7
——: *Cherubini* (Stuttgart, 1925)
A. Schmitz: 'Cherubinis Einfluss auf Beethovens Ouvertüren', *NBJb*, ii (1925), 104–18
G. Saponaro: 'Luigi Cherubini (1760–1842): note biografiche', *Bollettino bibliografico musicale*, v (1930), 9–31
A. Capri: 'Luigi Cherubini nel centenario della morte (1842–1942)', *Musica*, i (Florence, 1942), 72–101
G. Confalonieri: *Prigionia di un artista: il romanzo di Luigi Cherubini* (Milan, 1948)
M. J. S. Selden: *The French Operas of Luigi Cherubini* (diss., Yale U., 1951)
V. G. Haft: *Cherubini: a Critical Biography* (diss., Columbia U., 1952)
A. Damerini: 'Rivive *Medea* di Cherubini', *RMI*, lvi (1954), 61–7
F. Schlitzer, ed.: *I musicisti toscani*, i, Chigiana, xi (1954)
——: *Ricerche su Cherubini: note in margine ad un libro di G. Confalonieri* (Siena, 1954)
M. Cooper: 'Cherubini's *Medea*', *Opera*, x (1959), 349–55
C. Schröder: 'Chronologisches Verzeichnis der Werke Luigi Cherubinis unter Kennzeichnung der in der Musikabteilung der Berliner Staatsbibliothek erhaltenen Handschriften', *BMw*, iii (1961), 24–60
M. Chusid: 'Schubert's Overture for String Quartet and Cherubini's Overture to *Faniska*', *JAMS*, xv (1962), 78–84
A. Damerini, ed.: *Luigi Cherubini nel II centenario della nascita* (Florence, 1962)
C. F. Reynolds: *Luigi Cherubini* (Ilfracombe, 1963)
B. Deane: *Cherubini* (London, 1965)
A. L. Ringer: 'Cherubini's *Médée* and the Spirit of French Revolutionary Opera', *Essays in Musicology in Honor of Dragan Plamenac* (Pittsburgh, 1969), 281–99
S. C. Willis: *Luigi Cherubini: a Study of his Life and Dramatic Music, 1795–1815* (diss., Columbia U., 1975)
E. J. Dent: *The Rise of Romantic Opera*, ed. W. Dean (Cambridge, 1976)
S. C. Willis: 'Cherubini: from *Opera Seria* to *Opéra Comique*', *Studies in Music*, vii (London, Ont., 1982), 155–82
V. Della Croce: *Cherubini e i musicisti italiani del suo tempo* (Turin, 1983)
G. Buschmeier: *Die Entwicklung von Arie und Szene in der französischen Oper von Gluck bis Spontini* (Tutzing, 1991)

STEPHEN C. WILLIS

Chest voice (Fr. *voix de poitrine*; Ger. *Bruststimme*; It. *voce di petto*). A term that is used in two connections (leaving aside the anatomical conditions under which the chest voice functions): the lower part of the female vocal range and the upper part of the male. In both instances it applies to a certain type of voice production and its resulting sound, which is quite distinct from that of the head voice (*voce di testa*).

A male singer can extend his upward range by using the head voice or the FALSETTO, which may be strengthened and developed as a mixed tone so that the falsetto element is to a greater or lesser extent disguised. Alternatively he may use the chest voice, which produces the ringing high notes of the characteristic modern operatic voice. The tenor roles in operas by composers such as Bellini have high notes which are sometimes so frequent and beyond normal reach of the non-falsetto male voice that it seems likely that they would have been sung originally with the head voice. Tenors would not then have extended their chest voice much beyond *g′* or *a♭′*. The sensation caused among the Parisian public when Gilbert Duprez (1806–96) produced the *c″*s in *Guillaume Tell* with full chest voice (*do di petto* or *ut de poitrine*) is evidence that the previous general practice, and that of his predecessor in the role, Adolphe Nourrit, had been to use the head voice. Since then the ability to produce ringing high notes in the so-called chest voice has been virtually essential for any tenor hoping to make a career in Italian opera.

In the female voice the term denotes a tone more akin to the normal level of the speaking voice. The lower notes of the soprano are generally weak and colourless unless the chest voice is brought into play. Where its use becomes controversial and even dangerous is when it is extended much higher than *e♭′*. Beyond this, the effect can be strident and vulgar, though in certain passages in *verismo* operas it may well be exciting. A further danger to the voice itself is that the break in register cannot then be smoothed over, and the notes immediately above this extended chest register are weakened. It is the Latin races that have gone furthest in this use of the chest voice in women: the singing of Maria Callas provides an example of the excitements of a bold and colourful chest voice – which may also, however, have contributed to the deterioration of her voice as an evenly tempered instrument. J. B. STEANE

Chevalier, Mlle [Fesch, Marie-Jeanne] (*b* Paris, 12 Sept 1722; *d* after 1789). French soprano. She was recruited for the Paris Opéra and sang her first major role (Cybele) in Lully's *Atys* (1740). In addition to the title roles she took in Destouches' *Issé* (1741 and 1757), Lully's *Armide* (1746 and 1761), *Alceste* (1758) and Desmarets and Campra's *Iphigénie en Tauride* (1762, with additions by P.-M. Berton), she created J.-M. Leclair's Circe (*Scylla et Glaucus*, 1746), Rameau's Erinice (*Zoroastre*, 1749), Zirphile (*Acante et Céphise*, 1751), Phoebe (revised version of *Castor et Pollux*, 1754) and roles in Dauvergne's *tragédies lyriques* of the early 1760s. She appeared in numerous other operas, among these Bertin de la Doué's *Ajax* (1742; Cassandra), Lully's *Thésée* (1744; Medea), Marais' *La mort d'Hercule* (1744, as restaged under Berger; Dejanira) and Campra's *Tancrède* (1750 and 1764; Clorinde). She retired in 1766.

La Borde (1780) said she had 'une belle représentation, un jeu noble, et une manière aisée de chanter la musique de son temps'. She bridged the gap between the generation of Antier, Lemaure and Pélissier (all of whom disappeared from the scene in the 1740s) and that of Arnould and Lemière.

*

ES (B. Horowicz)
A. Pougin: *Un ténor de l'Opéra: Pierre Jélyotte et les chanteurs de son temps* (Paris, 1905), 107–10 PHILIP WELLER

Chevreuille, Raymond (*b* Watermael-Boitsfort, Brussels, 17 Nov 1901; *d* Montignies-le-Tilleul, 9 May 1976). Belgian composer. He abandoned studies at the Brussels Conservatory, and thereafter was self-taught. From 1934 his works were regularly performed at ISCM festivals, and in 1950 he was awarded the Italia Prize for *D'un diable de briquet*. He was a member of the Belgian Royal Academy (1973). As a music engineer with Belgian radio, he exploited radio's technical possibilities in two works written for the medium: *D'un diable de briquet*, for large forces, and *L'élixir du révérend père Gaucher*, written for a small ensemble. In *L'élixir* the amount of vocal music is considerably reduced by the use of spoken text. By manipulating pre-recorded passages, using different speeds and juxtaposing two recordings, he creates new effects with timbres, rhythms and tessitura. Such passages alternate with more traditionally produced material, creating a diversity through which Chevreuille seeks to strengthen their expressiveness. *Atta Troll*, for three singers and 11 instrumentalists, is similar to *L'élixir* in its economy of forces and rhythmic complexity.

broadcast by Belgian radio unless otherwise stated

Jean et les Argayons, op.7, 1934 (ballet chanté, P. Chevreuille), unperf.
D'un diable de briquet, op.45 (conte symphonique, R. Chevreuille, after H. C. Andersen), 21 July 1950
L'élixir du révérend père Gaucher, op.48 (jeu radiophonique, Chevreuille, after A. Daudet), 5 May 1952
Atta Troll, op.51 (chamber op, 1, Chevreuille, after H. Heine: *Atta Troll, ein Sommernachtstraum*), 10 Jan 1954

*

R. Wangermée: *La musique belge contemporaine* (Brussels, 1959)
D. von Volborth-Danys: *CeBeDeM and its Affiliated Composers* (Brussels, 1977–80) HENRI VANHULST

Chezy, Helmina [Wilhelmina] (**Christiane**) **von** [née Klencke] (*b* Berlin, 26 Jan 1783; *d* Geneva, 28 Jan 1856). German poet and librettist. She is best known for her libretto of *Euryanthe* for Weber and her play *Rosamunde*, for which Schubert wrote incidental music; she also provided the text for E. J. O. von Hettersdorf's Singspiel *Eginhard und Emma* (1812, Amorbach). Between two brief, unhappy marriages she lived with Friedrich and Dorothea Schlegel in Paris and steeped herself in Romantic literature. In 1810 she returned to Germany with her two young sons and led an unsettled existence but made a wide circle of friends and acquaintances. She was not, and never claimed to be, a gifted dramatist: she received the commissions for *Euryanthe* and *Rosamunde*, both performed in Vienna in 1823 to severe criticism, on the strength of her poetry. From 1823 to 1833 von Chezy lived in Austria, some of the time in Vienna. By now very fat, ill-dressed and decidedly eccentric, she was the object of some ridicule, yet she won the affection of many, especially young artists and intellectuals, for whom she kept open house in Vienna. ELIZABETH NORMAN McKAY

Chiabrera, Gabriello ['Il Savonese'] (*b* Savona, 8 June 1552; *d* Savona, 11 Oct 1638). Italian poet and librettist. In his brief autobiography, he stated that he was educated at the Jesuit College in Rome until the age of 20, when he entered the service of Cardinal Cornaro. After being involved in a duel, he left Rome and returned to his birthplace, where he spent the next decade pursuing his literary studies. He passed his later years in Florence (1595–1633) and Savona, enjoying the patronage of the Grand Dukes of Tuscany, Carlo Emmanuele I of Savoy, Vincenzo Gonzaga and Pope Urban VIII, all of whom he celebrated in his occasional verse. He also eulogized many of his contemporaries, among them Corsi, Rinuccini, Caccini and Tasso.

Although Chiabrera wrote in almost every literary genre of his day, his most important contribution was in the field of lyric and dramatic poetry intended for music. Influenced by the humanist theories of the Pléiade and by the strophic forms of the more popular vein of the Italian Renaissance, he experimented with the metrical patterns and simple strophic verse adapted by Ronsard from classical models, as well as with the varied stanza types of earlier Italian poets, such as Sannazaro, Serafino Aquilano, Lorenzo de' Medici and Poliziano. After publishing several collections of poetry (two books of *Canzonette* in 1591, *Scherzi e canzonette morali* and *Maniere de' versi toscani* in 1599) he was celebrated as a modern Pindar and as the creator of a new lyric style in Florence. The short, varied verses and novel, often symmetrical internal schemes of his canzonettas and *scherzi* (the latter a term he introduced) were natural aids to musical organization and attracted many song-writers in the early 17th century, such as Caccini, Peri, Monteverdi (the majority of the *Scherzi musicali* of 1607 are to Chiabrera's texts), Rasi, Landi and others. Although his theoretical works (*L'Orzalesi*, *Il Geri* and *Il Bamberini*) remained unpublished until 1826, they reveal an attitude of conscious reform aimed at greater simplicity and immediacy of appeal than the Petrarchan-style lyrics of his contemporaries.

A member of the Florentine Accademia degli Alterati, Chiabrera was also among the literary figures who frequented Corsi's salon in the 1590s and was one of the first poets to experiment with the new dramatic genre, the libretto. His *Il rapimento di Cefalo*, set largely by Caccini, was the most spectacular event of the Florentine wedding celebrations of 1600. He visited Mantua in 1602 and 1605 and provided the prologue and *intermedi* to Guarini's *L'idropica*, presented during the Gonzaga court festivities in 1608. Also in that year, for the wedding of Cosimo II in Florence, he wrote a 'canzona sopra il balletto a cavallo' and two 'favolette da rappresentarsi cantando', one of which was probably *Il pianto d'Orfeo*. Other librettos from this period are *Oritia* and *Il Polifemo geloso* (both published only in 1615, with *Il pianto*), and *La Galatea* (1614, revised as *Gli amori di Aci e Galatea* and set by Santi Orlandi for a performance in Mantua in 1617). Probably somewhat later are *Angelica in Ebuda* (1615) and *La vegghia* [*veglia*] *delle Grazie* (or *Il ballo delle Grazie*), the latter produced in Florence in 1615 with music in part by Peri. Two other librettos, *Amore sbandito* and *La pietà di Cosmo*, are lost.

Chiabrera's influence on his contemporaries may be seen in the fact that certain formal features of Rinuccini's expanded *Dafne* libretto of 1608 and of Striggio's *Orfeo* resemble those in *Polifemo* and *Galatea*, particularly in the use of specific strophic forms and unifying choral structures. His varied treatment of text and experimentation with new strophic designs have also been credited with fostering the musical separation between recitative and aria in the operas and chamber cantatas of the mid-17th century and with providing the basis for the psychological portrayal of their characters.

A. Solerti: 'Le "favolette da recitarsi cantando" di Gabriello Chiabrera', *Giornale storico e letterario della Liguria*, iv (1903), 227–37

——: *Gli albori del melodramma* (Milan, 1904), iii

F. Neri: *Il Chiabrera e la Pleiade francese* (Turin, 1920)

C. Calcaterra: *Poesia e canto: studi sulla poesia melica italiana e sulla favola per musica* (Bologna, 1951)

A. M. Nagler: *Theatre Festivals of the Medici* (New Haven, CT, 1964), 96ff

G. Getto: *Barocco in prosa e in poesia* (Milan, 1969), 123–62

S. Leopold: '"Quelle bazzicature poetiche, appellate ariette": Dichtungsformen in der frühen italienischen Oper (1600–1640)', *HJbMw*, iii (1978), 101–41

B. R. Hanning: *Of Poetry and Music's Power: Humanism and the Creation of Opera* (Ann Arbor, 1980)

S. Leopold: 'Chiabrera und die Monodie: die Entwicklung der Arie', *Studi musicali*, x/1 (1981), 75–106

Chiabrera e il suo tempo: Savona 1988

BARBARA R. HANNING

Chiamata (It.: 'call'). A 17th-century Italian term designating a military trumpet fanfare (see Girolamo Fantini's trumpet method *Modo per imparare a sonare di tromba*, 1638). Examples are occasionally found in early 17th-century Italian operas, such as the five-part instrumental 'Chiamata alla caccia' from the first act of Cavalli's *Le nozze di Teti e di Peleo* (1639), a piece similar in style to the opening toccata of Monteverdi's *Orfeo* (1607).

H. Goldschmidt: *Studien zur Geschichte der italienischen Oper im 17. Jahrhundert*, i (Leipzig, 1901), 402

E. Wellesz: 'Cavalli und der Stil der venezianischen Oper von 1640–1660', *SMw*, i (1913), 1–103, esp. 55

Chiara, Maria(-Rita) (*b* Oderzo, 24 Nov 1939). Italian soprano. She studied in Venice and Turin, making her début in 1966 at La Fenice as Desdemona. Engagements followed at S Carlo, Rome, La Scala and Verona Arena. She has also sung in Berlin, Hamburg, Munich, Vienna, Zürich, Geneva, Brussels, Barcelona, Rio de Janeiro and Buenos Aires. She made her Covent Garden début as Liù in 1973, her American début in Chicago as Manon Lescaut and her Metropolitan début as Violetta in 1977. Her roles include Mathilde (*Guillaume Tell*), Elsa, Massenet's Manon, Micaëla, Adriana Lecouvreur, Maddalena (*Andrea Chénier*), Tosca, Suor Angelica, Butterfly, Leonora (both *Il trovatore* and *La forza del destino*) and Aida, which she sang at Luxor (1987). Her beautiful, refined voice is best displayed in Puccini and Verdi.

ELIZABETH FORBES

Chiari, Pietro (*b* Brescia, Dec 1712; *d* Brescia, Aug 1785). Italian librettist. After a brief military career Chiari settled in Venice in 1746, where he wrote comedies, *romanze* and polemics under the Arcadian name of Egerindo Criptonide. In 1749 he joined the S Samuele theatre where he wrote for the Imer-Casali company of *commedia dell'arte* players; in 1753 he took a similar post at the S Angelo, which Goldoni had recently abandoned for the competing theatre, the S Luca. Chiari's blatant parodies of Goldoni aroused fury, and the literary war between the two marked the apogee of Chiari's fame. In summer 1754 Chiari went to Modena as court poet to Francesco III. A return to the Venetian stage in 1760 was not a success, and it was at this point that he took to writing opera librettos, usually for Galuppi and Traetta. His most popular included *Il marchese villano*, set by Galuppi and later by Paisiello, Piccinni, Nasolini and others under a variety of titles, and *La sposa fedele* (though no contemporary published libretto carries an attribution to Chiari), later translated into German for performances in Vienna.

Alcimena principessa dell'Isole Fortunate o sia L' amore fortunato ne' suoi disprezzi (dramma), Galuppi, 1749; *Le nozze di Paride* (spettacolo poetico e musicale), Galuppi, 1756; *Cleopatra, regina d'Egitto* (pubd Venice, 1761); *La bella Girometta*, Bertoni, 1761; *Il caffè di campagna* (dg), Galuppi, 1761; *Il marchese villano* (dg), Galuppi, 1762 [many settings, some as Il marchese Tulipano, Il matrimonio inaspettato, La lavandara/lavandaia astuta, I raggiri fortunati] (comp. unknown, Milan, 1764, and Sinigaglia, 1764; N. Piccinni, 1772; Caruso, 1775; Perez, 1776; Paisiello, 1779; Nasolini, 1790 and 1795)

L' astrologa, N. Piccinni, 1762; *La donna Girandola*, S. Perillo, 1763; *La francese a Malghera*, Traetta, 1764; *L' ingannatore ingannato*, Bertoni, 1764; *Le serve rivali* (dg), Traetta, 1766; *La sposa fedele*, P. A. Guglielmi, 1767 or 1765; *Le donne sempre donne*, A. Lucchesi, 1767; *Amore in trappola*, Traetta, 1768; *Il carnovale*, A. Boroni, 1769 (M. Vento and F. Gassmann, 1771); *L'amore senza malizia*, B. Ottani, 1768; *Amor lunatico* (dg), Galuppi, 1770; *Le orfane svizzere*, Boroni, 1770; *Le contadine furlane*, Boroni, 1771; *Il ciarlatano in fiera* (dg), Gazzaniga, 1774

*

F. Stefani, ed.: 'Memorie per sevire all'istoria dell' inclita città di Venezia, di G. Zanetti', *Archivio veneto*, xxix (1885), 93–148
G. F. Sommi Picenardi: *Un rivale del Goldoni* (Milan, 1902)
G. G. Bernadi: 'L'opera comica veneziana del sec. xviii', *Atti dell' Accademia virgiliana di Mantova* (Mantua, 1908)
G. Ortolani: *Settecento: per una lettera dell' Ab. Chiari* (Venice, 1908)
——: 'Note in margine alla riforma goldoniana', *RIM*, i, (1940), 39–71
——: *La riforma del teatro nel settecento e altri scritti*, ed. G. Damerini (Venice, 1962)
E. Theil and G. Rohr: *Libretti: Verzeichnis der bis 1800 erschienen Textbücher* (Frankfurt, 1970)
P. Weiss: *Carlo Goldoni, Librettist: the Early Years* (diss., Columbia U., 1970)
C. Alberti: 'Pietro Chiari e il teatro europeo del settecento', *Un rivale di Carlo Goldoni, l' Abbate Chiari e il teatro europeo del settecento: Venice 1985*
R. Turchi: *Il teatro italiano*, iv: *la commedia del settecento*, i (Turin, 1987), 393ff
PATRICIA LEWY GIDWITZ

Chiarini, Pietro (*b* Brescia, early 18th century; *d* ?Cremona, after *c*1765). Italian composer. Fétis gave his birthdate as 1717. His activity as an opera composer is attested by the surviving librettos of works produced at Venice, Verona and Genoa from 1738 to 1746. A solitary libretto of 1754 places him at Cremona, as does the title of a keyboard sonata published in 1765. His collaboration with Goldoni in 1741–2 was first elucidated by Ortolani in his edition of Goldoni's complete works; Walker's further researches into the tangled history of *Il finto pazzo* and its later version *Amor fa l'uomo cieco* succeeded in establishing Chiarini's share in their music. Walker also concluded that the comic intermezzo *Il geloso schernito*, previously ascribed to Pergolesi (and published as such in the composer's complete works), was in fact by Chiarini; there can be no doubt that this is music of a later vintage, and of less importance, than Pergolesi's.

lost unless otherwise stated

Argenide (dramma per musica, A. Giusti), Venice, S Angelo, aut. 1738
Achille in Sciro (dramma per musica, 3, P. Metastasio), Venice, S Angelo, carn. 1739, aria *GB-Lbl*
Arianna e Teseo (after Pariati: *Teseo in Creta*), Brescia, 1739
Issipile (dramma per musica, Metastasio), Brescia, Erranti, carn. 1740
Statira (dramma per musica, C. Goldoni), Venice, S Samuele, May 1741
Il finto pazzo (int, Goldoni, after T. Mariani: *La contadina astuta*), perf. with Statira [rev. of G. B. Pergolesi: Livietta e Tracollo]; rev. as Amor fa l'uomo cieco (int), perf. with Artaserse
Artaserse (dramma per musica, 3, Metastasio), Verona, Accademia Filarmonica, carn. 1741–2, aria *I-Gl*
Ciro riconosciuto (dramma per musica, Metastasio), Verona, Accademia Filarmonica, carn. 1743
I fratelli riconosciuti (dramma per musica, ? after F. Silvani: *La verità nell'inganno*), Verona, Accademia Filarmonica, Jan 1743
Meride e Selinunte (dramma per musica, A. Zeno), Venice, S Giovanni Grisostomo, carn. 1743–4
Alessandro nell'Indie (dramma per musica, Metastasio), Verona, Accademia Filarmonica, carn. 1744–5
Il geloso schernito (int, 3), Venice, S Moisè, aut. 1746, *F-Pc* [wrongly attrib. Pergolesi], ed. in *Opera omnia di Giovanni Battista Pergolesi*, iii [iii/1] (1939)
Didone abbandonata (Metastasio), Brescia, Erranti, 1748; Cremona, private perf., carn. 1756
La donna dottoressa (int), Cremona, 1754

Music in: Ezio, Cremona, Nuovo, 1757

*

FétisB
G. Ortolani and others, eds.: *Carlo Goldoni: Opere complete*, xxvi (Venice, 1928), xxxiii (1934), xxxvii (1951)
F. Walker: 'Two Centuries of Pergolesi Forgeries and Misattributions', *ML*, xxx (1949), 297–320
——: 'Goldoni and Pergolesi', *MMR*, lxxx (1950), 200–05
A. G. Berti: *Cronistoria del Filarmonico* (Verona, 1963)
P. Weiss: *Carlo Goldoni, Librettist: the Early Years* (diss., Columbia U., 1970)
PIERO WEISS

Chicago. City in Illinois, ranked the third largest city in the USA. The history of opera in Chicago can be divided into two periods. From 1850 to 1910 opera was presented by touring companies, mostly from New York. Since 1910, with a few exceptions, opera has been produced by resident companies of which the oldest, the Lyric Opera of Chicago (founded 1954 as the Lyric Theatre), is artistically the most important. The Lyric operates from September to February in the Civic Opera House with an annual budget of nearly $20 million. A younger company, Chicago Opera Theatre (founded 1974), has a well-established audience for a spring season of opera in English, with an emphasis on works (many from the 20th century) best suited to a smaller theatre.

The first operatic performance in the city was in Rice's Theater on 29 July 1850, when a touring company of Eliza Brienti and Messrs Manvers and Guibel gave Bellini's *La sonnambula* with a hastily recruited local chorus and orchestra. The public responded enthusiastically, but the run ended on the second night when the theatre caught fire during the second act. Opera returned in 1853, and from 1858 onwards operatic performances were a regular part of the music calendar. By 1875 more than 60 operas had been heard in the city, many of them recent works. *La traviata*, for example, reached Chicago in 1859, six years after its Italian première. Gounod's *Faust* was first sung in 1864, and Wagner entered the repertory when *Tannhäuser* was performed in 1865. Light opera by British, French and Viennese composers was also popular. When in 1865 Crosby's Opera House opened with 3000 seats, Chicago had a theatre larger than La Scala. In addition to opera it housed concerts by Theodore Thomas and his touring orchestra. It was destroyed in 1871 when almost the entire city burnt to the ground. The theatres were quickly rebuilt, and opera resumed in 1872. With the opening of the Metropolitan Opera House in New York, troupes from that theatre began regular visits to Chicago in 1884.

In 1889 Chicago built essentially the first civic cultural centre in the USA: the Auditorium, at Michigan Avenue and Congress Street, a 4000-seat house intended for a resident symphony orchestra and an opera company, neither of which yet existed. The Chicago SO was founded by Thomas in 1891, but the Auditorium was seen as a western branch of the New York Metropolitan until the new century. Seasons of a month or more were offered, and the 1889 repertory included the first Chicago performance of Wagner's *Ring* cycle and Verdi's newest opera, *Otello*, with Francesco Tamagno.

From the beginning, Chicago has had an audience for opera that in its enthusiasm and dedication is unlikely to be surpassed anywhere in the world. Not surprisingly, after the founding of the orchestra there was demand for a resident opera company. The demise of Oscar Hammerstein's Manhattan Opera Company created an opportunity and made available some extraordinary artists, chief among them Mary Garden, who was to be a central figure in Chicago opera for 21 years. In autumn 1910 the first season of the Chicago Grand Opera Company, formed with the financier Harold McCormick as president and Cleofonte Campanini as musical director, presented her in *Pelléas et Mélisande*, *Louise* and *Salome* (all sung in French). A landmark in the Garden seasons was the première of Prokofiev's *The Love for Three Oranges* (in French, conducted by the composer) in 1921 during her one season as general director of the company.

Opera in Chicago from 1850 to 1910, and, in the case of touring companies, as late as the 1960s, was commercial theatre, mounted by an impresario with the expectation of making a profit. The concept of opera as a subsidized art form that cannot possibly pay its way dates from the first resident company. The primary reason for the change was a dramatic increase in production costs. Musicians and stagehands no longer worked for a pittance, the public demanded scenery and costumes better suited to the work at hand than stock items from a warehouse, and more and more opera called for the services of a stage director and, in consequence, more rehearsal time.

Between 1910 and 1946 there were some seven opera companies in the Chicago area (several of them successive names for the same, reorganized company). All shared artists with the Metropolitan and leading European theatres, all presented a diversified repertory and all ceased production because of financial difficulties. The first, already mentioned as the Chicago Grand Opera Company, gave performances in the Auditorium between 1910 and 1913. The Ravinia Opera began producing a summer opera festival in the suburb of Highland Park in 1912 and continued until the Depression forced closure after the 1931 season. In 1915, the Chicago Grand Opera Company was reorganized as the Chicago Opera Association and functioned in the Auditorium until 1921. Reorganized again as the Chicago Civic Opera, it presented seven more seasons in the Auditorium, in 1929 transferring to the new Civic Opera House at Madison Street and Wacker Drive, where it presented three seasons to 1931. The company was finally dissolved in 1932. The Auditorium, though abandoned by the resident companies in 1929, remained in use beyond its centenary, housing large musicals such as *The Phantom of the Opera*.

The second Chicago Grand Opera Company lasted three seasons in the new theatre, 1933–5, and was succeeded for the next four seasons by the Chicago City Opera Company. A final reorganization in 1940 produced the Chicago Opera Company, which gave six seasons in the Civic Opera House before its demise after the 1946 series. The Chicago SO took part in one fully staged operatic performance in 1947 but declined to become further involved in operatic activities, except for opera in concert form. From 1947 to 1953 the city was again dependent on imported opera, with frequent visits from both the New York City Opera and the Metropolitan.

The Civic Opera House at Madison Street and Wacker Drive, Chicago: drawing, 1928

In its earlier years, Chicago opera generally represented the most utilitarian aspect of 19th-century staging. From the 1930s to the 1960s it might be seen as a sort of living museum of the better aspects of the 19th-century theatre. But with the Lyric in the 1970s it moved fully into the 20th century, using the full resources of modern stagecraft.

The Lyric Theatre, renamed Lyric Opera of Chicago in 1956, was founded by Carol Fox, Lawrence V. Kelly and Nicola Rescigno. The success of two performances of *Don Giovanni* in February 1954 made an autumn season possible, which in turn attracted immediate attention by presenting the American début of Maria Callas, who came to the new company because it would pay higher fees than the Metropolitan. She sang in *Norma* on the opening night in November 1954, followed by *La traviata* and *Lucia di Lammermoor*. For the opening night of the second season in October 1955 she returned to sing *I puritani*, and continued with *Il trovatore* and her only stage appearances in *Madama Butterfly*. A reorganization put Fox in charge (Kelly and Rescigno continued their operatic careers in Dallas), and the company continued with Renata Tebaldi, Birgit Nilsson and Inge Borkh among its sopranos. Notable on the artists' roster of the early Lyric seasons were

Giulietta Simionato, Jussi Björling, Giuseppe Di Stefano, Tito Gobbi and Boris Christoff. Sir Georg Solti was principal conductor, 1956–7. Other memorable conductors of the early seasons were Artur Rodzinski, Tullio Serafin, Dimitri Mitropoulos, Josef Krips and Bruno Bartoletti, principal conductor from 1964 and later artistic director. It was essentially an Italian company (often called 'La Scala West'), with nearly 70% of its repertory Italian. Fox looked to Europe for her singers, establishing a tradition that continues of turning to Germany, Austria and Italy for new talent. As the Lyric progressed into the 1960s its repertory became more cosmopolitan. There is now nearly equal emphasis on all the major areas of operatic literature and a commitment to present more works by Americans and by 20th-century composers: Fox was succeeded by her associate Ardis Krainik in 1981, who demonstrated a dedication to artistic innovation. Her introduction of surtitles attracted thousands of new subscribers.

A critical factor in financing opera in the USA, where support from all levels of government may be less than 5% of the budget, is maintaining a reasonable balance between box-office income and contributions from private philanthropy. Since the early Chicago opera companies were dealing with a relatively small audience, there was a limit to box-office revenue. Two or three performances might exhaust the potential public for a work. If production costs were high, the demands on philanthropic support might be unreasonable. The Lyric Theatre began with the same pattern as its predecessors: in the 1955 season 16 works were prepared to fill a schedule of 25 performances, a disastrous formula. By 1963, its tenth season, the Lyric was selling 34 performances from a repertory of eight operas. The achievement of the Lyric was to retain the support of those who had traditionally been operagoers while recruiting a large number of middle-class subscribers with growing musical interests. By the 1980s ten or more performances of a popular opera were feasible and about 60% of the budget was generated by ticket sales. In the 35th season of the Lyric, 1989–90, with extraordinary casts in a repertory of eight works (including Jessye Norman in *Alceste*, Placido Domingo in *La fanciulla del West* and Anna Tomowa-Sintow in *Yevgeny Onegin*), every ticket for a series of 65 performances in a 3500-seat theatre was sold. The company's first commission of a new work from an American composer was William Bolcom's *McTeague*, after the novel by Frank Norris, for performance in autumn 1992.

*

F. Ffrench, ed.: *Music and Musicians in Chicago* (Chicago, 1899)

G. Upton: *Musical Memories: my Recollections of Celebrities of the Half-Century 1850–1900* (Chicago, 1908)

C. Hacket: *The Beginning of Grand Opera in Chicago* (Chicago, 1913)

E. C. Moore: *Forty Years of Opera in Chicago* (New York, 1930)

R. Davis: *Opera in Chicago: a Social and Cultural History* (New York, 1966)

C. Cassidy: *Lyric Opera of Chicago* (Chicago, 1979)

ROBERT C. MARSH

Chierici, Sebastiano. *See* CHERICI, SEBASTIANO.

Child performers. Opera does not readily lend itself to being sung by pre-adolescent children: their voices may sound sweet in church but are rarely strong enough to hold their own in a theatre among those of adults. Child characters are accordingly few and hard to cast: Yniold in *Pelléas et Mélisande*, whose childishness is insisted upon, usually sounds weak if sung by a treble, and looks buxom if by a woman; worse difficulties arise with the two important child characters in *The Turn of the Screw*, where Miles must be a treble and Flora a soprano older than the character. The Three Boys of *Die Zauberflöte* are in practice most often sung by women. Choruses of children are not uncommon: Act 1 of *Carmen* provides a well-known example.

Up to 1830–40, when orchestral writing in opera grew heavier, light voices could cope with many parts. Average life expectancy was about half that of today and young people started careers earlier. An opera début between 16 and 19 was common for women and, in Italy, for castratos, whose vocal development had not been interrupted by puberty. Some (such as Girolamo Crescentini) began as early as 13 or 14, but these were regarded as young adults. The cult of children in the theatre flowed from the new sense, identified with Rousseau, of childhood as a special and valuable stage. Spectacular 19th-century opera productions often used children as dancers or extras to rouse sentiment or amusement, whether the story called for them or not – a practice kept up by some modern opera houses even though the engagement of child performers is now strictly regulated by law, alternative casts have to be used and, in Britain, a children's adviser employed. These regulations had to be fought for over many years against the public's tendency to regard children as 'cute' without inquiring into their conditions of work.

A special case are the children's companies, mainly Italian, which between about 1790 and 1920 performed operas with all the parts sung by pre-pubertal children. Teacher-impresarios took on the children of poor families for whom even modest opera earnings outstripped what they could have got in other jobs. The companies performed mainly comic operas, but one at least put on *Rigoletto* and *Lucia di Lammermoor*. They toured successfully in Italy and the Americas, running their seasons like any other company except that the parts were shared out among more singers. No member of these troupes is known to have gone on to an adult career as a soloist.

*

J. Rosselli: '"Cuteness was All" – Operatic Shirley Temples', *Opera*, xl (1989), 30–34

JOHN ROSSELLI

Children's opera. Since medieval times children have participated in musical dramas, whether such involvement originated within a church, a school or, later, a theatrical context. This article primarily discusses the history and development of operas for children to perform, rather than works that are particularly suitable for children to watch, such as Humperdinck's *Hänsel und Gretel* or Menotti's *Help, Help, the Globolinks!* Because of the very close links between school music education and the writing and performing of operas for children, especially from the end of the 19th century onwards, much of the article is concerned with the later history of the genre.

1. Up to the late 19th century. 2. 20th century.

1. UP TO THE LATE 19TH CENTURY. At certain medieval festivals, choirboys in France and England would elect their own boy bishops and might enact their own *ludi theatrales*. Thus, church records of 1497 tell us that at St Martin of Tours, on the second day of Advent, masked 'innocentes' would go into the city, where farces, moralities and miracles would be played – certainly with

music. In Tudor times, choristers' masques were often played at court, the Children of Paul's appearing before Queen Elizabeth more often than any other company. In the mid-16th century, they and the Children of the Chapel Royal began to give regular performances in private theatres, and occasionally to visit the provinces, forming what were virtually professional companies. Many of the boys were also skilled instrumentalists and music played a vital part in their plays. The more elaborate were almost little operas, with songs, dramatic musical interludes, entr'actes and sometimes a final choral prayer. The last boys' company was dissolved in 1608.

During the 17th century French Jesuit colleges began to interpolate musical *intermèdes*, including ballets and vocal music, between the acts of the Latin plays performed at their biannual prizegivings. These were sung in French, and together formed independent music dramas based on themes related to those of the plays. *Le duel de la juste rigueur et la clémence*, composed by M. Intermet and staged at Avignon in 1622 in the presence of Louis XIII, was one of the first of a series of such school entertainments and has good claim to be considered as the first French opera of any description. The Collège Louis-le-Grand in Paris, which housed up to 3000 students, employed Marc-Antoine Charpentier, who composed many such *intermèdes* including *David et Jonathas* (1688), the music of which happily survives. Although these works were lavishly produced with the help of professional musicians and dancers, they were also true school operas, being designed in the first place 'de donner de la bonne grace' to the pupils and to interest their parents in the activities of the colleges.

In 17th-century England masques were occasionally presented at private schools. The music of James Shirley's *Cupid and Death* (*c*1656), and of Thomas Duffett's *Beauties Triumph* (?1676), written for a girls' boarding school in Chelsea, has vanished without trace. Purcell's *Dido and Aeneas*, which was first performed at Josias Priest's girls' school in Chelsea in the summer of 1689, is thus the first English school opera of which we have full knowledge. Whether or not it was originally intended for school use it is in many ways ideally suited for performance by children. The plot is simple and affecting, word-setting relates closely to the patterns of natural speech, and there are several short and simple solo parts with plenty of chorus work and many opportunities for lively action.

After the Italian operatic invasion and the commercialization of London's opera houses, the art of opera lost its aristocratic aura and gained a doubtful moral reputation. Perhaps for these reasons, no school operas seem to have been written or performed in England during the 18th or early 19th centuries, though adult operas or plays with music were occasionally performed privately with children's casts, in England and elsewhere. Thus, in 1731 Dryden's *Indian Emperor* was acted and sung by children at a party given for the ten-year-old Duke of Cumberland. In Austria, the Empress Maria Theresa's birthday was celebrated at Schönbrunn in 1751 with a children's performance of Giuseppe Bonno's *Il re pastore*. In the late 1770s Charles Dibdin wrote short all-sung operas for performance by children at the newly founded Royal Circus theatre; he also engaged and coached the children. However, his poor financial management soon doomed the enterprise. A few professional children's companies operated sporadically in various parts of Europe during the 18th and 19th centuries, and even in the 20th, performing works from the adult repertory. A children's company which presented *HMS Pinafore* and *The Pirates of Penzance* at the Savoy Theatre in London in the 1880s was soon disbanded. But the 48-strong Compagnia dei Lillipuziani, which left Italy in 1912, probably driven out by the pressure of social disapproval, was still working in South America in 1920, its repertory including *Tosca*, *Rigoletto*, *Lucia di Lammermoor* and *La traviata*.

2. 20TH CENTURY. In England, the Education Act of 1870 which made class singing compulsory in all state schools increased the demand for choral works suitable for school use. In the years that followed, the operas of Gilbert and Sullivan – tuneful, witty and free of all moral taint – restored the art to respectability and provided influential models for composers of school operas. By the early 1900s Novello, England's leading publisher of educational music, were advertising more than 50 school operettas as well as a number of 'cantatas with action'. Most had spoken dialogue; the longest ran for as much as an hour and a half and almost all advertised that orchestral parts could be hired. Some fairy-tale operas derive at several removes from Mendelssohn; but the strongest influence, on librettos and on music, was that of Gilbert and Sullivan, whose idiom Gustav Holst adopted wholesale in his school operetta *The Idea*. Several composers of repute (among them Frederic Cowen, Arthur Somervell, Walford Davies and Percy Fletcher) contributed to the repertory. Many of these operettas contain songs and ensembles or choruses of considerable if conventional charm, but the feebleness, facetiousness or complexity of their librettos would render most unperformable in a later age.

The development of new and enlightened teaching methods in experimental schools in the Weimar Republic opened the way for the children's operas of Hindemith, Weill and Egk, whose artistic philosophies led them to take the composition of didactic works for the schoolroom as seriously as their work for concert hall or opera house. Hindemith described his *Lehrstück* (1929) as a training work 'intended to implicate all people present in the actual performance and not in the first place to make any definite impression as a musical or literary utterance'. The order of pieces could be changed, omissions, transpositions and additions could be made. Some scandal was caused by a scene in which two clowns cure a giant of his aches and pains by sawing off his limbs; but in fact the plot is no more gruesome than those of some of the English fairy-tale operettas mentioned above. When composing *Wir bauen eine Stadt* (1930), Hindemith would go each day to the Berlin school which was to give the first performances and make a note of the children's suggestions, and declared that he had never had so hard a task or such uncompromising critics.

Weill's and Brecht's *Der Jasager* (1930) was similarly didactic in approach and was practically designed so that it could be performed in many alternative instrumentations. Here too the children's cooperation was invited, and Brecht provided an alternative ending for the opera at the suggestion of the students of the Karl-Marx School in Berlin, though Weill did not set this to music. By 1932 *Der Jasager* had been produced in more than 300 German schools. Weill's *Down in a Valley* (1948) is musically less remarkable; but its dramatic effectiveness and extreme practicality quickly established it as the most popular of all youth operas. In the USA alone it received over 6000 school performances in its first nine years.

In 1932 *Der Jasager* was performed at the Henry Street Settlement Music School in New York; in 1937 the same school staged the first American school opera of consequence, Copland's *The Second Hurricane*, which bears signs of Weill's influence, and which Copland was to play through to Britten when he visited England in the summer of 1939. Britten's lyrical and dramatic gifts, his ability to write original and personal music using the simplest formulae, his Purcellian feeling for verbal inflection, and his ability to enter into the child's world assure his unique position as composer of music for children. While *Wir bauen eine Stadt* is hardly more than a collection of action songs, characteristically Hindemithian but robustly designed for practical use, each of Britten's children's operas is a musico-dramatic entity, precisely conceived in a manner which allows no reshuffling of its constituent elements. Each of the three establishes its own distinct genre. In *The Golden Vanity* (1966), written for the fully professional Vienna Boys' Choir, children shoulder full responsibility for the performance and play adult roles. In the two other operas, children's voices form part of a wider timbral palette, and the diatonic innocence of their music is contrasted with the music of the adults' world. *The Little Sweep* (1949) calls for trained children of nerve and stamina who can hold their own alongside adult singers, while in *Noye's Fludde* (1958) only elementary skills are demanded of young singers and instrumentalists and little responsibility is placed on their shoulders.

In 1969 a children's opera company was established in Tashkent with 86 boy and girl singers, several Uzbek composers being enlisted to provide a repertory. In the West children's opera has received no such direct state support. But in the last 40 years the expansion of school music departments and growing public interest in opera have encouraged many distinguished British composers to enter the field. Almost as importantly, poets and playwrights of comparable status have sometimes provided librettos. Many lines of approach have been suggested (see John 1971), and many sub-species of children's opera have come into existence.

Among British school operas designed primarily for school use, the finely crafted works of Alan Bush and Richard Rodney Bennett deserve special mention. John Gardner, John McCabe and Stephen Oliver are among those who have composed operas or music-theatre works on a larger scale, often including parts for adults, for schools festivals and children's theatre groups. Herbert Chappell and Andrew Lloyd Webber pioneered the way for composers of jazz and pop opera and school musicals, while Jeremy James Taylor's *The Ballad of Salomon Pavey* even includes parts for a consort of early instruments. Malcolm Williamson's 'Cassations' are made up of a few quickly learned songs which can be put together to form an opera in the course of a morning's rehearsal. Henze's *Pollicino* includes parts for 20 'musically completely innocent' singers and for a number of equally innocent players; the children studied intensively for three months before the first performance in Montepulciano in 1980.

Composers who have written for particular groups include Peter Maxwell Davies, whose three children's operas were first performed by local schoolchildren in Kirkwall, Orkney (*The Two Fiddlers*, 1978, has become especially well known); and Alan Ridout, who composed several operas for the near-professional choirboys of Canterbury. Children at the specialist Purcell School have written, orchestrated and performed their own opera. At the other end of the spectrum, David Bedford and others have broken away from convention in their use of free notations which encourage improvisation, with parts for non-music-readers and for toy and home-made instruments. Several opera companies run school projects in which children, guided by professionals, create their own workshop operas; Nordoff's and Robbins's musical plays complement their own therapeutic work with severely afflicted children.

Many operas which never reach the publishers' lists are written by teachers or local composers working in closest touch with the performers, the success of such projects often depending less on the quality and originality of music and libretto than on the enthusiasm of teachers and commitment of children. Adult operas also form part of the school repertory. Gilbert and Sullivan operas have for long been staple fare in secondary schools; works as diverse as Gluck's *Alceste* and *My Fair Lady* have been performed with enthusiasm and understanding, while Weill's *Threepenny Opera* is more popular in English and American schools than *Der Jasager*.

Children's operas do not transpose readily from one environment to another. Even Copland's brilliant and individual *The Second Hurricane* is so American in spirit and in the language of its libretto as to be almost unperformable in Britain, though Jonathan Elkus is among those who have had success on both sides of the Atlantic. Yet the composers of viable school operas have some things in common. Copland said of his that 'the musical challenge ... was to see how simple I could be without losing my identity'; Weill, that 'simple music can only be written by the simple musician ... simple works are not minor works': words which apply equally to the children's operas of Purcell, Britten, and to a select few of their successors.

See also CHILD PERFORMERS.

*

E. K. Chambers: *The Medieval Stage* (Oxford, 1903), 347ff

'Aktuelle Zwiegespräch zwischen Kurt Weill und Dr Hans Fischer', *Die Musikpflege*, i (1930), 48–52; trans. in K. H. Kowalke: *Weill in Europe* (Ann Arbor, 1979), 520–27

W. Mellers: 'Music for 20th-Century Children', *MT*, cv (1964), 342–5, 421–7, 500–05

R. W. Lowe: *Marc-Antoine Charpentier et l'opéra de collège* (Paris, 1966)

M. Shapiro: *Children of the Revels: the Boy Companies of Shakespeare's Time and their Plays* (New York, 1967)

H. Cole: 'Music (and especially Opera) for Children', *MT*, cxii (1971), 849–50

M. John, ed.: *Music Drama in Schools* (Cambridge, 1971)

H. W. Henze: '*Pollicino*: an Opera for Children', *MT*, cxxi (1980), 766–8

J. Rosselli: '"Cuteness was All" – Operatic Shirley Temples', *Opera*, xl (1989), 30–34

HUGO COLE

Chile. In contrast with other Latin American nations, where the capitals monopolized operatic life, in Chile the second largest city and chief seaport, Valparaíso, was visited by almost as many touring companies up to 1900 as was the capital, Santiago. *L'inganno felice*, sung in the 'Teatro de la calle de San Juan de Dios núm. 8' at Valparaíso on 26 April 1830 by a travelling Italian troupe headed by Domenico Pezzoni, inaugurated the Rossini vogue in Chile. *La gazza ladra* followed on 16 May, and between June 1830 and February 1831 the same troupe gave these and five more Rossini operas in the Teatro Principal at Santiago, following them with works by Mercadante and Paini.

The next Italian company, directed by Rafael Pantanelli, arrived from Lima in May 1844. During its first two seasons at Santiago it offered nine operas by Donizetti, seven by Bellini, five by Rossini and one each by Luigi Ricci and Pacini. In 1847 Pantanelli's company performed at the newly erected Teatro de la Victoria in Valparaíso, scheduling for 18 September the première of the first opera composed in Chile, *Telésfora*, with both libretto (in Spanish) and music by the Bavarian-born Aquinas Ried. Because of difficulties with the language the performance was first postponed and then cancelled. In 1860 Ried composed a second opera, *Il granatiere*, this time to an Italian libretto, and in 1868 the first act of a third, *Diana* (in Spanish). After 18 months at Valparaíso, members of Pantanelli's company went to Copiapó, where they performed operas by Bellini and Donizetti in an elegant theatre built in 1847.

In 1850 a company from Lima headed by Antonio Neumane arrived at Valparaíso, where it gave first performances in Chile of operas by Auber, Donizetti, Nicolai, Ricci, Gualtiero Sanelli and Verdi. Throughout the rest of the 19th century and into the 20th Chile continued to receive visiting troupes, but native singers began to appear more often with them. In 1861 the contralto Isabel Martínez de Escalante, a native of Valparaíso, joined the company that visited Chile that year. Another notable Chilean opera singer, also from Valparaíso, was the soprano Rosita Jacoby, who sang in Italy before returning to South America, and later Chileans who won fame abroad include Renato Zanelli, Nazzareno de Angelis, Carlo Galeffi and Ramón Vinay, who sang at the Metropolitan Opera, New York, before making his Santiago début in 1948.

The first Mozart opera to be performed in Chile was *Don Giovanni*, on 18 October 1870 in Santiago; Wagner entered the repertory with *Lohengrin* (in Italian) in 1885. It was not until ten years later that an opera by a native Chilean was seen, *La florista de Lugano* by Eliodoro Ortiz de Zárate; its libretto, like that of his *Lautaro* (1902), was in Italian. In 1904 Remigio Acevedo, a native of Santiago, returned after two years' study at Milan with a three-act opera, *Caupolicán*, but this did not receive its première until 1942, 31 years after the composer's death.

Meanwhile Italian companies continued to dominate the operatic stage in Chile, and in 1911 Mascagni conducted his *Iris* and other operas in Santiago and Valparaíso. An opera season was put on by a group of Chileans at the Teatro Unión Central in Santiago in 1922, but only isolated attempts were made to perform native works. These include Próspero Bisquert's *Sayeda* (1929), Pablo Garrido's *La sugestión* (1961) and Roberto Puelma's *Ardid de amor*, given its première at the Teatro Municipal, Santiago, in 1972, 16 years after its composition.

For further information on operatic life in the country's principal centre *see* SANTIAGO.

*

J. Zapiola: *Recuerdos de treinta años (1810–1840)* (Santiago, 1872–4, 6/1928)
R. Hernández Cornejo: *Los primeros teatros en Valparaíso* (Valparaíso, 1928)
E. Pereira Salas: *Los orígenes del arte musical en Chile* (Santiago, 1941)
D. Quiroga: 'Aspectos de la ópera en Chile en el siglo XIX', *Revista musical chilena*, nos.25–6 (1947), 6–13
E. Pereira Salas: 'El centenario del Teatro municipal', *Revista musical chilena*, no.52 (1957), 30–35
——: *Historia de la música en Chile, 1850–1900* (Santiago, 1957)
'Opera', *Revista musical chilena*, no.78 (1961), 88–9
M. Cánepa Guzmán: *La ópera en Chile (1839–1930)* (Santiago, 1976)
S. Claro-Valdés: *Oyendo a Chile* (Santiago, 1979)

ROBERT STEVENSON

Chimenti [Chementi], **Margherita** ['La Droghierina'] (*b* Rome; *fl* 1734–46). Italian soprano. She sang male parts in operas by Pergolesi and Leo in Naples (1734–5) and appeared in an opera at Venice (1736). She spent two seasons at the King's Theatre in London (1736–8), first with the Opera of the Nobility, then with Heidegger and Handel, again generally in male roles, making her début in Hasse's *Siroe* and appearing in operas by Broschi, Pescetti, Veracini and Duni. She created the parts of Adolfo in Handel's *Faramondo* and Atalanta in *Serse*, and appeared in two pasticcios, one of them Handel's *Alessandro Severo*. Mrs Pendarves called her 'a tolerable good woman with a pretty voice'. Her Handel parts indicate a limited technique and the compass (*c♯′* to *d″*) of a mezzo-soprano. After leaving London she sang at Livorno (1739–40), Florence (1741 and 1743–4, when Horace Mann considered her 'not worth hearing'), in three operas in Venice in 1741–2, and in Duni's *Catone in Utica* in Naples in 1746. WINTON DEAN

China. Piccinni's first biographer, P. L. Guinguené, writing in 1801, reported with some reservations that a production of *La buona figliuola* had been given by Italian Jesuits at the imperial court in Beijing (Peking) before 1778. If that is true, it was the first Western opera heard in China. After the Treaty of Nanking (1842), Europeans and Americans began establishing themselves in the international concessions in Shanghai, which rapidly became the leading banking and commercial centre of China. The American soprano Emma Eames was born in 1865 in Shanghai, the daughter of an American lawyer practising there. Two European-style theatres, the Lyceum and the larger Olympic, were built there in the latter half of the 19th century. In 1883–4 C. Daron, director of the Saigon Opera, took his troupe to perform in Shanghai; according to the *Gazzetta musicale di Milano*, Donizetti's *La fille du régiment* was performed in 1898. Pollard's Lilliputian Opera Company performed there at least twice, in 1897 and 1903. In October 1919 the Russian Grand Opera Company gave a six-week season that began at the Lyceum and transferred to the Olympic; altogether 19 operas (probably all sung in Russian) were given, including *Lakmé*, *The Queen of Spades*, Rubinstein's *The Demon*, *La Juive*, *The Tsar's Bride* and many works from the Italian repertory. Other touring companies that appeared in Shanghai included Carpi's Italian Grand Opera Company, which gave a ten-day season at the Olympic in 1923, and the Gonsalez brothers' Italian Opera Company, which performed at the Olympic in 1925.

The Central Opera was formed in Beijing in 1958. This company, closely associated with the Beijing Conservatory (devoted to Western music), performs only Western-style opera, not traditional Chinese Beijing Opera. Its productions have included *Madama Butterfly* (1958), *Moloda hvardiya* ('The Young Guard') by the Ukrainian composer Yuly Meytus, the comic opera

Arshin mal alan ('The Travelling Salesman') by the Azerbaijani composer Uzeir Hajibeyov, the operetta *The Little Spotted Calf* by the Hungarian Otto Vinize and *La traviata* (in a production based on old Russian photographs and documents), as well as patriotic works by local composers – *The Red Guard on the March*, *Youth of Today* and *Strong Lust in the Royal Family*. All works are sung in Chinese.

In 1981, under a Franco-Chinese cultural agreement, the French conductor Jean Périsson, who had re-formed the Beijing SO and the Shanghai SO together with René Terrasson, the director of the Strasbourg Opera, and with Jacqueline Brumaire as répétiteur, prepared a new production of *Carmen*, translated into Mandarin Chinese by Sun Hui-shuang. There were three alternating Chinese casts. Ai-Lan Zhu, who later sang Pamina at Glyndebourne (1990, 1991), was a member of the Central Opera and among those who sang Micaëla. The first performance took place on 1 January 1982 at the Bridge of Heaven Theatre, where the company performs along with a number of other dramatic troupes. 24 more performances followed, principally for the Chinese musical and theatre milieux. A further 38 were given in 1985–6, conducted by Zheng Xiao, China's first woman conductor. In autumn 1986 the production toured to Hangzhou and Shanghai; it was relayed by Chinese Television and Radio and commercially recorded. A second Franco-Chinese production, of Gounod's *Roméo et Juliette*, planned for 1983–4, failed to materialize. In 1986 Gino Bechi directed *Gianni Schicchi* and *La bohème* for the Central Opera. *La belle Hélène* was given by another Western-style company, Shanghai Opera, on 5 March 1986 at the Meigi Theatre during the third Shanghai Festival.

In 1987 the Beijing Central Opera made its first visit abroad, to Japan, and in 1988 presented *Madama Butterfly* and *Carmen*, with its own orchestra, at the Lyric Theatre of the Academy of the Performing Arts during the Hong Kong Festival. *Carmen* was praised by audiences and critics but *Butterfly* was not. In 1988 too the company made its European début at the Savonlinna Festival in Finland, presenting *Madama Butterfly* with Li Dan-dan in the title role; the company's orchestra was conducted by the German-trained Tang Muhai.

*

C. Pitt: 'Opera in China', *Opéra international* (forthcoming)

CHARLES PITT

Chinzer [Chintzer, Ghinzer, Kinzer], **Giovanni** (*b* Florence, 18 Sept 1698; *d* after 1749). Italian composer. The word 'corazza' (cuirassier), used in connection with his name, suggests a link between his family (of German origin) and the Swiss Guard of the Grand Duke of Tuscany. On 13 December 1719 he joined a company of Florentine musicians. His activity as an opera composer and impresario was mostly in Florence, at the Cocomero theatre, and in other Tuscan cities (Lucca, Pisa and Pistoia). After 1738 he is described in some librettos as 'professore di tromba' by imperial appointment, and after 1743 as 'maestro di cappella della Real Brigata de' Carabinieri di Sua Maestà Cattolica'. The publication of his instrumental music in Paris around 1750 suggests that he was in France at that time. His name is linked especially with comic opera: he continued the tradition of Florentine *commedia per musica* until its popularity was supplanted by the Neapolitan variety.

La serva favorita (G. C. Villifranchi), Florence, Cocomero, carn. 1727
Amor vince l'odio ovvero Timocrate [Act 1] (A. Salvi), Florence, Cocomero, carn. 1731 [Acts 2 and 3 by L. Bracci]
La commedia in commedia (?Vanneschi), Florence, Cocomero, aut. 1731
La vanità delusa (? F. Vanneschi), Florence, Cocomero, aut. 1731
Pimpinone (scherzo drammatico, rev. Vanneschi), Florence, Abbozzati, 1735
Il Temistocle (P. Metastasio), Pisa, Pubblico, carn. 1737
Chi non sa fingere non sa godere, Florence, Cocomero, carn. 1738
La contadina nobile (int), Pisa, Pubblico, sum. 1741
Atalo (F. Silvani), Venice, S Cassiano, carn. 1742; rev. as La verità nell'inganno, Munich, aut. 1747
Demofoonte (dm, Metastasio), Rimini, Pubblico, spr. 1743 [recits. only]
Arias in *A-Wn*, *B-Bc*, *F-Pa*, Pn and *GB-Lbl*

*

DBI (B. M. Antolini)
L. Nerici: *Storia della musica in Lucca* (Lucca, 1880)
A. Segré: *Il Teatro Pubblico di Pisa nel seicento e nel settecento* (Pisa, 1902)
A. Chiappelli: *Storia del teatro in Pistoia dalle origini alla fine del secolo XVIII* (Pistoia, 1913)
A. Pellegrini: *Spettacoli lucchesi nel secoli XVII–XIX* (Lucca, 1914)
R. L. Weaver and N. W. Weaver: *A Chronology of Music in the Florentine Theater*, i: *1590–1750* (Detroit, 1978)

FRANCESCO GIUNTINI

Chiocchetti, Pietro Vincenzo (*b* Lucca, 1680; *d* Lucca, 2 Feb 1753). Italian composer. Between 1710 and 1722 there were at least five different performances of his sacred works in Lucca; after this his musical activity there seems to have ceased, beginning again in 1741 after the performance of his opera *Solone*. His music was also heard in Venice, Bologna and above all Genoa, where between 1724 and 1740 there were at least 23 performances of his operas and oratorios in the two theatres, the S Agostino and the Falcone, and in the church of S Filippo Neri. In addition, Chiocchetti is listed as *direttore della musica* of S Agostino in a libretto of the opera *Arrenione* (1724). Perhaps on this evidence, Gerber and others have attributed the music to Chiocchetti; in his capacity as *maestro al cembalo* he could have composed some of its arias. Except for two arias, only the librettos remain as evidence of his prolific activity in opera and oratorio.

dm – *dramma per musica*

L'ingratitudine castigata [Alarico] (dm, 3, F. Silvani), Ancona, Fenice, 1719; rev. Genoa, Falcone, aut. 1726, lib. *I-Bc*, *SA*
Ricimero (dm), Genoa, S Agostino, aut. 1724, lib. *SA*
L'impresario delle Canarie (int, P. Metastasio), Genoa, S Agostino, carn. 1726
Partenope (dm), Genoa, S Agostino, carn. 1726, lib. *Mb*, *SA*
Andromaca (dm, 3, A. Zeno), Reggio Emilia, Pubblico, April 1726, lib. *Bc*, *MOe*, *Vgc*, *Vnm*
? Artaserse (dm, 3, Metastasio), Genoa, S Agostino, spr. 1730
L'innocenza giustificata (Silvani), Genoa, Falcone, aut. 1731
La clemenza di Tito (dm, 3, Metastasio), Genoa, S Agostino, ? carn. 1735; Genoa, Falcone, sum. 1736, lib. *US-Wc*
Demofoonte (dm, 3, Metastasio), Genoa, Falcone, 1735, lib. *I-Vgc* [according to Giazotto, perf. S Agostino, carn. 1735]
Solone (dm, 2), Lucca, Corte, 1741, lib. *Rsc*, *Vgc*, *US-Wc* [for the renovation of the Comizi of the Serenissima Repubblica di Lucca; according to Sonneck (1914), collab. G. Puccini and D. Pierotti]

Doubtful: Arrenione (3, Silvani), Genoa, aut. 1724, lib. *I-SA*; La Griselda (dm, 3, ? Zeno), Genoa, Falcone, spr. 1728, lib. *Mb*

*

AllacciD; *GerberL*; *GerberNL*
L. Nerici: *Storia della musica in Lucca* (Lucca, 1879), 276, 293, 299, 365, 373
R. Giazotto: *La musica a Genova nella vita pubblica e privata dal XIII al XVIII secolo* (Genoa, 1951), 333–4
C. Bongiovanni: *Il fondo musicale dell'archivio capitolare del duomo di Genova* (Genoa, 1990), 34–9

CARMELA BONGIOVANNI

Chiodi, Buono Giuseppe (*b* Salò, Lombardy, 20 Jan 1728; *d* Santiago, 7 Sept 1783). Italian composer, active in Spain. A priest, he was apparently *maestro di cappella* at Bergamo Cathedral when he was appointed to the equivalent post at Santiago di Compostela in 1769. Besides numerous sacred works, he wrote at least two operas, *De las glorias de España la de Santiago es la mejor* (1773) and *La birba* (1774). Nothing survives of the first, a kind of oratorio or 'poema sacro-melodramático' to a libretto by Amo y García de Lois. *La birba*, in three acts, was composed for the feast of St James the Apostle, and from surviving parts (in *E-SC*) it was evidently a comic opera, possibly the first ever performed in Santiago. The many arias and eloquent duets are particularly brilliant and carry the whole action; the few recitatives that survive are unusually elaborate for the time. M. PILAR ALEN

Chishko, Oles' [Olexander] **Semenovych** (*b* Dvurchnyy Kut, nr Kharkiv, 20 June/2 July 1895; *d* Leningrad [now St Petersburg], 4 Dec 1976). Ukrainian composer and singer. He studied composition and singing in Kharkiv and had already written two operas before he enrolled in 1930 at the Leningrad Conservatory, where his composition teacher was Pyotr Ryazanov. From 1926 to 1931 he sang (tenor) in the opera theatres of Kharkiv, Odessa and Kiev and, with the exception of the war years, from 1931 to 1948 he was in the Maliy theatre company and the Philharmonic Society in Leningrad. In 1944–5 and from 1948 to 1965 he taught composition at the Leningrad Conservatory.

As an opera composer, Chishko was drawn to heroic and revolutionary themes. He is best known for *Bronenosets 'Potyomkin'* ('The Battleship Potyomkin'), based on the same incident during the abortive 1905 Russian revolution as Eisenstein's famous film. Begun in the early 1930s at the request of the Academic Theatre of Opera and Ballet, Odessa, it was produced by a creative 'brigade' at the Kirov Theatre between 1933 and its première in 1937. Chishko's assured lyrical skills produced a tuneful, folk-based work in the vein of the period Socialist realist 'song opera', although his work suffered from a lack of convincing musical characterization, symphonic development and dramatic conviction. Nonetheless, the opera was widely performed; the subject matter and the lyrical writing contributed to its reputation as one of the most popular early Soviet operas on a revolutionary theme.

Yudif' [Judith] (3, Chishko), open rehearsal, Novorossiysk, L. V. Kichi Vocal Studio, 25 June 1923
V plenu u yablon' [In the Captivity of the Apple-Trees] (5, Chishko, after I. Dniprovsky), Odessa, 8 April 1931
Bronenosets 'Potyomkin' [The Battleship Potyomkin] (4, S. D. Spassky), Leningrad, Kirov, 21 June 1937; rev. (V. F. Chulisov), Leningrad, Maliy, 30 Dec 1955
Doch' Kaspiya [The Caspian Daughter], 1942
Makhmud Tarabi (4, Aybek [M. Tashmukhammedov]), Tashkent, Uzbek Theatre, 25 Dec 1944
Lesya i Danila [Lesya and Danila], 1958
Irkutskaya istoriya [The Irkutsk Story], 1961, inc.
Soperniki [The Rivals], 1964 LAUREL E. FAY

Chisholm, Erik (*b* Glasgow, 4 Jan 1904; *d* Cape Town, 8 June 1965). Scottish conductor and composer. He studied with Herbert Walton and Lev Pouishnoff, and at the Scottish Academy of Music from 1918 to 1920. In the late 1920s he toured Canada and the USA as a pianist, before returning to study composition with Tovey at Edinburgh University. Always an ardent and energetic promoter of new music, he founded the Active Society for the Propagation of Contemporary Music (1929). As conductor of the Glasgow Grand Opera Society (1930–39) he presented, semi-professionally, many British premières (*Les Troyens*, *Béatrice et Bénédict*, *Idomeneo*), and during these years he also founded the Barony Opera Society. He spent the war years as conductor of the Carl Rosa Opera company (1940) and was then musical director of the Entertainments National Services Association (ENSA) for South East Asia.

In 1946 Chisholm was appointed director of the South African College of Music at the University of Cape Town. There he founded the University Opera Company (1951) and the University Opera School (1954), both under the direction of the baritone Gregorio Fiasconaro. Chisholm and Fiasconaro gave great impetus to opera in South Africa: productions (usually conducted by Chisholm) included the premières of Joubert's *Silas Marner* and of Chisholm's own *Dark Sonnet*, *The Inland Woman* and *The Pardoner's Tale*, as well as many South African premières. A tour of Britain under Chisholm (1956–7) included the British stage première of Bartók's *Bluebeard's Castle*.

A prolific composer, Chisholm used Celtic forms and idioms in much of his earlier work; later he sometimes incorporated aspects of Hindu music into his moderately dissonant style. Probably it was as an opera composer that he produced his best work: this is particularly evident in the trilogy *Murder in Three Keys* and in the three acts that constitute *Canterbury Tales*. The latter is arguably his best stage work and a good example of his dramatic flair. In it he used a free modification of Schoenberg's 12-note technique and ingeniously incorporated Ars Nova devices and adaptations of 14th-century tunes. He prepared his own librettos for all his operas. His writings include *The Operas of Leoš Janáček* (Oxford, 1971).

librettos by the composer

The Feast of Samhain (comic op, 3, after J. Stephen), 1941
The Inland Woman, 1951 (1, after M. Lavin), Cape Town, 21 Oct 1953
Murder in Three Keys (trilogy), New York, Cherry Lane, 6 July 1954
Dark Sonnet (1, after E. O'Neill: *Before Breakfast*), Cape Town, 20 Oct 1952
Black Roses (1, after T. S. Eliot), New York, Cherry Lane, 6 July 1954
Simoon (1, after A. Strindberg), New York, Cherry Lane, 6 July 1954
Canterbury Tales (3, after G. Chaucer)
Act 1 The Wyf of Bathes Tale, 1962
Act 2 The Pardoner's Tale, Cape Town, Little, Nov 1961
Act 3 The Nonnes Preestes Tale, 1961
The Importance of being Earnest (3, after O. Wilde), 1963
The Midnight Court (ballad op, after B. Merryman)
The Wolfings (3, after W. Morris)

*

G. Pulvermacher: 'Chaucer into Opera', *Opera*, xiii (1962), 187–8
K. Wright: 'Erik Chisholm: a Tribute', *Composer*, no.17 (1965), 34–5 CAROLINE MEARS, JAMES MAY

Chi soffre speri [*L'Egisto, ovvero Chi soffre speri* ('Egisto, or Who Suffers May Hope')]. *Commedia musicale* in three acts by VIRGILIO MAZZOCCHI and MARCO MARAZZOLI to a libretto by GIULIO ROSPIGLIOSI after Giovanni Boccaccio's *Il decamerone* (book 9); Rome, Palazzo Barberini, 12 February 1637 (revised version, Rome, Teatro Barberini, 27 February 1639).

An impoverished Italian nobleman, Egisto (soprano), hopes to win the hand of a rich widow, Alvida (soprano), who has an ailing son. Egisto proves his love for her by destroying his family tower, for which Alvida has expressed dislike, and by sacrificing his beloved hunting falcon to be the main course of a dinner he prepares for her. In the ruins of the tower is found a cache of jewels, which restores Egisto's wealth. In the falcon is found a curative bloodstone that restores the health of Alvida's son. While Egisto is trying to please Alvida, one of her young servants, Lucinda, disguised as a man, Armindo (soprano), tries to discourage him, because she loves Egisto herself. She in turn, in her disguise, is being amorously pursued by a young lady, Eurilla (soprano). As Alvida looks more and more favourably on Egisto, Lucinda/Armindo despairs and attempts suicide. Fortunately she does not succeed, and the crisis reveals her to be Egisto's long-lost sister, restored to him with the family fortune. Egisto gains a sister as well as a wife.

Supporting the principal characters through their tribulations are a host of servants and friends, most notably Zanni (tenor) and Coviello (tenor) from Egisto's household. They are stock, masked characters from the Italian *commedia dell'arte*, along with their two little boys (in the 1639 version), Colello and Fritellino (both sopranos). They contrast Boccaccio's suburban tale of love and courtship with their impertinent dialect joking and emotional exaggerations, and spout folk proverbs and puns as well as literary quotations and sing popular songs. They advise Egisto about his strategies to win Alvida, stagger about complaining of hunger, trick cheese from a shepherd and weep for the falcon. In the 1639 version, they dominate the first two *intermedi*, especially the second, which represents an open-air market in the town of Farfa, where Zanni and Coviello have gone to shop. 'La fiera di Farfa' is basically a festive, scenic madrigal for ten voices of merchants and shopkeepers hawking their wares. (Some were apparently actual merchants of slippers, hats and dolls, whose lines were sung behind the set.) During a dance a scuffle breaks out and is resolved as market day draws to a close with the setting sun, a theatrical effect engineered by Gian Lorenzo Bernini.

Zanni and Coviello, who have entered opera from another social sphere, serve as the lively link between the nobility and townspeople of the romantic plot and the *rustici* or ordinary folk who populate the opera. The emotional focus of the drama, however, is on the disguised Lucinda, unhappy throughout, who has an expressive solo scene in each act.

* * *

Critics have long considered *Chi soffre speri* to be one of the precursors of later *opera buffa*. This is partly because of the presence of the comic servants in 20 of the 35 scenes, although they are not involved in a subplot of their own. The libretto was not the first for Rome on a secular subject, but it was one of the earliest to discard pagan mythology and characters as well as the apparatus of stage magic and machinery expected for gods and sorceresses. At the same time, the chorus, the staple of ancient tragedy and Renaissance pastorale, disappears. The lack of a chorus, perhaps more than the inclusion of comedians, places the libretto in the comic genre. Although *Chi soffre speri* was not the first opera in Rome with dialect-speaking, comic characters (that honour belongs to Castelli's *Primavera urbana*, 1635), it was the earliest for which the music (the 1639 version) has survived.

The greatest part of the opera is in recitative dialogue; examples of recitative in *Chi soffre speri* by Mazzocchi and Marazzoli have been cited as foreshadowing later *recitativo secco*. The text setting, however, is not so much 'dry' as imitative of ordinary speech, as opposed to the highly poetic or theatrical declamation elicited in earlier opera. In this, the music signals a trend towards increased stage naturalism. One result is a distinct reduction in the lyricism of the recitative; another is the emergence of musical characterization in the style of recitative 'speech'. This is made possible by the differences in social status of the cast. All characters sing repeated notes over sustained bass notes, but Zanni's manner is more singsong (ex.1), while Egisto's loftier

['After (the falcon) was buried, I felt like sugaring pastries, which I did with my own hands in an instant!']

speech reflects his upper-class locution and more coherent language (ex.2). The Farfa vendors offer

['What tricks do you have in store? Why won't there ever be peace for me, Fortune inexorable and proud?']

musical versions of their cries (ex.3). The duets and songs, while expressive, are largely *divertimenti* and do not attempt to reveal the personal feelings of the characters. They cluster at the beginnings of Acts 2 and 3 since the ends of these acts have swift turns of events that only in later opera could be unified musically by the ensemble finale.

Ex.3

(a)

['Chick peas! Chick peas! a pastime . . .']

(b)

['Straw hats! Straw hats!']

The 1639 *intermedi* to *Chi soffre speri* survive and are noteworthy because they are connected to the acts. Zanni, Coviello and Fritellino appear in the first two; Clori (from Act 3) and Eurilla are named in the third. In each case, characters present in the last scene of each act make a natural transition into the *intermedio*. The *intermedi* included dances and special imitations of nature (rain, hail, sunrise and sunset) as well as the only scene change, to the market at Farfa. Despite their clearly pastoral nature, they were also performed between the acts of the other Barberini opera of the 1639 season, Mazzocchi's *San Bonifatio*, set not in medieval Italy but in early Christian Rome. MARGARET MURATA

Chivot, Henri Charles (*b* Paris, 13 Nov 1830; *d* Paris, 19 Sept 1897). French librettist. With Alfred Duru, and occasionally others, Chivot wrote over 40 librettos for light operas and *opérettes* at the height of the Parisian operetta. Of these, the ones that have held their place in the French repertory most successfully are Offenbach's *La fille du tambour-major*, Audran's *Le grand Mogol* and *La mascotte* and Lecocq's *Les cent vierges*. The duet for the turkey-girl and the shepherd, 'J'aime bien mes dindons' from *La mascotte*, with its imitation turkey-gobbling noises, remains one of the most effective moments in all *opérette*.

selective list from over 40 works, all with Alfred Duru

Le carnaval d'un merle blanc, Lecocq, 1860; *Fleur-de-thé*, Lecocq, 1868; *L'île de Tulipatan*, Offenbach, 1868; *Le rajah de Mysore*, Lecocq, 1869; *Les cent vierges* (with Clairville), Lecocq, 1872; *Les braconniers*, Offenbach, 1873; *La blanchisseuse de Berg-op-Zoom*, Vasseur, 1875; *Le grand Mogol*, Audran, 1877; *Madame Favart*, Offenbach, 1878; *Les noces d'Olivette*, Audran, 1879; *La fille du tambour-major*, Offenbach, 1879; *La mascotte*, Audran, 1880; *La princesse des Canaries*, Lecocq, 1883; *La cigale et la fourmi*, Audran, 1886; *Surcouf*, Planquette, 1887; *La petite fronde*, Audran, 1888; *La fille à Cacolet*, Audran, 1889

*

StiegerO

E. N. Stoullig and E. Stoullig: *Les annales du théâtre et de la musique* (Paris, 1875) PATRICK O'CONNOR

Chlubna, Osvald (*b* Brno, 22 June 1893; *d* Brno, 30 Oct 1971). Czech composer. He studied at the Czech Technical College (1911–13) and the Commerical Academy (1913–14), then at the Brno Organ School with Janáček (1914–15) and in Janáček's master classes (1923–4). Until 1953 he earned his living as a bank clerk; he also taught at the conservatory (1919–35, 1953–9) and at the Janáček Academy (1956–8), and was active in various musical organizations.

Chlubna's music is lyrical and reflective, stimulated by nature and celebrating the working life of contemporary man. After a transitional phase influenced by the musical developments of around 1930, Chlubna developed into a romantic figure, the essence of his art lying in a sense of serenity expressed with great warmth. He favoured larger forms (including symphonic cycles, which show his best work) and, although he did not have an outstanding dramatic gift, he strove throughout his life to compose operas. Of his stage works the first, a conversation piece, *Pomsta Catullova* ('Catullus's Revenge', 1917), won a certain acclaim, as did the amorous and accessible comedy *Freje pana z Heslova* ('The Affairs of the Lord of Heslov', 1940) and the comedy *Kolébka* ('The Cradle', 1952).

An outstanding orchestrator, Chlubna was responsible for the scoring of the last act of Janáček's first opera, *Šárka*, and with Bakala he prepared *From the House of the Dead* for its première in 1930, supplying the opera with an optimistic ending. Criticized for this arrangement, Chlubna clarified his approach in *Opery Leoše Janáčka na brněnské scéně* ('Janáček's Operas in the Brno Theatre'; ed. V. Nosek, Brno, 1958). Chlubna's multi-volume work on Janáček's style in relation to European 20th-century music remains in MS.

Pomsta Catullova [Catullus's Revenge] op.4, 1917 (1, J. Vrchlický), Brno, Provincial, 30 Nov 1921; rev. version, 1959

Alladina a Palomid čili Síla touhy [Alladina and Palomid, or The Power of Desire] op.16, 1921–2 (3, after M. Maeterlinck), Brno, Provincial, 31 Jan 1925

Ňura op.31, 1928–30 (2, Chlubna, after O. Dymov), Brno, 30 May 1932

V den počátku [In the Day of the Beginning] op.43 (1, Chlubna, after A. Hartley), Brno, Provincial, 1935

Freje pana z Heslova [The Affairs of the Lord of Heslov] op.53, 1939 (3, Chlubna, after F. L. Stroupežnický: *Paní mincmistrová*), Brno, Provincial, 1949

Jiří z Kunštátu a Poděbrad [Jiří of Kunštát and Poděbrady] op.52, 1942 (3, Chlubna, after Jirásek: *Maryla*), unperf.

Kolébka [The Cradle] op.81 (3, Chlubna, after Jirásek), 1953

Eupyros op.98 (3, Chlubna), unperf.

*

J. Racek: *Leoš Janáček a současní moravští skladatelé* [Janáček and Contemporary Moravian Composers] (Brno, 1940)

L. Kundera: 'Osvald Chlubna', *České umění dramatické*, ed. J. Hutter and Z. Chalabala (Prague, 1941), 359–62 JAN TROJAN

Chollet, Jean Baptiste (**Marie**) (*b* Paris, 20 May 1798; *d* Nemours, 10 Jan 1892). French tenor. He studied in Paris and from 1823 to 1826 sang baritone roles in Switzerland and Le Havre, at the Opéra-Comique and in Brussels. In 1826 he joined the Opéra-Comique as a tenor and appeared in the première of Hérold's *Marie*; he remained until 1832, and created the title roles in Auber's *Fra Diavolo* (1830) and Hérold's *Zampa* (1831), the latter demanding a range from *G* to *d*♭''. He sang successively at Brussels and The Hague (1832–4), returning in 1835 to the Opéra-Comique, where he created Chapelou in Adam's *Le postillon de Lonjumeau* (1836) and remained until 1847. His voice deteriorated after an illness in 1844, and he spent the last, unsettled years of his career alternating theatre direction with singing. Chollet was capable of both powerful and light vocalization: his virtuosity in *fioriture* reminded Bellini of Rubini. Like many tenors of his day he used falsetto, particularly in cadenzas.

*

A. Laget: *Chollet* (Toulouse, 1880) PHILIP ROBINSON

Chookasian, Lili (*b* Chicago, 1 Aug 1921). American contralto. She studied with Philip Manuel and made her début in 1959, singing Adalgisa with the Arkansas Opera Theater, Little Rock. She made her European début in 1961 at Trieste as Herodias. After further study, with Rosa Ponselle, she made her Metropolitan début as La Cieca (*La Gioconda*, 1962), and sang at Bayreuth (1965). During the next 15 years her roles included Geneviève, Mistress Quickly, Ulrica, Azucena, Amneris, Auntie (*Peter Grimes*) and La Frugola, the Princess and Zita (*Il trittico*). She has also sung with the New York City Opera (*The Medium*, 1963) and with many other leading companies, including those of Mexico City and Hamburg (both in *Aida*) and Buenos Aires, as well as at the Salzburg Festival. She created the role of the Queen in Pasatieri's *Inez de Castro* (April 1976) at Baltimore. Her dark rich voice and strong sense of character were vividly displayed when she sang Maddalena in *Andrea Chénier* at the Metropolitan Opera in 1977. RICHARD LeSUEUR, ELIZABETH FORBES

Chopelet [Choplet], **Pierre** (*fl* 1690–1713). French *haute-contre.* According to the Parfaict brothers (*Histoire de l'Académie Royale de Musique*, *F-Pn*), he was a small man with a long face and beautiful eyes whose voice was 'assez gracieuse'. He began his career as a dancer, and made his début as a singer in 1690 as Envy in a revival of Lully's *Cadmus et Hermione*. He created the roles of Don Pédro in Campra's *L'Europe galante* (1697), Telamon in Campra's *Hésione* (1700) and Apollo and Dardanus in Gatti's *Scylla* (1701); he also sang the main roles in revivals of Lully's *Amadis* (1701), *Phaëton* (1702) and *Acis et Galatée* (1702). In 1702 the partial loss of his voice, through illness, forced him to sing minor roles for the remainder of his career; in spite of this restriction, he sang more than 30 roles in 21 different operas between 1703 and 1713. He retired from the Opéra in 1713 after creating the role of the Sacrificer in Campra's *Télèphe*. JAMES R. ANTHONY

Chopin. Opera in four acts by GIACOMO OREFICE to a libretto by Angiolo Orvieto; Milan, Teatro Lirico, 25 November 1901.

Chopin gives a wildly inaccurate account of the composer's life, but it contains a good deal of his music: nocturnes, mazurkas, the *Berceuse*, a barcarolle and the Fantasie on Polish Airs op.13. Act 1 is set in Poland one Christmas night with Chopin (tenor) in love with Stella (soprano), the first woman to arouse his passion. Later, in Paris (Act 2), Chopin's friend Elio (baritone) tells a group of schoolchildren of Poland's past glory, thereby so arousing Chopin that he runs into the house and creates a nocturne. The composer succeeds in beguiling the teacher, Flora (mezzo-soprano). In Act 3, set in Majorca, Chopin and Stella (rather than George Sand) are reunited and accompanied by their daughter Grazia (silent role), but the youngster dies of exposure during a thunderstorm. The parents and assorted Majorcans grieve. Back in Paris, Chopin, knowing his end is near, has no wish to die alone. Stella arrives opportunely from Poland, and Chopin expires in her arms. Orefice is a facile melodist, but his orchestrations of Chopin's piano music are brash. The most eloquent moment in the score is the finale to the Majorcan act. WILLIAM ASHBROOK

Chorale. A congregational hymn of the German Protestant church service. Chorales have been used allusively in opera. In *Die Zauberflöte* (1791) Mozart quotes the melody of 'Ach Gott von Himmel sieh darein', sung by the two Armed Men and accompanied in the contrapuntal manner of a Bach chorale prelude. In Meyerbeer's *Les Huguenots* (1836) the hymn 'Ein feste Burg ist unser Gott' stands, as so often, for the Protestant faith. Wagner set the opening, church scene of *Die Meistersinger* (1868) with 'Da zu dir der Heiland kam' sung by the full congregation. Gerald Barry's *The Intelligence Park* (1990) is based throughout on Lutheran chorales. JULIAN BUDDEN

Chorley, Henry F(othergill) (*b* Blackley Hurst, nr Billinge, Lancs., 15 Dec 1808; *d* London, 16 Feb 1872). English writer and critic. He received some musical training from Jakob Zeugheer (J. Zeugheer Herrmann), and wrote the libretto for Zeugheer's opera *Angela of Venice* (*c*1825). For a while he worked as a clerk in a firm of merchants, a position he detested. In 1830 he began to write articles and reviews for the new weekly *The Athenaeum* and in 1834 joined its staff in London. There he began a long career as the author of plays, novels, poems and essays; he also wrote librettos for Emanuele Biletta (*White Magic*, 1852), Vincent Wallace (*The Amber Witch*, 1861) and Sullivan (*The Sapphire Necklace*, *c*1862), and translated operas by Auber, Cimarosa, Gluck, Gounod, Mercadante and Meyerbeer. His contributions to *The Athenaeum* included weekly notices of musical events in London. His enthusiasms were mainly for opera, especially the works of Rossini, Meyerbeer and Gounod. His translation of Gounod's *Faust* was performed frequently at Her Majesty's Theatre during the 1864 season, and was the version long used in the Schirmer vocal score. In 1847 he attempted to persuade Mendelssohn to set his own adaptation of Shakespeare's *The Winter's Tale*.

Along with J. W. Davison, Chorley was the most influential of the mid-Victorian musical journalists in the eyes of his contemporaries. His books, though hastily put together, have contributed largely to later generations' understanding of mid-Victorian musical taste. His masterpiece, *Thirty Years' Musical Recollections* (London, 1862), a year-by-year summary of London operatic seasons from 1830 to 1860, contains informative digressions on contemporary singers and composers and chronicles Chorley's belief that, because of Benjamin Lumley's poor management, Her Majesty's Theatre declined until, after 1847, it was gradually supplanted as the principal opera house of London by the Royal Italian Opera at Covent Garden.

Chorley retired from *The Athenaeum* in 1868, though he continued to contribute occasional reviews and letters. He was said to be moody, quarrelsome and eccentric, and alienated his many musical and literary friends (excluding Dickens, dedicatee of his novel *A Prodigy: a Tale of Music*, 1866). At the end of his life he was working on a study of Rossini's music and his own autobiography; substantial portions of the autobiography were used in Hewlett's compilation.

DNB (R. Garnett); *Grove2* (J. Marshall)
G. Linley: *Musical Cynics of London* (London, 1862)
H. Hewlett, ed.: *Henry Fothergill Chorley: Autobiography* (London, 1873)
C. Santley: *Student and Singer: Reminiscences* (London, 1892)
R. C. Lehmann: *Memories of Half a Century* (London, 1908)
L. A. Marchand: *The Athenaeum: a Mirror of Victorian Culture* (Chapel Hill, NC, 1941) ROBERT BLEDSOE

Chorus (Fr. *choeur*; Ger. *chor*; It. *coro*). A group of singers with more than one individual singing each part. The choruses in opera usually represent collective entities such as priests, peasants, nymphs of the woods, and so forth. The term also refers to the music sung by a chorus. Choruses may sing in unison or their music may be divided into two, three, four or occasionally more individual parts assigned from among the four vocal ranges, soprano or treble, contralto, tenor and bass. In the 17th and 18th centuries, parts were written in the clefs named for each vocal range. Choruses were accompanied by basso continuo alone or with additional instruments. Texturally, choruses range from homophonic and antiphonal to imitative and contrapuntal.

1. Up to 1800. 2. After 1800.

1. Up to 1800. From the inception of opera around 1600, choruses played an important role, offering a break from the prevailing monody. Choruses took the form of madrigal-style pieces (such as 'Ahi, caso acerbo', in Monteverdi's *Orfeo*, 1607) or strophic ones (such as 'Vanne Orfeo'). Members sang in unison using recitative style or provided four-part homophonic refrains for intervening solo sections. They commented on the situation, supported solo roles, expressed a mood, accompanied dance and functioned as an active participant in the dialogue. At Rome, in the middle of the 17th century, choruses were still one of the regular components of opera, often closing one or more of the acts as well as the opera itself. These closing pieces often took the form of large concerted, polyphonic works (for example in Luigi Rossi's *Il palazzo incantato*, 1642). Within the operas themselves, polyphonic madrigals with continuo accompaniment enhanced intensely emotional scenes. In Venice, by the middle of the century, the chorus had all but disappeared from opera; only a vestigial *coro* for the assembled cast remained to celebrate the happy ending.

In France choruses became an important part of the *divertissements* in Lully's operas. *Divertissements* combined machine spectacle with homophonic chorus, choral-solo rondeaux and dance. They remained a part of the genre into the next century, where they are still a strong presence in the operas of Rameau (e.g. *Dardanus*). In England, Purcell's operas and semi-operas have Italian-derived madrigals, echo choruses and strophic choruses coexisting with French-inspired choral-solo rondos (*see* Dido and Aeneas). Handel's operas mostly have only concluding choruses, sung by the principals.

As a result of the Arcadian reform of the opera libretto in the early 18th century, choruses very nearly disappeared from the Italian operatic repertory though they can still be found in celebratory pieces and theatrical entertainments such as *feste teatrali*, serenatas and *azioni teatrali*, where they were often combined – as in Mozart's *Ascanio in Alba* and Gluck's *Orfeo ed Euridice* – with other spectacular elements such as stage effects, pantomime and dance. In opera, works on pastoral subjects, such as Metastasio's *Olimpiade*, *Nitteti* and *Achille in Sciro*, were more likely to have one or more choruses. They also occurred at the beginning of ceremonial or triumphal scenes, where they assisted in establishing the mood and swelling the crowd. These choruses were usually simple homophonic pieces though Metastasio provided texts suitable for setting antiphonally or in combination with the principals in solo or ensemble, where the chorus sang the refrains for strophic pieces or functioned as the tutti in rondo forms. For *Achille in Sciro* (1736, Vienna) and *Romolo ed Ersilia* (1765, Innsbruck), Metastasio wrote early examples of choral introductions; these take the form of a small chorus with tutti refrain. Choruses in Metastasian librettos were often cut when performed in Italian theatres.

Choruses became a distinctive feature of the French-inspired, 'reform' operas originating in Parma and Vienna in the 1760s and 70s. In Parma, the Italian composer Traetta composed several operas on texts that Frugoni derived from operas by Lully and Rameau. These follow the French dramaturgical forms and use chorus in the French way, as part of the *divertissements* and spectacle scenes and in combination with soloists (as in *Ippolito ed Aricia*). French-inspired operas performed in Vienna, Stuttgart, Mannheim and St Petersburg to texts by Marco Coltellini, Verazi and Calzabigi combined typically French subject matter and spectacular elements such as choruses with italianate dramaturgical practices. Here choruses appear alone, in combination with soloists and ensembles, and as components in spectacle scenes, introductions, scene complexes and finales. Gluck, in his *Alceste* (1767), goes furthest in assimilating the chorus into the action; with a small number of principals it naturally assumes greater prominence. Verazi, in *Fetonte* (1768) and *Calliroe* (1770), takes a more Italian approach. The final movements of the opening sinfonias become choruses with soloists; in *Fetonte*, the chorus participates as 'humankind' in the action ensemble finale (the first ever appended to an *opera seria*).

In the late 1780s choruses begin to reappear in operas within a purely italianate context, and Metastasio's choruses were often restored to their former positions. During the 1790s choruses became a common element in Italian opera after more than 100 years of almost total absence. Two operas led the way. Francesco Bianchi's *Alonso e Cora* (1786), written for Venice to a text by Giuseppe Foppa, opened with an extensive introductory chorus with solos and duos. Choruses also participated in scene complexes at the close of the first and last acts. This became a common practice in the 1790s. Tarchi's *Il conte di Saldagna* (1787), set for Milan to a text by Moretti, went even further: choruses occur singly, assert themselves within scenes as characters, alternate with solo voices, follow ensembles and combine with dance. Gazzaniga's *Gli Argonauti in Colco* (1790), set for Venice to a text by Sografi, established a new fluidity of construction in which the chorus functioned as a freely participating character unencumbered by formal restraints.

2. After 1800. Operas of the post-Revolutionary and neo-classical periods virtually all have a notable choral dimension in keeping with the ideals that they express: 'Ah! welche Lust' in Beethoven's *Fidelio* (1805) is an outstanding example. Among the earliest choral numbers to achieve popularity on their own are the 'Coro delle tenebre' in Rossini's *Mosè in Egitto* (1818), the 'Coro dei Bardi' in his *La donna del lago* (1819) and Weber's Huntsmen's Chorus in *Der Freischütz* (1821). In Italian opera the distribution of voices until about 1870 was SSTTBB, the men outnumbering the women in such a way as to permit double choruses, either male or mixed, such as 'Qual v'ha speme?' in Verdi's *Giovanna d'Arco* (1845). Several operas contain only a male chorus, for example Rossini's *Tancredi* (1813) and *Il barbiere di Siviglia* (1816), Donizetti's *Torquato Tasso* (1833) and Verdi's *Rigoletto* (1851).

Choral scenes are an essential feature of mid-century grand opera from Spontini onwards and in works of a specifically nationalist tendency in which the 'hero' may be a whole people. Verdi is generally credited with pioneering the unison chorus, as in 'Va pensiero sull'ali dorate' (*Nabucco*, 1842), 'O Signore, dal tetto natio' (*I Lombardi*, 1843) and 'Si ridesti il Leon di Castiglia' (*Ernani*, 1844), all of which embodied for their audience the spirit of the Risorgimento. As they faced a Neapolitan firing squad the patriots who had joined the insurgents led by the Bandiera brothers chanted the chorus 'Chi per la patria muore' from Mercadante's *Donna Caritea* (1826). The vast majority of 19th-century operas, in whatever language, open with a choral scene, often encapsulating one or more solo items (*see* INTRODUZIONE), and indeed throughout the period a chorus is often used to define an opera's ambience as well as to provide a pedestal for a principal's aria. Huge ensembles with two choruses in conflict are to be found in grand opera on the Meyerbeerian model, including Meyerbeer's *Les Huguenots* (1836), Wagner's *Rienzi* (1842) and Verdi's *Les vêpres siciliennes* (1855) and *Aida* (1871). A particularly impressive instance occurs in Act 3 of Wagner's *Der fliegende Holländer* (1843), where the jollity of the Norwegian sailors is turned into terror by the cries of the Dutchman's crew.

The chorus has a prominent role in the early Wagner canon, including *Tannhäuser* (1845) and *Lohengrin* (1850). In the *Ring* it appears only in *Götterdämmerung*. The choruses in Act 3 of *Die Meistersinger* (1868) have a consciously national character, such as those of Musorgsky's *Boris Godunov* (1869, 1874), several operas by Rimsky-Korsakov, Smetana's *The Bartered Bride* (1866) and *Libuše* (1881) and Borodin's *Prince Igor* (1890). The Polovtsian Dances from *Prince Igor* provide a unique instance of a choral ballet couched in a flamboyantly exotic style. During the 19th century, choruses in a national idiom were increasingly used to evoke a particular ambience, sometimes with the aid of authentic folksongs, such as the Ukrainian melodies of Tchaikovsky's *Cherevichki* (his 1887 revision of *Vakula the Smith*, 1874) and 'Slava' in the coronation scene of *Boris Godunov*. Examples from Italian opera of the so-called 'veristic' period include the Alsatian folksong in Mascagni's *L'amico Fritz* (1891), the French revolutionary songs in Giordano's *Andrea Chénier* (1896), and the Song of the Volga Boatmen in his *Siberia* (1903). By this time, however, with the passing of 'grand opera', the chorus had resumed a more modest function. Famous choruses from the latter part of the century include 'Gloire immortelle à nos aieux', from Gounod's *Faust* (1859), the Easter Hymn from Mascagni's *Cavalleria rusticana* (1890) and the Inno del Sole from his *Iris* (1898).

The use of a wordless chorus to convey atmospheric effects such as the howling of the wind appears to originate in 'C'est la corvette' (*Haydée*, Auber, 1847) as a couplet refrain. The device was put to genuine dramatic effect in Act 3 of *Rigoletto*. To the same family belongs the Humming Chorus in Puccini's *Madama Butterfly* (1904).

Among 20th-century composers to have made extensive use of the chorus are Strauss, Britten, Poulenc, Prokofiev and Henze; none has substantially enlarged the chorus's function, although Britten's handling of a male chorus (the crew of a ship) in *Billy Budd* (1951) and Poulenc's and Puccini's of a female (the inhabitants of a convent) in *Dialogues des Carmélites* (1957) and *Suor Angelica* (1918) break new ground, as does Prokofiev's use of choral epigraphs in *War and Peace* (concert performance, 1944). The 'Female Chorus' and 'Male Chorus' in Britten's *The Rape of Lucretia* (1946) are not choruses but solo singers who comment on the action in a manner akin to that of a Greek chorus. A similar function is performed by the chorus in Stravinsky's opera-oratorio *Oedipus Rex* (1928).

D. J. Grout: 'The Chorus in Early Opera', *Festschrift Friedrich Blume* (Kassel, 1963), 151–61

M. McClymonds: 'Mattia Verazi and the opera at Mannheim, Stuttgart, and Ludwigsburg', *Studies in Music from the University of Western Ontario*, vii/2 (1982), 99–136

——: 'The Venetian Role in the Transformation of Italian Opera Seria during the 1790s', *I vicini di Mozart: Venice 1987*, i, 221–40

MARITA P. McCLYMONDS (1), JULIAN BUDDEN (2)

Chorus master. The person who instructs and sometimes recruits the opera chorus. There seems to be no evidence of a chorus master so called before 1800, even in *tragédie lyrique*, where the chorus mattered, let alone in *opera seria* (which had no chorus until its latter years) or comic opera (where choruses were generally short and simple). Such work was presumably done by the chief répétiteur. Venetian documents of 1756 suggest the presence of a chorus leader, in effect a labour contractor – an ambiguous role which later chorus masters easily slipped into, at once recruiters, paymasters and sometimes defenders in labour disputes. A probable example is the chorus trainer who in 1838 worked for three Florence theatres at once: the leading impresario Alessandro Lanari was advised to get his own musical director to train the chorus for Mercadante's *Il giuramento*, a work thought to require special care. A chorus master is recorded at Venice from 1807, at Bologna from 1817 (in 1822–6 he doubled as chief répétiteur). Weber, as director from 1817 of the German opera in Dresden, secured, as one of his first acts, the appointment of a chorus master; the more demanding writing for the chorus in Romantic opera, where it stood for the collective voice of the community, required it. The impact of Parisian grand opera about 1850–60 made a chorus master a necessity everywhere. In modern opera houses with unionized choruses he is generally an official. He may be a former singer or conductor; past chorus masters have included singing teachers and composers, among them Delibes.

Contracts: A. Codognato and chorus members, 30 Nov 1756 (*I-Vas*, Capi del Consiglio dei Dieci, Mazzetti b.2)

Letter: A. Gazzuoli to A. Lanari, 29 Dec 1838 (*Fn*, Carteggi Vari 365/59)

L. Trezzini, ed.: *Due secoli di vita musicale: storia del Teatro Comunale di Bologna*, ii: S. Paganelli: *Repertorio critico degli spettacoli e delle esecuzioni musicali dal 1763 al 1966* (Bologna, 1966)

M. Girardi and F. Rossi, eds.: *Il Teatro La Fenice: cronologia degli spettacoli 1792–1936* (Padua, 1989)

JOHN ROSSELLI

Christelflein, Das ('The Christmas Elf'). *Spieloper* in two acts, op.20, by HANS PFITZNER to his own libretto after the play by Ilse von Stach; Dresden, 11 December 1917.

Pfitzner turned here to a fairy-tale for children, recasting his incidental music for the play, *Das Christelflein* (Munich, 11 December 1906), as an opera with spoken dialogue. A romantically naive melodic style is adopted for the Christmas eve encounter of a local landowner's family with pagan personifications of Nature, the Old Fir Tree (bass) and the Elf (soprano), with Knecht

Ruprecht (Teutonic 'Father Christmas', baritone) and with the Christ Child (soprano). The latter ensures that the Gumpachs' dying daughter gets her Christmas tree before he permits the inquisitive Elf to take her place in heaven, thereafter becoming 'Christ-Elflein'.

PETER FRANKLIN

Christiania. OSLO.

Christie, John (*b* Eggesford, Devon, 14 Dec 1882; *d* Glyndebourne, 4 July 1962). English opera enthusiast, founder in 1934 of GLYNDEBOURNE festival opera, husband of the soprano AUDREY MILDMAY and father of Sir George Christie, his successor as director of Glyndebourne.

Christie, Nan [Agnes] **(Stevenson)** (*b* Irvine, Strathclyde, 6 March 1948). Scottish soprano. She studied in Glasgow at the Royal Scottish Academy of Music and Drama. In 1970 she joined Scottish Opera, singing Flora (*The Turn of the Screw*), Yniold, Papagena, Blonde and Xenia and creating Galla in Hamilton's *The Catiline Conspiracy* (1974). With English Music Theatre she created Sophia Western in Stephen Oliver's *Tom Jones* (1976), also singing Pamina and Sandrina (*La finta giardiniera*). At Glyndebourne she sang Isotta in *Die schweigsame Frau* (1977), Despina (1978) and Nightingale and Fire in *L'enfant et les sortilèges* (1988). Her roles at Frankfurt have included Oscar, Gilda, Susanna and Marie in Zimmermann's *Die Soldaten* (1981). For the ENO she has sung Zdenka (*Arabella*), Eurydice (*Orphée aux enfers*), Adele (*Die Fledermaus* and *Le comte Ory*) and the Queen of Night. She has also sung in Paris, Brussels and Zürich, and in 1991 returned to Scottish Opera as Birdie Hamilton in Blitzstein's *Regina*. The role of Zerbinetta is one that well displays her range and flexibility.

ELIZABETH FORBES

Christie, William (Lincoln) (*b* Buffalo, NY, 19 Dec 1944). American conductor. He studied the piano and organ in Buffalo, then went to Harvard University, taking a degree in art history, before going to Yale School of Music, where he studied the harpsichord and musicology. He was briefly director of music at Dartmouth College, New Hampshire, but in 1971 moved to Europe, settling in Paris, where he worked chiefly as a harpsichordist. His successful work with ensembles led him in 1979 to found Les Arts Florissants, named after a small-scale opera by M.-A. Charpentier, one of the composers for whom Christie has shown special sympathies. The group has performed, as well as concert and sacred music, several stage works, among them Landi's *Sant'Alessio*, Luigi Rossi's *Orfeo*, Rameau's *Pygmalion* and music by Purcell; their urbane, graceful and stylish performances have won them warm praise, especially in the French repertory, where performances and recordings of Charpentier's *Médée* and Lully's *Atys* (given in the composer's tercentenary year, 1987, in Paris and elsewhere) have set new standards in the performance of French opera of the middle Baroque.

STANLEY SADIE

Christina [Christina Alexandra] (*b* Stockholm, 8 Dec 1626; *d* Rome, 19 April 1689). Queen of Sweden and patron of opera. She succeeded her father Gustavus II Adolphus in 1632, assuming power when she reached her majority in 1644. She abdicated in 1654 after her conversion to Catholicism and moved to Rome, where she became one of the outstanding figures in the city's cultural life. Her journey south took her to Innsbruck, where she made a public confession and where Cesti's opera *Argia* was performed in her honour. On her arrival in Rome (December 1655) celebrations organized by the nobility and the ecclesiastical authorities began almost immediately, reaching a peak in the ensuing carnival, known thereafter as 'the Queen's Carnival'. In early 1656 the Barberini family presented three lavish Marazzoli operas (*La Vita humana*, *Dal mal il bene* and *Le armi e gli amori*); the Pamphilis put on three entertainments, including Tenaglia's *Il giudizio di Paride*.

Almost immediately, Christina showed herself eager to become one of the leading artistic patrons and founded the Accademia Reale, a literary society with keen musical interests. She left Italy three times: once for a journey to France (July 1656 to 19 May 1658), then twice for journeys to Sweden (July 1660 to 20 June 1662; May 1666 to 22 November 1668). In June 1662, when she was on her way back to Italy, Cesti's *La magnanimità di Alessandro* was performed at Innsbruck in her honour. She always had musicians and singers in her service, and there was a room in her palace known as the Teatro della Commedia, though only a few performances are known to have taken place there. In Carnival 1666, when the Colonna family was away in Venice, she presented an opera, *Amore e fede* (with music perhaps by A. M. Abbatini); musicians from the Colonna household took part, along with singers from the Sistine Chapel, De Vecchi and Mario Savioni. For Carnival 1669 she arranged for the performance of Italian and Spanish comedies and Alessandro Melani's *L'empio punito*, to the cost of which (more than 6000 scudi) she contributed.

Christina's greatest period as a patron coincided with the opening of the first public theatre in Rome, the Tordinona; she agreed to be its patron and subscribed annually by renting five boxes with a private entrance at a cost of 500 scudi. In the four years the theatre was active (1671–4), nine operas were staged, five of which were dedicated to her. The theatre was inaugurated with Cavalli's *Scipione affricano* and a prologue and two intermezzos by Stradella. As was customary, the prologue indicated by heraldic allusions the two patrons of the theatre, Christina and the Altieri pope, Clement X; but the work, performed by many of the queen's musicians, had only a lukewarm reception. In 1673 G. A. Boretti's *Eliogabalo* and Bernardo Pasquini's *L'Amor per vendetta, overo L'Alcasta* were performed; their dedications mention Christina's patronage. The two operas performed the following year, Antonio Sartorio's *Massenzio* and G. M. Pagliardi's *Caligula delirante*, were also dedicated to her, though she disapproved of the latter work.

The celebration of Holy Year in 1675 interrupted the activity of the Tordinona. Pope Innocent XI, elected in 1676, prohibited all forms of public theatre and reduced the queen's revenues so that she could no longer finance the theatre regularly and could only subsidize individual productions. In 1679 she met the expenses of Alessandro Scarlatti's first opera, *Gli equivoci nel sembiante*; the composer then became her *maestro di cappella* and on 3 February 1680 his *L'honestà negli amori* was produced in her palace. Pasquini's *Il Lisimaco* (1681) was dedicated to Christina and perhaps also produced in her palace; her name also occurs in the libretto of Scarlatti's *Il Pompeo*, performed in Naples in 1684. In February 1687, when an embassy arrived in Rome with the intention of reopening diplomatic relations between England and the Holy See, she arranged for the performance in her palace of Pasquini's cantata *L'accademia per musica in onore di Giacomo II*, her last splendid musical occasion. After Christina's death, many of her books and manuscripts went to the Vatican Library.

*

G. Gualdo-Priorato: *Historia della Sacra Real Maestà di Christina Alessandra Regina di Svetia* (Rome, 1656)
A. Cametti: 'Cristina di Svezia: l'arte musicale e gli spettacoli teatrali in Roma', *Nuova antologia*, xvi (1911), 641–56
A. Sandberger: 'Beziehungen der Königin Christina von Sweden zur italienischen Oper', *Bulletin de la Société 'Union musicologique'*, v (1925), 121–73
A. Cametti: *Il teatro Tordinona, poi di Apollo* (Tivoli, 1938)
P. Bjurström: *Feast and Theatre in Queen Christina's Rome* (Stockholm, 1966)
G. Hilleström: 'Alessandro Scarlatti et son opéra *L'honestà negli amori*, dédié à la Reine Christine', *Queen Christina of Sweden: Documents and Studies*, ed. M. von Platen (Stockholm, 1966), 130–37
G. Masson: 'Papal Gifts and Roman Entertainments in Honour of Queen Christina's Arrival', ibid, 244–61
M. Murata: 'Il carnevale a Roma sotto Clemente IX Rospigliosi', *RIM*, xii (1977), 83–99
M. Murata: *Operas for the Papal Court, 1631–1668* (Ann Arbor, 1981)
F. D'Accone: Introduction to A. Scarlatti: *Gli equivoci nel sembiante* (Cambridge, MA, 1982)
L. Lindgren: 'Il dramma musicale a Roma durante la carriera di Alessandro Scarlatti (1660–1725)', *Le muse galanti*, ed. B. Cagli (Rome, 1985), 35–57 CATERINA PAMPALONI

Christiné, Henri (*b* Geneva, 27 Dec 1867; *d* Nice, 25 Nov 1941). French composer of Swiss birth. Originally a schoolmaster in Geneva, Christiné married a café-concert singer and left Switzerland to settle in France where his songs, composed first for his wife and later for such metropolitan stars as Mayol, Dranem and Fragson, put him in the forefront of popular songwriters in France in the years before World War I. During the 1900s he wrote several *opérettes* for the Scala in Paris, but it was his first commission from the powerful producer Gustave Quinson which secured his theatrical fame. *Phi-Phi* was a small-scale *opérette-bouffe*, set in ancient Greece (with modern connotations) and written for a tiny cast featuring André Urban as the sculptor Phidias and Alice Cocéa as the courtesan Aspasie, and a reduced orchestra. It was a sensational hit at the Bouffes-Parisiens and set a new fashion in music-theatre styles for the postwar era. Witty, jazzy, risqué musical plays replaced the classic French *opérettes* as the entertainment of *les années folles*, with Christiné as one of the era's most regular and favoured composers. *Dédé*, which starred Maurice Chevalier, *P. L. M.*, *J'adore ça!*, *Arthur* and others in the same vein successfully followed the long-running *Phi-Phi* and, when the fashion returned to larger-scale shows in the 1930s, Christiné collaborated with Tiarko Richepin on two shows for the Théâtre du Châtelet. It is, however, his *chansons*, and his small-scale jazz-age *opérettes* – above all *Phi-Phi* with its gay, sparkling music and hilarious text by Albert Willemetz and Fabien Sollar – which remain his outstanding works.

opérettes, and first performed in Paris, unless otherwise stated

Pas de revue! (revue), Geneva, 10 Feb 1894
Service d'amour (M. Dunan), Scala, 17 Feb 1903
Mam'zelle Chichi (2, C. Esquès), Scala, 2 July 1904
Les vierges du harem, 1907
Cinq minutes d'amour (2, Esquès), Scala, 29 Feb 1908
Phi-Phi (3, A. Willemetz and F. Sollar), Bouffes-Parisiens, 11 Nov 1918
Dédé (3, Willemetz), Bouffes-Parisiens, 10 Nov 1921
Madame (Willemetz and Y. Mirande), Daunou, 14 Dec 1923
J'adore ça! (comédie musicale, 3, Willemetz and Saint-Granier), Daunou, 14 March 1925
P. L. M. (3, Rip), Bouffes-Parisiens, 21 April 1925
J'aime (3, Willemetz and Saint-Granier), Bouffes-Parisiens, 23 Dec 1926
Arthur (A. Barde), Daunou, 5 Sept 1929
Encore cinquante centimes (Barde), Nouveautés, 17 Sept 1931, collab. M. Yvain
La Madone du promenoir (Barde, Saint-Granier and F. Mayol), Concert Mayol, 4 Nov 1933
Au temps des merveilleuses (Willemetz, A. Mouëzy-Eon and A. Fontanes), Châtelet, 22 Dec 1934, collab. T. Richepin
La poule (H. Duvernois and Barde), Nouveautés, 9 Jan 1936, collab. L. Lajtai
Yana (Willemetz, Mouëzy-Eon, H. Wernert and Lehmann), Châtelet, 18 Dec 1936, collab. Richepin

*

ES (E. Haraszti)
F. Bruyas: *Histoire de l'opérette en France, 1855–1965* (Lyons, 1974)
R. Traubner: *Operetta* (New York, 1983) KURT GÄNZL

Christmas Carol, A. Opera in two acts by THEA MUSGRAVE to her own libretto after CHARLES DICKENS; Norfolk, Virginia, 7 December 1979.

The miser, Scrooge (baritone), is forced by the Spirit of Christmas to contemplate the tragic consequences of his inhumanity. He undergoes a change of heart and makes such amends as he can to his victims.

The composer has added two extra scenes to Dickens's story: in the first, the ambitious young Scrooge sadly rejects his first love, Belle (soprano); in the second, the Cratchit family mourn the death of Tiny Tim. The opera is scored for chamber orchestra and a cast of 12 playing 36 characters. The three Spirits of Christmas are reduced to one, played by a silent mime, while the words of Marley's ghost are spoken, not sung. The carol *God Rest ye Merry Gentlemen* is sung at the end of the opera and also appears, variously transformed or fragmented, in earlier scenes. *Twinkle, twinkle, little star* is used as a leitmotif for Belle. *A Christmas Carol* is the most straightforwardly tuneful of Musgrave's operas; the elements of grotesquery and caricature in Dickens's story are played down, Scrooge emerging as an almost believable human character. HUGO COLE

Christmas Eve [*Noch' pered rozhdestvom*]. 'Carol come-to-life' (*bïl'-kolyadka*) in four acts by NIKOLAY ANDREYEVICH RIMSKY-KORSAKOV to his own libretto after the eponymous story in NIKOLAY VASIL'YEVICH GOGOL's collection *Evenings on a Farm near Dikanka* (ii, 1832); St Petersburg, Mariinsky Theatre, 28 November/10 December 1895.

Composed in 1894–5, almost immediately after Tchaikovsky's sudden death, *Christmas Eve* was at least the fourth opera on Gogol's tale to be performed, the others being *Vakula the Smith* by Tchaikovsky, its reincarnation as *Cherevichki* ('The Slippers'), and *Vakula kuznets* ('Vakula the Smith') by Nikolay Solov'yov, written to the same libretto as Tchaikovsky's and for the same contest (for the plot, *see* CHEREVICHKI). 'Please note', Rimsky-Korsakov wrote sententiously to Alexander Glazunov, 'my opera is called *Christmas Eve*, not *Cherevichki* and not *Vakula kuznets*'. But in fact he used the Gogol tale as little more than a springboard for another essay in pantheistic ur-Slavonic mythology in the manner of *The Snow Maiden* – at the other end, so to speak, of the solar calendar.

Rimsky-Korsakov's contemporaries were on the whole unsympathetic to this heavily mythologized treatment of Gogol's rather innocent tale, and the opera did not hold the stage. In his autobiography Rimsky conceded that he had been carried away, 'but this mistake gave me the chance to write a lot of interesting music'. It is indeed the fantastic music that lives in *Christmas Eve*, carrying to a new power the extravagant if schematic harmonic and colouristic invention that was Rimsky's special genius (see ex.1 for an instance in which a

Ex.1 Introduction to Act 2, end

characteristic circle of minor 3rds gives rise to a sequential passage that is almost wholly referable to the so-called 'octatonic' scale of alternating tones and semitones). The orchestration is also full of new and ingenious artifices (and a new instrument, the celesta, henceforth Rimsky's magic colour *par excellence*).

The opera's stage career was especially frustrating to Rimsky-Korsakov because a pair of grand dukes, attending the dress rehearsal, took offence at the inclusion in the cast of Empress Catherine II (as in Gogol's tale; Yakov Polonsky, Tchaikovsky and Solov'yov's librettist, had prudently replaced her with an unnamed 'Highness'). They demanded that her part be hastily written out of the opera, and in consequence the offended composer boycotted the première. (One of the noblemen, the Grand Duke Vladimir Alexandrovich, was the employer of Modest Solov'yov, brother of the composer of one of the competing operas.) At the first performance the opera was conducted by Eduard Nápravník, with Ivan Yershov as Vakula and Fyodor Stravinsky as Panas (alternating with Fyodor Shalyapin in the first production). RICHARD TARUSKIN

Christmas Rose, The. Opera in three scenes by FRANK BRIDGE to a libretto after a children's play by Margaret Kemp-Welch and Constance Cotterell; London, Royal College of Music, 8 December 1931 (student production).

This operatic Nativity play concerns the two children Miriam (soprano) and her young brother Reuben (mezzo-soprano) who are told to stay behind as their father (bass-baritone) and his fellow shepherds follow the star to Bethlehem after the visitation of the angels. Disappointed, they decide to make their own way there but arrive exhausted at the stable only to realize, heartbroken, that they have come empty-handed. Then Christmas roses push through the snow where Miriam's tears had fallen; these are their gifts for the child. Bridge clothes the story in radiant music, expertly crafted and with moments of exhilaration worthy of his rhapsody *Enter Spring*. STEPHEN BANFIELD

Christofes, Fritz. *See* FRIEDRICHS, FRITZ.

Christoff, Boris (Kirilov) (*b* Plovdiv, 18 May 1914). Bulgarian bass. He first studied law, but was heard in the famous Gusla Choir by King Boris of Bulgaria who sent him to Rome to study singing with Riccardo Stracciari; he continued in Salzburg with Muratti. Returning to Italy in 1946, he made his début as Colline at Reggio Calabria. The following season he sang Pimen

Boris Christoff in the title role of Musorgsky's 'Boris Godunov'

at both Rome and La Scala. He first sang Boris in 1949 at Covent Garden; he repeated the role in many leading houses, including La Scala and the Opéra, and in 1974 sang it at Covent Garden to celebrate the 25th anniversary of his first appearance there. His repertory included Khan Konchak, Rocco, King Mark, Hagen and Gurnemanz, the title role in Handel's *Giulio Cesare*, and most of Verdi's leading bass roles. He made his American début as Boris at San Francisco in 1956 and sang at Chicago from 1957 to 1963.

Hailed by many as Shalyapin's successor because of his identification with the great singing-acting parts in the Russian repertory, Christoff was also an outstanding Verdi singer, notably as Philip II in *Don Carlos* at Covent Garden (1958). His voice, though not large, was of fine quality, smooth, round, well projected and perfectly controlled. His many recordings include two of *Boris Godunov* in which he sings three roles, Boris, Pimen and Varlaam. He was able, through his personal magnetism and theatrical skill, to generate tension whenever he was on stage. His dramatic powers, and his ability to give words their fullest meaning and expressive weight, placed him among the great singing actors of his day.

*

G. Lauri-Volpi: *Voci parallele* (Milan, 1955)
J. Bourgeois: 'Boris Christoff', *Opera*, ix (1958), 692–7
F. F. Clough and G. J. Cuming: 'Boris Christoff: Discography', *Audio & Record Review*, iv/1 (1964–5), 73–4
O. Deykova: *Boris Christoff* (Sofia, 1966)
J. B. Steane: *The Grand Tradition* (London, 1974), 364ff

HAROLD ROSENTHAL/R

Christophe Colomb ('Christopher Columbus'). Opera in two parts by DARIUS MILHAUD to a libretto by Paul Claudel; Berlin, Staatsoper, 5 May 1930 (revised version, Graz, Oper, 27 June 1968).

The 27 scenes of Claudel's libretto move back and forth in time to form a mosaic of contrasting episodes which illustrate important incidents and personalities in Columbus's story. The work exists in two versions. In the first, after an introductory processional, Columbus (baritone) is seen dying in poverty in the garret of an inn in Valladolid. Flashbacks recount the events of his life, and the opera concludes with his entry into Paradise in the wake of his patroness, Isabella of Spain (soprano).

Concert performances made Milhaud dissatisfied with this plan, and for stage productions in Graz and Wuppertal (1968–70) he reversed the order of the two parts and made various changes, none of which, however, drastically affected the musical aspect. The second version opens with the news of Columbus's discovery of America and traces the subsequent troubles, jealousies and disappointments leading to his death. Then follows the scene at the Valladolid inn, and a review and examination of Columbus's character, his quelling of the mutiny and discovery of the New World and, finally, a setting of the *Te Deum*.

The production requirements are among the most elaborate and spectacular of any 20th-century opera. There are four solo roles, a huge chorus on which great demands of both technique and stamina are made (and which alternately forms part of the action and stands outside it like a Greek chorus), a large orchestra in the pit with a small group off stage, and film images projected on to a screen behind the stage. Additionally, Milhaud requires simultaneous representation on different platforms, as well as actors for the spoken scene of the sailors' revolt. The episodes are linked by a narrator who, often supported by choral speech, declaims against a complex rhythmic background of percussion (much simplified and partly dispensed with in the revised version). The action is part realistic, part allegorical, part stylized, part expressionistic; Columbus appears not only as himself but also as his conscience, his *alter ego* and, in one scene, as a youth, a grown man and his shadow. Predictably Claudel made much use of religious symbolism, the names 'Christophe' (bearer of Christ) and 'Colomb' (dove, symbol of the Holy Ghost) lending themselves conveniently to this purpose.

Christophe Colomb has been criticized (not least by Claudel) on grounds of excessive complexity, disjointedness and pretentiousness; certainly its diversity of elements and mechanical imponderables make a smooth-running production almost impossible. Television, with its great technical versatility and flexibility, might be a more promising medium. What cannot be impugned is the quality of the music, which is on a high level of inspiration throughout and represents virtually every facet of Milhaud's characteristic style.

CHRISTOPHER PALMER

Christophorus [*Christophorus, oder Die Vision einer Oper* ('Christophorus, or The Vision of an Opera')]. Opera in a prologue, two acts and an epilogue by FRANZ SCHREKER to his own libretto; Freiburg, 1 October 1978.

Dedicated to Schoenberg, *Christophorus* dramatizes Schreker's response to mid-1920s criticism. Partly realistic (the second act features a night club with adjoining opium den) and partly fantastic, it represents an opera-within-an-opera, with passages of spoken dialogue, and draws economically on a range of contemporary musical manners, dissonant and tonal. Anselm (tenor) is a music student instructed to write a string quartet on the legend of St Christopher. Instead, he decides to compose an opera with characters based on friends and acquaintances, but he loses control of Christoph (baritone), as fact and fantasy interweave in ever more complex and disturbing ways. Only in a string-quartet movement can he both express and control the essence of the myth.

PETER FRANKLIN

Christou, Jani (*b* Heliopolis, Egypt, 8 Jan 1926; *d* Athens, 8 Jan 1970). Greek composer. He studied in Alexandria and Cambridge, and later in Italy under Frazzi and Lavagnino. He settled in Greece in 1960. The leading Greek composer of his day, using an avant-garde idiom characterized by its energy and intensity and a strongly dramatic element, he is believed to have written a trilogy of operas, *La ruota della vita* (*Una mamma*; *Savitri*; *Il trionfo della morte*), to a libretto by Domenico de Paulis, of which only the text (1955) and some sketches survive, and a three-act 'space opera', *The Breakdown*, to his own libretto, surviving in 16 pages of full score. There is also a lost opera-oratorio, *Gilgamesh*, from the 1950s. Of a large number of small-scale avant-garde music-theatre projects, most of which he called *anaparastasis* ('re-enactments'), he finished only four, all with marked psychoanalytical associations. At the time of his death he was working on an opera on Aeschylus's *Oresteia*, for six soloists, a 24-voice mixed chorus and an ensemble of 12 actors with tapes and visual effects. In the 1960s he also wrote incidental music, mostly for Greek tragedies, for productions at Epidaurus, London and Athens.

GEORGE LEOTSAKOS

Chueca, Federico (*b* Madrid, 5 May 1846; *d* Madrid, 20 July 1908). Spanish composer and conductor. He studied the piano and theory at the Madrid Conservatory but then, at his parents' insistence, turned to medicine. Barbieri brought him back to a musical career when he conducted a series of Chueca's waltzes, *Lamentos de un preso*, which commemorated a student escapade. For a time he was forced to earn his living as a café pianist, but in due course he became conductor of the orchestra at the Teatro des Variedades. His first theatrical success was *La canción de la Lola* (1880), which ran for two years at the Teatro des Variedades and remained sufficiently well-known for Falla to quote it 37 years later in *El sombrero de trés picos*. Chueca composed about 40 zarzuelas, mostly in the one-act *género chico*, many of them in collaboration with Joaquín Valverde. He had a prodigious fund of melodic ingenuity, producing music that was enormously uplifting and cheerful, full of original and amusing touches. He was able to capture the local flavour of regions as far apart as Asturias and Andalusia and won lasting popularity in the entire Spanish-speaking world with music that transferred readily to street organs and café pianos. *La Gran Vía* (1886), a topical revue, ran uninterruptedly for four years at the Teatro Apolo and was also produced in Italy, France and England, while the march from *Cádiz* (also 1886) was itself the subject of a zarzuela by Estellés and the younger Valverde in 1896 and became the *de facto* Spanish national anthem during the Spanish-American War of 1898.

zarzuelas (selective list); unless otherwise stated, in one act, first performed in Madrid, and published in vocal score shortly after

El sobrino del difunto; Tres ruinas artisticas; Bonito país; Locuras madrileñas; Los barrios bajos, collab. J. Valverde *padre* and Rogel; El bautiza de Pepín, collab. Bretón and Valverde; Turcos y rusos; Un maestro de obra prima; Un crimen misterioso; ¡A los toros!, 1878, collab. Valverde; Majas y toreros, ?1878, collab. Valverde; La ferias (sainete lírico, M. Barranco y Caro), Buen Retiro, 3 July 1878, collab. Valverde; Escenas madrileñas; La función de mi pueblo, 1879, collab. Valverde; La canción de la Lola (sainete lírico, R. de la Vega), Alhambra, 25 May 1880, collab. Valverde

La venta del pillo; La plaza de Antón Martín; Panchita en el muelle de la Habana; R. R.; Luces y sombras (gacetilla cómico-lírico, S. Lastra, A. Ruesga and E. Prieto), Variedades, 1882, collab. Valverde; Fiesta nacional (acontecimiento cómico-lírico, T. Luceño and J. de Burgos), Variedades, 25 Nov 1882, collab. Valverde; Nuestro prologo; La abuela; De la noche a la mañana (sueño cómico-lírico, Lastra, Ruesga and Prieto), Variedades, Dec 1883, collab. Valverde; Un domingo en el Rastro

Caramelo (juguete cómico-lírico, Burgos), 1883–4, collab. Valverde; ¡Hoy sale, hoy! (sainete lírico, Luceño and Burgos), Variedades, 16 Jan 1884, collab. Barbieri; Vivitos y coleando (pesca cómico-lírica, Lastra, Ruesga and Prieto), Variedades, March 1884, collab. Valverde; Agua y cuernos (revue, Burgos and M. Pina), Buen Retiro, July 1884, collab. Valverde; Medidas sanitarias, collab. Valverde; Remifá; En la tierra como en el cielo, collab. Valverde; La Gran Vía (revista madrileña cómico-lírico-fantástico-callejera, F. Pérez y González), Felipe, 2 July 1886, collab. Valverde

Cádiz (episodio nacional cómico-lírico-dramático, 2, Burgos), Apolo, 20 Nov 1886, collab. Valverde; El año pasado por agua (Vega), Apolo, 1 March 1889, collab. Valverde; De Madrid á Paris (viaje cómico-lírico, J. Jackson Veyán and E. Sierra), Felipe, 12 July 1889, collab. Valverde; Le magasin de musique (Prieto and Barbera), Lisbon, Coliseo, Aug 1889, collab. Valverde; El arca de Noé (problema cómico-lírico, Ruesga and Prieto), Zarzuela, 26 Feb 1890, rev. as Fotografías animadas, Príncipe Alfonso, 1897

El chaleco blanco (episodo cómico-lírico, M. Ramos Carrión), Felipe, 26 June 1890; De Madrid á Barcelona (Perillán y Buxó), 1890, collab. Valverde; La caza del oso, ó, El tendero de comestibles (viaje-cómico-lírico, Jackson Veyán and Sierra), Apolo, 6 March 1891, collab. Valverde; Los descamisados (sainete lírico, C. Arniches and J. López Silva), Apolo, 31 Oct 1893; Las zapatillas (Jackson Veyán), Apolo, 5 Dec 1895; El coche correo (sainete lírico, Arniches and López Silva), Apolo, 4 April 1896

Agua, azucarillos y aguardiente (pasillo veraniego, Ramos Carrión), Apolo, 23 June 1897; El mantón de Manila (F. Irayzoz), Apolo, 11 May 1898; Los arrastraos (sainete lírico, Jackson Veyán and López Silva), Apolo, 28 May 1899 [?rev. as El capote de paseo, 1901]; La alegría de la huerta (A. Paso and E. García Alvarez), Eslava, 20 Jan 1900; El capote de paseo (Jackson Veyán and López Silva), Eslava, 1901 [?rev. of Los arratraos]; El bateo (sainete lírico, A. Domínguez and Paso), Zarzuela, 17 Nov 1901

La corría de toros, 1902; La borracha (zarzuela, Jackson Veyán and López Silva), 1904; Chinita (sainete lírico, L. Ibañez), ?1907, collab. P. Córdoba; El estudiante (zarzuela cómica, López Silva), Gran, 19 April 1907, collab. L. Fontanals; Las mocitas del barrio (A. Casero and A. Larrubiera), Lara, 29 March 1913; A la exposición; Los caramelos; El cofre misterioso; Lección conjugal

*

L. Carmena y Millán: 'Federico Chueca', *Cosas del pasado: musica, literatura y tauromaquia* (Madrid, 1904), 99–101, 157–61

'Chueca (Federico)', *Enciclopedia universal ilustrada europeo-americana* (Barcelona, 1907–30), xvii, 687–8

E. Cotarelo y Mori: *Historia de la zarzuela, ó sea el drama lírico* (Madrid, 1934)

J. Deleito y Piñuela: *Origen y apogeo del 'género chico'* (Madrid, 1949)

A. Fernández-Cid: *Cien años de teatro musical en España (1875–1975)* (Madrid, 1975)

J. Arnau and C. M. Gomez: *Historia de la zarzuela* (Madrid, 1979)

R. Alier and others: *El libro de la zarzuela* (Barcelona, 1982, 2/1986 as *Diccionario de la zarzuela*)

ANDREW LAMB

Chukhadjian, Tigran. *See* TCHUKHATJIAN, TIGRAN.

Church opera. *See* SACRED OPERA.

Chusid, Martin (*b* Brooklyn, 19 Aug 1925). American musicologist. He taught at the University of Southern California (1959–63), then at New York University, where he was chairman of the department of music from 1967 to 1970 and in 1976 was appointed director of the American Institute for Verdi Studies. He has been editor of the *Verdi Newsletter* since 1981. Chusid's main areas of research are the music of Schubert and opera, particularly the operas of Mozart and Verdi. He published *A Catalog of Verdi's Operas* (Hackensack, NJ, 1974) and, with William Weaver, edited *The Verdi Companion* (New York, 1979). He is involved with the new critical edition of Verdi's works, for which he edited *Rigoletto* (Chicago, 1983). PAULA MORGAN

Chute de la maison Usher, La ('The Fall of the House of Usher'). Unfinished opera by CLAUDE DEBUSSY to his own libretto after the tale by EDGAR ALLAN POE; New Haven, Yale University, 25 February 1977 (staged performance in a reconstruction by Carolyn Abbate).

Debussy wrote out three separate librettos, each presenting a different slant on Poe's tale, which in its original version is narrated by Roderick Usher's friend and includes only one speech for Usher himself. While the first and second versions of Debussy's libretto were conceived in three scenes, the third condenses the action into two (see E. Lockspeiser, *Debussy et Edgar Poe*, 1962, for a complete transcription). Debussy amplified the characters of Usher, the family physician and Lady Madeline, who does not speak in the original. He turned the physician into Roderick's rival in his incestuous love for Madeline, and added an episode where he buries Madeline alive while she is in a trance. Debussy also strengthens the eerie half-mad quality of Madeline by giving her a poem to sing, 'The haunted palace', recited by Roderick in Poe's original. This is inserted in the first scene, where she is dimly seen in the background.

In the second scene, Debussy gives Roderick an extended monologue in which he confesses his inner torments, to himself and then to the friend, dwelling on the links between his state of mind and the crumbling stones of the house. The friend entreats him to leave, but Roderick explains that the 'all-powerful presence of the stones has for many years directed the destiny' of the Usher lineage. The doctor enters with the news of Madeline's death. A storm is gathering, and the friend reads a medieval tale, 'The Mad Tryst'. Echoing a line from the tale, a dull metallic noise is heard; Roderick realizes what the physician has done and, listening to the sounds from beneath, hears her climbing the stairs; at his final words, 'Madman! Madman! I tell you she is behind this very door!', the force of the storm causes the panelling and the windows to collapse, revealing the white figure of Lady Madeline covered in blood. She falls upon Usher, dragging him to the floor, and a blood-red moon appears; all that remains is a stagnant pool and the ruins of the house.

Debussy's sketches leave considerable problems for anyone attempting a reconstruction. He intended the work for a soprano, three baritones and full orchestra. There are more than 14 manuscripts containing sketches at different stages of development; no edition could ever be more than an amalgam of unfinished material. However, the work reveals a side of Debussy that did not emerge elsewhere, though certain works, notably *Pelléas*, contain Poeian elements. The music Debussy completed displays a degree of dissonance not sustained in his other works, as well as some orchestral indications: Debussy was particularly proud of his use of 'the low notes of the oboe with violin harmonics'.

According to a letter from André Suarès to Romain Rolland, Debussy was engaged on a 'symphony on psychological themes from Poe' as early as 1890. His letters contain allusions to Poe, often identifying the 'neurasthenia' of Poe's characters with his own psychological state. He seems to have begun work on the libretto of *La chute* in 1908, having left his other Poe project, *Le diable dans le beffroi*, unfinished. The earliest surviving sketches seem to date from 1909, when he also presented a copied-out version of the prelude to Emma Bardac as a birthday gift. There are also sketches for the end of the piece, in the form of a melodrama in which blocks of music accompany spoken recitation. Several versions of Madeline's song were sketched, including a florid version for high soprano (placed in the next scene in the reconstruction by Juan Allende-Blin, 1979, Paris). It was apparently not until 1916 that Debussy again began work in earnest, and a substantial short score from this period is a main source: it is, however, confused by the existence of other manuscripts from this period. There are also sections for which no music has survived; in some modern revivals these have been spoken to preserve the continuity.

It is widely agreed that the work is too incomplete to be convincing in a reconstruction. Though Debussy left passages of striking music, there are large sections that were never sufficiently developed to do justice to Poe's chilling tale. Debussy summed up his difficulties in 1911: 'For a single bar that is alive', he wrote to André Caplet, 'there are 20 stifled by the weight of what is known as tradition'. Dukas later confirmed that Debussy was still dissatisfied with his musical responses to the text, and it remains an open question whether, even had he lived longer, he would have brought either this or his other Poe setting, *Le diable dans le beffroi*, to fruition. RICHARD LANGHAM SMITH

Cialli [Ciallis], **Rinaldo** (*fl* Venice, 1684–98). Italian librettist. Little is known about him other than that he was a priest. He wrote six librettos for various Venetian theatres and at least two oratorios. The first two and last two librettos are based on history, but *La fortuna tra le disgrazie* is entirely his own invention. Set in Persia in its original production at the Teatro S Angelo, it was set in Sicily when it was restaged a year later at the Teatro S Salvatore for, as the letter to the reader asserts, the setting is not an essential element of the drama. A detailed description of the original staging is found in *Pallade veneta* (January 1688). *Falsirena*, based on Marino's *Adone*, proved to be his greatest success; it was restaged in Venice the year after its première and in eight other Italian cities during the next decade. The original production boasted spectacular stage effects, for which Tomaso Bezzi was responsible. Cialli's last libretto marked Lotti's début as an opera composer.

Ariberto e Flavio regi de' longobardi, Lonati, 1684; *Le generose gare tra Cesare e Pompeo*, D. Gabrielli, 1686; *La fortuna tra le disgrazie*, Biego, 1688; *Falsirena*, M. A. Ziani, 1690 (also as Marte deluso); *Creonte*, Ziani, 1690; *Il trionfo dell'innocenza*, Lotti, 1693

*

AllacciD
C. Ivanovich: *Minerva al tavolino* (Venice, 1681, 2/1688)
G. Bonlini: *Le glorie della poesia e della musica* (Venice, 1730)
A. Groppo: *Catalogo di tutti drammi per musica recitati ne' teatri di Venezia* (Venice, 1745)
M. A. Zorzi: 'Saggio di bibliografia sugli oratorii sacri eseguiti a Venezia', *Accademie e biblioteche d'Italia*, iv (1930), 226–46, 394–403, 529–43; v (1931), 79–96, 493–508; vi (1932), 256–69
E. Selfridge-Field: *Pallade veneta: Writings on Music in Venetian Society, 1650–1750* (Venice, 1985) HARRIS S. SAUNDERS

Ciampi, Francesco (*b* ? Massa or Pisa, ?*c*1690; *d* after 1764). Italian composer. He served the Duke of Massa as a composer and violinist, and was a member of the Bologna Accademia Filarmonica. In 1735 he was *maestro di cappella* at the church of S Angelo Custode in Rome. He composed ten *opere serie* in all. Burney had high praise for some of his sacred music.

Sofonisba (G. M. Tommasi), Livorno, 1715
Tamerlano, Massa, Ducale, 1716
Timocrate, Massa, Ducale, 1716
Il Teuzzone (A. Zeno), Massa, Ducale, carn. 1717
L'amante ravveduto (A. Zaniboni), Bologna, 1725
Ciro (?P. Pariati), Milan, Ducale, 28 Aug 1726
Lucio Vero, Mantua, 1726
Zenobia, Mantua, 1726
Onorio (D. Lalli and B. Boldini), Venice, S Giovanni Grisostomo, aut. 1729; ov., 10 arias *GB-Lbl*
Demofoonte (P. Metastasio), Rome, Tordinona, 5 Feb 1735; 1 aria *I-Mc*

*

BurneyH
G. Storza: 'Un musico di Alderamo di Cybo Duca di Massa', *Giornale storico della Lunigiana*, xi (1920), 150–53

Ciampi, Vincenzo (Legrenzio) (*b* Piacenza, ?1719; *d* Venice, 30 March 1762). Italian composer. His place and date of birth, from Fétis, may be incorrect; he was frequently called a Neapolitan on librettos. He studied in Naples with Leo and Durante, and his first six comic operas were performed there (1737–45). He was at Palermo for half the 1746–7 opera season, composing his first *opera seria* and serving as *maestro al cembalo* for another, and was then *maestro di coro* at the Ospedale degli Incurabili, Venice. In 1748 he worked with Goldoni on comic operas in Venice; one of these, *Bertoldo, Bertoldino e Cacasenno* (probably given on 26 December 1748), was highly successful in Paris in 1753 and through Favart's parody *Ninette à la cour* (1755) influenced the development of *opéra comique*. In the autumn of 1748 Ciampi went to London as composer and music director to a company under G. F. Crosa that gave the first season of Italian comic operas there, at the King's Theatre. These included *Gli tre cicisbei ridicoli*, in which the favourite song 'Tre giorni son che Nina' has sometimes been attributed to Ciampi, but on dubious grounds, according to Walker. In summer 1749 the company visited Brussels, but it is uncertain whether Ciampi was with them. He was in Venice in autumn 1749, composing comic operas with Goldoni. Back in London for the 1749–50 season, he moved with the Crosa company to the Little Theatre in the Haymarket after a dispute between Crosa and the director Vanneschi at the King's. Eight performances of his *Il negligente* (first performed in Venice that autumn) were given between 21 November and 16 December. In January they returned to the King's, giving comic operas and two *opere serie* by Ciampi. The season was cut short in April by the impresario's bankruptcy, whereupon the company returned to the Little Theatre for four performances. There was no Italian opera in London in the next three seasons but Ciampi remained there.

His opera *Didone* was given nine times in the 1753–4 season, but a version of *Bertoldo* put on in December 1754 seems not to have repeated its successes on the Continent, being given only three times. The extent of Ciampi's association with the Italian opera seasons in London in this period is not known. By the end of 1756 he seems to have been back in Venice, as he resumed his operatic career there.

Ciampi's music is typical of that of many composers of his era in combining what are now considered old-fashioned (Baroque) elements with modern (*galant*) ones. Even when using Baroque material, he often cast it in the regular, short-breathed phrases of the *galant* style, though on occasion – as in the aria 'Se resto sul lido' in *Didone* (which Burney considered the best of his London *opere serie*) – he achieved an effect of majesty and broad rhythmic sweep. He was an agreeable and tuneful, if not a distinguished, composer, and Burney's judgment of his vocal works is still valid: 'they are not without merit; he had fire and abilities, but there seems something wanting, or redundant, in all his compositions; I never saw one that quite satisfied me, and yet there are good passages in many of them ... The comic songs of *Il negligente* are infinitely better than his serious, and convince me that his *genre* was buffo'.

dm – *dramma per musica* ob – *opera buffa*

Da un disordine nasce un ordine (ob, G. Federico), Naples, Fiorentini, aut. 1737
La Beatrice (ob, Federico), Naples, Nuovo, carn. 1740
La Lionora (ob, Federico), Naples, Fiorentini, wint. 1742 [parti buffe by Logroscino, parti serie by Ciampi]
La Flaminia (dm), Naples, Nuovo, spr. 1743
L'Arminio (dm, F. Navarra), Naples, Fiorentini, aut. 1744
L'amore ingegnoso (ob, A. Palomba), Naples, Fiorentini, aut. 1745
Artaserse (dm, P. Metastasio), Palermo, S Cecilia, 1747
L'Adriano (dm, Metastasio), Venice, S Cassiano, carn. 1748, *I-MOe*; rev. London, 1750, Favourite Songs (London, 1750)
La scuola moderna, ossia La maestra di buon gusto [after G. Cocchi: La maestra] (dramma giocoso, C. Goldoni), Venice, S Moisè, aut. 1748
Bertoldo, Bertoldino e Cacasenno (ob, Goldoni), Venice, S Moisè, ?26 Dec 1748, *MOe*; as Bertoldo in corte, Paris, 1753, *F-Po*; as Bertoldo, Bertoldino e Cacasenno alla corte del rè Alboino, London, 1755, *B-Lc**; Favourite Songs (London, 1755 and 1762)
La favola de' tre gobbi (intermezzo, Goldoni), Venice, S Moisè, carn. 1749, *Pn*; rev. as Li tre gobbi rivali amanti di Madama Vezzosa, Venice, aut. 1756; as Les trois bossus, Paris, Jan 1762; as I tre gobbi innamorati, Parma, carn. 1773; as Li tre difettosi rivali in amore (lib. rev. S. Prettini), aut. 1782
Il negligente (ob, Goldoni), Venice, S Moisè, aut. 1749; rev. London, 1750; as Il trascurato, Lodi, 1751; *D-Wa*, Favourite Songs (London, 1750)
Il trionfo de Camilla (dm, S. Stampiglia), London, King's, 31 March 1750, Favourite Songs (London, 1750)
Didone (dm, Metastasio), London, King's, 5 Jan 1754, Favourite Songs (London, 1754)
Catone in Utica (dm, Metastasio), Venice, S Benedetto, 26 Dec 1756, *A-Wn*
La clemenza di Tito (dm, Metastasio), Venice, S Moisè, carn. 1756–7; *I-Gl, Mc, MAav, P-La* (1759, Reggio Emilia)
Il chimico (ob), Venice, S Samuele, carn. 1756–7, *I-Fc*
Arsinoe (dm, G. B. Galliani), Turin, Regio, carn. 1758, *P-La*
Gianguir (dm, A. Zeno), Venice, S Benedetto, 26 Dec 1759
Amore in caricatura (ob, Goldoni), Venice, S Angelo, 18 Jan 1761, *La*
Antigona (dm, G. Roccaforte), Venice, S Samuele, April 1762

Arias in: Gli tre cicisbei ridocoli, 1749; Le caprice amoureux, ou Ninette à la cour, 1755; Les amants trompés, Paris, 1756; Tolomeo, 1762; The Maid of the Mill, 1765; The Summer's Tale, 1765; Lionel and Clarissa, 1768; The Captive, 1769; The School for Fathers, or Lionel and Clarissa, 1791
Arias, duets etc.: *GB-Lbl, I-Bc, Gl, Mc, Nc, Tf, Vqs*

*

BurneyH; *FétisB*
W. B. Squire: 'Tre giorni son che Nina', *MT*, xl (1899), 241–3
O. G. Sonneck: 'Ciampi's "Bertoldo, Bertoldino e Cacasenno" and Favart's "Ninette à la cour": a Contribution to the History of Pasticcio', *SIMG*, xii (1910–11), 525–64; repr. in *Miscellaneous Studies on the History of Music* (London and New York, 1921)
C. Anguissola: *Vincenzo Legrenzio Ciampi: musicista piacentino del settecento* (Piacenza, 1934, 2/1936)
F. Walker: 'Tre giorni son che Nina; an Old Controversy Reopened', *MT*, xc (1949), 432–5
A. L. Bellina: Preface to G. Cocchi: *La maestra*, DMV, xix (1987)

DENNIS LIBBY (text, with SASKIA WILLAERT), JAMES L. JACKMAN (work-list)

Ciannella, Giuliano (*b* Palermo, 25 Oct 1943). Italian tenor. He studied with Carlo Bergonzi, making his début in 1974 at Milan (Teatro Nuovo). He first sang at La Scala in 1976 as Cassio, the role of his Metropolitan début (1979). He has appeared widely in Italy and in Philadelphia, Chicago, San Francisco, Geneva and Paris as well as at Covent Garden, where he sang Manrico in 1985. His repertory includes Rodolfo, Pinkerton, Cavaradossi, Ruggero (*La rondine*), Faust, Don José, Chénier and Enzo; but his fine voice and fierce attack are best displayed in Verdi: as the Duke (*Rigoletto*), Macduff, Don Carlos, Alfredo and Ernani, and as Radames, which he sang at Luxor in 1987.

ELIZABETH FORBES

Cibber, Susanna Maria (*b* London, bap. 28 Feb 1714; *d* London, 30 Jan 1766). English actress and mezzo-soprano, sister of the composer Thomas Arne. Her brother taught her to sing and she first appeared in two seasons of English operas backed by her father, when she sang in Lampe's *Amelia* (March 1732), Handel's *Acis and Galatea*, J. C. Smith's *Teraminta* and her brother's *Rosamond*. In March 1733 she sang for Handel in *Deborah*. She then worked with the Drury Lane company, singing between the acts and in musical afterpieces. After her marriage to Theophilus Cibber his father Colley coached her for her first acting role, the heroine of the tragedy *Zara* (January 1736). She scarcely sang on the stage again, becoming the greatest tragic actress of her generation. A lawsuit brought by her husband against her lover caused a scandal in 1738 and she left the stage until the 1741–2 season when she acted in Dublin and sang there in concerts organized by Handel. She resumed her acting career in London, and sang in two of Handel's oratorio seasons; Burney wrote of her singing of Micah in *Samson*, a role Handel designed for her: 'her voice was a thread, and her knowledge of Music very inconsiderable, yet from her intelligence of the words and native feeling, she sung ... in a more touching manner, than the finest opera singer I ever heard'.

*

BDA; *BurneyH*; *LS*

C. Burney: 'Mrs Cibber', *Rees's Cyclopaedia*, viii (London, 1802–20)

Anon.: *An Account of the Life of Susanna Maria Cibber* (London, 1887)

M. Sands: 'Susanna Maria Cibber', *MMR*, lxxii (1942), 157–9, 174–7

J. Herbage: 'The Truth About Mrs Cibber', *MMR*, lxxviii (1948), 59–65

P. Lord: 'The English-Italian Opera Companies 1732–3', *ML*, xlv (1964), 239–51

M. Nash: *The Provoked Wife: the Life and Times of Susannah Cibber* (London, 1977)

OLIVE BALDWIN, THELMA WILSON

Ciboulette. *Opérette* in three acts by REYNALDO HAHN to a libretto by Robert de Flers and Francis de Croisset; Paris, Théâtre des Variétés, 7 April 1923.

Hahn's most successful and durable work for the stage, *Ciboulette* was at once an innovation, the beginning of a long series of light operas written in a nostalgic vein for the Paris stage, and a homage to Offenbach, Hervé and Olivier Métra (who appears as a character). Set in 1867, the story tells of the romantic adventures involving the aging poet Duparquet (baritone) – Rodolphe of Murger's *Vie de Bohème* 30 years on – and the market-girl Ciboulette (soprano) and her fickle suitor Antonin (tenor). In the first act Duparquet regrets that things are not what they were when he was young and in love; even lovers' quarrels had more spice to them ('Bien des jeunes gens'). The secondary couple, Zénobie (soprano) and Roger (baritone), sing a love duet which is a deliberate parody of 'Toi! Vous!' in Massenet's *Manon*. Ciboulette's character, her entrance aria 'Moi j'm'appell' Ciboulette' and her dialogue with the other market-women are reminiscent of Offenbach's *Mesdames de la Halle*. In Act 2 the action moves from Paris to a farm near Aubervilliers where the characters have come for a day-trip and where their sentimental adventures become further complicated by the predicament of Ciboulette, whose uncle has arranged a troupe of eight suitors for her hand. Duparquet tells of his own sad love for Mimi ('C'est tout ce qui me reste d'elle') and the act ends in a series of misunderstandings which separate the lovers. All ends happily in Act 3, which takes place in Olivier Métra's studio some months later: Antonin has disengaged himself and is reunited with Ciboulette, who has become an operetta singer, Conchita Ciboulera. She serenades the company with a Métra waltz, 'Amour qui meurs! Amour qui passes!'

In *Ciboulette* Hahn made use of his long study of Parisian popular music and, despite his reputation for preciousness, produced a vigorous and tuneful operetta which has proved the equal of the most successful works in the genre by his predecessors and contemporaries. At the première Ciboulette was sung by Edmée Favart, Zénobie by Jeanne Pierat, Antonin by Henry Defreyn, Duparquet by Jean Périer and Roger by Jean Calain; Paul Letombe conducted. Hahn supervised a film version in the 1930s, since when the work has been revived many times, famous Ciboulettes including Denise Duval, Geori Boué and Mady Mesplé.

PATRICK O'CONNOR

Ciccerelli [Cicarelli, Cicciarelli, Ceccherelli], **Chiara** (*fl* 1796–1808). Italian singer. She appeared in three operas in Genoa (1796), ten in Venice (1798–1800), 13 at La Scala (1802–3) and one more in Genoa (1807–8). She played both comic and serious parts. She may have been related to the singer Giuseppe Ciccerelli, who appeared in 21 operas in Venice, 1796–1800 (in four of them with her), and to Gaetano Ciccerelli, who sang in the revival of Cimarosa's *Gli Orazi ed i Curiazi* at La Fenice, Venice, in 1797.

COLIN TIMMS

Ciccimarra, Giuseppe (*b* Altamura, Apulia, 22 May 1790; *d* Venice, 5 Dec 1836). Italian tenor. He was engaged for many years in Naples, where he took part in six Rossini premières: at the Teatro del Fondo he sang Iago in *Otello* (1816); at the S Carlo he sang Goffredo in *Armida* (1817); Aaron in *Mosè in Egitto* and Ernesto in *Ricciardo e Zoraide* (1818); Pylades in *Ermione* (1819) and Condulmiero in *Maometto II* (1820). He sang Nathan in Mayr's oratorio *Atalia* (1822) at the S Carlo in a performance directed by Rossini and described by Donizetti in a letter to the composer. He retired in 1826.

ELIZABETH FORBES

Ciccolino [Ciecolino]. *See* RIVANI, ANTONIO.

Ciceri, Pierre-Luc-Charles (*b* St-Cloud, 17 Aug 1782; *d* St-Chéron, Seine-et-Oise, 22 Aug 1868). French stage designer and painter. After his training as a singer at the Paris Conservatoire was broken off because of an accident, he began in 1802 to take instruction in drawing and painting from the architect and stage designer F. J. Belanger. By 1806 he had entered the Paris Opéra studio as 'peintre des paysages'; about 1818 he was accepted into the circle of 'peintres en chef', and from 1824 to 1847 he was effectually head of that institution. He also worked as stage designer for other Parisian theatres, and was active in Kassel (1810), St-Cloud (1813) and London (1815). After an early phase in which he carried on the traditional forms of neo-classicism, culminating in the designs for Spontini's *Olimpie* (1819, with Degotti), he developed during the time of the Bourbon restoration a style of scenery design which reflected technical and economic developments and the discovery of national historical and cultural consciousness. It combined the progressive technique of gas lighting (first in *Aladin, ou La lampe merveilleuse*, 1822, with Daguerre; music by Isouard and Benincori) and the effective use of the new panorama and diorama, as well as the moving panorama, with neo-Baroque mechanical effects (volcanic eruption in *La muette de Portici* by Auber, 1828, after the model by Sanquirico in Milan) and the accurate, detailed depiction of historical epochs in stage scenery (e.g. Meyerbeer's *Robert le diable*). Ciceri's effective scenography corresponded exactly with the intentions of Romantic music drama, and it was above all through his ability to conceive stage design as the integrating element of theatrical production that he became the dominating figure of Romantic stage art and the prophet of an age of 'spectacles purement oculaires' (Théophile Gautier, 1858). A commercial scenic studio founded by him in 1822, which made scenery for theatres at home and abroad, contributed substantially to the international fame of the style of setting developed in Paris.

For illustration *see* GRAND OPÉRA, fig.4; *GUSTAVE III*; *MUETTE DE PORTICI, LA*, fig.2; and *OLIMPIE*.

*

I. Guest: 'Stage Designers, vi: Pierre Ciceri', *Ballet and Opera*, viii/7 (1949), 20–28
B. V. Daniels: 'Cicéri and Daguerre: Set Designers for the Paris Opéra, 1820–1822', *Theater Survey*, xxii (1981), 69–90
N. Wild: *Décors et Costumes du XIXe siècle*, i: *Opéra de Paris: Catalogues de la Bibliothèque de l'Opéra* (Paris, 1987)
C. Join-Diéterle: *Les décors de scène de l'Opéra de Paris à l'époque romantique* (Paris, 1988)
R. Wilberg: *The 'Mise-en-scène' at the Paris Opéra–Salle le Peletier (1821–1873) and the Staging of the First French Grand Opéra: Meyerbeer's 'Robert le Diable'* (diss., Brigham Young U., 1990)

MANFRED BOETZKES

Cicognini, Giacinto Andrea (*b* Florence, 1606; *d* Venice, *c*1650). Italian playwright and librettist. His father was the poet and playwright Jacopo Cicognini (1577–1633). Although he earned a law degree from the University of Pisa in 1627, he chose instead to pursue a career as a playwright. One of the most important figures in 17th-century Italian drama, Cicognini fused comic and tragic elements and, like his father, introduced Spanish influence, drawing on the works of authors such as Calderón de la Barca and Tirso de Molina. Cicognini's first libretto, *Il Celio*, appeared in Florence in 1646. That same year he moved to Venice, where his remaining librettos were written and originally staged. He participated in the meetings of the Accademia degli Incogniti, whose members shaped the direction of Venetian opera during the 1640s. Two of Cicognini's operatic works, *L'Orontea* and *Il Giasone* (both 1649), were the most popular of the century; they were performed throughout Italy for more than three decades, and *L'Orontea* was presented in Innsbruck (1656), Hanover (1678) and Wolfenbüttel (1686). His works were discussed by such literary critics as G. M. Crescimbeni and Stefano Arteaga. Cicognini's librettos are known for their intermingling of comic, satiric and tragic elements, their comic characterizations and their variety of verse forms.

Il Celio (dramma musicale), N. Sapiti and B. Baglioni, 1646 (Cavalli, 1652, as Veremonda, l'amazzone di Aragona); *Il Giasone* (dramma musicale), Cavalli, 1649; *L'Orontea* (dramma musicale), F. Lucio, 1649 (F. Cirillo, 1654; Cesti, 1656; F. Vismarri, 1660); *Gl'amori di Alessandro Magno e di Rossane* (dramma musicale, completed by unidentified author after Cicognini's death), Lucio, 1651 (B. Ferrari, 1656; G. A. Boretti, 1668, as Alessandro amante)

*

L. Grashey: *Giacinto Andrea Cicogninis Leben und Werke, unter besonderer Berücksichtigung seines Dramas 'La Marienne ouvero il maggior mostro del mondo'* (Leipzig, 1909)
R. Verde: *G. A. Cicognini* (Catania, 1912)
A. Belloni: *Storia letteraria d'Italia: il seicento* (Milan, 1929)
A. M. Crinò: 'Documenti inediti sulla vita e l'opera di Jacopo e di Giacinto Andrea Cicognini', *Studi secenteschi*, ii (1961), 255–86
W. C. Holmes: 'Giacinto Andrea Cicognini's and Antonio Cesti's *Orontea* (1649)', *New Looks at Italian Opera: Essays in Honor of Donald J. Grout* (Ithaca, NY, 1968), 108–32
L. Bianconi and T. Walker: 'Dalla *Finta pazza* alla *Veremonda*: storie di Febiarmonici', *RIM*, x (1975), 379–454
W. C. Holmes: 'Yet Another "Orontea": Further Rapport Between Venice and Vienna', *Venezia e il melodramma nel seicento: Venice 1972*, 199–225
L. Bianconi: *Il seicento* (Turin, 1982; Eng. trans., 1987)
E. Rosand: *Opera in Seventeenth-Century Venice: the Creation of a Genre* (Berkeley, CA, 1991)

BETH L. GLIXON

Cid, Der ('The Cid'). *Lyrisches Drama* in three acts by PETER CORNELIUS (i) to his own libretto after Guillén de Castro y Bellvís's *Las mocedades del Cid*, Pierre Corneille's *Le Cid* and Johann Gottfried Herder's *Der Cid*; Weimar, Hoftheater, 21 May 1865.

The tales of the 11th-century Christian hero, the Cid, provided Cornelius with ample material for a historical drama, with battles between the Spanish crusaders and the Moors being offset by the personal story of Chimene's desire for revenge for the Cid's murder of her father. Although the composer researched widely before writing his libretto, he gave second place to historical aspects, stressing the psychological battle within Chimene herself. Like Wagner's Isolde, she loves the object of her vengeance and longs for her own death as well as his, as the only way of resolving her conflicting emotions.

In Act 1 Fernando, the king of Castilia (tenor), seeks to give judgment in Chimene's case against the Cid, Ruy Diaz (baritone); although the people of Burgos sing choruses in praise of the Cid, Chimene (soprano) gains centre stage as she describes her feelings over her father's death ('Gedenkst du, König'). Revenge seems uppermost in her heart, despite pleas for reconciliation from the bishop, Luyn Calvo (bass). Her demands are stilled only by news of the Moors' invasion, requiring that the Cid lead his country in a different kind of revenge ('Der Schrei Castiliens in Gefahr betaubt der eignen Klage Ton').

As Chimene is alone in her castle in Act 2, her love for the Cid emerges more clearly ('Lasst mich nicht einsam'), though visits from Alvar Fanez (tenor), who promises to kill the Cid for her during battle, and later from the bishop, intensify the fluctuations of her heart. When Ruy Diaz himself appears, driven by love to ask for her blessing, they share the torment of their feelings ('O bange Fahrt auf dunklen Wellen'); as he leaves, Chimene is finally led to express openly her desire for his victory ('Ewiger! Blick' auf ihn!').

Act 3 opens with the crowd celebrating the triumph of the Cid over the Moors ('Heil ihm der Gott zum Sieg erkor'). Alvar Fanez appears instead of the hero, however, and Chimene fears that her revenge has been fulfilled ('Weh! dass du so erfüllt mein Los'). She can no longer hide her love from the world; when Ruy Diaz finally enters, the barrier of pride is removed and their union is blessed by the bishop, the king and the crowd ('Durch Kampf und Sieg').

Cornelius expended much effort on the opera from 1860 to 1865, hoping it would bring him popular success, but *Der Cid* received only two performances in his lifetime, in Weimar on 21 and 31 May 1865. Hermann Levi published his own revised version of the work in 1891 and conducted it in Munich in 1893. It was not until 9 and 10 June 1904 that the original opera was revived by Max Hasse in the Hoftheater, Weimar; in 1905 it was published as part of the collected edition of Cornelius's works. Subsequent performances have been rare. Aspects of the work's style, the stately choruses and many march-like rhythms, are highly reminiscent of *Lohengrin*, but in comparison with Wagner's music Cornelius's lacks dramatic tension. Even at points of crisis the characters tend to lapse into lyrical melodies, which though coloured by chromatic harmonies and expressive orchestral touches fail to further the dramatic action. AMANDA GLAUERT

Cid, El. Libretto subject used in many periods. Its chief source is PIERRE CORNEILLE's tragedy *Le Cid*; earlier sources are the plays of Guillén de Castro y Bellvís (1569–1631), *Las mocedades del Cid* and *Las hazañas del Cid*, and popular Spanish ballads. All recount the exploits of Rodrigo (or Ruy) Diaz de Vivar, a Spanish warrior of the 11th century (called El Cid after the Arabic *sidi*, 'lord'). Librettos on the subject have been written in Italian (as *Il Cid*, *Il Cidde* or *Il gran Cid*) and German (as *Der Cid*) as well as French (as *Le Cid*); some operas are entitled *Cimene*, *Chimène* or *Rodrigue et Chimène*.

The subject of Corneille's play was rarely used by Italian librettists, perhaps because, even watered down, Chimène's pursuit of vengeance against Rodrigue through most of the work made difficult the contriving of amorous encounters between them, as the genre required. A three-act libretto by Alborghetti had a few settings between 1715 and 1741, most notably by Gasparini (1717, Naples, as *Il gran Cid*) and Leo (1727, Rome, as *Il Cid*). In the 1760s a three-act libretto by Giovacchino Pizzi, a prominent Roman Arcadian, brought the subject its greatest Italian currency. Its characters include Rodrigo (primo uomo), Climene (prima donna), the king Fernando (tenor), Duarte (secondo uomo), Elvira (seconda donna) and Armindo (ultima parte). Pizzi's libretto seems to have been first set by Piccinni (1766, Naples, as *Il gran Cid*), later by Carlo Franchi (1769, Turin, as *Il gran Cidde Rodrigo*), Bianchi (1773, Florence, as *Il gran Cidde*), and Antonio Rosetti (1780, Naples, as *Il gran Cid*), but the Italian composer most involved with the subject was Sacchini, who set it three times. After Sacchini there was little important operatic treatment of the subject until the second half of the 19th century. Giovanni Pacini composed an *Il Cid* for La Scala in 1853; *Der Cid* by Cornelius, given at Weimar in 1865, had limited success. Massenet's *grand opéra Le Cid*, however, which follows Corneille's play fairly closely, was popular in Paris for more than 30 years after its première in 1885. Bizet in 1873 and Debussy in 1890 both began *Cid* operas (*Don Rodrigue* and *Rodrigue et Chimène*) which they did not complete.

See also CID, DER [Cornelius]; CID, LE [Massenet]; CIDDE, IL [Sacchini]; and RODRIGUE ET CHIMÈNE [Debussy]. For a list of operas based on Corneille's *Le Cid*, *see* CORNEILLE, PIERRE.

DENNIS LIBBY

Cid, Le. *Opéra* in four acts and ten scenes by JULES MASSENET to a libretto by Adolphe d'Ennery, ÉDOUARD BLAU and LOUIS GALLET after PIERRE CORNEILLE's drama (1637); Paris, Opéra, 30 November 1885.

The first performance of *Le Cid* confirmed Massenet's reputation as a successful opera composer, marking as it did his return to the Opéra for the first time since *Le roi de Lahore* eight years previously and coming a year after the double triumph of *Manon* by the Opéra Comique and the first performances in Paris of *Hérodiade* (Théâtre Italien). The De Reszke brothers Jean (tenor) and Edouard (bass) sang in *Hérodiade* and both were engaged for *Le Cid*.

After a conventional sonata-form overture, rare in French opera, the action follows the outlines of Corneille's play. In the first act preparations are in hand for the investiture of Rodrigue (tenor) as a knight of St James of Compostella. Chimène (soprano) tells her father, the Count of Gormas (bass), of her love for Rodrigue and receives his blessing. She is joined by the Infanta (soprano), also in love with Rodrigue but barred by rank from marrying him, and they sing a tender duet ('Laissez le doute dans mon âme'). Rodrigue is duly invested ('O noble lame étincelante'). The Count, confident of being appointed guardian of the king's son, learns that Rodrigue's father Don Diègue (bass) has been preferred and insults him in public. Don Diègue incites his son to avenge his honour before revealing the identity of the proposed victim.

In the second act Rodrigue provokes the Count to a duel and kills him. Chimène interrupts a ballet-fiesta with her public accusation of Rodrigue and demands for justice. A Moorish envoy declares war, and Rodrigue begs to be allowed to lead the Spanish forces, promising to return to whatever punishment the king sees fit. The third act is launched with the most famous number in the score, Chimène's 'Pleurez, pleurez mes yeux', and she voices her operatically conflicting emotions in an extended duet of farewell with Rodrigue. On the battlefield Rodrigue prays for victory ('O souverain, ô juge, ô père') and is reassured by a vision of St James. In the final act news is brought of his death in battle, but after Chimène and Don Diègue have reacted at some length this proves to be false: he returns in triumph and Chimène forgives him.

* * *

Le Cid was Massenet's last attempt at a conventional Meyerbeerian *grand opéra*. While he catches the scale of the work efficiently enough – his ease when writing in 9/8 or 12/8 time comes in useful when setting the lines by Corneille that survive in the libretto – he is patently less at home with stage fanfares, triple choruses and the whole paraphernalia of the form than with more intimate subjects. Comparison between Rodrigue's investiture and Radames's is instructive. The successful numbers (much recorded) are good – the energetic 'O noble lame' (reprised before the third-act battle), the Prayer with its humming-chorus background, Chimène's 'Pleurez' – and the justly famous second-act ballet is one of Massenet's best. But having to write for the comparatively heroic voices of Jean de Reszke and Fidès Devriès (the first Chimène) finds Massenet oddly inflexible in his response, and the role of Don Diègue is longer than it needs to be dramaturgically simply because Edouard de Reszke was available. The reminiscence motifs are short-breathed, and applied rather than integrated, very much after the manner of Debussy's 'visiting-card' jibe at *Das Rheingold*.

The loyalty of the De Reszke brothers and Pol Plançon (Count of Gormas) ensured considerable success for *Le Cid* both in France and America, and it achieved 150 performances at the Opéra by 1919. It has since lapsed from the repertory, not least because of difficulties of casting. There is an incomplete live recording (1976) with Placido Domingo in the title role.

For illustration *see* STAGE DESIGN, fig.11. RODNEY MILNES

Cidde, Il. Opera by ANTONIO SACCHINI to a libretto by GIOACCHINO PIZZI; Rome, Teatro Argentina, Carnival 1769.

Sacchini composed three operas to the story of EL CID. The first (given in 1769, not, as is sometimes stated, 1764), is said not to have been a success, although it was also given at Lisbon in 1773 and, apparently as a vehicle for its Roman primo uomo, Guarducci, at Perugia in 1779. The presence of Guarducci's cantabile aria 'Se placate alfin vi miro' in manuscript aria collections suggests that it enjoyed some popularity. *Il Cid*, Sacchini's second treatment of the subject, was the major work of his first season at the King's Theatre, London (1773), and was a success, receiving 22 performances, far more than any other opera of the season. It was set to a three-act libretto by the London theatre poet Bottarelli that reflects considerable influence of Pizzi, including the same cast of characters (Climene becomes Cimene), as well as some differences of emphasis, particularly scenes of spectacle, including a triumphal march, choruses, and ballets, designed to maintain the interest of a public that knew little Italian. (*Il gran Cid*, a setting by Paisiello of a revised version of Bottarelli's libretto, was produced in Florence in 1775 as a vehicle for its London primo uomo, Millico.) Finally, Sacchini returned to the subject again early in his Paris period, with *Chimène*, a three-act *tragédie lyrique* to a French libretto by Guillard. As might be expected, this libretto has the closest resemblance to Corneille's tragedy, while accommodating the French taste for choral singing and ballet. The solo vocal numbers are in a hybrid Italo-French style. With Saint-Huberty in the title role the work had its première before the court at Fontainebleau (1783) and then was given at the Paris Opéra. Its success was moderate (57 performances, and four more in 1808); Piccinni's *Didon*, first performed a month earlier, was more successful. The principal characters are Chimène, Rodrigue (tenor), Elvire, Rodrigue's father, Don Diègue (baritone), the king (tenor), and Don Sanche (tenor). Notwithstanding frequent assertions to the effect that the French opera is based on music from the London one, there appear to be no musical interrelationships of any substance among Sacchini's three *Cid* operas, although since the London one does not survive complete (unusually extensive excerpts were published) this cannot be asserted with absolute certainty. DENNIS LIBBY

Ciesinski, Katherine (*b* Newark, DE, 13 Oct 1950). American mezzo-soprano. Her teachers included Margaret Harshaw at the Curtis Institute. After winning competitions in Geneva and Paris, she gained wide recognition as Erika in a television broadcast of *Vanessa* from Spoleto in 1978. Her Santa Fe début was in 1979 as Countess Geschwitz in the first American performance of the three-act version of Berg's *Lulu*. Her European début, as Annina (*La traviata*) in Aix-en-Provence in 1976, was followed by engagements in many European cities, as well as in China and Israel. She made her début at the Metropolitan Opera as Nicklausse in 1988 and returned the following season in *Bluebeard's Castle*. She created roles in *The Aspern Papers* (1988, Dallas) and *La Célestine* (1988, Paris). Possessed of a generous but essentially lyrical voice, she employs her dramatic intensity and incisive musicianship for a dramatic repertory encompassing Brangäne, the Composer, Laura, Lucretia, Marina, Octavian and Waltraute, as well as roles in works by Cavalli, Handel and Mozart. Her recordings include *Ariane et Barbe-bleue*, *War and Peace* and Gounod's *Sapho*.
CORI ELLISON

Ciesinski, Kristine (Frances) (*b* Newark, DE, 5 July 1952). American soprano, sister of Katherine Ciesinski. She studied in Boston and won the International Singing Competition at Geneva in 1977. Engaged at the Landestheater in Salzburg (1979–81) and, since 1985, at Bremen, she has also appeared in Baltimore, Milwaukee, Frankfurt, and Munich. She sang Donna Anna for Scottish Opera (1985) and Berlioz's Cassandra (*La prise de Troie*) for Opera North (1986) and the WNO (1987). She made her London début in 1989 with the ENO as Ann Maurrant in Weill's *Street Scene*, returning in 1990 as Lady Macbeth, a role she repeated with huge success on the ENO tour of the USSR, and as Marie (*Wozzeck*). Her repertory includes the title role of *Iphigénie en Tauride*, Countess Almaviva, Donna Elvira, Fiordiligi, Leonore, Medea (Cherubini), Senta, Eva, Marguerite, Manon Lescaut (Puccini), Wally and Salome, a role that effectively displays her strong voice and dramatic temperament. ELIZABETH FORBES

Cifra, La ('The Cipher'). *Dramma giocoso* in two acts by ANTONIO SALIERI to a libretto by LORENZO DA PONTE after GIUSEPPE PETROSELLINI's libretto *La dama pastorella*; Vienna, Burgtheater, 11 December 1789.

The plot is a conventional *opera buffa* story related to those of Piccinni's *La buona figliuola* and Guglielmi's *La pastorella nobile*. Eurilla (soprano), a shepherdess, unaware that she is really Olimpia, a nobleman's daughter, is surrounded by *buffo* characters: the sly peasant Rusticone (bass), who tries to pass her off as his daughter; his real daughter Lisotta (soprano), a shrew convinced that she herself is of noble blood; and the silly peasant Sandrino (bass), who makes fumbling attempts to woo Lisotta. Only Milord Fideling (tenor), who arrives on the scene in search of the lost Olimpia, can awaken in Eurilla/Olimpia the vague feelings of her noble heritage.

Da Ponte arranged the libretto from an intermezzo Salieri had set ten years earlier in Rome. Salieri described the Act 1 finale as 'un misto di buffo, mezzo carattere, serio', and this description applies equally well to the whole opera. The music is an effective mix of serious and comic, noble and pastoral. Compound metre and the key of G contribute to the rustic opening of the *introduzione*, while the rondò of Eurilla/Olimpia in Act 2, 'Sola e mesta fra tormenti', is in the style of *opera seria*. Salieri wrote the role for Adriana Ferrarese, who was to be Fiordiligi in Mozart's *Così fan tutte*, first performed less than two months after *La cifra*. Both librettist and composer made the most of Ferrarese's ability to present comic and serious situations with equal effectiveness. There are musical reminiscenses of 'Sola e mesta fra tormenti' in 'Per pietà, ben mio, perdona', her rondò in *Così fan tutte*. JOHN A. RICE

Cigna, Gina [Sens, Genoveffa; Sens, Ginetta] (*b* Paris, 6 March 1900). Italian soprano of French birth. She studied with Calvé, Darclée and Storchio. In 1927 she made her début at La Scala as Freia, under the name Genoveffa Sens. In 1929, as Gina Cigna, she returned there and sang every season until 1943, establishing herself as a leading Italian dramatic soprano. She was particularly admired as La Gioconda and Turandot and in Verdi; she also took part in important revivals of *Alceste* (1935) and *L'incoronazione di Poppea* (1937) at Florence, and was the Kostelnička in the first staged performance in Italy of *Jenůfa* (1941, Venice). Cigna made her Covent Garden début as Marguerite in *La damnation de Faust* in 1933 and returned there in 1936, 1937 and 1939. She sang at the Metropolitan (1937–8) and also in San Francisco and Chicago. In 1947 she retired. She was a highly dramatic and musical singer, though her voice inclined to hardness and unsteadiness.

GV (R. Celletti; R. Vegeto) HAROLD ROSENTHAL/R

Cigna-Santi, Vittorio Amedeo (*b* ?Poirino, nr Turin, *c*1730; *d* after 1795). Italian librettist and scholar. Very little is known about his life and activities. Conflicting accounts report his birth as early as 1725, but this is contradicted by later reports of his age. He published only a few known celebratory poems before being appointed principal librettist in the Teatro Regio, Turin, from 1754–5, a post he was to keep for nearly 30 years. A volume of poetry published in 1760 ascribes his education to the Accademia dei Trasformati of Milan. Most of the original librettos he wrote for Turin achieved at least modest success outside the city as well, such as *Mitridate re di Ponto*, later set by Mozart for Milan in 1770. His most successful libretto, *Motezuma*, is typical of his dramaturgical style and was adapted and set, after its première in a version by G. F. Majo for Turin in 1765, by Mysliveček, Paisiello, Galuppi, Sacchini, Anfossi, Insanguine and Zingarelli over the next 16 years (the Zingarelli version was revised and re-staged by Haydn in 1785). Cigna-Santi's poetry is clearly less polished and elegant than that of either Zeno or Metastasio, whom he imitates. The choice of Montezuma as a subject is itself telling; influenced by the wave of exotic settings popular in the 1760s and 70s, it concerns a warrior (Cortez) who, by deception and with financial motives, seeks to destroy the kingdom of Montezuma – not a very appropriate Arcadian idea. The usual balance among five to seven roles is also strained, with the three main characters almost entirely dominant. Arias are sometimes overplayed in the drama for simple effects, and motivation for the characters' actions is not always clear. Metastasio found Cigna-Santi's poetry worthy of public praise, as he reported in a letter to Tommaso Filipponi on 27 February 1760. *Alcina e Ruggero*, his last *dramma per musica*, was staged primarily for visual display, with spectacular effects and intricate machines, a kind of production Cigna-Santi later defended. By his own account he spent much of his energy adapting other librettos for local performance. In 1777 he was nominated a 'poeta della società' of the Cavalieri. Outside the theatre his interests were wide-ranging; he produced a translation of Seneca, and for his studies in history and genealogy was named by the king in 1785 as 'istoriografo del supremo Ordine della Sma Annunziata'.

dm – *dramma per musica*

Andromeda (dm), Cocchi, carn. 1755 (Colla, 1771; G. Gazzaniga, 1775, as Perseo ed Andromeda); *Enea nel Lazio* (dm), Traetta, 1760; *Ifigenia in Aulide* (dm), Bertoni, 1762 (C. Franchi, 1766); *Ercole sul Tago* (serenata per musica), L. X. Santos, 1765; *Motezuma* (dm), G. F. Majo, 1765 (Mysliveček, 1771; Paisiello, 1772; Galuppi, 1772; Sacchini, 1775; Anfossi, 1776; Insanguine, 1780; Zingarelli, 1781); *Mitridate re di Ponto* (dm), Q. Gasparini, 1767 (Mozart, 1770); *Issea* (favola pastorale), Pugnani, 1771 (comp. unknown, London, as Apollo e Issea); *Tamas Kouli-Kan nell'India* (dm), Pugnani, 1772 (Guglielmi, 1774); *L'isola di Alcina* (dm), Alessandri, 1775, as Alcina e Ruggero DALE E. MONSON

Cigoli [Cardi, Ludovico] (*b* Castelvecchio di Cigoli, nr Pisa, 21 Sept 1559; *d* Rome, 8 June 1613). Italian scene designer and deviser of displays. A pupil of B. Morellone in Empoli, he went to Florence in about 1568 to study 'lettere umane'. He matriculated in 1578 at the

Cigoli's design for the figure of Lucifer in the fourth intermedio for Bargagli's comedy 'La pellegrina', performed in Florence, 2 May 1589 for the marriage of Ferdinando I de' Medici and Christine of Lorraine: pen, sanguine and watercolour

Accademia del Disegno and collaborated with A. Allori and B. Buontalenti in displays for the festive Medici entertainments. Most of his drawings are at the Uffizi, among them the preparatory study for the figure of Lucifer which appeared in the fourth *intermedio* of *Pellegrina*, the *commedia* by G. Bargagli performed on 2 May 1589 for the marriage of the Grand Duke Ferdinando I and Christine of Lorraine. Cigoli collaborated with Buontalenti, who was commissioned to re-equip the Medici theatre at the Uffizi, creating scenery, costumes and machinery for the intermezzos.

At the turn of the century, Cigoli was one of the most important Florentine artists and intellectuals and a member of several academies. In 1600 he provided the stage sets for Jacopo Peri's *Euridice*, written to celebrate the marriage of Maria de' Medici to Henri IV of France. In 1608, for the marriage celebration of Cosimo II de' Medici and Maddalena, Cigoli prepared drawings for a production of *Argonautica* and is also thought to have participated in the *Ballo e giostra dei venti* performed on 27 October in the same year. In 1610 he was still in the employ of the Medici.

Imitation of nature and constant reference to the best examples of the Renaissance characterize Cigoli's eclectic and anti-mannerist style; he was an initiator of the new Baroque art. The novel characteristics of his output are found particularly in his scene designs and displays and he influenced the designers G. Parigi and J. Callot.

His treatise, *Prospettiva pratica*, dating from the early 17th century, remains in manuscript. In it Cigoli expounds a method to enlarge the stage floor, thereby extending planes and enhancing the grandeur and receding effect and thus stressing the illusory and virtuoso nature of stage perspective.

DBI (M. L. Chappel)
G. Gaetà Bertelà and A. Petrioli Tofani, eds.: *Feste e apparati medicei da Cosimo I a Cosimo II* (Florence, 1969) [exhibition catalogue]
F. Marotti: *Lo spazio scenico, teorie e tecniche scenografiche in Italia dall'età barocca a settecento* (Rome, 1974), 43–50
A. Matteoli: *Lodovico Cardi-Cigoli pittore e architetto* (Pisa, 1980)
A. M. Petrioli Tofani and others: *Firenze e la Toscana dei Medici nell'Europa del Cinquecento* (Florence, 1980), 103–7, 354, 384, 390–92, 400, 650–58 [exhibition catalogue]
A. Morrogh: *Disegni di architetti fiorentini 1540–1640* (Florence, 1985) [exhibition catalogue]
A. Petrioli Tofani: 'Drawings by Cigoli for the 'Entrata' of 1608', *Burlington Magazine*, cxxvii (1985), 785–6; cxxviii (1986), 103–9
M. L. Chappel and others: *Il seicento fiorentino, arte a Firenze da Ferdinando I a Cosimo II* (Florence, 1986), 55–8, 110–29
F. Faranda: *Ludovico Cardi detto il Cigoli* (Rome, 1986)
M. Sellink: 'Lucifer', *Bulletin van het Rijksmuseum*, xxxv/2 (1987), 91–104
MARINELLA PIGOZZI

Cikker, Ján (*b* Banská Bystrica, 29 July 1911; *d* Bratislava, 21 Dec 1989). Slovak composer. At the Prague Conservatory he studied composition, conducting and the organ, and attended Novák's master classes (1930–36); at the same time he studied musicology at Prague University, and then went to the Vienna Academy (1936–7). He taught at the Bratislava Conservatory (1938–51), then at the Bratislava Academy (VŠMU), and was literary adviser on opera to the Slovak National Theatre (1945–8). He won many awards and prizes.

Cikker was among the most productive of Slovak opera composers. His first two operas constitute modern equivalents of the 'national' operas of the 19th century, and they often cite folk dances, sometimes in metamorphosed versions. *Juro Jánošík* tells the story of the Robin Hood-like Slovak bandit national hero, Jánošík. *Beg Bajazid* ('Bajazet Bey') is set during the period of the Hungarian wars with the Turks. Its eponymous hero is a Slovak who had been abducted to Turkey as a child. In the epilogue he returns with his family to his homeland together with liberated Slovaks. Cikker's third opera, *Mr Scrooge*, marks a turning point in his operatic compositions. His musical techniques have now become less traditional and the expression richer. Tonic centres are still apparent, though they are often concealed, and the work contains many polytonal passages; sometimes, however, the music is conventional, especially when strong human emotions are being expressed. From *Vzkriesenie* ('Resurrection') onwards Cikker wrote his own librettos; only in *Rozsudok: Zemetrasenie v Chile* ('The Sentence: Earthquake in Chile') did he insert some text by another, the poet Milan Rúfus. *Resurrection* marks the zenith of Cikker's work; the musical expression has clear links with that of *Mr Scrooge*, but it is more concentrated, and the vocal line sometimes merges into *Sprechgesang*. The extraordinary effectiveness of the work lies particularly in its dynamism, in the psychologically well-timed alternation of tension and relaxation, of climaxes and anticlimaxes. Dramaturgically new are the so-called 'intermezzos', monologues delivered by the main characters that probe into their conscious and subconscious minds and function as short-cuts in the narrative. Each of the three acts has a triadic conception, as each consists of two scenes divided by an intermezzo. The final catharsis, the death of Katuša (Cikker chooses a tragic ending here, similar to that of *Mr Scrooge*), expresses both Tolstoy's and the composer's humanism. A salient feature of *Hra o láske a smrti* ('The Play of Love and Death') is the invisible choruses which, like the choruses of classical drama, function as authorial commentary. *Coriolanus*, although derived from Shakespeare's play, puts greater stress on the role of the plebs; as the chorus the plebs constitute a second protagonist beside the eponymous hero (as in Musorgsky's *Boris Godunov*, except that Cikker's opera is made up of fairly short scenes). *Coriolanus* is distinguished from the earlier operas by its sharper, more transparent, orchestral sound (thanks largely to the revisions made by the conductor Zdeněk Košler). *The Sentence: Earthquake in Chile*, based on Kleist's novella *Das Erdbeben in Chile*, is structured like a single act of *Resurrection*. It deals with the love of a poor teacher for the daughter of a rich aristocrat. In the orchestra large-scale, grand effects give way to more chamber-music-like combinations of instruments. Cikker's remaining operas continue this trend; *Obliehanie Bystrice* ('The Siege of Bystrica'), loosely based on a novel by the Hungarian writer Kálmán Mikszáth, is a grotesque, bizarre work with lyrical and comic elements; *Zo života hmyzu* ('From the Life of the Insects') is a metaphor or allegory of tripartite structure with a prologue and epilogue after the comedy, usually known as *The Insect Play*, by the Čapek brothers.

See also CORIOLANUS; *HRA O LÁSKE A SMRTI*; and *VZKRIESENIE*.

librettos by the composer unless otherwise stated; first performed in Bratislava, Slovak National Theatre, unless otherwise stated

Juro Jánošík (Š. Hoza), 10 Nov 1954; 2nd version, 7 May 1956
Beg Bajazid [Bajazet Bey] (J. Smrek), 16 Feb 1957
Mr Scrooge, 1957–9 (Cikker and Smrek, after C. Dickens: *A Christmas Carol*); as Evening, Night and Morning, Kassel, Staats, 5 Oct 1963
Vzkriesenie [Resurrection] (3, after L. N. Tolstoy), Prague, National, 18 May 1962 (Bratislava, 1962)
Hra o láske a smrti [The Play of Love and Death] (1, after R. Rolland: *Le jeu de l'amour et de la mort*), as Das Spiel von Liebe und Tod, Munich, National, 1 Aug 1969 (Kassel and Basle, 1968)
Coriolanus (3, after W. Shakespeare), Prague, Smetana, 4 April 1974
Rozsudok: Zemetrasenie v Chile [The Sentence: Earthquake in Chile] (after H. von Kleist: *Das Erdbeben in Chile*), 8 Oct 1979
Obliehanie Bystrice [The Siege of Bystrica] (after K. Mikszáth), 8 Oct 1983
Zo života hmyzu [From the Life of the Insects] (after K. Čapek and J. Čapek), 21 Feb 1987

*

PEM (I. Vojtěch)
J. Kresánek: 'Nad dielom pätdesiatročného Jána Cikkera' [On the Works of the Fifty-year-old Ján Cikker], *Slovenská hudba*, v (1961), 295–302
P. Faltin: 'Sonda do svedomia' [Conscience-Searching], in J. Cikker: *Vzkriesenie* (Bratislava, 1963), 114–38 [lib.]
L. Polyakova: 'Cheshskaya i slovatskaya opera XX. vyeka', *Sovietsky kompozitor* (Moscow, 1983), 183–267
I. Vajda: *Slovenská opera* (Bratislava, 1988), 61–117, 236–8
LADISLAV BURLAS, IGOR VAJDA

Cilea, Francesco (*b* Palmi, Reggio Calabria, 23 July 1866; *d* Varazze, Savona, 20 Nov 1950). Italian composer. The son of an impoverished lawyer, he was educated at a boarding school in Naples from the age of seven. The influence of Francesco Florimo, the famous archivist and friend of Bellini, helped him to enter the Naples Conservatory in 1879, where his teachers were Paolo Serrao, Beniamino Cesi and Giuseppe Martucci and his fellow pupils included Umberto Giordano. There he made rapid progress, becoming a *maestrino* in 1885. His Suite for Orchestra (1887) was awarded a government prize, and several of his piano pieces were published by Ricordi in Italy and Bote & Bock in

Germany. His opera *Gina* was performed at the Conservatory on 9 February 1889, his final year. Despite a poor libretto, the editor Sonzogno thought sufficiently well of it to commission from Cilea an opera on a fashionable low-life subject. *La Tilda* was given with moderate success at the Teatro Pagliano, Florence, on 7 April 1892 under Rodolfo Ferrari with Fanny Torresella as protagonist. Sonzogno included it in his Italian opera season mounted later that year in Vienna, where it gained the gratifying approval of Hanslick. Cilea spent three years over the composition of his next opera, *L'arlesiana*, to a libretto taken from Alphonse Daudet's play for which Bizet had provided incidental music. The text of Rosa Mamai's aria ('Esser madre è un inferno') was supplied by Grazia Pierantoni, the wife of the senator in whose house Cilea was staying at the time. The opera was well received at its première at Sonzogno's Teatro Lirico, where it helped to launch the young Caruso on his international career. Not until the following year, however, did *L'arlesiana* achieve its definitive three-act form.

In 1900 Cilea began work on his most famous opera, *Adriana Lecouvreur*, whose subject appealed to him because of its 18th-century ambience and its mixture of comedy and pathos. Its première proved another triumph for Caruso as well as for the composer. At a season of Cilea's operas launched by Sonzogno at the Théâtre Sarah Bernhardt, Paris, in 1904, Alfred Bruneau singled out *Adriana Lecouvreur* as preferable to all other works from the Italian GIOVANE SCUOLA. A projected collaboration with Gabriele D'Annunzio on a *Francesca da Rimini* came to nothing, owing to Sonzogno's failure to meet the poet's financial demands. In his search for a subject that would offer a choral dimension Cilea turned to *Gloria*, a story of star-crossed lovers set in 14th-century Siena at the time of the siege. Despite the advocacy of Toscanini the opera failed at its première; nor did the revised version fare substantially better. Two more abortive operatic attempts were to follow, *Ritorno ad amore* and *Il matrimonio selvaggio*. By now Cilea had effectively ceased to compose, his only other work of substance being the 'poema' *Il canto della vita*, to a text by Sem Benelli, written to commemorate the Verdi centenary in 1913. The previous year Leopoldo Mugnone had conducted a revival of *L'arlesiana* in Naples, at which he had omitted Rosa Mamai's aria and her subsequent scene with L'Innocente. This so incensed Cilea that he withdrew the score from circulation for the next 24 years. It would not be heard again until 1936, once more at Naples, and in 1937 in Milan, for which occasion Cilea added a prelude based on themes from the opera.

Until his retirement in 1935 Cilea pursued a distinguished career in musical education. From 1890 to 1892 he taught harmony and the piano at the Naples Conservatory; from 1896 to 1904 he held the chair of harmony and composition at the Istituto Reale (later Conservatorio) of Florence. In 1913 he assumed the directorship of the Palermo Conservatory, passing to that of the Naples Conservatory in 1916, a post which he held for nearly 20 years. He was elected to the Academy in 1938.

Of the composers of the 'giovane scuola' Cilea had a lighter, more delicate touch than most. His operas, while allowing room for the detachable number, are motivically organized, even if the motifs themselves are rarely very theatrical (the 'poison' theme in *Adriana Lecouvreur* usually passes unnoticed as such). A competent pianist, his orchestral writing frequently shows traces of piano figuration; indeed, *Adriana Lecouvreur* has been described as the best orchestral score ever written for piano. Cilea was undoubtedly more of an all-round musician than most of his contemporaries, whose interests were principally operatic. Among his gods were Paisiello and Bellini, and although his melodic style mostly conforms to the slow swirl of Mascagni and his school, it never descends to brutal excess. If *Adriana Lecouvreur* remains his most popular opera, largely through its perennial appeal to the prima donna, his best-loved single aria is 'È la solita storia del pastore' from *L'arlesiana*, which remains one of the gems of the tenor repertory.

See also ADRIANA LECOUVREUR; ARLESIANA, L'; and GLORIA.

Gina (3, E. Goliciani), Naples, Conservatory, 9 Feb 1889
La Tilda (3, A. Graziani [A. Zanardini]), Florence, Pagliano, 7 April 1892
L'arlesiana (4, L. Marenco, after A. Daudet), Milan, Lirico, 27 Nov 1897; rev. version (3), Lirico, 22 Oct 1898
Adriana Lecouvreur (4, A. Colautti, after E. Scribe and E. Legouvé), Milan, Lirico, 6 Nov 1902
Gloria (3, Colautti), Milan, Scala, 15 April 1907; rev. version (lib. rev. E. Moschino), 1932
Il matrimonio selvaggio, 1909 (G. di Bognasco), unperf.
Ritorno ad amore (R. Simoni), inc.

*

E. Moschini: *Sulle opere di Francesco Cilea* (Milan, 1932)
Gajanus: *Francesco Cilea e la sua opera* (Bologna, 1939)
R. de Rensis: *Francesco Cilea* (Palmi, 1950)
T. d'Amico: *Francesco Cilea* (Milan, 1960)

JULIAN BUDDEN

Cillario, Carlo Felice (*b* S Rafael, Argentina, 7 Feb 1915). Argentinian conductor of Italian parentage. He moved with his parents to Italy when eight years old, studied at the Conservatorio G. B. Martini at Bologna and began his career as a solo violinist, turning to conducting in 1942 at the Odessa Opera. After forming and working with concert orchestras in Italy and Argentina he became increasingly involved with opera, making his British début at Glyndebourne in 1961 (*L'elisir d'amore*) and in the USA at the Chicago Lyric Opera (*La forza del destino*). His Covent Garden début was in 1964, with Callas and Gobbi in the Zeffirelli production of *Tosca*, earning him critical approval for his disciplined control and the expressive orchestral playing. Besides frequent engagements with major European and American opera companies (including La Scala, the Metropolitan and San Francisco) he was the music director for the Elizabethan Opera Trust in Sydney, 1970–71, and since 1988 has been principal guest conductor and music adviser to Australian Opera. He has also conducted regularly at the Stockholm Royal Opera and at Drottningholm. Mainly working in Italian and French opera, he has been widely praised for his sensitive support for singers, in conjunction with firm orchestral direction.

NOËL GOODWIN

Cimador [Cimadoro], **Giambattista** [Giovanni Battista; J. B.] (*b* Venice, 1761; *d* Bath, 27 Feb 1805). Italian composer. Born of a noble family, he studied the violin, cello and piano. In 1789 his *Ati e Cibele*, a *favola per musica* in two short scenes, was performed in Venice. This was soon followed by *Pimmalione*, a monodrama after Rousseau for tenor and orchestra with a small part for soprano, and *Il ratto di Proserpina*. Choron and Fayolle reported that, dissatisfied with *Pimmalione*, Cimador burnt the score and renounced composition; however, the work survived (parts of it were even published later in London and Vienna) and achieved considerable popularity throughout Europe as a concert piece for both male and female singers, being revived as late as 1836.

In 1791 Cimador moved to London, where he taught singing and was, as is recorded in *The Gentleman's Magazine*, 'a celebrated vocal performer'. He visited Bath in 1794 with Haydn, who referred to him as a violin virtuoso and composer. On 14 May 1795 *Ati e Cibele* was given its first London performance at the King's Theatre, with pantomime and dances by Noverre, for the benefit of Morichelli, who sang Cibele. Extracts from *Pimmalione* were given there on 8 June 1797, and Cimador appeared as a pianist during the season 1799–1800.

In about 1800 he entered into partnership with the Italian music publisher Tebaldo Monzani. Together they issued periodical collections of Italian and English vocal music, and, as The Opera Music Warehouse, they published Mozart's great operas, advertising that 'any of the songs, Duetts, Trios, Overtures ... may be had Single & the whole of Mozart's Pianoforte Compositions, published in Numbers'. Many of these were arranged or provided with piano accompaniments by Cimador.

Although Gerber suggested that Cimador patterned himself after Haydn, his compositions owe more to the early works of Mozart. Choron and Fayolle, writing mainly of *Pimmalione*, summed up Cimador as 'a musician of no great scientific acquirement although his works are full of fire and imagination'; Fétis however pronounced the work merely mediocre.

Ati e Cibele (favola per musica, 2, A. Pepoli), Venice, Accademia dei Rinnovati, spr. 1789

Pimmalione (scena drammatica, S. A. Sografi, after J.-J. Rousseau), Venice, S Samuele, 26 Jan 1790, *A-Wn**, *B-Bc*, *Lc*, *D-B*, *Mbs*, *F-Pc**, *I-Bc*, *Fc*, *Gl*, *Li*, *Mc*, *Nc*, *PAc*, *PLcon*, *Rrai*, *Rsc*, *Vlevi*, *Vnm*; arias (London, 1797), ov. and 4 arias (Vienna, n.d.)

Il ratto di Proserpina (favola per musica, 2, M. Botturini), Venice, Accademia dei Rinnovati, carn. 1791

*

FétisB; *GerberNL*

Obituary, *Gentleman's Magazine*, lxxv (1805), 290

A. Choron and F. Fayolle: *Dictionnaire historique des musiciens* (Paris, 1810–11)

H. C. R. Landon, ed.: *The Collected Correspondence and London Notebooks of Joseph Haydn* (London, 1959)

RODNEY SLATFORD, MARITA P. McCLYMONDS

Cimarosa, Domenico (*b* Aversa, 17 Dec 1749; *d* Venice, 11 Jan 1801). Italian composer. He was a central figure in opera, particularly comic opera, of the late 18th century.

1. LIFE. The son of Gennaro and Anna di Francesco Cimmarosa (as his name is spelt on his baptismal certificate), he was taken from Aversa to Naples a few days after his birth. His father was employed as a stonemason in the construction of the Capodimonte Palace; in the course of work he lost his life in a fall from scaffolding. At first Cimarosa studied music in his spare time with Father Polcano, organist at the monastery of S Severo de' Padri Conventuali. In 1761 he was admitted to the Conservatorio di S Maria di Loreto. During his 11 years there he studied with Manna, Sacchini, Fenaroli and possibly Piccinni. Cimarosa, who excelled as a composer, also had singing lessons from the castrato Giuseppe Aprile, who later sang the role of Annio in the Roman performance of *Caio Mario* (1780).

During his student days Cimarosa composed a number of sacred motets and masses, but with the première in 1772 of his first *commedia per musica*, *Le stravaganze del conte*, performed at the Teatro dei Fiorentini in Naples with the farsetta *Le magie di Merlina e Zoroastro*, his fame as a composer began to spread. Influenced by the tradition of the *commedia dell'arte*, the farsetta, which constituted Act 3 and included characters such as Dottor Balanzoni and Pulcinella, was the first of a number of similar intermezzos and farsettas that he was to write throughout his career. His works soon became popular in Rome, where his comic intermezzos were performed by a cast of five male singers at the Teatro Valle. *Il ritorno di Don Calandrino*, *L'italiana in Londra*, *Le donne rivali* and *Il pittore parigino* were given there between 1778 and 1781. Goethe was quite charmed by *L'impresario in angustie*, which he heard during his visit to Rome in 1787. In his *Italienische Reise* Goethe commented on the humour in the Act 1 finale in which the poet (centre stage) is being criticized by the impresario and the prima donna on one side of the stage, and the composer and the seconda donna on the other. Serious operas, including *Caio Mario* (1780) and *Alessandro nell'Indie* (1781), also had their premières in Rome, at the Teatro delle Dame and the Teatro Argentina.

On 10 July 1780 *L'italiana in Londra* was the first of Cimarosa's operas to be given at La Scala in Milan, initiating a tradition of performances of his works that lasted well into the 19th century. Throughout the 1780s he was affiliated with the royal chapel in Naples, and the libretto to *I due supposti conti* (1784, Milan) lists him as *maestro di cappella* to the Neapolitan royal chapel and as *maestro* of the Ospedaletto conservatory, Venice. Because he composed a large number of operas during this time for other Italian cities, including Livorno, Milan and Florence, he was frequently absent from his regular duties in Naples and Venice.

In 1787 Cimarosa accepted the position of *maestro di cappella* at the St Petersburg court of Catherine II, an invitation probably extended at the recommendation of the Duke of Serra Capriola, the ambassador in Russia of the Kingdom of the Two Sicilies. On their way to St Petersburg Cimarosa and his wife visited Livorno as guests of Grand Duke Leopold of Tuscany, who later, as emperor (1790–92), played a role in Cimarosa's successful sojourn in Vienna. At Parma he paid a visit to the Duchess Maria Amalia (daughter of Maria Theresa and wife of Ferdinand of the Bourbons), and spent 24 days in late August and September in Vienna, where he was presented to Joseph II. During this period the emperor repeatedly invited Cimarosa to sing and play for him. All of these contacts strengthened his ties with the Viennese court. From Vienna Cimarosa visited Warsaw and finally arrived in St Petersburg on 3 December 1787.

At the court of Catherine II Cimarosa succeeded a line of Italian composers that included Manfredini, Galuppi, Traetta and Sarti. His operas were presented at the Hermitage and the theatre at Gatchina, the sumptuous palaces of the empress. His serious opera *Cleopatra* and two previously written comic operas, *Le donne rivali* and *I due baroni di Rocca Azzurra*, were adjusted for performances in Russia. Shortly after Cimarosa's arrival, however, the empress engaged Martín y Soler as her second *maestro di cappella*. His operas seemed to have met with greater success at the Russian court than Cimarosa's. The magnificence and splendour of

Catherine's court began to fade by 1791 when economic crises had forced the empress to release most of the Italian singers. Cimarosa, who could not bear the harshness of the Russian winters, left the court in June 1791. After spending three months in Warsaw, he arrived in Vienna, shortly after the death of Joseph II.

It had been known for some time that Cimarosa's contract in Russia was nearing an end and that he was planning to return to Naples because of poor health. Joseph II had intended to employ him as soon as he reached Vienna, and in 1789 a number of Cimarosa's works were given at the Burgtheater in preparation for his return. Between May and September *I due supposti conti* was revived with a new cast, and *I due baroni di Rocca Azzurra*, for which Mozart composed the aria 'Alma grande e nobil core' (K578), was also presented. Upon his arrival in Vienna Cimarosa was appointed Kapellmeister by Leopold II and was commissioned to write an opera, *Il matrimonio segreto*, to a text by Giovanni Bertati based on Colman and Garrick's *The Clandestine Marriage*. The opera, performed at the Burgtheater on 7 February 1792, was so successful that Leopold II ordered that it be repeated that same evening in his private chambers. Cimarosa, whom Joseph Weigl described as having a jovial and friendly personality, enjoyed great popularity among Viennese society and often entertained his hosts by performing at the keyboard. During his two years in Vienna he composed two more operas (*La calamita dei cuori*, which was a failure, and *Amor rende sagace*), and reworked his *Il pittore parigino*.

In 1792 he returned to Naples where he was appointed *maestro della cappella Reale*. In addition to composing new operas, he reworked *L'italiana in Londra* and *I due baroni*, adding sections in Neapolitan dialect. The most important works written during this last phase of his career were *Le astuzie femminili* (1794) and two serious operas, *Penelope* (1794) and *Gli Orazi ed i Curiazi* (1796), the last for La Fenice in Venice. In the 1790s Italy was experiencing reverberations of the French Revolutionary Wars that shook Europe. In 1796 the French captured Venice. Three years later, liberal leaders under the auspices of the French established the Parthenopean Republic after the Bourbon king was forced to flee Naples. Cimarosa, whose republican sentiments were evident in his opera *Gli Orazi ed i Curiazi*, composed a patriotic hymn to a text by Luigi Rossi for the burning of the royal flag. When the Parthenopean Republic fell in June and the Bourbon troops returned, Cimarosa was forced to leave Naples. In an attempt to regain the favour of the king, he wrote a cantata praising the king, but Ferdinand IV had Cimarosa arrested on 9 December. The composer was spared the death sentence only because of the intervention of powerful friends. Upon his release from prison he left his native city in 1800 and went to Venice, where he started to write an opera, *Artemisia*, but he died before finishing it.

2. OPERAS. Cimarosa was among the most successful composers of his epoch. His facility at writing music resulted in the creation of almost 60 stage works, most of which were comic pieces. His operas were performed on all the major European stages, including Prague, Copenhagen, Stockholm, St Petersburg, Hamburg, London and Berlin. His works were particularly popular in Vienna and at Eszterháza. In Vienna, for example, *Le trame deluse* was repeated 16 times in 1787, and *Il pittore parigino* 27 times in Cimarosa's revised version of 1792. At Eszterháza between 1783 and 1790, Haydn conducted performances of 13 operas by Cimarosa, and many of them were given several times. *L'italiana in Londra* was repeated there at least 14 times in five years. Although Cimarosa revised some of his earlier compositions to suit the Neapolitan tastes his music had a broad, international appeal. Some of his operas were still being played in Naples as late as 1811, and his *Gli Orazi ed i Curiazi* and *Il matrimonio segreto* were given in Venice throughout the early 19th century.

Cimarosa was also admired by a number of 19th-century commentators. Eugène Delacroix preferred Cimarosa's music to Mozart's, and Stendhal wrote that he would rather be hanged than be forced to state which of the two he preferred. Hanslick praised Cimarosa's wonderful facility, masterly compositional strokes and good taste. Goethe, who first heard Cimarosa's music in Rome, wrote to Schiller in 1788 from Naples, praising one of Cimarosa's operas (probably *Il marito disperato*, performed there as *La gelosia punita*). Upon his return to Weimar Goethe directed performances of *Le trame deluse* and *Il matrimonio segreto*. He also created the pasticcio *Die theatralischen Abenteuer* (1791), from Cimarosa's *L'impresario in angustie*, incorporating parts of Mozart's *Der Schauspieldirektor* in 1797.

Cimarosa's operas are based on librettos by a number of authors; this accounts for the uneven quality of the texts. Giuseppe Palomba and Giuseppe Maria Diodati furnished the largest number, with 13 and seven, respectively. Both librettists created characters who speak in Neapolitan dialect, and Palomba's texts also intermingle broken Spanish and French words with *lazzi* ('tricks') from the *commedia dell'arte*. His plots feature multiple disguises and bizarre intrigues and complications. Cimarosa's *Le trame deluse*, a setting of Diodati's text, became one of his most successful operas. The language of *Penelope* is in the dignified style of Metastasio, though by avoiding pomposity and including ensembles Diodati indicated new stylistic tendencies. G. B. Lorenzi, Antonio Sografi, Giuseppe Petrosellini, Angelo Anelli and Giovanni Bertati were among Cimarosa's other librettists. In *Il matrimonio segreto* Bertati provided an excellent plot, devoid of disguises and excessive complications.

Despite the often mediocre and occasionally grotesque quality of the texts, Cimarosa was always able to write music suffused with lightness, elegance and finesse. The orchestration of his earlier works consisted primarily of strings, oboes, horns and trumpets, and only occasionally bassoons and flutes. The orchestra functioned as a vehicle for vocal accompaniment, with the strings providing most of the activity. During his Russian sojourn he began to use clarinets, and his orchestration generally acquired a fuller and richer sonority. This is evident in *Il matrimonio segreto*, where the large orchestra provides colour and exhibits independent motivic and rhythmic material that serves as commentary on the action. Cimarosa seldom wrote stylized da capo arias. His arias are sectional, with contrasting tempos, metre and keys to accommodate changes of mood and situation in the text. This freedom from a structural mould creates the effect of spontaneity and flexibility. The last section of an aria is frequently in a fast tempo in the manner of a cabaletta. Cavatinas also occur frequently.

One of Cimarosa's strengths was the composition of witty and vivacious ensembles. *Il matrimonio segreto*, an ensemble opera in the style of Mozart's *Le nozze di*

Figaro, is composed of eight arias, four duets, three trios, a quartet, a quintet and two finales featuring all six characters. Frequently his operas begin with a trio or a quartet, and he excelled at creating large-scale chain finales. Although Cimarosa's characters do not display layers of Mozartian complexity, he was capable of depicting human emotions in a touching but not over-sentimental manner, as in the opening duet 'Cara non dubitar' from *Il matrimonio segreto*.

Cimarosa's harmonic vocabulary is diatonic and unadventurous; the strength of his music lies in the richness of his melodic invention, the brilliance and energy of his rhythmic and melodic motifs and his constantly lively accompaniments. He expanded the parameters of *opera buffa* by creating a genre permeated with sentiment, simplicity, elegance and delicacy. The freshness and vigour of his music was unmatched by his Italian contemporaries.

See also ASTUZIE FEMMINILI, LE; BALLERINA AMANTE, LA; CONVITO, IL; DUE BARONI DI ROCCA AZZURRA, I; DUE SUPPOSTI CONTI, I; GIANNINA E BERNARDONE; GIUNIO BRUTO; IMPRESARIO IN ANGUSTIE, L'; ITALIANA IN LONDRA, L'; MAESTRO DI CAPPELLA, IL; MARITO DISPERATO, IL; MATRIMONIO SEGRETO, IL; ORAZI ED I CURIAZI, GLI; PENELOPE; PITTORE PARIGINO, IL; and TRAME DELUSE, LE.

NC – *Naples, Teatro S Carlo*
NFI – *Naples, Teatro dei Fiorentini*
NFO – *Naples, Teatro del Fondo*
NN – *Naples, Teatro Nuovo*
RV – *Rome, Teatro Valle*
WB – *Vienna, Burgtheater*

cm – *commedia per musica* dg – *dramma giocoso*
dm – *dramma per musica* fm – *farsa/farsetta per musica*
int – *intermezzo in musica* ob – *opera buffa*

Le stravaganze del conte (cm, 3, P. Mililotti), NFI, carn. 1772, *I-Nc**, *Rmassimo*; Act 3 = Le magie di Merlina e Zoroastro [Le pazzie di Stellidaura e Zoroastro] (fm)

La finta parigina (cm, 3, F. Cerlone), NN, carn. 1773, *Nc**, *Rmassimo*

La donna di tutti i caratteri (cm, 3, A. Palomba), NN, 1775 [rev. of music by P. Guglielmi]

I sdegni per amore (cm, 1, G. Mililotti), NN, Jan 1776, *Nc**, *Rmassimo*

I matrimoni in ballo (fm, 1, P. Mililotti), NN, carn. 1776 [with I sdegni per amore]; rev. as La baronessa stramba [as Act 3 of Il credulo], NN, 1786, *F-Pn*, *I-Nc**

La frascatana nobile [La finta frascatana] (cm, 3, P. Mililotti), NN, wint. 1776, *F-Pn*, *I-Nc**, *Rmassimo*

I tre amanti (int, 2, G. Petrosellini), RV, carn. 1777, *D-Dlb*, *F-Pn*, *I-Nc**, *Rmassimo*, *RU-SPtob*; as Le gare degl'amanti (dg), Nice, Maccarani, spr. 1783

Il fanatico per gli antichi romani (cm, 3, G. Palomba) NFI, spr. 1777, *F-Pn*, *I-Nc**

L'Armida immaginaria (dg, 3, Palomba, after T. Tasso: *Gerusalemme liberata*), NFI, sum. 1777, *F-Pn*, *I-Nc**, *Rmassimo*

Gli amanti comici, o sia La famiglia in scompiglio (dg, 2, Petrosellini), NFI, 1778; Cremona, carn. 1796; as Il matrimonio in commedia, Livorno, spr. 1797; as La famiglia stravagante, ovvero Gli amanti comici (fm), Macerata, carn. 1798

Il ritorno di Don Calandrino (int, 2, ?Petrosellini), RV, carn. 1778, *D-Dlb*, *Hs*, *Wa*, *F-Pn*, *GB-Lcm*, *I-Nc**, *RU-SPtob*; as Armidoro e Laurina (dg), Livorno, 1783

Le stravaganze d'amore (cm, 3, P. Mililotti), NFI, wint. 1778, *F-Pn* (rev.), *I-Nc**, *Rmassimo*, *US-Wc*

Il matrimonio per raggiro (dg, 2), Rome, *c*1778–9, RV, carn. 1802, *A-Wgm*, *B-Bc* (no ov.), *D-B* (2 copies, both in It. and Ger.), *Dlb*, *I-Bc* (inc.), *Fc*, *Rmassimo*, *Rsc*, *S-Skma*, *Uu*, *US-Bp*, *Wc*

L'infedeltà fedele (cm, 3, G. Lorenzi), NFO, 20 July 1779, *D-Dlb*, *I-Nc**, *Rmassimo* [for inauguration of NFO]

L'italiana in Londra (int, 2, Petrosellini), RV, 28 Dec 1779, *A-Wn* (2 copies), *B-Bc* (inc.), *CS-Pnm*, *D-Dlb*, *Hs*, *DK-Kk* (2 copies, 1 in Danish), *F-Pn*, *Po*, *H-Bn*, *I-CR*, *Fc* (3 copies), *Gl*, *Mc*, *MOe* (in Ger.), *Nc**, *PAc*, *Rmassimo*, *Rsc*, *P-La*, *RU-SPtob*, *US-Wc* (in Fr.); as La virtù premiata (dg), Genoa, aut. 1794

Le donne rivali (int, 2, ?Petrosellini), RV, carn. 1780, *F-Pn*, *GB-Lbl*, *I-Fc*, *Mc*, *Nc**, *Rmassimo*, *RU-SPtob*; as Le due rivali (cm), Monza, aut. 1791, collab. other composers; as Le due fidanzate (cm), Moscow, Imperial, 10 June 1789

Caio Mario (dm, 3, G. Roccaforte), Rome, Dame, carn. 1780, *F-Pn*, *I-Mc*, *Nc*, *Rmassimo*, *RU-SPtob*

I finti nobili (cm, 3, Palomba), NFI, carn. 1780, *F-Pn* (Acts 1, 2), *I-Nc**, *Rmassimo*; Act 3 = Gli sposi per accidente (fm), *Nc**

Il falegname [Il falegname] (cm, 3 or 2, Palomba), NFI, 1780, *A-Wn* (2 copies, 1 rev. in It. and Ger.), *D-B*, *Dlb*, *F-Pc* (pts only), *Pn*, *H-Bn*, *I-Mc* (inc., pts only), *Nc**, *Rmassimo*, *P-La*; as L'artista (dg, 2), Treviso and Udine, 1789

Il pittore parigino (int, 2, Petrosellini), RV, 2 Jan 1781, *A-Wn*, *B-Bc* (rev.), *D-B*, *Dlb*, *Rtt*, *F-Pn*, *GB-Lcm* (rev.), *H-Bn*, *I-Fc*, *Gl*, *Nc**, *Rmassimo*, *P-La*, *RU-SPtob*, *US-Bp*, *Wc*; as Il barone burlato (cm, 3, G. Bonito, after Petrosellini), NN, 1784, with addns by F. Cipolla; as Le brame deluse (dg), Florence, 1787

Alessandro nell'Indie (dm, 3, P. Metastasio), Rome, Argentina, 11 Feb 1781, *I-Nc**, *Rmassimo*

Giunio Bruto (dramma tragico per musica, 2, Eschilo Acanzio [G. Pindemonte]), Verona, Accademia Filarmonica, aut. 1781, *H-Bn*, *I-Fc*, *Nc**, *Rmassimo*

Giannina e Bernardone (dg, 2, F. Livigni), Venice, S Samuele, aut. 1781, *A-Wgm*, *Wn*, *B-Bc*, *D-Dlb*, *Rtt*, *F-Pn* (inc.), *H-Bn*, *I-Fc*, *Gl*, *Mc*, *Mr*, *Nc**, *Rmassimo*, *Tf*, *P-La*, *RU-SPtob*, *S-Skma*, *St* (2 copies, 1 inc.), *US-BE*; as Il villano geloso (int), Venice, 1786

L'amante combattuto dalle donne di punto (cm, 3, Palomba), NFI, 1781; as La biondolina, NFI, 1781, *Nc**, *Rmassimo*; as La giardiniera fortunata (2), NN, 1805, *Nc*

Il capriccio drammatico (cm, 1, G. M. Diodati), ?Turin, ?1781, or London, 1794 [related to L'impresario in angustie, 1786]

Il convito (dg, 2, Livigni), Venice, S Samuele, carn. 1782, *CH-Zz* (in Ger.), *D-B* (2 copies, 1 in Ger.), *Dlb*, *DO* (in Ger.), *Rtt*, *F-Pn*, *GB-Lbl*, *I-Fc*, *Gl*, *Nc**, *OS*, *Rmassimo*, *Tf*, *Vnm*, *P-La*, *US-Wc*; as Der Schmaus, Frankfurt, 1784

L'amor costante (int, 2), RV, carn. 1782, *A-Wn*, *F-Pn*, *H-Bn*, *I-Mc*, *Nc**, *Rmassimo*, *P-La*, *RU-SPtob*; as Giulietta ed Armidoro (dg), Dresden, 1790, *D-Dlb*

L'eroe cinese (dm, 3, Metastasio), NC, 13 Aug 1782, *F-Pn*, *I-Fc*, *Mc* (rev.), *Nc** (and 2 copies), *Rmassimo*, *P-La*

La ballerina amante (cm, 3, Palomba), NFI, 6 Oct 1782, *A-Wgm*, *B-Br*, *D-Dlb*, *F-Pn* (3 copies), *H-Bn*, *I-Fc*, *Nc** (and copy), *Rmassimo*, *P-La*, *RU-SPtob*, *US-Bp*; as L'amante ridicolo (dg, 2), Rovigo and Ferrara, 1789

Il morbo campano (dm), Chiavenna, Uccelloppoli, 1782

La Circe (dm, 3, D. Perelli), Milan, Scala, carn. 1783, *F-Pn* (inc.), *I-Nc**, *Rmassimo*, *P-La*

I due baroni di Rocca Azzurra (intermezzo comico per musica, 2, Palomba), RV, carn. 1783, *A-Wn* (with addl aria by Mozart), *B-Bc*, *CS-Pnm*, *D-Dlb*, *DK-Kk* (Act 2), *F-Pc*, *Pn*, *GB-Lbl* (with addns), *H-Bn*, *I-Fc* (2 copies), *MOe*, *Nc** (and copy), *Rmassimo*, *P-La*, *RU-SPtob* (in Russ. as Dve nevesty, also pts as I due baroni), *US-Bp*; as cm, lib rev., NFO, 1793; as La sposa in contrasto, Modena, 1802

La villana riconosciuta (cm, 3, Palomba), NFO, 1783, *F-Pn*, *I-Nc** (and copy), *Rmassimo*; as La villanella rapita, Berlin, 1793

Oreste (dm, 2, L. Serio), NC, 13 Aug 1783, *F-Pn*, *I-Nc** (and copy), *Rmassimo*, *P-La*

Chi dell'altrui si veste presto si spoglia (cm, 2, Palomba), NFI, 1783, *B-Bc*, *D-Dlb*, *F-Pn* (3 copies), *H-Bn*, *I-Fc*, *Nc** (and 2 copies), *PAc*, *Rmassimo*, *P-La*, *RU-SPtob*, *US-Wc*; as Nina e Martuffo (1), NN, 1825, *I-Nc*

I matrimoni impensati [La bella greca] (int, 2), RV, carn. 1784, *Mc*, *Nc**, *Rmassimo*

L'apparenza inganna, o sia La villeggiatura (cm, 2, Lorenzi), NFI, spr. 1784, *Fc*, *Nc**, *Rmassimo*

La vanità delusa [Il mercato di Malmantile] (dg, 2, C. Goldoni), Florence, Pergola, spr. 1784, *F-Pc*, *Pn* (2 copies), *I-Fc*, *Nc* (partly autograph), *Rmassimo*, *US-Bp*, *Wc*

L'Olimpiade (dm, 3, Metastasio), Vicenza, Eretenio, 10 July 1784, *F-Pn*, *GB-Lbl*, *Lcm*, *I-Bc*, *Fc*, *Nc* (partly autograph), *PAc*, *Rmassimo*, *Vnm* (2 copies), *P-La*, *S-Skma*, *US-Bp* [for inauguration of Eretenio theatre]

I due supposti conti, ossia Lo sposo senza moglie (dg, 2, A. Anelli), Milan, Scala, 10 Oct 1784, *A-Wn*, *D-Dlb*, *F-Pn* (3 copies), *H-Bn*, *I-CMbc*, *Fc*, *Nc**, *PAc*, *Rmassimo*, *P-La*, *RU-SPtob*, *US-Bp*, *Wc*; as Lo sposo ridicolo (fm), RV, 1786

Artaserse (dm, 3, Metastasio), Turin, Regio, 26 Dec 1784, *I-Nc**, *Rmassimo*, *P-La*, *RU-SPsc*

Il marito disperato [Il marito geloso] (dg, 2, Lorenzi), NFI, 1785,

CS-Pnm (inc.), *D-B* (rev. in Ger.), *F-Pn* (rev.), *H-Bn*, *I-Fc*, *NC**, *Rmassimo*, *US-Bp*; as Die bestrafte Eifersucht, Berlin, 1794; as L'amante disperato, NFO, 1795, *I-Nc*

La donna sempre al suo peggior s'appiglia (cm, 3, Palomba), NN, 1785, *F-Pn*, *I-Nc**, *Rmassimo*

La figlia di Peste, 1785, excerpts *GB-Lbl*

Il credulo (cm, 3, Diodati), NN, carn. 1786 [Act 3 = La baronessa stramba, 1776], *D-Dlb*, *F-Pn* (2 copies), *GB-Lbl* (? partly autograph), *H-Bn*, *I-Fc* (no ov.), *Mc* (2 copies), *Nc*, (4 copies, 1 partly autograph), *Rmassimo*, *RU-SPtob*, *US-Bp*, *Wc*; as Il credulo deluso (dg), Modena, 1791

Le trame deluse, ossia I raggiri scoperti (cm, 3, Diodati), NN, 7 Dec 1786, *A-Wn*, *D-B*, *Dlb*, *Hs*, *F-Pc*, *Pn* (inc.), *I-Fc*, *Mc* (2 copies), *Nc** (and 2 copies), *PAc*, *Rmassimo*, *Rsc*, *S-Skma*, *US-Bp*; as L'amor contrastato (cm, 3, Palomba), NFI, 1788; as Li raggiri scoperti (dg), Bologna, 1799

L'impresario in angustie (fm, 1 or 2, Diodati), NN, 1786 [preceded by Il credulo], *A-Wn*, *D-B* (2 copies in Ger.), *Dlb*, *HR* (inc.), *Hs*, *Mbs*, *F-Pc*, *Pn*, *GB-Cpl*, *Lbl*, *Lcm*, *H-Bn*, *I-Bc*, *Fc* (3 copies), *Gl*, *Mc* (2 copies), *Nc** (and copy), *Rmassimo*, *Rsc*, *Tf*, *P-La*, *RU-SPtob* (pts only), *S-St* (pts only, in Swed.), *US-Bp* (2 versions), *Wc*; as Die theatralischen Abenteuer (1, Goethe), Weimar, 1791

Volodimiro (dm, 3, G. Boggio), Turin, Regio, carn. 1787, *I-Nc**, *Rmassimo*, *P-La*

Il fanatico burlato (cm, 2, F. S. Zini), NFO, 1787, *A-Wn* (rev.), *F-Pn*, *I-Fc* (as La burla felice), *Mc* (Act 1), *Nc**, *Rmassimo*, *US-Bp*, *Wc*; as Der adelsüchtige Bürger, Mannheim, 1791

La felicità inaspettata (azione teatrale, 2, F. Moretti), St Petersburg, Hermitage, March 1788, *B-Bc*, *D-SWl*, *F-Pn* (2 copies), *I-Fc*, *Nc**, *RU-SPtob* (pts only)

La vergine del sole (dramma serio, 3, Moretti), ?St Petersburg, Hermitage, ?1788, St Petersburg, Kamennïy, 26 Oct 1789, *D-SWl* (in 2 acts), *F-Pn*, *I-Fc*, *Nc** (and copy), *Rmassimo*, *RU-SPtob* (inc.), *US-Wc*

La Cleopatra (dramma serio, 2, Moretti), St Petersburg, Hermitage, 27 Sept 1789, *B-Bc*, *Br*, *F-Pn*, *I-Fc* (as Cleopatra e Marc' Antonio), *Nc**, *Rmassimo*, *RU-SPsc*, *SPtob*

Il matrimonio segreto (melodramma giocoso, 2, G. Bertati, after G. Colman (i) and D. Garrick: *The Clandestine Marriage*), WB, 7 Feb 1792, *A-Wgm* (orch pts), *Wn*, *B-Bc* (rev. as Sophie et Dorval), *Br*, *CS-Pnm*, *D-B* (3 copies), *Dlb*, *DK-Kk* (in It. and Dan.), *F-Pn*, *GB-Lbl* (2 copies), *T*, *I-BGi*, *Fc* (several copies), *Gl* (2 copies), *Mc* (3 copies, 1 inc.), *Nc** (and several copies), *PAc*, *PCcon*, *Rmassimo*, *Rsc*, *Vc*, *RU-Mk* (in Russ., It. and Fr.), *SPtob* (inc.), *S-St* (2 copies, 1 in Swed.), *US-BE*, *LOu*

La calamita dei cuori (dg, Goldoni), WB, 1792

Amor rende sagace (dg, 1, Bertati), WB, 1 April 1793, *I-BZtoggenburg*, *RU-SPtob* [related to Le astuzie femminili, 1794]

I traci amanti (cm, 2, Palomba), NN, 19 June 1793, *A-Wn*, *B-Br*, *D-Dlb*, *F-Pn* (2 copies), *I-Fc* (2 copies), *Mc*, *Nc** (and copy), *Rmassimo*, *US-Bp*; as Il padre alla moda, ossia Lo sbarco di Mustanzir Bassà (dg), Padua, 1795; as Gli turchi amanti (dg), Lisbon, 1796

Le astuzie femminili (cm, 2, Palomba), NFI, 26 Aug 1794, *A-Wgm* (Act 1), *B-Bc* (inc.), *Br*, *D-B* (in It. and Ger.), *Dlb*, *F-Pn* (2 copies, 1 rev.), *GB-Lbl*, *I-Fc* (2 copies), *Nc**, *Rmassimo*, *Rsc* (in 3 acts, inc.)

Penelope (dm, 2, Diodati), NFO, carn. 1795, *B-Bc*, *Br*, *CS-Pnm*, *D-Dlb*, *Sl* (as Ulysses), *F-Pn*, *GB-Lbl* (2 versions), *I-CR*, *Fc* (2 copies), *Gl*, *Mc*, *Nc** (and copy), *PAc* (in 1 act), *Vnm*, *S-St* (inc.), *US-Bp*, *Wc*

Le nozze in garbuglio (cm, 2, Diodati), Messina, Monizione, May 1795

L'impegno superato (cm, 2, Diodati), NFO, 21 Nov 1795, *D-Dlb*, *F-Pn* (rev., inc.), *I-Fc*, *Mc*, *Nc* (2 copies, 1 partly autograph), *Rmassimo*, *US-Bp*, *Wc*

I nemici generosi (fm, 2, ?Petrosellini), RV, carn. 1796, *A-Wn*, *B-Bc* (Act 2), *D-Dlb*, *F-Pc*, *Pn* (in 1 act), *GB-Lbl* (in 1 act), *I-Fc*, *Nc* (3 copies, 1 partly autograph), *Rmassimo*, *P-La*, *RU-SPtob* (2 copies), *S-Skma* (2 copies), *US-Bp*, *Wc*; as Il duello per complimento (1), Venice, 1797

Gli Orazi ed i Curiazi (tragedia per musica, 3, S. A. Sografi), Venice, Fenice, 26 Dec 1796, *A-Wgm*, *Wn* (rev. in Ger.), *B-Bc*, *CS-Pnm*, *D-B* (in It. and Ger.), *Dlb*, *Mbs* (rev.), *DK-Kk* (2 copies), *F-Pn* (several copies), *GB-Lbl* (4 copies, 1 arr.), *Lcm*, *I-Bc*, *Fc* (2 copies), *Gl*, *Mc*, *Msartori*, *Nc* (several copies in 2 or 3 acts), *OS* (2 copies), *PAc* (2 copies), *Rsc* (3 copies), *Tn* (Act 2), *Vc*, *Vnm*, *RU-SPtob* (2 copies), *US-BE*, *LOu*, *Wc*; ed. G. Morelli and E. Surian (Milan, 1985)

La finta ammalata (fm, 1), Lisbon, S Carlos, 1796, perf. with V. Fabrizi: Il convitato di pietra (fm, 1)

Achille all'assedio di Troja (dm, 2), Rome, Argentina, carn. 1797, *I-Nc* [related to Gli Orazi ed i Curiazi, 1796]

L'imprudente fortunato (dg, 2), RV, carn. 1797, *A-Wgm*, *D-Dlb*, *F-Pc*, *Pn*, *I-Fc*, *Nc* (ov. autograph), *Rmassimo*, *US-Bp*, *Wc*

Artemisia regina di Caria (dramma serio per musica, 2, M. Marchesini), NC, sum. 1797, *A-Wn*, *F-Pn* (2 copies), *GB-Lbl*, *I-Gl* (Act 1), *Nc* (2 copies, 1 partly autograph)

L'apprensivo raggirato (cm, 2, Diodati), NFI, 1798, *CS-Pnm*, *F-Pn*, *I-Fc*, *Nc*, *RU-SPtob*

Artemisia (dramma tragico per musica, 3, Cratisto Jamejo [G. B. Colloredo]), Venice, Fenice, carn. 1801 [not completed by Cimarosa], *A-Wgm*, *Wn*, *B-Br*, *CS-Pnm*, *D-Dlb*, *GB-Lbl*, *I-Fc*, *Nc** (and copy), *PAc* (2 copies), *Rmassimo*, *Rsc*, *S-St*

Undated, doubtful etc.: Assalonte, *B-Bc*; La discordia fortunata (cm, 3), *F-Pn*; L'ajo nell'imbarazzo (ob, 1), *US-Wc*; Le donne vendicate (commedia, 2), *I-Fc*; Il cavalier del dente (dg, 3), *Gl*; La Molinara, *PAc* (inc.); La contessina (dg, 3, M. Coltellini, after Goldoni), Bologna, Zagnoni, sum. 1778, collab. G. Astarita and F. L. Gassmann, *Pn*; Il matrimonio per industria (commedia, 2), ?Naples, ?1778, *F-Pn*; L'avviso ai maritati (fm, 1, ?F. Gonnella), ?NFI, ?1780, *Pn*; Il vecchio burlato (dg), Venice, 1783; Angelica e Medoro (dramatic cantata, Metastasio), collab. Millico, ?1783; Li finti conti, Turin, Gallo-Ughetti, spr. 1785; I fratelli papamosche, Turin, Gallo-Ughetti, spr. 1785; Le statue parlante (int), Correggio, 1785; Gli amanti alla prova (Bertati), Naples, 1786; L'impostore punito (3), Turin, Carignano, 1786–7; Il maestro di cappella (comic monologue), *c*1786–92, vs *D-B* (in Ger.), *I-Rsc* (Leipzig, 1810); Gli inimici generosi, excerpts *US-Bp*; La scuffiara, 1788; Il matrimonio per susurro; Contrattempi, Bonn, 1793; La pupilla astuta (cm, 2, Palomba), NFO, 1794; La serva innamorata (commedia, 2, Palomba), NFI, 1794; Attilio Regolo (dramma serio, 3, ?Metastasio), Reggio Emilia, carn. 1797; Le nozze di Lauretta (dg, 2, G. Caravita), Turin, ?1797; Semiramide (3, Metastasio), NFI, 1799; Il conte di bell'amore; L'arte contro l'arte, Alexandria, carn. 1800; Il nuovo podestà (commedia, 2), Bologna, Comunale, spr. 1802; Tito Vespasiano (dramma serio, 2), Lisbon, S Carlos, 1821

Music in: Les folies amoureuses, 1823; La fausse Agnès, 1824; Bernabo, 1856

*

FlorimoN; *RosaM*

I. T. F. C. Arnold: 'Domenico Cimarosa', *Gallerie der berühmtesten Tonkünstler des achtzehnten und neunzehnten Jahrhunderts*, ii (Erfurt, 1810)

G. Terracina da Manfredonia: 'Domenico Cimarosa', *Biografia degli uomini illustri del regno di Napoli*, v, ed. Martuscelli (Naples, 1818)

Stendhal: *Vie de Rossini* (Paris, 1824; Eng. trans., 1956, 2/1970)

——: *Rome, Naples et Florence en 1817* (Paris, 1826)

P. Cambiasi: 'Notizie sulla vita e sulle opere di Domenico Cimarosa', *Gazzetta musicale di Milano*, lv (1900), 639–40, 657–8, 671–3, 688–9; lvi (1901), 6–7, 21–3, 34–6, 58–60, 75–7, 120–22

M. S. Trevisan: *Nel primo centenario di Domenico Cimarosa* (Venice, 1900)

Aversa a Domenico Cimarosa: nel primo centenario della sua morte (Naples, 1901)

A. Eisner-Eisenhof and J. Mantuani: *Katalog der Ausstellung anlässlich der Centenarfeier Domenico Cimarosas* (Vienna, 1901)

F. Polidoro: 'La vita e le opere di Domenico Cimarosa', *Atti della Accademia Pontaniana*, xxxii (1902), 1–54

M. Morris: 'Goethe als Bearbeiter von italienischen Operntexte', *Goethe Jb*, xxvi (1905), 3–51

R. Vitale: *Domenico Cimarosa, la vita e le opere* (Aversa, 1929)

G. Biamonti: *Il matrimonio segreto di Domenico Cimarosa* (Rome, 1930)

A. Della Corte: 'Cimarosa nel '99 e nella fortuna postuma', *RaM*, ix (1936), 280–83

M. Tibaldi-Chiesa: *Cimarosa e il suo tempo* (Milan, 1939)

C. Engel: 'A Note on Domenico Cimarosa's *Il matrimonio segreto*', *MQ*, xxxiii (1947), 201–6

Per il bicentenario della nascita di Domenico Cimarosa 1749–1949 (Aversa, 1949)

W. Dean: 'The Libretto of *The Secret Marriage*', *Music Survey*, iii (1950), 33–8

F. Schlitzer: *Goethe e Cimarosa* (Siena, 1950)

R.-A. Mooser: *Annales de la musique et des musiciens en Russie au XVIIIe siècle*, ii (Geneva, 1951)

U. Prota-Giurleo: 'Nuovi contributi alla biografia di Cimarosa', *La Scala*, lxxvii (1956), 36–41
A. Mondolfi: 'Aspetti e caratteri livornesi in un capolavoro napoletano', *Rivista di Livorno*, iv (1958)
A. Mondolfi-Bossarelli: 'Due varianti dovute a Mozart nel testo del *Matrimonio segreto*', *AnMc*, no.4 (1967), 124–30
D. Bartha: 'Haydn's Italian Opera Repertory at Esterháza Palace', *New Looks at Italian Opera: Essays in Honor of Donald J. Grout* (Ithaca, NY, 1968), 172–219
H.-B. Dietz: 'A Chronology of Maestri and Organisti at the Cappella Reale in Naples, 1745–1800', *JAMS*, xxv (1972), 379–406
G. Barblan: 'Un Cimador che divenne Cimarosa', *Quadrivium*, xiv (1973), 197–206
J. E. Johnson: *Domenico Cimarosa (1749–1801)* (diss., University College, Cardiff, 1976)
F. Lippmann: 'Haydns "La fedeltà premiata" und Cimarosas "L'infedeltà fedele"', *Haydn-Studien*, v (1982), 1–15
——: 'Über Cimarosas Opere Serie', *AnMc*, no.11 (1982), 21–60

GORDANA LAZAREVICH, JENNIFER E. JOHNSON (work-list)

Cincinnati. American city in Ohio. Opera began there in October 1801 when *The Poor Soldier*, with music by William Shield in collaboration with John O'Keeffe, was performed near a frontier fort, the nucleus of the rapidly growing town. In the first half of the century operas were performed in English, including, in the 1830s, Henry R. Bishop's versions of *Il barbiere di Siviglia*, *Der Freischütz*, *Le nozze di Figaro* and *La sonnambula*. Later, with the arrival of many European immigrants, especially Germans, and with the rise of a second-generation educated leisured class, Cincinnati became more sophisticated enjoying annual, and sometimes biannual, visits from the many repertory opera companies touring America; frequent visitors were the Strakosch Italian Opera, Richings English Opera, the Parepa-Rosa Opera, Maurice Grau's Great French Opera, Abbott Grand English Opera, the Damrosch Opera and (in the 20th century) the Metropolitan Opera House Company.

Though these visits continued into the 1920s and occasionally beyond, a permanent Cincinnati Opera company began as an experiment in summer 1920 at the Cincinnati Zoo. The original band shell at the zoo was replaced by a covered pavilion, open at the sides and with boxes at the rear, seating 2800. Intervals in the early years were extended to 45 minutes so that the audience could attend the neighbouring ice show. Summer thunderstorms sometimes soaked the patrons sitting at the sides, and singers and musicians often competed with the sounds of sea lions, peacocks and ducks on a nearby lake. Despite the inconvenience of dressing rooms in outdoor tents behind the stage and of performing sometimes in intense heat in heavy costumes, the best-known artists in America returned often. Jan Peerce and Dorothy Kirsten made their operatic débuts there, and Gladys Swarthout, Risë Stevens, Roberta Peters and Sherrill Milnes all sang leading roles there. Fausto Cleva first conducted at the zoo in 1927 and was Music Director from 1934 to 1963.

In the early years the eight-week summer season comprised six operas, though it was later extended to include between ten and 15. After 51 seasons at the zoo, the company moved in 1972 to the modernized 3600-seat Music Hall (built in 1878 to house the Cincinnati May Festival), which the opera shares with the symphony orchestra and the ballet. It is now the second oldest professional opera company in the USA. Five operas and one operetta or musical comedy are staged during the year, with four productions in the early summer. James de Blasis has been Artistic Director since 1973.

The Public Library of Cincinnati and Hamilton County has a card index file, complete from 1920, of the Cincinnati Opera by season, opera title, artist and role, as well as a collection of the programme booklets for 1929 and from 1936 to the present. All of these are continually updated.

*

R. Robertson: *Musical History of Cincinnati* (thesis, Cincinnati Conservatory of Music, 1941)
Twenty-fifth Anniversary Season Souvenir Booklet [Cincinnati Summer Opera Association pubn] (Cincinnati, OH, 1946)
'*The Poor Soldier* – a Revival of an old Comic Opera to be staged in Cincinnati', *Bulletin of the Historical and Philosophical Society of Ohio*, ix (1951), 235–6
J. E. Holliday: 'Cincinnati Opera Festivals during the Gilded Age', *Cincinnati Historical Society Bulletin*, xxiv (1966), 131–49
——: 'Grand Opera Comes to the Zoo', ibid, xxx (1972), 7–20
O. M. Gale: 'The Cincinnati Zoo – One Hundred Years of Trial and Triumph', ibid, xxxiii (1975), 87–119
H. Board: 'Ralph Lyford's Lyric Dream', *Cincinnati Horizons*, v (1976), 30–33
J. E. Holliday: 'Three World Premières of Grand Opera', *Cincinnati Historical Society Bulletin*, xxxvi (1978), 117–23
L. R. Wolz: *Opera in Cincinnati: the Years before the Zoo, 1801–1920* (diss., U. of Cincinnati, 1983) SAMUEL F. POGUE

Cinese smarrita, La. Opera by Giuseppe Scarlatti; *see* *ISOLA DISABITATA, L'* (i).

Cinesi, Le ('The Chinese Ladies'). *Azione teatrale* in one act by CHRISTOPH WILLIBALD GLUCK to a libretto by PIETRO METASTASIO; Vienna, Schlosshof, 24 September 1754.

In a city in China, Lisinga (contralto), a Chinese girl of noble birth, and her two friends Sivene (soprano) and Tangia (contralto) are trying to while away their boredom when Lisinga's brother Silango (tenor) appears, returned from a trip to Europe. They decide to pass the time by play-acting. Lisinga begins with Andromache's tragic aria following Hector's death in the Trojan War. Sivene wants to play the nymph Licoris, who mocks the affections of the shepherd Tirsis; her aria is preceded by one for her real-life lover Silango who, as Tirsis, declares his feelings for her half-playfully, half-seriously. Finally, Tangia plays a young coquette who has just returned from Europe, a parody of Silango. Since the friends cannot agree which scene was acted the best, they all join in a ballet, which ends the opera.

Gluck wrote *Le cinesi* for performance before the Empress of Austria, Maria Theresa, and her husband, and the production, in the theatre of Gluck's employer Prince von Saxe-Hildburghausen at Schlosshof, was extremely lavish, to judge from the account left by Dittersdorf in his autobiography. The subject and the exotic production reflected the fascination for *chinoiserie* in the 18th century, and to an extent this is reflected in Gluck's music which used small bells, triangles, small hand-drums and tambourines in the opening sinfonia. It is the first of Gluck's comic operas and its four arias show Gluck's masterly characterization in its succession of dramatic, amorous, pastoral and *buffo* styles. JEREMY HAYES

Cinti-Damoreau [née Montalant], **Laure (Cinthie)** (*b* Paris, 6 Feb 1801; *d* Paris, 25 Feb 1863). French soprano. She studied the piano at the Paris Conservatoire and singing with Plantade, and made her début at the Théâtre Italien in Martín y Soler's *Una cosa rara* (8 January 1816). In 1819 she was engaged with

Laure Cinti-Damoreau, who created leading roles in all Rossini's operas for Paris: engraving

the newly formed company at the Théâtre Louvois, where her roles included Cherubino and Rosina. In 1822–3 she sang at the King's Theatre, London. Her mastery of florid singing, learnt from colleagues at the Théâtre Italien, led to her engagement in 1826 at the Opéra where she remained until 1835, with an interruption in 1827 when she sang in Brussels and married the tenor V. C. Damoreau (1793–1863). She created the principal soprano roles in *Le siège de Corinthe*, *Moïse*, *Le comte Ory*, *Guillaume Tell* and *La muette de Portici*, and Isabelle in *Robert le diable*. Although she was the Opéra's most highly paid singer, she accepted a better offer from the Opéra-Comique, where in 1836–7 she appeared in three new operas by Auber. She taught at the Conservatoire (1833–56) and published a *Méthode de chant* (1849). Her voice, outstanding for its purity of tone and intonation, was likened to a perfect piano, and her ornamentation was stylish and varied. She was a Rossini rather than a Meyerbeer singer, lacking Falcon's emotional and dramatic power; but she successfully redirected her career elsewhere when Falcon threatened to eclipse her at the Opéra.

For further illustration *see* COMTE ORY, LE.

*

A. de Rovray: 'Laure Cinti-Damoreau', *Le moniteur universel* (1865), March–June [in 5 pts]

A. Caswell: 'Mme Cinti-Damoreau and the Embellishment of Italian Opera in Paris: 1820–1845', *JAMS*, xxviii (1975), 459–92

PHILIP ROBINSON

Cioè, Il. Opera by Leonardo Leo; *see* AMOR VUOL SOFFERENZA.

Ciottolino. *Fiaba musicale* in three scenes by LUIGI FERRARI TRECATE to a libretto by GIOVACCHINO FORZANO; Rome, Palazzo Odescalchi, Sala Verdi, 8 February 1922.

This disarmingly simple little opera – originally presented by the famous puppet theatre the Teatro dei Piccoli di Podrecca and also performable by children – won immediate success, running initially for 70 consecutive evenings. Child audiences responded readily to Forzano's cautionary tale about a little boy (Ciottolino, soprano) who dreams that he becomes King of the Fairies but runs into difficulties when it is found that he cannot read and has a bad temper (he wakes up just in time to avoid being eaten by an Ogre (bass)). Ferrari Trecate's unpretentious, conservative music has real charm. Melodies that often recall nursery songs are gracefully woven into a continuous musical texture, which is skilfully scored for small orchestral forces. There are some mild touches of parody. Though now rather dated, *Ciottolino* is still occasionally heard in Italy.

JOHN C. G. WATERHOUSE

Ciprandi, Ercole (*d* after 1790). Italian tenor. He sang in several London seasons (1754–6, 1764–6), first appearing as Danaus in *Ipermestra* by Hasse and Lampugnani; he earned praise – in Burney's words – for singing with 'much taste and feeling', distinguished himself in J. C. Bach's aria 'Non sò d'onde viene', originally written for Raaff, and appears to have been regarded as a conscientious artist. He went on singing in leading Italian opera houses (Turin, Milan and Rome) until at least 1774. He was sometimes described as Milanese; the date of birth given in previous works of reference, *c*1738, is hardly consistent with his singing tenor leads in London in 1754.

*

BurneyH

F. C. Petty: *Italian Opera in London 1760–1800* (Ann Arbor, 1980), 207

JOHN ROSSELLI

Cirillo [Cerilli], **Francesco** (*b* Grumo Nevano, nr Naples, 4 Feb 1623; *d* after 1667). Italian composer and singer. He came from the 'Terra di Lavoro', where the *comici dell'arte* of Campania traditionally originated. At the age of 12 he was sent to Rome; Prota-Giurleo's attempted reconstruction of his Roman years is entirely hypothetical. According to his marriage contract of 5 June 1654 he had then been in Naples for about three years; he must have worked there with the Febiarmonici, a group of singers from northern Italy who produced the first operas given at Naples. A contract of June 1655 mentions him among the members of the 'Accademia de' musici, detta de' Febi Armonici'. This group may have included some of the earlier company, although they now (from April 1654) performed in the first public opera house at Naples, the Teatro S Bartolomeo, rather than in the royal palace, where the viceroy, Count d'Oñate, had sponsored the earliest Neapolitan opera performances.

Among the earliest operas given at S Bartolomeo were *Orontea regina d'Egitto* in 1654, 'arricchita di nuova musica da Francesco Cerilli Napolitano' (Allacci), and *Il ratto d'Elena* (to a libretto by Gennaro Paolella) in January 1655, one of the first originally written for Naples, also with music by Cirillo. The latter is heavily dependent on Venetian models (the theme is comparable to that of Giulio Strozzi's libretto *La finta pazza*) but with an excessive number of arias and canzonettas. Cirillo presumably continued to work for the opera in Naples for several years, probably more as a music director and arranger of operas imported from Venice than as a composer: Prota-Giurleo's attributions are all incorrect or at least purely conjectural. Cirillo sang the baritone roles of Dario and Nicarco in *Statira* (1666) and the tenor or comic falsetto part of the *vecchia* Ceffea in *Scipione* (1667), both by Cavalli.

The Neapolitan *Orontea* (score in *I-Nc*) bears no musical relationship to that of Cesti (see Osthoff, Stalnaker, and Walker 1984), which was supposed for a long time to have been set and performed in Venice in 1649. It now seems clear that Cesti's *Orontea* originated in Innsbruck in 1656, whereas the original Venetian setting, now lost, may have been by Francesco Lucio, the composer of another opera performed at Naples in 1654, *Gli amori d'Alessandro Magno* (see Walker 1972 and 1984). Thus it is impossible to ascertain whether the Neapolitan *Orontea* contains any music from the Venetian *Orontea* or was entirely reset by Cirillo. Cirillo's importance as the 'primo operista napoletano' rests primarily on certain forms of theatrical production and his role in the selection of repertory. His musical style is rather superficial and rudimentary compared with that current at Venice, to judge from the few scenes of *Orontea* that, because they correspond to changes in the Venetian text, are surely his.

*

AllacciD; *CroceN*

N. d'Arienzo: 'Origini dell'opera comica', *RMI*, ii (1895), 597–628

U. Prota-Giurleo: *Francesco Cirillo e l'introduzione del melodramma a Napoli* (Grumo Nevano, 1952)

W. Osthoff: 'Neue Beobachtungen zu Quellen und Geschichte von Monteverdis "Incoronazione di Poppea"', *Mf*, xi (1958), 129–38

W. P. Stalnaker jr: *The Beginnings of Opera in Naples* (diss., Princeton U., 1968)

T. Walker: 'Gli errori di *Minerva al tavolino*: osservazioni sulla cronologia delle prime opere veneziane', *Venezia e il melodramma nel seicento: Venice 1972*, 7–16

L. Bianconi and T. Walker: 'Dalla "Finta pazza" alla "Veremonda": storie di Febiarmonici', *RIM*, x (1975), 379–454; Eng. trans. in preface to DMV, i (forthcoming)

D. A. D'Alessandro: 'L'opera in musica a Napoli dal 1650 al 1670', *Seicento napoletano: Arte, costume, ambiente* (Milan, 1984), 409–430, 543–9

T. Walker: '"Ubi Lucius": Thoughts on Reading "Medoro"', in preface to F. Lucio: *Il medoro*, DMV, iv (1984), pp. cxxxi–clx

LORENZO BIANCONI

Ciro in Babilonia [*Ciro in Babilonia, ossia La caduta di Baldassare* ('Cyrus in Babylon, or The Fall of Belshazzar')]. *Dramma con cori* in two acts by GIOACHINO ROSSINI to a libretto by Francesco Aventi partly based on the biblical story of Belshazzar's feast; Ferrara, Teatro Comunale, ?14 March 1812.

The Babylonian king Baldassare [Belshazzar] (tenor) is attracted to Amira (soprano), the wife of the Persian king Cyrus (contralto) whom Belshazzar has defeated. Cyrus's attempts to free his wife, and his young son imprisoned with her, are thwarted when his disguise as a visiting ambassador fails. He is thrown into prison while Belshazzar, determined to win over Amira, prepares a lavish wedding feast. A great storm erupts during which a message is written on the wall of the banqueting hall: 'God has numbered the days of your kingdom and brought it to an end. You have been weighed in the balance and found wanting'. The prophet Daniel (baritone) interprets this as divine anger, but the Magi advise Belshazzar to sacrifice important Persian prisoners to the gods. As Cyrus, Amira and their son are led to execution news arrives of the routing of Babylonian defences by the Persians; Belshazzar is deposed and Cyrus placed on his throne.

The work contains some sporadically fine music in Rossini's early manner but is vitiated by a poorly planned libretto that gives the future composer of such works as *Mosè in Egitto* and *Ermione* few opportunities for dramatically extended writing. The *aria del sorbetto* of the seconda donna, Argene (soprano), is written on a single repeated B♭.

RICHARD OSBORNE

Ciro riconosciuto ('Cyrus Recognized'). Libretto by PIETRO METASTASIO, first set by Antonio Caldara (1736, Vienna).

It was foretold that Astiage [Astyages], King of Media, would lose his throne to a descendant; consequently he exiled his son-in-law, Cambise [Cambyses], and ordered that his grandson, Cyrus, should be killed by Arpago [Harpagus], his adviser. Pitying the infant, Harpagus left him with the shepherd Mitridate [Mithridates] who raised Cyrus as his son, Alceo [Alcaeus]. 15 years later, when Harpagus confessed, his own son was executed.

ACT 1 It is rumoured that Cyrus is still alive but that an impostor, who claims the throne, is also using his name. Mandane, wife of Cambyses and mother of Cyrus, learns from Harpagus that her husband has secretly returned, and that Cyrus awaits Astyages at the Persian border. Mandane sends a greeting to her son, unaware that it is actually the impostor who is waiting. At Mithridates' hut, Alcaeus learns his real identity and goes to find his mother. Cambyses enters Media and, hearing the king approach, hides inside the hut where he overhears Astyages order Cyrus's execution. Cambyses makes an attempt on the life of the sleeping Astyages but Mandane intervenes, then recognizes her husband, as does the king, who has him arrested. Cyrus/Alcaeus appears, having killed the impostor; Mandane, believing her son dead, orders Cyrus's arrest.

ACT 2 Mithridates, fearing for Alcaeus, reveals his true identity to Mandane. Meanwhile, Astyages has Alcaeus released from prison. Cambyses arrives as Cyrus/Alcaeus departs and convinces Mandane that Alcaeus is not their son but his murderer. The two plot an ambush, and Cambyses leaves to make preparations.

ACT 3 Harpagus confirms Mithridates' story to Mandane who, horrified, reveals the plot. Cambyses and Cyrus enter fighting, and as Mandane stops them, the king arrives. He learns that Cyrus still lives and demands to know his whereabouts; Harpagus answers that Cyrus is being crowned at the temple. There, Mandane and Cyrus rescue Astyages from Mithridates and from Harpagus, who has seized the opportunity for personal vengeance. Remorseful, Astyages surrenders his throne to Cyrus.

* * *

The most complete outlines of the classical narrative on which this plot is based are to be found in Herodotus, *Historiae* (book 1) and Justin's epitome of the Trogus, *Historiae* (book 1). Further mentions occur in Ctesias, *La Persica* (books 6–7) and Valerius Maximus, *Historiae* (book 1). More contemporary with Metastasio is *Amasis* (1701), a drama by Joseph de la Grange-Chancel in which the inability of a father and a mother to recognize their own son is also important to the action. Caldara's setting served to celebrate the birthday of the Empress Elisabeth, consort of Emperor Charles VI, in 1736. With fewer than 30 subsequent settings, *Ciro riconosciuto* gained only moderate popularity in comparison with other Metastasian texts. Leo is credited with having introduced the chorus into the opera at Naples with revivals of this opera and *Olimpiade* in 1742–3. At the time that Jommelli went to Venice to prepare his 1749 setting of the text, Metastasio wrote to Farinelli that he found in

Jommelli's work 'all the harmony of Hasse, with all the grace, expression and invention of Vinci'. Two years later, after seeing sections of Hasse's score for Dresden (1751), and hearing reports about the work, the poet expressed his admiration for Hasse's ability always to surpass his previous efforts. It was in this opera of Hasse that his wife, Faustina Bordoni (as Mandane), made her last operatic appearance. In London, Cocchi's *Ciro riconosciuto* (1759) came to be regarded as his best Italian opera to have been written for that city.

For a list of settings *see* METASTASIO, PIETRO. DON NEVILLE

Cisneros, Eleonora de [Broadfoot, Eleanor] (*b* Brooklyn, 1 Nov 1878; *d* New York, 3 Feb 1934). American mezzo-soprano. She studied with Francesco Fanciulli and Adeline Murio-Celli in New York and later with Angelo Tabadello in Paris. Jean de Reszke arranged for her to sing at the Metropolitan, where during the 1899–1900 season she performed Rossweise (*Die Walküre*) and Amneris on tours and in New York. She claimed to be the first American-trained singer to perform at the Metropolitan. At Turin in 1902 she sang Brünnhilde, Ortrud, Venus, Delilah and Amneris. From 1904 to 1908 she sang regularly at Covent Garden. At La Scala she created Candia in Franchetti's *La figlia di Iorio* (1906), also singing in the first performances there of *The Queen of Spades* (1906), *Salome* (1906) and *Elektra* (1909). She appeared at Hammerstein's Manhattan Opera House (1906–8) and then with the Chicago-Philadelphia Opera Company (singing Amneris at the company's opening in Chicago in 1910) until 1916. In 1911 she performed in London and Australia with the Melba Opera Company. She continued to sing, mostly in Europe, into the 1920s. With a large, statuesque bearing and a voice of remarkable volume and range, she sang Santuzza, La Gioconda and Kundry, as well as mezzo-soprano roles such as Carmen, Laura (*La Gioconda*), Urbain (*Les Huguenots*) and Azucena. SUSAN FEDER

Città di Castello. City in Umbria, Italy. At Carnival 1629, to celebrate the marriage of Vittoria and Gianfrancesco Vitelli, the tourney *Il toro celeste* was staged with musical intermezzos by Pietro Gambari (libretto in *I-CCc* and *Vgc*). The Accademia degli Illuminati was formed in 1650 and 12 years later it commissioned the architect A. Gabrielli to build the Teatro degli Illuminati. The theatre was inaugurated on 25 August 1666 with the opera *Il trionfo della religione cattolica in Inghilterra*, to a text by F. I. Lazzari, the academy's principal (music by G. P. Almeri, G. B. Giansetti and G. Micarelli). In August 1669 another opera to a text by Lazzari was performed, *Le gelosie di Bacco* (composer unknown), and in 1673 a religious drama by him, *La cena di Baldasare*. In 1678 and 1679 *L'Attenaide* and *Il Cambise* (librettos in *I-Bu*) respectively were performed by a company working under the auspices of Louis XIV. On 10 August 1682 another religious drama by Lazzari was performed, *San Crescentiano*, with music by Pier Francesco Cappelletti.

Operatic productions suffered a decline in the 18th century, owing to the dilapidated state of the theatre (*L'impresario delle Canarie*, 1769; *I trionfi della Virtù*, 1771; P. A. Guglielmi's *Gli Uccellatori*, Carnival 1772). Restoration work was carried out under the architect Giacomo Mancini and the theatre was reopened for Carnival 1789 with the pasticcio *Il geloso*. But after 1800, local production of musical drama was abandoned in favour of visits by national touring companies presenting works by Rossini, Bellini, Donizetti, Verdi, Boito and Puccini.

*

F. I. Lazzari: *Serie de' Vescovi e breve notitia del sito, origine, diocesi, governo, santi, prelati, famiglie, e persone nobili di Città di Castello* (Foligno, 1693), 51–7

G. Mancini: *Memorie di alcuni artefici del disegno si antichi che moderni che fiorirono in Città di Castello* (Perugia, 1832), 173–7

A. Rosini: *Il teatro degli Accademici Illuminati in Città di Castello* (Città di Castello, 1935)

G. Ciliberti: 'La cappella musicale della cattedrale di Città di Castello nei secoli XVII-XVIII', *Annali della Facoltà di lettere e filosofia dell'Università degli studi di Perugia*, ix (1985–6), 43–140

B. Brumana and G. Ciliberti: 'Musica e torneo nel seicento: fonti per uno studio dei libretti e delle musiche', *La società in costume: giostre e tornei nell'Italia di antico regime* (Foligno, 1986), 167–81

GALLIANO CILIBERTI

City Opera. American company, founded in New York in 1943 as the City Center Opera Company; *see* NEW YORK, §3.

Civic Opera House. Theatre opened in CHICAGO in 1929 and used by a succession of local companies including, from 1956, the Lyric Opera.

Claflin, (Alan) Avery (*b* Keene, NH, 21 June 1898; *d* Greenwich, CT, 9 Jan 1979). American composer. He studied law and banking, and for 35 years worked for the French American Banking Corporation in New York. He studied music with A. T. Davison at Harvard University and was influenced by encounters with Satie, Auric, Poulenc and Milhaud in Paris after World War I. Many of his works date from after his retirement (1954) from the bank, of which he was president. They display a well-crafted, conservative, decidedly French-influenced style. Virgil Thomson praised his operas as having 'undeniable quality', and described *La grande Bretèche* (1946–8) as 'unashamedly romantic and passionate ... grateful to sing'. Of the four operas, only *La grande Bretèche* and excerpts from *Hester Prynne* have been performed; none is published. *The Fall of Usher* and *Hester Prynne* (1929–33) in particular reveal Claflin's mastery of both dramatic development and musical form. His assured and colourful orchestration and the singable melodies have obvious 19th-century roots, but his personal synthesis of these sources is impressive. In 1978 Claflin wrote: 'It seems to me that the conservative trend is here to stay for a good while. In the course of this I suspect that, one of these days, my music will really be "discovered"'.

The Fall of Usher, 1920–21 (1, A. Claflin, after E. A. Poe)

Hester Prynne (3, D. Claflin, after N. Hawthorne), Act 2 scene ii perf. Hartford, CT, 15 Dec 1934

La grande Bretèche, 1946–8 (1, G. R. Mills, after H. Balzac), NBC Opera Theater, 3 Feb 1957

Uncle Tom's Cabin, 1964 (3, D. Claflin, after H. E. B. Stowe)

*

V. Thomson: *American Music Since 1910* (New York, 1971), 132, 142

Avery Claflin (New York, 1975) [brochure, incl. biography, list of works, discography; pubn of BMI]

BARBARA A. PETERSEN

Clairville [Nicolaie, Louis François] (*b* Lyons, 28 Jan 1811; *d* Paris, 7 Feb 1879). French librettist. He began his career writing melodramas for the Théâtre du Luxembourg, of which his father was impresario, then continued at other theatres, notably the Ambigu, before finding his métier as librettist of light operas and *opérettes*, mostly written in collaboration with other authors, including Chivot and Duru. His most enduring contributions to the *opérette* are the librettos of Lecocq's *La fille de Madame Angot* (1872) and Planquette's *Les cloches de Corneville* (1877); the latter was received by the Stoullig brothers as 'a curious mixture of operetta and melodrama ... *La dame blanche* transported into the world of *Le roi d'Yvetot*', but like *Angot* it has retained its grip on the affection of the French audience for over a century. His nephew Charles Clairville (*b* Paris, 27 Nov 1855) wrote librettos for Varney (*Riquet à la houppe*, 1889) and Messager (*Miss Dollar*, 1893).

selective list from about 30 librettos

Daphnis et Chloé, Offenbach, 1860; *Les cent vierges* (with Chivot and Duru), Lecocq, 1872; *Don César de Bazan* (with Chantepie), Massenet, 1872; *La fille de Madame Angot* (with Siraudin and Koning), Lecocq, 1872; *Jeanne, Jeannette et Jeanneton* (with Delacour), Lacome, 1876; *Les cloches de Corneville* (with Gabet), Planquette, 1877; *Pâques fleuries* (with Delacour), Lacome, 1879; *Le moulin joli*, P. J. A. Varney, 1894

*

ES; *StiegerO*

E. N. Stoullig and E. Stoullig: *Les Annales du Théâtre et de la Musique* (Paris, 1875)

PATRICK O'CONNOR

Clapisson, (Antonin [Antoine-]) **Louis** (*b* Naples, 15 Sept 1808; *d* Paris, 19 March 1866). French composer. He was a professional violinist before entering the Paris Conservatoire (1830), where he studied with Habeneck and Reicha. He continued playing in theatre orchestras to earn money, first at the Théâtre Italien and then (from 1832) at the Opéra. In 1862 he returned to the Conservatoire as a professor of harmony and curator of the historical instrument collection he had assembled.

Clapisson deliberately sought popularity at the beginning of his career by writing songs, chansonnettes and other vocal pieces. His début at the Opéra-Comique in 1838 came about when he accepted the libretto of *La figurante*, already refused by Monpou because of a two-month deadline. *La figurante* was well received and *La perruche* (1840) remained in the repertory, but it was *Gibby la cornemuse* (1846) that finally brought him financial security. Clapisson wrote his best work, *La fanchonnette*, two years after his election to the Institut (in 1854, in competition with, and defeating, Berlioz). It has an improbable libretto, but is full of effective orchestration and graceful tunes that flatter the central character (played originally by Caroline Carvalho). Although this work retained some popularity during the 19th century, most of Clapisson's music did not long survive him. Even in his lifetime he was not regarded as truly original, but as talented, with clever ideas that did not always compensate for weak librettos.

opéras comiques unless otherwise stated; all printed works published in Paris

POC – *Paris, Opéra-Comique* PL – *Paris, Théâtre Lyrique*

La figurante, ou l'Amour et la danse (5, E. Scribe and J.-H. Dupin), POC (Nouveautés), 24 Aug 1838 (1839)
La symphonie, ou Maître Albert (1, J.-H. Vernoy de Saint-Georges), POC (Nouveautés), 12 Oct 1839 (1840)
La perruche (1, Dumanoir [P. F. Pinel] and Dupin), POC (Favart), 28 April 1840, *F-Po* (inc.); (1840)
Le pendu (1, P. F. A. Carmouche and F. de Courcy), POC (Favart), 25 March 1841, *Pc**; (1841)
Frère et mari (1, T. Polak and A. Humbert), POC (Favart), 7 July 1841 (1841)
Le code noir (3, Scribe, after Mme Reybaud: *L'Epave*), POC (Favart), 9 June 1842 (1842)
Les bergers-trumeau (opéra bouffon, 1, C.-D. Dupeuty and Courcy), POC (Favart), 10 Feb 1845
Gibby la cornemuse (3, A. de Leuven and Brunswick [L. Lhérie]), POC (Favart), 19 Nov 1846 (n.d.), vs (1851)
Don Quichotte et Sancho (scène musicale, 1, F.-A. Duvert, after M. de Cervantes), POC (Favart), 11 Dec 1847
Jeanne la folle (opéra, 5, Scribe), Paris, Opéra, 6 Nov 1848, *Po**
La statue équestre (1, Scribe), ?Lyons, 1850
Les mystères d'Udolphe (3, Scribe and G. Delavigne, after A. Radcliffe), POC (Favart), 4 Nov 1852, vs (1853)
La promise (3, De Leuven and Brunswick), PL, 17 March 1854 (1854)
Dans les vignes (1, Brunswick and A. de Beauplan), PL, 31 Dec 1854, vs (1855)
Le coffret de Saint-Domingue (1, E. Deschamps), Paris, Salle Herz, 25 May 1855, vs (1854/5)
Les amoureux de Perrette (1), Baden-Baden, mid-Aug 1855
La fanchonnette (3, De Leuven and Saint-Georges), PL, 1 March 1856 (1856)
Le sylphe (2, Saint-Georges), Baden-Baden, 11 Aug 1856, aria *Pc**; (n.d.)
Margot (3, Saint-Georges and De Leuven), PL, 5 Nov 1857 (1858)
Les trois Nicolas (3, Scribe, B. Lopez and G. de Lurieu), POC (Favart), 16 Dec 1858, vs (1859)
Mme Grégoire, ou La nuit du mardi-gras (3, Scribe and H. Boisseaux), PL, 8 Feb 1861
La poularde de Caux (opérette, 1, De Leuven and V. Prilleux), Paris, Palais-Royal, 17 May 1861, vs (1861), collab. F.-A. Gevaert, E. Gautier, F. Poise, A. Bazille and S. Mangeant
Le baron de Trenck, ?1866 (3), unperf.

*

F. Clément and P. Larousse: *Dictionnaire lyrique* (Paris, 1867–81, 2/1892, 3/1905 ed. A. Pougin as *Dictionnaire des opéras*)
A. Soubies and C. Malherbe: *Histoire de l'Opéra-Comique: la seconde Salle Favart (1840–1860)*, i (Paris, 1892)
——: *Histoire de l'Opéra-Comique, la seconde Salle Favart (1860–1887)*, ii (Paris, 1893)
A. Soubies: *Les membres de l'Académie des beaux-arts*, iii (Paris, 1911), 158–62
C. Le Senne: 'Période contemporaine: Clapisson', *EMDC*, I/iii (Paris, 1921), 1758–9
P. Landormy and J. Loisel: 'Institut de France: Clapisson', *EMDC*, II/vi (Paris, 1931), 3512
M. Curtiss: *Bizet and his World* (New York, 1958)

LESLEY A. WRIGHT

Claque. An organized body of operagoers who hire themselves out to provoke or prolong applause (or to boo, hiss, catcall or whistle at the rivals of the artist they support). It is distinct from (but may shade into) factions of admirers who applaud (or boo) out of conviction or friendship with management or artists. Faction thrives when opera rouses strong passions in a knowledgeable audience; a listless or ill-informed public provides suitable conditions for a claque. Hence the true claque flourished at the Paris Opéra at least from the 1830s, and at the New York Metropolitan for most of this century; two managers of these houses admitted that they had on occasion used it. The claque also thrived in modern Rome with its audience dominated by bureaucrats. The organizing principle was the payment by management or artists of a claque leader, both in money and in tickets which he gave out or sold at minimal prices to a semi-permanent group of underlings; these he marshalled in the theatre to provide degrees of applause in accordance with a tariff. On special occasions the underlings might be paid. The claque leader Auguste Levasseur (*d* 1844) was a well-known Paris figure who took a dispassionate view of his business. Italy, where faction was common, did not develop a true claque until the turn of the 19th and 20th centuries; in Vienna the early 20th-century claque leader Schostal is said to have cared about artistic standards. Some sort of claque is probably endemic in many opera houses.

Correspondence: G. Grisi to M. Accursi, *c*1834 (*US-NYp*)
H. Berlioz: *Les soirées de l'orchestre* (Paris, 1852; Eng. trans., 1956, 2/1973), 7th evening
L. Véron: *Mémoires d'un bourgeois de Paris* (Paris, 1853–5), iii, 261–2, 313–21
C. de Boigne: *Petits mémoires de l'Opéra* (Paris, 1857), 86–91
J. Lan: *Mémoires d'un chef de claque* (Paris, 1883)
Letter: to G. Gatti-Casazza, 30 April 1920 (New York, Metropolitan Opera Archives)
J. Wechsberg: *Looking for a Bluebird* (London, 1946), 72–97
W. L. Crosten: *French Grand Opera: an Art and a Business* (New York, 1948), 41–8
G. Forzano: *Come li ho conosciuti* (Turin, 1957), 11
M. Labroca: *L'usignolo di Boboli* (Venice, 1959), 162–6
R. Bing: *5,000 Nights at the Opera* (New York, 1972), 219–25, 245
F. Possenti: 'La "claque" a teatro', *Strenna dei Romanisti*, xxxvii (1976), 453–6
J. Rosselli: *The Opera Industry in Italy from Cimarosa to Verdi* (Cambridge, 1984), 159–60 JOHN ROSSELLI

Clarey, Cynthia (*b* Smithfield, VA, 25 April 1949). American mezzo-soprano. She studied singing at Howard University, Washington, DC, and the Juilliard School, and obtained early experience with the Tri-Cities Opera Company in Binghamton, New York. Her widespread American engagements have ranged from Cavalli to Offenbach and include the title role in *The Voice of Ariadne* (Musgrave) with the New York City Opera, and parts in the American première of Tippett's *The Ice Break* at Boston (1979) and in Miki's *An Actor's Revenge* at St Louis, as well as Baroque and Classical repertory. She shared the title role in Peter Brook's production of *La tragédie de Carmen* in Paris (1982) and on tour abroad; her British début was as Octavia in *L'incoronazione di Poppea* at Glyndebourne (1984), where she also sang Serena in *Porgy and Bess* under Rattle (1986). In 1985–7 she appeared at the Wexford Festival. Her voice commands a wide range with ease and fluency, sustained with musical perception and dramatic credibility. NOËL GOODWIN

Clari, Giovanni Carlo Maria (*b* Pisa, 27 Sept 1677; *d* Pisa, 16 May 1754). Italian composer. He studied composition in Bologna with G. P. Colonna. His first opera, the three-act 'scherzo drammatico' *Il savio delirante* (A. Saratelli; lib. *I-Bc*), was performed with two intermezzos to great acclaim at the Teatro del Pubblico on 27 January 1695, when he was 17. From 1703 to 1724 he was *maestro di cappella* at Pistoia Cathedral, during which time he composed his only other opera, the *dramma per musica Il principe corsaro* (3, ? G. B. Giardini; lib. *I-Bc*, *Fn*, *MOe*, *Rn*), staged in 1717 at the Teatro Cocomero, Florence. He spent the rest of his life in Pisa as a *maestro di cappella* and wrote the works for which he enjoyed most fame, his elegant chamber duets and trios. All the music from his operas is lost.

*

BurneyH; *MGG* (E. C. Saville)
C. Ricci: *I teatri di Bologna nei secoli XVII e XVIII* (Bologna, 1888), 374
F. Baggiani: *Giovan Carlo Maria Clari: musicista pisano del '700* (Pisa, 1977)
R. L. Weaver and N. W. Weaver: *A Chronology of Music in the Florentine Theater 1590–1750* (Detroit, 1978) COLIN TIMMS

Clarissa. Opera in two acts, op.30, by ROBIN HOLLOWAY after Samuel Richardson's novel; London, Coliseum, 18 May 1990.

Holloway was first drawn to Richardson's novel (reputedly the longest in the English language) in 1968, working intermittently on the libretto and the score without commission or prospect of performance until its completion in 1976 – a notable act of faith. Act 1 presents Clarissa's oppression by her family who seek to compel her into an arranged marriage, her rescue by the attractive rake Lovelace, his immurement of her in a London brothel and her temporary escape. In Act 2, the recaptured Clarissa continues to resist his advances – the true psychological complexity of their relationship being suggested in an extended 'dream ballet' – until he rapes her; the final scene presents her renunciation, death and apotheosis.

Though Holloway retains Richardson's 18th-century diction, his setting is the reverse of neo-classical: a post-Wagnerian flux of leitmotifs, symbolic key contrasts and quotations from Wagner, Debussy and Hugo Wolf. The surgings of a large orchestra and the transformations of an elaborate mise-en-scène, which Holloway confesses was partly inspired by the films of Fellini, are intended alike to focus obsessively on the central triangle of Clarissa (soprano), Lovelace (tenor) and Clarissa's confidante, Anna (coloratura soprano). All three roles are highly demanding. Holloway wrote a substantial *Clarissa Symphony* which is based on extracts from the opera. BAYAN NORTHCOTT

Clark, Graham (*b* Littleborough, 10 Nov 1941). English tenor. After singing Jeník and Riccardo (*Ballo*) with Gemini Opera, in 1975 he joined Scottish Opera, singing Brighella (*Ariadne auf Naxos*), Malcolm, Jaquino, Ernesto, David, Pedrillo and the Italian Singer (*Der Rosenkavalier*). He sang Bomarzo in the British première of Ginastera's opera for the ENO (1976) and Tonio (*La fille du régiment*) in Vancouver (1977). Over the next ten years his roles for the ENO included Almaviva, Hoffmann, Peter Quint, Count Ory, Rodolfo, Grigory, Vašek, Hermann (*The Queen of Spades*), Alexey (*The Gambler*), Albert Gregor (*The Makropulos Affair*), Mephistopheles (Busoni's *Doktor Faust*) and Don Juan (*The Stone Guest*). At Bayreuth (1981–9) he has sung David, Loge and Mime. He made his Metropolitan début in 1985 as Števa (*Jenůfa*), returning in 1989 as Herod. With a powerful, high-lying voice, he excels in character roles. ELIZABETH FORBES

Clarke, (James) Hamilton (Smee) (*b* Birmingham, 25 Jan 1840; *d* Banstead, 9 July 1912). English composer and conductor. After early instruction from his father, he studied to be a land surveyor, but then embarked instead on a musical career and held various appointments as organist and conductor, notably in Oxford and, succeeding Sullivan, in Kensington. He conducted at a number of London theatres, including the Opera Comique, where he had charge of a portion of the original run of *The Sorcerer* (1877). In 1878 he became musical director at the Lyceum Theatre, where he composed incidental music; in 1893 he was appointed principal conductor of the Carl Rosa company.

He composed scores for six short operettas produced by German Reed at St George's Opera House; of these, *Nobody's Fault* (1881) and *A Pretty Bequest* (1885) achieved the longest runs. He was a close associate of Sullivan and arranged overtures for several Savoy operas, including *The Sorcerer* (revised version, 1884) and *The Mikado* (1885). FREDRIC WOODBRIDGE WILSON

Clarke, Henry Leland (*b* Dover, NH, 9 March 1907). American composer. His studies at Harvard University (1924–9, 1931–2, 1944–7) included a course in composition with Gustav Holst. He also studied in Paris with Nadia Boulanger (1929–31) and in New York and Bennington with Hans Weisse and Otto Luening (1932–8). He held several teaching posts, retiring from the University of Washington, Seattle, in 1977 as professor emeritus.

Clarke has written two operas, of which the first, *The Loafer and the Loaf* (1, E. Sharp; Stockbridge, MA, July 1954) is described by the composer as 'an incredible episode in one act'. The plot, focussing on the question of who is more likely to steal a loaf of bread, the well fed or the hungry, is an extended dialogue between a prosperous citizen, the champion of right versus wrong, and a poet's wife, who represents the voice of reason and moderation. The music is essentially tonal and makes apt use of musical quotation, with some experimentation with chromaticism and atonality. The vocal lines are rhythmically complex and feature the wide leaps that became characteristic of his later work in the genre.

Lysistrata (1968–72; 2, J. Stevenson, after Aristophanes; Marlboro, Vermont, 9 November 1984) effectively uses a tableau-like staging for the soloist versus Greek chorus setting. The musical style is essentially atonal, with some use of speech-song in the vocal lines. The dramatic character of Lysistrata is portrayed by the wide range and leaps in her vocal lines, in vivid contrast to her comic foils, whose vocal parts are set in a more tonal idiom with frequent use of patter. This work shows the full development of Clarke's 'word tones', in which a specific pitch is assigned to each word of the text, that particular pitch being used at each occurrence of the same word. JAMES P. CASSARO

Claudine von Villa Bella **(i)** ('Claudine of Villa Bella'). *Schauspiel mit Gesang* in one act by IGNAZ VON BEECKE to a libretto by JOHANN WOLFGANG VON GOETHE; Vienna, Burgtheater, 13 June 1780.

In this unruly *Sturm und Drang* drama Goethe 'sought to work with romantic subjects', as he put it, 'and contemplated uniting noble sentiments with vagabond activities'. Donna Claudine (soprano) returns the love of the awkward young Don Pedro (tenor) and rejects the passionate nocturnal advances of his brother Crugantino (tenor), a reprobate who has fallen in among vagabonds. Crugantino wounds Pedro in a duel and has him carried off; Claudine follows in male attire and confronts Crugantino. A general mêlée develops, guards arrest everyone and in the final prison scene Pedro is restored to Claudine.

In Beecke's opera the music is most prominent in choral scenes, in Crugantino's dramatic Romanze 'Es war ein Buhle frech genug' and in the extensive finale to Act 2. Contrary to expectations at Vienna, Beecke's setting failed and was dropped after only two performances. THOMAS BAUMAN

Claudine von Villa Bella **(ii)**. Singspiel in three acts by JOHANN FRIEDRICH REICHARDT to a libretto by JOHANN WOLFGANG VON GOETHE; Charlottenburg, Schlosstheater, 29 July 1789.

Goethe rewrote his first two librettos during his Italian journey, in 1787–8. In line with his new allegiance to *opera buffa*, he rewrote *Claudine* entirely in verse, reduced the cast and toned down considerably the original storm-and-stress traits of the libretto (*see* CLAUDINE VON VILLA BELLA (i)). Only three numbers survived intact; even Crugantino's famous Romanze 'Es war ein Buhle frech genug' was sacrificed. Reichardt went over his composition with the poet at Goethe's house and the simple, lied-like style he maintained throughout the work shows that he was prepared to observe the restricted role the poet demanded from the music. For the première at Charlottenburg he left Goethe's blank verse unset, but composed it as recitative for a revival under Goethe's direction at Weimar in 1795. THOMAS BAUMAN

Claudius [*Die verdammte Staat-Sucht, oder Der verführte Claudius* ('The Accursed Lust for Power, or Claudius Betrayed')]. *Sing-Spiel* in three acts by REINHARD KEISER to a libretto by HINRICH HINSCH; Hamburg, Theater am Gänsemarkt, 1703.

The action centres on Messalina (soprano), wife of the Emperor Claudius, and her scandalous love affair with Silius (tenor), a Roman nobleman. Despite the efforts of Narcissus (soprano) and others to warn him, Claudius (bass) refuses to believe Messalina unfaithful. Eventually a group of conspirators resolves to kill the lovers, but before they can act Silius and Messalina exchange marriage vows in a bacchanalian ceremony, and the people hail Silius as emperor. In the end Claudius's supporters prevail, and Messalina is turned over to the Vestal Virgins (rather than being summarily executed as in Tacitus), while Silius goes into exile. In a magical subplot Calpurnia (soprano), who has also been smitten with Silius, consults various supernatural authorities in search of a cure for love, finally finding it in the cave of a fury (Erynnis, soprano), who restores her feelings for her betrothed, Callistus (contralto).

Claudius was the earliest Hamburg opera to include arias in Italian as well as German, an innovation for which Keiser seems to have been personally responsible. The musical style is marked by an abundance of popular melody, often in 6/8 or 12/8 time, and sparing use of coloratura. In 1726, Keiser extensively reworked the opera, but the music of this version is lost. Handel modelled several numbers in his first opera, *Almira* (1705, Hamburg), on specific pieces in *Claudius* and also borrowed heavily from Keiser's score in many of his later works. JOHN H. ROBERTS

Claussen, Julia (*b* Stockholm, 11 June 1879; *d* Stockholm, 1 May 1941). Swedish mezzo-soprano. She studied in Stockholm, making her début in 1903 at the Royal Opera, where she was engaged until 1912. She sang in Berlin, London, Vienna, Paris, Brussels and Chicago (1913–17); her Covent Garden roles (1914) were Ortrud and Amneris. She made her Metropolitan début in 1917 as Delilah and was engaged there for 15 years; her repertory included Gluck's Orpheus, Léonore (*La favorite*), Fidès (*Le prophète*), Carmen, Marina (*Boris Godunov*), Brangäne, Kundry and Fricka. She also sang Brünnhilde (*Die Walküre*), but the part lay too high for her rich-toned voice, which was strongest in the lower register. ELIZABETH FORBES

Clay, Frederic Emes (*b* Paris, 3 Aug 1838; *d* Great Marlow, 29 Nov 1889). English composer. His father, James Clay, was MP for Hull and a published amateur composer, while his grandmother, Miss Mortellari (later Signora Woolrych), achieved distinction as an opera singer. Frederic was educated largely at home, before studying harmony and counterpoint with Molique in London. A promising career in the Treasury Department supported his early compositions and also a brief period of further study with Hauptmann in Leipzig in

1863. In 1862 he made his public début at Covent Garden with *Court and Cottage* and it was during the rehearsals of his first real success, *Ages Ago* (1869), that Clay introduced his librettist, W. S. Gilbert, to his close friend Arthur Sullivan. In 1873, a comfortable legacy from his father enabled him to devote his attention completely to composition and in 1877 he tried his fortune in the USA, achieving only moderate success. On his return to England in 1881, he found a new librettist in George Sims but, after the second performance of *The Golden Ring* on 4 December 1883, Clay collapsed; he was paralysed for the rest of his life. Six years later, he was found drowned in his bath. He never married.

Most of Clay's works were written for the stage, although he wrote many popular songs, some hymns and two cantatas, one of which, *Lalla Rookh*, included the famous 'I'll sing thee songs of Araby'. Rooted firmly in the Victorian tradition, he was a thoroughly accomplished craftsman, although he never felt at ease in recitative. His melodies are always fresh and graceful; his harmonic treatment, though sometimes strikingly original, owes much to Rossini and Auber. Successful though he was, he never really broke away from the drawing-room ballad and, lacking Sullivan's sense of fun and powers of invention, remained largely in his shadow. His works have recently enjoyed renewed popularity on both sides of the Atlantic.

first performed in London unless otherwise stated; vocal score published in London soon after first performance

The Pirate's Isle (operetta, ? B. C. Stephenson), private perf., 1859, lost

Out of Sight (operetta, 1, Stephenson), Feb 1860

Court and Cottage (operetta, 1, T. Taylor), CG, 22 March 1862, lost, 1 song pubd

Constance (op, 1, T. Robertson), CG, 23 Jan 1865

The Bold Recruit (operetta, 1, Stephenson), Canterbury, Theatre Royal, 4 Aug 1868, *GB-Lbl**, vs

Ages Ago (musical legend, 1, W. S. Gilbert), Gallery of Illustration, 22 Nov 1869, autograph (private collection)

The Gentleman in Black (musical legend, 2, Gilbert), Charing Cross, 26 May 1870

In Possession (operetta, 1, R. Reece), Gallery of Illustration, 20 June 1871, lost

Babil and Bijou, or The Lost Regalia [tableaux 5–8] (fantastic music drama, 5, J. R. Planché, after D. Boucicault), CG, 29 Aug 1872, collab. Hervé, J. Rivière and J. J. de Billemont

Happy Arcadia (op, 1, Gilbert), Gallery of Illustration, 28 Oct 1872

The Black Crook (grand opéra-bouffe féerie, 4, H. Paulton and J. Paulton, after T. Cogniard: *La biche au bois*), Alhambra, 23 Dec 1872, collab. G. Jacobi, songs (London, *c*1875); rev. version, Alhambra, 3 Dec 1881

Oriana (romantic legend, 3, J. Albery), Globe, 16 Feb 1873, lib. pubd

Don Juan (Christmas extravaganza, 7 scenes, H. J. Byron), Alhambra, ? 19 Jan 1874, collab. Jacobi, incl. music by Lecocq and Offenbach

Cattarina, or Friends at Court (comic op, 2, Reece), Manchester, Prince's, 17 Aug 1874, songs (London, 1874)

Green Old Age (musical improbability, Reece), Vaudeville, 31 Oct 1874, ?unpubd

Princess Toto (comic op, 3, Gilbert), Nottingham, Theatre Royal, 26 June 1876, autograph (private collection)

Don Quixote (grand comic and spectacular op, 3, H. Paulton and A. Maltby), Alhambra, 25 Sept 1876

The Merry Duchess (sporting comic op, 2, G. R. Sims), Royalty, 23 April 1883, songs (London, 1883)

The Golden Ring (fairy op, 3, Sims), Alhambra, 3 Dec 1883, ?unpubd

On the March (musical comedy, 2, C. Clay, W. Yardley and Stephenson), music arr. E. Solomon and J. Crook, Sheffield, Theatre Royal, 18 May 1896

*

GänzlBMT

'Mr Frederic Clay', *The Ray* [Boston] (11 March 1880)

'Our Celebrities at Home, cccxvi: Mr. Frederic Clay at Clarence Chambers', *The World* (18 April 1883)

G. R. Sims: *My Life* (London, 1917)

T. Searle: *Bibliography of W. S. Gilbert* (London, 1931)

J. W. Stedman: *Gilbert before Sullivan* (Chicago, 1969)

CHRISTOPHER KNOWLES

Clayton, Thomas (*b* London, bap. 28 Oct 1673; *d* London, bur. 23 Sept 1725). English composer. A violinist, he joined his father William Clayton in the Royal Private Musick in 1689, obtaining a full place in 1693. He inherited property from both parents (his father died in 1697 and his mother in 1700) and also received his father's music books and instruments and his shares in the Drury Lane theatre. By autumn 1704 he had been to Italy to study music, although he was in England to sign each year for the livery payment due to him on 30 November.

On 28 October 1704 the *Diverting Post* reported that two operas, one of them by Clayton, were being prepared for the opening of Vanbrugh's new playhouse in the Haymarket. However, Clayton's opera, *Arsinoe, Queen of Cyprus* (*GB-Lbl*), was put on by Christopher Rich's company at Drury Lane on 16 January 1705. It was the first all-sung opera in the Italian style to be performed on the English stage and was a considerable success for two seasons. The libretto by Stanzani had originally been set by Franceschini in 1676, and it is not clear whether Clayton set the English translation by Peter Motteux or asked Motteux to fit English words to his setting of the Italian. Later in the century Burney and Hawkins were united in their scorn of its music, and the anonymous author of *A Critical Discourse upon Opera's in England* (1709) wrote that 'it ought to be called the Hospital of the old Decrepid *Italian* Opera's'. This critic claimed that the success of *Arsinoe* 'encouraged the Author to Compose another worse than the first'. (It also enabled Clayton to resign from the Private Musick in 1706.) His second opera was *Rosamond*, to an original English libretto by Joseph Addison. It was first performed at Drury Lane on 4 March 1707 and was a complete failure, receiving only three performances. Clayton's music has always been held responsible for this, but Addison's libretto is far from perfect, and its flattery of the Duke of Marlborough alienated the Tories. In 1709 the Whig Lord Wharton was appointed Lord Lieutenant of Ireland and Addison became his Principal Secretary, accompanying him on visits to Ireland in 1709 and 1710. They took Clayton with them and he organized operatic entertainments at Dublin Castle.

By that time opera in London was being performed in Italian. Addison and Steele, in *The Tatler* and later *The Spectator*, mounted a rearguard action against the absurdity of this, and Steele backed Clayton in a series of concerts at York Buildings between 1710 and 1712 which featured Clayton's settings of English poetry. In these concerts Clayton was joined by Haym and Dieupart, who had assisted in the production of *Arsinoe*. The resentment of the three musicians at their exclusion from the current operatic scene is shown in their letter to *The Spectator* in December 1711. At Steele's request, John Hughes adapted Dryden's *Alexander's Feast* for setting by Clayton (1712) and Hughes later sent Steele detailed criticism of Clayton's music. Hughes admitted that the words were generally 'naturally enough expressed' but added: 'If the music in score, without the words, does not prove itself by the rules of composition, which relate to the harmony and motion of different notes at the same time, the notes in the singing parts will not suffice, though they express the words ever so naturally'.

Clayton's preface to the libretto of *Arsinoe* began: 'The Design of this Entertainment being to introduce the Italian manner of Musick on the English Stage' and concluded: 'if this Attempt shall ... be a Means of bringing this manner of Musick to be us'd in my Native Country, I shall think all my Study and Pains very well employ'd'. He is certainly remembered for this achievement – and for being himself a very indifferent composer.

See also ARSINOE and ROSAMOND.

BurneyH
A Critical Discourse upon Opera's in England (London, 1709)
Memoirs of the Life of ... Wharton (London, 1715)
J. Duncombe, ed.: *Letters by Several Eminent Persons ... Including the Correspondence of John Hughes, Esq.* (London, 1772)
R. Fiske: *English Theatre Music in the Eighteenth Century* (London, 1973, 2/1986)
R. D. Hume: 'Opera in London, 1695–1706', *British Theatre and the Other Arts, 1660–1800*, ed. S. S. Kenny (London and Washington DC, 1984), 67–91
A. Ashbee: *Records of English Court Music*, ii: *(1685–1714)* (Snodland, Kent, 1987)

OLIVE BALDWIN, THELMA WILSON

Cledière, Bernard (*fl* 1673–80). French *haute-contre*. Recruited in Languedoc together with Beaumavielle, he sang at the Paris Opéra in Lully's *Cadmus* (1673, the Sun and First Prince), *Alceste* (1674, Admetus), *Thésée* (1675 and 1677; title role), *Atys* (1676 and 1682; title role), *Isis* (1677, Mercury) and *Bellérophon* (1679 and 1680, St Germain; title role). By 1682 he had left the Opéra to join the *musique du roi*. His position as principal *haute-contre* passed to the high *haute-taille* Dumesnil, with whom he had shared the role of Alpheius (*Proserpine*) in 1680; Cledière had sung it at St Germain, while Dumesnil, making his début, had taken it over for the Paris performances. PHILIP WELLER

Clément, Edmond (*b* Paris, 28 March 1867; *d* Nice, 24 Feb 1928). French tenor. He studied singing at the Conservatoire and made his début at the Opéra-Comique in 1889 in Gounod's *Mireille*. He took part in the premières of Saint-Saëns' *Phryné* and Bruneau's *L'attaque du moulin* as well as the first performances in Paris of *Falstaff* and *Butterfly*. In 1896 he was in the first *Don Giovanni* ever given at the Opéra-Comique, and in 1904 sang Don José in the 1000th performance of *Carmen* at that theatre. In 1909 he made his début at the Metropolitan in *Werther* and appeared in the only performances there of *Fra Diavolo* (1910). With the Boston Opera Company in 1912 he sang his first Hoffmann, a performance reputedly ideal in its mixture of masculinity and dreaminess, with finely shaded singing. His Don José also developed into a masterly portrayal. He returned to France to fight in World War I and was wounded; later he devoted himself to teaching, but gave a memorable last recital at the age of 60 in Paris, in November 1927. His recordings are models of their kind, with slim, clearly defined tone, a polished style and unostentatious personal charm.

J. B. Steane: *The Grand Tradition* (London, 1974)
M. Scott: *The Record of Singing* (London, 1977)

J. B. STEANE

Clementi, Aldo (*b* Catania, 25 May 1925). Italian composer. His music of the 1960s and 70s hardly seemed to prefigure a move into the opera house. After conventional studies with Alfredo Sangiorgi and Petrassi, the combined influences of fragmented serial counterpoint, absorbed from Maderna, and of abstract painting led him to devise complex structures from interweaving canonic lines that rotated quietly upon themselves, inviting exploration of an austere, intricate, but static musical universe. Initially, Clementi's materials were atonal, but from 1970 on he submitted borrowed tonal fragments to the same procedure. These, being multiply transposed, produce densely chromatic textures in which familiar gestures momentarily appear.

However, in 1980 Clementi took fragments from Nello Sàito's Freudian drama, *Es*, and constructed from them a framework that complemented his working methods. The resultant 'rondeau in one act', also entitled *Es*, was given its first performance at the Teatro La Fenice, Venice, on 28 April 1981. It sets out a circular dramatic proposition. Three women – Tuni, a secretary, Rica, a housewife, Mina, an artist – wait for, and fantasize about, a possibly imaginary Don Juan figure. This is not an exercise in empathy with fully rounded operatic characters: on the contrary, three of the repeated behavioural traits that an author might use to create a 'character' for each woman are instead assigned to three separate singers identically dressed and in an identical environment (piled one above the other in Uberto Bertacca's striking designs for La Fenice). The three sopranos representing Tuni are in offices, the three mezzo-sopranos representing Rica in kitchens, the three contraltos representing Mina in studios. Each rights a constantly falling object within her environment, re-enacting the myth of Sisyphus by way of underlining the circularity of her self-torture.

The six scenes of *Es* are identical in structure, but of cumulative intensity. Each begins with a waltz-canon that transforms, in calculated irony, materials from the six-verse chorale 'Jesu meine Freude' (a hymn of longing for Jesus). The nine performers sing or speak fragments from Sàito's text, or dissolve into hysterical laughter. Each waltz-canon is followed by a dance collage to which the performers gyrate mechanically, each pursuing her own rhythm, and accompanied by her own offstage instrument. Each scene ends with the austere consolation of an ever denser, slower, and longer instrumental berceuse – the last, a 45-part canon at the unison, involving the voices as well. This closing gesture is precipitated by the intervention of the recorded voice of an old woman, Matrax (spoken role), who spells out the self-renewing folly of romantic obsession.

A. Clementi: 'Alcune idee per un nuovo teatro musicale contemporaneo', *Il verri*, new ser., no.16 (1964)
R. Garavaglia: 'Io e l'Es di Aldo Clementi', *Laboratorio musica* (1981), Jan
D. Osmond-Smith: 'Au creux néant musicien: Recent Work by Aldo Clementi', *Contact*, no.23 (1981), 5–9
A. Clementi: 'Ancora sul teatro musicale', *Musica/Realtà*, v/Aug (1984)
R. Cresti: *Aldo Clementi* (Milan, 1990)

DAVID OSMOND-SMITH

Clementin [Clementino; Hader, Clementin; Hadersberg, Clementin von] (*b* *c*1655; *d* ?St Cloud, nr Paris, before 14 Feb 1714). Austrian soprano castrato. He served in Leopold I's Hofkapelle in Vienna from 1672 to 1687. J. H. Schmelzer commented in 1678 that he had a good voice. He sang at the Munich court in 1682, and in Steffani's *Servio Tullio* and Bernabei's *Ascanio in Alba*, both performed in 1686 for the wedding of the Elector of Bavaria, Maximilian II Emanuel; he entered service there in 1687 and became the leading castrato. According to archival sources, it seems that he composed the three-act festive opera *Eraclio*, performed on 5 February 1690 for Leopold I's visit. In 1692, after Maximilian became governor of the Spanish Netherlands, Clementin, now ennobled as Clementin von Hadersberg, was summoned to Brussels. He was held in great esteem by Maximilian and remained in the elector's service during the latter's exile (from 1704). His vocal range was *d′ to a″*.

*

E. Straub: *Repraesentatio Maiestatis oder churbayerische Freudenfeste* (Munich, 1969), 260

R. Münster: 'Die Musik am Hofe Max Emanuels', *Kurfürst Max Emanuel: Bayern und Europa um 1700* (Munich, 1976), 296, 299, 305, 310 ROBERT MÜNSTER

Clement IX, Pope. *See* ROSPIGLIOSI, GIULIO.

Clemenza di Scipione, La ('The Clemency of Scipio'). *Opera seria* in three acts by JOHANN CHRISTIAN BACH; London, King's Theatre in the Haymarket, 4 April 1778.

Scipio (tenor) has taken Carthage after a long siege. Among the prisoners are Arsinda (soprano), a Spanish princess, and Idalba (soprano), her friend, who is in love with the Roman general Marzio [Marcius] (soprano castrato). Luceio [Luceius] (soprano castrato), a Celtiberian prince, who is betrothed to Arsinda, finding that she has been captured, hurries to the Roman camp under an assumed name in an attempt to ransom her. When ransom is refused, he attempts to take her by force but is captured. First Scipio and then Marcius offer Luceius his liberty in exchange for his vow of allegiance to Rome, but he refuses. Finally he is brought to the Temple of Vengeance to be killed and once again he refuses to swear. Arsinda threatens to kill herself if he is not released at once; Scipio relents and grants Luceius his freedom unconditionally. Moved by his generosity Luceius and Arsinda both now swear loyalty to Rome. Scipio embraces them and also gives the marriage of Marcius and Idalba his blessing.

Bach's last Italian opera was composed to an anonymous libretto, thought by contemporaries to have been the work of a foreign (presumably Italian) diplomat in London. The simplicity of the plot and the directness of the language of the texts of the arias and ensembles show it to be a work in a post-Metastasian mould. The total absence of da capo or dal segno arias is another notably progressive feature. The original cast included Valentin Adamberger (Scipio), later to be the first Belmonte in Mozart's *Die Entführung aus dem Serail* (1782, Vienna), the Mannheim soprano Franziska Danzi (Arsinda), who on 3 August of the same year took part in the inauguration of the Teatro alla Scala, Milan, and Francesco Roncaglia (Luceius), who had created roles in both of Bach's Mannheim operas. The aria for Danzi, 'Infelice, in van m'affanno', with obbligato parts for flute, oboe, violin and cello, may have been the model for 'Martern aller Arten' in *Die Entführung*. The other vocal numbers are of more modest proportions. Bach makes two attempts at thematic integration: once by anticipating the melodic material of the aria 'Nel partir, bell'idol mio' in the preceding accompanied recitative but, more importantly, by using the opening motifs of the single-movement overture not only in the accompanied recitative in the first scene of Act 1 but also as the basis of the final chorus of the entire opera.

La clemenza di Scipione was revived in a two-act version in 1805 as a vehicle for Mrs Billington, and ran for 18 performances. ERNEST WARBURTON

Clemenza di Tito, La ('The Clemency of Titus'). Libretto by PIETRO METASTASIO, first set by Antonio Caldara (1734, Vienna). The title *Tito Vespasiano* was used for a later version of this libretto.

Titus Vespasian, Emperor of Rome, has succeeded to the throne that his father, Vespasian, usurped from the Emperor Vitellius.

ACT 1 Vitellia, daughter of Vitellius, reminds Sesto [Sextus], her lover, that Titus not only occupies a throne that is rightfully hers, but that he has also chosen a foreigner, Berenice, as consort. She then alludes to the conspiracy against Titus that only awaits Sextus's orders for its implementation. Loyal to Titus, Sextus hesitates; Annio [Annius], Sextus's friend, bears news that Titus will choose a new consort. The choice falls upon Servilia, sister of Sextus; but since she is in love with Annius, Titus releases her. Vitellia, hearing that a new consort has been chosen, incites Sextus to move against Titus. Publio [Publius], captain of the guard, and Annius now announce a third choice: Vitellia herself. She implores them to find Sextus quickly so that the conspirators' action can be halted.

ACT 2 But it has already begun. Sextus, distraught at seeing the Capitol in flames, hastens to save Titus, but believes he is too late when he comes upon a mortally wounded figure clad in the royal robes. Assuming full responsibility, Sextus prepares to kill himself. Annius, however, reveals that Titus lives: it was Lentulus, a conspirator, who had been struck down. Sextus, summoned by Titus, exchanges cloaks with Annius, since his own bears the badge of the conspirators. Thus, when Annius later appears before Titus, he is arrested for treason. He remains silent but is released when the dying Lentulus tells all. Sextus is arrested.

ACT 3 Annius begs Titus to pardon Sextus, who has been found guilty by the Senate. Brought before Titus, Sextus says nothing in order to protect Vitellia. He thus momentarily angers Titus, who signs the death warrant but then destroys it. Vitellia, believing that Sextus is to die on her account, makes a full confession to Titus who bestows a general pardon and urges her union with Sextus.

* * *

With some 40 different settings, *La clemenza di Tito* ranks well among Metastasio's more popular dramas. Classical sources for the plot include Cassius Dio, *Historiarum* (Xiphilinus, *Epitome*, book 66); Suetonius, *Vita* (Titus); Victor, *De Caesaribus* (nos.9–10); Victor, *Vita* (chap. 21); and Zonaras, *Annals* (book 11). The action of Metastasio's drama, with its theme of princely magnanimity, closely parallels that of Corneille's *Cinna* (1641), while Racine's *Bérénice* and Corneille's *Tite et Bérénice*, both produced in 1670, dramatize the all-important dismissal of Berenice. There is also a distinct correspondence between Vitellia's position in relation to Titus and Sextus in Metastasio's drama and Hermione's situation with regard to Pyrrhus and Orestes in Racine's *Andromaque* (1667). Metastasio wrote his drama to be set for the name-day celebrations of Emperor Charles VI in 1734, and it provides an excellent example of a work designed for imperial propaganda and the general moral enlightenment of the court. In a form adapted by

Caterino Mazzolà, it was still sufficiently apposite politically and appropriate allegorically to serve as part of the celebrations surrounding the coronation of Emperor Leopold II in Prague in 1791, when it was set by Mozart. Hasse's first setting (as *Tito Vespasiano* and with Metastasio's text considerably altered) served for the inauguration of the Teatro Publico in Pesaro. When Gluck set the libretto for Naples in 1752, his treatment of Sextus's aria 'Se mai senti' attracted attention for its general structure, the independence of its obbligato lines and its lack of coloratura passages, conditions that made possible a ready transference of the music to *Iphigénie en Tauride* (1779) for Iphigenia's 'O malheureuse Iphigénie'. Bernasconi's version for Munich (1768) is noteworthy for its extensive use of accompanied recitative and the fullness of the orchestral accompaniments.

For a list of settings *see* METASTASIO, PIETRO. DON NEVILLE

Clemenza di Tito, La ('The Clemency of Titus'). *Opera seria* in two acts, K621, by WOLFGANG AMADEUS MOZART to a libretto by PIETRO METASTASIO (*see* CLEMENZA DI TITO, LA above) adapted by CATERINO MAZZOLÀ; Prague, National Theatre, 6 September 1791.

Tito [Titus Flavius Vespasianus] *Roman Emperor*	tenor
Vitellia *daughter of the deposed Emperor Vitellius*	soprano
Servilia *sister of Sextus, in love with Annius*	soprano
Sesto [Sextus] *friend of Titus, in love with Vitellia*	soprano castrato
Annio [Annius] *friend of Sextus, in love with Servilia*	soprano
Publio [Publius] *prefect of the praetorian guard*	bass

Senators, ambassadors, praetorian guards, lictors, people of Rome

Setting Rome, AD *c*80

Although mostly composed after *Die Zauberflöte*, *La clemenza di Tito* was performed first. Its gestation has been dated back to 1789, when Mozart was in contact with the impresario Guardasoni, but the subject cannot have been chosen then. It has also been suggested that Vitellia's Act 2 rondò may be a revision of the 'rondo with obbligato basset-horn' sung by Josepha Duschek in Prague on 26 April 1791; there is, however, no positive evidence. Guardasoni obtained an open commission from the Bohemian Estates only in July, for an opera designed to celebrate Leopold II's coronation as King of Bohemia, and to some degree adapted to his particular taste.

Metastasio's libretto, already set by more than 40 composers, was 'ridotta a vera opera' ('reduced to a proper opera'), as Mozart wrote in his catalogue. Only seven arias and one chorus (designated 'Metastasio' below) were unchanged; Metastasio's aria and recitative texts were manipulated in the ensembles and finales devised by Mazzolà. Reduced by a third, the libretto gains clarity and the musical numbers pertinence, at the expense of dramatic weight.

Mozart probably composed all of *La clemenza* between late July and September 1791. He arrived in Prague on 28 August and despite illness finished work on the eve of the performance. The chief artistic drawback of the short time available was that Mozart subcontracted the simple recitatives, almost certainly to Süssmayr. The choruses and ensembles were worked out with Mazzolà in Vienna and written there, as were some arias. The singer Mozart knew best was Antonio Baglioni (Titus), two of whose arias were written in Vienna; the only ensemble composed in Prague (the trio early in Act 2) probably replaced intended arias for Vitellia (Maria Marchetti-Fantozzi) and Sextus (Domenico Bedini). Problems in these roles are apparent from surviving sketch and autograph material. Mozart began by assuming that Sextus would be a tenor, and Vitellia's 'Non più di fiori', the Act 2 rondò, is distinctly lower in tessitura than the rest of the role. The remainder of the cast was Carolina Perini (Annius, the travesty role); one Signora Antonini (Servilia); and a well-known *buffo* singer, Gaetano Campi (Publius).

The reception was modest until a triumphant last night was reported to Mozart (who had left Prague on 15 September) on the day of the première of *Die Zauberflöte* (30 September). Concert performances of extracts and of the whole opera were arranged by Constanze Mozart for her own benefit. In Vienna on 29 December 1791 and in later performances Aloysia Lange sang Sextus. After a further performance in Vienna in 1795 Constanze took the work to Graz, Leipzig and Berlin, herself singing Vitellia. In 1796 the German translation by Rochlitz was performed in Dresden and used in most German centres (including Vienna) within the next 15 years. The first performance outside Germany and Austria was also the first of any Mozart opera in London, on 27 March 1806, for the benefit of Mrs Billington. Performances followed in all the main European centres, usually in Italian (1809, Naples; 1816, Paris and Milan; 1817, in Russian, St Petersburg). Until about 1830 *La clemenza di Tito* was one of Mozart's most popular operas; it then went into eclipse. It has never fully entered the modern repertory and is often described as unworthy of Mozart, hastily assembled for a commission he could not refuse. Critical estimates have risen since World War II, and it is now seen as a positive step towards further reform of *opera seria*.

Despite its lack of overt thematic connection with the rest of the opera the overture has been described as a dramatic argument according to Gluck's principles (Floros 1964; Heartz 1978). It is a broadly conceived sonata with reversed recapitulation, the second theme in primary woodwind colours preceding the reprise of the majestic opening.

ACT 1 *Vitellia's apartments* Titus is in love with the Jewish queen Berenice; Vitellia denies being jealous, but believes she, an emperor's daughter, should be his consort. Overtly motivated by the need to avenge her father, she induces Sextus to lead an assassination plot. A loyal friend of Titus, he adores her blindly and cannot resist her commands. He begs her to say how he can please her, for she is his destiny (duet, 'Come ti piace, imponi'). Driving the music to the dominant with tremolando, she asks why he is delaying; he requests only a tender glance. In the Allegro, both admit to the confusion of their feelings. Annius reports that Titus has dismissed Berenice for reasons of state. Vitellia allows herself to hope, and tells Sextus to suspend the plot. In measured tones (a slow minuet) she declares that to win her he must not exhaust her with suspicions (Metastasio: 'Deh se piacer me vuoi'). The following Allegro returns to the opening words; its principal message, conveyed in a capricious mixture of sturdy rhythms and decorative flourishes, is that doubt encourages deception. Annius asks Sextus for his sister's hand, which he gladly grants in the duettino ('Deh prendi un dolce amplesso'), a winning expression of brotherly affection.

Before the Roman forum Senators and delegates from the provinces gather at the heart of the Imperial city. Titus enters in state, with lictors, guards and citizens. A march leads directly to a chorus in praise of Titus (Metastasio: 'Serbate, o dei custodi'). After formal expressions of homage from Publius and Annius, Titus replies that his sole aim is to be a good father to his people. The chorus is repeated; Titus calls for Sextus, and the stage is cleared during a repeat of the march. Private conversation (with Annius present) reveals the intimacy of Sextus and Titus. The emperor must publicly deny his love for Berenice by taking a Roman wife; who better than his friend's sister? Annius bravely eulogizes the emperor's choice. In a mellow Andante (Metastasio: 'Del più sublime soglio') Titus declares that the only happiness afforded by supreme power is to reward virtue. Annius reveals the emperor's decision to Servilia; the exquisite melody of their farewell (duet, 'Ah perdona al primo affetto') touches a nerve of painful tenderness within this severely political opera.

A garden in the Imperial palace on the Palatine To Publius Titus expounds his philosophy of disarming enmity by forgiveness. Servilia dares to confess that she and Annius are in love; he thanks heaven for her frankness, and releases her (Metastasio: 'Ah, se fosse intorno al trono'). The sweep of the melody in this short Allegro conveys his open-hearted nature; if the throne were flanked by such honesty, the cares of office would turn to joy. Vitellia bitterly compliments Servilia who, piqued, does not reveal her refusal. Deaf to reason, Vitellia upbraids Sextus for dilatoriness: Titus must die. Before embarking on his fatal mission he asks again for the loving glance which destroys his loyalty and assures his happiness (Metastasio: 'Parto, parto'). This aria with basset clarinet obbligato is in three sections, accelerating, as sentiment yields to determination, from a nobly extended Adagio through an impassioned Allegro ('Guardami, e tutto obblio') to a brilliant conclusion. Publius and Annius announce to Vitellia that she is the emperor's chosen consort (trio, 'Vengo! aspettate!'); the others mistake her confusion for excess of joy and comment sympathetically, but she is terrified that it is too late to stop the plot (her frantic message recalling Sextus ended Metastasio's first act). This gripping movement is dominated by Vitellia's agitation, expressed in gasping phrases and, when the musical line is more sustained, cruelly high tessitura (touching *d'''*).

A portico before the Capitol Sextus has launched the conspiracy, but is wracked by guilt (obbligato recitative); his weakness has made him a traitor. He cannot turn back; the Capitol is already in flames. The bulk of the finale is an action ensemble. Sextus, in words Metastasio intended as recitative, seems to begin an aria (a prayer for Titus's safety), but to Annius he babbles of his shame and rushes away; Annius is prevented from following by the need to keep Servilia out of danger. Cries of horror are heard from the offstage chorus; Publius appears, fearing for Titus, then Vitellia, frantically searching for Sextus. He returns, looking for a place to hide; all believe Titus dead. Sextus is about to confess when Vitellia silences him. In a concluding Andante all the characters and the distant chorus join in lamenting the murderous treachery.

ACT 2 *Palace gardens* Annius tells Sextus that Titus is alive. Sextus admits that he instigated the plot, refusing to give any reason. Annius gently urges him to throw himself on the emperor's mercy ('Torna di Tito a lato'), his concern enhanced by his repetition, to the end, of 'torna' ('return'). Vitellia warns Sextus too late; Publius comes with guards to arrest him (trio, 'Se a volto mai ti senti'). The principal melodic ideas belong to Sextus, bidding Vitellia a lingering farewell; the music darkens suddenly as her admiration for his devotion conflicts with her fear that he will implicate her. In the Allegretto, Sextus asks Vitellia to remember his love; she is gripped with remorse; Publius, though touched, remains firm (Metastasio's second act ends here).

A large room, with a writing-table The chorus (patricians, praetorian guards and people) thank Fate for sparing Titus ('Ah grazie si rendano'). In the middle section of this ironically serene Andante, Titus thanks them for their loyalty. He tries to understand the conspirators; Lentulus (who led the attack) is clearly guilty; perhaps he has accused Sextus to protect himself. In a short aria (Metastasio: 'Tardi, s'avvede') Publius bluffly comments that the good-natured find it hard to believe others capable of betrayal. A moment later he returns with Sextus's confession and news of his condemnation by the Senate. Annius pleads for mercy ('Tu fosti tradito'): Titus has been betrayed, but hope remains if he consults his heart (an episode in Metastasio in which Annius is accused is omitted). Bitterly hurt, Titus condemns his own hesitation in signing the death warrant, but the word 'death' stops him short (obbligato recitative, 'Che orror! che tradimento!'). He sends for Sextus; incisive orchestral gestures yield to sustained harmonies as he persuades himself that he cannot refuse the hearing which justice offers the meanest citizen. Publius brings in Sextus. The first speeches are sung aside (trio, 'Quello di Tito è il volto'). Sextus's fear appears in string tremolandos, his desperation in wide intervals and an anguished turn to the minor: can this be the face of Titus? Titus can barely recognize his guilt-ridden friend; Publius witnesses the emperor's tangled emotions. Titus commands Sextus to approach, but he is rooted to the spot. The ensemble freezes in the Allegro, Sextus's angular line again dominating while the others comment on his evident terror. Titus reduces Sextus to tears of contrition by addressing him kindly. But Sextus, protecting Vitellia, cannot justify his treachery. Titus dismisses him coldly. Gathering his feelings into a nobly arching melody, Sextus asks Titus to remember their earlier friendship (rondò, 'Deh, per questo istante solo'). In the Allegro the boundaries of the tonic (A major) are twice burst by cries of despair (in C and F majors); its gentler principal melody ('Tanto affanno soffre un core') becomes hectic in the faster coda. Titus signs the fatal paper, then tears it up; he is no Brutus, and cannot begin a career of tyranny by executing a friend. He tells Publius only that Sextus's fate is settled (Metastasio: 'Se all' impero, amici dei'); if the noble gods require an emperor to be cruel, they must deprive him of empire or give him another heart. This is the only aria in the modern equivalent of da capo form (section *A* ends in the dominant, *B* uses a contrasting tempo, *A′* resolves, rather than repeating, *A*); its weight, balanced by considerable

'La clemenza di Tito' (Mozart), final scene of Act 2: design by Giorgio Fuentes for the 1799 production at the Nationaltheater, Frankfurt

floridity, prepares fully for Titus's renunciation of revenge, while underlining his strength of purpose in a march-like coda.

Publius tells Vitellia he has heard nothing of the emperor's conversation with Sextus. Annius and Servilia ask the empress-designate to help. Servilia's lightly-scored minuet (Metastasio: 'S'altro che lagrime') is a gentle but penetrating plea; weeping is not enough to save Sextus. Moved by Sextus's constancy, Vitellia is at the point of decision (obbligato recitative, 'Ecco il punto, o Vitellia'); can she betray him to die alone? No chains of flowers will accompany the descent of Hymen (rondò, 'Non più di fiori'); the music, with basset-horn obbligato, paints the serene image which she must renounce. Her despair breaks out in the Allegro ('Infelice! qual orrore!'); she cannot live knowing the horror of what she has done. The aria merges into a transition with the character of a slow march.

A public place, before a temple The chorus acclaims the god-like emperor ('Che del ciel'). Annius and Servilia ask for mercy, but Titus addresses Sextus with severity. Before he can pronounce sentence (which all assume will be death) Vitellia intervenes, claiming sole responsibility for the conspiracy. Titus is bewildered; he was about to absolve one criminal, and another appears (obbligato recitative, 'Ma, che giorno'). But he defies the stars to deter him; all must be forgiven. In the finale they praise him and he rewards them with his confidence; may he die when Rome's good is not his chief concern. Chorus and principals together ask the gods to grant him long life.

* * *

La clemenza di Tito, like several of its predecessors, ends in forgiveness, here predicated in the title. The goodness of Titus (in contrast to his counterparts in *Lucio Silla* and *Die Entführung*) is so strongly presented in his arias that the outcome of his struggle in Act 2 is inevitable; his role is close to Metastasio's conception and his music has a correspondingly old-fashioned cut. Vitellia is capricious in the opening scenes, selfish but perplexed about her own motivation in the Act 1 trio, yet capable of noble renunciation ('Non più di fiori'). Sextus is an equally rewarding role, with two large arias and the dominant part in several ensembles. Titus's instruction, in Metastasio, that Vitellia must marry Sextus is omitted; it is, perhaps, too neat a solution.

As in *Così fan tutte*, several of the musical numbers are very brief, allowing the expansion of crucial arias and the first-act finale within a short opera. The use of accompanied recitative is traditional, but the arias range from *buffo* simplicity for Servilia and Publius, through the more developed but still direct style of Annius, to the fully elaborated arias of the three main characters: of these two are rondòs, and two have obbligatos for Anton Stadler. In the context of *opera seria*, however, the highest originality lies in the ensembles. There is a strong predilection for movements with two tempos (the usual slow–fast reversed in the first finale). While the folklike duets of the first act approach the style of *Die Zauberflöte*, the trios show that *buffo* textures are equally suited to tragic situations. The first finale is unique in Mozart's output, bridging the gap between Gluck and the 19th century in the realism of its opening, its stark modulation from E♭ to G♭ (by implied C and G minors and B♭, bars 17–24), and its offstage chorus and tremolando; compared to *Idomeneo*, the sparing use of such effects corresponds to the absence of a supernatural dimension to the plot.

Had he lived to prepare further performances, Mozart would surely have replaced Süssmayr's simple recitatives (which do not always end in an appropriate key). He might have increased the orchestrated recitative to a quantity approaching that in *Così* and, as he had planned for *Idomeneo*, rearranged the vocal forces, with a tenor Sextus. Now that performances and recordings, and a general revival of 18th-century repertory, encourage reassessment of its virtues, *La clemenza di Tito* clearly appears a conception not fully realized, but still masterly and amply rewarding study and performance.

JULIAN RUSHTON

Clendining [née Arnold], **Elizabeth** (*b* Stourhead, Wilts., *c*1768; *d* Edinburgh, 16 July 1799). English mezzo-soprano. She moved to Dublin with her father, a cathedral singer, and sang in concerts there before her marriage. In December 1791 her husband was in a debtors' prison and she went first to London, where despite Mrs Billington's help she failed to find engagements, and then to Bath. Rauzzini taught her and promoted her career so that she was able to raise the money to free her husband. She made a successful London début in Shield's *Hartford Bridge* (1792) and sang at Covent Garden for six seasons. She was praised for her taste, for the fullness of her middle and lower voice and the sweetness of her upper notes. In summer 1797 she sang opposite Incledon at the Crow Street Theatre, Dublin, and in 1798 took up an engagement at Edinburgh, where she died after a protracted illness.

BDA; *LS*
J. Roach: *Authentic Memoirs of the Green Room* (London, 1796)
The Thespian Dictionary (London, 1802, 2/1805)
M. Kelly: *Reminiscences* (London, 1826, 2/1826); ed. R. Fiske (London, 1975)
T. J. Walsh: *Opera in Dublin 1705–1797* (Dublin, 1973)

OLIVE BALDWIN, THELMA WILSON

Cleofide ('Cleophis'). *Opera seria* in three acts by JOHANN ADOLF HASSE to a libretto by PIETRO METASTASIO adapted by MICHELANGELO BOCCARDI; Dresden, Hoftheater, 13 September 1731 (revised with Metastasio's original title, ALESSANDRO NELL'INDIE, Venice, Teatro S Giovanni Grisostomo, 4 November 1736).

In the 4th century BC, Alessandro Magno [Alexander the Great] (tenor) and his invading Greek armies confront the Indian rulers Poro [Porus] (contralto) and Cleophis (contralto) at the river Hydaspes; but it is Porus's recurring jealousy, Cleophis's fidelity and Alexander's clemency that are central to the plot. At different times, Alexander grants every other character his liberty (Cleophis twice, Porus three times). Seeing Alexander as a rival for Cleophis's heart, Porus craves her reassurances. In truth, Alexander does fall in love and offer her marriage; but Cleophis remains faithful to Porus.

Disguises, mistaken identities, reports of drownings, intrigues and domestic squabbles threaten to eclipse political issues and transform the libretto into a comic entertainment. But the incidents invented by Metastasio neither mask nor subvert the libretto's elegant poetry or the logical construction of relationships among the characters which builds dramatic tension and guarantees a firm basis for Hasse's serious musical style. Nonetheless, the music for the Dresden production highlights the amorous elements and at times achieves coquettish freshness. Reinhard Strohm (in an essay for the excellent recording by the Rheinische Kantorei Dormagen, directed by William Christie) argues that this opera, Hasse's first as Kapellmeister to the Saxon court, literally belonged to the court, which explains why it was never performed elsewhere in this form. The Elector of Saxony, Friedrich August (the 'Strong'), would have been identified with Alexander the Great, Porus possibly with Hasse himself, and Cleophis with the Crown Princess Maria Josepha as well as Hasse's wife Faustina, who sang the role. Unusually, Hasse borrowed some 15 arias from earlier works, and fitted three of Metastasio's aria texts for *Alessandro nell'Indie* to music from his earlier operas. Metastasio's recitatives were sharply truncated: speeches declaiming virtues were shortened but amorous discussions were spared.

Hasse's setting of *Alessandro nell'Indie* for Venice in 1736 is almost completely different. It uses a libretto presumably by Metastasio or reworked by DOMENICO LALLI that was printed in the Venetian edition of Metastasio's works published by Bettinelli. However, one element borrowed from Boccardi's libretto of 1731 is the accompanied recitative and aria near the end of Act 2: though text and music are changed, Cleophis still calls upon the ghost of her beloved Porus with eerie, dramatic effect. Remarkably, half of the Venetian cast journeyed to Naples to open the carnival season with this work. Vittoria Tesi (Cleophis), Angelo Amorevoli (Alexander) and Margharita Giacomazzi (Erissena [Eryxene]) sang in both the Dresden and the Venice productions, but Giovanni Carestini, in residence at Naples, replaced Castore Antonio Castorini as Porus. Hasse's music was revived at Ferrara in 1737 (with additions by Vivaldi), at Venice in 1738 and 1743, at Verona in 1740 and 1754, at Lucca in 1759 and in Berlin in 1777.

SVEN HANSELL

Cleopatra. Libretto subject used in many periods. The story is based on historical figures and events recounted in Plutarch's *Lives* and other ancient writings; WILLIAM SHAKESPEARE's play has been an influential source. Operas on the subject are also entitled *Cleopatra regina d'Egitto*, *La morte di Cleopatra* and *Antony and Cleopatra*. The story should be distinguished from those of other librettos treating an earlier episode in her life, in which Cleopatra is paired with JULIUS CAESAR.

Set in 32 BC, the plot centres on the love between Cleopatra VII, Queen of Egypt, and Marcus Antonius [Mark Antony]. With Octavian, Antony rules as one of the Roman triumvirate. In a mutually beneficial political alliance, Antony establishes an amorous relationship with Cleopatra and eventually joins her in Alexandria. When he divorces his wife Octavia, sister of Octavian, the Romans declare war on Egypt and defeat Antony's army and the Egyptian fleet at the battle of Antioch. But Antony commits suicide before the Romans reach Alexandria, and in order to avoid the humiliation of being their prisoner Cleopatra poisons herself with the bite of an asp.

The first known libretto on the topic was published as early as 1628 in Bologna, as a 'tragedia' by Giovanni Capponi. Antonio Canazzi, who set Carlo Bartolomeo Torre's libretto (1653, Milan), was apparently the first composer to write an opera on the subject. Only a few other versions have survived from the late 17th and early 18th centuries, but in the last quarter of the 18th century interest in the subject was revived with a succession of *Cleopatra* operas by Carlo Monza (1775, Turin), Anfossi (1779, Milan), Cimarosa (1789, St Petersburg), Nasolini (*La morte di Cleopatra*, 1791, Vicenza), P. A. Guglielmi (*La morte di Cleopatra*, 1796, Naples), Weigl (1807, Milan) and Paer (1808, Paris). The subject became popular again in the second half of the 19th century, especially in Italian versions by Lauro Rossi (1876, Turin) and Melesio Morales (1891, Mexico City). Around the turn of the century several composers, including August Enna (1894, Copenhagen) and Massenet (1914, Monte Carlo), wrote *Cleopatra* operas. Mattheson's *Die unglückselige Cleopatra, Königin von Egypten* (1704, Hamburg) was the first German version of the subject, and since then at least a dozen other German composers, including Franz Danzi (1780, Mannheim), Julius Sulzer (1878, Vienna) and Theo Goldberg (1952, Karlsruhe) have used it. Two American composers have written English versions that were first given at the Metropolitan Opera, Henry

Hadley's *Cleopatra's Night* (1920) and Samuel Barber's *Antony and Cleopatra* (1966). Altogether there have been more than 50 dramatic works based on this story; in some productions the ancient Egyptian setting has inspired exotic scenery and spectacle. Almost all end with the death of Cleopatra; in this respect the subject stands firmly in the tradition of operas with tragic heroines, such as Dido and Ariadne.

See also ANTONY AND CLEOPATRA [Barber]; CLEOPATRA (i) [Mattheson]; and CLEOPATRA (ii) [Anfossi]. For a list of operas based on Shakespeare's *Antony and Cleopatra*, *see* SHAKESPEARE, WILLIAM.

PAUL CORNEILSON

Cleopatra (i) [*Die unglückselige Cleopatra, Königin von Egypten, oder Die betrogene Staats-Liebe* ('The Unfortunate Cleopatra, Queen of Egypt, or The Fraudulent State Love Affair')]. *Drama per musica* in three acts by JOHANN MATTHESON to a libretto by FRIEDRICH CHRISTIAN FEUSTKING; Hamburg, 20 October 1704.

The libretto is loosely based on Roman history and the account of Mark Antony by Plutarch. In addition to Cleopatra (soprano), Marcus Antonius [Mark Antony] (tenor) and their children Candace (soprano), the young Cleopatra (Egyptian princess) and Ptolemaeus [Ptolemy] (alto; Egyptian prince), the cast includes Archibius (baritone), governor of Alexandria; Dercetaeus (tenor), freed servant of Antony; Caesar Augustus (baritone); Mandane (soprano), an Armenian princess in love with Ptolemy; Juba (tenor), Mauritanian crown prince; Proculejus (alto), Roman general; and Nemesis (soprano), goddess of vengeance.

Act 1 takes place after the disastrous battle at Actium where Antony led his and the Egyptians' combined naval forces to defeat by the Romans of Augustus. Antony has fled to an island, where he swears he will become, like Timon of Athens, misanthropic and never again be lured into the arms of Cleopatra. The latter, however, arrives and quickly persuades her lover to rejoin her in another attempt to drive out the Romans from Egypt. Secondary pairings of lovers are established: Mandane (who is in the Roman camp) loves Ptolemy, but in their first encounter in Act 1 she finds him, she thinks, in the company of another woman, not recognizing Candace as his sister. Juba, also from the Roman camp, is attracted to Princess Candace. The Roman general Proculejus also loves Mandane. During a battle between Egyptian and Roman forces at the gates of Alexandria, Juba willingly surrenders to Antony, hoping thus to be brought close to Candace. The act ends with Caesar Augustus plotting to deceive both Antony and Cleopatra by offering his former Roman general freedom if he will lay down his arms, open Alexandria to the Romans, and hand over Cleopatra to him.

Act 2 opens with a banquet given by Cleopatra in Antony's honour, where the entertainment is supplied by a ballet of chimney-sweeps. Juba is brought forward in chains and, despite the pleas of Candace and Ptolemy, is condemned to death. Proculejus brings Augustus's offer to Antony, who rejects it. In turn Proculejus approaches Cleopatra with a letter from Augustus in which he professes his love for her and his wish to make her queen of the Roman world if she will abandon Antony. The act ends with a scene in which Ptolemy visits Mandane while she sleeps. He thinks he hears her profess her love for Proculejus in a dream. When she has awoken, the confusion continues, and she is unaware that Ptolemy has not been unfaithful. They sing a duet in which they accuse each other of unfaithfulness and treachery.

Act 3 begins as Antony is informed of the fall of Pharos (the peninsula protecting the harbour of Alexandria) and the surrender of the Egyptian fleet to the Romans. Further, he is told (falsely) that Cleopatra has committed suicide. Antony in remorse kills himself. Following a scene in which Candace goes to Juba in his prison cell to swear eternal fidelity, and a solo scene for Cleopatra as she reflects on Antony's suicide, the opera shifts to the streets of Alexandria and the triumphal entrance into the city of Caesar Augustus. Cleopatra, her children and Archibius all come humbly to pay homage to him. He asks for Cleopatra's love, and she promises him her heart and her bed. Mandane finally learns the truth about the relationship of Candace and Ptolemy, Juba is freed from prison and the two pairs of lovers are united. The scene moves to the temple of Isis where, after one last meeting with Augustus, Cleopatra is left alone to contemplate the latter's treachery. In a particularly beautiful scene she bids farewell to the world and commits suicide through the bite of asps hidden in a fruit basket. However, the tragedy of Antony and Cleopatra does not end the opera. Augustus reappears with all of the surviving main characters. He gives his blessing to the nuptials of the two young couples, and agrees to be the guardian of the children of Antony and Cleopatra. The opera ends with a ballet for the Egyptian and Roman lords and ladies.

Die unglückselige Cleopatra is the only extant score from among Mattheson's seven works composed (with one exception) for the Hamburg opera theatre. It has a peculiar fame in biographies of Handel, for it was during a performance of this opera that an altercation arose between Mattheson and his young friend Handel (for further details, *see* MATTHESON, JOHANN). Mattheson's score exhibits a general tunefulness of the arias, with frequently strophic, folk-like structure, and the avoidance of any kind of vocal virtuosity. There is a strong French influence evidenced in the use of French ballet dances and dance scenes, and the overall general character of the music is more French than Italian. There are many examples of arias of affective pathos and lyrical beauty which underscore the composer's conviction that all music must be a *redende Kunst* – an art of rhetorical persuasiveness.

See also CLEOPATRA above. GEORGE J. BUELOW

Cleopatra (ii). *Dramma serio* in three acts by PASQUALE ANFOSSI to a libretto by MATTIA VERAZI; Milan, Teatro alla Scala, Carnival 1779.

Anfossi was the most experienced of the composers with whom Verazi worked in Milan. His setting has a tightly knit tonal plan, based on C major and E♭ major and their dominants, and his short-breathed, declamatory vocal lines, *forte-piano* accents, stark contrasts between tutti textures in vocal caesuras and thin accompaniments, well-placed chromatic and modal inflections, quick responses to contrasting ideas and emotions and long crescendos make him an excellent interpreter of Verazi's dramatic aria texts. Marcantonio [Mark Antony] (soprano castrato) has the only two-tempo rondò, 'Ah basta: vi credo', though other ternary arias – both *ABA′* and *ABB′* – end faster than they begin. There are two fine 'ombra' arias for the prima donnas (both sopranos), 'Partirò: ma squalid' ombra' for Ottavia [Octavia] and Cleopatra's cavatina and aria concluding Act 2, in which solo wind colour, syncopations, tremolos, oscillating figuration, chromaticism, modal contrast and dotted rhythms induce visions of spectres. The rare duet for two men that serves both as an opening cavatina to the opera and as an exit piece two scenes later is a conventional static ensemble. There are also two multi-sectional action ensembles similar to comic opera finales: the short finale of Act 3, beginning just before the fatal poison takes effect, and the central sextet of Act 2, which begins as a duet and encompasses three scenes and four entrances (anticipating the action sextet in Act 2 of Mozart's *Don Giovanni*).

See also CLEOPATRA above. MARITA P. MCCLYMONDS

Clerici, Carlo Andrea (*b* ?Milan or Bergamo; *fl* 1662–1718). Italian singer. His name first appears in 1662, when he sang at Piacenza in Isidoro Tortona's *Andromeda*. His career was based in Parma, where he was in the service of the court from 1 July 1671 until 29 April 1718, apart from a period between 15 January 1707 and 1713; he was also one of the musicians in the Steccata chapel from 3 April 1670 to the end of April 1696. As well as appearances in the theatres of Parma (1677, 1679, 1681, 1689–90, 1692), he performed in Piacenza, Modena, Venice and Crema; in 1692 he took the leading role in Pietro Porfirii's revision of Carlo Pallavicino's *Vespasiano* at Fabriano and in 1696 was Ugone in Alessandro Scarlatti's *Flavio Cuniberto* and Ariberto in Pallavicino's *Il re infante* in Rome.

PAOLA BESUTTI

Clerici, Roberto (*fl* 1711–48). Italian designer. He was a theatre painter in Vienna in 1711, and in 1716 he supplied an immense perspective view of a royal palace for a revival of Haym's *Pyrrhus and Demetrius* at the King's Theatre, London. This scene, advertised as containing about a thousand yards of painting, was re-used for a revival of *Cleartes* on 30 March 1717. On 21 March 1719 he provided for a concert at the King's Theatre a 'Magnificent Triumphant Scene' which exceeded any previous one by 30 feet. When the Royal Academy of Music was founded in 1719 Clerici was appointed its decorator and machinist, and when the Academy took over the running of the operas at the King's Theatre he provided scenery for Giovanni Porta's *Numitore* (2 April 1720). By 1735 he was working in Portugal and in 1740 was responsible for decors at the Comédie Française. He is last heard of in Parma in 1748. SYBIL ROSENFELD

Clerici, Sebastiano. *See* CHERICI, SEBASTIANO.

Clerico, Francesco (*b* Milan, ?1755; *d* after 1838). Italian dancer, choreographer and composer. A pupil of Noverre, he danced at the Kärntnertortheater in Vienna in 1775 and presented his first choreography at the Teatro S Agostino in Genoa during Carnival 1776. Most of Clerico's works were created for the opera houses in Venice, where he worked during the 1780s at S Samuele, S Benedetto and S Moisè, and later in his career at the Fenice, and in Milan, where from 1790 he graced the stage of La Scala for nearly 40 years. He also created ballets for opera houses in Turin, Rome, Brescia, Padua, Bologna, Parma and Florence, and returned to work in Vienna, 1798–1800. Clerico often danced in his own ballets with his brother Gaetano and sister Rosa (who in 1786 married the choreographer and dancer Lorenzo Panzieri). Their exceptional abilities as dancers, according to Ritorni, contributed in part to the success of Clerico's ballets. Not only was he a renowned choreographer and dancer, but he also composed the music for many of his ballets. He was considered the heir to Angiolini, and an important precursor of Viganò. His enormous output totals nearly 80 ballets, many of which were restaged throughout Italy and in foreign theatres.

DBI (L. Tozzi); *ES* (M. L. Aguirre) [with list of ballets]
C. Ritorni: *Commentarii della vita e delle opere coreodrammatiche di Salvatore Viganò e della coreografia e de' corepei* (Milan, 1838)
O. Schneider: 'Clerico, Francesco', *Tanz Lexikon* (Mainz, 1985)
K. K. Hansell: 'Il ballo teatrale e l'opera italiana', *SOI*, v (1988), 175–306

IRENE ALM

Cleva, Fausto (Angelo) (*b* Trieste, 17 May 1902; *d* Athens, 6 Aug 1971). American conductor of Italian birth. He studied at the Trieste Conservatory and at the Verdi Conservatory in Milan, where he made his début conducting *La traviata* at the Teatro Carcano. Emigrating to the USA in 1920 (he became an American citizen in 1931), he was engaged by the Metropolitan Opera the same year, first as chorus master and later as conductor: he conducted over 650 performances there between 1950 and 1971. From 1934 to 1963 he was music director of the Cincinnati Summer Opera, and at the San Francisco Opera he conducted in the 1942–3 season and again between 1949 and 1955. As artistic director of the Chicago Opera Company, 1944–6, he played an important part in the postwar raising of the city's operatic standards. He made guest appearances with opera companies in Verona, Havana, Toronto, Montreal and Stockholm, and at the 1959 Edinburgh Festival, where he conducted the Swedish Royal Opera in *Rigoletto*. A widely admired operatic maestro in the familiar Italian mould, Cleva was made an honorary Commendatore by the Italian government.

BERNARD JACOBSON

Cleveland. American city in the state of Ohio. The first opera performed was mounted within two decades of Cleveland's incorporation as a city (1836). As in other areas of music there during the 19th century, the German community led the way. In January 1858 the Cleveland Gesangverein produced Flotow's *Alessandro Stradella*, conducted by Fritz Abel at the 2000-seat Academy of Music (built 1853) on Bank (now West Sixth) Street. The opera was repeated as part of the second Cleveland Saengerfest on 14 June 1859, and again on the occasion of the Gesangverein's 25th anniversary in 1878.

In 1872 Cleveland's foremost choral director, Alfred Arthur, presented Auber's *Fra Diavolo* at the Academy of Music. Other operas followed, including Arthur's own *The Water Carrier* in 1876 at the luxurious 1600-seat Euclid Avenue Opera House (built 1875) on Sheriff (East Fourth) Street. Cleveland's numerous immigrant communities made their contribution: in 1898 the oldest Czech singing society in the USA, the Lumir-Hlahol-Tyl Society (founded in Cleveland in 1867), presented Smetana's *Bartered Bride*. Ferdinand Puehringer, Reinhold Henninges, Max Faetkenheuer and others were active in producing opera as well as composing it. An interesting topical example is Puehringer's *The Hero of Lake Erie*, from the 1920s, on a plot concerning the battle of Lake Erie in 1813. Meanwhile visiting opera companies came in profusion, especially during the

1890s. The playbills for the Euclid Avenue Opera House for 1890–91 show at least ten companies on hand, each for a short season. The New York Metropolitan, which first brought *Il barbiere di Siviglia*, *Carmen*, *La traviata* and *Faust* in 1899, became the city's most illustrious visitor, appearing nearly every year until its last visit in 1986. 'Opera Week' at the Public Auditorium (9000 seats, including special seating for the Metropolitan) became a major event.

During the 1930s Arthur Rodzinski presented opera at the 2000-seat Severance Hall (built 1930). Though the emphasis was on Wagner, in January 1935 he gave Shostakovich's *Lady Macbeth of the Mtsensk District* (subsequently taking this production to the Metropolitan Opera House in New York). On 28 May 1963, during the fifth May Festival of Contemporary Music, the first performance of Robert Ward's *The Crucible* was given in the same hall. Its success encouraged the organization in 1964 of Lake Erie Opera Theater, managed by Howard Whittaker, the director of the Cleveland Music School Settlement. This group was active during the late 1960s, presenting important works in Severance Hall each September, including *The Rake's Progress*, *Dialogues des Carmélites* and *Albert Herring*. Continuing the tradition in Severance Hall, James Levine conducted concert performances of opera there in the early 1970s. Christoph von Dohnányi gave two performances of *Die Zauberflöte* with the Cleveland Orchestra at Blossom Music Center in 1985, and Cleveland State University has presented premières of works by the Cleveland composers J. D. Bain Murray (*The Legend*, 1987; *Mary Queen of Scots*, 1991) and Edwin London (*The Death of Lincoln*, 1988).

The city currently supports two local companies. Lyric Opera Cleveland (director Michael McConnell) offers a broad-based repertory during the summer at Kulas Auditorium (541 seats) in the Cleveland Institute of Music. Opera Cleveland, under its general director David Bamberger, celebrated its 15th anniversary season in 1990–91 with five works, each given two or three performances at the State Theater (3100 seats) in Playhouse Square Center.

*

F. K. Grossman: *A History of Music in Cleveland* (Cleveland, 1972)

J. H. Alexander: *It Must Be Heard: a Survey of the Musical Life of Cleveland, 1936–1938* (Cleveland, 1981)

——: 'Music', *The Encyclopedia of Cleveland History* (Bloomington, IN, 1987)

J. HEYWOOD ALEXANDER

Clifton, Arthur [Corri, P(hilip) Antony] (*b* Edinburgh, ?1784; *d* Baltimore, 19 Feb 1832). American composer and singer of British birth, son of Domenico Corri. As P. Antony Corri he was well established as a composer in London by about 1808–13, when a great many of his piano pieces and songs were published. He was one of the organizers of the Philharmonic Society in 1813, and sang in its first concerts. Some time afterwards he emigrated to the USA (apparently because of marital problems), where he appeared in New York and Philadelphia, and had settled in Baltimore by November 1817. Christened Arthur Clifton on 31 December 1817, he married Alphonsa Elizabeth Ringgold on 1 January 1818. He held positions as organist and choirmaster in Baltimore from 1818 until his death. He taught singing and probably also the piano, appeared in concerts as a singer and pianist, and was a theatre music director for at least two seasons. He continued to compose songs and piano pieces. His opera *The Enterprise, or Love and Pleasure* (W. H. Hamilton; Baltimore Theatre, 27 May 1822) was more ambitious than the usual English ballad opera yet probably lacked the recitatives of Italian opera. Many of the songs are relatively simple, in the ballad opera tradition, and were written for actor-singers; others, such as the vocally demanding Recitative and Bravura 'Awake the Note of War' (sung by Mrs Burke), show the italianate style of Clifton's father. The work is of interest as a rare example of American opera at this date; 18 numbers from it were published separately in 1823.

*

J. H. Hewitt: *Shadows on the Wall* (Baltimore, 1877)

W. D. Gettel: 'Arthur Clifton's *Enterprise*', *JAMS*, ii (1949), 23–35

L. Keefer: *Baltimore's Music* (Baltimore, 1962)

J. B. Clark: 'Works of A. Corri/A. Clifton', *Sonneck Society Newsletter*, xii (1986), 46–7

M. F. Schleifer, ed.: *American Opera and Music for the Stage: Eighteenth and Nineteenth Centuries*, Three Centuries of American Music, v (Boston, 1990) [incl. a repr. of numbers from *The Enterprise*]

J. BUNKER CLARK

Clive [née Raftor], **Kitty** [Catherine] (*b* London, 1711; *d* Twickenham, 6 Dec 1785). Anglo-Irish soprano and actress. She received musical instruction from Henry Carey and in 1728 became a member of the Drury Lane company, until 1743, when she moved to Covent Garden for two unhappy seasons, returning to Drury Lane until her retirement from the stage in 1769. She sang in the first performance of Arne's *Alfred* at Cliveden (1740).

Kitty Clive made her reputation in ballad opera. She enjoyed sensational success in Cibber's *Love in a Riddle, or Damon and Phillida* (1729), Coffey's *The Devil to Pay* (1731), and as Polly in *The Beggar's Opera* (1732), appearing for many years in these and similar pieces. She also sang in stage works of a more serious character, by Arne (including *Comus*, *Rosamond* and *The Judgment of Paris*), Lampe, Galliard and Boyce. She played many Shakespeare parts and sang regularly between acts, including music by Handel, who composed songs for her and engaged her for his oratorio season in 1743. He wrote the part of Dalila in *Samson* for her (compass *c'* to *a''*). She was a great comic actress, especially in what were called 'singing chambermaid' parts. She played 'country girls, romps, hoydens and dowdies, superannuated beauties, viragos and humourists', and was a brilliant mimic, of Italian opera singers in particular. According to Burney, 'her singing, which was intolerable when she meant it to be fine, in ballad farces and songs of humour was … every thing it should be'.

*

P. Fitzgerald: *The Life of Mrs. Catherine Clive … together with her Correspondence* (London, 1888)

WINTON DEAN

Cloches de Corneville, Les ('The Bells of Corneville'). *Opéra-comique* in three acts by ROBERT PLANQUETTE to a libretto by CLAIRVILLE and Charles Gabet; Paris, Folies-Dramatiques, 19 April 1877.

The libretto of *Les cloches de Corneville*, originally intended for Hervé, was entrusted by the director of the Folies-Dramatiques, Louis Cantin, to the then inexperienced Planquette. It combined the story of the return of the long-lost Marquis of Corneville (baritone) to his ancestral castle, and the discovery of the equally lost heiress, Germaine (soprano), both cheated out of their inheritance by the miserly steward Gaspard (actor/baritone). The comic pretensions of the servant girl Serpolette (soprano), and the cowardly Lothario, Jean Grenicheux (tenor), enhanced a tale full of colourful action which included ghosts, a particularly graphic and genuine mad scene, and a lively depiction of a hiring fair.

Planquette's music, among the most happily tuneful and enticing of its genre, follows one hit song and splendid ensemble with another. It is said that the British manager, Alexander Henderson, bought the rights to the piece after hearing only Germaine's celebrated 'Chanson des cloches', with its 'digue-digue-don' refrain, but there are many other highlights of equal value in the work, notably the vigorous chorus with baritone, 'C'est la salle de mes ancêtres', Grenicheux's beautiful, ingenuous 'Va petit mousse', the Marquis's picaresque 'J'ai fait trois fois le tour du monde', Serpolette's sparky 'Dans ma mystérieuse histoire' and Germaine's lyrical 'Ne parlez pas de mon courage'.

In a show where every one of the principals has star material, it is, however, very often the actor playing Gaspard who makes the most impact with his two dramatic set-piece scenes, his capture among the hoarded gold by what he believes to be ghosts at the end of Act 2, and his third-act mad scene and confession. Shiel Barry, the Irish-Australian actor who played the role in London, made almost a whole career of the part thereafter.

A triumph in Paris, the work broke all records in London and was produced world-wide for half a century. At the first performance the cast included Juliette Girard as Serpolette and Simon-Max as Grenicheux; Gaspard was played by M. Milher, the Marquis by M. Vois and Germaine by Mlle Gélabert.

KURT GÄNZL

Closed number. SET PIECE.

Cluj-Napoca (Ger. Klausenburg; Hung. Kolozsvár). City in Romania (Transylvania). The name Cluj was adopted when the city became part of Romania in 1918, and Cluj-Napoca in 1975. With 450 000 inhabitants it is one of the most highly developed cultural centres in the country. The first permanent theatre was established in 1792, directed by the literary man János Kótsi Patkó and supported by Baron Miklós Wesselénjyi; the company performed there in the winter months, in a repertory including works by Hungarian and Transylvanian composers (József Chudy and others) as well as the standard international fare (Gluck, Méhul, Dittersdorf, Paisiello), all sung in Hungarian. The company split in 1815 and the part remaining in the city principally toured until the establishment in 1821 of the Hungarian National Theatre in Farkas Street (cap. 1200). József Ruzitska became conductor and his *Béla futása* ('Bela's Escape'), the first true opera in Hungarian and the most popular Hungarian opera before Erkel, had its première there in 1822, in a repertory that included operas by Grétry, Méhul, Rossini and Weber. The city retained its importance as a centre of Hungarian operatic life until World War I, and a new National Theatre was built there in 1906.

When the city became a part of Romania, an Opera Română was opened (1919); a Hungarian Opera House (Opera Maghiară) was established in 1948, and there is an opera studio at the Gheorghe Dima Conservatory (1958). Artists who have visited the city include Alfred Piccaver, John Sullivan, Jovita Fuentes, Traian Grozăvescu, Tomel Spătaru, Ana Rozsa-Vasiliu, Lucia Stănescu and Aldo Protti; Pietro Mascagni, Jonel Perlea and Jean Bobescu are among those who have conducted there. Opera premières have included works by Felice Lattuada, Sabin Drăgoi, Nicolae Bretan, Paul Constantinescu, Emil Mouţia, Tudor Jarda, Gheorghe Dumitrescu and Cornel Ţăranu. Once a year the international Festivalul Toamna Muzicală Clujeană (Autumn in Cluj Festival) is held.

Z. Ferenczi: *A kolozsvári színészet és színház története* [History of Theatrical Art and Theatre in Kolozsvár] (Kolozsvár, 1897)

I. Gherghel: *Viaţa muzicală în Ardealul de după unire: activitatea Operei române din Cluj* [Musical Life in Transylvania after the Union: Romanian Operatic Activity in Cluj] (Cluj, 1939)

J. Janovics: *A Farkas utcai színház* [The Farkas Street Theatre] (Budapest, 1941)

I. Lakatos: *A kolozsvári magyar zenés színpad* [The Hungarian Music Theatre of Kolozsvár] (Bucharest, 1977)

V. Cosma: *Romània muzicală* (Bucharest, 1980)

VIOREL COSMA

Cluytens, André (*b* Antwerp, 26 March 1905; *d* Paris, 3 June 1967). French conductor of Belgian birth. After studying at the Antwerp Royal Conservatory he became a répétiteur at the Royal Theatre, Antwerp, where his father was principal conductor. His own début took place there in 1927 with *Les pêcheurs de perles* and he then became a resident conductor. In 1932 he was appointed music director at the Toulouse opera house, and from 1935 he conducted opera at Lyons, Bordeaux and Vichy. After settling in Paris he became music director at the Opéra-Comique in 1947. Cluytens became the first French conductor at Bayreuth (*Tannhäuser*, 1955) and he returned several times in later years. He also conducted Wagner more widely, including the *Ring* and *Parsifal* at La Scala. From 1959 he was under regular contract at the Vienna Staatsoper.

B. Gavoty: *André Cluytens* (Geneva, 1955)

NOËL GOODWIN

Coates, Albert (*b* St Petersburg, 11/23 April 1882; *d* Milnerton, nr Cape Town, 11 Dec 1953). English conductor and composer. The son of English parents, in 1902 he entered the Leipzig Conservatory to study the cello and piano, but became most influenced by Nikisch's conducting classes. He was engaged as répétiteur at the Leipzig Opera under Nikisch, then went as conductor successively to Elberfeld (1906–8), Dresden (as assistant to Schuch) and Mannheim. An invitation to conduct *Siegfried* at St Petersburg led to his appointment as principal conductor at the Mariinsky Theatre there for five years; this brought him into close contact with leading Russian musicians, particularly Skryabin, whose music he championed. First conducting at Covent Garden in 1914 (*Tristan und Isolde*), he shared performances of the *Ring* with Nikisch, and returned there frequently during Beecham's opera seasons before settling in South Africa in 1946. He wrote two operas: *Samuel Pepys*, produced at Munich in 1929, and *Pickwick*, staged at Covent Garden in 1936 as the main novelty of a season by the short-lived British Music Drama Opera Company, for which he was chiefly responsible in association with Vladimir Rosing.

Although unsuccessful in the theatre, *Pickwick* had the distinction of being the first opera to be shown on television; several scenes from it were included in the BBC's newly opened service in November 1936, in advance of its stage première.

H. Rosenthal: *Two Centuries of Opera at Covent Garden* (London, 1958)

S. Robinson: 'Albert Coates', *Recorded Sound*, lvii–lviii (1975), 382–405 [with discography by C. Dyment]

MICHAEL KENNEDY

Coates, Edith (Mary) (*b* Lincoln, 31 May 1908; *d* Worthing, 7 Jan 1983). English mezzo-soprano. She studied at Trinity College of Music, London. In 1924 she joined the Old Vic opera chorus and was soon singing small roles. When the company moved to Sadler's Wells in 1931 she became its leading mezzo-soprano, singing in the first English performances of *The Snow Maiden* (as Lehl) and *The Tale of Tsar Saltan*, both in 1933, and appearing as Eboli in 1938. In 1945 she created Auntie in *Peter Grimes*. Having made her Covent Garden début in 1937 she became a member of the company in 1947, remaining until 1967. Though not invariably successful in dramatic parts like Azucena, Fricka, Amneris and Carmen, she had striking acting ability and stage presence. She created roles in *The Olympians* (1949) and *Gloriana* (1953) and sang the Countess in the first production in English of *The Queen of Spades* (1950). In 1966 she created Grandma in Grace Williams's *The Parlour* for the WNO. She was made an OBE in 1977.

*

C. Hardy: 'Edith Coates', *Opera*, ii (1950–51), 69–72

HAROLD ROSENTHAL/R

Coates, John (*b* Girlington, Yorks., 29 June 1865; *d* Northwood, Middlesex, 16 Aug 1941). English tenor. Initially he sang as a baritone with the Carl Rosa company, then (1893) studied with William Shakespeare, who pronounced his voice a tenor; but he continued to appear as a baritone in operetta and musical comedy, touring the USA and England with the D'Oyly Carte company before retiring to study the tenor repertory. In 1901 he made his Covent Garden début as Faust and sang Claudio in the first performance of Stanford's *Much Ado about Nothing*. From 1902 to 1907 he appeared in Cologne and other German cities. He sang Mark in the British première of *The Wreckers* at His Majesty's Theatre in 1909, when he returned to Covent Garden singing Faust and Lohengrin; he sang Don José and Pedro in the British première of *Tiefland* (1910) for the Beecham Opera and Tannhäuser and Tristan for Raymond Roze's English opera season (1913). He toured with the Moody-Manners company, until it was disbanded in 1916, singing Siegfried, Tristan and other roles. Coates's voice, capable of astonishing variety of colour, showed outstanding intelligence and subtlety coupled with a rare imagination.

*

G. Moore: 'John Coates', *Am I Too Loud?* (London, 1962), 38–49
'John Coates', *Record Advertiser*, ii/3 (1971–2), 2–6 [with discography]

GERALD MOORE, ELIZABETH FORBES

Cobb, James (*b* 1756; *d* 1818). English librettist. He served most of his life in the secretary's office of the East India Company, and wrote about two dozen theatrical pieces, tailoring his work particularly for the performers at Drury Lane. Although his dialogue lacked grace and his plots simplicity, his librettos exploited his professional knowledge of exotic locales such as India and Turkey, allowing Sheridan, the manager at Drury Lane, much scope for grand spectacle. *The Haunted Tower* (1789), Drury Lane's runaway success, featured a lavish medieval ox-roast. *Ramah Droog* (1798) had an elaborate parade of the rajah's hunting-party.

Cobb's emphasis on spectacle allowed music a greater role in storytelling than with earlier comic operas. With his principal collaborator Stephen Storace, he shifted the emphasis of musical theatre from light comedy centred on dialogue to emotional drama relying on music.

comic operas unless otherwise stated

The Wedding Night (afterpiece), S. Arnold, 1780; *The Strangers at Home*, T. Linley the elder, 1785 (abridged by Cobb, 1792, as The Algerine Slaves, afterpiece); *Love in the East, or The Adventures of Twelve Hours*, Linley, 1788; *The Doctor and the Apothecary* (afterpiece, after G. Stephanie), S. Storace, 1788; *The Haunted Tower*, Storace, 1789; *The Siege of Belgrade* (after L. da Ponte), Storace, 1791; *The Pirates*, Storace, 1792; *The Cherokee*, Storace, 1794 (rev. 1802, as Algonah, addns by M. Kelly); *The Glorious First of June* (afterpiece, with R. B. Sheridan and others), Storace, 1794; *The Shepherdess of Cheapside* (afterpiece), 1796; *Ramah Droog, or Wine does Wonders*, J. Mazzinghi and W. Reeve, 1798 (abridged 1805); *Paul and Virginia* (afterpiece), Mazzinghi and Reeve, 1800; *A House to be Sold* (afterpiece), Kelly, 1802; *The Wife of Two Husbands* (afterpiece), Mazzinghi, 1803

*

M. Kelly: *Reminiscences* (London, 1826, 2/1826); ed. R. Fiske (London, 1975)
R. Fiske: 'The Operas of Stephen Storace', *PRMA*, lxxxvi (1959–60), 29–44
A. Garlington, jr: 'Gothic Literature and Dramatic Music in England: 1781–1802', *JAMS*, xv (1962), 48–64
R. Fiske: *English Theatre Music in the Eighteenth Century* (London, 1973, 2/1986)
E. White: *A History of English Opera* (London, 1983)
L. Troost: *The Rise of English Comic Opera: 1762–1800* (diss., U. of Pennsylvania, 1985)

LINDA V. TROOST

Cobelli, Giuseppina (*b* Maderno, Lake Garda, 1 Aug 1898; *d* Barbarano di Salò, 10 Aug 1948). Italian soprano. She studied in Bologna and Hamburg, making her début at Piacenza in 1924 as La Gioconda. After a season in the Netherlands, she was engaged by La Scala, making her début as Sieglinde (1925). Her roles included Isolde, Kundry, Fedora, Eboli, Margherita, Minnie and Adriana Lecouvreur, in which part she gave her last Scala performance in 1942. She created Silvana in Respighi's *La fiamma* (1934, Rome) and in 1937 sang Octavia (*L'incoronazione di Poppea*) at the Florence Festival. A beautiful woman with a highly individual voice, she had a dramatic temperament that expressed a special affinity for *verismo* heroines.

HAROLD ROSENTHAL/R

Coblenz. KOBLENZ.

Coburg. Town in central Germany. Its earliest theatrical performances took place in the 1680s, and some 33 different companies, many of them short-lived or travelling troupes, appeared in the town in the late 18th and early 19th centuries. It was not until 1827 that the court theatre of the duchy of Saxony was founded with a permanent company. *Fidelio* was given on 24 June 1832. In 1837 the foundation stone was laid for a new theatre in the classical style in the Schlossplatz, with Vincenz Fischer-Birnbaum as architect. It opened on 17 September 1840 with Auber's *Le lac des fées*; Lortzing's *Zar und Zimmermann* was staged on 2 May 1841. Wagner's music was much performed under Duke Ernst II, who composed music himself and was in touch with Wagner; there were productions of *Tannhäuser*, *Rienzi*, *Der fliegende Holländer* and *Lohengrin*. In 1874 Wagner visited Coburg to discuss scenery for the Bayreuth *Ring* with the court scene painter Brückner. The Coburg company mounted *Die Meistersinger* in 1889 and the *Ring*, without *Die Walküre*, in 1906–7. A suggestion that the company be dissolved for financial reasons had been silenced by popular protest. During World War I productions continued with only a few restrictions and on 1 November 1918 *Der Rosenkavalier* was given with the composer conducting. After 9 August 1919 the theatre was renamed the Coburgische Landestheater. *Parsifal* was staged on 25 December 1920. After 1921, with some interruptions, May festivals were held, and Wagner festivals after 1925. Then came the economic crisis; a merger with the Bamberg theatre failed, and in 1929 the Society of the Friends of the Coburg Regional Theatre was founded. There was an extensive repertory until 1944, with about 25 plays, 20 operas and 12 operettas a season. Even in the final period of wartime activity, in 1943–4, there were still 389 performances. The theatre closed on 1 September 1944, and opened again on 2 October 1945. It then gave plays by Goethe and Molière, operas (*Die Entführung aus dem Serail*, *Rosenkavalier*) and operettas (*Die Csárdásfürstin*, *Gräfin Mariza*). Celebrated artists such as Margarete Klose regularly gave guest performances in Coburg. The theatre was extensively renovated during the period 1969–76; it now has 557 seats. The season runs from the end of August to the beginning of July, and the repertory consists principally of opera (particularly German *Spieloper*) and operetta. KLAUS J. SEIDEL

Cocchi, Gioacchino (*b* ?Naples, *c*1720; *d* ?Venice, after 1788). Italian composer. Since he always called himself a Neapolitan, it is improbable that he was born at Padua, as Gerber stated. Annotations in the Österreichische Nationalbibliothek manuscript 19083 suggest that he studied with Giovanni Veneziano, perhaps at the Conservatorio di S Maria di Loreto in Naples. Between 1740 and 1750 he established himself as a composer of comic intermezzos and of operas, both serious and comic. Among these works, all produced at Naples or Rome, was the greatest success of his career, *La maestra* (1747), which was widely performed: as *La scaltra governatrice* it was the only full-length comic opera given by Bambini's Bouffons in Paris between 1752 and 1754.

A visit to Venice in 1749–50 resulted in Cocchi's appointment as choir director at the Ospedale degli Incurabili, a post he held until 1757. He continued to compose opera both in Venice and on the mainland but never again matched the international success of *La maestra.* Goldoni furnished him with four librettos, one of them, *La mascherata* (1750), among the librettist's best, but none of them held the stage for long.

In 1757 Cocchi went to the King's Theatre, London, as opera composer and music director; during the next five seasons he supervised the production of *opere serie*, composed several himself and contributed to pasticcios. Burney had few kind words for these productions, particularly for two comic operas from the very end of Cocchi's tenure (they evidently paled beside Galuppi's, then popular in London). After being replaced at the King's by J. C. Bach in 1762, Cocchi remained in London for about ten more years. Much in demand as a singing teacher, he published several collections of chamber arias and duets. For some years he directed the subscription concerts organized by Mrs Cornelys at Carlisle House, Soho Square, where the Mozarts met him in 1764 or 1765.

About 1772 Cocchi, now well off, returned to Venice. He did not, as has been alleged, resume his post at the Incurabili. This was held by Galuppi until the orphanage was dissolved in 1776. A manuscript *Dixit Dominus* (*A-Wn* 19084) is dated 1788. After that, Cocchi passes from sight. The date commonly given for his death, 1804, comes from the notoriously inaccurate Fétis.

Cocchi's reputation was considerable in his day. He was a solid craftsman, who aspired, according to the dedication of his op.63, to 'quella naturalezza e facilità che caratterizza il vero', an ideal that placed him among the progressive composers of the pre-Classical period. It is probable, as Burney supposed, that his inspiration ran dry in his later years; yet Burney's strictures seem excessive, and a juster estimate of Cocchi's music will surely emerge from an examination of his earlier works.

See also MAESTRA, LA and MATTI PER AMORE, LI.

LKH – *London, King's Theatre in the Haymarket*
NFI – *Naples, Teatro dei Fiorentini*

La Matilde (commedia, ? A. Palomba), NFI, wint. 1739, lib. *I-Nn*
Adelaide (os, 3, A. Salvi), Rome, Dame, carn. 1743, aria *D-Dlb*, *GB-Cfm*
L'Elisa (ob, 3, Palomba), NFI, aut. 1744
L'Irene (ob, D. Canica), NFI, spr. 1745
I due fratelli beffati (ob, 'E. Pigrugispano'), Naples, Nuovo, wint. 1746
Bajazette (os, 3, A. Piovene), Rome, Dame, 1746
L'ipocondriaco risanato (int), Rome, Valle, 1746
La maestra (ob, 3, Palomba), Naples, Nuovo, spr. 1747; rev. as La scuola moderna o sia La maestra di buon gusto (Goldoni, after Palomba), Venice, aut. 1748, addl music by V. Ciampi; rev. version, NFI, carn. 1751, collab. Cordella and Latilla; as La scaltra governatrice, Paris, 1753, *F-Po*, ov., arias (Paris, n.d.); rev. version, Venice, 1754, *I-MOe* (*R*1987 Acts 1 and 3: DMV, xix)
Merope (os, 3, A. Zeno), Naples, S Carlo, 20 Jan 1748, *Mc*
Arminio (os, Salvi), Rome, Argentina, carn. 1748, arias, duet *D-Dlb*
Siface (os, 3, P. Metastasio), Naples, S Carlo, carn. 1749, aria *MOe*
La serva bacchettona (ob, 3, Palomba), NFI, spr. 1749
Il finto turco (ob, Palomba), NFI, aut. 1749, lib. *I-Nn*; rev. version, NFI, wint. 1753, collab. Errichelli
Farsetta in musica (? A. Lungi), Rome, Valle, 1749
Siroe (os, 3, Metastasio), Venice, S Giovanni Grisostomo, carn. 1750, arias *I-Nc*, *Vc*, *Vmc*
La Gismonda (ob, 3, Palomba), NFI, spr. 1750
Demofoonte (os, Metastasio), Venice, 1750
Le donne vendicate (ob, 3, Goldoni), Venice, S Cassiano, carn. 1751
La mascherata (ob, 3, C. Goldoni), Venice, S Cassiano, carn. 1751
Nitocri (os, 3, Zeno), Turin, Regio, 26 Dec 1751, *Rsc*, *Tf*
Sesostri, re d'Egitto (os, 3, P. Pariati), Naples, S Carlo, 30 May 1752, ov. *Vc* (Padua, 1856)
Il finto cieco (ob, 3, P. Trinchera), Naples, Nuova, aut. 1752, *GB-Lbl*, Favourite Songs (London)
Il tutore (ob), Rome, Valle, 1752, *Lbl*
Semiramide riconosciuta (os, 3, Metastasio), Venice, S Cassiano, carn. 1753, *D-Dlb*, *Wa*, *GB-Lcm*, *Lbl*, *I-BGi*; rev. version, London, 1771, Favourite Songs (London, 1771)
Rosmira fedele (os, 3, S. Stampiglia), Venice, S Samuele, Ascension Fair, 1753, aria *D-SWl*
Il pazzo glorioso (ob, 3, A. Villani), Venice, S Cassiano, aut. 1753
La serva astuta (ob, Palomba), NFI, 1753, collab. Errichelli
Le nozze di Monsù Fagotto (int, 2, ?Lungi), Rome, Valle, carn. 1754
Il terrazzano (int), Florence, Cocomero, carn. 1754
Tamerlano (os, Piovene), Venice, 1754, collab. G. B. Pescetti, *D-Wa*
Li matti per amore (ob, 3, P. Fegejo [Goldoni], after G. A. Federico: *Amor vuol sofferenza*), Venice, S Samuele, aut. 1754, *A-Wn* (*R*1982: IOB, lxxvi); rev. as Il signor Cioè, Modena, Rangoni, 1755
Andromeda (os, 3, V. A. Cigna-Santi), Turin, Regio, carn. 1755, excerpts *I-Tf*
Il cavalier errante (ob, A. Medici), Ferrara, Bonacossi, carn. 1755
Artaserse (os, 3, Metastasio), Reggio Emilia, Pubblico, May 1755, arias *PLcon*
Zoe (os, 3, F. Silvani), Venice, S Benedetto, 26 Dec 1755
Emira (os, 3), Milan, Regio Ducal, Jan 1756
Demetrio (os, 3, Metastasio), LKH, 1757, arias *Fc*, Favourite Songs (London, 1757)

Zenobia (os, 3, Metastasio), LKH, 10 Jan 1758, Favourite Songs (London, 1758)
Issipile (os, 3, Metastasio), LKH, 14 May 1758, *D-Hs*, *EIRE-Dam*, *GB-Lbl*, *Lcm*, *US-Wc*; Favourite Songs (London, 1758)
Farnace (os), 1759, *B-Bc*, *GB-Lbl*; Favourite Songs (1759)
Ciro riconosciuto (os, 3, Metastasio), LKH, 3 Feb 1759, Favourite Songs (London, 1759)
La clemenza di Tito (os, 3, Metastasio), LKH, 15 Jan 1760, Favourite Songs (London, 1760)
Erginda (os, 3, after M. Noris), LKH, May 1760
Antigona (os), London, 1760
Tito Manlio (os, 3, Noris), LKH, 7 Feb 1761, Favourite Songs (London, 1761)
Alessandro nell'Indie (os, 3, Metastasio), LKH, 13 Oct 1761, Favourite Songs (London, 1761)
La famiglia in scompiglio (ob, ? G. Petrosellini), LKH, spr. 1762, Favourite Songs (London, 1762)
Le nozze di Dorina (ob, 3, Goldoni), LKH, spr. 1762
Anagilda, *D-Wa*

Doubtful: L'impostore (ob), Barcelona, S Cruz, 1752, collab. G. Scarlatti; Gli amanti gelosi (ob), LKH, 17 Dec 1753; La burla da vero (int), Madrid, Buen Retiro, 23 Sept 1754; Antigono, Bergamo, 1754 (attrib. Cocchi in catalogue of *US-BE*); Le nozze di Ser Niccolò (farsetta), Rome, Pace, 1760; Il cavalier Bertone (int, A. Belmuro), Madrid, Buen Retiro, 23 Sept 1784

*

BurneyH; *FétisB*
D. Martuscelli, ed.: Preface to *Biografia degli uomini illustri del regno di Napoli*, vi (Naples, 1819), §C, no.27
G. Hardie: 'Neapolitan Comic Opera, 1707–1750: Some Addenda and Corrigenda for *The New Grove*', *JAMS*, xxxvi (1983), 124–7
A. L. Bellina: '"La maestra" esaminata', introduction to G. Cocchi: *La maestra*, DMV, xix (1987), pp.vii–lxiv PIERO WEISS

Coccia, Carlo (*b* Naples, 14 April 1782; *d* Novara, 13 April 1873). Italian composer. The son of the violinist Gaetano Coccia, who later led the S Carlo orchestra, he was taught by Fenaroli at the Conservatorio di S Maria di Loreto, Naples. He became a protégé of Paisiello, who got him the post of *maestro accompagnatore al pianoforte* to Joseph Bonaparte, King of Naples, 1806–8. His first opera, *Il matrimonio per lettera di cambio* (1807, Rome), failed, but Paisiello gave him further encouragement, and he went on to produce 21 more during the following decade (between 1809 and 1817, working mostly in Venice). He was most successful in the sentimental *opera semiseria*, including *Clotilde* (1815, Venice), frequently given in Italy until the 1840s. Italian contemporaries admired *Clotilde* for its use of the chorus as an active participant in the drama, and compared Coccia with Mayr, although the opera failed in Paris and Dresden in 1822. Like many middle-ranking composers, Coccia was often accused of plagiarism; Meyerbeer praised the Act 1 finale of *Fajello* for its expressive declamation and theatricality, but lamented that Coccia had incorporated phrases from Spontini's *La vestale*. Coccia was never regarded as a leading composer and his superficial approach was frequently commented on; *La donna selvaggia* is said to have been composed in 12 or 16 days.

Coccia had come to prominence when Italian opera was at a very low ebb, and like many of his contemporaries he soon found his work eclipsed by Rossini's. In 1820 he became composer and *maestro concertatore* at the S Carlos, Lisbon, where he produced some new operas and an allegorical cantata, *O genio lusitano* (1821). From 24 January 1824 he was *maestro al piano* at the King's Theatre, London, and taught harmony and singing at the new RAM. He is said to have come to appreciate the German classics during his time in London, so that his later operas are informed with a greater seriousness. For Giuditta Pasta in 1827 he composed *Maria Stuarda*, his first opera since 1821. The *Harmonicon* (v, 1827, p.150) considered him 'a scientific and sensible musician', praising the 'undeviating correctness' of *Maria Stuarda*, a judgment that accurately reflects its four-square, diatonic progressions and melodies. Audiences reportedly found the opera too sombre and melancholy, but the *Harmonicon* ascribed its failure and the allegations of plagiarism to backstage intrigues.

Coccia returned to Italy and in 1828 produced *L'orfano della selva*, which made little impression though Bellini (a severe judge) considered it a competent *opera semiseria*. Similarly, his later *opere serie* frequently met with critical esteem rather than popular acclaim ('Il maestro è chiaro ... ma oscura è la sua musica', wrote the *Gazzetta di Milano* about his *Enrico di Monfort*, in 1831). On 30 May 1834 he became *maestro direttore della musica* at the S Carlo, Naples, but it seems to have been an unhappy time and he was replaced by Pietro Romani the following year. In a letter of 3 June he was forced to defend himself in *L'omnibus* against criticism concerning alterations made to Mercadante's *I Normanni a Parigi*. The Neapolitans also treated his own opera, *Marfa*, very badly. By far the most successful of his later operas was *Caterina di Guisa* (1833, Milan), modern in style, which he successfully revised for Turin in 1836 and revived at La Scala. With this *melodramma*, written to a libretto by Romani (one of the first taken from a French Romantic literary source), he was once again in the mainstream of current operatic developments. This opera apart, Coccia was generally more conservative than his younger contemporaries and invariably regarded as a learned composer. After 1841, just before Verdi became a dominant force, he stopped composing operas altogether.

In 1836 Coccia had become inspector of music and director of the singing school of the Accademia Filarmonica, Turin, a new conservatory, and in 1840 he succeeded Mercadante as *maestro di cappella* at S Gaudenzio in Novara. He remained there, writing sacred music until his death a day short of completing 91 years. He survived long enough to write a *Lacrymosa* for unaccompanied choir as part of the requiem organized by Verdi to commemorate Rossini.

Coccia's early prominence was based on the *opera semiseria*, not long before tastes moved towards *opera seria*. During the 1810s, his music assumed many of the mannerisms of Rossini, including 'open' declamatory melodies, with patter songs for basses and florid decorations for soprano lines. In comparison with Rossini's music, Coccia's suffers from a poverty of rhythmical inventiveness. In his operas of the 1830s, he was quick to learn from the developments in the Romantic *melodramma* made by Bellini and Donizetti. In *Caterina di Guisa*, he integrated the drama and the traditional movements of Rossinian aria forms with more success, even using ariosos within the recitatives. However, Coccia was resolutely faithful to Rossini's tonal closure of arias and duets, and developed any further musico-dramatic continuity only in his works of 1838–41.

The works of his maturity reveal a conscientious musician, but one whose melodic style lacked the Romantic fervour necessary to compete with Bellini and Donizetti. Although he managed to throw off Rossini's highly decorative *canto fiorito*, Coccia's melodies were generally diatonic, and frequently triadic, even as late as *La solitaria delle Asturie* (1838, Milan). He often cast arias in Bellini's concise *AA'BA'* form, but usually avoided the expressive appoggiaturas that were so much a feature of current Romantic style. *Caterina di Guisa* is his most notable work since for once his language sounds modern; he achieved an impassioned declamation in the dramatic duet closing Act 1. In this opera he produced a Romantic *melodramma* considerably in advance of those by Mercadante, the composer he otherwise most resembles. Similarly, in the arioso and cavatina for the *musichetto* Arturo, Coccia achieved a convincing post-Rossinian style.

In his final *opera seria*, *Giovanna II, regina di Napoli* (1840, Milan), Coccia went back to the melodic dissonance of Romantic *melodramma* of ten years earlier. Unfortunately the work was not successful, partly because of its rhythmic monotony, but mostly because the composer retained melodic thumbprints from M his earlier days, no longer suitable for modern singers. Writing for Erminia Frezzolini (Verdi's Joan of Arc), he reverted to vocal decorations rather than using the broadly spanned melodies characteristic of the times.

See also CATERINA DI GUISA.

mel – *melodramma*

Il matrimonio per lettera di cambio (burletta per musica, G. Checcherini), Rome, Valle, 14 Nov 1807

Il poeta fortunato, ossia Tutto il mal vien dal mantello (mel giocoso, G. Gasbarri), Florence, Intrepidi, spr. 1808, *F-Pn* (partly autograph), *I-Mr*

L'equivoco, o Le vicende di Martinaccio (dg, Gasbarri), Bologna, Marsigli, carn. 1809

Voglia di dote e non di moglie (dg, F. Aventi), Ferrara, Comunale, carn. 1809, vocal pts *Fc*

La verità nella bugia (farsa, G. Foppa), Venice, S Moisè, Oct 1809, *Mr*

Una fatale supposizione, ovvero Amore e dovere (farsa per musica, Foppa), Venice, S Moisè, 19 Jan 1811, *Mr**, *Fc*, *Nc*, *US-Bp*

I solitari (G. Rossi), Venice, S Moisè, 1 Nov 1811

Il sogno verificato (os, L. Prividali), Venice, Fenice, 23 Jan 1812, *I-Mr**

Arrighetto (dramma per musica, 1, A. Anelli), Venice, S Moisè, 9 Jan 1813, *Mr*

La donna selvaggia (dramma semiserio, 2, Foppa), Venice, S Benedetto, 24 June 1813, *Mr**, *F-Pn*, ov. (Milan, 1815); rev. version, Naples, S Carlo, spr. 1841, *I-Nc*; also as Matilde (dramma eroicomico), Florence, Pergola, spr. 1814, and as La selvaggia

Il crescendo (Rossi), Venice, S Moisè, 16 Feb 1814

Carlotta e Werter (dramma per musica, Gasbarri), Florence, Cocomero, aut. 1814, *F-Pn*, duet (Milan, 1828)

Evellina (mel eroico, 2, Rossi), Milan, Rè, 26 Dec 1814, *Pn**, *I-Mr*

Euristea (dramma per musica, Foppa), Venice, Fenice, 21 Jan 1815, *Mr**

Clotilde (mel semiserio, 2, Rossi), Venice, S Benedetto, 8 June 1815, *F-Pn*, *I-Bc*, *Fc*, *Mr*, *Nc*, *Mc*, *Rsc*, duet (London, ?1825; Milan, 1839)

I begl'usi di città (dg, 2, Anelli), Milan, Scala, 11 Oct 1815, *Mr**

Teseo e Medea (dramma per musica), Turin, Regio, 26 Dec 1815

Rinaldo d'Asti (dramma buffo, J. Ferretti), Rome, Valle, 17 Feb 1816

Etelinda (mel semiserio, 2, Rossi), Venice, S Benedetto, 26 June 1816, *Mr**; rev. version, Trieste, 1816

Claudina in Torino (dramma per musica, 2, Foppa), Venice, S Moisè, 20 Dec 1816, *Mr**, *F-Pn*

Fajello (dramma tragico, 2), Florence, Cocomero, 23 Oct 1817, *Pn*, *I-Fc*, aria (Milan, 1819); rev. as Gabriella di Vergy, Trieste, Nuovo, Sept 1818

Donna Caritea, regina di Spagna (os, ? P. Pola), Genoa, Agostino, 3 Jan 1818

Atar (drama serio, 2, F. Romani), Lisbon, S Carlos, 13 May 1820

La festa della rosa (drama jocoso, 2, Rossi), Lisbon, S Carlos, 13 Aug 1821, *Mr*, duet (Milan, 1824)

Mandane, regina della Persia (os, 2, L. Romanelli), Lisbon, S Carlos, 4 Nov 1821

Elena e Costantino (semiseria, 2, A. L. Tottola), Lisbon, S Carlos, 6 Feb 1822, *Mr*; possibly as Elena e Virginio, Trieste, sum. 1818

Maria Stuarda, regina di Scozia (os, 3, P. Giannone), London, King's, 7 June 1827, excerpts (London, 1827; Milan, 1828)

L'orfano della selva (mel comico, 2, Rossi), Milan, Scala, 15 Nov 1828, *Mr**, excerpts (Milan, 1828); rev. version, Naples, Fondo, aut. 1829, *Mr**, *Nc*

Rosmonda (mel serio, 2, Romani), Venice, Fenice, 28 Feb 1829

Edoardo in Iscozia (dramma per musica, 2, D. Gilardoni), Naples, S Carlo, 8 May 1831, *F-Pn*, *I-Mr*, *Nc*, inc. vs (Milan, 1831)

Enrico di Monfort (mel, 2, Rossi), Milan, Scala, 12 Nov 1831

Caterina di Guisa (mel, 2, Romani, after A. Dumas *père*: *Henri III et sa cour*), Milan, Scala, 14 Feb 1833, *Mr**, *Nc*, vs (Milan, 1833/*R*1986: IOG, iv); rev. version, Turin, Carignano, aut. 1836, *Mr**, vs (Milan, 1836/*R*1986: IOG, iv)

La figlia dell'arciere (mel tragico, 3, Romani and D. M. Andreotti), Naples, S Carlo, 12 Jan 1834, *Mr**, *Nc*, excerpts (Milan, 1834)

Marfa (mel, 2, E. Bidera), Naples, S Carlo, 13 July 1835, *Mr*, 2 arias (Milan, 1835)

La solitaria delle Asturie, ossia La Spagna ricuperata (mel, 2, Romani), Milan, Scala, 6 March 1838, *Mr**, excerpts (Milan, 1838); rev. version, Genoa, Carlo Felice, 10 Feb 1839, *Mr**, inc. vs (Milan, 1838–40)

Giovanna II, regina di Napoli (mel, 3, Rossi), Milan, Scala, 12 March 1840, *Mr**, excerpts (Milan, 1840; Naples, ?1840; London, *c*1840)

Il lago delle fate (mel, 4), Turin, Regio, 6 Feb 1841

*

FlorimoN

J. Ebers: *Seven Years of the King's Theatre* (London, 1828), 342

'Biographische Notizen und Verzeichniss der Compositionen des Herrn Coccia', *AMZ*, xxxv (1833), cols.361–3

'Carlo Coccia', *Iconografia musicale, ovvero Ritratti e biografie di vari dei più celebrati maestri, professori e cantanti moderni* (Turin, 1838), 18

G. Carotti: *Biografia di Carlo Coccia* (Turin, 1873)

O. Chilesotti: 'Carlo Coccia', *I nostri maestri del passato* (Milan, 1882)

G. Carli Ballola and G. Salvetti: 'L'ottocento minore', *Storia dell'Opera*, ed. G. Barblan and others, i/2 (Turin, 1977), 393–495, esp.407

P. Gossett: Introduction to C. Coccia: *Caterina di Guisa*, IOG, iv (New York and London, 1986)

A. Weatherson: 'English Legend, French Play, Two Italian Composers', *Donizetti Society Journal*, vi (1988), 107–21

SIMON MAGUIRE

Coccodrillo, Il ('The Crocodile'). Opera in four acts and two parts by VALENTINO BUCCHI to a libretto by the composer and Mauro Pezzati after FYODOR MIKHAYLOVICH DOSTOYEVSKY's novella *The Crocodile*; Florence, Teatro della Pergola, 8 May 1970.

Il coccodrillo draws freely on Dostoyevsky's novella. The plot links a sequence of 32 numbers. At its centre is the Official (tenor), 'class beta, fourth grade', symbolizing modern bureaucratic alienation, who, together with the Wife (soprano) and a friend, Teodoro (baritone), goes to the 'Città della Domenica' (Sunday City), a place of forgetfulness 'where silence is a punishment, since anyone who listens to it is killed by the noise'. In Act 2 the three are welcomed by the Hostess (spoken); then the Singer (female voice) appears and intones the 'Song of Coexistence' to words by Franco Fortini, and the Proprietor (bass) introduces a further attraction, a crocodile. The Official leaves the stage with the Proprietor, who later announces to the Wife and Teodoro that the Official has been swallowed by the crocodile. In Act 3 in his new home in the crocodile's belly, the Official feels anything but imprisoned: on the contrary, he feels sheltered and at ease and is finally able to see life clearly and live it creatively, imposing his rule on the world and ever after acting as a communal menace. In this situation, the attempts by his Wife and the Prime Minister (spoken) to make him see reason count for nothing. The opera ends with the death of the crocodile, heightened by the entry of the chorus (which has an important dramatic function in the work).

In creating this bitterly ironic metaphor of contemporary life, in which echoes of 1960s social criticism can be heard, Bucchi consciously embraced a total conception of music theatre which is essentially new compared with his previous theatrical works. He takes the resources of contemporary avant-garde theatre and absorbs them, pragmatically and without going to extremes, into his creative world. Compared with his earlier opera *Il contrabbasso*, *Il coccodrillo* makes expressive use of a wider range of theatrical and musical techniques, from mime and speech to film and recorded music. In increasing the orchestral forces to a total of 48, Bucchi does not abandon his typical chamber-group divisions (which may owe something to Monteverdi's *Orfeo*, of which he made a realization). And with *Il coccodrillo* there appears the liking for micro-intervals that was to characterize his exploration of a new musical language in the early 1970s. RAFFAELE POZZI

Cochereau, Jacques (*d* Paris, 17 July 1734). French *haute-contre*. Having left the army to join the Opéra at Lille, he married an opera singer and moved to Paris, where he made his début at the Opéra in 1702. Initially singing minor parts, he was quickly pressed into more important Lully roles: Perseus (1703 and 1710 revivals), Mercury (*Isis*, 1704 and 1717), Bellérophon (1705 and 1718), Admetus (*Alceste*, 1706 and 1716), Renaud (*Armide*, 1713), Phaethon (1710), Alpheius (*Proserpine*, 1715) and Médor (*Roland*, 1716). He also sang in the revivals of Destouches' *Amadis de Grèce* (1711), Desmarets' *Didon* (1704; Aeneas), Marais' *Alcide, ou la mort d'Hercule* (1705 and 1716; Hercules), Collasse's *Thétis et Pélée* (1699 and 1708; Peleus, with Desmatins and Journet respectively) and Desmarets and Campra's *Iphigénie en Tauride* (1711; Pylades, with Journet). Cochereau created such leading roles as Orestes in Bouvard and Bertin de la Doué's *Cassandre* (1706) and Idamantes in Campra's *Idoménée* (1712). Yet he apparently never overcame his native timidity, 'ce qui jeta du froid dans son jeu' (Parfaict). He retired during the 1718–19 season, when his position within the company passed to Muraire.

*

E. Campardon: *L'Académie royale de musique au XVIIIe siècle*, i (Paris, 1884), 131–8 PHILIP WELLER

Cochran, William (*b* Columbus, OH, 23 June 1943). American tenor. He studied at the Curtis Institute with Martial Singher. In 1969 he sang Froh with the San Francisco Opera in Los Angeles. After winning the Lauritz Melchior Heldentenor Foundation Award, he became a member of the Frankfurt Opera (1970), and also sang in Munich, Hamburg and Vienna. He made his Covent Garden début in 1974 as Laca (*Jenůfa*) and in 1977 sang Tichon (*Kát'a Kabanová*) at San Francisco. In 1984 he sang Bacchus at the Metropolitan. In addition to the Wagnerian heroic tenor roles, his repertory includes Idomeneus, Jason (Cherubini's *Médée*), Aeneas (*Les Troyens*), Otello, Canio, Herod, Bacchus and Grigory (*Boris Godunov*). His strong, well projected voice and fine musicianship have also been effectively displayed in Janáček's *The Makropulos Affair*, Busoni's *Doktor Faust*, Shostakovich's *Lady Macbeth of the Mtsensk District* and *The Nose*, Zimmermann's *Die Soldaten*, Stravinsky's *The Rake's Progress*, and as Alviano Salvago in Schreker's *Die Gezeichneten*, which he sang at Düsseldorf in 1989. A singer of tremendous energy and commitment, he is also an excellent actor.

ELIZABETH FORBES

Cocomero. Theatre in FLORENCE, in the via del Cocomero, opened perhaps as early as 1654. In the 18th century it served as the national theatre of Tuscany; it was twice restored in the 19th, and in 1859 renamed after G. B. Niccolini. Opera ceased to be performed there in 1935.

Cocteau, (Clément Eugène) Jean (Maurice) (*b* Maisons-Laffitte, Paris, 5 July 1889; *d* Milly-la-Forêt, Seine-et-Oise, 11 Oct 1963). French writer, film-maker, designer and aesthetic activist. *Les mariés de la tour Eiffel* (1920–21), a play-ballet for which five of Les Six wrote short pieces, embodied the anti-Romantic, Gallic, pro-Satie principles of his manifesto *Le coq et l'arlequin*. Other stage pieces with individual members of the group followed throughout the 1920s, but Cocteau was becoming more attached to the straight theatre. It was the plain, direct quality of his compressed translation of *Antigone* (later set as an opera by Honegger) that persuaded Stravinsky to approach him for the text of the opera-oratorio *Oedipus rex* (1927). Cocteau found his contribution reduced almost to nothing, however, for two rewritings were required, the text was cut, and it was translated into Latin. All that was left was the vernacular narration, whose alienating effect supported Stravinsky's distanced, liturgical treatment of the myth. Cocteau was director and designer for a revival of *Oedipus rex* in Paris in 1952.

Librettos: *Paul et Virginie* (oc, with R. Radiguet), Satie, 1920, lost; *Oedipus rex* (opera-oratorio), Stravinsky, 1927; *Le pauvre matelot*, Milhaud, 1927

Plays set as operas: *Antigone* (1922), Honegger, 1927; *La voix humaine* (1929), Poulenc, 1959

*

J. Cocteau: *Le coq et l'arlequin: notes autour de la musique* (Paris, 1918) [repr. in *Le rappel à l'ordre* (Paris, 1926) and in *Oeuvres complètes*, ix (Paris, 1950)]
——: 'La collaboration Oedipus rex', *ReM*, no.212 (1952), 51–2
V. Rašín: '"Les Six" and Jean Cocteau', *ML*, xxxviii (1957), 164–9
I. Stravinsky and R. Craft: *Dialogues and a Diary* (New York, 1963)
L'avant-scène, nos.365–6 (1966) [Cocteau number, incl. documentation of *Les mariés de la tour Eiffel*]

PAUL GRIFFITHS

Coelho, Rui (*b* Alcácer do Sal, 3 March 1892; *d* Lisbon, 5 May 1986). Portuguese composer and conductor. He studied at the Lisbon Conservatory and later with Humperdinck in Berlin (1910–13) and with Paul Vidal in Paris. In Portugal he often appeared as a pianist and conductor, mainly for his own works. He worked for Portuguese radio and was music critic for several Lisbon newspapers.

In spite of his contact with European musical trends of the 1910s, Coelho made almost no use of 20th-century techniques. He composed in a nationalist manner, trying to renew and to make known the Portuguese spirit in his instrumental music and in his works for the stage. For that purpose he created (1934) the Acção Nacional de Opera, a foundation for the promotion of Portuguese opera that, in fact, presented only his own works. Coelho has often been inaccurately called the creator of Portuguese national opera. Nevertheless, he gave a strong impulse to dramatic genres and towards fostering a new interest in national subjects. In his operas Coelho used only Portuguese texts on national subjects, literary, historic and popular. *O serão da infanta* (1913) was the first Portuguese opera to be sung in Portuguese at its première; *Belkiss* (1923) was awarded a prize in an international composition competition in Spain in 1924. Coelho also wrote the first Portuguese ballets of the 20th century, but while these and his orchestral works are still played, his operas are no longer performed.

operas, first performed in Lisbon, Teatro de S Carlos, unless otherwise stated

O serão da infanta (A. L. Vieira), 1913
Auto do berço (1, A. C. Oliveira), 1920
Crisfal (écloga, 1, Vieira), 1920
Rosas de todo o ano (1, J. Dantas), 1921
Belkiss, 1923 (3, E. de Castro), 9 June 1928
Inês de Castro (3, A. Ferreira and A. Patrício), 15 Jan 1927
Cavaleiro das mãos irresistíveis (1, Castro), 1927
Freira de beja (1, R. Chianca), 1927
Entre giestas (3, C. Selvagem), Lisbon, Coliseu, 1929
Tá-mar (3, A. Cortês), Lisbon, 1936
Bocage (opereta), Lisbon, Eden, 1937
Dom João IV (3, S. Tavares), 1 Dec 1940
A feira (G. Vicente), 1943
A rosa de papel (1, Coelho, after A. S. Rita), 18 Dec 1947
Auto da barca do inferno (1, Coelho, after Vicente), 1950
Inês Pereira (3, G. Saviotti, after Vicente), 5 April 1952
O vestido de noiva (1, C. Oulmont), 4 Jan 1959
Auto da alma (1, Coelho, after Vicente), Queluz, Palácio, 1960
Orfeu em Lisboa, 1964–6 (3, Coelho)
A bela dama sem pecado (parábola, 1, Oulmont), 1969
Auto da barca da glória (Vicente), 1970
O rouxinol cativo, n.d.
Soror Mariana (1, Dantas), n.d.

*

M. A. L. Cruz: *História da música portuguesa* (Lisbon, 1955)
J. F. Branco: *História da música portuguesa* (Lisbon, 1959)
Rui Coelho: sua acção e sua obras de 1910 a 1967 (Lisbon, 1967)

ADRIANA LATINO

Coerne, Louis (Adolphe) (*b* Newark, NJ, 27 Feb 1870; *d* Boston, 11 Sept 1922). American composer. He spent his early childhood in France and Germany; later his family moved to Boston, where he studied the violin with Franz Kneisel and composition with Paine at Harvard (1888–90). From 1890 to 1893 he studied the organ and composition in Munich with Rheinberger, and subsequently held appointments as organist and conductor in Buffalo, New York, and Columbus, Ohio. In 1899 he returned to Germany, where he composed the three-act opera *Zenobia* to a libretto by Oskar Stein, and was back in the USA to teach at Smith College in 1903–4.

Zenobia op.66 was published in Leipzig in 1903 and produced at the Stadttheater in Bremen on 1 December 1905, the first serious opera by an American to be performed in Europe. The German critics, intrigued at the prospect of hearing the work, received it with considerable enthusiasm. The libretto concerns the historical encounter of the Roman general Aurelian and the beautiful Zenobia, Queen of Palmyra, treating it with artistic licence. The first act, devoted largely to choruses and dances of celebration by the temporarily victorious army of Palmyra, is closest in character to grand opera. The later acts concentrate almost entirely on the emotional situation of the principal characters. Coerne's score combines elements of traditional operatic spectacle with Wagnerian leitmotif technique.

Following the successful production of *Zenobia*, Coerne returned to Harvard University, where he earned the first doctorate in the field of music to be granted by an American institution and became the first professor of music at Connecticut College. In addition to *Zenobia* and to songs, organ pieces, choral, chamber and orchestral works, Coerne wrote three works for the theatre, none of them produced or published – an opera in English, *A Woman of Marblehead*, and two operettas, *Jungfer Königin* (also known as *The Maiden Queen*) and *The Bells of Beaujolais*. Coerne's MSS are held at Connecticut College (*Woman of Marblehead*, full score and vs), the Boston Public Library (*Jungfer Königin*, vs) and the Library of Congress.

STEVEN LEDBETTER

Coertse, Mimi (Maria Sophia) (*b* Durban, 12 June 1932). South African soprano. After initial studies in Johannesburg she was a pupil of Maria Hittorf and Joseph Witt in Vienna (from 1954). She made her début at the Vienna Staatsoper in 1956 as the Queen of Night, a role with which she achieved considerable fame and which she sang in most of the major opera houses in Europe. From 1957 until her return to South Africa in 1973 she was associated principally with the Vienna Staatsoper. Notable performances there included the title role in the Viennese première of Strauss's *Die schweigsame Frau* (1968) and appearances in his *Die ägyptische Helena* and *Daphne*. Among her roles were Flotow's Martha, Fiordiligi, Gilda, Musetta and Countess Almaviva, which she sang in Pretoria in 1989.

JAMES MAY

Coffey, Charles (*b* Ireland, late 17th century; *d* London, 13 May 1745). Irish playwright and librettist. He appears to have been treated with some consideration by theatre managers, and frequently had a benefit. His fifth BALLAD OPERA, *The Devil to Pay*, failed in its full-length form (Drury Lane, 6 August 1731) because the audience thought Lady Loverule's greedy chaplain was in bad taste, but when cut to an afterpiece it was, after *The Beggar's Opera*, the most successful ballad opera of the century. The music was arranged by Seedo, and in Nell Jobson (the surly cobbler's wife) Mrs Kitty Clive found her favourite role. The plot tells how bad-tempered Lady Loverule and sweet-tempered Nell are suddenly exchanged in their marital beds by the magic powers of a 'doctor', who is furious at being refused lodging late at night in both their houses. Helped by John Mottley, Coffey based his libretto on *The Devil of a Wife* (1686) by Thomas Jevon, who in turn had been helped by Thomas Shadwell. It formed the basis of Balfe's comic opera *The Devil's in it* (1852); translated into German it became an influential Singspiel, *Der Teufel ist los*, and the basis of a ballet by Adolphe Adam, *Le diable à quatre* (1845).

Of Coffey's other ballad operas, the following were published with their tunes: *The Beggar's Wedding* (Little Theatre, 29 May 1729; earlier in Dublin); *The Female Parson* (Little Theatre, 27 April 1730); *The Boarding School* (Drury Lane, 29 Jan 1733); and *The Merry Cobler* (Drury Lane, 6 May 1735). The last was an unsuccessful sequel to *The Devil to Pay*. Facsimile editions of several of Coffey's operas are included in Rubsamen.

*

A. H. Scouten and L. Hughes: 'The Devil to Pay: A Preliminary Check List', *Library Chronicle* [pubn of the U. of Pennsylvania], xvi (1948), 15–24
——, eds.: *Ten English Farces* (Austin, 1948) [incl. edn of *The Devil to Pay*]
W. H. Rubsamen, ed.: *The Ballad Opera* (New York, 1974)

ROGER FISKE

Cogan [Coogan], **Philip** (*b* ?Cork, 1748; *d* Dublin, 3 Feb 1833). Irish composer. Nothing is known of his youth beyond the fact that he was a member of the choir of St Finbar's Cathedral in Cork. In 1772 he appears to have moved to Dublin, where he held posts at both cathedrals, as a chorister and organist. His obituary in *Freeman's Journal* states that he obtained the degree of music doctor, but there is no trace of his name in the records of Dublin University. Though he was usually referred to as 'Dr Cogan', most of his publications are ascribed to 'Mr Cogan'.

He acquired a distinguished reputation as a keyboard player, composer and teacher; his pupils included Michael Kelly, William Rooke and Thomas Moore. Kelly (in his *Reminiscences*, 1826) referred to him as 'an hospitable worthy fellow highly esteemed by all his connexions'.

Cogan's earliest composition seems to have been incidental music for the pantomime *The Rape of Proserpine* (Dublin, 9 February 1776), followed by the comic opera *The Ruling Passion*, to a libretto by Leonard McNally (first performed at the Capel Street Theatre, Dublin, on 24 February 1778). He collaborated on another comic opera, *The Contract*, to a libretto by Robert Houlton, with Stevenson and Giordani (Smock Alley, Dublin, 1782; M. Laurent provided ballet music). This was later revived as *The Double Stratagem* (Capel Street, 1784). None of Cogan's stage music is extant, though some of his published songs may have been composed for the theatre.

BRIAN BOYDELL

Cohan, George M(ichael) (*b* Providence, RI, 3/4 July 1878; *d* New York, 5 Nov 1942). American composer and singer. From boyhood he toured with his parents and sister in a vaudeville act, played the violin in a pit orchestra, and wrote sketches and songs. His patriotic vaudeville sketches gradually developed into works recognized as significant forerunners of American musical comedy. For *Little Johnny Jones* (1904) Cohan wrote book, lyrics and music, as well as taking the leading role with the songs 'Yankee Doodle Boy' and 'Give my regards to Broadway'. He wrote various other shows in similar vein, continuing also as a performer up to the Rodgers and Hart political satire *I'd Rather be Right* (1937). Cohan was an untrained musician, and his scores never pretended to be more than vehicles for spirited, morale-boosting songs. As a composer of such, and for bringing vaudeville elements into mainstream musical theatre, he remains justly celebrated.

musical comedies, words by Cohan; performances in New York unless otherwise stated

The Governor's Son, Hartford, CT, 11 Feb 1901 (Savoy, 25 Feb 1901); Running for Office, 14th Street, 27 April 1903 (rev. as The Honeymooners, Aerial Gardens, 3 June 1907); Little Johnny Jones, Hartford, CT, 10 Oct 1904 (Liberty, 7 Nov 1904); Forty-Five Minutes from Broadway, Columbus, OH, Sept 1905 (New Amsterdam, 1 Jan 1906); George Washington jr, Herald Square, 12 Feb 1906; The Talk of New York, Knickerbocker, 3 Dec 1907; Fifty Miles from Boston, Garrick, 3 Feb 1908; The Yankee Prince, Knickerbocker, 20 April 1908; The American Idea, New York, 5 Oct 1908; The Man who Owns Broadway, New York, 11 Oct 1909; The Little Millionaire, Cohan, 25 Sept 1911; The Voice of McConnell, Manhattan Opera, 25 Dec 1918; The Royal Vagabond, Cohan and Harris, 17 Feb 1919, collab. A. Goetzl; Little Nellie Kelly, Liberty, 13 Nov 1922; The Rise of Rosie O'Reilly, Liberty, 25 Dec 1923; The Merry Malones, Erlanger, 26 Sept 1927; Billie, Erlanger, 1 Oct 1928

G. M. Cohan: *Twenty Years on Broadway and the Years it Took to Get There* (New York, 1924)
W. Morehouse: *George M. Cohan: Prince of the American Theater* (Philadelphia, 1943)
J. McCabe: *George M. Cohan: the Man who Owned Broadway* (New York, 1973)

ANDREW LAMB

Coignet, Horace (*b* Lyons, 12 May 1735; *d* Lyons, 29 Aug 1821). French composer. A businessman and clerk in Lyons, and from about 1794 musical director of the city, he was an amateur composer and a competent violinist. He wrote little music for the stage but holds an honourable place in French music by virtue of his connection with J.-J. Rousseau. They met in Lyons on Good Friday, 1770; Rousseau, impressed by Coignet's *opéra comique Le médecin d'amour* (1758, Paris), invited Coignet's collaboration in a melodrama, *Pygmalion*. Rousseau, who favoured the form as he regarded French as a poor language for singing, had already written the text, and asked Coignet to compose the score, excluding two sections (part of the overture and the scene where the sculptor puts the finishing touches to the statue) which he wished to compose himself. The work was privately performed at the Hôtel de Ville, Lyons, in 1770, and subsequently at the Comédie-Française, Paris (30 October 1775). The score, which achieved considerable success, was later widely supposed to be Rousseau's own; several later composers wrote alternative versions.

*

Notice, *Gazette universelle de Lyon* (26 Oct 1821)
A. Mahul: *Annuaire nécrologique*, ii (1822)
H. Coignet: 'Particularités sur J.-J. Rousseau pendant le séjour qu'il fit à Lyon en 1770', *Oeuvres inédites de Rousseau*, ed. V. D. de Musset-Pathay, i (Paris, 1825), 461ff [orig. in Mahul (1822), also in *Tablettes historiques et littéraires* (Lyons, 28 Dec 1822)]
A. Jansen: *Jean-Jacques Rousseau als Musiker* (Berlin, 1884)
E. Istel: *Jean-Jacques Rousseau als Komponist seiner lyrischen Scene 'Pygmalion'* (Leipzig, 1901) [see also *Annales de la Société Jean-Jacques Rousseau 1905*, 141–72; rejoinders ibid, *1907*, 119–55]
A. Sallès: 'Horace Coignet et le Pygmalion de Rousseau', *Revue musicale de Lyon* (24 and 31 Dec 1905)
L. Vallas: *Un siècle de musique et de théâtre à Lyon* (Lyons, 1932)

ROGER J. V. COTTE

Colas Breugnon [*Kola Bryun'on: Master iz Klamsi* ('Colas Breugnon: Master of Clamecy')]. Opera in a prologue and three acts, op.24, by DMITRY BORISOVICH KABALEVSKY to a libretto by V. G. Bragin after the short novel by ROMAIN ROLLAND; Leningrad, Malïy Opera Theatre, 22 February 1938 (as *Master iz Klamsi*).

Colas Breugnon	baritone
Selina	mezzo-soprano
Jacqueline	soprano
Gifflard	low bass
Chamaille *the Curé*	bass
Robinet	tenor
Duke d'Asnois	tenor
Mademoiselle de Termes	soprano

Townspeople, soldiers, guests, servants, musicians

Setting Clamecy, Burgundy, in the 16th century

Kabalevsky began the composition of his first opera in 1936. He had the support of Rolland, who granted both him and the librettist generous latitude with the literary original. When the work was completed a year later, Rolland was disappointed by the liberties they had actually taken; he found that little of the specifically

Burgundian character of his original had been preserved in the libretto, though he was impressed with the music and its fidelity to French national colour. In fact, though Kabalevsky made a detailed study of French folk music, he opted against period stylization or wholesale quotation from native sources, trying to convey instead a more generalized spirit. The flaws in the dramaturgy did not escape critics and, shortly after its première, Kabalevsky resolved to revise the work to bring it closer to Rolland's intentions. This revision was completed only in 1968 as Kabalevsky's op.90, and was first performed in Leningrad at the Malïy Opera Theatre on 16 April 1970. In the interim, however, music from the opera was popularized in a suite of symphonic extracts. The overture in particular, with its sparkling and transparent orchestration, became a concert-hall favourite. Among the most important new features in the revised version of the opera are the addition of a prologue, the incorporation of scenes between Colas, his wife and grandchild, and the transformation of Colas' revenge against the Duke, in Act 4, from the level of physical violence into the realm of art. Kabalevsky was awarded the Lenin Prize for *Colas Breugnon* in 1972.

PROLOGUE Colas Breugnon, master carpenter and craftsman of the town of Clamecy, is a carefree spirit, incurable optimist and master of his own fate. With a glass of wine in hand he begins to reminisce about his past. (Scenes in the opera are linked by instrumental and sometimes choral interludes, making the course of the action seamless.)

ACT 1.i *The vineyards around Clamecy* The harvesters sing a song about springtime, 'Cherez les gustoy' ('Through the thick woods'), a graceful chorus for women's voices which shows the influence of French popular song. Young Colas flirts with and teases proud Selina, calling her a little weasel. The headstrong girl threatens him with her watering can and succeeds in chasing him off, only to lament his lack of persistence in 'Noch' i den'' ('Night and Day') before she falls asleep. Colas returns and cannot resist the temptation to embrace the sleeping girl. Overcome with passion, he tries to run away but is intercepted by Gifflard, the Duke's sycophant, who is also in love with Selina, and who taunts Colas. Their brawl is curtailed at the ominous announcement that the Duke has returned from Paris with a new garrison of soldiers.

1.ii *In front of the Duke's castle* The Duke cannot understand why his subjects greet him with apprehension. The Curé brushes over the awkward moment by summoning the musicians, including Colas (who plays the flute), to serenade the Duke. Mademoiselle de Termes notices Colas and asks him what he can do. The impudent craftsman catalogues his many skills in an energetic, syncopated rondo, 'Vskapïvat', vspakhivat'' ('To dig, to plough'). Mlle de Termes is entranced when she sees a fountain sculpted by Colas, and demands that he show her all his handiwork in the castle. Jealously, Selina watches them depart and, accompanied by the chorus, she sings a ballad about a cowardly knight, to the strains of a lilting waltz, 'Luga vechernïye myagki' ('The evening meadows are soft'). Her jealousy is fanned by Gifflard, and when the giddy Colas returns, she refuses to dance with him. Instead, Jacqueline – who has loved Colas from a distance – begs him to dance. Colas returns to the castle and the drunken Curé, reminiscent of a Musorgskian character type, emerges from the castle and collapses under a tree. The sounds of Colas' flute and women's laughter from the castle prompt Selina to cast her lot with the exultant Gifflard.

ACT 2.i *Colas Breugnon's workshop* Many years later, Colas puts up patiently with the scolding and nagging of his wife, Jacqueline. He has not forgotten his early love and, together with his apprentice Robinet, he is sculpting his masterwork, a statue of Selina. When fanfares announce the arrival of the Duke, Colas quickly hides the statue, but Gifflard finds it and the Duke promptly appropriates it for his castle. Colas accepts his loss with stoicism, reasoning in the song 'Chyornaya zala' ('The dark hall') that at least his work will be protected in the castle. Chased by his parishioners, the Curé takes refuge with Colas, whose mood changes abruptly as the two begin to drink; he regales his friend with a jaunty drinking song, 'Za Provansom' ('Beyond Provence'). Jacqueline and Robinet join in the festivities

'Colas Breugnon' (Kabalevsky): Act 2 scene i (Colas Breugnon's workshop) of the original production at the Malïy Opera Theatre, Leningrad, 22 February 1938

and their songs mingle. Suddenly Jacqueline screams. A procession of mourners eerily intoning the *Dies irae* is heard. The soldiers have brought the plague to the town. Jacqueline scoops up her granddaughter and all rush out to save themselves except Colas, who remains behind defiantly as the choral *Dies irae* swells.

2.ii *A shed outside Clamecy* Colas, sick and alone, contemplates his approaching death with Musorgskian introspection and delirium in the song 'Noch' tyanetsya' ('The night drags on'), culminating in a twisted dance of death. As he collapses, he sees stars and hears miraculous music. When the Curé arrives, he discovers Colas alive and ready to be revived with a swig of wine. Breathlessly, Robinet reports that the soldiers have burnt everything, that all he could save was Colas' flageolet. More gravely, the Curé prepares Colas for the imminent death of his wife. When he tells him that his granddaughter is also dying, Colas, although still frail, sets out with determination.

2.iii *A room in a stranger's house* Jacqueline bids farewell to Colas with tenderness, confessing her lifelong love and her envy of his eternal laughter. When it becomes clear that her granddaughter has been spared, Jacqueline dies. Colas dedicates himself solemnly to the future of his granddaughter in the song 'Slavnaya zverushka' ('Glorious little creature').

2.iv *Outside Selina's house* Colas and Selina meet unexpectedly. Against a nostalgic reprise of the harvesters' song from Act 1, they make awkward conversation until Selina demands a kiss. The two review the silly mistakes of their youth and Selina finally confesses her love, singing 'Ya lyubila tebya' ('I loved you'). Colas is philosophical: 'Maybe it's better this way. It's not possible to love one's whole life.' He kisses her and continues on his way. In the interlude between scenes, Colas hears that the Duke and Gifflard are burning and terrorizing the town. Disregarding the risks, he decides to go to the castle.

ACT 3.i *A hall in the Duke's castle* The Duke watches Clamecy burn in the distance. Gifflard slyly informs the Duke that Colas is inciting the townspeople to rebellion. In a spiteful frenzy, the Duke and Gifflard set about hacking and burning all Colas' creations. When Colas arrives they refuse to admit him until the last piece – his precious statue of Selina – has been destroyed. After his initial shock, Colas laughs in the Duke's face. He resolves to fulfil his promise of revenge on St Martin's Day.

3.ii *A field in front of the castle* The citizens of Clamecy are gathered in their holiday regalia. They dance and sing in honour of St Martin. The Duke and his guests appear and a herald announces, to drumroll, that Colas' monument in honour of the Duke will be unveiled. The citizens sing a hymn of praise to their city, 'O, slavnïy grad Klamsi' ('O, glorious city of Clamecy'), and the Curé blesses the hands that created the monument. As anticipation reaches its peak, the veil falls to reveal a heroic likeness of the Duke sitting backwards on a donkey. The hysterical Duke disappears into the castle accompanied by the laughter and rejoicing of his subjects. Colas concludes: 'Life is good, friends. There's only one bad thing – it's too short. Oh, how I wish it could be longer!' LAUREL E. FAY

Colas et Colinette, ou Le bailli dupé ('Colas and Colinette, or The Duped Bailiff'). Comic opera 'en prose, mêlée d'ariettes' in three acts by JOSEPH QUESNEL to his own libretto; Montreal, Théâtre de Société, 14 January 1790.

Although the work is the first known Canadian opera, its slight story has nothing to do with Canadian rural themes; like its music, it owes much to 18th-century French *opéra comique*. The shepherdess Colinette (soprano), ward of the country squire Monsieur Dolmont (bass), wants to marry the honest young shepherd Colas (tenor) rather than the rich, crotchety and conniving old bailiff (bass), who tricks Colas into volunteering for the army. The bailiff is foiled in his attempt to elope with Colinette and all ends happily with Dolmont giving the young lovers permission to marry. First performed as an afterpiece to Molière's *Le médecin malgré lui* – possibly with Quesnel playing the violin – and repeated a month later, *Colas et Colinette* was subsequently given in Quebec city twice in 1805 and twice in 1807. The libretto was published in 1808 but the score remained unpublished at Quesnel's death in 1809. Helmut Kallmann discovered an incomplete manuscript in the Archives du Séminaire de Québec in 1952. From the surviving vocal parts and a second violin part, the composer Godfrey Ridout reconstructed the full score of 14 musical numbers and added an overture based on the extant tunes. The Ridout version had its première on 6 October 1963 for Toronto's Ten Centuries Concerts and has since been performed in various Canadian cities, including Vancouver and Montreal, and in Belgium and Italy.

The lively original melodies owe something to Grétry, whom Quesnel acknowledged in an autobiographical poem as the leading French composer. Although Ridout's scoring deftly sets off the simple tunes and retains the music's charm and freshness, he drew on more knowledge of Mozart than Quesnel would have had.

GAYNOR G. JONES

Colasse, Pascal. *See* COLLASSE, PASCAL.

Colautti, Arturo (*b* Zara, 1851; *d* Rome, 9 Nov 1914). Italian writer and librettist. His later works praise the Irredentist movement which urged Italy's intervention against Austria in World War I on account of territorial disputes on the north-east border. In the sphere of music theatre, Colautti supplied opera librettos with an essentially naturalistic flavour for a variety of composers; the most successful was *Adriana Lecouvreur* (Cilea, 1902). His poems were also set, by F. P. Tosti.

Doña Flor, Westerhout, 1896; *Fedora*, Giordano, 1898; *Adriana Lecouvreur*, Cilea, 1902; *Gloria*, Cilea, 1907; *Paolo e Francesca*, Mancinelli, 1907; *Fasma*, P. La Rotella, 1908; *Fior di neve*, L. Filiasi, 1911; *Morgana*, R. de Micro, 1911; *Esmeralda*, M. Zanon, 1912; *Rudello*, G. Ottolenghi, 1914; *Colomba*, Westerhout, 1923

*

D. Novak Colautti: *Arturo Colautti* (Milan, 1939)
B. Croce: *La letteratura della nuova Italia*, vi (Bari, 1940), 170–71

RAFFAELE POZZI

Colbran, Isabella [Isabel] (**Angela**) (*b* Madrid, 2 Feb 1785; *d* Castenaso, Bologna, 7 Oct 1845). Spanish soprano. After study with Pareja, Marinelli and Crescentini, she made her début in Spain (1806), and then went to Italy, where she sang at Bologna (1807). In 1808 she sang at La Scala, and in 1811 she was engaged for Naples by the impresario Barbaia; she remained there for over a decade. A highly dramatic singer who excelled in tragedy, especially in Spontini's *La vestale* and Mayr's *Medea in Corinto*, she strongly influenced the operas that Rossini composed for Naples.

Isabella Colbran in the title role of Simon Mayr's 'Saffo': portrait (1817) by Heinrich Schmidt

Elisabetta, regina d'Inghilterra (1815), *Otello* (1816), *Armida* (1817), *Mosè in Egitto*, *Ricciardo e Zoraide* (1818), *Ermione*, *La donna del lago* (1819), *Maometto II* (1820) and *Zelmira* (1822) all contained parts written to display her special vocal and dramatic gifts. Colbran and Rossini, who had lived together for some years, were married at Castenaso in 1822. *Semiramide*, the final opera that he composed for her, was produced at La Fenice in 1823. The following year she accompanied Rossini to London and, after a disastrous appearance as Zelmira, retired from the stage. She and Rossini were formally separated in 1837. In her prime, she was greatly admired in Italy for the brilliance and power of her voice and the command of her stage presence.

ES (R. Celletti)
Stendhal: *La vie de Rossini* (Paris, 1824; Eng. trans., 1956)
C. Ricci: *Rossini: le sue case e le sue donne* (Milan, 1889)
G. Radiciotti: *Gioacchino Rossini: vita documentata* (Tivoli, 1927–9)
G. H. Johnston [Lord Derwent]: *Rossini and some Forgotten Nightingales* (London, 1934)
H. Weinstock: *Rossini: a Biography* (New York, 1968)
R. Osborne: *Rossini* (London 1986, 2/1987) ELIZABETH FORBES

Cold, Ulrik (Thestrup) (*b* Copenhagen, 15 May 1939). Danish bass. He studied at Copenhagen, where he sang with the university opera, notably as Seneca in Monteverdi's *L'incoronazione di Poppea*. From 1969 to 1971 he was engaged at Kassel, and then returned to Copenhagen, becoming director of the Royal Theatre there (1975–7). His repertory includes Wagner's Fasolt, King Mark, Pogner, Amfortas and Gurnemanz, Verdi's Padre Guardiano (*Forza*) and Falstaff, and the title role of Massenet's *Don Quichotte*, which he sang at the Komische Oper, Berlin, in 1971. His warm-toned, resonant voice and dignified stage presence make him an ideal Sarastro, the role in which he made his American début at San Francisco (1980). In 1981 he sang Allazim (*Zaide*) at Wexford and in 1987, Méphistophélès (Gounod's *Faust*) for the ENO, returning in 1990 as the General (*The Gambler*). ELIZABETH FORBES

Cole, Hugo (*b* London, 6 July 1917). English composer. He was educated at Winchester and King's College, Cambridge, where he read natural sciences. Already an accomplished cellist, he entered the RCM in 1944 to study the instrument as well as composition with Herbert Howells. He played in various London orchestras and also studied with Boulanger in Paris. Since 1964 he has been a music critic for *The Guardian*.

Cole's music has something of the same quality as his criticism. It is fresh, never short of good ideas and, if limited in expressive and structural scope, never pretentious. The clarity of his writing, its uncomplicated rhythms, and the general familiarity of his idiom – basically neo-classical and recognizably English in spite of the echoes of Copland – have made him a particularly successful composer of operas and other pieces for young and amateur performers.

Asses' Ears (children's op, 3 scenes, H. Cole), London, Wimbledon, Rokeby School, 12 Dec 1950
A Statue for the Mayor (children's op, 3, Cole), London, Wimbledon High School, 17 July 1952
Persephone (children's op, 3, Cole), London, Wimbledon High School, 14 July 1955
Flax into Gold, 1957 (children's op, 3 scenes, C. Storr), Oxford, 1966
The Tunnel (3, Cole), London, John Lewis auditorium, 24 Oct 1960
The Falcon (chamber op, 1, N. Platt, after G. Boccaccio), Bath, Shawford Mill, 29 Aug 1968
The Fair Traders (boys' op, 3 scenes, Cole), Wokingham, Town Hall, 30 Aug 1971 GERALD LARNER

Cole, Vinson (*b* Kansas City, MO, 20 Nov 1950). American tenor. He studied at the Curtis Institute, Philadelphia, singing Werther in 1975 before becoming a Santa Fe apprentice. In 1976 he sang Belmonte for the WNO and created Innis Brown in Ulysses Kay's *Jubilee* at Jackson, Mississippi. At St Louis (1976–80) he sang Count Ory, Ernesto and Tamino. In 1981 he sang Nicolai's Fenton for the New York City Opera and Rodolfo at Santa Fe. He has sung in Salzburg, Paris, Marseilles, Boston, Stuttgart and Naples. His roles have included Paolino (*Il matrimonio segreto*), Faust, Nadir, Des Grieux (*Manon*), Gennaro (*Lucrezia Borgia*), Percy (*Anna Bolena*), Lensky and Gluck's Orpheus, which perfectly displays the elegant style of his singing and the evenness of his lyrical voice. ELIZABETH FORBES

Coleman [Colman]. English family of musicians active in the 17th century.

(1) **Charles Coleman** (*d* London, bur. 8 July 1664). Composer, instrumentalist and singer. He sang Hymen in Robert White's masque *Cupid's Banishment* (1617) and appeared as singer and player in Shirley's *The Triumph of Peace* (1634). He wrote instrumental music for Davenant's *First Daye's Entertainment at Rutland-House* and for the work generally considered to be the first English opera, *The Siege of Rhodes* (1656). Songs and instrumental music by him survive in manuscript and published song books. During the Commonwealth he earned his living by teaching, but was otherwise a member of the King's Musick, as was his son Charles

(bap. 27 Feb 1620; *d* 1694), who played the bass viol in Crowne's court masque *Calisto* (1675).

(2) **Edward Coleman** (*b* London, bap. 27 April 1622; *d* Greenwich, 29 Aug 1669). Tenor and composer, son of Charles Coleman. He taught music during the Commonwealth and wrote songs, including one for Shirley's *The Contention of Ajax and Ulysses.* In 1656 he sang in *The First Daye's Entertainment at Rutland-House* and took the part of Alphonso in *The Siege of Rhodes.* He was a member of the King's Musick and Chapel Royal from 1660 but Pepys noted that his voice was 'quite spoiled' in October 1665.

(3) **Catherine Coleman** (*d* after 1669). Singer, wife of Edward Coleman. In *The Siege of Rhodes* (1656) she sang the heroine Ianthe (wife of Alphonso, played by her husband) and so became one of the first women to appear on the public stage in England. At Pepys's house in 1665 she sang extracts from this opera 'very finely, though her voice is decayed as to strength; but mighty sweet'.

*

BDA
E. J. Dent: *Foundations of English Opera* (Cambridge, 1928)
I. Spink: *English Song: Dowland to Purcell* (London, 1974, 2/1986), 115–18, 125
OLIVE BALDWIN, THELMA WILSON

Coleman, Cy [Kaufman, Seymour] (*b* Bronx, NY, 14 June 1929). American composer. He gave his first piano recital when he was six and studied in New York at the High School of Music and the College of Music. He initially played for nightclubs and worked for television and radio, becoming known as a songwriter. He went on to write Broadway musicals that reflected his heterogeneous background and which included effective parodies of classical styles as well as hit songs. *Wildcat* (1960) was an unpretentious Broadway-style vehicle for Lucille Ball; *Little Me* (1962), to a book by Neil Simon, was a very amusing burlesque of the celebrity biography with astutely witty musical illustrations; *Sweet Charity* (1966, after a Fellini film) was a brassy Tin Pan Alley entertainment, with much emphasis on dance, imitated less winningly in *Seesaw* (1973). Among the most versatile of Broadway composers, Coleman then wrote a small-scale comedy with songs, *I Love my Wife* (1977), which enjoyed a long run, a dazzling operetta burlesque, *On the Twentieth Century* (1978), and, in *Barnum* (1980), a surprisingly moving piece of spectacular razzmatazz which has been played more widely outside the USA than any other of his works. His more recent compositions, however, have failed to attract Broadway production.

Coleridge-Taylor, Samuel [Taylor, Samuel Coleridge] (*b* London, 15 Aug 1875; *d* Croydon, 1 Sept 1912). English composer. His father, a native of Sierra Leone, was a doctor. Until recently it was thought that Samuel's mother, an Englishwoman, was left to bring him up on her own when her husband returned to Africa, but Butterworth has suggested that Samuel was fostered by a member of the Coleridge family. Samuel entered the RCM as a violin student. He began to study composition with Stanford in 1892, was awarded an open scholarship for composition in 1893 and won the Lesley Alexander composition prize in 1895 and 1896. He left the RCM in 1897 and became well known as a composer of choral works and incidental music for the theatre. But his operatic output consists of only one opera, *Thelma* op.72 (in 3 acts, 1907–9; not published), of which only the prelude was performed; the 'operatic romance' *Dream Lovers* op.25 (1, P. L. Dunbar; Croydon, Public Hall, 16 Dec 1898), set in Madagascar and concerned with black consciousness; and the cantata-operetta *The Gitanos* op.26 for female school voices (E. Oxenford; London, 1898), though he had also had hopes of the cantata *Endymion's Dream* op.65 (C. R. B. Barrett; Brighton, 5 Feb 1910) being staged at Her Majesty's Theatre by Beerbohm Tree. His fame rests chiefly on the cantata *Hiawatha's Wedding Feast* (1898). In addition to composing, Coleridge-Taylor was an excellent conductor; and he visited the USA in 1904, 1906 and 1910 at the invitation of the Coleridge-Taylor Choral Society, founded in Washington, DC, in 1901 for black singers. His early death from pneumonia seems to have been partly a result of overwork.

His son Hiawatha (*b* Croydon, 15 Oct 1900; *d* London, 20 Jan 1980) conducted Coleridge-Taylor's ballet music in the staged performances of *Hiawatha* at the Albert Hall, the first of which took place on 19 May 1924.

*

W. C. Berwick Sayers: *Samuel Coleridge-Taylor, Musician: His Life and Letters* (London, 1915, 2/1927)
A. Coleridge-Taylor: *The Heritage of Samuel Coleridge-Taylor* (London, 1979)
J. Green and P. McGilchrist: 'Samuel Coleridge-Taylor: a Postscript', *The Black Perspective in Music*, xiv/3 (1986), 259–66
S. Butterworth: 'Coleridge-Taylor: New Facts for Old Fiction', *MT*, cxxx (1989), 202–4
J. Green: '"The Foremost Musician of his Race": Samuel Coleridge-Taylor of England, 1875–1912', *Black Music Research Journal*, x/2 (1990), 233–52
STEPHEN BANFIELD

Colette [Gauthier-Villars, Sidonie Gabriel] (*b* St Sauveur-en-Puisaye, 28 Jan 1873; *d* Paris, 3 Aug 1954). French writer. After she married the music critic known as Willy (Henri Gauthier-Villars) she became prominent in Parisian musical circles, and her association with the world of music continued long after their divorce. She was the librettist of Ravel's *L'enfant et les sortilèges*, but the collaboration involved little personal contact and it was not until after Ravel had finished the opera that she came to know him. Her infamous 'Claudine' novels, which Willy published under his own name, created a vogue, one result of which was the operetta *Claudine* by Rodolphe Berger. Music criticisms signed 'Claudine' were probably Colette's work and on several occasions she was sent to the same concert as Debussy to produce a different viewpoint.

*

H. Jourdan-Morhange: *Ravel et nous* (Geneva, 1945)
Colette: *En pays connu* (Paris, 1949) [memoirs relating to Ravel and *L'enfant et les sortilèges*]
——: *Lettres à ses pairs* (Paris, 1973) [letters to Ravel]
M. Crosland: 'Colette and Ravel: the Enchantress and the Illusionist', *Colette, the Woman, the Writer*, ed. E. Eisinger Mendelson and M. Ward McCarty (Pennsylvania, 1981), 116–24
RICHARD LANGHAM SMITH

Coletti [Colletti], **Agostino Bonaventura** (*b* Lucca, *c*1680; *d* Venice, 1752). Italian composer. He was an organist in Lucca, but by 1699 he had settled in Venice and in the same year was accepted as a member of the Accademia Filarmonica of Bologna.

He wrote his earliest dramatic work, *Bruto e Cassio*, in 1699 for the festivities celebrating the election of the city councillors in Lucca, referred to as the *Tasche*. His first standard opera was a small-scale pastoral for Rovigo in 1700. Six years later, he provided the music for the 1706–7 season at the Teatro S Angelo, the least prestigious of the large Venetian theatres. For the autumn production he arranged Mancia's *Paride in Ida*, another pastoral. The carnival production, *Ifigenia*, was his only fully-fledged serious work. Aside from the three operas of his Venetian years, his professional commitments before 1714 are unclear. From 7 December 1714 he served as third organist at St Mark's, and from 21 May 1736 he served as first organist and assistant *maestro di cappella*. In the 1720s, he provided dramatic compositions for three successive *Tasche* (1723, 1726, 1729). The music of his operas is not known to survive.

The cantatas of Coletti's op.1 (1699) show that his style resembled that of contemporary Venetian opera composers. Arias are usually in da capo form, often beginning with a motto. The focus is on the vocal part, the continuo sharing the same declamatory style as the voice.

Bruto e Cassio (componimento per musica, Contarini), Lucca, Dec 1699
Prassitele in Gnido (dramma pastorale, 3, A. Aureli), Rovigo, Manfredini, carn. 1700
Paride in Ida (dramma pastorale, 3, F. Mazzari), Venice, S Angelo, aut. 1706, collab. C. Mancia, perf. with intermezzos, Lesbina e Milo
Ifigenia (dramma per musica, 3, A. Aureli, after P. Riva), Venice, S Angelo, 3 Jan 1707
Muzio Scevola (componimento per musica), Lucca, Dec 1723
Codro re d'Atene (componimento per musica), Lucca, Dec 1726
Timoleonte cittadino di Corinto (componimento per musica), Lucca, Dec 1729

*

L. Nerici: *Storia della musica in Lucca* (Lucca, 1879)

HARRIS S. SAUNDERS

Coletti, Filippo (*b* Anagni, 11 May 1811; *d* Anagni, 13 June 1894). Italian baritone. He studied with Alessandro Busti in Naples and made his début there (1834) at the Teatro del Fondo in *Il turco in Italia*. Engaged by the Teatro S Carlo, he created Lusignano in *Caterina Cornaro* (1844) and Gusmano in *Alzira* (1845). In 1844 he created Carlo in *Ernani*. His engagement by Lumley to sing at Her Majesty's Theatre, London (1840), led to riots, the public evidently considering it an attempt to displace Tamburini, their favourite baritone. When Tamburini defected to Covent Garden (1846) Coletti was re-engaged by Lumley, and he sang Francesco opposite Jenny Lind in the première of *I masnadieri* (1847). Later he sang in the first Rome performance (1851) of *Rigoletto* (given under the title *Viscardello*). He retired from the stage in 1869. First in bel canto roles, then in Verdi, his performances were distinguished by their dramatic integrity and eschewal of mere virtuosity.

*

H. Chorley: *Thirty Years' Musical Recollections* (London, 1862)
B. Lumley: *Reminiscences of the Opera* (London, 1864)

HAROLD ROSENTHAL/R

Colgrass, Michael (Charles) (*b* Chicago, 22 April 1932). American composer. He graduated from the University of Illinois (BMus 1956), and studied composition with Milhaud, Riegger and Foss, among others. The recipient of many grants, fellowships and commissions, he is particularly well known for his orchestral and percussion works. In 1978 he won the Pulitzer Prize for his percussion piece with orchestra, *Déjà vu*.

Colgrass has written three operas, *Virgil's Dream* (1967), *Nightingale, Inc.* (1971) and *Something's Gonna Happen* (1978). *Virgil's Dream* is described by the composer as 'a satiric fantasy for musical chamber theatre'. 'Musical chamber theatre' is intended to indicate that the small ensemble of instrumentalists, singers and actors tell the story interchangeably, instrumentalists taking speaking roles, actors singing roles, and singers playing props. The story focusses on a child prodigy who is offered an insurance policy protecting his dream of a concert career against damage, loss or theft. The musical style is heavily influenced by jazz, with the absence of a conductor achieving a certain spontaneity in performance; some aleatory devices are used. The harmonic language is mainly atonal, with sections of tonal stability. Verbal clarity is the central driving force. *Something's Gonna Happen*, commissioned under a grant from the Ontario Arts Council, is a modern-day version of Jack and the Beanstalk. The Opera for Youth Publisher's Reading Clinic characterizes the work as a 'fanciful score in which plot, character and music combine artistically to make an exceptionally fine children's opera'. Tone clusters and syncopated rhythms are used within a basically tonal harmonic language. Some jazz influence is felt, especially in dance numbers, and the simple instrumental support (piano with obbligato flute) adds to the work's accessibility.

Virgil's Dream (music-theatre work, 1, M. Colgrass), Brighton, April 1967, vs (New York, 1976)
Nightingale, Inc., 1971 (comic op, 1, Colgrass), Champaign, IL, 1975
Something's Gonna Happen (children's musical, 1, Colgrass), Toronto, Huron Elementary School, May 1978, vs (New York, 1982)

JAMES P. CASSARO

Colini [Collini], **Filippo** (*b* Rome, 21 Oct 1811; *d* ? May 1863). Italian baritone. In both contemporary and modern sources he is sometimes confused with Virgilio Collini or Filippo Coletti. He studied with Camillo Angiolini at the Collegio Romano. Early in 1835 he appeared at the opera house in Fabriano, and during the autumn made his début at the Teatro Valle, Rome. Thereafter he was engaged at major Italian theatres in Palermo (1838–41, 1852–4), Naples (1841–2, 1848, 1855–7), Genoa (1842–3, 1854–5), Milan (1844–5) and Rome (1844, 1845–6, 1848–9, 1849–50), among others, and in Paris and Vienna.

During his early career his repertory consisted mainly of works by Donizetti, especially *Torquato Tasso*; later he concentrated on Verdi's operas, in particular *Nabucco*, *Ernani* and *Luisa Miller*. He sang Luigi XIV in the première of Campana's *Luisa di Francia* (1844), Severo in Donizetti's *Poliuto* (1848) and Inquaro in Eugenio Terziani's *Alfredo* (1852), and he created roles in three Verdi operas: Giacomo in *Giovanna d'Arco* (1845), Rolando in *La battaglia di Legnano* (1849) and Stankar in *Stiffelio* (1850). The gracefulness, flexibility and delicacy of his high baritone voice is said to have compensated for his meagre interpretational abilities.

*

ES (R. Celletti); *GSL*
A. Ghislanzoni: *Gli artisti da teatro*, vi (Milan, 1865), 63
G. Monaldi: *Cantanti celebri (1829–1929)* (Rome, 1929), 64

ROBERTA MONTEMORRA MARVIN

Coliseum. London theatre, home since 1968 of the English National Opera (Sadler's Wells Opera until 1974); *see* LONDON, §II, 2.

Colla, Giuseppe (*b* Parma, 4 Aug 1731; *d* Parma, 16 March 1806). Italian composer. According to Pelicelli, he was born on 4 August 1739. The occurrence of six arias by him in the opera *Caio Fabricio* (mainly by Jommelli) at Mannheim in 1760 suggests that he visited Germany. In 1766 he became *maestro di cappella* at the court of Duke Ferdinand of Parma, where from 1780 until his death he was also concert leader at the Teatro Ducale. He taught the duke and, after 1785, his son Prince Ludovico.

Colla had a long liaison with the celebrated soprano LUCREZIA AGUIARI, who sang his operas and little else in many northern Italian cities in the 1770s. The couple also visited Paris and London, where they appeared at the Pantheon Theatre during the 1775 season. Burney wrote that 'she sung hardly any other Music while she was here than her husband's, Signor Colla, which, though often good, was not of the original and varied cast which could supply the place of every other master, ancient and modern'.

Except for a single antiphon of 1757, none of the sacred music that Fétis claimed Colla wrote can be found today. On the other hand, scenographic drawings in pen and acquarelle by the Galliari brothers for *Andromeda* (1771, Turin) and *Didone* (1773, Turin; for illustration *see* OPERA SERIA, fig.4) have been discovered (in *I-Ms*, *Tmc*, *GB-Lva*, the Pinacoteca, Bologna, and the Pogliaghi Collection, near Varese). Most of his operas survive in scores copied for the library of King José of Portugal, now in the Ajuda Palace, Lisbon. Fétis cautioned that this composer should not be confused with another Giuseppe Colla of early 19th-century Milan, whose works Ricordi published.

opere serie unless otherwise stated

Adriano in Siria (P. Metastasio), Milan, Regio Ducal, 31 Dec 1762, arias *I-Nc*, *P-La* (2 copies)
Tigrane (F. Silvani), Parma, Ducale, 1766 or 1767, arias *I-PAc*
Enea in Cartagine (G. M. Orengo), Turin, Regio, 26 Dec 1769, *Tf*, *P-La* (1 complete copy, 1 of Act 2)
Licida e Mopso (pastorale), Colorno, 1769, *A-Wn*
Vologeso (A. Zeno), Venice, S Benedetto, 24 May 1770
L'eroe cinese (Metastasio), Genoa, S Agostino, 8 Aug 1771, arias *I-Gl*, *MAav*
Andromeda (V. A. Cigna-Santi), Turin, Regio, 26 Dec 1771, *D-Bds*, *I-Tf*, *P-La* (1 complete copy, 1 of Act 3)
Didone (Metastasio), Turin, Regio, carn. 1773, *I-Tf*, *P-La* (2 copies), arias *D-MH*, *I-Gl*
Tolomeo (L. Salvoni), Milan, Regio Ducal, 26 Dec 1773, *F-Pn*, *P-La*, 1 aria *GB-Lbl*
Sicotencal (C. Olivieri), Pavia, Quattro Signori, spr. 1776

6 arias in Caio Fabricio, Mannheim, 1760, *D-B*

*

BurneyH; *FétisB*
J. Harris, Earl of Malmesbury, ed.: *A Series of Letters of the First Earl of Malmesbury*, i (London, 1870), 297
A. Della Corte: 'Musiche italiane e francesi alla corte di Parma', *La stampa* (Turin, 22 Jan 1929)
N. Pelicelli: 'Musicisti in Parma nel sec. XVIII', *NA*, xi (1934), 239–81, esp. 272
M. Viale Ferrero: *La scenografia del '700 e i fratelli Galliari* (Turin, 1963), 227, 236, 245, 247, 250, 252ff, 265, 274ff
J. Jaenecke: *Die Musikbibliothek des L. Freiherrn von Pretlack* (Wiesbaden, 1973), 190, 262 SVEN HANSELL

Collasse [Colasse]**, Pascal** [Paschal, Pasquier] (*b* Reims, bap. 22 Jan 1649; *d* Versailles, 17 July 1709). French composer. His career was dominated by his association with Jean-Baptiste Lully, whose influence can be said to have worked both to the benefit and to the detriment of the younger man. At first a pupil and friend of Lully's, and helped by him to secure musical appointments at court, Collasse replaced Lallouette as Lully's secretary and as *batteur de mesure* at the Académie Royale de Musique (the Opéra); in both these positions he was ideally placed to learn the craft of *tragédie en musique* as devised and solely practised by Lully.

Among the tasks of Lully's secretaries was to take down the music he dictated and to write the inner parts of his instrumental numbers and choruses. When Lully died in 1687, Collasse was entrusted with the completion of his *Achille et Polyxène*, for which Lully had composed only an overture and the first act. This production was only a modest success. Just over a year later, however, the fortunes of the Académie seemed to improve with the resounding success of Collasse's *Thétis et Pélée*, the first performance of which took place just four days after the composer's marriage to the daughter of the theatre designer Jean Berain. The king attended a performance of *Thétis* at the Trianon a month later (the *Mercure galant* made a particular point of mentioning that this was, unusually for a concert performance, done in costume), and expressed his appreciation of the music. Subsequent revivals of the opera maintained its popularity and put it among the very few operas produced in France between *Armide* and *Hippolyte et Aricie* that had anything like the durability of their Lullian models.

Nothing that Collasse later wrote was able to reproduce this success, although his next opera, *Enée et Lavinie*, did well at first. Soon, however, verses lampooning the work and its authors began to circulate. Fontenelle was criticized for making the action too dependent on interventions and for the poor quality of his verse, which, like that of every other librettist of the period, was unfavourably compared with that of Lully's librettist, Quinault. The exception in a run of failures for Collasse was the *Ballet des saisons* (1695); the public's reception of it showed a taste for a new operatic form, the *opéra-ballet*, which was to emerge fully fledged two years later with Campra's *L'Europe galante*.

Although the year 1696 saw Collasse securing further royal appointments, it was otherwise a disastrous year for him. *Jason* survived less than a month, one writer providing an obituary: '*Jason* expired yesterday, leaving just 700 livres, and the *parterre* and the *loges* will sing the Libera [me] for him with little regret'. A second opera, *La naissance de Vénus*, fared little better, and in between the two, Collasse was the object of a bitter attack by *Jason*'s librettist, Jean-Baptiste Rousseau, who accused him of plagiarizing Lully. He was granted a privilege to found an opera company at Lille; this too was to end in disaster when the theatre burnt down. Titon du Tillet paints a sad picture of the latter part of Collasse's life: 'We would have had yet more works by this musician ... if he had not had the urge and the misfortune to search for the philosopher's stone; ... this research served only to ruin him and weaken his health'. Collasse's last opera, *Polyxène et Pyrrhus* (1706), failed miserably; his state of mind probably did not allow him to enjoy the success of the revival of *Thétis et Pélée* in 1708, and he died just over a year later.

Collasse had to choose whether to strike out on his own and make radical changes, or keep closely to the model he had inherited. Given Lully's popularity, the first path might have been suicidal; the safer way, however, left him open to the charge of plagiarism. In the preface to *La naissance de Vénus*, he carefully explained that he had incorporated 13 instrumental items by Lully, printing only their incipits. In other works he was suspected, probably unjustly, of doing more than this.

Le Cerf's verdict was that while Collasse had indeed used airs by Lully, he had not concealed the fact.

Despite his setbacks, Collasse was still able to make some innovations. *Achille et Polyxène* already shows a substantial increase in the number of dances, presaging the development of the *opéra-ballet*. Vocal lines sometimes show a freer use of decoration than Lully had permitted, and scene types from Lully's operas are used to great effect; episodes such as the temple scene in *Achille et Polyxène*, involving a disclosure made by an oracle, became extremely popular. A feel for instrumental colour is also often apparent: in *Enée et Lavinie* Collasse used a crumhorn and *taille de hautbois*, contrasting flutes and recorders in one scene with oboes in the next (the oboes accompanying the oracle), and specifying with unusual precision changes of dynamics and scoring for the repeats of dance movements. Most startling, however, is the *tempête* in *Thétis et Pélée*. The rushing scales and tremolando effects in the outer parts and the way the storm is sustained through subsequent choral and vocal scenes mark a significant departure from Lully. The notational complications completely defeated the antiquated movable type of the Ballard publishing house, and so the 'tempête' in the full score of 1689 was engraved. Although Collasse did not write a full-scale *tempête* again, other composers began to use the orchestra freely for descriptive effects suggesting both natural and supernatural phenomena, and it is perhaps in the handling of the orchestra that Collasse made his most important contribution to the slow process of change in the *tragédie en musique* after Lully.

See also *Ballet des saisons* and *Thétis et Pélée*.

Achille et Polyxène (tragédie en musique, prol., 5, J.-G. de Campistron), Paris, Opéra, 23 Nov 1687 (Paris, 1687) [ov., Act 1 by Lully]

Divertissement, ou Impromptu de Livry (F. C. Dancourt), July 1688, *F-Pn*

Thétis et Pélée (tragédie en musique, prol., 5, B. le Bovier de Fontenelle), Paris, Opéra, 11 Jan 1689 (Paris, 1689); rev. version, Opéra, 16 April 1708, with airs nouveaux (Paris, 1708) by J.-B. Stuck and A. Campra

Sigalion, ou Le secret (ballet, after Latin tragedy: *Polymnestor*), Paris, Collège Louis-le-Grand, 17 Aug 1689, *Pn*

Amarillis, 1689 (pastorale, J. Pic), unperf., *Pa*

Enée et Lavinie (tragédie en musique, prol., 5, Fontenelle), Paris, Opéra, 7 Nov 1690 (Paris, 1690/*R*1972)

Ballet de Villeneuve St-Georges (ballet, 3 entrées, Banzy), Villeneuve St-Georges, 1 Sept 1692, *Pn*

Astrée [et Céladon] (tragédie en musique, prol., 3, J. de La Fontaine), Paris, Opéra, 25 Nov 1692, *Pn*

Ballet des saisons (opéra-ballet, prol., 4 entrées, Pic), Paris, Opéra, 14, 15 or 18 Oct 1695, reduced score (Paris, 1695, 2/1700)

Jason, ou La toison d'or (tragédie en musique, prol., 5, J.-B. Rousseau), Paris, Opéra, 6/15 Jan 1696, *Pa*, *Pn*

La naissance de Vénus ('opéra', prol., 5, Pic), Paris, Opéra, 1 May 1696, *Pn*, reduced score (Paris, 1696), incl. some items by Lully

Canente [Picus et Canente] (tragédie en musique, prol., 5, A. H. de Lamotte), Paris, Opéra, 4 Nov 1700, *Pn*, *Po*

L'Amour et l'Hymen (divertissement, prol., 8 scenes), private perf., 1701, for marriage of the Prince of Conti

Polyxène et Pyrrhus (tragédie en musique, prol., 5, J.-L.-I. de La Serre), Paris, Opéra, 21 Oct 1706 (Paris, 1706)

Music in: Lully: Atys, Rennes, 1689; Télémaque, ou Les fragmens des modernes, 1704

*

Recueil général des opéra (Paris, 1703–46)

J.-L. Le Cerf de la Viéville: *Comparaison de la musique italienne et de la musique françoise* (Brussels, 1704–6)

E. Titon du Tillet: *Description du Parnasse françois* (Paris, 1727)

C. Parfaict and F. Parfaict: *Histoire de l'Académie royale de musique depuis son établissement jusqu'à présent* (MS, 1741, *F-Pn*)

[J.-B. Durey de Noinville]: *Histoire du théâtre de l'Académie royale de musique en France* (Paris, 1757)

A. Jal: *Dictionnaire critique de biographie et d'histoire* (Paris, 1867, 2/1872)

T. de Lajarte: *Bibliothèque musicale du Théâtre de l'Opéra: catalogue* (Paris, 1878)

M. Teneo: 'Miettes historiques: Correspondance théâtrale du XVIIe siècle', *Le mercure musicale*, i (1905), 577–83, 620–27; ii (1906), 21–8, 71–8

L. de La Laurencie: 'La musique française de Lulli à Gluck: première partie: l'opéra de 1687 à 1787', *EMDC*, I/iii (1921), 1362–1457

C. Masson: 'Journal du Marquis de Dangeau, 1684–1720: extraits concernant la vie musicale à la cour', *RMFC*, ii (1962), 193–228

J. R. Anthony: 'The French Opéra-ballet in the Early 18th Century: Problems of Definition and Classification', *JAMS*, xviii (1965), 197–206

A. Ducrot: 'Les représentations de l'Académie royale de musique à Paris au temps de Louis XIV (1671–1715)', *RMFC*, x (1970), 19–55

M. Benoit: *Musiques de cour: chapelle, chambre, écurie, 1661–1733* (Paris, 1971)

G. Sadler: Introduction to P. Collasse: *Enée et Lavinie* (Farnborough, 1972)

J. R. Anthony: *French Baroque Music from Beaujoyeulx to Rameau* (London, 1973, 2/1978)

R. M. Isherwood: *Music in the Service of the King* (Ithaca, NY, and London, 1973)

E. Lemaître: *L'orchestre dans le théâtre lyrique français chez les continuateurs de Lully, 1687–1715* (thesis, Paris Conservatoire, 1977)

J. de La Gorce: 'L'Académie royale de musique en 1704, d'après des documents inédits conservés dans les archives notariales', *RdM*, lxv (1979), 170–91

C. Wood: *Jean-Baptiste Lully and his Successors: Music and Drama in the 'tragédie en musique' 1673–1715* (diss., U. of Hull, 1981)

——: 'Orchestra and Spectacle in the *tragédie en musique*, 1673–1715: oracle, *sommeil* and *tempête*', *PRMA*, cviii (1981–2), 25–46

J. de La Gorce: 'Documents de critique musicale et théâtrale: dix lettres extraites de la correspondance entre Ladvocat et l'Abbé Dubos (1694–1696)', *XVIIe siècle*, cxxxix (1983), 267–82

E. Lemaître: 'Le premier opéra-ballet et la première tempête: deux originalités de l'oeuvre de Pascal Colasse', *XVIIe siècle*, no. 139 (1983), 243–55

R. Fajon: *L'opéra à Paris du Roi-Soleil à Louis le Bien-aimé* (Geneva, 1984)

W. Weber: '*La musique ancienne* in the Waning of the Ancien Régime', *Journal of Modern History*, lvi (1984), 58–88

CAROLINE WOOD

Collier, Marie (*b* Ballarat, 16 April 1927; *d* London, 7 Dec 1971). Australian soprano. She studied in Melbourne, making her début there in 1954 as Santuzza, then touring as Magda in *The Consul*. After further study in Milan and London, she joined Covent Garden in 1956 where she sang 293 performances in 15 seasons. Her roles included Musetta, Giulietta, Liù, Butterfly, Manon Lescaut, Giorgetta, Elisabeth de Valois, Aida, Jenůfa, Marie (*Wozzeck*), Lisa (*Queen of Spades*), Gutrune, Chrysothemis (which she recorded for Solti), Hecuba in *King Priam* (a role she created in Coventry in 1962) and Katerina Izmaylova in the first British staging of Shostakovich's opera (1963). At Sadler's Wells she sang Venus, Concepcion, Kát'a and Tosca. In 1965 she took over from Callas as Tosca at Covent Garden. She made her San Francisco début in 1964 as Katerina, returning as Minnie, Emilia Marty and the Woman (*Erwartung*). In 1967 she created Christine in Levy's *Mourning Becomes Electra* at the Metropolitan, later singing Santuzza and Musetta. Her vibrant, lustrous voice, flamboyant personality and acute instinct for drama were spectacularly displayed as Renata in Prokofiev's *The Fiery Angel* (first British staging, New Opera Company, 1965) and as Emilia Marty.

*

A. Blyth: 'Marie Collier', *Opera*, xix (1968), 953–7

ALAN BLYTH

Collin [Colin] **de Blamont, François** (*b* Versailles, 22 Nov 1690; *d* Versailles, 14 Feb 1760). French composer. Encouraged by Lalande from his 'tender childhood', Collin showed early promise, and help from influential friends led to prestigious appointments at court such as *surintendant de la musique de la chambre* (1719). Although passed over as *sous-maître de la chapelle* in 1723 in favour of Bernier, Campra and Gervais, he became *maître de musique de la chambre* on Lalande's death in 1726. The post of *surintendant* carried with it responsibility for music on great state occasions, and Collin was not slow to assert his precedence over the *sous-maîtres*. He failed to reach the levels of invention of most of his contemporaries, but this did not prevent some of his mature works for the stage from becoming popular, and remaining in the repertory for long periods. Particularly successful, thanks in part to the experienced librettist, Fuzelier, was *Les festes grecques et romaines*; the preface lays claim to the creation of a new genre, the *ballet-héroïque*. While Voltaire was scornful of the work ('at the Opéra, it was whistled by all honest people'), the *Mercure* declared in 1733 that 'never has a revival at the Opéra been more brilliant nor more applauded'. Substantial excerpts from *Les caractères de l'amour* were in the repertory of the Esterházy court ensemble by 1759.

See also FESTES GRECQUES ET ROMAINES, LES.

Les festes grecques et romaines (ballet-héroïque, prol., 3 (later 4) entrées, L. Fuzelier), Paris, Opéra, 13 July 1723 (Paris, 1723); rev. (? with changes by B. de Bury), 11 June 1733, Recueil des Airs ajoutées aux Fêtes grecques et romaines (Paris, *c*1733); 4th entrée added, Paris, Opéra, 9 Feb 1734 (Paris, *c*1734); *F-Pn*

Le retour des dieux sur la terre (divertissement, prol., 5 scenes, A. Tannevot), Fontainebleau, Sept 1725 (Paris, 1727)

Le Caprice d'Erato, ou Les caractères de la musique (divertissement, prol., 1, Fuzelier), Paris, Opéra, 28 Sept 1730 (Paris, 1730) [substituted for prol. of Marais' Alcyone from 8 Oct 1730]

Diane et Endymion (pastorale héroïque, prol., 5 entrées, B. Le Bovier de Fontenelle), Paris, Opéra, 17 May 1731, *Pc*; (Paris, 1731)

Les caractères de l'amour (ballet-héroïque, prol., 3 (later 4) entrées, S.-J. Pellegrin and ? M. A. Barbier), Dec 1736; Paris, Opéra, 15 April 1738 (Paris, 1738); 4th entrée (M. de Bonneval) added, 6 Jan 1739; *Pn*

Jupiter, vainqueur des Titans (tragédie lyrique, prol., 5, Bonneval), Versailles, 11 Dec 1745, lib. (Paris, 1745); collab. Bury

Les fêtes de Thétis (ballet-héroïque, prol., 2 entrées, P.-C. Roy), Versailles, 14 Jan 1750, *Pn*; Entrée 2 by Bury, dances by E. C. Hesse

Divertissements (music lost): Les présents des dieux (idylle héroïque, Pellegrin), 1727; Les fêtes du labyrinthe, 1728 [according to Fétis]; Ballet & Concert du Parnasse (pastiche, prol., 5 entrées), Versailles, 21 Sept 1729 [entrées by Collin de Blamont, Lully, Campra, Destouches and Mouret]; Le jardin des Hesperides (ballet), Compiègne, 27 Aug 1739; Zéphire et Flore, Fontainebleau, 16 Nov 1739; Bazile et Quitterie (ballet, Greffec), Versailles, 7 March 1740; L'heureux retour de la reine, 1744 [according to Fétis]; Les regrets des beaux-arts [according to Fétis]; Il pastor fido [according to Fétis]

*

FétisB
E. Titon du Tillet: *La Parnasse françois* (Paris, 1732–55)
M. Marais: *Journal et mémoires* (Paris, 1863–8)
J. Vasseur: 'Notice sur Collin de Blamont', *Mémoires de la Société des sciences morales de Seine-et-Oise*, xiii (1883), 373
P. Fromageot: *Les compositeurs de musique versaillais* (Versailles, 1906)
L. de La Laurencie: 'La musique française de Lulli à Gluck', *EMDC*, I/iii (1921), 1386–7
P.-M. Masson: 'Le "Ballet héroïque"', *ReM*, ix/8 (1927–8), 132–54
L. Vallas: *Un siècle de musique et de Théâtre à Lyon 1668–1789* (Lyons, 1932)
N. Dufourcq, ed.: *La musique à la Cour de Louis XIV et de Louis XV d'après les Mémoires de Sourches et Luynes 1681–1758* (Paris, 1970)
C. Massip: *François Collin de Blamont: musicien du roi* (diss., Paris Conservatoire, 1971)
J. E. Morby: 'The Great Chapel-Chamber Controversy', *MQ*, lviii (1972), 383–97
L. Sawkins: 'The Brothers Bêche: an Anecdotal History of Court Music', *RFMC*, xxiv (1986), 192–221
——: 'Classic and Baroque: Paris and the Esterházy court', *Haydn Society Newsletter*, x (1990), 5–17

LIONEL SAWKINS

Collingwood, Lawrance (Arthur) (*b* London, 14 March 1887; *d* Killin, Perthshire, 19 Dec 1982). English conductor and composer. He was a choirboy at Westminster Abbey, organ scholar at Exeter College, Oxford (1908–12), and then a student at the St Petersburg Conservatory, where his teachers included Nikolay Tcherepnin and Maximilian Steinberg. He graduated in 1917 and after military service in Britain returned to Petrograd as an assistant to Albert Coates, at that time a conductor at the Mariinsky Theatre. In 1920, back in London, he joined the music staff at the Old Vic, which at that period presented opera as well as plays. In 1931, when Sadler's Wells Theatre opened as an extension of that management, he became principal conductor of opera, and was largely responsible for the development of the company's repertory and standards. He shared with Coates the first performances in Britain of Rimsky-Korsakov's *The Tale of Tsar Saltan* (1933) and conducted the first performance outside Russia of *Boris Godunov* in Musorgsky's original score (1935). From the 1941–2 season until 1947 he was the company's musical director. In 1974 he emerged from retirement to conduct students of the London Opera Centre in *Le nozze di Figaro*.

Of Collingwood's own two operas, *Macbeth* had its première at Sadler's Wells on 12 April 1934 and *The Death of Tintagiles* received a concert performance as a tribute to him at Sadler's Wells Theatre on 16 April 1950. As a conductor he made many recordings of operatic selections for HMV. He was made a CBE in 1948.

*

D. Arundell: *The Story of Sadler's Wells* (London, 1965, 2/1978)

ARTHUR JACOBS

Collins, Anne (*b* Durham, 29 Aug 1943). English contralto. She studied in London at the RCM, making her début in 1970 as the Governess (*The Queen of Spades*) with Sadler's Wells (later the ENO), for whom she has sung Akhrosimova in *War and Peace* (1972) and Beroe in *The Bassarids* (1974), both British stage premières, as well as Ulrica, Erda, Podtochina (*The Nose*) and Mistress Quickly. She sang Mrs Page (*Die lustigen Weiber von Windsor*) at Wexford (1976) and made her Covent Garden début in 1977 as Anna (*Les Troyens*). For the WNO she has sung Filip'yevna (*Yevgeny Onegin*) and Sosostris (*The Midsummer Marriage*); in 1986 she sang Florence Pike (*Albert Herring*) at Glyndebourne and in 1990 the Nurse (*Ariane et Barbe-bleue*) with Opera North. Her repertory includes Mrs Herring, Auntie (*Peter Grimes*) and Handel's Dejanira (*Hercules*). A versatile singer with a strong, even voice, she is equally at home in Wagner and in Gilbert and Sullivan.

ELIZABETH FORBES

Collins, Kenneth (*b* Birmingham, 21 Oct 1935). English tenor. A member of the Covent Garden chorus, in 1963 he sang Pedrillo for the WNO. In 1970 he took over Arturo (*Lucia di Lammermoor*) at Covent Garden and sang Marcello in Leoncavallo's *La bohème* at Camden. He returned to the WNO in 1971 as Radames, subsequently singing Rodolfo, Cavaradossi, Des Grieux, Calaf, Chénier, Nadir, Erik, Manrico, Don Carlos, Carlo (*I masnadieri*), Riccardo and Ernani. For the ENO his roles have included Henri (*Les vêpres siciliennes*). He has sung at the New York City Opera, in Buenos Aires as Pollione and for Australian Opera, Sydney. His ringing voice and fierce attack are best suited to Verdi, especially such roles as Don Alvaro.

ELIZABETH FORBES

Colman. English family of theatre managers and librettists.

(1) **Francis Colman** (*b* ?Tiverton, Devon, *c*1690; *d* Pisa, 20 April 1733). Diplomat and opera lover. His marriage to Mary Gumley brought him into the family of William Pulteney (later the Earl of Bath), through whose influence he was appointed special envoy to Vienna in 1721. Three years later he was transferred to the court of the Grand Duke of Tuscany, at Florence, where he remained until his death. Letters to Handel and to Owen Swiney show that he helped re-engage Senesino for London in 1730. He adapted the libretto for Handel's *Arianna in Creta* (1734, London), but never heard it sung. He is believed by some to be the author of the 'Opera Register' (*GB-Lbl*), a brief record of operatic performances in London, 1712–15 and occasionally to 1734.

(2) **George Colman** (i) ('the elder') (*b* Florence, bap. 18 April 1732; *d* Paddington, London, 14 Aug 1794). Playwright, librettist and theatre manager, son of (1) Francis Colman. Named in honour of George II (godfather to children of His Majesty's envoys), he was brought up under the guardianship of his uncle, the Earl of Bath, who paid for his education in the law. He was more attracted to the theatre, however, and with considerable skill established himself as a writer in London. One of his best plays, co-written with David Garrick, was *The Clandestine Marriage* (Drury Lane, 20 Feb 1766); winning great critical and popular acclaim, it later became the basis for Cimarosa's *Il matrimonio segreto* (1792). Meanwhile he wrote works for Covent Garden, of which he was manager from 1767 to the spring of 1774, including the burletta *The Portrait* and the pantomime *Mother Shipton* (both 1770 with music by Samuel Arnold); he also adapted pieces for Arne in 1771–3. Later he managed the Haymarket Theatre, employing Arnold as house composer.

(3) **George Colman** (ii) ('the younger') (*b* London, 21 Oct 1762; *d* London, 26 Oct 1836). Librettist, playwright and theatre manager, son of (2) George Colman (i). Though trained for the law, like his father he was drawn to the stage. His three-act comedy *Two to One* (1784) was the first of his several pieces to be set by Arnold (their *Inkle and Yarico* of 1787 became one of the most popular comic operas of the age). He increasingly took over the Haymarket management after his father's stroke in 1785, and collaborated with both Stephen Storace, adapting Godwin's novel *Caleb Williams* for Storace's *The Iron Chest* (1796), and Michael Kelly, notably on the popular *Blue Beard, or Female Curiosity* (1798). He was Examiner of Plays (official censor for the London stage) from 1824.

BDA; *DNB* (J. Knight); *LS*
G. Colman (ii): *Random Records* (London, 1830)
'George Colman', *The Annual Biography and Obituary*, xxi (1837), 265–88
R. B. Peake: *Memoirs of the Colman Family* (London, 1841)
E. R. Page: *George Colman the Elder* (New York, 1935)
J. F. Bagster-Collins: *George Colman the Younger, 1762–1836* (New York, 1946)
K. Sasse: 'Opera Register from 1712 to 1734 (Colman-Register)', *HJb*, v (1959), 199–223

OLIVE BALDWIN, LEANNE LANGLEY, THELMA WILSON

Colmar. Town in Alsace, eastern France. At times it has been under German rule. In 1768 a theatre was created in the building of the tailors' corporation, in which both French and German operas were given alongside plays. The present beautiful little Théâtre Municipal (cap. 780) in the rue Interlinden was built by the architect Boltz and decorated by the artist Boulangé; it opened in 1849. Since 1972 Colmar, with Strasbourg and Mulhouse, has formed part of the Opéra du Rhin; the town receives one or two performances each of six or seven productions mounted from October to May. For productions too big to fit into the small theatre, the Colmar public are taken to Strasbourg by special trains and coaches. This association with Strasbourg dates back almost to the very beginning of Colmar's operatic history. During the German occupation (1940–45), when the stage was modernized, an independent company was formed but it has never been really viable. The Atelier Lyrique (opera workshop) of the Opéra du Rhin is established in Colmar under the direction of Pierre Barrat.

*

1974–1984: l'Atelier lyrique du Rhin à dix ans (Colmar, 1984)
L. J. Brote: 'L'Opéra du Rhin: l'art lyrique régionalise', *Le théâtre lyrique français*, ed. D. Pistone (Paris, 1987), 383–94
M.-N. Rio: 'L'atelier lyrique du Rhin', ibid, 395–400

CHARLES PITT

Cologne (Ger. Köln; It. Colonia). City in western Germany, in North Rhine-Westphalia. It is one of the oldest cities north of the Alps, but the absence of a courtly or aristocratic tradition meant that it remained culturally provincial for centuries, in opera as in other areas. Early dramatic performances included 16th-century mystery plays. At the end of the 16th century and during the first half of the 17th visiting English actors performed plays, sometimes with music; their repertory probably included plays with songs. Italian opera companies often visited the city from the beginning of the 18th century including, in 1757, that of Angelo Mingotti; it performed on a specially built stage in the Heumarkt. Dramatic performances also took place in the city's own hall in the Quartermarkt. The first permanent theatre (cap. 3000), the Deutsche Schaubühne, built by Joseph von Kurz, opened on 19 May 1768 with *La serva padrona* (probably not Pergolesi's) and remained in use until 1783. In the second half of the 18th century opera companies performed French works by Philidor, Grétry, Favart and others, as well as the new German Singspiels of Hiller, Neefe and Benda. In 1781 Johann Heinrich Böhm acquired the right to stage musical performances, and two years later his company moved into the new theatre building in the Komödienstrasse. The composers most often performed were Paisiello, Salieri, Traetta, Sarti and Piccinni. Although opera was performed with increasing frequency, Joseph Gregor Lang could still write in his book *Reise auf dem Rheine* (1790): 'Cologne is at least a century behind the rest of Germany where culture is concerned'.

In 1805 the theatre was refitted, the first company to occupy it being the Bergisches Theater. In the 1820s Albert Lortzing was a member of the Cologne company as 'young lover and second tenor'. The building in the Komödienstrasse was demolished in 1828 and replaced by a theatre with 1540 seats which opened on 19 January 1829 with Spohr's *Jessonda* and burnt down 30 years later. After its reconstruction in 1862, it was again destroyed by fire in 1869.

On 1 September 1872 the Theater in der Glockengasse, with 1266 seats, opened with *Der Freischütz*. Later outstanding events included the first performances in Cologne of *Das Rheingold* and *Die Walküre*. In 1884 Engelbert Humperdinck came to Cologne as assistant Kapellmeister of the opera, but he stayed for only one season. After 1895, singers including Carl Burrian and Hermann Jadlowker joined the Cologne Opera company, and among its most famous guests were Nellie Melba and Francesco Tamagno, Verdi's first Otello.

Plans for a new theatre began at the end of 1896. Built in the neo-Gothic style, the Neues Theater opened in 1902 and was equipped with the most up-to-date technology of the time. In 1902–3 the repertory consisted of 53 works. A festival was held for the first time in 1905, with an emphasis on German opera. After 1906 the Neues Theater was used exclusively for opera. Bruno Walter and Lovro von Matačić began their theatre careers there as co-répétiteurs. Otto Klemperer was involved with the Cologne Opera from 1917 to 1924, as head of productions as well as conductor. The house was famous between the wars for its productions of contemporary opera, such as Korngold's *Die tote Stadt* (1920), which had simultaneous premières in Cologne and Hamburg. In 1924 the Hungarian-born Eugen Szenkar took up the post of principal musical director of the Cologne Opera. He was responsible for the first performance in Cologne of *The Love for Three Oranges*. The opera house was destroyed in an air raid on 14 May 1944.

The postwar season began on 17 August 1945 in the great hall of the university, which had served as a temporary theatre in the last months of the war. The first opera produced, in September, was *Madama Butterfly*. While Herbert Maisch was Intendant the Kammerspiele was opened with 400 seats; by 1957 it had given seven premières, including K. A. Hartmann's *Simplicius Simplicissimus* (1949), Henze's *Ein Landarzt* (1953), Krenek's *Tarquin* (1950) and Hermann Reutter's *Die Witwe von Ephesus* (1954). Performances of works banned under the Nazis could now be given, including Milhaud's *Christophe Colomb* (1950), Weill's *Aufstieg und Fall der Stadt Mahagonny* (1951), Hindemith's *Mathis der Maler* (1953) and Schoenberg's *Die glückliche Hand* (1954). A number of first German performances are further evidence of the adventurous nature of the repertory; they include Britten's *The Rape of Lucretia* (1948), Bernstein's *Trouble in Tahiti* (1955) and Stravinsky's *The Rake's Progress* (1956).

After three years of building work the Grosses Haus, the present opera house (1346 seats), opened on 8 May 1957 with Weber's *Oberon*. The first German performances of Poulenc's *Dialogues des Carmélites* and the première of Wolfgang Fortner's *Bluthochzeit* (1957) maintained the company's reputation for producing contemporary opera.

In 1959 Oscar Fritz Schuh became Generalintendant of the Cologne theatres, with Wolfgang Sawallisch as director of music and Caspar Neher as principal stage designer (after his death he was succeeded by Teo Otto in 1962). Schuh took up his post with the ambitious aim of making Cologne the cultural centre of the Federal Republic of Germany. Although he set high standards in his four years in Cologne, with Wieland Wagner directing Wagner's *Ring* even before he staged the work in Bayreuth, Schuh's plans proved too demanding for Cologne. His successor was Arno Assmann, who engaged István Kertész for the Cologne Opera and appointed Hans Neugebauer principal dramatic director. The high point of his directorship was the première of Zimmermann's *Die Soldaten* (1965), conducted by Michael Gielen and directed by Neugebauer. Claus Helmut Drese became Generalintendant, 1968–75. Under his aegis Kertész and Jean-Pierre Ponnelle began their collaboration on an internationally famous cycle of Mozart operas.

In 1975 the post of Generalintendant was discontinued, and it was decided to keep the theatrical departments separate. Michael Hampe was appointed Intendant and has moved towards the stagione system, as well as leaving his mark on the aesthetic profile of the house as head of productions. In 1977 he appointed John Pritchard principal musical director, and after Pritchard's death James Conlon took over the post in 1989, as principal conductor. The Cologne Opera has given successful guest performances on the international level. Besides Hampe, the most important directors have been Ponnelle and Harry Kupfer.

*

C. Niessen: *Ist Köln eine Theaterstadt?* (Emsdetten, 1963)

I. Scharberth: *Oper in Köln* (Cologne, 1985)

C. H. Hiller: *Vom Quartermarkt zum Offenbachplatz: ein Streifzug durch vier Jahrhunderte Musiktheatralischer Darbietungen in Köln* (Cologne, 1986)

IMRE FABIAN

Colomba [Colombo, Columba], **Innocente** [Innocenzo] (**Giovanni Battista**) (*b* Arogno, 1717; *d* Arogno, 1793). Italian stage designer. In his youth he studied art with his uncle, Luca Antonio, and in 1737 emigrated to Germany, where he worked in Brunswick, Hamburg, Hanover, Kassel, Mainz, Mannheim and Munich. In Frankfurt he devised *mises-en-scène* for the election of Charles VII (1742). At Stuttgart he was architect and perspective painter at Carl Eugen of Württemberg's court and designed magnificent scenery for operas by Jommelli, such as *L'asilo d'amore* (1758), *Alessandro nell'Indie* (1760), *Demofoonte* (1764) and *Vologeso* (1766) and for ballets by Noverre. In 1764 he worked at the Nuovo Teatro, Como, where he also painted the decoration of the auditorium. In 1770–71 he was active at the Teatro Regio in Turin and had a stormy disagreement with the stage superintendent, G. B. Filippo Nicolis di Robilant, about the scenery for Paisiello's *Annibale in Torino*. He then moved to London, where he was responsible for the scenery and acted as machinist in many productions at the King's Theatre in the Haymarket; he designed scenery for 23 operas, including Domenico Corri's *Alessandro nell'Indie* (1774), Piccinni's *La donna di spirito* (1775), Sacchini's *Didone* (1775), *Amore soldato* (1778) and *Enea e Lavinia* (1779) and Grétry's *Zémire et Azor* (1779). His scene drawings in the Landesbibliothek, Stuttgart, and those formerly in the Pogliaghi collection in Varese (present whereabouts unknown), present imaginative structural and decorative portrayals, often inspired by Piranesi engravings, with a precise and clear line. He was also a landscape painter.

For illustration *see* PAISIELLO, GIOVANNI.

*

Nuove di diverse corti e paesi, ossia gazzetta di Lugano (31 Dec 1754)

Uriot: *Description des fêtes données à l'occasion du jour de naissance de son altesse ... Le Duc de Würtemberg et Teck* (Stuttgart, 1764)

G. A. Oldelli: *Dizionario storico-ragionato degli uomini illustri del Canton Ticino* (Lugano, 1807), 72ff

H. Tintelnot: *Barocktheater und barocke Kunst* (Berlin, 1939), 105ff

S. Rosenfeld and E. Croft Murray: 'A Checklist of Scene Painters Working in Great Britain and Ireland in the 18th Century', *Theatre Notebook*, xix (1964–5), 6–64, esp. 20

M. Viale Ferrero: *Storia del Teatro Regio di Torino*, iii: *La scenografia dalle origini al 1936* (Turin, 1980)

MERCEDES VIALE FERRERO, SYBIL ROSENFELD

Colombeau, Jules-Adenis. *See* ADENIS, JULES.

Colombia. For discussion of opera in Colombia *see* BOGOTÁ.

Colón. Theatre in BUENOS AIRES, the most important opera house in South America. Two different buildings have borne the name, the first from 1857 to 1889, the second from 1908.

Colonello, Attilio (*b* Milan, 9 Nov 1930). Italian stage designer and director. He studied architecture with Gio Ponti and Ernesto Rogers in Milan. His first important commission was *La traviata* (1956) for the Florence Festival, followed by Boito's *Mefistofele* (1958) at La Scala. Other Milan designs include an unremarkable *Don Pasquale* (1965) and two productions for Margherita Wallmann – the première of Pizzetti's *Clitennestra* (1965) and another *Don Pasquale* (1973). Dallas Civic Opera gave Colonello his American début with an acclaimed *Otello* of Piranesian grandeur in 1962, followed a year later by an impressive *L'incoronazione di Poppea*. He then designed three controversial productions for the Metropolitan Opera – a Jacobean *Lucia di Lammermoor* for Wallmann (1964) and, for Nathaniel Merrill, a 19th-century *Luisa Miller* (1968) and a gloomy *Il trovatore* (1969).

Colonello has worked for the major Italian regional companies, but most frequently for S Carlo, where he began in 1964 with another Wallmann production, an elegantly gothic *Roberto Devereux*, then designed his own productions of *Adriana Lecouvreur* (1966), the première of Jacopo Napoli's *Barone avaro*, and *Samson et Dalila* (both 1970), *Carmen* (1975), *La Gioconda* (1977) and *I puritani* and *Luisa Miller* (both 1988).

He has had his most impressive run of successes in the Verona Arena, beginning with a splendid *Nabucco* in 1962 and *Cavalleria rusticana*, *La bohème* and a Herbert Graf production of *Mefistofele* in 1964. He then designed *Carmen* (1965), *Rigoletto* (1966), a Graf *La forza del destino* and a Merrill *Andrea Chénier* (both 1967), the 100th Verona *Aida* (1968) and *Un ballo in maschera* (1972). In 1984 he returned to design and direct *I Lombardi*, rimming the arena bowl with a vast mosaic to create a stunning backdrop (see illustration).

Colonello's style looks backwards to the architectural grandeur of his neo-classical inheritance, besides identifying itself with the lavish splendour of the contemporary Italian school, best illustrated by Franco Zeffirelli and Luchino Visconti. He is sometimes criticized for his lack of period accuracy and attention to detail.

For further illustration *see* VERONA, fig.2. DAVID J. HOUGH

Colonna, Giovanni Paolo (*b* Bologna, 16 June 1637; *d* Bologna, 28 Nov 1695). Italian composer. He studied composition in Rome with Abbatini, Benevoli and Carissimi and became second organist of S Petronio in Bologna in 1661 and *maestro di cappella* there from 1674, holding similar posts at other churches. A founder-member and several times president of the Accademia Filarmonica, he was a noted teacher, numbering Giovanni Bononcini, Tosi, Clari, Urio, Silvani, G. C. Predieri, Andrea Fiorè and the castrato Cavalletti among his pupils.

Scene from Colonello's production of Verdi's 'I Lombardi alla prima crociata' in the Verona Arena, 1984

Only one of his operas survives complete. His substitute arias for a Bologna revival in 1680 of Freschi's *Tullia superba* are remarkable for their demanding florid vocal writing as well as their strictly imitative orchestral textures (including trumpets), their chromaticism and their ingenious bass lines; the thematic invention is effective and rhythms are varied. Similar features are found in his oratorio scores.

Le contese di Pallade e Venere sopra il bando d'Amore (dramatic cantata, Bianchini), Bologna, Palazzo Pubblico, 29 Nov 1666
L'alloro trionfante (dramatic cantata, T. Stanzani), Bologna, Accademia degli Unanimi, Feb 1672, collab. G. Vitali and others
Le stelle combattute dagli elementi (torneo or masque), Ferrara, S Lorenzo, early 1676, *GB-Cfm*
Pelope e Ippodamia (drammetto, A. M. Campeggi), Bologna, Palazzo Campeggi, 1678
Amilcare di Cipro (dramma per musica, A. Gargieria), Bologna, Malvezzi, 1 Dec 1692

Arias in D. Freschi: Tullia superba (dramma per musica, A. Medolago), Bologna, Sala, 1680, *I-MOe*

CARLO VITALI

Colorado Springs. American town in central Colorado. It is the location of the Colorado Opera Festival, founded in 1970 at Colorado College and associated with that institution until it became independent, with its own board of directors, in 1978. Dedicated to the 'imaginative and professional presentation of a well-rehearsed and varied repertoire', the company originally offered three productions each summer. The repertory is broadly standard, but has included the American stage premières of Traetta's *Il cavaliere errante* (1971) and Handel's *Serse* (1978) as well as the regional première of the original version of *Boris Godunov* (1976). During the 1980s the schedule was reduced to the presentation of a single opera because of financial problems, but the numerous educational projects were maintained. In 1982 the company, whose general director and co-founder is Donald P. Jenkins, moved to the new Pikes Peak Center, a 1900-seat house built by El Paso County.

WES BLOMSTER

Coloratura (It.: 'colouring'; Ger. *Koloratur*). Florid figuration or ornamentation, particularly in vocal music. Coloratura is thus defined in several early non-Italian music lexicons, such as those of Praetorius (1618), Brossard (1703) and Walther (1732), where the term is dealt with briefly and always with reference to Italian usage. In the principal Italian treatises on singing, however (G. Caccini, 1601/2; P. F. Tosi, 1723; Mancini, 1774; M. Garcia, 1840), the term never occurs; it is likewise absent from the vocabulary of such English authors as Burney and Chorley, who wrote extensively about Italian singing at a time when ornamentation was of utmost importance. In German, 'coloratura' (or 'Koloratur') has long been used as a generic term for ornamentation. 16th-century German organ composers, for example, described an ornamented melody as 'colloratum'. Mattheson (1739) equated 'Coloraturen' with 'Zierathen', the term under which he listed all the principal ornaments.

The term is now widely used to denote passages of florid vocal music, operatic roles of which such passages are a prominent part and singers who specialize in them. Most frequently the singer in question will be a high soprano, and the role in question one that has been regarded as properly hers, such as the Queen of Night in *Die Zauberflöte*. In recent times the coloratura mezzo-soprano has achieved greater prominence, with singers such as Marilyn Horne engaged in the revival of the operas which Rossini wrote for this kind of voice. There is no reason why it should not be applied to the tenor or any other type of voice used to sing elaborately decorative music; Rossini, Bellini and others call for elaborately ornamented lines even from deep basses.

The root of the Italian term is that of 'colour', and it is sometimes supposed that the word should imply a 'coloured' kind of singing. This would be misleading if understood as referring to vocal 'coloration', an art which many singers cultivate to aid the expressiveness of their performances. It is then argued that, since the mastery of florid music should be part of any singer's training, there is no need for a term that tends to place technically skilled singers in some kind of specialist category. For the type of singer commonly called a 'coloratura soprano' (Amelita Galli-Curci, Lina Pagliughi or Beverly Sills, for example) the term 'soprano leggiero' should be sufficient. This argument is obviously up against the barrier of usage; and it is also based on a mistaken idea of the derivation of 'coloratura'. The 'colouring' implied in this, as in *Koloratur*, is more akin to 'colouring' as practised in the traditional art of rhetoric; here the 'colours' were figurative or other expressions used to embellish the argument. Similarly, in music, decorative passages in the melodic line were said to be 'figured'. 'Coloratura', then, decorates passages or performances that are then said to be 'figured' or 'coloured' in this sense, and viewed in that light the 'coloratura' soprano is quite properly a singer who has acquired an exceptional facility in such work.

Most frequently coloratura singers are those with high, light voices since these are the most readily flexible type. The success of Maria Callas in roles which had previously been the province of such voices enlarged the perception of the 'coloratura soprano'. To some, it seemed that she had virtually created a new voice type, the dramatic coloratura. Joan Sutherland also showed that the requisite range and flexibility could exist in a voice of very considerable power, and, to a greater extent than Callas, she preserved the sweetness and purity of timbre traditionally associated with the *soprano leggiero*. These exceptionally gifted and famous singers have certainly been influential in securing the wider acceptance of 'coloratura' as central to an opera singer's art rather than a fringe activity for specialists. Another influence has been the resurgence of interest in Baroque operas, especially those of Handel, which clearly cannot be sung adequately except by singers soundly trained in florid work. The opening up of the Rossini repertory and other bel canto operas of the early 19th century has strengthened this, as has the steady increase of familiarity with the whole output of Mozart. Interest in medieval music, too, has involved the singing of elaborate melismas, and modern composers such as Tippett have been more ready than their predecessors to include florid passages in their writing for voice. At least the era has passed when a coloratura soprano was one who sang a few arias such as the 'Shadow' song from *Dinorah* and a great many songs about birds.

J. B. STEANE, OWEN JANDER

Coltellini, Celeste (*b* Livorno, 26 Nov 1760; *d* Capodimonte, Naples, 24 or 28 July 1829). Italian mezzo-soprano, daughter of Marco Coltellini. She studied with Manzuoli in Florence and Mancini in Vienna. In 1780 she made her début at La Scala, Milan, and also went to Venice; in 1781 she appeared in Naples. At the instigation of Joseph II she went to Vienna in 1785, performing in a Cimarosa opera. She appeared further in Naples in the late 1780s; Paisiello wrote for her *Nina, o sia La pazza per amore* (1789, Caserta). In 1791 she retired from the stage. She was admired for her musical refinement, expressiveness and excellent acting. RUDOLPH ANGERMÜLLER

Coltellini, Marco (*b* Livorno, 13 Oct 1719; *d* St Petersburg, Nov 1777). Italian librettist. He was an abbot but later married and had four daughters, including the singer Celeste Coltellini. He lived in Livorno, where he was close to the large English community, and in 1752 or 1753 briefly visited England with the Earl of Essex. After ten years of literary activity he began writing opera librettos. His first full-length work, *Almeria*, based on Congreve's *The Mourning Bride*, was performed in Livorno in 1761. He dedicated the work to Metastasio, who criticized the over-complex plot but was 'seduced by his poetic vivacity and by the magic of his beautiful writing', which he found 'live, harmonious, and full of images and ideas' (letter to Coltellini, dated 25 May 1761). By 1763 he was working in Vienna where he produced a series of librettos that show the influence of Algarotti and his fellow Livornese Calzabigi, who called Coltellini his disciple. The first of these, *Ifigenia in Tauride*, was set by Traetta (1763). Predating Calzabigi's libretto for Gluck's *Alceste* by four years, Coltellini's *Ifigenia* was the first full-length Viennese opera to incorporate French elements – chorus, ballet, scene complexes and multiple ensembles – into an italianate dramaturgical framework. It was successful and highly influential in Italy, where Gluck's *Alceste* remained an occasional novelty. Similar works for Vienna followed: *Alcide negli orti esperidi* (set by Majo, 1764), *Telemaco* (Gluck, 1765), *Amore e Psiche* (Gassmann, 1767) and *Armida* (Salieri, 1771). The staged assassination of Thoas in *Ifigenia* and the three tragic deaths in *Piramo e Tisbe* (Hasse, 1768) represented radical departures from the rules of 18th-century dramaturgy.

Coltellini could not have become Metastasio's successor, since Metastasio retained his position as imperial court poet until his death in 1782. Coltellini may have held the lesser post of imperial theatre poet. In 1772 he was called to the Russian court; on his way there he visited Berlin, where he discussed opera reform with Frederick the Great, to whom he dedicated his first St Petersburg libretto, *Antigona*, a *tragedia per musica* set by Traetta (1772). This masterpiece epitomized a decade of effort to revitalize Italian serious opera, which had begun in 1763 with Traetta's *Ifigenia in Tauride*. He produced only one other new work for that court, *Lucinda ed Armidoro* (Paisiello, 1777), though he probably revised his *Amore e Psiche* (1773) and *Armida* (1774) for productions there. He was probably also responsible for the version of Metastasio's *Nitteti* set by Paisiello (1777), notable for the addition of some scenes containing ballets and choruses.

Coltellini was a more elegant poet than Calzabigi, but he tended towards prolixity and did not always adhere to Calzabigi's central principle of presenting the drama in a series of tableaux so striking and self-explanatory in themselves that the text became of secondary importance. He sometimes preferred to work within the formal structure of the *opera seria*, which he modified and enhanced. In so doing he made elements of Viennese reform accessible to the Italian theatre, paving the way for a new style of opera in the 1790s. His elegant style attracted such discriminating composers as Gluck and Hasse. His *Contessina* was particularly successful; Gassmann's setting received many revivals, and the libretto was subsequently set by other composers, notably Piccinni.

From 1762 to 1770 Coltellini owned, but did not himself operate, the most important press in Livorno, which published the works of Algarotti. It is not unlikely that Coltellini held liberal political views, and it is possible that he wrote satires against Maria Theresa and Catherine II. But the claim that Catherine had him poisoned is unfounded.

L'Almeria (os, after W. Congreve: *The Mourning Bride*), G. F. de Majo, 1761; *Ifigenia in Tauride* (os), Traetta, 1763 (Galuppi, 1768; P. Marinelli, 1775; C. Monza, 1784; A. Tarchi, 1786); *Alcide negli orti esperidi* (os), G. de Majo, 1764; *Telemaco, ossia L'isola di Circe* (os), Gluck, 1765; *L'infedeltà delusa* (dg), ?1765 (J. Haydn, 1773; M. Nerí Bondi, 1783); *Armida* (festa teatrale), G. Scarlatti, 1767; *Amore e Psiche* (festa teatrale), Gassmann, 1767 (Traetta, 1773; G. Schuster, 1780); *Piramo e Tisbe* (int tragico), Hasse, 1768; *La finta semplice* (dg, after Goldoni), Mozart, 1769

La contessina (dg, after Goldoni), Gassmann, 1770 (Astarita, 1772; G. Rust, 1774, as Il conte Baccellone; Piccinni, 1775); *Armida* (os), Salieri, 1771 (? Sarti, 1786); *Il filosofo inamorato* (dg, after Goldoni: *Filosofia ed amore*), Gassmann, 1771; *Antigona* (tragedia), Traetta, 1772 (D. Bortnyansky, 1776, as Creonte; Campobasso d'Alessandro, 1789; P. Winter, 1791); *Lucinda e Armidoro* (azione teatrale), Paisiello, 1777; *Il tutore e la pupilla, ovvero Amor vuol gioventù* (int), G. Moneta, 1785

*

S. Arteaga: *Le rivoluzioni del teatro musicale italiano* (Bologna, 1783–8)
F. Mazzei: *Memorie della vita e delle peregrinazioni* (Lugano, 1845–6)
F. Pera: *Ricordi e biografie* (Livorno, 1867)
R.-A. Mooser: *Annales de la musique et des musiciens en Russie au XVIIIe siècle* (Geneva, 1948–51)
M. McClymonds: 'The Venetian Role in the Transformation of Italian Opera Seria during the 1790s', *I vicini di Mozart: Venice 1987*, 221–40 DENNIS LIBBY, MARITA P. McCLYMONDS

Columbus. American city, capital of Ohio. The first professional opera productions were concert performances given from 1956 by the Columbus SO under Evan Whallon. He expanded the orchestra from 45 players to 65 and brought in leading singers to perform in the Veterans Memorial Theatre (4000 seats), beginning in 1957 with a semi-staged *Così fan tutte* featuring Phyllis Curtin and David Lloyd. In 1958 Elisabeth Schwarzkopf sang scenes from *Rosenkavalier*. In 1959 George London performed excerpts from *Boris Godunov* and Eileen Farrell arias from Cherubini's *Médée*. By the mid-1970s an audience for three complete stage productions a year existed in the area. In 1981 Opera Columbus became an official offshoot of the Columbus SO. Whallon left the orchestra in 1982. Initial performances were in the Ohio Theatre, a converted Loews cinema and vaudeville house (2800 seats). But bookings by other companies forced Opera Columbus to move to a renovated cinema, the Palace, in 1984. In 1986 the company gave the première of Thomas Pasatieri's *Three Sisters* and subsequently recorded it. In 1987 they staged the first complete Wagner opera in Columbus, *Tristan und Isolde*, conducted by Christian Badea in a production by the Argentine designer Roberto Oswald. A period of rapid growth led to a pattern of four productions each season, but in 1991 the company announced a $1.7 million accumulated deficit against a $1.3 million budget and ceased activities briefly before reorganizing them on a more modest scale. NANCY MALITZ

Coluzzi, Niccolò (*fl* 1730s). Italian librettist. Little is known about his life except that he was active in Turin and was associated with the Teatro Capranica in Rome in the 1730s; it is uncertain whether he was house poet there or whether his employment was on a temporary basis. An early libretto, *Germanico in Germania* for Porpora (1732), bears his name, a rare distinction; this text was also set by Bernasconi (1744) and Carlo Monza (1770). An anonymous libretto for Bernardino Ottani's *Arminio* (1781) has also been ascribed to him.

*

E. Greppi and A. Giulini, eds.: *Carteggio di Pietro e di Alessandro Verri*, ii (Milan, 1910), 95; iii (1910), 156; xi (1940), 215

E. Celani: 'Musica e musicisti in Roma (1750–1850)', *RMI*, xviii (1911), 1–63

G. Pavan: 'Saggio di cronistoria del teatro musicale romano: il teatro Capranica', *RMI*, xxix (1922), 425–44

G. Papini: *Il Teatro Carignano dal 1608 ai giorni nostri* (Turin, 1935)

M.-T. Bouquet and A. Basso: *Storia del Teatro Regio di Torino* (Turin, 1977–) PATRICIA LEWY GIDWITZ

Colzani, Anselmo (*b* Budrio, nr Bologna, 28 March 1918). Italian baritone. He studied in Bologna and made his début there at the Teatro Comunale in 1947 as the Herald (*Lohengrin*). He first sang at La Scala in 1952 as Alfio (*Cavalleria rusticana*) and in 1955 took part in the stage première of Milhaud's *David*. He made his American début in 1956 at San Francisco as Luna, also singing Scarpia, Amonasro and Giovanni (*Francesca da Rimini*). In 1959 he created Marino in Luciano Chailly's *Riva delle Sirti* at Monaco. He made his Metropolitan début in 1960 as Boccanegra and remained with the company for 16 seasons, singing more than 200 performances, while continuing to appear at all the leading Italian theatres. His repertory included Enrico Ashton, Riccardo (*I puritani*), Nabucco, Germont, Don Carlo (*La forza del destino*), Iago, Falstaff, Marcello, Jack Rance, Carlo Gérard (*Andrea Chénier*) and Michonnet (*Adriana Lecouvreur*). He had a powerful, full-toned voice heard to best advantage in *verismo* operas. ELIZABETH FORBES

Comaschino, Il. *See* ARNABOLDI, CRISTOFORO.

Comédie-ballet (Fr.). A French Baroque stage work which combined spoken, or later sung, *comédie* and ballet.

As Molière stressed in his preface to *Les fâcheux* (1661), his artistic aim was for a more integrated spectacle, one in which vocal music and dance complemented the principal intrigue conveyed through the spoken dialogue. In partnership with Lully (from 1663 to 1670), he created the most enduring examples of the genre. In the course of this period there was a gradual breaking down of the compartmentalization of *intermède* and dialogue in favour of a more flexible structure: music was increasingly assigned a more prominent role. The last of their collaborations, *Le bourgeois gentilhomme* (1670), whose subject, a rich bourgeois and his efforts to become a cultivated gentleman, provided ample scope for Lully (in scenes where the titled character seeks to be a patron or student of the arts with comic results) – so much so that the critic of the *Gazette de Paris* found the intrigue of the *comédie* too accessory. After falling out with Lully, Molière turned to Marc-Antoine Charpentier, whose *Le malade imaginaire*, revised three times to avoid legal entanglements with Lully, achieved a notable success.

In the 18th century few works of this type were called *comédies-ballets* (Voltaire's *La princesse de Navarre* with music by Rameau, 1745, is a hybrid between *tragédie* and *comédie-ballet*, though termed the latter; *see* PARIS, fig.3); nonetheless, the model of Molière and his musicians was an important legacy. Incidental music (instrumental and vocal) supporting elements of the plot and characterization was a feature of French spoken theatre well into the 19th century.

While some scholars restrict the term *comédie-ballet* to works conforming to the Molière-Lully model, for 18th-century authors it also aptly designated a type of *opéra-ballet*, with no spoken dialogue and in three or four acts with a prologue. Rather than being composed of separate entrées, it had principal characters that appeared in all the acts and a continuous, though dramatically slight, plot. A. C. Destouches' *Le carnaval et la folie* (1703) was the most popular example: the antics of Folly, her betrothal to Carnival, and the vicissitudes of their engagement (in part because of Momus's meddling) provide ample opportunity for the satirical treatment of lyric conventions for love and comic portrayal of the gods. The humour was broader than in other *opéras-ballets* and, of course, in strong contrast to the dignity of tone sought in *tragédies lyriques*. As well as solo *airs* and *ariettes*, choruses and dances for disparate groups (sailors, music students, Folly's disciples) ensure a colourful scenic display and musical variety.

*

L. de Cahusac: 'Comédie ballet', *Encyclopédie, ou Dictionnaire raisonné des sciences, des arts et des métiers*, ed. D. Diderot and others (Paris, 1751–80)

J. R. Anthony: *French Baroque Music from Beaujoyeulx to Rameau* (London, 1973, 2/1978; Fr. trans., 1981, with addl bibliography)

R. M. Isherwood: *Music in the Service of the King* (Ithaca, NY, 1973)

J. S. Powell: *Music in the Theater of Molière* (diss., U. of Washington, 1982) M. ELIZABETH C. BARTLET

Comédie en musique. *See* COMÉDIE LYRIQUE.

Comédie-Italienne. Italian company based in Paris from 1716 and resident at the Hôtel de Bourgogne. Also known as the Théâtre Italien, it merged with the Opéra-Comique in 1762; *see* PARIS, §§2 (iii) and 3 (i).

Comédie larmoyante (Fr.: 'tearful comedy', 'sentimental comedy'). Term for a type of opera, normally *opéra comique*, borrowed from the spoken theatre (where the model was a type of verse-drama created by Nivelle de La Chaussée, 1692–1754) and popular in the late 18th century. Analogous with the Italian *opera semiseria*, it progressed by way of tears to a happy outcome and emphasized sentimentality while possessing moral overtones. The mid-century paintings of Jean-Baptiste Greuze were influential in shaping this type of *sensibilité*. Marmontel was particularly associated with tearful comedies; *Lucile*, set by Grétry (1769), is a classic example. English literature, in particular Richardson's novel *Pamela*, stood behind other early works of the kind. A later example, Dalayrac's *Nina, ou La folle par amour* (1786), also probably draws inspiration from English sources. Such literary connections and subject matter place the *comédie larmoyante* as a precursor of the *drame lyrique*.

Comédie lyrique [*comédie en musique*; *comédie mise en musique*] (Fr.). A type of French opera whose subject matter, treatment and tone reflect, more or less strongly, the norms of the current spoken *comédie*. In the 18th century *comédie lyrique* was applied to both *opéras* (e.g. Mouret's *Les amours de Ragonde*, 1742, and Grétry's *Colinette à la cour, ou La double épreuve*, 1782) and *opéras comiques* (e.g. Dezède's *Alexis et Justine*, 1785). The term *comédie* [*mise*] *en musique* was almost always restricted to the latter. In *opéras* authors sought to emphasize the difference between their works, with contemporary or exotic settings and lighter plots, and the usual fare at the Opéra, such as *tragédies lyriques*. In *opéras comiques* (most prevalent in the 1780s and 1790s) they wanted to avoid the most common designation of the previous generation, *comédie mêlée d'ariettes*; they believed the style of their texts more 'correct' in a tone of 'comique bourgeois' or more rarely 'comique noble' rather than the 'comique bas', the plot construction more regular and coherent (judged by *comédie* standards) and the music more varied and extensive – and certainly not described adequately by 'ariette'. In both a middle ground between the noble *tragédie lyrique* (with its classical settings) and the *comédie mêlée d'ariettes* (with its often stylized comic character types) was sought, although specific instances show that application was not always rigid or consistent. By the 19th century the neutral term 'opéra' was generally preferred, but *comédie lyrique* still occasionally appears (as for Massenet's *Thaïs*, 1894).

See also COMÉDIE-BALLET.

*

J. F. Marmontel: 'Comédie', 'Comique', *Encyclopédie, ou Dictionnaire raisonné des sciences, des arts et des métiers*, ed. D. Diderot and others (Paris, 1751–80)

M. Bobillier [M. Brenet]: *Dictionnaire pratique et historique de la musique* (Paris, 1926)

M. ELIZABETH C. BARTLET

Comédie mêlée d'ariettes (Fr.: 'comedy mixed with little songs'). The most frequently used term for French operas with spoken dialogue during the late *ancien régime*.

At first, it was applied to works which parodied music from Italian *opera buffa* (e.g. C.-S. Favart's *Le caprice amoureux, ou Ninette à la cour*, 1755), although another common term was *opéra bouffon*. Soon it came to be the designation for works with newly composed pieces (in contrast with the *opéra comique* in the conventional 18th-century sense, which used vaudevilles). Its ready acceptance was due to its combination of two key features of the new genre: 'ariettes' indicating the prominence of short vocal pieces in simple forms and 'comédie' pointing to the librettists' desire to match the standards of spoken theatre – i.e. to produce a more 'regular', moral work, as defined in French dramatic theory, with a more coherent plot and in a politer tone than was usual in *opéra comique en vaudevilles*. Among the subjects that proved popular were rural stories, in which idealized naive love triumphs in spite of the efforts of those in power (as in Egidio Duni's *La clochette*, 1766), and bourgeois comedy, where the happiness of virtuous people seems threatened (as in A.-E.-M. Grétry's *Lucile*, 1769), as also did some with effects of magic and fairy-tale plots (e.g. F.-A. D. Philidor's *Le bûcheron*, 1763). The *comédie mêlée d'ariettes* was sometimes a vehicle for the introduction to the French stage of foreign models, particularly English. Monsigny's *Le roi et le fermier* (1762, strictly speaking called a 'comédie mêlée de morceaux de musique' by its librettist, M.-J. Sedaine, who objected to 'd'ariettes') and Grétry's *Les fausses apparences* (1778) are fine examples.

During the 1780s and 90s the term, like the *villageois*, magical and sentimental subjects associated with the genre, gradually declined in popularity for new works, although old favourites remained a significant part of the repertory. Furthermore, with its stress on 'ariettes', more and more authors agreed with Sedaine that it seemed inappropriate for works in which substantial airs and ensembles were assuming an increasingly important role. (As well as *comédie mise en musique*, COMÉDIE LYRIQUE, *comédie mêlée de musique*, DRAME LYRIQUE, *drame mis en musique*, *opéra* (*see* OPÉRA (i)) and FAIT HISTORIQUE were frequent choices.)

For bibliography *see* OPÉRA COMIQUE. M. ELIZABETH C. BARTLET

Comédie mise en musique. *See* COMÉDIE LYRIQUE.

Comédie-parade (Fr.). A type of 18th-century play or *opéra comique* almost always in one act and using characters from the *commedia dell'arte* tradition (such as Pierrot, Columbine and Cassandre). In keeping with this the humour is broad and very close to farce. As *opéras comiques*, *comédies-parades* could either re-use pre-existing music in vaudeville fashion (for example, *Les docteurs modernes* by J.-B. Radet and P.-I. Barré, 1784) or be newly set (such as Champein's *Les amours de Colombine*, 1785). They were popular at the fair theatres in the mid-century and at the Comédie-Italienne (later called the Opéra-Comique) up to the 1780s. By the 1790s the genre had virtually disappeared, although old favourites like Grétry's *Le tableau parlant* (to a libretto by L. Anseaume, 1769) were sometimes revived and there was the occasional new one, such as Méhul's *L'irato, ou L'emporté* (to a libretto by B.-J. Marsollier des Vivetières, 1801).

*

L. de Tressan: 'Parade', *Encyclopédie, ou Dictionnaire raisonné des sciences, des arts et des métiers*, ed. D. Diderot and others (Paris, 1751–80)

M. ELIZABETH C. BARTLET

Comedy of Errors, The. *See* *EQUIVOCI, GLI*.

Comelli-Rubini, Adelaide [Chaumel, Adèle] (*b* c1796; *d* Romano, Bergamo, 30 Jan 1874). French, later Italian, mezzo-soprano. She studied in Paris, where she sang under her real name of Chaumel. Going to Italy, she was engaged at Naples as Comelli and, after her marriage to the tenor Giovanni Battista Rubini, appeared as Comelli-Rubini. In 1820 she sang Calbo in the first performance of Rossini's *Maometto II* at S Carlo. At the Teatro del Fondo in 1828 she created Matilde in Donizetti's *Gianni di Calais* and Nina in his *Il giovedì grasso*. She appeared at the King's Theatre in London with her husband in 1831, when her voice was not greatly admired.

For illustration *see* RUBINI, GIOVANNI BATTISTA.

ELIZABETH FORBES

Comes [Gomez, Gomes], **Pietro** (*fl* Naples, 1739–55). Italian composer. According to Eitner he was born 'near Naples', and Florimo referred to him as a singer. Librettos of his works call him a *maestro di cappella*. At first glance his list of works, entirely in the field of comic opera in Naples, is impressive, but examination of the librettos suggests that Comes was an undistinguished musician called upon when better and more expensive talent was not desired or available. It is probably significant that, except for his last opera, all his commissions came from the least important and least successful of the Neapolitan theatres, the Teatro della Pace.

His first opera, *La taverna di Mostacchio* (1739), is a resetting of *La Rina* (original music by N. Pisano, 1731); Scherillo believed *Le fenziune abbentorate* (1745) was a rewriting of F. A. Tullio's libretto *Lo finto Armenio* (by A. Orefice, 1717) and an unsuccessful attempt to bring an old-fashioned work up to date; *La vennegna* (1747) was, as its librettist admitted, written out of season and in a hurry; *Il nuovo Don Chisciotte* (1748) was a new version of *Il fantastico* (by L. Leo, 1743); and for *Rosmonda* (1755) Comes was commissioned to write only part, in collaboration with Logroscino, Traetta and Carlo Cecere.

Although none of Comes's music survives, the librettos of his works are of historical interest, incorporating developments of Neapolitan *opera buffa* during the 1740s: the move away from Neapolitan dialect for all characters, incorporation of plot elements drawn from literary romance, character satire instead of pure domestic farce and (to judge by their reduction in quantity) elaboration of the individual musical numbers.

opere buffe, first performed at the Teatro della Pace, Naples, unless otherwise stated

La taverna di Mostacchio (B. Saddumene), Dec 1739; rev. of N. Pisano's La Rina, 1731
Li despiette d'ammore (A. Palomba), spr. 1744
La fenziune abbentorate (P. Trinchera), wint. 1745
La vennegna (Trinchera), 1747
Lo chiacchiarone (Palomba), wint. 1748
Il nuovo Don Chisciotte (G. Federico, possibly with addns by Palomba), wint. 1748; rev. of Leo's Il fantastico, 1743
La Rosmonda (Palomba), Naples, Nuovo, carn. 1755; collab. Logroscino, Traetta and C. Cecere [recits. by Comes]

*

EitnerQ; *FlorimoN*
M. Scherillo: *L'opera buffa napoletana durante il settecento: storia letteraria* (Naples, 1883, 2/1917)
V. Viviani: *Storia del teatro napoletano* (Naples, 1969), 327ff

JAMES L. JACKMAN

Comic opera. A musico-dramatic work of a light or amusing nature. The term does not have any precise historical meaning; it may, for example, be applied equally to an Italian intermezzo, *farsa* or *opera buffa*, a French *opéra comique* (though many *opéras comiques* are serious or tragic works), a German Singspiel, a Spanish zarzuela or an English opera of a light character. It is often applied to operetta or *opéra bouffe* and may be applied to musical comedy. Most comic operas in languages other than Italian have spoken dialogue rather than continuous music.

See FARSA; INTERMEZZO; OPÉRA BOUFFE; OPERA BUFFA; OPÉRA COMIQUE; OPERETTA; SINGSPIEL; and ZARZUELA.

Comissiona, Sergiu (*b* Bucharest, 16 June 1928). Romanian conductor. After studying conducting at the Bucharest Conservatory and then with Silvestri and Lindenberg, he made his début with the Romanian State Opera orchestra in 1946. Two years later he was appointed assistant conductor of the Romanian State Ensemble of musicians, chorus and dancers, and was its musical director (1950–55). He was principal conductor of the Romanian State Opera (1955–9), winning the 1956 conducting competition at Besançon. From 1962 to 1966 he was a frequent guest conductor with the Royal Ballet at Covent Garden. For the next years he worked with orchestras in the USA and Europe, returning to Covent Garden as an opera conductor with *Il barbiere di Siviglia* in 1975 and making his New York début with *La fanciulla del West* in 1977; he conducted *Don Giovanni* at the Metropolitan in 1989. He became an American citizen in 1976 and was musical director of New York City Opera, 1987–8. Comissiona is a colourful performer, his gestures instinctively dramatic and choreographic.

ELLIOTT W. GALKIN/R

Scene from a commedia dell'arte performance (Harlequin distracts Pantaloon while passing Rosaura a letter from her lover): drawing by Giuseppe Zocchi (1711–67)

Commedia dell'arte. A semi-improvised theatrical entertainment, popular in Italy from the early 16th century to about 1750, which influenced the development of opera. The term originally meant 'professional theatre' (as opposed to the learned plays performed by aristocratic amateurs). By the late 16th century several troupes toured with both literary plays and others based on a plot outline on which the company improvised, using a stock of fixed gestures, verse tags and jokes. These semi-improvised shows often had one or two pairs of 'serious' lovers surrounded by comic old men and servants wearing masks; the masked characters became stereotyped figures, identified with regions and dialects of Italy (Pantaloon, Harlequin, Brighella etc.).

Performances included songs and dances as part of the action and also as intermezzos between scenes. Virginia Andreini, from a leading troupe, was enough of a virtuoso singer to create at short notice the title part in Monteverdi's early opera *L'Arianna* (1608). *Commedia dell'arte* had an obvious influence on the stock characters and situations in the comic scenes of 17th-century Italian operas and in later comic operas. The episodic form of Venetian opera owes much to it;

Pirrotta has argued that the operatic aria developed from its songs and stock scenes (*lazzi*) and so did the cult of the performer and of a deliberately non-realistic theatricality.

The 'fables' of CARLO GOZZI, a deliberate revival of *commedia dell'arte*, have provided a basis for several operas. In *Ariadne auf Naxos* Hofmannsthal and Strauss juxtaposed operatic and *commedia dell'arte* conventions.

See DONNA SERPENTE, LA; FEEN, DIE; KÖNIG HIRSCH; LOVE FOR THREE ORANGES, THE; and TURANDOT (ii).

*

N. Pirrotta: 'Commedia dell'arte and Opera', *Music and Culture in Italy from the Middle Ages to the Baroque* (Cambridge, MA, 1984), 343–60

P. Weiss: 'Venetian Commedia dell'Arte "Operas" in the Age of Vivaldi', *MQ*, lxx (1984), 195–217

M. P. Borsetta: *Teatro dell'arte e teatro d'opera nella prima metà del seicento* (diss., U. of Bologna, 1986) JOHN ROSSELLI

Commedia per musica (It.: 'comedy through music'). A term used for comic opera, particularly in Naples, in the 18th century. Sometimes the form 'commedia in musica' was used. It seems to have indicated no nuance of genre as compared with 'opera buffa' or 'dramma giocoso'. In the 19th century it denoted a species of comic opera in which spoken dialogue in Neapolitan *patois* replaced recitative. A late example is Luigi Ricci's *La festa di Piedigrotta* (1852). *See* OPERA BUFFA.

Commonwealth of Independent States. For information on opera in this country, the former Union of Soviet Socialist Republics, see under the names of individual republics and cities.

Compadecida, A ('Our Lady of Mercy'). Opera in three acts by JOSÉ SIQUEIRA to his own libretto after Ariano Suassuna's play *O auto da Compadecida*; Rio de Janeiro, Teatro Municipal, 11 May 1961.

The libretto presents a vividly satirical and amusing story of popular customs and characters of north-east Brazil, such as the clown Palhaço (spoken), João Grilo (tenor), Chico (baritone), Padre João (tenor), Antonio Morais (bass), Severino de Araujo (spoken) and the bandit Cangaceiro (tenor), combined with the bishop Bispo (bass), Demônio (the Devil; bass), Jesus Christ, as Manuel (tenor), and the Virgin Mary, A Compadecida (soprano). Although a secular story in which Our Lady of Mercy emerges to perform miracles, the setting stresses the idiosyncrasies of local human types. Siqueira called the work 'a comedy set to music', for which he used elements of comic opera (such as the alternation of sung and spoken passages) and musical motifs identified with specific characters and objects. João Grilo and Chico, the central roles, are characterized by folksong themes from the region of Paraíba. The work is an attempt to transfer the Iberian medieval *auto* tradition, of compositions of religious or allegorical character, to the environment of north-east Brazil. GERARD BÉHAGUE

Company. Though the term has at times been used of TRAVELLING TROUPES, in English it is more often applied to groups of singers who put on opera in a single theatre.

In Italy, where public opera was for many years given only during a season of about two months, a company was as a rule the group of singers contracted for that season only, most of whom moved on after it had ended. At most, the Naples royal theatres (S Carlo and Fondo) between about 1740 and 1860 engaged artists for a year. Opera houses capable of fielding two groups of soloists (the S Carlo and La Scala, Milan, in most years) were said to have a 'double company'. After the breakdown of the seasonal system in the late 19th century a company was a group assembled, however briefly, to perform an opera or operas (*see* SEASON).

In Central Europe, where opera was long centred on courts, companies were more nearly permanent. At Eszterháza during Haydn's tenure the median length of stay of Italian singers was between two and three years, but German singers stayed much longer (as did a very few Italians). Haydn could therefore count on a known array of (by and large mediocre) resources. In Paris, singers engaged by the opera houses under royal or, after the Revolution, government patronage were paid monthly salaries and approximated to the condition of civil servants; some stayed on for many years. Provincial French opera houses from the late 18th century to the early 20th usually engaged a company once a year for a season that might last from four to ten months. Much the same was and to some extent is still true of Central Europe. Since the 1950s, however, singers have been highly mobile; even those formally attached to a company (those of the two London opera houses included) may at times perform elsewhere.

*

J. Rosselli: *The Opera Industry in Italy from Cimarosa to Verdi: the Role of the Impresario* (Cambridge, 1984), 4–8, 127

J. Mongrédien: *La musique en France des Lumières au romantisme (1789–1830)* (Paris, 1986) JOHN ROSSELLI

Comparsa (It.: 'appearance'). A walk-on part ('extra', 'supernumerary'); its performer is not required to sing or to speak. An early example is Vespone (*La serva padrona*, Pergolesi, 1733), a servant who is even required to put on a disguise. Ceremonial scenes in *opera seria* and grand opera feature numerous *comparse* in the form of pages, footmen, soldiers, guards, lower nobility and functionaries of various types. Historical figures may sometimes appear as *comparse*, as in Giordano's *Andrea Chénier* (1896). A favourite *comparsa* is the executioner, as in *Les vêpres siciliennes* (1855), *Tosca* (1900) and *Turandot* (1926). In *Rigoletto* (1851), which has only a male chorus, all the women at the Mantuan court except the Countess of Ceprano are of necessity *comparse*. JULIAN BUDDEN

Compiègne. Town in France, 60 km north of Paris, with a famous royal and imperial chateau. Louis-Philippe installed a theatre seating 500 in the palace, where opera was given. In 1867, Napoleon III ordered his architect, Gabriel-Auguste Ancelet, to build a new court opera, the Théâtre Impérial, seating 800; it was on the site of the Carmelite convent that inspired Poulenc's *Dialogues des Carmélites*. Just outside the palace perimeter, it was connected by a gallery that crosses the rue d'Ulm. With the collapse of the Second Empire in 1870, the interior decoration was never completed. Newly restored and dedicated to the performance of French music, the theatre reopened on 21 September 1991 with Saint-Saëns' *Henry VIII*, in the framework of a festival of 19th-century music. CHARLES PITT

Componimento (It.). A term signifying 'composition', usually in reference to a dramatic poem to be set to music as a SERENATA. It occurs with particular frequency in the repertory of the Viennese court during the Baroque period. *Componimenti da camera* (or *per camera*) were written by Zeno, Pariati and Metastasio; *componimenti drammatici* by Metastasio; *componimenti per musica* by Stampiglia and Cupeda.

MICHAEL TALBOT

Comprimario (It.: 'subprincipal'; Fr. *coryphée*). A 19th-century term denoting a secondary, supporting role. A *comprimario* part might be assigned a cantabile, a *romanza* or a solo part in a duet or ensemble, but not a full-length, two-movement aria. Examples include Isacco (*La gazza ladra*, 1817), Smeton (*Anna Bolena*, 1830), Agnese (*Beatrice di Tenda*, 1833), and Medora (*Il corsaro*, 1848). Later in the century the term was extended to any character of the slightest scenic importance, however little he or she might have to sing, e.g. Flora Bervoix (*La traviata*, 1853). JULIAN BUDDEN

Comte Ory, Le ('Count Ory'). *Opéra* in two acts by GIOACHINO ROSSINI to a libretto by EUGÈNE SCRIBE and CHARLES-GASPARD DELESTRE-POIRSON after their own play; Paris, Opéra, 20 August 1828.

In 1817 Scribe and Delestre-Poirson wrote a one-act vaudeville on the exploits of the libidinous Count Ory, a real-life Don Juan who became the subject of a popular late 18th-century ballad. Rossini, in his turn, had written a coronation entertainment in 1825 for Charles X, *Il viaggio a Reims*, one of the supreme masterpieces of occasional music but a piece too closely tied to the circumstances of its composition to survive as an opera-house repertory work. For *Le comte Ory*, the music was adapted and extended and the one-act vaudeville turned into a two-act drama to make a work that is not only astonishingly cogent in its own right but also one of the wittiest, most stylish and most urbane of all comic operas.

'Le comte Ory' (Rossini): scene from Act 2 (the Countess's bedchamber), with Cinti-Damoreau (the Countess), Jawureck (Isolier, centre) and Adolphe Nourrit (Count Ory) in the original production at the Paris Opéra (Salle Le Peletier), 20 August 1828; lithograph by C. Deshayes after Ciceri

The setting is the castle of Formoutiers about the year 1200. The Count of Formoutiers and his men have left for the Holy Land, leaving the Countess Adèle (soprano) exposed to the wiles of young Count Ory (tenor) and his henchmen, led by the trusty Raimbaud (baritone). Ory establishes himself outside the castle as a hermit; and although the villagers, among them the Countess's stewardess Ragonde (mezzo-soprano), are taken in by this, Ory's tutor (baritone) is more than a little suspicious. Isolier, Ory's page (mezzo-soprano – an obvious forerunner of Oscar in Verdi's *Un ballo in maschera*), has himself been smitten by the Countess's beauty and, failing to recognize his master through the hermit's outfit, confides in him his plan to enter the castle disguised as a pilgrim. Ory approves the idea, but once inside the castle, he solemnly advises the Countess to be wary of young Isolier. Ory's own advances are progressing very satisfactorily when he is unmasked by his tutor. But, with a day to go before the return of the crusaders, Ory determines to make a further assault.

At the start of Act 2, the women angrily discuss Ory's dissimulation. A storm breaks and cries are heard from a band of 'pilgrims' – in reality, Ory and his men disguised as nuns – outside the castle. The pilgrims are given shelter and, on Raimbaud's initiative, soon discover the castle's wine cellars, a discovery which leads to an uproarious scene in which spirited carousings alternate with solemn prayer whenever strangers approach. This time, though, Isolier has his wits about him; he recognizes Ory and to ingratiate himself with the Countess lays a trap, luring Ory into a secret assignation. In the darkness of the bedchamber, misled by the Countess's own voice, Ory mistakenly addresses his amorous overtures to his page. Trumpet calls announce the arrival of the crusaders, leaving Ory and his men no alternative but to make good their escape.

* * *

Though sometimes designated an *opéra comique*, *Le comte Ory* is a uniquely Rossinian creation with skilfully structured ensembles and a sophistication in the orchestral and vocal writing that transcends anything to be found in the works of such composers as Auber or Hérold. It is a wry and witty piece that appropriates and develops the gentle guying of the romantic sensibility of *Il viaggio a Reims* while developing in the famous Act 2 trio, newly written, a degree of vocal and instrumental sensibility and sophistication that even Berlioz was bound to marvel at. The critic Henry Chorley noted that 'there is not a bad melody, there is not an ugly bar in *Le comte Ory*', adding that there is in the piece 'a felicitous curiousness in the modulations ... a crispness of finish, a resolution to make effects by disappointing the ear, which not only bespeaks the master's familiarity with the greatest classical writers, but also a wondrous tact in conforming to the taste of the new public whom he was to fascinate'. RICHARD OSBORNE

Comunale (It.: 'communal'). Name used in Italy for theatres built by or for a community or municipality. Florence and Modena have theatres of this name, but the best known is the Teatro Comunale of Bologna, built in 1757 (*see* BOLOGNA).

Comus. Masque in three acts by THOMAS AUGUSTINE ARNE to a libretto by John Dalton after John Milton; London, Drury Lane, Theatre Royal, 4 March 1738.

A lady (soprano) is lost in the wood where the magician Comus (tenor) lives; disguised as a shepherd he lures her to his palace. The lady's two brothers are warned by a spirit that she is in Comus's power. They are accosted by Comus's crew. The spirit provides the brothers with a magic potion to overcome Comus's spell. A feast is prepared in Comus's palace and the lady, spellbound, is entertained in song and dance. Comus presses her to drink from his cup but the brothers rush in and drive him away. The nymph Sabrina (soprano) releases the lady from her spell and the triumph of virtue is celebrated in a final chorus.

Comus was Arne's first and most enduring stage success, regularly revived throughout his life. The freshness of his lyric style in songs such as 'Now Phoebus sinketh in the West' and 'Would you taste the noontide air' remained unsurpassed in his later work. Arne's autograph score is lost, but a copy, made in about 1785 (*GB-Lbl*), includes the recitatives and choruses, omitted from the published score (1740), as well as some pieces from Handel's *L'Allegro* that supplement Arne's limited chorus writing. JOHN A. PARKINSON

Concato, Augusta (*b* Verona, 1895; *d* Carate Brianza, June 1964). Italian soprano, wife of NINO PICCALUGA.

Concertato. *See* PEZZO CONCERTATO.

Concert performance (It. *opera di concerto*). The performance of an opera without costume or, normally, any dramatic action. While the giving of concert performances has normally been regarded as a 20th-century procedure, designed to give a little-known opera a hearing without incurring the heavy expense involved in staging it, there are earlier precedents. Handel performed his opera *Imeneo* in a concert-room in Dublin during his 1741–2 visit, in concert form. Mozart's revival of *Idomeneo* in Vienna in 1786, at the Auersperg Palace, is generally thought to have been a concert performance. A number of Russian operas, either because they were left incomplete, such as Musorgsky's *The Fair at Sorochintsï* (1911), or for political reasons, such as Prokofiev's *War and Peace* (1944), were first given in concert form, partly as a try-out and partly to test public reaction before embarking on the expense of staging. Sometimes performances originally given on stage have been repeated in concert performance to bring them to a wider audience; this has happened several times at the London Promenade Concerts, particularly with performances originating at Glyndebourne, which are sometimes given 'semi-staged' on a platform, with basic acting and the use of some gesture and movement (and possibly with members of the cast costumed in a way that indicates their relative social station).

Conchita. Opera in four acts by RICCARDO ZANDONAI to a libretto by Maurice Vaucaire (translated into Italian and supplemented by Carlo Zangarini) after Pierre Louÿs's novel *La femme et le pantin*; Milan, Teatro Dal Verme, 14 October 1911.

The opera has six scenes: the Factory, Intermezzo in the street, Conchita's house, the 'Baile' (a small cabaret theatre), the Gate, Mateo's house. Louÿs's perverse and sensual Conchita (soprano), a more ambivalent version of Carmen, teases her lover Mateo (tenor) in a series of disturbing episodes but never yields to him until the end, after a severe beating. The other characters are secondary figures, set in a Spanish atmosphere which is also vividly evoked by the orchestral writing, the most attractive aspect of the opera, while the vocal parts are often in *verismo* style. This was the composer's second important opera, after *Il grillo del focolare*, and his first real success; he returned to Spanish themes in two later operas, *Una partita* and *La farsa amorosa*. Vocally the most interesting numbers are the duets between the lovers, and among Conchita's arias the first-act 'Ier dalla fabbrica', over a Spanish ostinato rhythm.

RENATO CHIESA

Concone, (Paolo) Giuseppe (Gioacchino) (*b* Turin, 12 Sept 1801; *d* Turin, 1 June 1861). Italian composer and singing teacher. After a short career as a singer, he turned to teaching and became one of the most influential singing instructors of his time. From 1837 to 1848 he taught in Paris, where he published many books of vocal exercises, some of which are still used. He composed two operas: *Un episodio del San Michele*, produced at Turin on 8 June 1836, and *Graziella*, which was not performed. His output also included songs and duets. After the Revolution of 1848, Concone returned to Turin, where he was organist and *maestro di cappella* at the Sardinian court. ELIZABETH FORBES

Conductor (Fr. *chef d'orchestre*; Ger. *Dirigent*; It. *direttore d'orchestra*). The opera conductor's role combines two functions: the conductor sets tempos and beats time visibly for singers and instrumentalists; the conductor controls or collaborates with others in many areas of musical and dramatic interpretation. The word acquired its present meaning during the 19th century, when the practice of conducting, in opera and on the concert platform, emerged in its modern form.

1. History and role. 2. The conductor as interpreter.

1. HISTORY AND ROLE. There is little information about how the earliest operas, at the beginning of the 17th century, were directed. The instrumental forces required for such works as Monteverdi's *Orfeo* (1607) and Landi's *Sant'Alessio* (1632) are small enough for the musicians to have followed the singers directly and to have played the ritornellos without visual signals. The practice of time-beating, however, was already well established in choral singing. 16th- and 17th-century treatises describe how to mark the beat with the hand, and contemporary drawings and engravings show time-beaters directing singers by waving a sheaf of rolled-up music. An engraving of the première of Lully's *Alceste* (1674) shows a man, perhaps Lully himself, standing among the instrumentalists, facing the stage and beating time in this manner; this is perhaps the earliest record of time-beating in an opera performance. (The report of Lully's striking his foot with a staff while beating time, and contracting fatal gangrene, refers to a performance of his *Te Deum*, not to an opera.) There is no record of time-beating in Italian opera of the 17th century. Pay lists show that the composer was often present at the keyboard; presumably he exercised a certain amount of leadership.

As opera orchestras grew in size during the 18th century, and as the relation between voices and instruments in Italian opera became more complex, a system of dual leadership developed in which the performance was directed by both the harpsichordist and the first violinist. The harpsichordist, called the *maestro*, was often the composer; it was the custom at many opera houses for the composer to preside at the harpsichord for the first three performances of an opera. He directed by playing the bass part and its chordal realization; occasionally he marked the tempo by waving his hands or stamping his feet (Schönfeld). The first violinist, called *capo d'orchestra* (*Konzertmeister* in Germany, leader in England), led by playing his part loudly and with broad physical gestures (*Wahrheiten*). Some sources suggest that the *maestro* was responsible primarily for the singers, the *capo d'orchestra* for the instrumentalists; other sources, particularly towards the end of the 18th century, complain that the lines of authority were blurred and that dual leadership created confusion (Schönfeld). At the Paris Opéra in the 18th century, a *batteur de mesure* marked time audibly by striking a large stick against a music stand or the front of the stage. Despite the complaints of Rousseau and many others, this practice continued into the 19th century. It is, however, likely that the audible beat was intermittent rather than constant and that it functioned mainly to coordinate the chorus and dancers on the stage rather than to control the solo singers or the instrumentalists.

Baton conducting became prevalent in opera during the first half of the 19th century. Sometimes the time-beater was the *maestro* who left his keyboard, as B. A. Weber did in Berlin from 1792; sometimes it was the leading violinist who abandoned playing and directed with his bow, like François-Antoine Habeneck in Paris in the 1820s. The old system of dual leadership persisted, however – in England and in Germany until the 1830s and 40s, in Italy until the 1860s. As time-beating developed into conducting, conductors began to assume control of more aspects of performance. At Dresden in the 1820s Weber rehearsed interpretation, told the singers how to move on the stage and supervised the scenery, costumes and effects. By the second half of the 19th century the role and authority of the conductor had become securely enough established that such men as Wagner, Michael Costa, Angelo Mariani and Mahler could become famous as conductors apart from their activities as instrumentalists or composers. In the first half of the 20th century conductors played a dominant role in opera houses – choosing which operas to perform, selecting singers and controlling all aspects of the production, musical and dramatic. Arturo Toscanini was famous for keeping his singers under tight control; Herbert von Karajan and Erich Kleiber often directed the operas they conducted.

The shift after World War II from repertory companies to companies that change casts for each production significantly altered the role of the opera conductor. Like leading singers and directors, conductors have become increasingly mobile, conducting different productions, with different casts, in different cities, all within short periods of time. Typically an opera company or festival will have one principal conductor, who conducts two or three operas a year but also conducts elsewhere. The remainder of the season is handled by assistants and guests, who fly in to conduct single productions. Opera conductors tend to be specialists, who start out as répétiteurs (pianists accompanying and coaching singers), then move up through a series of assistantships and guest appearances in increasingly important theatres. Opera conductors sometimes move into orchestral conducting on the concert stage, but it is less common for orchestral conductors to move into opera, perhaps because opera requires experience with singers and stagecraft.

One consequence of mobility is that, although the modern opera conductor retains great authority and a wide scope of responsibility, he or she needs to collaborate with others in many aspects of production. The conductor has primary responsibility for giving the beat to the orchestra and singers and for tempos, balance and other matters of interpretation. He collaborates with the director in the overall conception of the opera and in details of blocking, timing and stage business. He collaborates with the chorus master and with répétiteurs to rehearse the singers in advance of full-scale rehearsals. He collaborates with management to select which operas will be performed and which singers engaged. He is usually responsible for the musical text – including transpositions, which he works out with the singers, and cuts, which he works out with the director. If the opera is to be recorded or videotaped, he works with engineers and producers, both before the performance and afterwards when the sound is mixed and takes are spliced. The division of authority and responsibility in these matters varies considerably from one opera house to another and one production to another, according to local tradition and the personalities involved.

2. The conductor as interpreter. It was mainly through Wagner's operas that the great German interpretative school of conducting evolved; and all German conductors of any consequence since their time have been Wagnerians, many of them continuing, establishing or re-establishing the great operatic traditions of various German cities. In Munich, Franz Lachner, who built up the reputation of the Bavarian opera during his period as conductor and later director, 1836–68, staged *Tannhäuser* and *Lohengrin* in the 1850s. From 1860 Wagner himself, through his relationship with King Ludwig II, put Munich at the centre of operatic history and controversy. A Wagner interpretative dynasty was created, with Hans von Bülow as conductor 1865–9, Franz Wüllner 1869–71, Hermann Levi 1872–96 and Richard Strauss 1896–8. Felix Mottl, an Austrian who assisted Wagner and Richter at the first Bayreuth Festival, conducted at Bayreuth between 1886 and 1902, but made his chief mark at Karlsruhe, 1881–1903, where he had conducted the first complete performance (on successive evenings) of Berlioz's *Les Troyens* in 1890. From 1903 to 1911 he was chief conductor at the Munich Opera (he died after collapsing during a performance of *Tristan und Isolde*).

Bülow, who had been inspired to take up conducting when he heard Liszt direct *Lohengrin* in Weimar (1850), studied with Wagner. Although he conducted little opera after leaving Munich in 1869, he passed on his knowledge to his young protégé, Richard Strauss. Combining conducting with composition, Strauss was one of several conductors of the 1890s who took the opportunity of the centenary (1891) of Mozart's death to revive interest in such operas as *Così fan tutte*. Strauss had been conductor at Weimar, 1889–94, where he conducted (without the customary cuts) *Tannhäuser*, *Lohengrin* (including its 100th Weimar performance) and *Tristan und Isolde*. In 1893 he conducted the first performance of Humperdinck's *Hänsel und Gretel* and, the following year, of his own first opera, *Guntram*. In

1894 he also conducted *Tannhäuser* at Bayreuth. Two years later, at the age of 32, he was appointed chief conductor of the Berlin court opera.

After Spontini, who as conductor of the Berlin court opera (1819–41) had played a part in establishing the mystique surrounding the figure of the conductor, the Berlin Opera had been conducted by Meyerbeer from 1842 to 1848 and for a year by Otto Nicolai. A lean spell had been partly relieved by Felix Weingartner and Carl Muck in the 1890s. Strauss, succeeding Weingartner, held the post until 1908, continuing as chief guest conductor until 1919. His repertory ranged from *Tristan und Isolde* to *Die lustige Witwe*, including of course his own operas (though none had its première in Berlin). Not until after World War I, when the court opera became the Staatsoper, did Berlin follow an adventurous policy. Leo Blech, conductor 1918–23, was followed by Erich Kleiber, whose nine-year tenure until the Nazis came to power (1933) saw the first performance of Berg's *Wozzeck* in 1925 and the staging of operas by Busoni, Janáček and Krenek. Also active in Berlin, at the progressive Kroll theatre, opened in 1924 and closed by the authorities in 1931, was Otto Klemperer, who revived neglected works such as Verdi's *Luisa Miller* and staged contemporary operas by Hindemith, Milhaud, Weill, Stravinsky, Schoenberg and Janáček.

Dresden's earlier operatic eminence was revived with the rebuilding of Semper's opera house in 1878. Ernst von Schuch, appointed chief conductor in 1882 and remaining until his death in 1914, was an outstanding Wagner interpreter; he also introduced Puccini to the Dresden repertory and conducted the premières of four Strauss operas, *Feuersnot*, *Salome*, *Elektra* and *Der Rosenkavalier*. After Fritz Reiner's tenure, 1914–22, Fritz Busch continued the Strauss tradition and also inaugurated the German Verdi revival. Further Strauss premières followed under Karl Böhm. In the post-1945 period, conductors working in Dresden included Joseph Keilberth (1945–8), Rudolf Kempe (1949–52), Franz Konwitschny (1953–5) and Otmar Suitner (1960–64), under whom the Mozart-Wagner-Strauss tradition continued. But the true home of the Strauss tradition increasingly became Munich after the appointment there of Clemens Krauss in 1937, although Strauss Weeks had begun as early as 1919 while Bruno Walter was conductor and continued during the regime of Hans Knappertsbusch, 1922–34. When Krauss left in 1944, Georg Solti (1946–52), Kempe (1952–4) and particularly Wolfgang Sawallisch, from 1971, increased Munich's operatic importance, spicing the Mozart-Wagner-Strauss axis with forays into the contemporary scene.

Wagner's own tradition is, of course, most securely nurtured at Bayreuth itself at the annual (since 1951) summer festival. After Hans Richter and Levi, the conductors appearing there have included most of the great Wagner interpreters of the past century, notably Mottl, Strauss, Muck, Arturo Toscanini, Wilhelm Furtwängler, Knappertsbusch, Krauss, Herbert von Karajan, Kempe, Sawallisch, Böhm, Horst Stein, Boulez, Carlos Kleiber and Solti. One name absent from the list is that of Gustav Mahler, generally regarded as one of the greatest opera conductors of any period. Although Wagner had allowed a Jewish conductor, Levi, to work at Bayreuth, his widow Cosima showed no inclination to follow his example. Mahler's operatic apprenticeship had begun at Bad Hall in 1880 and continued at Olomouc, Kassel, Prague and Leipzig. He first conducted the *Ring* in Leipzig, as second conductor to Artur Nikisch, and then in Budapest, where he was chief conductor, 1888–91. After six successful years in Hamburg, Mahler in 1897 achieved his ambition of becoming director of the Vienna court opera. His ten-year 'reign', studded with controversy, proved to be one of the legendary operatic directorships. Like his friend Strauss, he was equally effective in Mozart and Wagner. He built an ensemble of singers flexible to all his demands in a widely varied repertory, introduced adventurous directors, and transformed the design and lighting of opera productions.

Mahler's arrival in Vienna displaced Richter, who had been musical director there since 1875 and had established a Wagner tradition. One of Mahler's assistant conductors, as he had been in Hamburg, was Bruno Walter, but the succession in 1907 went to Weingartner. Vienna's next 'golden period', at a time of economic recession and inflation, was the joint directorship of Strauss and Franz Schalk, 1919–24, when many operas received first Vienna performances. In spite of its fame as a musical centre and of its roll-call of great singers, Vienna never established an operatic tradition as specific as those of Munich or Dresden. One goes to Bayreuth for Wagner, to Salzburg for Mozart, to Munich for Strauss. As in Mahler's time, opera politics have bedevilled most of the conductors appointed at Vienna, among them Krauss, Walter, Böhm, Karajan, Lorin Maazel and Claudio Abbado. All the great operatic interpreters have conducted in Vienna; but none except Mahler – not even Karajan – has had the full control necessary for the foundation of a cohesive policy, and even Mahler was eventually defeated by 'the system'. To establish the Mahlerian operatic regime he desired, Karajan had to go to his native city of Salzburg, where he was artistic director of the festival from 1964 until his death in 1989, continuing its Mozart-Strauss tradition and establishing in addition an Easter festival (initially for Wagner productions).

The establishment of operatic interpretation as an art in Italy was achieved by two 19th-century conductors. Angelo Mariani's conducting of Verdi was apparently so exciting that he was once threatened with imprisonment for inciting rebellion. He also conducted the Italian premières of *Tannhäuser* and *Lohengrin*. Franco Faccio, 19 years his junior, was chief conductor at La Scala, Milan, 1871–90, during which time he conducted the first performances of Verdi's *Otello* (1887), Ponchielli's *La Gioconda* (1876) and Puccini's *Edgar* (1889). But both were eclipsed by Toscanini, who conducted the first performance of Puccini's *La bohème* in 1896 and the Italian première of *Götterdämmerung* the next year. His tyranny and fanaticism ensured brilliant performances during his three stormy spells as conductor at La Scala, 1898–1902, 1906–8 and 1920–29. His successor from 1909 to 1914 and at intervals thereafter until 1947 was Tullio Serafin, who introduced operas by Berg and Britten to Italy. From 1932 to 1954 La Scala was the preserve of Victor de Sabata, whose Verdi and Wagner performances had a dramatic intensity no less impressive than Toscanini's. Both Karajan and the American Leonard Bernstein enjoyed success at La Scala in the 1950s. Carlo Maria Giulini, Claudio Abbado and Riccardo Muti have continued the Verdi-Puccini tradition while widening the repertory to admit contemporary operas.

The traditions of operatic conducting in France are less clearly defined. The leading figure during the era of *grand opéra* was François-Antoine Habeneck, who directed the premières of, among other works, *Guillaume Tell*, *Les Huguenots*, *La Juive* and *Benvenuto Cellini*; he was principal conductor at the Opéra, 1824–46. Few others of any real eminence held positions as conductor at either the Opéra or the Opéra-Comique until the time of André Messager, at the Opéra-Comique, 1898–1904, and the Opéra, 1907–14; he conducted the premières of *Pelléas et Mélisande*, Charpentier's *Louise* and Massenet's *Grisélidis* as well as his own lighter operas; he was also a Wagnerian, championed Russian music and Mozart, and revived interest in Gluck and Rameau. Since his time, however, there have been few French conductors of international distinction at the two main houses in Paris, although Jean Fournet, D.-E. Inghelbrecht, Eugène Bigot, Roger Désormière, André Cluytens and Georges Prêtre have contributed to the continuance of French traditions.

Messager was also for six years (1901–7) manager and conductor of Covent Garden, London. Until the arrival of Britten, Tippett and the post-1945 operatic resurgence in Britain, the conducting of opera in London and elsewhere was mainly in the hands of imported guests, from Michael Costa (1833–79) and Carl Rosa to Richter, Mahler, Walter and many of the names mentioned above; and in the years since World War II distinguished Covent Garden musical directors have included Erich Kleiber, Rafael Kubelík and Georg Solti. Noted British interpreters of opera have included Percy Pitt, Thomas Beecham, John Barbirolli and Colin Davis. Beecham spent much time in the opera house and was an outstanding interpreter of Mozart, French opera, Strauss and Delius; Davis, at Covent Garden from 1971 to 1986, achieved special distinction in Mozart, Berlioz and Stravinsky. A British tradition of the conducting of Mozart, Strauss and Rossini developed at Glyndebourne, first under the imported guidance of Fritz Busch and Vittorio Gui but followed by John Pritchard and Andrew Davis, together with Bernard Haitink. Elsewhere, at the English National Opera (formerly Sadler's Wells) and in the regions, such conductors as Colin Davis, Reginald Goodall (a remarkable Wagnerian), Alexander Gibson, Charles Mackerras, Mark Elder, Richard Armstrong and David Lloyd-Jones have contributed valuably to the rise of opera as a force in British cultural life. Benjamin Britten, an outstanding conductor of his own and others' music, left authoritative accounts of his works through his recordings, though he conducted his operas in the theatre infrequently.

The leading conductors of Russian opera, even Russian nationalist opera, in its heyday were in fact foreigners. Catterino Cavos conducted the première of Glinka's *A Life for the Tsar*, Karl Albrecht that of his *Ruslan and Lyudmila*. The Czech Eduard Nápravník was the dominant conductor in St Petersburg from the end of the 1860s until the mid-1890s and in his capacity as chief conductor at the Mariinsky Theatre directed the premières of most of the principal operas by the Five (the 'Mighty Kuchka' – Balakirev, Borodin, Cui, Musorgsky and Rimsky-Korsakov) as well as several by Dargomïzhky, Rubinstein and Tchaikovsky. Among his successors at the Mariinsky was the Englishman Albert Coates. The leading conductor at the Bol'shoy in Moscow during the last two decades of the century was Ippolit Altani; he was succeeded, though for less than two years (1904–6), by Rakhmaninov. In the 20th century eminent figures have included Emil Cooper, who had charge of the Russian operas given in Dyagilev's Paris seasons before working in Moscow and, in the years after the 1917 Revolution, in Petrograd; Samuil Samosud, who was at the Mariinsky Theatre at the time of the Revolution, then at the Maliy until 1936, when it was regarded as 'the laboratory of Soviet opera' (he directed there the premières of Shostakovich's *The Nose* and Dzerzhinsky's *Quiet Flows the Don*, and was later to conduct that of part of Prokofiev's *War and Peace*), and who also had periods in Moscow at the Bol'shoy and then the Stanislavsky-Nemirovich-Danchenko Theatre; Samosud's successor at the Maliy, Boris Khaikin, who conducted several Prokofiev premières as well as works by Kabalevsky and Dzerzhinsky; Alexander Melik-Pashayev, a conductor of particular vitality who worked at the Bol'shoy over three decades; and his successor there, Yevgeny Svetlanov, noted for his fresh, colourful interpretations. The longest-serving chief conductor at the Bol'shoy is Yury Simonov, who was the youngest holder of the post when appointed in 1969. In 1985 he was succeeded by Alexander Lazarev. Mstislav Rostropovich, working chiefly in the USA, has upheld the tradition of free and dramatic direction of the Russian repertory.

A strong and continuous interpretative tradition has long existed in Prague, where nationalism gradually ousted German influences in the opera house. Smetana conducted there from 1866 to 1874, introducing his own operas and those of Dvořák and Fibich. From 1900 to 1920, the National Theatre productions were conducted by Karel Kovařovic, a notable interpreter of French opera and of Wagner and Strauss but also a devoted advocate of Smetana and Dvořák and, less devotedly, of Janáček. He was succeeded by a composer-conductor, Otakar Ostrčil, who was director from 1920 to 1935 and introduced Janáček's operas to the capital; he conducted complete cycles of the operas of Smetana, Dvořák and Fibich as well as the Prague première of Berg's *Wozzeck*. His work was carried on by Václav Talich from 1935 to 1945 and, in intervals between falling out of favour with the regime, in the postwar period. Since 1945, Czech interpretative tradition – particularly with regard to the operas of Janáček – has persisted through František Jílek, Bohumil Gregor, Václav Neumann, Jaroslav Krombholc, Zdeněk Košler and (outside Czechoslovakia) Rafael Kubelík. Prague's strong German tradition, fostered by Mahler, Seidl and Klemperer, survived in the Neue Deutsche Theater, built in 1887 (a century after Mozart's success in Prague with the première of *Don Giovanni*). Alexander Zemlinsky was conductor there from 1911 to 1927 and, when he joined Klemperer at the Kroll in Berlin, was followed by George Szell, under whose directorship operas by Weill, Krenek and Shostakovich were performed.

American operatic tradition, too, was nurtured by foreign or foreign-born conductors, not only in New York but in Chicago, San Francisco and elsewhere. The New York Metropolitan Opera's German tradition derived from Walter Damrosch (1884–91) and was continued by Anton Seidl, Alfred Hertz and Artur Bodanzky. The last, a Mahler protégé, conducted German opera at the Metropolitan from 1915 to 1939. In 1908 the company retained the services of both Mahler (to 1910) and Toscanini (to 1915), but the concert hall claimed both in due course. Serafin, de Sabata, Walter, Dimitri Mitropoulos and others were frequent visitors in the inter-war years to the USA. Of American-born conductors, Leonard Bernstein worked in Vienna and Milan more often than at the Metropolitan; inspired by his example, the next generation of American conductors, notably James Levine (at the Metropolitan), Julius Rudel (at New York City Opera) and such younger conductors as Dennis Russell Davies, Kent Nagano, John DeMain and the British-born Donald Runnicles are building an American interpretative tradition, heard not only at the Metropolitan and in Chicago and San Francisco but also in Bayreuth, Salzburg, Vienna and elsewhere.

Since the 1970s a new tradition, of period-style performance of operas of the Baroque and Classical eras, has begun to develop in several European countries and the USA, as historical knowledge of the early repertory widened and as tastes started to move away from the elaborate realizations of Monteverdi and others so popular in the late 1960s – and, at the other end of the period, from the heavy, string-based orchestral sound traditional in Mozart. A central figure in this movement has been Nikolaus Harnoncourt, conducting operas in Vienna and Zürich, where his performances of Monteverdi and Mozart in particular attracted attention in the early 1970s. Others have included, in the Low Countries, René Jacobs, in a wide repertory of 17th- and early 18th-century operas; Arnold Östman, conductor at the Drottningholm court opera house, noted for his swift, pointed Mozart interpretations; in Britain, John Eliot Gardiner, who has conducted period orchestras in operas by Rameau, Gluck and Mozart with particular dramatic energy; in Paris, William Christie, whose polished performances have set new standards in the French Baroque repertory, and Jean-Claude Malgoire, a vigorous interpreter of that repertory and also the operas of Handel, which have also been performed with lightness and vitality by period groups directed by Nicholas McGegan in Hungary and the USA and Sigiswald Kuijken in the Low Countries.

*

J. -J. Rousseau: *Dictionnaire de musique* (Paris, 1768; Eng. trans., 1771), 52–4, 355

Wahrheiten die Musik betreffend, gerade herausgesagt von einem teutschen Biedermann (Frankfurt, 1777)

[J. F. von Schönfeld]: 'Ueber den Vortrag, oder Exekuzion', *Jb der Tonkunst von Wien und Prag, 1796*, 171–8

M. M. von Weber: *Carl Maria von Weber: the Life of an Artist* (London, 1865)

B. Geissmar: *The Baton and the Jackboot* (London, 1944)

A. Carse: *The Orchestra from Beethoven to Berlioz* (Cambridge, 1948)

D. Wooldridge: *Conductors' World* (London, 1970)

H. C. Schonberg: *The Great Conductors* (London, 1973)

D. Koury: *Orchestral Performance Practices in the Nineteenth Century: Size, Proportions, and Seating* (Ann Arbor, 1986)

D. K. Holoman: 'The Emergence of the Orchestral Conductor in Paris in the 1830s', *Music in Paris in the Eighteen-Thirties*, ed. P. Bloom (Stuyvesant, NY, 1987), 387–430

N. Zaslaw: 'Lully's Orchestra', *Lully: Heidelberg and St Germain-en-Laye 1987*, 539–79

E. Galkin: *The History of Orchestral Conducting* (New York, 1988)

E. Bowles: *Musical Ensembles in Festival Books, 1500–1800* (Ann Arbor, 1989)

M. Chusid: 'A Letter by the Composer about *Giovanna d'Arco* and Some Remarks on the Division of Musical Direction in Verdi's Day', *Performance Practice Review*, iii (1990), 7–57

L. Jensen: 'The Emergence of the Modern Conductor in 19th-Century Italian Opera', *Performance Practice Review*, iv (1991), 34–63

N. Lebrecht: *The Maestro Myth: Great Conductors in Pursuit of Power* (London, 1991)

For further bibliography see articles on individual conductors.

JOHN SPITZER, NEAL ZASLAW (1), MICHAEL KENNEDY (2)

Conforto [Conforti], **Nicola** (*b* Naples, 25 Sept 1718; *d* ?Madrid, after 1788). Italian composer. He studied with Francesco Mancini in Naples. His first *opere buffe*, mounted at Naples and Rome in 1746–7, were so successful that in 1750 he was invited by the S Carlo to set Metastasio's *Antigono* (also successfully produced in London in 1757). In 1751 he was commissioned by the Austrian ambassador at Naples to compose a cantata, *Gli orti esperidi*, for the birthday of Maria Theresa. In the same year Farinelli commissioned him to compose a setting of Metastasio's *La festa cinese* to celebrate the name-day of Ferdinand VI at the Spanish court. This was followed by commissions to compose Metastasio's *Siroe* for the same occasion the following year, and *L'eroe cinese* for the king's birthday in 1754. The success of these works at Madrid was such that he received an appointment to compose operas for the court.

After arriving at Madrid (14 October 1755) he composed two *opere serie* which were sumptuously mounted the following year – *La ninfa smarrita* and the first setting of Metastasio's *Nitteti*. His annual salary was then nearly doubled, and he received a grant to bring his wife, the singer Zeffirina Anselmi, and two sons from Italy. After Charles III came to the Spanish throne in 1759 Conforto's importance declined. From then on he wrote occasional festive music and enjoyed the title of the king's *maestro de capilla*, but wrote no large-scale theatrical works.

Conforto wrote brilliant, pleasing melodies similar to those of Corradini, Mele, David Perez and other Neapolitan composers who were brought to the Iberian peninsula. In collaboration with the castrato Farinelli, who was then the manager of the court theatres at Aranjuez and Buen Retiro, he played an important part in establishing the taste for Italian opera in Spain: his works were sung in Italian by Italian singers (except for the tenor roles assigned to Raaff) with bilingual librettos for those ignorant of the language. He did not ally himself with national currents, and remained in Spain for business rather than artistic reasons.

La finta vedova (commedia, 2, P. Trinchera), Naples, Fiorentini, carn. 1746, *F-Pc*

La finta tartara (farsa, 2, A. Valle), Rome, Valle, carn. 1747

L'amore costante (tragicommedia, 2, C. De Palma), Naples, Fiorentini, aut. 1747

Antigono (dramma, 2, P. Metastasio), Naples, S Carlo, Dec 1750, *A-Wn*, *I-Nc*, *P-La*, Favourite Songs (London, 1757)

La festa cinese (componimento drammatico, 1, Metastasio), Aranjuez, 30 May 1751

Gli inganni per amore (commedia), Naples, Fiorentini, spr. 1752, lib. *I-Nn*

Siroe (dramma, 3, Metastasio), Madrid, Buen Retiro, 30 May 1752, *P-La*

La cantarina (int, 1, D. Macchia), Madrid, 1753

La commediante (commedia, 2, A. Palomba), Naples, Fiorentini, carn. 1754

Ezio (dramma, 3, Metastasio), Reggio Emilia, Moderno, May 1754, *D-Dlb*, *I-Nc*, *Mc*

L'eroe cinese (Metastasio), Madrid, Buen Retiro, 23 Sept 1754, *P-La*

Adriano in Siria (dramma, 3, Metastasio), Naples, S Carlo, 4 Nov 1754, *I-Nc*, *P-La*; rev. Madrid, Buen Retiro, 23 Sept 1757, *La*

La finta contessina, Naples, Fiorentini, 1754, *F-Pc* [perf. date according to Stieger]

Livia Claudia vestale (dramma, 3, A. Guidi), Rome, Dame, carn. 1755, *I-Nc*, *P-La*

La ninfa smarrita (dramma, 1, G. Bonecchi), Aranjuez, 30 May 1756

Nitteti (dramma, 3, Metastasio), Madrid, Buen Retiro, 23 Sept 1756, *I-Nc*

La forza del genio, o sia Il pastor guerriero (commedia, 2, Bonecchi), Aranjuez, 30 May 1758, *P-La*, 1 act *GB-Lcm*

Aria for Semiramide, *Nc*; aria for Alessandro Severo, cited in Breitkopf catalogue of 1765

*

ES (J. Subirá); *StiegerO*
L. Carmena y Millán: *Crónica de la ópera italiana en Madrid desde el año 1738 hasta nuestros días* (Madrid, 1878), 13ff
E. Cotarelo y Mori: *Orígenes y establecimiento de la ópera en España hasta 1800* (Madrid, 1917)
J. López-Calo and J. Subirá: 'L'opera in Spagna', *Storia dell'opera*, ed. G. Barblan and A. Basso, ii/1 (Turin, 1977), 489–536
E. Casares, ed.: F. Asenjo Barbieri: *Documentos sobre música española y epistolario* (*Legado Barbieri*) (Madrid, 1988), 164

ROBERT STEVENSON

Congreve, William (*b* Bardsley, Yorks., bap. 10 Feb 1670; *d* Bath, 19 Jan 1729). English dramatist and librettist. His stage career began in the 1690s with two comedies for the United Company at the Theatre Royal, *The Old Batchelour* and *The Double-Dealer*, both of which had music by Henry Purcell. After the Actors' Rebellion of 1694–5 and the establishment of the theatre in Lincoln's Inn Fields, Congreve left the Theatre Royal with the rebel troupe, which opened with his *Love for Love* (1695), one of the biggest successes of the period. At Lincoln's Inn Fields Congreve became close friends with the house composer John Eccles and his protégée, the actress-singer Anne Bracegirdle. Eccles wrote the music for Congreve's comedy *The Way of the World* (1700), not much of a success at its première but now recognized as a great play. In 1701 a group of noblemen organized a contest to encourage English opera composers and commissioned Congreve to write a libretto, *The Judgment of Paris*, which all contestants were to set. Congreve expected his friend Eccles to win, aided by casting Mrs Bracegirdle as Venus, but a rank outsider, John Weldon, received first prize. Shortly thereafter, Congreve formed a partnership with the playwright and architect John Vanbrugh to build a replacement for the tiny Lincoln's Inn Fields playhouse and the derelict Dorset Garden theatre. The result was the magnificent Queen's Theatre in the Haymarket, which opened in April 1705. Congreve, who had hoped the new theatre would revitalize English spoken drama, soon became disillusioned and dropped out of the partnership after the financially disastrous first season. But he was not opposed to opera and sometime during 1705–6 wrote *Semele*, which has been described as the finest libretto in the English language. It was set by Eccles, who finished the score in November or December 1706, but was not performed, being pushed aside by *Thomyris*, an Italian pasticcio. Congreve published the libretto of *Semele* in 1710, and Handel transformed it into a secular oratorio in 1743.

Congreve's *The Mourning Bride* formed the basis of Coltellini's *Almeria*, set by de Majo in 1761.

*

J. C. Hodges: *Congreve the Man* (New York, 1941)
William Congreve: Letters and Documents, ed. J. C. Hodges (New York, 1964)
B. Trowell: 'Congreve and the 1744 Semele libretto', *MT*, cxi (1970), 993–4 [also 1219]
Vice Chamberlain Coke's Theatrical Papers, 1706–1715, ed. J. Milhous and R. D. Hume (Carbondale, IL, 1982)

CURTIS PRICE

Conklin, John (*b* Hartford, CT, 22 June 1937). American stage designer. He is one of the principal figures in American stage design, both for opera and for the theatre, and has designed for the Metropolitan, San Francisco Opera, Houston Grand Opera, the Opera Theatre of St Louis, Glimmerglass Opera and Seattle Opera, among others. For San Francisco he designed the *Ring* (1985) and for Seattle Francesca Zambello's production of *War and Peace* (1990). His style is conceptual and semiotic rather than painterly or literal, and in its open approach to the design possibilities has had an enormous influence. He designed the costumes for Robert Wilson's production of *Die Zauberflöte* at the Paris Opéra Bastille in 1991. Conklin is professor at the Tisch School of the Arts at New York University.

For illustration *see* CORIGLIANO, JOHN.

PATRICK J. SMITH

Conlon, James (Joseph) (*b* New York, 18 March 1950). American conductor. He studied at the Juilliard School, New York, and made his début conducting *Boris Godunov* at the 1971 Spoleto Festival in Italy. After receiving the conducting award of the American National Orchestral Association, he conducted the first performance of Barber's revised version of *Antony and Cleopatra* at Juilliard in 1975 and made his Metropolitan début in 1976 with *Die Zauberflöte*. His British opera début was in *Macbeth* with Scottish Opera in the same year, followed by *Don Carlos* at Covent Garden in 1979. He has returned there several times, as well as working at the Paris Opéra and the Maggio Musicale, Florence. Conlon's opera engagements in the USA have included a three-year Verdi cycle at Chicago Lyric Opera, 1988–90. He recorded *La bohème* for Luigi Comencini's 1988 film. He became chief conductor at the Cologne Opera in 1989, having made his début there the previous year in Harry Kupfer's production of *Lady Macbeth of the Mtsensk District*, and has been much praised for fiery, alert and well-disciplined performances.

NOËL GOODWIN

Connecticut Opera. American company based in HARTFORD.

Connell, Elizabeth (*b* Port Elizabeth, 22 Oct 1946). Irish soprano of South African birth. She studied at the London Opera Centre, making her début as a mezzo-soprano in 1972 at Wexford as Varvara (*Kát'a Kabanová*). With Australian Opera (1973–4) she sang Venus, Kostelnička and Amneris. With the ENO (1975–80) she sang Eboli, Azucena, Herodias (*Salome*), Kabanicha, Eglantine (*Euryanthe*), Rossini's Isabella, Bartók's Judith, Sieglinde, Donna Elvira and Marina. Her Covent Garden début was in 1976 as Viclinda (*I Lombardi*). At Bayreuth (1980–82) she sang Ortrud and Brangäne. In 1983 she became a soprano. She has sung at La Scala, the Metropolitan, Geneva, Munich, Amsterdam, Hamburg, Glyndebourne, Vienna and San Francisco. Her roles include Fiordiligi, Vitellia, Electra (*Idomeneo*), Marie (*Wozzeck*), Elisabeth (*Tannhäuser*), Leonora (*Il trovatore*), Leonore (*Fidelio*), Reiza (*Oberon*), Norma, Senta and Ariadne. A highly dramatic singer, she excels in such roles as Lady Macbeth and Medea.

ELIZABETH FORBES

Conner, Nadine (*b* Los Angeles, 20 Feb 1913). American soprano. She studied in California and with Florence Easton in New York. She first appeared as Marguerite, in Los Angeles in 1940, and made her Metropolitan début in 1941, as Pamina. She was best known for her Mozart roles, including Zerlina and

Susanna, but sang in New York until 1958 as Marguerite, Violetta, Mimì, Gilda, Rosina and Sophie (*Der Rosenkavalier*). She appeared in concert with Bruno Walter and made films with Lauritz Melchior.

DAVID CUMMINGS

Conradi [Conradine], Madame (*b* Dresden, *c*1680; *d* after 1719). German soprano. The daughter of a barber, she sang at the Hamburg Gänsemarkt Opera before 1700. Walther (1732) described her as 'a virtuoso singer' and 'an excellent actress in the Hamburg theatre'. According to Mattheson, she knew scarcely a note of music; she learnt her music by heart from his singing to her. In his translation of Mainwaring's biography of Handel (1761), Mattheson described her as 'almost perfect in her beauty of person', with 'a remarkably fine voice' and with a range *a–d″* 'at the same strength ... this made her the most distinguished of female singers'.

In 1705 she made guest appearances, with Mattheson, at the Brunswick Opera. In 1706 and 1708 she sang at the weddings of the Prussian Crown Prince and the King of Prussia in Berlin, in Stricker's *Sieg der Schönheit über die Helden* and *Alexanders Heirat mit Roxane*. She retired from the theatre in 1709 and married a Count Gruzewska in 1711.

HANS JOACHIM MARX

Conradi, August (*b* Berlin, 27 June 1821; *d* Berlin, 26 May 1873). German composer. He studied harmony and composition with Karl Friedrich Rungenhagen, the director of the Berlin Singakademie. In 1843 he was appointed organist of the Invalidenhaus, Berlin, and wrote his first symphony. In Weimar he assisted Liszt as a copyist, first in early 1844, and again in 1848–9. Meanwhile, his operetta *Rübezahl* was produced in Berlin by amateurs in 1846 and repeated professionally in Stettin the following year. He held several conducting posts: at Stettin from the winter of 1849, in Berlin, Düsseldorf and Cologne from 1851, and back in Berlin from 1856. It was for Berlin theatres that he regularly turned out his operas and more than a hundred operettas, vaudeville sketches, farces and variously named dramatic tableaux.

Muza Hayrredin, die letzte Maurenkönigin (grosse Oper, 4, G. Bouillon), ?Berlin, 1852

Die Braut des Flussgottes (komische Oper, 2, after J. C. Grünbaum), Berlin, Kgl Opernhaus, 21 March 1859

Das schönste Mädchen im Städtchen (komische Oper, 2, A. von Winterfeld), Berlin, Friedrich-Wilhelmstädtisches, 10 June 1868

Aschenbrödel, oder Der gläserne Pantoffel (Märchen, 5, after E. Pasqué and E. Pohl), Berlin, Victoria, 4 Oct 1868

Schneewittchen (Märchen, 4, Pasqué and K. Brandt), Berlin, Victoria, 30 Oct 1869

Das Wunderhorn (Märchen, 4, Pasqué and Brandt), Berlin, Victoria, 17 Dec 1870

Die weisse Katze (Zaubermärchen, 3, after A. L'Arronge), Berlin, Victoria, 15 June 1872

Faust und die schöne Helena (Feerie, 4, Pasqué, Brandt and E. Jacobson, after A. R. Lesage), Berlin, Victoria, 18 Jan 1873

*

StiegerO

Obituary, *Neue Berliner Musikzeitung*, xxvii (1873), 181

G. R. Kruse: 'August Conradi', *Die Musik*, xii/4 (1933–4), 3–13

E. Dellé: *Das Victoria-Theater in Berlin (1859–91)* (diss., Free U. of Berlin, 1954)

L. Richter: 'Das Berliner Couplet der Gründerzeit', *Studien zur Trivialmusik des 19. Jahrhunderts*, ed. C. Dahlhaus (Regensburg, 1967), 199–217

E. Wischer: *Das Wallner-Theater in Berlin (1855–68)* (Munich, 1967)

HUMPHREY SEARLE/R

Conradi, Johann Georg (*d* Oettingen, 22 May 1699). German composer. His father, the organist Caspar Conrad, had settled in Oettingen, a small court town to the south of Ansbach, no later than 1644. Johann Georg probably received much of his musical training from his father. In 1671 he became director of music to the court of Oettingen-Oettingen. In 1683 he went as Kapellmeister to the more illustrious court at Ansbach, where Margrave Johann Friedrich fostered a rich musical establishment. During this period many of Lully's operas appear to have been performed at the court, which would explain the strong French stylistic characteristics of Conradi's later operas. The court orchestra was disbanded when the margrave died in 1686, and in March 1687 Conradi found new employment as Kapellmeister at Römhild, the residence of Duke Heinrich of Saxe-Gotha. By mid-1690 Conradi was living in Hamburg, where almost immediately he was appointed music director at the famous opera house on the Gänsemarkt. For about two and a half years his operas dominated the repertory, for which he wrote nine works. By 1698 he had returned to Oettingen as Kapellmeister.

Conradi's music typifies the creativity of the German Kapellmeister-composer of the late 17th century. When employed at small Protestant courts, he composed sacred music in various forms, including cantatas in German and psalms and other biblical text settings in Latin. He also wrote occasional pieces for ceremonies and festivities. However, like several other German composers of the period – Franck, Förtsch and, slightly later, Keiser – he was attracted to opera and to Hamburg, which boasted the only professional, public opera house in the German-speaking lands. One must assume, despite the lack of sources, that Conradi had written operas before going to Hamburg; otherwise he would hardly have been appointed to the position of composer and musical director of so famous a theatre. The titles of his Hamburg operas, all to librettos by Postel, are given by Mattheson in *Der musicalische Patriot*. The only extant score from among the nine known to have been performed in Hamburg is his first, *Die schöne und getreue Ariadne* (1691). It is specially important because it is the earliest surviving opera composed for Hamburg, and it permits a critical evaluation of Conradi's contribution to the history of opera in Germany.

Ariadne consists of a cosmopolitan mixture of Venetian, German and French musical styles, although the French spirit dominates everything but the recitatives. The score proves that it was Conradi rather than his successor in Hamburg, J. S. Kusser, who introduced French musical influences to Hamburg. The opening bars of the overture immediately suggest the style of Lully in their French ceremonial pomp and the characteristic dotted rhythms. Another French element is the numerous variations on chaconne basses; the closing scene, for example, is a movement marked 'Passacaille', consisting of 78 variations over a four-bar ground – the conventional four-note descending tetrachord common in earlier Italian operas as well as in those of Lully. These constantly unfolding variations over a stereotyped bass are reminiscent of Purcell's extended ground-bass pieces. Another extended variation movement begins the long solo scene for Ariadne at the start of Act 2: some 200 bars over a ten-bar chaconne bass.

With its largely simple, unornamented melodies the prevailing vocal style also suggests French musical taste.

The arias are usually rather short and often in some form of written-out *ABA* structure. There are a number of mellifluous duets. The orchestra plays an active role, although scoring is seldom specified. About half of the 38 arias in the three acts have orchestral accompaniment, and the orchestra also takes part in solo ensembles as well as in some of the recitatives and ariosos. The score is decidedly lyrical, less than a third of it consisting of recitative. The recitatives are, however, of particular musical and historical importance. Conradi employed a highly dramatic, emotion-laden style, which fully observes the rhetorically expressive emphases of Postel's poetry. The recitatives show that Conradi must have known Venetian opera as well as those of French composers. *Ariadne*, according to Mattheson, 'had paid for itself very well, and received much applause'. As late as 1722 Keiser revised the score extensively for a revival in Hamburg.

See also SCHÖNE UND GETREUE ARIADNE, DIE.

all but the first item in three acts, to librettos by C. H. Postel, and performed in Hamburg, Theater am Gänsemarkt; scores lost unless otherwise stated

Templum Martis oder Auffzug, Ansbach, 1683, lib. lost
Die schöne und getreue Ariadne, 1691, *US-Wc*
Diogenes Cynicus, 1691; also attrib. J. P. Förtsch
Der fromme und friedfertige König der Römer Numa Pompilius, 1691
Der tapffere Kayser Carolus Magnus und dessen erste Gemahlin Hermingardis, 1692
Der Verstöhrung Jerusalem erster Theil, oder Die Eroberung des Tempels, 1692
Der Verstöhrung Jerusalem ander Theil, oder Die Eroberung der Burg Zion, 1692
Der grosse König der africanischen Wenden Gensericus als Rom- und Karthagens Überwinder, 1693; also attrib. J. S. Kusser
Der königliche Printz aus Pohlen Sigismundus, oder Das menschliche Leben wie ein Traum, 1693
Der wunderbar-vergnüte Pygmalion, 1693

*

J. Mattheson: *Der musicalische Patriot* (Hamburg, 1728)
H. C. Wolff: *Die Barockoper in Hamburg* (Wolfenbüttel, 1957)
H. R. Jung: 'Johann Georg Conradi', *BMw*, xiii (1971), 31–55; xiv (1972), 1–62
G. J. Buelow: 'Die schöne und getreue Ariadne (Hamburg, 1691): a Lost Opera by J. G. Conradi Rediscovered', *AcM*, xliv (1972), 108–21

GEORGE J. BUELOW

Constanţa. Port city in Romania, on the western coast of the Black Sea. It was well known in antiquity as the Greek city of Tomis, and was named after Constantine the Great in the 4th century AD. For centuries it was part of the Ottoman empire. From 1877 plays and performances by opera companies were given regularly; in 1957 the Teatrul Liric (Lyric Theatre) was founded as a permanent state institution for music and dance. An annual season (1 June to 1 September) includes performances in Romanian, Italian and German, with many foreign guest performers. In addition, a festival called Luna Muzicii de Operă şi Balet (Month of Opera, Music and Ballet) has been held since 1974 and is the only one of its type in Romania. The repertory of the Lyric Theatre includes the standard French and Italian works; the company has also given world premières of operas by Sergiu Sarchizov, Teodor Bratu, Elly Roman, Viorel Doboş, Iulius Szarvady and others. The ensemble has toured Austria, Bulgaria, Italy, Switzerland, Belgium, Germany and the Netherlands.

*

V. Cosma: *România muzicală* [Musical Romania] (Bucharest, 1980)

VIOREL COSMA

Constantinescu, Paul (*b* Ploieşti, 30 June 1909; *d* Bucharest, 20 Dec 1963). Romanian composer. He studied at the Bucharest Conservatory (1929–33) and in Vienna (1933–5), where his teachers included Joseph Marx, then taught at the Bucharest Academy of Church Music (1937–41) and at the Conservatory (1941–63). His researches into folk music and Byzantine chant greatly influenced his own compositions, which include orchestral, choral and chamber works, as well as two operas. He managed to establish an individual style that served as the foundation for a national school and pointed the way for the next generation. *O noapte furtunoasă* ('A Stormy Night') is a two-act comic opera, with a libretto by the composer after Ion Luca Caragiale's play, first given at the Bucharest Opera on 25 October 1935, and revised in 1950. The lyric drama *Pană Lesnea Rusalim* (in three acts and five scenes, to a libretto by Victor Eftimiu) had its first performance at the Romanian Opera in Cluj-Napoca on 27 June 1956. Here the composer successfully integrates folk-music elements (the carol, the ballad, the dirge) and makes effective use of orchestral colour to highlight the text.

*

O. L. Cosma: *Opera românească* [The Romanian Opera] (Bucharest, 1962)
V. Tomescu: *Paul Constantinescu* (Bucharest, 1967)

VIOREL COSMA

Constantino, Florencio (*b* Bilbao, 1869; *d* Mexico City, 19 Nov 1919). Spanish tenor. While working as a ship's engineer he discovered a voice of great natural beauty and after a brief period of training made a successful début at Montevideo in 1892. He gained a reputation in Italy, Germany and Spain, and in 1906 a promising career opened up in the USA. He went to the Manhattan Opera Company in 1908, singing in *Rigoletto* with Tetrazzini, and was especially admired for his exquisite style in *I puritani*. He sang at the Boston Opera Company's opening night in 1909 and appeared regularly, giving his last performances in the USA in 1915. Shortly afterwards he went to Mexico City where he died in a hospital for the destitute, having been found lying in a street. His many recordings show some of the grace and much of the beautiful tone for which he was famous.

*

GV (R. Celletti; R. Vegeto)

J. B. STEANE

Consul, The. Musical drama in three acts by GIAN CARLO MENOTTI to his own libretto; Philadelphia, Shubert Theatre, 1 March 1950.

The Philadelphia première was a try-out for a Broadway run that began on 15 March 1950 at the Ethel Barrymore Theatre with Thomas Schippers conducting. It was enormously successful and that year won the New York Drama Critics' Circle Award for the best musical play and the Pulitzer Prize for Music. It enjoyed a run of 269 performances in New York and the following year was produced at La Scala, Milan, and in London, Zürich, Berlin and Vienna.

The action takes place in Magda Sorel's shabby apartment and in the waiting-room of a consulate in a large anonymous European city; the time is 'the present'. The opera begins in the dark and empty apartment with the sound of a gramophone recording of a French popular song drifting through the open windows from a café below. Suddenly the orchestra plays, loud and dissonant and at a much faster tempo as John Sorel (baritone), wounded, rushes in and falls to the floor; his meeting of freedom fighters has been raided by the secret police. Magda, his wife (soprano), and his Mother (contralto) rush in from the other side of the room. Thus the stage is set for a grim, intense drama.

John hides as the police arrive. After they have left he says he must flee to a neighbouring country and that Magda must go to the consulate for a visa. In the next scene Magda encounters bureaucratic delays. She pleads with the Secretary (mezzo-soprano) but the Consul does not appear. She also meets people in the same predicament as herself, most notable among them the Magician, Nika Magadoff (tenor).

Act 2 also opens with the offstage recording of the French song. The Mother sings a lullaby to Magda's dying baby while Magda sleeps and has a hallucinatory nightmare. A stone crashes through a window. This was a prearranged signal for them to send for the glass-cutter Assan (baritone), who will bring news of John. Assan arrives after a further visit by the secret police agent (bass) and tells them that John is hiding out in the mountains. Meanwhile, the Mother notices that the baby has died. The major part of the second scene (in the waiting-room) is dominated by the Magician, who performs tricks, hypnotizes the waiting people and leads them into a waltz. After a bitter argument with the Secretary Magda has a grand climactic aria, 'To this we've come'. Finally, the Secretary says that Magda can see the Consul as soon as an important visitor leaves. When she discovers that the visitor is the secret police agent Magda faints.

Act 3 begins at the consulate. While the waiting continues, one person, Vera Boronel (contralto), obtains her papers. In counterpoint to this Assan arrives to tell Magda that John wants to come back. This frightens them both, but Magda gives Assan a note for John that will supposedly solve the problem. She then rushes off, forgetting her handbag. John appears and is arrested. The Secretary promises him that she will telephone his wife. A funeral march in quintuple time leads into the final scene, which is devoted to Magda's suicide by gas: it includes a hallucinatory visitation of all the characters and a dance of death led by the Magician. At the moment of death the telephone rings.

The Consul is replete with powerful theatrical effects and some of Menotti's strongest and most dissonant music. While much of the music is traditionally tonal, often with a modal flavour, there is a considerable increase over earlier works in the amount and the level of dissonance, as at the orchestral opening. Several passages could be classified as atonal. Certain familiar Menotti devices are used: parallel chords, frequent triads, sequences and pedals. BRUCE ARCHIBALD

Contadina astuta, La. Intermezzo by Pergolesi; *see* LIVIETTA E TRACOLLO.

Contadina in corte, La ('The Country Girl at Court'). *Opera buffa* in two acts by ANTONIO SACCHINI to a libretto by NICCOLÒ TASSI; Rome, Teatro Valle, Carnival 1765.

This opera enjoyed more than 20 productions between its première and the mid-1780s, reaching a wide variety of cities from Rome to Warsaw. The version Sacchini set originally is a four-voice intermezzo about a country girl, Sandrina (soprano), engaged to Berto (bass), but seduced by Ruggiero (tenor), who is from a higher social class. Sandrina's friend, Tancia (soprano), also loves Berto, but this affection is not reciprocated. The story describes Sandrina's seduction by Ruggiero and the material wealth he can offer; Berto plots to win Sandrina back, while Tancia encourages her to stay with Ruggiero. Ruggiero keeps her in the end, and Berto is paid to marry Tancia. Sacchini's setting is full of charming melodies but also includes a melodramatic accompanied recitative for Berto when he realizes he has lost Sandrina.

A related text was also set by Giacomo Rust (1763, Venice) and by Pasquale Anfossi (1775, Venice), as *La contadina incivilita*; both these settings have seven characters rather than four. Ruggiero (here called Rinaldo) is provided with a comparably high-born betrothed, Clarice (soprano), Sandrina is given a low-born lover, Menichino (tenor), and there is also a servant, Fabio (bass), who instructs Sandrina in proper court behaviour. In this version Sandrina does not have the heart to leave her lover, and everyone marries a partner of the proper status. Some of the librettos with this expanded cast mention Sacchini as the composer; he may have revised his work, or it may be that these operas are pasticcios based on Sacchini's intermezzo.

MARY HUNTER

Contarini, Marco (*b* ?Piazzola sul Brenta, nr Padua, 20 Feb 1632; *d* Padua, ?17 ?May 1689). Italian patron of the arts. He came of a wealthy family and built two theatres on his estate, PIAZZOLA SUL BRENTA. There he commissioned and produced operas and other entertainments during the 1670s and 80s, engaging several of Venice's leading composers, notably Carlo Pallavicino and Domenico Freschi. His collection of over 100 manuscript scores of the period 1639–85 (now in *I-Vnm*) is a major source of 17th-century Venetian opera.

C. Ivanovich: *Minerva al tavolino* (Venice, 1681)
T. Wiel: *I codici musicali contariniani del secolo XVII nella R. Biblioteca di San Marco in Venezia* (Venice, 1888)
P. Camerini: *Piazzola* (Milan, 1925)
T. Walker: 'Gli errori di "Minerva al tavolino": osservazioni sulla cronologia delle prime opere veneziane', *Venezia e il melodramma nel seicento: Venice 1972*, 7–20
——: '*Ubi Lucius*: Thoughts on Reading *Medoro*', in A. Aureli and F. Lucio: *Il Medoro*, DMV, iv (1984), pp. cxxxi–clxiv

THOMAS WALKER

Conte di Saldagna, Il ('The Count of Saldagna'). *Tragedia* in three acts by ANGELO TARCHI to a libretto by FERDINANDO MORETTI; Milan, Teatro alla Scala, 10 June 1787.

Ramiro, the Count of Saldagna (soprano castrato), has secretly married Cimene (soprano), sister of Alfonso II, King of Asturia and Leone (bass). Alfonso disapproves of their marriage, believing Ramiro beneath his sister's station. He wishes to honour the request of Abdala, ambassador of the Moors (tenor), and marry her to their king. Angry at learning of the secret marriage, he takes Ramiro prisoner. With his counsellor Consalvo (soprano castrato), he devises a diabolical plot to take vengeance: Ramiro is pardoned, and a public celebration is arranged, but the celebratory cup is poisoned, and Ramiro dies a prolonged death before the horrified company.

The finest work of the innovatory librettist Moretti, it ranks among the earliest Romantic or Revolutionary operas in its treatment of historical subject matter without regard for the traditional rules of good taste: the ruler no longer stands for rectitude but commits a foul betrayal. The opera is also among the first to infuse a plot based on historical subject matter with French spectacular elements, usually reserved in Italian opera for works on legendary or mythological topics. Tarchi's musical setting – with its use of chorus in dialogue with the principals, its many ensembles, and its *divertissements* of chorus, dance, marches and battle scenes – contributes to the richness and spectacle of the work. The scoring of the recitatives with strings (and sometimes wind) throughout makes it unique in Italian *opera seria*.

MARITA P. McCLYMONDS

Conte lyrique (Fr.: 'lyric tale'). Term used in the late 19th century for a particular kind of *opéra comique*; *see* OPÉRA COMIQUE, §6.

Contes d'Hoffmann, Les ('The Tales of Hoffmann'). *Opéra fantastique* in five acts by JACQUES OFFENBACH to a libretto by JULES BARBIER after the play by Barbier and MICHEL CARRÉ based on the stories of E. T. A. HOFFMANN; Paris, Opéra-Comique (Salle Favart), 10 February 1881.

Hoffmann *a poet*	tenor
Olympia *a doll* Antonia *Crespel's daughter* Giulietta *a courtesan* Stella *a prima donna*	soprano
Nicklausse *a friend of Hoffmann* The Muse A Ghost *Antonia's mother*	mezzo-soprano
Counsellor Lindorf Coppélius *a maker of eyes* Dr Miracle Captain Dapertutto *a magician*	bass or baritone
Spalanzani *a physician*	tenor
Crespel *a violin maker, Antonia's father*	bass or baritone
Andrès *Stella's servant* Cochenille *Spalanzani's servant* Frantz *Crespel's servant* Pitichinaccio *Giulietta's servant*	tenor
Luther *innkeeper*	baritone
Nathanaël (*students*)	tenor
Wolframm (*students*)	baritone
Hermann (*students*)	baritone
Wilhelm (*students*)	baritone
Peter Schlemil	baritone

Students, tavern waiters, guests of Spalanzani, gamblers, valets, spirits of beer and wine

Setting Nuremberg, Paris, Munich, Venice in the early 19th century

The opera is based upon an 1851 play in which the poet E. T. A. Hoffmann is portrayed as a participant in various of his own stories. His spiritual and moral decline is depicted through successive loves – a frivolous infatuation with a mechanical doll, Olympia, genuine but thwarted love with the singer Antonia, and idle tarrying with the courtesan Giulietta. The three acts depicting these episodes are framed by a prologue and epilogue. In them Hoffmann is depicted telling these stories while awaiting his latest love, the prima donna Stella, who is finally recognized as a combination of the three earlier loves. Similarly, his constant companion Nicklausse is revealed as a personification of his poetic muse. To emphasize these unities, his various loves are properly sung by a single singer, as are Nicklausse and the Muse and also Hoffmann's four adversaries Lindorf, Coppélius, Dr Miracle and Dapertutto. At the première Hoffmann was sung by Jean-Alexandre Talazac, with Adèle Isaac as his lovers, and the bass Alexandre Taskin as the villains.

Offenbach seemingly regarded *Les contes d'Hoffmann* as a last chance for recognition as a composer of serious opera rather than of the frivolous and apparently ephemeral *opéras bouffes* for which he was best known. While coping with other pressing commissions, he devoted to it a considerable part of his energies during what were to prove the last few years of his life. Along the way the plan for the opera underwent some fundamental changes. Offenbach designed it first for the Théâtre de la Gaîté-Lyrique, with recitatives, a baritone Hoffmann and lyric soprano lovers. Then he was forced to rework it for the Opéra-Comique with spoken dialogue, a tenor Hoffmann and a coloratura soprano.

When Offenbach died the opera was in rehearsal and the music apparently conceived in its entirety, including the orchestration, although some detailed working out of the fourth act (Giulietta) and the final act (epilogue) remained to be done. Ernest Guiraud was brought in to produce a finished version, but before the opera reached production crucial changes were made. First, the mezzo-soprano Alice Ducasse was replaced and her combined role of Nicklausse and the Muse divided between a young soprano, Marguerite Ugalde, and an actress. Then dissatisfaction with some aspect of the Giulietta act caused its deletion at the première, with some of its numbers dispersed to other acts. Even when the Giulietta act was finally performed and published, it was placed before the Antonia act, perhaps to mask its less than fully finished state. Successive editions of the score have provided varying texts, some with recitatives evidently by Guiraud.

Some of the original material may possibly have been destroyed in the fire at the Salle Favart on 25 May 1887. Certainly the opera's association with the horrific fire at the Ringtheater in Vienna on 8 December 1881, when it was about to receive its second Viennese performance, gave it a reputation for bad luck that slowed its international acceptance. Only after a spectacular production in Berlin in 1905 did it really establish its international popularity. By then it had been subjected to further rewriting for a production at Monte Carlo in 1904. At the instance of the director, Raoul Gunsbourg, the Giulietta act was built up by inserting two new passages with music fashioned by ANDRÉ BLOCH to words apparently by the original librettist's son, Pierre Barbier.

Using music from *Le voyage dans la lune* (1875), they fashioned a new aria 'Scintille, diamant' for the baritone Maurice Renaud in the role of Dapertutto, and also added a 'septet' (actually for six solo voices and chorus), 'Hélas, mon coeur s'égare encore', built on the theme of the barcarolle, to provide a brilliant climax. These changes were perpetuated in the 1907 Choudens score, which also transferred Dapertutto's original aria 'Tourne, tourne, miroir' to Coppélius with different words as 'J'ai des yeux, de vrais yeux' and added a further passage to the Giulietta act in which Hoffmann discovers the loss of his reflection. In this form the opera has retained widespread popularity for its spectacular staging and for individual numbers such as Hoffmann's 'Legend of Kleinzach', Olympia's 'Doll's Song' and,

Poster for Offenbach's 'Les contes d'Hoffmann', printed by Lemercier for Choudens at the time of the original production at the Opéra-Comique, Paris, in 1881

above all, the 'Barcarolle' – one of the world's most popular melodies, which Offenbach had taken from an earlier work, *Les fées du Rhin*. During the 20th century the work has been produced repeatedly at opera houses throughout the world, often with the various leading soprano roles assigned to different singers – a fundamental denial of the opera's dramatic unity, but a rare opportunity to parade multiple leading ladies in a single opera.

Since World War II numerous attempts have been made to restore Offenbach's original conception. Thanks especially to the conductor and Offenbach scholar Antonio de Almeida, important manuscript sources have continued to be uncovered into the 1980s. These have been used for new performing editions by Fritz Oeser (Vienna, 1976) and Michael Kaye (Los Angeles, 1988). Oeser published important material for the first time, notably numbers for Nicklausse and the Muse, but added accretions of his own to those of Guiraud, whereas Kaye confined himself to authentic Offenbach. It remains to be seen to what extent these versions will finally replace the traditional text; but it is anyway impossible to produce a 'definitive' text for an opera of which some parts were composed two or three times over but which lacked the final finish and pruning. However, key elements of the restorations – the original order of acts, a single soprano heroine and single baritone villain, the identification of Nicklausse with the Muse, the restoration of the music for the latter, and the dropping of alterations by Pierre Barbier and Bloch – must be observed to give a faithful representation of Offenbach's conception.

Act 1 (Prologue) *Luther's tavern close to the opera house in Nuremberg* In the moonlight an invisible chorus of spirits of beer and wine sets the scene ('Glou, glou, glou'). Hoffmann's Muse bemoans the poet's dissolute life ('La vérité, dit-on, sortit d'un puits') and assumes the identity of his student friend Nicklausse. Counsellor Lindorf, a powerful local politician with designs on Hoffmann's current lover, Stella ('Dans les rôles d'amoureux langoureux'), succeeds in obtaining the key to her dressing-room from her servant Andrès. A rowdy bunch of students arrive ('Jusqu'au matin remplis mon verre'), followed by Hoffmann, who is in an agitated state. They persuade him to tell his story of the dwarf Kleinzach ('Il était une fois à la cour d'Eisenach'), but his mind (and the song) wanders to his dreams of a beautiful woman before he is persuaded to resume the story. Seeing Lindorf, Hoffmann recognizes him as his perpetual adversary in his love affairs and foresees another disaster. Prevailing upon Hoffmann to tell the stories of his loves, the students recharge their glasses and settle down for the evening.

Act 2 (Olympia) *The laboratory of the physicist Spalanzani* The eccentric inventor Spalanzani is hoping that his latest invention, a mechanical doll, will earn enough money to recoup the losses sustained from the bankruptcy of his banker. He is worried, though, that his former partner Coppélius may claim part of the proceeds. Hoffmann arrives as a pupil of Spalanzani, who talks of his 'daughter' Olympia. Spalanzani leaves to prepare for the arrival of his guests, and Hoffmann's heart leaps when, behind a curtain, he sees what he takes to be the sleeping figure of the daughter. Nicklausse vainly attempts to make light of his infatuation ('Une poupée aux yeux d'émail'). Coppélius enters with a collection of optical instruments, including a pair of magic spectacles which make anything seen through them beautiful ('Je me nomme Coppélius'). When Spalanzani returns, Coppélius demands a share of the profits from the mechanical doll, whose eyes he has supplied. To get rid of him, Spalanzani gives him a worthless cheque as the guests enter to a stately minuet ('Non aucun hôte vraiment'). Spalanzani presents his 'daughter', who attracts admiration with a coloratura aria ('Les oiseaux dans la charmille'), punctuated from time to time by pauses for her to be recharged. Hoffmann, deceived by his magic spectacles into believing her human, is completely bewitched and sings a rapturous romance ('Ah! vivre deux'). The guests return from dinner and begin waltzing ('Oui, pauvres fous'), but a furious Coppélius enters; he has discovered the cheque to be worthless and vows vengeance. Hoffmann is left breathless by his animated dance with Olympia, who then retires to her room. From it comes the sound of breaking machinery as Coppélius destroys Spalanzani's invention and the object of Hoffmann's infatuation. The guests gather around Hoffmann, mocking his foolishness.

Act 3 (Antonia) *A room in Crespel's house in Munich* The walls of the room are decorated with Crespel's musical instruments and a portrait of his dead wife. Seated at the piano, his daughter Antonia sings a nostalgic song about a lost love ('Elle a fui, la tourterelle') but afterwards collapses exhausted. Her father rushes in to remind her that she has inherited her mother's fatal chest complaint and that to continue singing will mean an early death. Crespel has hurried to Munich to protect Antonia from the influence of her lover Hoffmann, and he instructs his old servant Frantz not to open the door. However, Frantz is deaf and befuddled ('Jour et nuit je me mets en quatre'), and soon Hoffmann and Nicklausse gain admission. Nicklausse tries out a violin ('Vois sous l'archet frémissant') and Hoffmann sits at the piano and sings a snatch of a love song ('C'est une chanson d'amour'). Antonia appears and, despite Nicklausse's efforts, she joins Hoffmann in the song. She tells him she has been forbidden to sing and, when her father returns, flees to her room. Hoffmann hides and overhears an exchange with the mysterious Dr Miracle, whom Crespel accuses of being responsible for his wife's death and seeking to bring about his daughter's. However, Miracle claims that he alone can cure her ('Pour conjurer le danger'). After their departure, Hoffmann persuades Antonia to agree to give up singing, but no sooner has Hoffmann left than Miracle reappears and urges her to sing, conjuring up the voice of her dead mother ('Chère enfant!'). Seizing a violin, Miracle leads them in a frantic trio, which leaves Antonia exhausted. Crespel and Hoffmann rush in, but both despair as Miracle declares Antonia dead.

ACT 4 (Giulietta) *A palace overlooking the Grand Canal in Venice* To the strains of a barcarolle ('Belle nuit, ô nuit d'amour') a gondola carrying Nicklausse and the courtesan Giulietta draws up outside the palace. A wild party is in progress, and Hoffmann sings a vigorous drinking song ('Amis, l'amour tendre et rêveur, erreur!'). Giulietta provocatively introduces Hoffmann to her current lover, Schlemil. Despite Nicklausse's warnings against her charms, Hoffmann rises to the bait. The magician Dapertutto enters and tempts Giulietta in a sinister aria ('Tourne, tourne, miroir'). He promises her a diamond ring if, as she has already done with Schlemil, she will obtain for him Hoffmann's other self – in the form of his reflection. Left alone with Giulietta, Hoffmann expresses his passion for her ('O Dieu! de quelle ivresse') and a rapturous duet follows. When she asks for his reflection to remember him by, he agrees, finding that he is indeed no longer visible in the mirror. Schlemil arrives and finds them together, and Giulietta flees to her boudoir. Schlemil challenges Hoffmann to a duel, and Schlemil is killed. Hoffmann takes the key to Giulietta's boudoir from around Schlemil's neck only to find her throwing her arms around her servant Pitichinaccio. Nicklausse drags Hoffmann away as Dapertutto adds to the mocking laughter.

ACT 5 (Epilogue) *Luther's tavern in Nuremberg* At the end of his melancholy tale Hoffmann seeks solace in wine, until the revelries are interrupted by the entrance of Stella, fresh from her triumph in the opera house. Hoffmann, however, merely sees in her his three lost loves and rejects her. She leaves on Lindorf's arm as the poet sinks into a drunken stupor. Nicklausse remains and, metamorphosing afresh into Hoffmann's Muse, tells him to rekindle the fire of his creative genius ('Des cendres de ton coeur'). A final chorus ('On est grand par l'amour') points the moral that one is enriched by love and sadness.

* * *

On the face of it, *Les contes d'Hoffmann* represents a stark contrast to the frivolous *opéras bouffes* that represent Offenbach's other claims to enduring fame. He was, though, thoroughly at home in opera composition, and throughout his career he had composed more consistently serious works for occasional productions at opera houses. Moreover *Hoffmann* has plentiful moments when the music of *Orphée aux enfers*, *La belle Hélène* and *La Périchole* are close at hand. The fact that the music for 'Scintille, diamant' could be lifted straight from an operetta for one of the more sinister moments shows how much the effect created by Offenbach's music depended on its lyrics and context. *Les contes d'Hoffmann* cannot rival the dramatic power of Bizet's *Carmen*, but Offenbach's thorough technique, his popular touch, and the particular appeal of the Hoffmann creation have combined to provide a work of endless fascination to audiences. ANDREW LAMB

Contessina, La ('The Young Countess'). Libretto by CARLO GOLDONI, first set by Giacomo Maccari (1743, Venice); new version by MARCO COLTELLINI, first set by Florian Leopold Gassmann (1770, Mährisch-Neustadt [now Uničov]).

Goldoni's three-act *commedia per musica* features clever social criticism of the sort often seen in his spoken pieces. Lindoro, son of the rich Venetian merchant Pancrazio, has fallen in love with the Countess, presenting himself as a Milanese marquis, as she will not condescend to marry a tradesman. Her proud father, Count Baccellone Parabolano, approves the match, pending proof of Lindoro's nobility. Pancrazio's direct approach to the Count on behalf of his son is rudely rebuffed, so in the second act he impersonates, with studied affectation, the marquis's many-titled father, Marquis Cavromano. Meanwhile, the Contessina offends Lindoro by favouring a (fictitious) proposition from a would-be *cicisbeo*, relayed by the Count's boatman Gazzetta. In the final act, the undisguised Pancrazio shocks Baccellone with his claim to be the father of the groom, but the Count allows the ceremony to proceed, to avoid embarrassment in front of the guests.

In reworking Goldoni's libretto Coltellini retained the basic plot and characters (making Gazzetta a shop assistant and adding an impertinent maid, Vespina), and even some scenes and locutions, while providing for the ensembles and finales expected in a modern comic opera. In his version the Count's plebeian origins are made known not by an aside but by Gazzetta's entrance disguised as a rustic claiming relation to Count Baccellone. Gazzetta also impersonates a 'Marchese ridicolo' whom the Contessina decides to take on as a *cavaliere servente*.

La contessina was much performed in both versions of the libretto, often with significant changes or additions. Besides Maccari, composers of the original text included Lampugnani in 1759, Gherardeschi in 1766 and Kärzinger in 1775; Coltellini's libretto was also set by Gennaro Astarita and Marcello Bernardini (both in 1773), Giacomo Rust (*Il Conte Baccellone*, 1774) and Niccolò Piccinni (1775). There is a German translation by J. A. Hiller (of which only the arias survive) and a version with music by Wenzel Müller (*Die Gräfin, oder Der übelangebrachte Stolz*, 1786, Vienna). An adaptation, *Il superbo deluso*, with Gassmann's music, was first given in 1772. BRUCE ALAN BROWN

Conti, Carlo (*b* Arpino, Frosinone, 14 Oct 1796; *d* Arpino, 10 July 1868). Italian composer. He studied in Naples, with Zingarelli at the Reale Collegio di Musica di S Sebastiano and with J. S. Mayr. From 1819 to 1821 he taught at S Sebastiano. His earliest compositions were performed while he was a student; among them the *opera semiseria Le truppe in Franconia* (1819) was especially praised by Rossini. Conti quickly made a name for himself as an opera composer, winning fame above all for *L'Olimpia* (1826). At his father's request he gave up composing operas and returned to Arpino in 1831. He became an honorary member, and later president, of the Royal Academy of Arts in Naples and was professor of counterpoint and composition, and later assistant director, at the Conservatorio di S Pietro a Majella. He was elected an associate member of the Institut de France.

Conti's works are remarkable for their refined orchestration and technical command. He faithfully adhered to Rossini's operatic style in his theatrical works. Florimo attributed to Conti the farce *I Metastasiani*, for which no dates are known, and, on the basis of a letter by the composer, the opera *Sansone*, first performed at the S Carlo.

ob – *opera buffa* os – *opera seria*
oss – *opera semiseria*

Le truppe in Franconia (oss, 1), Naples, Reale Collegio di Musica di S Sebastiano, 1819
La pace desiderata (oss, 2), Naples, Nuovo, aut. 1820
Misantropia e pentimento (oss, 2, G. Checcherini), Naples, Nuovo, 4 Feb 1823
Il trionfo della giustizia (2, Checcherini), Naples, Nuovo, wint. 1823
L'Olimpia (os, 2, A. L. Tottola), Naples, S Carlo, 28 Oct 1826
L'audacia fortunata (oss, 2, J. Ferretti), Rome, Valle, carn. 1827
I finti sposi (oss, 2), Rome, Valle, carn. 1827
Bartolomeo della Cavalla, ovvero L'innocente in periglio (oss, 2, Ferretti), Rome, Valle, 10 Sept 1827
Gli Aragonesi in Napoli (ob, 2, Tottola), Naples, Nuovo, 29 Dec 1827
Alexi (os, 2, Tottola), Naples, S Carlo, 6 July 1828, collab. N. Vaccai
Giovanna Shore (os, 3, F. Romani), Milan, Scala, 31 Oct 1829

Doubtful: I Metastasiani, 1 scene and aria *I-Nc*; Sansone

*

DBI (F. Bussi); *ES* (F. Schlitzer); *FlorimoN* FRANCESCO BUSSI

Conti [Contini], **Francesco Bartolomeo** (*b* Florence, 20 Jan 1681; *d* Vienna, 20 July 1732). Italian composer. He first went to Vienna in April 1701, as associate theorbist at the Habsburg court, where he proved himself a master of dramatic composition in the operas, intermezzos, cantatas and oratorios he composed between 1706 and 1732. Music historians arbitrarily place him within the same stylistic framework as Fux and Caldara; but he does not belong with those whose works reflected the conservative musical taste of Charles VI. His operas and intermezzos are well-conceived, entertaining works in a style similar to that developing simultaneously in Naples with Vinci, Hasse and Pergolesi.

Over half of Conti's operas were created for Vienna's carnival season; he held a veritable monopoly on this coveted event from 1714 to 1725. His other dramatic works were designed for celebrations honouring members of the imperial family, most of them for the birthday (28 August) or name-day (19 November) of Empress Elisabeth Christina. Conti's operas for special events were limited, with few exceptions, to a single performance, whereas those for Carnival not only had two or more productions each season but also were repeated in Breslau, Brussels, Brunswick and Hamburg in either their original form or in revisions for German-speaking audiences.

In 1708 Conti was promoted to principal theorbist, a position he held until 1726. His talent as a theorbist and mandolin player was acknowledged beyond Vienna: he entertained Queen Anne in London in 1703 and 1707, was elected to membership in the Accademia Filarmonica of Bologna in 1708 and earned the title 'first theorbist of the world' for his part in the performance of Fux's *Costanza e fortezza* in Prague in 1723. By using the mandolin and theorbo as obbligato instruments in several of his operas and oratorios, Conti found opportunities for solo performances in his own works. The performance of *Galatea* in 1719 is the only occasion on which he paired these two instruments; it was given five days before his son Ignazio received a court appointment, suggesting that the unique scoring was intended for a father-and-son performance.

Long before the Habsburg court officially recognized Conti as a composer, he had distinguished himself with several successful productions. Little is known about this formative stage in his career. That Alessandro Scarlatti was influential is highly probable, for his name appears with Conti's in at least two works: a pasticcio oratorio (1708, Florence) and an intermezzo (*Vespetta e Milo*, 1717, Dresden). In 1713 Conti was appointed court composer, a position he held concurrently with that of theorbist, the combined stipends making him one of the highest-paid musicians in Vienna. His financial status was further enhanced by his second and third marriages, both to court prima donnas.

Among works brought to the imperial stage shortly after this second appointment was his untitled intermezzo with two characters, Dorimena and Tuberone, performed with the opera *L'Atenaide* (1714) by M. A. Ziani, Negri and Caldara. 'Dorimena and Turberone' may well have been the first intermezzo staged in Vienna independent of its host opera, and may have instituted the staging of independent intermezzos in Hamburg when it was repeated there in 1719. It underscores Conti's penchant for comedy and parody and his skill in writing *buffo* bass arias. In this, as in his other intermezzos, there is a variety of aria types, frequent use of accompanied recitative, at least one duet or trio in each part of the intermezzo, and even dance.

Conti collaborated with several librettists, notably Stampiglia, Pariati, Zeno and Metastasio. Pariati provided the greatest number of librettos, and those designated 'tragicommedia' offered Conti additional possibilities for bringing comedy to the stage. In these three- or five-act works comic characters not only form an integral part of the plot but also have their own separate scenes. His best known *tragicommedia* was *Don Chisciotte in Sierra Morena* (1719), a satire on *opera seria* and its heroic arias. The popularity of this work, featuring parts for a baritone and two basses, generated more than 25 productions outside Vienna (principally in Hamburg) between 1720 and 1737. He also collaborated with the scene designers Ferdinando, Giuseppe and Antonio Galli-Bibiena, and the composer Nicola Matteis (the younger), whose ballet music appears in the extant scores, often notated in full score rather than in the skeleton two-part arrangement common to manuscripts of the period.

Conti's musical style balances a zest for experimentation with a keen sense for clarity of design articulated by thematic and tonal principles. Nowhere is this more apparent than in his overtures and arias. In the overtures he developed concepts that evolve into fully recognizable sonata forms in both the first and third movements of the customary fast–slow–fast pattern. In the arias his handling of the ritornello principle in da capo structures moves his music towards the threshold of the Classical style. The aria accompaniments are exceptionally diverse in texture and scoring. His preference for bassoon and lower strings (baryton, viola da gamba, cello) as obbligato instruments extends even to the viola, which comes to the fore as a proponent of melodic material in *Meleagro* and as a supporter of the harmonic foundation in *Teseo*.

Most of the carnival operas conclude with a dance-like choral finale in triple time, sung by the principals; these are well-defined da capo or through-composed numbers which convincingly establish the inevitable *lieto fine*. In the one-act operas numbers sung by a separate chorus abound. In *Galatea* (1719) the chorus opens and concludes the opera, serving throughout as commentator and protagonist. Scoring for choral numbers varies considerably from the normal SATB ensemble doubled by instruments to a two-part male chorus accompanied by seven orchestral parts.

No new works by Conti were heard in Vienna between 1727 and 1731, when many of his operas were staged in other cities (often in translated, revised or pirated versions). Only *Sesostri* was revived in Vienna during Carnival 1729. Illness had momentarily curtailed Conti's activities; his duties as composer were absorbed by others, including his son Ignazio, already in the employ of the court. *Issipile*, Conti's last opera for Vienna and his sole collaboration with Metastasio, signals a change in the composer's style: arias are fewer in number but greater in length; emphasis shifts from male to female voices (no bass role is included); the amount of accompanied recitative increases substantially; scoring is limited to the three- or four-part strings reinforced by woodwind; and the overture and opera share thematic material. A more sensitive moulding of text and music pervades the score. *Issipile* gives clear evidence that Conti's popularity did not depend solely on his trademark of comic episodes and *buffo* bass arias; it received posthumous productions in Brunswick (1733, 1736), Jaroměřice (1733) and Hamburg (1737).

dm – *dramma per musica* int – *intermezzo*

first performed in Vienna, at court, unless otherwise stated; MSS in A-Wn and elsewhere (see Williams 1983)

Clotilde (G. Neri), ?carn. 1706, lost; songs (London, 1709)
Il trionfo dell'amicizia e dell'amore (dramma pastorale, 3, F. Ballerini), carn. 1711; rev. as Il trionfo dell'amore e della costanza, with addns by R. Keiser, Hamburg, Jan 1718, *D-SWl*
Circe fatta saggia (serenata, 1), 28 Aug 1713
Alba Cornelia (dm, 3, S. Stampiglia), carn. 1714; rev. version, Breslau, carn. 1726
I Sattiri in Arcadia (favola pastorale, 3, P. Pariati), 28 Aug 1714
Il Ciro (dm, 3, Pariati), carn. 1715, *MGs*; with Bagatella, Mamalucca, Pattatocco (int, 2, Pariati)
Teseo in Creta (dm, 3, Pariati), 28 Aug 1715; with Galantina, Pampalugo (int, 2, Pariati)
Il finto Policare (tragicommedia, 3, Pariati), 24 Jan 1716
Sesostri, re di Egitto (dm, 3, Pariati), 24 Jan 1717; with Grilletta, Pimpinone (int, 3, Pariati)
Astarto (dm, 3, A. Zeno and Pariati), carn. 1718; with Farfalletta, Lirone, Terremoto (int, 3, Pariati)
Amore in Tessaglia (componimeno da camera, 1, Pariati), 28 Aug 1718
Don Chisciotte in Sierra Morena (tragicommedia, 5, Zeno and Pariati), carn. 1719, *A-Wn* (*R*1982: IOB, lxix); rev. with addns by Mattheson, Hamburg, 1720, *D-MGs*; ov. in Williams (1983)
Cloris und Thyrsis, Hamburg, 26 April 1719, *MGs*
Galatea vendicata (festa teatrale, 1, Pariati), 19 Nov 1719
Alessandro in Sidone (tragicommedia, 5, Zeno and Pariati), carn. 1721; rev. version, Brunswick, Aug 1726; ov. in Williams (1983)
La via del saggio (componimento da camera, 1, Pariati), 1 Oct 1721, *MGs*
Archelao, re di Cappadocia (tragicommedia, 5, Pariati), carn. 1722
Pallade trionfante (festa teatrale, 1), 19 Nov 1722; ov. in Williams (1983)
Creso (tragicommedia, 5, Pariati), carn. 1723
Il trionfo della fama (serenata, 1, F. Fozio), Prague, 4 Nov 1723; ov. in Williams (1983)
Penelope (tragicommedia, 3, Pariati), carn. 1724
Meleagro (festa teatrale, 1, Pariati), 19 Nov 1724
Griselda (dm, 3, Zeno), carn. 1725; with Erighetta, Don Chilone (int, 3)
Isicratea (festa teatrale, 1, Pasquini), 19 Nov 1726
Issipile (dm, 3, P. Metastasio), carn. 1732; rev. version, Hamburg, 20 Feb 1737, *MGs*; ov. in Williams (1983)

Other intermezzos: Dorimena, Tuberone (2, Pariati), perf. with Ziani, Negri and Caldara: L'Atenaide, 19 Nov 1714; Act 3 of Vespetta e Milo (3, Stampiglia and Ballerini), perf. with Lotti: Giove in Argo, Dresden, 1717 [Acts 1 and 2 by A. Scarlatti]

*

S. Molitor: 'Ehrenrettung des Wielands kaiserlichen Hofcompositeurs in Wien Francesco Conti', *AMZ*, xl (1838), 153–8
L. von Köchel: *Die kaiserliche Hof-Musikkapelle in Wien von 1543 bis 1867* (Vienna, 1869)
A. von Weilen: *Zur Wiener Theatergeschichte* (Vienna, 1901)
J. Schneider: *Francesco Conti als dramatischer Componist* (diss., U. of Vienna, 1902)
R. Haas: 'Die Musik in der Wiener deutschen Stegreifkomödie', *SMw*, xii (1925), 3–64
——: 'Wiener deutsche Parodieopern um 1730', *ZMw*, viii (1926), 201–25
F. Hadamowsky: 'Barocktheater am Wiener Kaiserhof: mit einem Spielplan (1625–1740)'; *Jb der Gesellschaft für Wiener Theaterforschung 1951/52* (Vienna, 1955), 69–117
A. Wulff: 'Zur Deutung der Barockoper: *Il trionfo dell'amicizia e dell'amore* (Wien 1711)', *Musik und Geschichte: Leo Schrade zum sechzigsten Geburtstag* (Cologne, 1963), 96–145
H. Williams: *Francesco Bartolomeo Conti: his Life and Operas* (diss., Columbia U., 1964)
S. Kunze: 'Die Entstehung eines Buffo-Librettos: Don-Quijote-Bearbeitungen', *DJbM*, xii (1967), 75–95
C. Troy: *The Comic Intermezzo* (Ann Arbor, 1979)
H. M. Brown: Introduction to F. Conti: *Don Chisciotte in Sierra Morena*, IOB, lxix (1982)
H. Williams: Introduction and Thematic Index in F. B. Conti: 'Nine Sinfonie', *Italians in Vienna*, The Symphony 1720–1840, ser. B, ii (New York, 1983) [incl. addl source information]

HERMINE W. WILLIAMS

Conti, Gioacchino ['Egizziello', 'Gizziello'] (*b* Arpino, 28 Feb 1714; *d* Rome, 25 Oct 1761). Italian soprano castrato, probably the son of Nicola Conti. His nickname derived from Domenico Gizzi, who taught him singing; it was sometimes corrupted to Egizziello. His début at Rome in Vinci's *Artaserse* (1730) was a spectacular success. He sang at Naples in operas by Vinci (1732–3), and in Vienna (1734), Genoa, Venice (1735, two operas, including Leo's *La clemenza di Tito*) and other Italian cities. In 1736 he was engaged by Handel for London and made his Covent Garden début in a revival of *Ariodante*; a week later he created the role of Meleager in *Atalanta*. The press reported that he 'met with an uncommon Reception'; the poet Gray admired him 'excessively' in every respect except the shape of his mouth, which 'when open, made an exact square'. According to Jennens Handel considered him 'a rising genius'. The next season, Conti appeared in Handel's new operas *Arminio* (as Sigismond), *Giustino* (Anastasius) and *Berenice* (Alessandro) and in several revivals.

Conti sang in Rome in 1738 and 1741, at Padua in 1739 in Lampugnani's *Didone abbandonata*, and in 1742 in Florence, where he made a great impression but was taken seriously ill. He may have gone to Lisbon in 1743. He sang at the S Carlo, Naples, in 1746 in Duni's *Catone in Utica* and Jommelli's *Eumene*. In 1747 the theatre engaged both Conti and his rival Caffarelli; the rivalry caused much excitement. He was often heard at Venice, in operas by Jommelli, Hasse and Pescetti (1746–7, 1749–50), and appeared at Lucca (1749) and Padua (1751, in Galuppi's *Artaserse*). From 1752 to 1755 he was employed by the Lisbon court theatre and sang in many operas, most of them by Perez; he is said to have narrowly escaped with his life from the Lisbon earthquake (1755), and 'was impressed with such a religious turn by the tremendous calamity, that he retreated to a monastery, where he ended his days' (Burney), but not before he had imparted much sage and practical counsel to Guadagni. His retirement may, however, have been due to ill health.

Conti was one of the greatest of 18th-century singers. He was an exceptionally high soprano with a compass of at least two octaves (*c′* to *c‴*) and the only castrato for whom Handel wrote a top C. The four parts Handel composed for him indicate brilliance, flexibility and unusual powers of pathetic and graceful expression. In character Conti was the antithesis of Caffarelli, being as gentle as the latter was overbearing. WINTON DEAN

Conti, Ignazio Maria (*b* 16 July ?1699; *d* Vienna, 28 March 1759). Italian composer, son of F. B. Conti. From 24 November 1719 until his death he held the title *Hofscholar* as theorbist at the Habsburg court in Vienna. He never received a major appointment there, even though petitions were filed on his behalf by Fux in 1739. He held no official position as a composer, although his music was performed at court. The focus of his writing was sacred music. His few theatre works, all performed in Vienna (MSS in *A-Wn*), include two *feste teatrali*, *Pieria* (19 Nov 1728) and *Clelia* (19 Nov 1733), and other serenata-type compositions: *Dialogo tra l'Aurora ed il Sole* (*servizio da camera*; 15 Oct 1727), *Pastorale* (*festa da camera*; 26 July 1734), *La fortuna annichilata della prudenza* (*festa da camera*; 26 July 1735), *La liberalità di Numa Pompilio* (*servizio da camera*; 1 Oct 1735) and *Dafne in Alloro* (serenata). All except the last have librettos by G. C. Pasquini and were written to honour Charles VI, Elisabeth Christina and Maria Theresa on their birthdays and name-days. His style of composition echoes his father's, with attention to melody (voice doubled by violins), well-defined structure and variety of instrumental accompaniment.

For bibliography *see* CONTI, FRANCESCO BARTOLOMEO.

HERMINE W. WILLIAMS

Conti, Nicola [Niccolò] (*fl* Naples, 1733–54). Italian composer. He studied, according to Villarosa (*Memorie dei compositori*, 1840), with Durante and was later *maestro di musica* of 'many Neapolitan churches'. He was organist in the royal chapel. Although he wrote several operas, he composed mainly sacred music; his works were still sufficiently admired at the end of the century for a quintet, probably from one of his operas, to be incorporated into the pasticcio *L'ape musicale, ossia Il poeta impresario* (text, L. da Ponte; 1792, Trieste) and for Reichardt to praise the serious fervour expressed in his arias. It is uncertain whether he was the Nicolò Conti who sang in Brescia in 1747 and at the Teatro di S Samuele in Venice in 1749; he may have been the father of the soprano castrato Gioacchino Conti. His opera scores are lost. His serious style can be studied only from his oratorios, written about the same time, which impressed for their harmonic treatment and their tonal control; arias are in full da capo form and show Conti's predilection for concertato effects with contrasts in scoring, texture, dynamics, melodic style and key. He used much accompanied recitative, but was less skilful in his handling of declamation than of harmony. *Attalo, re di Bitinia*, performed in Naples in spring 1751 and sometimes ascribed to Nicola, was by Giuseppe Conti.

performed in Naples unless otherwise stated

L'Ippolita (ob, G. A. Federico), Fiorentini, spr. 1733
Cajo Marzio Coriolano (os, P. Pariati), S Bartolomeo, carn. 1734
?Berenice (os, B. Vitturi), Rome, Capranica, 7 Jan 1749
L'Olindo [most of Acts 1 and 2] (ob, A. Palomba), Fiorentini, spr. 1753; rest, incl. sinfonia, by M. Capranica
Arias in *D-Dlb*, *F-Pn*, *GB-Lbl*, *Lkc*, *I-Gl*, *Mc*; duet, *Mc*

JAMES L. JACKMAN

Contini, Domenico Filippo (*fl* 1669–87). Italian librettist. He may have been a native of Ancona (and possibly a relative of the Roman architect G. B. Contini, according to D'Accone), and was an abbot, who from 1676 to 1685 was patronized by the Colonna, Barberini and Orsini families. By far his most successful libretto was *Gli equivoci nel sembiante*, set by Alessandro Scarlatti as his first opera. Like Contini's other works it is a pastoral comedy, with four rustic characters in generalized settings, and was intended for a chamber production, without machines or choruses. Although the plot is conventional – an intricate web of intrigue and misunderstanding – the text is free from exaggerated similes and other 'Baroque' devices. Contini aimed at realism, as in *La donna ancora è fedele*, where the two cavaliers are tenors (not castratos). His works may have been produced on numerous occasions that are not documented by printed librettos; the only evidence that performances were given by a travelling troupe is found in the dedication to the 1691 edition of *Gli equivoci nel sembiante*, which may have been given in and around Venice throughout the 1690s.

In amor vince chi fugge, P. F. Corsi, 1669; *La donna ancora è fedele* (dramma per musica), B. Pasquini, 1676 (A. Scarlatti, 1698); *Gli equivoci nel sembiante* (dramma per musica), A. Scarlatti, 1679 (1679, as L'errore innocente, overo Gli equivoci nel sembiante; 1681, as L'amor non vuol inganni; 1690 and later, as Gli amori fortunati negl'equivoci); *Dalla padella alla bragia* (comedia), A. Olivieri, 1681; *Più timore che danno* (trattenimento drammatico), Bracciano, 1685 (G. della Porta, 1697, as Eurillo, overo La costanza negl'amori fra pastori)

Doubtful: *L'onestà nelli amori*, A. Scarlatti, 1680 (rev. G. Fabbrini, 1690; ? A. Caldara, 1705) [lib. attrib. 'Felice Parnaso', possibly by G. F. Bernini; see D'Accone, 30–33]

P. Mandosio: *Bibliotheca romana seu romanum scriptorum centuriae*, ii (Rome, 1692), 311
G. F. Crain jr: *The Operas of Bernardo Pasquini* (diss., Yale U., 1965)
U. Kirkendale: 'The Ruspoli Documents on Handel', *JAMS*, xx (1967), 235, 258–64
R. L. Weaver and N. W. Weaver: *A Chronology of Music in the Florentine Theater, 1590–1750* (Detroit, 1978)
F. A. D'Accone: *The History of a Baroque Opera: Alessandro Scarlatti's 'Gli equivoci nel sembiante'* (New York, 1985)
S. Franchi: *Drammaturgia romana: repertorio bibliografico cronologico dei testi drammatici pubblicati a Roma e nel Lazio, secolo XVII* (Rome, 1988)

LOWELL LINDGREN

Contini, Francesco Bartolomeo. *See* CONTI, FRANCESCO BARTOLOMEO.

Continuo [basso continuo] (It.; Fr. *basse continue*; Ger. *Generalbass*; sometimes Eng. 'thoroughbass'; It. *partimento*). Extemporized chordal accompaniment from a figured or unfigured bass, a technique that was symbiotic with the growth of opera; continuo was assumed in almost all ensemble scoring, was essential to Italian monody and was the basis of simple recitative until the 19th century. The 17th century showed a preference for multiple chordal instruments, often used in alternation; 18th-century *opera seria* used a smaller continuo ensemble of harpsichord(s) and theorbo, normally grouped with both a cello and a double bass, and *opera buffa* a single keyboard plus string bass. The contribution of continuo is most apparent in *recitativo semplice* (now usually called *secco*) and arias without obbligato instruments.

Continuo realization is essentially (and ideally) an improvised art, and since opera in particular is an arena of professionals, much remains undocumented or ambiguous; most figured-bass methods were published to teach elementary harmony rather than accompaniment. Areas of debate include not only where and when the various instruments played, but also the manner of realization: types of arpeggiation and imitation, placing of cadences, doubling of the vocal line, addition of dissonances and acciaccaturas, and ornamentation or simplification of the written bass are questions on which authorities signally fail to agree.

The continuo element would never have been a foreground component, nor would it have competed with other members of the orchestra, except in the rare cases when it was elevated to obbligato status. Exceptions such as Handel's famous 'cembalo solo' in *Rinaldo*, as published by John Walsh (1711), or the fortepiano obbligato in Reichardt's *Die Geisterinsel* (1798), should not be models for the present-day interpreter; the primary job of continuo is accompaniment.

1. The 17th century. 2. The 18th century. 3. The 19th and 20th centuries.

1. THE 17TH CENTURY. The earliest staged works in Italy call for a variety and multiplicity of instruments which were used for descriptive purposes and positioned for spatial effect. Peri, in *Euridice* (1600), lists a *gravicembalo*, chittarone and *liuto grosso*, Cavalieri (*Rappresentatione di Anima, et di Corpo*, 1600) 'una lira doppia, un Clavicembalo, un Chitarone ... o Tiorba ... un Organo suave con un Chitarone'. The listed instrumentation of Monteverdi's *Orfeo* (1607) implies three distinct continuo groups each with a viola da gamba as string bass: two with harpsichord, *organo di legno* and chittarone, a third with *arpa doppia* and chittarone. A regal is added for exotic (underworld) effect (recommended also by Doni, 1640, and Cesti, in his opera *Il pomo d'oro*, 1667), although the total number of keyboard players required is only two. Scenic placement (sometimes antiphonal, as also suggested for his ballet *Tirsi e Clori*, 1615) is as important in Monteverdi's instructions as sonority. With the combination of organ and theorbo frequently recommended in Italy (see Monteverdi's letter of 1611), it is possible that, instead of playing chords, the plucked instrument played the bass line as an alternative to a string bass. The assumption of a string bass, unsupported by many 17th-century Italian sources for church or chamber music, is legitimate for opera.

Ex.1 Monteverdi: *Orfeo*, Act 5, realization from Williams: *Figured Bass Accompaniment* (1970)

Precise playing instructions are sparse; Marco di Gagliano (*Dafne*, 1608) asks that harmony support the voice without obscuring the words and that the playing be without ornament, but repeating the notes that are sung. (Such doubling is mentioned in all periods, from Viadana, 1602, to Kollmann, 1801.) Few secular examples survive; lute and keyboard parts from the *Intermedii* of 1589, madrigals by Luzzaschi and other works leave the voice free in bravura passage-work, but double the vocal line elsewhere. The use of 'compound figures' in early Italian bass parts (figures larger than 8, from 9 to 18) indicates the actual pitch of notes in the right hand, and most Italian writers before 1700 allow simple ornaments (turns, slides, *cambiate* and appoggiaturas). At perfect cadences, 4–3 suspensions were formulaic, although they are frequently omitted today (ex.1).

In France, Lully's opera orchestra employed two *clavecins*, two theorbos, two lutes, two *basses de violes* and one or two *basses de violon* (the double bass did not secure a position at the Opéra until the 1720s). From his figured *basse continue* parts it is clear that continuo accompanied the voice and the three-part *ritournelles*, but was silent during the independent *symphonies* (including the overture) and many of the *airs de ballet*. Although this practice was not strictly observed outside Paris (and instructions exist for the realization of unfigured basses), its influence lasted throughout Rameau's career.

English operatic experiments followed the French in plurality of continuo instruments; Locke's music for *The Tempest* (1674) calls for 'a Band of 24 Violins, with the Harpsicals and Theorbo's which accompany the Voices'. Elementary instructions for playing a continuo part are contained in the same author's *Melothesia* (1673), Prencourt's 'Rules' (recorded by North) and the method attributed to John Blow (see Arnold 1931). Purcell's instrumental arrangements of his theatre and vocal music suggest a greater harmonic interest than the sparse figuring would indicate, and his solo keyboard

Performance of an opera on an oriental subject, possibly in the original Eszterháza opera house (the continuo instruments can be seen on the left of the orchestra pit): gouache (second half of the 18th century) by an unknown artist

arrangements show a partiality for rich, measured arpeggiation in the lute style. Like the French orchestra, his theatre band would not have included a string bass at 16-foot pitch on the continuo line; instrumental interludes may also have been played without continuo.

2. THE 18TH CENTURY. After 1700, as Italian *opera seria* and later *buffa* swept Europe, national differences in continuo formation were reduced, and (except in Paris) chordal instruments were expected to play continuously unless otherwise instructed; the organ was no longer associated with the theatre style and the opera continuo section stabilized at one or two harpsichords, sometimes with a theorbo (except in France). Numerous theatre plans and illustrations show a central keyboard instrument, facing the stage, played by the conductor, and a second at the side played by the 'accompanist', each supported by a cello and a double bass (*see* ORCHESTRA, fig.9). The inclusion of double bass in this grouping was not constant, and the evidence for its use is often unclear; it is usually possible to be specific only about the presence or absence of the cello.

French performance material shows that in Rameau one cello and keyboard played the recitatives; C. P. E. Bach (1753) makes a similar recommendation, Quantz (1752) adds a double bass. In England, Handel was reported (by a French observer in 1728) as using a cello, two harpsichords and an archlute for the recitatives, with the chords played 'en coupant le son' (i.e. not sustained), and Quantz illustrates two harpsichords and one theorbo in his opera seating plan. Some illustrations (e.g. Ghezzi's caricature of Logroscino, or the Covent Garden riots of 1763) show continuo harpsichords in performance with their lids closed.

Most instructions on performance, after dealing with finding the right harmony, discuss texture and the varied spreading of chords. Arpeggiation, 'the proper genius' of the harpsichord (North), carried two meanings: an idiomatic quick spread, or a more measured rhythmic pattern, repeated ad libitum. The rapid spread explains why some French considered the Italians to play without arpeggiation (Saint-Evremond 1739; Rameau 1760), while others complain of 'unceasing, busy figurations, the broken chords, the ever-rolling arpeggios' (Le Cerf 1704–6). For those French who equated arpeggiation with the *style luthée*, suitable to the slower delivery of French *récit*, a fast Italian arpeggio with passing dissonances would have seemed rough and almost instantaneous. Saint-Lambert (1707) provides a summary of techniques: broken chords in recitative may be dwelt on 'while the voice sings several notes unsupported', single notes may be reiterated 'but so judiciously that it seems as though the harpsichord did it by itself', or a continuous repetitive arpeggiation, 'almost like musketry fire', may be used for a few bars. Repercussion of chords is 'almost invariably used in accompanying a chorus', while imitation between the soloist and the accompanist's right hand is appropriate in arias without obbligato instrument.

Many sources mention the Italians' lavish use of passing notes and acciaccaturas, especially in 'recitatives and serious songs' (Gasparini 1708) for rich effects and greater volume; '*Acciaccature* ... rightly placed, have a wonderful Effect', a secret that 'has been in use above a

Ex.2 from Geminiani: *A Treatise of Good Taste* (1749)

Ex.4 from Telemann: *Generalbass-Übungen* (1733-4)

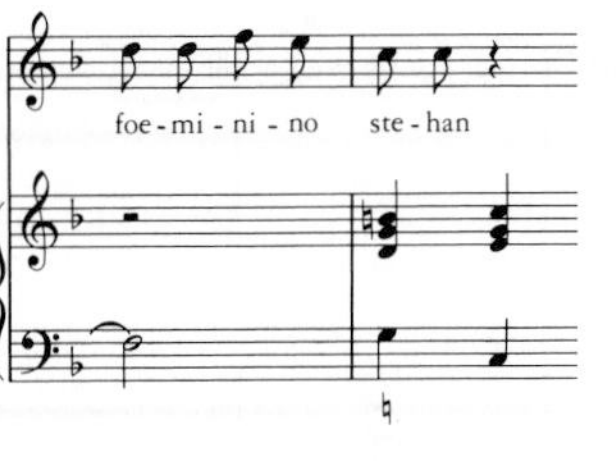

hundred years' (Geminiani 1748 and 1749). The interpolated notes could be a *tierce coulé*, or the note below the tonic; Manfredini (1775) also allows chromatic passing notes. The 'full-voiced', mature Italian style is discussed by Gasparini, Geminiani and Pasquali (1757), among others, but a simpler style (reported by Rousseau, 1782) was preferred for maximum clarity in *opera buffa* (ex.2).

Variety of accompaniment was recommended in recitatives: Pasquali advised that chords be spread, whether the text is 'common, tender or passionate'. For anger or surprise, use little or no arpeggio, both hands striking 'almost at once'. The last chords should be abrupt if the sense has come to a cadence (ex.3).

Recitative chords, even when the bass line is notated in long notes, are frequently to be played short (C. P. E. Bach, 1762: 'Even if the score expresses tied white notes, the sharply detached execution is retained'), and in opera until about 1750 the first of two cadential chords was played with, not after, the final syllables of the singer. Telemann included this instruction in his *Singe-, Spiel- und Generalbass-Übungen* (1733–4) and Quantz reiterates its use as a means of hastening the action (ex.4).

Heinichen (1728) admits the harmonic clash that is created but calls it a licence sanctioned by long usage in the theatre, an observation borne out by similar cadences in recitatives accompanied by full strings. (The term *cadenza tronca* was used ambiguously to mean both 'foreshortened cadence' and 'interrupted cadence'). By the 1760s the delayed cadence was considered normal, even in opera (C. P. E. Bach and Marpurg), and by Classical times it was universal.

Rameau's later operas show a steadily decreasing use of continuo, and his younger contemporaries (Dauvergne, La Borde, Philidor) omit figuring from all instrumental movements and choruses and many fully scored arias. In 1770, when Rameau's *Zoroastre* was revived, there was no keyboard, according to Grimm, and none of Gluck's operas performed in Paris in the 1770s contained *secco* recitative.

After the mid-century, a single keyboard (harpsichord or later fortepiano) was the most typical in opera layouts (see illustration opposite), normally with cello and

Ex.3 from Pasquali: *Thorough-Bass made Easy* (1757, ?4/*c*1790)

Ex.5 A. F. C. Kollman: *A Second Practical Guide to Thorough-Bass* (London, 1807)

double bass. A continuo realization was assumed throughout, not merely for the *secco* recitative; even in *Die Entführung aus dem Serail* (1782), a Singspiel with spoken dialogue, Mozart took his place at the 'clavier' (letter of 19 November 1782), and a Hungarian observer mentions the composer directing *Figaro* from the fortepiano (1786). *Secco* recitative was accompanied by simple short chords, the occasional rhythmic links in the bass being played *tasto solo*, and cadences were delayed. Kollmann (1801) continued a long tradition (Quantz, C. P. E. Bach, Telemann, Löhlein) of recommending giving the singer's note at the top of the preceding chords (ex.5).

Possible models for ensemble continuo are Mozart's own realization for the tuttis in his Piano Concerto in C K246, the contemporary realization for parts of his Piano Concerto in C K415/387*b* and Salomon's optional piano parts for his quintet arrangements of Haydn symphonies.

3. THE 19TH AND 20TH CENTURIES. *Secco* recitative ceased to play a part in serious opera after the 1820s, although it continued in comic opera through the 1850s and 60s, when there was a revived vogue for *opera buffa* (Donizetti's *Il campanello di notte*, 1835, is the last of his operas to use *secco*). La Scala employed two 'cembalo' players in the 1850s and listed a 'primo contrabasso al cembalo' in 1869, although the instrument in question was probably a piano. Turin Opera listed the position of 'maestro al cembalo' and 'cembalista' until 1845. Vissian's *Dizionario* (1846) significantly refers to 'recitativo accompagnato dal basso e dal piano'. Rossini, and his contemporaries, 'presided at the pianoforte' (Hogarth's *Memoirs*, 1851), on which they presumably accompanied the recitatives. In the absence of a keyboard, continuo accompaniment was supplied by spread chords from double bass and cello. (Meyerbeer includes what must be a parody of such a passage, with figured bass, in *Les Huguenots*.) The chordal and plucked techniques (described in such tutors as those of Baillot, Levasseur, Catel and Baudiot, 1804, and J. Fröhlich, *c*1819) were famously demonstrated by Robert Lindley and Dragonetti in London, and used (according to Bernard Shaw) for a performance of F. and L. Ricci's *Crispino e la comare* in London as late as 1891. A later solution was to rescore *secco* passages with string accompaniment (as late as 1975, in Raymond Leppard's arrangements of Monteverdi and Cavalli for Glyndebourne). Strauss's reworkings of Gluck (*Iphigenie auf Tauris*, 1900) and Mozart (*Idomeneo*, 1931) eliminated all *secco* recitative. For Classical and Baroque opera the temporary use of the piano (e.g. at Glyndebourne, 1935–6) gave way to the reinstatement of the harpsichord (without cello in 1951, with cello in 1956). We have yet to see any widespread adoption of the traditional cello and double bass grouping with the continuo keyboard, or the presence of continuo in Classical orchestral numbers.

*

PRIMARY SOURCES

L. da Viadana: *Cento concerti ecclesiastici* (Venice, 1602)
A. Agazzari: *Del sonare sopra il basso* (Siena, 1607, 2/1609)
G. B. Doni: *Annotazioni sopra il Compendio de' generi e de' modi della musica* (Rome, 1640)
L. Penna: *Li primi albori musicali per li principianti della musica figurata* (Bologna, 1672, 5/1696)
M. Locke: *Melothesia or Certain Rules for Playing upon a Continued-Bass* (London, 1673)
F. E. Niedt: *Musicalische Handleitung* (Hamburg, 1700)
J. L. Le Cerf de la Viéville: *Comparaison de la musique italienne et de la musique françoise* (Brussels, 1704–6)
M. de Saint-Lambert: *Nouveau traité de l'accompagnement du clavecin, de l'orgue* (Paris, 1707, ?2/1725; Eng. trans., 1984)
F. Gasparini: *L'armonico pratico al cimbalo* (Venice, 1708, 6/1802; Eng. trans., 1963)
J. D. Heinichen: *Der Generalbass in der Komposition* (Dresden, 1728; partial Eng. trans., 1966)
G. P. Telemann: *Singe-, Spiel- und Generalbass-Übungen* (Hamburg, 1733–4)
'Lettre sur les Opera', *Oeuvres de Monsieur de Saint-Evremond* (Amsterdam, 1739)
F. Geminiani: *Rules for Playing in a True Taste* (London, ?1748)
——: *A Treatise of Good Taste in the Art of Musick* (London, 1749)
J. J. Quantz: *Versuch einer Anweisung die Flöte traversiere zu spielen* (Berlin, 1752, 3/1789; Eng. trans., 1966)
C. P. E. Bach: *Versuch über die wahre Art das Clavier zu spielen* (Berlin, 1753–62, 2/1759–97; Eng. trans., 1949, 2/1951)
F. W. Marpurg: *Handbuch bey dem Generalbass* (Berlin, 1755–8)
N. Pasquali: *Thorough-Bass made Easy, or Practical Rules for Finding and Applying its Various Chords* (Edinburgh, 1757, ?4/*c*1790)
J.-P. Rameau: *Code de musique pratique* (Paris, 1760)
V. Manfredini: *Regole armoniche* (Venice, 1775, 2/1797)
J.-J. Rousseau: 'Accompagnement' and 'Récitatif – accompagné, mesuré', *Encyclopédie méthodique*, xxxvi/1–2 (Paris, 1782)
D. G. Türk: *Kurze Anweisung zum Generalbass-Spielen* (Leipzig and Halle, 1791, 2/1800)
M. P. King: *Thorough Bass made Clear to every Capacity* (London, *c*1796, 2/*c*1810)
A. F. C. Kollmann: *A Practical Guide to Thorough-Bass* (London, 1801)

MODERN STUDIES

F. T. Arnold: *The Art of Accompaniment from a Thorough-Bass as Practised in the 17th and 18th Centuries* (London, 1931)
J. Wilson, ed.: *Roger North on Music* (London, 1959)
G. J. Buelow: 'The Full-Voiced Style of Thorough-Bass Realization', *AcM*, xxxv (1963), 159–71
S. H. Hansell: 'The Cadence in 18th-century Recitative', *MQ*, liv (1968), 228–48
P. Williams: *Figured Bass Accompaniment* (Edinburgh, 1970)
W. Dean: 'The Performance of Recitative in Late Baroque Opera', *ML*, lviii (1977), 389–402
G. Sadler: 'The Role of the Keyboard Continuo in French Opera, 1673–1776', *EMc*, viii (1980), 148–57
M. Collins: 'Cadential Structures and Accompanimental Practices in Eighteenth-Century Italian Recitative', *Opera & Vivaldi*, ed. M. Collins and E. Kirk (Austin, 1984), 211–32
M. Cyr: 'Declamation and Expressive Singing in Recitative', ibid, 233–57
T. Borgir: *The Perfomance of the Basso Continuo in Italian Baroque Music* (Ann Arbor, 1987)
H. M. Brown and S. Sadie, eds.: *Performance Practice: Music after 1600* (London, 1989)

P. J. Rogers: *Continuo Realization in Handel's Vocal Music* (Ann Arbor, 1989) CHRISTOPHER HOGWOOD

Contrabbasso, Il ('The Double-Bass Player'). 'Grottesco' in one act (three scenes) by VALENTINO BUCCHI to a libretto by Mario Mattolini and Mauro Pezzati after ANTON PAVLOVICH CHEKHOV's short story *Romance with a Double Bass*; Florence, Teatro Comunale, 20 June 1954.

The plot of *Il contrabbasso*, set in an 'imaginary 19th century', centres on the vicissitudes of the hero, a Double-Bass Player (bass or baritone) who, wandering by a river with his instrument in its heavy case, comes upon a Princess (soprano). She, unaware of his presence, undresses to bathe, and the musician, struck by her beauty, also decides to take a swim. Two Robbers help themselves to both sets of clothes. The Princess, seeing the Double-Bass Player hiding behind a bush in embarrassment, supposes that he has stolen hers and demands them back. He denies the accusation and suggests that the Princess take refuge in his instrument case; this is then taken, for a joke, by a group of his fellow musicians, who carry it to a party at the Princess's castle.

In the castle the Princess's Father (comic bass) and her Fiancé (tenor) are impatiently awaiting her return. To while away the time the Fiancé shows off his knowledge of music by playing some of the instruments, and when he opens the double-bass case he discovers the naked Princess. She silences their scandalized surprise by telling them that she met a satyr by the river and escaped by hiding in the case.

In the final scene, which returns to the riverside, the Gendarme (bass), the Priest (tenor) and a small crowd (mixed chorus) listen in the moonlight to a lament which arouses their fear. It is the Double-Bass Player, at whose spectral appearance they all flee, leaving the disconsolate musician alone with his music.

The tragicomic action of this 'grottesco', a humorous but bitter metaphor for the solitude of the musician in the contemporary world, shows Bucchi's characteristic essentiality and clarity of style. Each dramatic situation is treated expressively yet incisively, for example through the double-bass theme and its successive variations and the repeated use of dance rhythms, such as the Bolero which accompanies the first appearance of the Princess in the opening scene, and, later, the Dance of the Robbers. According to Fedele D'Amico, *Il contrabbasso*'s economy of musical means, evident in the structure of the work and in the orchestral writing, is also influenced to some extent by the Italian comic tradition and by Stravinsky's neo-classical style.

RAFFAELE POZZI

Contralto (It.; Fr. *alto*; Ger. *Alt*). A voice normally written for in the range *g–e″*, which may be extended at either end. In modern English parlance it denotes the lowest female voice (it is used in that sense in this dictionary). It derives however from the 15th-century 'contratenor altus' ('high contratenor'), through the 16th-century abbreviation 'contr'alto'; the term 'alto' tended to be preferred in the 16th century, particularly for falsettists, and 'contralto' was applied to a low female or castrato voice. With the disappearance of the castrato it came to be reserved for the female voice.

1. Before 1800. 2. After 1800: voice types. 3. After 1800: singers and roles.

1. BEFORE 1800. In opera, the contralto has always had to struggle for existence in the shade of the more glamorous soprano voice, although composers have repeatedly shown a singular appreciation of the lower voice's potentialities. As early as Monteverdi's *L'incoronazione di Poppea* (1643) the most haunting lyrical music in the score, the lullaby 'Oblivion soave', is assigned not to a soprano but to Poppaea's nurse, the contralto Arnalta. Throughout the 17th century the contralto was cast as the nurse, the maid or the lady-in-waiting. In some such roles she came to be depicted as a crone and cherished for her capacity as a comic figure. In Cesti's *Orontea* (1656), for example, Aristea introduces herself by declaring that in spite of her age she is ready for love, and she woos the youthful Ismeno (who is actually a woman disguised as a boy).

The contralto as comic crone became a stock figure in the operas of Alessandro Scarlatti. In *La principessa fedele* (1710), Gerina flirts with the comic Turk, Mustafà; in *Tigrane* (1715), Dorilla flirts with the comic bass Orcone, and her comic function is stressed by her silly asides to the audience. The comic contralto emerged as the constant companion of the comic bass (Scarlatti called the pair the 'due dei baffi'); the popularity of their duet was such that Scarlatti often included three or four in an opera. The celebrated contralto Maria Antonia Marchesini built her career on this role type and Scarlatti composed several roles for her. The comic contralto, however, tended to disappear in the 18th century as, with the rise of the comic intermezzo and the *opera buffa*, the traditional *basso buffo* was normally paired with a soprano, representing a pert young girl.

Scarlatti did not entirely neglect the more serious type of contralto role; Princess Cunegonda in *La principessa fedele* has no fewer than eight arias, though this may be connected with the fact that the character is a Bohemian princess in male disguise. But it is in the operas of Handel that sympathetic and wide-ranging contralto parts are readily found. In his early London period he wrote for Anastasia Robinson, noted for her charm and expressiveness; she created many roles, including Zenobia (*Radamisto*, 1720) and Cornelia (*Giulio Cesare*, 1724), and was also much admired as Bononcini's Griselda (1722). Her successors included Anna Vincenza Dotti (Eduige in *Rodelinda*, 1725), who also sang male roles, Antonia Margherita Merighi (Rosmira in *Partenope*, 1730; Erissena in *Poro*, 1731; Amastris in *Serse*, 1738), Francesca Bertolli (her nine new Handel roles included Gandartes in *Poro* and Medoro in *Orlando*, 1733; she specialized in male roles) and Maria Caterina Negri (Polinesso in *Ariodante* and Bradamante in *Alcina*, both 1735). Handel wrote many male roles for contraltos.

The contralto voice was virtually unknown in France; the French *bas-dessus* is of mezzo-soprano rather than contralto pitch and quality. It scarcely appears in the operas of Gluck and indeed is rare throughout the Classical period; there is no true contralto role in any Mozart opera.

2. AFTER 1800: VOICE TYPES. In Germany, where the *Fächer* (categories of voice) are usually so firmly defined, the contralto and mezzo-soprano have both been commonly designated 'Alt'. In Italy a clear distinction has traditionally been made, as it has until recently in Britain, where one of the most notable changes regarding singers in the 20th century has been the movement

away from 'contralto' towards 'mezzo-soprano'. In the early years, following on from 19th-century practice, most female singers were described as soprano or contralto; by 1950 there were more who would use the term 'mezzo-soprano', and within a few decades the acknowledged contralto became a rarity. This change has coincided with the growth of opera as a prospective field for British singers who in earlier times would have been confined far more to song and oratorio.

This tendency has been an international one, in which no doubt the repertory itself has been a factor. Roles that call specifically for a deep voice are relatively few. Ulrica, the fortune-teller in *Un ballo in maschera*, is exceptional among Verdi's operas, and in Wagner the goddess Erda in *Das Rheingold* and *Siegfried* is the single major role in which a true contralto is essential. Formerly, singers listed as contralto (often quite rightly) would also take parts such as Azucena and Amneris, Carmen and Delilah. The first of these would often be an almost complete success when sung by a contralto: the highest notes might give difficulty or be omitted, but the stage character and a good deal of the music would benefit from the richness of true contralto tone. Amneris in *Aida* is a different matter, for if the repeated demands for high notes were to be met by a contralto it was likely to be either by the production of power without resonance or (in the German school particularly) by a lightening of tone at the very points where the full body of sound was most needed. In the French operas, disadvantage lay not so much in the demands upon the voice as in its quality and perceived character.

To a rather greater extent than with the bass among men, the contralto is generally considered an unromantic voice. This has not always been so. Such composers as Bizet and Saint-Saëns must have thought that the deeper voice could be sufficiently seductive. Yet the formidable females of the Gilbert and Sullivan operettas are invariably allotted to the contralto, and this must have coincided with a general feeling, even at that time, that this was appropriate casting. In Italian opera the contralto voice increasingly came to be used (apart from travesty roles) for elderly, usually unpleasant but sometimes comic characters: for instance, the Princess in *Suor Angelica* or Zita in *Gianni Schicchi*. The position is much the same in German and French opera (only in Russian opera are younger characters frequently sung by the contralto; the supply of youthful-sounding voices for roles such as Olga in *Yevgeny Onegin* or Pauline in *The Queen of Spades* seems limitless).

It is just such an 'image', the caricature of dowager duchess or gorgon aunt, that the sound of the true contralto voice risks evoking; and it can hardly be denied that a major contribution towards this state of affairs was made by the most famous contralto active in the present century, Dame Clara Butt. The justice of this in relation to Butt's art may be questionable, but in the general public mind it is the sound of her voice celebrating the 'mother of the free' that colours the notion of the word 'contralto'. Not unnaturally, singers have tended to shun it, and many, such as Janet Baker, who would almost certainly have described themselves as contralto in an earlier generation, have preferred the description of mezzo-soprano. Recent developments in musicology have tended to encourage this process, as in the revival of a taste for the operas of Rossini with their brilliant opportunities for the lower-voiced coloratura singer. Similarly, as the knowledge of Handel's operas has grown, and with it the frequency of performance, the need for flexible voices in the lower female range has favoured the mezzo, who is thought more likely to be skilled in the performance of rapid runs over a wide range. This, however, may overlook an important part of the contralto tradition, for the voice can be as fluent and agile as any other. An outstanding example in modern times has been Marilyn Horne, who though generally categorized as a mezzo has much of the full contralto quality in her voice. Recordings show that remarkable facility was also attained by earlier contraltos such as Ernestine Schumann-Heink, Sigrid Onegin and (not least) by Clara Butt herself.

3. AFTER 1800: SINGERS AND ROLES. Napoleon, attending a gala performance in 1800 at La Scala in celebration of his victory at Marengo, heard the contralto Josephina Grassini and remarked on 'the beauty of her stage appearance and the sublime accents of her voice'. When she made her London début four years later, the *Daily Advertiser* noted that 'the lady's voice is of the counter-alto kind, and much deeper than we have hitherto been accustomed to in a female'. For Grassini's benefit, later in the season, Winter composed *Il ratto di Proserpina*, in which she took the title role and Elizabeth Billington, a soprano with a superb voice but a rather ugly appearance, sang Ceres, giving rise to Lord Mount Edgecumbe's famous dictum that 'no doubt the deaf would have been charmed by Grassini and the blind must have been delighted with Mrs Billington'.

In Rossini's first great success, *Tancredi* (1813), the title role was created in Venice by Adelaide Malanotte, who scored a triumph with the aria 'Di tanti palpiti': her superb coloratura technique – she had studied with Crescentini – and her fine voice with its perfect intonation were greatly admired by Hérold. In Rome Rossini found another coloratura contralto, Geltrude Righetti, whose powerful and rich-toned voice, with a compass *f*–*b*♭″, and phenomenal technique inspired him to write Rosina in *Il barbiere di Siviglia* (1816) and the title role of *La Cenerentola* (1817) for her. Benedetta Rosamunda Pisaroni, who sang in three Rossini premières, started her career as a soprano, but when illness caused her to lose her top notes she developed her middle and lower registers to become a powerful, flexible contralto; as well as creating Zomira in *Ricciardo e Zoraide* (1818), Andromache in *Ermione* (1819) and Malcolm Graeme in *La donna del lago* (1819), she was an admired Arsace in *Semiramide*.

Marietta Brambilla, with a range *g*–*g*″, made her début at the King's Theatre, London, as Arsace; she sang Maffio Orsini in the first performance of *Lucrezia Borgia* (1833) at La Scala and created Pierotto in *Linda di Chamounix* (1842) in Vienna. Marietta Alboni, with a similar range and an even richer, more powerful and more flexible voice, had studied Rossini's contralto roles with the composer; she sang Arsace at the opening of the Royal Italian Opera at Covent Garden (1847), scoring a tremendous personal success; Meyerbeer had transposed the role of Urbain in *Les Huguenots* from soprano to contralto and composed the aria 'Non! – non, non, non, non, non! Vous n'avez jamais, je gage' in Act 2 for Alboni. Though reputed to dislike playing travesty roles, she sang the baritone part of Don Carlo in *Ernani* when neither Tamburini nor Ronconi would sing it. Anna Petrova, a Russian contralto who specialized in travesty roles, created two in Glinka's operas, Vanya in *A Life for the Tsar* (1836) and Ratmir in *Ruslan and Lyudmila* (1842). Her voice, full, rich-toned but without plumminess, was also effectively displayed as Bellini's Romeo, Arsace and Pippo in *La gazza ladra*.

Meyerbeer included a magnificent contralto role in *Le prophète*; Fidès, the mother of the self-styled prophet John of Leyden, was created in Paris in 1849 by Pauline Viardot, who also sang the role in London. A singer greatly admired for her artistry and musicality by many composers, most particularly by Berlioz, who adapted Gluck's Orpheus for her to sing at the Opéra (1859), she was less popular with the public, who did not find her voice sufficiently sweet-toned; when she sang Verdi's Lady Macbeth (transposed down a major 3rd, according to the conductor Luigi Arditi) in Dublin, a role well suited to her dramatically, the opera was not liked.

The title role of Massenet's *Hérodiade* (1881) was first sung by Blanche Deschamps, a French contralto with a rich and powerful voice and a fiery temperament, who also created Uta in Reyer's *Sigurd* (1884), Margared in Lalo's *Le roi d'Ys* (1888), Franck's Hulda (1894) and the Mother in *Louise* (1900). Deschamps-Jehin, as she became, was the first Delilah and Fricka at the Opéra; her immense repertory ranged from Hatred in Gluck's *Armide* to Fidès and Carmen. Massenet wrote two other dramatic roles for her, Madame de la Haltière in *Cendrillon* (1899) and the Baroness in *Chérubin* (1905). Another contralto with a powerful voice, a wide compass and an enormous repertory, covering both the mezzo and the contralto range, Ernestine Schumann-Heink, was the first Clytemnestra in *Elektra* (1909). Renowned as an interpreter of Wagner, she sang Erda, Fricka, Waltraute, Ortrud, Brangäne, Magdalene and other roles at Bayreuth, Covent Garden and the Metropolitan, where she took her farewell as Erda (*Siegfried*) in 1932 at the age of 70.

Schumann-Heink was one of the last, probably the greatest and certainly the most versatile of the dramatic contraltos. Composers continued to write parts for the contralto voice, but they were usually character roles, such as Margret in *Wozzeck* and the Theatrical Dresser/High-School Boy/Groom in *Lulu*. In his later operas Strauss provided several: the Widow Zimmerlein in *Die schweigsame Frau*, Gaea in *Daphne*, Leda in *Die Liebe der Danae* and the major role of Clairon in *Capriccio*, more usually sung by a mezzo. Prokofiev, continuing the Russian tradition of writing contralto roles for younger characters, contributed Blanche in *The Gambler* and Princess Clarice in *The Love for Three Oranges*, while Shostakovich cast Sonyetka in *Lady Macbeth of the Mtsensk District* as a contralto. Leokadja Begbick in *Der Aufstieg und Fall der Stadt Mahagonny* and Kabanicha in *Káťa Kabanová* are very effective contralto roles, also frequently sung by mezzos.

In *Peter Grimes* the only contralto part is that of Auntie, hostess of The Boar, but in Britten's next opera, *The Rape of Lucretia*, he wrote the title role for a contralto, Kathleen Ferrier, who sang it with unforgettable poignancy and dignity. Ferrier's other great role was Gluck's Orpheus, to which she also brought deep emotional commitment. Tippett wrote a very strong role vocally for a contralto, Sosostris in *The Midsummer Marriage*, while Poulenc provided the most dramatic opportunity for the contralto voice in Madame de Croissy, the First Prioress in *Dialogues des Carmélites*; this role, created at La Scala by Gianna Pederzini (a magnificent Mistress Quickly, and Madame Flora in *The Medium*), was first sung in Paris by Denise Scharley (a fine Ulrica and Amneris), while in the opera's American première at San Francisco, Claramae Turner (who had created Madame Flora) made an impressive Madame de Croissy.

See also ALTO; CASTRATO; MEZZO-CONTRALTO; and MEZZO-SOPRANO.

For bibliography *see* SINGING: A BIBLIOGRAPHY.

OWEN JANDER, J. B. STEANE, ELIZABETH FORBES

***Contratador de diamantes,* O** ('The Diamond Contractor'). Opera in three acts by FRANCISCO MIGNONE to a libretto by Gerolamo Bottoni after Afonso Arinos' play; Rio de Janeiro, Teatro Municipal, 20 September 1924.

The action takes place in Diamantina (Minas Gerais, Brazil), in the 18th century. Felisberto Caldeira (baritone), a diamond contractor, wants to fight for the freedom of the land. Cotinha (soprano), his niece, is in love with Camacho (tenor) and in an effective duet, they express their mutual love. Mestre Vicente (tenor) tells Camacho that he has learnt of a diabolic plot against Caldeira. The Magistrado (baritone), representative of the Portuguese kingdom, declares his attention to Cotinha but she despises him so he promises revenge. In front of the church, on a day of festivity, a procession passes and sacred choruses are heard; the *Congada*, a Brazilian dramatic folk dance, is performed. Suddenly, a crowd emerges from the church, outraged that the Magistrado kissed Cotinha in front of the altar. Her uncle intervenes but the Magistrado calls the royal dragoons and orders his imprisonment. Caldeira shouts that the thought of freedom of his people will not die with him. Later, on the banks of the river Ribeirão do Inferno, a song accompanies the arrival of the miners. Caldeira, condemned to exile, is taken to the border, dreaming of a liberated Brazil.

Mignone wrote this opera while studying at the Milan Conservatory under Ferroni. It is strongly influenced by late Romantic Italian opera with the orchestra assuming an important role. Although local musical elements are minimized, the Act 2 ballet, *Congada*, achieved great popularity as an orchestral piece. GERARD BÉHAGUE

***Convenienze teatrali,* Le** ('The Usages of the Stage'). *Melodramma comico* originally in one act, later expanded to two as a *dramma giocoso* and retitled *Le convenienze ed inconvenienze teatrali* ('The Usages and Misusages of the Stage'), by GAETANO DONIZETTI to his own libretto after SIMEONE ANTONIO SOGRAFI's plays *Le convenienze teatrali* (1794) and *Le inconvenienze teatrali* (1800); Naples, Teatro Nuovo, 21 November 1827 (revised version, Milan, Teatro Cannobiana, 20 April 1831).

In the one-act version, a provincial opera company is preparing to rehearse a new work, *Romilda ed Ersilio*. When Luigia, the seconda donna (soprano), hears the prima donna Corilla (soprano) rehearse her *sortita*, she is disgruntled because her role is not more conspicuous and sends for her mother, Mamm'Agata (baritone). When this harridan appears she turns everything upside down, insisting on an aria for her daughter and even describing the instrumental effects it should contain. Proclo (bass), a member of the company and Corilla's father, fatuously insists on his daughter's merits, an attitude which inspires a furious duet for the prima donna and Mamm'Agata, after which the former refuses to participate further. When the Impresario (bass) is wondering what is to be done, Mamm'Agata volunteers to audition for Corilla's role by singing a version of the

Willow Song from Rossini's *Otello* (badly misremembered). In despair, they begin the rehearsal, managing part of a recitative, chorus and funeral march, but time has passed and now they must prepare for the performance. In the *finaletto* the troupe express their uncertainty about the opera's reception.

In the two-act version, a few numbers are removed and others substituted, and recitatives take the place of spoken dialogue. Notable in Act 2 are a duet for Mamm'Agata and the Impresario, and a trio which boasts a new character, a German tenor almost totally ignorant of Italian. He takes the place of the contralto *musico* of the one-act version. The prima donna's name is changed, as is her entrance aria. A more substantial finale takes the place of the earlier *finaletto*.

Of the 20 operas from the first decade of Donizetti's career, none has equalled *Convenienze* for its popularity since its first 20th-century revival in 1962. It has appeared in many countries in a number of translations and under various titles, including *Viva la mamma*.

WILLIAM ASHBROOK

Converse, Frederick Shepherd (*b* Newton, MA, 5 Jan 1871; *d* Westwood, MA, 8 June 1940). American composer and administrator. At Harvard College (1889–93) he studied with John Knowles Paine, and later he took composition lessons with George Chadwick; from 1896 to 1898 he studied in Munich. He taught at the New England Conservatory of Music (1900–02) and at Harvard (1903–7) and quickly gained a reputation as one of America's outstanding composers.

In 1905 he wrote the music for Percy MacKaye's play *Jeanne d'Arc* and this led to further collaborations. Converse became vice-president of the Boston Opera Company which, at its peak (1909–14), rivalled the Metropolitan Opera. He oversaw several performances of his own works, including the Romantic opera *The Pipe of Desire*, which was completed in 1905 and received its première in 1906 in Boston. The work was staged at the Metropolitan on 18 March 1910 (in a double bill with *Pagliacci*), the first American opera to be performed there; Mahler, the principal conductor, had preferred it to several other American works. At that time, a controversy was raging in New York and Boston over the validity of singing opera in English, and Converse often voiced his belief that Americans could compose serious operas in English. No resources were spared in the preparation and production. Except for the English soprano Leonora Sparkes, all the singers of leading roles were Americans. The work, conducted by Alfred Hertz, was well received by the audience; most critics, however, attacked the undramatic libretto and criticized the score for its lack of originality, though Converse's skilful and effective orchestration was praised. In its 1910–11 season, the Boston Opera produced *The Pipe of Desire* with *Cavalleria rusticana* and gave the première of Converse's *The Sacrifice* (3 March 1911). The libretto (by Converse with assistance from John Albert Macy for the lyrics) was based on Henry Augustus Wise's story *Los gringos*. The plot, set in Southern California in 1846, is a love triangle between Chonita, a Mexican girl (soprano), Captain Burton, an American officer (baritone), and Bernal, a Mexican officer. Though the opera was enthusiastically received by the audience, newspaper reviews were mixed. Three months later, Converse collaborated with MacKaye on *Beauty and the Beast*, based on stories from *The Thousand and One Nights*; it was completed in 1913 but never performed, possibly because it calls for elaborate and expensive settings. (The libretto was published, 1917, as *Sinbad the Sailor*.)

In 1912, Converse and MacKaye began work on *The Immigrants*, a lyric opera prompted by Converse's visit to Naples in 1909, which portrays the plight of Italians who emigrated to the USA in the early part of the 20th century in hope of a better life. The score was completed in 1914, but the demise of the Boston Opera Company that year and the advent of World War I dampened interest and it was never performed. Converse returned to the New England Conservatory in 1920 as head of the theory department, and from 1931 until his retirement in 1938 was Dean of the Faculty. He was elected to the American Academy of Arts and Letters in 1937. Converse was one of the earliest American composers to write operas and symphonic poems; his music was widely performed during his lifetime.

The Pipe of Desire [Iolan] op.21 (romantic op, 1, G. E. Barton), Boston, 31 Jan 1906 (New York, 1908)
The Sacrifice op.27 (3, Converse, lyrics by J. A. Macy), Boston, Opera, 3 March 1911 (New York, 1910)
Beauty and the Beast, 1913 (prol., 3, P. MacKaye), unperf., unpubd
The Immigrants [The Emigrants], 1914 (lyric drama, 3, MacKaye), unperf., *US-Wc*

R. Severance: *The Life and Works of Frederick Shepherd Converse* (diss., Boston U., 1932)
R. J. Garofalo: *The Life and Works of Frederick Shepherd Converse (1817–1940)* (diss., Catholic U. of America, Washington DC, 1969)

ROBERT GAROFALO

Convery, Robert (*b* Wichita, KS, 4 Oct 1954). American composer. He studied at Westminster Choir College, the Curtis Institute and the Juilliard School. His principal composition teachers were Ned Rorem, David Diamond and Vincent Persichetti. He has been a resident artist or composer at the artists' colony Yaddo (1986), Phillips Exeter Academy (1988 and 1991), Dickinson College (1989–90) and with the New York Concert Singers (1991–3). *Pyramus and Thisbe* (1982), produced in a workshop at the O'Neill Theater Center, is a comic farce in two scenes, employing recitative and aria, adapted by the composer from Shakespeare's *A Midsummer Night's Dream*. Britten-like in its transparency of texture, each section of the music is organically constructed on a single musical cell. Each character is identified with an instrument of the orchestra and developed through a distinct melodic style. Convery received both the Charles Miller-Alfredo Casella Award and the Charles E. Ives Award for the work. *The Blanket* (1986), first performed at the Spoleto Festival, Charleston, is written in a carefully organized post-Menotti idiom. A model of musical economy, it contains three arias and one duet within its 16-minute length.

all librettos by the composer

The Lady of Larkspur Lotion (1, after T. Williams), Spoleto, Chiesa di S Eufemia, 15 July 1980
Pyramus and Thisbe (2 scenes, after W. Shakespeare), workshop perf., Waterford, CT, O'Neill, May 1982; Philadelphia, Curtis Institute, 23 March 1983
The Blanket (1), Charleston, SC, Emmett Robinson, 31 May 1988

ELLWOOD J. ANNAHEIM

Convitato di pietra, Il ('The Stone Guest'). Libretto subject used chiefly in the 18th and 19th centuries. This was the most common Italian title for the Don Juan story; operas on the subject are also entitled *Don Giovanni* and *Il dissoluto punito*.

The first important literary source is Tirso de Molina's play *El burlador de Sevilla y Convidado de piedra* ('The Trickster of Seville, or The Stone Guest'), published in 1630. Spoken dramas on the story were produced by Molière (*Don Juan, ou Le festin de pierre*, 1665) and Goldoni (*Don Giovanni Tenorio; o sia Il dissoluto*, 1736), but the legend circulated more widely in fairground and carnival performances. In Italy these drew upon the characters of *commedia dell' arte*, while in France they took the form of *comédies en chansons*, with improvised or popular songs interpolated into the rather simple plot. The stone guest of the title is the statue of the Commendatore [Commander]. Early in most tellings of the story (though not necessarily in the opening scene) the Commendatore, trying to protect his daughter from seduction or rape by Don Juan, is killed by the latter in a duel. In the final scene the Commendatore's stone statue comes to life, accepts Don Juan's invitation to dinner, appears at his house and drags the licentious and (usually) unrepentant, blaspheming nobleman to hell. Some version of the episodes involving the Commendatore, his daughter Donna Anna and her betrothed Don Ottavio (as these characters are named in many of the settings) is to be found in virtually all presentations. Other common features are Don Juan's comic servant, who frequently sings an aria cataloguing his master's many conquests; a peasant wedding in which Don Juan attempts to seduce the bride; and one or more previously seduced and abandoned ladies who continue to pursue him. In general, the story consists of a loosely connected string of incidents with little overall organization apart from that implicit in the opening and closing scenes with the Commendatore.

The first known operatic setting is *L'empio punito* (1669, Rome), with a libretto by Filippo Acciaiuoli and music by Alessandro Melani. The 18th century saw an increasingly frequent association of the story with the musical theatre. It was told in several ballets, including Gluck's *Don Juan, ou Le festin de pierre* (1761, choreographed by Gasparo Angiolini), and appeared even more widely in operas, especially towards the end of the century (usually under the title *Il convitato di pietra*). These included a three-act *dramma tragicomico* by Vincenzo Righini, to a libretto by Nunziato Porta (1776, Prague); Giuseppe Calegari's two-act *dramma giocoso* to a libretto by Pietro Pariati (1777, Venice); a one-act *opera buffa* by Giacomo Tritto (libretto by G. B. Lorenzi, 1783, Naples); *Don Juan albo Ukarany libertyn* ('Don Juan or The Rake Punished') by Joachim Albertini (1783, Warsaw: a Polish translation by W. Bogusławski of a three-act Italian libretto, perhaps Porta's); and no fewer than four versions in 1787: Vincenzo Fabrizi's setting of Lorenzi's 1783 libretto (Rome); Giuseppe Gazzaniga's one-act *dramma giocoso Don Giovanni* to a libretto by Giovanni Bertati (Venice); Francesco Gardi's *Il nuovo convitato di pietra*, a two-act *opera tragicomico* with a libretto by Giuseppe Foppa (also Venice); and the best-known setting, Da Ponte and Mozart's *dramma giocoso* or *opera buffa*, *Il dissoluto punito o sia Il Don Giovanni* (Prague). 19th- and 20th-century composers to tackle the subject include Ramón Carnicer (libretto after Bertati and Da Ponte, 1822, Barcelona) and Giovanni Pacini (Bertati's libretto, 1832, Viareggio), both using the title *Don Giovanni Tenorio*; A. S. Dargomïzhsky, in *Kamennïy gost* ('The Stone Guest'), a setting of a text by Alexander Pushkin, the music completed by Cui and orchestrated by Rimsky-Korsakov (1872, St Petersburg); Filippo Marchetti (*Don Giovanni di'Austria*, to a libretto by C. D'Ormeville, 1879, Rome); Felice Lattuada (*Don Giovanni*, to a libretto by A. Rossato after the play by José Zorrilla y Moral, 1929, Naples); and G. F. Malipiero (*Don Giovanni*, to a libretto by Malipiero after Pushkin, 1963, Naples).

See also DON *GIOVANNI* (i) [Gazzaniga]; DON *GIOVANNI* (ii) [Mozart]; and *STONE GUEST, THE* [Dargomïzhsky]. For bibliography on the origins of the story *see* MOZART, WOLFGANG AMADEUS.

JOHN PLATOFF

Convitato di pietra, Il. Opera by Giuseppe Gazzaniga; *see* DON *GIOVANNI* (i).

Convito, Il ('The Banquet'). *Dramma giocoso per musica* in two acts by DOMENICO CIMAROSA to a libretto by FILIPPO LIVIGNI; Venice, Teatro S Samuele, Carnival 1782.

Massimo (bass) is holding a banquet for some friends and dressing for the occasion with the help of his servant Ceccho (tenor). Among the guests are the widow Alfonsina (soprano), who still mourns her departed husband Barbaló, and Eleonora (soprano), who loves Count Polidoro (bass). The Cavaliere del Lampo (tenor), who arrives at the banquet uninvited, is looking for a suitable matrimonial candidate. All three men are amorously disposed towards Alfonsina, but she favours Massimo because he resembles her late husband. She entrusts her dilemma to the statue of Amor in the garden. Count Polidoro and the Cavaliere del Lampo disguise themselves as statues, so that when Alfonsina talks to the oracle they can advise her not to marry Massimo. After a nocturnal scene of disguise and mistaken identities, three happy couples are ready for the wedding ceremonies: Eleonora and Count Polidoro, Alfonsina and the Cavaliere del Lampo, and Alfonsina's maid Lisetta (soprano) and Ceccho.

This was not one of Cimarosa's most successful operas. It did not attain as many performances as Livigni and Cimarosa's other comic opera, *Giannina e Bernardone*, given in Venice the previous year, despite the fact that it contains a similar oracle scene. The music and text satirize Metastasian *opera seria* in Alfonsina's aria 'Son Didone abbandonata' in Act 1.

GORDANA LAZAREVICH

Conyngham, Barry (*b* Sydney, 27 Aug 1944). Australian composer. After an initial involvement with jazz and popular music, he read law at the University of Sydney, where he later studied composition with Peter Sculthorpe. Further compositional studies took him to Japan (1970), where he studied with Toru Takemitsu, to the University of California at San Diego (1972) and Princeton (1973) on a Harkness Fellowship and to the University of Aix-Marseilles in France (1974). He was appointed lecturer in composition at the University of Melbourne in 1975 (reader, 1984) and in 1990 became professor of creative arts at Wollongong University. A composer of great energy and diversity, he has written prolifically for orchestra, chamber ensembles and chorus. In addition to his six operas, his theatre works include *Mirror Images* (1974–5) for four actors and instrumental ensemble and works for modern dance. Employing a wide range of sources, his music is accessible, vigorous and formal; its logic is both aural and mathematical, characterized by readily recognizable ostinato figuration. Conyngham is a post-serial lyricist, and the linear elements of his work remain embedded in a tonally centred matrix.

See also BENNELONG; EDWARD JOHN EYRE; and FLY.

Edward John Eyre (1, M. Oakes, incl. extracts from E. J. Eyre's journal), Sydney, U. of NSW, Science Theatre, 1 May 1971
Ned Mark II, 1975–8 (2, A. Seymour), unperf.
The Apology of Bony Anderson (1, M. Copland), U. of Melbourne, Union, Oct 1978; rev. as Bony Anderson, Sydney, Cell Block, 30 June 1979
Fly (2, Copland), Melbourne, Victorian Arts Centre, State, 25 Aug 1984
The Oath of Bad Brown Bill (children's op, 2, Copland and S. Axelson), Melbourne, Victorian Arts Centre, Studio, 6 Jan 1985
Bennelong (puppet op, 13 scenes, Copland), Groningen, Netherlands, State, 21 April 1988

*

J. Murdoch: 'Barry Conyngham', *Australia's Contemporary Composers* (Melbourne and Sydney, 1972), 64–9
V. Plush: 'The Creative Force of Barry Conyngham', *Stereo FM Radio* (1976), Jan, 10–11
D. Symons: 'Barry Conyngham', *Australian Composers in the Twentieth Century*, ed. D. Tunley and F. Callaway (Melbourne, 1978), 212–18
G. Skinner: 'Barry Conyngham', *APRA Journal*, iii/1 (1983), 11–14
B. Conyngham: 'Music with an Australian Accent', *Australian Society* (1989), Feb, 35–7
THÉRÈSE RADIC

Cook [Cooke] [first name unknown] (*fl* 1701–18). English bass. He is named as the performer of a song in the musical periodical *Mercurius musicus* (1701), but his first recorded stage appearance was in 1703. He sang in revivals of both the Eccles and Leveridge *Macbeth* music. In the early operas in the Italian style he played the comic roles of Delbo in Clayton's *Arsinoe* (1705), the satyr in Fedeli's *The Temple of Love* (1706) and Brennus in Scarlatti's *Pyrrhus and Demetrius* (1708). With the triumph of opera in Italian he appeared only in concerts until January 1715, when he was in *The Island Princess*. He remained on the stage until May 1716, singing Jupiter in Turner's *Presumptuous Love* and the lion in Leveridge's burlesque opera *Pyramus and Thisbe*. In 1718 he and his wife Mary, an actress and singer, were in Penkethman's company at Greenwich.

*

BDA; *LS* OLIVE BALDWIN, THELMA WILSON

Cook, Deborah (*b* Philadelphia, 6 July 1938). American soprano. She studied in Philadelphia, making her début in 1971 with Glyndebourne Touring Opera as Zerbinetta. After engagements at Bremen and Munich, she joined the Hamburg Staatsoper and sang at Frankfurt, Stuttgart and Berlin. She created Rachel in *We Come to the River* at Covent Garden in 1976, returning as the Fiakermilli (*Arabella*) in 1977. She sang the title role in *Lucia di Lammermoor* for Northern Ireland Opera (1976) and at Buxton (1979). Her repertory included Konstanze, the Queen of Night (Winter's in *Das Labyrinth* as well as Mozart's), Norina, Adina, Prascovia (*L'étoile du nord*) and Dinorah, which she also recorded. The flexibility of her light, pure-toned voice and the accuracy of her singing were equally admirable in contemporary and Classical roles.

ELIZABETH FORBES

Cook, Thomas Aynsley (*b* London, July 1831 or 1836; *d* Liverpool, 16 Feb 1894). English bass. He studied in Germany with the elder Joseph Staudigl. After appearing in Germany, he made his English début in Manchester in 1856 with Lucy Escott's National English Opera Company, subsequently touring the USA with Escott. In 1862 he joined the Pyne-Harrison Company, appearing with it and the Royal English Opera Company at Covent Garden until 1866 in works by Balfe, Benedict and Wallace; Devilshoof in *The Bohemian Girl* was probably his most famous role. At the Gaiety Theatre (1870–71) he sang Van Bett in the first performance in England of *Zar und Zimmermann* as well as roles in *Zampa* and *Fra Diavolo*. In 1875 he joined the Carl Rosa Opera Company. He had a powerful voice of agreeable quality; his singing and acting were marked by abundant energy and spirit.

HAROLD ROSENTHAL/R

Cook, Will Marion [William Mercer] (*b* Washington DC, 27 Jan 1869; *d* New York, 19 July 1944). American composer and conductor. He studied the violin and enrolled at the Oberlin Conservatory in 1884 but left to go to Berlin to study with Joseph Joachim. He returned in the early 1890s and studied at the National Conservatory, New York, where his teachers included Dvořák and John White. He began to conduct and to write musical comedies, and planned to stage original operatic scenes at the Chicago World's Fair in 1893, though these were probably never produced. In Chicago he met Paul Laurence Dunbar, with whom he later wrote a sketch, *Clorindy, the Origin of the Cakewalk*. Featuring black vaudeville performers, *Clorindy* opened in a Broadway roof garden in 1898, inaugurating a string of similar acts created and directed by African-Americans. From 1900 to 1910 Cook was the principal arranger and conductor of musical comedies for the cakewalk-comedy team of Bert Williams and George Walker. Cook's most celebrated musical comedy, *In Dahomey* (1902), like all of his shows, included popular songs in traditional forms as well as more extended choral scenes. It enjoyed a London run, a performance at Buckingham Palace and tours in Britain and the USA which lasted until 1906. After 1910 Cook wrote for the Lafayette Theatre, Harlem, and from 1922 he worked as a promoter and touring conductor in the USA and as accompanist, adviser and coach to many young musicians.

Cook was a charismatic and animated conductor, and his musicals were noted for casts that mirrored his enthusiasm – the performers danced vigorously as they sang, a novel choreographic twist that was widely imitated. He skilfully built ambitious climaxes into his shows in a fashion comparable to contemporary operetta finales. The original syncopated melodic idiom of his music was akin to ragtime, though richer in romantic, chromatic harmony, and some of his texts were derived from black folklore. Although he often expressed an intention to write full-fledged operas, apparently none were completed.

musical comedies, first performed in New York, unless otherwise stated

Clorindy, the Origin of the Cakewalk (1, P. L. Dunbar), Casino Roof, 5 July 1898
Jes' Lak White Fo'ks (1, Dunbar), sum. 1898
In Dahomey (3, Dunbar and J. Shipp), Stamford, CT, 12 Sept 1902; rev. version (prol., 2)
The Southerners (2, W. Mercer and R. Grant), New York Theatre, 23 May 1904
Abyssinia (3, B. Williams and Shipp), Majestic, 20 Feb 1906
Bandanna Land (3, Shipp), Majestic, 3 Feb 1908
The Traitor (playlet, 2 pts., A. Creamer), Lafayette, 17 March 1915
Darkydom (2, H. Troy, L. Walton and J. R. Europe), Lafayette, 23 Oct 1915
Swing Along (1, W. Vodery), Lafayette, 1 April 1929
The Cannibal King (Dunbar and J. R. Johnson), ?unperf.

M. Cuney-Hare: *Negro Musicians and their Music* (Washington DC, 1936)
W. M. Cook: 'Clorindy, the Origin of the Cakewalk', *Theatre Arts*, xxxi (1947), 61–5, repr. in *Readings in Black American Music*, ed. E. Southern (New York, 1971, 2/1983), 227–33
E. Southern: *The Music of Black Americans: a History* (New York, 1971, 2/1983)
H. Sampson: *Blacks in Blackface* (Metuchen, NJ, 1980)
J. Green: 'In Dahomey in London in 1903', *The Black Perspective in Music*, xi (1983), 22–40
A. Woll: *Dictionary of the Black Theatre* (Westport, CT, 1983)
K. Bloom: *American Song: the Complete Musical Theatre Companion, 1900–1984* (New York, 1985)
M. Carter: *Will Marion Cook: Afro-American Violinist, Composer and Conductor* (diss., U. of Illinois, 1988)
T. Riis: *Just Before Jazz: Black Musical Theater in New York, 1890 to 1915* (Washington DC, 1989)
A. Woll: *Black Musical Theatre: from Coontown to Dreamgirls* (Baton Rouge, LA, 1989)

THOMAS RIIS

Cooke, Deryck (Victor) (*b* Leicester, 14 Sept 1919; *d* Croydon, 27 Oct 1976). English writer on music. He studied at Cambridge and worked in various capacities in the music department of the BBC from 1947, with a break from 1959 to 1965. He worked mainly on the music of the later 19th century, especially Wagner, Bruckner, Mahler and Delius; he published many articles and reviews in journals and symposia. His most important single achievement, besides his performing version of Mahler's Symphony no.10, was his book *The Language of Music* (London, 1959), in which he boldly and ingeniously argued that music was literally a language of the emotions. What was to have been an extended study of the *Ring*, based on rigorous musico-dramatic analysis of the kind he applied in his commentary for the 1959–65 recording by Solti, was incomplete at his death but parts were published as *I Saw the World End* (London, 1979).

Cooke, Thomas Simpson [Tom] (*b* Dublin, 1782; *d* London, 26 Feb 1848). Irish singer and composer. He received instruction in composition from Tommaso Giordani. At 15 he was appointed leader of the orchestra at the Crow Street Theatre, Dublin, a position he held for several years; he also kept a music shop (1806–12). On one of his benefit nights he announced himself to sing the part of the Seraskier in Storace's *The Siege of Belgrade*, an experiment that proved successful and led to his moving to London; he made his first appearance, in the same role, at the English Opera House (Lyceum) on 13 July 1813. On 14 September 1815 he appeared as Don Carlos in *The Duenna* at Drury Lane, where he continued as a principal tenor for nearly 20 years. He composed music for over 50 productions at Drury Lane during the same period, including an *Oberon* in opposition to Weber's opera in 1826.

In 1821 Cooke was called 'director of the music at Drury Lane Theatre'. From about 1823 he was alternately singer and leader of the orchestra. From 1828 to 1830 he was one of the musical managers of Vauxhall Gardens. When Alfred Bunn became lessee of both Covent Garden and Drury Lane, he engaged Cooke as director of the music and conductor. A member of the Philharmonic Society, Cooke was well known as a singing teacher and a musician of great versatility.

His theatrical music, composed for 'operas' that were essentially plays interspersed with songs and only rarely outlasted one season, shows no more dramatic sense than Bishop's. The most elaborate pieces are strophic arias designed for (written-out) florid variation, but these increasingly gave way to simpler ballads and sentimental and comic songs; after 1830 his major works were adaptations. The manuscripts of most of the librettos have survived (*US-SM* and *GB-Lbl*).

selective list; printed works published in London unless otherwise stated

DBCS – *Dublin, Theatre Royal, Crow Street*
LCG – *London, Covent Garden* LDL – *London, Drury Lane*

The Hunter of the Alps (musical play, W. Dimond), DBCS, 1805, ov. and 1 song (Dublin, *c*1805)
The Five Lovers (comic op), DBCS, 1806, ov. (*c*1806)
The First Attempt, or The Whim of the Moment (comic op), DBCS, 1807
Selima and Azor (2, G. Collier), LCG, 5 Oct 1813, collab. H. R. Bishop and T. Welsh, after T. Linley (i)
Rugantino, or The Bravo of Venice (musical play, after G. de Pixérécourt: *L'homme à trois visages*), DBCS, *c*1813
Frederick the Great, or The Heart of a Soldier (operatic anecdote, S. J. Arnold), London, Lyceum, 4 Aug 1814 (1814)
The King's Proxy, or Judge for Yourself (comic op, Arnold), London, Lyceum, 19 Aug 1815
The Magpie, or The Maid of Palaiseau (musical play, T. J. Dibdin, after L.-C. Caigniez: *La pie voleuse*), LDL, 12 Sept 1815
Frightened to Death! (operatic farce, 2, W. C. Oulton), LDL, 27 Feb 1817
The Innkeeper's Daughter (musical play, 2, G. Soane), LDL, 7 April 1817
The Falls of Clyde (musical play, Soane), LDL, 29 Oct 1817
Amoroso, King of Little Britain (burlesque, J. R. Planché), LDL, 21 April 1818
Sigesmar the Switzer (musical play, C. E. Walker), LDL, 26 Sept 1818
The Heroine, or A Daughter's Courage (musical play, R. Phillips), LDL, 22 Feb 1819
The Jew of Lubeck, or The Heart of a Father (musical play, H. M. Milner), LDL, 11 May 1819
David Rizzio (R. Hamilton and C. Dibdin), LDL, 17 June 1820, collab. T. Attwood, J. Braham and W. Reeve
Justice, or The Caliph and the Cobbler (musical play, J. S. Faucit), LDL, 28 Nov 1820, collab. C. E. Horn
The Kind Imposter (operatic farce, after C. Cibber: *She Wou'd and she Wou'd not*), LDL, 8 May 1821, collab. Horn
Grand Coronation of King George IV (pageant, Elliston), LDL, 1 Aug 1821 (1821), partly adapted
Geraldi Duval, the Bandit of Bohemia (musical play, Walker), LDL, 8 Sept 1821
The Veteran Soldier, or The Farmer's Sons (comic op, 3, E. Knight), LDL, 23 Feb 1822, lib. pubd as The Veteran, collab. J. Whitaker and J. Perry
The Two Galley-Slaves, or The Mill of St Aldervon (melodrama, J. H. Payne), LCG, 6 Nov 1822, collab. Horn
A Tale of Other Times, or Which is the Bride? (musical play, T. J. Dibdin), LDL, 19 Dec 1822, collab. Bochsa
Sweethearts and Wives (comic op, J. Kenney), London, Haymarket, 7 July 1823, collab. Whitaker, Nathan and Perry
Actors al fresco (burletta, W. T. Moncrieff), London, Vauxhall Gardens, 1823, collab. J. Blewitt and Horn; rev. as vaudeville, Vauxhall Gardens, 9 June 1827
Abou Hassan (Dimond, after F. K. Hiemer), LDL, 4 April 1825, part pubd (*c*1825), after Weber: Abu Hassan
Faustus (romantic drama, 3, Soane and D. Terry, after J. W. von Goethe), LDL, 16 May 1825, collab. Bishop and Horn [ov. from Weber's Euryanthe]
The Coronation of Charles X, in Five Minutes too Late, or An Elopement to Rheims (spectacle, 1, G. Colman (ii)), LDL, 5 June 1825, collab. Bishop and Horn
The Wager, or The Midnight Hour (comic op, after Mrs Inchbald), LDL, 23 Nov 1825
Malvina (G. Macfarren), LDL, 28 Jan 1826 (1826)
Benyowsky, or The Exiles of Kamschatka (operatic play, 3, Kenney, after A. von Kotzebue), LDL, 16 March 1826, collab. Horn, M. Kelly, B. Livius, J. Stevenson
Oberon, or The Charmed Horn (fairy-tale, Macfarren), LDL, 27 March 1826
The White Lady, or The Spirit of Avenel (S. Beazley, after E. Scribe), LDL, 9 Oct 1826, after Boieldieu: La dame blanche
The Boy of Santillane, or Gil Blas and the Robbers of Asturia (musical play, Macfarren), LDL, 16 April 1827, collab. Blewitt

Isidore de Merida, or The Devil's Creek (Dimond), LDL, 29 Nov 1827, collab. Braham, after Storace: The Pirates
The Taming of the Shrew (operatic farce, F. Reynolds, after D. Garrick: *Catherine and Petruccio*, 1756, and Shakespeare plays), LDL, 14 May 1828, collab. Braham, incl. music by Rossini
Peter the Great, or The Battle of Pultawa (musical play, T. Morton and Kenney, after F. du Petit-Méré), LDL, 21 Feb 1829, collab. Dr Carnaby
Thierna-na-Oge, or The Prince of the Lakes (musical play, Planché), LDL, 20 April 1829
Masaniello (Kenney, after Scribe), LDL, 4 May 1829, part pubd (*c*1829), collab. Livius, after Auber
The Dragon's Gift, or The Scarf of Flight and the Mirror of Light (musical play, Planché), LDL, 12 April 1830
Gustavus III, or The Masked Ball (Planché, after Scribe), LCG, 13 Nov 1833, part pubd (*c*1833), after Auber: Gustave III
The Challenge (Milner and Planché, after de Planard: *Le pré aux clercs*), LCG, 1 April 1834, after Hérold
The Red Mask, or The Council of Three (Planché, after A. Berrettoni: *Il bravo*), LDL, 15 Nov 1834 (*c*1834), after Marliani
Lestocq, or The Fête of the Hermitage (Macfarren and A. Bunn, after Scribe), LCG, 21 Feb 1835, part pubd (*c*1835), after Auber
The Jewess (Planché, after Scribe), LDL, 16 Nov 1835, after Halévy: La Juive
The Siege of Corinth (Planché, after L. Balocchi and A. Soumet), LDL, 8 Nov 1836, after Rossini
The Child of the Wreck (musical play, Planché), LDL, 7 Oct 1837
Prologue to Handel: Acis and Galatea, LDL, 5 Feb 1842
The Follies of a Night (vaudeville, Planché), LDL, 5 Oct 1842

*

DNB (J. A. Fuller Maitland); *NicollH*
T. S. Cooke: 19 autograph letters, 1821–42, *US-Ws*
G. A. Macfarren: 'Cooke, Thomas Simpson', *The Imperial Dictionary of Universal Biography*, ed. F. Waller (London, 1857–63)

BRUCE CARR

Cooper, Emil (Albertovich) (*b* Kherson, 8/20 Dec 1877; *d* New York, 19 Nov 1960). Russian conductor. He studied composition with Fuchs, and worked further with Taneyev and Nikisch. His conducting début was at Odessa in 1896, and after four years with the Kiev opera company (1900–04), he became conductor at the Zimin Opera Theatre, Moscow, where he gave the première of Rimsky-Korsakov's *The Golden Cockerel* (1909). Moving to the Russian Imperial Opera, Moscow, in 1910 he conducted the company's first performances of the *Ring* and new works by Medtner, Myaskovsky, Rakhmaninov, Skryabin and others. Dyagilev engaged him to conduct the Russian operas he first took to Paris in 1908 and 1909, including *Boris Godunov* with Shalyapin, which Cooper conducted again on his (and Shalyapin's) London début at the Theatre Royal, Drury Lane, in 1913.

After the Revolution Cooper went to the State (Mariinsky) Theatre, Leningrad, though in 1922 he decided to leave the USSR; he based himself in Paris but undertook widespread tours before becoming music director of Riga Opera (1925–8). He was principal conductor of Chicago Civic Opera from 1929 to 1932, then lived in Europe until 1939, when he returned to Chicago. He moved to the Metropolitan (1944–50) where he conducted the New York premières of *Peter Grimes* (1948) and *Khovanshchina* (1950, in a severely edited version). His New York performances were regarded as honest and dependably musical rather than inspired, and sometimes thought to be dull or brutally forthright. From 1950 Cooper was conductor of the Montreal Opera Guild, where he broadened the repertory with works previously unperformed there, including operas by Prokofiev and Menotti.

M. MONTAGU-NATHAN/NOËL GOODWIN

Cooper, Martin (Du Pré) (*b* Winchester, 17 Jan 1910; *d* Richmond, Surrey, 15 March 1986). English writer on music. He studied at Oxford and then with Egon Wellesz in Vienna (1932–4). On his return he became music critic of the *London Mercury* and the *Daily Herald*, also contributing to *The Spectator*, 1947–54. In 1950 he joined the *Daily Telegraph*, serving as chief critic, 1954–76. He was editor of the *Musical Times* from 1953 to 1956 and a member of the editorial board of *The New Oxford History of Music*. Cooper's special interests were French and Russian music since the mid-18th century and German music of the early Romantic period. His rare ability to discuss a particular topic in a wide cultural context was combined with writing of clarity and elegance. While Cooper's book on French music is probably his most important contribution to the literature, his early studies of Gluck and *opéra comique* contain much perceptive critical writing. An accomplished linguist, he undertook much translation in his late years. Two collections of his writings have been published (1966, 1989).

Gluck (London, 1935)
Bizet (London, 1938)
Opéra comique (London, 1949)
French Music from the Death of Berlioz to the Death of Fauré (London, 1951)
Russian Opera (London, 1951)
Ideas and Music (London, 1966)
ed.: *The Modern Age (1890–1960)*, NOHM, x (1974) [incl. 'Stage Works: 1890–1918', 145–207]
Judgements of Value (Oxford, 1989)

STANLEY SADIE

Cooper, The. Comic opera in two acts by THOMAS AUGUSTINE ARNE to his own libretto after NICOLAS-MÉDARD AUDINOT and Antoine François Quétant's *Le tonnelier*; London, Theatre Royal in the Haymarket, 10 June 1772.

Martin (baritone), an old cooper, is in love with his ward Fanny (soprano), but her affections are fixed on Colin (tenor), Martin's assistant. The old man looks for an excuse to dismiss his young rival but Colin enlists the aid of his uncle Jarvis (bass), to whom Martin owes money. Colin's nocturnal meeting with Fanny is interrupted by Martin, who is alarmed by the sight of a barrel (Colin's hiding place) apparently coming to life. The arrival of Jarvis, who demands repayment, forces Martin to allow his ward to marry Colin.

The opera's simple melodic style shows the influence of Dibdin. An amusing feature is Fanny's recitative 'He's gone to bed', in which the accompanying crotchets are marked 'play to the steps of her feet'. The work had an initial run of nine performances and the vocal score was published by Napier in 1772.

JOHN A. PARKINSON

Cooperstown. American town in New York State. It is the home of Glimmerglass Opera, founded in 1975 with the declared purpose of providing a showcase for young talent, which has become one of the leading summer opera festivals in the north-eastern USA. Its setting on Otsego Lake ('Glimmerglass' in the writings of James Fenimore Cooper) among the foothills of the Catskill Mountains about 13 km north of Cooperstown has led to its being called the American Glyndebourne. Offering at least three productions each summer since 1981 (six to eight performances of each opera since 1985), Glimmerglass presented its first commissioned work and world première, William Schuman's *A Question of Taste*, in 1989. The company had revived Schuman's only other opera, *The Mighty Casey* (1953), in 1986.

Glimmerglass is one of only a handful of American companies to own and operate its own purpose-built theatre, the 896-seat Alice Busch Opera Theater (with additional space for 24 wheelchairs), opened in 1987. Its unique design incorporates two-storey motorized side walls that roll back for ventilation and reveal the site's pastoral charm. Four large boxes on the side of the hall hold 60 seats. The company's repertory has been cautiously daring; Douglas Moore's rarely performed *Gallantry* and Mozart's *Der Schauspieldirektor* (both 1981), Mozart's *Il rè pastore* (1991), and the Schuman offerings mentioned above, have complemented a mixture of more traditional works. Glimmerglass productions are sung in English, reflecting the company's intention of making opera widely accessible.

ROBERT V. PALMER

Copenhagen (Dan. København). Capital of Denmark. Throughout most of the 16th century and part of the 17th Latin schools presented plays with music, chiefly in squares and in the town hall. In the second half of the 17th century ballets with operatic elements were given; *Der lobwürdige Cadmus*, with music by Kaspar Förster (*d* 1673), was performed in 1663 on a temporary stage in the Fredensborg Dyrehave ('deer park'), and in 1683 *Kong Dan* ('King Dan') was given at the Charlottenborg Palace. The first full-length opera, *Der vereinigte Götterstreit*, with music by Povl Christian Schindler, was performed on 15 April 1689 in a temporary theatre connected to the Sophie Amalienborg Palace for the birthday of Christian V. At the second performance, attended by court officials and the upper bourgeoisie, a fire broke out, leaving the theatre and castle in ashes and causing the death of nearly 200 spectators. Ballet and opera performances were later given in the banqueting hall of Copenhagen Castle (where the Christiansborg Palace now stands).

Inspired by his journey to Italy and France in 1692–3, Frederik IV had an opera house built in 1701–2 on the corner of Bredgade and Fredericiagade. Probably designed by the architect Johan Conrad Ernst, it was intended for the general public as well. Its period of activity was short; in 1717 it was rebuilt as the cadet academy (today it houses the high court). The court Kapellmeister was Bartolomeo Bernardi, whose opera *Il gige fortunato* was performed at Frederiksborg Palace in 1703 to celebrate several royal birthdays. In 1710 a stage was built in Copenhagen Castle and in 1721–3 a troupe from Hamburg organized by Johann Kayser, together with local Danish singers, performed a repertory including works by Reinhard Keiser, whose *Ulysses* was mounted in 1722 for the birthday of Frederik IV.

During the reign of the Pietist Christian VI (1730–46) the theatres were closed. But soon after Frederik V succeeded to the throne he summoned Pietro Mingotti's troupe to Copenhagen, where from 1747 to 1756 they gave a series of opera performances at Charlottenborg Palace on Kongens Nytorv and later, from 1752, in the Danske Skueplads ('Danish Theatre') building, also on Kongens Nytorv; this second venue, built by Nicolai Eigtved in 1748 with 800 seats, was to become the Kongelige Teater ('Royal Theatre') in 1770. Mingotti's first season lasted three months and included 39 performances. Gluck, music director for the company in 1748–9, composed *La contesa de' numi* for performance at Charlottenborg on the crown prince's birthday in 1749. In 1766 Nicolas-Henri Jardin built a court theatre in the riding grounds of Christiansborg Palace, where operas were given until 1786. During most of this period Eigtved's theatre was used chiefly for plays. But in 1773 it was enlarged by C. F. Harsdorff and a singing school was established under the direction of Michel Angelo Potenza. In 1819 Giuseppe Siboni became director of the reorganized school, which contributed to a rise in the standard of performance.

In addition to productions at the Kongelige Teater a number of new works were performed elsewhere by visiting troupes. At Vesterbro's Nye Teater ('New Theatre'), built in 1834 between the Frihedsstøtten and the present Tivoli, Philippo Pettoletti engaged the Schleswig-Holstein court theatre company, giving operas between 1834 and 1836. From 1842 to 1854 an Italian company favoured by Christian VIII performed regularly at the Hofteater (court theatre, renovated in 1842 by Jørgen Hansen Koch); the season ran from November to the end of April.

In 1874 the company of the Kongelige Teater moved into new premises (designed by Vilhelm Dahlerup and Ove Petersen), built next to the old theatre, now destroyed. Under the conductor Holger Simon Paulli, Wagner's operas were introduced beginning with *Lohengrin* in 1870, and similar efforts continued in the following years. Johan Svendsen's appointment as conductor in 1883 ushered in a flourishing period for the opera as well as for the court orchestra, culminating in productions of *Die Walküre* (1902), *Siegfried* (1903), *Götterdämmerung* (1905) and *Das Rheingold* (1908); the complete *Ring* was performed six times during the period 1909–12.

In 1931 the Kongelige Teater gained an additional auditorium, the Nye Scene ('New Stage'), known as the 'Stærekassen' ('nesting box'), designed by Holger Jacobsen with about 960 seats. For six days of the week the opera company used it, and on the remaining day it was used by the state broadcasting network for concerts. After two seasons this dual usage was abandoned and the radio network took over the building. But in 1945–6 it reverted to theatrical use. Between 1981 and 1985 the older, original stage (the Gamle Scene), now used chiefly for opera and ballet, was rebuilt (by the architect Nils Koppel) to expand the orchestra pit, accommodate more staff and modernize the technical facilities. It has about 1400 seats. Since about 1785 the seasons at the Kongelige Teater have run from September (at first the middle, later the beginning of the month) until about 1 June. In some years festivals have also been arranged for a few weeks in the summer (for example on Nielsen's centenary in 1965). The standard repertory is performed, as well as 20th-century works including Werle's *Animalen* and Nørgård's *Siddharta*.

Besides the Kongelige Teater's activities, some smaller opera enterprises have made their mark in Copenhagen, including the Operaselskabet ('Opera Company') of 1932, which staged the first Danish production of Weill's *Mahagonny* at the Nye Teater in 1933. The Student Opera (later incorporated into the Dramatic Music Theatre) presented a remarkable production of Monteverdi's *L'incoronazione di Poppea* in the 1960s.

*

T. Overskou: *Den danske Skueplads, i dens historie fra de første spor af danske skuespil indtil vor tid* [The Danish Theatre: its History from the Beginning of Danish Acting up to the Present Day] (Copenhagen, 1854–76)

V. C. Ravn: 'Den tydske opera i Kjøbenhavn i aarene 1721–1723' [German Opera in Copenhagen, 1721–3], *For ide og virkelighed* (1873), 513–51

L. Bobé: *Operahusets brand paa Amalienborg den 19de April 1689: et mindeskrift samlet efter trykte og utrykte kilder* [The Opera House Fire at the Amalienborg on 19 April 1689: a Memorial based on Published and Unpublished Sources] (Copenhagen, 1889); repr. in *Fra renaissance til empire: kulturhistoriske afhandlinger* (Copenhagen, 1916), 55–78
P. Hansen: *Den danske Skueplads: illustreret theaterhistorie* [The Danish Theatre: an Illustrated History] (Copenhagen, 1889–96)
K. Gjellerup: 'Richard Wagner og Danmark', *Nordisk tidskrift för vetenskap, konst och industri* (1896), 444–56
A. Aumont and E. Collin: *Det danske Nationalteater 1748–1889: en statistisk fremstilling af Det kongelige Teaters historie fra skuepladsens aabning paa Kongens Nytorv 18. December 1748 til udgangen af sæsonen 1888–89* [The Danish National Theatre, 1748–1889: a Statistical Account of the Royal Theatre's History from its Opening on Kongens Nytorv on 18 December 1748 to the End of the Season 1888–9] (Copenhagen, 1896–9)
J. Clausen: 'Musik paa Friluftsteatret' [Music at the Open-Air Theatre], *Teatret*, xiv/17 (1915), 130–36
E. H. Müller: *Die Mingottischen Opernunternehmungen, 1732–1756* (Dresden, 1915)
A. Hammerich: 'Gluck som kapelmester i København: en episode fra opera seria-tiden', *Vor fortid: Tidsskrift for dansk kulturhistorie*, i (1917), 433–48
R. Neiiendam: *Det kongelige Teaters historie 1874–1922* (Copenhagen, 1921–70)
T. Krogh: 'De første forsøg paa at skabe en opera i det danske sprog' [The First Attempt to Create an Opera in Danish], *Aarbog for musik 1922*, 123–58
——: *Zur Geschichte des dänischen Singspiels im 18. Jahrhundert* (Copenhagen, 1924)
——: 'Det tyske operaselskabs besøg i København under Fr. IV' [The German Opera Company's Visit to Copenhagen under Frederik IV], *Aarbog for musik 1924*, 88–160
K. Riisager: 'Opera og dobbeltscenen', *Teatret*, xxix/1 (1929), 30–31
K. Atlung: *Det kongelige Teater 1889–1939: en statistisk-historisk fremstilling*, i: *del Repertoiret* [The Royal Theatre 1889–1939: a Statistical Historical Account, i: Repertory] (Copenhagen, 1942) [incl. a register of composers]
O. Mackeprang: 'Pietro Mingottis operaopførelser i København 1747–56', *Historiske meddelelser om København*, iv/2 (1949), 1–52
T. Roepstorff: *Operahuset i København: bygningens historie* [The Opera House in Copenhagen: the Building's History] (Copenhagen, 1970)
G. Schepelern: *Italienerne paa Hofteatret* (Copenhagen, 1976)
G. Leicht and M. Hallar: *Det Kongelige Teaters repertoire 1889–1975* (Odense, 1977)
CLAUS RØLLUM-LARSEN

Copland, Aaron (*b* Brooklyn, New York, 14 Nov 1900; *d* Westchester, NY, 2 Dec 1990). American composer. He studied harmony and counterpoint with Rubin Goldmark and then became a pupil of Nadia Boulanger in France, 1921–4. As well as influencing his work she introduced him to Koussevitzky, the newly appointed conductor of the Boston SO, who championed his music when he returned to the USA. Copland's reputation rests mainly on his instrumental works, especially the orchestral and ballet music, though he was also active as a lecturer, author and conductor. He was a leading figure at the Tanglewood Music Center for 21 summers, first as Koussevitzky's assistant and later as chairman of the faculty. As his conducting career escalated in the 1960s and 70s, his composing decreased. Many tributes, awards and honorary degrees attest to Copland's stature as a composer and as a dedicated advocate of contemporary music and of American composers. His works are marked by rhythmic vitality and a distinctive personal signature. Following the jazz-orientated pieces of the 1920s, he produced several important compositions in an abstract and difficult style. In the 1930s and 40s he turned to a more accessible idiom, frequently adapting and including folktunes, as in the ballet scores that are among his most popular works. He returned to a more austere style for his last symphonic pieces of the 1960s.

Copland's first opera, *The Second Hurricane* (1937), is to a libretto by the dance critic and poet Edwin Denby. It was intended for high school students of the Henry Street Settlement and is simple in plot and musical style. Included are choruses for students and parents and such characters as Butch, Fat, Gip and Queenie. Set in the Midwest, it is a story about co-operation between youngsters of different races and personalities in the face of natural disaster. The subtitle 'play opera' refers to the spoken roles. Among the wide variety of numbers are the revolutionary song 'The Capture of Borgoyne', and 'Queenie's Song', for high soprano. The opera's première on 21 April 1937 at the Grand Street Playhouse, New York, was conducted by Lehman Engel and directed by Orson Welles. It has since been produced only occasionally, but Leonard Bernstein prepared a television version (1960) and conducted and narrated a recording. Copland's only full-length opera, *The Tender Land* (1954), was commissioned for television. The libretto is by Horace Everett (pseudonymn for Erik Johns). Set on a modest farm in the Midwest during the Depression, it concerns the rebellion and awakening sexuality of an adolescent girl. The music is melodious and folksy, the language informal and colloquial. After the opera was rejected by NBC television, the New York City Opera staged it on 1 April 1954. It received mixed reviews, and Copland and Johns prepared a revised version that has been produced by college opera workshops and small companies. An orchestral suite and two choruses, each of which may be performed separately or together, have been heard more frequently.

See also TENDER LAND, THE.

A. Berger: *Aaron Copland* (New York, 1953)
E. Johns: 'The Tender Land', *Center: a Magazine of the Performing Arts* (1954), March, 14
J. F. Smith: *Aaron Copland: his Work and Contribution to American Music* (New York, 1955)
A. Copland: *Copland on Music* (New York, 1960), 129–38
W. H. Mellers: 'The Tender Land', *MT*, ciii (1962), 245–6
——: 'The Teenager's World', *MT*, cv (1964), 500–05 [on *The Second Hurricane*]
A. Copland and V. Perlis: *Copland: 1900 through 1942* (New York, 1984)
V. Perlis: 'A New Chance for *The Tender Land*', *New York Times* (26 April 1987)
A. Copland and V. Perlis: *Copland: Since 1943* (New York, 1989)
VIVIAN PERLIS

Copley, John (Michael) (*b* Birmingham, 12 June 1933). English director. He studied at the National School of Opera in London under Joan Cross, who along with Tyrone Guthrie and Frederick Ashton exerted a strong influence on his work. He appeared as the Apprentice in *Peter Grimes* at Covent Garden in 1950 and later became a stage manager for Sadler's Wells Opera, where his first production was *Il tabarro* in 1957. He worked as an assistant to the director Christopher West at Covent Garden and during the 1960s was responsible for revivals of innumerable standard repertory works. His first major production there was *Così fan tutte* (1968), followed by *Le nozze di Figaro* (1971), *La bohème* (1974, with subsequent revivals) and *Semele* (1982). He was appointed resident director of the Royal Opera in 1971, later principal resident director (until 1988). He also directed regularly for the ENO – *Carmen*

(1969), *La traviata* (1973), *Der Rosenkavalier* (1975) and *Giulio Cesare* (1979). During the 1980s his essentially elegant style and taste for lavish visual settings fell out of favour in the UK, but he has worked regularly and fruitfully abroad, most notably with *The Midsummer Marriage* (1983, San Francisco), *Yevgeny Onegin* (1983, Ottawa), *Peter Grimes* (1986, Sydney), *Ariodante* (1987, Santa Fe) and *Semiramide* (1990, New York, Metropolitan). His greatest strength lies in his sensitive direction of singers, especially the less experienced, whom he has always helped to appear at ease on stage. His admiration for the work of Frederick Ashton has led to a distinctly 'balletic' outline to stage movement in his productions. RODNEY MILNES

Coppola, Pietro (Antonio) (*b* Castrogiovanni [now Enna], 11 Dec 1793; *d* Catania, 13 Nov 1877). Italian composer. His first teachers were his father and his brother. He then studied for a short time at the Naples Conservatory. From about 1810 he was a music teacher in Catania, where his family lived, and later *maestro concertatore* at the theatre there. His first operas, *Il figlio del bandito* (1816), *Artale d'Aragona* (?1816) and *Il destino* (1825), performed in Naples and Catania, did not make his name widely known.

He moved to Naples (1832) and in 1835 his opera *La pazza per amore*, a reworking of Lorenzi's libretto for Paisiello's *Nina* of 45 years before, was such a success in Rome that within a few years it had been performed in most of the theatres of Italy, as well as in Vienna, Berlin, Paris, Lisbon, Havana and Mexico City. In the next three years Coppola took advantage of this success with four more operas, written for Turin, Vienna and Milan, none of which was very successful. From 1839 to 1843 he was music director of the Lisbon opera house, the Teatro de S Carlos, where he produced his earlier operas and two new ones, *Giovanna I* (1840) and *Inès de Castro* (1841). From 1843 he was again in Italy; three new operas were performed in Rome and Palermo, but in 1850 he took up his old post in Lisbon and held it until 1871. During this period he revised his earlier works and composed a Portuguese comic opera, *Oaunel de Salamão* (1853). He returned finally to Italy in 1871 and was *maestro di cappella* in the cathedral of Novara, where he composed a large amount of church music. In 1873 he moved to Catania, where he was made honorary director of the municipal musical organizations.

Coppola was the typical exporter of a provincial and derivative operatic product, one largely outside the progressive path of Italian opera in his time. A facile melodist in the Bellinian vein, even neo-Neapolitan in *La pazza per amore*, he was less successful when later he attempted Romantic subjects and brilliant comedy.

His father, Giuseppe Coppola (*b* Naples; *d* Catania, *c*1810), was composer of a number of operas given in Naples about 1790 (including *I due fratelli perseguitati*, to a libretto by G. Palomba; *Le nozze disturbate*, G. Bertati; and *La giornata critica di Don Gianpicone*); he moved to Sicily in the 1790s and held positions at the theatre in Catania.

Il figlio del bandito (ob, 2, G. Checcherini), Naples, Fondo, 18 Jan 1816
Artale d'Aragona, Catania, Comunale, ?1816
Il destino, Catania, Comunale, Aug 1825
Il gondoliere di Venezia, ossia Gli sdegni amorosi (int, C. Goldoni), Naples, Fondo, 1825
Achille in Sciro (3, P. Metastasio), Catania, Comunale, 1828
La pazza per amore [Nina] (melodramma semiserio, 2, J. Ferretti, after G. E. Lorenzi), Rome, Valle, 14 Feb 1835, *I-Mr**, vs (Milan, n.d.); rev. 1871
Gl'Illinesi (melodramma serio, 2, F. Romani), Turin, Regio, 26 Dec 1835
La festa della rosa ossia Enrichetta di Bajenfeld (melodramma giocoso, 2, Ferretti), Vienna, Kärntnertor, 29 June 1836, vs (Milan, ?1850)
La bella Celeste degli Spadari (C. Bassi), Milan, Cannobiana, 14 June 1837
Il postiglione di Longjumeau (melodramma comico, 2, Bassi), Milan, Scala, 6 Nov 1838
Giovanna I regina di Napoli (4, A. Pendola), Lisbon, S Carlos, 11 Oct 1840
Inès de Castro (tragedia lirica, 3, S. Cammarano), Lisbon, S Carlos, 26 Dec 1841
Il folletto (melodramma giocoso, 2, Ferretti), Rome, Valle, 18 June 1843
L'orfano guelfa (dramma lirico, 3, G. Solito), Palermo, Carolino, carn. 1846, vs (Milan, ?1845)
Fingal (Solito), Palermo, Carolino, Oct 1847, duet (Milan, 1844)
Oaunel de Salamão [L'anello di Salomone] (2, M. Leal), Lisbon, Langerais, 23 June 1853

*

DEUMM (G. P. Minardi); *ES* (E. Zanetti); *FlorimoN*; *MGG* (A. Mondolfi-Bossarelli)
A. Cametti: 'Les rossiniens d'Italie', *EMDC*, I/ii (1921), 864–5
GIOVANNI CARLI BALLOLA

Copyright (Fr. *droit d'auteur*; Ger. *Urheberrecht*; It. *proprietà litteraria, diritti d'autore*). The legal right in literary, musical and artistic property.

1. Introduction. 2. Great Britain. 3. United States of America. 4. Other countries. 5. International conventions.

1. INTRODUCTION. Copyright protection is offered to original literary, musical and artistic works according to the national law of each country, with the result that the basis and extent of such protection for the same work may differ from one country to another. However, a large number of countries are party to one or more of the international copyright conventions which aim to make the basic principles of copyright protection common to all signatory states and to ensure that works by nationals of those states will be treated in any one country in the same way as those of its own citizens.

The present article describes copyright law as it affects the publication and performance of opera. However, many copyright laws fail to deal specifically with opera, which often derives its protection from laws framed to cover printed books, printed music and dramatic representations of any kind.

2. GREAT BRITAIN. Before any legal copyright system was instituted several countries had set up a system of privileges which reserved the rights over literary property to the Crown. In an attempt to secure a monopoly over the printing of books in England, for example, Henry VIII prohibited their importation altogether and established a system of privileges, the granting of which was the prerogative of the monarch. As commercial printing developed, opportunities to profit from an author's genius increased and from 1679 the Stationers' Company, set up by the Crown, was granted the right to control the printing of books in the interest of its members. This right, later referred to as 'copyright', was a source of profit for the king, who reaped the rewards of others' labour.

This unjust situation was terminated in 1709 by the introduction of the first true copyright act, which replaced the unrestricted and perpetual right which an author had to his work at common law. The act of 1709 gave protection to an author against the unauthorized printing of a book or musical composition for a period of 21 years if the work had already been published, and for 14 years for works published after the introduction of the act. Unpublished works were also protected for 14 years. If the author was still alive when protection expired, he could renew it for a further similar period. Publications covered by the act included dramatic compositions and therefore opera, which was just then beginning to make its appearance on the commercial stage in London. The remedies for infringement of the act's provisions were the forfeiting of all illegal copies and a fine of one penny for each sheet. Half of this amount went to the Crown and the rest to the author or the person who had sued on his behalf.

The earliest form of protection given to the performance, as distinct from the publication, of opera was afforded by the Dramatic Copyright Act of 1833. Section 1 of the act stipulated that the author of 'any tragedy, comedy, play, opera, farce or any other dramatic piece or entertainment' was to have the sole liberty of representing it or causing it to be represented at any place of dramatic entertainment. The act granted an exclusive right of public performance to the author for 28 years, with a reversionary period for the rest of his life provided the work was printed and published. The same protection was extended to works printed and published during the ten years preceding the passing of the act. The act did not, however, extend to the performance of musical compositions as a whole, which meant that an opera composer enjoyed a measure of protection not granted to composers of instrumental music.

In the case of Planché *v.* Braham (1837: *Law Journal Reports*, xvi, 25) an action was brought under the 1833 act for the singing of three songs from the libretto of Weber's *Oberon* written by the party suing (1838: exported in *Bingham's New Cases*, iv, 17). The point at law was whether or not there had been a representation of part of the opera, and thereby an infringement. The court refused to interfere with the decision of the jury in favour of the plaintiff: there had indeed been a representation of part of the opera. It was also held that it was piracy to make a piano arrangement from an opera (see Wood *v.* Boosey, 1877: *Law Reports*, Queen's Bench, iii, 223), to base quadrilles and waltzes on melodies from a copyright opera (see D'Almaine *v.* Boosey, 1835: *Yange and Collyers Reports*, Exchequer, 228) and to construct a full score from a non-copyright piano arrangement of a copyright opera (see Boosey *v.* Fairlie, 1877: *Law Reports*, Chancery Division, vii, 301). The penalty for an infringement of the 1833 act was a fine of 40 shillings for each unauthorized representation of the work or damages amounting to the full benefit received from such representations (or the full loss to the composer), whichever was the greater.

A further act of 1842 extended this protection to musical compositions generally, and the combined effect of both acts was, firstly, to grant to the author of any unprinted and unpublished dramatic piece (including an opera) or musical composition the sole and perpetual right to its performance; and, secondly, to grant to the author of any published dramatic piece or musical composition the same copyright in respect of performance as obtained in respect of publication, i.e. for 42 years or for the life of the author and seven years thereafter, whichever was the longer. (These provisions also extended to the author's assignees.) Other provisions of the act included the procedure for registering the various details of the piece, and for assigning copyright in its publication independently of the performing rights. The act was not immune to abuse, however, and a certain Wall became notorious for purchasing performing rights and then enforcing payment of the £2 penalty from those who, in all innocence, put on a public performance without his permission. Such abuse prompted the framing of the Copyright (Musical Compositions) Act of 1882 (amended in 1888), which required that a notice of the reservation of the rights of public performance be printed in every copy of the work. The 1888 act also provided for penalties against a proprietor, tenant or occupier of a place of dramatic entertainment who knowingly permitted an unauthorized performance.

To combat the practice of street hawkers selling copies of songs and musical pieces in breach of the existing laws, the Musical (Summary Proceedings) Act 1902 and the Musical Copyright Act 1906 were passed. In 1911 the term of copyright was extended to the life of the author and 50 years thereafter in conformity with international agreements (see §5). All these acts (except for certain provisions of the Copyright Act 1911) were finally repealed by the Copyright Act 1956, and this in turn was replaced on 1 August 1989 by the Copyright, Designs and Patents Act 1988.

Much of the new act restated existing law, especially as it relates to copyright itself, but the 1956 act remains relevant to works originating before 1 August 1989, just as the 1911 Act is still relevant to works copyrighted before the 1956 act came into force. The 1988 act does not specifically protect opera, but it does protect its constituent parts, the libretto and the music, separately. Additional copyrights will usually be created in the course of an opera's production, since the designs for sets and costumes will probably be protected if they were initially created in the form of drawings etc. Copyright may also exist in the typographical arrangement of a published edition of an opera, to the extent that it does not merely reproduce the arrangement of a previous edition.

The 1988 act also contained provisions new to British law, in particular by providing for the protection of 'moral rights', including those commonly known as the rights of 'paternity' and 'integrity'. The right of paternity entitles the author to be identified as such whenever the work is published, performed or otherwise commercially exploited, provided that right has been appropriately 'asserted' in writing. The right of integrity entitles the owner of the copyright not to have a work altered or adapted in such a way as to distort or mutilate it. Both rights subsist for as long as the copyright remains in force. A third moral right, which subsists until 20 years after a person's death, is not to have a literary, dramatic, musical or artistic work falsely attributed to that person. None of these rights can be assigned during the person's lifetime, but they will form part of his estate after his death.

3. United States of America. Literary piracy was for a long time difficult to combat in the USA. As there were different laws for different states, a work protected in one state might be reprinted immediately in an adjoining one. By the time the American constitution was drafted 12 out of the 13 states had passed copyright laws, some of which afforded protection to authors from another state on a reciprocal basis. Section 8 of the constitution stated that 'Congress shall have the power to promote

the progress of science and the useful arts by securing for a limited time to authors and inventors the exclusive right to their respective writings and discoveries'. In 1790 the Copyright Act, which mirrored English law, gave protection to an author for 14 years, and for a further 14 years if he were still living. It did not, however, protect foreign authors. A further act of 1831 secured copyright for 28 years and for the author's surviving wife or children for a further 14 years. The penalty for infringement was confiscation of the pirated work and 50 cents for every sheet in the offender's possession.

It was not until 1891 that American law provided protection for foreign works, and then only if the work were published in the USA and registered there. Section 729 of the penal code of 1899 stated that 'any person who causes to be publicly performed for profit any unpublished, undedicated or copyrighted (dramatic or) musical composition known as an opera without the consent of its owner or who knowing that such (dramatic or) musical composition is unpublished, undedicated or copyrighted permits, aids or takes part in such performance shall be guilty of a misdemeanour'.

In 1903 Wagner's heirs sought the aid of the American courts in the case of Wagner *v.* Caried (1903: *Federal Reports*, cxxv, 798). The exclusive right of publication and possession of *Parsifal* had been assigned by Wagner to the publishers B. Schott & Sons. The contract reserved the performance rights to Wagner, whose representatives brought an action to restrain the defendant from producing the work on stage in America. It was agreed that the notice printed in the published score would have been sufficient to protect the performing rights under German law, but an edition printed in 1902 had not been copyrighted in the USA, although copies had been sold there. The reservation of right was treated as a nullity and the effect of publication was to dedicate the work to the public. The note was deemed ineffective.

The Copyright Act of 1909 froze American law until 1976, when a law was passed which was more in keeping with those of other countries. On 1 March 1989 the USA became a member of the Berne Copyright Union (see §5) and the 50-year period was adopted. The country is also party to the Universal Copyright Convention.

4. OTHER COUNTRIES.

(i) France. Along with Britain, France took the lead in copyright legislation. Until the Revolution stage performances were controlled by a system of royal privileges, and in 1669 Pierre Perrin was granted an exclusive privilege to establish Académies d'Opéra in France. Lully took advantage of Perrin's being cheated by his collaborators after the successful staging of *Pomone* in 1671 to buy the privilege from him and then succeeded, with a series of restrictive patents and ordinances from the king, in stifling all rivalry to his own operatic ventures. His privilege was passed on to his heirs, and Anne Danican Philidor was obliged to pay Lully's son-in-law Francine 10 000 *livres* annually for three years for permission to perform complete musical works (and even then not operatic extracts) at the Concert Spirituel.

The system of privileges was swept away, along with the monarchy, by the Revolution. In 1791 the right of public performance was introduced, and in 1793 the first French copyright law gave an author the exclusive right to enjoy the fruits of his work for life, and his heirs or assignees the right to enjoy the same for ten years after his death. In 1810 the posthumous rights were extended to the widow for life and to the children for 20 years after the deaths of both parents. In the case of works printed or performed abroad, infringements of the copyright could still be proceeded against in the French courts, provided that two copies of the work had been registered in France. In 1825 the period of protection after an author's death was extended to 50 years.

(ii) Italy. The first copyright laws in Italy were also enacted after the French Revolution. A law of 1810 gave protection to an author's widow and his sons for a period of 20 years after his death. In 1811 the King of the Two Sicilies decreed that the authors of musical and theatrical works (presumably including operas) could claim damages for 'abusive use of the property of others in the event of performance of their works taking place without their consent'. The law remained basically unchanged until 1925, when Italy passed what was perhaps the most progressive copyright law then in force; it abolished all formalities for the acquisition of copyright, increased the period of protection to 50 years after the author's death and also recognized the author's 'moral rights' (see §2). Italian law also deals with the division of royalties between an opera composer and his librettist where no agreement exists: it gives three-quarters to the composer and one quarter to the librettist.

(iii) Germany and Austria. Piracy of works in Germany was widespread during the revival of German literature in the 18th century. Control was exercised by a system of privileges like those of England and France, but the system was made difficult to operate by the large number of independent principalities and it was not until 1832 that reciprocity was achieved between the different German states. In 1835 it was declared in Austria that the acts of the Germanic Diet would extend to all parts of the Austrian Empire. In 1837 the rest of Germany, soon followed by Austria, adopted the Prussian law, which gave protection to the author for his lifetime and to his heirs (hitherto without rights in Austria) for 30 years thereafter. This was extended in 1934 to the 50-year period of the Berne Convention (see §5) and in 1965 to 70 years.

(iv) Scandinavia and Spain. In Denmark the length of copyright protection was until 1838 unlimited, provided the work had been kept in print; but then the period was reduced to 30 years, though protection lapsed if the work was out of print for five years. Norway, Sweden and Spain also offered perpetual copyright until 1879, when Spain reduced the period to 50 years after the author's death; the period is now 80 years. In 1837 Sweden had made a similar reduction to 20 years, with the additional proviso that if the author's heirs or assignees failed to keep the work in print the copyright reverted to the state.

(v) Russia and Japan. In the 18th century Russia worked a system of privileges similar to those operating in Europe. Literary and musical success was recognized by certain titles of rank and honour. The copyright law of 1830 gave an author the sole liberty of printing and disposing of his works during his lifetime and extended this to his heirs or assignees for 25 years after his death; publication of an edition during the last five years of this period secured protection for a further ten years.

Performing rights were assigned to the author by separate licences. Both Tsarist and Soviet Russia remained outside the Berne Copyright Union, but in 1973 the Soviet Union became a party to the Universal Copyright Convention (see §5). Until then the only international agreement by the USSR was with Hungary.

The Japanese copyright law of 1869 regulated publishing activities in much the same way as they were regulated in Great Britain. A licence conferred protection for the author's lifetime. The Copyright Act 1899 incorporated the provisions of the Berne Convention and made Japan a member of the Berne Copyright Union (see §5); it is also a party to the Universal Copyright Convention. The Japanese copyright act of 1970 protects also moral rights (see §2) and neighbouring rights (that is, rights relating to performance and recording and certain subsidiary and derivative rights).

(vi) British Dominions. As long as British law extended to Australia and Canada, authors in those countries enjoyed the same copyright protection as British authors. The Australian Copyright Act 1905 made the same distinction between copyright in books or artistic works and the performing rights in such works as did the British acts of 1833 and 1842; and the Copyright Act 1968 is very similar to the UK act of 1956. Canada's copyright laws are based on the British act of 1911 and provide for a register which, although not compulsory, provides *prima facie* evidence of the facts registered. The New Zealand statute of 1962–71 resembles that of Australia.

5. International conventions. By the 19th century some kind of reciprocal copyright agreement between different nations was seen as a commercial necessity; public ridicule (as suffered by Beckmesser in *Die Meistersinger*) could not remain the only weapon against plagiarism of a stranger's work. In Great Britain from 1844 onwards a series of international copyright acts extended protection to works published in certain foreign countries which accorded reciprocal rights to British authors. Until then the general rule was that a foreign author or composer would have to be domiciled in Britain to receive the benefit of British copyright laws.

It was France and Britain who took the lead in the drafting of international copyright law as we know it today. In 1852 these two countries signed a convention which conferred reciprocal protection in the property of literature, drama, music, engraving and sculpture. Its aim was to prevent piratical translations and unauthorized imitations or adaptations in both countries. In the case of stage works protection was conferred by the process of registration at specified places within three months of the first representation; English works had to be deposited at the Bibliothèque Nationale in Paris and at the Ministry of the Interior. The smallest infringement of the registration procedure could invalidate the entry, and numerous works (including Gounod's *Faust*) were allowed to slip into the public domain for this reason. Britain made similar treaties with Hamburg in 1853, Belgium in 1854, Prussia in 1855 and Spain in 1857.

The International Copyright Act 1886, which abolished geographical limitations (that is, it extended protection to all countries that had copyright treaties with Great Britain), was followed in December 1887 by the Berne Convention, the first important international treaty on copyright, which gave its name to the Berne Copyright Union. This treaty, revised at Paris in 1896, at Berlin in 1908, at Rome in 1928, at Brussels in 1948, at Stockholm in 1967 and at Paris in 1971, gave authors of works first published or performed in a member state the same protection in other member states as would be enjoyed if the works had first been published or performed there. The original parties to the convention included, as well as Britain, Belgium, France, Germany, Italy and Spain; the majority of western European countries are now party to it, as are certain eastern European states, Canada, Australia, Japan and (since 1 March 1989) the USA. Russia (and later the Soviet Union) remained outside.

A wider range of countries adhere to the Universal Copyright Convention, signed at Geneva in 1952 and revised at Paris in 1971, which offers a lower level of protection; many countries are members of both this and the Berne Copyright Union.

Grove6 (E. P. Skone James, P. Kleiner and M. B. Nimmer)

E. P. Skone James: *Copinger and Skone James on Copyright* (London, rev. 11/1971)

M. B. Nimmer: *Nimmer on Copyright* (New York, 1973)

H. I. L. Laddie and others: *The Modern Law of Copyright* (London, 1980)

W. R. Cornish: *Intellectual Property, Patents, Copyright Trade Marks and Allied Rights* (London, 2/1989)

JOY BRERETON, AMANDA MICHAELS

Coq d'or, Le. Opera by Nikolay Rimsky-Korsakov; *see* GOLDEN COCKEREL, THE.

Coquard, Arthur(-Joseph) (*b* Paris, 26 May 1846; *d* Noirmoutier, Vendée, 20 Aug 1910). French composer. In 1865–6 he studied with César Franck at the Jesuit College before taking up a legal career; he continued to practise law until 1881. On returning to composition he wrote a number of stage works as well as music for solo voice and orchestra. His interest in classical literature and French classical drama is reflected in his incidental music although for his operas, such as *L'épée du roi* (1884), he chose more contemporary subjects. He assisted in the orchestration of Franck's *Hulda* and *Ghiselle* (Act 4) and completed, from sketches, Lalo's *La jacquerie* (1895, Monte Carlo), an outstanding achievement. His magnum opus was *La troupe Jolicoeur* of 1902, for which he also wrote the libretto (although his daughter Cécile wrote the prologue), a tale of circus life inspired no doubt by the contemporary naturalism of Zola's novels. He was a music critic for several journals and was director of music at the national institute for young blind people, 1892–9. Much of Coquard's music is characterized by a straining after expressiveness, reflecting the influence of Franck. He lacked, however, the sustaining power necessary for large-scale works and the effect of the whole is often stilted.

all printed works published in Paris

Cassandre (drame lyrique), 2, H. de Bornier, after Seneca: *Agamemnon*), Paris, Société Chorale d'Amateurs, 13 May 1881

L'épée du roi (oc, 2, A. Silvestre), Angers, Municipal, 20 March 1884 (n.d.)

Le mari d'un jour (oc, 3, A. d'Ennery and Silvestre), Paris, OC (Favart), 4 Feb 1886, vs (?1886)

Pompée (drame lyrique, 3, H. Moreau), Paris, Société Chorale d'Amateurs, 13 April 1888

L'oiseau bleu (fantaisie poétique, 2, S. Arnaud), Paris, d'Application, 6 March 1894 (n.d.)

La reine de Beauce, 1897–8 (comédie musicale, 3)

Jahel (drame lyrique, 4, Arnaud and L. Gallet), Lyons, Grand, 24 May 1900 (n.d.)

La troupe Jolicoeur (comédie musicale, prol., 3, A. Coquard and C. Coquard, after H. Cain), Paris, OC (Favart), 30 May 1902 (n.d.)
Isdronning, 1903 (oc, 2, Mme Coquard-Fournery)

*

N. Dufourcq: *Autour de Coquard, César Franck et Vincent d'Indy* (Paris, 1952) JOHN TREVITT

Cora och Alonzo ('Cora and Alonzo'). *Tragédie lyrique* in three acts by JOHANN GOTTLIEB NAUMANN to a libretto by Gudmund Göran Adlerbeth after JEAN FRANÇOIS MARMONTEL's *Les Incas, ou la Destruction de l'empire du Pérou*; Stockholm, Royal Opera Theatre, 30 September 1782.

Zulma (soprano), high priestess of the sun at the Incas' palace in Quito, prepares the reluctant Cora (soprano) to become one of the chaste and celibate sun maidens. The Inca Atilba (tenor) entertains a Spanish knight, Alonzo (tenor), and allows him to witness Cora's initiation; his heart is captured by her. She faints as she takes the oath of celibacy, and a volcano erupts and blots out the sun, spreading terror among the Incas. Cora later finds Alonzo alone and declares her love, but Zulma surprises them together and the guards seize them, as the penalty for consorting with a sun maiden is death. Palmor (bass), Cora's father, offers his life in exchange for hers, but Zulma insists that only Cora's sacrifice will stop the disasters. The Spaniards invade the palace and free Alonzo, but he asks that his countrymen yield to Atilba and the Incas, and then pleads for Cora's life. The people, whose sympathy is with the sun maiden, rise up against the priests of the sun, and Cora and Alonzo are united.

The planned première of *Cora och Alonzo* was postponed when Naumann left Stockholm before completing the work in 1778; he arranged a concert version in Dresden in 1780. In 1782 the new Royal Opera in Stockholm was completed and the opera intended for its inauguration, J. M. Kraus's *Aeneas i Cartago*, was cancelled; Naumann's *Cora och Alonzo* replaced it and remained in the repertory until 1832, with more than 50 performances. Musically, the work owes much to Gluck, with large choruses and ballets integrated into the drama, colourful orchestration and striking harmonies. Naumann's Italian heritage is evident in the long coloratura passages and lyrical melodies.

BERTIL H. VAN BOER

Corbelli, Alessandro (*b* Turin, 21 Sept 1952). Italian baritone. After studying with Giuseppe Valdengo, he made his début in 1974 at Bergamo and Treviso as Marcello and has since sung widely in Italy, Germany, Geneva, Vienna and Paris. He sang Pacuvio (*La pietra del paragone*) at the Piccola Scala and in Edinburgh (1982), then Dandini in Philadelphia (1984) and at Glyndebourne (1985). He made his Scala début in 1983 and his Covent Garden début in 1988 as Taddeo (*L'italiana in Algeri*). His repertory includes Sharpless (his Opéra début role, 1983), Silvio (his Vienna Staatsoper début, 1987), Mozart's, Paisiello's and Rossini's Figaro, Papageno, Guglielmo, Raimbaud (*Le comte Ory*), Malatesta, Sergeant Belcore and Escamillo. He has a flexible voice and his natural gifts incline towards comedy. ELIZABETH FORBES

Corbett, William (bap. ?London, 18 July 1680; *d* London, 7 March 1748). English composer. He came to attention as a theatre composer in 1703 with suites of incidental music and songs for productions of the Lincoln's Inn Fields company. Later he worked at the Queen's Theatre at the Haymarket, writing suites for Granville's semi-opera *The British Enchanters* (February 1706) and an unnamed production (1708); as a violinist he played a prominent role in its orchestra (though he was not its leader, as Burney maintained) at least between 1707 and 1710. He left England for Milan in 1716 and lived mostly in Italy (spying, it is said, on the Old Pretender) until he retired, probably in 1731. Corbett's suites are accomplished essays in the post-Purcell idiom, though they also contain some up-to-date italianate features.

*

BDA; *BurneyH*; *HawkinsH*; *LS*
M. Tilmouth: 'A Calendar of References to Music in Newspapers Published in London and the Provinces (1660–1719)', *RMARC*, no.1 (1961)
R. Fiske: *English Theatre Music in the Eighteenth Century* (London, 1973, 2/1986)
C. A. Price: *Music in the Restoration Theatre* (Ann Arbor, 1979)
J. Milhous and R. D. Hume, eds.: *Vice Chamberlain Coke's Theatrical Papers 1706–1715* (Carbondale and Edwardsville, IL, 1982)
O. Edwards: 'Espionage, a Collection of Violins, and *Le Bizzarie Universalie*: a Fresh Look at William Corbett', *MQ*, lxxiii (1989), 320–43

PETER HOLMAN

Corbisieri [Corbisiero], **Francesco** (*b c*1730; *d* Naples, after 1802). Italian composer. A pupil of Lorenzo Fago and G. G. Brunetti at the Turchini conservatory in Naples, he was appointed to the royal chapel in 1764 and remained there more than 38 years, rising from the rank of supernumerary organist to vice-*maestro* (1779). He composed two comic operas for Naples, *La Mergellina* (F. Cerlone; 1771, Act 1 *I-Nf**) and *La maestra* (C. Goldoni; Nuovo, winter 1773), and another for Salerno, *L'osteria di Pausilippo* (Cerlone; winter 1775), but his church music is more important.

*

ES ('Corbisiero, Antonio'; F. Schlitzer); *StiegerO*
U. Prota-Giurleo: 'Breve storia del teatro di corte', *Il teatro di corte del Palazzo reale di Napoli* (Naples, 1952), 131

HANNS-BERTOLD DIETZ

Corbisiero, Antonio (*b* Marzano di Nola, 21 May 1720; *d* Naples, 7 Jan 1790). Italian composer. From 1733 to 1739 he studied in Naples at the Conservatorio della Pietà dei Turchini with Nicola Fago, Andreo Basso, Leonardo Leo and Lorenzo Fago. He then settled in Naples as a composer and *maestro di canto*. In autumn 1749 his first opera, the comedy *Monsieur Petitone* on a libretto by Antonio Palomba, was produced at the Teatro Nuovo. During the early 1750s he composed three additional comic operas for Neapolitan theatres, *Il mercante innamorato* (P. Trinchera; Fiorentini, autumn 1750), *Lo finto innamorato* (Trinchera, based on his libretto to *La vennegna*; Nuovo, autumn 1751) and *La finta marchesa* (1754). Thereafter he composed only sacred music.

*

FlorimoN; *StiegerO* HANNS-BERTOLD DIETZ

Cordans, Bartolomeo (*b* Venice, *c*1700; *d* Udine, 14 May 1757). Italian composer. He became a member of the Franciscan order at an early age, but probably left it sometime before being nominated *maestro di cappella* at Udine Cathedral in 1735 (a position he retained until his death). In Udine he composed no operas; his eight known operas date from his years in Venice. In the mid-1740s he became a member of the Accademia Filarmonica in Bologna, and after the papal encyclical of

1749 he increasingly composed in a contrapuntal style. His portrait is in the castle museum, Udine.

opere serie unless otherwise stated; all first performed in Venice

Ormisda (A. Zeno), S Cassiano, carn. 1728
La generosità di Tiberio [Act 3] (N. Minato), S Cassiano, aut. 1729 [Acts 1 and 2 by S. Lapis]
Silvia (E. Bissaro), S Moisè, aut. 1730
Romilda (C. Pagani-Cesa), S Moisè, carn. 1731
Attanaganamenone (ob, G. B. Buini), S Moisè, spr. 1731
Fidarsi è bene ma non fidarsi è meglio (ob, Buini), S Moisè, spr. 1731
Sponsali d'Enea (F. Passarini), S Angelo, spr. 1731 [also attrib. M. Fino]
Rodelinda (A. Salvi), S Moisè, aut. 1731

*

A. Costadoni: 'Vita del reverendissimo padre D. Romano Merighi', *A. Calogerà: Raccolta di opuscoli scientifici e filologici*, xxv (Venice, 1742), 116
J. B. de La Borde: *Essai sur la musique ancienne et moderne* (Paris, 1780), iii, 182
SVEN HANSELL

Cordeiro da Silva, João. *See* SILVA, JOÃO CORDEIRO DA.

Cordella, Giacomo (*b* Naples, 25 July 1786; *d* Naples, ? 8 May 1846 [or ? 8 Aug 1846, 8 May 1847]). Italian composer. His teachers were Fenaroli and Paisiello. At the age of 18 he composed a sacred cantata and at about the same time Paisiello secured him a commission for his first opera, the *farsa Il ciarlatano*, for Venice, where it had a good reception; it was also performed in Milan, Turin, Padua and the Netherlands. Cordella is said to have returned to Paisiello for further study. He composed fewer than 20 operas, often at widely spaced intervals, and only three after 1826. Except for two disastrous attempts at *opera seria* he worked, generally with success, in the comic or semi-serious genres. His greatest success was *Una follia*, first given in 1813 at Naples, where most of his operas had their premières. His other vocal works include substitute arias; one for Weigl's *Amor marinaro* led to the attribution to him of an opera with this title. According to a biographical notice of 1825 (*AMZ*, xxvii, col.717), he had by then also composed many sacred works.

He held appointments at the Naples royal chapel and the conservatory and was music director (sometimes jointly) at the S Carlo from about 1832 to 1843. According to Florimo, he was a good organist, and his biography states that he made a special study of accompanying singers. About half his operas are extant in the Naples Conservatory library, many in autograph.

His father Geronimo (or Girolamo) Cordella, was also a composer, active in Naples and Tuscany; his operas include *La Faustina* (1747, Naples), *Il cicisbeo impertinente* (1754, Pisa) and *Le virtuose ridicoli*, *La donna capricciosa* and *La madamigella* (all 1756, Livorno).

Il ciarlatano ossia I finti savoiardi (L. G. Buonavoglia), Venice, S Moisè, 26 Dec 1804
L'albergatrice scaltra, Naples, S Carlo, 27 June 1807
Annibale in Capua, Naples, S Carlo, 21 Oct 1809
L'isola incantata, Naples, Nuovo, 1809
Una follia (commedia per musica, A. L. Tottola), Naples, Fiorentini, 1813
L'avaro (G. Palomba), Naples, aut. 1814
L'azzardo fortunato (commedia per musica, Tottola), Naples, carn. 1815
Il contraccambio (C. Sterbini), Rome, Valle, carn. 1819
Lo scaltro millantatore (G. Palomba), Naples, Nuovo, 16 July 1819
Lo sposo di provincia (G. Schmidt), Rome, Argentina, 1821
Il castello degli Invalidi, Naples, Nuovo, 1823
Il frenetico per amore, Naples, aut. 1824
Alcibiade (L. Prividali), Venice, Fenice, carn. 1825
Gli Avventurieri (melodramma giocoso, F. Romani), Milan, Cannobiana, 6 Sept 1825
La bella prigioniera, Naples, Fondo, 1826
Il marito disperato (commedia giocosa per musica, A. Passaro, after G. B. Lorenzi), Naples, Fondo, Lent 1833
I due furbi (A. Palomba, rev. A. Passaro), Naples, Nuovo, 16 July 1835
Matilde di Lanchefort (melodramma storico, Passaro), Naples, Fondo, spr. 1838
Amor marinaro, n.d.
Doubtful: Partenope, 1840

*

ES (F. Schlitzer); *FétisB*; *FlorimoN*
DENNIS LIBBY/R

Corder, Frederick (*b* London, 26 Jan 1852; *d* London, 21 Aug 1932). English translator and composer. He studied in London at the RAM, then with Ferdinand Hiller in Cologne. His first work for the stage, the grand opera *Le morte d'Arthur* (4, Corder, after T. Malory), had its première in Brighton in 1879. During the next five years he wrote several operettas which were also performed there; he also wrote librettos, of which *Sisyphus, King of Ephyrus* was set by Baron Bódog Orczy in 1882. Unable to support himself by composition, he turned more seriously to literary work, often in collaboration with his wife Henrietta Louisa (née Walford). Their pioneering translations of Wagner did much to spread an appreciation in England of the composer Corder admired above all others. The first, *Parsifal* (1879), reflects much of the manner of Wagner's original, but misses the complexity and subtlety of a drama whose real depths of meaning they hardly discerned. The *Ring* (1882–5) was for long the preferred English version, both for reading and in performance (e.g. *Die Walküre* at Covent Garden in 1895). Though no longer acceptable by reason of its many contortions of language in the attempt to match Wagner's *Stabreim*, it is remarkably faithful to the detail and much of the spirit of the German; its most crucial fault is that what is archaic in German sounds merely quaint in English. There are also translations of *Die Meistersinger von Nürnberg* (1882), *Tristan und Isolde* (1882) and *Lohengrin* (1906).

Of Corder's own operas, only the romantic opera *Nordisa* op.17 (3, Corder) met with any success, being widely performed after its première (26 January 1887), which was given by the Carl Rosa Opera Company at the Royal Court Theatre, Liverpool. But after the death of Carl Rosa, Corder was forced to abandon his hopes of a career as a composer for an established English opera, and turned to teaching; he was a professor of composition at the RAM from 1888 (curator, 1889). Among his writings is the book *Wagner and his Music*, published in London in 1912. JOHN WARRACK

Cordovano, Il ('The Cordovan'). Opera in one act by GOFFREDO PETRASSI to a libretto by Eugenio Montale after MIGUEL DE CERVANTES's *Entremes del viejo celoso*; Milan, Teatro alla Scala, 12 May 1949 (revised version, Milan, Piccola Scala, 18 February 1959).

The story is set in 17th-century Córdoba. The crusty septuagenarian Cannizares (bass) has taken a young wife Donna Lorenza (soprano) whom he keeps as a virtual prisoner at home to prevent possible illicit liaisons. Hortigosa (contralto), a neighbour, aided by Lorenza's young niece Cristina (soprano leggero), smuggles a comely youth (silent role) into the house for Lorenza's pleasure by using a cordovan leather mat for concealment. When Cannizares goes to investigate the ecstatic sighs coming from his wife's room he receives a basin of water in the face and the youth escapes in the confusion. Attracted by the commotion, the town guard arrives with a group of passing musicians who sing a moralizing chorus to the, by now, pacified company.

The cast of characters reminiscent of those of the *commedia dell'arte* act out a story similar to that used by Ravel in *L'heure espagnole.* Musically the characters are clearly defined by instrumental motto themes and distinctive modes of vocal declamation. The overall style of chromaticized neo-classicism can accommodate polytonality, octophonic and other 'alternating' scales, and even a 12-note chord (as Cannizares's rage reaches its peak). A busily contrapuntal orchestral part overwhelmed the voices in early performances; Petrassi therefore prepared a reduced-orchestra version in 1958 which went some way to rectifying the problem.

ALASDAIR JAMIESON

Corelli, Franco [Dario] (*b* Ancona, 8 April 1921). Italian tenor. He studied at Pesaro and made his début in 1951 at Spoleto in *Carmen*, subsequently appearing in various Italian theatres. In 1954 he sang at La Scala, returning there until 1965. He was first heard at Covent Garden in 1957 (*Tosca*), then at the Berlin Städtische Oper (1961) and at the Vienna Staatsoper (1963). After his Metropolitan début as Manrico (1961), he was engaged every year in New York. He appeared at the Paris Opéra and the Vienna Staatsoper in 1970 and at the Verona Arena in 1970 and 1972.

The possessor of a large, remarkably dark-coloured voice, he was limited at first to *verismo* roles in the middle of the tenor range. But later he developed a strong and extended upper register and acquired the ability to inflect and vary his tone. Long the finest exponent of the Italian *spinto* tenor repertory (Ernani, Manrico, Radames, Don Alvaro, Calaf), he successfully tackled some extremely difficult roles at La Scala between 1958 and 1962: Gualtiero in *Il pirata*, Poliuto, and Raoul in *Les Huguenots*. His handsome stage presence and, in certain operas (especially *Carmen*), his effective acting, added to his reputation.

GV (R. Celletti, with discography)
C. L. Osborne: 'Franco Corelli', *High Fidelity*, xvii/2 (1967), 63–7
R. Celletti: 'Franco Corelli', *Discoteca* no.111, (1971), 14

RODOLFO CELLETTI

Corena, Fernando (*b* Geneva, 22 Dec 1916; *d* Lugano, 26 Nov 1984). Swiss bass. He studied with Enrico Romani in Milan. After his début in 1937 he returned to Zürich for the war but made a postwar début in Trieste in 1947 (Varlaam). He appeared throughout Italy in roles as disparate as Escamillo, Sparafucile and Scarpia, and in 1949 sang in the première of Petrassi's *Il cordovano* at La Scala. The *buffo* repertory soon became his abiding speciality, however; he made his Metropolitan début as Leporello in 1954, becoming the logical and worthy successor to Salvatore Baccaloni. He sang in Edinburgh two years later (Verdi's Falstaff) and at Covent Garden as Dr Bartolo in 1960 and 1969. He also appeared in Vienna, at the Salzburg Festival, in Berlin, Buenos Aires, Verona and Amsterdam; his other notable roles included Don Pasquale, Gianni Schicchi, Dulcamara, Don Alfonso, Sulpice in *La fille du régiment*, Mustafà and Lescaut in *Manon*. With the passing of time, Corena made up in comic invention for what he may have begun to lack in vocal opulence. His wit, style and flair for improvisation remained exemplary.

MARTIN BERNHEIMER

Corfu (Gk. Kerkyra). Capital city of the island bearing the same name and of the Ionian Islands; under Venetian rule for 400 years (until 1797), they were the only part of Greece to avoid Ottoman occupation. Folk, popular and church music constitute the background against which opera became virtually a cult among the Ionian population.

Corfu represents the earliest and most prominent Greek operatic centre as well as one of the most important in the eastern Mediterranean and the Balkans. The S Giacomo Theatre (now the Town Hall) was completed in 1691; the earliest opera performances date from 1733, introduced by the impresario Carlo Grassi. The only work identified as having been given there in the 18th century is Ferdinando Robuschi's *Castrini, padre e figlio* (2, F. Ermioneo; 1788, Venice), performed in autumn 1788 (as brought to light by the scholar Yorgos Konstantzos).

Both plays and operas were staged, the main season running from 26 December to Lent; there may also have been autumn performances. Opera companies were Italian. The theatre was enlarged under British rule and, used almost exclusively by Italian companies, became the focus of social life in the Ionian Islands and the heart of a remarkable musical culture. Soon after 1800 many Ionian composers appeared, writing operas and influencing musical life, education and composition on the Hellenic mainland. From 1840 Corfu musicians participated in the theatre orchestra. After a poor performance of Verdi's *La battaglia di Legnano* by an Italian troupe in 1855, an all-Greek opera company was mooted, but the plan never materialized; nonetheless by 1867, in the première of Xyndas's comic opera *O ypopsifios vouleftis* ('The Parliamentary Candidate'), all the participants were Corfiots.

The 12 known scores by Mantzaros for voices and orchestra include *Don Crepuscolo* (1815), the earliest extant opera by a Greek and the first 19th-century work known to have been performed at the S Giacomo. A contemporary MS list of Italian librettos of operas staged in the period 1823–89 shows seven by Greek composers: Carrer's *Isabella d'Aspeno* (1853) and *Rediviva* (1856), Xyndas's *Anna Winter* (1855), Padovanis's *Dirce* (1857), Eduardo Lambelet's *Olema la schiava* (1857) and *Il castello maledetto* (1862) and Samaras's *Flora mirabilis* (1889). Zingarelli, the spiritual mentor of Mantzaros, is not represented, but works by his pupils Persiani (*Inès de Castro*, 1837) and Speranza (*I due Figaro*, 1841) were given there. Donizetti and Verdi are the composers most fully represented.

During the 19th century opera spread to the other Ionian islands. The earliest known performances of opera on Zakinthos (It. Zante) were in 1813 (see Zois 1898); opera on Kefallinia began in 1838 with performances by visiting Italian companies, subsidized by the British authorities (see Evanghelatos 1970). There were also performances in Lefkas (Leucadia) on the visit of the British High Commissioner in the 1830s. The second half of the 19th century saw the openings and closings of several small theatres on both islands; the two most important theatres, the Kefalos on Kefallinia (inaugurated 1858, cap. 500) and the Foscolo on Zakinthos (inaugurated 1875; cap. *c*750), were destroyed in the earthquakes of August 1953 and have not been replaced.

The construction of a larger, modern theatre in Corfu began in 1893. The Dhimotikon Theatron (Municipal

Theatre), 39 metres high with 64 boxes in three tiers, a gallery and a large stage, was inaugurated with *Lohengrin* in 1902. After 1900, when the Elliniko Melodrama company from Athens came to life, companies, mainly Italian, alternated with Greek opera and operetta presentations. Another theatre, the Phoenix, had both winter (500 seats) and open-air summer (*c*1050 seats) premises; it was active between 1895 and 1945, with operetta companies appearing in the larger venue. Visits by Italian companies were almost completely suspended from 1923, when the Fascists bombarded the city and occupied the island. The Municipal Theatre was heavily damaged by fire in 1943, when it seems that the theatre archives as well as Ionian composers' manuscripts were destroyed; the building was demolished in 1952.

Regolamento per il teatro di San Giacomo in Corfù, pubblicato per ordine del prestantissimo Reggente (Corfu, 1834)

L. H. Zois: 'Historike selidhes Zakinthou: to theatron', *Attiki Iris*, nos.5–11 (1898)

L. S. Vrokinis: *Peri tis ikodomis tis en to kerkyraiko asti stoas (Loggia) ke tis is theatron metatropis aftis, 1663–1799* [On the Edifice of the Arcade – Loggia – in the City of Corfu and its Transformation into a Theatre, 1663–1799] (Corfu, 1901); repr. in *Kerkyraika hronika*, xvii (1979), 263–81

T. N. Synadinos: *Istoria tis neoellinikis moussikis, 1824–1919* [History of Modern Greek Music, 1824–1919] (Athens, 1919)

N. A. Laskaris: *Istoria tou neoellinikou theatrou* [History of Modern Greek Theatre] (Athens, 1938–9)

S. G. Motsenigos: *Neoelliniki moussiki, symvoli is tin istoriantis* [Modern Greek Music: a Contribution to its History] (Athens, 1958)

S. A. Evanghelatos: *Historia tou theatrou en Kefallinia, 1600–1900* (diss., Athens U., 1970)

D. C. Kapadohos: *To theatro tis Kerkyras sta mesa tou xix eonos* [The Corfu Theatre during the Middle of the 19th Century] (Athens, 1991)

GEORGE LEOTSAKOS

Corghi, Azio (*b* Cirié, nr Turin, 9 March 1937). Italian composer. Although initially attracted to painting, he took a piano diploma at the Turin Conservatory in 1961, then studied composition with Bruno Bettinelli at the Milan Conservatory, where he now teaches composition. An early fascination with Berg and Debussy laid the foundations for his mature synthesis of linear logic and sophistication of timbre. He first broached the problems of musical theatre in two experimental works, *Symbola* (1971) and *Tactus* (1974). The interaction of musical and physical gesture explored in these works flowed into two ballets with voices, *Actus III* (1978) and *Mazapegul* (1986). Both underlined Corghi's abiding interest in Italian folk music and poetry. Meanwhile, his first full-scale opera, *Gargantua* (to a libretto by Augusto Frassineti, after Rabelais), achieved substantial success at its première at the Teatro Regio, Turin, on 2 May 1984. It was followed by a commission from La Scala resulting in *Blimunda*, first performed at the Teatro Lirico, Milan (20 May 1990).

While *Symbola* and *Tactus* both dissolve texts into phonemes, *Gargantua* marks a conscious return to verbal coherence and delight in theatrical narrative. Rooted in Bakhtin's rich commentaries on Rabelais, it sidesteps gratuitous musical rollicking in favour of a Stravinskian overview of the human carnival. *Blimunda*, based on José Saramago's *Memorial do convento*, continues this vein of polished, humane operatic fantasy. Corghi's musicological work includes critical editions of Rossini's *L'italiana in Algeri* and Puccini's *Tosca*.

'Azio Corghi', *Notiziario degli Edizioni Suvini Zerboni* (Feb 1987)

DAVID OSMOND-SMITH

Cori, Angelo Maria (*b* Rome; *d* ?London, after 1741). Italian teacher of languages and editor of librettos. He was in London by 1723, when he published *A New Method for the Italian Tongue: or, a Short Way to Learn It*. Its title-page identifies him as 'a Roman, Master of the Latin, Spanish and Italian Languages; living at Mr. Wallis's in Lisle-Street, near Leicester-Fields', and its list of subscribers includes Ariosti, Bononcini, Geminiani, J. J. Heidegger and John Rich, the poet Paolo Antonio Rolli and many diplomats (including Riva of Modena). Rolli refers to Cori as Padre or Fra 'Ciro' in five extant epigrams and declares that he was defrocked and became a freemason. Rolli also describes him and the aged 'Roscio' (Giacomo Rossi) as teachers of Mongolese Italian who exercised their poetic ability where the 'cembalo alemanno' ('German harpsichord') had banished good sense. Cori as well as Rossi may thus have adapted texts for Handel in the 1730s.

Rolli further refers to Cori as a wretched amender of librettos for the Opera of the Nobility, for which Cori had adapted at least the six texts he dedicated to noblewomen; these include *Merope* by Zeno and five works by Metastasio, from which he cut about two-thirds of the recitative and replaced one-third of the aria texts. He rewrote *Issipile* for Sandoni in the 1734–5 season and *Adriano in Siria* for Veracini in 1735–6. In 1736–7 he reworked four: *Merope*, a pasticcio; *Demetrio* for Pescetti; *La clemenza di Tito* for Veracini; and *Demofoonte* for Egidio Duni. Since Rolli provided the Nobility with only one text in 1736–7, it seems likely that Cori supplanted him as poet for the company during this its fourth and final season. Rolli's bitter dislike shows through in epigrams that characterize Cori as a ridiculous and arrogant pedant who dressed like a cavalier, served as a go-between in illicit love affairs, and married and ultimately lived in servants' quarters with a poor but beautiful woman who 'gave pleasure' to his patrons.

During the period 1737–9 Cori and Pescetti produced *Arsace*, based on Rolli's version of 1721; *La conquista del vello d'oro*, based on a rewritten version of 1717, produced in Reggio Emilia; and *Angelica e Medoro*, based on a serenata by Metastasio. The last work was sponsored by Charles Sackville, Lord Middlesex, who managed four operatic seasons between 1739 and 1744. On Sackville's behalf, 'Angelo Corri' was granted a licence to produce operas at the Haymarket on 3 January 1740. The last known reference to him is in Walpole's letter of Christmas eve 1741, which identifies him as 'prompter' and factotum for the opera.

H. Walpole: *Letters*, ed. P. Cunningham, i (London, 1861), 107–8

S. Fassini: *Il melodramma italiano a Londra nella prima metà del settecento* (Turin, 1914)

P. A. Rolli: *Liriche*, ed. C. Calcaterra (Turin, 1926)

O. E. Deutsch: *Handel: a Documentary Biography* (London, 1955)

J. W. Hill: *The Life and Works of Francesco Maria Veracini* (Ann Arbor, 1979)

C. Taylor: 'From Losses to Lawsuit: Patronage of the Italian Opera in London by Lord Middlesex, 1739–45', *ML*, lxviii (1987), 1–25

LOWELL LINDGREN

Corigliano, John (Paul, jr) (*b* New York, 16 Feb 1938). American composer. He received his first formal training at Columbia University (BA 1959), where he was a pupil of Otto Luening; he later studied with Vittorio Giannini at the Manhattan School and privately with Paul Creston. From 1959 to 1964 he worked

John Conklin's design for John Corigliano's 'The Ghosts of Versailles': Act 1 scene i from the première at the Metropolitan Opera, New York, 1991, with (downstage, left) Håkon Hagegård as Beaumarchais and Teresa Stratas as Marie Antoinette

in New York as a music programmer, first for WQXR-FM and later for WBAI-FM. He has also been an associate producer of music programmes for CBS television (1961–72) and music director for the Morris Theater in New Jersey (1962–4). Since 1968 he has taught composition, first at the College of Church Musicians, Washington, DC, and later at the Manhattan School (from 1971) and Lehman College, City University of New York (from 1974).

Corigliano has composed a wide range of instrumental music in traditional forms (his concertos are frequently played by major orchestras), and much vocal music, mostly for four-part choirs. Behind the composition of these works is a philosophy that music should be written for both willing performers and audiences. His musical style is often lyrical, with tonal harmonies, brilliant orchestrations, virtuoso instrumental writing and some bombastic touches; serial techniques, atonality and disjunct melodic movements are sometimes employed for piquant contrast. He often quotes from other composers, or from historical styles, to produce a pastiche-like texture. Corigliano believes that film music has fundamentally changed contemporary listening habits, and it is to those who have a particular taste for this genre that his music, which is accessible, eclectic and frequently referential, would be most likely to appeal.

Corigliano has written three large-scale dramatic works. *Naked Carmen* (composed in 1970), an 'electric rock opera', came out of his experimentation beginning in the late 1960s with non-traditional performing forces. This one-act work, based on Bizet's opera, uses synthesizers, amplified instruments, kazoos, an orchestra, and singers from rock, soul and opera genres. Co-written with the record producer David Hess, *Naked Carmen* has been issued as an LP although it has never been performed live. The score to Ken Russell's film *Altered States* (1980) is an integral part of the film's effect, and won for Corigliano an Academy Award nomination.

The Ghosts of Versailles is his most ambitious operatic project to date. A large-scale, two-act opera to a libretto by William M. Hoffman, it was commissioned in May 1980, completed in April 1987 and first performed with stage designs by John Conklin at the Metropolitan Opera in 1991 (the first new opera given there since 1967; see illustration); it was enthusiastically received. The plot, which borrows its characters from the third play of Beaumarchais' 'Figaro' trilogy (*La mère coupable*) and which includes the playwright himself, takes place in three worlds: the ghostly, the theatrical and the historical. Beaumarchais, one of the spirits inhabiting Versailles, falls in love with Marie Antoinette and contrives a new play in order to change history and prevent her beheading, only to have his efforts undone by the disillusioned revolutionary Figaro. Hoffman has said that 'the opera is primarily a love story, but it is also about the French Revolution, the nature of revolution in general, the nature of love and the nature of time' (*New York Times*, 15 December 1991). Corigliano's music invokes and parodies Mozart, Rossini, Strauss, Turkish dances and other historical idioms; at the other end of the spectrum, he uses 12-note techniques, quarter-tone dissonances and a style that 'creates a sense of displacement, nostalgia and loss, tinged with an almost overly sweet pop sentimentality' (*New York Times*, 21 December 1991).

D. James: 'Between the Frames: John Corigliano and *Altered States*', *Fanfare*, v/4 (1982), 64

A. Kozinn: 'Rushing in where Copland Feared to Tread', *New York Times* (15 Dec 1991)

E. Rothstein: 'For the Met's Centennial, a Gathering of Ghosts', *New York Times* (21 Dec 1991) DALE COCKRELL

Coriolanus. Music drama in three acts by JÁN CIKKER to a libretto by the composer based on WILLIAM SHAKESPEARE's tragedy, with lines from EURIPIDES, SOPHOCLES and Palladius; Prague, Smetana Theatre, 4 April 1974.

The plot follows Shakespeare's original. Enraged by what he considers the ingratitude of the plebs, Coriolanus (baritone) joins forces with the Volscians under their leader Tullus Anfidius (tenor) and besieges Rome. The intercession of his mother, Volumnia (contralto), and his wife, Virgilia (soprano), however, cause him to yield. Accused of treachery by Anfidius, he is murdered by the Volscians.

Cikker's sixth opera is similar to Musorgsky's *Boris Godunov* in that the chorus becomes a second protagonist. The structure of the work is symmetrical: the first and third act each have six scenes. The musical language is basically modal but makes much use of chromaticism. Zdeněk Košler, the conductor of the première, had a considerable influence on the orchestration.

IGOR VAJDA

Cork. City in the south of Ireland, the second city of the Republic. The first regular theatre, funded by the owners of the Smock Alley Theatre in Dublin, opened in 1713 in Dingle Lane. It was small and by 1760 had been replaced by the Theatre Royal, managed by Spranger Barry, in what is now Oliver Plunkett Street; the performance on the second night was of *The Beggar's Opera.* Regular performances were given until 1840, when the theatre was gutted by fire after a performance of Bellini's *La sonnambula.* It was rebuilt by 1860 and continued until 1877, when the theatre became the General Post Office. Theatrical activity then transferred to the Athenaeum in Emmet Place, which was renamed the Cork Opera House and Theatre Royal and regularly presented opera, amateur and professional, until 1955, when it burnt down; it reopened in 1965. In the early 20th century there were regular visits from the touring companies run by Horace Lingard, Carl Rosa, Moody and Manners, and Joseph O'Mara; grand opera has been performed intermittently by local companies since the 1950s. Amateur opera began in 1880 with the Pinafore Club, which is still in existence, inspired by the visit of Richard D'Oyly Carte's company in 1879.

JAMES N. HEALY

Cormon, Eugène [Piestre, Pierre-Etienne] (*b* Lyons, 5 May 1810; *d* Paris, March 1903). French playwright and librettist. During his long and prolific career (1832–78) he used his mother's name, Cormon. He wrote more than 135 plays and librettos, normally with a collaborator such as Laurencin (P.-D.-A. Chapelle), A.-P. d'Ennery or Michel Carré. One of his dramas, *Philippe II, roi d'Espagne* (1846), later served as a source for the libretto of Verdi's *Don Carlos* (1867).

Cormon began writing librettos in the mid-1840s, and in 1847 he provided Maillart with the book for *Gastibelza*, an ephemeral success which opened Adolphe Adam's Opéra National. With Maillart he also produced a more enduring contribution to the repertory, *Les dragons de Villars.* Critics often praised his works for the charm of their dialogue and well-planned scene structure, and he is supposed to have regretted that such a talented beginner as Bizet had to work with one of his weakest efforts, *Les pêcheurs de perles* (1863).

Cormon was a stage director at the Opéra (1859–70), where he was responsible for Meyerbeer's *L'Africaine* (1865), and later became the administrator of the Théâtre du Vaudeville, succeeding Léon Carvalho in 1874–5.

Gastibelza, ou Le fou de Tolède (drame lyrique, with A.-P. d'Ennery), Maillart, 1847; *Marie-Thérèse* (with Dutertre), N. Louis, 1847; *Le moulin des tilleuls* (oc, with J. de Maillan), Maillart, 1849; *Les deux sergeants* (oc, with Saint-Amand), Louis, 1850; *Le chien du jardinier* (oc, with Lockroy [J. P. Simon]), Grisar, 1855; *Les dragons de Villars* (oc, with Lockroy), Maillart, 1856; *Le mariage extravagant* (oc), E. Gautier, 1857

Le roi Don Pèdre (oc, with E. Grangé [Basté]), Poise, 1857; *Le nid de cicognes,* C.-L.-A. Vogel, 1858; *Quentin Durward* (oc, with M.-F. Carré), Gevaert, 1858; *Le diable au moulin* (oc, with Carré), Gevaert, 1859; *Le château trompette* (oc, with Carré), Gevaert, 1860; *La comète de Charles-Quint* (oc, with J. Méry), A.-J. Vivier, 1860; *Le docteur Mirobolan* (oc, with H. Trianon), Gautier, 1860; *Les pêcheurs de Catane* (drame lyrique, with Carré), Maillart, 1860; *Les deux amours* (with A. Achard), Gevaert, 1861

Jocrisse (oc, with Trianon), Gautier, 1862; *Les pêcheurs de perles* (with Carré), Bizet, 1863; *Le docteur Magnus* (with Carré), E. Boulanger, 1864; *Lara* (oc, with Carré), Maillart, 1864; *Le trésor de Pierrot* (oc, with Trianon), Gautier, 1864; *Le captif*, E. Lassen, 1865; *José Maria* (oc, with H. Meilhac), J. Cohen, 1866; *Les bleuets* (oc, with Trianon), Cohen, 1867

Robinson Crusoé (oc, with H.-J. Crémieux), Offenbach, 1867; *Le premier jour de bonheur* (oc, with D'Ennery), Auber, 1868; *Rêve d'amour* (oc, with D'Ennery), Auber, 1869; *Déa* (oc, with Carré), Cohen, 1870; *Madame Turlupin* (oc, with C. Grandvallet), Guiraud, 1872; *La filleule du roi* (oc, with R. Deslandes), Vogel, 1875; *Suzanne* (oc, with Lockroy), Paladilhe, 1878

*

DBF (P. Faure)
G. Vinot: 'Cormon', *La grande encyclopédie* (Paris, 1887–1901)
G. Vapereau: *Dictionnaire universel des contemporains* (Paris, 6/1893)
M. Curtiss: *Bizet and his World* (New York, 1958)
T. J. Walsh: *Second Empire Opera* (London, 1981)

LESLEY A. WRIGHT

Cornacchioli, Giacinto (*b* Ascoli Piceno, *c*1598–9; *d* ?Ascoli Piceno, after 1 Sept 1673). Italian composer. His career and the circumstances surrounding his only known work, the 'favola boschereccia' *Diana schernita,* remain obscure. Published in Rome in 1629, the score (in *I-Rsc*) is not listed under either Cornacchioli's name or that of the librettist Giacomo Francesco Parisani in *Apes urbanae* (Rome, 1633, a bibliography of works by writers in the Barberini circle), despite its dedication to Taddeo Barberini. Apart from the score, the only other trace of Cornacchioli in Rome is as witness to a will drafted by composer Luigi Rossi in December 1647 (not 1653, as often reported), before Rossi's second trip to Paris.

The straightforward libretto of *Diana schernita,* in five short acts without scene divisions, its mythological plot, small cast of four soloists, and modest scenic and instrumental demands all suggest a private production, perhaps for an academy, of which Johann Rudolph, Baron of Hohen-Rechberg, in whose residence it was performed, may have been a member.

Amore [Cupid] (soprano) is resentful towards the goddess Diana (contralto) for misdirecting him into a cavern. He takes revenge by helping Pan (bass) fulfil his lust for Diana and by causing the death of Endimione [Endymion] (tenor), her lover. Disguised as Actaeon, Endymion is turned into a stag when he surprises Diana bathing. Diana flees into a grotto to dress, but Cupid has poisoned the water with love, so that Pan, hiding in the grotto, can embrace her. The nymphs bear in the slain stag: to Diana's infidelity is added the death of the youth she had loved. The uncertain moral tone of Endymion's death and Pan's conquest is ambiguously amended by the transformation of the stag into a lily, which three bees (the Barberini emblem) lift into the silver clouds above.

Cornacchioli animated his recitatives with surprisingly mobile harmonic rhythm and frequent arioso passages. The two formal arias, sung by Endymion and Diana, are of four strophes in variation; Endymion has one additional recitative soliloquy (Act 3) and Diana a recitative lament (Act 4). Nothing unusual in Cornacchioli's musical setting supports the interpretation of this score as either a comedy or a parody of the early Florentine *favola in musica.*

H. Goldschmidt: *Studien zur Geschichte der italienischen Oper im 17. Jahrhundert*, i (Leipzig, 1901), 35–8, 185–7
R. Rolland: *Histoire de l'opéra en Europe avant Lully et Scarlatti* (Paris, 1931), 158–60
V. Frajese: 'Giacinto Cornacchioli nell'inizio del seicento musicale romano', *Rivista filarmonica ascolana*, i (1955), 20–31
J. E. Rotondi: *Literary and Musical Aspects of Roman Opera, 1600–1650* (diss., U. of Pennsylvania, 1959)

MARGARET MURATA

Corneille, Pierre (*b* Rouen, 6 June 1606; *d* Paris, 1 Oct 1684). French poet and dramatist, considered the creator of French classical tragedy. He was educated by Jesuits, studied law and purchased a position in the municipal offices of Rouen which he retained until 1650. The success of his first biographical play, *Mélite* (1629), persuaded him to continue writing and over the next five years he wrote the seven comedies that established his reputation, though they are less important than his subsequent serious dramas. His most famous play, *Le Cid* (1636), which drew on the work of Guillén de Castro, was followed by three plays with political themes, *Horace* (1640), *Cinna* (1640–41) and *Polyeucte* (1641–2), after which he experimented with new forms of drama while continuing to write more conventional tragedies and tragicomedies. The plays of his declining years are characterized by relaxed pacing, unusual locales (as in the African setting of *Sophonisbe*, 1663), a mixture of comedy and tragedy, and the abandonment of Alexandrine verse. Corneille wrote a total of 33 plays, including eight comedies and 23 tragedies or tragicomedies, as well as a *tragédie-ballet*, *Psyché*, with Molière and Quinault, which was set by Lully (1671) and served as the basis for the collaboration of Lully and Thomas Corneille on a later *tragédie lyrique* of the same name.

Many of Corneille's plays are dramas of moral or psychological conflict in which action is replaced by reaction. He used his legal skills to present both sides of an issue and to offer alternative solutions to a controversial situation. In *Horace*, for example, the champions chosen by Rome and Alba to represent them in single combat happen to be linked by ties of marriage. Corneille's main characters are larger than life, independent and idealistic, and demonstrate high ethical standards when placed in situations where passion conflicts with duty or reason; the resolution of that conflict forms the denouement of the play (e.g. in *Nicomède*, 1651). Many of his subjects are classical, often deriving from Roman history.

Two of Corneille's plays, *Andromède* (1649) and *La toison d'or* (1660), were intended to be performed with music; both are machine plays and therefore written with spectacle in mind. The requirements of drama, however, are not superseded by those of spectacle, as the action of the machines is incorporated into the play so as to meet the demands of classical drama that the action be serious and concern people of high moral standing, and that the unities of time, place and action be respected. By design, the music has only an incidental role. In the preface to *Andromède* Corneille stated that no words of significance should be sung, since in his opinion the sung words could never be properly heard by the audience; music, therefore, was restricted to choruses and airs. He defined *Andromède* as 'une tragédie avec musique' rather than 'une tragédie en musique'. Corneille used this play as a means of attacking the florid excesses of Luigi Rossi's *Orfeo* (1647, Paris). He particularly condemned the musical portrayal of the principal characters' emotions, which seemed to be more important than the plot and, indeed, than the characters themselves. Dassoucy, who composed the music for *Andromède*, disagreed with Corneille; he was a strong admirer of the Italian operatic style in general and of Rossi in particular.

Protagonists with high ethical standards provide heroes who are ideal for *opera seria*. It is not surprising, therefore, that even before the end of the 17th century English, French and Italian librettists turned to Corneille for inspiration. *Airs sérieux* with texts based on *Le Cid* were set as early as 1681 by Charpentier. Other composers to use texts based on this drama include Handel (*Flavio, re de' longobardi*, 1723) and Massenet (*Le Cid*, 1885). Sacchini's *Il Cidde* was performed in Rome in 1769; it was later rewritten (1773, London) and then again as *Chimène* (1783, Fontainebleau).

Corneille's next great tragedy, *Horace* (1640), provided the subject for Salieri's *Les Horaces* (1786) and Cimarosa's *Gli Orazi ed i Curiazi* (1796). *Polyeucte* served Salvatore Cammarano, who wrote the libretto for Donizetti's *Poliuto* (1838, banned by the censors in Naples and not performed until 1848). Gounod also set a *Polyeucte* libretto, but his opera of 1878 was unsuccessful. *Pertharite* (1651) reached the opera stage through several *Rodelinda* texts, one version of which, by Nicola Haym, was used by Handel for his London opera of 1725.

Metastasio saw in Corneille the greatness of Sophocles and turned to his tragedies several times. In Metastasio's opinion, Corneille's plays 'filled the minds of the spectators with radiant ideas'. *Artaserse* has marked similarities with *Le Cid*, and *Catone in Utica* was apparently influenced by both *La mort de Pompée* (1642–3) and *Sertorius* (1662). There is a notable resemblance between the plots of *Demetrio* and Corneille's *Don Sanche d'Aragon*, and it is possible that Metastasio drew characters and incidents from *Sophonisbe* when adapting *Siface* from Domenico David's *La forza del virtù*. A particularly striking analogy arises between Metastasio's *La clemenza di Tito* and Corneille's *Cinna* and *Tite et Bérénice* (1670), and the plight of the heroine in Metastasio's *Zenobia* parallels that of *Polyeucte*. Other librettists who drew upon Corneille include Benedetto Pasqualigo (*Berenice*, *Cimene*), Antonio Salvi (*Rodelinda, Adelaide*) and Mattia Verazi (*Sofonisba*).

See also CID, EL.

Médée (play, 1634): M.-A. Charpentier, 1693; J.-F. Salomon, 1713 (as Médée et Jason); Cherubini, 1797

Le Cid (play, 1637): C. F. Pollarolo, 1706 (as Flavio Bertarido, re dei langobardi); Stuck, 1715 (as Il Cid); F. Gasparini, 1717 (as Il gran Cid); Handel, 1723 (as Flavio, re de' longobardi); Leo, 1727; Piccinni, 1766 (as Il gran Cid); C. Franchi, 1769 (as Il gran Cidde Rodrigo); Sacchini, 1769 (rev. 1773; rev. 1783 as Chimène); Bianchi, 1773 (as Il gran Cidde); Paisiello, 1775 (as Il gran Cid); A. Rosetti, 1780 (as Il gran Cid); Aiblinger, 1821 (as Rodrigo und Chimene); Schindelmeisser, 1846 (as Die Rächer); Pacini, 1853 (as Il Cid); L. T. Gouvy, 1863; P. Cornelius (i), 1865; Massenet, 1885; Pizzetti, before 1915; Wagenaar, 1915

Horace (play, 1640): Tosi, 1688 (as Orazio); Bertoni, 1746 (as Orazio e Curiazo); Salieri, 1786 (as Les Horaces); Cimarosa, 1796 (as Gli Orazi ed i Curiazi); Portugal, 1798 (as Gli Orazi e i Curiazi); Mercadante, 1846 (as Orazi e Curiazi)

Cinna (play, 1641–2): De Luca, C. F. Pollarolo and G. Bononcini, 1697 (as La clemenza d'Augusto); Caldara, 1734 (as La clemenza di Tito); Hasse, 1735 (as Tito Vespasiano, ovvero La clemenza di Tito); Graun, 1748; Asioli, 1793; Portugal, 1793; Paer, 1795; F. Bianchi, 1798

Polyeucte (play, 1642–3): Donizetti, comp. 1838, perf. 1848 (as Poliuto; rev., 1840, as Les martyrs); Gounod, 1878

La mort de Pompée (play, 1644): Graun, 1742 (as Cesare e Cleopatra)

Héraclius (play, 1646–7): P. A. Ziani, 1671

Andromède (play, 1649–50): Mattioli, 1665 (as Perseo); J. W. Franck, 1675 (as Die errettete Unschuld); M.-A. Charpentier, 1682; Lully, 1682 (as Persée); Philidor, 1780 (as Persée)

Nicomède (play, 1651): C. Grossi, 1677 (as Il Nicomede in Bitinia)

Perthарite (play, 1651): Perti, 1710 (as Rodelinda, regina de' longobardi); Handel, 1725 (as Rodelinda, regina de' longobardi); Cordans, 1731 (as La Rodelinda); Graun, 1741 (as Rodelinda, regina de' langobardi)

La toison d'or (play, 1660): Draghi, 1678 (as La conquista del vello d'oro); Collasse, 1696 (as Jason, ou La toison d'or); Keiser, 1720 (as Jason, oder Die Eroberung des güldenen Flüsses

Sophonisbe (play, 1663): Caldara, 1708; Galuppi, 1753; Galuppi, 1764

Agésilas (play, 1666): Andreozzi, 1788 (as Agesilao, re di Sparta); Isola, 1790 (as Lisandro)

Attila (play, 1667): P. A. Ziani, 1672

Tite et Bérénice (play, 1670): Freschi, 1680 (as Berenice vendicativa); Bronner, 1702; Ruggieri, 1711 (as Le gare di politica e d'amore); Caldara, 1714 (as Tito e Berenice); Orlandini, 1725; Araia, 1730; Ferrandini, 1730; Handel, 1737; Galuppi, 1741; ?Piccinni, 1764; Rust, 1785–6; Nasolini, 1793 (as Tito e Berenice); P. Raimondi, 1824 (as Berenice in Roma); Magnard, 1909

Psyché (tragédie-ballet, 1671, with Molière and Quinault): Locke, 1675

*

M. Ecorcheville: *Corneille et la musique* (Paris, 1906)

H. Prunières: *L'opéra italien en France avant Lulli* (Paris, 1913)

L. M. Armour: 'Les musiciens de Corneille, 1650–1699', *RdM*, xxxvii (1955), 43–75

M. Turnell: *The Classical Moment: Studies of Corneille, Molière and Racine* (London, 1963)

H. T. Barnwell, ed.: *P. Corneille: Writings on the Theatre* (Oxford, 1965)

C. Girdlestone: *La tragédie en musique (1673–1750) considérée comme genre littéraire* (Geneva, 1972)

C. Delmas: Introduction to P. Corneille: *Andromède: tragédie* (Paris, 1974)

R. B. Moberly: 'The Influence of French Classical Drama on Mozart's *La clemenza di Tito*', *ML*, lv (1974), 286–98

R. Strohm: '"Tragédie" into "Dramma per musica"', *Informazione e studi vivaldiani*, ix (1988), 14–24; x (1989), 57–101; xi (1990), 11–25; xii (1991), 47–74

ALISON STONEHOUSE

Corneille, Thomas [M. de l'Isle] (*b* Rouen, 20 Aug 1625; *d* Les Andelys, 8 Dec 1709). French playwright and librettist. Although overshadowed by his brother Pierre, he was a prolific and successful writer who embraced virtually all dramatic genres of the period. With Donneau de Visé he edited the *Mercure galant*, and his election in 1684 to the Académie Française encouraged scholarly pursuits.

Corneille's background made him an obvious substitute for Quinault, Lully's principal librettist, who in the late 1670s was in disgrace at court. Like Quinault he had made his name in spoken drama, and he had collaborated with Donneau de Visé on machine plays such as *Circé* and *L'inconnu* (both 1675) with incidental music by Marc-Antoine Charpentier. A number of his dramas have been the source of operas, including Alessandro Melani's *Il carceriere di se medesimo* (1681), to a libretto by Ludovico Adimari after Corneille's *Geôlier de soi-mesme*, and J.-B. Lemoyne's *Nephté* (1789), to a libretto by F.-B. Hoffman after Corneille's *Camma*. In addition Corneille was responsible for three librettos. The revision of the *tragédie-ballet Psyché* (Lully, 1678), possibly undertaken with Fontenelle, preserves some of the original text and music, yet reveals Corneille's familiarity with the characteristics of the *tragédie en musique*. The language, however, is at times too complex and less lyrical than Quinault's, and the work betrays the difficulty of integrating the *divertissements*, a problem also evident in the *tragédie en musique Bellérophon* (Lully, 1679), possibly written with Boileau and Fontenelle. A third *tragédie en musique*, *Médée* (Charpentier, 1693), is considered by Girdlestone (1972) one of the best 17th-century French librettos. It demonstrates Corneille's versatility, particularly in finding the right balance between tragedy and spectacle and in allowing Medea to develop into a complex character who spearheads a fine, subtle climax.

*

C. Parfaict and F. Parfaict: *Histoire du théâtre français depuis son origine jusqu'à présent* (Paris, 1734, 3/1745–49)

——: *Histoire de l'Académie royale de musique* (MS, 1741, *F-Pn* nouv. acq.fr.6532)

H. de la Motte: 'Examen de l'opéra de Psiché', *Mercure de France* (April 1757), ii, 47–57

J. Carlez: 'Pierre et Thomas Corneille: librettistes', *Mémoires de l'Académie nationale des sciences, arts et belles-lettres de Caen* (1881), 137–74

G. Reynier: *Thomas Corneille: sa vie et son théâtre* (Paris, 1892)

P. Mélèse: *Répertoire analytique des documents contemporains … concernant le théâtre à Paris sous Louis XIV, 1659–1715* (Paris, 1934)

S. Spycket: 'Thomas Corneille et la musique', *XVIIe siècle*, xxi–xxii (1954), 442–55

D. A. Collins: *Thomas Corneille: Protean Dramatist* (The Hague, 1966)

C. Girdlestone: *La tragédie en musique (1673–1750) considérée comme genre littéraire* (Geneva, 1972)

C. J. Gossip: 'Vers une chronologie des pièces de Thomas Corneille', *Revue d'histoire littéraire de la France*, lxxiv (1974), 665–78, 1038–58

H. Schneider: 'Zur Rezeption von Molières und Lullys "Psyché"', *Stimmen der Romania: Festschrift T. W. Elwert* (Wiesbaden, 1980), 389–403

M. Turnbull: *A Critical Edition of 'Psyché', an Opera with Words by Thomas Corneille and Philippe Quinault and Music by Jean-Baptiste Lully* (diss., U. of Oxford, 1981)

——: 'The Metamorphosis of *Psyché*', *ML*, lxiv (1983), 12–24

L'avant-scène opéra, no.68 (1984) [*Médée* issue]

H. W. Hitchcock: 'Charpentier's *Médée*', *MT*, cxxv (1984), 563–7

A. Parmley: *The Secular Stage Works of Marc-Antoine Charpentier* (diss., U. of London, 1985)

V. Kapp: 'Thomas Corneille: librettiste', *Les écrivains français et l'opéra*, ed. J.-P. Capdevielle and P.-E. Knabe (Cologne, 1986), 49–59

R. Strohm: '"Tragédie" into "Dramma per musica"', *Informazione e studi vivaldiani*, ix (1988), 14–24; x (1989), 57–101; xi (1990), 11–25; xii (1991), 47–74

T. MICHAEL TURNBULL

Cornelius, (Carl August) Peter (i) (*b* Mainz, 24 Dec 1824; *d* Mainz, 26 Oct 1874). German composer. Born into a theatrical family, he was trained from early years as an actor. His interests in literature grew alongside his musical talents, causing him many doubts over the direction of his career; he worked both as a violinist in the Mainz theatre orchestra and as an actor in the Nassau court theatre troupe. After the death of his father in 1843, Cornelius travelled to Berlin for theoretical musical studies with Siegfried Dehn, though with the emphasis on contrapuntal skills much of his talent remained unfulfilled. He was left to explore his poetic gifts separately through contacts with the poets Eichendorff and Heyse and others in the Berlin literary circle.

In 1849 came the first hints that opera might unite Cornelius's talents; he sketched the libretto for a one-act comic opera, though he failed to complete any of the music. The example of Wagner's music dramas already fascinated him and in 1852 he sought out Liszt in Weimar as one of the most important figures of the New

German School. Weimar proved an important spiritual home for Cornelius, offering him the chance to work with Liszt as writer and translator, as well as composer. Liszt encouraged him to use his poetic sensibilities as the foundation for his work, although this found an outlet in songs and church music before opera. Cornelius's operatic aspiration was to raise the level of comic opera as Wagner had raised tragedy, yet steering clear of any Wagnerian profundities. Indeed, when Cornelius eventually began work on *Der Barbier von Bagdad* in 1855, he looked to the Turkish colouring of Mozart's *Die Entführung*, to Berlioz's *Benvenuto Cellini* and even to Rossini for inspiration; he wrote the opera as a conscious answer to Rossini's *Il barbiere di Siviglia*.

Despite its mixed pedigree, *Der Barbier von Bagdad* was greeted as the first operatic product of the Lisztian school, arousing anti-Liszt demonstrations at its première in Weimar in 1858. Liszt in fact sought to bring the work more into line with Wagnerian principles by encouraging Cornelius, in 1873, to write a second overture quoting the opera's music in leitmotivic fashion. With his next operas, *Der Cid* and *Gunlöd*, Cornelius entered directly the Wagnerian territory of historical drama and myth. Moreover, in 1861, shortly after beginning work on *Der Cid*, he moved to Vienna and found himself in daily contact with Wagner, as friend and counsellor. But Cornelius saw *Der Cid* as a sign that he was no longer afraid of being drawn into imitating Wagner, and could accept the challenge of writing a heightened emotional drama in the mould of Beethoven's *Fidelio* or Weber's *Euryanthe*. He refused to respond to Wagner's invitation to follow him to Munich until 1865, when *Der Cid* was entirely finished; even then he accepted his posts as répétiteur and later teacher at the Munich Königliche Musikschule reluctantly.

Many, including Wagner himself, questioned whether Cornelius did not lose his true operatic path during these battles for independence. The widely contrasting operatic plans he entertained before composing *Der Cid* and *Gunlöd* reveal his uncertainty; at one point he planned to set E. T. A. Hoffmann's work, at another he worked on an operatic cycle called *Tiroler Treue*. The dramatic structure of *Der Cid* shows that Cornelius was not primarily concerned with what would be effective on the stage. Despite the poetic craft and psychological insight of the libretto, he failed to make the most of the story's dramatic conflicts, such as the impact of the Cid's political mission on the confused feelings of the heroine Chimene. *Gunlöd*, which Cornelius began soon after the completion of *Der Cid* but left unfinished at his death, represented little advance in this respect. The opera centres almost entirely on the feelings of Gunlöd, with the epic background in the *Edda* legends remaining largely incidental.

While both *Der Cid* and *Gunlöd* show a debt to the style of *Lohengrin*, as seen in the many march- or hymn-like passages, the treatment of such material is quite different. Cornelius's music tends towards lyrical expression, rather than the creation of large-scale dramatic tensions. He conceived his music in song-like units, though within these he moved flexibly from recitative to aria styles, often balancing deftly between the two. The freedom and originality of his style is best appreciated in *Der Barbier von Bagdad*, where his concern with musical detail suited the nature of the plot, much of its humour arising from intimate details of speech and gesture. The oriental-style peculiarities of speech are brought alive by harmonic and rhythmic twists, and by the sharply coloured orchestral punctuation. The freedom of his harmonic modulations, his frequent changes of metre and separation of orchestral colours all suggest the influence of Berlioz. Though he used melodic reminiscences to point his stories, the music's continuity and structure did not depend upon them; he relied little on motivic development in the Wagnerian manner, but rather on the creation of a continuous flow of inventive detail. *Der Barbier von Bagdad* was something of an isolated achievement for Cornelius, but its impact on Wagner's *Die Meistersinger* and Wolf's *Der Corregidor* suggests that he fulfilled his ambition to set new standards for German comic opera.

See also Barbier von Bagdad, Der; Cid, Der; and Gunlöd.

Edition: *P. Cornelius: Musikalische Werke*, ed. M. Hasse and W. von Baussnern (Leipzig, 1905–6) [H]

Der Barbier von Bagdad (komische Oper, 2, Cornelius, after *The Thousand and One Nights*), Weimar, Hof, 15 Dec 1858 (Leipzig, 1886), orig. version H iii

Der Cid (lyrisches Drama, 3, Cornelius, after G. de Castro, P. Corneille and J. G. Herder), Weimar, Hof, 21 May 1865 (Munich, 1891), orig. version H iv

Gunlöd, 1866–74 (3, Cornelius, after the *Edda*), inc.; completed K. Hoffbauer (Frankfurt, 1879), Weimar, Hof, 6 May 1891; completed W. von Baussnern, H v, Cologne, 15 Dec 1906

*

A. Sandberger: *Leben und Werke des Dichtermusikers Peter Cornelius* (Leipzig, 1887)
R. Batka: 'Der Cid', *Kranz* (Leipzig, 1903), 237–42
M. Hasse: *Peter Cornelius und sein Barbier von Bagdad* (Leipzig, 1904)
E. Janowitzer: *Die Opern von Peter Cornelius* (diss., U. of Vienna, 1921)
M. Klein: *Die dramatischen Dichtungen von Peter Cornelius* (diss., U. of Tübingen, 1921)
H. Paulig: *Peter Cornelius und sein 'Barbier von Bagdad'* (diss., U. of Cologne, 1923)
E. Newman: 'Barber von Bagdad', *Opera Nights* (London, 1943), 53–76
L. Wurmser: 'Cornelius and his "Barber"', *Opera*, xvi (1965), 868–73
M. R. Griffel: *'Turkish' Opera from Mozart to Cornelius* (diss., Columbia U., 1975), 391–429
H. Federhofer, ed.: *Peter Cornelius als Komponist, Dichter, Kritiker und Essayist* (Regensburg, 1977)
G. Wagner: *Peter Cornelius: ein Verzeichnis seiner musikalischen und literarischen Werke* (Tutzing, 1986) AMANDA GLAUERT

Cornelius, Peter (ii) [Petersen, Lauritz Peter Corneliys] (*b* Labjerggaard, Jutland, 4 Jan 1865; *d* Snekkersten, nr Copenhagen, 30 Dec 1934). Danish baritone, later tenor. He studied with Nyrop, and made his début in Copenhagen in 1892 as Escamillo, then continued to sing baritone roles including Kothner, Don Giovanni, Amonasro and Iago. After further study he made his tenor début in 1899 as the Steersman in *Der fliegende Holländer*. In 1902 he sang Siegmund and by 1914 he had added Siegfried, Lohengrin, Walther, Tannhäuser and Tristan to his repertory. He sang Siegfried at Bayreuth (1906) and at Covent Garden (1908–9), where he also sang Renaud in a revival of the first British production of Gluck's *Armide*. He made guest appearances in Paris, Budapest, Karlsruhe, Stockholm and Oslo. He retired in 1922, but in 1927 sang Tannhäuser when the tenor engaged fell ill. He made many recordings, the best of them in the period 1907–12. HAROLD ROSENTHAL/R

Cornelys, Theresa [Imer, Teresa; Mme Trenti] (*b* Venice, 1723; *d* London, 19 Aug 1797). Italian singer. She made her début in Venice about 1741–2, then appeared in Vienna (1744–5), London (1746) and

Hamburg (1748), and was with the Mingottis and Gluck in Copenhagen in 1749. About 1757 she was given the direction of all theatres in the Austrian Netherlands, but this venture left her bankrupt and she fled to Holland where she sang as 'Mme Trenti'.

In 1759 she returned to London, where she spent the rest of her life, known as 'Mrs Cornelys'. She renovated Carlisle House, Soho Square, and began a series of evening entertainments including concerts, but in 1771 she incurred the wrath of the law with her 'Harmonical Meetings', a poorly disguised effort to stage operas outside the opera house (directed by Giardini, composed by Vento, and with Gaetano Guadagni among the singers). She was declared bankrupt in 1772, and after further adventures died in the Fleet prison.

MURRAY R. CHARTERS

Coronaro. Italian family of composers and musicians.

(1) **Antonio Coronaro** (*b* Vicenza, 29 June 1851; *d* Vicenza, 24 March 1933). Composer. He studied in Vicenza and was organist at the cathedral there from 1885 until his death; he also taught the piano, harmony, counterpoint and composition. Three of his five operas were performed; *Seila*, the first, was his only success. The plot is from the biblical story of Jephtha and is treated in the manner of a grand opera, with choruses shouting 'Vittoria', marching bands on stage and ballets. Critics considered Coronaro too much under the influence of Verdi and Gomes. He also composed piano pieces, songs and sacred works.

Seila (3, A. Boni), Vicenza, Eretenio, 18 Jan 1880
La maliarda (2), Vicenza, Eretenio, carn. 1884
Il falco di Calabria (3), Vicenza, Patronato Leone XIII, 15 Jan 1903
Edwart, unperf.
Olinta e Simone, unperf.

(2) **Gaetano Coronaro** (*b* Vicenza, 18 Dec 1852; *d* Milan, 5 April 1908). Composer and conductor, brother of (1) Antonio. He began as a classics scholar, but soon turned to music, studying at first in Vicenza and from 1871 at the Milan Conservatory with Franco Faccio. For his graduation in 1873 he wrote an eclogue, *Un tramonto*, to a libretto by Boito. This short work proved tremendously successful, being performed as far away as Moscow and Chicago and winning the Giovannina Lucca prize. This prize enabled Coronaro to study abroad; a trip to Germany produced a passion for Wagner. On his return to Milan in 1876 Coronaro began a successful career as teacher, conductor and composer. From 1879 he taught at the conservatory, where he was professor of composition from 1894. He conducted at La Scala, in 1879 deputizing for Faccio.

The success of *Un tramonto* encouraged Coronaro to write operas, but only the first of the five he composed, *La creole* (1878, Bologna), had a very favourable reception, and one was never performed. *Un tramonto* is a simply structured pastorale, with a hunters' chorus and a storm and four numbers in classic recitative-aria format; the finale is more ambitious, making use of an unaccompanied offstage chorus and the return of earlier melodic ideas. *La creole*, a grand opera with *verismo* overtones, was considered more original, even though it showed the influence of Wagner, Meyerbeer and Verdi. It presents a love triangle in which the contralto villainess, in a jealous rage, pushes the soprano heroine off a cliff at the end of Act 2. This premature gesture leaves little for the final act except the avenging of the murder during the heroine's funeral cortège. Critics have held Coronaro to be tied to a Verdian tradition, more an assimilator than a creator of styles. He also composed sacred, chamber and orchestral music.

Un tramonto (eclogue, 1, A. Boito), Milan, Conservatorio di Musica, 8 Aug 1873, vs (Milan, 1873)
La creole (3, E. Torelli-Viollier), Bologna, Comunale, 27 Nov 1878, *I-Mr**, vs (Milan, 1879)
Il malacarne (3, S. Interdonato), Brescia, Grande, 20 Jan 1894
Un curioso accidente (ob, 1, V. Tedeschi-Treve, after C. Goldoni), Turin, Emanuele, 11 Nov 1903
Enoch Arden (A. Fogazzaro, after A. Tennyson), 1905
La signora di Challant (G. Giacosa), unperf.

(3) **Gellio Benevenuto Coronaro** (*b* Vicenza, 30 Nov 1863; *d* Milan, 26 July 1916). Composer, brother of (1) Antonio and (2) Gaetano Coronaro. He studied at the Bologna Conservatory. Like his brother Gaetano he won great acclaim and a prize for a one-act graduation composition, the idyll *Jolanda* (1883). He had considerable success as a pianist and conductor. His opera *La festa a marina* (1893, Venice) won first prize in the third Sonzogno competition, but subsequent theatrical ventures failed. *La festa a marina* was considered a poor, if slavish, imitation of *Cavelleria rusticana*; its *verismo* plot, set in Calabria, presents the treacherous wife slain on stage, 'uttering gurgling sounds as she falls with cut throat'. The tunes are passable, however, and the drama is punctuated with effective offstage choruses, sung with ironic indifference to the foreground tragedy of the principals. Coronaro had three other operas performed; *Claudia* (1895, Milan) was published. He also composed keyboard, chamber and sacred works, and songs.

Jolanda (1, G. Chiericato), Bologna, Liceo Musicale, 24 June 1883
La festa a marina (bozzetto lirico, 1, V. Fontana), Venice, Fenice, 21 March 1893, vs (Milan, 1893)
Minestrone napoletano (operetta), Messina, 1893
Claudia (dramma lirico, 3, G. D. Bartocci-Fontana, after G. Sand), Milan, Lirico, 5 Nov 1895, vs (Milan, 1894)
Bertoldo (ob, 3, M. Basso), Milan, Fossati, 2 March 1910

*

E. Oddone: *Gaetano Coronaro* (Rome, 1922)
G. Mantesi: *Storia musicale vicentina* (Vicenza, 1956)

MARVIN TARTAK

Coronatione di Poppea, La. Opera by Claudio Monteverdi; *see* INCORONAZIONE DI POPPEA, L'.

Corradi, Giulio Cesare (*b* Parma; *d* ?Venice, 1701 or 1702). Italian librettist. By the 1690s Coronelli had included him in a list of poetry instructors, along with Zeno, Silvani and others. He wrote 22 librettos for Venetian theatres between 1675 and 1702. His career as an original librettist began with two large-scale works for the Teatro S Salvatore, set by Giovanni Legrenzi. His first, *La divisione del mondo* (1675), pays homage to the Venetian nobility (to whom the libretto is dedicated), and its theme, the division of the universe among Jupiter, Neptune and Pluto, gave rise to magnificent spectacle (such as the gods' battle with the Titans) and numerous love entanglements; Guido Rangoni, the theatre's director in 1675, was responsible for the elaborate production. Surviving designs for Corradi's second work, *Germanico sul Reno* (1676, in *F-Po*), make clear the mechanisms behind such spectacle. Corradi had a long-standing association with theatres owned by the Grimani family; he wrote three works for the first four seasons (1678–81) of their new, luxurious theatre, the S Giovanni Grisostomo, and from 1686 to 1693 provided librettos for their older theatre, SS Giovanni e Paolo.

Corradi played no role in the efforts made in the 1690s to elevate libretto style, even though he did introduce serious elements into three works around 1690: deaths take place on stage in *Il gran Tamerlano*, *L'amor di Curzio per la patria* and *Alboino in Italia*. His works emphasize lively character interaction; they have some historical basis, except for *La divisione del mondo* and two works that draw upon Tasso, *La Gierusalemme liberata* and *Gli avvenimenti d'Erminia e di Clorinda*. The last two were of contemporary relevance because of the ongoing struggle of Venice against the Turks. The subjects of his first two works for the S Giovanni Grisostomo, *Vespasiano* and *Nerone*, were well suited to the pre-eminence of that theatre; he used Vespasian and Nero – touchstones of theatricality in the ancient world – to exploit spectacular features of the modern stage. *Vespasiano* was subsequently presented in several other Italian cities, particularly for the opening of new theatres.

drammi per musica unless otherwise stated

La schiava fortunata (rev. of G. A. Moniglia: *Semiramide*), M. A. Ziani, 1674; *La divisione del mondo*, Legrenzi, 1675; *Germanico sul Reno*, Legrenzi, 1676; *Vespasiano*, C. Pallavicino, 1678 (J. W. Franck, 1681, as Vespasian; Ariosti, 1724); *Nerone*, Pallavicino, 1679 (Strungk, 1693, as Nero); *Creso* (dramma da rappresentarsi), Legrenzi, 1681; *I due Cesari*, Legrenzi, 1683; *L'amazone corsara, ovvero L'Alvilda regina de' Goti* (dramma da rappresentarsi in musica), Pallavicino, 1686

La Gierusalemme liberata (dramma da rappresentarsi in musica), Pallavicino, 1687 (Ger., 1695, as Armida; Schürmann, 1722, as Das eroberte Jerusalem, oder Armida und Rinaldo); *L'inganno regnante, ovvero L'Atanagilda regina di Gottia*, Ziani, 1687; *Il gran Tamerlano*, Ziani, 1689; *L'amor di Curzio per la patria* (dramma da rappresentarsi in musica), Alghisi, 1690

Il trionfo della continenza, Alghisi, 1690; *Alboino in Italia*, G. F. Tosi and C. F. Pollarolo, carn. 1691; *Iole regina di Napoli*, Pollarolo, 1692; *Gli avvenimenti d'Erminia e di Clorinda*, Pollarolo, carn. 1693; *Amage regina de' Sarmati*, Pollarolo, 1693; *Domizio*, Ziani, 1696; *Primislao primo re di Boemia*, Albinoni, 1697; *Tigrane re d'Armenia*, Albinoni, 1697; *Egisto re di Cipro*, Ziani, 1698; *Aristeo*, A. Pollarolo, 1700; *La pastorella al soglio* (opera postuma), various comps., 1702 (A. Orefice, 1710; Orlandini, 1717; as La pastorella as soglio, ovvero Odoardo re d'Inghilterra, 1728)

*

DBI (M. Capucci)

V. Coronelli: *Guida de' forestieri* (Venice, 1700)

H. C. Wolff: *Die venezianische Oper in der zweiten Hälfte des 17. Jahrhunderts: ein Beitrag zur Geschichte der Musik und des Theaters im Zeitalter des Barocks* (Berlin, 1937)

R. Brockpähler: *Handbuch zur Geschichte der Barockoper in Deutschland* (Emsdetten, 1964)

H. S. Saunders: *The Repertoire of a Venetian Opera House (1678–1714): the Teatro Grimani di San Giovanni Grisostomo* (diss., Harvard U., 1985)

E. Rosand: *Opera in Seventeenth-Century Venice: the Creation of a Genre* (Berkeley, 1991) HARRIS S. SAUNDERS

Corradini [Coradini, Coradigni]**, Francesco** [**Francisco**] (*b* Venice, *c*1700; *d* Madrid, 14 Oct 1769). Italian composer. His first known opera, *Lo'ngiegno de le femmine*, an *opera buffa* in Neapolitan dialect, was successfully performed in Naples in 1724, and followed by two additional stage works in 1725. He then left Italy for Spain, where he first found employment as *maestro di capilla* to the viceroy Prince of Campoflorido in Valencia. There he wrote the three-act comedy *Folla real*, performed at the viceroy's palace during festivities honouring the birthday of Queen Isabella (Farnese). Corradini's name has thus become associated with a three-act pastoral melodrama *La Dorinda*, which according to its anonymous score (*E-Mn*) had also been mounted at the Palacio Real, but for a celebration of the queen's name-day; this however appears to be a pasticcio (it includes an aria from Feo's *Siface* of 1723). In 1729 Corradini moved to Madrid, and for the next 15 years he virtually dominated the public theatrical scene with his successful Spanish operas, zarzuelas and music for popular *comedias*, *sainetes* and *autos sacramentales* in the Italian style. His scores for the comedies *Eco y Narcisco* and *Las Mascaras* are characterized by catchy tunes with regular phrase structures and simple harmonic vocabulary that reflect the public taste of the time. In 1747, under King Ferdinand VI, he joined G. B. Mele and the *primo maestro* of the *capilla real*, Francesco Corselli, as a director of the orchestra at the royal theatre in the palace of Buen Retiro managed by Farinelli, and collaborated with them in setting a Spanish translation of Metastasio's *La clemenza di Tito* and then Rolli's *Polifemo*. Corradini did not die in 1749, as has been stated, but he withdrew from the operatic scene and dedicated himself to his duties as *maestro de musica de camera* of the queen dowager, Isabella Farnese, a position to which he had been appointed in 1747; he also served as music teacher of the infanta Maria Antonia. After the death of Queen Isabella in 1766 he retired with a royal pension. His will, signed five days before his death, shows that he was a native of Venice, not of Naples (as has always been assumed).

performed in Madrid unless otherwise stated

as – *auto sacramentale* com – *comedia*
ob – *opera buffa* zar – *zarzuela*

Lo'ngiegno de le femmine (ob, F. A. Tullio), Naples, Fiorentini, 1724

L'aracolo de Dejana (ob, Tullio), Naples, Nuovo, carn. 1725

Il premio dell'innocenza, ovvero Le perdite dell'inganno (dramma per musica, C. de Palma), Naples, Nuovo, Dec 1725, lib. *I-Bc*

El amor más fino y constante, Valencia, Olivera, 27 Jan 1729

Amado y aborrelido, Valencia, Olivera, 24 Nov 1729

Con amor non hay libertad (melodrama armónica, 2), Cruz, 22 Jan 1731

Templo y monte de Filis y Demofonte (zar, J. de Cañizares), Príncipe, 27 Oct 1731

La sirena de Trinacria (zar), 1732

La immunidad del sagrado (as), ?12 June 1732

Milagro es hallar verdad (zar, 2, Cañizares), Príncipe, 28 Nov 1732

Gloria de Jésus cautivo y Prodigos de su rescate (com, A. Azevedo), Dec 1732

Santa Gertrudis (com de santo), Cruz, 22 Dec 1732 [Act 2]

La boba discreta (com, Cañizares), Príncipe, 7 Feb 1733

La vacante general (auto, P. Calderón de la Barca), 12 June 1733

El dia mayor de los dias (auto, Calderón), Cruz, 1733

Eco y Narcisco (com, Calderón), Cruz, 22 Jan 1734, *E-Mm*

Non hay que temer a la estrella si domina Venus bella (com), Príncipe, 26 Feb 1734

Vencer y ser vencido: Anteros y Cupido (zar, 2, J. de Anaya y Aragonés), Príncipe, 14 Feb 1735

Trajano en Dacia y Cumplir con amor su honor (op, 2), Caños del Peral, sum. 1735; rev. version, Cruz, 21 Sept 1737

Las prodigiosas señales del nacimiento de Cristo (auto), Cruz, 8 Oct 1735

Dar el ser el hijo al padre (melodramma armónica, 2), Príncipe, 31 Jan 1736

El ser noble es obrar bien, Caños del Peral, Nov 1736

La Clicie (dramma armónica, Cañizares), Príncipe, carn. 1739

La mágica Florentina (com), carn. 1739

El mágico broacario (com), carn. 1739

La Elisa [Burlas y veras de amor: La Elisa] (op, 2, Cañizares), Príncipe, 30 Jan 1739; rev. version, Cruz, Nov 1739

La semilla y la cizaña (auto, Calderón), 1739

Las peñas de Montserrat (com), 1739 [bailes]

El anillo de Giges (com, Cañizares), Príncipe, 1740

Don Juan de Espina en Madrid (com), 1740, *Mm*
A falta de hechieros lo quieren ser los gallegos (com), ? Nov 1740 or Oct 1741
Don Juan de Espina en Milan (com), 1741
El Thequeli (dramma scenico, N. A. Solano y Lobo), Caños del Peral, 1744, lib. *Mm*
La más heroica amistad y el amor más verdadero (os, M. Guerrero, after P. Metastasio: *L'olimpiade*), Caños del Peral, Aug 1745
La Briseida (?os or serenata), Cruz, 14 Aug 1745; rev. Príncipe, 23 May 1746 [3 arias]
Margarita de Cortona, Príncipe, 26 Dec 1745
San Francisco de Paula (com de santo), Príncipe, 30 May 1746
Nuestra Señora de la Salceda (? as or com, Calderón), 1746
El jardín de Falerina (? auto or com), 1746
La cura y la enfermedad (auto, Calderón), 1746
La clemencia de Tito [Act 2] (os, I. de Luzán y Suelves, after Metastasio), Buen Retiro, carn. 1747 [Act 1 by F. Corselli, Act 3 by G. B. Mele]
El Polifemo [Act 2] (os, P. Rolli), Buen Retiro, 20 Jan 1748 [Act 1 by Corselli, Act 3 by Mele]
El asombro de Jerez: Juana la Rabicortona (com), Príncipe, 1748
Nuestra Señora de Milagro (com de santo), 1749
Las mascaras (com) [bailes], *Mm*

Doubtful: Folla real (ob, 3), Valencia, Palacio del Viceré, 25 Oct 1728; La Dorinda (melodrama pastoral), ?pasticcio, Valencia, Palacio Real, 19 Nov [without year], *Mn*

*

ES (J. Subirá)
M. Scherillo: *L'opera buffa napoletana durante il settecento* (Naples, 2/1916)
E. Cotarelo y Mori: *Orígenes y establecimiento de la ópera an España hasta 1800* (Madrid, 1917)
J. Subirá: *La música en la Casa de Alba* (Madrid, 1927), 240–42
——: *Historia de la música teatral en España* (Barcelona, 1945), 102–4, 112–15
H. Anglés and J. Subirá: *Catálogo del la Biblioteca nacional de Madrid* (Barcelona, 1946), 371–2
C. Morales Borrero, ed.: *Fiestas reales en el reinado de Fernando VI: manuscrito de Carlos Broschi Farinelli* (Madrid, 1972), 23
W. M. Bussey: *French and Italian Influences on the Zarzuela 1700–1770* (Ann Arbor, 1982), 11, 63, 113, 171–2

HANNS-BERTOLD DIETZ

Corrado, Gioacchino (*b* Naples; *fl* 1705–44). Italian bass. He was principal *buffo* singer in Naples when Leo, Sarri, Mancini, Hasse, Vinci and Pergolesi were composing there. After performing in comic operas at the Teatro dei Fiorentini he specialized in the intermezzo repertory from 1711 (Mancini's *Lidia e Ircano*) to 1736 at the Teatro S Bartolomeo. When Charles III of Bourbon banned intermezzos from the royal theatre, Corrado continued his career in comic opera at the Fiorentini and the Nuovo theatres, and sang at the S Carlo on the only occasion that a *commedia in musica* was staged there (Auletta and Federico's *La locandiera* in 1738). He visited Venice in 1725, singing Sarro's *L'impresario delle Canarie*, and brought back the texts of many Venetian intermezzos which were then staged in Naples. He created the role of Uberto in Pergolesi's *La serva padrona* (1733).

*

F. Piperno: 'Buffe e buffi', *RIM*, xviii (1982), 240–84
——: 'Note sulla diffusione degli intermezzi di J. A. Hasse', *AnMc*, no.25 (1987), 287–303
——: 'L'intermezzo a Napoli negli anni di Pergolesi: Gioacchino Corrado e Celeste Resse', *Pergolesi Studies*, iii (forthcoming)

FRANCO PIPERNO

Corrêa de Azevedo, Luiz Heitor. *See* AZEVEDO, LUIZ HEITOR CORRÊA DE.

Corregidor, Der ('The Magistrate'). Opera in four acts by HUGO WOLF to a libretto by Rosa Mayreder after Pedro de Alarcón's novel *El sombrero de tres picos*; Mannheim, Nationaltheater, 7 June 1896.

Don Eugenio de Zuniga *Corregidor*	tenor
Juan Lopez *mayor*	bass
Pedro *his secretary*	tenor
Tonuelo *a mayoral official*	bass
Repela *Don Eugenio's servant*	bass
Tio Lukas *the miller*	baritone
Frasquita *his wife*	mezzo-soprano
A Neighbour	tenor
Donna Mercedes *Don Eugenio's wife*	soprano
Duenna *her servant*	alto
Manuela *Juan Lopez's maid*	mezzo-soprano
A Nightwatchman	baritone

The bishop and his retinue, servants of the Corregidor and the mayor, police constables, musicians

Setting The region of Andalusia, in 1804

Although Wolf first considered treating Alarcón's novel operatically in 1888, it was not until 1895 that he settled on Rosa Mayreder's libretto as a suitable adaptation. Work then proceeded swiftly, and the whole opera was written between March and December 1895. Despite Wolf's many ambitions for his work, the authorities in Vienna and Berlin refused to stage the première and there were problems during the rehearsals at Mannheim. While Joachim Romer (Lukas) and Hans Rüdiger (the Corregidor) had some knowledge of Wolf's style, Hohenleitner (Frasquita) and Karl Marx (Repela) found the difficulties of their parts almost insuperable. Wolf disputed the tempos set by the conductor, Hugo Röhr, and at one point threatened to withdraw the opera. The work was performed only twice at Mannheim and had to wait until 29 April 1898 before its next performance, in Strasbourg; by then Wolf had made cuts and revisions in the final act. Mahler conducted the opera in Vienna on 18 February 1904, in his own three-act version, with Bertha Förster-Lauterer (Frasquita), Hans Breuer (Corregidor) and Leopold Demuth (Lukas). (Falla's ballet on the same story dates from 1919.)

Performances of *Der Corregidor* have continued to be rare. There was a Salzburg Festival performance conducted by Bruno Walter in 1936 with Novotná, Gunner Graarud and Jerger Zec. The 1944 recording, conducted by Elmendorff with Teschemacher (Frasquita), Erb (Corregidor) and Josef Herrmann (Lukas), was followed in 1987 by a version conducted by Albrecht, with Soffel, Werner Hollweg and Fischer-Dieskau in the major roles.

ACT 1 *The courtyard and wine arbour of the mill* The prelude establishes the magisterial dignity of the Corregidor, Don Eugenio de Zuniga, and contrasts the rising sequences of his unbridled passions with song-like phrases conveying the domestic bliss of Tio Lukas and Frasquita. As Lukas discusses the blessings of marriage with a neighbour, the miller's motif picks up the simple style of a song accompaniment. As Frasquita herself enters, a flow of lyrical variations reveals the depth of their love. The comedy begins as Repela announces with mock solemnity the arrival of his lecherous master ('Schreckliche Müllerin'). With Lukas's connivance, Frasquita plays up to the Corregidor with a fandango and a seductive song from Wolf's Spanish songbook, *In dem Schatten meiner Locken*. The Corregidor expounds his love with expansive phrases ('Süsse Zauberin'), yet at their climax Frasquita dodges his embrace and he slips from his stool; mocking references to the dignified

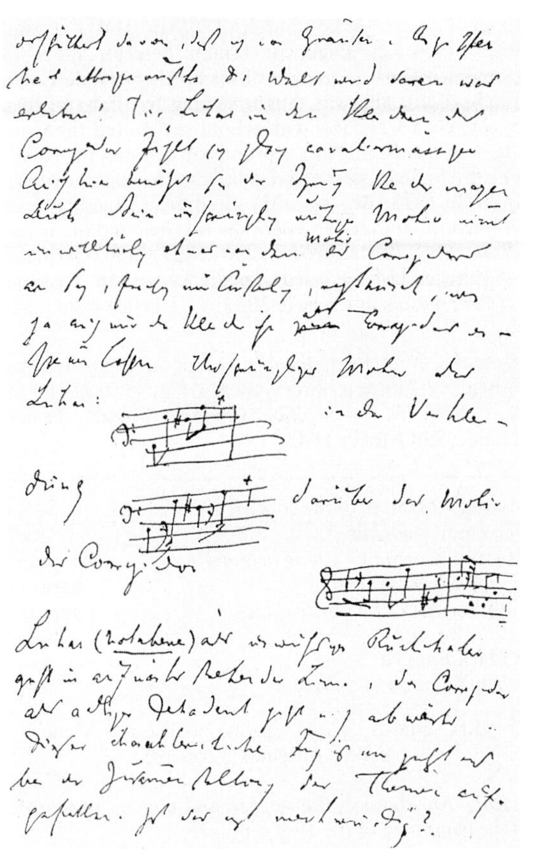

Autograph letter from Wolf to Rosa Mayreder (8 June 1895) referring to the way in which the motifs of Lukas and the Corregidor are combined as Lukas dresses in the Corregidor's clothes in Act 3 scenes iii–iv of Wolf's opera

motif in the prelude are heard in the orchestra. A polite conversation restores some order, but Lukas and Frasquita cannot entirely conceal their glee, nor the Corregidor his desire for revenge. Any battle of wits is postponed by the march-like procession of the bishop, arriving to sample the miller's hospitality.

ACT 2.i–vi *The mill's kitchen* By the evening fireside, Frasquita and Lukas reaffirm their love with the prelude's song-phrases ('In solcher Abendfeierstunden'). The idyll is disturbed by the knocking of the drunken but insistent Tonuelo, calling Lukas away to wait upon the mayor, Juan Lopez. Frasquita continues her household tasks, singing to allay her anxiety ('Flackerschein, ich blase'). The underlying conspiracy surfaces as the Corregidor himself appears, his ardour still burning although he has fallen into the mill-stream on the way to Frasquita's door. As the confrontation gathers pace, he faints and Frasquita escapes, leaving him to regain some composure by reflecting on the fickleness of women ('Herz, verzage nicht geschwind') – a second quotation from Wolf's Spanish songbook.

2.vii–xi *A room in the mayor's house* A dance-like orchestral interlude sets the mood for a drinking party at the mayor's house. As Lukas arrives, he soon appreciates the situation and adds his own drinking song ('Ich hab' dich zum Beistand erwählt') to the one already heard from Pedro ('Ich und mein holdselig's Weibchen'). His captors believe in his exaggerated drunkenness, naively wishing him a good night's sleep with another song ('Don Rodrigo'). He then escapes; Manuela is left to try to raise the spirits of Tonuelo and Pedro to a more heroic level as Lukas's empty bed is discovered ('Also auf, ihr beiden Helden').

ACT 3.i–ii *Two paths through moonlit countryside* In her flight to find Lukas, Frasquita hears strange night noises, one of which is Lukas himself passing in the opposite direction, unseen by her. The atmospheric tone-painting and Frasquita's romantic reflections on the moon ('Neugier'ge Mond') are upset by the unwelcome entry of Repela, sent by his master and now persisting with his own advances in a sharply ironic duet with her ('Muss es denn sein').

3.iii–vi *The mill's kitchen* After an interlude, continuing to depict Frasquita in flight, now closely followed by Repela, the tone of the opera changes drastically, from farce to tragedy. In seeking his wife, Lukas catches a glimpse of the Corregidor in his bed and believes Frasquita to have been unfaithful. As he conceives the idea of seeking revenge by donning the Corregidor's clothes and seducing Donna Mercedes, the mood of his motif changes from its former ponderous despair and it combines triumphantly with the Corregidor's own. On waking, the Corregidor has to wear Lukas's clothes and he is comically apprehended by the mayor's party (including Frasquita), who have come in search of the miller. The Corregidor attempts to regain his magisterial dignity as all agree in march-like tones to accompany him in pursuing Lukas to town ('Euer Gnaden, unterthänigst').

ACT 4 *The street in front of the Corregidor's house* Roused by the Corregidor's efforts to enter his own house, Donna Mercedes refuses to recognize him, saying her husband is already in bed ('Mein Gatte, der Corregidor'). The rich harmonies and chorale-like texture of her music set her apart from the rest of the ensemble, and the contrapuntal complexity of the music grows as each character seeks the truth. Even though Frasquita's innocence is quickly established, Mercedes stops her servants from telling how they foiled Lukas's plan until the husbands retire to exchange clothes, so that only Frasquita hears the full account. At the close, Frasquita and Lukas are reunited, to reminiscences of their love music, but Mercedes continues to ignore the Corregidor's urgent questions about his honour. His wrath is finally silenced before his wife's greater dignity and he joins the general hymn in honour of her and the new day ('Guten Morgen, edle Donna!').

* * *

With all the twists in its plot, *Der Corregidor* has been likened to a Mozart comic opera; the battle for ascendancy between Lukas and the Corregidor is certainly reminiscent of the relationship between master and servant in *Le nozze di Figaro*. Wolf aspired to a light conversational style in his opera, in contrast with the heightened tone of Wagnerian music drama. The speed of the action inspired the composer to a stream of melodic invention while also revealing his lack of experience of long-term dramatic pacing. He skilfully extended each lyrical idea to fit the narrative or dovetailed it into a new one, but he still conceived each operatic scene as a chain of song-like units rather than a single musical sweep. With such dramatic failings *Der Corregidor* cannot be acknowledged as the perfect antidote to Wagner, yet it continues to be respected as the confirmation of Wolf's skill and resources as a song composer.

AMANDA GLAUERT

Corri, Domenico (*b* Rome, 4 Oct 1746; *d* Hampstead, London, 22 May 1825). Italian composer. After studying with Porpora in Naples, he returned to Rome, where his opera *La raminga fedele* was produced in 1770. Mentioned favourably in Charles Burney's writings, he was invited by the Musical Society of Edinburgh to conduct their concerts (from 1771); he remained in Edinburgh about 18 years. He quickly established business enterprises and became manager of the Vauxhall pleasure gardens and the Theatre Royal in Edinburgh. The latter enterprise failed in 1779 and Corri turned to music publishing, working in London from about 1790. His firm specialized in the publication of single numbers from operas and solo songs; for a time Lorenzo da Ponte was associated with it. In 1806 Corri's most successful opera, *The Travellers*, was produced, and he appears to have continued as a composer and teacher for another decade.

A competent composer, Corri completed four operatic works. Within an unsophisticated style he could display a neat sense of musical characterization, as in the quartet 'Past ten o'clock' from *In and Out of Tune*, where the calls of the Night Watchmen are humorously intermingled with a singer's sol-fa exercises. In *The Travellers*, which includes scenes set in China and Turkey, Corri indulged in pseudo-Oriental music, albeit at the expense of harmonic interest. Among his other works are music for a play and other stage productions, and writings on music, of which *The Singer's Preceptor* (London, 1810) contains his autobiography to that date and much valuable information about performing practices (*see* ORNAMENTATION, §2).

Several members of his family were also musicians, among them his daughter the pianist, harpist and composer Sophia Giustina Corri (*b* Edinburgh, 1 May 1775; *d* after 1828), wife of J. L. Dussek, who sang in operas in London, his son Philip Antony Corri (who later took the name ARTHUR CLIFTON) and his niece FRANCES CORRI. Rosalie Corri (*b* 1803), sister of Frances, was a soprano who sang in London in 1820–21 and at the Teatro Re in Milan in 1823. Patrick Anthony Corri (1820–76), son of Domenico's son Haydn Corri (1785–1860), a singer, conductor and composer, was father of Haydn Woulds Corri (1845–76), a baritone. Sons of William Charles Cunningham Corri (1834 or 1835–93), a son of Domenico's son Montague Philip Corri (*c*1784–1849), included Charles Montague Corri (1861–1941), a conductor of opera at the Old Vic Theatre, London, and Clarence Collingwood Corri (1863–1918), composer of the operettas *The Dandy Fifth* (1898) and *In Gay Piccadilly* (1901). Ghita Auber Corri (1869 or 1870–1937), granddaughter of Haydn Corri, sang in the Carl Rosa Opera Company.

La raminga fedele (ob), Rome, Pace, carn. 1770, lost

Alessandro nell'Indie (os, P. Metastasio), London, King's, 3 Dec 1774, songs (London, 1774)

The Cabinet (comic op, T. J. Dibdin), London, CG, 9 Feb 1802, vs (London, 1802); collab. J. Braham, J. Davy, J. Moorehead and W. Reeve

The Travellers, or Music's Fascination (A. Cherry), London, Drury Lane, 22 Jan 1806, vs (London, 1806)

In and Out of Tune (operatic farce, D. Lawler and Cherry), London, Drury Lane, 1 March 1808, vs (London, 1808)

*

A. Obertello: 'Una famiglia di musicisti italiani in Inghilterra', *Nuova antologia* (1930), July–Aug, 244–62

W. C. Smith: *The Italian Opera and Contemporary Ballet in London 1789–1820* (London, 1955)

PETER WARD JONES

Corri, Frances (*b* Edinburgh, 1795 or 1801; *d* after 1833). Scottish singer of Italian descent, niece of Domenico Corri (daughter of his brother Natale Corri, 1765–1822). She was taught singing by Braham, then by Angelica Catalani, with whom she toured the Continent in 1815–16. After a promising début at the King's Theatre in 1818 she sang regularly in the company until 1820. In 1821 she left for the Continent, singing first in Munich, then in Italy, where she married and made her home. She also toured Spain (1827) and Germany (1830); her last recorded appearance was in Rossini's *La Cenerentola* at Lucca in 1833. PETER WARD JONES

Corsaro, Il ('The Corsair'). Opera in three acts by GIUSEPPE VERDI to a libretto by FRANCESCO MARIA PIAVE after BYRON's poem *The Corsair*; Trieste, Teatro Grande, 25 October 1848.

Corrado *Captain of the corsairs*	tenor
Giovanni *a corsair*	bass
Medora *Corrado's young beloved*	soprano
Seid *Pasha of Coron*	baritone
Gulnara *Seid's favourite slave*	soprano
Selimo *an Aga*	tenor
A Black Eunuch	tenor
A Slave	tenor

Corsairs, guards, Turks, slaves, odalisques, Medora's maids, Anselmo (a corsair)

Setting An island in the Aegean and the city of Coron, at the beginning of the 19th century

Verdi had toyed with setting Byron's poem as early as 1844 and kept the subject in mind during the years immediately following. In 1845 he considered using it to fulfil a commission from Her Majesty's Theatre in London: Piave wrote the libretto, but the London trip was postponed. A year later Verdi showed his continuing enthusiasm for the topic by asking Piave not to give the libretto to any other composer. Eventually, Verdi wrote the opera to fulfil the final part of a long-standing contract with Ricordi's rival publisher Francesco Lucca, a man with whom Verdi had had unfortunate dealings ever since Lucca and Ricordi had come to legal blows over the rights to *Nabucco* in 1842. Anxious above all to be rid of his obligation, Verdi set Piave's libretto in the winter of 1847–8, giving the opera to Lucca without any idea of where or when it would first be performed. For a composer who in all previous operas had taken an enormous, often fanatical interest in the details of his creations' first staging, such indifference is suspicious: many have seen it as an indication that Verdi had little faith in his new opera. Lucca eventually placed the opera at the Teatro Grande in Trieste, but Verdi did not even trouble to attend the first performances. The première, whose cast included Gaetano Fraschini (Corrado), Achille De Bassini (Seid) and Marianna Barbieri-Nini (Gulnara), was poorly received and managed only a few revivals before it disappeared from the repertory. It has rarely been revived in modern times.

The prelude, based on material from the opera, is one of extreme contrasts, with the opening orchestral storm music followed by a lyrical subject of great simplicity.

ACT 1.i *The corsairs' island in the Aegean* A boisterous offstage chorus of corsairs introduces Corrado, who bemoans his life of exile and crime in the Andante 'Tutto parea sorridere', an aria that delicately hovers between Italian formal convention and the French two-verse variety. A letter containing military intelligence is presented to Corrado, who resolves to set sail, rallying his troops with the cabaletta 'Sì: de' Corsari il fulmine'; in the manner of Verdi's earliest successes, the chorus joins the soloist for the final lines.

1.ii *Medora's apartments in the old tower* Medora, awaiting Corrado's arrival, takes up her harp and sings a two-verse *romanza*, 'Non so le tetre immagini', full of vague forebodings though not without elaborate vocal ornament. Corrado enters and a conventionally structured duet finale closes the act. The first lyrical movement, 'No, tu non sai', a dissimilar type in which Medora's disturbed chromatic line is settled by Corrado's reassuring melodic stability, is unusual in its progressive deceleration of tempo; the cabaletta, 'Tornerai, ma forse spenta', which sees Corrado about to depart yet again, is more traditionally paced, with a final Più mosso in which the couple sings an extended passage in 3rds and 6ths.

ACT 2.i *Luxurious apartments in Seid's harem* A chorus of odalisques, graced with high woodwind local colour, introduces Gulnara, who hates Seid and seeks to escape from the harem. Her cavatina, 'Vola talor dal carcere', is conventionally scored but has much of that harmonic and orchestral density we expect from post-*Macbeth* Verdi. She agrees to attend a banquet of Seid's and in the cabaletta 'Ah conforto è sol la speme' prays that Heaven will take pity on her.

2.ii *A magnificent pavilion on the shores of the harbour of Coron* After a brief chorus of greeting, Seid salutes his followers and joins them in a solemn hymn to Allah, 'Salve Allah!', a number whose rhythmic cut is more than a little reminiscent of the famous choruses in *I Lombardi* and *Ernani*. A Dervish appears, asking for protection from the corsairs. He and Seid have time for the brief first movement of a duet, 'Di': que' ribaldi tremano', before flames are seen and offstage cries signal an attack. The Dervish throws off his disguise to reveal himself as Corrado, who calls for his followers. In an extended battle sequence, Corrado and his troops attempt to save the women of the harem, a delay in the attack that causes their defeat and the wounding of Corrado. In the ensuing Andante of the concertato finale, 'Audace cotanto mostrati pur sai?', Seid derides the fallen hero, Corrado is defiant and Gulnara and the odalisques find their amorous feelings aroused by these handsome would-be saviours. More prisoners are brought on, but Seid is above all happy to have Corrado in his power and leads off the stretta 'Sì, morrai di morte atroce', promising his prisoner an agonizing death.

ACT 3.i *Seid's apartments* The baritone has so far seen little of the vocal limelight, and room is now made for a full-scale double aria. In the Andantino, 'Cento leggiadre vergini', Seid regrets that of all the women available to him, the one whom he loves has spurned him. As in Corrado's Act 1 aria, though even more economically, the aria is notable for its orchestral reprise of the main melody. In the cabaletta 'S'avvicina il tuo momento', a movement more reminiscent of *Oberto* than of the post-*Macbeth* style, Seid looks forward to Corrado's grisly death.

Gulnara enters to plead for Corrado's life. The first movement of the ensuing duet, 'Vieni, Gulnara!', is a free dialogue over a complex orchestral melody of a kind later to be made famous in the Rigoletto-Sparafucile duet. But Seid will not be persuaded and eventually concludes that Gulnara must love Corrado. His anger bursts forth in the duet cabaletta, 'Sia l'istante maledetto'.

3.ii *Inside a prison tower* A sombre prelude featuring solo cello and viola introduces Corrado, alone and in chains. He laments his fate in a spare but expressive recitative before falling asleep. Gulnara steals in and awakens him. In the long, expressive and unusually free first movement of their duet, 'Seid la vuole', Gulnara offers Corrado a means of escape, saying that she herself will kill Seid. Corrado's personal honour obliges him to refuse her help, and he further distresses her by admitting his love for Medora. Gulnara departs, and the orchestra sounds a reprise of the stormy music first heard in the prelude to Act 1. As the storm subsides, Gulnara returns to announce that Seid is dead. Corrado now assures her of his protection and in the cabaletta 'La terra, il ciel m'abborrino' they prepare to escape together.

3.iii *The corsairs' island* (as 1.i) An orchestral prelude featuring fragments of Medora's Act 1 *romanza* introduces Corrado's beloved, near death and without hope of seeing him again. But suddenly a ship is sighted, Corrado and Gulnara arrive, and the lovers are in each other's arms. Corrado and Gulnara relate something of their adventures before Medora leads off the Andante concertato, 'O mio Corrado, appressati', whose opening melody appeared in the prelude to the opera. Corrado and Gulnara heighten the emotional temperature by protesting at fate, but Medora's strength fails. In an agony of despair, Corrado flings himself from the cliffs.

* * *

It is important to recall that the libretto to *Il corsaro* (and therefore its essential dramatic structure) was fixed as early as 1846, some time before Verdi worked on *Macbeth*: much of the opera seems rather old-fashioned in relation to the works that surround it in the Verdian canon. It is also – perhaps for this reason, perhaps (as mentioned earlier) because of Verdi's feud with the publisher Lucca – an uneven work, with an element of the routine in certain passages. On the other hand, there are many moments, particularly in the final act, that stand comparison with the best operas of this period, and some formal experiments – strange and elliptical as they may be in their dramatic context – that were to bear much fruit in the years to come. ROGER PARKER

Corselli [Courcelle], **Francesco** [Francisco] (*b* Piacenza, *c*1702; *d* Madrid, 3 April 1778). Italian composer of French parentage. In 1727 he succeeded Giacomelli as *maestro di cappella* of the Steccata Church at Parma and from that year until 1733 was *maestro di cappella* to the Duke of Parma, later Charles III of Spain. His first two operas were produced at Venice in 1731 and 1732, and an oratorio was given at Parma in 1733. In 1734 he was appointed a suffragan royal *maestro de capilla* at Madrid and in 1737 coadjutor; from 1734 he was also music teacher of the royal children and from 1738 to 1778 titular *maestro* of the royal chapel and rector of the choir school, writing much sacred music. From 1735 to 1748 he composed six operas (or possibly seven; see Asenjo Barbieri) mounted with utmost splendour, the last two in collaboration with other Italians in Madrid;

in 1750 he had a serenata staged there. He was extremely handsome and affable, and his charm and compatibility permitted his serving with unvarying satisfaction monarchs as diverse as Philip V, Ferdinand VI, Charles III and their consorts. His other assets included a fine tenor voice and an ability to play both the violin and the harpsichord. He married a Frenchwoman in 1738 and had four daughters.

His extant stage works are in the vein of Leo, Durante, Lotti, Galuppi and Pergolesi – these being among the 19 Italian composers whose works he recommended acquiring after a fire in 1734 had destroyed the archive in the old Royal Alcázar at Madrid.

three-act opere serie, performed in Madrid, unless otherwise stated

Venere placata (C. N. Stampa), Venice, Grimani di S Samuele, Ascension 1731, frags. *D-Bds*

Nino (I. Zanelli and V. Cassani), Venice, S Angelo, carn. 1732

La Cautela en la amistad y el robo de las Sabinas (2, J. de Agramont y Toledo), Caños del Peral, sum. 1735 [sung by women only, drawn from the Cruz and Príncipe companies]

Alessandro nelle Indie (P. Metastasio, trans. G. Val), Buen Retiro, 9 May 1738

Farnace, Buen Retiro, 4 Nov 1739

Achille in Sciro (Metastasio), Buen Retiro, 8 Dec 1744

La clemenza di Tito [Act 1] (I. de Luzán y Suelves, after Metastasio), Buen Retiro, carn. 1747 [Act 2 by F. Corradini, Act 3 by G. B. Mele]

Il Polifemo [Act 1] (P. Rolli), Buen Retiro, carn. 1748 [Act 2 by Corradini, Act 3 by Mele]

Doubtful: Romula, Buen Retiro, 19 Aug 1735; Polifemo, 20 Oct 1739

*

ES ('Courcelle, Francesco'; J. Subirá)

L. Carmena y Millán: *Crónica de la ópera italiana en Madrid desde el año 1738 hasta nuestros días* (Madrid, 1878), pp.xxxvi, 10–13 [lists singers]

O. G. T. Sonneck: *Catalogue of Opera Librettos* (Washington DC, 1914), i, 796, 1124

E. Cotarelo y Mori: *Orígenes y establecimiento de la ópera en España hasta 1800* (Madrid, 1917)

J. Subirá: *La música en la Casa de Alba* (Madrid, 1927), 227ff

——: *El teatro del Real palacio* (Madrid, 1950), 24, 43

N. A. Solar-Quintes: 'El compositor Francisco Courcelle: nueva documentación para su biografia', *AnM*, vi (1951), 179–204

F. Asenjo Barbieri: *Biografías y documentos sobre músicos españoles (Legado Barbieri)*, ed. E. Casares (Madrid, 1986), 156–7

ROBERT STEVENSON

Corsi, Emilia (*b* Lisbon, 21 Jan 1870; *d* Bologna, 17 Sept 1927). Italian soprano. She studied with her father, the tenor Achille Corsi, and made her début at Bologna in 1887 as Micaëla (*Carmen*). After singing at Parma, Palermo and Bergamo, she was engaged at La Scala, where she sang Lisa in the first Milan performance of Tchaikovsky's *The Queen of Spades* (1906) and also Agathe (*Der Freischütz*). She appeared in Russia and at Warsaw sang Camille in Hérold's *Zampa* (1906). Having started as a light, coloratura soprano, she graduated to heavier roles such as La Gioconda, Puccini's Manon Lescaut and Sieglinde. She retired in 1910.

ELIZABETH FORBES

Corsi, Giovanni (*b* Verona, 1822; *d* Monza, 4 April 1890). Italian baritone. He made his début in 1844 at Milan as Dandini (*La Cenerentola*) and from 1847 sang regularly at La Scala. He also appeared at the Théâtre Italien, Paris, where he sang Rigoletto in the first Paris performance of Verdi's opera (1857). His younger brother, Achille Corsi (*b* Legnano, 1840; *d* Bologna, 15 April 1906), was a tenor who made his début at La Scala in 1859 as Arvino (*I Lombardi*) and sang until 1882, specializing in Rossini roles.

ELIZABETH FORBES

Corsi, Jacopo (*b* Florence, 1561; *d* Florence, 29 Dec 1602). Italian patron of opera. He belonged to an up-and-coming Florentine family whose ventures in banking, wool and silk made him one of the wealthiest merchants in the city. A renowned patron of the arts, particularly music, he maintained a salon which was a focal point of Florentine artistic endeavour in the 1590s. His interests were prompted by the perceived requirements of noble behaviour and by the need to make his mark in Florentine society. Both factors clearly influenced the two main musical works to emerge from his patronage, *Dafne* (1598) and *Euridice* (1600), the first operas.

Corsi was taught the lute, keyboard, singing and composition by Luca Bati and Cristofano Malvezzi. He was also associated with Giovanni de' Bardi, whose 'Camerata' motivated musical debate in Florence in the 1580s, and with Bardi's protégé Vincenzo Galilei. Clearly Corsi knew Bardi's and Galilei's views on the defects of modern music and on the need to revive classical practice, and he supported a singer-composer associated with Bardi, Giulio Caccini. When Bardi left Florence for Rome in 1592, Corsi became the leading music patron in the city; he played host to numerous visiting artists, poets and musicians (including Torquato Tasso, Gabriello Chiabrera, Carlo Gesualdo and Alfonso Fontanelli). He also developed a close relationship with the poet Ottavio Rinuccini and the musician Jacopo Peri, both of whom joined Corsi in business. Doubtless he encouraged Rinuccini's attempts to revive the performance of classical drama (with *Dafne*): Corsi began composing the music before approaching Peri (some survives in *B-Bc* and *I-Fn*). The opera was performed privately in Carnival 1598, and before the court in the carnivals of 1599 and 1600.

Corsi's provision of court entertainments dated back to the mid-1580s; he often contributed to Medici wedding festivities and other civic entertainments, presumably to gain favour with the Grand Duke. He also played a major part in the diplomatic negotiations for the marriage of Maria de' Medici to Henri IV of France. In return, Corsi was invited to provide a second collaboration between Rinuccini and Peri, *Euridice*, for the wedding festivities in 1600; he played the harpsichord in the performance on 6 October. The prestige to be gained from the opera was doubtless enhanced by its veneer of humanist respectability.

Euridice was not a success: a private entertainment was ill suited to princely modes of celebration. Moreover, Corsi must have known that the notion of reviving antiquity was spurious: *Dafne* and *Euridice* are pastorals, not tragedies. But this is not to deny his significant contribution to the arts in Florence. His untimely death was much lamented and his fame as a patron was recalled in dedications through the early 17th century.

*

N. Pirrotta: 'Temperaments and Tendencies in the Florentine Camerata', *MQ*, xl (1954), 169–89; repr. in N. Pirrotta: *Music and Culture in Italy from the Middle Ages to the Baroque* (Cambridge, MA, 1984), 217–34

W. V. Porter: 'Peri and Corsi's *Dafne*: Some New Discoveries and Observations', *JAMS*, xviii (1965), 170–96

F. W. Sternfeld: 'The First Printed Opera Libretto', *ML*, lix (1978), 121–38

T. Carter: 'Music and Patronage in Late Sixteenth-Century Florence: the Case of Jacopo Corsi (1561–1602)', *I Tatti Studies: Essays in the Renaissance*, i (1985), 57–104

TIM CARTER

Cortes [Kortes], **Sergey** (*b* San Antonio, Chile, 1935). Belorussian composer. He was brought up in Argentina in the family of his mother and studied composition with Y. Fisher, a graduate of the St Petersburg Conservatory. Since 1955 he has lived in Minsk. After graduating from the Belorussian Conservatory he worked as director of music in theatres, as principal musical editor of the film studio Belorusfilm, then as director of the opera theatre. Most of his compositions are vocal works, including monologues, romances and oratorios. Characteristic of his music is recitative-like melody reminiscent of the narrative style of the ballad.

The libretto, by Viktor Khalip, of his opera *Giordano Bruno* (1977, Belorussian Theatre of Opera and Ballet) is based on the trial of the philosopher and on known events from the last years of his life. The dramatic construction (prologue, two acts – consisting of six scenes – and epilogue) relates to the 'theatre of representation', in which action is combined with discussion of it – a continuation of the tradition of the opera-oratorios of Stravinsky, Milhaud and Honegger. In the musical language there are aleatory elements, 12-note writing and polytonality as well as diatonic music, and links with Orff and Prokofiev can be detected. Better known is Cortes's second opera, *Matushka Kurazh* ('Mother Courage'; 2, S. Shteyn and V. Khalip, after B. Brecht; Kaunas Musical Theatre, Lithuania, 1982). The subject matter and song texts of Brecht's play are retained in the opera, but sometimes their placing is altered. The image of Mother Courage as a tradeswoman is softened and made more humane by Cortes. At the same time, the universal significance of the work is strengthened: concrete events are projected into the fate of humanity, which is suffering from the horrors of war. It is natural, therefore, that alongside the simplicity of style, both in the plot and in the music (which features rhyming couplets in the songs, orchestral doubling and ostinato), Cortes also uses contrapuntal techniques, colouristically differentiated orchestration, tone clusters, and aleatory and symphonic episodes. The work was also performed (1984) as *Markitantka* ('The Camp-Follower') at the Moldavian Theatre of Opera and Ballet in Kishineu.

MARINA NEST'YEVA

Cortese, Luigi [Louis] (*b* Genoa, 19 Nov 1899; *d* Genoa, 10 June 1976). Italian composer. He studied in Genoa, graduated in mathematics (1924) and then pursued his music studies in Paris under Gédalge and in Rome under Casella. From 1939 he held various posts in Genoa, ending (1951–64) as director of the Liceo Musicale; he was also active as a lecturer, pianist, private teacher and critic. It was some time before he found an individual style, after wavering between French influences (his mother was French) and various aspects of Casella. Even the dramatic oratorio *David* (1936–8), his first major composition and one of his finest achievements, is still eclectic: the plaintive, wayward chromaticisms suggest parallels with Martin, and the dissonances are at times fierce, but beneath the chromatic surface there is a more conservative substratum, sometimes relatable to Pizzetti. Thereafter his basic style remained unchanged, gaining in consistency and refinement of detail but sometimes at the expense of imaginative tension. *Prometeo*, for instance, is similar to *David* in idiom, but dramatically static and more impressive orchestrally than vocally (some of its best parts have been gathered into a powerful orchestral suite, 1947); while *La notte veneziana*, in keeping with its more sentimental subject matter, 'softens' the oratorio's style, introducing lyrical elements which at times recall Puccini. On the whole, opera was not an area in which Cortese gave of his best, and the uniformly slow and melancholy *Le notti bianche* proved even less successful than its predecessors.

Prometeo op.18, 1941–7 (3, L. Cortese, after Aeschylus), Bergamo, Novità, 22 Sept 1951

La notte veneziana op.32, *c*1953–5 (radio op, 2, G. Pacuvio, after A. de Musset), RAI, 20 Nov 1955; stage, Genoa, Politeama Margherita, 6 May 1972

Le notti bianche op.51, 1968–70 (2, Cortese, after F. M. Dostoyevsky: *White Nights*), Milan, Piccola Scala, 30 April 1973

*

R. Malipiero: 'Lettera da Bergamo', *RaM*, xxi (1951), 316–19 [on *Prometeo*]

M. Pincherle: 'Musiciens italiens à Gênes et à Paris', *Nouvelles littéraires*, no.1444 (1955), 8 [partly on *Prometeo*]

E. Frassoni: 'Sorridente filosofia lagunare', *La notte veneziana* (Genoa, Teatro Comunale, 1971–2) [programme book]

D. de' Paoli: 'Da Genova – "Il castello di Barbablu" di Béla Bartók e "La notte veneziana" di Luigi Cortese', *NRMI*, vi (1972), 247–8

——: 'Le notti bianche', *Teatro alla Scala: la stagione lirica 1972–3*, 709–11 [programme book]

——: 'Luigi Cortese (1899–1976)', *NRMI*, xi (1977), 220–31

——: 'Ricordo di Luigi Cortese', *Notiziario delle edizioni Suvini Zerboni*, no.5 (1977), 5–16

R. Iovino and D. Prefumo: *Luigi Cortese: la vita e l'opera* (Genoa, 1979) [esp. 'Le opere per il teatro', 91–105]

JOHN C. G. WATERHOUSE

Cortez, Viorica (*b* Bucium, Iaşi district, 26 Dec 1935). Romanian mezzo-soprano. She was trained at the Iaşi and Bucharest conservatories and sang with the Bucharest Opera until 1970. A mezzo-soprano of wide compass with a strong, colourful tone, she has won praise for her unaffected yet dramatic portrayal of Carmen (Covent Garden from 1968, La Scala, Metropolitan, Chicago). Her other roles include Amneris and Eboli, Venus and Kundry, Delilah, Charlotte and Stravinsky's Jocasta; she sang Dulcinée in the new production (1974) of Massenet's *Don Quichotte* at the Opéra. In 1990 she sang Gertrude (Thomas' *Hamlet*) at Turin and created the title role of Tutino's *La Lupa* at Livorno.

VIOREL COSMA

Cortis [Corts], **Antonio** (*b* on board ship between Oran, Algeria, and Altea, 12 Aug 1891; *d* Valencia, 2 April 1952). Spanish tenor. He studied in Madrid, where he sang in the chorus at the Teatro Real. At first he sang minor roles, then began to assume leading roles (Cavaradossi, Don José and Turiddu) in Barcelona and Valencia. In 1917 he sang for the first time in South America, where his roles included Beppe (*Pagliacci*). He was a regular guest at the Teatro Costanzi, Rome (1920–23); he also appeared in Milan, Naples and Turin, and in 1927 sang Radames at the Verona Arena. He sang at Chicago (1924–32) and San Francisco (1924–6). His roles in the USA included Edgardo, Manrico, Radames, Chénier, Canio, Cavaradossi, Des Grieux (*Manon Lescaut*), Enzo (*La Gioconda*) and Don José. His only Covent Garden season was in 1931 when he sang Calaf, and Hippolytus in Romani's *Fedra* opposite Ponselle. After 1935 he sang only in Spain, making his last stage appearance in 1951 at Saragossa as Cavaradossi. His voice was similar to Caruso's and he was known as the 'Caruso espagnol'.

'Antonio Cortis', *Record Collector*, xx (1971–2), 53–70 [with discography by J. Léon and J. Dennis] HAROLD ROSENTHAL/R

Cortolezis, Fritz (*b* Passau, Lower Bavaria, 21 Feb 1878; *d* Bad Aibling, 13 March 1934). German composer. After studying with Thuille and others in Munich, from 1903 to 1912 he held a number of positions, mainly as choirmaster, in various opera houses: Schwerin, the Nationaltheater in Berlin, Regensburg, Munich, and the Kurfürstenoper in Berlin. He became general music director at the Hoftheater in Karlsruhe in 1913, and from 1925 to 1928 he conducted opera in Breslau. Cortolezis was notably responsible for many early performances of Strauss's operas. Selections from three light operas are among his published works.

Rosemarie (Operette, 3), Bremen, 1919
Das verfemte Lochen (komische Oper, 3, B. Dovsky), Rostock, 1924
Der verlorene Gulden (Spieloper, 3, Dovsky), Breslau, 1928
Das kristallene Herz, 1934 (Märchenoper), inc.

*

MGG (A. Ott)
F. Cortolezis: 'Gedanken über eine stilgerechte Aufführung des "Fidelio"', *NBJb*, iii (1927), 91–102
W. Zentner: 'Todesfälle: Fritz Cortolezis', *ZfM*, ci (1934), 464–6
WILLIAM D. GUDGER

Cortona, Il. *See* CECCHI, DOMENICO.

Cortoni, Arcangelo (*fl* 1756–77). Italian tenor. He made his *opera seria* début at Bologna in May 1756, but did not then begin a sustained career. During the period 1760–68 he was with Jommelli's company at Stuttgart (except for 1762, when he sang in Florence, Venice and Genoa). From autumn 1769 he appeared in major Italian theatres, including four seasons at the S Carlo, Naples, where he sang in all three of Jommelli's late Neapolitan operas. He is not found after 1777. Jommelli praised his technical skill (as did Burney), mentioning particularly his bravura abilities; but he also commanded a grand, energetic style of declamation and, as shown by the long solo final scene of Jommelli's *Ifigenia in Tauride*, must have been a considerable actor.
DENNIS LIBBY

Coruña, La [Corunna]. *See* LA CORUÑA.

Cosa rara, Una [*Una cosa rara, o sia Bellezza ed onestà* ('A Rare Thing, or Beauty and Honesty')]. *Dramma giocoso* in two acts by VICENTE MARTÍN Y SOLER to a libretto by LORENZO DA PONTE after Luis Vélez de Guevara's play *La luna della Sierra*; Vienna, Burgtheater, 17 November 1786.

A royal hunting party, consisting of Queen Isabella (soprano), Prince Giovanni (tenor) and the equerry Corrado (tenor), arrives at a village in the mountains and is drawn into a local crisis. The marriage plans of Lilla (soprano), the village beauty, and Lubino (bass), a mountaineer, are thwarted by Tita (bass), Lilla's brother, who wants to marry her forcibly to the mayor Lisargo (bass). Lilla beseeches the Queen for help, but before she can intervene, Ghita (soprano), Tita's betrothed, prevails upon him to abandon his unhappy scheme. The Queen commands that the double wedding take place that very day. Meanwhile the Prince, who has earlier pleaded his love to Lilla, renews his wooing; he is aided by Corrado, who is secretly wooing her himself. They harass the two couples with serenades, disguises and threats. Despite Lilla's constancy, the furious and jealous husband is driven to appeal to the Queen for help. Corrado is punished, after which the Queen and Prince depart amid rejoicing.

For his second collaboration with Martín, Da Ponte chose a Spanish subject in honour of the composer and his patron, the wife of the Spanish ambassador, who supplied authentic folk costumes for the production. Da Ponte generally followed his model, a rural *comedia* dating from after 1614, in plot and structure, while compressing three acts into two. He retained the unusual positioning of a wedding at the end of Act 1 (instead of at the end of the drama), and also followed Vélez by incorporating popular Spanish songs into the drama, providing texts for Martín to set in a Spanish folk idiom (the Prince's serenade, with its unusual syncopated rhythms and three-bar phrases, and the

'Una cosa rara' (Martín y Soler): title page of the German version, 'Lilla, oder Schönheit und Tugend' (Munich: M. Götz, c1790)

seguidilla, with its obbligato mandolin). From the play's juxtaposed dramatic modes (historical, farcical, pastoral), Da Ponte selected the pastoral and made it dominant in the libretto. Accordingly, he reduced the sharp contrast among Vélez's characters: Queen Isabella, while still recognizable as the popular 15th-century monarch, appears without her historical trappings (retinue, ceremonial scene), the comic shepherd couple lose their boorishness, the Prince takes on some of Corrado's power and Corrado takes on some of the Prince's innocence. Lilla and Lubino remain unchanged as the ideal shepherd couple.

The original singers, familiar from Mozart's Da Ponte operas, included Nancy Storace (Lilla), Stefano Mandini (Lubino), Francesco Benucci (Tita), Dorothea Bussani (Ghita), Luisa Laschi (Queen Isabella), Vincenzo Calvesi (Prince Giovanni), Michael Kelly (Corrado) and Johann Hoffmann (Lisargo).

The opera was so popular that it 'almost threw the city into a frenzy'; 'everyone praised such grace, such sweetness, such melody'. Mozart quoted it in the *Don Giovanni* supper scene. A good example of what so enchanted audiences is Lilla and Lubino's reconciliation duet, 'Pace, caro mio sposo'; according to Kelly, it was 'completely the rage all over Ireland, England, and Scotland for many, many years'. It typifies Martín's style with its melody-dominated texture, its periodic phrasing and its pastoral 6/8 *andante sostenuto* metre. The voices take the melody in turn and finish in parallel 3rds. Its charm moved the Viennese theatregoer Zinzendorf to declare it too erotic for young people. A legend persisted for years that the waltz originated in the opera's final scene. But on the contrary, the warm response of the already waltz-crazed Viennese to the 3/8 contredanse passage in the finale probably prompted its repetition at the end (in a revision), so that the two shepherd couples who had danced the seguidilla concluded the opera by dancing a waltz. DOROTHEA LINK

Così fan tutte [*Così fan tutte, ossia La scuola degli amanti* ('All Women do the Same, or The School for Lovers')]. *Opera buffa* in two acts, K588, by WOLFGANG AMADEUS MOZART to a libretto by LORENZO DA PONTE; Vienna, Burgtheater, 26 January 1790.

Fiordiligi	*ladies from Ferrara,*	soprano
Dorabella	*sisters, living in Naples*	soprano
Guglielmo	*an officer, Fiordiligi's lover*	bass
Ferrando	*an officer, Dorabella's lover*	tenor
Despina	*maidservant to the sisters*	soprano
Don Alfonso	*an old philosopher*	bass

Soldiers, servants, sailors, wedding guests

Setting Naples, in the 18th century

Così fan tutte was commissioned following the successful revival of *Le nozze di Figaro* in August 1789. The libretto is original; there is no hard evidence for the theory that it was based on a recent Viennese scandal. It has a mythological and literary ancestry in the Procris story, and in Boccaccio, Shakespeare (*Cymbeline*) and Cervantes, all of whom anticipate elements of the plot: the trial of female constancy and the wager. The use of two couples may derive from Marivaux (Steptoe 1981).

Così fan tutte was rehearsed at Mozart's apartment on 31 December, and in January with Haydn present. It received five performances before the death of Joseph II on 20 February closed the theatres; five more followed from June to August. There is little information about its genesis or reception. The cast was Da Ponte's mistress, Adriana Ferrarese del Bene (Fiordiligi), Susanna in the 1789 *Figaro*; Louise Villeneuve (Dorabella); Vincenzo Calvesi (Ferrando); and three stalwarts from the 1786 *Figaro*, Dorotea Bussani (Despina), Francesco Benucci (Guglielmo) and Francesco Bussani (Alfonso).

Performances followed in 1791 in Prague, Leipzig and Dresden, and in German in Frankfurt (as *Liebe und Versuchung*), Mainz and Amsterdam. At Leipzig in 1794 and in other centres it appeared as *Weibertreue, oder Die Mädchen sind von Flandern*, translated by C. F. Bretzner, author of the source of *Die Entführung aus dem Serail*. Numerous German productions followed throughout the 19th century, but no opera of Mozart received such frequent 'improvement' or so many alternative titles besides the standard German *So machen es alle*. The alleged immorality of the libretto encouraged such treatment; some adaptations had the ladies learn of the plot and avenge themselves by turning the tables on their lovers. Critical opinion suggested that it was one of Mozart's weaker pieces, and the music appeared in pasticcios or with a completely different story; as late as 1909 in Dresden a new libretto was based on Calderón de la Barca by K. Scheidemantel. Today the opera is given in its original form, even with the restoration of Mozart's own cuts. *Così* was the second opera performed at Glyndebourne (1934) and productions since World War II are too numerous to mention; it is by now as much a repertory piece as the other Mozart-Da Ponte operas.

The short introduction to the overture concludes with a motto, a double cadence of striking simplicity (*piano*, interrupted, then *forte*, perfect), later sung to the words of the title. The sonata-form Presto mockingly tosses a figure among the woodwind, its cadence taken from Basilio's line 'Così fan tutte le belle' (*Figaro*, the Act 1 trio, 'Cosa sento!'). The motto reappears just before the end.

ACT 1 *A coffee-house* Ferrando and Guglielmo proclaim the virtues of the sisters Dorabella and Fiordiligi, to whom they are betrothed; Alfonso is sceptical (trio, 'La mia Dorabella'). The young men prepare to defend the ladies' honour with swords, but the diatonic brilliance of music shared by all three argues no great discord. Alfonso declines to fight, but calls them simpletons to trust female constancy: a faithful woman is like a phoenix; all believe in it but none has seen it (his mocking *pianissimo* unison cadence resembles the motto). The others insist that the phoenix is Dorabella/Fiordiligi (trio, 'È la fede delle femmine'). Alfonso wagers 100 zecchini that fidelity will not endure a day of the lovers' absence; he will prove it if they promise to obey him while wooing each other's betrothed in disguise. Ferrando plans to spend his winnings on a serenade, Guglielmo (the first division between them) on a meal; Alfonso listens politely (trio, 'Una bella serenata'). An extended orchestral coda closes a scene of purely *buffo* electricity.

A garden by the sea [morning] The girls sing rapturously of their lovers (duet, 'Ah guarda sorella'); Dorabella (surprisingly, in view of the sequel) touches a note of melancholy before they launch into voluptuous coloratura in 3rds, united in loving the idea of loving.

Autograph score of Mozart's 'Così fan tutte' (beginning of Act 1 scene i), composed 1789

Alfonso appears, the prolonged F minor cadences of his tiny aria ('Vorrei dir') choking back the awful news: their lovers are to leave for active service. The men take solemn leave with only hints at lyricism (quintet, 'Sento, o Dio'). The girls' agitation is coloured by the dominant minor; Alfonso quells any premature delight at this evidence of love. Ferrando's lyricism (to a motif from the trio, 'Una bella serenata') now matches the girls'; Guglielmo sings with Alfonso (this inevitable consequence of differences in tessitura continually invites differentiation of character). The girls declare they will die; in a prepared speech (duettino, 'Al fato dan legge') the men promise to return. A march is heard (chorus, 'Bella vita militar'). They embrace, promising a daily letter, their rapturous indulgence in misery (particularly intense in the melodic line, taken by Fiordiligi) counterpointed by Alfonso's efforts not to laugh (quintet, 'Di scrivermi ogni giorno'). The men embark (reprise of the chorus); Alfonso joins a moving prayer for their safety (trio, 'Soave sia il vento'), the orchestra evocative yet sensuous. Alfonso prepares for action (arioso); 'He ploughs the waves, sows in sand, traps the wind in a net, who trusts the heart of a woman'.

A furnished room Despina has prepared the ladies' chocolate and is sampling it when they burst in. Dorabella explains their despair, but her extravagant grief leaves her barely coherent (obbligato recitative and the first real aria, 'Smanie implacabili'). Despina cannot take them seriously; surely they can find other lovers. In the teeth of their protests she inverts Alfonso's creed (aria, 'In uomini'): men, especially soldiers, are not expected to be faithful; women should also use love to enjoy themselves. Alfonso bribes Despina to assist him, without revealing the plot. The men enter as 'Albanians', their bizarre disguise impenetrable even to the sharp-witted Despina (sextet, 'Alla bella Despinetta'). Recovering from laughter, she helps them to plead with the ladies (Alfonso being concealed); they are rejected in a furious Allegro. Alfonso claims them as his friends, but after the men's voices unite, turning recitative towards arioso, Fiordiligi articulates her constancy in a powerful recitative and aria ('Come scoglio'); she stands firm as a rock in tempestuous seas. The three sections grow in brilliance and versatility; near the start, after leaps of a 10th and 12th, she ascends majestically over two octaves (the total range is *a-c‴*); near the end she takes the bass line. Guglielmo's patter-song in praise of his own appearance (especially the moustaches) finds no favour ('Non siate ritrosi'; there is a longer, rejected alternative, 'Rivolgete a lui lo sguardo', K584). As the outraged girls depart, the men bubble with delight (trio, 'E voi ridete?'), a brilliant hocket covering Alfonso's insistence that the more the girls protest, the more sure is their fall. Guglielmo wonders when they can get lunch; Ferrando enjoys the atmosphere of love ('Un' aura amorosa'), muted violins and clarinets supporting his ardently extended line.

The garden [afternoon] At the beginning of the finale, the girls unwittingly share Ferrando's mood of longing, spinning a tender D major melody to a gently ironic rococo decoration of flutes and bassoons. How their fate has changed! Their sighs are displaced by fear when the men rush in drinking poison, to music (in G minor) suddenly suggestive of tragic violence. Alfonso and Despina go for help, instructing the ladies to nurse the men, who are thoroughly enjoying themselves; yet minor modes prevail as never before in Mozart's finales. Despina, to a pompous G major minuet, appears disguised as the doctor, invoking Mesmer as she magnetizes out the poison. The key abruptly changes to B♭: the men profess to believe they are in paradise. In the final Allegro (in D) the men request a kiss and are again rebuffed.

ACT 2 *A room* Despina tries to persuade her shocked employers that there is no harm in a little flirtation. In Mozart's slyest *buffo* soprano aria ('Una donna a quindici anni'), she explains that a young girl who knows the arts of attracting men can have them at her mercy. The girls agree that there can be no harm in a little light flirtation, and they select partners (duet, 'Prenderò quel brunettino'). Dorabella will take the brown-haired one (Guglielmo), Fiordiligi the blond (Ferrando;

thus they fall in with the men's plan); and they prepare to amuse themselves.

Furnished garden by the sea [early evening] The serenade on wind instruments, repeated by the lovers and chorus ('Secondate, aurette amiche'), is a prayer for success in love. The four meet but are tongue-tied; Alfonso and Despina give a lesson in etiquette (quartet, the ladies silent, 'La mano a me date'), and join their hands. The couples prepare to walk round the garden. Guglielmo is all too successful in winning Dorabella's heart and a mark of her favour, replacing Ferrando's portrait by his own gift, a pendant heart (duet, 'Il core vi dono'). The gently bantering 3/8, in F major, matches Dorabella's innocent flirtatiousness; Gugliemo can hardly believe his success, but falls comfortably in with her mood. Fiordiligi rushes in, pursued by Ferrando: she has seen in him temptation, a serpent, a basilisk; he is stealing her peace. He protests that he wants only her happiness and asks for a kindly glance, noting that she looks at him and sighs. Her lovely soul will not long resist his pleading; otherwise her cruelty will kill him ('Ah lo veggio quell'anima bella'). In this lightly flowing rondo, as in 'Un'aura amorosa', woodwind are added only at the reprise; the ending achieves an unexpected intensity. This aria is traditionally omitted, but without it Ferrando's exit is inexplicable. Fiordiligi wrestles with her conscience, her obbligato recitative ('Ei parte') running a gamut of feeling while traversing tonal space from B♭ to E. In her deeply expressive rondò ('Per pietà, ben mio') the elaborate wind parts (notably the horns) have an *opera seria* formality; sheer musical beauty articulates her cry of despair, as she asks her absent lover's forgiveness. There has been no simple recitative since before the duet for Guglielmo and Dorabella; the symmetry of the couplings breaks down in over 400 bars of continuous music.

Dorabella's fickleness rouses Ferrando to fury (obbligato recitative, 'Il mio ritratto! Ah perfida!'). Guglielmo tries to console him by adopting Alfonso's philosophy (aria, 'Donne mie la fate a tanti'); he is fond of women and defends their honour, but their little habit of deceiving men is reprehensible. The restless perpetual motion conveys Guglielmo's confidence that the tragedy will not befall him. Ferrando's feelings are in turmoil (obbligato recitative, 'In qual fiero contrasto'). An obsessive orchestral figure projects shame ('Alfonso! how you will laugh!') and anger ('I will cut the wretch out of my heart') beyond the decorum of comedy. In a cavatina ('Tradito, schernito') he denounces Dorabella's treachery but admits (clarinets entering as C minor turns to E♭ major) that he still loves her. Alfonso and Guglielmo overhear the reprise in which the E♭ melody recurs in C, oboes replacing clarinets: this new instrumental colour (his previous arias used no oboes) may be prophetic. His pride piqued, he agrees to a further attack on Fiordiligi.

A room, with several doors, a mirror, and a table Despina praises Dorabella's good sense; Dorabella answers Fiordiligi's protests in a graceful 6/8 aria ('È amore un ladroncello') which, despite its sophisticated instrumentation, shows her conversion to Despina's easy virtue; love is a thief, a serpent, but if you let him have his way, he brings delight. Alone, Fiordiligi resolves to repel her new suitor; sadistically observed by the men, she prepares to join her lover at the front, and orders Despina to bring his uniform. She launches an aria ('Fra gli amplessi'), but as she quickens the tempo from Adagio Ferrando joins in, changing the dominant (E) from major to minor. Her anguished plea (Allegro) moves to C major, with a striking allusion to Ferrando's first phrase in the Act 1 trio for the men, 'Una bella serenata'. (The keys and key-scheme parallel the seduction trio of *Don Giovanni.*) Ferrando's lyricism outdoes hers. The note of true ardour is intensified when the acceleration of tempo is halted by a Larghetto (back in A); it is hard not to believe that Ferrando is genuine. Despite a high *a″* on 'crudel', Fiordiligi's responses are tremulous; the solo oboe rises above her, speaks for her, as she admits defeat ('hai vinto'). The fourth (Andante) section of this greatest of Mozart's duets combines their voices in an intimacy never vouchsafed to Dorabella and Guglielmo. The latter is enraged; Ferrando is ironic; Alfonso tells them their only revenge is to marry their 'plucked crows'. Women are always accused of fickleness, but he forgives them; they are not responsible for their own nature ('Tutti accusan le donne'). All three sing the motto from the overture: 'Così fan tutte'.

A reception room prepared for a wedding An Allegro, resembling the opera's opening number, begins the finale, as Despina orders the servants to a prepare a feast (brief choral response) and Alfonso applauds their work. The chorus greets the couples; in their carefree response the accident of casting matches the composer's dramatic insight by bringing Fiordiligi and Ferrando together in expansive coloratura. With Dorabella they sing the toast, a ravishing canon in A♭; Guglielmo, whose range prevents him from following on, mutters curses. In the strangest of the 3rd-related modulations of Mozart's finales, Alfonso enters in E major, with Despina disguised as a notary. Coughing formally, she reads the marriage contract; the ladies sign it. But then the Act 1 march in D, associated with the officers' departure, is heard. Consternation: their lovers are returning (this peripeteia moves from D to E♭). The Albanians are hidden, and the men reappear jauntily as their old selves, pretend puzzlement at their reception, drag out the notary, revealed as Despina, and find the marriage contract: indignation, confession, blame (on Alfonso), threats of revenge. Returning half-changed into Albanians, Ferrando greets Fiordiligi (apparently quoting earlier music subsequently abandoned), Guglielmo greets Dorabella (quoting their love duet), and both address the flabbergasted Despina as the doctor (quoting the first finale). Alfonso calms them down; the ladies beg pardon; the men condescend to forgive, and all agree to follow Alfonso's idea of reason: to laugh when there is cause to weep, and so find equilibrium.

* * *

Only the present century has taken a serious interest in *Così fan tutte*. At first it was considered a heartless farce clothed in miraculous music, a view supported by its obvious artificiality (the lovers' disguises, the 24-hour time-scale). A number of cuts, particularly of Act 2 arias, became customary. Recently directors and critics have sought deeper meanings, and even questioned the restoration of the original pairing of lovers, which it seems legitimate to assume from the conventionality of the conclusion but which is not specified in the libretto or clarified by the music.

Così has been seen as revealing a dark side to the Enlightenment, an anti-feminist sadism (Ford 1991). Yet by any showing the most admirable character is Fiordiligi. The girls develop more than the men. Dorabella at least learns to understand her own lightness;

and 'Fra gli amplessi' suggests that Fiordiligi has matured through learning the power of sexuality. There is little sign that Guglielmo learns anything in the school for lovers, even that those who set traps deserve to get caught, although his vanity is wounded as deeply as his purse. Ferrando, however, comes to live as intensely as Fiordiligi, and may appear to have fallen in love with her. To suggest that they should marry (leaving Guglielmo for Dorabella) is, however, still less satisfactory than reversion to the original pairings. The conclusion represents not a solution but a way of bringing the action to a close with an artificiality so evident that no happy outcome can be predicted. The music creates this enigma, but cannot solve it.

By standards other than Mozart's, the instrumentation in *Così* would be of novel richness. The invention of B♭ trumpets allows their substitution for horns in 'Come scoglio' and 'Ah lo veggio', divorced from the timpani; three other numbers also use trumpets without horns. The resourceful use of woodwind, application of string mutes, and exploration of a wider than usual range of keys and key relations, creates an unprecedentedly voluptuous colouring (E major and A♭ major are juxtaposed in the second finale, the former used in three other numbers, a concentration unusual in Mozart).

Much of the style of *Così* has been attributed to parody, but a stylistic mixture had long been a feature of *opera buffa*. Guglielmo sings pure *buffo* arias, but all Ferrando's strike serious notes reflected in their variety of form. The girls' first arias overplay feelings which will not endure: Dorabella's prolonged cadences in 'Smanie implacabili' recall Alfonso's mock-seriousness in 'Vorrei dir'. 'Come scoglio' is sometimes considered pure parody, Fiordiligi's second aria 'Per pietà' essentially serious; yet the latter has equally wide leaps and even more florid instrumentation, the differences in perception of them being explicable by the fact that one administers a rebuff to the 'Albanian' strangers, and the other, following a disturbing attack on her loyalty to Guglielmo, is an internal monologue.

There are fewer arias in *Così* than in the other Da Ponte operas, but they are correspondingly more important in unfolding the inner drama. The increased number of ensembles is balanced by the brevity of several of them, not only the sparkling *buffo* trios for the men but also 'Soave sia il vento', a gem in which even Alfonso appears moved; it bids farewell to innocence as well as to the lovers. There is a marked increase in the amount of obbligato recitative, which with the tone of some of the arias (notably Fiordiligi's) brings *Così* closer to *opera seria* than the other Da Ponte operas.

Così fan tutte is likely to remain a disturbing experience because of, not despite, its aesthetic attractions. The libretto may be Da Ponte's most original, but its superb pacing does not mask its potential triviality. Mozart found in it ways to seek out hitherto unplumbed depths in the human psyche, making the uncut whole, for an increasing number of commentators, the profoundest of his Italian comedies. JULIAN RUSHTON

Cossack beyond the Danube, A. Opera by S. S. Gulak-Artemovsky; *see* *ZAPOROZHETS ZA DUNAYEM*.

Cosselli, Domenico (*b* Parma, 27 May 1801; *d* Marano, nr Parma, 9 Nov 1855). Italian baritone. After studying in Parma he joined the chorus of the Teatro Ducale there in 1820. By 1823 he was singing leading roles in *Tancredi* and *La Cenerentola*, and he became a Rossini specialist. He appeared at all the chief Italian theatres, singing in *Le comte Ory*, *Zelmira* and *Semiramide*. He created roles in several operas by Donizetti: Olivo in *Olivo e Pasquale* (1827, Rome), Azzo in *Parisina* (1833, Florence) and Enrico Ashton in *Lucia di Lammermoor* (1835, Naples). He also sang several Bellini roles: Valdeburgo in *La straniera* (1832, Venice); Ernesto in *Il pirata* and Filippo in *Beatrice di Tenda* (1834, Naples); and Riccardo in *I puritani* (1837, Faenza). In 1843 he retired from the stage. ELIZABETH FORBES

Cossira [Coussival], **Emile** (*b* Orthez, Basses-Pyrénées, 1854; *d* Quebec, Feb 1923). French tenor. He studied in Bordeaux and made his début in 1883 at the Opéra-Comique in Grétry's *Richard Coeur-de-Lion*. From 1888 to 1891 he was engaged at the Paris Opéra, making his début as Fernand in *La favorite*. He also sang Vasco da Gama, Raoul, Romeo, Faust and Edgardo there and created the title role of Saint-Saëns' *Ascanio* (1890). In 1891 he sang at Covent Garden as Romeo, Faust and Don José. Returning in 1894, he took part in the first British performance of Bruneau's *L'attaque du moulin*. The same year he sang Tristan in the first French-language performance of *Tristan und Isolde* at Brussels. In 1896 he sang Walther (*Die Meistersinger*) at Lyons. He had a fine voice and sang with style.

ELIZABETH FORBES

Cossotto, Fiorenza (*b* Crescentino, Vercelli, 22 April 1935). Italian mezzo-soprano. A pupil of Ettore Campogalliani, she made her début in 1957 at La Scala (as Sister Mathilde in the première of *Dialogues des Carmélites*), returning there almost continuously up to the 1972–3 season and appearing in *La favorite*, *Les Huguenots*, *Il trovatore*, *Aida*, *Don Carlos*, *Barbiere*, *Cavalleria rusticana* (Santuzza), *Norma* and other operas. She began her international career in 1958, singing Jane Seymour in Donizetti's *Anna Bolena* at the Wexford Festival. In 1959 she first appeared at Covent Garden (Neris in Cherubini's *Médée* with Callas) and then sang in Barcelona, Vienna, Paris, Chicago (1964) and New York (Amneris at the Metropolitan, 1968), as well as in all the leading Italian theatres. She has a full, resonant voice, particularly clear and easily produced in the top register. Temperamentally suited to the vigorous and forceful utterances of Azucena, Eboli and Amneris, she also shows a special aptitude for coloratura singing, above all as Adalgisa.

GV (G. Gualerzi; R. Celletti) RODOLFO CELLETTI

Cossutta, Carlo (*b* Trieste, 8 May 1932). Italian tenor. He studied in Buenos Aires, making his début at the Teatro Colón in 1958 as Cassio and in 1964 creating the title role of Ginastera's *Don Rodrigo*. In 1964 he made his European début at Covent Garden as the Duke in *Rigoletto*. He returned as Don Carlos, Gabriele Adorno, Manrico and Turiddu and, in 1974, for his first Otello; in these roles his generous volume, ringing tone and sturdy manner won praise. He made his American début in 1963 at Chicago as Abdallo (*Nabucco*) and his Metropolitan début in 1973 as Pollione (*Norma*). He has sung widely in the USA and Europe and in 1974 he sang Radames with La Scala in Moscow.

HAROLD ROSENTHAL/R

Costa, Anna Francesca [Checca] (*fl* 1640–54). Italian soprano, sister of Margherita Costa. One of the most admired singers of the decade 1640–50, she owed much of her fame to her success at the French court between 1645 and 1647. She was in the service of Gian Carlo de' Medici in Florence but in October 1644 left for Paris, where she was warmly welcomed by Cardinal Mazarin and the queen. During Carnival 1645 she sang in an opera performed privately in the Palais Royal and in Carnival 1646 she appeared in Cavalli's *Egisto*. In Paris she also sang in Sacrati's *La finta pazza* (1645) and in Luigi Rossi's *Orfeo* (Eurydice), which had many successful performances between 3 March and 1 May 1647. She returned to Italy with letters of recommendation from Mazarin and was in Rome until 1650, when she went to Florence in the service of Leopoldo and Cardinal Gian Carlo de' Medici. In 1652 she signed the dedication of an opera performed in Bologna (*Ergirodo*, composer unknown) and in 1654 she sang in Florence in Cesti's *Alessandro vincitor di se stesso*. Letters of recommendation dated 1654 indicate that she went again to Paris. She was the mistress of the Prince of Wales (later Charles II) during his Parisian exile.

*

L. Bianconi and T. Walker: 'Dalla *Finta pazza* alla *Veremonda*: storie di Febiarmonici', *RIM*, x (1975), 379–454

M. Mabbett: 'Italian Musicians in Restoration England', *ML*, lxvii (1986), 237–47, esp. 245

PAOLA BESUTTI

Costa, Giovanni Francesco [Gianfrancesco] (*b* Venice, 1711; *d* Venice, Oct or Nov 1772). Italian engraver and stage designer. A pupil of G. Mengozzi Colonna, Costa was famous as an engraver (*Delle delicie del fiume Brenta*). As designer he worked principally in Venice (at the S Angelo, S Benedetto, S Giovanni Grisostomo and S Samuele theatres), though he was also active in Vicenza (Teatro delle Grazie) and Padua (Teatro Obizzi). In Turin (Teatro Regio) he worked either on his own (Gluck's *Poro*, Carnival 1745) or with Giambattista Crosato. In his later years he was assisted by his son Tommaso and other young sons. He designed the Teatro S Benedetto in Venice, with U-shaped auditorium and five tiers of boxes, and the scenery for the inaugural opera (Gioacchino Cocchi's *Zoe*, 26 December 1755) and many others in the following years (including Gian Francesco Majo's *Antigono*, 26 December 1767). The theatre was destroyed by fire on 5 February 1774. No scene drawings by Costa survive, but two series of engravings by him (*Aliquot aedificia* and *Rovine d'archi e templi*), with fantastic compositions of architecture and ruins, show his liking for picturesque landscapes and his interest in classical antiquity. He also wrote an important theoretical treatise, *Elementi di prospettiva* (Venice, 1747).

*

F. Mauroner: 'Gianfrancesco Costa', *Print Collector's Quarterly* (1940), 469–95

M. Viale Ferrero: 'Scenografia', *Mostra del barocco piemontese* (Turin, 1963), i, 28 [exhibition catalogue]

M. T. Muraro: 'Teatro di San Benedetto', *I teatri pubblici di Venezia (secoli XVII-XVIII)* (Venice, 1971), 149–50 [exhibition catalogue]

M. Viale Ferrero: 'Appunti di scenografia settecentesca in margine a rappresentazioni di opere in musica di Gluck e balli di Angiolini', *Chigiana*, xxix–xxx (1975), 513–34

——: *Storia del Teatro Regio di Torino*, iii: *La scenografia dalle origini al 1936* (Turin, 1980)

F. Mancini, M. T. Muraro and E. Povoledo: *I Teatri del Veneto*, ii: *Verona, Vicenza, Belluno* (Venice, 1985)

MERCEDES VIALE FERRERO

Costa, Giovanni Maria (*b* Genoa, ?1581; *d* in or after 1656). Italian composer. He spent his working life at Genoa, where he appears to have been organist of the cathedral in the late 16th century and at the convent of S Brigida from 1601. According to the title-page of his *Primo libro de madrigali* (Venice, 1640) he was *maestro di cappella* to the republic of Genoa. When over 70 he composed the opera *Ariodante* (G. A. Pisani [G. A. Spinola], after L. Ariosto; lib. *I-Nc*, *Rc*) and the intermezzo *Gl'incanti di Ismeno* (Spinola), which were performed together at the Teatro del Falcone, Genoa, in 1655–6. Giazotto says that Costa also set Spinola's *Aspasia* in 1656 and/or 1660; the drama was certainly performed at Genoa in 1695, but the music may have been by Geronimo Maria Costa (*b* Genoa, 1655).

*

AllacciD

R. Giazotto: *La musica a Genova nella vita pubblica e privata dal XIII al XVIII secolo* (Genoa, 1951)

C. Sartori: *I libretti italiani a stampa dalle origini al 1800*, i (Cuneo, 1990)

COLIN TIMMS

Costa, (Maria) Margherita [Margarita] (*b* Rome; *fl* 1629–57). Italian singer and poetess, sister of Anna Francesca Costa. Her rather chequered career as a talented courtesan led her from Rome through Florence (1629), Rome (1644), Turin (1645) and Paris (1647) before returning again to her native city; her patrons included the Medici (in particular, Grand Duke Ferdinando II), the Barberini and Cardinal Mazarin. Her rivalry with another Roman soprano, Cecca del Padule, was reputed to have inspired Domenico Mazzocchi's *La catena d'Adone* (1626), although she did not take part in the performance. Costa's numerous publications include poetry, letters, a comedy (*Li buffoni*, Florence, 1641), a libretto for a *Festa reale per balletto a cavallo* (Paris, 1647, with a dedication to Mazarin: it had been offered to Grand Duke Ferdinando II in 1640), and two opera librettos, *La Flora feconda* (Florence, 1640) and *Gli amori della luna* (Venice, 1654).

*

DBI (M. Capucci); *ES* (N. Pirrotta)

A. Ademollo: *I primi fasti della musica italiana a Parigi (1645–1662)* (Milan, n.d.)

H. Prunières: *L'opéra italien en France avant Lully* (Paris, 1913)

D. Bianchi: 'Una cortigiana rimatrice del Seicento: Margherita Costa', *Rassegna critica della letteratura italiana*, xxix (1924), 1–31, 187–203; xxx (1925), 158–211

L. Bianconi and T. Walker: 'Dalla *Finta pazza* alla *Veremonda*: storie di Febiarmonici', *RIM*, x (1975), 379–454, esp.443

TIM CARTER

Costa, Sir **Michael (Andrew Agnus)** [Michele Andrea Agniello] (*b* Naples, 4 Feb 1808; *d* Hove, 29 April 1884). English conductor and composer of Italian birth. His teachers included Niccolò Zingarelli and the castrato Girolamo Crescentino. While he was still a student four of his operas and a cantata were performed in Naples. He went to England in 1829, and soon became the director of London's leading musical organizations through a combination of technical skill, a dominant personality and favourable circumstances. In 1830, as *maestro al piano* at the King's Theatre, he encountered the customary divided leadership, the orchestra being 'presided over' by a pianist and 'led' by a violinist; in 1832 he became director of music. At this time he probably introduced authoritative conducting with a baton and by 1833 he was both director and conductor of the Italian opera at the King's Theatre. The press almost immediately praised the discipline and ensemble of his baton-conducted band and hailed the improved standard of orchestral playing, but his compositions found no widespread favour with the public. Rossini's judgment in 1856 speaks for itself: 'Good old Costa has sent me an oratorio score and a Stilton cheese; the cheese was very fine'. *Malek Adel*, his most successful opera, contains no innovative music whatsoever. The score is vigorous and noisy, but exhibits a lack of melodic inspiration (an unusual defect in an Italian composer). The one number touched by genuine emotion is Mathilde's preghiera 'Tu mi creasti l'anima', which could pass for Donizetti.

When he resigned from the theatre (now Her Majesty's) in 1846, Costa took 53 of its 80-member orchestra with him and founded the Royal Italian Opera in the following year at the newly renovated Covent Garden Theatre. In 1846 he also accepted the conductorship of the Philharmonic Society, stipulating absolute control over the orchestra. Critical praise was high; in 1848 Davison wrote, 'In speaking of the orchestra of the Royal Italian Opera, we take off our critical hat, and make low obeisance ... it is almost unnecessary to add that it will be the finest orchestra in the world, without making any exception whatever'. By the end of his career, however, his tastes had become obsolete; Shaw put it neatly: 'Costa ... allowed the opera to die in his grasp whilst it was renewing its youth and strength all over Germany.'

Costa continued to conduct the Philharmonic Society until 1854 (he was succeeded for one uneasy season by Wagner) and remained at Covent Garden until a dispute with the manager Frederick Gye in 1868. He then returned to Her Majesty's in the Haymarket and, from 1871 until its amalgamation with the Covent Garden company ten years later, was its musical director, working with the impresario Henry Mapleson. Costa also made a nationwide reputation as a conductor of oratorio. As well as operas, he composed ballets and oratorios. He received many awards and was knighted in 1869.

Il delitto punito (2), Naples, Conservatorio, 1826
Il carcere d'Ildegonda (D. Gilardoni), Naples, Nuovo, 1827
Il sospetto funesto (3), Naples, Conservatorio, 1827
Malvina (2, G. Schmidt), Naples, S Carlo, Jan 1829; rev. as Malek Adel (os, 3, C. Pepoli, after S. Cottin: *Mathilde*), Paris, Italien, 14 Jan 1837, vs (London, 1837)
Don Carlos (tragedia lirica, 3, L. Tarantini), London, Her Majesty's, 29 June 1844, vs (London, 1844)

Italian recitatives in: Der Freischütz [as Il Franco arciere], London, CG, 16 March 1850; Fidelio, London, CG, 27 May 1851; Les deux journées, London, Drury Lane, 20 June 1872

*

H. Davison: Review in *Musical World* (12 Feb 1848)
B. Lumley: *Reminiscences of the Opera* (London, 1864)
H. Berlioz: *Mémoires* (Paris, 1870), ii, 313–14; Eng. trans. (1969), 466–7
J. E. Cox: *Musical Recollections of the Last Half-century* (London, 1872), i, 175–81; ii, 60–71, 160–61, 173, 364–9
H. Davison: *From Mendelssohn to Wagner* (London, 1912), 109
N. T. Portacci: *Michele Costa* (Taranto, 1934)
G. B. Shaw: *Music in London 1888–89* (London, 1937)
A. Della Corte: *L'interpretazione musicale e gli interpreti* (Turin, 1951), 137–9
F. Walker: 'Rossiniana in the Piancastelli Collection II: Correspondence with Costa', *MMR*, xc (1960), 203–13

NIGEL BURTON, KEITH HORNER

Costa Mesa. City in California. It is the home of the Orange County Performing Arts Center, opened in October 1986. In February 1987 a new professional opera company, Opera Pacific, opened with Gershwin's *Porgy and Bess*. The founder and general director, David DiChiera, established a pattern of three or four productions annually, including at least one American musical. An early milestone was the 1989 *Norma*, with Joan Sutherland in one of her last performances on stage. By 1990 Opera Pacific had become one of the largest professional opera companies in the USA. The company, which offers a training programme for young singers, plays in the Performing Arts Center's Segerstrom Hall, a 3000-seat auditorium with an unusual seating configuration: four seating trays with side walls that barely rise above the head level of seated patrons are positioned asymmetrically and at different heights from the stage, which shrinks and expands by means of a hydraulically adjustable back wall; the width and height of the proscenium arch are also adjustable.

NANCY MALITZ

Costantini, Livia. *See* NANNINI, LIVIA DOROTEA.

Costanza e Fortezza ('Constancy and Fortitude'). *Festa teatrale* in three acts, K315, by JOHANN JOSEPH FUX to a libretto by PIETRO PARIATI; Prague, amphitheatre of Hradschin [now Hradčany] Castle, 28 August 1723.

Livy's history was the source for this rather freely adapted story of the siege of Rome by the Etruscans at the end of the sixth century BC. Tito Tarquinio [Titus Tarquinius] (soprano), an Etruscan, is trying to reconquer the Roman throne with the help of the Etruscan king Porsenna [Porsena] (alto), who has fallen in love with Valeria (soprano), the daughter of the Roman consul Publio Valerio [Publius Valerius] (bass). Tarquinius loves Clelia [Cloelia] (alto), who is also a Roman; both girls are captives of the Etruscans. Orazio [Horatius] (tenor), Cloelia's betrothed, defends a bridge over the Tiber single-handed; it is torn down behind him and he jumps into the river, but is rescued. Muzio [Mucius] (alto), Valeria's lover, is captured by the Etruscans as he stabs a man he believes to be Porsena, but who is only his treasurer; in expiation he burns his own hand. Because of this heroism he is released by Porsena. Tarquinius tries to take Cloelia by force, and she is about to stab him when Valeria's brother Erminio [Herminius] (soprano), also in love with Cloelia, intervenes. The consul offers peace; Porsena accepts and withdraws his support of Tarquinius.

The *licenza* is a hymn in honour of Empress Elisabeth Christine, whose birthday was the occasion for the original open-air performance, and also of Prague – Emperor Charles VI and his wife were in Prague for their coronation as king and queen of Bohemia. Pariati chose Charles's device, 'Constantia et Fortitudine', as title and cornerstone of the plot, and there are many symbolic allusions to contemporary history and politics. The production, according to J. J. Quantz, included about a hundred singers and some two hundred instrumentalists (with such guests as Quantz, C. H. Graun and S. L. Weiss), and was conducted by the vice-*maestro di cappella*, Caldara. Though one of Fux's principal works, its style is not typical of his operas: it has an unusual number of mostly homophonic choruses, elaborate polyphony in the aria accompaniments (Quantz compared it with church style), and frequent use is made of wind soloists.

For illustration *see* GALLI-BIBIENA, fig.2 and PRAGUE, fig.1.

HERBERT SEIFERT

Costanzi. Theatre in Rome, opened in 1880; renovated in 1926–7 and reopened in 1928 as the Teatro Reale dell'Opera. *See* ROME, §3(iii).

Costanzi, Giovanni Battista [Giovannino del Violoncello, Giovannino da Roma] (*b* Rome, 3 Sept 1704; *d* Rome, 5 March 1778). Italian composer. He was probably a pupil of G. L. Lulier. He entered the service of Cardinal Pietro Ottoboni in Rome in 1721, and in 1737 he was made *capo d'istromenti* (Corelli's former position). After the brilliant success of his opera *Carlo Magno* in 1729, he was appointed to a number of the most important posts of *maestro di cappella* in Rome, including S Lorenzo in Damaso in 1731 and St Peter's (Cappella Giulia) in 1755. His growing reputation as a cellist and composer brought him a succession of honours.

Costanzi was among the most prolific composers of the 18th century, but only part of his output has survived. To judge from what remains, operas and dramatic cantatas predominated until about 1740, but later he concentrated on religious music. The surviving opera arias show a mastery of vocal writing and subtle instrumental scoring.

all performed in Rome

L'amor generoso, Capranica, 7 Jan 1727, arias *US-NH*
Rosmene, Pace, 8 Jan 1729, arias *GB-Cfm, I-Rc*
Carlo Magno (P. Ottoboni), Cancelleria, 1729, *F-Pn, I-Rvat*
Eupatra, Valle, 3 Jan 1730, arias *Rc*
Il trionfo della Pace, Residenza del Duca di Saint'Aignon, 25 Aug 1739
Intermezzi in musica (G. Palladio), Rome, carn. 1746

Arias for Sarro's La Partenope, Tordinona, 13 Feb 1734, 1 aria *Rc*; act 2 of La Flora, 14 Feb 1734

*

A. Cametti: 'Musicisti del settecento in Roma: G. B. Costanzi, violoncellista e compositore', *Musica d'oggi*, vi (1924), 6, 39–43

HANS JOACHIM MARX

Costume. The history of costume on the Western operatic stage is traced by referring to a variety of sources: original costumes, contemporary illustrations, commemorative portraits, designers' drawings, inventory lists and wardrobe accounts, theatrical costume books, and memoirs, essays and programmes.

1. The Renaissance. 2. 17th century. 3. 18th century. 4. 19th century. 5. 20th century.

1. THE RENAISSANCE. Records of the earliest operas, staged in Florence, do not mention the costume designer, but Bernardo Buontalenti is a possible candidate. He had been responsible for the machinery, settings and costumes of all the Medici theatrical events since succeeding Giorgio Vasari in 1574, the most spectacular being the six *intermedi* of 1589. By good fortune, costume drawings attributed to Buontalenti survive for more than a hundred *intermedi* characters. After the production, the Medici had the costumes put away in cupboards and regularly looked after, which implies that they were also used regularly. Eight years later, two of the 1589 creative ensemble, the poet Ottavio Rinuccini and the composer Jacopo Peri, altered and expanded the third *intermedio*, *Il combattimento pitico d'Apollo*, renaming it *Dafne*, for a performance at the palace of Jacopo Corsi. Among the guests was Giovanni de' Medici, so it is possible that Buontalenti's 1589 designs for Apollo and the Delphic singers (fig.1), if not the actual costumes, were seen in this, the first opera.

For inspiration, Buontalenti had books of engravings, drawings, paintings and literary sources. A costume that was recognizably classical had been established in the sophisticated courts of Italy by the 15th century. So successful was it that it has been used ever since throughout Europe, sometimes elaborated, but never seriously altered. The first Renaissance theorist to consider the costumes of actors was G. B. Giraldi Cinthio, in his *Discorsi* of 1554. He refers to the ancient Greek division between comedy and tragedy: while actors could suitably appear in a comedy dressed as private citizens, in tragedy they should always be in costumes lordly and magnificent ('grandi e magnifici'). This distinction between comic and tragic applied to opera, thus maintaining 'rules' of costume constant for all theatre. Giraldi Cinthio also recommends the national dress of people from distant countries, because the novelty arouses the admiration of the audience and thus its attention.

The next commentary is by a practical man of the theatre at the Gonzaga court of Mantua, Leone de' Sommi. In the third dialogue of his four *Dialoghi in materia di rappresentazioni sceniche* (*c*1565) he dismisses the clothing traditions of the Roman stage: white costumes for old men, colourful garments for the young, yellow clothes for prostitutes and twisted cloaks for pimps and parasites. Sommi believed that each character should be different and individual in his costume so that the audience could easily recognize him. The ancients had portrayed character types, but Sommi wanted individuals on the stage. Also, it was most important for the stage to look magnificent and for all actors to appear in dress as fine as money could buy ('vestir nobilmente'). Sommi believed that sumptuous clothes enhanced a comedy and still more a tragedy, which must never be presented in modern dress. The ideal look of the Renaissance was Roman, and Roman themes and costume, if not the clothing traditions of the Roman stage, dominated opera for the following two centuries. Some tragedies, written on Turkish themes, required 'foreign and strange' robes and turbans for the men and veils for the women, providing beauty as well as novelty on the stage.

Males taking female roles could wear masks and papier mâché breasts and chests ('poppe e petti di cartone'). Musicians shared the stage with singers and were costumed in the same manner, their instruments decorated in appropriate disguises. Musicians as Tritons blew wind instruments disguised as conch shells; in pastoral settings, musicians as satyrs played instruments covered with foliage.

2. 17TH CENTURY. Theatrical convention may be described as a kind of tacit agreement between stage and stalls, providing a short cut for the designer. In 20th-century films, the good guy in a Western wears white, the bad guy black. Buonarroti, in his report of Caccini's *Il rapimento di Cefalo* (Florence, 1600), confirms that costume conventions for familiar characters had been established. Dawn is a beautiful young woman with golden wings, dressed in an iridescent white robe with a reddish cast. Oceanus, his bristly beard streaked with moss, wears a royal crown and, on his shoulders, a soft cape decorated with marine ornamentation (see fig.7*b* for a costume for Neptune, *c*1760). His Tritons are rough creatures of the deep, with scaly, bluish-green skin, blowing conchs and lashing the water with their forked tails. Cupid is a winged, blindfolded boy with an

arrow in his hand, the quiver slung across his back, soaring on his cloud like a bird through the air. Night is wreathed with poppies and sheathed in black veils and a blue mantle spangled with stars. Black wings sprout from her shoulders. She holds two small children in her arms, one white, the other black. These are her sons, Sleep and Death. (Mozart's Queen of Night has yet to be seen with sons.) Mercury has his winged helmet and caduceus. Fame, with great wings and hair streaming (like gossip) in the wind, holds the traditional trumpet and an olive branch. Her robe is wrought all over with eyes. Buonarroti declared that Caccini's opera could confidently be compared to the spectacles of ancient Rome (see Nagler, 96–100).

Princes financed their court operas for invited guests. When in 1637 in Venice opera was first organized as a commercial venture, open to all who could afford to pay, the costumes were apparently no less splendid; according to the description for the first such entertainment, Francesco Manelli's *Andromeda*, Dawn 'was dressed entirely in cloth of silver ... Juno came out on a golden car drawn by her peacocks, blazing in a coat of cloth of gold with a superb variety of jewels on her head or in her crown' (Worsthorne, 25). Five years later, in 1642, it was said of Francesco Sacrati's *Bellerofonte* (Teatro Novissimo, Venice) that 'the audience admitted that a royal court could not have arranged it with greater propriety and beauty' (ibid, 177).

Throughout the Baroque period, Roman dress meant noble character. It was adopted for the monarchy in portraiture by Charles Le Brun, favourite painter of Louis XIV, and for every west European ruler from Sweden to Austria. Roman dress did not go out of date, unlike fashionable clothes that changed every season, so was ideal for a portrait meant to last. But as prevailing fashion always influences historical reconstructions, it did not seem at all incongruous in the 1650s for an operatic hero in Roman dress to wear a periwig. On the contrary, it showed him to be of the upper class, for a periwig cost more than a working man earned in a year; on stage and off, the periwig distinguished gentlemen from artisans and labourers at a glance.

Menestrier (1682) decreed rules for specific characters (quoted in Beaumont, p.xix):

> The costume of Spring should be green sprinkled with flowers, and a garland of roses. Winter should be dressed in white with a long beard, a furred costume, and appear sluggish in his movements. The dress of Summer should be isabel colour, which is that of the harvest; she must wear a crown of ears of corn on her head and carry a scythe. That of Autumn should be olive colour or that of dead leaves, with a cornucopia full of fruit, and a garland of vine leaves.
>
> Winds should be dressed in feathers on account of their lightness; the Sun in cloth of gold with a gilt head-dress, the Moon in cloth of silver; both wear a mask, one with golden rays, the other with silver.
>
> Time should be dressed in four colours denoting the four seasons. For head-dress he should wear a clock-face marking the hours, wings on his back and head, an hour glass in one hand and a scythe in the other. Night should be dressed in black powdered with stars, and wear a crescent moon on her head. Cupid should be dressed in rose-coloured material, covered with flaming hearts, his eyes bandaged, a bow in his hand and a quiver on his back.

If not a heroic figure in Roman dress, an allegorical or mythological creation, or a foreigner, the performer wore contemporary dress.

Baroque operas included many balletic interludes and *divertissements* to amuse the audience and give the singers a rest. Menestrier recommends that in each scene the dancers should be dressed alike, and that they should not appear twice in the same costume. He suggests successive entrées of soldiers, shepherds, gods from ancient legend, thieves, animals, genii, American Indians, Persians and Moors. The expense of such a quantity of costumes could not be borne by individual performers, so managements paid for opera-ballet clothing (unlike the system in French drama). Wardrobe stocks, full of costly clothes, were only occasionally replenished. In his *Roscius anglicanus* (London, 1708) John Downes, prompter at the Duke of York's playhouse at Dorset Garden and later at the Lincoln's Inn Fields Theatre, recorded just 12 productions that had new clothes in the 45 years from about 1660 to 1705. Shadwell and Locke's semi-opera *Psyche* (1675) 'came forth in ... new Cloaths' and Purcell's *Fairy-Queen* (1692) 'was Superior ... especially in Cloaths'. Although no iconography exists, it is thought the 'Cloaths' were similar to those of earlier masques, known through the drawings of Inigo Jones (for illustration *see* MASQUE). Michael Ayrton based his costumes for the 1948 Covent Garden production of *The Fairy-Queen* on these. On the opening of the new opera house in the Haymarket in 1705 (the Queen's – later King's – Theatre), the Lincoln's Inn Fields company moved in with 'half a Score of their Old Plays, Acted in old Cloaths' from their previous playhouse. Economy was essential for a company to remain solvent. When possible, the theatre would borrow or purchase cheaply the cast-offs of the nobility.

The theatre architect or decor and machinery designer may well have had a hand in designing costumes. Such work was not often credited and, unless costume drawings are extant, there is no way of knowing the creator. For instance, it is assumed but not certain that costumes were designed by the famous stage designer and machinist Giacomo Torelli, who worked in Venice (1641–*c*1645) and Paris (1645–*c*1659). The 17th-century artists known to have designed both settings and costumes include Inigo Jones, who introduced Italian design to London (he was involved in more than 40 productions between 1605 and 1640); Count Filippo d'Agliè in Turin (1640–67), as shown in Tommaso Borgonio's illustrations; Ludovico Burnacini in Vienna (*c*1656–1705) and Jean Berain in Paris (1673–1711; fig.4). Specialists in costume drawings include Pompeo Caccini in Rome for Filippo Vitali's *Aretusa* (1620), Stefano della Bella in Florence (1650 to the early 1660s; fig.3), and in Paris Daniel Rabel (1614–34), Henri de Beaubrun (1651) and Henry de Gissey (*c*1653–1673).

3. 18TH CENTURY. Leading singers in the 18th century were commonly allowed new clothes, which they could choose themselves, while the rest of the cast were dressed from the wardrobe. The variety available is indicated in an inventory of old stock from Drury Lane, taken in 1714 and cited by Rosenfeld: it includes ten Roman shapes and Persian vests, 50 very old Roman, Persian, Chinese and shepherds' dresses, 24 Spanish dresses, three suits of dancing clothes trimmed with copper, a set of woman's clothes of copper and silk, and 18 singers' and dancers' costumes from Purcell's opera *King Arthur* (1691) valued at 2s. 6d. each.

In addition to its breathtaking quality, magnificence served a practical purpose. Theatre had come indoors, and performances took place by candlelight. Costumes were less visible in the soft glow, so glitter was important to reflect light. Where genuine gold and silver were not affordable, copper and artificial tinsel were

(a)

1. Costume drawings attributed to Bernardo Buontalenti for the third intermedio (Apollo's slaying of Python), Uffizi Theatre, Florence, 2 May 1589: (a) Apollo, a dancer. In 'Dafne' (1598), Apollo probably wore such a golden wig and costume in the solar colours of gold, red and sky-blue. As the hero who slays Python, he wears Roman armour. The long, musculated cuirass of gilded leather has a short, scalloped skirt, an interpretation of the Roman fringed skirt of protective leather strips. Underneath, he wears a belt with three vertical protective lappets hanging below a second scalloped fringe; his blue knee-length tunic has a scalloped hem (scallops, tassels and fringes were favourite Renaissance theatrical devices), and each sleeve is caught up by a brooch in a Renaissance conception of the Roman short sleeve. Bare arms and legs were acceptable in ancient Greece and Rome, but not to Renaissance eyes. His over-all tights are scarlet, as is the short mantle. The gilded classical boots have an open trellis pattern cut in thin leather and sewn with jewels, a Renaissance style so successful it was to last for the next 200 years. Apollo is masked, as were all the performers. (b) Delphic singers, 18 couples in all. This design was for two couples, whose robes differed only in colour and decoration. The intermedi's deviser, Giovanni de' Bardi, prescribed Hellenic costumes ('abiti tendenti al greco'), and some sort of 'cose marine' to refer symbolically to the founding of Delphi by a son of Neptune. Buontalenti provided headpieces and handpieces of coral branches and seashells. Because Greece was under Turkish domination and not safe for Italian artists to visit, an ancient dress worn east of Rome had to be devised. The result was a combination of Near Eastern costume and the lightweight fabrics, folded and girded to make layers, as seen carved on Roman statues. The man wears a long-sleeved oriental tunic, overlaid with a skirt and a pseudo-shepherd's coat, girded with an oriental sash, and decorated in the Mannerist fashion with braid, scallops, jewels and tassels. By convention he is masked and wears classical boots. 'She' is a male singer provided with moulded papier-mâché breast pieces, and dressed in a girded bodice with fashionable short puffed sleeves, and three tiers of skirts. The floating veils are also a theatrical convention. Both decorum and disguise are served by over-all tights and mask. The chorus in 'Dafne' (1598) may have worn costumes of this design.

(b)

2. *Preliminary sketches by Terence Emery for Monteverdi's 'Orfeo', Palazzo Vecchio, Florence, 19 June 1984 (Early Opera Project). No iconography survives for the original 1607 production. Emery's reconstruction, inspired by 16th- and 17th-century drawings, is inscribed (left to right, top half): Franco-florentine Early 17th C.; lots of vermilion & white; older shepherd; shepherdesses; Apollo; Red; gold Pluto; Charon; and (lower half): Aged shepherds?; Apollo; Poss Helmet; Apollo Helmet – Breastplate; Botticelli, Shades; Terence Emery '84.*

3. *(opposite) Brown-ink and watercolour drawings by Stefano della Bella for Cavalli's 'Hipermestra', Teatro della Pergola, Florence, 12 June 1658. Costumes were an important part of the production by the Accademia degli Immobili, and a 'considerable expense'. Their design was entrusted to four members of the Immobili noted for learning in the classics; however, the Medici sense of opulence overcame historical accuracy, resulting in highly decorative costumes that must have delighted the audience.*

(a) Hypermnestra's first and grandest appearance in Act 1 scene i is described in G. Rucellai's 'Descrizione' (1658; trans. D. Henderson, 1990): 'beautiful of figure and royally apparelled, she appears in a sumptuous gown and mantle of the lightest cloth-of-silver shot through with threads of gold, its train, which covered a considerable part of the floor, delicately held by a close-following page; the lofty sweep of her hair sparkled with gems, while many strands of pearls, so white that Eritrean shells seemed to have only just now surrendered them, encircled her neck and decorated her bosom in an abundance justly due a new bride and queen'. On her richly embroidered sky-blue dress, the pointed bodice is in the new fashion, with the seams bound in gold braid. The soft drape across her bosom is of apricot muslin, the train of peach muslin. Her blackamoor's colours are also blue and peach. Hypermnestra's white high-necked chemise has theatrical 'historical' sleeves. Full sleeves held in at two points on the arm were fashionable at the end of the 15th century, and long strip sleeves pendant from the upper armband had been in fashion about 1628. The fantastic headdress is of matching blue, with gold trim and black feathers.

(b) Delmiro, general of the armies of Egypt, described by Rucellai: 'in the most noble of military uniforms, on his breast a shining silver cuirass and at his left side a gem-encrusted sabre, his shoulders sumptuously cloaked in a white satin cape wondrously embroidered, while from his helmet the most graceful of white feathers waft delicately'. He wears a contemporary metal breastplate and helmet, a quantity of gold and pink plumes with a central black tuft of feathers adding at least 15 cm to his height. The splendidly theatrical Roman tunic in pale gold has neckline pleating and full sleeves held in below the elbow, with a border of embroidery at the hem. The sword belt slung around his hips causes the tunic to billow, and a long, dark gold mantle hangs from his shoulders. His boots are in the theatrical tradition of the 1589 Apollo.

(c) Venus, whose arrival by chariot in the Prologue is described by Rucellai: 'a snow-white cloud ... rises on high; bordered in gold and quite apart from everything surrounding it, the cloud is crowned by the Goddess of Cyprus, flame-coloured and costumed in magnificent embroidery, girt about resplendently with ribbons of richest gold'. Her fashionable gown is in pale gold muslin with a rose-pink muslin skirt, embroidered and bejewelled for additional glitter. Theatrical long strip sleeves with a dagged edge are pendant from just below her elbow. Dagging, a late 15th-century fashion, is repeated on her mantle. The headdress, inspired by her marine nativity, is shaped like the lip of a conch shell, encircled by pearls, and crowned with a starfish and plume.

(a)

(b)

(c)

4. Designs by Jean Berain for operas by Lully.

(a) The goddess Cybele (Mlle de Saint Christophle) in 'Atys', St Germain-en-Laye, 10 January 1676; drawing from the workshop of Jean Berain. Cybele is the ancient Phrygian earth mother, ruler of all nature. Her sceptre, plumed headdress and train denote a queen. The short classical overskirt is modelled on the Roman tunic. Her gown has a theatrical fringe at the hem and tasselled sleeves, taken from the medieval Fool's costume. Traditionally, Cybele's dress is predominantly green and decorated with flowers; Berain uses stylized acanthus leaves and flowerets in vivid hues of red shot with gold, blue, white, grey and black.

(b) Pluto (sung by Gaye) in 'Proserpine', St Germain-en-Laye, 3 February 1680; drawing by Jean Berain. Pluto, King of the underworld, wears a radiated gold crown with black and fire-red plumes, rubies and diamonds. The seducer of Persephone is portrayed sympathetically, as a handsome young gallant, in accordance with contemporary taste; he is luxuriously dressed in a close-fitting jacket, with his cravat tied in a pretty bow and ribbons decorating his sleeves. The boots and the theatrical classical Roman skirt and mantle, both fringed in gold, are extremely ornate. His role is identified by the red, black, grey and gold colours, and accessories like the decorative demon's masks and hand-held fork.

5. Costume drawings by Antonio Bertoli, Vienna c1740, reveal the predominant influence of 18th-century French design. Irrespective of character, all costumes have particularly rich ornamentation in keeping with the period's fashion, with sumptuous mantles, belts and boots, and variegated velvets and satins. The width of hoops under ladies' skirts is matched in the flared skirts of men's jackets.

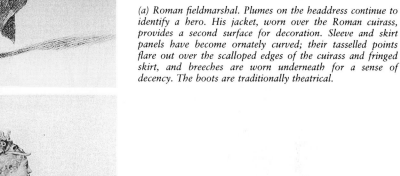

(a) Roman fieldmarshal. Plumes on the headdress continue to identify a hero. His jacket, worn over the Roman cuirass, provides a second surface for decoration. Sleeve and skirt panels have become ornately curved; their tasselled points flare out over the scalloped edges of the cuirass and fringed skirt, and breeches are worn underneath for a sense of decency. The boots are traditionally theatrical.

(b) Athene/Minerva. The goddess, warrior for Justice, carries a spear and shield as delicate as her helmet is petite. The Rococo ensemble is enriched by decorations associated with her mythological past: the serpent-haired head of Medusa, owls (which are sacred to her), olive branches and serpents (symbolizing wisdom) and cobwebs (denoting her role as patron of spinning and weaving).

6. Two singers in a scene from an unknown opera painted by Louis-René Boquet, c1750, in brown-toned watercolours. The plumes, coronet, train and sceptre identify a prince, who is making a declaration, on his knees, to his young princess. The width of their skirts, matching their outstretched arms, has reached its limit. Her sumptuous dress is adorned with garlands and rocailles.

(a)

(b)

7. Engravings by Jean Baptiste Martin from his designs for the Paris Opéra, 1748–c1757, published in 'Gallerie des modes et costumes français, dessinés d'après nature' (1779): (a) Medea in Charpentier's 'Médée'. The wand indicates a sorceress; her fashionably cut dress is overlaid with ornamentation to suit her character: the bat is associated with Night and dark deeds. She has a lavish powdered wig and headdress of plumes and heron feathers. A similar gouache, 'Médée dans l'opéra de Thésée' (Musée de l'Opéra, Paris), is thought to be of Mlle Chevalier in the 1744 revival of Lully's opera. (b) Neptune in 'Different Operas and Pieces'. He has a flowing beard and moustache, and as King of the Oceans wears a radiated crown decorated with pearls and plumes. His closely fitted tunic with tonnelet is embellished with sea plants, coral, pearls and shells. The royal mantle has an overall scalloped shell design.

8. *Iphigenia and Achilles in Gluck's 'Iphigénie en Aulide'.*

(a) Sophie Arnould as Iphigenia in the première, Académie Royale de Musique, Paris, 19 April 1774. The reform movement partially succeeded with this costume of classical Greek simplicity. However, fashionable taste prevails in the straw bonnet wreathed with roses, worn over the himation (veil). The engraving identifies the opera as 'Iphigénie en Tauride' but Sophie Arnould had retired the year before the première of Gluck's 'Iphigénie en Tauride' (1779). It may be an earlier French setting by Desmarets and Campra in 1704 and revived in 1762 (revised by Berton), when it is likely that Sophie sang Iphigenia. If this was her costume in 1762, it was very daring.

(b) Achilles (sung by Lavigne), Théâtre de l'Académie Impériale de Musique, Paris, 2 May 1809. Historical accuracy has supplanted the tradition that all heroes don Roman dress. Achilles wears a classic white Greek chiton ornamented with gold motifs at the neck, sleeve and hemlines. His battle helmet and armour are copied faithfully from 5th- and 4th-century BC *sculptures of Greek warriors; their golden colour suggests burnished brass reflecting the crimson of the crest and mantle.*

allowed. Rock crystal served as diamonds, and sequins covered the fabrics so that they shone all over. Predominant colours were strong and bright, such as white, yellow, scarlet or orange. Fine materials of silk, satin, velvet and damask were essential. Chinese opera today, in a continuous tradition dating from the 12th century, dresses in fine fabrics of bright colours; sequins and pheasant-tail feathers signify rank in the manner of Baroque opera's sequins and ostrich feathers. 18th-century fashion added long cuffed sleeves and hoops to Roman armour, while decency added knee-breeches underneath the hoop. Heroines, as ladies of quality, adopted panniers that grew wider each season. Men's coat-tails flared out correspondingly. From 1708 to the 1780s the emphasis in dress both off and on the stage was on width.

Two satirical engravings are the only extant pictures that might represent Handel's London productions, renowned for their scenic splendours and 'heroic habits'. Senesino, the alto castrato famous for his heroic roles, appears in both scenes wearing traditional Roman armour; no doubt he sang the title role in *Giulio Cesare in Egitto* (1724) in such a costume. The soprano Francesca Cuzzoni is also in traditional operatic dress: her fashionable hoop is roughly the shape of a rounded dome, its inspiration attributed by the anonymous author of the poem *The Art of Dress* (London, 1717) to St Paul's Cathedral. Cuzzoni has a plumed headdress with veil and mantle carried by her page. The dress decorations are too indistinct to identify a role, and it is certain only that she is a heroine (for illustration *see* SENESINO). Horace Walpole described her thus in the title role of Handel's *Rodelinda*, 1725 (quoted in W. Dean and J. M. Knapp, *Handel's Operas 1704–1726*, Oxford, 1987, pp.589–90):

> She was short and squat, with a doughy cross face, but fine complexion; was not a good actress; dressed ill; and was silly and fantastical. And yet on her appearing in this opera, in a *brown silk gown*, trimmed with silver, with the vulgarity and indecorum of which all the old ladies were much scandalised, the young adopted it as a fashion, so universally, that it seemed a national uniform for youth and beauty.

Historical clothes were attempted for special characters. Medieval dress was ignored because it was 'uncivilized'. 15th- and 16th-century dress was used without discrimination, for the audience did not demand historical accuracy. In *Henry IV* (part 1) Sir John Falstaff had a costume based on 16th-century lines that included a bonnet with heroic plumes, a doublet and a ruff, and trunk-hose. By the mid-18th century thigh exposure was unacceptable, so he acquired knee-breeches. However, the style of the breeches was not contemporary and close-fitting, but that of the baggy 1630s. They made padding for his character both easier and more convincing, with the addition of Cavalier boots to conceal a skinny lower leg. Rococo artists thought the most elegant and timeless dress was that of the 1630s, as painted by Anthony van Dyck. After 1731 the Van Dyck style became a new form of 'historical' costume, popular both for masquerades and for the stage. The scale of the original was reduced for both sexes, reflecting the vogue for petite dimensions: lace collars were smaller, sleeves were narrower, high waists were dropped to the normal waistline, and men's breeches stopped at the knee instead of the top of the calf. The slash – a slit in the outer garment through which puffed the undergarment, generally of silk – was 'historical', so was used everywhere. In October 1793 the actor John Philip Kemble performed Hamlet in a black satin Van Dyck costume that became traditional for the role.

When Haydn was at Eszterháza the costumes, illumination and all scenic effects for operas were under the supervision of the painter Pietro Travaglia. Prince Nikolaus himself approved each production's wardrobe estimate by the theatre manager; in his 'Instruction' dated 14 February 1779, the prince wrote: 'With a view to fixing future expenses, the wigmaker is to receive a florin, the tailor 30 kreuzer and Mrs Handl [wardrobe mistress] likewise 30 kreuzer for each opera performance' (Horányi 1962, p.119). A painting of 1775 shows a comic scene of a lady in contemporary Rococo dress and eight men in typical Turkish costumes. Staging was often lavish: Haydn's *Armida* (1784; for illustration *see* HAYDN, JOSEPH) required as 'supers' six stage musicians, four girls and 34 grenadiers dressed in Roman and Turkish costumes. Some costume sketches for this have survived (a satyr and a nymph are reproduced in colour in Horányi). For Sarti's *Didone abbandonata*, also produced at Eszterháza in 1784, at least 60 performers appeared on stage in Roman, Turkish, Moorish and Trojan dresses, accompanied by sham elephants, tigers and lions.

In the late 18th century, neo-classical taste simplified theatre costume. Powdered hair went out in the 1780s, as did wigs, except for elderly men. The republican toga replaced the Baroque ideal of imperial Roman armour. The plumed helmet and cuirass were retained for military figures, but the hooped skirt was gone, replaced by knee-breeches. It took 20 years to reduce the female shape to a classical, slender line. By 1776 the bustle was fashionable for daytime, but full hoops were still worn in the evening. Not until the turn of the century did fashion and artistic theory agree on the classical look. In 1734 the French dancer Marie Sallé had played Galatea, a Greek statue, in the ballet *Pigmalion* at Covent Garden. Correctly observing that Greek statues did not have hoops, she wore a simple muslin gown with loose drapery, and slippers without the usual high heels. She created a sensation, but not a reform in costume. Rather like the 20th-century Windmill Theatre nudes, her scanty dress was acceptable only in immobility.

The most significant contribution to costume reform during the second half of the 18th century was made by the ballet teacher Jean-Georges Noverre in his *Lettres sur la danse* (1760). He wanted ballet to be more than a pretty diversion in opera and to tell a story of its own. Noverre wrote that uniformity in sets and costumes deprived the stage picture of dramatic effect. If everything glittered with equal gaudiness, no part could be subordinate to another. So, if the set was rich, the costumes should be simple, and vice versa. Male dancers at the Paris Opéra were still wearing masks, which Noverre thought ridiculous and restrictive: 'away with those lifeless masks but feeble copies of nature'. They disappeared for solo performers in 1773, but his other ideas of abolishing the hoop, the panniers and the tall wigs were adopted more slowly. The first woman who dared to appear in an opera with bare arms and legs is acknowledged to be Mademoiselle Huberty in Niccolò Piccinni's *Didon* (1783). Louis-Gabriel Moreau, 'Dessinateur du Cabinet du Roi', designed for her a loose tunic of fine linen caught by a belt beneath her bosom, a purple cloak, laced sandals for her otherwise bare feet and a crown with a long veil (for illustration *see* DIDON (ii)). Noverre and Louis-René Boquet created their *ballets en action* (dances linked with the plot of the opera) at the Württemberg court at Stuttgart, at the courts of Vienna, Turin and Milan, at the Paris Opéra and in London. There, intermittently from 1787 to 1793, Noverre was choreographer at the King's Theatre. Copies of Boquet's drawings were used by costume makers in the opera houses of Stockholm and Lisbon.

Viennese opera production was lavish in Mozart's day. The engravings by Josef and Peter Schaffer (1795) of six scenes of an early staging of *Die Zauberflöte* (reproduced in colour in Angermüller) are well known (for illustration *see* ZAUBERFLÖTE, DIE), but for the earlier operas no original costume illustrations appear to survive. In Italy there was less emphasis on magnificence in production. Maximilien Misson, in his *Nouveau voyage d'Italie* (The Hague, 1691; Eng. trans., 1695, 4/1714), had written of Venetian opera that 'the Habits are poor, there are no Dances, and commonly no fine Machines, nor any fine Illuminations'. The Lisbon court ordered costumes from the Milan tailors Motta and Mazza for Jommelli's *Olimpiade* in 1774 and complained that those for the nymphs and shepherds were too light and poorly ornamented.

18th-century designers for both stage and costume include Filippo Juvarra in Rome and Turin (1708–14), Alessandro Mauro in Venice, Dresden, Rome and Turin (*c*1709–1748), and in Paris Claude Gillot (*c*1697–*c*1721), François Boucher (1744–8), Jean Baptiste Martin (1748–*c*1758; fig.7) and Boquet (1760–82; fig.6). Specialists in costume design include Antonio Daniele Bertoli in Vienna (*c*1731–1743; fig.5), Francesco Ponte in Dresden (*c*1760; for illustration *see* ATTILIO REGOLO and BORDONI, FAUSTINA) and Leonardo Marini in Turin (1769–98).

4. 19TH CENTURY. The practice of women appearing in breeches parts continued, and Lucia Vestris was a sensation as Macheath in a revival of Gay's *The Beggar's Opera* at the Haymarket Theatre in 1820. But the emerging Victorian image of women as helpless angels meant that serious singers took male heroic roles less often. Travesty roles such as Cherubino were intended to be cross-dressed and the practice continues today in costumes for Siebel, Octavian and the 'principal boy' in British Christmas pantomimes, where the hero is a female in tight breeches.

After neo-classical purity, magnificent splendour returned to enchant the audience. Throughout the 19th century costumes and settings were rarely by one designer, sets being painted by scenic artists; costume designers were seldom credited. The Esterházy theatre at Eisenstadt staged Isouard's opera *Cendrillon* in 1810, less than four weeks after the prince had seen it in Paris. He brought costume models from Paris to be copied, and for the first time velvet gowns embroidered with gold and silver threads appeared on a German stage, according to the manager Heinrich Schmidt. But 'economic difficulties' forced the prince to close his theatre in 1813.

The commercial theatres of Paris became the centre of operatic life in Europe. The production book, published after an opera was successful, included notes and illustrations of the original set and costume designs. These guided productions elsewhere and Parisian design concepts became world famous. Engravings of performers in costume at the Opéra, the Opéra-Comique, the Théâtre Italien and the Théâtre Lyrique show no particular 'house style'. The distinctions in costume were still those of character recommended by Sommi in the 16th century; servant- and peasant-girls, in either *grand opéra* or *opéra comique*, could be identified by mid-calf or ankle-length skirts, while ladies' gowns touched the floor.

The Romanticism of the 19th century made antiquarian research fashionable, and by 1815 several books on historical costume had appeared. The past fascinated the 19th century, as it had the 16th. Sir Walter Scott's popular novels, set in the Middle Ages and the 16th and 17th centuries, contained elaborate descriptions of ancient dress. Rossini, Bizet and Donizetti all set Scottish and English stories, as the 200-year interest in Roman themes faded. Rossini's *La donna del lago* (Naples, Teatro S Carlo, 24 September 1819) is set in Scotland during the first half of the 16th century. Accurate, traditional costumes were designed for the London première in 1823 at the King's Theatre, according to John Ebers, manager 1821–7 (*Seven Years of the King's Theatre*, p.119):

> A good deal of care was used in Mounting this opera. The characters were clothed in the tartans of their various clans, according to the information received from natives of Scotland, who were consulted for the purpose. The heron's plume and golden chain of the Scottish King were lent to me by a lady of distinguished rank.

Ebers wrote that before his management 'the same scenes, the same dresses, and the same decorations figured in every performance, till the eye was wearied and the imagination disgusted by seeing different countries and ages all exhibiting the same scenes and costumes' (ibid, 73). His reforms of the wardrobe and scenery provided up to four costume changes for the principals in each production. The 1827 season included an opera by Coccia, *Maria Stuarda, regina di Scozia* (to a libretto by P. Giannone); Ebers estimated that £2000 was spent on the scenery and costumes alone: 'The dresses of the principal characters, The Queens Mary and Elizabeth, Leicester, and Burleigh, were studiously magnificent' (ibid, 343). James Robinson Planché, antiquarian scholar, author and designer, brought the 12th century to the stage in 1823 at Covent Garden for Shakespeare's *King John*, clothing the entire cast, not just the leading roles, in historical costume.

By 1850 Her Majesty's Theatre possessed more than 5000 costumes in stock and the season's outlay for 'unmade fabric' was £1400, according to Shirley Brooks in the *Morning Chronicle* (20 March 1851). He reported that the wardrobe mistress spent considerable time in historical research before making the costumes, and the audiences were 'shown robes and garments not only in the form the nobles and ladies of olden days wore them, but of materials as rich and costly as theirs'. The ideal was to create an illusion of reality on the stage. It became possible to dress any period anywhere, since illustrated manuscripts survived from the Middle Ages and explorers were taking photographs in remote regions. Verdi took inspiration from 4000 years of history – from ancient Egypt in *Aida* (1871) and biblical times in *Nabucco* (1842), 13th-century Sicily in *Les vêpres siciliennes* (1855) and contemporary Paris in *La traviata* (1853). But tragedy, unlike *opera buffa*, could not yet be staged in contemporary dress, so the première of *La traviata* was set in the early 1700s and the following year was taken 75 years further back. In London the censors would not allow sin to be contemporary on the stage, so their Violetta (1856) also wore 1630s dress.

9. Miss Hughes as Reiza in Weber's 'Oberon'. Miss Hughes was a contemporary of Mary Anne Paton, who sang Reiza in the first performance (Covent Garden, London, 12 April 1826) so this dress is likely to be similar to the original. The opera is set in the 9th century, but her silhouette and ringlets are in the height of 1826 fashion. As the daughter of a caliph, she wears a turban headdress, with plumes pinned centre front and a veil (the floating veil is also a theatrical convention for a heroine). Other Turkish touches are her transparent sleeves and crescent moon decoration.

10. Costume drawings for Bellini's 'I puritani', Théâtre Italien, Paris, 24 January 1835, reflecting the supporters of Cromwell during the English Civil War, dressed c1630. Men's historical costume and hairstyle is usually modified less than women's by current fashion. Sir Giorgio's moustache and locks are in period, but Elvira's cap and hair are fashionably styled. (a) Sir Giorgio (first sung by Luigi Lablache). (b) Elvira (first sung by Giulia Grisi). She has fashionably sloping shoulders and a fitted waist. Her lace collar is a compromise between the very wide look of 1835 and period accuracy. Slashing on the bodice denotes 'period', and the tasselled points are 'theatrical'.

(a)

(b)

(a)

(b)

11. The title roles in Wagner's 'Tristan und Isolde': costume drawings by Franz Seitz for the première, Munich, 10 June 1865. 12th-century dress has been chosen for the legend, with Celtic ornamentation in gold and precious stones. (a) Tristan (sung by Ludwig Schnorr von Carolsfeld). His costume, sword and shield are those of a Crusader. (b) Isolde (sung by Malvine Schnorr von Carolsfeld). Historical reconstruction is inevitably influenced by contemporary taste. Women's medieval dress was close-fitting and floor length; Isolde's costume is neither, but nevertheless is very bold, considering the great width of crinoline skirts in 1865.

12. Nellie Melba as Violetta in Verdi's 'La traviata', Théâtre de la Monnaie, Brussels, 9 November 1887. She inscribed the photograph given to Jean Worth: '1850 – costumes – bravo!'. However, a crinoline would have appeared ugly and absurd in 1887 when fashionable dress was straight and stiff with a right-angled back bustle. Worth created a sensitive compromise which had the character of the 1850s without being too wide for contemporary taste. The ball gown, in soft green velvet veiled with pink chiffon and trimmed with light fur, had the characteristic off-the-shoulder neckline and tiered skirt. Melba agreed to her hair being dressed low on the neck, interwoven with flowers at the nape, in the style associated with the Empress Eugénie. Prima donnas travelled with their own gowns, and Melba probably wore this in Palermo, New York, London, Amsterdam, Rotterdam and Philadelphia, 1892–1910.

Puccini also ranged far and wide, from Japan, China and the California gold rush, to Napoleonic Rome and the 19th-century Paris of Louis Philippe. Wagner looked to the Middle Ages with meticulous attention to costume details for *Rienzi* (1842), *Tannhäuser* (1845), *Lohengrin* (1850) and *Die Meistersinger* (1868). With *Tristan* (1865) he went back to Celtic myth (fig.11), and for the *Ring* (1869–76) to the ancient Teutonic gods. German and Scandinavian tribes had not left statues of their gods as examples, so a costume was invented. Wagner favoured the 7th-century look, when Vikings and Saxons had been victorious, and sketched tunics down to the calves, elongated shields and winged helmets. He dressed his warrior maiden, Brünnhilde, in a corselet of chain mail, with flowing hair and winged helmet – dramatic, but historically inaccurate (fig.23*a*). This 19th-century version of Viking dress became traditional at Bayreuth, but designers for other productions often gave the Teutonic gods medieval dress.

In May 1865 August Bournonville, guiding genius of Copenhagen's Royal Danish Ballet, wrote (*Mit Theaterliv*, Copenhagen, 1847–77; Eng. trans., 1979, pp.157–9):

It is Paris, of course, that has led the way for the enormous progress made in the so-called *mise-en-scène* ... The Opéra ... displayed such magnificence in the way of scenery and costumes that it literally crushed the lyric drama ... one must do justice to one branch of the stage that has made real progress, namely the costuming. Nowadays it has become an actual science, and in the research as well as its application the French set us an example worth following. I dare say that what is suitable to the character still has a hard fight to wage against that which is becoming, while the correctness of a costume must combat what is merely brilliant. Ideas of what is *beautiful* are continuously dependent upon the whims of *fashion*, but the true magic of a play is realized only when the situation is supported by a faithful picture of time and place. Unfortunately, I have all too often had to recognize that only with the utmost difficulty are the demands of the ballet, and especially of modern dancing, reconciled with authentic costume. But where all theory finally breaks down is with *the prima donnas*, both in drama and in opera. As a rule, they give their imaginations such free play that they go beyond the bounds of history and geography. There is nothing to be done about this. Try to persuade them and you are laughed at. Give an order and they go into convulsions. Tell them that their talent is beneath contempt; they will let it pass. But call to their attention the extravagance of their toilette; they will never forgive you for it!

Interest in nationalism was reflected in new Slavonic operas. Smetana's *The Bartered Bride* (1866) called for Czech peasant costume. In St Petersburg, operas based on Russian history required native peasant dress and Russian historical costume. These presented no costume difficulties for Russian designers and could be copied for productions elsewhere. The robe worn by Fyodor Shalyapin in the coronation scene of *Boris Godunov* is so like the genuine article that the London Theatre Museum suggests it was made by the ecclesiastical tailors in St Petersburg. Shalyapin carried his operatic wardrobe with him, the usual practice of the great soloists. Nellie Melba, Adelina Patti, Emma Albani and Emma Eames went to the leading fashion designer Charles Frederick Worth for their gowns and also for their theatrical costumes (fig.12). Worth, and his son Jean P. Worth, had a rare talent for adapting historical periods to the prevailing ideal of elegance. In *Melodies and Memories* (1925) Melba recalled that

Some of the dresses which Worth made for me were dreams of beauty. In particular, there was an exquisite coat of cloth of gold, hand-painted and sewn with jewels, which I wore in *Lohengrin*. It was so lovely that when I appeared in Russia before the Tsar and Tsarita [1891] they sent for me after the second act, and one of the first actions of the Tsarita was to bend over my cloak and take it in her hands and to stroke it, saying: 'How perfectly lovely this is'.

The permissiveness allowed to the principal singers could lead to an extravagance in their dress that was not compatible with other costumes on stage. Adelina Patti, appearing at Covent Garden as Violetta in 1895, is said to have worn a magnificent white dress studded with 3700 diamonds worth £200 000 (H. Klein: *The Reign of Patti*, 1920, p.328). Costume design improved at Covent Garden after Attilio Comelli was engaged in 1898. He worked prolifically for 22 years (fig.14) and many of his productions stayed in the repertory until after World War II. His 1899 *Bohème* was not replaced until 1974, by Julia Trevelyan Oman's designs (fig.21). The earliest *verismo* opera, *Carmen* (1875), required believable costumes for poor people. Not the fare expected from the Opéra-Comique, it was initially unpopular; for the successful 1883 production, two Spanish painters, Ignacio Zuloaga and Ermenegildo Anglada, were engaged to provide the Mediterranean ambience and authentic costumes for the gypsies, cigarette-girls, whores, smugglers and soldiers.

The earliest master of operetta, Jacques Offenbach, delighted Paris by making the gods of Olympus dance the cancan. After *Orphée aux enfers* (1858) and *La belle Hélène* (1864) in ancient Greek dress, Offenbach turned to the contemporary scene and an international variety of dress. The star of *La Grande-Duchesse de Gérolstein* (1867), Hortense Schneider, was regally dressed in a ball-gown embroidered with her 'national' flowers and an ermine cloak, designed by Worth exactly like those he supplied to the real duchesses in the audience. Strauss's *Die Fledermaus* (1874) allowed for a variety of costume, as did Lehár's *Lustige Witwe* (1905). The ladies' dresses for Gilbert and Sullivan's *Patience* (which opened at the Savoy Theatre, London, in 1881) were designed by Gilbert, while Richard D'Oyly Carte wrote to the theatrical costume house L. & H. Nathan, Tichborne Street, asking to be 'furnished with 16 Dragoon Officers' costumes complete – tunic, trousers, helmet, plume, pouch-belt and pouch, gauntlets, waist belt, sword, knot and spurs for the sum of £12.10.0d each'. This was the beginning of a long association for the firm with the Savoy operas. (The designers Peter Goffin, Wilhelm, Charles Ricketts and George Sheringham took their drawings to Nathans' to be realized.) The costumes for *Patience* were the first ever to be seen by electric light, installed initially in the Savoy Theatre following the invention of J. W. Swan's incandescent bulb. The brightness showed up far more detail and did not kill green and blue as gaslight and candlelight had done. Indeed, white fabrics shone so much that they had to be replaced by cream ones, and massive amounts of sequins and metallic embroidery were no longer needed for visibility.

By the turn of the century musical comedy had emerged, with its chorus of girls dressed for frivolous glamour and a bit risqué. Audiences expected to be delighted by at least five costume changes, and the more the merrier. A chorus-line of butterflies might metamorphose into flowers, birds, marine creatures, nationalities, bathing beauties, 'Farmerettes', 'Prince Charmings', and models in high-fashion day dresses and evening gowns. F. Osmond Carr's *In Town* (1892, Prince of Wales Theatre) and Ivan Caryll's *The Shop Girl* (1894, Gaiety Theatre) were set, as the titles suggest, in London. The USA introduced Gustave

Kerker's *The Belle of New York* (1897), and London responded with Leslie Stuart's *The Belle of Mayfair* (1906).

At the end of the 19th century a reaction against naturalism began in Russia and Europe. At his Private Russian Opera in Moscow, Savva Mamontov engaged artists more interested in primitive Russian paintings, icons and peasant art than in historical accuracy. They wanted tonal harmony of decor and costume, so they often hand-painted the furs, armour and designs on to cloth and canvas, or specially dyed silks and velvets. The aim was to create an imaginative stage picture that enhanced the mood of the opera: Rimsky-Korsakov's *Snow Maiden* was given brilliantly coloured fairy-tale sets and costumes by Viktor Vasnetsov in 1885.

5. 20TH CENTURY. After the success of *Boris Godunov* in Paris in 1908, with costumes designed by Alexander Golovin and Ivan Bilibin, Dyagilev presented in the following year the Polovtsian Dances from *Prince Igor* with scenery and costumes by Nicholas Roerich, *Ivan the Terrible* with costumes by Dmitry Stelletsky, and the orgy scenes and finale from Serov's opera *Judith* with costumes by Léon Bakst. Western Europe had not seen such brilliant colouring since the 18th century; the bold, sensuous and imaginative design thrilled audiences and its influence was immediate. Roerich designed *The Snow Maiden* for the Opéra-Comique in Paris (1908) and for Chicago (1921–2), where it became the striking success of the season. Russian artists, active internationally, were led by Bakst, Alexandre Benois, Boris Anisfeld, Mikhail Larionov, Natal'ya Gontcharova, Konstantin Korovin, Sergey Sudeykin and Mstislav Dobuzhinsky. From its opening in 1883 until World War I, the Metropolitan Opera House often duplicated European productions and ordered costumes from abroad. Designers also were imported, including Hans Kautsky, Mariano Fortuny, Paul Paquereau, Antonio Rovescalli and Vittorio Rota. In Milan and New York, Alfredo Edel brought a stylistic and craftsman-like conception.

The animal kingdom had appeared in non-singing roles – as a lion in Handel's *Alcina* (1735), as 'wild animals' in *Die Zauberflöte* (1791) and as a magpie calling the single word 'Ninette' in Rossini's *La gazza ladra* (1817). However, an animal costume that permits singing poses a unique challenge. The dragon (Fafner in disguise) was the first to sing, in Wagner's *Siegfried* (1876) with costumes by Carl Emil Doepler. Rimsky-Korsakov's *The Tale of Tsar Saltan* (1900), designed by Mikhail Vrubel', included a swan (princess in disguise) and a bumble-bee (Guidon in disguise). The next operatic creatures to sing were, appropriately, birds: the title role in Rimsky-Korsakov's *The Golden Cockerel* (1909), designed by Ivan Bilibin, and in Stravinsky's *The Nightingale* (1914), designed by Alexandre Benois; Henri Matisse designed the famous 1920 production. All creatures great and small were to follow – Albert Wolff's *L'oiseau bleu* (1919), designed by Boris Anisfeld; Stravinsky's *Renard* (1922), designed by Mikhail Larionov (for illustration *see* STAGE DESIGN, fig.18); Janáček's *The Cunning Little Vixen* (1924), designed by Eduard Milén; Ravel's *L'enfant et les sortilèges* (1925), with decor by Alphonse Visconti and costumes by Georgette Vialet; Britten's *Noye's Fludde* (1958), designed by Ceri Richards; Andrew Lloyd Webber's musical *Cats* (1981), designed by John Napier; Knussen's *Where the Wild Things Are* and *Higglety Pigglety Pop!* (both 1984, Glyndebourne), with librettos and designs by Maurice Sendak; and Birtwistle's *Yan Tan Tethera* (1986, Opera Factory), designed by David Roger with sheep masks by Arianne Gastambide.

The first American operettas were as European as the origins of their composers. There was 15th-century French costume for Rudolf Friml's *Vagabond King* (1925), 1860s German dress for Sigmund Romberg's *Student Prince* (1924) and Arab robes for his *Desert Song* (1926). Regional USA was represented on stage by American-born composers, notably in Jerome Kern's *Show Boat* (1927), with settings by Josef Urban and costumes by John Harkrider; Gershwin's *Porgy and Bess* (1935), with settings by Sudeykin and costumes by the Theatre Guild Workroom under the supervision of Jean Tate; and Rodgers's *Oklahoma!* (1943), with settings by Lemuel Ayres and costumes by Miles White.

What the 19th century termed realism, the early 20th century called mere imitation. Historically precise details were replaced by designs inspired by the music and the libretto for an individual, overall concept. Georg Fuchs, founder of the Munich Artists' Theatre in 1908, advocated 'stylized' period dresses that were a creative synthesis of all the years of fashion in all the places pertinent to the opera, rather than an exact historical dating. Thus, the costumes for Mozart's *Le nozze di Figaro* (1784), with a libretto by Da Ponte based on Beaumarchais' play – a continuation of the story of the barber of Seville – should contain elements of fashion from about 1700 to 1784 in both Spain and France, with a court atmosphere of Maria Theresa's Vienna, and hints of Salzburg and Ceneda, Italy. Stylized and exaggerated modern costumes were used in the 1920s by the 'constructionists', who sought to eliminate emotional content; they harmonized scenery and costumes by including the same motifs in both. (These ideas were followed in the designs by Pet Halmen (costumes) and Jean-Pierre Ponnelle (sets) for the 1985 Bayerische Staatsoper production of Hindemith's *Cardillac* in Munich; see fig.24.)

The revolt against realism was furthered by Max Reinhardt, whose productions of the classical operettas of Offenbach were brilliant successes; Ernst Stern designed *Orphée aux enfers* for Berlin in 1906, and Max Rée the 1921 Copenhagen production. At the request of Richard Strauss and Hugo von Hofmannsthal, Reinhardt directed the premières of *Der Rosenkavalier* (1911), with designs by Alfred Roller (for illustration *see* ROSENKAVALIER, DER), and, as a finale to Molière's *Le bourgeois gentilhomme*, *Ariadne auf Naxos* (1912), with designs by Ernst Stern (fig.13). Stern (*My Life, My Stage*, p.127) considered that *Le bourgeois gentilhomme* was

> a social and moral satire abounding textually in drastic persiflage of a particular epoch, and I therefore decided that the costumes in our production of it must be characteristic of the period around 1700. At the same time, I argued, my operatic types must look as French society of 1700 would have expected its mythological figures to look on the stage.

Creating a period view of a still earlier time is historical authenticity of a kind the Romantics never attempted. Pet Halmen designed costumes for Mozart's *Mitridate, rè di Ponto* in Jean-Pierre Ponnelle's production (1983, Schwetzingen Festival), using the mixture of Roman heroic dress, women's hoops and tall wigs that Mozart knew in 1770. Stern could usually do what he liked with

13. Costume drawings by Ernst Stern for the first production of Richard Strauss's 'Ariadne auf Naxos', Hoftheater, Stuttgart, 25 October 1912. The mythological theme abounds in 'delightful and charming anachronisms' (E. Stern, 'My Life, My Stage', London, 1951, p.127). He fuses an 18th-century theatrical view of ancient costume and hairstyles with fashionable touches of 1912. (left) Ariadne (sung by Maria Jeritza). The mantle frames her face like a Madonna, then swirls around her in gay abandon. Her chiton exposes a shoulder, leg and bare feet. (centre) Bacchus (sung by Herman Jadlowker). A handsome young man, he raises both hands and a staff in the pose of a French dancing master. His curls are crowned with stylized vine leaves and the Greek chiton is girded with an 18th-century sash. The weighted corners of his mantle and his sandals are in the antique style. (right) A Dryad. Her fan-shaped cap is topped with plumes and arcs of vine leaves and her arms are adorned with sleeve flounces, vines and ribbons in the style of 1700. Her bare shoulders are evocative of evening wear in 1912; the pointed bodice and bustle-like draperies are in the 1700 style and the softly pleated underskirt and sandals are ancient Greek.

(a)

(b)

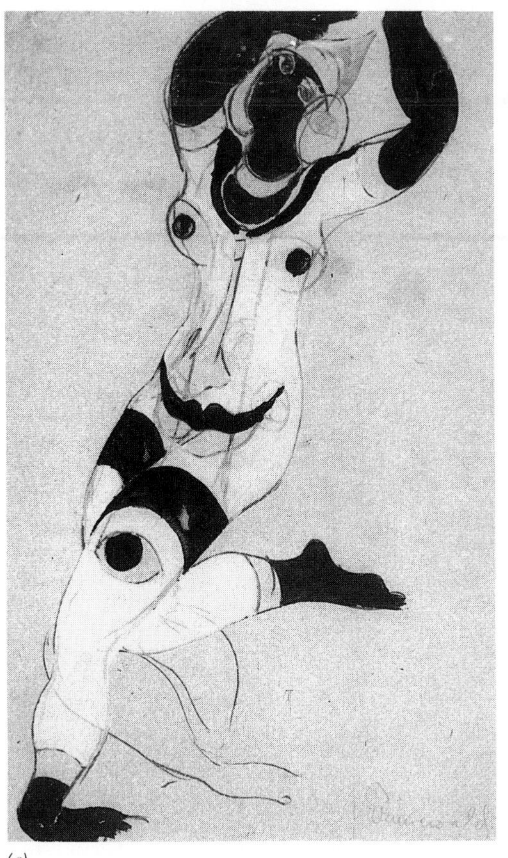

(a) (b)

15. Costume drawings by Isaac Grünewald for dancers in Saint-Saëns' 'Samson et Dalila', Stockholm Royal Opera, 21 March 1921. Grünewald, living in Paris during the 1920s, was an admirer of Matisse and Dufy. (a) Female dancer. The man's moustachioed face projected on to her body is both erotic and humorous. Her leotard and cap are posterpaint-blue with black and white decoration. (b) Male dancer. Bold abstract patterns express strength and power. His robe is purple with a black and gold design.

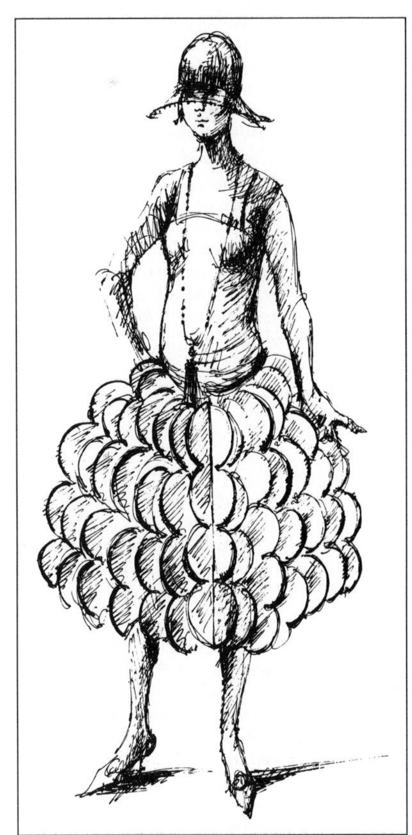

16. Costume drawing by Irene Sharaff for a dancer in 'Billion Dollar Baby', a Broadway musical set in the 1920s, written by Betty Comden and Adolph Green, with a score by Morton Gould and choreography by Jerome Robbins, 1945. Sharaff used a newly invented plastic for the transparent cloche hats, thereby allowing the short haircuts and 'bangs' of the chorus girls to be seen.

14. (opposite) Costume drawings by Attilio Comelli for Verdi's 'Aida', Covent Garden, London, 14 May 1914: (a) Aida (sung by Emmy Destinn). Photographs show 19th-century Aidas with well rounded curves, as was the fashion. This slender Aida, in keeping with the change in fashion, is realistically more like ancient Egyptian paintings of beautiful women. She wears a pale gold sleeveless dress, with pleated skirt edged in red. Both the overskirt and circular head covering are royal blue, dotted in gold. The detail drawing shows the decorative red and blue edge of the draped overskirt. Her fringed red sash is held in place with a blue ribbon, tied in a bow. Both collar and head circlet are made of gold, set with turquoise stones, and the snake bracelets are gold. White veils, falling from the back of her circlet to the hipline, are drawn up across her arms and attached to the bands across the bodice. (b) Ramfis (sung by Adamo Didur). This unsigned drawing may be a copy; construction details have been added in pencil. The robe, shoes and cloak are white with gold for the protective falcon wings and lotus and papyrus emblems of Upper and Lower Egypt. The cap, with its long flaps, is red and the sash is yellow with an orange and gold design. His false symbolic beard denotes wisdom.

(a)

(b)

17. *Costume drawings by Oliver Messel for two Rossini operas at the 1954 Edinburgh International Festival (Glyndebourne Festival Opera): (a) Countess Adèle (sung by Sari Barabas) in 'Le comte Ory'. Her headdress and sky-blue dress, with gold decoration and sleeve linings, are based on the medieval Lady and the Unicorn tapestries and Flemish and Netherlandish painting. In the neo-romantic tradition, Messel was known for his poetic imagination and sense of elegance, and was meticulous in selecting fabrics and colours. (b) Dr Bartolo (sung by Ian Wallace) in 'Il barbiere di Siviglia'. He wears a white wig and shirt with an outfit of dark brown and black. For this opera buffa, Messel selected the colours from a Goya painting: yellows, orange, warm browns, blood-red, grey-blue, and black.*

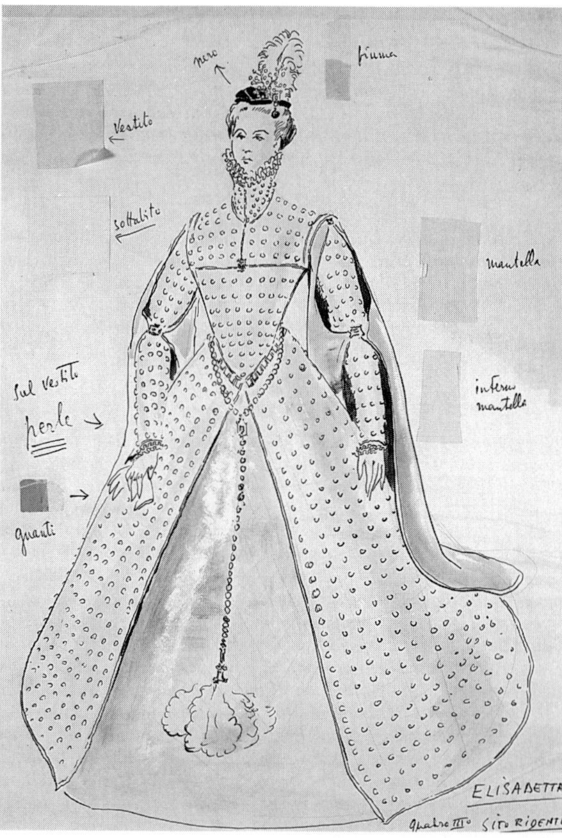

18. *Costume drawings by Maurizio Chiari for Verdi's 'Don Carlos', Act 2 scene ii, Covent Garden, London, 9 May 1958, directed and designed by Luchino Visconti. He provided a realistic and lavish evocation of 16th-century Spain.*

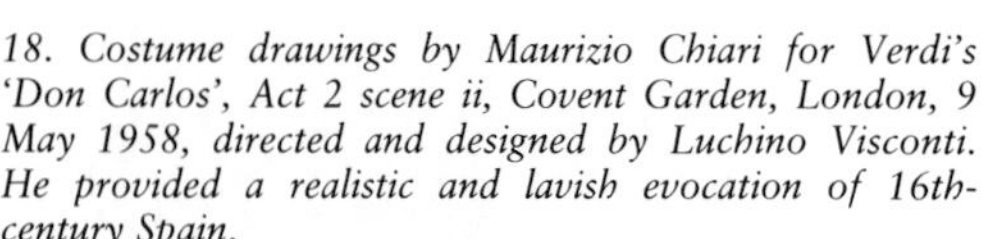

(a) Elisabeth de Valois (sung by Gré Brouwenstijn). Notes for the dressmaker instruct that pearls are to be sewn on her pale pink silk dress. She has a white silk underdress, pale blue cloak with shell-pink lining and medium blue gloves. Her tiny black cap is decorated with a chartreuse feather and a gold and pearl ornament; Visconti changed his mind about the feather fan attached to the decorative chain around her waist and crossed it out. For further illustration see BROUWENSTIJN, GRÉ.

(a)

(b)

19. Maria Callas as Floria Tosca in Puccini's 'Tosca', Covent Garden, London, 21 January 1964, directed by Franco Zeffirelli; a classic production known the world over, not least for the red (sometimes known as Callas) dress of Act 2: (a) Costume drawing by Marcel Escoffier. The Empire-style gown, designed for unadorned velvet, is simplicity itself. (b) Maria Callas on stage, illustrating the transformation of her costume from drawing to making. Glamour has been added by gold braid on the neckline and Empire waist, and by the diamond and ruby tiara, drop earrings and necklace.

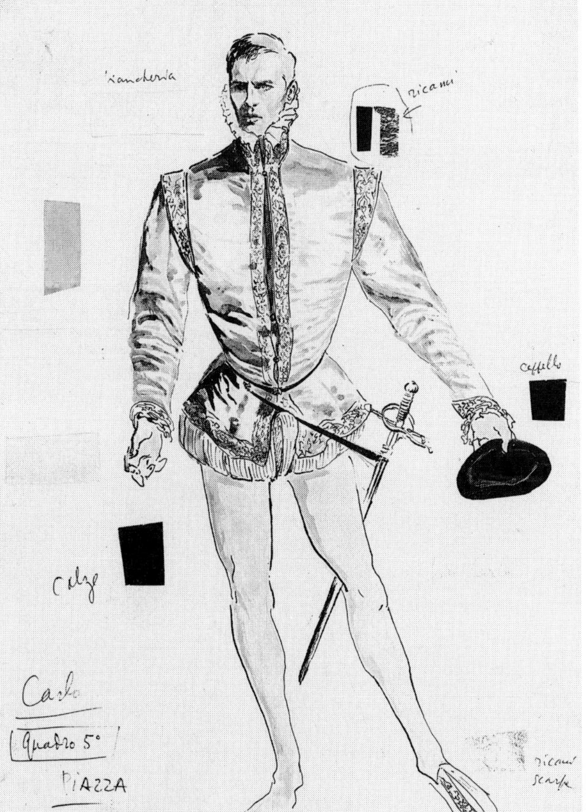

18 (b) Don Carlos (sung by Jon Vickers) dressed in pale peach linen, a yellow ochre jacket and bright yellow breeches with decoration of dark brown and gold. Cap and tights are dark brown and his shoes have gold decoration.

(a)

(b)

20. Costume designs by Tanya Moiseiwitsch for a production by Tyrone Guthrie of Britten's 'Peter Grimes', Metropolitan Opera, New York, 20 January 1967. In her creation of an 1830s North Sea fishing community, each person is individually costumed. (a) Ellen Orford (sung by Lucine Amara). The gentle schoolmistress is dressed in royal blue with black trimming, white dickey and cuffs, straw bonnet and a black shawl. (b) Peter Grimes (sung by Jon Vickers) wears green wellington boots with grey socks folded over the tops, and otherwise is all in black: sweater, trousers, coat and cap. The fishing net was specially woven in twine thick enough to be visible to the audience. For further illustration see VICKERS, JON.

21. Costume drawings by Julia Trevelyan Oman for Puccini's 'La Bohème', Covent Garden, London, 6 February 1974. In this, the first new production of the opera at Covent Garden since it was originally staged in 1899, Oman has depicted the period most precisely. (a) Rodolfo (sung by Placido Domingo) wears a romantic-style soft shirt and characteristic long jacket, plaid waistcoat and narrow plaid trousers.

(a)

(b)

22. Tristan and Isolde in Wagner's opera, produced by Michael Hampe, designed by Mauro Pagano: a co-production of the Paris Opéra, 28 January 1985, and Cologne Opera, 9 March 1986. The drawings exemplify Pagano's neo-romantic style. (a) Tristan (sung by René Kollo and Spas Wenkoff) in three costume variations and undergarment. Although based on medieval design, his poncho, boots, and leather and metal gear are all part of the 1980s fashion scene. (b) Isolde (sung by Ute Vinzing and Jeannine Altmeyer) at the end of Act 1, with a pattern for her medieval-inspired gown.

21 (b) Mimì (sung by Katia Ricciarelli) has her hair parted in the middle, and a shawl envelops her narrow shoulders.

23. Three designs for Brünnhilde in Wagner's 'Die Walküre', illustrating the influence of contemporary fashion.

(a) Amalie Materna in the original production of the complete 'Ring' cycle, Bayreuth, 1876, with costumes designed by Carl Emil Doepler. The winged helmet and chain mail had been suggested by Wagner. Her silhouette and draped skirt with a train were fashionable in 1876.

(b) Lucienne Bréval, Paris Opéra, 1908. Her dress is based on the design by Charles Bianchini for her performance in the first Paris production (12 May 1893). The components of her costume are retained in the hourglass female shape of the belle époque.

(c) Costume drawing for Catarina Ligendza by Peter Sykora, Deutsche Oper, Berlin, 6 October 1984. Brünnhilde continues to be identified by her helmet, but the wings are stylized and made of metal. Black leather and metal studs, from breastplate to military greatcoat, are used exclusively. Leather trousers, high fashion in 1984, contribute to the military look. Her golden hair provides the only colour.

(a)

(b)

(c)

(a)

(b)

24. Costume drawings by Pet Halmen for Ladies and Gentlemen of the Court in Hindemith's 'Cardillac', Bayerische Staatsoper, Munich, 1985. With Jean-Pierre Ponnelle, director and set designer, he moved the period flavour from Louis XIV to pre-revolutionary Paris for that period's extravagance. The costumes are a startling pastiche of the 1750s, 1920s and early 1980s. (a) Ladies of the Court. The headdresses combine 18th-century court wigs, 1920s hair-ornament feathers and 1980s punk flavour. From neck to waist, the gowns are 1920s. The skirts have 1750s hoops, but are decorated with 1920s constructionist designs. The 1980s chunky-style jewellery is worn in 1920s fashion. The fan, muff and shoes are about 1750. (b) Gentlemen of the Court. Stylized 18th-century hats meet high collars, so no hair or wig is seen. The coats are cut in 18th-century fashion, but the exaggerated and asymmetrical collars, lapels and skirt panels again express 1920s constructionist ideas. The shirts, with high 18th-century necklines, are similar to 20th-century polo-necks. Breeches, stockings and shoes are 18th-century.

the costumes since Reinhardt's principal interest lay in the staging, but the designer credits Reinhardt with introducing him to the psychological importance of colour. For instance, Reinhardt saw Iago in green, 'glistening like a reptile'.

In 1912 the Russian expressionist painter and art theorist Kandinsky published an experimental 'colour opera', *Der gelbe Klang*, which proved influential; it consists of a series of six 'images' with an introduction. He believed that changes in colour and light acquire an 'independent significance' equal to that of music and dance in stimulating the inner experiences of the spectator. Colour was used brilliantly by Irene Sharaff. She designed costumes for many successful musicals (fig.16) and for Villa-Lobos's operetta *Magdalena* (1948), set in Latin America and Paris about 1911. In *Broadway & Hollywood* (p.43) she wrote of the opportunity this work allowed for her

to key a number in one basic colour ... the period costumes, and the clothes of the tribe living along the Magdalena River had a uniformity in silhouette and proportions – including derby hats worn by the women – that had to be followed fairly closely. The freedom in designing the costumes was in the colors and there was opportunity for gaiety and drama. In the production number at the edge of the jungle, the singers and dancers, the entire ensemble of the large company, poured slowly on the stage in every conceivable hue and tone of red. Underlying the music ... the reds sang out in unison. This saturation of reds and the power in color were never more vividly illustrated for me than in that number.

Cecil Beaton used a black and white palette to stunning effect in the stylized ladies' dresses of the Ascot scene in Lerner and Loewe's *My Fair Lady* (1956). In his introduction to *Cecil Beaton's Fair Lady* (London, 1964) he wrote of his excitement for the stage assignment:

At first the Producer, Herman Levin, and the Director, Moss Hart, had considered that our venture should be costumed in the period around 1904. This was the epoch in which all recent musicals had automatically been costumed ... But so frantic was my appeal for the re-creation of the world I knew before it disappeared in the first World War, that I was given the reins. ... When I told Moss of my intention to make Ascot entirely black and white – an idea that had originated with the famous Black Ascot after King Edward [VII]'s death [1910] – he was worried. 'You're sure it won't look like a comic strip?'

The production epitomized Beaton's romantic notion of the theatre, 'which at its finest should be an opulent cornucopia showering the spectator with golden illusions not to be found at home'.

In Bernstein's *West Side Story*, produced on Broadway in 1957 and as a film in 1961, Sharaff used colour for historical and psychological effect (*Broadway & Hollywood*, pp.100–01):

I relied on colour to contrast the two gangs, with touches in their outfits that were taken from Renaissance clothes ... teen-age boys one saw on the streets of New York had arrived at a uniform of their own ... of blue jeans or chinos, T-shirts, windbreakers, and sneakers ... For the Sharks, the Puerto Rican gang, I used sharp purple, pink-violet, blood red, and black; for the Jets ... I chose muted indigo blues, musty yellows, and ochre. The colors seemed to suit their physical appearance ... [the Puerto Rican] outfits gave them an aggressive quality ... The modern windbreaker with a hood, particularly when worn with tight-fitting jeans, has a silhouette and line resembling that of figures in Florentine Renaissance paintings ... The one article of clothing of ethnic character the Puerto Rican girls wore was the rebozo, the long woollen stole with fringed ends worn around the shoulders and sometimes also over the head in Mexico and the Caribbean area. In the last scene, when the hero was shot, the rebozos over the girls' heads made them look like traditional figures of mourning.

This adaptation of a period's silhouette has been a favourite 20th-century device. The great success of Nigel Playfair's revival of *The Beggar's Opera* in 1920 (at the Lyric Theatre, Hammersmith) was due in part to Claud Lovat Fraser's designs. In keeping with the opera's subject, he eliminated sentiment by eliminating period flowered and figured materials. The colours were clear and hard within a historically correct outline of hoops, wigs, hats, shoes and wide-cuffed sleeves.

Virgil Thomson asked Florine Stettheimer, the painter of *Cathedrals of Fifth Avenue*, to design his *Four Saints in Three Acts* (1934), set in 16th-century Spain. Stettheimer's great cellophane cyclorama dazzled under clear white, then sky-blue, light. Scenic textures of lace, feathers, gilt, glass and transparency, together with vivid costumes for the all-black cast (the two St Theresas wore cardinal's robes of red or white for the different acts) were a theatrical sensation on Broadway and an inspiration to designers (for illustration *see* FOUR SAINTS IN THREE ACTS).

Opera costume designers usually emerge from among stage designers, fashion designers and fine artists. An artist, if untrained in cutting and sewing fabric, may not perceive difficulties in transferring two-dimensional drawings to three-dimensional singers. Often designs need to be modified in collaboration with experienced wardrobe personnel, to ensure ease of movement and comfort for the performer. The importance of this working relationship is not always acknowledged. The composer can be a visual artist as well: Lou Harrison was responsible for the shadow figures and the decoration of the large stage (built by William Colvig) for the première of his puppet opera *Young Caesar* (1971).

During the second half of the 20th century the influence of the director and the designer increased. At times the two jobs have merged to create a director-designer – and the result is a unity of vision: notable productions include Wieland Wagner's *Ring* cycles, Zeffirelli's *La bohème* (1963, La Scala), Everding's *Tristan und Isolde* (1974, Bayreuth) and Ponnelle's *Idomeneo* (1982, Metropolitan Opera). The dual role has been taken also by Philip Proust, Pier Luigi Pizzi, Sandro Sequi, Ezio Frigerio, Achim Freyer, Stefanos Lazaridis, Tom Cairns and David Fielding. A diversity of design styles, including realism, neo-historicism, expressionism, symbolism and surrealism, has been used to make opera exciting for modern audiences, to 'test the present against the past'.

Wieland Wagner knew opera to be a non-realistic art form and decided to abolish the kitsch realism of a German past (whether authentic or legendary) to achieve a timeless effect, inspired by ancient Greek theatrical design. Lighting could focus on the central action and be an eloquent asset to both situation and character. Brünnhilde was costumed in magnificent colour and classic simplicity, without her traditional metallic brassière and helmet. This abstract, non-realistic approach prepared the way for Götz Friedrich's production of the *Ring* cycle for the Royal Opera at Covent Garden (1974–6), with sets and lighting by Josef Svoboda and costumes by Ingrid Rosell. A science fiction fantasy was created using laser beams, mirrors and high-intensity spots of white and brilliantly coloured light. Characters were costumed symbolically to illuminate their relationships: Froh as a 'drag queen' with a tendency to hysteria and Loge as a weird isolationist manipulating the gods. Friedrich's later Covent Garden production (1990–91), which had received its première by the Deutsche Oper, Berlin, in

25. *Costume designs by Maria Björnson for Janáček's 'The Cunning Little Vixen' in a joint production by Scottish Opera and the WNO, first shown at the Edinburgh Festival in 1980: Toad, Caterpillar and Cricket (above; played by children from local South Wales schools); Cock (sung by Richard Morton) and Hens (sung by Diane Fuge and members of the WNO female chorus). Björnson's costume drawings illustrate the essence of each animal adapted to human shape and characteristics; the use of make-up, rather than masks, ensures the singers' comfort. Movement, choreographed by Stuart Hopps, is suggested in their stance: Toad is waterproof in goggles, sou'wester and wellington boots; Caterpillar undulates like his accordion; Cricket bows across taut 'legs'; Cock struts in crested bowler and spats as the housewife Hens gossip and fuss in hairnets, curlers and aprons.*

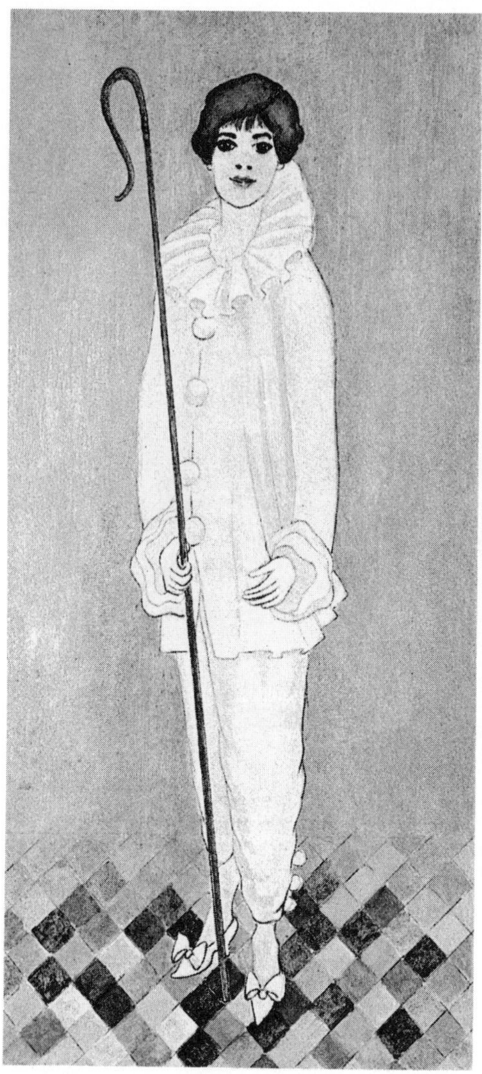

26. Two costumes for Berg's 'Lulu': (left) Jocelyn Herbert's design for the title role (sung by Carole Farley and Teresa Stratas) in a production by John Dexter, Metropolitan Opera, New York, 18 March 1977 (first version), 12 December 1980 (reconstructed version); colour lithograph. The image of Lulu as Pierrot is a symbol of untainted innocence. (right) Anna Panagulias as Lulu in a production by Lotfi Mansouri with costumes by Bob Mackie, San Francisco Opera, 9 September 1989. This was the operatic début for fashion designer Mackie; Lulu's 1930s gown for Act 3 scene i is in black velvet trimmed with fox fur and diamond crystal hand-beading. On the opening night some opera patrons wore Mackie dresses, recalling the glamorous era of Worth in Paris.

1984, was designed by Peter Sykora. The scenic concept is a 'time tunnel' of no fixed historical time or place. Every character is 'both present and past', reflecting the epic dimensions of the *Ring*, in which, according to Friedrich, 'the beginning is the end and the end is a new beginning' (*Kennedy Center Opera House 1989*, programme booklet, p.20). The costumes, therefore, juxtapose elements of different periods in an attempt to create a time-allusive ambience (fig.23*c*).

Luchino Visconti and his disciple Franco Zeffirelli delighted in lavishly detailed, realistic stagings and gorgeous, elaborately ornamented costumes (figs.18 and 19). Visconti said that he set *La traviata* (1955, La Scala; designed by Lila de Nobili) in 'La belle époque' because he thought Maria Callas looked especially beautiful in gowns of that period. Neo-romantic design, sometimes called 'nostalgic historicism', was exemplified in Oliver Messel's work (fig.17). Designers who have excelled in this style are David Walker, Peter Rice, Bob Crowley, Carlo Savi, Mauro Pagano (fig.22) and Tony Walton.

The team of Tyrone Guthrie, director, and Tanya Moiseiwitsch, designer, presented the first Covent Garden performances of Britten's *Peter Grimes* in 1947 and, for the 1967 season, were invited to produce it at the Metropolitan Opera (fig.20). There they were successful in creating a heightened realism, a stylized naturalism to evoke the sea and the harsh life of a fishing community in East Anglia. The costumes, in natural brown and grey dyes, seemed part of the landscape; Ellen Orford's royal blue dress was the only bright note.

Designers capable of creating in a diversity of styles choose the one most appropriate to the director's interpretation. Ita Maximowna, Jocelyn Herbert (fig.26), Jürgen Rose, John Bury, John Conklin, Maria Björnson (fig.25), William Dudley and Sue Blane are renowned for their eclecticism. For example, Blane designed realistic costumes for Trevor Nunn's production of *Porgy and Bess* (1986, Glyndebourne); stylized, dapper English 1920s costumes for Jonathan Miller's *Mikado* (1986, ENO); symbolic settings and costumes for Giles Havergal's *Nozze di Figaro* (1987, WNO); Ukrainian fairy-tale sets and costumes for David Pountney's *Christmas Eve* (1988, ENO); and fantastically surreal costumes for Richard Jones's *Love for Three Oranges* (1988, Opera North).

Artists, however, contribute unique styles. The Metropolitan Opera asked two famous painters to create their own individual fantasy worlds for *Die Zauberflöte*: Marc Chagall in 1967, and David Hockney in 1981. The director Peter Brook asked Salvador Dali to design *Salome* for Covent Garden (1949) because he considered that the surrealist's 'natural style has both what one might call the erotic degeneracy of Strauss and the imagery of Wilde' (*The Shifting Point: Forty Years of Theatrical Exploration, 1946–1987*, London, 1988, p.170). It proved too outrageous and was abandoned after six performances. The ENO chose the satirical cartoonist Gerald Scarfe for Offenbach's *Orphée aux enfers* in 1985. His witty designs, realized by Kandis Cook, delighted audiences.

Directors may change the period of an opera in order to gain fresh insights and the costume designer must then help to overcome anachronisms. For instance, Jonathan Miller's *Rigoletto* (1982, ENO) was transposed from a Renaissance court to 'Little Italy' in New York in the 1950s with the Duke of Mantua as 'Duke', a Mafia boss. The 'court jester' title role was interpreted as that of chief bartender, the butt of everyone's jokes in Duke's hotel headquarters. For Act 1 scene i Rigoletto stood out visually in his white barman's jacket (with black bow-tie and trousers) designed by Rosemary Vercoe, providing a 'shock of recognition'. Similarly, Miller and the designer Stefanos Lazaridis set *Tosca* (1986, Maggio Musicale Fiorentino) in fascist Rome; Peter Sellars, with his costume designer Duná Ramicová, put Handel's *Giulio Cesare in Egitto* (1985, Pepsico Summerfare Festival) into a 20th-century world dominated by Ronald Reagan, and *Die Zauberflöte* (1990, Glyndebourne) in the beach culture of southern California. For this setting, as exotic as Mozart's Egypt, the Three Boys have multicoloured Bermuda shorts and skateboards, Tamino wears a T-shirt and denims, Pamina is in a scarlet, princess-line dress and hippy beads, and Sarastro is a guru in a long robe and a stole.

Designers, as well as singers, travel the world. José Varona exemplifies the late 20th-century international designer – his work spans four continents, and he is noted in the worlds of opera, ballet and Shakespeare. Born in Argentina, he established himself in Buenos Aires during the late 1950s, then worked in Caracas and Rio de Janiero. From 1962 he designed operas in many centres in North America and (from 1969) Europe, and he has worked for Australian Opera in Sydney. Costumes also travel: David Hockney's designs for *The Rake's Progress* at Glyndebourne in 1977 were also created for La Scala – the costumes were later bought by San Francisco Opera and are now available on hire worldwide (for illustration *see* HOCKNEY, DAVID).

Co-production, a late 20th-century imaginative invention, allows companies to share the original cost of sets and costumes and, usually, engage their own singers. For example, Opera America, comprising 123 member-companies, is developing networks: Syracuse's *Porgy and Bess* was shared by Hartford and Buffalo.

GENERAL

J. Gregor: *Wiener szenische Kunst*, ii: *Das Bühnenkostüm in historischer, ästhetischer und psychologischer Analyse* (Zürich, 1925)

C. Fischer: *Les costumes de l'opéra* (Paris, 1931)

T. Komisarjevsky: *The Costume of the Theatre* (London, 1931)

N. M. Lobanova: *Russkiy istoricheskiy kostyum dlya stseni* (Moscow, 1945)

C. W. Beaumont: *Ballet Design: Past & Present* (London, 1946)

O. Strunk: *Source Readings in Music History from Classical Antiquity to the Romantic Era* (London, 1952)

J. Laver: *Costume in the Theatre* (London, 1964)

M. Monteverdi, ed.: *Catalogo del Museo Teatrale alla Scala*, iii: *Scenografia e costumi* (Milan, 1975)

E. Berckenhagen and G. Wagner: *Bretter, die die Welt bedeuten* (Berlin, 1978)

L. Van Witsen: *Costuming for Opera: Who Wears What and Why* (Bloomington, IN, 1981)

D. de Marly: *Costume on the Stage 1600–1940* (London, 1982)

THE RENAISSANCE

G. B. Giraldi Cinthio: *Discorsi intorno al comporre de i romanzi, delle comedie, e delle tragedie, e di altre maniere di poesie* (Venice, 1554); ed. G. Antimaco, *G. B. Giraldi Cinthio: Scritti estetici*, Biblioteca rara, lii–liii (Milan, 1864)

A. Warburg: 'I costumi teatrali per gli intermezzi del 1589', *Commemorazione della riforma melodrammatica* (Florence, 1895), 103–46; rev. with notes by G. Bing, in A. Warburg: *Gesammelte Schriften*, i (Leipzig, 1932), 259–300, 394–438

A. M. Nagler: *Theatre Festivals of the Medici, 1539–1637* (New Haven, CT, 1964)

S. M. Newton: *Renaissance Theatre Costume and the Sense of the Historic Past* (New York, 1975)

17TH CENTURY

C. F. Menestrier: *Des ballets anciens et modernes selon les règles du théâtre* (Paris, 1682, 4/1686)

J. Gregor, ed.: *Ludovico Burnacini: Maschere*, Monumenta scenica, i (Vienna, 1924)

S. T. Worsthorne: *Venetian Opera in the Seventeenth Century* (Oxford, 1954)

P. D. Massar: 'Costume Drawings by Stefano Della Bella for the Florentine Theater', *Master Drawings*, viii (1970), 243–66

F. Lesure: *L'opéra classique français: XVII et XVIII siècles* (Geneva, 1972)

M. F. Christout: *The Ballet de Cour in the 17th century* (Geneva, 1987)

M. M. McGowan: *The Court Ballet of Louis XIII: a Collection of Working Designs for Costumes, 1615–33* (London, 1987)

18TH CENTURY

J. Messelreuter: *Neu-eröffneter Masquen-Saal* (Bayreuth, 1723)

T. Jefferys: *A Collection of the Dresses of Different Nations, Ancient and Modern … to which are added the Habits of the Principal Characters on the English Stage* (London, 1757–72)

J.-G. Noverre: *Lettres sur la danse et sur les ballets* (Lyons and Stuttgart, 1760, 2/1783; Eng. trans., 1783, enlarged 1803, and 1930)

J. Gregor, ed.: *Antoine Daniel Bertoli: desseins*, Monumenta scenica, iii (Vienna, 1925; Eng. trans., 1925)

S. Rosenfeld: 'The Wardrobes of Lincoln's Inn Fields and Covent Garden', *Theatre Notebook*, v (1950–51), 15–19

M. Horányi: *Eszterházi vigassàgok* (Budapest, 1959; Eng. trans., 1962, as *The Magnificence of Eszterháza*)

J. de La Gorce: *Berain, dessinateur du Roi Soleil* (Paris, 1986)

R. Angermüller: *Mozart: die Opern von der Uraufführung bis heute* (Fribourg, 1988; Eng. trans., 1988)

19TH CENTURY

A. Martinet, ed.: *La petite galerie théâtrale, ou Recueil des différents costumes d'acteurs des théâtres de la capitale* (Paris, 1796–1843) [1637 engravings]

G. Englemann: *Recueil des costumes de tous les ouvrages dramatiques, représentés avec succès sur les grands théâtres de Paris* (Paris, 1819–22) [374 engravings]

C. Brühl: *Neue Kostüme auf den beiden königlichen Theatern in Berlin* (Berlin, 1819–31)

J. Ebers: *Seven Years of the King's Theatre* (London, 1828)
Galerie dramatique: costumes des théâtres de Paris (Paris, 1844–70) [1000 engravings]
G. Zeh: *Das bayreuther Bühnenkostüm* (Munich, 1973)
W. Weaver, ed.: *Verdi: a Documentary Study* (London, 1977)
D. de Marly: *Worth: Father of Haute Couture* (London, 1980)
M. Viale Ferrero and G. Marchesi: *Settantaquattro figurini inediti di Alfredo Edel* (Parma, 1984)
N. Wild: *Décors et costumes du XIXe siècle*, i: *Opéra de Paris* (Paris, 1987)

20TH CENTURY

S. Dark: 'Art of Theatrical Disguise', *Cassell's Magazine* (1902), July; repr. as 'Comelli' in *About the House: the Magazine of the Friends of Covent Garden*, iv/9 (1975), 46–51
E. Mandinian: *Purcell's The Fairy Queen as presented by the Sadler's Wells Ballet and the Covent Garden Opera: a Photographic Record by Edward Mandinian, with essays by E. J. Dent, Constant Lambert, and Michael Ayrton* (London, 1948)
E. Stern: *My Life, My Stage* (London, 1951)
H. Rischbieter, ed.: *Art and the Stage in the 20th Century: Painters and Sculptors Work for the Theater* (Greenwich, CT, 1968)
S. Marešová: *Czech Stage Costumes/Le costume tchèque de théâtre* (Prague, 1972)
I. Sharaff: *Broadway & Hollywood: Costumes Designed by Irene Sharaff* (New York, 1976)
D. Herbert, ed.: *The Operas of Benjamin Britten: the Complete Librettos Illustrated with Designs of the First Productions* (London, 1979)
R. Monti and M. Bucci, eds.: *Visualità del 'Maggio': Bozzetti, figurini e spettacoli 1933–1979* (Florence, 1979)
J. Bowlt: *Russian Stage Design: Scenic Innovation, 1900–1930, from the Collection of Mr. and Mrs. Nikita D. Lobanov-Rostovsky* (Jackson, MS, 1982)
D. Harris: 'The Original Four Saints in Three Acts', *Drama Review*, xxvi (1982), 102–30
I. Maximowna: *A Picture Book of Set Design: Sketches, Scene Photos and Costume Models* (Tübingen, 1982)
G. Taborelli, ed.: *La danza, Il canto, L'abito: Costumi del Teatro alla Scala, 1947–1982* (Milan, 1982)
M. Friedman: *Hockney Paints the Stage* (London, 1983)
R. Pinkham, ed.: *Oliver Messel* (London, 1983)
F. Corsaro and M. Sendak: *The Love for Three Oranges: the Glyndebourne Version* (New York, 1984)
R. Strong: 'The Rule of Taste: Design at Glyndebourne, 1935–84', *Glyndebourne: a Celebration* (London, 1984), 88–100
R. Jacobson: *Magnificence Onstage at the Met: Twenty Great Opera Productions* (New York, 1985)
D. Bablet and E. Billeter, eds.: *Die Maler und das Theater im 20. Jahrhundert* (Frankfurt, 1986)
The Operatic Muse: an Exhibition of Works from the Robert L. B. Tobin Collection (San Antonio, TX, 1986)
S. M. Winkelbauer: *Wake up and Dream!: Costume Designs for Broadway Musicals 1900–1925 from the Theatre Collection of the Austrian National Library* (Vienna, 1986)
M. Kahane: *Les artistes et l'Opéra de Paris: dessins de costume 1920–1950* (Paris, 1987)
M. Pozharskaya and T. Volodina: *Russkiye sezonï v Parizhe* (Moscow, 1988; Eng. trans., 1990, as *The Art of the Ballets Russes: the Russian Seasons in Paris 1908–29*)
J. Cavanagh: *British Theatre: a Bibliography, 1901–1985* (Mottisfont Abbey, Hants, 1989)
J. Goodwin, ed.: *British Theatre Design: the Modern Age* (London, 1989)

SIDNEY JACKSON JOWERS

Cotapos (Baeza), Acario (*b* Valdivia, 30 April 1889; *d* Santiago, 22 Nov 1969). Chilean composer. Self-taught in composition, he settled in New York (1917–27), where he was an associate of Varèse, Cowell and Copland. He was among the founders of the International Composers' Guild and of the League of Composers. Thereafter he lived in France (1927–34) and Spain (1934–8), working on the ambitious opera *Voces de gesta*, a lyric tragedy based on Valle Inclán's poems. There is no evidence that the piece was completed, though an orchestral suite was performed in Spain (1934) and a scene, *Los invasores*, in Chile (1942). Cotapos returned to Chile in 1939, and there he finished the opera *El pájaro burlón*, for which he wrote his own libretto. In 1960 he received the Chilean National Arts Prize. His music is highly coloured and imaginative, as dramatic and intense as it is formless and complex, and usually very dense in harmony and orchestration.

*

D. Quiroga: 'Acario Cotapos: La creación viviente', *Revista musical chilena*, no.76 (1961), 33–42 [Cotapos issue]

JUAN A. ORREGO-SALAS

Cotogni, Antonio (*b* Rome, 1 Aug 1831; *d* Rome, 15 Oct 1918). Italian baritone. He studied in Rome, making his début there in 1852 at the Teatro Metastasio as Belcore. He sang at La Scala and in Bologna as Posa in the first Italian performance of *Don Carlos* (1867). At Covent Garden (1867–89) he made his début as Valentin and sang a great many roles, including Don Giovanni, Papageno, Mozart's and Rossini's Figaro, William Tell, Enrico Ashton, Belcore, Malatesta, Alphonse (*La favorite*), Hoël, Hamlet, Nevers, Nélusko, Mercutio, Germont, Amonasro, Luna, Rigoletto and Escamillo, and Barnaba in the first London performance of *La Gioconda* (1883). He gave his farewell at St Petersburg in 1898. A versatile artist, whose flexible voice was ideally suited to Italian opera, he also sang Telramund.

ELIZABETH FORBES

Cotrubas, Ileana (*b* Galati, 9 June 1939). Romanian soprano. She studied in Bucharest and made her début there in 1964 as Yniold. After further study in Vienna, she sang with the Frankfurt Opera (1968–71). She first sang at Salzburg in 1967 as the Second Boy (*Die Zauberflöte*), returning for Bastienne, Konstanze and Pamina. She made her Glyndebourne début in 1969 as Mélisande, later singing Calisto, Susanna and Titania. In Vienna she sang Zerlina, Sophie and Nedda. At Covent Garden, where she first appeared in 1971, her roles included Tatyana, Violetta, Adina, Norina, Amina and Antonia, and she sang Manon at the Paris Opéra in 1974. She sang Mimì at La Scala in 1975 as well as for her 1977 début at the Metropolitan, where she subsequently sang Gilda, Micaëla and Ilia. Taking on heavier roles, she sang Elisabeth de Valois at Florence, Marguerite at Hamburg (1985), Amelia (*Simon Boccanegra*) at Naples, Magda (*La rondine*) in Chicago (1986), Alice Ford at Monte Carlo (1987) and Desdemona at Barcelona (1988). She retired in 1989, having recorded many of her Mozart roles. Her sweet-toned, agile voice and gentle personality conveyed vulnerability and pathos to great dramatic effect.

*

A. Blyth: 'Ileana Cotrubas', *Opera*, xxvii (1976), 428–33
——: 'Cotrubas Says Farewell', *Opera*, xl (1989), 410–12

ALAN BLYTH

Cottini [Cottina], **Antonio** [Galli, Antonio Pietro] (*b* ?Ferrara or Modena; *fl* 1661–1708). Italian bass. Known as Cottini during the early stages of his career, he is first heard of in 1661 in Florence, where he sang Zeffiro in Jacopo Melani's *Ercole in Tebe*. In 1668–9 he was active in Hanover and he was in Ferrara in 1675 as a signatory to the dedication of M. G. Peranda's oratorio *Il sacrificio di Iephte*. On 8 January 1676 he received the title 'servant' from Duke Ferdinando Carlo Gonzaga of Mantua, but when he performed in P. A. Ziani's *Attila* in Milan on 19 January 1677 he styled himself 'virtuoso of the Duke of Modena'. That year he also sang the leading role in Legrenzi's *Germanico sul Reno* in Milan and Modena. In 1680 he was in Dresden and he subsequently performed in Reggio Emilia, Modena, Milan, Turin, Genoa and Venice. He was also an impresario and as such signed the dedications of operas performed at Modena in 1697 and 1703–4. He was married to the singer Francesca Sarti.

*

S. Durante: 'Alcune considerazioni sui cantanti di teatro del primo settecento e la loro formazione', *Antonio Vivaldi: teatro musicale cultura e società: Venice 1981*, ii, 427–81

P. Besutti: *La corte musicale di Ferdinando Carlo Gonzaga ultimo duca di Mantova: musici, cantanti e teatro d'opera tra il 1665 e il 1707* (Mantua, 1989)

PAOLA BESUTTI

Countertenor. Male voice of between tenor and alto pitch; its normal range is approximately *g* to *d″* or *e″*. Its uses in opera fall under three headings: roles in Baroque opera that were sung originally by a castrato, roles written specifically for the voice since its re-emergence (about 1950) as a generally acceptable solo instrument, and other roles, mostly 'travesti' parts usually taken by women but found suitable by those countertenors who are considered to have power and range of voice sufficient to undertake them.

The nature of the voice and the correctness of its description by the term 'countertenor' have been much disputed. The word arises from its use in medieval and Renaissance polyphonic music and refers to the voice-part written 'against' (*contra*) the tenor. Unlike terms such as 'alto' and 'bass', it does not describe the voice but, like 'tenor' itself, indicates a function. The French term HAUTE-CONTRE compromises in this respect, with the 'contre' relating to its part in the counterpoint and the 'haute' specifying a voice of high pitch. Theories abound as to whether the *haute-contre* is historically a high tenor, or one who has smoothed his passage into the falsetto, or whether it is essentially the same as the countertenor of modern times, who may or may not be identical with the voice known for many years, mostly in church music, as 'alto'. It is a matter of dispute whether the true countertenor necessarily uses falsetto or is simply an extended tenor.

The renaissance of the countertenor in Britain was closely associated with the specially gifted singer Alfred Deller (1912–79), who was an 'alto' in the choir of St Paul's Cathedral. When he began his career as a soloist, he worked with the composer Michael Tippett, and between them it was agreed that a return to the term 'countertenor' would be appropriate, largely because the repertory they were immediately concerned with was drawn from Purcell (himself a countertenor) and his contemporaries, writing at a time when that was the word in use.

In revivals of such works as Purcell's *The Fairy-Queen*, the new generation of countertenor soloists led by Deller played a prominent part. They have continued to do so, and have increasingly shown ability to cope with the contralto or mezzo-soprano (and formerly castrato) roles in the operas of Handel and other Baroque composers. Countertenors have sung and recorded many of Handel's roles, for example in *Giulio Cesare*, *Tamerlano* and *Orlando*. Most staged revivals also use countertenors, several of whom have developed the volume and penetrative quality of tone necessary to be effective in a large theatre.

Modern composers of opera have also shown interest in this newly available voice. Britten wrote the role of Oberon in *A Midsummer Night's Dream* for Deller, who sang it in the première at Aldeburgh in 1960. This remains the countertenor's most attractive operatic part: the American Russell Oberlin succeeded Deller in early performances, and the leading British countertenor since Deller, James Bowman, has sung it in at least ten different productions. Other modern operas using the voice include Britten's *Death in Venice*, Weir's *A Night at the Chinese Opera* and Glass's *Akhnaten*. An imaginative feature of Reimann's *Lear* is the casting of Edgar as a countertenor, particularly effective in the howling of 'poor Tom'.

There has also been a movement to extend the countertenor's sphere so as to include such roles as Gluck's Orpheus, Pharnaces in Mozart's *Mitridate*, Orlofsky in *Die Fledermaus* and the Tsar's son in *Boris Godunov*. All of these are in the stage repertory of the remarkable singer Jochen Kowalski (*b* 1954), who has claimed for the voice dramatic and emotional qualities, dissociating it from the main British line from Deller onwards.

*

J. Hough: 'The Historical Significance of the Counter-tenor', *PMA*, lxiv (1937–8), 1–24

F. Hodgson: 'The Contemporary Alto', *MT*, cvi (1965), 293–4

G. M. Ardran and D. Wulstan: 'The Alto or Countertenor Voice', *ML*, xlviii (1967), 17–22

O. Baldwin and T. Wilson: 'Alfred Deller, John Freeman and Mr Pate', *ML*, l (1969), 103–10

P. Giles: *The Counter Tenor* (London, 1982)

L. F. Wiens: *A Practical and Historical Guide to the Understanding of the Counter Tenor Voice* (diss., Indiana U., 1987)

P. Giles: *A Basic Counter-Tenor Method* (London, 1988)

N. Kimberley: 'Beautiful Freaks', *Opera Now* (1991), June, 13–15

P. Giles: *Counter-Tenors and Countertenors* (forthcoming)

For further bibliography *see* SINGING: A BIBLIOGRAPHY.

J. B. STEANE

Coup de glotte (Fr.; Ger. *harte Einsatz*; It. *colpo della glottide*). A term, meaning literally a blow or 'strike' of the glottis, used to describe a way in which singers may make a note first sound. It is frequently called a method of 'attack', though that word itself is possibly misleading and, since the area is a somewhat controversial one among teachers of singing, it may even be said to beg the whole question. The practical question is how a note should be initiated when it is to be sung on a syllable that starts with a vowel and, usually, when it is the first of a phrase or is in some way isolated. The dilemma was formulated influentially by one of the most famous teachers of singing, Manual García (1805–1906), who wrote of the *coup de glotte* and advocated it. Controversy has arisen over two points: what he meant by it, and whether he was right. The glottal attack results from the pressure of breath against the closed glottis, and was illustrated by García by reference to a slight cough (by means of which the reader or pupil could become aware of the glottis and its action). Sung or spoken in this way, the vowel-sound 'ah' begins with a very slightly percussive sound. The opposite method is referred to as 'the soft attack', has more in common with the whisper than the cough, and is introduced by a light aspirate. This would certainly be anathema to the García school, but, since the glottal attack as described can be harmful to the voice if used habitually, it is argued that this is not what García had in mind either. Franklyn Kelsey (*The Foundations of Singing*, 1950) argued that the stroke of the glottis, correctly used in line with García's known methods, is 'essentially a gentle and skilful gesture into a light pressure' rather than 'a kind of explosive release from heavy pressure'.

J. B. STEANE

Courcelle, Francesco. *See* CORSELLI, FRANCESCO.

Couroupos, Yorgos (*b* Athens, 1 Jan 1942). Greek composer. He studied the piano at the Athens Conservatory and composition with Olivier Messiaen at the Paris Conservatoire (1968–72). After holding posts with the National Lyric Theatre, Athens, he was appointed director of the Calamata Municipal Conservatory in 1985. He often uses ancient Greek subjects for inspiration and conceives of music primarily as dramatic expression; this dictates the use of a wide range of elements: clusters, percussive rhythms, drones as tonal centres, micro-intervals and phonemes, as well as natural sounds and traditional elements. He has written more than a dozen musical theatre works (staged mostly in France and Crete), among which should be noted his 1975 musical spectacle *Dieu le veut*. His first opera, *Labyrinthos*, is to a libretto by Periklis Korovessis. His second, the one-act chamber opera *Pylades*, to a libretto by Yorgos Heimonas after Sophocles and Euripides, was given its first performance at the Athens Concert Hall on 31 May 1992. Its dramatic pacing and the masterful vocal writing, which follows the inflections of the Greek language, represent a milestone in the history of Greek opera after Manolis Kalomiris. GEORGE LEOTSAKOS

Cousin Jacques. *See* BEFFROY DE REIGNY, LOUIS-ABEL.

Cousser, Jean Sigismond. *See* KUSSER, JOHANN SIGISMUND.

Coutts, Francis Burdett Money. *See* MONEY-COUTTS, FRANCIS BURDETT.

Couzinou, Robert (*b* 1888; *d* Paris, 1958). French baritone. His début at the Opéra-Comique in 1912 led to a long engagement at the Opéra where he sang in a large repertory, appearing in the Paris premières of *L'heure espagnole*, *Parsifal* and *Turandot*. At the Metropolitan he sang with Caruso in *Samson et Dalila* (1918) and at Covent Garden in the London première of Mascagni's *Iris* in 1919. At Monte Carlo he appeared in Lully's *Armide et Renaud*. His most successful roles included Rigoletto, Iago and Hamlet. A firm, well-directed voice and a sense of style distinguish his recordings; he was also a fine actor with a dignified stage presence.

J. B. STEANE

Covarrubias, Manuel (*fl* Mexico City, 1838–44). Mexican composer. His *Reinaldo y Edina* (completed 1838) was the first known opera to be written in Mexico by a native of the country. For this three-act work he used a libretto by the 22-year-old Gabino F. Bustamante from Querétaro. In 1842 V. G. Torres's *Panorama de las Señoritas*, a Mexico City periodical, included the following comment on Covarrubias's second opera, *La sacerdotisa peruana* ('The Peruvian Priestess'): 'we see an extraordinary talent; although the author lacks contrapuntal learning, he has orchestrated the three acts of an opera that is full of melancholy and entirely new ideas'. In 1844 Covarrubias's overture *La Palmira* was the first work in the opening-night concert at the Gran Teatro de S Anna at Mexico City (10 February). Lack of later references suggests that he died very young.

*

G. Orta Velázquez: *Breve historia de la música en México* (Mexico City, 1970), 272, 278

G. Carmona: *Periodo de la independencia a la revolución (1810 a 1910)*, La música de México: Historia, iii (Mexico City, 1984), 39, 64–5

ROBERT STEVENSON

Covent Garden. Area in London that gives its name to the city's principal opera house. The first theatre on the site, the Theatre Royal, was built in 1732, and the present one, the third, in 1858; it is now the Royal Opera House. *See* LONDON, §II, 2.

Covered tone (Fr. *voix sombrée*; Ger. *gedeckte Ton*; It. *voce cuperta*). Although 'open' and 'covered' would seem to be layman's terms and their manifestations in singing easy to recognize, the technique of 'covering' and the need for it are probably understood properly only by singers themselves. As voices ascend in the scale, reaching the higher notes of the singer's range, the method of voice production is gradually modified, partly so as to ensure a musically pleasing sound rather than a shout, partly to protect the voice, and also to secure a greater concentration of tone. This may involve modifications of the vowel sound, shading the brighter vowels towards those that are 'darker' and less open. It will also be a difficult exercise, during the course of which the singer seems to him or herself to be producing thinner, less powerful and excitingly resonant sounds in the upper notes than would otherwise have been possible. A further difficulty lies in the areas of the voice called the *passaggi*, the 'passage' notes where the 'registers' change. The process has to be smoothed over; and training, which aims at the perfection of a seamless scale, lays a special emphasis on the importance of 'covering' at these points. J. B. STEANE

Cowan, Richard (*b* Euclid, OH, 24 Dec 1957). American baritone. He studied at Indiana State University and made his début with Opera Theater of Michigan as Angelotti (*Tosca*). In 1985 he made his European début in Florence as the Animal Tamer/Athlete (*Lulu*), returning in 1988 to create Wolfgang in Bussotti's *L'ispirazione*. He sang Masetto at Aix-en-Provence (1986). At Chicago he has sung the Animal Tamer/Athlete (1987), Masetto and Escamillo (1990), and Antony in Barber's *Antony and Cleopatra* (1991). In San Francisco (1989) he again sang the Animal Tamer/Athlete. He made his Metropolitan début as Don Giovanni (1990), then sang Schaunard, the role he took in Luigi Comencini's film of *La bohème* in 1987. His repertory also includes Mozart's Figaro and Guglielmo, Germont, Ford, Sharpless and John the Baptist. In 1990 he married the American soprano Constance Hauman. An excellent actor with a fine stage presence, he has a strong, lyrical voice. ELIZABETH FORBES

Coward, Sir Noël (Pierce) (*b* Teddington, Middlesex, 16 Dec 1899; *d* Blue Harbour, Jamaica, 26 March 1973). English composer and writer. He was born into a family of amateur musicians; his early talents as a singer and entertainer were actively encouraged. His initial career was as a professional actor and playwright, as well as a composer of songs. He produced his first fully integrated musical score, the operetta *Bitter-Sweet*, in 1929, by which time he was regarded on both sides of the Atlantic as an important spokesman of his generation. Remarkably prolific, he continued to pour out plays, revues, musicals, songs, poetry, short stories, novels and autobiography.

Almost wholly self-taught as a composer, Coward depended on the services of an amanuensis for the proper notation of his scores (though not for their composition), and on professional orchestrators for their final presentation. Inevitably this limited his capacity for large-scale musical organization, but that deficiency is more than offset by outstanding melodic gifts and a very fresh way of handling the harmonic and rhythmic clichés of popular music. The waltz and military march are obvious influences, as are music-hall songs and the operas of Gilbert and Sullivan. The best Coward tunes are closely wedded to their words and match verbal dexterity with unexpected turns of phrase which, though never compromising the instantly memorable melodic shape, lift them out of the ordinary. Their intrinsic worth is such that they have withstood many varied and often inappropriate kinds of arrangement and orchestration. A latterday Gilbert and Sullivan, he is the only English composer able to stand on equal terms with his great American contemporaries in this field. His songs epitomize their period.

selective list; librettos by Coward unless otherwise stated

Bitter-Sweet (operette, 3), Manchester, Palace, 2 July 1929; Conversation Piece (romantic comedy with music, 3), London, His Majesty's, 16 Feb 1934; Operette (2), Manchester, Opera House, 17 Feb 1938; Pacific 1860 (musical romance, 3), London, Drury Lane, 19 Dec 1946; Ace of Clubs (musical play, 2), Manchester, Palace, 16 May 1950; After the Ball (musical play, 2), Liverpool, 1 March 1954; Sail Away (musical comedy, 2), Boston, Colonial, 9 Aug 1961; The Girl who Came to Supper (musical, 2, Coward and H. Kurnitz), New York, Broadway, 8 Dec 1963

*

N. Coward: *Present Indicative* (London, 1937, 2/1986)
——: *Future Indefinite* (London, 1954, 2/1986)
R. Mander and J. Mitchenson: *Theatrical Companion to Noël Coward* (London, 1957)
S. Morley: *A Talent to Amuse* (London, 1969)
C. Castle: *Noël* (London, 1972)
C. Lesley: *The Life of Noël Coward* (London, 1976)
C. Lesley, G. Payn and S. Morley: *Noël Coward and his Friends* (London, 1979)
G. Payn and S. Morley, eds.: *The Coward Diaries* (London, 1982)

MICHAEL HURD/R

Cowell, Henry (Dixon) (*b* Menlo Park, CA, 11 March 1897; *d* Shady, NY, 10 Dec 1965). American composer. A champion of modern music, he founded the journal *New Music* in 1927 and in 1929 became the first American composer to visit the USSR. He taught at the University of Southern California and the Peabody Conservatory, and lectured throughout the world. Cowell's lifelong fascination with innovatory sonorities and folk and ethnic styles is manifest in his vast output, which includes music for orchestra, band, chorus, chamber ensemble, solo piano and voice.

Although Cowell composed extensively for films, dance and stage plays, he wrote only two operas. *The Building of Bamba*, to a libretto by the poet John O. Varian, is according to the composer 'an Irish mythological opera'. It was produced on 18 August 1917, at the Halcyon Sanatorium near Pismo Beach, California, during the annual convention of the Temple of the People, a theosophist cult. The work, scored for soloists, mixed chorus and two pianos, was reviewed as a 'Mystery Play presented in terms of music, color and fire'. Of the original 14 numbers, only nine survive, in pencil sketches dated July 1917 (*US-Wc*). Among missing manuscripts is the prelude, *The Tides of Manaunaun*, composed in 1911–12, one of the earliest and most often played of Cowell's 'tone cluster' piano pieces.

Cowell's more ambitious operatic undertaking, *O'Higgins of Chile*, was composed in 1949 to a Ditson Fund commission on a libretto by Elizabeth Lomax. The action, which takes place from 1818 to 1822, is based upon the true story of General Bernardo O'Higgins, who became a leader of the South American rebels against Spanish rule, captured Santiago and proclaimed Chilean independence. The opera requires a large cast of 18 solo roles, dancers, onstage instrumentalists and several choruses. Cowell intended the staging to be 'emotional, poetic and distorted rather than representational ... to underline the tragic, ironic, lyric and comic content of the opera'. The work is essentially tonal with occasional spoken dialogue, folklike passages with Spanish inflections ('Fiesta', Act 3) and touches of humour (Mariana's 'Lemon Song', 1.iii). For political reasons, the opera was never performed and remains unorchestrated (vs, *US-Wc**).

*

Review of 'The Building of Bamba', *The Temple Artisan*, xviii/4 (1917), 244
R. C. B. Brown: 'Henry Cowell is Back with New Projects', *San Francisco Chronicle* (31 May 1925)
M. L. Manion: *Writings about Henry Cowell: an Annotated Bibliography*, ISAMm, xvi (Brooklyn, NY, 1982)
W. Lichtenwanger: *The Music of Henry Cowell: a Descriptive Catalogue*, ISAMm, xxiii (Brooklyn, NY, 1986)

ELISE K. KIRK

Cowen, Sir **Frederick Hymen** [Hyman Frederick] (*b* Kingston, Jamaica, 29 Jan 1852; *d* London, 6 Oct 1935). English pianist, conductor and composer. He was taken to England at the age of four. A precocious child, at eight he composed an operetta to a libretto by his cousin Rosalind. In 1865 he won the Mendelssohn Scholarship but relinquished it because his parents would not give up their control of him. He studied at the Leipzig Conservatory (1865–6) and the Stern Conservatory, Berlin (1867). His reputation as a composer was firmly established by his *Scandinavian Symphony* (1880), and he held many senior conducting posts in Great Britain between 1884 and 1923, though after the war he devoted much of his time to editorial and educational work. He received an honorary MusD from Cambridge in 1900 and from Edinburgh in 1910, and was knighted in 1911.

Cowen's operatic works fall into two clearly divided periods, the first of which proved to be the more successful. His tiny 'comedietta' *One Too Many* (1874) demonstrates a felicitous, light, sure touch which was later to desert him, though not before he had written his finest opera, *Pauline* (1876). Solidly based on contemporary French and Italian models, *Pauline* marks an advance on the operas of Balfe and Wallace in its sophisticated lyricism and dramatic directness. The baritone Charles Santley, for whom Cowen wrote the role of Claude Melnotte, felt that the audience would have preferred a tenor as the hero, and that he did not do justice to the part. Although the opera was only partially successful, Cowen responded positively to the libretto, characterizing his heroine as a credible prototype of Victorian womanhood.

The spirit of the English 'Renaissance' was alien to Cowen's nature, and in his three operas of the 1890s he unwisely tackled 'grand' subjects which over-inflated his slender muse. *Signa* (1893), a setting of an Italian *verismo* story, drew one or two moments of genuine passion from him, and he was unlucky that Richard D'Oyly Carte's ill-fated Royal English Opera House venture, for which the opera was originally intended, foundered before it was ready for production. *Thorgrim* (1890) and *Harold* (1895) are flawed by their sense of stylistic uncertainty: they inhabit a no-man's-land between lyrical number opera and quasi-Wagnerian synthesis. Thorgrim himself is clearly intended as a second Siegfried, but instead emerges as an unintentionally humorous parody of him. Where individual numbers do impress they still fail to relate to their dramatic context: Thorgrim's 'Why wanders Thorvald from the stream' is a case in point. Such librettos inevitably fostered unconvincing music; *Pauline* apart, Cowen's best work is probably to be found in his delightfully narcissistic orchestral pieces *The Language of Flowers* (1880) and *The Butterfly's Ball* (1901).

See also PAULINE.

all publications are vocal scores, published in London

Garibaldi, or The Rival Patriots (drawing-room operetta, 2, R. Cowen), 1860 (1860)

One Too Many (comedietta, 1, F. C. Burnand), London, St George's Hall, 24 June 1874 (1898)

Pauline (4, H. Hersee, after E. Bulwer-Lytton: *The Lady of Lyons*), London, Lyceum, 22 Nov 1876 (1876)

Thorgrim (4, J. Bennett, after Icelandic saga: *Viglund the Fair*), London, Drury Lane, 22 April 1890 (1890)

Signa (3, G. A. A' Beckett, H. A. Rudall and F. E. Weatherly, after Ouida); It., Milan, Dal Verme, 12 Nov 1893; reduced to 2 acts, London, CG, 30 June 1894 (1894)

Harold, or The Norman Conquest (4, E. Malet), London, CG, 8 June 1895 (1895)

Untitled: comedy opera (3), *GB-Lbl** [dated 7 April 1921], unperf.

*

DNB (J. M. Levien); *LoewenbergA*

C. Willeby: *Masters of English Music* (London, 1893), 173–256

R. A. Streatfield: *The Opera: a Sketch* (London, 1896), 320–22

'Frederick Hymen Cowen', *MT*, xxxix (1898), 713–19

J. A. Fuller Maitland: *English Music in the XIXth Century* (London, 1902), 189, 227–8

E. Walker: *A History of Music in England* (Oxford, 1907, enlarged J. A. Westrup, 3/1952), 318, 327–8

J. Bennett: *Forty Years of Music 1865–1905* (London, 1908), 376–8

C. Santley: *Reminiscences of My Life* (London, 1909), 129–30

F. H. Cowen: *My Art and My Friends* (London, 1913), 237–70

G. B. Shaw: *Music in London 1890–94* (London, 1932), iii, 261–3

Obituaries: *The Times* (7 Oct 1935), 17; *MT*, lxxvi (1935), 1008

G. B. Shaw: *London Music in 1888–89* (London, 1937), 222, 366, 371, 375

F. Howes: *The English Musical Renaissance* (London, 1966), 64–5

G. Hughes: *Sidelights on a Century of Music 1825–1924* (London, 1969), 180–87

N. M. Burton: 'Opera: 1865–1914', *Music in Britain: the Romantic Age, 1800–1914*, ed. N. Temperley (London, 1981), 342–5

E. W. White: *A History of English Opera* (London, 1983)

——: *A Register of First Performances of English Operas and Semi-Operas* (London, 1983) JENNIFER SPENCER, NIGEL BURTON

Cowie, Edward (*b* Birmingham, 17 Aug 1943). English composer. After studies at Trinity College of Music in London and at the universities of Southampton and Leeds, he worked privately with Fricker, Goehr and Lutosławski. He is a painter and ornithologist as well as a composer. He came to prominence in the early 1970s with a remarkable series of works that successfully fused multifarious talents from a number of disciplines. His four-act opera *Commedia* (1974–8, libretto by D. Starsmeare), the principal outcome of this period, was first given in German (as *Kommödianten*), at the Staatstheater, Kassel, on 10 June 1979; the British première followed three years later (17 February 1982, London, Sadler's Wells). Cowie has described it (*Opera*, xxx, 1979, pp.534–5) as a fantasy-opera, using traditional *commedia dell'arte* characters to construct a black, almost tragic comedy framed by the cycle of the four seasons. His music, freely atonal, is impressionistic and improvisatory in effect, following the dictates of invention rather than established formal archetypes, and frequently deriving in detail from the observation of natural phenomena. NICHOLAS WILLIAMS

Cox, Jean (*b* Gadsden, AL, 14 Jan 1922). American tenor. He studied at the University of Alabama and the New England Conservatory of Music and in Rome with Luigi Ricci and Bertelli. He made his début in 1951 at Boston as Lensky and his European début in 1954 as Rodolfo at Spoleto. After engagements at Kiel (1953–4) and Brunswick (1955–9), he was engaged by the Mannheim Opera, which became his base. He first sang at Bayreuth in 1956 as the Steersman, returning as Lohengrin (1967), Parsifal (1968), Walther (1969) and Siegfried (1970–75), the last a role he also sang at La Scala, Covent Garden, Munich, Florence and Naples. As Siegfried he looked and moved well; though lacking the full vocal resources for the part, in 1983 he was recalled to Bayreuth to replace a colleague in *Götterdämmerung*. He made occasional appearances in the USA, notably in Chicago (1964–73), where he sang Bacchus, Erik and Siegfried, and the Metropolitan, where he made his début in 1976 as Walther. His repertory also included Don Carlos, Otello, Samson, Števa (*Jenůfa*), Apollo (*Daphne*), Sergey (*Lady Macbeth of the Mtsensk District*) and the Cardinal (*Mathis der Maler*).

HAROLD ROSENTHAL/R

Cox, John (*b* Bristol, 12 March 1935). British director. He was educated at Oxford, and after periods of training at Glyndebourne, the Theatre Royal in York and BBC TV, made his professional début with Ravel's *L'enfant et les sortilèges* for Sadler's Wells Opera in 1965. He was director of production at Glyndebourne, 1971–81, general administrator and artistic director of Scottish Opera, 1981–6, and was appointed production director of the Royal Opera, Covent Garden, in 1988. During his time as assistant producer at Glyndebourne he came under the influence of Carl Ebert and Günther Rennert, and developed his gift for sharply observed social comedy, most notably in the series of Strauss productions there – *Ariadne auf Naxos* (1971), *Capriccio* (1973), *Intermezzo* (1974), *Die schweigsame Frau* (1977), *Der Rosenkavalier* (1980) and *Arabella* (1984) – for which he is perhaps most famous. He also produced *Il turco in Italia* there (1970), the first British performance of Einem's *Der Besuch der alten Dame* (1973), *The Rake's Progress* (1975) and *Die Zauberflöte* (1987), the last two designed by David Hockney. He has also worked widely in Europe, Australia and the USA (*Daphne* in Munich, *Don Carlos* in San Francisco, *Un ballo in maschera* in Sydney). His production of *Patience* was one of the ENO's longest-running operetta successes. RODNEY MILNES

Cox and Box [*Cox and Box; or, the Long-Lost Brothers*]. Operetta in one act by ARTHUR SULLIVAN to a libretto by F. C. BURNAND after J. Maddison Morton's farce *Box and Cox*; private performance, London, probably 26 May 1866.

The farcical plot revolves around the efforts of Bouncer (baritone) to keep apart his lodgers, Cox (tenor) and Box (baritone), to whom he lets the same room in turn by night and by day. It was Sullivan's first operetta, written for a social gathering at Moray Lodge, Kensington, when the composer improvised a piano accompaniment. It was orchestrated for a benefit performance at the Adelphi Theatre (13 May 1867), an overture and more vocal music being added a few months later. Wider popularity followed Thomas German Reed's production (29 March 1869) at the Royal Gallery of Illustration. Much of the music exploits Sullivan's gift for stylistic burlesque and two of the numbers, the lullaby 'Hush'd is the bacon' and 'The buttercup dwells' gained popularity, with different lyrics, as drawing-room songs. A shortened version, prepared for the 1921 D'Oyly Carte revival, forms the basis for most contemporary performances.

DAVID RUSSELL HULME

Crabbé, Armand (**Charles**) [Morin, Charles] (*b* Brussels, 23 April 1883; *d* Brussels, 24 July 1947). Belgian baritone. He used the name Charles Morin when appearing in small roles. He studied in Brussels and with Cottone in Milan and made his début at the Monnaie in 1904 as the Nightwatchman in *Die Meistersinger*. From 1906 to 1914 he sang at Covent Garden, where his roles included Valentin, Alfio, Silvio and Ford; he returned in 1937 as Gianni Schicchi. At La Scala he sang Rigoletto, Marcello, Beckmesser, Lescaut and the title role of Giordano's *Il re* (1929), which he created. He joined Hammerstein's Manhattan Opera in 1907 and appeared at Chicago (1910–14), and at the Teatro Colón, Buenos Aires, in the 1920s. One of his most successful roles was Mârouf, which Rabaud transposed for him from tenor to baritone. Crabbé continued to appear until the early 1940s, mainly in Antwerp. He published *Conseils sur l'art du chant* (Brussels, 1931) and *L'art d'Orphée* (Brussels, 1933).

W. R. Moran: 'Notes from a Wandering Collector', *Record News*, iv (1959–60), 28–35 [with partial discography]

HAROLD ROSENTHAL/R

Crabbe, George (*b* Aldeburgh, 24 Dec 1754; *d* Trowbridge, 3 Feb 1832). English poet. First apprenticed to a doctor, he went to London in 1770 to pursue a literary career. He was befriended by the political philosopher Edmund Burke, who helped him to publish his work and advised him to become a clergyman. In 1781 he became curate at Aldeburgh, and from 1782 to 1785 was chaplain to the Duke of Rutland at Belvoir. Crabbe published very little after this period until the appearance of a new volume in 1807 and, in 1810, his major poem about the life of a country town, *The Borough*. This includes the tale 'Peter Grimes', on which Benjamin Britten – also a native of Suffolk and drawn by Crabbe's atmospheric evocation of its coastal life – based his 1945 opera of the same name.

ANTHONY PARR

Cracow. KRAKÓW.

Craig, Charles (**James**) (*b* London, 3 Dec 1920). English tenor. In 1947 he joined the Covent Garden Opera chorus, subsequently making his début as a principal tenor with the touring Carl Rosa Opera in *La bohème* (1953). He moved to the Sadler's Wells Opera in 1956, and first sang at Covent Garden as a principal in 1959 (*Madama Butterfly*). His roles there have included Pollione (*Norma*, 1979) and Puccini's Des Grieux, and for the ENO he has sung Radames (1980), Cavaradossi and Otello (1981). He has been a guest principal at many of the major opera houses in Europe and North and South America. His singing developed a typically italianate fervour and a true sense of operatic style in a repertory of nearly 50 roles.

NOËL GOODWIN

Craig, Edward (**Henry**) **Gordon** (*b* Stevenage, 16 Jan 1872; *d* Vence, France, 29 July 1966). English stage designer. He was the son of the architect and designer E. W. Godwin and the actress Ellen Terry, and is best known for his revolutionary theories and scene projects which have influenced virtually all 20th-century theatrical art. Like Adolphe Appia, he was among the first to design neutral, non-specific settings – screens 'painted' with light to meet the symbolic, poetic requirements of each moment – and in his 'Über-Marionette' theory he was the originator of the concept of the actor as a controlled instrument without egoism, the ideal tool of a higher directorial purpose.

Craig's earliest and arguably most artistically successful realized productions were those he directed from 1900 to 1903 for the Purcell Operatic Society, including Purcell's *Dido and Aeneas* and *The Masque of Love* (an adaptation of *Dioclesian*), and Handel's *Acis and Galatea*. These productions, which marked the beginning of the contemporary revival of English opera, aroused great interest. For *Dido and Aeneas* he created a proscenium of unusual proportions and, by abandoning wings and borders and using only a vast sky-cloth which disappeared out of view of the audience, gave the illusion for the first time of vast scale and space appropriate to the staging of lyric drama. In *Acis and Galatea* the giant was effectively suggested by a shadow projected by an offstage actor, moving in front of a naked electric light. Colour schemes and textures in the costumes and also uses of coloured light heralded reforms to be seen in opera in the next quarter-century. In all these productions, both soloists and chorus eschewed 19th-century conventions and were produced to act and move in a style consonant with the mood of the piece. Craig pub-

Etching (1907) by Edward Gordon Craig from his collection of designs entitled 'Scene' (London, 1923), in which he developed his system of 'screens'

lished his theories in *The Art of the Theatre* (London, 1905) and further explained them in *On the Art of the Theatre* (London, 1911), *Towards a New Theatre* (London, 1913), *Scene* (London, 1923) and in the periodical *The Mask* (1908–29).

One of Craig's most remarkable projects, inspired by the influence of Martin Shaw, was Bach's *St Matthew Passion*, an idea that consumed his interest for over 14 years. He even constructed a model of the playing area, unsuited to any conventional theatre, with towering flights of steps, platforms and chambers on which the epic could be enacted with stylized movement and changes of light.

See also STAGE DESIGN, §6.

*

ES (N. Marshall)
M. F. Shaw: *Up to Now* (London, 1929)
J. Leeper: *Edward Gordon Craig: Designs for the Theatre* (Harmondsworth, 1948)
D. Bablet: *Edward Gordon Craig* (Paris, 1962; Eng. trans., 1966)
I. W. K. Fletcher and A. Rood: *Edward Gordon Craig: a Bibliography* (London, 1967)
E. A. Craig: *Gordon Craig: the Story of His Life* (London, 1968)
M. P. Loeffler: *Gordon Craigs frühe Versuche zur Überwindung des Bühnenrealismus* (Berne, 1969)
D. Oenslager: *Stage Design* (London, 1975)

PAUL SHEREN

Cranmer, Arthur (Henry) (*b* Birmingham, 5 May 1885; *d* Harlech, 20 Aug 1954). English baritone. He sang the part of Dalua in Boughton's *The Immortal Hour* during its run in London in 1922 some 500 times. Later he joined the British National Opera Company and took part in the opera festivals organized by Napier Miles at Bristol, excelling as the visitor in Miles's *Markheim*. His gift for conveying a sense of mystery made him particularly successful in Stanford's *The Travelling Companion*, at Bristol and at Sadler's Wells, but he also played Rossini's Dr Bartolo and Mozart's Don Alfonso.

Cras, Jean (Emile Paul) (*b* Brest, 22 May 1879; *d* Brest, 14 Sept 1932). French composer. He was one of the few private pupils of Henri Duparc, with whom he began lessons in 1901. He later made a career in the Navy, reaching the rank of vice-admiral. His only opera, *Polyphème* (5, after A. Samain's verse play), tells the well-known story of Polyphemus's attempt to steal Galatea (soprano) from Acis (tenor). The opera is notable for its development of the character of the unfortunate cyclops Polyphemus (baritone) and includes ballets and various subsidiary characters. With its impressionistic orchestral evocations of the sea and extended lyrical melodies, the work has a striking chromatic restlessness reminiscent of Chausson and Duparc. It was first performed at the Opéra-Comique on 29 December 1922 and was revived two years later.

*

M. Cras: 'Regard sur Jean Cras', *Zodiaque*, cxxiii (1980), Jan, 3–12

RICHARD LANGHAM SMITH

Crass, Franz (*b* Wipperfürth, 9 Feb 1928). German bass-baritone. He made his first appearance at the age of 11 as the Second Boy in *Die Zauberflöte*. He then studied at the Cologne Musikhochschule, and made his début at Krefeld in 1954 as the King in *Aida*. Engagements followed at Hanover and Cologne; after 1964 he divided his time between Hamburg, Munich, Frankfurt and Vienna, with guest appearances in leading European theatres. Crass first appeared at Bayreuth in 1959 as King Henry (*Lohengrin*) and returned each year until 1973, singing the Dutchman, Biterolf, Fasolt, King Mark and Gurnemanz. He sang at Salzburg as Rocco and Sarastro and at La Scala as Don Fernando (*Fidelio*). In 1966 he sang Barak in the British première of *Die Frau ohne Schatten*, given by the Hamburg Staatsoper at Sadler's Wells. His repertory included Nicolai's Falstaff, Philip II and Bartók's Bluebeard. Crass possessed a beautifully schooled voice of lyric rather than dramatic quality.

HAROLD ROSENTHAL/R

Crawley, Clifford (*b* Dagenham, 29 Jan 1929). English composer and teacher. He studied at the GSM and Durham University, and privately with Lennox Berkeley and Humphrey Searle. In England he held teaching positions at various schools, becoming head of the music department at St Osyth's College of Education. He moved to Canada in 1973 to be professor of composition in the School of Music at Queen's University, Kingston in Ontario. He has conducted the Kingston Symphony Educational Concerts (1974–9) and the Eastern Ontario Concert Orchestra. Crawley has a special interest in music education. In addition to children's musicals, he has written a number of serious operas, some of which are intended for young people. He aims to write in an accessible style; his music for children is simple but similar to music for adults. *The Slaughter of the Innocents* (1975, Leicester) is in the tradition of Britten's *Noye's Fludde*: there are three distinct levels of difficulty in the vocal and instrumental parts so that few professional performers are needed.

The Slaughter of the Innocents (short Christmas op, 1, R. Wright), Leicester Cathedral, 6 May 1975
The Creation (2, D. Gordon), Kingston, Ont., St George's Cathedral, 12 May 1978
The Trouble with Heroes, 1980 (short op, 1, after G. Vanderhaeghe), unperf.
Barnardo Boy (2, D. Helwig), Kingston, Ont., Grand, 12 May 1982
Pied Piper (Helwig), excerpts with pf acc., CBC, 1990

F. R. C. CLARKE, RUTH PINCOE

Crébillon, Prosper Jolyot de (*b* Dijon, 13 Jan 1674; *d* Paris, 17 June 1762). French dramatist. He studied law at Dijon and by 1703 was living in Paris. He became a member of the Académie Française in 1731 and was appointed theatre censor in 1733. His nine tragedies, based on subjects from classical antiquity, are melodramatic and exploit violence and romantic entanglements; they were highly regarded during his lifetime. *Idoménée* (1705), his first work, was a source for Campra and Danchet's *Idoménée*, which in turn served for Mozart and Varesco's *Idomeneo*. His masterpiece, *Rhadamiste et Zénobie*, was first performed in 1711; there are notable similarities between it and Metastasio's *Zenobia*, as also between Crébillon's *Xerces* (1714) and Metastasio's *Artaserse*. Other plays by Crébillon on which operas were based were *Semiramis* and *Pyrrhus*.

*

J. de Crébillon: *Théâtre complet* (Paris, 1923)
H. C. Lancaster: *Sunset: a History of Parisian Drama in the Last Years of Louis XIV, 1701–1715* (Baltimore, 1945)
P. O. Le Clerc: 'Voltaire and Crébillon père: History of an Enmity', *Studies on Voltaire and the Eighteenth Century*, cxv (Banbury, 1973) [whole issue]

ALISON STONEHOUSE

Crémieux, Hector-Jonathan (*b* Paris, 10 Nov 1828; *d* Paris, 30 Sept 1892). French playwright and librettist. After studying law he entered the civil service, but with the encouragement of the Duke of Morny he soon began to take an active interest in the theatre. His first work, *Fiesque*, first performed in 1852, was a five-act historical drama after Schiller. Crémieux realized before long, however, that he would do better with comedy, especially if it had the support of music and spectacle. For his *Aladin, ou La lampe merveilleuse* (1863), which was classed as 'une féerie', no fewer than 20 tableaux were required. He had his greatest successes with *opéra comique* librettos for Offenbach and Hervé who responded to his gift for parody, his irrepressible cheekiness and his skill in pacing. As was habitual in France at the time, he most often collaborated, generally with Ludovic Halévy (under the joint pseudonym Paul d'Arcy) for his best work (notably *Orphée aux enfers*, Offenbach, 1858), but also with Louis-Adolphe Jaime, Albert de Saint-Albin, Philippe Gille and others. It is hard to be sure exactly what his contribution was to these various partnerships, though Halévy, who for career reasons did not at the time wish to draw attention to his involvement in comic opera, is known to have allowed Crémieux more than his fair share of the credit for the libretto of *Orphée aux enfers*. In general terms, it appears likely that Crémieux did not so much provide original ideas as develop those proposed by his fertile-minded collaborators and organize them into effective plots. Crémieux stopped writing in 1887 to become secretary-general of the Société des Dépôts; when it crashed five years later he committed suicide.

Le savetier et le financier (opérette, with E. About), Offenbach, 1856; *Une demoiselle en loterie* (opéra bouffe, with L.-A. Jaime), Offenbach, 1857; *Orphée aux enfers* (opéra bouffon, with L. Halévy), Offenbach, 1858; *Ma tante dort* (oc), L. H. J. Caspers, 1860; *La baronne de San Francisco* (opérette, with Halévy), Caspers, 1861; *La chanson de Fortunio* (oc, with Halévy), Offenbach, 1861; *Le pont des soupirs* (opéra bouffe, with Halévy), Offenbach, 1861; *Le roman comique* (opéra bouffe, with Halévy), Offenbach, 1861

Les eaux d'Ems (opérette, with Halévy), Delibes, 1861; *Une fin de bail* (oc, with Halévy [collab. as P. d'Arcy]), P. J. A. Varney, 1862; *Jacqueline* (opérette, with Halévy [collab. as P. d'Arcy]), Offenbach, 1862; *Les bergers* (oc, with P. Gille), Offenbach, 1865; *Geneviève de Brabant* (opéra bouffe, after Jaime and E. Tréfeu), Offenbach, 1867; *Robinson Crusoé* (oc, with E. Cormon), Offenbach, 1867; *Le petit Faust* (opéra bouffe, with Jaime), Hervé, 1869; *Les Turcs* (opéra bouffe, with Jaime), Hervé, 1869

Le trône d'Ecosse (opéra bouffe, with Jaime), Hervé, 1871; *La jolie parfumeuse* (oc, with E. Blum), Offenbach, 1873; *La veuve du Malabar* (opéra bouffe, with A. Delacour), Hervé, 1873; *Bagatelle* (oc, with Blum), Offenbach, 1874; *La famille Trouillat, ou La rosière d'Honfleur* (oc, with Blum), Vasseur, 1874; *La belle poule* (opéra bouffe, with A. de Saint-Albin), Hervé, 1875; *Le manoir du Pic-Tordu* (oc, with A. Mortier, Saint-Albin and C.-L.-E. Nuitter), Serpette, 1875; *La foire Saint-Laurent* (opéra bouffe, with Saint-Albin), Offenbach, 1877

Doubtful: *M. Choufleuri restera chez lui le ...* (opéra bouffe, ? with Halévy and E. de l'Epine), Offenbach and Saint-Rémy, 1861

CHRISTOPHER SMITH

Cremona. City in Lombardy, northern Italy. Operatic activity began in 1670 with performances for the aristocracy in a small private theatre of the Marchesa Ariberti; these were closely linked to the predominantly Venetian repertory of the Teatro Ducale in Milan. Public theatre was inaugurated in 1747 with a Bolognese comic opera at the Teatro Nazari, built on what is now the Corso Vittorio Emanuele through the initiative of a group of nobles headed by the Marchese G. B. Nazari; it was designed by Giovanni Battista Zaist with 100 boxes in four tiers, but built with 75 boxes in three tiers and a gallery. On Nazari's death in 1783 it was renamed the Teatro della Nobile Associazione, having been acquired by a syndicate of aristocrats who managed it from 1785 until it burnt down in 1806. 18th-century playbills usually indicate a single carnival season of two operas, until 1765 mainly *opera buffa* brought by impresarios from Bologna.

The new Teatro della Concordia, designed by Luigi Canonica on the model of the Teatro Carcano in Milan (102 boxes in four tiers, and a gallery), was built on the Nazari site and opened in 1808 with Paer's *Il principe di Taranto*. It was destroyed by fire in 1824, rebuilt by Luigi Voghera and Faustino Rodi, and reopened in 1825 with Rossini's *La donna del lago*. From 1817 a supplementary autumn opera season was often organized for the September fair.

In the widespread financial difficulties which followed the unification of Italy, productions at the Concordia decreased despite the presence of Ponchielli (1864–71) as conductor and coordinator. From 1870 it had competition from the private Teatro Ricci in what is now via Battisti, which presented popular entertainment including operetta. When this burnt down in 1896 it was replaced by the Politeama Cremonese (1200 seats, 40 boxes, two galleries; renamed the Verdi in 1901), whose owners presented operas in different seasons from those of the Concordia (renamed the Ponchielli in 1892).

Despite the grandiose productions of the Fascist era (a party official of national renown, Farinaci, directed the Ponchielli for many years), operatic activity declined during the 20th century, as exemplified by the brevity of the postwar annual seasons – ten days in February–March – at the Ponchielli. Renovated in 1969, it has enjoyed a more lively and lengthy activity in recent years as part of an operatic circuit with nearby Lombardy cities.

E. Santoro: *Il teatro di Cremona* (Cremona, 1969–72)

R. Monterosso: 'Il teatro d'opera a Cremona nel sec. XVIII', *Quadrivium*, xii (1971), 211–27

ALESSANDRO ROCCATAGLIATI

Cremonini, Clementina (*fl* 1763–6). Italian soprano. She sang with the Italian opera company in London between 1763 and 1765 and in concerts, including the first London appearance of the young Mozarts. She was in J. C. Bach's *Orione* and *Adriano in Siria* and took the lead in two English operas at Drury Lane in 1764, *The Royal Shepherd* (Rush) and *Almena* (M. Arne and Battishill). The prompter Hopkins noted that she sang 'very fine', while Burney wrote that she was 'a good musician, with a modern style of singing, but almost without voice'. She left London to sing in Dublin, disappearing from the records after October 1766.

BDA; *BurneyH*; *LS*

T. J. Walsh: *Opera in Dublin 1705–1797* (Dublin, 1973)

OLIVE BALDWIN, THELMA WILSON

Crescentini, Girolamo (*b* Urbania, 2 Feb 1762; *d* Naples, 24 April 1846). Italian soprano castrato and composer. After his studies in Bologna under Lorenzo Gibelli he made his début in 1776, in Fano, in female roles and in 1781, in Treviso, as primo uomo. He sang in Naples (1787–9) and in the most important Italian theatres, in London (1785) and from 1798 to 1803 in Lisbon, where he was also manager of the S Carlos Theatre. In 1805 he was in Vienna and from 1806 to 1812 in Paris at Napoleon I's court as singing teacher to the royal family. When he returned to Italy he was appointed singing teacher at the Bologna Conservatory and from 1825 at the Naples Royal Conservatory. His style can be placed in the general return to *patetico* at the end of the 18th century and his ornamentation was never immoderate. Stendhal said that no composer could have written the infinitely small nuances that formed the perfection of Crescentini's singing in his aria 'Ombra adorata aspetta', inserted into Zingarelli's *Giulietta e Romeo*. Isabella Colbran was among his pupils.

Besides his operatic arias he composed didactic and vocal chamber works, which were famous throughout the 19th century. He was a member of the Accademia di Santa Cecilia (Rome) and the Accademia Filarmonica of Bologna.

Arias: 'Ombra adorata aspetta' (scena ed aria), for Zingarelli's Giulietta e Romeo (Naples, n.d.); 'Fra tanti affanni miei', Lucca, 1786, *I-PAc*; 'Ah spiegarmi in tal momento' (scena e rondò), Reggio Emilia, 1787, *PAc*; 'Fin da primi anni' (cavatina), *Mc*; 'Non temer dell'Indo', *Bc*; 'Oh Dio mancar mi sento', *Bc*; 'Grazie vi rendo, oh dei' (cavatina seria), *FZc*; 'Sommo ciel che il cor', for Giulietta e Romeo, *Nc*; 'Vieni agli amplessi miei', for Salieri's Axur, *Nc*

*

DBI (M. Borgato); *ES* (C. Sartori)
C. I. Ruders: *Viagem em Portugal* (Stockholm, 1805–9; Port. trans., 1981), 90ff
Stendhal: *Vie de Rossini* (Paris, 1823), 115
R. Edgcumbe: *Musical Reminiscences* (London, 1834), 45–6
AMZ, xxxix (1837), 614–17 [autobiographical letter]
N. E. Cattaneo: 'Un necrologico epigramma-errata corrige', *Gazzetta musicale di Milano*, v (1846), 220–21
F. Romani: 'Girolamo Crescentini', *Gazzetta musicale di Milano*, v (1846), 180–81
F. da Fonseca Benevides: *O Real Teatro de São Carlos de Lisboa* (Lisbon, 1883), 57–9, 62, 72–3
N. Lucarelli: *Girolamo Crescentini: la vita, la tecnica vocale analizzata attraverso alcune sue arie tipiche* (diss., U. of Perugia, 1984)

NICOLA LUCARELLI

Creso ('Croesus'). Libretto by GIOACCHINO PIZZI, first set by Niccolò Jommelli (1757, Rome).

The story is taken from Herodotus. The Persian princess Cratina tells Croesus, last king of Lydia, that his daughter Ariene has fallen in love with Ciro [Cyrus], betraying Prince Euriso, to whom she has been promised. Croesus vows to punish his daughter by death, while Cratina vows revenge on Cyrus, who has sworn his love to her. Euriso (disguised as Rodaspe) goes to Cyrus's camp offering to trade Ariene for Cratina, but he refuses. Ariene is unable to convince Euriso that she is faithful.

In the second act Croesus and Euriso's plot to assassinate Cyrus fails, and they are captured in the enemy camp as Croesus is about to murder Ariene. Sibari, Cyrus's captain, reveals his love for Ariene, who remains faithful to her father and Euriso, and tries to rescue them.

As the third act begins, Cyrus plans to send Euriso, unarmed, into exile and is about to burn Croesus, who predicts that Cyrus will suffer the same fate. Ariene vows she will save her father or die with him. Cyrus allows Croesus to live, gives Ariene to Euriso and offers his love to Cratina.

Earlier librettists had also adapted the Croesus story: Bostel for Keiser (1711) and Pariati for Francesco Conti (1723). Later settings of Pizzi's libretto include those by Sacchini (1765, Naples) and Anfossi (1787, Rome). Most revisions affect the problematic relationship between Euriso and Ariene. An English translation of Sacchini's setting was produced in London in 1777–8 and in 1781 as *Euriso*.

For a list of settings *see* PIZZI, GIOACCHINO.

MARY ANN PARKER

Creso ('Croesus'). *Opera seria* in three acts by ANTONIO SACCHINI to a libretto by GIOACCHINO PIZZI (*see* CRESO above); Naples, Teatro S Carlo, 4 Nov 1765.

This was Sacchini's most widely performed *opera seria*, with at least ten productions between 1765 and 1781, including one with the title *Euriso* (1781, London). At the time of its composition, aria forms in *opera seria* were in transition. Arias *dal segno* with the sign in *A′* were the norm, but those with the sign at the beginning of the vocal part can also be found in the opera, alongside more modern through-composed rounded ternary arias, shortened rondos (*ABAB*) and a nascent two-tempo rondò for Euriso (soprano), 'Poveri affetti miei', where the reprise remains in the new tempo. The duet concluding Act 1 is through-composed, as is the trio in Act 2. The latter moves from three parts to two to one as first Croesus (tenor), the father of Ariene (soprano), and then her betrothed, Euriso (soprano castrato), denounce Ariene and leave. This form may have reached Naples through Majo, who composed a quartet of diminishing forces for his *Ifigenia in Tauride* at Mannheim in 1764, or through Traetta, whose *Didone abbandonata* was performed in Naples early the same year. The Mannheim court poet Verazi had first used such ensembles in *Sofonisba*, a collaboration with Traetta (1762).

Sacchini's arias have the broad melodic style and minimal accompaniments common among the younger composers of the 1760s and thereafter, but they still show careful attention to orchestration and accompaniment styles, which vary in subsequent repetitions. Winds take an active role in vocal caesuras and ritornellos. They provide the sounds of birds and breezes in Euriso's 'M'ucciderà' (Act 3.v) and underscore Ariene's pleas for pity in her obbligato recitative during the last scene, where she has not one but two cavatinas.

MARITA P. McCLYMONDS

Crespin, Régine (*b* Marseilles, 23 Feb 1927). French soprano. She studied with Jouatte and Cabanel at the Paris Conservatoire and made her operatic début at Mulhouse in 1950, as Elsa, the role of her Opéra début the same year (10 August). In the next six years, despite further appearances in Paris (as Vita in d'Indy's *L'étranger*, Desdemona and Gounod's Marguerite), her career was more successfully advanced in the provinces, in French opera (Salome in *Hérodiade*, Brunehild in Reyer's *Sigurd*) and in the German and Italian roles, sung in French, with which her international reputation was later made – notably Sieglinde, the Marschallin and Tosca. In 1956 she returned to the Opéra as Weber's Reiza; subsequent successes there led to engagements at Bayreuth, as Wieland Wagner's 'Mediterranean enchantress', Kundry (1958–60), and Sieglinde (1961), and at Glyndebourne (1959–60) as the Marschallin. In this role, an aristocratic, rather melancholy elegance of style and a delicate mastery of nuance, both vocal and dramatic, won her wide praise, particularly in Berlin, Vienna and New York (Metropolitan début, 1962). At Covent Garden she played the Marschallin (début 1960), Tosca, Elsa and, less happily, Beethoven's Leonore. Her repertory also included Ariadne and Carmen (Metropolitan, 1975). By the time of her retirement from the operatic stage, in 1991, she had gained a considerable reputation as a teacher of singing at the Paris Conservatoire.

Crespin was the first French singer after Germaine Lubin to command the heroic roles of German and

French opera with equal authority; she was distinguished for a classical nobility of style in French roles such as Julia in *La vestale*, Berlioz's Dido and the titular heroines of *Iphigénie en Tauride* and Fauré's *Pénélope*. She sang Madame Lidoine at the Paris première of *Dialogues des Carmélites* (1957), and Phaedra in the 1959 La Scala revival of Pizzetti's opera. She took the title roles in Offenbach's *La Grande-Duchesse de Gérolstein* (1983) and Menotti's *The Medium* (1986), both at San Francisco. She sang Madame de Croissy (*Carmélites*) at the Metropolitan (1987) and made her last stage appearance as the Countess (*The Queen of Spades*) at the Opéra in 1989. Although her vocal timbre was not ideally suited to Italian opera, she was a moving Amelia (*Ballo*), Desdemona, Gioconda and Tosca. Her singing was notable for a remarkable finesse of diction, phrase shaping and tone-colour; in her prime, the eloquence of her soft high phrases was matched by few other singers.

*

GV (F. Serpa; R. Vegeto)
A. Natan: *Prima donna* (Basle, 1962)
A. Tubeuf: 'Régine Crespin', *Opera*, xv (1963), 227–32
H. D. Rosenthal: 'Mediterranean', *ON*, xxx/22 (1965–6), 14
J. B. Steane: *The Grand Tradition* (London, 1974), 483ff

MAX LOPPERT

Cricchi [Cricca], **Domenico** (*b* Bologna, *fl* 1726–59). Italian bass. He was a performer of comic intermezzos in Italy and Europe. From 1726 to 1735 he performed mainly in northern Italy in works by Hasse with Rosa Ruvinetti Bon, but when she married he began to work with other partners including Maria Ginevra Magagnoli and extended his repertory to include intermezzos by Pergolesi. He was largely responsible for their wide popularity, and also for introducing the duet 'Per te ho io nel core' (*Flaminio*, Act 3 scene x) to end *La serva padrona* instead of the original finale 'Contento tu sarai'. Towards the end of his career he sang again with Ruvinetti Bon in northern and eastern Europe, in St Petersburg (1745–7), Dresden (1747), Berlin (1748–52) and Vienna (1759). They thus contributed to the diffusion of the intermezzos of Hasse, Pergolesi and Orlandini and laid the foundations for the success of *opera buffa*.

*

G. Lazarevich: 'Haydn and the Italian Comic Intermezzo Tradition', *Internationaler J. Haydn Kongress: Vienna 1982*, 376–84
F. Piperno: 'Buffe e buffi', *RIM*, xviii (1982), 240–84
——: 'Gli interpreti buffi di Pergolesi', *Studi pergolesiani*, i (1986), 166–78
——: 'Note sulla diffusione degli intermezzi di J. A. Hasse', *AnMc*, no.25 (1987), 287–303

FRANCO PIPERNO

Crimi, Giulio (*b* Paterno, nr Catania, 10 May 1885; *d* Rome, 29 Oct 1939). Italian tenor. He studied in Catania and made his début in *Il trovatore* at Palermo in 1910. He then sang throughout Italy, appearing at La Scala in *Aida* and *La battaglia di Legnano* in 1916. His international career began in 1914 with highly successful performances as Puccini's Des Grieux in Paris and London, where he also sang in the British première of Montemezzi's *L'amore dei tre re*. He appeared in Buenos Aires in 1916, and then in Chicago in the American première of Mascagni's *Isabeau*. He joined the Metropolitan, where a major event in his first year was the world première of Puccini's *Trittico* (1918): he appeared in both *Il tabarro* and *Gianni Schicchi*. Back in Italy he enjoyed a last success in *L'Africaine* at the Costanzi, Rome, in 1924, and then retired to teach, his most famous pupil being Tito Gobbi. On recordings, Crimi's full-bodied voice impresses favourably – less so the style and reliability of its usage.

J. B. STEANE

Crispino e la comare ('Crispino and the Fairy'). *Melodramma fantastico-giocoso* in four acts by LUIGI RICCI and FEDERICO RICCI to a libretto by FRANCESCO MARIA PIAVE, after the old Venetian comedy *Il medico e la morte, ossia Il dottore ciabattino*; Venice, S Benedetto, 28 February 1850.

The plot is a mixture of medical satire and fantasy. Crispino (baritone) is a Venetian shoemaker; his wife Annetta (soprano) a seller of broadsides. Unable to pay his debts, Crispino determines to drown himself, but the Comare (mezzo-soprano) offers to save him if he will become a doctor and gives him a bag of gold. To the outrage of other practitioners, Crispino achieves a number of miraculous cures, successes that win him the approval of the general public. His accomplishments go to his head, and he turns pretentious and overbearing. The Comare reappears and threatens him with death. Promising to reform, Crispino is restored to his loving family.

The Riccis' score is studded with infectious melodies, largely in dance rhythms, but it is old-fashioned in its use of predictably symmetrical forms. Annetta, a role performed by Patti, Tetrazzini and Galli-Curci, has the most grateful arias, particularly 'Io non sono più l'Annetta', in Act 2. A once-famous *buffo* speciality was the trio of the squabbling doctors, 'Di Pandolfetti medico' (Act 3). The work, which was staged in Paris in 1869 as *Le docteur Crispin* (translated by Nuitter), possesses a naive charm and humour that justifies its occasional revival.

WILLIAM ASHBROOK

Crispo ('Crispus'). *Drama* in three acts by GIOVANNI BONONCINI to a libretto by Gaetano Lemer; Rome, Sala del Federico Capranica, Carnival 1721 (new version, with alterations to the libretto by PAOLO ANTONIO ROLLI, London, King's Theatre, 10 January 1722).

The Empress Fausta (contralto), the wife of Costantino [Constantine] (contralto; changed to bass in the 1722 production) and mother of Costante [Constans] (?soprano; soprano), is horribly in love with her stepson Crispus (contralto; mezzo-soprano), who repulses her advances. Constans and Crispus both love Olimpia (?soprano; soprano), who chooses the latter. Fausta wrongly accuses Crispus of her own crime, then stages a meeting in which she pretends to push him away from her while Constantine observes from a distance. The emperor therefore orders that Crispus take poison, which he does. After a mad scene Fausta recovers and confesses her guilt. Constans, who saved Crispus from death by poison, demands Olimpia as his reward until Fausta reminds him that only Crispus, whose great mercy saved even her, deserves Olimpia. The most noble Crispus was portrayed by Antonio Bernacchi in Rome and by Senesino in London. The villainous Fausta was portrayed by Giovanni Carestini in Rome and by Anastasia Robinson in London; for the revival in autumn 1722 Robinson was replaced by Margherita Durastanti.

The only known score was destroyed during World War II, but aria collections contain 15 of the 36 arias in the Roman libretto and 20 of the 29 heard in London. Bononcini's wife, Margherita Balletti, reported that the opera triumphed in Rome because its unequalled beauties were no longer heard. This may well mean that Bononcini's gentle tunes were outmoded for composers and listeners who preferred astonishing, concerto-like figuration in both vocal and violin parts. In London Bononcini's *Crispo*, *Griselda* and *Astarto* accounted for 40 of the 62 performances given by the Royal Academy of Music during 1721–2, its only profitable season, which represented the peak of Bononcini's success in England. One of the tuneful airs, 'Se vedete i pensier miei', was sung even by Tom, the servant in Richard Steele's *The Conscious Lovers* (1722).

LOWELL LINDGREN

Crist, Richard (*b* Harrisburg, PA, 21 Oct 1947). American bass. He studied at the New England Conservatory and made his début in 1972 in *Les Troyens* with the Opera Company of Boston. Further roles with this company have included Wesener in the American première of Zimmermann's *Die Soldaten* (1983) and the Judge, which he created, in DiDomenica's *The Balcony* (1990). He made his Metropolitan début in 1985 as Dr Grenvil, and has sung with the companies of Philadelphia, San Francisco and San Diego. His repertory includes Osmin, Leporello, Sarastro, Rocco, Cardinal Brogni and Gremin, as well as Samuel (*Ballo*), which he sang with Hamburg Opera in 1984. His extensive experience of performing 20th-century music includes appearances as Arnold, in the Italian and British premières of Henze's *The English Cat*, and Mizhuyev in the American première of Shchedrin's *Myortvïe dushi* (1988).

Cristiani, Stefano (*b* Bologna, *c*1770; *d* ?Mexico, after 1825). Italian composer and conductor. He was probably a pupil at the Bologna Conservatory and later studied with Paisiello and Cimarosa. In 1798 he was musical director at La Scala and his first opera, *La citta nuova*, was performed there. He went to Barcelona in 1803 and then lived in Madrid (1803–11) and Cuba (1811–22), composing several Spanish operas. In 1823 he was living in Mexico as a piano teacher and composer.

all lost

MDCP – *Madrid, Teatro de los Caños del Peral*

La citta nuova (2), Milan, Scala, 9 Sept 1798
L'amante democratico (2, G. D. Boggio), Turin, Carignano, early 1799
L'amore prigioniero (1, P. Metastasio), Barcelona, Principal, 28 Jan 1803
El criado de dos amos (2), MDCP, 9 Aug 1803
Ramona y Roselio, o Los ladrones compasivos (2, F. Copons), MDCP, 21 Oct 1803
La biblioteca de los zapatos (2), MDCP, 12 Nov 1803
Saul (2, F. Sánchez Barbera, after V. Alfieri), MDCP, 6 March 1805
Quien ha hace la paga (2), MDCP, 10 July 1810
Un loco no hace un ciento (2, ? after G. Foppa), Havana, Principal, 19 Aug 1817
El vinagrero (2), Havana, Principal, 20 Oct 1817
Clarice (2), Havana, Principal, 19 Dec 1817
El solitario (3), Mexico City, Nuevo Coliseo, 2 Dec 1824

JOSÉ ANTONIO GONZÁLEZ

Cristoforeanu, Florica (*b* Rîmnicul Sărat, 16 May 1887; *d* Rio de Janeiro, 1 March 1960). Romanian mezzo-soprano. She studied singing in Bucharest and Milan (at the Giuseppe Verdi Conservatory with Vanerí Filippi and Bodrilla), making her début as Lucia at Capodistria in 1908. After touring widely in western Europe she was in Bucharest for performances in operetta, 1909–13, then sang throughout Europe, notably at Barcelona, and also at the Teatro Colón, Buenos Aires. At La Scala (début, Santuzza, 1927) she sang Salome under Strauss (1928), Mariola in the première of Pizzetti's *Fra Gherardo* (1928), Carmen, Fedora, Conchita (Zandonai) and Charlotte. She had a repertory of more than 90 roles, embracing mezzo, dramatic, lyric and coloratura parts in opera and operetta, including Wally, Tosca and Magda de Civry (*La rondine*). In Bucharest her Butterfly, Minnie, Kundry and Adriana Lecouvreur were especially admired. Her range, both vocal and dramatic, was exceptional, enhanced by a rich timbre and an intense commitment. She wrote a book of memoirs, *Amintiri din cariera mea lirică* (1964).

VIOREL COSMA

Cristoforo Colombo ('Christopher Columbus'). *Dramma lirico* in four acts and an epilogue by ALBERTO FRANCHETTI to a libretto by LUIGI ILLICA; Genoa, Teatro Carlo Felice, 6 October 1892 (revised version in three acts and an epilogue, Milan, Teatro alla Scala, 17 January 1923).

At the court in Salamanca in 1487 a council of geographers evaluates the claim of Columbus (baritone) to have discovered a new route to India. Roldano Ximenes (bass) tries to sabotage the project with tales of sea monsters. Queen Isabella (soprano) reveals her vision of a land beyond the Atlantic. Act 2 takes place on the *Santa Maria* and *Pinta* five years later. As the crew realize that the compass has stopped functioning correctly, the situation on the *Santa Maria* begins to border on mutiny; incited by Ximenes they try to throw Columbus overboard. At sunrise a cry from the *Pinta* announces the discovery of the new continent. In Act 3 the Spaniards are killing the people of Xaragua, in the West Indies, in their search for gold; Yanika (mezzo-soprano), the daughter of the old Cacique (bass), implores the princess Anacoana (mezzo-soprano) to avenge her father's murder. Act 4 opens with the arrival of the Spanish ambassador Bobadilla (bass). Through Ximenes's false allegations Columbus is captured and taken back to Spain. In the epilogue, in the monastery crypt at Medina del Campo in 1506, Columbus, broken by his imprisonment, learns of Isabella's death and dies in the arms of Fernando Guevara (tenor), the commander of the king's guard.

Of the many librettos on the discovery of the Americas, Illica's was the first to encompass both the discovery and Columbus's death. His vision of vast spaces on stage, disposition of crowd scenes and carefully crafted dialogue constitute a landmark in the history of the Italian libretto. Franchetti's music exploited the possibilities inherent in the text to create large-scale scenes for the chorus, complex ensembles and numerous orchestral interludes. More than in the works of his contemporaries the musical discourse unfolds without interruption, revealing an indebtedness to Wagner's technique of orchestral commentary.

At its première *Cristoforo Colombo* won immediate international success. Subsequent revisions, made partly to reduce the playing time, began in 1895 with the condensing of Acts 3 and 4 into one act; for the 1923 production Franchetti wrote a new third act to replace the original Acts 3 and 4.

JÜRGEN MAEHDER

Critic, The [The Critic, or, An Opera Rehearsed]. Opera in two acts, op.144, by CHARLES VILLIERS STANFORD to a libretto by Lewis Cairns James after RICHARD BRINSLEY SHERIDAN's play; London, Shaftesbury Theatre, 14 January 1916.

Sheridan's first act, set in the house of the critic Dangle, is dispensed with. His second and third acts are the play itself, the comically bad tragedy *The Spanish Armada*, in rehearsal in the theatre. Here it is presented as an opera with the essentials of Sheridan's text retained together with the spoken interjections by the author Puff, the composer (appropriating Dangle's part), the critic Sneer (spoken) and the under-prompter Mr Hopkins (spoken). The conductor (dressed and characterized as Thomas Linley) also adds comments about orchestral misreadings and retakes, all of which are precisely notated in the score. For the overture the orchestra is directed to tune up and practise listed passages.

Stanford enjoys quoting from Handel, Beethoven, Parry and his own song 'Drake's drum' and providing pantomime for a silent character and a mad scene for Tilburina (soprano), daughter of the Governor of Tilbury Fort (baritone), after the death of her lover, the imprisoned Spaniard Don Ferolo Whiskerandos (tenor). But the comic subtlety which raises the work high above burlesque is that he shows how well the awful script can function as a libretto for beautiful, serious music.

STEPHEN BANFIELD

Criticism. Etymologically, the central concept of criticism is judgment, discrimination, discernment. As such it is distinct from the descriptive reporting which has a necessary place in journalism. Yet in practice both are essential to genuine criticism. Just as description by itself, whether of performance or performer, shirks the prime critical task, so criticism unanchored in detailed observation turns into ineffectual theorizing.

1. The role of criticism. 2. The Baroque era. 3. 'Reform'. 4. Early Romanticism. 5. The age of Wagner. 6. After Wagner: psychology, history, ideology. 7. Recent trends.

1. THE ROLE OF CRITICISM. To some extent criticism can be categorized by the subject-matter it has chosen to address at different periods and in different contexts. At the most humble and familiar level it is concerned with individual performances (necessarily live until recently, but now also recorded, which brings a new historical element into play). It is aimed principally at potential audiences, but serves also as part of the civilized discourse by which reputations are made and unmade and, incidentally, as a permanent record. The greater part of the reviews printed in the regular press necessarily come under this heading, but although regular press criticism existed in a few centres, notably Paris, even in the 18th century, it is essentially a product of the commercialization (one might almost say industrialization) of opera performance that came about in the first decades of the 19th century, and brought in its wake a demand for consumer information and consumer protection. Of the vast amount of such criticism printed in the last 200 years much is inevitably trivial, though even that has begun in recent years to take on a certain importance as a result of the historicizing of the repertory.

The critic of individual performances transcends the limits of his subject-matter only insofar as he chooses to deal with the work itself, as opposed to an individual manifestation of it. The two functions are, of course, by no means incompatible: in fact one might reasonably maintain that valid judgment of an individual performance must always depend on some notion of an ideal one, and the competent critic is precisely the one whose experience has enabled him to form such an ideal standard of reference. It is true that the constraints of regular press criticism rarely allow time or space for much consideration of the work rather than its performance, except when the opera itself is new or unfamiliar. Nevertheless the critic, relying on the shared experience of his readers, can sometimes provide new insights and readjust old attitudes in very few words. By and large, though, operas themselves, as opposed to performances of them, are most likely to be subjected to critical evaluation either in monographs on individual composers or in those rare books and essays that seek to examine the genre as a whole.

The most general, and historically the most influential, category of criticism is that which attempts to consider not merely what opera is and historically has been, but also (the critical component) what it might and should be. This class of writing depends for its vitality on some sense of urgency in writer and reader alike, and has therefore tended to appear either when rival trends were in conflict or when historical conditions have called opera's social underpinnings into question – as in the mid-18th century, for example, or at the present day. Yet even in the years of opera's most widespread popularity the artistic vision of an individual such as Wagner could compel him to reassess the entire possibilities of the genre – an intellectual effort that must, however self-serving, be described as criticism.

Opera is inherently a mixed medium, a type of drama compounded primarily of words and music, but also including, from its earliest days, elements of visual spectacle both animate (choreography) and inanimate (scenery) which can be grouped together under the heading of 'production'. Over the centuries the balance between these elements has shifted constantly and those shifts have often been accompanied by written manifestos, complaints and justifications that constitute some of the most famous of all critical writings on opera. In fact it is tempting to see all the famous critical debates on the nature of opera as stemming from the contradictory needs of those refractory partners, words and music – linked by a contract that has constantly to be rewritten.

2. THE BAROQUE ERA. In a sense opera as a genre might even be said to have been born of criticism, or at least out of a feeling that the potentiality of music to achieve specific dramatic effects was being inadequately used; the practice of Peri and Caccini is in this sense based on the 'critical' thought of the scholars Girolamo Mei and Vincenzo Galilei. At one level their concern to emulate the ancient Greeks gives rise to an emphasis on emotional effectiveness, so that Monteverdi's setting of Ariadne's lament, for example, is universally praised for its ability to bring tears to the audience's eyes (Gagliano, preface to the score of *Dafne*). At a more general level, however, it leads to a constantly recurring need throughout the 17th century, and even well into the 18th, to justify opera's existence as a genre. As Rosand has remarked, in her study of Venetian opera:

> Its failure to conform to the standard [i.e. Aristotelian] laws of genre or kind rendered opera suspect; it was continually called upon to define and redefine, to explain and justify itself: music with words or words with music; classical drama *redivivus*, declaimed in the manner of the ancient poets, or irrational entertainment performed by characters who inexplicably (and ridiculously) sing instead of speak.

This concern for justification was intensified when the clash of national cultural traditions came into play. In the land of its birth, opera seems to have won general acceptance by the latter half of the 17th century, and foreigners who observed it on its home ground (e.g. Coryat, Maugars) were happy enough to take it on its own terms. However, when the attempt was made to import it into countries with strong cultural traditions of their own, resistance was naturally much stronger. Corneille, tentatively essaying the new genre in his *Andromède* (1649–50), took care to give 'nothing of importance' to his singers, as the sense of the words would be obscured. The Lully-Quinault collaborations from 1672 onwards soon drew the fire of critics such as Boileau, La Bruyère and Fénelon, who saw in them only the degradation of the classical French tragedy (though La Bruyère did see some justification for opera in its ability to depict the *merveilleux*). However, the classic statement of this French resistance is perhaps that of Saint-Evremond. He casts it in high-mindedly intellectual terms: while music has its virtues, it offers too much to the senses, too little to the intellect, for opera to be worthy of comparison with the spoken tragedies of Corneille and Racine. So far from music's enhancing the drama, for Saint-Evremond it can only mar it. In this rationalistic view, choruses may be permitted in quasi-liturgical situations, and solo song for lyrical effusions of love or lamentation: for the rest music, together with 'machines', must be excluded from drama as unnatural and ridiculous.

This attitude was later taken up, though with different nuances, by Addison in England, Gottsched in Germany, and by Rousseau and the Abbé Arnaud in France again, often with acknowledgment of Saint-Evremond. It represents, of course, a denial of the essential feature of the opera as invented by the Italians, namely that it should be in music throughout, and raises the perennial question whether all elements of a drama are susceptible of expression in music. To this attitude may be attributed the emergence of the French *opéra comique* in the middle of the century and the rapid growth of its popularity both at home and, usually in translated form, in other countries too.

The contrast between French and Italian styles implicit in Saint-Evremond (who was writing in English exile) becomes the central issue in Raguenet's *Paralèle des italiens et des françois* (1702; translated into English in 1709). While admitting that French operas excel in their dramaturgy and their *mise-en-scène*, Raguenet, who had visited Italy in 1698, unequivocally praises the Italians for their musical variety, brilliance and expressiveness. He was answered by Le Cerf de la Viéville (the representative of an older standpoint) in a series of publications which defend the virtues of Lullian opera, as he sees them: an artful simplicity, achieved through instinct (feeling) refined by the 'rules' of codified experience (i.e. tradition), and immune to the vulgar bravura of the Italians. The fact that the Raguenet *Paralèle* was still considered sufficiently vital to be worth publishing 20 years later in the first German musical periodical, Mattheson's *Critica musica* (1722–5), suggests that more was at stake than a merely local matter of aesthetic preference. In that, the controversy directly raises a question of continuing importance throughout the history of opera: given the fact that opera is drama conveyed through music, to what extent should each of the two elements be constrained by the other?

The quarrel between the respective champions of Lully and Rameau in the 1740s was essentially a restatement of the same positions, with the Lullistes standing for what they saw as a noble simplicity of music properly subordinated to the text, while the Ramistes defended the newer master's much greater musical richness and complexity. More important, though, because of its more lasting effects on the development of opera, was the so-called QUERELLE DES BOUFFONS in the following decade.

In spite of the fact that French criticism in the 18th century was conducted by and for a small educated élite, it contained a distinct political element, and never more so than in the Querelle des Bouffons, a pamphlet war that flourished between 1752 and 1754. At the start this was not so much a dispute between rival national schools as between social classes and the modes of theatrical entertainment that typified their respective tastes – the courtly *tragédie lyrique* and the bourgeois *opéra comique*. The latter had achieved great popularity in the hands of Favart well before the middle of the century, but the superior musical quality of the Italian works brought to Paris by Bambini's company in the early 1750s at last provided a handy stick with which to beat the court opera on superficially aesthetic grounds. It is only because of the implicit social content of this dispute that a writer as cultivated as Grimm, the editor of the *Correspondance littéraire*, who was quite able to appreciate Rameau's musical qualities, found himself drawn into the conflict on the side of the 'reformers', in spite of the seeming irrelevance of comparing a comic style with a serious one. But however unfair the victory won by Rousseau and the Encyclopedists, it did encourage a generation of younger French composers to take the new genre of *opéra comique* seriously, as its immensely rapid development in the hands of Philidor and Monsigny demonstrated during the following decade. In Vienna too, newly sympathetic to French trends in the wake of Kaunitz's alliance of the Catholic powers, it was quickly taken up by the adaptable Gluck, who had hitherto moved within a completely Italian musical orbit. For once a critical movement seems actually to have stimulated a creative one, if only by articulating the need for it.

3. 'REFORM'. Meanwhile in Italy a precisely opposite movement was taking shape, though drawing to the same ultimate conclusion, namely the rapprochement of the Italian and French, the serious and comic styles. The rigidity (and therefore absurdity) of the *opera seria* conventions had already become obvious enough to be satirized by Benedetto Marcello in his *Teatro alla moda* (*c*1720). Now, a generation later, a serious and knowledgeable opera-lover like Algarotti, friend of both Voltaire and Frederick the Great, looked to save it rather than satirize it; his immensely influential *Saggio sopra l'opera in musica* (1755), impregnated with the ideals of the Enlightenment, recommends imbuing it with precisely those features of the *tragédie lyrique* which up-to-date French intellectuals were busily rejecting. Although he justified the 'exotic' and spectacular elements as appropriate to the genre (Algarotti remains a courtier at heart), all elements of the work, including the music, were once more to be subordinated to the unifying poetic idea. He was able to put some of his ideas into practice at Parma, but Algarotti's illness and early death meant that his ideals were realized elsewhere and by other hands, notably though not solely by Gluck in his Vienna *Orfeo* (1762) and *Alceste* (1767). Gluck's literary collaborator Calzabigi – only two years younger

than Algarotti, but much longer-lived – certainly had a hand in the famous preface to the score of *Alceste*, for it manifests a viewpoint that can already be detected in the preface to his complete edition of Metastasio (1755); it remains one of the most important documents in the history of operatic criticism.

The reintroduction to Paris in the 1770s of this new type of neo-classical *tragédie lyrique* with an Italian accent (purged of what Rameau's opponents had seen as his musical extravagance) gave rise to the third of the great critical pamphlet wars of the French 18th century, the struggle between the adherents of Gluck and Piccinni; but this seems almost entirely a matter of shadow-boxing, since the motivations behind it were even more palpably extra-musical than they had been 20 years earlier. Piccinni's practice in the serious field (and it was as a tragedian that he was matched against Gluck) is not so much different as simply inferior.

The most distinguished critical writer on opera of the time was the ex-Jesuit Arteaga. His subtle but essentially reactionary writings hark back to an ideal of antique perfection whose closest modern approximation he finds in the works of Metastasio – dramas made for music in such a way that the respective potential of each art can be realized in controlled alternation rather than fused into a single experience. Arteaga remained a somewhat isolated figure, but the last half-century of the *ancien régime* is nevertheless one of the few periods in musical history when criticism can be said to have had much effect on the course of operatic composition. A small but highly motivated and articulate audience was able to impress its taste (and by no means only its musical taste) on the composers who served it, and in so doing perhaps prepared the ground for Mozart's extraordinarily various achievements in the field of opera.

It seems unlikely that Mozart himself was much influenced by any critical writing on opera; eager to please, he simply took advantage of whatever stylistic possibilities came to hand, mastering them and improving them with an increasingly sure instinct for dramatic effectiveness. Those possibilities included the traditional Italian forms, the Germanized *opéra comique*, the Frenchified *opera seria*, and ultimately combinations of those styles that are unique to himself and completely transcend their models. But just as Mozart was very little indebted to the critical writing of his contemporaries, so he provoked very little articulate commentary from them. The operas of his maturity coincided with the disappearance of precisely that circle of articulate, cosmopolitan critics whose reactions we might most wish to have; the complacent remarks of Count Zinzendorf, or even the reported opinions of the Emperor Joseph II, are no substitute for the sophisticated critical intelligence of Parisian connoisseurs. Though the obituary tributes make it clear that Mozart's stature was already widely recognized by his death, it is only in the generation after it that we find much critical writing of any interest about his operas, and then from representatives of the new wave of literary romanticism. Goethe came to be fully aware of Mozart's operatic genius, and in the following generation Stendhal's youthful enthusiasm for Rossini, though indelibly expressed, gradually gave way to a mature admiration for the older composer; but it is in the new wave of German-language musical periodicals that most of the detailed critical examination of his music appeared.

4. Early Romanticism. E. T. A. Hoffmann, who began writing in the Leipzig *Allgemeine musikalische Zeitung* in 1809, brought nearly as much hero-worship to Mozart as to Beethoven, and his writings about his music, notably the well-known short story *Don Juan* (1813), naturally emphasize the demonic elements in that opera, though in a way that might have surprised the composer. Hoffmann was also characteristic of the Romantic movement in being one of the first composers to publish music criticism. As composers, with other creative artists, came to be considered less as craftsmen or entertainers, on however high a plane, than as spiritual leaders of mankind, an element of propaganda for the progressive creeps in – quite explicitly in the critical writings of Weber, Hoffmann's junior by ten years. Weber's passionate concern for the future of German opera sometimes led him into unfairness in his judgments of other national styles, but his views on the potentialities of the genre often anticipate those of Wagner in the following generation. By the 1830s the lead in opera had shifted definitively to Paris, and Schumann, writing first in the *Allgemeine musikalische Zeitung* and later in his own *Neue Zeitschrift für Musik*, showed little interest in a genre which he evidently associated with meretricious glamour and virtuosity. Berlioz, however, as we know from his *Mémoires*, had received some of the most intense musical experiences of his youth in the opera house, and was constantly drawn to it both as composer and as critic. His regular contributions to the Paris *Journal des débats* are always brilliantly expressed and often trenchant, but contain much generous insight. Gluck and his epigone Spontini are treated with great understanding, as might be expected. Of the great operatic composers of the past it is Mozart for whom Berlioz seems to lack immediate sympathy; clearly the traditional national prejudices – French for verbal drama, Italian for melodic expansion – lived on in the new age of Romanticism. As might be expected, it is not only in his musical style but also in his musical specificity that Berlioz outshines the other Parisian critics, such as the ineffectual opera-doctor Castil-Blaze (responsible for mangling Weber's *Freischütz*, among other works) and the ex-singer Scudo, for whom the apogee of Romanticism was represented by Meyerbeer. Among the composer-critics of the 19th century, Berlioz is at once the most spontaneous and the most open-minded in his treatment of opera, and honest enough to admit, towards the end of his life, that Wagner's later music, specifically *Tristan* (which he never saw on the stage), was no longer comprehensible to him.

5. The age of Wagner. Wagner's own earliest critical writings, reports sent back to the Dresden *Abendzeitung* when he was a young man in Paris, contain praise for several composers whom he was later to scorn, including Meyerbeer, Halévy and Auber; the revolution of taste which had driven Rossini into retirement after *Guillaume Tell* and established the new style of Parisian grand opera satisfied his aesthetic needs for the time being. But only briefly. The 1840s, and his own 30s, were for Wagner a period of intense and often painful development, so that his exile from Germany and from practical work in the theatre after the 1849 revolution in Saxony appear in retrospect to have been a providential opportunity for him to catch up with his own ideas. The theoretical writings of the next few years, though turgid and repetitive in expression and characteristically

prophetic in tone (something which served him ill among foreign critics who perforce often judged him by them rather than by staged performances of his works), represent the most sustained attempt in history to examine the entire nature, actual and potential, of opera. *Oper und Drama*, in particular, makes clear that Wagner's basic critical tenet involved a revaluation of the relation between music and drama. According to his diagnosis music, a means of expression, had been allowed to become an end, at the expense of drama – and this applied not merely to the older 'singer's opera', with which so many of his contemporaries were still satisfied, but also to the sensational grand operas that had succeeded them. This doctrine would seem to place Wagner wholeheartedly in the tradition of the literary, 'French' school of writers about opera, but his musical genius soon carried him, after this necessary intellectual house-cleaning, to a position which balanced the claims of music and drama in a quite new way – a way, in fact, which remained unique to himself since it involved the 'composition' of the drama as well as of the music.

The works embodying this revolutionary reassessment of what opera could and should be resulted in a watershed in opera criticism. Viewed from the perspective of the late 20th century, when we can understand how necessary it was for composers who came after Wagner to reject his domination, the difficulty with which that domination was achieved can easily be forgotten, but a brief examination of the critical writing of the time confirms it. In England, for example, where his early Romantic operas were not given until the 1870s (and then in Italian) and the later works only in the following decade, the most prominent critics, H. F. Chorley of *The Athenaeum* and J. W. Davison of *The Times*, were almost entirely uncomprehending. Chorley's taste had been formed in the days of the 'singer's operas' of Rossini, Bellini, and to some extent Donizetti; his genuine connoisseurship in that field even impeded his acceptance of Verdi. Davison's experience was perhaps wider, but his sympathies even narrower, and he was particularly offended by the prophetic strain in Wagner's writing. It is true, as Langley suggests ('Italian Opera and the English Press, 1836–1856', *Periodica musica*, vi (1988), 3–8), that other critics were less hidebound, though many were shocked by what they felt to be the immorality of the stories, but it was not until the decade after Wagner's death that the young Bernard Shaw would trounce the resisters with his unique combination of musical sensitivity, insight into the drama, and wit.

In Italy, where resistance to Wagner might be expected to have been at its strongest, at least two influential critics, the scholarly Abramo Basevi, author of a fine early study of Verdi, and Filippo Filippi, the critic of *La perseveranza*, showed themselves well aware of his stature, even though the former felt his influence was a dangerous one for Italian composers. In the German-speaking countries the battle for and against Wagner was waged more heatedly. K. F. Brendel, who took over the editorship of Schumann's *Neue Zeitschrift für Musik* in 1845 and held it until his death in 1868, made of it a beacon for the radical Romantics promoted by Liszt at Weimar, Wagner among them. In so doing he enraged its founder and his followers, such as the violinist Joachim and the young Brahms, though Brahms himself had far more respect for Wagner than he had for Liszt, and indeed than Wagner had for him. The resistance to Wagner found its most articulate and influential voice in Eduard Hanslick, honorary reader at Vienna University and for many years the critic of the *Presse* and *Neue freie Presse*. His treatise *Vom Musikalisch-Schönen* ('Of the Beautiful in Music'), first published in 1854 and often reprinted, established his credentials as an aesthetician before he was 30. Unfortunately its central argument that music's beauty resides essentially in its formal and not its expressive properties, though well worth making, blinded him to the virtues of much new music and of Wagner's operas in particular. Hanslick's unyielding conservatism, combined with his undeniable authority, did much to prolong and embitter the struggle for and against Wagner in the German-speaking world. It also helps to explain the savagery with which the opposing point of view was put by the young Hugo Wolf in the articles he wrote for the *Wiener Salonblatt* in the 1880s.

Perhaps the most confused and interesting of the critical reactions to Wagner's operatic methods were those in the Slavonic countries, where they became entangled in the arguments for and against nationalism in music and correspondingly intensified. In Russia A. N. Serov saw in the Wagner of *Oper und Drama* a kindred spirit, for whom drama must always take precedence over music, a prescription that suited his own slender gifts as a composer. His schoolfellow and sometime friend V. V. Stasov, on the contrary, regarded Wagner's methods as completely opposed to the interests of Balakirev's nationalist circle of composers, of which he was an enthusiastic and increasingly conservative champion. In Bohemia, however, yet another composer-critic, namely Smetana, demonstrated in his epic operas on Czech historical themes that there was no inherent contradiction between nationalist and Wagnerian aspirations.

In France a small number of sophisticated enthusiasts were among the earliest champions of the mature Wagner. Baudelaire's highly laudatory essay on his Paris concerts of 1860 (which included the *Tristan* prelude) and the *Tannhäuser* production of the following year, inaugurated an alliance between Wagner and the French literary avant-garde which reached its apogee in the founding in 1885 of the *Revue wagnérienne*, dominated by members of Mallarmé's poetic circle. Young composers such as Chabrier, Chausson and d'Indy were all profoundly influenced by their experiences of Wagner's operas at Munich and Bayreuth, yet this rapid and fervent acceptance led, for the most radical of them all, to an equally instinctive rejection. For Debussy Wagner quickly came to seem too 'composed', too full of a music that draws attention to itself rather than to the drama. His criticisms, in other words, can be understood as rejecting the mature Wagner's practice in favour of his original theory – or, perhaps more convincingly, returning to the traditional French principle of the primacy of the word. This, in any case, is what he demonstrates in his only completed opera, and also, though more indirectly, in his own, very individual journalistic criticism, published in the *Revue blanche*.

6. After Wagner: psychology, history, ideology. The shift in subject matter from the mythological or symbolic to the socially and psychologically realistic around the turn of the century, although it had a precursor in Bizet's *Carmen* (originally and appropriately an *opéra comique*), was essentially a reflection of the contemporary drama, as mediated through national

taste. The two most successful opera composers of the period were both affected by this movement: Puccini was drawn to situations involving the victimization of pathetic 'little women', while Strauss revelled for a while in the challenge of depicting pathological characters. Each was roundly criticized on grounds of taste, despite the difference in their musical vocabularies. And there are in fact underlying similarities, even of technique: Debussy's operatic aesthetic was a distillation of Wagner's, Puccini's a dilution, and Strauss's an amplification of it.

Although none of the successful opera composers of the early 20th century was able to exert Wagner's tight intellectual control over his librettos (drama seems almost to drown in Strauss's music-saturated operas), many opera critics of the period tended to write as if Wagner had established the only viable convention and pointed the only way forward. The violent shift of taste brought about by World War I shattered any such comfortable consensus. One of the many facets of 'neo-classicism' was a revulsion from the musical continuity and omniscient commentary of the Wagnerian synthesis. The operas of Mozart and Verdi (though some of these had of course never lost their popularity except in intellectual circles) began to be reassessed, and those of Handel to be revived, at least in Germany. A new generation of composers at the same time proclaimed the virtues not of expression but of objectivity.

The critics best able to adapt to this new multiplicity of operatic conventions, all competing within a single repertory, were those who could bring to bear on it a long historical perspective. It is no accident that several of the foremost critics of the day were scholars of distinction, among them Ernest Newman in England (Gluck, Wagner), Henry Prunières in France (Monteverdi and the early Baroque) and Alfred Einstein in Germany (Gluck, Mozart). At a later date Martin Cooper (Gluck, the *opéra comique*) and Winton Dean (Handel, Bizet) carried on the tradition of the scholar-critic, as did Paul Henry Lang in the USA. In the years since World War II the advent of the various new sound-recording formats has enlarged the accessible repertory still further, and imposed on the critic a still greater need for breadth of sympathy. It has also, incidentally, provided him with an armoury of information on performance practice that makes possible a far more objective vocal connoisseurship than has ever existed in the past. The present situation demands of the practical critic an ability to judge not by a single aesthetic, let alone ideological, yardstick, but with reference to the intentions of the composer and the conventions within which he worked.

Under the mid-century totalitarian regimes in Germany, the Soviet Union and elsewhere, ideological criticism was for the first time applied not only to the dramatic subject matter of operas (as had frequently been the case in the past) but also to their musical style. Works by Weill, Hindemith, Krenek were denounced and banned by the Nazis, while in Russia Stalin's cultural henchman Zhdanov dutifully attacked the 'formalism' of Shostakovich and Prokofiev, as well as many lesser composers. But censorship is to criticism what propaganda is to education; cynics may profess that no hard and fast line divides them, but in practice the distinction is rather easily made. And there is in fact a good deal in common between good teaching and good criticism, however informally the latter may be conducted.

7. RECENT TRENDS. The most influential recent book on opera criticism, at least in the English-speaking world, has been Joseph Kerman's *Opera as Drama* (1956, 2/1989). In it Kerman re-emphasizes the view that opera is a form whose dramatic potential deserves to be taken seriously (a view not likely to be contested by any reasonably educated person), and, more controversially, that its drama is realized above all by and through its music – in brief, 'the composer is the dramatist'. According to this view, the quality of an opera depends above all on its music, and although this has been questioned more recently by historians who have concentrated on other, particularly literary, aspects of operatic practice, it seems to be borne out by empirical observation of the way in which the standard repertory has evolved. Although throughout operatic history individual singers and, in more recent years, director-producers have been able to ensure an audience for whatever they do, the central repertory has been shaped by public admiration for its music, not its librettos or its staging.

To the revised second edition of his book Kerman appends a suggested methodology for opera criticism, based on his analysis of the contributions music makes to drama: namely intensity and specificity of characterization, articulation (which he would prefer to call generation) of the action, and the establishment of an atmosphere or sonorous 'world' in which this particular drama belongs. Unexceptionable as these principles may be in the judging of works (rather than performances), Kerman's own application of them points up certain problems. Above all, the critic is liable to be constrained by his own conception of what is truly 'dramatic', either in text or music. A degree of subjectivity is of course inherent in the whole critical exercise, and provocative judgments are necessary, even desirable, as a challenge to too easily accepted consensus opinion. More serious, however, is the dismissal of an entire repertory (e.g. Baroque opera) on the ground that its style 'lacks the flexibility required to respond very far to action'. Here one senses that the theory which has been devised to validate and refine response to a canonical repertory is also being used to justify a lack of response to a less familiar one. More fruitful in the long run would seem to be those studies (Dean on Handel, Ashbrook on Donizetti, Budden on Verdi are three recent examples) which attempt to achieve empathy with the composer's creative intentions by a patient examination of his works, and then to communicate it by informed advocacy. But such advocacy too depends on an initial commitment to the music, and is thus as vulnerable to the charge of subjectivity as informed rejection. The truth is that no criticism can be completely objective, only more or less well-founded, and more or less persuasively expressed.

One of the most conspicuous recent developments in opera criticism is the increasing attention paid to it in academic circles. Not that traditional musicology ever eschewed criticism completely; the writings of Abert and Dent on Mozart's operas constitute criticism of the most genuine kind, and both were professors. But for every Abert or Dent there have been many scholars who saw as their main task the purely philological one of establishing accurate texts (insofar as the concept of accuracy is applicable to an art-form as subject to circumstance as opera; *see* EDITING), or of gathering reliable biographical data. More recently, stimulated by comparable developments in the study of literature, there has been a proliferation within the universities of new critical approaches to opera. Regrettably, these have tended to separate into mutually exclusive camps: on the one hand are those (relatively few) for whom music is a purely autonomous entity, on whose formal properties alone the value of the work depends; on the other, those for whom the most interesting aspect of an opera lies in its context (biographical or social) or its interpretation (psychological, political, cultural). No doubt all of these approaches can make a contribution to our understanding, yet practised in isolation from one another they give rise to strange distortions. Of them all it is perhaps the purely music-theoretical that is least appropriate to opera, since even the operas of such composers as Wagner and Schoenberg hardly aim at the tightness of organization that tend to be the theorist's criterion of excellence; to look for it in Mozart or Verdi, let alone lesser composers, may yield interesting insights, but at the expense of concentrating on a side-issue. Yet if formalism is not much practised today in opera criticism, the opposite trend is rampant and multifarious. Following the lead of academic literary criticism, scholars have subjected the operatic repertory to every kind of interpretation – psychological (both Freudian and Jungian), political (usually some variety of Marxist), sociological, and in the broadest sense cultural. At a slightly earlier date the German political philosopher and would-be composer Theodor W. Adorno had brought most of these disciplines to bear in his writings on music, and particularly opera, but for the reader who happens not to share his strongly marked political and sociological attitudes, these seem to distort rather than illuminate his critical judgments (as for example in the study *In Search of Wagner*).

There are at least two main objections to the current frenzy of reinterpretation. The first is that many of its exponents tend to fasten on the literary component of opera to the virtual exclusion of the music (this has been particularly noticeable in some feminist writing); in this sense they are as one-sided, and hence as sterile in terms of genuine appreciation, as the proponents of the musical autonomy they reject. The second is that their eager revisionism is offset by a remarkable conservatism in the choice of works they choose to discuss. This is perhaps natural; there is after all little temptation to reinterpret a work for which no standard interpretation has evolved. But the tendency constantly to re-examine a restricted number of canonical works, foremost among them the best-known operas of Mozart, Verdi and Wagner, lends a certain ingrown quality to much of the newer academic criticism of opera – a characteristic reflected in the hermetic jargon in which it is sometimes cast.

It begs, moreover, a fundamental question that has perhaps received too little explicit consideration: for whom is criticism written? If for the relatively restricted world of professional academics, there can be little harm (if not much profit) in the constant refinement, through analysis and polemic, of our appreciation of a canonical repertory. Ultimate truth, which would presumably involve sharing both composer's and librettist's conscious and unconscious intentions, may never be reached, but at least it is possible to persuade oneself that it lies somewhere ahead. But opera is a genre that depends for its very existence on a nexus of public support; it seems, then, that an equally valuable form of criticism, at least in practical terms, may be that which has traditionally addressed itself not to the academic but to the lay audience which collectively supports the whole edifice. The arrival of complete opera recordings in convenient format has made the notion of a standard repertory almost obsolete. It is true that the greatest and most popular works (often the same) are available in many recordings while others can be found in only one, but to anyone capable of reading a record catalogue Henze's operas are now as accessible as Mozart's, and at least one or two of Vivaldi's as accessible as those of Verdi. In face of this unprecedented and almost overwhelming availability, it seems self-indulgent for critics to spend their time skating ever more fantastic figures on the surface of familiar works when the unfamiliar cry out for elucidation and assessment. It is for this reason that the painstaking work of the best traditional critics, armed with a trained literary and musical sensitivity as well as a wide experience of the genre in all its forms, and willing to meet the challenge of everything that comes their way, seems unlikely soon to be outmoded.

M. Graf: *Composer and Critic: Two Hundred Years of Musical Criticism* (New York, 1945)

A. R. Oliver: *The Encyclopedists as Critics of Music* (New York, 1947)

R. Giazotto: *Poesia melodrammatica e pensiero critico nel settecento* (Milan, 1952)

Opera, iii (1952), 137–61; see also p.655 [symposium on opera criticism]

J. Kerman: *Opera as Drama* (New York, 1956, 2/1989)

D. Arundell: *The Critic at the Opera* (London, 1957)

G. Flaherty: *Opera in the Development of German Critical Thought* (Princeton, 1978)

C. Dahlhaus: *Vom Musikdrama zur Literaturoper: Aufsätze zur neueren Operngeschichte* (Munich and Salzburg, 1983)

A. Groos and R. Parker, eds.: *Reading Opera* (Princeton, 1988)

C. Abbate: *Unsung Voices* (Princeton, 1991)

R. Donington: *Opera and its Symbols: the Unity of Words, Music and Singing* (New Haven, 1991)

For further bibliography *see* Libretto (ii), §III, esp. G.

JEREMY NOBLE

Crivelli, Gaetano (*b* Brescia, 20 Oct 1768; *d* Brescia, 16 July 1836). Italian tenor. After making his début at Brescia in 1794, he appeared at Verona, Palermo, Venice and Naples, where he studied with Nozzari and Aprile. In 1805 he sang at La Scala in operas by Mayr and Pavesi. He appeared in Paris in 1811 in Paisiello's *Pirro* and as Don Ottavio. He made his London début at the King's Theatre in 1817 as Ulysses in Cimarosa's *Penelope*. He also sang in Paer's *Griselda*, in the first London performance of *Don Giovanni*, and in *Così fan tutte* and *La clemenza di Tito*. Returning to Italy, he appeared at La Fenice where he sang Adriano in the first performance of Meyerbeer's *Il crociato in Egitto* (1824). Adriano became his favourite role, and he sang it at his farewell in 1831.

ELIZABETH FORBES

Croatia. During the 16th and 17th centuries artistic activity in Croatia was concentrated along the Adriatic coastal strip, where Italian influence brought about an early awareness of opera. In 1617 Paskoj Primović published his translation of Rinuccini's *Euridice*, working from Peri's score; Junije Palmotić's play *Atalanta* (1629) was furnished with music, now lost. But the absence of strong centres of patronage meant that throughout the 17th and most of the 18th century opera was given only sporadically. From the second half of the 18th century inland Croatia and particularly Zagreb played a dominant role. Drama and opera became especially important during the movement for national cultural emancipation that developed in the 19th century when the arts were powerful weapons against Austrian and Hungarian domination. In the 1840s Romantic opera had an auspicious start in the works of Vatroslav Lisinski, though his early death and the unfavourable political climate delayed further development until 1870, when Ivan Zajc abandoned a promising career in Vienna and accepted the directorship of the Croatian National Opera. The repertory was based on the standard Italian and German works, and Zajc's own operas enjoyed great popularity, since like the Verdi Risorgimento works they reflected the ideology of the Croatian movement for cultural emancipation. The generation of composers that came immediately after Zajc (Blagoje Bersa, Josip Hatze) showed readiness to accept newer tendencies – Wagnerian elements, naturalism and *verismo*.

The composers active after World War I endeavoured to create an original style based on folk music: a belated reaction against the cosmopolitan language of Zajc and Bersa, this occasionally dulled creativity, forcing them into an ideological mould. Antun Dobronić avoided the term opera, labelling his works 'stage symphony' or 'musical stage mystery', while Božidar Širola and Jakov Gotovac showed a preference for comic opera. Other notable works came from Krešimir Baranović and Fran Lhotka.

The ideology of socialist realism adopted by the Yugoslav state after 1945 was abandoned in the 1950s, when a variety of individual styles emerged. Ivo Brkanović and Ivo Tijardović continued in the style established in the pre-war period, while Boris Papandopulo, Ivo Lhotka-Kalinski and Natko Devčić successfully refined their earlier eclectic styles and moved towards a cautious modernism. There has also been a sustained interest in Shakespeare: in Krešimir Fribec's *Romeo i Julija* (1954–5), which uses serial technique, only the two main characters act, while the chorus provides a commentary; Stjepan Šulek followed his *Koriolan* (1958) with the highly acclaimed *Oluja* ('The Tempest', 1969); Igor Kuljerić wrote *Rikard III* (1987) to a commission by the Zagreb Biennale of Contemporary Music. Milko Kelemen's innovatory *Der neue Mieter* (1964) and *Der Belagerungszustand* (1970), though written to German commissions, received their Croatian premières at the Zagreb Biennale in 1965 and 1971 respectively.

There are permanent opera companies in Zagreb, Rijeka, Split and Osijek. Operetta has been popular especially in Zagreb, Osijek and Split; Ivan Zajc, Srećko Albini and Ivo Tijardović have enjoyed considerable success in the genre. Opera has played an important part in the summer festivals in Dubrovnik, Split and Opatija.

For further information on operatic life in the country's principal centres *see* DUBROVNIK; OSIJEK; SPLIT; and ZAGREB.

*

Hrvatsko narodno kazalište: sto godina opere [Croatian National Theatre: a Hundred Years of Opera] (Zagreb, 1971)
J. Andreis: *Music in Croatia* (Zagreb, 1974)
D. Cvetko: *Musikgeschichte der Südslawen* (Kassel and Maribor, 1975)
J. Sivec: *Opera skozi stoletja* [Opera through the Centuries] (Ljubljana, 1976)

BOJAN BUJIC

Croce, Elena [Viviani, Elena Croce] (*fl* 1708–20). Italian soprano. She sang in operas by Caldara and Lotti at Venice in 1708 and in A. Scarlatti's *L'amor volubile e tiranno* at Naples in 1709. Probably early in 1710 she replaced Margherita Durastanti as Agrippina in some performances of Handel's opera at Venice. She sang there again, as Elena Croce Viviani, in 1712 and 1713. She sang at the King's Theatre, London, in pasticcios and Haym's adaptation of A. Scarlatti's *Pirro e Demetrio* in 1716, and in 1719–20 at Munich.

WINTON DEAN

Crociato in Egitto, Il ('The Crusader in Egypt'). *Melodramma eroico* in two acts by GIACOMO MEYERBEER to a libretto by GAETANO ROSSI; Venice, Teatro La Fenice, 7 March 1824.

Palmide *daughter of Aladino*	soprano
Aladino *Sultan of Damietta*	bass
Felicia *a relative of Adriano in male attire*	contralto
Adriano de Montfort *Grand Master of the Knights of Rhodes*	tenor
Osmino *a vizier*	tenor
Alma *confidante of Palmide*	soprano
Mirva *Palmide's son*	silent
Armando D'Orville *a knight disguised as Elmireno*	soprano castrato

Christian slaves and knights, Egyptians, imams and emirs

Setting Damietta in the 13th century

Il crociato was Meyerbeer's most successful, as well as his last, opera for an Italian stage. The part of Armando was written for the castrato Giovanni Battista Velluti, which makes the work noteworthy as the last major opera with a role for that voice type. Following its Venetian première, *Il crociato* took other houses by storm: within a little over a year productions were mounted in Florence, Trieste, Padua, Parma and London. The work then served as Meyerbeer's entrée to Paris, where it was first performed at the Théâtre Italien on 25 September 1825 with the soprano Giuditta Pasta in the role of Armando and Nicholas Levasseur as Aladino.

The source history of *Il crociato* is complicated, since Meyerbeer made revisions for many of the early productions. No one production may be taken as the definitive version. A major problem at the first run in Venice (followed in the plot summary below) was the role of Felicia, which had been belatedly inserted into a fully formed plot; it was scarcely effective to have Felicia heroically address the Egyptian populace when the knights first disembark, only to have her fade in importance by the second act. In performances at other centres Meyerbeer reworked that scene for Adriano (the most convincing version) or, when the earlier Armando-Palmide duet was cut (as in London), for Armando. A concluding rondò for Velluti ('Rapito io sento il cor') was replaced early on with a new final duet for Palmide and Armando, 'Ravisa qual alma'. The Act 1 trio containing the canzonetta 'Giovinetto cavalier' was modified from a dramatic situation, where Palmide and Felicia are joined by Armando, to one where Armando and Palmide are interrupted by Felicia. Meyerbeer was unhappy about certain aspects of the Parisian production: a fine aria, Palmide's 'D'una madre disperata', was not performed during that run and one of the most spectacular effects in earlier Italian productions, the appearance of two *bande* in the Act 1 finale, was also not realized. Pasta did not sing Armando's

'Il crociato in Egitto' (Meyerbeer), Act 1 scene iii (the port of Damietta): design by Alessandro Sanquirico for the first Milan production at La Scala, 2 March 1826

rondò, 'Il dì rinascerà', near the end of the opera but was given a new entrance aria, 'Ah come rapida fuggì la speme'.

ACT 1.i *A courtyard in the palace of the sultan* The opera opens with an elaborate pantomime instead of an overture: Christian slaves emerge from their cells for a day's hard labour, overseen by Arabian custodians. The pantomime merges into the first part of a multi-sectional vocal introduction, and the arrival of Palmide is heralded with a stately triplet motif over a tonic pedal. She sings a solo embedded in the introduction ('I doni d'Elmireno'), first presenting gifts from Elmireno (alias Armando) to the slaves and then, in an *a parte* cabaletta, singing of her love for him. For the cabaletta reprise she is joined by her father Aladino, who informs her that Elmireno will return victorious from his campaigns that day. Trumpets signal the arrival of a delegation from the Knights of Rhodes, and in the stretta of the introduction all sing with eager anticipation of peace. Aladino tells his daughter that he intends to give her in marriage to Elmireno. Osmino is angry since he desires Palmide and the throne for himself; Palmide is distressed because she has already secretly married Elmireno and borne a son, Mirva.

1.ii *The sultan's gardens* Slaves attend to Palmide and Mirva. Suddenly Armando appears, ahead of his troops, and sings of his love for his son in the cavatina 'O figlio dell'amore'. He reveals to Palmide that he is not Elmireno, but a knight of the Order of Rhodes, and that before he had assumed an Egyptian disguise he was in love with Felicia. Palmide reproaches Armando in a duet with *agitato* syncopations in the orchestra and vehement octave leaps on the word 'barbaro', and both bemoan a bleak future in a slow section with parallel singing.

1.iii *The port of Damietta* A chorus heralds the arrival of the European ships; string tremolos and weak-beat accents translate musically the 'placid murmurs of the waves'. Felicia disembarks first, bearing the offer of peace from the knights and, in a cavatina, 'Pace io reco', remembering that it was on this soil that her beloved Armando perished.

1.iv *A remote part of the shore* Adriano chances on Armando, whom he soon recognizes as his nephew. With raging coloratura in the first section of a duet, he chastises Armando for having sided with the enemy. Armando reveals that his heart no longer belongs to Felicia; in the slow section he sings of the grief he would bring Palmide if he were to abandon her, and Adriano responds by reminding him of his mother. His argument proves persuasive: the following section brings a reversal in Armando's position when he decides to return home, and leads to a cabaletta of reconciliation.

1.v *The sultan's gardens* Felicia comes upon Palmide and learns that Mirva is the fruit of her union with Armando. She prepares to give up Armando for ever, sadly remembering the canzonetta 'Giovinetto cavalier' with which he first courted them both. This stirs memories in Palmide, who sings another stanza of the song. Armando is suddenly heard echoing the final phrase. Felicia stands in the shadows, voicing her sorrow, as he rushes in to embrace Palmide for the last time.

1.vi *Aladino's palace* Preparations have been made for the peace delegation and the wedding of Elmireno and Palmide. The sultan's imams march in to a broad melody in equal notes, and the Christian knights enter with their own march in contrasting metre, tempo and character. The appearance of Armando dressed in European garb brings an explosion of sound (using diminished harmonies) from the assembled masses. Armando, Adriano, Palmide and Felicia each sing the same melody to voice their different perspectives; these statements are separated by angry interjections from Aladino, who never sings the strain. When the sultan moves to stab Armando, Felicia throws herself in front of him. This spawns the slow section of the finale, a canon of consternation and confusion, after which Aladino orders that all the knights be imprisoned. Egyptians and knights form separate groups, each accompanied by its own *banda* as it asserts the justice of its cause.

ACT 2.i *The palace* Osmino is angered that Palmide prefers a Christian to him; he has discovered the parentage of Mirva and instructs a group of emirs to spread sedition through the sultan's lands. Felicia enters and in an aria, 'Ah ch'io l'adoro ancor', she sings of both her continued love for Armando and her will to save him.

2.ii *The sultan's gardens* Reminded of Armando by her surroundings, Palmide gives expression to her sorrow ('Tutta qui parla ognor'). Osmino appears with the sultan, who has been told about the child and has come to execute him. Palmide offers her own life instead in a dramatic aria, 'D'una madre disperata', with grand unison triadic passages and fanfare motifs around held notes in the voice; the argument is summed up musically with declamation on repeated notes that gives way to concluding coloratura. Aladino is profoundly moved; he embraces Mirva and sends for Armando and Adriano. Following Palmide's cabaletta of joy, the sultan informs the knights that all the Christians will be set free. Adriano learns of the parentage of Mirva and repudiates Armando.

2.iii *A remote part of the shore* Osmino and a group of emirs plan to monitor the actions of Armando and Palmide in a chorus in which quiet *divisi* writing gives way to a boisterous unison passage as the triumph of Osmino is anticipated. They hide themselves and Armando and Palmide appear. He beseeches her to flee with him. Adriano and other knights arrive, and Palmide agrees to swear before the Christian God to leave her homeland. Armando sings a prayer ('O cielo clemente'), the slow part of a multi-sectional number; he is joined first by Palmide and then by Adriano and Felicia. Aladino suddenly enters and is horrified to see his daughter in a Christian rite and prepared to abandon him. He orders all the Christians to be captured and executed, unleashing an agitated stretta. Alone, Osmino revels in a plan to arm the Christian knights in order to depose Aladino and secure the throne for himself.

2.iv *A prison* In a highly charged accompanied recitative Adriano bids his brethren embrace their fate heroically. To the sound of harps and trombones he warns them that the hour of death is near; they softly echo his words. Momentarily alone, Armando longs for Palmide (rondò, 'Il dì rinascerà'). Osmino and the emirs enter; during a soft, staccato chorus they offer swords to the knights. Aladino appears and orders Osmino to execute the Christians. Instead, Osmino attacks the sultan. Contrary to Osmino's plans, however, Armando urges his brethren to defend Aladino. Moved by Armando's action, Aladino sanctions the marriage of Palmide and Armando and permits them to return to Europe with the knights.

* * *

As a launching point for Meyerbeer's systematic campaign to gain an Opéra commission by attracting attention at lesser theatres, *Il crociato* served its purpose well (there followed a Parisian staging of *Margherita d'Anjou* in 1826 and, shortly after, negotiations with the Opéra-Comique for the soon-to-be re-routed *Robert le diable*). The work underlines the connection between French grand opera and the Italian repertory in that some of its material prefigures *Les Huguenots* – Meyerbeer's first complete work conceived from the start for the Opéra – including the religious conversion of the romantic female lead, juxtaposition and combination of musically contrasting choral groups, and a conspiracy scene. This last also points up the distance yet to be travelled: it is a relatively small-scale piece compared to the later Consecration of the Swords and is generated by the ire of a single individual rather than by entrenched historical forces. The size of the introduction of the first act in *Il crociato* relative to contemporaneous Italian standards also anticipates grand opera practice, as do some effects of orchestration. In other respects – its elaborate vocal ornamentation, forms, and lightly episodic nature – the opera is more characteristically Italian, and it is ultimately most useful to adopt a critical position informed by an understanding of an ultramontane operatic culture dominated by Rossini.

STEVEN HUEBNER

Croesus [*Der hochmüthige, gestürtzte und wieder erhabene Croesus* ('The Proud, Overthrown and Again Exalted Croesus')]. *Singe-Spiel* in three acts by REINHARD KEISER to a libretto by LUCAS VON BOSTEL after NICOLÒ MINATO's *Creso*; Hamburg, Theater am Gänsemarkt, 1711 (revised version, Hamburg, 6 December 1730).

The story of Croesus, the fabulously wealthy King of Lydia in the 6th century BC, was interwoven by Minato with an ingenious intrigue of his own invention centred on Croesus's son Atis. In the opening scene Croesus (tenor) glories in his wealth and power and refuses to heed the warnings of his resident philosopher Solon (tenor) that happiness can be fleeting. The Median princess Elmira (soprano) loves Atis (soprano), a mute, and spurns the attentions of the wicked Prince Orsanes (bass). Croesus goes to war against Cyrus, King of Persia (bass), leaving Eliates (tenor) in charge. He is defeated, and a Persian soldier is about to kill him when Atis – suddenly able to speak – cries out, revealing the king's identity. While Croesus remains a prisoner, Atis returns to court disguised as a peasant boy, Ermin, convincing everyone he is not who he appears to be because he can talk. Orsanes, seeing a way to seize power, engages Ermin to kill Atis and take his place. Atis then starts posing as himself by pretending to be mute, though he refuses to take orders from Orsanes. As Ermin, he also makes advances to Elmira to test her fidelity. Cyrus finally decides to put Croesus to death on a funeral pyre and invites the Lydian court to watch. When Solon appears, Croesus recalls his words of warning, and Cyrus is so moved at the thought that he too might one day fall from power that he restores Croesus to his throne. Atis and Ermin are revealed as one and the same, and Croesus agrees to the marriage of Atis and Elmira. In addition to the main action there is some broad clowning by the comic servant Elcius (tenor), who sings partly in dialect.

The original German version of this libretto dates from 1684, when it was set for Hamburg by J. P. Förtsch. Probably because of the high esteem in which it was held, Italian arias were not added, either in 1711 or in 1730, and even the final version retained the formal variety of early Hamburg opera, with relatively few numbers in da capo form. Only the extensively revised score of 1730 survives complete. Essentially a comedy but with some moments of noble pathos for Croesus himself, this is perhaps Keiser's greatest work.

For illustration *see* HAMBURG, fig.1. JOHN H. ROBERTS

Croiza [Conelly], **Claire** (*b* Paris, 14 Sept 1882; *d* Paris, 27 May 1946). French mezzo-soprano. She made her début in Nancy in 1905 (in De Lara's *Messalina*). The following year she began her long association with the Théâtre de la Monnaie, Brussels (début as Delilah, 1906), where her wide repertory included Berlioz's Dido, Clytemnestra in *Iphigénie en Aulide* and Strauss's *Elektra*, Erda, Carmen, Donizetti's Léonor, Charlotte and Fauré's Penelope. At the Paris Opéra she appeared in 1908, as Delilah. At Rouché's Théâtre des Arts in 1913 she sang in the d'Indy editions of *Poppea* and Destouches' *Les éléments* and an act of Gluck's *Orphée*. She sang the title role in Gustave Doret's *La tisseuse d'orties* at its first performance in 1927 at the Opéra-Comique, and in the first staged performance of Debussy's *La damoiselle élue* in 1919 at the Théâtre du Vaudeville.

From 1922 Croiza taught at the Ecole Normale and from 1934 at the Conservatoire; Micheau, Jansen, Maurane and Souzay were among her pupils. Her instinct for the French language and her intelligence, clarity of tone and passionate reserve caused her to be admired as much by poets as by musicians; in 1924 Paul Valéry hailed her as possessing 'la voix la plus sensible de notre génération'. Among French composers Saint-Saëns, d'Indy and Fauré admired her unreservedly, and of the next generation Debussy and Roussel. Her silvery yet warm tone, and that 'volupté du son' based on pure, perfect utterance of the words, can be heard on her records.

H. Abraham: *Un art de l'interprétation ... Claire Croiza* (Paris, 1954) [based on notes of Croiza's teaching made at her classes]

B. Bannerman: 'Recollections of Claire Croiza', *British Institute of Recorded Sound Bulletin*, no.1 (1956), 12–29 [with discography]

MARTIN COOPER

Croll, Gerhard (*b* Düsseldorf, 25 May 1927). Austrian musicologist of German origin. He studied with Rudolf Gerber at the University of Göttingen where he took the doctorate in 1954; from that time his field of interest has been Italian Baroque opera and music of the Classical era. After four years on a scholarship he published editions of Steffani's *Tassilone* and, for the Neue Mozart-Ausgabe, *Der Schauspieldirektor* (followed some 25 years later by *Die Entführung aus dem Serail*). In 1958 he became assistant lecturer at the University of Münster, where he completed the *Habilitation* in 1961 (*Agostino Steffani: Studien zur Biographie, Bibliographie der Opern und Turnierspiele*; extracts in *Festschrift Karl Gustav Fellerer*, Regensburg, 1962). He was appointed to the new chair of musicology at Salzburg in 1966. Having prepared *Le cinesi* for the Gluck complete edition in 1958, he became editor-in-chief in 1960, going on to prepare editions of *La danza* (1969), *Iphigenie auf Tauris* (1965), *Iphigénie en Tauride* (1973) and *Alceste* (1988). He has been president of the Internationale Gluck-Gesellschaft since 1987.

RUDOLF KLEIN

Crooks, Richard (Alexander) (*b* Trenton, NJ, 26 June 1900; *d* Portola Valley, CA, 1 Oct 1972). American tenor. He studied with Sidney H. Bourne and Frank La Forge, and first sang in opera at Hamburg as Cavaradossi in 1927. Appearances with the Berlin Staatsoper and in other European centres followed, in roles such as Walther and Lohengrin. He made his American opera début in 1930 in Philadelphia as Cavaradossi, and his Metropolitan début as Massenet's Des Grieux in 1933. He sang leading lyric roles, mostly French and Italian, with the company and elsewhere in the USA for the next ten seasons, then pursued a concert career. Crooks had a beautiful voice which, though limited in the upper register, was admired for its consistently high standard of tone and production. He was a sound musician but an indifferent actor.

S. Sheldon: 'Richard Crooks', *Record News* [Toronto], ii (1957–8), 307–23 [with discography]

K. S. Mackiggan: 'Richard Crooks', *Record Collector*, xii (1958–60), 125–42, 147–55, 258–61; xx (1971–2), 258–70 [with discography by C. I. Morgan]

C. I. Morgan: 'Richard Crooks: a Biography', *Record Advertiser*, ii/6 (1971–2), 2–12; iii/1 (1972–3), 2–16 [with discography]

MAX DE SCHAUENSEE/R

Crosato, Giambattista [Giovanni Battista] (*b* Venice, 1685/6; *d* Venice, 15 July 1758). Italian painter and stage designer. He was well known as a fresco painter (the ballroom ceiling in Palazzo Rezzonico, Venice and frescoes in the Palazzina di Caccia, Stupinigi, Turin). In the theatre he painted figures in collaboration with specialists in perspective. Nothing is known of his activity before 1729, when he was working on the sacristy of S Maria dei Servi, Venice, but it is possible that he was collaborating with Alessandro Mauro (i) and Romualdo Mauro on theatre decoration before then; there is documentary evidence that he was among their associates at the Teatro Regio, Turin, during Carnival 1730–31. He was at the Regio again for the 1742–3 season, collaborating with G. F. Costa (Pietro Auletta's *Caio Fabricio* and Nicolò Jommelli's *Tito Manlio*) and in 1749–50 with G. Mengozzi Colonna (Giuseppe Scarlatti's *Siroe* and D. M. B. Terradellas's *Didone*). A set design by him (with architectural features drawn by a perspective artist) in the Galleria Sabauda, Turin, reproduces the first scene of *Siroe*, showing the Temple of the Sun and the accompanying dramatic action; this corresponds perfectly to that prescribed by Metastasio's libretto and it is interesting to note the dramatic gestures of the actors, which are much more dynamic and lively than is usually supposed to have been the case in operatic performance in the middle of the 18th century (for illustration *see* SIROE RE DI PERSIA). Other evidence of Crosato's activity in Turin is provided by two exquisite sketches for curtains: *The Sacrifice of Iphigeneia* (Turin, Museo Civico) and *Diogenes Searching for an Honest Man* (Turin, Galleria

'Diogenes Searching for an Honest Man': design by Giambattista Crosato for a curtain, probably for the Teatro Carignano, Turin (mid-18th century)

Sabauda), the latter probably for the Teatro Carignano (see illustration).

*

G. Fiocco: *Giambattista Crosato* (Venice, 1941)
A. Griseri: *Le metamorfosi del barocco* (Turin, 1967)
M. Viale Ferrero: 'Giovanni Battista Crosato e la sua attività di scenografo al Teatro Regio di Torino', *Venezia e il melodramma nel settecento*, ed. M. T. Muraro (Florence, 1978), 47–62
——: *Storia del Teatro Regio di Torino*, iii: *La scenografia dalle origini al 1936* (Turin, 1980) MERCEDES VIALE FERRERO

Crosby, John O('Hea) (*b* New York, 12 July 1926). American conductor and administrator. He studied music theory and composition at Yale and later at Columbia University, and then worked as accompanist for Columbia Opera Workshop and American Theatre Wing. In 1956 he founded the Santa Fe Opera, where he has conducted a wide repertory, including many works by Richard Strauss; he has also conducted in other cities in the USA and Canada. He is president emeritus of the Manhattan School of Music, and was president of Opera America, 1976–80.

See also SANTA FE.

Cross, Joan (*b* London, 7 Sept 1900). English soprano. She studied at Trinity College of Music with Dawson Freer. In 1924 she joined the chorus of the Old Vic, soon undertaking such roles as Cherubino and the First Lady (*Die Zauberflöte*). She was principal soprano of Sadler's Wells Opera, 1931–46; she sang Kupava in the English première of *The Snow Maiden* and Militrisa in *The Tale of Tsar Saltan* (both 1933). She made her Covent Garden début in 1931 as Mimì. At the reopening of Sadler's Wells Theatre in 1945 she created Ellen Orford; she also created the Female Chorus in *The Rape of Lucretia* (1946), Lady Billows in *Albert Herring* (1947), Elizabeth I in *Gloriana* (1953) and Mrs Grose in *The Turn of the Screw* (1954). A founder-member of the English Opera Group, she began directing opera in 1946 with *Der Rosenkavalier* at Covent Garden and subsequently worked with the Norwegian National Opera. In 1948 together with Anne Wood she founded the Opera School, later the London Opera Centre.

A singer of sincerity, intelligence and technical skill, she was a complete operatic performer for whom words and music were of equal importance.

*

GV (E. Lockspeiser; J. B. Richards)
C. Hardy: 'Joan Cross', *Opera*, i (1950), 22–28
Harewood: 'Joan Cross – a Birthday Celebration', *Opera*, xli (1990), 1032–8 HAROLD ROSENTHAL/R

Cross, Letitia (*b* *c*1681; *d* London, 4 April 1737). English soprano, actress and dancer. She was 'the girl' in Purcell's theatre company in 1695 during the last few months of his life. She sang in his *Indian Queen* and *Bonduca*, and he wrote Dorinda's song 'Dear pretty youth' in *The Tempest* for her. As Altisidora in *Don Quixote* she sang his last theatre song, 'From rosy bowers'. In 1698 she went to France with 'a certain baronet', returned to the London stage in December 1704 and the following month played Dorisbe in Clayton's *Arsinoe*, the first English opera in the Italian style. She resumed her old acting roles – parts which fitted her vivacious personality – and frequently appeared as a dancer. She had a small role in *Almahide* (1710), was Mercury in Turner's *Presumptuous Love* (1716) and continued to sing Purcell's music, notably

Cupid in the *Timon of Athens* masque and the frost music from *King Arthur*. After 1725 she made only one benefit appearance.

LS
O. Baldwin and T. Wilson: 'Purcell's Sopranos', *MT*, cxxiii (1982), 602–9
C. A. Price: *Henry Purcell and the London Stage* (Cambridge, 1984)
OLIVE BALDWIN, THELMA WILSON

Crosse, Gordon (*b* Bury, 1 Dec 1937). English composer. He studied at Oxford University with Egon Wellesz, graduating in 1961, after which he spent a further two years doing research into early 15th-century music. In 1962 he studied with Goffredo Petrassi in Rome. Returning to England, he taught in the extra-mural department of Birmingham University, and in 1966 became Haywood Fellow in Music, also at Birmingham. In 1969 he became Fellow in music at the University of Essex, in 1973 was composer-in-residence at King's College, Cambridge, and in 1977 he became visiting professor in composition at the University of California.

Admired from an early stage in his career for the quality of his word-setting – his children's piece *Meet my Folks!* (1964), a 'theme and relations' with words by Ted Hughes, is a particularly vivid example – Crosse seemed to have the potential for making a valuable contribution to the English operatic repertory. Indeed, his first work of that kind, a severely economical treatment of Yeats's *Purgatory* (1966), is remarkable for both its dramatic effectiveness and its reflection in musical terms of the poet's fatalistic symbolism. He suffered a setback, however, in attempting to supply what he described as a 'comic supplement' to *Purgatory* in *The Grace of Todd* (1967–8), although the weakness was not so much his often witty score as David Rudkin's ill-structured and laborious libretto.

Crosse's major operatic enterprise, *The Story of Vasco*, which took him five years to complete (1968–73), is brilliantly successful in creating a musical equivalent of the 'tissue of images' which Georges Schehadé, the author of the French text which Ted Hughes translated and adapted for the libretto, considers to be the essential nature of the play. The abrupt but hypnotic cutting between pictures of, say, the harshness of war and its absurdities, or the innocence and disillusion of dreamers and idealists who are caught up in it, is articulated in the score with every appearance of spontaneity within an effortlessly flexible serial organization.

Misunderstood by some critics, who identified an apparent failure in character development and dramatic pacing, *The Story of Vasco* has remained Crosse's one full-scale opera and his most important work in any medium. While still involved with *Vasco* he completed *Wheel of the World* (1969–72), an 'entertainment' adapted from three of Chaucer's *Canterbury Tales*, for performance by young people (described by the composer as 'a kind of music theatre, not opera'), and in 1973 he added an operatic morality play *Potter Thompson* (with a text by Alan Garner) to an already distinguished catalogue of pieces for children.

See also PURGATORY and STORY OF VASCO, THE.

Purgatory op.18 (1, after W. B. Yeats), Cheltenham, Everyman, 7 July 1966
The Grace of Todd op.20 (1, D. Rudkin), Aldeburgh, Jubilee Hall, 7 June 1969; rev. 1974
Wheel of the World (entertainment, 1, D. Cowan, after G. Chaucer: *The Canterbury Tales*), Oxford, 5 June 1972
The Story of Vasco op.29 (3, T. Hughes, after G. Schehadé: *L'histoire de Vasco*), London, Coliseum, 13 March 1974
Holly from the Bongs (nativity op, 1, A. Garner), Manchester, 9 Dec 1974
Potter Thompson, 1972–3 (music drama, 1, Garner), London, St Mary Magdalene, Munster Square, 9 Jan 1975

GERALD LARNER

Crouch [née Phillips], **Anna Maria** (*b* London, 20 April 1763; *d* Brighton, 2 Oct 1805). English soprano and actress. She was articled to Thomas Linley and made her début as Mandane in *Artaxerxes* on 11 November 1780. She sang and acted at Drury Lane with summer seasons in Ireland and the provinces until her retirement in 1801, although her later career was dogged by ill-health. Two years after her marriage in 1785 she met the tenor Michael Kelly and they were living together long before the legal separation from her husband in 1791. They appeared together in stage works, oratorios and concerts, and moved in brilliant social and artistic circles. Among the parts she created were Lady Elinor in Storace's *The Haunted Tower*, Catherine in his *Siege of Belgrade* and the title role in his *Lodoiska*. Sainsbury's *Dictionary* (1825) records that she had a 'remarkably sweet voice and a naive affecting style of singing' together with 'extraordinary personal charms'.

BDA; *DNB* (W. Squire); *LS*
'Mrs. Crouch', *Thespian Magazine*, i (1792), 14–15
A. Pasquin [pseud. of J. Williams]: *The Children of Thespis*, i (London, 13/1792)
J. Roach: *Authentic Memoirs of the Green Room* (London, 1796)
'Memoirs of Mrs. Crouch', *European Magazine*, xlviii (1805), 323–6
M. J. Young: *Memoirs of Mrs Crouch* (London, 1806)
M. Kelly: *Reminiscences* (London, 1826, 2/1826); ed. R. Fiske (London, 1975)
W. Oxberry: 'Memoir of the late Mrs. Anna Maria Crouch', *Dramatic Biography*, v (1826), 235–46
W. Robson: *The Old Play-Goer* (London, 1846)
OLIVE BALDWIN, THELMA WILSON

Crozier, Eric (*b* London, 14 Nov 1914). English librettist and director. His literary gifts, sensitivity to words and musical acumen have made him an outstanding librettist, his collaboration with Britten producing several masterly works. A passion for the theatre began with visits to the Everyman Theatre in Hampstead and St Pancras People's Theatre, and was nurtured by his introduction to Chekhov, whose style inspired him. He studied at the Royal Academy of Dramatic Art for two years, and in 1934 won a scholarship to the British Institute in Paris, where his experiences laid the foundations for much of his subsequent career. He encountered La Compagnie des Quinze, a group of young players founded by Jacques Copeau 'with the declared aim of bringing back truth, beauty and poetry to the French stage'. He also translated plays and gave English lessons. His friendship with the actor Stephen Haggard led to his appointment as one of the first producers for BBC Television. Following the outbreak of World War II he worked with Tyrone Guthrie at the Old Vic (based in Burnley), then with Sadler's Wells, where his first production was *The Bartered Bride* (1943). In 1945 he produced *Peter Grimes* at Sadler's Wells; after dissension within the company, he left and became co-founder with Britten of the English Opera Group (1947) and of the Aldeburgh Festival (1948). Thus an important collaboration began. His first libretto, *Albert Herring* (1947), was based on Maupassant's short story *Le rosier de Madame Husson*. Its great success – despite the hostility of many critics and the lofty disapproval of John Christie of Glyndebourne – led to *Let's Make an Opera* (1948), which was subsequently pared down to the central story *The Little Sweep*. With E. M. Forster he wrote *Billy Budd* (1951), based on the novel by Herman Melville; originally in four acts, it was reduced to two in 1960. He also wrote the libretto for Lennox Berkeley's *Ruth* (1956). He directed the premières of *Peter Grimes* (1945, London; 1946, Tanglewood) and *The Rape of Lucretia* (1946, Glyndebourne). His opera translations include *The Bartered Bride*, *Otello*, *Falstaff* and *La traviata* (all with Joan Cross), *Idomeneo*, *Salome* and *Die Frau ohne Schatten*. Most recently, he has been a tutor at the Britten-Pears School for Advanced Musical Studies at Snape Maltings, with his wife, Nancy Evans, who succeeded Peter Pears as director. She retired in 1990; both were appointed OBE in 1991. Crozier has also written books for children and is an accomplished broadcaster.

*

S. Wadsworth: 'The Go-Between: the Collaboration that gave us *Billy Budd*', *ON*, xliv/20 (1979–80), 11–14

J. K. Law: 'Linking the Past with the Present: a Conversation with Nancy Evans and Eric Crozier', *OQ*, iii/1 (1985), 72–9

D. Mitchell: 'The Serious Comedy of *Albert Herring*', *Glyndebourne Festival Opera 1986*, 105–11 [programme book]

J. K. Law: 'Daring to Eat a Peach: Literary Allusion in *Albert Herring*', *OQ*, v/1 (1987–8), 1–10

J. M. THOMSON

Crusell, Bernhard Henrik (*b* Nystad, Finland, 15 Oct 1775; *d* Stockholm, 28 July 1838). Swedish composer and translator of Finnish birth. The son of a poor bookbinder, he received his earliest musical education from a clarinettist of the Nyland regimental band. In 1788 he joined the military at Sveaborg, and in 1790 moved to Stockholm where he was appointed court musician and studied composition with Daniel Böritz and G. J. Vogler. He was made chief conductor of the Royal Guard band in 1818, and three years later joined the Gothic Society, which led him to associate with literary figures such as Pixérécourt, Tegnér and Runeberg, and provided the stimulus to translate opera texts for the Swedish stage. In 1822 he travelled to Dresden and spent several weeks with Weber; on his return he was appointed deputy Kapellmeister at the Royal Opera in Stockholm. Crusell wrote a single opera in three acts, *Den lilla slavinnan* ('The Little Slave Girl'), to a text by Pixérécourt (trans. U. Mannerhjerta and G. Lagerbjelke; *S-St*, excerpts published, Stockholm, 1824). First produced at the Royal Opera on 18 February 1824, and with music resembling Weber's, it was given 34 times over the next 14 years. He retired in 1829 and, though best known as a clarinet virtuoso, in 1837 was inducted into the Wasa Order for his service in the translation of opera librettos into Swedish, including works by Mozart, Rossini, Spohr and Auber.

*

F. Dahlström: *Bernhard Henrik Crusell* (Helsinki, 1976)

——: *Bernhard Crusell: Tonsättare, Clarinettvirtuos* (Stockholm, 1977)

BERTIL H. VAN BOER

Cruvelli [Crüwell], **(Jeanne) Sophie (Charlotte)** (*b* Bielefeld, 12 March 1826; *d* Nice or Monaco, 6 Nov 1907). German soprano. A pupil of Francesco Lamperti, she made her début at La Fenice in 1847 as Odabella (*Attila*). She repeated the same role in Udine, followed by Lucrezia (*I due Foscari*). Verdi's early operas suited her voice, which was large and powerful if not always under perfect control, and in 1848 she sang Elvira (*Ernani*) and Abigaille (*Nabucco*, given as *Nino*) at Her Majesty's Theatre in London, as well as Leonore (*Fidelio*) and Countess Almaviva. She appeared in Milan in 1850, adding Donizetti's *Linda di Chamounix* and Verdi's *Luisa Miller* to her repertory. She made her Paris début in 1851 as Elvira, and at the Théâtre Italien she also sang in *Norma*, *La sonnambula*, *Fidelio* and *Semiramide*. In 1854 she transferred to the Opéra (her performance is reported in *Dwight's Journal*, iv (1853–4), 150–51), appearing as Valentine (*Les Huguenots*), Julia (*La vestale*) and Rachel (*La Juive*). She then returned to London, where she sang in Rossini's *Otello*, in *Fidelio* and as Donna Anna at Covent Garden. She created Hélène in *Les vêpres siciliennes* at the Paris Opéra in 1855, then retired the following year.

ELIZABETH FORBES

Cruz-Romeo [Cruz-Romo, Cruz-Romero], **Gilda** (*b* Guadalajara, 12 Feb 1940). Mexican soprano. She studied at the Mexico City Conservatory and made her début with the National Opera as Ortlinde (*Die Walküre*) in 1962. In 1969 she sang in *Mefistofele* with New York City Opera, and in 1970 made her Metropolitan début as Butterfly followed by continuing engagements as Nedda, Leonora (*Il trovatore*), Desdemona, Elisabeth de Valois and Puccini's Manon Lescaut, among other roles. She achieved particular success as Tosca and Aida, singing the latter role in her Covent Garden début (1972) and at La Scala (1973). She toured to Moscow with the La Scala company in 1974, and appeared at the Vienna Staatsoper, as Leonora (*Forza del destino*), and in Australia, South America and the USSR. In 1987 she sang Cherubini's Medea at Bridgeport, Connecticut, and Matilde in the first American performance of Mascagni's *Silvano* at Englewood, New Jersey, in 1989; she also sang in several seasons at the Verona Arena. A dramatic soprano of strongly expressive vocal timbre and stage presence, she developed a career as a concert soloist as well as an opera singer.

NOËL GOODWIN

Cry of Clytaemnestra, The. Chamber opera in one act by JOHN C. EATON to a libretto by Patrick Creagh after AESCHYLUS's *Agamemnon*; Bloomington, Indiana University Opera Theater, 1 March 1980.

The opera compresses the events of Aeschylus's play into a densely woven 80-minute sequence. The story is unfolded through the distorted visions of Clytemnestra (mezzo-soprano), who recalls and anticipates past and future events in dream-like succession. Although the music proceeds without a break, the opera divides into a series of relatively discrete 'scenes' that present the essential action: the decision of Agamemnon (baritone) to sacrifice his daughter Iphigenia (coloratura soprano) in order to escape Aulis; Iphigenia and her brother Orestes (lyric tenor) as children at play, the former expressing concern for her father's fate; Iphigenia's murder; Agamemnon's betrayal of his wife Clytemnestra with Cassandra (soprano), who prophesies his death; Clytemnestra's betrayal of Agamemnon with Aegisthus (tenor); Aegisthus's conflict with Clytemnestra's daughter Electra (dramatic soprano); and Clytemnestra's murder of Agamemnon.

The music of the opera is intensely expressive, reflecting the psychological focus of the dramatic presentation. Scored for a 17-piece chamber orchestra (plus electronic tape), the work employs microtonal tuning in both equal-tempered quarter-tone tuning and, more occasionally, just intonation. Eaton distinguishes the two types for dramatic effect, associating the former with states of extreme psychological conflict and the latter with innocence and purity. Formally the opera is organized around a series of recurring, piercing cries emitted by Clytemnestra as she recalls the dreadful events that have overtaken her life. These provide an important element of musical unity and also serve to articulate the overall shape, punctuating the dramatic continuity; they also undergo transformations that mirror Clytemnestra's shifting psychological orientation: from anguished horror at the opening in reaction to the sacrifice of her daughter, to 'pure and terrifying' exaltation at the end as she prepares for her husband's return and murder. All are characterized by intense microtonal inflexions and by extreme timbral and phonetic articulations. The innocence of Iphigenia, on the other hand, is underscored by introducing her, immediately following Clytemnestra's opening howl, with a simple vocalise based on the 'pure' consonances of the natural overtone series.

Despite the complexity of its music, *The Cry of Clytaemnestra* has an immediate dramatic impact. The instrumental writing is virtuoso, incorporating a variety of colouristic effects, yet the focus is consistently on the voice, which carries the essential musical argument throughout. Aided in part by the relative modesty of the resources required, the opera has received a number of productions since the Indiana première, most notably in New York and California. ROBERT P. MORGAN

Csárdásfürstin, Die ('The Csárdás Princess'). Operetta in three acts by EMMERICH KÁLMÁN to a libretto by LEO STEIN and BÉLA JENBACH; Vienna, Johann Strauss-Theater, 17 November 1915.

In an intimate Budapest café-cabaret the singer Sylva Varescu (soprano) bids farewell to her faithful public before an American tour. A party is thrown for her by two men-about-town admirers, Count Boni Káncsiánu (tenor or baritone *buffo*) and Feri von Kerekes (tenor or baritone *buffo*). Sylva is in love with Prince Edwin von und zu Lippert-Weylersheim (tenor), who has a marriage contract drawn up to join them together before her departure. However, his parents oppose their son's marriage to a mere cabaret singer and consider him engaged to his cousin, Countess Stasi (soubrette soprano). Wedding invitations have already been printed, and when Sylva sees one she departs in sadness without signing Edwin's contract. Two months later, at a ball given by the Lippert-Weylersheims in Vienna to announce Edwin's engagement to Stasi, Sylva turns up, posing as Boni's wife. Edwin resumes his relationship with her and seeks to get his parents to agree to their marriage by announcing his engagement to Countess Káncsiánu. Sylva, unwilling to go along with the deception, reveals herself as the cabaret singer. Only when it transpires that the old Princess Lippert-Weylersheim (spoken), Edwin's mother, was herself at one time a cabaret singer are objections to their marriage finally waived.

Kálmán's best-known work was first heard with Mizzi Günther (the original Merry Widow) as Sylva and was produced in the USA as *The Riviera Girl* and in Britain as *The Gipsy Princess*. Highlights of a colourful and richly melodic score, mixing Hungarian and Viennese rhythms, include Boni's and Feri's march song with male chorus 'Die Mädis vom Chantant', Boni's song with female chorus 'Ganz ohne Weiber geht die Chose nicht' and the waltz duets 'Machen wir's den Schwalben nach' (Edwin and Stasi) and 'Tausend kleine Engel singen' (Edwin and Sylva). ANDREW LAMB

Császár, György (*b* 1813; *d* Pest, 20 Aug 1850). Hungarian composer. He was at first a violinist and later musical director at the National Theatre in Pest. He is remembered for his two operas, *A kunok* ('The Cumanians'; Pest, 16 September 1848) and *Morsinai Erzsébet* ('Elizabeth of Morsina'; Pest, 14 February 1850), of which the former was in the local repertory for more than half a century. Both operas draw their plots from Hungarian history and contain Hungarian elements within a basically italianate melodic style.

Csiky, Boldizsár (*b* Tîrgu-Mureş, 3 Oct 1937). Romanian composer of Hungarian descent. He studied music in Tîrgu-Mureş (1953–5) and at the conservatory in Cluj (1956–61), and later became secretary and music director of the Tîrgu-Mureş Philharmonic Society. In 1966 he composed *Görög Ilona* (1967, Tîrgu-Mureş), a chamber opera using pantomime and folktunes; he also wrote music for plays (by Goldoni, Hašek, Zsigmond Moricz, Vasile Alecsandri and Ion Creangă), including some with extended ballet episodes and some for the puppet theatre. His style, which is rooted in the Bartók tradition, is characterized by concision, attractive instrumental writing and a daring modern harmonic language. VIOREL COSMA

Cuba. The earliest known opera performance in Cuba, of a setting of Metastasio's *Didone abbandonata*, took place in the newly inaugurated Teatro Coliseo, Havana, on 12 October 1776. The first notice in a periodical, dated 17 December 1791, announced Grétry's *Zémire et Azor* in a Spanish translation; until 1832 all opera performances were sung in Spanish except those by visiting French companies in 1800–02 and 1824.

The first Italian opera company opened in Havana in 1834. During the course of the century the genre was taken up in the cities of Matanzas, Santa Clara, Cienfuegos, Trinidad, Camagüey and Santiago de Cuba. Between 1846 and 1930 many Italian and some French companies visited Cuba almost every year, performing mainly works by Rossini, Bellini, Donizetti, Verdi, Meyerbeer, Gounod and Puccini.

Cuban composers who wrote operas during this period include Gaspar Villate, whose works belong firmly in the European tradition and had European premières (1877–85). The influence of native Cuban music, however, can be felt in varying degrees in the operas of Sánchez de Fuentes (who had five premières in Havana), Ignacio Cervantes, Hubert De Blanck and Laureano Fuentes. The most important Cuban opera of these years, Mauri's *La esclava*, received its first performance in 1921. The Cuban zarzuela tradition, to which *La esclava* belongs, is distinct from the Spanish one in its use of Afro-American rhythms.

A Russian company visited Cuba in 1930 and introduced operas by Borodin, Musorgsky and Rimsky-Korsakov. Shortly after that, however, economic circumstances caused a collapse in operatic activity. From 1939 some private institutions began to offer short opera seasons which included the first performances in Cuba of *Tristan und Isolde* (1948) and works by Menotti and Britten. After the revolution of

1959, the State began to support opera and created the Opera de Cuba, which has mounted productions of the standard Italian repertory as well as premières of Cuban works, for example Jorge Berroa's *Soyan* (1980) and Sánchez Ferrer's *Ecue-Yamba-O* (1986). The first Festival Internacional Lírico in 1989 included the first performance of the opera *Ernest Hemingway* by the Armenian composer Yuri Ghazaryan.

For further information on operatic life in the country's principal centre and for bibliography *see* HAVANA.

*

E. Tolón and J. A. González: *Operas cubanas y sus autores* (Havana, 1943)
A. Carpentier: *La música en Cuba* (Mexico City, 1946, 2/1979)
J. A. González: *La composición operística en Cuba* (Havana, 1986)

JORGE ANTONIO GONZÁLEZ (with CHARLES PITT)

Cuberli [Tervell], **Lella** (*b* Austin, TX, 29 Sept 1945). American soprano. She studied at Dallas and Milan, making her début in 1975 as Violetta in Budapest. She has sung in Florence, Turin, Bologna, Naples, Venice, Brussels, Paris and Vienna. She sang Adalgisa at Martina Franca (1977), Konstanze at La Scala (1978), where she also sang in Handel's *Ariodante*, and Mozart's Countess Almaviva at both Aix-en-Provence (1985) and Salzburg (1986). Her repertory includes Donna Elvira, Fiordiligi, Junia (*Lucio Silla*), Paisiello's Rosina and Nina, Lucia, Desdemona and Mélisande, as well as the Rossini roles in which she excels: Semiramis (the role of her Metropolitan début, 1990), Ellen (*La donna del lago*), Fiorilla, Elizabeth, Amenaide (*Tancredi*) and Mathilde (*Guillaume Tell*), which she sang at Covent Garden (1990).

*

L. Bloch-Morhange: *Vies de divas* (Paris, 1990)

ELIZABETH FORBES

Cuclin, Dimitrie (*b* Galaţi, 24 March 1885; *d* Bucharest, 7 Feb 1978). Romanian composer. After studies at the Bucharest Conservatory (1903–7) and at the Schola Cantorum in Paris (1908–14) with d'Indy, he became professor at the Bucharest Conservatory and at the City Conservatory of Music in New York. His deep concern with drama was a particular characteristic of his first years as a composer, and he wrote his own librettos to five operas. The huge proportions of these works, which require large instrumental and vocal forces, have made stage productions impossible, although his style is known for its traditional tonal character and its references to folk music.

all to librettos by Cuclin

Soria, 1911 (madrigal op, 5)
Traian and Dochia, 1921 (4)
Agamemnon, 1922 (5, after Aeschylus)
Bellérophon, 1925 (4)
Meleagridele, 1930 (prol., 3, epilogue), broadcast, Bucharest, Romanian Television, 1980

*

O. L. Cosma: *Opera românească* [Romanian Opera] (Bucharest, 1962)

VIOREL COSMA

Cud mniemany [*Cud mniemany, czyli Krakowiacy i górale* ('The Supposed Miracle, or the Kracovians and the Highlanders')]. Singspiel in four acts by JAN STEFANI to a libretto by Wojciech Bogusławski, probably after Antoine-Alexandre-Henri Poinsinet's play *Le sorcier*; Warsaw, National Theatre, 1 March 1794.

The plot is conventional. A young girl, Basia (soprano), and her stepmother, Dorota (soprano), are in love with the same boy, Stach (tenor). Dorota tries to arrange for Basia to marry someone else (a mountaineer), but after several complications Basia remains with her lover and all ends happily. The opera's significance lies in the texts of its songs rather than in the plot. These deal with patriotic sentiments, the lack of independence and a dislike of foreign powers – themes close to the heart of Polish audiences during the years of the Partitions.

Musically the work is in a simple, early Classical idiom, with spoken dialogue interspersed with arias that are generally strophic and based on folkdance rhythms. Some make use of Polish folksong, while others became so popular that they were later thought to be folksongs. *Cud mniemany* was by far the most popular opera at the end of the 18th century and the beginning of the 19th and became a model for a national operatic style. It has remained in the repertory in Poland. JIM SAMSON

Cuénod [Cuenod], **Hugues** (**Adhémar**) (*b* Corseaux-sur-Vevey, 26 June 1902). Swiss tenor. He studied in Geneva, Basle and Vienna, making his début in 1928 at the Théâtre des Champs-Elysées, Paris, in the French première of Krenek's *Jonny spielt auf*. A specialist in character roles, he created Sellem in *The Rake's Progress* in 1951 at La Fenice. He made his Glyndebourne début in 1954 as Sellem, going on to sing over 470 performances there: as Don Basilio and Don Curzio (*Figaro*), Dr Caius, Dancing Master (*Ariadne auf Naxos*), Lucan (*L'incoronazione di Poppea*), Monsieur Taupe (*Capriccio*), Torquemada (*L'heure espagnole*), Monostatos, Erice (*Ormindo*), Triquet (*Yevgeny Onegin*), Schmidt (*Werther*), Linfea (*Calisto*) and the Cock (*The Cunning Little Vixen*). At Covent Garden he sang the Astrologer in *The Golden Cockerel* (1954) and Vašek in *The Bartered Bride* (1958). He sang Triquet at Geneva in 1986 and in 1987 (aged 85) made his Metropolitan début as Emperor Altoum (*Turandot*) and sang Monsieur Taupe at Glyndebourne. He was a subtle, stylish singer, as effective in Monteverdi or Cavalli as in Ravel or Stravinsky, and used his high, light tenor with exquisite taste as can be heard on his many recordings. ALAN BLYTH

Cui, César Antonovich [Kyui, Tsezar' Antonovich] (*b* Vilna [now Vilnius], 6/18 Jan 1835; *d* Petrograd, 26 March 1918). Russian composer and critic of French-Lithuanian descent.

1. Life, writings. 2. Operas.

1. LIFE, WRITINGS. A military engineer by training, he was professor of fortifications at the Academy of Military Engineering in St Petersburg (from which he had graduated in 1857), eventually achieving the rank of general (1904). He had briefly studied music theory (1850) with Moniuszko before moving to St Petersburg to pursue his engineering career.

In 1856 Cui met Balakirev. The two formed the nucleus of what would later become known as the New Russian School (the 'Mighty Kuchka' or 'The Five'), which originated not as a company of musical nationalists but as a sort of Russian 'Davidsbund' – a maverick faction waging war against dogmatic authority (as represented by the newly professionalized and academicized musical life of St Petersburg under the aegis of Anton Rubinstein) on the one hand and against the philistinism of aristocratic 'melomanes' on the other. In this spirit Cui – like Schumann, his musical idol, before him – embarked on a secondary career in musical journalism. He became the music critic for the *Sankt-peterburgskiye vedemosti*, the leading St Petersburg daily, in 1864, holding the position for 13 years, after which he wrote more or less regularly for a variety of newspapers and magazines until the end of the century, including (1878–80) the *Revue et gazette musicale de Paris*, for which he prepared a series of outrageously partisan critical essays that were issued in book form as *La musique en Russie* (Paris, 1880). (The largest Russian-language anthology of his criticism, *Izbrannïye stat'i*, 1952, is skewed towards his less interesting – because indiscriminately conservative and increasingly provincial – later writings, which best served the purposes of the Stalinist musical establishment.)

Both as critic and as composer, Cui was primarily interested in opera and other forms of vocal music. He bitterly opposed the officially supported Italian opera company in St Petersburg, which he saw as thwarting the prospects of native talent. This principled opposition amounted in practice to a blind antagonism towards Italian music and its representatives, both creative and executive. He saw the emergent Russian school as a yet more idealistic offshoot of the German, as represented by Weber, Schumann and (honorifically) Meyerbeer. He saw musical progress as consisting in harmonic exploration, melody having been exhausted by the Italians. Despite this, he (like most other Russian composers) resisted Wagner as 'unmusical'.

Against the encrusted routines and codes of the Italian opera Cui upheld an un-Wagnerian ideal of formal freedom epitomized in the later work of Dargomïzhsky, particularly *The Stone Guest*, which Cui completed (and Rimsky-Korsakov orchestrated) after the composer's death in 1869. (Almost half a century later he also completed Musorgsky's *Fair at Sorochintsï*.) The highest form of dramatic music, Cui thought, was a kind of infinitely flexible, prosodically impeccable lyric arioso which he called 'melodic recitative'; this kind of writing, rather than one based on elaborate musical numbers, best guaranteed that 'vocal music correspond strictly to the meaning of the text', as he put it in 1881 in a eulogy on Musorgsky (whose *Boris Godunov* he had notoriously abused seven years earlier). Cui's theoretical thinking is epitomized in a testamentary article of 1887, 'A Few Words about Contemporary Operatic Forms' (see Taruskin 1981). It has been observed that the operatic manner Cui advocated was well suited to the technique and resources of autodidacts such as Dargomïzhsky, Musorgsky and himself.

Although he signed his articles ***, the identity of the outspoken critic for the *Sankt-peterburgskiye vedomosti* was never in doubt. Because of his bully pulpit and his seniority within the New Russian School, Cui's voice possessed an authority in his day of which his present reputation gives no inkling. (In his one surviving letter to Musorgsky, for example, Dargomïzhsky referred to his addressee as a 'Cui-composer'.) In mid- to late 19th-century Russia he was a major, much-discussed operatic figure, despite the conspicuous failure of his actual operatic works to achieve repertory status.

2. Operas. There were 15 operas, the first begun in the year of Glinka's death and the last completed in the year of the first performance of *The Rite of Spring*. Cui's basic approach and style never wavered over this vast span of years. From first to last his music was a dilute compound of Schumann and Auber (*Genoveva*, amazingly, was his favourite opera), his structures petty and schematic (couplets *à la vaudeville* are never far away, even in his 'melodic recitatives'), his character portrayal banal and shallow. Despite his membership in the Balakirev circle, he had no affinity for Russian themes – how could he have, he once exclaimed, when he was 'd'origine mi-française, mi-lithuanienne et je n'ai pas le sens de la musique russe dans mes veines'. He was at his best in treacly love duets, which gave Vladimir Stasov an excuse to dub him a 'realist' after all:

> True, Cui's talent was always directed almost exclusively towards the portrayal of amorous feeling, in all its varied manifestations (jealousy, despair, self-sacrifice etc.), and therefore, it would seem, must appear one-sided; but the portrayal of this feeling reaches such a depth with Cui, and such keen force, as has not been equalled not only by any of his comrades in the Russian school but perhaps in the whole realm of music.

Cui evaluated himself rather differently, seeing his highest achievement in the 'ideal union of word and music', which made him in his own eyes the first (and only) Russian composer to have written a real opera. He made this claim in connection with *Saratsïn* ('The Saracen', 1899), by which time he was regarded even by Rimsky-Korsakov as a walking anachronism.

Cui's subject matter is stereotypically Romantic, with a preference for French source material: V. Hugo (*Angelo, tyran de Padoue*), Dumas *père* (*Charles VII chez ses grands vassaux*), J. Richepin (*Le flibustier*), G. de Maupassant (*Mam'zelle Fifi*), P. Mérimée (*Matteo Falcone*), C. Perrault (*Le chat botté*, *Chaperon rouge*). The Richepin opera, to a French libretto by the author of the original play, was composed for the Opéra-Comique and has never been professionally staged in Russia. Of Cui's three Pushkin operas, only *Kapitanskaya dochka* ('The Captain's Daughter') has a Russian setting. *Kavkazskiy plennik* ('The Captive in the Caucasus') is an exercise in orientalism, while *Pir vo vremya chumï* ('A Feast in Time of Plague'), set in Renaissance Italy, is drawn from the same set of 'Little Tragedies' in verse as *The Stone Guest* and emulates Dargomïzhsky's score in being a verbatim setting of the original without any mediating libretto. By the turn of the century Cui and his works had been forgotten by the theatres. His letters of the period are full of forced-jocular references to himself as 'pariah', 'boycott victim' and the like. Stimulated by friendship with Nadezhda Dolomanova, a pioneer in pre-school music education, he turned to composing little fairy-tale operas for (and capable of being performed by) children. The last of them, *Ivanushka-durachok* ('Ivanushka the Little Fool') features an exuberant rhythm band in its orchestra.

The one opera of Cui's that deserves honourable mention in any history of the genre in Russia is *Vil'yam Ratklif* ('William Ratcliff'), after Pleshcheyev's verse translation of Heine's famous highlands horror-tragedy. It was the first opera by any of the 'kuchkists' to achieve production and was therefore taken, both within and outside the group, to be a programmatic embodiment of their operatic ideals. The composer's most ambitious score, it was a benchmark in the employment of leitmotifs and reminiscences (more or less decreed by the nature of the original play, a *Schicksalsdrama*, or 'drama of fate', in which the events unfold in roughly reverse order by means of narratives and flashbacks). Although even by 1869 the subject and its treatment struck many as stilted, and although the opera's musical textures (like Schumann's) are hopelessly turgid and its orchestration inept, it remained a treasured memory for all the 'kuchkists'. For Balakirev it was 'the best opera after [Glinka's] *Ruslan*', and Musorgsky paid it the tribute of emulation in *Boris Godunov* (compare the structure of his second act with Cui's, or his title character's monologues with Ratcliff's melodramatic scene 'At the Black Stone'). It is in fact a key to the musico-dramatic aesthetic of the New Russian School, for what made the 'kuchka' in the days of *Ratcliff* truly a *kuchka* – a united 'little band' – was their common devotion to operatic reform, to the 'freedom of operatic forms, the equality of text and music, indeed the complete merger of text and music', as Cui himself summed it up. His early contribution to the furtherance of these aims was in its day an indispensable, even crucial one.

See also ANDZHELO; KAVKAZSKIY PLENNIK; MLADA (i); SÏN MANDARINA; and WILLIAM RATCLIFF.

in order of composition; autograph scores of works first given at St Petersburg, Mariinsky Theatre, in RU-Ltob

Kavkazskiy plennik [The Captive in the Caucasus], Acts 1, 3, 1857–8, Act 2, 1881–2 (3, V. A. Krïlov, after A. Pushkin), St Petersburg, Mariinsky, 4/16 Feb 1883, vs (St Petersburg, 1882)

Sïn mandarina [The Mandarin's Son], 1859 (oc, 1, Krïlov), St Petersburg, Artists' Club, 7/19 Dec 1879, vs (St Petersburg, 1859)

Vil'yam Ratklif [William Ratcliff], 1861–8 (3, A. N. Pleshcheyev, Krïlov, after H. Heine), St Petersburg, Mariinsky, 14/26 Feb 1869, vs (St Petersburg, 1869)

Andzhelo [Angelo], 1871–5 (4, V. P. Burenin, after V. Hugo), St Petersburg, Mariinsky, 1/13 Feb 1876, vs (St Petersburg, 1876); rev., Moscow, Bol'shoy, 4/17 Jan 1901

Mlada, 1872 (op-ballet, 4, Krïlov), Act 1 only, concert perf. Petrograd, Feb 1917, vs (St Petersburg, 1911) [other acts by Rimsky-Korsakov, Borodin and Musorgsky, incidental ballet music by Minkus]

Le flibustier, 1888–9 (comédie lyrique, 3, J. Richepin), Paris, OC (Favart), 22 Jan 1894, vs (Paris, 1894)

Pir vo vremya chumï [A Feast in Time of Plague], 1895–7, 1900 (dramatic scenes, 1, Pushkin's 'little tragedy'), Moscow, New, 11/24 Nov 1901, vs (Leipzig, 1901)

Saratsïn [The Saracen], 1896–8 (4, after A. Dumas *père*: *Charles VII chez ses grands vassaux*), St Petersburg, Mariinsky, 2/14 Nov 1899, vs (Moscow, 1899)

Mademuazel' Fifi [Mam'zelle Fifi], 1902–3 (1, Cui, after G. de Maupassant and O. Metenier), Moscow, Hermitage, 4/17 Nov 1903, vs (Moscow, 1903)

Snezhnïy bogatïr' [Hero of the Snows] (children's op, 1, M. Pol'), Yalta, 15/28 May 1906, vs (Moscow, 1906; rev. lib, 1953)

Mateo Falcone (dramatic scene, after P. Mérimée, trans. V. A. Zhukovsky), Moscow, Bol'shoy, 14/27 Dec 1907, vs (Moscow, 1907)

Kapitanskaya dochka [The Captain's Daughter], 1907–9 (4, Cui, after Pushkin), St Petersburg, Mariinsky, 14/27 Feb 1911, vs (Moscow, 1910)

Krasnaya shapochka [Red Riding-Hood], 1911 (children's fairy-tale op, 2, M. Pol', after C. Perrault), vs (Moscow, 1912 [in magazine *Svetlyachok*])

Kot v sapogakh [Puss in Boots], 1913 (children's fairy-tale op, 1, Pol', after Perrault), Tiflis, State, 30 Dec 1915/12 Jan 1916, vs (Moscow, 1913 [*Svetlyachok*])

Ivanushka-durachok [Ivanushka the Little Fool], 1913 (children's fairy-tale op, 1, N. Dolomanova), vs (Leipzig, 1914)

*

C. Cui: *La musique en Russie* (Paris, 1880) [incl. 'Notice biographique' on Cui by C. Bellaigue]

N. Rimsky-Korsakov: '"Vil'yam Ratklif" Ts. A. Kyui', *N. A. Rimsky-Korsakov: Muzïkal'nïye stat'i i zametki (1869–1907)* [Articles and Notes on Music], ed. N. Rimskaya-Korsakova (St Petersburg, 1911), 15–46

C. Cui: *Muzïkal'no-kriticheskiye stat'i* [Critical Articles on Music], i (Petrograd, 1918)

——: *Izbrannïye stat'i* [Selected Articles], ed. Yu. A. Kremlyov (Leningrad, 1952) [incl. memoir, 'Pervïye kompozitorskiye shagi Ts. Kyui' [Cui's First Steps as a Composer], 1909]

V. Stasov: 'Dvadtsat' pyat' let russkogo iskusstva: nasha muzïka' [25 Years of Russian Art: Our Music], *Izbrannïye sochineniya* [Selected Works], ed. E. D. Stasova and others (Moscow, 1952), ii, 522–68

——: 'Tsezar' Antonovich Kyui', ibid, iii, 387–408

C. Cui: *Izbrannïye pis'ma* [Selected Letters], ed. M. O. Yankovsky (Leningrad, 1955)

A. Gozenpud: *Russkiy opernïy teatr XIX veka (1857–1872)* [Russian Operatic Theatre of the 19th Century] (Leningrad, 1971), chap. 9 [on *William Ratcliff*]

G. Abraham: 'Heine, Queuille, and "William Ratcliff"', *Musicae Scientiae Collectanea: Festschrift Karl Gustav Fellerer zum 70. Geburtstag* (Cologne, 1973), 12–25 [repr. in Abraham, *Essays on Russian and East European Music* (Oxford, 1985), 56–67]

A. Gozenpud: *Russkiy opernïy teatr XIX veka (1873–1889)* (Leningrad, 1973), chap. 8 [on *Andzhelo*]

R. Taruskin: '"Kuchkism" in Practice: Two Operas by César Cui', *Opera and Drama in Russia as Preached and Practiced in the 1860s* (Ann Arbor, 1981) [chap.6, pp.341–426, and appx D: Love Duets from *Andzhelo*, pp.519–41]

G. Metzner: 'Heine in der Musik: Bibliographie der Heine-Vertonungen', iii: *Komponisten C-F* (Tutzing, 1989) [essay on *William Ratcliff*]

RICHARD TARUSKIN

Cullis, Rita (*b* Poulton Cum Spital, nr Birkenhead, 25 Sept 1952). English soprano. She studied in Manchester, making her début in 1974 as Second Boy (*Die Zauberflöte*) with the WNO, for which she sang (1976–84) Miss Wordsworth, Xenia, Leïla, Musetta, the Governess, Liù, Tatyana, Gilda, Lenio (*The Greek Passion*), Pamina and Ellen Orford. At Buxton she sang Elisetta (*Il matrimonio segreto*) in 1981 and Lucinda (*La buona figliuola*) in 1985; for Glyndebourne Touring Opera (1984–8), Countess Almaviva and Kát'a; for Opera North (1985–6), Jenifer (*The Midsummer Marriage*) and Christine (*Intermezzo*), while for the ENO her roles have included the Composer, the Fox, Donna Anna and Fiordiligi. In 1989–90 she returned to the WNO for Agathe and the Marschallin and in 1991 she sang Countess Almaviva in Toronto. A powerful actress, she has a vibrant, warm-toned voice.

ELIZABETH FORBES

Culshaw, John (Royds) (*b* Southport, 28 May 1924; *d* London, 27 April 1980). English record and television producer. Self-educated in music, he joined the Decca company in 1946. In just over 20 years he supervised the recording of more than 30 operas, including the first commercial recording of Wagner's *Ring* cycle, with Georg Solti conducting the Vienna PO, a project he described in vivid detail in his book *Ring Resounding* (London, 1967). The sessions on *Rheingold* in 1958 crowned what he had been developing over his previous opera recordings, the idea of a total production in sound, meticulously observing the composer's directions, often transcending what was possible in the opera house. That historic recording led not just to the rest of the *Ring* tetralogy but to equally spectacular recordings of other Wagner works, Strauss and others.

In all his projects he was a persuader rather than a dictator (unlike his older rival in EMI, Walter Legge), getting his way by diplomacy. He persuaded Kirsten Flagstad, well into retirement, to sing Fricka in *Das Rheingold*, and it was through Culshaw above all that Benjamin Britten – who was deeply suspicious of recording – agreed to conduct the first recordings of most of his operas. When in 1967 Culshaw left Decca to become head of music for BBC television, it was one of his prime aims to present Britten's operas in that medium, and he did so with memorable results. After leaving the BBC in 1975, he worked as a freelance, writing and broadcasting prolifically as well as producing records. When he died at 55, he had nearly completed his lively autobiography, published posthumously under the title *Putting the Record Straight* (London, 1981). He also wrote a book on Rakhmaninov (London, 1949) and *Reflections on Wagner's Ring* (London, 1976). Culshaw's great achievement was to develop the concept of opera recording as an art form distinct from live performance. EDWARD GREENFIELD

Cummings, Conrad (*b* San Francisco, 10 Feb 1948). American composer. He studied at Yale University, SUNY at Stony Brook and Columbia University, and at Tanglewood and Stanford University. He then worked at the Columbia-Princeton Electronic Music Center, Brooklyn College and IRCAM, and from 1980 taught at the Oberlin Conservatory of Music.

Cummings's first opera, *Eros and Psyche* (1983), was commissioned by Oberlin College to celebrate its 150th anniversary. Described as a 'post-modern' opera with definite neo-Baroque tendencies, it was modelled mostly after Handel's operas, with other inspirations ranging from the Baroque to current performance art and minimalism. The work's basic premise is a recurring Cummings theme: resolution of conflicts, but with a trace of humour. *Cassandra* (1984–5) was withdrawn: but a dramatic scene with the same title was developed from it.

The chamber works *Positions 1956* and *Insertions*, for his own Cummings Ensemble (soprano, baritone, violin/viola, cello, flutes, saxophone/clarinet and synthesizer, all amplified), are operatic studies on the subjects of sex, war and politics. *Photo-Op*, a 50-minute 'imaginary unstaged opera' (also for the Cummings Ensemble), further explores in its surrealistic view of a national political convention the merging of political and personal, public and private themes; the composer has continued to develop the work for fully staged performance. By creating a laboratory setting with a small group (but expanding it to operatic scope through amplification) Cummings has freed himself to deal with highly charged and controversial subjects. Potent dramatic imagery and simple, direct tunefulness characterize these three works, which can be performed as a trilogy.

In 1989 Cummings began work on an opera dealing with the American involvement with Vietnam and fusing historical scenes with Vietnamese and American fables, which he described as 'epic in historical scope yet intimate in the treatment of individual characters'.

Eros and Psyche (3, Cummings, after Apuleius), Oberlin, Opera Theater, 16 Nov 1983
Cassandra, 1984–5 (3, Cummings), withdrawn; rev. as dramatic scene, 1986
Positions 1956 (chamber op, M. Korie, after popular sex manuals of the 1950s), New York, Knitting Factory, 11 March 1988
Insertions (chamber op, J. Siena, H. Reznikov, M. Blumenthal and V. Seth), New York, Knitting Factory, 18 March 1988
Photo-Op (imaginary unstaged op, Siena), New York, Knitting Factory, 19 May 1989 BARBARA A. PETERSEN

Cunitz, Maud (*b* London, 3 April 1911; *d* Baldham, nr Munich, 22 July 1987). German soprano. She studied in Nuremberg, joining the chorus at the Opera there in 1931. She made her début as a soloist in 1934 at Gotha, then sang at Coburg, Lübeck, Magdeburg and Stuttgart. In 1944 she sang Elisabeth (*Tannhäuser*) at the Vienna Staatsoper, where she was later engaged (1946–9). In Salzburg (1943–6) she sang Donna Elvira, Zdenka (*Arabella*) and Octavian as well as Semele in the public dress-rehearsal of *Der Liebe der Danae* in 1944. In 1946 she joined the Staatsoper in Munich and in 1953 made her London début with that company at Covent Garden as the Countess in the British première of *Capriccio* and as Arabella. Her repertory included Agathe, Elsa, Countess Almaviva, Ariadne, Leonora (*Il trovatore* and *La forza del destino*), Aida, Desdemona, Butterfly and Micaëla. She was a reliable if not particularly colourful singer. ELIZABETH FORBES

Cunningham, Arthur (*b* Piermont, NY, 11 Nov 1928). American composer. He began to write music for his own jazz band at the age of 12. He attended Fisk University (BA 1951), the Juilliard School (1951–2) and Columbia University Teachers College (MA 1957). In 1951 the National Association of Negro Musicians sponsored a concert of his music. During his service in the US army (1955–7) he composed for army bands, musical shows and television.

His seven completed stage works, written between 1963 and 1973, include rock operas, musical plays, incidental music and a theatre piece. The librettos draw heavily on African and Afro-American subjects and children's fantasies. Cunningham's musical style is eclectic, integrating such contemporary 20th-century phenomena as jazz, rock and gospel, as well as traditional techniques and serialism. His *Ostrich Feathers* (1965) anticipated the vogue of rock-opera composition in the USA during the late 1960s and early 70s. *Night Song* (1973), a theatre piece with a text in Swahili, Gullah (Sea Islands) and English, was commissioned for the American bicentenary by Cheyney State College, Pennsylvania, but never performed.

Patsy Patch and Susan's Dream (rock musical for children, Cunningham), Orangeburg, NY, 27 April 1963
The Beauty Part (musical show with improvised pf acc., S. J. Perelman), Blauvelt, NY, Rockland County Playhouse, 13 Aug 1963
Violetta, 1963 (musical, after J. Audiberti: *Le mal court*)
Ostrich Feathers (rock musical play for children, B. Brenner), New York, Martinique Theatre, 16 Nov 1965
His Natural Grace [Louey, Louey], 1969 (mini rock op, 1, Cunningham), excerpts perf.
Night Song, 1973 (theatre piece), unperf.
House by the Sea (1, Cunningham), inc.

*

SouthernB
E. Southern: *The Music of Black Americans: a History* (New York, 1971, 2/1983)
C. Laverne: *Black Idioms in Opera as Reflected in the Works of Six Afro-American Composers* (diss., U. of Southern California, 1974)
A. Tischler: *Fifteen Black American Composers: a Bibliography of their Works* (Detroit, 1981) JOSEPHINE WRIGHT

Cunning Little Vixen, The [*Příhody Lišky Bystroušky* ('The Adventures of the Vixen Bystrouška')]. Opera in three acts by LEOŠ JANÁČEK to his own libretto after Rudolf Těsnohlídek's novel *Liška Bystrouška*; Brno, National Theatre, 6 November 1924.

Těsnohlídek's novel came about as a text which the Brno newspaper *Lidové noviny* commissioned to go with a collection of drawings made many years earlier by the painter Stanislav Lolek (fig.1 overleaf). These told the story of a clever vixen reared as a cub by a forester but who escapes and raises a family. Těsnohlídek's *Liška Bystrouška* was serialized in *Lidové noviny* between 7 April and 23 June 1920, though it was not until 1921 (when the novel was published in book form) that Janáček began to consider making an opera out of it. He began work on 22 January 1922 and after completing an early draft of Act 1 (26 March 1922) he contacted Těsnohlídek for his permission and got him to write the text for the Forester's song in Act 2. Janáček

Bystrouška ('Little Sharp Ears') [the Vixen]	soprano
(as a cub)	child soprano
(as a young woman)	dancer
Fox [*Zlatohřbítek*, 'Golden-back']	soprano
Forester	baritone
Schoolmaster } Mosquito }	tenor
Badger } Priest }	bass
Blue Dragonfly	dancer
Cricket	child soprano
Grasshopper	child soprano
Frog	child soprano
Forester's Wife } Owl }	contralto
Lapák *the dog*	mezzo-soprano
Frantík *a boy*	soprano
Pepík	soprano
Cock } Jay }	soprano
Chocholka *the hen*	soprano
Pásek *an innkeeper*	tenor
Woodpecker	contralto
Harašta *a poultry dealer and poacher*	bass
Mrs Pásková	soprano

Hens, creatures of the forest, offstage chorus, fox cubs (children)

Ballet: midges, squirrels, hedgehog

(The cast-list specifies that four pairs of characters should be sung by the same singers: Schoolmaster/Mosquito; Priest/Badger; Forester's Wife/Owl; Cock/Jay.)

Setting A forest near Brno, a farmyard at the Forester's lodge and Pásek's inn; about 1920

made his own libretto: Acts 1 and 2 correspond roughly to the novel; Act 3 is a free amalgam of passages from the novel and other elements. Janáček completed the opera on 10 October 1923 and Universal Edition published a vocal score (made by Janáček's pupil Břetislav Bakala) in July 1924, some months ahead of the Brno première on 6 November under František Neumann. The Prague première followed on 18 May 1925 under Ostrčil. Max Brod's German version took considerable liberties in attempting to clarify and unify the plot, with a much more tangible relationship between the Vixen and Terynka, a young girl talked about by the humans but never seen. The German première (Mainz, 13 February 1927) was not particularly successful and the opera had to wait until Felsenstein's celebrated production at the Komische Oper in Berlin in 1956 to enjoy international acclaim (for illustration *see* HEINRICH, RUDOLF).

ACT 1 *A wooded glen, a sunny summer afternoon* During the orchestral prelude the Badger emerges from his sett, smoking a pipe. Flies swirl round and dance, followed by the Blue Dragonfly. They disperse as the Forester approaches. Tired from the heat he lies down and dozes off. The Cricket and Grasshopper make music (a delicately-scored waltz) and are joined by the tipsy Mosquito. The Frog tries to catch the Mosquito but has himself attracted the attention of the young Vixen; in his efforts to escape her, he lands on the Forester's nose. The Forester wakes up, seizes the Vixen and takes her home 'for the children'. The music of the

1. *One of the drawings by Stanislav Lolek that inspired Rudolf Těsnohlídek's novel 'Liška Bystrouška', on which the libretto of Janáček's 'The Cunning Little Vixen' is based*

opening prelude returns as the Blue Dragonfly searches vainly for the Vixen.

The yard of the Forester's lodge; autumn, in afternoon sun After a short prelude the Vixen and Lapák the dog discuss their lack of experience in love. When Lapák makes advances to the Vixen she knocks him over. Pepík and Frantík run out and torment the Vixen. She attacks Pepík and attempts to escape but is tied up by the Forester. In a substantial interlude, night falls and the Vixen dreams she is a young girl. The dawn breaks; whole-tone harmonies give way to a radiant B♭ major and a soaring new theme.

Lapák and the Cock advise the Vixen to submit to captivity, while the Hens (a two-part chorus) industriously lay eggs. The Vixen rebukes the Hens for their slavish devotion to the Cock and in disgust at their reactionary attitudes feigns suicide. Intrigued, the Cock approaches, is seized by the Vixen and is killed. In the commotion which follows (an energetic finale) the Forester tries to beat the Vixen but she bites through her leash and escapes into the woods.

ACT 2 *The Badger's sett in the wood, late afternoon* The music of the prelude provides material for the subsequent scene in which the Vixen disturbs the Badger and then mockingly criticizes him, encouraged by the chorus of forest animals. Physically beaten by the enraged Badger, the Vixen retaliates by fouling his sett. This forces the Badger to leave and the Vixen promptly occupies it. An interlude leads into the next scene.

A room inside the inn 'U Pásků' ['At the Páseks'] The Schoolmaster and Forester are playing cards. The Priest joins them as the Forester, teasing the Schoolmaster about rumours of his impending marriage, sings a song about Veronika, a woman loved and lost, 'Bývalo' ('It used to be'). To get his own back the Schoolmaster taunts the Forester with the Vixen's escape. Hearing the cock crow, the Schoolmaster and then the Priest leave. The Forester reflects drily on the Schoolmaster's infatuation but leaves abruptly when

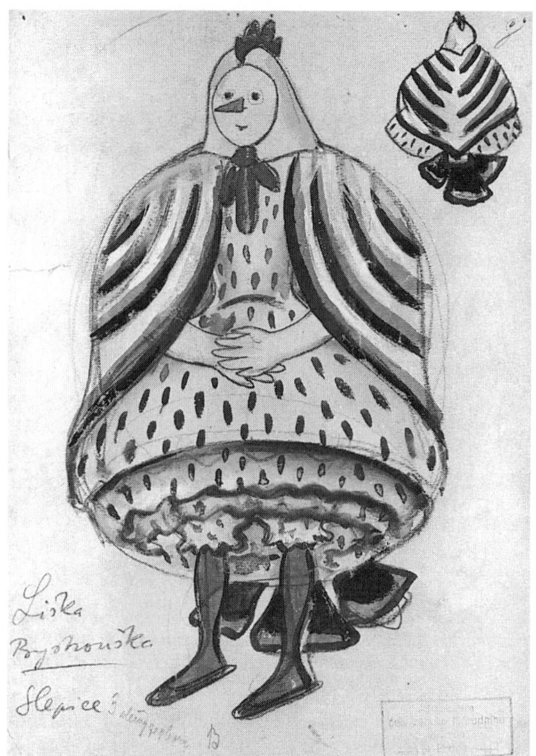

2. *'The Cunning Little Vixen' (Janáček): costume design for a hen by Josef Čapek for the first Prague production, 18 May 1925*

Pásek reminds him of the Vixen's escape. An interlude leads into a scene in the forest.

The forest, a path leading uphill with sunflowers growing against the fence; a moonlit night The Schoolmaster drunkenly makes his way home, regretting his unsteady gait. The Vixen, who has watched his antics, hides behind a sunflower which the Schoolmaster mistakes for Terynka, the young woman he admires from afar. He declares his love for her and, in attempting to embrace the sunflower, falls over the fence. The Vixen escapes and now observes the approaching Priest. He remembers bitterly his deception by a young girl when he was a student. The Forester is heard searching for the Vixen. She runs off, the Schoolmaster and Priest take fright (singing together briefly) and make their separate ways home as two shots ring out. The Forester comes out from the trees, convinced that he saw the Vixen.

The Vixen's burrow in the moonlight A gentle vocalise for offstage chorus opens the scene. The Vixen approvingly observes the Fox, who approaches and strikes up a conversation. The Vixen boasts of her home and her past exploits at the Forester's (a set-piece narrative condensing many chapters of the novel and establishing her fearless and assertive personality). Impressed, the Fox introduces himself and then dashes off while the Vixen, in a lyrical interlude, muses on her 'beauty'. The Fox returns with a freshly killed rabbit, which they share. In further conversation they admit to each other their sexual inexperience. When the Fox makes advances the Vixen at first rejects them but this prompts him to a passionate declaration of his love. She is won over: her 'Chcu!' ('I want!') is heard over languorously sensuous music and they go into her burrow. Time passes (a repeat of the Blue Dragonfly music from Act 1) and the Owl and the Jay comment censoriously on the turn of events. Soon the Vixen comes out again crying; she whispers something to the Fox and he decides they must be married at once. The opening offstage chorus (now designated 'the voice of the forest') returns to provide a background to the ceremony celebrated by a Woodpecker. Then the chorus music accelerates into an exuberant and substantial dance to close the act.

ACT 3 *A clearing in the forest; autumn, noon, a clear sky* An assertive, mostly minor-key, prelude announces the approach of Harašta, who sings a three-stanza song 'Déž sem vandroval' ('When I went a-wandering'). He notices a dead hare on the path but is surprised by the Forester, whom he tells of his impending marriage to Terynka. The Forester warns him about poaching and examines the dead hare. He notices a fox-trail and, convinced that it is the Vixen's, sets a trap for her. The Forester and Harašta leave the clearing separately.

Immediately the Fox Cubs run on. Their song – a two-stanza folk-text 'Běží liška k Táboru' ('A vixen runs to Tábor'), in a delightful Lydian setting – develops into a suspicious investigation of the baited hare. With the help of the Vixen and the Fox they contemptuously recognize it as a trap. Surrounded by their many children, the Vixen and Fox look forward to breeding again in May. Over their lyrical duet the voice of Harašta is heard again singing another folk-text, 'Když jsem já šel okolo' ('When I went round the green grove'). He enters with a pannier full of poultry. The Vixen lies down in his path and feigns injury. Harašta reaches for his gun but the Vixen lures him away until he stumbles, and bloodies his nose. Meanwhile the Vixen and her family devour the contents of the pannier. Angered, Harašta fires wildly, the foxes scatter but the Vixen lies dying.

A bowling alley in the garden at 'U Pásků; unaccustomed quiet The prelude develops into a nostalgic Adagio (marked both 'espressivo' and 'dolcissimo'). Time has passed. Only the Forester and the Schoolmaster are left at Pásek's inn. The Forester teases the Schoolmaster about his encounter with the sunflower, but is immediately sympathetic when he sees his friend grieving over Terynka's wedding. The Priest has moved to a new parish and has written that he is lonely (the nostalgic music of the prelude flowers into a new variant). The Forester complains of getting old like his dog, Lapák. He leaves, and a brief interlude follows based on the new nostalgic variant. Soon it gives way to vigorous music chiefly for horn quartet (a post-première addition to help with the scene change).

A wooded glen as in the opening scene, the sun shining after a shower The Forester is walking home. He notices a fungus growing and is reminded of happily picking mushrooms with his wife on their honeymoon. He contemplates the scene in one of the most lyrical outpourings of Janáček's late operas, 'Je to pohádka či pravda?' ('Is it a fairy-tale or true?'), expressing his love for the sunlit evenings in the forest and imagining the seasonal return of the fairy spirits and the unearthly joy which they bring to mankind. He falls asleep and the animals from the opening scene return. In his dream the Forester sees a vixen-cub, looking exactly like the Vixen Bystrouška herself. As he reaches out towards her he catches hold of a frog instead – the grandson (it explains) of the one which landed on his face in Act 1. In silent reverie the Forester lets his gun slip to the ground.

* * *

Janáček wrote *The Vixen* on the eve of his 70th birthday and in this, his sunniest work, he came to terms with his years and his inevitable death. Thus he boldly introduced the death of the Vixen into the opera, but without fuss or pathos, and ended the opera with an evocation of its beginning and a strong message of renewal into which death is subsumed. The images emphasized in his libretto and in his music are cyclical; the seasons come and go, and though the humans get older, they are juxtaposed against images of youth. The children's voices that Janáček carefully specified help to underline this point. Their enlargement of the vocal spectrum, together with the inventive use of mime and ballet, also serves to portray the animal world.

For a page from the autograph score *see* JANÁČEK, LEOŠ, fig.1.

JOHN TYRRELL

Cunning Man, The. Comic opera in two acts arranged by CHARLES BURNEY after JEAN-JACQUES ROUSSEAU's *Le devin du village*; London, Drury Lane Theatre, 21 November 1766.

Burney admired Rousseau's *intermède* as an example of the ideal union of the sister arts of music and poetry. He began his adaptation in King's Lynn some time before 1760 and completed it in London in 1766 at the prompting of David Garrick. Burney's adaptation 'totidem syllabis' incorporates new recitatives, faithful to the spirit of the originals and making musical reference to them, and two new airs to facilitate the division of Rousseau's one act into two.

According to Burney's memoirs, the part of the Fortune Teller (bass) was given to Samuel Champness, 'a Cathedral singer, but little acquainted with secular Music, and no actor'. Colin (tenor) was sung by Joseph Vernon, 'with an inferior ten[or] voice, but with more knowledge of m[usic] and a much better actor'. The part of Phoebe (soprano) was given to Elizabeth Wright, a 'brilliant performer'. Fanny Burney reported that 'the drama was too denuded of intricacy or variety for the amusement of John Bull; and the appearance of only three interlocutors caused a gaping expectation of some followers, that made every new scene begin by inflicting disappointment'. Moderately successful nonetheless, *The Cunning Man* received 14 performances in 1766 and two more in 1768. Several collections and arrangements of the music were published, and at least six printings of the libretto appeared during the 18th century, the latest in 1792.

See also DEVIN DU VILLAGE, LE.

KERRY S. GRANT

Cunning Peasant, The [*Šelma sedlák*]. Comic opera in two acts by ANTONÍN DVOŘÁK to a libretto by Josef Otakar Veselý; Prague, Provisional Theatre, 27 January 1878.

Veselý's plot resembles that of the Beaumarchais–Da Ponte *Le nozze di Figaro*. It involves a Prince (baritone) who attempts to seduce a lowly young woman, Bětuška (soprano), who is already in love with a young man, Jeník (tenor). The Princess (soprano) is involved in a plot to expose the philandering of her husband. In Act 2 scene viii, the Princess reveals her identity after having disguised herself as Bětuška during the Prince's attempted seduction. In the end, the Prince asks for forgiveness and swears fidelity, and a farm is presented to Jeník and Bětuška.

At times, especially in Act 1 scenes i and ii, the resemblance to Smetana's *The Bartered Bride*, accepted as the classic of Czech comic opera by Dvořák, is marked. For the most part the musical language is entirely characteristic of Dvořák and a number of characterizations look forward to later operas, most notably *The Jacobin*: the depiction of the Prince anticipates Bohuš. The lovers Jeník and Bětuška resemble Jeník and Mařenka in *The Bartered Bride*. The melodic inspiration never flags, and Dvořák incorporates elements of classical pastiche in the depiction of Martin (bass), the cunning peasant of the title, who had planned Bětuška's marriage to a rich farmer. In its day, this was one of the most popular of Dvořák's operas; its popularity declined only with the première of his next comic opera, *The Jacobin*.

JAN SMACZNY

Cupeda, Donato (*b* ?Naples, *c*1661; *d* Vienna, 27 Dec 1704). Italian librettist. He was appointed substitute for the court poet Minato on 1 Jan 1694 by Emperor Leopold I and succeeded to that position in March 1698, by which year he was also a member of the emperor's literary academy. In his first year at court he wrote only the text for an oratorio and a dramatic chamber composition. The preface to the carnival opera of 1695, *Amore dà senno*, describes the work as his first opera libretto (earlier dates cited by Weilen are incorrect). Until his early death Cupeda wrote texts for three-act operas, serenatas and cantatas set by Antonio Draghi, C. A. Badia, Giovanni Bononcini, Marc'Antonio Ziani, J. J. Fux and Attilio Ariosti. The subjects of his librettos are taken from mythology and from Greek, Roman and medieval history. They are reworked with considerable freedom; love affairs and comic episodes, for example, increase in importance.

Amore dà senno, overo Le sciocchezze d'Hippoclide (drama musicale), A. Draghi, 1695; *La finta cecità di Antioco il Grande* (drama per musica), Draghi, 1695; *La magnanimità di Marco Fabrizio* (opera in musica), Draghi, 1695; *L'Adalberto, overo La forza dell'astuzia femminile* (drama per musica), Draghi, 1697; *Bacco, vincitore dell'India* (festa teatrale), C. A. Badia, 1697; *L'amare per virtù* (drama per musica), Draghi, 1697; *L'idea del felice governo* (serenata), Badia, 1698

L'Arsace, fondatore dell'imperio de' Parthi (drama per musica), A. Draghi and C. D. Draghi, 1698; *La forza dell'amor filiale* (drama per musica), A. Draghi and C. D. Draghi, 1698; *La fede publica* (drama per musica), G. Bononcini, 1699; *Il commun giubilo del mondo* (musica da camera), Badia, 1699; *L'Alceste* (drama per musica), A. Draghi, 1700; *La costanza d'Ulisse* (drama per musica), Badia, 1700; *Il Gordiano Pio* (drama per musica), M. A. Ziani, 1700

Gli ossequi della notte (serenata), Ziani, 1701 (J. J. Fux, 1709); *Gli affetti più grandi, vinti dal più giusto* (dramma per musica), Bononcini, 1701; *L'offendere per amare, overo La Telesilla* (drama per musica), Fux, 1702; *Il Romolo* (drama per musica), Ziani, 1702; *I gloriosi presagi di Scipione Africano* (trattenimento musicale), A. Ariosti, 1704; *Il fiore delle eroine* (trattenimento per musica), Bononcini, 1704; *Caio Popilio* (trattenimento musicale), Ziani, 1704; *Il ritorno di Giulio Cesare, vincitore della Mauritania* (festa per musica), Bononcini, 1704

*

A. von Weilen: *Zur Wiener Theatergeschichte: Die vom Jahre 1629 bis zum Jahre 1640 am Wiener Hofe zur Aufführung gelangten Werke theatralischen Charakters und Oratorien* (Vienna, 1901)

F. Hadamowsky: 'Barocktheater am Wiener Kaiserhof. Mit einem Spielplan (1625–1740)', *Jb der Gesellschaft für Wiener Theaterforschung 1951–52*, 7–96

K. Jekl: *Die Italiener in Wien in der ersten Hälfte des 18. Jhdt* (diss., U. of Vienna, 1953), 10–12

H. Seifert: 'Die Aufführungen der Opern und Serenate mit Musik von Johann Joseph Fux', *SMw*, xxix (1978), 14–27

——: *Neues zu Antonio Draghis weltlichen Werken* (Vienna, 1978)

——: *Die Oper am Wiener Kaiserhof* (Tutzing, 1985)

HERBERT SEIFERT

Cupid and Death. Masque in five entries by JAMES SHIRLEY with music by Christopher Gibbons and MATTHEW LOCKE; London, 26 March 1653 (revised version, London, Leicester Fields, 1659).

Cupid and Death was staged as an entertainment for the Portuguese ambassador, the Condé de Penaguiõ, who was in London before signing a peace treaty between King John IV and Oliver Cromwell on 10 June 1654. The producer was 'Mr Luke Channen', presumably the dancing-master Luke Channell. Shirley had written several Stuart masques, including *The Triumph of Peace* (1634), which was bitterly attacked by the Puritans for its extravagance.

Avoiding any hint of the decadent splendours of the court masque, Shirley shaped Aesop's allegorical fable into a series of antimasques. Cupid and Death stay in the same inn during bad weather. Though principally speaking characters, they make their first appearance in dances. As a joke, the Chamberlain of the inn decides to exchange their arrows while they are asleep. The next day Cupid unintentionally murders many young lovers, while Death's arrows rejuvenate the old and infirm, as an astonished Mother Nature looks on. Hoping to avenge the prank, Death strikes the Chamberlain, who immediately makes love to his trained apes. Into this ribald confusion descends Mercury upon a cloud to restore order: Cupid is banned from court and banished to cottages, while Death, though his power to kill is restored, must henceforth avoid contact with 'persons in whose breast divine marks of art or honour shine'. The masque ends with a scene in Elysium for the slain lovers.

The plot unfolds through spoken dialogue, recitative, formal songs, choruses and, most important, ballet. Besides Cupid and Death, Folly, Madness, Despair and others express themselves through speech and dance, while Nature (soprano) and Mercury (bass) are restricted to singing. The Chamberlain (tenor) both speaks and sings. Nothing is known of the music of the first production, since the only source is Locke's autograph manuscript of the 1659 version (*GB-Lbl* Add.17799 – a 'short score' which lacks most tenor and viola parts). It clearly shows the division of labour, but whether Locke had any involvement with the first production is uncertain. He seems to have revised Gibbons's score, adding or replacing some pieces and converting much of the original spoken dialogue in the fifth entry into recitative: in fact, only a few lines of dialogue remain in the fourth and fifth entries, and from Mercury's entrance *Cupid and Death* becomes to all intents and purposes an opera.

Gibbons's pieces (confined to songs, choruses and dances in the second entry and a single duet and chorus in the fifth) are melodically bland and contrapuntally stiff. Locke's music is much more varied and directly illustrative of the action. Most remarkable are his recitatives for Nature and Mercury (particularly the latter's 'Hence, ye profane'). In these florid, declamatory songs Locke took care to place the main embellishments over the least important words, a style of prosody which recalls the earliest operatic monodies of Peri and Caccini.

CURTIS PRICE

Cupido [*Der sich rächende Cupido* ('The Avenging Cupid')]. *Musicalisches Schau-Spiel* in three acts by REINHARD KEISER to a libretto by JOHANN ULRICH VON KÖNIG, partly after FRANCESCO DE LEMENE's *Endimione*; Hamburg, Theater am Gänsemarkt, 9 July 1724.

The goddess Diana (soprano), sworn enemy of love, threatens with death any of her followers who succumb to it. To prove his power, Cupid (soprano) shoots her with one of his arrows, and she falls madly in love with Endimion [Endymion] (contralto), a beautiful young man she finds sleeping in the woods. Another arrow wounds her disciple Aurilla (soprano), who also develops a passion for Endymion, spurning the pleas of the lovesick Tirsis (bass). Endymion, however, has no interest in either lady and constantly searches for his lost love Dorinda. After various absurd misunderstandings, it is finally revealed that Dorinda is his dog. The 'comic hunter' Sylvano (tenor), having captured Cupid in his net like a bird, offers him to Diana, and Cupid persuades her to release him in exchange for making Endymion love her. Aurilla, previously turned into a tree by Diana for loving Endymion, is freed and happily united with Tirsis.

Cupido is a revised version of *Die entdeckte Verstellung, oder Die geheime Liebe der Diana* ('The Pretence Exposed, or Diana's Secret Love'; 1712, Hamburg). Much of the music seems to have been newly composed or substantially rewritten (the 1712 version is largely lost), and the score also includes seven Italian arias by other composers, apparently added at the singers' request. The title role was sung by Keiser's 11-year-old daughter, Sophia Dorothea Louisa. With its witty libretto, colourful stage pictures, numerous homophonic choruses, and special profusion of melody, *Cupido* is one of Keiser's most appealing works.

JOHN H. ROBERTS

Curci [Curcio], **Giuseppe** (*b* Barletta, 15 June 1808; *d* Barletta, 5 Aug 1877). Italian composer and singing teacher. He went to Naples as a student at the Conservatorio di S Sebastiano, where he studied with Ferno, Tritto and Pietro Raimondi. When that institution was abolished in 1826, he transferred to S Pietro a Majella, where his principal instructors were Zingarelli (for composition) and Crescentini (for voice); he remained there under special dispensation until 1835. Two of his earliest stage works were written for the *teatrino* at the conservatory. These comic works were sufficiently well received to win him a chance to compose for the Teatro Nuovo, Naples, where his *Il ciabattino e la morte* (1832) dealt with the same subject that was to serve the Ricci brothers much more successfully as *Crispino e la comare* (1850). In 1834, Curci brought out on the same stage *Il sarto e i tabarri*. After having his cantata *Ruggiero* performed at the S Carlo in January 1835, he moved to northern Italy in search of the success that had so far eluded him. At Turin, his *Il proscritto* won some favour, while *Don Desiderio*, produced at the Apollo, Venice, for Carnival 1837, managed to enjoy a short-lived vogue. By 1840 he had renounced the stage to become a teacher of voice in Vienna, Pest, Paris (where he remained for eight years) and England, and he published two volumes of *solfeggi*. In the mid-1850s he returned to his native town, managing the Teatro Piccinni at Bari for a year, but devoting himself chiefly to instruction, and turning out a quantity of sacred music. As an opera composer, Curci mastered the then current conventions, but sadly he lacked genuine originality or any strong feeling for theatrical values.

*

ES (F. Schlitzer)

F. De Filippis and R. Armese: *Cronache del Teatro di S Carlo*, i (Naples, 1963), 71, 148

WILLIAM ASHBROOK

Curcio, Giuseppe Maria (*b* Naples, *fl* 1780–1809). Italian composer. The librettos of his operas indicate that he was a member of the Accademia Fiorentina degli Armonici from 1797 and at the beginning of the 19th century was also *maestro di cappella* of Fermo Cathedral. He wrote both serious and comic operas, performed in Naples, Rome, Florence, Turin, Livorno and Lisbon, and ballets (for F. Robusti's *La Briseide*, 1791, Naples).

I matrimoni per inganno (ob, G. Palomba), Naples, Fondo, 1779
La scaltra in amore (ob, P. Mililotti), Naples, Fondo, 1780
I matrimoni per sorpresa (int), Rome, Capranica, carn. 1781
Il millantatore (ob, Palomba), Naples, Fondo, 1781
Solimano (os, G. Migliavacca), Turin, Regio, 1782
La Nitteti (os, P. Metastasio), Naples, S Carlo, 20 Jan 1783, *I-Nc*
Le convulsioni (ob, Palomba), Naples, Fiorentini, 1787, *Mc**
Emira e Zopiro (os), Florence, Pergola, 8 Sept 1795
La presa di Granata [La conquista di Granata] (os, M. Ballani), Livorno, Avvalorati, aut. 1795
Il trionfo di Scipione in Cartagine (os, C. Mazzini), Florence, Pergola, 1795
Giulio Cesare in Egitto (os, F. Ballani), Rome, Argentina, 1796
Zulema [Gonzalvo di Cordova] (os, O. Balsamo), Naples, S Carlo, 13 Aug 1797, *Nc*
Le nozze a dispetto (ob, Palomba), Naples, Fondo, 1797, *Nc*
I supposti deliri di donna Laura (ob), Rome, Valle, 18 April 1798
La disfatta dei Macedoni (os), Rome, Alibert, aut. 1798
Il fanatico per l'astronomia [L'astronomo burlato], Rome, Tordinona, Oct 1799
Ifigenia in Aulide (os, G. Moretti), Florence, Pergola, aut. 1799, *PAc*
Argea, ovvero Sicione liberata (os, G. Boggio), Florence, Pallacorda, 1799
Roma liberata (os, F. Ballani), Rome, Alibert, spr. 1800
Chi la fa la paga (ob), Rome, Capranica, carn. 1804
Amazilde, Rome, Argentina, 27 Dec 1809

*

ES (F. Schlitzer); *DBI* (B. M. Antolini); *FlorimoN*
I. Mamczarz: *Les intermèdes comiques italiens au XVIIIe siècle en France et en Italie* (Paris, 1972)
R. Zanetti: *La musica italiana del settecento* (Milan, 1978)

RENATO BOSSA

Curioni, Alberico (*b* Milan, *c*1785; *d* Torno, Como, March 1875). Italian tenor. He sang from an early age in the major Italian cities, including Milan, Naples, where he created Alberto in Rossini's *La gazzetta* (1816), and Pesaro, where he sang Giannetto in *La gazza ladra* (1818). He made his London début in 1821 at the King's Theatre as Mozart's Titus and sang there until 1837. His roles included Rossini's Otello, Agorante (*Ricciardo e Zoraide*) and King James (*La donna del lago*), Carolino (Mayr's *Il fanatico per la musica*), Ferrando, Pollione, and Adriano in the London première of *Il crociato in Egitto* (1825). He created Orombello in *Beatrice di Tenda* (1833, Venice). Reputed to have a 'sweet, mellifluous-toned voice', he also had a fine stage presence. ELIZABETH FORBES

Curioni, Rosa (*fl* 1753–62). Italian mezzo-soprano. She sang in Perez's *Merope* and Latilla's *Antigona* at Modena in 1753 and in Cocchi's *Antigono* at Bergamo in 1754. In the same year she was engaged as seconda donna for the King's Theatre, London, and made her début in *Ipermestra* by Lampugnani and Hasse. She specialized in male roles, playing the Emperor Valentinian in Hasse's *Ezio* in 1755. The part of Lysander in J. C. Smith's *The Fairies* (1755), written for her, was sung by Guadagni, but she did create Ferdinand in Smith's *The Tempest* (1756), and sang in oratorios under Handel. She sang the title role in Traetta's *Didone abbandonata* at Venice in 1757; back in London for the 1761–2 season, she appeared in four operas and was described as musician to Duke Clemens of Bavaria. WINTON DEAN

Curioso indiscreto, Il ('Unwise Curiosity'). *Dramma giocoso* in three acts by PASQUALE ANFOSSI to a libretto possibly by GIOVANNI BERTATI after an episode in MIGUEL DE CERVANTES's *Don Quixote*; Rome, Teatro delle Dame, Carnival 1777.

The plot is set in motion by the insatiable curiosity of the Marchese Calandrino (bass), who wants to test the fidelity of his betrothed, Clorinda (soprano), by having his friend, the Contino (tenor), woo her. She falls in love with the Contino, and the rest of the story concerns the complications arising from the Contino's previous involvement with Emilia (soprano), the attachment of Aurelio (tenor) to Emilia, and Clorinda's attempts to help Aurelio. Two servants, Prospero (bass) and Serpina (soprano), complete the cast. The opera is marked by an unusual number of Anfossi's characteristically mellifluous tunes for both pairs of lovers.

Rudolph Angermüller (1989) has posited Giuseppe Petrosellini as the librettist; since there is no indisputable evidence of Bertati's authorship, the attribution to him must be doubtful. Anfossi's opera had immediate success, playing in most of the major Italian cities north of Rome in the four years after its première, and travelling to Paris (1778) and Prague (1780). For the 1783 production in Vienna, Mozart wrote three insertion arias (K418–20), two for Aloysia Lange and one for the tenor Valentin Adamberger (which was not performed). In response to criticisms that he was 'correcting' Anfossi's opera, Mozart had a notice placed in later copies of the libretto that his insertions were not intended to damage Anfossi's reputation. To announce insertion arias in a libretto was extremely unusual; the fact that Mozart felt obliged to explain them indirectly reflects the relative standings of Anfossi and Mozart in Vienna at that time. MARY HUNTER

Curlew River. Parable for church performance by BENJAMIN BRITTEN to a libretto by WILLIAM PLOMER; Orford Church, Suffolk, 12 June 1964.

This is the first of Britten's three 'parables', single-act chamber operas of about an hour's duration for a small group of male singers and instrumentalists (23 performers in all, in the case of *Curlew River*), dressed as monks or lay brothers, and performing without conductor. Though inspired by Japanese noh theatre (*Curlew River* derives its plot from the play *Sumidagawa*, which Britten saw in Tokyo in 1956), the parables are made specifically Christian by their texts and modes of presentation. They are notable for their close coordination of movement, gesture and music, and provide clear evidence of Britten's disenchantment, in the 1960s, with many aspects of conventional opera. The music, deriving from the plainchant of a framing processional hymn, is both more concentrated in form and less dependent on conventions of tonal harmony than in Britten's earlier operas.

After the hymn 'Te lucis ante terminum' and a preliminary homily from the Abbot (bass), the various characters assume appropriate masks and costumes. The action centres on the ferry crossing the Curlew River. The Ferryman (baritone) explains that people are gathering to pray at the shrine of someone buried on the far bank a year ago, a shrine credited with miraculous healing powers. When the Madwoman (tenor) approaches she is first mocked, but then allowed to join the travellers. As the company crosses the river, to brilliantly graphic 'water music', the Ferryman tells the story of the shrine, and the woman, who sings one of Britten's most poignant laments, is convinced that the grave is her son's, murdered by a traveller who abducted him. As she joins in prayer at the tomb the voice of the Spirit of the Boy (treble) is heard. Then he is seen, his presence consoling his mother, who is restored to sanity; as the Abbot observes in his final statement, 'a woman was healed by prayer and grace, a woman with grief distraught'. The story concluded, the monks move away from the acting area, recapitulating the processional hymn. The pervasive influence of this chant on the music of *Curlew River* can be traced not only in the actual intervals of the melodic lines but also in the elaborate counterpoint (at times free in rhythm and coordination) of the ensembles, through which the ritual quality of the work is most vividly conveyed. ARNOLD WHITTALL

Curphey, Margaret (*b* Douglas, Isle of Man, 27 Feb 1938). British soprano. She studied at the Birmingham School of Music. After touring with Opera for All, she joined Sadler's Wells in 1965. A full and flexible lyric soprano enabled her to play a wide range of parts, from Mimì, Pamina and Violetta to Ellen Orford, Elisabeth de Valois and Santuzza, all sung with taste and distinction and acted with reserve. In Wagner, however, she progressed from a capable, vocally well-projected Eva (notably at the first Coliseum performances in August 1968), Elsa and Gutrune, to a Sieglinde (first London appearance, 1975) of rich vocal amplitude and real pathos. She undertook her first *Walküre* Brünnhilde two months later and a complete Brünnhilde in autumn 1977, but retired because of ill-health. MAX LOPPERT

Currie, Russell (*b* North Arlington, NJ, 3 April 1954). American composer of Scottish descent. He graduated from Brooklyn College, CUNY (1981), where he studied composition with Robert Starer and the piano with Paul Jacobs. In 1988 he founded Orra, an organization whose purpose is to produce contemporary music and develop interdisciplinary arts projects that combine music with dance, film, plays, photography and painting, and he is director of the music-theatre programme at the 3rd Street School in New York.

Currie's compositions include music for several films and a number of chamber works, but his major focus has been chamber opera. His trilogy, *The Cask of Amontillado* (1982), *A Dream within a Dream* (1984) and *Ligeia* (1986), is derived from short stories by Edgar Allan Poe. The works were commissioned by the Bronx Arts Ensemble and the first two (staged in 1984 and 1985 respectively) were produced together in 1988 by Jersey Lyric Opera (5 June) and by Orra at Symphony Space, New York (10 June); *Ligeia* was revised and expanded in 1990.

Through his arching lines, lean though colourful orchestration and cool eclecticism, Currie sustains the ominous moods of Poe's allegory about man's tormented inner life. With suggestions of *Wozzeck*, Currie conjures up musical images of madness not unlike those of Alban Berg, another admirer of Poe. Currie's fourth opera, *Rimshot*, portrays the banishment and return to celebrity of a rock drummer. It melds music, text, costumes, movement and visual effects in a music-theatre work that the composer claims 'takes opera as its starting point'.

The Cask of Amontillado (chamber op, 1, C. Laanes, after E. A. Poe), concert perf., New York, Fordham U., 3 April 1982; stage, New York, TOMI Theater, 22 March 1984 [pt 1 of trilogy]

A Dream within a Dream (chamber op, 1, R. Kornfeld, after Poe: *The Fall of the House of Usher*), concert perf., New York, Wave Hill, 29 April 1984; stage, New York, Lehman Center for the Performing Arts, 15 June 1985; rev., concert perf., New York, Merkin Concert Hall, 11 May 1986 [pt 2 of trilogy]

Ligeia (op/fantasy, 2, Kornfeld, after Poe), concert perf., Riverdale, Young Men's-Young Women's Hebraic Association, NJ, 5 April 1987; rev. 1990 [pt 3 of trilogy]

Rimshot (music-theatre work, 6 scenes, R. Singer), New York, Pace Downtown, 10 May 1990

*

R. H. Kornick: *Recent American Opera: a Production Guide* (New York, 1991) ELISE K. KIRK

Curtain (Fr. *rideau*; Ger. *Vorhang*; It. *sipario*). A hanging screen of cloth separating the stage from the auditorium, capable of being removed during the action, or any concealing drapery. The word is used by extension for the end of an act or scene, when the curtain might fall (hence the cue 'curtain') and the theatrical effect at the end of an act (hence 'strong curtain').

Though the ancient Greeks probably invented the theatrical curtain, its first certain use dates from Roman times, when it was hung before the *scaenae frons* and dropped as the performance began, revealing the splendour of the façade and whatever scenery was set up. The curtain, having fallen into a trough, could be raised on poles to conceal the stage again. This system was revived in Italian Renaissance theatres with their picture-frame stages, perhaps as early as 1515 (and it was used as a gag in the modern musical *A Funny Thing Happened on the Way to the Forum*). For Renaissance and Baroque operas, scene shifts were accomplished with sliding wings and shutters painted in perspective; changes took place *a vista* – in full view of the audience – and were part of the spectacle. 'Discovered' scenes were revealed by opening painted shutters. The curtain was not used except at the beginning and end of a performance or whenever the stage needed to be covered so that a tableau might be arranged. The classical tradition of the front curtain's dropping instead of rising did not last beyond the Renaissance, when roller curtains were introduced; keeping the stage visible during scene shifts was given up in the 19th century with the advent of realistic, three-dimensional scenery, the difficult changing of which was better left hidden. Some contemporary designers abjure the curtain and realism and prefer darkening the stage for shifts, covering changes with projections on a front scrim (a gauze curtain stretched across the proscenium opening), staging visible scene changes, or using a 'unit' setting for the whole performance.

By the time opera developed, two curtain types had been established: traverse (draw) and flown (drop). Variations on these have evolved, the tableau being the most popular in opera houses because of its graceful sweeping up and to the sides. Curtains are frequently made of a rich-looking fabric, often velour; the Metropolitan Opera House has one of gold patterned silk damask. Sometimes lavish and decorative curtains are abandoned for austere productions to which they are not well suited.

In addition to a theatre's main curtain (sometimes rigged to operate mechanically as draw, drop, tableau or

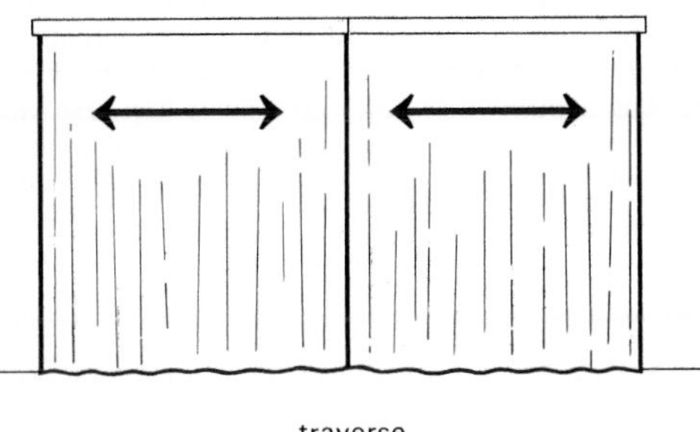
traverse

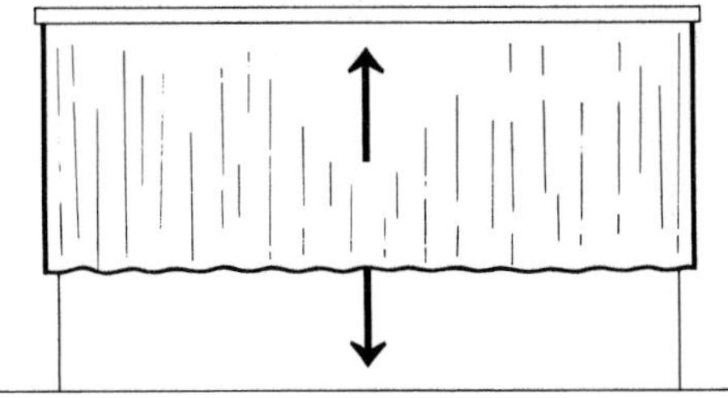
flown

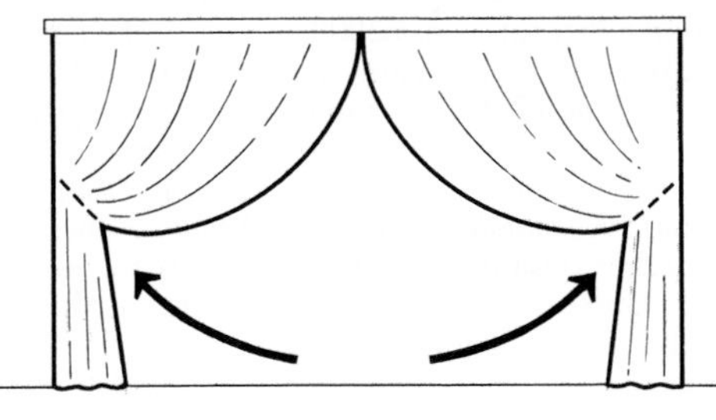
tableau

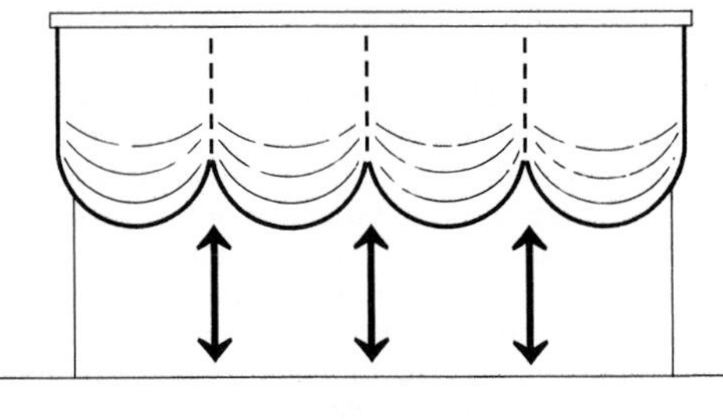
contour

The four principal curtain actions

contour), a designer may add a special show curtain for use between acts and scenes. Curtains can be treated as scenic units and painted, or within settings they can cover alcoves or windows. A stage can be hung completely with curtains to form a standard wing-border-drop setting, and backstage curtains are regularly used to mask back- and above-stage areas.

For further illustration *see* CROSATO, GIAMBATTISTA.

EDWARD A. LANGHANS

Curtain call. At the end of a performance, the cast of the opera traditionally take a bow, together with the conductor and, on first nights of a new production, the director, designer, chorus master and, if there is one, the choreographer. In some houses, or on special occasions, curtain calls may be taken after each act.

Depending on the performance traditions of the opera house or, in recent years, the whim of the director, the individuals may bow first at the end of the performance, before the ensemble, especially if the opera has ended with a solo or duet that arouses enthusiastic applause. For instance, at the Opéra Bastille, in its initial series of performances of Berlioz's *La prise de Troie*, Grace Bumbry, who sang Cassandra, took a solo bow immediately at the end of the final scene. The order in which individual performers may appear before the curtain is dictated by their voice types, basses, baritones, contraltos and mezzos usually taking their bows before tenors and sopranos, but it is usual for the artist singing a title role to come last. This may be excepted if there is a star singer in one of the other parts, for instance the soprano who sings the Marschallin may sometimes take the final curtain call, after the artist who has sung the title role in *Der Rosenkavalier*. In Russia it is traditional for the players to return the audience's applause at the final curtain call, and in many houses the public will bring flowers to throw on the stage, or be presented formally as tributes, handed to the artists by a flunkey. It is said that at La Scala, during her stormy reign there, Maria Callas, who was very shortsighted, could pick out by their scent the flowers from the vegetables that her detractors hurled across the footlights. An artist who fears that his or her reception may be unfavourable may choose not to take a solo curtain call. Some directors have refused to allow more than a single ensemble curtain call.

As a dramatic device, the curtain call features in scenes in Cilea's *Adriana Lecouvreur*, Noël Coward's *Operette* and Leoncavallo's *Pagliacci*. In Offenbach's *Belle Lurette*, the curtain call is the subject of an aria, 'On s'amuse, on applaudit'. The largest number of curtain calls ever – 165 – was achieved, according to the *Guinness Book of Records*, by Luciano Pavarotti, after a performance of *L'elisir d'amore* in Berlin in 1988.

See also CLAQUE and PRIMA DONNA.

PATRICK O'CONNOR

Curtain tune. Term used for an overture in certain English plays and semi-operas of the late 17th century; *see* ACT MUSIC.

Curtin [née Smith], **Phyllis** (*b* Clarksburg, WV, 3 Dec 1922). American soprano. She studied singing with Olga Averino and later with the bass Joseph Regneas. Her first important opera appearances were with the New England Opera Theatre in Boston as Lisa in *The Queen of Spades* and Lady Billows in *Albert Herring*, followed in 1953 by a début with the New York City Opera in von Einem's *Der Prozess*. Her varied roles at the City Opera over the next ten years included all the major Mozart heroines, Violetta, Salome, Walton's Cressida and Susannah in Floyd's opera, a role she created. Engagements in Vienna, Buenos Aires and Frankfurt, and with the Metropolitan (début, 4 November 1961), La Scala and Scottish Opera in the 1960s brought her international repute. She retired from singing in public in 1984. If she lacked the star qualities of more celebrated operatic sopranos, Curtin's singing was always much respected for its cultivated musicality, interpretative grace and vocal purity. PETER G. DAVIS

Curtis, Alan (Stanley) (*b* Mason, MI, 17 Nov 1934). American musicologist, harpsichordist and conductor. He studied at Michigan State University and at the University of Illinois (PhD 1963); from 1957 to 1959 he studied in Amsterdam with Gustav Leonhardt. In 1960 he joined the University of California at Berkeley, becoming professor in 1970. An early advocate of the historically informed performance of music of the 17th and 18th centuries, he has achieved a considerable reputation as a harpsichordist and conductor in the USA and in Europe. Among his recordings are Monteverdi's *Poppea*, Cavalli's *Erismena* and Handel's *Admeto* and he has conducted operas by Rameau (*Dardanus*), Landi (*Il Sant'Alessio*), Jommelli (*La schiava liberata*) and Cesti (*Il Tito*); in 1984 he conducted Gluck's *Armide* on the opening of the restored Bibiena Theatre in Bologna. Curtis's edition of *Poppea* was published in 1989; he has also edited *La schiava liberata*, with Marita McClymonds, and he conducted the modern première (1982, Netherlands Opera). PHILIP BRETT

Cuvilliéstheater. Munich theatre, originally built at the Bavarian court by François Cuvilliés and opened in 1753; it is also known as the Residenztheater. *See* MUNICH, §§2 and 3(i).

Cuyás y Borés, Vicenc (*b* Palma de Mallorca, 6 Feb 1816; *d* Barcelona, 7 March 1839). Spanish composer. He abandoned medical studies in Barcelona to undertake musical composition with Ramón Vilanova. At 19 he attracted attention with a symphony dedicated to the actress Matilde Díez performed at the Principal (sometimes called Santa Cruz) theatre. Composing under the influence of Bellini, Cuyás left unfinished *Ugo conte di Parigi* (to a libretto by Romani) in order to complete in record time the two-act *La Fattucchiera* (Romani, after Arlincourt: *Ismalie, ou L'amour et la mort*; MS score in Villanueva y Geltrú, Biblioteca-Museo Balaguer). Romani's libretto had previously been set by Mercadante (1832) and Carnicer (1838) as *Ismalia, ossia Morte ed amore*. Cuyás's opera was a resounding success at its opening at the Principal in Barcelona on 17 June 1838, and the audience called for the 22-year-old composer to appear on stage. The denouement, in which the heroine Ismalia, victimized by the vengeful sorceress, joins the shade of her deceased lover, particularly moved the public. The opera was given 20 performances the first season and seven the next. Cuyás had, however, undermined his health and contracted tuberculosis. Friends who gathered at his bedside the night of 7 March 1839 reported that the composer's death coincided with the closing scene of the final performance. (A third Romani setting, *El sonámbulo*, was never finished.)

*

LaborD

B. Saldoni: *Diccionario biográfico-bibliográfico de efemérides de músicos españoles* (Madrid, 1868–81), ii, 42, 79

F. Pedrell: *Diccionario biográfico y bibliográfico de músicos y escritores de música españoles, portugueses e hispano-americanos antiguos y modernos* (Barcelona, 1897), 465–72

R. Mitjana: 'La Musique en Espagne', *EMDC*, I/iv (1920), 2317

J. Subirá: *La ópera en los teatros de Barcelona*, ii (Barcelona, 1946), 16–18 JOHN DOWLING

Cuzzoni, Francesca (*b* Parma, 2 April 1696; *d* Bologna, 19 June 1778). Italian soprano. Her parents were Angelo, a professional violinist, and Marina Castelli. She was a pupil of Francesco Lanzi; her first known appearance was in an anonymous *La virtù coronata, o Il Fernando* (1714, Parma). She sang in 1716–17 at Bologna in operas by Bassani, Buini, Gasparini and Orlandini and by 1717–18 was 'virtuosa di camera' to the Grand Princess Violante of Tuscany, singing at Florence, Siena, Mantua, Genoa and Reggio Emilia in operas by Orlandini, C. F. Pollarolo and Vivaldi (*Scanderbeg*). She made her Venice début in 1718 as Dalinda in Pollarolo's *Ariodante*, with Faustina Bordoni as Ginevra; the future rivals appeared there again in two operas the following year. Cuzzoni sang at Florence and Milan in 1719, at Turin, Bologna and Florence in 1720, at Padua in 1721 and in five more operas at Venice in 1721–2; in Orlandini's *Nerone* she played Poppaea, with Faustina as Octavia and Diana Vico as Agrippina.

She went to London at the end of 1722, having married the composer and harpsichordist Pietro Giuseppe Sandoni on the way. Her reputation preceded her. Her King's Theatre début on 12 January 1723 as Teofane in Handel's *Ottone* was sensational. The part had not been composed for her and at rehearsal she refused to sing her first aria, 'Falsa immagine', until Handel threatened to pitch her out of the window; but her triumph was complete. At her benefit on 25 March 'some of the Nobility gave her 60 Guineas a Ticket' (in addition to her salary of £2000 a season). She remained a member of the company until the Royal Academy closed in June 1728 and sang in every opera: Handel's *Flavio* (Emilia), *Giulio Cesare* (Cleopatra; she and Senesino had an outstanding success), *Tamerlano* (Asteria), *Rodelinda* (title role), *Scipione* (Berenice), *Alessandro* (Lisaura), *Admeto* (Antigona), *Riccardo Primo* (Costanza), *Radamisto* (Polissena in the 1728 revival), *Siroe* (Laodice) and *Tolomeo* (Seleuce), Ariosti's *Coriolano*, *Vespasiano*, *Aquilio Consolo*, *Artaserse*, *Dario*, *Lucio Vero* and *Teuzzone*, Bononcini's *Erminia*, *Farnace*, *Calpurnia* and *Astianatte*, and the pasticcios *Elpidia* and *Elisa*. The exuberance of her admirers soon led to quarrels, first with the partisans of Senesino and later with those of Faustina Bordoni, who made her London début in *Alessandro* in 1726. The rivalry between the two great sopranos was notorious and became a public scandal when ovations, whistles and catcalls in turn led to a scuffle on stage during *Astianatte* on 6 June 1727. Cuzzoni was dismissed by the Academy, but reinstated when the King threatened to withdraw his subsidy. The final Academy season seems to have been less cantankerous, despite (or because of) the satirical portrait of the ladies as Polly and Lucy in *The Beggar's Opera*.

Cuzzoni spent winter 1728–9 in Vienna at the invitation of Count Kinsky, the imperial ambassador in London; she made a great impression but was not engaged for the opera because she demanded an exorbitant salary. She sang at Modena and Venice in 1729. Heidegger wished to engage both prima donnas for the Second Royal Academy that autumn, but Handel, who according to Rolli had never liked Faustina and wanted to forget Cuzzoni, preferred new voices. In 1730–31 Cuzzoni sang at Piacenza, Bologna, in Hasse's *Ezio* and Sarro's *Artemisia* at Naples, and in three operas, including Hasse's *Artaserse*, in Venice. During 1731–2 she appeared again in Venice and Florence in operas by Hasse and her husband, and at Genoa in the carnival seasons of 1733 and 1734, still in close association with Sandoni. She was one of the first singers approached by the Opera of the Nobility, in opposition to Handel in 1733; she arrived in April 1734 and joined the cast of Porpora's *Arianna in Nasso*. She sang in four more operas by Porpora (*Enea nel Lazio*, *Polifemo*, *Ifigenia in Aulide* and *Mitridate*), Hasse's *Artaserse*, Handel's *Ottone* (her old part, but under Nobility management), Sandoni's *Issipile*, Veracini's *Adriano in Siria*, the pasticcio *Orfeo* and Francesco Ciampi's *Onorio*. She seems to have aroused less enthusiasm on this visit.

Cuzzoni sang in Leo's *Olimpiade* and Caldara's *Ormisda* at Florence in 1737–8; the following carnival season she performed operas by Leo and Arena in Turin, receiving the huge sum of 8000 lire. Later in 1739 she was at Vienna, and in September 1740 she was a member of Angelo Mingotti's opera company at Hamburg. She sang in Amsterdam in 1742 with the Wolfenbüttel Kapellmeister Giovanni Verocai (she and Sandoni had now separated) and is said to have published there a new setting of Metastasio's *Il Palladio conservato* (no copy is known). After 1749 she was plagued with debts and an aging voice; her time was spent alternately in prison for debt or giving concerts to pay her debtors. In February 1750 she performed in Paris before the French queen; in 1750 and 1751 she revisited London and sang at concerts, but was coldly received. She spent her last years in Bologna, supporting herself, it is said, by making buttons. She died in obscurity and extreme poverty.

Cuzzoni in her prime was by universal consent a superb artist. Burney expressed the views of various writers, including Tosi, Quantz and particularly Mancini (*Pensieri e riflessioni pratiche sopra il canto figurato*, 1774):

> It was difficult for the hearer to determine whether she most excelled in slow or rapid airs. A native warble enabled her to execute divisions with such facility as to conceal every appearance of difficulty; and so grateful and touching was the natural tone of her voice, that she rendered pathetic whatever she sung, in which she had leisure to unfold its whole volume. The art of conducting, sustaining, increasing, and diminishing her tones by minute degrees, acquired her, among professors, the title of complete mistress of her art. In a cantabile air, though the notes she added were few, she never lost a favourable opportunity of enriching the cantilena with all the refinements and embellishments of the time. Her shake was perfect, she had a creative fancy, and the power of occasionally accelerating and retarding the measure in the most artificial and able manner, by what the Italians call *tempo rubato*. Her high notes were unrivalled in clearness and sweetness; and her intonations were so just and fixed, that it seemed as if it was not in her power to sing out of tune.

Tosi praised her 'delightful soothing *Cantabile*', and contrasted her pre-eminence in 'Pathetick' with Faustina's dramatic fire in 'Allegro'. Quantz, who heard her often in 1727, said that 'her style of singing was innocent and affecting', and her graces 'took possession of the soul of every auditor, by her tender and touching expression'. She could move an audience to tears in such simple arias as 'Falsa immagine' and Rodelinda's 'Hò perduto il caro sposo'. She was probably at her best on her first visit to London, and the wonderful series of parts Handel wrote for her, especially Cleopatra, Asteria, Rodelinda and Antigone, seems perfectly calculated to bring out the qualities mentioned above. They call for a fluid use of the whole compass from *c′* to *b″* (Quantz said she sang up to *c‴*) and offer repeated openings for her famous trill, which was slow and sensuous. Cuzzoni was the first female high soprano to distinguish herself in prime roles. Although not inclined to extremely fast passage-work, she was capable of singing coloratura arias extremely difficult for their variety of rhythm and figuration, such as 'Sprezzando il suol' in Porpora's *Enea* or 'Da tempeste' in *Giulio Cesare*; features include short florid passages, unexpectedly rising to the higher register and then abruptly truncated on a staccato note (usually *a″* or *b″*). Other arias, such as 'Conservati fedele' in Hasse's *Artaserse* or the Largo 'Ombre, piante', again in *Rodelinda*, show an equally definite propensity to the noble and the pathetic. Cuzzoni was neither a great actress nor a beautiful woman. Horace Walpole, with reference to *Rodelinda*, said:

> she was short and squat, with a doughy cross face, but fine expression; was not a good actress; dressed ill; and was silly and fantastical. And yet on her appearing in this opera, in a *brown silk gown*, trimmed with silver, with the vulgarity and indecorum of which all the old ladies were much scandalized, the young adopted it as a fashion, so universally, that it seemed a national uniform for youth and beauty.

The best likeness of Cuzzoni is a print after Seeman, reproduced in Hawkins's *History*. She appears in many caricatures, including two operatic scenes engraved by Vanderbank (1723) and Goupy (1729) and original drawings by A. M. Zanetti (two in the Cini collection, *I-Vgc*) and Marco Ricci (two at Windsor Castle).

*

DBI (B. M. Antolini) — WINTON DEAN, CARLO VITALI

Cvejić [Tzveych], **Biserka** (*b* Krilo-Jesenice, nr Split, 5 Nov 1923). Croatian mezzo-soprano. She studied with Josip Rijavec at the Academy of Music in Belgrade and in 1950 sang Maddalena with the Belgrade Opera. She made her official début (as Charlotte in Massenet's *Werther*) with the same company in 1954, remaining a member until 1959. She sang with the Vienna Staatsoper, 1959–79, and the Zagreb Opera, 1975–8, and during this period appeared at a number of important opera houses, including the Metropolitan, the Arena in Verona, La Scala and Covent Garden. Her dramatic voice was even, polished, technically assured and ideally suited to such roles as Verdi's Amneris, Eboli and Azucena, Bizet's Carmen and Saint-Saëns' Delilah. She retired from the stage in 1990. ROKSANDA PEJOVIĆ

Cymon. Dramatic romance in five acts by MICHAEL ARNE to a libretto by DAVID GARRICK after JOHN DRYDEN's play *Cymon and Iphigenia*; London, Theatre Royal, Drury Lane, 2 January 1767.

In this Arcadian romance 'simple Cymon' (tenor), a prince held captive by the enchantress Urganda (soprano), falls in love with the shepherdess Sylvia (soprano). Urganda threatens Sylvia with dire punishment but is foiled by the superior power of the magician Merlin (tenor), and the lovers are finally united. This was Michael Arne's most successful work, with 64 performances in seven seasons. A vocal score was published in 1767; for a later revival three new songs, one by Dibdin, were added. Sylvia's aria 'This cold flinty heart' was popular and frequently reprinted, as was 'Care flies from the lad that is merry', sung by the shepherd Linco (tenor). A revival on 17 January 1778 advertised 'a new overture and additional airs and choruses' all by Arne. A revival by Sheridan's Drury Lane company in 1791 included music by Stephen Storace and Thomas Shaw. As late as 1827 Bishop revived the work at Covent Garden. Arne's vocal style is unfailingly inventive, if not original, and he succeeds in writing music appropriate to each character and situation. JOHN A. PARKINSON

Cyrano de Bergerac. *Commedia eroica* in four acts by FRANCO ALFANO to a libretto by HENRI CAIN after Edmond Rostand; Rome, Teatro Reale (as *Cyrano di Bergerac*, Italian translation by C. Meano and F. Brusa), 22 January 1936 (original French, Paris, Opéra-Comique, 29 May 1936).

In Act 1, set in the Hôtel de Bourgogne, Paris, in 1640, Cyrano (tenor), captain of the Gascon cadets, poet and swashbuckler, struts among the assembled company, throwing out an actor who has cast eyes on his beloved cousin Roxane (soprano), duelling with a Viscount who has dared to refer to his huge nose and composing a poem the while. On hearing that a gang of ruffians has waylaid a comrade, he sets out to deal with them single-handed. Act 2 begins in the bakery of Ragueneau (baritone), where Cyrano meets Roxane; she confides to him her love for a new recruit, Christian de Neuveville (tenor), and commends him to her cousin's care. Sick at heart, he agrees to her request. A fellow-officer, Carbon (bass), enters with a crowd at his heels to congratulate Cyrano on his latest exploit; they sing a duet with chorus in praise of the Gascon cadets ('Ce sont les cadets de Gascogne'). Christian is presented to Cyrano, who promises to help him win Roxane's hand, putting his poetic gifts at the young man's service. After sending her love-letters written by Cyrano, Christian determines to press his suit in person; at Roxane's window, he expresses himself so ineptly that she retires in dudgeon. At Cyrano's suggestion he then calls Roxane on to the balcony while his captain feeds him suitably poetic lines, eventually delivering them himself in Christian's voice; Roxane at once yields to her young lover. The third act is set during the siege of Arras, where Cyrano heartens the demoralized cadets by bidding an old shepherd pipe to them a song from the Dordogne, and mercilessly exposes the cowardice of their commander De Guiche (baritone), one of Roxane's unsuccessful suitors. Christian receives a visit from Roxane, now his wife, whom the perennial gallantry of the Spaniards has permitted to cross the enemy lines. She tells him that his letters (written by Cyrano) have so touched her that she would adore him even if he were as ugly as sin. Realizing the full import of her words, Christian sadly tells Cyrano that it is he whom Roxane really loves; but then the trumpets summon them to battle and Christian is killed. Act 4 is set 15 years later; Roxane has retired to a convent. Cyrano arrives, pale and haggard, mortally wounded in an affray. Roxane produces Christian's last letter to her, which Cyrano reads aloud; as he does so, she recognizes the voice she heard long ago beneath her balcony. To a reminiscence of the love scene from Act 2, Cyrano dies in her arms.

Cyrano de Bergerac is cast in the spare, neo-classical style of Alfano's later years. The idiom remains diatonic, with abundant use of parallel discords; the vocal writing owes something to Debussy's *Pelléas et Mélisande*.

JULIAN BUDDEN

Cythère assiégée ('Cythera Besieged'). *Opéra comique* in one act by CHRISTOPH WILLIBALD GLUCK to a libretto by CHARLES-SIMON FAVART (1748) after Favart and Christophe Barthélemy Fagan's *opéra comique Le pouvoir de l'Amour ou Le siège de Cythère* (1743); Vienna, Burgtheater, spring 1759 (revised, by Favart, as an *opéra-ballet* in three acts, Paris, Opéra, 1 August 1775).

Favart's text (originally in vaudevilles and prose, only the former in 1748) is a loose parody of Quinault and Lully's *Armide* of 1686, as is confirmed by Cochin's frontispiece to the libretto, engraved after Boucher's painting *Armide et Renaud*. In a clear sexual allegory, the Scythian warriors Brontès and Barbarin (baritones) and Olgar (tenor in Vienna, *haute-contre* in Paris) assail the fortifications of Cythera, but fall captive to the charms of the nymphs Cloé, Daphné and Carite (in the 1775 version, also Doris; all sopranos), in successive scenes. Gluck's 1759 setting features vocal and dance airs, alternately voluptuous and martial, and at times combined in large-scale tableaux; a powerful central choral confrontation; and a closing *ballet général*. His use of Turkish instruments for the Scythians foreshadows his musical characterization of this group in *Iphigénie en Tauride*.

The 1775 version is a thorough reworking, with even greater emphasis on spectacle, and much new and borrowed music. In revising some of his original *airs nouveaux*, Gluck vitiated their Bohemian (and martial-sounding) tonic accents, apparently out of consideration for proper French declamation. BRUCE ALAN BROWN

Czaar und Zimmermann, oder Die zwei Peter. Original title of Albert Lortzing's *ZAR UND ZIMMERMANN*.

Czech Republic.

1. The 18th century. 2. 1807–90. 3. After 1890.

1. THE 18TH CENTURY. Opera became an important genre in the Czech lands (*see also* SLOVAKIA) only in the 18th century, by which time the Habsburg domination of Bohemia and Moravia was so complete that their inhabitants had virtually lost the most important aspects of their national identity – their language (Czech) and their religion (an indigenous and early type of Protestantism based on the teachings of Jan Hus). By 1781, when Joseph II proclaimed religious freedom, only 2% of Czechs professed to be Protestants, and by then Czech too was virtually extinct as a language of artistic and learned discourse, despite the high status and culture it had achieved by the 17th century. Schooling was in German, and Czech survived only in the country, fostered largely by nationalistically inclined school teachers. The result was that German affected the lives and even the works of the earliest generations of Czech opera composers. František Škroup, the composer of the first professional Czech opera, wrote only three Czech operas but eight German ones. Among his successors Dvořák wrote his first opera, and Fibich all his juvenille operas, in German. Smetana, the 'father of Czech music' and the most fervent Czech patriot among musicians of his generation, was educated in German, and found this the most natural language for correspondence and even for his diary. It was not until his fourth opera that he learnt how to overcome problems of misplaced stress in his setting of Czech.

Consequently, although many operas were written in the 18th century and early 19th by Czech composers such as Mysliveček, Gassmann, Koželuch, the Benda family, Gyrowetz, Wranitzky, Tomášek, Rösler and others, they were in Italian (or later in German and French), not in Czech. In the 18th century the Czech capital, Prague, could be considered operatically as just another German city, with opera sponsored by a few noblemen (especially Count Franz Anton Sporck) and with regular tours by Italian travelling companies (impresarios included Antonio Denzio, Santo Lapis, the Mingottis, G. B. Locatelli, Giuseppe Bustelli and Pasquale Bondini). When, in the 19th century, the linguistic battle for opera began, it was a German opera company, not a Czech one, that ousted the regular Italian company at the Prague Estates Theatre in 1807. The theatre's first music directors were Wenzel Müller (until 1813) and Weber (1813–16), known for their later promotion of German-language opera in Vienna and Dresden respectively. What distinguished the Czechs was the quality of their music education. Music was taught at even the most humble rural schools, a fact commemorated in their different ways by both Burney and Wagner. It was Prague, not Vienna, where Mozart's music achieved cult status, and two of his mature operas were commissioned by the Estates Theatre.

The only Czech 'operas' from the 18th century were amateur affairs, usually short and undemanding. Some, such as the group of 'Haná Singspiels', traded on the distinctive Moravian dialect of the Haná region. Others such as *Pargamotéka* (1747) and *Landebork* (?1757–8) had a political slant (proclaiming loyalty to the dynasty). These two works originated in a monastery near Olomouc and are thought to be by a Cistercian monk, Father Alanus Plumlovský. Monks, often coming from rural backgrounds, would have been more likely than other educated classes to know Czech at this time; the use of the vernacular may have been considered simply an entertaining diversion rather than an early expression of patriotism.

From 1785 Czech actors in the German drama company at the Estates theatre began to perform the first plays in Czech. With influential support from Joseph II, the company, known as the Vlastenské Divadlo (Patriotic Theatre), became independent and for the next 20 years presented works (including Singspiels and plays with music) in German or Czech according to demand. The repertory from the early 1790s included a number of Czech adaptations of Viennese Singspiels: Ignaz Umlauf's *Die Bergknappen*, Dittersdorf's *Hieronymus Knicker* and, in 1794, Mozart's *Die Zauberflöte*. Of the known repertory to 1807, 57 musical works are recorded as being performed in Czech.

2. 1807–90. After the demise of the Patriotic Theatre no Czech professional stage performances took place in Prague until 1824, when the playwright Jan Nepomuk Štěpánek was appointed at the Estates Theatre expressly to foster Czech theatre. The Czech company there worked under peculiar restraints: performances in Czech were generally restricted to weekend matinées (between 1824 and 1834 only 320 Czech performances took place). Nevertheless a demanding repertory was given (a third were operas by composers such as Mozart, Rossini, Cherubini, Méhul, Weber and Spohr) and, with the Czech national revival well under way, audiences for Czech performances were constantly increasing. It was during this period that the first professional Czech operas were written, notably by František Škroup, none of them performed frequently enough, however, to constitute a continuous tradition of indigenous Czech opera.

Although Czech performances flourished in the years around the 1848 revolution, substantial progress came only when political conditions had relaxed sufficiently in 1862 to allow the opening of a purely Czech theatre, the Provisional Theatre. The true beginnings of a continuous tradition of Czech opera can be traced to here. Although, as its title suggests, the Provisional Theatre was intended as a temporary institution, 20 years passed before it was replaced; most of the operas of Smetana and his immediate contemporaries (Skuherský, Šebor, Bendl, Blodek, Rozkošný, Hřímalý) were written for the Provisional Theatre and its loyal band of soloists.

Until a body of Czech opera had been built up, foreign operas in translation dominated the repertory. German opera (with the exception of those by composers with Czech links – Mozart, Weber, Gluck) was unacceptable; Italian opera (Rossini to early Verdi) was popular and particularly suited the italianate training of the singers and the smallness of the stage and orchestra. French opera was encouraged as an antidote to the other two traditions (among others by Smetana during his time as music director at the theatre, 1866–74) and, despite the difficulty of presenting grand opera in such modest circumstances, Meyerbeer became an integral part of the repertory. Grand opera had a discernible impact on the earliest operas written for the Provisional Theatre, but so did Italian operatic conventions. There are traces of the cantabile–cabaletta and the concertato finale in several of Smetana's operas; for all his reservations Smetana sometimes employed coloratura and, with a couple of exceptions (notably *Dalibor*), he wrote for light italianate voices rather than heavy dramatic ones.

A Czech dimension derived from the subject matter: historical operas, usually serious, were based on Czech medieval and mythical history, while operas based on folklore, usually comedies, celebrated rural life. Much emphasis was placed in conservative circles on the use of folk music, but this was resisted by Smetana (whose use of folksong is minimal) – although he was prepared to base numbers on dance patterns such as the slow-waltz *sousedská* and the polka. His operas also contain several named dances; *The Bartered Bride*, with its *skočná*, polka and furiant, is the best-known example.

The most valuable source of Czechness was the Czech language itself, which, unlike almost all other European languages, regularly stresses the first syllables of words. The syncopations produced by long, unstressed vowels and short, stressed vowels make the sound of Czech particularly distinctive. These characteristics were muted in many early Czech operas, however, by incompetent word-setting, by the survival of a type of prosody based not on stress but on vowel length and by librettists' determination to use iambs, considered 'high style' but which go against the rhythmic character of the language. The most Czech-sounding librettos Smetana set were those such as *The Bartered Bride* and *The Two Widows*, which rely heavily on trochees.

The death of Smetana in 1884 and the move to the large, well-equipped National Theatre (permanently in 1883) brought to an end this type of specifically Czech opera. In his long operatic life Dvořák kept mostly to Czech or Slavonic subjects, but the next generation of Czech opera composers, Fibich, Foerster and Ostrčil, were far more apt to explore non-Czech subjects and take a more Wagnerian approach to the orchestra and vocal conventions. There is no evidence that this appeared to the public; the most popular operas by these composers were those based on Czech subjects. Yet considerable influence was still wielded by critics such as Hostinský and Nejedlý, who attempted to mould Czech tastes into what they considered a 'progressive' line, a view that led to their wholesale rejection of Dvořák and his pupils.

3. After 1890. The period from about 1890 to 1940 was the heyday of Czech operatic performance, with strong artistic leadership given by several successive composer-conductors (Kovařovic and Ostrčil in Prague; Neumann in Brno), a wealth of fine singers, many of whom (Burian, Destinn) made international careers, and innovatory directors (Pujman) and stage designers (Čapek, František Muzika). The German Theatre in Prague, under a distinguished series of conductors (Mahler, Much, Schalk, Blech, Klemperer and Kleiber), continued to serve the highly cultured German minority until its expulsion in 1945. Apart from Kovařovic and Ostrčil, prominent Czech opera composers of the period include Foerster, Novák, Jeremiáš, Karel, Hába and E. F. Burian. The best-known Czech composers of the period, however, were all outside the mainstream. Martinů had settled in Paris in 1923 and, although he wrote some operas in Czech for Prague, his work was increasingly in other languages and for other publics. Weinberger had an international success with his opera *Švanda dudák* ('Schwanda the Bagpiper') but for all its assiduous milking of Czech sentimental-nationalist formulae it failed to attract much of a local following. Janáček's career was centred on the Moravian capital, Brno, and he was over 60 before Prague eventually got round to staging his masterpiece, *Jenůfa*, in 1916. Janáček's early operas had been based on Czech nationalist models but thereafter he was his own man, with a musical language shaped by the much richer, eastward-looking traditions of Moravian folk music, an interest in fashionable European opera composers and his own considerable dramatic gifts. No later Czech opera composer matched his stature.

Although the postwar Communist administration provided generous funding enabling the continuation of opera in many centres (Prague, Brno, Plzeň, Ostrava, Ústí nad Labem, Liberec, České Budějovice, Opava and Olomouc), operatic achievements were notably fewer, with no strong artistic personalities emerging either as conductors or composers and a gradual decline in vocal standards. The most productive and performed Czech composer of the period was Jiří Pauer; others include Josef Berg, J. F. Fischer, Luboš Fišer, Jan Hanuš, Karel Horký, Ilja Hurník, Ivo Jirásek, Iša Krejčí, Otmar Mácha and Evžen Zámečník.

For further information on operatic life in the country's principal centres *see* Brno; České Budějovice; Jaroměřice nad Rokytnou; Kuks; Liberec; Olomouc; Opava; Ostrava; Plzeň; Prague; Teplice; and Ústí nad Labem.

*

O. Teuber: *Geschichte des Prager Theaters: von den Anfangen des Schauspielwesens bis auf die neueste Zeit* (Prague, 1883–8)
O. Hostinský: *Bedřich Smetana a jeho boj o moderní českou hudbu* [Smetana and his Struggle for Modern Czech Music] (Prague, 1901, 2/1941, ed. B. Hostinský)
V. A. J. Hornové: *Česká zpěvohra* [Czech Opera] (Prague, 1903)
Z. Nejedlý: *Česká moderní zpěvohra po Smetanovi* [Modern Czech Opera after Smetana] (Prague, 1911)
J. Hutter and Z. Chalabala, eds.: *České umění dramatické*, ii: *zpěvohra* [Czech Dramatic Art, ii: Opera] (Prague, 1941)
L. Novák: *Stará garda Národního divadla* [The Old Guard at the National Theatre] (Prague, 1944)
V. H. Jarka, ed.: *Kritické dílo Bedřicha Smetany* [Smetana's Works of Criticism] (Prague, 1948)
M. Očadlík: *Smetanovi libretisté* [Smetana's Librettists] (Prague, 1948)
——: 'Soupis českých tištěných operních textů' [Catalogue of Czech Printed Operatic Texts], *MMC*, vii (1958) [whole vol.]
E. Hermannová and V. Lébl: *Soupis české hudebně dramatické tvorby* [A List of Musico-Dramatic Works] (Prague, 1959)
P. Eckstein: *Czechoslovak Opera: a Brief Outline* (Prague, 1964)
——: *Die tschechoslowakische zeitgenössischer Oper/The Czechoslovak Contemporary Opera* (Prague and Bratislava, 1967)
F. Černý, ed.: *Dějiny českého divadla* [The History of Czech Theatre] (Prague, 1968–)
J. Vratislavský: *Neumannová éra v brněnské opeře* [The Neumann Era in the Brno Opera] (Brno, 1971)
L. Jehne: 'K problematice smetanovských hlasových oborù a pěveckých typù' [The Problem of Smetana's Voice Categories and Types of Singers], *HV*, xi (1974), 125–34
J. Sehnal: 'Počátky opeory na Moravě' [The Beginnings of Opera in Moravia], *O divadle na Moravě*, ed. E. Petrù and J. Stýskal (Prague, 1974), 55–77
E. Bejlovcová: *Hudebně dramatická tvorba skladatelů českého původu ve fondech pražských hudebních archivů a knihoven 1769–1871* [Musico-Dramatic Works by Composers of Czech Origin in the Collections of Prague Archives and Libraries, 1769–1871] (diss., Charles U. of Prague, 1979)
M. Pospíšil: 'Balada v české opeře 19. století' [The Ballad in Czech 19th-Century Opera], *HV*, xvi (1979), 3–25
J. Trojan: *Ceské zpěvohry 18. století* [Czech 18th-Century Operas] (Brno, 1981)
P. Daněk and J. Vyšohlídová: 'Dokumenty k operní soutěži o cenu hrabětě Harracha' [Documents concerning Count Harrach's Opera Prize Competition], *MMC*, xxx (1983), 147–75
Divadlo v české kultuře 19. století: Plzeň 1983 (Prague, 1985)
L. Polyakova: *Cheshkaya i slovatskaya opera XX. veka* [Czech and Slovak Opera of the 20th Century], i (Moscow, 1983)
L. Šíp: *Ceská opera a její tvůrci: průvodce* [Czech Opera and its Creators: a Guide] (Prague, 1983)
H. Havlíková and others, eds.: *Katalog dramatickýchděl* [Catalogue of Stage Works] (Prague, 1984; Ger. trans., 1985)
B. Srba: 'Bedřich Smetana a soudobá divadelní konvence' [Smetana and the Theatrical Conventions of his Time], *OM*, xvii (1985), 71–81, 97–107
O. Hostinský: *Z hudební bojů let sedmdesátých a osmdesátých: výbor z operních a koncertních kritik* [From the Musical Battles of the 1870s and 80s: a Selection of Opera and Concert Reviews], ed. E. Vítová (Prague, 1986)
J. Tyrrell: *Czech Opera* (Cambridge, 1988)
F. Černý: *Kalendárium dějin českého divadla* [A Calendar of the History of the Czech Theatre] (Prague, 1989) JOHN TYRRELL

Czerwenka, Oskar (*b* Vöcklabruck, nr Linz, 5 July 1924). Austrian bass. He studied in Vienna, making his début in 1947 at Graz as the Hermit (*Der Freischütz*). In 1951 he joined the Vienna Staatsoper, remaining a member of the company for 30 years. He first sang at Salzburg in 1953, creating two minor roles in von Einem's *Der Prozess* and returning for Mozart's Bartolo and Truffaldino (*Ariadne auf Naxos*). He sang Baron Ochs, his most famous role, at Glyndebourne in 1959 and made his Metropolitan début, also as Ochs, in 1960, later singing Rocco. At Hamburg he created Jacobowsky in Klebe's *Jacobowsky und der Oberst* (1965), repeating it in New York (1967). His repertory included Osmin, van Bett (*Zar und Zimmermann*), Kecal, Mustafà (*Italiana in Algeri*), Don Pasquale, Daland, Waldner (*Arabella*), Morosus (*Die schweigsame Frau*), La Roche (*Capriccio*) and Abu Hassan (*Der Barbier von Bagdad*), which he recorded for Leinsdorf. He had a fine, dark-coloured voice and, though apt to overplay his comic roles, he could be an effective actor.

ALAN BLYTH

Czibulka, Alphons (*b* Szepesvárally a [now Spišská Nová Ves, Slovakia], 14 May 1842; *d* Vienna, 27 Oct 1894). Hungarian composer. At the age of 15 he was performing as a pianist in Russia; then he became a music teacher, and later a conductor in Wiener Neustadt (1864–5), Innsbruck, Trieste and at the Carltheater in Vienna. He then entered military service, becoming bandmaster of several Austro-Hungarian infantry regiments. During the 1880s and early 1890s he conducted 'Monster Concerts' in the Prater in Vienna, and he composed much successful dance and salon music, and several operettas, of which the first, *Pfingsten in Florenz* (1884), was the most successful. Around 1889–90 he arranged dances on themes from *The Yeomen of the Guard* and *The Gondoliers* (for Bosworth & Co.), at the time when these works were being performed in Germany.

operettas

Pfingsten in Florenz (3, R. Genée and J. Riegen), Vienna, An der Wien, 20 Dec 1884; Der Jagdjunker der Kaiserin (3, F. Zell and Genée), Berlin, Walhalla, 3 Dec 1885; Der Glücksritter (3, Genée, W. Mannstädt and B. Zappert, after A. Dumas *père*), Vienna, Carl, 22 Dec 1887; Gil Blas von Santillana (3, Zell and M. West), Hamburg, Carl Schultze, 23 Nov 1889; Der Bajazzo (3, V. Léon and H. von Waldberg), Vienna, An der Wien, 7 Dec 1892; Monsieur Hannibal (3, Mannstädt and K. Dreher), Munich, Gärtnerplatz, 5 Sept 1893 ANDREW LAMB

Czyż, Henryk (*b* Grudziądz, 16 June 1923). Polish composer and conductor. After reading law and philosophy at Toruń University he studied conducting and composition at the Poznań Conservatory. Although his compositional output is relatively small, his three stage works form an important contribution and display a talent for comedy tinged with melancholy, and a musical language influenced by jazz, blues and dance. *Białowłosa* ('The Girl with the Flaxen Hair') is an unusually philosophical musical comedy: its science-fiction heroine, untainted by human evils, arrives from another planet and is confronted by the turmoil of contemporary urban existence. In drawing his other two librettos from Mrożek and Gałczyński, Czyż aligned himself with the surreal tradition of 20th-century Polish literature.

Białowłosa [The Girl with the Flaxen Hair] (morality op, 2, Czyż, after D. Baduszkowa), Warsaw, State, 24 Nov 1962; rev. version, Łódź, Wielki, 2 Oct 1971

Kynolog w rozterce [Cynologist at a Loss] (comic op, 1, S. Mrożek), Polish TV, 1965; stage, Kraków, Miejski, 19 Nov 1967

Inge Bartsch (op-musical, 2, L. Janowicz, after K. I. Gałczyński), Warsaw, Wielki, 11 Dec 1982 ADRIAN THOMAS

D

Dabadie, Henri-Bernard (*b* Pau, 19 Jan 1797; *d* Paris, May 1853). French baritone. He studied at the Paris Conservatoire and made his début in 1819 at the Opéra as Cinna in Spontini's *La vestale*. During the 16 years he sang at the Opéra, he created several roles in operas by Rossini: Pharaoh in *Moïse et Pharaon* (1827), Raimbaud in *Le comte Ory* (1828) and William Tell (1829). He sang Pietro in the first performance of Auber's *La muette de Portici* (1828). Having created Belcore in Auber's *Le philtre* (1831) in Paris, he sang the same role at the première of Donizetti's *L'elisir d'amore* (1832) in Milan. Back at the Opéra he sang Count Dehorn in the first performance of Auber's *Gustave III* (1833) and created Ruggiero in Halévy's *La Juive* in 1835, the year of his retirement. His wife, the soprano Louise Dabadie, frequently sang with him.

For illustration *see* GUILLAUME TELL (ii). ELIZABETH FORBES

Dabadie [née Zulme Leroux], **Louise** (*b* Boulogne-sur-Mer, 20 March 1804; *d* Paris, Nov 1877). French soprano. From 1824 to 1835 she sang at the Paris Opéra, appearing frequently with her husband, the baritone Henri-Bernard Dabadie. She created Sinais in Rossini's *Moïse et Pharaon* (1827), Jemmy in *Guillaume Tell* (1829) and Arvedson in Auber's *Gustave III* (1833). She also sang Julia in Spontini's *La vestale*, Amazily in the same composer's *Fernand Cortez* and Adèle in Rossini's *Le comte Ory*. ELIZABETH FORBES

Da capo (It.: 'from the head'). An instruction, often abbreviated 'D.C.', placed at the end of the second (or later) section of a piece of music, indicating that the performer is to return to the head of the piece and recapitulate the first section (or part of it). A pause sign or the word *fine* ('end') may mark the point at which the piece is to end. The da capo aria, in which the first (or *A*) section is recapitulated, normally in ornamented form, after the second (*B*) section, was central to opera from the late 17th century to the middle of the 18th, when it was succeeded by the DAL SEGNO aria and other types. It is commonly represented *ABA* or *ABA'*, although in its material and treatment of the text it can be regarded as a five-part form (*AA'BAA'*). See ARIA, §2(i), and ORNAMENTATION, §1.

Daddi, Francesco (*b* Naples, 1864; *d* Chicago, 1945). Italian tenor, later bass. He trained as a singer and pianist at the Naples Conservatory and made his stage début at Milan in 1891. The following year at the Dal Verme he sang Beppe in the première of *Pagliacci*, and this was also his role in his single season at Covent Garden in 1900. He sang in the shared première of Mascagni's *Le maschere* at Rome in 1901. Having become one of Italy's leading comprimario tenors, he emigrated to the USA in 1907, singing with the Manhattan Company, usually in small parts but also as Corentin in *Dinorah* with Tetrazzini. From 1911 to 1920 he appeared regularly in Chicago, where he enjoyed considerable success in comic bass roles such as Dr Bartolo in *Il barbiere di Siviglia*. His recordings, made as a tenor, include Beppe's Serenade in *Pagliacci* and many Neapolitan songs graced by an agreeable lyric voice and an idiomatic sense of style. J. B. STEANE

Dafne ('Daphne'). Opera in a prologue and six scenes by MARCO DA GAGLIANO to a libretto by OTTAVIO RINUCCINI after OVID's *Metamorphoses*; Mantua, February 1608.

Dafne is a slightly revised and expanded version of Rinuccini's earliest opera libretto on the same subject, which in Peri and Corsi's setting (Carnival 1598, Florence) is generally considered the first opera.

Ovid (tenor) as Prologue explains the cautionary nature of his tale: never underestimate the power of Love. The first scene presents the Pythic combat, in which Apollo (tenor) slays Pitone [Python], the monstrous dragon who has been menacing the nymphs and shepherds of an unspecified pastoral landscape (this scene is a reworking of Rinuccini's third *intermedio* from the spectacular Florentine wedding festivities of 1589). The second scene is the confrontation between Apollo and Amore [Cupid] (soprano): Apollo, fresh from his victory in battle, boasts of his prowess as an archer and taunts the little god of love about his small bow and arrows, whereupon Cupid vows to his mother Venere [Venus] (soprano) that he will avenge his scorned bow by wounding Apollo. The third scene is the encounter in the forest: now the victim of Cupid's revenge, Apollo falls hopelessly in love with Daphne (soprano), a nymph and follower of Diana. Remaining true to her vows of chastity, Daphne dismisses Apollo's suggestion that they join together in the hunt. In the fourth scene Cupid boasts to Venus of his conquest of Apollo. The fifth scene centres on the expressive recitative narration by the shepherd-messenger Tirsi [Thyrsis] (alto castrato) (first sung by the Florentine male alto Antonio Brandi, who in Gagliano's preface to the published score received the highest praise among all the performers in 1608). He describes how Daphne, fleeing from Apollo's amorous advances, prayed for some means of escape and was immediately transformed into a laurel tree ('Quando la bella ninfa'). The final scene consists of Apollo's monologue: he laments his loss of Daphne but then adds an encomium ('Ninfa sdegnosa e schiva') in which he consecrates the laurel to himself as a symbol of victory. A small chorus of nymphs and shepherds punctuates the end of each scene (except the third) with commentary, while various members of the chorus take part as soloists in the action.

On a symbolic level the story is about the nature of art in general and, by extension, about the power of the new art-form in particular. This is confirmed by the identification of Ovid/Prologue with Apollo/poet in the original production; according to the composer's preface, Ovid was crowned with laurel and held a lyre and bow, as did Apollo in the last scene (it is not unlikely that the same singer, Francesco Rasi, performed both tenor roles, just as Daphne and Venus were sung by the same soprano, Caterina Martinelli). Thus, although Apollo the dragon-slayer is in his turn vanquished by Love, Apollo the poet-musician rises above his despair by immortalizing Daphne in his encomium and conferring on her transformed state the honour of always remaining green. In this way he sublimates his defeat in love into a poetic statement about the power of art to overcome the limitations and frustrations of life. Apollo is therefore the real protagonist of *Dafne*, as well as a figure who had long been associated iconographically (through the laurel) with the Medici, the ruling Florentine family and patrons of the earliest operatic productions, as well as of Gagliano and his librettist.

Rinuccini's libretto is a mixture of lyrical verse forms, some of which were adopted by other librettists: free rhyme patterns for conversational and narrative passages, and more formal, strophic schemes for the prologue, choruses and several arias. Gagliano's musical recitative style owes a great deal to Peri's original formulation, except that he increased the recitational flow by reducing the rhythmic prominence of the verse-endings and by relying more on the force and logic of harmonic progressions than on the structure and rhyme scheme of the verse.

Gagliano's description of the production of 1608, included in his preface to the published score, is the most informative document of its kind in the history of early opera. In addition to details of the staging, he discussed ornamentation and other contemporary performance practices. He also acknowledged the collaboration in three of the songs of a fellow academician and 'great protector of music' – undoubtedly Cardinal Ferdinando Gonzaga, the patron of Gagliano's Accademia degli Elevati.

BARBARA R. HANNING

Dafni **(i)** ('Daphnis'). *Favola boschereccia per musica* in three acts by Alessandro Scarlatti (*see* SCARLATTI family, (1)) to a libretto, probably by Eustachio Manfredi, extensively reworked by Francesco Maria Paglia; Posillipo, near Naples, residence of the viceroy, 5 August 1700.

The action of this pastoral comedy takes place in Arcadia, and the plot extends the eternal triangle to a polygon. Galatea (soprano) is attracted to Daphnis (alto castrato) but betrothed to Fileno (tenor). Fileno for his part is in love with Nerina (soprano), who nurtures a passion for Galatea. Tirsi (soprano castrato) is also in love with Nerina, while Dameta (bass), the supposed father of Galatea, spends much of his time trying to win over the opera's other comic character, Selvaggia (soprano). After a series of accidents and misunderstandings the denouement is reached when Galatea, who has attempted suicide by drowning, is rescued by the river-god Alfeo, who reveals that she is his daughter and the sister of Fileno. Galatea is then united with Daphnis and Nerina with Tirsi, leaving Fileno the loser along with Dameta, who fails to win Selvaggia's affection.

Dafni was composed to celebrate the birthday of Maria de Giron y Sandoval, wife of the viceroy, the Duke of Medinaceli, and the libretto opens with a prologue in her honour which is absent from the only surviving score, copied in 1724. Tailored for a private and possibly ad hoc theatre, the opera requires only a single set and an orchestra of strings, one or two flutes and continuo. Except for the three-movement 'Preludio', the musical substance is provided by the recitative-aria (or duet) unit and a final *coro*. The recitative is of the 'semplice' type, accompanied by continuo only, and the arias are nearly all in ternary (da capo or dal segno) form. Handel drew on a number of them for his opera *Faramondo* and other works composed in the 1730s.

MALCOLM BOYD

Dafni **(ii)** ('Daphnis'). *Poema pastorale* in three acts by GIUSEPPE MULÈ to a libretto by Ettore Romagnoli; Rome, Teatro Reale dell'Opera, 14 March 1928.

In the fascist period this was generally regarded as Mulè's most important opera, and was quite often performed in Italy. Since then it has fallen into neglect, like all its composer's works, for reasons that have as much to do with his political record as with artistic considerations (its revival at Palermo in March 1991 was the first for 37 years). Yet there is nothing remotely 'fascist' about the opera's subject, or about its music.

The work portrays the tribulations of the musically gifted Sicilian shepherd Dafni [Daphnis] (tenor) and his beloved Egle [Aegle] (soprano). Not only are the couple's lives repeatedly disrupted by the ribald antics of Sileno [Silenus] (baritone) and his company of satyrs, but their love arouses the jealousy of Venere [Venus] (soprano), who decrees that henceforth they must wander the world, endlessly seeking each other without success. Eventually they glimpse one another across an abyss, into which Aegle then falls when fleeing from the satyrs. Moved at last to pity, the goddess prevents her death; but Daphnis has meanwhile been mortally wounded in his own attempt to save her. The lovers are briefly reunited before he dies.

Though uneven in quality (the first act probably being the best), the music of *Dafni* has a real if modest individuality. Fresh modal melodies redolent of Sicilian folk music interact with a gently piquant harmonic vocabulary in which tritones, augmented triads and 'exotic' augmented 2nds often figure prominently.

JOHN C. G. WATERHOUSE

Da Gagliano, Marco. *See* GAGLIANO, MARCO DA.

Daguerre, Louis-Jacques-Mande (*b* Corneilles, Seine-et-Oise, 18 Nov 1787; *d* Bry-sur-Marne, 10 July 1851).

Stage design attributed to Daguerre for the original production of Isouard and Benincori's 'Aladin, ou La lampe merveilleuse' (Act III scene i, showing the throne room and, through the arches, a courtyard with fountains), performed at the Paris Opéra in 1822

French stage designer and inventor. After attending school in Orléans, he was apprenticed to the Paris Opéra's scene painter Degotti (1803–07); in 1810 he married an Englishwoman, Louise Arrowsmith. From 1807 to 1815 he collaborated with Pierre Prévost on panoramas of Rome, Naples, London, Jerusalem and Athens. As a scene painter at the boulevard theatre Ambigu-Comique (1816–22), he made many experiments with light to create spectacular landscapes with coloured filters (in *Le songe, ou La chapelle de Glenthorn*, 1818, there was a summit view of a crumbling Gothic chapel in changing moonlight). He was also a scene painter at the Paris Opéra (1819–22), where his and Ciceri's lavish setting for Nicolas Isouard and Angelo Benincori's *Aladin, ou La lampe merveilleuse* was the first to use gas lighting (1822).

Daguerre invented the diorama (1822), a 'drama of light', which usually consisted of backdrop paintings on transparent cloths lit by movable coloured filters. Dioramas became a feature of 19th-century pantomime decor, especially in London at Drury Lane and Covent Garden. He also developed the photographic process that bears his name, daguerreotype. *L. J. M. Daguerre: the History of the Diorama and the Daguerreotype*, a biography by Helmut and A. Gernsheim, was published in New York in 1969. DAVID J. HOUGH

Dahlhaus, Carl (*b* Hanover, 10 June 1928; *d* Berlin, 13 March 1989). German musicologist. He studied at the universities of Göttingen and Freiburg (1947–52), and took the doctorate at Göttingen in 1953 with a dissertation on Josquin. From 1950 to 1958 he was Dramaturg at the Deutsches Theater in Göttingen; in the early 1960s he worked as a music critic before taking up his first university post, at Kiel, in 1962. He later held posts at Saarbrücken University and the Technical University of Berlin, and was visiting professor at Princeton in 1968.

Dahlhaus's extensive writings reveal a strong interest in opera and a special concern with Wagner. His preferred literary medium became the relatively brief essay in which there is often a striking contrast between the wide-ranging account of a historical or philosophical topic and the presentation of detailed comments on extracts from particular compositions. Dahlhaus was never much concerned with biographical, anecdotal aspects of music history, and as chief editor of the complete Wagner edition (Mainz, 1970–) he supervised the most thoroughgoing attempt so far undertaken to deduce Wagner's intentions from his sketches and other sources. In a late article, 'What is a Musical Drama?' (1989), Dahlhaus declared that the primary concern of 'a theory of opera intended to provide a foundation for the interpretation of a single work according to its individuality' should be to show the ways in which music 'realizes the elements in the action'; and he also argued that 'the history of opera, considered from the point of view of realizing dramatic intentions, is best written as a history of the evolution of musical means available to serve that end'. At the heart of Dahlhaus's work is his view of Wagner's development of such musical means – more flexible forms and phrase structure, less stable tonality, various leitmotif techniques – to realize the new dramatic intentions of his later music dramas. Dahlhaus also explored the wider and more fundamental question of Wagner's pivotal position in the history of opera, with the result that his sometimes provocative, invariably stimulating accounts of other opera composers often place them in a Wagnerian perspective. Dahlhaus provided relatively few demonstrations of close, extended analysis; but these writings too, especially sections of *Wagners Konzeption des musikalischen Dramas* (1971), are remarkable in their technical penetration and musical pertinence. With Sieghart Döhring, Dahlhaus was the editor of *Pipers Enzyklopädie des Musiktheaters* (Munich, 1986–).

'Wagners Begriff der "dichterisch-musikalischen Perioden"', *Beiträge zur Geschichte der Musikanschauung im 19. Jahrhundert*, ed. W. Salmen (Regensburg, 1965), 179–95

'Formprinzipien in Wagners "Ring des Nibelungen"', *Beiträge zur Geschichte der Oper*, ed. H. Becker (Regensburg, 1969), 95–129

ed.: *Das Drama Richard Wagners als musikalisches Kunstwerk* (Regensburg, 1970)

ed.: *Richard Wagner: Werk und Wirkung* (Regensburg, 1971)

Wagners Ästhetik (Bayreuth, 1971)

Wagners Konzeption des musikalischen Dramas (Regensburg, 1971)
'Motive der Meyerbeer-Kritik', *Jb des Staatlichen Instituts für Musikforschung 1978*, 35–42
Richard Wagner's Music Dramas (Cambridge, 1979)
'Zum Affektbegriff der frühdeutschen Oper', *HJbMw*, v (1981), 107–11
'Tonalität und Form in Wagners "Ring des Nibelungen"', *AMw*, xl (1983), 165–73
'Die romantische Oper als Idee und Gattung', *Jb der Akademie der Wissenschaften in Göttingen 1983*, 52–64
Vom Musikdrama zur Literaturoper: Aufsätze zur neueren Operngeschichte (Munich and Salzburg, 1983)
'Webers "Freischütz" und die Idee der romantischen Oper', *ÖMz*, xxxviii (1983), 381–8
with J. Deathridge: *The New Grove Wagner* (London, 1984)
'Regietheater', *Musica*, xxxviii (1984), 227–30
'Wagner, Meyerbeer und der Fortschritt', *Festschrift Rudolf Elvers* (Tutzing, 1985), 103–16
ed.: *Die Musik des 18. Jahrhunderts* (Laaber, 1985) [incl. 'Revolutionsoper und symphonische Tradition', 345–56]
'Tragödie, Tragédie, Reformoper: zur *Iphigénie in Aulis* von Euripides, Racine und Gluck', *Oper als Text*, ed. A. Gier (Heidelberg, 1986), 95–100
'Wagners Stellung in der Musikgeschichte', 'Die Musik', 'Die musikalische Wirkung', *Richard-Wagner-Handbuch*, ed. U. Müller and P. Wapnewski (Stuttgart, 1986), 60–85, 197–221, 675–97
Klassische und romantische Musikästhetik (Laaber, 1988)
Nineteenth Century Music (Berkeley, 1989)
'What is a Musical Drama?', *COJ*, i (1989), 95–111

HANS HEINRICH EGGEBRECHT, ARNOLD WHITTALL

Daija, Tish (*b* Shkodër, Albania, 13 Jan 1926). Albanian composer. His father played in a local folk-orchestra, which met regularly in the family home. Daija was encouraged in music at school by the music master Prenkë Jakova and he began writing songs as a child. From 1950 to 1956 he studied composition in Moscow with Vladimir Fere. He was director of the Ansamblin Shtetëror të Këngëve e Valleve Popullore (State Ensemble of Folksong and Dance), a professional folksong and dance company in Tirana, from 1962 to 1980 and has since worked as a composer.

In 1957 he wrote his first stage work, the operetta *Lelja*. This was soon followed by the two-act opera *Pranvera* ('Spring'), to a libretto by the poet Llazar Siliqi; it was first performed at the Theatre of Opera and Ballet in Tirana on 12 June 1960. The opera deals with the national struggle against fascism and the subsequent 'spring of freedom'. Daija's musical style, as with all Albanian composers, is firmly rooted in the folk music of the country.

His second opera, *Vjosa* (also to a libretto by Siliqi), was first performed on 9 February 1980 at Tirana. The story promotes the idea of the unity of the Albanian people, the governing working class with the cooperative peasantry. It tells of a girl, Vjosa, who goes to work as a volunteer with the peasants in a remote mountain region. She meets Muj, and so begins a story of true love as a union of ideals. The pastoral scenes use the typical rhythms and timbres of the *lahouta*, a type of lute, and the *çifteli*, a long-necked two-stringed instrument, and throughout the opera the music is developed from national folksongs and dances.

*

S. Kalemi: *Arritjet e artit tonë muzikor* [The Arrival of our Musical Art] (Tirana, 1982)
J. Emerson: *Albania: the Search for the Eagle's Song* (Studley, Warwicks., 1990)

JUNE EMERSON

Daisi ('Twilight'). Lyric-dramatic opera in three acts by ZAKHARY PETROVICH PALIASHVILI to a libretto by V. Guniya after verses by Shota Rustaveli, N. Baratashvili, Akvsenti Tsereteli and Vazha Pshavela; Tbilisi, Georgian National Opera House, 19 December 1923.

Paliashvili's second opera, *Twilight* was the first opera to appear in Soviet Georgia and draws on motifs from Georgian folk legends. Set in late 18th-century Georgia, the story combines romantic and heroic themes, effectively playing off the dramatic conflict between love and patriotic duty. As in his earlier *Abesalom da Eteri* ('Abesalom and Etery'), Paliashvili fused features of his Georgian musical heritage – characteristic modal inflections, genre writing, melismatic vocal lines and ornamentation – into a harmonically traditional structure inherited from 19th-century Russian opera. The poetic expressivity of the melodies, with their exotic flavour, has contributed significantly to the opera's continued popularity.

In a courtyard at dusk Nano (mezzo-soprano) looks forward eagerly to the approaching holiday, but her friend Maro (soprano) is subdued. While her beloved, Malkhaz (tenor), has been away in distant lands, Maro has become betrothed to the military officer Kiazo (baritone), whom she does not love. Nano gives her the good news that Malkhaz has returned, and his carefree song is heard in the distance. When the lovers meet, Maro is sad and distracted; she confesses to Malkhaz that she has become betrothed to another. The peasants begin their festivities, and Nano ensures that Maro and Malkhaz are included in the dancing, observed by the elderly Tsangala (bass) who threatens to tell Kiazo. Nano chases him away. As evening falls, church bells summon the people to the festival. Malkhaz tries to detain Maro, but she runs away.

In Act 2 the festivities continue in the churchyard. Night has fallen and the people have begun to disperse when Kiazo arrives. Tsangala informs him that Maro is unfaithful and in love with Malkhaz; the irate Kiazo swears vengeance against his rival. Maro emerges from the church, terrified that the two will meet, and begs Malkhaz to avoid Kiazo. Nano warns the lovers that Kiazo is approaching. A confrontation is avoided only by the news of a sudden enemy attack; Kiazo takes his place at the head of the troops and rouses them to battle.

Act 3 opens with Kiazo, overcome by jealousy, abandoning his troops and returning to confront Maro. She confesses that she does not love him and, provoked by his reproaches, flings her engagement ring at him. Malkhaz appears and the rivals draw their sabres. Seeing the soldiers on their way to battle, the combatants take pause, but their personal feud overwhelms them. In the duel, Malkhaz is fatally wounded. Kiazo is branded with shame by the troops and, conscious of his disgrace, vows to lay down his life to expiate the crime. Maro's lament for her beloved and a choral funeral march yield to the confident swell of the orchestral conclusion as the troops depart to defend their country. LAUREL E. FAY

Dalayrac [D'Alayrac], **Nicolas-Marie** (*b* Muret, Haute Garonne, 8 June 1753; *d* Paris, 26 Nov 1809). French composer. His father was a king's counsellor and a wealthy aristocrat either by birth or through personal ennoblement. Nicolas' musical talents were cultivated at Toulouse College, where he went from the age of eight, and, on his return to Muret six years later, in singing lessons and playing the violin in a local orchestra. He was obliged by his father to study law, in which he qualified by the age of 21. In 1774 he went to Versailles, where a commission had been obtained for him as a sub-lieutenant in the personal guard of the Count of Artois, later Charles X. In Paris, Dalayrac encountered influential musicians and musical amateurs such as the Baron de Bésenval and the Chevalier de Saint-Georges; he later received composition lessons from Honoré Langlé. Grétry reported in his *Mémoires* that Dalayrac was admitted to his study, but was not a formal pupil.

Dalayrac's earliest compositions were violin duos and string trios and quartets, some of which are lost. Surviving sets of quartets start with op.4. He had lifelong masonic connections, but none of his masonic music has been preserved (Porset 1991).

In 1781 Bésenval asked Dalayrac to set *Le petit souper* and *Le chevalier à la mode* to music for private stage performance. They were well received, and the following year, under Marie Antoinette's protection, *L'éclipse totale* became Dalayrac's first public opera. He rapidly consolidated his position, and by 1786 could be viewed as Grétry's successor. Before the Revolution his chief successes were *Nina* (1786), *Azémia* (1786) and *Les deux petits Savoyards* (1789). Most of his output was published in full score; Beethoven possessed copies of *Les deux petits Savoyards* and *La soirée orageuse*.

From about 1790 Dalayrac was obliged to spell his name in a non-aristocratic manner (rather than D'Alayrac). In 1792 he married the actress Gilberte Sallarde, who later, during the Directory and Consulate, presided over a lively salon. In the difficult days of 1793–5 Dalayrac's musical popularity seems to have guided him safely through. He wrote one or two Republican songs, but his most usual contribution was indirect: others adapted his popular operatic tunes to Republican words. The ubiquitous 'Veillons au salut de l'Empire', for example, was originally from his *Renaud d'Ast* (1787). In 1795 he was a signatory with the foremost Parisian composers to a prospectus for Republican music. Yet his success set him somewhat apart from the 'Conservatoire school' (Méhul, Cherubini, Gossec etc.) and he could afford not to join the Conservatoire staff.

In 1798 Dalayrac was awarded membership of the Swedish Royal Academy, and in 1804 he was made one of the first members of the Légion d'honneur. He put particular effort into *Le poète et le musicien*, which was intended for Napoleon's coronation anniversary (4 December 1809), but caught a fever and died before the destined day. Pixérécourt stressed the composer's modest, friendly nature and restrained style of living. That Dalayrac never received a government annuity was ascribed by Pixérécourt to his retiring disposition. A marble bust of the composer by Pierre Cartellier, funded by subscription, was placed in the foyer of the Opéra-Comique in 1811.

Dalayrac's work, almost totally within the *opéra comique* tradition, formed a logical continuation of Grétry's. He wrote mainly for the same company that held Grétry's allegiance, the Comédie-Italienne. Like Grétry, he tackled a wide range of dramatic subjects, while never tiring of the appeal of comedy. *Azémia*, for example (partly inspired by Shakespeare's *The Tempest*), portrayed young love, exotic scenery and final rescue from a remote island. *Nina* showed the woman 'crazed for love'. *Sargines*, set in the Middle Ages, centred on King Philip-Augustus (1165–1223) and the battle that decisively broke Anglo-Angevin power in France. (It stands as a pro-monarchist statement on the eve of the Revolution.) *Raoul, sire de Créqui* shows the rescue of a medieval 'good seigneur' from atrocious conditions of imprisonment, and emphasizes the affection of his people. *Camille* and *Léon* share strong elements of Gothic fantasy: the former, the story of an imprisoned wife, was also taken up by Ferdinando Paer in a successful setting (1799). On the other hand, works like *Maison à vendre* provided light musical settings that acted as a vehicle for comic intrigue. To some extent, Dalayrac always adapted his musical style according to the subject. *Sargines* is consistently striking for its warlike and patriotic idiom.

Although Dalayrac was a skilled composer of ensembles, his more memorable music was designed for solo voice. He provided a new generation of French singers with up-to-date lyricism modelled on foundations laid down by Paisiello and Sacchini, and he cultivated, more particularly, a naively tuneful style, as accomplished as it was popular. This is typified by the lilting 6/8 melody 'Quand le bien-aimé reviendra' from *Nina*; adapted for liturgical use, it became, at Berlioz's first communion in 1815, one of his early musical experiences. At least four songs were parodied on the same melody and published. In 1810 *Azémia* and *Gulistan* were revived in Paris, and a music journalist could still rhetorically ask 'who does not know by heart' music from the former, such as 'Ton amour, ô fille chérie', 'Aussitôt que je t'apperçois' and 'J'ai peur et ne sais pas pourquoi'. Dalayrac's increased use of italianate melody later in his career was criticized by Martine (1813), but there is conspicuously virtuoso solo writing already in Verseuil's aria 'Quel moment' in *Les deux petits Savoyards*. In general, his musical style became more lightweight, with shorter phrases and, typically, triplet accompaniment figures.

Poisson de La Chabeaussière (in the dedicatory epistle of *Azémia*) and Marsollier des Vivetières (1825) paid tribute to the composer's active and astute contribution to the dramatic planning of various operas. Pixérécourt, another of his librettists, wrote Dalayrac's biography. Yet it was for the redoubtable François-Benoît Hoffman that Dalayrac produced possibly his most polished score, *Léon* (1798). It is meticulously planned with regard to its key scheme, recurring themes for the two moral messages of the fable and three recurring motifs associated with the lovers. Then, in *Léhéman* (1801), eight recurring elements are found, including the *romance* 'Un voyageur s'est égaré' ('A pilgrim lost'). Carl Maria von Weber, in his review, found 'especially interesting' the *romance*'s 'interweaving with the progress of the whole plot' which forges a conceptual and musical unity throughout.

Dalayrac seems never to have left France, but his works were very popular abroad, especially in Germany, Scandinavia and Russia. A few were adapted in England; they were known in Vienna; Beethoven played in the Bonn orchestra when *Nina, Azémia* and *Les deux petits Savoyards* were in repertory; and Weber conducted *Adolphe et Clara* and *Les deux petits Savoyards* in Prague in 1814. *Camille* and *Adolphe et Clara* were still sung in Paris in the 1840s; *Maison à vendre* was probably the universal favourite, revived in Paris up to 1853.

The orchestration of Dalayrac's operas is resourceful rather than brilliant. Woodwind solos are favoured, particularly those for bassoon, and muted strings are often found in *romances*. *Col legno* is used in *Une heure de mariage*. *Lina* (1807) provides perhaps the first printed indication anywhere in a full score of soft-ended timpani sticks, in calling for 'baguetes garnies'. In *Léhéman* offstage trumpet-calls in the first finale announce the capture of Léhéman's ally by the enemy. This 'warning' technique was afterwards used by Méhul in *Héléna*, and subsequently by Beethoven in *Fidelio*.

See also DEUX PETITS SAVOYARDS, LES and NINA, OU LA FOLLE PAR AMOUR.

first performed in Paris unless otherwise stated; printed works are full scores published in Paris

PCI – *Comédie-Italienne* PFE – *Théâtre Feydeau*
OC – *Opéra-Comique*

A trompeur trompeur et demi (proverbe, 1, Desfontaines [F.-G. Fouques]), Brunoy, 23 Nov 1780
Le petit souper, ou L'abbé qui veut parvenir (oc, 1, E. L. Billardon de Sauvigny), private perf., 1781 (*c*1781)
Le chevalier à la mode (oc), private perf., 1781
L'éclipse totale (cmda, 1, A. E. X. Poisson de La Chabeaussière, after La Fontaine), PCI, 7 March 1782, *F-A*, *Mc*, inc. orch pts *Pc*
Le corsaire (cmda, 3, Poisson de La Chabeaussière), Versailles, 7 March 1783; rev. version, PCI, 19 May 1785 (*c*1785); rev. as Le corsaire algérien, ou Le combat naval, PCI, 1 July 1793
Mathieu, ou Les deux soupers (cmda, 3, Poisson de La Chabeaussière), Fontainebleau, 11 Oct 1783; rev. as Les deux tuteurs (2), PCI, 8 May 1784 (1785)
L'amant statue (cmda, 1, Desfontaines), PCI, 4 Aug 1785 (1785)
La dot (cmda, 3, Desfontaines), Fontainebleau, 8 Nov 1785 (1786)
Nina, ou La folle par amour (cmda, 1, B.-J. Marsollier des Vivetières), PCI, 15 May 1786 (1786)
Azémia, ou Le nouveau Robinson (oc/roman lyri-comique mêlé d'ariettes, 3, Poisson de La Chabeaussière), Fontainebleau, 17 Oct 1786; rev. as Azémia, ou Les sauvages (cmda, 3), PCI, 3 May 1787 (*c*1787)
Renaud d'Ast (cmda, 2, P.-Y. Barré and J.-B. Radet, after La Fontaine: *L'oraison de Saint Julien*), PCI, 19 July 1787 (*c*1787)
Les deux sérénades (cmda, 2, J.-F.-T. Goulard), PCI, 23 Jan 1788
Sargines, ou L'élève de l'amour (comédie mise en musique, 4, J.-M. Boutet de Monvel), PCI, 14 May 1788 (*c*1788)
Fanchette, ou L'heureuse épreuve (cmda, 2, Desfontaines), PCI, 13 Oct 1788; rev. version (1), 1801; rev. version (2), Oct 1810, *Pn**
Les deux petits Savoyards (cmda, 1, Marsollier des Vivetières), PCI, 14 Jan 1789 (*c*1789)
Raoul, sire de Créqui (cmda, 3, Boutet de Monvel, after F. Arnaud: *Le sire de Créqui*), PCI, 31 Oct 1789 (*c*1789); rev. as Bathilde et Eloi, OC (Favart), 9 Nov 1794
La soirée orageuse (cmda, 1, Radet), PCI, 29 May 1790 (*c*1790)
Le chêne patriotique, ou La matinée du 14 juillet 1790 (comédie, 2, Boutet de Monvel), PCI, 10 July 1790
Vert-vert (divertissement mêlé d'ariettes, 1, Desfontaines), PCI, 11 Oct 1790
Camille, ou Le souterrain (comédie mêlée de musique, 3, Marsollier des Vivetières), PCI, 19 March 1791 (*c*1791)
Agnès et Olivier (comédie héroïque, 3, Boutet de Monvel, after J. Cazotte: *Olivier*), PCI, 10 Oct 1791
Philippe et Georgette (cmda, 1, Boutet de Monvel, after C. Villette), PCI, 28 Dec 1791 (1794)
Tout pour l'amour, ou Roméo et Juliette [Juliette et Roméo] (comédie, 4, Boutet de Monvel), PCI, 7 July 1792, *A*, *Pn*
Ambroise, ou Voilà ma journée (cmda, 2, Boutet de Monvel), PCI, 12 Jan 1793, rev. (1), 20 Jan 1793, MS (private collection); (*c*1798)
Asgill, ou Le prisonnier de guerre (drame lyrique, 1, Marsollier des Vivetières), OC (Favart), 2 May 1793; rev. as Arnill, ou Le prisonnier américain (comédie, 2), OC (Favart), 9 March 1795; rev. version (1), 17 March 1795, *A*, *Mc*
Urgande et Merlin (comédie, 3, Boutet de Monvel), OC (Favart), 14 Oct 1793
La prise de Toulon (tableau patriotique mêlé d'ariettes, 1, L.-B. Picard), PFE, 1 Feb 1794, *Pn*
Le congrès des rois (cmda, 3, Desmaillot [A. F. Eve]), OC (Favart), 26 Feb 1794, collab. H.-M. Berton, Blasius, Cherubini, Devienne, Deshayes, Grétry, Jadin, Kreutzer, Méhul, Solié, Trial
L'enfance de J. J. Rousseau (cmda, 1, F.-G.-J.-S. Andrieux), OC (Favart), 23 May 1794
Les détenus, ou Cange, commissionnaire de Lazare (fait historique, 1, Marsollier des Vivetières), OC (Favart), 18 Nov 1794, *A*
La pauvre femme (comédie, 1, Marsollier des Vivetières), OC (Favart), 8 April 1795, *A*, *US-NYp*
Adèle et Dorsan (comédie, 3, Marsollier des Vivetières), OC (Favart), 27 April 1795 (*c*1795); later reduced to 2 acts
La famille américaine (comédie, 1, J.-N. Bouilly), OC (Favart), 20 Feb 1796 (*c*1796)
Marianne, ou L'amour maternel [La tendresse maternelle] (comédie, 1, Marsollier des Vivetières), OC (Favart), 7 July 1796 (*c*1796)
La maison isolée, ou Le vieillard des Vosges (comédie, 2, Marsollier des Vivetières), OC (Favart), 11 May 1797 (1797)
La leçon, ou La tasse de glaces (comédie, 1, Marsollier des Vivetières, after Carmontelle), PFE, 24 May 1797 (*c*1797)
Gulnare, ou L'esclave persanne (comédie, 1, Marsollier des Vivetières, OC (Favart), 30 Dec 1797 (1798)
Alexis, ou L'erreur d'un bon père (cmda, 1, Marsollier des Vivetières), PFE, 24 Jan 1798 (1798)
Primerose [Roger, ou Le page] (opéra, 3, E.-G.-F. Favières and Marsollier des Vivetières, after Morel de Vindé), OC (Favart), 8 March 1799
Léon, ou Le château de Monténéro (drame, 3, F.-B. Hoffman, after A. Radcliffe: *The Mysteries of Udolpho*), OC (Favart), 15 Oct 1798 (*c*1798)
Adolphe et Clara, ou Les deux prisonniers (comédie, 1, Marsollier des Vivetières), OC (Favart), 10 Feb 1799 (*c*1799)
Laure, ou L'actrice chez elle (1, Marsollier des Vivetières), OC (Favart), 27 Sept 1799
Le rocher de Leucade (oc, 1, Marsollier des Vivetières), OC (Favart), 14 Feb 1800
Une matinée de Catinat, ou Le tableau (comédie, 1, Marsollier des Vivetières), PFE, 1 Oct 1800 (*c*1800)
Maison à vendre (comédie, 1, A. Duval), OC (Favart), 23 Oct 1800 (1800)
Léhéman, ou La tour de Neustadt (opéra, 3, Marsollier des Vivetières), OC (Feydeau), 12 Dec 1801 (*c*1802)
L'antichambre, ou Les valets maîtres (1, L. E. F. C. Mercier-Dupaty), OC (Feydeau), 27 Feb 1802; rev. as Picaros et Diégo, ou La folle soirée (opéra bouffon, 1), OC (Feydeau), 3 May 1803 (1803)
La boucle de cheveux (opéra, 1, Hoffman), OC (Feydeau), 30 Oct 1802 (*c*1802)
La jeune prude, ou Les femmes entre elles (comédie mêlée de chants, 1, Mercier-Dupaty), OC (Feydeau), 14 Jan 1804 (*c*1804)
Une heure de mariage (comédie mêlée de chants, 1, C.-G. Etienne), OC (Feydeau), 20 March 1804 (*c*1806)
Le pavillon du calife, ou Almanzor et Zobéide (opéra, 2, E. Morel de Chédeville, J.-B.-D. Després and J.-M. Deschamps), Opéra, 20 April 1804, frags. *F-Pn*; rev. as Le pavillon des fleurs, ou Les pêcheurs de Grenade (comédie lyrique, 1, R. C. G. de Pixérécourt), OC (Feydeau), 13 May 1822 (n.d.)
Gulistan, ou Le hulla de Samarcande (oc, 3, Etienne and Poisson de La Chabeaussière), OC (Feydeau), 30 Sept 1805 (*c*1805)
Deux mots, ou Une nuit dans la forêt (comédie, 1, Marsollier des Vivetières, ? after M. G. Lewis: *The Monk*), OC (Feydeau), 9 June 1806 (*c*1806)
Koulouf, ou Les Chinois (oc, 3, Pixérécourt), OC (Feydeau), 18 Dec 1806 (*c*1807)
Lina, ou Le mystère (opéra, 3, J. A. de Réveroni Saint-Cyr), OC (Feydeau), 8 Oct 1807 (*c*1808)
Elise-Hortense, ou Les souvenirs de l'enfance (cmda, 1, Marsollier des Vivetières), OC (Feydeau), 26 Sept 1809 (n.d.)
Le poète et le musicien, ou Je cherche un sujet (comédie mêlée de chant, 3, Mercier-Dupaty), OC (Feydeau), 30 May 1811 (1811)

*

A. D'Origny: *Annales du Théâtre Italien depuis son origine jusqu'à ce jour* (Paris, 1788)
A.-E.-M. Grétry: *Mémoires, ou Essais sur la musique* (Paris, 1789, enlarged 2/1797), iii, 265
R. C. G. de Pixérécourt: *Vie de Dalayrac* (Paris, 1810)
J.-D. Martine: *De la musique dramatique en France* (Paris, 1813), 107–8, 262ff
B.-J. Marsollier [des Vivetières]: *Oeuvres choisies*, i (Paris, 1825), 6
A. Fourgeaud: *Les violons de Dalayrac* (Paris, 1856)
A. Adam: *Souvenirs d'un musicien* (Paris, 1857, 2/1871), 217–66
A. Pougin: 'Deux musiciens journalistes: épisode de la vie de Berton et de Dalayrac', *Le ménestrel*, xxxiii (1866–7), 308
M. Tourneux, ed.: *Correspondance littéraire, philosophique et critique par Grimm, Diderot, Raynal, Meister, etc.* (Paris, 1877–82)
A. Pougin: *L'opéra-comique pendant la Révolution de 1788 à 1801* (Paris, 1891)
H. Quittard: 'La "Nina" de Dalayrac', *RHCM*, viii (1908), 154
G. Cucuel: *Les créateurs de l'opéra-comique français* (Paris, 1914), 199–220
H. Radiguer: 'La musique française de 1789 à 1815', *EMDC*, I/iii

(1921), 1562–1660, esp. 1600–04
J. Tiersot: *Lettres de musiciens écrites en français du XVe au XXe siècle*, i (Turin, 1924), 258ff
E. C. van Bellen: *Les origines du mélodrame* (Utrecht, 1927), 106, 133, 164, 171
B. Connell: *Portrait of a Whig Peer* (London, 1957), 235
L. J. Moss: *The Solos of the One-Act Opéras-comiques by Nicolas Dalayrac (1753–1809)* (diss., New York U., 1969)
D. Charlton: *Orchestration and Orchestral Practice in Paris, 1789–1810* (diss., U. of Cambridge, 1973)
——: 'Motif and Recollection in Four Operas of Dalayrac', *Soundings*, vii (1978), 38–61
G. Luciani: 'Aspetti della vita teatrale a Chambéry durante l'Impero e la Restaurazione', *Chigiana*, new ser., xiii (1979), 239–64
K. Pendle: '*A bas les couvents!* Anticlerical Sentiment in French Operas of the 1790s', *MR*, xlii (1981), 22–45
J. Warrack, ed.: *Carl Maria von Weber: Writings on Music* (Cambridge, 1981)
J. B. Kopp: *The 'Drame Lyrique': a Study in the Esthetics of Opéra-Comique, 1762–1791* (diss., U. of Pennsylvania, 1982)
K. Pendle: 'A Working Friendship: Marsollier and Dalayrac', *ML*, lxiv (1983), 44–57
D. Charlton: *Grétry and the Growth of Opéra-Comique* (Cambridge, 1986)
F. Karro-Pelisson: 'Le musicien et le librettiste dans la nation: propriété et défense du créateur par Nicolas Dalayrac et Michel Sedaine', *Fêtes et musiques révolutionnaires: Grétry et Gossec*, Etudes sur le XVIIIe siècle, xvii, ed. R. Mortier and H. Hasquin (Brussels, 1990), 9–52
Nicolas Dalayrac, musicien murétain, homme des lumières: Muret 1990 [incl. C. Porset: 'Nicolas Dalayrac et la Loge des Neuf Soeurs', 65–71]
D. Charlton: 'On Redefinitions of "Rescue Opera"', *Music and the French Revolution*, ed. M. Boyd (Cambridge, 1992), 169–88
M. Couvreur: 'La folie à l'Opera-Comique: des grelots de Momus aux larmes de Nina', *L'opéra-comique en France des origines à 1789*, ed. P. Vendrix (Liège, 1992)

DAVID CHARLTON

Dal Barba, Daniel [Daniele] **(Pius)** (*b* Verona, 5 May 1715; *d* Verona, 26 July 1801). Italian composer. He made his singing début in Verona in Pietro Chiarini's *I fratelli riconosciuti* (1743), followed by a leading part in *Il Siroe* (1744) and in his own *opera seria Il Tigrane* (1744). During a stay in Venice in 1746–7, he sang in several *opere buffe* at the Teatro S Angelo and composed a parody, *Il gran Tamerlano*. He then appeared in the Trent summer opera productions *Artaserse* and *Il Demetrio* before taking up a two-year post at the Trent Bishopric.

In 1749 Dal Barba became *maestro di cappella* of the Filarmonica and Filotima academies in Verona; several operas and intermezzos came from his association with the former. From 1770 to 1779 he was *maestro di cappella* at Verona Cathedral. His sacred and instrumental works display technical competence and an intimate familiarity with current idioms and popular taste. All his operatic music is lost, but the printed librettos survive, chiefly in the Biblioteca Civica, Verona.

Il Tigrane (os, 3, ? C. Goldoni), Verona, Filarmonico, carn. 1744
Il gran Tamerlano (parody, 1, 'Verdacchi Predomosche'), Venice, Vendramin, aut. 1746
Lo starnuto d'Ercole (int, 5), Verona, Seminario, *c*1748
Il finto cameriere (int, 3, Dal Barba), Verona, S. E. Capitanio, carn. 1749
Ciro in Armenia (os, 3, G. Manfredi), Verona, Nuovo, carn. 1750
Artaserse (os, 3, P. Metastasio), Verona, Nuovo, carn. 1751
Alessandro nell' Indie (os, 3, Metastasio), Verona, Filarmonico, 1761

*

G. Gagliardi: *Attori e spettatori a Verona nel secolo XVIII* (Verona, 1907), 15–16
C. Garibotto: 'Spettacoli lirici al Filarmonico nel settecento', *Atti dell'Accademia d'agricoltura, scienze e lettere di Verona*, 5th ser., i (Verona, 1924), 33, 38, 40; xii (Verona, 1934)
V. C. Mazzanti: 'Un teatro veronese anteriore al Filarmonico', *Atti dell'Accademia d'agricoltura, scienze e lettere di Verona*, 5th ser., i (Verona, 1924), 77, 88
C. Garibotto: 'Teatri privati a Verona nel settecento', *Atti dell'Accademia d'agricoltura, scienze e lettere di Verona*, 5th ser., iv (Verona, 1927), 114
T. Lenotti: *I teatri di Verona* (Verona, 1949), 9–10, 16–17, 89
M. Dubiaga jr: *The Life and Works of Daniel Pius Dal Barba (1715–1801)* (diss., U. of Colorado, 1977)

MICHAEL DUBIAGA JR

Dalberg [Dalrymple], **Frederick** (*b* Newcastle upon Tyne, 7 Jan 1908; *d* South Africa, May 1988). South African bass of English birth. He studied in Dresden, making his début in 1931 at Leipzig as Monterone (*Rigoletto*), later singing King Henry (*Lohengrin*), Osmin, Sarastro, Philip II and many Wagner roles. He appeared at Munich, Dresden, Vienna and Berlin, where he spent the war years. At Bayreuth (1942–4 and 1951) he sang Hagen, Fafner and Pogner. After an engagement at Munich, he joined Covent Garden in 1951. There he created John Claggart in *Billy Budd* (1951), Sir Walter Raleigh in *Gloriana* (1953) and Calkas in Walton's *Troilus and Cressida* (1954). He sang the Doctor in the British stage première of *Wozzeck* (1952) and his repertory included King Mark, Hunding, Caspar, Pizarro, Ochs, Kečal, Sparafucile and Mozart's Bartolo. From 1957 to his retirement in 1970 he was engaged at Mannheim, where, as well as Daland, Gurnemanz and Fasolt, his roles included Don Pasquale, Boris and Dikoj (*Kát'a Kabanová*). He created Cousin Brandon in Hindemith's *Long Christmas Dinner* (1961). A most versatile singer, he excelled in German roles. His daughter Evelyn (*b* Leipzig, 23 May 1939) sang in Europe and South Africa as a mezzo-soprano.

ELIZABETH FORBES

Dale, Laurence (*b* Pyecombe, Sussex, 10 Sept 1957). English tenor. He studied at the GSM, making his début in 1981 with the ENO as Camille. He sang Don José in Peter Brook's version of *La tragédie de Carmen* in Paris (1981–2) and New York (1983), Romeo at Basle and Ramiro at Glyndebourne (1983), and then Pong (*Turandot*) in Los Angeles and at Covent Garden (1984). For the WNO he has sung Don Ottavio, Ferrando, Gabriel von Eisenstein and Alfredo, and for Opera North, Tamino, Jeník and Belmonte. He has also sung at Lyons, Amsterdam, Geneva and Brussels as well as at Aix-en-Provence, where he took part in *Les Indes galantes* (1990). His repertory includes Monteverdi's Orpheus, Lensky, Jaquino and Gonzalve (*L'heure espagnole*). His high-lying and sweet-toned voice is particularly suited to French music. ELIZABETH FORBES

Dalgerie. Tragic opera in one act by JAMES PENBERTHY to a libretto by Mary Durack after her novel *Keep him my Country*; Perth, Australia, Somerville Auditorium, 22 January 1959.

Dalgerie (soprano), an aboriginal woman with leprosy, waits to see her former white lover and employer, Stan (baritone), before she dies. There is a series of flashbacks to the events leading to the present. Because a marriage between Dalgerie and Stan is forbidden by tribal law, she performs love magic to ensure that 'though they may be parted in life, their spirits can be united in death'. Dalgerie resists tribal love rituals (played by a band of aborigines) and Stan tries to take her away from them, but she realizes that she now belongs to Julunggal, the snake. Dalgerie leaves the district and spreads a rumour that she has died. In their final meeting she reassures Stan that they will be reunited, and then dies in his arms. Penberthy's score makes use of driving rhythmic and melodic ideas from aboriginal music, combined with his own romantic idiom that he feels is a response to the mystical and melancholic qualities of the Australian landscape. *Dalgerie* has the distinction of being the first opera to be staged in the Sydney Opera House, in two matinée performances for schoolchildren (23 and 24 July 1973); at the official opening of the house on 25 July 1973, it shared a double bill with Sitsky's *The Fall of the House of Usher*. MICHAEL HANNAN

D'Alibert, Giacomo. *See* ALIBERT, GIACOMO D'.

Dalibor. Opera in three acts by BEDŘICH SMETANA to a libretto by JOSEF WENZIG; Prague, New Town Theatre, 16 May 1868.

Vladislav *Czech king*	baritone
Dalibor *a knight*	tenor
Budivoj *commander of the king's castle guard*	baritone
Beneš *a gaoler*	bass
Vítek *Dalibor's messenger*	tenor
Milada *sister of the Burgrave of Ploškovice*	soprano
Jitka *a country girl on Dalibor's estates*	soprano
Zdeněk *a musician (vision)*	silent

Judges, the king's soldiers, Dalibor's messengers and servants, the people, priests

Setting 15th-century Prague, partly in the castle and its environs, partly in the lower town

Dalibor was one of Josef Wenzig's six plays and opera librettos based on Czech history. As a Czech sympathizer but German-speaker he wrote in German and his *Dalibor* and *Libuše* texts had to be translated into Czech. This was undertaken by his pupil Ervín Špindler, who preserved the line lengths and metres of the original so that, it is claimed, the operas could be performed in either Czech or German (an odd concept for such nationalist works). It seems more likely that Špindler had little option as far as *Dalibor* is concerned since Smetana began composition on 15 April 1865, even before Wenzig finalized his text (Wenzig's completed German text is dated 16 June 1865). According to references in his letters, Smetana completed Act 1 in sketch by 12 October 1865 and on 3 April 1866 he was working on Act 2. The full score is dated as follows: Act 1, 15 September 1866; Act 2, 24 October 1867; Act 3, 29 December 1867.

Dalibor was first performed on the day of the ceremonial laying of the foundation stone of the National Theatre on 16 May 1868, by which time Smetana had become chief conductor at the Provisional Theatre and conducted the opera's première. By the next performance it was clear that the work was not popular with audiences and it was attacked in the press for not sounding sufficiently 'Czech'. Its lack of success encouraged Smetana to make revisions. He made two cuts, amounting to over 70 bars, in the Act 2 scene between Dalibor and Milada and revised and extended the end of Act 3. These changes, made in 1870, had no effect on the opera's fortunes; it was given a few times and then disappeared from the repertory. Its later popularity with Czech audiences dates from 5 December 1886 when it was performed for the first time at the Prague National Theatre.

ACT 1 *The castle courtyard* There is no overture. A 22-bar prelude, introducing the motto theme (ex.1) of

this predominantly monothematic opera, leads into a sombre chorus of 'people', waiting to hear Dalibor's fate. Individual sentiments are voiced by Jitka, an orphan whom Dalibor has cared for. The brief recapitulation of the choral-orchestral opening brings Jitka to a decision: Dalibor will be freed, and her new sentiments are conveyed by the joyous Allegro variant of ex.1, 'Ze žaláře' ('A glow beckons from jail', ex.2).

Four offstage trumpets announce the arrival of King Vladislav. His entry music, based on a descending variant of ex.1 (ex.3), is slow-paced, finely gradated and

surprisingly long: 57 bars. Although about to judge Dalibor and thus placed in opposition to the opera's hero, Vladislav is depicted sympathetically and in the round. As he describes Dalibor's crime (disturbing the peace of the land, attacking the castle of Ploškovice and killing the Burgrave there), his solo goes through eight tempo changes, but the dominant manner is his first: 'con espressione' and *maestoso*.

Before sentencing Dalibor, the court invites Milada, sister of the murdered Burgrave, to speak. She is introduced by a solo harp cadenza, soon joined by a pair of clarinets. One of the glories of the Czech repertory, her speech is a substantial, multi-section declamation, its tempos and expression reflecting the different moods of the words as she pleads for vengeance and describes in vivid language the battle in which her brother fell. The part is written for a dramatic soprano with a strong lower register but capable of a thrilling climactic cry of 'Dalibor' to a top B. At the end her voice combines with that of Jitka in a new variant of ex.1 expressing the two women's different reactions. This duet provides a link to the third important entrance: that of Dalibor himself to a brief *maestoso* transformation of ex.1. All, including Milada, comment on his calm and noble bearing.

In recitative, Vladislav describes Dalibor's crime and invites his response. Far from denying the crime, Dalibor describes his friendship with the musician Zdeněk (ex.4, a *dolce* version of ex.1 with throbbing

triplet accompaniment) and then (Marziale) how Zdeněk fell in battle in Dalibor's longstanding feud with the Burgrave. In a strongly declamatory passage Dalibor declares how, even had the king stood in his way, he would have avenged his friend's death. The judges (a unison bass chorus) pronounce that Dalibor has condemned himself to death, and confer with the king.

A lyrical episode follows: a 6/8 Lento (including a variant of ex.1) in which Dalibor reveals himself untroubled by his probable fate since his life has been empty since the death of Zdeněk. Milada, whose voice occasionally mingles with his, is appalled. Then Dalibor's sentence is confirmed by one of the judges; he is to languish in gaol until he dies. His response is ecstatic: over ex.4 he sings 'quasi in exaltazione' that he looks forward to seeing Zdeněk again. Twice the chorus punctuate his solo with their astonishment at his noble bearing.

Milada is quite overcome. In a violent change of mood (Presto) she begs Vladislav to pardon him but, as the judges explain, Dalibor has threatened the king and must die. Vladislav himself, in a *tranquillo* passage with solemn brass accompaniment, declares that the law must be upheld. To a repeat of his entrance music, he withdraws with his retinue. The people disperse, leaving Milada and Jitka.

In a passionate 6/8 Presto Milada describes her feelings, 'Jaká, jaká to bouře ňadra mi plní' ('What a storm fills my breast!'). On her last word her voice combines with that of Jitka, who has observed her growing love for Dalibor and suggests action. This is agreed in an extended duet repetition of ex.2 as Jitka describes her plan for rescuing Dalibor from prison. Milada takes up her part; the two voices combine in what is in effect a vigorous cabaletta, a joyful pendant to their duet before Dalibor's entrance.

Act 2.i *A road in the lower town, with an inn* A new atmosphere is suggested by a brief prelude and by the strophic offstage chorus for soldiers – one of the few parts of the opera whose 'Czechness' appealed to its early audiences. Jitka meets her lover Vítek, their unanimity reflected in the intertwining 3rds and 6ths of their duet. Jitka then describes how Milada has dressed as a boy and with harp in hand has charmed her way into the castle in search of Dalibor. The soldiers come out of the tavern; their chorus is heard again with added parts for the two soloists. As they go off a long orchestral interlude covers the scene change and introduces the subdued mood of the next scene; a chromatic figure leads into a Largo with ostinato quavers in the bass.

2.ii *An inner room in the castle* Budivoj questions Beneš the gaoler about his new assistant, a 'poor musician', then, warning him to be vigilant over Dalibor, he departs. The chromatic figure and ostinato quavers of the prelude return to preface Beneš's aria about the hard life of a gaoler ('Ach, jak těžký žalářníka život jest'), a simple *ABA* structure against the quaver ostinato.

To exuberant music (Moderato, with frequent triplets in the voice part) Milada, now dressed as a boy, runs in with food for her new employer. Before he eats, Beneš goes to fetch his old violin (Dalibor has asked for a violin to relieve his boredom). Left alone, Milada expresses her agitation at the thought of seeing Dalibor (scena) and, to a surging orchestral accompaniment, her feelings of 'unbounded joy' ('Radostí nesmírnou') in the following aria. Beneš returns with a lamp and a violin for Milada to take to the prisoner, and, after a brief duet passage, both go off. An extended interlude includes Milada's harp cadenza from Act 1 and a new version of ex.4.

2.iii *A dark prison* Dalibor has woken from a dream about Zdeněk; in a broad Andante amoroso he expresses his thoughts about embracing him. His reverie is interrupted by the arrival of Milada. Dalibor is thrilled with the violin and cries out to Zdeněk; only then does he notice the 'boy' and asks who he is. To the passionate theme from her first solo in Act 1 Milada reveals herself; regretting her earlier pleas for vengeance, she has come to try and rescue him. Then in an Andante (a slow, major-key variant of ex.1) she begs forgiveness. They vow faithfulness to one another and the act concludes with their Largo duet 'Ó nevýslovné štěstí lásky' ('O the unutterable happiness of love'), in which their voices intertwine as artlessly as those of the younger lovers at the beginning of the act. An orchestral postlude concludes with the Zdeněk variant (ex.4) of the motto theme.

Act 3.i *The royal chamber, brightly lit* The prelude includes Vladislav's march (ex.3), Beneš's quaver ostinato and a new *maestoso* theme. Budivoj warns King Vladislav of a rebellion by Dalibor's people and Beneš describes how his harp-playing assistant has disappeared, leaving instead a purse and a note telling him to keep silent. They withdraw. While his advisers confer, Vladislav sings a lyrical aria about the burdens of office. His advisers decree that Dalibor must die that day and Vladislav reluctantly gives instruction to Budivoj. The interlude begins with the motto theme in its original form and key (ex.1), passing on to Vladislav's march (ex.3), the concluding duet of Act 2, and Jitka's 'freedom' motif (ex.2).

3.ii *Dalibor's prison* Dalibor, now unfettered, sings a vigorous aria contemplating his impending freedom, 'Ha, kým to kouzlem' ('What magic is this'). His exultation is shortlived; just as he is about to give a signal on his violin, Budivoj appears with his soldiers and takes him off, to the strains of a march.

3.iii *In front of the prison; night, faint moonlight* Milada, Jitka, Vítek and their company are waiting for Dalibor's signal. When instead they hear an offstage chorus of monks, Milada realizes that they have been betrayed and, sword in hand, she leads her soldiers into the castle. All return, with Dalibor now bearing the mortally wounded Milada. They bid farewell to one

'Dalibor' (Smetana): drawings after the original production at the New Town Theatre, Prague (16 May 1868)

another, and Milada dies. Budivoj and his soldiers emerge and celebrate their victory. Dalibor throws himself into battle with them and dies joyfully with the thought that Zdeněk and Milada await him.

* * *

With Milada's Leonore-like bid to rescue Dalibor from his prison, this opera has been criticized for being a Czech *Fidelio*. There are, however, striking differences. This is not an opera about marital fidelity or the brotherhood of man. Dalibor shows more interest in his dead friend Zdeněk than in his would-be rescuer Milada. With its continuous scene-change music and thematic metamorphosis, the opera's aesthetic is that of Liszt and early Wagner, not of Beethoven. And in supplying Dalibor with a violin, the opera reinforces a favourite myth about the Czechs being good musicians. As Beneš, the music-loving gaoler who supplies the instrument for his charge, declares: 'What Czech does not love music?'. JOHN TYRRELL

Dalis, Irene [Yvonne] (*b* San Jose, CA, 8 Oct 1925). American mezzo-soprano. She studied in New York and Milan, and in Berlin with Margarete Klose. Her début was at the Oldenburg Landestheater in 1953 as Eboli; she repeated this role for her Metropolitan Opera début in 1957 and later took 21 other roles in 19 seasons there. Her European career included work in West Berlin, 1955–60, and Hamburg, 1967–71. In 1958 she made her British début at Covent Garden, singing Ortrud, and the next year sang the Nurse in the first American production of *Die Frau ohne Schatten* at San Francisco. She had notable success at Bayreuth, first as Ortrud in 1961 and later the same year as the first American Kundry there. She retired to San Jose in 1977, became a professor of voice studies at the University of California and started a professional company which in 1984 evolved into Opera San José; the company gives five productions a season, as well as educational and schools' performances, under her artistic direction. Besides having an international reputation in Wagner, she was much admired as Amneris, Azucena, Clytemnestra, Delilah, Electra (Strauss), Lady Macbeth and the Kostelnička (*Jenůfa*); her voice, displaying contralto depth and richness, was more sensuous than brilliant in timbre. NOËL GOODWIN

Dallapiccola, Luigi (*b* Pisino d'Istria, 3 Feb 1904; *d* Florence, 19 Feb 1975). Italian composer. He grew up in a disputed territory (then part of the Austrian empire), a circumstance that seems to have had a significant effect on his character in later life. Pisino was a frontier town and a crossroads of cultures. Dallapiccola's father was headmaster of the only Italian-language school in the region, and he gave his son a wide-ranging education steeped in the classics (this was to bear fruit later in works such as *Marsia* and *Ulisse*). During World War I, the school was considered subversive, and following its closure Dallapiccola and his family were interned at Graz. The intense concern with liberty which was to characterize his later work dates from this time. While in Graz, he grew to love opera, and after a performance of *Der fliegende Holländer* in 1917 determined to become a composer. Immediately after the war, Dallapiccola came to know the music of Debussy (*Pelléas* in particular impressed him) and he developed an enthusiasm (shared by many leading Italian composers of the day) for early Italian music, notably that of Monteverdi – he published a realization of *Il ritorno di Ulisse* in 1942 – and Gesualdo.

In 1922 Dallapiccola moved to Florence, where he studied with Vito Frazzi at the conservatory, subsequently making the city his home for the rest of his life. Following a performance there of *Pierrot lunaire* in 1924, putting him in touch with the music of the Second Viennese School, he taught himself 12-note technique. He worked slowly and painstakingly in the absence of any literature on the subject, and in isolation, as his enthusiasm was not shared by the Italian musical establishment, and during the Fascist period performances of such music were rare and scores hard to come by. Through the examples of Berg and, during the 1940s and 50s, Webern, he gradually forged a language of his own, amalgamating Germanic serial and developmental procedures with a characteristically Italian feel for melody. He became the principal pioneer of dodecaphony in Italy and also encouraged other Italian composers, playing a major part in getting them re-admitted to the ISCM in 1946. From 1934 to 1967 he taught at the Florence Conservatory while gaining international recognition as a lecturer on his many visits abroad (notably in the USA).

Dallapiccola's first acknowledged works, dating from the early 1930s, are in general contrapuntally conceived, often juxtaposing a somewhat archaic diatonicism with bold and intense chromaticism; he later described this music as 'anecdotal'. Mussolini's Ethiopian campaign of 1935 led Dallapiccola to reconsider his role as a composer, as he himself put it: 'the world of ... carefree serenity closed for me, without the possibility of return ... I had to find other timber in other woods'. His subsequent music combined impassioned political protest with an increasingly refined serial technique. In his first stage work, *Volo di notte* (1937–8), Dallapiccola incorporated material from his *Tre laudi*, settings of the 13th-century mystic poet Jacopone da Todi. This re-use of music originally associated with medieval religious texts in an opera about night flying is typical of Dallapiccola, who tended towards a religious interpretation of everyday existence. *Volo di notte* is, however, unique in Dallapiccola's output in that it takes as its ostensible subject matter an aspect of contemporary technological advance; in his later operas *Il prigioniero* and *Ulisse*, as well as the ballet *Marsia* and the *sacra rappresentazione Job*, he had recourse to historical, mythological or biblical sources, thus making his symbolism less specifically tied to time or place.

The *Canti di prigionia* were conceived in 1938 (when Mussolini adopted Hitler's race policies) and were directly inspired by events during the early years of World War II; Dallapiccola chose texts by Mary Stuart, Boethius and Savonarola that predated such events but seemed to 'mirror a perennial human condition' in their concern with liberty and trust in God. The *Canti* end positively in tone ('Let the foe rise up, I fear nothing'), but their sequel, *Il prigioniero* (1944–8), Dallapiccola's second opera, is more pessimistic. Musically its idiom is dodecaphonic, though often the series contain diatonic segments, giving the music a goal-directed, almost romantic character. Both music and text are concentratedly symbolic; the three series represent hope, prayer and freedom, and other motifs come to the fore symbolizing the liberty for which the prisoner yearns, spurred on by the false friendship of the gaoler. At the end this freedom is found to be nothing but an illusion and, as the offstage chorus sings words from the Prayer of Mary Stuart (canto i), the prisoner is led off to the fire, his hope and prayer come to nothing. His final words are a question ('la libertà?') which, writing in 1960, Dallapiccola said he hoped one day to be in a position to answer. That day came in 1968, at the end of *Ulisse*.

The composer's next stage work, *Job* (1950), again deals with a crisis of faith. It is his first major work to be based largely on a single series, and its melodic writing is more angular than that of *Il prigioniero*. By making doubt, and the solitude that comes with it, the central theme of his dramatic works, while also exploring religious and philosophical topics, leaving them unresolved, Dallapiccola considered his operas to fall within the tradition of Busoni's *Doktor Faust* and Schoenberg's *Moses und Aron*. After *Job* Dallapiccola continued to refine his dodecaphonic technique, and by the mid-1950s his style had reached a state of stability: the influence of Webern became absorbed into a personal language now of exceptional sensitivity, from which all tonal references had been expunged. In his choice of texts he was nevertheless guided by the same concerns. Dallapiccola later refined his ideas in a series of works about death which culminated in *Ulisse*, a long-meditated project that, taking Homer's *Odyssey* as its model, traces Ulysses' career through times of doubt and solitude to the point where he discovers God. *Ulisse* is Dallapiccola's only full-length opera and was composed over eight years. It follows the example of Dante and Tennyson in making the Greek hero a searcher after truth, and both musically and philosophically it has much in common with *Moses und Aron*. It was deliberately conceived as a summation of Dallapiccola's work. Most of the themes and imagery he had used from the 1930s are present, and the epilogue, in which Ulysses – restless and searching even after reaching Ithaca – contemplates the stars, is a collage of quotations from earlier works.

After *Ulisse* Dallapiccola devoted himself to teaching and to adapting his most important articles and lectures for publication (1970). In his meditation on death, *Sicut umbra* (1970), the star symbolism that was so important in his three operas appears as a graphic image: the music is notated so that the figures look in the score like well-known constellations. In 1972 Dallapiccola's health began to deteriorate and he completed no more compositions.

See also JOB; PRIGIONIERO, IL; ULISSE; and VOLO DI NOTTE.

Volo di notte, 1937–8 (1, Dallapiccola, after A. de Saint-Exupéry: *Vol de nuit*), Florence, Pergola, 18 May 1940, vs (Milan, 1940), full score (Vienna, 1964)

Il prigioniero, 1944–8 (prol., 1, Dallapiccola, after V. de l'Isle-Adam: *La torture par l'espérance* and C. de Coster: *La légende d'Ulenspiegel et de Lamme Goedzak*), RAI, 1 Dec 1949; stage, Florence, Comunale, 20 May 1950 (Milan, 1948)

Job (sacra rappresentazione, 1, Dallapiccola, after Bible), Rome, Eliseo, 30 Oct 1950 (Milan, 1951)

Ulisse, 1960–68 (prol., 2, epilogue, Dallapiccola, after Homer: *The Odyssey*), Berlin, Deutsche Oper, 29 Sept 1968 (Milan, 1971)

*

L. Dallapiccola: '*Volo di notte* di L. Dallapiccola', *Scenario*, ix (1940), 176–7

A. Mantelli: 'Lettera da Firenze: Volo di notte di Dallapiccola', *RaM*, xiii (1940), 274

F. Ballo: *Arlecchino di Ferruccio Busoni, Volo di notte di Luigi Dallapiccola, Coro di morti di Goffredo Petrassi* (Milan, 1942)

L. Dallapiccola: 'Per la prima rappresentazione di Volo di notte', *Letteratura*, vi/3 (1942), 10

R. Vlad: 'Il Prigioniero', *Fiera letteraria*, iv/49 (1949), 7

M. Mila: '*Il prigioniero* di Luigi Dallapiccola', *RaM*, xx (1950), 303–11

R. F. Goldman: 'Current Chronicle: New York', *MQ*, xxxvii (1951), 405–10 [on *Canti di prigionia* and *Il prigioniero*]

L. Dallapiccola: 'The Genesis of the *Canti di prigionia* and *Il prigioniero*', *MQ*, xxxix (1953), 355–72

G. Gavazzeni: 'Volo di notte di Dallapiccola', *La musica e il teatro* (Pisa, 1954), 221–37

J. Rufer: 'Luigi Dallapiccola: "Il prigioniero"', *Oper im XX. Jahrhundert*, ed. H. Lindlar, Musik der Zeit, vi (Bonn, 1954), 56

K. H. Wörner: 'Dallapiccolas *Job*', *Melos*, xxi (1954), 208–10

A. Jacobs: 'Luigi Dallapiccola and the Stage: Job', *The Listener* (17 Sept 1959), 460

L. Dallapiccola: 'The Birth-pangs of Job', *Musical Events*, xv/5 (1960), 26
——: 'A Composer's Problem', *Opera*, xii (1961), 8–11
F. D'Amico: 'Liberazione e prigionia'; 'La verità di Dallapiccola', *I casi della musica* (Milan, 1962), 139–42; 152–5
G. Ugolini: '*Il prigioniero* di Luigi Dallapiccola', *RaM*, xxxii (1962), 233–41
J. C. G. Waterhouse: 'Dallapiccola, Luigi: *Volo di notte*', *ML*, xlvi (1965), 86–8
D. Drew: 'Dallapiccola's Odyssey', *The Listener* (17 Oct 1968), 514–15
L. Dallapiccola: 'Nascita di un libretto d'opera', *NRMI*, ii (1968), 605; repr. in Dallapiccola (1970), 171–87; Eng. trans., abridged, *The Listener* (23 Oct 1969), 553–4
M. Mila: 'Dallapiccola und seine Bühnenwerke', *Opern Journal* (1968–9), no.2, pp.4–11
'Opinioni: il giudizio sull'*Ulisse* di Dallapiccola e sulla prima rappresentazione mondiale alla Deutsche Oper di Berlino nei principali commenti della stampa italiana ed internazionale', *NRMI*, ii (1968), 1269–78
A. Böhm: 'Die Heimkehr des Odysseus in Eyvind Johnsons "Strändernas svall"', *Istituto universitario orientale: annali (sezione germanica)*, xiii (Naples, 1970), 23–79, esp. 45ff
L. Dallapiccola: *Appunti, incontri, meditazioni* (Milan, 1970)
'Opinioni: I commenti della stampa italiana alla "prima" in Italia dell'*Ulisse* di Luigi Dallapiccola', *NRMI*, iv (1970), 205–9
J. C. G. Waterhouse: 'A Concern for Freedom', *Times Literary Supplement* (19 Nov 1971) [on *Appunti, incontri, meditazioni*]
F. Nicolodi, ed.: *Luigi Dallapiccola: saggi, testimonianze, carteggio, biografia e bibliografia* (Milan, 1976)
L. Dallapiccola: *Parole e musica* (Milan, 1980; trans., and selections ed. R. Shackelford, 1987, as *Dallapiccola on Opera: Selected Writings*)
D. Kämper: 'Uno sguardo nell'officina: gli schizzi e gli abbozzi del *Prigioniero* di Luigi Dallapiccola', *NRMI*, xiv (1980), 227–39
——: *Gefangenschaft und Freiheit: Leben und Werke des Komponisten Luigi Dallapiccola* (Cologne, 1984)
——: *Luigi Dallapiccola* (Florence, 1985)
M. Venuti: *Il teatro di Dallapiccola* (Milan, 1985)

ANTHONY SELLORS

Dallapozza, Adolf (*b* Bozen, 14 April 1940). Austrian tenor. He studied in Vienna while singing in the Volksoper chorus and made his début in 1962 as Ernesto. Engaged in Vienna for some 20 years, he sang at the Volksoper and Staatsoper in a varied repertory that included Ferrando, Tamino, Jaquino, Tonio (*La fille du régiment*), Werther, Wilhelm Meister, the Baron (*Der Wildschütz*), Don Gaston (*Die drei Pintos*), Albert Herring, the Man with a Donkey (*Die Kluge*), Camille (*Die lustige Witwe*) and many other operetta parts. He also sang in Munich and Hamburg and at La Scala (as Jaquino). Among his other roles were Monteverdi's Orpheus, Don Narciso, Elvino, the Italian Singer (*Der Rosenkavalier* and *Capriccio*) and Sutermeister's Romeo. A versatile artist, he had a voice not large but well projected.

ELIZABETH FORBES

Dall'Argine, Costantino (*b* Parma, 12 May 1842; *d* Milan, 1 March 1877). Italian composer and conductor. He studied composition at Busseto and at the Milan Conservatory. He became famous for his ballets, of which he wrote more than 30; they owed their success to a facile brilliance conforming to the taste of the day: *Brahma* was acclaimed as a symbol of traditional Italian music in opposition to Boito's avant-garde tendencies when it was performed with his *Mefistofele* at La Scala (7 and 8 March 1868). Dall'Argine composed three operas. Two were performed in Milan in 1867: *I due orsi* (ob, 3, A. Ghislanzoni; S Radegonda, 14 Feb) and *Il diavolo zoppo* (A. Scalvini; Fossati, 10 Dec). His unsuccessful attempt to set *Il barbiere di Siviglia* (C. Sterbini; Bologna, Comunale, 11 Nov 1868; vs, Bologna, *c*1870) aroused sharp but short-lived controversy, followed by rapid and complete oblivion for this mediocre score, dedicated to Rossini. Dall'Argine had a successful career as a theatre conductor.

ES (C. Sartori)

FRANCESCO BUSSI

Dalla Rizza, Gilda (*b* Verona, 12 Oct 1892; *d* Milan, 4 July 1975). Italian soprano. She studied with Alerano Ricci at Bologna, making her début there in 1912 as Charlotte. She created Magda in *La rondine* at Monte Carlo (1917) and was also the first Italian Suor Angelica and Lauretta (1919, Rome); at the first Covent Garden performances (1920) she failed to repeat her successes in these roles. After a performance of *La fanciulla del West* at Monte Carlo in 1921 Puccini said 'At last I've seen my Fanciulla'; although he wrote Liù with her in mind, the role was created by another singer. Having first appeared at La Scala in 1915 as Yaroslavna (*Prince Igor*), she was engaged there from 1923 to 1939; her Violetta caused a sensation. She created 13 of the 58 roles in her repertory, including Zandonai's Giulietta and Mariella in Mascagni's *Il piccolo Marat*; she was the first Italian Arabella at Genoa in 1936. She retired from the stage in 1939, but played Angelica once more during the 1942 Puccini celebrations at Vicenza. A beautiful woman, generally considered a great singing actress, she was called the 'Duse of the Lyric Theatre'.

GV (E. Gara; R. Vegeto)
M. J. Matz: 'Gilda dalla Rizza', *ON*, xxxiv/13 (1969–70), 22–3

HAROLD ROSENTHAL/R

Dallas. American city. It was founded in 1841 as a trading post and has grown to be one of the two largest urban centres in Texas. Field's Theatre (1873), a second-floor room in a frame building located on the south side of Main Street between Lamar and Austin streets, later renamed the Dallas Opera House, was the site of the first operatic production with orchestra, Flotow's *Martha* (1875). Lacking even one dressing-room, and with access to the backstage area through a window, the theatre was immediately inadequate. A new Dallas Opera House (1883, destroyed by fire in 1901) was constructed on the south-west corner of Commerce Street and Austin Street. It opened with Gilbert and Sullivan's *Iolanthe*, presented by the Chicago Ideal Opera Company. The third Dallas Opera House (on Main Street and St Paul Street; cap. 1700) was completed in 1904. In 1905 the Metropolitan Opera Company of New York included Dallas in a 16-city national tour of Wagner's *Parsifal*. The Metropolitan was not to appear again in Dallas for 34 years, but other touring companies helped to build an audience for opera. Between 1911 and 1924 the Chicago Opera Company brought such artists as Tetrazzini in *Lucia di Lammermoor*, Shalyapin in *Boris Godunov* and Boito's *Mefistofele*, and Mary Garden (*Thaïs* and *Salome*). After the Dallas Opera House burnt down in 1921 some touring groups used the Fair Park Coliseum (cap. 3000). In the 1930s and 40s the San Carlo Opera Company brought popular operas to Dallas, staging them in the more intimate Majestic Theatre (1925 Elm Street; cap. 1500).

Through the efforts of Arthur L. Kramer and the Dallas Grand Opera Association, the Metropolitan added Dallas to its roster in 1939. Grace Moore sang Manon, Melchior and Rethberg were heard in

Tannhäuser. *Otello* and *Bohème* (the latter prefaced by the fourth-act prelude and ballet from *Carmen*) completed the repertory heard at Fair Park Music Hall (opened 1925, cap. 4100). The Metropolitan continued to present a season of four operas each spring until 1982 (except for 1941–3, 1961, and 1972, when the Music Hall was closed for renovation).

The impresario Lawrence Kelly and the conductor Nicola Rescigno, who had lost an operatic power struggle in Chicago, chose Dallas as a suitable arena for their considerable talents, and the Dallas Civic Opera was inaugurated on 21 November 1957 with a gala concert by Maria Callas. The following night the first operatic production, *L'italiana in Algeri* (not staged in America since 1919), featured the mezzo-soprano Giulietta Simionato, with stage design and direction by Franco Zeffirelli in his American début. In subsequent seasons Callas sang Violetta, Lucia and Cherubini's Medea; Joan Sutherland made her American stage début (1960) in Handel's *Alcina*, and also appeared in *Don Giovanni* and *Lucia di Lammermoor*; other important American débuts were those of Luigi Alva, Teresa Berganza, Montserrat Caballé and Jon Vickers. Each season consisted of three or four productions, scheduled during the autumn to fit in with the commitments of the Dallas SO, Fair Park Music Hall, and imported key figures such as the Scala chorus masters Norberto Mola and Roberto Benaglio and the prompter Vasco Naldini. Popular operas from the standard Italian repertory were presented in glittering productions, as were less familiar works, particularly Baroque operas (*L'incoronazione di Poppea*, *Dido and Aeneas*, *The Fairy-Queen* and *Giulio Cesare*).

After Kelly's death in 1974, Rescigno was both general and artistic director for three seasons and continued to conduct a majority of the performances, including the first American staging of a Vivaldi opera (*Orlando furioso*, 1980). 1975 saw the company's first Wagner production (*Tristan und Isolde*), with Jon Vickers. In 1977 Plato Karayanis was named general director. The company changed its name to the Dallas Opera in 1981, the 25th-anniversary season, during which a *Ring* cycle was begun with *Die Walküre*; *Rheingold* (1982), *Siegfried* (1984) and *Götterdämmerung* (1985) followed. Spring seasons (1984–6) in the renovated Majestic Theatre gave opportunities for opera of a more intimate nature, including works by Monteverdi, Cimarosa, Rossini, Menotti, Thomson and Britten. Dallas Opera's first commissioned work, *The Aspern Papers* by Dominick Argento, had its première in 1988. The 1989 season was the company's first without the Dallas SO (unavailable because of an expanded subscription series). Joan Sutherland opened it with her American stage farewell performances; at the season's end, the resignation of Rescigno signalled the end of an era. With its own orchestra and the increased availability of space, Dallas Opera added a fifth production to its schedule and extended its season for an additional winter month.

Both the University of North Texas (Denton) and Southern Methodist University (Dallas) support opera workshops which annually stage complete operas as well as scenes. John Burrows, director of opera at SMU from 1980 to 1983, founded Dallas's second opera company, Public Opera, which gave its first season in summer 1984, with three productions at the Plaza Theatre (a small former cinema near SMU). In 1987 the company changed its name to Lyric Opera of Dallas and in 1988 moved to the Majestic Theatre. The repertory, all sung in English, usually includes at least one Gilbert and Sullivan work, an opera from the standard repertory, and a less familiar work – Rimsky-Korsakov's *Mozart and Salieri*, Offenbach's *La grande-duchesse de Gérolstein* and the Dallas composer Robert X. Rodriguez's *The Ransom of Red Chief* (première, 1986) have been given.

*

J. W. Rogers: *The Lusty Texans of Dallas* (New York, 1951)
Q. Eaton: *Opera Caravan* (New York, 1957)
J. Ardoin and G. Fitzgerald: *Callas* (New York, 1974)
J. Ardoin: 'The Kelly Years', *ON*, xxxix/5 (1974), 14–19
'Dallas Civic Opera Annals 1957–1974', *ON*, xxxix/5 (1974), 20 [diary of perfs.]
S. Acheson: *Dallas Yesterday* (Dallas, 1977)
J. Ardoin: *The Callas Legacy* (New York, 1977, 2/1982)
M. Seal: 'The Met in Dallas', *Bravo: the Dallas Grand Opera Celebrates the First 100 Years of the Metropolitan Opera* (Dallas, 1984), 10–13
R. Pines: 'A Glittering Beginning', *Dallas Opera Magazine*, x/6 (1987), 33–5
C. Noden-Skinner: 'Music in Dallas from 1916 to 1926', *Essays on Music History: a Birthday Tribute for Herbert Turrentine* (Dallas, 1988), 73–87

LARRY PALMER

Dal male il bene ('From Ill comes Good'). *Dramma musicale* in three acts by ANTONIO MARIA ABBATINI and MARCO MARAZZOLI to a libretto by Giacomo and GIULIO ROSPIGLIOSI after Antonio Sigler de Huerta's *No ay bien sin ageno daño*; Rome, Palazzo Barberini alle Quattro Fontane, 12 February 1654.

In a comedy of romantic misunderstandings, Don Diego (tenor) believes his Elvira (soprano) has taken up with Don Fernando (alto), who is only a stranger trying to help her. Diego's sister Leonora (soprano), in love with the dashing Fernando without knowing he feels the same about her, visits him disguised as a youth and believes he is courting Elvira. Elvira deceitfully tells Fernando that Leonora and Diego are lovers. The intrigues are compounded by the advice and collusion of Tabacco (baritone), Fernando's man, and Marina (soprano), Leonora's servant, but everything is sorted out in the end.

Though not the first opera to have comic characters, *Dal male il bene* is among the first to have comedy inherent in its plot; it has no elements of pastorale, classical *favola*, the supernatural or spectacle. The plot's twists are emphasized by the comings and goings in the apartments of Fernando and Diego, with transitions aired in a street set. Unusually specific stage directions and a detailed 'director's sheet' have survived, giving actors' cues, directions for actions and descriptions of the characters' emotions.

The libretto's language and the dialogue's pacing retain 17th-century Spanish and Italian decorum. The aristocrats' speech is lofty, even when they are angry, jealous or doubtful. Tabacco and Marina are colloquial and witty, without any stock-comic attributes. With only 18 lyrical numbers in 36 scenes, much of the score is in rapid and natural recitative, at its most expressive in Donna Elvira's sharply drawn character. Four duets offer lyric contemplation on the vicissitudes of love. The most notable solo arias are sung by Tabacco and define his insouciant wisdom.

The opera was staged twice in Rome in 1656, in different palaces. Most of the extant documentation, in large part published by Giorgina Masson (1966) and Galliano Ciliberti (1986), pertains to these performances.

MARGARET MURATA

Dal Monte, Toti [Meneghelli, Antonietta] (*b* Mogliano Veneto, 27 June 1893; *d* Treviso, 25 Jan 1975). Italian soprano. She studied in Venice with Barbara Marchisio and made her début at La Scala in 1916 as Biancafiore in Zandonai's *Francesca da Rimini.* In 1922 she sang Gilda at La Scala, and thereafter concentrated on the light soprano repertory, with occasional appearances in lyric roles (she was noted as Adina, Violetta and Butterfly); she sang in the première of Giordano's *Il re* in 1929. In the USA she sang Lucia and Gilda at the Metropolitan (1924) and appeared with the Chicago Opera (1924–8). Her only Covent Garden appearances were in 1925 as Lucia and Rosina, after which she joined Melba's company for the latter's farewell tour.

*

A. C. Renton: 'Toti dal Monte', *Record Collector*, iv (1949), 147–50 [with discography by G. Whelan]
T. Dal Monte: *Una voce nel mondo* (Milan, 1962) [autobiography]
D. Reutlinger: 'The Maestro's Singers: Toti Dal Monte, Soprano', *Il maestro*, i/3–4 (1969), 2–4 [with discography]

HAROLD ROSENTHAL/R

Dalmorès, Charles [Brin, Henry Alphonse] (*b* Nancy, 21 or 31 Dec 1871; *d* Los Angeles, 6 Dec 1939). French tenor. He began his musical career as an orchestral horn player in Paris, where he was at first refused admission to the Conservatoire because he was 'too good a musician to waste his time in being a mediocre singer'. He made his operatic début at Rouen, in 1899, as Siegfried. He then went to the Brussels Opera, and in 1904 first sang at Covent Garden, in *Faust.* He appeared in the British premières of Massenet's *Hérodiade*, Saint-Saëns' *Hélène*, Charpentier's *Louise* and Laparra's *Habanera*, as well as in the world première of Leoni's *L'oracolo* (1905). He also made a special study of Wagner, under Franz Emmerich, and in 1908 sang Lohengrin at Bayreuth. One of the most valued singers in Oscar Hammerstein's company at the Manhattan Opera House, New York (1906–10), he made his début there as Gounod's Faust and later sang Don José, Manrico and Pelléas among other roles. He sang regularly with the Boston and Philadelphia-Chicago companies, and as a member of the Chicago Opera (1910–18), where his roles included Tristan and Parsifal. He later taught in France and the USA. A sensitive musician and a colourful personality, he was also admired for his acting. His recordings show that his powerful voice was used with much technical accomplishment and a sense of style. J. B. STEANE

Dal Pane [Da'l Pane, Del Pane], **Domenico** (*b* Rome, *c*1630–33; *d* Rome, 10 Dec 1694). Italian soprano castrato. As a boy soprano at S Maria Maggiore in Rome (1641–6), he boarded and studied with A. M. Abbatini. By 1645 he had acquired a patron in Cardinal Rinaldo d'Este, then Cardinal Protector of France. He was a regular occasional singer in various Roman musical establishments until at least 1682, but served mainly in the Sistine Chapel (1654–79); during this time he also served Olimpia Aldobrandini Pamfili and became a priest. He sang with the Imperial Chapel in Vienna (1650–54) and visited Germany in 1672. He also composed madrigals and sacred vocal music.

He sang the solo prologue in a 1644 play at the Seminario Romano (*Crispo*, with music by Carlo Cecchelli) and may be the 'castrato d'Abbatini' who sang the prologue to *Dal male il bene* in 1656. As d'Este's protégé he had two roles in Luigi Rossi's *Orfeo* (1647, Paris) in which, as Proserpina, his singing on behalf of Eurydice affects Pluto more than does Orpheus's. As Colpa in Marazzoli's *La vita humana* (1656, Rome) and Beatrice in Abbatini's *La comica del cielo* (1668, Rome) he played forceful, dramatic roles in a consistently high soprano tessitura.

MARGARET MURATA

Dal Prato [Del Prato], **Vincenzo** (*b* Imola, 5 May 1756; *d* Munich, 1828). Italian castrato. He studied with Lorenzo Gibelli and made his début at the opera house in Fano in 1772. After touring extensively in Germany and the Netherlands, he sang at Stuttgart in 1779 for the future Russian Tsar Paul I. In 1780 Dal Prato was appointed to the court of Carl Theodor, the Elector of Bavaria, in Munich, where he spent the rest of his career. His voice was apparently a high mezzo. His most famous role was Idamantes in Mozart's *Idomeneo* (1781), and he also sang in Salieri's *Semiramide* (1782), Holzbauer's *Tancredi* (1783) and Vogler's *Castore e Polluce* (1787). Mozart complained about the inexperienced singer's poor stage presence and had to teach Dal Prato his music. But Dal Prato was apparently eager to learn, and Mozart referred to him as his 'molto amato castrato Dal Prato'. His singing was admired more for its grace and polished execution than its power or dramatic qualities.

*

F. J. Lipowsky: *Baierisches Musiklexikon* (Munich, 1811), 253–5
F. Haböck: *Die Gesangkunst der Kastraten* (Vienna, 1923)
——: *Die Kastraten und ihre Gesangkunst* (Stuttgart, 1927)
E. Anderson, ed.: *The Letters of Mozart and his Family* (London, 1938, 3/1985)
A. Heriot: *The Castrati in Opera* (London, 1956), 120–21

PAUL CORNEILSON

Dal Re, Vincenzo. *See* RE, VINCENZO.

Dalrymple, Frederick. *See* DALBERG, FREDERICK.

Dal segno (It.: 'from the sign'). An instruction, often abbreviated 'D.S.', placed at the end of the second (or later) section of a piece of music, indicating that the performer is to return to the sign at an earlier point and recapitulate the ensuing music up to a pause sign or the word *fine* ('end'). It was initially used, with the sign placed at the first vocal entry, simply to eliminate the repeat of the opening ritornello ('Dal segno al fine'). The 'dal segno aria' proper, however, came to succeed the DA CAPO aria about the middle of the 18th century; here the sign would lead the singer to a later point, usually the beginning of the second solo section or that point in the second solo where the music returns to the tonic key. *See* ARIA, §2(ii).

Dalton, Andrew (*b* Melbourne, 29 Sept 1950). Australian countertenor. He studied in Brisbane and made his début in 1974 at Vadstena, Sweden, in Provenzale's *La Stellidaura vendicata.* He has sung with Scottish Opera, at Berne, Amsterdam, Venice, Innsbruck, Paris, Geneva, Munich, Buxton and Lausanne. His repertory includes Monteverdi's *Orfeo* and *Il ritorno d'Ulisse*, Cavalli's *Egisto*, Handel's *Ariodante* and *Agrippina*, Conti's *Don Chisciotte*, Gluck's *Orpheus*, Jommelli's *La schiava liberata* and also *Fetonte* (1988, La Scala). His voice is particularly suited to Baroque music, but Britten's Oberon, which he has sung in Basle, Lübeck, Karlsruhe, Linz and Cologne, is among his best roles. ELIZABETH FORBES

D'Alvarez [Alvarez de Rocafuerte], **Marguerite** (*b* Liverpool, 1886; *d* Alassio, 18 Oct 1953). Mezzo-soprano of Peruvian parentage. She studied in Brussels and made her operatic début at Rouen as Delilah in 1907 or 1908. In 1909 she joined Hammerstein's Manhattan Opera Company, first appearing as Fidès in *Le prophète*. With the Boston Opera Company in 1913 she made a strong impression as the Mother in Wolf-Ferrari's *I gioielli della Madonna* and at Covent Garden in 1914 her Amneris in *Aida* won acclaim for the power, rich quality and ease of her singing. She appeared as Carmen at La Scala and as Léonor in *La favorite* at Marseilles. After 1918 she sang principally in concerts, giving her last London recital in 1939. She appeared in the film *Pandora and the Flying Dutchman* and wrote a colourful autobiography, *Forsaken Altars* (London, 1954), published also as *All the Bright Dreams* (New York, 1956). Her recordings show an exceptionally rich and well-produced voice but are too few to do justice to her wide repertory. J. B. STEANE

Dal Verme. Theatre in Milan, opened in 1872. It functioned as an opera house until 1930, when it became a cinema. *See* MILAN, §3.

Dam, José Van. *See* VAN DAM, JOSÉ.

Damase, Jean-Michel (*b* Bordeaux, 27 Jan 1928). French composer. Born into a musical family, he studied composition with Büsser, and has written much attractive, elegant music, close to the traditions of the Conservatoire. He won the Prix de Rome in 1947 and has since written prolifically for the stage, orchestra and chamber ensembles.

During the 1970s he was resident conductor at the Grand Théâtre in Bordeaux where several of his operatic works were performed. Particularly important are his collaborations with Jean Anouilh. *Eugène le mystérieux* (1964) puts a novelist on stage with his own characters and includes quotations of music by Liszt, Adam and Offenbach. *L'héritière* (1974) is the story of a girl who is abandoned by her suitor when he hears that she will be disinherited; the music is witty and often sardonic. *Madame de ...* , which uses some pastiche, is set in an age of drawing-room elegance before World War I, while in *Eurydice* (1972), a full-scale opera with a large cast (after Anouilh's *Point of Departure*), the Orpheus myth is transferred to a Paris railway station. Eurydice, in order to purify herself from an excess of lovers, attempts suicide.

La tendre Eléonore, 1958 (opéra-bouffe, 1, L. Masson), Marseilles, Opéra, 18 Jan 1962
Colombe (comédie lyrique, 4, J. Anouilh), Bordeaux, Grand, 5 May 1961
Eugène le mystérieux (feuilleton musical, 2, M. Achard, after E. Sue), Paris, Châtelet, 7 Feb 1964
Le matin de Faust (légende dramatique, 3, Y. Gautier and F. Dereyne), Nice, Opéra, 15 Jan 1966
Madame de ... (roman musical, 1, Anouilh, after L. de Vilmorin), Monte Carlo, Opera, 26 March 1970
Eurydice (comédie lyrique, 3, Anouilh), Bordeaux, Grand, 26 May 1972
L'héritière (4, L. Ducreux, after adaptation by R. and A. Goetz of H. James: *Washington Square*), Nancy, Grand, 13 March 1974

*

M. Mari: 'Quarante ans de créations françaises à Monte-Carlo', *Le théâtre lyrique français 1947–85*, ed. D. Pistone (Paris, 1987), 339–46 RICHARD LANGHAM SMITH

Damask Drum, The. Opera by Paavo Heininen. *See* *SILKKIRUMPU*.

Dambis, Pauls (*b* Riga, 30 June 1936). Latvian composer. He graduated from the Latvian State Conservatory in 1962. From 1965 to 1969 he was a producer for Latvian television, from 1968 to 1978 deputy chairman of the Soviet Latvian Composers' Union and from 1984 to 1989 chairman of the Latvian Composers' Union. In addition, he has taken part in folklore expeditions for the Latvian Academy of Sciences. His opera *Ikars* ('Icarus', 1970; 2, J. Peters) was first performed in Riga in 1976. Based on the legend of a 17th-century peasant who descends from a church spire on wings he has made himself, it is a drama of ideas on the relationship between a genius and conservative society that combines oratorio style with expressionist recitatives. Dambis's television mono-opera *Vēstules nākamībai* ('Letters to the Future'; 1, V. Oga) appeared in 1972. In the opera *Karālis Līrs* ('King Lear', 1983; 3, after W. Shakespeare) Renaissance and classical features are heard alongside expressionist elements. A composer of striking individuality, he is notable for his use of innovatory timbres and textures in chamber and choral music, especially in works freely based on Latvian folk texts and melodies.

*

I. Zemzare: *Paula Dambja spēles* [Games of Pauls Dambis] (Riga, 1990) JĒKABS VĪTOLIŅŠ, ARNOLDS KĻOTIŅŠ

Dame. Theatre in Rome, originally known as Teatro Alibert, renovated and opened in Carnival 1726. *See* ROME, §2.

Dame blanche, La ('The White Lady'). *Opéra comique* by ADRIEN BOIELDIEU to a libretto by EUGÈNE SCRIBE after WALTER SCOTT's novels *Guy Mannering*, *The Monastery* and *The Abbot*; Paris, Opéra-Comique (Salle Feydeau), 10 December 1825.

The opera is set in Scotland in 1753. Dickson (tenor), a tenant farmer on the estate of the late Count Avenel, and his wife Jenny (mezzo-soprano) are about to celebrate the baptism of their young son when they realize that there is no godfather. A young officer in the English army, Georges [George] Brown (tenor), offers his services. Dickson tells Brown that the castle is going to be auctioned by the corrupt steward, Gaveston (baritone), who intends to buy it and the title himself. Jenny sings the Ballad of The White Lady ('D'ici voyez ce beau domaine'), the 'White Lady' being the guardian spirit of the Avenels. Dickson receives a letter from the White Lady summoning him to the castle. As he is too frightened to obey, Brown volunteers to go instead.

In the castle Anna (soprano), an orphan brought up by the Count and Countess Avenel (who both died in exile), tells the old housekeeper Marguerite (mezzo-soprano) how she looked after a wounded soldier who reminded her of Julien, the missing Avenel heir. Gaveston announces his plans for the auction the following morning. Brown arrives, seeking shelter for the night. Left alone, he sings a cavatina, 'Viens, gentille dame'. The White Lady, who is Anna veiled and in disguise, enters. She recognizes Brown as the soldier she cared for in Hanover. Tomorrow he must obey her implicitly. Brown promises to do so.

Next morning the auction takes place. Dickson, on behalf of the Avenel tenants, bids against Gaveston but soon reaches his limit. Prompted by Anna, Brown enters the auction, outbids the steward and buys the castle for 500 000 francs. If that sum is not paid before midday he goes to prison.

Anna and Marguerite search for the statue of the White Lady in which is hidden the fortune of the Avenels. Brown has the strange feeling that he recognizes the castle. Overheard by Anna, Gaveston receives the news that George Brown (although unaware of it) is Julien Avenel. As midday strikes, the White Lady arrives with the treasure-chest. Gaveston tears off her veil and reveals Anna. Julien is told of his identity; he and Anna, once childhood sweethearts, are reunited.

La dame blanche, enormously popular in France during most of the 19th century, reached its 1000th performance by the Opéra-Comique in 1862. Boieldieu's delightful score is full of striking numbers, including Jenny's ballad, Brown's entrance aria and, in particular, the music sung by Anna, much of it very florid and preceded by harp arpeggios whenever the White Lady appears. The auction scene, an ensemble in the Italian style, is the musical centre of the opera; it has an intensity of dramatic expression rarely equalled and never surpassed in *opéra comique* of that period, either by Boieldieu himself or by any of his contemporaries.

For illustration *see* OPÉRA COMIQUE, fig.2. ELIZABETH FORBES

Damiani, Victor (*b* Montevideo, 1897; *d* Cerro Colorado, FL, 28 Jan 1962). Uruguayan baritone. After studying in Montevideo and Louvain, he made his début at 22 in Chile and Buenos Aires as Amonasro. He sang at the Solís in Montevideo and the Colón with Toti Dal Monte and Miguel Fleta in 1924, and with them opened the 1925 season at the Madrid Teatro Real. He sang 11 different roles at La Scala under Toscanini and Panizza, 1927–9. In 1930–31 he sang at the Teatro Reale, Rome; his last Italian appearance was in 1949 at the Teatro Massimo, Palermo, in *Tosca*, *Otello* and *Andrea Chénier*. The most acclaimed and internationally known of all Uruguayan singers, he died on stage during a concert performance. Damiani had a warm and resonant voice of extraordinary power, and was an outstanding actor, especially in such Verdi roles as Rigoletto, Germont, Renato, Amonasro and Luna.

SUSANA SALGADO

D'Amico, Fedele (*b* Rome, 27 Dec 1912; *d* Rome, 10 March 1990). Italian music critic, son of the theatre historian and critic Silvio D'Amico. After taking a law degree and studying music in Rome, he took up journalism. Besides working as music critic for several papers and journals in Rome, including *Voce operaia* (1943–4), *Vie nuove* (1948–54), *Il contemporaneo* (1954–9) and *L'espresso* (from 1967), he held editorial positions on *La rassegna musicale* (1941–4), *Enciclopedia dello spettacolo* (music and dance section, 1944–57) and *Nuova rivista musicale italiana* (from 1967). He also worked as an administrator and music consultant for organizations such as the Società Italiana per la Musica Contemporanea (1949–59), the publishing firm Il Saggiatore (1958–66) and the Teatro dell'Opera, Rome (1963–8). In 1963 he began teaching music history at the University of Rome, becoming full professor in 1977, a position he held until his retirement in 1988. In 1985 he was artistic director of the Maggio Musicale in Florence. He published biographies of Rossini (Turin, 1939) and Musorgsky (Turin, 1940) as well as a collection of essays, *I casi della musica* (Milan, 1962), and translated librettos for works by Mozart, Boccherini, Henze, Janáček, Weill, Hindemith, Stravinsky and Shostakovich. A member of several academies, he received the Penna d'Oro in 1989.

CAROLYN GIANTURCO

Dammtor [Theater am Dammtor]. Theatre in Hamburg, opened in 1827 as the Neues Stadt-Theater in the Dammtorstrasse; it was renamed the Hamburgische Staatsoper in 1934, destroyed in 1943 and rebuilt in 1955. *See* HAMBURG, §2.

Damnation de Faust, La ('The Damnation of Faust'). *Légende dramatique* in four parts by HECTOR BERLIOZ to a libretto by the composer and Almire Gandonnière after GÉRARD DE NERVAL's French translation of JOHANN WOLFGANG VON GOETHE's *Faust*; concert performance, Paris, Opéra-Comique (Salle Favart), 6 December 1846 (adapted as a fully staged opera in five acts by Raoul Gunsbourg for the Monte Carlo Opéra, 18 February 1893).

La damnation de Faust began to emerge in late 1845 when Berlioz undertook to revise and expand his *Huit scènes de Faust* of early 1829 into an 'opéra de concert', a natural outgrowth of the sorts of issues he had treated in his 'symphonie dramatique' *Roméo et Juliette* of 1839. He began to use the term 'légende' in late 1846. The *dramatis personae* are Faust (tenor), Méphistophélès (baritone or bass), Brander (bass) and Marguerite (mezzo-soprano), with a chorus and a children's chorus. *La damnation de Faust* was an artistic success but a failure at the box office. In late 1847, Berlioz briefly entertained the notion of rewriting the work as *Méphistophélès*, an opera for the bass Pischek with new texts by Scribe, but the idea was abandoned after a brief exchange of correspondence with the librettist in November and December 1847.

It was with his *version scénique* of Berlioz's masterpiece – somewhat shortened, and with the scenes reordered, and with Jean de Reszke as Faust at the première – that Raoul Gunsbourg established the Monte Carlo Opéra as one of the leading companies in Europe; his reign there endured for more than half a century. Within a year the staged version of *La damnation de Faust* had been presented in Milan, Strasbourg, Liverpool, Moscow and New Orleans. It was revived at Monte Carlo in 1902, with Melba and Jean de Reszke, and given in 1903 for the centenary of Berlioz's birth.

See also FAUST. D. KERN HOLOMAN

Damonte, Magali. *See* CHALMEAU-DAMONTE, MAGALI.

Damrosch, Leopold (*b* Posen [now Poznań], 22 Oct 1832; *d* New York, 15 Feb 1885). German conductor and composer. After studying at Berlin University, he abandoned a career in medicine in favour of music, becoming a pupil of Ries, S. W. Dehn and Böhmer. At first he conducted in Germany, mainly in Breslau; a Library of Congress inventory lists an opera *Romeo und Julia*, to his own libretto after Shakespeare, as having been performed there in 1862. Moving to New York in 1871, he was instrumental in the establishment of German opera at the Metropolitan, which had opened with a financially disastrous Italian season. Having formed a plan for German opera, he gathered a company of German singers and the season opened on 17 November

1884, ending on 11 February 1885. Damrosch conducted all the performances but the last, which took place a few days before his death.

Damrosch, Walter (Johannes) (*b* Breslau [now Wrocław], 30 Jan 1862; *d* New York, 22 Dec 1950). American conductor and composer of German birth. The son of Leopold Damrosch, he began his musical studies in Germany, moving to the USA with his family in 1871. By the age of 18 he was already conducting an oratorio society. When his father began a series of performances of German opera at the Metropolitan Opera in 1884, Walter, already a devotee of Wagner, became his assistant, and continued as assistant to Anton Seidl until 1891. From 1894 to 1899 he directed the Damrosch Opera Company in New York, which offered strong competition to the Metropolitan.

A highly influential figure in American musical life, Damrosch wanted to compose, but the demands of his conducting activities – notably with the New York Symphony (later Philharmonic) Society – forced composition into second place. He nonetheless completed three works for the stage. *The Scarlet Letter*, after Nathaniel Hawthorne's novel, was given its stage première by the Damrosch Opera Company in 1896 with a fine cast including the baritone David Bispham; Seidl called it a 'New England Nibelung trilogy', and Damrosch himself later agreed that it was over-influenced by Wagner. In 1900 he began work on *Cyrano de Bergerac*, to a libretto based on Rostand's play. He worked on it for a dozen years, breaking off to compose *The Dove of Peace*, a satirical comic opera (1912), which met with only qualified success. *Cyrano* was finally produced in New York, at the Metropolitan, only the fourth American opera to be heard there; though criticized for its length (four hours, after extensive cutting), it was praised for its orchestration and choral writing. Damrosch's autobiography, *My Musical Life*, was published in 1923.

Damrosch's last opera, composed between 1935 and 1937 (though he had considered the subject for two decades), was *The Man Without a Country*, based on the 1963 novel by Edward Everett Hale. The libretto by Arthur Guiterman, a writer better known for light verse than for serious efforts, was conventional: he introduced 'romantic interest' and the protagonist's heroic death in battle, neither of which figures in the novel. The score, which included some spoken passages, similar to the melodrama in the second act of *Fidelio*, was warmly received on the opening night, under the composer's direction. However, Olin Downes found the work 'melodious, but along too well-trodden paths', and it was not revived after the first run of performances.

The Scarlet Letter (G. P. Lathrop, after N. Hawthorne), Boston, 10 Feb 1896

Cyrano de Bergerac, 1900–12 (W. J. Henderson, after E. Rostand), New York, Met, 27 Feb 1913

The Dove of Peace (comic op, W. Irwin), Philadelphia, 15 Oct 1912

The Man Without a Country (A. Guiterman, after E. E. Hale), New York, Met, 12 May 1937

*

O. Downes: 'Music of the Times: New Opera at the Metropolitan', *New York Times* (9 May 1937)

——: 'Damrosch's Work Traditional Opera', *New York Times* (13 May 1937)

G. Damrosch Finletter: *From the Top of the Stairs* (Boston, 1946)

G. Bordman: *American Musical Theatre: a Chronicle* (New York, 1978), 281

STEVEN LEDBETTER

Damrosch Opera Company. American company formed and directed by Walter Damrosch, 1894–9, to perform German opera (especially Wagner) in New York and elsewhere after the Metropolitan Opera resumed performance of the French and Italian repertory. During its 1884–5 season the Metropolitan Opera Company, under the direction of Leopold Damrosch, was also sometimes referred to as the Damrosch Opera Company. *See* TRAVELLING TROUPES, §5(vi).

Damse, Józef (*b* Sokołów, nr Stryj, 26 Jan 1789; *d* Rudna, nr Warsaw, 15 Dec 1852). Polish composer. From 1809 to 1812 he was a clarinettist, trombonist and military bandmaster, from 1813 a singer and actor, first in Vilnius and then in Warsaw, where he began to compose operas. He wrote 40 comic operas and burlesques, 16 melodramas and three operas. He was not a composer with high artistic aspirations and, particularly in his stage works, he pandered to the lowest tastes of the public, though there are reminiscences of Mozart and Rossini operas known in Warsaw at the time, as well as popular melodies. In 1829 his *Chłop milionowy* ('The Millionaire Peasant'), based on a play by Raimund, created a sensation in Warsaw.

selective list; all first performed in Warsaw

Klarynecik magnetyczny [The Magnetic Clarinet] (comic op, 3, L. Dmuszewski), 26 Aug 1820

Dawne czasy [Old Times] (K. Godebski), National, 26 April 1826, collab. J. Stefani

Chłop milionowy, czyli Dziewczyna ze świata czarownego [The Millionaire Peasant, or The Girl from Fairyland] (melodrama, 3, Damse, after F. Raimund: *Das Mädchen aus der Feenwelt, oder Der Bauer als Millionär*), 26 Nov 1829

Oblubienica z Lammermooru [The Bride of Lammermoor] (after W. Scott), March 1832

Zamek Kenilworth [Kenilworth Castle] (after Scott), 1832

Bankocetle przeciete, czyli Aktorowie na prowincji [Snipped Banknotes, or Actors in the Provinces] (comic op, 2, S. Doliwa Starzyński), 20 April 1836

Kontrabandzista [The Smuggler] (3, S. Bogusławski, after Scott), 1 June 1844

ALINA NOWAK-ROMANOWICZ

Dan, Ikuma (*b* Tokyo, 7 April 1924). Japanese composer. He studied composition with Kan'ichi Shimofusa at the Tokyo Music School, and after graduating in 1945 studied further with Saburō Moroi and Yamada. In 1950 he made a successful début as a composer with his First Symphony, written for an NHK competition. In 1953 he formed the Sannin no Kai (Group of Three) with Akutagawa and Mayuzumi. Besides operas he has composed six symphonies and many vocal-orchestral works, as well as music for theatre, films and television.

The first of Dan's five operas, *Yūzuru* ('The Twilight Heron', 1952), was an immediate success and, with its simple lyricism and straightforward sentiment, became the most popular opera by a Japanese composer. It won a number of prizes, including the Kōsaku Yamada Prize, the Mainichi Music Prize and the Iba Opera Prize. By 1989 the work had received 550 performances and had been heard in Europe and the USA as well as in Asia. His second opera, *Kikimimi zukin* ('The Listening Cap', 1955), is based, like the first, on a folktale by Kinoshita and makes effective use of folk material. With *Yō Kihi* ('Yang Kwei-fei', 1958), he attempted a full-scale tragedy based on the true story of Yang Kwei-fei, the famous Chinese beauty who became a mistress of Emperor Xuan-zong. His fourth opera, *Hikarigoke* ('Luminous Moss', 1972), which won an Art Festival Prize, created a sensation for its dramatic narration of a shocking story of stranded men resorting to cannibalism. The composer returned to a folk subject with *Chanchiki* (1975), the story of a fox who tries to teach his way of life to his son; it was performed at Belgrade, Budapest, Luxembourg and Dresden during autumn 1989.

See also YŪZURU.

Yūzuru [The Twilight Heron] (1, J. Kinoshita), Osaka, Asahi Hall, 30 Jan 1952, vs (Tokyo, 1955); rev. version, Zürich, 27 June 1957, vs (Tokyo and London, 1976)
Kikimimi zukin [The Listening Cap] (3, Kinoshita), nr Osaka, Takarazuka, 18 March 1955
Yō Kihi [Yang Kwei-fei] (3, J. Osaragi), Tokyo, Sankei Hall, 11 Dec 1958
Hikarigoke [Luminous Moss] (2, T. Takeda), Osaka, International Festival Hall, 27 April 1972, vs (Tokyo, 1984)
Chanchiki (2, Y. Mizuki), Tokyo, Metropolitan Festival Hall, 13 Oct 1975, vs (Tokyo, 1980)

MASAKATA KANAZAWA

Danaïdes, Les ('The Danaids'). *Tragédie lyrique* in five acts by ANTONIO SALIERI to a libretto by MARIE FRANÇOIS LOUIS GAND LEBLANC ROULLET and Tschudi after RANIERI DE' CALZABIGI; Paris, Opéra, 26 April 1784.

Set in ancient Greece, *Les Danaïdes* is a gruesome story of vengeance, deception and murder. Danaus (baritone) and his daughters, the Danaids (chorus of sopranos and altos), swear an oath of friendship to the sons of Aegyptus, brother and arch-enemy of Danaus. Aegyptus is dead; the eldest of his sons, Lyncée [Lynceus] (tenor), now leads the family. As part of the treaty of friendship, Lynceus and his brothers are engaged to be married to the Danaids, Lynceus himself to Hypermnestre [Hypermnestra] (soprano), the eldest. Lynceus and Hypermnestra sing of their love for one another in the duet 'Oublions tous ces jours de peine'.

In a dungeon Danaus reveals to his daughters that he deceitfully arranged the reconciliation with Aegyptus's sons as part of his plan to avenge the wrongs committed against him by Aegyptus. He commands his daughters to kill their husbands; all except Hypermnestra swear an oath to Nemesis, goddess of vengeance, promising to do so. Danaus confronts Hypermnestra, demanding that she too promise to kill her husband. He refers to the prediction of an oracle: if his vengeance is not complete he will be killed by one of Aegyptus's sons. Left alone, Hypermnestra faces her dilemma: if she saves Lynceus by warning him of her father's plan, her father will be killed; if she obeys her father, she will have to kill the man she loves. In the aria 'Foudre céleste je t'appelle' she asks the gods to strike her dead.

Amid the dancing and singing of the wedding celebrations Hypermnestra comes close to telling Lynceus of her father's intentions. She pleads unsuccessfully with Danaus for mercy. In private she tells Lynceus that they must separate, without telling him why. Suddenly the cries of Lynceus's brothers are heard off stage as the Danaids attack them. Lynceus flees.

When Hypermnestra tells her father that she saved Lynceus he is outraged. The Danaids enter with bloody swords; Danaus orders them to find Lynceus and kill him. Lynceus attacks the palace, slaughtering the Danaids. Hypermnestra faints. The palace is destroyed, the ruins engulfed in flames. A change of scene reveals the Danaids imprisoned in the underworld with Danaus chained to a rock, his entrails devoured by a vulture; a chorus of Furies promises them unending torment.

Salieri's music combines the nobility and simplicity of Gluckian melodies with the warmth and lyricism of the Italian masters of *tragédie lyrique*, Piccinni and Sacchini. The music for the wedding festivities in Act 3 shows him expertly employing the conventions of French ballet and choral music. Arias range from elaborate italianate *arie di bravura* like Hypermnestra's 'Foudre céleste je t'appelle' to short, intensely lyrical numbers like Lynceus's 'A peine aux autels d'Hyménée'. At the same time Salieri did full justice to the libretto's horror and violence: the overture's slow introduction in D minor, orchestrated with trombones, anticipates the infernal music of Mozart's *Don Giovanni*, and the music for the underworld scene, in C minor, makes effective use of syncopation, sforzandos, tremolo, diminished 7th chords and full orchestra (with trombones) to produce an overwhelming evocation of demonic terror.

Les Danaïdes was an immediate and lasting success. It was performed 127 times at the Opéra into the 1820s, when it delighted the young Berlioz shortly after his arrival in Paris. He wrote of the performance in his memoirs (1870; trans. D. Cairns 1969, pp. 54–5):

> The pomp and brilliance of the spectacle, the sheer weight and richness of sound produced by the combined chorus and orchestra, the pathos of Mme Branchu [as Hypermnestra], her extraordinary voice, and rugged grandeur of Dérivis [as Danaus], Hypermnestre's aria (in which I detected, imitated by Salieri, the characteristics of Gluck's style) ... and finally the tremendous bacchanal and the sad sensuous ballet music which Spontini added to his fellow-countryman's score, excited and disturbed me to an extent which I will not attempt to describe.

JOHN A. RICE

Dance. Dance in opera ranges from the simple act-ending ballets of early Italian opera or the interlude-like *divertissements* of 17th-century French spectacles to the integral use of choreography as a dramatic or expressive element in 20th-century opera.

1. The 17th century. 2. The 18th century. 3. The 19th century. 4. After 1900.

1. THE 17TH CENTURY. Early opera owed a clear debt to Renaissance *intermedi* and pastoral plays, both of which involved music and dance. Not surprisingly, dance quickly found its way into opera as the genre developed. The nobility, for whom dance was an essential means of expression, often danced either solo or ensemble pieces in court *intermedi*, and remained a strong resource as dance was incorporated into opera. Although 17th- and 18th-century polemics frequently dealt with issues such as the primacy of music over text or vice versa, the role of dance in opera was seldom the centre of controversy (at least until Noverre's *Lettres sur la danse* of 1760 and Angiolini's *Lettere ... à Monsieur Noverre* of 1773). Its role in 17th-century Italian opera has been little studied, at least in part because ballets were not generally central to the action of the drama itself and ballets indicated in librettos are often lacking from extant scores. Moreover, contemporary eyewitness accounts seldom provide much information about dancing, and choreography for specific operatic dances is scarce. In England and at the court of Savoy (Turin), opera eventually superseded court ballets and masques, but only late in the 17th century. Much the same can be said about France, where a strong tradition of *ballet de cour* (to *c*1661), followed by *comédie-ballet*, forestalled the advent of the *tragédie lyrique*. As opera became established in France and England, composers including Lully and Purcell embraced aesthetic approaches to dance in opera different from those found in Italy.

Dance in early Italian operas occurred predominantly between acts, at the end of the opera or in scenes involving pastoral characters. It generally added little to the progress of the drama, instead highlighting an emotion, appearing as a separate episode or enhancing a situation of the opera plot (such as a combat). In early Florentine operas by Peri and Caccini based on the Orpheus myth, Eurydice invites nymphs and shepherds assembled for her wedding day to join in a dance, and Peri's version even ends with a ballo. Monteverdi's *Orfeo* (1607, Mantua) concludes with a *moresca* for nymphs and shepherds, who have just sung a joyful chorus, while other opportunities for dancing come not in named dances but during instrumental ritornellos in pastoral scenes. Domenico Mazzocchi, working in Rome, honoured this tradition by including modest dancing in his *La catena d'Adone* (1626). When Adonis and Falsirena appear (Act 1 scene iii), the *argomento* indicates that Ballerini 'make dances interrupted by songs'. No independent instrumental music is present in the printed score, so it seems most likely that the dancing occurred during the triple-metre choruses. Stefano Landi used ballets at the ends of acts to highlight the plot in his Roman opera *Il Sant'Alessio* (1632). Dance figures prominently in Act 3, where a chorus of Angels sings while a troupe of Virtues dances. Evidence exists that dancing to instrumental music replaced sung choruses in other operas at the papal court (*c*1631–68). Most dances are brief, single-movement pieces.

In Venetian opera from 1637 to the 1680s dance requirements varied from opera to opera; some contained virtually no dancing while in others it figured prominently. Francesco Manelli's *Andromeda*, the opera that inaugurated the Teatro Novissimo di S Cassiano in 1637, required a variety of dances, according to the printed Venetian scenario (Worsthorne 1955). At the conclusion of Act 1, for example, the dancers included three youths dressed as *amori*, six of Andromeda's ladies who 'for joy at killing a boar, did a light and wonderful ballet with such varied and different weavings of paces that truly one was able to call it a leaping labyrinth', and 12 wood nymphs who 'made a very eccentric and tasteful ballet of movements and gestures' to close the act. We are told that the effect of the last dance, which like the others was created by the famous G. B. Balbi, was such that 'there were no eyes that did not weep the passing of this dance'. We know also from a printed scenario that Monteverdi, in his *Le nozze d'Enea con Lavinia* (1641, Venice; music lost), used dance in *intermedi* between the acts and also within the drama itself. Venetian operas of the 1640s often included ballets which were loosely linked to the plot at the ends of the first two acts. When court operas such as Cesti's *L'Argia* (1656, Innsbruck; revised for Venice, 1669) or *L'Ercole in Tebe* (1661, Florence, music by Jacopo Melani; reset for Venice by G. A. Boretti in 1671) were prepared for Venetian performance, some choruses, machines and dances were pruned.

As Venetian opera developed, however, the importance of dance declined. Whether for economic or artistic reasons, the requirements of commercial theatres differed from those with court traditions. In the next three decades, as Venetian opera flourished, dances appeared in many of Cavalli's nearly 30 operas, though like choruses they are of little dramatic importance or interest. Except for various correntes, an occasional ballo, or a few pieces surviving only as bass lines, most dance music called for in the librettos is not contained in extant music. The role of dance in Venetian opera during the waning years of the 17th century, as seen in the works of Giovanni Legrenzi, Carlo Pallavicino and Carlo Francesco Pollarolo, changed little.

Two assessments of ballet in late 17th-century Venetian opera, both by French travellers, are hardly complimentary. Limojon de St Didier (*c*1680) noted that 'the Ballets or Dancings between the Acts are generally so pittiful, that they would be much better omitted; for one would imagine these Dancers wore Lead in their Shoes, yet the Assembly bestow their Applauses on them, which is merely for want of having seen better' (quoted in Grout 1947). A decade later, Maximilien Misson, no doubt accustomed to the prominance of dance in French opera, said that 'there are no Dances' (Grout). The italophile François Raguenet, in his famous *Paralèle* (1702; Eng. trans. 1709), noted that Italian dancers are 'the poorest Creatures in the World; they are all of a Lump, without Arms, Legs, a shape or air'.

Italian opera also flourished in Vienna at the Habsburg court of Leopold I (reigned 1657–1705). There ballet, whether for dancers or for noble horsemen in a *balletto a cavallo*, was much appreciated. But an important distinction obtained: in Italy most ballet music seems to have been written by the original opera composer himself, while in Vienna its composition was conventionally the domain of a second composer. Thus in Cesti's famous *Il pomo d'oro*, first performed in Vienna in 1668, ballets concluding each of the five acts were composed not by Cesti but by Johann Heinrich Schmelzer. Schmelzer's ballets, which emphasized spectacle, included groups of up to eight dances with no fixed sequence such as that found in later dance suites. A triple ballet of short pieces (16–48 bars each) ending Act 5 includes a gran ballo, aria, branle di Morsetti, sarabanda per la terra, balletto per il mare, trezza, aria viennense and gigue. According to Viennese custom, the ballet music was not copied into opera manuscripts but remained separate. This practice, also common in mid-18th-century Italy, explains the loss of so much ballet music.

The first operas in France were Italian operas imported by Cardinal Mazarin. An astute judge of French taste, Mazarin commissioned a few operas (notably Luigi Rossi's *Orfeo*) and had others modified to emphasize rapid set changes, ballets and machines. *La finta pazza* (music by Francesco Sacrati, performed December 1645), for example, was expanded to include ballets for monkeys, eunuchs, Indians and ostriches, with choreography and costumes by Balbi; the sets were designed by Giacomo Torelli (Anthony 1973; for illustration *see* BALBI, GIOVAN BATTISTA). By 1654 an attempt had been made to wed Italian opera to French *ballet de cour* in Carlo Caproli's *Le nozze di Peleo e di Teti*, again with sets by Torelli. Ballet *entrées*, occasioned by the Italian text, were inserted between scenes (see fig.1 overleaf). It was prophetic that Jean-Baptiste Lully, a principal architect of French opera, not only danced in this production but also contributed ballet music, as he was later to do for Cavalli's *Serse* (November 1660) and *Ercole amante* (February 1662).

In 1673, when Lully turned to writing *tragédies lyriques*, he and his librettist Quinault, considering opera an institution of the state, developed a 'form' including an encomiastic prologue (extolling Louis XIV) and five acts. Dance, previously the mainstay of earlier Lully court entertainments, was ubiquitous in the new

1. Set design by Giacomo Torelli for 'Le nozze di Peleo e di Teti', performed in Paris in 1654: drawing showing the third entry depicting the pearl fishers dancing to entertain Thetis who has been forced ashore by a storm stirred up by Neptune (on chariot, right)

genre. Lully treated it as both 'an expressive medium and a legitimate dramatic agent' (Anthony 1973). His *tragédies* include bourrées, sarabandes, canaries, gigues, chaconnes, passacailles and other dances. Gavottes, and above all minuets, are most popular; dancing was especially prominent in the *divertissements* found in many acts. Later writers such as the Abbé Dubos (*Réflexions critiques*, 1719) inform us of 'some ballets almost without dance, but rather composed of gesture and of demonstrations; in a word, a pantomime', citing among other examples the funeral ceremonies in *Psyché* and *Alceste* and a ballet for the 'Songes funèstes' in *Atys* (Act 4).

England, like France, had a rich 17th-century tradition of dancing. Court masques and later theatre masques, in which dance was central, provided the heritage for the operas of the Restoration (1660–*c*1700), by Blow (*Venus and Adonis*, *c*1682), Grabu (*Albion and Albanius*, 1685) and Purcell (*Dido and Aeneas*, 1689). In *Dido*, which leant heavily on continental traditions, dances are both numerous and integrated into the action. The 1689 libretto indicates 11 dances in the opera proper: three each in the outer acts and five in the middle. In Act 2, dances such as the Sailor's Dance have strong rhythmic patterns and symmetrical phrase structure, while others, like 'Jack of Lanthorn' for the Witches, contain sections of varying lengths, contrasting tempos and inconsistent rhythmic patterns, which suggest the possible use of pantomime. Some choruses, such as 'Fear no danger', were also danced. With the invasion of England by Italian opera in the early 18th century, the efficacy of the masquing traditions Purcell had so skilfully integrated into his theatrical works underwent re-examination.

2. The 18th century. As the new century began, the legacies of dance in Italian and French opera contrasted greatly with each other. In France Lully's rich influence was felt by many composers. In Italy, however, what little dance survived in operas had become stylized; the reforms of Zeno and of Metastasio left little room for ballet to flourish. One measure of the prominence and function of dance in 18th-century opera is the extent to which French influence is found. But the 18th century also presents paradoxes occasioned by regional idiosyncrasies, the quirks of rulers or composers, the spectre of 'reform', and the rise of highly skilled, sometimes peripatetic, virtuoso dancers. For example, sung comedy was used at S Carlo in Naples to end acts until the advent in 1735 of Charles III, who dictated that ballets should be substituted; in England, ballet was not generally a focal point of Handelian opera, yet prominent ballet music (admittedly written specifically for Marie Sallé) occurs in *Ariodante* and *Alcina* (both 1735). Moreover, the 18th century was an era during which the influence of important choreographers such as Franz Hilverding (1710–68) and Gasparo Angiolini (1731–1806) transcended national borders, as did that of Jean-Georges Noverre (1727–1810). Significant reform in opera, most visible in the work of Noverre, had particular ramifications for the second half of the century.

In France a new genre, the *opéra-ballet*, was created by André Campra, whose *L'Europe galante* of 1697 was a lighter work in which dance and singing were combined, with greater emphasis placed on *divertissements*. Critics such as Rémond de Saint-Mard (*Réflections sur l'opéra*, 1749) lamented this tendency to elevate dance above the drama itself, but with the rise of such virtuoso dancers as Michel Blondi (1675–1737), Françoise Prévost (1680–1741) and Jean Balon, French audiences flocked to the opera, despite the critics' views. Jean-Joseph Mouret, in *Les fêtes de Thalie* (1722), used dance to highlight regional colour, thus adding another forum for virtuoso solo dancing. The challenge left by Lully's legacy was met most artistically by Jean-Philippe Rameau, whose own ventures into the realm of large-scale theatrical entertainments began in 1733 with *Hippolyte et Aricie*. His five *tragédies lyriques* and six *opéras-ballets* (1735–48) all use dance prominently. Marie-Anne Camargo, Marie Sallé and Gaetano Vestris, three of the most famous 18th-century dancers, took part in some of his works. The excellence and vitality of Rameau's dance music and his interest in fusing dance and drama paralleled the mid-century fascination with virtuoso dancing. Rameau's chief librettist, Louis de Cahusac, also wrote a treatise (*La danse ancienne et moderne*, 1754) in which he argued that art should imitate nature and that dance should not be used solely as ornament. Rameau's marvellous tambourins and rigaudons, with their innovatory instrumental writing, provided new vehicles for dancing, and his character dances (particularly those in *Les fêtes d'Hébé*) required virtuoso dance techniques. (For an illustration of his *La princesse de Navarre see* ORCHESTRA, fig.6.)

During the second half of the 18th century, French opera houses continued to present operas by Lully and Rameau, as well as new works, and to export both dancers and choreographers. The most influential figure who studied in Paris was Noverre. Nurtured by the teaching of the ballet-masters Marcel and Louis Dupré, the music of Rameau and the dancing of the extraordinary Marie Sallé, Noverre also worked in London (Drury Lane, with Garrick), Stuttgart and Milan. His most important post was that of ballet-master to the imperial family in Vienna, a city second only to Paris in dance at that time. Between 1767 and 1774 he staged nearly 40 ballets and choreographed several Gluck operas including *Alceste*. Noverre's theory of how dance should relate to opera is adroitly summarized in Letter VIII of his *Lettres sur la danse* (quoted from the anonymous English translation of 1783):

> As long as the Ballets at the opera are not intimately connected with the drama, so as to bear a part in its exposition, intrigue, and denouement, they will ever be disagreeable and unentertaining. Each of the Ballets ought, in my opinion, to be of itself a scene that might serve as a link to connect the first with the second act, this with the third &c. ... The poet should write those scenes; the musician translates his meaning, and the dancers explain it, by their action, with proper energy.

Noverre's concept, in which dance, ballet and pantomime worked together in unity, acquired the name *ballet d'action*. Moreover, his insistence on other reforms, such as the elimination of stereotyped or unwieldy costumes, and of masks and unnecessary head-dresses, led dance in opera still farther from its traditional base. But Noverre's claim to have invented the concept of *ballet d'action* did not go unchallenged.

France, though a dominant force in 18th-century dance, was not the sole national catalyst determining European taste. Austria and Italy too made important contributions through Hilverding and Angiolini, both of whom travelled widely. After his first Viennese appointment Hilverding worked in Russia from 1759 to 1764, brought by the Empress Elisabeth to reorganize the ballet. He contributed substantial ballets, each with its own plot and music by a secondary composer, to follow the first two acts of an opera. For example, he choreographed 'L'enlèvement de Proserpine' (music by Carlo Bellozzi) and 'Ballet à l'Angloise' (music by A. Sacco), which were added to *Lo speziale* (Carlo Goldoni's libretto set by Vincenzo Pallavicini and Domenico Fischietti in 1758). Aside from ballets for operas by Traetta and other Italians, Angiolini's collaboration with Gluck in Vienna is most noteworthy. His choreography for Gluck's renowned ballet *Don Juan* was followed by that for Gluck's first version of *Orfeo ed Euridice*. This opera is particularly important for its integration of ballet into the second act. In an entry to hell followed by a scene set in the Elysian fields, Gluck provides a magnificent opportunity for dances that interpret and further the dramatic action. A reviewer of the 1762 première (probably the librettist Calzabigi himself, according to Heartz 1975) remarked that

2. Marie Sallé: engraving (1733) by Nicolas IV de Larmessin after N. Lancret

'Angiolini has used his skills in a new way, namely in bringing the dances together with the choruses and the action in such a way as to provide a magnificent model for the future'. Gluck's last triumph, *Iphigénie en Tauride* (1779), composed for Paris rather than Vienna, flew in the face of Grimm's opinion that 'French opera is a kind of drama in which the fate of all characters is to see everyone dancing around' (*Correspondance littéraire*). Gluck, with his librettist Guillard, used dance sparingly but with great dramatic flair, as in the Scythian dance in Act 1, with its accompaniment including bass drum, cymbals, triangle and piccolo, and in the scene in Act 2 where the Eumenides surround an unconscious Orestes and torment him in a pantomime ballet. *Iphigénie* represents 'the high point of tragic ballet in the service of Gluck's Gesamtkunstwerk' (Nettl 1963).

In London during the late 18th century, dance was a frequent addition to performances of Italian operas at the King's Theatre and the Pantheon. Italian *opera seria* in London resisted change, ignoring the reforms of Gluck (Price 1989), and would, in the words of the early 19th-century visitor Christian Goede, have been instantly 'abandoned, notwithstanding the talents of the singers and the beauty of the music, if dancing were not the powerful magnet which attracts the Londoners' (quoted by Wiley 1992). London theatres employed many important French and Italian choreographers and dancers including Charles Didelot and Jean Dauberval to perform the works of Noverre and others. Native English composers such as Joseph Mazzinghi, however, were sometimes hired to arrange music for ballets and to compose substitute arias at theatres such as the Pantheon.

At about the same time, the function and placement of dance in opera changed little in the works of Mozart. His early operas such as *Lucio Silla* (1772, Milan) contain ballets following each act according to standard Italian conventions. But in later, more mature operas Mozart and his librettists seldom gave much prominence to ballet music. Only in *Idomeneo* (1781, Munich), no doubt composed under Gluck's influence, did Mozart write important ballet music. The composer concluded his opera with a chaconne followed by other dances in which trios of instruments for solo dancers and full orchestra for the *corps de ballet* are ingeniously alternated. Despite his friendship with Noverre, his own ability to dance and his fluency in writing dance music, Mozart turned to expressive means other than dance in operas from *Le nozze di Figaro* onwards. Only the banquet scene in *Don Giovanni*, with its introduction of dance music played by multiple orchestras, gives us a precious glimpse of how original Mozart could be in providing a brief opportunity for dancing within the opera proper.

As royal patronage of artistic institutions fell victim to the French Revolution, as the great French heritage of operas from Lully to Rameau was removed from the active repertory, and as composers wrestled with the legacy of Metastasio, the reforms of Gluck and the late operas of Mozart, the final decade of the century saw little development in either the place or function of dance in opera.

3. THE 19TH CENTURY. In the 19th century dance in opera varied from brief digressions to extended ballets; it enhanced atmosphere, provided local colour and celebrated ritual. The prominence and style of dancing could vary from one production to the next depending on the performers, who might be extras, choristers, singing principals or professional dancers.

The style of dance music is a response to the technique of the dance, more intricate steps tending to require simpler accompaniment. Thus opera dances, at extremes, may press the limits of a composer's individual style or lapse into the simple, clichéd manner of specialist ballet music, which accompanied choreography based on the *danse d'école* during much of the century. Most opera dances are parenthetical to the plot; occasionally they have an effect on the singing principals, and exceptionally they are central to the story or contribute to characterization. The operatic tradition, which in this context refers to the practice of the Paris Opéra, also affects a work's dances.

Compared with the Scythians in Act 1 of Gluck's *Iphigénie en Tauride*, the Romans in Spontini's *La vestale* (1807) and the Spaniards and Aztecs in his *Fernand Cortez* (1809, rev. 1817) perform more dances, of greater length and more complex repetition schemes, to richer scoring. The larger dimensions of Spontini's work, a response to the tastes of the Napoleonic age, nevertheless yield in dramatic involvement to Gluck, whose dancing Eumenides in a pantomime ballet (Act 2 of *Iphigénie en Tauride*) interact with a principal character, Orestes, causing his troubled dream. In *Fernand Cortez* Spontini includes dancers in juxtapositions of stage activity that diversify spectacle without advancing the drama: the women of Amazily's retinue dance with Spanish soldiers at the same time as a group of principals sing, separately, of the Spaniards' fate. The scale and pageantry of Spontini's dances were echoed by later masters, notably Meyerbeer and Wagner. Spontini's juxtapositions, if not Berlioz's in *Roméo et Juliette*, may have inspired the merging of the Norwegian sailors' dance with the music for the Dutchman's crew in Wagner's *Der fliegende Holländer* (1843).

Describing the ballets in revolutionary and Napoleonic grand opera, Winton Dean has written: 'A very mild exoticism emerges mouse-like from a welter of brass and percussion' (NOHM, viii, 96). The dances Rossini wrote for his adaptations and original work at the Opéra after the monarchy was restored (1826–9) reveal no greater distinction, and contribute little to the historical record other than the fact that Rossini composed them. A number of factors account for this: the pressure of dance technique to force music into an expressively neutral style, the composer's lack of concern or knowledge about musical shadings appropriate to ethnic or antique settings, modern ignorance of the visual component of the dances (which was better equipped than music to convey local colour), and the state of present-day critical sensitivities, several generations removed from what 19th-century audiences deemed artistic.

Their vivacious musical style and suitability to dramatic context make the bolero and tarantella of Auber's *La muette de Portici* (1828) exceptional for their time (see fig.3), to say nothing of the opera's leading female role, Fenella, a silent character whose part, assigned throughout the century to a ballerina, is expressed mimetically. Possibly indebted for this unusual casting to Weber's *Silvana* (whose title role is also a mute girl who dances), *La muette* enjoyed remarkable success for decades, but its very novelty discouraged imitators.

Three works of Giacomo Meyerbeer produced for the Opéra, *Robert le diable* (1831), *Les Huguenots* (1836)

3. Costume designs by Hippolyte Lecomte for two Spanish dancers in the Act 1 Bolero of the original production of Auber's 'La muette de Portici' at the Paris Opéra, 29 February 1828

and *Le prophète* (1849), warrant emphasis for the importance of their dances, which by their longevity in Paris and wide dissemination abroad influenced other composers. In addition, they illustrate the principal types of opera dance in the 19th century.

The Ballet of Nuns in Act 3 of *Robert* affirmed the stature that classical dancing had always enjoyed at the Opéra, as well as the anticlericalism fashionable since the Revolution: a group of nuns, who offended heaven during life, rise from their graves and perform a bacchanale, during which Robert is enticed to steal a magic branch (for illustration *see* GRAND OPÉRA, fig.4). Here, as in Auber's *La muette*, a ballerina took the leading part, and in response to the recently appointed director Louis Véron's initiative to use the best collaborators, Filippo and Marie Taglioni, father and daughter, were engaged as choreographer and principal dancer. The nocturnal setting of the stage, in a moonlit cemetery filled with spectral women, produced an effect of mystery and *frisson* to which the Taglionis returned in ballet proper with *La sylphide* (1832), the first so-called white ballet, and which Jean Coralli and Jules Perrot, on a story by Théophile Gautier, immortalized in *Giselle*, to Adolphe Adam's music (1841).

While *Robert* gave impetus for a new development in the history of ballet, the reciprocal influence of ballet on opera is also important, and sensed most strongly in the dance music. Specialist ballet composers of this period developed a musical accompaniment for classical steps that was superior to the crude pastiche used at the beginning of the century, though it often lacked the character and sophistication brought to dance music by more illustrious figures. Solo dances call for light textures and prominent instrumental obbligatos (a violin, cello or flute), harmony is simple, phrasing regular and metre often pronounced, and in fast tempos the pace is steady and the rhythm that of a popular dance, while the singing melody of solo Adagios recalls Italian opera and is rhythmically flexible.

Such music served the dance first, and the dramatic atmosphere of the opera, as best it could, second. The precedence of choreography explains why music so little reinforces stage atmosphere in the bacchanale of *Robert*. Yet its priority was lasting: composers of more pronounced creativity than Meyerbeer, in ballet sequences of comparable scale and choreography, still distinguish the ballet music from the rest of the opera, such as Verdi in *Les vêpres siciliennes* (1855) and *Don Carlos* (1867). Composers were expected to write in the specialist manner when the style of dancing required it.

Les Huguenots contains one dance (discounting danced activity in the wedding procession at the end of Act 3, which is called for in a rubric but otherwise not specified). Its several parts, played without a break, have different metres, regular phrasing, vivacious motifs and bright scoring. The pause it creates in the story, apparently gratuitous, in fact contributes to dramatic tension, as the dance delays an altercation between the Huguenot Marcel and his Catholic antagonists, Saint-Bris and Nevers, allowing ill-feeling between them to fester. It is performed by gypsies and set on the left bank of the Seine, though the music, while lively and attractive, has no particular local flavour. In French opera this dance stands between the Aztecs of Spontini and the allurements of Lillas Pastia's tavern in *Carmen*; in opera generally, it is the kind of dance encountered most often: brief, engaging, colourful, a respite from heavier fare.

The skaters' ballet in Act 3 of *Le prophète* is offered on the merest dramatic pretext: women cross a frozen lake (on roller skates in the first production) to deliver food to the Anabaptist military camp, then doff their skates and dance with the soldiers. Given the villainy and bloodthirstiness of the story, this ballet suite serves the same function in *Le prophète* as the gypsy dance in *Les Huguenots* – it offers relief. The music, some of Meyerbeer's most delightful, consists of a waltz, redova, pas de quatre and galop, presented in utter disregard of period and locale. Such bright dance suites were especially popular later in the century, in Mediterranean

4. The bacchanal in the Venusberg from Wagner's 'Tannhäuser': watercolour by Michael Echter after a performance given at the Munich Hoftheater (using the 1861 Paris version), 1 August 1867, with choreography by Lucile Grahn

settings by Verdi (*Aida*, 1871), Goldmark (*Die Königin von Saba*, 1875), Anton Rubinstein (*Neron*, 1875–6) and Massenet (*Hérodiade*, 1881).

The success of French grand opera, and the expectation that it include ballets, caused many of the century's greatest composers to add or augment dances in earlier works being produced at Paris for the first time, notably Berlioz (for Weber's *Der Freischütz*, 1841), Verdi (*Jérusalem* [revision of *I Lombardi*], 1847; *Il trovatore*, 1857; *Otello*, 1894) and Wagner (*Tannhäuser*, 1861; see fig.4).

Elsewhere opera dances might follow Parisian fashion, sometimes directly but more often in extraordinary transformations, or keep faith with a different operatic tradition, or perhaps evolve from a mixture of established practice and new stimuli, of which the expression of national identity was the most important.

In Italy, where they had never been institutionalized, opera dances occurred less frequently than in France, suites in the French manner being rare (Rossini's *Armida*, 1817; Donizetti's *L'assedio di Calais*, 1836). The demand for dancing was met by an independent ballet tradition, marked later in the century by the rise of the *féerie*, of which Luigi Manzotti's *Excelsior* (1881) was a model for the rest of Europe.

When not composing for Paris, Giuseppe Verdi used dance, typically accompanied by a chorus, in festive settings made ambivalent by the actions of principal characters. It could be a cover for skulduggery (*Rigoletto*, 1851; *Un ballo in maschera*, 1859) or reveal tragedy, poignantly so when, to the sound of a waltz, Violetta offers Alfredo a flower to keep until it withers, a metaphorical prediction of their own relationship (*La traviata*, 1853). Elsewhere dance conveys the essence of contrasting dramatic situations, as in *Ernani* (1844), in which Verdi distinguishes Elvira's imminent wedding to Silva, whom she does not love, by a crude galop, from her subsequent wedding to Ernani, whom she does love, by a more elegant polonaise.

Giacomo Puccini employed dance more to sustain atmosphere and to jest than to comment directly on the drama. In Act 2 of *Manon Lescaut* (1893), for example, the dancing lesson recalls Molière, and the altered octaves of the organ grinder's dance in *Il tabarro* (1918) verge on the grotesque. A waltz is played in the festive scenes of *La bohème* (1896) and *La rondine* (1917), the latter Puccini's most traditional invocation of dance, as it marks the flowering love of Magda and Ruggero. But the customary rubato afforded 'Quando me 'n vo'' in performance renders meaningless the instruction that it be played in the tempo of a slow waltz, though such indulgence is in keeping with Musetta's character. Exceptional in Puccini is the waltz Minnie and Johnson perform in *La fanciulla del West* (1910), the melody of which becomes a reference, subsequently invoked many times, to Minnie's love.

Even after the Napoleonic invasions, French opera continued to affect opera in German-speaking lands, owing to French taste at important courts (Berlin, Vienna) and in important composers (Spontini, Weber, Spohr, Wagner), and to the widespread popularity of French theatre (including *opéra comique*) as a repertory to perform and borrow. While some important German operas omit dances entirely (*Fidelio*, *Lohengrin*, Schumann's *Genoveva*), others call for ballets in the French manner – Weber's *Euryanthe* (1823) for a production in Berlin, Wagner's *Rienzi* (1842) and *Tannhäuser* (1845), Lortzing's *Undine* (1845) and Nicolai's *Die lustigen Weiber von Windsor* (1849), in which dance is the vehicle for Falstaff's punishment in the final scene.

Coincident with French influence, German patriotism after Napoleon's defeat affirmed the distinctive attributes of German opera that had been developing in the 18th century. Fired by the perception of simplicity identified with 'das Volk', composers added rustic dances to rural settings and moralizing plots to form the central image of native German opera from Weber's *Der Freischütz* (1821) to Humperdinck's *Hänsel und Gretel* (1893). Virtually all of Lortzing's domestic comedies, starting with *Die beiden Schützen* (1837), present dances in this spirit, though these may betray a French lineage by the title 'Ballett' (*Casanova*, 1841), or may be identified simply by rubric (Georg's aria, a Tempo di polacca, in Act 1 of *Der Waffenschmied*, 1846; the *Tanz* at the beginning of *Der Wildschütz*, 1842). If Wagner had truly sought a *Gesamtkunstwerk*, he might have constructed more librettos including dance; as matters stand, it has no place in music drama apart from the Dance of the Apprentices in Act 3 of *Die Meistersinger von Nürnberg* (1868).

After the phenomenal success of *Der Freischütz*, composers in countries outside the operatic mainstream began to make comparable assertions of national identity. They used dance in different ways, combining it with other indigenous musical intonations and subject matter, inevitably blended, for lack of adequate precedent, with devices borrowed from the standard repertory. The *csárdás* at the wedding festivities in Act 3 of Ferenc Erkel's *Hunyadi László* (1844) is a case in point, as are the celebrated polka, furiant and Dance of the Comedians in Smetana's *The Bartered Bride* (1866). Moniuszko used dance in *Halka* (1858) to distinguish noble (the mazurka played in honour of Zofia and Janusz) from peasant (the Highlander Dances). In Act 4 Jontek, Halka's beau before she fell in love with Janusz, who has dishonoured her, sings a meditative *dumka* in which he affirms his steadfast love. This aria, in the spirit of a dance-song, is the point of departure for the opera's denouement, as Halka, finally aware of Janusz's betrayal, lapses into dementia and commits suicide.

In Russia Glinka's *A Life for the Tsar* (1836) and *Ruslan and Lyudmila* (1842) also enjoy prestige as national monuments, but their dances only partly justify this status. In *A Life*, dances of striking national character that identify the Polish invaders – the brilliant choral polonaise, the mazurka and *krakowiak* – are juxtaposed with classical dances requiring specialist ballet music, without the slightest concern for the absurdity of ballerinas accompanying armies into war. The same disparity of musical style distinguishes the Turkish and Arabian dances and Lezginka in *Ruslan* from the classical dances of the Naina's maidens, though here logic is suspended because all the characters are fantastic.

Glinka's bow to the French tradition was not imitated (though Tchaikovsky presented a vignette of French ballet in the *intermède* of *The Queen of Spades*, 1890), but his more exotic dances cast a wide shadow across Russian opera, in brilliant individual dances (as in Rimsky-Korsakov's *The Snow Maiden*, 1882), in ballets Meyerbeerian in scale but oriental in atmosphere (Borodin's *Prince Igor*, 1890), or in evocations of Poland as a contrast to Russia (Musorgsky's *Boris Godunov*, where the vision-like polonaise quotes the opening fanfares from its counterpart in *A Life for the Tsar*).

In Tchaikovsky's *Yevgeny Onegin* (1879) the choral waltz and the cotillion of Act 2 not only enhance a characteristic setting, but also provide the impetus for the tragedy that comes later in the act. Offended that the flirtatious Olga has yielded his place beside her in the cotillion to Onegin, Lensky challenges Onegin to the duel in which the young poet dies. In the next act a polonaise and écossaise form the background against which Onegin, bored at first, is overcome with love for Tatyana, whose rebuff shatters him at the end of the opera. The keys of the dances reinforce a network of dramatically significant tonal relationships: the cotillion starts in G, a key associated with Onegin, and moves to E minor, a key associated with the workings of fate, when Onegin angers Lensky to the point of making his challenge; the écossaise, which frames Onegin's revelation of love for Tatyana, is in B♭, a key associated with rejection since Onegin rejected Tatyana in Act 1. The dances are basic to the musico-dramatic sense of the opera.

4. After 1900. Practices of the 19th century continue to be followed in the 20th as circumstances warrant, but dance is also variously adapted to diverse musical styles and operatic subject matter. Moreover, the musical and film have opened new outlets for dance in theatrical genres adjacent to opera. Within opera, new tendencies have emerged.

One is to leave dancing to the singers. Jules Massenet, whose earlier operas are rich in dances, wrote them for *Le jongleur de Notre Dame* (1902) and *Don Quichotte* (1910) but assigned to the jongleur Jean and to Dulcinée choreographic responsibilities he had previously spared even seductresses such as Thaïs and Esclarmonde. The most notorious dancing part in Richard Strauss's operas is the title role in *Salome* (1905), though her counterparts in *Elektra* (1909) and *Daphne* (1938) must also dance, as do Zerbinetta and the quartet of *commedia dell'arte* players in *Ariadne auf Naxos* (1912), who are called on to dance as they sing about the healthy effects of dancing. Brief dances in passing are assigned to singers in such stylistically diverse works as Fauré's *Pénélope* (1913) and Schoenberg's *Von heute auf morgen* (1930), the last a criticism of the modishness fashionable in the decades after World War I. Choruses continue to dance as well (*Porgy and Bess*, 1935; *The Rake's Progress*, 1951).

A second tendency is for dance to make its point without dancing. In all the waltzes of *Der Rosenkavalier* (1911), Strauss calls on no one to dance except Annina, for a moment in Act 3. The foxtrot and 'Tango-Angèle' convey the tsar's anti-regal ambitions and heighten tension in Kurt Weill's *Der Zar lässt sich photographieren* (1928), while the slow waltz played in the same composer's *Aufstieg und Fall der Stadt Mahagonny* (1930), as Jake eats himself to death, heightens the effect of neurotic excess. Among many uses of dance in *Wozzeck* (1925) are the playing of a Ländler during the scene-change before Wozzeck discovers Marie with the Drum Major in the tavern, and of a polka in the course of the tavern scene following Marie's murder.

Post-tonal idioms have proved to be perfectly compatible with effective opera dances (the Butchers' Dance and orgy scene in Schoenberg's *Moses und Aron*, comp. 1930–32; the circus show and final scene of Henze's *Der junge Lord*, 1965), and are part of an array of innovations using dance and choreography in 20th-century opera. Others include Dyagilev's experimental staging in 1914 of Rimsky-Korsakov's *The Golden Cockerel* (1909), in which the singers stood on the sidelines, yielding centre stage to dancers who acted the parts; Maurice Grosser's superimposition of a scenario on to Virgil Thomson's *Four Saints in Three Acts* (1934) after the composer had finished it, making it both an opera and a choreographic spectacle; and Britten's assignment of dancers in *Death in Venice* (1973) to the parts of Tadzio and several of his circle, whose movements, neither wholly balletic nor freely naturalistic, call for the collaboration of a choreographer (see fig.5).

5. The games of Apollo from Britten's 'Death in Venice' (Act 1 scene vii): scene from the original production by the English Opera Group at The Maltings, Snape, Suffolk, June 1973, with Peter Pears as Aschenbach (seated) and Robert Huguenin as Tadzio (carried)

More conventional uses of dance form a counterpoint to such innovations throughout the century. Ravel emphasized the whimsical phantasmagoria of *L'enfant et les sortilèges* (1925) with dances for the armchair, wallpaper figures, frogs and Monsieur Arithmétique with his numerals. Britten made the masque in *Gloriana* (1953) a double gesture of homage, to the first Queen Elizabeth on stage, and to the second by composing the opera for her coronation festivities. The dance inaugurating the temple of Akhetaten in Glass's *Akhnaten* (1984) has countless precedents in similar celebrations, and the lengthy interpolated ballet in Adams's *Nixon in China* (1987) echoes an honoured tradition in the City of Lights.

*

A. Coeuroy: 'Wagner et le ballet', *ReM*, iii (1921–2), 110–17

D. J. Grout: *A Short History of Opera* (New York, 1947, 2/1965)

R.-A. Mooser: *Annales de la musique et des musiciens en Russie au XVIIIme siècle* (Geneva, 1948–51)

I. Guest: *The Ballet of the Second Empire 1858–1870* (London, 1953)

——: *The Ballet of the Second Empire 1847–1858* (London, 1955)

W. C. Smith: *The Italian Opera and Contemporary Ballet in London 1789–1820* (London, 1955)

S. T. Worsthorne: *Venetian Opera in the Seventeenth Century* (Oxford, 1955)

V. Krasovskaya: *Russkiy baletnïy teatr vtoroy polovinï XIX veka* [Russian Ballet Theatre of the Second Half of the 19th Century (Moscow and Leningrad, 1963), 26–62

P. Nettl: *The Dance in Classical Music* (New York, 1963)

J. R. Anthony: 'The French Opera-Ballet in the Early 18th Century: Problems of Definition and Classification', *JAMS*, xviii (1965), 197–206

I. Guest: *The Romantic Ballet in Paris* (London, 1966)

J. R. Anthony: 'Some Uses of the Dance in the French Opéra-Ballet', *RMFC*, ix (1969), 75–90

A. Porter: 'Verdi's Ballet Music, and "La Pérégrina"', *2° congresso internazionale di studi verdiani: Verona 1969*, 355–67

P. Miguel: *The Ballerinas: from the Court of Louis XIV to Pavlova* (New York, 1972)

M. Robinson: *Naples and Neapolitan Opera* (Oxford, 1972)

J. R. Anthony: *French Baroque Music from Beaujoyeulx to Rameau* (New York, 1973, 2/1978)

R. Fiske: *English Theatre Music in the Eighteenth Century* (Oxford, 1973, 2/1986)

M. H. Winter: *The Pre-Romantic Ballet* (London, 1974) [incl. lengthy bibliography]

D. Heartz: '"Orfeo ed Euridice": some Criticisms, Revisions, and Stage-Realizations During Gluck's Lifetime', *Chigiana*, xxix–xxx (1975), 383–94

W. Hilton: *Dance of Court & Theater: the French Noble Style 1690–1725* (Princeton, 1981)

M. Murata: *Operas for the Papal Court 1631–1668* (Ann Arbor, 1981)

M. Conati: 'Ballabili nei "Vespri" con alcune osservazioni su Verdi e la musica popolare', *Studi verdiani*, i (1982), 21–46

J. Milhous: 'David Garrick and the Dancing Master's Apprentice', *Essays in Theatre*, ii (1983), 19–31

S. Pitou: *The Paris Opéra: an Encyclopedia of Operas, Ballets, Composers, and Performers*, i: *Genesis and Glory, 1671–1715* (Westport, CT, 1983)

C. Price: *Henry Purcell and the London Stage* (Cambridge, 1984)

D. Lawton: '"Le Trouvère": Verdi's Revision of "Il Trovatore" for Paris', *Studi verdiani*, iii (1985), 79–119

S. Pitou: *The Paris Opéra: an Encyclopedia of Operas, Ballets, Composers, and Performers*, ii: *Rococo and Romantic, 1715–1815* (Westport, CT, 1985)

R. Ralph: *The Life and Works of John Weaver* (Brooklyn, New York, 1985)

H. Seifert: *Die Oper am Wiener Kaiserhof im 17. Jahrhundert* (Tutzing, 1985)

J. R. Anthony and others: *The New Grove French Baroque Masters* (London, 1986)

M. Little: 'Recent Research in European Dance, 1400–1800', *EMc*, xiv (1986), 4–14

C. Price: Introduction to H. Purcell: *Dido and Aeneas* (New York, 1986)

J. Sasportes: 'Marmontel, musa dei balli a Venezia', *L'opera tra Venezia e Parigi: Venice 1986*, 91–104

L. Bianconi: *Music in the Seventeenth Century* (Cambridge, 1987)

E. T. Harris: *Henry Purcell's Dido and Aeneas* (Oxford, 1987)

R. Harris-Warrick: 'Contexts for Choreographies: Notated Dances Set to the Music of Jean-Baptiste Lully', *Jean-Baptiste Lully: St Germain-en-Laye and Heidelberg 1987*, 433–55

J. Schwartz and C. Schlundt: *French Court Dance and Dance Music: a Guide to Primary Source Writings 1643–1789* (Stuyvesant, NY, 1987)

J. Chazin-Bennahum: *Dance in the Shadow of the Guillotine* (Carbondale, IL, 1988)

K. K. Hansell: 'Il ballo teatrale e l'opera italiana', *SOI*, v (1988), 175–306

M. E. Smith: *Music for the Ballet-Pantomime at the Paris Opéra, 1825–1850* (diss., Yale U., 1988)

R. J. Wiley: 'The Dances in *Eugene Onegin*', *Dance Research*, vi (1988), 48–60

C. Price: 'Italian Opera and Arson in Late Eighteenth-Century London', *JAMS*, xlii (1989), 55–107

S. Pitou: *The Paris Opéra: an Encyclopedia of Operas, Ballets, Composers, and Performers*, iii: *Growth and Grandeur, 1815–1914* (Westport, CT, 1990)
E. Rosand: *Opera in Seventeenth-Century Venice: the Creation of a Genre* (Berkeley, 1991)
M. Little and C. G. Marsh: *La danse noble: an Inventory of Dances and Sources* (New York, forthcoming)
R. J. Wiley: Preface to C.-L. Didelot: *Flore et Zéphire, Sapho et Phaon and Ken-si and Tao*, MLE, D3 (forthcoming)

CARL B. SCHMIDT (1, 2), ROLAND J. WILEY (3, 4)

Danchet, Antoine (*b* Riom, Auvergne, 7 Sept 1671; *d* Paris, 21 Feb 1748). French librettist. At an early age he exhibited a 'happy disposition for letters'. He studied first with the Oratorians of Riom, then in Paris with the Jesuits. A Latin poem on the taking of Mons won him a chair of rhetoric at Chartres in 1692. After a year he returned to Paris. In 1696 he found employment as tutor to two children in the home of Colbert de Turgis, receiving a pension of 200 *livres*. But the great success of his first opera, *Hésione* (1700), alarmed the puritanical de Turgis family; he refused to stop writing librettos, and a trial ensued that was decided in his favour.

Danchet first collaborated with André Campra on a *divertissement*, *Vénus, feste galante*, performed on 27 January 1698 at the home of the Duchesse de la Ferté. Between 1698 and 1740 Danchet provided Campra with librettos for 18 works: eight *tragédies en musique*, three *opéras-ballets*, three *divertissements*, two *fragments* and two ballets. In addition he supplied Campra with eight cantata texts and wrote four five-act tragedies for the theatre. The Académie des Inscriptions, Médailles et Belles-Lettres admitted Danchet in 1705 and he achieved the rank of associate the following year. In 1712 he was elected to the Académie Française. From 1727 he took charge of the *Mercure de France*, which he directed until his death. He married in 1728 Marie Thérèse de La Barre, who bore him several children. His health began to decline in 1746; ravaged by severe rheumatism, he died at the age of 76.

Abbé Sabatier found Danchet's serious poetry 'weak, languid, deprived of imagery and colour'; on the other hand Houdar de Lamotte (*L'Europe galante*) considered him the 'first of our Lyric Poets' after Quinault (a sentiment shared by Girdlestone). *Idomenée*, *Télèphe* and *Camille, reine des volsques* are true tragedies. *Camille*, a political tragedy, minimizes the role of the supernatural. Girdlestone observed that 'for the music, the best *tragédies* are *Hésione*, *Tancrède* and *Alcine*; for the libretto, *Idomenée*, *Télèphe* and *Camille*'. He did not include here *Achille et Déidamie* (1735), a weak work for which librettist and composer were accused of 'completely drowning the subject in *divertissements*. No one wished to honour it by calling it a tragedy'.

In *Les fêtes vénitiennes* music and text are equal partners; the work conforms exactly with Rémond de Saint-Mard's definition of *opéra-ballet*: 'Each act must be made up of a fast moving, light and, if you wish, a rather *galant* intrigue ... two or three short scenes and the rest of the action in *Ariettes*, *Fêtes*, *Spectacles* and other such agreeable things'. The format of *opéra-ballet* gave Danchet an opportunity to test his original dramatic ideas. Thus in the third entrée of *Les fêtes vénitiennes* he fashioned the action to accommodate an 'opera' within an *opéra-ballet*. It is subdivided into four scenes; the first two have an identity separate from the entrée, and the third serves as a *divertissement* for both the 'opera' and the entrée. The action of the two is co-ordinated from this point to the end of the entrée.

div – *divertissement* obl – *opéra-ballet*
tm – *tragédie en musique*

Vénus, feste galante (div), Campra, 1698; *Apollon et Daphné* (div), J.-B. Lully, arr., 1698; *Hésione* (tm), Campra, 1700; *Aréthuse, ou La vengeance de l'Amour* (ballet), Campra, 1701; *Les fragments de Monsieur de Lully* (fragment), Lully, arr. Campra, 1702; *Tancrède* (tm), Campra, 1702; *Les Muses* (obl), Campra, 1703; *Iphigénie en Tauride* (tm, prol. only, text by J.-F. Duché de Vancy), Desmarets, completed Campra, 1704; *Télémaque, ou Les fragments des modernes* (fragment), Campra, M.-A. Charpentier, Collasse, Desmarets, Marais and J.-F. Rebel, arr. Campra, 1704

Alcine (tm), Campra, 1705; *Le triomphe de l'amour* (obl), Campra, 1705; *Les fêtes vénitiennes* (obl), Campra, 1710; *Idomenée* (tm), Campra, 1712; *Les amours de Vénus et Mars* (ballet), Campra, 1712; *Télèphe* (tm), Campra, 1713; *Camille, reine des volsques* (tm), Campra, 1717; *Les muses rassemblées par l'Amour* (div), Campra, 1724; *Achille et Déidamie* (tm), Campra, 1735; *Les nopces de Vénus* (div), Campra, 1740; *Les fêtes d'Euterpe* (ballet, with C.-S. Favart and F.-A.-P. de Moncrif), Dauvergne, 1758; *Alphée et Aréthuse* (intermède), Dauvergne, 1762

*

ES

R. de Saint-Mard: *Réflexions sur l'opéra* (Paris, 1741)
'Discours sur la vie et les Ouvrages de M. Danchet servant de Préface', *Théâtre de M. Danchet* (Paris, 1751)
A. Sabatier: *Les trois siècles de la littérature française* (Amsterdam, 1774)
L. de La Laurencie: 'Notes sur la jeunesse d'André Campra', *SIMG*, x (1908–9), 159–258
H. C. Lancaster: *Sunset: a History of Parisian Drama in the Last Years of Louis XIV, 1701–1715* (Baltimore, 1945), 130–34
——: *French Tragedy in the Time of Louis XV and Voltaire, 1715–1774* (Baltimore, 1950)
C. Girdlestone: *La tragédie en musique (1673–1750) considérée comme genre littéraire* (Geneva, 1972)
S. Pitou: *The Paris Opera: an Encyclopedia of Operas, Ballets, Composers, and Performers*, i: *Genesis and Glory, 1671–1715* (Westport, CT, 1983)

JAMES R. ANTHONY

Danco, Suzanne (*b* Brussels, 22 Jan 1911). Belgian soprano. She received her entire musical education at the Brussels Conservatory, studying the piano and the history of music as well as singing; and the unusual breadth of her culture was shown by her command of many different styles. In opera she was best known for her Mozartian interpretations, notably of Fiordiligi and Donna Elvira, which were applauded in Italy as well as at the festivals of Edinburgh, Glyndebourne and Aix-en-Provence. In England she sang parts as different as those of Mimì (1951, Covent Garden) and Marie in a BBC concert performance of *Wozzeck*; and she made an exquisite heroine in Ansermet's first recording of *Pelléas et Mélisande*. Her versatility was the more remarkable in that her clear, cool soprano offered no great richness or variety of colour; but it had been admirably trained, and could manage the roulades of Mozart as easily as the most difficult intervals of Berg.

DESMOND SHAWE-TAYLOR

D'Andrade [De Andrade], **Francisco** (*b* Lisbon, 11 Jan 1859; *d* Berlin, 8 Feb 1921). Portuguese baritone. He studied in Milan with Sebastiano Ronconi and made his début in 1882 at San Remo as Amonasro. He sang in Spain and Portugal and in Italy, where he appeared at the Teatro Costanzi, Rome, and at La Scala, Milan. In 1886 he made his London début at Covent Garden as Rigoletto; during his five-year association with the Royal Italian Opera he also sang Renato (*Un ballo in maschera*), Don Carlo (*Ernani*), Valentin, Barnaba (*La Gioconda*), Don Giovanni, Mozart's and Rossini's Figaro, Amonasro, Germont, Count di Luna, Alphonse (*La favorite*), Hoël (*Dinorah*), Riccardo (*I puritani*),

Telramund, Escamillo, Nevers (*Les Huguenots*), Zurga, Count Almaviva and Enrico Ashton. With his brother António, a tenor, D'Andrade took part in the first performance of *Donna Bianca* (1888, Lisbon) by the Portuguese composer Alfredo Keil. D'Andrade sang regularly at Frankfurt (1891–1910) and, having first visited Berlin in 1889, became a member of the Hofoper (later Staatsoper), from 1906 to his retirement in 1919. A very elegant and cultured singer, he had a beautiful, evenly produced voice with a powerful upper register. Among his most admired characterizations was Don Giovanni, which he sang at the 1901 Salzburg Festival.

*

M. Moreau: *Cantores de ópera portugueses*, i (Lisbon, 1981), 607–817 ELIZABETH FORBES

D'Angeri, Anna (*b* Vienna, 14 Nov 1853; *d* Trieste, 14 Dec 1907). Italian soprano. After study with Mathilde Marchesi she made her début in 1872, as Sélika in *L'Africaine* at the Teatro Sociale in Mantua. Sensational success followed at the Vienna Hofoper, where she sang until 1880. She appeared in London from 1874, notably as Ortrud and Venus in the British premières of *Lohengrin* and *Tannhäuser*. An admired Leonora (*Il trovatore*), Elvira (*Ernani*) and Elisabeth de Valois, she was chosen by Verdi to appear as Amelia in the revised version of *Simon Boccanegra* (1881, La Scala). She was sought for the role of Desdemona in the première of *Otello* but by this time she had retired, having married Vittorio Dalem, the director of the Teatro Rossetti in Trieste. DAVID CUMMINGS

D'Angri, Elena. *See* ANGRI, ELENA.

Daniel-Lesur [Lesur, Daniel Jean Yves] (*b* Paris, 19 Nov 1908). French composer. He had early lessons with Tournemire and then studied at the Paris Conservatoire (1919–29), his subsequent career including work as an organist, as a teacher at the Schola Cantorum (1935–64) and as a musical administrator. Like his contemporary Messiaen, he stood out in the 1930s against the prevailing neo-classical currents, and pursued a serious-minded, modally shaded style that might suggest the Tournemire pupil. His single opera *Andrea del Sarto* (1961–8) was the culmination of a long involvement with the de Musset play: he had written incidental music for it in 1947, followed by a symphonic poem two years later. The opera has its moments of orchestral bravura, but its more permanent qualities are of sombre meditation on the life of the artist. Cast in two acts, to the composer's own libretto, it had its first performance at the Marseilles Opera on 24 January 1969.

PAUL GRIFFITHS

Daniels, Barbara (*b* Newark, OH, 7 May 1946). American soprano. After studying at the Cincinnati College-Conservatory, she made her début in 1973 with the West Palm Beach Opera as Mozart's Susanna. In 1974 she was engaged at Innsbruck, where her roles included Fiordiligi and Violetta, then in 1976 she moved to Kassel, adding Liù and Massenet's Manon to her repertory; there she also took part in the première of Walter Steffan's *Unter den Milchwald* (1977). She made her Covent Garden début in 1978 as Rosalinde (*Die Fledermaus*) and sang Norina at the Kennedy Center, Washington, DC (1979), and Zdenka at San Francisco (1980), before making her Metropolitan début in 1983 as Musetta. Since 1978 she has sung at Cologne, where her roles have included Elisetta (*Il matrimonio segreto*), Lady Harriet (*Martha*), Micaëla, Musetta and Mrs Alice Ford. A lyric soprano whose repertory includes Mimì, Marguerite, Butterfly, Minnie, which she sang at the Metropolitan (1991), and Jenůfa, she also has a facility for coloratura, which she demonstrated with great success as Adèle in *Le comte Ory* at Zürich (1981) and as Handel's Agrippina at Schwetzingen (1985).

ELIZABETH FORBES

Dan'kevych, Kostyantyn Fedorovych (*b* Odessa, 11/24 Dec 1905; *d* Kiev, 26 Feb 1984). Ukrainian composer and conductor. After graduating from the Odessa Institute of Music and Drama (now the Odessa Conservatory) in 1929, he joined its faculty; he was a professor and director there from 1948 to 1951, when he was invited to the Kiev Conservatory. From 1956 to 1967 he was head of the Composers' Union of the Ukraine. He wrote symphonies, symphonic poems, chamber music, songs and film scores, but his fame rests primarily on his operas; *Bohdan Khmel'nyts'ky* (1951), about the struggle of the Ukrainian peasants against the Polish aristocracy in the 17th century, achieved international recognition in its second (1953) version. In 1939 he composed a highly successful ballet, *Lileya* ('Lily'). M. Mykhaylov wrote a monograph on Dan'kevych (Kiev, 1959).

See also BOHDAN KHMEL'NYTS'KY.

Trahediina nich [Tragic Night] (4, V. Ivanovych and Dan'kevych, after O. Bezymens'ky), Odessa, 1935

Bohdan Khmel'nyts'ky, 1948–50 (4, V. Vasylevska, after O. Korniychuk), Kiev, 29 Jan 1951; rev. Kiev, 1953, vs (Kiev, 1954); rev. 1977, Dnipropetrovsk, 1978

Nazar Stodolya (3, L. Predslavych, after T. H. Shevchenko), Kharkiv, 28 May 1960, vs (Kiev, 1962) VIRKO BALEY

D'Annunzio, Gabriele (*b* Pescara, 12 March 1863; *d* Gardone Riviera, 1 March 1938). Italian writer. A strong influence on Italian music in the early 20th century, he frequently wrote about music and musicians, for example in the odes to Bellini and Verdi in the second book of *Laudi* (Milan, 1904) and the passages on Monteverdi and Wagner in the novel *Il fuoco* (1896–8). It has often been said that to have recognized Monteverdi's stature before 1900 itself revealed a searching mind, and that D'Annunzio was also ahead of his time in admiring Wagner as an artist while refusing to accept his philosophy and theories. But it has recently been shown (see Tedeschi) that these 'advanced' opinions were plagiarized, mainly from Romain Rolland. Nevertheless throughout his life – from his passionate concert-going in Rome around 1880 to his retirement in the Vittoriale, where he even had his own string quartet – D'Annunzio sought the company of musicians and won their respect with his appearance of knowledge and penetrating insight.

D'Annunzio collaborated directly with composers on several occasions. *Parisina* was originally drafted in 1906 as a libretto for Puccini, but was eventually set by Mascagni instead; and *Fedra*, although initially conceived as a play, was written with the idea of then adapting it as a libretto for Pizzetti, with whom D'Annunzio was for a time on very close terms. Pizzetti's elaborate incidental scores for *La nave* (1908) and *La pisanelle, ou La mort parfumée* (as *La pisanella*, 1913) were commissioned as integral parts of the dramas' conceptions, while the texts were being written; this was also the case with Debussy's music for *Le martyre de St*

Sébastien (1911). Other composers who used adaptations of D'Annunzio plays as opera librettos included Franchetti, Zandonai, Montemezzi and G. F. Malipiero. Furthermore, many Italian composers were influenced in a more general way by the hedonistic aesthetic of 'dannunzianesimo', that cult of the elaborately picturesque, the exotic, the selfconsciously archaic, the gratuitously barbaric and the sensual. The music of Respighi, in particular, often came remarkably close to the D'Annunzian spirit: his regular librettist, Claudio Guastalla, was a disciple of D'Annunzio.

La città morta (play, 1898): R. Pugno and N. Boulanger, comp. 1911 as La ville morte
Francesca da Rimini (play, 1901): Zandonai, 1914
La figlia di Iorio (play, 1904): Franchetti, 1906; Pizzetti, 1954
La fiaccola sotto il moggio (play, 1905): Pizzetti, comp. 1914–15 as Gigliola, unfinished
Sogno d'un tramonto d'autunno (play, 1905): R. Torre Alfina, comp. before 1913; G. F. Malipiero, 1963 [comp. 1913(?–14)]
La nave (play, 1908): Montemezzi, 1918
Fedra (play, 1909): Pizzetti, 1915
Parisina (op, 1913): Mascagni, 1913

*

'Gaio': 'D'Annunzio, Mascagni e "Parisina" ', *Il marzocco* [Florence], xviii/51 (1913), 3
A. Calza: 'Wagner e D'Annunzio: il critico contro il librettista', *Harmonia* [Rome], ii/1–2 (1914), 18–23
G. Donati-Petténi: *D'Annunzio e Wagner* (Florence, 1923)
G. M. Gatti: 'Gabriele D'Annunzio and the Italian Opera-Composers', *MQ*, x (1924), 263–88
I. Pizzetti: ' "Fedra": memorie e appunti del musicista per la biografia del poeta', *Scenario*, vii (1938), 199–203
L. Tomelleri, I. Pizzetti and others: *Gabriele d'Annunzio e la musica* (Milan, 1939); also in *RMI*, xliii (1939), 161–301
D. de' Paoli: 'Gabriele d'Annunzio, la musica e i musicisti', *Nel centenario di Gabriele d'Annunzio* (Turin, 1963), 41–125 [RAI pubn]
R. Chiesa: 'La *Francesca da Rimini* di D'Annunzio nella musica di Riccardo Zandonai', *Quaderni dannunziani* [Brescia], nos.32–3 (1965), 320–54
E. Paratore: 'Introduzione a *La figlia di Iorio* di Pizzetti', *Studi dannunziani* (Naples, 1966), 331–7
A. Marchetti: 'Carezze e graffi di D'Annunzio a Puccini', *NRMI*, viii (1974), 536–9
R. Tedeschi: *D'Annunzio e la musica* (Scandicci, Florence, 1988)

JOHN C. G. WATERHOUSE

Danon, Oskar (*b* Sarajevo, 7 Feb 1913). Yugoslav conductor and composer. He studied in Prague at the conservatory and the university. From 1938 he established himself as an orchestral and theatrical conductor in Sarajevo. In 1945 he was appointed director and conductor of the Belgrade Opera, but in 1960 he gave up administrative responsibilities in favour of full-time conducting.

Although Danon had already conducted performances of *The Bartered Bride* in Prague, his international fame began in 1958 with the Belgrade Opera performances of *Prince Igor* and *Don Quichotte* at Lausanne and Paris. He conducted the company in *The Love for Three Oranges* with great success at the 1959 Wiesbaden Festival and *Boris Godunov* (in Rimsky-Korsakov's edition) at the Paris Opéra in 1960. The Belgrade company's proficiency in the Russian repertory was particularly valued at a time when the West had virtually no contact with Soviet operatic enterprise. Although the company performed at home in Serbo-Croat, it was engaged to record in Russian. Danon's conducting of *Prince Igor* was the first complete recording of it to reach the West (1955), followed in 1956 by Glinka's *A Life for the Tsar*. At the 1962 Edinburgh Festival he was much commended for his vigorous and varied conducting of the Belgrade company in *Don Quichotte*, *Prince Igor* and the first performances in Britain of Prokofiev's *The Gambler* and *The Love for Three Oranges*. Later the same year he conducted *Prince Igor* in the Chicago Lyric Opera season. Outside the Slavonic repertory he conducted *Tristan und Isolde* (1969, Barcelona), *Arabella* (1970, Amsterdam) and other works. He continued to conduct regularly in Belgrade, opening the restored National Theatre in 1990 with Konjović's *Knez od Zete* ('The Prince of Zeta'). His compositions include incidental music for Shakespeare and other drama productions.

ARTHUR JACOBS

Dante Alighieri (*b* Florence, May or June 1265; *d* Ravenna, 14 Sept 1321). Italian poet. He was the author of the *Commedia* (known since the 16th century as *La divina commedia*), a narrative poem that has provided material for more than 20 operas: the best-known are *Gianni Schicchi* (1918, music by Puccini, libretto by Giovacchino Forzano) and *Francesca da Rimini* (1914, music by Zandonai, libretto by Tito Ricordi after the play by Gabriele d'Annunzio).

Inferno, the first part of the *Commedia*, with its themes of sin and damnation, held a strong attraction for artists and composers of the neo-Gothic and early Romantic period. The second and third parts, *Purgatorio* and *Paradiso*, have exercised less theatrical appeal, although Cammarano's libretto for Donizetti's *Pia de' Tolomei* ultimately derives from the *Purgatorio*. The stern figure of Virgil, who in the *Inferno* accompanies the frightened Dante through hell, and the dramatic tales related by the sinners were potentially the stuff of 19th-century opera. The famous illustrations by Gustave Doré in an edition of the *Inferno* published in 1861, many of them like stage sets, fostered a familiarity with Dante's imaginary world.

Operas inspired by Dante himself include Godard's *Dante et Béatrice* (1890), Nouguès's *Dante* (1914) and John Foulds's *The Vision of Dante* (1905–8).

all from the poem Commedia
Inferno, v:97–142 (Francesca da Rimini episode): Generali, 1829; Mercadante, 1830–31; Morlacchi, comp. 1836; Goetz, 1877; Cagnoni, 1878; A. Thomas, 1882; Nápravník, 1902; Rakhmaninov, 1906; Mancinelli, 1907, as Paolo és Francesca; Ábrányi, 1912, as Paolo és Francesca; Zandonai, 1914
Inferno, xxx:32–3, 42–5 (Gianni Schicchi reference): Puccini, 1918
Inferno, xxxiii:1–75 (Ugolino episode): Dittersdorf, 1796
Purgatorio, v:130–36 (Pia de' Tolomei episode): Donizetti, 1837

BARBARA REYNOLDS

Danton and Robespierre. Grand opera in three acts by JOHN C. EATON to a libretto by Patrick Creagh; Bloomington, Indiana University Opera Theater, 21 April 1978.

The opera treats in telescopic fashion the struggle between the title characters during the period immediately following the French Revolution: Danton (tenor) rouses the people to patriotic fury, urging them to repel an army of Prussian, Austrian and emigré troops advancing towards Paris. Robespierre (baritone), becoming increasingly more inflexible in his commitment to the revolution, plots the September massacres. Danton, having called for an end to the Reign of Terror, is opposed by Robespierre who, joined by St Just (bass) and Couthon (tenor), signs an act of indictment against him. Danton is brought before the Revolutionary Tribunal and eventually executed. With the terror at its height, a conspiracy is launched against Robespierre, who, after condemnation by the full Assembly, unsuccessfully attempts to take his own life. As the opera ends he is executed. Woven between the epic scenes presenting these events are several more intimate ones depicting Danton's relationship with his first wife Gabrielle (soprano) and her confidante Louise (soprano), whom, following Gabrielle's death, Danton marries.

Eaton's music, joining vocal, orchestral and electronic components in a richly spun fabric, captures the violence, fury, exaltation and fear of the post-revolutionary period with remarkable precision. The crowd scenes, some devoted to the people, others depicting political assemblies, rank among his finest creations. Microtonality, a constant feature in Eaton's mature music, is put to effective use to symbolize the conflict between Danton and Robespierre and their embodiment of the opposition of humanistic pragmatism and unbending idealism. Danton is conceived as a multidimensional figure, with music rich in tonal nuance and microtonal inflection. Robespierre's growing inflexibility is mirrored by his being associated with just intonation (employed here by Eaton for the first time), which becomes increasingly dissonant as it moves further away from his home key of C major. This idea is realized musically in a tonal, triadically harmonized chorale, played by an appropriately tuned electronic synthesizer, which begins in C and then modulates through more distant keys, eventually reaching an extreme of F♯ major. The pure C major opening thus gives way to increasingly oppressive dissonant 'beating', produced by the overtones of the out-of-tune triads. Four complete statements of the chorale are heard during the opera, each assuming a different character in response to the changing dramatic context and collectively integrating the musical and dramatic structure.

ROBERT P. MORGAN

Dantons Tod ('Danton's Death'). Opera in two parts (six scenes) by GOTTFRIED VON EINEM to a libretto by BORIS BLACHER and the composer after GEORG BÜCHNER's drama of 1835; Salzburg, Festspielhaus, 6 August 1947.

The action takes place in Paris in 1794 against the background of the French Revolution. In Part 1 scene i, various deputies sit with their female accomplices at a gambling table. Camille Desmoulins (tenor) brings news that Robespierre (tenor) has instigated the arbitrary execution of 20 people. An attempt is made to persuade Danton (baritone) to attack the tyrannical moral preacher in the Convention, but Danton, though no friend of Robespierre, shows little inclination to do so. In the street outside, the prompter, Simon (*buffo* bass), beats his wife for allowing their daughter to consort with rich cavalrymen. A quarrel ensues and a young man, taken for an aristocrat, is nearly hanged by a howling mob. Robespierre appears and tries to mobilize public feeling for his own ends. Danton, who is also present, cannot conceal his distaste for Robespierre's methods. After Danton leaves, Saint-Just (bass) advises Robespierre to destroy his rival and his supporters. Robespierre agrees but wants his youthful friend Desmoulins saved. However, when he finds out that Desmoulins has publicly attacked him in a newspaper article, he has no alternative but to plan his conviction. In scene iii Danton, who is staying as a guest at the house of Desmoulins and his wife Lucile (soprano), discovers that he will be arrested. He declines an offer to escape, claiming that he is weary. Lucile has a premonition that her husband will also be caught up in Danton's overthrow despite his youthful friendship with Robespierre.

In Part 2 of the opera, Danton and Desmoulins have been taken to prison. The people still discuss whether Danton's arrest was justified, but the view put about by Robespierre that he is in reality an aristocrat seems to prevail. Inside the gaol Desmoulins, thinking of Lucile, passionately clings to life, and Danton finds it difficult to calm him down when Lucile appears in front of the prison and agitatedly asks whether all the prisoners will be executed. Danton is subsequently arraigned before the Revolutionary Tribunal and accused of conspiring with enemies of the country. He passionately refutes these accusations and the favour of the mob seems to turn towards him. Saint-Just presents new evidence of Danton's guilt to the president of the Tribunal. At this point, Danton accuses Robespierre of treachery and the assembly breaks up in wild tumult. After an instrumental interlude, the scene changes to the Square of the Revolution. Robespierre has emerged victorious. Danton and his followers are to be executed. The mob hurls abuse at the condemned. As the crowd disperses and the executioners wipe the blood from the guillotine, Lucile, who is near to madness, appears shouting 'Long live the King!' and delivers herself to the executioners.

Dantons Tod, von Einem's first opera, was written between 1944 and 1946. The initial inspiration for the work was the unsuccessful assassination attempt on Hitler in 1944. Both the composer and Blacher immersed themselves in Büchner's drama, reducing the original 32 scenes to six and amalgamating the episodes which involve the mob so that they play a central role in the action. The musical idiom is by no means innovatory, owing much to composers as different as Strauss, Hindemith, Stravinsky and Blacher himself. Nevertheless, these influences are absorbed into a style that has sufficient flexibility and individuality to deal with the great range of emotions demanded by the text. Von Einem's harmonic language is firmly based on tonality despite occasional dissonant passages. His vocal writing is rarely melodic, relying to a large extent on the use of parlando. This is further emphasized by the way in which the central figures of the drama are deliberately undercharacterized, so that the masses who control the Revolution stay in the foreground. Apart from the five powerful brass chords which open and close the opera, and certain individual tonal colourings such as the muted trumpets which accompany Robespierre, there is little evidence of the use of specific leitmotifs, nor is there any intense thematic development in the symphonic manner. The most exciting section of the opera occurs in the Tribunal Scene (Part 2 scene ii), where the brilliant and often complex choral writing charts the volatile opinions of the mob with astonishing precision. *Dantons Tod* was acclaimed after its first performance and secured international recognition for its composer. It was regarded by many to be an epoch-making work and remains the most consistently impressive of his operatic compositions. ERIK LEVI

Danzi. German family of musicians.

(1) **Franziska** [Francesca] (**Dorothea**) **Lebrun** [née Danzi] (*b* Mannheim, bap. 24 March 1756; *d* Berlin, 14 May 1791). Soprano. She was the daughter of the Mannheim cellist Innozenz Danzi and Barbara Toeschi.

She made her début in Gassmann's *L'amore artigiano* in May 1772, and Burney heard her in Sacchini's *La contadina in corte* in August that year. She soon gained a leading position in the Mannheim court opera, singing the role of Parthenia in Schweitzer's *Alceste* (1775, Schwetzingen) and the role of Anna in Holzbauer's *Günther von Schwarzburg* (1777). Schubart claimed that she could sing up to *a'''* with clarity and distinctness, and that she was capable of executing the most difficult coloratura. She took the lead in four *opere serie* in London (1777–8), then appeared in the inaugural performance of Salieri's *Europa riconosciuta* that opened La Scala, Milan (1778). She was in London again for two seasons from November 1779; her husband, Ludwig August Lebrun (1752–90), wrote some ballet music for operas at the King's Theatre, and she published two sets of sonatas for keyboard and violin. Burney remarked that her vocal abilities were superior to those of other women on the London stage, but that, 'travelling with her husband, an excellent performer on the hautbois, she seems to have listened to nothing else ... [and has] copied the tone of his instrument so exactly, that when he accompanied her in divisions of thirds and sixths, it was impossible to discover who was uppermost'. She returned to Munich, where the former Mannheim court had moved, but also travelled with her husband, singing as a guest artist in operas and concerts in Vienna and Verona; she spent 1786–7 at S Carlo, Naples, sang in Vogler's *Castore e Polluce* during Carnival 1787 in Munich, and was a guest artist in Berlin, 1789–90.

Her daughter Rosine Lebrun (1783–1855) was also successful as an opera singer and was a member of the Munich theatre company, 1801–30.

*

BurneyGN; *BurneyH*
Musikalische Real-Zeitung, iii (1789), no.52, col.415; iv (1790), no.1, col.7; no.4, col.30; no.17, col.128
Musikalische Korrespondenz der Teutschen filarmonischen Gesellschaft (6 Jan 1791, 16 Feb 1791)
C. F. D. Schubart: *Ideen zu einer Ästhetik der Tonkunst* (Vienna, 1806)
F. J. Lipowksy: *Baierisches Musiklexikon* (Munich, 1811)

(2) **Franz (Ignaz) Danzi** (*b* Schwetzingen, bap. 15 June 1763; *d* Karlsruhe, 13 April 1826). Composer, brother of (1) Franziska Lebrun. He studied the piano, the cello and singing with his father and at the age of 15 joined the celebrated Mannheim orchestra. When the Elector Palatine Carl Theodor transferred his court to Munich in 1778, Danzi remained in Mannheim, in the orchestra of the newly established Nationaltheater. He studied composition with G. J. Vogler and before leaving Mannheim wrote a duodrama, a Singspiel and incidental music for at least eight plays.

In 1784 he was appointed to replace his father as principal cellist in the court orchestra at Munich. Although he wanted to compose operas for the court, Danzi received no major commissions until 1789; *Die Mitternachtstunde* (formerly dated 1788) was not performed until 1798. In 1790 he married the singer Margarethe Marchand (see (3) below). The couple visited Hamburg, Leipzig, Prague, Florence and Venice, spending two years in the Guardasoni company. In 1796 they returned to Munich. After the successful première of *Die Mitternachtstunde*, Danzi was appointed vice-Kapellmeister on 18 May 1798 and placed in charge of German opera and church music.

The next few years were marked by a series of personal and professional setbacks. Danzi's father died in 1798, and his wife died in 1800 after a long illness. The death of Carl Theodor in 1799 had a greater impact on Danzi's career: the new elector, Maximilian IV Joseph, was less sympathetic to German opera and imposed financial restrictions on the theatres. Further, Danzi faced opposition from rivals, including the new intendant Joseph Marius Babo and the Kapellmeister Peter Winter. When his serious German opera, *Iphigenie in Aulis*, was finally given in 1807, it was poorly prepared and had only two performances; bitter and disappointed, Danzi left Munich for the Rhineland.

In October 1807, the King of Württemberg offered Danzi the position of Kapellmeister at Stuttgart. There Danzi met Carl Maria von Weber and encouraged the younger composer as he completed his Singspiel *Silvana*. In 1811 the king established an institute for music: Danzi was appointed a director, to teach composition and supervise instruction on wind instruments. He left Stuttgart in 1812 to become Kapellmeister in Karlsruhe. The musical organization there was inexperienced and weak, and Danzi spent the rest of his tenure trying to build a respectable company. He remained an active correspondent with Weber and directed his operas soon after their premières. Danzi also wrote regularly for the *Allgemeine musikalische Zeitung* and *Aurora*; his libretto *Die Opernprobe* was set to music by Poissl.

Although he is remembered mainly for his chamber music, Danzi was in fact one of the most important German opera composers of Mozart's generation. His early dramatic work, *Cleopatra*, has many of the *Sturm und Drang* qualities of the operas performed at Mannheim in the late 1770s. In an approbatory essay on *Iphigenie*, Friedrich Rochlitz placed it beside Schweitzer's *Alceste* and Holzbauer's *Günther von Schwarzburg* in the tradition of serious German opera. Danzi's comic operas are more successful: *Die Mitternachtstunde* and *Der Kuss* rank alongside the best of Winter's and Weigl's works in this genre. Colourful orchestration, chromatic harmonies and cantabile melodic writing are distinguishing features of Danzi's operas. In choosing exotic subjects and folk tales, he anticipated Weber and later German Romantic opera composers.

See also BERGGEIST, DER; KUSS, DER; and MITTERNACHTSTUNDE, DIE.

Cleopatra (duodrama, 1, J. L. Neumann), Mannheim, National, 30 Jan 1780, *D-B*, *US-Wc*
Azakia (Spl, 3, C. F. Schwan), Mannheim, National, 6 June 1780
Der Sylphe, by 1785 (Operette, 1, F. L. W. Meyer), ?Munich, 1788
Der Triumph der Treue (Spl, 2, J. F. von Binder, after C. M. Wieland: *Oberon*), Munich, 7 Feb 1789
Der Quasimann (komische Oper, 2, M. G. Lambrecht), Munich, Aug 1789, 1 aria *A-Wgm*
Die Mitternachtstunde (Spl, 3, Lambrecht, after Dumaniant [A.-J. Bourlin]: *La guerre ouverte*), Munich, Hof, 16 Feb 1798, *D-B*, *Mbs*, vs (Bonn, *c*1800)
Der Kuss (tragisch-komische Oper, 3, Lambrecht), Munich, Hof, 27 June 1799, *US-Wc*, vs, 1 aria, 2 duets (Munich, *c*1799)
El Bondokani [Der Calif von Bagdad] (Spl, 1, Lambrecht), Munich, Hof, 20 Aug 1802
Iphigenie in Aulis (grosse Oper, 3, K. Reger), Munich, Hof, 27 Jan 1807, vs, 2 arias and a march (Munich, *c*1807)
Dido (melodrama, 1, G. Reinbeck), Stuttgart, 18 Dec 1811
Camilla und Eugen, oder Der Gartenschlüssel (Spl, 1, F. C. Hiemer), Stuttgart, 15 March 1812, *D-B*, *Sl*
Der Berggeist, oder Schicksal und Treue [Rübezahl] (romantische Oper, 2, C. von Lohbauer), Karlsruhe, Hof, 19 April 1813, *Mbs**
Malvina (grosse Oper, 2, G. C. Römer), Karlsruhe, Hof, 26 Dec 1814
Turandot (Spl, 2, after C. Gozzi), Karlsruhe, Hof, 26 Dec 1816, *Mbs*
L'Abbé de l'Attaignant, oder Die Theaterprobe (Spl, 1, Hiemer), Karlsruhe, Hof, 14 Sept 1820

*

F. J. Lipowsky: *Baierisches Musiklexikon* (Munich, 1811)

Neuer Nekrolog der Deutschen, Jg.4: 1826 (1828)
F. Rochlitz: 'Franz Danzi', *AMZ*, xxviii (1826), cols.581–7; repr. in *Für Freunde der Tonkunst*, iii (Leipzig, 1830), 170–86
M. M. von Weber: *Carl Maria von Weber*, i (Leipzig, 1864)
H. Giehne: 'Franz Danzi', *Badische Biographien*, i (Heidelberg, 1875), 159–60
E. Reipschläger: *Schubaur, Danzi und Poissl als Opernkomponisten* (diss., U. of Rostock, 1911)
M. Herre: *Franz Danzi: ein Beitrag zur Geschichte der deutschen Oper* (diss., U. of Munich, 1930)
P. M. Alexander: *The Chamber Music of Franz Danzi: Sources, Chronology, and Style* (diss., Indiana U., 1986)

(3) **(Maria) Margarethe Danzi** [née Marchand] (*b* Frankfurt, 1768; *d* Munich, 11 June 1800). Soprano, wife of (2) Franz Danzi. The daughter of the singer and theatre manager Theobald Hilarius Marchand, she was acquainted with the theatre early in life, and appeared on the Mannheim stage as early as 1777. Together with her younger brother Heinrich she received tuition from Leopold Mozart at his home in Salzburg from 1781 to about 1785. She made her début at Munich in Carnival 1788 as Telaira in Vogler's *Castore e Polluce*. She married Franz Danzi in 1790 and began a successful career with him; from 1796 she was prima donna of the German Theatre in Munich. She also composed, mainly for the violin. ROLAND WÜRTZ (1,3), PAUL CORNEILSON (2)

Danzig (Ger.). GDAŃSK.

Daphne. *Bukolische Tragödie* in one act by RICHARD STRAUSS to a libretto by JOSEPH GREGOR; Dresden, Staatsoper, 15 October 1938.

Daphne	soprano
Peneios *a fisherman, her father*	bass
Gaea *her mother*	contralto
Leukippos *a shepherd*	tenor
Apollo	tenor
Four Shepherds	tenor, baritone, two basses
Two Maids	sopranos

Shepherds, herdsmen and women

Setting An olive grove by the river Peneios in mythological Thessaly, with Mount Olympus in the background

When Nazi anti-Semitism made it impossible for Stefan Zweig to continue as Strauss's librettist after *Die schweigsame Frau*, Zweig passed on his sketch for a one-act work, *1648* (*see* FRIEDENSTAG, its ultimate title), to his friend and chosen successor Gregor. While Gregor developed it he was also writing his own text for *Daphne*, which Strauss wanted as a companion piece. The composer began the *Daphne* score in earnest only when *Friedenstag* was almost done, and the latter had its première nearly three months before Karl Böhm conducted the integral double bill – which proved to be unfeasibly lengthy. (Margarete Teschemacher was the heroine, Torsten Ralf Apollo, Martin Kremer Leukippos; Cebotari sang Daphne at the first Berlin performance.) On reading Gregor's sketch, Zweig expected *Daphne* to make an evening by itself, like *Salome* or *Elektra*: he was quite right, and in most recent revivals the opera has been so performed.

Strauss had no great opinion of Gregor, despite sharing his hellenophilia, and treated his first draft to unsparing criticism. More politely, Zweig backed the composer's suggestions and offered more of his own. In due course Gregor's orotund Zeus-figure was expunged, along with an improbable Medusa ballet, and Daphne herself – reluctant adolescent, sex-shy nature-lover – was brought into much sharper psychological focus. At substantial cost, indeed, to the 'Apollonian' versus 'Dionysiac' polarity which the composer claimed to be the real, Nietzschean topic of the opera: Daphne's overbearing seducer is no Apollonian devotee of calm beauty and order, nor is there anything remotely Dionysiac about her hapless childhood swain.

The hardest blow for Gregor must have been losing his sententious pageant-finale (meant to parallel the choral close of *Friedenstag*), where all the voices would variously celebrate Daphne's transformation into a laurel tree. It never convinced Strauss, and when the conductor Clemens Krauss suggested instead a purely musical transformation – Daphne's wordless voice interleaved with orchestral intimations of Nature – he saw the point at once. He notified Gregor that his elaborate moral-drawing would not be needed: 'Der Baum allein singt!' Without doubt, that was the saving of *Daphne*. In 1943 Strauss made decent amends to his author with a glowing cantata-version of the scene, *An den Baum Daphne* (for *a cappella* double chorus and boys' choir), which sets a new, simpler Gregor description to music derived from the opera.

An oboe begins the pastoral prelude in G, redolent of glades and brooks and in fact Daphne; other woodwind join in. As the curtain rises on sunset, an alphorn (when available!) summons shepherds to the Dionysiac feast; four of them hail the night before hurrying off to collect their herds and anoint themselves. Alone, young Daphne wishes that day would go on forever ('O bleib, geliebter Tag!'). She knows that the feast will be coarse and crude; she loves only simple Nature – meadows, trees, all the works of the sun-god. In the dark, only the beloved tree of her childhood consoles her. (Strauss sets this soliloquy in ravishing textures, alive with solo-string whispers.) To her dismay, Leukippos springs out from behind it to plead his adoration, which also began in their childhood. What Daphne loved was the bloom of his cheeks, the sisterly tenderness of his eyes, his flute playing; now, unfortunately, he has become a man (he breaks his flute to prove it). With his hopes for the feast-night dashed, he retreats.

Gaea has overheard this with regret, and tells Daphne that the gods will one day make her heart open like a blossom. (The *Ur*-Gaea was the earth-goddess, as Peneios was a river-god; though Gregor's text presents them merely as imposing elders, the contralto role is mysterious and Erda-like down to an extraordinary E♭.) Her daughter likes the floral imagery, but she refuses the human raiment Gaea's maids bring her for the feast and runs away. In a scherzo-interlude the maids chatter about the waste of gown and jewels, and then persuade poor doe-eyed Leukippos to masquerade in them in the hope of catching Daphne unawares.

Now Peneios assembles the shepherds ceremonially, and alarms them by inviting the gods too to their banquet. At once an eerie, crackling storm blows up; Apollo strides in, disguised as a simple cattleman. A randy steer chased his cows hither and yon, he says, and only now have he and his men managed to settle them nearby. The nervous shepherds, much relieved, repeat 'Einen brünstigen Stier!' (very like the vassals in

Götterdämmerung) and go off to feast. Apollo berates himself for his whimsical deception, but is immediately riveted by the appearance of Daphne in the moonlight with a welcoming cup. Her plea for endless day had reached his ear; now, to her delight, he calls her 'Sister' – but innocent raptures soon lead to a more-than-brotherly embrace. (Strauss was proud of this highly charged passage, which recalls Parsifal's erotic initiation by Kundry's kiss.) She recoils in confusion, as the Dionysian crowd returns with torches.

There is lascivious ritual cavorting by masked 'rams' and 'bacchantes'. In his maiden guise, Leukippos silently invites Daphne to join the dance; as she nearly succumbs, jealous Apollo erupts and denounces her 'playmate'. Leukippos, unmasked but undaunted, demands in the name of Dionysus that the stranger reveal himself too. That he does, amidst terrible darkening and thunder, and when Leukippos remains bravely defiant the god draws his bow to shoot him dead.

Daphne is overwhelmed not only by grief but also by remorse: why did she reject Leukippos's staunch love? Guilty and deeply moved, Apollo implores his fellow gods that Leukippos shall be Dionysus's flautist on Olympus, and that with Zeus's blessing chaste Daphne shall become the sacred laurel tree, her twigs crowning every hero. The god and the crowd fade into the dark while Daphne calls out to her 'green brothers' ('Ich komme, ich komme'). As the moonlight returns, so do the magical F♯ murmurings of her earlier soliloquy; from the miraculous tree, her wordless voice soars in timeless, haunting communion with the oboe.

* * *

If *Daphne* is too long for half an evening, it is also – and to positive effect – too short for a whole one. Had the unimaginative Gregor spread the action over two acts, it might have been epically dire; but compressed into one it makes a concise frieze, almost cartoon-like, with expanded panels only for Daphne's initial soliloquy and the concluding transformation. (Sliding down from dewy G major to visionary F♯ intimations, the soliloquy mirrors the progress of the whole opera from prelude to final *Verwandlung*.) The principal roles pose problems. Besides Gaea's subterranean range, there is the strenuous Apollo to contrast with the lyrical Leukippos, whose brave rhetoric must overreach his insipid musical material – nothing less than a Fritz Wunderlich will do – and a Daphne who can sound sweetly serene in an extravagantly high register. Strauss's delight in chamber writing for the opera house rose to new subtleties here, prefiguring the late joys of *Capriccio* and his woodwind concertos. DAVID MURRAY

Da Ponte, Lorenzo [Conegliano, Emmanuele] (*b* Ceneda [now Vittorio Veneto], 10 March 1749; *d* New York, 17 Aug 1838). Italian librettist. His involvement in the remarkable flowering of *opera buffa* in Vienna from 1783 to 1790 and his collaborations with Martín y Soler, Salieri and, above all, Mozart make him arguably the most significant librettist of his generation: his three librettos for Mozart (*Le nozze di Figaro*, *Don Giovanni* and *Così fan tutte*) are justifiably regarded as peaks of the genre.

1. LIFE. Da Ponte's biographers rely largely on his *Memorie*. Written from the age of 60 onwards as an apologia for a life plagued by (often self-induced) misfortune, they present a carefully constructed image of the man and his work. Accounts of raffish adventures in the manner of his friend Casanova mix with vainglorious statements of achievement and accusations of treachery by friend and foe; sometimes fact can only with difficulty be separated from fiction.

Born Emmanuele Conegliano, Da Ponte adopted the name of the Bishop of Ceneda, Lorenzo da Ponte, when his father, a Jewish tanner, converted to Christianity in 1763. Da Ponte's early training in Ceneda and Portogruaro prepared him for the priesthood (he was ordained in 1773) and for teaching (at seminaries in Portogruaro, 1770–73, and Treviso, 1774–6). However, his penchant for liberal politics and married women led to a ban on his teaching in the Veneto and, on 17 December 1779, a 15-year exile from Venice. He went first to Gorizia and then to Dresden, believing that his friend, the poet and librettist Caterino Mazzolà, would secure him a court post: in Dresden he worked with Mazzolà translating and arranging plays and librettos (including Quinault's *Atys*; Da Ponte had already collaborated with his brother, Girolamo, on a translation of J.-F. de La Harpe's *Le comte de Warwick* in 1780). Mazzolà then provided Da Ponte with a recommendation to Salieri in Vienna: he arrived there in late 1781, meeting Metastasio just before his death. Da Ponte attracted the favour of Joseph II, and when Joseph abandoned his pursuit of German opera and revived the Italian company (in 1783), Da Ponte was appointed poet to the court theatre.

Da Ponte's facility for versifying, his ready wit and sound knowledge of languages made him an ideal theatre poet. His work included translating texts from French to Italian, reworking old librettos for revivals and providing new works (themselves often adaptations) for Viennese composers. His first new libretto for Salieri as musical director of the company, *Il ricco d'un giorno*, was a failure (Da Ponte blamed the music). But in 1786 his position was assured by the success of his *Il burbero di buon cuore* for Martín y Soler. That year saw a remarkable output of six librettos, including *Le nozze di Figaro* for Mozart and the hugely popular *Una cosa rara* (again set by Martín y Soler).

Da Ponte had an uneasy relationship with Count Rosenberg, director of the theatre, and his rivalry with the poet Giambattista Casti found expression in satirical poems (notably the *Epistola nell'Abate Casti*, Vienna, 1786) and even on the stage. Nor did Da Ponte's arrogance (see Michael Kelly's *Reminiscences*, 1826) help matters. He managed to regain Salieri's favour, providing *Axur, re d'Ormus* (based, like *Figaro*, on Beaumarchais) at the same time as writing *L'arbore di Diana* for Martín y Soler and *Don Giovanni* for Mozart; he later produced three other librettos for Salieri. He also published a volume of *Saggi poetici* (Vienna, 1788). In 1789 Da Ponte was involved in the revival of *Figaro*, probably providing the new texts for arias to be sung by his mistress, Adriana Ferrarese (the new Susanna), and he also wrote *Così fan tutte* in that year (Ferrarese was Fiordiligi). In addition, he claims to have saved the Italian opera in Vienna from threatened closure. However, the death of his patron Joseph II on 20 February 1790 and court intrigue on the succession of Leopold II led to his dismissal (for which he blamed Salieri, among others) in 1791.

The poet was denied permission to return to Venice, and although a reported meeting (in Trieste) with the short-lived Leopold II and the support of Leopold's successor Francis II went some way towards healing the rift, he never re-established himself in Vienna. Instead, having 'married' an Englishwoman, Ann (Nancy) Grahl, on 12 August 1792, he set off for Paris and then, discouraged by the unstable political situation there, headed for London. Doubtless he hoped to join forces with his former colleagues in Vienna, the singer Michael Kelly and the composer Stephen Storace. After a futile year attempting to establish Italian opera in Brussels, Rotterdam and The Hague, he was appointed to the King's Theatre, Haymarket, by the new manager, William Taylor. While there Da Ponte arranged operas by Cimarosa and others, collaborated again with Martín y Soler on two operas during the composer's stay in London from 1794 to 1796, and also provided librettos for Francesco Bianchi. A trip to Italy in 1798 to recruit singers for the theatre reunited him with his family and his beloved Venice, although his old enemies forced a quick departure. His return to London saw his position blocked by intrigue – he was dismissed in 1799 – and the King's Theatre in financial disarray: his unwise involvement in Taylor's dubious dealings led to Da Ponte's declaring himself bankrupt in February 1800. He was reinstated at the theatre in 1801 and collaborated with Peter Winter on three new operas, but, pursued by creditors, he followed Nancy to America in 1805.

Da Ponte became a grocer and general merchant in New York, then Sunbury (Pennsylvania) and Philadelphia, supplementing his income with private teaching and dealing in Italian books (an activity begun in London). He also produced an early version (1807) of what was to become a compendious autobiography. Returning to New York in 1819, he determined to bring Italian culture to his newly adopted country (he took American citizenship) through teaching and book-dealing; he also occupied the (largely honorary) post of Professor of Italian at Columbia College in 1825 and from 1827 until his death. The publication both of a complete version of the *Memorie* (1823–7) and of a volume of *Poesie varie* (New York, 1830) seems to have formed part of this endeavour; he also issued other translations (e.g. of Byron), catalogues and miscellaneous prose (including a *Storia della lingua e della letteratura italiana in New York*, 1827). His interest in opera revived in his later years; he saw *Don Giovanni* performed by Manuel García's visiting company in 1826, and a new edition of *Figaro*, *Don Giovanni*, *Axur* and his tragedy *Il Mezenzio*, reportedly the only dramatic works from his European period that he had with him in America, was published that year. Notwithstanding his grief at Nancy's death (he issued a volume of commemorative verse in 1832), Da Ponte became financially involved in the ill-fated tour of the Montresor company in 1832–3 (he published an account in 1833) and acted briefly as manager of the newly built Italian Opera House. The initiative brought financial loss, and also a sense that his life's work had been for nothing – a projected final volume of the *Memorie* was never completed – although by all accounts his elaborate funeral offered significant recognition of his achievement.

2. Works. Accounts of Da Ponte's working methods rely heavily on the *Memorie*, and one need not set much store by his claim of writing *Axur, re d'Ormus*, *L'arbore di Diana* and *Don Giovanni* concurrently, sustained by his snuff-box, a bottle of Tokay and the ministrations of a 16-year-old Calliope ('whom I would have liked to love simply as a daughter, but ...'). However, the *Memorie* offer intriguing insights into theatre life in Vienna, London and New York, as well as into Da Ponte's own perception of his art: 'poetry is the door to music, which can be very handsome, and much admired for its exterior, but nobody else can see its internal beauties if the door is wanting'. He also made comments on contemporary librettists (whom he generally derided) and on the composers with whom he worked. Da Ponte was well aware of the different talents of his collaborators and carefully crafted his librettos to suit their needs. Although an obvious admirer of Mozart, he was less enthusiastic than one might expect (which may reflect Mozart's mixed critical reception in the early 19th century), while he praised Salieri (with only a little irony) as an educated and worthy *maestro di cappella*. But his favourite composer seems to have been Martín y Soler: Da Ponte viewed *L'arbore di Diana* as his best libretto. Other composers such as Vincenzo Righini and Francesco Piticchio are roundly dismissed.

The prodigiousness of Da Ponte's output was doubtless due to his facility as a poet: significantly, he was a skilled improviser. But it also reflects his reliance on existing works: nearly all his librettos involve some adaptation, and he appears less happy when inventing original dramatic situations. However, adaptation was common in the period, and Da Ponte's skill lay in his precise knowledge of the dynamics of opera: he condensed situations, pinpointed characters and focussed the action in a manner allowing the composer freedom to create drama through music. Beaumarchais, Da Ponte reported, admired the libretto of *Le nozze di Figaro* for 'contracting so many *colpi di scena* in so short a time, without the one destroying the other'. Even if the remark is apocryphal, it reflects Da Ponte's perception of his achievement.

Da Ponte had a profound sense of the literary and dramatic traditions within which he was working. He claimed to have admired Metastasio from childhood; echoes of and quotations from Metastasio abound in his librettos. But Da Ponte took his heritage further back still to the Renaissance. His linking of *Axur* with Tasso, *L'arbore di Diana* with Petrarch and *Don Giovanni* with Dante is no coincidence: as his later teaching proved, he was intimately familiar with Italian Renaissance poetry. Again, references and quotations in his librettos emphasize the point: Dante, Petrarch, Boccaccio, Ariosto, Sannazaro, Tasso and Guarini all make appearances (and Da Ponte arranged Guarini's celebrated pastoral play *Il pastor fido* for Salieri in 1789). Moreover, Da Ponte made careful use of rhyme and metre as well as complex syntactical and rhetorical patterns. The rich resonances and subtle structures give his librettos a literary emphasis that sets them apart from the workaday efforts of his contemporaries. He was well aware of his skill: his texts often refer to, as they deliberately surpass, verse by Bertati, Casti and Mazzolà.

Two dramatists rarely mentioned in the *Memorie* are Goldoni and Carlo Gozzi, perhaps because they were too close to home. Da Ponte's first success, *Il burbero di buon cuore*, was an adaptation of Goldoni, and from him Da Ponte learnt the secret of comic pacing, of lexical manipulation (in particular, witty '-ino' and '-etto' diminutives) and of taut poetic structures. The debt is particularly apparent in *Don Giovanni*, notwithstanding its more immediate borrowings from Giovanni Bertati's recent 'Don Giovanni' libretto (set by Gazzaniga; Da Ponte later reworked this version in

London). Da Ponte's 'dramma giocoso' (the term itself derives from Goldoni) owes much to Goldoni's play *Don Giovanni Tenorio*, as well as to Molière, and Leporello's opening solo has clear echoes of *Il servitore di due padroni*. Da Ponte claimed that the mixture of comedy and seriousness in the opera was his idea, not Mozart's, and it relates directly to Goldoni's notion of a new kind of drama for the 18th century.

As for Gozzi (whom he knew in Venice in the late 1770s), Da Ponte entered his fantasy world in *L'arbore di Diana*, while Gozzi's *Le droghe d'amore* (1777) may have influenced *Così fan tutte*. In *Così* (which the librettist always called *La scuola degli amanti*), Da Ponte's sense of literary play reaches its peak. It is perhaps best viewed as an opera about opera – failure to do so accounts for the oft-perceived 'problems' of the work – in the vein of Casti's *Prima la musica e poi le parole* (there are echoes in the text). Da Ponte ranked the libretto below *Figaro* and *Don Giovanni*, probably because of the opera's poor critical reception, but, as Dent realized, it contains his best work. Attempts to find a single source for the story have largely failed (but there are roots in Ovid, Boccaccio and particularly Ariosto). However, Da Ponte clearly placed the drama in the time-honoured tradition of the pastoral (in Act 1 Don Alfonso quotes directly from Sannazaro: 'Nel mare solca e nell'arena semina'). He also revelled in the allegorical play of essentially abstract characters and situations. Whether or not Mozart fully grasped this aspect of the libretto is another matter; moreover, opera was soon to move in very different directions. But *Così* marks an eloquent testament both to Da Ponte's literary heritage and to opera in the Age of Enlightenment.

LIBRETTOS

La scuola degli gelosi [rev. of C. Mazzolà lib. for Salieri], Vienna, 22 April 1783

Ifigenia in Tauride [trans. of N.-F. Guillard and M. F. L. G. L. Roullet lib. for Gluck: Iphigénie en Tauride], Vienna, 14 Dec 1783

Il ricco d'un giorno (dg, after G. Bertati), Salieri, Vienna, 6 Dec 1784

Il burbero di buon cuore (dg, after C. Goldoni: *Le bourru bienfaisant*), Martín y Soler, Vienna, 4 Jan 1786

Il finto cieco (commedia per musica, after M.-A. Legrand: *L'aveugle clairvoyant*), Gazzaniga, Vienna, 20 Feb 1786

Le nozze di Figaro (commedia per musica, after P.-A. Beaumarchais: *La folle journée, ou Le mariage de Figaro*), Mozart, Vienna, 1 May 1786, rev. with 2 new arias, Vienna, 29 Aug 1789

Il demogorgone, ovvero Il filosofo confuso (dg, ? after G. Brunati), Righini, Vienna, 12 July 1786

Una cosa rara, o sia Bellezza ed onestà (dg, after L. Vélez de Guevara: *La luna de la Sierra*), Martín y Soler, Vienna, 17 Nov 1786

Gli equivoci (dramma buffo, after W. Shakespeare: *The Comedy of Errors*), Storace, Vienna, 27 Dec 1786

Il Bertoldo (dg, after Brunati), Piticchio, Vienna, 22 June 1787

L'arbore di Diana (dg), Martín y Soler, Vienna, 1 Oct 1787

Il dissoluto punito, o sia Il Don Giovanni (dg, after Bertati lib. for Gazzaniga: Don Giovanni Tenorio, o sia Il convitato di pietra), Mozart, Prague, 29 Oct 1787, rev. Vienna, 7 May 1788 (Carnicer, Barcelona, 20 June 1822, as Don Giovanni Tenorio)

Axur, re d'Ormus (dramma tragi-comico, after Beaumarchais lib. for Salieri: Tarare), Salieri, Vienna, 8 Jan 1788

Il talismano [rev. of Goldoni lib. for Salieri], Vienna, 10 Sept 1788

Il pastor fido (dramma tragicomico, after B. Guarini), Salieri, Vienna, 11 Feb 1789

L'ape musicale (commedia per musica, after Goldoni), Vienna, 27 Feb 1789 [pasticcio incl. music by Anfossi, Cimarosa, Gassmann, Gazzaniga, Giordani, Martín y Soler, Mombelli, Mozart, Paisiello, Piccinni, Salieri, Tarchi]; Vienna, 23 March 1791, as L'ape musicale rinnovata; Trieste, 1792, as L'ape musicale, ossia Il poeta impresario; New York, 1830

La cifra (dg, after G. Petrosellini lib. for Salieri: La dama pastorella), Salieri, Vienna, 11 Dec 1789

Così fan tutte, o sia La scuola degli amanti (dg), Mozart, Vienna, 26 Jan 1790

Nina, o sia La pazza per amore [rev. of G. Carpani lib. for Paisiello], Vienna, 13 April 1790, addl items by Weigl

La quacquera [quakera] spiritosa [rev. of G. Palomba lib. for P. A. Guglielmi], Vienna, 13 Aug 1790

La caffettiera bizzarra (dg, after Goldoni), Weigl, Vienna, 15 Sept 1790

Il matrimonio segreto [rev. of Bertati lib. for Cimarosa], London, 11 Jan 1794

I contadini bizzarri [rev. of T. Grandi lib. for Sarti: Le gelosie villane], London, 1 Feb 1794, addl items by Paisiello

Il capriccio drammatico [rev. of G. M. Diodati lib. for Cimarosa: L'impresario in angustie], London, 1 March 1794

Il Don Giovanni [rev. of Bertati lib. for Gazzaniga], London, 1 March 1794, addl items by Sarti, Federici and Guglielmi

La bella pescatrice [rev. of F. S. Zini lib. for P. A. Guglielmi], London, 18 March 1794

La prova dell'opera, London, 1 April 1794 [pasticcio with music by ?Cimarosa]

La Semiramide [rev. of Moretti lib. for F. Bianchi: La vendetta di Nino], London, 26 April 1794

La Frascatana [rev. of F. Livigni lib. for Paisiello], London, 5 June 1794

La scuola de' maritati [*La capricciosa corretta*, *I sposi in contrasto*, *La moglie corretta*] (dg), Martín y Soler, London, 27 Jan 1795

Alceste, o sia Il trionfo dell'amore conjugale [rev. of R. de' Calzabigi lib. for Gluck], London, 30 April 1795

L'isola del piacere, or The Island of Pleasure (ob), Martín y Soler, London, 26 May 1795

Le nozze dei contadini spagnuoli (int), Martín y Soler, London, 28 May 1795

La bella Arsene [trans. of C.-S. Favart lib. for Monsigny], addl items by Mazzinghi, London, 12 Dec 1795

Antigona (os), Bianchi, London, 24 May 1796

Il tesoro (ob), Mazzinghi, London, 14 June 1796

Zemira e Azor [trans. of J.-F. Marmontel lib. for Grétry], London, 23 July 1796

Il consiglio imprudente (ob, after Goldoni: *Un curioso accidente*), Bianchi, 20 Dec 1796

Evelina, or The Triumph of the English over the Romans [trans. of Guillard lib. for Sacchini: Arvire et Eveline], London, 10 Jan 1797

Merope (os, after Voltaire), Bianchi, London, 10 June 1797

Cinna (os, ? after A. Anelli), Bianchi, London, 20 Feb 1798

Angelina, ossia Il matrimonio per susurro [rev. of C. P. Defranceschi lib. for Salieri: Angiolina], London, 29 Dec 1801

Armida (os), Bianchi, London, 1 June 1802

La grotta di Calipso (dramma), Winter, London, 31 May 1803

Castor e Polluce, o Il trionfo dell'amor fraterno, or The Triumph of Fraternal Love (os), Winter, London, 22 March 1804

Il ratto di Proserpina, or The Rape of Proserpine (os), Winter, London, 3 May 1804

Lost: *Eco e Narciso*, *Il disinganno de' morti*

WRITINGS

Storia compendiosa della vita di Lorenzo da Ponte scritta da lui medesimo a cui si aggiunge la prima letteraria conversazione tenuta in sua casa, il giorno 10 di marzo dell'anno 1807, in New York, consistenti in alcuni composizioni italiane ... tradotto in inglese dai suoi allievi (New York, 1807)

An Extract from the Life of Lorenzo da Ponte with the History of Several Dramas Written by him, and among Others, il Figaro, il Don Giovanni and La scuola degli amanti, Set to Music by Mozart (New York, 1819)

Memorie di Lorenzo da Ponte da Ceneda scritte da esso (New York, 1823–7, enlarged 2/1829–30); ed. C. Pagnini (Milan, 1971); Eng. trans., ed. L. A. Sheppard (London, 1929), ed. A. Livingston and E. Abbott (Philadelphia, 1929)

*

DBI (G. Scarabello)

G. Casanova: *Mémoires* (Leipzig, 1826–38); ed. R. Vèze (Paris, 1924–35)

M. Kelly: *Reminiscences of Michael Kelly, of the King's Theatre, and Theatre Royal, Drury Lane* (London, 1826, 2/1826/R1968 with introduction by A. H. King); ed. R. Fiske (London, 1975)

J. Bernardi: *Cenni storici intorno la chiesa e diocesi di Ceneda* (Ceneda, 1842)

E. Masi: *L'Abbate L. da Ponte* (Bologna, 1881)

A. Marchesan: *Della vita e delle opere di Lorenzo da Ponte* (Treviso, 1900)

E. J. Dent: *Mozart's Operas: a Critical Study* (London, 1913, 2/1947, 3/1955)
H. Boas: 'Lorenzo da Ponte als Wiener Theaterdichter', *SIMG*, xv (1913–14), 325–38
E. Istel: *Das Libretto: Wesen, Aufbau und Wirkung des Opernbuches, nebst einer dramatischen Analyse des Librettos von Figaros Hochzeit* (Berlin and Leipzig, 1914)
P. Molmenti, ed.: *Carteggi casanoviani* (Milan, 1917–19)
H. Abert: *W. A. Mozart* (Leipzig, 1919–21, 3/1955–6)
R. Payer von Thurn: *Joseph II als Theaterdirektor: ungedruckte Briefe und Aktenstücke aus den Kinderjahren des Burgtheaters* (Vienna, 1920)
J. L. Russo: *Lorenzo da Ponte: Poet and Adventurer* (New York, 1922)
G. Gugitz: *Denkwürdigkeiten des Venezianers Lorenzo da Ponte* (Dresden, 1924) [incl. detailed list of writings]
A. Livingston: *Da Ponte in America* (Philadelphia, 1930)
F. Nicolino: 'La vera ragione della fuga di Lorenzo da Ponte da Venezia', *Archivio storico italiano*, 7th ser., xiv (1930), 129–38
C. Pagnini: *Lorenzo da Ponte e il contribuito di Trieste alla propaganda italiana in America* (Parenzo, 1934)
G. Andrees: *Mozart und Da Ponte* (Leipzig, 1936)
B. Ziliotto: 'Lorenzo da Ponte e Giuseppe de Coletti', *Archeografo triestino*, iv/1–2 (1938–9)
A. Loewenberg: 'Lorenzo da Ponte in London: a Bibliographical Account of his Literary Activity, 1793–1804', *MR*, iv (1943), 171–89
H. R. Marraro: 'Documents on Da Ponte's Italian Library', *Publications of the Modern Language Association of America*, lviii (1943), 1057–72
D. Rossetti: *Scritti inediti pubblicati dal Municipio di Trieste*, ii: *Epistolario*, ed. C. Pagnini (Udine, 1944)
P. S. Orsi: 'Il bando da Venezia di Lorenzo da Ponte', *Ateneo veneto*, cxxxvi/2 (1952), 129–31
F. Gaeta: 'Un ignorato episodio della vita dell'abate Lorenzo da Ponte', *Giornale storico della letteratura italiana*, cxxxi (1954), 195–208
P. Nettl: 'Frühe Mozartpflege in Amerika', *MJb 1954*, 78–88
A. Fitzlyon: *The Libertine Librettist: a Biography of Mozart's Librettist Lorenzo da Ponte* (London, 1955/R1982 as *Lorenzo da Ponte: a Biography of Mozart's Librettist*)
W. C. Smith: *The Italian Opera and Contemporary Ballet in London 1789–1820: a Record of Performances and Players with Reports from the Journals of the Time* (London, 1955)
P. Lecaldano: *Lorenzo da Ponte: tre libretti per Mozart* (Milan, 1956)
W. Freitag: 'Lorenzo da Ponte in Amerika', *Musica*, xiv (1960), 560–65
C. Pagnini: *Bibliografia Dapontiana* (Trieste, 1960)
K. M. Pisarowitz: 'Da Ponte in Augsburg', *Acta mozartiana*, ix (1962), 68–70
A. Livermore: 'Così fan tutte: a Well-Kept Secret', *ML*, xlvi (1965), 316–21
O. Michtner: 'Der Fall Abbe da Ponte', *Mitteilungen des Österreichischen Staatsarchivs*, xix (Vienna, 1966), 170–209
A. Rosenberg: *Don Giovanni: Don Juans Gestalt und Mozarts Oper* (Munich, 1968)
O. Michtner: *Das alte Burgtheater als Opernbühne: von der Einführung des deutschen Singspiels (1778) bis zum Tod Kaiser Leopolds II. (1792)* (Vienna, 1970)
P. J. Smith: *The Tenth Muse: a Historical Study of the Opera Libretto* (London, 1971)
S. Kunze: *Don Giovanni vor Mozart: die Tradition der Don-Giovanni-Opern im italienischen Buffa-Theater des 18. Jahrhunderts* (Munich, 1972)
D. Goldin: 'Mozart, Da Ponte e il linguaggio dell'opera buffa', *Venezia e il melodramma nel settecento: Venice 1975*, ii, 213–77
S. Kunze: 'Elementi veneziani nella librettistica di Lorenzo da Ponte', ibid, 279–92
L. Zorzi: '"Teatralità" di Lorenzo da Ponte tra *Memorie* e libretti d'opera', ibid, 313–21
G. Schmidgall: *Literature as Opera* (New York, 1977)
F. Petty: *Italian Opera in London, 1760–1800* (Ann Arbor, 1980)
B. Brophy: 'Da Ponte and Mozart', *MT*, cxxii (1981), 454–6
D. Goldin: 'Da Ponte librettista fra Goldoni e Casti', *Giornale storico della letteratura italiana*, clviii (1981), 396–408
A. Steptoe: 'The Sources of *Così fan tutte*: a Reappraisal', *ML*, lxii (1981), 281–94
D. Goldin: 'Aspetti della librettistica italiana fra 1770 e 1830', *AnMc*, no.21 (1982), 128–91
——: *La vera Fenice: libretti e librettisti tra sette e ottocento* (Turin, 1985)
S. Hodges: *Lorenzo da Ponte: the Life and Times of Mozart's Librettist* (London, 1985) [incl. detailed list of writings]
M. Hager: 'Die Opernprobe als Theateraufführung: eine Studie zum Libretto im Wien des 18. Jahrhunderts', *Oper als Text: romanistische Beiträge zur Libretto-Forschung*, ed. A. Gier (Heidelberg, 1986), 101–24
T. Carter: *W. A. Mozart: 'Le nozze di Figaro'* (Cambridge, 1987)
A. Steptoe: *The Mozart-Da Ponte Operas: the Cultural and Musical Background to 'Le nozze di Figaro', 'Don Giovanni', and 'Così fan tutte'* (Oxford, 1988)
D. Heartz: 'The Poet as Stage Designer: Metastasio, Goldoni, and Da Ponte', *Mozart's Operas*, ed. T. Bauman (Berkeley, 1990), 89–105
D. Link: *The Da Ponte Operas of Vicente Martín y Soler* (diss., U. of Toronto, 1991)

TIM CARTER

Dara, Enzo (*b* Mantua, 13 Oct 1938). Italian bass. After working as a journalist, he studied singing at Mantua with Bruno Sutti and made his début as Colline in 1960 at Fano. His main career began after military service when he sang Dulcamara at Reggio Emilia in 1967. After appearing as Mustafà (*L'italiana in Algeri*) at the 1969 Spoleto Festival he made his début at La Scala the next year as Bartolo, the part he sang for his Metropolitan Opera début in 1982 and with the Royal Opera at Covent Garden in 1985; he had previously appeared in that house in 1976 with the La Scala company as Dandini. Other engagements have included the Bol'shoy Opera, Moscow, the Vienna and Munich Staatsopern and Buenos Aires, mostly in 18th- and early 19th-century *buffo* roles. In 1990 he sang Don Pasquale in Venice and Selim in Madrid. His vivid sense of comedy is informed by musicality and agile technique.

NOËL GOODWIN

D'Arcais, Francesco, Marquis of Valverde (*b* Cagliari, 15 Dec 1830; *d* Castel Gandolfo, 14 Aug 1890). Italian critic and composer. In 1853 he became music critic for the *Rivista contemporanea* of Turin and of *L'opinione* in Rome, with which he was associated for 36 years; he also wrote for the *Gazzetta musicale di Milano* and other periodicals. Originally hostile to Wagner and Boito, he came to admire both. He joined a 'league of orthography' which was directed against the claques then powerful in the Rome theatres and which upheld an ideal of the theatre as 'art'. He composed vocal and dramatic music, including three comic operas: *I due precettori* (Turin, Rossini, 1858), *Sganarello* (Milan, Re, 1861) and *La guerra d'amore* (Florence, Niccolini, 7 December 1870).

SERGIO MARTINOTTI

Darcis [d'Arcis, d'Arcy], **François-Joseph** (*b* Vienna, 1759–60; *d* ?Moscow, *c*1783). French composer. A child prodigy, he was taken to Paris about 1769 and entrusted to the tutelage of Grétry. His first stage work, *Le bal masqué*, a one-act *opéra comique*, was given in 1772 before the royal family at Versailles; Grimm (or Diderot), who heard it at the Comédie-Italienne, said that 'the music ... by a 12-year-old scamp named Darcis ... is pitiable from start to finish ... Not the shadow of talent ... He could spend 20 years with Grétry and would come out as inept as he went in'. The public liked it well enough to support a run of six performances and a revival. A second one-act *opéra comique, La fausse peur*, which opened in 1774, had more success: the *Mercure de France* (October 1774) called the *airs* 'agreeable and effective; the piece has action and humour that give it appeal in the provinces'.

By the time it was revived, in 1778, Darcis' parents had sent him to Russia, his amorous exploits having given much cause for concern. In 1778 *L'intendant*, on a Russian libretto by N. Nikolev, was given at the Grand Theatre in Moscow: it was a brilliant success, and there are records of performances for 21 years, rare for a Russian comic opera of the period. But not even Russian winters could cool Darcis' passions: apparently in the wake of some scandal he was killed either in a duel with a Russian officer or by his own hand.

The style of Darcis' *ariettes* is hardly different from that of his sonatas, and both are very like those of the young Mozart. The writing is mostly in two parts, the accompaniments to formula, the phrases clear and symmetrical with little contrast. As well as stage works, Darcis composed keyboard works and a *Quintetto concertant*.

all printed works published in Paris

Le bal masqué (oc, 1, B.-J. Marsollier des Vivetières), Versailles, 31 March 1772, *F-Pc*, Ariettes détachées du Bal masqué (n.d.)

La fausse peur (comédie with ariettes, 1, Marsollier des Vivetières), Paris, Comédie-Italienne, 18 July 1774 (engraved after Oct 1774), excerpts pubd separately

L'intendant (bagatelle dramatique avec chants, 1, N. Nikolev), Moscow, Grand, July 1778, lost

*

DBF (M. Briquet)

A.-E.-M. Grétry: *Mémoires, ou Essais sur la musique* (Paris, 2/?1796–7), 382ff

M. Tourneux, ed.: *Correspondance littéraire, philosophique et critique par Grimm, Diderot, Raynal, Meister etc.* (Paris, 1877–82), ix, 481–2

R.-A. Mooser: *Annales de la musique et des musiciens en Russie au XVIIIme siècle* (Geneva, 1948–51) DAVID FULLER

Darclée, Hariclea (*b* Braila, 10 June 1860; *d* Bucharest, 10 or 12 Jan 1939). Romanian soprano. She studied in Paris with J.-B. Faure, making her début in 1888 at the Opéra in *Faust*. In 1890 she sang at La Scala in *Le Cid* and was immediately engaged by all the leading Italian theatres. Between 1893 and 1910 she appeared in Moscow, St Petersburg, Lisbon, Barcelona, Madrid and Buenos Aires, returning several times to La Scala. Her repertory ranged from the coloratura (Gilda, Ophelia) to the dramatic roles (Valentine, Aida), including many others in the Franco-Italian lyric repertory: Violetta, Desdemona, Manon, Manon Lescaut, Mimì, Santuzza, Wally, Iris and Tosca (she created the last three).

Among her exceptional qualities were power, beauty of tone, evenness, agility and excellent technique. She was extremely handsome, with a stage presence as elegant as her vocal line. A certain coldness of temperament, however, diminished her conviction in the *verismo* repertory. She sang until 1918, appearing as late as 1916 as Santuzza.

*

GV (R. Celletti; R. Vegeto)

G. Monaldi: *Cantanti celebri* (Rome, 1929), 245

W. Ashbrook: *The Operas of Puccini* (New York, 1968)

RODOLFO CELLETTI

***Dardanus* (i)**. *Tragédie en musique* in a prologue and five acts by JEAN-PHILIPPE RAMEAU to a libretto by CHARLES-ANTOINE LE CLERC DE LA BRUÈRE; Paris, Opéra, 19 November 1739.

The appearance of *Dardanus*, Rameau's fifth opera, marked the climax of the Lulliste–Ramiste dispute, involving cabal and counter-cabal. The opera was given

Vénus [Venus]	soprano
L'Amour [Cupid]	soprano
Iphise *daughter of Teucer*	soprano
Teucer *king of Phrygia*	bass
Anténor [Antenor] *a neighbouring prince*	bass
A Phrygian Woman	soprano
Isménor [Ismenor] *magician and priest of Jupiter*	bass
Dardanus *son of Jupiter and Electra*	haute-contre
A Phrygian	bass
First Dream	soprano
Second Dream	haute-contre
Third Dream	bass
A Pleasure	soprano

Retinue of Venus and Cupid, Sports and Pleasures, retinue of Jealousy, people, warriors, magicians, Phrygians, Dreams

Setting Ancient Phrygia

with a strong cast including Jélyotte (Dardanus) and Pélissier (Iphise), Le Page (Teucer and Ismenor) and the dancers Dupré and Mlles Sallé and Barberine. Yet although it consisted of some 26 performances, this first run was judged a limited success. The work was criticized for its absurd plot and its abuse of the supernatural, an abuse frankly admitted in the libretto. Rameau and La Bruère, with help from Pierre-Joseph Pellegrin, subsequently revised it to the extent of giving the last three acts an entirely new plot. This version, eventually staged in 1744, at first excited little comment, even though the title-page of the new edition describes it, without too much exaggeration, as a 'nouvelle tragédie'. Revived in 1760 with further though less extensive changes, *Dardanus* was acclaimed as one of Rameau's finest achievements and remained in the Opéra's repertory until August 1771. The libretto, adapted by Nicolas-François Guillard, was reset by Sacchini (1784).

In Greek legend, Jupiter's son Dardanus founded the royal house of Troy. In this he was assisted by the Phrygian king Teucer, whose daughter he then married. La Bruère's libretto invents a pre-history to these events, in which Dardanus is at war with Teucer.

PROLOGUE *Cupid's palace on Cythera* Venus invites the Pleasures to reign in Cupid's palace. To her chagrin, they cause the god and his retinue to fall asleep. She summons Jealousy to reawaken them, whereupon mortals of all ages pay homage to Cupid.

ACT 1 *A place filled with the mausolea of Phrygian warriors killed fighting against Dardanus* Iphise, desolate, tries to banish thoughts of love for her father's enemy, Dardanus; her tortured emotions are revealed in a rich-textured monologue 'Cesse, cruel Amour', remarkable for its dissonant harmony and anguished appoggiaturas. Teucer arrives with news of a military alliance. He horrifies his daughter by revealing that she is to be betrothed to Antenor, the Phrygians' new ally. On the tombs of illustrious warriors, Teucer and Antenor swear allegiance ('Mânes plaintifs', a stern but compelling duet with orchestral accompaniment, its changes of pace reflecting the singers' growing excitement). With the Phrygian warriors, they invoke the gods' aid ('Mars, Bellone, guidez nos coups'), the urgency of their prayer underlined by grimly repeated chords.

ACT 2 *A solitary place with a temple in the distance* Ismenor, entering to an energetic prelude which continues intermittently during the ensuing recitative, reveals the extent of his magic powers. When Dardanus appears, the magician warns that he is on enemy territory; nevertheless, as a priest of Dardanus's father Jupiter, Ismenor agrees to help when Dardanus reveals his love for Iphise. To demonstrate what his power could accomplish, the magician causes an eclipse of the sun; his invocation ('Suspends ta brillante carrière') gains immense strength from its rich web of double-stopped strings and bold vocal leaps. In a grim, incantatory chorus, 'Obéis aux lois des enfers', Ismenor's magicians warn Dardanus of the perils ahead, whereupon Ismenor gives Dardanus a magic ring that disguises him as the magician himself. In turn Antenor and Iphise come to consult this pseudo-Ismenor. Antenor asks him for assistance in the battle against Dardanus, while Iphise beseeches his help in exorcising her love for this enemy of her father. In so doing, she unwittingly reveals the state of her emotions. Overjoyed, and to Iphise's consternation and embarrassment, Dardanus appears in his own form and declares his love.

ACT 3 *A balcony in Teucer's palace* Iphise reveals that Dardanus has been captured. In 'O jour affreux!', a monologue of tragic intensity, fixed form is abandoned in favour of freely developing declamation underpinned by fragments of the long opening *symphonie*. The Phrygians' celebrations (which include a *parodie*, 'Paix favorable', of Rameau's keyboard piece *Le niais de Sologne*) are interrupted with news that Neptune has sent a sea monster to avenge this impious imprisonment of a son of Jupiter. Antenor resolves to fight the monster.

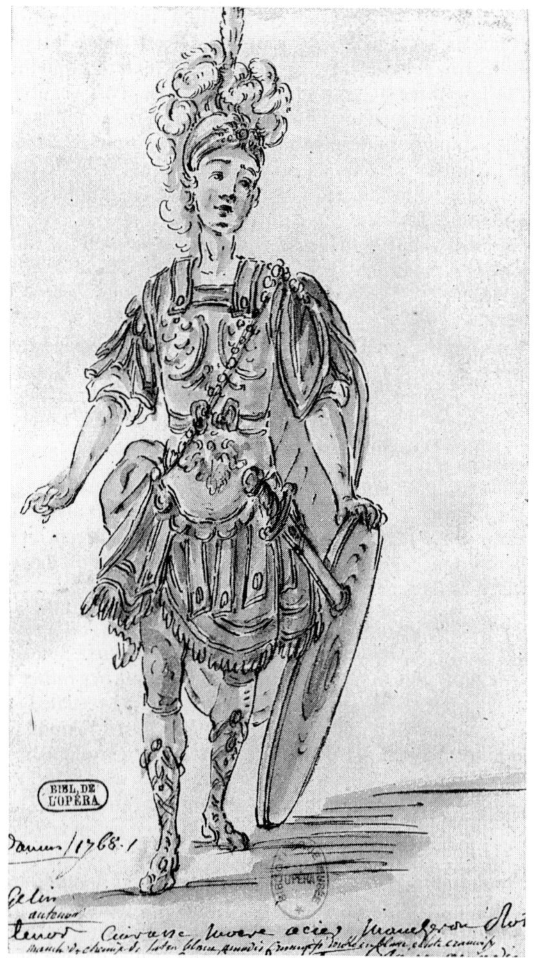

1. Design by Louis-René Boquet for the costume of Antenor (sung by Nicolas Gélin) in the 1768 revival of Rameau's 'Dardanus' at the Paris Opéra

ACT 4 *A ravaged sea shore* By now, Dardanus has escaped. As he sleeps he is visited by Venus and her attendant Dreams who perform a *divertissement*; this includes the famous 'Trio des songes', whose slurred pairs of crotchets look back to the *sommeils* of Lully's day. The Dreams exhort Dardanus to confront the sea monster. This he does during a graphically portrayed tempest, killing the monster and in the process rescuing Antenor. Dardanus (who, in the darkness, remains incognito) takes advantage of his rival's gratitude to extract a promise that Iphise may if she wish refuse Antenor's hand. As a pledge Antenor gives Dardanus his sword.

ACT 5 *Teucer's palace* Teucer and his court welcome Antenor, believing him to have slain the monster. He, however, is embarrassed by their reception, especially when he learns of Neptune's decree – that he who slays the monster will marry Iphise. Dardanus appears and reveals his identity. Producing Antenor's sword as a token, he claims Iphise's hand. Venus descends and effects a reconciliation between the enemy factions. Cupid erects a temple in which to celebrate the marriage of Dardanus and Iphise.

* * *

On a purely musical level the original version of *Dardanus* is, without doubt, one of Rameau's most inspired creations, encompassing the widest emotional range of all his works. The two superb ceremonies in Acts 1 and 2 – the first where Teucer and Antenor pledge allegiance, the second where Ismenor demonstrates his occult power – contain music of immense strength and amazing harmonic richness. Moreover, the Dream sequence, Iphise's two tortured monologues, her consultation with the pseudo-Ismenor and Dardanus's encounter with the sea monster, are all among Rameau's very finest scenes, while the ballet music is of a high order throughout. Sadly, however, the momentum generated by such music is continually checked by the plot's ill-motivated twists and turns and by increasingly puerile supernatural interventions.

In revising the libretto for the 1744 revival La Bruère simplified the plot and eliminated supernatural excesses. In the process he provided the drama with greater human interest, and the action is now firmly focussed on the conflicting emotions of the principal characters. In Act 3 the jealous Antenor devises a plan to murder the captive Dardanus without appearing to be the perpetrator. In the following act he visits Dardanus in prison and foretells his rescue but warns that his liberator will instead become the victim; as a consequence, when Iphise gives Dardanus the chance to escape, he refuses. It is Antenor, remorseful and now mortally wounded, who eventually makes possible Dardanus's escape. In the ensuing battle (represented as an entr'acte between Acts 4 and 5) Dardanus defeats Teucer, but the king defiantly refuses to give him Iphise's hand. Only when the despairing hero asks to be struck down with

2. 'Dardanus' (Rameau): model of the set for the Act 5 finale (a palace surrounded by clouds) for the revival at the Paris Opéra (Palais-Royal), 15 April 1760

his own sword does Teucer relent. As in the original, Venus descends to celebrate the union.

Musically, it is true, the revision entails the removal of many beautiful or powerful passages, among them the dream sequence, the monster scenes and Iphise's second monologue (her first is drastically curtailed, too). But the prologue and Acts 1 and 2 remain largely intact, while the large quantity of new music in later acts generally maintains a level scarcely below that of the original. Dardanus's F minor prison monologue 'Lieux funestes', with its incomparable bassoon obbligato, develops an almost Beethovenian intensity. Moreover it is wonderfully contrasted with the ethereal music for Ismenor that immediately follows. There have been few modern revivals of *Dardanus*. Charles Bordes presented a concert performance of the 1739 version at the Schola Cantorum, Paris, on 26 April 1907, and a staged production at Dijon in December of the same year. In 1983 the Paris Opéra staged a conflation of the 1739 and 1744 versions, which involved some rewriting of the plot. For all its dramatic superiority, however, the 1744 version has never been revived in modern times, largely because there exists no adequate modern edition.

GRAHAM SADLER

***Dardanus* (ii).** *Tragédie* in four acts by ANTONIO SACCHINI to a libretto by NICOLAS-FRANÇOIS GUILLARD after CHARLES-ANTOINE LE CLERC DE LA BRUÈRE; Versailles, 18 September 1784.

Dardanus, Sacchini's third French opera, was completed in 1784 and performed at Versailles, then in Paris (30 November). Sacchini suffered from the hostility aroused by the queen's predilection for foreigners, and only the revised three-act version (1785, Fontainebleau; 1786, Paris) was adequately performed and properly appreciated.

Guillard's adaptation blends both versions but is based principally on the revised version of Rameau's opera (1744). The title-page of the printed score reads only 'paroles de M. Guillard', but most of the text is by La Bruère. Guillard omitted the Prologue, altered the order of events in Act 3, and skilfully compressed Acts 4 and 5 into one act while losing nothing essential to the action. The intervention of Venus is replaced by the reappearance of Isménor [Ismenor] (bass), prepared by an impressive invocation, with trombones, in Act 2. Iphise (soprano) and Anténor [Antenor] (bass) have the most developed roles, the latter enhanced musically at the expense of Teucer (bass), and dramatically by attributing some of his villainy to Arcas (tenor).

Sacchini's penchant for arioso (already apparent in *Chimène*) suited this type of libretto; although his recitative is seldom as expressive, some short numbers match Rameau's in intensity (notably Iphise's first scene). There are several full-scale arias, by now conventional at the Opéra, in which his lyricism finds fuller expression. Musically, this is perhaps the finest resetting of an old libretto after Gluck's *Armide*.

JULIAN RUSHTON

Dargomïzhsky, Alexander Sergeyevich (*b* Troitskoye, Tula district, 2/14 Feb 1813; *d* St Petersburg, 5/17 Jan 1869). Russian composer. The outstanding figure in Russian opera between Glinka's lapse into creative impotence and the advent of Tchaikovsky and the Five, Dargomïzhsky had an influence, and has a historical importance, out of all proportion to the frequency with which his music was ever performed.

He was born to wealth and leisure, his father being a highly placed civil servant and his mother the former Princess Kozlovskaya. He spent his first four years on the family estate near Smolensk before moving to St Petersburg at the end of 1817. In the capital he received his education from private tutors, including instruction in piano, violin and singing. Among his piano teachers was Franz Schoberlechner, a Viennese composer whose Russian-born wife was a leading singer in a short-lived Italian operatic venture in St Petersburg (1828–31) under the direction of Luigi Zamboni, the creator of Rossini's Figaro. Dargomïzhsky must have heard his teacher's *Il desertore per l'amore* at its 1830 première. More to the point, he heard his first authentic performances of Mozart's *opere buffe* alongside works of Vincenzo Fioravanti, Generali, Mercadante, Morlacchi and Pacini, but mainly Rossini, of whose operas no fewer than 17 were given in the Russian capital during those three seasons.

By then the young Dargomïzhsky had already begun to compose. His earliest piano pieces date from the winter of 1824–5, his earliest romances from 1827. In the same year he was enrolled in the first of several civil-service sinecures that guaranteed him a comfortable existence for life. In 1835 he met Glinka, who had just returned to St Petersburg from Italy, and from his first round of studies with Siegfried Dehn in Berlin. Glinka not only fired his younger friend's ambitions to compose; he also showed him the notebooks reflecting his harmony and counterpoint studies. This vicarious course with Dehn via Glinka constituted Dargomïzhsky's professional education, such as it was, in composition.

Given his background, it is natural that his first inclination was to write an Italian opera. He chose *Lucrezia Borgia* as his subject, but was dissuaded from it by Vasily Zhukovsky, a great lyric poet and also an official in Tsar Nikolay I's secret police, who convinced Dargomïzhsky that such a subject could never clear the censorship. It was at this point (1837 or 1838) that Dargomïzhsky settled on *Esmeralda*, Victor Hugo's verse libretto after his own *Notre-Dame de Paris*, written two years earlier for Louise Bertin, whose setting had been produced at the Paris Opéra in 1836. Dargomïzhsky finished his setting, to an abridgment of the original French text, by the end of 1841. The next year he made a Russian singing translation, with the help of two assistants, to facilitate production at home. (The other major work of the period was a cantata, *Torzhestvo Vakkha*, 'The Triumph of Bacchus', on some early anacreontic verses of Pushkin; in 1848 he expanded the piece into a 'lyrical opera-ballet'.)

Now began the composer's education in the facts of Russian artistic life. As early as 1827 a ukase had come down from the throne which set up a flagrantly discriminatory schedule of fees for theatrical authors and artists, whereby payments to Russian artists and authors were limited to pittances while the emoluments of foreign authors were subjected to no restrictions. This would not have mattered much to a man of means like Dargomïzhsky, but *Esmeralda* could not have been worse timed. In 1843, G. B. Rubini had been invited by the Imperial Theatres directorate, on the tsar's behalf, to establish an all-star Italian opera company in St Petersburg. By the time the bureaucratic (i.e. censorship) formalities had been cleared with respect to *Esmeralda*'s libretto, the Italians had come to town, and (as we learn from an agonized letter from Alexander Serov to Vladimir Stasov, dated 14/26 September 1844), 'until the craze for the Italians is past, Gedeonov [Intendant of the Imperial Theatres] will not accept any opera from anyone for anything on any terms, on account of which Dargomïzhsky has received a point-blank refusal'. The Italian craze would not pass for decades. By 1846 the Russian opera troupe had been formally 'banished' to Moscow, leaving the St Petersburg operatic stage entirely in the hands of the foreign troupe; until 1850 the Russian troupe would appear in the Russian capital only for short guest seasons in the spring, after the Italians had gone home. Russian composers were in a double bind. Some (e.g. Alexey L'vov and Feofil Tolstoy) had tried to turn the new state of affairs to their advantage by writing Italian operas for the Italian singers. But the aristocratic 'melomanes' who made up the Italian opera audiences railed at having domestic imitations diluting their subscriptions, and the tsar obliged by forbidding performances of operas by Russian composers at the Italian opera. In effect Russian composers were barred from their country's best venue, the Bol'shoy Kamennïy ('Great Stone') theatre in St Petersburg, and from access to the best singers performing in Russia.

So it was that *Esmeralda* saw the light of day only in 1847 and in Moscow (*The Triumph of Bacchus* was not produced until 1867, also in Moscow, by which time it was a decided anachronism). When the Italian baritone Tamburini tried to secure it for his benefit, in 1851, he was refused because of the ban. Under the circumstances, it is not surprising that Dargomïzhsky's personal taste for Italian opera soured. In 1844, the year of his opera's initial rejection, he wrote to his father about Donizetti's *Linda di Chamounix*: 'About this there is nothing much to say. First of all, you'll hear it in St Petersburg; but second, once a medal or a coin has been stamped out and described, is there any need to describe the next medal or coin that issues from the same die and the same machine?' The 'realist' ferment had begun, at first as a ferment of sour grapes.

The letter had been posted in Paris, during Dargomïzhsky's first trip abroad (1844–5). He met Meyerbeer in Berlin, Fétis and Vieuxtemps in Brussels, Halévy and Auber in Paris, Donizetti in Vienna. Partly as a result, one has to think, of his hopeless situation vis-à-vis official institutions at home, he began to react negatively to grand opera despite his new acquaintances and to respond with enthusiasm to the Parisian vaudevilles, admiring their topical 'bite and wit'. This concern for topicality expressed in satire became a regular feature of his songs on his return home. His vocal music began to show the influence of conversational speech contours and tempos. This new departure in realism (à la Daumier, one might say) conditioned his further operatic work. Its French sources were reflected in Dargomïzhsky's penchant even in the late 1850s and 60s for texts by Béranger, translated in the pages of a St Petersburg satirical journal, *Iskra* ('The Spark'), with whose editors he was on intimate terms.

The great project of Dargomïzhsky's middle period, and his most enduring work for the stage, was the opera *Rusalka*, after Pushkin's unfinished verse tragedy of the same name, on which he worked from 1848 to 1855. Anything but realistic in impulse, Pushkin's play was a romantic Singspiel libretto in the tradition of Kauer's *Das Donauweibchen*, long a Russian favourite. Dargomïzhsky's opera could be seen as the culmination of a long line of German and Russian water-nymph operas. Yet the accent with him (as, arguably, with Pushkin) is not on the supernatural aspect of the subject, or on the means of its embodiment in 'fantastic' music, but on the highly charged confrontations of the main characters – a Kievan Prince, a Miller and the latter's daughter (Natasha in the opera), whom the Prince seduces and abandons, and who, having thrown herself into the Dnepr, becomes the queen of the river nymphs (*rusalki*) and lures her tormentor to his doom.

In a letter to Prince Vladimir Odoyevsky, Moscow's leading musical connoisseur, written at the height of his labours on the opera, Dargomïzhsky summed up his attitude towards *Rusalka* and what he took to be his task and achievement as a Russian composer:

The more I study the components of our national music, the more varied the aspects I discern in them. Glinka, who alone up to now has given Russian music a grand scale, in my opinion, has as yet touched only one of its sides – the lyrical side. His dramaturgy is too plaintive, the comic aspect loses its national character … To the extent that I am able I am working, in my *Rusalka*, to develop our dramatic components.

Both the comic and the dramatic 'components' in *Rusalka* intersect at fullest strength on the character of the Miller. His main aria, which opens the opera, is cast in a jolly comic-opera patter style, but one not so obviously modelled on the *opera buffa* as is, for example, Farlaf's rondo in *Ruslan and Lyudmila*, which must have been in Dargomïzhsky's mind when he criticized Glinka's handling of 'the comic aspect'. Otherwise the Miller takes part only in ensembles. The most striking of these is his duet with the Prince in Act 3, which begins with a lengthy accompanied recitative set directly to Pushkin's original verses, in which the bereft and demented father, thinking himself a raven, pathetically recounts his daughter's suicide. It amounts to a veritable mad scene.

The vast historical importance of this passage for Russian opera was catalysed by Alexander Serov, Russia's leading music critic by the time of *Rusalka*'s première in 1856. In a mammoth review which appeared in ten instalments in the St Petersburg weekly, *Teatral'nïy i muzïkal'nïy vestnik* ('The Theatrical and Musical Courier'), Serov raved about Dargomïzhsky's success in realizing the greatest of all music's potentials, that of combining with words to produce a 'dramatic truth' greater than either art could achieve alone. After a 'theoretical' evaluation of the composer's achievement along these lines, he proceeded to a minute *explication de texte* that impressed many readers, among them Dargomïzhsky himself. He sent Serov revealing congratulations for the latter's 'penetration of my innermost and even unconscious thoughts'; for he had not thought the Act 3 duet anywhere nearly so important. (His own favourite part of *Rusalka* was the Act 4 finale, where he had had not only to write the music – uncharacteristically complex and 'symphonic' music, in which he took especial pride – but also to give the drama the ending Pushkin's torso lacked.) He immediately acceded to the critic's view; starved as he was for approbation, he was exceptionally vulnerable to the influence of those who praised him.

For even *Rusalka* earned him at first no more than a *succès d'estime*. At the time of its première, the Russian Opera had returned to St Petersburg from its temporary exile but was still barred from the main theatre. Its rather skimpy performance schedule was worked into the time available between dramatic spectacles at the so-called Alexandrinsky Theatre, the chief house for Russian drama, and between the clowns and the bareback riders at the Circus Theatre, which eventually became its home. *Esmeralda* had its St Petersburg première at the Alexandrinsky in 1851; *Rusalka*, done at the barn-like, smelly Circus in 1856, was wrecked by the hall's size and acoustics. The composer became even more embittered. He affected to renounce opera altogether ('You have to pose, accept subjects from the Tsar [as Glinka had done], seek a brilliant production, write about yourself in the papers … I could never accustom myself to this'). His letters began filling up with the slogans for which he is so well remembered, unwittingly echoing Serov's *Rusalka* review:

I do not deceive myself. My artistic plight in St Petersburg is not an enviable one. The majority of our music lovers and newspaper hacks do not recognize inspiration in me. Their routine view seeks out melodies that flatter the ear, which I do not pursue. I am not about to lower music to the level of a pastime for their sake. I want sound directly to express the word. I want truth.

These maverick views coincided with those of the young 'Davidsbund' that was forming in St Petersburg around Mily Balakirev in the late 1850s, and for his last decade Dargomïzhsky was a kind of father figure or patron saint to the New Russian School, the 'Mighty Kuchka' or the Five. He also began to receive some official recognition as a musical presence in the Russian capital and was able to act as mediator among the warring factions in St Petersburg musical politics. When Anton Rubinstein founded the Russian Musical Society in 1859, under the patronage of the Grand Duchess Elena Pavlovna, Tsar Alexander II's German-born aunt, he named Dargomïzhsky to the otherwise almost exclusively aristocratic board; in 1867 Dargomïzhsky became president of the society's St Petersburg branch and invited Balakirev to conduct its concerts. In 1864–5 he went abroad for another extended tour, this time hearing his music performed in Brussels under the aegis of the Countess Mercy Argenteau. After his return home he experienced an unexpected triumph, when *Rusalka* was revived to great acclaim in the new, luxurious Mariinsky Theatre (built in 1860 after the Circus Theatre burnt down), since which time it has never left the Russian repertory.

In this last, happiest phase of his career, Dargomïzhsky planned three operas, of which two (*Mazepa*, after Pushkin; *Rogdana*, on a fairy-tale subject) were scarcely begun. The one realized notion, and the most radical by far, was that of setting *Kamennïy gost'* ('The Stone Guest'), Pushkin's 'little tragedy' on the Don Juan theme, to music directly as it stood, without any mediating libretto. Actually, this meant setting Pushkin's text in the way many passages in *Rusalka*, including the duet for the Prince and the Miller, had already been set. Thus it can be seen as another response to Serov's compliments of 1856; and if so, then Serov was the unwitting catalyst of that most fabled of all operatic cult-objects – one, moreover, whose intimacy could not have been more alien to Serov's own bloated operatic style and philosophy. By the late 1860s, however, Serov and Dargomïzhsky were no longer close; César Cui, a member of the Balakirev circle who had embarked on a Schumannesque career of partisan music criticism in 1864, had become Dargomïzhsky's press champion. Thanks to him, by the time it was a half-finished pencil sketch *The Stone Guest* was already a legend. Cui knew well whereof he wrote: the opera was given a great many run-throughs, at various stages of its gestation, at 'kuchkist' soirées, the composer taking the part of Don Juan, Musorgsky that of Leporello, Dargomïzhsky's singing-pupil Alexandra Purgold both female roles, and her sister Nadezhda – the future Mme Rimsky-Korsakov – accompanying.

A full-length 'numberless' opera (but for two interpolated songs), it exemplified for the 'kuchkists' the true music of the future (the Wagnerian being of course the false), for it embodied what they saw as the most salubrious of all possible operatic reforms. That is to say, it did away with artificial 'form' while retaining the traditional lyric style. Set throughout in a kind of heightened arioso (or 'melodic recitative', as Cui called it), consisting of romance-like vocal phrases set to a figurative and harmonically regular accompaniment, *The Stone Guest* might best be viewed as a gigantic through-composed art song in which the whole shaping force, save at the pettiest level, is exercised by the text. Its manner was very influential on Musorgsky, who paid heartfelt tribute to the late Dargomïzhsky in a pair of dedications as the 'great teacher of musical truth'. Many of Dargomïzhsky's individual expressive phrases are indeed inspired *trouvailles*, extraordinarily memorable and seemingly definitive. To those who understand and love the words on which it was modelled, *The Stone Guest* can seem a masterpiece; to others it can seem only 'a famous but rather dull opera'. Export is out of the question.

Like all of Dargomïzhsky's operas, *The Stone Guest* had a chequered stage career. The composer did not live to complete it. The end of the first act, and patches elsewhere, were supplied by Cui, and the whole was orchestrated by Rimsky-Korsakov. The posthumous première in 1872 was preceded by a noisy fund-raising campaign led by Vladimir Stasov, which led ultimately to the abrogation of the archaic pay scale of 1827. The work has hung on ever since at the fringes of the Russian repertory, dutifully revived from time to time and soberly praised before taking another dip in Lethe.

See also ESMERALDA; RUSALKA (ii); and STONE GUEST, THE.

Esmeralda, 1838–41 (4, V. Hugo, trans. Dargomïzhsky, N. Aksel [N. F. Lindfors] and A. P. Bashutsky, after *Notre-Dame de Paris*), Moscow, Bol'shoy, 5/17 Dec 1847, vs (Moscow, 1961)

Torzhestvo Vakkha [The Triumph of Bacchus], 1843–8 (lyric op-ballet, 1, after A. Pushkin), Moscow, Bol'shoy, 11/23 Jan 1867, vs (Moscow, 1969)

Rusalka, 1848–55 (4, Dargomïzhsky, after Pushkin), St Petersburg, Circus, 4/16 May 1856, vs (St Petersburg, 1858), full score (Moscow, 1949)

Mazepa, 1859 or 1860 (after Pushkin), inc., duet and mad scene (St Petersburg, 1872)

Rogdana, 1860–67 (magic op, Dargomïzhsky, after A. F. Weltman: *Ratibor Kholmogradskiy* and other sources), inc., excerpts (St Petersburg, 1872, 1875)

Kamennïy gost' [The Stone Guest], 1866–9 (3, Pushkin), inc., completed Cui and Rimsky-Korsakov, St Petersburg, Mariinsky, 16/28 Feb 1872, vs (St Petersburg, 1872), rev. (St Petersburg, 1906), full score (Leningrad, 1929)

*

LIFE AND WORKS

N. Findeyzen, ed.: *A. S. Dargomïzhsky (1813–1869): avtobiografiya, pis'ma, vospominaniya sovremennikov* [Autobiography, Letters, Reminiscences of Contemporaries] (Petrograd, 1921)

C. Cui: 'K kharakteristike Dargomïzhskogo' [Towards an Evaluation of Dargomïzhsky; orig. pubd 1909], *Izbrannïye stat'i* [Selected Articles], ed. Yu. A. Kremlyov (Leningrad, 1952), 527–40

V. Stasov: 'Aleksandr Sergeyevich Dargomïzhsky: materialï dlya ego biografii' [Material for his Biography; orig. pubd 1875], *Izbrannïye sochineniya* [Selected Works], ed. E. D. Stasova and others (Moscow, 1952), i, 269–70

——: 'Dvadtsat' pyat' let russkogo iskusstva: nasha muzïka' [25 Years of Russian Art: our Music; orig. pubd 1882], *Izbrannïye sochineniya*, ed. E. D. Stasova and others (Moscow, 1952), ii, 522–8

M. Pekelis: *Aleksandr Sergeyevich Dargomïzhsky i ego okruzheniye* [Dargomïzhsky and his Milieu] (Moscow, 1966–83)

——: 'Dramaturgicheskiye iskaniya poslednego perioda' [Dramaturgical Endeavours of the Late Period], *SovM* (1980), no.5, pp.100–08

OPERAS

Esmeralda

M. Pekelis: 'Stsenicheskaya istoriya Esmeral'dï' [The Stage History of *Esmeralda*], *Muzïkal'naya zhizn'* (1958), no.15, pp.20–22

——: 'Pervaya opera Dargomïzhskogo' [Dargomïzhsky's First Opera], *A. S. Dargomïzhsky: Esmeralda* (Moscow, 1961) [introduction to vocal score]

Rusalka

C. Cui: '"Rusalka", opera Dargomïzhskogo' [1865], *Muzïkal'no-kriticheskiye stat'i* [Critical Articles on Music] (Petrograd, 1918), i, 41–55

A. Serov: '"Rusalka": opera A. S. Dargomïzhskogo' [1856], *Izbrannïye stat'i* [Selected Articles], ed. G. N. Khubov (Moscow and Leningrad, 1950), i, 254–338

C. Cui: '"Rusalka", opera A. S. Dargomïzhskogo' [1888], *Izbrannïye stat'i* [Selected Articles], ed. Yu. A. Kremlyov (Leningrad, 1952), 390–404

A. Gozenpud: *Russkiy opernïy teatr XIX veka (1836–1856)* [Russian Operatic Theatre of the 19th Century] (Leningrad, 1969), 355–454

——: *Russkiy opernïy teatr XIX veka (1857–1872)* [Russian Operatic Theatre of the 19th Century] (Leningrad, 1971), 108–23

The Stone Guest

G. Abraham: 'The Stone Guest', *Studies in Russian Music* (London, 1935), 121–8

B. Levik: *'Kamennïy gost'' Dargomïzhskogo – 'Motsart i Sal'yeri' N. Rimskogo-Korsakova – 'Skupoy rïtsar'' S. Rakhmaninova* (Moscow and Leningrad, 1949)

C. Cui: '"Kamennïy gost'" Pushkina i Dargomïzhskogo' [1868, 1872], *Izbrannïye stat'i* [Selected Articles], ed. Yu. A. Kremlyov (Leningrad, 1952), 143–7, 206–9 [two different articles]

V. Stasov: 'Avtograf A. S. Dargomïzhskogo, pozhertvovannïy v Publichnuyu biblioteku' [An Autograph of Dargomïzhsky, Donated to the Public Library; orig. pubd 1872], *Izbrannïye sochineniya* [Selected Works], ed. E. D. Stasova and others (Moscow, 1952), i, 217–18

M. Druskin: *Voprosï muzïkal'noy dramaturgii operï* [Questions on Musical Dramaturgy in Opera] (Moscow, 2/1953)

D. Rabinovich: 'K vozobnovleniyu *Kamennogo gostya*' [On the Revival of *The Stone Guest*], *SovM* (1960), no.1, pp.62–5

N. Balagovidova: 'Kamennïy gost'' [*The Stone Guest*], *SovM* (1963), no.7, pp.87–92

A. Gozenpud: '"Kamennïy gost'" Dargomïzhskogo', *Russkiy opernïy teatr XIX veka (1857–1872)* [Russian Operatic Theatre of the 19th Century] (Leningrad, 1971), 276–327

G. Belyanova: 'Osnovnïye zakonomernosti formoobrazovaniya v opere Dargomïzhskogo "Kamennïy gost'"' [Basic Formal Principles in Dargomïzhsky's Opera *The Stone Guest*], *Stranitsï istorii russkoy muzïki* [Pages from the History of Russian Music] (Leningrad, 1973), 18–36

M. Geylig: 'Nekotorïye osobennosti dramaturgii "Kamennogo gostya" Dargomïzhskogo' [Some Dramaturgical Peculiarities in Dargomïzhsky's *The Stone Guest*], *Voprosï opernoy dramaturgii* [Questions of Operatic Theory] (Moscow, 1975), 145–68

J. Baker: 'Dargomïzhsky, Realism, and *The Stone Guest*', *MR*, xxxvii (1976), 193–208

A. Tsuker: 'Kamennïy gost' kak muzïkal'naya kontseptsiya' [*The Stone Guest* as a Musical Conception], *SovM* (1980), no.5, pp.108–13

R. Taruskin: '*The Stone Guest* and its Progeny', *Opera and Drama in Russia* (Ann Arbor, 1981), 249–340

RICHARD TARUSKIN

D'Arienzo, Marco (*b* Naples, 24 April 1811; *d* Naples, 24 April 1877). Italian librettist. He was by profession a tax collector but between 1834 and 1837 he contributed regularly to the periodical *L'omnibus*. He had a facility for writing librettos, producing 30 between 1837 and the end of his life. His particular talent was for comedies and farces, and some two-thirds of his output was for the Teatro Nuovo. Only one libretto – *Pelagio*, set by Mercadante – was for the Teatro S Carlo, but he wrote several librettos for Lauro Rossi, for performance in Turin, and a number for student use at the conservatory in Naples. His comic works often had involved plots, but they were witty and well presented; and his best work (for example, *Piedigrotta* for Luigi Ricci) has a light and truly Neapolitan touch.

cm – *commedia per musica* mel – *melodramma*

Il conte di Saverna (mel), P. Fabrizi, 1837; *Il feudatario di Margate* (mel), G. Moretti, 1839; *Il portatore d'acqua* (mel), Fabrizi, 1840; *Il proscritto* (mel), M. Aspa, 1841; *Guglielmo Colmann* (mel), Aspa, 1842; *Gli zingari* (cm), Vincenzo Fioravanti, 1844;

Leonora (mel), Mercadante, 1844; *Chi cenerà?* (commedia, with A. de Leone), Fioravanti, 1844; *Il figlio dello schiavo* (mel), G. Puzone, 1845; *Le due guide* (mel), De Giosa, 1847; *Policarpio* (cm), Moretti, 1849; *Delfina* (mel), Lillo, 1850; *Le precauzioni [Il carnevale di Venezia]* (cm), E. Petrella, 1851; *La bottega di caffè* (cm), A. Barbati, 1852; *Piedigrotta* (cm), L. Ricci, 1852, as La festa di Piedigrotta; *La figlia del pilota* (mel), R. Gianetti, 1852

Violetta (mel), Mercadante, 1853; *Gismondo Rethel*, G. Benzi, 1853; *L'alchimista* (mel), Lauro Rossi, 1853; *Il festino* (cm), Moretti, 1854; *Il marinaio di Nisida* (azione melodrammatica), A. Candeloro, 1854; *La colomba di Barcellona* (mel, with R. d'Ambra), Gianetti, 1855; *Il traviato* (azione melodrammatica), Claudio Conti, L. Vespoli and others, 1855; *Pelagio* (tragedia lirica), Mercadante, 1857; *La cantante* (mel), Vespoli, 1858; *Ser Pomponio* (cm), F. de Tommasi, 1859; *La figlia del marinaio* (mel), Conti, 1866; *La contessa di Mons* (mel), Rossi, 1874; *Cleopatra* (mel), Rossi, 1876; *Napoli di carnevale* (op giocosa), De Giosa, 1876; *Mario Menzikoff*, F. Ferrari, 1877

*

A. Martorana: *Notizie biografiche e bibliografiche degli scrittori del dialetto napoletano* (Naples, 1847)

V. Viviani: 'Libretti e librettisti', *Cento anni di vita del Teatro S Carlo, 1848–1948*, ed. F. de Filippis (Naples, 1948), 29–39

JOHN BLACK

D'Arienzo, Nicola (*b* Naples, 24 Dec 1842; *d* Naples, 25 April 1915). Italian composer and teacher, nephew of the librettist Marco d'Arienzo. Because of early paternal opposition he first studied music secretly with Vincenzo Fiore Vanti (counterpoint) and Giovanni Moretti (instrumentation); he later made rapid progress, aided by Mercadante. His first opera, *Monzù Gnazio*, a comic opera in Neapolitan dialect, was performed in 1860. During the next 20 years he wrote seven more, all in the comic or semi-serious genres; *Il cuoco* (1873) was the most widely performed and *La figlia del diavolo* (1879) the most controversial, because of its *verismo* tendencies. After 1880 he had only one more opera performed, devoting himself mostly to instrumental and sacred music and to teaching and writing.

Arienzo taught harmony and counterpoint at the music school of the Real Albergo dei Poveri in Naples from 1872 to 1874, then at the S Pietro a Majella Conservatory (1875–1911, temporary director from 1909), where Leoncavallo was among his pupils. In 1878 he published his *Introduzione del sistema tetracordale nella musica moderna*, which attempts to formulate a new harmonic system based on a scale related to the Phrygian mode and which he linked historically to Neapolitan folk music with its flattened Neapolitan 2nd. He claimed to have put this system into use in *La figlia del diavolo*. He later published historical and critical studies, most notably on the old Neapolitan *opera buffa*.

Monzù Gnazio, o La fidanzata del parrucchiere (A. Passaro), Naples, Nuovo, 1860

I due mariti (A. Spadetta), Naples, Bellini, 1 Feb 1866; rev. version, Milan, Re, 1871, vs (Milan, ?1876)

Le rose (Spadetta), Naples, Bellini, Feb 1868

Il cacciatore delle Alpi (Spadetta), Naples, Collegio de' Nobili a Vico Nilo, 23 June 1870

Il cuoco e il segretario (Spadetta), Naples, Rossini, 11 June 1873

I viaggi (Spadetta), Milan, Castelli, 28 June 1875

La figlia del diavolo (A. Landi), Naples, Bellini, 16 Nov 1879

I tre coscritti (L. E. Bardare), Naples, Real Albergo dei Poveri, 10 Feb 1880

La fiera (S. Di Giacomo), Naples, Nuovo, Feb 1887

Unperf.: Rita di Lister, before 1875 (M. d'Arienzo); Lesbo di Rodio (N. d'Arienzo); Capitan Fracassa

*

M. Caputo: 'Nicola D'Arienzo', *Gazzetta musicale di Milano*, xlii (1887), 135

A. Della Corte: 'Un maestro: Nicola D'Arienzo', *RMI*, xxii (1915), 327–41

ANDREA LANZA

D'Arkor, André (*b* Liège, 23 Feb 1901; *d* Brussels, 19 Dec 1971). Belgian tenor. He was trained in Liège and made his début there as Gérald in *Lakmé* in 1924, moving then to Lyons and Ghent. In 1930 he became principal lyric tenor at La Monnaie, Brussels, and in his 17 years there sang more than 40 roles, taking part in several premières, including that of Lattuada's *Le preziose ridicole*. In 1937 he sang in Lehár's *Der Zarewitsch* and in 1940 in *Das Land des Lächelns*. He appeared at the Opéra-Comique, Paris, in 1931 as Des Grieux in *Manon*. He later became director of the Théâtre Royal de Liège; during his 20 years there more than 50 new productions were mounted. He was an accomplished singer with admirably even voice-production and an extensive upper range, features well represented in his recordings.

J. B. STEANE

Darmstadt. City in western Germany. From 1567 to 1918 it was the residence of the landgraves of Hesse, and also, from 1806, that of the grand dukes of Hessen-Darmstadt; it was the regional capital from 1918 to 1945 and has since been a centre of local government. Its musical and theatrical traditions date from the 17th century, when Singballette, tournaments and masquerades were performed. In 1670 a comedy theatre was established in a converted riding school. Among works performed there were *Triumphierendes Siegesspiel der wahren Liebe* (1673) by Wolfgang Carl Briegel, Hofkapellmeister from 1671 to 1709, and Lully's *Acis et Galatée* (1687). Under Count Ernst Ludwig, himself a composer, court music flourished, particularly opera. In 1709 the count appointed as Hofkapellmeister Christoph Graupner, who composed at least three operas for Darmstadt.

Under Grand Duke Ludwig I (1790–1830) the court opera reached its peak. The Hofkapelle, often conducted by Ludwig himself, comprised 89 musicians in addition to a chorus of 54 and included many fine singers. Georg Joseph Vogler was Hofkapellmeister and director of a music school, and Weber and Meyerbeer were among his pupils. In 1819 the Grossherzogliches Hoftheater (1400 seats) was opened with a performance of *Fernand Cortez* by Spontini, who spent a year in the city before going to Berlin in 1820. The theatre burnt down in 1871; it was replaced in 1879 and further renovated in 1904–5. Important Wagner productions, directed by Louis Schindelmeisser in collaboration with the scene designer Carl Barndt (who had worked in Bayreuth), were mounted after 1850. Conductors have included Kleiber (1912–19), Weingartner (1914–19), Szell (1921–2), Böhm (1927–31) and Hans Schmidt-Isserstedt (1931–3). The last grand duke, Ernst Ludwig (1892–1918), was sympathetic towards modern art, and a tradition of contemporary opera production grew up, with such directors as Carl Ebert (1927–31) and Arthur Maria Rabenalt working in Darmstadt.

The theatre was destroyed in an air raid in September 1944, but by 15 December 1945 performances had resumed again, in the Orangeriehaus; other temporary stages were found in the city hall and in the castle. During the 1950s artists such as Erika Köth, Christa Ludwig and Sandor Konya were part of the company. Gustav Rudolf Sellner was Intendant, 1951–60. The new Grosses Haus (956 seats) opened on 6 October 1972 with *Fidelio*. Since then, Darmstadt's operatic tradition has been enriched by the city's associations with contemporary music, particularly that of the avant garde. Kurt Horres, Intendant from 1974 to 1984, paid special attention to modern music theatre; his successor was Peter Brenner. The company gives an average of 215 performances each season, including the standard repertory. Interesting productions in recent years have been the first performance in West Germany of Cerha's *Baal* (1981) and the première of Peter Maxwell Davies's *Resurrection* in 1988.

*

E. Pasqué: *Geschichte der Musik und des Theaters am Hof zu Darmstadt* (Darmstadt, 1853)
W. Kleefeld: *Landgraf Ernst Ludwig von Hessen-Darmstadt und die deutsche Oper* (Berlin, 1904)
H. Kaiser: *Barocktheater in Darmstadt* (Darmstadt, 1951)
——: *Modernes Theater in Darmstadt* (Darmstadt, 1955)
——: *Vom Zeittheater zur Sellner-Bühne* (Darmstadt, 1961)
——: *Das Grossherzogliche Hoftheater zu Darmstadt, 1810–1910* (Darmstadt, 1964) SABINE SONNTAG, ERNST THOMAS

D'Arquier, Joseph. *See* ARQUIER, JOSEPH.

Darwish [Darweesh], **Sayed** [Sayyid] (*b* Alexandria, 17 March 1892; *d* Alexandria, 15 Sept 1923). Egyptian composer and singer. He is the most popular figure in Egyptian music. Darwish began his career as a singer-composer performing at modest local cafés and attributing his vocal compositions to famous composers. An important turning-point came when he went to Cairo, probably in 1917, and Salama Higazy introduced him to his theatre public. Although his first 'operetta', *Faysouzshah*, was a failure, he soon achieved success, becoming the favourite composer in this genre and even forming his own (short-lived) troupe. A prolific composer, he wrote his 28 operettas in six years. They owed their immense popularity to their social and patriotic subjects, their workers' songs and their vivid musical characterizations, essentially Egyptian and strongly reminiscent of folk music. Darwish may have been influenced by the Italian opera performed in Cairo: he admired Verdi and had planned, just before his early death, to study in Italy. His most popular operettas were *El-ashara'l tayyiba* (1920), *Sheherazade* (1921) and *El-barooka* (1921); the latter two were performed by his own troupe. With the exception of *Abdel-Rahman El-Nasser* (5, A. Allam; Cairo, 3 Jan 1921), based on the history of Córdoba, the stage works all have substantial comic elements.

*

M. A. Hammad, ed.: *Sayed Darwish: hayat wa nagham* [Darwish: Life and Music] (Cairo, 1970)
H. Darwish: *Min agl aby Sayed Darwish* [For my Father, Sayed Darwish] (Cairo, 1990) SAMHA EL-KHOLY

Dauberval [d'Auberval, D'Oberval], **Jean Bercher** (*b* Montpellier, 19 Aug 1742; *d* Tours, 14 Feb 1806). French dancer, teacher and choreographer. He danced in Lyons in 1757 under Noverre, who described his pupil as a joyful and dramatically expressive dancer. Within two years Dauberval was ballet-master for the Turin opera house. In 1761 he made a successful début at the Paris Opéra in Rameau's *Zaïs*. He performed under Noverre in Stuttgart, 1762–4, appeared at the Haymarket, London, in 1764 and returned in 1766 to the Opéra, where he was appointed assistant ballet-master in 1770. He danced in many revivals of works by Lully and Rameau, and in the premières of Dauvergne's *Polyxène* (1763), Louis Granier's *Théonis* (1767), P.-M. Berton and J. B. de La Borde's *Adèle de Ponthieu* (1772) and Gossec's *Sabinus* (2nd version; 1774). From 1781 to 1783 he shared the title of ballet-master with Maximilien Gardel; he was ousted as a result of political intrigues.

Dauberval then went to Bordeaux, where his years at the Grand Théâtre, 1785–91, were his most fertile period. His ballets, including *Le déserteur* (1785; based on Monsigny's opera), came to be staged throughout Europe. In 1784, 1791–2 and 1796 he returned to London, where he choreographed new ballets at the Pantheon and Haymarket theatres, including dances for Sacchini's *Armida* (1791). He was equally facile in comically realistic *ballets villageoises* and more classically orientated *ballets anacréontiques*. He often worked with Barthélemon, composer at the Haymarket Theatre, but usually arranged his own accompaniments; Bournonville claimed that his use of 'patchwork' arrangements severely limited the beauty of his dances. His best-known ballet is *La fille mal gardée* (1789).

*

A. Bournonville: *Mit theaterliv* (Copenhagen, 1847–77; Eng. trans., 1979)
A. Jullien: 'Un mariage chorégraphique: Mlle Théodore et Dauberval', *L'Opéra secret au XVIIIe siècle* (Paris, 1880), 163–202
I. Guest: 'The Legacy of Dauberval', *Ballet Annual*, xv (1961), 104–8 MAUREEN NEEDHAM COSTONIS

Dauer, Johann [Joseph] **Ernst** (*b* Hildburghausen, 1746; *d* Vienna, 12 Sept 1812). German tenor. He began his career in 1768, and in 1771 was engaged in Hamburg, where he sang in Singspiels. In 1775 he went to Gotha and in 1777 to Frankfurt and Mannheim. In 1779 he was engaged at the court theatre in Vienna, initially singing in the Singspiel company (making his début as Alexis in Monsigny's *Le déserteur*) and, the following year, also acting in the spoken theatre company. He created Pedrillo in Mozart's *Die Entführung aus dem Serail* (1782) and Sturmwald in Dittersdorf's *Der Apotheker und der Doktor* (1786). He was a useful though uninspired performer: according to the actor F. L. Schröder, 'He touched the heart in neither serious nor comic roles. His manner was a little cold and remote; his movement somewhat wooden' (quoted by O. Michtner, *Das alte Burgtheater als Opernbühne*, Vienna, 1970, pp.369, 521). He played secondary lovers, character roles and sturdy, unpolished lads.

CHRISTOPHER RAEBURN, DOROTHEA LINK

Daussoigne-Méhul, Louis Joseph (*b* Givet, Ardennes, 10 June 1790; *d* Liège, 10 March 1875). Franco-Belgian composer. He was Etienne-Nicolas Méhul's nephew and later his adopted son. Admitted to the Paris Conservatoire in 1799, he studied with Adam, Catel, his uncle and Cherubini and won the Prix de Rome in 1809. After studying in Italy he was appointed professor of harmony at the Conservatoire in 1816. His early operas met with moderate success, but *Les deux Salem*, first performed at the Opéra in 1824, was a failure. His recitatives for Méhul's *Stratonice* (performed in this version at the Opéra on 30 March 1821) and his additional numbers for his uncle's *Valentine de Milan* (Feydeau, 28 November 1822) show a style almost identical with Méhul's. He was director of the Liège Conservatory, 1827–62; among his pupils was César Franck. He also contributed various articles to the *Bulletins de l'Académie royale de Belgique* in Brussels, including 'L'essai philosophique sur l'origine, le caractère et les transformations de la musique théâtrale'. Among his works are several operatic transcriptions for piano.

Le faux inquisiteur (oc, 3, J.-P.-G. Viennet), Paris, OC (Feydeau), Dec 1817

Aspasie et Périclès (opéra, 1, Viennet), Paris, Opéra, 17 July 1820
Les deux Salem (opéra féerie, 1, P. de Lespinasse, after Plautus: *Menaechmi*), Paris, Opéra, 12 July 1824

Unperf.: Les amants corsaires (oc, 3, Viennet); Robert Guiscard (opéra, 3, N.-F.-G. Saulnier); Le testament (oc, 1, B.-J. Marsollier des Vivetières)

Dauvergne [D'Auvergne], **Antoine** (*b* Moulins, 3 Oct 1713; *d* Lyons, Feb 1797). French composer. He began his career as a violinist in Moulins and Clermont-Ferrand before moving to Paris in the late 1730s. According to Pierre de Bernis, he studied composition with Rameau. In 1739 he became a violinist in the *chambre du roi*. He joined the Opéra orchestra in 1744 and by 1752 had assumed some of the conducting responsibilities. His first stage work, *Les amours de Tempé*, a ballet in four acts, was presented at the Opéra in 1752; the reviewer of the *Mercure de France* commented favourably on Dauvergne's solid instrumental pieces, knowledge of harmony and taste. His greatest success and most important opera, *Les troqueurs*, followed in 1753, and established a theatrical career which was to last over 20 years.

In 1755 Dauvergne was appointed composer and master to the *chambre du roi*. After seven years as a co-director of the Concert Spirituel, an appointment he held for 11 years, he became a director of the Opéra in 1769. While there he was closely involved in the negotiations with Gluck (1772–4). Dauvergne was against bringing Gluck and his operas to Paris, so Gluck himself wrote to Dauvergne, enclosing the first act of *Iphigénie en Aulide* as a sample. Although Dauvergne conceded the novelty and potential of Gluck's work, he continued to discourage the composer by demanding five other operas. Marie Antoinette intervened, however, and the première of *Iphigénie* at the Opéra in 1774 was a triumph.

Dauvergne's 1773 arrangement of Destouches' *Callirhoé* was poorly received, and this was his last dramatic setting. Nevertheless, he was named composer to the Opéra in March 1776, and the following month resigned as director. In 1780 he became a director again, but shortly thereafter numerous musicians complained in writing of his perpetual nagging and inept management; he resigned in 1782, but in 1785 became director for the third time. Another series of letters, critical of his age, taste and management, made this term as unpleasant as the last. Disillusioned, and in financial and other difficulties, he retired in 1790.

Dauvergne's early works include violin sonatas, *Concerts de simphonies* and many motets (all lost). Of his stage works, only *Les troqueurs* is important historically and musically. Based on a La Fontaine tale, it was the first thoroughly French comic opera constructed on Italian models; all of the music was original and recitative replaced the usual spoken dialogue. Italian influence is revealed in the opening sinfonia, in the remarkable action ensemble – a quartet – that concludes the work, and by such devices as tremolos, widely varied dynamics and large melodic leaps. *Les troqueurs* was an instant success, enjoyed numerous revivals, was presented in several European capitals and was parodied at least twice. According to Maret, Rameau admired the work: 'Forecasting to what degree of perfection this form might be carried in the future, he [Rameau] would think with emotion of the progress that taste for this opera would bring about in good music'. La Borde regarded Dauvergne's other operas highly: 'The arias are pleasing and often of great beauty. He combines great talent and modesty'.

first performed in Paris unless otherwise stated; all printed works published in Paris

Les amours de Tempé (ballet-héroïque, 4, L. de Cahusac), Opéra, 7 Nov 1752 (*c*1753)
Les troqueurs (intermède, 1, J.-J. Vade, after La Fontaine), Foire St Laurent, 30 July 1753 (*c*1755), excerpts also pubd
La coquette trompée (comédie lyrique, 1, C.-S. Favart), Fontainebleau, 13 Nov 1753 (n.d.)
La sibylle (ballet, 1, F.-A. P. de Moncrif), Fontainebleau, 13 Nov 1753
Enée et Lavinie (tragédie lyrique, 5, B. L. de Fontenelle), Opéra, 14 Feb 1758 (1762)
Les fêtes d'Euterpe (ballet, 3, Favart, A. Danchet and Moncrif), Opéra, 8 Aug 1758 (*c*1759); incl. La coquette trompée, La sibylle
Le rival favorable (entrée added to Les fêtes d'Euterpe, P. N. Brunet), Italien, 14 April 1760
Canente (tragédie, prol., 5, A. H. de Lamotte), Opéra, 11 Nov 1760 (*c*1761)
Hercule mourant (tragédie lyrique, 5, J. F. Marmontel), Opéra, 3 April 1761, *F-Po*
Alphée et Aréthuse (ballet, 1, Danchet), Choisy-le-Roi, 15 Dec 1762
Polyxène (tragédie lyrique, 5, N.-R. Joliveau), Opéra, 11 Jan 1763 (*c*1763)
Le triomphe de Flore, ou Le retour de printemps (ballet-héroïque, 1, Vallier [L. Tolmer]), Fontainebleau, 29 Oct 1765
La Vénitienne (comédie-ballet, 3, Lamotte), Opéra, 3 May 1768, selected airs (1768)
La tour enchantée (ballet figuré, 1, Joliveau), Versailles, 20 June 1770
Le prix de la valeur (ballet-héroïque, 1, Joliveau), Opéra, 4 Oct 1771
Le Sicilien, ou L'amour peintre (comédie-ballet, 1, F. Levasseur, after Molière), Versailles, 10 March 1780
La mort d'Orphée (tragédie, Marmontel), unperf.
Sémiramis (tragédie, P.-C. Roy), unperf.

Other stage music: new airs for Lully: Persée, 1758, collab. F. Rebel, F. Francoeur and B. de Bury; airs for Linus (opéra, C.-A. Le Clerc de la Bruère), 1758, inc., *F-Pn*, collab. J.-C. Trial and P.-M. Berton; arr. of Collin de Blamont: Fêtes grecques et romaines, 1770; arr. of A. C. Destouches: Callirhoé, 1773

*

Les spectacles de Paris [title varies] (1752–94, 1800–01, 1815)
Etat actuel de la musique du roi et des trois spectacles de Paris (Paris, 1759–60, 1767–78)
H. Maret: *Eloge historique de M. Rameau* (Paris, 1766)
F. J. de Pierre de Bernis: 'Eloge de M. LeClair', *Nécrologe des hommes célèbres de France* (Paris, 1767)
J.-B. de La Borde: *Essai sur la musique*, iii (Paris, 1780), 378ff
E. du Fournel du Roure de Paulin: *La vie et les oeuvres d'Antoine d'Auvergne* (Paris, 1911)
L. de La Laurencie: 'Deux imitateurs français des Bouffons: Blavet et Dauvergne', *Année musicale*, ii (1912), 65–125

MICHAEL A. KELLER

Davaux [D'Avaux, Davau], **Jean-Baptiste** (*b* La Côte-St-André, 19 July 1742; *d* Paris, 2 Feb 1822). French composer. He was an 'amateur' in the 18th-century sense of the term, in that he held no post in any orchestra, chapel or opera company. He was secretary in various princely households and then, after the Revolution, in the service of the state. The main body of his instrumental work dates from before 1789; under the Empire 'brilliant concerts' were given in his salon. The music of his two *opéras comiques* had some success because of the prestige he enjoyed as a violinist and a composer of orchestral and chamber music. Adverse criticism in the reviews of the period was directed at the librettos, described as long and tedious; the music was praised for its orchestral effects but condemned for its lack of originality and character. The one notable feature in the manuscript (which is not definitive) of *Cécilia* is the presence of *récitatif mesuré* in the third finale.

Théodore, ou Le bonheur inattendu (cmda, 3, B.-J. Marsollier des Vivetières, after H. Kelly: *False Delicacy*), Fontainebleau, 4 March 1785, excerpts arr. pf (Paris, 1785 and n.d.)

Cécilia, ou Les trois tuteurs (3, Descombles, after F. Burney), Paris, Comédie-Italienne, 14 Dec 1786, *F-Pc* (partly autograph)

MICHEL NOIRAY

Davenant, Sir **William** (*b* Oxford, 1606; *d* London, 1667). English dramatist and theatre manager. Said (without proof) to have been William Shakespeare's illegitimate son, Davenant succeeded Ben Jonson as poet laureate in 1637 and remained staunchly loyal to the Stuart royal family. He contributed to the last of their court masques and later spent time with Charles II during his exile on the Continent. In spite of the ban on plays and public theatres during the Commonwealth, he returned to England in the mid-1650s in the hope of initiating some kind of theatrical activity. In 1656 at a makeshift theatre in Rutland House, Charterhouse Yard, he offered a series of musical entertainments with rudimentary scenery. One of these was *THE SIEGE OF RHODES*, a full-length rhymed play 'sung in *Recitative Musick*', the music being composed and partly performed by leading musicians of the day, including Henry Lawes and MATTHEW LOCKE. This, the first full-length English opera, seems to have been created from necessity to circumvent the ban on spoken drama rather than from conviction. At the Restoration in 1660, Davenant's theatrical enterprise and loyalty were rewarded when Charles II granted him a theatre patent which allowed him to establish the Duke's Company of actors. According to the terms of the patent, Davenant was given the rights to several of Shakespeare's plays, which he freely adapted with musical episodes, a practice which eventually led to the development of SEMI-OPERA. He also revived *The Siege of Rhodes* after the Restoration, but it was then 'acted as a just *Drama*' (that is, as a spoken play rather than an opera). JOHN DRYDEN had great respect for Davenant, whom he credited with the invention of the heroic rhymed play.

*

A. Harbage: *Sir William Davenant: Poet Venturer (1606–1668)* (Philadelphia, 1935)

J. Freehafer: 'The Formation of the London Patent Companies in 1660', *Theatre Notebook*, xx (1965–6), 6–30

R. D. Hume: *The Development of English Drama in the Late Seventeenth Century* (Oxford, 1976)

E. W. White: *A History of English Opera* (London, 1983)

CURTIS PRICE

Davico, Vincenzo (*b* Monaco, 14 Jan 1889; *d* Rome, 8 Dec 1969). Italian composer. He studied in Turin with G. Cravero and then in Leipzig with Reger. From 1918 to 1940 he lived in Paris, composing, while also conducting in Italy and elsewhere. When he returned to Italy he worked at the RAI and also contributed to many Italian and foreign journals.

Davico's theatre music comprises three works, the lyric drama *La dogaressa* (1920), the *beffa lirica Berlingaccio* (composed in 1931) and the one-act opera *La principessa prigioniera* (1940). The most characteristic feature of these works is Davico's preference for light vocal lyricism, harmonic freshness and elegant orchestral writing influenced by impressionist, late 19th-century French music. Because of the crepuscular tones of his chamber music Davico has been described as a delicate miniaturist, and so his theatre music, necessarily of larger musical and dramatic dimensions, does not show him at his most typical.

La dogaressa (dramma lirico, 1, G. M. Gatti), Monte Carlo, 26 Feb 1920

Berlingaccio, 1931 (beffa lirica, 3, G. Pierotti della Sanguigna), unperf.

La principessa prigioniera (1, G. Gros, trans. Pierotti della Sanguigna), Bergamo, Donizetti, 29 Sept 1940

*

ES (G. Graziosi)

A. Picchi: 'La principessa prigioniera', *Augustea* (1940)

G. Cogni: 'Ricordo di Davico', *Rassegna musicale Curci*, xxiii/2 (1970), 39–40

RAFFAELE POZZI

David, Domenico (*b* Veneto region; *d* Venice, 30 June 1698). Italian librettist. A doctor of medicine, he belongs, with Zeno, to the first generation of reform librettists. He was among the earliest members of the Accademia degli Animosi, in which he used the name Osiro Cedreatico, and was patronized by several important Italian families. Although his lyric poetry dates from the 1670s, he did not enter the operatic field until 1691 when he wrote *L'amante eroe* for the Teatro S Salvatore. His other two librettos were for the Teatro S Giovanni Grisostomo.

David's dramas stand out in the company of contemporary Venetian music dramas because of their pronounced moral tone and the purposeful disposition of the dramatic action. In the letter to the reader in *L'amante eroe*, he expressed concern about the excessive number of arias and the need for more recitative 'in order to move the affections'. Metastasio's first libretto, *Siface* (F. Feo, Naples, Teatro S Bartolomeo, spring 1723), is largely a rewriting of *La forza della virtù*.

L'amante eroe, M. A. Ziani, 1691; *La forza della virtù*, C. F. Pollarolo, 1693 (?Severo di Luca, 1699, as Creonte tiranno di Tebe; Keiser, 1700, as La forza della virtù, oder Die Macht der Tugend; 1717, as La virtù coronata); *Amor e dover*, Pollarolo, 1696

*

AllacciD; *ES* (E. Zanetti)

G. M. Crescimbeni: *Notizie istoriche degli Arcadi morti*, iii (Rome, 1721)

G. Bonlini: *Le glorie della poesia e della musica* (Venice, 1730)

A. Groppo: *Catalogo di tutti i drammi per musica recitati ne' teatri di Venezia* (Venice, 1745)

N. Burt: 'Opera in Arcadia', *MQ*, xli (1955), 145–70

R. S. Freeman: *Opera without Drama: Currents of Change in Italian Opera, 1675–1725, and the Roles played therein by Zeno, Caldara, and Others* (diss., Princeton U., 1967)

K. Leich: *Girolamo Frigimelica Robertis Libretti (1694–1708): ein Beitrag insbesondere zur Geschichte des Opernlibretto in Venedig* (Munich, 1972)

H. S. Saunders: *The Repertoire of a Venetian Opera House (1678–1714): the Teatro Grimani di San Giovanni Grisostomo* (diss., Harvard U., 1985)

C. Sartori: *I libretti italiani a stampa dalle origini al 1800* (Cuneo, 1990–)

HARRIS S. SAUNDERS

David, Félicien(-César) (*b* Cadenet, Vaucluse, 13 April 1810; *d* St Germain-en-Laye, 29 Aug 1876). French composer. Orphaned at the age of five, he was sent in 1818 to the *maîtrise* of St Sauveur in Aix-en-Provence; he was soon composing motets, hymns and a string quartet. In 1825 he went to the Jesuit college of St Louis at Aix and began to discover the music of *opéras comiques* (in the guise of church music) as well as the sacred works of Haydn, Mozart and Cherubini. From 1828 he worked as assistant conductor in the Aix theatre, as a lawyer's clerk and then as *maître de chapelle* at the *maîtrise* of St Sauveur. His inclination was more towards church music than the theatre, although he wrote a number of nocturnes and *romances* in conformity with the fashion of the day.

After a year, he moved to Paris and studied with Millault, Fétis and Benoist at the Conservatoire, and privately with Reber. Hampered by poverty, he left prematurely in 1831 to give his life yet another new direction by joining the Saint-Simonians. Whether from a lack of direction in his musical studies or from sympathy with Saint-Simon's doctrines, David became the most prominent musician in a sect whose programme of equality and social realignment received considerable encouragement from the July Revolution of 1830. The Saint-Simonians split late in 1831; David followed 'Père' Enfantin to Ménilmontant, outside Paris, where he composed music for the cult's ceremonies.

When the community was disbanded by government order in 1832, David left with a small band of friends to preach the Saint-Simonian gospel to the orient with the hope of restoring Egypt to its ancient prosperity. They sailed on 22 March 1833 to Constantinople, Smyrna, Jaffa, Jerusalem and finally Egypt, where the ardour of their mission was gradually superseded by the fascination of the East, at least in David's mind, for he clearly recognized a powerful source of musical inspiration in the customs, religions and landscape of the countries he visited. The journey was one of adventure and discovery. David devoted much time to composing songs and piano pieces, mainly of an oriental mould. He stayed nearly two years in Cairo, giving music lessons and exploring the desert, returning to France in June 1835.

In Paris the following year David published at his own expense a collection of *Mélodies orientales* (for the piano) which had little success; a public that enjoyed Hugo's *Orientales* had not yet developed more than a passing taste for musical orientalism. He now settled in Igny, turning his attention to instrumental music, as well as writing many songs. In 1841 David moved to Paris and in July 1844 he produced *Le désert*, an *ode-symphonie* that met with immediate success and initiated a series of descriptive works exploring the French passion for oriental subjects, a predilection that can be heard in the music of Reyer, Gounod, Bizet, Delibes, Saint-Saëns, Roussel and Messiaen, among others. Riding on its success, he toured Germany and Austria in 1845, meeting Mendelssohn in Frankfurt and Meyerbeer in Berlin, and attending the Beethoven celebrations in Bonn.

After a series of concert works, David ventured finally to write for the stage, and his *La perle du Brésil* appeared at the Opéra-National (later the Théâtre Lyrique) in 1851; making much of a storm at sea and Brazilian local colour, it has more decorative than dramatic vitality, but remained in the repertory for over 30 years. Zora's coloratura aria with flute obbligato, 'Charmant oiseau', became quite widely known. *Herculanum*, his next opera (1859), though more stagily Meyerbeerian, is not among his best works. It was first conceived as a melodrama entitled *La fin du monde*, with a finale depicting the Last Judgment, and was later reworked by Méry into a grand opera, whose first title was *Le dernier amour*. *Herculanum* contrasts the Christian and pagan worlds and ends with the cataclysmic eruption of Vesuvius. The more modest *opéra comique Lalla-Roukh* (1862) was much more appropriate to David's gifts, as Berlioz recognized; its delicate evocation of Thomas Moore's Kashmir, its dreamy atmosphere and aromatic orchestration mark it as his masterpiece. It quickly became popular and established David's success. *La captive*, similarly set in the East, was withdrawn from rehearsal in 1864 at the request of the librettist and never performed. *Le saphir* (1865), based on Shakespeare's *All's Well that Ends Well*, responded with only moderate success to Auber's *mot* 'I wish he'd get off his camel' by eschewing any kind of exotic or descriptive element. Discouraged, David never again wrote for the stage.

In 1867 David was awarded a prize of 20 000 francs by the Académie des Beaux Arts for *Herculanum* and *Lalla-Roukh*, and in 1869 he succeeded Berlioz as a member of the Institute and also as librarian of the Conservatoire, an office which he discharged with even less devotion and interest than his predecessor. He retained his Saint-Simonian faith; yet apart from the music specially written in 1832 there is no trace of social dogma or idealism in his work, and he seems to have been content to exploit his talent for the picturesque and the evocative. In some respects his music echoes Berlioz, especially *Harold en Italie*, but his Romanticism did not extend to the dynamic imagination of the *Symphonie fantastique* or *La damnation de Faust*, and he showed no awareness of the richer harmonic language of Chopin and Liszt. Rather his music falls into the French tradition of being agreeable diversion, strongly coloured but emotionally naive; in this he preceded and greatly influenced a whole school, including Gounod, Thomas, Lalo, Saint-Saëns, Massenet and, probably most strongly, Delibes. Dumesnil regarded David as second only to Berlioz among French composers of his time, and even if this implies much about the state of French music in this period, it is a judgment with which few would wish to quarrel.

all first performed in Paris; all printed works published in Paris

La perle du Brésil (oc, Gabriel, S. Saint-Etienne), Opéra-National, 22 Nov 1851 (1852); rev. 1859–61 (1873)

Le fermier de Franconville, ?1857 (oc, 1, ? A. de Leuven), unperf., *F-Pc*

Herculanum (opéra, J. Méry and T. Hadot), Opéra, 4 March 1859 (1859)

Lalla-Roukh (oc, H. Lucas and M. Carré, after T. Moore), OC (Favart), 12 May 1862 (*c*1863)

La captive (oc, Carré), *c*1860–64, unperf., *Pc*, vs (1883)

Le saphir (oc, Carré, Hadot and de Leuven, after W. Shakespeare: *All's Well that Ends Well*), OC (Favart), 8 March 1865, vs (1865)

*

PEM (A. Gerhard, H. Schneider)

S. Saint-Etienne: *Biographie de Félicien David* (Marseilles, 1845)

H. Berlioz: 'Première représentation de *La perle du Brésil*', *Journal des débats* (27 Nov 1851)

E. de Mirecourt [C. J. B. Jacquot]: *Félicien David* (Brussels, 1854, 3/1869)

H. Berlioz: 'Première représentation d'*Herculanum*', *Journal des débats* (12 March 1859)

T. Gautier: *Histoire de l'art dramatique en France depuis vingt-cinq ans*, vi (Brussels and Paris, 1859), 273–9

H. Berlioz: 'Première représentation de *Lalla Roukh*', *Journals des débats* (23 May 1862)

A. Azevedo: *Félicien David: coup d'oeil sur sa vie et son oeuvre* (Paris, 1863)

P. Scudo: *La musique en l'année 1862* (Paris, ?1863), 26–38

E. Reyer: *Notes de musique* (Paris, 1875)

C. Saint-Saëns: *Harmonie et mélodie* (Paris, 1885)

A. Jullien: *Musiciens d'aujourd'hui*, 2nd ser. (Paris, 1894), 113–27

R. Brancour: *Félicien David* (Paris, 1909)

R. Dumesnil: *La musique romantique française* (Paris, 1944)

M. J. Achter: *Félicien David, Ambroise Thomas, and French Opéra Lyrique 1850–1870* (diss., U. of Michigan, 1972)

P. Besnier: 'Musique pour la fin du monde', *Missions et démarches de la critique: mélanges offerts à J. A. Vier* (Paris, 1973), 171–82

P. Gradenwitz: 'Félicien David (1810–1876) and French Romantic Orientalism', *MQ*, lxii (1976), 471–506

T. J. Walsh: *Second Empire Opera: the Théâtre Lyrique, Paris 1851–1870* (London, 1981)

G. Favre: *Musiciens méditerranéens oubliés* (Paris, 1985)

D. V. Hagan: *Félicien David, 1810–1876: a Composer and a Cause* (Syracuse, NY, 1985)
R. P. Locke: *Music, Musicians, and the Saint-Simonians* (Chicago and London, 1986)
J.-P. Bartoli: 'A propos de deux ouvrages sur Félicien David et les Saint-Simoniens: une lettre inédite de David', *RdM*, lxxv (1988), 65–76
R. P. Locke: 'David and *Aida*', *MT*, cxxix (1988), 282 [letter to the editor]
——: 'Félicien David, compositeur saint-simonien et orientalisant', *Les Saint-Simoniens et l'Orient: vers la modernité*, ed. M. Morsy (Aix-en-Provence, 1990), 135–54 HUGH MACDONALD (text), RALPH P. LOCKE (work-list)

David, Karl Heinrich (*b* St Gall, 30 Dec 1884; *d* Nervi, Italy, 17 May 1951). Swiss composer. He studied the violin and composition at the Cologne Conservatory and in Munich with Thuille, and thereafter worked as a conductor in minor theatres. He later taught in Basle, and was an editor and music critic in Zürich, where he lived from 1918. He left a large and varied output, including several operas, ballets and other stage pieces.

Tredeschin, 1919 (after G. Bundi), unperf.
Aschenputtel (dramatisches Märchenspiel, after J. L. and W. C. Grimm), Basle, 1921
Der Sizilianer (comic op, 1, after Molière), Zürich, 1924
Traumwandel (2, lyrische Oper, after I. Turgenev), Zürich, 1928
Weekend, 1931–2 (Szenen mit Musik, 4), unperf.

*

K. H. David: 'Autobiographische Skizze', *SMz*, lxxxv (1945), 16–18
Der Schweizerische Tonkünstlerverein: Festschrift zur Feier des 50jährigen Jubiläums (Zürich, 1950)
W. Schuh: 'Karl Heinrich David zum Gedächtnis', *SMz*, xci (1951), 303–4 PETER ROSS

David, Léon (*b* Les Sables d'Olonne, Vendée, 18 Dec 1867; *d* Les Sables d'Olonne, 27 Oct 1962). French tenor. He studied in Nantes and in Paris, making his début in February 1892 at Monte Carlo as Euxenos in Desjoyeaux's *Gyptis*. In June the same year he began a long engagement at the Opéra-Comique, Paris, by singing Iopas in *Les Troyens*. His repertory included Almaviva, George Brown (*La dame blanche*), Gerald (*Lakmé*), Des Grieux (*Manon*), Wilhelm Meister (*Mignon*), Nadir, Vincent (*Mireille*), Werther and Don José. Between 1900 and 1907 he sang at the Théâtre de la Monnaie, where his roles included Belmonte and Dimitri (Alfano's *Risurrezione*). In 1913 he created Paco in Falla's *La vida breve* at Nice. His voice, a lyric tenor, was of beautiful quality. ELIZABETH FORBES

Davide [David], **Giacomo** (*b* Presezzo, Bergamo, 1750; *d* Bergamo, 31 Dec 1830). Italian tenor. He was self-taught as a singer, but studied composition in Naples. After making his début in 1773 at the Regio Ducal Teatro, Milan, in the première of Gazzaniga's *Zon Zon*, he sang in Turin, Venice, Bologna, Lucca, Rome, Parma and at La Scala, where he took part in the premières of Cimarosa's *Circe* and Sarti's *Idalide* (1783), Mayr's *Lodoiska* (1799) and many other operas. He appeared in Naples, Padua, Florence, Genoa, Trieste and St Petersburg in works by Guglielmi, Paisiello, Bertoni, Federici and Portugal. With a powerful, extremely flexible voice, he was able to compete with the castratos in florid music and far exceed them in his dramatic intensity. ELIZABETH FORBES

Davide [David], **Giovanni** (*b* Naples, 15 Oct 1790; *d* St Petersburg, 1864). Italian tenor. Son and pupil of the tenor Giacomo Davide, he appeared with his father at Siena in 1808 in Mayr's *Adelaide di Guesclino*. Engagements in Brescia, Padua and Turin followed, and in 1814 he created Narciso in *Il turco in Italia* at La Scala, the first of many Rossini premières in which he took part. Two years later he went to Naples and sang in the first performances of *Otello* (as Roderigo), *Ricciardo e Zoraide*, *Ermione*, *La donna del lago* and *Zelmira*. He also appeared in *Tancredi*, *La gazza ladra*, *Matilde di Shabran*, *Bianca e Falliero*, *Mosè in Egitto*, *Semiramide* and *Otello* (in the title role). In 1830 he appeared in Paris, and the following season in London, but by then his voice, notable for its extreme agility and amazing compass of three octaves up to *b♭''*, was beginning to decay. After his retirement he went to St Petersburg to direct the Italian opera. ELIZABETH FORBES

Davidenko, Alexander Alexandrovich (*b* Odessa, 1/13 April 1899; *d* Moscow, 1 May 1934). Soviet composer. From 1918 he studied at the Odessa conservatory and from 1922 at the Moscow conservatory with Glier. For a number of years he headed Prokoll, a 'production collective' whose aim was to write music in the spirit of the new revolutionary era and to propagate it widely; he made arrangements of revolutionary and other Russian songs. Most of his other compositions are choral. His music has a vividly expressed folksong element, with bold melodic outlines and polyphony which combines Russian folk with Western traditions. Although dated in theme, his choral works, which influenced Shostakovich and other Soviet composers, have retained their value.

In 1930 Davidenko began work on the opera *1919 god* ('The Year 1919'), which he did not complete. The first act was performed in 1931 by the workers' opera group of the aviation equipment factory in Moscow. He began composing another opera, *1905 god* ('The Year 1905'; vs, Moscow, 1963), in 1933 in collaboration with Boris Shekhter. The libretto, written by S. Mstislavsky from a scenario devised in collaboration with K. S. Stanislavsky, was the first on the subject of the 1905 uprising. The music was completed by Shekhter in 1935, after Davidenko's death, and a radio adaptation of the work was broadcast that year. Of the three acts that make up *1905 god*, Davidenko alone composed the first scene, the whole of Act 2, the first scene of Act 3 and extensive choral scenes; he was also responsible for fragments pertaining to the characterization of the main roles. Davidenko's vocal and choral style in this work continues the tradition of Musorgsky; his colourful harmony is reminiscent of Puccini.

*

V. Bely: 'Tvorchestvo Aleksandra Davidenko' [The Work of Alexander Davidenko], *SovM* (1952), no.9, pp.22–7
A. Davidenko: *Vospominaniya, stat'i, materiali* [Reminiscences, Articles, Materials] (Leningrad, 1968) GALINA GRIGOR'YEVA

David et Jonathas ('David and Jonathan'). Sacred opera in five acts by MARC-ANTOINE CHARPENTIER to a libretto by François Bretonneau; Paris, Collège Louis-le-Grand, 28 February 1688.

The drama is set in the Holy Lands during biblical times. King Saul (bass), on the eve of his battle against the Philistines, consults a Witch (*haute-contre*), who in turn summons the ghost of Samuel (bass); Samuel predicts defeat. David (*haute-contre*), banished from the camp of the Israelites by Saul, has joined the Philistine army. In spite of his desire for peace, David is forced to fight against the Israelites and his beloved friend Jonathas [Jonathan] (soprano), son of Saul. When he sees his sons dying and himself about to be captured,

Saul falls on his sword. Jonathan, mortally wounded, dies in David's arms, while the Israelites proclaim David to be Saul's successor as their king.

David et Jonathas served as a five-part *intermède* to the spoken tragedy *Saül* of Pierre Chamillart. It is the sole surviving example of a type of sacred opera which arose from the longstanding Jesuit practice of performing an interlude of music and dance between the acts of a Latin biblical drama. *Celse Martyr* (1687), Charpentier's earlier attempt at writing a similar operatic *intermède* for another sacred tragedy, is lost. *David et Jonathas* enjoyed a lasting success among the Jesuits, and it was revived at Louis-le-Grand in 1706, at the Collège d'Harcourt in 1715 and at Jesuit colleges at Amiens and La Flèche in 1741. A profoundly meditative work which marshals the resources of opera (airs, ensembles, choruses, symphonies and dances) to different ends, *David et Jonathas* is virtually devoid of action and recitative. Instead, it offers a dramatically static but emotionally vivid series of psychological tableaux of each of the principal characters. *Saül* (spoken in Latin) and *David et Jonathas* (sung in French) present the same story from different and often contradictory viewpoints; the two works are interwoven with one another in such a way that the opera provides a lyrical reflection on the actions (and their consequences) that take place in the Latin tragedy. As multi-level theatre, *David et Jonathas* represents a daring attempt to offer an original alternative to the Lully-Quinault model of *tragédie lyrique*.

JOHN S. POWELL

Davidoff [Levinson], **Alexander** (*b* Poltava, 4 Sept 1872; *d* Moscow, 28 June 1944). Russian tenor. He studied in Odessa and Kiev, joining the opera at Tbilisi in 1893. His Moscow début was with Savva Mamontov's Private Russian Opera in 1896, and with this company in early 1898 he took the title role in the première of Rimsky-Korsakov's *Sadko*. From 1900 to 1912 he sang at the Mariinsky in St Petersburg, appearing first as Hermann in *The Queen of Spades*, the opera with which he became most closely associated until increasing deafness brought his career to an end. His voice, which was that of a lyric tenor, was heavily taxed by roles such as Otello and Canio, yet his contemporary, Sergey Levik, held that his special ability lay in bringing lyric qualities to such roles. He also sang in Paris, where in 1934 he briefly became director of the Opéra Russe. Recordings show him as an unusually interesting and often stylish singer, at his best both graceful and expressive.

J. B. STEANE

Davïdov, Stepan Ivanovich (*b* nr Chernigov, 1/12 Jan 1777; *d* Moscow, 10/22 May 1825). Russian composer, conductor and pedagogue. He received his early training (from the age of nine) as a member of the court chapel choir at St Petersburg. From 1795 to 1801 he studied with Giuseppe Sarti. In 1797 he succeeded Bortnyansky as conductor of the chapel choir, and held the post for three years; his numerous sacred choruses must date from this tenure. From 1800 to 1810 (interrupted by sick leave in 1804–6) he taught 'singing and music' at the imperial theatre school and composed on demand for the Russian troupe in the capital. After an undocumented period, in 1814 he took up a similar post in Moscow, where he spent the rest of his life. His chief contractual duty at this time was as official operatic renovator: 'If the director or his staff shall decide to modify an old opera or to insert a new aria, song or any other sort of composition, then making the tunes and the accompanying parts at the behest of the director or staff shall be the responsibility of Mr Davïdov'.

Because of the nature of his official duties, Davïdov left a wealth of miscellaneous music for the stage, but only two fully fledged operas. Both were Singspiels, and both were sequels to Ferdinand Kauer's phenomenally popular Singspiel *Das Donauweibchen*, first performed at St Petersburg (in N. S. Krasnopol'sky's translation) in 1803, during Davïdov's first stint as staff composer there. He was required to furnish six supplementary numbers for the sake of local colour. An immediate sequel (1804), also based on Kauer's music, had additional numbers by Catterino Cavos, another staff composer for the St Petersburg stage. In 1805 and again in 1807 Davïdov was commissioned to write wholly new sequels. The earlier of these was *Lesta, ili Dneprovskaya rusalka* ('Lesta, or The Dnepr Water Nymph'), a three-act work to a libretto by Krasnopol'sky (25 October/6 November 1805). It is the first Russian Romantic opera and held the stage until the 1850s, furnishing an immediate precedent not only for Pushkin's dramatic poem entitled *Rusalka* but also for Dargomïzhsky's opera on Pushkin's text. Davïdov's second sequel was *Rusalka* (1807), to a libretto by Alexander Shakhovskoy, again in three acts.

Besides producing quantities of theatrical ephemera, including incidental music and choruses to neo-classical tragedies, Davïdov wrote complete scores to several ballets, and a number of patriotic 'divertissements' (displays of national costume, song and dance) that were popular in the aftermath of the Patriotic War. (One of them, *Lukashka, ili Svyatochnïy vecher*, 'Lukashka, or A Yuletide Evening', was billed as a one-act opera but did not differ materially from the others.) Davïdov's was an all-purpose theatrical style, reminiscent at its best of Mozart and Rossini, with admixtures of folksong and indigenous sentimental romance as his subjects required. Some of his tunes have entered the oral tradition.

See also LESTA, ILI DNEPROVSKAYA RUSALKA.

A. Rabinovich: *Russkaya opera do Glinki* [Russian Opera Before Glinka] (Moscow, 1948) [incl. excerpt from *Lesta* in full score]
A. Glumov: *Muzïka v russkom dramaticheskom teatre* (Moscow, 1955)
P. Grachov: 'S. I. Davïdov', *Ocherki po istorii russkoy muzïki 1790–1825*, ed. M. Druskin and Yu. V. Keldïsh (Leningrad, 1956), 263–82
A. Gozenpud: *Muzïkal'nïy teatr v Rossii* (Leningrad, 1959)
S. L. Ginzburg: IRMO [incl. excerpts from *Lesta* in vs]
L. Fyodorovskaya: *Kompozitor Stepan Davïdov* (Leningrad, 1977)
Yu. V. Keldïsh: 'S. I. Davïdov', *Istoriya russkoy muzïki*, iv (Moscow, 1986), 145–67

RICHARD TARUSKIN

Davies, Arthur (*b* Wrexham, 11 April 1941). Welsh tenor. He studied at the RNCM. He made his début with the WNO in 1972 as Squeak (*Billy Budd*); over the next 12 years he sang some 35 roles with the company, including Nemorino, Almaviva, Ferrando, Nadir, Albert Herring, Yannakos (Martinů's *The Greek Passion*), Jack (*The Midsummer Marriage*), Quint, Nero, the Fox, Jeník, Rodolfo and Don José. After his Covent Garden début in Henze's *We Come to the River* (1976) he sang Alfredo, Števa (*Jenůfa*), Pinkerton and Foresto in *Attila* (1991). His roles for the ENO include the Duke, Essex (*Gloriana*), Don Ottavio, Faust, Gabriele Adorno, Werther, Turiddu and Riccardo (*Un ballo in maschera*). For Scottish Opera he has sung David and Cavaradossi.

His once light, lyric voice has grown heavier while retaining its flexibility, as he demonstrated when he sang Gaston for Opera North in the British stage première of Verdi's *Jérusalem* (1990). ELIZABETH FORBES

Davies, Cecilia (*b c*1757; *d* London, 3 July 1836). Irish soprano. As a child she toured with her elder sister Mary Ann (Marianne), a glass harmonica player. After 1767 the family went to the Continent. In Vienna Cecilia studied for a year with Hasse; she then insisted on trying her luck in Italy, though he thought her unready. In 1772 she sang Bradamante in Hasse's *Ruggiero* at Naples and Florence; each time she seems to have failed, though she claimed a success marred by cabal. When she sang in opera in London in 1773–4 and 1776–7 she was highly praised by Burney and others; Walpole, a dissenter, wished 'she had less top to her voice and more bottom' (see Matthews). After another failed continental tour, and some London concert and oratorio performances up to 1791, her later years were spent in poverty.

*

BurneyH
Correspondence: Cecilia and Mary Ann Davies and J. A. Hasse to G. M. Ortes, 1770–78 (*I-Vmc* Cod. Cicogna 3197–8 bis)
B. Matthews: 'The Davies Sisters, J. C. Bach and the Glass Harmonica', *ML*, lvi (1975), 150–70 JOHN ROSSELLI

Davies, Dennis Russell (*b* Toledo, OH, 16 April 1944). American conductor. He studied with Morel and Jorge Mester at the Juilliard School and in 1968 made his conducting début in New York with the Juilliard Ensemble (which he co-founded with Berio and directed from 1968 to 1974). In 1970 he conducted the première of Berio's *Opera* at Santa Fe, and in 1973 his European career was launched when Maderna chose him as his replacement to conduct *Pelléas et Mélisande* at the Netherlands Opera. He made his Bayreuth début with *Der fliegende Holländer* in 1978, since when his career has been based in Germany. In 1980 he became music director of the Stuttgart Staatsoper, the only American to run a German opera house at the time. A strong supporter of American minimalist and eclectic music, he was responsible for the world première at the Staatsoper of Glass's *Akhnaten* (1984), which he recorded. Davies has also been a champion of Henze: he conducted the world première of *The English Cat* (1983, Schwetzingen Festival) and the first complete performance of the original five-hour version of *König Hirsch* (1985, Stuttgart). Before leaving Stuttgart in 1987 he conducted the German première of Viktor Ullmann's *Der Kaiser von Atlantis*, which the composer had written and rehearsed while interned in the concentration camp at Theresienstadt. He then became Generalmusikdirektor of the city of Bonn, where his responsibilities included the Oper der Stadt Bonn. He made his début with the Lyric Opera of Chicago in 1987 conducting Cerha's completed version of Berg's *Lulu*. Recent world premières conducted by Dennis Russell Davies include Manfred Trojahn's *Enrico* (1991, Schwetzingen) and Bolcom's *McTeague* (1992, Chicago). NANCY MALITZ

Davies, (Albert) Meredith (*b* Birkenhead, 30 July 1922). English conductor and organist. He was an organ scholar of Keble College, Oxford, and worked as an organist and choral conductor until a performance of Britten's *Spring Symphony* won the composer's approval and led to his engagement to conduct *The Rape of Lucretia* and *A Midsummer Night's Dream* at successive Aldeburgh festivals, 1960–61, and elsewhere (he conducted the North American première of the latter at Vancouver in 1961). He continued to work with Britten as music director of the English Opera Group, 1963–5, and conducted *Peter Grimes* both at Covent Garden and at Sadler's Wells, where he also conducted Delius's *A Village Romeo and Juliet* in 1962. In 1967 he conducted the première of Berkeley's *Castaway* at Aldeburgh. His recordings include Vaughan Williams's *Riders to the Sea* (1970) and *Sir John in Love* (1975), *A Village Romeo and Juliet* (in performance, 1962; studio, 1972) and *Fennimore and Gerda* (1976). Davies was principal of Trinity College of Music, London, from 1979 to 1988. He was made a CBE in 1982.

ARTHUR JACOBS

Davies, Sir **Peter Maxwell** (*b* Manchester, 8 Sept 1934). English composer. He studied at Manchester University and the RMCM (1952–7), where his fellow students included Goehr and Birtwistle, with whom he formed the New Music Manchester Group. His first acknowledged compositions date from that student period and show how an awareness of the current avant garde (Boulez, Stockhausen, Nono) was already fused with thematic material and technical devices derived from early English composers. He refined those techniques during studies with Petrassi in Rome (1957–9), and in works such as *St Michael* for 17 wind instruments (1957) and *Prolation* for orchestra (1958) established himself as one of the leading British composers of the postwar generation.

Davies began the composition of his first opera, *Taverner*, during two years spent in Princeton on a Harkness Scholarship from 1962 (where he studied with Roger Sessions and Earl Kim). He completed the score in 1968, though he had to reconstruct part of it in 1970 after a fire destroyed the manuscript. Before its completion, however, his music, and his concepts of musical theatre, had undergone a radical change of direction. In 1967 with Birtwistle he established a performing group, the Pierrot Players, based on the instrumentation of Schoenberg's *Pierrot lunaire*, with the specific intention of exploring the possibilities of small-scale music theatre. (He re-formed the group on his own in 1971 as the Fires of London.) In his setting of Trakl, *Revelation and Fall*, composed in 1966, he had already begun to blur the distinctions between concert and dramatic works: at the first performance the solo soprano wore a scarlet nun's habit and was required to scream through a megaphone at the climax of the work. In *Eight Songs for a Mad King* (1969) the protagonist is the insane George III, who talks and sings to his caged birds, represented by the instruments of the ensemble. In *Vesalii icones* (1969) a solo male dancer presents images from the anatomical drawings of Vesalius, while a solo cello offers its own musical commentary; the whole sequence is superimposed on the imagery of the Stations of the Cross. The two latter scores represent Davies's reappraisal of musico-dramatic conventions at its sharpest and most effective, while their moral preoccupations were those explored in *Taverner*. Subsequent dramatic forays, such as *Miss Donnithorne's Maggot*, *The Medium* and *The No. 11 Bus*, broke no new ground, and lacked much of the theatrical force of their predecessors.

In 1970 Davies moved to Orkney, and the islands' landscape and their culture, especially as reflected in the writings of George Mackay Brown, produced a sea-change in his music. The reorientation, from the expressionist extremes of his music of the late 1960s towards a style of softer edges and more emphasis on instrumental colour and harmonic clarity, was charted in his ensemble and orchestral pieces of the early 1970s, and led eventually to the flexible musical style established in his four symphonies and subsequent orchestral works. The Orkney period produced two chamber operas, however: *The Martyrdom of St Magnus*, based on Mackay Brown's novel on the history of Orkney's patron saint, and *The Lighthouse*, Davies's own speculative retelling of an incident on the Flannan Isles in the early 1900s. In both works some traces of the emotional extremes of music-theatre pieces surface, and the music is still founded in plainchant transformations, but in *The Martyrdom*, in particular, the influence of Britten's church parables can be felt.

Although an opera based on the life of St Francis of Assisi is in progress, Davies has returned to the opera house only once since *Taverner*, with *Resurrection*, composed for Darmstadt in 1988. Again the work has roots in Davies's past; he had begun to plan it in the early 1960s, as a comic counterpart to *Taverner*. Its story of the 'Hero' from a north of England working-class background, made to conform to the narrow morals of a sick commercialized society, has clear autobiographical elements. Yet the musical mixture of pastiche and parody, music hall and revue, overlaid with the constant intrusions of television advertising clichés, seemed insubstantial and dramatically thin at the first performance.

Davies was knighted in 1987.

See also LIGHTHOUSE, THE; MARTYRDOM OF ST MAGNUS, THE; and TAVERNER.

librettos by the composer unless otherwise stated

Taverner, 1962–8 (2, after 16th-century documents), London, CG, 12 July 1972
Notre Dame des fleurs, 1966 (mini-op), London, Queen Elizabeth Hall, 17 March 1973
Eight Songs for a Mad King (R. Stow), London, Queen Elizabeth Hall, 22 April 1969
Blind Man's Buff (masque, after nursery rhymes and G. Büchner: *Leonce und Lena*), London, Round House, 29 May 1972
Miss Donnithorne's Maggot (Stow), Adelaide, 9 March 1974
The Martyrdom of St Magnus (chamber op, 9 scenes, after G. Mackay Brown: *Magnus*), Kirkwall, St Magnus Cathedral, 17 June 1977
The Two Fiddlers (children's op, after Mackay Brown), Kirkwall, 16 June 1978
Le jongleur de Notre Dame (masque), Stromness, 18 June 1978
Cinderella (children's op), Kirkwall, 21 June 1980
The Lighthouse (chamber op, prol., 1), Edinburgh, Moray House, 2 Sept 1980
The Rainbow (music theatre for children), Kirkwall, 20 June 1981
The Medium (music theatre), Stromness, 21 June 1981
Songs of Hoy (masque), Stromness, 21 June 1982
The No.11 Bus (masque), London, Queen Elizabeth Hall, 20 March 1984
Resurrection (prol., 1), Darmstadt, Staats, 18 Sept 1988

*

S. Pruslin, ed.: *Peter Maxwell Davies: Studies from Two Decades* (London, 1979)
P. Griffiths: *Peter Maxwell Davies* (London, 1982)

ANDREW CLEMENTS

Davies, Ryland (*b* Cwm, Ebbw Vale, 9 Feb 1943). Welsh tenor. He studied at the RMCM, where he made his début in 1964 with the WNO as Rossini's Almaviva. At Glyndebourne he sang in the chorus, making his solo début in 1965 as the Major-domo (*Rosenkavalier*). Over the next 25 years he sang Nemorino with the Glyndebourne touring company, Belmonte, Lensky, Ferrando, Flamand (*Capriccio*), Tamino, Lysander, the Prince (*The Love for Three Oranges*) and Tichon (*Kát'a Kabanová*). In 1967 he sang Essex (*Gloriana*) at Sadler's Wells and in Lisbon. He made his Covent Garden début in 1969 as Hylas (*Les Troyens*), then sang Don Ottavio, Ernesto, Fenton, Enéas (*Esclarmonde*) and Ferrando, the role of his San Francisco (1970), Paris Opéra (1974) and Metropolitan (1975) débuts. He sang Cassio (*Otello*) at Salzburg (1970), Pelléas at Stuttgart (1979), Berlin (1984) and Hamburg, and Weber's Oberon at Montpellier (1987). He had a sweet-toned, lyrical voice and excellent diction, as demonstrated in his performance as Armand de Clerval in Massenet's *Thérèse* and in his Mozart recordings. ALAN BLYTH

Davies, Tudor (*b* Cymmer, Glam., 12 Nov 1892; *d* Penault, Mon., 2 April 1958). Welsh tenor. He studied first while working in a coalmine, and later at the RCM with Gustave García. He joined the British National Opera Company and made his Covent Garden début in 1921 as Rodolfo in *La bohème*, a role he repeated, opposite Melba, the following year. He created Hugh the Drover in Vaughan Williams's opera at His Majesty's Theatre in 1924, and in 1925 sang in the first performance, at Manchester, of Holst's *At the Boar's Head*. With the Sadler's Wells Company (1931–41) and later the Carl Rosa (1941–6) he appeared in a wide range of roles until his retirement in 1946. His voice came under strain, but in his prime, as records show, he sang with ringing, incisive tone and lively temperament.

*

A. D. Hillier and J. Jarrett: 'Tudor Davies: a Biography and Discography', *Record Advertiser*, ii (1971–2), no.4, pp.2–21; no.5, pp.2–9 J. B. STEANE

Davis, Andrew (Frank) (*b* Ashridge, Herts., 2 Feb 1944). English conductor. He studied at the RCM and at King's College, Cambridge, where he was an organ scholar. He is well known for his interpretations of *Der Rosenkavalier* and *Salome* at Covent Garden, and his *Ariadne auf Naxos* at the Metropolitan was particularly well received. He has enjoyed a close association for many years with the Glyndebourne Festival Opera where he triumphed with *Kát'a Kabanová* in 1988. He became musical director there, succeeding Bernard Haitink, in 1989, and had an immediate success with *Jenůfa*. In the 1988–9 season he conducted *La clemenza di Tito* for the Chicago Lyric Opera and in 1990 the British première of Tippett's *New Year* for Glyndebourne. He was appointed CBE in 1992.

KENNETH LOVELAND

Davis, Anthony (*b* Paterson, NJ, 20 Feb 1951). American composer. A graduate of Yale University, where he was the first Lustman Fellow, he gained international recognition in the 1970s as a virtuoso pianist and as the director of Episteme, a chamber ensemble specializing in improvisation. His first opera, *X: the Life and Times of Malcolm X*, was developed at Philadelphia's American Music Theater Festival and first performed on 28 September 1986 at the New York City Opera, conducted by Christopher Keene and directed by Rhoda Levine. Its stark and powerful libretto, by the poet and writer Thulani Davis, the composer's cousin, is based on a story by the composer's brother, Christopher Davis; in a series of fast-moving vignettes it sketches the galvanic life and career of the controversial American black activist Malcolm X (1925–65). Featuring a dark, atonal palette, complex rhythmic patterns and poignant lyricism, *X* is stylistically typical of Davis's works. It is influenced by classical, popular and non-Western sources; historical Afro-American music, including swing, scat, modal jazz and rap, and the libretto's emulation of contemporaneous literary styles, help re-create the 'sound' of Malcolm's era. Although *X*'s score includes some improvisatory passages, it is mainly constructed on traditional operatic lines.

Davis's futuristic second opera, *Under the Double Moon*, set to a libretto by the science-fiction writer Deborah Atherton, deals with human choice and change on the planet Undine. More intimate and lyrical than *X*, it draws musical inspiration from Balinese sources. Commissioned by the Opera Theatre of St Louis, *Double Moon* was conducted by William McGlaughlin and directed by Rhoda Levine at its first performance there on 15 June 1989. Both of Davis's operas exemplify his aesthetic desire to create an authentic American operatic art-form through the use of vernacular musical styles, as well as his attempt to break down the divisions between popular culture and serious art.

*

G. Blair: 'Evening the Score', *New York Daily News Magazine* (28 Sept 1986)

J. Rockwell: 'Malcolm X – hero to some, racist to others – is now the stuff of opera', *New York Times* (28 Sept 1986)

K. R. Schwarz: ' ... and an Opera from Outer Space', *New York Times* (11 June 1989)

R. H. Kornick: *Recent American Opera: a Production Guide* (New York, 1991), 76–7

MARY LOU HUMPHREY

Davis, Sir **Colin (Rex)** (*b* Weybridge, 25 Sept 1927). English conductor. He studied the clarinet at the RCM, but as he was not a pianist he was barred from the conducting class and could not become a répétiteur. Instead he gained practical experience conducting the Chelsea Opera Group, in Mozart performances at Oxford and Cambridge in the early 1950s which drew praise for their vivacity and sensitivity. He achieved prominence when he replaced Klemperer in a concert performance of *Don Giovanni* at the Royal Festival Hall in 1959, following his début in 1958 at Sadler's Wells Opera (*Die Entführung*), where he was named chief conductor in 1959 and music director, 1961–5. There he conducted a wide variety of operas, introducing Weill's *Mahagonny*, Pizzetti's *Assassinio nella cattedrale* and Janáček's *The Cunning Little Vixen* to the British public, and conducting the première of Bennett's *The Mines of Sulphur* (1965).

Davis replaced an ailing Beecham for *Die Zauberflöte* at Glyndebourne in 1960 and made his Covent Garden début in 1965 with *Le nozze di Figaro*. He conducted *Peter Grimes* for his début at the Metropolitan Opera in 1967. In 1971 he succeeded Solti as music director of the Royal Opera, after establishing his authority in Berlioz with *Les Troyens* there in 1969 and his support for Tippett in the première of *The Knot Garden* (1970), followed in 1977 by *The Ice Break*, which is dedicated to him. In that year he became the first British conductor at Bayreuth (*Tannhäuser*), and he led the Royal Opera tours to La Scala (1976) and South Korea and Japan (1979).

During his 15 years at Covent Garden Davis conducted more than 30 operas, including the first British production in 1981 of the completed three-act *Lulu:* He had particular successes in Mozart, Berlioz and Tippett, but it was some time before he mastered the long lines of Verdi and the sonorities and rhythmic breadth of Wagner: his *Ring* performances (1974–6) failed to win unanimous approval.

After leaving Covent Garden, Davis worked mainly in the symphonic repertory, notably in Munich, Dresden and Vienna, where he also had success at the Staatsoper from 1986. He returned often to the Royal Opera House, conducting Mozart operas and some Puccini, and in 1990 received the house's 25-year silver medal. He was made a CBE in 1965 and knighted in 1980, and has received comparable honours from France (Légion d'honneur), Germany (Order of Merit) and Italy (Commendatore).

Davis has recorded more than 20 operas, among them all of Berlioz, the principal operas of Mozart (including *Figaro* twice, *Idomeneo* twice and *La clemenza di Tito*), Britten's *Peter Grimes* and Tippett's *The Midsummer Marriage* and *The Knot Garden*. His *Tannhäuser* at Bayreuth was filmed, and his video films include *The Turn of the Screw*.

*

H. Matheopoulos: 'Sir Colin Davis', *Maestro: Encounters with Conductors of Today* (London, 1982), 147–66

A. Clark: 'The Age of Reason', *Classical Music* (15 Sept 1990), 11–13

NOËL GOODWIN

Davis, John (*b* Paris, 1773; *d* Mandeville, LA, 13 June 1839). Entrepreneur and impresario of French birth. He arrived in New Orleans in 1809; in 1819 he completed the rebuilding of the Théâtre d'Orléans (destroyed by fire in 1816), which under his management became a centre of musical and theatrical life in New Orleans. His opera company used French singers, instrumentalists and dancers, and mounted 464 performances of 140 operas during its first five years, including American premières of works by Auber, Boieldieu, Spontini, Rossini, Hérold, Isouard and Donizetti. Between 1827 and 1833 Davis took the company on six tours to New York, Philadelphia, Boston and Baltimore, to great acclaim. Although most of the touring repertory had been performed in New Orleans, the first northeastern performances of much of it have been erroneously cited as American premières. In 1837 a management crisis and advancing illness forced Davis to retire; his son, Pierre Davis, succeeded him as director of the Théâtre d'Orléans.

*

J. S. Kendall: *The Golden Age of the New Orleans Theatre* (Baton Rouge, LA, 1952)

J. Belsom: *Reception of Major Operatic Premières in New Orleans during the Nineteenth Century* (thesis, Louisiana State U., 1955)

S. Chevalley: 'Le Théâtre d'Orléans en tournée dans les villes du nord, 1827–1833', *Comptes rendus de l'Athenee louisianais* (New Orleans, 1955), 27–71

H. A. Kmen: *Music in New Orleans: the Formative Years, 1791–1841* (Baton Rouge, LA, 1966)

JOHN JOYCE, KATHERINE K. PRESTON

Davis [Davies, Davys], **Mary** [Moll] (*b c*1650; *d* after 1698). English soprano, dancer and actress. She appeared on stage from the early 1660s and was particularly praised, by Pepys and others, for her dancing. Late in 1667 her singing of 'My lodging it is on the cold ground' so pleased Charles II that it 'Rais'd her from her Bed on the Cold Ground, to a Bed Royal' (Downes, p.24; 1987 edn, p.55). She sang and danced at court, appearing in Crowne's masque *Calisto* in 1675 and singing Venus in Blow's *Venus and Adonis* (*c*1682), in which her daughter by the king, Lady Mary Tudor, was Cupid.

*

BDA; *LS*
J. Downes: *Roscius Anglicanus* (London, 1708); ed. J. Milhous and R. D. Hume (London, 1987)
J. H. Wilson: *All the King's Ladies* (Chicago, 1958)
O. Baldwin and T. Wilson: 'An English Calisto', *MT*, cxii (1971), 651–3
R. Luckett: 'A New Source for Venus and Adonis', *MT*, cxxx (1989), 76–9 OLIVE BALDWIN, THELMA WILSON

Davy, Gloria (*b* New York, 29 March 1931). American soprano. She studied with Belle Julie Soudent at the Juilliard School. In 1953 she scored a notable success in a world tour of *Porgy and Bess* and then sang the Countess in the American première of *Capriccio* at the Juilliard in 1954. She made her European début in 1957 at Nice as Aida, the role in which she also made her débuts at the Metropolitan (1958), the Vienna Staatsoper (1959) and Covent Garden (1960). Her other roles included Pamina, Nedda and Leonora (*Il trovatore*). She appeared in Milan, Brussels and Berlin, where she was engaged at the Deutsche Oper (1963–8). She had a lyrical voice and an appealing stage presence.
RICHARD BERNAS, ELIZABETH FORBES

Davy, John (*b* Upton Hellions, nr Crediton, 23 Dec 1763; *d* London, 22 Feb 1824). English composer. He was brought up by a Devon blacksmith who played the cello, and by the age of 12 was an articled pupil of William Jackson, organist of Exeter Cathedral. Later he moved to London where he played the violin in the Covent Garden orchestra. His first two theatrical scores, the opera *A Pennyworth of Wit* (which had no spoken dialogue) and the ballet *Alfred the Great*, were for Sadler's Wells. He was 37 before he had a chance to write an opera for a West End theatre, *What a Blunder!*, his most ambitious work. It had the usual spoken dialogue, a heroine called Leonora and a Spanish setting; the songs and ensembles are unremarkable, but the overture is among the best of its time. The themes are interesting and tautly developed with adventurous modulations in the Viennese style. (The work survives only in piano arrangement.) Davy's natural bent was for instrumental music, but he had to spend most of his creative energy collaborating with indifferent composers in a succession of trivial Covent Garden operas, ballets and pantomimes, and as he lost heart his own contribution lapsed into near nonsense. Between 1808 and 1818 he composed hardly anything. His last theatre score, for *The Tempest*, was no more than a pastiche. By this time Davy was drinking too much, and he died in poverty.

all first performed in London; all printed works published in London

LCG – *Covent Garden* LLH – *Little Theatre, Haymarket*

A Pennyworth of Wit, or The Wife and the Mistress (T. J. Dibdin), Sadler's Wells, 18 April 1796
What a Blunder! (comic op, 3, J. G. Holman), LLH, 14 Aug 1800, vs as op.5 (1800)
The Cabinet (comic op, Dibdin), LCG, 9 Feb 1802, vs (1802); collab. Braham, Corri, Moorehead and Reeve
The Caffres, or Buried Alive (E. Eyre), LCG, 2 June 1802
The Miller's Maid (F. Waldron), LLH, 25 Aug 1804
Thirty Thousand, or Who's the Richest? (Dibdin, after M. Edgeworth), LCG, 10 Dec 1804, vs (1805); collab. Braham and Reeve
Spanish Dollars, or The Priest of the Parish (A. Cherry), LCG, 9 May 1805, vs (1805)
The Blind Boy (melodrama, W. B. Hewetson), LCG, 1 Dec 1808, ov., background music and song (1806)
The Lord of the Manor (3, J. Burgoyne), LCG, 24 Oct 1812, *GB-Lcm*; after Jackson's opera; collab. Bishop, Doyle, Reeve, R. Welsh
The Farmer's Wife (comic op, 3, C. Dibdin jr), LCG, 1 Feb 1814; collab. Bishop, Reeve and others
Rob Roy Macgregor, or Auld Lang Syne (I. Pocock, after W. Scott), LCG, 12 March 1818, vs as op.15 (1819); 1 chorus by Bishop
The Fisherman's Hut (melodrama, J. Tobin), Drury Lane, 20 Oct 1819, songs (1819); collab. M. P. King
Women's Will – a Riddle (E. L. Swift), LCG, 20 July 1820, vs as op.16 (*c*1820)
The Tempest (after W. Shakespeare), LCG, 15 May 1821, ov. and addl music to F. Reynolds's version, with other music by H. Purcell, T. A. Arne and T. Linley (ii), vs (1821)

*

DNB (G. Goodwin)
The Thespian Dictionary (London, 1805)
Obituary, *Gentleman's Magazine*, xciv (1824), 280–81
ROGER FISKE

Dawson, Lynne (*b* York, 3 June 1956). English soprano. She studied at the GSM. She made her début as the Countess with Kent Opera in 1986 and sang Monteverdi's Orfeo (a role she later recorded) at Florence the following year. Her other roles have included Zdenka in *Arabella* (1988) and Xiphares in *Mitridate* (1991), both at the Châtelet, Paris; Pamina for Scottish Opera (1988) and Konstanze at La Monnaie (1990); and Teresa (*Benvenuto Cellini*) at Amsterdam in 1991. She is a good linguist and has brought particular conviction and charm to the roles of Angelica in Handel's *Orlando*, Pamina, and Sandrina in Mozart's *La finta giardiniera*. Her warmly coloured, clear-textured voice, with its sensitively controlled vibrato, is admirably suited to the Baroque and Classical repertory. Her unaffected personality and interpretative freshness communicate themselves strongly in English Baroque operas, her recordings of which include *Venus and Adonis*, *Dido and Aeneas*, *The Fairy-Queen* and *Timon of Athens*.
NICHOLAS ANDERSON

Dayton. American city, in Ohio. It is the home of the Dayton Opera Association, formed in 1960 by William Reiley, a Methodist minister who had been transferred from Toledo, and his wife, Mildred, a member of the Toledo Opera chorus. They convinced the director of the Toledo Opera, Lester Freedman, that he should create a second company to share production costs. The Dayton Opera opened with single performances at the Memorial Hall of *Tosca*, *Il barbiere di Siviglia* and *Rigoletto*. In 1975 the Dayton Performing Arts Fund was established to stabilize arts organizations in the city. The company's season expanded to four productions in 1976, including *Aida* with Martina Arroyo. In 1981 David DiChiera, general director, of the Michigan Opera Theatre in Detroit, was named artistic director, and production sharing was transferred from Toledo to Detroit. By 1984 the Dayton Opera had settled into an annual pattern of 12 performances of three productions, including one light opera or musical. By 1990 the company was attracting 24 000 patrons annually. The company's home, Memorial Hall, is a proscenium house, built in 1910, with 2489 seats. In 1991 Jane D. Nelson was named general director and the company cut its ties with Detroit.
NANCY MALITZ

Dead Souls. Opera by R. K. Shchedrin; *see* MYORTVÏYE DUSHI.

De Ahna(-Strauss), Pauline (*b* Ingolstadt, 4 Feb 1863; *d* Garmisch, 13 May 1950). German soprano. She studied in Munich, then took lessons with Richard Strauss at Feldafing (1887); she made her début in 1890 as Pamina at Weimar. In 1891 she appeared at Bayreuth, singing Elisabeth (*Tannhäuser*) and a flowermaiden (*Parsifal*). In 1894 at Weimar she created Freihild in *Guntram*, the first opera by Richard Strauss, whom she subsequently married. Her repertory also included Agathe, Leonore (*Fidelio*), Donna Anna, and Ada in *Die Feen*, which she sang in Munich (1896). She retired from the stage in 1897 and is immortalized as Christine Storch in her husband's opera *Intermezzo*. The echo of her beautiful voice can be heard in the series of superb roles for soprano in Strauss's later operas from Salome to the Countess Madeleine in *Capriccio*.

For illustration *see* STRAUSS, RICHARD, fig.1. ELIZABETH FORBES

De Amicis [De Amicis-Buonsollazzi], **Anna Lucia** (*b* Naples, *c*1733; *d* Naples, 1816). Italian soprano. She began performing in comic operas with her family in the 1750s in Italy, Paris and Brussels, then in 1762 made her London début at the King's Theatre. Following her début as a serious singer in J. C. Bach's *Orione* (1763), she left comic opera. As prima donna in Milan (1764–5), Venice (1764), Innsbruck (1765) and Naples (1766), she became involved in theatrical disputes and wished to retire. But after marriage (1768) to a Florentine physician she resumed her career, singing in Venice (1768–9, 1770–71) and Naples (1769–70, 1771–2, in Jommelli's *Armida abbandonata* and *Ifigenia in Tauride*). Mozart praised her highly, and in the role of Junia she ensured the success of his *Lucio Silla* in Milan (1772). Engagements in Naples (1773–6), Turin (1776–9) and the Italian première of Gluck's *Alceste* (1778, Bologna) concluded her brilliant career, though she sang for at least another ten years in private Neapolitan productions.

De Amicis amazed listeners with her vocal agility. Burney described her as the first to sing staccato divisions, and the first to 'go up to E flat in altissimo, with true, clear, and powerful *real* voice'. She was equally impressive as an actress: Metastasio wrote that 'among the dramatic heroines ... there was absolutely no one but the signora De Amicis suited to portray the character ... with the fire, the boldness, the frankness, and the expression necessary'.

BurneyH; *ES* (U. Prota-Giurleo and E. Zanetti); *LS*
E. Anderson, ed.: *The Letters of Mozart and his Family* (London, 1938, 3/1985)
B. Brunelli, ed.: *Tutte le opere di Pietro Metastasio*, iv–v (Milan, 1954) KATHLEEN KUZMICK HANSELL

Dean, Stafford (Roderick) (*b* Kingswood, Surrey, 20 June 1937). English bass. He studied with Gordon Clinton at the RCM and privately with Howell Glynne and Otakar Kraus. After touring with Opera for All, he made his Glyndebourne début in 1964 (Lictor in *L'incoronazione di Poppea*). His first role at Sadler's Wells the same year was Zuniga (*Carmen*), followed by, among others, Daland, Sparafucile, Colline and Pluto in Monteverdi's *Orfeo*. At Covent Garden he has played Masetto (début 1969), the He-Ancient (*The Midsummer Marriage*), Publius (*La clemenza di Tito*), Le Bailli (*Werther*), Don Alfonso, Alfonso (*Lucrezia Borgia*), Bottom and Gesler (*Guillaume Tell*) in 1990; but the two parts that have most advanced an international career have been Leporello (in London, Stuttgart and San Francisco) and Figaro (for Scottish Opera, widely in Europe and, in February 1976, at the Metropolitan). His sonorous, dark tone lends individuality to good-humoured, sturdily conceived portrayals such as Osmin (1982, Scottish Opera), Ptolemy in *Giulio Cesare* (1985, Zürich) and Don Pedro in *Béatrice et Bénédict* (1990, ENO). MAX LOPPERT

Dean, Winton (Basil) (*b* Birkenhead, 18 March 1916). English writer on music. A son of Basil Dean, the theatre producer, he studied at King's College, Cambridge (MA 1941), and privately with Philip Radcliffe. At Cambridge he saw and participated in some of the Handel oratorio stagings of the 1930s, which implanted a deep feeling for Handel as a dramatic composer. After World War II he became known as a writer on music and especially on 19th-century opera, publishing a study of Bizet (1948) notable for its balanced criticism and penetrating discussion of the composer as a musical dramatist. His regular opera criticism (in the *Musical Times* and *Opera*) has been notable for its vigorous yet elegant expression and its clear view of the nature of musical drama.

Dean's most important works are *Handel's Dramatic Oratorios and Masques* (1959) and (with J. Merrill Knapp) his study of Handel's operas up to 1726, which set new standards in Handel scholarship with their combination of criticism and source study, and did much to influence the revival of Handel's dramatic works. He has prepared a number of editions, including (in collaboration with Sarah Fuller) Handel's *Giulio Cesare in Egitto*. While Handel remains at the centre of his studies, he has written with distinction on other topics, notably French opera in the post-Revolution period and Italian opera in the decades preceding Verdi. He contributed on early 19th-century opera to the eighth volume of the *New Oxford History of Music*.

Bizet (London, 1948, enlarged 2/1965 as *Georges Bizet: his Life and Work*, 3/1976)
Handel's Dramatic Oratorios and Masques (London, 1959)
Handel and the Opera Seria (Berkeley, 1969)
with J. M. Knapp: *Handel's Operas, 1704–1726* (Oxford, 1987)
Essays on Opera (Oxford, 1990) STANLEY SADIE

De Andrade, Francisco. *See* D'ANDRADE, FRANCISCO.

De Angelis, Nazzareno (*b* Rome, 17 Nov 1881; *d* Rome, 14 Dec 1962). Italian bass. After singing as a boy chorister in Rome, he studied with Ricci and Prati. He made his début in 1903 at Aquila in *Linda di Chamounix*. During the 1906–7 season he appeared at La Scala in *La Gioconda*, *Tristan* and *Aida*, among other operas; he sang there nearly every year until 1914, then occasionally between 1918 and 1933, in *La vestale* (1908), *Les vêpres siciliennes* (1909), *Médée* (1910), *Norma* (1912), *Nabucco* (1913), *L'amore dei tre re* (the first performance, 1913), *Mosè* (1918), *Mefistofele* (1918), *Die Walküre* (1924) – all, with *Il barbiere di Siviglia* and *Don Carlos*, strong points of his repertory. Between 1909 and 1925 he sang in South America and between 1910 and 1920 at the Chicago Auditorium. He retired in 1938. De Angelis's voice was large in volume and range, with a rich timbre skilfully varied by inflection and shading. A vigorous actor and a master of phrasing, he was the finest Italian bass between 1910 and 1930.

GV (R. Celletti; R. Vegeto) RODOLFO CELLETTI

De Araújo, João Gomes. *See* GOMES DE ARAÚJO, JOÃO.

Death in Venice. Opera in two acts (17 scenes), op.88, by BENJAMIN BRITTEN to a libretto by MYFANWY PIPER based on THOMAS MANN's novella *Der Tod in Venedig*; Snape, the Maltings, 16 June 1973.

Gustav von Aschenbach *a novelist*	tenor
The Traveller *who also sings:*	
The Elderly Fop The Old Gondolier The Hotel Manager The Hotel Barber The Leader of the Players The Voice of Dionysus	bass-baritone
The Voice of Apollo	countertenor
The Polish Mother	
Tadzio *her son* Jaschiu *his friend*	choreographed

Youths and girls, hotel guests and waiters, gondoliers and boatmen, street vendors, touts and beggars, citizens of Venice, choir in St Mark's, tourists, followers of Dionysus

Choreographed roles: Tadzio's two sisters, his governess, other boys and girls, strolling players, beach attendants

Setting Munich and Venice

Britten had *Death in Venice* in mind as an operatic subject for many years, and in September 1970, very soon after the completion of *Owen Wingrave*, he invited Myfanwy Piper to write the libretto. She had finished a draft of Act 1 by September 1971, and it seems probable that Britten began the music that December, using preliminary sketches made during an autumn visit to Venice. The opera was complete by the end of 1972, although some quite significant changes were still to come, and additional modifications were made between the première and the publication of the vocal score in 1975.

Of all Britten's operas, *Death in Venice* is the most dependent on the particular vocal qualities of Peter Pears, to whom it is dedicated. The intimate, intense character of the music reflects the refinement and delicacy of the Pears sound at that relatively late stage of his career, and the musical idiom – an economical blend of Britten's personal adaptation of 12-note features in association with those fundamental elements of tonal harmony that he never abandoned – is the fullest demonstration of the flexibility and focus of Britten's own late style. Not surprisingly, Pears was an indispensable asset to early revivals of the work after the première, as was John Shirley-Quirk in the bass-baritone roles. The opera's Covent Garden première was in October 1973 and its Metropolitan première in October 1974. A recording, conducted by Steuart Bedford, was made at Snape in April 1974.

ACT 1.i *Munich* The 'master writer' Aschenbach is weary and unable to work, but affirms his belief in order rather than passion. A traveller appears, whose account of the mysterious marvels of distant places stirs Aschenbach's desire to 'travel to the south'. In the first of the 'quasi parlando' recitatives with piano that are a special feature of the work (the pitches moulded to the inflections of Pears's speaking voice), Aschenbach persuades himself that such a journey may restore his 'flagging inspiration'.

1.ii *On the boat to Venice* This scene is punctuated by a haunting refrain on the word 'Serenissima' (adapting the 'magic' motif of the traveller's music from scene i). Among the predominantly young and lighthearted passengers is an elderly fop, rouged and dressed in a forlorn attempt to belie his age. Aschenbach is apprehensive that Venice will not provide its usual welcome. The scene ends with an interlude in barcarolle style, called 'overture', evoking the waters and bells of the city.

1.iii *The journey to the Lido* Aschenbach's belief in the healing powers of Venice is restored, despite the sinister refusal of his gondolier to obey orders, or wait to be paid. In a lyrical arioso Aschenbach muses on the fact that a black gondola is 'a vision of death itself'.

1.iv *The first evening at the hotel* The manager sings the praises of his establishment. To an expansive, consonant yet tonally unstable motif the obsequious manager shows the writer the view of the beach from his room, then leaves Aschenbach to reflect in recitative on his aims and ambitions as a creative artist. After a while he is drawn back to the view before him. Among the hotel guests from various countries who pass he notices a Polish family, including a boy of great physical beauty (characterized by a sinuous modal motif on the vibraphone) whose name, he learns, is Tadzio. Aschenbach meditates on the irresolvably ambiguous relation between the artist's sense of beauty and his desire to achieve a purely formal perfection.

1.v *On the beach* Aschenbach finds the atmosphere oppressive and cannot work, but nevertheless wishes to remain in Venice. As he watches, Tadzio arrives on the beach with his family and plays with other children, who accept him as their leader. Aschenbach reflects that he feels 'a father's warmth' for a beauty 'I might have created'.

1.vi *The foiled departure* Crossing from the Lido to Venice proper, which is crowded and stifling, Aschenbach resolves to leave. Back at the hotel he informs the manager of his decision, but after crossing to the city once more to take the train back to Germany, he learns that his baggage has been sent to Como. He returns to the hotel, both angry and delighted that his departure has been prevented. Seeing Tadzio on the beach, he makes a firm decision to stay on.

1.vii *The games of Apollo* Aschenbach witnesses beach sports in which Tadzio takes part: the games are presented in choreographed form with a choral commentary and apostrophes from the voice of Apollo (for illustration *see* DANCE, fig.5). At the end Tadzio's victory is celebrated, and Aschenbach exclaims ecstatically that 'the boy ... shall inspire me ... The power of beauty sets me free'. He develops this theme in an extended lyrical outpouring, and is forced to recognize the truth. As Tadzio passes him on his way into the hotel and smiles at him, Aschenbach confesses – though the boy cannot hear him – 'I love you!'

ACT 2 In a recitative, Aschenbach attempts to come to terms with his love, and regrets his inability even to speak to Tadzio.

2.viii *The hotel barber's shop* He hears the first rumours of a sickness that is causing people to leave Venice, but the barber becomes evasive when questioned.

2.ix *The pursuit* Aschenbach crosses to the city and learns that 'citizens are advised to take precautions against infection', but that 'rumours of cholera' are being denied. His only concern is that the Polish family should not hear such rumours; he begins to follow them about the city and, finally, back to the hotel, still without making any direct contact with Tadzio.

2.x *The strolling players* Aschenbach is with other hotel guests on the terrace after dinner. A troupe of actor-singers presents a parody of courtship, with its leader adding a mock lament, 'So I shall never be able to marry'. Aschenbach accosts the leader, seeking the truth about the possible plague. Once again, the answers are worryingly evasive, and the leader's final song, with its chorus of mocking laughter, turns into a sinister attack on the hotel guests.

2.xi *The travel bureau* Aschenbach arrives as a crowd of visitors seeks information and an early escape from Venice. At first the clerk offers the usual evasive responses, but in the end he admits to Aschenbach that 'death is at work. The plague is with us'. He advises him to leave before the city is blockaded.

2.xii *The lady of the pearls* Aschenbach rehearses how he might warn Tadzio's mother of the danger, but when she appears in the hotel he cannot speak to her. In despair and joy he realizes that all he cares about is his love for Tadzio.

2.xiii *The dream* In a feverish sleep, Aschenbach seems to hear a debate between Apollo and Dionysus: with the victory of Dionysus his followers sing and dance in triumph. Waking, he recognizes that he can 'fall no further'.

2.xiv *The empty beach* Aschenbach watches as Tadzio and a few friends begin to play their beach games, only to abandon them and run off.

2.xv *The hotel barber's shop* He submits to the kind of rouging and hair-colouring that marked the elderly fop in scene ii.

2.xvi *The last visit to Venice* Aschenbach is almost hysterically exuberant in his new guise. Once again he follows the Polish family through the city, ever more strongly convinced that Tadzio understands his feelings and is encouraging him. He buys some strawberries, but they are musty and overripe. Bitterly he recalls his proclamation of his own creative beliefs from scene i, and in an understated yet supremely eloquent arioso summarizes the celebrated Platonic exchange between Socrates and Phaedrus which traces the path from the sensual discovery of beauty to the abyss of passion.

2.xvii *The departure* This begins with a richly orchestrated fantasia on the 'view' motif from scene iv. The hotel manager and a porter discuss the departure of the guests. Aschenbach learns that the Polish family is about to leave, and the manager assumes that Aschenbach himself will soon follow them. Tadzio and a few other children play on the beach, and this time the game turns rough, with Tadzio being knocked down, his face pressed into the sand by Jaschiu. As Aschenbach cries out the boy gets up, unharmed. Aschenbach calls Tadzio's name, and, when the boy beckons him, collapses and dies in his chair. To a short postlude combining Tadzio's unearthly theme and the melody from scene vii for Aschenbach's phrase about the indissoluble fusion of feeling and thought, 'Tadzio continues his walk far out to sea'.

* * *

Britten's *Death in Venice* will always seem disconcerting to those who believe that Mann's claustrophobically intense story demands a music of Bergian expressionistic force – or Mahlerian nostalgia, as in Visconti's film – to do it justice. Yet Britten's relatively narrow range of tone colours, with the dry piano of Aschenbach's recitatives at one extreme and the gamelan-style tuned percussion for Tadzio and the beach games at the other, together with his unfailingly concise musical forms, bring Aschenbach's inhibitedness and obsession with the structures of art unerringly into the dramatic foreground. It is clear that we are seeing Venice solely through Aschenbach's eyes, and the simplicity with which the enticing Tadzio and Aschenbach's own fumbling attempts to express love are represented demonstrate how justified Britten was in trusting his own aesthetic principle and in 'tear[ing] all the waste away'. Only a deeply prejudiced ear could mistake this directness and economy for blandness or superficiality, and the opera's hushed ending is an inspired synthesis of the work's most memorable qualities – intensity and restraint. ARNOLD WHITTALL

Death of Dido, The. Masque in two entertainments by JOHANN CHRISTOPH PEPUSCH to a libretto by Barton Booth after VIRGIL's *Aeneid*, book iv; London, Drury Lane, 17 April 1716.

Pepusch's only substantial contribution as a composer of extended musical dramas for the theatre is four masque-type afterpieces, written during the period 1714–16 while he was musical director at Drury Lane. *The Death of Dido*, the last of them, has four principal characters: Dido (soprano), Aeneas (mezzo-soprano, sung as a travesty role), Mercury (tenor) and Doris (soprano). The librettist, Barton Booth (1681–1733), though well known in 1716 as an actor and theatre manager, had no experience in writing for the stage, and *Dido* was to be his only dramatic piece. He nevertheless managed to develop a tender love story within a compact and fast-moving plot.

Pepusch's music for *The Death of Dido*, like that of his earlier masques, is distinctly and intentionally italianate, employing parlando recitatives, da capo arias, and Italian orchestration of strings and woodwinds. Though only a few of the arias appeared as printed broadsheets, a full manuscript score survives (*GB-Lam*). The two-movement overture is simple in construction: short, thinly scored and favouring three-part textures. The musical highlight comes in the Second Entertainment, when Aeneas accepts that his divine mission must supersede his love for Dido in 'Let me die renowned in story', an intimate aria of fragile beauty. In Dido's lament, 'Oh, I feel the friendly blow', occasion- al suspensions in the flute obbligato and voice provide the desired effect, but the aria is not as memorable as 'Welcome, gentle death' in Pepusch's *Venus and Adonis* (1715), and certainly bears no comparison with the famous lament in Purcell's *Dido and Aeneas* (1689).

Pepusch's *Dido* was not performed again in the 18th century after 1716. However, it had a modern revival at Holme Pierrepont Hall, Nottingham, 14–19 September 1981. D. F. COOK

Deathridge, John (William) (*b* Birmingham, 21 Oct 1944). English musicologist. He studied at Oxford University with Egon Wellesz and Frederick Sternfeld, completing in 1973 a dissertation on the sketches of Wagner's *Rienzi* which was later published (Oxford, 1977). During the 1970s and early 80s he lived in Germany, continuing his research on Wagner and working as an organist, conductor and broadcaster. He returned to England in 1983 to become a Fellow of King's College, Cambridge, and has been a visiting professor at Princeton University (1990–91) and the University of Chicago (1992). His *New Grove Wagner* (with Carl Dahlhaus) appeared in 1984, and the *Verzeichnis der musikalischen Werke Richard Wagners und ihre Quellen* (with Martin Geck and Egon Voss) in 1986; these, as well as numerous articles, reviews and radio programmes on Wagner, have assured him an important place among Wagner scholars of his generation. His other interests include the symphonic repertory of the 19th century and 20th-century opera.

De Bassini, Achille (*b* Milan, 5 May 1819; *d* Cava de' Tirreni, 3 Sept 1881). Italian baritone. He made his début in 1837 at Voghera in the title role of Donizetti's *Belisario*. Engaged at La Scala, he sang William Tell, Figaro (*Barbiere*) and Don Carlo (*Ernani*) there. He created roles in four Verdi operas: the Doge in *I due Foscari* (1844, Rome); Seid in *Il corsaro* (1848, Trieste); Miller in *Luisa Miller* (1849, Naples); and Melitone in *La forza del destino* (1862, St Petersburg). In 1859 he sang at Covent Garden as Germont, Rodolfo (*La sonnambula*) and Luna, and in Mercadante's *Il giuramento*. His wife, the soprano Rita Gabussi-De Bassini (*b* Bologna *c*1815; *d* Naples, 26 Jan 1891), sang at La Scala and at S Carlo, where she created the title role of Mercadante's *Medea* (1851). Their son, Alberto De Bassini (*b* Florence, 14 July 1847; *d* after 1890), made his début as a tenor in 1869 at Venice, then sang widely in Italy and in Russia. In 1890 he became a baritone and later sang with touring companies in the USA.

ELIZABETH FORBES

De Begnis, Giuseppe. *See* BEGNIS, GIUSEPPE DE.

De Blanck, Hubert (*b* Utrecht, 11 June 1856; *d* Havana, 28 Nov 1932). Dutch composer, later naturalized Cuban. He attended the Liège conservatory and began a career as a pianist, touring extensively in Europe. In 1880 he went to Latin America, then the following year to the USA. He visited Cuba in 1883 and decided to settle there. In 1885 he founded the first Cuban conservatory, which he directed until his death. He wrote three operas, all to librettos by Ramón Espinosa de los Monteros. Only the second, *Patria*, in two tableaux, was performed (the prelude and second tableau at the Teatro Tacón, Havana, on 1 December 1889, the complete work at the Teatro Payret, Havana, on 21 September 1905). *Patria* is set in Cuba during the 1895 war. Although it observes late 19th-century operatic conventions its music has an originality in which no influences are discernible and includes such Cuban forms as the *criolla* and habanera, as well as quoting part of the Cuban national anthem. *Actea* (composed *c*1892), also in two tableaux, takes as its subject Nero's participation under an assumed name in the Olympic games; *Hicaona*, written about seven years later, is set in pre-Columbian Cuba and is in three acts.

O. Martinez: *Hubert de Blanck, vida y obra* (Havana, 1956)
J. Ardévol: *Introducción a Cuba: la música* (Havana, 1969)
A. Carpentier: *La música en Cuba* (Havana, 2/1979)
J. A. González: *La composición operística en Cuba* (Havana, 1986)

JORGE ANTONIO GONZÁLEZ

Dèbora e Jaéle ('Deborah and Jael'). Opera in three acts by ILDEBRANDO PIZZETTI to his own libretto, freely based on *Judges* iv and v; Milan, Teatro alla Scala, 16 December 1922.

Pizzetti's adaptation, begun in 1915, of the well-known Old Testament story preserves the external outline of the original (Jael does indeed end up driving a tent-peg into the sleeping Sisera's skull); but the motivation is completely transformed and the distribution of good and evil almost reversed. Deborah (mezzo-soprano) is depicted as the inflexible representative of the established Jewish law, whereas Sisera (tenor) – who is here himself the King of Canaan – is a far more complex and interesting character. Having been to Greece in Phoenician ships, he has begun to develop an alternative vision of life which makes him feel estranged from his own people. Jael (soprano) too, in a more purely instinctive way, senses that the old law is not the absolute truth, but needs to be superseded by something higher. Consequently, when sent by Deborah to persuade Sisera to lead his army into a situation where defeat will be inevitable, she finds that there is a bond of sympathy between her and the king which quickly gives rise to a conflict between love and duty. Later, when (as in the biblical story) the defeated Sisera takes refuge in Jael's tent, their love is renewed; and the king then falls asleep, profoundly exhausted. The victorious Israelites are heard closing in from all sides; whereupon Jael, in panic, decides to kill Sisera herself before he awakes, rather than expose him to the worse death that would await him if he were found there alive.

Although neither the logic of the plot nor Pizzetti's literary style stands up entirely to detailed scrutiny, the effect in the theatre is profoundly moving, thanks to some of the most evocative music by any Italian composer of the 20th century. The methods used in the composer's earlier opera *Fedra*, though preserved in principle, are reinforced by important new elements. The chorus has a still more prominent part than in the earlier opera, sometimes dwarfing the individual characters: this is especially the case in the darkly turbulent first half of Act 1, where a debt to *Boris Godunov* is evident in the complex subdivision of the choral body into interacting groups. Another important new influence is that of Bloch – appropriately enough in a work on a biblical subject. Again there are occasional longueurs: Pizzetti's penchant for longwinded ethical discourses weighs heavily, for example, on Deborah's harangue in the latter part of Act 1. Yet although the opera (whose music was composed during 1917–21) is not all on a level with its best parts, its exceptionally high standing with Italian critics up to the early 1960s is as understandable as its total neglect since then is outrageous.

The changing fortunes of *Dèbora e Jaéle*, indeed, reflect the drastic fluctuations of Pizzetti's Italian reputation in a particularly extreme form. By the time of the work's première he was already being hailed in influential quarters as 'doubtless the greatest musician in Italy today' (G. M. Gatti, writing in 1921), and *Dèbora* soon came to be regarded, despite some dissentient voices, not only as its composer's masterpiece but as one of the supreme peaks in 20th-century Italian opera. In 1956 – by which time the work had been revived many times in Italy, though relatively seldom staged abroad – it was still possible for a large and mixed panel of leading Italian critics to vote it into third place (which it shared with *Salome*) in a choice of the 20 most important and durable operas of the century: only *Pelléas et Mélisande* and *Wozzeck* were awarded more votes. Yet by 1980, Pizzetti's centenary year, his reputation had declined to such a degree that neither *Dèbora* nor any of his other operas was revived in any of Italy's numerous opera houses. A more balanced reassessment is overdue. JOHN C. G. WATERHOUSE

Debrecen. City in eastern Hungary. The first opera performances were given in summer, between 1798 and 1808, by a company from Kolozsvár (now Cluj-Napoca, Romania). It performed Singspiels including, in 1799 (six years after the Buda première), the first Hungarian opera, József Chudy's *Pikkó Hertzeg és Jutka Perzsi*. After summer 1808 the troupe stayed for the whole of 1809 instead of returning to Kolozsvár. Although Debrecen had its own theatre company from 1810, and from 1814 to 1824 shared one with Nagyvárad (now Oradea, Romania), no opera performances are recorded. In 1830 a first-rate company from Kassa (now Košice, Czechoslovakia) presented three Rossini operas in Debrecen, and in 1836 a company from Nagyvárad stayed for several months, performing *Tancredi*, *Freischütz*, József Ruzitska's *Béla futása* ('Béla's Escape'), *Die Schweizerfamilie*, *Der Dorfbarbier* and *Il barbiere di Siviglia*.

The present theatre, the Csokonai Színház (cap. 1500), opened in 1865; it has been frequently restored, most recently in 1958–61. Three companies performed there in the 19th century; none was successful, partly because the best soloists had left for Budapest. The first company presented, as well as the standard Italian repertory, Erkel's *Hunyadi László*, *La muette de Portici*, *Les Huguenots* and *Martha*. Opera performances have been given continuously except during 1881–98, World War I and 1945–52.

In 1949 all theatres became state-owned. The opera section of the Csokonai resumed operations in 1952. Each season eight to ten operas are given; the company also tours. Apart from the standard repertory (mostly Italian) it has presented *Amelia al ballo* (1962), *A Midsummer Night's Dream* (1962), *Mahagonny* (1966) and *Our Man in Havana* (1967).

*

T. Hegyi: *A debreceni szinészet és színház története a legrégibb időktől a kiegyezésig* [History of Performance and Theatre in Debrecen from Oldest Times to the Compromise of 1867] (Debrecen, 1939)

J. Breuer, ed.: *Debrecen zenei élete a századfordulótól napjainkig* [The Musical World of Debrecen from the Turn of the Century to the Present] (Debrecen, 1975)

F. Katona, ed.: *A debreceni színészet története* [History of Performance in Debrecen], i: *1866–1974* (Debrecen, 1976)

Gy. Kertész, M. Lázár, N. Péteri and E. Szabó: *25 éves a debreceni opera* [25 Years of the Debrecen Opera] (Debrecen, 1977)

Á. Gupcsó: 'Zenés színjátszás Debrecenben (1798–1810, 1833–1841)' [Music Theatre in Debrecen], *Zenetudományi dolgozatok* [Budapest] (1980), 259–74; (1981), 101–15; (1985), 113–32; (1986), 65–91 DEZSŐ LEGÁNY

Debussy, (Achille-)Claude (*b* St Germain-en-Laye, 22 Aug 1862; *d* Paris, 25 March 1918). French composer. He completed only one true opera, *Pelléas et Mélisande*, but throughout his life he was constantly planning other theatrical projects. Reaching various stages of fruition, they range from an almost complete conventionally heroic opera in three acts (*Rodrigue et Chimène*) to one-act pieces more in the genre of music theatre, such as the two plays after Edgar Allan Poe, *La chute de la maison Usher* and *Le diable dans le beffroi*. In many of the unfinished projects it is unclear to what extent Debussy envisaged a theatrical presentation, but it is clear that plans for several other operas were at one time or another in his mind.

Debussy's response to literature was encouraged during his teens by his liaison with the singer Marie-Blanche Vasnier, for whom he composed many songs during the early 1880s. In these he confronted the problem of a musical response to the themes and images of contemporary French poetry, notably that of the so-called Parnassians Théodore de Banville and Leconte de Lisle. In turn he moved on to settings of Baudelaire and of the newly emerging symbolists, Verlaine and Mallarmé. Responding to this literature, sharing a distaste for reality and preferring a language of suggestion and symbol, he moved from the *mélodie* to larger-scale dramatic cantatas and eventually to melodrama-type works combining recitation and musical accompaniment.

Among the early projects was the setting of part of Banville's play *Diane au bois*. Not only was it important as a precursor to the *Prélude à l'après-midi d'un faune*; it also caused Debussy to formulate principles concerning the qualities of a libretto suitable for musical setting and ways of approaching the task. In a celebrated interview of the late 1880s with his teacher Ernest Guiraud (Eng. trans. in Lockspeiser 1965–6), he described his ideal text. At the time, it seemed to relate to *Diane au bois*, whose stage directions possibly indicate that he had a staged performance in mind, but his response to the question of what would constitute the ideal librettist would seem more precisely to apply to *Pelléas*:

> One who only states half of what is to be said, and allows me to graft my dream on to his. One who conceives his characters as out of place and out of time, and who does not force on me a 'big scene'. One who, here and there, will allow me the freedom to have a little more art than he – to finish off his work.

Also important among the works from this time is the cantata *La damoiselle élue*, a setting of a celebrated poem by Dante Gabriel Rossetti. Commentators have rightly stressed this work, with its musical portrayal of the pre-Raphaelite *ange-femme*, as embodying an important prototype for the character of Mélisande.

By 1890 Debussy was working on his first real opera, a version of *El Cid* to a libretto supplied by Catulle Mendès. Entitled *Rodrigue et Chimène*, the heroic text with ample military scenes for chorus had none of the qualities already isolated by Debussy as essential for his ideal libretto, and he eventually abandoned the work. In his next venture, the proposed *Prélude, interludes et paraphrase finale* on Mallarmé's *Prélude à l'après-midi d'un faune*, Debussy found a literary source far more in tune with his ideals. Apparently conceived as an accompanimental paraphrase to Mallarmé's extended *eclogue*, it was eventually distilled into the orchestral piece widely considered to be Debussy's first seminally important work.

It was in 1893 that he first read Maurice Maeterlinck's play *Pelléas et Mélisande*. As far as opera was concerned, this was without doubt the most important literary encounter of his life. He began work almost immediately on a setting which bore little relation to the established traditions of 19th-century opera but which has taken its place as one of the most

'Pelléas et Mélisande' (Debussy), Act 1 scene i (a forest; design by Lucien Jusseaume) from the original production at the Opéra-Comique (Salle Favart), Paris, 30 April 1902, with the themes from the orchestral prelude in Debussy's hand: from 'Le théâtre' (June 1902)

frequently performed and highly regarded operas of the 20th century. Making only a few cuts in the text, the work eschews both aria and recitative in their conventional forms, and uses a kind of declamation which only in the most emotional (or symbolic) moments extends into more melodic writing. Instead, most of the musical interplay of motifs and evocation is assigned to the orchestra – the 'décor orchestral', as Debussy himself called it.

In an era when French opera was selfconscious about its debt to Wagner, Debussy's music was for a long time considered to be wholly anti-Wagnerian, an idea fostered by the composer himself in interviews, letters and music-critical writings. Closer analysis has revealed a far more complex relationship between Wagner and Debussy. Although *Pelléas* has many aspects – of prosody, harmony and orchestration in particular – that are not at all Wagnerian, it does have a system of leitmotifs related to its symbolic underlay, although they are more those of *Tristan* and *Parsifal* than the character-linked motifs of Wagner's earlier operas. In addition, Wagner's chromatic harmony, and in particular his use of the half-diminished or so-called *Tristan* chord, is reflected in much of Debussy's harmony in *Pelléas*, though he isolates such devices from the slow-moving forward flow of Wagner's own style.

Debussy was never to complete any sequel to *Pelléas*. Although many theatrical projects are to be found among his abandoned works, none of them is a true opera. The most complete is the problematic *La chute de la maison Usher*, based on Poe's tale. He worked on this over many years and left three versions of the libretto (which he wrote himself) as well as many manuscripts containing small sections of music in various stages of completion. No less important in illuminating Debussy's literary preoccupations, but far less complete, is his other unfinished work based on a Poe tale, *Le diable dans le beffroi*, which he was working on only a month after the first performance of *Pelléas* in 1902. Debussy was adamant in his belief that he should not attempt to capitalize on the success of *Pelléas* by writing a sequel in a similar vein. In a letter to André Messager in 1903 he wrote:

> As for those people who are kind enough to hope that I can never progress from *Pelléas*, they are deliberately shutting their eyes to the truth. They simply do not know that if that were the case I would immediately take up the indoor cultivation of pineapples, considering that the most odious path would be to start all over again in exactly the same way.

Debussy's final phase of music for the theatre coincided with the rising popularity of contemporary ballet, and he wrote several works in that genre during the years following *Pelléas*. Although there were clearly plans for an operatic sequel to *Pelléas*, none progressed far beyond the planning stage except for *La chute de la maison Usher*. Possible reasons were that Debussy's health was declining and literary tastes were changing. Some of his works originally conceived for concert performance were presented in some kind of staged production, the most celebrated being Nizhinsky's interpretation of the *Prélude à l'après-midi d'un faune*. The *scène lyrique L'enfant prodigue* and the symphonic suite *Printemps* were at one time or another treated in this way.

See also CHUTE DE LA MAISON USHER, LA; PELLÉAS ET MÉLISANDE; and RODRIGUE ET CHIMÈNE.

Diane au bois, 1883–6 (after a comédie-héroïque by T. de Banville), inc.; pf reconstruction by E. Lockspeiser, BBC radio, 9 Nov 1968

Rodrigue et Chimène, 1890–92 (3, C. Mendès, after G. de Castro), inc.; extracts with pf reconstruction by R. Langham Smith, Paris, Bibliothèque Nationale, 22 June 1987

Pelléas et Mélisande, 1893–5, 1901–2 (5, M. Maeterlinck, abridged Debussy), Paris, OC (Favart), 30 April 1902; vs, with original short interludes (Paris, 1902); expanded interludes arr. pf (Paris, 1905); rev. vs with expanded interludes (Paris, 1907); full score (Paris, 1905, rev. 1966); sketches (Geneva, 1977) [facs.]

La chute de la maison Usher, 1908–17 (2 scenes, Debussy, after E. A. Poe), inc., originally planned as 3 scenes; text and facs. in Lockspeiser: *Debussy et Edgar Poe* (Monaco, 1962); reconstruction by C. Abbate, New Haven, 25 Feb 1977; reconstruction by J. Allende-Blin, vs (Paris, 1979)

PROJECTED WORKS

Florise, *c*1882 (Banville)

Hymnis, *c*1882 (Banville), frags. incl. one song and an *Ode bacchique*

Salammbô, *c*1886 (G. Flaubert)

Axël, *c*1887–9 (J. M. M. P. A. de Villiers de l'Isle-Adam), scene i completed, lost

La princesse Maleine, 1891 (op, Maeterlinck)

Cendrelune, 1895–8 (fairy-tale op, P. Louÿs)

La grande bretèche, 1895 (Debussy, after H. de Balzac)

Les uns et les autres, 1896 (comedy in verse, 1, P. Verlaine)

Le chevalier d'or, 1897 (Rosicrucian pantomime, J.-L. Forain), musical plan completed

Amphion [Orphée], *c*1900 (experimental ballet and later op, P. Valéry)

Le diable dans le beffroi, 1902–12 (Poe), scenario and sketches extant, in Lockspeiser (1962)

Joyzelle, ?1903 (Maeterlinck)

Don Juan, *c*1903, mentioned by Albert Carré

Dionysos, 1904–5 (J. Gasquet)

L'histoire de Tristan, 1907–12 (op, 4, G. Mourey), one theme quoted by Debussy in a letter to Durand

Orphée-roi, 1907–16 (op, V. Segalen)

L'orestie, 1909 (op, L. Laloy, after Aeschylus)

Crimen amoris, rev. as Fêtes galantes, 1912–15 (opéra-ballet, C. Morice), sketches extant

Drame indien, *c*1914 (G. d'Annunzio)

*

J. Durand: *Quelques souvenirs d'un éditeur de musique* (Paris, 1924–5)

M. Emmanuel: *Pelléas et Mélisande* (Paris, 1926)

J. Durand, ed.: *Lettres de Claude Debussy à son éditeur* (Paris, 1927)

D.-E. Inghelbrecht: *Comment on ne doit pas interpréter 'Carmen', 'Faust' et 'Pelléas'* (Paris, 1933)

J. André-Messager, ed.: *L'enfance de 'Pelléas': lettres de Claude Debussy à André Messager* (Paris, 1938)

G. Gatti-Casazza: *Memories of the Opera* (New York, 1941)

J. Chailley: 'Le symbolisme des thèmes dans *Pelléas et Mélisande*', *L'information musicale*, no. 64 (1942), 889–90

A. Cortot: 'Un drame lyrique de Claude Debussy: *Rodrigue et Chimène*', *Inédits sur Claude Debussy*, ed. A. Hoérée (Paris, 1942), 12–16

P. Dukas: *Chroniques musicales sur deux siècles* (Paris, 1948)

M. Garden and L. Biancolli: *Mary Garden's Story* (London, 1952)

A. Goléa: *Pelléas et Mélisande* (Paris, 1952)

R. Cogniat: *Cinquante ans de spectacles en France: les décorateurs de théâtre* (Paris, 1955)

J. Kerman: *Opera as Drama* (New York, 1956, 2/1989)

M. Dietschy: *La passion de Claude Debussy* (Neuchâtel, 1962; Eng. trans., 1990)

M. Garden: *Souvenirs de Mélisande* (Liège, 1962)

E. Lockspeiser: *Debussy et Edgar Poe* (Monaco, 1962)

——: *Debussy: his Life and Mind* (London, 1965–6)

G. Favre, ed.: *Correspondance de Paul Dukas* (Paris, 1971)

F. Lesure, ed.: *Claude Debussy: Monsieur Croche et autres écrits* (Paris, 1971, 2/1987; Eng. trans., 1977)

C. Abravanel: *Claude Debussy: a Bibliography* (Detroit, 1974)

F. Lesure: *Debussy*, Iconographie musicale (Geneva, 1975)

R. Orledge: 'Debussy's "House of Usher" Revisited', *MQ*, lxii (1976), 536–53

J. Allende-Blin: 'Eine Dokumentation: "La chute de la maison Usher"', *Musik-Konzepte*, i–ii (1977) [Debussy issue], 3–9, 10–41 [lib.]

F. Lesure: *Catalogue de l'oeuvre de Claude Debussy* (Geneva, 1977)

——, ed.: *Esquisses de 'Pelléas et Mélisande'* (Geneva, 1977) [facs.]
L'avant-scène opéra, no.9 (1977) [*Pelléas et Mélisande* issue]
R. Holloway: *Debussy and Wagner* (London, 1979)
G. O'Connor: *The Pursuit of Perfection: a Life of Maggie Teyte* (London, 1979)
F. Lesure, ed.: *Claude Debussy: lettres 1884–1918* (Paris, 1980; Eng. trans., 1987)
C. Abbate: '*Tristan* in the Composition of *Pelléas*', *19th Century Music*, v (1981–2), 117–41
R. Langham Smith: 'Debussy and the Pre-Raphaelites', *19th Century Music*, v (1981–2), 95–109
N. John, ed.: *Pelléas et Mélisande*, ENO Opera Guides, ix (London, 1982)
R. Orledge: *Debussy and the Theatre* (Cambridge, 1982)
R. Terrasson: *'Pelléas et Mélisande' ou l'initiation* (Paris, 1982)
R. Howat: *Debussy in Proportion* (Cambridge, 1983)
D. Grayson: *The Genesis of Debussy's 'Pelléas et Mélisande'* (Ann Arbor, 1986)
J. Pasler: '"Pelléas" and Power: Forces behind the Reception of Debussy's Opera', *19th Century Music*, xi (1987–8), 147–77
R. Langham Smith: '"Rodrigue et Chimène": genèse, histoire, problèmes d'édition', *Cahiers Debussy*, xii–xiii (1988–9), 67–81
——: 'Un primo sguardo al "Rodrigue et Chimène" di Debussy', *Studi su Debussy: Quaderni di Musica/realtà*, xxi (1989), 194–222
R. Nichols and R. Langham Smith: *Pelléas et Mélisande* (Cambridge, 1989)
J. Briscoe: *Claude Debussy: a Guide to Research* (New York, 1990)
——: 'To invent New Forms: Debussy's Diane au bois', *MQ*, lxxiv (1990), 131–69 RICHARD LANGHAM SMITH

De Camp, Maria Theresa (*b* Vienna, 17 Jan 1775; *d* Addleston, Surrey, 3 Sept 1838). English actress, singer and dancer. Her father, an orchestral flute player, brought his family to London and she danced on stage as a child, gradually taking juvenile acting and singing parts. From 1790 she built up a repertory of roles in musical pieces, an early success being Macheath in a travesty *Beggar's Opera*. Hard-working, intelligent and lively, she had parts in many operas by Storace and Kelly. C. H. Wilson wrote, 'she sings so well, acts so well, dances so well, and looks so well, that she is deservedly a great favourite of the town'. After marrying Charles Kemble in 1806 she generally acted with him but made few appearances after 1813.

*

BDA; *DNB* (J. Knight); *LS*
'Miss De Camp', *Thespian Magazine*, iii (1794), 79–80
C. H. Wilson: *The Myrtle and Vine* (London, 1802)
R. Fiske: *English Theatre Music in the Eighteenth Century* (London, 1973, 2/1986) OLIVE BALDWIN, THELMA WILSON

De Castris [De' Massimi], **Francesco** [Cecchino, Checchino] (*b* Roman Campagna, *c*1650; *d* Rome, late Nov or early Dec 1724). Italian soprano castrato. In Rome he served Cardinal Camillo Massimi until 1677 (hence his nickname). By 1679, when he sang in two operas in Bologna, he was based in Ferrara in the service of Marquis Ippolito Bentivoglio, under whose patronage he often appeared in the Venetian theatres of S Giovanni Grisostomo and S Salvatore; he also sang at St Mark's. His Venetian period is marked by a close connection, both personal and professional, with Giovanni Legrenzi. In 1687 he entered the employ of Ferdinando de' Medici in Florence, where from 1696 he sang in operas by C. F. Pollarolo, A. Scarlatti, Perti and others. His good looks and diplomatic abilities made him a powerful favourite; he was master of the revels and conducted court missions. The decline of his voice – which he admitted in his correspondence with Perti, 1700–01 (*I-Bc*), when he asked for his roles in *Lucio Vero* and *Astianatte* to be adapted – and the hostility provoked by his position at court caused Ferdinando to exile him to Rome; there he lived in the Medici palace (1703–11), still carrying out diplomatic missions for his patron and receiving a good pension from Florence. In his younger years (*c*1680) De Castris's compass was limited (approximately *d*♯′ to *g*″), and he apparently tended to stay within the higher register with coloratura passages. He mostly took the roles of seductive women, or rejected male lovers and political conspirators; later he turned to heroic characters. He should not be confused with Francesco Castri from Bologna, Domenico Cecchi ('il Cortona') or Francesco de Grandis from Verona ('Checchino').

*

C. Ricci: *I teatri di Bologna nei secoli XVII e XVIII* (Bologna, 1888)
R. Lustig: 'Per la cronistoria dell'antico teatro musicale: il teatro della villa medicea di Pratolino', *RMI*, xxxvi (1929), 259–66
M. De Angelis: 'Il teatro di Pratolino tra Scarlatti e Perti: il carteggio di G. A. Perti con il principe Ferdinando de' Medici', *NRMI*, xxi (1987), 605–40 CARLO VITALI

Decembrists, The [*Dekabristï*]. Opera in four acts by YURY ALEXANDROVICH SHAPORIN to a libretto by Vsevolod Rozhdestvensky after Alexey Tolstoy; Moscow, Bol'shoy Theatre, 23 June 1953.

Kondraty Fyodorovich Rïleyev *a poet*	baritone
Pavel Ivanovich Pestel' *Colonel of the Vyatka Regiment*	bass
A. A. Bestuzhev *Captain of the Dragoon Life Guards*	bass
Prince Trubetskoy *Colonel of the Preobrazhensky Life Guards*	baritone
Pyotr Grigor'yevich Kachovsky	tenor
Yakubovich *Captain in a Dragoon Regiment*	bass
Prince Dmitry Alexandrovich Shchepin-Rostovsky *Staff Captain in the Moscow Guards*	tenor
Princess Ol'ga [Olga] Mirnova *Prince Dmitry's mother*	mezzo-soprano
Madame Orlova *a neighbour*	mezzo-soprano
Yelena *her daughter*	soprano
Mariya Timofeyevna *Princess Olga's housekeeper*	soprano
Stesha *a gypsy*	mezzo-soprano
Rostovtsev *an officer of the Yeger'skiy Regiment*	tenor
Nicholas I *Tsar of Russia*	bass
Count Benkendorf	bass
Governor-General	bass
Metropolitan Serafim	tenor
Sergeich *porter at the fortress of SS Peter and Paul*	bass
Major-Domo	spoken
Nightwatchman	bass
First Peasant	tenor
Second Peasant	bass

People, soldiers, workers, peasants, serfs, girls, gypsies, watchmen, police, guests

Setting Russia in 1825, during the reigns of Alexander I and Nicholas I

The story of the Decembrist uprising in St Petersburg occupied Shaporin for most of his career, and he made several attempts at an opera on this theme. The first version, based on an idea by Alexey Tolstoy and begun in 1920, was named *Polina Gyobel'* ('Paulina Goebbel') after the revolutionary sympathizer who married the

Decembrist Annenkov and went with him into exile. Its première was given in Leningrad in 1925, on the 100th anniversary of the uprising. Shaporin continued to work on the opera, however, seeking advice from several writers, particularly the musicologist and composer Boris Asaf'yev. In 1935 a commission from the Moscow Bol'shoy spurred him to intensify his efforts, and some scenes were tried out in Moscow soon afterwards, but the dramatic shape and emphasis continued to change right up to the première in 1953. The love story remained but assumed only secondary importance, and the character of Pestel' was introduced. At the same time Shaporin was persuaded that it would be ideologically, if not historically, correct to give a greater role to the masses. The chorus therefore plays a far more important part in the final version, underlining the work's involvement with the mainstream Russian tradition: comparisons with Musorgsky, Tchaikovsky and particularly the Borodin of *Prince Igor* have been frequent, in terms of both style and structure. At its première *The Decembrists* was recognized as a major contribution to Soviet opera as well as the high point of Shaporin's career. It quickly established a secure place in the Soviet repertory. A recording, with the Orchestra and Chorus of the Bol'shoy Theatre, Moscow, conducted by Alexander Melik-Pashayev, was issued in 1958.

ACT 1.i *The country estate of Princess Olga, seen from the terrace of the house* Serf girls are singing of their wretched condition. Mariya Timofeyevna rebukes them; they change to a happier song as the Princess arrives. The Princess says she will sell the girls and tells them to be quiet: they bore her; everything bores her. Princess Olga learns that her son is in the fields talking to the peasants. Prince Dmitry enters, depressed, and the Princess dispatches the girls. Dmitry cannot bear to see his people so wretched; where, his mother asks, did he get such ideas? All is well in Russia; the Tsar takes care of his people. But Dmitry says he is a detested tyrant. It emerges that Dmitry is in love, with a girl not of good family but to him the embodiment of virtue.

A neighbour, Madame Orlova, arrives with her daughter Yelena; Dmitry's excitement at her arrival reveals her as his inamorata. The Princess asks Orlova if she has come to borrow more money; they go indoors. Dmitry declares his love, but Yelena tries to stop him: 'I am not rich enough for you.' Princess Olga dismisses the Orlovas, refusing to lend them money, and tells Dmitry he must get this nonsense out of his head.

A fellow officer, Pestel', enters; he hopes Dmitry has not lost his revolutionary fervour. He suspects that one of their number, Prince Trubetskoy, wants to 'fob off the people' with a constitutional monarchy where a republic is the only answer. Dmitry swears allegiance. Pestel' gives him a letter for the poet Rïleyev in St Petersburg and concludes with a hymn to the Republican cause.

1.ii *An inn on the Moscow–St Petersburg road, a room reserved for 'better-class' people; outside, a fair* Kachovsky tells Trubetskoy that the fair is full of police and counsels secrecy. Yakubovich enters with a group of gypsy musicians to act as a screen for their plotting; Stesha sings a wild song to the chorus. Dmitry enters. Trubetskoy tells them that the Tsar has left St Petersburg; everywhere misery increases. Bestuzhev appears suddenly with the news that the Tsar has committed suicide; surely now is the time to strike? Trubetskoy protests that they are not ready, but Bestuzhev's call is eagerly taken up. Another conspirator, Rostovtsev, unconvinced, slips away unnoticed.

1.iii *The fairground outside the inn* Night is falling. Rumours of the Tsar's death are spreading, though most people are more concerned with eating and drinking. Trubetskoy and Yakubovich are seen leaving the inn. The police arrive and close the fair. People are wondering about the Tsar's successor. Gradually the stage goes quiet. Dmitry enters with a letter from Yelena and the lovers sing rapturously. Dmitry tells Yelena that he must go to St Petersburg but promises to be true for ever.

ACT 2.i *St Petersburg* On the evening before the uprising the conspirators are meeting in Rïleyev's apartment. Kachovsky claims that the army, which the next day will swear allegiance to the Tsar, is with them. But Rïleyev is troubled by the absence of Trubetskoy, who was to lead them tomorrow. Trubetskoy arrives: Grand Duke Constantine has refused the throne, which will go to his brother Nicholas. Rïleyev says this makes no difference, but Trubetskoy points out that they cannot hope for strong military support. Rostovtsev arrives, denouncing both plan and conspirators, but escapes when Yakubovich threatens to kill him.

As dawn breaks, Trubetskoy is again put forward as leader. Looking across the river to the Winter Palace, the company express their hatred of tyranny and slavery.

2.ii *A room in the Winter Palace* Nicholas, newly crowned, is pondering the situation. St Petersburg is in turmoil. He calls the Governor-General: 'This is revolution', he says; 'talk to them, then send in the clergy. If that does not succeed, prepare the guns.'

2.iii *The Senate Square with the monument to Peter the Great; crowds of people and workers* Troops led by Dmitry and Bestuzhev arrive and are greeted by Rïleyev. The Tsar however is still in power. A procession of priests enters, but quickly leaves in the face of the crowd's hostility. Trubetskoy arrives secretly but leaves when he sees the mood of the crowd; the others await him with mounting anxiety. The Governor-General orders the rebel troops back to barracks, but Kachovsky shoots him; the crowd, rushing forward, is routed by the Tsar's artillery; Dmitry is wounded. As darkness falls an old soldier laments the bloodshed, and the chorus joins him.

ACT 3 *A crowded ballroom in St Petersburg* A ball celebrates the crushing of the revolution; Princess Olga is among the revellers. Yelena enters, masked, to ask the Tsar if she may accompany Dmitry in his exile to Siberia. She is rebuffed by the Princess: her son is a traitor. A waltz strikes up and the Tsar enters, also masked. He persuades Yelena to dance with him; he will grant her what she wishes. Count Benkendorf addresses the masked Tsar as 'Sire' and Yelena realizes who her partner is. She makes her request; the Tsar is not pleased, but he has committed himself. Having given his permission, he orders Yelena to leave.

ACT 4.i *A dungeon in the Peter and Paul Fortress* Rïleyev, alone, is thinking of the failure of the uprising; perhaps his daughter will live to see better times. The names of the Decembrists are called for execution. Last on the list is Pestel', who embraces Rïleyev and joins him in an expression of faith in Russia's future.

4.ii *The courtyard of the Peter and Paul Fortress* The porter Sergeich sings of past campaigns and of the dreadful weather. Dmitry and Bestuzhev are led out. Dmitry is in despair; but at the last minute Yelena appears with her good news and they leave together.

4.iii *The road to Siberia* Peasants are seen with their children, singing of their hard life (to the tune of the serf girls at the beginning of Act 1). Dmitry and Bestuzhev enter with the other exiles singing a Hymn to Liberation, sure that their names will live as the first to rise against the Tsar.

Though hardly on a par with the greatest achievements of Shostakovich and Prokofiev, in its way *The Decembrists* is a remarkable work. It manages to evoke the sound worlds and melodic styles of Tchaikovsky, Musorgsky and Rimsky-Korsakov without sounding merely derivative, while containing just enough passing harmonic astringency to remind the listener that the work was actually written in the 20th century. The vocal writing is sympathetic, the orchestral contribution has colour, atmosphere and, in places, real intensity of feeling, and the handling of the plot has dramatic pace. However difficult it may be to disagree with Gerald Abraham's reservation that *The Decembrists* lacks 'some element that can be isolated and labelled "unmistakable Shaporin" ', this opera still stands some way above the average operatic product of the years of Soviet socialist realism. STEPHEN JOHNSON

Decision, The. Opera in three acts by THEA MUSGRAVE to a libretto by Maurice Lindsay; London, Sadler's Wells (New Opera Company), 30 November 1967.

The opera is based on an incident which took place in a Scottish mining village in 1835, when the miner John Brown was trapped underground for 23 days before being rescued alive, only to die shortly after. In the first scene John Brown (baritone) protests against the hardships endured by miners and warns of an impending roof fall. Later action takes place on two levels, as the trapped miner relives his past in a series of flashbacks. The manager of the mine (baritone) is reluctant to organize a dangerous rescue operation, but a group of miners led by John Brown's father (baritone) attempts to find the victim. The decision of the title rests with the foreman, Wayson (tenor), whose dead wife, Kate (soprano), had been Brown's lover. When Wayson hears distant tappings from the trapped man he is faced with the choice of revenging himself by leaving Brown to die or of organizing a search; he takes the latter course.

Musgrave has emphasized the vital role of the chorus in her opera: 'the rescue aspects of the story are less important than the social and personal predicaments involved ... the crowd come to understand that only by standing together can they improve conditions in the mines'. HUGO COLE

De Fabritiis, Oliviero (Carlo) (*b* Rome, 13 June 1902; *d* Rome, 12 Aug 1982). Italian conductor and composer. He studied at the Rome Conservatory with Refice and made his début in 1920 at the Teatro Adriano, Rome. After an engagement at Salerno he was artistic secretary at the Teatro dell'Opera in Rome (1932–43), where he conducted frequently, and in 1938, with Toti dal Monte and Gigli in *Lucia di Lammermoor*, he inaugurated the summer performances at the Baths of Caracalla. De Fabritiis conducted many operas with Gigli in Europe and the Americas, and also Gigli's famous recordings of *Andrea Chénier*, *Tosca* and *Madama Butterfly*. As well as conducting most of the standard Italian repertory he gave the premières of operas by Mascagni, Pizzetti, Rossellini, Zafred and others. He first appeared in Britain at the 1963 Edinburgh Festival in *Adriana Lecouvreur* with the San Carlo company from Naples, and made his Covent Garden début in 1965 with *Simon Boccanegra*. A conductor of characteristic italianate warmth of expression, he was skilled at balancing vocal consideration with instrumental detail.

PIERO RATTALINO

De Ferrari, Serafino (Amedeo) (*b* Genoa, 1824; *d* Genoa, 27 March 1885). Italian composer and conductor. After studying in Genoa and Milan he appeared in public as a pianist, organist and conductor. From 1852 he conducted several opera seasons in Amsterdam. He became director of singing at the Teatro Carlo Felice in Genoa and later at the Teatro Carignano in Turin. From 1873 until his death he was director of the Civico Istituto di Musica in Genoa.

Except for *Il matrimonio per concorso* (1858), which was hindered by a poor libretto, De Ferrari's operas were generally successful; *Pipelet* (1855), usually considered his finest, and *Il menestrello* (1859) were performed abroad as well as throughout Italy. However, these works, though elegantly written, charming and melodious, were not original enough to maintain their popularity. De Ferrari's other works include sacred music, cantatas, songs and chamber music.

Catilina (G. B. Casti), 1852, unperf.

Don Carlo (os, 3, G. Pannacchi), Genoa, Carlo Felice, 12 Feb 1854, excerpts (Turin, n.d.); rev. as Filippo II (R. Berninzone), Carlo Felice, Dec 1856

Pipelet, o Il portinaio di Parigi (ob, 3, Berninzone, after E. Sue: *Mystères de Paris*), Venice, S Benedetto, 25 Nov 1855, vs (Milan, n.d.)

Il matrimonio per concorso (ob, 3, D. Bancalari and D. Chiossone), Venice, Fenice, 7 Aug 1858, excerpts (Milan, n.d.)

Il menestrello (ob, 3, Berninzone), Genoa, Doria, 17 April 1859; rev. Genoa, Paganini, 23 July 1861, vs (Turin, 1862)

Il cadetto di Guascogna (commedia lirica, 3, Berninzone), Genoa, Carlo Felice, 9 Nov 1864; rev. Turin, Rossini, spr. 1873, vs (Turin, n.d.)

*

ES (C. Sartori) FRANCESCO BUSSI

Deffès, Pierre-Louis (*b* Toulouse, 25 July 1819; *d* Toulouse, 10 June 1900). French composer. Following initial studies at the Toulouse Conservatoire, he went to Paris in 1839, entering the Conservatoire as a composition pupil of Halévy. He won the Prix de Rome in 1847, and on his return journey from Rome travelled through Germany; it is possible that his contact with Ems, where a number of his works received their premières in the 1860s, was made at this time. He later returned to Toulouse and became head of the Conservatoire.

Like many composers after him, Deffès found that winning the Prix de Rome did not guarantee success on the lyric stage, and none of his works stayed long in the repertory. Fétis said of Deffès's first stage effort, *L'anneau d'argent*, that it lacked novelty, and this applies to much of his music. His most successful piece was *Le café du roi*, which enjoyed Paris revivals in 1868, 1876 and 1889. The majority of his works are slight, one-act pieces to texts by indifferent librettists. Shakespeare's *The Merchant of Venice* seems to have fired his imagination late in life, and he produced the five-act *Jessica*, based on Shakespeare's play, in 1898.

There may also have been an intermediate three-act version, mentioned by Pougin (in *FétisBS*).

all printed works published in Paris

L'anneau d'argent (oc, 1, J. Barbier and L. Battu), Paris, OC (Favart), 5 July 1855, vs (1855)
La clé des champs (oc, 1, H. Boisseaux), Paris, OC (Favart), 10 May 1857, vs (1857)
Broscovano (oc, 2, E. Scribe and Boisseaux), Paris, Lyrique, 29 Sept 1858, vs (1859)
Les petits violons du roi (oc, 3), Paris, Lyrique, 30 Sept 1859
Le café du roi (oc, 1, H. Meilhac), Ems, Casino, 17 Aug 1861, vs (1862)
Les Bourguignonnes (oc, 1, Meilhac), Ems, Casino, 19 July 1862, vs (1863)
La boîte à surprises (1, A. P. Deforges and Laurencin [A. Chapelle]), Ems, Casino, 30 July 1864
Passé minuit (1, E. Lockroy and A. Bourgeois), Paris, Bouffes-Parisiens, 24 Nov 1864
Lanterne magique (opérette, 1, Auguste Carré), unperf., vs (1865)
Valse et menuet (oc, 1, J. Adenis and J. Méry), Ems, Casino, 27 July 1865
Le fantôme du Rhin (oc, 1, Adenis and Méry), Ems, Casino, Aug 1866
La comédie en voyage (oc, 1, Adenis and Méry), Ems, Casino, 27 July 1867
Les croqueuses de pommes (opérette, 5, E. Grangé and E. Abraham), Paris, Menus-Plaisirs, 29 Sept 1868, vs (1868)
Petit bonhomme vit encore (2), Paris, Bouffes-Parisiens, 19 Dec 1868
La trompette de Chamboran (oc, A. de Leuven and Adenis), Dieppe, Casino, 8 Aug 1877
Cigale et bourdon (opérette, 1, J. Maillet), Paris, Salle Tailbout, 3 Feb 1878; cited in *StiegerO*
Les noces de Fernande (oc, 3, V. Sardou and E. de Najac), Paris, OC (Favart), 19 Nov 1878, vs (1878)
Colombine (Adenis), Paris, OC (Favart), Oct 1890; cited in *FétisBS*
Jessica (opera, 5, Adenis and Boisseaux, after W. Shakespeare: *The Merchant of Venice*), Toulouse, Capitole, 25 March 1898

Unperf., unpubd: La nuit de noces (3, Sardou); Riquet à la houppe (opéra-comique-féerie, 3)

*

FétisB; *FétisBS*; *StiegerO* JOHN WAGSTAFF

Deflo, Gilbert (*b* Menen, 22 Sept 1944). Belgian director. He studied at Brussels and in Milan with Strehler. His first production in 1974 was *The Love for Three Oranges* at Frankfurt, where he also staged *Boris Godunov*. In Hamburg he directed *Pelléas et Mélisande* and Ligeti's *Le Grand Macabre* (1978); at Nuremberg, the première of Zemlinsky's *Der Traumgörge*; in Amsterdam, the première of Gilse's *Thijl* (1980); and for the WNO, *Die Frau ohne Schatten* (1981). At the Théâtre de la Monnaie, Brussels (1981–90), he staged *Don Carlos*, *Idomeneo*, *Cendrillon*, *Der fliegende Holländer*, *Tristan und Isolde*, *Les contes d'Hoffmann*, *The Cunning Little Vixen*, *Der Rosenkavalier* and *Simon Boccanegra*. For Scottish Opera he directed *Aida*. He staged the première of Liebermann's *La forêt* at Geneva (1987). Deflo is most effective when directing highly dramatic works such as *Le Grand Macabre* or *Die Frau ohne Schatten*. ELIZABETH FORBES

Defossez, René (*b* Spa, 4 Oct 1905; *d* Etterbeek, Brussels, 20 May 1988). Belgian composer. After studies at the Liège conservatory he was a composition pupil of Rasse; in 1935 he won the Belgian Prix de Rome. He taught at the conservatories of Liège and Brussels (1946–73). From 1936 to 1959 he was conductor of the Théâtre Royal de la Monnaie and subsequently appeared as a guest conductor in Europe and the USA. He was elected to the Belgian Royal Academy in 1969 and helped establish the Opéra de Chambre de Belgique in 1972. His earliest works have a distinctly impressionist quality. Later he moved towards an eclectic neoclassical style, including novel touches within strictly conventional moulds. Defossez composed a number of operettas under the pseudonym Chamaré.

Le subterfuge improvisé (comédie musicale, 1, R. Lebrun), Belgian Radio, 4 Oct 1941
A chacun son mensonge (chamber op, after E. Labiche), Belgian Television, Nov 1964
Thriller (chamber op, C. Fraikin), Brussels Conservatoire, 26 Jan 1976

Arr.: Les surprises de l'amour [after Poise: La surprise de l'amour], Belgian Television, 1961 HENRI VANHULST

Defranceschi, Carlo Prospero (*fl* 1798–1800). Italian librettist active in Prague and later Vienna. Virtually nothing is known about him apart from his librettos for comic operas by Jan Josef Rösler in Prague and Paer and Salieri in Vienna. His libretto *Angiolina* (1800) carries the remark, 'The poetry is in great part by Sig. Carlo Prospero Defranceschi, Candidate in Jurisprudence'. Salieri's setting of the libretto was produced a year later in London, with Defranceschi's text much altered by Da Ponte.

Defranceschi's alterations to Shakespeare's *Merry Wives of Windsor* for Salieri's *Falstaff* of 1799 reveal a poetic-dramatic hand of considerable skill, able to reconcile a rambling Elizabethan comedy with the conventions of Viennese *opera buffa*. Within the two-act plan he develops sharp contrasts among the five principals (Falstaff and the two married couples), which are turned to account in the musical variety inspired from Salieri and in the lively ensembles and finales.

Psiche e Amore, J. J. Rösler, 1797; *La pace de Klentsch*, Rösler, 1798; *Falstaff, ossia Le tre burle* (dramma giocoso per musica), Salieri, 1799; *Il morto vivo* (ob), Paer, 1799; *Angiolina, ossia Il matrimonio per susurro* (ob), Salieri, 1800; *Cesare in Farmacusa* (drama eroicomico per musica), Salieri, 1800

THOMAS BAUMAN

De Freitas, Frederico (Guedes). *See* FREITAS, FREDERICO DE.

De Frumerie, (Per) Gunnar (Fredrik). *See* FRUMERIE, GUNNAR DE.

De Fuentes, Eduardo Sánchez. *See* SÁNCHEZ DE FUENTES, EDUARDO.

De Gamerra, Giovanni (*b* Livorno, 1743; *d* Vicenza, 29 Aug 1803). Italian librettist. A cleric, he served in the Austrian army (1765–70) after studying law at Pisa and produced many plays and poems, including a *poema eroicomico* in seven volumes. After 1771, when he was appointed poet to the Regio Ducal Teatro in Milan, his literary output was dominated by librettos. Some of his early serious librettos – *Lucio Silla*, *Erifile* and *Medonte re d'Epiro* – were set repeatedly by leading composers. De Gamerra's flirtation, during the French Revolution, with revolutionary politics nearly cost him his career: in 1791 Emperor Leopold II urged his brother Ferdinand, governor of Milan, not to engage him as librettist for La Scala, describing him as 'fanatic to excess, hot-headed, imprudent concerning ... liberty, very dangerous' (letter, Vienna, Haus-, Hof- und Staatsarchiv). In 1793, however, he was appointed house librettist for the court theatres in Vienna, and during the next decade he collaborated with Salieri and Weigl as well as providing librettos for Winter, Paer and Mayr. He is also said to have made the first Italian translation of *Die Zauberflöte*.

De Gamerra's librettos are in many ways typical of late 18th-century developments in Italian musical drama. They are the product of a poet steeped in the traditions of Metastasian opera but eager to incorporate ideas of the kind proposed by Calzabigi, Verazi and other innovators. In 'Osservazioni sull'opera in musica', published in 1771 in his *Armida* libretto (of which no setting is known), he argued in favour of more 'spectacle' in *dramma per musica* in the form of chorus, ballet and elaborate scenery, and he put those ideas into practice with tableaux like the dimly lit *ombra* scene among the funeral urns in Act 1 of *Lucio Silla* and, in *Pirro*, with large-scale action ensembles including an assassination attempt on stage. In his late librettos De Gamerra adapted to Viennese taste by combining comic and serious elements.

See also ERIFILE.

dm – *dramma per musica*

Lucio Silla (dm), Mozart, 1772 (Anfossi, 1774; J. C. Bach, 1775; Mortellari, 1779); *Il Sismano nel Mogol* (dm), Paisiello, 1773 (Zannetti, 1775, as Sismanno nel Mogole); *Erifile* (dm), ? Mysliveček, 1773 (Sacchini, 1778; F. Bianchi, 1779; ? Alessandri, 1780; Sarti, 1783; G. Giordani, 1783; C. Monza, 1786); *La calamita de' cuori* (dg, after C. Goldoni), Salieri, 1774; *Medonte re d'Epiro* (dm), Alessandri, 1774 (Mortellari, 1775, as Arsace; Sarti, 1777; Bertoni, 1777; G. Radicchi, 1778; Insanguine, 1779; Mysliveček, 1780; Andreozzi, 1783; P. A. Guglielmi, 1788, as Arsace; A. Pio, 1790; G. Giordani, 1791); *La finta scema* (commedia per musica), Salieri, 1775; *Daliso e Delmita* (azione pastorale), Salieri, 1776 (F. Bianchi, 1789)

Pirro (dm), Paisiello, 1787 (Zingarelli, 1791); *Cleomene* (dm), Sarti, 1788; *Adrasto re d'Egitto* (dm), Tarchi, 1792; *Gli amanti in Tempe* (azione pastorale), Andreozzi, 1792; *Giulietta e Pierotto* (dg per musica), J. Weigl, 1794; *Eraclito e Democrito* (commedia per musica), Salieri, 1795; *Palmira regina di Persia* (dramma eroicomico), Salieri, 1795; *I due vedovi* (commedia per musica), Winter, 1796; *Il moro* (commedia per musica), Salieri, 1796; *I tre filosofi*, Salieri, 1797 [unfinished]; *I solitari* (os), Weigl, 1797; *L'amor marinaro, ossia Il corsaro* (dg per musica), Weigl, 1797; *L'accademia del maestro Cisolfaut*, Weigl, 1798; *Achille* (melodramma eroico), Paer, 1801; *Ercole in Lidia* (dm), Mayr, 1803

*

ES

G. De Gamerra: 'Osservazioni sullo spettacolo in generale, … per servire allo stabilmento del novo Teatro nazionale', *Novo teatro di Giovanni de Gamerra* (Venice, 1790), i

E. Masi: 'Gio. De Gamerra o il segreto d'un cuor sensibile', *Studi e ritratti* (Bologna, 1881), 267–97

——: 'Giovanni de Gamerra e i drammi lagrimosi', *Sulla storia del teatro nel secolo XVIII* (Florence, 1891), 281–354

I. Sanesi: *La commedia* (Milan, 1935), 442–6

D. Heartz: 'Mozart and his Italian Contemporaries: La clemenza di Tito', *MJb 1978–9*, 275–93

K. Hansell: Preface to W. A. Mozart: *Lucio Silla*, NMA, II: 5/vii (1986)

C. Esch: *'Lucio Silla': vier Opera-seria-Vertonungen aus der Zeit zwischen 1770 und 1780* (diss., U. of Göttingen, 1991)

JOHN A. RICE

Degiardino, Felice. *See* GIARDINI, FELICE.

De Giosa, Nicola (*b* Bari, 3 May 1819; *d* Bari, 7 July 1885). Italian composer and conductor. In 1834 he obtained a free place at the Naples Conservatory, where his teachers included Zingarelli and later Donizetti and Pietro Raimondi. In 1841 he left because of disagreements with the director Mercadante and composed the *opera buffa La casa di tre artisti* (1842, Naples). As *L'arrivo del signor zio* it was repeated in Genoa (1846) and at the Teatro Re in Milan, where it caused a controversy between supporters of the old Neapolitan school and the new style of Verdi, whose *I due Foscari* was also being given.

De Giosa's *opéra comique La chauve-souris* was not performed (though it was parodied by Enrico Golisciani for Naples in 1875 as *Il pipistrello*); but his series of works in the best tradition of Neapolitan *opera buffa* culminated in *Don Checco* (1850, Naples), his masterpiece and one of the greatest successes in the history of opera in Naples. His later comic operas declined in quality, but remained in demand in Italy, the most successful being *Napoli di carnevale* (1876, Naples). Beginning with *Folco d'Arles*, his several attempts at serious opera, which appeared as pale imitations of Donizetti, had little success.

In his middle years he reduced his activity as a composer in favour of conducting; he was particularly admired for his orchestral balance and ensemble. From 1860 he conducted several seasons at S Carlo, and then at La Fenice, in Cairo, at the Colón in Buenos Aires and finally (1876) at the Politeama in Naples. His other works include church and orchestral music and many songs which made him celebrated as a salon composer.

La casa di tre artisti (ob, 3, A. Passaro), Naples, Nuovo, July 1842, excerpts (Naples, n.d.); as L'arrivo del signor zio, Genoa, Carlo Felice, aut. 1846, *I-Mr**; as La soffitta degli artisti, Rome, Argentina, Jan 1847

Elvina (opera semiseria, 3, A. Spadetta), Naples, Nuovo, 11 May 1845, *Mr**, *Nc*, excerpts (Naples and Milan, n.d.)

Ascanio il gioielliere (opera semiseria, 3, G. S. Giannini), Turin, Angennes, June 1847, *Mr**, vs (Milan, n.d.)

La chauve-souris, ?1847 (oc, 3, P. J. B. Choudard Desforges), unperf.; in It. as Il pipistrello (parody, adapted E. Golisciani), Naples, Società Filarmonico a Pizzofalcone, 28 Jan 1875

Le due guide (melodramma, 4, M. d'Arienzo), Livorno, Avvalorati, carn. 1848, excerpts (Naples, n.d.)

Don Checco (ob, 3, Spadetta), Naples, Nuovo, 11 July 1850, *Mr**, vs (Milan and Naples, n.d.)

Folco d'Arles (melodramma tragico, 3, S. Cammarano, after V. Hugo: *Ruy Blas*), Naples, S Carlo, 22 Jan 1851, *Nc*, vs (Naples, n.d.); rev. version, Florence, 1867

Guido Colmar, o Diego Garias (os, 3, D. Bolognese), Naples, S Carlo, 27 Nov 1852, *Nc*, vs (Naples, n.d.); rev. as Silvia (tragedia lirica), Naples, S Carlo, 1864, vs (Milan, ?1866)

Elena, 1853, unperf.; rev. as Il bosco di Dafne (dg, 3, M. A. Bianchi), Naples, S Carlo, 16 April 1864, *Nc*

Ida di Benevento [L'assedio di Bari], ?1854 or ?1858, unperf.

Ettore Fieramosca (os, 3, Bolognese), Naples, S Carlo, 10 Feb 1855, *Nc*

Un geloso e la sua vedova (opera comica, 3, E. Del Preite), Naples, Nuovo, 8 Jan 1857, *Mr**, vs (Naples, 1857)

Isella la modista (melodramma giocoso, 3, L. Tarantini), Naples, Fondo, 15 June 1857, *Nc*

Il gitano, 1859, unperf.; as Lo zingaro, vs (Naples, n.d.)

Napoli di carnevale (ob, 3, Arienzo), Naples, Nuovo, 28 Dec 1876, *Mr**, vs (Milan, n.d.)

Il conte di S Romano (os, 4, Golisciani), Naples, Bellini, 12 May 1878, *Mr**, vs (Milan, n.d.)

Rabagas (opera comica, 4, Golisciani, after V. Sardou), Rome, Argentina, 23 March 1882

Unperf., n.d.: La schiava polacca; Il capitan Mario; Giovanna di Navarra; Osman II; Satana

Contribs to: Il biglietto del lotto stornato, 1846; Gli speculatori, 1872

*

ES (E. Zanetti); *FlorimoN*

A. Acuto: 'Nicola De Giosa', *Gazetta musicale di Milano*, xl (1885), 331, 345

ANDREA LANZA

Degrada, Francesco (*b* Milan, 23 May 1940). Italian musicologist. After studying at both Milan Conservatory and University, he taught at the conservatories of Bolzano (1965–6), Brescia (1967–8) and Milan

(1966–74). In 1964 he became lecturer in music history at the University of Milan, and in 1980 full professor. He is on the editorial board for the critical edition of Verdi, and is a member of the Institute of Verdi Studies, the Vivaldi Institute and the Pergolesi Research Center. In addition to many articles, he has written books on Baroque and Romantic opera, and edited books on Vivaldi and Pergolesi.

ed.: *Al gran sole carico d'amore: per un nuovo teatro musicale* (Milan, 1975)
Macbeth: un'opera sperimentale (Milan, 1975)
ed.: *Sylvano Bussotti e il suo teatro* (Milan, 1976)
L'opera a Napoli nel settecento (Turin, 1977)
'L'opera napoletana', *Storia dell'opera*, ed. A. Basso and G. Barblan, i (Turin, 1977), 237–320
ed., with M. T. Muraro: *Antonio Vivaldi da Venezia all'Europa* (Milan, 1978)
ed.: *Vivaldi veneziano europeo: Venice 1978*
Il palazzo incantato: studi sulla tradizione del melodramma dal barocco al romanticismo (Fiesole, 1979)
ed., with R. De Simone, D. Della Porta and G. Race: *Pergolesi* (Naples, 1986) CAROLYN GIANTURCO

De Grandis, Francesco (*fl* 1685–1729). Italian soprano castrato. He is first found in opera in 1685 at Modena, Reggio and Milan (listed as in the service of Marchese Luigi Canosa). In 1687–92 he was in the service of the Vienna court, also making appearances at Piacenza, Genoa and Parma in 1689–90. He resumed his Italian career in 1692 and was for a long time in the service of the Duke of Modena, intermittently singing leading roles elsewhere until 1720. His last known opera performance was at Reggio in 1723, although he was still singing in Modena in 1729. He was a skilled singer, commanding a variety of vocal genres (range approximately *d'* to *a''*, but remaining mostly in the *f'* to *f''* octave). DENNIS LIBBY

De Grandis, Renato (*b* Venice, 24 Oct 1927). Italian composer. He studied composition and musicology with Malipiero in his native city until 1951, and attended masterclasses in Siena. In 1945 he won the Italian radio prize, and in 1953 the national first prize for composition. From 1956 onwards he was intensively involved with 12-note technique and with serial and aleatory composition. He lived in Darmstadt from 1959 until the early 1980s, when he moved back to Venice.

Music drama is the focal point of De Grandis's composition, which is marked stylistically by Italian and Dutch vocal polyphony of the 15th and 16th centuries. For all its experimental features, his operatic writing is clearly part of a continuing tradition and strives in particular to perpetuate the *opera buffa* style. His earliest operas have never been performed, but his chamber opera *Il cieco di Hyuga*, written in 1959 on the subject of a Japanese noh play, was broadcast and later staged. In this work extremely complex polyphony, which also provides a kind of acoustic outline of the imaginary musical space, is combined with aleatory techniques in the handling of the four soloists and the small instrumental ensemble. More traditional are the operatic farces *Gloria al re* (1967, better known as *Es lebe der König*) and *Das wahrhaftige Ende des Don Giovanni* (1973), in which De Grandis derives elements of plot and techniques from *opera buffa* and combines them skilfully and effectively with 20th-century theatrical and musical techniques, sometimes used ironically.

La fanciulla del lago, 1951 (De Grandis), unperf.
Il gave, 1952 (De Grandis), unperf.
Il pastore, 1954 (De Grandis), unperf.
Il cieco di Hyuga, 1959 (chamber op, after noh), as Der Blinde von Yuga, Westdeutscher Rundfunk, 1964; concert perf., Darmstadt, 1968; stage, Bonn, 19 April 1969
Gloria al re, 1962 (farsa, 3, De Grandis), as Es lebe der König, Kiel, 1967
Bilòra, 1966 (De Grandis), unperf.
Eduard und Kunigunde (1), Wiesbaden, aut. 1971
Das wahrhaftige Ende des Don Giovanni, oder Das Abenteuer einer Wiedergeburt (farsa, 1, De Grandis), Bonn, 29 April 1973
Die Schule der Kahlen (1, De Grandis), Karlsruhe, 26 Nov 1976

*

W. Konold: 'Der Weg des Renato de Grandis zu einer neuen Kantabilität', *Melos*, xxxviii (1971), 1–6 WULF KONOLD

De Grecis, Nicola (*b* Rome, 1773; *d* 1826 or later). Italian bass. He made his début in 1795 at Rome. In 1805 he sang in Mayr's *Elisa* and in the première of Generali's *Don Chisciotte* at La Scala. In 1807 he took part in the first performance of Pietro Carlo Guglielmi's *La guerra aperta* at the Teatro Valle, Rome. After appearing at La Scala in Farinelli's *La locandiera* (1808), he sang in three Rossini premières at the Teatro S Moisè, Venice: as Mr Slook in *La cambiale di matrimonio* (1810); as Blansac in *La scala di seta* (1812); and as Gaudenzio in *Il Signor Bruschino* (1813). He also sang in Rossini's *La gazza ladra*, *Cenerentola*, *La pietra del paragone*, *Matilde di Shabran*, *Barbiere* and *L'italiana in Algeri*. At La Scala he sang in the first performances of Mercadante's *Elisa e Claudio* (1821) and, as Don Meschino, of Donizetti's *Chiara e Serafina* (1822). At Turin he sang in the première of Vaccai's *La pastorella feudataria* (1824). He retired in 1826.

ELIZABETH FORBES

De Grey, (Constance) Gladys, Countess [Marchioness of Ripon] (*b* London, 24 April 1859; *d* London, 27 Oct 1917). English patron of London opera seasons from 1887 to 1914. A daughter of Sidney Herbert (Lord Herbert of Lea), Secretary of War during the Crimean War, and a close friend of the Prince and Princess of Wales, she ensured the social success of the 1887 opera season given by Augustus Harris at Drury Lane through her stipulation that he engage Jean de Reszke, then known in London only as a baritone. When Harris took over Covent Garden in 1888, she exerted great influence over the management committee or syndicate (on which her husband sat, as well as, after Harris's death, her close collaborator H. V. Higgins) because she could persuade fashionable people to subscribe to the season in advance. She was partly responsible for the break with the tradition of giving all operas in Italian; she imposed the re-engagement of Melba after her initial near-failure, and later sustained Melba's virtual control over casting. Herself unmusical, she was fired by enthusiasm for her friends among musicians.

*

E. F. Benson: 'Three Great Ladies and Others', *As we Were* (London, 1930)
H. Rosenthal: *Two Centuries of Opera at Covent Garden* (London, 1958)
J. Hetherington: *Melba* (London, 1967) JOHN ROSSELLI

De Hita, Antonio Rodríguez. *See* RODRÍGUEZ DE HITA, ANTONIO.

Dehn, Paul (Edward) (*b* Manchester, 5 Nov 1912; *d* Chelsea, London, 30 Sept 1976). English librettist. He was educated at Shrewsbury School and Brasenose College, Oxford. His connection with the theatre began in 1951 when he wrote sketches for revues at the Lyric

Theatre. He wrote the libretto for Lennox Berkeley's opera *A Dinner Engagement*, first performed at the Aldeburgh Festival in 1954. A further Aldeburgh connection followed in 1967 when he was librettist for two one-act operas, Berkeley's *Castaway* and Walton's *The Bear*, the latter an adaptation of a vaudeville by Chekhov. MICHAEL KENNEDY

Deiber. *See* TEYBER family.

Deidamia. Opera in three acts by GEORGE FRIDERIC HANDEL to a libretto by PAOLO ANTONIO ROLLI; London, Lincoln's Inn Fields Theatre, 10 January 1741.

Deidamia was Handel's last opera. He completed the autograph score on 20 November 1740, though new settings of three of the arias for Neraea (sung by Maria Monza) were probably composed later. Achilles was written for Miss Edwards (later Mrs Mozeen), Deidamia for Elisabeth Duparc ('La Francesina'), Ulysses for the castrato Giovanni Andreoni and the bass roles for Henry Reinhold (Lycomedes) and William Savage (Phoenix). Like its companion *Imeneo*, *Deidamia* seems to be a deliberate attempt at a lighter style of opera, perhaps in emulation of similar pieces promoted by Lord Middlesex at the Little Theatre in the Haymarket the previous two seasons; but it failed to recapture the waning public interest in Handel's operas. It received only three performances, two at Lincoln's Inn Fields in a mixed season of opera, ode and oratorio, and the third and last (on 10 February) at the Little Theatre, the only occasion Handel ever performed there; the significance of the change of venue is not known.

Deidamia was first revived at Halle in 1953. Two years later Edward J. Dent recommended it for the first production of the newly formed Handel Opera Society and provided the English translation used by the society for the first British revival at St Pancras Town Hall on 3 June 1955. Dent's attachment to the piece, also evident in his account of it in *Handel: a Symposium* (ed. G. Abraham, 1954), was no doubt prompted by its clearly expounded story and detached manner, factors which make it particularly acceptable to those unsympathetic to heroic *opera seria* and which gave it a certain vogue in the 1950s and 60s. More recent criticism has ranked it among the duller Handel operas, but it remains a good choice for performance by modest forces in a small theatre.

Rolli's libretto appears to be an original treatment of the post-Homeric myth of Achilles' boyhood, though earlier operatic versions exist. The young Achille [Achilles] (soprano), threatened by a prediction that he will die in the Trojan war, has been disguised as a girl named Pyrrha and brought up on the island of Scyros with Deidamia (soprano), the daughter of King Licomede [Lycomedes] (bass). Deidamia has discovered Achilles' true identity and the pair have become lovers. Ulisse [Ulysses] (mezzo-soprano), disguised as Nestor's son Antilochus, Nestor himself (silent) and the Greek ambassador Fenice [Phoenix] (bass) come to Scyros to find Achilles. Lycomedes, faithful to a promise given to Achilles' father, says Achilles is no longer on the island. Achilles shows his prowess in the hunt, occasioning wondering remarks from Deidamia's companion Neraea (soprano). The disguised Ulysses pays court to Deidamia, inflaming Achilles' jealousy. Lycomedes orders a royal hunt, during which Achilles' skills easily reveal his identity to the Greeks. Ulysses and Phoenix both make ambiguous overtures to 'Pyrrha', who rather enjoys the flattery, but Deidamia becomes fearful of losing her lover. More sincerely, Phoenix declares his love for Neraea. Ulysses offers gifts to Lycomedes' family, giving 'Pyrrha' a choice of fine silks and ornaments, or shield, helmet and sword. As Achilles fatally chooses the latter an alarm sounds. Ulysses calls for heroes to defend Greece: Achilles throws off his disguise and declares himself ready. Lycomedes seeks to allay Deidamia's grief by explaining that Achilles is doomed to die. She seeks consolation by turning to Ulysses, but he now reveals his own identity and his fidelity to his wife Penelope. Achilles dismisses Deidamia's fears for him: the future is unknown and they must 'enjoy the good the present hour brings along'. As the Greeks depart for Troy Ulysses joins the hands of the lovers: Deidamia's constancy shall be the reward of Achilles' valour.

* * *

Rolli's wry, occasionally cynical, treatment of the late classical story more or less precludes strong emotional involvement with any of the characters, and Handel does not go far to encourage it except in two grief-stricken arias for Deidamia, the second of which ('M'ai resa infelice') effectively abandons da capo format in favour of alternating fast and slow sections with a key structure adumbrating sonata form. The music is never less than sturdily pleasant, however, with a fine aria for Lycomedes as he pleads old age as an excuse for not joining the hunt ('Nel riposo') and an amusing mock-heroic piece for Achilles when he brandishes the sword offered by Ulysses ('Ai Greci questa spada'). A slow march for trumpets and drums at the start of the opera for the disembarkation of the Greek visitors and a hunting chorus with horns add colour to the score. Chrysander's Händel-Gesellschaft edition (1885) gives the opera as performed (except for some cuts indicated by Handel in Ulysses' aria 'Come all'urto'); the 'A' versions of Neraea's arias were discarded before performance. ANTHONY HICKS

Deirdre. Opera in three acts by HEALEY WILLAN to a libretto by John Coulter after the ancient tales of the Red Branch Knights of Ulster; Toronto, MacMillan Theatre, 2 April 1965 (original version broadcast on CBC radio, 20 April 1946).

The plot concerns the tragedy of a foundling girl, Deirdre (soprano), her refusal to marry her guardian, King Conochar (baritone), and her elopement with Naisi, a prince of Ullah (tenor). Other principal characters include the Druid leader, Cathva (bass), and Deirdre's nurse, Levercham (contralto). The story ends with the deaths of Deirdre and Naisi and the destruction of Conochar's kingdom. *Deirdre of the Sorrows* (the opera's original title) was initially commissioned as a full-length radio opera by the Canadian Broadcasting Corporation. Subsequently, now called *Deirdre*, it was revised for stage production in 1962 and again in 1964–5 (the latter being the published version).

Although Willan generally followed the Wagnerian tradition of music drama in *Deirdre*, his treatment of leitmotifs (comparatively few, used sparingly) is more akin to that of Elgar. The musical idiom is typical of the turn of the century. A sombre yet moving work, it exhibits certain stylistic elements first discernible in Wagner, but also Willan's own distinctive musical character. F. R. C. CLARKE

Déjanire ('Dejanira'). *Tragédie lyrique* in four acts by CAMILLE SAINT-SAËNS to a libretto by LOUIS GALLET and the composer after SOPHOCLES' *Trachiniae*; Monte Carlo, 14 March 1911.

In 1898 Saint-Saëns had already treated the subject of Hercules in two symphonic poems when he composed incidental music for Gallet's tragedy *Déjanire*, played at the open-air theatre at Béziers (for illustration *see* SAINT-SAËNS, CAMILLE). In winter 1909–10 he adapted the work as an opera for production in Monte Carlo. Since Gallet had died in 1898 Saint-Saëns did the adaptation himself, writing assonant rather than rhyming verse. The plot has some features in common with that of Handel's *Hercules*. It recounts the jealousy of Dejanira (soprano) for the passion felt by Hercule [Hercules] (tenor) for Iole (soprano), who in turn loves Hercules' friend Philoctète [Philoctetes] (baritone). When Hercules discovers this he spares Philoctetes' life only on condition that Iole consent to marry him. At their marriage ceremony, Iole gives Hercules Dejanira's poisoned tunic and brings about his death, a moment which drew from Saint-Saëns some unusually harsh dissonances. Some scenes are mildly modal, to evoke the ancient world, and there is a good deal of pageantry, a remnant of the opera's origins as a large-scale outdoor production. Both Dejanira and Hercules have forceful, strongly dramatic roles, and there is an interesting role for the ancient prophetess Phénice (contralto).

HUGH MACDONALD

Dekabristï. Opera by Y. A. Shaporin; *see DECEMBRISTS, THE.*

De Konink [Kooninck], **Servaas.** *See* KONINK, SERVAAS DE.

De Koven, (Henry Louis) Reginald (*b* Middletown, CT, 3 April 1859; *d* Chicago, 16 Jan 1920). American composer. In 1872 he went to England and in 1880 took the BA in modern history from Oxford University. He had studied the piano with Wilhelm Speidel at Stuttgart and after graduating returned there to study the piano and harmony with Siegmund Lebert and Dionys Pruckner. He pursued further theory studies with J. C. Hauff at Frankfurt, and learnt singing with Luigi Vannuccini at Florence and composition with Richard Genée at Vienna. In 1882 he returned to the USA, working in business before turning to composition full time. He was a music critic (1889–1912) for *Harper's Weekly*, the *New York World*, *New York Herald*, *New York Journal* and the *Chicago Evening Post*. He also founded and conducted the Washington SO (1902–4).

De Koven is best known for his operettas. His three most successful works, *Robin Hood* (1891), *Rob Roy* (1894) and *The Highwayman* (1897), have British settings; most of the others are set in Europe or the Far East. At a time when Gilbert and Sullivan and continental operettas dominated the American musical stage, *Robin Hood*, which blended elements of both, ushered in an era of American contributions from John Philip Sousa and Victor Herbert and paved the way for later works by George M. Cohan and Jerome Kern. Although contemporary critics frequently found de Koven's style derivative, audience reaction made *Robin Hood* one of the most successful operettas of its day, and de Koven's works became the repertory mainstay of the Bostonians, a prominent operetta troupe. The interpolated song 'Oh, promise me' from *Robin Hood* has remained a popular wedding ballad. De Koven explored a variety of musical theatre styles throughout his career, his output including several extravaganzas for Florenz Ziegfeld at the turn of the century. His often folklike melodies reveal a fragile lyricism, and although his harmonies are rarely adventurous, he used chromaticism tellingly in his oriental settings.

At the end of his career, when his reputation had been eclipsed by younger composers, de Koven wrote two operas. *The Canterbury Pilgrims*, loosely derived from Chaucer, followed Percy MacKaye's play of the same title. It had its première at the Metropolitan on 8 March 1917. The success it seemed likely to enjoy was probably hindered by the USA's entrance into World War I. The three-act folk opera *Rip Van Winkle*, based on Washington Irving's *The Legend of Sleepy Hollow*, opened at the Chicago Opera on 2 January 1920, shortly before de Koven's death. As late as the 1940s de Koven's operettas were still being revived, especially *Robin Hood*, which has entered the amateur repertory.

most MSS in US-Wc and WM

The Canterbury Pilgrims (4, grand op, P. MacKaye, after G. Chaucer: *The Canterbury Tales*), Met, 8 March 1917, vs (Cincinnati, 1917)

Rip Van Winkle (3, folk op, MacKaye, after W. Irving: *The Legend of Sleepy Hollow*), Chicago, Opera, 2 Jan 1920, vs (New York, 1919)

operettas in three acts, to librettos by H. B. Smith, unless otherwise stated; dates are of first New York performance unless otherwise stated; printed works published in vocal score in New York in year of first performance unless otherwise stated

co – *comic opera*

The Begum (Hindoo co), Fifth Avenue, 21 Nov 1887, excerpts (Philadelphia, 1887); Don Quixote (co), Boston, Boston Theatre, 18 Nov 1889 (1890); Robin Hood (co), Standard, 28 Sept 1891; The Fencing Master (co), Casino, 14 Nov 1892; The Knickerbockers (co), Garden, 29 May 1893 (1892); The Algerian (comedy op), Garden, 26 Oct 1893; Rob Roy (romantic co), Herald Square, 29 Oct 1894; The Tzigane (Russian co), Abbey's, 16 May 1895, unpubd; The Mandarin (Chinese co), Herald Square, 2 Nov 1896; The Paris Doll (operatic comedy), Hartford, CT, Parson's, 14 Sept 1897, unpubd; The Highwayman (romantic co), Broadway, 13 Dec 1897 (1898); The Three Dragoons (co), Broadway, 30 Jan 1899 (Cincinnati, 1899)

The Man in the Moon (spectacular fantasy, L. Harrison and S. Stange), New York Theatre, 24 April 1899, unpubd, collab. L. Englander and G. Keller; Papa's Wife (comedy with music), Manhattan, 13 Nov 1899, unpubd; The Man in the Moon, Jr. (spectacular fantasy, 3, Harrison and Stange), New York Theatre, 23 Dec 1899, unpubd, collab. Englander and F. Solomon; From Broadway to Tokio (spectacular fantasy, Harrison and G. V. Hobart), New York Theatre, 23 Jan 1900, collab. A. B. Sloane; Foxy Quiller (co), Broadway, 5 Nov 1900; The Little Duchess (musical comedy), Casino, 14 Oct 1901; Maid Marian (co), Garden, 27 Jan 1902 (1901); The Jersey Lily (musical comedy, Hobart), Victoria, 14 Sept 1903, unpubd, collab. W. Jerome and J. Schwartz

Red Feather (co, 2, book C. Klein, lyrics C. E. Cook), Lyric, 11 Nov 1903; Happyland, or The King of Elysia (co, 2, F. Ranken), Lyric, 2 Oct 1905; The Student King (romantic light op, Ranken and Stange), Garden, 25 Dec 1906; The Girls of Holland (fantastic light op, Stange), Lyric, 18 Nov 1907, unpubd; The Golden Butterfly (co), Broadway, 12 Oct 1908 (1909); The Beauty Spot (musical play, 2, J. W. Herbert), Herald Square, 10 April 1909; The Yankee Mandarin (co, 2, E. Paulton), Boston, Majestic, 12 June 1909 (1908); The Wedding Trip (opéra bouffe, Smith and F. de Gresac), Broadway, 25 Dec 1911; Her Little Highness (musical play, C. Pollock and R. Wolf), Liberty, 13 Oct 1913; Yesterday (musical romance, prol., 2, G. MacDonough), Washington DC, Belasco, 16 March 1917, unpubd

Inc., unpubd: Cupid, Hymen and Co., *c*1885; Fort Caramel, *c*1886; The Dey, *c*1891; Ollolla, *c*1907

*

A. F. de Koven: *A Musician and his Wife* (New York, 1926)

J. Stedman: '"Then Hey! For the Merry Greenwood": Smith and de

Koven and Robin Hood', *Journal of Popular Culture*, xii (1978), 432–45 ORLY LEAH KRASNER

De Kruyf, Ton. *See* KRUYF, TON DE.

Delalande, Michel-Richard. *See* LALANDE, MICHEL-RICHARD DE.

Delannoy, Marcel (*b* La Ferté-Alain, Essonnes, nr Paris, 9 July 1898; *d* Nantes, 14 Sept 1962). French composer. He intended to become an architect but his interests turned to painting and finally Honegger encouraged him to become a composer. He was mainly self-taught, although he took instruction from Roland-Manuel and others. Delannoy's first important work, *Le poirier de misère*, attracted much attention when it was staged by the Opéra-Comique in 1927. In this work, based on a Flemish legend, he cultivated a direct and unpretentious style, echoing, although not quoting, folksong. The 'Danse macabre' from the last act displays the characteristic features of his style: constancy of rhythmic pattern (here syncopated), polytonal polyphony of lines and chords, vivid instrumental colour and continually striking melodic spontaneity. Always attracted by the theatre, he sought to provide it with new forms: the *chanson de geste Le fou de la dame* is based on a blues of winning charm; *Ginevra* evokes a theme of courtly love by drawing on the style of Renaissance chansons; and *Puck* uses a mobile declamation oscillating between speech and song. Though slightly influenced by Honegger, Delannoy pursued an individual path and remained on the edge of contemporary currents.

Le poirier de misère, 1925 (oc, 3, J. Limozin and A. de la Tourrasse), Paris, OC (Favart), 21 Feb 1927
Le fou de la dame (chanson de geste, Limozin and Tourrasse), Geneva, 1929 (concert perf.); stage, Paris, OC (Favart), 2 June 1930
Philippine [Lola-Lolette] (operetta, 2, Limozin and H. Lyon), Paris, Champs-Elysées, Oct 1937
Ginevra (oc, 3, J. Luchaire, after G. Boccaccio), Paris, OC (Favart), 25 July 1942
Puck, 1943–5 (opéra féerique, 3, A. Boll, after W. Shakespeare: *A Midsummer Night's Dream*), Strasbourg, Municipal, 29 Jan 1949

*

P. Landormy: *La musique française après Debussy* (Paris, 1943)
A. Boll: 'Marcel Delannoy: musicien de théâtre', *ReM*, no.209 (1949), 22–9
——: *Marcel Delannoy* (Paris, 1957) ARTHUR HOÉRÉE/R

Delaporte, Francis. *See* LAPORTE, PIERRE FRANÇOIS.

De Lara [Cohen], **Isidore** (*b* London, 9 Aug 1858; *d* Paris, 2 Sept 1935). English composer and singer. In 1874 he entered the Milan Conservatory, where he studied composition with Alberto Mazzucato (winning the gold medal) and singing with Francesco Lamperti. After further studies with Lalo in Paris, de Lara returned to London in 1877, where he was appointed professor of singing at the GSM. At first known as a singer and songwriter, he soon turned his attention to the stage, producing *The Royal Word* (in which he played the part of Charles II, 1883), *Wrong Notes* (1883) and *Minna, or The Fall from the Cliff* (1886). On the suggestion of Victor Maurel he transformed his cantata *The Light of Asia*, based on the life of Buddha, into an opera and secured its production (in Italian) at Covent Garden in 1892. The following year his *Amy Robsart* was given in French at the same theatre, and a year later at Monte Carlo. De Lara then settled at Monte Carlo, and it was there, under the patronage of the Princess of Monaco, that he enjoyed the most successful phase of his career. *Moïna* was produced there in 1897, as was *Messaline*, his most popular work, in 1899. The 1908 Paris production of *Sanga* was granted a state subsidy on being 'counted as the work of a French composer' by the French Minister of Fine Arts. During World War I de Lara again returned to London, where he established a fund for the relief of distressed musicians, in support of which he organized some 1400 concerts with British artists and promoted new British works. In the 1920s he strove to establish an English national opera, but without success.

Although French influences (Massenet especially) predominate in de Lara's operas, he was a truly eclectic composer. His style may be said to have developed, but it never really settled down. *Amy Robsart* exhibits his main characteristics: the musical vocabulary bubbles along in a state of constant flux in order that it may strike any attitude required at a moment's notice. Massenet's diatonic succulence is present but not his Gallic sophistication or bittersweet tenderness, and de Lara is exposed as a latter-day Meyerbeer in that he produces effects without causes. His orchestration, however, is excellent: tasteful, kaleidoscopic, and highly original. It is therefore all the more regrettable that a man with so fine a musical ear so frequently failed to engage his musical intellect; a work such as *Messaline* relies too heavily on cheap perfumes, and, at the moments when the music should attempt to rise to dramatic greatness, it degenerates into synthetic posturings.

See also AMY ROBSART and MESSALINE.

printed works published in vocal score in Paris unless otherwise stated

The Royal Word (comic op, 1, H. Hersee), London, Gaiety, 17 April 1883
Wrong Notes (comic op), private perf., 1883
Minna, or The Fall from the Cliff (comic op, H. S. Edwards), London, Crystal Palace, 1886
La luce dell'Asia (sacred legend, 3, W. Beatty-Kingston, after E. Arnold, It. trans. G. Mazzucato), London, CG, 11 June 1892 (London, 1891) [rev. of de Lara: The Light of Asia, 1891 (cantata)]; as Le réveil de Bouddha (trans. P. Milliet), Ghent, 2 Dec 1904
Amy Robsart (3, A. H. G. Harris and F. E. Weatherly, after W. Scott: *Kenilworth*, Fr. trans. Milliet), London, CG, 20 July 1893 (1894); with orig. Eng. text, Croydon, Grand, 14 May 1920
Moïna (drame lyrique, 2, L. Gallet), Monte Carlo, Casino Municipal, 11 March 1897 (1896)
Messaline (tragédie lyrique, 4, P. A. Silvestre and E. Morand), Monte Carlo, Casino Municipal, 21 March 1899 (1899)
Sanga (drame lyrique, 3, Morand and P. de Choudens), Nice, Municipal, 21 Feb 1906 (1906); rev. version (4), Paris, OC (Favart), 1908 (?1908)
Soléa (drame lyrique, 4, J. Richepin, after de Lara, Ger. trans. O. Neitzel), Cologne, Stadt, 19 Dec 1907 (1907)
Les trois masques (drame lyrique, 4, C. Méré, It. trans. A. Colautti), Marseilles, Grand, 24 Feb 1912, full score (1912); Eng. trans., Greenock, 27 June 1919
Naïl (drame lyrique, 3, J. Bois), Paris, Gaîté, 22 April 1912 (1911); Eng. trans., London, CG, 18 July 1919
Les trois mousquetaires (oc, 6 scenes, H. Cain and L. Payen, after A. Dumas *père* and A. Maquet), Cannes, Casino Municipal, 3 March 1921 (London, 1921); Eng. trans., Newcastle upon Tyne, 2 May 1924
Prince Marcocana, Aix-les-Bains, Sept 1927
A fehér vilorlás [Le voilier blanc], Budapest, 24 May 1933

*

GänzlBMT; *LoewenbergA*; *StiegerO*
L. de Fourcaud: 'Messaline', *Théâtre*, xvi (1899), 18–22
I. de Lara: *Many Tales of Many Cities* (London, 1928)
G. B. Shaw: *Music in London 1890–94* (London, 1932)
Obituary, *MT*, lxxvi (1935), 944

T. Beecham: *A Mingled Chime* (London, 1944)
U. Manferrari: *Dizionario universale delle opere melodrammatiche* (Florence, 1954)
H. Rosenthal: *Two Centuries of Opera at Covent Garden* (London, 1958)
E. W. White: *A History of English Opera* (London, 1983)
T. Hirsbrunner: 'Isidore de Lara: Messaline', *PEM*, iii, 412–14

NIGEL BURTON, SUSAN THACH DEAN

Delavigne, Germain (*b* Giverny, Eure, 1 Feb 1790; *d* Montmorency, 30 Nov 1868). French playwright and librettist. He was the elder brother of Casimir Delavigne, who under the Restoration made his name with patriotic verses and then became a successful dramatist, presenting liberal ideas in tragedies that combined classical tradition with nicely judged novelty in subject, theme and technique. On one occasion Germain worked with Casimir on a libretto, *Charles VI*, which was set to music by Halévy in 1843. His usual collaborator, however, was Eugène Scribe, whom he had met when both were schoolboys at the Collège Ste-Barbe in Paris. A large number of *comédies-vaudevilles* appeared under their joint names; these lighthearted little plays, often with some particular relevance to the topic of the hour, were interspersed with songs, which were frequently sung to popular tunes. They also collaborated on librettos for two of the most flagrantly Romantic, and most successful, operas of their time, *La muette de Portici* (Auber, 1828) and *Robert le diable* (Meyerbeer, 1831). A taste for the Gothic is further evident in such works as *Les mystères d'Udolphe* (Clapisson, 1852) and *La nonne sanglante* (Gounod, 1854).

CHRISTOPHER SMITH

Del Campo, Conrado. *See* CAMPO, CONRADO DEL.

De Leeuw, Ton. *See* LEEUW, TON DE.

De Lemene, Francesco. *See* LEMENE, FRANCESCO DE.

De Leone, Francesco Bartolomeo (*b* Ravenna, OH, 28 July 1887; *d* Akron, OH, 10 Dec 1948). American composer of Italian parentage. He studied at the Dana Institute of Music in Warren, Ohio, and from 1903 to 1910 at the Naples Conservatory. His three-act operetta *A Millionaire's Caprice* received its première there in 1910. Returning to the USA, De Leone settled in Akron, where he established the music department at the University of Akron and founded the De Leone School of Music. He received the David Bispham Memorial Medal for his opera *Alglala*, which concerns a lady descended from an Indian tribe that once lived in Ohio. He also composed four sacred music dramas.

A Millionaire's Caprice [Capriccio di miliardario] (operetta, 3), Naples, Granville-Fournier Opera, 26 July 1910
Alglala (1, C. Fanning), Akron, All-American Opera Company, 23 May 1924, vs (New York, 1924)
Princess Ting-Ah-Ling (operetta, 2, C. O. Roos and J. Roos), vs (New York, 1930)
New York (lyric drama, 3, C. Menzalora), 1942, MS, vs *US-Wc*
Pergolesi (3, N. Buonpane), MS, U. of Akron
Cave Man Stuff (operetta), MS, U. of Akron

THOMAS WARBURTON

Delestre-Poirson, Charles-Gaspard (*b* Paris, 22 Aug 1790; *d* Paris, 19 Nov 1859). French theatre manager, playwright and librettist. His earliest work was an *Ode sur le mariage de S. M. l'Empereur* (1810), but after the fall of Napoleon he devoted his energies exclusively to the theatre. His favourite dramatic form was the brief *comédie-vaudeville* and, like many of his contemporaries, he often worked with collaborators, notably Eugène Scribe and Mélesville. Among the relatively small number of his opera librettos the most famous is that of the two-act *Le comte Ory*, written with Scribe and set to music by Rossini. First performed in 1828, it is based on a one-act *comédie-vaudeville*, also the product of collaboration between Delestre-Poirson and Scribe, dating from 1816. This so-called 'Anecdote from the 11th century' pokes fun at the 'troubadour' medievalism that was a feature of early Romanticism in France. In December 1820 Delestre-Poirson became manager of the new Gymnase-Dramatique (sometimes called the Théâtre de Madame); he retired from this post in 1844.

*

F. Pupil: *Le style troubadour, ou La nostalgie de bon vieux temps* (Nancy, 1985)

CHRISTOPHER SMITH

De Leuven, Adolphe. *See* LEUVEN, ADOLPHE DE.

Delibes, (Clément Philibert) Léo (*b* St Germain du Val, 21 Feb 1836; *d* Paris, 16 Jan 1891). French composer. His mother, an able musician, was the daughter of an opera singer and niece of the organist Edouard Batiste. Léo's operatic career began in 1849 with his appearance in the première of Meyerbeer's *Le prophète*, which employed some choristers from the Madeleine. He studied at the Paris Conservatoire, but won no prizes there. He was already attracted to the theatre, working as accompanist and later chorus master at the Théâtre Lyrique, and also supplying light music for the highly successful Folies-Nouvelles. His first stage work, *Deux sous de charbon, ou Le suicide de bigorneau*, was an 'asphyxie lyrique' in one act, the first of many operettas appearing over the next 14 years. Many were written for the Bouffes-Parisiens, Offenbach's theatre, including his second piece, *Deux vieilles gardes*, which enjoyed enormous success, largely through his gift for witty melody and lightness of touch.

In 1864 Delibes became chorus master at the Opéra, which provided an opportunity to compose for ballet. *Coppélia* (1870), in particular, brought him fame and success, and it strengthened his determination to elevate his dramatic standing and work on a larger scale. *Le roi l'a dit* (1873, Opéra-Comique), a more sophisticated comedy than anything he had done before, was followed by a second successful ballet, *Sylvia*, in 1876. He then embarked on a grand opera in a Meyerbeerian style, *Jean de Nivelle*. This too was a success, although it was only once revived. His librettists, Gondinet and Gille, then supplied him with *Lakmé*, his greatest operatic achievement, staged at the Opéra-Comique in 1883 in a particularly splendid production. Delibes' last years were honoured and comfortable, but his output and his confidence declined drastically and he had not orchestrated his next opera, *Kassya*, at his death in 1891. It was performed in 1893 with Massenet's orchestration.

His early music belongs to the tradition of Boieldieu, Hérold and Adam, but once he had broken out of the milieu of operetta, kinships with Meyerbeer, Bizet and Lalo are to be discerned. Delibes and Bizet had much in common and admired each other's work but were never close friends. Both were feeling their way to a more fluent and expressive harmonic style without leaning on Wagner. Delibes always retained his early qualities of wit, elegance and lightness. *Jean de Nivelle* combines a weightier tone after the manner of Meyerbeer and Lalo with a disconcertingly light style in such pieces as 'Moi! j'aime le bruit de bataille'. The chorus 'Nous sommes les reines d'un jour' is set to shifting time signatures and a modal melody of striking originality. *Kassya* has a Galician setting with oriental inflections in the music. The vocal writing is of the highest quality, and there is a fine close to the first scene of Act 3, with snow falling on the deserted stage. Tchaikovsky's unqualified admiration for Delibes was based on the operas as well as the ballets.

See also LAKMÉ and ROI L'A DIT, LE.

all printed works published in Paris
PBP – *Paris, Bouffes-Parisiens*

Deux sous de charbon, ou Le suicide de bigorneau (asphyxie lyrique, 1, J. Moineaux), Paris, Folies-Nouvelles, 9 Feb 1856
Deux vieilles gardes (opérette bouffe, 1, de Villeneuve and Lemonnier), PBP, 8 Aug 1856, vs (1856)
Six demoiselles à marier (opérette bouffe, 1, E. Jaime and A. Choler), PBP, 12 Nov 1856, vs (?1856)
Maître Griffard (oc, 1, Mestépès), Paris, Lyrique, 3 Oct 1857, vs (1857)
La fille du golfe (oc, 1, C. Nuitter), vs (1859)
L'omelette à la Follembuche (opérette bouffe, 1, E. Labiche and M. Michel), PBP, 8 June 1859, vs (1859)
Monsieur de Bonne-Etoile (oc, 1, P. Gille), PBP, 4 Feb 1860, vs (1860)
Les musiciens de l'orchestre (opérette bouffe, 2, A. Bourdois), PBP, 25 Jan 1861, collab. J. Erlanger and J.-L.-A. Hignard
Les eaux d'Ems (comédie, 1, H. Crémieux and L. Halévy), Ems, Kursaal, sum. 1861, vs (1861 or 1862)
Mon ami Pierrot (opérette, 1, Lockroy), Ems, Kursaal, July 1862
Le jardinier et son seigneur (oc, 1, M. Carré and T. Barrière), Paris, Lyrique, 1 May 1863, vs (1863)
La tradition (prol. en vers, H. Derville), PBP, 5 Jan 1864
Grande nouvelle (opérette, 1, A. Boisgontier), vs (1864)
Le serpent à plumes (farce, 1, Gille and N. Cham), PBP, 16 Dec 1864, vs (1864)
Le boeuf Apis (opéra bouffe, 2, Gille and E. Furpille), PBP, 25 April 1865
Malbrough s'en va-t-en guerre, Act 4 (opérette, 4, Siraudin, Williams and Busnach), Paris, Athénée, 13 Dec 1867, collab. Bizet, E. Jonas and I. Legouix
L'écossais de Chatou (opérette, 1, Gille and A. Jaime), PBP, 16 Jan 1869, vs (1869)
La cour du roi Pétaud (opéra bouffe, 3, Gille and Jaime), Paris, Variétés, 24 April 1869, vs (1869)
Le roi l'a dit (oc, 3, E. Gondinet), OC (Favart), 24 May 1873, vs (1873), full score (*c*1890)
Jean de Nivelle (opéra, 3, Gondinet and Gille), OC (Favart), 8 March 1880, vs (1880)
Lakmé (opéra, 3, Gondinet and Gille, after P. Loti: *Rarahu*), OC (Favart), 14 April 1883, vs (1883)
Kassya (drame lyrique, 4, H. Meilhac and Gille), OC (Lyrique), 24 March 1893, vs (1893) [orchd Massenet]

Le Don Juan suisse (opéra bouffe, 4), lost; La princesse Ravigote (opéra bouffe, 3), lost; Le roi des montagnes (oc, 3), sketches

*

E. Hanslick: 'Jean de Nivelle von Léo Delibes', *Aus dem Opernleben der Gegenwart* (Berlin, 1884), 47–56
A. Pougin: 'Léo Delibes', *Revue encyclopédique* (1 March 1891), 294
E. Guiraud: *Notice sur la vie et les oeuvres de Léo Delibes* (Paris, 1892)
A. Jullien: *Musiciens d'aujourd'hui*, 2nd ser. (Paris, 1894), 261–89
H. Maréchal: *Souvenirs d'un musicien* (Paris, 1907)
A. Pougin: *Musiciens du XIXe siècle* (Paris, 1911)
J. Tiersot: *Un demi-siècle de musique française (1870–1917)* (Paris, 1918)
O. Séré: *Musiciens français d'aujourd'hui* (Paris, 1921)
J. Loisel: *Lakmé de Léo Delibes* (Paris, 1924)
H. de Curzon: *Léo Delibes* (Paris, 1926)
P. Landormy: *La musique française de Franck à Debussy* (Paris, 1943)
A. Boschot: *Portraits de musiciens*, 2nd ser. (Paris, 1947)
P. Lalo: *De Rameau à Ravel* (Paris, 1947)
A. Coquis: *Léo Delibes: sa vie et son oeuvre (1836–1891)* (Paris, 1957)
M. Curtiss: *Bizet and his World* (New York, 1958)
G. Hughes: 'Delibes and Le roi l'a dit', *Sidelights on a Century of Music (1825–1924)* (London, 1969), 116–24
W. Studwell: *Chaikovskii, Delibes, Stravinskii: Four Essays on Three Masters* (Chicago, 1977)
——: *Adolphe Adam and Léo Delibes: a Guide to Research* (New York, 1987)

HUGH MACDONALD

De Lima, Jerónimo Francisco. *See* LIMA, JERÓNIMO FRANCISCO DE.

De Literes, Antonio. *See* LITERES, ANTONIO DE.

Delius, Frederick [Fritz] **(Theodore Albert)** (*b* Bradford, 19 Jan 1862; *d* Grez-sur-Loing, 10 June 1934). English composer of German descent. Only one of his six completed operas seems likely to hold the stage, but the three precursors to *A Village Romeo and Juliet* and Delius's other operatic projects of the late 19th century show his determination to succeed as an opera composer. He had already seen some Wagner, but regular opera-going became possible only when he began studying in Leipzig (1886). His early Paris years were dominated by the idea of writing a grand opera 'with processions, pageants, and dancers'.

An operatic possibility of 1888, to be based on Bulwer Lytton's *Zanoni*, took shape instead as a draft for a play with incidental music; some of the resulting mood pictures were absorbed into *Irmelin* and *The Magic Fountain*. The following year he informed Grieg that he was writing incidental music to Ibsen's *Emperor and Galilean*; it appears not to have survived. In October 1889 Sinding sent Delius a book on Tiberius and Cleopatra, possibly requested with a view to an opera. Some time later Delius was in correspondence with Ibsen about an opera based on *The Feast of Solhaug*; for this Delius drafted a four-part choral song and made other sketches.

Following Wagner's example, Delius usually wrote his own librettos. The text for *Koanga* was by Charles Keary, and the French libretto of *Margot la rouge* was by Berthe Gaston-Danville ('Mme Rosenval'), but the rest were Delius's own. *Fennimore and Gerda* was set in German, and Delius's wife Jelka was on hand to translate both *Koanga* and *A Village Romeo and Juliet* for their German premières.

Despite Wagnerian aspirations, Delius assessed rightly the nature of his own operatic gift. He was happiest at scene painting, least good with violent action. Effortlessly he could evoke a variety of moods, conjure up an atmosphere of legendary romance, yearn for the unattainable, lament a passing glimpse of happiness. *Irmelin* (1890–92) has many *Tristan* echoes, but in the Delius opera little happens. The unfolding of the story is controlled by a Voice in the Air, assuring the princess that the right man will eventually come, and the Silver Stream, which leads Nils to Irmelin and the palace. It is a fairy-tale in music, set in never-never land, lovely, insubstantial, and with no character development.

In the next two operas, *The Magic Fountain* (composed 1893–5) and *Koanga* (1895–7), Delius enshrined different aspects of his experience as an orange-planter in Florida. The hero of the former was eventually called Solano (Delius's plantation had been 'Solano Grove'), but he began as Ponce, a clear reference to Ponce de León, who discovered Florida in his search for the fountain of eternal youth. Delius's reading of

Fenimore Cooper led him to endorse the idea of the 'noble savage', and the Indian princess Watawa came to symbolize Delius's distaste for the brutality of the Spanish conquistadores. During 1894 Delius heard much Wagner, in Bayreuth and Munich; *The Magic Fountain* has a network of leitmotifs more elaborate than was usual for Delius. The music incorporates ideas from the *Florida* suite (1888), and Watawa's motif was later used in *Sea Drift* (1903–4).

The music of *Koanga* owes much to Delius's experience of black slave song. In Acts 1 and 2 there are traditional tunes with harmonies such as he had heard improvised on the plantation. The art of Delius, with its powerful sense of nostalgia, was finely adapted to champion the lot of the deprived, contrasting a bitter present with lost happiness. It was now, in February 1896, that he wrote to his friend Jutta Bell: 'I have a vague idea of writing 3 works: One on the Indians, one on the Gypsies and one on the Negroes'. The well-known dance from the opera, 'La calinda', derives from the *Florida* suite, and as early as the London concert performance of May 1899 the prelude to Act 2 of *The Magic Fountain* was substituted for the Act 3 *Koanga* prelude. In 1897 Delius produced incidental music to Gunnar Heiberg's satiric drama, *Folkeraadet*; he achieved a *succès de scandale* in Christiania (now Oslo) by much mocking use of the Norwegian national anthem.

Though Delius can hardly be said to have fulfilled his 'trilogy' idea, there is an undoubted gypsy element in the vagabonds of *A Village Romeo and Juliet* (first performed as *Romeo und Julia auf dem Dorfe*), and in the dispossessed Dark Fiddler, so much more important in the opera than in the Keller novel on which it was based. The helplessness of the main characters, Sali and Vreli, is even more pronounced than in *Irmelin*; but Delius now has the artistry to invest it with an almost unbearable poignancy. Nature has run wild in the Fiddler's disputed territory and in the Paradise Garden of the last scene, just as it did in the Everglades of *The Magic Fountain* and in the exotic settings of *Koanga*. In the background are the snow mountains that formed an inspiration to Delius throughout his working life.

The last two operas, each in their own way, attempted a new line. *Margot la rouge* (composed 1902), a one-act shocker set in a Paris café, was a conscious assault on the Italian *verismo* market. In this it failed, if only because gratuitous violence was more convincingly done by others. It is significant, though, that Delius thought of following *Margot* with a setting of Wilde's *Salome*; he also knew that much of the *Margot* music was too good to lose. Strauss wrote *Salome*; but Delius used *Margot* excerpts to set the Whitman text of his *Idyll* (1932).

Just as *A Village Romeo and Juliet* was divided into six 'scenes' (nos.2 and 5 end 'attacca'), *Fennimore and Gerda* (composed 1908–10) became a sequence of 11 'pictures'. Some of these were linked, and Delius specified only brief pauses (usually three minutes) between the separate ones. Like *Margot*, the new work was on a near-contemporary subject, and again a love triangle ended disastrously. Each 'picture' makes a telling dramatic point, and there is a new stringency in the harmonic language; but the strength of *Fennimore and Gerda* lies in the marvellous subtlety of the interludes that act as index to the growing emotional tension or set the scene for what is to come. The two Gerda scenes are idyllic and quintessential Delius; but they provide no adequate foil to the Fennimore tragedy and offer a happy ending too easily obtained.

Delius considered two further operatic projects, *Deirdre of the Sorrows* (J. M. Synge's last play), and Emily Brontë's novel *Wuthering Heights*, the latter to be treated as a series of 'pictures' in the manner of *Fennimore and Gerda*. His last completed work for the stage was the incidental music to Flecker's *Hassan* (1920–23), one of his greatest successes, and perhaps the nearest he ever came to the 'processions, pageants, and dancers' of his early ambitions.

See also FENNIMORE AND GERDA; *IRMELIN*; *KOANGA*; *MAGIC FOUNTAIN, THE*; *MARGOT LA ROUGE*; and *VILLAGE ROMEO AND JULIET, A*.

Irmelin, 1890–92 (3, Delius), Oxford, New, 4 May 1953, vs (London, 1953)

The Magic Fountain, 1893–5 (lyric drama, 3, Delius), BBC Radio, 20 Nov 1977, vs (London, 1979)

Koanga, 1895–7 (lyric drama, prol., 3, epilogue, Delius and C. F. Keary, after G. W. Cable: *The Grandissimes*), inc. concert perf., London, St James's Hall, 30 May 1899; stage, Elberfeld, Stadt, 30 March 1904, vs (London, 1935), full score (London, 1980)

Romeo und Julia auf dem Dorfe [A Village Romeo and Juliet] (lyric drama, 6 pictures, Delius, after G. Keller), Berlin, Komische Oper, 21 Feb 1907 (Berlin, 1910)

Margot la rouge, 1902 (lyric drama, 1, Mme Rosenval [B. Gaston-Danville]), St Louis, 8 June 1983, vs (Paris, 1905)

Fennimore and Gerda, 1908–10 (11 pictures, Delius, after J. P. Jacobsen: *Niels Lyhne*), Frankfurt, Opernhaus, 21 Oct 1919, vs (Vienna and Leipzig, 1919), full score (Vienna and New York, 1926)

*

C. Palmer: 'Delius and Poetic Realism', *ML*, li (1970), 404–14

W. Randel: '"Koanga" and its Libretto', *ML*, lii (1971), 141–56

R. Threlfall: 'Delius: Late Swallows in Florida', *Composer*, no.51 (1974), 25–7

——: 'The Early History of Koanga', *Tempo*, new ser., no.110 (1974), 8–11

C. Redwood: 'Delius as a Composer of Opera', *A Delius Companion*, ed. C. Redwood (London, 1976), 217–38

——: 'Delius's "Magic Fountain"', *MT*, cxviii (1977), 909

R. Threlfall: 'Delius's Unknown Opera: The Magic Fountain', *SMA*, xi (1977), 60–73

D. Redwood: *Flecker and Delius: the Making of 'Hassan'* (London, 1978)

L. Carley: *Delius: a Life in Letters* (London, 1983–8)

ROBERT ANDERSON

Della Casa, Lisa (*b* Burgdorf, nr Berne, 2 Feb 1919). Swiss soprano. She studied with Margarete Haeser in Zürich and made her début at Solothurn-Biel as Butterfly in 1941. At the Stadttheater, Zürich (1943–50), she sang such diverse roles as Serena (*Porgy and Bess*), Pamina and Gilda, and created the Young Woman in Burkhard's *Die schwarze Spinne* (1949). She first appeared at Salzburg in 1947 as Zdenka (*Arabella*) and the following summer returned to sing the Countess (*Capriccio*). In 1951 she made her British début as Countess Almaviva at Glyndebourne; later that year in Munich she sang Arabella, the role with which she was most closely associated and which she sang at her Covent Garden début in 1953 with the Bayerische Staatsoper, and repeated in 1965. She became a member of the Vienna Staatsoper in 1947 and in 1952 sang Eva at Bayreuth. In 1953 she created the three female roles in *Der Prozess* at Salzburg. She sang at the Metropolitan (1953–68), making her début there as Countess Almaviva, and at San Francisco (1958). Best known in the Strauss repertory, Della Casa graduated from Sophie through Octavian to the Marschallin; she also sang Ariadne, Chrysothemis and Salome. She could spin out Strauss's soaring line with a smooth legato, and the limpid silvery quality of her voice made her an admirable Mozart singer. Her beauty and natural charm enhanced her vocal gifts.

*

GV [with discography by R. Vegeto]
A. Natan: 'Della Casa, Lisa', *Primadonna: Lob der Stimmen* (Basle, 1962) [with discography]
G. Fitzgerald: 'Lisa Della Casa', *Opera*, xix (1968), 185–91
D. Debeljević: *Ein Leben mit Lisa Della Casa, oder 'In dem Schatten ihrer Locken'* (Zürich, 1975) HAROLD ROSENTHAL/R

Della Corte, Andrea (*b* Naples, 5 April 1883; *d* Turin, 12 March 1968). Italian musicologist and critic. Self-taught in music, he was professor of music history at the Turin Conservatory (1926–53) and at Turin University (1939–53). His main occupation, however, was journalism, as contributor to various Neapolitan papers from 1906 and as music critic of *La stampa*, 1919–67, a post to which he brought a professionalism hitherto unknown in Italy. As a musicologist his chief interest was opera history, and he made valuable contributions to the knowledge of Neapolitan opera, Gluck and above all Verdi, increasing awareness of the organic unity of Verdi's dramas to which Toscanini's reform of interpretation was also greatly contributing.

Paisiello (Turin, 1922)
L'opera comica italiana del '700 (Bari, 1923)
Nicolò Piccinni (Bari, 1928)
Canto e bel canto (Turin, 1934) [edn of treatises by Tosi and Mancini]
Pergolesi (Turin, 1936)
Ritratto di Franco Alfano (Turin, 1936)
with G. Pannain: *Vincenzo Bellini* (Turin, 1936)
Un italiano all'estero: Antonio Salieri (Turin, 1937)
Tre secoli di opera italiana (Turin, 1938)
Verdi (Turin, 1939)
Le sei più belle opere di Verdi (Milan, 1947, 3/1958)
Gluck (Florence, 1948)
Baldassare Galuppi (Siena, 1949)
with G. Barblan: *Mozart in Italia* (Milan, 1956)
Drammi per musica dal Rinuccini allo Zeno (Turin, 1958)
Toscanini visto da un critico (Turin, 1958) GIORGIO PESTELLI

Della-Maria, (Pierre-Antoine-)Dominique (*b* Marseilles, 14 June 1769; *d* Paris, 9 March 1800). French composer. He was a child prodigy who excelled at the mandolin and cello; an opera by him, performed at the Théâtre de Marseille when he was 18, showed undoubted talent. To complete his studies he spent ten years in Italy, where he wrote six comic operas including *Il maestro di cappella* (performed in 1792); Paisiello, his last teacher there, was very fond of him.

Della-Maria arrived in Paris in 1796. He was fortunate enough to be helped by the dramatist Alexandre Duval, who gave him a script intended for the Théâtre-Français; he turned this into a libretto for *Le prisonnier* and wrote the music in one week. The finest singers of the Opéra-Comique, including Elleviou and Mme Dugazon, were engaged for its performance. From its première in 1798 the work was immensely successful, the *airs* becoming particularly popular. The public welcomed Della-Maria's original, brilliant and fluid melodic style in contrast to the heavier music of his contemporaries. He did not continue to write in this manner, however, and his subsequent works were less successful; *La fausse duègne* was not performed until after his death (1802).

Della-Maria's charm and talent made him a famous and cherished figure in Paris, and he was a member of the Marseilles Academy. His sudden death at the age of 30 shocked the musical world; Dalayrac delivered a funeral oration and Duval had a tomb erected on his Romainville estate near Paris.

opéras comiques, first performed in Paris, unless otherwise stated; all printed works published in Paris

Il maestro di cappella (dg), Naples, 1792
Chi vuol non puole (dg, 2), Vicenza, Nuovo, sum. 1795, *F-Pn*
Il matrimonio per scommessa, ossia La guerra aperta (?dg, F. Casari), Venice, S Samuele, aut. 1795
Le prisonnier, ou La ressemblance (opéra, 1, A. Duval), OC (Favart), 29 Jan 1798 (1798)
Le vieux château, ou La rencontre (opéra, 1, Duval), 15 March 1798 (*c*1798)
Jacquot, ou L'école des mères (2, J. Desprès and C.-J. Rouget de Lisle), OC (Favart), 28 May 1798
L'opéra comique (oc, 1, A. Ségur and E. Dupaty), OC (Favart), 9 July 1798 (*c*1798)
L'oncle valet (opéra, 1, Duval), OC (Favart), 8 Dec 1798 (*c*1799)
La maison du Marais (3, Duval), OC (Favart), 8 Nov 1799
La fausse duègne (3, G. Montcloux d'Epinay), OC (Feydeau), 24 June 1802 [completed by Blangini]

*

E. Dupaty: 'Della-Maria', *Courrier des spectacles* (4 germinal VIII [25 March 1800])
A. Duval: 'Notice sur le compositeur Della-Maria', *Décade philosophique* (10 germinal VIII [31 March 1800]), 35
N. F. Framery: *Notice sur le musicien Della-Maria mort depuis peu* (Paris, 1800)
A. Duval: Preface to *Le prisonnier*, *Oeuvres complètes d'Alexandre Duval*, ii (Paris, 1822)
A. Pougin: 'Della Maria', *Revue et gazette musicale*, xxvi (1859), 245–8
M. de Thémines: 'Della Maria', *L'art musical*, xviii (1879), 305, 315 PAULETTE LETAILLEUR

Della Valle, Pietro (*b* Rome, 11 April 1586; *d* Rome, 21 April 1652). Italian author, librettist and composer. A nobleman, well grounded in practical music, he wrote the verse for a short musical tableau executed in Rome during Carnival 1606. Five characters sang Paolo Quagliati's monodic setting at several outdoor sites atop a festive cart. Later given a chamber performance, the piece was published as *Carro di fedeltà d'Amore* (Rome, 1611).

After 12 years in the Mediterranean and middle-eastern lands, Della Valle returned to Rome in 1626, his personal and musical life indelibly marked by his travels. In 1628 he married Maria Tinatin di Ziba and the next year commemorated the birth of their first child with a *veglia*, or festive ball, that included a three-act musical representation entitled *La valle rinverdita.* Della Valle's libretto specifies costumes, scene changes and special stage effects; in unrhymed verse it recalls the death of his first wife and celebrates his marriage to Maria. The prosody moves from solemn to musical over the three acts, closing with all the allegorical figures dancing round the cradle. Neither composer nor date of performance is known from the published libretto (Venice, 1633).

As well as composing oratorios and experimenting with unusual temperaments, Della Valle sponsored dramatic performances with music at his home in 1634 and 1635 (the latter directed by Stefano Landi) as well as *Il trionfo dell'autunno* in 1644 (text by Ottaviano Castelli, music by Angelo Cecchini).

*

P. Della Valle: 'Della musica dell'età nostra ...', *Trattati di musica di G. B. Doni*, ed. A. F. Gorio (Florence, 1763), ii, 249–64 [modern edn in Solerti 1903]
A. Ademollo: *I teatri di Roma nel secolo decimosettimo* (Rome, 1888), 2–4, 45
A. Solerti: *Le origini del melodramma* (Turin, 1903), 148–85 [incl. text of *Carro di fedeltà d'Amore*]

——: 'Lettere inedite sulla musica di P. della Valle', *RMI*, xii (1905), 271–338 [incl. text of *La valle rinverdita*]
U. Rolandi: 'Il primo "librettista" romano ed il suo primo libretto per musica', *Rassegna dorica*, ii (1930–31), 6–14
V. Gotwals and O. Keppler: *La sfera armoniosa and Il carro di fedeltà d'Amore* (Northampton, MA, 1957)
A. Della Corte: 'Il valore artistico del "Carro di fedeltà d'Amore"', *Sborník prací filosofické fakulty brněnské university*, F9 [Festschrift for Jan Racek] (Brno, 1965), 55–8
A. Ziino: 'Pietro della Valle e la "musica erudita": nuovi documenti', *AnMc*, no.4 (1967), 97–111
——: '"Contese letterarie" tra Pietro della Valle e Nicolò Farfaro sulla musica antica e moderna', *NRMI*, iii (1969), 101–20

MARGARET MURATA

Delle Dame. Theatre in Rome, originally known as Teatro Alibert, renovated and opened in Carnival 1726. *See* ROME, §2.

Deller, Alfred (George) (*b* Margate, 31 May 1912; *d* Bologna, 16 July 1979). English countertenor. He sang in Canterbury Cathedral choir before forming his own group, the Deller Consort, devoted mainly to the performance of early music. Britten wrote the part of Oberon in *A Midsummer Night's Dream* for him, and he sang in the first performances in 1960 and in the recording. He was noted for his smooth, light and lyrical voice, his command in dramatic arias and florid passages, and some tendency towards vocal mannerism. His singing did much to encourage the revival of the high male voice. DAVID SCOTT

Deller [Teller, Döller, Töller], **Florian Johann** (*b* Drosendorf, bap. 2 May 1729; *d* Munich, 19 April 1773). Austrian composer. Initially he probably studied in Vienna; in 1756 he took lessons in counterpoint and composition from Jommelli, who was principal conductor at Stuttgart. As a violinist in the dancing classes of the ballet-masters Michel dell'Agatha and François Sauveterre, he gained an insight into dance technique and its musical requirements; J.-G. Noverre, who arrived in Stuttgart in 1760, soon recognized Deller's talent for composing ballet music, and is said to have considered him his most able collaborator (see Schubart).

After Noverre left Stuttgart in 1767, Deller turned his hand to writing comic operas, including *Le contese per amore* and *Il maestro di cappella*. After 20 years of service in Stuttgart and many years of complaining of his low position there, he was finally released in the summer of 1771 and made his way to Vienna, where *Il maestro di cappella* was performed at the Burgtheater on 31 December 1771. He also wrote several instrumental works, but it is for his ballet music that he is chiefly remembered.

Il tamburo notturno (ob), Grafeneck, 1765 [possibly by Rodolphe]
Il maestro di cappella (dg, A. Palomba), Vienna, Burg, 31 Dec 1771; 5 arias, duet, *A-Wn*; only lib. pubd
Le contese per amore (dg, 3), *D-Dlb*, ?unperf.; Ger. trans. as Eigensinn und Lauen der Liebe, Bonn, 1782, lib. (Frankfurt and Leipzig, 1783)

Doubtful: La contadina nella corte (comic op; see Abert, 1907); 5 other comic operas, Württemberg, 1770

*

C. F. D. Schubart: *Ideen zu einer Ästhetik der Tonkunst* (Vienna, 1806), 151ff
J. Sittard: *Zur Geschichte der Musik und des Theaters am württembergischen Hofe* (Stuttgart, 1890–91)
J. J. Olivier: *Les comédiens français dans les cours d'Allemagne au XVIIIe siècle*, i (Mannheim, 1901), iv (Kassel, 1905)
K. Schiffmann: *Drama und Theater in Oesterreich ob der Enns bis zum Jahre 1803* (Linz, 1905), 126ff
H. Abert: 'Die dramatische Musik', *Herzog Karl Eugen von Württemberg und seine Zeit*, ed. Württembergischer Geschichts- und Altertums Verein (Esslingen, 1907–9), 557–611
R. Krauss: *Das Stuttgarter Hoftheater von den ältesten Zeiten bis zur Gegenwart* (Stuttgart, 1908)

FRIDERICA DERRA DE MORODA

Delle Sedie, Enrico (*b* Livorno, 17 June 1822; *d* La Garenne-Colombes, nr Paris, 28 Nov 1907). Italian baritone. He studied with Galeffi and made his début at San Casciano in 1851 as Nabucco, repeating the role shortly afterwards at Pistoia. The following year he appeared at Florence in *Rigoletto* and in 1855 at the Cannobiana, Milan, in *I puritani* and Federico Ricci's *Corrado d'Altamura*. He sang at La Scala in 1859 and made his London début in 1861 at the Lyceum Theatre as Luna (*Il trovatore*). He also sang Renato in the first London performance of *Un ballo in maschera*, a part he repeated at the Théâtre Italien, Paris, and at Covent Garden in 1862. His other roles included Rossini's Figaro, Malatesta (*Don Pasquale*), Plumkett (*Martha*), Germont (*La traviata*) and Don Giovanni. From 1867 to 1871 he taught singing at the Paris Conservatoire. Although his voice was small, his style and musicianship were regarded as outstanding. He wrote two treatises on singing (1876, 1886) as well as the book *Riflessioni sulle cause della decadenza della scuola di canto in Italia* (Paris, 1881).

*

A. Bonaventura: *Musicisti livornesi* (Livorno, 1930)
E. Gara: *L'impresario in angustie* (Milan, 1940)

ELIZABETH FORBES

Dellinger, Rudolf (*b* Graslitz [now Kraslice], Bohemia, 8 July 1857; *d* Dresden, 24 Sept 1910). German composer and conductor. The son of a woodwind instrument maker, he attended the music school in Graslitz for three years and then (1874–9) studied the clarinet with Julius Pisarowitz at the Prague Conservatory. In 1880 he became theatre conductor in Brno and was subsequently at various German theatres before he went to the Carl Schultze-Theater in Hamburg in 1883. There he met the singer Anna Maria Eppich (1864–1919), whom he married after the wide success of his first operetta *Don Cesar*; this work, which used the same story as Wallace's *Maritana*, was performed throughout Germany and Austria and as far afield as the USA. In 1893 Dellinger became chief conductor at the Residenz-Theater in Dresden, where further operettas by him were produced with limited success. In later years he suffered from financial worries, and in December 1909 he had a mental breakdown which led to his death. Besides his operettas, he composed marches and songs.

all three-act operettas

DRT – *Dresden, Residenz-Theater*
HCS – *Hamburg, Carl Schultze-Theater*

Don Cesar (O. Walther, after P. Dumanoir and A.-P. d'Ennery: *Don César de Bazan*), HCS, 28 March 1885, vs (Hamburg, 1885)
Lorraine (Walther), HCS, 2 Oct 1886, vs (Hamburg, 1886)
Kapitän Fracassa (F. Zell and R. Genée, after T. Gautier), HCS, 2 March 1889, vs (Hamburg, 1889)
Saint Cyr (Walther, after A. Dumas *père*, A. de Leuven and Brunswick: *Les demoiselles de Saint-Cyr*), HCS, 10 Jan 1891, vs (Hamburg, 1891)
Die Chansonette (V. Léon and H. von Waldberg), DRT, 16 Sept 1894, vs (Leipzig, 1894)
Jadwiga (R. Pohl and P. Hirschberger, after E. Scribe: *Les diamants de la couronne*), DRT, 5 Oct 1901, vs (Leipzig, 1901)

Der letzte Jonas (Pohl and W. Ascher), DRT, 2 April 1910

*

A. John: 'R. Dellinger, der Komponist des Don Cesar', *Literarisches Jb*, ii (Eger, 1892)
R. Dellinger: 'Autobiographie', *Bildende Geister*, ii (Berlin, 1906)
E. Gierach: 'R. Dellinger', *Sudetendeutsche Lebensbilder*, ii (Reichenberg, 1930)
R. C. Dellinger: 'R. Dellinger, der letzte klassische Komponist der Operette', *Sudetendeutsche Monats-Heft*, i (Reichenberg, 1936)
K. M. Pisarowitz: 'R. Dellinger', *Deutsche Korrespondenz*, xxvii (Bonn, 1957)

ANDREW LAMB

Dello Joio, Norman (*b* New York, 24 Jan 1913). American composer. At 12 he began his professional career as an organist, following in the family tradition. His musical education included composition studies with Bernard Wagenaar at the Juilliard Graduate School (1939–41) and with Hindemith at Yale (1941–3). The main musical influences on him were 19th-century Italian opera, Roman Catholic church music and 1930s jazz. A synthesis of these elements forms the basis of his operatic vocabulary. He has received many awards including the Pulitzer Prize for music (1957) and he was elected to the National Institute of Arts and Letters in 1961.

Dello Joio's first opera, *The Triumph of Joan* (1950), was withdrawn but was reworked for television as *The Trial at Rouen* (1956). Another revised version, *The Triumph of St Joan* (1959), won him his second New York Music Critics' Circle Award. His one-act melodrama *The Ruby* (1955) is based on Edward Dunsany's play *A Night at an Inn*; the story concerns four English seamen who steal a giant ruby out of an idol, and the consequences of their theft. Dello Joio's use of recitative and dissonant harmonic language match the *Sturm und Drang* of the libretto. Tension recedes during the love scene, and the vocal writing becomes Puccinian in its lyricism. In his use of three 'theme cells', Dello Joio's structure reveals an economy of means similar to that of his instrumental works. He himself believes his finest operatic writing is in the three-act *Blood Moon* (1961) which is based on the true story of the 19th-century actress Ada Mencken, an octoroon who loved a white man; one writer described it as the 'Traviata' of the Deep South. Although the music was conservative the subject matter was not, and its première was not a success. Unlike his other operas, *Blood Moon* contains traditional set numbers, letting the characters express single emotions with arched melodies. The most notable dramatic works Dello Joio has written for television are *All is Still* (1971), a monodrama based on a letter from Mozart to his father, and *The Louvre*, which won an Emmy award in 1965.

The Triumph of Joan (3, J. Machlis), Bronxville, NY, Sarah Lawrence College, 9 May 1950, withdrawn; rev. as The Trial at Rouen (2, Dello Joio), NBC TV, 8 April 1956 (New York, 1958); rev. as The Triumph of St Joan, New York City Opera, 12 April 1959
The Ruby (1, W. Mass, after E. Dunsany: *A Night at an Inn*), Bloomington, Indiana U., 13 May 1955
Blood Moon (3, G. Hoffman), San Francisco, Opera, 18 Sept 1961

*

E. Downes: 'Opera about Joan', *New York Times* (14 May 1950)
N. Dello Joio: 'Challenge of Joan', *New York Times* (1 April 1956)
M. Powell: 'Current Chronicle', *MQ*, xlii (1956), 383–6
E. Downes: 'The Music of Norman Dello Joio', *MQ*, xlviii (1962), 149–72
T. A. Baumgardner: *Norman Dello Joio* (Boston, 1986) [incl. catalogue of works and discography]

MARJORIE MACKAY-SHAPIRO

Delmas, Jean-François (*b* Lyons, 14 April 1861; *d* St Alban de Monthel, 29 Sept 1933). French bass-baritone. He studied at the Paris Conservatoire and in 1886 made his début as Saint-Bris in *Les Huguenots* at the Opéra. There he remained until 1927, singing in every season. He appeared in the premières of many French operas including *Thaïs*, in which he was the original Athanaël in 1894. He was also the Opéra's first Hans Sachs, Wotan, Hagen and Gurnemanz. His sonorous bass voice had an extensive upper range which enabled him to sing baritone roles such as Iago. He also appeared at Monte Carlo, but though of international calibre confined his career to France. His recordings are early and surprisingly few but show a commanding manner and a magnificent voice. J. B. STEANE

Delmas, Marc (Marie-Jean-Baptiste) (*b* St Quentin, 28 March 1885; *d* Paris, 30 Nov 1931). French composer. He studied at the Paris Conservatoire with Leroux and others, winning the Prix de Rome in 1919. His music shows unusual robustness of picturesque and dramatic gesture; perhaps for this reason he had considerable success with works for the stage, including operas and incidental music. His lyric drama *Cyrca* won him the Prix de la Ville de Paris (1925). His writings include books on Bizet (1930), Gustave Charpentier (1931) and Massenet (1932).

Jean de Calais (1), Calais, Grand, 21 Feb 1907
Laïs (drame lyrique, 3, C. Pontier and L. Lacrie), Dijon, 4 Feb 1908
Stéfano (drame lyrique, 1, A. Boucheron), St Quentin, 7 Feb 1911
Anne-Marie (légende bretonne, 3, E. Roussel and A. Coupel), Paris, Conservatoire, 12 Nov 1911; Tourcoing, 1922
Camille, 1911 (oc, 1, P. Spaak), Paris, OC (Favart), 11 Oct 1921
Cyrca, 1921 (drame lyrique, 3, P. Bérel and Boucheron), *c*1925; as ballet, Paris, Opéra, 16 Dec 1927
Iriam (conte persan, 3, Bérel), Bordeaux, Grand, 7 Feb 1923
Le masque (comédie lyrique, 4, Bérel), Nice, Casino Municipal, 9 April 1926
La giaour (drame lyrique, 3, Chékri-Ganem and A. Peytel, after Byron), Vichy, Casino, 21 June 1928
Quand on conspire (comédie lyrique, R. Escholier), *c*1930
Sylvette (opérette, 3, R. Peters, M. Carré and C. Roland), Paris, Trianon Lyrique, 12 Feb 1932, collab. H. Fevrier

Undated: Roquelaure (opérette, P. Veber)

*

Une heure de musique avec Marc Delmas, Collection du musicien, xiv (Paris, *c*1930)

PAUL GRIFFITHS

Del Monaco, Giancarlo (*b* Venice, 27 Dec 1943). Italian director, son of Mario Del Monaco. After studying languages and music, he made his début as a stage director in 1964 at Siracusa, with *Samson et Dalila*. He then worked as an assistant to Günther Rennert, Wieland Wagner and Walter Felsenstein in Stuttgart (1965–8). He was an assistant stage director at the Vienna Staatsoper (1968–70), principal stage director at Ulm (1970–73), Intendant at Kassel (1980–82) and director of the Macerata Festival (1986–8), before being appointed Intendant at Bonn from 1992. He has staged productions for all the major opera houses in the German-speaking world, particularly the Staatsoper in Munich and the Zürich Opera. A versatile director, he prefers to work within a traditional visual framework, and gives his productions a solid dramatic foundation.

ANDREW CLARK

Del Monaco, Mario (*b* Florence, 27 July 1915; *d* Mestre, nr Venice, 16 Oct 1982). Italian tenor. He studied at Pesaro and the Rome Opera School. In 1939 while still a student he sang Turiddu at Pesaro, making

Mario Del Monaco as Verdi's Otello

his official début in 1941 at the Teatro Puccini, Milan, as Pinkerton. His international career began in 1946 when he sang Radames at the Verona Arena and Cavaradossi, Canio and Pinkerton at Covent Garden with the S Carlo company. He made his American début in 1950 at San Francisco as Radames and Chénier, and his New York début in the same year as Puccini's Des Grieux at the Metropolitan, where he sang until 1959. His most famous role was Otello, which he sang throughout Europe (including Covent Garden in 1962) and North America. His repertory also included Aeneas (*Les Troyens*), which he sang at La Scala in 1960, and Siegmund, while Loris (*Fedora*) was a favourite role in the later years of his career. He possessed a thrilling natural voice of enormous power, though his reluctance to sing below *mezzo-forte* was sometimes criticized. A volume of autobiography, *La mia vita e i miei successi*, including a list of his roles, was published in Milan in 1982.

*

GV (E. Gara; R. Vegeto)
F. Nuzzo: 'Mario Del Monaco', *Opera*, xiii (1962), 372–6
A. Chedorge, R. Mancini and J.-L. Caussou: 'Mario Del Monaco', *Opéra* (Paris, 1965) HAROLD ROSENTHAL/R

Delna [Ledan], **Marie** (*b* Meudon, nr Paris, 3 April 1875; *d* Paris, 23 July 1932). French contralto. After studying with Rosine Laborde she made her début at the age of 17 as Dido in *Les Troyens* at the Opéra. The following year she sang Charlotte in the French première of *Werther* and in 1894 created the role of Marcelline in Bruneau's *L'attaque du moulin*, in which she also appeared in London (1894) and New York (1910). She was also Mistress Quickly in the French première of *Falstaff*. On her marriage in 1903 she retired, but resumed her career in 1908. An acrimonious season at the Metropolitan was offset by success in Italy, and after her retirement from opera in 1922 she continued to give concerts. Her firm, opulent voice can be heard in a few rare recordings. J. B. STEANE

De Los Angeles, Victoria. *See* LOS ANGELES, VICTORIA DE.

Del Prato, Vincenzo. *See* DAL PRATO, VINCENZO.

Del Puente, Giuseppe (*b* Naples, 30 Jan 1841; *d* Philadelphia, 25 May 1900). Italian baritone. After making his début at Iaşi, Romania, he sang in Spain (1870) and Rome (1873). He was first heard in London at Drury Lane in 1873 and sang one performance of *Rigoletto* at La Scala in 1875. During 1878 he sang Escamillo in the first performances of *Carmen* in London (Her Majesty's Theatre) and New York (Academy of Music). He sang Valentin in *Faust* at the opening night of the Metropolitan (22 October 1883), also appearing in the first New York performance of *La Gioconda* as Barnaba and in several other roles during the inaugural season. In 1885 he sang Escamillo at the S Carlo, Assur (*Semiramide*) at Covent Garden and Lescaut in the first New York performance of Massenet's *Manon* (Academy of Music). He continued to sing in London until 1888 and in America until 1895. A stylish singer, he did not have a remarkable voice but was admired for his forthright interpretations, especially of the French repertory.

*

J. H. Mapleson: *The Mapleson Memoirs* (London, 1888); ed. H. Rosenthal (London, 1966)
W. H. Seltsam: *Metropolitan Opera Annals* (New York, 1949)
H. Rosenthal: *Two Centuries of Opera at Covent Garden* (London, 1958) ELIZABETH FORBES

Del Re, Vincenzo. *See* RE, VINCENZO.

Giuseppe De Luca in the title role of Verdi's 'Rigoletto'

De Luca, Giuseppe (*b* Rome, 25 Dec 1876; *d* New York, 26 Aug 1950). Italian baritone. After lengthy vocal studies with Venceslao Persichini, he made his operatic début at Piacenza on 6 November 1897 as Valentin in *Faust*. In 1902 he sang the leading baritone role in the first performance of Cilea's *Adriana Lecouvreur* at the Teatro Lirico, Milan, and in the two following years took part in the premières at La Scala of Giordano's *Siberia* and Puccini's *Madama Butterfly*. He remained at La Scala for eight seasons, but the greater part of his career lay in the USA. For 20 consecutive seasons (1915–35) he was an invaluable member of the Metropolitan's company, gradually assuming all the leading roles of the Italian repertory. His complete mastery of the art of singing enabled him to retain his powers almost unimpaired to an advanced age – as was observed when, after an absence of 25 years, he made an unheralded appearance at Covent Garden in 1935 as Rossini's Figaro. This, together with Rigoletto (in which he made his Metropolitan farewell in 1940), ranked among his favourite roles. His many gramophone records, both the brilliant early Fonotipias and the mature Victors made between 1917 and 1930, are models of classical style and the bel canto tradition.

*

A. Favia-Artsay: 'Giuseppe De Luca', *Record Collector*, v (1950), 56–69 [with discography] DESMOND SHAWE-TAYLOR

De Luca [Di Luca], **Severo** [Saverio] (*fl* 1685–1720). Italian composer. His dramatic works include at least three operas (two of which were collaborations), nine serenatas and two oratorios. According to Valesio, he was Neapolitan and was in the service of the Spanish ambassador in Rome. This assertion is supported by his dramatic works: the first, *L'Epaminonda* (1685), his only complete opera, was produced in Naples, and four of his Roman serenatas as well as his final opera, *La clemenza d'Augusto* (1697; only Act 1 is by him) were commissioned by Spanish ambassadors or members of their families. He was *maestro di cappella* at S Giacomo degli Spagnoli, and may have been quite old (as well as neglectful of his duties) by 13 January 1720, when the church named Giuseppe Valentini as his *coadjutore*. A controversy resulted, Valentini was ousted, and De Luca retained control over music at the church.

L'Epaminonda (melodramma, A. Perrucci), Naples, Regal Palazzo, carn. 1685

La costanza nell'amor divino, overo La Santa Rosalia [Act 1] (dramma sacro per musica, 3, P. Ottoboni), Rome, ? Palazzo della Cancelleria, ? carn. 1696, arias *F-Pn*, *GB-Ob* and *I-PAVu*; rev. as L'amante del cielo (Ottoboni), Rome, Collegio Nazareno, carn. 1699, *Rps* [Act 2 by F. C. Lanciani, Act 3 by F. Gasparini]

La clemenza d'Augusto [Act 1] (dramma per musica, 3, C. S. Capece), Rome, Tordinona, 4 Feb 1697, *E-Mn*, arias *GB-Ob* [Act 2 by C. F. Pollarolo, Act 3 by G. Bononcini]

*

F. Valesio: *Diario di Roma*, ed. G. Scana and G. Graglia (Milan, 1977–9)

E. Careri: 'Giuseppe Valentini (1681–1753): documenti inediti', *NA*, new ser., v (1987), 98–9, 112

S. Franchi: *Drammaturgia romana: repertorio bibliografico cronologico dei testi drammatici pubblicati a Roma e nel Lazio, secolo XVII* (Rome, 1988) LOWELL LINDGREN

De Lucia, Fernando (*b* Naples, 11 Oct 1860; *d* Naples, 21 Feb 1925). Italian tenor. He made his début in *Faust* at S Carlo on 9 March 1885. He was at first best known in *tenore di grazia* roles, especially as Almaviva, but from the 1890s he became equally famous as the impassioned tenor heroes of the new *verismo* school such as Turiddu and Canio. His Metropolitan career was confined to one season (1893–4); at Covent Garden he was highly successful around the turn of the century, and was the first to sing Rodolfo and Cavaradossi in Italian at that house. Between 1902 and 1922 he made some 400 gramophone records; these have become historically significant because of his free, spontaneous and vivid treatment of musical text and ornament, which forms a link with mid-19th-century style.

*

GV (R. Celletti; R. Vegeto)

M. Henstock: 'Fernando De Lucia', *Record Collector*, xxx (1985), 101–39, 149–212 [annotated discography]

——: *Fernando De Lucia* (London, 1990) [with discography]

DESMOND SHAWE-TAYLOR

De Lussan, Zélie (*b* Brooklyn, NY, 21 Dec 1861; *d* London, 18 Dec 1949). American mezzo-soprano of French descent. She was taught by her mother, herself a singer, and first appeared on stage at the age of nine. She gave public concerts when 16 and made her official stage début at Boston in 1884, as Arline in *The Bohemian Girl*. In 1888 she sang in London as Carmen, a role she is said to have sung more than a thousand times, and in which many considered her the equal of Calvé. She also became famous for her Zerlina in *Don Giovanni*, and in 1897 was London's first Musetta in *La bohème*. Her Metropolitan début in 1894 as Carmen was no less successful, and she appeared there for a further three seasons in roles including Nannetta, Zerlina and Nedda. In 1910 she sang Cherubino in Beecham's Mozart season at His Majesty's and Gertrude in *Hamlet* at Covent Garden; she also worked with smaller companies such as the Carl Rosa and Moody-Manners, with which she sang until 1913. She taught for many years in England, retaining the vitality and charm of her personality well into old age. Her recordings are few but show something of her rich voice and lively temperament. J. B. STEANE

Delvincourt, Claude (*b* Paris, 12 Jan 1888; *d* Orbetello, Tuscany, 5 April 1954). French composer. In addition to studying law, he was a pupil of Büsser and others; at the Paris Conservatoire in 1913 he won the Prix de Rome jointly with Lili Boulanger. He was sent as a recruit to the front at Argonne in 1914, working with a group of sound therapists. In 1915 he was severely wounded; his convalescence lasted until 1920. He was appointed director of the Versailles Conservatory in 1931, and in 1941 he took over the direction of the Paris Conservatoire.

Delvincourt's works include *La femme à barbe* (opéra bouffe, 2, A. de la Tourrasse; Versailles, Montpensier, 9 June 1938) and *Lucifer* (1, R. Dumesnil, after Byron: *Cain*; Paris, Opéra, 14 Dec 1948), in which choreographic scenes combine with sung roles. His music is marked by a Cartesian control which does not preclude depth of feeling or humour. After Debussy and Ravel, he was one of the most ardent of French composers in trying to recapture the spirit of the Middle Ages and the Renaissance. ALAIN LOUVIER

Del Violone [Violoncello], **Giovanni.** *See* LULIER, GIOVANNI LORENZO.

De Macchi, Maria. *See* MACCHI, MARIA DE.

DeMain, John (*b* Youngstown, OH, 11 Jan 1944). American conductor. He joined the NET opera project as assistant conductor to Peter Herman Adler in 1969, and in 1972 won the Julius Rudel Award to be an apprentice at New York City Opera. Three years later he was named music director of the Texas Opera Theater, the touring arm of Houston Grand Opera. In 1976 he conducted the Houston production of *Porgy and Bess*, which he also took to Broadway and recorded, winning a Grammy in 1977 for the best opera recording. The following year he became principal conductor of the Houston company; he was promoted to music director in 1980. With that organization he has been involved in many world premières including Floyd's *Willie Stark* (1981), Bernstein's *A Quiet Place* (1983), John Adams's *Nixon in China* (1987), Glass's *The Making of the Representative for Planet 8* (1988), Tippett's *New Year* (1989) and Moran's *Desert of Roses* (1992). He became artistic director of the company's New World programme in 1990, opening the European opera tradition to multi-cultural influences; his first project was a reworking of Astor Piazzolla's tango opera *Maria de Buenos Aires* which received its North American première in 1991. He was music director of Opera Omaha (1983–91), where he co-founded the Fall Festival, presenting new and rarely staged works. He was also principal conductor of the Chautauqua Opera (1982–7), and has conducted at the Wexford Festival, Washington Opera and Juilliard Opera Theatre. NANCY MALITZ

De Majo, Gian Francesco. *See* MAJO, GIAN FRANCESCO DE.

De Majo, Giuseppe. *See* MAJO, GIUSEPPE DE.

De Marchi, Emilio (*b* Voghera, nr Pavia, 6 Jan 1861; *d* Milan, 20 March 1917). Italian tenor. His voice was discovered during military service. He made his début at the Dal Verme, Milan, in 1886 as Alfredo, and sang in leading houses throughout Italy and Spain. In 1890 he was a member of the distinguished Italian company that visited Buenos Aires, and the following year made his début at La Scala. He was Puccini's choice for the coveted role of Cavaradossi in the première of *Tosca* (Rome, 1900), which he also sang at Covent Garden (1901, 1905) and the Metropolitan. In New York he was an admired Radames, and in 1902 sang the title role in the house première of *Ernani*. In his last seasons at La Scala his roles included Max in *Der Freischütz* (1905) and Licinius in Spontini's *La Vestale* (1909). He made no commercial recordings, but a few fragments from *Tosca* recorded on cylinder at the Metropolitan carry dramatic conviction and ring out well on the high notes. J. B. STEANE

De' Massimi, Francesco. *See* DE CASTRIS, FRANCESCO.

De Méric [Bonnaud], **Joséphine** (*b* Strasbourg, 22 March 1801; *d* London, 26 Dec 1877). French soprano. As Mlle Bonnaud she sang in amateur concerts in Strasbourg; she made her operatic début in 1823 at the Théâtre Italien in Paris in *Tancredi* (Amenaide). Her greatest successes were in Italy, where she first sang in 1825 (at the Cannobiana and La Scala in Milan). After a disappointing reappearance in Paris and a short season in Lisbon, she took leading roles at the King's Theatre, London, in 1832–3 singing Giulietta in the London première of Bellini's *I Capuleti e i Montecchi* opposite Pasta's Romeo. From 1834 to 1844 she sang mainly in Italy, and was particularly renowned for her Sandrina in Luigi Ricci's *Un avventura di Scaramuccia*. De Méric compared her distinctive and wide-ranging voice to the sound of a clarinet. Her marriage to the impresario Joseph Glossop in 1827 was possibly bigamous: he is not known to have divorced his first wife, Elizabeth Feron. In later years de Méric was known as the wife of the Italian tenor Timoleone Alexander. She is sometimes confused with Henriette Méric Lalande (both were referred to as Mme [de] Méric), to whom she was no relation. Her daughter by Glossop, Emilie de Méric Lablache (*b* Paris, 6 Oct 1830; *d* after 1900), was an operatic contralto; she married Nicolas Lablache, a son of the great bass, in 1854. D. J. CHEKE

De Mesquita, Henrique Alves. *See* MESQUITA, HENRIQUE ALVES DE.

Demetrio ('Demetrius'). Libretto by PIETRO METASTASIO, first set by Antonio Caldara (1731, Vienna). Versions of the libretto were also set as *Alceste, Cleonice* and *Demetrio, rè della Siria*.

ACT 1 Cleonice, newly crowned Queen of Syria, is urged by her people to choose a husband. She complains about this pressure to Olinto, a nobleman, who reveals his hopes to be the chosen king. Cleonice spurns him, however, because she secretly loves the commoner Alceste [Alcestes], of whom there has been no word since he fought beside her father, Alexander Balas, against the armies of Crete. Balas was slain in this battle, and it is suspected that Alcestes has met the same fate. Alcestes is in truth Demetrius, son of the former King of Syria, whose throne Balas usurped. His identity, however, is known only to his tutor, Fenicio, Olinto's father. Alcestes' sudden return incites Cleonice to insist upon no social barriers in her choice of consort. This granted, she still dismisses Alcestes, believing that she has now placed her personal desires ahead of her duty.

ACT 2 After an unsuccessful attempt to see Cleonice, Alcestes is ordered by the jealous Olinto to leave the country. Informed of this incident, Cleonice sends for Alcestes who proclaims his love for her. She explains that affairs of state compel her to reject his devotion, and the lovers bid each other a tender farewell.

ACT 3 As Alcestes is preparing to depart, Cleonice arrives and commands him to stay: she has decided to relinquish the throne to Fenicio and leave with Alcestes. Fenicio refuses the throne and reveals Alcestes' identity. Alcestes, hailed as Demetrius, marries Cleonice and takes his rightful place as King of Syria.

* * *

In addition to Metastasio's *argomento*, accounts in Appian, *Historia* (book 11); Diodorus Siculus, *Bibliotheca* (book 32) and Justin's epitome of the Trogus *Historiae* (books 35–6) identify the Demetrio of this drama as Demetrius II (named 'Nicator') who was exiled by his father, Demetrius Soter, King of Syria, to escape the onslaught of Alexander Balas, usurper of the Syrian throne. The young Demetrius subsequently overthrew Balas and regained his royal position. The plot that Metastasio built upon this narrative closely parallels that of Corneille's *Don Sanche d'Aragon* (1649), and the text was set to celebrate the name-day of Emperor Charles VI in 1731. *Demetrio* was Metastasio's first drama for the Viennese court and although, as he himself pointed out, it lacks bold dramatic strokes, it was enthusiastically received and Caldara's music was praised. In 1732, Giovanni Giai set it for Rome, where women were not permitted on the stage; the list of stage directions that Metastasio sent to Marianna Benti-Bulgarelli, his first Dido, suggests that she was involved with the direction. Included in Metastasio's instructions are suggestions for the blocking of the Alcestes-Cleonice farewell scene near the end of Act 2 which, the poet adds, when staged in this way, had brought tears to the eyes of his Viennese audiences.

With over 50 different settings between 1731 and 1840, *Demetrio* won a secure place among the more popular of Metastasio's dramas. Half of these settings were composed by 1750, with Milan, Naples, Rome and Venice becoming the main centres of *Demetrio* premières. In 1732, Antonio Bernacchi sang Alcestes in two new settings, Hasse's for Venice and Schiassi's for Milan. In the former, Faustina Bordoni appeared as Cleonice, a role played by Antonia Negri in the latter. Giuseppe Aprile and Caterina Gabrielli are to be found paired during the 1760s, and in 1770, Gabrielli sang with Gasparo Pacchierotti in a pasticcio version at Palermo. Giovanni Carestini, Farinelli and Senesino were all to play Alcestes, and to this list can be added Venanzio Rauzzini, Alcestes for the première of Bernasconi's setting (1772, Munich). Bianchi's setting (1774, rev. 1780) includes an early example of an action-ensemble finale in a serious opera.

For a list of settings *see* METASTASIO, PIETRO. DON NEVILLE

Demetrio e Polibio ('Demetrius and Polybius'). *Dramma serio* in two acts by GIOACHINO ROSSINI to a libretto by Vincenzina Viganò-Mombelli; Rome, Teatro Valle, 18 May 1812.

Rossini's first attempt at a full-scale opera, though not his first work to be staged, this *dramma serio* was assembled piecemeal during Rossini's student years in Bologna and completed by 1808. The opera's title refers not to the young lovers but to their fathers, the kings of Syria and Parthia. As often in myth and fairy-tale, the two men are radically opposed in temperament. The kindlier Polybius (bass) is a father twice over: father to his daughter Lisinga (soprano) and adopted father to her lover Siveno (contralto), the estranged son of Demetrius (tenor), now living in the Parthian court. Demetrius, the villain of the piece, turns up in disguise and demands Siveno's return to Syria. His seizing of Lisinga and Polybius's tit-for-tat arrest of Siveno precipitate the opera's one moment of dramatic confrontation and the famous quartet 'Donami ormai Siveno'. Otherwise, the highlight of the score is the duet for the young lovers, 'Questo cor ti giura amore', a charming and characteristic invention that Rossini was to redeploy on several subsequent occasions.

RICHARD OSBORNE

De Mey, Guy (*b* Hamme, 4 Aug 1955). Belgian tenor. He studied at the Brussels Conservatory, and at Amsterdam with Erna Spoorenberg and Stella Dalberg. Later teachers included Peter Pears and Eric Tappy. His operatic career has been varied and he has proved himself a fluent interpreter of styles ranging from the 17th century to the 20th, but it is in Baroque opera that he has gained widest recognition. He sang the title role in Lully's *Atys* in Paris (1987), Florence and New York. Other roles include Alidoro in Cesti's *Orontea* (1986, Innsbruck), Rameau's Hippolytus (1987, Reggio Emilia), Aegeus in Cavalli's *Giasone* (1988, Innsbruck) and Eurymachus in Monteverdi's *Il ritorno d'Ulisse in patria* (1989, Mezières). His recordings include Monteverdi's *Orfeo* and *L'incoronazione di Poppea*, *Orontea*, Cavalli's *Serse* and *Giasone*, *Atys*, Handel's *Alessandro*, Telemann's *Der geduldige Socrates* and Rameau's *Platée*. NICHOLAS ANDERSON

DeMezzo, Pietro (*b* Venice, *c*1730; *d* ?Venice, after 1794). Italian baritone. His ability to execute florid coloratura led him to specialize in serious operatic roles and sacred music (he sang in the choir of St Mark's), and he appeared frequently at the Venetian theatres in the spring and autumn seasons, singing in other Italian cities (including Naples, Rome, Parma, Turin, Milan, Mantua and Verona) during Carnival. He created Alexander in Gluck's *Il rè pastore* in Vienna (1756). Towards the end of his career he sang increasingly in Venetian operas; he also taught singing and composed nearly 200 vocal exercises and other vocal works. SVEN HANSELL

Demian, Wilhelm [Vilmos] (*b* Braşov, 22 June 1910). Romanian composer and conductor. He studied at the Astra Conservatory in Braşov (1925–8), and continued his composition studies with Richard Stöhr at the Hochschule für Musik in Vienna (1929–33). After working as an orchestral conductor in Cluj, he came to prominence as a conductor at the Hungarian Opera House there (1949–79), writing the opera *A kelepcel Capcana* ('The Trap', 1, A. Sinberger; Cluj, 1965) and, among other musicals, *Atenţie se filmează* ('Attention, they are Shooting a Film', 1967; 3, Ö. Sárossy and B. Horváth; Cluj, 1976); both were staged at the Hungarian Opera. He also composed incidental music. His works have well-balanced architectonic structures and masterly orchestration, employing a wide range of instrumental colours to depict Transylvanian folklore. Their simple vocal textures and restrained modern harmony have made them readily accessible.

VIOREL COSMA

Demiriş, Okan (*b* Istanbul, 9 Feb 1940). Turkish composer. He studied at the Istanbul Municipal Conservatory and the State Conservatory in Ankara, and became interested in the folk music of eastern Turkey. He then began working in various musical institutions while teaching at the Istanbul State Conservatory of Turkish Music. He became leader of the Istanbul State Opera orchestra in 1969, and conductor in 1980; he has had periods as director of the Istanbul State Opera, including an appointment from 1991. Demiriş has composed three operas: *Murat IV* (15 May 1980, Istanbul) is in the repertory of both the Istanbul and Ankara Operas, and has been performed at two Istanbul International Festivals and at the Izmir Festival. *Karyagdi Hatun* followed on 26 December 1985 and *Yusuf ile züleyha* ('Joseph and his Brothers') on 24 March 1990. The leading soprano roles were created by Demiriş's wife, Leyla Demiriş, a soloist with the Istanbul Opera. FARUK YENER, CHARLES PITT

Demitz, Heinz-Jürgen (*b* Hanover, 1946; *d* ?Hanover, Nov 1989). German baritone. He studied in Hanover, making his début there in 1975, and, after engagements at Bremerhaven and Wuppertal, returned there in 1979. He also sang in Hamburg and Dortmund. His repertory included Papageno, Guglielmo, Don Alfonso, Yevgeny Onegin and Donner, which he sang at Bayreuth (1983); later he took on Kurwenal, Amfortas, Gunther, Hans Heiling, Barak, Amonasro and the Dutchman, which he sang at Trieste (1986). He created the title roles of Boehmer's *Dr Faustus* at the Paris Opéra, Sutermeister's *Le roi Bérenger* at Munich (both 1985) and the Town Governor in Cerha's *Der Rattenfänger* at Graz (1987). Tall and imposing with a strong voice, he had not yet reached his full potential at the time of his early death.

ELIZABETH FORBES

Democrito corretto ('Democritus Corrected'). *Opera giocosa* in two acts by CARL DITTERS VON DITTERSDORF to a libretto by Gaetano Brunati after J. F. Regnard's verse comedy *Le Démocrite amoureux*; Vienna, Burgtheater, 24 January 1787.

The philosopher Democritus (bass), given to a simple rural life, finds himself out of place amid the intrigues and gallantries at the court of Prince Lisandro [Lysander] (tenor) in Athens. Secretly in love with the country girl Egeria (soprano), Democritus sees his inclinations quickly overshadowed by those of Lysander, who, after winning her heart, discovers that Egeria is actually of royal birth.

In contrast to the immediate triumphs scored in 1786 by Dittersdorf's first two German operas for Vienna (*Der Apotheker und der Doktor* and *Betrug durch Aberglauben*), *Democrito corretto*, his only opera for the Italian company at the Burgtheater, failed roundly and was withdrawn after two performances. Da Ponte claimed that the Emperor Joseph II found Brunati's libretto so utterly wretched that he ordered that no work by him was ever again to appear in his theatre. Nonetheless, *Democrito corretto* achieved great favour on many stages as a German opera, appearing in no fewer than six translations and adaptations (one of these, *Silene*, by Dittersdorf himself).

THOMAS BAUMAN

Demofoonte ('Demophoön'). Libretto by PIETRO METASTASIO, first set by Antonio Caldara (1733, Vienna). Versions of the libretto were also set as *Demofoonte, rè di Tracia*, *Démophon*, *Demophontes*, *Dirce* and *L'usurpatore innocente*.

ACT 1 It has been decreed in Thrace that, until such time as one who would unknowingly usurp the throne has been identified, a virgin of noble birth must be sacrificed each year to Apollo. Demophoön, King of Thrace, aware that the death penalty threatens anyone not of royal birth who weds the heir to the throne, has arranged for the union of his son, Timante [Timanthes], with Creusa, Princess of Phrygia. Timanthes, however, has secretly married Dircea [Dirce], daughter of the noble Matusio [Mathusius], and by her has a son. Creusa arrives, accompanied by Timanthes' younger brother, Cherinto [Cherinthus], who has fallen in love with her. Timanthes begs Creusa to reject him. Offended, she orders Cherinthus to avenge her by killing his brother. Demophoön, meanwhile, has named Dirce as the next sacrificial victim in defiance of a plea from Mathusius to have her exempted. A warning from Mathusius comes too late and Dirce is imprisoned.

ACT 2 Confessing that he loves Dirce, Timanthes pleads with Demophoön for her release. When Demophoön agrees, on condition that Timanthes marry Creusa, Timanthes is forced to plan a rescue attempt. Meanwhile Dirce, resigned to her fate, bids Creusa care for Timanthes. Creusa determines to save Dirce and

'Demofoonte', Act 2 scene ix (TIMANTHES: 'Come, my all, come: you are safe'): engraving from the 'Opere' of Pietro Metastasio (Paris: Hérissant, 1780–82)

turns to Cherinthus for help. She is in love with him, but duty forbids her to reveal the fact. Timanthes fails in his attempt to free Dirce and, when circumstances force him to reveal the secret of their marriage, both are condemned.

ACT 3 In response to Creusa's pleas, Demophoön releases Timanthes and Dirce. Overjoyed, Timanthes offers to abdicate in favour of Cherinthus, but is cast into despair when a document is produced that proves Dirce to be Demophoön's daughter and thus, supposedly, his own sister. But a second document reveals that Timanthes is the son of Mathusius. The innocent usurper is thus identified, Creusa can marry Cherinthus and in doing so honour her pledge to marry the heir to the throne; and the union of Dirce and Timanthes can remain sacrosanct.

* * *

Metastasio's plot derives from a macabre tale described in the Hyginus *Poetica* (book 2, no.40) in which a certain Mastusius murders the king's daughters in revenge for the sacrifice of his own, mixes their blood with wine, then serves it to the king. Contemporary critics praised Metastasio for the purgation of such barbarities and set him above the ancient writers for so doing. Several of the actions that Metastasio wove around the Hyginus tale may well have been suggested by Antoine Houdar de Lamotte's *Inès de Castro* (1723), a drama based on the passionate relationship between Inês and Prince Pedro, son of Afonso IV of Portugal. Other themes, such as the need to placate a deity and the union of a couple of specified lineage, have been traced to Guarini's *Il pastor fido* (1590), while the theme of incest that momentarily touches Timanthes as a result of unsuspected family relationships has been linked to Tasso's *Il rè Torrismondo* (1587), itself an imitation of Sophocles' *Oedipus rex*. Metastasio wrote his text for a setting that celebrated the name-day of Emperor Charles VI in 1733; as with his other dramas, critics commented on it as a literary work, using as criteria their notions of Aristotelian principles. The poet, although generally praised, is still to be found, for example, defending himself against accusations of character inconsistencies.

As a libretto, *Demofoonte* ranks in popularity with Metastasio's top six works, beside *Olimpiade* and second only to *Artaserse* and *Alessandro nell'Indie*. The popularity of Latilla's setting for Venice (1738) helped launch his career; and Gluck achieved significant operatic acclaim with his setting for Milan (1742). Jommelli was to provide four different renderings, and for Galuppi success was assured with his setting for Madrid (1749, in a production supervised by Farinelli). Berezovsky's version for Livorno (1773) is claimed to be the first opera by a Russian (Ukrainian) composer to be given in Italy, and a two-act version of Portugal's setting for Milan (1794), performed in Rio de Janeiro, was one of the first operas performed in that city. A French adaptation by Desriaux was set by J. C. Vogel (1789) for the Paris Opéra. Cherubini's *Démophoon* (1788), to a text by Marmontel, is a more independent work.

For a list of settings *see* METASTASIO, PIETRO. DON NEVILLE

Demofoonte ('Demophoön'). *Opera seria* in three acts by NICCOLÒ JOMMELLI to a libretto by PIETRO METASTASIO (*see* DEMOFOONTE above); Naples, Teatro S Carlo, 4 November 1770.

Jommelli had already written three different settings of this text: for Padua (1743), for Milan (1753), and for Stuttgart (1764; repeated with some new music in 1765). The opera for Naples (1770) was an almost entirely new setting. In the versions for Stuttgart and Naples, a new trio for Dircea [Dirce], Matusio [Mathusius] and Timante [Timanthes] (all sopranos) was added at the end of Act 1, and Metastasio's original duet was retained to conclude Act 2. These later operas contain liberal amounts of dramatically powerful obbligato recitative, occasionally programmatic and frequently employing wind instruments. Although written only five years apart, these two versions differ in style to a remarkable degree. The setting for Naples is more intense, rhythmically complex and chromatic than the Stuttgart version. After attending a rehearsal in Naples, Charles Burney commented on the opera in his journal: '[It] is in a difficult style, more full of instrumental effects than vocal. Sometimes it may be thought rather *recherchée* but it is admirable in the *tout ensemble*: masterly in modulation, and in melody full of new passages'. MARITA P. MCCLYMONDS

Demon, The [*Demon*]. Opera in a prologue, three acts and apotheosis by ANTON GRIGOR'YEVICH RUBINSTEIN to a libretto by Pavel Alexandrovich Viskovatov (based on a scenario worked out by the composer with Apollon Nikolayevich Maykov and modified) after the poem ('oriental tale') by MIKHAIL YUR'YEVICH LERMONTOV (1839); St Petersburg, Mariinsky Theatre, 13/25 January 1875.

Rubinstein composed this opera at a time when Lermontov's romantic tale of supernatural seduction, with its Mephistophelian hero and its exotic setting, was perhaps the most popular narrative poem in Russia. Banned as sacrilegious until 1860 (as at first was the opera), it concerns the love of a fallen angel for a Caucasian princess (Tamara, daughter of Gudal), whom he pursues to a monastery, whither she has retreated to mourn her bridegroom (whom the Demon has killed) and to escape the unseen spirit's luring speeches. Their single face-to-face encounter ends with a kiss by which the Demon takes possession of the mortal beauty, killing her; yet her suffering has redeemed her soul in the sight of God, and the Demon is cheated at the last of his own redemption through love of her. The original cast included Ivan Mel'nikov in the title role, Osip Petrov as Gudal, Wilhelmina Raab as Tamara and Fyodor Komissarzhevsky as Sinodal; Eduard Nápravník conducted.

Although Rubinstein called his work a 'fantastic opera' because of its supernatural title character, it is stylistically remote from the fantastic strain of Russian opera. It is chiefly concerned with the psychological and emotional portrayal of the Demon (and, secondarily, of Tamara), treated musically in 'human' terms deriving from the idiom of the contemporary Russian romance, the vehicle for the setting of lyric poetry. The Demon, cast as a lyric baritone, makes his appeals to Tamara (soprano) in a series of passionate outbursts, the first of which – 'Ditya, v ob'yat'yakh tvoikh voskresnu k novoy zhizn' ya' ('Child, in thy embraces I shall be reborn to new life') – in Act 1 provides the opera's main recalling theme, which reaches its fullest statement in the Demon's most extended set piece, the so-called 'first romance' in the Act 2 finale, 'Ne plach', ditya' ('Do not weep, child'). The opera's most frequently detached number (and a Shalyapin speciality), this romance is actually sung offstage ('heard' by Tamara alone), while the assembled characters on stage are in the process of singing a lament for Prince Sinodal (tenor), the bridegroom. It is immediately followed by a second romance, 'Na vozdushnom okeane, bez rulya i bez vetril' ('On an airy ocean, without rudder or sail').

Tamara's main set piece is also a romance – 'Noch' tepla, noch' tikha' ('The night is warm, the night is still') – sung at the beginning of the monastery scene in Act 3, otherwise given over in its entirety to an astonishing 25-minute seduction duet, with a text almost entirely from Lermontov, who cast the analogous scene in his poem in the form of a dramatic dialogue. It consists of a veritable medley of romances (the largest being the Demon's famous 'Oath'), the characters for the most part alternating rather than joining their voices – and when they do sing together, they sing in opposition rather than in concert, for this is no ordinary love scene. Nor is the opera, its accessibility notwithstanding, at all conventional. Its enormous influence on Tchaikovsky's *Yevgeny Onegin* – that other seemingly traditional but utterly eccentric romance-opera – is instantly apparent to anyone who knows both works.

The other conspicuous stylistic strain in *The Demon* is that of 'oriental' (i.e. conventionalized Islamic) genre-painting, deriving (as in so many other Russian operas) from Glinka's *Ruslan and Lyudmila*. The whole role of Sinodal, confined to the last scene in Act 1, is cast in this decorative idiom (which of course further de-emphasizes him as a character). It contains the oft-excerpted arioso 'Obernuvshis' sokolom' ('In the guise of a hawk'). The other 'oriental' numbers include the girls' chorus 'Khodim mï k Aragve svetloy' ('We are going to the bright Aragva'), based on a Georgian folksong, and the caravan chorus 'Nochen'ka tyomnaya' ('Dark night'), both in Act 1, and the Act 2 ballet.

RICHARD TARUSKIN

Demougeot, Marcelle (*b* Dijon, 18 June 1876; *d* Paris, 24 Nov 1931). French soprano. She studied with Charles Laurent in Dijon, and at the Paris Conservatoire. After her début at the Opéra (as Donna Elvira, 1902) she became the best-known French Wagnerian singer of her generation, singing Brünnhilde and appearing as Kundry in the local première of *Parsifal* (1914). A wide vocal range enabled her also to sing Fricka in *Das Rheingold*. At the Monte Carlo Opera she sang in the première of *Déjanire* by Saint-Saëns. She remained a member of the Opéra until 1925 and in 1930 sang Brünnhilde in Strasbourg.

DAVID CUMMINGS

Dempsey, Gregory (*b* Melbourne, 20 July 1931). Australian tenor. At first a baritone, he made his tenor début in 1954 at Melbourne as Don Ottavio. In 1962 he was engaged at Sadler's Wells Opera where he created Boconnion in Bennett's *The Mines of Sulphur* (1965). He also sang with Scottish Opera and the WNO, and made his American début in 1966 at San Francisco as Gregor (*The Makropulos Affair*). He first appeared at Covent Garden in 1972, as Števa (*Jenůfa*). His wide repertory included Aeneas (*Les Troyens*), Don José, David (*Die Meistersinger*) and Mime, which he sang in the ENO *Ring* cycle (1973). His roles in 20th-century operas included the Drum Major (*Wozzeck*), Peter Grimes, Skuratov (*From the House of the Dead*), Tom Rakewell, Dionysus (*The Bassarids*), the Shepherd (*King Roger*) and Mark (*The Midsummer Marriage*), which he sang in Adelaide in 1978. His voice had the strength for dramatic roles, the wide range required by modern works and the versatility of a character tenor.

ELIZABETH FORBES

De Muro, Bernardo (*b* Tempio Pausania, Sardinia, 3 Nov 1881; *d* Rome, 27 Oct 1955). Italian tenor. At the Accademia di S Cecilia in Rome he trained first as a baritone, then as a dramatic tenor. His début in 1910 at the Costanzi, Rome, in *Cavalleria rusticana* involved encores of each of his solos. His greatest success came with his début at La Scala in 1912 as Folco in the première of Mascagni's *Isabeau*. De Muro made that role his own, singing it 382 times, the final occasion being at the Caracalla, Rome, in 1938. He was only five feet tall but had a stentorian voice, sometimes compared with that of Francesco Tamagno. At La Scala he also sang in *Carmen*, *Don Carlos* and the première there of Rimsky-Korsakov's *The Maid of Pskov*. Although he sang Otello's solos impressively on records he would never undertake the part on stage because of his physique. He enjoyed great success in South America and later in the USA, where he sang for the last time at an open-air performance of *Carmen* at the age of 63. His earlier recordings, made in 1912, show his magnificent voice at its best and also preserve something of his famous role in *Isabeau*.

*

B. de Muro: *Quand'ero Folco* (Milan, 1955)

E. Arnosi and J. A. Léon: 'Bernardo de Muro', *Record Collector*, xviii (1968–9), 52–69, 274; xix (1970–71), 92–5; xx (1971–2), 166 [with discography by J. A. Léon]

J. B. STEANE

Demuth [Pokorny], **Leopold** (*b* Brno, 2 Nov 1861; *d* Czernowitz [now Chernovtsy, Ukraine], 4 March 1910). Moravian baritone. He studied at the Vienna Conservatory and in 1889 at Halle made his stage début in the title role of Marschner's *Hans Heiling*. He sang at the Leipzig Opera, 1891–7, and for a season at Hamburg. In 1898 he joined the Hofoper at Vienna, where he sang 68 roles as a leading member of the company under Mahler. At the Bayreuth Festival of 1899 he sang Hans Sachs and Gunther. He was Vienna's first Falstaff in 1904, and in 1910 its first Scarpia. He also appeared in the world première of Goldmark's *Ein Wintermärchen* (1908). A busy concert artist, he had a large repertory of lieder; it was during a concert, in which he was said to have been in excellent form, that he died of a heart attack. His sturdy voice, wide range and remarkable versatility are well represented in his many recordings.

*

C. Norton-Welsh: 'Leopold Demuth', *Record Collector*, xxi (1973–4), 245–69 [with discography]

J. B. STEANE

Dene, Jozsef (*b* Budapest, 31 March 1938). Hungarian bass-baritone. He studied in Budapest and was engaged at the Hungarian State Opera, where in 1969 he sang Alberich (*Das Rheingold*). In 1970 he began a connection with Zürich, which has continued for some 20 years. At the Berlin Komische Oper he sang Mozart's Figaro (1975). He has sung at San Francisco, Bayreuth, the Metropolitan and La Scala. His repertory includes Monteverdi, Mozart, Rossini, Verdi, Wagner, Janáček, Delius and Berg, but his versatility also extends to contemporary works: in 1982 he sang Gloucester in Reimann's *Lear* at the Paris Opéra, and he created roles in Boehmer's *Dr Faustus* (1985, Paris) and Cerha's *Der Rattenfänger* (1987, Graz).

ELIZABETH FORBES

Den Haag (Dutch). HAGUE, THE.

Denhof Opera Company. A company formed by Ernst Denhof (*d* 1936), an Austrian-born musician living in Edinburgh, to give performances of the *Ring* in English. The 1910 series under Michael Balling was so successful that Denhof decided to tour the provinces; the company visited Leeds, Manchester and Glasgow in 1911, and Hull, Leeds, Liverpool, Manchester and Glasgow in 1912, using local orchestras. The repertory was expanded to include the first performances in English of *Elektra*, as well as productions of Gluck's *Orfeo ed Euridice*, *Der fliegende Holländer* and *Die Meistersinger*. In 1913 the first productions in English of *Der Rosenkavalier* and *Pelléas et Mélisande* were given, as well as performances of *Die Zauberflöte*. After two weeks in Birmingham and one in Manchester, Denhof, with losses of £4000, was unable to continue, and Beecham, one of the conductors for the 1913 season, took over the company. It formed the nucleus of what eventually became the Beecham Opera Company (*see* LONDON, §II, 1).

HAROLD ROSENTHAL

Denisov, Edison (Vasil'yevich) (*b* Tomsk, 6 April 1929). Russian composer. He taught himself the mandolin, guitar and later the clarinet before taking piano lessons at the Tomsk College of Music (1946–50). His early attempts at composition he sent to Dmitry Shostakovich, who recognized his talent and encouraged him to continue his musical studies. After graduating from the mathematical and technical department of Tomsk University in 1951, Denisov entered the Moscow Conservatory where he studied composition with V. Y. Shebalin and piano with V. S. Belov, graduating in 1956. In 1960 he was appointed to teach instrumentation and score reading there.

His first opera, *Ivan-soldat* ('Soldier Ivan'), dates from 1959 and is based on traditional Russian stories. His next two operas both received their premières in 1986: *L'écume des jours* (1977–81) was inspired by the writings of the French jazz musician and existential poet Boris Vian, and incorporates plainchant, jazz and a quotation from Wagner in its depiction of a pair of young intellectuals in 1940s Paris. *Quatre filles*, based on Picasso's painting *Les demoiselles d'Avignon*, failed to reach the stage for some years because of protracted negotiations with Picasso's heirs.

An important influence on Denisov's musical thinking was Filip Gershkovich, a pupil of Berg and Webern, who inspired the leading talents of the younger Soviet avant garde, including Al'fred Shnitke, Andrey Volkonsky and Viktor Suslin, with the ideas of the Second Viennese School. Thereafter, Denisov saw serialism as an essential school of musical discipline for a young composer, and rapidly assimilated the techniques adopted by the Soviet avant garde so much later than their European contemporaries, after the pressures of the Stalinist era had eased. His early works reflect the stylistic example of Boulez – his *Solntse inkov* ('Sun of the Incas') is dedicated to Boulez – but they were received with extraordinary hostility from the reactionary Soviet Composers' Union under Tikhon Khrennikov, which placed many obstacles in his way: performance of his works at home and in other Socialist countries was banned, as was quotation from them, and he was forbidden to make contacts or travel abroad. Consequently his music almost disappeared from sight in his own country, being kept alive only through the interest shown in it by other countries.

Denisov's compositions are marked by a curious sense of 'weightlessness', based partly on a systematic use of interlocking semitones. His serial technique proceeds logically by small steps in microtones, and is precisely notated; his style is thus rather laconic, strictly economical and logical. Attesting his mathematical training he has said, 'I am concerned not only with beauty of sound... but with beauty of ideas, as mathematicians understand it, or as it was understood by Bach and Webern.'

See also ÉCUME DES JOURS, L'.

Ivan-soldat [Soldier Ivan], 1959 (Denisov, after Russ. traditional stories)

L'écume des jours, 1977–81 (3, Denisov, after B. Vian), Paris, OC (Favart), 15 March 1986; as Pena dney, Perm, 1989; as Der Schaum der Tage, Gelsenkirchen, 16 March 1991 (Hamburg, 1990); excerpts first perfd as Colin et Chloé, concert suite, Moscow, 17 Oct 1983

Quatre filles (1, Denisov), Bonn, Oper, 4 Oct 1986; as Chetïre devushki, Moscow, Forum, 1990

*

B. Schwarz: *Music and Musical Life in Soviet Russia 1917–1970* (London, 1972; Ger. trans., enlarged, 1982 as *Musik und Musikleben in der Sowjetunion 1917 bis zur Gegenwart*)

D. Gojowy: *Neue sowjetische Musik der 20-er Jahre* (Laaber, 1980)

E. Denisov: *Sovremennaya muzïka i problemï evolyutsii kompozitorskoy tekhniki* [Contemporary Music and the Problems of the Development of Composers' Techniques] (Moscow, 1986)

D. Schostakowitsch: 'Briefe an Edison Denissow', *Musik des Ostens*, x (1986), 181–206

H. Danuser, H. Gerlach and J. Köchel, eds.: *Sowjetische Musik im Licht der Perestrojka* (Laaber, 1990)

J. Milojković-Djurić: *Aspects of Soviet Culture: Voices of 'Glasnost', 1960–1990* (New York, 1991) DETLEF GOJOWY

Denize, Nadine (*b* Rouen, 6 Nov 1943). French mezzo-soprano. She studied in Paris, where she made her début at the Opéra in 1967 as Marguerite (*La damnation de Faust*). At the Opéra-Comique she sang Charlotte (*Werther*), a role she repeated at Aix-en-Provence (1979). She has appeared widely in France, in Düsseldorf, Hamburg, Vienna, Chicago, Philadelphia and at La Scala, where she sang Cassandra in *Les Troyens* (1982). Her repertory includes Carmen, Octavian, Eboli, Neris (*Médée*), Mother Marie (*Dialogues des Carmélites*), Concepcion, Kundry, Brangäne and Ortrud, which she sang at Strasbourg in 1985. At the opening of the Bastille in 1990 she sang Anna (*Les Troyens*). A fine actress, she has a warm-toned, soft-grained voice. ELIZABETH FORBES

Denmark (Dan. Danmark). Operatic activity in the 17th century was largely confined to vocal elements in court ballets and in other entertainments associated with the royal palaces in and around Copenhagen. Schütz's extended spells in Denmark in the 1630s and 40s doubtless brought German influence to bear on court drama and music, and the first full-length opera to be performed, P. C. Schindler's *Der vereinigte Götterstreit* (1689, Copenhagen), was in German. An opera house was completed in Copenhagen in 1702, and guest performances of operas by German and Italian composers, notably Reinhard Keiser, were given both there and at court.

From the 1740s onwards touring Italian opera companies visited the Danish court; one of these was directed by Giuseppe Sarti who, with his librettist N. K. Bredal, took the first steps towards a Danish-speaking national opera by mounting a strongly italianate pasticcio *Gram og Signe* (1756). J. E. Hartmann showed himself more independent in his Singspiels to texts by Johannes Ewald, *Balders død* ('The Death of Balder', 1779) and *Fiskerne* ('The Fishermen', 1780): although he was influenced by Gluck, Hartmann's orchestration in *The Death of Balder* is individual and characterful, and its dark-coloured mood can be perceived as 'nordic'. The most significant feature of Danish opera in the decades around 1800 was the growth of the Singspiel. J. A. P. Schulz's *Høstgildet* ('Harvest Home', 1790) and *Peters bryllup* ('Peter's Wedding', 1793) show influences from *opéra comique* as well as indigenous folksong. The most important opera of the period is F. L. A. Kunzen's *Holger Danske* ('Ogier the Dane', 1789), which contains features from both Gluck and *opéra comique*. In the Singspiels *Dragedukken* ('The Dragon Doll', 1797) by Kunzen and *Ungdom og galskab* ('Youth and Folly', 1806) by Edouard Du Puy influences from Mozart's operas can be heard; the latter work moreover displays an elegant mixture of French and Danish styles. C. E. F. Weyse's Singspiels *Sovedrikken* ('The Sleeping-Draught', 1809), *Faruk* (1812), *Ludlams hule* ('Ludlam's Cave', 1816), *Floribella* (1825) and *Festen paa Kenilworth* ('The Feast at Kenilworth', 1836) show an advance on those of Schulz and Kunzen; the influence of Mozart is again evident, and that of Dittersdorf too.

While Weyse enjoyed only limited success with his operas, Friedrich Kuhlau made his mark as a noteworthy opera composer with *Røverborgen* ('The Robbers' Castle', 1814) and *Lulu* (1824). The former combines traits from Italian opera and *opéra comique*, whereas the latter, besides adhering to the Italian opera tradition, is influenced by Weber's operatic style. J. P. E. Hartmann's first opera, *Ravnen* ('The Raven', 1832), is informed by a rich harmonic language reminiscent of Spohr and Weber, while his second, *Korsarerne* ('The Corsairs', 1835), develops the style of Kuhlau's *Røverborgen*, with elements from *opéra comique*. His third, and last completed opera, *Liden Kirsten* ('Little Christine', 1846), is his masterpiece, displaying Romantic folk elements. His *Kong Saul* (*c*1865) includes extensive choral parts.

The most significant Danish Romantic opera is Peter Heise's *Drot og marsk* ('King and Marshal', 1878), which with its folk and medieval elements can be linked to *Little Christine*, and it also includes a number of passages of great dramatic power. Folk elements also inform Asger Hamerik's unfinished opera *Tovelille* (1865) while his one-act opera *La vendetta* (1870) – composed and performed in Italy – anticipates *verismo*. In the operas of P. E. Lange-Müller there are influences from folk music (*Tove*, 1878), *opéra comique* (*Spanske studenter*, 1883), Heise (*Fru Jeanna*, 1891) and Wagner (*Fru Jeanna*, and *Vikingeblod*, 1900). In C. F. E. Horneman's *Aladdin* (1888) the oriental colouring and the effective choruses are particularly striking.

Although the works so far referred to attracted little attention outside Denmark, August Enna's *Heksen* ('The Witch', 1892) captured a European audience. It contains elements from Danish balladry and from Verdi and Wagner, welded into a highly effective dramatic style. In *Aucassin og Nicolette* (1896) Enna moved towards *opéra comique*, while in many of his later operas he was strongly influenced by *verismo*.

Danish opera was decisively enriched and renewed by Carl Nielsen's two operas. *Saul og David* (1902) breaks with the influences of Wagner and *verismo* and shows in its large-scale choral sections the influence of Handel's oratorios; the solo roles display, on the one hand, dramatic strength and expressive power and, on the other, extraordinary lyric charm. *Maskarade* (1906), with its wit, charm and fluent dialogues, proclaims a kinship first and foremost with Mozart; it is the archetypal Danish comic opera and is a popular repertory piece in Denmark.

Late Romantic opera in Denmark is represented primarily by Hakon Børresen. His *Den kongelige gaest* (1919) is a conversation piece with influences from Richard Strauss, while *Kaddara* (1921), which is set in Greenland, contains a number of exotic elements. In the operas of Paul von Klenau a development can be traced from the sonorous and melodic *Kjarten und Gudrun* (1918) through number-opera pastiche in *Die Lästerschule* (1926) to the almost film-like *Michael Kohlhaas* (1933) and *Rembrandt van Rijn* (1937), these last two works being marked by frequent changes of scene and violent scenic effects.

Whereas Finn Høffding's *Kejserens nye klaeder* ('The Emperor's New Clothes', 1928) bears obvious traces of pastiche, and his *Kilderejsen* ('Spring Journey', 1942) appears to build on the wit and lyricism of Nielsen's *Maskarade*, Poul Schierbeck's *Fête galante* (1931) shows traits from Nielsen mixed with elements from Puccini and Strauss. Ebbe Hamerik was the most prominent Danish opera composer in the inter-war period. His *Stepan* (1924) has typically colourful late Romantic orchestration, and *Marie Grubbe* (1940) is strongly nationalist in tone and contains elements of folk music. His last opera, *Drømmerne* ('Dreams'; produced posthumously in 1974), involves actors in the deployment of the text, and there are many rapid changes of scene.

School opera was developed by, among others, Karl S. Clausen (*Klokken*, 'The Clock', 1934), Høffding (*Pasteur*, 1935) and Erling Brene (*Drengen med fløjten*, 'The Boy with the Flute', 1951, and *Under piletraeet*, 'Under the Willow Tree', 1955). Short opera is prominent in the work of Svend S. Schultz (among others *Solbadet* 'The Sunbath', 1949, and *Høst*, 'Harvest', 1950). Two important works from the 1960s are Niels Viggo Bentzon's *Faust III* (1964), which, in a style owing something to improvisation, combines elements from folk ballads, jazz and 12-note music, and Poul Rovsing Olsen's *Belisa* (1966), in which the prevailing lyricism includes touches of oriental colouring. The work of both Ib Nørholm and Per Nørgård has been central to Danish opera since the 1960s. Nørholm used collage technique in his television opera *Invitation til skafottet* ('Invitation to the Scaffold', 1965), while in the chamber opera *Den unge park* ('The Young Park', 1970) he made use of a type of leitmotif technique. Later operas by him are *The Garden Wall* (*Havemuren*; 1976) and *Sandhedens haevn* ('Truth's Revenge'; 1986). Nørgård's *Gilgamesh* (1973) is a large-scale opera in which his concept of an 'infinite series' is combined with a rhythmic hierarchy based on the golden section, together with harmonic structures derived from the overtone and postulated undertone scale. His *Det guddommelige tivoli* ('The Divine Circus', 1982), which portrays episodes from the life of the schizophrenic artist Adolf Wölfli, makes use of, among other features, Balinese instruments and rhythms; *Siddharta* (1983) is an opera-ballet in which Nørgård further developed the techniques used in *Gilgamesh*.

For further information on operatic life in the country's principal centres *see* ÅRHUS; COPENHAGEN; and ODENSE.

*

C. Thrane: *Fra hofviolonernes tid* (Copenhagen, 1908)

G. Lynge: *Danske komponister i det tyvende aarhundredes begyndelse* [Danish Composers at the Start of the 20th Century] (Copenhagen, 2/1917)

T. Krogh: 'De første forsøg paa at skabe en opera i det danske sprog' [The First Attempt to Create an Opera in the Danish Language], *Aarbog for musik 1922*, 123–58

——: *Zur Geschichte des dänischen Singspiels im 18. Jahrhundert* (Copenhagen, 1924)

——: 'Aeldre dansk teatermusik', *Musikhistorisk archiv*, i (1931), 1–100

E. Jacobsen and V. Kappel: *Musikkens mestre: dansk komponister* (Copenhagen, 1947)

F. Törnblom: *Operaens historie* (Copenhagen, 1967)

B. Wallner: *Vår tids musik i Norden: från 20-tal till 60-tal* [The Music of our Time in the North: from the 1920s to the 60s] (Stockholm, 1968)

K. A. Bruun: *Dansk musiks historie fra Holberg-tiden til Carl Nielsen* (Copenhagen, 1969)

N. Schiørring: *Musikkens historie i Danmark* (Copenhagen, 1977–8)

M. Andersen: 'Dansk nutidsopera 1940–1989: fornyelse, kontinuitet, bredde ...' [New Danish Opera 1940–89: Renewal, Continuity, Breadth ...], *Dansk musiktidsskrift*, lxiii (1988–9), 226–8

CLAUS RØLLUM-LARSEN

De Nobili, Lila (*b* Lugano, 3 Sept 1916). Italian painter and designer. She studied at the Académie Ronson, Paris, and the Accademia di Belle Arti, Rome; in 1945 she settled in Paris. After an early career as a fashion

Lila De Nobili's set for 'La traviata', Act 2 scene i (a country house near Paris), from Visconti's production at La Scala, Milan, 1956 (with Maria Callas as Violetta)

illustrator and interior decorator she designed a series of plays for the French director Rouleau and in 1956 was invited by Visconti to design his famous production of *La traviata* with Callas at La Scala. Other notable operatic productions have been Zeffirelli's *Aida* (1963, Teatro alla Scala), set and costumed in the Second Empire taste of the original production, and his enduring *Rigoletto* (1964, Covent Garden).

De Nobili's work exemplifies the return to the realistic, 19th-century stage picture fashionable in the late 1950s and the 1960s. She undertook only a few selected productions, but her individual style, characterized by an elegiac, hazy romanticism (as also in Ashton's ballet *Ondine*, 1958, Covent Garden), and a refined and fastidious sensibility allied to a ruthless perfectionism in execution, have ensured her cult status among fellow designers. In the late 1960s she retired from the stage to concentrate on her painting.

*

ES (R. Lucchese) MARINA HENDERSON

Dent, Edward J(oseph) (*b* Ribston, Yorks., 16 July 1876; *d* London, 22 Aug 1957). English musicologist and translator. He studied at Cambridge with Charles Wood and Stanford. In 1902 he was elected a Fellow of King's College, Cambridge, then worked as a music critic in London (from 1918) before returning to Cambridge as professor of music in 1926. He was a director and later governor of Sadler's Wells Opera and a director of Covent Garden Opera Trust.

At Cambridge, Dent opened up wide areas of the repertory that were then little known. He worked especially on 18th-century Italian opera, and the fruits of his study appeared in a long series of articles and most notably in his books on Alessandro Scarlatti and Mozart's operas, both of which testify to his keen judgment and careful scholarship. He contributed an edition of the masque *Cupid and Death* to Musica Britannica in the hope that it would stimulate stage productions.

Dent was involved in the historic production of *Die Zauberflöte* at Cambridge in 1911, when the work was still practically unknown to the British public. His translation of it was the first in a long series that did much to bring opera to a wider audience. As an excellent linguist, with an easy literary style and a sensitivity to the needs of the theatre and the voice, he was well equipped to produce translations that were worthy of the originals and conveyed the course of the drama stylishly and idiomatically. They include, besides many of the repertory classics, *Les Troyens* and *Benvenuto Cellini*, Busoni's *Doktor Faust*, *Turandot* and *Arlecchino*, Auber's *Fra Diavolo*, *Háry János* and Handel's *Deidamia*. Dent's translations have of necessity been modified or superseded over the years, but his achievement in having immeasurably raised the status of the translator remains undiminished.

Alessandro Scarlatti (London, 1905, rev. 2/1960 by F. Walker)
Mozart's Operas: a Critical Study (London, 1913, 2/1947, rev. 1991; Ger. trans., 1923)
Foundations of English Opera: a Study of Musical Drama in England during the Seventeenth Century (Cambridge, 1928)
Ferruccio Busoni: a Biography (London, 1933, 2/1966)
Handel (London, 1934)
Opera (Harmondsworth, 1940, 5/1949)
A Theatre for Everybody: the Story of the Old Vic and Sadler's Wells (London, 1945, 2/1946)
ed. W. Dean: *The Rise of Romantic Opera* (Cambridge, 1976)

*

J. A. Westrup: 'Dent as Translator', *MR*, vii (1946), 198–204
W. Dean: 'Edward J. Dent: a Centenary Tribute', *ML*, lvii (1976), 353–61
H. Carey: *Duet for Two Voices* (Cambridge, 1979)
ANTHONY LEWIS, NIGEL FORTUNE

Denver. American city, the state capital of Colorado. It was founded in 1858. Mining wealth and civic pride supported opera as an important element of entertainment in Denver, and the city enjoyed regular opera seasons from 1864 to the turn of the century. All early performances were by travelling companies, among them the Gruenwald company (1864), the Howson (or Hawson) Opera Troupe (1869), 'Grand Opera Concerts' (1871), Mlle Marie Aimée and her French Opera Bouffe Company (1872), the Ware-Linton Opera Company (1875), Oates Comic Opera (1876) and the Richings-Bernard company (1877). In 1881 H. A. W. Tabor financed a Grand Opera House (he had already built one in Leadville, Colorado). It was located at 16th and Curtis streets, and opened amid great fanfare with Emma Abbott heading her own company in Wallace's *Maritana*. On 23 January 1882 the *Denver Tribune* announced 'Colorado's First Original Opera', a collaboration between Stanley Wood (libretto) and W. F. Hunt (music) called *Brittle Silver*. In a burst of enthusiasm the newspaper printed the entire libretto.

At the turn of the century national monetary reform and the change to the gold standard placed great strain on the financing of opera and most classical music. Touring companies still appeared, but not regularly. Denver's theatres came under the control of east-coast syndicates which preferred their own theatre productions to opera. The operatic dark ages in the city lasted until the 1929 Depression, although the building of the Denver Civic Auditorium in 1908 gave a home to travelling companies. Conceived as a multi-purpose auditorium, it seated 2200, with traditional boxes; later remodellings stripped away the box seats. Located at 14th and Curtis streets, it became the cornerstone for a complex serving most of Denver's musical and theatrical needs. Local opera was produced from 1915 under the direction of the Rev. Joseph J. Bosetti, whose Denver Grand Opera Company continued sporadically until 1951.

A new age of opera began with the founding of the Central City Opera House Association which, despite its name, has always had its headquarters in Denver. The mining town of Central built its opera house in 1878. Under Denver patronage a summer festival in Central was planned and inaugurated in 1932 (*see* CENTRAL CITY). At the same time, the Denver (now Colorado) SO was formed. The desire for locally produced opera in the capital has been frustrated more than once, however. The most notable of the attempts to establish a company was the Denver Lyric Opera (1958–71), which gave the première of Dominick Argento's *Colonel Jonathan the Saint* (1971). The Denver Lyric Opera Guild continues as a support organization for all opera in the area, in addition to sponsoring auditions and an annual scholarship programme for Colorado singers. Further operatic ventures were undertaken by the University of Denver, Loretto Heights College and Colorado Women's College.

Finally, in 1981 Nathaniel Merrill, an experienced director at the Metropolitan Opera, announced plans for Opera Colorado. The company opened in 1983 in what is still a unique venue in the USA, Boettcher Concert Hall, constructed to a 'vertical surround' design in which the audience completely surrounds the stage. Opera Colorado has turned this to advantage, achieving an intimacy unmatched in grand opera anywhere (the most distant seat is only 26 metres from the stage; the orchestra is beneath it). Imaginative stage design for 365-degree viewing, and staging aimed at unusual viewpoints, have gained the company a fiercely loyal following. During the first two weeks of May the company offers four performances of two operas, using international singers and the Colorado SO. All productions are in the original language with 'SurRound' titles for translation. The hall, which seats 2400 on several banked tiers and is located at 13th and Curtis streets, is part of the Denver Performing Arts Complex which incorporates the old Auditorium Theater. In 1991 Denver opened a new proscenium theatre, the 2800-seat Buell Theatre, in the Performing Arts Complex. Its first performances featured Opera Colorado, which announced plans to offer performances regularly both there in the autumn and in the Boettcher Concert Hall in the spring.

Denver and Colorado have inspired several operatic plots. The most famous is that of Douglas Moore's *The Ballad of Baby Doe*, set entirely in Colorado and commissioned by the Central City Opera; the opera was given its première in July 1956. Operatic works have also been written by the resident composers Normand Lockwood, Cecil Effinger and Mary Davis.

*

F. H. Johnson: *Denver's Old Theater Row* (Denver, 1970)

S. A. Linscome: *A History of Musical Development in Denver, Colorado, 1858–1908* (diss., U. of Texas, 1970)

G. Giffin: 'The Pride of Gregory Gulch', *ON*, xli/1 (1976–7), 20–22

GLENN GIFFIN

Denza, Luigi (*b* Castellammare di Stabia, 24 Feb 1846; *d* London, 26 Jan 1922). Italian composer. From 1862 he studied composition under Mercadante and Serrao at the Naples Conservatory. In 1876 his *opera seria Wallenstein* (4, A. Bruner), after Schiller's trilogy, was produced in Naples (Mercadante, 13 May). He later settled in London and became a director of the London Academy of Music and professor of singing at the RAM. He composed more than 500 songs, partsongs and cantatas to Italian, French and English texts; he is best remembered for the Neapolitan song *Funiculì funiculà*. His melodic style has much in common with that of Ciro Pinsuti; he wrote in an overtly populist vein which anticipated the sugary Hollywood idiom of the 1920s.

NIGEL BURTON, KEITH HORNER

Denzio [Denzi], **Antonio** (*b* Venice, ?*c*1690; *d* ?Moscow, after 1763). Italian tenor, impresario and librettist. He sang at Venice and elsewhere in Italy between 1715 and 1723, at first taking leading roles such as Artabanus in Vivaldi's *La costanza trionfante degli amori e degli odii* (Venice, Carnival 1716), but within a few years singing only minor parts. In 1724 the impresario Antonio Maria Peruzzi engaged Denzio to assemble a company of singers in Venice and bring them to Prague, where they performed in the theatres of Count Franz Anton von Sporck. Peruzzi's financial mismanagement of the company led to his being replaced as impresario by Denzio late in that year; in the next ten years Denzio staged 57 productions of operas and sacred dramas in Prague, including works by Vivaldi and Albinoni as well as by the troupe's composers, Antonio Bioni and Giovanni Antonio Guerra. Denzio's own librettos included *La pravità castigata* (1730), the first known operatic treatment of the Don Juan story.

In late 1734 Denzio was briefly imprisoned for debt and gave up the leadership of the company. He then worked in Venice as an impresario and singer; in the 1740s he directed ballets and pantomimes in Germany, with disastrous financial results. He was appointed court poet to Empress Elizabeth of Russia in 1755, and wrote librettos for comic intermezzos and serenatas performed at St Petersburg. He left court service in 1758 or 1759 but apparently remained in Russia.

*

O. Teuber: *Geschichte des Prager Theaters*, i (Prague, 1883)

R.-A. Mooser: *Annales de la musique et des musiciens en Russie au XVIIIme siècle*, i (Geneva, 1948)

P. Kneidl: 'Libreta italské opery v Praze v 18. století, 1', *Strahovská knihovna*, i (1966), 97–131

T. Volek and M. Skalická: 'Vivaldis Beziehungen zu den böhmischen Ländern', *AcM*, xxxix (1967), 419–28

D. Freeman: *The Opera Theater of Count Franz Anton von Sporck in Prague* (New York, 1990)

MICHAEL TALBOT

Denzler, Robert (*b* Zürich, 19 March 1892; *d* Zürich, 25 Aug 1972). Swiss conductor. He studied at the Zürich Conservatory and then in Cologne while working as a répétiteur at the opera house and the Bayreuth Festival. At that time (1911–12) he started appearing as a conductor and was engaged as director of music at Lucerne (1912) and as conductor of the Zürich Opera (1915). Following his time as chief conductor of the Berlin Städtische Oper (1927–32), he returned in 1934 to Zürich, where he conducted the premières of Berg's *Lulu* and Hindemith's *Mathis der Maler*. Denzler was renowned as an interpreter of classical opera, contemporary music and, above all, Wagner. JÜRG STENZL

De Pablo, Luís. *See* PABLO, LUÍS DE.

De Paolis, Alessio (*b* Rome, 5 March 1893; *d* Queens, NY, 9 March 1964). Italian tenor. He studied in Rome, making his début in 1919 at Bologna as the Duke (*Rigoletto*). In 1921 he sang Fenton (*Falstaff*) at La Scala, and for a decade continued to appear as a lyric tenor throughout Italy. In 1933 he turned to character roles. He made his New York début in 1938 as Cassio (*Otello*) at the Metropolitan, where he gave well over a thousand performances of 50 roles in the next 26 seasons. His repertory included Shuysky, Goro (*Madama Butterfly*), Spoletta, Don Basilio, the Astrologer (*The Golden Cockerel*), Gherardo (*Gianni Schicchi*) and Monsieur Triquet (*Yevgeny Onegin*), which he sang shortly before his death.

ELIZABETH FORBES

De Pasquali, Bernice. *See* PASQUALI, BERNICE DE.

De Pirro, Nicola (*b* Nocera, Cosenza, 28 April 1898; *d* Rome, 3 July 1979). Italian administrator. From his youth he supported the populist wing of the fascist movement. In 1925, under Mussolini's dictatorship, he became the founder-director of the fascist trade union for theatre workers; later he headed the inspectorate that dealt with newly nationalized opera houses, as well as the consortium that was supposed to control their repertory. From 1935 to the fall of the regime in 1943 he was the head of theatre administration in the Ministry of Press and Propaganda (later Ministry of Popular Culture). 'Among the more intelligent and competent' fascist bureaucrats (Sachs), he tried to reconcile the aims of bringing opera to the masses and of encouraging young composers; in 1942 his office financed the first Italian production of *Wozzeck*, at that time banned in Germany. His most notable achievement was the Carro di Tespi, a network of well-organized summer touring companies which from 1930 gave open-air opera performances; in 1937 they gave 75 performances in 42 provinces, before audiences totalling about half a million.

*

ES ('Carro di Tespi'; R. Volpini)
N. De Pirro: *Il teatro per il popolo* (Rome, 1938)
L. Trezzini and A. Curtolo: *Oltre le quinte: idee, cultura e organizzazione musicale in Italia* (Venice, 1983), 42–4
F. Nicolodi: *Musica e musicisti nel ventennio fascista* (Fiesole, 1984)
H. Sachs: *Music in Fascist Italy* (London, 1987) JOHN ROSSELLI

De Reszke. Polish family of singers.

(1) **Jean de Reszke** (*b* Warsaw, 14 Jan 1850; *d* Nice, 3 April 1925). Tenor. He studied with Ciaffei and Cotogni as a baritone, making his début (under the name of Giovanni di Reschi) at La Fenice, Venice, in 1874 as Alphonse XI (*La favorite*), the role of his London début at Drury Lane the same year. He also sang Valentin and Don Giovanni. In 1876 (now as Jean de Reszke), he sang Melitone (*Forza*) and Rossini's Figaro in Paris, then retired to restudy as a tenor with Sbriglia. His first appearance as a tenor, in the title role of *Robert le diable* at Madrid in 1879, was not a success and he did not sing again until 1884, when he made a triumphant reappearance as John the Baptist in the first Paris performance of Massenet's *Hérodiade*, at the Théâtre Italien. The following year he created the title role in *Le Cid* at the Opéra, where he was engaged for five seasons, singing Radames, Vasco da Gama (*L'Africaine*) and the title roles of *Le prophète* and *Faust*.

Edouard de Reszke (left) as Don Diègue and Jean de Reszke as Rodrigue in the original production of Massenet's 'Le Cid' at the Paris Opéra in 1885

In 1887 he made his tenor début in London at Drury Lane as Radames, later singing Lohengrin (his first Wagnerian role) in Italian. During the next four years he sang Vasco da Gama, Raoul (*Les Huguenots*), Faust, Lohengrin, Riccardo (*Un ballo in maschera*), Romeo, Walther, Don José and Otello at Covent Garden. He made his American début in 1891 at Chicago as Lohengrin, then sang for the first time at the Metropolitan as Romeo. In 1894 he sang Werther in Chicago, New York and London. Taking on the heavier Wagner roles, he sang Tristan (1895), young Siegfried (1896) and Siegfried in *Götterdämmerung* (1898). His last new role was Canio (1902). His beautiful voice, fine musicianship and handsome appearance made him unsurpassed in the French repertory, as well as in the Wagner roles he sang with such distinction.

(2) **Edouard de Reszke** (*b* Warsaw, 22 Dec 1853; *d* Garnek, Poland, 25 May 1917). Bass, brother of (1) Jean de Reszke. He studied with Steller and Coletti, and made his début as the King in the first Paris performance

of *Aida* at the Opéra in 1876. He was then engaged for two seasons at the Théâtre Italien. He sang Indra in Massenet's *Le roi de Lahore* at Milan (1879) and made his London début at Covent Garden in the same role (1880). He also sang Saint-Bris (*Les Huguenots*), Rodolfo (*La sonnambula*) and Don Basilio (*Il barbiere di Siviglia*). In 1881 he sang Fiesco in the first performance of the revised version of *Simon Boccanegra* at La Scala, Milan, where he also appeared as Silva (*Ernani*). He sang Alvise in the first London performance of *La Gioconda* (1883).

He sang in *Hérodiade* and *Le Cid* in Paris with Jean, and thereafter his career closely followed that of his brother, in London, Chicago and New York. His vast repertory included Méphistophélès, Friar Laurence (*Roméo et Juliette*), Don Pedro (*L'Africaine*), Rocco and Leporello, which he sang at a special centenary performance of *Don Giovanni* at the Opéra in 1887. His huge voice and giant stature made him a magnificent exponent of Wagner roles, and he sang Daland, King Henry (*Lohengrin*), Hans Sachs, King Mark, the Wanderer (*Siegfried*) and Hagen. He retired in 1903, soon after his brother.

(3) **Josephine de Reszke** (*b* Warsaw, 4 June 1855; *d* Warsaw, 22 Feb 1891). Soprano, sister of (1) Jean and (2) Edouard de Reszke. After studying at the St Petersburg Conservatory, she made her début in Venice in 1874 in *Il Guarany* by Carlos Gomez. She made her Paris début in 1875 at the Opéra as Ophelia (Thomas' *Hamlet*) and sang there for a decade in such roles as Marguerite, Mathilde (*Guillaume Tell*), Valentine (*Les Huguenots*), Rachel (*La Juive*), and both Isabelle and Alice in *Robert le diable*. She created the part of Sitâ in *Le roi de Lahore* (1877). In 1881 she sang Aida at Covent Garden, but was not a success and cancelled her contract. She sang Salome at some of the Paris performances of *Hérodiade* in 1884, when all three de Reszkes were on stage together.

*

C. Leiser: *Jean de Reszke and the Great Days of Opera* (London, 1933)
P. G. Hurst: *The Age of Jean de Reszke* (London, 1958)

ELIZABETH FORBES

Dérivis. French family of singers.

(1) **Henri-Etienne Dérivis** (*b* Albi, 2 Aug 1780; *d* Livry, Seine et Oise, 1 Feb 1856). Bass. He made his début in 1803 at the Paris Opéra, where he was engaged until 1828. He created the Pontifex Maximus in Spontini's *La Vestale* (1807) and the High Priest in the same composer's *Fernand Cortez* (1809). He took part in the first performances of Cherubini's *Les Abencérages* (1813) and of Spontini's *Olympie* (1819). He sang Mahomet II in Rossini's *Le siège de Corinthe* (1826) and many other roles, including Sarastro in a reworking of Mozart's *Die Zauberflöte*, *Les mystères d'Isis*.

(2) **(Nicholas) Prosper Dérivis** (*b* Paris, 28 Oct 1808; *d* Paris, 11 Feb 1880). Bass, son of (1) Henri-Etienne Dérivis. He studied in Paris and made his début there at the Opéra in 1831. During the next 20 years he sang an enormous repertory, including Bertram (*Robert le diable*), William Tell, Leporello, Don Giovanni and Balthazar (*La favorite*). He sang a Herald in the first performance of *La Juive* (1835) and later took the part of Cardinal Brogny in that opera. He created Nevers in *Les Huguenots* (1836), Balducci in *Benvenuto Cellini* (1838) and Félix in Donizetti's *Les martyrs* (1840). At La Scala he sang Zaccaria in the first performance of *Nabucco* (1842) and Pagano at the première of *I Lombardi* (1843). He created the Prefect in Donizetti's *Linda di Chamounix* in Vienna (1842). In 1851 he sang Zacharie in Meyerbeer's *Le prophète*.

(3) **Maria Dérivis** (*b* *c*1845; *d* in or after 1877). Soprano, daughter of (2) Prosper Dérivis. She made her début in 1869, sang Marguerite in Gounod's *Faust* at the Paris Opéra in 1873 and was engaged at the Théâtre de la Monnaie from 1875 to 1877, singing Mireille, Isabelle (*Le pré aux clercs*) and the title role in *Dinorah* (*Le pardon de Ploërmel*). ELIZABETH FORBES

Dermota, Anton (*b* Kropa, Slovenia, 4 June 1910; *d* Vienna, 22 June 1989). Slovene tenor. He first appeared in Cluj in 1934, then was invited by Bruno Walter to Vienna, where in 1936 he made his début as the First Man in Armour (*Die Zauberflöte*) and went on to sing Alfredo; the same year he had sung Zorn (*Die Meistersinger*) at Salzburg, where in 1938 he sang Belmonte and Don Ottavio. In 1947 he appeared at Covent Garden with the Vienna Staatsoper as Don Ottavio, Ferrando and Narraboth. Although he won most renown as a Mozart tenor, Dermota also appeared in the Italian and German repertory, and in 1955 was accorded the honour of singing Florestan at the reopening of the Vienna Staatsoper; in 1956 he took part in the première there of Martin's *Der Sturm*. His large repertory included the title role in Pfitzner's *Palestrina* and Lensky in *Yevgeny Onegin*. He made guest appearances in most leading European opera houses. His singing was always flexible and musicianly; the voice itself had a touch of reediness.

*

GV (F. Serpa; R. Vegeto) HAROLD ROSENTHAL/R

Dernesch, Helga (*b* Vienna, 3 or 13 Feb 1939). Austrian soprano and mezzo-soprano. After studying at the Vienna Conservatory she was engaged by the Berne Opera, making her début in 1961 as Marina (*Boris Godunov*). Engagements followed at Wiesbaden (1963–5) and Cologne (1965–8). At Bayreuth, where she first appeared in 1965, she sang Freia, Gutrune and Eva. With Scottish Opera she sang Gutrune (1968), her first Leonore (1970), Brünnhilde, Isolde, Ariadne, the Marschallin and Cassandra (*Les Troyens*). At the Salzburg Easter Festivals she appeared as Brünnhilde (*Siegfried* and *Götterdämmerung*), Leonore and Isolde. At Covent Garden, where she made her début in 1970 as Sieglinde, she sang Chrysothemis, the Dyer's Wife and, in 1987, the Nurse (*Die Frau ohne Schatten*). She made her Chicago (1971) and Vienna Staatsoper (1972) débuts as Leonore. She created the title role of Fortner's *Elisabeth Tudor* at Berlin in 1972 and Goneril in Reimann's *Lear* in 1978. She then began to sing mezzo roles, including Clytemnestra, Herodias, Adelaide (*Arabella*), Mistress Quickly, Erda and Fricka. In 1985 she sang Marfa (*Khovanshchina*) at the Metropolitan and in 1986 created Hecuba in Reimann's *Troades* in Munich. Her voice has great richness and power, and her strikingly handsome stage appearance and intense acting make her a compelling performer.

*

T. Smillie: 'Helga Dernesch', *Opera*, xxiv (1973), 407–12

HAROLD ROSENTHAL/R

De Rogatis [Rogati], **Francesco Saverio** (*b* Naples, 1745; *d* Naples, 1827). Italian poet. He studied at the

Collegio Calasanzio in Rome, where he joined the Arcadian Academy under the pastoral name Argesio Ginesio. He returned to the University of Naples and pursued studies in poetry with the court poet Saverio Mattei, a close friend of Niccolò Jommelli. Mattei introduced De Rogatis to the *drammatico-lirico* style. De Rogatis's drama, based on Tasso's *Gerusalemme liberata*, had already achieved some notoriety when the need for a new libretto for Jommelli arose. The libretto, *Armida abbandonata* (facs. in IOB, xciii, 1983), is unusually rich in spectacular effects including ballet, chorus and machine spectacle. In 1773 elements of De Rogatis's libretto were combined with parts of another on the subject by the Turin librettist Jacopo Durandi to produce a composite on which Haydn's *opera seria Armida abbandonata* was ultimately based. Other settings were made by Naumann, Gazzaniga, Tozzi, Mortellari, Bertoni, Cherubini and Zingarelli.

*

Marchese de Villarosa: 'Necrologia', *Poesie varie del Signor Francesco Saverio de Rogati* (Naples, 1842), 5–8

M. McClymonds: *Niccolò Jommelli: the Last Years, 1769–1774* (Ann Arbor, 1980)

——: 'Haydn and his Contemporaries: "Armida abbandonata"', *International Joseph Haydn Congress: Vienna 1982*, 325–32

MARITA P. McCLYMONDS

De Rogatis, Pascual. *See* ROGATIS, PASCUAL DE.

Déry (Schenbach-Széppataky), Róza (*b* Jászberény, 1793; *d* Miskolc, 1872). Hungarian soprano. She studied singing with Gáspár Pacha. Between 1815 and 1850 she performed with various companies in towns throughout Hungary including Buda, Kassz, Arad, Pozsony and Nagyvárad. She made a lasting impression with her acting ability and captivating singing. Her best-known operatic roles were Jutka in László Kelemen's *Pikkó Hertzeg és Jutka Perzsi*, Norma and Rosina; she also sang in performances of *Die Zauberflöte* and *L'italiana in Algeri*. Her diary, published in 1899, remains an important literary work. Eniko Balkány wrote a monograph on her (1937).

Derzhinskaya, Kseniya Georgiyevna (*b* Kiev, 25 Jan/6 Feb 1889; *d* Moscow, 9 June 1951). Russian soprano. She studied singing in Kiev, and from 1913 to 1915 sang at the Moscow opera house Narodnïy Dom. She was a soloist at the Bol'shoy from 1915 to 1948, and was greatly influenced by Stanislavsky and the conductor Václav Suk. Under the latter she sang Lisa (*The Queen of Spades*), Nastas'ya (Tchaikovsky's *The Enchantress*), Fevroniya (Rimsky-Korsakov's *The Legend of the Invisible City of Kitezh*) and Ortrud. Other roles included Mariya (Tchaikovsky's *Mazepa*), the Snow Maiden and Gounod's Marguerite. She was one of the outstanding Russian singers of her time, distinguished by the wide range and beautiful timbre of her strong voice, the completeness of her interpretations and her dramatic gift. Her portrayals of Russian women were particularly successful. In 1926 she sang in a concert performance of *Kitezh* at the Paris Opéra, with great success.

*

E. Groshyova: *Kseniya Georgiyevna Derzhinskaya* (Moscow, 1952)

I. M. YAMPOL'SKY

De Sabata, Victor (*b* Trieste, 10 April 1892; *d* Santa Margherita Ligure, 11 Dec 1967). Italian conductor and composer. After studying composition with Giacomo Orefice at the Milan Conservatory, he won considerable success with his opera *Il macigno* (La Scala, 1917). In 1918 he was engaged by the Monte Carlo Opera, where he conducted the première of *L'enfant et les sortilèges* and the French première of Puccini's *La rondine*. Making his La Scala début in 1930 with *La fanciulla del West*, he soon became permanently attached there; his *Tristan und Isolde*, staged in December that year, was a great success and he came to be considered an outstanding interpreter of it. With singers from La Scala he visited Berlin, Munich (1939), London and Edinburgh (1950), though poor health restricted his conducting activities and from 1953 he served as artistic director of and then consultant to La Scala.

Blessed with an outstandingly exact and critical ear, De Sabata was a gifted, original and fascinating conductor whose often incandescent performances resembled Toscanini's. From his large repertory he preferred Verdi's later works and liked Boito's *Mefistofele* and, in Italian translation, Saint-Saëns' *Samson et Dalila*. He was a typical product of the Italian culture that, after Wagner, had absorbed Strauss and the French impressionists and had witnessed the rise of the Italian *verismo* school. De Sabata's few recordings include *Tosca*, made with Callas, Di Stefano and Gobbi.

*

F. Aprahamian: 'Victor de Sabata: a Memoir', *Opera*, xix (1968), 155–7

T. Celli: *L'arte di Victor de Sabata* (Turin, 1978) [with discography by L. Bellingardi]

PIERO RATTALINO

Desaides, Nicholas. *See* DEZÈDE, NICOLAS.

De Santi, Anna (*b* Florence, *c*1772; *d* nr Dresden, 2 June 1802). Italian soprano, wife of GAETANO ANDREOZZI.

De Santis, Luigi (*fl* Naples, 1790s). Italian poet. His principal claim to fame is an updated version of *Ines de Castro*, which Cosimo Giotti had written for Florence with music by Gaetano Andreozzi in 1783. In his rewritten version of 1794 De Santis provided Francesco Bianchi with multiple ensembles – an introductory quintet, several duets, and two ensemble finales (a trio and a sextet) – newly fashionable in *opera seria*. With an early Romantic plot based on medieval Spanish history, Bianchi's opera enjoyed a number of revivals and pasticcios in the 1790s. The libretto was later set by Nasolini, Ignazio Gerace and Giustino Cervellini. De Santis wrote one other libretto, the comic opera *La guerra aperta*, set by Francesco Ruggi for Naples in 1796.

MARITA P. McCLYMONDS

Désaugiers [Des Augiers, Desaugiers], **Marc-Antoine** (*b* Fréjus, 1742; *d* Paris, 10 Sept 1793). French composer. Little is known about his career, except that a deformity of the left hand prevented him from performing instrumentally. His first stage work performed at the Comédie-Italienne, *Le petit Oedipe* (1779), suffered from a clumsily allegorical libretto, but *Florine* (1780) brought him some celebrity, no doubt because of its high proportion of numbers of a sentimental nature; the Count's aria 'Ce fut par la faute du sort', in particular, contains a good example of the type of melody with regular, symmetrical phrasing liked by the French at the beginning of the 1780s. Although the music of *Les deux sylphes* is relatively uninteresting, the *comédie Les deux jumeaux de Bergame* of 1782 contains two pieces – the serenade 'Daigne écouter l'amant fidèle et tendre' and the final vaudeville – which remained popular until the beginning of the 19th century. Désaugiers received no further commissions from the Comédie-Italienne and did not come to the fore again until new theatres were created under the Revolution. His last three operas are chiefly in comic vein, and show to what extent French composers had assimilated the techniques of Italian *opera buffa*. Mastery of the form is evident, for instance, in the second finale of *Le rendez-vous* (1790), which is divided into seven successive movements strictly determined by the development of the dramatic action. A peculiarity of the tonal pattern of this finale (B♭–E♭–c–C–F–B♭) is that in part it follows the circle of 5ths, a procedure employed by Désaugiers again in the first finale of *Le médecin malgré lui* (A–D–G–C–A). Désaugiers had only one work produced at the Opéra, *Erixène* (1780), but nonetheless showed great interest in the pastoral genre, as the large number of manuscripts preserved in the library of the Paris Conservatoire proves.

all first performed in Paris; all printed works published in Paris

PCI – *Comédie-Italienne*

Le petit Oedipe, ou Agenor et Zulma [parody of J.-F. Ducis: Oedipe chez Admète] (comédie pastorale mêlée d'ariettes et de vaudevilles, 1, Landrin), PCI (Bourgogne), 22 May 1779, excerpts (1779; n.d.)

Florine (cmda, 3, B. Imbert), PCI (Bourgogne), 15 June 1780, *F-Pc** (in 2 acts, with many alternative items), excerpts (1780)

Erixène, ou L'amour enfant (pastorale, 1, N. F. Guillard, after C. H. Voisenon: *Colin Maillard* and B. Guarini: *Il pastor fido*), Opéra, 24 Sept 1780, *Po*, excerpts (1780)

Les deux sylphes (comédie semi-lyrique, 1, Imbert), PCI (Bourgogne), 18 Oct 1781 (1782), airs (n.d.)

Les deux jumeaux de Bergame [Les jumeaux] (comédie, 1, J. P. Florian), PCI (Bourgogne), 6 Aug 1782 [lib. incl. 3 musical items]; full setting (cmda, 1), unperf., *Pc**; excerpts (1782, 1783 and n.d.)

L'auteur satirique (comédie, 1, J. B. D. Desprès, after Voisenon: *L'art de guérir l'esprit*), PCI (Favart), 24 June 1783, *Pc* (MS 14010), air (n.d.) [lib. incl. 2 musical items]; full setting (cmda, 1), unperf., *Pc** (MS 13890)

Jeannette et Lucas, ou Le secrétaire de sa prétendue (comédie mêlée de chants, 2), Beaujolais, 18 Feb 1788

La jeune veuve curieuse (1), Beaujolais, 5 July 1788, 1 air (1788)

Le rendez-vous (comédie, 2, P.-D. de Villers), Français Comique et Lyrique, 31 July 1790 (n.d.), *Pc**

L'amant travesti (opéra bouffon, 2, A.-D. Dubreuil, after J. de La Fontaine: *Le muletier*), Monsieur, 2 Nov 1790, *Pc* (partly autograph)

Le médecin malgré lui (opéra bouffon, 3, M.-A. M. Désaugiers, after Molière), Feydeau, 26 Jan 1792, *Pc**

Unperf. (autographs in *Pc* unless otherwise stated): L'absence de Nina, ou Les rigueurs de l'absence (scène lyrique); Le bal (comédie, 1, ? J.-F. Regnard); Bélisaire, 1787 (tragédie lyrique, 3, A. F. Désaugiers, after J. F. Marmontel), *Po*, frag. *Pc*; Cadmus et Hermione (tragi-comédie, 3, ? after P. Quinault); Coridon et Phylis; Doris et Phylamon, ou Les trompeurs trompés (comédie lyrique, 1, Legrand); Echo et Narcisse (pastorale-héroïque, 1, C. de Laurès); La fête cauchoise, ou Le mariage de Toinette (cmda, 1); Mirzelle (opéra-féerie, 1, Voisenon); Philémon et Baucis (1, after La Fontaine); Zadir et Zilla (comédie semi-lyrique, 1)

*

A. Choron and F. Fayolle: *Dictionnaire historique des musiciens* (Paris, 1810–11)

J. T. Merle: 'Notice sur la vie et les ouvrages de M. A. Désaugiers', *Chansons et poésies diverses de Marc-Antoine Désaugiers*, iv (Paris, 1827)

MICHEL NOIRAY

Deschamps-Jehin, (Marie) Blanche (*b* Lyons, 18 Sept 1857; *d* Paris, June 1923). French contralto. She studied in Lyons and Paris, and made her début in 1879 as Mignon at the Théâtre de la Monnaie, where she also created Massenet's Herodias (1881) and Uta in Reyer's *Sigurd* (1884). At the Opéra-Comique, Paris, she created Margared in *Le roi d'Ys* (1888), Madame de la Haltière in Massenet's *Cendrillon* (1899) and the Mother in *Louise* (1900). At Monte Carlo she sang the title role in the first performance of Franck's *Hulda* (1894) and created the Baroness in Massenet's *Chérubin* (1905). She made her début at the Paris Opéra in 1891 as Léonor (*La favorite*), later singing Fidès, Amneris, Hedwige (*Guillaume Tell*), Delilah, Gertrude (*Hamlet*), Ortrud, Fricka, and Véronique in the first performance of Bruneau's *Messidor* (1897). Her repertory also included Carmen, Azucena, Brangäne and Erda. Her voice, a true contralto, was rich-toned and flexible.

ELIZABETH FORBES

Desclauzas, Marie [Malvina-Ernestine Armand] (*b* Paris, 1840; *d* Nogent-sur-Marne, 9 March 1912). French soprano. She studied at the Conservatoire, made her début as an actress at Reims when she was 15, and soon went to Paris. She then went into operetta, and made a successful visit to the USA in 1869, returning to Paris in 1870. With the Humbert company at the Brussels Fantaisies-Parisiennes, she was cast as Mlle Lange in the first production of Lecocq's *La fille de Madame Angot* (1872); when the show was taken to Paris the composer insisted that she be retained, and she repeated her enormous success at the Théâtre des Folies-Dramatiques. She began to use her talent for comedy in character roles, first at the Renaissance, Paris, then elsewhere, including Hervé's *Alice de Nevers* (1875) and works by Lecocq, of which the most notable was the Directrice in Lecocq's *Le petit duc* (1878), which she played for some 20 years. Such was her personality and effectiveness that female character roles in *opérette* became known as 'les rôles de Desclauzas'.

Desderi, Claudio (*b* Alessandria, 9 April 1943). Italian bass-baritone. He studied in Florence and made his début in 1969 with the Maggio Musicale in Edinburgh as Gaudenzio (*Il Signor Bruschino*). He has sung at all the major Italian theatres, including La Scala, with whose company he went to Covent Garden in 1976 as Alidoro and Dandini. In 1977 he sang Martio in the modern version of Landi's *Sant'Alessio* at Salzburg. He made his Glyndebourne début as Rossini's Bartolo (1981), returning as Don Magnifico (1983), Mozart's Figaro (1984), Don Alfonso (1987) and Falstaff (1988). He has sung at Chicago, Dallas, Washington, DC, Geneva, Brussels and the Paris Opéra. He made his début with the Royal Opera in 1987 as Figaro, returning as Don Alfonso (1989). His repertory includes Count Robinson (*Il matrimonio segreto*), Leporello, Gianni Schicchi, Dulcamara, the Viceroy (*La Périchole*), Nick Shadow and Rossini's Macrobio (*La pietra del paragone*), Mustafà (*L'italiana in Algeri*), old Bruschino and Raimbaud (*Le comte Ory*). A fine comic actor with superb diction, he also conducted *Rigoletto* in Belfast (1977) and Mozart's Da Ponte operas in Italy and London (1989–91).

ELIZABETH FORBES

De Segurola, Andrés. *See* SEGUROLA, ANDRÉS DE.

Déserteur, Le ('The Deserter'). *Drame* in three acts by PIERRE-ALEXANDRE MONSIGNY to a libretto by MICHEL-JEAN SEDAINE; Paris, Comédie-Italienne (Hôtel de Bourgogne), 6 March 1769.

Le déserteur was inspired by an incident that occurred in 1767 at Compiègne where Louis XV was undertaking a military inspection. With the announcement that a deserter had been condemned to death, the wife of the

Maréchal de Ségur, the camp commandant, threw herself at the king's feet and obtained a pardon for him. Although the touching nature of this anecdote is retained in the libretto, much of the plot is Sedaine's own invention, and it is not the Maréchale de Ségur who saves his life but the soldier's fiancée, Louise. Act 1 takes place in the country near the village where Louise (soprano) lives; the girl is waiting for her fiancé, Alexis (baritone), who is to visit her while on leave. However, the local seigneur's wife, a malevolent duchess, has decided to put Alexis's love to the test. Accordingly, when he approaches the village he sees a wedding procession with Louise herself as the bride. Although this is no more than an unkind practical joke, Alexis, an impetuous character, reacts violently; in his despair he crosses the Flemish frontier in the sight of four soldiers and is arrested for desertion. In Act 2 he is visited in prison by Louise; he learns from her that she was a most reluctant party to the scene staged by the Duchess and that she still loves him. But it is too late: Alexis is condemned to death. During Act 3 Courchemin (baritone), a military police sergeant, brings news that the king has allowed a young woman (Louise) to soften his heart and has pardoned a man condemned to death. Louise arrives at the prison just in time to see her fiancé, but she faints, and comes to her senses only after Alexis has left for the place of execution. Once she regains consciousness she hurries to the public square, and the opera ends with general rejoicing.

A plot of this nature was so remote from the usual subject matter of the *opéra comique* that Sedaine called his work a *drame*, thus clearly establishing its relationship with the plays and theoretical writings of Diderot. It is true that the comic element is still quite prominent, largely owing to the presence in Alexis's prison of the dragoon Montauciel (tenor), who acts as a foil to the serious characters. However, Sedaine's main achievement, certainly working in close collaboration with Monsigny, was to devise a libretto particularly favourable to musical innovation. For instance, composer and librettist avoid giving Alexis a big aria of despair at the end of the first act, as this would have entailed dangerous anticipation of the remaining acts; instead, they place the decisive moment when Alexis deserts at the heart of a long musical sequence linking a vehement recitative to an aria concluding in the dominant key and a part-comic, part-tragic quintet in which the young man defies the border guards. The end of the second act is equally striking: two comic characters, Louise's cousin Bertrand (tenor) and Montauciel, each sing a song, and these are then superimposed independently in a duet. (Cherubini later set himself a similar exercise in the first act of *Lodoïska.*) The opera's conclusion consists of an unbroken sequence linking four successive episodes: an aria for Alexis, a recitative by Louise, an ensemble in accompanied recitative style and a chorus alternating with the soloists and replacing the traditional final vaudeville.

'Le déserteur' (Monsigny), Act 3: aquatint by Duhamel after F. M. Queverdo (c1787)

A similar search for complexity is found in the purely musical elements, such as the programmatic content of the overture (which begins and ends with the theme of the final chorus) and the use of entr'actes as thematic reminders: the first entr'acte takes up the music of Louise's first aria and the second, marked *andante amoroso*, is built on the theme of the aria in which Alexis reads Louise's letter (2.ii). More subtly, Monsigny three times associates the character of Louise with the key of A major, in two of her arias (1.i and 2.viii) and in a quotation made by Courchemin in the middle of his big narrative (3.viii). Another characteristic of the work is the frequent introduction of a break in continuity within the same piece, producing an emotional effect suited to the intolerable situation of the character concerned. This procedure occurs in Alexis's first aria (1.iv), before the drama itself has even begun. Monsigny employs it again when Alexis is reading Louise's letter (2.ii), the result being a curious formal pattern approaching that of the rondo: *ABACD* (*andante amoroso*) *E* (recitative *presto*) *A′*; other examples of sudden changes of direction occur in the fugal trio (2.xi) and in arias in the final act for Alexis (scene iv), Courchemin (scene vi) and Louise (scene x). On each occasion these interruptions of the musical discourse correspond to a real dramatic necessity, and unite with various other procedures to represent, in 1769, the height of expressiveness, at least in the context of French musical language. It is not surprising, therefore, that *Le déserteur* soon came to be considered Sedaine and Monsigny's masterpiece, marking both the apex of the *opéra comique* of the 1750s and 60s and the point of departure for new experiments in the serious vein. MICHEL NOIRAY

Deshayes [Des Hayes, Deshays], **Prosper-Didier** (*b* mid-18th century; *d* Paris, 1815). Composer and dancer active in France. He was ballet-master at the Comédie-Française by 1764 and was an *adjoint* at the Opéra in 1774. He made his début as an opera composer in 1785 with the popular but slight *Le faux serment, ou La matrone de Gonesse*. Only this *opéra comique* and the *drame Zélia* (1791), after Goethe's *Stella*, were published as scores.

Deshayes usually wrote arias in the conventional three-part – often da capo – form; some, however, are more closely linked to the dramatic text, with relatively independent sections following each other within a regular and simple harmonic order. His motivic inventions do not appear to be inspired by the dramatic situations, and motivic developments are even less noticeable. All the more surprising, therefore, is the scale and dramatic complexity of *Zélia*. The heroine gives lodging to a distressed woman and her child who turn out to be the wife and daughter of Zélia's former lover, who returns after years of absence. After the three principal characters have either fainted or attempted suicide a happy ending is finally brought about. The second finale of this *opéra comique* gives a good idea of Deshayes' dramatic style. Rather than inventing a continuous musical flow in accordance with the unfolding drama, Deshayes organized his score by means of a series of motivic gestures, each of which is played in sequences a number of times and is then replaced by another gesture. The stiffness of this procedure is partly compensated for by an abundance of special sound effects.

Deshayes' stage works were performed at 11 different theatres, indicating the difficulty of fostering close links with a particular theatre in the aftermath of the French Revolution.

all performed in Paris; all printed works published in Paris

Le faux serment, ou La matrone de Gonesse (cmda, 2, L. H. Dancourt), Beaujolais, 31 Dec 1785 (1786), excerpts (1786 and n.d.)

La défaite du serpent Python par Apollon (scène lyrique, 1, Renou), Société des Enfants d'Apollon, 1 June 1786

Le paysan à prétention (opéra bouffon, 1, Eyrand), Beaujolais, 12 June 1786, romance (n.d.)

L'auteur à la mode, ou Le mari complaisant (cmda, 2, Durival), Beaujolais, 23 Dec 1786, excerpts (1786, 1787, n.d.)

Berthe et Pépin (cmda, 3, Pleinchesne, after C.-J. Dorat: *Les deux reines*), Italien, 3 Nov 1787

Delie, ?1787 (ballet-héroïque, 1), unperf., *F-Pc**

La chute de Phaëton (scène lyrique, 1, Renou), Société des Enfants d'Apollon, 12 June 1788

Adèle et Didier (oc, 1, Boutillier), Italien, 5 Nov 1790

Zélia, ou Le mari à deux femmes (drame, 3, P.-U. Dubuisson, after J. W. von Goethe: *Stella*), Louvois, 29 Oct 1791 (n.d.)

La suite de Zélia (3, Dubuisson), Louvois, 25 Feb 1792

Mélite, ou Le pouvoir de la nature (cmda, 3, Desfontaines, after M. de Cervantes: *Leocadia*), Italien, 19 March 1792

La fin du jour (opéra-vaudeville, 1, Rouhier-Deschamps), Palais-Variétés, 2 Aug 1793

Le mariage patriotique (cmda, 2, Rouhier-Deschamps), Cité-Variétés, 19 Dec 1793

Le petit Orphée (opéra-vaudeville, 4, Rouhier-Deschamps), Palais-Variétés, 1793 [parody of Gluck: Orfeo ed Euridice]

Le congrès des rois (cmda, 3, Desmaillot [A. F. Eve]), OC (Favart), 26 Feb 1794, collab. Dalayrac, Grétry, Méhul and 8 others

Arlequin imprimeur, ou Pourquoi écoutait-il? (comédie mêlée de vaudevilles, 1, Lepitre), Cité-Variétés, 16 June 1794

Bella, ou La femme à deux maris (3, A. Duval), Amis de la Patrie (Louvois), 15 June 1795

Don Carlos (fait historique, 2, F. P. A. Léger and A. P. Dutremblay), OC (Favart), 11 Jan 1800

Henri de Bavière (3, Léger and Dutremblay), Molière, 22 Aug 1804

*

A. Duval: 'Notice sur *Bella*', *Oeuvres complètes d'Alexandre Duval*, ii (Paris, 1822)

E. Campardon: *L'Académie royale de musique au XVIIIe siècle* (Paris, 1884)

MICHAEL FEND (text), MICHEL NOIRAY (work-list)

Deshevov, Vladimir Mikhaylovich (*b* St Petersburg, 30 Jan/11 Feb 1889; *d* Leningrad [now St Petersburg], 27 Oct 1955). Russian composer. Between 1908 and 1914 he studied composition and the piano at the St Petersburg Conservatory, where his teachers included Alexander Winkler, Leonid Nikolayev, A. K. Lyadov and V. P. Kalafati. After demobilization from wartime service he helped organize musical activities for the fledgling Soviet state, in 1921 founding a People's Conservatory in Sevastopol' of which he became director. From 1923 to 1933 he taught in Leningrad music schools and was active in music theatre. Deshevov's most famous work was *Rel'sï* ('Rails') for piano (1926), which illustrated the aesthetic appeal of urban industrialism. He is credited with the score for one of the first ballets on a Soviet subject, *Krasnïy vikhr'* ('Red Whirlwind'), staged in 1924, as well as with one of the earliest operas on a revolutionary theme, *Lyod i stal'* ('Ice and Steel', 4, B. A. Lavrenyov). Staged at the State Academic Theatre of Opera and Ballet in Leningrad on 17 May 1930, it was produced also in Odessa and Moscow. He began another opera, *Golodnaya step'* ('The Hungry Steppe'), in 1931. Originally commissioned by the State Academic Theatre of Opera and Ballet, the story portrays the struggle by progressives to introduce new agricultural methods in Uzbekistan. The commission was subsequently withdrawn and the work left incomplete. From the 1930s Deshevov concentrated on incidental, radio and film music.

See also LYOD I STAL'.

*

V. M. Deshevov: 'Muzïka i dram-teatr' [Music and Drama Theatre], *Zhizn' iskusstva*, no.50 (1929), 3

D. Shen: *Vladimir Mikhaylovich Deshevov: ocherk zhizni i tvorchestva* [Vladimir Mikhaylovich Deshevov: a Study of his Life and Works] (Leningrad, 1961)

L. Nikitina: 'Vladimir Deshevov: 20-e godï' [Vladimir Deshevov: the 20s], *SovM* (1980), no.1, pp.85–90

LAUREL E. FAY

Desmarets [Desmarest, Desmaretz, Desmarais], **Henry** (*b* Paris, Feb 1661; *d* Lunéville, 7 Sept 1741). French composer. Little is known of his early musical life other than that he was one of the boy pages of Louis XIV's musical establishment. There, directly under the influence of Pierre Robert and Henry Du Mont at an important period in the development of the *grand motet*, he probably also encountered Lully, who used the chapel pages to augment his performances. In 1680 Desmarets was referred to as an 'ordinaire de la musique du Roy', so he had clearly stayed on the Versailles musical scene after leaving the chapel at the age of 17. Titon du Tillet mentioned an *idylle* written by him for the birth of the Duke of Burgundy in 1682; this was a form to which he would regularly return.

Desmarets was unsuccessful in a contest in 1683 for a post as *sous-maître* at the royal chapel, but later got himself involved in writing motets for one of the successful competitors, Goupillet, to pass off as his own. The deception was not revealed until 1693 when Desmarets, complaining that he had not been paid sufficiently, exposed Goupillet. Desmarets gravitated increasingly towards secular forms of composition. It seems that he wanted to study in Italy; this plan was scotched by Lully, who did not want a promising disciple already well grounded in the French style to be corrupted by over-exposure to Italian music. Some measure of court favour can be inferred from the private performance of his first opera, *Endymion* (lost), which took place over several days in the king's apartments, one or two acts at a time, in February 1686, and pleased the dauphine so much that she commanded another performance a few days later. The diarist Dangeau, who relates these events, refers more than once to the composer as 'le petit Marais' (not to be confused with the violist and composer Marin Marais), conveying perhaps the memory of Desmarets as a boy, his shortness of stature and the court's affection for him. Writing for the stage of the Académie was barred to Desmarets at the time, of course, since Lully enjoyed a complete monopoly; the gap left by his untimely death in March 1687 began to be filled only tentatively by the next generation.

The librettos of Desmarets' earliest surviving *tragédies en musique*, *Circé* and *Didon*, were written by Mme de Saintonge, with whom Desmarets seems to have continued collaborating, even though the many *idylles* in her collected works have no composer cited. *Théagène et Cariclée* followed in 1695. Du Tralage cynically declared that *Didon* succeeded with the public because it was copied from Lully, that *Circé*, less closely modelled on Lully, was less successful, and that *Théagène*, in which the composer went his own way, was not successful at all. The ballet *Les amours de Momus* was eclipsed by another important precursor of the *opéra-ballet*, Collasse's *Ballet des saisons* (1695), partly because its designation as a 'ballet' was criticized. One commentator pointed out that it had a continuous plot divided into acts and scenes; he suggested that were it not for the fact that 'no blood is spilt', *Les amours de Momus* could be described as a *tragédie*. Desmarets began work on another opera, *Vénus et Adonis*, in 1695, and was apparently at the same time in dispute with Collasse as to who should set Duché's *Iphigénie en Tauride*; this was to be left unfinished by Desmarets and completed by Campra.

Within months of the death of his first wife in August 1696, Desmarets had fallen in love with his pupil, the 18-year-old daughter of Jacques de Saint-Gobert, director of taxation for Senlis. The couple's lurid story, replete with all the ingredients of romantic fiction, is detailed by Antoine (1965). The upshot was a long legal battle, at the end of which in August 1699 the couple fled the country, Desmarets being condemned to death in his absence and hanged in effigy. The composer began his exile in Brussels. His friend and fellow chapel page, the composer Jean-Baptiste Matho, obtained a letter of recommendation for him from the Duke of Burgundy to the new king of Spain, Philip V, and Desmarets moved to the Spanish court in 1701 and married Mlle de Saint-Gobert. Six years later, again with support from connections in France, he secured an appointment as *surintendant de la musique* at the court of Lorraine, which was closely modelled on the court of Louis XIV, his duties encompassing both religious and secular music.

Although he mounted a production of his own *Vénus et Adonis* for the court at Lunéville in 1707, Desmarets' operatic activities focussed chiefly on revivals of operas by Lully at both Lunéville and Nancy (the libretto of a new prologue for a production of *Armide* in 1710 is extant). Whether the concentration on Lully (still a guaranteed success in Paris) was due to modesty, royal preference or pressure of work is not known. During this time he continued to write occasional pieces and, more important, motets. However favourable the musical climate in Lorraine, Desmarets cherished the hope that he would be allowed to return to his native land. A petition to Louis XIV on his behalf by Matho in 1712 was rejected, but Desmarets was finally pardoned by the regent in 1720. When Lalande died in 1726, Desmarets actively sought his post of *sous-maître*, but was unsuccessful. Perhaps the taint of scandal attached to his name was still too strong for a chapel appointment to be deemed appropriate. His wife died in the following year and he ended his days in Lorraine.

Like his contemporaries, Desmarets worked within the framework that Lully had established, while developing certain aspects of it. The *sommeil* in Act 3 of *Circé* is closely modelled on the one in Lully's *Atys*. Desmarets made effective use of orchestrally accompanied recitative, with the strings taking over from the continuo at telling moments such as the one in *Didon* (1.ii) where Dido relates the events of the hunt and storm. Invocations of oracles and spirits and their pronouncements are a feature of nearly all Desmarets' *tragédies en musique*; characteristically they are treated with a low-lying accompaniment, often with an obsessive rhythmic pattern and in what for its time was a remote key, F minor. His soliloquies use effective changes of style and texture (e.g. from continuo to string accompaniment or from *air* to recitative and back) to illustrate the uncertainties and changes of mood being expressed. Desmarets' particular contribution to another contemporary trend, an enthusiasm for bass voices and low sonorities, is a type of chorus in which a single melody line is directed to be sung by the basses only, for example the *songes affreux* in *Circé*, an idea which was subsequently taken up by other composers.

See also Didon (i).

first performed in Paris, Académie Royale de Musique (the Opéra), unless otherwise stated

tm – *tragédie en musique*

Idylle sur la naissance du duc de Bourgogne, ?1682, lost
Endymion (tm, prol., 5), Versailles, 16–23 Feb, 5 March 1686, lost
La Diane de Fontainebleau (divertissement, Maurel), Fontainebleau, 2 Nov 1686, *Pa*
Didon (tm, prol., 5, L.-G. G. de Saintonge), 11 Sept or 5 June 1693, *Pn*, vs and reduced inst score (Paris, 1693)
Circé (tm, prol., 5, Saintonge), 11 Nov 1694 (Paris, 1694)
Théagène et Cariclée (tm, prol., 5, J.-F. Duché de Vancy), 12 April 1695, reduced score, abridged (Paris, 1695)
Les amours de Momus (ballet, prol., 3, Duché de Vancy), 12–14 June 1695, reduced score (Paris, 1695)
Vénus et Adonis (tm, prol., 5, J.-B. Rousseau), March, April or July 1697, reduced score (Paris, 1697)
Les festes galantes (ballet, prol., 3, Duché de Vancy), 10 May 1698, reduced score (Paris, 1698)
Divertissement representé à Barcelone pour le mariage de leurs majestez catholiques en octobre 1701 (Saintonge), music lost, attrib. Desmarets
Iphigénie en Tauride (tm, prol., 5, Duché de Vancy and A. Danchet, after Euripides), 6 May 1704, extracts (Paris, 1704), reduced score (Paris, 1711), completed by A. Campra
Le temple d'Astrée (divertissement, 5 scenes, du Tremblay), Nancy, 9 Nov 1709, only lib. extant
Diane et Endymion (tm, prol., 5, Saintonge), Nancy, Jan 1711, music lost, attrib. Desmarets
Divertissement for the Elector of Bavaria, Namur, 1712, lost
Divertissement for fête of the Duke of Lorraine (prol., 6 scenes, Cusson), Lunéville, 15 Nov 1717, only lib. extant; rev. as Divertissement for marriage of the Prince of Lixheim, Nancy, 1721
Renaud, ou La suite d'Armide (tm, prol., 5, S.-J. Pellegrin, after T. Tasso), 5 March 1722, reduced score (Paris, 1722)

Music in: Télémaque, ou Les fragmens des modernes (1704); Armide (revival 1710)
Doubtful: Plutus, ou Le triomphe des richesses (ballet), Paris, Collège Louis-le-Grand, 5 Aug 1682, *F-Pn* (attrib. 'Desmatins'); Idylle sur la naissance de Monseigneur le Dauphin (Paris and Lyons, 1730)

*

Recueil général des opéra (Paris, 1703–46)
C. and F. Parfaict: *Histoire de l'Académie royale de musique depuis son établissement jusqu'à présent* (MS, 1741, *F-Pn*)

E. Titon du Tillet: *Le Parnasse françois*, suppl. i (Paris, 1743)
[J.-B. Durey de Noinville]: *Histoire du théâtre de l'Académie royale de musique en France* (Paris, 1757)
T. de Lajarte: *Bibliothèque musicale du Théâtre de l'Opéra: catalogue* (Paris, 1878)
J. N. du Tralage: *Notes et documents sur l'histoire des théâtres de Paris au XVIIe siècle ...* (Paris, 1880)
A. Jacquot: *La musique en Lorraine* (Paris, 2/1882)
M. Brenet: 'Un compositeur oublié du XVIIIe siècle: Henri Desmarets (1662–1741)', *Le ménestrel*, xlix (1882–3), 305–07, 313–15, 321–3, 329–31
M. Teneo: 'Miettes historiques: correspondance théâtrale du XVIIe siècle', *Mercure musical*, i (1905), 577–83, 620–27; ii (1906), 21–8, 71–8
L. de La Laurencie: 'La musique française de Lulli à Gluck: première partie: l'opéra de 1687 à 1787', *EMDC*, I/iii (1921), 1362–1457
P.-M. Masson: 'Le ballet héroïque', *ReM*, ix/7–11 (1928), 132–54
C. Masson: 'Journal du marquis de Dangeau, 1684–1720: extraits concernant la vie musicale à la cour', *RMFC*, ii (1961–2), 193–228
M. Antoine: *Henry Desmarest* (Paris, 1965)
A. Ducrot: 'Les représentations de l'Académie Royale de Musique à Paris au temps de Louis XIV (1671–1715)', *RMFC*, x (1970), 19–55
J. R. Anthony: *French Baroque Music from Beaujoyeulx to Rameau* (London, 1973, 2/1978)
R. M. Isherwood: *Music in the Service of the King* (Ithaca, NY, and London, 1973)
E. Lemaître: *L'orchestre dans le théâtre lyrique français chez les continuateurs de Lully, 1687–1715* (thesis, Paris Conservatoire, 1977)
J. de La Gorce: 'L'Académie royale de musique en 1704, d'après des documents inédits conservés dans les archives notariales', *RdM*, lxv (1979), 170–91
C. Wood: *Jean-Baptiste Lully and his Successors: Music and Drama in the 'tragédie en musique' 1673–1715* (diss., U. of Hull, 1981)
——: 'Orchestra and Spectacle in the *tragédie en musique*, 1673–1715: oracle, *sommeil* and *tempête*', *PRMA*, cviii (1981–2), 25–46
J. de La Gorce: 'Documents de critique musicale et théâtrale: dix lettres extraites de la correspondance entre Ladvocat et l'Abbé Dubos (1694–1696)', *XVIIe siècle*, no.139 (1983), 267–82
R. Fajon: *L'opéra à Paris du Roi-Soleil à Louis le Bien-aimé* (Geneva, 1984)
W. Weber: '*La musique ancienne* in the Waning of the Ancien Régime', *Journal of Modern History*, lvi (1984), 58–88

CAROLINE WOOD

Desmatins, Mlle (*fl* 1682–*c*1708). French soprano. She made her début in a minor role in Lully's *Persée* (1682), and sang the confidante Sidonie to Le Rochois' Armide in 1686. Desmatins herself sang Armide in 1703. Roles she created include Briseis (Lully and Collasse's *Achille et Polyxène*, 1687) and Juno (Collasse's *Enée et Lavinie*, 1690). In 1697 she played the first of the Hesperides in the prologue and alternated with Le Rochois in the title role of Destouches' *Issé*. She sang Medea in Lully's *Thésée* in 1698 (a role sung previously by St Christophle and Le Rochois) and the title role in the 1699 revival of Collasse's *Thétis*. In 1704 she created the title role in Desmarets and Campra's *Iphigénie en Tauride*, took the title role in the revival of Destouches' *Didon* and sang Io in the revival of Lully's *Isis*. The following year she sang Lully's Angélique (*Roland*) and Sthenobea (*Bellérophon*); in 1706 she sang his Alcestis and created the title role in Marais' *Alcyone*. She disappeared from cast lists in 1707–8, whereupon most of her roles passed to Mlle Journet.

PHILIP WELLER

Des Moines Metro Opera. American company founded in 1973 and based in INDIANOLA.

Desormery [Désormerie], **Léopold-Bastien** (*b* Bayon, Lorraine, *c*1740; *d* nr Beauvais, *c*1810). French composer. According to Fétis he studied music at the archiepiscopal school of Nancy. By 1762 he was a singer and composer in Lyons, where his pastoral *La bergère des Alpes* was performed in the following year. By 1764 he was a *pensionnaire* of the Lyons opera. He was on the staff of a small music school in Lyons (1765) and was also a musician at the cathedral. He sang comic parts in Mâcon and by 1770 had become a *comédien* in Strasbourg. That year he was co-winner of the Parisian Concert Spirituel annual prize for 'musique latine'. He then moved to Paris and was an actor at the Théâtre Italien from about 1774 to 1778. During these years he also sang in and wrote sacred works for the Concert Spirituel, and in quick succession composed several stage works, including *Euthyme et Lyris* (1776, 22 performances) and the highly successful *Myrtil et Lycoris* (1777, 63 performances) for the Opéra. Unable to repeat his former successes he abandoned his artistic career and devoted himself to teaching, retiring to the vicinity of Beauvais. Shortly before his death he attempted another theatrical work, but it was not performed.

La bergère des Alpes (pastorale, P. J. B. Nougaret, after J. F. Marmontel), Lyons, Jan 1763 [cited by Léris]
Hylas et Eglé (ballet-héroïque, 1, J.-J. Le Franc de Pompignan), Paris, Opéra, 16 Feb 1775, collab. Le Gros, rev. of Grenet's ballet Hylas
La fête de village (oc, 2, Dorvigny), Paris, Hôtel de Bourgogne, 28 June 1775, air in *Mercure de France* (July 1778)
Euthyme et Lyris (ballet-héroïque, 1, M. J. Boutillier), Paris, Opéra, 1 Oct 1776, *F-Po*, airs (Paris, n.d.)
Myrtil et Lycoris (pastorale, 1, Boutillier and Boquet de Liancourt), Fontainebleau, 14 Nov 1777, *Po* (Paris, *c*1777)
Les montagnards, *c*1808 [cited by Fétis]
Le mendiant (comédie, 3), ariettes (Paris, n.d.)

FétisB
A. de Léris: *Dictionnaire portatif historique et littéraire des théâtres* (Paris, 2/1763), 724
Mercure de France (June 1770, Oct 1774, March 1775, Sept 1784, May 1790)
Affiches, annonces et avis divers (4 June 1793)
L. Vallas: *Un siècle de musique et de théâtre à Lyon 1688–1789* (Lyons, 1932)
C. Pierre: *Histoire du Concert spirituel 1725–1790* (Paris, 1975)

ROGER J. V. COTTE

Désormière, Roger (*b* Vichy, 13 Sept 1898; *d* Paris, 25 Oct 1963). French conductor and composer. He studied at the Paris Conservatoire and with Koechlin and made his conducting début in 1921. A resident conductor at the Opéra-Comique from 1937 (where he added works by Chabrier, Ravel and Richard Strauss to the repertory), he served as the theatre's director, 1944–6, and additionally as associate director at the Opéra, 1945–6. He was much admired for his sensitive performances of Debussy's *Pelléas et Mélisande*, which the Opéra-Comique brought to Covent Garden in 1949. The onset of an aphasic disorder in 1950 forced his premature retirement.

D. Mayer and P. Souvchinsky: *Roger Désormière et son temps* (Monaco, 1966)

NOËL GOODWIN

Desportes, Yvonne (Berthe Melitta) (*b* Coburg, Germany, 18 July 1907). French composer. She studied under the Gallons and Dukas at the Paris Conservatoire, winning the Prix de Rome in 1932. From 1943 she taught at the Conservatoire. She composed two operas and three ballets; large-scale choral and orchestral pieces also form a large part of her output, much of which makes notable use of percussion. Her first opera, *Maître Cornélius* (1939; 3, M. Belvianes, after H. de Balzac), was accepted by the Paris Opéra, but after the Liberation it was rejected and has not been performed. *Le forgeur de merveilles* (3, Desportes, after F.-J. O'Brien), accepted by Opéra de Lyon, was broadcast on French radio on 30 June 1967, with Jean Giraudeau.

ALAIN LOUVIER

Despréaux, Jean-Etienne (*b* Paris, 31 Aug 1748; *d* Paris, 26 March 1820). French composer and administrator. His father, Jean-François Despréaux (1693–1768), was a wind player at the Opéra and the Concert Spirituel. His brothers were also composers. Jean-Etienne was a dancer at the Opéra from 1764 until 1781, when he retired; he returned briefly as a *directeur de la scène* in 1792. He was later an inspector at the Opéra and taught *maintien* and dancing at the Conservatoire from 1807 to 1815. His major works are parodies of popular operas by F.-A. Philidor, Piccinni, Rameau, Boieldieu and others. Despréaux and the dancer Marie Madeleine La Guimard performed together in these pieces and were married in 1789. He may have been the Despréaux who, on attending an opera at Versailles, asked for a seat where he could hear the music but not the words, because 'I greatly esteem the music of Lully, but have contempt for the verses of Quinault' (*Almanach des spectacles*, 1772).

all parodies, with librettos by Despréaux; all printed works published in Paris

Romans [N. Piccinni: Roland], Versailles, 30 May 1778 (?1778)
Momie [C. W. Gluck: Iphigénie en Aulide], Choisy, Aug 1778 (1778)
Berlingue [F.-A. Philidor: Ernelinde], Choisy, 13 Sept 1778 (1778)
Christophe et Pierre-Luc [J.-P. Rameau: Castor et Pollux], Versailles, 1780 (1780)
Syncopé, reine de mic-mac [Piccinni: Pénélope], Versailles, 31 Jan 1786 (1786)
Jenesaiki, ou Les exaltés de Charenton [A. Boieldieu: Béniowski], Paris, Vaudeville, 21 June 1800, collab. R. A. de Chazet, M. Dieulafoy and P.-Y. Barré
La tragédie au vaudeville [J.-F. Ducis: Otello, and other plays], Paris, 18 March 1801, collab. 7 others

ES (M.-F. Christout); *MGG* (P. Chaillon-Guiomar)
A. Firmin-Didot: 'Souvenirs de Jean-Etienne Despréaux ... (d'après ses notes manuscrites)', *Revue d'art dramatique*, xxix (1893), 257–63, 341–51; xxx (1893), 10–26, 90–106
S. Travers: *Catalogue of Nineteenth Century French Theatrical Parodies* (New York, 1941)

MICHAEL BARNARD

Desprez, Louis-Jean (*b* Auxerre, May 1743; *d* Stockholm, 17 March 1804). French stage designer, architect and engraver. He studied in Paris with J.-F. Blondel and Pierre Desmaisons and from 1771 taught at the Ecole Militaire. He won the Académie's Grand Prix de Rome in 1776 and lived from 1777 in Italy, where he made many drawings from nature for Richard de Saint-Non's *Voyage pittoresque de Naples et de Sicilie* (1781–5); from 1779 he was in Rome and often worked as a scene painter at the Teatro Alibert. In 1784 he was summoned to Stockholm by Gustavus III as scenic director at the Royal Opera House. As a stage designer, artistic director of court festivals, authority on architecture and a member of the Swedish Academy, he exerted a powerful influence on cultural development in Sweden until his employer's death in 1792. During a stay in London (1789) he sketched plans for the rebuilding of the Italian opera house, the King's Theatre, which had been destroyed by fire.

Desprez' work on the *Voyage pittoresque* had aroused his interest in the history and cultural traditions of antiquity and the Middle Ages and had revealed his mastery of the depiction of effect-laden romantic landscapes. This was reflected in his designs for more than 15 opera productions: they rejected the academic classicism of his French teachers, admitted the influence of contemporary Italian stage design and supported Gustavus III's endeavours to establish a Swedish national opera. His designs for J. G. Naumann's national historical opera *Gustaf Wasa* (1786; for illustration *see* GUSTAF WASA) show him to have been an important innovator for the operatic stage: his atmospheric landscapes and architectural compositions, his effective tableaux and his emotionally expressive crowd scenes anticipated principles of stage design that were to be a feature of Romantic opera.

Set design by Louis-Jean Desprez for O. Åhlström's 'Frigga' (the sacred grove surrounding the temple of Frigga in Old Uppsala) for the original production at the Stockholm Royal Opera in 1787: watercolour

ES (D. Bablet)
A. Beijer: 'Ett regihistoriskt dokument', *Dikt och studie* (Uppsala, 1922), 71
N. G. A. Wollin: *Gravures originales de Desprez ou exécutées d'après ses dessins* (Malmö, 1933)
——: *Desprez en Italie: dessins topographiques et d'architecture, décors de théâtre et compositions romantiques exécutées 1777–1784* (Malmö, 1935)
——: *Desprez i Sverige* (Stockholm, 1936; Fr. trans., 1939) [incl. catalogue of scene designs]
A. Beijer: *Slottsteatrarna på Drottningholm och Gripsholm* (Stockholm, 1937), 139ff
M. Fuchs: 'Un livre sur le décorateur Desprez', *Bulletin de la Société des historiens du théâtre*, xxvi (1937), 53–5
P. Bjurström: *Teaterdekoration i Sverige* (Stockholm, 1964), 33ff, 172f [with Eng. summary]
B. H. Wiles: 'An Unpublished Stage Design by Desprez and its Source: Polignano a Mare', *Festschrift Ulrich Middeldorf* (Berlin, 1968), 503–5
Louis-Jean Desprez, 1743–1804: peintre, graveur, architecte et décorateur de théâtre en Italie et en Suède (Paris, 1974) [exhibition catalogue]
MANFRED BOETZKES

Dessau. City in eastern Germany, an industrial centre in the Halle district. In the 1770s musical scenes, operas and operettas were performed in the open air and in the theatre of Wörlitz castle (60 seats). In 1775, after an outdoor performance of Anton Schweitzer's *Elysium*, Friedrich Wilhelm Rust started an amateur society that performed Singspiels by J. A. Hiller, Dittersdorf, Mozart and others in a private house. In 1798 F. W. von Erdmannsdorff was commissioned by Prince Leopold Friedrich Franz to build the Hoftheater (1000 seats), one of the largest theatres in Germany at that time, together with those of Berlin and Bayreuth. It opened on 26 December 1798 with K. A. von Lichtenstein's *Bathmendi*, directed by the composer and conducted by Kapellmeister Konrad Jacobi.

A strong Wagnerian tradition began in 1857 with *Tannhäuser*, produced by Eduard Thiele, who was appointed Hofkapellmeister in 1856 when the theatre reopened as the ducal court theatre after a fire. His production of *Die Meistersinger* in 1869 directly after its Munich première won the approval of Wagner, who recommended the 'remarkable little court theatre' of Dessau as a model; on 8 March 1872, after a performance of Gluck's *Orfeo*, Wagner commented that he had 'never seen a nobler and more perfect performance as a whole'. The cult of Wagner at Dessau brought prominent Bayreuth artists to give guest performances there, and conversely Wagner recruited musicians from Dessau for Bayreuth. August Klughardt (Hofkapellmeister, 1882–1902) continued the Wagnerian tradition, and at the end of the century Dessau was often called the 'Bayreuth of the North'. The Kapellmeister Franz Mikorey (1902–17), along with the Dramaturg Artur Seidl (1903–19), followed the same line. After World War I the theatre resumed activity as the Friedrichstheater; after World War II it became the Landestheater. Conductors included Knappertsbusch (1919–22), Artur Rother (1927–34; he gave the first performance of Wagner-Régeny's *La sainte courtisane* in 1930) and Helmut Seydelmann (1934–51). In 1922 the theatre burnt down, and the new Dessau Theater was opened in 1938. Following war damage in 1944 it was rebuilt (1245 seats) and reopened on 16 August 1949 with *Die Zauberflöte*. The Intendant Willy Bodenstein revived the company's Wagnerian tradition, and Heinz Röttger (Generalmusikdirektor, 1954–77) organized Wagner Festival weeks and staged the first performances of his own operas *Die Frauen von Troja* (1962) and *Der Weg nach Palermo* (1965). Music-theatre works have also been presented since 1983 in the Theater im Bauhaus, where the Dessau Landestheater has given performances since 1977.

*

W. Hosäus: 'F. W. Rust und das Dessauer Musikleben 1766–1796', *Mitteilungen des Vereins für Anhaltische Geschichte und Altertumskunde*, iii (1881), 265–332
M. von Prosky: *Das Herzogliche Hoftheater zu Dessau von seinen Anfängen bis zur Gegenwart* (Dessau, 1894)
M. Hasse: *Dessau, ein norddeutsches Bayreuth* (Oldenburg and Berlin, 1914)
G. Eisenhardt: 'Dessau', *Bedeutende Musiktraditionen der Bezirke Halle und Magdeburg* (Halle and Magdeburg, n.d.)
DIETER HÄRTWIG

Dessau, Paul (*b* Hamburg, 19 Dec 1894; *d* Königs Wusterhausen, nr Berlin, 27 June 1979). German composer. He studied the violin in Berlin and later became a conductor. An opera enthusiast from his youth, he was co-répétiteur in Hamburg in 1912 and conducted operetta at the Tivoli Theatre, Bremen, in 1913 before becoming conductor and composer at the Hamburg Kammerspiele in 1918. Klemperer engaged him as co-répétiteur and conductor in Cologne in 1919, and in 1925, through Bruno Walter, he was appointed principal conductor at the Städtische Oper, Berlin. One of his first attempts at composition was the opera *Giuditta*, begun in 1910–12 but not completed. During the 1920s he attempted, unsuccessfully, to write operas on texts by Grillparzer, Eichendorff and Upton Sinclair, finding more success writing and directing film music. In 1931, however, he completed a radio operetta, *Orpheus 1930/31*. Obliged to emigrate in 1933, he became a committed supporter of Judaism. He moved to Paris and, influenced by René Leibowitz, adopted 12-note technique.

In 1939 Dessau emigrated to the USA. He met Brecht in New York in 1943, and began working with him (having already composed the songs for the Paris première of *Furcht und Elend des Dritten Reiches* in 1938). Adopting Brecht's methods of epic drama, applicable and relevant to both music and theatre, he wrote the music for *Mutter Courage und ihre Kinder* in 1946. His first planned collaboration with Brecht, the opera *Die Reisen des Glücksgotts*, begun in Hollywood in 1945, remains a fragment. In 1949, after his and Brecht's return to Germany, Dessau composed *Das Verhör des Lukullus*, from a radio play written by Brecht at the beginning of World War II. A 'trial performance' in 1951 led to changes, and the work had its official première later that year as *Die Verurteilung des Lukullus*. Dessau's last Brecht opera, *Puntila*, was written in 1956–9 following discussions with the dramatist shortly before his death in 1956. Continuing to be influenced by Brecht's ideas, Dessau subsequently composed *Lanzelot* (1969), *Einstein* (1971–3) and *Leonce and Lena* (1977–8). All these works had their premières at the Deutsche Staatsoper, Berlin, and from *Puntila* onwards they were directed by Dessau's wife Ruth Berghaus.

Giuditta, which Dessau began at the age of 15, follows the principles of Wagnerian music drama and combines eclectic influences ranging from Puccini to Richard Strauss. Like many composers of his generation, Dessau went through an expressionist phase, but he was more inclined to adopt fashionable neoclassical genres in the 1920s. He showed his dramatic gift at that time in large-scale film scores. His radio operetta *Orpheus 1930/31*, revived by Hans Werner Henze in the late 1970s for his festival at Montepulciano, plays parodistically with the requirements of the 'Neue Sachlichkeit' school of neo-realism; it introduces the noise of trams, the rattling of cars and howling factory sirens, while its musical parodies range from *Carmen* to *Orphée aux enfers*.

After Dessau had discovered 12-note technique for himself, he was sometimes diverted from using it by his encounter with Jewish folklore and by the populist requirements of Brecht; however, his angular, sharply accented and expressively charged musical language brought him into conflict with the doctrines of Socialist realism, which favoured easier listening and recommended 19th-century musical models. At the end of the 1950s Dessau returned to 12-note technique, seeking to link progressive left-wing political awareness with advanced artistic methods; thus he incurred further hostile criticism, although many young composers saw him as an example to be followed.

In the 1970s such debates over cultural policy were largely discontinued, for strategic reasons. Dessau became a state artist and received honours, although his creative talents had not really been properly encouraged. An increasing tendency towards quotation and adaptation may be observed in the later works. Quotations ranging from Bach to Richard Strauss feature in *Einstein* as Brechtian alienation effects. In the main part of the opera (as in *Lukullus*) the orchestra dispenses with violins, oboes, clarinets and horns; in the intermezzos the addition of these instrumental colours may be understood as implying criticism, for the orchestral colouring too is involved in the intended caricature of 'hotchpotch' opera. The posthumously produced opera *Leonce und Lena* imparts a pessimistic tone to its subject with the filigree-like working of the music: the cheerful cantabile in which the eponymous couple indulges sounds distorted and broken, and wherever pleasure in music-making appears it is to be distrusted: gaiety is turned on its head and transformed into something destructive.

See also LANZELOT; PUNTILA; and VERURTEILUNG DES LUKULLUS, DIE.

Giuditta, 1910–12 (M. May), inc., unperf.
Orpheus 1930/31 (heiteres Hörspiel, R. Seitz), Berlin, 1931; rev. as Orpheus und der Bürgermeister
Das Verhör des Lukullus (12 scenes, B. Brecht), Berlin, Staatsoper, 17 March 1951 ('trial perf.'); rev. as Die Verurteilung des Lukullus, Berlin, Staatsoper, 12 Oct 1951 (Berlin, 1961)
Puntila, 1956–9 (13 scenes, epilogue, P. Palitzsch and M. Wekwerth, after Brecht: *Herr Puntila und sein Knecht Matti*), Berlin, Staatsoper, 15 Nov 1966 (Berlin, 1959)
Lanzelot (15 scenes, H. Müller and G. Tscholakowa, after J. Schwarz: *Der Drache*, and H. C. Andersen), Berlin, Staatsoper, 19 Dec 1969 (Berlin, 1970)
Einstein (prol., 3, 2 ints, epilogue, K. Mickel), Berlin, Staatsoper, 16 Feb 1974 (Berlin, 1973)
Leonce und Lena (prol., 2, T. Körner, after G. Büchner), Berlin, Staatsoper, 24 Nov 1979 (Berlin, 1978)

*

F. Hennenberg: *Dessau–Brecht: musikalische Arbeiten* (Berlin, 1963)
——: *Paul Dessau: eine Biographie* (Leipzig, 1965)
G. Rienäcker: 'Zu einigen Gestaltungsproblemen im Opern-schaffen von Paul Dessau', *Sammelbände zur Musikgeschichte der DDR*, ii (Berlin, 1971), 100–43
——: 'Zur Dialektik musikdramaturgischer Gestaltung: analytische Notate zum 12. Bild der Oper *Lanzelot* von Paul Dessau', *DJbM*, xviii (1973)
P. Dessau: *Aus Gesprächen* (Leipzig, 1974)
——: *Notizen zu Noten* (Leipzig, 1974)
F. Hennenberg: *Für Sie porträtiert: Paul Dessau* (Leipzig, 1974, 2/1981)
——, ed.: P. Dessau: *Opern* (Berlin, 1976)
FRITZ HENNENBERG

Dessì [Dessy], **Daniela** (*b* Genoa, 14 May 1957). Italian soprano. She studied at the Parma Conservatory with Carla Castellani and at the Accademia Chigiana, Siena. Her career began with concert singing and sacred music, and she turned increasingly to opera after her début in 1979 as Serpina in Pergolesi's *La serva padrona* with Opera Giocosa at Genoa. She also sang Lauretta (*Gianni Schicchi*) there the same year, but then concentrated on earlier opera, including works by Cimarosa, Monteverdi (*L'incoronazione di Poppea*), Handel, Jommelli and Paisiello. Her success as Desdemona at Barcelona with Placido Domingo led to her American début in the same role with him in Los Angeles.

Engagements throughout Italy and elsewhere in Europe embraced a wider and growing repertory of Mozart, Rossini, Donizetti, Verdi and Puccini roles, in which she is admired for depth of passionate feeling combined with sensitivity to verbal inflection. She has made a number of recordings including Gilda (*Rigoletto*) with Muti and the title role in Donizetti's *Alina, regina di Golconda* (both 1989), as well as Italian issues of Cimarosa, Pergolesi (*Adriano in Siria*), Traetta and Vivaldi among others. NOËL GOODWIN

Dessus (Fr.: 'top'). The highest voice in a vocal or instrumental ensemble in French sources from the 17th century to the early 19th. Divided textures employ *premier dessus* (*c'–b''*) and *second dessus* (*b–g''*), or *haut-dessus* and *bas-dessus*. Throughout the period, pitch was as much as a whole tone lower than that now used. Although the term 'soprano' was understood in France at least as early as Brossard's *Dictionaire* (1703), it was identified largely with Italian singers. Rousseau (1768) defined 'dessus' but not 'soprano' (though under 'Castrato' he referred to 'the part called *dessus* or *soprano*'). *Dessus* continued in France as the normal term for the highest voice as late as the first edition of Rossini's *Guillaume Tell* (1829), even though French terms for some other voices (*haute-contre*, *taille*, *basse-taille*) had long been obsolete.

After *Ercole amante* (1662), the last of the imported Italian productions instigated by Mazarin, which had employed castratos as soprano soloists, solo *dessus* parts were always assigned to women singers in French opera. However, falsettos (*faussets* or *faucets*), and sometimes boys (*pages*), augmented the women for minor roles and for the *dessus* line of the chorus of the Paris Opéra. French court performances of opera from Lully to the Revolution followed similar practices, but in the chorus, castratos (already on the payroll of the royal chapel) were also used.

See SOPRANO, §1. LIONEL SAWKINS

Destinn [Kittl], **Emmy** [Destinnová, Ema] (*b* Prague, 26 Feb 1878; *d* České Budějovice, 28 Jan 1930). Czech soprano. She studied singing with Marie Loewe-Destinn, adopting her teacher's name in gratitude; in later life she used only the Czech form of her stage name. She made her début on 19 July 1898 as Santuzza in Berlin, where she remained for ten years and was highly successful in a wide repertory. After a much acclaimed Senta at Bayreuth in 1901, she was greatly

Emmy Destinn as Senta in Wagner's 'Der fliegende Holländer' at Bayreuth in 1901: photograph from 'Le théâtre' (September 1901)

admired at Covent Garden (début as Donna Anna in 1904), especially as Aida and Butterfly, and at the Metropolitan (début as Aida in 1908), where she created Minnie in *La fanciulla del West* (1910). During World War I her position as a declared sympathizer with the Czech national movement led to her internment in her own castle of Stráž nad Nežárkou. After the war she appeared again both at Covent Garden and at the Metropolitan. She was one of the greatest artists of her generation, and left over 200 gramophone records, of which the best are impressive.

A. Rektorys: *Ema Destinnová* (Prague, 1936) [incl. bibliography and discography]

A. Rektorys and J. Dennis: 'Emmy Destinn', *Record Collector*, xx (1971–2), 5–47, 93–4 [with discography]

DESMOND SHAWE-TAYLOR

Destiny. Opera by Leoš Janáček; *see* OSUD.

Destouches, André Cardinal (*b* Paris, bap. 6 April 1672; *d* Paris, 7 Feb 1749). French composer. Although opera composers in the two generations after Lully enjoyed nothing like his power and royal protection, Destouches came nearest to being a royal favourite. This degree of privilege and recognition may have had something to do with his social status as well as with the merits of his compositions, but the diarist the Marquis de Dangeau referred more than once to Louis XIV's liking for Destouches' music and his encouragement to the young composer to carry on.

1. LIFE. The son of a wealthy Parisian merchant, Etienne Cardinal, Seigneur des Touches et de Guilleville, he took the patronym Destouches after his father's death in 1694. He had rather unlikely beginnings for a composer: after finishing his Jesuit schooling, he accompanied Father Gui Tachard on a voyage to Siam in 1687–8 and may have been considering entering the Church. Four years later he enlisted in the second company of the King's Musketeers, leaving it in 1694 to devote himself to music, his talent having apparently revealed itself only at that relatively late stage. During the rest of his musical life, Destouches was not allowed to forget his brief army career, critics dubbing him the 'mousquetaire musicien', suggesting that he take up his musket again and unfairly taunting him with charges of amateurism.

The young man soon made influential friends, notably the future Prince of Monaco, Antoine de Grimaldi, who was responsible for introducing him at court and with whom he sustained a long correspondence until the prince's death in 1731. Le Cerf de la Viéville referred to him always as 'Mr des Touches' (uniquely among the many composers he discussed) and said that he began to compose operas without knowing how to read and write music. His cousin was one of the major librettists of the period, Houdar de Lamotte, and it has been suggested that Lamotte's libretto for what is generally regarded as the first *opéra-ballet*, *L'Europe galante* (1697), was originally offered to Destouches but appropriated by the senior composer André Campra, who permitted Destouches to compose just three *airs* for it. Destouches' own operatic career was assured after the success of a concert performance of his pastorale, *Issé*, before the court at Fontainebleau in the same year; the king ordered it to be performed again at the Trianon with the addition of a prologue and a ballet, and gave the composer 200 louis d'or, saying that no opera since Lully had given him so much pleasure. On 30 December *Issé* opened at the Opéra, where it was an immediate success and subsequently enjoyed several revivals. Regardless of the state of Destouches' compositional technique when he arrived on the scene, his talents were quickly recognized, the *Gazette d'Amsterdam* referring to him as 'a new Lully' in court *divertissements* even before *Issé*; Le Cerf, writing in 1704, described *Issé* as 'one of the most pleasing operas to have appeared since Lully'.

The custom of presenting an opera at court before its Paris première, which had begun with Lully's *Thésée* in 1675 and had continued with one or two exceptions until *Acis et Galatée*, switched briefly after Lully's death to one of putting on the new work at court later (Collasse's *Thétis* and *Enée*), and then died out, no opera being given at court between 1691 and 1697. With the advent of Destouches, the original practice enjoyed a modest revival (embracing his first three *tragédies* and *Le Carnaval et la Folie*), although it was concert versions, rehearsals or excerpts that were given (it is not always possible to be certain which), rather than complete stage presentations. Sometimes a work was played serially over several days: *Marthésie*, for example, some of which was heard at Fontainebleau on 27 September 1699, was according to Dangeau ordered to be played again at the king's supper 'beginning next Wednesday', with 'only one act a day to be performed'.

After a dormant period about which virtually nothing is known, Destouches emerged with more specific posts at the Opéra and at court – inspector general and later director at the former (1713, 1728), *surintendant* and then *maître de musique de la chambre* at the latter (1718, 1727). The *tragédie en musique* was however in its greatest decline since the death of Lully; Destouches abandoned the genre altogether after *Sémiramis* (1718). The *opéra-ballet Les élémens*, written nominally in collaboration with Lalande but almost certainly largely by Destouches, was his last major success, although revivals of his earlier works continued. His later career was concerned mainly with the organization of concerts for the queen, which he directed for 20 years, and with the revision and revival of earlier successes.

2. OPERAS. In his serious operas, Destouches (like contemporaries such as Collasse, Desmarets and Campra) worked broadly within the framework and conventions of the *tragédie en musique*, modifying it to encompass the small changes which the tastes of the conservative public and critics would permit. Sometimes the Lullian sources for particular scenes are obvious: presumably both librettist and composer would have expected an audience to recall Roland's madness (*Roland*, Act 4) and Armide's destructive fury (*Armide*, 5.v) when watching the gradual deterioration of the heroine's reason towards the end of *Marthésie*. Soliloquies featured increasingly in the operas of this period; four of the acts in *Omphale*, for example, open with them. Destouches was particularly resourceful in handling different types of declamation and in varying the accompaniment between continuo and strings to reflect the dilemmas commonly expressed in such scenes. A dramatic example occurs in the opening scene of the third act of *Télémaque*, for the magician Adraste: Destouches used rapid changes of style and orchestral texture to evoke the horror of the surroundings and the character's progression from despair to an avowal of revenge. Another common feature is the ceremonial set piece built up around elements of magic or the supernatural, invoking oracles or provoking the apparitions of *ombres* of the departed. *Omphale* (4.iii–v) has an unusually extended scene of this kind, except that the revelation is of the future to Argine by the spirit of Tiresias. Destouches' approach to recitative, for many the most admired feature of Lully's operas, was drawn more from the *petit air* than from Lully's constantly changing, flexible metres. Whole dialogue scenes in *Amadis de Grèce* and *Omphale* are carried on in this manner.

The reworking of *Issé* for the 1708 revival reflects the changes in style that were taking place in the second decade after Lully's death. A comparison of the revised version with the 1697 original shows more colourful and characteristic dances, enlargement of the *divertissements* (hence the expansion to five acts), longer choruses with more contrapuntal writing and the addition of ritornellos, and enriched accompaniments to the more important vocal *airs*, both harmonically and in instrumental colour. The additional *air* 'Chantez oiseaux' (5.i) shows the growing influence of the cantata. Only the recitative survives virtually unchanged. When Grimm chose Destouches' *Omphale* as the target of a late salvo in the long-running dispute between Lullistes and Ramistes (*Lettre sur Omphale*, 1752), he admitted that his own view of the recitative as sad and expressionless was not the commonly held opinion.

Although Destouches made a significant contribution to the *tragédie en musique*, in the end his efforts in areas closely related to the opera but not bound by all its stultifying conventions had the greatest impact, creating or paving the way for the *pastorale-héroïque* and *ballet-héroïque*.

See also AMADIS DE GRÈCE; CALLIRHOÉ; ELÉMENS, LES; and ISSÉ.

all printed works first published in Paris

Issé (pastorale-héroïque, prol., 3, A. H. de Lamotte), Fontainebleau, 7 Oct, and Versailles, Trianon, 17 Dec 1697 (concert perfs.), staged Paris, Opéra, 30 Dec 1697 (1697); rev., with 2 addl acts, 1708 (2/1724/*R*1984: FO, xiv)

Amadis de Grèce (tragédie en musique, prol., 5, Lamotte), Paris, Opéra, 26 March 1699, reduced score (1699, 3/1712/*R*1967)

Marthésie, reine des Amazones (tragédie en musique, prol., 5, Lamotte), Fontainebleau, Oct 1699, and Paris, Opéra, 29 Nov 1699, reduced score (1699)

Omphale [Hercule et Omphale] (tragédie en musique, prol., 5, Lamotte), Paris, Opéra, 10 Nov 1701, reduced score (1701)

Le Carnaval et la Folie (comédie-ballet, prol., 4, Lamotte), Fontainebleau, 14 Oct 1703 (concert perf.), staged Paris, Opéra, 3 Jan 1704 (*c*1703), reduced score (1738); Act 3 perf. separately as Le professeur de folie (divertissement), Paris, Opéra, 17 Sept 1706, reduced score (1711)

Callirhoé (tragédie en musique, prol., 5, P.-C. Roy), Paris, Opéra, 27 Dec 1712 (1712, 2/1713)

Télémaque et Calypso (tragédie en musique, prol., 5, S.-J. Pellegrin), Paris, Opéra, Nov/Dec 1714, reduced score (1714, 2/1715, 3/1728)

Sémiramis (tragédie en musique, prol., 5, Roy), Paris, Opéra, ?4 Dec 1718, reduced score (1718)

Les élémens (opéra-ballet, prol., 4 entrées, Roy), Paris, Tuileries, 31 Dec 1721; Paris, Opéra, 29 May 1725, *F-Pn* (*R* forthcoming: FO, xvi), selections (1725), score (2/1742); collab. Lalande

Les stratagèmes de l'amour (ballet-héroïque, prol., 3 entrées, Roy), Paris, Opéra, 19/28 March 1726, reduced score (1726)

*

Recueil général des opéra (Paris, 1703–46)

J.-L. Le Cerf de la Viéville: *Comparaison de la musique italienne et de la musique françoise* (Brussels, 1704–6)

C. and F. Parfaict: *Histoire de l'Académie royale de musique depuis son établissement jusqu'à présent* (MS, 1741, *F-Pn*)

F. M. Grimm: *Lettre de M. Grimm sur Omphale, tragédie lyrique* (Paris, 1752)

E. Titon du Tillet: *Le Parnasse françois*, suppl. ii (Paris, 1755)

[J.-B. Durey de Noinville]: *Histoire du théâtre de l'Académie royale de musique en France* (Paris, 1757)

T. de Lajarte: *Bibliothèque musicale du Théâtre de l'Opéra: catalogue* (Paris, 1878)

V. d'Indy: Introduction to A. C. Destouches: *Les éléments* (Paris, *c*1880)

J. A. Carlez: *La Sémiramis de Destouches* (Caen, 1892)

G. Pellissier: 'Famille, fortune et succession d'André Cardinal Destouches', *Mémoires de la Société de l'histoire de Paris*, xxvi (1899), 25–58

V. d'Indy: 'Lulli, Destouches, Rameau et leurs librettistes', *Minerva*, ii/May–June (1902), 234

M. Brenet: 'Destouches et son opéra d'Issé', *Courrier musical*, xi (1908), 661–5

K. Dulle: *André Cardinal Destouches (1672–1749): ein Beitrag zur französischen Operngeschichte* (diss., U. of Leipzig, 1909)

L. de La Laurencie: 'La musique française de Lulli à Gluck, première partie: l'opéra de 1687 à 1787', *EMDC*, I/iii (1921), 1362–457

A. Tessier: 'Correspondance d'André Cardinal des Touches et du Prince Antoine Ier de Monaco (1709–1731)', *ReM*, viii/1–2 (1926), 97–114; viii/3–5 (1927), 104–17, 209–24; viii/6–8 (1927), 149–62

P.-M. Masson: *L'opéra de Rameau* (Paris, 1930)

——: 'La "Lettre sur Omphale" ', *RdM*, xxiv (1945), 1–19

R. Girardon: 'André Destouches à Siam', *Mélanges d'histoire et d'esthétique musicales offerts à Paul-Marie Masson*, ii (Paris, 1955), 95–102

R. P.-M. Masson: 'André Cardinal Destouches: surintendant de la Musique du Roy, directeur de l'Opéra', *RdM*, xliii (1959), 81–98

C. Masson: 'Journal du Marquis de Dangeau, 1684–1720: extraits concernant la vie musicale à la cour', *RMFC*, ii (1962), 193–228

D. R. B. Kimbell: 'The Amadis Operas of Destouches and Handel', *ML*, xlix (1968), 329–46

A. Ducrot: 'Les représentations de l'Académie royale de musique à Paris au temps de Louis XIV (1671–1715)', *RMFC*, x (1970), 19–55

M. Benoit: *Musiques de cour: chapelle, chambre, écurie, 1661–1733* (Paris, 1971)
J. R. Anthony: *French Baroque Music from Beaujoyeulx to Rameau* (London, 1973, 2/1978)
R. M. Isherwood: *Music in the Service of the King* (Ithaca, NY, and London, 1973)
E. Lemaître: *L'orchestre dans le théâtre lyrique français chez les continuateurs de Lully, 1687–1715* (thesis, Paris Conservatoire, 1977)
C. Wood: *Jean-Baptiste Lully and his Successors: Music and Drama in the 'tragédie en musique' 1673–1715* (diss., U. of Hull, 1981)
——: 'Orchestra and Spectacle in the *tragédie en musique*, 1673–1715: Oracle, *sommeil* and *tempête*', *PRMA*, cviii (1981–2), 25–46
L. E. Brown: 'Departures from Lullian Convention in the *tragédie lyrique* of the *préramiste* Era', *RMFC*, xxii (1984), 57–78
R. Fajon: *A. C. Destouches et l'évolution du répertoire de l'Académie royale de musique en France* (diss., U. of Paris, 1984)
——: Introduction to A. C. Destouches: *Issé*, FO, xiv (1984)
——: *L'opéra à Paris du Roi-Soleil à Louis le Bien-aimé* (Geneva, 1984)
W. Weber: '*La musique ancienne* in the Waning of the Ancien Régime', *Journal of Modern History*, lvi (1984), 58–88
L. Rosow: 'André Cardinal Destouches: *Issé: pastorale héroïque*', *JAMS*, xl (1987), 548–57 [review of facs. edn]
——: 'From Destouches to Berton: Editorial Responsibility at the Paris Opéra', *JAMS*, xl (1987), 285–309
CAROLINE WOOD

Destouches, Franz Seraph von (*b* Munich, 21 Jan 1772; *d* Munich, 10 Dec 1844). German composer. In 1787 he had some lessons from Haydn in Vienna, and in 1797 was appointed music director at Erlangen. Shortly afterwards he joined the orchestra of the Weimar theatre (then under Goethe's direction) as second leader; there he wrote the incidental music for several plays by Schiller and others by Kotzebue and Zacharias Werner.

Destouches succeeded J. F. Kranz as first leader in 1804, but left Weimar in 1810 to become professor of music at Landshut. From 1826 to 1842 he was conductor at Homburg in Hesse and then retired to his native town. Besides his works for the stage he wrote sonatas, concertos, a mass and an oratorio.

Die Thomasnacht (J. Destouches), Munich, Hof, 31 Aug 1792, *D-Ds*
Das Missverständnis (komische Oper, P. A. Wolff), Weimar, 27 April 1805
Die bluhende Aloë (komische Oper, Wolff), *c*1805
Der Teufel und der Schneider (U. von Destouches), Munich, 1851

*

E. von Destouches: 'Franz Destouches', *Allgemeine Zeitung*, lxiv, suppl. (Munich, 1904)

Deszczyński, Józef (*b* Vilnius, 1781; *d* Horodyszcze, 1844). Polish composer. He worked in Vilnius as a music master. His first stage work, *Dworek na gościńcu* ('The Manor House by the Wayside'), a one-act comic opera to a libretto by L. Dmuszewski, was performed in Warsaw on 27 January 1809. The following year a three-act melodrama, *Egbert, czyli Połączenie się Anglików* ('Egbert, or The Union of the English'; after R. C. G. de Pixérécourt, trans. J. Wolski), was staged in Vilnius (30 January). From 1814 he was conductor of a private orchestra in Horodyszcze on the estate of Count Ludwik Rokicki and during this time he staged operas by Salieri, Boieldieu and others in the neighbouring town of Mińsk.

*

K. Michałowski: *Opery polskie* (Kraków, 1954)
ALINA NOWAK-ROMANOWICZ

Detmold. Town in Westphalia, north-western Germany. Musical works were performed in the old Komödienhaus from 1778 onwards. On 8 November 1825 the Hoftheater, on the site of the present Detmold theatre, opened with *La clemenza di Tito*. Albert Lortzing performed as singer and actor in Detmold between 1826 and 1833, and Wilhelmine Schröder-Devrient was a member of the company for some time; the presence of Brahms as music tutor and choral director to the princely court, 1857–9, also made a mark on the town's musical life. The Hoftheater continued until 1912, and was replaced in 1919 by the Lippesches Landestheater (676 seats), which opened on 28 September with Lortzing's *Undine*. Undamaged in World War II, the theatre became active again in 1950, staging both drama and musical performances. Of the company's approximately 530 performances annually, over half are operatic. It also makes regular and frequent provincial tours. In 1975 a cooperative arrangement was made with the town of Gütersloh nearby, enabling Detmold to stage such large-scale works as *Tannhäuser* and *Turandot*. In 1982 the first performance in German of Menotti's *Le dernier sauvage* was directed by the composer.

*

B. Wiesener and O. Röhler, eds.: *150 Jahre Theater in Detmold: zum Jubiläum des Landestheaters* (Detmold, 1975)
SABINE SONNTAG

De Totis, Giuseppe Domenico (*b* Rome, 1644–5; *d* Rome, 4 Nov 1707). Italian librettist. Crescimbeni stated that he wrote dramatic poetry, studied law, became a prelate in about 1690 and was immediately granted posts at the papal court through Cardinal Pietro Ottoboni's influence. De Totis took the name 'Filedo Nonacrio' as a member of the Arcadian Academy and was secretary of the Accademia degli Umoristi. According to Crescimbeni 'the sweetness of the verse' and 'the propriety of the sentiment' in his dramas ameliorated 'some corruptions of the century in which he flourished'. He invented a type of *melodramma* called 'spada e cappa' ('cloak and dagger'); *Idalma* and *Tutto il mal* are his contributions to this genre. Both are comedies featuring ordinary people so inextricably involved in love entanglements that swords are drawn and lives are threatened. De Totis directed *Tutto il mal* for the stage (see Lindgren and Schmidt), as he presumably did all his dramas. The most splendidly produced was certainly *La caduta del regno dell'amazzoni*, a *festa teatrale* with 14 stage sets (for illustration *see* FONTANA, GIROLAMO), ten special effects created by stage machinery, four ballets, a prologue, two intermezzos and an epilogue. Like his other operas, its musical core consisted of set pieces (66) for eight singers. His first four operas were each produced in five or more cities, but only one, *La Rosmene*, was revived after 1696. All were written for productions in either Rome or Naples. He was also known for nine oratorio texts.

La Rosmene, o vero L'infedeltà fedele (melodramma), Vigna di Porta Pia, 1677 (A. Scarlatti, 1686; G. Vignola, 1709); *Idalma, o vero Chi la dura la vince* (commedia per musica), B. Pasquini, 1680; *Tutto il mal non vien per nuocere* (commedia per musica), Scarlatti, 1681; *Aldimiro, o vero Favor per favore* (melodramma), Scarlatti, 1683; *Psiche, o vero Amore innamorato* (commedia per musica), Scarlatti, 1683; *Fetonte* (dramma per musica), ? Scarlatti, 1685; *La caduta del regno dell'amazzoni* (festa teatrale), Pasquini, 1690; *Agrippina*, G. L. Lulier, comp. 1691 (?B. Sabadini, 1714, as La virtù coronata, ossia Il Fernando)

*

P. Mandosio: *Bibliotheca romana seu romanum scriptorum centuriae*, i (Rome, 1682), 317
G. M. Crescimbeni: *Notizie istoriche degli Arcadi morti*, iii (Rome, 1721), 9–13, 378

G. F. Crain jr: *The Operas of Bernardo Pasquini* (diss., Yale U., 1965)
L. E. Lindgren and C. B. Schmidt: 'A Collection of 137 Broadsides Concerning Theatre in Late Seventeenth-Century Italy: an Annotated Catalogue', *Harvard Library Bulletin*, xxviii (1980), 196
S. Franchi: *Drammaturgia romana: repertorio bibliografico cronologico dei testi drammatici pubblicati a Roma e nel Lazio, secolo XVII* (Rome, 1988) LOWELL LINDGREN

Detroit. American city in the state of Michigan. Founded in 1701, it had little significant musical life before 1850. The first local attempts at opera were unstaged Italian works presented by the Detroit Philharmonic Society in 1855. Albert Lortzing's *Zar und Zimmermann*, given by the Harmonie Society in 1866, was the first opera staged by local performers. In 1869 the Detroit Opera House was built; with a seating capacity of over 2000, it was the largest hall the city had known. It was demolished on 4 May 1966, after which various theatres were used for operatic performances. The Masonic Auditorium (built in 1928) is used for many musical events, among which was an annual visit by the Metropolitan Opera (discontinued after the 1985 season). Thaddeus Wronski organized the Detroit Civic Opera Company in 1928; it was later associated with the Detroit SO in productions that were also presented in New York and Chicago, and continued until 1937. The Piccolo Opera Company was formed in 1961 to perform operas in English for schools and other organizations. The Overture to Opera series was organized in 1963 by David DiChiera, while he was on the faculty of Oakland University. Backed by the Detroit Grand Opera Association, the programme consisted of staged scenes and one-act operas which were given in schools and community centres throughout the state.

The Michigan Opera Theatre was also founded (in 1971) by DiChiera, who became its artistic director. It is resident in Detroit and tours throughout Michigan. It has its own orchestra and presents five works each season. Repertory includes American works (the première of Pasatieri's *Washington Square* was given in 1976), Mozart and Verdi, and works of national or ethnic schools, such as Tigranyan's *Anoush* (North American première, 1981) and Moniuszko's *The Haunted Manor* (American première, 1982). The company sponsors an opera-in-residence programme, whereby members visit colleges for a week and work with students to produce an opera. Singers who established their careers with the company include Kathleen Battle, Maria Ewing, Leona Mitchell, Carmen Balthrop and Vinson Cole. With the appointment of DiChiera in 1985 as general director of Opera Pacific (Costa Mesa, California) there began a beneficial three-way collaboration between that company, Michigan Opera Theatre and Dayton Opera (of which DiChiera is artistic director), both in productions and in educational programmes. In 1990 the Michigan Opera Theatre undertook a campaign to raise funds for the purchase and refurbishing of Grand Circus Theater in central Detroit, which will provide a permanent home for the troupe.

*

M. Teal: *Musical Activities in Detroit from 1701 through 1870* (diss., U. of Michigan, 1964) MARY D. TEAL

Dettmer, Wilhelm Georg (*b* Breinum, nr Hildesheim, 29 June 1808; *d* Frankfurt, 28 May 1876). German bass. He studied in Hanover, making his début in 1834 at Brunswick in Winter's *Das unterbrochene Opferfest*. He then sang at Breslau, Kassel (where he studied under Spohr's supervision), Frankfurt and the Hofoper at Dresden, where he created Colonna in *Rienzi* (1842) and the Landgrave in *Tannhäuser* (1845). Returning to Frankfurt in 1849, he sang there for 25 years and took his farewell in 1874 as Stadinger in *Der Waffenschmied*.

ELIZABETH FORBES

D'Ettore, Guglielmo. *See* ETTORE, GUGLIELMO.

Deus ex machina (Lat.: 'god from the machine'). A term used by historians of drama to denote a god who by a theatrical machine (Gk. *mechane*, Lat. *machina*) is hoisted on to the stage to resolve the plot, to 'untie the knot' (*dénouement*). Such endings, whether they occur in ancient Greek tragedy or in operatic librettos, are usually unforeseen and sudden, and by extension the term is frequently used to signify any arbitrary resolution of a plot (Paul Valéry has said that all endings are arbitrary). As a rule, the reversal of fortune is from sadness to happiness, and the 'deus ex machina' conclusion is therefore a subdivision of the LIETO FINE.

The two treatises on literary criticism that have been used for thousands of years to debate such matters are Aristotle's *Poetics* and Horace's *Art of Poetry*. Both Aristotle (1454b) and Horace (192) deal with the main artistic problem of the 'deus ex machina', namely that playwrights often use the device in a manner that leads to an unreasonable and implausible conclusion (Russell and Winterbottom 1972, pp.111, 284). Of the ancient Greek tragedians, it is Euripides in whose works a deity most frequently makes an appearance (*theophania*) to bring about the reversal of fortune: it has been reckoned that this happens in nine out of his 16 extant plays (Grube 1941). To take as an example his *Iphigenia in Tauris*, a plot well known in the history of opera, Iphigenia and Orestes are to die, when Athena intervenes at the play's end. It does not matter whether the goddess is hoisted by a crane or a pulley (*mechane*), or whether she appears on a high platform suitable for the appearance of deities (*theologeion*), as long as her intervention is both sudden and crucial (Pickard-Cambridge and Lucas 1970). Certainly, appearance by virtue of a theatrical contraption, such as a cloud machine, would appeal to the playwrights and librettists of the Baroque, with their proverbial fondness for stage machinery to bring about the miraculous, supernatural effects which abound in their mythological plots.

Parenthetically we should note that the 'deus ex machina' makes his powerful impact not only at the end of a drama, but in several instances intervenes earlier. For example, in Monteverdi's *L'incoronazione di Poppea* (1642) Cupid appears in the finale of the second of three acts to prevent the assassin from murdering Poppaea; and in the first scene of the final act of Gluck's *Paride ed Elena* (1770) Athena appears to prophesy the fall of Troy, which casts a sombre light on the festive finale of the second and final scene. Still, in the history of drama as well as of opera the most important and prominent function of the ancient theatrical device is to bring about the conclusion of the plot.

We may instance here the operas of Gluck, since he still partakes of the traditions of mythological subject matter and court entertainment so characteristic of Peri and Monteverdi, of Lully and Rameau. Also, Gluck and his librettists were in touch with the Italian and French Aristotelians, whose study of the ancient tragedies and of Aristotle's views of the essential ingredients of tragedy exercised so powerful an influence on opera in the 17th and 18th centuries. There is – above all – Gluck's *Orfeo ed Euridice* (1762), where the god Cupid appears twice, at the conclusion of the first and the last acts, to wrench the plot from despair to hope and happiness. (For similar scenarios from Monteverdi, Landi, Buti and Keiser to Stravinsky, *see* ORPHEUS. The deities who save Orpheus differ: they include Apollo, Mercury, Jupiter and Pluto.)

Among other mythological plots, relevant here, are those of Alcestis, Ariadne, Echo and Iphigenia: all of them fairly popular in the history of opera, with relevant examples easily culled from standard reference works, and most of them treated by Gluck, who, together with Euripides, must rank as a key figure in the dramatic history of divine or at least numinous intervention.

The myth of Alcestis is a case in point. Its treatment extends from Quinault's libretto (Lully, 1674) to Hofmannsthal (for Wellesz's opera, 1924) and Thornton Wilder (the basis for Talma's opera, 1962). But nobody demonstrates the powerful role of the 'deus ex machina' device better than Gluck. In Euripides, Alcestis is rescued from the underworld by Hercules. But Gluck's librettist, Calzabigi, expressly substituted for Hercules ('in luogo d'Ercole') Apollo, descending on a cloud, to bring about the miracle. And in the French revision of 1776, where Hercules is reinstated, the final appearance of Apollo has been maintained, unnecessarily as some critics have argued (Winterfeld 1851; Weismann 1962; Finscher 1964).

The story of Echo and Narcissus looms large in the history of music, partly because of the acoustical and musical possibilities inherent in the myth. Rinuccini's libretto, rejected by Monteverdi (*see* LIETO FINE), is followed by a variety of operas in the 17th and 18th centuries, and in our age Britten's *Six Metamorphoses after Ovid* for solo oboe re-evoke the plot. Gluck's librettist radically departed from Rinuccini's tragic finale: Echo and Narcissus live happily ever after, resurrected and reunited by Cupid, seemingly in as capricious a manner as in the composer's *Orfeo*.

Some 40 operas deal with the myth of Iphigenia, who is twice snatched from death by a 'deus ex machina'. At Aulis it is Artemis (Diana) who prevents her from being sacrificed by her father, and at Tauris it is Athena (Minerva) who rescues her and her brother Orestes. Both in the history of drama (Euripides to Goethe) and of opera (Löwe, Keiser and Caldara to Traetta, Galuppi and Cherubini) the fascinating problem is how to make these external interventions plausible in psychological and atmospheric terms, how to 'internalize' them. (It is a challenge not wholly different from the treatment of magic potions in librettos from Cavalli to Wagner.) Suffice it to say that for centuries critics have praised Gluck's *Iphigénie en Tauride* (1779) as a masterpiece of dramatic and musical construction where divine intervention does not vitiate theatrical verisimilitude. In the earlier *Iphigénie en Aulide* (1774), Gluck's judgment seems hesitant. In the first version it is the goddess's representative, the priest Calchas, who pronounces the pacification of Diana. But in the revision of 1775 the goddess herself appears. Whatever the merits of either procedure, throughout the history of libretto construction numinous symbols (priests, prophets, oracles) are frequently substituted for the *deus*.

Such substitutions occur more frequently in operas by the younger composers who succeeded (and imitated) Gluck. In Mozart's *Idomeneo* the god Neptune (or at least his oracle) brings about the conclusion. But the final *coup de théâtre* may also be produced by a bolt of lightning or, more characteristically, by an act of clemency. Magnanimity, in operas composed after the French Revolution, is usually not divine, but nevertheless sudden, unexpected, and effects a hairbreadth escape, as so many French rescue operas demonstrate: probably the best-known example is the intercession of the minister of state in Beethoven's *Fidelio*. One could argue that this minister as well as the forgiving emperor in Mozart's *La clemenza di Tito* are functionally, if not factually, the equivalent of *deus ex machina* (acclaimed, incidentally, as in Gluck, by the chorus).

Such substitutions explain, at least partially, the popularity of a dramatic device from Rinuccini to Hofmannsthal. At its best it never descends to a merely mechanical contrivance. In fact its persistence throughout the 18th century, in spite of the growth of rationalism and empiricism, attests to the strength of the classical tradition in that age, which otherwise tended to treat myths as superstitions. But by the 19th century the intellectual foundations had been severely attenuated, and the social bases for flattering analogies between a benign god and a wise prince largely removed. It remained for the 20th century to rediscover symbolic and archetypal significances of the 'deus ex machina' in the wake of Freud, Jung and Lévi-Strauss.

See also FINALE; LIETO FINE; and ORPHEUS, for historical information and additional bibliography.

C. von Winterfeld: *Alceste 1674, 1726, 1769, 1776 von Lully, Händel und Gluck* (Berlin, 1851) [also discusses Alcestis plot in Handel's *Admeto*]

J. M. A. Grube: 'Prologues and Epilogues', *The Drama of Euripides* (London, 1941), 63–79

T. B. L. Webster: *Greek Theatre Production* (London, 1956, 2/1970)

H. J. Rose: *Handbook of Greek Mythology* (London, 6/1958)

W. Weismann: 'Der *deus ex machina* in Glucks *Iphigenie in Aulis*', *DJbM*, vii (1962), 7–17

L. Finscher: 'Gluck und das *lieto fine*', *Musica*, xviii (1964), 296–301 [queries Weismann 1962]

D. W. Lucas, ed.: *Aristotle: Poetics: Introduction, Commentary* (Oxford, 1968, 2/1972), 24, 163ff

H. Hunger: *Lexikon der griechischen und römischen Mythologie* (Vienna, 6/1969) [mentions operas based on Greek myths]

A. W. Pickard-Cambridge and D. W. Lucas: 'Tragedy', *Oxford Classical Dictionary*, ed. N. G. L. Hammond and H. H. Scullard (Oxford, 2/1970)

O. Kuhn: *Mythos … Studien zur Gestaltung des Alkestis-stoffes bei … Hofmannsthal, T. S. Eliot und Thornton Wilder* (Munich, 1972)

A. Lesky: *Die tragische Dichtung der Hellenen* (Göttingen, 3/1972)

D. A. Russell and M. Winterbottom, eds.: *Ancient Literary Criticism: the Principal Texts in New Translation* (Oxford, 1972)

P. Weiss: 'Baroque Opera and the Two Verisimilitudes', *Essays in Honor of Paul Henry Lang* (New York, 1984), 117–26

FREDERICK W. STERNFELD

Deutekom, Cristina [Engel, Stientje] (*b* Amsterdam, 28 Aug 1932). Dutch soprano. She studied at the Amsterdam Conservatory, joined the chorus of the Nederlandse Opera and, after singing small roles with the company, scored a major success in 1963 as the Queen of Night, which quickly took her to débuts in the same role in Munich and Vienna, at the Metropolitan Opera (1967) and Covent Garden (1968), and in the 1971 recording under Solti. Her virtuosity and flexibility in coloratura technique, in spite of occasional hardness in tone, brought her further success as Donna Anna, Armida (Rossini), Konstanze, Fiordiligi, Duchess

Hélène (*Les vêpres siciliennes*), Elvira (*I puritani*), Lucia and Norma as well as Odabella (*Attila*) which she recorded in 1973. NOËL GOODWIN

Deutsch, Max (*b* Vienna, 17 Nov 1892; *d* Paris, 22 Nov 1982). French composer of Austrian origin. He studied at the University of Vienna (1910–15) and with Schoenberg (1913–20), also serving in World War I. During the 1920s he worked as a theatre conductor in several European countries; in 1923 his one-act opera *Schach* was performed in Berlin. He moved to Paris in 1924. In 1934–5 he held a chair at the University of Madrid, then worked as a pianist and revue composer in Paris before volunteering for service in World War II. Later he was professor of composition at the Ecole Normale de Musique, his pupils including Bussotti. He composed two further stage works, the *légende dramatique La fuite* (Tzara; 1946, Paris) and the opera *Apothéose*, to his own libretto (*c*1972). PAUL GRIFFITHS

Deutsche Oper am Rhein. Company formed in 1956 by the theatrical merger of DÜSSELDORF and Duisburg.

Deutsche Oper Berlin. Opera company and theatre; *see* BERLIN, §3(ii).

Deutsche Staatsoper. Opera company and theatre which in 1919, as the Staatsoper, replaced the former Berlin Hofoper; *see* BERLIN, §3(i).

Deux aveugles, Les ('The Two Blind Men' [*The Blind Beggars*]). *Bouffonerie musicale* in one act by JACQUES OFFENBACH to a libretto by Jules Moinaux; Paris, Théâtre des Bouffes-Parisiens (Salle Lacaze), 5 July 1855.

On a Paris bridge two blind musicians are begging, Patachon (tenor) playing the trombone and Giraffier (baritone) the mandolin. They play cards to decide which shall have the bridge to himself, but each cheats outrageously, revealing that neither is really blind. Consisting of just an overture and four short numbers interspersed with humorous exchanges, the work was the success of the opening evening of the Théâtre des Bouffes-Parisiens, not least for the bolero for the pair, 'La lune brille, le ciel scintille', with Pradeau taking the part of Patachon and Berthelier that of Giraffier.

ANDREW LAMB

Deux comtesses, Les. Intermezzo by Giovanni Paisiello; *see* DUE CONTESSE, LE.

Deux journées, Les ('The Two Days' [*The Water Carrier*]). *Comédie lyrique* in three acts by LUIGI CHERUBINI to a libretto by JEAN-NICOLAS BOUILLY; Paris, Théâtre Feydeau, 16 January 1800.

Bouilly claimed to have based his libretto on a historical incident during the French Revolution's Reign of Terror. Since those days were still fresh in people's minds, and since censorship was prevalent, he moved the story to 1647 and the Fronde, a chapter in French history similar to the Revolution. The play opens in the house of the Savoyard water carrier Mikéli (baritone), who is hiding Armand (tenor) and Constance (soprano), a parliamentarian and his wife, proscribed by recent edict of Cardinal Mazarin. In the strophic aria 'Guide mes pas', Mikéli asks for divine assistance in his task; probably the most popular piece in the opera, its melodic shape strongly resembles an old French dance entitled 'Tourdion' from a 1530 publication by Pierre Attaingnant. Constance and Armand enter disguised as military officers but quickly assume roles as members of Mikéli's family to avoid discovery by soldiers who arrive to search the house. As they leave, Mikéli's father Daniel (bass) and his children Marcélina (soprano) and Antonio (tenor) return. Antonio recognizes Armand as the benefactor of his youth, and the act ends as the whole family prepares to assist Constance and Armand.

Act 2 takes place before the gates of Paris. Constance, disguised as Marcélina, and Antonio enter on their way to Gonesse. The guards prevent their departure, but they leave safely after assurances from the Commandant (bass), who participated in the house search, and from Mikéli, who arrives with his water barrel to a reprise of 'Guide mes pas' from Act 1. After sending the soldiers on a false path in search of Armand, Mikéli turns his water barrel around with the back facing the portal. Armand jumps out and runs into the woods as the soldiers return to continue their search outside Paris. Act 3 moves to Gonesse where the inhabitants are celebrating the marriage of Antonio to a local girl. The festivities are interrupted by the soldiers. Mikéli hides Armand in a tree trunk while Constance continues to masquerade as Antonio's sister. When the soldiers try to seduce her, Armand leaps from the tree. Just as he is arrested, Mikéli runs in to announce that the queen and cardinal, intimidated by the populace, have lifted the proscription against Armand. The opera ends as everyone sings of the virtues of humanitarianism.

With this opera Cherubini experienced a success which he never repeated in his lifetime. This was partly due to the libretto, judged by Beethoven and Goethe to be one of the finest of the period. Beethoven considered Cherubini the greatest living operatic composer on the basis of *Les deux journées*, and Mendelssohn remarked that the first three bars of the overture were worth more than the whole of the Berlin opera's repertory. The story is an example of the 'rescue' plot with some up-to-date heroism, fraternity and equality to make it digestible by post-revolutionary audiences. The initial production, in which the part of Constance was created by Julie-Angélique Scio, ran for over 200 performances and had been revived four times by 1842, the year of Cherubini's death. It was presented in German-speaking countries throughout the 19th century, including a performance conducted by Cherubini in Vienna on 5 August 1805 for which he worked some changes. Musically, the opera was successful because Cherubini conformed to the French concept of the *opéra comique* – short musical numbers with an emphasis on spoken dialogue and ensemble (only two of the 15 musical items are arias). Although it was Cherubini's most popular dramatic work, *Les deux journées* contains none of the innovations that characterize his other efforts in the genre.

The subtitle *Le porteur d'eau*, sometimes encountered, was merely a French translation of the title under which the work was first presented in English and appears on neither the first libretto nor the first edition of the score. STEPHEN C. WILLIS

Deux petits Savoyards, Les ('The Two Little Savoyards'). *Comédie mêlée d'ariettes* in one act by NICOLAS-MARIE DALAYRAC to a libretto by BENOÎT-JOSEPH MARSOLLIER DES VIVETIÈRES; Paris, Comédie-Italienne, 14 January 1789.

The action takes place near Lyons, at the chateau of Verseuil. Verseuil (tenor; a part originally written for J.-P. Solié) has made his fortune in America, but his only brother has died and his family become lost. Two young brothers from Savoy (Michel and Joset, both travesty sopranos) appear in national costume; they and their mother (who does not appear in the opera) are wandering entertainers. The Bailli (baritone) regards Savoyards as troublesome foreigners, but Verseuil finds the boys interesting and honest. With a view to adopting them, he interviews them separately. The brothers try to escape, after which it is discovered that they are in fact Verseuil's nephews.

Marsollier's plot forms part of a common strain of sentimental 'humanity' operas, some portraying children. But the enduring success of *Les deux petits Savoyards* came also from the attraction of regional accents and character, and folktunes like 'Escouto d'Jeannetto' (treated in piano variations by Eberl, Hummel and F. J. Kirmair) and 'Une petite fillette'. The opera was seen in Germany 'throughout the 19th century' according to Loewenberg (*Annals of Opera*, 1943).

DAVID CHARLTON

Devčić, Natko (*b* Glina, 30 June 1914). Croatian composer. He studied at the Zagreb Academy of Music, in Vienna and later in New York, where he worked on electronic music (1967–8). From 1947 to 1980 he was professor and head of the department of composition and conducting at the Zagreb Academy. After an early nationalistic phase, which reached its high point in the popular *Istarska suita* for orchestra (1948), he came more and more to use novel techniques, though still retaining some contact with the features of Istrian folk music, as in the opera *Labinska vještica* ('The Witch of Labin'; D. Robić; Zagreb, 25 December 1957). This work is based on the historical character Matija Vlačić (Flacius Illyricus), who was born near Labin in Istria; the music is notable for its pandiatonic treatment of the Istrian mode and for the prominent role of the chorus. Devčić's other compositions include vocal works (some with speaker) and dance pieces.

*

K. Kovačević: 'Labinska vještica Natka Devčića' [The Witch of Labin by Natko Devčic], *Zvuk* (1958), nos.21–3, pp.33–41

——: *Hrvatski kompozitori i njihova djela* [Croatian Composers and their Works] (Zagreb, 1960), 117–26

I. Supičić: 'Estetski pogledi u novijoj hrvatskoj muzici: pregled temeljnih gledanja četrnaestorice kompozitora' [Aesthetic Approaches in Contemporary Croatian Music: a Survey of the Basic Views of 14 Composers], *Arti musices*, i (1969), 23–61

J. Andreis: *Music in Croatia* (Zagreb, 1974)

N. Gligo: *Varijacije razvojnog kontinuiteta: skladatelj Natko Devčić* [Variations in a Developing Continuity: the Composer Natko Devčic] (Zagreb, 1985) [Ger. summary]

KREŠIMIR KOVAČEVIĆ/KORALJKA KOS

Devienne, François (*b* Joinville, Haute-Marne, 31 Jan 1759; *d* Paris, 5 Sept 1803). French composer. He achieved early fame as a flautist, bassoonist and composer of chamber and orchestral works, many of which he performed at the Concert Spirituel in Paris. He remained active as an instrumentalist throughout his life and was employed as bassoonist from 1789 to 1801 at the Théâtre de Monsieur (later the Théâtre Feydeau), the establishment for which he wrote most of his stage works. His theatrical career spanned only the closing decade of the 18th century and was concentrated exclusively on the *opéra comique*.

Devienne, along with Berton and Dalayrac, favoured the type of *opéra comique* that remained light and sentimental in character, drawing on everyday situations for its subject matter and using figures from the less elevated orders of society, as opposed to the type that emphasized serious elements at the expense of comic intrigue, preferred by such contemporaries as Cherubini, Méhul and Le Sueur. The topics he chose give scope for a natural grace and freshness, to which he added directness of expression and an imaginative sense of the theatre. He was a skilful melodist and excelled in combining simplicity with vocal display. His harmonic language is pure, his instrumental writing carefully conceived and often rich and sonorous, enhancing the melodic interest without overwhelming the voices.

Les comédiens ambulans, *Le valet de deux maîtres* and *Les visitandines* were Devienne's most successful stage works. *Les visitandines*, performed more than 200 times (as late as 1920 in Paris), was particularly popular during the Revolution period for its anti-clerical sentiments – a heroine rescued from religious seclusion and the mockery of religious figures through transvestite disguises – as well as for its broad humour and musical charm.

opéras comiques unless otherwise stated; all first performed in Paris

Le mariage clandestin (1, Vicomte de Ségur), Montansier, 11 Nov 1790, 1 air pubd

Les précieuses ridicules (1, P.-L. Moline, after Molière), Montansier, 9 Aug 1791

Encore des Savoyards, ou L'école des parvenus (1, J.-B. Pujoulx), OC (Favart), 8 Feb 1792

Les visitandines (2, L. B. Picard), Feydeau, 7 July 1792; rev. in 3 acts, 1793 (Paris, *c*1792)

L'enlèvement des Sabines (pièce en vaudevilles, 2, Picard), Feydeau, 31 Oct 1792 [doubtful]

Les quiproquos espagnols (2, J.-E. Dejaure), Feydeau, 10 Dec 1792

Le congrès des rois (cmda, 3, Desmaillot [A. F. Eve]), OC (Favart), 26 Feb 1794; collab. Dalayrac, Grétry, Méhul and 8 others

Rose et Aurèle (1, Picard), Feydeau, 8 Aug 1794 (Paris, *c*1795)

Agnès et Félix, ou Les deux espiègles (3, C.-A. Demoustier), Feydeau, 22 Aug 1795

Volécour, ou Un tour de page (1, E.-G.-F. Favières), OC (Favart), 22 March 1797

Les comédiens ambulans (2, Picard), Feydeau, 28 Dec 1798 (Paris, *c*1799)

Le valet de deux maîtres (1, J.-F. Roger, after C. Goldoni), Feydeau, 2 Nov 1799 (Paris, *c*1800)

*

MGG (M. Briquet and S. Wallon)

A. Pougin: *Devienne* (Paris, 1864); serialized in *Revue et gazette musicale de Paris*, xxxi (1864), 241, 251, 308, 324, 355, 364

G. Chouquet: *Histoire de la musique dramatique en France depuis ses origines jusqu'à nos jours* (Paris, 1873)

M. Tourneux, ed.: *Correspondance littéraire, philosophique et critique par Grimm, Diderot, Raynal, Meister, etc.* (Paris, 1877–82)

E. Humblot: *Un musicien joinvillois … François Devienne* (St Dizier, 1909)

J. Tiersot: *Lettres de musiciens écrites en français du XVe au XXe siècle*, i (Turin, 1924)

W. Montgomery: *The Life and Works of François Devienne, 1759–1803* (diss., Catholic U. of America, 1975)

ELISABETH COOK

Devil and Daniel Webster, The. Folk opera in one act by DOUGLAS S. MOORE to a libretto ('book') by Stephen Vincent Benét after his own short story; New York, Martin Beck Theater, 18 May 1939.

Moore and Benét called this work a folk opera 'because it is legendary in its subject matter and simple in its musical expression'. In fact, it is a musical, albeit an unorthodox one, with no overture, only one act, and much of the spoken dialogue accompanied by music. The opera may be performed either with full orchestra (wind in pairs) or a reduced ensemble with solo winds.

It is set in the home of farmer Jabez Stone (bass) of Cross Corners, New Hampshire, in the 1840s. After 12 introductory bars the curtain rises on the wedding reception of Jabez and his new wife Mary (mezzo-soprano). Jabez, we learn, has worked his way out of poverty with surprising speed and become state senator for the district. Indeed, he is such a hot political prospect that his name has been suggested for governor, and the Secretary of State, Daniel Webster (baritone), has agreed to appear at the wedding. Webster's arrival is marred, however, by the sudden unmanageability of the violinist's instrument. When the Fiddler (spoken role) comments that 'the very devil' has got into his instrument, Mr Scratch (tenor) appears, introducing himself as a Boston lawyer and claiming to be an old friend of the bridegroom. Under the pretence of fixing the fiddle, he plays a devilishly Stravinskian accompaniment to a nasty ballad of death and despair ('Young William was a thriving boy'), which Webster interrupts in a fury.

The Fiddler, much antagonized, opens the box Scratch brought with him, releasing a mothlike lost soul which cries for help and reveals that Jabez, too, has sold his soul to the Devil. The crowd recoils from Jabez, but Mary and Webster refuse to desert him. He explains that in a weak moment he sold his soul to escape his grinding poverty, and that the debt is due this day. Webster attempts to cheer him up with a tall story ('I've got a ram, Goliath') and Mary offers up a prayer ('Now may there be a blessing').

Webster insists on a trial of the case, allowing Scratch any judge and jury he likes provided they are American. Scratch packs the court with the spirits of outlaws and villains, but when Webster appeals to their love of freedom they find for Jabez. Webster grabs Scratch by the collar and summons the neighbours to drive him out of New Hampshire.

For all its American ballads and fiddle tunes, *The Devil and Daniel Webster* follows an English model, *Ruddigore*, which it resembles in numerous particulars (for example, the male chorus from hell who sit in judgment on the protagonist). The extensive use of melodrama, the Devil's fiddling, and the folktale ambience all echo Stravinsky's *Histoire du soldat*; Stravinsky returned the compliment by using *The Devil and Daniel Webster* as one of his models for *The Rake's Progress*. ANDREW STILLER

Devil and Kate, The [*Čert a Káča*]. Comic opera in three acts by ANTONÍN DVOŘÁK to a libretto by Adolf Wenig after a Czech folktale; Prague, National Theatre, 23 November 1899.

Jirka *a shepherd*	tenor
Káča [Kate] *a middle-aged spinster*	mezzo-soprano
Her Mother	mezzo-soprano
Marbuel *a devil*	bass
Lucifer	bass
Door-Keeper Devil	bass
Sentry Devil	bass
Princess	soprano
Chambermaid	soprano
Marshal	bass
Musician	tenor

Peasants, young boys and girls, musicians, devils, courtiers and people (offstage)

Setting a country inn on a summer evening; hell; the Princess's castle

The Devil and Kate was the first opera to be completed by Dvořák after *The Jacobin* (1888). In the intervening years, he made extensive revisions to *Dimitrij* and *The Jacobin*, and sketches for unfinished projects, including an opera based on Longfellow's *Song of Hiawatha*. The subject of *The Devil and Kate* continues Dvořák's interest in Czech folklore, which first emerged in his four symphonic poems based on ballads by K. J. Erben, composed after his return from the USA in 1896.

Based on a story in Božena Němcová's *Folk Tales and Legends* (1845), which was later used as the basis of a drama by J. K. Tyl (1850) and a poem by Ladislav Quis (1883), the libretto of *The Devil and Kate* was written by Adolf Wenig; under the title *Ovčák* ('The Shepherd'), the text had won first prize in a competition for new librettos organized by the National Theatre in 1898. František Rieger, who had helped the composer with the revision of *The Jacobin*, recommended the work to Dvořák.

The story of *The Devil and Kate* is virtually unique in Czech comic opera in being without love interest. Apart from this, the characters and the setting of the outer acts accord well with the nationally inspired conventions of Czech comic opera. Dvořák apparently made sketches for the opera in 1897, before the libretto had been entered for the competition. Abandoning these ideas, he began work on a continuous sketch on 9 May 1898, after some brief preliminaries begun on 5 May 1898. The sketch of the first act was completed on 14 May and the full score on 1 July. The second and third acts were completed on 29 September 1898 and 5 February 1899 respectively. Following the third performance of the opera on 29 November 1899, Dvořák added 20 bars to the end of Act 2 in order to improve the pacing.

The première was given under the National Theatre's chief conductor and Dvořák's friend, Adolf Čech. The cast included some of the company's finest singers: Bohumíl Pták (Jirka) and Ružena Maturová (Princess), who later created the roles of Rusalka and Armida. The opera was an immediate success and has remained popular in Czechoslovakia. A production in German translation took place at Bremen on 27 April 1909, but the opera did not reach Vienna until 11 January 1924, when it was given by the Olomouc company; a production at the Volksoper followed on 19 February 1932. The first professional performance in English was at the Wexford Festival on 20 October 1988; the production was later presented at the St Louis Festival (14 June 1990).

The overture is Dvořák's longest and most developed since the one he wrote for *Vanda* in 1879. Arranged in a loose rondo, with a slow introduction and apotheosis, the music is based entirely on material from the opera.

ACT 1 *A country inn on a summer evening* The act is not divided into scenes. A long introduction leads to the rise of the curtain revealing musicians and a chorus of young men. This passage, in which the orchestra imitates the sound of bagpipes being played on stage, has clear parallels with the first scene of *The Bartered Bride*. The chorus asks the shepherd Jirka why he must leave his merrymaking and taunts him about Kate's amorous intentions towards him. Jirka tells of his taskmaster, the estate steward, and sings an expressive song, 'Já ubohej ovčáček' ('I, an unhappy shepherd'). Meanwhile, Kate and her mother arrive. During a vigorous waltz, she is ignored by the local lads and, with her passion for the dance, declares that she would willingly dance with the Devil. On cue, the devil Marbuel, dressed as a huntsman, appears and introduces himself. Marbuel asks about the happiness of the village folk under the Princess and her steward with a view to exacting retribution from the oppressors, but is readily diverted into drinking beer and flirting with Kate. They dance, and Marbuel asks Kate to run away with him. Jirka announces that he has been sacked by the steward, who told him to 'go to hell'. Marbuel persists in his suit of Kate, and in a marvellously evocative arioso describes his home, 'Je sic to trochu daleko' ('It is a little far'). Kate is quickly convinced and agrees to go; she and Marbuel disappear through a hole in the floor. Jirka resolves to follow the pair and bring Kate back.

ACT 2 *Hell* After a substantial prelude and chorus, Lucifer asks what has become of Marbuel. Marbuel appears with Kate, who scolds him: 'You promised me castles, yet you drag me to hell!'. As Kate distracts Marbuel with her scolding, Jirka appears at the gates. Kate refuses to go with him back to earth, and Jirka suggests they give her gold, abundant in hell, to get rid of her. She disappears in pursuit of gold while Marbuel reports on his mission. Lucifer decides that the Princess must be dragged down to hell and the steward warned. The problem at hand, however, is Kate who refuses to leave. Jirka agrees to help and after a substantial ballet dances Kate out of hell.

ACT 3 *In the Princess's castle* Disturbed by a guilty conscience, the Princess sings an aria, 'Jak smutno v zámku' ('How sad it is in the castle'). Fearful of hell, she agrees to Jirka's demand to abolish serfdom and rule her subjects well. In order to foil Marbuel and save the Princess, Jirka hides Kate behind a door to wait for the unfortunate devil. When he appears, Kate leaps on him and he disappears in fright. The Princess rewards her with a new house and money, and all ends happily.

* * *

The static quality of the opera is much enlivened by Dvořák's witty, almost telegraphic word-setting (in places anticipating Janáček), effective set pieces and sharp characterization, especially in the title roles. The opera is through-composed, although some of the numbers, including a long and brilliant ballet, are detachable. The simplicity of the melodic writing, frequently in balanced, symmetrical phrases, looks back to Dvořák's earlier comic operas. The recrudescence of Wagnerian harmony and the use of leitmotif are incidental features in a work which is completely characteristic of Dvořák's maturity. Particularly effective is the exquisite orchestration in such passages as Marbuel's arioso in Act 1 and the numbers built on sweeping ostinatos, such as the prelude to Act 2.

JAN SMACZNY

De Villati, Leopoldo. *See* VILLATI, LEOPOLDO DE.

Devils of Loudun, The. Opera in three acts by KRZYSZTOF PENDERECKI to a libretto by the composer after John Whiting's dramatization of ALDOUS HUXLEY's novel *The Devils of Loudun*, based on Erich Fried's German translation of the play; Hamburg, Staatsoper, 20 June 1969.

The Devils of Loudun is Penderecki's first and most popular opera and has had many new productions in Europe and the USA. The subject not only inspired Huxley and Whiting but also spawned Ken Russell's film *The Devils*. With its unabashed exploration of lust, blasphemy, exorcism and religious persecution, it fitted Penderecki's taste for vivid musical and dramatic extremes. Moreover, in two large-scale choral works – the *St Luke Passion* (1963–6) and *Dies irae* (1967), written in memory of those murdered at Auschwitz – he had recently developed both his musical language and his control of extended structures.

The principal story draws on contemporary accounts of the trial of Father Grandier in 1634, when he was accused of bewitching the nuns of St Ursula's Convent, and principally its prioress, Jeanne. A subplot, concerning Grandier's stand against a royal command (instigated by Cardinal Richelieu to limit provincial power) to tear down the walls of Loudun, threads its way through the opera and further contributes to Grandier's isolation and downfall. Penderecki originally cast the story in three acts with 30 short scenes, but he added two further scenes to Act 2 in 1975. He created an overarching dramatic framework by anticipating in the opera's first scene the final procession of Grandier (baritone) to the stake. At the beginning of the opera, Jeanne (dramatic soprano) has a vision of Grandier's final moments, although the real seeds of his destruction are sown when this vision moves to show Grandier embracing the pretty young widow Ninon (contralto). As the opera progresses, Jeanne's erotic fantasies concerning Grandier assume demonic aspects and become public knowledge. Although Grandier is innocent of corrupting Jeanne and her nuns, his weakness for other members of the opposite sex – Ninon and Philippe (high lyric soprano), the young girl whose pregnancy he disowns – accelerates his end in the eyes of some of the local citizens.

The plotting against Grandier is led by Adam, the town chemist (tenor), and Mannoury, the surgeon (baritone), whose malicious gossiping is woven through Act 1, gradually attracting other interests. These centre on the church in the persons of Fathers Barré (bass), Rangier (*basso profondo*) and Mignon (tenor), and on the agent of the subplot, De Laubardemont (tenor), the king's special commissioner, who eventually takes the lead in Grandier's downfall.

The opera is headed by a quotation from St Chrysostomus: 'Daemoni, etiam vera dicenti, non est credendum' (The devil cannot be believed even when he tells the truth). The message here, however, is that utterances forced out by exorcism or torture are automatically deemed to be truthful, an attitude that is open to distortion and injustice and one that links this work with Penderecki's *Dies irae* and all that its background evokes. Yet the plot is very simple, with few twists or turns. The interest therefore lies in its pacing, its characterization and in the dramatic elements that Penderecki chose to emphasize.

The sequence of scenes is dramatically assured, their sound-world clearly delineated. Penderecki uses the chorus and orchestra as characterizing agents, sometimes with tutti textures familiar from earlier works (witness the portrayal of demons in Act 2, scene ix) or as distinctive components of the pervading dramatic recitatives, as in the five scenes in Act 1 involving Adam and Mannoury. Most of the scenes are compact (the opera lasts under two hours), although Penderecki dwells longer on the more ghoulish moments, such as the torturing of Jeanne (2.i), her public exorcism (2.x) or the

'The Devils of Loudun' (Penderecki): scene from the original production at the Hamburg Staatsoper, 20 June 1969

drawing of Grandier's fingernails (3.ii) and the breaking of his legs (3.v).

Penderecki's fascination with the lurid may seem gratuitous. But the opera's singleminded message has a graphic power that goes some way towards overcoming its sense of voyeurism. The minor characters are given due attention, though musical as opposed to dramatic characterization of the principals is not Penderecki's primary compositional focus. This lies more in the contrasts of pace and of vocal and instrumental textures, all of which are particularly effective in the interlocking structure of Act 1, the developing drama of Act 2, and the simple effectiveness of the two split-level scenes in Act 3. Above all, the atonal musical language is still fresh and adaptable, distinguishing *The Devils of Loudun* from its successors. ADRIAN THOMAS

Devil's Wall, The [*Čertova stěna*]. Comic-romantic opera in three acts by BEDŘICH SMETANA to a libretto by ELIŠKA KRÁSNOHORSKÁ; Prague, New Czech Theatre, 29 October 1882.

The 'Devil's Wall' is a group of rocks sticking out of the river Vltava at Vyšší Brod. According to Czech folk tradition these are the remains of an attempt by the Devil to dam the river and flood the land around it. Krásnohorská built on this legend when she invented the plot of Smetana's final opera, set in the middle of the 13th century. Rejected by his beloved many years earlier, Vok Vítkovic of Rožmberk (baritone) has not married. His courtiers are anxious that he should have an heir and do their best to provide him with one: the opera opens, after a brief potpourri prelude, with the return of the knight Jarek (tenor) after just such a quest and his account of its failure to Míchálek (tenor), the Rožmberk castellan. The hermit Beneš (bass), on the other hand, is anxious for Vok to stay single and his wealth to go to a monastery of which Beneš will be abbot. In this he is assisted by Rarach (bass), a devil usually seen – confusingly – in the shape of Beneš, though he is recognizable through his pantomime-devil laugh, heard over augmented triads (ex.1).

Other residents of Vok's court include his young nephew Záviš (contralto) and Míchálek's daughter, Katuška (soprano). Katuška and Jarek are lovers, but Jarek has vowed not to marry before Vok does. Further complications arise when Vok offers to marry Katuška, a proposal that Míchálek takes more seriously than intended. News comes that Vok's former beloved has died and has entrusted her daughter Hedvika (soprano) to his care. Vok's recollection of his love stirs up the best-known aria of the opera, 'Jen jediná mé ženy' ('Only one woman's pretty face has so moved me'), an aria loaded with personal significance for Smetana.

Act 2 depicts Jarek's continuing efforts to find a wife for Vok (frustrated again by Rarach, this time disguised as a shepherd), Míchálek's posturing as the potential father-in-law of Vok and the arrival of Hedvika. Beneš sees her as a threat to his plans and, with Rarach, gets Vok to announce that he will end his days in the monastery. In the most substantial concertato ensemble of the piece, 'Blaha lásky' ('The bliss of love'), the company urge him to reconsider. Vok relents: he will marry any girl who, out of love, comes to him at the monastery.

The action of Act 3 was confused by cuts which Smetana made to the libretto, but its chief incidents include Beneš's confession of his sins to Míchálek, the arrival of a chorus of village maidens as hopeful brides for Vok (a plan thwarted by their menfolk), the Lisztian 'infernal dance' for Rarach's minions leading to the orders by Rarach (now seen in his devilish form) for the damming of the river. Realizing Vok's danger and, at the same time, her love for him, Hedvika makes the perilous journey to him over the rocks above the rising water. Vok is moved by Hedvika's gesture and his marriage to her allows Jarek to marry Katuška. No longer guiltily impotent, Beneš makes the sign of the cross over the Devil's work; the wall breaks and the waters return to their course. The opera ends with the arrival of the king's messengers calling Vok to take up the highest office of the land.

The composition of the opera (autumn 1879 to 17 April 1882; prelude, June 1882) was much affected by Smetana's worsening illness. It is hardly the 'comedy' that he asked his librettist for and its musical realization is inconsistent and at times perfunctory. Nevertheless it is an innovative score and a deeply felt one with Smetana identifying strongly with its isolated hero, Vok, and writing some of his most poignant music for him.

JOHN TYRRELL

Devil Take her, The. Opera in a prologue and one act by ARTHUR BENJAMIN to a libretto by Alan Collard and John B. Gordon with additional lyrics by Cedric Cliffe after BEN JONSON and others; London, Royal College of Music, 1 December 1931.

This is a version of the classic comedy, in which a man married to a silent woman lives to regret the day she regains the power of speech. It is set in 15th-century London. The husband is a Poet (tenor) who speaks the prologue before the curtain while the orchestra is instructed to hold specified chords of the overture. Other principal roles are the Wife (mezzo), the Doctor doubling the Devil (bass), a Neighbour (baritone) and a Maid (soprano), with ten supporting roles. The duration is about 50 minutes and the music is continuous, breaking into arioso and ballad-song, and coloured by character and situation to express satirical comment on the story. The première was conducted by Thomas Beecham and directed by the co-librettist, John B. Gordon.

NOËL GOODWIN

Devin du village, Le ('The Village Soothsayer'). *Intermède* in one act by JEAN-JACQUES ROUSSEAU to his own libretto; Fontainebleau, 18 October 1752.

The shepherds Colin (tenor) and Colette (soprano), the Soothsayer (baritone) and a chorus of villagers form the cast of this story of young love reconciled. Thanks to the Soothsayer's intelligence (rather than his magic arts) Colin, lured away by the advances of the lady of the manor, is made to realize that Colette is his only real treasure. The pretence that Colette has likewise given her affections to a courtier hastens Colin's return, and the concluding reconciliation is celebrated in songs and village dances.

Le devin was staged at the Paris Opéra on 1 March 1753, parodied at the Comédie-Italienne by C.-S. Favart and Harny de Guerville (*Les amours de Bastien et de Bastienne* of August 1753), and several years later adapted by Charles Burney as *The Cunning Man* (London, Drury Lane, 21 November 1766). The work's importance was, however, disproportionate to its length and musical weight. It appeared just at the time when, in the Querelle des Bouffons, the French *tragédie lyrique* was being compared unfavourably (by Rousseau among others) with the Italian *opera buffa* as a model of operatic style. Although Rousseau claimed to have written only 'French' music (*Dictionnaire de musique*, 'Copiste'), his simple melodic approach in *Le devin* was inspired by the *buffo* manner, and this work, consisting entirely of *airs*, recitatives, choruses and dances, allowed the Opéra to meet a demand for lighter, shorter works in French without compromising dramatic principles. The freshness and simplicity of the human story also had a strong appeal: idealized though it was, Rousseau lent a new conviction to the old pastoral convention that rural simplicity is preferable to metropolitan sophistication. This gave considerable impetus in the 1750s to the theme of *paysannerie*, particularly in the *opéra comique*.

A theatrical innovation in the final celebrations, at least in the printed score (Paris, 1753), is a mime scene in which Colette, after resisting money and jewels from the Courtier (silent), is reunited by him with Colin. (The idea of power used wisely reappears in later 18th-century works such as *Die Entführung aus dem Serail* and *Le nozze di Figaro*.) Rousseau exchanged many ideas with Diderot, and practised what his friend was later influentially to preach in favour of tableau and mime in both spoken and sung drama. Rousseau's mime was not included in early performances, probably not because its subject was too delicate for court eyes, but because the Opéra preferred a *divertissement* without dramatic action. Following the first court performance, Colette's opening air, 'J'ai perdu mon serviteur', was

'Le devin du village' (J.-J. Rousseau): engraving (1779) by P. A. Martini after J. M. Moreau

Admission ticket designed by John Devoto for a performance (unstaged) of Handel's 'Hercules' given on 21 February 1752

rumoured to have been sung all day, and out of tune, by Louis XV. Colin's *romance*, 'Dans ma cabane obscure', with its archaic simplicity and trochaic rhythms in 3/4 time, had a lasting influence on the *opéra comique*, though this example of the form is not a narrative as Rousseau's own definition requires (*Dictionnaire de musique*, 'Romance'). The final round-dance for the two lovers, with choral refrain 'Allons danser sous les ormeaux', seals both the social and the musical atmosphere of the work, thoroughly vindicating the composer's claim in his preface to have attained the elusive goal of 'Unité de mélodie' (*Dictionnaire*).

Rousseau's own honeymoon with the Opéra did not last. Following a scathing attack on French opera in his *Lettre sur la musique française* at the end of 1753, his right to complimentary tickets for life was withdrawn. The orchestra burnt him in effigy in 1754. He strove for a number of years thereafter to retrieve his score of *Le devin* since, in his view, the company had broken its word. The work itself was performed regularly in Paris until 1829, when, it is said, Berlioz, in a puff of powder from a periwig thrown onto the stage, temporarily exploded its reputation. For many years Rousseau was accused by some of not being the composer, but early 20th-century scholarship has disproved all the competing theories. There is now a consensus of agreement with Gluck's remark to Salieri about the *intermède*'s uniquely individual and cohesive style.

PHILIP E. J. ROBINSON

Devisenarie (Ger.: 'motto aria'). Term used for an ARIA, in the Baroque period, in which a 'motto' ('Devise') is given out initially by the singer, taken up in the accompaniment and then continued by the voice.

Devlin, Michael (Coles) (*b* Chicago, 27 Nov 1942). American bass-baritone. He studied in Louisiana and New York, making his début in 1963 at New Orleans as Spalanzani. Engaged in 1966 at the New York City Opera, he sang in the première of Ginastera's *Bomarzo* (1967) at Washington, DC, and in the American première of Reimann's *Melusine* (1972) at Santa Fe, where he has also sung Don Giovanni, Yevgeny Onegin, Altair (*Die ägyptische Helena*) and the Commandant (*Friedenstag*). He first sang at Glyndebourne in 1974, Covent Garden in 1977 and the Metropolitan in 1978. He has appeared at San Francisco, Dallas, Frankfurt, Aix-en-Provence, Paris and Amsterdam, where in 1977 he created the title role of *Axel* (de Leeuw and van Vlijmen). His roles include Escamillo, Golaud, Count Almaviva, Alfonso, Nick Shadow, Ford, Wotan and also the four villains in *Les contes d'Hoffmann*, which best display his dramatic talent as well as his fine voice.

ELIZABETH FORBES

DeVol, Luana (*b* St Bruno, nr San Francisco, 30 Nov 1942). American soprano. She studied in San Diego, London and San Francisco. She made her European début in 1983 at Stuttgart as Leonore and was then engaged at Aachen (1984) and Mannheim (1986). She has sung Agathe and Euryanthe at the Deutsche Oper, Berlin; Ariadne in San Francisco; Irene (*Rienzi*) in Hamburg; Senta at Bregenz and Ellen Orford and Chrysothemis at Zürich. In 1990 she sang the *Siegfried* Brünnhilde at Mannheim and Isolde at St Gallen. Her roles include Elsa, Reiza and Leonora (*La forza del destino*). She has a large, clear-toned voice whose dramatic strength has not dispelled its lyrical sweetness and brilliance.

ELIZABETH FORBES

Devoto, John (*fl* 1708–52). Decorative and scene painter. He was probably born in France. In 1708 he was working as Gerard Lanscroon's assistant in England,

and in 1718 he was a 'history painter' in London with his own apprentice. He thus decorated walls in noble homes with architectural scenes and landscapes that used foreshortening, perspective and other techniques vital to scene painting. He is known to have painted scenes for various productions at Drury Lane in 1723–*c*1733, Goodman's Fields in 1735–46, Norwich in 1739 and New Wells, Clerkenwell, in 1740–42.

Most of Devoto's extant stage designs are small sketches in a volume containing 92 of his drawings (London, British Museum, Department of Prints and Drawings). His earliest dated designs are of 1719–20, and they include copies of Filippo Juvarra's scenes for Filippo Amadei's *Teodosio il giovane* (1711, Rome) and a Bibienesque scene. Perhaps Devoto hoped for employment by the newly founded Royal Academy of Music at the King's Theatre, but the earliest – and only – evidence of his scene painting for that opera house is a notice in the *Daily Post* of 26 February 1728 (see Gibson) offering a reward of one guinea for the return of his 'Opera Drawings' depicting a garden and a palace, which were perhaps intended for Handel's *Lotario* (1729). In 1729–30 he copied designs by Pietro Righini for Vinci's *Medo* (1728, Parma) and by the Valeriano brothers for Porpora's *Ezio* (1728, Venice), so he may well have designed further operas for Handel, such as *Ezio* of 1732 (see Lindgren). His last fully dated works are admission tickets for Handel's *Hercules* (21 February 1752, see illustration) and *Samson* (11 March 1752).

*

BDA; *ES* (H. R. Beard)
O. E. Deutsch: 'Ink-Pot and Squirt-Gun', *MT*, xciii (1952), 401–3
E. Croft-Murray: *John Devoto: a Baroque Scene Painter* (London, 1953)
S. Rosenfeld and E. Croft-Murray: 'A Checklist of Scene Painters Working in Great Britain and Ireland in the 18th Century', *Theatre Notebook*, xix (1964–5), 51–2
E. Croft-Murray: *Decorative Painting in England, 1537–1837*, ii: *The Eighteenth and Nineteenth Centuries* (London, 1970), 200–01
S. Rosenfeld: *Georgian Scene Painters and Scene Painting* (Cambridge, 1981)
L. Lindgren: 'The Staging of Handel's Operas in London', *Handel Tercentenary Collection*, ed. S. Sadie and A. Hicks (London, 1987), 102–19
E. Gibson: *The Royal Academy of Music, 1719–28: the Institution and its Directors* (New York, 1989), 263–6

LOWELL LINDGREN

Devrient, Eduard (Philipp) (*b* Berlin, 11 Aug 1801; *d* Karlsruhe, 4 Oct 1877). German theatre historian, librettist and baritone. He studied at the Berlin Singakademie and on 18 April 1819 sang the part of Thanatos in Gluck's *Alceste*; after appearing as Masetto he was engaged as a baritone at the Königliche Oper. In 1822 he toured to Dresden, Leipzig, Kassel and Frankfurt. After losing his voice through overwork following his performance as Bois-Guilbert in Marschner's *Der Templer und die Jüdin* in 1831 he concentrated on acting. In 1844 he became chief producer and actor at the Dresden Hoftheater. He resigned in 1846 and worked as a writer until his appointment as director of the Karlsruhe Hoftheater in 1852; he retired in 1870.

Although Devrient was successful as an opera singer (in works by Gluck, Mozart, Beethoven, Spohr, Weber, Marschner, Rossini and Auber), actor and playwright, his principal contributions lie in his work as a theatre reformer, historian and librettist, and in his efforts towards the Bach revival. His libretto *Hans Heiling*, originally written for Mendelssohn (1827), was later revised for Marschner; Devrient sang the title role at the first performance (1833, Berlin). Two of his works, *Die Kirmess* and *Der Zigeuner*, were set by Taubert and first performed at Berlin. Among his writings, *Das Nationaltheater des neuen Deutschlands: eine Reformschrift* (1849) and *Geschichte der deutschen Schauspielkunst* (1848–74) are particularly important.

*

ES (F. d'Amico)
E. Kilian: *Beiträge zur Geschichte des Karlsruher Hoftheaters unter Eduard Devrient* (Karlsruhe, 1893)
R. K. Goldschmit: *Eduard Devrients Bühnenreform am Karlsruher Hoftheater* (Leipzig, 1921)
F. Rein: *Eduard Devrient als Oberregisseur in Dresden von 1844–6* (diss., U. of Erlangen, 1931)
J. Bab: *Die Devrients* (Berlin, 1932)
R. Kabel, ed.: *Eduard Devrient aus seinen Tagebüchern* (Weimer, 1964)

GAYNOR G. JONES

Devriès [De Vries]. Dutch family of singers.

(1) **Rosa de Vries-van Os** [neé van Os] (*b* Deventer, 1828; *d* Rome, 1889). Soprano. She made her début in 1846 at The Hague as Rachel (*La Juive*). From 1849 to 1851 she appeared with the French Opera in New Orleans, singing Fidès in the American première of *Le prophète*. In 1853 she sang Norma at Toronto; after further touring in the USA and Canada, in 1855 she went to Italy. She sang at the Lyceum Theatre, London, in 1856 and at La Scala, as Abigaille (*Nabucco*), Joan of Arc and Lady Macbeth, in 1858. At S Carlo she took part in the first performance of Viveconte's *Luisa Strozzi* (1862); she returned to La Scala for Mercadante's *Il bravo* (1863).

(2) **Jeanne Devriès** (*b* New Orleans, before July 1850; *d* 1924). Soprano, daughter of (1) Rosa de Vries-van Os. She studied with Duprez in Paris, making her début there in 1867 at the Théâtre Lyrique as Amina (*La sonnambula*). The same year she created Catharine in Bizet's *La jolie fille de Perth* and also sang Lady Harriet (*Martha*), Zerlina and Rosina. After an engagement at the Théâtre de la Monnaie she sang mostly in France, excelling in coloratura roles such as Amina and Marguerite.

(3) **Fidès Devriès** (*b* New Orleans, 22 April 1851; *d* 1941). Soprano, daughter of (1) Rosa de Vries-van Os. She studied in Paris and made her début in 1869 at the Théâtre Lyrique in Halévy's *Le val d'Andorre*. After singing at the Théâtre de la Monnaie, in 1871 she was engaged at the Paris Opéra, making her début as Marguerite, later singing Isabelle (*Robert le diable*), Inès (*L'Africaine*) and Ophelia, which she sang in the 100th performance of *Hamlet* (1874). At the Théâtre Italien she sang Amelia (*Simon Boccanegra*) and Salome (*Hérodiade*), then in 1885 she created Chimène in Massenet's *Le Cid* at the Opéra. She sang Elsa in the first Paris performance of *Lohengrin* at the Eden-Théâtre in 1887. In Monte Carlo she added Aida, Violetta and Leïla (*Les pêcheurs de perles*) to her repertory and in 1889 took her farewell to the stage as Gilda.

(4) **Maurice Devriès** (*b* New York, 1854; *d* Chicago, 1919). Baritone, son of (1) Rosa de Vries-van Os. He made his début in 1874 at Liège as Nevers (*Les Huguenots*). He was engaged at the Théâtre de la Monnaie, where in 1884 he created Gunther in Reyer's *Sigurd*. After singing in France and Italy, he went to

New York and made his Metropolitan début in 1895 as Mercutio (*Roméo et Juliette*). He also sang Bustamente in the first American performance of Massenet's *La Navarraise*. His repertory included William Tell and Telramund.

(5) **Hermann Devriès** (*b* New York, 28 Dec 1858; *d* Chicago, 24 Aug 1949). Baritone, son of (1) Rosa de Vries-van Os. He studied with J.-B. Faure in Paris, where he made his début in 1878 at the Opéra as Méru in *Les Huguenots*. He sang other minor roles such as Wagner (*Faust*), Selva (*La muette de Portici*) and Polonius (*Hamlet*), then in 1880 made his Opéra-Comique début as Lothario (*Mignon*), a role he repeated over 50 times. After singing at the Théâtre de la Monnaie, in 1888 he appeared at Chicago and New York. He sang at Covent Garden in 1899, then toured the USA with the Savage Grand Opera Company.

(6) **David Devriès** (*b* Bagnères-de-Luchon, 1881; *d* Neuilly-sur-Seine, 1934). French tenor of Dutch extraction, son of (4) Maurice Devriès. He studied at the Paris Conservatoire and made his début in 1904 as Gérald (*Lakmé*) at the Opéra-Comique, where he was engaged for many years. In 1906 he created Philodemus in Erlanger's *Aphrodite*, and he was particularly successful as George Brown in the 1909 revival of Boieldieu's *La dame blanche*. His roles included Almaviva (*Il barbiere*), Don José, Julien (*Louise*), Pinkerton, Des Grieux (*Manon*), Vincent (*Mireille*), De Nangis (*Le roi malgré lui*), Jean Gaussin (*Sapho*), Armand (*Thérèse*), Werther, Araquil (*La Navarraise*), Cavaradossi, Rodolfo and Alfredo. In 1909–10 he sang with the Manhattan Opera Company in New York and Philadelphia, making his début as Ange-Pitou (*La fille de Madame Angot*). He also sang Strauss's Aegisthus and Narraboth and, with the permission of MARY GARDEN, Jean in *Le jongleur de Notre-Dame*. In 1910 he sang Pelléas at Covent Garden, and in 1913 Nicias (*Thaïs*) at Monte Carlo and Paco in the première (in French) of *La vida breve* at Nice. He appeared with the Brussels Opera in the 1920–21 season. He excelled in French music and was a fine example of the elegance and accomplishment of the French school of his time.

ELIZABETH FORBES

Dew, John (*b* Santiago de Cuba, 1 June 1944). British director. After studying in Germany with Felsenstein and Wieland Wagner, he directed *The Rake's Progress* at Ulm in 1971, then staged a Mozart cycle and a Wagner cycle (culminating with *Götterdämmerung*) at Krefeld. Appointed head of production at Bielefeld (1981), he has since staged Brand's *Maschinist Hopkins*, Musgrave's *Mary, Queen of Scots*, Schreker's *Irrelohe* and *Der singende Teufel*, Korngold's *Das Wunder der Heliane*, Hindemith's *Neues vom Tage*, Antheil's *Transatlantic*, Krenek's *Der Sprung über den Schatten*, Stephan's *Die ersten Menschen*, Boito's *Nerone*, Delius's *Fennimore and Gerda*, Adams's *Nixon in China*, Wellesz's *Die Bakchantinnen* and other 20th-century operas. At the Deutsche Oper, Berlin (1987), he directed *Les Huguenots* (staged at Covent Garden in 1991) and the première of Neikrug's *Alamos* (1988). Dew's habit of updating operas often succeeds, as in a production of *La Juive* set in Nazi Germany, but *Les Huguenots*, transplanted to a divided Berlin, lost all point in London.

ELIZABETH FORBES

De Waart, Edo (*b* Amsterdam, 1 June 1941). Dutch conductor. The son of a choral singer, he studied the oboe at the Amsterdam Conservatory, joining the Amsterdam PO in 1961 and the Concertgebouw Orchestra two years later. Meanwhile, he studied conducting with Franco Ferrara; he made his conducting début with the Netherlands Radio PO. He was appointed assistant conductor of the New York Philharmonic in 1965 and of the Concertgebouw Orchestra the following year, and in 1967 became co-conductor of the Rotterdam PO with Jean Fournet, whom he later succeeded as musical director (1973–9).

By then he had begun conducting opera – Menotti's *The Saint of Bleecker Street* (1970, Netherlands Opera) – and he made his American opera début with the Santa Fe Opera (*Der fliegende Holländer*, 1970), which started a continuing association with that company. His other opera performances included *Der Rosenkavalier* (1975, Houston), *Ariadne auf Naxos* (1976, Covent Garden), and *Lohengrin* (1979, Bayreuth Festival opening). Named principal guest conductor of the San Francisco SO in 1975, he became its musical director in 1977, a position he held until June 1985, rebuilding the orchestra significantly.

In June 1985 he conducted a *Ring* cycle for the San Francisco Opera, and then served one year as the music director of the Netherlands Opera before assuming the directorship of the Minnesota Orchestra. He has conducted *Nixon in China* for the Brooklyn Academy of Music (1987) and for the Holland Festival and Metropolitan Opera (1988); his recording of it was highly praised. With the Dutch Radio PO he has conducted, in concert, *Götterdämmerung*, *A Life for the Tsar* and Schreker's *Die Gezeichneten* (1989). He is a consistent conductor with a clear, straightforward manner, producing performances of integrity and high quality, and specializing in large Romantic works.

ROBERT COMMANDAY

Dexter, John (*b* Derby, 2 Aug 1925; *d* London, 23 March 1990). English director. He began his career in the spoken theatre, gaining attention at the English Stage Company (1957–72); in 1963 he became associate director of the National Theatre. His first operatic staging was *Benvenuto Cellini* for Covent Garden in 1966, followed by productions of other operas in Hamburg (1969–72) and Paris (1973). Opera direction began to interest Dexter increasingly during this period, and in 1974 the post of director of production was created for him at the Metropolitan Opera, a position he held until 1981.

During his seven years at the Metropolitan, Dexter staged many important 20th-century works never before presented by the company. These included highly praised productions of *Lulu*, *Dialogues des Carmélites*, *Billy Budd*, *Aufstieg und Fall der Stadt Mahagonny*, and a triple bill of three contemporaneous French works: Satie's *Parade*, Poulenc's *Les mamelles de Tirésias* and Ravel's *L'enfant et les sortilèges*. His rather chilly productions of works from an earlier age – *Aida*, *Rigoletto*, *Les vêpres siciliennes*, *Le prophète*, *La forza del destino*, *Don Pasquale* and *The Bartered Bride* – were less favourably regarded.

Dexter's productions for the Metropolitan tended to be tightly organized, schematized conceptions, and their effect derived mainly from his clever manipulation of soloists and chorus within the context of a highly structured set design. He always collaborated closely with favourite designers and achieved some of his most successful work with such kindred spirits as Jocelyn Herbert, David Hockney and David Reppa. His crisp, unsentimental approach often produced striking theatrical results in contemporary operas, but the same techniques could just as frequently stifle the warmer, more passionately emotive spirit of the Romantic 19th-century repertory. After leaving the Metropolitan, Dexter returned to theatre direction, most notably with a highly successful Broadway play that has distinct operatic resonances – David Henry Hwang's *M. Butterfly*. PETER G. DAVIS

De Zárate, Eliodoro Ortiz. *See* ORTIZ DE ZÁRATE, ELIODORO.

Dezède [D. Z., Dezèdes, Desaides, De Zaides], **Nicolas** [?Alexandre] (*b* ?1740–45; *d* Paris, 11 Sept 1792). Composer, active in Paris. The mystery of Dezède's ancestry has never been unravelled; he may have been the illegitimate son of a German prince, and his education was well provided for. He signed his works 'D.Z.', these being the only letters he knew his name contained. After going to Paris to complete his musical education, and in need of funds after the cessation of an annuity, he formed a successful partnership with Jacques Marie Boutet de Monvel.

Monvel was responsible for the librettos of Dezède's most successful works; none of his remaining stage works had more than a few performances, and several were heavily criticized for faulty dramaturgy. Monvel, who subsequently worked with Dalayrac, specialized in rustic subjects, but with an up-to-date moral slant, as found in *Julie* (1772) and *Les trois fermiers* (1777). The popular success of *Blaise et Babet* (1783) was also due to deft characterization, especially the candour and naivety of the main couple. *Alexis et Justine* (1785) was a sentimental tale in the mould of Sedaine's *Félix, ou L'enfant trouvé*. *Zulima* (1778) and *Alcindor* (1787) were escapist 'magic' operas.

In other works, too, Dezède sided with the liberal forces of revolution. *Péronne sauvée* (1783; based on the siege of Péronne in 1536) focussed on a working-class wife, the historical Marie Fouré, who heroically attacks an English soldier and alerts the French to defend the city walls. Later, Dezède became involved in *opéra comique* projects at the Comédie-Française (renamed Théâtre de la Nation), writing both words and music for three works: *Les trois noces* (1790), *Ferdinand* (1790) and *Paulin et Clairette* (1792). *Les trois noces* was a true successor to Monvel, for it showed rural unrest being quelled by news of the king's (actual) appearance before the National Assembly on 4 February 1790, to take the Civic Oath.

Dezède's music was always recognized for the tunefulness of the simpler melodies, in *romances*, vaudevilles and other set pieces. Mozart paid 'Lison dormait dans un bocage' (from *Julie*) the compliment of his nine variations (K264); comparable melodies are 'Faut attendre' and 'Sans un petit brin d'amour' from *Les trois fermiers* (Lesure lists other popular printed extracts).

However, Dezède was not a naive musician. He tended towards a rich contemporary style, German-influenced and sometimes Italian-sounding in the vocal writing. Phrase structures are symmetrical, orchestration is varied and colourful, and the idiom follows that of the Mannheim school. *Julie* already shows Dezède's use of minor-mode expression and off-beat accentuation. *Les trois fermiers* extended his use of chromatic and dissonant harmony, and betrayed a penchant for strong tutti writing. This 'noisy' tendency in his work was regularly criticized in the *Correspondance littéraire*. In *Blaise et Babet* Dezède began to inject more naturalistic verbal rhythms into his vocal line and to temper the general sophistication with 'rustic' musical formulas. But the overall effect was still of mannered and polished entertainment, though the result was seen as subversive in certain quarters: 'By a peculiarity hardly appropriate to the [peasant] characters, the arias are more elegant than the ordinary dialogue' (*Mémoires secrets*).

An experimental feature of one of the works for which Dezède wrote the music and the text (perhaps *Les trois noces*) was the use of prose for operatic musical setting. The attempt, which was perhaps not repeated in French until Gounod's abortive *George Dandin* (1874), is reported in Ducray-Duminil (1798) as follows: 'A little play with music by him was performed, in which the sung part was unrhymed; he had composed music even to bare prose, without metre or hemistich. This bizarre trial was unsuccessful'.

Blaise et Babet, with 145 performances to the end of 1791, was one of the two most popular operas at the Comédie-Italienne during the 1780s. *Les trois fermiers* was less so, but it received 165 performances between 1777 and 1791. Dezède's music was widely known outside France, from Russia to the Americas.

Dezède's daughter Florine (*b* ?1766; *d* by 1792) composed the *comédie mêlée d'ariettes Lucette et Lucas* (1, N. J. Forgeot), first given by the Comédie-Italienne at the Hôtel de Bourgogne on 8 November 1781. It was quite successful, being performed until 1792 and published in score (Paris, 1786).

See also BLAISE ET BABET; JULIE; and TROIS FERMIERS, LES.

first performed in Paris unless otherwise stated; all printed works published in Paris

PCI – *Comédie-Italienne*

Julie (cmda, 3, J. M. B. de Monvel), PCI (Bourgogne), 28 Sept 1772 (*c*1773)

L'erreur d'un moment, ou La suite de Julie (cmda, 1, Monvel), PCI (Bourgogne), 14 June 1773 (*c*1774)

Le stratagème découvert (cmda, 2, Monvel), PCI (Bourgogne), 4 Oct 1773

Les trois fermiers (cmda, 2, Monvel), PCI (Bourgogne), 24 May 1777 (1777)

Fatmé, ou Le langage des fleurs (comédie-ballet, 2, J. P. A. Razins de Saint-Marc), Fontainebleau, 30 Oct 1777

Zulima, ou L'art et la nature (oc, 3, P. de Montignac, after de Lanoue [J.-B. Sauvé]: *Zélisca*), PCI (Bourgogne), 9 May 1778

Le porteur de chaise [Jérôme le porteur de chaise; Jérôme et Champagne] (comédie-parade, 2, Monvel), PCI (Bourgogne), 10 Dec 1778; rev. (1), 11 Jan 1781

Cécile (cmda, 3, Mabille, after Mme Riccoboni: *Lettres de Milady Catesby*), Versailles, 24 Feb 1780; PCI (Bourgogne), 26 Feb 1780, *F-Pn*

A trompeur, trompeur et demi, ou Les torts du sentiment (cmda, 1, E. L. Billardon de Sauvigny), PCI (Bourgogne), 3 May 1780

Blaise et Babet, ou La suite des trois fermiers (cmda, 2, Monvel), Versailles, 4 April 1783; PCI (Favart), 30 June 1783 (1784)

Péronne sauvée (opéra, 4, Billardon de Sauvigny), Opéra, 27 May 1783, *Pc*, *Po*

Le véritable Figaro, 1784 (oc, 3, Billardon de Sauvigny) [unperf. because it libelled Beaumarchais; see Tourneux, Nov 1784]

Alexis et Justine (comédie lyrique mêlée d'ariettes, 2, Monvel, after *The Thousand and One Nights*, Versailles, 14 Jan 1785; PCI (Favart), 17 Jan 1785 (1785)

Alcindor (opéra-féerie, 3, M. A. J. Rochon de Chabannes), Opéra, 17 April 1787, *Po*

Auguste et Théodore, ou Les deux pages (comédie mêlée de chant, 2, L. F. Faur, after J. J. Engel: *Der Edelknabe*), Comédie-Française, 6 March 1789
Les trois noces (pièce champêtre, 1, Dezède), Nation, 23 Feb 1790
Ferdinand, ou La suite des deux pages (comédie, 3, Dezède), PCI (Favart), 19 June 1790
Paulin et Clairette, ou Les deux espiègles (comédie, 2, Dezède), Nation, 5 Jan 1792
La fête de la cinquantaine (opéra, 2, Faur), Amis de la Patrie, 9 Jan 1796 (1796)

Unfinished: Amadis (opéra); Inez de Castro (opéra)

*

[L. Petit de Bachaumont and others]: *Mémoires secrets pour servir à l'histoire de la république des lettres en France* (London, 1777–89)
A. D'Origny: *Annales du Théâtre italien depuis son origine jusqu'à ce jour* (Paris, 1788)
F. G. Ducray-Duminil: 'Sur Dezède', *Courrier des spectacles* (22 pluviôse VI [10 Feb 1798])
A. Pougin: 'Dezède', *Revue et Gazette musicale de Paris*, xxix (1862); also pubd separately (Paris, 1862)
M. Tourneux, ed.: *Correspondance littéraire, philosophique et critique par Grimm, Diderot, Raynal, Meister, etc.* (Paris, 1877–82)
A. Danicourt, ed.: *Péronne sauvée* (Péronne, 1879)
C. D. Brenner: *The Théâtre Italien: its Repertory 1716–1793* (Berkeley, 1961)
F. Lesure: *Catalogue de la musique imprimée avant 1800 conservée dans les bibliothèques publiques de Paris* (Paris, 1981)
D. Charlton: *Grétry and the Growth of Opéra-Comique* (Cambridge, 1986)
——: 'The Dramaturgy of *Grand Opéra*: Some Origins', *IMSCR*, xiv *Bologna 1987*, 853–8
H. Macdonald: 'The Prose Libretto', *COJ*, i (1989), 155–66
M. Noiray: 'Les créations d'opéra à Paris de 1790 à 1794', *Orphée phrygien: les musiques de la Révolution*, ed. J. R. Julien and J. C. Klein (Paris, 1989), 193–203

DAVID CHARLTON

De Zumaya, Manuel. *See* ZUMAYA, MANUEL DE.

D'Hèle [Hales, ?Hall], **Thomas** (*b* ?Gloucester, *c*1741; *d* Paris, 27 Dec 1780). English or Irish librettist. According to the *Correspondance littéraire*, he entered military service and was sent to Jamaica during the Seven Years War. After extended travels in Europe he arrived in Paris around 1770, and met Jean-Baptiste Suard, whose special interest was English writing. Suard apparently made him a close friend, and recommended him to Grétry as a man of wit and originality (Garat 1820). He had by then very little money, and was known for his eccentricity. Grétry called him 'as phlegmatic as he was tender in affairs of the heart', and noted that he turned author 'from necessity'.

D'Hèle had completed *Le jugement de Midas*, based on an English burletta by Kane O'Hara, when he first came to Grétry to discuss another libretto derived from an English source, *L'amant jaloux*. Grétry already knew D'Hèle's acute dramatic judgment at first hand from discussions in the theatre, and they formed an immediate partnership. D'Hèle's three librettos for Grétry are remarkable achievements of refinement and comedy. The first two utterly transform their English originals through polished, economical stagecraft, and create dialogue that was quickly recognized as an exemplar of ironic humour. The musical portions, if not predominant, are incorporated with skill, taking extensive responsibility for the drama in the ensembles. All three librettos created memorable characters and situations.

D'Hèle died after an illness; the projects left unfinished included a commission from Marie Antoinette. Earlier in 1780 he and Cailhava had revised Colalto's virtuoso comedy *Les trois jumeaux vénitiens* for the actor Volange. This revival took place on 22 February 1780.

Le jugement de Midas (cmda), Grétry, 1778; *Les fausses apparences, ou L'amant jaloux* (cmda), Grétry, 1778; *Les événements imprévus* (cmda), Grétry, 1779

*

T. D'Hèle: 'Roman de mon oncle', *Correspondance littéraire* (July 1777); repr. in Van de Weyer (1854)
'Notice sur M. D'Hèle', *Le nécrologe des hommes célèbres de France, par une société de gens de lettres*, xvii (Paris, 1782), 273–6
A. D'Origny: *Annales du Théâtre italien depuis son origine jusqu'à ce jour*, ii (Paris, 1788), 122–4, 128, 145–6
A.-E.-M. Grétry: *Mémoires, ou Essais sur la musique* (Paris, 1789, enlarged 2/1797)
D. J. Garat: *Mémoires historiques sur le XVIII siècle*, i (Paris, 1820), 298
P. M. M. Lepeintre Desroches: *Suite du répertoire du théâtre français* (Paris, 1822–3), lvi, 85
S. Van de Weyer: 'Lettres sur les Anglais qui ont écrit en français: Thomas Hales', *Philobiblion Society: Bibliographical and Historical Miscellanies*, i (London, 1854), 1–99
M. Tourneux, ed.: *Correspondance littéraire, philosophique et critique par Grimm, Diderot, Raynal, Meister, etc.* (Paris, 1877–82) [necrology in April 1781 issue]
A.-E.-M. Grétry: *Réflexions d'un solitaire*, ed. L. Solvay and E. Closson (Brussels and Paris, 1919–22), iii, livre 5, chap.10
C. D. Brenner: *A Bibliographical List of Plays in the French Language 1700–1789* (Berkeley, 1947, 2/1979)
P. Culot: *Le jugement de Midas: opéra-comique d'André-Ernest-Modeste Grétry* (Brussels, 1978) [incl. lib. and part facs.]
D. Charlton: *Grétry and the Growth of Opéra-Comique* (Cambridge, 1986)

DAVID CHARLTON

Diable à quatre, Le [*Le diable à quatre, ou La double métamorphose* ('The Devil to Pay, or The Wives Metamorphosed')]. *Opéra comique* in three acts by CHRISTOPH WILLIBALD GLUCK and others to a libretto by MICHEL-JEAN SEDAINE and Pierre Baurans after the ballad opera by CHARLES COFFEY; Laxenburg, 28 May 1759.

Claude-Pierre Patu's translation of Coffey's ballad opera of 1731 formed the basis for Sedaine's *opéra comique* (in prose, vaudevilles and *ariettes* parodied by Baurans), which was first performed at the Foire St Laurent, Paris, in 1756. For the Viennese version Gluck reset several musical numbers and wrote new accompaniments to some vaudevilles and *ariettes* (e.g. by Vincenzo Ciampi and Giuseppe Scarlatti). As transplanted to French soil, the story concerns the shrewish Marquise and the good-natured Margot (both sopranos), whose cobbler husband Jacques (baritone) regularly beats her. The Marquise interrupts a party offered by the Marquis (*haute-contre*) to his neighbours and domestics, breaking a blind hurdy-gurdy player's instrument over his head and insulting an astrologer who has sought shelter there. This 'Docteur' (tenor) punishes the Marquise by magically transporting her to Margot's humble cottage (and Margot to the chateau), and by causing their features to be transposed. While the Marquise suffers the indignity of being whipped and forced to work by her 'husband' Jacques, Margot marvels at her new surroundings, and enchants the Marquis and servants with her reformed character. The Doctor eventually reverses his spell, judging the Marquise sufficiently punished, and the opera ends with a general *contredanse*.

Sedaine's libretto was admired for its successful combination of ribald comedy and high moral tone. Gluck's often folklike music was much appreciated in Vienna; Haydn, who heard it in 1761, quoted Margot's 'Je n'aimais pas le tabac beaucoup' in his Symphony no.8, *Le soir*, of the same year. BRUCE ALAN BROWN

Diaghilev [Diaghileff], **Sergey Pavlovich.** *See* DYAGILEV, SERGEY PAVLOVICH.

Dialogues des Carmélites ('Dialogues of the Carmelites'). Opera in three acts by FRANCIS POULENC to his own libretto after Georges Bernanos' play; Milan, Teatro alla Scala, 26 January 1957.

The Marquis de la Force	baritone
Blanche de la Force *his daughter*	soprano
The Chevalier de la Force *his son*	tenor
Madame de Croissy *Prioress*	contralto
Madame Lidoine *the new Prioress*	soprano
Mother Marie of the Incarnation *assistant Prioress*	mezzo-soprano
Sister Constance of St Denis *a young nun*	soprano
Mother Jeanne of the Child Jesus *dean of the community*	contralto
Sister Mathilde	mezzo-soprano
Mother Gerald } *old nuns*	sopranos, mezzo-sopranos, contraltos
Sister Claire } *old nuns*	
Sister Antoine (Portress) } *old nuns*	
Sister Catherine	
Sister Felicity	
Sister Gertrude	
Sister Alice	
Sister Valentine	
Sister Anne of the Cross	
Sister Martha	
Sister St Charles	
Father Confessor of the Convent	high baritone
First Officer	tenor
Second Officer	baritone
Gaoler	baritone
Thierry *a valet*	baritone
M. Javelinot *a physician*	baritone

Officials of the municipality, officers, police, prisoners, guards

Setting Chiefly the Carmelite convent at Compiègne, later Paris during the French Revolution and the subsequent Terror, 1789–94

The story of the Compiègne Carmelites was first told by one of their number, Mother Marie of the Incarnation of God, who survived the Terror and lived until 1836. The publication of her *Relation* led to the beatification of the nuns in 1906. In 1931 their story was turned into a novel by the German Catholic convert Gertrude von Le Fort; the heroine Blanche de la Force was her invention. In 1947 the Austrian priest and French resistance fighter Father Brückberger devised a cinematic scenario on the subject and engaged the French novelist Georges Bernanos to write the dialogue. Just as Gertrude von Le Fort had written herself into her heroine (she named her 'de la Force'), so Bernanos, then suffering from terminal cancer, concentrated on the crisis of faith of the dying Prioress (even giving her his precise age, 59) as well as exploring his own religious obsessions. His work was deemed uncinematic but it eventually surfaced as a stage play, in which form Poulenc saw it in the early 1950s. When Ricordi suggested it as an opera Poulenc seized the chance enthusiastically; but despite rapid composition (1953–6) the première was postponed because of legal wrangles over the rights to the piece.

The opera was first performed (in Italian) at La Scala in a production by Margherita Wallmann. The cast included Virginia Zeani (Blanche), Leyla Gencer (the new Prioress), Eugenia Ratti (Constance) and Fiorenza Cossotto (in the small part of Mathilde); the conductor was Nino Sanzogno. The Paris première was given a few months later (June 1957) with Poulenc's intended cast of Denise Duval (Blanche), Régine Crespin (the new Prioress), Rita Gorr (Mother Marie) and Liliane Berton (Constance); Pierre Dervaux was the conductor. The producer was again Wallmann, and for reasons of staging, extra orchestral interludes were composed for this production; Cologne, San Francisco and American television followed in the same year. The first Covent Garden cast (1958) included Elsie Morison, Joan Sutherland and Jeannette Sinclair with Kubelik conducting. Notable recent productions include that of John Dexter, seen in America and Paris, often with Crespin as the old Prioress, a role which she recreated in Wallmann's 1983 production at Covent Garden with Felicity Lott (Blanche), Pauline Tinsley (Mother Marie), Valerie Masterson (the new Prioress) and Lillian Watson (Sister Constance).

ACT 1.i *The library of the Marquis de la Force* The opera opens in a mood of anxiety. The Chevalier de la Force voices his fears for his sister Blanche, whom he knows to be easily frightened, for her carriage has been held up by a protesting crowd. In a breathless Allegro, the Chevalier's father, the Marquis, recalls the Royal Fireworks Panic he and his wife were caught up in 19 years earlier, when his wife died giving birth to Blanche. Blanche appears, seemingly composed: only the shifting unrelated harmonies of her music betray her inner uncertainty. On her way to bed she is terrified by a shadow on the wall; she returns and with a mixture of resignation and resolution expresses her resolve to take the veil and join the Carmelite order.

1.ii *The parlour of the Carmelite convent* Some weeks later the Prioress, seated because of her age and infirmity, is interviewing Blanche. In a long flowing arioso (underpinned by the anxious rising minor 3rd which permeates the whole opera) she reminds her of the nature of their order. As the scene continues the tone changes into rapid recitative (more violent minor 3rds in the orchestra) as the interview becomes more like an interrogation to discover Blanche's true reasons. The order can protect nobody; it is a house of prayer which must be protected by its own members. The Prioress's music switches rapidly from brusque accusatory outburst to lyrical and loving lines when prayer is discussed. Blanche's resolve survives this ordeal and touches the Prioress, who gives her blessing.

1.iii *Inside the convent* An austere plainsong ritornello leads to a surprising scherzo as we meet young Sister Constance, Blanche's complete opposite. She is a peasant girl, fun-loving and frothy, who can speak of life and death with the same levity with which she treats the convent chores. She shocks and disarms Blanche by admitting her premonition, her happy premonition, that she and Blanche will both die young, and on the same day.

1.iv *The infirmary* A plangent clamour of bells introduces the Prioress's death scene, one of the most protracted, and realistic, in all opera. Over a steady ostinato rhythm she veers from visionary calm to delirium and agony-induced profanity: 'who am I to concern myself with God – let him first concern himself

'Dialogues des Carmélites' (Poulenc): scene from the original production at La Scala, Milan, 26 January 1957

with me'. The loyal and stolid Mother Marie is in attendance, chiefly concerned with avoiding a scandal. The Prioress consigns Blanche, her youngest and thus most beloved daughter, to Marie's particular care. Blanche appears twice – firstly to receive a blessing, then, mysteriously unbidden, at the end of the tortuous scene to witness the Prioress's last undignified agony.

ACT 2.i *The chapel* A simple and moving requiem sung for the dead Prioress is interrupted by the jagged music of terror. Blanche has been left alone to watch over the body and runs away in panic. She is admonished and forgiven by the ever-watchful Marie. In an interlude the music regains its calm as Constance voices her thought, central to Bernanos' theology, that perhaps we die not for ourselves but for others. Perhaps we even die each other's deaths, so the Prioress's agony might afford a poor sinner an easy passing: 'Perhaps the Lord God gave her the wrong death, as a cloakroom attendant might give you the wrong coat'.

2.ii *The chapter room* In the opera's most extended arioso the new Prioress warns the convent of the adversity ahead. The simple harmonies and rhythmic implacability underline her strength and humility. The scene closes with a moving *Ave Maria.* Panic intrudes in a brief interlude in which a stranger is announced – Blanche's brother. Mother Marie allows the interview on the condition that she can be present.

2.iii *The parlour* In an extended duet, the nearest thing to a traditional love duet in the opera, the Chevalier begs his sister to leave with him. As an aristocrat and a nun she is doubly in danger from the encroaching Terror. Poulenc's harmonic restraint is loosened to produce music of Puccinian intensity as Blanche, by turns aloof, agitated and affectionate, restates her desire to stay, to die if need be.

2.iv *The sacristy* The act ends with a finale of Verdian dimensions. It opens with the Father Confessor leading the sisters in the opera's third prayer, an intense and sensual *Ave verum corpus.* He then bids them farewell; he has been forced to go into hiding. The Prioress warns the sisters against easy pride, the temptation of martyrdom. These are timely words as an angry crowd is heard followed by knocks at the door. Commissars enter and read a decree of expulsion from the convent. Their grotesquerie is compounded when one of their number admits that he is secretly sympathetic but in these dangerous times is forced to 'howl with the pack' (collaboration was still a recent memory when this work was written). Amid the general stupefaction Blanche is given a statue of the Infant Jesus. However a second wave of terrifying noise from the street causes her to drop the statue, smashing it on the stone floor.

ACT 3.i *The chapel* A stately sarabande (Mother Marie's motif) bears witness to the sisters' strength in adversity. The convent is devastated, desecrated. In the absence of the Prioress, Mother Marie proposes that the sisters take the vow of martyrdom. To ensure complete assent she proposes a secret vote. There is one dissenting vote, Blanche's, thus rendering the decision invalid. Constance rushes forward claiming the vote was hers, and that she has now reconsidered. The vote is allowed to stand and Blanche, without the courage either to live or to die, runs away. An interlude shows the nuns in numb disbelief as they hear their community declared illegal in any form. In a lyrical codetta the Prioress agrees to endorse the vow made in her absence. It was, after all, made to God.

3.ii *The library of the Marquis* We see and hear Blanche at her most tortured and traumatized. Her father has been guillotined, his house ransacked. She is living there as a servant. Mother Marie arrives; her music is a rock in Blanche's sea of troubles. She tells Blanche that she may have saved her life but not her soul. In a spoken interlude with ad libitum percussion set near the Bastille, Blanche hears that the Compiègne Carmelites have been arrested.

3.iii *The conciergerie* In an arioso of ineffable calm the Prioress tries to fill her imprisoned charges with strength and courage. The music is interrupted, becomes frenzied and chattery as a gaoler enters and delivers their death sentence. The Prioress concludes her interrupted aria with a loving, maternal blessing. An interlude reveals Mother Marie at the height of anguish because she is not with her condemned sisters. The

Father Confessor calms her. If God has another destiny for her, that is His will.

3.iv *Place de la Révolution* The final prayer of the opera, the *Salve regina*, is sung to music of great lyrical beauty. Over a rhythmic ostinato (again based on minor 3rds) the nuns' voices rise and fuse as they sing their way to the scaffold. A crowd looks on, murmuring and gasping as, one by one, the nuns are guillotined. Blanche appears, now transfigured and fearless. Constance sees her and walks to the scaffold, her face irradiated with joy. Blanche sings alone until she too is guillotined. Dumbfounded, the crowd disperses.

* * *

Poulenc used to apologize for the unashamedly old-fashioned musical language of his opera. 'It seems,' he wrote, 'that my Carmelites can only sing tonal music. You must forgive them.' He acknowledged his debt to the past in the work's dedication: to Musorgsky, Monteverdi, Debussy and Verdi. He could have added Stravinsky, but in a sense such a debt is reflected in most of his output. The carefully placed and prosodically precise recitatives are redolent of *Pelléas et Mélisande* and *Poppea*, the epic sweep of *Boris Godunov* and *Don Carlos*. The orchestration is extravagant (triple wind, two harps, piano – and guillotine) but sparingly deployed, often in sections. The tessituras are equally carefully planned: Poulenc's grand operatic models are Amneris (Mother Marie), Kundry (old Prioress), Desdemona (new Prioress), Thaïs (Blanche) and Zerlina (Sister Constance). The opera's musical language is further enriched by a series of motifs which stand not only for various characters but also for the qualities those characters embody, even when perceived in other people. Thus, when the first Prioress tells Blanche to be steadfast, the orchestra seems to say, 'be just like Mother Marie'. When the second Prioress sings of her love for the sisters we hear music used by Blanche when singing to her brother. This sharing of musical material runs throughout the work and seems a felicitous musical analogue for Bernanos' view of martyrdom: the transference of grace, the universality of suffering. As Sister Constance says in the opera, 'Perhaps we do not die for ourselves, but for each other, or even instead of each other. Who knows?' JEREMY SAMS

Diamant des Geisterkönigs, Der ('The Diamond of the King of the Spirits'). *Zauberspiel* in two acts by JOSEPH DRECHSLER to a libretto by FERDINAND RAIMUND after a story in *The Thousand and One Nights*; Vienna, Theater in der Leopoldstadt, 17 December 1824.

Raimund's second play is a localization of an oriental tale. Eduard (spoken), the son of a magician, will be able to gain his paternal inheritance only if he can find a girl who has never told a lie; his comic servant Florian (tenor) is exposed to agonized writhings each time Eduard fails in his quest. Eduard finally learns that his true love, Amine (spoken), means more to him than a diamond, and Florian is also rewarded with the hand of the cook, Mariandel (soprano). The magic framework contains transparent satirical references to the contemporary Viennese political scene, but the work is best loved for Drechsler's delightful music, the principal numbers of which were published in a handsome vocal score by Diabelli. These include the charming tenor and soprano duet 'Mariandel, Zuckerkandel', the polacca 'Die Ehre ist fürwahr nicht klein', a lengthy quodlibet for Florian (Raimund's own part), and an extended finale ('Der kleine Liebesgott'), as well as six choruses and 12 further vocal numbers, some 25 musical items all told. The piece, performed in the Theater in der Leopoldstadt/Carl-Theater 160 times up to 1854, was adapted in Danish by Hans Andersen and in English by William and Robert Brough, and was used by Hofmannsthal as the basis for his 'fantasy on a theme from Raimund', *Der Sohn des Geisterkönigs* (1917). *Der Diamant des Geisterkönigs* continues to have a place in the Austrian repertory to this day.

PETER BRANSCOMBE

Diamond, David (Leo) (*b* Rochester, NY, 9 July 1915). American composer. In the 1930s his teachers included Bernard Rogers (at the Eastman School), Roger Sessions (in New York) and Nadia Boulanger (France). In Paris, the contacts he made with André Gide, Ravel, Roussel and Stravinsky broadened his artistic and philosophical ideas. He began to receive commissions, and after a period in Italy he taught composition at Salzburg, and in the USA at Harvard University and, from 1973, at the Juilliard School.

Diamond's symphonies, quartets and songs are the core of a large and varied output. Clear structures and meticulous craftsmanship, brilliant writing for the orchestra and an intensely individual lyricism – occasionally austere but more often romantically tinged – mark his symphonic and chamber works and have assured his position as a 20th-century classicist. He has proved proportionately reticent with theatre music, however, making early operatic attempts with incomplete and unperformed scenes based on texts of Lawrence and Yeats. In 1958 he wrote a two-hour musical comedy, *Mirandolina*, in a German-language adaptation by Pinkas Braun of Goldoni's play; and in 1965 his chamber operetta *The Golden Slippers* had a few performances in a small upper Broadway theatre. But his sole big venture, *The Noblest Game*, based on a modern libretto by Katie Loucheim, was finished in 1975 after four years' labour, then consigned to a drawer. The work is scheduled for performance by the New York City Opera in 1993–4.

David, 1935 (D. H. Lawrence), inc., withdrawn
Twisting of the Rope, 1940 (W. B. Yeats), inc., withdrawn
Mirandolina, 1958 (musical comedy, 4, P. Braun, after C. Goldoni), unperf.
The Golden Slippers (musical folk play, 2, S. Citron, after B. Pérez Galdós), New York, 5 Dec 1965
The Noblest Game, 1971–5 (prol., 2, K. Loucheim), unperf.

NED ROREM, FRANCIS THORNE

Diavolessa, La ('The She-Devil'). *Dramma giocoso* in three acts by BALDASSARE GALUPPI to a libretto by CARLO GOLDONI; Venice, Teatro S Samuele, November 1755.

Giannino (bass) is despondent because Dorina (alto) will not marry him in his poverty. Falco (tenor), a Neapolitan innkeeper, sends them to Don Poppone (bass); they will pose as Turkish mystics who can help Poppone find buried treasure in his basement. When they arrive they are mistaken for the Roman Count Nastri (alto) and his wife the Countess (soprano), whom Poppone was expecting; when the noble couple arrive they are mistaken for the announced Turks. In a mystic seance Giannino and Dorina, disguised as devils, demand money in exchange for the location of the treasure; just as they are paid the lights go out. The servant Ghiandina (soprano) confronts Giannino and Dorina; she knows all and will see that they are punished. Falco surprises Giannino with a letter attesting his inheritance of enough money to marry Dorina. They give Poppone back his due, the real count and his wife return to Rome and all is forgiven. Dorina's aria 'Si distingue dal nobile il vile' (1.vii) was largely borrowed from Galuppi's *Alessandro nell'Indie*. The second finale, the seance, evokes mysterious and eerie powers through musical imagery. DALE E. MONSON

Diavolo nel campanile, Il ('The Devil in the Belfry'). *Grottesco* in one act by ADRIANO LUALDI to his own libretto after EDGAR ALLAN POE's short story; Milan, Teatro alla Scala, 21 April 1925 (revised version, Florence, Teatro Comunale, 21 May 1954).

Poe's brief 'absurdist' tale portrays an utterly self-contained Dutch village (Vondervotteimittiss), in which the community is so obsessively governed by punctuality and unchanging routines that total chaos ensues when a mysterious diabolical outsider tampers with the town clock, making it strike 13. To turn this simple idea into a sufficient (if controversial) basis for his opera, Lualdi invented many details, some of which parody stock situations of traditional comic opera; and he matched the resultant quirky assemblage with a bizarre score in which multiple musical parodies create reckless stylistic non-sequiturs, ending in a deliberate musical chaos (with several superimposed tonalities) to underline the grotesque turmoil on the stage. The opera was originally composed during 1919–23, but in 1952 Lualdi added a new ending, which features a clever parody of 12-note technique entitled 'Passacaglia del mondo alla rovescia': here time is supposed to run backwards, and the devil – horrified by what he sees and hears – is eventually defeated. JOHN C. G. WATERHOUSE

Díaz, Justino (*b* San Juan, Puerto Rico, 29 Jan 1940). American bass. He studied with Frederick Jagel and first appeared with the New England Opera Theater in 1961 as Giorgio. He made his Metropolitan début in 1963 (Monterone) as a winner of the Auditions of the Air; the 30 roles he sang there included Colline, Sparafucile, Mozart's Figaro and Don Giovanni, and Antony, which he created in Barber's *Antony and Cleopatra* on opening night at Lincoln Center in 1966, the year he sang Escamillo at Salzburg. Subsequent appearances have included La Scala, Hamburg and Vienna. He created Francesco in Ginastera's *Beatrix Cenci*, which inaugurated the Kennedy Center Opera House in Washington (1971), made his Covent Garden début as Escamillo in 1976 and returned as Iago in 1990. Díaz is a leading bass at the Metropolitan; his evenly produced, warm *basso cantante* has also been heard at Philadelphia (Don Giovanni, 1980), San Francisco (Scarpia, 1982), Milan (Count Asdrubale in *La pietrà del paragone*, 1982) and Cincinnati (Attila, 1984). His recordings include roles in *Médée*, *La Wally* and *Lucia di Lammermoor*, and he played Iago in Zeffirelli's film of *Otello*.

*

J. W. Freeman: 'No Short Cut', *ON*, xxxi/9 (1966–7), 16
R. Zachary: 'Song and Dance', *ON*, xxxvi/11 (1971–2), 14–15
RICHARD BERNAS, ELIZABETH FORBES

Dibák, Igor (*b* Spišská Nová Ves, Slovakia, 6 July 1947). Slovak composer. He studied in Bratislava with Cikker and later became an editor for Slovak television. He has written two short neo-classical comic operas. *Svietnik* ('The Candelabra') was first performed at the Slovak National Opera, Bratislava, on 12 June 1977. Its libretto (by the composer) is based on Chekhov's short story, *Proizvedeniye iskusstva* ('The Objet d'art'). While preserving a Russian flavour, the opera pinpoints some universal truths by poking fun at human failings; it also has an element of theatre within theatre: two performers can play all four main roles between them. The music is deftly woven from dozens of different motifs, and the distortion of diatonic chords through dissonance reveals the influence of Stravinsky's neo-classicism. The comic *Silvester* ('New Year's Eve'), to a libretto by Peter Štrelinger and the composer, contains elements of operetta; written for Slovak television, it was broadcast on 30 December 1988.

*

I. Vajda: *Slovenská opera* (Bratislava, 1988), 194–5, 243–4
IGOR VAJDA

Dibdin, Charles (*b* Southampton, bap. 15 March 1745; *d* London, 25 July 1814). English composer, dramatist, actor, singer and entertainer. He was the 12th child of a parish clerk and a sorely tried mother who produced at least 14 children. His own claim to have been educated at Winchester College is not supported by the school records, though he did have lessons from two successive organists of Winchester Cathedral. As a composer he was self-taught; he himself thought that he had learnt to compose by scoring Corelli's concertos from the separate parts and from reading Rameau's *Traité de l'harmonie* in English, but he must have learnt mainly from his practical experience in the theatre. By the age of 15 he was singing occasionally in such Covent Garden operas as required a chorus, supplementing his income by working for the music publisher John Johnson. The variety of his talents was already astonishing. He was only 18 when he published, more or less in full score, *A Collection of English Songs and Cantatas*, and a year later John Beard, the manager of Covent Garden, accepted *The Shepherd's Artifice*, an all-sung pastoral for which Dibdin wrote both words and music; he sang the leading role himself.

At this period Dibdin seldom wrote his own librettos. From 1767 to 1772 he was lucky enough to have as his collaborator Isaac Bickerstaff (1733–*c*1808), an Irishman who had previously written *Thomas and Sally* and *Love in a Village* for Arne as well as *The Maid of the Mill* for Arnold. His characterization and dialogue are reminiscent of Sheridan, who was in fact a good deal influenced by Bickerstaff's *Lionel and Clarissa*. Bickerstaff went to France in 1772, to escape prosecution for a homosexual offence, but before then Dibdin and he had created comic operas of a promise that cannot be paralleled in 18th-century England. The first was *Love in the City* (1767), which has an unusual libretto about London tradesmen; the novelty of this theme deprived the opera of the success it deserved. It was followed the next year by *Lionel and Clarissa* and *The Padlock*. Beard did not at first trust Dibdin to compose such operas in their entirety, and in any case the huge success of *Love in a Village* had aroused a taste for pastiche; Dibdin composed no more than the finales and two or three songs for *Love in the City*. What Dibdin called the Boxing Trio in the Act 2 finale must have struck a new note in English opera, for the heroine, Priscilla Tomboy, had to sing while engaged in some spirited fisticuffs in the street. Dibdin was the only English composer before Storace to write dramatic ensembles of this kind, and he did so frequently.

Charles Dibdin as Mungo in 'The Padlock', first performed at Drury Lane, London, 3 October 1768: anonymous engraving

Dibdin first showed his unfortunate capacity for irritation when he suddenly left Covent Garden in summer 1768 and signed on for a seven-year spell at Drury Lane. He was free to write trifles for other theatres in the summer, and to make what he could from publishing his operas. The only Dibdin opera to survive orchestrally is *The Recruiting Sergeant* (1770), though the published full score omits the wind parts in the songs (wind parts for two of them, however, are in *GB-Lbl*). This and *The Ephesian Matron* were written for Ranelagh Gardens, where for two summers Dibdin was in charge of the music. His next major work, *The Wedding Ring* (1773), the libretto of which derives from Goldoni's *Il filosofo di campagna*, was not a success. The splendid 'action' quartet at the end of Act 1 passed unnoticed because the audience was obsessed by the erroneous belief that the words were by the disgraced and despised Bickerstaff. Garrick was more tolerant and quietly accepted from Bickerstaff in France a play called *The Sultan*, for which Dibdin wrote some unpublished music (1775). He and Bickerstaff had already created one 'harem' opera, *The Captive* (1769), and Dibdin wrote another on his own, *The Seraglio* (1776); their influence on the librettos of Mozart's 'harem' operas has been debated, but inconclusively.

During the 1770s Dibdin composed a number of 'dialogues' for the entertainments at Sadler's Wells. These dialogues were all-sung operas on cockney themes, each lasting about 15 minutes; the first was *The Brickdust Man* (1772). Only six dialogues are known to have been published, and of these only four are extant. Dibdin also sang at Ranelagh Gardens. He published some of his Ranelagh songs and then, thinking well of them, wrote an afterpiece, *The Waterman* (1774), round the most successful. The charming libretto about working-class Londoners was his own, and the result was a lasting success. No other operatic successes came his way, apart from *The Quaker* (1775); the rest of his career was a long decline caused not, as might be thought, by writing his own librettos – he could always write natural, easy dialogue – but by his increasingly truculent and quarrelsome behaviour.

Many of his troubles were matrimonial. He was married in his teens to a woman named Elizabeth, by whom he had a daughter. He soon abandoned his wife and, after an affair with a Miss Burgess, began living with a pantomime dancer, Harriet Pitt, who bore him two sons, Charles Isaac Mungo (1768–1833), who managed and then owned Sadler's Wells (1800; 1803–19), and Thomas John (1771–1841), who wrote opera librettos for Covent Garden. He then left Harriet and took up with an indifferent Drury Lane singer called Anne Wyld. Garrick, godfather to one of Dibdin's sons, consequently refused to re-engage him when his seven years had expired. By summer 1776 Dibdin's debts had risen to £800; he fled to France to avoid imprisonment, taking Miss Wyld and their daughter with him, and spent most of the next two years in Nancy.

In France Dibdin made efforts to repay his debts. He wrote as prolifically as ever, sending by post a stream of dialogues to King (at Sadler's Wells), and an opera libretto (*The Gipsies*) to Samuel Arnold, who had been so kind as to complete *The Seraglio* for him when he made his escape. He also laid up a store of dialogue operas based on French librettos which he translated and reset. At Drury Lane Thomas Linley (i), now in charge of music, made an unexpected success of *The Quaker*, whose single performance in Garrick's day had been unremarked in the confusion of Dibdin's perfidy and Garrick's imminent retirement. *The Quaker* contains a delightfully individual patter song, 'Women are Will o' the Wisps', and some experimental ensembles in which the dialogue flows at the speed of recitative, virtually no words being repeated. Nearly all the music is of interest, apart from the overture. Dibdin's overtures were always poor; his strength lay in his dramatically motivated vocal lines, always so easy to sing in character.

In 1778 Dibdin returned to London and was employed by Thomas Harris at Covent Garden. Dibdin tried the experiment of publishing his Covent Garden music, not opera by opera, but in monthly anthologies drawn from several works, calling them *The Monthly Lyrist* (later *The Lyrist or Family Concert*; 1780–81); both this series and the *Lyric Remembrancer* (1799) collapsed from lack of response. In 1781, already out of patience with Dibdin, Harris proposed an operatic version of Dryden's *Amphitryon*, to be called *Jupiter and Alcmena*. After a disagreement about payment, Dibdin left. None of the playhouses would employ him, except to write the occasional afterpiece opera – six in the next 30 years, all of them worthless.

Dibdin now joined Charles Hughes, owner of a riding school, and together they persuaded a group of businessmen to put up £15 000 for the building of a new theatre, the Royal Circus, south of the Thames near St George's Circus. Entertainments alternated between riding displays and short all-sung operas and ballets performed mainly or entirely by children. Dibdin engaged and coached the children, and wrote the entire repertory, words and music; he also mismanaged the theatre's business arrangements. This, coupled with difficulties over getting the theatre licensed, landed the proprietors in debt. Dibdin, also in debt, chose this moment to ask the proprietors for a substantial loan. They sacked him, and by February 1784 he was in the King's Bench, the debtors' prison, and writing an angry little book about what had happened (*The Royal Circus Epitomised*).

In summer 1787 he decided to emigrate to India. To raise money for the voyage, he made a nine-month tour of English provincial towns, singing his own songs interspersed with spoken patter at the pause marks. He wrote a very readable book about his tour in the form of a series of letters, which contains a great deal of interesting, if not always reliable, information about his life, his music and his finances. But when he set out on his voyage he found the sea not at all to his liking, and disembarked at Torbay. It now occurred to him to present his one-man entertainments in London. He gave his 'Table Entertainments' (generally a mixture of narration and singing by a single person seated behind a table and facing an audience, but their title apparently had little significance in Dibdin's case) from January 1789 until the middle of 1805 when he retired, having been promised a pension; when the pension was cut off he returned to his table entertainments for a few more disconsolate seasons. He had started them in the King Street auction rooms, Covent Garden, to an audience of not much more than a dozen, but they soon became popular, and on 31 October 1791 he proudly opened a tiny theatre off the Strand, the Sans Souci, specially built to his own requirements. He even had enough money to start his own publishing 'warehouse', and in 1796 he moved both theatre and warehouse to his new Sans Souci Theatre in Leicester Square.

The songs he composed and published at this time run into hundreds. They celebrate such contemporary events as establishing a 'telegraph' across the Channel and a parachute descent in 1802, but the more popular ones were those in which Dibdin could parade his humorous accents and spoken patter. During this period he was also writing vast quantities of prose (including a periodical called *The Bystander* and three novels). He wrote an uninteresting *Complete History of the English Stage*, an autobiography greatly padded out with his own song lyrics, a textbook called *Music Epitomised* (1804, which had reached its 12th edition by 1835), and, most remarkable of all, his *Observations on a Tour through ... England and ... Scotland* (1801–2). He undertook this and other tours in order to present his table entertainments outside London, and the surprising aspect of this volume is that it is illustrated with sepia prints taken from paintings by Dibdin himself. Those of the Lake District and the Scottish mountains bear little resemblance to their alleged subjects; nevertheless, Dibdin was skilled in painting as in so many other activities.

In 1842 George Hogarth (Charles Dickens's father-in-law) published a massive volume called *The Songs of Charles Dibdin*. It was impossible for him to include all the music, but he tried to include all the lyrics, and they fill 306 closely printed two-column pages. Few famous poets wrote as much, though quantity is no recompense for quality. Dibdin died in Camden Town, destitute and friendless. According to Hogarth, he had married Miss Wyld when his first wife died; she at least stayed by him, as did one of their daughters.

See also EPHESIAN MATRON, THE; LIONEL AND CLARISSA; and PADLOCK, THE.

performed in London unless otherwise stated; all printed works published in London; vocal scores and librettos published soon after first performance unless otherwise stated

LCG – *Covent Garden* LDL – *Drury Lane*
LLH – *Little Theatre in the Haymarket* LRC – *Royal Circus*
LRG – *Ranelagh Gardens* LSW – *Sadler's Wells*
aft – *afterpiece* a-s – *all-sung*
pan – *pantomime*

The Shepherd's Artifice (aft, a-s, 2, Dibdin), LCG, 21 May 1764, 2 songs (1764)
Love in the City (comic op, 3, I. Bickerstaff), LCG, 21 Feb 1767 [incl. music by G. Cocchi, F. H. Barthelemon, Galuppi, Jommelli, Pergolesi]; 1 song pubd (Dibdin) (Dublin, n.d.); reduced (aft, 2) as The Romp, or A Cure for the Spleen by T. Lloyd, Dublin, Capel Street, 23 Jan 1771
The Village Wedding (aft, J. Love), Richmond, 18 July 1767
The Sailor's Reception (pan, Love), Richmond, 15 Sept 1767
Lionel and Clarissa, or A School for Fathers (comic op, 3, part pasticcio, Bickerstaff), LCG, 25 Feb 1768; rev. as A School for Fathers, LDL, 8 Feb 1770
The Padlock (aft, 2, Bickerstaff, after M. de Cervantes: *El celoso extremeno*), LDL, 3 Oct 1768, ov. (1768)
Damon and Phillida (aft, 2, Dibdin, after C. Cibber), LDL, 21 Dec 1768
The Ephesian Matron, or The Widow's Tears (aft, a-s, 1, Bickerstaff, after Petronius: *Satyricon*), LRG, 12 May 1769
The Captive (aft, 2, part pasticcio, Bickerstaff, after J. Dryden), LLH, 21 June 1769
The Jubilee (aft, 2 pts, part pasticcio, Bickerstaff and others, based on D. Garrick's Shakespeare entertainment at Stratford), LDL, 14 Oct 1769; vs contains cantata Queen Mab in full score
Interlude in Amphitryon, or The Two Sosias (a-s, J. Hawkesworth, after Dryden), LDL, 23 Nov 1769
The Maid the Mistress (aft, a-s, Bickerstaff, after G. A. Federico), LRG, 28 May 1770; rev. as He Wou'd if he Could, or An Old Fool Worse than Any (burletta, 2), LDL, 12 April 1771
The Recruiting Sergeant (aft, a-s, 1, Bickerstaff), LRG, 20 July 1770; wind pts for songs not in full score, some pts in *GB-Lbl*
The Institution of the Garter (aft, a-s, 3 pts, Garrick, after G. West), LDL, 28 Oct 1771
Amelia (aft, 2, part pasticcio, R. Cumberland), LDL, 14 Dec 1771
The Pigmy Revels (pan, Messink), LDL, 26 Dec 1772; no lib.
The Brickdust Man (dialogue, Bickerstaff), LSW, 1772; vs incl. ov.
The Palace of Mirth (dialogue, Dibdin), LSW, 1772; vs pubd, no copy known
The Wedding Ring (aft, 2, Dibdin, after C. Goldoni), LDL, 1 Feb 1773, ov. *Lbl* Add.30950
The Ladle (dialogue, Dibdin, after M. Prior), LSW, 12 April 1773
The Grenadier (dialogue, ?Garrick), LSW, 19 April 1773
The Vineyard Revels (dialogue pan), LSW, 3 May 1773; vs pubd, no copy known
The Mischance (dialogue, Dibdin, based on 'The Barber of Bagdat'), LSW, 12 July 1773
The Trip to Portsmouth (aft, 1, G. A. Stevens), LLH, 11 Aug 1773; collab. T. Arne
The Deserter (aft, 2, Dibdin, after M.-J. Sedaine), LDL, 2 Nov 1773; Monsigny's opera with new music by Dibdin and 2 airs by Philidor
A Christmas Tale (entertainment, 5 pts, Garrick, after C.-S. Favart, Fletcher and Dryden), LDL, 27 Dec 1773
The Waterman, or The First of August (ballad op, 2, Dibdin), LLH, 8 Aug 1774
The Cobler, or A Wife of Ten Thousand (ballad op, 2, Dibdin, after Sedaine), LDL, 9 Dec 1774; no vs
The Quaker (aft, 2, Dibdin, after C. Shadwell), LDL, 3 May 1775, vs (1777); incl. song by T. Linley (i)
The Sultan, or A Peep into the Seraglio (aft, 2, Bickerstaff, after Favart), LDL, 12 Dec 1775; no vs
The Blackamoor Wash'd White (aft, 2, H. Bate Dudley), LDL, 1 Feb 1776, Act 1 vs (1776), ov. pubd in pts but no set known
The Metamorphoses (aft, 2, Dibdin, after Molière: *Le sicilien* and *George Dandin*), LLH, 26 Aug 1776; no vs
The Seraglio (aft, 2, Dibdin), LCG, 14 Nov 1776; completed by S. Arnold
Yo Yea, or The Friendly Tars (dialogue, Dibdin), LSW, 18 Aug 1777; 3 songs (1777)

Poor Vulcan (aft, burletta, a-s, 2, Dibdin, after P. A. Motteux), LCG, 4 Feb 1778; vs omits all recits. from Act 2 and some from Act 1
Rose and Colin (aft, 1, Dibdin, after Sedaine), LCG, 18 Sept 1778; no vs
The Wives revenged (aft, 1, Dibdin, after Sedaine), LCG, 18 Sept 1778; no vs
Annette and Lubin (aft, 1, Dibdin, after Favart), LCG, 2 Oct 1778, finale *Lbl* Add.30955; no vs
The Medley (pan, Dibdin), LCG, 14 Oct 1778; rev. as The Mirror, or Harlequin Everywhere (3 pts), LCG, 30 Nov 1779
The Touchstone (pan, 2 pts, Dibdin), LCG, 4 Jan 1779; unusual for its spoken dialogue
The Chelsea Pensioner (aft, 2, Dibdin, after J. F. Marmontel), LCG, 6 May 1779, ov. and 6 vocal items in The Lyrist; no vs
Plymouth in an Uproar (aft, 2, E. Neville), LCG, 20 Oct 1779, ov. and 1 song in The Lyrist; no vs
The Shepherdess of the Alps (3, Dibdin, after Marmontel), LCG, 18 Jan 1780; no vs
The Islanders (3, Dibdin, after G. F. P. Saint-Foix), LCG, 25 Nov 1780, ov. and 12 songs in The Lyrist (1780–81); only song texts pubd, no vs; shortened as The Marriage Act (aft, 2), LCG, 17 Sept 1781; no vs
Harlequin Freemason (pan, Dibdin), LCG, 29 Dec 1780, ov. and songs in The Lyrist; no vs
Jupiter and Alcmena (3, Dibdin, after Dryden: *Amphitryon*), LCG, 27 Oct 1781, MS lib. *US-SM*, no vs
The Graces (1, Dibdin), LRC, 1782, lib. pubd; no music known
The Talisman (of Orosmanes) (pan, Dibdin), also called The Magic of Orosmanes, LRC, 28 March 1783, 1 song (1783), another with recit. *GB-Lbl* Add.30951, lib. pubd
Robin Hood (pan, Dibdin), 9 June 1783, ov. and background music *Lbl* Add.30950
Pandora (pan, Dibdin), LRC, 14 July 1783, several MS items *SOp* (with other unidentified Dibdin music), 2 lyrics in Hogarth
The Long Odds (serenata, Dibdin), LRC, 27 Oct 1783, at least 7 songs *Lbl* Add.30951–3, MS lib. *Lbl* Add.30964
The Lancashire Witches (pan, Dibdin), LRC, 27 Dec 1783, piece for woodwind *Lbl* Add.30952; song texts pubd, no copy known
The Cestus (serenata, 1, Dibdin), LRC, 1783, vs without linking recits. (1783)
The Saloon (interlude, Dibdin), LRC, 2 Feb 1784, 3 song texts in Hogarth
Liberty Hall (aft, 2, Dibdin), LDL, 8 Feb 1785, ov. *Lbl* Add.30950
The Life, Death, and Renovation of Tom Thumb (burletta, Dibdin), LRC, 28 March 1785, songs *Lbl* Add.30952, lib. pubd
Clump and Cudden (interlude, Dibdin), LRC, May 1785; 1 song in Lyric Remembrancer (1799), others *Lbl* Add.30954–5, 4 song texts in Hogarth
The Benevolent Tar, or The Miller's Daughter (1, Dibdin), LRC, 1785, songs *Lbl* Add.30951–2, 30955 and in Hogarth, lib. pubd
Harvest Home (aft, 2, Dibdin), LLH, 16 May 1787, songs *Lbl* Add.30951 and 30955
The Provocation (ballet pan, J. Byrne), LCG, 4 Oct 1790
A Loyal Effusion in honour of His Majesty's Birthday (aft, 1, Dibdin), LCG, 4 June 1794, MS lib. *US-SM*, no vs
Hannah Hewitt, or The Female Crusoe (aft, 2, Dibdin), LDL, 7 May 1798, MS lib. *SM*, no vs; only 1 perf.
The Broken Gold (ballad op, 2, Dibdin), LCG, 8 Feb 1806, MS lib. *GB-Lbl* Add.30963, only song texts pubd
The Round Robin (aft, C. I. M. Dibdin), LLH, 21 June 1811, songs *Lbl* Add.30952–3

Other operas, inc. and unperf., incl. MS libs. to Hassan and The Cake House, *Lbl*
Hogarth gives lyrics from the following Sadler's Wells dialogues of which no music survives: England against Italy, 1773; None so Blind as Those who Wont See, 1773; The Imposter, 1776; The Razor-Grinder, 21 April 1777; She is Mad for a Husband, 1777; The Old Woman of Eighty, 1777; other titles in *The Musical Tour* and *Grove5*, but nothing is known of these works
Other pieces, for the Royal Circus, from which nothing survives, listed in Dibdin's *The Musical Tour, The Professional Life* etc.

*

BDA; *LS*
ABCdario Musico (London, 1780)
Charles Dibdin: a Collection of over One Hundred Letters, Portraits, Manuscripts, & Playbills relating to Charles Dibdin and his Family (*US-CA*, Theatre Collection)
C. Dibdin: *The Royal Circus Epitomised* (London, 1784)
——: *The Musical Tour of Mr. Dibdin* (Sheffield, 1788)
——: *A Complete History of the English Stage* (London, 1797, 1800)
——: *The Professional Life of Mr. Dibdin* (London, 1803, enlarged 2/1809)
The Thespian Dictionary (London, 1805)
W. Kitchener: *The Sea Songs of Charles Dibdin: with a Memoir of his Life and Works* (London, 1823)
G. Hogarth: *The Songs of Charles Dibdin* (London, 1842) [incl. memoir and notes, historical, biographical and critical]
E. M. Lockwood: 'Charles Dibdin's Musical Tour', *ML*, xiii (1932), 207–14
E. R. Dibdin: *A Charles Dibdin Bibliography* (Liverpool, 1937)
——: 'Charles Dibdin as a Writer', *ML*, xix (1938), 149–70
H. G. Sear: 'Charles Dibdin: 1745–1814', *ML*, xxvi (1945), 61–5
P. A. Tasch: *The Dramatic Cobbler: the Life and Works of Isaac Bickerstaff* (Lewisburg, PA, 1971)
R. Fiske: *English Theatre Music in the Eighteenth Century* (London, 1973, 2/1986)
R. Fahrner: *The Theatre Career of Charles Dibdin the Elder (1745–1814)* (New York, 1989) [incl. chronological list of Dibdin's staged works, 215–27] ROGER FISKE/IRENA CHOLIJ

Dibuk, Il ('The Dybbuk'). Opera in a prologue and three acts by LODOVICO ROCCA to a libretto by RENATO SIMONI after Shalom Anski's play *Tzvishen tzvei Velter* (1920); Milan, Teatro alla Scala, 24 March 1934.

In the 1930s *Il Dibuk* enjoyed what some saw as the biggest success won by a new Italian opera since Puccini's *Turandot*; and it has remained easily the best-known of Rocca's works. Undoubtedly much of the credit must go to the unusually striking libretto – and, indeed, to the extraordinary, justly famous Yiddish play (usually known as *The Dybbuk*) on which it was based. Set in a close-knit 19th-century east European Jewish community, the plot centres on a young couple, Hanan (tenor) and Leah (mezzo-soprano), who have been solemnly promised to each other by their fathers before they were born, and who are, moreover, deeply in love. But Leah's father Sender (baritone) breaks his promise by making her marry another man, thus causing Hanan to die of grief. In keeping with an old Jewish superstition, the young man gets his revenge while the wedding is in progress, by entering Leah invisibly in the form of a 'dybbuk', making her behave as if possessed by an evil spirit. Only after much striving does the Rabbi Ezriel (bass) succeed in driving out this 'demon'; and even then Hanan is not finally defeated: as soon as Leah has been left on her own, he appears as a visible ghost and, after an extended duet, takes her away to be united with him in the land of the dead.

Composed in 1928–30, the music of *Il Dibuk* covers a wide spectrum of styles. The darkly modal, quasi-Russian choral writing is repeatedly tinged with oriental inflections reminiscent of Bloch; the orchestration is colourful and sometimes appropriately macabre; in the more intense dramatic scenes the level of dissonance sometimes rises startlingly, with harsh note-clusters, abrupt outcrops of parallel 2nds, etc.; yet there are also reversions – notably in the final duet – to a more traditional, sentimental Italian manner. In purely musical terms the juxtapositions may sometimes seem arbitrary, even crude; but their dramatic effectiveness is often striking. The opera has continued to be revived occasionally in Italy into the 1980s, although it may now seem rather faded when compared (for example) with Prokofiev's *The Fiery Angel*, which was still unknown at the time of *Il Dibuk's* première and which treats comparable subject matter with a unifying genius that Rocca lacked. JOHN C. G. WATERHOUSE

DiChiera, David (*b* McKeesport, PA, 8 April 1935). American administrator and composer. He studied the piano and composition in Los Angeles and in 1958 went to Italy, where he was engaged in research into unpublished 18th-century Italian opera. In 1960 he returned to Los Angeles and began teaching there; he moved to Michigan in 1962 and the following year established the educational programme 'Overture to Opera', bringing opera performances to schools and community centres throughout the state. He founded and became director of the Michigan Opera Theatre (1971) and the Music Hall Center for the Performing Arts (1973). Under DiChiera the Opera Theatre staged revivals of American operas by Gershwin, Blitzstein, Gruenberg and others, and the première of Pasatieri's *Washington Square* (1976); in 1981 the company began a series of national operas, including American premières of works by Tigranyan and Moniuszko. DiChiera was president of Opera America from 1979 to 1983 and artistic director of Dayton Opera from 1981; in 1985 he founded and became general director of Opera Pacific. His one-act children's opera, *Rumpelstiltskin*, composed in collaboration with his wife, Karen DiChiera, to a libretto by Joan Hill, was given its first performance in Detroit in 1977.

Dickens, Charles (*b* Portsmouth, 7 Feb 1812; *d* Gad's Hill, nr Rochester, 9 June 1870). English writer. He wrote the libretto for John Hullah's 'operatic burletta' *The Village Coquettes*, produced at St James's Theatre in December 1836, while his first novel, *The Pickwick Papers*, was appearing in monthly instalments. Although references to opera in his novels are infrequent, he often attended performances at Covent Garden and Her Majesty's Theatre, and in letters praised Mario, Grisi, Lind and Viardot (especially as Fidès in Meyerbeer's *Le prophète*). In Paris he was moved to tears by a performance of Berlioz's version of Gluck's *Orfeo* in November 1862 (with Viardot in the title role) and, a few months later, by Gounod's *Faust*. As editor of the journals *Household Words* and, later, *All the Year Round*, he published articles about opera from time to time, and in 1869 published in *All the Year Round* several attacks on Wagner, probably written by his friend Henry Fothergill Chorley.

Although there have been many dramatizations of Dickens, these have been principally in the form of stage plays or films, which give more obvious scope for his colourful and topical writing and especially his social commentary than opera can readily accommodate; there are no settings of his novels as operas from his own time, and not until the 20th century have composers shown an interest in using his works (and then only a limited selection of them).

The Pickwick Papers (novel, 1836–7): C. Wood, 1922 (as A Scene from Pickwick); A. Coates, 1936 (as Pickwick)
Barnaby Rudge (novel, 1841): J. Edwards, 1901 (as Dolly Varden)
The Old Curiosity Shop (novel, 1841): L. Landi, 1916 (as Nelly)
A Christmas Carol (novel, 1843): B. Herrmann, 1954; J. Cikker, 1963 (as Mr Scrooge); L. Liviabella, 1963 (as Canto di Natale); T. Musgrave, 1979
Martin Chuzzlewit (novel, 1844): C. Wood, 1924 (as The Family Party)
The Cricket on the Hearth (novel, 1845): G. Gallignani, 1873 (as Il grillo del focolare); K. Goldmark, 1896 (as Das Heimchen am Herd); R. Zandonai, 1908 (as Il grillo del focolare); A. Mackenzie, 1914
A Tale of Two Cities (novel, 1859): A. Benjamin, 1957

J. T. Lightwood: *Charles Dickens and Music* (London, 1912)
C. Cudworth: 'Dickens and Music', *MT*, cxi (1970), 588–90

ROBERT BLEDSOE

Dickie, Brian (*b* Newark-on-Trent, 23 July 1941). English administrator. Educated at Trinity College, Dublin, he began a long association with Glyndebourne Festival Opera in 1962. In 1967 he was appointed administrator of Glyndebourne Touring Opera; during this period he was also artistic director of the Wexford Festival Opera (1967–73) and artistic adviser to the Théâtre Musical de Paris (1973–81). In 1981 he became general administrator of Glyndebourne Festival Opera and is credited with raising musical standards by securing Haitink as the festival's music director and engaging Rattle to conduct the touring company. Dickie developed a reputation for encouraging adventurous staging and new works: Knussen's *Where the Wild Things Are* (definitive version, 1984) and *Higglety Pigglety Pop!* (preliminary version, 1985) had sets designed by Maurice Sendak, and the world première of Nigel Osborne's *The Electrification of the Soviet Union* (1987) was directed by Sellars. Dickie became general director of the Canadian Opera Company in Toronto in 1989, since when his aim has been to feature Canadian artists and composers. He presented world premières of John Oliver's *Guacamayo's Old Song and Dance* (1991) and Somers's *Mario and the Magician* (1992). He was also vice-president of the Theatrical Management Association (1983–5) and chairman of the Theatres' National Committee (1980–85). He married the American soprano Nancy Gustafson. NANCY MALITZ

Dickie, Murray (*b* Bishopton, Renfrewshire, 3 April 1924). Scottish tenor. After study with Dino Borgioli and Guido Farinelli, he sang Almaviva in *Barbiere* at the Cambridge Theatre, London, in 1947. In 1949 he joined the Covent Garden company, singing Don Basilio in *Figaro*, the Curé in Bliss's *The Olympians*, Tamino, and David in Beecham's *Meistersinger* performances. He sang Pedrillo at Glyndebourne in 1950, joined the Vienna Staatsoper in 1952 and has appeared at the festivals of Salzburg and Edinburgh, and at La Scala, Buenos Aires and the Metropolitan (début 1962 as David). Although primarily a *buffo* tenor of vitality and charm, he has also sung such parts as Faust and Don Ottavio. From 1975 he was active as an opera director.

PETER BRANSCOMBE

Dickons [née Poole], **Maria** [Martha] **(Francis) Caroline** (*b* 1776; *d* 1833). English soprano. In 1793 she played Ophelia in *Hamlet*, primarily to sing Purcell's 'Mad Bess' song, and in 1794 she sang in Shield's *The Travellers in Switzerland*. After a brief retirement she returned to Covent Garden as a successful Mandane in Arne's *Artaxerxes* (1807). She made her début at the King's Theatre in 1812 as the Countess in the London première of Mozart's *Figaro*; the following year she sang Giaconda in P. C. Guglielmi's *Le due nozze*. At Drury Lane in 1815 she sang in S. J. Arnold's *The Unknown Guest*; notices were mixed, but Leigh Hunt thought her the best female singer in English opera. She retired from the stage in 1820.

*

LS
L. Hunt: 'Musical Sketches', *Examiner* (12 Feb 1815)
'Sketch of Maria Dickons', *Theatrical Inquisitor* (1819), 83–5
T. Fenner: *Opera in London: Views from the Press, 1785–1830* (Carbondale, IL, forthcoming) THEODORE FENNER

Dictionaries and guides. Opera dictionaries and guides fall into a number of different categories. First, chronologies: some of the earliest Italian and French examples take this form, and the usefulness of such a format has been demonstrated in the 20th century by Alfred Loewenberg's *Annals of Opera 1597–1940*. Second, dictionaries ordered alphabetically by title, composer or librettist: Franz Stieger arranged his *Opern-Lexikon* by all three. Third, guides to the operatic repertory including plot summaries and discussion of the music: Gustav Kobbé's *Complete Opera Book* is the best-known example in English; in Germany, publication of *Pipers Enzyklopädie des Musiktheaters* began in 1986. Fourth, guides to national or local schools of opera composition. Fifth, guides to one composer's operatic output or detailed studies of a single opera: of this last kind the Cambridge Opera Handbooks are a valuable recent example, but their origins can be traced back a long way. In the late 18th and early 19th centuries opera librettos occasionally included quite detailed introductory material outlining the background and plot of an opera. Finally, an exclusively 20th-century phenomenon is the publication of guides to opera recordings, such as *Opera on Record* edited by Alan Blyth.

1. DICTIONARIES.

(i) Early history. The earliest opera dictionaries appeared in the second half of the 17th century, the work of Italian writers. In the 18th century the first French dictionaries were published, along with one Russian dictionary.

The first attempt at an opera dictionary was published in Rome. This was *Drammaturgia ... divisa in sette indici* by Leone Allacci, a Greek theologian who from 1616 worked in the Vatican Library, becoming chief curator in 1661. *Drammaturgia* was published in Rome in 1666 and lists dramatic works of all kinds, including opera librettos, published in Italy, along with numerous unpublished works. A second edition, by Giovanni Cendoni, Apostolo Zeno and others, was published in Venice in 1755. This much expanded edition makes the significant addition of the composers' names in the section devoted to *drammi per musica*.

Cristoforo Ivanovich was the librettist for a number of operas, but his most significant contribution to operatic history is 'Le memorie teatrali di Venezia', a catalogue of Venetian opera performances from 1637 to 1681 published as an appendix to his *Minerva al tavolino* and updated for the second edition (Venice, 1681, 2/1688). This is an important, if rather inaccurate, source of information about the operatic repertory of 17th-century Venice. Subsequent chroniclers drew extensively on Ivanovich's work, notably Giovanni Carlo Bonlini. His catalogue was called *Le glorie della poesia e della musica contenute nell'estatta notizia de' teatri della città di Venezia, e nel catalogo purgatissimo dei drammi quivi sin'hora rappresentati, con gl'auttori della poesia e della musica e con le annotazioni ai suoi luoghi propri.* It was published anonymously in Venice in 1730 and consists of a detailed chronological listing of 658 operas performed in Venice between 1637 and 1730, together with their librettists and composers. There are two indexes, one by title, the other by librettist. Some surviving copies have a loosely inserted supplement for the year 1731 bringing the total number of operas to 672. Bonlini's work was continued by Antonio Groppo, who published a *Catalogo di tutti drammi per musica recitati ne' teatri di Venezia dall'anno 1637 ... fin all'anno presente 1745* (Venice, *c*1745).

The earliest French opera dictionaries appeared in the 18th century, beginning with Maupoint's *Bibliotheque des theatres, contenant le catalogue alphabetique des piéces dramatiques, opera, parodies, & opera comiques; & le tems de leurs représentations* (Paris, 1733). This is arranged alphabetically by work and gives the composer, librettist and first performance. Sometimes the names of performers and their roles are also included. The appendices include chronological listings of operas and composers. The following 30 years saw the publication of several important French theatre and opera catalogues of which the most notable were the *Histoire du théâtre de l'Opéra en France* by J.-B. Durey de Noinville (Paris, 1753, with L. Travenol, 2/1757), the *Dictionnaire portatif des théâtres ... de Paris* by A. de Léris (Paris 1754, 2/1763), the *Dictionnaire des théâtres de Paris* by Claude and François Parfaict (Paris, 1756, 2/1767–70, with G. d'Abguerbe) and, perhaps the most detailed of all, *Ballets, opéra, et autres ouvrages lyriques par ordre chronologique* by Louis, Duke of La Vallière (Paris, 1760), which attempted to do for the Parisian musical theatre what Bonlini and others had done for the Venetian. In addition, La Vallière gave details of publications, an unusual and useful feature. The book also includes an index of composers and titles. 1776 saw the publication of the *Dictionnaire dramatique* by J. de la Porte and S. R. N. Chamfort. The first Russian theatre chronology to include operatic works was published in Moscow in 1787. This was the anonymous *Dramaticheskiy slovar', ili Pokazaniya po alfavitu vsekh rossiyskikh teatral'nïkh sochineniy* ('Dictionary of the Theatre, or Alphabetical List of All Russian Theatrical Works').

(ii) Since 1800. The 19th century saw the publication of two of the most important opera dictionaries, one French and one German. Félix Clément and Pierre Larousse issued their *Dictionnaire lyrique, ou Histoire des opéras* in Paris in 1867–9 (4 suppls. to 1881, 2/1897 ed. A. Pougin as *Dictionnaire des opéras*, suppl. 1904, 3/1905). Clément (1822–85) was in some ways a surprising compiler of an opera dictionary; he had studied classics as well as the organ and composition, and his musical career was almost exclusively as a church musician, as organist at the Sorbonne and as the organizer of concerts at the Ste Chapelle. The *Dictionnaire lyrique* is not without problems. Dates are often inaccurate, and it includes music which is not strictly operatic, such as incidental music to plays. Its tone (as well as its policy on inclusions and omissions) is fiercely partisan, flying the flag on behalf of French opera and saving its most savage condemnation for Wagner. Even so, the work is valuable, not least for the view it gives of French operatic taste, as well as for its useful detail. Arthur Pougin's revisions correct some of the inaccuracies. Pougin himself produced a valuable work on all aspects of the French theatre in his *Dictionnaire historique et pittoresque du théâtre* (Paris, 1885), which includes entries on many features of operatic life, especially in France. Hugo Riemann (1849–1919) produced, with his *Opern-Handbuch* (Leipzig, 1887, 2/1893, suppl. 1979 by Franz Stieger), the first significant German-language opera dictionary.

Entries are arranged in a continuous alphabetical sequence including composers, titles and librettists.

The early years of the 20th century saw the publication of several important new dictionaries. In Italy, Carlo Dassori produced his *Opere e operisti (dizionario lirico 1541–1902)* (Genoa, 1903, 2/1906), which comprises an alphabetical listing by composer and title of 3628 composers and 15 406 operas. In the USA John Towers compiled his more comprehensive *Dictionary-Catalogue of Operas and Operettas which have been Performed on the Public Stage* (Morgantown, WV, 1910). This includes alphabetical listings by title and composer along with a list of 'libretti, with the number of times they have been set to music for the public stage'. Towers lists 28 015 operatic works.

The indefatigable Franz Stieger (1843–1938) compiled the information for his *Opern-Lexikon* from the last decades of the 19th century until the 1920s. Three each of its 11 volumes are devoted to listings by title, composer and librettist, and two to supplements. Publication was planned in the 1920s, but it was not until 1975 that it got under way, at Tutzing, the final volume appearing in 1983. The work contains details of about 60 000 works, including some oratorios and ballets.

As a student, Alfred Loewenberg went to as many opera performances as possible and began to accumulate a vast amount of information on operatic history. When he was forced by the Nazi regime to leave Germany in 1935, he settled in London and there completed his research. The result was the first detailed opera chronology to appear in English: *Annals of Opera 1597–1940* (Cambridge, 1943, 2/1955, 3/1978). Arranged year by year, this not only gives details of composer, librettist and place of first performance of some 4000 operas but also much information about revivals, alternative titles, revised versions and translations. The book includes indexes of operas, composers and librettists, as well as a general index. It is in fact a most enjoyable chronology to read, not least on account of the fascinating minutiae of operatic history with which Loewenberg peppered his text. The original edition was superseded by the two published after Loewenberg's death, the second edition revised by Frank Walker and the third revised and expanded by Harold Rosenthal. Slonimsky (in the seventh edition of *Baker's Biographical Dictionary*) described the book as 'a unique achievement'.

Two important Italian publications appeared in the 1950s and 60s. Umberto Manferrari compiled a *Dizionario universale delle opere melodrammatiche* (Florence, 1954–5), listing about 30 000 works arranged by composer, and Aldo Caselli produced his *Catalogo delle opere liriche pubblicate in Italia* (Florence, 1969), listing Italian first performances from the beginning of opera to the 20th century arranged alphabetically by composer and place. The most substantial dictionary of Italian theatre of all kinds is the nine-volume *Enciclopedia dello spettacolo* (Rome, 1954–62, suppls. 1963 and 1966, index 1968; material on opera edited by Fedele D'Amico), which includes a vast range of information about composers, singers, librettists, cities, individual opera houses and other operatic topics.

In 1978 publication started in Vienna of *Opern-Uraufführungen: ein internationales Verzeichnis von der Renaissance bis zur Gegenwart*, compiled by Clemens Gruber. This is arranged by language areas; the first two volumes to appear (vols.ii and iii) list works by German, Austrian and Swiss composers from 1800 to 1899 and from 1900 to 1977. The most recent attempt in the apparently irresistible quest for truly comprehensive documentation of opera is the *Edwin Mellen Opera Reference Index*, compiled by Charles H. Parsons (Lewiston, NY, 1986–). By the end of 1990, 12 of the projected 22 volumes had appeared. These include catalogues of composers and librettists, a geographical index of premières, a list of opera subjects and discographies. Volumes planned include an index of casts, a catalogue of printed opera scores and an opera bibliography.

A number of general opera dictionaries have been produced in the second half of the 20th century. In the USA, David Ewen compiled his *Encyclopedia of the Opera* (New York, 1955); a completely revised edition was published in 1971 as *New Encyclopedia of the Opera*. In England, Harold Rosenthal and John Warrack compiled the *Concise Oxford Dictionary of Opera* (London, 1964, 2/1979, repr. with corrections 1985), which sets high standards of accuracy within its relatively modest dimensions. Later, Leslie Orrey edited *The Encyclopedia of Opera* (London, 1976), a well-illustrated opera dictionary. *The Dictionary of Opera* by Charles Osborne was published in London in 1983. In Germany, Horst Seeger compiled his *Opern Lexikon* (Berlin, 1978, 4/1989), a general dictionary including entries on singers, publishers and miscellaneous operatic information as well as the more usual composers, librettists and titles.

In addition to these wide-ranging volumes there is a large number of specialist chronologies and dictionaries, dealing with the operatic repertory of a particular country or city, or with one aspect of opera (such as librettos or singers). Taddeo Wiel compiled *I teatri musicali veneziani nel settecento: catalogo delle opere in musica rappresentate nel secolo XVIII in Venezia (1701–1800)* (Venice, 1897), which gives useful details of principal singers and dancers as well as librettists, composers and titles. Similar work was done for opera in Naples by Benedetto Croce in *I teatri di Napoli* (Naples, 1891, abridged and rev. 2/1916 as *I teatri di Napoli dal Rinascimento alla fine del secolo decimottava*, 4/1947), in Bologna by Corrado Ricci in *I teatri di Bologna nei secoli XVII e XVIII* (Bologna, 1888) and in Venice by Giovanni Salvioli (writing as L. N. Galvani) in *I teatri musicali di Venezia nel secolo XVII (1637–1700)* (Milan, 1879). Other local chronologies include *A Register of First Performances of English Operas and Semi-Operas from the 16th Century to 1980* by Eric Walter White (London, 1983) and *Twentieth Century Opera in England and the United States* by Cameron Northouse (Boston, 1976), a chronology of first performances of 20th-century English and American operas between 1900 and 1974. For London opera performances up to 1800, by far the most comprehensive information is to be found in *The London Stage, 1660–1800* (Carbondale, IL, 1960–68, index 1979). This lists all performances in London theatres by date and includes a vast range of additional information about casts, box-office receipts and much else. Each year has a useful prefatory essay. R.-A. Mooser compiled *Opéras, intermezzos, ballets, cantates, oratorios joués en Russie durant le XVIIIe siècle* (Geneva, 1945, 3/1964), a dictionary of early operatic activity in Russia, and G. B. Bernandt produced his *Slovar' oper, vpervïye postavlennïkh ili izdannïkh v dorevolyutsionnoy Rossii i v SSSR (1736–1959)* ('Dictionary of Operas First Performed or Published in Pre-Revolutionary Russia and the USSR'; Moscow, 1962).

Specialist reference works with a particular focus on singers include the *Grosses Sängerlexikon* compiled by K. J. Kutsch and Leo Riemens (Berne, 1987, suppl. 1991) and the *Dictionnaire des chanteurs de l'Opéra de Paris* by Jean Gourret (Paris, 1982). A useful source of information on modern opera performers and others is the directory *Who's Who in Opera: an International Biographical Directory of Singers, Conductors, Directors, Designers and Administrators*, edited by Maria F. Rich (New York, 1976); it also includes entries on 101 opera companies.

Printed librettos have also been a fruitful area of study. In 1914 the Library of Congress issued a *Catalogue of Opera Librettos Printed Before 1800* by Oscar Sonneck (Washington DC, 1914). The most recent successor to this is the remarkable work of Claudio Sartori being published as *I libretti italiani a stampa dalle origini al 1800: catalogo analitico con 16 indici* (Cuneo, 1990–), an immense and extremely detailed catalogue arranged alphabetically by opera. Librettos printed since 1800 have received much less attention until recently. The *Catalogo dei libretti per musica dell'ottocento (1800–1860)* by Francesco Melisi (Lucca, 1990) lists the collection in the Biblioteca del Conservatorio di S Pietro a Majella, Naples. It is arranged alphabetically by opera and includes indexes of composers, singers, choreographers, costume designers, directors, dedicatees, towns and theatres.

2. GUIDES. The 19th century saw the publication of a vast range of popular guides to the operatic repertory, mostly concerned with plot summaries rather than detailed discussion of the music. These guides, many with a bias towards operas of the country in which they were published, were intended for the enthusiastic operagoer rather than the scholar, and so great was the demand that foreign-language editions of some were prepared. Of these, one of the most delightful is *The New Opera Glass* by F. Charley (Leipzig, 1877; ed. with introduction by R. Elkin, London, 1951). This aimed to give English-speaking visitors to German opera houses 'the plots of the popular operas of modern times' and does so in such quaint English that it has become something of a collector's item.

The first really substantial English-language guide to opera plots was the *Complete Opera Book* by Gustav Kobbé (New York and London, 1919). It was an immediate success and went through more than 20 impressions by 1950. Several revised and enlarged editions compiled by the Earl of Harewood were published between 1954 and 1976 (the ninth, as *The New Kobbé Complete Opera Book*), and a tenth appeared in 1987 (as *Kobbé's Complete Opera Book*). Few of the many subsequent imitators of Kobbé, especially in English and German, attempted to match the scope or detail of his work, although some guides have a stronger emphasis on certain aspects of the repertory. In 1986 publication began in Munich and Zürich of a much more comprehensive and ambitious work, the eight-volume *Pipers Enzyklopädie des Musiktheaters: Oper, Operette, Musical, Ballett*, edited by Carl Dahlhaus and Sieghart Döhring. This is arranged alphabetically by composer and contains detailed discussion of both the plot and the music of each opera; it also includes details of first performances and subsequent productions, and it is lavishly illustrated. *The Opera Companion to Twentieth Century Opera* by George Martin (New York, 1979) includes detailed synopses of 78 works.

Studies of the operas of a particular country are often historical or stylistic surveys rather than guides. Some, however, provide valuable lists and statistics. For example, *Czech Opera* by John Tyrrell (Cambridge, 1988) includes a useful list of Czech operas mentioned in the text of the book, with dates of first performances, publication and recordings. Some national studies are arranged by composer, one example being the highly detailed *Die deutsche Oper der Gegenwart* by C. Niessen (Regensburg, 1944), an impressively full account of operas composed, mainly, during the Nazi era.

Literature on the operatic works of particular composers proliferated at the end of the 19th century, especially with hundreds of volumes on the operas of Wagner. Books on individual operas have their origins in the introductions found in some early printed librettos. Early in the 19th century, librettos for performances at the Royal Opera House, Covent Garden, occasionally included biographical information about the composers as well as plot summaries. Among the most recent examples of studies of particular works, the Cambridge Opera Handbooks (usually containing detailed musical analyses as well as essays on the genesis and reception history of the work) and the guides produced by the ENO and the Royal Opera House (including a complete libretto with English translation as well as essays and articles) display a high level of scholarship.

Operatic recordings are discussed at length by various authors in the three volumes of *Opera on Record*, edited by Alan Blyth (London, 1979–84), and in Blyth's own *Opera on CD* (London, 1992). Detailed discographies are to be found in volumes x and xi of the *Edwin Mellen Opera Reference Index* (1990).

DICTIONARIES AND GUIDES: SELECTIVE LIST

L. Allacci: *Drammaturgia* (Rome, 1666); enlarged G. Cendoni, A. Zeno and others as *Drammaturgia di Lione Allacci accresciuta e continuata fino all'anno MDCCLV* (Venice, 1755)

C. Ivanovich: *Minerva al tavolino* (Venice, 1681, 2/1688)

[G. C. Bonlini]: *Le glorie della poesia e della musica contenute nell'estatta notizia de' teatri della città di Venezia, e nel catalogo purgatissimo dei drammi quivi sin'hora rappresentati con gl'auttori della poesia e della musica e con le annotazioni ai suoi luoghi propri* (Venice, 1730, suppl. 1731)

Maupoint: *Bibliotheque des theatres contenant le catalogue alphabetique des piéces dramatiques, opera, parodies, & opera comiques; & le tems de leurs représentations* (Paris, 1733)

A. Groppo: *Catalogo di tutti drammi per musica recitati ne' teatri di Venezia dall'anno 1637 … fin all'anno presente 1745* (Venice, c1745)

J.-B. Durey de Noinville: *Histoire du théâtre de l'Opéra en France* (Paris, 1753, with L. Travenol, 2/1757)

[A. de Léris]: *Dictionnaire portatif des théâtres … de Paris* (Paris, 1754, 2/1763)

[C. Parfaict and F. Parfaict]: *Dictionnaire des théâtres de Paris* (Paris, 1756, 2/1767–70, with G. d'Abguerbe)

[Louis, Duke of La Vallière]: *Ballets, opéra, et autres ouvrages lyriques par ordre chronologique* (Paris, 1760)

A. G. Contant d'Orville: *Histoire de l'opéra bouffon: contenant les jugements de toutes les pieces qui ont paru depuis la naissance jusqu'à ce jour* (Amsterdam, 1768)

J. de la Porte and S. R. N. Chamfort: *Dictionnaire dramatique* (Paris, 1776)

Dramaticheskiy slovar', ili Pokazaniya po alfavitu vsekh rossiyskikh teatral'nïkh sochineniy [Dictionary of the Theatre, or Alphabetical List of All Russian Theatrical Works] (Moscow, 1787)

F. Gleich: *Wegweiser für Opernfreunde* (Leipzig, 1827)

J. B. Giraldon, ed.: *Les beautés de l'opéra, ou chefs-d'oeuvre lyriques* (Paris, 1845) [incl. essays by T. Gautier, J. Janin and P. Chasles]

C. Heath: *Beauties of the Opera and Ballet* (London, 1845)
F. Clément and P. Larousse: *Dictionnaire lyrique, ou Histoire des opéras* (Paris, 1867–9, 4 suppls. to 1881, 2/1897 ed. A. Pougin as *Dictionnaire des opéras*, suppl. 1904, 3/1905)
F. Charley: *The New Opera Glass, or Opera as she is Wrote* (Leipzig, 1877); ed. with introduction by R. Elkin (London, 1951, 2/1952)
L. N. Galvani [G. Salvioli]: *I teatri musicali di Venezia nel secolo XVII (1637–1700)* (Milan, 1879)
F. E. Carleton: *Operas: their Writers and their Plots* (Philadelphia, 1882)
A. Pougin: *Dictionnaire historique et pittoresque du théâtre* (Paris, 1885)
G. P. Upton: *The Standard Operas: their Plots and their Music* (Chicago, 1886, enlarged 2/1919)
H. Riemann: *Opern-Handbuch* (Leipzig, 1887, 2/1893, suppl. 1979 by F. Stieger)
C. Ricci: *I teatri di Bologna nei secoli XVII e XVIII* (Bologna, 1888)
F. R. Chesney: *Operatic Tales* (London, 1889)
O. Neitzel: *Die Führer durch die Oper des Theaters der Gegenwart* (Leipzig, 1890–93)
C. Annesley: *The Standard Operaglass, Containing the Detailed Plots of One Hundred Celebrated Operas* (New York, 1891, 6/1937 as *The Home Book of Opera*)
B. Croce: *I teatri di Napoli* (Naples, 1891; abridged and rev. 2/1916 as *I teatri di Napoli dal Rinascimento alla fine del secolo decimottava*, 4/1947)
W. Lackowitz: *Der Operettenführer* (Berlin, 1894, 8/1908)
R. A. Streatfield: *The Opera: a Sketch of the Development of Opera* (London, 1896, 5/1925)
T. Wiel: *I teatri musicali veneziani nel settecento: catalogo delle opere in musica rappresentate nel secolo XVIII in Venezia (1701–1800)* (Venice, 1897)
M. Kalbeck: *Opern-Abende* (Berlin, 1898)
J. W. Buel: *The Great Operas* (London, 1899)
E. Singleton: *A Guide to the Opera* (New York, 1899)
G. P. Upton: *The Standard Light Operas: their Plots and their Music* (Chicago, 1902)
C. Dassori: *Opere e operisti (dizionario lirico 1541–1902)* (Genoa, 1903, 2/1906)
A. E. Bergh: *The Opera: Comprising the Romantic Legends, Stories and Plots of Famous Operas and Biographies of the Composers* (London, 1909)
L. L. Melitz: *The Opera Goers' Complete Guide* (New York, 1909, 2/1926)
E. Singleton: *A Guide to Modern Opera* (New York, 1909)
J. C. Hadden: *Favorite Operas from Mozart to Mascagni: their Plots, History and Music* (London and New York, 1910)
H. E. Krehbiel: *A Book of Operas: their Histories, their Plots and their Music* (New York, 1910)
H. L. Mason: *Opera Stories ... of over 100 Operas and Ballets, also Portraits of Leading Singers* (Boston, 1910, 2/1923)
J. Towers: *Dictionary-Catalogue of Operas and Operettas which have been Performed on the Public Stage* (Morgantown, WV, 1910)
E. Combe: *Les chefs-d'oeuvre du répertoire: opéra, opéra-comique, opérette* (Paris, 1914)
O. G. T. Sonneck: *Catalogue of Opera Librettos Printed Before 1800* (Washington DC, 1914)
H. E. Krehbiel: *A Second Book of Operas: their Histories, their Plots and their Music* (New York, 1917)
M. Chop: *Führer durch die Opernmusik* (Berlin, 1918)
G. Kobbé: *Complete Opera Book* (New York and London, 1919, 10/1987 as *Kobbé's Complete Opera Book*, rev. Earl of Harewood)
L. L. Melitz: *Führer durch die Operetten* (Berlin, 1921)
A. Eisenmann: *Das grosse Opernbuch* (Stuttgart, 1923)
M. F. Watkins: *First Aid to the Opera-Goer* (New York, 1924)
F. H. Martens: *The Book of the Opera and the Ballet and History of the Opera* (New York, 1925)
——: *A Thousand and One Nights of Opera* (New York and London, 1926)
W. Rieck: *Opera Plots: an Index to the Stories of Opera, Operettas, Ballets, etc., from the Sixteenth to the Twentieth Century* (New York, 1927) [see also Drone 1978]
G. R. Kruse, ed.: *Reclams Opernführer* (Leipzig, 2/1928, 3/1930)
E. Newman: *Stories of the Great Operas and their Composers* (New York, 1928)
J. Kapp: *Das Opernbuch* (Leipzig, 1929)
M. S. Teasdale: *Handbook of 20th Century Opera: 20th Century Opera at Home and Abroad* (New York, 1938)
J. Hutter and Z. Chalabala, eds.: *České umění dramatické*, ii: *Zpěvohra* [Czech Dramatic Art: Opera] (Prague, 1941)
A. Loewenberg: *Annals of Opera 1597–1940* (Cambridge, 1943, 2/1955 ed. F. Walker, enlarged 3/1978 by H. Rosenthal)
E. Newman: *Opera Nights* (London, 1943)
C. Niessen: *Die deutsche Oper der Gegenwart* (Regensburg, 1944)
R.-A. Mooser: *Opéras, intermezzos, ballets, cantates, oratorios joués en Russie durant le XVIIIe siècle* (Geneva, 1945, 3/1964)
D. Brook: *Companion at Opera* (London, 1947)
M. J. Cross: *Complete Stories of the Great Operas* (Garden City, NY, 1947, enlarged 3/1955, ed. K. Kohrs)
L. Biancolli, ed.: *The Opera Reader* (New York, 1953)
H. Bauer: *Taschenlexikon für Opern, Operetta und Ballette* (Frankfurt, 1954)
E. Newman: *More Opera Nights* (London, 1954)
S. and S. D'Amico, eds.: *Enciclopedia dello spettacolo* (Rome and Florence, 1954–62, suppls. 1963 and 1966, index 1968) [operatic material ed. F. D'Amico]
U. Manferrari: *Dizionario universale delle opere melodrammatiche* (Florence, 1954–5)
K. Blaukopf: *Grosse Oper, grosse Sänger* (Stuttgart, 1955)
R. A. Bradford: *Opera, Once Over Lightly* (New York, 1955)
D. Ewen: *Encyclopedia of the Opera* (New York, 1955, enlarged 2/1963, ?3/1971 as *New Encyclopedia of the Opera*)
H. Schnoor: *Oper, Operette, Konzert* (Gütersloh, 1955, 2/1979 as *Mosaik-Opernführer*, rev. S. Pflichte)
Decca Book of Opera (London, 1956)
G. von Westermann and K. Schumann: *Knaurs Opernführer* (Munich, 1957, 3/1981; Eng. trans., rev., 1964, as *Opera Guide*)
P. Czerny, ed.: *Opernbuch* (Berlin, 1958, 5/1961)
F. Fellner: *Opera Themes and Plots* (New York, 1958)
The London Stage, 1660–1800 (Carbondale, IL, 1960–68, index 1979)
Q. Eaton: *Opera Production: a Handbook* (Minneapolis, 1961)
E. Krause: *Oper A–Z: ein Opernführer* (Leipzig, 1961, 3/1978)
G. Martin: *The Opera Companion* (New York, 1961)
F. L. Moore, ed.: *Crowells' Handbook of World Opera* (New York, 1961)
A. Ross: *The Opera Directory* (London, 1961)
G. B. Bernandt: *Slovar' oper, vpervïye postavlennïkh ili izdannïkh v dorevolyutsionnoy Rossii i v SSSR (1736–1959)* [Dictionary of Operas First Performed or Published in Pre-Revolutionary Russia and the USSR] (Moscow, 1962)
W. Brockway and H. Weinstock: *The World of Opera: the Story of its Origins and the Lore of its Performance* (New York, 1962)
M. Lubbock: *The Complete Book of Light Opera* (London, 1962)
G. Marek: *Opera as Theater* (New York, 1962)
A. Natan: *Primadonna: Lob der Stimmen* (Basle, 1962)
M. Otaguro: *Kageki daijtin* [Dictionary of Opera] (Tokyo, 1962)
J. Mattfeld: *A Handbook of American Operatic Premieres, 1731–1962* (Detroit, 1963)
A. Natan: *Primo uomo: grosse Sänger der Oper* (Basle, 1963)
R. Celletti, ed.: *Le grandi voci: dizionario critico-biografico dei cantanti con discografia operistica* (Rome, 1964)
A. Jacobs and S. Sadie: *The Pan Book of Opera* [also pubd as *The Opera Guide* and *Opera: a New Guide*] (London, 1964, enlarged 2/1984)
H. Rosenthal and J. Warrack: *Concise Oxford Dictionary of Opera* (London, 1964, 2/1979, repr. with corrections 1985)
K. J. Kutsch and L. Riemens: *Kleines Sängerlexikon* (Berne, 1966; Eng. trans., 1969, as *A Concise Biographical Dictionary of Singers*)
A. Caselli: *Catalogo delle opere liriche pubblicate in Italia* (Florence, 1969)
H. S. Sharp and M. Z. Sharp: *Index to Characters in the Performing Arts*, ii: *Operas and Musical Productions* (New York, 1969)
T. Besterman: *Music and Drama: a Bibliography of Bibliographies* (Totowa, NY, 1971)
M. Sénéchaud: *Le répertoire lyrique d'hier et d'aujourd'hui: opéras, opéra-comiques, drames lyriques, comédies musicales et ballets dramatiques* (Paris, 1971)
J. Drinkrow: *The Vintage Operetta Book* (Reading, 1972)
J. Wechsberg: *The Opera* (New York, 1972)
A. H. Drummond: *American Opera Librettos* (Metuchen, NJ, 1973)
K. Harris: *Opera Recordings: a Critical Guide* (New York, 1973)
P. H. Highfill jr, K. A. Burnim and E. A. Langhans: *A Biographical Dictionary of Actors, Actresses, Musicians, Dancers, Managers & Other Stage Personnel in London, 1660–1800* (Carbondale and Edwardsville, IL, 1973–)

Y. Karakandas: *Apanda tou lyrikou theatrou* [Everything about Lyric Theatre] (Athens, 1973)
H. Barlow and S. Morgenstern: *A Dictionary of Opera and Song Themes* (London, 1974, 2/1976)
I. Bontinck-Küffel, K. Blaukopf and M. Wagner, eds.: *Opern auf Schallplatten (1900–1962): ein historischer Katalog vollständiger oder nahezu vollständiger Aufnahmen* (Vienna, 1974)
H. Dostal: *Oper und Ballett im Film* (Vienna, 1974; incl. Eng. and Fr. versions)
K. J. Kutsch and L. Riemens: *Unvergängliche Stimmen: kleines Sängerlexikon* (Berne, 1975, 2/1982)
P. Várnai: *Operalexikon* (Budapest, 1975)
F. Stieger: *Opern-Lexikon* (Tutzing, 1975–83)
R. Celletti: *Il teatro d'opera in disco* (Milan, 1976)
A. Jefferson: *The Glory of Opera* (London, 1976)
C. Northouse: *Twentieth Century Opera in England and the United States* (Boston, 1976)
L. Orrey, ed.: *The Encyclopedia of Opera* (London, 1976)
M. F. Rich, ed.: *Who's Who in Opera: an International Biographical Directory of Singers, Conductors, Directors, Designers and Administrators* (New York, 1976)
E. Forbes: *Opera from A–Z* (London, 1977)
R. May: *A Companion to the Opera* (Guildford, 1977)
R. Mezzanotte, ed.: *L'opera: repertorio della lirica dal 1597* (Milan, 1977; Eng. trans., 1977, as *Simon and Schuster Book of the Opera*, and 1979, as *Phaidon Book of the Opera*; Fr. trans., 1979)
M. Scott: *The Record of Singing* (London, 1977–9)
G. M. Bordman: *American Musical Theatre: a Chronicle* (New York, 1978, 2/1986)
J. M. Drone: *Index to Opera, Operetta and Musical Comedy Synopses in Collections and Periodicals* (Metuchen, NJ, 1978) [continuation of Rieck 1927]
H. Seeger: *Opern Lexikon* (Berlin, 1978, 4/1989)
F. von Stranz: *Die grosse Opernführer* (Munich, 1978)
C. Gruber: *Opern-Uraufführungen: ein internationales Verzeichnis von der Renaissance bis zur Gegenwart* (Vienna, 1978–)
P. Gammond: *Illustrated Encyclopedia of Recorded Opera* (London, 1979)
G. Martin: *The Opera Companion to Twentieth Century Opera* (New York, 1979)
A. Payne: *Grands opéras du répertoire: résumés, analyses musicales, discographie* (Paris, 1979)
A. Blyth, ed.: *Opera on Record* (London, 1979–84)
N. Amadé: *Operaritkaságok* [Opera Rarities] (Budapest, 1980)
P. Brunel and S. Wolff, eds.: *L'Opéra* (Paris, 1980)
F. Endler: *Endlers Opern-Führer* (Vienna and Stuttgart, 1980)
A. Rich: *Opera* (Poole, 1980)
K. Pahlen: *Oper der Welt* (Zürich, 1981, 4/1987)
D. Zöchling: *Die Oper: Westermans farbiger Führer durch Oper, Operette und Musical* (Brunswick, 1981)
J. Gourret: *Dictionnaire des chanteurs de l'Opéra de Paris* (Paris, 1982)
A. Hostomská: *Příběhy, pověsti a pohádky paní hudby* [Stories, Legends and Fairy Tales set to Music] (Prague, 1982)
C. Marinelli: *Opere in disco da Monteverdi a Berg* (Florence, 1982)
G. Lanza Tomasi: *Guida all'opera da Monteverdi a Henze* (Milan, 1983)
C. Osborne: *The Dictionary of Opera* (London, 1983)
B. Regler Bellinger and others: *Knaurs grosser Opernführer* (Munich, 1983)
B. Shteynpress: *Operniye prem'yeri XX veka, 1901–1940: Slovar'* [New Opera Productions of the 20th Century, 1901–1940: a Dictionary] (Moscow, 1983)
F.-R. Tranchefort: *L'Opéra* (Paris, 1983)
E. W. White: *A Register of First Performances of English Operas and Semi-Operas from the 16th Century to 1980* (London, 1983)
S. Pitou: *The Paris Opera: an Encyclopedia of Operas, Ballets, Composers and Performers* (Westport, CT, 1983–)
R. F. P. Fellers: *The Metropolitan Opera on Record: a Discography of Commercial Recordings* (Westport, CT, 1984)
G. A. Marco: *Opera: a Research and Information Guide* (New York, 1984)
M. W. Andreasen: *Politikens opera leksikon* (Copenhagen, 1985)
A. Farkas: *Opera and Concert Singers: an Annotated International Bibliography of Books and Pamphlets* (New York, 1985)
S. Neef: *Handbuch der russischen und sowjetischen Oper* (Berlin, 1985)
J. L. DiGaetani: *An Invitation to the Opera* (New York, 1986)
K. Gänzl: *The British Musical Theatre*, i: *1865–1914*, ii: *1915–1984* (London, 1986)
P. Kornehof: *Winkler Prins encyclopedie van de opera* (Amsterdam, 1986)
C. Dahlhaus and S. Döhring, eds.: *Pipers Enzyklopädie des Musiktheaters: Oper, Operette, Musical, Ballett* (Munich and Zürich, 1986–)
C. H. Parsons: *Edwin Mellen Opera Reference Index* (Lewiston, NY, 1986–)
D. Hamilton, ed.: *The Metropolitan Encyclopedia of Opera* (London and New York, 1987)
K. J. Kutsch and L. Riemens: *Grosses Sängerlexikon* (Berne, 1987, suppl. 1991)
J. Lazarus: *The Opera Handbook* (Harlow, 1987)
R. May: *A Guide to the Opera* (Twickenham, 1987)
E. Mordden: *A Guide to Opera Recordings* (New York, 1987)
H. Wagner: *Handbuch der Oper* (Wilhelmshaven, 1987)
R. Turnbull: *The Opera Gazetteer* (London, 1988)
J. Anderson: *Bloomsbury Dictionary of Opera and Operetta* (London, 1989)
Earl of Harewood: *Kobbé's Illustrated Opera Book* (London, 1989)
S. G. Pallay: *Cross Index Title Guide to Opera and Operetta* (New York, 1989)
M. R. Griffel: *Operas in German: a Dictionary* (New York, 1990)
M. Hamilton: *A–Z of Opera* (New York, 1990)
F. Melisi: *Catalogo dei libretti per musica dell'ottocento (1800–1860)* (Lucca, 1990)
C. Sartori: *I libretti italiani a stampa dalle origini al 1800: catalogo analitico con 16 indici* (Cuneo, 1990–)
F. M. Stockdale and M. R. Dreyer: *The Opera Guide* (London, 1990)
J. P. Crouch: *The Opera Lover's Guide to Europe* (New York and Toronto, 1991)
R. H. Kornick: *Recent American Opera: a Production Guide* (New York, 1991)
A. Blyth: *Opera on CD* (London, 1992)
S. Sadie, ed.: *The New Grove Dictionary of Opera* (London, 1992)
J. Warrack and E. West, eds.: *The Oxford Dictionary of Opera* (Oxford, 1992)

NIGEL SIMEONE

Didelot, Charles-Louis (Frédéric) (*b* Stockholm, 1767; *d* Kiev, 7/19 Nov 1837). French choreographer. After studying in Stockholm and Paris, he travelled widely; Swift traced his dances in operas at Stockholm (1787), Bordeaux (1790) and Paris (1791, 1793), but his most extensive engagements were in London (1796–1801, 1812–14) and St Petersburg (1801–12, 1816–30). As a choreographer at the King's Theatre, Didelot was no doubt involved with opera – a repertory of continental masterpieces leavened by pasticcios and new works by resident composers. In Russia his work is traceable in state records, performance sources and personal accounts. Between 1806 and 1827 he created dances for 25 operas, mostly by French composers, including six by Boieldieu (who worked in St Petersburg, 1804–11), Spontini's *La vestale* and *Fernand Cortez* and works by Grétry, Isouard, Catel, Rodolphe Kreutzer and Auber. Didelot also choreographed operas by Mozart and Winter and five operas by the russified Italian Catterino Cavos. Of special interest is his conversion of Boieldieu's opera *Le calife de Bagdad* into a ballet; his pupil Adam Glushkovsky left a partial account of this adaptation.

*

Yu. Slonimsky: *Didlo: Vekhi tvorcheskoy biografii* [Didelot: Landmarks of a Creative Biography] (Leningrad and Moscow, 1958)
M. G. Swift: *A Loftier Flight: the Life and Accomplishments of Charles-Louis Didelot, Balletmaster* (Middletown, CT, 1974)
A. P. Glushkovsky: 'Recollections of the Great Choreographer Ch. L. Didelot and some Deliberations Concerning the Art of Dance', *A Century of Russian Ballet: Documents and Accounts, 1810–1910*, trans. R. J. Wiley (Oxford, 1990), 5–49

ROLAND JOHN WILEY

Diderot, Denis (*b* Langres, 5 Oct 1713; *d* Paris, 31 July 1784). French philosopher and critic, best known as principal editor of the *Encyclopédie* but also an in-

Denis Diderot, engraving by Van Loo

fluential writer on music. Born into a bourgeois family and educated by Jesuits, he was a writer of immense knowledge, energy and determination, who was imprisoned briefly for his philosophical views yet showed a spirit of tolerance that set him apart from most of his friends and colleagues. An intimate of Friedrich Grimm and, initially, of Jean-Jacques Rousseau (their views later diverged), he was at first a warm supporter of Rameau although, while remaining one of the few sane voices in the Querelle des Bouffons, he sided with the *coin de la reine* as a champion of Italian opera. As chief architect of the *Encyclopédie*, a task that occupied him for some 20 years, he had a strong impact on the musical thought of his own and subsequent times. Various theatrical 'reforms' of the mid-18th century followed his lead: his ideas on declamation, realism and gesture were known to Noverre, Algarotti, Jommelli, Traetta and Gluck among others.

Theatrical criticism is strewn throughout Diderot's voluminous writings on all subjects and in his fiction. His early satire, *Les bijoux indiscrets* (1748), contains a chapter on opera in which Lully ('Utmiutsol') is compared with Rameau ('Utremifasollasiututut'). The merits of both emerge although Diderot's preference is for Rameau, who is praised for his harmonic richness and fine sense of nuance in distinguishing between delicate shades of feeling. Diderot's later difficulties with Rameau were provoked by the composer's refusal to write the music articles in the *Encyclopédie*. These subsequently passed to Rousseau, whom Rameau viewed with hostility. In the early volumes Rameau is repeatedly cited as the supreme authority in musical matters; when the composer, enraged by the attacks on French music during the Querelle des Bouffons (by Grimm and Rousseau in particular), reacted to the 'errors' in the *Encyclopédie* by an attack on the whole enterprise, Diderot, as editor-in-chief, was forced to rebut. He did so in the preface to the sixth volume (1756) but restrained his pen out of deference and respect for the composer.

At about this time Diderot began to turn his attention to the theatre. Two plays, *Le fils naturel* (1757) and *Le père de famille* (1758), were inspired by a belief that the theatre should become more social and less aristocratic in its orientation; they led to the birth of the *drame bourgeois*, a literary genre that influenced the style and subject matter of the nascent *opéra comique* and eventually produced a musical equivalent, the *drame lyrique*. Each play was accompanied by an essay ('Entretiens sur Le fils naturel' and 'De la poésie dramatique' respectively); these ranged over the need for reform in every aspect of the theatre, especially the lyric theatre and, with Diderot's next essay *Le neveu de Rameau*, written shortly after 1760 (but not published until 'discovered' and translated by Goethe over 40 years later), represent the most coherent consideration of dramatic theory published in 18th-century France.

Drawing on innovations that had recently taken place on the English stage, particularly on the part of the celebrated actor David Garrick, Diderot's aim was to combat the lack of reality he perceived in French theatre. He criticized the 'déclamation maniérée, symétrisée et si éloignée de la vérité' that had been in vogue for many years ('De la poésie'). In *Le neveu* – presented as a dialogue between 'Le philosophe' and Rameau's disreputable nephew, a gifted but shallow performer of 'modern' (Italian) music – he advocated a more natural declamatory style where the melody was tailored closely to the accents of speech, imitating nature and speaking to the heart. He also argued for greater realism in the physical conduct of actors: 'C'est à l'acteur à convenir au rôle, et non pas au rôle à convenir à l'acteur' ('De la poésie'). Gesture, he believed, should play an important part in the dramatic development of a work, allowing the verbal element to be more frequently subordinated to the visual: the most effective way to communicate a message was to 'suggest it by means of a memorable image' (Kopp 1982). Allied to this was the idea that stage decorations and costumes should reflect the subjects they portrayed: 'ce qui montre surtout combien nous sommes encore loin du bon goût et de la vérité, c'est la pauvreté et la fausseté des décorations, et le luxe des habits' ('De la poésie').

Diderot's desire to create a more realistic type of drama closely coordinating visual, aural and literary aspects meant that works needed to be represented, not simply 'read', in order to come alive and reach as wide an audience as possible. In choosing to focus on characters drawn from the daily experience of his middle- and lower-class audiences rather than on stereotypes from the mythological or historical past, he was able to create effective outlets for the discussion of contemporary social, political and religious issues and, in this way, achieved another important objective in enlightening and educating the public he served. Most importantly, however, Diderot's reforms, which inspired many artists throughout Europe, radically altered the way in which stage works were conceived and represented since they called for a closer and more creative collaboration between composers, librettists and actors.

WRITINGS

(only those relating to opera included)

Edition: *Oeuvres complètes de Diderot*, ed. J. Assézat and M. Tourneux (Paris, 1875–7/R1966)

Les bijoux indiscrets (Paris, 1748)

Lettre sur les aveugles à l'usage de ceux qui voient (London, 1749)

Lettre sur les sourds et les muets à l'usage de ceux qui entendent et qui parlent (Paris, 1751)

Arrêt rendu à l'amphithéâtre de l'Opéra (Paris, 1753) [also attrib. d'Holbach]

Au petit prophète de Boehmischbroda [Grimm] (Paris, 1753) [also attrib. d'Holbach]

Les trois chapitres ou La nuit du mardi-gras au mercredi des cendres (Paris, 1753) [also attrib. d'Holbach]

Avertissement au Tome VI, Preface of the *Encyclopédie*, vi (Paris, 1756)

Le fils naturel, ou Les épreuves de la vertu (Paris, 1757) [incl. 'Entretiens sur Le fils naturel']

Le père de famille (Paris, 1758) [incl. 'De la poésie dramatique']

Le neveu de Rameau (MS, *c*1760, *US-NYpm*) [ed. J. Fabre, Geneva, 1950, 2/1963; Ger. trans., 1805; Eng. trans., 1965]

*

R. L. Evans: *Diderot et la musique* (diss., U. of Birmingham, 1932)

A. R. Oliver: *The Encyclopedists as Critics of Music* (New York, 1947)

J. Thomas: 'Diderot, les Encyclopédistes et le grand Rameau', *Revue de synthèse*, xxviii (1951), 46–67

R. Mortier: *Diderot en Allemagne* (Paris, 1954)

J. Doolittle: *Rameau's Nephew: a Study of Diderot's 'Second Satire'* (Paris, 1961)

H. G. Farmer: 'Diderot and Rameau', *MR*, xxii (1961), 181–8

D. Heartz: 'From Garrick to Gluck: the Reform of Theatre and Opera in the Mid-Eighteenth Century', *PRMA*, xciv (1967–8), 111–27

P. H. Lang: 'Diderot as Musician', *Diderot Studies*, x (1968), 95–107

S. Sacaluga: 'Diderot, Rousseau, et la querelle musicale de 1752: nouvelle mise au point', ibid, x (1968), 133–71

E. Fubini, ed.: *Gli illuministi e la musica* (Milan, 1969)

D. Heartz: 'Les lumières: Voltaire and Metastasio; Goldoni, Favart and Diderot', *IMSCR*, xii: *Berkeley 1977*, 233–8

——: 'Diderot et le Théâtre lyrique', *RdM*, lxiv (1978), 229–51

J. Kopp: *The Drame Lyrique: a Study in the Esthetics of Opéra-Comique, 1762–1791* (diss, U. of Pennsylvania, 1982)

E. Fubini: *Les philosophes et la musique* (Paris, 1983)

B. Didier: *La musique des lumières* (Paris, 1985)

DANIEL HEARTZ/ELISABETH COOK

Dido, Königin von Carthago ('Dido, Queen of Carthage'). *Singe-Spiel* in three acts by CHRISTOPH GRAUPNER to a libretto by HINRICH HINSCH; Hamburg, Theater am Gänsemarkt, spring 1707.

Dido, upbraided by Juno in a dream, fears that Aeneas will abandon her. Her sister Anna tries to cheer her up; she herself feigns indifference to the advances of Juba, Prince of Tyre. Meanwhile, Dido's confidante Iras tries in vain to move the cold heart of Achates, and the Numidian king Hiarbas [Iarbas] finds his love for Dido spurned now that Aeneas is on the scene. Secretly among her retinue, Iarbas orders a messenger to ask for her hand and, when refused, to announce hostilities. Dido calls for a sacrifice, and choice falls by lot on Iarbas himself, who accepts his fate. But a bolt of lightning halts the proceeding. Meanwhile, visitations from Mercury and Venus have induced Aeneas to leave for Italy, using the opportunity of a mock sea battle. Dido, stricken, mounts an altar to Hecate and falls on Aeneas's sword; Iras, seeing Achates flown as well, follows suit. Anna accepts her sister's crown and sceptre and gives her heart at last to Juba.

Although rife with subplots, the libretto is wholly serious, in line with recent trends in Italy. Graupner's opera, his first for Hamburg, mixes 29 German and 16 Italian arias with 12 ensembles. Dido, in contrast to the others, sings mostly in the minor mode.

THOMAS BAUMAN

Dido, Queen of Carthage. Mainpiece opera in three acts by STEPHEN STORACE to a libretto by PRINCE HOARE after PIETRO METASTASIO's *Didone abbandonata* (*see* DIDONE ABBANDONATA below); London, King's Theatre in the Haymarket, 23 May 1792.

When Storace's *Dido* was performed in 1792 it was the first full-length all-sung English opera to be produced in London for more than 20 years. It was also Storace's only serious opera. A complete libretto was published by the theatre for the première, but the music is lost. The work ran for only five performances and received much adverse criticism, most of it directed at the long recitatives and the total length of the opera. That the recitative was drastically shortened after the first night did not appease critics or audiences, who preferred spoken dialogue. *Dido* was produced by the Drury Lane company at the King's Theatre, to which it moved while its own theatre was being rebuilt. Storace may have been prompted to compose an all-sung opera because the King's Theatre had better acoustics for singing than for speech. He wrote the title role for the German soprano Gertrud Elisabeth Mara, and used two of his regular singers for the other main characters, Anna

Maria Crouch in the breeches role of Aeneas (soprano) and Michael Kelly as Iarbas (tenor).

The widow Dido (soprano) has built the city of Carthage on land bought from Iarbas, an African king. She has rejected his offer of marriage and is in love with Aeneas. The opera opens with Aeneas preparing to sail with his troops for Italy. Iarbas, disguised as his own ambassador, continues to try for Dido's hand in marriage and for Aeneas's death. Iarbas's assistant Abdalla (tenor), who has fallen in love with Dido's companion Anna (soprano), disapproves of his master's fraudulent approach and prevents him from killing Aeneas. Aeneas meanwhile is still determined to leave. Dido, realizing that she must either return Iarbas's love or sacrifice her life and realm, asks Aeneas to kill her. He refuses to do so and finally leaves for Italy. Iarbas attacks and sets fire to Carthage, and in despair Dido prepares to die. The opera ends with a masque entitled *Neptune's Prophecy*, in which Neptune (bass) and Venus (soprano) rise from the fire, call Aeneas and his son Ascanius (boy soprano) to their presence, and prophesy their futures. The masque appears to have been designed for the début of Thomas Welsh, a treble of remarkable prowess.

Although no music survives, it is known from the playbill that Storace both provided original music and adapted compositions by Salieri and others. The libretto shows that *Dido* consisted almost entirely of exit airs, with ensembles restricted to the three finales. The solos were meticulously apportioned between the main characters and carefully spaced according to the conventions of *opera seria*. Such a pattern was unlike what Storace's usual audience had come to expect, so it is not surprising that the work was a failure. Storace never again used recitative or an *opera seria* libretto for his English audience. JANE GIRDHAM

Dido and Aeneas. Tragic opera in three acts by HENRY PURCELL to a libretto by NAHUM TATE after the same poet's play *Brutus of Alba* and VIRGIL's *Aeneid*; first known performance at a girls' boarding school at Chelsea, before December 1689.

Dido *Queen of Carthage*	soprano
Belinda *her confidante*	soprano
Aeneas *a Trojan prince*	baritone
Sorceress	baritone/mezzo-soprano
Spirit *in form of Mercury*	alto
Sailor	soprano

Choruses of courtiers, witches, sailors and cupids

Setting Dido's palace at Carthage; a nearby cave; a grove; the quayside

The only known performance during Purcell's lifetime was at Chelsea, in a boarding school run by Josias Priest, a famous dancer and choreographer. This took place some time before December 1689, when Thomas D'Urfey's spoken epilogue was published in his collection of *New Poems*. Allusions in both the prologue and epilogue suggest that the première probably happened in springtime, but the year is uncertain. On stylistic grounds, the opera could have been composed by 1685 or perhaps even earlier.

Nahum Tate based the libretto on his five-act tragedy *Brutus of Alba, or The Enchanted Lovers* (1678), which he had originally called 'Dido and Aeneas', and various translations of the fourth book of Virgil's *Aeneid*. The libretto is highly condensed and elliptical; certain key events, such as the manner of Dido's death, are unspecified or (as in the case of the lovers' debauched night in the cave) discreetly glossed over.

The opera was obviously written in response to John Blow's *Venus and Adonis* (*c*1683), on which Tate and Purcell relied for broad structure (three-act tragedy with allegorical prologue, in imitation of *tragédie lyrique*) and details of dramatic form: both works use dance to articulate the story; in each the chorus plays several different roles (courtiers, huntsmen, cupids, witches, sailors etc.); and Purcell largely adopted Blow's style of arioso recitative and even alluded to his teacher's opera in Act 2 scene ii (the grove) where Aeneas displays a boar's head trophy impaled upon his spear (Adonis was killed by the Aedalian boar).

The early performance history of the two operas may have similar parallels. *Venus and Adonis* was composed for the private entertainment of Charles II and then adapted for the girls of Priest's school in April 1684, with the part of Adonis (originally a baritone) being transposed up an octave and sung by Priest's daughter. Following this pattern, *Dido and Aeneas* too may have been written for a court performance and later arranged for schoolgirls. This hypothesis would help explain several discrepancies between the libretto printed for the Chelsea amateur production ('perform'd by young gentlewomen') and the earliest surviving score, which includes a baritone Aeneas as well as countertenor, tenor and bass chorus parts which could hardly have been executed by Priest's young pupils. Furthermore, the fairly elaborate stage directions in the Chelsea libretto ('*Phoebus* Rises in the Chariot'; '*Venus* Descends in her Chariot'; '*Cupids* appear in the Clouds o'er [Dido's] Tomb') would probably have been unrealizable by a boarding school and may therefore relate to an earlier professional or court performance.

Allusions in the libretto itself offer several hints at the occasion for which *Dido and Aeneas* may have been composed, but none is sufficiently topical to be taken as hard evidence of one date or another. The prologue (the music of which is lost) seems to refer to the Glorious Revolution of 1688, with Phoebus and Venus representing William and Mary, the new political order; the Act 1 chorus 'When monarchs unite, how happy their state, / They triumph at once o'er their foes and their fate' would also appear to compliment the new king and queen. But the opera itself, in which the prince deserts his queen with tragic consequence, would have been offensive during any part of the reign of William and Mary. In a poem of about 1686 Tate himself alluded to James II as Aeneas, who is misled by the evil machinations of the Sorceress and her witches (representing Roman Catholicism, a common metaphor at the time) into abandoning Dido, who symbolizes the British people. The same symbolism may apply to the opera, but the poem brings us no closer to the date of the première.

The style of the music suggests a date closer to 1685 than to 1689. It is generally simpler than that of the music Purcell is known to have composed around 1690. (Of course, that could be taken as evidence that *Dido* was written for a school performance.) The airs are only moderately decorated; the choruses are brief and not developed contrapuntally; there is a heavy reliance on ground basses; and there are passages of peculiar voice spacing and modal part-writing. None of these

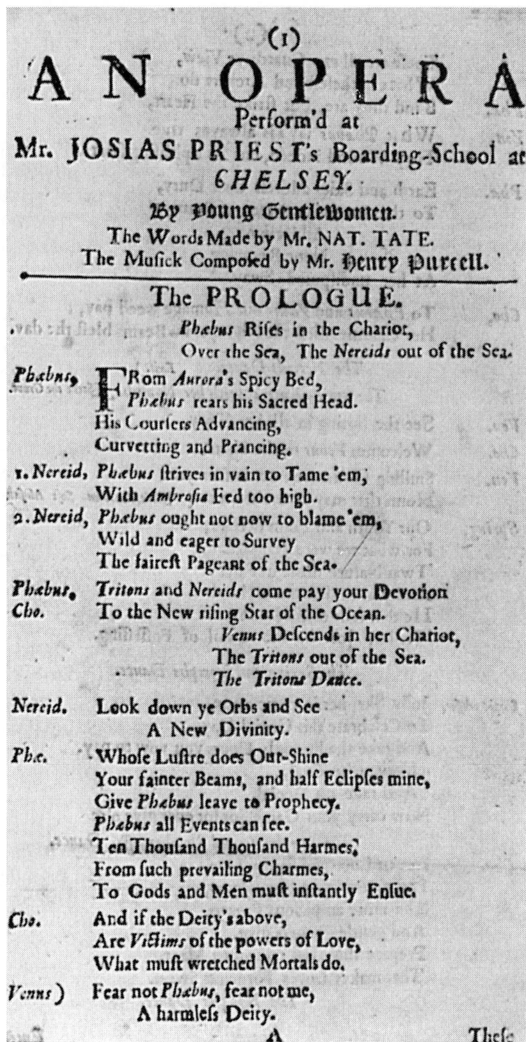

(1)

AN OPERA

Perform'd at

Mr. JOSIAS PRIEST's Boarding-School at

CHELSEY.

By Young Gentlewomen.

The Words Made by Mr. NAT. TATE.

The Musick Composed by Mr. Henry Purcell.

The PROLOGUE.

Phœbus Rises in the Chariot,
Over the Sea, The *Nereids* out of the Sea.

Phœbus, FRom *Aurora*'s Spicy Bed,
Phœbus rears his Sacred Head.
His Coursers Advancing,
Curvetting and Prancing.

1. *Nereid,* *Phœbus* strives in vain to Tame 'em,
With *Ambrosia* Fed too high.

2. *Nereid,* *Phœbus* ought not now to blame 'em,
Wild and eager to Survey
The fairest Pageant of the Sea.

Phœbus, *Tritons* and *Nereids* come pay your Devotion

Cho. To the New rising Star of the Ocean.

Venus Descends in her Chariot,
The *Tritons* out of the Sea.
The Tritons Dance.

Nereid. Look down ye Orbs and See
A New Divinity.

Phæ. Whose Lustre does Out-Shine
Your fainter Beams, and half Eclipses mine,
Give *Phœbus* leave to Prophecy.
Phœbus all Events can see.
Ten Thousand Thousand Harmes,
From such prevailing Charmes,
To Gods and Men must instantly Ensue.

Cho. And if the Deity's above,
Are *Victims* of the powers of Love,
What must wretched Mortals do.

Venus) Fear not *Phœbus*, fear not me,
A harmless Deity.

A These

Opening page of Nahum Tate's libretto for Purcell's 'Dido and Aeneas', printed for the performance by the girls of Josias Priest's boarding school, Chelsea (before December 1689)

characteristics are often found in Purcell's later music. But, because *Dido* is Purcell's only true opera, it is difficult to find suitable pieces with which to compare it, so the stylistic evidence too is inevitably inconclusive.

There is no other recorded performance of the opera during Purcell's lifetime and it seems to have attracted no contemporaneous comment, unless Dryden's remark of about 1695 – that the story of Aeneas at Carthage is too big a subject even for an opera – is a veiled criticism. The first piece from the opera to be published was Dido's aria 'Ah! Belinda' (in *Orpheus britannicus*, 1698), transposed up a tone from C to D minor. In 1700 the opera was incorporated into an adaptation of *Measure for Measure* given by Thomas Betterton's troupe at the theatre in Lincoln's Inn Fields. Apparently arranged by John Eccles (who wrote the act music for the play), the prologue was transformed into the finale and the second scene of Act 2 was enlarged. On this occasion, the Sorceress was sung by a Mr Wiltshire, a bass-baritone, who also impersonated the sailor at the beginning of Act 3. This casting may reflect Purcell's conception of the role of the Sorceress as a baritone, since on the Restoration stage witches and sorceresses were almost always acted by men. *Dido and Aeneas* was revived in 1704 in conjunction with other plays and then disappeared until being rediscovered in the late 18th century and adapted as a concert piece.

The earliest score (the Tenbury College manuscript now in the Bodleian Library) dates from after 1777 and differs from the Chelsea and 1700 *Measure for Measure* librettos in several important ways: the score lacks the prologue and the end of the second act; the acts and scenes are somewhat differently disposed, though the running order is the same as in the Chelsea libretto and that described below; the Sorceress is a mezzo-soprano; several dances, including the final Cupids' Dance, are omitted. This manuscript may have been copied from a score used for a performance after 1700 and is likely to be several stages removed from Purcell's lost autograph. Though unquestionably a masterpiece and one of the greatest of all musical tragedies, *Dido and Aeneas*, as it has come down to us, is a mutilated fragment of Purcell's original. There is no reason to believe, however, that the basic musical text lacks authority; the complex and subtle rhythms of the vocal lines, the frequent dissonances (especially false relations) and meticulous word underlay are all perfectly characteristic. Even the notation of the manuscript – time and key signatures, the use of accidentals etc. – is unmodernized and typical of late 17th-century practice.

ACT 1 *The palace* Dido, the widowed Queen of Carthage, has been entertaining Prince Aeneas after his escape from the sack of Troy. Though encouraged by her confidante Belinda and other courtiers, she is reluctant to express her love for Aeneas, but whether she hesitates out of respect for her late husband or duty to the State is not made clear by the libretto. Aeneas presses his suit and, after token resistance, Dido gives in, as her courtiers celebrate the prospect of a royal union. The exceptionally severe C minor overture is in the French style, except that the opening slow section is not repeated and leads without pause into a nervous canzona built on an obsessively oscillating motif of a 3rd. The act opens with Belinda's arietta 'Shake the cloud from off your brow', which is joined to the chorus 'Banish sorrow, banish care', in the same style but to different music. This pairing of air and chorus is the basic dramatic unit of the opera. The first substantial piece is Dido's aria, 'Ah! Belinda, I are press'd'. Built over a three-bar ground bass, it is actually a miniature da capo aria, complete with an opening declamatory passage (the aria proper begins at the third line 'Peace and I are strangers grown'), modulation to the minor dominant, reprise and orchestral postlude. The act continues swiftly in arioso with frequent choral interjections. The recitative, modelled on the declamatory airs of Henry Lawes, Matthew Locke and especially the very similar passages in Blow's *Venus and Adonis*, is characterized by plastic vocal lines invariably set in duple metre over bass lines which begin in long notes and then move on in measured crotchets and quavers. Significant words are highly decorated, but never so artificially that one loses sight of the human drama that the recitatives convey. With an unerring sense of pace and the need for contrast, Purcell punctuates the emotional exchanges with formal set pieces, such as 'Fear no danger to ensue', a carefree triple-metre duet and chorus in the French style. Aeneas's first appearance (in recitative) is brusque and perfunctory, the real conquest being conveyed by the exquisitely dissonant E minor chorus 'Cupid only throws the dart', the only piece in the first act which is not in the key of C minor or major. Dido's submission is unvoiced but, as Belinda remarks, 'her eyes confess the flame her tongue denies'. The act concludes with a rejoicing chorus, 'To the hills and the vales', and the Triumphing Dance, another ground.

ACT 2.i *The cave* In sharpest contrast to the formal, courtly rejoicing at the end of the first act, the second finds the Sorceress with her coven of witches (or 'enchantresses', as Tate called them), plotting Dido's death. Their hatred is without motive and unexplained, the Sorceress's malevolence replacing Aeneas's destiny as the engine of the impending tragedy. She is nevertheless an imposing character, who sings only in recitative accompanied by four-part strings, her evil utterances being answered by cackling acolytes in 'Ho, ho, ho!' choruses. When the Sorceress imagines the royal couple hunting, the strings flourish D major arpeggios which are both vivid and eerie. The Sorceress unfolds a plot: she will conjure a storm to ruin the hunt and drive the royal party back to Carthage; one of her witches will then appear to Aeneas in the shape of Mercury and command him to sail away. The scene continues with the noble (and therefore slightly incongruous) chorus 'In our deep vaulted cell', cast in the then popular form of a series of echoes; Purcell's original touch is to contrive false echoes which are altered in subtle and weird detail. The same is true of the much more boisterous Echo Dance of Furies which concludes the scene.

2.ii *The grove* In the only moment of repose in the taut drama, Dido and Aeneas are entertained after the hunt (and their first night together) by Belinda and the chorus in the languid 'Thanks to these lonesome vales', then by the Second Woman who sings another piece on a ground bass, 'Oft she visits this lone mountain'. The latter recounts the tale of Actaeon, who was killed by his own hounds – an ominous foreshadowing. The moment of tranquillity is shattered when Aeneas displays the head of the wild boar he has just killed and the Sorceress's storm breaks out. The courtiers are sent running for cover, singing the difficult contrapuntal chorus 'Haste, haste to town'. Left behind, Aeneas is confronted by the false Mercury, who orders him to sail that night. He responds in a recitative, 'Jove's commands shall be obey'd', his only substantial solo, in which he dreads having to break the news to Dido. While the recitative expresses true anguish, Aeneas remains the least developed of the main characters, a gullible, perfidious weakling, though Purcell manages to find some sympathy for his predicament. In the libretto the second scene of Act 2 concludes with a chorus and dance of witches gloating over their deception, though no music survives. The act thus ends abruptly and in a different key from that in which it began, which is unusual for Purcell.

ACT 3.i *The ships* In an ironic juxtaposition, Aeneas's men are preparing to set sail, having heard of his decision to leave even before Dido has been told. They will 'take a boozy short leave' of their nymphs as Aeneas has resolved to abandon his queen. Though the air and chorus 'Come away, fellow sailors' is a jolly sea shanty, it cynically presages the descending chromatic tetrachord through which Dido will later die. The Sorceress and the witches demonically celebrate the success of their plot in a series of ariettas, duets and a chorus ('Destruction's our delight, delight our greatest sorrow') in the same vein as before. The scene concludes with a freakish Witches' Dance, its piecemeal construction and rapid changes of mood being reminiscent of Jacobean antimasque dances: 'Jack of the Lanthorn leads the Spaniards out of their way among the Inchantresses'. The exact meaning of this choreography is unclear, but one should appreciate the balletic aspect of the opera, in which dance is used both to entertain and to advance the plot.

3.ii *The palace* The final meeting of Dido and Aeneas takes place in a remarkable recitative, 'Your counsel all is urg'd in vain', in which Dido mocks Aeneas's hollow protestations of fidelity and then dismisses him after the two have joined in a brief, bitter duet. But she realizes that 'death must come when he is gone', and time seems to ebb away during the deceptively brief chorus 'Great minds against themselves conspire'. The most famous piece in the opera, the lament 'When I am laid in earth', is built on a five-bar ground bass, a descending chromatic tetrachord, a cliché Purcell borrowed from contemporary Venetian opera. But with the soft, four-part string accompaniment, the miraculous avoidance of cadences in expected places, Dido's impassioned yet plaintive cries of 'Remember me' and the final ritornello during which she dies, Purcell achieved one of the great moments in opera, a tragic love-death, pathos without sentimentality. During the final chorus, 'With drooping wings', cupids appear in the clouds and scatter roses on Dido's tomb.

* * *

Tate's libretto has been criticized for extreme compression of the story, under-development of the character of Aeneas and poor poetry ('Our plot has took/The queen's forsook'). But the pace and concision of the drama are manifest and the short, irregular and sometimes unscanning lines (which Dryden advocated as being ideal for opera) obviously appealed to Purcell, whose flexible phrases always capture the meaning of the words and touch the passions. The reliance on Blow's *Venus and Adonis* should not be underestimated, for in that brilliantly original work Tate and Purcell found a model which they followed faithfully. But what distinguishes *Dido* from its predecessor is that *Venus and Adonis* has practically no arias, whereas in *Dido* the drama gravitates towards them – quite apart, that is, from the quality of the music and the human scale of the tragedy it conveys. CURTIS PRICE

Di Domenico, Gianpaolo. *See* DOMENICO, GIANPAOLO DI.

Didon **(i)** ('Dido'). *Tragédie en musique* in a prologue and five acts by HENRY DESMARETS to a libretto by LOUISE-GENEVIÈVE GILLOT, Dame de SAINTONGE; Paris, Opéra, 11 September (?5 June) 1693.

Dido (soprano), the widowed Queen of Carthage, about to marry Enée [Aeneas] (*haute-contre*), confides her doubts to her sister Anne (soprano). Jupiter promises to intervene on behalf of his son Iarbas (bass), rejected by Dido; Venus is equally vigilant over her son Aeneas. Dido persuades Aeneas to disobey the gods' command to leave, brought by Mercury; but in a storm, Mercury reappears and Aeneas finally decides he must go. Dido has his belongings burnt and, haunted by the reproaches of the ghost of her first husband, kills herself. Among the work's five major soliloquy scenes is one for Aeneas; in allowing us some insight into his dilemma,

Didon can be said to present a more rounded picture than Purcell's *Dido and Aeneas*. CAROLINE WOOD

Didon (ii) ('Dido'). *Tragédie lyrique* in three acts by Niccolò Piccinni (*see* PICCINNI family, (1)) to a libretto by JEAN FRANÇOIS MARMONTEL; Fontainebleau, 16 October 1783.

The sixth and most successful of the nine serious French operas that Piccinni wrote during his sojourn in Paris, *Didon* continued to be performed there until 1836 and received performances in French and German translation throughout Europe during the first quarter of the 19th century. It is based on Virgil's story of Dido, Queen of Carthage, and her love for the Trojan prince Aeneas. At the beginning of Act 1 Dido explains to Enée [Aeneas] (tenor) the external obstacle to their union: Iarbe [Iarbas] (bass), the neighbouring king, has threatened that Dido shall cease to reign unless she becomes his queen. Iarbas, disguised as one of his own subjects, repeats his conditions, adding that a Trojan king on Dido's throne is unacceptable. Dido remains firm, and, after she leaves, Aeneas and Iarbas (having revealed his identity) confront each other. The act ends with Iarbas fulminating. Act 2 begins with Aeneas revealing to Dido's sister Elise (soprano) that he must continue on to Italy and establish a new empire for his descendants. He sings an aria excusing his departure, 'Didon me sera toujours chère, mais je suis père, et je suis roi'. He asks Elise to tell the bad news to Dido, but she begs him at least to defend them from the wrath of Iarbas. When Dido and Aeneas meet again, she plans to announce their betrothal, before Iarbas invades. Guilt-ridden, Aeneas leaves. Iarbas tells Dido that Aeneas is a traitor, but she does not believe him. A ceremonial scene follows, after which Aeneas reveals his plans to Dido, with predictable results. The third act begins with a solo for Dido, in which she worries about Aeneas's safety as he battles with Iarbas. After a grand victory scene, Aeneas tells Dido that it is his destiny to leave. Dido, alternately grief-stricken and enraged, has a powerful effect upon Aeneas, who does not resolve to go until the ghost of his father Anchises appears and orders him to obey the gods' command. A storm ensues, in which there is general confusion, and Aeneas departs. Dido watches him from a distance; she arranges a pyre on which to burn his armour and other effects but climbs on to it herself. A chorus of priests of Pluto and female attendants of Dido swear eternal hatred towards Aeneas.

Mme de Saint-Huberty in the title role of Piccinni's 'Didon', which she created in Paris, 1783: engraving after Dutertre from 'Costumes et annales des grands théâtres de Paris' (1786)

Each act is constructed to include one major confrontation: in Act 1, the duet between Aeneas and Iarbas (1.v); in Act 2, the series of exchanges between Dido and Aeneas, culminating in the final number; and in Act 3, the scene between Dido and Aeneas that ends with her curse (3.iii). While the first two acts include ensembles for the principals, the last act, in which Iarbas is dead and Dido and Aeneas are concerned with their individual fates, has only solos and choruses. The scenes are continuous, on the whole moving from one number to the next compellingly and seamlessly. The most striking example of this is in the last number of Act 2, which begins as a duet for Dido and Aeneas, 'Tu sais si mon coeur est sensible', and with the addition of Elise becomes a trio, during which the lovers quarrel; the trio is then interrupted by the entrance of the chorus, announcing the invasion of Iarbas, shouting 'Aux armes'. This number mixes the French concept of continuity and the italianate finale.

Many of the arias are in *ABA* form, but other forms include the short modulating arias so beloved by the Piccinnistes (e.g. Dido's 'Nous allons la revoir, cette grotte charmante') and a two-part structure in which the second half makes reference to, but does not repeat, the material of the first (e.g. Aeneas's 'Je lui rends sa liberté'). Iarbas, whose basic position does not change in the course of the opera, sings in the most clearly defined forms; his 'O Jupiter ô mon père' at the end of Act 1, for example, is built on sonata-like lines but without development and with a coda.

Piccinni's musical style in this opera is quite varied. Heroic numbers such as Dido's 'Ni l'amante' and Iarbas's arias are similar to ones of comparable expressive content in contemporary Italian operas. (Dido's 'Ni l'amante', in which she promises to stand firm, begins with the same melodic figure as Fiordiligi's aria 'Come scoglio' in Mozart's *Così fan tutte*.) Other numbers have an almost Gluckian terseness (e.g. Dido's 'Ah qu'il vive') or a French melodic simplicity (e.g. Dido's 'Je veux si tel est mon malheur'). Diminished 7th chords and Neapolitan progressions are frequently used to underline the sentiment or the dramatic situation, and remote keys and unusual modulations are common. Although there are individual moments of great effectiveness, the opera succeeds through the tightness of its dramatic construction and its concentration on the central relationship between Dido and Aeneas.

MARY HUNTER

'Didone abbandonata', opening of Act 3 scene i from the 'Opere' of Pietro Metastasio (Venice: Zatta, 1781–3) with (left) an engraving of the final scene (DIDO: *'Fall, Carthage; let the royal palace burn, and its ashes shall be my tomb')*

DIDONE Atto III.
P. Ant.º Novelli inv.
G. Zuliani sc.
Precipiti Cartago,
Arda la Reggia e sia
Il cenere di lei la tomba mia.
DIDONE Scena Ult.

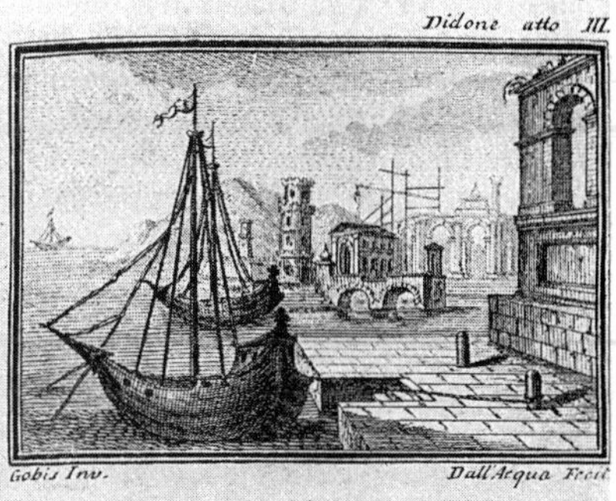

ATTO III.

SCENA PRIMA.

Porto di mare con navi per l'imbarco d'ENEA.

ENEA con ſeguito di Troiani.

Compagni invitti, a tollerare avvezzi
E del Cielo, e del mar gl'inſulti, e l'ire,
Deſtate il voſtro ardire,
Che per l'onda infedele
E' tempo già di riſpiegar le vele.
Andiamo, amici, andiamo.
Ai Troiani navigli

Fre-

Didone ('Dido'). Opera in a prologue and three acts by FRANCESCO CAVALLI to a libretto by GIOVANNI FRANCESCO BUSENELLO after VIRGIL's *Aeneid*; Venice, Teatro S Cassiano, 1641.

The second collaboration between Cavalli and Busenello, loosely based on Virgil's *Aeneid*, follows the escape of Enea [Aeneas] (tenor) from the burning Troy to Carthage, where he falls in love with and then abandons Dido (soprano), who, contrary to Virgil, accepts the hand of Iarba [Iarbas], King of the Getuli (alto), rather than death on the pyre. Act 1 of this rather uneven work contains some of the most powerfully dramatic recitative Cavalli ever wrote. Among the outstanding musico-dramatic numbers are two strophic laments (also in Act 1) of Cassandra (soprano) and her mother Ecuba [Hecuba] (mezzo-soprano), both based on variations of the descending tetrachord ostinato; three consecutive strophic arias, one for Dido and two for Iarbas, at the beginning of Act 2, in which Iarbas woos Dido, is rejected, and departs; a charming trio for three court ladies (sopranos), also in Act 2, in which they describe Aeneas's effect on Dido; a strophic aria for Anna (soprano), Dido's nurse, in which she encourages her mistress to yield to her feelings for Aeneas; Aeneas's beautiful, strophic lullaby-farewell recitative and aria sung to the sleeping Dido in Act 3 as he prepares to follow the command of Mercurio [Mercury] (alto) that he leave Carthage; and Dido's desperate recitative lament as she prepares to stab herself. Iarbas, who has gone mad with grief at being rejected by Dido, is cured in time to interrupt her suicide, and the two sing a final love duet. ELLEN ROSAND

Didone abbandonata ('Dido Abandoned'). Libretto by PIETRO METASTASIO, first set by Domenico Sarro (1724, Naples).

ACT 1 In spite of their mutual love, Enea [Aeneas] has resolved to separate from Dido, Queen of Carthage. Iarba [Iarbas], King of the Moors, arrives disguised as his own minister, Arbace [Arbaces], to offer peace on behalf of his king in return for Dido's hand and the life of Aeneas. His offer rejected, Iarbas instructs his confidant, Araspe [Araspes], to kill Aeneas; Araspes refuses, but is arrested along with Iarbas when the latter makes a thwarted attempt himself. Iarbas reveals his identity and departs under escort. Aeneas tells Dido of his intention to leave, but falters when she accuses him of treachery and ingratitude.

ACT 2 Araspes, now released, declares his love for Selene, Dido's sister – who, herself in love with Aeneas, rejects him. Meanwhile, Aeneas gains a pardon from Dido for Iarbas, unaware that the king has already been set free by Osmide [Osmidas], a confidant of Dido who has offered his services to the Moorish king in the hope of gaining Dido's throne. Dido pretends to accept the offer of marriage from Iarbas; Aeneas's jealous anger reassures her of his love, and with renewed hopes of detaining him she again spurns Iarbas.

ACT 3 Aeneas is preparing to depart when Iarbas challenges him to a duel. Fighting breaks out between Trojans and Moors but subsides when Aeneas, the victor, spares the life of his challenger. Selene, in a final attempt to hold Aeneas, confesses her love for him, but to no avail. The Trojan fleet sets sail. Araspes announces that the Moors have set fire to the city, but Dido still spurns the offer of Iarbas even as the flames engulf her palace. She now learns of Osmidas's treachery and her sister's secret love for Aeneas. With life and empire in ruins, she hurls herself into the flames.

* * *

Didone abbandonata, Metastasio's first original drama and the work that launched his career, was written under the guiding hand of Maria Anna Benti (La Romanina), the celebrated singer-actress who created the role of Dido and who was partnered at the time by Nicolini, the equally famous castrato who had been Handel's first Rinaldo. The plot is drawn from Virgil's *Aeneid* (book 4) and Ovid's *Phastus* (book 3), and the popularity of the subject for both spoken and musical drama provided several works that Metastasio may have used as models. Possibilities from among the spoken dramas include George de Scudéry's *Didon* (1635) and Antoine-Jacob de Montfleury's tragedy, *L'ambigu comique, ou Les amours de Didon et d'Aenée* (1673); possible librettos range from G. F. Busenello's *La Didone* (1641) to Louise-Geneviève Gillot Saintonge's *Didon* (1693). *Didone abbandonata* ranks among Metastasio's six most popular dramas, with settings stretching from 1724 well into the 19th century. Vinci (1726, Rome) was particularly praised for his rendition of Dido's defiance of Iarbas ('Son regina', 1.v) and Jommelli for his portrayal of the final catastrophe (1747, Rome). This conclusion, which contains the aria 'Vado ... ma dove?', was altered by Francesco Algarotti for Hasse (1742, Hubertusburg) since the stage could not accommodate the final burning of Carthage. In this version, Dido leaves the action after a new aria, 'Ombra cara', inserted three scenes from the end. It is likely that, as from the Dresden performance (1743), Hasse's opera was performed with both 'Ombra cara' and the original ending. Other successful settings include Schiassi's for Bologna (1735) and Joseph Schuster's for Naples (1776), his first serious Italian opera and a work significant to the establishment of his popularity in Italy. In 1751 Metastasio sent a shortened version of *Didone abbandonata* to Farinelli in Madrid, where the supervision of theatre performances was one of his many tasks.

For a list of settings *see* METASTASIO, PIETRO. DON NEVILLE

Didone abbandonata (i) ('Dido Abandoned'). *Dramma per musica* in three acts by LEONARDO VINCI to a libretto by PIETRO METASTASIO (*see* DIDONE ABBANDONATA above); Rome, Teatro delle Dame, 14 January 1726.

The innovatory tragic finale of Metastasio's version of the story was probably based on similar finales in Antonio Salvi's *Arsace* and Piovene's *Tamerlano*. The libretto was revised by Metastasio specifically for Vinci, the revisions conditioned by the demands of the composer, the singers and the Roman audience.

Because only a month separated the production of Vinci's *Didone abbandonata* from, on one side, his *Astianatte* (Naples, December 1725) and, on the other, *Siroe re di Persia* (Venice, February 1726), there was some compositional overlap. Vinci appears to have composed the arias up to Act 2.i at some time in 1725, using the original libretto. However, interrupted by the composition and production of *Astianatte*, work on *Didone abbandonata* did not resume until December, when Vinci arrived in Rome and began collaborating with Metastasio. The poet wrote several parody texts for Acts 2 and 3, allowing Vinci to incorporate arias he had already composed for *Ifigenia in Tauride*, *Astianatte* and even the still unperformed *Siroe*. The success of their first collaboration is attested by the Jesuit priest and historian Cordara, who reported that 'every scene produced one continued applause', and that the response to 'the spirited air, "Son regina" ... seemed to shake the theatre to its foundation'. Algarotti later hailed Dido's death scene as a model for dramatic declamation, asserting that 'Virgil himself would be pleased to hear a composition so animating and so terrible'. *Didone abbandonata*, along with *Siroe*, represents the first important manifestation of the early Classical style in Vinci's works. Handel not only produced a pasticcio version but borrowed several themes, a fact that did not go unnoticed by Jennens, who provided him with the Vinci score. KURT MARKSTROM

Didone abbandonata (ii) ('Dido Abandoned'). *Dramma per musica* in three acts by GIUSEPPE SARTI to a libretto by PIETRO METASTASIO (*see* DIDONE ABBANDONATA above); Copenhagen, Theatre on Kongens Nytorv, winter 1762.

Sarti's 13th opera for the Danish court closely follows Metastasio's libretto of 1724. While some 18th-century composers cut the libretto of *Didone abbandonata* extensively, reducing the importance of some secondary characters, Sarti retained Metastasio's rich characterizations for the roles of Dido (soprano), Selene (soprano), Enea [Aeneas] (soprano), Iarba [Iarbas] (tenor), Osmida [Osmidas] (tenor) and Araspe [Araspes] (bass). Most of the aria texts are set as da capo; only in Dido's arias, as if to distinguish the title role from the rest, did Sarti make a sustained effort to break away from the da capo mould. The most remarkable of Dido's arias, 'Non ha ragione, ingrato', near the end of Act 1, vividly reflects Dido's conflicting feelings of anger and love through its succession of tempos (fast–slow–fast–slow–fast), and through its melody in G minor in which obsessive dwelling on E♭ makes the chromatic pitches C♯ and B♮ all the more poignant. Aeneas's Act 1 aria 'Quando saprai chi sono' is typical of the prevailing aria structure and melodic style of the opera. It is a da capo aria (labelled 'dal segno') whose vocal line opens with three two-bar phrases, the third of which repeats the words of the second, answering it tonally. This kind of phrasing (*abb'*) is typical of such Neapolitan composers as Pergolesi and Vinci, who were among the first to set Metastasio's early librettos in the 1720s and 30s. By repeatedly adopting the style for this libretto in particular, Sarti placed himself in the Neapolitan tradition of serious opera. He set *Didone abbandonata* to music again later in his career (June 1782, Padua), shortly after the première of his most successful opera, *Giulio Sabino*. JOHN A. RICE

Didur, Adam [Adamo] (*b* Wola Sekowa, nr Sanok, 24 Dec 1874; *d* Katowice, 7 Jan 1946). Polish bass. He studied in Lwów with Wysocki and in Milan with Emmerich. He made his début in 1894 in Rio de Janeiro, and sang at the Warsaw Opera, 1899–1903. After appearances in Spain he sang at La Scala (1904–6), and in Russia (1909). In 1905 he made his Covent Garden début as Colline in *La bohème*, returning in 1914 to sing Baron Archibaldo in the British première of Montemezzi's *L'amore dei tre re*. Having made his American début in 1907 at the Manhattan Opera House as Alvise Badoero (*La Gioconda*), he joined the Metropolitan Opera, where he was engaged for 25 seasons; he made his début there in 1908 as Ramfis, and sang Mozart's Figaro and Count Almaviva as well as Boris (1913), Baron Archibaldo (1915), Galitsky and Konchak in *Prince Igor* (1915), all American premières. His voice had a black timbre of a certain biting quality and he was a splendid actor. After retiring he returned to Poland.

*

L. de Noskowski: 'Adamo Didur', *Record Collector*, xvi (1964–6), 4–23 [with discography by J. Dennis]

LEO RIEMENS, ELIZABETH FORBES

Dieter, Christian Ludwig (*b* Ludwigsburg, 13 June 1757; *d* Stuttgart, 15 May 1822). German composer. He was educated at the military academy of the Duke of Württemberg, which bound him to serve at the ducal court for the rest of his life. As well as receiving a thorough general education, he studied composition with Antonio Boroni and Agostino Poli, both Kapellmeister to Duke Carl Eugen. *Der Schulze im Dorfe* (1779), his first German opera, enjoyed great local popularity, as did most of his later ones, despite his patron's pronounced preference for Italian opera. (Dieter's setting of Bretzner's original *Belmont und Constanze*, for example, was said to have been responsible for the very late arrival of Mozart's *Die Entführung aus dem Serail* on the Stuttgart stage, in 1795.) Until 1789 Dieter set mainly works by the most successful north German librettists and local imitators. He left the texts unaltered, but he bent the musical practices of Hiller, Wolf and André to local taste by supplementing lieder in popular style with large-scale arias, written in the tradition of Jommelli, and more colourful orchestration. His facility, however, lay in comic situations rather than the elevated style at which his compatriot Zumsteeg excelled.

In 1789 Dieter, like many other German composers, abandoned northern texts and turned to works conceived in the spirit of the Viennese popular theatre, which allowed greater scope for comic and broadly farcical scenes. His reputation as a composer remained a local though an abiding one: in 1802 Stuttgart audiences still looked forward eagerly to the last of his dozen operas, *Des Teufels Lustschloss*.

See also BELMONT UND CONSTANZE (ii).

all first performed at Stuttgart by the Herzogliche Nationale Schaubühne and, unless otherwise stated, in the Kleines Theater an der Planie

Der Schulze im Dorfe, oder Der verliebte Herr Doctor (komische Oper, 3, G. E. Heermann), Ducal, 10 May 1779
Der Irrwisch, oder Endlich fand er sie (Spl, 3, C. F. Bretzner), 27 Nov 1779, *D-DS*
Laura Rosetti (Schauspiel mit Gesang, 3, B. C. d'Arien), 9 Feb 1781
Belmont und Constanze, oder Die Entführung aus dem Serail (komische Oper, 3, Bretzner), 27 Aug 1784, *SWl* (2 copies)
Der Rekruten-Aushub, oder Die Familien-Heirath (Operette, 2), 1785
Die Dorfdeputirten (komische Oper, 2, Heermann, after C. Goldoni: *Il feudatorio*), Oct 1786
Das Freyschiessen, oder Das glükliche Bauernmädchen (Operette, 2, J. A. Weppen), 31 Aug 1787
Glücklich zusammengelogen (Spl), 1787/8
Der Luftballon (Spl, E. Schikaneder), 1789
Der Eremit auf Formentara (Spl, 2, A. von Kotzebue), 10 Jan 1791
Elisinde (komische Oper, 3, C. A. Vulpius), 1794
Des Teufels Lustschloss (Spl, 2, Kotzebue), 1802

*

H. Abert: 'Die dramatische Musik', *Herzog Karl Eugen von Württemberg und seine Zeit* (Esslingen, 1905), 588–98
W. Preibisch: 'Quellenstudien zu Mozarts *Entführung aus dem Serail*', *SIMG*, x (1908–9), 430–76
K. Haering: 'Christian Ludwig Dieter: Hofmusiker und Singspielkomponist, 1757 bis 1822', *Schwäbische Lebensbilder*, i (1940), 98–104

THOMAS BAUMAN

Dietsch [Dietch, Dietzch, Dietz], **(Pierre-)Louis (-Philippe)** (*b* Dijon, 17 March 1808; *d* Paris, 20 Feb 1865). French composer. According to Fétis, he was a choirboy at Dijon Cathedral and from 1822 a pupil at Choron's Institution Royale de Musique Classique et Religieuse in Paris. In 1830 he entered the Conservatoire, studying with Reicha. He was active in Parisian churches and orchestras and in 1840 became chorus master at the Opéra on Rossini's recommendation. He taught at the Ecole Niedermeyer (Choron's Institution revived) after 1853 until his death. He succeeded Girard as conductor at the Opéra in 1860 but left after three years when he (or an orchestra member) had a disagreement with Verdi during a rehearsal of *Les vêpres siciliennes*.

Dietsch's opera *Le vaisseau fantôme, ou Le maudit des mers* (2, P. Foucher and H. Révoil; *F-Po*) was first performed on 9 November 1842 at the Opéra. Wagner's assumption that Foucher and Révoil based their libretto on his scenario for *Der fliegende Holländer* (recently sold to the Opéra) has gained common currency. In fact, *Le vaisseau fantôme* bears only a passing resemblance to the *Höllander*, and was based on a variety of sources including Captain Marryat's *The Phantom Ship* and Scott's *The Pirate*. In 1861 Dietsch conducted the infamous Paris première of *Tannhäuser*, provoking Wagner's wrath through his incompetence and unwillingness to accept help.

Dietsch's compositions, mostly sacred works, are well constructed but conservative and unimaginative. Berlioz found *Le vaisseau fantôme* excessively solemn; other reviewers considered it an admirable achievement, though somewhat academic. The work was criticized for its two-act structure, thought to be inadequate for so portentous a subject. Dietsch may have written a ballet for a performance of Weber's *Der Freischütz* in 1841.

*

MGG (E. Haraszti)
L. Escudier: 'L'orchestre de l'Opéra', *Art musical*, iii (1863), 271–2
G. Servières: *Tannhäuser à l'Opéra en 1861* (Paris, 1895)
E. Newman: *The Life of Richard Wagner*, iii (London, 1945)
E. Haraszti: 'Pierre-Louis Dietsch und seine Oper', *Mf*, viii (1955), 39–58
G. Leprince: '*The Flying Dutchman* in the Setting by Philippe Dietch', *MQ*, l (1964), 307–20
B. Millington: '"The Flying Dutchman", "Le vaisseau fantôme" and other Nautical Yarns', *MT*, cxxvii (1986), 131–5

JEFFREY COOPER, BARRY MILLINGTON

Di Gatti, Theobaldo. *See* GATTI, THEOBALDO DI.

Di Giacomo, Salvatore (*b* Naples, 12 March 1860; *d* Naples, 5 April 1934). Italian poet, novelist, playwright, writer on music and theatre historian. In 1880 he gave up studying medicine to become a journalist. Besides his work as director of the Lucchesi Theatre library in Naples he was also artistic director of the Collezione Settecentesca, published by Sandron of Palermo. In 1929 he was awarded the title Accademico d'Italia.

In his musical research Di Giacomo concentrated on opera and particularly on musical life in Naples from the 16th century to the 18th; his book on the four Neapolitan conservatories (1924–8) remains a standard reference work, and many of his articles on opera were reprinted in a collected edition of 1946. His literary writings, admired by Croce, are characterized by vivid realism and spontaneity of expression; they chiefly depict small-scale but highly emotional situations. Those that provided inspiration for musical settings (for several of which he wrote the librettos himself) include various collections of poems and the dramas *Malavita* (in collaboration with G. Cognetti, from the novella *Il voto*, 1889), *A San Francisco* (from a short poem of the same title, 1896), *Assunta Spina* (1909) and *Quand l'amour meurt* (1911).

La fiera, N. D'Arienzo, 1887; *Malavita* (with G. Cognetti), Giordano, 1892; *A San Francisco*, C. Sebastiani, 1896 (J. Napoli, 1982); *L'abate*, W. Borg, 1898; *Giorgetta la merciaia*, M. Forte, 1903; *'O mese mariano*, Giordano, 1910; *Rosaura rapita*, V. Valente, 1910; *'O munasterio*, P. H. Allen, 1913; *Zi' Munacella*, G. Pietri, 1934, as Maristella

*

B. Croce: 'Note sulla letteratura italiana, vi: Salvatore Di Giacomo', *La critica* [Bari], i (1903), 401–25, 438–41
K. Vossler: *Salvatore Di Giacomo: ein neapolitanischer Volksdichter in Wort, Bild und Musik* (Heidelberg, 1908)
G. A. Borgese: 'Il teatro di Salvatore Di Giacomo', *La vita e il libro*, i (Turin, 1910, 2/1923), 119–24
H. Bacaloglu: *Naples et son plus grand poète* (Naples, 1911)
L. Russo: *Salvatore Di Giacomo* (Naples, 1921, repr. 1945)
B. Croce: *Letteratura della Nuova Italia* (Bari, 3/1929), 73
F. T. Marinetti: *L'originalità napoletana del poeta Salvatore Di Giacomo* (Naples, 1936)
A. Bellucci: *Un furto digiacomiano nell'Archivio dei Girolamini* (Naples, 1956)
U. Prota Giurleo: *Ricordi digiacomiani* (Naples, 1956)

FERRUCCIO TAMMARO

Di Giovanni, Edoardo. *See* JOHNSON, EDWARD.

Dignum, Charles (*b* Rotherhithe, *c*1765; *d* London, 29 March 1827). English tenor and composer. As a boy he sang in a Roman Catholic chapel and was taught by Samuel Webbe and then Thomas Linley (i). He made a successful début as Thomas in the pasticcio *Love in a Village* at Drury Lane in 1784 and remained there, singing in many English stage works, until his retirement in 1812. His short, plump figure and abundant good nature fitted him for roles such as Tom Tug in Dibdin's *The Waterman* and Crop in Storace's *No Song No Supper*. Dignum wrote tunes for sentimental and patriotic ballads which were published with accompaniments by his composer friends. He was a leading oratorio soloist, singing in the first English performance of Haydn's *Creation* (1800).

*

BDA; *DNB* (W. B. Squire); *LS*
J. Roach: *Authentic Memoirs of the Green Room* (London, 1796)
'Mr. Charles Dignum', *European Magazine*, xxxiv/Dec (1798), 363–4
C. H. Wilson: *The Myrtle and Vine* (London, 1802)
T. Gilliland: *Dramatic Mirror*, ii (London, 1808)
J. Boaden: *Memoirs of the Life of John Philip Kemble*, i (London, 1825)
J. Sainsbury, ed.: *A Dictionary of Musicians* (London, 2/1825)

OLIVE BALDWIN, THELMA WILSON

Dijon. City in eastern France, historically the principal city of Burgundy. After witnessing operatic productions by touring companies during the late 17th century, in 1717 the town council bought one of the local gaming-houses, the 'tripot de Barres', and turned it into the first local theatre, in which opera was on the bill. By 1809 the council had adopted the plans of a local architect, Jacques Cellerier, to build the current Grand Théâtre (cap. *c*1000) next to the old palace of the dukes of Burgundy (today the Préfecture). The foundation stone was laid in 1810, but owing to the political situation the work was not completed until 1828. Inspired by the Greek Antique style in vogue at the time, with its façade peristyle of Corinthian columns and its interior decoration by Moench in blue, white and gold, it is a fine example of its period. Here audiences heard the standard operatic repertory during the 19th century and, in 1907, a production of Rameau's *Dardanus* directed by d'Indy. The opera company is now the last in France to be run by an impresario (from 1974 the bass Pierre Filippi) under the concession system, with a municipal subsidy. It is one of the most hardworking of the French opera houses. The season runs from October to April, when productions of seven or eight operas are each given two performances (Friday evenings and Sunday matinée), together with productions of as many operettas, performed more frequently.

*

L. de Gouvenain: *Le théâtre à Dijon, 1422–1790* (Dijon, 1888)
L. Vallas: '*Dardanus* à Dijon', *Revue musicale de Lyon*, v (1907), 297
A. Cornerau: 'La première salle de spectacles de Dijon', *Mémoires de l'Académie des sciences, arts et belles-lettres de Dijon* (1923), 289–304

CHARLES PITT

Di Lelio, Umberto (*b* 1894; *d* Milan, 1946). Italian bass. After appearing at various Italian theatres, including the Teatro Massimo, Palermo (1920), he was engaged at La Scala, where he made his début in 1922 as Klingsor and continued to sing until 1941. He created Hever in *Dèbora e Jaéle* (1922) and sang a wide variety of roles, including Sparafucile, Varlaam (*Boris Godunov*), Stromminger (*La Wally*), Pistol, Baron Ochs, Dukas' Bluebeard, the Wanderer (*Siegfried*), Sulpice (*La fille du régiment*), Mozart's Count Almaviva, Galitsky (*Prince Igor*) and Tsar Saltan (1929) in the Italian première of Rimsky-Korsakov's opera. He sang Count Robinson in *Il matrimonio segreto* at Salzburg (1931), took part in the Italian première of *Arabella* at Genoa (1936) and sang Don Pasquale and Ramfis at Covent Garden (1937). Though best known for *buffo* roles, such as Rossini's Don Basilio, he was equally impressive as a Wagnerian.

ELIZABETH FORBES

Dimitrescu, Constantin (*b* Blejoi, Prahova district, 19 March 1847; *d* Bucharest, 9 May 1928). Romanian composer and conductor. He studied music at the conservatory in Bucharest (1864–6) and then in Vienna (1867–9) and Paris (1870) before working as a cello teacher at the conservatory in Bucharest and as cellist and conductor of the Bucharest PO (1870–1916). From 1893 to 1900 he conducted the National Theatre orchestra in Bucharest. As a composer he was prominent in the field of musical fairy-tale and national operetta; he achieved his greatest success in the musical theatre with the comic opera *Nini* (1897). He also wrote music for plays by Victorien Sardou, Molière, François Coppée, Shakespeare, Ibsen, V. Alecsandri, B. P. Haşdeu and others.

unperformed unless otherwise stated

Patru săbii [Four Swords], 1883
Sergentul Cartuş [Sergeant Cartridge], 1883 (operetta, 2, I. Apostolini)
Renegatu [The Renegade] (M. Dimitriade), 1886 (Bucharest, 1893)
Sanda (comic op, 2), 1886
Ali Baba inţara minunilor [Ali Baba's Dream], 1894
Nini (comic op, 3, D. Ionescu-Zane), Bucharest, National, 20 Feb 1898
Sînziana şi Pepelea [Sinziana and Pepelea], 1899 (musical fairy play, 5, V. Alecsandri)

*

T. Moisescu and M. Păun: *Opereta: ghid* [Operetta: Guide] (Bucharest, 1969)

E. Dolinescu: *Compozitorul Constantin Dimitrescu* [The Composer Constantin Dimitrescu] (Bucharest, 1977) VIOREL COSMA

Dimitrescu, Giovanni [Ioan] (*b* Iaşi, 30 Dec 1860; *d* Hove, 4 March 1913). Romanian tenor. He studied at the conservatory in Iaşi and at the conservatory in Bucharest with George Stephănescu. He built up a wide repertory at the Romanian Opera House in Bucharest and the National Theatre in Iaşi in such operas as *Otello*, *Aida*, *Un ballo in maschera*, *Rigoletto*, *Pagliacci*, *Margherita d'Anjou*, *Les Huguenots*, *Tannhäuser* and *La Juive* and later toured widely. Primarily a dramatic tenor with a metallic, penetrating timbre, a phenomenal range and perfect technique (he was once described as having 'two larynxes'; *Il piccolo*, 1899), he also sang lyrical roles with a rare purity of sound. He was a peerless interpreter of Meyerbeer's operas. In 1913, exhausted by mental and physical pressures induced by 120 performances in a single year, he committed suicide.

*

Revista teatrale melodramatico [Milan] (21 March 1910) VIOREL COSMA

Dimitrij. Grand opera in four acts by ANTONÍN DVOŘÁK to a libretto by MARIE ČERVINKOVÁ-RIEGROVÁ; Prague, New Czech Theatre, 8 October 1882 (revised version, Prague, National Theatre, 7 November 1894).

Jov *the patriarch of Moscow*	bass
Prince Vasilij Šujský	baritone
Petr Fedorovič Basmanov *leader of the tsar's army*	bass
Xenie Borisovna *daughter of Boris Godunov*	soprano
Dimitrij Ivanovič	tenor
Marfa Ivanovna *his supposed mother, widow of Ivan the Terrible*	contralto
Marina Mníškova *wife of Dimitrij*	soprano
Něborský } *soldiers from the Polish retinue*	baritone
Bučinský }	baritone

People of Moscow, Boyars, princes, Polish retinue, soldiers, dancers, attendants

Setting Moscow in the years 1605 and 1606

Marie Červinková-Riegrová originally wrote the libretto of *Dimitrij* (completed in December 1880) for Karel Šebor. After the failure of Šebor's setting of her first libretto, *Zmařená svatba* ('The Frustrated Wedding'), in 1879 and his procrastination over setting the second, *Dimitrij*, Červinková-Riegrová (at the prompting of her father František Rieger) offered it to Dvořák.

The plot is constructed as a four-act grand opera in the manner of Scribe and is based on Ferdinand Mikovec's *Dimitr Ivanovič*, an adaptation of Schiller's incomplete *Demetrius*, with additional material from Ostrovsky's *Dimitrij Samozvanec and Vasilij Šujskij*. Dvořák began work on the sketch on 8 May 1881 and completed the full score on 5 September 1882. The overture was written between 5 and 23 September 1882. During the composition Dvořák requested more ensembles from his librettist.

The première was a great success, but in 1883, at Hanslick's suggestion, Dvořák persuaded Červinková-Riegrová to alter Act 4 scene iv in order to remove the assassination of Xenie. This was followed by further slight revisions in 1885 before publication. The revised version of the opera was given at the National Theatre in Prague on 28 November 1885.

A much more radical musical revision of the work was prompted by a performance in Vienna on 2 June 1892, during a National Theatre tour, when *Dimitrij* did not enjoy the success of the Smetana operas presented there. Influenced in some measure by the ardent Wagnerian Anton Seidl, Dvořák reworked the opera partly on Wagnerian lines and attempted to introduce greater realism. This recomposition took place between 28 March and 31 July 1894 in New York, and early in 1895 in Prague. The new version was performed at the National Theatre in Prague on 7 November 1894. There is no evidence that Dvořák disliked the new version, but the publication in 1912 of the vocal score edited by Kovařovic, mostly based on the 1885 version, suggests that the earlier *Dimitrij* was widely preferred. The British première of *Dimitrij*, largely based on the 1885 version and in a translation by John Tyrrell, was given by Nottingham University on 30 January 1979.

While the more severe commentators, notably Zdeněk Nejedlý, were inclined to condemn the retrospective qualities of *Dimitrij*, the opera was an undeniable success in Dvořák's lifetime. In its earlier forms, *Dimitrij* was valued principally for the set pieces in each act and its remarkable lyricism.

The synopsis that follows is that of the 1885 and 1894 versions.

ACT 1 *A square in Moscow, in front of the Kremlin* Immediately after the death of Boris Godunov, the Polish army led by Dimitrij, the supposed son of Ivan the Terrible and pretender to the crown of Russia, is advancing on Moscow. The fear and uncertainty of the people are expressed in a fine double chorus (reduced to a single chorus in the final version). Jov, the patriarch, announces that the Boyars will support Xenie and Fedor, the children of Boris. At this proclamation Basmanov reveals that the army has turned to Dimitrij who even now comes to greet his mother Marfa, the widow of Ivan the Terrible. Šujský laments the fate of Russia and offers refuge to Xenie, who is fleeing from the crowd that has just murdered her brother Fedor. The army arrives and Dimitrij greets the Kremlin. His sincerity wins over the doubtful Marfa. Although she knows he is not her son, she is impressed by him and sees the chance of revenge on her old enemies. She acknowledges him publicly and Dimitrij enters the Kremlin to general rejoicing. The action of this first act, moving in clear stages towards the climax, is matched by equally clear musical gestures. Solo statements are lyrical and broadly developed, and important exchanges are set to traditionally conceived accompanied recitative. The opening chorus, march and stretta conclusion have enormous cumulative power.

ACT 2 *Inside the Kremlin* Dimitrij celebrates his wedding to Marina, a member of the Polish princely family, the Sandomírský, and asks her to take Russian nationality. Marina refuses and Dimitrij leaves. At a ball Marina encourages the Polish faction in a choral ballet characterized by mazurka rhythms, set partly to themes taken from Dvořák's first Slavonic dance (op.46). The Russians lament their fate and a quarrel ensues; at the height of it Dimitrij appears and quells the riot.

The vault of the tsars Dimitrij is alone on stage. Xenie, fleeing from the Poles, laments her fate. She is molested by two Polish retainers. Dimitrij drives them away and in an extended duet confesses his love

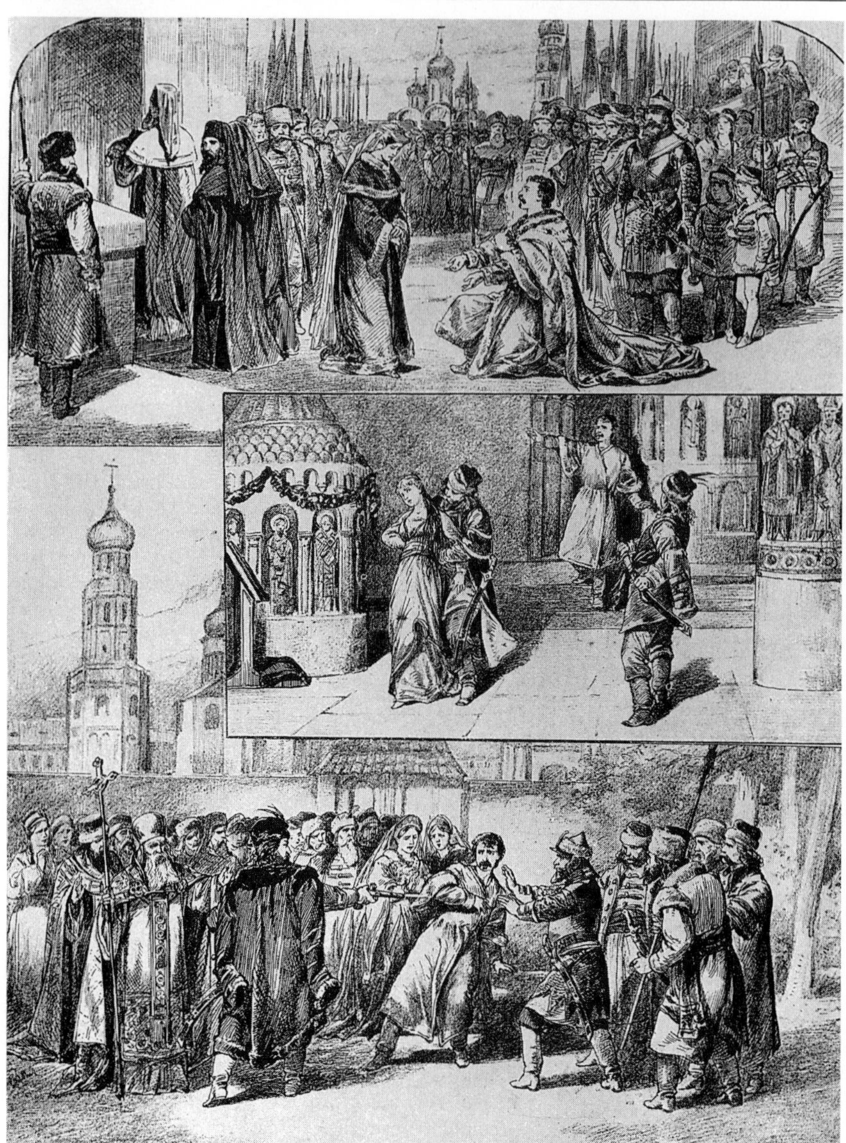

'Dimitrij' (Dvořák): scenes from the original production at the New Czech Theatre, Prague, 8 October 1882; engraving after Emanuel Zillich from 'Světozor', xvii (1884)

for Xenie, whom he was watching earlier. They hide as conspirators, led by Šujský, enter. Dimitrij discovers their plot to reveal him as a pretender. Making his presence known, he impresses the conspirators enough for some of them to join him; Šujský is arrested. Dvořák's tonal structure reinforces this conventional unmasking to great effect. The extended duet between Dimitrij and Xenie is Dvořák's most successfully sustained love scene up to this time.

ACT 3 *A vaulted hall in the Kremlin* Dimitrij thinks lovingly of Xenie. A delegation of Boyars led by Basmanov acclaims Dimitrij, and Jov requests that Marina join the Orthodox Church. This suggestion provokes the Polish army, and Dimitrij hopes that his union with Xenie may be permitted. Xenie enters and pleads for the life of Šujský, whom Dimitrij pardons, to the outrage of the Poles and the approbation of the Russians. Dvořák's handling of this complex scene with double chorus preserves the contrast between groupings and suggests a wide range of emotion. In a fit of jealousy Marina reveals to Dimitrij that he is really the serf Griška Otrepěv. Dimitrij resolves to prevent disorder by continuing to rule and rejects Marina who, overcome by his dignity, begs for mercy.

ACT 4 *A courtyard in Šujský's house* Xenie is troubled by her love for Dimitrij. He joins her, and his avowal of love leads to another fine extended duet. He allays her fears and prepares to divorce Marina. As he leaves it becomes clear that Marina has heard all. Marina confronts Xenie and, impressed by her modesty and moved by her earlier misapprehension that the man she loved was in fact the tsar, prevents her Polish followers from attacking her. Xenie asks the patriarch Jov to take her into a nunnery. Dimitrij tries to repudiate Marina, who reveals that he has no rightful claim to the throne. Šujský calls on Marfa to swear that Dimitrij is indeed her son. The ensuing ensemble and chorus (removed in the final version) is one of the glories of the opera. Dimitrij prevents Marfa from swearing falsely, and Šujský shoots him. Basmanov, Jov and the chorus lament Dimitrij's death, praising his goodness and bravery.

* * *

Although *Dimitrij* is fundamentally a grand opera, Dvořák uses motifs both as reminiscences and, at various stages, as part of the textural fabric. Each character has considerable credibility, and dramatic exchanges are dealt with efficiently, but Dvořák is at his best in the concerted passages. In the principal choruses, duets and above all the concluding ensemble Dvořák's ability to create broad, stirring paragraphs, in which the abstract musical design supports a generalized emotion rather than a dramatic moment, emerges as his most potent operatic quality. JAN SMACZNY

Dimitrova, Ghena (*b* Beglej, Pleven, 6 May 1941). Bulgarian soprano. After studies at the State Conservatory she joined the National Opera and made her début as Abigaille at Sofia in 1966. In 1970 success in an international competition in Sofia brought her engagements in Italy (her first Turandot, 1975, Treviso), France and Spain, five seasons at the Teatro Colón, Buenos Aires (from 1975), and her Vienna Staatsoper début (1978). Her American début was at Dallas in 1981 as Elvira (*Ernani*). In 1983 she first appeared at La Scala and Covent Garden, on both occasions as Turandot; she had made her London début earlier that year in a concert performance of *La Gioconda* with Domingo. She sang Lady Macbeth on the Royal Opera tour to Greece in 1986, and Aida in the 'on-site' production at Luxor, 1987. In 1988 followed her début at the Metropolitan Opera, as Turandot, which she also sang with the company of La Scala in Korea and Japan that year. Dimitrova is a powerful *lirico spinto* soprano whose often thrilling singing compensates for some lack of dramatic involvement at times.

*

H. E. Phillips: 'Crisis of Will', *ON*, lii/11 (1987–8), 27–9

NOËL GOODWIN

Dimmler [Dimler, Dümler], **Franz Anton** (*b* Mannheim, 14 Oct 1753; *d* Munich, 7 Feb 1827). German composer. He was a composition pupil of G. J. Vogler. From 1767 he played the horn in the Mannheim orchestra; after the court moved to Munich in 1778, he was a double bass player in the Munich orchestra. Various members of his family were also musicians in Mannheim and Munich.

As a composer Dimmler wrote mainly theatrical works, including several Singspiels for Munich in the late Mannheim tradition: *Der Guckkasten* (1797, Hoftheater), *Der Schatzgräber* (*Les fosseyeurs*; 1798, Schloss Seefeld; *F-Pc*) and *Die Zobeljäger* (mentioned in Lipowsky). He also composed incidental music and many ballets (now lost) which were well thought of in their time. His extant music is primarily instrumental.

*

F. J. Lipowsky: *Baierisches Musiklexikon* (Munich, 1811)
F. Walter: *Geschichte des Theaters und der Musik am kurpfälzischen Hofe* (Leipzig, 1898) ROLAND WÜRTZ

Di Murska, Ilma (*b* Zagreb, 4 Jan 1836; *d* Munich, 14 Jan 1889). Croatian soprano. She studied in Vienna and Paris with Mathilde Marchesi and in 1862 made her début as Lady Harriet (*Martha*) in Florence. After singing in Budapest, Berlin, Hamburg and Vienna, she made her London début at Her Majesty's Theatre in 1865 as Lucia. She sang with Mapleson's company until 1873, notably as Senta in the English première of *Der fliegende Holländer* (1870), sung in Italian and the first Wagner opera to be heard in London. Considered one of the finest interpreters of the Queen of Night, she also sang Konstanze, Amina, Marguerite de Valois, Dinorah, Isabella (*Robert le diable*) and Ophelia. Her voice had a compass of nearly three octaves, and her acting was said to have been original, though sometimes bordering on the extravagant.

*

H. Sutherland Edwards: 'A Flight of Prime Donne', *The Prima Donna*, ii (London, 1888), 59, 124, 179, 215
B. Marchesi: *Singer's Pilgrimage* (London, 1923), 32, 113
H. Klein: 'Ilma Di Murska', *Great Woman Singers of my Time* (London, 1931), 67, 80, 93, 136
H. Rosenthal, ed.: *The Mapleson Memoirs: the Career of an Operatic Impresario 1858–88* (London, 1966)

HAROLD ROSENTHAL/R

Dinner Engagement, A. Opera in two scenes, op.45, by LENNOX BERKELEY to a libretto by PAUL DEHN; Aldeburgh, Jubilee Hall, 17 June 1954.

The opera is set in the kitchen of a Chelsea house belonging to the impoverished Earl of Dunmow (baritone), who has known better days as Envoy Extraordinary to the Grand Duchy of Monteblanco. With his wife, the Countess (soprano), and assisted by their hired help Mrs Kneebone (contralto), they are preparing dinner for the Grand Duchess of Monteblanco (contralto) and especially for her son Phillipe (tenor), whose interest in things gastronomic (and whose considerable fortune) they are hoping to divert towards their daughter Susan (soprano). At the most inconvenient moment, with Susan in a temper and badly made up and with the entrée just beginning to burn, the royal party arrives through the outer door of the kitchen.

The Grand Duchess kindly pretends not to notice that she is in a kitchen. After presenting her hosts with some *pâté de foie gras* as a souvenir of Monteblanco, she goes out with them to inspect the 'grounds'. Phillipe at once falls in love with Susan, and is even further encouraged by finding she has heard of cold cherry soup. He declares his love by singing a Monteblancan shepherd's song ('Mon aimée attend la lune'), his mother insists on an immediate engagement, and three of the arias are finally woven together into a septet of rejoicing. Berkeley matches Dehn's witty, vernacular libretto with a number of musical parodies and with an overall style that Dehn rightly judged to be lighter, simpler and more continuously melodic than was the composer's wont.

ROGER NICHOLS

Dinorah [*Le pardon de Ploërmel* ('The Pilgrimage of Ploërmel')]. *Opéra comique* in three acts by GIACOMO MEYERBEER to a libretto by MICHEL CARRÉ and JULES BARBIER after Carré's play *Les chercheurs de trésor*; Paris, Opéra-Comique (Salle Favart), 4 April 1859.

The opera opens in the Breton village of Ploërmel during the annual pilgrimage to the chapel of the Virgin. Dinorah (soprano) has gone mad because her bridegroom Hoël (baritone) disappeared following a storm that interrupted their wedding on the same day the previous year. Hoël returns to the village, having discovered the whereabouts of some treasure, but does not recognize Dinorah. He enlists Corentin (tenor) to help him recover the riches, but not without sinister intent since, according to legend, the first to touch them will perish. In Act 2 they descend upon the cache in a mysterious valley and Dinorah happens upon the scene. From her Corentin learns about the legend surrounding the lode, and both Hoël and he invite the other to inspect it first. The demented girl, in pursuit of her pet goat, steps on a tree trunk spanning a river as it is hit by lightning. When she is swept away in the current, Hoël finally recognizes her and leaps to her rescue. In the last act Hoël admits that love is more important than riches, Dinorah comes to believe that her period of madness was a dream, and the two are married.

The work, originally called *Le pardon de Ploërmel*, was planned as a one-act *opéra comique* and enlarged to three acts at Meyerbeer's request. The composer converted the original spoken dialogue into recitatives for performances in other countries, where the opera often became known as *Dinorah*. The most famous number is the heroine's coloratura waltz aria in Act 2, 'Ombre légère qui suis mes pas', during which she dances with her own shadow. A more convincing musical portrayal of her madness is the Act 1 ternary *berceuse* 'Dors, petite', containing a middle section with volatile changes of mood. The overture is innovatory in that it features participation of the chorus, a prayer to the Virgin sung behind the curtain that alternates with procession and storm music in the pit. This has a real musico-dramatic function: when Dinorah sings that the events of the opera were but a dream, the prayer and procession are heard again, suggesting that, instead of a full year, perhaps little real time has elapsed between events depicted in the overture and the end of the work.

STEVEN HUEBNER

Dioclesian [*The Prophetess, or The History of Dioclesian*]. Semi-opera in five acts by HENRY PURCELL to words adapted by THOMAS BETTERTON from the play of John Fletcher and Philip Massinger; London, Queen's Theatre, Dorset Garden, late May 1690.

This cynical and morbidly humorous tragicomedy, originally produced in 1622, is concerned with a struggle for political power in ancient Rome. The prophetess Delphia has predicted that Diocles, a common soldier, will become emperor after he kills 'a mighty boar'. Believing this to be highly improbable, Diocles mockingly promises to marry Delphia's ugly niece Drusilla when the prophecy is fulfilled. Shortly thereafter he discovers that the captain of the guard Volutius Aper ('the boar') has murdered the old emperor and, on avenging the murdered ruler, Diocles is elected co-emperor. Pompously renaming himself 'Dioclesian', he conveniently forgets his promise to Drusilla and transfers his affections to the beautiful Princess Aurelia. The angry prophetess disrupts the wedding ceremony by conjuring up a dreadful monster and thunder and lightning. Delphia further spoils Diocles' chances with the princess by casting a spell to make her fall in love with his nephew and rival Maximinian; the prophetess then helps the invading Persians to defeat the Roman army. Shocked into action, Diocles counterattacks and routs the invaders. With great humility, he cedes his half of the throne to Maximinian, honours his original promise to marry Drusilla and retires to Lombardy to dedicate his life to virtue.

In revising Fletcher and Massinger's play, Betterton's main task was to create situations for Purcell's music. The first inserted scene (which includes 'Great Diocles the boar has kill'd' and 'Let the soldiers rejoice') praises Diocles for avenging the emperor's murder and celebrates his enthronement. It was rightly criticized at the time for holding up the plot:

How ridiculous is it in that Scene in the *Prophetess*, where the great Action of the *Drama* stops, and the chief Officers of the Army stand still with their Swords drawn to hear a Fellow Sing 'Let the soldiers rejoice' – faith in my mind 'tis as unreasonable as if a Man shou'd call for a Pipe of Tobacco just when the Priest and his Bride are waiting for him at the Altar.

Yet the subdued music perfectly captures the idea of 'the king is dead, long live the king'. This scene contrasts sharply with the music heard later at the celebration of the victory over the Persians, 'Sound Fame', a virtuoso air on a ground bass for countertenor with trumpet obbligato. Besides the famous strophic song 'What shall I do to show how much I love her', which is ill-suited to its dramatic context, other notable pieces in the play proper include the intricately contrapuntal Dance of Furies and the Butterfly Dance, which are vividly descriptive of the special choreography.

The longest and most important scene of the semi-opera is the final masque, ostensibly performed to welcome Diocles into rural retirement, but actually a self-contained, through-composed pastoral. One of Purcell's greatest works, it remained popular well into the 18th century. The theme is Cupid's taming of an ill-tempered Jove, depicted in a series of five scenes or entries preceded by an invocation of the nymphs and fauns. High points are the boisterous trio of Baccanalians ('Make room for the great god of wine'), the sensual dialogue for a shepherd and his lass ('Tell me why') and the C major chaconne 'Triumph, victorious Love' for countertenor, tenor and bass with brilliant antiphonal passages for trumpets, oboes and strings. From this plotless miscellany emerges a highly unified score in which the contrasting heroic and pastoral modes gradually converge.

CURTIS PRICE

Diodati, Giuseppe Maria (Rossi) (*fl* late 18th century). Italian librettist. He was the house poet of the Teatro Nuovo in Naples, his surviving librettos (which bear his signature or the stamp G.M.D.) belonging to the period 1786–98. His association with Cimarosa (for whom he wrote over two-thirds of his extant texts) established him as a leading librettist of the period. His other major association was with the Neapolitan Giacomo Tritto. Several of his librettos achieved considerable success: *Il credulo* and *Le trame deluse*, both set by Cimarosa in 1786, were performed in major Italian centres, though the success of the latter must be attributed to the music if we are to believe Count Zinzendorf, who was unsparing in his treatment of Diodati's contribution. On the other hand, Goethe so admired *L'impresario in angustie* that he translated it into German and arranged both text and music for performance (with musical additions of his own) in Weimar in 1791.

commedie per musica unless otherwise stated

Il capriccio drammatico (commedia), Cimarosa, ?1781; *Il credulo*, Cimarosa, 1786; *Le trame deluse, ossia I raggiri scoperti*, Cimarosa, 1786; *L'impresario in angustie* (farsa per musica), Cimarosa, 1786 (Fioravanti, 1798); *Il Corrivo*, G. Giordani, 1787; *L'incontro per accidente*, Fabrizi, 1788; *I sposi in Rissa* (farsa), F. A. Speranza (D. Bernardo di Fraja, 1791); *Il cartesiano fantastico*, Tritto, 1790; *Le astuzie in amore*, Tritto, 1790; *Le nozze in garbuglio*, Tritto, 1793 (Cimarosa, 1795); *L'impostore smascherato*, Tritto, 1794; *Gli amanti in puntiglio*, Tritto, 1794; *Penelope* (dramma per musica), Cimarosa, 1795; *L'impegno superato*, Cimarosa, 1795; *L'apprensivo raggirato*, Cimarosa, 1798; *Paolo e Virginia*, P. C. Guglielmi, 1817

*

CroceN

M. Morris: 'Goethe als Bearbeiter von italienischen Operntexten', *Goethe Jb*, xxvi (1905), 3–51

M. Scherillo: *L'opera buffa napoletana durante il settecento* (Palermo, 1916)

A. Della Corte: *L'opera comica italiana nel '700* (Bari, 1923)

PATRICIA LEWY GIDWITZ

Dippel, Andreas (*b* Kassel, 30 Nov 1866; *d* Hollywood, CA, 12 May 1932). American tenor and impresario. He studied in Kassel, and later in Berlin, Milan and Vienna. He made his début as Lyonel in *Martha* at Bremen in 1887, remaining there for five years, and sang at Bayreuth (1889), Breslau (1892–3) and the Vienna Hofoper (1893–8), and appeared at Covent Garden, 1897–9, as Lohengrin, Siegmund and Radames. He made his début at the Metropolitan Opera on 26 November 1890 in the title role of Franchetti's *Asrael*, and sang with the company from 1898 to 1908. Although his voice was unremarkable, Dippel was a versatile artist: he was the Metropolitan's standby tenor, with a repertory of more than 150 operatic roles, most notably his Wagnerian portrayals, particularly of Tristan and Siegfried. In 1908 he was appointed administrative manager of the Metropolitan. After two years he left and became director of the Philadelphia-Chicago Opera Company, but he resigned in 1913 although that venture, unlike the previous one, was a financial success. He then formed his own touring light-opera company and in 1924 started another group, which presented German operas in the American Midwest. DEE BAILY

Dirindina [*La Dirindina*]. *Farsetta per musica* in two parts by Domenico Scarlatti (*see* SCARLATTI family, (2)) to a libretto by GIROLAMO GIGLI; scheduled for performance at Rome, Teatro Capranica, Carnival 1715 (performance cancelled).

Don Carissimo (baritone), a singing-master, lusts after his pupil Dirindina (soprano). She arouses Carissimo's jealousy by showing affection towards Liscione (tenor or soprano), a castrato who comes to tell her that she has been offered a part at the Milan opera. In Part 2 Carissimo interrupts Liscione rehearsing Dirindina in the part of Dido and, taking as real what he sees and hears, intervenes to save his pupil from 'suicide'. Liscione and Dirindina mock his stupidity.

Gigli's pungent satire on serious opera and those who performed it aroused the hostility of the original cast, who manoeuvred to have both performance and publication banned. (That casting problems had arisen even before Scarlatti completed the score is suggested by the fact that Liscione's music is written in the tenor clef in Part 1 and in the soprano clef in Part 2.) Originally intended as intermezzos for Scarlatti's *Ambleto*, *La Dirindina*, which shows a lively feeling for the *buffo* style, was replaced by a pastoral piece for two singers (composer unknown). The earliest known performance took place at the Teatro S Samuele, Venice, in 1725, but it is not certain whether this was with Scarlatti's music. MALCOLM BOYD

Disertore, Il ('The Deserter'). Libretto subject used in the late 18th century and the early 19th, based on the *opéra comique* LE DÉSERTEUR by PIERRE-ALEXANDRE MONSIGNY to a libretto by MICHEL-JEAN SEDAINE (1769, Paris), and on a play of the same name by Louis Sébastien Mercier (1770, Paris).

The first Italian operatic version was written by C. F. Badini for P. A. Guglielmi (1770, London). Badini acknowledged his indebtedness to 'the French' in the plan of the drama but asserted his independence as far as the individual numbers are concerned. His version is a fairly typical *opera buffa*, which distributes the dramatic attention more equally among the characters than does Sedaine's work. The story begins with a feast, purporting to be the wedding of the heroine, Rosetta, to Beltramino. It is in fact a joke designed to test the constancy of Rosetta's real lover, Alessio, who is deemed to have deserted the army by virtue of having strayed from the barracks to see Rosetta. Alessio is sentenced to death, but Rosetta obtains a last-minute pardon from the King.

The other significant Italian operatic version of this plot was a text by Bartolomeo Benincasa, set first by Alessandro Bianchi (1785, Venice), and based on the Mercier play. This libretto concerns the love between Adelina and Gualtieri (Mercier's Clary and Durimel). Gualtieri has deserted the army after being imprisoned for insubordination; he is found guilty and sentenced to death. It turns out, however, that Ormondo, the commander who must give the order to fire, is Gualtieri's long-lost father. He faints before he can carry out the order, allowing Adelina to arrive with a pardon from the King. The happy end of Benincasa's libretto differs from Mercier's play, in which the hero dies; the last-minute pardon follows the comic opera and a 1772 Italian 'translation' of the play, in which the commanding officer is moved by the pleas of the family to commute Durimel's sentence. In a preface to his libretto Benincasa expounded his views on the need for an intermediate form of drama between tragedy and comedy, somewhat akin to the French *comédie larmoyante*, of which this libretto was intended to be exemplar and standard-bearer.

The comic plot was set by Sacchini in 1774 (only the libretto is extant) as *Il disertore per amore*, and by Gazzaniga in 1779 as *Il disertore francese*, a *dramma giocoso*; Francesco Bianchi's 1784 setting, and Angelo Tarchi's of 1789, are both based on the Mercier play and are designated *dramma serio*, as is a pasticcio of 1790. The story appeared as *Il disertore olandese* in 1795 (no composer named) and as a *dramma giocoso*, *Il disertore francese* (set by Leali, in 1800, and combining elements of both the comic and serious traditions). The title was also used for many ballets. MARY HUNTER

Disingannati, I ('The Undeceived'). *Commedia per musica* in three acts by ANTONIO CALDARA to a libretto by GIOVANNI CLAUDIO PASQUINI after MOLIÈRE's play *Le misanthrope*, with ballet music by Nicola Matteis; Vienna, Hoftheater (Teatrino), 8 February 1729.

In adapting Molière's play Pasquini retained its basic plot and principal characterizations while broadening its social appeal. The vain and coquettish Celimene (soprano) and her sycophants, the poet Trigeno (soprano), the fawning Filindo (alto) and the affected Acasto (alto), ridicule the ideals of the sincere Elianta (soprano). Alceste (tenor), though loved by Elianta and vowing to relinquish the hypocrisies of society, is ensnared by Celimene only to be humiliated when she refuses to abandon the world he despises. Pasquini adds three comic characters derived from other plays by Molière: Anselmo (bass), Elianta's over-protective and doddering elderly brother; Geronzio (bass), an unsuccessful alchemist in love with Elianta, and Dorina (soprano), Celimene's *cameriera*, a pert realist in a rather precious domain.

More or less free from the constraints which the personal tastes of his patrons imposed on his writing of *opera seria*, Caldara appears to have used the carnival operas as opportunities for experiment and development. *I disingannati* is probably one of his most accessible operas. It differs from most of his *seria* settings not so much in any reduction of the accompanying forces (the string orchestra in three or four parts remains the basis) as in a lightening of vocal lines by the removal of extravagant bravura and the injection of *galant* traits.

Caldara seems to have found Pasquini's taut dialogue particularly congenial. The fast-paced action brings a high proportion of *allegro* arias (23 of the 26 numbers); the characters' cut-and-thrust exchanges produce five ensembles – more than in any of the *opere serie*. Nine arias without opening ritornellos further maintain the momentum of his vivacious melodic style. Dorina in particular is skilfully drawn, her plain-speaking and commonsense nature reinforced by the forthright motifs, balanced phrases and strongly cadenced lines of her three arias (e.g. 'Una donna ch'abbia l'arte', 2.xii). Anselmo and Geronzio provide the comic ensembles; the patter argument of 'Vedette peccato!' (2.xvi) is pure intermezzo. A more sophisticated humour emerges as Caldara tilts at the affectations and grand manner of *opera seria* in, for example, Celimene's powerful but empty 'Lusingo tutto quanti' (1.i) and Acasto's self-pitying 'Gonfio torrente' (2.xiv). BRIAN W. PRITCHARD

Dissoluto punito, Il. Opera by W. A. Mozart; *see* DON GIOVANNI (ii).

Di Stefano, Giuseppe (*b* Motta Santa Anastasia, nr Catania, 24 July 1921). Italian tenor. He studied in Milan with Luigi Montesanto. He made his début in 1946 at the Teatro Municipale, Reggio Emilia, as Massenet's Des Grieux, and first sang at La Scala in 1947. He made his Metropolitan début in 1948 as the Duke in *Rigoletto* and continued to appear there until 1965. Until 1953 he sang lighter roles such as Wilhelm Meister (*Mignon*), Elvino (*La sonnambula*), Mascagni's Fritz and Nadir. His singing at that time was notable for its beautiful tone and the use of an exquisite *pianissimo*, the voice possessing a rich, velvety sound. As he began to take on heavier parts his singing became rougher and less elegant, and the voice larger and less pure. By 1957 he had added Don José, Canio, Turiddu, Radames, Don Alvaro (*La forza del destino*) and Osaka (*Iris*) to his repertory; thus, when he made his British début at Edinburgh in 1957, his Nemorino had less vocal charm than had been expected. He sang Cavaradossi at Covent Garden in 1961, but during the 1960s his appearances became sporadic.

*

GV (R. Celletti; R. Vegeto)
R. Bing: *5000 Nights at the Opera* (London, 1972), 145ff

HAROLD ROSENTHAL/R

Dittersdorf, Carl Ditters von [Ditters, Carl] (*b* Vienna, 2 Nov 1739; *d* Neuhof, Pilgram, Bohemia, 24 Oct 1799). Austrian composer. He was the outstanding representative of German opera in Vienna between Mozart's *Die Entführung aus dem Serail* (1782) and *Die Zauberflöte* (1791).

1. LIFE. Ditters (his surname up to 1773) was born into comfortable middle-class circumstances and received as a child a sound education that included private instruction in music. His gift for the violin earned him an appointment at the age of 11 in the splendid musical household of Prince Joseph Friedrich of Sachsen-Hildburghausen, where his musical studies continued – now including composition with the prince's Kapellmeister, Giuseppe Bonno. In 1761 the prince returned to Saxony to assume the regency of Hildburghausen and dissolved his orchestra; through his efforts many of his musicians, including Ditters and Gluck, found employment with the court theatre under Count Giacomo Durazzo. Together with his brother, Ditters accompanied Gluck to northern Italy in 1763 for the première of Gluck's *Il trionfo di Clelia* (Bologna, 14 May).

After Durazzo's departure in 1764, Ditters decided against continuing under his successor, Count Sporck, and instead accepted the post of Kapellmeister to the Bishop of Grosswardein in April 1765. He put to use the theatrical experience he had gained in Vienna and Italy, writing and arranging Italian comic operas for the bishop's theatre. In 1769 Maria Theresa ordered the theatre to be closed, apparently because comic operas had been given there during Lent. Ditters's travels after this event brought him into contact with Prince-Bishop Schaffgotsch of Breslau, who hired him in November 1769. Ditters quickly gained great favour with his new employer. He proposed that an old tower in the residence at Johannisberg be converted into a theatre, and organized a small opera company (16 musicians and four singers) to perform there. The 'Turm-Theater' was inaugurated on 1 May 1771 with Ditters's *Il viaggiatore americano in Joannesberg*; the cast included the composer's future wife, the Hungarian-born Nicolina Trink, whom he had first met at Grosswardein. Ditters remained in Johannisberg until 1776, save for a trip to Vienna in 1773, where his oratorio *Esther* was performed. At that time he also received a patent of nobility from Maria Theresa, secured through the exertions of his employer as a prerequisite to naming him *Amtshauptmann*. Ditters, now with the added surname 'von Dittersdorf', regarded his ennoblement as the most important event in his life. He wrote nine Italian comic operas for the Johannisberg theatre. Unlike his earlier operas for Grosswardein, all of them are extant, mostly by virtue of copies the composer sent to Joseph Haydn at Eszterháza, where four of them were performed (though with extensive cuts).

In 1776 the prince-bishop closed the Turm-Theater as an economy measure. Little is known of Dittersdorf's activities during the next decade. Wartime duties preoccupied him from 1778 to 1782 during the War of the Bavarian Succession. In 1784 we hear of him in Vienna, at the famous evening of quartet-playing with Haydn, Mozart and Vanhal described by Michael Kelly (*Reminiscences*, London, 1826). In 1786 he was again in Vienna to conduct his oratorio *Giobbe*, commissioned by the Tonkünstler-Sozietät. In July of that year his first German opera, *Der Apotheker und der Doktor* (now usually known as *Doktor und Apotheker*), had its première at the Burgtheater, where the German troupe under imperial supervision was temporarily performing. The opera became the greatest popular triumph of Dittersdorf's career: over the next 12 years it was performed 72 times at the imperial theatres in Vienna. The immediate stir it created there led to commissions for two further operas. *Betrug durch Aberglauben*, produced by the German company at the Kärntnertor that October, proved nearly as successful, but *Democrito corretto*, given at the Burgtheater the following January by the emperor's Italian company, was a failure. In various German translations, however, it enjoyed popularity on other stages. Thereafter Dittersdorf's operas were all German. Further triumphs at Vienna – notably *Die Liebe im Narrenhause*, *Das rote Käppchen* and *Hieronymus Knicker* – established him as the dominant figure in German opera in both Austria and Germany during the later 1780s.

The 1790s marked a sharp decline in both Dittersdorf's popular fortunes and his health. By 1794, now 55, he was suffering from advanced gout, and he retired to quarters at Schloss Rothlhotta, the Bohemian estate of Baron von Stillfried. By now Vienna and other leading stages where German opera was cultivated were dominated by new fashions – heroic-comic spectacles and magic operas – but in the provinces Dittersdorf was far from forgotten. Duke Friedrich August of Oels, who had established a theatre at his small Silesian court in 1793, commissioned seven German operas from him between 1794 and his own death in 1798. When his health permitted, Dittersdorf travelled to Oels to supervise rehearsals. Unlike his earlier German operas for Vienna, his works for Oels remained local phenomena: only one, *Das Gespenst mit der Trommel*, saw a further production elsewhere, at the National Theatre, Berlin, in 1795. In his autobiography, dictated to his son during his final months in 1799, Dittersdorf said nothing about his last operas and his association with Oels.

2. WORKS. Two years after Dittersdorf's death, his autobiography was brought out at Leipzig. In his introductory remarks the editor, Carl Spazier, summed up the composer's contribution to the German operatic stage:

> He is for us in a certain sense what Grétry is for France. His dramatic works have for the most part natural life, cheer, character, and truth, and especially a certain affability and popularity that addresses an emotion directly.

Dittersdorf's training equipped him with a mastery of up-to-date *opera buffa* style that he displayed to advantage in his Italian operas for Johannisberg. But his reputation as an opera composer was made when he fused this Italian manner with German musical and theatrical traditions. Spazier's words aptly capture the cheerful, popular style that resulted.

In his most successful German operas for Vienna, Dittersdorf showed a strong preference for tunes built up from two-bar phrases with a generous amount of repetition. 3/8 and 2/4 metres predominate. Slow arias appear infrequently; rather, the composer favoured a slow–fast pattern. Key is coordinated with metre in establishing familiar aria- and lied-types for characters equally familiar in 18th-century repertories. Elaborate bravura arias are restricted to the female characters, a direct reflection of the capabilities of the personnel in the German company that played at the Kärntnertor between 1786 and 1790.

Dittersdorf reserved his most resourceful harmonic language and some of his most telling musical strokes for his finales, where situation rather than character guided his imagination. His sections are shorter than Mozart's, but there are more of them, and they often collide with jarring harmonic shifts (D minor to F♯ minor, for example). The minor mode, which he by and large avoided in his arias, comes into its own in his finales. The orchestra plays a fairly neutral role, hammering away at continuous patterns built from familiar motivic prototypes and only occasionally offering pithy commentary of its own on the goings-on. Dittersdorf's finales are among the longest in any operas written during the 1780s (the Act 1 finale of *Die Liebe im Narrenhause*, for instance, runs to 1150 bars) – a marked departure from German opera of earlier years.

His introductory ensembles, on the other hand, tend towards the dramatically static tableau.

The librettos Dittersdorf set all tread well-travelled 18th-century paths: they are, by and large, dramas of common sense in which greed or jealousy or superstition receives a benign correction, inevitably paving the way to matrimonial bliss for a pair of young lovers. Enlightenment ideals occasionally share the stage with the shortcomings of the age – from the traditional comic exploitation of the hard of hearing in *Hieronymus Knicker* to the darker ridicule of the mentally infirm in *Die Liebe im Narrenhause*. For several of his operas Dittersdorf himself wrote or adapted the libretto, with indifferent results.

When the Viennese suburban theatres turned to a newer style of popular opera (a trend culminating in *Die Zauberflöte*), Dittersdorf continued to cling to the style of text as well as music on which he had made his reputation in the 1780s. Magic, knight-errantry and spectacle remained foreign to his art. When in 1792 F. W. Gotter sent him a draft of *Die Geisterinsel* (an adaptation of Shakespeare's *The Tempest* originally intended for Mozart), Dittersdorf at first offered suggestions for revisions and excisions to bring it into line with his own operas, and finally returned the text itself unset two years later. His late operas for Oels speak with the same italianate accents on virtually the same Enlightenment themes as in his Viennese operas. A rather pathetic attempt to sell copies of the scores in 1798 went unanswered, and Dittersdorf died the next year an impoverished, embittered man.

See also BETRUG DURCH ABERGLAUBEN; DEMOCRITO CORRETTO; DOKTOR UND APOTHEKER; GESPENST MIT DER TROMMEL, DAS; HIERONYMUS KNICKER; LIEBE IM NARRENHAUSE, DIE; and ROTE KÄPPCHEN, DAS.

all premières in Johannisberg given at the Turm-Theater, all those in Oels at the Herzogliches Hoftheater; see Horsley (1988)

[Amore in musica] (Ger. version, trans. Dittersdorf), Grosswardein, ?1771

Il viaggiatore americano in Joannesberg (farce, 2, S. I. Pintus), Johannisberg, 1 May 1771

L'amore disprezzato (operetta buffa, 1), Johannisberg, 1771, *A-Wgm*

Il finto pazzo per amore (operetta giocosa, 2), Johannisberg, 3 June 1772, *H-Bn*

Il tutore e la pupilla (dg, 3), Johannisberg, 1 May 1773, *Bn**

Lo sposo burlato (operetta giocosa, 2), Johannisberg, 1773 or 1775, *Bn*; as Der gefoppte Bräutigam (trans. Dittersdorf), Vienna, Kärntnertor, Sept 1783

Il tribunale di Giove (serenade with prol., 1), Johannisberg, 1774, *GB-Lcm*

Il Maniscalco (operetta giocosa, 2), Johannisberg, 1 May 1775, *H-Bn**

La contadina fedele (op giocosa, 2, ?Dittersdorf), Johannisberg, 20 Feb 1776, *Bn**

La moda, o sia Gli scompigli domestici (dg, 2), Johannisberg, 3 June 1776, *Bn**

L'Arcifanfano, re de' matti (op giocosa, 3, C. Goldoni), Johannisberg, late 1776, *Bn**

Il barone di rocca antica (operetta giocosa, 2, ? G. Petrosellini), Johannisberg, by 1776, *Bn**

I visionari, comp. 1770–76, ?unperf.

Der Apotheker und der Doktor [Doktor und Apotheker] (komisches Spl, 2, G. Stephanie the younger, ? after 'Graf von N**': *L'apoticaire de Murcie*), Vienna, Burg, 11 July 1786, *A-Sca*, *Wgm*, *Wn* (2 copies), *B-Bc*, *D-B*, *Dlb*, *SWl*, *H-Bn*, vs (Mainz, *c*1786; Vienna, 1787; Berlin, 1943); adapted as The Doctor and the Apothecary (musical entertainment, 2), London, Drury Lane, 1788

Betrug durch Aberglauben [Die Schatzgräber, Der glückliche Betrug, Die dienstbaren Geister] (komisches Spl, 2, F. Eberl), Vienna, Kärntnertor, 3 Oct 1786, *A-Sca*, *Wn* (2 copies), *D-B*, *Mbs*, vs (Leipzig, *c*1930)

Democrito corretto (op giocosa, 2, G. Brunati, after J. F. Regnard: *Le Démocrite amoureux*), Vienna, Burg, 24 Jan 1787, *A-Wgm*, *Wn* (2 copies), *D-B*, *Mbs*; 6 Ger. versions, incl. Silene (trans. Dittersdorf); Der neue Demokrit (trans. H. G. Schmieder); Demokrit der Zweyte (adapted by ? F. L. Schröder), Hamburg, 27 July 1791

Die Liebe im Narrenhause (komische Oper, 2, Stephanie the younger), Vienna, Kärntnertor, 12 April 1787, *A-Wgm*, *Wn*, *D-B* (*R*1986: GOB, xv), *Mbs*, *Rp*, *F-Pc* (vs), *GB-Lbl*; as Orpheus der Zweyte (adapted by F. L. Schröder), Hamburg, 1788; vs (Mainz, 1790)

Das rote Käppchen, oder Hilft's nicht, so schadt's nicht [Die rote Kappe; Das Rotkäppchen] (Spl, 3, Dittersdorf, after F. Livigni: *Giannina e Bernardone*), Vienna, Kärntnertor, 1788, *A-Wgm* (2 copies), *D-B*, *LÜh* (Act 1 only); text rev. C. A. Vulpius, Weimar, Hof, 7 June 1791, *Mbs*, vs (by Ignaz Walter, Mainz, 1792; Leipzig, 1792)

Hieronymus Knicker [Lucius Knicker; Chrisostomus Knicker] (komisches Spl, 2, Stephanie the younger), Vienna, Leopoldstadt, 7 July 1789, *A-Wgm*, *D-B*, *Mbs* (2 copies), *US-Wc*, vs (Mannheim, *c*1791; Leipzig, n.d.); text rev. Vulpius, Weimar, Hof, 1791; text rev. A. F. von Hofmann as Hokus Pokus, oder Die Lebensessenz, Salzburg, 1792

Die Hochzeit des Figaro (komisches Spl, 2, Dittersdorf, after P.-A. Beaumarchais), Brno, 1789

Der Schiffspatron, oder Der neue Gutsherr (Spl, 2, J. F. Jünger, rev. Dittersdorf, after G. F. W. Grossmann), Vienna, Wieden, 1789, *A-Wgm*, *D-Dlb*, *Mbs*, vs (Leipzig, 1793); as Der Gutsherr, oder Gürge und Hannchen, Dresden, 1799

Der Teufel ein Hydraulikus (3, J. F. E. Albrecht, after P. Weidmann: *Der Bettelstudent*), Grätz, 1790, *Dlb*

Hokus-Pokus, oder Das Gaukelspiel (Spl, 2, Dittersdorf and Vulpius), Breslau, Wäsersches, 4 Nov 1791, *Dlb** [damaged]

Das Gespenst mit der Trommel [Geisterbanner] (deutsches komisches Spl, 2, Dittersdorf, after Goldoni: *Il conte Caramella*), Oels, 16 Aug 1794, *A-Wgm* (Act 2 only), *D-B*, *Dlb**

Don Quixote der Zweyte [Don Chisciotto] (komisches Spl, 2, Dittersdorf, after M. de Cervantes), Oels, 4 Feb 1795, *Dlb**, *US-Wc* (copy of preceding)

Gott Mars, oder Der eiserne Mann [Der Hauptmann von Bärenzahn, Der Wechsel Gott Mars] (komisches Spl, 2, Dittersdorf), Oels, 30 May 1795, *D-Dlb** (dated 1791)

Der Durchmarsch (J. B. Paneck, after F. X. Girzig: *Die christliche Judenbraut*), Oels, 29 Aug 1795

Der Schach von Schiras (komisches Spl, 2, Dittersdorf, after A. von Kotzebue: *Sultan Wampum*), Oels, 15 Sept 1795, *Dlb**

Die befreyten Gwelfen [Die Gwelfen] (prol., 1), Oels, 29 Oct 1795, *Dlb**

Ugolino (tragische Oper, 2, Dittersdorf, after H. W. von Gerstenberg, and Dante: *Commedia*), Oels, 11 June 1796, *Dlb**

Die lustigen Weiber von Windsor (Spl, 2, G. C. Römer, after W. Shakespeare), Oels, 25 June 1796, *Dlb**, *US-Wc* (copy of autograph)

Der schöne Herbsttag (Dialog, 1, after P. Metastasio: *Il vero omaggio*), Oels, 29 Oct 1796, *D-Dlb**

Der Ternengewinnst, oder Der gedemütigte Stolz [Terno secco] (komisches Spl, 2, Dittersdorf), Oels, 11 Feb 1797, *Dlb**

Der Mädchenmarkt (Spl, 3, C. A. Herklots, after G. F. Poullain de Saint-Foix: *La colonie*), Oels, 18 April 1797, *Dlb**; as Il mercato di ragazze, Oels, 1798

Die Opera Buffa (komisches Spl, 2, C. F. Bretzner), Vienna, Kärntnertor, 1798, *A-Wn**

Don Coribaldi, ossia L'usurpata prepotenza, comp. *c*1798 (drama, 2), unperf.

Music in: Der Fürst und sein Volk, 1791

*

[C. Ditters von Dittersdorf, attrib.]: 'Von dem wienerischen Geschmack in der Musik', *Wiener Diarium*, suppl. no.26 (18 Oct 1766)

'Korrespondenz des Herrn v. Dittersdorf mit einem Freunde über musik. Gegenstände', *AMZ*, i (1798–9), 138–41, 201–5

Karl von Dittersdorfs Lebensbeschreibung, seinem Sohne in die Feder diktiert (Leipzig, 1801; ed. N. Miller, Munich, 1967; Eng. trans., 1896)

C. Krebs: *Dittersdorfiana* (Berlin, 1900)

K. M. Klob: *Drei musikalische Biedermänner: Ignaz Holzbauer, Karl Ditters von Dittersdorf, Michael Haydn* (Ulm, 1911)

K. Holl: *Carl Ditters von Dittersdorfs Opern für das wiederhergestellte Johannisberger Theater* (diss., U. of Bonn, 1913)

L. Riedinger: 'Karl von Dittersdorf als Opernkomponist', *SMw*, ii (1914), 212–349

J. Thamm: 'Die erste Johannisberger Oper Dittersdorfs: Il viaggiatore americano in Joannesberg', *Der Oberschlesier*, xxi (1939), 577–83

J. Platoff: *Music and Drama in the 'Opera Buffa' Finale: Mozart and his Contemporaries* (diss., U. of Pennsylvania, 1984)

T. Bauman: *North German Opera in the Age of Goethe* (Cambridge, 1985)

P. J. Horsley: *Dittersdorf and the Finale in Late-Eighteenth-Century German Comic Opera* (diss., Cornell U., 1988)

D. Heartz: 'Ditters, Gluck und der Artikel "Von dem wienerischen Geschmack in der Musik (1766)"', *Gluck-Studien*, i (1989), 78–80

THOMAS BAUMAN

Divall, Richard (*b* 9 Sept 1945). Australian conductor. He studied with Charles Mackerras, Nikolaus Harnoncourt, Reginald Goodall and Joseph Post. He was director of the innovatory Young Opera Company of Sydney, 1968–72, and musical director of the Queensland Opera Company, 1971–2. In 1972 he was appointed music director of the Victoria State Opera; he conducted the first opera performed in the State Theatre of the Victorian Arts Centre, Melbourne, *Don Carlos*, on 1 August 1984, and the world première of the 1841 version of *Der fliegende Holländer* in the new Schott edition at that theatre on 9 November 1987. Divall has been active in the editing and performance of Australian colonial music and of Classical and pre-Classical operas, particularly those of Gluck, Rameau and Handel. His large repertory includes all the Monteverdi and Mozart operas. He has conducted for the BBC, the Netherlands Opera and at the Hong Kong Festival. In Australia he has conducted opera at four Adelaide Festivals and is a regular guest conductor for the Australian Opera and the ABC. In 1981 he was made an OBE and in 1989 a Commendatore al Merito of the Order of Malta.

THÉRÈSE RADIC

Divertissement (Fr.). In its most basic meaning, 'entertainment' or 'diversion'; specifically, in French opera of the 17th, 18th and 19th centuries, a group of dances and vocal numbers (*choeurs dansés* nearly always and solos frequently) or an independent opera almost always in one act, in which ballet had a prominent role and whose dramatic content was slight, or a short ballet, often written to celebrate a special occasion. In the 17th and 18th centuries *divertissements* were frequently added to plays.

Royal and aristocratic households of the Middle Ages and the Renaissance used music and dancing both as entertainment and as ostentatious display of rank and wealth. Important events like princely marriages and royal state entries were celebrated with appropriate pageantry: *divertissements* included masquerades, balls, parades, banquets and commemorative spectacles in which music had a significant role. Within this culture and society the *intermède* and *ballet de cour*, both also called *divertissements* by contemporaries, developed.

Courtly entertainment reached an apogee during the reign of Louis XIV. The king took a personal interest and ensured that the entertainment offered to his courtiers and visitors was a constant reminder of his power and magnificence as ruler of France, the acknowledged cultural centre of Europe. *Petits divertissements* were those given on a fairly regular basis or for annual events, such as the king's name-day: operas, *ballets de cour*, dinner music, masked balls, games with vocal and instrumental music in the background, promenades with wind serenades and fanfares, mock tournaments and fireworks displays. *Grands divertissements* included the same components but were presented even more lavishly. They were organized around a central theme, honoured individuals or commemorated special events and lasted several days. New entertainments were essential. That in 1664, for example (with the Ruggiero-Alcina episode of Ariosto's *Orlando furioso* as its main theme), in honour of the two queens (Anne of Austria and Marie-Thérèse) featured two new *comédies-ballets* by Molière and Lully: *Les plaisirs de l'île enchantée* and *La princesse d'Elide* (see Isherwood 1973). *Divertissements* remained a significant part of court life until 1789.

Given the cultural milieu of the court, it is little wonder that Baroque operas and *comédies-ballets* reflected the contemporary aesthetics of entertainment; their *divertissements* were formalized miniatures of the courtly model. Visual display (in dances, costumes, stage sets and machines) supported by appropriate music provided contrast with and relief from dramatic developments. With the *fin heureuse* of the *tragédie lyrique*, *divertissements* became an expression of rejoicing and the conventional conclusion of the opera. It was also part of the librettist's art to find other suitable places. In *Alceste* (1674), Philippe Quinault had a *divertissement* celebrating Glory dominate the prologue; in another in Act 1 the people and minor sea divinities celebrate conjugal love (interrupted by threats from Thetis); a *pompe funèbre* for Alcestis (middle of Act 2) and a *fête infernale* for the creatures of the Underworld (middle of Act 3) provide local colour and spectacle. The final one, after Alcestis's rescue from Hades, consists of a *choeur dansé*, two dances for shepherds, an *air*, another dance and a final *choeur dansé* – all illustrating the general theme, the triumph of love. So popular did *divertissements* become that they were an important model for the *opéra-ballet*, which in turn influenced later *tragédie lyrique*.

By the time of Rameau, *divertissements*, as dramatically static scenes, were placed at or near the ends of acts, and virtually every act had a substantial one – so much so that, in the opinion of some critics, the drama was overshadowed, though others found (and spectators agreed) that they were of great interest, combining the best that the French lyric stage had to offer. Both sides noted the increased emphasis on the *divertissement*. The connection between *divertissements* and the main action was sometimes slight. To the elements found in Lully were added italianate *ariettes*, showing off the virtuosity of the singer. Rameau's *Castor et Pollux* (1737) is representative: the entire prologue is virtually a *divertissement*, and in the course of the opera Castor is welcomed back as a conquering hero, tempted by Celestial Pleasures to renounce his decision to take his brother's place in the Underworld, challenged by demons and welcomed by Happy Shades – all in *divertissements* in which he, though present, is a passive observer. The final one, ordered by Jupiter, commemorates the elevation of the brothers' constellation with singing and dancing by Stars and Planets.

In part in reaction to late Baroque opera, Gluck and other late 18th-century composers sought to restore primacy to the drama; however, they did not ignore the potential contribution of *divertissements*, but insisted that they serve dramatic ends. Spectacle became much shorter and more fully integrated. The joyous *fête* to welcome Iphigenia contrasts ironically with the reality (Agamemnon has already been informed that he must sacrifice her) and with the heroine's vague feelings of foreboding (Gluck's *Iphigénie en Aulide*, 1774). In his *Iphigénie en Tauride* (1779), Spontini's *La vestale* (1807) and numerous other works, spectacle was used to establish a pseudo-religious atmosphere. In nearly all operas of the Classical period, the only substantial *divertissement* was the final one, after the conclusion of the dramatic action – an arrangement that permitted authors to conform to their artistic credo and yet meet their audience's expectations for pageantry.

With the rise of *grand opéra*, authors sought to use spectacle in innovatory and melodramatic ways. Meyerbeer and Scribe were masters of the art: examples include the ghostly nuns' orgy and seemingly successful seduction of the hero in *Robert le diable* (1831) and the innocent pastimes of the peasant skaters, sharply contrasted with the bloodthirsty Anabaptists, in *Le prophète* (1849). Since tragic endings were generally preferred, the conventional placement for the main *divertissement* was the third act, although there was

Conclusion of the third day of the 1664 grand divertissement at Versailles: eruption of the palace of the sorceress Alcina on the enchanted island; engraving by Israel Silvestre

some flexibility and additional ones might appear elsewhere. (To credit the fiasco of the Parisian version of Wagner's *Tannhäuser* in 1861 principally to the composer's failure to meet audience expectations for a third-act ballet is to oversimplify a complex social and political, as well as musical, event.)

Divertissement was also a term used to describe a short work in which dance was featured prominently and whose main theme was rejoicing. It was thus a favourite choice for *pièces de circonstance*. It could take the form of an *opéra* (Lully's *Eglogue de Versailles*, 1685; Gossec's *Le triomphe de la République*, 1793), an *opéra comique* (e.g. Propiac's *Les trois déesses rivales*, to a libretto by J. de Piis, 1788), a work in vaudevilles (*Le mai des jeunes filles, ou Un passage de militaires* by P.-I. Barré, J.-B. Radet and N. Desfontaines, 1807) or a ballet (R. Kreutzer's *La fête de Mars*, choreography by Gardel, 1809).

*

A. Félibien: *Les divertissemens de Versailles* (Paris, 1676)

L. de Cahusac: 'Divertissement', *Encyclopédie, ou Dictionnaire raisonné des sciences, des arts et des métiers*, ed. D. Diderot and others (Paris, 1751–80)

Castil-Blaze [F. H. J. Blaze]: *Dictionnaire de musique moderne* (Paris, 1821, 2/1825)

J. R. Anthony: *French Baroque Music from Beaujoyeulx to Rameau* (London, 1973, 2/1978; Fr. trans., 1981, with addl bibliography)

R. M. Isherwood: *Music in the Service of the King* (Ithaca, NY, 1973)

P. Russo: 'L'isola di Alcina: funzioni drammaturgiche del *divertissement* nella *tragédie lyrique* (1691–1735)', *NRMI*, xxi (1987), 1–15

M. ELIZABETH C. BARTLET

Djamileh. *Opéra comique* in one act by GEORGES BIZET to a libretto by LOUIS GALLET, after Alfred de Musset's story *Namouna*; Paris, Opéra-Comique (Salle Favart), 22 May 1872.

Commissioned for the Opéra-Comique in 1871, *Djamileh* was originally planned in two acts but then reduced to one. It had ten performances in 1872 but was not revived in Paris until 1938 even though it enjoyed considerable success outside France. Du Locle, director of the Opéra-Comique, had himself suggested the name 'Djamileh' to replace Musset's 'Namouna'.

Set in the palace of Haroun (tenor) in Cairo, the opera tells of his eternal quest for pleasure and his habit of acquiring a new slave girl every month. Djamileh (mezzo-soprano), who is due to be discarded when the new girl arrives, has fallen in love with Haroun, so with the help of Splendiano (baritone), Haroun's servant, she disguises herself as the incoming slave girl and thus wins Haroun's heart. The story's fanciful improbability belongs to the tradition of *opéra comique*, with opportunities for oriental melodies and dances, a comic servant and a dash of real passion. The overture and nine numbers are interspersed with dialogue and *mélodrame*.

Bizet's score is full of inventive touches, especially in its use of chromatic colour, widely mistaken for Wagnerism in 1872. In the final duet the music takes on a more serious and passionate tone, and Djamileh is characterized from the beginning by a darkly expressive melody. Her main solo, the 'Ghazel', blends exotic colour, chromatic side-slips, suppressed passion and the key of D minor to give a strong foretaste of the Habanera in *Carmen*.

HUGH MACDONALD

Dlugoszewski, Lucia (*b* Detroit, 16 June 1934). American composer. Although she began composing at three, and studied both the piano and composition as a child, she first pursued a medical career. She left Wayne State University in 1949 and went to New York to study the piano with Grete Sultan and composition with Felix Salzer at the Mannes School of Music; she later studied with Edgard Varèse (1951–4). As early as 1949 she had developed an advanced style using 'everyday sounds', but by 1954 her quest for a music stripped of outside associations led her to write for conventional instruments in unconventional ways and to invent instruments of her own. Between 1958 and 1960 she developed about a hundred new percussion instruments, made for her by the sculptor Ralph Dorazio.

In 1952 she began an association with the choreographer Erick Hawkins, becoming music director of his dance company in 1954 and providing all its music until 1972. She also provided music for productions by the Living Theater. She was virtually ignored by the music world until Virgil Thomson began to champion her work in 1965.

Among Dlugoszewski's many dance and music-theatre pieces are several which approach the realm of opera, and one specifically designated as such: *The Heidi Songs* (1970, rev. 1989), which sets Ashbery's 'Animals of All Countries' after the fashion of kabuki drama (or, to a lesser degree, Stravinsky's *Renard*), with movement and song assigned to different performers. *Tiny Opera* (1953) is a theatre piece for four poets, moving voice, dancers and piano.

Dlugoszewski's music is based on an elaborate and sophisticated aesthetic, outlined in her essay, 'What is Sound to Music?' (1973) and derived from Taoism, Zen Buddhism and the philosophy of F. S. C. Northrop. Although these ideas seem to synthesize those of Partch and Cage, they are in fact an independent, self-consistent formulation. She identifies a large number of abstract aesthetic states which provide titles for many of her works (e.g. *Tender Theater Flight Nageire*) and supply a basis for composition reminiscent of the Baroque doctrine of the affections.

*

P. Reps: *Accordingly, the Music of Lucia Dlugoszewski (Suchness Concert), in Unwrinkling Plays* (Rutland, VT, 1965)

A. Hughes: 'And Miss Dlugoszewski Experiments – a Lot', *New York Times* (7 March 1971)

L. Dlugoszewsi: 'What is Sound to Music?', *Main Currents in Modern Thought*, xxx/1 (1973), 1–11

T. Johnson: 'Lucia Dlugoszewski', *HiFi/MusAm*, xxv/6 (1975), MA4–5

J. Highwater: 'Dlugoszewski Ascending', *New York Arts Journal*, viii/3 (1981)

J. Dunning: 'The Composer who Energizes the Erick Hawkins Dancers', *New York Times* (7 Dec 1988)

ANDREW STILLER

Dłuski, Erazm (*b* Szczuczyńce, 1857; *d* Otwock, 26 Feb 1923). Polish composer. At the St Petersburg Conservatory he studied the piano with Anton Rubinstein, composition with Nikolay Solov'yov and orchestration with Rimsky-Korsakov. In 1891 he won first prize in the conservatory's annual Rubinstein Composers' Competition. On graduating he became the director of a local orchestra and worked as an accompanist and singing teacher. He moved to Warsaw in 1919 and was co-director of the opera class at the conservatory from 1920. He was made an honorary professor of the Brussels Conservatory.

Dłuski's two piano sonatas were performed by Rubinstein. However, his main interest was in operatic and vocal music. He composed five operas, of which only one, *Urwasi*, was performed in its entirety (Lwów, 1902; a concert performance had been given there in June 1901); the opera is characterized by many orientalisms and rich orchestration influenced by Rimsky-Korsakov. It was well received in St Petersburg (25 March 1902). *Kobieta z kindżałem* ('The Woman with a Dagger') was scheduled for performance in St Petersburg during the 1903–4 season, but it is not known whether or not it was given. *Romano* was staged in 1890 before its completion (1895).

Romano, 1895 (4), 1890, inc., lost
Urwasi, 1900 (2, after Kalidasa: *Vikrama and Urvasi*), Lwów, 25 Feb 1902; Biblioteka Teatru Lwowskiego, vs (Lwów, n.d.)
Madame Sans Gêne (after V. Sardou), unperf.
Narzeczona z Koryntu [The Bride of Corinth], unperf.
Kobieta z kindżałem [The Woman with a Dagger], 1902 (1, after A. Schnitzler), ? St Petersburg, 1903–4

*

SMP; *PSB* (W. Poźniak)
W. Poźniak: 'Opera po Moniuszce' [Opera after Moniuszko], *Z dziejów polskiej kultury muzycznej* [From the History of Polish Musical Culture], ii (Kraków, 1966), 265–328, esp. 301–2

ZOFIA CHECHLIŃSKA

Dneprovskaya rusalka. Opera by S. I. Davïdov; *see* LESTA, ILI DNEPROVSKAYA RUSALKA.

Dnepr Water Nymph, The. Opera by S. I. Davïdov; *see* LESTA, ILI DNEPROVSKAYA RUSALKA.

Dobbs, Mattiwilda (*b* Atlanta, GA, 11 July 1925). American soprano. She studied with Lotte Lehmann in California and with Pierre Bernac in Paris, making her début at the 1952 Holland Festival as Stravinsky's Nightingale. In 1953 she sang Zerbinetta at Glyndebourne and in 1954 made her Covent Garden début as the Queen of Shemakha (*The Golden Cockerel*). She went on to sing at the Metropolitan, where she made her début as Gilda (1956) and was particularly well known for her Olympia. She also sang at La Scala, the Paris Opéra and the principal European festivals. In 1967 she sang and recorded Konstanze under Menuhin in the Phoenix Opera production, one of her last important appearances. Her small but buoyant voice, finished technique and lively interpretations survive on a small number of recordings; perhaps the best of these is the first, a fresh and elegant performance of Leïla (*Les pêcheurs de perles*) conducted by René Leibowitz.

RICHARD DYER, ELIZABETH FORBES

Dobronić, Antun (*b* Jelsa, Hvar Island, 2 April 1878; *d* Zagreb, 12 Dec 1955). Croatian composer. After working for 14 years as a teacher he studied composition with Vítězslav Novák and others at the conservatory in Prague (1910–12), and from 1922 to 1940 was professor at the Academy of Music in Zagreb. His studies in Prague had a decisive influence on his aesthetic views, and he became one of the most prominent representatives of the so-called national style in Croatian and Yugoslav music between the two world wars. He sought to realize his ideas not only in his compositions but also through writings and polemics. Believing that the fulfilment of the national style lay in a synthesis of the sophistication of Western European art music with the primitiveness and strength of the national folk idiom, he developed a technique based on a predominantly polyphonic treatment of melodies, many of them of folk origin or in folk style. A prolific composer, he left 12 works for the musical stage. Opera was an outdated form in his opinion; he searched for original solutions to the problems of content and form in each work, in most cases defining the genre with a subtitle.

unperformed unless otherwise stated

Dubrovački diptihon [The Dubrovnik Diptych] (scenic sym., 2 pts): 1 Suton [The Dusk], 1917 (1, after I. Vojnović); 2 Novela od Stanca [The Joke about Stanac], 1920 (1, after M. Držić)
Mara, 1928 (musical-scenic mysterium, introduction, 2, epilogue, after M. Begović)
Udovica Rošlinka [The Widow Rošlinka], 1931 (musical comedy, 3, after C. Golar), Zagreb, 23 May 1934
Požar strasti [The Fire of Passion], 1933 (musical-scenic tragedy, 3, after J. Kosor)
Rkač, 1935 (musical-scenic lyrics, 3, after P. Petrović: *Rkač*), Zagreb, 1 Dec 1938; later retitled Goran
Ekvinocij [Equinox], 1938 (scenic sym., 4, with int, after Vojnović)
Ognjište [The Fireside], 1942 (mysterium, introduction, 2, interludium, epilogue, after M. Budak)
Pokladna noć [Carnival Night], 1945 (mono-opera for Bar, musical-scenic satire, 3, after Z. Veljačić), Rijeka, 19 Feb 1955
Sluga Jernej [The Servant Jernej], 1946 (scenic oratorio, 3, with preludes and interludes, after I. Cankar)
Vječnaja pamjat [Eternal Memory], 1947 (musical-scenic satire, 2 pts): 1 Medvjed [The Bear] (1, after A. P. Chekhov); 2 Balerina [The Ballerina] (1, after N. V. Gogol)
Mati [Mother], 1948 (musical-scenic epic, 2, after M. Gorky)
Mali kadija [The Little Cadi], 1954 (musical-scenic tale, children's op, 2, interlude, after J. Truhelka and *The Thousand and One Nights*)

*

K. Kovačević: *Hrvatski kompozitori i njihova djela* [Croatian Composers and their Works] (Zagreb, 1960), 127–43
J. Andreis: *Music in Croatia* (Zagreb, 1974)
M. Miletić: 'Antun Dobronić, 1878–1955', *Zvuk* (1979), no.3, pp.50–58
K. Kos: 'Slovensko selo u djelu "Vdova Roślinka" Cvetka Golara i Antuna Dobronića' [The Slovenian Village in *The Widow Roślinka* by Cvetko Golar and Antun Dobronić], *Slovenska opera v evropskem okviru* [Slovenian Opera in a European Context] (Ljubljana, 1982), 132–42
S. Majer-Bobetko: 'Neke glazbenoestetske koncepcije mladoga Dobronića' [Some Musical-Aesthetic Ideas of the Young Dobronić], *Arti musices*, xiii/1 (1983), 55–67

KORALJKA KOS

Dobroven [Dobrowen; Barabeichik], **Issay Alexandrovich** (*b* Nizhniy Novgorod, 15/27 Feb 1891; *d* Oslo, 9 Dec 1953). Norwegian conductor of Russian birth. At the Moscow Conservatory he studied the piano with Igumnov and composition with Taneyev before becoming a pupil of Leopold Godowsky in Vienna. He began conducting in Moscow, but after the Revolution settled in Germany. Between the wars he held appointments at Berlin and Dresden (from 1924); Sofia (Bulgarian Opera, 1927–8); Frankfurt and San Francisco (from 1930); and the Budapest Opera (1936–9). Specializing in Russian music, he conducted the German première of *Boris Godunov* in Dresden in 1922. In the mid-1930s he went to Oslo and became a Norwegian citizen. He escaped in 1940 to Sweden, where he was engaged at the Stockholm Royal Opera. After 1945 he resumed travelling, and in 1949 he initiated a notable series of Russian operas at La Scala, putting into practice his long-standing concern for the integration of music and drama by directing as well as conducting. His last operatic engagement was a revival of *Boris Godunov* at Covent Garden (1952–3).

NOËL GOODWIN

Dobrski, Julian (*b* Nowe, 31 Dec 1811 or 1812; *d* Warsaw, 2 May 1886). Polish tenor. He studied in Warsaw with C. E. Soliva. After making his début in *Il barbiere di Siviglia* at the Wielki Theatre, Warsaw, on 20 September 1832, he performed there in operas by Bellini, Donizetti, Meyerbeer, Weber, Hérold, Auber, Halévy and Verdi. He sang in Turin and Genoa

(1846–8) and was forced to leave his native country after taking part in the spring revolution of 1848. On 1 January 1858 he created Jontek in the revised *Halka* at the Wielki; Moniuszko transformed a melody in mazurka rhythm into the Act 4 aria 'Szumią jodły' ('Fir Trees Sway') specially for him. He captivated audiences by the beauty of his tone as well as the dramatic power of his performances. On 25 February 1858, after a performance of *Ernani*, he received in tribute to his 25 years on the stage a solid gold diamond-encrusted wreath, engraved with the titles of all the operas in which he had appeared. In 1861 he again incurred the displeasure of the authorities for his patriotic attitude and was prematurely dismissed from the Wielki Theatre. However, in 1865 he returned to Warsaw to sing and gave his last operatic performance there that year, in Halévy's *La Juive*. He had taught since 1861, and later he held important teaching posts in Warsaw.

IRENA PONIATOWSKA

Dobrzyński, Ignacy Feliks (*b* Romanów, Volhynia, 25 Feb 1807; *d* Warsaw, 9 Oct 1867). Polish composer. He was brought up at Romanów, where his father was master of the chapel of Count Iliński. After 1825 Dobrzyński studied with Józef Elsner at the conservatory in Warsaw, where he was later active as a teacher, critic, impresario, pianist and conductor; he was director of the Warsaw Opera from 1852 to 1855.

As a composer Dobrzyński followed the Viennese Classical tradition, though his musical language incorporates elements of Polish folk music. In 1838 he completed his first stage work, *Monbar, czyli Flibustierowie* ('Monbar, or The Filibusters'; 3, S. Pruszakowa and L. Paprocki, after K. van der Velde: *Der Flibustier*; Warsaw, 10 January 1863; arr. pf (Warsaw, 1860)). Dobrzyński's two other works for the theatre were both dramas in three acts: *Konrad Wallenrod* (K. Kaszewski and J. Królikowski, after A. Mickiewicz), which, although never completed, was performed in Warsaw on 19 June 1859, and *Burgrafowie* ('The Burgraves'; Kaszewski, after V. Hugo), performed in Warsaw on 22 September 1860.

ALINA NOWAK-ROMANOWICZ

Dobson, John (*b* Derby, 17 Nov 1930). English tenor. He studied in London and Italy, making his début in 1956 at Bergamo as Pinkerton. In 1959 he sang Godvino (*Aroldo*) at Wexford and joined the Royal Opera, for whom he has sung over 85 roles in 30 years. For the WNO he sang Alfredo (1963) and Luigi (*Il tabarro*, 1966). His Covent Garden repertory included David, Loge, Mime, Jaquino, Andres (*Wozzeck*), Turiddu, Rodolfo, Pang, Robert Boles (*Peter Grimes*), Snout, Shuisky, Sellem (*The Rake's Progress*) and Spalanzani. He created Paris in *King Priam* at Coventry (1962), Luke in *The Ice Break* (1977) and sang in the British première of Berio's *Un re in ascolto* (1989). A totally reliable singer, he was a splendid character actor.

ELIZABETH FORBES

Doche, Joseph-Denis (*b* Paris, 22 Aug 1766; *d* Soissons, 20 July 1825). French composer. He was trained as a choirboy at Meaux Cathedral and at the age of 19 was *maître de chapelle* at Coutances. He returned to Paris in 1791 and three years later became a viola player, then a cellist and double bass player, at the Théâtre du Vaudeville, where several of his works had their first performances; from 1810 he was deputy director and from 1815 director until his retirement eight years later.

His son Alexandre-Pierre-Joseph Doche (1799–1849) was a violinist and musical director at the Théâtre du Vaudeville, in succession to his father; he went to St Petersburg in 1848. Two one-act *opéras comiques* by him were given in Paris, *Le veuf de Malabar* (1846) and *Alix* (1847), by the Opéra-Comique at the Salle Favart.

first performed in Paris unless otherwise stated

Adèle et Didier, 1791

La haine aux femmes (vaudeville, J. N. Bouilly and M. J. Pain), 1800

Point de bruit (opéretta, 2, Tournay), Porte-St-Martin, 25 Oct 1802

Fanchon la vielleuse (vaudeville, 3, Bouilly and Pain), Vaudeville, 19 March 1803, vs (Paris, *c*1803)

Les deux sentinelles (oc, 1, Henrion), Gaîté, 26 Sept 1803

Le poète satirique (vaudeville, 1, Bouilly), Vaudeville, 30 Nov 1803

Lantara (mélodrame, P. Y. Barré and others), Vaudeville, 2 Oct 1809

La belle au bois dormant (féerie, 2, Bouilly and T. M. Dumersan), 1811

Unperf.: Les trois Derville, 1818 (oc); Les deux Edouard (mélodrame)

Docteur Miracle, Le. *Opérette* in one act by GEORGES BIZET to a libretto by Léon Battu and LUDOVIC HALÉVY; Paris, Bouffes-Parisiens, 9 April 1857.

In 1856 Offenbach announced a competition for an *opéra comique* to be played at his theatre, the Bouffes-Parisiens. The jury of eminent figures from the world of opera were unable to agree on a winner out of the six finalists, so the settings by Bizet and Lecocq were awarded a shared first prize. The two works were staged alternately in April 1857 with the same cast in both, each work receiving 11 performances. Bizet's opera was not revived until 1951.

The opera consists of an overture and six numbers for a cast of four singers. It relates how a 'podestat' (a mayor or magistrate) (baritone) wishes to protect his daughter Laurette (soprano) from the attentions of a soldier, Silvio (tenor). Disguised as a servant Silvio makes an omelette for the family dinner. He is discovered and sent away, so he leaves a message that the omelette was poisoned and that only Dr Miracle can cure them. Draped in black and speaking Latin, the doctor extracts the promise of Laurette's hand in exchange for the cure. Laurette agrees to the sacrifice, upon which the doctor reveals himself as Silvio in disguise.

Both libretto and music conform to prevailing tastes in *opéra comique*, with hints of Offenbach's new manner. At the age of 18 Bizet had a polished command of this fluent, tuneful style, although his word-setting is still rather stiff. The centrepiece of the comedy is the 'Omelette Quartet' with its solemn and mock-heroic invocations to a poorly cooked omelette.

HUGH MACDONALD

Doese, Helena (*b* Göteborg, 13 Aug 1946). Swedish soprano. She studied in Göteborg and in Rome with Luigi Ricci, making her début as Aida at Göteborg in 1971. She then joined the Berne Opera for three seasons (to 1975), during which time she made her British début at Glyndebourne in 1974 as Countess Almaviva and her Covent Garden début the same year as Mimì. As a member of the Stockholm Royal Opera from 1975, she sang a variety of roles including Kát'a in a production by Joachim Herz and an acclaimed Eva (*Die Meistersinger*) for Götz Friedrich. Her American début was at San Francisco in 1982 as Countess Almaviva, and she has sung Aida with Australian Opera. Other roles associated with her are Agathe, Donna Anna, Amelia (*Simon Boccanegra*), Ariadne, Chrysothemis, Fiordiligi, Gutrune and Sieglinde. During the 1980s she became a principal with the Frankfurt Opera. A lyric soprano of expressive character and engaging stage personality, she has made video recordings as Mimì, Eva and Donna Anna and is frequently heard as a concert soloist. NOËL GOODWIN

Dohnányi, Christoph von (*b* Berlin, 8 Sept 1929). German conductor. After studying law in Munich, he entered the Musikhochschule there in 1948 and won the Richard Strauss Conducting Prize in 1951, his final year. He joined his grandfather, the composer Ernő Dohnányi, in the USA, where he attended conducting courses given by Bernstein. In 1952 he was engaged by Solti as chorus master and conductor at the Frankfurt Opera. He was Generalmusikdirektor in Lübeck (1957–63), Kassel (1963–6) and Frankfurt (1968–75), and held a similar post at the Hamburg Staatsoper (1977–84), transferring thence to the Cleveland Orchestra. Dohnányi conducted the premières of Henze's *Der junge Lord* (1965, Berlin) and *The Bassarids* (1966, Salzburg Festival), and has appeared frequently at major European festivals, in Munich and Vienna, and in the USA at the Metropolitan and the San Francisco Opera. He first appeared at Covent Garden conducting *Salome* (1974), and has returned for much-admired accounts of *Wozzeck*, *Die Frau ohne Schatten*, *Die Meistersinger* and a new production of *Fidelio* (1990). Dohnányi is one of the most successful German conductors of the postwar era. He has been praised particularly for his technical ability, orchestral control and innate musicianship, most notably when he conducted Schoenberg's *Moses und Aron* at Frankfurt and Vienna in the 1970s. On occasion he has been criticized for a want of breadth in his readings of Romantic works. HANSPETER KRELLMANN, ALAN BLYTH

Dohnányi, Ernő [Ernst von] (*b* Pozsony [now Bratislava], 27 July 1877; *d* New York, 9 Feb 1960). Hungarian composer. His formal education in music was brief yet of great significance: he was the first Hungarian of extraordinary talent who chose to attend the Music Academy of Budapest. His meteoric rise began in London, and by 1899 he was a world celebrity as both a pianist and a composer, acclaimed by Brahms himself. In 1905 Joachim invited him to the Hochschule in Berlin, and during the ten years he taught there he composed some of his finest works, while continuing his concert tours in Europe and the USA.

In 1915 Dohnányi returned to Budapest and undertook the reshaping of Hungarian musical life. For 25 years he was chief conductor of the Hungarian Philharmonic Society (1919–44); he was also music director of Hungarian radio (1931–44) and director of the Liszt Academy (1934–41), where his masterclasses were the training ground for many artists. In 1944 Dohnányi left Hungary and eventually settled in the USA at Tallahassee, teaching at Florida State University.

Dohnányi remained outside the stylistic revolutions of the 20th century, evolving a language entirely his own. Friendships in literary circles during periods of residence in Vienna (1901–2 and 1903–5) awakened his interest in the stage. The first result was a mime play, *Der Schleier der Pierrette* (1908–9), based on a drama by Arthur Schnitzler. It offered an opportunity to combine elements of abstract and programme music and was a great success in Dresden, Berlin and Budapest. In Vienna Elsa Galafrès took the part of Pierrette, and the friendship that developed between her and Dohnányi eventually led to their marriage. Victor Heindl, another poet friend in Vienna, supplied the libretto for *Tante Simona* (1911–12), a comic opera in one act which, despite charming sections, did not enjoy lasting success. During this period Dohnányi also began work on two full-length operas. Awareness of his increased interest in the musical theatre prompted offers from the Budapest Opera of the post of director, but he repeatedly declined the post.

A vajda tornya ('The Vaivode's Tower', 1915–22) is about the building of a tower as a last defence; an evil spirit destroys it every time it nears completion. To placate the spirit, the first woman who crosses the bridge over the moat must be walled in alive, and this is the lovely daughter-in-law of the old chieftain, who has to carry out the sacrifice. The German and French co-authors set the story in Albania, but since a similar legend was very much alive in Transylvania (then part of Hungary), Dohnányi moved the setting there, reworking the text himself. The opera follows Romantic traditions, but Dohnányi's voice is unmistakable. It displays his outstanding melodic gift and the transparent orchestration is clearly the work of a master chamber musician. This is the only full-length Hungarian opera written in the first half of the 20th century.

Der Tenor (1920–27), on the other hand, is one of the few true comic operas of the century. Based on Carl Sternheim's *Bürger Schippel*, it tells the story of a typical German civic vocal quartet whose leading tenor dies and there is no one to replace him but Schippel, the drunken flautist of the nearby tavern. Schippel is naturally expected to remember his place in social intercourse, but complications arise when he decides that he wants to marry the daughter of the quartet's wealthiest member. The opera mirrors three layers of society and the relationships between them. Notable is the servility of the burghers towards the duke, seen against their constant humiliation of Schippel. The composer offers his best work here: the music sparkles with wit and abounds in lyricism. The work was an instant success in Hungary and throughout Germany. Its run came to an end when Dohnányi refused to substitute a non-Jewish alternative for the Mendelssohn song quoted in the finale. The first postwar revival was undertaken by BBC radio, followed by Hungarian Television.

Tante Simona op.20, 1911–12 (komische Oper, 1, V. Heindl), Dresden, Kgl, 22 Jan 1913

A vajda tornya [The Vaivode's Tower] op.30, 1915–22 (romantikus opera, 3, V. Lányi, after H. H. Ewers and M. Henry), Budapest, Magyar Királyi, 18 March 1922

Der Tenor op.34, 1920–27 (komische Oper, 3, E. Góth, after C. Sternheim: *Bürger Schippel*), Budapest, Magyar Királyi, 9 Feb 1929

*

L. Podhradszky: 'The Works of Ernő Dohnányi', *SM*, vi (1964), 357–73

B. Vázsonyi: *Dohnányi Ernő* (Budapest, 1971)

BÁLINT VÁZSONYI

Doktor Faust **(i).** *Original-Oper* in four acts by IGNAZ WALTER to a libretto by Heinrich Gottlieb Schmieder after the plays Maler Müller's *Fausts Leben*, Gotthold Ephraim Lessing's *Doctor Faust*, JOHANN WOLFGANG VON GOETHE's *Faust: ein Fragment* and Friedrich Maximilian Klinger's *Fausts Leben, Thaten und Höllenfahrt*;

first version, Bremen, 28 December 1787; second version, Hanover, 8 June 1798; revised version, with a new text by Christian August Mämminger, Regensburg, Hoftheater, 10 October 1819.

Walter probably began work on the opera during his association with Schmieder at the Nationaltheater in Mainz from 1788 to 1792. Only the musical texts of Schmieder's libretto survive. A copy of these from the original production (now in *US-Wc*) carries handwritten notes indicating that Walter himself, one of Germany's leading tenors, took the part of Faust (with his wife, the soprano Juliane Browne Roberts, cast as the Queen of Aragon). The texts include several direct appropriations from Goethe (including the *Romanze* 'Es war ein König in Tule' in Act 1 and Gretchen's aria 'Meine Ruh ist hin' in Act 4). In the concluding graveyard scene Faust places the unconscious Gretchen on a gravestone; then, called to a reckoning by Leviathan (Mephistopheles), he is surrounded by a demons' chorus and dragged off to hell.

See also FAUST. THOMAS BAUMAN

Doktor Faust **(ii).** Opera by FERRUCCIO BUSONI to his own libretto based on the 16th-century puppet plays; Dresden, Sächsisches Staatstheater, 21 May 1925.

Docktor Faust	baritone
Wagner *his famulus*	bass
Mephistopheles	tenor
The Duke of Parma	tenor
The Duchess of Parma	soprano
Master of Ceremonies	bass
Gretchen's Brother	baritone
A Lieutenant	tenor
A Theologian	baritone
A Law Student	baritone
A Scientist	baritone
Prologue	speaker
Helena [Helen of Troy]	dance or mime
Three Students from Cracow	male voices
Five Spirit Voices *servants of Lucifer*	male voices
Four Students in Wittenberg	male voices
Three Voices from On High	female voices

Churchgoers, spirit voices, soldiers, courtiers, Catholic and Protestant students, huntsmen, peasants

Setting Wittenberg and Parma in the 16th century

Busoni considered several subjects, including the Wandering Jew, Leonardo da Vinci and Don Juan, before finally deciding on Faust. He wrote the libretto between 1910 and 1915, the most significant portion coming to him impulsively at Christmas 1914. The first draft was published in 1917 (in *Die weissen Blätter*) and a revised version in 1920 (by Kiepenheuer, Berlin). Work on the score was begun in 1916, although the first musical studies for the opera date from 1912. Ill-health began to impede Busoni's progress from 1921, and when he died in 1924 two substantial passages were still incomplete, the apparition of Helen to Faust in scene ii and the closing scene.

For the première, in Dresden, the missing music was provided by Philipp Jarnach. Robert Burg sang the title role and Theo Strack, Mephistopheles; Fritz Busch conducted an ensemble which also included Meta Seinemeyer (Duchess of Parma), Paul Schöffler and Erna Berger. An abridged disc recording with Dietrich Fischer-Dieskau in the title role, conducted by Ferdinand Leitner, was issued in 1969. In 1974, hitherto unknown sketches for the missing scenes were acquired by the Staatsbibliothek Preussischer Kulturbesitz, Berlin, from Philipp Jarnach. Antony Beaumont's new completion, based on this material, was first performed at the Teatro Comunale in Bologna on 2 April 1985.

The opera begins with a Symphonia in which distant bell sounds are followed by music which vacillates between darkness (the *Nocturne symphonique*) and light (an Easter chorale). Invisible voices chime out the word 'Pax' as if bells.

PROLOGUE ('Der Dichter an die Zuschauer') In ten verses of *ottava rima*, the poet outlines the genesis of the libretto and stresses its puppet origins.

PRELUDE 1 *Faust's study in Wittenberg, at Easter* Wagner admits the three students from Cracow, who present Faust with a magic book. The music is largely adapted from Busoni's *Sonatina seconda* for piano, composed in 1912, the work in which he made his closest approach to atonality.

PRELUDE 2 *The same scene at midnight* With the aid of the book, Faust summons the servants of Lucifer. Mephistopheles, the highest of six spirit voices, claims to be 'swifter than the thoughts of mankind'. He draws up the traditional pact, which Faust signs with his own blood, while a distant chorus of worshippers sings the creed. Faust collapses.

The opening adagio in C♯ minor returns at the central point of the scene and again, in C major, at the close. Mephistopheles' first utterances, rising to a bloodcurdling high C, are followed by a brilliant scherzo. The adagio music encircles two sets of variations: orchestral variations to depict the increasing swiftness of the servants of Lucifer, and choral variations for the Easter music, which builds from a distant trio of solo voices to a clamorous setting of 'Et iterum venturus est' for double chorus, offstage brass, bells and organ.

SCENIC INTERMEZZO *A Romanesque chapel* Gretchen's brother vows to avenge himself on Faust; Mephistopheles engineers his brutal murder. A sombre D minor prelude for organ and orchestra in expanded rondo form is interrupted by a military march, which accompanies the six soldiers conjured up by Mephistopheles.

MAIN PLAY Scene i *The ducal park in Parma* At the climax of the Duke's wedding celebrations, the Master of Ceremonies presents Faust to the court as a celebrated magician. In three visions (Samson and Delilah, Solomon and the Queen of Sheba, Salome and John the Baptist), Faust expresses his love for the Duchess whom, with the aid of Mephistopheles, he soon succeeds in winning. The Duchess sings of her infatuation with Faust, then flees with him. Disguised as court chaplain, Mephistopheles advises the Duke to remarry, raising his clawed hand in ghastly benediction.

The scene opens with a *cortège* and continues with a brilliant ballet sequence. Busoni's Divertimento for flute op.52 provided the substance for the Duchess's solo scene, while the dialogue between the Duke and Mephistopheles is adapted from the Toccata for piano. A sombre symphonic intermezzo (a shortened version of the Sarabande from op.51) marks the turning-point in the drama.

'Doktor Faust' (Busoni), Main play, scene ii (a tavern in Wittenberg): design by Karl Dannemann for the original production at the Sächsisches Staatstheater, Dresden, 21 May 1925

Scene ii *A tavern in Wittenberg* Faust mediates in an argument between Catholic and Protestant students, but his words only lead to further uproar. Mephistopheles, disguised as a courier, brings the dead body of the Duchess's child. He sets it alight and out of the flames emerges Helen of Troy. Faust, unable to grasp the visionary figure, is confronted by the students from Cracow, who tell him that he is to die at midnight. He welcomes his final hour.

Busoni considered the students' dispute to be his most perfect operatic composition technically. Faust's monologue 'Traum der Jugend', in which he muses ecstatically on the achievements of generations not yet born, is a visionary episode, dating from the spring of 1923. This was the last music for the opera that Busoni lived to complete.

Scene iii *A street in Wittenberg* The nightwatchman (Mephistopheles) calls the hour. Students skittishly serenade Wagner, who has suceeded Faust as rector. Faust gives alms to a beggar woman: she is the Duchess, who urges him to 'finish the work before midnight'. He transfers his soul to the dead child and, as the nightwatchman calls the midnight hour, he falls dead. The child arises in his place and strides out into the night.

The first part of the scene is an extended scherzo. Faust's entry is followed by a succession of musical reprises. Busoni's score breaks off shortly before the reappearance of Helen, at bar 490.

* * *

The score is assembled from numerous musical studies, ranging from unfinished fragments (lieder, piano pieces etc.) to published works including the *Nocturne symphonique* op.43, the Sarabande and Cortège op.51, the *Tanzwalzer* op.53 for orchestra, the *Sonatina seconda* and Toccata for piano and several Goethe settings. Diverse as these sources are, they are unified by what Busoni described as his 'Faustian' musical vocabulary: tonal music of extreme harmonic subtlety, with predominantly polyphonic textures and clear but sophisticated orchestral sonorities.

Busoni distinguished between Wagnerian music drama and his own (epic) theatre, in which words and music are intended to fulfil their own, separate functions. In 1922 he published his essay 'Über die Partitur des "Doktor Faust"', in which he stressed that each section of his score is shaped into an organic if unorthodox symphonic form: the festivities at Parma (scene i) are cast in the form of a dance suite, while the tavern scene at Wittenberg (scene ii) features a scherzo, chorale and fugue. The introspective Faustian element is counteracted in each main scene by lighter, extrovert episodes. Hence the work can be understood as a modern mystery play, part folk festival, part Passion.

See also FAUST. ANTONY BEAUMONT

Doktor Faustus. Opera in two acts by GIACOMO MANZONI to his own libretto after THOMAS MANN's novel; Milan, Teatro alla Scala, 16 May 1989.

Mann's narrative is pared down to a central core. We are immediately confronted by the infection with syphilis of the composer Adrian Leverkühn (bass-baritone) by the prostitute whom he calls Hetaera Esmeralda (soprano). (Her name, translated into a note-sequence, is to permeate his music, as it does Manzoni's opera.) Leverkühn is visited by Him (the Devil), who spells out the price he must pay for the enjoyment of his genius: he must renounce love; tertiary syphilis will in due course consume him. Since He constantly changes shape, Manzoni uses a trinity of voices (bass, light tenor and soprano), each pursuing a more agile and elaborate vocal line than the last.

In Act 2 Echo, Leverkühn's nephew (treble), comes to stay. Together they listen to the 'Ariel Songs', on which Mann recorded that Leverkühn was working at the time of Echo's visit. Adrian's love for Echo is punished by the boy's grave illness, a tension made the more acute by the worldly chatter of the impresario, Saul Fittelberg, whose visit Manzoni interposes at this juncture. Echo dies. Between Acts 2 and 3 Manzoni evokes another of

'Doktor Faustus' (Manzoni): Act 1 scene iv from the original production, designed and directed by Robert Wilson, at La Scala, Milan, 16 May 1989, showing Wilson in the role of Serenus Zeitblom (right) observing Adrian Leverkühn as he composes

Leverkühn's compositions, the choral 'Doctor Fausti Weheklag'. At the start of Act 3 Leverkühn makes his manic confession before an increasingly embarrassed assembly of friends and associates, and submits to his fate. Serenus Zeitblom, Mann's narrator, and until now a silent witness, recounts the final decade of Leverkühn's life, passed in the mute, shattered abeyance of tertiary syphilis.

With its roots in the writings of Adorno and Schoenberg, both authoritatively translated by Manzoni, Mann's novel had long been a focus of obsessive interest for the composer. Before preparing his libretto Manzoni wrote the orchestral *Scene sinfoniche per il Doktor Faust* (1984). From these he developed musical materials for the opera, in which the texture-based idioms of previous works (tellingly used in the music accompanying Echo's illness) cede their central place to melody. The intensive thematic working, particularly of the Hetaera Esmeralda pitch sequence, reflects the praxis of Leverkühn/Schoenberg, but Manzoni used it to his own purposes, rather than as an evocation of early 20th-century modernism.

See also FAUST. DAVID OSMOND-SMITH

Doktor und Apotheker ('Doctor and Apothecary' [*Der Apotheker und der Doktor*]). *Komisches Singspiel* in two acts by CARL DITTERS VON DITTERSDORF to a libretto by GOTTLIEB STEPHANIE (the younger), purportedly after 'Graf von N**'s *L'apoticaire de Murcie*; Vienna, Burgtheater, 11 July 1786.

The village apothecary Stössel (bass) and his wife Claudia (contralto) hope to match their daughter Leonore (soprano) with the boisterous Captain Sturmwald (tenor). But she has fallen in love with Gotthold (tenor), the son of Stössel's sworn enemy, Doktor Krautmann (bass). Gotthold and his companion Sichel (tenor), who loves Stössel's niece Rosalie (soprano), contrive a wild-goose chase that plays on the apothecary's professional vanity in order to get him out of the way. Their tryst with the young ladies is interrupted by the appearance of Claudia, which sends them into hiding. The situation is further complicated by the return of Stössel with Sturmwald. Another attempt at infiltration – Sichel disguised as Sturmwald and Gotthold as a notary – secures the unwitting parents' signatures on marriage contracts joining the young lovers.

With his first comic opera for Vienna, Dittersdorf scored his greatest and most abiding triumph. *Doktor und Apotheker* (originally *Der Apotheker und der Doktor*) is the only German opera from Joseph II's Vienna apart from Mozart's *Die Entführung aus dem Serail* to have held the stage to the present day. At its première the Vienna *Realzeitung* declared it 'the one work among all new German operas that has earned and deserved the greatest applause. The music is very original and full of the most beautiful ideas – a true masterpiece of art.' At Vienna's imperial theatres alone it was performed 72 times between 1786 and 1798.

The score marked out the direction that Dittersdorf followed in all his subsequent operas for Vienna and Oels. Its arias are specially rich in comic strokes (Stössel's vainglorious 'Galenus und Hippocrates sind gegen mich nur Stümper') and cheerful warmth (Rosalie's 'Verliebte brauchen keine Zeugen'). The Act 1 finale, following the latest Italian practice, is a long, multi-sectional affair with surprising turns of events.

Doktor und Apotheker, unlike most German operas of the period, found its way very quickly to major theatres abroad as well as those in German-speaking lands. A considerably altered version with some new music by Stephen Storace enjoyed great success at Drury Lane in 1788. THOMAS BAUMAN

Dolcevillico, Francesco Saverio. *See* SÜSSMAYR, FRANZ XAVER.

Dolidze, Viktor Isidorovich (*b* Ozurgetu, 18/30 July 1890; *d* Tbilisi, 24 May 1933). Georgian composer. His early training was in banking; his musical interests grew, however, and before long he had learnt to play several instruments and organized an orchestra of mandolins and guitars in Tbilisi. He entered the Kiev Institute of Commerce while concurrently studying the piano and composition at the music school. After graduating from Kiev in 1917, he devoted himself to composition. His first big project was the comic opera

Keto da Kote ('Keto and Kote'), based on Akvsenti Tsarageli's comedy *Khanuma*; the earliest and still the most popular Georgian comic opera, it is the work for which he is chiefly remembered. Completed in 1917, it had its first performance in 1919, the year in which two other important Georgian operas, Paliashvili's *Abesalom da Eteri* ('Abesalom and Etery') and Arakishvili's *Tkmuleba Shota Rustavelze* ('The Legend of Shota Rustaveli'), first appeared. Dolidze wrote two more operas and left another, *Zamira*, incomplete at his death.

all librettos by the composer

Keto da Kote [Keto and Kote] (comic op, after A. Tsarageli: *Khanuma*), Tbilisi, 1919

Lellia (after Tsarageli: *Lezginskaya devushka Guldzhavar* [The Lezginka Girl Guldzhavar]), Tbilisi, 1922

Tsisana (after Ertatsmindeli), Tbilisi, 1929

Zamira, inc., excerpts Tbilisi, 1930

*

S. Korev: *'Keto i Kote' V. Dolidze* (Moscow, 1951)

STEPHEN JOHNSON

Dolores, La. Opera in three acts by TOMÁS BRETÓN to his own libretto after a play by Feliú y Codina; Madrid, Teatro de la Zarzuela, 16 March 1895.

Dolores (soprano) is a maid at an inn in mid-19th-century Calatayud. Her suitors include the army sergeant Rojas (bass), the young barber Melchior (bass), who boasts of having enjoyed her favours, and the wealthy Patricio (baritone), who organizes a festival in her honour. A further candidate, the innkeeper's young theology student nephew Lazaro (tenor), bravely rescues Rojas from an attacking bull but kills Melchior to protect Dolores from his advances. By taking the blame for the killing, Dolores demonstrates that she reciprocates Lazaro's affection, but Lazaro insists on shouldering responsibility as vengeance on Melchior for dishonouring her. The opera was produced in Lisbon, Vienna and Prague and was revived at the Teatro del Liceo, Barcelona, in 1975. Highlights of a work full of Spanish colour, rhythms and passion are the *jota* that ends Act 1 and the Act 3 duet for Lazaro and Dolores, 'Dí que es verdad que me quieres'. ANDREW LAMB

Domanda di matrimonio, Una ('A Marriage Proposal'). *Opera buffa* in one act by LUCIANO CHAILLY to a libretto by Claudio Fino and Saverio Vertone after ANTON PAVLOVICH CHEKHOV's play *The Proposal*; Milan, Piccola Scala, 22 May 1957.

The opera, composed in 1956, is set in the country house of the landowner Chabukov and centres on three characters: the property-owning neighbour Ivan Vassil'evich Lomov (tenor), Stefan Stefanovich Chabukov (baritone) and the latter's 25-year-old daughter, Natalya Stefanovna (lyric soprano). The plot revolves around the comic mishaps of Lomov, who wants to marry Natalya but, because of his timidity and awkwardness, cannot bring himself to ask for her hand. In spite of Chabukov's efforts to bring about their union, encounters between Lomov and the proud and argumentative Natalya always end in a quarrel, whether about property rights or about the prowess of their respective dogs. During one of these rows, Lomov faints. Recovering, he finds Natalya surprisingly demonstrative; Chabukov, exasperated by their arguing, asks them to marry. The two accept the idea but then again begin to quarrel.

Chailly adapts Chekhov's narrative to the customary self-contained numbers of *opera buffa*, with arias, duets and trios. The work as a whole has a rhythmic verve which – as Massimo Mila stressed – seems to wink at Rossinian precedents, within a stylistic context that makes complex references to a neo-classical mould.

RAFFAELE POZZI

Domanínská [Klobásková, Vyčichlová], **Libuše** (*b* Brno, 4 July 1924). Czech soprano. She studied at Brno Conservatory and with Řezníčková, made her début as Blaženka in Smetana's *The Secret* with the Brno Opera in 1945 and soon became a leading member of the company. Her soft, warm, youthful dramatic soprano voice, gifted in cantilena and capable of delicate expressive nuance, was primarily valuable in Smetana. But she won great success with Janáček's Jenůfa, Kát'a and the Vixen, in which the outstanding character of her voice was supported by sensitive dramatic feeling. In 1955 she joined the Prague National Theatre; with that company she sang at the Edinburgh and Holland festivals and the Helsinki Sibelius festival. She also appeared at the Teatro Colón, Buenos Aires, and as a regular guest at the Vienna Staatsoper, 1958–68. As well as her Czech roles, she sang in Russian and Soviet operas and in Verdi, Puccini and Mozart.

ALENA NĚMCOVÁ

Domenico [Dominici], **Gianpaolo di** [Paolo, Giampaolo de, Giovan Paolo de] (*fl* Naples, *c*1706–41). Italian composer. He was probably a Neapolitan; the librettos of his three comic operas name him as 'Vertuoso de cammera del la ... dochessa de Laurenzano', and he was paid 45 ducats for playing in the S Carlo orchestra in 1739–40. His first opera, *Lisa pontegliosa* (A. Piscopo; Naples, Fiorentini, winter 1719), though described by Scherillo as belonging to the pastoral variety of *opera buffa*, is more correctly categorized as an example of the customary Neapolitan domestic farce transferred to a pastoral setting, for in number of characters, plot and dramaturgy the work is far closer to the popular *chelleta pe' mmuseca* than to the traditional pastoral comedy. Both Domenico's other operas, *Li stravestemiente affortunate* (1719, F. A. Tullio; Naples, Fiorentini, November 1722) and *Lo schiavo p'amore* (Naples, Fiorentini, November 1724), rely heavily on the comic device of transvestite disguise, borrowed from literary romance. The libretto of the latter work contains an interesting letter by its unknown author (A. Palomba according to Manferrari) criticizing the public taste in comic opera. This taste, he said, requires that an *opera buffa* be short, yet contain many time-consuming arias; that the plot be complicated, but that there be little of the necessary recitative to develop such a plot; that the opera be highly amusing, yet be without any pungency of wit. Domenico also contributed, with Palella, Porpora and G. Signorille, to the *commedia per musica Il trionfo del valore* (A. Palomba, Naples, Nuovo, winter 1741).

*

CroceN; *EitnerQ*

M. Scherillo: *L'opera buffa napoletana durante il settecento: storia letteraria* (Naples, 1883, 2/1917)

U. Manferrari: *Dizionario universale delle opere melodrammatiche*, i (Florence, 1954), 316

V. Viviani: *Storia del teatro napoletano* (Naples, 1969), 317–20

JAMES L. JACKMAN

Domgraf-Fassbänder, Willi (*b* Aachen, 19 Feb 1897; *d* Nuremberg, 13 Feb 1978). German baritone. He studied with Jacques Stückgold and Paul Bruns in Berlin and Borgatti in Milan. He made his début at Aachen in 1922 as Count Almaviva. Engagements followed at the Deutsche Oper, Berlin, at Düsseldorf and at Stuttgart. In 1930 he became first lyric baritone at the Berlin Staatsoper, where he remained until 1946.

He first appeared in England at Glyndebourne on the opening night of the first season in 1934, when he sang Figaro. His warm and pleasing natural baritone made his Mozart singing particularly appealing, and his mercurial personality and good looks were an added attraction. He returned to Glyndebourne in 1935 and 1937 as Figaro, Guglielmo and Papageno, which he also sang at Salzburg. After the war he appeared in Hanover, Vienna, Munich and Nuremberg. He scored a great personal success in the title roles of Egk's *Peer Gynt* and of *Wozzeck*. HAROLD ROSENTHAL/R

Domingo, Placido [Plácido] (*b* Madrid, 21 Jan 1941). Spanish tenor. Taken by his family to Mexico in 1950, he studied the piano, conducting (under Igor Markevich) and finally singing. In 1957 he made his début as a baritone in the zarzuela *Gigantes y cabezudos*. His first important tenor role was Alfredo in Monterrey, Mexico, in 1961, the year he made his American début as Arturo (*Lucia di Lammermoor*) in Dallas. From 1962 to 1965 he was a member of the Israeli National Opera, singing some 300 performances of ten operas, some of them in Hebrew. In 1965 he made his New York début at the City Opera as Pinkerton and in 1966 sang the title role in the first North American performance of Ginastera's *Don Rodrigo*. He first sang at the Metropolitan as Maurizio (*Adriana Lecouvreur*, 1968), at La Scala as Ernani (1969), and at Covent Garden as Cavaradossi (1971). He scored great successes as Vasco da Gama (*L'Africaine*) at San Francisco in 1972, as Arrigo (*Les vêpres siciliennes*) in Paris and later in New York, and as Otello in Hamburg and Paris in 1975. That year he also sang Verdi's Don Carlos at Salzburg. In 1976 he appeared as Turiddu and Canio in a double bill in Barcelona – on one occasion singing the Prologue to *Pagliacci* when the baritone was taken ill; he repeated both roles at Covent Garden later that year. In 1982–3 at the Metropolitan he sang Paolo (Zandonai's *Francesca da Rimini*), Aeneas (*Les Troyens*) and Lohengrin; his repertory also includes Hoffmann, Don José, Pollione, Edgardo, Riccardo, Radames, Chénier, Don Alvaro (*La forza del destino*), Werther, Puccini's Des Grieux, Rodolfo, Calaf and Samson as well as Menotti's Goya, which he created in Washington, DC (1986), and Parsifal (1991, La Scala).

Domingo is widely regarded as the supreme lyrical-dramatic tenor of the late 20th century, a musician of considerable depth (he has conducted operas on several occasions), and an actor of exceptional passion and commitment as well as a singer of warmth, intelligence and fine taste. While his sympathies and his stylistic range are wide, he has become particularly identified with Verdi's Otello, a role of which he is generally felt to be the supreme exponent, and which he acted with great power in the Zeffirelli film (1986).

*

H. Rosenthal: 'Placido Domingo', *Opera*, xxiii (1972), 18–23
J. B. Steane: *The Grand Tradition* (London, 1974), 541–2
P. Domingo: *My First Forty Years* (New York, 1983)
D. Snowman: *The World of Placido Domingo* (New York, 1985)
HAROLD ROSENTHAL, ELIZABETH FORBES

Dominguez, Oralia (*b* San Luis Potosí, 15 Oct 1928). Mexican contralto. She studied at the Mexican National Conservatory and made her début with Mexico City Opera in 1950. Three years later she first appeared in Europe, at La Scala in *Adriana Lecouvreur*. Engagements at other leading opera houses followed, including S Carlo, Naples, the Vienna Staatsoper and Paris Opéra, and she made her Covent Garden début as Sosostris in the première of Tippett's *A Midsummer Marriage* (1955). She combines a well-trained and voluptuous voice of exotic timbre with agility of technique, which was heard to advantage in Rossini's *L'italiana in Algeri* at the 1957 Glyndebourne Festival, and her engaging sense of comedy made her a much admired Mistress Quickly in Verdi's *Falstaff* at Glyndebourne (1956–60) and Covent Garden (1967–8). Her recordings include roles in operas from Monteverdi to Wagner.

NOËL GOODWIN

Dominiceti, Cesare (*b* Desenzano del Guarda, 12 July 1821; *d* Sesto San Giovanni, Lombardy, 20 June 1888). Italian composer. He studied in Milan. His first opera, *I begli usi di città*, was successful in his native city in 1841, but failed in Venice later that year. His next, *La fiera di Tolobos* (1845, Brescia), was unsuccessful. *Due moglie in una* (1853, Milan), a *melodramma giocoso* in the Rossini style, was judged to have some originality, and another opera, *La maschera*, was performed at La Scala in 1854. Dominiceti went to South America as a conductor with a travelling opera company; he was abandoned in Bolivia by its impresario and for 18 years worked in a tin mine. He returned to Milan and resumed his musical career with *Morovico* (1873), but was considered out of date. From 1881, the year of his last opera (*L'ereditiera*, Milan), he was composition professor at the Milan Conservatory. His fame in later years rested on his ability as an orchestrator (he may have helped Boito with the scoring of the revised *Mefistofele*).

Of the three operas performed after his return, only *Il lago delle fate* (1878, Milan) had any success. Classified as a *dramma fantastico*, it was set in a gorge in the Black Forest. It is structured as an old-fashioned number opera, but uses harmonies that are modishly chromatic, and has an interesting delirium scene. Boito wrote a libretto, *Irám*, for him; according to Ricordi's 1875 catalogue the autograph score was then in its archives.

I begli usi di città (A. Anelli), Desenzano, Sociale, Oct 1841
La fiera di Tolobos (2, C. Bassi), Brescia, Grande, spr. 1845
Due mogli in una (melodramma giocoso, 2, Bassi), Milan, Filodrammatici, 30 June 1853, excerpts (Milan, n.d.)
La maschera (ob, F. Guidi), Milan, Scala, 2 March 1854
Morovico (3), Milan, Dal Verme, 4 Dec 1873
Il lago delle fate (dramma fantastico, A. Zanardini), Milan, Carcano, 18 May 1878, vs (Milan, 1881)
L'ereditiera (ob, Zanardini), Milan, Dal Verme, 14 Feb 1881

MARVIN TARTAK

Domino noir, Le ('The Black Domino'). *Opéra comique* in three acts by DANIEL-FRANÇOIS-ESPRIT AUBER to a libretto by EUGÈNE SCRIBE; Paris, Opéra-Comique (Salle Bourse), 2 December 1837.

The opera is set in Spain at the time of the Bourbon Restoration. During a masked ball at court, Horace de Massarena (tenor) confesses his love to Angèle (mezzo-soprano), a lady of the royal convent who is disguised in a black domino. She tells him that great obstacles stand in the way of their union. At midnight, she leaves the ball alone. After various adventures Angèle reaches the house of Count Juliano (tenor), a man of dubious reputation, and persuades his housekeeper, Jacinthe (soprano), to give her refuge. Juliano gives his friends a dinner after the ball, and Angèle, disguised as Jacinthe's niece from Aragon, serves the guests. The gentlemen press their attentions on her and she seeks the protection of Massarena, who locks her up in Jacinthe's room. When Gil-Perez (bass), administrator of the convent and Jacinthe's lover, forces his way in, he finds Angèle, and she manages to get the key of the convent from him.

Back in the convent, Brigitte (soprano) explains Angèle's absence by saying she is ill. Massarena asks the Abbess to help free him from his engagement to be married, and recognizes Angèle's voice among the singing nuns. He does not know her in her veil, but she learns that he is breaking his engagement for her sake. Ursule (soprano) brings Angèle news that she is heir to a large inheritance. The Queen gives Angèle her permission to marry, and all rejoice.

Le domino noir was Auber's most successful *opéra comique* in Paris, with over 1200 performances by 1909. The many surprising twists in its plot, a notable feature of *opéra comique*, also made it popular in Germany and England (the London première was on 18 January 1838), and it was translated into most European languages. Auber's music not only brings out the humour and wit of the libretto's couplets and features many dance rhythms, but also displays depths of expression, as in the minor-key section of the overture, in Massarena's 'Amour, viens finir mon supplice', and in Angèle's 'Le trouble et la frayeur' and its interpolated bolero, 'Flamme vengeresse'. Auber proved himself a shrewd dramatist in his use of parlando over an independent instrumental theme and in his choice of motifs to suit various situations. He imported a discreet Spanish flavour with two boleros and the popular *aragonese*, 'La belle Inès fait florès'. Angèle's bolero became a worldwide success as 'La gitana' or 'El jaleo de Jeres'. HERBERT SCHNEIDER

Dom Sébastien, roi de Portugal ('Dom Sebastian, King of Portugal'). *Opéra* in five acts by GAETANO DONIZETTI to a libretto by EUGÈNE SCRIBE after Paul-Henri Foucher's *Dom Sébastien de Portugal* (1838); Paris, Opéra, 13 November 1843.

The action of Donizetti's last opera is set in Lisbon and in the Moroccan desert in 1578. A fleet prepares to carry the crusade of the King of Portugal, Dom Sébastien (tenor; originally Gilbert Duprez), against the Moors. The Grand Inquisitor, Dom Juam de Sylva (bass), plans to betray his country to Spain during Sébastien's absence, in view of the weakness of the regent, Sébastien's uncle Dom Antonio (tenor). The poet Camoëns (baritone; originally Paul Barroilhet) asks the king to let him accompany the expedition. They are interrupted by the spectacle of a beautiful Moorish girl, Zayda (mezzo-soprano; originally Rosine Stolz), who although baptized a Christian is being led to the stake by the Inquisition. When the king inquires about her crime the Grand Inquisitor denounces her as an apostate. The king orders her to be freed and declares that he will return her to her father in Africa. Asked to deliver an augury for the expedition, Camoëns hints at disaster, as the sky grows ominously dark, but soon the sun shines again as the forces optimistically embark.

Near Fez, Ben-Selim (bass), Zayda's father, informs his daughter that she will marry the chieftain Abayaldos (baritone). Left alone, Zayda grieves as she thinks lovingly of the king (aria, 'Sol adoré de la patrie'). As part of the wedding preparations dancers entertain Zayda and her maidens. Abayaldos appears; angered by these diversions, he announces that the Portuguese are advancing towards the plain of Alcazar Kebir. He goes to meet them and after the battle, in which he is victorious, he and his warriors return to exterminate any survivors. Lying wounded amid the dead, Dom Henrique (bass) sacrifices himself to spare the king, lying unconscious nearby. Zayda appears, searching for Sébastien, and is appalled to discover him wounded (duet, 'Grand Dieu! sa misère est si grande!'); she confesses her love for him. Abayaldos returns and Zayda, knowing he is unaware of the identity of the Portuguese she has tended, consents to marry him if he will spare this man and repatriate him. Regaining consciousness, Sébastien meditates on his situation (aria, 'Seul sur la terre'), reminding himself that Zayda's love and his soldier's heart sustain him. The use of an extended, exquisitely crafted solo as an act finale represents a new level of achievement for Donizetti.

In Lisbon, Dom Antonio has declared himself king when he learns of the disaster of Alcazar Kebir. Abayaldos, jealously determined to murder the Christian he spared, is present in disguise, with Zayda. In the main plaza, Camoëns expresses his delight in returning to Portugal (aria, 'O Lisbonne'), even though he is now reduced to penury. He meets another veteran of the African campaign and soon realizes that it is Sébastien himself, altered by the rigours he has undergone. Camoëns is eager to restore him to the throne and believes other soldiers will rally to the cause. A massive funeral *cortège* starts to cross the square, the inquisitors denouncing the 'late' king's foolhardiness. Camoëns, impulsively defending Sébastien, is summarily seized; Sébastien comes forward to defend him, proclaiming his identity as king. Abayaldos, believing that he slew Sébastien at Alcazar Kebir, steps forward to denounce him as an impostor, and the Grand Inquisitor orders the king's arrest.

In the crypt where the Inquisition tries its cases, Sébastien, instead of answering charges, accuses the Inquisitors of treason. Zayda, who has asked to testify, tells of Dom Henrique's sacrifice and how she found and succoured Sébastien after the battle. General amazement is expressed in the septet 'D'espoir et de terreur', the last and arguably the finest of Donizetti's great concertatos. Abayaldos now reveals himself and charges Zayda with adultery; she confesses that she and the king love each other, and the Inquisitors sentence them both to death.

As part of his scheme to betray Portugal to the Spaniards, Dom Juam requires a deed of abdication signed by Sébastien. He tells Zayda that if she can make him sign it in one hour she will be spared; but she is happy to die for the man she loves (aria, 'Mourir pour ce qu'on aime'). She shows Sébastien the document; he spurns it, preferring to die to save his country. Dom Juam, off stage, says her hour is up; to spare her, the king secretly signs. Just then, Camoëns is heard outside (barcarolle, 'O matelots'); he has come with others to save the king and Zayda, and appears at the window with ropes to aid their escape. Outside, the Regent and Dom Juam coolly watch their descent and order soldiers to fire. The bodies of Zayda and Sébastien are pitched into the harbour below.

* * *

A monumental work, hampered by a ponderous, not entirely plausible libretto, *Dom Sébastien* reveals the

'Dom Sébastien, roi de Portugal' (Donizetti): scene from Act 3 (the Grand Inquisitor orders the arrest of Dom Sébastien) of the original production at the Paris Opéra (Salle Le Peletier), 13 November 1843; engraving from 'L'illustration' (25 November 1843)

development of Donizetti's international style. The flexible melodies and propulsive ensembles that were his trademark are now marked with new glints of local colour and a more subtle use of musical reminiscence, combined with a tone of authentic grandeur. The scene of the funeral *cortège* with its march (which haunted Mahler) is one of the true peaks of the much maligned genre of grand opera. *Dom Sébastien* (perhaps above all the late works) is in need of scholarly attention to clarify its confusing musical text, and of carefully prepared revivals, before it is likely to assume its true position among Donizetti's most ambitious and most compelling works. WILLIAM ASHBROOK

Doña Francisquita. Lyric comedy in three acts by AMADEO VIVES to a libretto by FEDERICO ROMERO and GUILLERMO FERNÁNDEZ SHAW, after Félix Lope de Vega's *La discreta enamorada*; Madrid, Teatro Apolo, 17 October 1923.

This work, one of the most distinguished scores in the zarzuela repertory, is set in carnival time in mid-19th-century Madrid; its plot is an elaborate amorous imbroglio. Francisquita (soprano), a pretty girl enamoured of the student Fernando (tenor), finds a pretext to talk to him; but he, ignoring the counsels of his friend Cardona (tenor), is infatuated with the actress Aurora (mezzo-soprano), though she is scornful of him. Fernando's widowed father Matías (bass) comes to court Francisquita (though her widowed mother (contralto) at first thinks that she herself is the object of his attentions); in an attempt to quicken Fernando's interest Francisquita pretends to accept him. Fernando decides to pretend to court Francisquita to make Aurora jealous. When, at a waterside festivity, Matías bids his son meet his supposed betrothed, the young man finds himself torn between the actress and the girl, who now feigns both indifference to him and an impatience to become 'Madame Francisquita'. Fernando succeeds in making Aurora furiously jealous by play-acting with Cardona, who has disguised himself as a woman. In the carnival atmosphere Fernando and Francisquita join in a mazurka together, while Matías, increasingly suspicious of his son, dances with Aurora. Misunderstandings thicken when the mother is tricked into believing that Fernando is interested in her rather than her daughter, but finally the two young people are brought together. LIONEL SALTER

Donalda [Lightstone], **Pauline** (*b* Montreal, 5 March 1882; *d* Montreal, 22 Oct 1970). Canadian soprano. She studied in Montreal and went to Paris in 1902, taking her stage name from her benefactor, Donald A. Smith (Lord Strathcona). After studies with Edmond Duvernoy and Paul Lhérie, she made her début as Massenet's Manon in Nice in 1904, and at Covent Garden in 1905 as Micaëla with Destinn and Dalmorès. Later she sang several roles there including Mimì with Caruso and was Ah-joe in the première of Leoni's *L'oracolo* (1905). In 1919 she was the first London Concepcion in Ravel's *L'heure espagnole*, at Covent Garden. She also sang at the Théâtre de la Monnaie in Brussels, the Opéra-Comique in Paris and the Manhattan Opera in New York; among her roles were Nedda, Carmen, Zerlina, Violetta and Eva. Her rich timbre and vivacious style won much admiration. She retired in 1922 and taught in Paris until 1937; she then returned to Montreal, where she founded the Opera

Guild in 1942. That organization gave several Canadian premières and she remained president until its demise in 1969.

A. E. Knight: 'The Life of Pauline Donalda', *Record Collector*, x (1955–6), 265–74 [with discography]
R. C. Brotman: *Pauline Donalda* (Montreal, 1975)

GILLES POTVIN

Donat, Zdzisława (*b* Poznań, 4 July 1939). Polish soprano. She studied at Warsaw and Siena, making her début in 1964 at Poznań as Gilda. Engaged at the National Opera, Warsaw, from 1971, she sang Konstanze at the Gärtnerplatz theatre, Munich (1974), at the Deutsche Oper, Berlin (1976), and at Bregenz (1980). Her repertory includes Violetta and Amina, but her best-known role is the Queen of Night, which she has sung at Vancouver, Salzburg (1979–84), Tokyo, Geneva, Munich, Buenos Aires, Düsseldorf, Covent Garden (1979), the Metropolitan Opera (1981) and Orange (1989). She has a light, high-lying voice of great flexibility and sings with impeccable intonation.

ELIZABETH FORBES

Donath, Helen (*b* Corpus Christi, TX, 10 July 1940). American soprano. Educated at Del Mar College, Corpus Christi, she made her début in 1961 as Wellgunde (*Das Rheingold*) at Cologne, where she was a member of the opera studio, and was engaged at Hanover from 1963 to 1967. She sang Pamina at the 1970 Salzburg Festival and made her American début a year later with the San Francisco Opera as Sophie, a role she also sang at her Chicago début three years later. She made her Covent Garden début as Anne Trulove (*The Rake's Progress*) in 1979, and has sung such roles as Susanna, Ilia (*Idomeneo*), Zerlina, Marzelline (*Fidelio*), Aennchen (*Der Freischütz*), Oscar, Micaëla, Mélisande, Mimì, Liù and Martinů's Julietta in many of the leading European houses. She has also sung Eva at Bayreuth, and the Governess in *The Turn of the Screw* at Los Angeles (1991). A most sensitive singer, she has moved from soubrette to lyric roles without losing the inherent purity of her voice.

ELIZABETH FORBES

Donatoni, Franco (*b* Verona, 9 June 1927). Italian composer. He studied at the Milan Conservatory and under Lino Liviabella in Bologna and Pizzetti at the Accademia di S Cecilia, Rome. From 1953 he attended courses at Darmstadt given by Bruno Maderna, which brought him into contact with the preoccupations of the avant garde. He taught at the conservatories of Bologna, Milan and Turin and at Bologna University, and also conducted composition classes at the Accademia di S Cecilia and at the Chigiana in Siena. In 1966 he was awarded the Marzotto Prize.

At the height of his powers Donatoni was influenced by John Cage's aleatory and indeterminate music, and he continued to explore its possibilities until the mid-1960s, when he found the means, in 'automatism', to reduce the compositional process to a mechanical transformation of earlier musical material (not necessarily of his own making). Automatism dominated the compositions of the 1970s, but by the end of the decade a different compositional trend was inaugurating a new and vital phase in Donatoni's music. The mechanical approach of the 1970s was now applied more flexibly, and to this stage in his development belongs his only work for the theatre, *Atem*, a two-act opera produced at La Scala on 14 February 1985; the title means 'breath' but can also be read backwards as 'meta' ('aim' or 'goal'). Donatoni's music was not originally intended for the theatre; it juxtaposes in a theatrical sequence excerpts from his own earlier compositions and some new pieces to form a kind of theatre of the mind.

The 16 sections of *Atem* cover 24 years of Donatoni's activity as a composer. The first, serving as a prologue, uses *Sezioni* (1960), the second is a new *Trio I* for bass and two instruments to a poem by Susan Park and the third recalls *Per orchestra* (1962). In parts 4–7 *Estratto II* (1970), *Doubles II* (1969), *Arie II* (words by Renato Maestri) and *In cauda I* (1982, by Brandolino Brandolini d'Adda) are manipulated in various ways. *Voci* (1972–3) serves as the prelude to the second act, which draws in turn on *She* (1982), *Diario '83* (1983), a new *Trio II* for contralto and two instruments to a poem by Fernando Pessoa, *Arie IV* (words by Tiziana Fumagalli), *Darkness* (1984; Donatoni added a spoken text by Park) and *Abyss* (1983, text again by Park). The work ends with an electronic section using material from the string quartet *The Heart's Eye* (1979–80) and *Darkness*.

The patchwork structure of Donatoni's *Atem*, the course (or 'meta') of which suggests a descent towards darkness, reflects its explicit anti-narrative intention, and the disguised re-use of closed numbers in effect negates any traditional kind of dramatic purpose. The rift between music and theatre, and the fact that they do not interact but run parallel with each other – the director Giorgio Pressburger based the events on stage on Donatoni's writings collected in *Antecedente X* (Milan, 1980) – seems to be a fundamental premise of *Atem*, and the opera is thus a confirmation of Donatoni's artistic credo and at the same time an extreme and isolated manifestation of it.

F. Donatoni: 'Atem', *Piano Time*, xxiii/Feb (1985), 19
E. Restagno, ed.: *Donatoni* (Turin, 1990), 181–3

RAFFAELE POZZI

Donauweibchen, Das ('The Nixie of the Danube'). Singspiel ('romantisch-komisches Volksmärchen mit Gesang') in three acts by FERDINAND KAUER to a libretto by KARL FRIEDRICH HENSLER, 'after a legend from prehistoric times'; Vienna, Theater in der Leopoldstadt, 11 January 1798.

Ritter Albrecht, attended by his timid comic servant Käsperle, is hunting in the forest while travelling to celebrate his nuptials with Countess Bertha. By the Danube he meets, and at first does not recognize, a beautiful girl – Hulda, the Nixie of the Danube, with whom he had spent a night of love five years before, after she had sheltered him from a storm. Hulda and their daughter, Lilli, of whose existence Albrecht had known nothing, strive by means of disguises and apparitions to win Albrecht's love, but he goes through with his marriage to Bertha, trying in vain to deny Hulda her demand for three nights of his love each year. A feature of the play is the series of 11 disguises in which Hulda appears, with or without her daughter. The work ends with a tableau: Hulda disappears into a grotto with Albrecht, to the consternation of the bride and assembled guests.

The reason for the open ending is apparent from the subtitle, 'First Part'; 'Part Two' followed less than five weeks later. The two parts enjoyed well over 200 performances at the Theater in der Leopoldstadt, there were further sequels there and elsewhere, and the work was popular for many years over much of Europe. E. T. A. Hoffmann referred to *Das Donauweibchen* in *Der goldne Topf* (1814), and Goethe localized it (as *Die Saalnixe*) in his novel *Die Wahlverwandtschaften* (1809). The Romantic elements of the story – love, apparitions, ballads, mystery, above all the figure of Hulda/Undine/Ondine/Rusalka – are echoed with simple directness and melodic charm in Kauer's extensive score, which contains 28 numbers. Hulda was created by Anna Gottlieb (Mozart's first Barbarina and Pamina) and Lilli by Wenzel Müller's six-year-old daughter Rösi (who as Therese Grünbaum went on to enjoy a successful operatic career). PETER BRANSCOMBE

Don Carlos. *Opéra* in five acts by GIUSEPPE VERDI to a libretto by JOSEPH MÉRY and CAMILLE DU LOCLE after FRIEDRICH VON SCHILLER's dramatic poem *Don Carlos, Infant von Spanien*; Paris, Opéra, 11 March 1867. Revised version in four acts (French text revised by Du Locle, Italian translation by Achille de Lauzières and Angelo Zanardini), Milan, Teatro alla Scala, 10 January 1884.

Philip II *King of Spain*	bass
Don Carlos *Infante of Spain*	tenor
Rodrigue *Marquis of Posa*	baritone
The Grand Inquisitor	bass
Elisabeth de Valois *Philip's queen*	soprano
Princess Eboli	mezzo-soprano
Thibault *Elisabeth de Valois' page*	soprano
The Countess of Aremberg	silent
The Count of Lerma	tenor
An Old Monk	bass
A Voice from Heaven	soprano
A Royal Herald	tenor
Flemish Deputies	basses
Inquisitors	basses

Lords and ladies of the French and Spanish court, woodcutters, populace, pages, guards of Henry II and Philip II, monks, officers of the Inquisition, soldiers

Setting France and Spain, about 1560

Schiller's *Don Carlos* had been suggested to Verdi – and rejected by him – as a possible subject for the Paris Opéra in the early 1850s, when negotiations were beginning for the work that would become *Les vêpres siciliennes*. In 1865, with another full-scale Verdi grand opera being planned for Paris's foremost theatre, the composer clearly saw new potential in the subject. Emile Perrin, the new director of the Opéra, had discussed various topics with Verdi, for the most part via the composer's French publisher and friend Léon Escudier. Verdi pronounced *King Lear*, ever near to his heart at this period, too lacking in spectacle for the Opéra; *Cleopatra* was better, but the lovers would not arouse sufficient sympathy. *Don Carlos*, however, was now 'a magnificent drama', even though Verdi immediately saw the need to add two new scenes to the scenario offered him: one between the Inquisitor and Philip, the other between Philip and Posa. As the libretto took shape, the composer took his usual active part in advising on everything from large structural matters to minute details of phrasing and vocabulary.

Verdi worked steadily on the opera during the first half of 1866 and arrived in Paris in July of that year with most of the score completed. Then came the notoriously long, arduous rehearsal period at the Opéra, during which Verdi made several important changes, including the addition of a scene for Elisabeth at the start of Act 5. As the rehearsals neared completion in February 1867 it became clear that the opera was far too long, and Verdi made substantial cuts, among which were the lengthy and impressive Prelude and Introduction to Act 1, part of the Philip-Posa duet in Act 2, and both the Elisabeth-Eboli and the Carlos-Philip duets in Act 4. The première, whose cast included Louis-Henri Obin (Philip), Paul Morère (Don Carlos), Jean-Baptiste Faure (Posa), Marie Sasse (Elisabeth) and Pauline Guéymard-Lauters (Eboli), was not a great success, and *Don Carlos* disappeared from the Opéra repertory after 1869.

Early Italian revivals, in a translation by Achille de Lauzières, were sometimes successful; but the opera's length continued to present problems, and it was frequently given in severely cut versions. In 1872 Verdi himself made further revisions, restoring and rewriting passages of the Philip-Posa duet and cutting a portion of the final duet between Carlos and Elisabeth. Then, in 1882–3, he made a thoroughgoing revision, in part to reduce the opera to more manageable proportions, in part to replace pieces he now found unsatisfactory. The most important cuts were the whole of Act 1 (though Carlos's aria was inserted into the following act), the ballet and its preceding scene in Act 3 and the Act 5 Chorus of the Inquisitors. Many other passages were revised, recomposed or reordered. The La Scala première of this new, four-act version, given in Italian translation, included Alessandro Silvestri (Filippo), Francesco Tamagno (Don Carlo), Paul Lhérie (Rodrigo), Abigaille Bruschi-Chiatti (Elisabetta) and Giuseppina Pasqua (Eboli). Some two years later a further version which restored the original Act 1 began to be performed and was published (we must assume with Verdi's approval).

It is important to bear in mind that, although the 1884 version was first given in Italian, the revisions Verdi made were to a French text: in other words, there is no 'Italian version' of *Don Carlos*, merely an 'Italian translation'. The following discussion will move through the opera by act, marking in italic the version to which various passages belong: *1867* means the version eventually performed at the Parisian première, *1884* the substantially revised four-act version. Where appropriate, French incipits are followed by their Italian equivalents.

ACT 1 *The forest at Fontainebleau*

1867 An impressive introductory chorus was cut during rehearsals, leaving the opera to start with a brief Allegro brillante; offstage fanfares and huntsmen's calls introduce Elisabeth, who (observed by Carlos) gives alms to the woodcutters and then departs.

Carlos, who has come incognito from Spain, has now seen for the first time his betrothed, Elisabeth, and in the brief, italianate aria 'Je l'ai vue' ('Io la vidi') he announces love at first sight. He is about to follow Elisabeth when a horn call tells him that night is falling. Thibault and Elisabeth, lost in the wood, appear, and Carlos offers help, introducing himself simply as 'a Spaniard'. Thibault goes off for assistance, so making way for the duet that will dominate this brief act. The opening movement, 'Que faites-vous donc?' ('Che mai fate voi?'), is formed from a series of contrasting episodes, the tension rising as Elisabeth eagerly questions this stranger about the Infante Carlos whom she is to marry. Carlos presents her with a portrait of her betrothed, which she immediately recognizes as the man before her. This precipitates the second movement, 'De quels transports' ('Di qual amor'), a cabaletta-like celebration of their good fortune, based on a melody that recurs through the opera as a symbol of their first love.

The joy is short-lived. Thibault returns to announce that Henry II has decided to give Elisabeth to Philip instead of to his son, so putting an end to the war between Spain and France. The couple express their horror in the restrained, minor-mode 'L'heure fatale est sonnée!' ('L'ora fatale è suonata!'), which is immediately juxtaposed with the major-mode offstage chorus of celebration, 'O chants de fête' ('Inni di festa'). The Count of Lerma arrives to request Elisabeth's formal approval of the match, a female chorus adding their pleas for peace. Elisabeth reluctantly accepts, and the stage clears to a triumphant reprise of 'O chants de fête'. Carlos is left alone to bemoan his fate.

ACT 2/1.i *The cloister of the Yuste monastery*
Both A solemn introduction for four horns precedes the offstage chorus 'Charles-Quint, l'auguste Empereur' ('Carlo, il sommo Imperatore'), a funeral dirge for Charles V. A solitary monk adds his prayer to theirs, but admits that Charles was guilty of folly and pride.

1867 Carlos enters: he has come to the monastery to forget the past. In a solemnly intoned, sequential passage, 'Mon fils, les douleurs de la terre', the monk tells him that the sorrows of the world also invade this holy place. The monk's voice reminds a terrified Carlos of the late emperor himself.

1884 Carlos's extended scena explores his anguish at losing Elisabeth and culminates in a revised version of 'Je l'ai vue' ('Io la vidi') from the original Act 1 (the act entirely omitted from this version). There follows a curtailed conversation with the monk.

1867 Rodrigue, Marquis of Posa, appears and is greeted by Carlos. Posa launches into a description of the battles in Flanders (a first portion of this part of the duet, beginning 'J'étais en Flandre', was cut from the 1867 version during rehearsals), and Carlos responds with a lyrical declaration of friendship, 'Mon compagnon, mon ami'. Carlos then admits his secret love for Elisabeth, now the wife of Philip his father. Posa reiterates his friendship in a reprise of 'Mon compagnon', advising Carlos to forget his sorrows in the battle for Flanders.

1884 The above-described portion of the duet was further condensed and enriched, with a skilful link from the scene with the monk, and with 'Mon compagnon' becoming 'Mon sauveur, mon ami' ('Mio salvator, mio fratel').

Both The final section of the duet, the cabaletta 'Dieu tu semas dans nos âmes' ('Dio, che nell'alma infondere'), is a 'shoulder-to-shoulder' number reminiscent of Verdi's earliest manner, the tenor and baritone vowing eternal friendship in parallel 3rds. In an impressively scored coda, Philip, Elisabeth and a procession of monks cross the stage and enter the monastery. Carlos and Posa join the chanting monks before a thrilling reprise of their cabaletta brings the scene to a close.

2/1. ii *A pleasant spot outside the Yuste monastery gates* Eboli and the other ladies-in-waiting are not allowed in the monastery, so they amuse themselves outside. The female chorus sets the scene with 'Sous ces bois au feuillage immense' ('Sotto ai folti, immensi abeti'), and then Eboli sings her famous 'Chanson du voile' (Veil Song), 'Au palais des fées' ('Nel giardin del bello'): the two-stanza song with refrain, packed with both harmonic and instrumental local colour, tells the story of Achmet, a Moorish king who one evening mistakenly wooed his own wife in the garden. A disconsolate Elisabeth appears, soon followed by Posa, who hands the queen a letter from her mother in which is hidden a note from Carlos. As Elisabeth reads, Posa makes courtly conversation with Eboli; but in the background of their dalliance we hear from Elisabeth that Carlos's letter asks her to trust Posa. At a word from Elisabeth, Posa begins his two-stanza cantabile *romance*, 'L'Infant Carlos, notre espérance' ('Carlo, ch'è sol il nostro amore'), in which he tells how Carlos, rejected by his father, requests an interview with his new 'mother'. In between stanzas, Eboli wonders whether Carlos's dejection has been caused by love for her, while Elisabeth trembles with confusion. With the completion of the second stanza, however, Elisabeth agrees to the interview; Posa and Eboli walk off together, and the ladies-in-waiting leave.

The ensuing duet between Carlos and Elisabeth, 'Je viens solliciter' ('Io vengo a domandar'), is one of Verdi's boldest attempts to match musical progress to the rapid alternations of spoken dialogue: there is little sense of a conventional four-movement form (except perhaps for a cabaletta-style ending), the duet instead passing through a rapid series of contrasting episodes, some sense of strictly musical connection coming from shared motifs. In a controlled opening, Carlos asks Elisabeth to intercede on his behalf with Philip, who will not allow him to leave for Flanders. Elisabeth agrees, but Carlos can restrain himself no further and pours out his love. Elisabeth at first attempts to deflect him, but eventually admits her feelings; Carlos falls into a swoon, and Elisabeth fears he is dying. As he awakens he begins a final, passionate declaration, 'Que sous mes pieds' ('Sotto al mio pie' '), but when he attempts to embrace his beloved, she recovers herself and angrily rejects him, telling him sarcastically that to claim her he must kill his father. Carlos rushes off in despair, just as Philip himself appears, angry that Elisabeth has been left alone. He orders her lady-in-waiting, the Countess of Aremberg, back to France; Elisabeth bids the Countess a tender farewell in the two-stanza, minor–major *romance*, 'O ma chère compagne' ('Non pianger, mia compagna'). Philip, left alone, gestures for Posa to remain with him.

1867 After a brief recitative, Posa begins the first movement of a duet by describing his soldierly life ('Pour mon pays') and narrating his journeys in war-torn Flanders ('O Roi! j'arrive de Flandre'). Philip stresses the need for political control, and sternly curbs Posa's idealism. The impasse produces a lyrical second movement, the Meno mosso 'Un souffle ardent', in which the two men are placed in patterned opposition before joining voice in a final section. Posa throws himself at Philip's feet: Philip forgives his rashness, but bids him beware the Inquisitor. The king then confides in Posa, beginning the closing cabaletta, 'Enfant! à mon coeur éperdu', with an admission of his troubled personal feelings.

1884 In this radical revision, virtually all trace of the conventional four-movement form disappears from the duet, being replaced by the kind of fluid dialogue we find in *Otello*. Posa's 'O Roi! j'arrive de Flandre' ('O signor, di Fiandra arrivo') is retained, but most of the remaining music is new. Particularly impressive is Philip's advice to beware the Inquisitor, in which solemn chords serve momentarily to halt the musical flow. Philip is more explicit about his fears, going so far as to mention Carlos and Elisabeth; but he closes the duet with yet another sinister reference to the power of the Inquisitor.

ACT 3/2.i *The queen's gardens*
1867 Festivities are in progress; Philip is to be crowned the next day. In a further essay in local colour, the offstage chorus sings 'Que de fleurs et que d'étoiles' to the accompaniment of castanets. Elisabeth appears with Eboli: the queen is already weary of the celebrations and changes masks with Eboli so that she can retire to seek religious consolation. When Elisabeth leaves, Eboli has a brief solo, 'Me voilà reine pour une nuit', which recalls the central section of the Veil Song. She writes a letter of assignation to Carlos, hoping to entice him.

The ensuing ballet, entitled 'La Pérégrina', tells of a fisherman who happens on a magic cave containing the most marvellous pearls in the ocean. He dances with the White Pearl; gradually the other pearls join in. Philip's page enters to the strains of a Spanish hymn played by the brass; he has come to find for his master the most beautiful pearl in the world. At the climax of the ballet, Eboli (posing as Elisabeth) appears as La Pérégrina: the page's search is at an end. Verdi's music for the ballet, some 15 minutes long, is the traditional mixture of orchestral sophistication and extreme musical simplicity.

1884 A short, understated prelude is based on the first phrase of Carlos's 'Je l'ai vue' ('Io la vidi'); it clearly belongs to Verdi's last manner, particularly in the overt use of thematic transformation and the ease with which it moves between distantly related keys.

Both Carlos enters, reading the letter of assignation; this briefly sets the scene for the ensuing ensemble, which follows the common Italian four-movement pattern, led off by a condensed series of contrasting lyrical episodes, each punctuated by some dramatic revelation. As Eboli appears, Carlos breaks into a passionate declaration of love, thinking she is Elisabeth. Eboli responds with matching phrases, but the lyrical development abruptly breaks down as she removes her mask. Eboli at first misconstrues Carlos's confusion, and attempts to reassure him: but she soon guesses the truth, and accuses him of loving the queen. At this point Posa arrives, and a brief transitional passage leads to the second main movement, 'Redoubtez tout de ma furie!' ('Al mio furor sfuggite invano'), in which the baritone's and mezzo's agitated rhythms are set against the tenor's long, impassioned melody. A brief transition movement during which Carlos restrains Posa from killing Eboli leads to the final stretta, 'Malheur sur toi, fils adultère' ('Trema per te, falso figliuolo'), in which Eboli brings down furious curses on the man who has rejected her. She rushes off, leaving Carlos and Posa; they act out a brief coda in which Carlos – after some hesitation – entrusts his friend with some secret papers. The scene concludes with a brash orchestral reprise of their earlier cabaletta, 'Dieu tu semas dans nos âmes' ('Dio, che nell'alma infondere').

3/2. ii *A large square in front of Valladolid Cathedral* This central finale, the grand sonic and scenic climax of *Don Carlos*, is formally laid out along traditional Italian lines but, in response to the added resources of the Opéra, is on a scale Verdi had never before attempted. The opening chorus, 'Ce jour heureux' ('Spuntato ecco il dì'), is a kind of rondo: the main theme, beginning with a motif formed around scale degrees 1, 3, 6 and 5, and making prominent use of dynamic triplet figures, alternates with a funereal theme to which monks escort heretics to the stake, and with a more lyrical idea in which the monks promise salvation to those who repent. A solemn procession fills the stage, after which a herald announces Philip, who appears on the steps of the cathedral. He is confronted by six Flemish deputies, escorted by Carlos. They kneel before him and, with a solemn prayer for their country, 'Sire, la dernière heure' ('Sire, no, l'ora estrema'), lead off a grand concertato movement in which all the principals join, Elisabeth, Carlos and Posa adding their pleas, while Philip and the monks stubbornly resist. A transitional movement begins as Carlos steps forward, asking to be sent to Flanders. When Philip refuses, Carlos threateningly draws his sword. No one dares intervene until Posa steps forward and demands Carlos's surrender. To a soft, veiled reprise of their friendship cabaletta, Carlos relinquishes his weapon, upon which Philip pronounces Posa promoted to a dukedom. The scene closes with a grand reprise of the opening choral sequence. As the heretics go to their death, a voice from heaven assures them of future bliss.

ACT 4/3.i *The king's study* The king, alone with his official papers, sings the famous 'Elle ne m'aime pas!' ('Ella giammai m'amò!'). As a complex psychological portrait, the aria has few rivals in Verdi. The king's mood swings from self-pity at his emotional isolation (an arioso accompanied by obsessive string figures and culminating in the passionate outburst of 'Elle ne m'aime pas!'), to a sombre meditation on his mortality (with mock-medieval 'horn 5ths' to accompany his picture of the stone vault in which he will lie), to a recognition of his power (a triplet bass melody hinting at the musical grandeur of the preceding concertato finale). But the aria closes with a reprise of its opening outburst: Philip's tragedy, at this point in the drama, is primarily a personal one.

The subsequent duet with the old and blind Grand Inquisitor, 'Suis-je devant le Roi?' ('Sono io dinanzi al Re?'), continues the aria's relative formal freedom, its sense that the music reacts immediately and flexibly to the shifting emotions of the dialogue. The opening orchestral idea, with its concentration on low strings, ostinato rhythms and restricted pitches, sets the scene for this power struggle between two basses. Philip seems in command as he asks the Inquisitor how to deal with Carlos; but, as the controlled opening gives way to freer declamation, the Inquisitor takes over, stating that Posa is the more serious threat and demanding that he be turned over to the Inquisition. Philip resists, but in an imposing declamatory climax the Inquisitor warns him that even kings can be brought before the tribunal. As the opening orchestral idea returns, Philip attempts to restore peace; but the Inquisitor is indifferent and leaves Philip in no doubt as to how the struggle will be resolved.

'Don Carlos' (Verdi), the concertato finale to Act 3: engraving from 'L'univers illustré' (1867) showing the original production at the Paris Opéra (Salle Le Peletier), 11 March 1867, with sets by Charles-Antoine Cambon and Joseph Thierry, and costumes by Alfred Albert

The Scène et Quatuor that follows (much revised for the 1884 version) is more conventionally structured. In the opening *scène*, set to the kind of lyrically enriched recitative that was now the Verdian norm, Elisabeth rushes in to announce the theft of her jewel case. Philip produces it and invites her to reveal its contents; when she refuses he breaks the lock and finds inside a picture of Carlos. In spite of her protestations, he accuses her of adultery; the queen faints, and Philip summons Posa and Eboli, who arrive to precipitate the formal quartet, 'Maudit soit le soupçon infâme' ('Ah! sii maledetto, sospetto fatale'). The ensemble is at first dominated by Philip, whose opening statements – fragmentary expressions of remorse – gradually form into a lyrical melody that interweaves with Posa's decision to take action and Eboli's cries of remorse. But towards the end Elisabeth's sorrowful lament takes on increasing urgency and focus.

Philip and Posa leave. Originally the scene continued with a duet for Elisabeth and Eboli, but this was cut during rehearsals for the 1867 première, when the cut extended some way into Eboli's confession; however, Verdi recomposed and expanded this for the 1884 version, in which Eboli first admits her love for Carlos and then, to a bare, almost motif-less rhythmic idea in the strings, reveals that she has been the king's mistress. Elisabeth orders Eboli to quit the court, and then departs. Eboli's ensuing aria, 'O don fatal' ('O don fatale'), in which she laments her fatal beauty, is cast in a conventional minor–major form, with the major section (in which she bids farewell to the queen) strongly reminiscent in its chromaticism and wide-spaced orchestral sonority of Verdi's last style. In a cabaletta-like coda, Eboli resolves to spend her final hours at court in an attempt to save Carlos.

4/3. ii *Carlos's prison* A string introduction of unusual depth and density introduces Posa to the waiting Carlos. Posa bids farewell to his friend in a rather old-fashioned *romance*, 'C'est mon jour suprême' ('Per me giunto è il dì supremo'), and then explains that he has been discovered with Carlos's secret papers. A shot rings out; Posa falls mortally wounded. After telling Carlos that Elisabeth awaits him at the monastery of St Yuste, he delivers a second *romance*, 'Ah! je meurs' ('Io morrò'), happy that he can die for Carlos's sake. A duet for Philip and Carlos that followed this episode (cut before the 1867 première, though Verdi drew on its material for the 'Lacrymosa' of the Requiem) was replaced with a riot scene (subsequently pruned for the 1884 version) in which Eboli appears at the head of a group intent on liberating Carlos. Philip also appears, but the crowd is silenced by the entry of the Inquisitor, who orders all to their knees before the king.

ACT 5/4 *The monastery at St Yuste* An impressive and extended orchestral prelude introduces Elisabeth at the tomb of Charles V. Her aria, 'Toi qui sus le néant' ('Tu, che le vanità'), is in French ternary form: the outer sections are a powerful invocation of the dead emperor, and their firm, periodic structure stabilizes the number, allowing for remarkable variety and musical contrast during the long central section in which the queen's thoughts stray to memories of the past. Carlos appears for their final duet (from here to the end of the opera, Verdi made a number of important revisions in 1884). The set piece begins with the conventional series of contrasting sections, in the most prominent of which,

'J'avais fait un beau rêve' ('Sogno dorato io feci!'), Carlos announces that he has done with dreaming and will now try to save Flanders. The final movement, 'Au revoir dans un monde' ('Ma lassù ci vedremo'), a kind of ethereal cabaletta in which the couple bid each other a tender farewell, is similar to the closing duet of *Aida* in its restraint and delicate orchestral fabric. As they say 'Adieu! et pour toujours' for the last time, Philip bursts in accompanied by the Inquisitor and various officials. The king tries to deliver his son to the priests, but Carlos retreats towards the tomb of Charles V. The tomb opens and the old monk appears, wearing the emperor's crown and mantle. He gathers Carlos to him and, with a few sententious words, draws him into the cloister.

* * *

Soon after the first Paris performances of *Don Carlos*, Verdi voiced his doubts about the Parisian tradition of grand opera. While he was always ready to praise the care with which productions were mounted – particularly in comparison with much of Italy, where he often judged standards to be unbearably low – he was also aware that the sheer size of the undertaking, the number of different demands that had to be catered for, could take their toll on a work's balance and coherence of effect. He might well have had *Don Carlos* in mind. As we have seen, the opera in rehearsal proved impracticably long; the subsequent cuts were made for practical rather than dramatic reasons, leaving the 1867 version with many inconsistencies and imbalances. Clearly some of the outstanding problems were put straight by the composer's revisions of the 1870s and 1880s; but even the final versions of the opera pose uncomfortable dramatic questions.

Possibly the most serious difficulty comes in the comparative weight assumed by various characters. Philip and Eboli are the most successful and well-rounded portraits, though arguably Elisabeth achieves her proper sense of importance by means of her magnificent fifth-act aria and duet. Posa's musical physiognomy is strangely old-fashioned: his music almost all dates from the earliest layers of the score, and even then recalls the Verdi of the early 1850s (or even 1840s). On the other hand, it can be argued that this sense of anachronism is in keeping with Posa's dramatic position – as a nostalgic look at youthful days of action within the context of sterner political realities. With Carlos, however, few would deny an unsolved problem: his musical portrait never seems to find a centre, a true nexus of expression such as each of the other principals eventually achieves.

It is perhaps an indication of our changing views and tastes that, in spite of these difficulties, *Don Carlos* has of late become one of the best-loved and most respected of Verdi's operas. The simple fact is, of course, that Verdi dedicated to the work some of his greatest dramatic music. One need think only of the magnificent series of confrontational duets that form such a great part of the drama. As has been noted briefly above, several of these break decisively with traditional models, forging for themselves a vital new relationship between musical and dramatic progress. It is for such moments that *Don Carlos* will be remembered and treasured, and they will surely continue to prove more powerful than any large-scale dramatic obstacles the work might present. ROGER PARKER

Dönch, Karl (*b* Hagen, 8 Jan 1915). German bass-baritone. He studied at the Dresden Conservatory and made his début in 1936 at Görlitz. In 1947 he joined the Vienna Staatsoper, where he was often heard as Beckmesser, a role he recorded under Knappertsbusch (1950) with Schöffler as Hans Sachs; further success came in 1951 as the Doctor (*Wozzeck*), which he recorded under Boulez (1966). He sang in the premières of Liebermann's *Penelope* at Salzburg (1954) and Frank Martin's *Der Sturm* at Vienna (1956). A versatile actor-singer who made much of comedy-character, he sang in major German theatres, at La Scala, and in New York and Buenos Aires. He was also in demand for operetta, and recorded several roles in the 1950s. He was director of the Vienna Volksoper from 1973 to 1987.

NOËL GOODWIN

Don Chisciotte ('Don Quixote'). Opera in six scenes by VITO FRAZZI to his own libretto after MIGUEL DE CERVANTES's romance *Don Quijote* and Miguel de Unamuno's *Vida de Don Quijote y Sancho* (1905); Florence, Teatro Comunale, 28 April 1952.

Frazzi's rather idiosyncratic adaptation of a few episodes from *Don Quijote* – ranging from the dream-vision of the hero (baritone) in the cave of Montesinos to the encounter with maese Pedro's prophesying ape and puppet show – is richer in dialogue than in visible action. The emphasis is less on the story's adventurous qualities than on some of its philosophical and psychological implications, which are underlined with the help of elements taken from Unamuno. Although this approach tends to limit the opera's impact in the theatre, its musical qualities are considerable: despite occasional excesses of recitative-like declamation, the score abounds in skilfully woven vocal ensembles, and in harmonic subtleties which sometimes reflect Frazzi's longstanding interest (quite independent of Messiaen's) in modes of limited transposition. Composed between 1940 and 1950, the six scenes may be performed separately or together. JOHN C. G. WATERHOUSE

Donets'k (Russ. Donetsk). City in south-eastern Ukraine, formerly Yuzovka (to 1924), Stalin (1924–35) and Stalino (1935–61). Opera was brought to the city by travelling companies until the Donets'kyy Muzychnyy Teatr was created in 1932; in 1940 the company moved into a new theatre (cap. 1054), and in 1941 was reorganized as the Donets'kyy Teatr Opery ta Baletu with singers from the Lugansk and Vinnetsk opera theatres. During World War II the theatre was closed but the company continued to perform elsewhere. The first opera produced at Donets'k was Glinka's *Ivan Susanin* in 1941. Other early productions included *Rigoletto*, *Pagliacci*, *Yevgeny Onegin* (1943), *Carmen* (1946) and *The Snow Maiden*. In the 1950s and 60s a number of new productions were added: *Don Carlos*, Orff's *Die Kluge* and *La fanciulla del West*. Among Ukrainian operas produced there were Mayboroda's *Yaroslav mudryy* ('Yaroslav the Wise') in 1973 and Mark Karmins'ky's *Desyat' dniv, shcho potryasly svit* ('Ten Days that Shook the World', 1970). Recent new productions have included *Tosca* (1988), Gulak-Artemovsky's *Zaporozhets za Dunayem* ('A Cossack beyond the Danube', 1989) and *La traviata* (1991). The season runs from September to July, with some nine opera productions as well as operetta and ballet. The company's ballet contingent received critical and popular acclaim during its 1989 American tour.

*

ME ('Donetskiy teatr operï i baleta') VIRKO BALEY

Don Giovanni (i) [*Don Giovanni, o sia Il convitato di pietra* ('Don Giovanni, or The Stone Guest'); *Don Giovanni Tenorio*]. *Dramma giocoso* in one act by GIUSEPPE GAZZANIGA to a libretto by GIOVANNI BERTATI; Venice, Teatro S Moisè, 5 February 1787.

This *opera buffa* has become widely known because Da Ponte's libretto for Mozart's *Don Giovanni* is based in part on Bertati's text. Originally performed as an opera within an opera (as the second part of *Il capriccio drammatico*, a pasticcio with music by G. Valentini and others), Gazzaniga's work was successful in its day, achieving at least 30 productions in the ten years after its première. Its cast includes Don Giovanni (tenor), his servant Pasquariello (bass) and Donna Anna (soprano), the daughter of the Commendatore (bass) and betrothed to Duca Ottavio (tenor). Donna Elvira (soprano) has promised herself to Giovanni, while the country girl Maturina (soprano), betrothed to Biagio (bass), is the current object of Giovanni's attentions. Donna Ximena (soprano), whom Giovanni has previously wooed, and Lanterna (tenor), another servant of Giovanni's, complete the cast. The plot is more compact than that of Da Ponte's and Mozart's opera, but there are many parallels between the two works. Pasquariello's catalogue aria to Donna Elvira, and the use of the same key for the Commendatore's death as for the statue's appearance (in this case E♭ minor) are two of the most obvious examples. One difference between Da Ponte's text and Bertati's lies in Da Ponte's omission of Bertati's crudely funny scene where Donna Elvira, Maturina and Donna Ximena discover their common expectations that Giovanni will marry them; this culminates in a duet for Donna Elvira and Maturina in which they call each other 'meatballs' and 'sardines' – a level to which Da Ponte's Elvira never quite descends. In Bertati's version, Donna Anna retires to a convent after the opening scene and thus does not supply the motivation for the action that she does in the Da Ponte-Mozart work. Gazzaniga's textures are slender and the opera moves at a lively pace with few suggestions of serious human emotion.

MARY HUNTER

Don Giovanni (ii) [*Il dissoluto punito, ossia Il Don Giovanni* ('The Libertine Punished, or Don Giovanni')]. *Opera buffa* in two acts, K527, by WOLFGANG AMADEUS MOZART to a libretto by LORENZO DA PONTE; Prague, National Theatre, 29 October 1787.

Don Giovanni *a young and extremely licentious nobleman*	baritone
Commendatore	bass
Donna Anna *his daughter*	soprano
Don Ottavio *her betrothed*	tenor
Donna Elvira *a lady from Burgos*	soprano
Leporello *Giovanni's servant*	bass
Masetto *a peasant, betrothed to Zerlina*	bass
Zerlina *a peasant girl*	soprano

Peasants, servants, demons

Setting A Spanish town (traditionally Seville), in the 16th century

The commission for *Don Giovanni* followed the triumphant production of *Le nozze di Figaro* in Prague (December 1786). The impresario Guardasoni probably asked Mozart to expand Bertati's one-act *Don Giovanni*, set by Gazzaniga for Venice in February 1787. Da Ponte's memoirs suppressed his indebtedness, but he improved Bertati in every respect and drew on other sources, notably Molière's *Dom Juan* and versions from popular theatre. About half the libretto, between the Act 1 quartet and the graveyard scene, is original.

Mozart began work during the summer, leaving for Prague on 1 October. This season in the Bohemian capital has the flavour of legend; but there is no reason to suppose that Mozart's compositional processes were abnormal, even in the late composition of the overture (on the eve of the performance, already twice postponed, or of the final rehearsal). He may have had to resist Bassi's demand for a big aria, and possibly did not know Baglioni when he composed 'Il mio tesoro'.

Mozart surely had in mind production in Vienna with the personnel of the original *Figaro*. The two casts are listed together:

	Prague 1787	*Vienna 1788*
Leporello	Felice Ponziani	Francesco Benucci
Anna	Teresa Saporiti	Aloysia Lange
Giovanni	Luigi Bassi	Francesco Albertarelli
Commendatore/ Masetto	Giuseppe Lolli	Francesco Bussani
Ottavio	Antonio Baglioni	Francesco Morella
Elvira	Caterina Micelli	Caterina Cavalieri
Zerlina	Caterina Bondini	Luisa Mombelli/ Therese Teyber

The new triumph in Prague was not repeated in Vienna, although *Don Giovanni* received more performances than *Figaro* had done in 1786. Mozart wrote a replacement aria for Ottavio, an additional *scena* for Elvira, so that her role became approximately equal to Anna's, and a *buffo* duet for Mombelli and Benucci. The final scene, after Giovanni's disappearance, may have been omitted.

Don Giovanni soon acquired a reputation for exceptional difficulty, derived from the superimposed dance metres of the first finale and the unprecedented harmonic richness of the second. Guardasoni gave it in Warsaw in 1789; and it made rapid progress in Germany as a Singspiel, becoming after *Die Entführung* the Mozart opera most performed in his lifetime. At least three translations were used: by H. G. Schmieder (Mainz and Frankfurt, early 1789); C. G. Neefe (Mannheim and Bonn, also in 1789); and F. L. Schröder, in four acts (Hamburg 1789; Berlin 1790). German was used in Prague in 1791, Vienna in 1792, and outside Germany in Amsterdam (1793) and St Petersburg (1797). *Don Giovanni* became popular in France, often in adapted versions (in French, arranged C. Kalkbrenner, 1805; in Italian, 1811; in both languages thereafter). An attempt at Florence in 1792 seems to have been frustrated by the first finale; the Italian première was at Bergamo in 1811, followed that year by Rome. In England there is some doubt over the earliest performances, which may have been partly amateur affairs. In 1817 it appeared at rival theatres in Italian and in English; it remained popular in both languages. The first American performances, in 1826, were by García's company in association with Da Ponte. Nearly every opera singer of note has been associated with one of the main roles, and 19th- and 20th-century productions are too numerous to detail.

The overture begins with the imposing music for the entrance of the 'stone guest'. Its emergence into the D major Allegro establishes the ambivalence of the opera, its perilous balance of humour and tragedy. The full sonata form has been interpreted as a portrait of Giovanni, or as justice (the heavy five-note figure) pursuing the mercurial seducer. There is no final cadence; the coda modulates to a new key (F major) for the opening scene.

ACT 1 *Courtyard of the Commendatore's house; night* Leporello is always on guard (*Introduzione*, 'Notte e giorno faticar'), but indulges in fantasy ('Voglio far il gentiluomo'). He hides at the approach of Anna, pursuing Giovanni (who conceals his face); the music is still formal despite its growing intensity (as often hereafter, Leporello comments in the background). Anna's father confronts Giovanni; musical formality yields to disordered gesture as they fight. The old man dies at a rare moment of stillness, even Giovanni being moved (in the short trio in F minor, he has a melody formerly sung by Anna in a faster tempo). Giovanni and Leporello escape. Anna returns and faints over the body (obbligato recitative and duet, 'Fuggi, crudele'); reviving, she responds to Ottavio's tender invitation to take him as husband and father by demanding an oath of vengeance. Their voices unite in powerful D minor cadences which form the first decisive closure of the opera.

A street; dawn Elvira, in travelling clothes, is pursuing her betrayer (aria, 'Ah, chi mi dice mai'); her sincere, slightly ridiculous pose is conveyed by a sweeping melodic line and formal orchestral gestures. Giovanni scents adventure; recognition comes too late to prevent his unctuous advance, which covers the cadence of the aria. He escapes her reproaches, leaving Leporello to show her the catalogue (aria, 'Madamina, il catalogo è questo'). Giovanni's conquests total 640 in Italy, 230 in Germany, 100 in France, 91 in Turkey, but in Spain, 1003. Bubbling patter is succeeded by a luscious minuet as Leporello details the types of women who have yielded; although willing to take anybody, Giovanni prefers the young beginner (an orchestral and tonal shiver underlines this depravity).

[Mid-morning] Peasants invade the stage (a bucolic G major chorus). Attracted to the bride, Zerlina, Giovanni invites them all to his house. He dismisses the jealous Masetto, who upbraids Zerlina in an action aria ('Ho capito, signor, sì') before being dragged away. Giovanni flatters Zerlina with an offer of marriage (duettino, 'Là ci darem la mano'). 'Vorrei, e non vorrei': held by the hand, and following his melodic lead, Zerlina still worries about Masetto, but her impending submission is not in doubt. Their voices join in a pastorale ('Andiam mio bene'). Elvira's homily to Zerlina ('Ah fuggi il traditor') is a very short aria of Baroque vigour and formality, ending with strident coloratura. Anna and Ottavio greet Giovanni as a friend; the devil is frustrating his every plan, but he offers his assistance with exaggerated courtesy. Elvira interrupts again; recognizing a social equal, she tells Anna in measured tones not to trust Giovanni (quartet, 'Non ti fidar, o misera'). Anna and Ottavio are puzzled; Giovanni tries to hush Elvira and explains that she is mad. In the course of a finely wrought ensemble her denunciation grows more vehement, even shameless. Giovanni's farewell is too effusive; Anna realizes, and explains to Ottavio, that it was he who tried to seduce her the previous night. Her harrowing description (obbligato recitative) revives the orchestral turbulence of the music after her father's death; her aria in D major ('Or sai chi l'onore') bespeaks her valiant determination to avenge her father. Ottavio can hardly believe Giovanni's villainy, but his role is to support Anna. (His exquisite aria, 'Dalla sua pace' K540*a*, was added for Vienna.) Giovanni congratulates Leporello on disposing of Elvira and prepares for a brilliant afternoon's work (aria, 'Fin ch'han dal vino'); wine will warm them up, they will mix the minuet, follia and allemande, and ten names will enter the catalogue.

Giovanni's garden [afternoon] In Mozart's most enchanting melodic vein, with cello obbligato, Zerlina wins Masetto back (aria, 'Batti, batti'; like 'Là ci darem' it begins in 2/4 and ends in a honeyed 6/8). When she hears Giovanni's voice she is too obviously aroused. The finale begins as Giovanni gives orders to his servants; then, espying Zerlina as she tries to hide, he resumes his blandishments. Masetto pops out of hiding; to the sound of a contredanse they go inside. Elvira leads Anna and Ottavio, masked, towards Giovanni's lair. Leporello sees them (the minuet is heard from the window), and they are invited in. Their short prayer accompanied by wind ('Protegga il giusto ciel') is a moment of stillness at the heart of one of Mozart's most active finales.

The ballroom To music resembling the earlier bucolic chorus, Giovanni and Leporello entertain the peasants. Masetto urges prudence. The central key-change from E♭ to C, resplendent with trumpets, greets the masked trio with the acclamation 'Viva la libertà!'. Now in G major, in a tour de force using three small stage bands, the ball resumes. The minuet is danced by Anna and Ottavio; on it is superimposed the contredanse in 2/4 with the same pulse (the 'follia' of Giovanni's aria) danced by Giovanni and Zerlina, and the 'teitsch' (Allemande) with a bar of 3/8 to the prevailing beat, which Leporello forces Masetto to dance. Giovanni drags Zerlina out. She screams; Masetto rushes after them; and as the violently interrupted tonalities return via F to the tonic C, Giovanni complacently blames Leporello and offers to kill him on the spot. Zerlina and the trio, unmasking, denounce him and he is momentarily nonplussed, but in a whirlwind ensemble he outfaces them all.

ACT 2 *A street* Giovanni scorns Leporello's furious attempts to resign (duet, 'Eh via buffone'). A purse changes hands, but when Leporello tells his master to give up women he claims to need them 'as much as the food I eat and the air I breathe'. His love is universal; faithfulness to one women betrays all the rest. Leporello is forced to change clothes for the seduction of Elvira's maid. It is twilight; Elvira, on a balcony, tries to repress her desire for Giovanni but her fluttering heart betrays her (trio, 'Ah taci, ingiusto core'). Giovanni adopts her melody, but in the more intense dominant (sonata form perfectly matches Mozart's dramatic requirements). In the middle section his ardour is extreme; exploring a remote key (C within the dominant region of A), he anticipates the melody of his serenade. She denounces him; he presses her; she weakens; though he pities her, Leporello is in danger of laughing aloud. She comes down to the disguised servant, who begins to enjoy the act. Giovanni chases them away and serenades the maid (canzonetta, 'Deh vieni alla finestra'). But Masetto and a group of peasants, bearing crude weapons, are after Giovanni's blood. The false Leporello sympathizes and in an action aria ('Metà di voi quà vadano') gives in-

Design by Leopold Peuckert for the graveyard scene in Mozart's 'Don Giovanni' (Act 2); this is the earliest known design for the opera (Prague, ?1790s)

structions on how to search the streets and recognize the villain. He keeps Masetto with him and gives him a beating. Hearing groans, Zerlina offers the balm only she can provide; a heart-easing melody in a gentle 3/8 invites Masetto to lay his hand on her bosom (aria, 'Vedrai, carino').

A courtyard at Anna's house Leporello, seeing lights, retreats with Elvira into the dark yard, intent on desertion. She begs him not to leave her; he gropes for the exit (sextet, 'Sola in buio loco'; in E♭). A moment of magic – soft trumpets and drums mark a key-change from the dominant (B♭) to D – brings Anna and Ottavio with servants and lights. His renewed plea for marriage, and her prevarication, unfold in long melodic spans which draw the tonality to C minor. Elvira's search for 'Giovanni', and Leporello's for the gate, are interrupted by Zerlina and Masetto. All denounce the betrayer, in a scene of unreality (for the true villain is absent) made pathetic by Elvira's plea for mercy, and comic by Leporello's terror and abject submission when he identifies himself. This movement resembles a short finale, for it ends with a huge ensemble of consternation. Then everybody turns on Leporello, who babbles excuses as he escapes (aria, 'Ah pietà, Signori miei'). Ottavio decides to go to the authorities; he asks the others to watch over Anna while he avenges her (aria, 'Il mio tesoro', a full-length virtuoso piece accompanied by muted strings and clarinets).

(In the Vienna version, Leporello escapes in a recitative, using only a motif from the Prague aria; Ottavio decides to go to the authorities. Then Zerlina drags Leporello back and ties him up, threatening dire punishments (duet, 'Per queste tue manine'); Leporello again escapes. Masetto claims to have prevented another of Giovanni's crimes. Elvira vents her mixed feelings: obbligato recitative, 'In quali eccessi' and aria, 'Mi tradì', a piece of vertiginous emotion embodied in perpetual-motion quavers.)

A graveyard [night] Giovanni escapes an adventure by leaping the wall. Leporello joins him, complaining that once again he has nearly been killed. Giovanni heartlessly narrates the conquest of Leporello's girl; his laughter is rebuked by the dead Commendatore (an oracular utterance, with trombones). They find the statue and Leporello is forced to read the inscription: 'I await vengeance on the villain who slew me'. Giovanni forces Leporello to invite the statue to supper. This most sinister situation is handled as a *buffo* duet ('O statua gentilissima') mainly reflecting the fear of Leporello as he approaches and retreats. The statue nods, then sings its acceptance; even Giovanni is puzzled and subdued, but he leads Leporello off to prepare the meal.

A darkened room in Anna's house Ottavio is again pressing his suit; he calls Anna cruel. She protests at the word (obbligato recitative, 'Crudele! Ah nò, mio bene'); society would frown on an immediate wedding. The recitative anticipates the Larghetto of the aria ('Non mi dir'), an undulating melody of great sweetness forming the slow section of a rondò. In the Allegro she hopes that heaven will take pity on her; the blossoming coloratura corresponds to the strength of her resolve. Ottavio is determined to share her martyrdom.

A dining-room in Giovanni's house (finale) Giovanni enjoys a meal without waiting for his guest; Leporello is frankly envious. A sequence of popular tunes (from Martín y Soler's *Una cosa rara*, Sarti's *Fra i due litiganti* and Mozart's *Figaro*) played by onstage wind band accompanies the farce of Leporello stealing food and being caught with his mouth full. Elvira bursts in, barely coherent; she is making a last appeal to Giovanni to reform. He laughs at her, tries to make her join him, and to a newly minted melody drinks a toast to wine and women, 'Sostegno e gloria d'umanità'. From outside, Elvira screams. Leporello investigates and returns in terror, babbling of a white stone man with huge strides. When knocking is heard he hides under the table and Giovanni opens the door. The overture music is reinforced by trombones as the statue enters to a crushing diminished 7th. His solemn grandeur, Giovanni's polite, then impatient responses, and Leporello's terrified asides, are musically characterized but subsumed to a harmonic development of unparalleled richness. The statue cannot take mortal food, but he invites Giovanni to sup with him. With admirable fearlessness, in a phrase of marked dignity, Giovanni accepts; but on grasping the statue's chilling hand he is overcome by his impending dissolution. Still refusing to repent, he is engulfed in flames. The chorus of demons exactly reflects the cadences of the vengeance duet, at the beginning of Act 1. The others rush on with the police, to find only Leporello, who stammers out enough for them to understand. In an extended Larghetto, Ottavio again pleads with Anna; she tells him to wait a year for their wedding. Elvira will go to a convent, Zerlina and Masetto will marry, Leporello will find another master. All join to point the moral in a bright fugato: 'This is the end of the evil-doer: his death is as bad as his life'.

* * *

There are two authentic versions of *Don Giovanni*, the differences mainly in the distribution of arias. Each has only one for Ottavio, since when including a new aria for Elvira (Cavalieri) in Act 2, Mozart omitted 'Il mio tesoro' as well as a short aria for Leporello. The concentration of arias in Act 2 which results from the common practice of including in succession those for Leporello, Ottavio and Elvira was never the authors' intention. The additional duet for Zerlina and Leporello, its coarseness perhaps designed to humour the Viennese, is generally omitted, but Elvira's 'In quali eccessi ... Mi tradì' is too good to lose; some 19th-century performances, including one that may have had Da Ponte's approval, removed it to Act 1.

In musical form and dramatic technique, particularly the proportion and design of arias and ensembles, *Don Giovanni* is largely modelled on *Figaro*. Exceptions include the 'Catalogue' aria, with its fast–slow tempo pattern; the first finale which besides the unique dance sequence covers a change of location; and the extended introduction, embedded in a vast structure extending from the overture to the end of the duet 'Fuggi, crudele'. The harmonic language associated with Don Giovanni's fall, including that duet and the second finale, marks a decisive departure from *buffo* norms (certainly not anticipated by Gazzaniga, whose setting may have influenced Anna's first entry). The designation 'dramma giocoso' used by Da Ponte (though not by Mozart) has no particular significance; the serious characters are as much embroiled in the intrigue as in *Figaro*.

The tragic elements nevertheless form a new synthesis of *buffo* and serious styles, and explain why *Don Giovanni* has gripped the imagination of writers and philosophers. In particular they have been attracted by the daemonic in Giovanni, and by the impossibility of penetrating a character so mercurial, whose music says so little about his motivation; even 'Fin ch'han dal vino' is a set of instructions to Leporello, though also an explosion from his joyous daemon. Whereas the other characters are remarkably three-dimensional, Giovanni adapts the style of each of his victims, including the Commendatore who brings out the heroic in him and Leporello whom he chaffs in pure *buffo* style. He woos Anna by courtly flattery, Zerlina by condescension, Elvira's maid by disguise; Elvira herself he evades or mocks, but he can also woo her with false ardour (in the trio at the beginning of Act 2).

Elvira, ignored in the 19th century, now seems the most interesting because psychologically the most complex of the women. Though the greatest singers, such as Patti, sometimes sang Zerlina, Anna attracted most interest; E. T. A. Hoffmann suggested that she had been seduced by Giovanni and was in love with him rather than Ottavio, a fantasy which received comic treatment in Shaw's *Man and Superman*. Stendhal and Kierkegaard used Giovanni to illustrate aspects of love and the erotic. Significantly Kierkegaard was aware of earlier dramatic treatments but derived his views from the music, not the libretto or the historical evolution of the character (B. Williams, in Rushton 1981).

Don Giovanni is governed by a single idea, Giovanni's flouting of society in pursuit of sexual pleasure, which binds together a disparate set of ambivalent or comic incidents. The libretto has been unfairly criticized; its episodic nature is a condition of the subject, in which respect it differs from *Figaro* and *Così*. Divine retribution appears like an act of God, or a different kind of life-force personified in the statue; what in previous treatments had been comic, perfunctory or merely gruesome, is raised to sublimity by Mozart's music.

See also CONVITATO DI PIETRO, IL. For further illustration *see* BASSI, LUIGI. JULIAN RUSHTON

Donington, Robert (*b* Leeds, 4 May 1907; *d* Firle, Sussex, 20 Jan 1990). English musicologist. He studied at the Queen's College, Oxford, and with Arnold Dolmetsch (the viol, the violin and the interpretation of early music). He subsequently divided his career between performance and scholarship. From 1961 he spent much of his time in the USA, and in 1964 he was appointed professor of music at the University of Iowa. He was awarded the OBE in 1979.

Donington was best known for his indispensable studies of instruments and of Baroque performance practice, but he also wrote substantially on opera. He was the author of a provocative study of symbolism in Wagner's *Ring*, based on Jungian myth analysis, and of two books on the history of opera. His writings contain valuable insights into the problems of Baroque performance practice and a commonsense attitude to their solution, with emphasis on good taste and instinctive musicianship. His discussion of early recordings and his applications to earlier periods of conclusions drawn from early 20th-century singing are stimulating if controversial.

The Interpretation of Early Music (London, 1963, 3/1974)
Wagner's 'Ring' and its Symbols: the Music and the Myth (London, 1963, 3/1974)
The Opera (London, 1978)
The Rise of Opera (London, 1981)
Opera and its Symbols: the Unity of Words, Music and Singing (New Haven, CT, 1991) HOWARD MAYER BROWN

Donizetti. Theatre in BERGAMO, Donizetti's birthplace, built as the Teatro Riccardi in 1791, rebuilt in 1801 and renamed the Teatro Donizetti in 1897 on the centenary of the composer's birth.

Donizetti, (Domenico) Gaetano (Maria) (*b* Bergamo, 29 Nov 1797; *d* Bergamo, 8 April 1848). Italian composer. In the years between the death of Bellini (1835) and for a few years after the emergence of Verdi with *Nabucco* (1842) Donizetti was the dominant figure in the world of Italian opera.

1. Education and early career. The fifth child of poor parents from Bergamo, Donizetti was born with no particular prospects. As a child he must have demonstrated innate musical ability because at nine he was admitted as a free student among the first group to attend the Lezioni Caritatevoli, a school started by Simon Mayr to train choristers and instrumentalists to participate in the music at S Maria Maggiore, where Mayr was *maestro di cappella*. There is no trace of other musicians in his family background but some propensity for music showed itself in Gaetano's generation. His elder brother Giuseppe (1788–1856) rose from a position as military bandsman to become chief of music for the Ottoman armies; the middle brother, Francesco (1792–1848), reputedly slow of intellect, mastered enough of the art of the bass drum to play with the Bergamo civic band.

The Lezioni Caritatevoli was instituted to fill the void left by the suppression of the church-run conservatories, after the banning of all such institutions in northern Italy during the Napoleonic period. For Donizetti the regime at Mayr's school included classes in singing (with Solari) and keyboard (with Gonzales, the first to recognize his unusual ability) and, later, in composition and theory, with Mayr himself. Although deficiencies in Donizetti's voice put his continuation as a pupil in doubt, Mayr was sufficiently convinced of the promise implicit in the youthful, rebellious musician that he exerted himself to retain his prize student and to open up opportunities for him. Mayr's end-of-term burletta, *Il piccolo compositore di musica* (1806), was designed to show off his students, and the title role was assigned to Donizetti.

It is difficult to overestimate the crucial role that Mayr played not only in Donizetti's education but also in easing the first steps of his professional career. Donizetti was fortunate in studying composition with one of the leading opera composers of the day, one whose major works were written precisely during the years Donizetti was his pupil. When Mayr became convinced that Donizetti needed further instruction, he arranged and partly underwrote Donizetti's two-year course at Bologna (1815–17) with Padre Stanislao Mattei (1750–1825), the teacher of Rossini and Morlacchi. It was Mayr, as well, who helped him with his first professional engagement, commissioned by Paolo Zancla, a Sicilian impresario then active in the Veneto, and it was Mayr who supplied him with his first librettist, Bartolomeo Merelli. Besides all this, Mayr believed in encouraging Donizetti to compose at every opportunity, and from this period (1817–21) come most of his non-operatic works: chiefly sacred and chamber music, including a sizable number of string quartets. The salon music, many vocal solos and duets to piano accompaniment, on the other hand, was produced throughout his career. Contrary to an erroneous but oft-repeated legend, Donizetti did not serve in the Austrian armed forces; a patroness in Bergamo paid for his military exemption.

Although Donizetti composed a number of operatic scenes to pre-existing librettos while he was Mattei's pupil in Bologna, none of these seems to have been publicly performed. His first opera to see the stage was *Enrico di Borgogna*, given at S Luca, Venice, on 14 November 1818, and it was judged successful enough to prompt a second work, a one-act farce *Una follia*, the following month. Two further works for Zancla's company followed in the next few years.

There seems little doubt that Mayr turned over to Donizetti a commission to write an opera for the Teatro Argentina in Rome for the carnival season of 1821–2. The fact that *Zoraide di Grenata* was the fourth and last of Merelli's texts set by Donizetti suggests that it was started in Bergamo under Mayr's watchful eye. The work proved unexpectedly successful because of a combination of unforeseen circumstances, among them the death of one of the leading singers shortly before the première, which involved Donizetti's changing and omitting some of the music at the last minute. In short, the public was so well disposed towards the young composer that at the third performance it gave him a genuine triumph, a torchlight procession in his honour. On this showing Donizetti won a contract with the leading impresario of the period, Domenico Barbaia, then principally active in Naples.

Naples was to be the chief but not the only arena of activity for Donizetti for the next 16 years. He arrived there early in 1822, during the last weeks of Rossini's tenure and on the eve of Barbaia's taking Rossini to Vienna for the Italian (April–July) season at the Kärntnertortheater. He left Donizetti behind as director of music at the Teatro Nuovo. Donizetti's first score for Naples was a two-act *dramma*, *La zingara*, which enjoyed a number of revivals; a septet in the second act was singled out for particular praise, proving Donizetti to be 'a worthy pupil' of Mayr. For the autumn season at La Scala, he was commissioned to write a *semiseria* to a libretto by Felice Romani, *Chiara e Serafina*, but the work produced at best a slight impression. It was to be eight years before Donizetti managed to win over the Milanese. Even less success attended his first opera written for the S Carlo, *Alfredo il grande*, doomed by a singularly maladroit libretto to survive for only two performances.

Donizetti's first work to achieve real hardihood was a two-act *melodramma giocoso*, *L'ajo nell'imbarazzo*, put on at the Teatro Valle in Rome in February 1824. It first revealed his contagious sense of humour and his way of humanizing comedy with touches of pathos. He had come to Rome at the end of 1823, first of all to supervise the mounting of a revised version of *Zoraide*, given again at the Argentina, with the role of Abenamet expanded for the star *musico* Benedetta Rosamunda Pisaroni, but this time the work was coldly received. During his stay in Rome Donizetti became closely attached to the Vasselli family, whose daughter Virginia was to become his wife in 1828. Her brother Antonio ('Toto') Vasselli, later Ricordi's Roman agent, became his closest friend.

During winter 1825–6 Donizetti was in Palermo as musical director of the Teatro Carolino. During this frustrating period his career seems to have stalled. He returned to Naples, where one of his first activities was to compose, without any contract or hope of performance, a setting of *Gabriella di Vergy* to a libretto earlier set by Carafa. This was an important step, for it was Donizetti's first effort to deal with a powerful tragic plot. *Gabriella* was also an augury for Donizetti's chief efforts in the next five years when he sought to enlarge his range by dealing with a wide variety of subjects and genres. It was not performed until 1869.

The earliest of the notable works in this phase of Donizetti's career is *Otto mesi in due ore* (1827), a subject that he kept returning to over the years, most notably as *Elisabeth* (an unperformed version of the latter work, apparently dating from Donizetti's Paris years, was lately rediscovered in the archives of Covent Garden). *Le convenienze teatrali*, a satire on provincial opera companies, has enjoyed great popularity since World War II (sometimes under an alternative title, *Viva la mamma*); *L'esule di Roma* contains the first of Donizetti's depictions of mental derangement; *Elisabetta al castello di Kenilworth* marks the composer's first encounter with the figure of Queen Elizabeth I and is his earliest score to contain two major female roles; *Imelda de' Lambertazzi*, his earliest experiment with a baritone hero, ends with a gruesome death scene. All these were first given in Naples.

2. THE ACHIEVEMENT OF FAME. In 1830 Donizetti was invited to Milan to participate in a special carnival season at the Teatro Carcano which opened with *Anna Bolena*, the leading roles being sung by Pasta, Rubini and Filippo Galli. Practically overnight he became an international figure, for the work was soon given in both Paris and London with Pasta and Rubini. This success improved Donizetti's working conditions, reducing his bondage to the Neapolitan theatres and leaving him freer to accept engagements elsewhere. *Fausta* was an impressive work, although its future was hindered by the censors, but it served to bring him once again into contact with Giuseppina Ronzi De Begnis, who became his ideal dramatic *soprano d'agilità*; some of his grandest female roles were conceived in terms of her voice. *Ugo conte di Parigi*, his first opera for La Scala since the ill-fated *Chiara*, ran afoul of the censors. It had the important effect, however, of stimulating Donizetti in his deliberate campaign throughout the rest of his Italian career to push the censors to the limits in his efforts to deal with powerful subjects.

Two months after *Ugo* he brought out *L'elisir d'amore*, one of his comic masterpieces and the greatest popular success he enjoyed. He came into contact with another singing actor who would powerfully stimulate him when he wrote *Il furioso nell'isola di San Domingo* and *Torquato Tasso*, both for the baritone Giorgio Ronconi. *Parisina* and *Rosmonda d'Inghilterra* were written for the impresario Lanari at Florence; the former brought him together with another potent singing actress, Karoline Unger, as well as the tenor Gilbert Duprez, the latter with Fanny Tacchinardi-Persiani, the greatest vocal technician of her generation. It is essential to stress the importance of this constellation of gifted singers because Donizetti's operas were composed with the capacities of the original cast in mind and aimed at winning immediate success with jaded audiences. Two other notable works of this period were *Lucrezia Borgia* and *Gemma di Vergy*.

In 1835 he wrote for the first time for Paris, absorbing the musical tastes of that city, when he presented *Marino Faliero* at the Théâtre Italien. On his return to Naples, he brought out *Lucia di Lammermoor*, arguably his finest score and one deeply in tune with the romantic sensibility of the age, writing once more for Persiani and Duprez. *Lucia* marked the beginning of his collaboration with Salvadore Cammarano, who was to remain his preferred librettist. *Maria Stuarda*, banned in Naples by the king, became briefly a *succès de scandale* at La Scala with Malibran in the title role, but there too it was suppressed by the authorities. *Belisario* was at first more readily accepted than *Lucia*, but within two years *Lucia* had made a permanent place for itself in the international repertory.

At this time Donizetti's parents died, within weeks of each other, and from then on his personal life was touched by tragedy. The following year his wife Virginia died during a harrowing cholera epidemic. Of his three children, two were stillborn and the other lived only a few days. A morbid streak becomes increasingly apparent in Donizetti's character, a symptom perhaps of the disease that in 1845 was to end his career.

L'assedio di Calais (1836, Naples) is significant because it reveals Donizetti's ambition to internationalize his style and win a contract to compose for the Paris Opéra. Both *Roberto Devereux* and *Maria de Rudenz* are evidence of the mature Donizetti's infatuation with strong dramatic subjects. The banning of *Poliuto* in summer 1838 marked the severing of Donizetti's ties with Naples, ties that had been weakened by the king's studied avoidance of confirming his appointment as director of the Naples Conservatory.

3. FINAL PERIOD AND LAST ILLNESS. Donizetti moved to Paris in autumn 1838, engaged by Duponchel to write three works for the Opéra. Eugène Scribe was to convert the three acts of *Poliuto* into a French *grand opéra* in four acts, as *Les martyrs*. Donizetti rearranged his score and added new music. This task only partially occupied him in 1839, for he also made a French adaptation of *Lucia* for the Théâtre de la Renaissance, composed two acts of *Le duc d'Albe*, which he never finished, slightly revised *Roberto Devereux* for its mounting at the Théâtre Italien, and completed *L'ange de Nisida*, also for the Renaissance. This last was not given because the management went bankrupt, and he salvaged much of the score for *La favorite*.

In 1840 he produced *La fille du régiment* at the Opéra-Comique, an accomplishment that called forth from Berlioz the quip: 'One can no longer speak of the opera houses of Paris but only of the opera houses of M. Donizetti'. *La fille* became one of the central works of the Comique for the rest of the century, testimony to the composer's success at mastering the French idiom. Next, he engaged in the frustrations of the three-month rehearsal period preceding the mounting of *Les martyrs*, with Dorus-Gras and Duprez, at the Opéra. He returned to Italy to prepare the *opera buffa* version of *La figlia del reggimento*, but before it was staged he was summoned back to Paris to put on *La favorite*, with Rosine Stoltz and Duprez. This grand but sober work proved the most substantial success of his serious French operas. Its last act was not, as popular legend has it, written in a single night; it was almost entirely derived from *L'ange de Nisida*.

No sooner was *La favorite* safely launched than Donizetti hurried back to Italy, where *Adelia* was staged at the Teatro Apollo in Rome, with Strepponi in the title role. He returned to France where he started composing *Maria Padilla*, in response to his first invitation to open a season at La Scala since the difficulties over *Maria Stuarda*. He contributed much to Gaetano Rossi's libretto. Beginning the season that in March 1842 saw the furore over Verdi's *Nabucco*, *Maria Padilla* proved a legitimate success with 26 performances, but in spite of many fine passages it never gained the reputation it merited.

Donizetti had been appointed musical director of the annual Italian season at the Kärntnertortheater in Vienna by his former librettist, Merelli, now the impresario of La Scala and lessee of the principal Viennese opera house; on his way there he stopped in

Bologna, at Rossini's invitation, where he conducted the Italian première of the *Stabat mater* (which he later directed in Vienna). His duties in Vienna involved not only preparing others' works but also supplying a new opera each year. His first, *Linda di Chamounix*, given with Tadolini, the favourite singer of Donizetti's last years, won such a substantial success that he was appointed Hofkapellmeister. Donizetti now returned to Paris, where he started to compose a *Caterina Cornaro*, but halted work when he learnt that Franz Lachner had written an opera on the same subject (1841, Munich). Instead, he accepted Crosnier's commission to supply an *opera buffa* for the principal quartet at the Théâtre Italien; this was to be *Don Pasquale*, that wonderful swan-song of a nearly moribund genre. Once this was staged, he returned to Vienna, where he brought out *Maria di Rohan*, another vehicle for Tadolini with Ronconi. At some point in 1843 he composed and orchestrated seven numbers of *Ne m'oubliez pas*, intended for the Opéra-Comique but left incomplete. All this while, he was engaged upon the composition of the sprawling, five-act *Dom Sébastien*, given in November with Stoltz and Duprez, the last of his works written for the Opéra. In some ways Donizetti's most monumental achievement, it is hampered by a devious and not always convincing text by Scribe.

It was during the turmoil of the rehearsal period for this last opera that the symptoms of Donizetti's illness unequivocally began to manifest themselves in sudden periods of apathy, inexplicable lapses of memory and moments of intense nervous excitement. For a time it was generally supposed that his condition was caused by overwork. He managed one last chore: the completion of *Caterina Cornaro*, now scheduled for the S Carlo, but he arranged a medical excuse to avoid going to Naples to supervise its production. In 1844, he took an extended trip through Italy, but his many friends were dismayed by his altered demeanour. In 1845 he returned to Vienna, where he oversaw a production of *Dom Sébastien*, adding some new music to the score. His final piece of work was to supply a new ending to *Caterina* for its production at Parma in February 1845.

In autumn that year Donizetti's condition worsened to the extent that his nephew Andrea was summoned from Constantinople to see what should be done to protect his famous uncle. After medical consultations he was diagnosed as suffering from cerebro-spinal syphilis, a finding that was confirmed at his autopsy. Not knowing what else to do, Andrea arranged his commitment to a sanatorium at Ivry. There Donizetti was confined for 17 months, then, through the intervention of a Viennese friend, Baron Lannoy, his nephew was summoned back to find a suitable apartment in Paris where Donizetti could be maintained and visited and taken out for drives. By now, Donizetti was paralysed and spoke only rarely and disjointedly. Among his visitors was Verdi, whose account of the meeting makes sad reading. Through the intervention of friends in Bergamo it was arranged, not without considerable interference, that Donizetti would be brought back to his birthplace, where he was cared for in the palace of the Baronessa Scotti; it was there that he died.

He was buried in the Valtesse cemetery, but in 1875 his remains were moved to S Maria Maggiore, where they were placed in front of the monument by Vincenzo Vela. The Istituto Musicale G. Donizetti in Bergamo, the continuation of Mayr's Lezioni Caritatevoli, contains a Museo Donizettiano with a collection of manuscripts, mainly juvenilia, and mementoes. His birthplace in the Via Borgo Canale is now a national landmark. The principal collections of Donizetti manuscripts are to be found at the Conservatorio di S Pietro a Majella in Naples, at Casa Ricordi in Milan, and at the Bibliothèque Nationale in Paris.

4. CHARACTER. Donizetti's copious correspondence gives considerable insight into his nature. He was by and large open and affectionate, supportive of his colleagues and capable of responding eloquently and sensitively when his feelings were aroused. Two particular passages may be quoted. One is his description, from a letter to Mayr (dated 15 July 1843), of the basement rooms in which he lived as a child: 'You went down cellar steps, where no glimmer of light ever penetrated. And like an owl I took flight'. The other, from the letter to his brother-in-law Vasselli (dated 3 July 1843) in which he gave his piano to his niece Virginia (named after Donizetti's wife):

> Do not sell the pianoforte for any price, for contained in it is my whole artistic life. From 1822 I have had the sound of it in my ears; there murmured the *Annas*, the *Marias*, the *Faustas*, the *Lucias*, the *Robertos*, the *Belisarii*, the *Marinos*, the *Martyrs*, the *Olivos*, *Ajo*, *Furioso*, *Paris*, *Castello di Kenilworth*, *Ugo*, *Pazzi*, *Pia*, *Rudenz* – Oh! let it live as long as I live! – With that piano I lived my time of hope, my married life, my lonely time. It heard my joys, my tears, my deluded hopes, my honours – it shared with me my sweating and my labour – my talent lived there, in that piano lives every period of my career.

One of Donizetti's most admirable traits was his constant affection for the man he called his 'second father', Mayr. His gratitude for his teacher's assistance coupled with the unpretentious way he told him of his works and of his hopes for them reveal one of the most likable sides of Donizetti's character. The letters he wrote to his brother-in-law in the devastating wake of Virginia's death expose great depth of feeling.

Donizetti's keen sense of theatrical values stemmed from his continuous immersion in the composition and rehearsing of his works. His intuitive understanding of what suited his gifts often caused him to participate in the preparation of the librettos he set and even prompted his writing three for himself: those of *Le convenienze*, *Il campanello di notte* and *Betly*.

5. OPERAS.

(i) General survey. Along with Bellini, Donizetti epitomized the Italian Romantic spirit of the 1830s. A more fragile spirit than its German or French counterpart, it declared itself through – and often in the teeth of – an operatic tradition of fixed, generic forms and vocal virtuosity, linked to the necessity of rapid production. If Bellini expressed Italian Romanticism in its most concentrated form, Donizetti compensated by a greater versatility and resource and a stronger feeling for dramatic movement. He also had the benefit of a more thorough musical training under Mayr and Mattei, and this contributed much to his superior fluency of technique and invention.

When Donizetti began his career in 1818, Italian music was wholly dominated by Rossini, whose formal, abundantly florid style all composers were bound to imitate since, as Pacini wrote, 'there [was] no other way of making a living'. Although reputedly desirous of reform, Donizetti conformed to this style without difficulty, whether in the *seria*, *buffa* or *semiseria* genre, and the 30 or so works produced over the next ten years, mainly for Naples and other cities in the south, all show nimble craftsmanship and melodic fertility. In the serious and 'semi-serious' operas there is as yet little trace of individuality, which, in all the principal voice parts, tends to sink under the weight of Rossinian *canto fiorito* and *solfeggi* (see ex.1, a passage for one of the

Ex.1

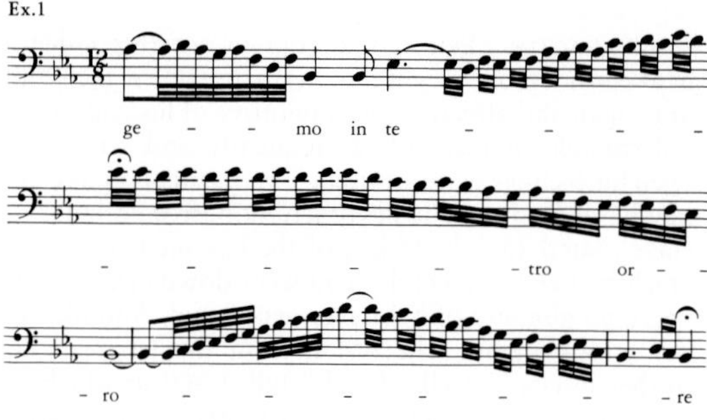

['I groan with dismal dread']

four virtuoso basses in the heroic opera *Otto mesi in due ore, ossia Gli esiliati in Siberia*, 1827).

It is his comedies, such as *L'ajo nell'imbarazzo* (1824), *Olivo e Pasquale* (1827) and *Il giovedì grasso* (1829), that afford the earliest glimpse of the true Donizetti. The first, in particular, shows that blend of humour and tenderness (here enhanced by the felicity of Ferretti's verse) that is the hallmark of his comic style. Even the routine syllabic setting for the two *buffi* is floated on a characteristically fresh melody embellished with light, faintly sensuous chromatic inflections (ex.2).

After 1828 Donizetti's own style began to take shape under the influence partly of Bellini's *Il pirata* (1827), which brought to Italian opera a new manner in which

Ex.2

[Giulio: 'By Jove, the teacher has lost his wits.' Gregorio: 'My friend thinks that my wits are gone.' Giulio: 'Or else he's a wolf in sheep's clothing.' Gregorio: 'Or he thinks I'm a wolf in sheep's clothing.']

fioritura was both reduced and subordinated to passionate expression, and partly of Rossini's monumental French operas, such as *Le siège de Corinthe* (1826) and *Moïse* (1827), which found their way to Italy in translation. Rossini's influence is noticeable in *L'esule di Roma* (1828), with its abundant choruses, and in *Il diluvio universale* (1830), an *azione tragico-sacra* whose melodic fertility amply repays its obvious debt to 'il nuovo *Mosè*'. Hints of Bellini are evident in *Alina, regina di Golconda* (1828), *Il paria* (1829) and *Elisabetta al castello di Kenilworth* (1829). The next operas are marked by a tendency for *canto fiorito* to disappear from the male voices or to be relegated to the cadenzas; at the same time, the melodies shed the declamatory element inherited from Rossini to become more lyrical and periodic in Bellini's manner, or else more vivid and concise in an anticipation of Verdi's.

During this period certain works stand out as landmarks. With *Anna Bolena* (1830) Donizetti came into his own as a tragic composer. Here, for the first time, the traditional procedures were put to recognizably personal use, in the service of a drama both powerful and swift. *L'elisir d'amore* (1832) saw the perfection of sentimental comedy in a pastoral setting and remains as much a classic of its genre as does Rossini's *Barbiere* of late Classical *opera buffa*. In *Lucrezia Borgia* (1833) Donizetti explored a vein of sensational melodrama in which convention was more radically modified than ever before: the concertato and stretta that were expected to end at least one act were reduced to a few pages at the end of the prologue, and not one of the duets is in the standard Rossinian three-part form that had generally served Donizetti until then. The first movement of that between Lucrezia and Alfonso ('Vi chiedo, o signore') takes the form of a dialogue; the duettino 'Qui che fai' in the same act is conducted as a series of 'parlanti' over a sinuous orchestral theme. Both served Verdi as models, in *Nabucco* and *Rigoletto* respectively.

The progress away from Rossini was gradual and not uniformly maintained. *Torquato Tasso* (1833) was more innovatory than *Rosmonda d'Inghilterra* (1834). Even *Lucia di Lammermoor*, generally considered the archetype of Italian Romantic opera, remains a curious blend of old and new, as may be seen by comparing the two duets 'Della tomba che rinserra' and 'Il pallor funesto orrendo'; the first is conceived lyrically throughout, the second is cast in a typically Rossinian mould of complex symmetries in which the architectural element takes precedence over the dramatic. The deeply pathetic sextet with its groundswell rising to climax (a legacy from Bellini that was seized on by the Italian Romantics) is framed by two movements built on the same orchestral theme – another device associated with Rossini, which artificially heightens the contrast between stasis and action. Similarly, though vocal coloratura is used effectively to depict the fragility of the heroine, some of the Mad Scene remains on a purely decorative level, even when shorn of the disfiguring cadenza for flute and voice added for or by Teresa Brambilla and still performed. The brilliant cabaletta 'Spargi d'amaro pianto' shows a curious indifference to the mood of Cammarano's text. Unlike Bellini's Elvira in similar circumstances, Lucia lacks the excuse of morbid euphoria for her roulades.

By 1837 drama has gained the upper hand in determining the structure of most duets. In *Roberto Devereux* (1837) the middle movement of that between

Nottingham and Sarah ('Nol sai che un nume vindice') is a dialogue over the funeral march that conducts Essex to the Tower of London, while the cabaletta allocates contrasted themes to the two soloists. Vocal virtuosity becomes increasingly functional. Unlike Bellini, Donizetti never wholly abandoned the declamatory flourish characteristic of the 1820s – hence, in ex.3, the

['O thou who dost awaken the lightning, and unleash the thundercloud, receive with pity my tears of sorrow.']

late but characteristic instance of an 'open' melody (to use Lippmann's useful term for a melody that begins with ornamental, declamatory gestures in free time and gradually takes on a regular periodic motion as it proceeds) in the heroine's cavatina from *Pia de' Tolomei* (1837), 'O tu che desti il fulmine'.

During the years from 1839 onwards Donizetti's style was further enriched as a result of his commissions for Paris and Vienna and the need to cater to audiences more sophisticated than those of Naples or Milan. All the foreign works apart from *Dom Sébastien* have full-length overtures, mostly worked out with considerable skill, though only four (those of *La fille du régiment*, *Maria di Rohan*, *Don Pasquale* and the one later appended to *Roberto Devereux*) are thematically associated with the operas to which they belong. In general, the orchestration is fuller, the harmony subtler and more varied. Donizetti took full advantage of the greater resources offered by the Paris Opéra (the overture to *Les martyrs* begins with a Maestoso for four bassoons). Yet apart from such obvious gallicisms as the trio 'Tous les trois réunis' in *La fille du régiment* (1840) – a counterpart to the stretta 'Venez amis, retirons-nous' from Rossini's *Le comte Ory* (1828) – and the portentous denunciation of Balthazar in *La favorite* (1840), which echoes that of Cardinal Brogni in Halévy's *La Juive*, his music did not change its physiognomy in response to a French text, as Verdi's so often did. Indeed, it is a French opera, *La favorite*, that supplies one of the most evocatively Italian arias in the tenor repertory – 'Spirto gentil', originally intended for the unfinished *Le duc d'Albe* (begun in 1839). Few would maintain that it gains anything by being sung in the original French. Only *Dom Sébastien*, with its preponderance of military rhythms and accompanimental 'tics', suggests a conscious attempt to imitate the grand manner of Meyerbeer.

The wider horizons offered by Parisian grand opera also benefited the last Italian operas, three of which were written for non-Italian audiences. *Linda di Chamounix* is Donizetti's ripest and most varied essay in the *semiseria* genre, including a hilarious scene for *buffo* bass and chorus, a melancholy ballad sung by a boy minstrel, a solemn prayer for bass and chorus that serves as an act-finale, a mad scene for the heroine and a 'theme song' (here a love duet), the singing of which by the hero recalls the distraught heroine to her right mind. In this work the current Italian idiom is sometimes invaded by harmonies of an almost Schumannesque sensibility (ex.4).

['(When I am near you) I forget everything at a smile from you, everything in you bestows love upon me']

Don Pasquale (1843), Donizetti's comic masterpiece, recovered for Italy the classical heritage of Mozart; it features a unique style of conversational recitative of freely floating lines with only an occasional string chord to underpin the modulations (until 20 years later composers were still using a continuo instrument for recitative in *opera buffa*). *Maria Padilla* (1841), *Caterina Cornaro* (mostly composed in 1842) and *Maria di Rohan* (1843) all hint at the way Donizetti's art would have evolved if his career had not been cut short. In the heroine's scena and cavatina in Act 1 of *Maria Padilla* the traditional Rossinian framework appears dissolved into an interplay of declamatory and lyrical elements, of vocal and orchestral melody sustaining a dramatic flow less urgent than Verdi's, yet no less continuous. *Maria di Rohan*, Donizetti's most concise tragedy, brought recitative into the heart of a formal number, thus achieving a variety of pace unusual for the time. All three works are free from the consciously grand manner that Mercadante had introduced with his *Il giuramento* (1837) and *Elena da Feltre* (1838). The most elaborate of Donizetti's concertatos is unfailingly limpid.

(ii) Melody, form, harmony. Donizetti's melodic style was of his time and place, with little to distinguish it from that of his contemporaries, who were all working in the same enclosed tradition and who, like their 18th-century forebears, availed themselves of a common stock of procedures. Donizetti had no such obvious traits as Bellini's 'heavenly length', his personal manner of articulating a melody or his continual use of simple discords on accented beats. Scholars such as Lippmann

and Ashbrook, however, have drawn attention to his use of graceful, rather sensuous chromatic passing notes in the course of plain diatonic melodies, a penchant for cadences and half-cadences that descend from the fifth to the third degree of the scale, a robust, popular quality in choral and stage-band music (a trait shared with Luigi Ricci and Verdi), and a fondness for lyrical melodies in triple or 6/8 time, often resulting in a characteristic mazurka-like setting of the ubiquitous octosyllabic verse (e.g. 'Da un tuo detto sol dipende', *Alina, regina di Golconda*; 'Per guarir di tal pazzia', *L'elisir d'amore*; and 'Sin la tomba è a me negata', *Belisario*). Notable above all was Donizetti's ability to generate long, satisfying periods from plain, often predictable extensions of a single rhythmic idea (e.g. 'Rayons dorés', *La favorite*; 'O luce di quest'anima', *Linda di Chamounix*; the prayer with chorus 'Deh, tu di un umile', *Maria Stuarda*; and Gennaro's solo 'Di pescator ignobile', *Lucrezia Borgia*, ex.5).

['I believed myself the son of a lowly fisherman, and lived my earliest years with him in Naples, when an unknown warrior came to rid me of my illusion.']

Another characteristic melody is that which, either through a natural abruptness or because it reaches its climax earlier than expected, exhausts its momentum in varied repetitions, shortenings or expansions of the cadential phrase (see 'Mentre il cor abbandonava', *Il diluvio universale*; and 'Tu che siedi in terzo cielo', *Fausta*). This design is especially effective in cabalettas, where the repetitions not only afford a basis for virtuosity but also prepare for the desired full stop and applause (see 'Spargi d'amaro pianto', *Lucia*; and 'Mon arrêt descend du ciel', *La favorite*). In general, however, Donizetti's achievement lay less in any specific contribution to the post-Rossinian tradition than in a wide-ranging invention within it. His cabalettas present every possible variety from the brilliant to the expressive and sentimental. His cantabiles exploit the standard binary form in many unpredictable guises. His use of quasi-recitative to diversify narrative arias is especially skilful (see 'Nella fatal di Rimini', *Lucrezia Borgia*; and 'Regnava nel silenzio', *Lucia*). Particularly affecting are those sudden modulations towards the end of a period, increasingly common in the later operas. The most magical instance occurs in the duet 'Signorina, in tanta fretta' in *Don Pasquale* (ex.6).

Donizetti often combined two forms within the same

['but it was necessary to obtain the effect; now we must ensure the success of our plan']

number. Leicester's cavatina 'Ah rimiro il bel sembiante' (*Maria Stuarda*) is half duet, half aria with *pertichini*. Sometimes he added a strophic dimension to his cantabiles, as in 'Ah non avea più lagrime' (*Maria de Rudenz*), or the famous minor–major *romanza* 'Una furtiva lagrima' (*L'elisir d'amore*), the first verse of which ends in the relative, the second in the tonic major. There is scarcely an opera from 1830 onwards that does not contain an unobtrusive novelty of form and texture, whether it be Guido's mournful cavatina 'Questo sacro augusto stemma' (*Gemma di Vergy*), sung over a pattering recital by Rolando and the chorus of the story of Joan of Arc; the clinching of a cabaletta with a phrase taken from the cantabile, as in the duet 'Fama! Sì, l'avrete' (*Anna Bolena*); or the sobbing transition from central ritornello to the second statement of the cabaletta 'Ugo è spento!' (*Parisina*). As might be expected, the French works make use of the ternary form with modulating middle section (see Zayda's two *romances* in *Dom Sébastien*); all the works of this period show a more frequent use of thematic reminiscence, which however nowhere approaches the quasi-symphonic concept of leitmotif.

In his view of opera Donizetti postulated the supremacy of the human voice and the vocally conceived period as its principle of organization; his harmony and scoring are conditioned accordingly. His tonal range is in general wider than Bellini's, his harmonies blander and yet more sophisticated (he was more sparing in the use of poignant discord). Like most of his Italian contemporaries he aimed at dramatic expression by means of vocal contour rather than harmonic nuance; hence the somewhat generalized emotion of the many cabalettas based on simple major-key harmonies in a tragic context. Nor did he fail to observe the unwritten law that any piece begun in the minor key must conclude unequivocally in the major, whether relative or tonic – a scheme that weakens many a rondò finale, even the remarkable stretta 'Come tigri di stragi anelanti' in Act 1 of *L'assedio di Calais*. Local colour is rare (the yodelling themes in *Betly* are an exception).

Autograph score of part of the Mad Scene from Act 3 of Donizetti's 'Lucia di Lammermoor' (composed 1835): a rudimentary outline for the cadenza can be seen on the extreme right; the cancelled line, originally intended for 'armonica' (glass harmonica), was transferred to the flute

There is nothing in *Il paria* to indicate that the drama is set in India. Only in the 'Danse arabe' in *Dom Sébastien* did Donizetti avail himself of the harmonic resources offered by the exotic, and, partly for this reason, his ballet music is in general trite and undistinguished.

(iii) Orchestration and vocal writing. In his scoring Donizetti followed Rossini's 'prismatic' treatment of the orchestra, tracing variegated patterns of wind colour over a neutral string background, pointing modulations with sustaining instruments, doubling melodic lines wholly or in part with solo flute, clarinet or trumpet, as the case may be. Concertante and obbligato instruments, always treated in bel canto style, frequently embellish a scena or form the basis of a prelude, with or without an accompanying harp. Instances include a glass harmonica (*Elisabetta al castello di Kenilworth* and also *Lucia*, where it was later replaced by a flute), clarinet (*Torquato Tasso*), harp (*Lucia*), bass clarinet (*Maria de Rudenz*) and trumpet (*Don Pasquale*). Tuttis are usually noisy and opaque, while lyrical accompaniments keep to a plain rhythmic pattern in a more popular variant of Rossini's manner and sometimes justify Wagner's famous gibe about the big guitar. But put any score of Donizetti's beside one of Mercadante's or Pacini's and what leaps to the eye is its spareness. It seems impossible that so few notes can make the effect that they invariably do. If in his early operas Donizetti's use of wind colour may appear ornamental and hedonistic, in his later works it can be powerfully evocative. Horns, for example, play an important role in establishing the atmosphere of *Lucia di Lammermoor*.

In his treatment of the voice Donizetti followed the lead first of Rossini, then of the Bellini of *La sonnambula* and after. He was particularly responsive to the individual qualities of the singers for whom he wrote: he never attempted, as Bellini once did, to impose a plain style on a florid singer. The agility of Tacchinardi-Persiani left its mark on *Rosmonda d'Inghilterra*, *Lucia* and *Pia*; the more dramatic talents of Pasta and Ronzi De Begnis were given full scope in the more directly expressive final scenes of *Anna Bolena*, *Maria Stuarda* and *Roberto Devereux*. Confronted by a mezzo-soprano with no flexibility whatever, such as Rosine Stoltz, creator of Léonor in *La favorite*, Donizetti eschewed all decoration to achieve a noble simplicity that pervades not only the heroine's part but the whole score, apart from the dispensable ballet. Except in *L'assedio di Calais* he followed the trend that was banishing the contralto or mezzo-soprano *en travesti* from hero to a subordinate position in the plot, such as that of the hero's or heroine's friend.

In the male parts *canto fiorito* gave way to a simpler eloquence in which syncopation usually replaces passage-work as a way of giving emphasis. Like Bellini, Donizetti treated his baritones and basses alike, but he was more successful in giving a high charge of irony to the singer's lyrical line (see 'Pour tant d'amour', *La favorite*), thereby foreshadowing Verdi. The growing incidence of important baritone roles in the later operas (in both *Maria de Rudenz* and *Maria Padilla* the baritone takes precedence over the tenor) was due to Giorgio Ronconi, who did more than any singer of his day to stimulate that forceful conception of the voice type associated with the young Verdi. For Donizetti, however, as for most of his contemporaries, the baritone remained essentially a *basso cantante* with a tessitura roughly a tone lower than that of his Verdian counterpart. On the other hand, the Donizettian tenor has a character of his own. A poet of the voice even when a villain (as in *Pia de' Tolomei*), he first takes shape in his less heroic aspects in *L'elisir d'amore*, to reach his fullest incarnation as Edgardo in *Lucia*, a role that provided two famous singers of the day with their respective sobriquets: 'the tenor of the curse' (Fraschini) and 'the tenor of the beautiful death' (Moriani). Capable of great force ('Maledetto sia l'istante', *Lucia*) and even virtuosity ('Trema Bisanzio!', *Belisario*), he excels in the portrayal of innocence betrayed. In his mature operas Donizetti's touch never failed with the tenor, yet his means were of the simplest (ex.7). Even that degree

['Adina, believe me, I beseech you, you cannot marry (him)']

of discord is exceptional; no composer was more adept at distilling sadness from the combination of tenor voice and plain major-key harmonies, as in 'Tu che a Dio spiegasti l'ali' (*Lucia*).

Donizetti's sculpting of a tenor melody can be traced in the sketches for Ernesto's aria 'Cercherò lontana terra' in *Don Pasquale* (published by Rattalino, 1970). These refute the notion that the composer always wrote uncritically and at breakneck speed. Indeed, they resemble Beethoven's sketches in their painstaking adjustment of detail. But a comparison with the few known sketches by Verdi is significant. While Verdi's alterations were all directed towards a more exact representation of a particular character in a particular situation, Donizetti was here concerned purely with perfection of melodic craftsmanship in relation to the portrayal of a tenor in distress.

6. Donizetti as a man of the theatre. Few of Donizetti's admirers would attempt to deny a certain generic quality in his art that recalls the outlook of a previous age. In general, the Romantic ethos insists on the unique unrepeatable masterpiece – a description that could be more easily applied to *Norma* than to any of Donizetti's serious operas. It is sometimes said that he needed the stimulus of a romantic story in order to give of his best. In fact he was at home in almost every field from theatrical satire (*Le convenienze teatrali*) to neo-classical tragedy without love interest (*Belisario*). For the comedies *Il campanello* and *Betly* he compiled his own librettos, while in *Don Pasquale* he rewrote so much of the text that the librettist refused to acknowledge paternity of it. But, as with Verdi, an unusual plot elicited unusual solutions. *Lucrezia Borgia* is matched in this respect by *L'assedio di Calais*, a patriotic grand opera on the French model, with which Donizetti hoped to 'introduce a new genre to Italy'. Of its many ensembles, not one is without some surprising feature, structural and harmonic, while the fact that the juvenile lead is a mezzo-soprano allows a play of 6ths and 3rds in his duet comparable to Bellini's 'Mira o Norma'. Yet the opera failed to circulate, doubtless because of its eccentric distribution (mezzo-soprano, baritone and bass principals, the last appearing only in Act 3; two *soprani comprimari*, including the heroine, and a host of secondary roles). Donizetti never continued along this path.

Too often the idealist in Donizetti was forced to yield to the practical man of the theatre. He might welcome the freedom from Italian operatic routine afforded him by the Parisian stage; he might express a preference for the tenor ending to *Lucrezia Borgia* as against the rondò finale that he had been obliged to write for Méric-Lalande in 1833. But like Rossini and generations of Italian composers before him, Donizetti believed that operas should be re-created strictly in terms of the resources available for each revival. He was always ready to adapt his scores to the demands of different singers, to expand secondary roles into principal ones, even altering the original voice type, and to provide alternative numbers for the principals themselves – a practice made all the easier by the fact that Italian opera during the 1830s was constructed from short, finite scenes. Sometimes the alternative pieces were derived from previous scores. Thus the cabaletta from a contralto and bass duet in *Imelda de' Lambertazzi*, 'Restati pur m'udrai', was transposed for soprano and tenor, fitted out with two preceding movements and introduced into *Anna Bolena* as an alternative to the much shorter duet for Anne and Percy that is printed in the definitive score ('S'ei t'aborre'). The entire duet was modified for *Marino Faliero* five years later. When Donizetti had no time to attend to the matter himself, he would advise the singer to use a 'pezzo di baule' (suitcase aria). Some of the transferences are difficult to account for except on grounds of convenience. Thus the Larghetto concertato in Act 2 of *Maria de Rudenz* ('Chiuse il dì per te la ciglia') was reproduced note for note as the Act 2 concertato of *Poliuto*, whence it passed into Act 3 of the French version, *Les martyrs*. A quartet finale from *Il paria* was carried over into *Torquato Tasso*. The duet cabaletta 'A consolarmi affrettisi', the 'theme song' of *Linda di Chamounix*, first appeared in *Sancia di Castiglia*, while the overture to the same opera (the slow introduction apart) was adapted from a string quartet written in 1836. The overture to *Les martyrs* derives mostly from one contributed by Donizetti to a composite cantata for the death of Malibran. Perhaps the most bizarre self-borrowing occurs in *La fille du régiment*, where what was once Noah's solemn invocation 'Su quell'arca nell'ira de' venti' (*Il diluvio universale*) was transformed into the jaunty 'Chacun le sait, chacun le dit'. *La favorite* was almost entirely compiled from music written for different contexts yet welded together with such skill that the listener is unaware of any incongruity. Indeed, the fact that so many of the themes are based on the ascending or descending scale gives the opera a distinctive character rare in Italian opera of the time. 'Spare-part' construction, limited range of harmony, total subordination of orchestra to voice and the artificiality that attaches to the use of set forms to clothe Romantic subjects all contributed to the low esteem in which Donizetti was held in the Wagnerian age and after.

As a composer of comedy, Donizetti's position has never been seriously challenged; both *Don Pasquale* and *L'elisir d'amore* have remained in the general repertory since they were composed. In the tragic genre he was both more and less than a great composer: he summed up within himself a whole epoch, yet not one of his tragic operas makes the impact one expects of an unqualified masterpiece – all are subject to lapses into routine craftsmanship. So central was he to the vitality of the tradition he served, however, that when he retired it began to decay. His lesser contemporaries, Mercadante and Pacini, lacking his certainty of aim, his sense of a just relation of means to ends, soon declined into mannerism and selfconsciousness. Only Verdi succeeded in putting the Donizettian heritage to a new and valid use. Donizetti's own works survive through the grace and spontaneity of their melodies, their formal poise, their effortless dramatic pace and above all the romantic vitality that underlies their veneer of artifice.

7. REPUTATION. Donizetti's reputation has undergone great fluctuations. When illness terminated his activity, he had achieved wide acceptance wherever Italian opera was performed; but from 1828 onwards, when he entered into direct competition with Bellini at the opening of the Teatro Carlo Felice, Genoa, he was often unfairly criticized by the friends and advocates of Bellini. Bellini's letters contain many uncharitable references to him. After Bellini's death at a cruelly early age, his friends resented Donizetti's survival and his popularity. The nature of Donizetti's illness was common knowledge, creating an aura of scandal in an age of prudery, and compromised his place in the regard of a public which largely adhered to an idealized image of composers.

With the development of the repertory system in Italy, replenished by the newer works of Verdi, the vogue for French works after 1860 and, later, the introduction of Wagnerian music dramas, the place of Donizetti in the scheme of things drastically diminished, except for a few staple items: *Lucia*, *La favorite* (or rather *La favorita*) and the comedies *L'elisir d'amore* and *Don Pasquale* proving the hardiest. Outside Italy the case was much the same. Donizetti was demoted from a dominant figure to merely one-third of a composite image 'Rossini-Bellini-Donizetti'; and he was generally accounted the least of these.

It was not until attention was focussed on him again – first in 1948 by the festivities on the centenary of his death, next by a series of revivals of by-then-forgotten scores begun in his native Bergamo in the 1950s, and capped by the staging of *Anna Bolena* at La Scala with Maria Callas in 1957 – that serious revaluation began. It was hastened by the advocacy of such singers as Leyla Gencer, Joan Sutherland and Beverly Sills, and of conductors, notably Gianandrea Gavazzeni, and the growth at the same time of Donizetti scholarship. Propitious to this Donizetti renaissance was the paucity of new, viable works entering the operatic mainstream. The replenishment of the repertory by the examination of the past has proved beneficial to Donizetti's reputation, and now that few of his 65 completed operas have remained unrevived it is clear that he forms a vital link between the opening of the 19th century and the development of Italian opera subsequent to his death in 1848. The amount of concrete evidence available to us at the end of the 20th century makes possible a clearer appreciation of his centrality to that tradition than at any time since his death.

See also *AJO NELL'IMBARAZZO,L'*; *ALINA, REGINA DI GOLCONDA*; *ANNA BOLENA*; *ASSEDIO DI CALAIS, L'*; *BELISARIO*; *BETLY*; *CAMPANELLO DI NOTTE, IL*; *CATERINA CORNARO*; *CONVENIENZE TEATRALI, LE*; *DOM SÉBASTIEN, ROI DE PORTUGAL*; *DON PASQUALE*; *DUCA D'ALBA, IL*; *ELISIR D'AMORE, L'*; *EMILIA DI LIVERPOOL*; *ESULE DI ROMA, OSSIA IL PROSCRITTO, L'*; *FAUSTA*; *FAVORITE, LA*; *FILLE DU RÉGIMENT, LA*; *FURIOSO NELL'ISOLA DI SAN DOMINGO, IL*; *GABRIELLA DI VERGY*; *GEMMA DI VERGY*; *LINDA DI CHAMOUNIX*; *LUCIA DI LAMMERMOOR*; *LUCREZIA BORGIA*; *MARIA DE RUDENZ*; *MARIA DI ROHAN*; *MARIA PADILLA*; *MARIA STUARDA*; *MARINO FALIERO*; *OLIVO E PASQUALE*; *PARISINA* (i); *PIA DE' TOLOMEI*; *POLIUTO*; *RITA*; *ROBERTO DEVEREUX*; *SANCIA DI CASTIGLIA*; *TORQUATO TASSO*; *UGO CONTE DI PARIGI*; *ZORAIDE DI GRENATA*.

mel – *melodramma*

NC – *Naples, Teatro di S Carlo*
NFO – *Naples, Teatro del Fondo*
NN – *Naples, Teatro Nuovo*
RV – *Rome, Teatro Valle*

MSS are autographs unless otherwise stated

title	*genre, acts*	*libretto*	*first performance*	*remarks; sources*
Il Pigmalione	scena drammatica, 1		Bergamo, Donizetti, 13 Oct 1960	comp. Bologna, 1816; *F-Pc*
L'ira d'Achille	1		unperf.	comp. Bologna, 1817; *Pc* (inc.)
Enrico di Borgogna	mel, 2	B. Merelli	Venice, S Luca, 14 Nov 1818	copy *Pc*
Una follia	farsa, 1	Merelli	Venice, S Luca, 15 Dec 1818	? also perf. as Il ritratto parlante; ov., copy *I-Bc*
Le nozze in villa	opera buffa, 2	Merelli	Mantua, Vecchio, carn. 1820–21	comp. Bergamo, 1819; as I provinciali, ossia Le nozze in villa, Genoa, 1822; copy *F-Pc*
Il falegname di Livonia, o Pietro il grande, czar delle Russie	opera buffa, 2	G. Bevilacqua-Aldovrandini, after A. Duval	Venice, S Samuele, 26 Dec 1819	*I-Mr*
Zoraide di Grenata	mel eroico, 2	Merelli	Rome, Argentina, 28 Jan 1822	rev. (J. Ferretti), Rome, 1824; *Mr*
La zingara	dramma, 2	A. L. Tottola	NN, 12 May 1822	copy *Nc*; vs (Paris, 1856)
La lettera anonima	dramma per musica, 1	G. Genoino	NFO, 29 June 1822	*Mr*; vs (Paris, 1856)
Chiara e Serafina, o Il pirata	mel semiseria, 2	F. Romani, after R. C. G. de Pixérécourt: *La cisterne*	Milan, Scala, 26 Oct 1822	*Mr*
Alfredo il grande	dramma per musica, 2	Tottola	NC, 2 July 1823	*Nc*, copy *F-Pc*
Il fortunato inganno	dramma giocoso, 2	Tottola	NN, 3 Sept 1823	*I-Nc*

title	genre, acts	libretto	first performance	remarks; sources
L'ajo nell'imbarazzo	mel giocoso, 2	Ferretti, after G. Giraud	RV, 4 Feb 1824	rev. as Don Gregorio, Naples, 1826; as Il governo della casa, Dresden, 1828; *Nc* (partly autograph), excerpts (Milan, ?1827, 1837), vs (Paris, 1856; Milan, 1878)
Emilia di Liverpool	dramma semiseria, 2	after S. Scatizzi: *Emilia di Laverpaut*	NN, 28 July 1824	rev. (G. Checcherini), Naples, 1828; also perf. as L'eremitaggio di Liverpool; *Nc*, copy *F-Pc*, vs (Paris, 1856)
Alahor in Granata	dramma, 2	M. A.	Palermo, Carolino, 7 Jan 1826	copy *US-Bm*
Elvida	dramma, 1	G. F. Schmidt	NC, 6 July 1826, rev.(3) *c*1838	*I-Nc*
Gabriella di Vergy	tragedia lirica, 3	Tottola, after P. Du Belloy	NC, 29 Nov 1869	orig. comp. 2 acts, 1826, rev. (3) *c*1838; rev. by others for 1869 perf., *BGi*
2nd version			Belfast, Whitla Hall, 9 Nov 1978	comp. *c*1838; *GB-Lu* (partly autograph)
Olivo e Pasquale	mel, 2	Ferretti, after S. A. Sografi	RV, 7 Jan 1827	*I-Nc*; excerpts (Milan, 1830), vs (Paris, 1856)
Otto mesi in due ore, ossia Gli esiliati in Siberia	op romantica, 3	D. Gilardoni, after Pixérécourt: *La fille de l'exilé*	NN, 13 May 1827	rev. (A. Alcozer), Naples, 1833; *Nc*; rev. by U. Fontana as Elisabeth, ou La fille du proscrit (A. de Leuven and Brunswick [L. Lhérie]), unperf., MS London, Royal Opera House (partly autograph), vs (Paris, ?1854)
Il borgomastro di Saardam	mel giocoso, 2	Gilardoni, after Mélesville [A.-H.-J. Duveyrier], J. T. Merle and E. Cantiran de Boirie	NFO, 19 Aug 1827	*Mr*, excerpts (Milan, 1830, 1833), vs (Paris, 1856)
Le convenienze teatrali	? mel comico/ giocoso, 1	Donizetti, after Sografi	NN, 21 Nov 1827	2-act version, Vienna, 1840; *F-Pc* (partly autograph), 2 excerpts (Milan, 1830 or 1831), vs (Paris, 1856), vs, ed. E. Riccioli (Florence, 1971)
2nd version: Le convenienze ed inconvenienze teatrali	dramma giocoso, 2		Milan, Cannobiana, 20 April 1831	
L'esule di Roma, ossia Il proscritto	mel eroico, 2	Gilardoni, after L. Marchionni: *Il proscritto romano*	NC, 1 Jan 1828	also perf. as Settimio il proscritto; *I-Mr*, excerpts (Milan, 1828; Naples, 1832), with new aria, Bergamo, 1840, vs (Milan, ?1840)
Alina, regina di Golconda	mel, 2	Romani, after M.-J. Sedaine	Genoa, Carlo Felice, 12 May 1828	rev. version, Rome, 1829; *Nc*, vs (Milan, 1842)
Gianni di Calais	mel semiseria, 3	Gilardoni, after C. V. d'Arlincourt	NFO, 2 Aug 1828	*Nc*, excerpts (Milan, 1830 or 1831)
Il paria	mel, 2	Gilardoni, after C. Delavigne	NC, 12 Jan 1829	*Nc*, scena ed aria (Milan, 1837), vs (Paris, 1856)
Il giovedì grasso, o Il nuovo Pourceaugnac	1	Gilardoni	NFO, 26 Feb 1829	*Nc*, vs, without recits. (Paris, 1856)
Elisabetta al castello di Kenilworth	mel, 3	Tottola, after V. Hugo: *Amy Robsart*, and E. Scribe: *Leicester* [itself after W. Scott: *Kenilworth*]	NC, 6 July 1829	*Nc*, vs (Paris, 1856)
I pazzi per progetto	1	Gilardoni	NC, 6 Feb 1830	*Nc*, vs (Paris, 1856)
Il diluvio universale	azione tragico-sacra, 3	Gilardoni, after Byron: *Heaven and Earth* and F. Ringhieri: *Il diluvio*	NC, 6 March 1830	*Nc*, excerpts (Milan, 1834), vs (Paris, 1856)
Imelda de' Lambertazzi	mel tragico, 2	Tottola	NC, 5 Sept 1830	*Nc*, excerpts (Milan, 1830)
Anna Bolena	tragedia lirica, 2	Romani, after I. Pindemonte and A. Pepoli	Milan, Carcano, 26 Dec 1830	*Mr*, vs (Milan, 1830 or 1831, 2/1876)
Gianni di Parigi	mel, 2	Romani, after Saint-Just	Milan, Scala, 10 Sept 1839	comp. 1831; *Nc*, vs (Milan, 1843)
Francesca di Foix	mel, 1	Gilardoni, after C.-S. Favart and Saint-Amans: *Ninette à la cour*	NC, 30 May 1831	*Nc*
La romanziera e l'uomo nero	1	Gilardoni	NFO, 18 June 1831	*Nc*, vs, without recits. (Paris, 1856)

title	genre, acts	libretto	first performance	remarks; sources
Fausta	mel, 2	Gilardoni and Donizetti	NC, 12 Jan 1832	ov. added, Milan, 1832; rev. version, Venice, 1834; *Nc*, vs (Milan, 1832 or 1833; Paris, ?1832)
Ugo conte di Parigi	tragedia lirica, 4	Romani, after H.-L.-F. Bis: *Blanche d'Aquitaine*	Milan, Scala, 13 March 1832	*Nc*, vs (Milan, 1832)
L'elisir d'amore	mel giocoso, 2	Romani, after Scribe: *Le philtre*	Milan, Cannobiana, 12 May 1832	*Nc* (Act 1), *BGi* (Act 2); vs (Milan, 1832, 2/1869), full score (Milan, 1916)
Sancia di Castiglia	tragedia lirica, 2	P. Salatino	NC, 4 Nov 1832	*Nc*, vs (Milan, 1833)
Il furioso nell'isola di San Domingo	mel, 2	Ferretti, after anon. play on M. de Cervantes: *Don Quixote*	RV, 2 Jan 1833	rev. version, Milan, 1833; *Mr*, excerpts (Milan, 1833), vs in 2 acts (Paris, *c*1845)
Parisina	mel, 3	Romani, after Byron	Florence, Pergola, 17 March 1833	*BGi* (*R*1981: ERO, xxv), vs (Milan, 1833, 2/1911)
Torquato Tasso	mel, 3	Ferretti	RV, 9 Sept 1833	*Mr*, vs (Milan, 1833; Naples and Rome, *c*1835; Paris, n.d.): also perf. as Sordello il trovatore
Lucrezia Borgia	mel, prol., 2	Romani, after Hugo	Milan, Scala, 26 Dec 1833	rev. version, Milan, 1840; *Mr*; vs (Milan, 1834, 2/1859 or 1860), full score (Naples and Milan, *c*1890)
Rosmonda d'Inghilterra	mel serio, 2	Romani	Florence, Pergola, 27 Feb 1834	*Nc*, excerpts (Milan, 1834, 1851 or 1852); rev. as Elenora di Gujenna, Naples, 1837, *Nc*, vs (Paris, ?1840)
Maria Stuarda	tragedia lirica, 2/3	G. Bardari, after F. von Schiller	Milan, Scala, 30 Dec 1835	comp. for Naples, 1834, banned by censor; *S-Smf*, excerpts (Milan, 1835), vs (Paris, 1866)
2nd version: Buondelmonte	tragedia lirica, 2	P. Salatino	NC, 18 Oct 1834	new lib. fitted to music for Naples perf., *I-Nc* (partly autograph), excerpts (Milan, 1834 or 1835)
Gemma di Vergy	tragedia lirica, 2	G. E. Bidera, after A. Dumas *père*: *Charles VII chez ses grands vassaux*	Milan, Scala, 26 Dec 1834	*Mr*, vs (Milan, 1835, 2/1870 or 1871)
Marino Faliero	tragedia lirica, 3	Bidera, after Delavigne	Paris, Italien, 12 March 1835	*Nc*, vs (Paris, n.d.; Milan, 1835 or 1836)
Lucia di Lammermoor	dramma tragico, 3	S. Cammarano, after Scott: *The Bride of Lammermoor*	NC, 26 Sept 1835	rev., Fr., Paris, 1839; autograph owned by Comune di Bergamo (*R* Milan, 1941), vs (Naples, ?1835; Milan, 1837, 2/?1857), full score (Milan, *c*1910)
Belisario	tragedia lirica, 3	Cammarano, after E. von Schenk, trans. Marchionni	Venice, Fenice, 4 Feb 1836	*Mr*, vs (Milan, 1836, 2/1870; Paris, ?1836)
Il campanello di notte	mel giocoso, 1	Donizetti, after Brunswick, M.-B. Troin and V. Lhérie: *La sonnette de nuit*	NN, 1 June 1836	*Nc*, vs (Naples and Rome, ?1836; Milan, 1839)
Betly, ossia La capanna svizzera	dramma giocoso, 1	Donizetti, after Scribe and Mélesville: *Le chalet*	NN, 21 Aug 1836	rev. (2 acts), Naples, 1837; *Nc*, vs (Naples, ?1836; Paris, ?1836; Milan, 1836 or 1837, 2/1877)
L'assedio di Calais	dramma lirico, 3	Cammarano, after Du Belloy	NC, 19 Nov 1836	*F-Pc*, ?*I-Nc*, vs (Milan, 1836)
Pia de' Tolomei	tragedia lirica, 2	Cammarano, after B. Sestini, and Dante: *Commedia*	Venice, Apollo, 18 Feb 1837	rev. version, Sinigaglia, 1837; *Nc*, excerpts (Milan, 1837; Paris, ?1837)
Roberto Devereux, ossia Il conte di Essex	tragedia lirica, 3	Cammarano, after F. Ancelot: *Elisabeth d'Angleterre*	NC, 28 Oct 1837	*Nc* (*R*1982: ERO, xxvi), vs (Naples, 1837; Milan, 1838/*R*1975, 2/1870 or 1871)
Maria de Rudenz	dramma tragico, 3	Cammarano, after A. Bourgeois, J.-G.-A. Cuvelier and J. de Mallian: *La nonne sanglante*	Venice, Fenice, 30 Jan 1838	*Vt*, vs (Milan, ?*c*1845; Paris, *c*1845; Leipzig, *c*1845)
Poliuto	tragedia lirica, 3	Cammarano, after P. Corneille	NC, 30 Nov 1848	comp. for S Carlo, 1838, banned by censor; *Nc*, vs (Milan, *c*1850)
2nd version: Les martyrs	grand opéra, 4	Scribe	Paris, Opéra, 10 April 1840	*Mr*; (Paris, 1840/*R*1982: ERO, xxvii), vs (Paris, ?1840/*R*1975; Milan, 1843)
La fille du régiment	opéra comique, 2	J. H. Vernoy de Saint-Georges and J.-F.-A. Bayard	Paris, OC (Bourse), 11 Feb 1840	*Nc*; (Paris, ?1840); It., Milan, 1840, vs (Milan, 1840 or 1841, 2/1879)

title	genre, acts	libretto	first performance	remarks; sources
L'ange de Nisida	3	A. Royer and G. Vaëz	unperf.	comp. 1839; also known as Silvia; rev. as La favorite; excerpts *F-Pc*
La favorite	opéra, 4	Royer and Vaëz (with addns by Scribe), after Baculard d'Arnaud: *Le comte de Comminges*	Paris, Opéra, 2 Dec 1840	Malfieri collection; (Paris, 1841/*R*1982: ERO, xxviii), rev. and expanded from L'ange de Nisida
Adelia, o La figlia dell'arciere	mel serio, 3	Romani and G. Marini, after anon. Fr. play	Rome, Apollo, 11 Feb 1841	*I-Nc*, vs (Paris, ?1843; Milan, n.d.)
Rita, ou Le mari battu	opéra comique, 1	Vaëz	Paris, OC (Favart), 7 May 1860	comp. 1841; *Nc*, vs (Paris, 1860); also perf. as Deux hommes et une femme
Maria Padilla	mel, 3	G. Rossi and Donizetti, after Ancelot	Milan, Scala, 26 Dec 1841	*Mr*, vs (Paris, ?1841; Milan, 1841 or 1842)
Linda di Chamounix	mel semiserio, 3	Rossi, after A.-P. d'Ennery and G. Lemoine: *La grâce de Dieu*	Vienna, Kärntnertor, 19 May 1842	rev. version, Paris, 1842; *Mr*, vs (Vienna and Milan, 1842; Paris, 1842)
Caterina Cornaro	tragedia lirica, prol., 2	G. Sacchèro, after Saint-Georges: *La reine de Chypre*	NC, 18 Jan 1844	comp. 1842–3; *Nc*, vs (Milan, 1845/*R*1974; Paris, 1845)
Don Pasquale	dramma buffo, 3	G. Ruffini and Donizetti, after A. Anelli: *Ser Marcantonio*	Paris, Italien, 3 Jan 1843	*Mr*; vs (Milan, 1843, 2/1871), full score (Milan, 1961)
Maria di Rohan	mel tragico, 3	Cammarano, after Lockroy [J. P. Simon] and Badon: *Un duel sous le Cardinal de Richelieu*	Vienna, Kärntnertor, 5 June 1843	rev. version, Paris, 1843; *Mr*, vs (Milan, 1843, 2/1870 or 1871; Ger., Vienna, ? 1843; Paris, n.d.)
Dom Sébastien, roi de Portugal	opéra, 5	Scribe, after P.-H. Foucher	Paris, Opéra, 13 Nov 1843	*F-Pc* (with unpubd addns), vs (Paris, ?1843; Milan, 1844, 2/1886), full score (Paris, 1843–4/*R*1980: ERO, xxix)

Inc. or unfinished: Olimpiade (P. Metastasio), duet, comp. Bologna, 1817, *I-BGi* (not autograph); Introduzione and aria [aria adapted from Le nozze in villa] in I piccioli virtuosi ambulanti (ob, 1), Bergamo, sum. 1819, pasticcio perf. by students of Mayr's school; La bella prigioniera (farsa, 1), comp. Naples, 1826, 2 nos., pf acc., *BGi*; Adelaide (comica), begun Naples, 1834, inc. autograph *F-Pc* [partly used in L'ange de Nisida]: Le duc d'Albe (op, 4, Scribe and C. Duveyrier), begun Paris, 1839, *I-Mr* (inc.), completed by M. Salvi and others as Il duca d'Alba, Rome, 1882, vs (Milan, 1881 and 1882), completed by T. Schippers, Spoleto, 1959; Ne m'oubliez pas (3, Saint-Georges), comp. Paris, 1843, 7 nos. *F-Pc*; La fidanzata, aria *Pc*

CATALOGUES

Ricordi di Gaetano Donizetti esposti nella mostra centenaria tenutasi in Bergamo nell'agosto–settembre 1897, raccolti da Giuseppe e Gaetano Donizetti, collezione di proprietà dei fratelli Giuseppe e Gaetano Donizetti (Bergamo, 1897, enlarged 2/1897)

C. Malherbe: *Centenaire de Gaetano Donizetti: catalogue bibliographique de la section française à l'exposition de Bergamo* (Paris, 1897)

G. Zavadini: *Catalogo generale: Museo donizettiano di Bergamo* (Bergamo, 1936)

V. Sacchiero and others: *Il Museo donizettiano di Bergamo* (Bergamo, 1970)

V. Sacchiero: 'Contributo ad un catalogo donizettiano', *CSD 1975* [see SPECIALIST PUBLICATIONS below], 835–941

L. Inzaghi: 'Catalogo generale della opera', *Gaetano Donizetti*, ed. G. Tintori (Milan, 1983), 133–278

SPECIALIST PUBLICATIONS

Studi donizettiani, no.1 (1962); no.2 (1972); no.3 (1978); no.4 (1988) [*SD*]

Donizetti Society Journal (1974–) [*DSJ*]

1° convegno internazionale di studi donizettiani: Bergamo 1975 [*CSD 1975*]

LETTERS

A. De Eisner-Eisenhof, ed.: *Lettere inedite di Gaetano Donizetti* (Rome, 1897)

F. Schlitzer: 'Curiosità epistolari inedite nella vita teatrale di Gaetano Donizetti', *RMI*, l (1948), 273–83

G. Zavadini: *Donizetti: vita, musiche, epistolario* (Bergamo, 1948)

G. Barblan and F. Walker: 'Contributo all'epistolario di Gaetano Donizetti', *SD*, no.1 (1962), 1–150

F. Speranza: 'Lettere inedite di Donizetti', 'Lettere inedite dirette a Donizetti', *SD*, no.2 (1972), 97–110, 111–29 [index, 131–2]

'An Unpublished Donizetti Letter', *DSJ*, ii (1975), 271–4 [letter to G. Peluti]

J. Commons: 'Una corrispondenza tra Alessandro Lanari e Donizetti (45 lettere inedite)', *SD*, no.3 (1978), 9–74

F. Lippmann: 'Autographe Briefe Rossinis und Donizettis in der Bibliothek Massimo, Rom', *AnMc*, no.19 (1980), 330–35

SD, no.4 (1988), 7–126 ['Lettere inedite o sparse di Donizetti con data', 7–78; 'Lettere inedite di Donizetti senza data o con data incompleta', 79–82; 'Lettere indirizzate a Donizetti', 83–90; 'Lettere di altri nelle quali si parla di Donizetti', 91–108; 'Lettere e articoli concernenti la malattia di Donizetti (1846–1847)', 109–20; index, 121–6]

LIFE AND WORKS

La MusicaE (G. Barblan)

F. Regli: *Gaetano Donizetti e le sue opere* (Turin, 1850)

G. Bonetti: *Gaetano Donizetti* (Naples, 1926)

G. Donati-Petteni: *Donizetti* (Milan, 1930, 3/1947)

G. Gavazzeni: *Gaetano Donizetti: vita e musiche* (Milan, 1937)

G. Monaldi: *Gaetano Donizetti* (Turin, 1938)

G. Zavadini: *Donizetti: vita, musiche, epistolario* (Bergamo, 1948)

L. Bossi: *Donizetti* (Brescia, 1956)

A. Geddo: *Donizetti: l'uomo, le musiche* (Bergamo, 1956)

H. Weinstock: *Donizetti and the World of Opera in Italy, Paris and Vienna in the First Half of the Nineteenth Century* (New York, 1963)

W. Ashbrook: *Donizetti* (London, 1965)

——: *Donizetti and his Operas* (Cambridge, 1982) [incl. full bibliography]

P. Mioli: *Donizetti: 70 melodrammi* (Turin, 1988)

BIOGRAPHICAL STUDIES AND MEMOIRS

L. Stierlin: *Biographie von Gaetano Donizetti* (Zürich, 1852)

T. Ghezzi: 'Ricordi su Donizetti', *Omnibus* [Naples] (7 March 1860)

L. Escudier: *Mes souvenirs* (Paris, 1863)

F. Cicconetti: *Vita di Gaetano Donizetti* (Rome, 1864)

A. Bellotti: *Donizetti e i suoi contemporanei* (Bergamo, 1866)

Cenni biografici di Gaetano Donizetti raccolti da un vecchio dilettante di buona memoria (Milan, 1874)

F. Alborghetti and M. Galli: *Gaetano Donizetti e G. Simone Mayr: notizie e documenti* (Bergamo, 1875)

P. Cominazzi: 'Sorsa attraverso le opere musicali di Gaetano Donizetti: reminiscenze', *La fama* (1875), no.35, pp.137–8; no.36, pp.141–2; no.37, pp.145–7; no.38, pp.149–51; no.39, pp.153–4; no.40, pp.157–9

G. Duprez: *Souvenirs d'un chanteur* (Paris, 1880)

E. Branca: *Felice Romani ed i più riputati maestri di musica del suo tempo* (Turin, Florence and Rome, 1882)

G. Cottrau: *Lettres d'un mélomane* (Naples, 1885)

A. Gabrielli: 'Le case di Donizetti a Napoli', *Fanfulla della domenica*, liii (1893)

E. Verzino: *Contributo ad una biografia di Gaetano Donizetti* (Bergamo, 1896)

C. Ricci: 'Donizetti a Bologna: appunti e documenti', *Gaetano Donizetti: numero unico nel primo centenario della sua nascita 1797–1897*, ed. P. Bettòli (Bergamo, 1897), 10–13

A. Cametti: *Un poeta melodrammatico romano: appunti e notizie in gran parte inedite sopra Jacopo Ferretti e i musicisti del suo tempo* (Milan, 1898)

G. Antonini: 'Un episodio emotivo di Gaetano Donizetti', *RMI*, vii (1900), 518–35

A. Gabrielli: *Gaetano Donizetti* (Rome and Turin, 1904)

A. Cametti: *Donizetti a Roma* (Turin, 1907)

A. Pougin: 'Donizetti', *Musiciens du XIXe siècle* (Paris, 1911)

U. Riva: 'Un bergomasco (Giuseppe Donizetti pascià), riformatore della musica in Turchia', *Rivista di Bergamo*, i (1922), 349–53

G. Caversazzi: *Gaetano Donizetti: la casa dove nacque, la famiglia, l'inizio della malattia* (Bergamo, 1924)

A. Codignola: *I fratelli Ruffini: lettere di G. e A. Ruffini alle madre dall'esilio francese e svizzero* (Genoa, 1925–31)

G. Caversazzi: *Gaetano Donizetti: discorso a cura della Congregazione di carità* (Bergamo, 1926)

F. Abbiati: 'La musica in Turchia con Giuseppe Donizetti, pascià', *Bergomum*, xxii/Nov (1928)

G. Donati-Petteni: 'Attraverso le biografie donizettiane', *Rivista di Bergamo*, viii (1929), 398–406

——: *Studi e documenti donizettiani* (Bergamo, 1929)

G. Rota-Basoni Scotti: 'Le memorie donizettiane della Baronessa Basoni Scotti', *Rivista di Bergamo*, viii (1929), 446–57

Donizetti l'uomo: Bergamo 1946–8

O. Tiby: 'Gaetano Donizetti a Palermo', *Annuario dell'Accademia di Santa Cecilia* (1949–51); pubd separately (Rome, 1951)

F. Schlitzer: *L'ultima pagina della vita di Gaetano Donizetti da un carteggio inedito dell'Accademia Chigiana*, Quaderni dell'Accademia Chigiana, xxviii (Siena, 1953)

A. Damerini: 'Vita tragica di Donizetti', *Melodramma*, i–ii (1954)

F. Schlitzer: *Donizetti, G.: episodi e testimonianze F. Fiorentino* (Naples, 1954)

——: 'Donizettiana', *Mondo teatrale dell'ottocento* (Naples, 1954), 49–122

——: *L'eredità di Donizetti: da carteggi e documenti dell'archivio dell'Accademia Chigiana*, Quaderni dell'Accademia Chigiana, xxx (Siena, 1954)

O. Tiby: *Il Real Teatro Carolino e l'ottocento musicale palermitano* (Florence, 1957)

G. Zavadini: *Donizetti l'uomo* (Bergamo, 1958)

A. Geddo: 'Para una iconografia de Donizetti', *Boletín de programas*, xx (1961), 86

F. Walker: *The Man Verdi* (London, 1962)

H. Weinstock: 'Chi era Marianna Donizetti?', *SD*, no.2 (1972), 41–6

G. Barblan: 'Donizetti in Naples', *DSJ*, i (1974), 105–19

L. Mikoletzky: 'Gaetano Donizetti und der Kaiserhof zu Wien: neue Dokumente', *AnMc*, no.14 (1974), 411–13

J. Allitt: *Donizetti and the Tradition of Romantic Love: a Collection of Essays on a Theme* (London, 1975)

G. Barblan: 'Gaetano Donizetti mancato direttore dei conservatori di Napoli e di Milano', *Il melodramma italiano dell'ottocento: studi e ricerche per Massimo Mila* (Turin, 1977), 403–12

G. Pillon: 'I diarii della follia di Gaetano Donizetti', *Il borghese* (31 July 1977)

R. Steiner-Isenmann: *Gaetano Donizetti: sein Leben und seine Opern* (Berne, 1982)

Musikrevy, xlvii (1992), 87–111 [18 short articles]

RECEPTION

A. Calzado: *Donizetti e l'opera italiana in Spagna* (Paris, 1897)

A. Centelli: 'La musica di Donizetti a Venezia', *Gaetano Donizetti: numero unico nel primo centenario della sua nascita 1797–1897*, ed. P. Bettòli (Bergamo, 1897), 13–15

C. Malherbe: 'Le centenaire de Donizetti et l'exposition de Bergame', *RMI*, iv (1897), 707–29

A. Pougin: 'Les opéras de Donizetti en France', *Gaetano Donizetti: numero unico nel primo centenario della sua nascita 1797–1897*, ed. P. Bettòli (Bergamo, 1897), 20–21

G. Pinetti: *Le opere di Donizetti nei teatri di Bergamo* (Bergamo, 1942)

A. Della Corte: 'Un secolo di critica per l'opera di Donizetti', *Melodramma*, i–ii (1954)

F. Lo Presti: 'La fortuna di Donizetti oggi in Inghilterra', *DSJ*, iv (1980), 231–8

J. Black: 'Donizetti and his Contemporaries in Naples 1822–1848: a Study in Relative Popularity', *DSJ*, vi (1988), 11–27

CRITICAL AND SPECIAL STUDIES

General

P. Scudo: 'Donizetti et l'école italienne depuis Rossini', *Critique et littérature musicales* (Paris, 1850, 3/1856), 75–97

H. F. Chorley: 'Donizetti's Operas', *Thirty Years' Musical Recollections*, i (London, 1862), 153–65

P. Bettòli: 'Le opere di Gaetano Donizetti: errori e lacune', *Gaetano Donizetti: numero unico nel primo centenario della sua nascita 1797–1897* (Bergamo, 1897), 26–7

E. C. Verzino: *Le opere di Gaetano Donizetti: contributo allo loro storia* (Bergamo and Milan, 1897)

L. Miragoli: *Il melodramma italiana nell'ottocento* (Rome, 1924)

G. Donati-Petteni: *Studi e documenti donizettiani* (Bergamo, 1929)

G. Barblan: *L'opera di Donizetti nell'età romantica* (Bergamo, 1948)

B. Dal Fabbro: 'Donizetti e l'opera buffa', *I bidelli del Walhalla* (Florence, 1954), 129–40

F. Schlitzer: *Mondo teatrale dell'ottocento* (Naples, 1954)

E. Dent: 'Donizetti: an Italian Romantic', *Fanfare for Ernest Newman* (London, 1955), 86–107; repr. in *DSJ*, ii (1975), 249–70

M. P. Boyé: 'Donizetti et l'opéra italien', *Revue de la Méditerranée*, nos.73–6 (1956), 240–54, 369–83, 486–95, 581–91; nos.77–82 (1957), 24–38, 177–84, 286–302, 415–35, 545–58, 623–34; no.83 (1958), 46–59

A. Geddo: 'Donizetti: ordine fra i suoi quartetti', *La Scala*, no.77 (1956), 63–6

G. Barblan: 'Il "Giovedi grasso" e gli svaghi "Farsaioli" di Donizetti', *Musicisti piemontesi e liguri*, Chigiana, xvi (1959), 109–14

——: 'Attualità di Donizetti', *L'opera italiana in musica … in onore di Eugenio Gara* (Milan, 1965), 59–73

F. Cella: 'Indagini sulle fonte francesi dei libretti di Gaetano Donizetti', *Contributi dell'Istituto di filologia moderna*, Fr. ser., iv (1966), 343–590

F. Lippmann: 'Die Melodien Donizettis', *AnMc*, no.3 (1966), 80–113

R. Celletti: 'Il vocalismo italiano da Rossini a Donizetti', *AnMc*, no.5 (1968), 267–94; no.7 (1969), 214–47

F. Lippmann: 'Gaetano Donizetti', *Vincenzo Bellini und die italienische opera seria seiner Zeit*, AnMc, no.6 (1969), 304–17

E. de Mura: *Enciclopedia della canzone napoletana* (Naples, 1969)

W. Dean: 'Some Echoes of Donizetti in Verdi's Operas', *3° congresso internazionale di studi verdiani: Milan 1972*, 122–47

F. Lippmann: 'Der italienische Vers und der musikalische Rhythmus: zum Verhältnis von Vers und Musik in der italienischen Oper des 19. Jahrhunderts', *AnMc*, no.12 (1973), 253–369; no.14 (1974), 324–410; no.15 (1975), 298–333

W. Dean: 'Donizetti's Serious Operas', *PRMA*, c (1973–4), 123–41

R. Angermüller: 'Il periodo viennese di Donizetti', *CSD 1975*, 619–97

F. L. Arruga: 'Appunti e prospettive sulle drammaturgia di Donizetti', *CSD 1975*, 743–73

W. Ashbrook: 'La struttura drammatica nella produzione di Donizetti dopo il 1838', *CSD 1975*, 721–41

L. Badacci: 'Donizetti e la storia', *CSD 1975*, 5–27

G. Bezzola: 'Aspetti del clima culturale italiano nel periodo donizettiano', *CSD 1975*, 29–42

C. Cassini: 'Il decennio della fortuna critica di Donizetti a Parigi', *CSD 1975*, 571–94

F. Cella: 'Il donizettismo nei libretti di Donizetti', *CSD 1975*, 43–50

J. Commons: 'Un contributo ad uno studio su Donizetti e la censura napoletana', *CSD 1975*, 65–106

——: 'Unknown Donizetti Items in the Neapolitan Journal "Il sibilo"', *DSJ*, ii (1975), 145–60

S. Döhring: 'La forma dell'aria in Gaetano Donizetti', *CSD 1975*, 149–78

A. Gazzaniga: 'Donizetti a Napoli: da "La zingara" a "L'Esule"', *CSD 1975*, 351–98

F. Lippmann: 'Donizetti e Bellini: contributo all'interpretazione dello stile donizettiano', *CSD 1975*, 179–99

——: 'Verdi und Donizetti', *Opernstudien: Anna Amalie Abert zum 65. Geburtstag* (Tutzing, 1975), 153–73

B. Zanolini: 'L'armonia come espressione drammaturgica in Donizetti', *CSD 1975*, 775–834

A. Zedda: 'La strumentazione nell'opera teatrale di Donizetti', *CSD 1975*, 453–542

J. Commons: 'Giuseppe Bardari', *DSJ*, iii (1977), 85–96

G. Gavazzeni: 'Brogliacco donizettiano', *Il melodramma italiano dell'ottocento: studi e ricerche per Massimo Mila* (Turin, 1977), 425–36

J. Black: 'Cammarano's Libretti for Donizetti', *SD*, no.3 (1978), 115–31

T. G. Kaufman: 'Italian Performances in Vienna 1835–1859', *DSJ*, iv (1980), 53–71

A. Weatherson: 'Donizetti in Revival', *DSJ*, iv (1980), 13–26

J. Black: *Donizetti's Operas in Naples* (London, 1982)

A. Gazzaniga: 'La geminazione nel linguaggio di Donizetti', *NRMI*, xviii (1984), 420–33

S. L. Balthazar: *Evolving Conventions in Italian Serious Opera: Scene Structure in the Works of Rossini, Bellini, Donizetti, and Verdi, 1810–1850* (diss., U. of Pennsylvania, 1985)

A. Gazzaniga: 'Appunti di Donizetti per una conferenza', *NRMI*, xix (1985), 291–7

C. Dahlhaus: 'Komödie mit Musik und musikalische Komödie: zur Poetik der komischen Oper', *NZM*, Jg.147 (1986), 24–7

W. Ashbrook: 'Donizetti and Romani', *Italica*, lxiv (1987), 606–31

S. Fayad: *Donizetti a Napoli (1822–1838)* (Naples, 1987)

N. L. Jennings: *Gaetano Donizetti (1797–1848): the Evolution of his Style Leading to the Production of 'Anna Bolena' in 1830* (diss., Michigan State U., 1987)

Anna Bolena

M. Ballini: 'Ritorno dell' "Anna Bolena"', *La Scala*, no.89 (1957), 17–22

P. Gossett: *Anna Bolena* (Oxford, 1985)

C. N. Gattey: 'Donizetti's "Anna Bolena": Historical Accuracy Considered', *About the House*, vii (1988), 11–17

Don Pasquale

W. J. Kleefeld: *Don Pasquale von Gaetano Donizetti* (Leipzig, 1901)

A. Lazzari: 'Giovanni Ruffini, Gaetano Donizetti e il *Don Pasquale*', *Rassegna nazionale* (1 and 16 Oct 1915)

C. B. Micca: 'Giovanni Ruffini e il libretto del Don Pasquale', *Rivista di Bergamo*, x (1931), 537–41

M. Rinaldi: 'Antonio e Pasquale', *La Scala*, no.9 (1950), 13–15

F. Walker: 'The Librettist of "Don Pasquale"', *MMR*, lxxxviii (1958), 219–23

P. Berri: 'Il librettista del "Don Pasquale": leggende, ingiustizie, plagi', *La Scala*, no.110 (1959), 19–24

H. Liebsch: 'Eine Oper – zwei Texte: textkritische Bemerkungen zu Donizettis "Don Pasquale"', *Musik und Gesellschaft*, xii (1963), 91–5

P. Rattalino: 'Il processo compositivo nel "Don Pasquale" di Donizetti', *NRMI*, iv (1970), 51–68, 263–80

——: 'Trascrizioni, riduzioni, trasposizioni e parafrasi del *Don Pasquale*', *CDS 1975*, 1015–34

L'avant-scène opéra, no.108 (1988) [*Don Pasquale* issue]

L'elisir d'amore

E. Prout: 'Auber's "Le philtre" and Donizetti's "L'elisir d'amore": a Comparison', *MMR*, xxx (1900), 25–7, 49–53, 73–6

E. Appelius: 'Il centenario dell' "Elisir d'amore"', *Rivista di Bergamo*, xi (1932), 195–7

G. Gavazzeni: 'Donizetti e l'Elisir d'amore', *RaM*, vii (1934), 44–50

La favorite

G. Barblan: *La favorita: mito e realtà* (Venice, 1965)

W. Ashbrook: 'La composizione di *La favorita*', *SD*, no.2 (1972), 13–27

R. Leavis: '*La favorite* and *La favorita*: One Opera, Two Librettos', *DSJ*, ii (1975), 117–29

W. Ashbrook: '*L'ange de Nisida* di Donizetti', *RIM*, xvi (1981), 96–114

P. Gossett: Introduction to *La favorite*, ERO, xxviii (1982)

H. R. Cohen, ed.: *The Original Staging Manuals for Twelve Parisian Operatic Premières/Douze livrets de mise en scène lyrique datants des créations parisiennes* (Stuyvesant, NY, 1991) [incl. production book for *La favorite*]

Lucia di Lammermoor

R. Barbiera: 'Chi ispirò la "Lucia"? ... il martirio di Gaetano Donizetti', *Vite ardenti nel teatro da archivii e da memorie (1700–1900)* (Milan, 1931), 147–75

G. Roncaglia: 'Il centenario di "Lucia"', *RMI*, xl (1936), 119–25

I. Pizzetti: 'Un autografo di Donizetti', *La musica italiana dell'ottocento* (Turin, 1947), 231–9

M. Baccaro: '*Lucia di Lammermoor*' *prima al S. Carlo di Napoli* (Naples, 1948)

F. Sacchi: 'Sensazionale tragedia in Scozia', *Melodramma*, i–ii (1954)

E. H. Bleiler: *Lucia di Lammermoor by Gaetano Donizetti* (New York, 1972) [incl. lib. and trans., introductory essays]

A. Gazzaniga: 'Un intervallo nelle ultime scene di "Lucia"', *NRMI*, xiii (1979), 620–33

J. N. Black: 'Cammarano's Notes for the Staging of *Lucia di Lammermoor*', *DSJ*, iv (1980), 29–44

L'avant-scène opéra, no.56 (1983) [*Lucia di Lammermoor* issue]

W. Ashbrook: 'Popular Success, the Critics and Fame: the Early Careers of *Lucia di Lammermoor* and *Belisario*', *COJ*, ii (1990), 65–81

Maria Stuarda

P. Schmid: '*Maria Stuarda* and *Buondelmonte*', *Opera*, xxiv (1973), 1060–66

J. Commons: '*Maria Stuarda* and the Neapolitan Censorship', *DSJ*, iii (1977), 151–67

J. Commons, P. Schmid and D. White: '19th Century Performances of *Maria Stuarda*', *DSJ*, iii (1977), 217–42

Other operas

H. Berlioz: '"La fille du régiment"', *Journal des débats* (16 Feb 1840); repr. in *Les musiciens et la musique* (Paris, 1903), 145–56

A. Cametti: *La musica teatrale a Roma cento anni fa: 'Olivo e Pasquale' di Donizetti* (Rome, 1927)

——: 'La musica teatrale a Roma cento anni fa: "Il corsaro" di Pacini, il "Furioso" e "Torquato Tasso" di Donizetti, "La sonnambula" di Bellini, la "Norma" di Bellini', *Reggia Accademia di Santa Cecilia, Roma: annuario* (1930–31), 445–89; (1933–4), 365–421

A. Capri: 'Linda di Chamounix', *La Scala*, no.31 (1952), 16–50

A. Pironti: 'Duca d'Alba', *La Scala*, no.34 (1952), 38–41

N. Gallini: 'Inediti donizettiani: ultima scena dell'opera "Caterina Cornaro"', *RMI*, lv (1953), 257–75

B. Becherini: 'Il "Don Sebastiano" di Donizetti al XVIII maggio musicale fiorentino', *RBM*, ix (1955), 143–53

U. Cattini: 'Note sul Roberto Devereux', *Ricordiana* (1957), Nov, 478–88

G. Barblan: 'Un personaggio di Cervantes nel melodramma italiano: "Il furioso all'isola di San Domingo"', *Musicisti lombardi e emiliani*, Chigiana, xv (1958), 85–94

J. Commons: 'An Introduction to "Il duca d'alba"', *Opera*, x (1959), 421–6

——: 'Emilia di Liverpool', *ML*, xl (1959), 207–28

G. Roncaglia: 'Ricuperato anche "Il furioso all'isola di S. Domingo" di Gaetano Donizetti', *La Scala*, no.115 (1959), 34–9

G. Barblan: 'Il nuovo finale dell'atto 1° della *Pia de' Tolomei*, con scritti di Donizetti e Cammarano', *SD*, no.1 (1962), 143–51

——: 'Una donizettiana farsa di costume: "Le convenienze e le inconvenienze teatrali"', *Le celebrazioni del 1963*, Chigiana, xx (1963), 217–36

——: 'Alla ribalta un'ottocentesca tragedia lirica: "Parisina d'Este" di Donizetti', *Chigiana*, xxi (1964), 207–38

——: 'Caracteristicas corais do "D. Sebastiano" de Donizetti', *Estudos italianos em Portugal*, xxiii (1964), 203

——: 'Lettura di un'opera dimenticata: "Pia de' Tolomei" di Donizetti (1836)', *Chigiana*, xxiv (1967), 221–43

J. Freeman: 'Donizetti in Palermo and *Alahor in Granata*', *JAMS*, xxv (1972), 240–50

P. Rattalino: 'Unità drammatica della *Linda di Chamounix*', *SD*, no.2 (1972), 29–40

J. Schapp: '*Il burgomastro di Saardam*', *DSJ*, i (1974), 51–7

J. Watts: '*L'ajo nell'imbarazzo*', *DSJ*, i (1974), 41–9

G. Barblan: '*Maria di Rohan*', *DSJ*, ii (1975), 14–33

G. Carli Ballola: 'Lettura del *Torquato Tasso*', *CSD 1975*, 201–13

J. Commons: 'The Authorship of *I piccioli virtuosi ambulanti*', *DSJ*, ii (1975), 199–207

J. Guaricci: '*Lucrezia Borgia*', *DSJ*, ii (1975), 161–77

M. F. Messenger: 'Donizetti, 1840: 3 "French" Operas and their Italian Counterparts', *DSJ*, ii (1975), 99–115

B. Sarnaker: 'Chi cantò l'*Esule di Roma*? ovvero, Parti in cerca di cantanti', *Il melodramma italiano dell'ottocento: studi e ricerche per Massimo Mila* (Turin, 1977), 413–24

D. White: 'Donizetti and the "Three Gabriellas"', *Opera*, xxix (1978), 962–70
J. N. Black: 'Cammarano's Self-Borrowings: the Libretto of *Poliuto*', *DSJ*, iv (1980), 89–103
T. G. Kaufman: '*L'esule di Roma*: a Performance History', *DSJ*, iv (1980), 104–9
P. Gossett: Introduction to *Parisina*, ERO, xxv (1981)
——: Introduction to *Les martyrs*, ERO, xxvii (1982)
——: Introduction to *Roberto Devereux*, ERO, xxvi (1982)
W. Ashbrook: 'Donizetti and Romantic Sensibility in Milan at the Time of *Maria Padilla*', *DSJ*, v (1984), 8–19
J. Black: '*Elisabeth d'Angleterre*, *Le comte d'Essex*, and *Roberto Devereux*', *DSJ*, v (1984), 135–46
——: 'The Revival of *Gemma di Vergy* at the S Carlo of Naples in June 1838', *DSJ*, v (1984), 82–7
J. Commons and J. Black: '*Il campanello di notte*: Further Evidence, Further Questions', *DSJ*, v (1984), 231–9
W. Crutchfield: 'A Donizetti Discovery', *MT*, cxxv (1984), 487–90 [*Elisabeth* (*Otto mesi*)]
T. Kaufman: '*Lucrezia Borgia*: Various Versions and Performance History', *DSJ*, v (1984), 37–81
F. Lo Presti: '*Le duc d'Albe*: the Livret of Scribe and Duveyrier', *DSJ*, v (1984), 243–316
R. Parker: '*Maria Padilla*: Some Historical and Analytical Remarks', *DSJ*, v (1984), 20–34
A. Bini: '*Otto mesi in due ore* ossia *Gli esiliati in Siberia*: vicende di un'opera donizettiana', *RIM*, xxii (1987), 183–260
W. Ashbrook: 'Popular Success, the Critics and Fame: the Early Careers of *Lucia di Lammermoor* and *Belisario*', *COJ*, ii (1990), 65–81
H. R. Cohen, ed.: *The Original Staging Manuals for Twelve Parisian Operatic Premières/Douze livrets de mise en scène lyrique datants des créations parisiennes* (Stuyvesant, NY, 1991) [incl. production book for *La fille du régiment*]

WILLIAM ASHBROOK (1–4, 7, work-list (with JOHN BLACK), bibliography), JULIAN BUDDEN (5, 6)

Donna del lago, La ('The Lady of the Lake'). *Melodramma* in two acts by GIOACHINO ROSSINI to a libretto by ANDREA LEONE TOTTOLA after WALTER SCOTT's poem *The Lady of the Lake*; Naples, Teatro S Carlo, 24 October 1819.

The opera is set in 16th-century Scotland, in the reign of James V. The Highlanders, led by Douglas, the father of Ellen, the so-called Lady of the Lake, are in revolt against the king. Ellen loves the impetuous Malcolm Graeme but has been promised in marriage to one of her father's confederates, the bellicose chieftain Roderick Dhu. Act 1 begins by picturesque Loch Katrine; peasants go about their work and a hunt is heard in the distance. A skiff approaches across the loch, rowed by Elena [Ellen] (soprano), singing one of the simplest and loveliest of Rossini cavatinas, 'O mattutini albori!'. As she steps ashore she is met by the king, Giacomo [James] (tenor), separated from the hunt; he introduces himself as Uberto. He is greatly struck by Ellen's beauty and accepts her offer of shelter; as they prepare to set out across the loch they express mutual tenderness in a duet. The hunt returns, framing the action (much as at the start of Act 2 of *Tristan und Isolde*), while the king learns to his dismay that Ellen is the daughter of the rebel Douglas; he is further unsettled by the news that she is destined to be the wife of Rodrigo [Roderick Dhu]. A tense duettino develops, growing into a full-blown duet that expresses conflicting emotions: Ellen's love for Malcolm, the king's deep affection for her.

After this long and imaginatively sustained opening movement, there is a rather more conventional scena, cavatina and cabaletta for Malcolm, a fresh-faced young warrior who, like Tancredi before him, is cast as a mezzo-soprano. Douglas (bass) also has a set-piece entrance aria in which he extols to Ellen the virtues of loyalty and obedience. She and Malcolm are left to ponder the age-old conflict between love and duty in a duet simply accompanied by strings, bassoons and clarinets. A warrior chorus is now heard as Roderick Dhu (tenor) arrives to claim his bride: his own music is florid and threatening, though there is a strain of tenderness in the lyrical middle section of his entrance aria as he reflects on the absent Ellen. Malcolm dedicates himself formally to the rebel cause but when mention is made of Ellen's impending marriage contention breaks out. The Act 1 finale gathers pace and intensity when it is reported that enemy forces are at hand. Thrusting emotion aside, Roderick calls for the symbolic raising of an ancient war shield. Priests are summoned for the famous Chorus of the Bards ('Già un raggio forier'), scored in Ossianic style for male voices, harp, violas, pizzicato cello and double bass. A meteor is sighted and taken as a good omen, generating a frenzy reflected in the writing as Rossini brings together the soloists, three choruses, orchestra with harp and an onstage military band.

Act 2 begins with a slow aria of great tenderness for the king, developing into a duet in which he openly declares his love while Ellen insists that there can be no more than friendship between them. Before she departs he insists on giving her a ring which, he says, will guarantee her royal protection. But their leave-taking is seen by Roderick and in a trio of gathering ferocity he demands to know the man's identity. To Ellen's consternation, James concedes that he is a follower of the king and in a moment that is as thrilling in the opera as it is in Scott's poem Ellen and James find themselves surrounded by soldiers who have been hidden in the bracken. After scenes for Douglas, now bent on surrender, and Malcolm, the action moves to the palace at Stirling. Douglas has been taken captive and Ellen arrives with the ring given her by the mysterious stranger. A voice is heard singing in a nearby room. Ellen recognizes both the voice and the melody; it is her own aubade, sung by the stranger she met on Loch Katrine. James now reveals his true identity, spares the lives of Douglas and Malcolm and, putting aside his own emotions, gives his blessing to the marriage of Ellen and Malcolm. So many emotions, 'Tanti affetti', now rush through Ellen's mind in one of those brilliant showcase arias that Rossini delighted in writing for heroines at the end of comic and serious works alike. It makes a luminous conclusion to one of the most lyrical and imaginative of all Rossini's scores. RICHARD OSBORNE

Donna serpente, La ('The Snake-Woman'). *Opera fiaba* in a prologue and three acts by ALFREDO CASELLA to a libretto by Cesare Lodovici after CARLO GOZZI's play of the same name (1762); Rome, Teatro Reale dell'Opera, 17 March 1932.

Being based on one of Gozzi's eccentric fantasy plays, *La donna serpente* (composed during 1928–31) invites comparison with several previous operas. Admittedly, only *Die Feen* derives from precisely the same source, and Casella's treatment of the subject could hardly be more different from the young Wagner's. However, he probably owed more to Puccini's *Turandot* than he would have acknowledged: for example, just as in that opera Gozzi's *commedia dell'arte* characters are thinly disguised by the 'Chinese' names Ping, Pang and Pong, so in *La donna serpente* the names of Truffaldino, Brighella, Pantalone and Tartaglia are quaintly perverted into their 'Caucasian' equivalents Alditrúf (tenor), Albrigòr (baritone), Pantúl (baritone) and Tartagíl (tenor). Moreover, Puccinian overtones can sometimes be sensed in the plaintive lyrical outpourings of Altidòr (tenor), King of Tiflis, as he laments the suffering caused by his mysterious queen's strange behaviour.

By and large, however, the work's uninhibited rejoicing in the unrealistic extravagances of its extraordinary plot suggests a closer kinship with the *Turandot* of Busoni, and still more with the racy, pungent humour of Prokofiev's Gozzi opera *The Love for Three Oranges*, which in general spirit (though not in musical language) may perhaps be regarded as *La donna serpente*'s closest precursor. Moreover, Casella himself acknowledged a debt to the fairy-tale operas of Rimsky-Korsakov; and the roots of certain more 'archaic' components in the work's make-up can be traced back to various earlier phases of Italian operatic history, from Monteverdi to Rossini.

Altidòr's queen is in fact the fairy Miranda (soprano); but since she has married him against the will of her father King Demogorgòn (baritone), she has been compelled – as a result of the strongest spell that Demogorgòn could cast in the circumstances – to conceal her identity for the first nine years and a day after the wedding. Moreover, when that long period is over, her father's magic then obliges her to test Altidòr's devotion to the utmost, through a series of wildly cruel and unpredictable acts: among other things, she has their children burnt to death and seemingly leads a Tartar army against her husband's kingdom. Understandably, Altidòr fails these tests: having previously sworn that in no circumstances will he ever curse Miranda, he eventually can stand no more and breaks his oath. As a result, Miranda turns into a snake: according to Demogorgòn's decree, she is to remain in that form for two centuries, and then finally return to fairyland. But Demogorgòn's magic is not invincible: the wizard Geònca (bass), who originally prevented the fairy king from obstructing Miranda's marriage outright, again comes to the royal couple's defence. After a stark confrontation between the voices of Demogorgòn and Geònca (heard through loudspeakers during the final act's central interlude), the last scene is set amid the Caucasus mountains. Here Altidòr defeats three monsters and passes through a great fire which destroys Miranda's snake-body and restores her to human shape. The spouses are reunited, their children are brought back to life, and all ends happily.

For all its stylistic eclecticism, *La donna serpente* has plentiful vitality, providing a compendium of many of the best aspects of Casella's music of the inter-war years. A large part is played by the chorus (the composer originally planned the work as a choral ballet), and the beautiful neo-madrigalian lament at the beginning of Act 3 is one of the opera's highlights. Much of the score, however, is fast-moving and streamlined in effect – sometimes pugnaciously neo-Baroque, sometimes of neo-Rossinian lightness (especially in the music associated with the *commedia dell'arte* characters who, as so often in dramas based on Gozzi, are unexplainedly caught up in the action without being central to it). The orchestration is resourceful and often imaginative, notably in the many 'magic' scenes.

In the theatre *La donna serpente* can undeniably create problems: the wilder flights of fantasy need careful handling, and only a visually lavish production can adequately match the glittering music. It is perhaps not surprising that even in Italy the work has rarely been staged, though quite often heard on the radio. However, in 1982 it was revived at Palermo, in a production which proved so effective that it would certainly have been followed up by other opera houses had not Casella's political record been anathema to the Communist party, which at that time controlled so much of Italy's operatic life.

JOHN C. G. WATERHOUSE

Donne curiose, Le [*Die neugierigen Frauen*] ('The Inquisitive Women'). Comic opera in three acts by ERMANNO WOLF-FERRARI to a libretto by Luigi Sugana after CARLO GOLDONI's play of the same name (1753); Munich, Residenztheater, 27 November 1903.

Though written in his mid-20s, this first of Wolf-Ferrari's five Goldoni operas is remarkably mature: many of the qualities that were to blossom so richly in *I quatro rusteghi* (1906) are already abundantly evident, expressed in only slightly less sure-footed terms. A major factor in this sudden arrival at maturity, after the inventive but rather uncontrolled eclecticism of the composer's first performed opera *Cenerentola*, was his profound responsiveness to the entire world of Goldoni – who, as well as being a playwright, was himself a distinguished *opera buffa* librettist. Being adapted from one of Goldoni's spoken dramas, however, *Le donne curiose* has only indirect links with the structural conventions of 18th-century opera; the musico-dramatic discourse crystallizes from time to time into more or less self-contained numbers, but the general approach has a flexibility which owes as much to Verdi's *Falstaff* as to true *opera buffa*.

As so often in Goldoni, the basic plot is no more than a simple springboard for a lighthearted, witty comedy of manners. Sugana's libretto, though it only intermittently uses actual words from the play, follows its outline fairly closely. The 'inquisitive women' of the title spend most of the opera trying to figure out what their menfolk get up to in a mysterious club from which ladies are rigidly excluded. Beatrice (mezzo-soprano) believes the men gamble, Rosaura (soprano) that they womanize; Eleonora (soprano) thinks they are alchemists hunting for the philosopher's stone, while the clever servant Colombina (soprano) suspects that they are digging for buried treasure. After persistent efforts and repeated setbacks the women at last gain furtive access to the club – only to find the men indulging in nothing worse than a slap-up dinner, prepared for them by Pantalone (*buffo* baritone) and Arlecchino (*buffo* bass) to celebrate the imminent marriage of Florindo (tenor) to Rosaura.

Despite its stylistic debts to earlier composers of Italian comic operas (from Pergolesi through Mozart and Rossini to Verdi), Wolf-Ferrari's music has many individual features. The orchestration, which uses relatively small forces with unusual delicacy and resourcefulness, has been particularly admired; while the harmonic and melodic idiom, though in no way revolutionary, has a subtly pervasive flavour of its own (which can all too easily be ruined, however, in a heavy-handed performance). Room is found for passing allusions to idioms as far apart as Handelian bravura and Venetian folksong; yet the overall effect remains surprisingly unified – more so, indeed, than in some later Wolf-Ferrari operas that have become much better known.

JOHN C. G. WATERHOUSE

Donnelly, Malcolm (*b* Sydney, 8 Feb 1943). Australian baritone. He studied in Sydney, where he made his début in 1966, and then in London before joining Scottish Opera (1972), with which he sang Count

'Donnerstag aus Licht' (Stockhausen): Act 1 scene ii (Moon-Eve) from the original production at La Scala, Milan, 3 April 1981

Almaviva, Malatesta, the Music-Master (*Ariadne auf Naxos*), James Stewart (Musgrave's *Mary, Queen of Scots*), Harašta (*The Cunning Little Vixen*) and Enrico Ashton. At Wexford (1977–8) he sang Herod (*Hérodiade*) and Sebastiano (*Tiefland*). For the ENO his numerous roles include Pizarro, Germont, Napoleon (*War and Peace*), Count di Luna, Ourrias (*Mireille*), Tonio, Mazeppa, Rigoletto, Scarpia, Ford, Simon Boccanegra and Macbeth. With Opera North he has sung the Dutchman, Prince Igor, Jack Rance and Captain Balstrode; he has also appeared with Australian Opera, most notably as Macbeth, a role well suited to his powerful voice and strong personality.

ELIZABETH FORBES

Donnerstag aus Licht ('Thursday from Light'). Opera in three acts, a greeting and a farewell by KARLHEINZ STOCKHAUSEN to his own libretto; Milan, Teatro alla Scala, 3 April 1981 (following an incomplete performance on 15 March 1981).

Donnerstag was the first opera of Stockhausen's *LICHT* cycle to be completed; it was composed from 1978 to 1981 (*Der Jahreslauf*, a scene from the as yet incomplete *Dienstag*, was composed in 1977). It will be performed fourth within the projected cycle of seven.

The framing format of Greeting and Farewell calls for special comment. Their function is both ceremonial and musico-structural. The Greeting, like an extended version of the traditional Bayreuth fanfare, welcomes the audience to the theatre, emphasizing both the festive and the ritual character of what is to follow. Its musical intent is more didactic than that of the Wagnerian Vorspiel; instead of foreshadowing the emotional climate of the following action (most of its music is actually drawn from Act 2), it serves to introduce (or reinforce) the main melodic 'formula' on which the opera is based, namely that associated with Michael (tenor/trumpet/dancer). Similarly, the Farewell will not seek to provide an extended coda or epilogue to the action of Act 3; it will restore a sense of ritual and ceremony (a sort of 'Ite missa est'), reminding the audience that what they have witnessed is only part of a larger dramatic and spiritual entity.

Donnerstag is also 'Michael's Day' (the archangel Michael being, along with Eve (soprano/basset-horn/dancer) and Luzimon/Lucifer, (bass/trombone/dancer/mime), one of the cycle's three principal characters/archetypes). The three acts portray his childhood (as incarnate human), his musical 'Journey around the Earth', and his return to his celestial residence.

Act 1, 'Michael's Youth', is openly autobiographical, being clearly based on the first 20 years of Stockhausen's life: his parents' poverty, his mother's death in an asylum, his father's death at the front and many other details are incorporated. In the opening scene ('Childhood') Michael is brought up by his parents Eve and Lucifer, and shows great aptitude in many fields. The hardships of daily life drive Eve to madness, and she is taken to an asylum. In the second scene ('Moon-Eve') Michael falls in love with Mondeva (Moon-Eve, another incarnation of Eve), who is half-woman and half-bird, while both his parents are killed. The final scene ('Examination') depicts Michael's triumphantly successful entrance examination to the High School of Music; a transformed Eve and Lucifer reappear as the jury.

Act 2, 'Michael's Journey around the Earth', is purely instrumental: Michael is represented by a solo trumpet, and the Earth by the orchestra. Michael plays inside an enormous rotating globe, from which he emerges at seven 'stations' to 'converse' with the other musicians seated at the base of the globe. At the sixth such station he hears the distant sound of a basset-horn, and signals for the globe to turn in reverse. Eve appears once more, now as seductress.

In the first scene ('Festival') of Act 3, 'Michael's Return Home', Michael returns to his 'heavenly residence', is greeted by Eve and the chorus, and presented with gifts, from the last of which (a miniature globe) a demon emerges and fights him. Then Lucifer enters mockingly; an argument ensues, and finally Lucifer is expelled. In the final scene ('Vision') Michael turns to the audience and explains both Lucifer's opposition to his (Michael's) decision to become incarnate as a human being, and his own mission of bringing 'celestial music to humans, and human music to the celestial beings'. As the audience leaves the theatre, the

'Thursday Farewell' is heard from the rooftops of the surrounding buildings.

The music of *Donnerstag* (and the subsequent *Licht* operas) is based on three melodic 'formulae' (an extension of Stockhausen's 'total serialization' of the 1950s) whose pitches, dynamics and rhythms also determine both the melodic/harmonic and formal structure of the whole work. The live vocal and instrumental music is supplemented in Acts 1 and 3 by tapes of instrumental and choral music (the latter may also be performed separately as 'Unsichtbare Chöre' – 'Invisible Choirs'). Altogether, 15 musical interpreters are called for (four solo voices, eight instrumentalists, three dancers), in addition to the chorus and orchestra.

A striking feature of *Donnerstag* is the relative autonomy and importance of purely instrumental music (e.g. the complete absence of vocal music in Act 2). Despite the music's highly organized and integrated structure, many items can also be performed separately as concert pieces (notably the piano part of 'Examination', as *Klavierstück XII*, and 'Michael's Journey around the Earth').

The scores of *Donnerstag*, published by the Stockhausen-Verlag, go far beyond the standard score format. They include not only many photographs of early productions, but also extremely detailed instructions concerning stage design, preparation of supplementary tapes, sound projection, and gestures (many of which are derived and developed from an earlier quasi-scenic work, *Inori*). The scores thus provide an authentic basis for all aspects of future performance practice.

RICHARD TOOP

Don Pasquale. *Dramma buffo* in three acts by GAETANO DONIZETTI to a libretto by GIOVANNI RUFFINI and the composer after ANGELO ANELLI's libretto for Stefano Pavesi's *Ser Marcantonio* (1810); Paris, Théâtre Italien, 3 January 1843.

Don Pasquale *an elderly bachelor*	bass
Dr Malatesta *his physician*	baritone
Ernesto *his nephew*	tenor
Norina *a youthful widow, Ernesto's beloved*	soprano
A Notary *Malatesta's cousin Carlino*	bass

Servants

Setting Don Pasquale's bourgeois villa in Rome and the adjacent garden, as well as Norina's house, in the mid-19th century

Don Pasquale was an instant success as introduced by the quartet of stars at the 'Italiens': Giulia Grisi (Norina), Luigi Lablache (Don Pasquale), Giovanni Matteo Mario (Ernesto) and Antonio Tamburini (Malatesta), with Federico Lablache, the great bass's son (Notary). The Italian première took place at La Scala, Milan, on 17 April 1843, with Ottavia Malvani (Norina), Napoleone Rossi (Pasquale), Leone Corelli (Ernesto) and Achille De Bassini (Malatesta). For its Viennese première, at the Kärntnertortheater on 14 May 1843 in Italian (a production prepared by Donizetti), he added to the score the baritone-*buffo* duet 'Cheti, cheti, immantinente', borrowing it from a discarded section of the unperformed *L'ange de Nisida*; *Don Pasquale* was sung on that occasion by Tadolini (Norina), Rovere (Pasquale), Salvi (Ernesto) and Ronconi (Malatesta). Its London première, at Her Majesty's on 19 June 1843, used the same cast as the Paris première, with one exception (Luciano Fornasari as Malatesta). It was first given in New York, in English, on 9 May 1846. As can be seen, *Don Pasquale* travelled across Europe at a remarkably rapid pace. Its popularity has continued undiminished, and it can truly be said never to have left the international repertory, being a particular favourite in German-language theatres.

Some memorable 20th-century revivals include those at the Metropolitan, 24 December 1904, with Sembrich, Arcangelo Rossi, Caruso and Scotti, and on 23 February 1935 with Bori, Pinza, Schipa and De Luca, conducted by Panizza. There was a notable revival at La Scala on 21 December 1904 with Storchio, Antonio Pini-Corsi, Sobinov and De Luca. A 1905 revival at Covent Garden featured Hermine Bosetti (Norina), Charles Gilibert (Pasquale) and Victor Maurel (Malatesta), but it was not heard there again until the coronation season of 1937, when it was performed by Mafalda Favero (Norina), Umberto di Lelio (Pasquale), Dino Borgioli (Ernesto) and Piero Biasini (Malatesta). It was a feature in the repertory at the Cambridge Theatre in London between 1946 and 1948, evenings made unforgettable by Noni's Norina, Tajo's Pasquale and Stabile's incomparable Malatesta. It had been introduced at Glyndebourne in 1938 by Fritz Busch, with Audrey Mildmay (Norina), Baccaloni (Pasquale), Borgioli (Ernesto) and Stabile (Malatesta). More recent exponents of the title role include Geraint Evans, Fernando Corena, Gabriel Bacquier, Renato Capecchi and Sesto Bruscantini.

ACT 1.i *A room in Pasquale's house* The action is preceded by a brilliant overture which gives prominence to two melodies heard later, Ernesto's serenade and Norina's self-characterizing aria, 'So anch'io la virtù magica'. The elderly Don Pasquale is determined to marry and sire an heir more direct than his nephew Ernesto, whom he plans to disinherit because of that young man's unreasonable infatuation with a youthful widow, Norina. To reassure himself about his generative powers, Pasquale consults Malatesta, who gives a favourable prognosis, but as he is a devoted friend to both Ernesto and Norina he starts to tell Pasquale about a young woman, a certain Sofronia, his own sister, who would be perfect for such a marriage – and she is beautiful besides (Larghetto cantabile, 'Bella siccome un angelo'). The old bachelor is delighted with what he takes to be the symptoms of a regained youth (Vivace, 'Un fuoco insolito'). Ernesto enters and is surprised at his uncle's exuberance and disconcerted when he hears that he plans to take a wife. Their duet, 'Prender moglie!', contrasts an elegiac melody for Ernesto, 'Sogno soave casto', with Pasquale's patter, half-rancorous, half-gleeful.

1.ii *A room in Norina's house* Norina, reading, laughs over a silly romantic tale; she knows her own ability to exert charm. The contrast in style between the slightly exaggerated, bel canto tale of chivalry (Andante, 'Quel guardo il cavaliere') and the good-humoured dance tune (Allegretto, 'So anch'io la virtù magica'), is not only a capital piece of musical characterization but also an implied musical criticism, vintage 1843, as this work was first played in contemporary dress rather than period costume. Malatesta visits her and together they plot in just what manner she should enact the supposed bride, a part she is ready and eager to play if it will help her ultimately to win Ernesto (duet, 'Pronta io son').

ACT 2 *A living-room in Pasquale's house* Ernesto is feeling sorry for himself, imagining his future as an exile and lamenting his lost love. His Larghetto, 'Cercherò lontana terra', is preceded by an eloquent introduction with a trumpet solo, and is a locus classicus of Donizetti's ability to write melodies grateful to the lyric tenor voice. Ernesto leaves just before Pasquale, afire with impatience to meet his bride, enters. Malatesta leads in a veiled lady, really Norina, who feigns terror but is actually so amused at Pasquale's antique gallantry that she can hardly keep herself from collapsing in laughter. Malatesta pretends to encourage her (trio, 'Via, da brava'). Later, he introduces a supposed notary, in reality his cousin Carlino, who takes down the marriage agreement Pasquale dictates, assuring Sofronia that she will be the absolute mistress of all his possessions. Just as the document is signed and the notary asks where the second witness might be, Ernesto storms in to take leave of Pasquale. He is enraged at the spectacle of Norina apparently in the act of marrying his testy uncle; Malatesta whispers an explanation and the young man remains to watch the fun (quartet, 'Ah, figliuol, non mi far scene'). As soon as the notary declares them man and wife, Sofronia turns into a shrew, reproving Pasquale's manners, demanding a *cavalier servente* and carrying on so outrageously that the old man seems turned to stone (quartet, 'È rimasto là impietrato'). The economy and unflagging comic afflatus of this second act, everywhere given tongue by melodic wit and allusiveness, stands as one of Donizetti's greatest achievements.

'Don Pasquale' (Donizetti): Act 3 scene ii from the London première at Her Majesty's Theatre, 19 June 1843, with (left to right) Giovanni Mario (Ernesto), Giulia Grisi (Norina), Luciano Fornasari (Malatesta) and Luigi Lablache (Don Pasquale); the same cast (with the exception of Fornasari) had sung in the original Paris production earlier that year, when the part of Malatesta was sung by Antonio Tamburini

ACT 3.i *A living-room in Pasquale's house* Sofronia has continued her high-handed ways, ordering jewels and clothes, hiring more servants. When she appears dressed to go out, Pasquale stops her (Allegro, 'Signorina, in tanta fretta'). She orders him to bed and, when he protests more urgently, slaps his cheek (Larghetto, 'È finita Don Pasquale'). He threatens her with divorce, and in an aside she expresses sympathy for the old fellow's pain; then as she blithely leaves she drops a note implying that she has a rendezvous in the garden that night. The stunned Pasquale summons Malatesta. The servants comment on the constant comings and goings in this unpredictable household ('Che interminabile andirivieni!'). Malatesta arrives and snatches a hasty word with Ernesto, stressing that Pasquale should not recognize him when he plays his part in the apparent assignation. Pasquale enters and recounts all his problems with his bride: her extravagance, her blow on his cheek and now infidelity. Malatesta struggles to keep a straight face. Then they plot how they will catch the lovers redhanded, the verve of their patter duet, 'Cheti, cheti, immantinente', catching the very spirit of the situation.

3.ii *Don Pasquale's garden* In the garden Ernesto sings a tender serenade, praising the balmy April night and longing for his beloved to appear ('Com'è gentil'). Norina steals in and they sing a rapturous duet (Notturno, 'Tornami a dir che m'ami'). Don Pasquale and Malatesta have observed this scene from behind a bush. The outraged 'husband' now storms out of hiding to confront Norina and order her to leave his house at once. When she adamantly refuses, Malatesta takes charge of the scene, with Pasquale's consent, and informs Sofronia that tomorrow Ernesto's bride Norina will be installed as mistress of the house. Sofronia says she would rather leave than live under the same roof as Norina. Malatesta then tells Pasquale that he can get rid of Sofronia only by marrying Norina to Ernesto that very evening. Pasquale agrees, and Ernesto is summoned and told to fetch Norina. When the supposed Sofronia turns out to be Norina herself, and the whole plot is explained to Pasquale, he accepts the situation with good grace. All comment on the fact that a man who marries in old age is asking for trouble (rondo, 'La morale in tutto questo').

* * *

Don Pasquale has been described as 'Mozartian', and clearly it shares certain characteristics with Mozart's approach: the characters are humanized, not mere farcical stereotypes, and the melodies mirror the emotions they express. This comparison is often made in apparent astonishment that a Donizetti could achieve such an irresistibly heartfelt comedy. Rather, it is more appropriate to describe the opera as supremely 'Donizettian', for it stands as a summation of all his most valuable qualities.

It is a 'romantic' comedy with 19th- rather than 18th-century values. The difference comes out in Norina's *sortita*. To an irresistible dance tune she laughs at sentimental tales and asserts her own ability to stimulate love. She does not rely on someone else to provide 'qualche ristoro', the relief that Mozart's Countess longs for; Norina, with a 'testa bizzarra' that goes along with her 'core eccellente', depends on her own very persuasive charm. The humour of the piece is compounded of high spirits, captivatingly revealed in the Norina-Malatesta duet and the Act 2 trio 'Sta a vedere', and of sympathy, as Norina feels sorry for the slap she gave Pasquale, 'È duretta la lezione' ('The lesson is a little bitter'), her words set to a melody of expansive tenderness. It is precisely Norina's capacity for tenderness that keeps her sense of humour within the bounds of good taste. And that good taste is found everywhere in the music, which contains not the faintest hint of vulgarity.

It used to be a matter of comment that Donizetti composed the opera in a remarkably short time, about two weeks. ('Composition', of course, did not include the orchestration, a chore to be accomplished during the rehearsal period.) That rapidity was possible because of several typically Donizettian attributes. Not only was he trained as a boy to think in terms of complete musical structures, but he also had the advantage of long experience in the theatre – *Don Pasquale* is after all his 64th opera. A further consideration helps explain his celerity. In the score he adapted a good deal of music that originally had been written for other contexts: duets from scores he had abandoned, salon songs, and (for the chorus of servants in the last act) a waltz he had written in an aristocratic lady's album. It is mistaken, however, to regard such heterogeneity of sources as something reprehensible; Donizetti worked with extraordinary concentration and was able to endow the mixture of new music and that adapted from other occasions with a freshness and piquancy that remain unimpaired to this day.

This concentration is also clear in the bounds of the work itself. With one exception, the whole action is carried by four principals, and in the organic growth of the extraordinary second act, expanding only so far as a quartet, the inventiveness is such that it produces the effect of a more complex concertato. The chorus has one moment of prominence in the last act, and then appears as background for Ernesto's serenade and the rondò-finale; everything else is for the four principals.

A particular feature of *Don Pasquale* is the natural melodiousness of the recitative, here accompanied by strings rather than employing the traditional harpsichord heretofore associated with *opera buffa*. There are other unusual aspects to the score. The Norina-Malatesta duet, although in two tempos, is in effect a continuously increasing outpouring of comic brio, made so by melodic reminiscence from the first section in the second, and by the harmonic echoes from one to the other (both being in F major). The natural sequence of one movement on the heels of another in the second act, from Pasquale's entrance to the conclusion, gives no sense of separate 'numbers' but achieves an effortless musical continuity. This spontaneity animates the encounter between Norina and Pasquale at the beginning of Act 3. Here, her waltz tune 'Via, caro sposino' has a simplicity that produces the effect of making it seem the inevitable mode of utterance for her character at that moment, and can be said to represent the distillation of Donizetti's comic style at its purest amalgam of humour and wry tenderness.

WILLIAM ASHBROOK

Don Perlimplin. Radiophonic opera by BRUNO MADERNA to his own libretto after FEDERICO GARCÍA LORCA's play; RAI, 12 August 1962.

Maderna's first completed dramatic work was cast in radiophonic form, the composer having spent several years working in the Studio di Fonologia Musicale of RAI. The plot concerns the middle-aged confirmed bachelor Don Perlimplin (flute), who succumbs to attempts to persuade him to marry a young girl, Belisa (soprano), persuasions largely conducted by the insistent Mother-in-Law ('Suocera'). Belisa receives love letters from an anonymous stranger, asking to meet her in the garden on her wedding night: when she meets him, he is revealed as none other than Don Perlimplin himself, his 'cuckoldry' being a ploy to make him realize fully his love for Belisa.

In the radio opera, Don Perlimplin never speaks, his words being simply 'expressed' through the part for solo flute; similarly, the Mother-in-Law's words become the brief utterances of a small group of wind instruments ('Suocera Sax'). The music contains many references to popular musical styles such as blues and rag, as well as taped music and radiophonic effects. The work was closely embedded in the radio medium but has on one occasion been performed as a concert piece. In its original form it won the Italia Prize for radio presentations in 1962.

RAYMOND FEARN

Don Procopio. *Opera buffa* in two acts by GEORGES BIZET to a libretto by CARLO CAMBIAGGIO after Luigi Prividali's libretto *I pretendenti delusi*; Monte Carlo, Opéra, 10 March 1906.

Bizet spent nearly three years (1857–60) in Italy as winner of the Prix de Rome. He composed *Don Procopio* in Rome in winter 1858–9 as an envoi for the French Academy, who responded with warm commendation. But it was not performed or published in his lifetime. The Choudens vocal scores contain extraneous recitatives and other interpolated material.

The libretto, an adaptation of Prividali's libretto set by Giuseppe Mosca in 1811, has certain similarities, as Bizet was well aware, to Donizetti's *Don Pasquale*. Don Andronico (bass) wants to marry his niece Bettina (soprano) to an old miser, Don Procopio (bass). To avoid this fate, and with the help of her brother Ernesto (baritone) and her lover Odoardo (tenor), she convinces Don Procopio that she is spendthrift and grasping, at which Don Procopio takes fright and offends his friend Don Andronico. The lovers are thus united.

The music, like the text, is wholly Italian, a style Bizet admired in Rossini and Donizetti, although he later spoke dismissively of it. His invention and wit are astonishing, since he infuses a familiar idiom – vocal coloratura, patter declamation, swift-moving ensembles, and so on – with frequent original touches, in harmony, orchestration and melodic style. His fluency and professionalism are remarkable. One piece, a march, was borrowed from the Symphony in C; other sections were later used in *Les pêcheurs de perles* and *La jolie fille de Perth*, including the famous Serenade from that opera.

HUGH MACDONALD

Don Quichotte. *Comédie-héroïque* in five acts by JULES MASSENET to a libretto by HENRI CAIN after Jacques Le Lorrain's verse play *Le chevalier de la longue figure* (1904, after MIGUEL DE CERVANTES: *Don Quixote*), Monte Carlo, Opéra, 19 February 1910.

Don Quichotte is the most successful of the six operas commissioned from Massenet by Raoul Gunsbourg for the Opéra de Monte Carlo. The title role was written for Shalyapin, a regular guest artist in Monaco, about whom Massenet was distinctly cool in his *Souvenirs*; the composer much preferred Vanni-Marcoux, who sang the role in Paris at the Gaîté Lyrique later the same year, with Lucien Fugère, another of his favourite singers, as Sancho. In both productions Dulcinée was sung by Lucy

Don Quichotte		bass
Sancho Panza		bass-baritone
La Belle Dulcinée		mezzo-soprano
Pedro	*Dulcinée's admirers*	soprano
Garcias	*Dulcinée's admirers*	soprano
Rodriguez	*Dulcinée's admirers*	tenor
Juan	*Dulcinée's admirers*	tenor
Chef des Bandits		baritone

Townspeople, bandits

Setting Spain

Arbell, the young mezzo with whom Massenet was infatuated. Both Shalyapin and Vanni-Marcoux left substantial recorded extracts. The opera maintained a precarious hold on the repertory after World War II, mainly as a star vehicle for Slavonic basses in the Shalyapin tradition (Boris Christoff, Miroslav Čangalović), and has since seen an upsurge in popularity both with audiences and with such basses as Ruggero Raimondi and Samuel Ramey. There is a good complete recording with Nicolai Ghiaurov, Gabriel Bacquier and Régine Crespin (1978).

ACT 1 *A square outside the house of La Belle Dulcinée* To the background of conventional pastiche-Spanish dance music Dulcinée, a capricious small-town tart, is serenaded by her four admirers. She replies with the first of two meditations on what life holds for women as the years pass by ('Quand la femme a vingt ans'). Don Quichotte and Sancho Panza are greeted with affection by the townspeople and scorn by the four admirers. Quichotte, who imagines Dulcinée to be his ideal of womanhood, serenades her with 'Quand apparaissent les étoiles', a typically self-generating Massenet melody, much reprised. It is interrupted by Juan, who challenges the old man to a duel. This is in turn interrupted by Dulcinée, who dismisses Juan and archly teases Quichotte for his adoration, eventually ordering him to prove his devotion by retrieving a pearl necklace stolen from her bedroom by the local bandit chief. The act ends with a rapt reprise of the Serenade.

ACT 2 *Open countryside, dawn* During his quest for the necklace, Quichotte composes a new serenade. Sancho, fearing the expedition to be a wild goose chase, launches into a comic tirade against womankind ('Comment peut-on penser du bien'), the text of which (though not the music) is a conscious echo of Leporello's Catalogue Aria. At its conclusion the mists rise and a line of windmills is revealed. Quichotte duly does battle with them.

ACT 3 *In the mountains, twilight* Still on the trail of the bandits, Quichotte falls asleep. Sancho flees when the bandits surround them, and Quichotte is quickly overcome. As they prepare to murder him, Quichotte consigns his soul to God in a prayer of sombre simplicity ('Seigneur, reçois mon âme'); shamed, the bandit chief asks the old man who he is, and is so moved by his reply ('Je suis le chevalier errant') that he returns the necklace. Quichotte, recalling how the oppressed and the criminal have always understood him, blesses the bandits as he leaves. This short act, lasting some 17 minutes, is one of Massenet's most perfectly crafted dramatic paragraphs, its control of mood from broad farce to religiosity to pure sentiment quite faultless.

'Don Quichotte' (Massenet): Lucy Arbell as Dulcinée and Fyodor Shalyapin as Don Quichotte in Act 4 of the original production at the Opéra, Monte Carlo, 24 February 1910; photograph from 'Le théâtre' (April 1910)

ACT 4 *Dulcinée's garden* Surrounded by her admirers, Dulcinée sings the second and more sombre of her meditations ('Lorsque le temps d'amour a fui') and longs for some new sensation to satisfy her hungry flesh. She then chases away her melancholy mood with a flamboyant song to her own guitar accompaniment ('Ne pensons qu'au plaisir d'aimer') and the company retires. Quichotte and Sancho enter. Imagining that marriage beckons and his days of knight-errantry are over, Quichotte promises Sancho a carefree retirement on his own island. Dulcinée returns. Quichotte produces the necklace in triumph and solemnly proposes marriage, much to the amusement of her entourage. Dulcinée dismisses them and in a tender duet ('Oui, je souffre votre tendresse') gently disabuses Quichotte of his folly. In her rejection of him lies proof of her affection: her function is to give love freely, and she could not bear to deceive him. The crestfallen Quichotte thanks her at least for her frankness. She leaves, but the guests return to mock the old man. Sancho rounds on them in a broad C major melody ('Riez, allez, riez du pauvre idéologue') and rebukes them for their cruelty before leading his dazed master away.

ACT 5 *A mountain pass, night* Propped up against a tree, Quichotte recognizes that he has long outlived his proper function and prepares to die. He reminds Sancho of his promise of an island ('Prends cette île'), the only island it is in his power to give – the island of dreams. In the planet Jupiter shining brightly in the heavens he seems to see a vision of Dulcinée as he dies.

* * *

Just as there was a strong element of autobiography in the verse play loosely based on Cervantes by the studiedly eccentric Jacques Le Lorrain, so there is in Massenet's setting. The 67-year-old composer, in poor health, portrayed himself (flatteringly) as the courtly, vague, otherworldly knight, and the ambitious Lucy Arbell (less flatteringly) as the tough but ultimately sensitive gold-digger. Of the four styles of music in the score, the pastiche-Spanish so beloved of French composers is the least interesting; like Meyerbeer before him, Massenet tended not to waste time on music he knew would serve as background to stage action. Dulcinée is drawn with that flirtatiousness and regret at lost youth that male composers flatter themselves to think appropriate to ladies of easy virtue: she is Thaïs's little sister. But Sancho's rumbustious, *opera buffa* idiom and the quirky, mock-academic musical language devised for Quichotte himself are perfectly judged. The opera starts weakly, but for a score of just two hours of music this is not too serious. The windmill scene, the prayer, the duet in which two utterly different worlds meet briefly before going their separate ways and, above all, the death scene show Massenet at his most sensitive and unobtrusively skilful. RODNEY MILNES

Don Rodrigo. Opera in three acts, op.31, by ALBERTO GINASTERA to a libretto by ALEJANDRO CASONA after a historical legend; Buenos Aires, Teatro Colón, 24 July 1964.

The setting is Toledo in the eighth century. Don Rodrigo (dramatic tenor), victorious over his foes, is with great pomp crowned King of Spain. By tradition a new king must add a new lock to an ancient chest in the Cave of Hercules, but Rodrigo instead commands it to be opened: in it he finds a parchment prophesying that the country will be invaded and he will be the last king of his dynasty. He falls in love with Florinda (dramatic soprano), who has been entrusted to his care by her father, his Berber ally Don Julián (baritone), governor of Ceuta; he seduces her but then ignores her. She writes to her father, urging him to avenge her; in response, Julián abandons his political alliance and opens the gates of Gibraltar (which until then he had protected from attack) to the Moors. At the battle of Guadalete, Rodrigo is defeated and wounded: he seeks refuge and forgiveness in the hut of a blind hermit. He dies penitent in the arms of the forgiving Florinda, his redemption a metaphor for the eventual Christian reconquest of Spain.

The work has nine scenes, which are structured dramatically as a palindrome centred on Scene 5 (the rape): Rodrigo's appearance in Scene 1 is counterbalanced by his death in Scene 9, his coronation in Scene 2 by his defeat in Scene 8, and so on. Each of the scenes, which are connected by orchestral interludes, is cast in a specific closed form (after the acknowledged model of Berg's *Wozzeck*), respectively: Scene 1, *Rondo*; Scene 2, *Suite in quattro pezzi*; Scene 3, *Melodramma*; Scene 4, *Caccia ed scherzo* (including a 'madrigale a cinque' for voice, flauto d'amore, viola d'amore, mandolin and harp); Scene 5, *Notturno e duo*; Scene 6, *Aria in cinque strofe*; Scene 7, *Tripartita* (here, to represent Julián's rebellion and the Moorish invasion, the chorus is divided between those shouting and those singing); Scene 8, *Canon ed aria* (the canon being rhythmic and treated in augmentation and diminution); and Scene 9, *Struttura d'arco* (culminating in the tolling of 25 bells directed to be played from the orchestra, stalls and gallery of the theatre).

Very large vocal and instrumental forces are called for: besides the bells just mentioned, Ginastera demands 18 horns (again divided into groups and distributed round the theatre) and a vast percussion section; as well as the three principal characters there are a further 16 roles (playable by 11 singers, including two children) and a large chorus. Serial techniques are employed with considerable virtuosity, and use is also made of note clusters and microtones. The basic note row is treated not only in its entirety but also, for dramatic characterization, in segments: the first four pitches are associated with heroism and Rodrigo, the second four with lyricism and Florinda, the last four with Julián and tragedy. Subsidiary motifs are also derived from these segments, making for an unusually unified musical structure to match the dramatic organization. *Don Rodrigo*, with Domingo in the title role, was given in the New York City Opera's first season in its new headquarters, the New York State Theater at Lincoln Center, on 22 February 1966. LIONEL SALTER

Donzelli, Domenico (*b* Bergamo, 2 Feb 1790; *d* Bologna, 31 March 1873). Italian tenor. After studying with Bianchi he made his début at Bergamo in 1808 in Mayr's *Elisa*. He then completed his studies in Naples with Viganoni and Crivelli. For the next decade he sang florid tenor roles throughout Italy, appearing in Rossini's *Tancredi*, the first performance of *Torvaldo e Dorliska* (1815, Rome), *L'inganno felice* and *La Cenerentola*. Then his voice began to grow heavier, and he turned to a different repertory. In 1825 he made his Paris début at the Théâtre Italien in the title role of Rossini's *Otello*. During six seasons in Paris he sang in the first performances of Rossini's *Il viaggio a Reims* (1825), Halévy's *Clari* (1829) and Bertin's *Fausto* (1831). He sang from 1829 at the King's Theatre, taking part in the first London performances of Bellini's *Il pirata* (1830) and *La straniera* (1832). He created Pollione in *Norma* at La Scala (1831), and later sang the role in London, Venice, Bologna, Trieste and Sinigaglia (Senigallia). He appeared in many Donizetti operas, including *Fausta*, *Anna Bolena*, *Parisina*, *Belisario*, *Lucia di Lammermoor* and *Roberto Devereux*. Two of the greatest successes of his later career were in Auber's *La muette de Portici* and Mercadante's *Il bravo*. He retired in 1844. ELIZABETH FORBES

Dooley, William (*b* Modesto, CA, 9 Sept 1932). American baritone. He studied in Rochester and Munich, and made his début in 1957 at Heidelberg as Posa. He was then engaged at Bielefeld (1959) and in 1962 joined the Deutsche Oper, Berlin, with which he has remained active. In 1964 he made his début at the Metropolitan Opera as Yevgeny Onegin; he sang there for 14 seasons, and also appeared in Santa Fe, Chicago, Vienna and Florence. Among his roles are Pizarro, Telramund, Kothner, the Dutchman, Amonasro, Macbeth, the four villains (*Les contes d'Hoffmann*), Escamillo and John the Baptist (*Salome*), but he excels in modern works. He created Cortez in Sessions's *Montezuma* (1964, Berlin); the Captain of the Guard in *The Bassarids* (1966, Salzburg); Mizoguchi in Mayuzumi's *Kinkakuji* (1976, Berlin); Oberlin in Rihm's *Jakob Lenz* (1979, Hamburg); Tiresias in Rihm's *Oedipus* (1987, Berlin); and Eagle in Marc Neikrug's *Los Alamos* (Berlin, 1988). He has also sung Wozzeck, Dr Schön,

Baron d'Houdoux (*Neues vom Tage*), Gorjančikov (*From the House of the Dead*), Nick Shadow and Major Mary (*Die Soldaten*). ELIZABETH FORBES

Doolittle, Quenten (*b* Elmira, NY, 21 May 1925). Canadian composer. He studied at Ithaca College, Indiana University and the Eastman School of Music; his composition teachers included John Weinzweig and Luigi Zaninelli. He taught at North Dakota State University (1958–60) and (from 1960) at the University of Calgary, where he was a professor until his retirement in 1988. He was also principal viola player of the Calgary PO (1965–72).

Doolittle began composing about 1965; he was influenced by serial and improvisational techniques, and his works are characterized by the juxtaposition of varying styles. His first opera, *Charlie the Chicken* (1975), is based on the play by Jonathan Levy, and has an overture (1978) which involves prepared tape and dummy figures which move and speak. He has also been involved in a series of interdisciplinary workshops exploring the possibilities of literature in terms of creative sound, drama and movement.

Charlie the Chicken (chamber op, 1, J. Levy), Toronto, Free, 19 June 1975
The Second Shepherds' Play (operetta/Christmas musical, 1, B. J. Wylie), Calgary, Pumphouse, Nov 1982
Silver City (2, J. Truss), Banff Centre, 1983; rev. 1984, Toronto, Comus Music Theatre, 1 March 1986
Boiler Room Suite (chamber op, 2, R. Deverell), Banff, 21 Sept 1989
RUTH PINCOE

Dopper, Cornelis (*b* Stadskanaal, nr Groningen, 7 Feb 1870; *d* Amsterdam, 18 Sept 1939). Dutch conductor and composer. He studied at the Leipzig Conservatory, where his teachers included Reinecke, but was for the most part self-taught. In 1896 he became coach and conductor at the Nederlandse Opera in Amsterdam. After the dissolution of the company in 1903, he became conductor of the Savage Opera Company which played in North America. He succeeded J. M. S. Heuckeroth as second conductor of the Concertgebouw (1908–31) alongside Mengelberg. His compositional output includes five operas, of which one remained incomplete.

Het blinde meisje van Castel Cuillé (M. C. Meursinge-Offers), The Hague, 17 Dec 1894
Frithjof, 1895 (B. Bueninck), unperf.
William Ratcliff op.2, 1896–1901 (2, H. Heine), Weimar, Hof, 19 Oct 1909
Het eerekruis (1, H. Engelen), Amsterdam, 9 Jan 1903
Don Quichotte, inc. ROGIER STARREVELD

Doppler, (Albert) Franz [Ferenc] (*b* Lemberg [now L'viv], 16 Oct 1821; *d* Baden, nr Vienna, 27 July 1883). Austrian composer. He was the son of a bandmaster and oboist, and as a child in Warsaw he heard many operas and ballets. When the Polish army was defeated in the War of Independence of 1830–31 the family fled to Kraków, then Lemberg and, in 1834, to Vienna, where Doppler gave many concerts as a flautist. He was appointed first flute at the Bucharest Opera and after a concert tour in Transylvania he became a member of the German Theatre orchestra in Buda. A second tour took him to Kassa (now Košice), Kiev, Odessa, Kishinev, Iaşi and Bucharest. From his childhood he had gained an awareness of folk music, customs, local colours and the style of contemporary operas.

In 1841 he was invited by Erkel to join the orchestra of the National Theatre in Pest (where he later became second conductor), at the same time taking lessons in harmony and orchestration from Erkel's father-in-law, György Adler. From 1841 to 1848 Doppler was also the bandmaster of the National Guard in Buda. He collaborated with Erkel in writing music for the folk plays *Két pisztoly* ('Two Pistols', 1844) and *A rab* ('The Prisoner', 1845), and in 1846 he began his first opera, *Benyovszky, vagy A kamcsatkai számű̋zött* ('Benyovszky, or The Exile of Kamchatka'), based on the life of the 18th-century historical figure. The opera reveals the influence of French and Italian composers and contains elements of characteristic Polish and Hungarian tunes and rhythmic patterns, all incorporated into a strong theatrical whole, skilfully orchestrated. Following the War of Independence (1848–9), when the Hungarians defeated the Habsburg armies but Russian intervention deprived Hungary of freedom, any implied criticism of the Habsburgs, Austrians or Russians was not tolerated; the opera was consequently banned on account of its Polish tunes and Hungarian hero. For ten years it could be revived only as *Afanasia* (the name of the heroine), with the hero's name altered.

Doppler's second opera, *Ilka és a huszártoborzó* ('Ilka and the Recruiting of the Hussars'), the first Hungarian comic opera permitted by the censor, remained in the repertory for half a century. It is an innocent love story set around 1813 when the Russians and Habsburgs were allies; much of the music derives from folk material. *Wanda* deals with the Turkish invasion of Vienna in 1683 and the city's liberation by the Poles, another subject which gave scope for the characterization of different peoples in the framework of a style derived from French and Italian opera. In 1858 Doppler went to Vienna as principal flautist of the Hofoper. His only German opera, *Judith*, was produced there in 1870.

first performed at the Hungarian National Theatre, Pest, unless otherwise stated

Benyovszky, vagy A kamcsatkai számű̋zött [Benyovszky, or The Exile of Kamchatka] (3, R. Köffinger, trans. B. Egressy, after A. von Kotzebue), 29 Sept 1847, *H-Bn*, arr. pf (Pest, n.d.)
Ilka és a huszártoborzó [Ilka and the Recruiting of the Hussars] (comic op, 2, J. Janotyckh von Adlersheim, trans. J. Szerdahelyi), 29 Dec 1849, *Bn*, arias arr. pf (Pest, n.d.)
Wanda (4, T. Bakody), 30 Dec 1850, *Bn*, arr. pf (Pest, n.d.)
Két huszár [Two Hussars] (3, J. Czanyuga), 12 March 1853, *Bn*, ov. arr. pf (Pest, n.d.)
Erzsébet [Elizabeth] (3, Czanyuga), 6 May 1857 [ov. and Act 1 only; Act 2 by F. Erkel, Act 3 by K. Doppler], *Bn*
Judith (4, S. H. Mosenthal), Vienna, Hofoper, 30 Dec 1870, vs (Vienna, 1870)

*

N. N.: 'Doppler Ferency', *Orszag Tükre* [Budapest] (10 Oct 1862)
A. Németh: *A magyar opera története a kezdetektől az Operaház megnyitásáig* [History of Hungarian Opera from its Beginnings to the Opening of the Opera House] (Budapest, 1987)
DEZSŐ LEGÁNY

Dorati, Antal (*b* Budapest, 9 April 1906; *d* Gerzensee, nr Berne, 13 Nov 1988). American conductor and composer of Hungarian birth. The son of professional musicians, he studied at the Liszt Academy in Budapest with Bartók, Kodály and Leo Weiner. In 1924 he became a répétiteur at the Budapest Royal Opera, where he made his conducting début the same year and remained for four years. In 1928 he became assistant to Fritz Busch at the Dresden Opera, then musical director at Münster (1929–33). He specialized in conducting for ballet, most notably with the Ballets Russes de Monte

Carlo (successor to the Dyagilev company), until 1945 when his appointment to the Dallas SO heralded a distinguished career as an orchestral conductor and trainer. He took American citizenship in 1947, and became a frequent guest conductor of opera in Europe and North America, making his Covent Garden début in 1962 with *The Golden Cockerel.* His recordings include a number of 20th-century operas, notably *Die ägyptische Helena*, and a Haydn series that did much to rekindle interest in previously neglected operas. Dorati's conducting was distinguished by vigorous direct rhythm and an acute ear for rich colour. He published a variety of compositions and an autobiography, *Notes of Seven Decades* (London, 1979). NOËL GOODWIN

D'Ordonez, Carlo [Karl von]. *See* ORDONEZ, CARLO D'.

Doret, Gustave (*b* Aigle, 20 Sept 1866; *d* Lausanne, 19 April 1943). Swiss composer. He studied in Berlin, and in Paris with Massenet. He made his career as a conductor in that city, becoming concert director of the Société Nationale and conducting regularly with the Opéra-Comique between 1907 and 1914, though he also worked abroad. His fame as a composer extended at the same time. The Opéra-Comique successfully gave his opera *Les armaillis* in 1906, and *La tisseuse d'orties* was produced in 1926. He was very much attracted to opera and wrote (with the playwright René Morax) several works for the Théâtre du Jorat, which opened at Mézières (Vaud) in 1908 with *Henriette.* These works created a form of popular theatre which met with great success in Switzerland, France and Belgium.

Doret received many honours, and throughout his life exercised a considerable influence on music in Switzerland through his uncompromising personality (notably in his writings) and his abilities as a conductor. His use of timbre and his unprepared modulations are reminiscent of Debussy, although he lacked Debussy's subtlety and mobility, and his lyrical lines betray the pupil of Massenet. He composed few purely orchestral works, showing a preference for vocal music through which he could express, in his individual voice, the spirit of his people as revealed in their historical dramas and legends.

En prison, 1892, unperf.
Maedeli (2, H. Cain and D. Baud-Bovy), 1901
Les armaillis (légende dramatique, 2, Cain and Baud-Bovy), Paris, OC (Favart), 23 Oct 1906, vs (Paris, 1906); rev. Geneva, Grand, 28 Nov 1913; rev. (3), Paris, OC, (Favart), 5 May 1930
Henriette (4, R. Morax), Mézières, Jorat, 1908
Le nain du Hasli (légende féerique, 2, Cain and Baud-Bovy), Geneva, Grand, 1908, vs (Paris, 1908)
Aliénor (légende, 5, Morax), Mézières, Jorat, 16 May 1910, vs (Paris, 1910)
Loys (3, P. Quillard), Vevey, 1911 (concert perf.) [Act 3 only]; stage, Brussels and Zürich, 1914
La nuit des quatre temps (4, Morax), Mézières, Jorat, 6 June 1912
Davel (5, Morax), Mézières, Jorat, 1923
La tisseuse d'orties (drame lyrique, 4, Morax), Paris, OC (Favart), 29 Nov 1926
La servante d'Evolène (Morax), Mézières, Jorat, 29 May 1937
Nérine, unperf.

*

L. Schneider: 'Les armaillis', *Le théâtre*, no.191 (1906), 8–10
J. Dupérier: *Gustave Doret* (Lausanne, 1932)
V. Vincent: *Le Théâtre du Jorat* (Neuchâtel, 1933)
G. Doret: *Temps et contretemps* (Fribourg, 1942)
W. Tappolet: 'Gustave Doret', *SMz*, lxxxiii (1943), 194–7
'Lettres inédites de Gustave Doret à René Morax', *Revue musicale de Suisse romande*, xix/3 (1966), 7–10
P. Meylan: 'Gustave Doret musicien de théâtre', *SMz*, cvi (1966), 293–7
R. Morax: 'L'oeuvre de Gustave Doret', *Revue musicale de Suisse romande*, xix/3 (1966), 3–4 PIERRE MEYLAN

Dorfbarbier, Der ('The Village Barber'). Singspiel in one act by JOHANN BAPTIST SCHENK to a libretto by JOSEF (? and PAUL) WEIDMANN after the latter's comedy of the same name; Vienna, Burgtheater, probably 6 November 1796. (The playbills for the Kärntnertortheater and Burgtheater respectively give 30 October 'zum ersten mal' and 7 November 'zum zweytenmal' 1796 as the dates of the first two performances; Schenk named 6 November 1798. The box-office records, perhaps the most reliable source, indicate 6 November 1796.)

Paul Weidmann's comedy had received a modest ten performances after its première on 18 June 1785 when (according to credible anecdote) his brother, the comic actor and singer Josef, suggested they should adapt it as a Singspiel; Johann Schenk undertook to set it to music. Though the first night showed above-average receipts it was 22 August 1797 before *Der Dorfbarbier* was heard again. It then became very popular, being frequently revived in Vienna (there were 332 performances at the court theatres up to 1891) and given in virtually every German-language house for much of the 19th century. It was also staged in Poland, Hungary, Russia, Bohemia, the Netherlands, Sweden and the USA, and is still occasionally revived in European houses.

The story, with touches of black comedy, is less predictable than is usual in this genre. Though the barber's foster-daughter Suschen (soprano) is in the end united with her Joseph (tenor), it takes a plot hatched by the schoolmaster (bass), and two supposed deaths, to outwit Lux, the barber (bass), who intends to marry his pretty ward himself. In the end, however, he is persuaded that the seemingly miraculous bacon-cure he prescribes for all ills will assure him greater immortality than would marriage to his ward.

The work's success is due above all to the well-drawn characters. The music is tuneful, lively, at times touching in its sentiment; and the parts of Lux, Adam (tenor), his cynical journeyman, and Suschen, provided generations of singing actors (Josef Weidmann, Hasenhut and later J. N. Nestroy) and opera singers (Weinmüller, Friedrich Baumann, Magdalena Willmann, Johann Michael Vogl, Maria Anna Gassmann) with ample opportunities for vocal and mimetic display. Though solo numbers predominate, there are skilful and quite ambitious ensembles, including a septet at the halfway mark and a brief concluding ensemble for all nine characters. Many anecdotes testify to its hold on audiences and performers, and in the 1840s it could not have seemed particularly surprising to find Beethoven's librettist G. F. Treitschke writing an article entitled 'Die Zauberflöte, Der Dorfbarbier, Fidelio' (*Orpheus*, ii, 1841, p.239). Weber, who conducted *Der Dorfbarbier* at Prague in 1816, seems to have recalled Suschen's Polacca, 'Mädchen kann man leicht betören', when writing Aennchen's music in *Der Freischütz* a few years later; and Lortzing, too, knew and appreciated it.

PETER BRANSCOMBE

Dorfgala, Die ('The Village Fête'). *Komische Operette* in three (later two) acts by ANTON SCHWEITZER to a libretto by FRIEDRICH WILHELM GOTTER; three-act version, Weimar, Hoftheater, 18 May 1772; two-act version, Hamburg, Theater am Gänsemarkt, 21 January 1779.

The young tutor Treumund (tenor) is in love with Klärchen (soprano), an innkeeper's daughter, but the scheming and now aging Frenchwoman Antoinette (soprano) aims to win him away. To that end she enlists the aid of the town busybody, Liese (soprano), whose husband the Schoolmaster (bass) is busy preparing a fustian musical play he has composed to celebrate the birthday of the local noblewoman. Liese hopes to engineer a match between her own buffoon of a son Christlieb (tenor) and Klärchen. Antoinette's claim to Treumund disintegrates, but an itinerant puppeteer, Niklas (tenor), turns out to be her first love from long ago.

Unlike Hiller's comic operas, Schweitzer's most successful venture into the field views rustic life with amused detachment, raised to parody in the rehearsal of the Schoolmaster's play about Samson and Delilah.

THOMAS BAUMAN

Dori [*La Dori*]. *Dramma musicale* in a prologue and three acts by ANTONIO CESTI to a libretto by GIOVANNI FILIPPO APOLLONI; Innsbruck, Hof-Saales, 1657.

A masterpiece of mistaken identities, secondary love intrigues, comic interludes, rapid-fire dialogues and unexpected resolutions, the plot is one of the most complicated of the mid-17th century. Before the opera begins, a marriage contract is signed between the rulers of Persia and Nicaea, designed to unite Dori (soprano), Princess of Nicaea, with Oronte (alto castrato), Prince of Persia. However, confusion over Dori's identity makes the contract impossible to fulfil. After being captured by pirates, she was washed ashore, recaptured and, disguised as a man, sold as a slave called Ali to her sister, Arsinoe (soprano), who is now betrothed to Oronte. Ali tries to persuade Oronte to marry Arsinoe, but fails when the ghost of his mother counsels him to be true to his father's wishes and to Dori. Later, Oronte finds Arsinoe in Ali's arms and accuses her of infidelity with a slave. Ali contemplates suicide by poison, but the nurse Dirce (alto), who has prepared a sleeping potion for the loutish servant Golo (bass), substitutes this potion for the poison. Oronte finally agrees to marry Arsinoe, but before the ceremony can take place Arsete (tenor) arrives with a message from Dori saying 'Willingly do I slay myself that Arsinoe may marry you'. Golo saves the day when he finds the apparently dying Ali and discovers the original contract in her pocket. As Arsete explains what has happened, it appears that Dori is dead. Oronte bewails her passing and Tolomeo (soprano castrato), who has spent most of the opera disguised as Celinda, threatens Oronte for his inconstancy. Oronte proclaims he would be constant still if Dori were alive, at which point she walks in and the opera ends with the couples, Tolomeo and Arsinoe, and Dori and Oronte, happily united in love.

Along with Cesti's *Orontea* and Cavalli's *Giasone*, *Dori* was among the most successful of 17th-century operas. Librettos document more than 30 productions, and other performances are known from contemporary accounts. Several reasons for such longevity are the even distribution of arias and duets throughout the three acts, an effective comic element and the high quality of the music itself.

CARL B. SCHMIDT

Dorilla in Tempe. *Melodramma eroico pastorale* in three acts, RV709, by ANTONIO VIVALDI to a libretto by ANTONIO MARIA LUCCHINI; Venice, Teatro S Angelo, 9 November 1726.

Dorilla in Tempe was performed several times in varying versions during the second half of Vivaldi's operatic career. The plot, which mixes pastoral and heroic elements, centres on the shepherd Nomio [Nomius] (alto), who is in fact Apollo in disguise. He falls in love with Dorilla (mezzo-soprano), daughter of Admeto [Admetus], King of Thessaly (bass), who is herself in love with the shepherd Elmiro (soprano). Admetus is forced by the gods to save his kingdom by offering his daughter as a sacrifice to the sea-serpent Pitone [Python], but she is rescued just in time by Nomius. Nomius claims the hand of Dorilla as his reward, but she remains reluctant and escapes with Elmiro. The pair are captured, and Elmiro is sentenced to death. Finally, however, the intervention of Nomius, revealing his divine identity, saves the situation and Dorilla and Elmiro are reunited.

The visual aspect of *Dorilla in Tempe* was important: there were elaborate sets by Antonio Mauro and sections of ballet (often involving choral music) choreographed by Giovanni Galletto. The opera was the first work by Vivaldi to include in its cast the mezzo-soprano Anna Girò. She sang the secondary role of Eudamia and went on to form a lifelong association with the composer. *Dorilla* was revived with an almost identical text at the small Teatro S Margherita, Venice, in 1728 and again at the Sporck Theatre, Prague, in spring 1732, this time with substantial alterations to the libretto. When the opera returned to the Teatro S Angelo in Carnival 1734, Vivaldi converted the work into a pasticcio using recent music by other composers, including Hasse, Giacomelli and Leo. The surviving score in Turin appears to be adapted with various insertions and deletions for the 1734 performance (it is from this score that the voice types above are taken). Unusually for Vivaldi's operatic scores, the sinfonia is clearly linked with the main opera: it follows the title-page instead of preceding it, and the music of its final movement – a C major version of the opening of the 'Spring' concerto, RV269 – reappears in the opera's opening chorus, appropriately in praise of spring. The pastoral nature of *Dorilla* is reflected in its choral and ballet music: this is particularly extensive for the elaborate celebrations at the end of Act 2, where a hunt is enacted to the inevitable horn accompaniment.

ERIC CROSS

Dorman, Mrs [Young, Elizabeth]. English contralto. *See* YOUNG family, (5).

D'Ormeville, Carlo (*b* Rome, 24 April 1840; *d* Milan, 29 July 1924). Italian librettist and impresario. He began his working life as a playwright and literary critic but in 1868 was appointed stage director at La Scala, in which capacity he assisted with the preparations for the première of *Aida* in Cairo. In the 30 years from 1862 he wrote nearly 30 librettos and translated a number of others. Until the end of his life he ran a theatrical agency sending opera companies to South America. His librettos, of which *Ruy Blas* was the most frequently heard, were thoroughly romantic, illuminated by the historical extravagances of Parisian grand opera, and often incorporated important ballets.

Iginia d'Asti, F. Sangiorgio, 1862; *Guisemberga di Spoleto* (tragedia lirica), Sangiorgio, 1864; *Le due amiche* (dramma lirico), T. Seneke, 1866; *Graziella* (idillio drammatico), D. Monti, 1869; *Ruy Blas* (dramma lirico), Marchetti, 1869; *Il Guarany* (opera-ballo, with A. Scalvini), Gomes, 1870; *Regina e favorita*, L. Sangermano, 1871; *Il conte Verde* (dramma lirico), G. Libani, 1873; *Giuseppe Balsamo* (op), Sangiorgio, 1873; *Gustavo Wasa* (dramma lirico), Marchetti, 1875; *Luigi XI*, L. Fumagalli, 1875; *Diana di Chaverny* (dramma lirico), Sangiorgio, 1875; *La lega* (dramma lirico), G. Josse, 1876; *Mattia Corvino*, Pinsuti, 1877

Lina (rev. of F. Guidi: La Savoiarda), Ponchielli, 1877; *Raggio d'amore* (dramma lirico), G. Litta, 1879; *Elda* (dramma fantastico), Catalani, 1880; *Gabriella di belle isole*, P. Maggi, 1880; *Don Giovanni d'Austria* (dramma lirico), Marchetti, 1880; *Sardanapolo* (opera-ballo), Libani, 1880; *Cordelia* (dramma lirico), Gobatti, 1881; *Ugo e Parisina*, G. B. Bergamini, 1881; *I Burgravi* (dramma lirico), A. Orsini, 1881; *Fernando de La Cruz*, M. Sansone, 1884; *Adelaide di Monferrato* (dramma lirico), L. Moroni, 1884; *Baldassare*, Villate, 1885; *Ines de Castro*, Villate, lost, ?unperf.; *Arminio* (dramma lirico), A. de Stefani, 1886; *Celeste*, D. Lamonaco and C. Biondi, 1892 JOHN BLACK

Dorn, Heinrich Ludwig Egmont (*b* Königsberg, 14 Nov 1804; *d* Berlin, 10 Jan 1892). German conductor, composer and journalist. He studied the piano, singing and composition in Königsberg and then moved to Berlin, where his first opera, *Rolands Knappen*, was produced successfully in 1826. He made his journalistic début around the same time as co-editor of the *Berliner allgemeine Musikzeitung*; among his writings is a defence of the beleaguered Gaspare Spontini. Over the next two decades he built a solid reputation as a conductor of opera, holding theatre posts at Königsberg (1828); Leipzig (1829–32), where he taught counterpoint to the young Schumann; Hamburg (1832); Riga (1834–43); and Cologne (1844–8). His most prestigious appointment (1849) was as co-conductor, with W. Taubert, of the Berlin Hofoper. After his retirement from that post in 1869, he remained active in Berlin for many years as a teacher and writer. Two of his sons, Alexander (1833–1901) and Otto (1848–1931), also made musical careers in Berlin.

In his later years Dorn was a particularly bitter critic of Wagner; his collected writings include negative reviews of *Tristan*, *Die Meistersinger* and the first Bayreuth festival. His enmity, reciprocated by Wagner, was partly personal. The two men had started out as friends, first in Leipzig, where Dorn conducted two of Wagner's student works, and later in Riga, where Wagner conducted Dorn's *Der Schöffe von Paris*. They then quarrelled over Wagner's dismissal from Riga, which Wagner believed Dorn had engineered. Nevertheless Dorn's friend Liszt persuaded him to conduct *Tannhäuser*, the first Wagner opera performed in Berlin, in 1855; and through much of his career Dorn seems to have been attracted by aspects of Wagner's style. His *Die Nibelungen* (1854), by far the most successful of his operas, even seeks to compete with Wagner: based on the medieval *Nibelungenlied*, a source approached by Wagner when sketching the *Ring* cycle, it uses an ambitious scheme of reminiscence motifs – which may also reflect the influence of Liszt, who conducted the opera's première at Weimar. Dorn's other operas are highly conservative, given equally to sentimentality and to light humour. They were overshadowed in popularity by his numerous collections of songs and salon pieces and by his patriotic choruses.

Rolands Knappen (komische Oper, 2, Dorn), Berlin, Königstädtisches, 15 July 1826, vs (Berlin, 1826)

Der Zauberer und das Ungetüm (melodrama, 3, Dorn and J. von Minutuoli), Berlin, 20 April 1827

Die Bettlerin (romantisch-komische Oper, 4, C. von Holtei), Königsberg, Stadt, 24 July 1828, vs (Leipzig, 1828)

Abu Kara (romantische Oper, 3, L. Bechstein), Leipzig, Stadt, 27 Sept 1831, vs (Leipzig, *c*1831)

Der Schöffe von Paris (komische Oper, 2, W. A. Wohlbrück), Riga, Stadt, 1 Nov 1838

Das Banner von England (romantische Oper, 4, K. Alt, after W. Scott), Riga, Stadt, 8 Nov 1841

Die Nibelungen (grosse romantische Oper, 5, E. Gerber, after the medieval saga), Weimar, Hof, 22 Jan 1854, vs (Berlin, 1854)

Ein Tag in Russland (komische Oper, 3, J. C. Grünebaum, after E. Scribe), Berlin, Hof, 19 Dec 1856

Gewitter bei Sonnenschein (Spl, 1, C. Nuitter), Dresden, 19 Sept 1865, vs (Berlin, 1866)

Der Botenläufer von Pirna (komische Oper, 3, M. Heydrich, after Mélesville [A.-H.-J. Duveyrier]), Mannheim, 3 Dec 1865, vs (Berlin, 1865)

Rosavra, unperf.; Artaxerxes, inc.; Das Schwanenmädchen, inc.

*

T. Kroyer: 'Die circumpolare Oper: zur Wagner geschichte', *JbMP 1919*, 16–33

H. Grohe: 'Heinrich Dorn: ein "Kollege" Richard Wagners', *NZM*, Jg.106 (1939), 706–8

A. Rauh: *Heinrich Dorn als Opernkomponist* (diss., U. of Munich, 1939)

A. P. Leverett: 'Liszt, Wagner, and Heinrich Dorn's *Die Nibelungen*', *COJ*, ii (1990), 121–44 ADELYN PECK LEVERETT

Dorset Garden Theatre. London theatre used in the 17th century for productions with music; *see* LONDON, §II, 2.

Dortmund. City in western Germany, in North Rhine-Westphalia. Its first operatic performances, *Die Zauberflöte* and operas by Dittersdorf, took place in September 1807 in the Gildenhaus, the 'National Theatre of the First Government'. After 1837 opera was performed in the Kühnscher Saal and from 1867 in the Gesellschaftscircus Carré, which was renovated four years later and opened on 28 September 1871 with *Der Freischütz*. A limited company was formed to maintain this theatre but was soon dissolved, and after 1875 theatrical performances resumed in the Kühnscher Saal. This burnt down in 1903, and the Theater am Hiltropwall opened with *Tannhäuser* on 17 September 1904; the Dortmund company cooperated with that in Essen until 1907. In 1925 Josef Krips became Kapellmeister, and around this time the company included Margarete Teschemacher and Karl Schmitt-Walter. The theatre was destroyed in an air raid on 6 October 1944. Postwar performances began in the main hall of the Pädagogische Akademie, but in 1948 it was decided to build a small theatre with the modest means available; the Kleines Haus (650 seats) opened on 12 November 1950 with *Fidelio*. The first plans for the building of the Grosses Haus were made in 1955, and the new theatre (1160 seats) opened on 3 March 1966 with *Der Rosenkavalier*. The leading performers were Elisabeth Grümmer, Kurt Böhme and Teresa Zylis-Gara, who, like Wolfgang Windgassen, started her career in Dortmund. The first Generalmusikdirektor was Wilhelm Schüchter (1966–74), who was succeeded by Marek Janowski, Hans Wallat and Klaus Weise. The season begins at the start of September and ends at the start of July, during which time there are usually five or six new opera productions. Notable recent events include the first performance in Germany of Petrassi's *Il cordovano* (1987) and a production of Rossini's seldom staged *La pietra del paragone* (1988).

*

A. Mämpel: *Das Dortmunder Theater* (Dortmund, 1935–6)

E. Elschner, ed.: *75 Jahre Theater in Dortmund 1904–1979* (Dortmund, 1979) SABINE SONNTAG

Dorus-Gras [née Van Steenkiste], **Julie(-Aimée-Josephe** [Joséphine]) (*b* Valenciennes, ?7 Sept 1805; *d* Paris, 9

Julie Dorus-Gras as Marguerite de Valois, the role she created in Meyerbeer's 'Les Huguenots' at the Paris Opéra, 29 February 1836: artist unknown (c1836)

Feb 1896). South Netherlands soprano. She studied at the Paris Conservatoire and made her début at the Théâtre de la Monnaie, Brussels, in 1825. She sang Elvire at the first Brussels performance of Auber's *La muette de Portici* (1829) and also took part in the historic performance of that opera in 1830 that sparked off the Belgian revolution. She was engaged at the Paris Opéra in 1831, making her début as Adèle (*Le comte Ory*) and during the next 15 years created many roles there, including Alice in *Robert le diable* (1831), Prince Eudoxie in *La Juive* (1835), Marguerite de Valois in *Les Huguenots* (1836) and Teresa in *Benvenuto Cellini* (1838). In 1847 she sang the title role of *Lucia di Lammermoor* in English at Drury Lane, with Berlioz conducting. In 1849, when she sang at Covent Garden in three of her most famous roles, Elvire, Alice and Marguerite de Valois, she was still, according to Chorley, 'an excellent artist, with a combined firmness and volubility of execution which have not been exceeded, and were especially welcome in French music'. She was not a particularly convincing actress, but the accuracy of her singing and the brilliance of her voice ensured her success.

*

T. Gautier: *L'histoire de l'art dramatique en France depuis vingt-cinq ans* (Paris, 1858–9)
H. F. Chorley: *Thirty Years' Musical Recollections* (London, 1862)
G. Chouquet: *Histoire de la musique dramatique en France depuis ses origines jusqu'à nos jours* (Paris, 1873)
S. Wolff: *L'Opéra au Palais Garnier (1875–1962)* (Paris, 1962)

ELIZABETH FORBES

Dostoyevsky, Fyodor Mikhaylovich (*b* Moscow, 30 Oct/11 Nov 1821; *d* St Petersburg, 28 Jan/9 Feb 1881). Russian novelist. A doctor's son, he first worked as a military engineer. In 1849 he was arrested for his participation in the Petrashevsky Circle, a socialist group, was condemned to death, reprieved at the last minute and exiled to Siberia; his experiences there led him towards a more fervent embrace of Orthodox Christianity. In 1859 he returned to St Petersburg and pursued a literary career, its furious pace driven by debts arising from compulsive gambling.

Considering his huge reputation and wide influence, it is at first surprising how little Dostoyevsky's work is reflected in Russian or Soviet opera. Yet reasons are easily surmised. Until the very late 19th century, novels were not normally considered suitable for operatic (or even dramatic) adaptation; and since the Revolution, Dostoyevsky, who was in his maturity a politically conservative thinker, has enjoyed an equivocal reputation in his homeland. The writer's own musical interests and predilections have been investigated by Gozenpud (1981).

As a central member in the 1860s of the literary circle known as the *pochvenniki* ('men of the soil'), Dostoyevsky was personally acquainted with the critic and composer Alexander Serov, who frequented their gatherings on account of his close friendship with the poet Appolon Grigor'yev. Dostoyevsky paid social calls on Serov as well, at one of which (1864) he met Tchaikovsky, then still a conservatory student, who remembered the great writer as one who spoke of music 'as a true littérateur, with neither musical education nor a natural ear'. As editor of the journals *Vremya* ('Time') and *Epokha* ('The Epoch'), Dostoyevsky published several of Serov's critical articles and is thought to have contributed to the scenario of his opera *Rogneda*, which reflects ideas on pacific Christianity that are close to those Dostoyevsky espoused.

The earliest opera to be based even indirectly on Dostoyevsky's fiction was *Yolka* ('The Christmas Party') by Vladimir Rebikov (1903, Moscow), to a libretto by S. Plaksin that conflates motifs from Dostoyevsky's story *The Boy at Christ's Christmas Party* (1876) with others from Andersen (*The Little Match Girl*) and Gerhart Hauptmann (*Hanneles Himmelfahrt*). In the years immediately preceding the Revolution, Nikolay Myaskovsky planned an opera on *The Idiot* (1869), for which Pyotr (later Pierre) Suvchinsky prepared a libretto in 1916, but he did not write it (or any opera). The same year, Prokofiev completed his opera *The Gambler*, after Dostoyevsky's grimly comic novella of social humiliation (1866). A difficult essay in avowedly anti-lyrical declamation 'à la Musorgsky', it was not produced until 1929, in Brussels. Soviet operas based on Dostoyevsky include Mikhail Tsvetayev's *Belïye nochi* ('White Nights', 1933), after the 1848 short story; Bogdanov-Berezovsky's *Nastas'ya Filippovna* (1964), after *The Idiot*; Butsko's *Belïye nochi* (1974); and Gleb Sedel'nikov's *Bednïye lyudi* ('Poor Folk', 1974), after Dostoyevsky's first novel.

Mahler's oft-cited remark – that for composers of the younger generation reading Dostoyevsky was more important than studying counterpoint – testifies to the writer's impact as a cultural phenomenon; but even in the West, musical dramatizations of his works have been rare and relatively insignificant. Pre-eminent is Janáček's *From the House of the Dead* (1930), after the novel in which Dostoyevsky memorialized his own Siberian imprisonment (1862). Another Czech composer, Otakar Jeremiáš, based an opera on *The Brothers Karamazov* (1880), as did the Dutchmen Daniel Ruyneman and Paul Coenen; Renzo Rossellini's *La leggenda del ritorno* is more freely based on the

Grand Inquisitor chapter in the novel. *Verlobung in Traum* (1933), by the German-speaking Prague composer Hans Krása, was an adaptation of Dostoyevsky's novella *Uncle's Dream* (1859). *Crime and Punishment* (1866) has been the basis for operas by Arrigo Pedrollo, Heinrich Sutermeister and Emil Petrovics, the last a monodrama. In *L'idiota* Luciano Chailly managed to reduce Dostoyevsky's visionary novel of perdition and expiation to a love triangle. *Myshkin*, an opera on the same subject by the American composer John Eaton, had its first showing on New York public television in 1973. Karel Kupka's adaptation of the novel (1962) has never been staged.

The fantastic tale *The Crocodile* (1865) has been used by Thomas Wagner and Valentino Bucchi. The story *A Gentle Creature* (1876) was turned into a chamber opera by John Tavener (1977). Most recently the early novella *The Double* (1846) has been adapted by Jan Klusák and again by Flavio Testi.

Dvoynik [The Double] (novella, 1846): J. Klusák; F. Testi, 1981, as Il sosia

Belïye nochi [White Nights] (short story, 1848): M. Tsvetayev, 1933; L. Cortese, 1973, as Le notti bianche; Yu. M. Butsko, 1973; S. Rajičić, 1985, as Bele noći; F. Mannino, 1989, as Le notti bianchi

Bednïye lyudi [Poor Folk] (novel, 1849): G. Sedel'nikov, 1974

Dyadyushkin son [Uncle's Dream] (novella, 1859): H. Krása, 1933, as Verlobung in Traum

Zapiski iz myortvogo doma [Notes from the House of the Dead] (novel, 1862): Janáček, 1930, as Z mrtvého domu [From the House of the Dead]

Igrok [The Gambler] (novella, 1866): Prokofiev, 1929

Prestupleniye i nakazaniye [Crime and Punishment] (novel, 1866): A. Pedrollo, 1926, as Delitto e castigo; H. Sutermeister, 1948, as Raskolnikoff; E. Petrovics, 1970, as Bün és bünhödés

Idiot [The Idiot] (novel, 1869): K. Kupka, 1962, unperf.; V. M. Bogdanov-Berezovsky, 1964, as Nastas'ya Filippovna; L. Chailly, 1970, as L'idiota; J. C. Eaton, 1973, as Myshkin; M. S. Vaynberg, 1986

Krokodil [The Crocodile] (fantastic tale, 1865): T. Wagner, 1963; V. Bucchi, 1970, as Il coccodrillo

Krotkaya [A Gentle Creature] (short story, 1876): J. Tavener, 1977, as A Gentle Spirit

Mal'chik u Khrista na yolke [The Boy at Christ's Christmas Party] (short story, 1876): V. I. Rebikov, 1903, as Yolka [The Christmas Party]

Brat'ya Karamazovï [The Brothers Karamazov] (novel, 1880): O. Jeremiáš, 1928, as Bratři Karamazovi; D. Ruyneman, 1928, as De gebroeders Karamasoff; P. Coenen, 1945, as Die Karamazows; R. Rossellini, 1966, as La leggenda del ritorno; A. N. Kholminov, 1985

*

V. Karatïgin: 'Dostoyevsky i muzïka', *Zhizn' iskusstva* (15 and 29 Nov, 13 Dec 1921); repr. in *Izbrannïye stat'i*, ed. Yu. A. Kremlyov (Moscow and Leningrad, 1965), 251–62

A. Gozenpud: *Dostoyevsky i muzïkal'no-teatral'noye iskusstvo* (Leningrad, 1981)

H. Robinson: 'Dostoevsky and Opera: Prokofiev's *The Gambler*', *MQ*, lxx (1984), 96–106

B. Shteynpress: 'Russkaya literatura v zarubezhnoy opere' [Russian Literature in Foreign Operas], *SovM* (1986), no.6, pp.93–6

RICHARD TARUSKIN

Dotti, Anna Vincenza (*b* Bologna; *fl* 1715–27). Italian contralto. In 1715 she sang at Livorno in Bononcini's *Camilla*; in 1715–16 she appeared in Florence and in 1716 at Bologna, Reggio Emilia and in Venice, where she sang in three operas, of which two were by Vivaldi. Between 1717 and 1720 she sang in nine operas in Naples, including the version of Handel's *Rinaldo* with additions by Leo at the royal palace in 1718, in which she was Almirena. From autumn 1724 she was for three seasons a member of the Royal Academy company in London as second woman to Cuzzoni, singing in Handel operas, Ariosti's *Artaserse*, *Dario* and *Lucio Vero*, Bononcini's *Astianatte* and the pasticcios *Elpidia* and *Elisa*. She created Irene in *Tamerlano* (1724) and Eduige in *Rodelinda* (1725), and appeared in revivals of *Giulio Cesare*, *Ottone* and probably *Floridante*. After Bordoni's arrival in spring 1726 Dotti was allotted less important parts; Handel gave her only one aria in *Alessandro* and *Admeto*, in both of which (as on other occasions) she played male roles. On leaving London she enjoyed considerable success at Brussels (autumn 1727). Her compass was narrow (*a* to *e''*), and her lower notes evidently weak. She is sometimes confused with Anna Maria Dotti, who sang in two operas at Venice in 1708. One of the two sang in Lotti's *Teuzzone* at Bologna in November 1711.

WINTON DEAN

Double bill. There is a long theatrical tradition of performing more than a single work in an evening; usually, in the 18th century, this would consist of a serious opera with an intermezzo or a ballet, or a mainpiece with an AFTERPIECE. The term properly refers, nowadays, to a performance of two short, usually one-act, operas together. The most popular double bill is *Cavalleria rusticana* and *Pagliacci* ('Cav and Pag'); others have included the two Ravel operas, *L'enfant et les sortilèges* and *L'heure espagnole*, and various pairs of one-act works, among them Schoenberg's *Erwartung*, Bartók's *Bluebeard's Castle*, Stravinsky's *The Nightingale* and his *Oedipus rex*, and operas from Puccini's *Il trittico*, originally composed as a triple bill but generally thought too long to be performed complete. Pergolesi's *La serva padrona*, originally composed as a pair of intermezzos for performance in a serious opera, is also a favourite for inclusion in double bills. A historic example is the performance of Mozart's *Der Schauspieldirektor* and Salieri's *Prima la musica, dopo le parole* in 1786 at opposite ends of the orangery at Schönbrunn Palace, Vienna; in the interval all the chairs were turned round.

Doubrava, Jaroslav (*b* Chrudim, 25 April 1909; *d* Prague, 2 Oct 1960). Czech composer. He studied composition privately with Otakar Jeremiáš from 1931 to 1937. Between 1945 and 1955 he worked for Czech Radio in various capacities including as head of music. Symphonic and stage works make up the bulk of his comparatively small output (as well as the operas, his three completed ballets are regularly performed). His polyphonic style owes much to that of Novák and Ostrčil, and the operas are characterized by a fastidiously crafted inventiveness of expression. His first opera was the three-act *Sen noci svatojanské* ('A Midsummer Night's Dream'), composed in the 1940s but not performed until 1969; it was followed by *Křest svatého Vladimíra* ('The Conversion of St Vladimir') and *Líný Honza* ('Lazy Honza'), both unfinished. Doubrava's Shakespeare treatment emphasizes the theme of romantic love in ariosos and dance scenes (the last three scenes of the play are omitted, and the opera begins with the scene of the rude mechanicals). The work was prepared for performance by Jiří Jaroch. Doubrava's masterpiece is the *Balada o lásce* ('Ballad of Love'), also known as *Láska čarovaná* ('Love Bewitched'), whose inspiration in folklore represented a new direction in his work. Its simple, essentially epic tale of the love of a country girl for a devil-may-care soldier grows out of the spirit of folk imagery and relies heavily on the chorus. The musical tableaux have a natural picturesque quality (refined in the act of composition), and their effect is deeply moving. The resulting work is a humanistic protest against war.

Sen noci svatojanské [A Midsummer Night's Dream], 1942–9 (op, 3, Doubrava and R. Vonásek, after W. Shakespeare), Opava, Nejedlý, 21 Dec 1969
Křest svatého Vladimíra [The Conversion of St Vladimir], 1949–50, inc. (op, 3, Doubrava, after K. Havlíček Borovský), unperf.
Líný Honza [Lazy Honza], 1952, inc. (op, 1, Vonásek and Doubrava, after J. Lada), unperf.
Balada o lásce [Ballad of Love]/Láska čarovaná [Love Bewitched], 1960 (opera-ballad, 3, J. Wenig and Doubrava, after Z. Winter), Prague, Smetana, 21 June 1962 [orchd J. Hanuš]

*

J. Hanuš: 'Profil jevištního díla Jaroslava Doubravy' [Profile of Doubrava's Stage Works], *HRo*, xiv (1961), 771–3
L. Šip: *Česká opera a její tvůrči* [Czech Opera and its Creators] (Prague, 1983), 265–8
HELENA HAVLÍKOVÁ

Douglas, Clive (Martin) (*b* Rushworth, Victoria, 27 July 1903; *d* Melbourne, 29 April 1977). Australian composer. He studied composition with A. E. H. Nickson at the Melbourne University Conservatorium (MusB 1934, MusDoc 1958). His compositional preference for orchestral music and opera reflected his long association with the Australian Broadcasting Commission as resident staff conductor (Tasmania, 1936–41; Brisbane, 1941–7; Sydney, 1947–53; Melbourne, 1953–66); he was awarded many prizes and commissions by the ABC and the Australasian Performing Rights Association. Among his works are four dramatic pieces for which he also wrote the texts and 24 documentary film scores. All reflect his conscious search for a truly Australian form of musical expression, either through the programmatic use of Aboriginal myth and legend or by the grafting of Aboriginal melodic and rhythmic material on to an essentially European style.

all to librettos by the composer; autograph MSS in AUS-Msl

The Scarlet Letter op.1, 1925–9 (after N. Hawthorne), inc., unperf.
Ashmadai op.12, 1929, 1934–5 (operetta, 1, after Byron: *Heaven and Earth*), private perf., 21 Sept 1935; broadcast, Melbourne, 17 Aug 1936
Bush Legend [Kaditcha] op.19 (operetta, 3 scenes), ABC Tasmania, 22 June 1938
Eleanor, Maid Rosamund and Henry of Anjou opp. 26–8, 1941–2 (lyric drama, 3), ABC Brisbane, 6 Jan 1943 [Act 1 only]

*

R. Covell: *Australia's Music* (Melbourne, 1967), 149–52, 261
A. D. McCredie: *Musical Composition in Australia* (Canberra, 1969), 10
G. Howard: 'Clive Douglas', *Australian Composition in the Twentieth Century*, ed. F. Callaway and D. Tunley (Melbourne, 1978), 37–43
KAY DREYFUS

Douglas, Nigel [Leigh Pemberton, Nigel Douglas] (*b* Lenham, Kent, 9 May 1929). English tenor. He studied in Vienna with Alfred Piccaver, making his début in 1959 at the Kammeroper as Rodolfo (*La bohème*), then singing at the Volksoper. Later he created L'Heureux in Sutermeister's *Madame Bovary* (1967, Zürich), Philip in Gardner's *The Visitors* (1972, Aldeburgh) and Basil in Mathias's *The Servants* for the WNO (1980), with which he also sang Alwa (*Lulu*), the Captain (*Wozzeck*), Loge and Herod. With the ENO he sang the Devil in Rimsky-Korsakov's *Christmas Eve* (1988) and the Earl of Kent in Reimann's *Lear* (1989), both first British stage productions. A noted exponent of Britten's operas, he has sung Peter Grimes, Vere, Aschenbach and Lechmere (*Owen Wingrave*), which he created both on BBC Television (1971) and at Covent Garden (1973), where he sang Herod in 1988. He also sings, translates and directs operetta. The dryness of his voice is offset by superb diction and the excellence of his acting.

ELIZABETH FORBES

Dourian, Ohan (*b* Jerusalem, 8 Sept 1922). Armenian conductor. In 1945 he graduated from the Jerusalem Conservatory, where he studied conducting with Walter Pfeffer and composition with Josef Grinthal; he then moved to Paris, where he continued his studies with Roger Désormière and Jean-Louis Martinet. In 1957 he became chief conductor of the Armenian PO in Erevan. In 1966 he was appointed director of the Armenian Television and Radio SO, simultaneously working at the Leipzig Opera. After serving as the director of the Spendiaryan Theatre, Erevan (1971–4), he moved to Marseilles. He has appeared as a guest conductor in Munich, Vienna, Amsterdam, the USA and South Africa. In September 1991 he again became music director of the Spendiaryan Theatre in Erevan.

Dourian's conducting, in the Romantic tradition, has been widely recognized for its strictness of conception and balance of form; his artistic temperament has led critics to compare him to Toscanini and Stokowski. He is noted for his interpretations of operas by Mozart, Verdi, Wagner, Gounod, Borodin, Puccini and contemporary composers. Dourian has also composed choral and symphonic works, many of which are based on national musical themes.

*

S. Sarkisyan: 'Ōperayi problemnerê aysor' [The Problems of Opera Today], *Sovetakan arvest* (1971), no.9, pp.16–19
SVETLANA SARKISYAN

Dourlen, Victor-Charles-Paul (*b* Dunkirk, 3 Nov 1780; *d* Batignolles, Paris, 8 Jan 1864). French composer. He studied at the Paris Conservatoire and in 1805 won the Prix de Rome with the cantata *Cupidon pleurant Psyché*. His comic opera *Philoclès*, performed in 1806 before his departure for Italy, gave further evidence of early mastery. The works he wrote as a student in Rome were well received, and at the same time he apparently also produced stage works for Paris. From 1812 he taught at the Conservatoire. Dourlen's compositions include songs and instrumental music. Of his operas, only *Le frère Philippe* had any success. It is a semi-farcical version of the old fable of the misogynist who has brought up his son in ignorance of women. The music is discreet and varied, with a sprinkling of Italianisms. It is fully within the early 19th-century *opéra comique* idiom. The music and librettos of most of Dourlen's stage works are lost.

all first performed in Paris, at the Opéra-Comique (Théâtre Feydeau) unless otherwise stated

Philoclès (2, J. Gensoul), 4 Oct 1806
Linnée, ou La mine de Suède (oc, 3, J. C. B. Dejaure), 10 Sept 1808
La dupe de son art, ou Les deux amants (oc, 1, L.-C. Sapey), 9 Sept 1809
Cagliostro, ou Les illuminés [Act 1] (oc, 3, J. A. de Réveroni de Saint-Cyr and E. Mercier-Dupaty), 27 Nov 1810, frags., sketches *F-Pc** [Acts 2 and 3 by A. Reicha]
Plus heureux que sage (oc, 1, Mézès), 25 May 1816
Le frère Philippe (oc, prol., 1, A. Duport), 20 Jan 1818 (Paris, 1818)
Marini, ou Le muet de Venise (oc, 3, E.-J.-B. Delrieu), 12 June 1819
La vente après décès (oc, 1, C.-G. Etienne), Gymnase-Dramatique, 1 Aug 1821
Le petit souper (1, J. B. R. B. V. d'Epagny), 22 Feb 1822

DAVID CHARLTON

Douthitt, Wilfried. *See* GRAVEURE, LOUIS.

Dow, Dorothy (*b* Houston, 8 Oct 1920). American soprano. She studied at the Juilliard School, making her début in 1946 at Buffalo as Santuzza. In 1947 she created Susan B. Anthony in Virgil Thomson's *The Mother of Us All* at Columbia University. Engaged at Zürich (1948–50), she sang Elisabeth (*Tannhäuser*) at La Scala (1950), returning for Marie (*Wozzeck*), La Gioconda, Chrysothemis, Danae and Walton's Cressida. She sang the woman in the American première of *Erwartung* (Washington, DC, 1951). At Glyndebourne she sang Lady Macbeth (1952) and Ariadne (1953). She sang Irmengard in Spontini's *Agnes von Hohenstaufen* at Florence (1954) and Renata in the first staged performance of Prokofiev's *The Fiery Angel* at Venice (1955). A most dramatic singer of imposing stage presence, she had an opulent voice that she used with great expressiveness. ELIZABETH FORBES

Dowd, (Eric) Ronald (*b* Sydney, 23 Feb 1914; *d* Sydney, 15 March 1990). Australian tenor. He made his début in 1948 at Perth as Hoffmann, then toured Australia, singing Lensky, Florestan, Alfredo, Cavaradossi, Lohengrin and other roles. In 1956 he joined Sadler's Wells, making his début as Canio, then sang Pinkerton, Oedipus, Peter Grimes, Tannhäuser, Idomeneus (which he also sang at Aix-en-Provence), Samson, the Witch (*Hänsel und Gretel*) and Jim Mahoney in the first British staging of *Aufstieg und Fall der Stadt Mahagonny* (1963). He made his Covent Garden début in 1960 as Walther, but could not finish the performance because of illness. Later he sang Peter Grimes, the Drum Major (*Wozzeck*), Canio, and Claudius in Searle's *Hamlet*, a role he created at the Hamburg Staatsoper (1968). He also created Mosbie in Goehr's *Arden must Die* (1969, Hamburg). He sang Aeneas in *Les Troyens* for Scottish Opera, at Covent Garden and in Boston. Returning to Sydney, he joined Australian Opera, singing Pierre in *War and Peace* at the opening of the new Sydney Opera House (1973) and Fatty in the Australian première of *Mahagonny* (1975). His virile, grainy tenor was used to expressive and dramatic effect as Peter Grimes and Aeneas, characters in the grip of an obsession.

ALAN BLYTH

Dowiakowska-Klimowiczowa, Bronisława (Apolonia Izabela) (*b* Warsaw, 9 Feb 1840; *d* Warsaw, 3 Feb 1910). Polish soprano. She studied with Quattrini and made her début in Warsaw on 20 April 1858 in Flotow's *Alessandro Stradella*, later singing in *Les Huguenots* and *Don Giovanni*. From 1859 she sang about a hundred roles in operas including all those of Moniuszko and others by Kurpiński, Auber, Hérold, Grossman, Bellini, Donizetti, Meyerbeer, Weber, Flotow, Halévy, Rossini, Marschner, Mozart, Verdi, Wagner and Bizet; she was the first Polish Marguerite in *Faust* (1865). Between 1873 and 1889 she made guest appearances in Lemberg (now L'viv), Kraków, Kiev, Odessa and Nice. Her compass was *a* to *e‴*, and to her brilliant technique was added notable clarity of enunciation. Her final appearance was as Mignon at the Warsaw Opera (2 September 1894).

*

J. Kleczyński: 'Bronisława Dowiakowska', *Echo muzyczne, teatralne i artystyczne*, xi (1894), 237–8 IRENA PONIATOWSKA

Downes, Sir Edward (Thomas) (*b* Birmingham, 17 June 1924). English conductor. He studied at Birmingham University and the RCM and conducted his first opera (*Le nozze di Figaro*) while a music lecturer at Aberdeen University. After further studies assisting Hermann Scherchen in Europe, he joined the Carl Rosa company, 1950–52, then Covent Garden in 1952 as répétiteur. His début there as a conductor was with *La bohème* in 1953, and the next year he drew attention with a new production of *Der Freischütz*. During 17 years on the music staff he conducted almost every work in the repertory, including the first Western production of Shostakovich's *Katerina Izmaylova* (1963), for which he translated the libretto. In 1966 he was named assistant to the musical director, Solti, and in 1967 he was the first British conductor to conduct a *Ring* cycle at Covent Garden since Beecham in 1939.

After conducting the first British staging of Searle's *Hamlet* (1969), Downes left staff work but continued to make frequent appearances, conducting the premières of Bennett's *Victory* in 1970 and Peter Maxwell Davies's *Taverner* in 1972. He then went to Sydney as music director of Australian Opera, 1972–6, where he conducted Prokofiev's *War and Peace* (in his own translation) as the official first operatic performance in the new Sydney Opera House (1973). He first appeared with the WNO in 1975 with *Der fliegende Holländer*, and in 1976 broadcast newly prepared versions of Wagner's *Rienzi*, *Die Feen* and *Das Liebesverbot* for the BBC. In 1977 he conducted 26 Wagner performances at the Paris Opéra, and the next year made his South American début in Buenos Aires at the Colón with *Don Giovanni*, followed by a tour conducting in various North American cities.

Downes undertook the completion of Prokofiev's unfinished opera *Maddalena*, of which he gave the première on BBC Radio in two performances, one in Russian, the other in his own translation (both 25 March 1979), and conducted the stage première at Graz two years later. The broadcast performances were with the BBC Northern Symphony (later BBC Philharmonic) Orchestra in Manchester, where he was principal conductor, 1980–91, and with which he also conducted radio broadcasts of Rimsky-Korsakov's *Legend of the Invisible City of Kitezh* (1986), *Christmas Eve* (1987), and in 1990 the first performance since the original one of Tchaikovsky's *Vakula the Smith* in its first (pre-*Cherevichki*) version, about which he wrote at length in *Opera* (xl, 1989, pp.1426–31). He has also made translations for *Jenůfa*, *Khovanshchina* and *The Nose*.

Not as ambitious as some, Downes took time to win eventual recognition as the foremost British conductor of Russian opera and of Verdi, especially the latter's early and middle-period works, combining detailed understanding of vocal technique with sensibility to musical line and texture. He was made a CBE in 1986 and knighted in 1991. That year he began his 40th consecutive season of Covent Garden performances as the newly appointed associate music director and principal conductor of the Royal Opera, appearing first in *Das Rheingold*. NOËL GOODWIN

Down in the Valley. Folk opera in one act by KURT WEILL to a libretto by Arnold Sundgaard; Bloomington, Indiana, School of Music, 15 July 1948.

The Leader (baritone) introduces the original folksong, 'Down in the Valley', accompanied by the chorus. The text of the song outlines the story: 'Brack Weaver ... died on the gallows one morning in May / He died for the love of sweet Jennie Parsons / He died for the slaying of Thomas Bouché / He broke loose from jail down at

Birmingham City / To spend his last hours with Jennie near home.' Brack's escape and flight to Jennie (lyric soprano) begin the action. As Brack (tenor or high baritone) reminisces, there is a flashback to the scene of his crime. Brack is jealous of Thomas Bouché (bass), who also has eyes for Jennie, and of whom her father approves for selfish business reasons. At the village dance, Bouché drunkenly pursues Jennie, fights with Brack, and is stabbed to death with his own knife. The scene shifts forward again to Brack and Jennie's brief reunion and finally to Brack's prison cell before his execution. The chorus concludes as it began.

Down in the Valley was initially conceived and recorded in 1945 as the model for a series of short radio operas. The series never materialized, however, because of the timidity of potential sponsors. In April 1948 Weill reworked the piece as a 'folk opera', transforming most of the spoken dialogue into recitative and melodrama. Like *Der Jasager*, it is intended for non-professional groups, requiring only simple staging, if any. 'It can be performed', Weill wrote in the preface to the vocal score, 'wherever a chorus, a few singers, and a few actors are available. In colleges and universities it should be produced through the combined efforts of both the drama and music departments.' Its eight scenes are through-composed, constituting in effect an expanded rondo which intersperses folksongs as set pieces ('Hop Up, my Ladies', 'Sourwood Mountain', and 'The Little Black Train'). 'The Lonesome Dove' is used twice, at the end of the first part and just before the final scene. As the original radio project had intended, the story is generated from a single folksong, 'Down in the Valley', which is used 19 times. The disjunction between the simplicity of the melodic material and the refinement of its compositional working is striking: Weill draws on an array of compositional idioms and techniques to vary each repetition of the principal tune in accordance with the requirements of the drama. The work's impact has been considerable. A notable instance of its influence is Copland's *The Tender Land*, which similarly transforms borrowed material. In its first nine years *Down in the Valley* is reported to have received more than 1600 productions and some 6000 performances, making it, after *Die Dreigroschenoper*, Weill's most frequently performed work. STEPHEN HINTON

D'Oyly Carte, Richard. *See* CARTE, RICHARD D'OYLY.

D'Oyly Carte Opera Company. The management, from 1879, under which the Gilbert and Sullivan operettas were presented in London and on tour by Richard D'Oyly Carte and his successors; *see* LONDON, §II, 1.

Draeseke, Felix (August Bernhard) (*b* Coburg, 7 Oct 1835; *d* Dresden, 26 Feb 1913). German composer. He entered the Leipzig Conservatory and studied composition with Julius Rietz. He wrote his own librettos, and also contributed to the *Neue Zeitschrift für Musik*, praising radical trends. After hearing *Lohengrin* at Weimar he wrote *König Sigurd* (1853–7), hailed by Liszt, whom he met in 1857, as 'a monumental work'; a Weimar production was planned but was cancelled when Liszt resigned in 1858. Wagner's *Tristan* prelude made an impression on Draeseke, who paid Wagner a lengthy visit in Lucerne (Wagner referred to him as 'a very gifted and not uncultured musician'). In 1862 Draeseke settled in Switzerland and taught at the Lausanne Conservatory (1864–74), with an interruption to direct the Munich Conservatory (1868–9) at von Bülow's invitation. During his years in Switzerland he abandoned much of his experimental, programmatic style in favour of classical forms and contrapuntal skills. He also suffered personal setbacks: an impairment of hearing (by 1865), a broken marriage engagement (1870), depression over his neglect as a composer and failure to secure a professorship at the Geneva Conservatory (1875). But with a legacy from his grandfather he returned to Germany in 1876 and composed prolifically.

Herrat (1877–9) was performed at Dresden in 1892 and was successfully revived there (1905) and at Coburg (1906). *Gudrun* (1879–84) was intended as the 'feminine' counterpart to the virtues of manliness and steadfast loyalty celebrated in *Herrat*. Another stage work of that time was a 'folk tale with music', *Der Waldschatzhauser* (1876–82). After a second period of deep depression, in 1894 he married a woman 24 years his junior; new-found happiness led to creative rejuvenation and completion of his largest work, *Christus* (planned 1864 and composed 1895–9), a prelude and trilogy of oratorios which he intended as an equivalent of Wagner's *Ring* cycle. The only subsequent stage work he saw performed was the comic opera *Fischer und Kalif* (1894–5), given at Prague in 1905. He returned to mythical opera with *Merlin* (1900–05), but died ten weeks before its première.

Draeseke's transition from Wagnerian radical to turn-of-the-century conservative is neatly illustrated in his pamphlet *Die Konfusion in der Musik* (1906), which attacks modern trends, notably the style of Richard Strauss. Virtually unknown outside Germany, his music was rarely performed, except for a few revivals around the centenary of his birth. However, a Draeseke Society was founded in Germany in the 1980s.

librettos by the composer

König Sigurd, 1853–7 (3, after E. Geibel: *Sigurd*), frag. perf. Meiningen, 1867
Herrat, 1877–9 (3), Dresden, 10 March 1892, vs (1893)
Gudrun, 1879–84 (3), Hanover, 11 Jan 1884, vs (Leipzig, 1885)
Bertran de Born, 1892–4, unperf.
Fischer und Kalif, 1894–5 (2), Prague, 15 April 1905
Merlin, 1900–05 (3, after K. L. Immermann: *Mythe*), Gotha, 10 May 1913, vs (1910)

*

MGG (H. Stephani)
O. zur Nedden: *Felix Draesekes Opern und Oratorien* (diss., U. of Marburg, 1925)
E. Roeder: *Felix Draeseke* (Dresden and Berlin, 1932–7)
Festschrift Felix-Draeseke-Feier der Landeshauptstadt Dresden (Dresden, 1935)
H. Stephani: 'Felix Draeseke: 1835–1913', *ZMw*, xvii (1935), 426–8
DEREK WATSON

Draghi, Antonio (*b* Rimini, *c*1634; *d* Vienna, 16 Jan 1700). Italian composer and librettist. Nothing is known of his life before Carnival 1657, when he took part in the Venetian performance of P. A. Ziani's opera *Le fortune di Rodope e di Damira* as a bass singer. He joined the newly founded Kapelle of the Empress Dowager Eleonora in Vienna in late 1657 or 1658 as one of 24 members who were especially important in the expanding operatic life of the imperial court. By 1661, the year of his marriage, he had begun writing librettos for operas commissioned by Eleonora each year for the birthday of her stepson, Emperor Leopold I. Their music was provided by her *maestri di cappella*, first Giuseppe Tricarico and after 1663 his successor P. A. Ziani (the latter had been engaged after the empress had sent

Draghi to Venice to negotiate with him in 1662). Beginning in 1665 Draghi also received orders for texts for carnival operas, and from 1666 he even composed the music for some of them. By 1668 he was Eleonora's vice-*maestro di cappella*, and between April and June 1669 he succeeded Ziani as full *maestro di cappella*, in preference to Legrenzi who had also been recommended. In promoting him, the empress was prompted by members of the imperial court as well as by her own knowledge of his merits and musical experience. He held this position until the end of 1681. In addition, in 1673 he was appointed *intendente delle musiche teatrali* to Leopold I, a post created seven years earlier for Antonio Cesti. Draghi deserved the title, having been entrusted since 1668 with the bulk of dramatic composition for both courts. On 1 January 1682 he reached the highest musical office in Austria, *maestro di cappella* of the imperial court, succeeding J. H. Schmelzer who had died of the plague in early 1680; he held the position until his death.

Draghi composed 118 operas and other secular stage works. Together with the court poet Nicolò Minato he provided most of the dramatic works, including *sepolcri* and oratorios, performed at the Habsburg court between 1668 and 1697; L. O. Burnacini was their theatre architect, stage and costume designer. This stable team guaranteed Leopold, for most of his reign, a steady series of opera productions without much change in style or quality. About half the secular stage works are three-act *drammi per musica*, which were mostly performed as carnival entertainments or on birthdays of the imperial family. The occasional works sometimes have prologues and always *licenze* as declarations of homage to the person honoured; almost all are furnished with ballets by J. H. or A. A. Schmelzer after each act. The other half of the operas are in only one act and bear various designations: a *festa teatrale* or *festa musicale* was usually given on the empress's birthday or name-day, an *introduzione per un balletto* on name-days, and a *trattenimento per musica* during Carnival. It is noteworthy that, owing to the war with the Turks and other political difficulties, Draghi's output between the carnivals of 1682 and 1692 consisted almost exclusively of one-act stage pieces and chamber works. The dramatic works for the chamber, usually performed without stage designs and costumes, have texts that are almost always mythological or allegorical; they bear designations including serenata, (*compositione per*) *musica da camera*, *introduzione per un balletto* and *trattenimento per musica*. They differ from the operas in that arias are at least as frequent as recitatives and are all in two strophes, separated by a ritornello usually for two violins and continuo (from 1685 also including a viola). Some of the open-air serenatas have unusually full instrumental accompaniment.

Draghi's arias often contain long virtuoso coloratura passages. The aria structure most often found in the early operas and chamber works is *ABB* (or a variant thereof); later the composer began to use da capo structure – sometimes varied, sometimes with a coda – and then to enlarge the first section and increase contrast between the two sections. In the late operas he introduced accompaniment by solo instrument or unusual combinations such as lute and three shawms (*La chioma di Berenice*, 1695 version); his later recitative tends towards smaller note values and more formulaic cadences, the vocal part falling a 4th or 3rd and the continuo finishing alone. In contrast to contemporary operas in Italy there are no strict ostinatos; only in *Chi più sa manco l'intende* (1669) and in the late operas are there rare *bassi quasi ostinati*. Laments are usually accompanied by violas.

Draghi wrote many elaborate ensembles, mostly duets, but also larger ones up to quintets, and some choruses in four or eight parts. In many of his operas there are single arias or scenes composed by Emperor LEOPOLD I, and in some of his late works, including the operas *L'Arsace* and *La forza dell'amor filiale* (both 1698) and the revival of *Sulpitia* in 1697, several arias were written by Carlo Domenico Draghi (1669–1711), Antonio's son, who held the post of imperial organist.

Domenico Federici, an Austrian librettist resident in Venice, remarked in a letter of 1670 to Leopold I that he thought Draghi the best *maestro di cappella* and a better

'Il fuoco eterno custodito dalle Vestali' (Antonio Draghi), Act 1 scenes xvii–xix (street in Rome at an embarkation point on the Tiber), first performed at the Hoftheater auf der Cortina, Vienna, 30 October 1674: engraving by M. Küsel after a design by Ludovico Burnacini

composer than Cavalli, Ziani and Legrenzi; even singers then in Vienna, he said, had written to their friends that they had never sung in Italy melodies as pure and noble as his (Dottori, ed. Cerboni Baiardi 1971); this might have been mere flattery, however. As a librettist, Draghi avoided historical plots, and in his first works invented new ones. His carnival operas *La mascherata* and *Comedia ridicula* included much criticism and satire and were the first thoroughly comic operas performed in Vienna; his serious librettos have comic scenes at the ends of the acts. Count Carlo de' Dottori, a poet himself, wrote in 1667 that Draghi had talent as a librettist and handled the stage well, but that he lacked certain skills and his verses jumped like an acrobat. Besides secular music, Draghi composed 41 sacred dramatic works (oratorios and *sepolcri*) and in his early years in Vienna wrote the librettos for four such pieces. His non-dramatic compositions consist of a few cantatas, including some for academy sessions, two masses, a *Stabat mater* and several smaller sacred works.

unless otherwise stated, librettos by N. Minato, works performed in Vienna, Hofburg, and MSS in A-Wn

dm – *dramma per musica*

La mascherata (compositione drammatica, 3, Draghi), Kleines Hof, 1 or 4 March 1666, Act 3 lost, 5 numbers ed. in Neuhaus, contribs. Leopold I

Vero amor fà soave ogni fatica (introduzione a un ballo, 1, Draghi), 6 Feb 1667, music lost, lib. *Wn*

Comedia ridicula (3, librettist not known), 11 or 13 Feb 1668, Act 3 lost

Gl'amori di Cefalo e Procri (rappresentazione drammatica, 1, Draghi), 9 June 1668

Achille riconosciuto (introduzione di un balletto, 1, F. Ximenes), Favorita, ? 12 June 1668, music lost, lib. *Wn*

Il Ciro vendicatore di se stesso (dm, 1, Ximenes), Amalienburg, 18 Nov 1668, pt 1 lost

Chi più sa manco l'intende, overo Gli amori di Clodio, e Pompea (dm, 3, Ximenes), Emperor's rooms, 21 Feb 1669, contribs. Leopold I

Achille in Sciro (prol., 1, Ximenes), ?Favorita, ? 21 May 1669, 7 numbers ed. in Neuhaus

Il Perseo (drama musicale, 3, A. Amalteo), 15 July 1669, Act 2 lost

Atalanta (dm, 3), 18 Nov 1669, Acts 1 and 3 lost

Le risa di Democrito (trattenimento per musica, 3), 17 Feb 1670, *Wn* (1673 version), lib. *CS-Pu*, contribs. Leopold I

Leonida in Tegea (dm, prol., 3), 9 June 1670, Act 3 lost; arr. M. A. Ziani, Venice, S Moisè, 9 Feb 1676; with rev. of Act 3, 11 Feb 1694, facs. in IOB, lxiv (1982); contribs. Leopold I

Iphide Greca (dm, 3), 12 June 1670, music lost, lib. *A-Wgm*; ?rev. version, 12 Jan 1696, Act 1 lost; contribs. Leopold I

Penelope [La casta Penelope] (dm, 3), 18 Nov 1670

L'avidità di Mida (trattenimento per musica, 3), Ritterstube, 8 Feb 1671

La prosperità di Elia Sejano (dm, 3), 9 June 1671, contribs. Leopold I

La gara dei genii (festa teatrale, 1), 14 July 1671, contribs. Leopold I

Cidippe (dm, 3), 18 Nov 1671, Act 2 lost, contribs. Leopold I

Gl'atomi d'Epicuro (dm, prol., 3), 9 June 1672

Gundeberga (dm, 3), 12 July 1672, Acts 1 and 3 lost, contribs. Leopold I

Sulpitia (dm, 3), 21 Nov 1672, Act 1 lost, contribs. Leopold I; with addns by C. D. Draghi, 27 Nov 1697, Act 1 lost

Il gioir della speranza (introduzione ad un balletto, 1), Emperor's rooms, 9 Feb 1673

Batto convertito in sasso (musica di camera, 1), Favorita, 9 June 1673

Provare per non recitare (composizione per musica, 1), Favorita, 15 Oct 1673, music lost, lib. *I-Rvat*, *Vnm*

Gl'incantesimi disciolti (introduzione d'un balletto, 1), Karlau bei Graz, 17 Oct 1673, contribs. Leopold I

La Tessalonica (dm, 3), rooms of Archduchess Maria Anna, 18 Nov 1673, music lost, lib. *D-W*, *I-Vnm*

La lanterna di Diogene (dm, 3), 30 Jan 1674, Act 1 lost, contribs. Leopold I

Le staggioni ossequiose (introduzione d'un balletto, 1), Stallburg, 12 April 1674

Il ratto delle Sabine (dm, 3), Cortina, 9–10 June 1674, Act 1 lost, contribs. Leopold I

Il trionfatore de' centauri (festa musicale, 1), Schönbrunn, zoo, 13 Aug 1674

Il fuoco eterno custodito dalle Vestali (dm, 3), Cortina, 30 Oct 1674, contribs. Leopold I

La nascita di Minerva (festa musicale, 1), 18 Nov 1674, music lost, lib. *A-Wn*

I pazzi Abderiti (dm, 3), Emperor's rooms, 23 Feb 1675, contribs. Leopold I

Pirro (dm, 3), Laxenburg, zoo, 30 May 1675, Act 1 lost

Zaleuco [Seleuco] (dm, 3), ? 17 June 1675, music lost, lib. *Wn*

Turia Lucretia (dm, 3), 18 Nov 1675, Act 3 lost

Sciegliere non potendo adoprare (prol., 1), 18 Nov 1676

Hercole acquistatore dell'immortalità (dm, 3), Linz, Landhaus, 7 Jan 1677

Chilonida (dm, 3), hall of Archduchess Maria Anna, 20 Feb 1677, contribs. Leopold I

Il silentio di Harpocrate (dm, 3), 27 Feb 1677, music lost, lib. *Wn*; ?rev. version, 22 Nov 1688, Act 3 lost

Adriano sul Monte Casio (dm, 3), 27 June 1677, contribs. Leopold I

Le maghe di Tessaglia (festa musicale, 1), Schönbrunn, park, 22 July 1677

Rodogone (dm, 3), Amalienburg, 18 Nov 1677, Act 2 lost

La fortuna delle corti (introduzione d'un balletto, 1, librettist not known), Stallburg, 1677

La conquista del vello d'oro (festa teatrale, 3), Wiener Neustadt, palace great hall, 8 Feb 1678, Act 1 lost

Leucippe Phestia (dm, 3), 14 June 1678, contribs. Leopold I

Il tempio di Diana in Taurica (festa musicale, 1), Schönbrunn, park, 1 Sept 1678

La monarchia latina trionfante (festa musicale, 1), Cortina, 8 Oct 1678, music lost, lib. *Wn*

Enea in Italia (dm, 3), Wiener Neustadt, palace great hall, 29 Oct 1678, Act 2 lost, contribs. Leopold I

Li favoriti dalla fortuna (festa musicale, 1), 22 Nov 1678

Baldracca (dm, 3), 22 Jan 1679, Act 1 lost

L'ossequio di Flora (introduzione a un balletto di giardinieri, 1), carn. 1679

La svogliata (trattenimento musicale, 1), carn. 1679

Curzio (dm, 3), intended for 10 Aug 1679, Acts 2 and 3 lost, contribs. Leopold I

I vaticini di Tiresia Tebano (festa musicale, 1), Prague, royal ballroom, 11 Jan 1680, contribs. Leopold I

La patienza di Socrate con due mogli (scherzo dramatico per musica, 3), Prague, royal ballroom, 29 Feb 1680, 1 scene ed. in GMB, contribs. Leopold I

La forza dell'amicitia (dm, 3), Linz, palace, 13 Feb 1681, Act 1 lost; ?rev. version, 13 Jan 1694, lost, lib. *Wn*

Temistocle in Persia (dm, 3), Wiener Neustadt, 30 June 1681, Acts 1 and 3 lost, contribs. Leopold I

La rivalità nell'ossequio (trattenimento musicale, 1), Schloss Frohsdorf, park, 22 July 1681, music lost, lib. *Wn*

Achille in Tessaglia (trattenimento musicale, 1, librettist not known), Mannersdorf, 26 July 1681, music lost, lib. *Wn*

L'albero del ramo d'oro (introduzione d'un ballo, 1), Ödenburg, 15 Nov 1681, ov. ed. in H. Botstiber: *Geschichte der Ouvertüre* (Leipzig, 1913)

Gli stratagemi di Biante (dm, 3), 15 Jan 1682, contribs. Leopold I

La chimera (drama fantastico musicale, 3), 7 Feb 1682; rev. version, 14 Feb 1692, Act 2 lost

Il tempio d'Apollo in Delfo (introduzione d'un balletto, 1), Laxenburg, 14 July 1682

Il giardino della Virtù (1), Emperor's rooms, 7 Jan 1683

Lo smemorato (trattenimento musicale, 1), Emperor's rooms, 28 Feb 1683

La lira d'Orfeo (trattenimento musicale, 1), Laxenburg, park, 9 June 1683

Gl'elogii (1), Linz, palace, 16 Jan 1684, contribs. Leopold I

Tullio Hostilio, aprendo il tempio di Giano (festa musicale, 1), Linz, 9 June 1684, music lost, lib. *Wn*

I varii effetti d'amore (introduzione ad un balletto, 1), 16 Jan 1685, music lost, lib. *Wn*

La più generosa Spartana (introduzione ad un balletto, 1), ? 10 June 1685

Il Palladio in Roma (dm, 3), 17 Sept 1685, contribs. Leopold I

Il rissarcimento della ruota della Fortuna (introduzione ad un balletto, 1), ? 15 Nov 1685

Lo studio d'amore (introduzione ad un balletto, 1), Emperor's rooms, 13 Jan 1686, contribs. Leopold I
Le scioccaggini degli Psilli (trattenimento musicale, 1), ? 24 Feb 1686
Il nodo gordiano (festa teatrale, 1), 11 June 1686, contribs. Leopold I
Le ninfe ritrose (introduzione d'un balletto, 1), Hofburg, park, 22 July 1686, contribs. Leopold I
Il ritorno di Teseo dal labirinto di Creta (introduzione d'un balletto, 1), ?7 Oct 1686
La grotta di Vulcano (introduzione d'un balletto, 1), ? 15 Nov 1686
La vendetta dell'Honestà (rappresentazione musicale, 1), 9 June 1687, music lost, lib. *Wn*
La gemma Ceraunia d'Ulissipone hora Lisbona (dramma musicale, 3), Heidelberg, Elector's palace, 1 and 3 July 1687, music lost, lib. *BR-Rn, US-Wc*
La vittoria della Fortezza (introduzione d'un balletto, 1), Bellaria, 22 July 1687, contribs. Leopold I
La fama addormentata e risvegliata (introduzione d'un balletto, 1), Pressburg, ?19 Nov 1687
Il marito ama più (festa musicale, 1), Pressburg, Count Pálffy's palace, 17 Jan 1688, contribs. Leopold I
Tanisia (dm, 3), 26 Feb 1688, contribs. Leopold I
La moglie ama meglio (festa musicale, 1), 10 June 1688, contribs. Leopold I
Pigmaleone in Cipro (festa musicale, 1), 13 Jan 1689, contribs. Leopold I
La Rosaura, overo Amore, figlio della Gratitudine (dm, 3, O. Malvezzi), 19 Feb 1689, Act 3 lost, contribs. Leopold I
Il Telemaco, overo Il valore coronato (composizione per musica, 1, Malvezzi), Augsburg, Fuggers' house, 21 Nov 1689, pt 1 lost, 23 arias *D-Mbs*
La regina de' volsci (dm, 3), Augsburg, Fuggers' house, 12 Jan 1690, 32 arias *Mbs*, contribs. Leopold I
Scipione preservatore di Roma (trattenimento musicale, 1), ? 26 July 1690, music lost, lib. *A-Wn*
La chioma di Berenice (festa musicale, 1), intended for 28 Aug 1690, contribs. Leopold I; rev. version, Favorita park, 4 Aug 1695, pt 2 lost, contribs. Leopold I
Li tre stati del tempo: passato, presente, e venturo (introduzione d'un balletto, 1), Neuburg, ?June 1691, music lost, lib. *I-Fn, Vnm*
Il ringiovenito (festa musicale, 1), Favorita, 18 June 1691, contribs. Leopold I
Il pellegrinaggio delle Gratie all'Oracolo Dodoneo (invenzione per una serenata, 1), Favorita park, 23 July 1691
Le attioni fortunate di Perseo (festa, 4), 28 Nov 1691, music lost, lib. *A-Wn*
Fedeltà e Generosità (festa teatrale, 1), 12 Jan 1692, contribs. Leopold I
Le varietà di fortuna in Lucio Iunio Bruto, l'autore della libertà romana (festa per musica, 3), Favorita, 18 June 1692, Acts 1 and 3 lost, contribs. Leopold I
Il merito uniforma i genii (introduzione d'un balletto, 1, ?Minato), Favorita park, 22 July 1692, music lost, lib. *Wn*
Il vincitor magnanimo Tito Quintio Flaminio (dm, 3), 27 Nov 1692, contribs. Leopold I
L'amore in sogno, overo Le nozze d'Odati, e Zoriadre (dm, 3), Favorita, 29 June 1693, Acts 1 and 3 lost, contribs. Leopold I
La madre degli dei (festa musicale, 1), Favorita park, 22 July 1693
L'imprese dell'Achille di Roma (festa per musica, 4, librettist not known), 22 Nov 1693, music lost, lib. *Wn*
Pelopida Tebano in Tessaglia (festa teatrale, 1), 25 Nov 1694, pt 1 lost
L'industrie amorose in Filli di Tracia (dm, 3), 16 Jan 1695, contribs. Leopold I
Amore dà Senno, overo Le sciocchezze d'Hippoclide (dm, 3, D. Cupeda), 6–12 Feb 1695, Acts 1 and 2 lost, contribs. Leopold I
La finta cecità di Antioco il grande (dm, 3, Cupeda), Favorita, 6 July 1695, Acts 2 and 3 lost, contribs. Leopold I
La magnanimità di Marco Fabrizio (3, Cupeda), 22 Nov 1695, contribs. Leopold I
Timone misantropo (dm, 3, librettist not known), carn. 1696, Act 1 lost, contribs. Leopold I
Le piramidi d'Egitto (trattenimento musicale, 1), 6 Jan 1697
L'Adalberto, overo La forza dell astuzia femminile (dm, 3, Cupeda), 12 Feb 1697, contribs. Leopold I
L'amare per virtù (dm, 3, Cupeda), Favorita, 30 June 1697, Act 2 lost, contribs. Leopold I
La tirannide abbatuta dalla virtù (festa musicale, 1), Favorita park, 11 Aug 1697, contribs. Leopold I
L'Arsace, fondatore dell'imperio de' parthi (dm, 3, Cupeda), Favorita, 3 July 1698, Acts 1 and 2 lost, collab. C. D. Draghi
Il delizioso ritiro di Lucullo (festa musicale, 1, librettist not known), Favorita park, 7 Aug 1698, music lost, lib. *Wn*
La forza dell'amor filiale (dm, 3, Cupeda), 27 Nov 1698, Act 3 lost, collab. C. D. Draghi, contribs. Leopold I
Le finezze dell'amicizia, e dell'amore (festa musicale, 1, librettist not known), 1 Aug 1699, music lost, lib. *Wn*
L'Alceste (dm, 3, Cupeda), 28 Jan 1700, music lost, lib. *Wn*

Music in: Ipermestra, 1671

Librettos for other composers (pubd and in *A-Wn* unless otherwise stated): *L'Almonte* (componimento drammatico), G. Tricarico, 1661; *L'Oronisbe*, P. A. Ziani, 1663; *L'invidia conculcata dalla Virtù, Merito, Valore della S. C. Mta di Leopoldo imperatore*, Ziani, 1664, lib. lost, score *Wn*; *La Cloridea*, Ziani, 1665; *L'Alcindo*, A. Bertali, 1665; *La Galatea*, Ziani, 1667; *Apollo deluso* (dm), G. F. Sances and Leopold I, 1669

*

L. von Köchel: *Die kaiserliche Hof-Musikkapelle in Wien von 1543 bis 1867* (Vienna, 1869)
A. von Weilen: *Zur Wiener Theatergeschichte: die vom Jahre 1629 bis zum Jahre 1740 am Wiener Hofe zur Aufführung gelangten Werke theatralischen Charakters und Oratorien* (Vienna, 1901)
M. Neuhaus: 'Antonio Draghi', *SMw*, i (1913), 104–73
E. Wellesz: 'Die Opern und Oratorien in Wien 1660–1708', *SMw*, vi (1919), 5–138
Z. Kalista, ed.: *Korespondence císare Leopolda I. s Humprechtem Janem Cernínem z Chudenic*, i (Prague, 1936), 134
F. Hadamowsky: 'Barocktheater am Wiener Kaiserhof: mit einem Spielplan (1625–1740)', *Jb der Gesellschaft für Wiener Theaterforschung 1951–52*, 7–96
H. Knaus: *Die Musiker im Archivbestand des kaiserlichen Obersthofmeisteramtes (1637–1705)* (Vienna, 1967–9)
G. Cerboni Baiardi, ed.: C. de' Dottori: *Lettere a Domenico Federici* (Urbino, 1971)
N. Hiltl: *Die Oper am Hofe Kaiser Leopolds I. mit besonderer Berücksichtigung der Tätigkeit von Minato und Draghi* (diss., U. of Vienna, 1974)
H. Seifert: *Neues zu Antonio Draghis weltlichen Werken* (Vienna, 1978)
——: 'Die Musiker der beiden Kaiserinnen Eleonora Gonzaga', *Festschrift Othmar Wessely zum 60. Geburtstag* (Tutzing, 1982), 527–54
——: 'Die Beziehungen zwischen den Häusern Pfalz-Neuburg und Habsburg auf dem Gebiet des Musikdramas vor und um 1700', *Mannheim und Italien: zur Vorgeschichte der Mannheimer*, ed. R. Würtz (Mainz, 1984), 12–31
——: *Die Oper am Wiener Kaiserhof im 17. Jahrhundert* (Tutzing, 1985)

HERBERT SEIFERT

Drăgoi, Sabin Vasile (*b* Selişte, Arad, 18 June 1894; *d* Bucharest, 31 Dec 1968). Romanian composer. He studied music in Iaşi (1918–19) with Alexandru Zirra, then at the Cluj Conservatory (1919–20); at the Prague Conservatory (1920–22) he studied with Vitězslav Novák (composition and orchestration) and Otakar Ostrčil (conducting). He taught in Timişoara and elsewhere and was prominent as an ethnomusicologist. Musical theatre attracted him considerably. Employing elements of ancient Romanian folklore (especially the carol, the ballad, the dirge and youth dances) and traditional psalmody, Drăgoi composed in a sonorous tonal language based on the diatonic modalism characteristic of the national schools of eastern Europe. His first opera, *Năpasta*, was the earliest Romanian opera in which motifs from peasant music were combined with rich harmonic and rhythmic resources, and it is built on the principle of variation rather than thematic development. Drăgoi also composed film music. Faithful to his own temperament, his works remain closer to the lyrical than to the dramatic; hence the clear, calm and luminous features of his entire output.

Năpasta [The Calamity] (musical drama, 3, Drăgoi, after I. L. Caragiale), Bucharest, 30 May 1928; rev. 1958, perf. Bucharest, 23 Dec 1961 (Bucharest, 1961)
Constantin Brâncoveanu, 1929 (musical mystery, S. Tudor, after hymn of St Demetrius the New), Bucharest, 25 Oct 1935
Kir Ianulea (comic fantasy op, 5 scenes, R. Urlăţianu, after Caragiale), Cluj, 22 Dec 1939
Horea, 1945 (historical op, 7 scenes, Drăgoi)
Păcală, 1956, rev. 1959 (comic op for children, 3, A. S. Drăgoi, after P. Dulfu), Braşov, 6 May 1962 (Bucharest, 1977)

*

O. L. Cosma: *Opera românească* [The Romanian Opera] (Bucharest, 1962)
N. Rădulescu: *Sabin Drăgoi* (Bucharest, 1971) VIOREL COSMA

Dragon of Wantley, The. Burlesque opera in three acts by JOHN FREDERICK LAMPE to a libretto by HENRY CAREY; London, Little Theatre in the Haymarket, 16 May 1737.

This was Lampe's first great success, and it came after about ten years' work in the London theatre as a bassoonist and composer. Carey, his regular collaborator, probably came from the Rotherham area of Yorkshire, and would therefore have known the local legend of Moore of Moore Hall and the dragon of Wantley or Wharncliffe, though it was also well known nationally through the ballad printed by Thomas D'Urfey in *Pills to Purge Melancholy* (1699) and by Ambrose Phillips in *A Collection of Old Ballads* (1723). The idea of turning the tale into a burlesque of Italian opera probably came from James Ralph, who published the synopsis of a possible libretto in *The Touchstone* (1728); Carey and Lampe worked on the text together, and apparently offered it to Charles Fleetwood at Drury Lane as early as 1734–5. It was a sensation when it eventually appeared: its text was reprinted 14 times in little more than a year; it transferred in the autumn to Covent Garden, and was pirated at Drury Lane and Bartholomew Fair, Smithfield (where it was done by 'Lilliputians'); and it held the stage until 1782.

The definitive three-act *Dragon of Wantley* as performed at Covent Garden (the Little Theatre production was advertised as being in two acts) opens with the locals fleeing at the approach of the Dragon (bass). Margery (soprano), a 'fair Maid', her father Gaffer Gubbins (tenor) and Mauxalinda (soprano) decide that Moore (tenor) is the man to rid them of the Dragon. Moore accepts the challenge in return for Margery's favours, which arouses the jealousy of Mauxalinda, his 'Cast off Mistress'. In Act 2 Margery recovers from a premonition of Moore's death only to meet Mauxalinda intent on revenge; Moore intervenes and then drinks 'Six Quarts of Ale, And one of *Aquae-vitae*' to prepare himself for battle. In Act 3 he appears in his suit of spiked armour, hides in a well and then kills the Dragon with a well-aimed 'Kick on the Back-side' while the orchestra plays a march-like 'Battle Piece'. He is reunited with Margery, who has been hiding up a tree, and all ends happily.

Like *The Beggar's Opera* a decade earlier, *The Dragon of Wantley* ridiculed Italian opera by transferring its artificial conventions and high-flown sentiments to a down-to-earth English situation. But Lampe added to the comedy by setting Carey's inane lines to seemingly serious music, with elaborate Handelian airs and powerful fugal choruses – laid out, in a manner peculiar to himself, in three parts for two trebles and bass. The work is his only opera to survive complete: it appeared in full score (London, 1738) without the recitatives, but they exist in a manuscript score (*GB-Lcm*). Several airs appeared in Bickham's contemporary series *The Musical Entertainer*, with engravings that seem to show scenes from an early production (for illustration *see* LAMPE, JOHN FREDERICK). PETER HOLMAN

Drake, Bryan (Ernest Hare) (*b* Dunedin, 7 Oct 1925). New Zealand baritone. He studied in New Zealand, making his début in 1948 as Escamillo, and then in London. At Covent Garden he created Donald (*Billy Budd*) in 1951. For the WNO (1956–72) his roles included Schaunard, Sharpless, Ferrando (*Il trovatore*), Germont, Pagano (*I Lombardi*), Monterone, Zaccaria and the title role of *Nabucco*, Gesler (*Guillaume Tell*), Macbeth and Mr Flint (*Billy Budd*). He created the Traveller in *Curlew River* (1964); the Abbot/Astrologer in *The Burning Fiery Furnace* (1966) and the Elder Son in *The Prodigal Son* (1968) at Orford Church; Joe Buston in Gardner's *The Visitors* (1972) and Mr Lamb in *The Voice of Ariadne* (1974) at Aldeburgh. He was director of opera at the RCM (1981–5), and voice consultant at the Britten-Pears School from 1987. A reliable artist, he had a voice well adapted to the Britten roles that he sang.

*

A. Simpson and P. Downes: *Southern Voices: International Opera Singers of New Zealand* (Auckland, 1992), 76–89
ELIZABETH FORBES

Dramatic soprano. A type of soprano voice. The term admits a wide variety of repertory and voice type. Any claimant to it must possess a powerful voice and a style capable of energetic emphasis; yet at one end of the spectrum is the singer whose best roles may be, for example, the respective Leonoras of *Il trovatore* and *La forza del destino*, and at the other is the singer who encompasses the heaviest of the Wagnerian soprano parts, Brünnhilde and Isolde. The first type may be described as lyric-dramatic and the second as heroic. The more narrowly defined dramatic soprano would then look for parts such as Aida, Lady Macbeth and Abigaille in Verdi, Senta, Elisabeth and Kundry in Wagner, Leonore in *Fidelio*, and the title roles in *Medea* and possibly *Turandot* (the last of these raises a problem for many dramatic sopranos on account of the high tessitura; it is beyond the reasonable ambitions of those who have an admixture of mezzo-soprano in the voice). Contrasted voices which might still come within the general category of dramatic soprano are, for instance, those of Jessye Norman (an exceptionally full-bodied sound, shaded towards the mezzo and nearer to the lyric-dramatic) and, in an earlier generation, Eva Turner, whose voice was pure soprano but of such penetrative power that the heaviest Wagnerian roles came within its scope and with such brilliance in the upper register that it was ideal for Turandot. J. B. STEANE

Dramaturg [dramaturge]. A German, now partly anglicized term for a person on the staff of a theatre or (more recently) of an opera house, whose responsibility it is to keep up with developments in the repertory and with new work; to suggest, sometimes to adapt texts for production, and to edit or write programmes and explanatory articles. In the 18th and early 19th centuries the Dramaturg often did the work now done by the producer or director, a figure who had not yet emerged. Later he became more of a literary adviser. Even in German opera houses the Dramaturg did not become established until after World War I and more so after World War II. In Britain the first person so styled was at the new National Theatre in the late 1960s. The ENO in 1985 renamed its existing editorial coordinator its 'dramaturge'; there had earlier been a 'director of drama and text'. In other companies the post may exist without the title. JOHN ROSSELLI

Drame lyrique (Fr.: 'lyric drama'). The term was used in two different periods.

In the late 18th and early 19th centuries it designated either an *opéra* or, more often, an *opéra comique* similar in subject and tone to the contemporary spoken *drame*. Unlike the *tragédie* and *tragédie lyrique*, whose plots were generally drawn from classical history and mythology and whose leading characters were upper-class, *drames* (both spoken and sung) had modern, usually European settings and featured among the cast bourgeois imbued with a Rousseau-like *sensibilité*. The tone, more serious than that of the *comédie* and related forms, was also strongly moralizing. Most *drames* revolved around a virtuous person threatened by a loss of wealth or social position or even life, and swift changes in fortune and melodramatic scenes were common. The earliest important example at the Comédie-Italienne was Monsigny's *Le déserteur* (libretto by Sedaine, 1769), in which the hero is under threat of execution but is saved by royal clemency at the last moment. In addition, the *drame lyrique* permitted an extension of the theatre's repertory by the introduction of historical or pseudo-historical subjects, as in J.-P.-E. Martini's *Henri IV* (libretto by B. F. de Rosoi, 1774), with the battle of Ivry as backdrop.

During the Revolution the number of *drames lyriques* greatly increased: Grétry, Le Sueur and Méhul, among others, wrote striking works in the genre. The term was rarer at the Opéra during this period, though occasionally found (e.g. Jadin's *Le siège de Thionville*, libretto by N.-F.-G. Saulnier and Dutilh, 1793); the principles of the *drame lyrique*, however, permeated works called 'opéra' or 'tragédie lyrique'. With the Consulate the Opéra-Comique turned to lighter fare, and *drames lyriques* gradually disappeared there (one of the last was Méhul's *Valentine de Milan*, probably written in 1807–8, première 1822), while at the Opéra the interest in European or modern historical subjects continued throughout the first three decades and was a major source for *grand opéra*.

In the late 19th and early 20th centuries 'drame lyrique' was applied to French operas influenced by the aesthetic ideals of Wagner (whose own works were usually termed 'drame musical' in French translation). They featured a continuous action, a prominent, symphonically treated orchestral part and a rich harmonic vocabulary. Some composers experimented with obvious Wagnerian devices, such as leitmotif, but more important for the essence of French *drame lyrique* was the avoidance of the pomp of *grand opéra* in favour of an intense psychological study. Massenet's *Werther* (1892), Bruneau's *Messidor* (1897), Chabrier's *Briséïs* (1899, incomplete) and Saint-Saëns' *Déjanire* (1911), among others, were called 'drame lyrique', but scholars often extend the term to similar works designated by the more neutral 'opéra'.

*

P. J. B. Nougaret: *De l'art du théâtre* (Paris, 1769)
B. F. de Rosoi: *Dissertation sur le drame lyrique* (The Hague and Paris, 1775 [1776])
E. Schuré: *Le drame musical* (Paris, 1875, 4/1930)
A. Bruneau: *Musiques d'hier et de demain* (Paris, 1900)
F. A. Gaiffe: *Le drame en France au XVIIIe siècle* (Paris, 1910)
O. Séré [J. Poueigh]: *Musiciens français d'aujourd'hui* (Paris, 1911, 8/1921)
V. d'Indy: *Richard Wagner et son influence sur l'art musical français* (Paris, 1930)
M. Cooper: *French Music from the Death of Berlioz to the Death of Fauré* (London, 1951)
S. Wolff: *L'Opéra au Palais Garnier, 1875–1962* (Paris, 1963)
J. B. Kopp: *The Drame Lyrique: a Study in Esthetics of Opéra-Comique, 1762–1791* (diss., U. of Pennsylvania, 1982)

M. ELIZABETH C. BARTLET

Dramma giocoso (It.: 'jocular drama'). Term used on Italian librettos in the second half of the 18th century to designate a comic opera. It was used as early as 1695, by G. C. Villifranchi (preface to *L'ipondriaco*), and became established as a descriptive term when regularly used, from 1748 onwards, by Carlo Goldoni. Its common use was for the type of libretto favoured by Goldoni and his followers in which character-types from serious opera ('parti serie') appeared alongside the standard peasants, servants, elderly buffoons and others traditional to comic opera ('parti buffe'), often with intermediate characters ('in mezzo carattere'). Notable early examples are Goldoni's *Il filosofo di campagna* (set by Galuppi in 1754) and *La buona figliuola* (set by E. Duni in 1756 and N. Piccinni in 1760); Haydn set three Goldoni *dramma giocoso* texts, *Il mondo della luna*, *Le pescatrici* and *Lo speziale*. It is however doubtful whether the *dramma giocoso* was considered a distinct musical genre at the time (*see* OPERA BUFFA). Certainly it was used interchangeably with other genre descriptions; Mozart's *Don Giovanni*, for example, is described on the libretto as a *dramma giocoso* and on the score as an *opera buffa*. There is reason to think that librettists favoured the term for their texts but that composers more often thought of their comic works simply as *opere buffe*.

*

D. Heartz: 'Goldoni, Don Giovanni and the Dramma Giocoso', *MT*, cxx (1979), 993–8; repr. in *Mozart's Operas* (Berkeley, 1990), 195–205

Dramma [drama] **per musica** (It.: 'play for music'). A phrase found on the title-page of many Italian librettos; it refers to a text expressly written to be set by a composer (e.g. *L'Erismena, drama per musica di Aurelio Aureli, Favola Seconda dedicata all'illustriss. Signor Giacomo Cavalli ... M DC LV*) and by extension also to the composition. The term was the one most commonly used for serious Italian opera in the 18th century (as opposed to the primarily modern term *opera seria*, with which it is in effect interchangeable).

Variants such as *dramma in musica* (referring rather to the setting than to the verbal text) or *dramma musicale* are also found. Some later writers have misinterpreted the term in the sense 'drama through music', and applied it to musico-dramatic effects achieved by the composer.

Dranishnikov, Vladimir Alexandrovich (*b* St Petersburg, 29 May/10 June 1893; *d* Kiev, 6 Feb 1939). Russian conductor and composer. He studied at the St Petersburg Conservatory with Lyadov and Shteynberg (composition) and Nikolay Tcherepnin (conducting). Having led the orchestra at the Mariinsky Theatre he was conductor from 1918, and music director from 1925 to 1936. A talented opera conductor, he achieved a sensitive integration of voices and orchestra to dramatic as well as musical purpose. Under his direction the theatre staged notable productions of *The Love for Three Oranges*, *Wozzeck* and the original version of *Boris Godunov* between 1926 and 1928. In 1936 he became artistic director and chief conductor at the Kiev Opera, where he staged many operas by Ukrainian composers. He composed several works himself, and wrote articles on the problems of operatic dramaturgy.

*

I. Belza: 'Vladimir Alexandrovich Dranishnikov', *Voprosï muzïkal'no-ispolnitel'skogo iskusstva* [Problems in the Art of Musical Performance], v, ed. A. A. Nikolayev and others (Moscow, 1969) I. M. YAMPOL'SKY

Dream on the Volga, A. Opera by A. S. Arensky; *see* *SON NA VOLGE.*

Drechsler, Joseph (*b* Vlachovo Březí, nr Strakovice, 26 May 1782; *d* Vienna, 27 Feb 1852). Bohemian composer. He moved to Vienna in 1807, becoming a répétiteur at the Hofoper in 1810, and in 1812 (or 1814) assistant Kapellmeister. In 1815 he opened a music school and took up his first church appointment.

Drechsler's 'grand military opera' *Pauline* was given at the Theater an der Wien on 23 February 1821. That year he was appointed a conductor at the Theater in der Josefstadt, where his music to Meisl's *Das Bild des Fürsten*, together with Beethoven's *Die Weihe des Hauses*, was performed on 3 October 1822 to celebrate the reopening of the theatre; in July 1823 Beethoven recommended him to the Archduke Rudolph. From 1824 to 1830 he was chief conductor and composer at the Theater in der Leopoldstadt, for which he composed many scores. Though the bulk of his output proved ephemeral, Drechsler enjoyed considerable success with his music to Gleich's *Der Berggeist* and *Ydor*, Bäuerle's *Gisperl und Fisperl*, and especially Therese Krones's *Sylphide* and two of Raimund's *Zaubermärchen*, *Der Diamant des Geisterkönigs* and *Das Mädchen aus der Feenwelt* (these last three totalled nearly 600 performances in 20 or 30 years in the Leopoldstadt Theatre alone). Drechsler's felicitous melodic gift and ability to convey romantic atmosphere and comedy raise him well above the average *Volkskomödie* composer. From 1830 he devoted himself mainly to his church duties and to teaching.

See also DIAMANT DES GEISTERKÖNIGS, DER and MÄDCHEN AUS DER FEENWELT, DAS.

all first performed in Vienna; many autographs in A-Wgm, Wn, Wst

WJ – *Theater in der Josefstadt* WK – *Kärntnertortheater*
WL – *Theater in der Leopoldstadt* WW – *Theater an der Wien*

Zspl – *Zauberspiel*

Die Feldmühle (Spl, 1), WK, 29 Sept 1812; Der verlorene Sohn (Melodram, 4, F. Rosenau), WL, 26 Feb 1819; Der Berggeist, oder Die drei Wünsche (Zspl, 3, J. A. Gleich), WL, 12 June 1819; Der Wunderdoktor (Operette, 1, Gleich), WL, 21 Jan 1820; Ydor, der Wanderer aus dem Wasserreiche (Zspl, 2, Gleich), WL, 19 Feb 1820; Der Tausendsassa (Posse, 2, A. Bäuerle), WL, 6 July 1820; Pauline, oder Mut und Liebe (grosse militärische Oper, 3, Ebersberg), WW, 23 Feb 1821; Das Vergissmeinnicht (Zspl, 2), WL, 4 Aug 1821; Amor der Heiratsstifter (Zauberposse, 2, Gleich), WL, 1 March 1822; Das Bild des Fürsten (Allegorie, K. Meisl), WJ, 3 Oct 1822; Die Schauernacht im Felsenthale (Zspl, 3, Gleich), WJ, 14 Nov 1822

Capricciosa, oder Hütchen dreh dich (Zspl, 2, F. X. Told), WJ, 8 March 1823; Die Wiener in Bagdad (Zspl, 3, Meisl), WL, 5 July 1823; Wann waren die guten Zeiten? (Feenmärchen, 3), WJ, 8 Nov 1823; Der Zauberschlaf, oder die 100jährige Träumerin (Feenmärchen, 2, G. Stiller), WJ, 22 April 1824; Frühling, Sommer, Herbst und Winter (Zspl, 4, J. Willmann), WJ, 31 May 1824; Der Feuervogel (Feenmärchen, 2, Gleich), WJ, 20 Nov 1824; Der Diamant des Geisterkönigs (Zspl, 2, F. Raimund), WL, 17 Dec 1824; Die Wunderbrille im Zauberwalde (Zspl, 2, Gleich), WL, 25 Feb 1825; Die Wölfin um Mitternacht (Märchen, 2, Meisl), WL, 11 March 1825; Gisperl und Fisperl (komisches Zspl mit Gesang, 3, Bäuerle), WL, 30 Sept 1825

Lisco und Saldino oder Der bezauberte Garten (Zaubermärchen, 2, J. Lhotsky), WL, 17 Nov 1825; Oskar und Tina, oder Der Kampf um die Schönheit im Reiche der Lügen (Phantasie-Gemälde mit Gesang 2, Meisl), WL, 27 Jan 1826; Das grüne Männchen, oder Der Vater von 13 Töchtern (Zspl, 2, Meisl), WL, 14 April 1826; Die Gratzer in Wien, oder Staberls neueste Possen (lokales Freskogemälde mit Gesang, 2, Bäuerle), WL, 31 May 1826; Die Abenteuernacht (Spl, 3, T. von Haupt and J. Lang), WL, 28 Sept 1826; Das Mädchen aus der Feenwelt, oder Der Bauer als Millionär (Zaubermärchen, 3, Raimund), WL, 10 Nov 1826; Die Fahrt nach der Schlangenburg, oder Das Ebenbild (Zaubermärchen, 3, Meisl), WL, 30 Jan 1827; Kabale und Liebe (parodistisches Zspl, 2, Bäuerle), WL, 16 March 1827; Die Benefizvorstellung (Posse, 2, Gleich), WL, 7 April 1827, collab. W. Müller and I. Schuster

Fee Sanftmuth und Fee Gallsucht (Märchen, 2, Meisl), WL, 20 April 1827; Sir Armand und Miss Schönchen (Zaubermärchen, 2, Meisl), WL, 6 Oct 1827; Die Kunst, sein Glück zu machen, oder Nichts geht über die Weiber (Zspl, 2, Bäuerle), WL, 28 Nov 1827; Sylphide, das Seefraulein (Zspl, 2, T. Krones), WL, 15 Feb 1828; Die Giraffe in Wien (modernes Gemälde , 2, Bäuerle), WL, 9 May 1828; Der Mann mit Millionen, jung, schön und doch nicht glücklich (Zspl, 3, Bäuerle), WL, 10 Jan 1829; Der Nebelgeist und der Branntweinbrenner (Zspl, 2, T. Krones), WL, 24 April 1829; Urgandas Prüfung, oder Der Wettstreit der Genien (Posse, 2, Meisl), WL, 3 Oct 1829; Die unheilbringende Zauberkrone (Zspl, 2, Raimund), WL, 4 Dec 1829

Fra Diavolo, oder Das Gasthaus auf der Strasse (Posse, 3, Meisl), WL, 24 Nov 1830; Mahiro, oder Der geraubte Marmorkopf (Zspl, 2, F. Tomaselli), WL, 29 Dec 1830; Der blaue Zwerg, oder Cajetan und Urschel (Zspl, 2, J. Krones), WL, 1 Dec 1831; Mimili (Aenneli), oder Die Rosenkönigin (Zspl, 2, J. Schickh), WL, 31 Oct 1832; Der Zauberwald (Zauberposse, Tomaselli), WL, 13 Nov 1832; Der Denkzettel (Posse, 2, E. Straube), WL, 19 Dec 1832; Die Fee Seifenblase, oder Bilder aus dem Leben eines Glücklichen (Zaubermärchen, 3, J. E. Gulden), WL, 20 Feb 1836; Die Brünnl-Nixe bei Sievering (Zauberposse, 2, Gulden and D. F. Reiberstorffer), WL, 23 April 1836

*

StiegerO; *WurzbachL*
C. Preiss: *Joseph Drechsler* (Graz, 1910) PETER BRANSCOMBE

Dreigroschenoper, Die ('The Threepenny Opera'). Play with music in a prologue and three acts by KURT WEILL (music), BERTOLT BRECHT (book) and Elisabeth Hauptmann (translation) after John Gay's *THE BEGGAR'S OPERA*; Berlin, Theater am Schiffbauerdamm, 31 August 1928.

First came the idea of adaptation. Having been alerted to the huge success of Sir Nigel Playfair's revival of John Gay's *The Beggar's Opera* at the Lyric Theatre, Hammersmith, which had opened on 5 June 1920, Brecht had his collaborator Elisabeth Hauptmann prepare a working translation of the piece in the winter months of 1927–8. Shortly afterwards he was approached by the young impresario Ernst Josef Aufricht who was looking for a play with which to launch his new company at the Theater am Schiffbauerdamm in Berlin. Brecht offered Aufricht *The Beggar's Opera*, even though work on it had scarcely begun. Between its inception early in 1928 and its first performance on 31 August eight or so months later, the 'play with music' underwent numerous and substantial reworkings, especially during the chaotic final month of rehearsal under the direction of Erich Engel. Apart from the Gay text, Brecht also used poems by François Villon (for

Jonathan Jeremiah Peachum *head of a band of beggars*	baritone
Frau Peachum	contralto
Polly *her daughter*	soprano
Macheath [Mac the Knife] *head of a band of street robbers*	tenor
Brown *London's chief of police*	baritone
Lucy *his daughter*	soprano
Jenny *a whore*	soprano
Trauerweidenwalter, Hakenfingerjakob, Münzmatthias, Sägerobert, Ede, Jimmy } *Macheath's men*	tenors and basses
Filch *one of Peachum's beggars*	spoken
Smith *first constable*	spoken
Moritatensänger (*ballad singer*)	baritone

Beggars, whores, constables

Setting Soho, London

which he was later charged with plagiarism, having failed to credit the German translator, K. L. Ammer) and Rudyard Kipling. Announced in May as *The Beggar's Opera*, the work initially bore the subtitle *Die Luden-Oper* ('The Pimps' Opera'). The title *Die Dreigroschenoper* did not emerge until a week or so before the première. There were also last-minute cast changes. Radical cuts were necessary. Most of the Kipling material, for example, was removed (only 'Pollys Lied', a translation of 'Mary, Pity Women!', remained). The ballad ('Moritat') of Mac the Knife (Mackie Messer) was the last interpolation of all, created to satisfy the vanity of the tenor Harald Paulsen as Macheath, but performed in the end by the ballad singer. The work was not expected to succeed. In the event, however, it proved to be the biggest theatrical success of the Weimar Republic, running for more than 350 performances over the next two years. The principal roles were created by singing actors from the spoken theatre (Lotte Lenya, Erich Ponto), cabaret (Rosa Valetti, Roma Bahn, Kurt Gerron) and operetta (Harald Paulsen). The Lewis Ruth Band, a seven-man outfit of versatile jazz studio musicians, named after the band's flautist and saxophonist, Ludwig Rüth, provided the instrumental accompaniment. Theo Mackeben directed from the piano. In its final form, revised by the composer immediately after the première, the full score requires a total of 23 instruments.

The *Dreigroschen* fever which gripped Germany from 1928 to 1930 soon spread to other countries. By 1933 Weill's publisher, Universal Edition, had licensed a total of 133 new productions worldwide. The work has been translated into most of the major languages, into English no less than eight times. 2611 consecutive performances were given at the Theatre de Lys, New York, in the mid-1950s, in the acclaimed production of Marc Blitzstein's translation and arrangement, making *The Threepenny Opera* for a while the longest-running musical show in history. The same production also marked the comeback of Lotte Lenya, Weill's widow, who had played Jenny at the Berlin première (for illustration *see* LENYA, LOTTE).

Weill's score, his second collaboration with Brecht, retains only one of the original airs arranged by Pepusch for *The Beggar's Opera* (no.3); the rest is a completely new composition. There are several versions of the book. The original 1928 libretto, which already departs significantly from Gay, was published in that year as loan material to theatres. It contains a certain amount of stage business deleted from all later editions of the text. The 'literary' version which Brecht prepared for the collected edition of his works (the *Versuche*) in 1931 is the one commonly used today, even though it was produced independently of the composer. The changes, some of them substantial, document an attempt to bring the piece into line with the author's latest theories of epic theatre; they also suggest a desire to appease Marxist critics, who had originally missed any 'modern social or political satire' and described Brecht as a 'bohemian'. In the postwar period Brecht presented yet another version entitled *Die Dreigroschen-Oper* (with the all-important hyphen) for copyright reasons, including revised song texts with references to the atrocities of National Socialism. Of the numerous recordings, the album of highlights made in December 1930 with members of the Schiffbauerdamm cast holds particular interest for the evidence it offers of 'authentic' performance practice.

Brecht devised captions for the stage version as part of the work's epic structure (displayed on screens in the theatre) and a narration for a concert version (published in Hinton 1990). The separate numbers were also originally displayed on screens.

PROLOGUE After the overture (no.1) the first caption reads: 'A fair in Soho. The beggars are begging, the thieves thieving, the whores whoring. A ballad singer sings the "Ballad of Mac the Knife"' (no.2, 'Die Moritat von Mackie Messer').

ACT 1.i The caption reads: 'To combat the increasing callousness of mankind Jonathan Jeremiah Peachum, a man of business, has opened a shop where the poorest of the poor can acquire the sort of appearance that can still touch the hardest of hearts' (no.3, 'Morgenchoral des Peachum': 'Peachum's Morning Hymn'). Jonathan Peachum learns from his wife that his daughter Polly is having a relationship with a certain young man. He tells her that his daughter's beloved, Macheath, is the notorious gang leader Mac the Knife (no.4, 'Anstatt dass-Song': 'Instead of Song').

1.ii At five o'clock the next afternoon, Mac the Knife is celebrating his marriage to Polly Peachum, in a stable fitted out with exclusive furnishings which his gang have stolen (no.5, 'Hochzeitslied': 'Wedding Song'). But he is not happy with the work of his gang. It is the work of apprentices, not of grown men. To clear the air and liven things up a little, Polly volunteers to sing a song (no.6, 'Seeräuberjenny': 'Pirate Jenny'). London's chief of police, Brown, arrives. The bandits call him Tiger Brown. He is a good friend of Mac the Knife, whose evil deeds he neither sees nor hears. Brown has come to congratulate Mac on his wedding (no.7, 'Kanonen-Song': 'Cannon Song') and then quickly takes his leave. He still has preparations to make for the coronation celebrations the following day. Once the bandits have also left, the wedding night begins, and Polly and Mac sing their 'Liebeslied' (no.8).

1.iii In his outfitting shop for beggars, Peachum realizes that the loss of his daughter spells utter ruin. Polly is received by her parents (no.9, 'Barbara Song') and the act ends with the 'Erstes Dreigroschenfinale' (no.10, 'First Threepenny Finale').

Design by Caspar Neher for the Act 3 finale of Weill's 'Die Dreigroschenoper' for a production at the Stadttheater, Cologne, 1930: pen, ink and watercolour

ACT 2.i On Thursday afternoon, Mac takes leave of his wife in order to flee from his father-in-law to Highgate moor. Jonathan Peachum wants to hand Mac over to the law. Mrs Peachum suspects that Mac is hiding out in Turnbridge with his whores and wants to bribe the girls to give him away. Polly, however, springs to his defence and points out that the chief of police is his best friend. She informs Mac of the danger, and advises him to flee. During his absence she will continue to run the business as captain of the gang. They take leave of each other in 'Melodram' (no.11*a*) and in 'Pollys Lied' (no.11*b*, 'Polly's Song'). (No.12, 'Die Ballade von der sexuellen Hörigkeit': 'The Ballad of Sexual Dependency', was cut from the 1928 version.)

2.ii The caption reads: 'The coronation bells had not yet died down and Mac the Knife was still sitting with the whores of Turnbridge. The whores betray him. It is Thursday evening.' Mac and the whore Jenny remember in a song the pleasant hours they have spent together (no.13, 'Zuhälterballade': 'Pimps' Ballad'). While Mac was singing, Jenny stood at the window and gave a signal to the constable.

2.iii Although betrayed by the whores, Macheath will be freed from prison through the love of another woman. Brown is unhappy; he could have spared his friend the trouble he is in (no.14, 'Die Ballade vom angenehmen Leben': 'The Ballad of the Easy Life'). Lucy and Polly meet in front of Mac's prison. Lucy, Brown's daughter, is secretly married to Mac. She and Polly sing the 'Eifersuchtsduett' (no.15, 'Jealousy Duet'). (No.15*a*, Lucy's aria, 'Eifersucht! Wut, Liebe und Furcht zugleich', was omitted on the first night but is usually included in modern performances and recordings and is the most overtly operatic number in the work.) The quarrel comes to an abrupt conclusion: Mrs Peachum appears and drags Polly off. Lucy stands her ground. Mac succeeds (with Lucy's help) in escaping from prison. He makes a beeline for the whores. When Peachum wishes to pay Mac a visit he finds only the police chief Brown. In order to frighten him about the consequences of his carelessness in letting Mac escape, Peachum tells him a story with an obvious reference to the coronation celebrations taking place the next day. Mac sings (with Mrs Peachum) the parable about what keeps man alive (no.16, 'Zweites Dreigroschenfinale': 'Second Threepenny Finale').

ACT 3.i That same night Peachum prepares to set off. His intention is to disturb the coronation procession with a demonstration of misery and squalor. He delivers a speech to his beggars but is arrested by Brown. Peachum, however, warns him about being too hasty (no.17, 'Das Lied von der Unzulänglichkeit menschlichen Strebens': 'The Song of the Insufficiency of Human Endeavour' and no.18, 'Salomon-Song': 'Solomon Song'). He has the police chief in the palm of his hand and blackmails him, thus forcing his own release. Moreover, he again puts Brown on the trail of Mac.

3.ii On Friday morning at six o'clock Macheath, who has gone again to the whores, is once again betrayed by them. He is to be hanged. Once more he tries, by means of bribery, to escape (no.19, 'Ruf aus der Gruft': 'Call from the Grave'). The bells of Westminster are ringing. All Mac the Knife's acquaintances have appeared in the prison to bid him farewell as he is taken to the gallows. He begs everyone for forgiveness (no.20, 'Grabschrift': 'Epitaph'). Unlike real life, however, *The Threepenny Opera* has a happy end. After 'Gang zum Galgen', (no.20*a*, 'Walk to the Gallows'), the king's mounted messenger saves Mac from execution (see illustration). The gratification of all concerned is expressed by Peachum:

> Now, ladies and gentlemen, in our show
> We should witness Mac's hanging
> For in the Christian world, as well you know,
> Nothing comes from nothing.

But lest you might be tempted
To accuse us of some crass collusion
Mac will now be exempted
We offer instead an alternative conclusion.
Mercy, it's said, tempers justice
In opera, that's par for the course
So let's have the theory in practice
And behold the King's envoy – on a horse.

The opera ends with the 'Drittes Dreigroschenfinale' (no.21, 'Third Threepenny Finale') and 'Schlussgesang' ('Chorale').

* * *

Die Dreigroschenoper has been described (H. Keller) as 'the weightiest possible lowbrow opera for highbrows and the most full-blooded highbrow musical for lowbrows'. For Weill it was not just 'the most consistent reaction to Wagner'; it also marked a positive step towards an operatic reform. By explicitly and implicitly shunning the more earnest traditions of the opera house, Weill created a mixed form which incorporated spoken theatre and popular musical idioms. Parody of operatic convention – of Romantic lyricism and happy endings – constitutes a central device. The through-composed music drama is replaced by the *Urform* ('prototype') of the number principle. Rather than carry the drama forward the music stops the action in its tracks in a way comparable to *opera seria*. Nor does it contribute to dramatic characterization in any general or substantial way. Often the protagonists merely 'adopt attitudes', to use Brecht's expression. The piece is a montage rather than an organic construction. The music even undermines the sense of the words. Writing to his publisher about the 'Zuhälterballade', for instance, Weill observed: 'The charm of the piece rests precisely in the fact that a rather risqué text … is set to music in a gentle, pleasant way.' The pervading tone is thoroughly ironic, a deliberately unsettling mixture of sentimentality and caustic social criticism.

If generic ambiguity is a key to the work's enduring success, it has also encouraged a performing tradition at odds with the composer's original intentions. Weill wrote for musically gifted all-round performers. Yet the work has more often than not been performed by actors who, of necessity, bellow and bark their songs rather than sing them. Any parodic and comic effects should result from an abundance – not a paucity – of musical talent.

STEPHEN HINTON

Drei Pintos, Die ('The Three Pintos'). Unfinished *komische Oper* in three acts, J Anh.5, by CARL MARIA VON WEBER to a libretto by Theodor Hell [CARL GOTTFRIED THEODOR WINKLER] after Carl Seidel's story *Der Brautkampf*; Leipzig, Neues Stadttheater, 20 January 1888, in a version completed by GUSTAV MAHLER.

In summer 1820, while in the final stages of writing *Der Freischütz*, Weber began to sketch *Die drei Pintos*, together with his incidental music to *Preciosa* (J279). But after the completion of *Preciosa* in July he left Dresden on a concert tour of north Germany and did not take up the opera again until January 1821. He continued to work on it sporadically for the rest of the year until, in November, he received an invitation to write a new opera for Vienna. In response to suggestions in the press that he was not capable of tackling anything more ambitious than Singspiel, he was concerned that the new opera should be something weightier than *Die drei Pintos*, and shortly afterwards embarked on the composition of *Euryanthe*. In autumn 1824 his interest in *Die drei Pintos* was rekindled, but with his decision to compose *Oberon* for London it was laid aside once more, and his death in June 1826 prevented further work on it.

Clarissa (soprano) has been promised by her father, Don Pantaleon de Pachero (bass), to Don Pinto de Fonseca (bass), the son of one of his old friends, whom Pantaleon, Clarissa and the maid Laura (soprano) have never seen. Travelling to Seville to marry Clarissa, Don Pinto meets a student, Don Gaston (tenor), who, together with his servant Ambrosio (bass) and the innkeeper's daughter Inez (soprano), makes Don Pinto drunk and steals his papers. Don Gaston intends to impersonate Don Pinto and marry Clarissa but, falling in with her lover Don Gomez (tenor), agrees to let Gomez impersonate Don Pinto. Their plans are disrupted by the arrival of the real Pinto and his father, but eventually matters are amicably resolved and Don Gomez is betrothed to Clarissa.

Weber sketched only seven of the 17 projected numbers. The sketched portion comprised the whole of the first act and the first number of Act 2. According to Weber's pupil, Julius Benedict, the entire first act was sufficiently complete in Weber's mind for him to play it through to him on the piano; but most of the sketches contain only the voice parts with a few hints of orchestration. Weber's widow sent the sketches to Meyerbeer with a view to his completing the opera, but, having done nothing with them for 20 years, he returned them to the Weber family in 1847. Eventually Weber's grandson, Carl, showed them to Mahler, who used them as a basis for his completion of the opera. He based the additional numbers that he was obliged to compose on other music by Weber. The scoring and a substantial portion of the music is Mahler's own, but he succeeded brilliantly in entering into the spirit of Weber's music.

CLIVE BROWN

Dresden. City in Germany on the River Elbe, founded by Margrave Dietrich of Meissen in the 12th century. Its distinguished operatic history began under the electors of the early 18th century, but its most important period as a European centre came later – first with three Wagner premières in the 1840s, and ultimately in the early 20th century, when between 1901 and 1938 the city was host to no fewer than nine Strauss premières.

1. Before 1815. 2. After 1815.

1. BEFORE 1815. French ballet with singing was established at court in 1581, and by the second half of the 17th century entertainments that mixed ballet and opera were common, in addition to *Wirtschaften* (masquerades). The first German opera, Schütz's lost *Dafne*, was performed at Schloss Hartenfels in Torgau on 13 April 1627 to celebrate the marriage of Elector Johann Georg I's daughter. Other operas and ballets marked official celebrations, including G. A. Bontempi's opera *Il Paride*, given on 3 November 1662 during the rule of Elector Johann Georg II, the first Italian opera ever performed in north Germany.

In 1664 construction began on a new playhouse (fig.1), designed by Wolf Kaspar von Klengel and inaugurated on 27 January 1667 with Bontempi's *Il Teseo*. The Comödienhaus seated nearly 2000 and included the most modern lighting and stage machinery. Here Elector Johann Georg III, even more Italophile than his father, established a permanent Italian opera company in 1685 which included Carlo Pallavicino as Kapellmeister and Margherita Salicola as prima donna.

She scored a brilliant triumph in Pallavicino's *La Gierusalemme liberata* (1687).

Operas were given during Carnival under Johann Georg III and his son Johann Georg IV (1691–4). His successor, Friedrich August I, dismissed the Italian company and replaced them with a troupe of French actors for whom he built a new Schauspielhaus at the Schiesshaus, where they gave plays and opera-ballets. In 1697 the elector converted to Catholicism and took the Polish crown. He had the old opera house converted to a Catholic chapel in 1708. J. D. Heinichen was appointed Hofkapellmeister in 1717; at the urging of Crown Prince Friedrich August II a new Italian opera company was established in the same year, including the composer Antonio Lotti, his wife Santa Stella Lotti and the alto castrato Francesco Bernardi, known as Senesino. The elector ordered a new opera house to be built; meanwhile a provisional stage was set up in the Redoutensaal, inaugurated on 25 October 1717 with Lotti's *Giove in Argo*. The French troupe was strengthened and an Italian company performing both comedies and comic operas was engaged. The new opera house (fig.2), built near the Zwinger pavilion at a cost of nearly 150 000 thaler, opened on 3 September 1719 with a repetition of *Giove in Argo*. Designed by the architect M. D. Pöppelmann and decorated by Alessandro Mauro, it was one of the largest in Europe, seating 2000 spectators. Usually, however, the court issued no more than 1400 tickets, which were distributed free of charge.

Later in September Lotti's *Teofane* was produced with great pomp to celebrate the marriage of the electoral prince, Friedrich August. Handel attended, and later had Stefano Pallavicino's libretto adapted by Haym for his own *Ottone* (1723). He also sought to engage some of the Dresden singers for London. The company experienced other difficulties as well, and when Senesino refused to sing in Heinichen's *Flavio Crispo* the elector dismissed all his Italian singers in disgust. A new group of younger singers was recruited beginning in 1725, including Anna Negri, Domenico Annibali and Giovanni Bindi. In 1731 Johann Adolf Hasse and his wife Faustina Bordoni were brought from Venice. Hasse scored a great success with *Cleofide* on 13 September, but returned with Faustina to Italy shortly thereafter.

An era of unstinted support for Italian opera began with the accession of Friedrich August II. He and his wife, the Austrian Archduchess Maria Josepha, took a keen and detailed interest in operatic affairs, as did their daughter-in-law Maria Antonia Walpurgis, eldest daughter of Carl VII, Elector of Bavaria. Hasse and Faustina were won back to Dresden by early 1734, and for the next 22 years Hasse wrote, rehearsed and conducted a new opera, and sometimes two, for carnival nearly every year; he was made Oberkapellmeister in 1750. A brief period of artistic rivalry with his former teacher, Porpora, who came to Dresden in 1747 as Maria Antonia's singing teacher, ended with Porpora's departure in 1752. Each year productions became more lavish. The set designer Giuseppe Galli-Bibiena arrived in 1747, and in 1750 supervised renovations to the opera house. Felice Salimbeni was engaged in 1751 and sang in Hasse's *Il Ciro riconosciuto* on 20 January, a high point in the composer's career. In summer 1754 *Il trionfo della fedeltà*, with both text and music by Maria Antonia, was produced for a small circle of courtiers; the composer herself sang the principal role. Rousseau, in his *Dictionnaire de musique*, praised the opera orchestra and Hasse's arrangement of it. Little store was set by the chorus, however; it was made up of students from the Kreuzschule, a practice that continued until Weber's time.

Outside court circles Italian operas were given before paying audiences in 1746 by the travelling company of Pietro Mingotti at a small theatre erected in the Zwinger. He returned the next summer (at which time his wife Caterina Regina was engaged by the court opera), when the troupe marked the marriage of the electoral prince with a performance of *Le nozze*

1. Interior of the Comödienhaus, Dresden, designed by Wolf Kaspar von Klengel and inaugurated in 1667: engraving by Lehmann and Optz

d'Ercole e d'Ebe by its conductor, Gluck. In 1755 a new theatre was built in the Zwinger, where the troupe of G. B. Locatelli performed comic operas, especially those of Galuppi, for two summers. Here a company of German actors under Pietro Moretti gave plays and comic operas from 1761 to 1763. The theatre, which seated only 350, was later acquired and rebuilt by the court as the Kleines Kurfürstliches Theater.

The Seven Years War wrought immediate and severe hardship on Dresden. The elector spent the war years in Poland, where opera performances continued. Hasse, whose manuscripts were destroyed in the 1756 bombardment of the city, left for Italy in December. The elector returned from Warsaw in 1763 and the opera house, used as a storage depot by the Prussians, was restored and opened with Hasse's *Siroe* on 1 August. In October Friedrich August II died, followed by his son in December, and under Friedrich August III, even before he came of age in 1768, pomp and extravagance became a thing of the past. The Italian opera and comedy were dissolved, as was the ballet. In 1765 an *opera buffa* troupe under Giuseppe Bustelli was installed at the little theatre, where it continued under partial court subvention until 1777. The company performed three times weekly – twice a week after 1774 – with a rapid turnover in the repertory.

Serious opera was mounted only rarely. It had formed the basis of the training of a new generation of local composers – Joseph Schuster, Franz Seydelmann and especially J. G. Naumann – but only Naumann had a serious opera produced at Dresden, *La clemenza di Tito* (1769). It marked the marriage of the new elector to Maria Amalia of Zweibrücken; Lorenzo Quaglio provided scenery, and the cast included Regina Mingotti, Giuseppe Tibaldi and Gasparo Pacchiarotti (Sesto). Naumann was appointed Kapellmeister in 1776 and, after periods in Stockholm and Copenhagen, Oberkapellmeister in 1786; 11 of his operas had their premières at Dresden, the last in 1801.

German companies had performed at their own financial risk for civic audiences at Dresden since mid-century, usually at the Theater auf dem Linckeschen Bade, east of the city. In 1770 the company of J. C. Wäser was allowed to perform at the court theatre on days when the Italian company was idle. The court began subsidizing German troupes with the engagement of the Döbbelin company from October 1774 to Easter 1775. The Seyler company brought German theatre and opera of the highest level to Dresden from October 1775 to Easter 1777, including Hasse's *Piramo e Tisbe* in translation. During the War of the Bavarian Succession the elector dissolved Bustelli's Italian *buffa* troupe and replaced it with a German company under Pasquale Bondini. After the war, in 1780, an Italian troupe under Antonio Bertoldi was reinstated with a greater subvention and more court involvement in personnel and repertory. In the same year Caterino Mazzolà was engaged as theatrical poet.

Italian comic opera dominated Dresden's theatrical life for the rest of the century. Even *Die Zauberflöte* was given in Italian in 1793. A troupe of German actors under Joseph Seconda played at the Linkesches Bad every summer from 1790 to 1817, but their efforts were overshadowed by the Italian *buffa* troupe under Joseph's brother Franz, active at the little court theatre from 1793 to 1814 with an annual subvention of 10 000 thaler. Operas in the *semiseria* vein appeared with the appointment of Ferdinando Paer, who succeeded Naumann as Kapellmeister from 1802 to 1806, including his *Leonora, ossia L'amore conjugale* (1804). In 1810 the position was given to Francesco Morlacchi, who held it until his death in 1841. E. T. A. Hoffmann served briefly as music director of Joseph Seconda's German company (1813).

Saxony's alliance with the French during the Napoleonic Wars proved ruinous to the country. The Russian government of Prince Repnin-Volkonsky, imposed by the Allies in 1814, suspended all theatrical privileges and combined the German and Italian companies with the Kapelle as a single Staatstheater, which lasted until the return of the king in 1815.

2. After 1815. After the return of Friedrich August III from Prussian captivity in 1815, Count Heinrich

2. Interior of the Dresden court theatre (designed by M. D. Pöppelmann, with interior decoration by Alessandro Mauro) during the performance of Lotti's 'Teofane' (13 September 1719) in celebration of the marriage of Crown Prince Friedrich August II: pen and ink drawing with wash by Carl Heinrich Jacob Fehling; for a further illustration see Teofane

3. 'Talestri, regina delle amazoni' (Maria Antonia Walpurgis): design for Act 3 scene i in the 1763 Dresden production; engraving by B. Muellers from the first edition of the score (Leipzig: Breitkopf, 1765)

Vitzthum was appointed the first Generaldirektor of the Königliche Kapelle and court theatre. At the same time the Staatstheater formed by Repnin was dissolved. The Dresden Hoftheater was actually founded on 1 January 1817, when the royal household took over the theatre in the city, the Kleines Hoftheater or Morettisches Theater (fig.4), as well as the Theater auf dem Linckeschen Bade, which remained in use until 1858. On 17 January 1817 Weber took up his post as music director and director of the newly founded German opera – the 'Deutsches Departement' as this new institution was officially called. However, the struggle for pre-eminence between the Italian opera, favoured at court, and the German opera, supported by the citizens, lasted until 1832, when the Italian court opera, directed since 1810 by Weber's adversary Francesco Morlacchi, was dissolved. Its last performance, on 31 March 1832, was of Mozart's *Don Giovanni*.

Weber's repertory, initiated with a production of Méhul's *Joseph* on 30 January 1817, consisted mainly of French *opéra comique* and similar works, with the aim of moving towards German works by Mozart, Beethoven (*Fidelio* was produced in 1823) and Weber himself. His own operas *Der Freischütz* (1822) and *Euryanthe* (1824) were written in Dresden but did not have their premières in the city. The engagement of Wilhelmine Schröder-Devrient provided Weber with a singer and actress of the first rank for his company. With his early death in 1826 hopes for further consolidation of the German opera at first seemed to have suffered a setback, but its triumph could not now be prevented. Marschner's brief period as music director (1824–6) had little effect, but Carl Gottlieb Reissiger (music director from 1826, Kapellmeister from 1828 and principal Hofkapellmeister, 1851–9) strongly influenced the musical life of Dresden for several decades. He gave a brilliant first performance of Weber's *Oberon* in 1828 and produced several operas of his own, including *Die Felsenmühle* (1831). During his period of office, 1843–9, Wagner was employed as conductor of both the opera and the orchestra. The Königliches Sächsisches Hoftheater, designed by Gottfried Semper

4. The first Dresden Hoftheater (also known as Morettisches Theater), before 1841: engraving by C. Breichburg

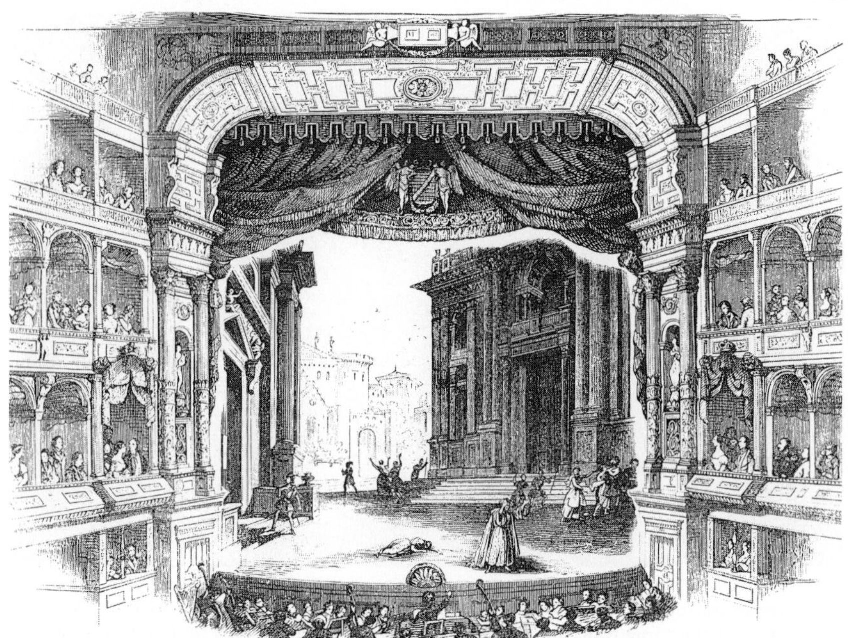

5. Interior of the Dresden Hoftheater (designed by Gottfried Semper) during the first performance of Wagner's 'Rienzi' (final scene of Act 4), 20 October 1842: engraving from the 'Illustrirte Zeitung' (Leipzig, 12 August 1843)

6. The Semper theatre engulfed by fire on 21 September 1869: wood engraving

and sometimes known as the Semper Opernhaus, was opened on 13 April 1841 with Weber's *Jubel* overture and Goethe's *Torquato Tasso*. Like the old court theatre, which was demolished at the same time, it had to accommodate both spoken drama and opera (including the German, Italian and French repertories). 17 years after Weber's death, Wagner became his true successor and continued his plans and ideas. It is significant that his probationary period as conductor began with *Euryanthe*.

Wagner's creative work in Dresden had been anticipated by the successful première there of *Rienzi* in 1842, for which Reissiger was responsible, and it marked a new era in the city's operatic history. *Der fliegende Holländer* also had its première there, on 2 January 1843, conducted by the composer. *Tannhäuser* was composed in Dresden and first performed on 19 October 1845, but the occasion was less successful. Meanwhile Wagner composed *Lohengrin* and the biblical scene *Das Liebesmahl der Apostel* (1843) and worked on the librettos of *Die Meistersinger* and the *Ring*. He gave fine productions of works by Gluck and conducted the orchestra, which he praised as a 'magic harp', in the remarkable 'rediscovery' of Beethoven's Ninth Symphony at the Palm Sunday concert in 1846. Outstanding singers of the time included Schröder-Devrient, Josef Tichatschek, Anton Mitterwurzer and Johanna Wagner. The composer was responsible for having Weber's mortal remains brought from London to Dresden in 1844, and he gave a memorial address at their burial. After the failure of the Dresden May Rising in 1849, the Schröder-Devrients, the Kapellmeister August Röckel, Semper and many others, including Wagner himself, had to flee the city. Wagner did not revisit it until 1862, by which time his music dramas had triumphed over the operas of Meyerbeer and become firmly established in the Dresden repertory.

In 1860–77 Julius Rietz was director of the Hofoper and the orchestra; he became the city's first Generalmusikdirektor in 1874. The first local performance of *Il trovatore* took place in 1860, with Ludwig Schnorr von Carolsfeld in the cast. On 21 September 1869 Semper's famous round theatre, then considered the most beautiful theatre in the world, was destroyed by fire, and from 2 December 1869 productions were staged in a temporary theatre specially constructed to the north-west of Semper's building. This was the so-called Bretterbude ('shack'), although it had four tiers of seats and could accommodate 1800 spectators. It was used until Semper's second theatre opened (with Weber's *Jubel* overture and Goethe's *Iphigenie auf Tauris*) on 2 February 1878, after nearly seven years of construction work. Spoken drama was also performed in the new theatre until 1895. In 1872, while the opera company was still playing in the 'Bretterbude', Ernst von Schuch made his first appearance in Dresden as Kapellmeister to the Italian operatic entrepreneur Pollini (with Désirée Artôt and her husband Mariano Padilla y Ramos). He was immediately appointed musical director in succession to K. A. Krebs, becoming Kapellmeister in 1873, director of the court opera in 1882 and Generalmusikdirektor in 1889; he was ennobled in 1898. Between 1877 and 1882 he was still subordinate to Franz Wüllner, Rietz's successor, but when Wüllner left Schuch reigned supreme until his death in 1914.

The brilliant Schuch era restored Dresden's status as one of the leading operatic cities of the world. The great conductor, who gave 51 premières and some 120 German or local first performances, began by championing late Wagner against the will of the court (he gave three complete *Ring* cycles in the late summer of 1886), and he had the support of a fine company of singers including Therese Malten, Heinrich Gudehus, Karl Scheidemantel and Karl Perron. He encouraged new operatic writing, whether from Italy (Verdi, Puccini – he gave the first German performance of *Tosca* in 1902 – and Mascagni), the Slavonic countries (Dvořák, Smetana, Paderewski and Rubinstein) or Germany, notably with the early operas of Richard Strauss. He thus made the public receptive to contemporary works and established the initially controversial Strauss on stage and in the concert hall. The première of *Feuersnot* on 21 November 1901 was the first in a series of Strauss premières on which the fame of the Dresden opera in the 20th century rested. Over four decades, nine of Strauss's 15 operas were first performed in Dresden. *Salome* in 1905 was followed by *Elektra* in 1909 and *Der Rosenkavalier* in 1911, to the success of which Max Reinhardt as director and Alfred Roller as stage designer contributed a great deal. Singers such as Marie Wittich, Carl Burrian, Margarethe Siems, Minnie Nast, Eva von der Osten and Friedrich Plaschke made up Schuch's famous Strauss ensemble, and under him the orchestra became world famous. During and after World War I the theatre had several fine conductors: Hermann Kutzschbach (1898–1906, 1909–36), Kurt Striegler (1909–45, 1952–3) and Fritz Reiner (1914–21), Schuch's immediate successor.

After the November Revolution of 1919 the Hoftheater became the Sächsisches Staatstheater. Fritz Busch was appointed Generalmusikdirektor and Operndirektor in 1922. He further raised the standard of the orchestra and encouraged performance of contemporary works, with premières of Busoni's *Doktor Faust* (1925), Weill's *Der Protagonist* (1926), Hindemith's *Cardillac* (1926), Othmar Schoeck's *Penthesilea* (1927), Heinrich Kaminski's *Jürg Jenatsch* (1929), Rezniček's *Spiel oder Ernst?* (1930), Striegler's *Dagmar* (1932) and Eugen d'Albert's *Mister Wu* (1932). He continued the Strauss tradition with the premières of *Intermezzo* (1924) and, with the composer conducting, *Die ägyptische Helena* (1928). Under Busch the Dresden Staatsoper became the force behind a German revival of Verdi, giving the first German performances of *La forza del destino* (1926) and *Macbeth* (1928). Busch also gave the first German performances of Puccini's *Turandot* (1926) and Wolf-Ferrari's *Sly* (1928), as well as the first performances in Dresden of many other operas, including Musorgsky's *Boris Godunov* (1923) and *Khovanshchina* (1927). With the Generalintendant Alfred Reucker, he reinvigorated the company, which in his time included Elisabeth Rethberg, Marta Fuchs, Maria Cebotari, Erna Berger and Paul Schöffler. Among directors of productions were Issay Dobroven and Otto Erhardt.

7. Richard Strauss with leading members of the Dresden Opera in 1910: (seated, left to right) Count Seebach (director-general), Strauss, Ernst von Schuch (conductor); (standing, left to right) Max Hasait (technical director), Otto Altenkirch (scenic artist), Max Reinhardt, Hugo von Hofmannsthal (librettist), Alfred Roller (set designer), Leonhard Fanto (costume designer) and George Toller (director)

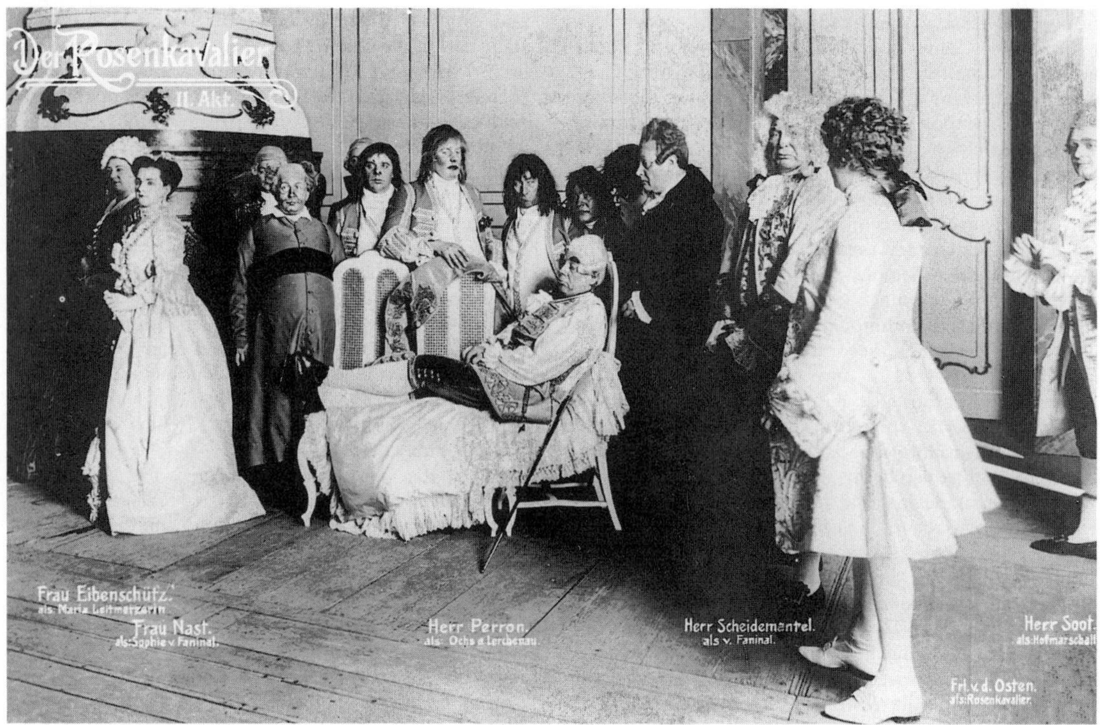

8. 'Der Rosenkavalier (Richard Strauss): scene from Act 2 of the original production at the Königliches Opernhaus, Dresden, 26 January 1911, with (left to right) Riza Eibenschütz (Marianne), Minnie Nast (Sophie), Carl Perron (Baron Ochs), Karl Scheidemantel (Faninal), Eva von der Osten (Octavian) and Fritz Soot (Faninal's Major-Domo)

The dismissal of Busch and Reucker from their posts in March 1933 was one of the first of the Fascist government's notorious attacks on culture. After a short interregnum, which saw the première of Strauss's *Arabella* (1933) under Clemens Krauss, Karl Böhm took over the direction of both opera and orchestra (1934–42) and succeeded in preserving their artistic reputation and encouraging new work in a very difficult time. In November 1935 the Staatsoper scored a success in London with productions of *Don Giovanni* and *Le nozze di Figaro*, *Tristan und Isolde* and Strauss's *Rosenkavalier* and *Ariadne auf Naxos*. Strauss's *Die schweigsame Frau*, which had its première in Dresden on 24 June 1935, was banned after the fourth performance because the librettist, Stefan Zweig, was Jewish. Other premières under Böhm included Wagner-Régeny's *Der Günstling* (1935), Strauss's *Daphne* (1938), Richard Mohaupt's *Die Wirtin von Pinsk* (1938) and Sutermeister's *Romeo und Julia* (1940) and he revived Orff's *Orfeo* in 1940. After Böhm's appointment to the Vienna Staatsoper in 1943 he was succeeded for a year, until the opera closed, by Karl Elmendorff, who was responsible for, among other things, the première of *Die Hochzeit des Jobs* by Joseph Haas. Singers in the war years and during the postwar period included Elisabeth Höngen, Christel Goltz, Elfride Trötschel, Elisabeth Reichelt, Helena Rott and Bernd Aldenhoff.

The last opera performance in the Semper theatre, after the proclamation of 'total war' by the Fascist regime, was of *Der Freischütz* on 31 August 1944. All Dresden's theatres were destroyed in the air raids of 13–14 February 1945. Performances resumed after the end of the war, at first in temporary accommodation in the Tonhalle (later the Kleines Haus) and the Bühlau Kurhaus. The first postwar opera performance was of *Le nozze di Figaro* on 10 August 1945, when an outstanding production team of Joseph Keilberth (director of the opera and orchestra, 1945–50), Heinz Arnold (principal director of productions until 1951) and the stage designer Karl von Appen set high standards for the revival of opera in Dresden. Special mention should be made of the remarkable new production of *Salome*, the first performance in East Germany of Orff's *Antigonae* (1950), and the first two postwar premières, Blacher's *Die Flut* (1947) and Robert Oboussier's *Amphytryon* (1951).

In 1947 the Saxon Landtag decided that the former 'Theatres of the Capital of Saxony' should be renamed the Dresden Staatstheater and Staatskapelle Dresden. In 1948, the 400th anniversary of the founding of the Kapelle, the rebuilt theatre was opened as the Grosses Haus of the Staatstheater with *Fidelio* (with Christel Goltz as Leonore; she also played the leading parts in *Salome* and *Antigonae*). The Staatsoper played in this theatre (1103 seats) until 1984, sharing it with spoken drama; the company also gave (and still does) some performances in the Kleines Haus (525 seats). Keilberth's successor was the young Rudolf Kempe, whose remarkable talent soon made its mark. His company included, as well as Goltz and Trötschel, Joseph Herrmann, Kurt Böhme and Werner Faulhaber. In 1953 Franz Konwitschny became Generalmusikdirektor, and Lovro von Matačić became head of music in 1956. With the appointment of Otmar Suitner in 1960, the Dresden Staatsoper again won fame beyond its own region. The same year saw the engagement of Siegfried Kurz (Generalmusikdirektor 1971, executive musical director 1975–83). Together with Rudolf Neuhaus, who had been at the opera since 1953, he influenced the musical side of many productions until the 1980s. In 1964 Kurt Sanderling became principal conductor; he was succeeded in 1966–8 by Martin Turnovský. Herbert Blomstedt held the post from 1975 to 1985, and he was followed by Hans Vonk until 1990. Hiroshi Wakasugi was then appointed permanent conductor, with Hans-E. Zimmer as executive general musical director. Singers such as Theo Adam, Eberhart Büchner, Reiner Goldberg, Klaus König, Peter Schreier, Gisela Schröter, Karlheinz Stryczek, Armin Ude, Siegfried Vogel and Ingeborg Zobel have begun their international careers in Dresden. With the appointment of Harry Kupfer as director of opera and principal director of productions (1972–81) and of Horst Seeger as Intendant (1973), Generalintendant (1979) and then Intendant of the opera company (1983–4), the Dresden Staatsoper increasingly shone as a leading East German company. Major annual tours, beginning in 1974, contributed to its standing, and on 24 June 1977 the foundation stone was laid for the rebuilding of Semper's opera house to a design essentially faithful to the original.

From 1978 guest performances at the Dresden Musical Festival (held in May and June) supplemented the productions of the Staatsoper itself. In 1983 the Staatstheater Dresden became two separate companies: the Staatsoper and the Staatsschauspiel (the Staatsoperette, performing operettas and musicals, had always been independent, and so, from 1946, had the Landesbühnen Sachsen, based nearby in Radebeul – the largest touring theatre company in East Germany, with a fine music section). The gala reopening of the Semper Oper (1309 seats) took place on 13 February 1985 with a production of *Der Freischütz* conducted by Wolf-Dieter Hauschild and directed by Joachim Herz, principal director of productions, 1985–91. In 1991 Christoph Albrecht was appointed Intendant, and the company was renamed the Sächsische Staatsoper.

Since the 1950s the Staatsoper has both reflected its Dresden traditions (in Weber, Wagner and Strauss) and encouraged contemporary opera, giving first performances in Germany, or East Germany, of works by Hartmann, Britten, Henze, Stravinsky and Schoenberg, while concentrating on the neglected Slavonic repertory (including the première of Juri Buzko's *Weisse Nächte* in 1973 and the first German performances of operas by Khrennikov, Cikker, Janáček, Moniuszko and Prokofiev) and on works by East Germans (including premières of operas by Fidelio F. Finke, Karl-Rudi Griesbach, Rainer Kunad, Udo Zimmermann and Siegfried Matthus). An opera studio for young singers, first set up in 1954, was revived in 1981.

*

M. Fürstenau: *Zur Geschichte der Musik und des Theaters am Hofe zu Dresden* (Dresden, 1861–2)

——: 'Die Theater in Dresden 1763 bis 1777', *Mittheilungen des Sächsischen Altertumsvereins*, xxv (1875), 44–78

C. Gurlitt: *Das neue Königliche Hoftheater zu Dresden* (Dresden, 1878)

R. Prölss: *Geschichte des Hoftheaters zu Dresden von seinen Anfängen bis zum Jahre 1862* (Dresden, 1878)

——: *Beiträge zur Geschichte des Hoftheaters zu Dresden in actenmässiger Darstellung* (Erfurt, 1879)

A. Kohut: *Das Dresdner Hoftheater in der Gegenwart* (Dresden, 1888)

H. von Brescius: *Die königliche sächsische musikalische Kapelle von Reissiger bis Schuch (1826–1898)* (Dresden, 1898)

R. Haas: 'Beitrag zur Geschichte der Oper in Prag und Dresden', *Neues Archiv für sächsische Geschichte und Altertumskunde*, xxxvii (1916), 68–96

E. H. Mueller von Asow: *Angelo und Pietro Mingotti: ein Beitrag zur Geschichte der Oper im XVIII. Jahrhundert* (Dresden, 1917)

R. Engländer: 'Das Ende der opera seria in Dresden: Naumanns "Clemenza di Tito" 1769', *Neues Archiv für sächsische Geschichte und Altertumskunde*, xxxix (1918), 311–24

E. H. Müller: *Die Mingottischen Operunternehmungen, 1732–1756* (Dresden, 1919)

O. Schmid: *Die Heimstätten der Dresdner Landestheater mit Berücksichtigung ihrer inneren Geschichte* (Dresden, 1919)

R. Engländer: 'Dresden und die deutsche Oper im letzten Drittel des 18. Jahrhunderts', *ZMw*, iii (1920), 1–21

——: *Johann Gottlieb Naumann als Opernkomponist (1741–1801)* (Leipzig, 1922)

——: 'Zur Musikgeschichte Dresdens gegen 1800', *ZMw*, iv (1922), 199–241

O. Erhardt, ed.: *Opernfestspiele Dresden: Gedenkbuch* (Dresden, 1928)

P. Adolf: *Vom Hof- zum Staatstheater Dresden* (Dresden, 1932)

O. Funke: *Festschrift zur Jahrhundertfeier der Dresdner Oper 1834–1934* (Dresden, 1934)

G. Pietzch: 'Sachsens Bedeutung für die deutsche Oper', *Blätter der Staatsoper Dresden 1936–7*, 19

——: *Sachsen als Musikland* (Dresden, 1938)

——: '125 Jahre Opernschaffen', *Die Musik*, xxx (1938), 467–71

H. Schnoor: *Dresden: vierhundert Jahre deutsche Musikkultur* (Dresden, 1948)

F. von Schuh: *Richard Strauss, Ernst von Schuh und Dresdens Oper* (Dresden, 1951, 2/1953)

A. Yorke-Long: 'Maria Antonia of Saxony', *Music at Court: Four Eighteenth Century Studies* (London, 1954), 73–93

W. Becker: *Die deutsche Oper in Dresden unter der Leitung von C. M. von Weber 1817–1826* (Berlin, 1962)

W. Höntsch and U. Püschel, eds.: *300 Jahre Dresdner Staatstheater* (Berlin, 1967)

E. Steindorf and D. Uhrig, eds.: *Staatskapelle Dresden* (Berlin, 1973)

S. Köhler: *Musikstadt Dresden* (Leipzig, 1976)

Unser Opernhaus: Führer durch die Semper-Oper (Dresden, 1984)

H. Seeger and M. Rank, eds.: *Oper in Dresden* (Berlin, 1985)

Semperoper Dresden (Dresden, 1985)

E. Steindorf: *Die Staatskapelle Dresden* (Leipzig, 1987)

W. Höntsch, ed.: *Das klingende Dresden* (Leipzig, 1989)

THOMAS BAUMAN (1), DIETER HÄRTWIG (2)

Dresden, Sem (*b* Amsterdam, 20 April 1881; *d* The Hague, 30 July 1957). Dutch composer. He studied at the Amsterdam Conservatory with Bernard Zweers and in Berlin with Pfitzner. In 1914 he founded the internationally reputed Madrigaal Vereeniging and in 1924 he became director of the Amsterdam Conservatory. He was director of the Royal Conservatory in The Hague (1937–49, except 1941–5). In addition to an operetta, *Toto* (1945), Dresden wrote a short one-act opera, *François Villon*, his last composition. Orchestrated by Jan Mul, it met with considerable success at its première on 17 June 1958 at the Koninklijke Schouwburg, The Hague, performed by Nederlandse Opera as part of the 1958 Holland Festival. The music is rather introverted and intellectually conceived, but is nevertheless lyrical and sometimes deeply moving.

*

J. Wouters: 'Composers' Gallery: Sem Dresden', *Sonorum speculum*, xxv (1965), 1–13

L. Samama: *Zeventig jaar Nederlandse muziek (1915–1985)* (Amsterdam, 1986), 47–8

LEO SAMAMA

Dresen, Adolf (*b* Eggesin, Pomerania, 31 March 1935). German director. He studied at the Karl Marx University in Leipzig. Although he had been brought up and educated in the former German Democratic Republic, he was permitted to emigrate (to Vienna) in 1977 and was launched almost immediately on an operatic career. He staged *Yevgeny Onegin* for the Hamburg Staatsoper in 1978. His double bill of Zemlinsky's *Der Zwerg* and *Eine florentinische Tragödie* for the Staatsoper in 1981 was highly acclaimed and was taken by the company to the Edinburgh Festival in 1983. It was later reproduced at Covent Garden (1985). He directed Musorgsky's *Boris Godunov* (1986) and Beethoven's *Fidelio* (1988) at the Théâtre de la Monnaie in Brussels, and *Fidelio* was borrowed by Covent Garden in 1990. Although Dresen cites Brecht as a major influence on his theatrical style, his productions are less overtly ideological than those of his compatriots Ruth Berghaus, Harry Kupfer and Götz Friedrich. In scenic terms he prefers an expressionistic naturalism to Berghausian abstraction or the Kupfer-Friedrich brand of contemporary visual translation. HUGH CANNING

Dressel, Erwin (*b* Berlin, 10 June 1909; *d* Berlin, 17 Dec 1972). German composer. He studied first in Berlin, where his incidental music to *Much Ado about Nothing* was used at the Staatstheater in 1923. After a period at the Schule am Goetheanum, Dornach, Switzerland, he returned to Germany and began a long-lasting collaboration for the stage with the poet Arthur Zweiniger. Their first success was the satirical opera *Der arme Columbus*, composed after a period when Dressel had served as theatre conductor in Hanover (1927–8). Subsequently he worked as a freelance composer, pianist and arranger of music for the radio. He was also music director for the Hamburg Junge Bühne (1946–8) and vocal coach at the Deutsche Staatsoper, Berlin (1948–9).

librettos by A. Zweiniger unless otherwise stated

Der arme Columbus, Kassel, 1928
Die Reise zum Christkind, 1928, unperf.
Der Kuchentanz, Kassel, 1929
Simplizius, 1929, unperf.
Der Rosenbusch der Maria, Leipzig, 1930
Die Mutter (dramatische Szene), Krefeld, 1930
Die Zwillingsesel, Dresden, 1932
Jery und Bätely (Dressel, after J. W. von Goethe), Berlin, Schubertsaal, 1932
Zweimal Karamazow (T. Burger and H. Elsner, after F. M. Dostoyevsky), Vienna, 25 Dec 1936
Das Urteil von Zalamea, 1938–41, unperf.
Die Laune des Verliebten (lyrische Oper, 1, after Goethe), Leipzig, Städtisches, 30 Oct 1949
Der Bär (after A. P. Chekhov), Berne, 1963 JOSEPH CLARK

Dresser, Marcia van (*b* Memphis, 4 Dec 1877; *d* London, 11 July 1937). American soprano. She sang small parts such as a flowermaiden (*Parsifal*) or a Valkyrie at the Metropolitan (1903–4), then went to Munich to study. Engaged at Dresden in 1907, she made her début as Elisabeth (*Tannhäuser*). She sang Sieglinde at Covent Garden (1909) and was engaged at Frankfurt (1910–14) before returning to the USA, where she sang for two seasons in Chicago, then left the operatic stage. Her voice, a lyric soprano, was not large, but she was greatly admired as a Mozart singer. ELIZABETH FORBES

Dreyer [Dreier], **Johann Conrad** (*b* Brunswick, 1672; *d* Lüneburg, 23 Jan 1742). German tenor. The son of a cobbler, he received his first musical training from Franciscus Günther, Kantor of Brunswick, later studying composition with Johann Theile. From Lent 1700 to about 1705 he sang tenor parts for Mattheson at the Hamburg Gänsemarkt Opera; the young Handel was also a member of the company. Mattheson wrote that he had never met a singer more theatrically gifted or 'who conducts himself more wisely, modestly, temperately, industriously, rationally and virtuously', or one who had 'a finer tenor voice and greater musical steadiness'. Dreyer described the Gänsemarkt Opera as a 'school' in Mattheson's sense of the term; he and Mattheson shared the leading male roles in operas by Keiser, Bronner and Mattheson himself. He probably sang in the first performances of Handel's *Almira* and *Nero* (both 1705). From about 1709 to 1713, Dreyer was one of the lessees of the Gänsemarkt Opera; then he became Kantor of the monastery of St Michael, Lüneburg, where he remained until his death.

*

J. Mattheson: *Der musicalische Patriot* (Hamburg, 1728), 349
——: *Grundlage einer Ehrenpforte* (Hamburg, 1740), 52–7
HANS JOACHIM MARX

Dreyfus, George (*b* Wuppertal, 22 July 1928). Australian composer of German birth. His family settled in Melbourne as refugees in 1939. He began his career as a bassoonist, after studying at the Melbourne University Conservatorium, but he was largely self-taught as a composer. His early works were in an advanced style, for woodwind and voice. In 1958 he formed the New Music Ensemble to promote performances of contemporary music and in 1970 established the Dreyfus Chamber Orchestra, the only group devoted to 19th- and 20th-century Australian music. Dreyfus's success in writing music for films and television enabled him to devote all his time to composition after 1965. His subsequent works include two symphonies, a sextet for didjeridu and wind, and pieces for performance by community groups.

Although Covell considered Dreyfus 'an operatic composer in the making' (1967), none of his operas has achieved a place in the repertory of a professional company, perhaps because he has eschewed large-scale opera and written for solo voices and chamber ensemble, without chorus. *Garni Sands* (1965–6), his most ambitious stage work, is set in an isolated colonial farm settlement. It concerns the love of the owner's daughter for one of her father's convict workers. The music matches the subject in both its grim and its lyrical aspects. Considerable demands are made on the eight voices; orchestral interludes link the five scenes, reflecting and carrying forward the action. It was performed by the University of New South Wales Opera in 1972, conducted by the composer; he also conducted the work in New York (Bel Canto Opera Company, 1975) and in Sydney (Opera Mode, 1985).

His one-act opera for schoolchildren, *The Takeover* (1969), concerns Aboriginal land rights; it was commissioned by the Australian Musica Viva Society and has been performed in schools and elsewhere. *The Gilt-Edged Kid* (1970) was described by its librettist as 'an Australian political fairy-tale [about] that most characteristic of antipodean sports, the leadership contest'. A black-humoured satire, commissioned but not accepted by the Australian Opera, it was given first in Melbourne in 1976 by GECKO, a temporary, non-professional company, and later in Sydney. The 'pantopera' *The Lamentable Reign of King Charles the Last* (1975), a political cartoon in musical form, was commissioned by New Opera, South Australia, and performed at the 1976 Adelaide Festival of Arts.

The music-theatre piece *The Sentimental Bloke* (1985) is based on the colloquial narrative poems of C. J. Dennis and uses Australian folktunes; it has been given in a number of Australian state capital cities and provincial centres.

Garni Sands, 1965–6 (2, F. Kellaway), Sydney, University of New South Wales Science Theatre, 12 Aug 1972, vs (Melbourne, 1972)

The Takeover (school op, 1, Kellaway), Canberra, 6 Oct 1969, vs (Melbourne, 1969)
The Gilt-Edged Kid, 1970 (1, L. Strahan), Melbourne, Montsalvat Great Hall, 15 May 1976 (Melbourne, 1976)
The Lamentable Reign of King Charles the Last (pantopera, 1, T. Robertson), Adelaide, Scott, 25 March 1976
The Sentimental Bloke (2, G. Blundell, after C. J. Dennis), Melbourne, Victorian Arts Centre Playhouse, 12 Dec 1985 (Melbourne, 1985)

*

R. Covell: *Australia's Music* (Melbourne, 1967), 266–7
J. Murdoch: *Australia's Contemporary Composers* (Melbourne and Sydney, 1972), 83–4
K. Lucas: 'George Dreyfus's *Garni Sands*: a Forward Step for Australian Opera', *SMA*, vii (1973), 78–87
F. Kellaway: 'Garni Sands', *Overland*, no.60 (1975), 28–30
K. Lucas: 'Dreyfus Opera in New York', *Opera Australia*, vi (1975), 12 [on *Garni Sands*]
F. Callaway and D. Tunley, eds.: *Australian Composition in the Twentieth Century* (Melbourne, 1978), 127–9

CHRISTOPHER SYMONS

Drey Töchter des Cecrops, Die ('The Three Daughters of Cecrops'). Opera in a prologue and five acts by JOHANN WOLFGANG FRANCK to a libretto by Aurora von Königsmark; Hamburg, Theater am Gänsemarkt, 1680 (enlarged version, Ansbach, ?1686).

The text is based freely on Greek legend. Cecrops (bass), first king of Athens, has three daughters: Aglaure [Aglauros] (soprano), Herse (soprano) and Pandrose [Pandrosus] (soprano). They are dedicated to serving the goddess Minerve [Minerva; Pallas Athene] (soprano). As Mercurius [Mercury] (alto) flies by and sees them he immediately falls in love with Herse. She has already attracted the love of Prince Pirante (tenor), son of the Phoenician king Agenora. Mercury promises the sister Aglauros great riches if she will enable him to fulfil his desire for Herse. Minerva, determined to prevent such shameful greed, engages Neid [Envy] (alto) to come to Aglauros at night and to instil in her such jealousy of her sister that she cannot fulfil her wicked promise to Mercury. When Mercury returns, Aglauros forcibly prevents him from entering her sister's chambers, and he punishes Herse by turning Aglauros into stone. Later, Minerva publicly declares that Herse will keep her vow to enter the goddess's service, thus frustrating Prince Pirante's amorous intentions. He, however, is later led at night by his servant Sylvander (tenor) to Pandrosus, wrongly supposing that he will be keeping a tryst with Herse. This brings about his marriage to Pandrosus, and the opera ends with the double wedding ceremony of the royal couple and of their respective servants, Sylvander and his beloved Philomene (alto).

Die drey Töchter des Cecrops is one of the earliest surviving German operas, by a composer of particular significance in the early development of Hamburg opera. Its recitatives are written in a highly expressive manner, with active harmonic support anticipating the arioso style, and are clearly separated from the arias. The latter are in various styles, often Venetian in character, although many have simply constructed lied-like melodies, some of which seem to be modelled on the German chorale. GEORGE J. BUELOW

Driessler, Johannes (*b* Friedrichsthal, Saarland, 26 Jan 1921). German composer. He went to the Cologne Musikhochschule in 1940, but his studies were almost immediately interrupted by the war. After his army service he helped to found the Nordwestdeutsche Musikakademie in Detmold in 1946, serving as deputy director from 1960 to 1983. Driessler's reputation rests largely on his church music, although he also developed a talent for choral composition in his operas; he is a traditional composer preferring a tonal contrapuntal style. His works have not won a lasting place in the German repertory.

Claudia Amata (lyrische Oper, G. Driessler), Münster, 1952
Prinzessin Hochmut (Märchenoper, Driessler), Kassel, 1952
Der Unfried (Jugendoper op), Naumburg, 1957
Doktor Luzifer Trux, 1958 (B. von Heiseler), unperf.

*

O. Riemer: 'Johannes Driessler als Opernkomponist', *Musica*, vi (1952), 398–406 HANSPETER KRELLMANN

Driscoll, Loren (*b* Midwest, WY, 14 March 1928). American tenor. He studied at Syracuse and Boston, where he made his début in 1954 as Dr Caius (*Falstaff*). In 1957 he sang Tom Rakewell at Santa Fe, returning for the American premières of Hindemith's *Neues vom Tage* (1961) and Henze's *Boulevard Solitude* (1967). He sang at the New York City Opera (1957–9) and at Glyndebourne as Ferrando in 1962 before joining the Deutsche Oper, Berlin. There he remained for over 20 years, singing in the première of Sessions's *Montezuma* (1964), creating Lord Barrat in *Der junge Lord* (1965) and singing Eumaeus in *Il ritorno d'Ulisse* (1968) and First Officer in Wilhelm Dieter Siebert's *Der Untergang der Titanic* (1979). At Salzburg he created Dionysus in *The Bassarids* (1966), also singing the role at La Scala and Santa Fe (1968). He made his Metropolitan début in 1966 as David (*Die Meistersinger*), created the Architect in Reimann's *Melusine* (1971) at Schwetzingen, repeating it at Edinburgh, and took part in the première of Nabokov's *Love's Labour's Lost* at Brussels (1973). A stylish singer, specializing in 20th-century music, he had a repertory which included Don Ottavio, Almaviva, Valzacchi (*Der Rosenkavalier*), Flamand (*Capriccio*), the Bishop of Budoja (*Palestrina*), Szokolay's Hamlet, Andres (*Wozzeck*) and the Painter (*Lulu*), which he recorded. ALAN BLYTH

Drogheda, 11th Earl of [Moore, Charles Garrett Ponsonby] (*b* London, 23 April 1910; *d* London, 24 Dec 1989). British financier and opera administrator. He was educated at Eton and Trinity College, Cambridge. In the early 1930s he helped to promote newly formed string quartets; after World War II he took part in the development of the Haydn-Mozart Society. He joined the board of Covent Garden in 1954 and was elected chairman in 1958, remaining in that post until 1974. He helped in engaging Georg Solti as musical director in 1961, and with him and Sir David Webster effected the transformation of the Royal Opera from a resident company based on British singers giving opera in repertory to an international company based on a *stagione* system and using the world's leading artists. He took a constant, positive interest in both the artistic and financial sides of running Covent Garden, including the creation of the Royal Opera House Benevolent Fund. Partly through his influence, opera and ballet were more widely accepted as part of the national heritage. A farewell gala in his honour was held at Covent Garden on 17 July 1974. His career outside music was mostly spent on the *Financial Times* (as managing director 1945–70, then as chairman), where he took a keen interest in the day-to-day running of the arts page. ALAN BLYTH

Droghierina, La. *See* CHIMENTI, MARGHERITA.

Drömmen om Thérèse ('Dream about Thérèse'). Chamber opera in two acts by LARS JOHAN WERLE to a libretto by Lars Runsten after EMILE ZOLA's short story *Pour une nuit d'amour*; Stockholm, Royal Opera (the Rotunda), 26 May 1964.

Told in flashback as Thérèse (soprano), a beautiful coquette, prepares for her wedding, the opera deals with the infatuation of Julien (baritone) for the haughty and unattainable Thérèse; however, when she kills her servant and lover Colombel (tenor) during the brutal love games in which they indulge, Thérèse in desperation promises Julien a night of love if he will dispose of the corpse by throwing it in the river. Julien does as she demands; then, overcome with horror and self-disgust, he drowns himself.

Staged in the round with the 26-piece orchestra arranged in groups outside the audience, the opera uses stereophonic tapes of electronic music, broadcast through speakers strategically placed to blend in, or contrast with, the live sound. If in the orchestral writing Werle follows the stylistic path of Boulez and Stockhausen, his own personal characteristics emerge most strongly in the highly dramatic and very singable vocal lines. ELIZABETH FORBES

Drot og marsk ('King and Marshal'). Tragic opera in four acts by PETER HEISE to a libretto by Christian Richardt; Copenhagen, Royal Theatre, 25 September 1878.

The plot is based on a dramatic event in Danish medieval history, the murder of King Erik V ('Glipping') in November 1286 in a barn in Jutland. Inspired by old ballads, and romantic plays and novels based on them in 19th-century Danish literature, Richardt succeeded in creating a highly effective libretto which suited Heise's 'song-drama' perfectly. The ladykiller King Erik (tenor) seduces the chaste Lady Ingeborg (soprano), wife of the king's chivalrous Lord Marshal Stig Andersen (baritone), and is slain by the marshal and his fellow conspirators, assisted by the treacherous Rane Jonsen (tenor), the king's valet. As a representative of the people and another victim of the king's charm, the pauper Åse (soprano) is given a central position in the opera, and her songs, known as 'Åse's Songs' and published separately, are woven into the dramatic conflict. With *King and Marshal* Danish opera took a decisive step away from the old-fashioned Singspiel tradition towards through-composed music drama, where music and text are given a dramatic unity; it was inspired not only by Weber and Marschner, but also by Meyerbeer and Verdi. NIELS MARTIN JENSEN

Drottningen av Golconda ('The Queen of Golconda'). 'Romantic opera' in three acts by FRANZ BERWALD to a text adapted by him from a libretto by J. B. C. Vial and E. G. F. de Favières for *Aline, reine de Golconde* by Henri-Montan Berton (*see* BERTON family, (2)), itself based on MICHEL-JEAN SEDAINE's libretto after Jean Stanislas de Boufflers' novel of the same title (1762); composed 1864–5, first performed Stockholm, Royal Opera, 3 April 1968.

Aline (soprano), the widowed Queen of Golconda, recognizes the new French ambassador as Saint Phar (baritone), whom she loved as a girl in Provence before she was abducted and sold as a slave to the elderly King of Golconda, who later married her. Aline, heavily veiled, remains unrecognized by Saint Phar, who delivers to her a treaty of friendship with France. Dressed in Provençal costume, she receives Saint Phar in her French Gardens and it becomes clear that he remembers and still loves her. During celebrations for the wedding of Aline's maid Zélie (mezzo-soprano) to Nadir (tenor) a revolution breaks out, led by the court official Sadomar (bass), and Aline and her court are held prisoner. Aline rejects Sadomar's suggestion that she become his consort. At Zélie's suggestion Saint Phar is helped to escape and he fetches help from the crew of his ship. After a short battle they defeat the rebels. Saint Phar describes his vision of Aline, whom he once loved. Throwing back her veil, Aline reveals her face. She and Saint Phar will reign together in Golconda.

In 1863 Berwald started work on an opera, *Slottet Lochleven* ('Lochleven Castle'), based on Scott's novel *The Abbot*. Then, in October 1864, Christine Nilsson, his former pupil and protégée, made a highly successful début at the Théâtre Lyrique, Paris. Berwald, who had long dreamt of having his operas performed in Paris, saw his chance and entirely recast the five-act sketch of *Lochleven Castle*. The tragic heroine, Mary Stuart, unsuited to the youthful Nilsson, became the Queen of Golconda who, in her brilliant opening aria, sings of her lost love and country to the music that originally expressed Mary's longing for her home in France. Many of the sections missing from the score of *Lochleven Castle* were probably transferred to *The Queen of Golconda*. The overture may be adapted from the tone poem *Ein humoristisches Capriccio*, dating from 1841. Aline's final aria, another very florid outburst, comes from the operetta *Jag går i kloster* ('I enter a convent'), written for Jenny Lind.

Nilsson, of course, never sang Aline because the opera was not in fact performed until 1968, the centenary of Berwald's death. At the first performance the title role was sung by Elisabeth Söderström, with Birgit Nordin as Zélie and Erik Saedén as Saint Phar. The first British performance was at Nottingham University in 1982. Although his treatment of the subject was old-fashioned even in the 1860s, *The Queen of Golconda* is Berwald's finest opera. Aline's music is embellished with the coloratura in which Nilsson excelled, but the scene in the French Gardens when Saint Phar sees what he imagines to be a vision of Aline is ravishingly beautiful; the faithful Zélie is nicely characterized, while Sadomar and his fellow conspirators huff and puff in the best tradition of *opéra bouffe*. ELIZABETH FORBES

Drottningholm. 18th-century opera house on Lake Mälaren, just outside Stockholm, in the Swedish royal palace. The first theatre there was built in 1754; it burnt down in 1762 and was then replaced by a larger building, designed by C. F. Adelcrantz and completed in 1766, with changes (including the addition of a foyer) in 1791 by L.-J. Desprez. Its heyday began in 1777 when Gustavus III, son of Queen Lovisa Ulrika, who originally commissioned the theatre, inherited the palace. The repertory included spoken drama, operas in French, Italian and Swedish and pantomime ballets. After the assassination of Gustavus in 1792 the theatre fell into disuse. Not until the 1920s was it investigated, by the theatre historian Anje Beijer. The original wooden machinery, by Donato Stopiani, was found to be in good working order, needing only to be fitted with new ropes (electrical wiring was also installed); it includes a windlass for changing the side flats, a wind machine, a thunderbox (containing rolling stones), two machines for flight chariots, rollers for clouds, a wave-machine,

1. *Interior of the Drottningholm court theatre (1766), designed by C. F. Adelcrantz; the setting is a park with a view of the royal palace across Lake Mälaren; for further illustration see* SEATING.

(a)

(b)

(c)

2. *Surviving stage machinery at Drottningholm, designed by the Italian engineer Donato Stopiani in 1766: (a) windlass and ropes (in the roof-space) for controlling the upper scenery borders; (b) spiral rollers for creating wave effects (see also fig.3a); (c) capstan (below stage) for operating the scenery flats; for diagrams see* MACHINERY, *figs.2 and 5, and for lighting equipment see* LIGHTING, *fig.1b*

3. *Examples of late 18th-century sets preserved at Drottningholm: (above) street scene with sea and a lighthouse, composed of seven pairs of flats, the wave machine and a backdrop; (below) rustic interior (the furnishings are painted on the flats and backdrop); see also* GALLI-BIBIENA, *fig.4*

trapdoors and footlights and sidelights, all of whose movement was controlled by wheel systems. Several original flats and backcloths survive, consisting of some 15 complete and 20 partial sets, by Desprez, Carlo Bibiena and J. D. Dugourc. The theatre has a single, raked floor (a central area was reserved as a 'royal box') with small side boxes; the main seating is on benches. The capacity is 454, in 32 rows, and the orchestra pit seats 30. The building is 57 metres by 23, with a stage depth (footlights to back wall) of 19.8 and a proscenium width of 8.8 and height of 6.6. Drottningholm is generally regarded as the best-preserved theatre of the 18th century, in particular for its machinery.

The theatre reopened for occasional performances in 1922. An annual festival was founded in 1953, in which some 50 performances are given in brief seasons between May and September, drawing chiefly on an 18th-century repertory, including works by Handel, Haydn, Gluck, Cimarosa and Mozart, as well as composers historically connected with Sweden such as Kraus and Naumann. Artistic directors have included Gustaf Hilleström (1946–67), Bertil Bokstedt (1968–79) and Arnold Östman (1980–91); Charles Farncombe was music director, 1970–79, followed by Östman. At performances the orchestra wears period costume, and period instruments have come to be preferred; Östman has made recordings, sound and video, of Mozart operas based on Drottningholm productions. Performances have not usually adopted period-style staging.

*

G. Hilleström: *Drottningholmsteatern förr och nu* [The Drottningholm Theatre, Then and Now] (Stockholm, 1956) [in Swed. and Eng.]

A. Beijer: *Drottningholm Slottsteater pa Lovisa Ulrikas och Gustaf IIIs tid* (Stockholm, 1981)

T. Rangström: *Drottningholm Slottsteater* (Stockholm, 1985) [illustrated guide, in Swed., Eng., Ger. and Fr.]

G. Kull: *Drottningholms Slottstheater: scenamaskineriet/ Drottningholm Court Theatre: the Stage Machinery* (Härnösand, 1987)

Scenery from Swedish Court Theatres (Stockholm, forthcoming)

For further bibliography *see* STOCKHOLM. STANLEY SADIE

Drury Lane. London theatre, properly called the Theatre Royal, Drury Lane; the first on the site was opened in 1663, and the present one in 1812. *See* LONDON, §II, 2.

Druzhba narodov. Opera by V. I. Muradeli; *see* *VELIKAYA DRUZHBA*.

Dryden, John (*b* Titchmarsh, Northants., 9 Aug 1631; *d* London, 1 May 1700). English writer and dramatist. A fine playwright and essayist, he also contributed significantly to the development of English opera both as theorist and as author of three important librettos, one of them, *King Arthur*, with music by Henry Purcell. Dryden's introduction to the professional stage was as a journeyman playwright for Sir William Davenant's Duke's Theatre in the early 1660s. This company specialized in plays with music; Dryden's early works, such as *The Indian Queen* (1664, with Sir Robert Howard), display a gift for writing lyrics and supernatural musical scenes. In collaboration with Davenant, Dryden adapted *The Tempest* (1667), in which Shakespeare's original requirements for music were greatly increased and new musical scenes added. Music continued to feature prominently in Dryden's plays, reaching an apogee with the brilliant conjuration scenes in *Oedipus* (1678, with Nathaniel Lee). He was appointed poet laureate in 1668.

Dryden's interest in opera as such began in 1674 when he wrote *The State of Innocence and the Fall of Man* (published in 1677), a libretto based on Milton's *Paradise Lost* (the old poet reportedly gave Dryden permission to dramatize his epic). Believing fervently that scenic spectacle should be an integral part of any opera, Dryden included elaborate stage directions which, given the bad financial state of the King's Company at the time, would have been unrealizable; *The State of Innocence* was never staged nor was it even set to music. This may have been just as well, because although the libretto is a remarkable poem, its undifferentiated verse and long lines would have presented most composers with difficulty. Dryden was aware of the problem, which he tackled in his next libretto, *Albion and Albanius* (1685). This began as a prologue to *King Arthur*, a SEMI-OPERA, but was expanded into an autonomous work at the request of Charles II, who wanted 'something at least like an opera' to celebrate his silver jubilee. In the preface to *Albion and Albanius* Dryden defines opera as 'a Poetical Tale, or Fiction, represented by Vocal and Instrumental Musick, adorn'd with Scenes, Machines, and Dancing' and suggests how this foreign medium might be adapted for English composers: he advocates short, unrhymed lines which avoid feminine endings for the 'recitative musick' and smoother, more lyrical poetry for what he called 'the songish part, for want of a proper English word'. In recognizing a clear distinction between recitative and aria, Dryden showed a knowledge of the latest trends in Italian opera. *Albion and Albanius*, the first full-length English opera to survive, was set by Luis Grabu, in whom Dryden expressed full confidence, defending his setting (in the style of Lully) against strong criticism: 'When any of our Country-men excel him, I shall be glad, for the sake of old *England*, to be shown my error'.

Dryden converted to Roman Catholicism shortly after the accession of James II (a Catholic) and was therefore dismissed as poet laureate at the Glorious Revolution of 1688 and stripped of his other offices. In spite of charges of 'trimming', his ill-timed conversion was genuine. In need of money, he turned once again to the theatre and wrote, among other plays, *Amphitryon* (1690). Greatly impressed by Purcell's semi-opera *Dioclesian* which had been staged the previous season (and having ghost-written the preface for Purcell), he invited the composer to provide music for his new play, graciously admitting that 'we have at length found an *English-man*, equal with the best abroad'. A year later Purcell wrote the music for *King Arthur* (1691), his only semi-opera conceived as such and not adapted from an existing play. The collaboration does not seem to have been entirely without tension. In the preface to *King Arthur* Dryden, while praising Purcell, complained that he was 'oblig'd to cramp my Verses' in order to make them 'harmonious to the Hearer ... because these sorts of Entertainment are principally design'd for the Ear and Eye'. Indeed, Purcell freely altered many of the great poet's lines. Although more than half of *King Arthur* consists of spoken dialogue, Dryden well understood a fundamental fact about the relationship between librettist and composer: 'my art, on this occasion, ought to be subservient to his'.

*

C. E. Ward, ed.: *The Letters of John Dryden* (Durham, NC, 1942)

E. N. Hooker and others, eds.: *The Works of John Dryden* (Berkeley and Los Angeles, 1956–)
C. A. Price: *Henry Purcell and the London Stage* (Cambridge, 1984)
J. Winn: *John Dryden and his World* (New Haven, 1987)

CURTIS PRICE

Drysdale, Learmont (*b* Edinburgh, 3 Oct 1866; *d* Edinburgh, 18 June 1909). Scottish composer. He studied composition with Corder at the RAM, 1887–92, and returned to Scotland in 1904. In 1896 he wrote the striking mystical play *The Plague*, in which speech and music were synchronized: this was produced in Edinburgh by Sir James Forbes Robertson. Two years later Drysdale's strong dramatic bent found full expression in the opera *The Red Spider*, based on themes of Devon folklore. The work toured Britain, receiving its 100th performance, at Dundee, with much acclaim. It was while still at work scoring the opera *Fionn and Tera* (1909) that Drysdale died of pneumonia. A young Scottish composer, David Stephen, undertook to complete the scoring, and Oscar Hammerstein planned to produce it at the London Opera House, but with the enterprise's collapse after one season, the plan was shelved.

mostly MS, at GB-Gu

The Plague (mystic musical play, 1, I. Robertson), Edinburgh, Royal Lyceum, Oct 1896
The Oracle, 1897 (comic op, 2, T. S. Pilieau and A. W. Gattie), MS lost
The Red Spider (romantic light op, 3, S. Baring-Gould), Lowestoft, Marina, 25 July 1898, 3 songs pubd
Hippolytus (2, Euripides, trans. G. Murray), Glasgow, Athenaeum Hall, Dec 1905
Fionn and Tera, 1909 (grand op, 2, Duke of Argyll), unperf.

Inc.: Flora Macdonald (romantic op, L. Drysdale); The Vikings (2, C. Burton and L. Tracy); The Girl from London (2, R. Rutter); In Office Hours (1, E. Kuhe); Long and Short (1, G. Thorne)

*

GänzlBMT
L. Drysdale: 'Scottish Composers', *Dunedin Magazine*, iii (1914–15), 15–30 [with list of works]
H. G. Farmer: *A History of Music in Scotland* (London, 1947), 521 ff

JEAN MARY ALLAN

Dua, Octave [Haegen, Leo van der] (*b* Ghent, 28 Feb 1882; *d* Brussels, 8 March 1952). Belgian tenor. He made his début as Jeník in the first performance in French of *The Bartered Bride* (1907, Brussels) and for a while continued to sing lyric roles. His real talent was as a comedian, character actor and comprimario tenor, in which capacity he sang with the Chicago company (1915–22) with a period at the Metropolitan (1919–21). In both cities he was particularly admired for his portrayal of Truffaldino in *The Love for Three Oranges*, which he sang at its première in Chicago in 1921. He also made a special place for himself in English operatic life, appearing in London first under Beecham in 1914, then as an 'outstanding' Torquemada in the English première of *L'heure espagnole* at Covent Garden in 1919, and in almost every season at Covent Garden and on tour from 1924 to 1939. Newman in *The Sunday Times* considered him 'without an equal today' in his field. Some early recordings show a pleasing voice, but essentially he was a stage artist and here the best testimonials are the tributes regularly paid him by the critics.

J. B. STEANE

Dubellamy, Charles Clementine [Evans, John] (*d* New York, 6 Aug 1793). English tenor and actor. After appearing in Norwich and briefly at the King's Theatre he was taken on by John Beard at Covent Garden, making his début there as Young Meadows in *Love in a Village* (November 1766). A handsome man, he was admired more for his singing than his acting. For nine seasons after Beard's retirement in 1767 he shared the tenor parts in English operas and afterpieces with George Mattocks, generally taking the subordinate role. He was the first Antonio in *The Duenna* and played Hastings in the première of *She Stoops to Conquer*. He sang in Haymarket summer seasons, appeared in burlettas at Marylebone Gardens (1774) and worked in Ireland and the provinces. From 1780 to 1782 he was at Drury Lane, where his last new role was Summers in the comic opera *The Fair American* by Thomas Carter; some time after that he moved to New York.

*

BDA; *LS*
D. Pinn: *Roscius* (Norwich, 1767, 2/1767)
W. Dunlap: *A History of the American Theatre* (New York, 1832, 2/1833)

OLIVE BALDWIN, THELMA WILSON

Dublin. Capital of the Republic of Ireland (Eire). After years of strife culminating in the Williamite war of the 1690s, Dublin settled down to a period in which the elegance and affluence associated with a colonial governing class provided an ideal background for the cultivation of the arts. As the second city in the British Isles at that period, both in population and in cultural reputation, Dublin attracted many musicians of European fame and developed a remarkably active musical life, reflecting the taste of London rather than that of the Gaelic majority in the country. The fashion for Italian opera, however, initiated in London in the second decade of the 18th century, did not reach Dublin until 1761, when the De Amicis travelling company gave a season of Italian burlettas at the Smock Alley Theatre (built 1662). These were mainly pasticcios, though they included Pergolesi's *La serva padrona*. The first *opera seria* was Tommaso Giordani's *L'eroe cinese*, given its première at the same theatre in May 1766. Dublin's first complete season of Italian opera, in which the evening's entertainment was devoted to one opera without the usual addition of a play or farce, took place in 1777, on the initiative of a number of nobility and gentry, in the Fishamble Street Theatre. Newly adapted from the previous Great Musick Hall, built in 1741 in time for Handel's visit and the first performance of *Messiah*, this theatre closed in 1798. The operas performed there included Piccinni's *La buona figliuola*, in which Michael Kelly made his début as a boy singer.

If Dublin's taste for Italian opera lagged many years behind that of London, English ballad opera evoked an enthusiastic response with the first production, at the Smock Alley Theatre, of *The Beggar's Opera* in March 1728; 40 performances were given before the end of that year, and the work remained a favourite for many decades. The staple fare of Dublin opera audiences in the 18th century consisted of English ballad and comic operas, with Lampe's *The Dragon of Wantley* and Arne's *Tom Thumb the Great* being particular favourites. More substantial offerings included Purcell's semi-operas *Dioclesian* and *King Arthur*, and Arne's masque *Comus* (repeated frequently after August 1741) and his *Artaxerxes* (48 performances in 1765–7). English translations of Gluck's *Orfeo ed Euridice*, Grétry's *Richard Coeur-de-lion* and Dittersdorf's *Doktor und Apotheker* were staged in 1762, 1787 (both

Smock Alley) and 1789 (Crow Street) respectively. Smock Alley closed in 1787.

The only theatre to survive after the 18th century, following the Act of Union in 1800, was Crow Street, which itself closed in 1820 and was supplanted the following year by the new Theatre Royal in Hawkins Street. This burnt down in 1880, but the Gaiety Theatre, open since 1871, was available to take its place. Seating 1075, this acoustically unsatisfactory theatre, with restricted stage space, has been the main house for operatic performances ever since.

In the 19th century it was chiefly Italian opera that established itself in Dublin. In the second decade, Mozart's *Così fan tutte*, *Don Giovanni* and *Figaro* were introduced without notable success; but with the advent of easier travel, touring opera companies paid regular visits and succeeded in implanting an enthusiasm for opera that left a permanent mark on Irish musical life. By 1840, audiences already familiar with Rossini could appreciate the full flowering of Italian opera with great singers in Bellini and Donizetti, followed in the 1850s by Verdi.

Of German opera sung in German there was none, though Weber's *Der Freischütz* and *Oberon* met with considerable success when produced in English soon after their original productions. Wagner's *Lohengrin* was given in Italian in 1875, and *Der fliegende Holländer* in English by the Carl Rosa company in 1878. French companies visited in 1824, 1850, 1870 and 1875, bringing operas by Boieldieu, Auber, Offenbach, Hérold and Halévy among others. The Irish composers Balfe and Wallace were very popular in Dublin, both receiving the ultimate compliment of having an opera performed in Italian.

The foremost organization for opera at present is the Dublin Grand Opera Society, which since 1941 has given two seasons annually at the Gaiety Theatre. The society has its own amateur chorus, and Radio Telefís Éireann (RTE) provides its orchestra; most of the principal singers are engaged from abroad. The standard Italian repertory generally predominates, though the society has staged Gerard Victory's *The Music hath Mischief* (1968).

With the formation of Irish National Opera an attempt was made to provide operatic experience for Irish singers and at the same time to take performances of the less complex operatic masterpieces to the smaller provincial towns. This organization was responsible for introducing to Dublin two new operas by Irish composers, James Wilson's *Twelfth Night* (1969) and A. J. Potter's *The Wedding* (1981), but a change in Arts Council policy resulted in its replacement by the Opera Theatre Company. Independent groups have staged first performances of two further operas by James Wilson, *The Hunting of the Snark* (1965) and *Letters to Theo* (1982). Among the city's many societies devoted to light opera, the foremost is the Rathmines and Rathgar Musical Society, founded in 1913.

*

A. E. Timlin: 'Opera in Dublin', *Music in Ireland*, ed. A. Fleischmann (Cork, 1952), 244–50

T. J. Walsh: *Opera in Old Dublin 1819–1838* (Wexford, 1952)

——: *Opera in Dublin 1705–1797* (Dublin, 1973)

——: 'Opera in Nineteenth-Century Dublin', *Four Centuries of Music in Ireland*, ed. B. Boydell (London, 1979), 45–9

B. Boydell: 'Music 1700–1850', *A New History of Ireland*, ed. T. W. Moody and W. E. Vaughan (Oxford, 1986), 568–628

——: *A Dublin Musical Calendar 1700–1760* (Dublin, 1988)

BRIAN BOYDELL

Dubois, Pierre Max (*b* Graulhet, 1 March 1930). French composer. He studied at the Paris Conservatoire (1949–53) and received his first commission from the RTF as early as 1949. He won the Prix de Rome in 1955 and the Grand Prix of the city of Paris in 1964; he has held appointments in Paris and Quebec, notably as professor of analysis at the Conservatoire. His output is mostly instrumental; the main influences on his music have been Milhaud, Françaix and Prokofiev. His only opera, *Comment causer*, is a one-act 'opéra-pouf' to a libretto by J. Tardieu. First given at the Théâtre Royal, Liège, on 14 October 1971, it is set in a salon in 1900 and tells of a count who visits his mistress while his wife is having tea with her. The moral of the tale is that smart people need only know how to converse in society: the count extricates himself with a string of polite formulae.

PAUL GRIFFITHS, RICHARD LANGHAM SMITH

Dubois, (François Clément) Théodore (*b* Rosnay, Marne, 24 Aug 1837; *d* Paris, 11 June 1924). French composer. He studied in Reims and at the Paris Conservatoire with Marmontel and Ambroise Thomas among others. Thoroughly steeped in the traditional harmonic and contrapuntal training of his day, he won the Prix de Rome in 1861 and was encouraged by Liszt. On his return to Paris he devoted himself to teaching, and published several treatises on compositional technique, which became widely used.

Despite his many church compositions he had considerable aspirations as an operatic composer. His first *opéra comique*, *La guzla de l'émir* (1873), is a modest work, in set pieces, telling of the Emir Hassan (tenor) who attempts to entice girls to his harem with the aid of his *guzla* (a single-string violin). Faintly oriental modal inflections contribute to the mood of the work but never disrupt its traditional basis.

Le pain bis (1879) is also a small-scale work, for four characters, composed in the set-piece couplets of operetta. To illustrate its theme of fickleness in love and in life, it tells of Dugazon (soprano), a lady from Lille, who used to like strawberries but now prefers brown bread. The *scène lyrique L'enlèvement de Proserpine*, a choral scene with some solos in tableau form, dates from the same year; it was probably intended for amateurs.

Aben-Hamet (1884), first sung in Italian, is far more substantial. It expands the oriental theme of *La guzla de l'émir* but is composed in a continuous lyrical narrative, incorporating arias, choruses and a dance sequence. Aben-Hamet (baritone), a Moorish warrior, goes to the Alhambra Palace in the hope of seeing the graves of the Arabic kings and avenging their conquest by the Christians. In the prologue he is in love with Alfaïma (soprano), daughter of the Sultane, Zuléma (contralto), but he later falls in love with Bianca (soprano), daughter of the Christian Duc de Santa-Fé (bass). Zuléma and Alfaïma have followed him and watch in horror as he betrays his ancestors by courting Bianca. They plan an insurrection with the help of gypsies (who later supply a balletic interlude). Aben-Hamet's sense of duty is reawakened when he learns that Bianca is to be married to Lautrec (tenor), a descendant of the Christian warrior El Cid. Fierce fighting breaks out and Aben-Hamet, wounded, dies singing fond farewells to Bianca. Although a note of realism is struck with the singing of Christian plainchant, Dubois' response to the chants of the muezzin and the gypsy dances is restricted to a few modal inflections. Paul Landormy (1943) was not alone in accusing Dubois of 'holding fast to his traditional doctrines without in the least illuminating them with personal fire'.

His other large-scale opera, *Xavière* (1895), is set in the Auvergne. Landry (tenor) is in love with the schoolteacher Xavière (soprano). Her mother Benoite (mezzo-soprano) would inherit if Xavière died, and she plots to kill her daughter with the aid of Landry's father, Landrinier (bass), who wants to marry Benoite. Local colour is introduced in the form of country dances and the choruses of chestnut gatherers. Xavière survives attacks under the guard of the priest Fulcran (baritone), and the opera has a happy end.

Dubois had two of his ballets performed at the Paris Opéra in 1883 but none of his operas was given there, apart from the prelude and second tableau from Act 3 of the otherwise unstaged *Miguela* (the same excerpt had been given by the Concerts Lamoureux in 1896).

performed in Paris unless otherwise stated; printed works published in Paris

La prova di un'opera seria, 1863, unpubd [composed in Rome]
La guzla de l'émir (oc, 1, J. Barbier and M. Carré), Athénée, 30 April 1873 (*c*1873)
Le pain bis (oc, 1, A. Brunswick and A. R. de Beauplan), OC (Favart), 26/27 Feb 1879 (1879)
L'enlèvement de Proserpine (scène lyrique, 1, P. Collin), 1879
Aben-Hamet (4, L. Détroyat and A. de Lauzières), Châtelet, 16 Dec 1884, vs (1884)
Xavière (idylle dramatique, 3, L. Gallet, after F. Fabre), OC (Lyrique), 26 Nov 1895, vs (1895)
Miguela (3), unperf. except for prelude and 2nd tableau from Act 3: concert perf., 23 Feb 1896; stage, Opéra, 18 May 1916

Unperf.: La fiancée d'Abydos; Le florentin

*

H. Imbert: *Nouveaux profils de musiciens* (Paris, 1892)
J. Tiersot: *Un demi-siècle de musique française* (Paris, 1918)
M. Widor: *Notice sur la vie et les travaux de Théodore Dubois* (Paris, 1924)
P. Landormy: *La musique française de Franck à Debussy* (Paris, 1943, 2/1948)
RICHARD LANGHAM SMITH

Dubosc, Catherine (*b* Lille, 12 March 1959). French soprano. She studied piano and cello at the Strasbourg conservatory, then singing with Gerda Hartmann. In 1980 she entered the Ecole Nationale d'Art Lyrique of the Paris Opéra, where her teachers were Denise Dupleix and Hans Hotter. She received further tuition from Eric Tappy at the Lyons Opéra before joining that company in 1985 for two seasons. She has sung many Mozart roles, including Susanna, Despina and Pamina, as well as Marzelline, Nannetta (Verdi's *Falstaff*) and Blanche de la Force in Poulenc's *Dialogues des Carmélites*. Other roles include Gretel (1987, Geneva) and Hypsipyle in Cavalli's *Giasone* (1988, Utrecht). She has also appeared at the Opéra-Comique and the Théâtre du Châtelet in Paris, and at Nancy, Montpellier, Avignon, Geneva, Edinburgh and Strasbourg. Her recordings include *Giasone*, Campra's *Tancrède*, Leclair's *Scylla et Glaucus*, Gluck's *Le rencontre imprévue* and Prokofiev's *The Love for Three Oranges*.

NICHOLAS ANDERSON

Dubrovnik. City on the coast of Croatia (formerly part of Yugoslavia). There have been close links between music and drama in Dubrovnik since the Middle Ages, when societies of young people performed mystery plays, masquerades and pastorals with music. The principal figure in the pastoral genre was the dramatist Marin Držić (1508–67); musical insertions are mentioned in his instructions to performers, though none of the music survives. Early translations of Italian librettos (e.g. Pasko Primović, *Euridice*, Venice, 1617) are evidence of the spread of Italian opera. The archives record a production of *Atalanta*, the first Croatian opera, in Dubrovnik in 1629 (Croatian text by Junije Palmotić; music, now lost, by Lambert Courtois the younger). After Palmotić (1606–57), Šiško Gundulić (1634–87) and Antun Gleđević (1659–1728), Dubrovnik writers concerned themselves less intensively with music theatre. Following the earthquake of 1667, in which any musical source material that may have existed was destroyed, native theatrical activity lessened. From 1681 onwards dramatic performances took place in the Orsan, formerly a shipyard. Italian companies performed contemporary works there until the mid-19th century.

Opera did not feature regularly in Dubrovnik, however, until the 20th century, as part of the International Summer Festival, founded in 1950. Two different approaches to presentation can be traced from that time: guest performances by prominent Yugoslav and international companies, and productions created for Dubrovnik that concentrate on the pre-Romantic repertory, which is exceptionally well suited to the historic and architecturally open backdrop of the city.

*

N. Beritić: 'Iz povijesti kazališne i muzičke umjetnosti u Dubrovniku' [On the History of Theatre and Music in Dubrovnik], *Anali historijskog instituta JAZU u Dubrovniku*, ii (1953), 339–56
J. Andreis: *Music in Croatia* (Zagreb, 1974)
M. Demović: 'Palmotićeva Atalanta prva hrvatska poznata opera' [Palmotić's *Atalanta*, the First Known Croatian Opera], *Marulić*, viii (1975), 35–56
B. Bujić: 'An Early Croat Translation of Rinuccini's "Euridice"', *MZ*, xii (1976), 16–30
M. Demović: *Glazba i glazbenici u Dubrovačkoj republici od početka XI. do polovine XVII. stoljeća* [Music and Musicians in the Republic of Dubrovnik from the Beginning of the 11th Century to the Mid-17th] (Zagreb, 1981)
——: *Glazba i glazbenici u Dubrovačkoj republici od polovine XVII. do prvog desetljeća XIX. stoljeća* [Music and Musicians in the Republic of Dubrovnik from the Mid-17th Century to the First Decade of the 19th] (Zagreb, 1989)
P. Selem: 'Opera', *Dubrovačke ljetne igre 1950–1989* [The Dubrovnik Summer Festival 1950–89] (Dubrovnik, 1989), 77–83 [retrospective festival programme book]
KORALJKA KOS

Dubrovsky. Opera in four acts, op.58, by EDUARD NÁPRAVNÍK to a libretto by MODEST IL'YICH TCHAIKOVSKY (assisted by Josef Paleček and advised by Ivan Vsevolozhsky) after Pushkin's unfinished novella; St Petersburg, Mariinsky Theatre, 3/15 January 1895.

Pushkin's melodramatic story of vengeance and star-crossed love was practically an operatic gala even before it was set to music: a landowner's son (Vladimir Dubrovsky, tenor in the opera), cheated out of his inheritance by Kirill Troyekurov (baritone), a false friend of his father Andrey (bass), becomes a 'noble outlaw' but is undone by love for Troyekurov's daughter, Masha (soprano). To be near her, he intercepts and impersonates a French tutor and gives her music lessons. That is one natural opportunity for the composer, to which Nápravník responded with some pretty vocalises and French salon ditties. There are also massed choral scenes: the elder Dubrovsky's wake, the robbers' den (including a funnier-than-intended scene with the hapless tutor, M. Desforges) and above all the younger Dubrovsky's first criminal act (turned by the librettist into the Act 1 finale), consisting of the lurid murder by arson of the rude bailiffs sent by the court to take possession of the Dubrovsky homestead on Troyekurov's behalf. The one decidedly unoperatic feature of the literary source was the way it ended, or rather broke off, with Masha married off to an old nobleman against her will and Dubrovsky narrowly escaping capture. Modest Tchaikovsky replaced this typically Pushkinian anti-climax with a gigantic love duet, reminiscent of the one he wrote for his brother's opera on *The Queen of Spades* (off which *Dubrovsky* seems in so many ways a chip), ending in a shoot-out and the hero's death in his beloved's arms.

The vocal writing is virtuoso, testifying to the opulence of the Imperial Russian Opera (where Nápravník was chief conductor) in its golden age. The title role, a showpiece for Nikolay Figner, remains one of the most characteristic Slavonic-tenor roles in the repertory. (This must partly account for the opera's somewhat improbable survival in post-revolutionary times; the unflattering portrayal of the social background, as embodied in Masha's father and her fiancé Prince Vereysky (bass), is undoubtedly another reason.) The Act 1 romance, 'O, day mne zabven'ye' ('O grant me oblivion'), a stylized lullaby ending *morendo* on a sustained high B♭, is a Russian concert favourite, recorded by Dmitry Smirnov, Sergey Lemeshev and Ivan Kozlovsky, among others. Troyekurov's role, too, demands a spectacular voice, a dramatic baritone with a high A♭; it was originally sung by Leonid Yakovlev. The original Masha was Medea Mei-Figner; Fyodor Stravinsky was Andrey Dubrovsky.

Nápravník's lavishly decorative score – unquestionably his finest, if unmistakably the work of a routinier – abounds in local colour and nature depiction (notably a 'night intermezzo' for strings in Act 4). Among the Russian folksongs quoted is 'Akh vï, seni, moi seni' ('Little doorstep mine'), made famous in the fourth tableau of *Petrushka*. RICHARD TARUSKIN

Duca d'Alba, Il [*Le duc d'Albe*] ('The Duke of Alba'). Opera in four acts partly composed by GAETANO DONIZETTI in 1839 to a libretto in French by EUGÈNE SCRIBE and Charles Duveyrier and later completed by a commission including Donizetti's pupil Matteo Salvi with the libretto translated into Italian by Angelo Zanardini; Rome, Teatro Apollo, 22 March 1882.

The work was originally intended for the Paris Opéra but the powerful Rosine Stoltz, the director's mistress, disliked her intended role of Hélène and Donizetti put the work aside when it was roughly half completed to work simultaneously on *L'ange de Nisida* and *La fille du régiment*. One aria originally intended for the voice of Gilbert Duprez, who in the natural course of events would have created the leading tenor part in 1840, was in fact sung by him in 1840 in the last act of *La favorite*; in its better-known Italian guise this aria begins 'Spirto gentil'. The aria that later replaced it in the 1882 *Il duca d'Alba*, at the start of Act 4 ('Angelo casto e bel', later recorded by Caruso and a few others), is familiar to those who know the farther reaches of the Italian tenor's repertory, but it was not composed by Donizetti though it is often ascribed to him. The tenor role was sung by Julian Gayarre in 1882.

The plot has to do with uprising against Spanish oppression in Flanders, a movement led by Amelia [Hélène] (soprano), the daughter of the late Egmont, and her lover Marcello di Bruges [Henri] (tenor). This young man is horrified when he discovers that he is the illegitimate son of their Spanish oppressor, the Duke of Alba (baritone). Amelia is bent on revenge for her father's death; when she attempts to assassinate the Duke, Marcello interposes himself and receives the fatal blow.

The plot was later reworked by Scribe and the action transferred to 13th-century Sicily to serve as the text for Verdi's *Les vêpres siciliennes* (1855).

WILLIAM ASHBROOK

Duché de Vancy, Joseph-François (*b* Paris, 29 Oct 1668; *d* Paris, 14 Dec 1704). French librettist. Unlike some of his contemporaries, he embarked on writing for the opera without first having essayed tragedy. As a young man he was appointed a *valet de chambre du roi*, which gave him good connections. After enjoying the protection of the Maréchal de Noailles, he came to the attention of Mme de Maintenon, who appointed him to St Cyr; like his predecessor Racine, he wrote scriptural *tragédies* for the young ladies. His *Iphigénie en Tauride* was completed by Campra in 1704 after Desmarets had been obliged to flee the country; Danchet wrote a new prologue, Duché by then having renounced the theatre. Although the opera was eventually successful, the quality of the libretto is mediocre, and it does not bear comparison with Guillard's much more celebrated version for Gluck. The melodramatic *Scylla* should be considered Duché's best work.

tragédies en musique unless otherwise stated

Céphale et Procris, Jacquet de la Guerre, 1694; *Les amours de Momus* (ballet), Desmarets, 1695; *Théagène et Chariclée*, Desmarets, 1696; *Les festes galantes* (ballet), Desmarets, 1698; *Scylla*, T. di Gatti, 1701; *Iphigénie en Tauride* (prol. A. Danchet), Desmarets, completed Campra, 1704

*

C. M. Girdlestone: *La tragédie en musique (1673–1750) considérée comme genre littéraire* (Geneva, 1972) CAROLINE WOOD

Due baroni di Rocca Azzurra, I ('The Two Barons from Rocca Azzurra'). *Intermezzo comico per musica* in two parts by DOMENICO CIMAROSA to a libretto by GIUSEPPE PALOMBA; Rome, Teatro Valle, Carnival 1783.

Franchetto (tenor) and his sister Sandra (soprano) are plebeians who aspire to marry into nobility. They scheme that Sandra shall marry Baron Totaro (baritone) and Franchetto marry Madama Laura (soprano). The simple-minded Totaro and his uneducated uncle Don Demofonte Cucuzzoni (bass) dress according to the latest Parisian fashion and believe that all women are infatuated with them. Totaro has come to claim his bride Laura, whom he has not met, which gives Franchetto the opportunity to show him a picture of Sandra, pretending that she is Laura.

This leads to a series of mistaken identities and to Totaro's confusion over which of the two women is his bride. Since both persistently claim to be Laura, Totaro and Franchetto decide to ask a soothsayer and a sorceress for advice. Laura and Sandra each appear in four disguises, persuading Totaro that his bride has multiplied into eight people – two brides, two ladies, two soothsayers and two sorceresses, all claiming to be Laura. The impasse is resolved by Laura's realization that the plot is a ruse invented by Franchetto. Laura finally marries Totaro and Sandra pairs with the rich Demofonte, leaving Franchetto as the odd man out.

This delightful plot, set to vivacious witty music, is a farce, full of slapstick humour, satirizing Demofonte's ignorance, crude language and vanity as he strives to follow the Parisian fashion and etiquette of the day.

Franchetto, the con-man, with his quick-witted sister Sandra, furthers the plot through scheming and deceit. The work presents excellent musical characterization through individual arias and a considerable number of ensembles.

After its première in Rome by an all-male cast the piece enjoyed 30 years on the European stage. At Modena in 1802 it was performed under the title *La sposa in contrasto, ossia I due baroni* ('The Mistaken Bride, or The Two Barons'). For the performance in Vienna (1789) Mozart provided new music for Laura's aria 'Alma grande e nobil core' (K578), which was sung by Louise Villeneuve. At the performance in Naples (1793) Cimarosa added two new Neapolitan characters. The Paris performance in 1802 contained additions by Valentino Fioravanti. GORDANA LAZAREVICH

Due cesari, I ('The Two Caesars'). *Dramma per musica* in three acts by GIOVANNI LEGRENZI to a libretto by GIULIO CESARE CORRADI; Venice, Teatro S Salvatore, Carnival 1683.

I due cesari was the S Salvatore's first production for Carnival 1683. With regard to spectacle, it was unable to compete with *Il re infante*, which was enjoying great success at the Teatro S Giovanni Grisostomo: there were only ten stage sets, compared to 12 in *Il re infante* and 11 in *Giustino*, which followed *I due cesari* at the S Salvatore on 12 February. According to Chassebras de Cramailles (*Mercure galant*, March 1683), the great number of beautiful voices compensated for the relative lack of splendour. He praised Clement Hader in particular for an aria he sang to the accompaniment of trumpets. Unfortunately, although 24 arias (roughly a third of the total) survive in three manuscript aria collections, no full score survives. The work was restaged in Milan at the Teatro Regio in 1687, when Giovanni Battista Speroni again assumed the role of Geta.

The main plot and counterplot alternate, coming together only at the end. The main plot focuses on matters of succession and has two historical characters: Bassianus Caracalla and Geta, the sons of Emperor Septimius Severus. The counterplot focuses on fanciful love interests; Onoria, daughter of the imperial librarian Evandro, eventually marries Bassiano (soprano castrato), but only after several assignations with her father's students Fabio (soprano castrato) and Lentulo. The main plot concerns the machinations of Bassiano to deny his brother Geta (soprano castrato) any part in ruling, contrary to the stipulations of their father, who had intended them to rule jointly. Leucipe, an English princess who is in love with Bassiano, eventually saves him. Geta is recognized as the legitimate ruler and forgives his brother. The happy ending contrasts with historical fact: Caracalla murdered the historical Geta. HARRIS S. SAUNDERS

Due contesse, Le ('The Two Countesses'). *Intermezzo per musica* in two acts by GIOVANNI PAISIELLO to a libretto by GIUSEPPE PETROSELLINI; Rome, Teatro Valle, 3 January 1776.

The rich and fickle Contessina di Bel Colone (soprano) is not treating the declared affections of Leandro (tenor) with enough seriousness. Her flirting with other men arouses his intense jealousy. While the Countess and Leandro are out of the house, Prospero (bass), the guardian of the house, and his cousin, the maid Livietta (soprano), receive the Cavaliere della Piuma (tenor), a widower who has come to visit the Countess. Livietta makes the Cavaliere believe that she is the Countess. When the real Countess unexpectedly returns, Livietta tells the Cavaliere that the new arrival is the slightly deranged maid pretending to be a countess. While the Cavaliere is temporarily foiled, the resulting mistaken identities aggravate Leandro's already rampant jealousy. Only upon Livietta's insistence that the Cavaliere immediately marry her does he become suspicious and confused about the identities of the two countesses. Livietta's ruse is discovered, leaving the Cavaliere free to marry the real countess, and, in a sudden reversal, Leandro pairs off with Livietta.

As was the custom in Rome, *Le due contesse* was performed by an all-male cast. Over the next ten years it was extremely popular, with performances in Vienna (1776 and 1787) and at Eszterháza (1779) under Haydn. Except for the transposition of several arias and the omission of two others, Haydn left the original music virtually intact. At the second performance in Vienna in 1787, however, the work acquired several substitute arias by Weigl and Rauzzini. It was also performed in 1778 in Paris as *Les deux comtesses* and in Dresden the same year as *Die zwei Komtessen*. GORDANA LAZAREVICH

Due Foscari, I ('The Two Foscari'). *Tragedia lirica* in three acts by GIUSEPPE VERDI to a libretto by FRANCESCO MARIA PIAVE after BYRON'S play *The Two Foscari*; Rome, Teatro Argentina, 3 November 1844.

Francesco Foscari *Doge of Venice*	baritone
Jacopo Foscari *his son*	tenor
Lucrezia Contarini *Jacopo's wife*	soprano
Jacopo Loredano *member of the Council of Ten*	bass
Barbarigo *senator, member of the Giunta*	tenor
Pisana *Lucrezia's friend and confidante*	soprano
Officer of the Council of Ten	tenor
Servant of the Doge	bass

Members of the Council of Ten and the Giunta, Lucrezia's maids, Venetian women, populace and masked figures of both sexes

Walk-on parts Il Messer Grande, Jacopo Foscari's two small children, naval commanders, prison guards, gondoliers, sailors, populace, masked figures, pages of the Doge

Setting Venice in 1457

Soon after the première of *Ernani* in Venice, Verdi agreed to write a new opera with Piave for the Teatro Argentina in Rome. The first choice was *Lorenzino de' Medici*, but this proved unacceptable to the Roman censors, and a setting of Byron's *The Two Foscari* was agreed upon. It is clear from Verdi's early descriptions that he conceived of the opera as in the *Ernani* vein (relatively small-scale, concentrating on personal confrontations rather than grand scenic effects), although he did urge Piave to attempt something grandiose for the first-act finale. The correspondence between composer and librettist reveals the extent to which Verdi intervened in the making of the libretto, a good deal of the large-scale structure of the opera being dictated by his increasingly exigent theatrical instincts. The composer was also concerned with matters of ambience and anxious to introduce certain moments in which scenic effects could be exploited.

Composing *I due Foscari* occupied Verdi for about four months (a long time by the standards of most of its predecessors). Its first performance was not a great success, possibly because the expectations of the audience had been driven too high by Verdi's enormous and widespread success with *Ernani*. The première cast included Achille De Bassini (Francesco Foscari), Giacomo Roppa (Jacopo) and Marianna Barbieri-Nini (Lucrezia). In 1846 Verdi supplied the famous tenor Mario with a replacement cabaletta for Jacopo in Act 1 (first performed at the Théâtre Italien, Paris).

The prelude depicts an atmosphere of stormy conflict before introducing two themes from the opera, the first a mournful clarinet melody to be associated with Jacopo, the second an ethereal flute and string passage from Lucrezia's cavatina.

ACT 1.i *A hall in the Doge's Palace in Venice* The curtain rises as the Council of Ten and the Giunta are gathering. Their opening chorus ('Silenzio ... Mistero') immediately casts over the opera a subdued yet menacing atmosphere, suggested musically by dark instrumental and vocal sonorities and by tortuous chromatic progressions. The prelude's clarinet melody is heard as Jacopo appears from the prisons to await an audience with the Council. In a delicately scored arioso he salutes his beloved Venice and begins the first section of a two-part cavatina. The first movement, 'Dal più remoto esilio', evokes local colour in its 6/8 rhythm, prominent woodwind sonorities and unusual chromatic excursions. The cabaletta, 'Odio solo, ed odio atroce', is routinely energetic, although it defies convention in allowing the tenor to linger over a high A♭ as the orchestra undertakes a reprise of the main theme.

1.ii *A hall in the Foscari Palace* Lucrezia, Jacopo's wife, enters to a rising string theme, associated with her at intervals through the opera. She is determined to confront the Doge in an attempt to save her husband, but first offers a prayer, 'Tu al cui sguardo onnipossente'. This preghiera exhibits a more highly ornamental vocal style than is usual in early Verdi, although the decoration is – typically for the composer – strictly controlled within fixed phrase lengths. The ensuing cabaletta, 'O patrizi, tremate l'Eterno', is novel in formal design, beginning with an arioso-like passage in the minor and dissolving into open-structured ornamental writing at the end.

1.iii *A hall in the Doge's Palace* (as 1.i) The Council has concluded its meeting and, in part with a return to the music of the opening chorus, informs us that Jacopo's 'crime' must be punished with exile.

1.iv *The Doge's private rooms* The Doge's Scena e Romanza opens with yet another theme that is to recur through the course of the opera, this time a richly harmonized melody for viola and divided cellos. The *romanza* 'O vecchio cor, che batti', in which the Doge apostrophizes his son, is clearly a companion piece to Jacopo's earlier 'Dal più remoto esilio' (notice, for example, the identical opening accompaniment figures), although the baritone father sings with far more direct emotional appeal than his tenor son. The ensuing finale of Act 1 is a lengthy scene between Lucrezia and the Doge, in which Jacopo's wife begs the Doge to show mercy. One of Verdi's finest early soprano-baritone duets, the number falls into the conventional four-movement pattern, but individual sections boast considerable inner contrast, responding closely to the differing emotional attitudes of the principals.

ACT 2.i *The state prisons* A fragmentary, highly chromatic prelude for solo viola and cello introduces Jacopo, alone in prison. He has a terrifying vision of Carmagnola, a past victim of Venetian law, and in the *romanza* 'Non maledirmi, o prode' begs the vision for mercy. 'Non maledirmi' is conventional in its move from minor to major, but has an unusual return to the minor as the vision of Carmagnola reappears to haunt the prisoner and eventually render him unconscious. Lucrezia, accompanied by her rising string theme, enters and, after reviving Jacopo, announces his sentence of exile. There follows one of Verdi's very rare love duets, this one laid out in the usual multi-movement form though without an opening 'action' sequence. The closing portions of the duet see an injection of local colour: gondoliers singing in praise of Venice interrupt husband and wife, giving them fresh hope for the future. The Doge now enters to bid a sad farewell to his son. The first lyrical movement of the ensuing trio, 'Nel tuo paterno amplesso', makes much of the contrast in vocal personalities – declamatory tenor, sustained, controlled baritone, breathless, distraught soprano – while the final stretta (in which the principals are joined by a gloating Loredano) simplifies matters by uniting Jacopo and Lucrezia in syncopated unison.

2.ii *The hall of the Council of Ten* An opening chorus, again partly built on material from Act 1 scene i, explains that Jacopo's crimes are murder and treason against the state. The Doge appears, soon followed by his son, who continues to protest his innocence. The Doge will not listen, but all are dumbfounded by the sudden appearance of Lucrezia, who has brought her children with her in a final plea for mercy. The stage is set for the concertato finale, 'Queste innocenti lagrime', led off by Jacopo, who is seconded by Lucrezia. This grandiose movement develops impressive momentum up to the final peroration (the passage sometimes termed 'groundswell'), but its last cadence is interrupted: Jacopo returns to the minor mode and intimate musical language of his opening phrases, and is in turn interrupted by a further tutti repetition of the 'groundswell' idea. The extreme juxtaposition creates sufficient dramatic charge to close the act without a traditional fast stretta.

ACT 3.i *The old piazzetta di S Marco* Local colour in the form of an 'Introduzione e Barcarola' begins the act, with gondoliers offering a more developed reprise of the music that had earlier interrupted the Jacopo-Lucrezia duet. Jacopo is brought forth for the final parting. His 'All'infelice veglio' is *romanza*-like in its progress from minor to major but is enriched by contributions from Lucrezia and, eventually, from the chorus, making the scene a fitting grand climax to the tenor's role.

3.ii *The Doge's private rooms* (as 1.iv) First comes a scena for the Doge in which he is presented with a deathbed confession revealing that Jacopo is innocent. But the message is too late: Lucrezia rushes on to announce that Jacopo died suddenly on leaving Venice. Lucrezia's aria 'Più non vive!' is, as befits this late stage of the drama, highly condensed, and is perhaps best considered a kind of bipartite cabaletta, allowing (as did her first-act aria) more room than is usual in early Verdi for ornamental flourishes. As she leaves, the Council of Ten appear, asking the Doge to relinquish his power. He answers in an impassioned aria, 'Questa dunque è l'iniqua mercede'. In many ways the most powerful section of the opera, this 'aria' is really a duet between the Doge and the male chorus: he in declamatory triplets demanding the return of his son; they in inflexible unison. The great bell of St Mark's sounds and, after a final apostrophe to Jacopo, the Doge falls lifeless to the ground.

* * *

I due Foscari, as Verdi himself was later to admit, suffers somewhat from being too gloomy in its general tone, in spite of periodic evocations of the Venetian lagoon. But the opera nevertheless offers several interesting experiments. Perhaps most striking is the use of recurring themes to identify the principals. These proto-'leitmotifs' are here perhaps applied too rigidly, serving ultimately to deny any sense of development or progression in the characters; but the experiment itself is significant, suggesting that Verdi was anxious to explore new means of musical and dramatic articulation. The increased importance of local colour is also notable in light of Verdi's future development. Although in *I due Foscari* the sense of a precise ambience seems imposed on the score rather than emerging from it, Verdi's awareness of the potential of this added dimension in musical drama was decisive; from this time onwards he would rarely employ local colour in quite the mechanical way he had in his earliest operas. ROGER PARKER

Due litiganti, I. Opera by Giuseppe Sarti; *see FRA I DUE LITIGANTI IL TERZO GODE.*

Duenna, The [*The Duenna, or The Double Elopement*]. Comic opera in three acts by THOMAS LINLEY (i) and THOMAS LINLEY (ii) to a libretto by RICHARD BRINSLEY SHERIDAN; London, Covent Garden, 21 November 1775.

Don Jerome	bass
Louisa *his daughter*	soprano
Ferdinand *his son*	tenor
Isaac Mendoza	tenor
Don Carlos	tenor
Margaret *Louisa's duenna*	mezzo-soprano
Clara *in love with Ferdinand*	soprano
Antonio *in love with Louisa*	tenor

maids, servants, friars and masqueraders

Setting Seville, mostly in and around Don Jerome's house

Sheridan began work on *The Duenna* in the spring of 1775, soon after the successful production of *The Rivals* in January. The influences on the new play came from Congreve and Wycherley, and perhaps also from Molière's *Le Sicilien* and Beaumarchais. More immediately it appears that he based the plot on the experiences of his own elopement with and marriage to Elizabeth Linley in 1772–3 and heightened the farce by interweaving two love affairs, thus making the father of the brother and sister concerned look even more ridiculous.

In spite of the plot, Sheridan seems to have managed to persuade his father-in-law, Thomas Linley (i), to provide music for the play, although the latter did not approve of Sheridan's methods of compiling his lyrics and music as he went along. Much preparation still remained to be done when Linley wrote to Garrick on 28 September 1775:

> ... as often as I am called upon, I have promised to assist Sheridan in compiling, I believe is the properest term, an opera, which, I understand from him, he has engaged to produce at Covent-Garden this winter. I have already set some airs which he has given me, and he intends writing new words to some other tunes of mine. My son has likewise written some tunes for him, and I understand he is to have others from Mr Jackson, of Exeter. This is a mode of proceeding in regard to his composition, I do not by any means approve of. I think he ought first to have got it entirely new set. No musician can set a song properly unless he understands the character and knows the performer who is to exhibit it. For my part, I shall be very unwilling for either my own name, or my son's, to appear in this business, and it is my present resolution to forbid it; for I have great reason to be diffident of my own abilities and genius, and my son has not had experience in theatrical compositions, though I think well of his invention and musical skill.

Many letters passed between London and Bath with Sheridan begging Linley to come to London to assist with rehearsals; he held out little hope of success without this assistance.

ACT 1 Antonio is discovered serenading Louisa by Don Jerome, who promptly locks her up to prevent her eloping and vows not to speak to her until she has married Isaac Mendoza, to whom he has promised her. The old Duenna contrives to be caught while acting as go-between for the lovers and is banished by Don Jerome; Louisa then leaves the house disguised in the Duenna's clothes and veil. Once outside she encounters her brother's mistress, Clara, who has escaped from her father and who announces her intention, in the hearing of Isaac who has just arrived, of entering the local nunnery. Louisa introduces herself to Isaac as Clara and asks his help in finding her lover Antonio. Isaac welcomes the opportunity to dispatch his rival and sends his friend Don Carlos in search of Antonio.

ACT 2 Don Jerome receives Isaac and praises the attractions of his daughter; explaining the vow of silence he has made, he sends Isaac alone to her chamber. There the horrified suitor discovers the old Duenna in Louisa's clothes, but, mindful of her wealth and warmed by her flattery of him, he resolves to ask Don Jerome to set a time for the marriage. Margaret reminds him of Don Jerome's vow and persuades him to elope with her. While in search of a priest Isaac meets Ferdinand and tells him of the presumed Clara's elopement with Antonio. Ferdinand sets off in pursuit of his supposed rival and, on entering the garden of the nunnery, sees him with Louisa (whom he takes to be Clara) on their way to the friary to be married. Clara approaches Ferdinand in the hope of a reconciliation after their quarrel on the preceding evening; he fails to recognize her in her nun's habit, but she is reassured of his love by his evident jealousy of Antonio, in search of whom he abruptly leaves her.

ACT 3 Don Jerome receives a letter from Isaac containing news of his elopement and one from Louisa asking her father's forgiveness for the rashness of her actions. This he gives freely, under the impression that the two have eloped with each other. At the friary Antonio and Louisa meet Isaac and Margaret before the priest who is to marry them. Ferdinand bursts in and challenges Antonio to a duel, but Clara enters soon afterwards and reveals her identity, whereupon the three couples are married. The opera ends with Don Jerome convinced of his folly and laughing at Isaac for becoming the dupe of his own knavery as he welcomes the neighbourhood to the wedding feast he has had prepared.

* * *

The music for the opera was primarily the responsibility of the elder Linley, who took suggestions from Sheridan and Sheridan's wife. Most of his own contributions (which amount to about half of the total) are in fact based on traditional tunes and works by other composers, notably the finale to Act 3, 'Come now for jest and smiling', for which he used the melody of Morley's ballett *Now is the month of maying*, a brilliant choice. Among the items that he allocated to his son Thomas (ii) are a larger number of newly composed pieces, including the overture and the air 'Sharp is the woe'; this is one of the younger Linley's finest songs, scored imaginatively for horns and strings. Certain lyrics that were set do not appear in existing copies of the play, and are thus not known apart from their musical settings. Only a few of the musical items were published in a vocal score, and none in full score. The overture was published only in parts (*c*1778) and not in score. Decorated versions of ten of the songs were later included in Domenico Corri's 'Select Collection' of arias and songs (3 volumes, *c*1785), while four of them were included in Thomas Busby's collection of songs 'as ornamented by Mrs Billington' (1801). Elizabeth Billington sang the part of Clara in some performances in the 1780s and 90s.

The Duenna was performed 75 times in its first season, a record for an 18th-century English opera, exceeding the *Beggar's Opera*'s 63 performances in 1728. It was performed more frequently than any other Sheridan play during the author's lifetime, and was heard intermittently at Covent Garden up to 1840. The *Songs* were in constant demand and reprinted many times over. There were six editions before the end of 1775, 15 by 1776, 25 by 1778 and a 30th in 1786. Sheridan's own first edition of the complete play appeared only in 1794, after many revisions.

On the first performance there was universal praise for Sheridan's script and a good deal of admiration for the music. The *London Chronicle* for 21–3 November 1775 wrote:

> The versification and matter of the songs are far above the usual vehicles of tunes, and the music is, on the whole, the most judicious association of songs, simple tunes, duets, glees etc. that we ever remember in the theatre; ... No piece which has been brought out for some time past, has ever met with the warm reception which the Duenna deservedly met with from a polite and judicious audience.

The *Morning Chronicle* for 22 November, however, complained that 'from redundancy of songs, and the dull music of some of them, it is rendered heavy and serious where the business of the scene should be sprightly and evidently laughable'. Thomas Moore (1825) later wrote that 'The Duenna is one of the very few operas in our language which combines the merits of legitimate comedy with the attractions of poetry and song', and William Hazlitt (1819) commented:

> The Duenna is a perfect work of art. It has the utmost sweetness and point. The plot, the characters, the dialogue, are all complete in themselves; ... and the songs are the best that were ever written, except those in 'The Beggar's Opera'. They have a joyous spirit of intoxication in them, and a strain of the most melting tenderness.

In the 20th century *The Duenna* has been revived in 1924 at Hammersmith in a version by Nigel Playfair with music by Alfred Reynolds 'after Linley'. Another version was broadcast by the BBC (Third Programme) on 7 March 1962, and yet another was produced in London by Opera di Camera on 16 March 1976. In addition Sheridan's libretto was the basis of Prokofiev's opera *BETROTHAL IN A MONASTERY* (1946).

GWILYM BEECHEY

Duen'ya ('The Duenna'). Opera by Sergey Prokofiev; *see BETROTHAL IN A MONASTERY.*

Duesing, Dale (*b* Milwaukee, 26 Sept 1947). American baritone. After studying at Lawrence University, he sang in Bremen (1972) and Düsseldorf (1974–5), where his roles included Dandini and the King (*Die Kluge*). In 1976 he took part in the première of Imbrie's *Angle of Repose* at San Francisco and sang Olivier (*Capriccio*) at Glyndebourne; he made his Metropolitan début in 1979 as Harlequin (*Ariadne auf Naxos*). He has also appeared at Chicago, Seattle, Santa Fe, Salzburg and La Scala. His repertory includes Monteverdi's Otho, Mozart's and Rossini's Figaro, Guglielmo, Papageno, Belcore, Pelléas, Wolfram, Yevgeny Onegin, Marcello, Demetrius and Billy Budd, the last a role particularly well suited to his vocal and dramatic gifts.

ELIZABETH FORBES

Due supposti conti, I [*I due supposti conti, ossia Lo sposo senza moglie* ('The Two Would-Be Counts, or The Bridegroom without a Wife')]. *Dramma giocoso per musica* in two acts by DOMENICO CIMAROSA to a libretto by ANGELO ANELLI; Milan, Teatro alla Scala, 10 October 1784.

Don Pantaleone (tenor) wants his sister Beatrice (soprano) to marry the peasant farmer Marcotondo (bass) in order to avoid having to part with a dowry. Pantaleone has forced Marcotondo to assume the identity of Count Farfallone. Beatrice, who has run away from home, is warned by Fidalma (soprano), secretly in love with Pantaleone, and her maid, Laurina (soprano), of impending danger if Pantaleone should discover her whereabouts. Complications arise when Count Caramella (bass), a rich farmer from Mantua, also disguised as Count Farfallone, challenges the other 'count', the cowardly Marcotondo, to a duel. After a series of confusions between the two counts Beatrice eventually marries Caramella, Fidalma marries Pantaleone, and Laurina marries Pipetto (tenor); all make fun of Marcotondo, who proposes to all three ladies but, rejected by them all, is destined to remain a bachelor.

This popular opera was performed in many European cities for over 24 years; it was given in Rome (1786) with the title *Lo sposo ridicolo*. Popular at the courts of Vienna (15 performances) and Eszterháza (seven performances), it was altered for both places. In Vienna the overture and two substitute arias from works by Paisiello were inserted, as well as two other arias by Francesco Bianchi and Michele Neri. At Eszterháza Haydn reworked Laurina's (there Laura's) aria in Act 1 'Se voi foste un cavaliere' and composed new music for Beatrice's aria 'Infelice sventurata'.

The music is generally vivacious, with some slapstick in the finale of Act 2. Folk elements occur in the opening orchestral contradanza, as well as in Caramella's cavatina 'Donne belle seguaci d'amore', sung to the accompaniment of a guitar. Also noteworthy is the duet for Beatrice and Caramella 'Nel veder quel tuo sembiante', with its charming heartbeat imitations at 'tiche, tache, toche, ta'.

GORDANA LAZAREVICH

Duet (Fr. *duo*; Ger. *Duett*; It. *duetto*). A composition for two voices, normally with accompaniment. The duet, the most popular type of operatic ENSEMBLE, has been used in opera since its inception.

1. Italian opera up to 1750. 2. French opera up to *c*1775. 3. The Classical period. 4. Since 1800.

1. ITALIAN OPERA UP TO 1750. In early Italian operas duets appeared both within concerted contexts and as expressions of emotion for pairs of characters. They might be assigned to any pair from the cast (or occasionally from the chorus); they might appear at any point in the opera, or be combined with an aria, or serve to conclude a scene, an act or the opera itself. Duets might be on any scale, from brief expressions of emotion of a few bars to long, multi-sectional pieces during which the plot advanced ('Scopriamli sì', *Ormindo*, Cavalli, 1644); they might be strophic pieces over a ground bass or might take more formal patterns – *ABA'*, *ABB'A* ('Auree trece inanella', *Ormindo*) *ABB'* ('Saett'amor', *Ormindo*), da capo. By the 1670s rounded ternary forms were generally favoured. Most duets began imitatively, but during the 1680s a new style started to appear in which each character sang first a short solo (often the same music but with different words); imitative dialogue then quickly led into duet textures. A da capo indication might replace the *A'* section of the rounded ternary ('Poco chiede la tua fede', *Eraclea*, A. Scarlatti, 1700). Duets were much used in comic scenes within serious operas, which commonly took the form of a dialogue followed by a duet; this might be quite brief and in any form ('Mi sento ardito', *Eraclea*).

During the first decades of the 18th century, when the main stream of Italian opera divested itself of comic elements, the *opera seria* became the principal entertainment of the evening, and comic diversions took the form of intermezzos, which served as entr'actes. These short episodes, also for two characters, usually a bass and a soprano, often ended with a duet finale in several sections, with a da capo ('Per te ho io nel core', *La serva padrona*, Pergolesi, 1733). After 1700, duets tended to begin with a long solo for each participant, usually singing a different strophe of poetry but set to the same music, a 4th or 5th apart in pitch; this is followed by a transitional section in which the voices have alternating short phrases and overlapping of parts or a section *a due* to lead to simultaneous cadences. Such patterns are found as early as 1718–19 in A. Scarlatti's *Telemaco* and *Marco Attilio Regolo*. By the 1730s duets were following the standard five-part da capo form, with the text sung twice through, with multiple settings of the words for the short phrases and the subsequent duo portions (*AA'*) followed by a contrasting B section and da capo (see 'Alma mia, dolce ristoro', *Admeto*, Handel, 1727). In *opera seria* from 1730 until about 1780, duets were virtually the exclusive province of the principal couple, normally a soprano and a castrato (soprano or alto); until the 1770s, the duet would usually be the only ensemble in an *opera seria*, where it might function as the finale to the first or second of the three acts ('Se viver non degg'io', *Mitridate, rè di Porto*, Mozart, 1770), although duets also appeared in the third act, typically at a lovers' reunion or their supposed last farewell ('Tu vuoi ch'io viva', *Artaserse*, Metastasio). In comic opera after 1750, when large ensemble finales became the norm, a duet for the principal *buffa* couple was usually the only other ensemble. Duets became more prevalent after 1760; an *opera giocosa* could have a duet for both the *buffa* and the *seria* couple, as well as an elaborate comic action piece (usually for two men), and one or more short duets might enliven the action (see *Il re alla caccia*, Galuppi, 1763). Comic duets, often composed to dialogue texts, were usually spirited and highly charged encounters, while those in serious opera were refined and elevated in tone. Comic duets were also more flexible in structure (often in binary or chain forms, to match the nature of the intrigue), whereas serious ones tended to take the same forms as were prevalent for arias.

2. FRENCH OPERA UP TO *c*1775. The duet is very much the most popular type of concerted number in the *tragédie lyrique*, accounting for nearly 90 per cent of all ensembles in the period from Lully to Rameau. There are usually three or four duets in each work, sited at various points within the action. Short duets are particularly common before the end of the 17th century (see *Alceste*, Lully, 1764). Vocal pairings are more diverse than in *opera seria*; as well as lovers' duets there are vengeance duets (usually for rejected suitors), confrontation duets (Rameau's *Zoroastre* includes two notable examples), pairings of hero or heroine with his or her confidant(e), and diverse combinations of secondary characters, especially in prologues and *divertissements*. These last tend to use longer verses as opposed to the quatrains generally favoured in other types of duet. Binary forms predominate, though rondeau forms also appear; by the end of the 17th century da capo and dal segno types are sometimes used, under the influence of Italian models. In Rameau's operas duets often appear as part of a larger design, alternating with solo or choral sections in ternary or rondeau structures ('Volez zéphirs' and 'Forêts paisibles', *Les Indes galantes*, 1735). Textures are mainly homophonic, though after 1700 some contrapuntal writing may be found in duets within the *tragédie* proper (as opposed to the prologues and *divertissements*; see *Hippolyte et Aricie*, Rameau, 1733).

Normally both characters sing the same words, simultaneously: *unanime* expression ensures the clarity of the text that was always a prerequisite in French opera. Divergent duets involving discord and contradiction were considered contrived, artificial and improper to the dignity of the *tragédie lyrique*. But Rousseau, writing on 'Duo' in the *Encyclopédie* in the light of Italian practices that were currently gaining a foothold in France, advocated not the French homophonic duet but the Italian-style dialogue duet as the clearest form of ensemble expression.

In *opéra comique* the duet is secondary in importance as compared with larger ensembles, though still predominant in the frequency of its occurrence. There is less emphasis on the lovers' duet; rather, the form is used to portray varied dramatic situations (see *Tom Jones*, Philidor, 1765), particularly to highlight dramatic irony and ambiguity. Almost half the duets are for singers of the same sex; forms become increasingly adaptable to dramatic exigency, and texts, often quite irregular in structure, tend to be laid out in dialogue form in the printed librettos.

3. THE CLASSICAL PERIOD. Reform thinking after the middle of the century affected the duet only marginally. In Traetta's *Ifigenia in Tauride* (1763, Vienna), the librettist, Coltellini, reintroduced the single-sex duet, probably from French opera, and Verazi followed suit a year later in his libretto on the same subject, set by G. F.

de Majo for Mannheim. Single-sex duets do not however become common in *opera seria* until the 1790s. In Majo's opera the duet, for Pylades and Orestes, includes interjections from a third character, Iphigenia – another practice reintroduced either from French opera or from early 18th-century Italian librettos, where the device is still found. In the 1790s a similar kind of duet with unequal participation becomes common – the aria with interjections or interruptions (*pertichini*) from one or more other characters. Also in the 1790s duets, like other types of ensemble, become more frequent as cavatinas and as components in scene complexes, as well as functioning as independent exit pieces either within an act or at its close.

The early 1760s saw a move towards the truncated forms that were becoming prevalent in arias – the 'da capo al segno' type ('Turna la pace', *Ippolito ed Aricia*, Traetta, 1759) and the simple dal segno (which returned to a point early in the *A′* section ('La destra ti chieda', *Demofoonte*, Jommelli, 1764). Many duets of the decade took through-composed forms, preceding arias by nearly ten years in this. Most composers simply set the text through once or twice, but by the late 1760s duets began to take the form *ABA′C* ('Ah! tornate, o Dio, serene', Jommelli, *Armida abbandonnata*, 1770) or *ABC* ('Se viver non degg'io', *Mitridate*, 1770), often with each section delineated by a change of tempo, metre or both. The *B* section used the first segment of text intended for setting *a due* and the *C* section was based on the final strophe. It was common for tempos to move from slow (Adagio or Larghetto) to moderate (Allegretto, for the *B* section) to fast (Allegro assai, for the *C* section; 'Cara, sarò fedele', *Armida*, Haydn, 1784), though on occasion the central section was the slowest ('Ich gehe, doch rate ich dir', *Die Entführung aus dem Serail*, Mozart, 1782). In duets for lovers, in particular, it was normal for the finale section largely to consist of music sung *a due* in 3rds or 6ths, symbolizing unanimity of purpose after the resolution of earlier difficulties or uncertainties; familiar examples are Mozart's 'Là ci darem' from *Don Giovanni* and 'Fra gli amplessi' from *Così fan tutte*. A high proportion of love duets in the Classical era were set in A major, a key that lends itself to the production of soft, sensuous, translucent textures (particularly by the use of flutes rather than oboes in conjunction with high-pitched horns). 'Che soave zeffiretto' from *Le nozze di Figaro* is a rare example of a duet portraying in its music the direction and reading-back of a letter.

4. Since 1800. In the 19th century, especially in Italy, the duet assumed an importance equal to that of the aria. In operas of Rossini's time and after, the 'grand duet' is normally articulated in three ample movements. The first, the *tempo d'attacco*, consists of two parallel stanzas for each singer in fast time, both ending with emphatic cadences, after which the music proceeds in dialogue, modulating to a new key in preparation for the slow central cantabile. This takes the form of a joint soliloquy, the voices sooner or later joining in 3rds (soprano and contralto or mezzo), 6ths (soprano and tenor) or 10ths (soprano and baritone) and finishing with a combined cadenza. There follows a swift *tempo di mezzo* during which some event will occur that provokes a decision and so detonates the final movement, or cabaletta. Classic instances of this formula include 'Ebben, a te; ferisci' (*Semiramide*, Rossini, 1823), 'Deh, con te li prendi' (*Norma*, Bellini, 1831) and 'Il pallor funesto orrendo' (*Lucia di Lammermoor*, Donizetti, 1835). Donizetti also employs a *tempo d'attacco* in dialogue from the outset, such as 'Soli noi siamo' (*Lucrezia Borgia*, 1833), a procedure followed by Verdi from early in his career, as in 'Guardami, sul mio ciglio' (*Oberto*, 1839), 'Donna, chi sei?' (*Nabucco*, 1842) and 'Ti colgo alfine' (*Attila*, 1846). Verdi's later duets adhere still more closely to the cut and thrust of the conversation, while mostly showing traces of an underlying tripartite design, for example 'Fatal mia donna! un murmure' (*Macbeth*, 1847), 'Pura siccome un angelo' (*La traviata*, 1853), 'Dinne, perchè in quest'eremo' (*Simon Boccanegra*, 1857) and even 'Già nella notte densa' (*Otello*, 1887). Throughout the period two-movement duets are to be found, occasionally without a *tempo d'attacco*, for example 'Ah se dei mali miei' (*Tancredi*, Rossini, 1813), more often without a cantabile, as in 'Va crudele, al Dio spietato' (*Norma*), 'Il più lieto dei viventi' (*Poliuto*, Donizetti, composed 1838) or 'Anima mia!' (*Alzira*, Verdi, 1845); there are also a number of duets that end as trios, such as 'Pensa che sol per poco' (*Elisabetta, regina d'Inghilterra*, Rossini, 1815), 'Vieni, cerchiam pe' mari' (*Il pirata*, Bellini, 1827) and 'Qui mi trasse amor possente' (*Ernani*, Verdi, 1843). Single-movement duets are rare outside *opera buffa* or *semiseria*; examples include 'Son geloso del zeffiro errante' (*La sonnambula*, Bellini, 1831) and 'Tornami a dir che m'ami' (*Don Pasquale*, Donizetti, 1843).

Outside Italy such formulae persist only in the Parisian grand operas of Rossini, Donizetti and Verdi, for example 'Oui, vous l'arrachez à mon âme' (*Guillaume Tell*, Rossini, 1829). Otherwise duets are much freer in form, consisting either of a single movement, such as 'O namenlose Freude' (*Fidelio*, Beethoven, 1805), 'Komm denn, unser Leid zu rächen' (*Euryanthe*, Weber, 1823) and 'Nuit d'ivresse et d'extase infinie' (*Les Troyens*, Berlioz, 1863), or as a succession of episodes which may be linked by an element of thematic recurrence, as in 'Que peut-il pour moi ce Dieu?' (*Faust*, Gounod, 1859), 'Parle-moi de ma mère' (*Carmen*, Bizet, 1875). A similar principle holds good for Russian and Czech opera as well as the early Wagner canon, for example 'Das süsse Lied verhallt' (*Lohengrin*, 1850). The extended dialogues of the music dramas, however, hardly qualify as duets, since they do not constitute independent formal units, the one possible exception being that of the lovers in Act 2 of *Tristan und Isolde* (1865) in which a three-part ground-plan is discernible – (*a*) 'Isolde! Tristan! Geliebter!'; (*b*) 'O sink hernieder, Nacht der Liebe'; (*c*) 'So stürben wir, um ungetrennt'.

From about 1870 onward the structure is governed by the sense of the text, the voices rarely uniting except in an amorous context. Favourite love duets not already mentioned include 'Parigi, o cara' (*La traviata*, Verdi, 1853), 'Son la vittima che geme' (*Un ballo in maschera*, 1859), 'O soave fanciulla' (*La bohème*, Puccini, 1896), 'Viene la sera' (*Madama Butterfly*, 1904), to which may be added two expressive of budding affection – 'Fresche scintillano' (*L'amico Fritz*, Mascagni, 1891) and 'Mir ist die Ehre widerfahren' (*Der Rosenkavalier*, Richard Strauss, 1911). Among those that exploit the perennial charm of two female voices in 3rds and 6ths are the cantabile 'Mira, O Norma' (*Norma*) and 'Sous le dôme épais' (*Lakmé*, Delibes, 1883). Duets between women who are rivals in love include 'Fu la sorte dell'armi a tuoi funesta' (*Aida*, Verdi, 1871) and 'L'amo come il fulgor del creato' (*La Gioconda*, Ponchielli, 1876), and for male voices 'Solenne in quest'ora' (*La forza del destino*, Verdi, 1862) and 'Au fond du temple saint' (*Les pêcheurs de perles*, Bizet, 1863).

*

E. J. Dent: 'Ensembles and Finales in Eighteenth-Century Italian Opera', *SIMG*, xi (1909–10), 543–69; xii (1910–11), 112–38
M. F. Robinson: *Naples and Neapolitan Opera* (Oxford, 1972)
H. Becker: 'Das Duett in der Oper', *Musik, Edition, Interpretation: Gedenkschrift Gunter Henle* (Munich, 1980), 82–99
S. L. Balthazar: 'The *Primo Ottocento* Duet and the Transformation of the Rossinian Code', *JM*, vii (1989), 471–97
E. Cook: *The Operatic Ensemble in France, 1673–1775* (diss., U. of East Anglia, 1989)

MARITA McCLYMONDS, ELISABETH COOK, JULIAN BUDDEN

Dufallo, Richard (John) (*b* East Chicago, IN, 30 Jan 1933). American conductor. He studied at the American Conservatory of Music, Chicago. His career has been mainly with symphony orchestras in the USA and (since 1971) also in Europe, with a special interest in contemporary music, but he has worked with Cincinnati Opera conducting *Boris Godunov* and with New York City Opera in *Il trittico*, and was director of the 'Mini-Met' series at the Metropolitan, 1972–4. His early experience as a clarinettist has been of practical help in new music, and his performances strive for the clearest emotional as well as musical impact. RICHARD BERNAS

Dufranne, Eva (*b* Belgium, 1857; *d* Paris, July 1905). Belgian soprano and mezzo-soprano. She studied in Brussels and then in Paris, making her début at the Opéra in 1880 as Rachel (*La Juive*). Apart from one season (1890–91) at the Théâtre de la Monnaie, she was engaged at the Opéra for the next 18 years, singing a wide variety of roles: Berthe (*Le prophète*), Alice (*Robert le diable*), Sélika (*L'Africaine*), Donna Elvira and Donna Anna, Massenet's Sapho, Xaima and Hermosa (Gounod's *Le tribut de Zamora*), Aida and Amneris, Elsa and Ortrud, Brünnhilde and Fricka (*Die Walküre*), Hilda and Uta (*Sigurd*), Catherine (Saint-Saëns' *Henry VIII*), Léonor (*La favorite*) and Gertrude (*Hamlet*). ELIZABETH FORBES

Dufranne, Hector (*b* Mons, 25 Oct 1871; *d* Paris, 4 May 1951). French bass-baritone. He made his début in 1898 at La Monnaie in Brussels, as Valentin in *Faust*, having studied at the Brussels Conservatoire with Désirée Demest. In 1900 he appeared as Thoas in *Iphigénie en Tauride* with the Opéra-Comique in Paris, where he became one of the leading and longest-serving members of the company. He sang in many premières, including those of *Grisélidis* (1901), *L'heure espagnole* (1911) and, at Monte Carlo, Massenet's *Thérèse* (1907). He was also the Opéra-Comique's first Scarpia in *Tosca* and the Opéra's first John the Baptist in *Salome* (1910). Above all, he was associated with the role of Golaud in *Pelléas et Mélisande*, which he sang at the première (1902) and in the first American production (New York, Manhattan, 1910). In 1914 he sang the role in his single appearance at Covent Garden and in 1939, for the last time, at Vichy. He won high praise for both his singing and his acting in New York and later became a favourite at Chicago, where he sang Celio in the world première of *The Love for Three Oranges* (1921), conducted by Prokofiev. At a private performance in Paris he took the part of Don Quixote in the stage première of Falla's *El retablo de maese Pedro* (1923). His admirable voice, well placed and finely produced, served him well through a long career and is impressively heard in some historically important recordings, particularly those of *L'heure espagnole* and *Pelléas et Mélisande* (1928).

J. B. STEANE

Dugazon. Term used in French opera since the late 18th century for the types of role, and the types of voice associated with them, originally sung by LOUISE-ROSALIE DUGAZON. The 'jeune Dugazon' represents a light, soubrette-like but expressive Romantic role, such as she sang until the late 1780s, and the 'mère Dugazon' the mature young woman she characteristically impersonated thereafter.

Dugazon [Gourgaud], **(Alexandre-Louis-)Gustave** (*b* Paris, ?1782; *d* Paris, ?1826). French composer, son of Louise-Rosalie Dugazon. He studied with Berton and Gossec at the Conservatoire, winning second prize in the Prix de Rome in 1806. *Le voisinage* (1800), a collaboration, was his first dramatic work. He wrote three other operas and four ballets, none successful, and published collections of romances and nocturnes and piano adaptations of arias by Rossini and others.

all performed in Paris

Le voisinage (oc, 1, J. B. Pujoulx), OC (Favart), 24 Jan 1800, collab. Bertaud, Dubuat, Pradher and Quinebaud
Le chevalier d'industrie (oc, 1, J. M. B. Saint-Victor), OC (Feydeau), 16 Nov 1804, collab. Pradher
Marguerite de Waldemar (oc, 3, Saint-Félix), OC (Feydeau), 12 Dec 1812
La noce écossaise (oc, 1, T. M. Dumersan), OC (Feydeau), 19 Nov 1814

*

J. J. Olivier: *Madame Dugazon de la Comédie-Italienne, 1755–1821* (Paris, 1917)

LELAND FOX

Dugazon [née Lefèbvre], **Louise-Rosalie** (*b* Berlin, 18 June 1755; *d* Paris, 22 Sept 1821). French soprano. The daughter of a dancer at the Paris Opéra, it was as a dancer that she first appeared, in 1767; her singing career began when Grétry included an *ariette* for her in *Lucile* (1769), and she made her mature début in 1774 as Pauline in his *Silvain*. She married the actor Jean-Baptiste-Henri Gourgaud, called Dugazon, in 1776, but they separated after three years and divorced in 1794. For political reasons she did not sing on the stage in 1792–4.

Dugazon was one of the most popular singers at the Opéra-Comique, where from 1776 she created some 60 roles, among them Dalayrac's Nina (1786), and sang many by Grétry, notably in *Les mariages samnites* (1778), *Aucassin et Nicolette* (1782), *Richard coeur-de-lion* (1784) and *Le comte d'Albert* (1788); her dramatic talents gave her singing an expressiveness and versatility that was highly acclaimed. Later she renounced romantic roles to play young matrons, for example in Méhul's *Euphrosine et Coradin* (1791). Her singing and her characteristic casting gave rise to the terms 'jeune Dugazon' and 'mère Dugazon'. Her last performance was in 1804, as Zémaïde in Boieldieu's *Le calife de Bagdad*; in that year the main performing troupes in Paris combined for her benefit at the Opéra. Three of her sisters sang and danced at the Opéra-Comique, and her son Gustav Dugazon was a composer.

See also DUGAZON.

*

ES (B. Horowicz)
A. Pougin: *Figures d'Opéra-Comique* (Paris, 1875), 5–75

Louise-Rosalie Dugazon in the title role of Dalayrac's 'Nina, ou La folle par amour' which she created in the original production at the Comédie-Italienne, Paris, 15 May 1786: engraving by Dutertre after Janninet from 'Costumes et annales des grands théâtres de Paris' (1786)

J. J. Olivier: *Madame Dugazon de la Comédie-Italienne, 1755–1821* (Paris, 1917)
H. LeRoux and A. LeRoux: *La Dugazon* (Paris, 1926)

LELAND FOX

Duhamel, Antoine (*b* Valmondois, 30 July 1925). French composer. The son of the writer Georges Duhamel and the actress Blanche Albane, he studied in Messiaen's analysis class and was later taught extensively by Leibowitz. His early works already showed a marked leaning towards the theatre and, more particularly, the cinema, and film music subsequently formed a large part of his output. In 1951–2 he was active at the Club d'Essai, which promoted new and unusual works; Duhamel himself mounted performances of little-known Baroque operas including Scarlatti's *Il trionfo d'onore* and Rameau's *Pygmalion*. It was in the 1960s that Duhamel was most active in film music, working for such celebrated directors as Godard and Truffaut and writing for television. Later in the 1960s he returned to concert music. *Lundi, Monsieur, vous serez riche* ran to over 100 performances in Paris and on tour. His eclecticism is particularly wide in *L'opéra des oiseaux*, where a mixture of the spoken word and singing includes old popular songs, pop music and free jazz, with orchestra and soloists dressed as birds who inhabit both stage and auditorium. *Le cirque impérial*, performed in the Music-Theatre series of the Avignon Festival, includes singers, acrobats and actors and is accompanied by a chamber group of 11 instruments. In *Gambara* Duhamel used Balzac's story of the self-destructive artist to 'speak to the public of the strange existence of a composer'. *Le transsibérien*, set on a train, tells the story of Cendrars' exile on the eve of the Russian revolution. Duhamel has also worked with group composition and realization, notably at the Avignon Festival, where in 1976 he directed *Les troubadours*. He has also directed several ballets and was responsible for the revival of Gervais' *Penthée* broadcast on 23 December 1980).

L'ivrogne, 1952 (after C. Baudelaire), Tours, 1984
Gala de cirque, (opéra-ballet), Strasbourg, Opéra, 1965
Lundi, Monsieur, vous serez riche (opéra, 2, R. Forlani), Paris, Renaissance, 23 Jan 1969
L'opéra des oiseaux (opéra, 1, S. Ouaknine and C. Ferris, after Aristophanes), Lyons, Opéra, 19 May 1971
Ubu à l'opéra (théâtre-musical, G. Wilson, after A. Jarry), Avignon, Festival, 16 July 1974
Gambara (opéra, 2, G. Dufour and R. Pansard-Besson after H. de Balzac), Lyons, Opéra, 2 June 1978
Le cirque impérial (théâtre-musical, C. Alranq), Avignon, Centre Dramatique La Courneuve, 30 July 1979
Les travaux d'Hercule (opéra pour la jeunesse, 1, Duhamel), Vaise (Opéra de Lyon), 15 June 1981
Le transsibérien (opéra ferrovière, B. Cendrars), (Bouffes du Nord), 29 Nov 1983
Le scieur de long (C. Ciccione and Duhamel, after Baudelaire), Tours, Opéra, 9 March 1984
Quatrevingt-treize (grand opéra, 2, G. Ben Aych, after V. Hugo), Fourvières (Opéra de Lyon), 10 July 1989
Les Aventures de Sinbad le marin, (opéra de chambre, M. Beretti), Colmar, Atelier Lyrique, 12 Feb 1991

RICHARD LANGHAM SMITH

Duhan, Hans (*b* Vienna, 27 Jan 1890; *d* Baden, nr Vienna, 6 March 1971). Austrian baritone. A singer with a thorough musical training (he studied the piano and the organ, as well as singing, at the Vienna Academy), he is remembered principally as the first artist to make complete recordings of *Winterreise* and *Die schöne Müllerin*. His career in opera, though it lasted from 1910 to 1940, was largely confined to Vienna and Salzburg where in addition to the usual baritone roles in Mozart he sang Pedrillo in *Die Entführung*. He made his début at Troppau and joined the Vienna Staatsoper in 1914. At the première of *Ariadne auf Naxos* (1916, revised version) he doubled as the Music Master and Harlequin. He was especially admired in Mozart and Lortzing, but the overuse of his light baritone voice in operas such as *Die Meistersinger* led to vocal difficulties and encouraged him to concentrate on lieder and teaching (among his pupils was the baritone Hermann Uhde). In later years he worked as stage director, conductor and composer. Recordings show a voice limited in colour as well as volume, though used with skill and intelligence. J. B. STEANE

Duisburg. Town in western Germany. It is the base, with DÜSSELDORF, of the Deutsche Oper am Rhein.

Dukas, Paul (Abraham) (*b* Paris, 1 Oct 1865; *d* Paris, 17 May 1935). French composer, teacher and critic. He studied at the Paris Conservatoire with Théodore Dubois (harmony), Georges Mathias (piano) and Guiraud (composition). From 1892 he wrote a great deal of music criticism, reflecting his wide sympathies and sound judgment. He taught at the Conservatoire for two periods (orchestration from 1910 to 1913 and composition from 1928); his pupils there, who included Messiaen, regarded him with esteem and affection. He also earned the gratitude of other musicians (Falla among them), not strictly pupils, to whom he gave advice and encouragement.

Dukas' first mature work, the concert overture *Polyeucte* (1891) was followed by a small number of compositions, including the symphonic scherzo *L'apprenti sorcier* (1897). His largest work, the three-act *Ariane et Barbe-bleue*, was first performed in Paris at the Opéra-Comique in 1907. The *poème dansé La péri* (1911–12), produced as a ballet but better known as a concert piece, is his last important work. Dukas' achievements may seem limited in quantity, but the quality is high and none of them are lightweight.

Dukas was a man of wide culture and superior intelligence, intensely self-critical with a vein of scepticism and perhaps self-doubt. He destroyed a number of works, both finished and unfinished (the latter, however, sufficiently advanced to be played and discussed in his own circle), because they did not meet his high standards. These apparently included an opera on Shakespeare's *The Tempest* and another ballet. With Saint-Saëns, he completed Guiraud's unfinished opera *Frédégonde* and assisted in the preparation of the complete edition of Rameau's works, begun in 1895. In the teeming, faction-ridden musical life of early 20th-century Paris, Dukas occupied a singular position, remaining on terms of close friendship with representatives of such varied schools of thought as Fauré (Conservatoire), d'Indy (Schola Cantorum) and the independent Debussy.

See also ARIANE ET BARBE-BLEUE.

*

G. Samazeuilh: *Paul Dukas* (Paris, 1913, 2/1936)
V. d'Indy: *Emmanuel Chabrier et Paul Dukas* (Paris, 1920)
O. Messiaen: 'Ariane et Barbe-bleue de Paul Dukas', *ReM*, no.166 (1936) [Dukas issue]
P. Dukas: *Ecrits sur la musique* (Paris, 1948)
G. Favre: *Paul Dukas: sa vie, son oeuvre* (Paris, 1948)
——: *L'oeuvre de Paul Dukas* (Paris, 1969)
——, ed.: *Correspondance de Paul Dukas* (Paris, 1971)
J. Helbé: *Paul Dukas (1865–1935)* (Paris, 1975)
P. Dukas: *Chroniques musicales sur deux siècles 1892–1932* (Paris, 1980)

RONALD CRICHTON

Duke, Vernon [Dukelsky, Vladimir Alexandrovich] (*b* Parfianovka, nr. Pskov, Russia, 10/23 Oct 1903; *d* Santa Monica, CA, 16 Jan 1969). American composer. He studied with Glièr and Dombrovsky at the Kiev Conservatory and then fled the Revolution with his family, settling first in Constantinople (1920–21) and then in New York (1922). In 1924 he was in Paris, where he was commissioned by Dyagilev to write a ballet based on his piano concerto; in Britain he wrote music for the stage before returning to New York, where he studied orchestration with Joseph Schillinger (1934–5). In 1948 he founded the Society for Forgotten Music. At George Gershwin's suggestion he adopted the pseudonym Vernon Duke for his popular songs and light music, continuing to use his Russian name for his other works until 1955. Duke developed two styles, one for his choral works, operas, ballets and orchestral and chamber compositions (championed in the USA and Europe by Koussevitzky) and another for his revues, musicals and film scores, for which he was better known. His most successful work was the musical play *Cabin in the Sky* (1940), which was performed on Broadway by an all-black cast that included Ethel Waters and choreographed by Balanchine. In many of his concert works Duke used a contrapuntal style; in his songs the melodic style is expansive, almost rhapsodic, and uses chromaticism and wide arpeggios. Besides an autobiography, *Passport to Paris* (1955), he wrote *Listen Here!: a Critical Essay on Music Depreciation* (1963) and Russian poetry.

musical comedies or musicals unless otherwise stated

The Yellow Mask (2, E. Wallace; lyrics D. Carter), Birmingham, Royal, 15 Nov 1927, London Carlton, 8 Feb 1928; Open your Eyes (2, F. Jackson; lyrics J. Dyrenforth and C. Knox), Edinburgh, Empire, 26 Aug 1929, collab. C. Gibbons; Cabin in the Sky (L. Root; lyrics J. T. Latouche), New York, Martin Beck, 25 Oct 1940; Banjo Eyes (J. Quillan and I. Elinson, after J. C. Holm and G. Abbott: *Three Men on a Horse*; lyrics Latouche and H. Adamson), New York, Hollywood, 25 Dec 1941

The Lady comes Across (F. Thompson and D. Powell; lyrics Latouche), New York, 44th Street, 9 Jan 1942; Jackpot (G. Bolton, S. Sheldon and B. Roberts; lyrics H. Dietz), New York, Alvin, 13 Jan 1944; Sadie Thompson (Dietz and R. Mamoulian, after S. Maugham: *Rain*; lyrics Dietz), New York, Alvin, 16 Nov 1944; Mistress into Maid (opera, Duke, after A. Pushkin), Santa Barbara, CA, 1958; Zenda (opera, E. Freeman; lyrics L. Adelson, S. Kuller and M. Charnin), San Francisco, Aug 1963

*

N. Slonimsky: 'Vladimir Dukelsky', *MM*, iv/3 (1927), 37
D. Ewen: *Popular American Composers* (New York, 1962, suppl. 1972)
Obituary, *New York Times* (18 Jan 1969)
A. Wilder: *American Popular Song: the Great Innovators, 1900–1950* (New York, 1972)
G. Bordman: *The American Musical Theatre* (New York, 1978)

RONALD BYRNSIDE/R

Duke Bluebeard's Castle. Opera by Béla Bartók; *see* BLUEBEARD'S CASTLE.

Du Locle, Camille (*b* Orange, 16 July 1832; *d* Capri, 9 Oct 1903). French theatre director and librettist. After serving as an assistant to his uncle Emile Perrin during his tenure as director of the Paris Opéra from 1862 to 1870, Du Locle administered the Opéra-Comique with Adolphe de Leuven from 1870 to 1874, and alone from 1874 to 1876. As a director he is best remembered for having mounted the première of Bizet's *Carmen* in 1875, a controversial production that met with little initial success. Du Locle also championed the works of Gounod at the Opéra-Comique following the demise of the Théâtre Lyrique in the late 1860s. 'At last [Boieldieu's] *La dame blanche* is no longer making money', he is said to have once exclaimed, with epigrammatic verve reflective of a fundamentally innovatory spirit. He was a close friend of Ernest Reyer, with whom he collaborated as librettist on *Sigurd* (1884) and *Salammbô* (1890). Following the death of Joseph Méry, Du Locle completed the libretto for Verdi's *Don Carlos* (1867). He developed close personal ties with Verdi and went on to provide a prose scenario for *Aida* and to prepare the French translation of that opera as well as those of *La forza del destino* and *Simon Boccanegra.*

STEVEN HUEBNER

Dumas [Davy de la Pailleterie], **Alexandre (i)** (*b* Villers-Cotterêts, Aisne, 24 July 1802; *d* Puys, nr Dieppe, 5 Dec 1870). French dramatist and novelist. He was known as Dumas *père*, having acknowledged his illegitimate son of the same name who also became a playwright. Dumas *père*'s sense of plot and theatre made his colourful plays and romances a rich source for librettists during and after his lifetime. Many of his plots were loosely based on historical events and characters, though he often altered fact to suit his dramatic purposes. He turned several of his novels, including *Le comte de*

Monte Cristo and *Les trois mousquetaires*, into plays, which sometimes served as a stepping-stone to their transformation into operas. He also collaborated on at least three librettos: with Nerval on *Piquillo* (set by Monpou, 1837); with Edouard Duprez on *Samson* (Gilbert Duprez, 1857); and with Adolphe de Leuven on *Le roman d'Elvire* (Ambroise Thomas, 1860) and probably, under the name 'de Beauplan', on *La bacchante* (Eugène Gautier, 1858).

Henri III et sa cour (play, 1829): Coccia, 1833, as Caterina di Guisa; Flotow, 1838, as Le comte de Saint-Mégrin; J. M. Josse, 1876, as La lega; P. and L. Hillemacher, 1886, as Saint-Mégrin
Charles VII chez ses grands vassaux (play, 1831): Donizetti, 1834, as Gemma di Vergy; Cui, 1899, as Saratsin [The Saracen]
Don Juan de Marana, ou La chute d'un ange (play, 1836): Enna, 1925; Goossens, 1937
Kean (play, 1836): F. Sangiorgi, 1855, as Edmondo Kean
Pascal Bruno (novel, 1838): Hatton, 1844
Mademoiselle de Belle-Isle (play, 1839): Samaras, 1905
Othon l'archer (novel, 1840): K. H. A. Reiss, 1856, as Otto der Schütz; Minchejmer, 1864, as Otton łucznik
Le chevalier d'Harmental (novel, 1842, with A. Maquet): Messager, 1896
Benvenuto Cellini (novel, 1843): Saint-Saëns, 1890, as Ascanio
Les demoiselles de Saint-Cyr (play, 1843, with A. de Leuven and Brunswick): Dellinger, 1891, as Saint Cyr; Humperdinck, 1905, as Die Heirat wider Willen; Chapuis, 1921
Les trois mousquetaires (novel, 1844): Xyndas, 1855, as Anna Winter; A. A. Visetti, 1871; R. Dionesi, 1888; De Lara, 1921; Benatzky, 1929
Le comte de Monte Cristo (novel, 1845–6): R. Dell'Aquila, 1876
Mémoires d'un médecin [Joseph Balsame] (play, 1848): Sangiorgi, 1873, as Giuseppe Balsamo; Litolff, 1876, as La mandragore
Le tulipe noir (novel, 1850): Flotow, 1876, as Il fiore d'Arlem
La dame de Monsoreau (novel, 1860): Salvayre, 1888

Dumas, Alexandre (ii) (*b* Paris, 27 July 1824; *d* Marly-le-Roi, 27 Nov 1895). French dramatist. Known as Dumas *fils*, he was the illegitimate son of Alexandre Dumas *père*. His direct contribution to musical theatre was less than that of his father, but his *La dame aux camélias* formed the basis of one of the most popular operas ever. In 1844 he embarked on a passionate liaison with Alphonsine Plessis, a noted *demi-mondaine* born in 1824 who preferred to be called Marie Duplessis. The couple soon parted, and on 3 February 1847 she died. Dumas composed some verses in her memory and then, in 1848, published the novel *La dame aux camélias* which, with its accent of truth, immediacy of emotion and clever use of realistic detail, started the process by which a brief affair would be transformed into a great tragic love story that has acquired the status of myth. Dumas next fashioned a drama of the same name out of his novel, and its first performance, on 2 February 1852 (Paris, Théâtre du Vaudeville), after delays caused by censorship, was a triumph. Among those whose interest was aroused was Verdi. He asked Francesco Maria Piave for a libretto based on the play, and *La traviata* had its première in Venice at La Fenice on 6 March 1853. Paris first heard the opera, under the title *Violetta*, at the Théâtre Lyrique on 27 October 1864. Dumas never equalled *La dame aux camélias*, but he continued to write novels and well-made plays in which his concern for the ills of contemporary society became more and more apparent. He was elected to the Académie Française in 1874.

*

H.-J. Neuschäfer and G. Sigaux, eds.: *Alexandre Dumas fils: La dame aux camélias; le roman, le drame, 'La traviata'* (Paris, 1981)
CHRISTOPHER SMITH

Dumesnil [Duménil, Dumény, Du Mesny, du Mény] (*fl* 1677–1700; *d* 1702). French tenor. His voice was discovered by Lully, who had him trained successfully in deportment and gesture, but unsuccessfully in musical notation. He had 'une très belle représentation' and acted nobly, yet all his life learnt his roles by rote. He made his début in 1677 as Triton in Lully's *Isis*, and sang Alpheius (Lully's *Proserpine*, 1680) in Paris, taking over from Cledière. He created Perseus (1682), Amadis (1684), Médor (*Roland*, 1685), Renaud (*Armide*, 1686) and Acis (*Acis et Galatée*, 1686) for Lully, as well as the roles of Achilles (Lully and Collasse's *Achille et Polyxène*, 1687), Peleus (Collasse's *Thétis et Pélée*, 1689), Aeneas, in both *Enée et Lavinie* (Collasse, 1690) and *Didon* (Desmarets, 1693), Bacchus (Marais' *Ariane et Bacchus*, 1696) and Amadis (Destouches' *Amadis de Grèce*, 1699). Perhaps his greatest success was as Phaethon (Lully, 1683). He sang the title roles in revivals of Lully's *Atys* (1689 and 1699) and *Thésée* (1688 and 1698).

His sonorous and prodigiously high tenor voice enabled him to pass for an *haute-contre*: in fact he was an 'haute-taille, des plus hautes' (Parfaict). His lack of technical musical ability apparently caused him to sing out of tune frequently, and he often appeared drunk on stage. He was obviously a gallant: the ribbons he took from the *actrices de l'Opéra* were many. However, he seems to have met his match in Mlle Maupin who, disguised as a man, ambushed and out-duelled him one night. She took his watch as a token – as in *Die Fledermaus* – with which to embarrass him the following day at the Opéra when he recounted the escapade. Dumesnil went to England to sing every Easter after the Académie season and returned each time with earnings of at least 1000 pistoles. He retired in 1700.

*

ES (B. Horowicz)
F. Parfaict and C. Parfaict: *Histoire de l'Académie royale de musique depuis son établissement jusqu'à present* (MS, 1741, *F-Pn*)
PHILIP WELLER

Dumitrescu, Gheorghe (*b* Oteşani, Vîlcea district, 28 Dec 1914). Romanian composer. At the Bucharest Conservatory (1934–41) he studied with Mihail Jora, Dimitrie Cuclin and Jonel Perlea. As violinist, composer and conductor at the Bucharest National Theatre (1936–46), and later as composer and artistic adviser to an army ensemble and as professor of harmony at the Bucharest Conservatory (1951–79), he has devoted his life to composition, and is one of the most prolific of contemporary Romanian composers. The genre that has principally challenged his creative power is dramatic music. At first he composed music for plays by Aeschylus, Sophocles, Shakespeare, A. Kiriţescu, Laurenţiu Fulga, Cezar Petrescu and Dinu Bondi; he then wrote both music and librettos for a series of operas, and has also written film music. His outlook is essentially large scale, with text and music working effectively together in each work. Almost all of the themes in the operas derive from traditional sources. The music uses descending unison phrases, chromatic passages based on the augmented 4th and the 5th, and grand, climactic finales. Dumitrescu's late works contain modal passages, polytonal chords and serial elements.

librettos by the composer unless otherwise stated

Tarşiţa şi Roşiorul, 1949 (operetta, 3, A. Kiriţescu), collab. V. Doboş

Ion Vodă cel Cumplit, 1955 (musical drama, 4, with G. Teodorescu), Bucharest, 12 April 1956
Decebal op.41, 1957 (musical tragedy, 4), Bucharest, 4 Oct 1969 (Bucharest, 1965)
Răscoala [The Uprising] op.48, 1959 (folklore musical drama, 4, after L. Rebreanu), Bucharest, 20 Nov 1959 (Bucharest, 1963)
Fata cu garoafe [Girl with Carnation] op.53 (4, N. Tăutu), Bucharest, 6 May 1961 (Bucharest, 1964)
Meşterul Manole [Master Builder Manole] op.103, 1967 (4, after Rom. legend), Craiova, 4 April 1980
Geniu pustiu [Solitary Genius] op.112, 1972 (4, after M. Eminescu), Cluj-Napoca, 12 March 1977
Vlad Ţepeş op.118 (musical drama, 4), concert perf., Bucharest, 6 Feb 1975
Orfeu op.133, 1978 (lyric tragedy, 4), concert perf., Bucharest, 22 April 1980
Luceafărul [The Evening Star] op.141 (ballet-opera, 4 scenes, after Eminescu), concert perf., Bucharest, 29 Dec 1981
Marea trecere [Great Love] op.143 (4), concert perf., Bucharest, 13 Dec 1982
Ivan Turbincă op.152, 1983 (3)
Prometheus op.157, 1985 (lyric tragedy, 4), concert perf., Bucharest, 15 Oct 1987
Mihai Viteazul [Michael the Brave] op.158, 1986 (lyric historical drama, 4)
Avram Iancu op.160, 1987 (musical drama, 4)
Voivodul Gelu op.161, 1988 (lyric tragedy, 4)
Supreme Sacrifice op.162, 1988 (opera-oratorio, 4 pts)

*

R. Gheciu: *Mit şi epopee* [Myth and Epos] (Bucharest, 1984)

VIOREL COSMA

Dümler, Franz Anton. *See* DIMMLER, FRANZ ANTON.

Dumme Gärtner aus dem Gebirge, Der [*Der dumme Gärtner aus dem Gebirge, oder Die zween Anton* ('The Foolish Gardener from the Mountains, or The Two Antons')]. Singspiel in two acts by BENEDIKT SCHACK and FRANZ XAVER GERL to a libretto by EMANUEL SCHIKANEDER; Vienna, Freihaus-Theater auf der Wieden, 12 July 1789.

This Singspiel (also known as *Die beyden Anton*) has an honoured place in the history of the Viennese popular theatre: it was the work that Schikaneder wrote for the reopening of the Theater auf der Wieden after his return from the provinces, and it marks the first appearance of the character of Anton, with which he hoped to outdo the popularity of the comic servant Kaspar (or Käsperle) in his rival Marinelli's Theater in der Leopoldstadt. In all, there were six sequels to *Der dumme Gärtner*; they enjoyed varying success but certainly did not endanger the popularity of Kaspar. The texts of most of the Anton plays are lost, but many of the songs survive, some in printed vocal score; the best-known is 'Ein Weib ist das herrlichste Ding auf der Welt', from the first sequel, *Die verdeckten Sachen* (26 September 1789), on which Mozart wrote his eight variations for keyboard K613 (dated 'im März 1791'). The romance 'Einst verliebte sich ein Jüngling' and the tempo di menuetto 'O Hochzeitstag, wann kommst du an?' from *Der dumme Gärtner* were favourites in their day. The later Anton plays were: *Was macht der Anton im Winter?* (1790), *Der Frühling, oder Der Anton ist noch nicht tot* (1790), *Anton bei Hofe, oder Das Namensfest* (1791), *Der Renegat, oder Anton in der Türkei* (1792) and *Das Häuschen im Walde, oder Antons Reise nach seinem Geburtsort* (1795).

PETER BRANSCOMBE

Dumont, Hyacinthe de Gauréault, Sieur de (*b* ?1647; *d* Paris, 19 March 1726). French administrator. An equerry of the dauphin and governor of Meudon, he went into partnership with JEAN-NICOLAS DE FRANCINE by letters patent of 30 December 1698, and shared the licence of the Opéra (Académie Royale de Musique) with him in the proportion of one quarter of the rights and profits to Dumont, the other three-quarters to Francine. From then on until his death his career was linked to Francine's.

Their period of management was one of great financial problems, made even worse by the financial burdens (such as artists' pensions, authors' royalties and the entertainment tax) on the Opéra after the death of Lully. Saint-Simon thought highly of Dumont, describing him as a 'great gentleman' who gained the confidence of the king, and 'who governed his private purse and, as a rule, his pleasures'.

*

Paris, Archives Nationales, Série AJ[13]1
F-Po, MS Amelot
J. Gourret: *Ces hommes qui ont fait l'Opéra* (Paris, 1984)

NICOLE WILD

Dun. French family of singers.

(1) **Jean Dun** (i) [*père*] (*d* Paris, 1735). His career as a bass at the Opéra, spanning 36 years, began in 1684 when he created the roles of Arcalaus and Florestan in Lully's *Amadis*. He appeared in more than 37 operas, often playing more than one character in the same work: in Campra's *opéra-ballet Les fêtes vénitiennes*, for example, he created roles in three entrées. He often reappeared in revivals over several years: he created the roles of Jupiter and the Oracle in Collasse's *Thétis et Pélée* in 1689, repeating them in 1699, and in the revivals of 1708 and 1712 he sang as a triton. He retired from the Opéra in 1720 after creating the role of Fabio in 1718 in the entrée 'La vieillesse' from Campra's *opéra-ballet Les âges*.

(2) Mlle **Dun** (*b* Paris; *d* Paris, 1713). Daughter of (1) Jean Dun. She made her début in the October 1708 revival of Destouches' *pastorale-héroïque Issé* as the first of the Hesperides. According to the brothers Parfaict (*Dictionnaire des théâtres de Paris*, Paris, 1756), she was 'très applaudie' as a performer of minor roles. She appeared in Marais' *Sémélé*(1709), Stuck's *Méléagre* (1709) and *Manto la fée* (1711), Campra's *Hésione* (1709), in Bertin's *Diomède* (1710) and Salomon's *Médée et Jason* (1713). Like her father she appeared in several entrées of *Les fêtes vénitiennes*, creating a total of six roles between June and December 1710. She was described by the Parfaicts as possessing a figure 'peu gracieuse' but having a tender and delicate voice coupled with good taste in her singing.

(3) **Jean Dun** (ii) [*fils*] (*b* Paris; *d* 1772). Son of (1) Jean Dun, and also a bass, he made his début at the Opéra singing in the trio of fates in a revival of Lully's *Isis* in 1717. In 1718 he created Valère in Campra's *Les âges*, singing opposite his father in the same entrée. Highly regarded, he sang in more than 20 operas, often appearing in more than one role in the same work. He created roles in four operas by Rameau: Jupiter and Pluto in *Hippolyte et Aricie*(1733), Osman-Bacha (*Les Indes galantes*, 1735), Jupiter in *Castor et Pollux* (1737), and Hymas and Eurilas (*Les fêtes d'Hébé*, 1739). A 1738 inventory of the Opéra described him thus: 'good musician, sings well, but he has not got a clear voice' (see G. Sadler, *EMc*, xi, 1983, pp.453–67). He retired from the Opéra as a singer in 1741 and soon

afterwards joined the orchestra there, playing the bass viol until 1759.

(4) Mlle **Dun** [née Catin] (*d* after 1756). Wife of (3) Jean Dun *fils*. She entered the Opéra in 1721 and was employed as a member of the chorus, although on occasion she was assigned such minor roles as an Amazon in Lully's *Bellérophon* (revival of 1728) and Terpsichore in Montéclair's *Jephté* (1732). JAMES R. ANTHONY

Dunayevsky, Isaak Iosifovich (*b* Lokhvitsa, province of Poltava, 17/30 Jan 1900; *d* Moscow, 25 July 1955). Russian composer. He studied the violin with Akhron at the Kharkiv Music School (1910–15), taught himself the piano, conducted student orchestras, and was a composition pupil of Bogatïryov at the Kharkiv Conservatory (1915–19). In the early 1920s he composed for the theatre and worked as a lecturer, journalist and director of amateur music studies. He was music director of the Ermitazh and Korsh theatres, Moscow (1924–9), and composer to the Moscow Theatre of Satire (1926–9). His first major success was with the operetta *Zhenikhi* ('The Bridegrooms', 1927), the forerunner of Soviet musical comedy. From 1929 to 1941 he was music director of the Leningrad Music Hall, a variety theatre, where his *Zolotaya dolina* ('The Golden Valley') was given in 1937, and he composed music for some 30 films. Dunayevsky's 12 operettas also include *Vol'nïy veter* ('Wild Wind'; 1947, Moscow) and *Belaya akatsiya* ('White Acacia', completed and given posthumously, 1955). His major contribution was in renewing Russian musical theatre by freeing it from Viennese operetta stereotypes. His songs invoke the vigorous, optimistic and enthusiastic spirit of the 1930s; the initial phrase of his 'Pesni o rodine' ('Song of the Motherland') from the film *Tsirk* ('Circus', 1936) became the call sign of Moscow radio.

*

M. Yankovsky: *I. I. Dunayevsky* (Leningrad and Moscow, 1940)
L. Danilevich: *I. I. Dunayevsky* (Moscow and Leningrad, 1947)
A. Chernov: *I. I. Dunayevsky* (Moscow, 1961)
I. I. Dunayevsky: *Vïstupleniya, stat'i pis'ma* [Speeches, Articles, Letters] (Moscow, 1961)
L. Mikheyeva: *I. I. Dunayevsky* (Leningrad, 1963)
D. M. Person, ed.: *I. I. Dunayevsky: noto-bibliograficheskiy spravochnik* (Moscow, 1971)

GENRIKH ORLOV, ANDREW LAMB

Duncan, Ronald (*b* Salisbury, Rhodesia [now Zimbabwe], 6 Aug 1914; *d* Barnstaple, Devon, 3 June 1982). English poet and dramatist. He was described by Ezra Pound as 'the lone wolf of English letters'. After 1945 he took part in the attempted renaissance of verse drama in England (he was initially influenced by T. S. Eliot), but the critical tide turned against these efforts in the late 1950s, and his plays are rarely if ever performed today. His *Collected Poems* were published in 1981. Among other activities, Duncan wrote librettos for Thomas Eastwood (*Christopher Sly*, 1960, and *The Rebel*, 1969), and collaborated with Benjamin Britten on a number of projects. He revised parts of Montagu Slater's libretto for *Peter Grimes* (1945), and provided the libretto for *The Rape of Lucretia* (1946); Britten subsequently wrote the incidental music for Duncan's verse play *Stratton* (1949).

*

E. Crozier, ed.: *The Rape of Lucretia: a Symposium* (London, 1948)
R. Duncan: *Working with Britten: a Personal Memoir* (Bideford, 1981)

ANTHONY PARR

Duncan, (Robert) Todd (*b* Danville, KY, 12 Feb 1903). American baritone. After attending Butler University, Indianapolis (BA 1925), and Columbia University Teachers College (MA 1930), he joined the voice faculty of Howard University in Washington, DC, where he remained until 1945. He made his début in 1934 as Alfio in *Cavalleria rusticana* with the Aeolian Opera in New York, and later became the first black member of the New York City Opera, where he first appeared as Tonio (1945). Also active in musical theatre, he created Porgy in Gershwin's *Porgy and Bess* at the Alvin Theatre, New York (1935), and in revivals. He appeared in the London production of *The Sun Never Sets* (1938) and as the Lord's General in Vernon Duke's *Cabin in the Sky* (1940, New York); his performance as Stephen Kumalo in Weill's *Lost in the Stars* (1949–50) won him the Donaldson and New York Drama Critics awards in 1950.

*

R. Abdul: *Blacks in Classical Music* (New York, 1977)
P. Turner: *Afro-American Singers* (Minneapolis, 1977)

DOMINIQUE-RENÉ DE LERMA

Dunhill, Thomas (Frederick) (*b* London, 1 Feb 1877; *d* Scunthorpe, Lincs., 13 March 1946). English composer. He studied composition with Stanford at the RCM from 1893. From 1899 to 1908 he was assistant music master at Eton College, concurrently teaching harmony and counterpoint at the RCM. His one-act opera *The Enchanted Garden* op.65 was performed privately at the RAM in March 1928. Two three-act light operas followed: *Tantivy Towers* op.73 (libretto by A. P. Herbert) was first performed at the Lyric Theatre, Hammersmith, on 16 January 1931, and *Happy Families* op.77 (R. Fyleman) at Guildford on 1 November 1933.

Duni, Antonio (*b* Matera, *c*1700; *d* ?Schwerin, after 1766). Italian composer. He was a son of Francesco Duni, *maestro di cappella* in Matera, and the elder brother of Egidio Duni and is said to have studied with Nicola Fago at the Turchini Conservatory in Naples. After a period at the archiepiscopal court in Trier he moved to Madrid, where he contributed to the development of a more operatic and italianized style of zarzuela with two works: *Locuras hay que dan juicio y sueños que son verdad* (libretto by A. de Zamora; 23 February 1726) and *Santa Ines de Montepoliciano* (M. F. de Armeso; 25 December 1727). He was apparently a friend of Farinelli and served the Duke of Osuna as *maestro di cappella* and music teacher. After a period of travelling around Europe (there are reports of him in Germany and Paris) he arrived in Schwerin in September 1755 as *maestro di cappella* of an Italian opera troupe. For the birthday of Princess Amalia in March the following year he wrote three arias for the two-act pasticcio intermezzo *L'amor mascherato* (MS at *B-Bc*), which seems to have enjoyed a modest success in other German cities. In September 1757, having lost his post in Schwerin by bringing a lawsuit against Peretti, the troupe's director, he went to Moscow, where he taught privately and at the university. After teaching in Riga in 1765–6 he returned to Schwerin and on 5 July 1766 petitioned the Duchess of Mecklenburg for a post and security for his family.

*

R.-A. Mooser: *Annales de la musique et des musiciens en Russie au XVIIIme siècle* (Geneva, 1948–51), i, 316

KENT M. SMITH

Duni, Egidio (Romualdo) [Duny, Egide (Romuald)] (*b* Matera, Basilicata, bap. 11 Feb 1708; *d* Paris, 11 June 1775). Italian composer. He was one of the most important *opéra comique* composers in the third quarter of the 18th century, contributing to the creation of a new style in that genre, the *comédie mêlée d'ariettes*, through the blending of Italian elements with the traditional French ones.

1. Life. Duni was the fourth son of Francesco Duni, *maestro di cappella* in Matera, and the younger brother of Antonio Duni. Little is known of his early training, which took place in Naples, though probably not with Durante as has previously been supposed. *Nerone*, his first opera, was staged during the Rome spring season of 1735, and after composing works for Rome and Milan in Carnival 1736 Duni went to London, where his *Demofoonte* was performed in an English version in May 1737. Further operas were written for Milan in 1739 and for Florence in 1740 and 1743. On 16 December 1743 Duni was appointed *maestro di cappella* of S Nicola di Bari and, with *Ipermestra* and *Ciro riconosciuto* (both 1748, Genoa), he came to the attention of the Duke of Richelieu and Philip, Duke of Parma. Soon after, he became court *maestro di cappella* in Parma and music teacher to the duke's daughter Isabella, later Empress of Austria.

With *Olimpiade* (Parma, Carnival 1755) Duni's career as an *opera seria* composer came to an end, while Goldoni's arrival in Parma in May 1756 led to his collaboration on Duni's last Italian opera, *La buona figliuola*, better known through Piccinni's later setting. The French atmosphere of the Parma court turned Duni's attention to the *opéra comique*, and he is often said to have written, during his stay there, the music for two Favart librettos in that genre, *La chercheuse d'esprit* and *Ninette à la cour*. This is highly doubtful in both cases (nor has it been proved that any of Duni's music was used in the pastiche *Ninette à la cour* performed in Paris in 1755). Jean Monnet, director of the Paris Opéra-Comique, reported in his memoirs that in autumn 1756 he received a request from Parma for a French libretto for Duni, who wished to write an opera for Paris. The result, after hesitation on Monnet's part, was Louis Anseaume's *Le peintre amoureux de son modèle*, for whose first performance on 26 July 1757 Duni went to Paris. This was a brilliant success and refuted Rousseau's claim that the French language was unsuitable for music: with its blend of vaudeville tunes and natural French expressive declamation within an Italian musical idiom, *Le peintre* served for several years as a model *opéra comique*.

Released with a pension from his post in Parma, Duni settled in Paris, married and, during 1758–60, strengthened his reputation with several successful *opéras comiques*. In 1761 he was appointed music director of the Comédie-Italienne but, ironically, a number of his new works for that theatre were not well received. In August 1761 he indignantly replied in the *Mercure de France* to hostile criticism of his *La bonne fille*, and a private letter dated January 1762, published by Tiersot, reveals that he was also in conflict with Favart at this time. However, his collaborations with Anseaume – *Mazet* (1761), *Le milicien* (1762) and *Les deux chasseurs et la laitière* (1763), the unusually dramatic *L'école de la jeunesse* (1765) and *La clochette* (1766) – were extremely successful. These works, as well as two ambitious collaborations with Favart, *La fée Urgèle* (1765) and *Les moissonneurs* (1768), were published in Paris and adapted, translated and imitated all over Europe. They held the stage in France until nearly the end of the century.

During the 18 months between the première of *La clochette* in July 1766 and that of *Les moissonneurs* in January 1768, Duni apparently made a visit to Italy. On his return to Paris he met with Grimm's harsh and unjust suggestion that he 'would do well to give up composition since his trip to Italy had not refreshed his head'. Despite similar but milder criticism, Duni's next work, *Les sabots* (1768) – the first of two collaborations

Scene from the title page of the score of Egidio Duni's 'L'isle des foux' (Paris, ?1760): engraving by F. J. Flipart after C. Cochin

with Sedaine – had a modest success, and on 26 November 1768 both he and Favart were given pensions by the Comédie-Italienne. After *Thémire* (1770) he retired, continuing to teach and occasionally to judge musical competitions.

2. WORKS. Scattered and poorly catalogued sources make a comprehensive view of Duni's Italian career difficult. The works for which most of the music survives – *Nerone*, *Catone in Utica* and *Olimpiade* – as well as substantial fragments from *Demofoonte* and *Ipermestra*, reveal a composer who, while always respecting the established formal and harmonic conventions of his day, nevertheless achieved effective dramatic characterization through grateful vocal phrases of considerable variety. Duni's principal importance, however, lies in his decisive role during the formative years of the *comédie mêlée d'ariettes*. He was fortunate in his collaboration with such leading librettists as Favart, Anseaume and, towards the end of his career, Sedaine. This undoubtedly aided his assimilation of the various currents of the French musical environment and, especially, his sensitivity to the demands of natural and expressive French musical declamation for which he earned Diderot's warm praise in *Le neveu de Rameau*.

Duni's early *comédies* gradually eliminated the vaudevilles that had formed the basis of much previous composition in the genre, and worked consistently towards the objective of *opéra comique* based entirely on original music by combining italianate *ariettes*, ensembles and recitatives with other more characteristically French elements – *couplets*, spoken dialogue and *divertissements*. Duni's treatment of the vocal ensemble was particularly innovatory and most apparent in his collaborations with Anseaume, who specialized in constructing elaborate concerted texts for several characters. *L'isle des foux* (1760) contains the first known sextet in an *opéra comique*, and *L'école de la jeunesse* (1765) is unprecedented in including one sextet and two septets. In addition, Duni and his librettists used the ensemble increasingly to further the dramatic intrigue, and two exceptional experiments in this respect are found in *La fille mal gardée* (1758) and *L'isle des foux*, where a single concerted movement spans successive scenes and introduces new characters. The latter work, alongside *Les deux chasseurs*, *Le rendez-vous* (both 1763) and *La fée Urgèle*, also reveals imaginative orchestral details (in spite of the small orchestra available), and these render criticisms of Duni's instrumental writing somewhat unjust. Dramatic characterization is especially effective in *Mazet*, where the protagonist is required to feign loss of speech; there are other fine moments in *Les deux chasseurs* and *La clochette*, both of which are enhanced by a liberal use of stage directions to encourage a more realistic acting style.

Duni's works, along with those of Gluck and Laruette, represent the earliest and finest examples of a new type of *opéra comique*. They gave the mid-18th-century Parisian public repeated exposure to what it wanted: French music with Italian spirit, usually in delightful pastoral settings touched by sentimentality. Ultimately, however, Duni failed to keep pace with the genre he had helped to create, and he was overtaken in popularity by composers such as Monsigny and Philidor. Grimm's initial admiration of him as the founder of a new musico-dramatic tradition in France gradually gave way to criticisms of his outdated style: 'our good father Duni is no longer young; he begins to lack ideas'. Symptomatic of these limitations (especially of his lack of harmonic originality) was Duni's refusal early in 1763 to undertake the correction in Paris of Gluck's *Orfeo ed Euridice*, in which he saw little except copying errors and passages of shocking violence. He knew his own abilities and sensed the needs of his audience to a remarkable degree: his success, therefore, was great, but died with the society that had fostered it.

See also ECOLE DE LA JEUNESSE, L'; FÉE URGÈLE, LA; and PEINTRE AMOUREUX DE SON MODÈLE, LE.

PCI – *Paris, Comédie-Italienne*

Nerone (os, 3, after F. Silvani: *La fortezza al cimento*), Rome, Tordinona, 21 May 1735, *I-Nc*
Adriano in Siria (os, 3, P. Metastasio), Rome, Tordinona, 27 Dec 1735
La tirannide debellata (os, 3, after A. Zeno and P. Pariati: *Flavio Anicio Olibrio*), Milan, Regio Ducal, carn. 1736
Demophontes, King of Thrace (os, 3, after Metastasio), London, King's, 24 May 1737, 6 arias (London, 1737)
La Didone abbandonata (os, 3, Metastasio), Milan, Regio Ducal, Jan 1739
Catone in Utica (os, 3, after Metastasio), Florence, Pergola, carn. 1740, *E-Mn*
Baiazette, o Tamerlano (os, 3, A. Piovene), Florence, Pergola, aut. 1743, 1 aria *D-ROu*
Artaserse (os, 3, Metastasio), Florence, Pergola, 1744, 2 arias *ROu*
Ipermestra (os, 3, Metastasio), Genoa, Falcone, carn. 1748
Ciro riconosciuto (os, 3, Metastasio), Genoa, Falcone, spr. 1748
Olimpiade (os, 3, after Metastasio), Parma, Ducale, carn. 1755, *F-Pc*
La buona figliuola [La Cecchina] (melodramma giocoso, 3, C. Goldoni), Parma, Ducale, 26 Dec 1756; rev. as La bonne fille, Paris, Comédie-Italienne, 8 June 1761
Le peintre amoureux de son modèle (oc, 2, L. Anseaume), Paris, Foire St Laurent, 26 July 1757 (Paris, ?1757); rev., Paris, Foire St Germain, Feb 1758
Le docteur Sangrado (oc, 1, Anseaume and J.-B. Lourdet de Santerre, after A.-R. Lesage: *Gil Blas*), Paris, Foire St Germain, 13 Feb 1758 (Paris, 1758), collab. J.-L. Laruette
La fille mal gardée, ou Le pédant amoureux (cmda, 1, Favart, M. J. B. Favart and Lourdet de Santerre), PCI, 4 March 1758 (Paris, ?1758) [parody of La Provençale (5th entrée in Mouret: Les fêtes de Thalie)]
La chute des anges rebelles (oc), Paris, Tuileries, Salle des Machines, 16 March 1758
Nina et Lindor, ou Les caprices du coeur (int, 2, ?C. P. Richelet), Paris, Foire St Laurent, 9 Sept 1758 (Paris, ?1758)
La veuve indécise (oc, 1, Anseaume, after J.-J. Vadé), Paris, Foire St Laurent, 24 Sept 1759 (Paris, ?1759) [parody of La veuve coquette (2nd entrée in Mouret: Les fêtes de Thalie)]
La boutique du poëte (oc), PCI, 8 Oct 1760
L'isle des foux (cmda, 2, Anseaume and P.-A. Lefebvre de Marcouville, after Goldoni: *Arcifanfano re dei matti*), PCI, 29 Dec 1760 (Paris, ?1760)
Mazet (cmda, 2, Anseaume), PCI, 24 Sept 1761 (Paris, ?1761)
La plaideuse, ou Le procès (cmda, 3, C.-S. Favart), PCI, 19 May 1762
La nouvelle Italie (comédie heroï-comique, 3, J. Galli di Bibiena), PCI, 23 June 1762, collab. A. J. Rigade
Le milicien (cmda, 1, Anseaume), Versailles, 29 Dec 1762; PCI, 1 Jan 1763 (Paris, ?1763)
Les deux chasseurs et la laitière (cmda, 1, Anseaume), PCI, 23 July 1763 (Paris, 1763)
Le rendez-vous (comédie, 1, P. Légier), PCI, 16 Nov 1763 (Paris, n.d.)
L'école de la jeunesse, ou Le Barnevelt françois (cmda, 3, Anseaume), PCI, 24 Jan 1765 (Paris, 1765)
La fée Urgèle, ou Ce qui plaît aux dames (cmda, 4, Favart, after Voltaire and G. Chaucer), Fontainebleau, 26 Oct 1765 (Paris, 1765)
La clochette (cmda, 1, Anseaume), PCI, 24 July 1766 (Paris, 1766)
Les moissonneurs (cmda, 3, Favart, after *Ruth*), PCI, 27 Jan 1768 (Paris, 1768)
Les sabots (oc, 1, M.-J. Sedaine, after J. Cazotte), private perf., Auteuil; PCI, 26 Oct 1768 (Paris, n.d.)

La rosière de Salency (cmda, 3, Favart), Fontainebleau, 25 Oct 1769, excerpts with lib. (Paris, 1769); collab. Blaise, Philidor, Monsigny and van Swieten
Thémire (pastorale mêlée d'ariettes, 1, Sedaine), private perf., Passy, Aug 1770; Fontainebleau, 20 Oct 1770; PCI, 26 Nov 1770; ariettes (Paris, n.d.)

Music in: The Noble Peasant (1784); The Crusade (1790)

Doubtful: Alessandro nell'Indie (os, Metastasio), ?1736; Armida (os), 3 arias *D-ROu*; Demetrio (os, Metastasio), Florence, ? carn. 1747, 6 arias *ROu*; La semplice curiosa (componimento drammatico, P. Pertici, after Favart: *La chercheuse d'esprit*), Florence, Cocomero, aut. 1751; L'embarras du choix (oc), PCI, 13 March 1758 [parody of Dauvergne: Enée et Lavinie]; Le retour au village, 1756–9 (oc, after Favart: *Le caprice amoureux, ou Ninette à la cour*), unperf. (Paris, n.d.); L'heureuse espièglerie, ?*c*1771 (oc, 1), unperf.

*

ES (E. Zanetti); *MGG* (M. Briquet)
E. R. Duni: 'A M. D. L. G. Pensionnaire adjoint au Mercure pour l'article des spectacles', *Mercure de France* (Aug 1761), 175–9
J. Monnet: *Supplément au roman comique, ou Mémoires pour servir à la vie de Jean Monnet* (London, 1772); ed H. d'Almeras (Paris, 1909)
'Eloge de Monsieur Duni', *Le nécrologe des hommes célèbres de France*, xi (1776), 165
C. Goldoni: *Mémoires* (Paris, 1787)
A.-E.-M. Grétry: *Mémoires, ou Essais sur la musique* (Paris, 1789, enlarged 2/1797)
C.-S. Favart: *Mémoires et correspondance littéraires, dramatiques et anecdotiques* (Paris, 1808)
F. M. Grimm: *Correspondance littéraire, philosophique et critique*, ed. M. Tourneux (Paris, 1877–82)
A. Pougin: 'Duni et les commencements de l'opéra-comique', *Le ménestrel*, xlvi (1879–80), 139
G. Sospizio: 'E. R. Duni e N. Piccinni', *L'avvenire di Sardegna della Domenica* (8 April 1884)
J. Tiersot: 'Lettres de musiciens écrites en français du XVe au XXe siècle', *RMI*, xvii (1910), 512; pubd separately (Turin, 1924), i, 82ff
G. Cucuel: *Les créateurs de l'opéra-comique français* (Paris, 1914)
D. Diderot: *Le neveu de Rameau*, ed. J. Fabre (Geneva, 1950, 2/1963; Eng. trans., 1965)
D. Heartz: 'Diderot et le théâtre lyrique: "le nouveau stile" proposé par *Le neveu de Rameau*', *RdM*, lxiv (1978), 229–52
K. M. Smith: *Egidio Duni and the Development of the Opéra-Comique from 1753 to 1770* (diss., Cornell U., 1980)
J. Kopp: *The Drame Lyrique: a Study in the Esthetics of Opéra-Comique, 1762–1791* (diss., U. of Pennsylvania, 1982)
E. Cook: *The Operatic Ensemble in France, 1673–1775* (diss., U. of East Anglia, 1989) KENT M. SMITH/ELISABETH COOK

Duniecki, Stanisław (*b* Lwów, 25 Nov 1839; *d* Venice, 16 Dec 1870). Polish composer. He studied the piano and composition under J. K. Kessler, then in Leipzig, Vienna, Brussels (with Fétis) and Paris, where he had lessons in orchestration from Berlioz. Returning to Poland in 1863, he took charge of the orchestra at a small Polish theatre in Czernowitz (now Chernovtsy). In 1864 he was appointed conductor at the Lwów theatre, where he staged his most famous operetta, *Paziowie Królowej Marysieńki* ('Queen Mary's Pageboys'), a work in the tradition of Jan Stefani and K. K. Kurpiński. Hoping that the operetta would be performed in Warsaw, Duniecki spent some time there reviewing for the weekly journal *Kłosy*. However, as the Warsaw Opera did not stage the work, he accepted the post of conductor at the Kraków theatre, where it was performed in 1865. Duniecki staged Moniuszko's *Halka* (1866) and *Verbum nobile* (1867), as well as several of his own operas, but despite his efforts the Kraków Opera did not survive. He left Poland in 1867, visiting Romania and Merano and finally settling in Venice. In 1866 he had begun work on an opera based on the Russian poem *Igor*, but he died before it was completed.

Smetana reportedly admired the melodic beauty of the arias and duets in *Paziowie*, *Odaliski* and *Pokusa*, as well as the orchestration, characterized by the predominance of wind over string instruments. Duniecki admired Wagner and apparently expressed interest in composing works in a serious style, but his limited compositional experience prevented him from achieving this goal; his musical style may be compared to that of Rossini and Offenbach, and includes elements from his national tradition. Duniecki also wrote articles about opera for the Polish periodicals *Kłosy* and *Kalina.*

lost unless otherwise stated

Korylla (operetta, 1, P. Duniecki, after Fr. novel), Lwów, Skarbek, 18 May 1859
Kowal z przedmieścia Pragi [The Blacksmith from the Prague Suburbs] (melodrama), Czernowitz, 1864
Nędznicy [The Scoundrels] (melodrama, W. Rapacki, after V. Hugo: *Les misérables*), Czernowitz, 1864
Paziowie Królowej Marysieńki [Queen Mary's Pageboys] (operetta, 2, P. Duniecki, after W. Pol: *Obrazy* [The Pictures]), Lwów, Skarbek, 16 Dec 1864, *PL-Kj*; extracts ed. J. Wildt (Kraków, 1870)
Dożynki, czyli Pierwsze wrażenia [The Harvest Festival, or First Impressions] (comic op, 2, J. Jasiński), Kraków, Old, 29 Oct 1865
Odaliski (operetta, 2, P. Duniecki), Kraków, Old, 9 Jan 1866
Pokusa [The Temptation] (comic op , 1, S. Duniecki), Kraków, Old, 24 April 1866; as Chochlik [The Gnome], Lwów, 1869; as Sotek [The Imp], Prague; as Der Teufel ist los, Poznań and Berlin; as Lucifer, Vienna
Doktor Pandolfo (operetta), Kraków, Old, 1866
Loczki panny Proci [Miss Procia's Curls], *c*1867 (melodrama)
Zemsta Stasi [The Vengeance of Stasia], *c*1867 (melodrama)
Igor, 1866–9 (P. Duniecki and J. Turski), inc.

*

PSB (J.W. Reiss); *SMP*
W. L. Anczyc: 'Stanisław Duniecki', *Tygodnik ilustrowany*, clxxii (1870), 177–8
S. Wasylewski: 'Sprawa Stanisława Dunieckiego', *Wiadomości literackie*, xxxi (1937), 2
J. W. Reiss: 'Stanisław Duniecki 1839–1870', *Poradnik muzyczny*, v/3d (1951)
I. Poniatowska: 'Duniecki, Stanisław', *Encyklopedia muzyczna PWM* (Kraków, 1979) IRENA PONIATOWSKA

Dunn, Geoffrey (Thomas) (*b* London, 13 Dec 1903; *d* London, 6 Sept 1981). English librettist, translator and tenor. He studied at the RAM and was later opera director there (1931–40). He sang with Nigel Playfair's company at the Lyric Theatre, Hammersmith, and took part in seldom heard works, including *Idomeneo*. In 1930 he helped form the Intimate Opera Company, for which he prepared several 18th-century English operas. Before World War II he wrote librettos for Easdale and Murrill, and later for Williamson's *English Eccentrics* (1964, Aldeburgh), *Julius Caesar Jones* (1966) and *Dunstan and the Devil* (1967). He gave up singing almost entirely to concentrate on acting, but appeared as Cardinal Pirelli in Sandy Wilson's *Valmouth* (1958, after Ronald Firbank's novel). His many translations extend from Berlioz's *Béatrice et Bénédict* and Bizet's *Les pêcheurs de perles* to Cavalli's *Calisto* and Dohnányi's *Der Tenor*, but his greatest impact was made with the Sadler's Wells operetta productions, notably of Offenbach's *Orphée aux enfers* (1960), *La vie parisienne* (1961), *La belle Hélène* (1963) and *Barbe-bleue* (1965). His lines are always musically phrased, apt for stage effect, and endlessly witty in rhyme and pun. ALAN BLYTH, ARTHUR JACOBS

Dunn, Mignon (*b* Memphis, TN, 17 June 1931). American mezzo-soprano. She studied singing in New York with Karin Branzell, making her début as Carmen in New Orleans. After engagements with several small companies she made her New York City Opera début as a Maid in *Troilus and Cressida* in 1956. After her first performance at the Metropolitan, two years later, as the Nurse in *Boris Godunov*, she became a mainstay of the company with more than 50 roles to her credit; these included Fricka, Amneris, Giulietta (*Les contes d'Hoffmann*), Delilah, Venus, Ortrud, Erda, Laura, Santuzza, Azucena, Marina, Anna (*Les Troyens*), Mother Marie, the Nurse (*Die Frau ohne Schatten*), Herodias, Adelaide (*Arabella*) and Carmen. She made her début at San Francisco as Brangäne in 1967 and subsequently appeared there as Baba the Turk (*The Rake's Progress*), Mlle Arvidson (Ulrica) and Erda. Dunn has performed virtually every important mezzo role, and her extensive career has included engagements with most of the leading opera companies. She performed and recorded Virgil Thomson's *The Mother of us All* singing Susan B. Anthony, and she created Madame Irma in Robert DiDomenica's *The Balcony* (1990, Boston). Her voice is a large, dramatic instrument, and as an artist she has an expressiveness that is best suited to the grand gesture.

*

R. Jacobson: 'The Other Valkyrie', *ON*, xxxviii/20 (1973–4), 16–18

J. Heimenz: 'Mignon Dunn', *HiFi/MusAm*, xxv/4 (1975), 18

RICHARD LeSUEUR, ELIZABETH FORBES

Dunn, Susan (*b* Malvern, AR, 23 July 1954). American soprano. After study at Indiana University she made her début as Aida at Peoria in 1982. She won the Richard Tucker Award in 1983 and in 1985 was heard as Sieglinde in Act 1 of *Die Walküre* at Carnegie Hall. Her pure, powerful, *spinto* voice is particularly admired in the roles of Leonora in *Il trovatore* and *La forza del destino*. Her roles also include Amelia (*Un ballo in maschera* and *Simon Boccanegra*). She first appeared in Europe in 1986, as Hélène in *Les vêpres siciliennes* (Bologna) and as Aida (La Scala). American engagements have taken her to Washington, Chicago, San Francisco, Houston and the Metropolitan (1989), where she sang Leonora (*Il trovatore*).

DAVID CUMMINGS

Duodrama. By extension of the term MONODRAMA, a two-character MELODRAMA, sometimes with a chorus, using spoken words alternating with or set over music, popular from the 1770s to the 1790s in the German theatre. The term was applied to Georg Benda's well-known melodramas *Ariadne auf Naxos* (1775) and *Medea* (1775), as well as to such works as *Inkle und Yariko* with music by F. W. Rust (1777); *Doktor Faust*, a comic duodrama with arias published by J. F. Schink in 1778, of which no musical setting is known; *Antonius und Cleopatra*, a 'Duodrama mit Gesang' composed by J. C. Kaffka (1779), half melodrama and half opera; *Emma und Edgar* (1780) with music by Franz Mezger; and *Pyramus und Thisbe* with music by J. B. Fuss (*c*1795).

For bibliography *see* MELODRAMA. ANNE DHU SHAPIRO

Duparc, Elisabeth ['Francesina'] (*d* ?1778). French soprano. Trained in Italy, she sang in several operas at Florence in 1731 and 1734–5. In 1736 she was engaged by the Opera of the Nobility for London, making her King's Theatre début in Hasse's *Siroe*, and singing in operas by Broschi, Pescetti, Veracini and Duni. The following season (1737–8) she appeared in operas by Pescetti and Veracini, the Handel pasticcio *Alessandro Severo* and Handel's new operas *Faramondo* (Clotilde) and *Serse* (Romilda). From then she was known almost exclusively as a Handel singer. She was his leading soprano at the King's Theatre in early 1739 and 1744–5, at Lincoln's Inn Fields in 1739–40 and 1740–41 and at Covent Garden in early 1744 and 1746. She sang in many oratorios, probably in *Giove in Argo* (1739), in *Imeneo* (Rosmene) and *Deidamia* (title role) in 1740–41, and created the roles of Semele (1744) and Iole in *Hercules* (1745).

Francesina's bright soprano improved greatly under Handel's tuition and she became a worthy successor to Strada and even Cuzzoni. Many of her arias resemble Cuzzoni's in their demand for rapid and agile decoration, frequent trills and a melodious warbling style; Handel gave her several bird songs. His high opinion of her powers of characterization and all-round musicianship is clear from the many superb parts he wrote for her. Burney ranked her as a singer of the second class, but also wrote of 'her lark-like execution', 'a light, airy, pleasing movement, suited to [her] active throat'. Her compass was *c'* to *b''*.

WINTON DEAN

Du Plessis, Christian Johannes (*b* Vryheid, 2 July 1944). South African baritone. He studied and began his career in South Africa, making his stage début with the Performing Arts Council of the Transvaal Opera in Johannesburg as Yamadori (*Butterfly*) in 1967. Further studies followed in London with Otakar Kraus, and he sang Mathieu in a concert performance of *Andrea Chénier* in 1970. He sang Valentin (*Faust*) at Barcelona in 1971, and was later a member of the ENO, 1973–81, his roles including Cecil (*Maria Stuarda*), Marcello and Posa. A warm-toned and polished stylist in the bel canto repertory, he made a speciality of lesser-known Bellini and Donizetti works in concert performances for the London Opera Society and stage productions by Opera Rara, for example in the title role of *Torquato Tasso* and as Corrado in *Maria de Rudenz* (Donizetti) and Ernesto in *Il pirata* (Bellini). He formally retired in 1988.

NOËL GOODWIN

Duponchel, Charles (Edmond) (*b* Paris, 25 July 1794; *d* Paris, 8 April 1868). French theatre director and administrator. After training as a painter and architect he achieved prominence as a *metteur en scène*, first at the Comédie-Française and then at the Opéra. His work as stage director for almost all operas given at the Opéra from Auber's *La muette de Portici* (1828) to Meyerbeer's *Le prophète* (1849) caused the impresario Alphonse Royer later to refer to him as the 'Alexander of the *mise-en-scène*'. Given the importance of stage spectacle in French grand opera, Duponchel contributed much to the success of major works by Meyerbeer and Halévy; he was instrumental in placing greater emphasis on local colour than had previously been the custom in Opéra productions. After the resignation of Louis Véron, in 1835 Duponchel became director of the Opéra, a position he filled, with considerably fewer financial rewards than his predecessor had, until 1840. Beginning in 1847 he participated for two years in a joint directorship of the house, first with Léon Pillet and Nestor Roqueplan, and then with Roqueplan alone.

STEVEN HUEBNER

Dupont, Alexis [Pierre-Auguste] (*b* ?Paris, 1796; *d* Paris, June 1874). French tenor. After graduating from the Paris Conservatoire in 1818, he began a career as a concert singer. He was engaged by the Opéra-Comique from 1821 to 1823, making his début as Azor in Grétry's *Zémire et Azor.* Following a trip to Italy for further vocal training, he sang at the Opéra in 1826 as Pylades in Gluck's *Iphigénie en Tauride*; for the next 14 years he enjoyed great success there. Auber composed the role of Alphonse in *La muette de Portici* for him. Dupont sang in the premières of Rossini's *Guillaume Tell* and Halévy's *La Juive*, and in the infamous Castil-Blaze revival of *Don Giovanni* (1834). According to Charles Hervey (*The Theatres of Paris*, Paris, 1846), his 'sweet but delicate' voice suffered against the power of the Opéra orchestra. He retired from opera in 1840, but continued to sing in public until 1856.

LAURIE C. SHULMAN

Dupont, Gabriel Edouard Xavier (*b* Caen, 1 March 1878; *d* Vesinet, nr Paris, 2 Aug 1914). French composer. A pupil of Massenet at the Paris Conservatoire, he achieved early success with his opera *La cabrera*, which in 1903 won a competition organized by the Milanese publisher Sonzogno. In keeping with the Italian taste of the period, it has strong *verismo* elements, and it is the only one of Dupont's stage works to have a contemporary setting. *La glu*, which followed some years later, is in a lighter vein; it met with little success and failed to achieve a performance in Paris. The character of Marie-des-Anges was played by Claire Friche, who also appeared in the première of Dupont's *La farce du cuvier* (1912, Brussels). According to Debussy's wife Emma Bardac, Debussy himself recommended it for performance at the Paris Opéra-Comique, but without success. Dupont's final stage work, completed just before he succumbed to the lung disease from which he had suffered for many years, was *Antar*, a much larger work than any of the preceding, and the only one of Dupont's works to reach the Paris Opéra (though its première was considerably delayed by the outbreak of World War I). An ambitious score, revived at the Opéra in 1924 and 1946, it reveals Dupont's considerable musical talent and dramatic instinct.

La cabrera (drame lyrique, 2, H. Cain), Milan, Lirico, 16 May 1904, vs (Milan, 1904)
La glu (drame musical populaire, 4, J. Richepin and Cain), Nice, Opéra, 24 Jan 1910, vs (Paris, ?1910)
La farce du cuvier (2, M. Lena), Brussels, Monnaie, 21 March 1912, vs (Paris, 1912)
Antar (conte-héroïque, 4, Chekri Ganem), Paris, Opéra, 23 Feb 1921, vs (Paris, 1921)

*

MGG (G. Ferchault)
E. Vuillermoz: '"Antar" de Gabriel Dupont à l'Opéra', *ReM*, ii (1921), 67–9
M. Dumesnil: 'Gabriel Dupont, Musician of Normandy', *MQ*, xxx (1944), 441–7
M. Kelkel: *Naturalisme, vérisme et réalisme dans l'opéra d'1890 à 1930* (Paris, 1984)

JOHN WAGSTAFF

Duprato, Jules Laurent (Anacharsis) (*b* Nîmes, 20 Aug 1827; *d* Paris, 20 May 1892). French composer. He studied at the Paris Conservatoire with Aimé Leborne and won the Prix de Rome in 1848. Having returned home via Germany, he turned to stage works, enjoying notable success with *Les trovatelles* (1854). Later works received less acclaim, although *Le sacripant* (1866) won him a prize of 1000 francs as the best work produced at the Fantaisies-Parisiennes. Pougin (Fétis) and others blamed Duprato's failures on poor librettists and bad luck, but the first charge is difficult to sustain, since Philippe Gille also provided librettos for *Manon* and Delibes' *Lakmé*, and Du Locle worked on *Don Carlos*. The teacher of Robert Planquette and Georges Douay, Duprato was appointed professor of harmony at the Conservatoire in 1871, and subsequently abandoned writing stage works. He seems to have suffered general ill-health, which led to long postponement of the première of *Le cerisier* and increasing paralysis in the last 20 years of his life.

The majority of Duprato's stage works are one-act pieces, employing few characters and much spoken dialogue. *La reine Mozab* appeared in *Le magasin des demoiselles* (an annual specializing in operettas for salon performance): it is little more than an appeal to French patriotism. *La fiancée de Corinthe* (dedicated to J.-B. Faure), on the other hand, displays more breadth of conception and employs flexible and effective recitative. A chorus in 5/8 metre recalls a similar number in *La déesse et le berger*, also classically inspired: although the rhythm used may have been intended to evoke early Greek music, the combination of note lengths used does not appear to have been notated by 19th-century writers on Greek music. Gustave Bertrand (*Le ménestrel*, October 1867) detected Gounod's influence in both works, while others saw an Italian influence in works such as *Salvator Rosa.*

unless otherwise stated, performed in Paris and printed works published in vocal score in Paris

Les trovatelles (oc, 1, M. Carré and J. Lorin), OC (Favart), 28 June 1854, (1854)
Pâquerette (1), OC (Favart), 20 June 1856, unpubd
M'sieu Landry (opérette, 1, C. Du Locle), Bouffes-Parisiens, 24 Nov 1856 (1856)
La reine Mozab (oc, 1, A. Carré), unperf. (1860)
Salvator Rosa (oc, 3, E. Grangé and H. Trianon), OC (Favart), 30 April 1861 (1861)
La déesse et le berger (oc, 2, Du Locle), OC (Favart), 21 Feb 1863 (1863)
Une promenade de Marie-Thérèse (opérette de salon, 1, P. Bogaerts), unperf. (1863)
Marie Stuart au chateau de Lochleven (opérette de salon, 1, Bogaerts), unperf. (*c*1863)
Le bonhomme hiver (oc, 1, Du Locle), unperf., ?unpubd [?1863]
Le baron de Groschaminet (opérette, 1, C.-L.-E. Nuitter), Fantaisies- Parisiennes, 24 Sept 1866 (1866)
Le sacripant (2, P. Gille), Fantaisies-Parisiennes, 24 Sept 1866 (?1866)
Le chanteur florentin (scène lyrique, 1, A. and E. Blau), Fantaisies-Parisiennes, 29 Nov 1866
La fiancée de Corinthe (1, Du Locle, after J. W. von Goethe), Opéra, 22 Oct 1867 (1868)
La tour du chien vert (opérette, 3, Gille), Folies-Dramatiques, 28 Dec 1871
Le cerisier (oc, 1, J. Prével, after J. de La Fontaine), OC (Favart), 15 May 1874 (?1874)
Gazouillette (oc), unperf.

Recits. and two arias for Balfe: The Bohemian Girl, vs (Rouen, 1862); recits. (unperf.) for Hérold: L'illusion

*

FétisBS
J. Ruelle: 'Jules Duprato', *L'art musical*, xxxi (1892), 74–5
P. Clauzel: 'Jules Duprato', *Mémoires de l'Académie de Nîmes*, 7e série, xvii (1894), 191
F. Bruyas: *Histoire de l'opérette en France* (Lyons, 1974)
H. R. Cohen, ed.: *Les gravures musicales dans L'illustration* (Quebec, 1982) [incl. photograph of Duprato and pictures of sets of *La déesse et le berger* and *La fiancée de Corinthe*]

JOHN WAGSTAFF

Duprez, Gilbert(-Louis) (*b* Paris, 6 Dec 1806; *d* Paris, 23 Sept 1896). French tenor and composer. His début at the Odéon (*Il barbiere di Siviglia*, 1825) and the première of his opera *La cabane du pêcheur* at Versailles the next year met with mixed success; he continued his studies in Italy after the Odéon closed in 1828. He soon distinguished himself as a *tenore di grazia*, but revealed his gifts as a dramatic tenor in Bellini's *Il pirata* at Turin in 1831. In the service of the impresario Alessandro Lanari, he enjoyed an almost uninterrupted run of successes in leading romantic roles, beginning with Arnold in the Italian première of *Guillaume Tell* (1831, Lucca), where he was the first tenor to sing the top high C as a chest note. Duprez scored a triumph as Percy in Donizetti's *Anna Bolena* in Florence in 1831 (repeating his success at his first appearance in Rome in 1834), before going on to create further Donizetti roles there – Ugo in *Parisina* (1833) and Henry II in *Rosmonda d'Inghilterra* (1834). The highlight of his stay in Italy was perhaps his creation of Edgardo in *Lucia di Lammermoor* (1835, Naples); apparently he advised his close friend Donizetti on the structure and composition of the last scene. With the interpretation of these roles his voice became progressively darker.

Returning to France, he was engaged at the Opéra, where he made his début in *Guillaume Tell* (1837), achieving immediate and overwhelming success with Paris audiences. His 'chest' C, in spite of the disappointment of Rossini, who compared it to 'the squawk of a capon with its throat cut', aroused wild enthusiasm and affected the taste of the public, who would listen to *Tell* only when Duprez was singing. He created leading roles in Halévy's *Guido e Ginevra* (1838), *La reine de Chypre* (1841) and *Charles VI* (1843), Berlioz's *Benvenuto Cellini* (1838), Auber's *Le lac des fées* (1839), Donizetti's *Les martyrs* (1840), *La favorite* (1840) and *Dom Sébastien* (1843) and Verdi's *Jérusalem* (*I Lombardi*) (1847), and established himself as Nourrit's successor in *Robert le diable*, *Les Huguenots*, *La Juive* and *La muette de Portici*. He also sang in London (1844–5, *Lucia*) and toured Germany (1850). He taught at the Paris Conservatoire (1842–50) and in 1853 founded his Ecole Spéciale de Chant; during this time his own operas were being staged in Paris.

According to Scudo, Duprez was already outstanding as a student for the breadth and incisiveness of his phrasing, though his voice then was not large. Gradually he became the first great *tenore di forza*, despite a vocal tessitura limited in its lower range (as shown in his refusal to sing Pollione in *Norma* at Rome in 1834). In France he was praised as the first true Romantic tenor and for his excellent declamation and the smoothness of his *canto spianato*; but his acting style was said to be exaggerated. Presumably through forcing his voice, and also because of the great number of performances he gave during his years in Italy where he had to sing as many as six times a week, a decline set in early; Berlioz greatly admired him in the vigorous music of *Benvenuto Cellini* in 1838, though noting (*Mémoires*) that his voice had coarsened somewhat. The story of the famous tenor's rise and fall in *Les soirées de l'orchestre* is largely based on Duprez's career. He composed a number of operas and his writings include *L'art du chant* (1845) and *Souvenirs d'un chanteur* (1880), a valuable account of his times and distinguished contemporaries.

In 1827 he married Alexandrine Duperron (*d* 1872), a soprano who made her début at the Odéon in 1827. She had a reasonably successful career, often singing with her husband during the Italian period. Her repertory included Imogene in *Il pirata* (1831, Turin) and Adalgisa (1834, Rome), a role in which she was warmly applauded. She retired from the stage about 1837. Their daughter Caroline (*b* Florence, 10 April 1832; *d* Pau, 17 April 1875) was a *soprano leggero* who also sang with her father, appearing in Paris and other French cities and (1851) in London; she created a number of roles at the Opéra-Comique.

For illustration *see* FAVORITE, LA.

La cabane du pêcheur (oc, 1, E. Duprez), Versailles, 1826
Le songe du comte Egmont (scène lyrique, E. Duprez), Brussels, Monnaie, 25 Dec 1842
L'abîme de la maladetta (oc, 3, E. Duprez and G. Oppelt), Brussels, Monnaie, 19 Nov 1851; rev. as Joanita, Paris, Lyrique, 11 March 1852
La lettre au bon Dieu (oc, 3, E. Scribe and F. de Courcy), Paris, OC (Favart), 28 April 1853
Jélyotte, ou Un passe-temps de duchesse (opérette, 1), Paris, private perf., 7 April 1854
Samson (opérette, 4, A. Dumas *père* and E. Duprez), Paris, concert perf., 1 Oct 1857
Jeanne d'Arc (grand op, 5, J. Méry and E. Duprez), Paris, Grand, 24 Oct 1865
La pazzia della regina (op, 2), Paris, private perf., 1877

Unperf.: Amelina (2); Tariotti (grand op); Zéphora (5)

*

ES (R. Celletti)
A. Elwart: *Duprez: sa vie artistique* (Paris, 1838)
L. Escudier and M. Escudier: *Etudes biographiques sur les chanteurs contemporains* (Paris, 1840)
E. Devrient: *Galerie des artistes dramatiques de Paris* (Paris, 1840–42)
H. Berlioz: *Les soirées de l'orchestre* (Paris, 1852; Eng. trans., 1956, 2/1973)
P. Scudo: *Critique et littérature musicales*, 2nd ser. (Paris, 1859)
N. Desarbres: *Deux siècles à l'Opéra* (Paris, 1868)
H. Berlioz: *Mémoires* (Paris, 1870, 2/1878; Eng. trans., 1969)
Jarro [G. Piccinni]: *Memorie d'un impresario fiorentino* (Florence, 1892)
U. Morini: *La Reale Accademia degli immobili ed il suo teatro 'La Pergola' (1649–1926)* (Pisa, 1926)
G. Monaldi: *Cantanti celebri* (Rome, 1929)
G. Landini: 'Gilbert-Louis Duprez ovvero l'importanza di cantar Rossini', *Bollettino del Centro rossiniano di studi* (1982), 1–3, 29
J. Rosselli: *The Opera Industry in Italy from Cimarosa to Verdi* (Cambridge, 1984)
R. Celletti: *Voce di tenore* (Milan, 1989)
S. Corti: *Edizione critica delle lettere del tenore G. L. Duprez nell'archivio dell'impresario teatrale Alessandro Lanari presso la Biblioteca nazionale di Firenze* (diss., U. of Pisa, 1991)

JOHN WARRACK, SANDRO CORTI

Dupuis, Albert (*b* Verviers, 1 March 1877; *d* Brussels, 19 Sept 1967). Belgian composer. His work began to attract notice while he was a student at the Verviers conservatory: a comic opera was performed at the town theatre when he was 18. He then attended courses given by d'Indy and others at the Schola Cantorum in Paris; he won the Belgian Prix de Rome in 1903. After a brief career as a conductor he was appointed director of the Verviers conservatory. In his compositions he remained faithful to the teaching of the Schola Cantorum. His 15 operatic pieces show the influence of Massenet, and it was to the theatre that his work was best suited.

Idylle, Verviers, 5 March 1895
Bilitis (comédie lyrique, 2, Dupuis), Verviers, Grand, 21 Dec 1899
Jean-Michel (nouvelle musicale, 4, G. Garnir and H. Vallier), Brussels, Monnaie, 5 March 1903
Martille (drame lyrique, 2, E. Cattier), Brussels, Monnaie, 3 March 1905
Fidélaine (conte lyrique, 3, H. Lejeune), Liège, Royal, 30 March 1910

Le château de la Bretêche (drame lyrique, 4, P. Milliet and J. Dor, after H. de Balzac), Nice, 28 March 1913
La chanson d'Halewyn (légende dramatique, 3, L. Solvay), Antwerp, Vlaamse Opera, 14 Feb 1914
La passion (drame lyrique, 4, J. Méry and P. de Choudens), Monte Carlo, 2 April 1916
La délivrance (drame réaliste, 2), Verviers, Grand, 19 Dec 1918
La barrière (drame lyrique, 3), Verviers, Grand, 26 Feb 1920
La victoire (tragédie antique, 4, H. Cain, after L. Payen), Brussels, Monnaie, 28 March 1923
Un drame sous Philippe II (drame lyrique, 4, Cain, after Porto-Riche), Liège, Royal, 29 Dec 1926
Hassan (conte oriental, 5 épisodes, Dor), Antwerp, Royal, 5 Nov 1931
Ce n'était qu'un rêve (comédie féerique, 1, V. Gille), Antwerp, Royal, 26 Jan 1932
Le poète et sa femme (drame poétique, 6 tableaux)

*

J. Dor: *Albert Dupuis* (Liège, 1935)
[R. Michel]: *Un grand musicien belge méconnu: Albert Dupuis* (Verviers, 1967)

HENRI VANHULST

Dupuis, José (*b* Liège, 18 March 1831; *d* Nogent-sur-Marne, May 1900). Belgian tenor. He studied at Liège and in 1854 went to Paris, where he sang at the Théâtre du Luxembourg. Engaged at the Théâtre des Variétés, he created roles in several of Offenbach's finest *opéras bouffes*: Paris in *La belle Hélène* (1864), the title role in *Barbe-bleue* (1866), Fritz in *La Grande-Duchesse de Gérolstein* (1867), Piquillo in *La Périchole* (1868) and Falsacappa in *Les brigands* (1869). He also sang in the premières of many other light operas, including Lecocq's *Le beau Dunois* (1870) and *Le grand Casimir* (1879), and Hervé's *La veuve de Malabar* (1873) and *Roussotte* (1881). He continued to appear as Paris and Fritz well into his fifties, by which time his sweet, clear tenor had roughened noticeably, leading him to add character roles such as Frimousse (Lecocq's *Le petit duc*) to his repertory in the later years of a long and remarkable career.

ELIZABETH FORBES, KURT GÄNZL

Du Puy, (Jean Baptiste) Edouard (Louis Camille) (*b* Baigory, Basse Navarre, *c*1770; *d* Stockholm, 3 April 1822). French composer and singer. He was brought up by a paternal uncle in Geneva and studied in Paris with Charles Chabran (C. F. Chiabrano) (violin) and J. L. Dussek (piano). In 1786 he was appointed musician to Prince Heinrich of Prussia at Rheinsberg; he became Konzertmeister in 1788 and studied under C. F. C. Fasch in Berlin. In 1792 he was banished from Rheinsberg because, in the spirit of Voltaire, he interrupted a Sunday service by riding into church on horseback. After working as a touring violinist in Poland and Germany he went to Stockholm in 1793, where he joined the opera orchestra. In 1795 he became a member of the Swedish Academy of Music. Two ballet pantomimes and others of his compositions were given at the Royal Opera. In 1799 he sang Pierrot in Grétry's *Le tableau parlant* and in D. Della-Maria's *Le prisonnier* and was given a 16-year contract. But political factors – in particular his threateningly emphatic diction of some lines in Gaveaux's *Le petit matelot* – led to his exile.

Du Puy went to Copenhagen, joining the opera orchestra and making his stage début as Firman in the Singspiel *Domherren i Milano* with music by Claus Schall, adapted from the comedy *Le souper imprévu, ou Le chanoine de Milan* by A. Duval. A high point in his stage career was the première of his *Ungdom og galskab* ('Youth and Folly') in 1806, for which he composed the music and sang the role of Ritmester Rose. In 1807 Du Puy directed the first performance of Mozart's *Don Giovanni* in Scandinavia, singing the title role himself. In 1809 he sang the first act of this opera with his pupil Crown Princess Charlotte Frederika (consort of Crown Prince Christian Frederik, afterwards Christian VIII) at Amalienborg Palace; but scandal broke out later in the year when Du Puy was discovered in bed with the princess and had to leave Denmark at two hours' notice.

He went to Paris, but with the election of Napoleon's commander Jean Baptiste Bernadotte to the Swedish throne he was able to return to Stockholm; he became court violinist and singer and from 1812 enjoyed high esteem as a conductor. He sang 18 roles at the Opera, including Mozart's Figaro and Don Giovanni and repeating the part of Ritmester Rose in *Ungdom og galskab*. Though not powerful, his voice (according to Beskow) had agility and a wide range in both tenor and baritone registers, and he always sang with verve and feeling. His music has fleeting charm, evident particularly in the graceful ballads and merry drinking-songs of the operas and *divertissements*. For many years the lively tunes in *Ungdom og galskab* assured his popularity in Denmark.

De ädelmodiga bönderna [The Noble Peasant] (scene, C. J. Lindegren), Stockholm, Arsenal, 10 Feb 1797 [perf. with N. Dezède: Les trois fermiers]
Ungdom og galskab, eller List over list [Youth and Folly, or Trick for Trick] (Spl, 2, N. T. Brunn, after J. N. Bouilly: *Une folie*), Copenhagen, Royal, 19 May 1806; as Ungdom och dårskap, eller List not list (trans. C. G. Nordfoss), Stockholm, Opera, 31 Oct 1814
Björn Jernsida (op, Valerius), inc.
Felicie, eller Den romanska flickan [Felicie, or The Maid of Rome] (comic op, 3, L. Hjortsberg, after E. Mercier-Dupaty), 19 Dec 1821

*

MGG (R. Cotte)
C. Palmstedt: *Edouard Du Puy, minnersteckning* (Stockholm, 1866)
B. von Beskow: *Lefnadsminnen* (Stockholm, 1870)
A. Buntzen: *Edouard Dupuy* (Stockholm, 1902)
R. Neiiendam: *Ungdom og galskab* (Copenhagen, 1923)
J. Neiiendam, ed.: Letters from Du Puy in *Personalhistorisk tidsskrift*, lvi (Copenhagen, 1935), 265–71
F. Eibe: 'Dupuy: forskningen', *Dansk musiktidsskrift*, xi (1936), 135–40
[F. Lauterbach:] *Edouard du Puy 1771–1822* (Copenhagen, 1949)
A. Kjaerulf: *Nordens Don Juan* (Copenhagen, 1952)

KLAUS NEIIENDAM

Dupuy, Martine (*b* Marseilles, 10 Dec 1952). French mezzo-soprano. In 1975 she won the International Singing Competition at Peschiera del Garda and sang Eurydice in Campra's *Le carnaval de Venise* at Aix-en-Provence. She has sung throughout Italy and at the Paris Opéra, Marseilles, Lausanne, Madrid, Buenos Aires and Salzburg; she made her Metropolitan début in 1988 as Handel's Sextus. Her repertory includes Mozart's Sextus and Cecilio (*Lucio Silla*), Vivaldi's Pharnaces, Monteverdi's Nero and Penelope, Bellini's Adalgisa and Romeo, Nancy (*Martha*), Ada (Donizetti's *Il diluvio universale*), Maffio Orsini and the Rossini roles that best display her strong coloratura technique: Cenerentola, Rosina, Arsace (*Semiramide*), Malcolm (*La donna del lago*), Isabella and Néocles (*Le siège de Corinthe*).

ELIZABETH FORBES

Duquesnoy [Lanetin, Lanctin], **Charles-François-Honoré** (*b* Beuzet, 18 May 1759; *d* Brussels, 9 May 1822). South Netherlands singer and composer. He was trained as a choirboy, and made his adult début in 1781 at the Paris Opéra, where he stayed for six years; in

1787 he became first countertenor at the Théâtre de la Monnaie in Brussels. He had started composing religious music at an early age but turned to opera in the early 1780s. In 1787 he produced in Brussels a two-act *opéra-ballet*, *Almanzor, ou Le triomphe de la gloire*, which must have been inspired by the repertory in Paris. Political problems in Brussels in 1794 induced him to change his name and leave for The Hague; he stayed there only a year before settling in Hamburg, where he and other musicians from the Monnaie set up a theatre for the large émigré public. In 1802 he returned to his native land, where he devoted himself wholly to religious music. Although Duquesnoy showed great facility in adapting to public taste and the prevailing performance conditions (and despite exerting a decisive influence on Roman Catholic church music in the Netherlands), his stage music does not depart in any way from the standard idioms of French opera between 1780 and 1800.

Diane jalouse, ou Le triomphe de l'amour (opéra, 1, H. D. C.), Bordeaux, 1784; cited in *StiegerO*
Almanzor, ou Le triomphe de la gloire (opéra-ballet, 2, d'Aumale de Corsenville), Brussels, 1787
Le mari vengé, ou Le mystificateur mystifié (oc, 3), Brussels, Monnaie, 1789
Le prix des arts, ou La fête flamande (opéra, 1), Brussels, 20 June 1791, *B-Ac*
L'hommage de Bruxelles (scène lyrique), Brussels, 1793, *Ac*
Le médecin et l'apothicaire (opéra, 3, after C. D. von Dittersdorf: Doctor und Apotheker), Brussels, 2 May 1794
La fête des mariages, ou Le tirage de la milice (oc), Hamburg, 1798
L'héroine villageoise (ballet-pantomime, 4), St Petersburg, Aug 1800, *F-Pn*
Le mari garçon (opéra), *B-Ac*

*

BNB (F. Loise)
A. Corbet: 'Onbekende werken van Charles Duquesnoy (1759–1822)', *RBM*, ii (1947–8), 44–54 PHILIPPE VENDRIX

Durán, Josep [Duran, José] (*b* ? Barcelona; *d* ?Barcelona, after 1791). Catalan composer. He was music master to the Marquéz de los Vélez from about 1755 and probably also *maestro de capilla* of Barcelona Cathedral. He studied in Naples, and possibly became a *maestro di cappella* there. His unashamed preference for Italian styles over Catalan or Spanish in his operas and church music precipitated a celebrated polemic about Spanish traditions, notably with the *maestro de capilla* of Toledo Cathedral, Jaime Casellas. In 1760 in Barcelona he gave the first performance of his opera *Antígona*, followed in 1762 by *Temístocles*, both to librettos (now in *E-Bc*) by Metastasio.

*

LaborD
E. Cotarelo y Mori: *Orígenes y establecimiento de la ópera en España hasta 1800* (Madrid, 1917), 233, 240–41
J. Subirá: *La ópera en los teatros de Barcelona*, i (Barcelona, 1946), 30, 37
A. Martín Moreno: *Historia de la música española*, iv: *Siglo XVIII* (Madrid, 1985), 94–5, 155–6, 372, 429 JACK SAGE

Durandi [Duranti, Giacomo], **Jacopo** (*b* Sant'Agata, Vercelli province, 25 July 1737; *d* Turin, 28 Oct 1817). Italian librettist. He provided librettos for *opere serie* performed at the Teatro Regio in Turin during a brief hiatus in Cigna-Santi's service there. His chief claim to fame is the seminal libretto *Armida* (based on TORQUATO TASSO's *Gerusalemme liberata*), which, together with an *Armida abbandonata* for Jommelli (1770, Naples), by an equally obscure Neapolitan poet, De Rogatis, spawned a series of operas on the Saracen witch Armida and the crusader Rinaldo including Haydn's great *opera seria* of that title. (Versions of this libretto after Sacchini's setting of 1772 combine elements from Durandi's libretto with that of De Rogatis.)

Typically for Turinese operas of the period, Durandi's librettos imbue traditional italianate formal designs with natural and man-made spectacle borrowed from Verazi's librettos for Stuttgart and Mannheim. The three-year residency of Innocente Colomba, former scene designer for Stuttgart and Ludwigsburg, may account for the appearance of some extravagant French-inspired machine spectacle in the form of an aerial ballet in the middle of Durandi's *Annibale in Torino*, an otherwise military opera replete with battle scenes and cavalry displays with elephants. This libretto enjoyed a revival in Turin 20 years later.

all opere serie

Ecuba, Celoniati, 1769; *Armida*, Anfossi, 1770 (Manfredini, 1770; Sacchini, 1772); *Berenice*, I. Platania, 1771; *Annibale in Torino*, Paisiello, 1771 (Zingarelli, 1792)

*

M.-T. Bouquet: *Storia del teatro regio di Torino*, i: *Il teatro di corte dalle origini al 1788* (Turin, 1976)
M. P. McClymonds: 'Haydn and his Contemporaries: "Armida abbandonata"', *Joseph Haydn: Vienna 1982*, 325–32
MARITA P. McCLYMONDS

Durastanti, Margherita (*fl* 1700–34). Italian soprano. Her first known appearances were in a pasticcio at Venice in 1700 and in an opera by M. A. Ziani at Mantua (where she may have been in court service) in 1700–01. From 1707 she was in the service of Marquis Ruspoli at Rome, her colleagues including Caldara and Handel, who composed for her many of his finest solo cantatas. She was prima donna at the S Giovanni Grisostomo theatre in Venice, 1709–12, where she sang in nine operas by Lotti and C. F. Pollarolo and created the title part in Handel's *Agrippina* (1709). She sang at Bologna and Reggio Emilia in 1710, Milan and Reggio Emilia again in 1713, Parma in 1714, Florence in 1715, and in 1715–16 in five operas at Naples, including A. Scarlatti's *Carlo rè d'Alemagna* and *La virtù trionfante*. Veracini engaged her for Dresden in 1719. Handel heard her there in Lotti's *Teofane* and engaged her for the Royal Academy in London, where she made her début in the first production, Porta's *Numitore*, in 1720, and played the title roles in Handel's *Radamisto* and D. Scarlatti's *Narciso*. The following season she sang in G. Bononcini's *Astarto*, the revival of *Radamisto* (now as Zenobia; her old role was taken by Senesino), *Arsace* (Orlandini-Amadei), the composite *Muzio Scevola* and *Odio ed amore*.

After singing in Munich (1721), Durastanti missed the London season owing to illness, but returned in 1722–4, appearing in Handel's *Floridante* (Rossane), *Ottone*, *Flavio* and *Giulio Cesare*, and in operas by Bononcini and Ariosti. She rejoined Handel's company in 1733–4, singing in *Ottone*, *Sosarme*, *Il pastor fido*, *Arianna*, and several pasticcios.

Durastanti had a longer personal association with Handel than any other singer. The parts he wrote for her, Agrippina, Radamisto, Cloelia in *Muzio Scevola*, Gismonda in *Ottone*, Vitige in *Flavio*, Sextus in *Giulio Cesare* and Tauris in *Arianna*, show an exceptionally wide range of character, suggesting that she was a gifted actress. Her voice was never a high soprano, and its compass gradually dropped from *d'* to *a''* in *Agrippina* to *b* to *g''* in 1733–4, when her tessitura was that of a mezzo-soprano. She frequently played male roles.

Burney said that her 'person was coarse and masculine', but she seems to have been a dramatic singer and a good musician.

*

U. Kirkendale: 'The Ruspoli Documents on Handel', *JAMS*, xx (1967), 222–73, 518 WINTON DEAN

Durazzo, Count **Giacomo** (*b* Genoa, 27 April 1717; *d* Venice, 15 Oct 1794). Italian impresario, poet and diplomat. He came from a noble Genoese family of Albanian origin that from the late 16th century produced two cardinals and eight doges (the latter including his older brother Marcello). Giacomo's early interest in the theatre was stimulated by a visit to Paris, during which he conceived his own reform dramas (e.g. *Armida*). The decisive event in his life was his appointment in 1749, suggested by Prince Kaunitz, as Genoan ambassador to Vienna. His marriage there in 1750 to Aloisia Ernestine Ungnad von Weissenwolf raised his Viennese social position. In February 1752 he was named assistant to Count Franz Esterházy as director of Viennese theatrical affairs, the Empress Maria Theresa's doubts about the appointment having been dispelled by Kaunitz. In spring 1754, on Esterházy's resignation, he became sole *directeur des spectacles*.

In this post Durazzo was responsible for the city's two large theatres (including their repertories and personnel), the 'French' Burgtheater and the 'German' Kärntnertor, each of which had its own actors, orchestra and ballet troupe; his fostering of the Kärntnertor resulted in a wider role for music in German plays and an improvement in the quality of ballets. After the burning of the Kärntnertor on 3 November 1761 (for which Durazzo was called to account before the empress), both troupes played alternately in the Burgtheater until the opening of the new Kärntnertor on 9 July 1763. Among the great singers engaged by Durazzo were Caterina Gabrielli (Kaunitz's favourite), Giacomazzi, Scotti and Guadagni. The ballet master was Gasparo Angiolini and the theatre engineer G. M. Quaglio. The theatrical situation he set up in Vienna, with his command of protocol and cultural politics, enabled him to build from one production to another, developing long-term artistic relationships among the creative talent that he drew to the 'French' theatre.

Durazzo's appointment in 1760 as *cavagliere di musica* brought violent opposition from the court Kapellmeister Reutter, whom Durazzo had estranged by inviting Gluck to serve as composer and conductor of court chamber and table music, instead of limiting his responsibilities to theatre and concert music. The quarrel became so bitter that Durazzo left Vienna and his post in summer 1761, but with Kaunitz's support he was able to return to both and to continue his patronage of Gluck.

In spring 1764 Durazzo combined a journey to Frankfurt for the coronation of Joseph II (3 April 1764) with a visit to Paris, accompanied by Gluck and Coltellini. In Frankfurt, because of the continued opposition of Reutter and various intrigues, he was finally forced to resign. The background is not clear. Durazzo's management of the finances may have played a part, especially those arising from his association with Favart. There may also be a connection with the departure from the theatre of the prima ballerina formerly protected by Durazzo, Louise Geoffroy-Bodin. Durazzo offered his resignation to Joseph II on 1 April 1764 and it was accepted (a few days earlier Joseph had recommended to the empress, who considered Durazzo 'a terrible busybody', that he be dismissed because he was 'dangerous' and 'already the cause of enough confusion'). Soon after, again through Kaunitz's influence, he was appointed ambassador of the Viennese court to Venice, a post he held until 1784. He performed artistic as well as diplomatic duties, and lived and entertained lavishly, receiving musicians such as the Mozarts in 1771 and Schuster in 1776. Little is known of his last ten years but part of the time was spent in Genoa.

Durazzo's achievements in Viennese theatre and concert life were widely recognized by his contemporaries, and the opposition and scepticism he sometimes faced only serve to stress the extent of his accomplishments. A determining factor in his work was Kaunitz's policy of alliance with France, which coincided with Durazzo's own artistic aims. The 'troupe de comédiens françois' brought to Vienna by Kaunitz in spring 1752 was provided by Durazzo with *opéras comiques* and vaudeville comedies imported from Paris (later with Favart's help) and arranged by Gluck. It was Gluck who helped Durazzo to achieve an independent *opéra comique*, following the Parisian model: the way led through an ever increasing number of inserted 'airs nouveaux' to *La rencontre imprévue* (7 February 1764; to a text by Dancourt), the last of eight entirely new *opéras comiques* composed by Gluck. This work remained popular for decades and was a stimulus for Mozart's *Die Entführung aus dem Serail*.

Of even greater importance was Durazzo's activity in serious opera. Einstein described him as the 'father of the idea of the Gluckian opera reform'. In *L'innocenza giustificata* (8 December 1755), the *festa teatrale* composed by Gluck, Durazzo combined aria texts from Metastasio with recitatives written by himself. This and his *Le cacciatrici amante*, set by Wagenseil (25 June 1755), which both relate to Parisian *opéra-ballet*, represented decisive breaks with the Metastasian tradition. (Two other texts written about the same time are shorter, more decorative works: *La gara*, set by Reutter, 1755, and *La joie imprévue*, 1756, given by children). He had Migliavacca revise to his specification, for Traetta, the text of his own earlier *Armida* (3 January 1761) in a form that was designed to combine French and Italian elements. But his ultimate triumph came in his recognition that Calzabigi, who came to Vienna at the beginning of 1761, would provide the ideal partner for Gluck and that their collaboration, in *Orfeo ed Euridice*, could form the model for a new Italian opera for the Viennese stage. This renewal of *opera seria* cannot be separated from the reform of stage dance. Here Durazzo had ideal partners, first in Hilverding and then in Angiolini, and again it must have been he who brought Angiolini and Gluck together in the ballet-pantomime *Don Juan* (17 October 1761) and the ballets in *Orfeo ed Euridice*.

The results of Durazzo's initiatives in *opera buffa* are probably already to be found in the parody of *La serva padrona* (with French text) put on by the children of the actors at the Burgtheater in December 1758 and in the production of a setting of *Il finto pazzo* on 31 December 1758. He engaged Giuseppe Scarlatti and encouraged Gassmann, whose talent for *opera buffa* he soon recognized. He did not, however, bring about the hoped-for link between Favart and Goldoni.

The anonymous *Lettre sur le méchanisme de l'opéra italien* (allegedly published in Naples and Paris, and dated 'Florence, 1 March 1756'), long ascribed to Josse de Villeneuve, has also been attributed to Durazzo (see Gentili-Verona 1969); but recent research (see Brown 1991) suggests that Durazzo is unlikely to have been the author himself – who was probably a Frenchman – although the *Lettre* may reflect views close to his own and there is reason to think that it may have been published with his financial support. The author, writing within a French frame of reference, set out to 'dissipate the marvellous vapour' surrounding Calzabigi's 'Dissertazione su la poesie drammatiche del sig. Abate Pietro Metastasio' (Paris, 1755). He postulated a conciliation between French and Italian opera that would take advantage of the best in both traditions, chided French critics for writing about Italian opera when they knew little of its working, and described its strengths and weaknesses (remarking on obbligato recitative as a little-used resource that unfailingly moved audiences); he takes up issues of the Querelle des Bouffons and ends with a discussion of modern French opera.

*

B. Benincasa: *Descrizione della raccolta di stampe di S.E. il Sig. Conte Jacopo Durazzo patrizio genovese ec.ec. esposta in una dissertazione sull'arte dell'intaglio a stampa* (Parma, 1784)

R. Haas: 'Josse de Villeneuves Brief über der Mechanismus der italienischen Oper von 1756', *ZMw*, vii (1924), 129–63 [incl. Ger. trans. of *Lettre*]

——: *Gluck und Durazzo im Burgtheater* (Vienna, 1925)

J. Witzenetz: *Le théâtre français de Vienne 1752–1772* (Szeged, 1932)

H. Bédarida: 'L'opéra italien jugé par un amateur français en 1756', *Mélanges de musicologie offerts à M. Lionel de la Laurencie* (Paris, 1933), 185–200

A. Einstein: *Gluck* (London, 1936, 2/1954)

A. Novotny: *Staatskanzler Kaunitz als geistige Persönlichkeit* (Vienna, 1947)

G. Gentili-Verona: 'Le collezioni Foa e Giordano della Biblioteca Nazionale di Torino', *Vivaldiana*, i (1969), 31–56

G. Zechmeister: 'Die Wiener Theater nächst der Burg und nächst dem Kärntnerthor von 1747 bis 1776', *Theatergeschichte Österreichs*, iii/2 (Vienna, 1971)

G. Croll: 'Neue Quellen zu Musik und Theater in Wien 1758–1763; ein erster Bericht', *Festschrift Walter Senn* (Munich and Salzburg, 1975), 8–12

W. Koschatzky: *Giacomo Conte Durazzo 1717 1794: zum Jubiläum des Wiener Burgtheaters 1776–1976* (Vienna, 1976) [exhibition catalogue]

P. Howard: *C. W. von Gluck: Orfeo* (Cambridge, 1981)

D. Heartz: 'Traetta in Vienna: *Armida* (1761) and *Ifigenia in Tauride* (1763)', *Studies in Music from the University of Western Ontario*, vii (1982), 65–88

A. Fabio Ivaldi: 'La famiglia di Giacomo Durazzo: i personaggi decisivi, l'ambienti genovese', *Teatro Comunale, Genoa 1987*, 103–222 [programme book for Gluck's *Alceste*]

B. A. Brown: 'Durazzo, Duni, and the Frontispiece to *Orfeo ed Euridice*', *Studies in Eighteenth-Century Culture*, no.19 (East Lansing, MI, 1989), 71–97

——: *Gluck and the French Theatre in Vienna* (Oxford, 1991)

GERHARD CROLL, DANIEL HEARTZ/R

Durban. City in the Republic of South Africa. It contains the headquarters of the Natal Performing Arts Council (NAPAC), established in 1963, which is responsible for opera and ballet performances in Natal. Before 1985 opera was presented at the Alambra Theatre; since then it has been performed at the Opera (1225 seats), which forms part of the Natal Playhouse theatre complex. There are normally two seasons a year. Performances are accompanied by the Natal PO, formed in 1983.

*

G. S. Jackson: *Music in Durban 1850–1900* (Johannesburg, 1970)

Duret, Cécile. *See* SAINT-AUBIN, JEANNE CHARLOTTE.

Durey, Louis (Edmond) (*b* Paris, 17 May 1888; *d* St Tropez, 3 July 1979). French composer. He resolved to devote himself to music after seeing *Pelléas et Mélisande* in 1907 and attended the Schola Cantorum until 1914. One of Les Six, he soon distanced himself from the group to pursue an independent path. Satie's simplicity and Stravinsky's polytonality formed the foundation for his work, but Durey's music always has a sober gravity that distinguishes him from these composers. His dramatic works include the comic opera *L'occasion* (1, after P. Mérimée; 1923–5), the monodrama *Judith* (1, F. Hebbel, trans. Gallimard and P. de Lanux; 1918), for solo voice and piano, and incidental music for Maeterlinck's *L'Intruse*. *L'occasion* was refused by the Opéra-Comique because of its libretto, which tells of a hypocritical priest who murders for love; it eventually received its première in a radio broadcast recorded in Strasbourg, 22–5 May 1974. As secretary-general of the Fédération Musicale Populaire and of the Association Française des Musiciens Progressistes, part of Durey's work was in the furtherance of his political aims.

*

'Louis Durey', *Courrier musical de France*, viii (1964), 265–8

F. Robert: *Louis Durey: l'aîné des Six* (Paris, 1968)

F. Robert: 'Le théâtre lyrique des Six', and '"L'occasion": extrait du Catalogue commenté de L. Durey', *Le théâtre lyrique français 1945–1985*, ed. D. Pistone (Paris, 1987), 276–93

ARTHUR HOÉRÉE

Durkó, Zsolt (*b* Szeged, 10 April 1934). Hungarian composer. He studied first at the Szeged and Budapest conservatories, then until 1960 at the Budapest Academy of Music with Ferenc Farkas. In 1961–3 he attended Petrassi's masterclasses at the Accademia di S Cecilia, Rome, and after returning to Budapest worked as a freelance composer. In 1971–7 he taught at the Budapest Academy of Music, and from 1982 he was a reader of new scores for Hungarian Radio. He has won many prizes.

Durkó played a leading part in the establishment of an internationally orientated style in Hungarian music after 1959. Despite his consistently atonal writing after his stay in Rome, he has always sought inspiration in ideas rooted in Hungarian history and consciousness, maintaining a position as a classicist striking a balance between the traditional and the new. His leanings towards vocal writing culminated in a triptych consisting of the two oratorios *Halotti beszéd* ('Burial Prayer', composed 1967–72) and *Széchenyi* (1981–2), with the three-act opera *Mózes*, begun in 1972, as the central section (libretto by the composer, after Imre Madách; Budapest, Hungarian State Opera House, 15 May 1977). The opera deals with the conflict between the heroic individual and the masses. Durkó employs the operatic framework to expand his well-tried harmonic and textural hallmarks into an expressive large-scale musical construction.

*

A. Boros: *Harminc év magyar operái 1948–1978* [30 Years of Hungarian Opera, 1948–78] (Budapest, 1979)

G. Staud, ed.: *A Budapesti operaház száz éve* [100 Years of the Budapest Opera House] (Budapest, 1984)

TIBOR TALLIÁN

Durme, Jef [Jozef] **van** (*b* Kemzeke-Waas, 7 May 1907; *d* Brussels, 28 Jan 1965). Belgian composer. He studied harmony with Edward Verheyden and counterpoint with Flor Alpaerts at the Antwerp conservatory. For further studies he went in 1931 to Vienna where he received advice from Alban Berg, and for a long time his style and technique were influenced by that composer. His five operas are dramas of ideas, particularly *Remous*, whose première was conducted by Hermann Scherchen.

Remous op.15 (opéra, 1, J. Weterings), Brussels, Palais des Beaux-Arts, 31 May 1935
La mort d'un commis-voyageur op.58, 1954–5 (opéra, 2, van Durme, after A. Miller: *Death of a Salesman*), unperf.
König Lear op.59, 1955–7 (opéra, 2, after W. Shakespeare), unperf.
König Richard der Dritte op.60, 1960–61 (opéra, 2, after Shakespeare), ?unperf.
Antonius und Kleopatra op.61, 1962–4 (opéra, 3, after Shakespeare), ?unperf.

*

I. de Sutter: 'Jef van Durme', *Vlaams muziektijdschrift*, xxii (1970), 71–5

CORNEEL MERTENS/R

Durón, Sebastián (*b* Brihuega, bap. 19 April 1660; *d* Cambó, 3 Aug 1716). Spanish composer. He was known in his day as a virtuoso organist and a prolific composer of sacred and secular works. After working as an organist and composer in cathedrals in several Spanish cities (Saragossa, Seville, Burgo de Osma and Palencia), he was engaged in 1691 as an organist in the Spanish royal chapel in Madrid, and subsequently became *maestro de capilla* and director of the royal choir school. According to court documents, he had by 1697 distinguished himself at court not only through his excellent sacred compositions, but also as a superior theatrical composer, deemed 'without equal'. After supplying music for a number of important productions, Durón was abruptly dismissed and exiled in 1706 because he had openly supported the Austrian cause against the Bourbon Philip V in the War of the Spanish Succession. In January 1707 he was still in Madrid and was further dishonoured for attempting to remove a great many scores 'of the best pieces' (including his own) from the music library of the royal chapel. He fled to France and ended his days in the service of Mariana of Neuburg.

Complete scores survive for one short opera, seven zarzuelas and one *comedia*. A few songs are preserved in loose scores from other works as well. His first theatrical score was probably the zarzuela *Salir el amor del mundo* to a text by the dramatist José de Cañizares, produced at the Madrid court in 1696. This was followed by music for other zarzuelas and *comedias* with texts by Cañizares and other fashionable dramatists: Antonio de Zamora, Marcos de Lanuza and Manuel de Vidal Salvador. The highly successful zarzuela *Veneno es de amor la envidia* was perhaps Durón's last composition for the Spanish stage. The première of this work, staged in the public Teatro de la Cruz on 22 January 1711 by the company of Joseph de Prado, took place well after Durón's exile, as did Prado's public performances of two other zarzuelas by Durón in Madrid in 1710 and 1711; Durón may have sent scores to Madrid from his place of exile, or left copies of these works with a trusted and well-placed friend in Madrid before his departure. Beyond Spain, some of Durón's zarzuelas were presented in privately sponsored performances in Lisbon (1718–23), and his music seems to have been fairly well known in Latin America, as copies of his cantatas and excerpts of theatrical songs are still preserved there.

Durón's one-act 'ópera scénica' *La guerra de los gigantes* was evidently composed as an aristocratic commission for the Count of Salvatierra, probably between 1700 and 1707. The story and five characters of the opera are taken from the legend of the revolt of the giants against the gods of Olympus. With no libretto surviving, it is difficult to know precisely if the manuscript score represents a complete opera and indeed whether it was fully sung in performance. Because the work has virtually no recitative and a flimsy plot that unfolds through a series of set pieces (largely strophic airs and four-part choruses), it is possible that it was actually a partly sung entertainment in the manner of a zarzuela or semi-opera, with spoken roles for additional secondary characters and further dramatic dialogue. Most contemporary works included eight or more characters: in Durón's own *Veneno es de amor la envidia*, perhaps his most italianate work, three of the eight characters have entirely spoken roles, two minor comic characters sing a few songs, and only the three supernatural principals sing their roles entirely.

Although his career as a composer of stage works was brief, Durón's contribution to the history of Spanish theatre music is important. His scores are the first to demonstrate the co-existence of native and imported musics that came to characterize musical life in Madrid in the early 18th century. Several years after Durón's death, his theatre music was still controversial; some nationalist critics held that by introducing contemporary foreign musical genres and styles to the Spanish stage he had opened the door to all sorts of modern abuses. His scores contain French minuets in addition to popular Spanish dance songs such as the seguidilla, and italianate da capo arias beside traditional Spanish airs and song forms. Beyond formal distinctions, Durón's approach to text setting and to the musical phrase also diverge considerably from the established Spanish techniques associated with the music of Hidalgo. For these new sounds, he was accused by later writers of having polluted the 'purely Spanish' style with capricious foreign 'barbarisms', to the detriment of traditional Spanish gravity.

Salir el amor del mundo (zar, 2, J. de Cañizares), Madrid, court, 1696, *E-Mn*; ed. Martín Moreno (1979)
Muerte en amor es la ausencia (comedia, 3, A. de Zamora), Madrid, 1697, *Mn*
Selva encantada de amor (zar), *Mn*
Apolo y Dafne (zar), collab. J. de Navas, *Mn*
El imposible mayor en amor, le vence amor (zar, Cañizares), Madrid, 1710, *P-EVp*
Las nuevas armas de amor (zar, Cañizares), Madrid, 1711, *E-Mn*, *P-EVp*; ed. Hart (1974)
Veneno es de amor la envidia (zar, Cañizares), Madrid, Cruz, 22 Jan 1711, *E-Mn*
El estrago en la fineza (zar, Cañizares), *P-EVp*
Amor es quinto elemento (Zamora), 1 song *E-Bc*, 1 song *Mn*
Los elementos de amor, voz, cristal, luz, y color (M. de Vidal Salvador), 1 song *Mn*
Acis y Galatea (zar, Cañizares), 1 song *Mn*
La guerra de los gigantes (ópera scénica), *Mn*

Attributed: Celos vencidos de amor (zar, M. de Lanuza), 1698; Júpiter y Yoo (zar, Lanuza, 1699), *Mn*

*

N. A. Solar Quintes: 'Nuevos documentos para la biografía del compositor Sebastián Durón', *AnM*, x (1955), 137–62
L. G. Siemens Hernández: 'Nuevos documentos sobre el músico Sebastián Durón', *AnM*, xvi (1961), 177–99
——: 'Nuevos aportaciones para la biografía de Sebastián Durón', *AnM*, xviii (1963), 137–59
A. Martín Moreno: 'El músico Sebastián Durón: su testamento y muerte: hacia una posible biografía', *AnM*, xxvii (1972), 163–88
G. Q. Hart: *A Study and Edition of the Zarzuela 'Las nuevas armas de amor', Libretto by José de Cañizares, Music by Sebastián Durón* (diss., U. of London, 1974)
A. Martín Moreno, ed.: *Salir el amor del mundo, zarzuela en dos*

jornadas, texto de José de Cañizares, música de Sebastián Durón (Malaga, 1979)
W. M. Bussey: *French and Italian Influence on the Zarzuela 1700–1770* (Ann Arbor, 1980)
L. K. Stein: 'Un manuscrito de música teatral reaparecido: "Veneno es de amor la envidia" ', *RdMc*, v (1982), 225–33

LOUISE K. STEIN

Du Roullet [Durollet], **Marie François Louis Gand Leblanc.** *See* ROULLET, MARIE FRANÇOIS LOUIS GAND LEBLANC.

Duru, Alfred (*b* Paris, 1829; *d* Paris, Jan 1890). French librettist. He collaborated with HENRI CHARLES CHIVOT on more than 40 light opera librettos.

Dushanbe. Capital of Tajikistan. Until 1929 it was known as Dyushambe, and from 1929 to 1961 as Stalinabad. The Tadzhikskiy Gosudarstvennïy Teatr (Tajik State Theatre), organized in 1929, oversaw some musical activities until a more formal musical group was created within the theatre in 1933. In 1934–5 the Tadzhikskiy Muzïkal'nïy Ansambl was formed with the assistance of a visiting Tajik-language Jewish theatre company from Samarkand. The establishment of the Tadzhikskiy Muzïkal'nïy Teatr in 1936 led to a number of 'musical dramas', including *Vosstaniye Vose* ('Vose's Uprising') in 1939 (with music by S. A. Balasanian). The Tadzhikskiy Teatr Operï i Baleta (Tajik Theatre of Opera and Ballet), formed in 1940, devoted itself to the creation of a national opera repertory with the encouragement of national and federal officials, giving premières of works by Balasanian, A. S. Lensky and I. R. Saifiddinov. The theatre has featured mostly native artists, trained in Moscow and Leningrad, since being renamed the Tazhikskiy Akademicheskiy Teatr Operï i Baleta imeni S. Ayni (Tajik Ayni Academic Theatre of Opera and Ballet) in 1954; performances of Russian and European classics are in Russian, while national works are presented in Tajik.

*

ME (I. G. Nisnevich; also 'Tadzhikskiy teatr operï i baleta', N. K. Nurdzhanov)
G. Bernandt: *Slovar' oper vpervïye postavlennïkh ili izdannïkh v dorevolyutsionnoy Rossii i v SSSR 1736–1959* [Dictionary of Operas First Performed in Pre-Revolutionary Russia and in the USSR 1736–1959] (Moscow, 1962), 537
N. Nurdzhanov: *Istoriya tadzhikskogo sovetskogo teatra (1917–1941 gg.)* [The History of Tajik Soviet Theatre (1917–41)] (Dushanbe, 1967)
——: *Tadzhikskiy teatr* (Moscow, 1968)
Yu. V. Keldïsh, ed.: *Istoriya muzïki narodov SSSR* [History of the Music of the Soviet Peoples], i-v (Moscow, 1970–74)
Muzïkal'naya zhizn' Sovetskogo Tadzhikistana: 1919–45 gg. [Musical Life in Soviet Tajikistan: 1919–45] (Dushanbe, 1974)

GREGORY SALMON

Düsseldorf. City in western Germany, in North Rhine-Westphalia. Its musical history was influenced chiefly by the princely courts. From the second half of the 17th century there were performances of music drama; in 1695 the city acquired its first opera house, which remained in use until 1738, when it was turned into a barracks. This theatre staged performances of the operas of Agostino Steffani, who initially came from Hanover on a diplomatic mission and then took over the management of the opera: two operas and a pasticcio with music from earlier works were given between 1707 and 1709. Handel visited Düsseldorf in 1711 to recruit the famous castrato Baldassari, then employed at the court, to perform in London. When the opera house was closed the Grupellos foundry was converted for use as a theatre in 1747, and despite its considerable drawbacks it staged performances of music drama by touring opera companies for almost a hundred years. The music festivals of the Lower Rhine, held from 1818 onwards, were a strong attraction: in 1833 Mendelssohn was appointed director of the 15th festival, and in 1850 Schumann came from Dresden as director of the orchestra and chorus.

The first Stadttheater was built in 1875. It was rebuilt in 1906, partly destroyed in 1943, restored in 1944 and completely rebuilt in 1956; it has 1342 seats. Düsseldorf had a flourishing theatrical life between 1946 and 1951 under the direction of Gustaf Gründgens, who staged *Figaro* and Offenbach's *Les brigands*. In 1956, under the directorship of Hermann Juch (1956–64), the previous theatrical union (1887–1921) with Duisburg, about 25 km from Düsseldorf, was revived to form the Deutsche Oper am Rhein. Within a short time Juch built up a repertory of 58 works, almost all of which were performed in both theatres. The Duisburg theatre (1118 seats) was built in 1912, destroyed in 1942 and rebuilt in 1950. Until 1942 Duisburg was an active centre, and many operas received their premières there, including Volkmar Andreae's *Ratcliff* (1914), Julius Weismann's *Schwanenweiss* (1923) and *Ein Traumspiel* (1925) and Max Brand's *Maschinist Hopkins* (1929). The first performance after the merger with Düsseldorf was of *Falstaff* on 30 September 1956, with Otto Wiener in the title role. A day earlier the association of the two theatres had been celebrated in Düsseldorf with a special performance of *Elektra* conducted by Karl Böhm, with Astrid Varnay in the title role.

Important premières and first German performances in Düsseldorf and Duisburg have included Liebermann's *Die Schule der Frauen* (1957–8), Krenek's *Karl V* (1957–8, première of the revised version), Sutermeister's *Titus Feuerfuchs* (1958), Krenek's *The Bell Tower* (1958, European première), Shostakovich's *Lady Macbeth of the Mtsensk District* (first staged performance in Germany) and *The Nose* (1963, first German-language performance), Giselher Klebe's *Die tödlichen Wünsche* (1959), Frank Martin's *Monsieur de Pourceaugnac* (1964), Schoenberg's *Moses und Aron* (1968), Cavalieri's *Rappresentatione di Anima, et di Corpo* (1971), Mozart's *Mitridate, re di Ponto* (1971), Britten's *Death in Venice* (1974), Kelterborn's *Ein Engel kommt nach Babylon* (1977) and Berio's *Un re in ascolto* (1988).

Under the artistic management of Grischa Barfuss, Intendant of the Deutsche Oper am Rhein for 22 years from 1964, there were notable cycles of the works of Janáček, Puccini and Rossini. Early in his career Carlos Kleiber was appointed conductor of the company (1956–64). Singers who began their careers in Düsseldorf have included Hildegard Behrens, Manfred Jung and Hermann Becht. Barfuss was succeeded as Intendant in 1986 by Kurt Horres. The Deutsche Oper am Rhein gives some 450 performances a season, 300 in Düsseldorf and 150 in Duisburg. It has a strength of about 185 (including dancers), and an orchestra of 131 in Düsseldorf and of 93 in Duisburg.

*

W. Horn and R. Wollhardt: *Rheinische Symphonie: 700 Jahre Musik in Düsseldorf* (Düsseldorf, 1987)
D. M. Weber: *Der städtische Musikverein zu Düsseldorf und die Düsseldorfer Oper in der Zeit von 1890 bis 1923* (Berlin, 1990)

SABINE SONNTAG

Dustmann-Meyer, (Marie) Louise (*b* Aachen, 22 Aug 1831; *d* Berlin, 2 March 1899). German soprano. She made her début in 1848 at the Theater in der Josefstadt, Vienna, then sang in Breslau, Kassel, Dresden and Prague. Engaged at the Vienna Hofoper from 1857 until her retirement in 1875, she had a wide repertory ranging from the Queen of Night, Donna Anna and Susanna to Senta, Elisabeth, Ortrud and Eva. She also sang both of Gluck's Iphigenias, Spohr's Jessonda, Linda (*Linda di Chamounix*), Norma, Valentine (*Les Huguenots*), Euryanthe, Reiza (*Oberon*), Anna (*Hans Heiling*), Marguerite (*Faust*) and Amelia (*Un ballo in maschera*). She sang Elsa in the first performance of *Lohengrin* heard by Wagner, who admired her enough to consider her as a possible creator of Isolde. Her opulent voice combined power, flexibility and dramatic conviction.
ELIZABETH FORBES

Dutillieu, Irene Tomeoni. *See* TOMEONI, IRENE.

Dutillieu [Dutilleu, Du Tilleul], **Pierre** (*b* Lyons, 15 May 1754; *d* Vienna, 28 June 1798). Italian composer of French descent. He was educated in Naples and worked in Italy, mainly at the Teatro del Fondo in Naples. In 1791 he and his wife, the singer Irene Tomeoni, were engaged at the Burgtheater in Vienna. He achieved little success with his operas in Vienna (though *Gli accidenti della villa* was performed many times in Naples up to 1814); his ballets were more favourably received. Among his other works are instrumental pieces and songs.

all opere buffe, first performed at Vienna, Burgtheater

Il trionfo d'amore (C. Mazzolà), 14 Nov 1791
Nannerina e Pandolfino, o sia Gli sposi in cimento (G. Bertati), 15 Dec 1792, excerpts in *A-Wgm*
Gli accidenti della villa (F. S. Zini), 19 Sept 1794, *I-Nc*
La superba corretta, 30 April 1795
Il nemico delle donne (Zini), 17 Aug 1797
GERNOT GRUBER

Dütsch, Otto Johann Anton [Dyutsh, Otton Ivanovich] (*b* Copenhagen, 1823; *d* Frankfurt, 21 April 1863). Russian composer and conductor of Danish birth. After graduating in 1847 from the Leipzig Conservatory, where his teachers included Felix Mendelssohn, he went to Russia. In 1852 he took a position with the Imperial Theatres in St Petersburg, working from then until 1863 chiefly as a conductor in various theatres, but also as a chorus master and accompanist for the Italian opera. In the last year of his life he taught theory at the newly established St Petersburg Conservatory.

Dütsch's brief career as a composer for the stage began with a one-act operetta, *Uzkiye bashmaki* ('Tight Shoes', St Petersburg, Alexandrinsky, 1851; revived, 1856, as *V derevne*, 'In the Country'). His major work was *Kroatka, ili Sopernitsï* ('The Croatian Girl, or The Rivals', 4, N. Kulikov; St Petersburg, Mariinsky, 9/21 Dec 1860), in which the great contralto Dar'ya Leonova sang the title role.

The plot revolves around a love triangle consisting of a Hungarian girl (Iliya), a Croatian girl (Ganksa) and an Austrian officer, set against a romantic background of popular insurrection. At first this was to have been the Hungarian uprising of 1848; but the censor having rejected so recent and dangerous an example, the setting was moved back (despite great harm to the coherence of the libretto) to the year 1644, a time of border warfare between Hungary and Croatia. Continuing official squeamishness about theatrical representations of political unrest probably accounted for the opera's short stage life, despite all precautions and notwithstanding a favourable reception by press and public. The music is attractively melodic and liberally tinged with national hues, especially of the Hungarian gypsy variety: Iliya's Act 2 aria with chorus borrows a theme from Liszt's Sixth Hungarian Rhapsody. The opera was cancelled after eight performances and was never shown again on the imperial stage, though there were subsequent private and amateur productions. Ganksa's sentimental Act 4 romance 'Chto zhizn' dlya nas' ('What is life to us') remained an extremely popular concert number in Russia well into the 20th century.

N. F. Findeyzen: 'Dyutshi – otets i sïn' [The Dütsches – Father and Son], *RMG*, iii/2 (1896), 4–10
A. A. Gozenpud: *Russkiy opernïy teatr XIX veka (1857–1872)* (Leningrad, 1971), chap.2
RICHARD TARUSKIN

Duval, Denise (*b* Paris, 23 Oct 1921). French soprano. She made her début at Bordeaux in 1943 as Lola (*Cavalleria rusticana*), then appeared at the Folies Bergères. In 1947 she made her début at the Opéra-Comique as Butterfly and was chosen by Poulenc to create Thérèse in *Les mamelles de Tirésias*. At the Opéra-Comique she also created Francesca in Hahn's *Le oui des jeunes filles* (1949). At the Opéra (where she made her début in 1947 as Salome in *Hérodiade*), she sang Thais, Rosenn (*Le roi d'Ys*), the Princess in Rabaud's *Mârouf*, Portia in Hahn's *Le marchand de Venise,* Ravel's Concepcion and Blanche in the Paris première of *Dialogues des Carmélites* (1957). She created Elle in *La voix humaine* (1959, Opéra-Comique) and repeated the role in the American première at Carnegie Hall and the British première with the Glyndebourne company at Edinburgh (1960). At Glyndebourne she sang Mélisande (1962). A very beautiful woman with great dramatic intelligence, she was a most gifted singing actress, as the roles composed for her by Poulenc demonstrate. She retired in 1965 owing to ill-health.
ANDRÉ TUBEUF, ELIZABETH FORBES

Dux, Claire (*b* Witkowicz, 2 Aug 1885; *d* Chicago, 8 Oct 1967). Polish soprano. She studied in Berlin and made her début in Cologne as Pamina in 1906, later becoming a member of the Royal Opera, Berlin, where she sang the leading lyrical German and Italian roles. In 1911 she made her London début with Beecham at His Majesty's Theatre; two years later she was Covent Garden's first Sophie in *Der Rosenkavalier*. In 1921 she went to the USA; she appeared frequently in Chicago, where she settled after retiring from the stage. Dux's voice was a lyric soprano of the utmost purity, controlled by a firm technique and capable of exquisite *pianissimo*. She was admired as an actress, and her Sophie, Eva and Pamina were particularly distinguished. Beecham called her 1914 Drury Lane Pamina 'the most exquisite exhibition of *bel canto* that London has heard for more than a generation' (*A Mingled Chime*, London, 1944).
ALAN BLYTH

Dvě vdovy. Opera by Bedřich Smetana; *see* *TWO WIDOWS, THE.*

Dvořáček, Jiří (*b* Vamberk, eastern Bohemia, 8 June 1928). Czech composer and teacher. He studied at the Prague Conservatory (1943–7) and at the Prague Academy (1949–53), where his composition teachers were Jaroslav Řídký and Václav Dobiáš. From 1953 he worked at the academy, at first as secretary to the composition department and then as lecturer in composition theory. He has progressed from a romantic, folkloric style to a dodecaphony that is only exceptionally atonal. His opera *Ostrov Afrodity* ('The Island of Aphrodite', 1967), for which he wrote his own libretto (after A. Parnis), was performed in Dresden in 1971. This work, inspired by the struggle for independence and social justice in Cyprus in 1955, reveals a wide range of stylistic influences. Its fluid recitative gives the music a somewhat cinematic, sub-pictorial quality.

*

ČSHS

L. Zenkl: 'O hudebni řeči Jiřího Dvořáčka' [On Dvořáček's Musical Speech], *HRo*, xxviii (1975), 403–6 OLDŘICH PUKL

Dvořák, Antonín (Leopold) (*b* Nelahozeves, nr Kralupy, Bohemia, 8 Sept 1841; *d* Prague, 1 May 1904). Czech composer. With Smetana and Janáček, he is regarded as one of the greatest composers of the nationalist movement in what was to become Czechoslovakia. He is usually associated with the composition of orchestral and chamber music, but after 1869 there was no single period of any length in his composing career when he was not engaged in some kind of operatic project. In an interview printed in the Viennese newspaper *Die Reichswehr* (1 March 1904) the composer stated: 'I proved many years ago that my main inclination was towards dramatic creation'. With 11 operas, Dvořák was, along with his friend Karel Bendl, one of the most prolific opera composers of the Czech national revival. Nevertheless, he frequently stood aside from trends adopted by his Czech contemporaries, and in many senses his operas were not typical of the revival. While his comic operas in general conform to the Czech village comedy established by Smetana in *The Bartered Bride*, none of his grand operas are based on Czech history or mythology. His most successful opera, *Rusalka*, was not typical of Czech opera in the 1890s and early 1900s, when many of his contemporaries were turning to *verismo* subjects.

1. EARLY YEARS AND INFLUENCES, 1841–78. After a highly traditional musical upbringing, in many ways little different from that of his 18th-century predecessors, Dvořák completed his studies at the Prague Organ School. The rigours of a conventional course of study notwithstanding, he was involved with opera from very early in his professional career. In September 1859, shortly after graduating from the Prague Organ School, he joined Karel Komzák's band of 18 players, which in November 1862 formed the basis of the orchestra of the newly founded Provisional Theatre under J. N. Maýr. During nine years as a viola player in the orchestra, Dvořák was exposed to a wide range of works. Under Maýr's directorship the repertory of the Provisional Theatre favoured Italian opera, and French grand opera increased in frequency and reached a position of considerable importance after Smetana took over the musical directorship in September 1866. German opera was represented by Beethoven, Weber, Lortzing, Flotow, Nicolai and, above all, Mozart, and an increasing number of operettas, mainly by Offenbach and Suppé, were given. In addition, Dvořák also participated in the premières of a number of native operas, including Smetana's *The Brandenburgers in Bohemia*, *The Bartered Bride* and *Dalibor* as well as the revival of Škroup's *Dráteník* ('The Tinker').

Although Wagner's musical style was a major influence on a number of Dvořák's operas, Wagner's operas were notably absent from the repertory of the Provisional Theatre, a matter of policy on Smetana's part. However, Dvořák played some of Wagner's music, including the overture to *Tannhäuser* and the preludes to *Tristan und Isolde* and *Die Meistersinger*, at a concert at the theatre conducted by the composer in 1863. Accounts of Dvořák attending the German Estates Theatre are contradictory, but it is not likely that he attended a performance of a music drama by Wagner. His early knowledge of Wagner's music stemmed from a study of the scores lent to him by Karel Bendl. Wagner's influence was most potent at the beginning and end of Dvořák's operatic career, though Wagnerian harmony can be found in many of his other operas. The more continuous texture and renewed interest in Wagnerian harmony in Dvořák's last three operas, and his revisions of *Jakobín* ('The Jacobin') and especially *Dimitrij* in the 1890s, mark a wholehearted return to his earlier fascination. Despite his interest in the ornamental aspects of Wagner's style, Dvořák did not make a conscious and thorough-going attempt at music drama in the manner of Fibich's *Nevěsta messinská* ('The Bride of Messina'). While he was prepared to defend Wagner's musical achievement, Dvořák never revealed his personal feelings about the composer's ideas on opera.

In many ways, Dvořák's attitude to Wagner reflects his general approach to operatic theory. Beyond practical questions concerning librettos, he was habitually reticent on aesthetic questions. He did not discuss opera to any great extent in his letters, and at a time when polemic concerning the nature of national opera was a regular part of musical life in Prague, he remained silent. While he stated that he considered opera to be 'The most suitable form for the nation', Dvořák's enthusiasm for opera seems to have sprung more from its potential for reaching a large audience than from the belief that opera could make a specific statement.

After Dvořák left the Provisional Theatre at the end of the season in July 1871, his operatic experience becomes harder to pinpoint. He admired *Carmen* and *Yevgeny Onegin*, and, in general, Verdi. Marginalia in Dvořák's score of Charpentier's *Louise* reveal a somewhat prurient interest in the musical language rather than a fascination with *verismo* drama. Given the decidedly archaic nature of Dvořák's last opera, *Armida*, his enthusiasm for *Les Huguenots*, revived in Prague in March 1903, is significant. A comprehensive statement about his tastes on the basis of the evidence available is impossible. The pattern that emerges, however, supported by his admiration for *Tannhäuser* over Wagner's later music dramas, reinforces the impression that Dvořák preferred works that mirror his own compositional tendency towards number opera.

The decision to set Körner's old-fashioned German libretto *Alfred der Grosse* might have been prompted in part by the fact that Czech works were being performed at the Provisional Theatre. The subject of the libretto, with its clear juxtaposition of the overbearing Danes and the downtrodden Britons who eventually triumph, would have had a clear resonance for Czech audiences (who were themselves hoping to achieve greater autonomy). While the German text would have excluded the work from performance in the Provisional Theatre, a number of German operas by Czechs were translated and included in the repertory. Although the composer's manuscript is dated 1870, the compositional process probably began in the late 1860s, when Dvořák was also engaged on his highly experimental string quartets in B♭, D and E minor. The existence of the score of *Alfred* was virtually unknown in Dvořák's lifetime, and apart from the strong possibility that he showed the work to Smetana, he never drew attention to the opera.

Only a relatively short time elapsed between the completion of *Alfred* and the commencement of his next opera, *Král a uhlíř* ('King and Charcoal Burner'), early in the spring of 1871. The opera was completed in December 1871 and was offered to the authorities of the Provisional Theatre. Unlike in the case of the composer's work on *Alfred*, the public was well informed (via the music journal *Hudební listy*) that Dvořák was engaged on a comic opera. In September 1873, however, the theatre authorities returned the manuscript, the complexities of the writing having proved too difficult for the company's performers. Dvořák, who had coached the singers, accepted the decision. He recomposed the work between April and November 1874, just after he had completed his Fourth Symphony. The opera was taken up again by the Provisional Theatre, and it was first performed with some success on 24 November 1874, three weeks after its completion.

Even before *King and Charcoal Burner* had been given, Dvořák began work on his next comic opera, *Tvrdé palice* ('The Stubborn Lovers'); he had received the libretto early in 1870. Although he worked on the opera between October and 24 December 1874 it was not performed until October 1881, after his next two operas, *Vanda* and *Šelma sedlák* ('The Cunning Peasant'), had had their premières at the Provisional Theatre.

After leaving the orchestra of the Provisional Theatre, Dvořák had sustained himself at first by piano teaching. On 17 November 1873 he married Anna Čermáková, and shortly afterwards he became organist at St Adalbert's Church. In 1875 he won the Austrian State Prize for the first time. He composed his grand opera *Vanda* in four months at the end of that year, which also saw the creation of the String Quintet in G op.77, the Moravian Duets op.20, the Serenade for strings op.22, the Piano Trio in B♭ op.21, the Piano Quartet in D op.23 and the first version of the Fifth Symphony op.76. Quite unintentionally, on the composer's part, the première of *Vanda* (17 April 1876) led to a disagreement between the Young Czech and Old Czech political parties. *Vanda* was the first opera to be directed by Rudolf Wirsing at a time when the Old Czech party was feeling that the Young Czechs were gaining too much control over the Provisional Theatre and the plans for the National Theatre. As a result the Old Czech press boycotted the première. Other reviews suggest that *Vanda* had a moderate success, but the first performance was the only occasion when the opera was given complete. The resources of the Provisional Theatre were inadequate for the conjuration scene in Act 3, and in subsequent performances, including a revival in 1880 for which Dvořák provided a new overture and small revisions, particularly to the final scene, the opera was given in four rather than five acts.

For all the deficiencies of structure and versification in the libretto of *Vanda*, Dvořák showed himself adept at handling the conventions of serious grand opera. Where there is drama in the libretto, he responded convincingly. He was also developing a melodic style of considerable originality, which he used as a means of unifying large stretches of music.

The completion of his next comic opera, *The Cunning Peasant*, in July 1877 marked the end of Dvořák's most intense period of operatic composition. Its première in January 1878 coincided with his growing international reputation. Late in 1877 Brahms had recommended that Simrock should publish Dvořák's Moravian Duets, and 1878 saw the composition, orchestration and publication of the first set of Slavonic Dances. Dvořák drew on his new-found interest in national elements in many parts of *The Cunning Peasant*, an opera that bears many resemblances in milieu and structure to Smetana's *The Bartered Bride*. Hostinský (1908) and Eliška Krásnohorská (in letters to Smetana) were the first to draw attention to the similarities between Dvořák's and Smetana's comic operas. For all its palpable debt to *The Bartered Bride*, *The Cunning Peasant* shows that Dvořák could handle comic situations in ensembles, was capable of effective characterization and was well aware of the uses of thematic reminiscence – all of which, coupled with his highly developed and accessible melodic gifts, were sufficient to disarm most criticism of the opera and guaranteed the work's popularity. Between its première in 1878 and the closing of the Provisional Theatre in 1883 *The Cunning Peasant* was the most frequently performed Czech comic opera apart from *The Bartered Bride*. Indeed, its popularity declined only with the appearance of *The Jacobin* in 1889.

2. Maturity, 1878–90. By 1880 Dvořák's operatic career must have seemed particularly buoyant. *The Cunning Peasant* was a success, and the composer's revised version of *Vanda* was given in June 1880 at a gala performance in the presence of the emperor. On completing *The Cunning Peasant* Dvořák began to search for a new libretto and in 1878 encouraged the playwright Julius Zeyer to write a text based on the legend of Šárka. The composer kept the libretto for three years without working on it and the project was finally shelved when he began to sketch *Dimitrij* on 8 May 1881. The libretto, by Marie Červinková-Riegrová, daughter of the Old Czech politician František Ladislav Rieger, had been given to Dvořák by Mayr. Although the first performance on 8 October 1882 was successful, Dvořák accepted Hanslick's advice and persuaded Červinková-Riegrová to join him in a major alteration to the fourth act. The revised version had its première in 1885.

Dvořák considered a number of subjects after *Dimitrij*, some of them non-Czech. He had been considering Červinková-Riegrová's libretto of *The Jacobin* since 1883, but did not start work on it until 1887. His inclination, in part fired by Hanslick, was towards a subject that would be of interest outside Bohemia. *The Jacobin*, with its traditional Czech setting and characterization, at first did not appeal to the composer. During the composition, between 10 November 1887 and 18 November 1888, however, he became very enthusiastic about the libretto and the character of the choirmaster, Benda, which became one of his most vivid musical evocations. The first performance of *The Jacobin* on 12 February 1889 was a major success and over the next five years it replaced *The Cunning Peasant* as Dvořák's most popular comic opera.

Dimitrij, *The Jacobin*, a revision of *King and Charcoal Burner*, and the overture and incidental music to František Šamberk's play *Josef Kajetán Tyl* (which includes Dvořák's only example of melodrama) make up the composer's entire output for the theatre in the 1880s. In the new version of *King and Charcoal Burner* the vocal lines were adapted to a more satisfactory versification of the libretto by V. J. Novotný, and the third act was made much neater by removing an unnecessary subplot from the original. This perceptible falling off in Dvořák's operatic output – compared to six operas in the 1870s – coincided with the dramatic advance of his fortunes abroad. Much of the decade was taken up with trips to England, for which he supplied orchestral and choral works such as the Seventh Symphony in D minor, the oratorio *Svatá Ludmila* ('St Ludmilla') and the Requiem.

3. Final years, 1891–1904. In January 1891 Dvořák began to teach composition at the Prague Conservatory. Of even greater significance for his career was the offer (on 5 June) of the directorship of the National Conservatory of Music of America in New York; Dvořák arrived in New York on 27 September 1892. Apart from the cantata *The American Flag* and the *Biblické písně* ('Biblical Songs'), the works he composed in the USA were exclusively instrumental; they included the Ninth Symphony ('From the New World') and the String Quartet in F op.96 ('The American').

Dvořák's patron in the USA, Mrs Jeannette Thurber, encouraged the composer to write an opera based on Longfellow's *Song of Hiawatha*. Numerous sketches, some of which found their way into the Ninth Symphony, testify to a more than passing interest on Dvořák's part, but the only substantial operatic project to be completed during his time there was a thorough revision of *Dimitrij*. Partly in response to criticism of the earlier versions as being too monolithic, and with the encouragement of Anton Seidl, Dvořák made the revision more fluent, more Wagnerian and more up-to-date. In the new version, first performed on 7 November 1894, he eschewed much of the lyricism of the original and removed the chorus and quintet from the final scene, one of his most effective operatic passages. In the 1890s he also made substantial revisions to the second and third acts of *The Jacobin*. In 1894 Červinková-Riegrová made some structural alterations, suggested by Dvořák, which greatly streamlined the final act. The composer worked on the new version in 1897, and it was performed with great success on 19 June the following year.

On his final return from the USA in April 1895 Dvořák turned away from abstract instrumental composition to concentrate on symphonic poems and opera. The shift towards the musical language of Wagner, apparent in the revisions of *Dimitrij* and to a lesser extent in *The Jacobin*, is even clearer in his last three operas, *Čert a Káča* ('The Devil and Kate'), *Rusalka* and *Armida*. Dvořák's use of ballads from K. J. Erben's *Kytice* ('A Garland of National Tales') as the basis for four symphonic poems is mirrored in the subjects of the librettos of *The Devil and Kate* and *Rusalka*. In 1900 Dvořák showed a passing interest in Karel Pippich's libretto *Vlasty skon* ('The Death of Vlasta'), making a few sketches before turning his attention to *Rusalka*, but his enthusiasm was fired at this stage less by heroic historical or mythological themes than by more folklike material.

Adolf Wenig's libretto, *The Devil and Kate*, occupied Dvořák from May 1898 to the end of February 1899. The musical substance of the opera, unique in 19th-century Czech comic opera for avoiding love interest, nevertheless draws on many common features of the style: attractive symmetrical melodies, bagpipe effects and a substantial ballet. In addition to externals commonly associated with Czech comic opera, the declamation is noticeably telegraphic, anticipating Janáček, and the characterization of the main comic figures is extremely sharp.

At a time when many of his contemporaries were turning to *verismo* subjects, Dvořák's adherence to the folktale was exceptional. It is significant that Jaroslav Kvapil failed to find a composer for his libretto *Rusalka* among the younger generation of Czechs. In transferring the main elements of Friedrich de la Motte Fouqué's *Undine* to the context of Bohemian mythology, Kvapil consciously modelled his characters on the demiurges in Erben's *Garland of National Tales*, material close to Dvořák's heart. The collaboration between composer and librettist, though not without disagreement, was extremely successful and resulted in Dvořák's most popular opera. As with *The Devil and Kate*, the continuous sketch of *Rusalka* is extremely fluent; the compositional process lasted from April to November 1900. The depth of characterization in Kvapil's libretto, which looks beyond simple folk archetypes, evoked from Dvořák music of genuine depth. The texture, though mostly continuous and clearly indebted to Wagner, relaxes with extended lyrical interludes, most notably Rusalka's Song to the Moon. The melodic substance, drawing on material sketched in the USA, is consistently distinguished, and the dramatic situations are well captured. Much of the opera, however, is meditative and provides the perfect vehicle for Dvořák's blend of the symphonic and the lyric.

The première of *Rusalka* in March 1901 was a major personal triumph and encouraged Dvořák to search for a new libretto. The success of Růžena Maturová in the title role undoubtedly contributed to the selection of a libretto that focussed almost entirely on a single female character. To an even greater extent than in Dvořák's previous two operas, Vrchlický's four-act libretto, based on Tasso's story of Armida and Rinaldo, was peripheral to the subject matter favoured by Czech composers at the turn of the century. Dvořák himself also had problems with the composition, as shown by an indecisive continuous sketch and a gestation period, from March 1902 to August 1903, much longer than for either *The Devil and Kate* or *Rusalka*. Difficulties over the first production and a less than successful première did not deter Dvořák from his pursuit of opera. According to his interview with *Die Reichswehr* only two months before his death, Dvořák was considering three librettos. His sketches for a poor libretto by Rudolf Stárek, based on the familiar legend of *Horymír*, offer no support for Janáček's suggestion that Dvořák was about to abandon the methods he had been cultivating.

4. Operatic style. Dvořák's operatic sympathies were wide and included the work of Bizet, Wagner, Verdi and Meyerbeer as well as his foremost Czech predecessor, Smetana. The influence of these and other composers overlaid a fundamental conservatism in Dvořák's approach, and he never wholly abandoned number opera. Unlike Fibich, Dvořák did not experiment with operatic form but was content to build on conventional

Ex.1

(a) *Alfred,* Act 1 scene i

['The people revel in the flush of victory; while I am pursued by the ghastly vision of last night']

(b) *Dimitrij,* Act 3 scene iii

['You are a serf, you are Griška Otrepěv!']

(c) *Armida,* Act 2 scene ii

['Enough of this waiting in the desert']

formulae rather than cultivate music drama and melodrama. Despite his appearing to be somewhat outside the Czech mainstream as perceived by Otakar Hostinský and others, Dvořák's success in opera, as measured by the number of performances in his lifetime, was second only to that of Smetana in his native land.

From an early stage, Dvořák's operas were seen in relation to Smetana's more fundamental contribution to Czech opera. After the première of *Rusalka*, Zdeněk Nejedlý headed a campaign against Dvořák, complaining that he was undramatic and old-fashioned in his adherence to French and Italian opera and that he negated the progressive achievement of Smetana. The aggravated hysteria of Nejedlý's attack has tended to dog studies of Dvořák's operas throughout the 20th century and has concealed a fundamental lack of understanding of the composer's aims. Unlike Smetana, Dvořák never intended to provide a body of operas central to the national repertory. In his serious operas, unique among his major contemporaries, he looked outside the conventions of the Czech tradition, basing them successively on English, Polish, Russian and oriental subjects. In *Vanda*, *Dimitrij* and *Armida*, Dvořák was content to work within the conventions of grand opera as practised much earlier in the century. His achievement in these serious works was less in the transformation of an older form than in the vigour with which he invested familiar formulae.

In their adherence to a rural or provincial milieu, Dvořák's comic operas approach the archetype established by Smetana in *The Bartered Bride*. But apart from the use of bagpipe effects in *King and Charcoal Burner* and (much later) in *The Devil and Kate*, and a general tendency to favour symmetrical melody, Dvořák's early comic operas marked an advance on Smetana's first two comedies, *The Bartered Bride* and *The Two Widows*, in having been conceived as through-composed from the start.

Dvořák's relations with his librettists were productive, particularly in the case of Marie Červinková-Riegrová, but were much less of an intense and mutually creative collaboration by comparison with Smetana and Eliška Krásnohorská. While Dvořák encouraged his librettists to provide him with subjects he wished to set – in 1881 he asked Josef Štolba, the librettist of *The Stubborn Lovers*, to write a comic text based on foreign history – he tended to accept what was offered without much thought to the final shape. In the case of some of the early operas, this resulted in his setting less than ideal librettos: *King and Charcoal Burner*, *Dimitrij* and *The Jacobin* required extensive revision at a later stage. Although Dvořák was rarely indecisive and never gullible, he could be impressionable. He was particularly sensitive to criticism and to the suggestions of his friends: Hanslick gave him advice about *Dimitrij*, Seidl spurred his renewed interest in Wagner, and František Šubert influenced his choice of librettos for the last three operas.

Compared with Fibich, Janáček and even Smetana, Dvořák could very easily be seen as a conservative. His adherence to grand-opera formulae and pursuit of the lyrical expansion afforded by dance – with the exception of *The Stubborn Lovers*, all of his operas include ballets – represent the broader aspects of an acceptance of tradition of which the hegemony of the set piece in his works was the most important internal feature.

Many dramatic, expressive and structural features of Dvořák's operatic style were fixed very early in his career. The use of ostinato figures to bind together large stretches of music involving different groupings of soloist and chorus prevalent in Dvořák's mature works can be found as early as *Alfred*. Similarly, the rhetoric of the recitative in major musical statements, deriving from earlier 19th-century practice, was fixed in *Alfred* and reappears at significant points in later operas (ex.1). The foundation of the musical expression of such powerful moments in the later operas, such as Rusalka's 'Ó marno to je' ('Oh, useless it is') and Armida's Act 2 aria, 'Slyš, z hlubin bídy svojí' ('Hear, from the depths of destitution'), is to be found in Vanda's superb aria, 'Bohové velci, bohové strašliví' ('Great gods, terrible gods'), composed as early as 1875. In the same way, the characterization of Bohuš in *The Jacobin* may be traced back through the Count in *The Cunning Peasant* and the King in the second version of *King and Charcoal Burner*.

From *Alfred* onwards, Dvořák made use of thematic reminiscence. Occasionally, and most notably in *Vanda*, the use of motivic recurrence in the early operas approaches leitmotif. In *Rusalka* and *Armida* the tendency is even more marked. Dvořák's use of thematic reminiscence, however, is at its most effective when making a clear dramatic point rather than creating a continuous texture. But the finest music in his operas is to be found in the extensive set pieces for soloists and chorus.

Judged from an international perspective, Dvořák was typical in adopting the hybrid forms of opera used widely in the late 19th century. Locally, this marked him as a conservative, but the strength and individuality of his three late operas have secured audiences in his native land and, apart from *The Bartered Bride*, *Rusalka* is the most frequently performed Czech opera.

See also Alfred; Armida (vii); Cunning peasant, the; Devil and kate, the; Dimitrij; Jacobin, the; King and charcoal burner; Rusalka (iii); Stubborn lovers, the; and Vanda.

Edition: *A. Dvořák: souborné vydání* [Complete Edition], ed. O. Šourek and others (Prague, 1955–) [AD] [vols. in progress are given in square brackets]

B – Burghauser thematic catalogue no.
first performed in Prague unless otherwise stated

B; op.	*title*	*genre, acts*	*libretto*	*composition; first performance*	*publication*	*remarks*	*AD*
16	Alfred	heroic op, 3	T. Körner	?1869–19 Oct 1870; Olomouc, Czech, 10 Dec 1938	ov., Berlin and Leipzig, 1912, and AD i/1, 1974	orig. text in Ger.; listed both as op. 1 and as op. 10	[i/1]
21	Král a uhlír [King and Charcoal Burner]	op, 3	B. J. Lobeský [Bernard Guldener]	?April–20 Dec 1871; National, 28 May 1929	vs, Prague, forthcoming		[i/2]
42; (14)	2nd version	op, 3	Lobeský	17 April–3 Nov 1874; Provisional, 24 Nov 1874		new setting of B 21, with new version of 'Ballad of King Mathias', comp. Dec 1880–Jan 1881 (B 115); rev. as B 151	[i/3]
151; 14	3rd version	comic op, 3	Lobeský, rev. V. J. Novotný	Feb–March 1887; National, 15 June 1887	vs, Prague, 1915, arr. Dvořák and R. Veselý	rev. of B 42	[i/3]
46; 17	Tvrdé palice [The Stubborn Lovers]	comic op, 1	J. Štolba	Oct–24 Dec 1874; New Czech, 2 Oct 1881	vs, Berlin, 1882		[i/4]
55; 25	Vanda	grand op, 5	V. Beneš-Šumavský and F. Zákrejs, after J. Surzycki	9 Aug–22 Dec 1875; Provisional, 17 April 1876	ov., Prague, forthcoming	rev. 1879, 1880 and 1883; ov. comp. 1879 (B 97)	[i/5]

B; op.	title	genre, acts	libretto	composition; first performance	publication	remarks	AD
67; 37	Šelma sedlák [The Cunning Peasant]	comic op, 2	J. O. Veselý	Feb–July 1877; Provisional, 27 Jan 1878	vs, Berlin, 1882; ov., Berlin, 1879		[i/6]
127; 64	Dimitrij	grand op, 4	M. Červinková-Riegrová	8 May 1881–23 Sept 1882; New Czech, 8 Oct 1882	vs, Prague, 1886, arr. Zubatý and J. Káan	rev. 1883 and 1885; rev. as B 186	[i/7]
186; 64	rev. version	grand op, 4	Červinková-Riegrová	28 March 1894–30 Jan 1895; National, 7 Nov 1894	vs, Prague, 1912, rev. K. Kovařovic	rev. of B 127	[i/8]
159; 84	Jakobín [The Jacobin]	op, 3	Červinková-Riegrová	10 Nov 1887–18 Nov 1888; National, 12 Feb 1889	vs, Prague, 1911, arr. Veselý rev. Kovařovic	rev. as B 200	i/10
200; 84	rev. version	op, 3	Červinková-Riegrová, rev. with F. L. Rieger	17 Feb–7 Dec 1897; National, 19 June 1898	vs, Prague, 1941	rev. of B 159	i/10
201; 112	Čert a Káča [The Devil and Kate]	comic op, 3	A. Wenig, after Cz. fairy-tale	5 May 1898–27 Feb 1899; National, 23 Nov 1899	vs, Prague, 1908		i/11
203; 114	Rusalka	lyric fairy-tale, 3	J. Kvapil, after F. de La Motte Fouqué: *Undine*	21 April–27 Nov 1900; National, 31 March 1901	vs, Prague, 1905, arr. J. Faměra		i/12
206; 115	Armida	op, 4	J. Vrchlický, after T. Tasso: *Gerusalemme liberata*	11 March 1902–23 Aug 1903; National, 25 March 1904	vs, Prague, 1941, arr. K. Šole		[i/13]

CATALOGUES

O. Šourek: *Dvořák's Werke: ein vollständiges Verzeichnis* (Berlin, 1917)

J. Burghauser: *Antonín Dvořák: thematický katalog, bibliografie, přehled života a díla* [Thematic Catalogue, Bibliography, Survey of Life and Work] (Prague, 1960, 2/forthcoming)

B. Červinková and others: *Antonín Dvořák: bibliografický katalog* (Prague, 1991)

SOURCE MATERIAL

O. Šourek: *Dvořák ve vzpomínkách a dopisech* (Prague, 1938, 9/1951; Eng. trans., 1954, as *Antonín Dvořák: Letters and Reminiscences*)

——: *Antonín Dvořák přátelům doma* [Dvořák to his Friends at Home] (Prague, 1941)

A. Hořejš: *Antonín Dvořák: the Composer's Life and Work in Pictures* (Prague, 1955)

J. Burghauser: *Král a uhlíř* (Prague, 1957) [critical edn of lib.]

O. Šourek: Preface to A. Dvořák: *Rusalka*, AD, i/12 (1960)

J. Burghauser: *Dimitrij* (Prague, 1961) [critical edn of lib.]

F. Bartoš: Preface to A. Dvořák: *Jakobín*, AD, i/10 (1966)

J. Clapham: 'Dvořák's Relations with Brahms and Hanslick', *MQ*, lvii (1971), 241–54; Cz. trans., *HV*, x (1973), 213ff [incl. orig. Ger. text of letters]

J. Burghauser: Preface to A. Dvořák: *Čert a Káča*, AD, i/11 (1976)

M. Kuna, ed.: *Antonín Dvořák, korespondence a dokumenty: korespondence odeslaná* [Antonín Dvořák, Correspondence and Documents: Correspondence Dispatched] (Prague, 1987–)

BIOGRAPHICAL AND CRITICAL STUDIES

E. Hanslick: 'Concerte', *Neue freie Presse* [Vienna] (23 Nov 1879); repr. in Hanslick: *Concerte, Componisten und Virtuosen* (Berlin, 1886, 4/1896); Eng. trans. as 'Anton Dvořák', *Musical Review* [New York] (11 Dec 1879); *Dwight's Journal of Music* (3 Jan 1880); *Musical Standard*, new ser., xviii (1880), 58

A. Piskáček: 'Dvořák v tvorbě operní' [Dvořák in his Operatic Works], *Dalibor*, xxvi (1904), 163–4, 187–90

K. Hoffmeister: 'Dvořákovy opery' [Dvořák's Operas], *Věstník pěvecký*, x (1905), 119–22

O. Hostinský: *Antonín Dvořák ve vývoji naší dramatické hudby* [Dvořák in the Development of our Dramatic Music] (Prague, 1908); repr. in *Antonín Dvořák: sborník statí o jeho díla a životě* [Dvořák Memorial Volume: Essays on his Work and Life] (Prague, 1912), 208–26

Dvořákův sborník' [Dvořák Memorial Volume], *HR*, iv (1910–11), 409–96 [28 articles by Šourek and others, incl. L. Janáček: 'Za Antonínem Dvořákem', 432, repr. in *Musikologie*, v (1958), 353–4, ed. B. Štědroň]

J. Bartoš: *Antonín Dvořák: kritická studie* (Prague, 1913)

L. Bráfová: *Rieger, Smetana, Dvořák* (Prague, 1913)

O. Šourek: *Život a dílo Antonína Dvořáka* [Life and Work of Dvořák] (Prague, 1916–33; i–ii, 3/1954–5; iii–iv, 2/1956–7)

K. Hoffmeister: *Antonín Dvořák* (Prague, 1924; Eng. trans., 1928)

O. Šourek: *Antonín Dvořák* (Prague, 1929, 3/1947; Eng. trans., 1952)

——: *Dvořákova čítanka: články a skadby* [Dvořák Reader: Articles and Works] (Prague, 1929)

O. Šourek and P. Stefan: *Dvořák: Leben und Werk* (Vienna, 1935; Eng. trans., 1941, as *Anton Dvořák*)

H. Sirp: *Anton Dvořák* (Potsdam, 1939)

V. Fischl, ed.: *Antonín Dvořák: his Achievement* (London, 1942)

J. M. Květ: *Mládí Antonína Dvořáka* [The Youth of Dvořák] (Prague, 1943, 3/1944)

A. Robertson: *Dvořák* (London, 1945, 2/1974)

I. Belza: *Antonin Dvorzhak* (Moscow, 1949, 2/1954)

O. Šourek: *Z Dvořákovy cesty za slávou* [Dvořák's Path to Fame] (Prague, 1949)

H. Boese: *Zwei Urmusikanten: Smetana – Dvořák* (Vienna, 1955)

R. Smetana: *Antonín Dvořák: o místo a význam Dvořákova skladatelského díla v českém hudebním vývoji* [Dvořák: the Place and Meaning of Dvořák's Compositions in the Development of Czech Music] (Prague, 1956)

J. Clapham: 'The Operas of Antonín Dvořák', *PRMA*, lxxxiv (1958), 55–69

——: 'Dvořák as a Composer of Opera', *The Listener* (22 Jan 1959)

K. B. Jirák: *Antonín Dvořák: 1841–1961* (New York, 1961)

A. Hetschko: *Antonín Dvořák* (Leipzig, 1965)

J. Burghauser: *Antonín Dvořák* (Prague, 1966; Eng. trans., 1967)

——: *Nejen pomníky* [Not Just Monuments] (Prague and Bratislava, 1966)

J. Clapham: *Antonín Dvořák: Musician and Craftsman* (London, 1966)

L. S. Ginzburg, ed.: *Antonin Dvorzhak: sbornik statyei* [Dvořák: a Collection of Articles] (Moscow, 1967)

J. Berkovec: *Antonín Dvořák* (Prague, 1969)

Z. Gulinskaya: *Antonin Dvorzhak* (Moscow, 1973)

J. Clapham: *Dvořák* (Newton Abbot and London, 1979)

OM, xv/3 (1983) [Dvořák issue]

H.-H. Schönzeler: *Dvořák* (London, 1984)

J. Smaczny: 'Word-Setting in the Late Dvořák Operas', *Colloquium Dvořák, Janáček and their Time: Brno XIX 1984*, 239–42

J. Clapham: 'Antonín Dvořák', *The New Grove Late Romantic Masters* (London and New York, 1985), 205–99 [incl. full list of works]
J. Tyrrell: *Czech Opera* (Cambridge, 1988)
M. Hallová, Z. Petrášková and J. Tauerová-Veverková, eds.: *Musical Dramatic Works by Antonín Dvořák* (Prague, 1989)

SPECIFIC WORKS

M. Lemarieová: *Dvořákova Rusalka* (diss., Charles U., Prague, 1952)
V. Tausky: 'Dvořák's "Rusalka" ', *Opera*, x (1959), 76–81
J. Smaczny: 'Armida – Dvořák's Wrong Turning?', *Zpráva* [London], iii/5 (1977), 10–14
M. Kuna and M. Pospíšil: 'Dvořák's *Dimitrij*: its History, its Music', *MT*, cxx (1979), 23–5
M. Kuna: 'Ke vzniku Dvořákova *Dimitrije*' [Towards the Origins of Dvořák's *Dimitrij*], *HV*, xviii (1981), 326–42
——: 'Ke zrodu Dvořákova Jakobína' [Towards the Origins of Dvořák's *The Jacobin*], *HV*, xix (1982), 245–68
J. Smaczny: 'Dvořák and *Rusalka*', *Opera*, xxxiv (1983), 241–5
M. Kuna: 'Od Matčiny písně k Dvořákovu Jakobínu' [From *The Mother's Song* to Dvořák's *The Jacobin*], *HV*, xxi (1984), 32–68
A. Stich: 'O libretu Dvořákova Dimitrije' [About the Libretto of Dvořák's *Dimitrij*], *HV*, xxi (1984), 339–52
H. A. Houtchens: *A Critical Study of Antonín Dvořák's 'Vanda'* (diss., U. of California, Santa Barbara, 1987)
J. A. Smaczny: *A Study of the First Six Operas of Antonín Dvořák: the Foundations of an Operatic Style* (diss., U. of Oxford, 1989)
——: '*Alfred*: Dvořák's First Operatic Endeavour Surveyed', *JRMA*, cxv (1990), 80–106
J. Burghauser, ed.: *Dvořák dramatik* (Prague, forthcoming) [incl. chaps. on each of the operas]

JAN SMACZNY

Dvořáková, Ludmila (*b* Kolín, 11 July 1923). Czech soprano. She studied in Prague, making her début in 1949 at Ostrava as Kát'a, then singing Jenůfa, Rusalka, Countess Almaviva, Aida and Leonora (*Il trovatore*). She moved to Bratislava (1952), then to Prague (1954), gradually undertaking heavier parts: Milada (*Dalibor*), Elisabeth, Leonore (*Fidelio*) and Senta. In 1960 she joined the Berlin Staatsoper, where she sang Octavian, Ariadne, Brünnhilde, Venus, Tosca, Elisabeth de Valois, the Marschallin and the Dyer's Wife. In 1965 she sang Katerina Izmaylova at the Vienna Staatsoper and made her Bayreuth début as Gutrune, returning there as Venus, Brünnhilde, Kundry and Ortrud. In 1966 she sang Leonore at the Metropolitan and made her Covent Garden début as Brünnhilde, later appearing as Leonore and Isolde. Her voice was full and warm, especially in the middle register, though not always easily produced at the top; in the late 1970s she began to sing mezzo roles such as Herodias and the Kostelnička.

*

A. Blyth: 'Ludmila Dvořáková', *Opera*, xxii (1971), 768–72

ALAN BLYTH

Dvorsky, Peter (*b* Partizánske, nr Topol'čany, 27 Sept 1951). Slovak tenor. He studied at the Bratislava Conservatory and the Scuola della Scala in Milan. After his début, with the Bratislava opera in 1972 as Lensky, he won the Moscow Tchaikovsky Competition in 1974 and the Geneva International Competition the next year. He first sang at the Vienna Staatsoper in 1977 (the Italian singer in *Der Rosenkavalier*), and appeared as Alfredo at the Metropolitan Opera the same year. In 1978 he sang Rodolfo at La Scala and the Duke in *Rigoletto* at Covent Garden, returning in 1988 as Lensky and as Riccardo (*Un ballo in maschera*); he has also appeared at the Bol'shoy and with the Chicago Lyric Opera as well as in most major European centres, including Salzburg (1989) where he sang Cavaradossi. A lyric tenor, he sings with strong dramatic feeling and much tonal beauty if variable technique.

NOËL GOODWIN

Dyagilev [Diaghilev], **Sergey Pavlovich** (*b* Grusino, Novgorod, 19/31 March 1872; *d* Venice, 19 Aug 1929). Russian impresario. A perceptive amateur of the arts gifted with a flair for organization and publicity, he was intimately involved in all aspects of the production, and even creation, of operas and ballets by composers including Stravinsky, Ravel and Prokofiev. In 1908, intent on introducing Russian opera to an enthusiastic crowd of Parisians, he imported Shalyapin, Natasha Yermolenko and an all-Russian cast for a production of Musorgsky's *Boris Godunov*. In the following year he returned to Paris to launch his Ballets Russes company, meanwhile offering Rimsky-Korsakov's *Maid of Pskov* and one act each from Glinka's *Ruslan and Lyudmila* and Serov's *Judith*, as well as excerpts from Borodin's *Prince Igor*, at the Théâtre du Châtelet. Among other Russian operas he presented were Musorgsky's *Khovanshchina* (1913, with alterations by Stravinsky) and Rimsky-Korsakov's *The Golden Cockerel* and *May Night* (both 1914). Owing to the difficulty of obtaining Russian singers after the Revolution, Dyagilev turned to French opera for his 1924 Monte Carlo season, which included Gounod's *Le médecin malgré lui*, *Philémon et Baucis* and *La colombe*, and Chabrier's *Une éducation manquée* (with new recitatives by Milhaud). Stravinsky, who had been associated with the Ballets Russes since 1910, composed three operas for the company: *Solovey* ('The Nightingale', Opéra, 26 May 1914), with sets and costumes by Alexandre Benois and choreography by Boris Romanov; *Mavra* (Opéra, 3 June 1922), with sets and costumes by Survage and direction by Bronislava Nizhinska; and *Oedipus rex* (Théâtre Sarah Bernhardt, 30 May 1927), composed for the 20th anniversary of Dyagilev's theatrical activity.

*

S. Lifar: *Serge de Diaghilev* (London, 1940)
R. Buckle: *Diaghilev* (London, 1979)
L. Garafola: *Diaghilev's Ballets Russes* (New York, 1989)

MAUREEN NEEDHAM COSTONIS

Dyck, Ernest Van. *See* VAN DYCK, ERNEST.

Dyer, Mrs. *See* HODGSON, MARY.

Dyutsh, Otton Ivanovich. *See* DÜTSCH, OTTO JOHANN ANTON.

Dzerzhinsky, Ivan Ivanovich (*b* Tambov, 27 March/9 April 1909; *d* Leningrad [now St Petersburg], 18 Jan 1978). Russian composer. He studied the piano at the First Music Tekhnikum in Moscow, 1925–9, and composition at the Gnesin Tekhnikum, 1929–30. He continued composition studies at the Leningrad Central Musical Tekhnikum (1930–32) before enrolling at the Leningrad Conservatory, where he studied with Pyotr Ryazanov and Asaf'yev (1932–4). From 1936 he occupied important positions in the Union of Soviet Composers, and he also served, periodically after 1946, as a deputy to the Leningrad City Soviet.

Dzerzhinsky's chief claim to fame was his first opera, *Tikhiy Don* ('Quiet Flows the Don'), composed while he was still a student and – after its initial failure in an opera competition – salvaged and improved with the help and sponsorship of Dmitry Shostakovich. When it was first staged in Leningrad in October 1935, *Quiet Flows the Don* won admirers for its freshness, the direct simplicity of its melodic language and the human depth in its treatment of a contemporary theme. In January

1936, the work assumed even greater symbolic significance when it was singled out by Stalin as a positive model for the future development of Soviet opera – often referred to as 'song opera' – counterbalancing it with the negative model of Shostakovich's hugely successful *Lady Macbeth of the Mtsensk District*.

Dzerzhinsky tried repeatedly throughout the rest of his life to recapture the formula of his initial success. While he composed symphonic works, three piano concertos, much choral music and songs, as well as incidental and film music, he devoted most of his energy to the operatic genre. In his operas, as well as in his non-operatic works, he was attracted to contemporary themes of patriotic import. His musical talents were limited, however, and his powers of invention really did not exceed the pretensions of song form. Some of his subsequent operas, including *Sud'ba cheloveka* ('The Fate of a Man', 1961), were orchestrated by others.

See also QUIET FLOWS THE DON and SUD'BA CHELOVEKA.

Tikhiy Don [Quiet Flows the Don], 1932–4 (4, L. I. Dzerzhinsky, after M. Sholokhov), Leningrad, Malïy, 22 Oct 1935, vs (Leningrad, 1934); rev. version, Leningrad, Malïy, 7 Nov 1947

Podnyataya tselina [Virgin Soil Upturned] (music drama, 4, L. I. Dzerzhinsky, after Sholokhov), Moscow, Bol'shoy, 23 Oct 1937, vs (Moscow, 1939); rev. version, Perm, 30 May 1964

Volochayevskiye dni [Volochayev Days], 1939

Krov' naroda [The Blood of the People] (3, I. I. Dzerzhinsky and E. A. Rïss), Orenburg, City Dramatic, 21 Jan 1942

Nadezhda Svetlova (lyrical scenes, 3, I. I. Dzerzhinsky, K. A. Lipskerov and Rïss, after K. Simonov), Orenburg, City Dramatic, 8 Sept 1943, vs (Moscow, 1943)

Metel' (v zimnyuyu noch') [The Blizzard (on a Winter's Night)] (comic op, 3, L. I. Dzerzhinsky, after A. S. Pushkin), Leningrad, Musical Comedy, 24 Nov 1946

Knyaz'-ozero [The Prince-Lake] (folk op, 4, epilogue, L. I. Dzerzhinsky, after P. Vershigora), Leningrad, Kirov, 26 Oct 1947

Daleko ot Moskvï [Far from Moscow] (4, L. I. Dzerzhinsky, after V. Azhaev), Leningrad, Malïy, 19 July 1954; rev. version, Leningrad, Malïy, 8 Nov 1954

Groza [The Storm], 1940–55 (4, L. I. Dzerzhinsky, after A. N. Ostrovsky), concert perf., Moscow, House of Actors, 17 April 1956

Sud'ba cheloveka [The Fate of a Man] (3, I. I. Dzerzhinsky, after Sholokhov), Moscow, Bol'shoy, and Leningrad, Kirov, 17 Oct 1961, vs (Leningrad, 1980)

Grigoriy Melekhov (3, I. I. Dzerzhinsky, E. A. Karetnikova, A. V. Sokolov and A. D. Churkin, after Sholokhov), Leningrad, Kirov, 4 Nov 1967, vs (Leningrad, 1970) [continuation of Quiet Flows the Don]

*

G. Abraham: *Eight Soviet Composers* (London, 1943), 79–88

O. M. Tompakova: *Ocherk o zhizni i tvorchestve I. I. Dzerzhinskogo* [Study of the Life and Work of I. I. Dzerzhinsky] (Leningrad, 1964)

S. V. Aksyuk, ed.: *Ivan Dzerzhinskiy; stat'i, vospominaniya* [Ivan Dzerzhinsky: Articles, Reminiscences] (Moscow, 1988)

LAUREL E. FAY